Who'sWho in America®

Who's Who in America®

2018

MARQUIS Who'sWho®

100 Connell Drive, Suite 2300, Berkeley Heights, New Jersey 07922
www.marquiswhoswho.com

Who's Who in America®

Table of Contents

Preface

> **"W**ho's Who in America** shall
> *endeavor to list those individuals who
> are of current national interest and inquiry either
> because of meritorious achievement or because of
> the positions they hold."— 1899*

Albert Nelson Marquis
Founder

Marquis Who's Who is proud to present the 71st edition of Who's Who in America. This 2018 compilation features over 5,900 profiles of prominent individuals representing virtually every major field of endeavor.

On the pages that follow, you will find Nobel and Pulitzer Prize winners, legendary athletes, best-selling authors, university presidents, accomplished artists, renowned entertainers, entrepreneurs and corporate executives, government and religious leaders, innovators/inventors, as well as professionals in the fields of education, law, medicine, broadcasting, publishing, information technology, and more.

As in all Marquis Who's Who biographical volumes, the individuals profiled in Who's Who in America are selected on the basis of current reference value. Factors such as position, noteworthy accomplishments, visibility, and prominence in a field are all taken into account.

Among our many new listees in the 71st edition are:

- **Ava DuVernay**, award-winning director and producer
- **Darius Adamczyk**, new chairman and CEO of Honeywell International
- **Madhav Rajan**, dean of the School of Business at the University of Chicago
- **Jose Altuve**, 2017 Most Valuable Player for the-world-champion Houston Astros
- **Veronica Roth**, award-winning author of the "Divergent" series

In an effort to further illuminate our biographical coverage we asked many of our listees to tell us in narrative form about the attributes that contributed to their success, why they chose the profession they did, and what they consider to be the highlight of their career. The result is thousands of biographies that now go beyond the facts of their lives to shed additional light on what makes these inspiring individuals tick.

In an effort to make Who's Who in America more user-friendly we are pleased to have made the following changes:

- Most abbreviations have been removed.
- The font size has been enlarged.
- An Index is included, featuring last name, first name, title, industry and corresponding page number.
- The book is now one volume.

While the vast majority of the individuals profiled are American, also included are the biographies of select individuals from around the world whose lives have had considerable impact and influence in America.

Biographical information is gathered in a variety of manners. In most cases, we invite our biographees to submit their biographical details. In some cases, though, the information is collected by our research and editorial staffs, which use a wide assortment of tools to gather the most complete, accurate and up-to-date information available.

While the Marquis Who's Who editors exercise the utmost care in preparing each biographical sketch for publication, it is inevitable in a publication involving so many profiles that occasional errors will appear. Users of this publication are urged to notify the publisher of any issues so that adjustments can be made, which will be reflected not only in all subsequent editions but which will also be immediately displayed via Marquis Biographies Online.

All of the profiles in Who's Who in America are available on Marquis Biographies Online (https://mbo.marquiswhoswho.com/) through a subscription. At the present time, subscribers to Marquis Biographies Online have access to all the names included in all of the Marquis Who's Who publications, as well as many new biographies that will appear in upcoming publications.

We sincerely hope that this volume will be an indispensible reference tool for you. We are always looking for ways to better serve you and welcome your ideas for improvements. In addition, we continue to welcome your Marquis Who's Who nominations.

Key to Information

Doe, John Anderson Jr., **T:** President **I:** Manufacturing **CN:** Doe Widget Company **OC:** Manufacturing executive **DOB:** 1/1/1930 **PB:** Syracuse **SC:** NY/USA **YOP:** 2018 **PT:** John Anderson Doe Sr.; Josephine Doe **MS:** Married **SPN:** Jane (Richards) Doe (September 23, 1952) **CH:** Jeremy; Robert; Annabelle **ED:** JD, Yale University (1987); MS in Physical Science, Massachusetts Institute of Technology (1968); BA in Physics, Yale University (1950) **CT:** Certification in Widget Manufacturing, National Widget Certification Board **C:** President, Doe Widget Company (1999-2017); Vice President of Production, Roe Manufacturing, Inc. (1980-1998); Production Manager, Roe Manufacturing, Inc. (1972-1980); Postgraduate Researcher, Massachusetts Institute of Technology (1968-1972) **CR:** Vice Chairman, Syracuse Chamber of Commerce (1990-2003) **CIV:** Volunteer, American Red Cross; Fundraiser, National Audubon Society **MIL:** Lieutenant, United States Army (1957-1965) **CW:** "Essentials of Widget Manufacturing" (1991) **AW:** Lifetime Achievement Award, Syracuse Chamber of Commerce (2014) **MEM:** National Audubon Society; American Widget Association **BAR:** American Bar Association; New York State Bar Association **MH:** Albert Nelson Marquis Lifetime Achievement Award (2016) **ACH:** Finding a new and innovative method of manufacturing widgets; Filing and registering six patents throughout his career **H:** Birdwatching; Watching sports; Spending time with his family **PA:** Independent **RE:** Presbyterian **BA:** 1600 Cliffside Drive, Suite 20, Syracuse, NY 13202 **ADD:** 2505 James Avenue, Syracuse NY 13206 **URL:** http://www.johndoewidgets.com

Key

T:	Title	**CR:**	Career Related
I:	Industry	**CIV:**	Civic
CN:	Company Name	**MIL:**	Military Service
OC:	Occupation	**CW:**	Creative Works
DOB:	Date of Birth	**AW:**	Awards
PB:	Place of Birth	**MEM:**	Memberships
SC:	State/Country of Origin	**BAR:**	Bar Admissions
YOP:	Year of Passing	**MH:**	Marquis Who's Who Honors
PT:	Parents	**ACH:**	Achievements
MS:	Marital Status	**H:**	Hobbies
SPN:	Spouse Name	**PA:**	Political Affiliations
CH:	Children	**RE:**	Religion
ED:	Education	**BA:**	Business Address
CT:	Certifications	**ADD:**	Personal Address
C:	Career	**URL:**	Website

In Memoriam

Marquis Who's Who
dedicates this registry to the memory
of the following listees:

Robert J. Banis

Anthony Michael Bourdain

John Britt

Barbara Bush

Chia-Hwa (Lydia) Chu Chang

Oscar De La Renta

Stephanie Anne Donoghue

Aretha Louise Franklin

Florence Griffith-Joyner

Clovis Haden

Barbara Stein Katz

Irving John Kern

Nancy Hay Knapp

Ursula Kroeber Le Guin

Alan Graham MacDiarmid

John McCain

Keith E. Melder

Stan Mikita

Al Oerter

Donald Milford Payne

Richard Thomas Reminger

Irwin Allen Rose

Philip Roth

Kate Spade

Keir B. Sterling

(William) Payne Stewart

Ray Thomas

Charles Hard Townes

Samuel Wagner

Subhashie Wijemanne

Tom Wolfe

Kenneth Rau Woolling

DISTINGUISHED LISTEES

71st Edition

David Aaronson

Title: Lawyer **Industry:** Law and Legal Services **Company Name:** American University Washington College of Law **Date of Birth:** 09/19/1940 **Place of Birth:** Washington **State:** DC **Parents:** Edward Allan Aaronson; May (Rosett) Aaronson **Marital Status:** Married **Spouse Name:** Laura Dine (1991) **Children:** Dara Prushansky (Stepchild); Jared Prushansky (Stepchild) **Education:** PhD, The George Washington University (1970); LLM, Georgetown University (1965); LLB, Harvard University (1964); MA, The George Washington University (1964); BA in Economics, The George Washington University (1961) **Certifications:** Maryland State Bar Association, Inc. (1975); Supreme Court of the United States (1969); The District of Columbia Bar (1965) **Career:** Professor, B.J. Tennery Scholar, American University Washington College of Law, Washington, DC (1970-Present); Professor, School of Justice, College of Public and International Affairs (1981-1992); Deputy Director, Law and Policy Institute, Jerusalem (1978); Partner, Aaronson and Aaronson (1967-1970); Research Associate, Patent Research Project, Department of Economics, The George Washington University, Washington, DC (1966); Associate, Firm, Aaronson and Aaronson, Washington, DC (1965-1967); Staff Attorney, Legal Intern Program, Georgetown Law, Washington, DC (1964-1965); Research Assistant, Office of the Commissioner, Bureau of Labor Statistics, United States Department of Labor, Washington, DC (1961) **Career Related:** Director, Advocacy LLM Program (2011-Present); Director, Trial Advocacy Program (2004-Present); Trustee, Montgomery-Prince George's Continuing Legal Education Institute (1983-1997); Co-director, Trial Advocacy Program (1982-2004); Visiting Professor, Faculty of Law, The Hebrew University of Jerusalem (1978); Founder, Prosecutor, Criminal Litigation Clinic (1972); **Civic:** Member, The Friendship Heights Village Council (1979) **Creative Works:** Author, "Maryland Criminal Jury Instructions and Commentary, Volume Two" (2017); Author, "Maryland Criminal Jury Instructions and Commentary, Third Edition, with Annual Supplements" (2009); Co-author, "The Insanity Defense: A Critical Assessment of Law and Policy in the Post-Hinckley Era" (1988); Author, "Public Policy and Police Discretion: Processes of Decriminalization" (1984); Co-author, "Decriminalization of Public Drunkenness: Tracing the Implementation of a Public Policy" (1981); Co-author, "Alternatives to Conventional Criminal Adjudication: Guidebook for Planners and Practitioners" (1977); Co-author, "The New Justice: Alternatives to Conventional Criminal Adjudication" (1977); Author, "Maryland Criminal Jury Instructions and Commentary" (1975); Contributor, Articles, Professional Journals **Awards:** B.J. Tennery Scholar (1990-Present); Pauline Ruyle Moore Scholar in Public Law (2011); Robert C. Heeney Award, Maryland State Bar Association, Inc. (1999); Scholar/Teacher of the Year Award, American University (1989); Pauline Ruyle Moore Scholar in Public Law (1983); Outstanding Teacher Award, American University Washington College of Law (1981); Outstanding Community Service Award (1980); Outstanding Teacher Award, American University Washington College of Law (1978); E. Barrett Prettyman Fellow, Georgetown University (1965); Honoree, Fourth Best Program in the Country, U.S. News & World Report L.P. **Membership:** Criminal Justice Section, Rules of Criminal Procedure and Police Practices, ABA (1991-Present); Criminal Law Section Council, Maryland State Bar Association, Inc. (1984-Present); Chair, ABA (2008); Co-chair, ABA (2007); Elected to Section Council, Criminal Justice Section, Association of American Law Schools (1999-2004); Chairman, Maryland State Bar Association, Inc. (1989-1990); Chairman, Criminal Code Review Committee, The District of Columbia Bar (1971-1973); Bar Association of Montgomery County; The American Law Institute; Phi Beta Kappa **Marquis Who's Who Honors:** Albert Nelson Marquis Lifetime Achievement Award (2017) **Shipping Address:** 5206 Westwood Dr, Bethesda, MD, 20816

George Gabriel Abdelsayed

Title: Gastroenterologist **Industry:** Medicine & Health Care **Place of Birth:** Cairo **Country of Origin:** Egypt **Parents:** Gabriel Abdelsayed; Tahani Abdelsayed **Education:** MD, New York Medical College, Valhalla, NY (1983); Degree, St. John's University, Summa Cum Laude (1979) **Certifications:** Certification in Sports Medicine (2007); Certification in Critical Care Medicine (2001); Certification in Geriatrics (1996); Certification, American Board of Nutrition (1992); Certification in Gastroenterology (1989); Medical Diplomate, American Board of Internal Medicine (1988) **Career:** Associate Clinical Professor, NYU Langone Health (2016-Present); Associate Professor of Medicine, Donald and Barbara Zucker School of Medicine at Hofstra (2016-Present); Associate Clinical Professor of Medicine, Yale School of Medicine (2008-2016); Assistant Clinical Professor of Medicine, Yale School of Medicine (2006-2008); Program Director, Chief of Gastroenterology Section, Bridgeport Hospital, Yale New Haven Health (2005-2012) **Career Related:** President, New Jersey Chapter, American Society for Parenteral and Enteral Nutrition, New Jersey Gastroenterology & Endoscopy Society (2003-2004); Chief of Gastroenterology and Endoscopy, Barnert Hospital (Now Community Healthcare Associates, LLC) (2001-2003); Physician-in-Chief, Pharmacy and Therapeutics Committee, Barnert Hospital (Now Community Healthcare Associates, LLC) (2000-2003); Private Practice, Paterson, NJ (1998-2005); New Jersey Society of Gastrointestinal Endoscopy (1997-1998); Associate Program Director of Medicine, St. Joseph's Hospital and Medical Center (1995-1998); Associate Chairman of Education, New Jersey (1995-1998); Chief, Gastroenterology Department, Methodist Hospital, Brooklyn, NY (1993-1995); Chairman, Department of Medicine, Barnert Hospital **Civic:** Physician-at-Large, North Hudson Community Action Corporation, Western New York, New Jersey (2000-2005); Deacon, Medical Consultant, Coptic Orthodox Church of North America, New Jersey **Awards:** Best Teacher Award, Methodist Hospital **Membership:** Honorary Member, Patient Care Committee, American College of Gastroenterology (2007-Present); Fellow, American College of Physicians; Fellow, American College of Gastroenterology **Marquis Who's Who Honors:** Albert Nelson Marquis Lifetime Achievement Award (2017) **Hobbies:** Tennis; Travel; Magic **Shipping Address:** 500 Central Ave Apt 1501, Union City, NJ, 07087

Ralph William Abelt

Title: Bank Executive **Industry:** Financial Services **Date of Birth:** 02/16/1929 **Place of Birth:** Elmhurst **State:** IL **Parents:** P. Alfred Abelt; Clara (Springhorn) Abelt **Marital Status:** Married **Spouse Name:** Patricia Mitchell (2/2/1952) **Children:** Susan E.; Christopher M.; Leslie A. **Education:** MBA in Finance, Indiana University (1953); BS in Finance, University of Colorado (1952) **Career:** President, Chief Executive Officer, Northeast Ohio Council (1988-1991); Chairman, Chief Executive Officer, Bank One Cleveland, NA (1983-1986); President, Chief Executive Officer, Director, Bank One of Northeastern Ohio, NA, Painesville, OH (1977-1983); Vice President of Commercial Banking, Continental Illinois, Chicago, IL (1953-1977); Accountant, Marion Hutchinson, C.P.A., Denver, CO (1952) **Career Related:** Director, Plasticolors, Inc., Ashtabula, OH (1987-1990) **Civic:** Director, Treasurer, Oro Valley Community Foundation, Tucson, AZ (2007-2009); Director, Knowledgeworks Foundation, Cincinnati, OH (1987-2007); Director, Holden Arboretum, Kirtland, OH (1986-2005); President, Executive Board Member, Area Vice President, Lake Erie Council, Boy Scouts of America, Painesville, OH (1981) **Military Service:** U.S. Marine Corps (1946-1948) **Marquis Who's Who Honors:** Albert Nelson Marquis Lifetime Achievement Award (2017) **To what do you attribute your success:** Mr. Abelt attributes his success to a high level of achievement, along with being in the right place at the right time. **Why did you become involved in your profession or industry:** Mr. Abelt became involved in his profession at the recommendation and urging of faculty at both the University of Colorado and Indiana University. **What do you consider to be the highlight of your career:** The highlight of Mr. Abelt's career was being named chairman and chief executive officer of a major bank in Cleveland, OH. **Hobbies:** Skiing; Golf; Game hunting; Bird hunting; Woodworking **Shipping Address:** 13500 N Rancho Vistoso Boulevard, Apt. 511, Oro Valley, AZ, 85755

Nels John Ackerson

Title: Chairman, Lawyer **Industry:** Law and Legal Services **Company Name:** Ackerson Kauffman Fex **Date of Birth:** 04/12/1944 **Place of Birth:** Indianapolis **State:** IN **Parents:** Ralph D. Ackerson; Mariel F. (Maze) Ackerson **Marital Status:** Married **Spouse Name:** Sharon Carroll Ackerson (6/11/1983) **Children:** Betsy Virginia Ackerson; Peter Nels Ackerson; Stacia Carroll Loveall (Stepdaughter); Joshua Michael Loveall (Stepson) **Education:** Honorary PhD, Purdue University (2006); JD, Harvard Law School, Harvard University, Cum Laude (1971); MA in Public Policy, Harvard University (1971); BS, Purdue University, with Distinction (1967) **Certifications:** United States Court of Appeals for the Fourth Circuit (1999); United States Court of Appeals for the Sixth Circuit (1996); United States Court of International Trade (1991); Supreme Court of the United States (1989); United States Court of Appeals for the District of Columbia Circuit (1985); Washington, DC (1985); Indiana (1971); United States District Court for the Southern District of Indiana (1971); United States Court of Appeals for the Seventh Circuit (1971) **Career:** Chairman, Ackerson Kauffman Fex, Washington, DC (2004-Present); Chairman, Class Corridor LLC (2001-Present); Partner, Director, Sommer Barnard Ackerson PC (2002-2004); Chairman, Ackerson & Bishop Chartered, The Ackerson Group, Chartered, Washington, DC (1991); Partner, Sidley & Austin (Now Sidley Austin LLP), Cairo, Washington, DC (1982-1991); Partner, Sidley, Austin & Naguib (Now Sidley Austin LLP), Cairo, Washington, DC (1982-1984); Partner, Campbell, Kyle & Proffitt, Noblesville, IN (1979-1982); Chief Counsel, Executive Director, United States Senate Subcommittee on Constitution, Washington, DC (1977-1979); Chief Counsel, United States Senate Subcommittee, Constitutional Amendments, Washington, DC (1976-1977); Associate, Barnes, Hickam, Pantzer & Boyd, Indianapolis, IN (1971-1976); Advisor, Harvard Advisory Mission to Republic of Colombia (1970) **Career Related:** Advisory Mission on to Republic of Colombia, Harvard University; Advisor, Communications Environmental and Land Use Law Report; Class Counsel, AT&T Fiber Optic Litigation Board **Civic:** Liberal Arts Advisory Council, Purdue University (1997-2000); Democratic Nominee for United States Congress, Fifth District, State of Indiana (1980) **Creative Works:** Board of Editors, "Harvard Law Review" (1968-1971), Author, Community Development Corporations **Awards:** Honorary PhD, Purdue University (2006); JD, Harvard Law School, Harvard University, Cum Laude (1971); MA in Public Policy, Harvard University (1971); BS, Purdue University, With Distinction (1967); **Membership:** President, American Chamber of Commerce in Egypt (1984); Litigation Section, ABA; Business and Banking Section, ABA; International Law Section, ABA; Administrative Law Section, ABA; American Agricultural Law Association; Center for National Policy; Food and Agriculture Committee, National Policy Association; Association of Trial Lawyers of America **Bar Admissions:** Indiana; Washington, DC; Supreme Court of the United States; United States Circuit Courts for the First, Second, Fourth, Fifth, and Seventh Circuits **Marquis Who's Who Honors:** Albert Nelson Marquis Lifetime Achievement Award (2017) **To what do you attribute your success:** Mr. Ackerson attributes his success to his parents, as well as his caring family and community; their examples shaped the best parts of his character and led him to believe that each of us has a skill or can develop a skill, whether humble or great, that can make a huge difference to another or to others. He also credits his farm community, church and teachers that shared in that humble, but inspiring, confidence, that urged him to develop skills to benefit his neighbors and country. **What do you consider to be the highlight of your career:** Mr. Ackerson's career, from my personal perspective has had several highlights: being chief of the United States Senate staff responsible for Title IX's successful amendments and Senate passage becoming law, being the author and chief of the United States Senate Staff responsible for the first legislation to stimulate production of biomass or alcoholic alternatives to petroleum fuels and leading the United States Senate Staff responsible for the passage of civil rights legislation and patent legislation. He is also proud of leading a class action counsel for landowners in multiple class actions nationwide seeking due process and fair compensation for taking of property for our nation's fiber optic and utilities networks. Mr. Ackerson has opened and managed the first American law firm office in Egypt – Sidley & Austin & Naguib – and was elected president of the American Chamber of Commerce in Egypt. **Hobbies:** Singing; Travelling; Public policy **Political Affiliations:** Democrat **Religion:** Presbyterian **Business Address:** 1300 Pennsylvania Ave NW Ste 700, DC, Washington, 20004 **Shipping Address:** 5275 Gulf of Mexico Dr Unit 202, Longboat Key, FL 34228

David Franklyn Adams

Title: Music Educator **Industry:** Education/Educational Services **Company Name:** An Achievable Dream Academy **Date of Birth:** 05/17/1939 **Place of Birth:** Albuquerque **State:** NM **Parents:** John Marian Adams; Mary Louise Adams; Kenneth Jewell; Peggy Crowther (Stepmother) **Marital Status:** Married **Spouse Name:** Vickie Sharon Mobley (6/8/1998); Gail Lenore Ingraham (6/10/1966, Divorced 10/28/1983) **Children:** Christina Ann Cox; Tamara Gail Olarte; Wendy Michelle Swoope **Education:** Diploma, Mesa College (1974) **Career:** Band Director, An Achievable Dream Academy, Newport News, VA (2001-Present); Director of Jazz Studies, Academy of Music, Norfolk, VA (1999-2000); Band Director, Teacher, Bosque Preparatory School (Now Bosque School) (1996-1998); Private Teacher, Musician, Albuquerque, NM (1990-1995); Counselor, Army Community Services (1988-1990); Acting Band Commander, United States Army Band, Fort Hamilton, NY (1986-1987); Rhythm Vocal Branch Head, Armed Forces School of Music, Norfolk, VA (1980-1986); Stage Band Director, First Army Band, Fort Carson, CO (1979-1980); Pianist, The United States Army Field Band (1977-1979); Pianist, The United States Air Force Bicentennial Band, Fort Meade, MD (1974-1976); Musician, Denver Affair, Las Vegas, NV (1969-1973); Band Director, Burlington High School, Burlington, CO (1967-1968) **Career Related:** Founder, Director, Producer, Young Razzcals Jazz Project (1992-Present); All-City Jazz Band Director, Virginia Beach City Public School (2002); Resident Jazz Musician (2001) **Civic:** Director of Aerospace Education, Civil Air Patrol, Albuquerque, NM (1990-1995); Mission Pilot, Civil Air Patrol, Norfolk, VA (1980-1990); Squadron Commander, Civil Air Patrol, Fort Meade, MD (1977-1979) **Military Service:** United States Army (1974-1990) **Creative Works:** Composer, "The Magic of Christmas"; Author, "The Reason for the Rhyme" **Awards:** Outstanding Leadership and Performance, Young Razzcals Jazz Project (2001-2002); Community Service Award, Arts Council Cooperative (1997); Frank G. Brewer Aerospace Award, National Civil Air Patrol (1995); Regional Civil Air Patrol (1995); Grover Loening Aerospace Award, Civil Air Patrol (1991) **Membership:** International Association of Jazz Educators; National Association of Music Education **Marquis Who's Who Honors:** Albert Nelson Marquis Lifetime Achievement Award (2017); Distinguished Humanitarian (2017) **To what do you attribute your success:** Mr. Adams attributes his success to loving what he does. **Why did you become involved in your profession or industry:** He loved trumpet. He had company over one night, where he lived on a farm and they all went on the front porch, turned on the radio and heard Louis Armstrong. **Hobbies:** Flying; Running; Writing; Scuba Diving; Hang Gliding **Shipping Address:** 5228 Dundee Ln, Virginia Beach, VA, 23464 **Website:** http://www.youngrazzcalsjazzproject.com

Erwin Ellery Adler

Title: Lawyer **Industry:** Law and Legal Services **Company Name:** Adler Law Group **Date of Birth:** 07/22/1941 **Place of Birth:** Flint **State:** MI **Parents:** Ben Adler; Helen M. (Schwartz) Adler **Marital Status:** Married **Spouse Name:** Stephanie Ruskin (6/8/1967) **Children:** Lauren; Michael; Jonathan **Education:** JD, Harvard University (1966); LLM, University of Michigan (1967); BA, University of Michigan, Cum Laude (1963) **Career:** Managing Partner, Adler Law Group (2004-Present); Partner, Management Committee, Richards, Watson & Gershon, Los Angeles, CA (1983-2004); Partner, Rogers & Wells, Los Angeles, CA (1981-1983); Partner, Lawler, Felix & Hall, Los Angeles, CA (1977-1980); Associate, Lawler, Felix & Hall, Los Angeles, CA (1973-1976); Associate, Pillsbury, Madison & Sutro, San Francisco, CA (1967-1973) **Career Related:** Presenter, Legal Issues including Preparation of Associated Written Materials for Various Continuing Legal Education Programs, University of California; Presenter, Legal Issues, Various Bar Associations, Other Organizations and Companies including Various National Conferences, Society of Claims Law Associates; Presenter, National Conferences, Excess/Surplus Lines Associates; Presenter, National Conference, Independent Underwriters Reinsurance Association **Civic:** Board of Directors, Children's Scholarships Inc. (1979-1980); Board of Directors, Hollywood Civic Opera Association (1975-1976) **Awards:** Recipient, President's Choice Award, Society of Claim Law Associates **Membership:** Vice Chairman, Appellate Advocacy Committee, ABA (1982-1987); The Phi Beta Kappa Society; The Honor Society of Phi Kappa Phi; Los Angeles County Bar Association **Bar Admissions:** Michigan (1966); California (1967) **Marquis Who's Who Honors:** Albert Nelson Marquis Lifetime Achievement Award (2017) **Religion:** Jewish **Business Address:** 350 S. Figueroa Street, Suite 520, Los Angeles, CA 90071 **Shipping Address:** 350 S. Figueroa Street, Suite 520, Adler Law Group, Los Angeles, CA, 90071 **Website:** http://www.adlerlawgroup.com

Kathryn Ann Adolph

Title: Passenger Service Employee **Industry:** Leisure, Travel & Tourism **Date of Birth:** 12/20/1945 **Place of Birth:** Hartington **State:** NE **Parents:** Edmund Leonard Arens; Elizabeth Claire Arens **Spouse Name:** Lester Leroy Adolph (1/2/1965, Divorced 1998) **Children:** Leslie Marie; Edmund Glenn **Education:** BS in Adult and Occupation Education, Kansas State University (1981) **Certifications:** Certificate in Supervisory, Metropolitan Community College **Career:** Passenger Service Employee, American Airlines, Kansas City, MO (2001-2008); Passenger Service Employee, Trans World Airlines, Kansas City, MO (1978-2001) **Creative Works:** Featured Guest, Industry Expert, Cable News Network **Marquis Who's Who Honors:** Albert Nelson Marquis Lifetime Achievement Award (2017) **Why did you become involved in your profession or industry:** Ms. Adolph became involved in her profession because it was a childhood dream of hers since she was four years old. When her mom asked her what she wanted to be when she grew up, she said that she wanted to work for Trans World Airlines and go to Switzerland. Ms. Adolph went into the airlines profession and was able to fulfill both of those dreams. **What do you consider to be the highlight of your career:** Ms. Adolph is most proud of her two children. They have become outstanding people with careers in information technology. She is also proud of the fact that she maintained a full-time career all while raising two children and earning a college degree from Kansas State University. **Hobbies:** Writing; Photography; Machine embroidery **Shipping Address:** 5809 Payne St, Shawnee, KS, 66226

David A. Affeldt

Title: Lawyer, Consultant **Industry:** Law and Legal Services **Date of Birth:** 01/15/1941 **Place of Birth:** Cedar Rapids **State:** IA **Parents:** Chester Nicholas Affeldt; Helen (May) Affeldt **Marital Status:** Widowed **Spouse Name:** Judy Cook (8/29/1964, Deceased 10/27/1998) **Children:** Christine Harmon **Education:** JD, University of Texas (1966); BA, University of Iowa (1963) **Career:** Consultant, National Aging Organizations (1980-Present); Special Assistant to Commissioner, Social Security Administration, Washington, DC (1979-1980); Chief Counsel, Senate Committee on Aging, Washington, DC (1970-1979); Legislative Aide to Congressman Neal Smith, United States House of Representatives, Washington, DC (1968-1969); Assistant Counsel, Iowa Senate, Des Moines, IA (1967); Assistant Attorney General, Iowa Department Justice, Des Moines, IA (1966) **Civic:** Consultant on Older American Issues, Pamela Harriman/Democrats for the 80s, Washington, DC (1982-1986) **Military Service:** District of Columbia National Guard (1968-1972); U.S. Army Reserve (1966-1968) **Creative Works:** Author, Numerous Reports on the Elderly; Author, "On the Other Side of Easy Street: A Report from the Villers Foundation" **Awards:** Resolutions and Certificates of Commendation, National Aging Organizations, United States Senate **Membership:** District of Columbia Bar **Bar Admissions:** United States District Court for the District of Columbia (1993); United States Court of Appeals for the District of Columbia Circuit (1993) **Marquis Who's Who Honors:** Albert Nelson Marquis Lifetime Achievement Award (2017) **Hobbies:** Reading; Swimming; Tennis; Travel; Mini-triathlons **Shipping Address:** 10404 Joiners Ln, Potomac, MD, 20854

Nkechi Agwu

Title: Mathematics Professor **Industry:** Education/Educational Services **Company Name:** CHI STEM TOYS Inc. **Date of Birth:** 10/08/1962 **Place of Birth:** Enugu **Country of Origin:** Nigeria **Parents:** Jacob Ukejeh Agwu; Europa Lauretta Durosimi Wilson **Marital Status:** Widowed **Spouse Name:** Nicholas C. B. Ogbonna (Deceased) **Children:** Ngozichuwkwuka Jacob Ayemere Durosimi Agwu **Education:** PhD, Syracuse University (1995); MS, University of Connecticut (1989); Honorary BS, University of Nigeria (1984) **Certifications:** Certified Public Notary, State of New York (2016-Present); Chaplaincy and Ministry Training, Worldwide Association of Small Churches (2016); Certified in First Aid, National Safety Council; Certified in CPR, National Safety Council **Career:** Pastor, Glorious Miracle Embassy International, Nigeria (2016-Present); Pastor, African Representative, Worldwide Association of Small Churches (Now Worldwide Association of Small Churches and Houses of Worship), United States (2016-Present); Director, Teaching Learning Center, Borough of Manhattan Community College, The City University of New York (1995-Present); Professor, Teaching Learning Center, Borough of Manhattan Community College, The City University of New York (1995-Present); Lecturer, Kaduna Polytechnic, Kaduna, Nigeria (1985-1987); Statistician, Federal Office of Statistics (Now National Bureau of Statistics), Enugu, Nigeria (1984-1985); Executive Secretary, CHI STEM TOYS Inc. **Career Related:** Educational Consultant, New Covenant Christian School, Bronx, NY (2017-Present); Educational Consultant, National Mathematics Centre, Abuja, Nigeria (2016-Present); Consultant, New Visions for Public Schools, New York City, NY (2000-2001); Educational Consultant, Algebra Project, New York City, NY (1998-2000) **Civic:** Bronx Volunteer Fire Patrol Company #4; Member, Community Emergency Response Team, Borough of Manhattan Community College, The City University of New York; Global Chaplain, Worldwide Association of Small Churches (Now Worldwide Association of Small Churches and Houses of Worship) **Creative Works:** Author, "God's Own: The Genesis of Mathematical Story-Telling"; Author, "The Grace of Dr. Mrs. Mojisola Olayinka Edema: A Visionary and a Reformer"; Author, "Woman Thou Art Loosed: Escaping the Limitations of Femininity"; Author, "Using a Threaded Discussion Web-Based Software to Teach Statistics"; Editor, The College Mathematics Journal; Editor, American Journal of Undergraduate Research **Awards:** Carnegie African Diaspora Fellowship (2016-2017); Chaplaincy Award, Worldwide Association of Small Churches (Now Worldwide Association of Small Churches and Houses of Worship) (2016); Carnegie African Diaspora Fellowship (2014); Fulbright Fellow, United States (2004); Visiting Fellow, Educational Testing Service (2003); Travel Award, International Conference on Technology in Collegiate Mathematics, Addison-Wesley (2002); Performance Excellence Award, Professional Staff Congress, The City University of New York (2000); INPUT Award, American Mathematical Association of Two-Year Colleges (2000); Mini-Grant, New York City Literary Assistance Center and Professional Development Consortium (1998-1999); Named, Project Kaleidoscope Faculty, Twenty-First Century Class of 1997 (1997-2002); Professional Development Award, Institute in the History of Mathematics and its Use in Teaching, Mathematical Association of America (1997-2001); Travel Award, American Mathematical Association of Two-Year Colleges (1997); Division K Travel Award for Dissertation Award and Syracuse University Creative Research Award for Dissertation, "Using a Computer Laboratory Setting to Teach College Calculus," UMI Dissertation Services, Ann Arbor, MI (1996); National Graduate Student Dissertation Travel Award, American Educational Research Association - Division K (1994); Teaching Assistantship, Syracuse University (1991-1995); Teaching Assistantship, University of Connecticut (1987-1991); Nigerian Federal Government Merit Award (1981-1984); Sierra Leone President's Bronze Award for Exemplary Community Service Working with the Disabled and Senior Citizens as an Interact Club Leader (1980) **Membership:** Lifetime Member, Global Chaplain, Pastor, African Representative, Worldwide Association of Small Churches (Now Worldwide Association of Small Churches and Houses of Worship); Lifetime Member, President, New York City Branch Leadership Corps, American Association of University Women; Social Advocacy Chair, Black Women for Black Girls Giving Circle; Lifetime Member, International Biographical Association; Lifetime Member, Mathematical Association of America; Lifetime Member, American Mathematical Association of Two-Year Colleges. **Hobbies:** Mathematical storytelling; Poetry; Creation of toys; Cultural games and artifacts; Singing; Dancing; Traveling; Proverbs **Religion:** Christian **Shipping Address:** 6 Rudd Place, Bronx, NY, 10473

Elizabeth Franz Albert

Title: Investor, Environmentalist **Industry:** Financial Services **Place of Birth:** Chicago **State:** IL **Parents:** Herbert George Franz; Louise Anders Franz **Marital Status:** Married **Spouse Name:** Henry Burton Albert **Education:** Coursework, Chevy Chase Junior College **Career:** Investor, Stock Market, Real Estate; Environmentalist **Career Related:** Breeder, Several Champion Miniature Poodles **Civic:** Former Member, Landmarks Preservation Council of Chicago **Creative Works:** Exhibitor, Portraits; Exhibitor, Still Life Paintings; Contributor, Biology Textbook; Editor, Biology Textbook **Membership:** American Farmland Trust; National Trust for Historical Preservation; Founding Member, Cousteau Society; Natural Resources Defense Council; Osprey Society, Environmental Defense Fund; Charter Member, National Museum of Women in the Arts; Chicago Symphony Orchestra Society; Life Member, Art Institute of Chicago **To what do you attribute your success:** She attributes her success to trying to be helpful in whatever way she can. That's why she was put here. It is her reason for living. **Why did you become involved in your profession or industry:** As a young woman, there were many things she wanted to do. She was diagnosed with Brucellosis, a terrible bacterial disease that she contracted by drinking unpasteurized milk when she was 16. At that time, milk was called certified milk to make sure that the cow was healthy and free of tuberculosis. Since Brucellosis was treated like a chronic disease, it changed her life entirely. She had wanted to be a doctor but was too sick. She wasn't able to do medicine or become a prima ballerina. She thought that she might go into ballet and then study medicine, but that did not come to be. She also thought about architecture at one point or being a couturier in Paris, but she was too sick. She could paint, however, even if she was sick. She was very blessed to also have the talent to paint. She wanted to study medicine most, but she became a painter. **Hobbies:** Music; Renovating houses; Antiques; Gardening; Reading **Political Affiliations:** Republican **Religion:** Episcopalian **Shipping Address:** 15420 W Little Saint Marys Rd, Mettawa, IL, 60048

Gifford Harry Albright, PhD

Title: Architectural Engineering Educator (Retired), Consultant **Industry:** Education/Educational Services **Company Name:** Pennsylvania State University **Date of Birth:** 02/14/1931 **Place of Birth:** Pottsville **State:** PA **Parents:** Harry Clayton Albright; Grace Reinhart Albright **Education:** MS, Massachusetts Institute of Technology (1955); BArch Engineering, Pennsylvania State University (1953) **Career:** Professor Emeritus of Architectural Engineering, Pennsylvania State University (1991-Present); Program Director, National Science Foundation, Washington, DC (1983-1988); Department Head of Architectural Engineering, Pennsylvania State University (1962-1983); Professor of Architectural Engineering, Pennsylvania State University, University Park, PA (1958-1991); Research Projects Director, United States Naval Civil Engineers Corps, Washington, DC (1956-1958) **Career Related:** Building Research Consultant, G. H. Albright Associates, State College, PA (1958-Present) **Civic:** Councilman, Triangle National Fraternity, Plainfield, IN (1982-1986); President, Pennsylvania State University Alumni Chapter, Triangle Fraternity (1965-1969); Chair, Building Code Appeals Board, Borough of State College, State College, PA (1965-1968) **Military Service:** Lieutenant Junior Grade, US Naval Reserve **Creative Works:** Author, "Planning Atomic Shelters: A Handbook"; Co-Author, "An Illustrated History of Tamaqua" **Membership:** Advisor, Construction Specification Institute (2004-2007); President, Pennsylvania State Retired Faculty Staff Club (2004-2005); Pennsylvania State Faculty Staff Club (1998-1999); American Society of Testing and Materials; American Concrete Institute; Earthquake Engineering Research Institute; American Society of Heating, Ventilation and Refrigeration Engineers; Associate, American Institute of Architects; Construction Industry Institute **Marquis Who's Who Honors:** Albert Nelson Marquis Lifetime Achievement Award (2017); Distinguished Humanitarian (2017) **Why did you become involved in your profession or industry:** Mr. Albright was inspired to pursue a career in architectural engineering by a shop teacher that he had in middle school named Pop Miller. He assigned Mr. Albright special assignments from a correspondence school in Scranton, Pennsylvania. **What do you consider to be the highlight of your career:** Mr. Albright is most proud of his time as a program director of the National Science Foundation in Washington, DC **Shipping Address:** 500 E Marylyn Ave Apt 407, State College, PA, 16801

Joseph William Albright

Title: Vice President for Schools/Facilities Technical Services **Industry:** Business Management/ Business Services **Company Name:** Sodexo **Date of Birth:** 02/03/1954 **Place of Birth:** Chillicothe **State:** OH **Parents:** Herman LeRoy Albright; Catherine Regina (Rieder) Albright **Marital Status:** Married **Spouse Name:** Iris J. Evans **Children:** Andrea Lyn; Jason Michael; James Darrell Evans; Marie Elizabeth Evans; Oksana Nelson; Beth Hood **Education:** MS in Industrial Engineering, University of Tennessee (2001); Master's Degree in Strategic Studies, U.S. Army War College (2000); BME, University of Dayton (1976); Postgraduate Coursework, University of Phoenix **Career:** Vice President for Schools/Facilities Technical Services, Sodexo (2012-Present); Founder, Performance-Based Solutions, Inc. (2008-2012); Managerial Consultant, Performance-Based Solutions, Inc. (2008-2012); Director, Situational Awareness, Office of Deputy Under Secretary of the Army for Business Transformation (2004-2009); Senior Logistician, Office of the Secretary of the Army, Washington, DC (2004-2005); Senior Logistics Analyst, Office of Deputy Under Secretary of the Army, Washington, DC (2002-2004); Industrial Operations Project Chief, Headquarters, U.S. Army (2000-2002); Office Deputy Chief Staff of Logistics, Headquarters, U.S. Army (2000-2002); Depot Maintenance Project Chief, Headquarters, U.S. Army (1998-1999); Deputy Support Operations Officer, Third Corps Support Command V, U.S. Army (1996-1998); Commander, Milan Army Ammunition Plant, Tennessee (1994-1996); Chief, Program Management Division (1993-1994); Technical Inspector, Division of Army Materiel Command, U.S. Army (1993-1994); Inspector General, Division of Army Material Command, U.S. Army (1990-1993); Technical Inspector, Division of Army Material Command (1990-1993); Commander, 96th Ordnance Co., U.S. Army (1988-1990); Assistant Executive Officer to Deputy Commanding General, Material Readiness Army Material Command, U.S. Army (1987-1988); Coordinator for Ammunition Logistics, U.S. Army (1985-1987); Material Officer, Third Ordnance Battalion, 59th Ordnance Brigade, U.S. Army (1982-1985); Research Engineer, Large Caliber Weapon System Laboratory (1980-1982); Chief, Integrated Logistic Support Office, Large Caliber Weapon System Laboratory (1980-1982); Operations Officer, Ninth Ordnance Co., U.S. Army, Germany (1979-1980); Accountable Officer, Ninth Ordnance Co., U.S. Army, Germany (1977-1979) **Career Related:** Vice President of Education Market Technical Services, Sodexo (2014-Present), Vice President, Technical Support Division, Sodexo (2012-2014); President, Managing Consultancy (2010-2011); Affiliate, Performance-Based Solutions, Inc. (2008-2010) **Military Service:** Civilian, U.S. Army (2004-2008); Colonel, Ordnance Branch, U.S. Army (1999-2004); Commissioned Second Lieutenant, Ordnance Branch, U.S. Army (1976) **Awards:** Distinguished Service Medal, Tennessee National Guard (1996); Distinguished Graduate, Ordnance Officer Advanced Course (1980); Distinguished Military Graduate (1976); Decorated Legion of Merit; Meritorious Service Medal; Army Commendation Medal; Army Achievement Medal **Membership:** Board of Leaders, Christian Athletes of West Tennessee (2010-Present); Chairman, Board of Directors, Organization of Hope (2010-Present); American National Standards Institute; National Fire Protection Association; American Society of Mechanical Engineers; Sons of the American Revolution; Life Member, U.S. Army Ordnance Corps Association; Pi Sigma Tau; Fellow, Christian Athletes of West Tennessee; Charter Member, Museum of the American Revolution; Charter Member, WWII Museum; Founding Member, Museum of the U.S. Army; Colonial Williamsburg Foundation; Ford's Theatre Foundation; U.S. Army War College **Marquis Who's Who Honors:** Albert Nelson Marquis Lifetime Achievement Award (2017) **Hobbies:** Reading; Gardening; Landscaping; Restoring antique furniture **Shipping Address:** 1070 Denney Dr, Milan, TN 38358

Gail Susan Alexander

Title: Psychiatrist **Industry:** Social Work **Marital Status:** Married **Spouse Name:** Joel Feiner (5/30/1992) **Children:** Deirdre McCormack, MD; Peter Alexander, MD; Margo Murray **Education:** MPH, School of Medicine, Yale University (1983); MD, New York University (1966); BA, Vassar College (1961) **Career:** Psychiatrist, Private Practice (2000-Present); Director, Training, Child Adolescent Psychiatry, University of Texas, Dallas, TX (1992-2000); Director, Outpatient, Child Adolescent Psychiatry, St. Luke's-Roosevelt Hospital, New York, NY (1991); Director, Health Service, State University of New York (1977-1987); Psychoanalyst, Dallas Psychoanalytical Center; Faculty, Dallas Psychoanalytical Center **Career Related:** Board of Examiners, American Board of Psychiatry and Neurology (1998); Education Committee, University of Texas Southwest Medical School, Dallas, TX (1992-2000); Clinical Professor, Psychiatry, University of Texas Southwest Medical Center, Dallas, TX; Fellow, American Psychiatric Association **Awards:** Best Doctors in Dallas, TX (2001-Present); Leading Doctors of the World **Membership:** Academy of Child and Adolescent Psychiatry **Marquis Who's Who Honors:** Albert Nelson Marquis Lifetime Achievement Award (2017) **Why did you become involved in your profession or industry:** Dr. Alexander was always interested in science, and became involved in medicine through this interest. She initially worked in internal medicine, and then became a psychiatrist after developing an interest in the interface between the body and the brain. **Hobbies:** Yoga; Reading; Hiking; Walking; Vegetable gardening; Her dog **Shipping Address:** 593 Prim Street, Ashland, OR, 97520

Gerald Lee Alexanderson

Title: Mathematician, Educator, Writer **Industry:** Education/Educational Services **Company Name:** Santa Clara University **Date of Birth:** 11/13/1933 **Place of Birth:** Caldwell **State:** ID **Parents:** Albert William Alexanderson; Alvina (Gertlar) Alexanderson **Education:** MS, Stanford University (1958); BA, University of Oregon (1955) **Career:** Leadership Board, College of Arts and Sciences, Santa Clara University (2010-2015); Vice Dean, College of Arts and Sciences, Santa Clara University (1990); Director, Department of Mathematics and Natural Sciences, Santa Clara University (1981-1990); Michael and Elizabeth Valeriote Professor, Santa Clara University (1979-2016); Professor, Santa Clara University (1972-1979); Associate Professor, Santa Clara University (1968-1972); Department Chairman, Santa Clara University (1967-2002); Coordinator, Honors Program, Santa Clara University (1965-1967); Assistant Professor, Santa Clara University (1962-1968); Instructor of Mathematics, Santa Clara University (1958-1962) **Career Related:** Associate Director, William Lowell Putnam Competition (1975-2017); Lecturer, Geneva (1964-1968); Lecturer, Stanford University (1958-1959) **Civic:** Chair, Board of Trustees, American Institute of Mathematics (1994-Present); Board of Directors, Stanford University Library Associates (1995-1998); Vice Chair, Board of Trustees, Santa Clara University (1984-1986); Trustee, Santa Clara University (1979-1986) **Creative Works:** Author, "G. H. Hardy Reader" (2016); Co-Author, "Fascinating Mathematical People" (2011); Co-Author, "Expeditions in Mathematics" (2011); Co-Author, "The Harmony of the World: 75 Years of Mathematics Magazine" (2007); Editor, Spectrum Book Series (2000-2016); Author, "The Random Walks of George Polya" (2000); Co-Author, "Lion Hunting and Other Mathematical Pursuits" (1995); Co-Author, "More Mathematical People" (1990); Co-Author, "Discrete and Combinatorial Mathematics" (1987); Co-Author, "The Polya Picture Album: Encounters of a Mathematician" (1987); Editor, Mathematics Magazine (1986-1990); Co-Author, "The Santa Clara Silver Anniversary Contest Book" (1985); Co-Author, "Mathematical People" (1985); Associate Editor, American Mathematical Monthly (1983-1986); Co-Author, "International Mathematical Congresses: An Illustrated History" (1983-1986); Associate Editor, Two-Year College Mathematics Journal (1979-1984); Co-Author, "First Undergraduate Course in Abstract Algebra" (1973); Co-Author, "Algebra Through Problem Solving" (1966); Editor, "The William Lowell Putnam Mathematical Competition, Problems and Solutions" (1965-1984); Author, "Algebra and Trigonometry" (1963); **Awards:** Haimo Award for Distinguished Teaching, Mathematical Association of America (2005); Yueh-gin Gung and Dr. Charles Y. Hu Award for Distinguished Service, Mathematical Association of America (2005); Distinguished Teaching Award, Mathematical Association of America (2004); Bayma Award for Scholarship, Santa Clara University (1996); Faculty Senate Professor, Santa Clara University (1990-1991); Meritorious Service Certificate, Northern California Section, Mathematical Association of America (1989); Alumni Achievement Award, University of Oregon (1989); **Membership:** Editorial Consultant Bulletin, American Mathematics Society (2006-Present); Chair, Carriage House Committee, Mathematical Association of America (2010-2013); Centennial Publications Committee, Mathematical Association of America (2009-2015); Chair, Secretary Search Committee, Mathematical Association of America (2008-2009); Chair, Euler Prize Committee, Mathematical Association of America (2005-2011); Chair, Development Committee, Mathematical Association of America (1999-2003); Chair, Washington Program Committee, Mathematical Association of America (1999-2000); Chair, Ad Hoc Building Committee, Phi Beta Kappa (1998-2000); Development Committee Chair, Phi Beta Kappa (1997-2002); Chair, Phi Beta Kappa (1997-2000); President, Mathematical Association of America (1997-1999); President-elect, Mathematical Association of America (1996-1997); Audit Committee, Phi Beta Kappa (1994-2000); Committee on Committees, Phi Beta Kappa (1994-2000); Trustee, Phi Beta Kappa Foundation, Phi Beta Kappa (1993-1996); Chair, Phi Beta Kappa (1993-1994); Committee on Publications, Phi Beta Kappa (1992-1994); Senator, Phi Beta Kappa (1991-2002); Committee on Associations, Phi Beta Kappa (1991-1997); Executive Committee, Mathematical Association of America (1990-2000); Secretary, Mathematical Association of America (1990-1996); Elected Fellow, Phi Beta Kappa (1989); Chair, 75th Anniversary Committee, Mathematical Association of America (1987-1990); Allendoerfer Prize Committee, Mathematical Association of America (1986-1990); Committee on Publications, Mathematical Association of America (1986-1990); **Hobbies:** Book collecting; Art collecting **Political Affiliations:** Democrat **Shipping Address:** 1133 Highland Avenue, Santa Clara, CA, 95050 **Website:** https://en.wikipedia.org/wiki/Gerald_L._Alexanderson

Lois Arlene Height Allen

Industry: Education/Educational Services **Date of Birth:** 09/02/1932 **Place of Birth:** Kenton **State:** OH **Parents:** Robert Harold Height; Frances (Sims) Height **Marital Status:** Married **Spouse Name:** James Pierpont Allen (6/14/1953) **Children:** Daniel Pierpont; Carole Elizabeth **Education:** MA, Ohio State University (1958); BS, Ohio State University (1954) **Career:** Private Music Teacher, Columbus, OH (1960-2014); Music Teacher, Ohio State University (1957-1959); High School Music Supervisor, Westerville, OH (1956-1957); High School Music Teacher, Junior and Senior, Upper Arlington High School, Columbus, OH (1954-1956) **Career Related:** Moderator, Mountview Baptist Church, Upper Arlington, OH (1996-1997); Executive Director, Battelle Scholars Program Trust Fund (1983-1986); Educational Radio Interviewer, WOSU (1972, 1971, 1970); Church Organist, Choir Director, Mountview Baptist Church, Upper Arlington, OH (1960-1977) **Civic:** President, Opera Columbus (2010-Present); Vice President, Opera Columbus (2008-Present); Publicity Director, Ohio Theatre Shop (1996-Present); Chairman, Education Committee, Opera Columbus Gala Committee (1991-Present); Member, Volunteer Council, American Symphony Orchestra League (1981-Present); Opera Columbus Gala Committee (2015); Committee Member, Columbus Symphony Gala Center (2015); Ambassador, Ohio State University School of Music (2013); Member, Staff Committee, Columbus Museum of Art Decorators Show House (2013); Board of Directors, President Ohio Theatre Shop (2008-2009); Organist, Glen Echo Presbyterian Church (2002-2004); Board of Trustees, Education Committee, Columbus Symphony (1992-2012); 1st Vice President, Member, Women's Board, Columbus Symphony (1992-2011); Board of Directors, President, Women's Board, Columbus Museum Art (1991-2015); Organist, Choir Master, The Church of St. Edwards (1990-1992); President, Volunteer Council, American Symphony Orchestra League (1987-1989); Member, Artistic Affairs Committee, American Symphony Orchestra League (1987-1989); President, Opera Columbus (1987-1988); Vice President, Women's Guild, Opera Columbus (1986-2015); Member, Executive Committee, American Symphony Orchestra League (1986-1988); Vice President, American Symphony Orchestra League (1983-1984); Trustee, Opera Columbus (1981-1985); Member, Mayor's Award Council Committee (1981-1984); Organist, Choir Director, North Congregational Church (1979-1985); President, Ohio State University Society of Friends of School Music (1977-1978); Trustee, Columbus Symphony Orchestra (1973-1981); General Chairman, Central Ohio Arts Festival (1972); Chairman, Fine and Applied Arts, Central Ohio Arts Festival (1971); Chairman, Juried Art Competition, Central Ohio Arts Festival (1970, 1969); Member, Sustaining Board, Maryhaven House for Alcoholic Women (1969-1973); Member, Project Hope, Central Ohio (1967-1973); Area Leader, Republican Party (1966-1968); Area Chairman, United Appeals of Franklin County (1966-1968); 1st Vice President, Member, Women's Board, Columbus Symphony (1965-1979) **Awards:** Music Educator Award, Columbus Symphony Orchestra (2005); Columbus Symphony Advocate Award (2002); Woman of Year, Rotary Club, Upper Arlington, OH (1995); Central Ohio Woman of Year, Kappa Delta (1970) **Membership:** Moderator, Mountview Baptist Church (1996-Present); Secretary, Ohio Organization of Orchestras (1979-1982); Treasurer, Ohio Organization of Orchestras (1976-1979); President, Ohio State University Alumnae of Franklin County Club (1971-1972, 1962-1964); Tau Beta Sigma; Delta Omicron; Kappa Delta; American Guild of Organists; Choristers Guild of America; Federation of American Baptist Musicians; Center for Science and Industry; Ohio State Historical Society; Rotary Club, Upper Arlington, OH; National Trust USA; Order of the Eastern Star; White Shrine of Jerusalem

Mary Margaret Allen Sochet, PhD

Title: Psychotherapist, Educator, Community Organizer **Industry:** Education/Educational Services **Company Name:** Human Resources Institute **Date of Birth:** 02/10/1938 **Place of Birth:** Plattsburgh **State:** NY **Parents:** Edwin Elisha Allen; Mary Elizabeth (Thomson) Allen **Marital Status:** Married **Spouse Name:** Marvin J. Sochet (1963) **Children:** Melorra Sochet; David Sochet **Education:** PhD in Human Development, New York University (1963); MA in Human Relations, New York University (1961); BS in Childhood Education, State University of New York at Plattsburgh (1958) **Certifications:** Diplomate, Institute for Practicing Psychotherapy **Career:** Staff Consultant, Human Resources Institute (1966-Present); Private Practice, Psychotherapy, New York, NY (1966-1982); Psychotherapist, Contemporary Guidance Services, Inc., New York, NY (1966-1978); Program Director, Newark Preschool Council (1965-1966); Acting Executive Director, Newark Preschool Council (1965-1966); Early Childhood Education Professor, Brooklyn College (1964-1971); Child Development and Psychology Professor, Brooklyn College (1964-1971); Teacher, New York City Public Schools (1962-1964); Kindergarten Teacher, Long Island Public Schools (1958-1962); Co-Chair, International NGO, "Perhaps Kids Meeting Kids Can Make a Difference"; Founding Member, Children's Free School Community Loft Neighbor's Network; Teacher, Professor, Program Director, Newark Pre-School Council; First Year Round Head Start Consultant, Human Resources Institute; Co-Developer, With Robert F. Allen, "Toward A Caring Community, A New Jersey Community Mental Health Program" **Career Related:** Writer in Field; Lecturer in Field; Educational Consultant in Field; Editorial Consultant in Field; Activist, Civil Rights, Human Rights, Peace Making, Community Organizing; Educator, Human Development, Social Relations, Psychotherapy; Consultative Status, United Nations **Civic:** Co-Chairman, Kids Meeting Kids (1983-Present); Founding Member, Neighbor's Network (1979-Present); Founding Member, Community Loft (1971-1974); Organizing Member, Children's Free School (1969-1981) **Creative Works:** Author, "Time Out, A Book of Poems and a Collection of Short Stories," Two Harbors Press (2012); Co-Author, "Toward a Caring Community" (1980); Contributor, Articles to Various Journals on Education, Social Class, Community Organization, Peace, School Integration, Children's Rights and Mental Health, Various Journals **Awards:** Honoree, Distinguished Worldwide Humanitarian Award (2017); Recipient, Founder's Day Award, New York University (1963); Recipient, Founder's Day Award, New York University (1963); Fellow, National Conference of Christian and Jews (Now National Conference for Community and Justice) (1961) **Membership:** American Psychological Association; Society for the Psychological Study of Social Issues; Psychologists for Social Responsibility; Educators for Social Responsibility; Fellow, National Conference of Christians and Jews; NGO Committee on UNICEF **Marquis Who's Who Honors:** Albert Nelson Marquis Lifetime Achievement Award (2017); Distinguished Humanitarian (2017) **What do you consider to be the highlight of your career:** The highlight of Dr. Sochet's career was working in Newark, New Jersey, during the early days of the Head Start Program. As part of this program, she worked closely with parents and families. Dr. Sochet also served as an organizing member of the Children's Free School and her work in this regard was later adapted in the book "Sharing Our Children." With colleagues, she developed a program, Project Smile, at Brooklyn College, where students became active agents of positive community change. With her family, Dr. Sochet developed "Kids Mentoring Kids Can Make a Difference," an international peace and children's rights organization. **Political Affiliations:** Democrat **Shipping Address:** 380 Riverside Dr Apt 8H, New York, NY, 10025

Chester Allan Alper

Title: Pediatrician, Educator **Industry:** Education/Educational Services **Company Name:** Boston Children's Hospital **Date of Birth:** 05/21/1931 **Place of Birth:** Brooklyn **State:** NY **Parents:** Jacob Julian Alper; Emma Ruth Alper **Marital Status:** Married **Spouse Name:** Natalie Carole Katz (9/3/1961) **Children:** Jonathan David **Education:** Research Fellow, Peter Bent Brigham Hospital, Boston, MA (1962-1964); Postdoctoral Research Fellow, Malmo Allmanna Sjukhus, Sweden (1960-1962); Assistant Resident, Harvard Service, Boston City Hospital, Boston, MA (1959-1960); Intern, Harvard Service, Boston City Hospital (1956-1957); MD, Harvard University, Cum Laude, Boston, MA (1956); AB, Harvard Medical School, Harvard University, Summa Cum Laude, Cambridge, MA (1952) **Certifications:** Diplomate, American Board of Internal Medicine (1964) **Career:** Professor of Pediatrics, Harvard Medical School, Harvard University (1975-Present); Vice President, CBR Institute of Biomedical Research, Immune Disease Institute, Inc., Boston, MA (1993-2009); Scientic Director, Center for Blood Research, Immune Disease Institute, Inc., Boston, MA (1972-1993); Member, Adjunct Faculty, The Rockefeller University, New York, NY (1989-1990); Associate Professor of Pediatrics, Harvard Medical School, Harvard University (1969-1975); Scientific Director, Blood Grouping Laboratory, Boston, MA (1971-1972); Scientific Director, Blood Research Institute, Boston, MA (1971-1972); Research Associate in Medicine, Children's Hospital, Boston, MA (1964-1970); Research Associate in Medicine, Harvard Medical School, Harvard University (1964-1969) **Career Related:** Scientific Director, Center for Blood Research (1971-1993) **Military Service:** Lieutenant, Naval Air Station, U.S. Naval Reserve, Brunswick, ME (1957-1959) **Creative Works:** Editorial Board Member, "Journal of Clinical Immunology" (1999-Present); Editorial Board Member, "Experimental and Clinical Immunogenetics," Basel, Switzerland (1992-2002); Editorial Board Member, "Tissue Antigens" (1990-2002); Editorial Board Member, "Immunogenetics" (1989-1997); Editorial Board Member, "Complement" (1982-1988); Editorial Board Member, "Journal of Immunology" (1977-1981); Editorial Board Member, "Clinical Immunology and Immunopatholgy" (1976-1996) **Awards:** Merit Award, National Institute of Allergy and Infectious Diseases, National Institutes of Health (1990-2000); Fellowship, John Simon Guggenheim Memorial Foundation (1989-1990); Detur Prize, Harvard University (1952) **Membership:** Henry Kunkel Society; The American Association of Immunologists, Inc.; Association of American Physicians; The American Society of Clinical Investigation; American Federation of Clinical Research **Marquis Who's Who Honors:** Albert Nelson Marquis Lifetime Achievement Award (2017); Distinguished Humanitarian (2017) **What do you consider to be the highlight of your career:** A highlight of Dr. Alper's career has been working on a model for type-I diabetes. After more than 55 years in the field, he believes that he is now doing his most important work yet. **Hobbies:** Music; Calligraphy; Cartooning **Political Affiliations:** Liberal **Business Address:** 25 Shattuck St, 25 Shattuck St, MA, Boston, 02115 **Shipping Address:** 161 Sewall Ave, Brookline, MA, 02446

Harvey Alpern

Title: Cardiologist **Industry:** Medicine & Health Care **Company Name:** Harvey L. Alpern Consulting **Date of Birth:** 06/01/1938 **Place of Birth:** Los Angeles **State:** CA **Parents:** Sander A. Alpern; Rose K. Alpern **Marital Status:** Divorced **Children:** David **Education:** Cardiology Fellow, St. Georges Hospital, London (1968-1969); Resident, Cardiology, Cedars-Sinai Medical Center, Los Angeles, CA (1967-1968); Resident, Internal Medicine, Cedars-Sinai Medical Center, Los Angeles, CA (1965-1967); Intern, Cedars of Lebanon Hospital, Los Angeles, CA (1964-1965); MD, University of Southern California (1964); BA, Pomona College (1960) **Certifications:** Diplomate, American Board of Internal Medicine; Diplomate, American Board of Cardiovascular Disease **Career:** Disability Medicine, Harvey L. Alpern Consulting, Inc. (2006-Present); Private Practice, Santa Monica, CA (1970-2007) **Career Related:** Medical Director, Executive Fit Health, San Francisco, CA (1985-1993); Board of Directors, Century City Hospital, Los Angeles, CA **Civic:** Active, Los Angeles-Guangzhou Sister City Association (1994-Present); Board of Directors, Los Angeles Business Council (1987-1996); Board of Directors, National Health Foundation, Los Angeles, CA (1985-1995) **Military Service:** Captain, U.S. Air Force Reserve (1965-1970) **Creative Works:** Contributor, Articles, Professional Journals **Membership:** Board of Directors, Los Angeles Chapter, American Heart Association, Inc. (1974-1975); Board of Directors, New West Symphony; Council on Clinical Cardiology, American Heart Association, Inc.; American College of Physicians; Board of Directors, California Society Industrial Medicine; Board of Directors, President, American Academy of Disability Evaluation Physicians; Fellow, American College of Cardiology; Fellow, American Heart Association, Inc.; Fellow, American Academy of Disability Evaluation Physicians **Marquis Who's Who Honors:** Albert Nelson Marquis Lifetime Achievement Award (2017); Distinguished Humanitarian (2017) **Hobbies:** Wine tasting **Religion:** Jewish **Shipping Address:** 1223 Wilshire Blvd PMB 756, Santa Monica, CA, 90403

Eleanor Breitel Alter

Title: Principal Attorney **Industry:** Law and Legal Services **Company Name:** Alter, Wolff & Foley LLP **Date of Birth:** 11/10/1938 **Place of Birth:** New York **State:** NY **Parents:** Charles David Breitel; Jeanne (Hollander) Breitel **Marital Status:** Married **Spouse Name:** Dr. Allan M. Lans **Children:** Richard B. Zabel; David B. Zabel **Education:** LLB, Columbia Law School, Columbia University (1964); Postgraduate Coursework, Harvard Law School, Harvard University (1960-1961); Honorary BA, University of Michigan (1960) **Career:** Partner, Alter, Wolff & Foley LLP (2016-Present); Partner, Kasowitz, Benson, Torres & Friedman, New York, NY (1997-2016); Partner, Rosenman & Colin LLP (1982-1997); Partner, Marshall, Bratter, Greene, Allison & Tucker (1974-1982); Associate, Marshall, Bratter, Greene, Allison & Tucker (1968-1974); Associate, Miller & Carlson (1966-1968); Attorney, Office of the General Counsel, Department of Insurance Department, State of New York (1964-1966) **Career Related:** Visiting Professor of Law, University of Chicago (1993); Visiting Professor of Law, University of Chicago (1990-1991); Ulysses S. Schwartz Fellow, School of Law, University of Chicago (1988); Adjunct Professor of Law, School of Law, New York University (1983-1987); Lecturer in Field **Civic:** Chairman of the Board, New York State Lawyers Fund for Client Protection (1985-2010); Board of Visitors, School of Law, University of Chicago (1984-1987); Trustee, Board Member, New York State Lawyers Fund for Client Protection (1983-2013) **Creative Works:** Featured, "Forbes Magazine" (2017); Board of Editors, New York Law Journal (1987-2015) **Membership:** Matrimonial Law Committee, Association of the Bar of the City of New York (2002-2005); Judiciary Committee, Association of the Bar of the City of New York (1996); Judiciary Committee, Association of the Bar of the City of New York (1994-1995); Chair, Nominating Committee, Association of the Bar of the City of New York (1994); Executive Committee, Association of the Bar of the City of New York (1991-1993); American Law Institute; Association of the Bar of the City of New York; Family Law Section, New York State Bar Association; American College of Family Trial Lawyers; American Academy of Matrimonial Lawyers; International Academy of Matrimonial Lawyers; American Council on the Teaching of Foreign Language **Bar Admissions:** State of New York (1965) **Business Address:** 810 7th Avenue, Suite 3600, New York, NY, 10019

Sylvester Chukwuemeka Amamilo

Title: Orthopedist, Consultant **Industry:** Medicine & Health Care **Date of Birth:** 10/20/1942 **Place of Birth:** Enugwu Ukwu, Ogbunike **Country of Origin:** Anambra/Nigeria **Parents:** Jeremiah Madueke Amamilo; Veronica Onuekwusie Amamilo (Nee Ndibe) **Marital Status:** Married **Spouse Name:** Ngozi I. Anerobi (4/16/1952) **Children:** Emeka; Chukwunonso (Deceased); Ikechukwu; Ifeatu **Education:** Master of Surgery in Orthopedic Surgery, University of Liverpool (1982); Bachelor of Medicine, Bachelor of Surgery in Medicine, University of Ibadan (1974); BSc in Zoology, University of Nigeria, with Honors (1966) **Certifications:** Certificate, College of the Immaculate Conception, Enugu, Nigeria (1960) **Career:** Consultant, Orthopedic Surgeon, London, England (1993-Present); Consultant, Orthopedic Surgeon, National Health Service (1993-2008); Senior Lecturer, University of Nigeria Medical School, Enugu, Nigeria (1985-1993); Consultant, University of Nigeria Medical School (Now Faculty of Medical Sciences), Enugu, Nigeria (1985-1993) **Creative Works:** Author, "The Role of Periosteum in Growth Plate Failure," Clinical Orthopedics and Related Research (1982); Contributor, Articles, Professional Journals **Awards:** Professional Excellence Award, Urunnebo (Obu Ozom) Community, Enugwu Ukwu (2016); Conferment of Chieftaincy Title and Membership of Enugwu Ukwu Traditional Cabinet, Enugwu Ukwu Community (2014); Best Science Graduate of the Year, University of Nigeria (1966); Dean of the Faculty of Science Prize, University of Nigeria; Certificate of Merit, University of Nigeria **Membership:** Girdlestone Orthopaedic Society, Oxford; Fellow, The Royal College of Surgeons of England; Fellow, Royal Society of Medicine; Fellow, British Orthopaedic Association; Fellow, International College of Surgeons, Chicago, IL **Marquis Who's Who Honors:** Albert Nelson Marquis Lifetime Achievement Award (2017) **To what do you attribute your success:** He attributes his success to obedience, motivation and devotion. **Why did you become involved in your profession or industry:** He became involved in his wish to become a doctor since he was five years old. He was advanced and molded by his peers. **What do you consider to be the highlight of your career:** The highlight of his career was his appointment as a Consultant Orthopaedic Surgeon which enabled him to be a Fellow of the British Orthopaedic Association, as well as receiving recognition and inclusion in Who's Who in the World Publications by Marquis Who's Who. **Where will you be in five years:** In five years, he will still be practicing Orthopaedics. **Hobbies:** Tennis; Chess; Guitar **Religion:** Christian **Business Address:** 1 Beaumont Square, London, United Kingdom, E1 4NL **Shipping Address:** Sunset House, 15A Sunset Ave, Woodford Green Essex, United Kingdom, IG8 0TH

Kent Tucker Andersen

Title: Investment Company Executive **Industry:** Financial Services **Company Name:** Above All Advisors **Date of Birth:** 06/05/1942 **Place of Birth:** Manchester **State:** CT **Parents:** Alfred Hans Andersen; Dorothy Emily (Ray) Andersen **Marital Status:** Married **Spouse Name:** Karen Ann Kirchofer (10/11/1963) **Children:** Heather Michele; Kristen Eileen **Education:** BA, Wesleyan University (1963); Coursework, Phillips Exeter Academy, Exeter, NH (1959) **Certifications:** Chartered Financial Analyst **Career:** Founder, Above All Advisors (2000-Present); Chief Investment Strategist, Cumberland Associates LLC, New York, NY (1997-1999); Managing Partner, Cumberland Associates LLC, New York, NY (1982-1996); Partner, Cumberland Associates LLC, New York, NY (1972-1999); Partner, Rudman Associates, New York, NY (1969-1972); Security Analyst, Smith Barney and Co., New York, NY (1968-1969); Actuarial Student, The Travelers Indemnity Company, Hartford, CT (1963-1966) **Career Related:** Wesleyan Investment Committee (2009-Present); Advisory Board, Value Investment Partners (2008-Present); Trustee, Wesleyan University (2009-2015) **Civic:** Chairman, Artificial Cell Technology (2006-Present); Director, Questech Corporation (2005-Present); Executive Committee, ifree (2005-Present); Trustee, Warren Congregational Church, Connecticut (2005-Present); Board of Directors, ifree (2001-Present); Board of Directors, GOPAC (1995-Present); Executive Committee, GOPAC (1993-Present); Executive Committee, Cato Institute, Washington, DC (1992-Present); Chairman, Investment Committee, Phillips Exeter Academy (1989-Present); Board of Directors, Cato Institute, Washington, DC (1987-Present); Board Vice President, Chairman, Executive Committee, Phillips Exeter Academy (1993-1999); Chairman, Phillips Exeter Academy (1992-1999); Trustee, Phillips Exeter Academy (1989-1999); Trustee, Martin Luther King Scholarship Fund Montclair (1989-1994); Admissions Representative, New Jersey Area (1983-1993); Trustee, YMCA of Montclair, North Essex, NJ (1980-1996); Trustee, First United Methodist Church of Montclair (1976-1994) **Military Service:** U.S. Public Health Service (1966-1968) **Awards:** Founder's Day Award, Phillips Exeter Academy (2007); Distinguished Alumnus Award, Wesleyan University (1988) **Membership:** Executive Committee, Club for Growth (1984-1994); President, Kappa Nu Kappa (1963); Society of Actuaries; New York Society Security Analysts; Institute of Chartered Financial Analysts **Marquis Who's Who Honors:** Albert Nelson Marquis Lifetime Achievement Award (2017) **Hobbies:** Running marathons **Political Affiliations:** Republican **Shipping Address:** 369 Lexington Ave Ste 305, Above All Advisors LLC, New York, NY, 10017

Allamay E. Anderson

Title: Healthcare Educator **Industry:** Education/Educational Services **Date of Birth:** 07/18/1933 **Place of Birth:** New York **State:** NY **Parents:** John Samuel Richardson; Charlotte Jane (Harrigan) Richardson **Marital Status:** Married **Spouse Name:** Diane Kay Swartz (7/19/2003); Edgar Leopold Anderson (4/14/1957, Divorced 4/14/1963) **Children:** David Lancelot **Education:** MEd, Fordham University (1984); BA, Queens College, The City University of New York (1975) **Certifications:** Certified in Professional Management, Adelphi University (1978) **Career:** Professional Development Consultant, New York, NY (1978-Present); Executive Board, School of Education Alumni Association, Fordham University (1997-2006); Retired, Manhattan High School (1995); Coordinator, AIDS Resource, Manhattan High School (1995); Special Education Teacher, Manhattan High School, New York, NY (1989-1995); Teacher, Home and Career Skills, Louis Armstrong Middle School (1988); Owner, AEA Development Service (1987-1997); Adjunct Lecturer, Home Economics, Queens College, The City University of New York (1987); Partner, Masiba Building Corp., Corona, NY (1975-1982); Staff, School Food Service Dietitian, Board of Education, New York, NY (1968-1988); Executive Board, NAACP **Career Related:** Elementary School Literary and Math Tutor, Kalamazoo Public Schools (2014-Present); Leadership Member, Western Michigan University Life Long Learning Academy Center of Gerontology (2011-Present); Board of Directors, Ecume Senior Center (2012) **Civic:** Bridges Chair, Srs. Dorie Miller (2003-2006); Assistant Presiding Partner, Dynamic Investors Club (1996-2007); Vestry Member, Grace Episcopal Church (1996-1999); Long Island Episcopal Cursillo (1991); Kwanzaa Advisory Committee Urban Coalition, Puerto Rico (1983); Vestry Member, Youth Ministries, Grace Episcopal Church (1982-1985); Officer, New York City Community Development Agency (1980-1983); School Coordinator, League For Better Community Life, Inc. (1977); Treasurer, Executive Board, League For Better Community Life, Inc. (1970-1976) **Awards:** Mothers Hope Award (2011); Clergy Award, Fordham University School of Education (2006); Appreciation Award, Langston Hughes Library Action Committee (2006); Salutatorian, Institute Senior Action (2005); Concourse Village Branch Positive Image Award, Key Women of America, Inc. (2005); Award, National Association Investment Clubs (2004); Community Service Award, New York State United Teachers (2001); Alumni Achievement Award, Fordham University School of Education (2000); Professional Award, Negro Business and Professional Women's Clubs (1998); Clergy Award, Fordham University School of Education (1996); Elmcor Community Service Award, Elmcor Youth & Adult Activities, Inc. (1989) **Membership:** Silver Life Member, NAACP (2007); Health Chair, NAACP (2003-2013); Women's History Month Honoree, NAACP (1996); Kwanzaa Chair, Langston Hughes Library Action Committee (1994-1997); Treasurer, Langston Hughes Library Action Committee (1989); Chairman Bylaws Committee, Home Economics Alumni Association, Queens College, The City University of New York (1982); Retired Teachers Chapter, United Federation Teachers; Vice President, Home Economics Alumni Association, Queens College, The City University of New York; National Association Investment Clubs; Greater New York Chapter, Association of Fundraising Professionals; Lifetime Member, Joint Public Affairs Committee, Older Adults; Negro Business and Professional Women's Clubs **Shipping Address:** 2077 Quail Cove Drive, Kalamazoo, MI, 49009

Frank Gist Anderson Jr.

Title: Professor of Humanities in Medicine (Retired) **Industry:** Education/Educational Services **Company Name:** Texas A&M University **Date of Birth:** 08/17/1928 **Place of Birth:** College Station **State:** TX **Parents:** Frank Gist Anderson; Helen Arnett Salyer **Marital Status:** Married **Spouse Name:** Jane Nugent Hafner (2003-Present); Velma Cartwright Gilmore (1953-2002) **Children:** Edith Anderson Wakefield; Frank Gist III **Education:** Resident, Mayo Foundation for Medical Education and Research, Rochester, MN (1958-1961); Intern, The University of Kansas Medical Center, Kansas City, KS (1954-1955); MD, The University of Texas Medical Branch at Galveston (1954); BS, Texas A&M University, College Station, TX (1950) **Certifications:** Certified, American Board of Ophthalmology (1971-Present) **Career:** Professor of Humanities in Medicine, Texas A&M University, College Station, TX (1996-2001); Clinical Professor of Ophthalmology, Texas A&M University, College Station, TX (1981-2001); Private Practice, Bryan, TX (1964-1993); Ophthalmologist, Kelsey-Seybold Clinic, Houston, TX (1961-1964) **Career Related:** Chief of Surgery, CHI St. Joseph Health, Bryan, TX (1988); President, Medical Staff, Humana Hospital (now College Station Medical Center), Bryan-College Station, TX (1983-1984); Visiting Ophthalmologist, King Khaled Eye Specialist Hospital, Riyadh, Saudi Arabia (1983); Chief of Surgery, Humana Hospital, Bryan-College Station, TX (1982-1983); Chief of Surgery, Humana Hospital, Bryan-College Station, TX (1978-1979); President, Medical Staff, CHI St. Joseph Health, Bryan, TX (1974); Chief of Surgery, CHI St. Joseph Health, Bryan, TX (1968) **Civic:** Chancellor's Council, Texas A&M University, College Station, TX (1996-2003); Delegate, Republican Party of the Texas State Convention, Fort Worth, TX (1990); President, Friends of the Medical Sciences Library, Texas A&M University, College Station, TX (1987-1988); A&M Legacy Society, Texas A&M University, College Station, TX **Military Service:** Captain, U.S. Army Medical Corps (1955-1957) **Creative Works:** Author, "The History of Medicine in Brazos County" (2001); Contributor, Articles, Professional Journals **Awards:** Honorary Member, Texas Medical Association (1994) **Membership:** Ophthalmology Delegate, House of Delegates, Texas Medical Association (1989); President, Brazos-Robertson County Medical Society (1978); Fellow, American College of Surgeons; Fellow, American Academy of Ophthalmology; Fellow, Texas Society of Ophthalmology and Otolaryngology; American Medical Association; Texas Longhorn Breeders Association of America; Diplomate, American Board of Ophthalmology; Former Member, Board of Directors, The Brazos Valley Symphony Orchestra; Former Member, Board of Directors, Opera and Performing Arts Society, Texas A&M University **Marquis Who's Who Honors:** Albert Nelson Marquis Lifetime Achievement Award (2017) **Why did you become involved in your profession or industry:** Dr. Anderson has wanted to be a physician since he was 16 years old, and some contacts from the military pointed him toward ophthalmology. **What do you consider to be the highlight of your career:** The highlight of Dr. Anderson's career was making the mid-career transition into new ultrasound cataract surgery methodologies that utilize inter-ocular lenses. **Hobbies:** Collecting U.S. commemorative stamps and U.S. gold and silver coins **Religion:** Presbyterian **Shipping Address:** 828 S Rosemary Dr, Bryan, TX, 77802

Jeffrey L. Anderson

Title: Distinguished Research Physician **Industry:** Medicine & Health Care **Company Name:** Intermountain Healthcare **Date of Birth:** 10/27/1944 **Place of Birth:** Salt Lake City **State:** UT **Parents:** Aldon Anderson, Jr.; Virginia (Weilenmann) Anderson **Marital Status:** Married **Spouse Name:** Kathleen Tadje (8/18/1967) **Children:** Russell; Nathan; Derek; Megan **Education:** Postdoctoral Fellow in Cardiology, School of Medicine, Stanford University (1976-1978); Resident, Internal Medicine, Massachusetts General Hospital, The General Hospital Corporation (1972-1974); MD, Harvard Medical School, Harvard University, Cum Laude (1972); BA in Chemistry, The University of Utah, Magna Cum Laude (1968) **Certifications:** Diplomate in Cardiac Electrophysiology, American Board of Internal Medicine (2002, 1992); Diplomate in Cardiovascular Subspecialty, American Board of Internal Medicine (1979); Diplomate, American Board of Internal Medicine (1975); Licensed to Practice Medicine, State of Utah (1973) **Career:** Distinguished Research Physician, Intermountain Heart Institute, Intermountain Medical Center, Intermountain Healthcare (2017-Present); Associate Chief, Cardiology, Intermountain Medical Center, Intermountain Healthcare (2007-Present); Co-Director, Cardiovascular Medicine, Intermountain Medical Center, Intermountain Healthcare (2007-Present); Professor, Internal Medicine, School of Medicine, The University of Utah (1989-Present); Vice-Chair, Research, Department of Internal Medicine, Intermountain Medical Center, Intermountain Healthcare (2008-2015); Co-Director, Cardiovascular Research, Intermountain Medical Center, Intermountain Healthcare (2007-2010); Associate Chief, Cardiology, LDS Hospital, Intermountain Healthcare (2002-2007); Co-Director, Cardiac Research, Intermountain Healthcare (2002-2007); Chief, Division of Cardiology, School of Medicine, The University of Utah (1984-2001); Executive Director, Cardiovascular Clinical Research, Merck Research Laboratories, Merck Sharp & Dohme Corp. (1998-1999); Staff Physician, LDS Hospital, Intermountain Healthcare (1980-1998); Associate Professor, Internal Medicine, School of Medicine, The University of Utah (1982-1989); Director, Coronary Care Unit, LDS Hospital, Intermountain Healthcare (1980-1989); Assistant Professor, Internal Medicine, School of Medicine, The University of Utah (1980-1982); Assistant Professor, Internal Medicine, Cardiology Division, Michigan Medicine, University of Michigan (1978-1980); Staff Physician, Michigan Medicine, University of Michigan (1978-1980); Staff Associate, Laboratory of Molecular and Cellular Biology, National Institutes of Health (1974-1976) **Creative Works:** Editorial Board Member, Cardiosource Clinical Trials, American College of Cardiology (2003-Present); Editorial Board Member, Journal of Thrombosis and Thrombolysis (1996-Present); Editorial Board Member, Evidence-Based Cardiovascular Medicine (1996-Present); Editorial Board Member, BioMedical International Journal (2013-2014); Associate Editor, Journal of Heart Failure, American College of Cardiology (2012-2016); Editorial Board Member, "Current Treatment Options in Cardioavascular Medicine" (2012); Head of Faculty, Cardiovascular Disorders Field, Faculty of 1000 (2009-2015); Editorial Board Member, Asian-Pacific Journal of General Practice (2009); Editorial Board Member, Open General/Internal Medicine Journal (2007); Editor-in-Chief, "Current Cardiology Reviews" (2005-2007); Associate Editor, MyAmericanHeart Website for Clinical Updates, American Heart Association, Inc. (2005) **Awards:** Legacy of Life Award, Intermountain Research and Education Foundation, Intermountain Healthcare (2015); Emeritus Alumni Merit of Honor Award, University of Utah (2014); Honoree, Highly Cited Researcher, Thomson Reuters (2014); Physician Volunteer of the Year Award, Western States Affiliate, American Heart Association, Inc. (2013); Honoree, Top One Percent of United States Cardiologists, U.S. News and World Report (2012); Honoree, Best Doctors in America (2005-2009); Gold Caduceus Award, Deseret Foundation, Intermountain Healthcare (2006); Heart of Gold Award, Utah Chapter, American Heart Association, Inc. (2004); Honoree, Elite Reviewer, American College of Cardiology (2004); Honoree, Christi U. Smith Endowed Chair in Cardiology Research (2000-2002); Laureate Award, Utah Chapter, American College of Physicians (2000); Honoree, Honorary Professor of Medicine, Xi'An Medical University (1997); Honoree, The Best Heart Doctors in America, Good Housekeeping (1996); Researcher of the Year Award, LDS Hospital, Intermountain Healthcare (1995) **Membership:** Clinical Policy Approval Committee, American College of Cardiology (2016-Present); Orchestra at Temple Square (2003-Present); Association of University Cardiologists (1996-Present); Lifetime Honorary Member, Board of Directors, Utah Affiliate, American Heart Association, Inc. (1994-Present); Heart Rhythm Society (1992-Present) **Marquis Who's Who Honors:** Albert Nelson Marquis Lifetime Achievement Award (2017) **Religion:** Latter Day Saints Church **Business Address:** 5121 S Cottonwood St, UT, Murray, 84107 **Shipping Address:** 2708 E Sherwood Dr, Salt Lake City, UT, 84108

Daniel Christopher Andreae

Title: Award Winning Health Educator, Distinguished Community Leader Industry: Education/Educational Services Company Name: University of Waterloo / University of Guelph Humber **Education:** Honorary LLD, Assumption University; Doctorate in Adult Education, University of Toronto; Master of Social Work, Clinical Specialization, Wilfrid Laurier University; Bachelor of Arts in Psychology, York University, with Honors; Coursework, The Centre for Mind Body Medicine, Washington, DC; Coursework, The Behavioral Medicine and Training Institute, Saybrook University; Coursework, Stress Management, Pain Management, Eating Disorders, Cardiac Care, The Benson Henry Mind Body Institute; Diplomas in Stress Management, Nutrition and Autism Awareness, Stonebridge Colleges, Cornwall, England; Food as Medicine Training, The Center for Mind Body Medicine, Washington, DC Certifications: Certified in Clinical and Applied Psychophysiology **Career:** Professor, University of Guelph-Humber; Adjunct Associate Professor, Rension University **Career Related:** Benson Henry Mind Body Institute Affiliated with Massachusetts General Hospital **Awards:** Member, President's Circle, Weizmann Institute of Science (2017); Honoree, Neuroscience Laboratory Dedication, Weizmann Institute of Science (2017); Honoree, Professional of the Year, Covington Who's Who Executive and Professional Registry (2015); Honoree, "Tier of Excellence" Lifetime Accomplishment, Oxford Who's Who (2015); Honoree, Leading Man, Weizmann Institute of Science (2014); Lyall Hallman Social Work Award (2008); Honoree, Canadian Social Worker of the Year (2006); Honoree, Ontario Social Worker of the Year (1999); Honoree, Alumnus of the Year, Wilfrid Laurier University (2001); Award of Merit, the Brain Injury Association of Canada; Champion of Change Award, Chair of the International Body Princess Yasmin Khan; Outstanding Service Award for Leadership, Alzheimer Society of Toronto; Ontario Medal of Citizenship, Lieutenant Governor of Ontario; Recipient, Inaugural June Callwood Outstanding Volunteer Award, Premier of the Province of Ontario; Queen Elizabeth Jubilee Medal; Canada 125 Medal; Governor General's Caring Canadian Award; Distinguished Teaching Award, University of Waterloo; Two Faculty of the Year Awards, University of Guelph-Humber; Faculty Mentoring Award; Inaugural Impact Award from Laurentian University. Membership: Honorary Patron, Brain Injury Canada; Former Chair, Patrons Council, Alzheimer Society; Chair, Advisory Council, National Eating Disorder Center of Toronto General Hospital; Special Advisor, Weizmann Canada; Health Advisor, Psychology Foundation of Canada Education; Governing Board, The Michener Institute University Health Network, Toronto, Canada Marquis Who's Who Honors: Albert Nelson Marquis Lifetime Achievement Award (2017); Distinguished Humanitarian (2017) **Why did you become involved in your profession or industry:** Dr. Andreae became involved in his profession because he has a passion for education and a dedication to lifelong learning. He believes that "education is not just an intellectual exercise, it is most effective when the head meets the heart and knowledge can be applied to enhance the quality of one's life on all levels; emotional, physical, spiritual and social." **What do you consider to be the highlight of your career:** The highlights of his career are mentoring and teaching students, as well as becoming the First Executive Director of the Alzheimer Society of Toronto. **Hobbies:** Travel; Reading: history, psychology, science and health; Baseball; Collecting important rare signatures **Shipping Address:** 1902-30 Wellington St E, Toronto, ON, Canada, M5E 1S3

John F. Andrews

Title: President **Industry:** Other **Company Name:** The Shakespeare Guild **Date of Birth:** 11/02/1942 **Place of Birth:** Carlsbad **State:** NM **Parents:** Frank Randolph Andrews; Mary Lucille (Wimberley) Andrews **Marital Status:** Married **Spouse Name:** Janet Ann Denton (10/15/1994); Vicky Roberta Anderson (8/20/1966, Divorced 1983) **Children:** Eric John; Lisa Gail **Education:** PhD, Vanderbilt University (1971); MA in Teaching, Harvard University (1966); AB, Princeton University (1965) **Career:** Advisory Council Member, The English-Speaking Union (2007-Present); President, The Shakespeare Guild (1992-Present); Executive Director, Washington Branch, The English-Speaking Union (2001-2007); Editor, The Everyman Shakespeare (1993-2000); Editor, The Guild Shakespeare (1988-1992); Deputy Director, Division of Education Programs, National Endowment for the Humanities (1984-1988); Executive Editor, Folger Books, Folger Shakespeare Library (1974-1984); Chairman, Folger Institute, Folger Shakespeare Library (1974-1984); Director of Academic Programs, Folger Shakespeare Library (1974-1984); Director of Graduate Studies in English, Florida State University (1973-1974); Assistant Professor of English, Florida State University (1970-1974); Instructor of English, University of Tennessee, Nashville (Now Tennessee State University) (1969-1970) **Career Related:** Founder, Gielgud Award for Excellence in the Dramatic Arts, The Shakespeare Guild (1994); Chairman, National Advisory Panel for The Shakespeare Plays (1979-1985); Publications Editor, Shakespeare: The Globe and the World Touring Exhibition (1978-1981); Board, Humanities Council, Washington, DC; Center for Political and Strategic Studies; Center for Renaissance and Baroque Studies, University of Maryland; New Mexico Humanities Council, KSFR-FM; Administrator, Program Grants, National Endowment for the Humanities, Andrew W. Mellon Foundation, Exxon Mobil Corporation, Metropolitan Life Insurance Company, Surdna Foundation; Consultant, Time-Life TV; Consultant, WNET/Thirteen Corporation for Public Broadcasting, Public Broadcasting Service; **Creative Works:** Editor-in-Chief, "Shakespeare's World and Work" (2001); Editor, "The Guild Shakespeare," Doubleday (1988-1992); Core Advisor, "The Shakespeare Hour," Public Broadcasting Service (1985-1986); Editor-in-Chief, Contributor, "William Shakespeare: His World, His Work, His Influence" (1985); Editor, "Shakespeare Quarterly" (1974-1985); Chair, Advisory Panel, "The Shakespeare Plays," Time-Life Television (1974-1985); Assistant Editor, "Shakespeare Studies" (1972-1974); **Awards:** Honorary Officer, Order of the British Empire (2000); Research Awards, Folger Shakespeare Library, Florida State University, National Endowment for the Humanities **Membership:** Trustee, Shakespeare Association of America (1979-1982); Council, Renaissance Society of America (1975-1984); Secretary, Florida State University Chapter, American Association of University Professors (1972-1974); Modern Language Association; Milton Society of America; National Council of Teachers of English; International Shakespeare Conference; The Literary Society; Cosmos Club **Marquis Who's Who Honors:** Albert Nelson Marquis Lifetime Achievement Award (2017) **Shipping Address:** 14 Via San Martin, Santa Fe, NM, 87506 **Website:** http://www.24-7pressrelease.com/press-release-service/434820

John Andrick

Title: Cultural Historian **Industry:** Education/Educational Services **Date of Birth:** 06/13/1948 **Place of Birth:** Bethany **State:** MO **Education:** PhD, Department of History, University of Illinois at Urbana-Champaign (2016) **Certifications:** Certified Powered Industrial Truck Operator, Raymond Corp. (2009) **Career:** Panel Moderator, Annual Conference, Phoenix, AZ (2016); Conference Co-organizer, Panel Synthesizer, University of California, Santa Cruz (2015); Panel Chair, Commentator, Annual Meeting, Organization of American Historians, Atlanta, GA (2014); Operations Facility Manager, University of Illinois Library High-Density Shelving Facility, Champaign, IL (2002-2012); Operations Manager, University of Illinois Library High-Density Shelving Facility (2003-2004); Bookstacks Space Manager, Circulation Department, University of Illinois Library (1988-2003); College Leader, Campus Charitable Fund, University of Illinois Library High-Density Shelving Facility; Speaker, Victorian Cultural History **Career Related:** Annual Meeting of American Association History of Medicine (2013); Visiting Teaching Associate, Social Studies Department, University High School, Urbana, IL (1994); Graduate Research Assistant, Campus-Wide Research Services Office, University High School (1982-1983); Acting Head, Social Studies Department, University High School, Urbana, IL (1979-1980); Graduate Teaching Assistant, U.S. History, EOP Rhetoric and Business and Technical Writing, University High School (1975-1982); Public School Teacher, Newton, IL **Civic:** Volunteer, North American Victorian Studies Association; Volunteer, Modernist Studies Association; Volunteer, Organization of American Historians **Military Service:** U.S. Army, Fairbanks, AK (1971-1973) **Creative Works:** Author, "Cultivating a 'Chairside Manner': Dental Hypnosis, Patient Management Psychology, and the Origins of Behavioral Dentistry in America, 1890-1910,' Journal of the History of the Behavioral (2013); Author, "Delsartean Hypnosis for Girls' Bodies and Minds: Annie Payson Call and the Lasell Seminary Nerve Training Controversy," History of Psychology (2012); Anonymous Peer Reviewer, History of Psychology (2012); Author, "Hypnosis and the Emmanuel Movement: A Medical and Religious Repudiation," American Journal of Clinical Hypnosis (1978); Contributor, Articles, Professional Journals Such as History of Behavioral Sciences, History of Psychology, Journal of Clinical Hypnosis **Awards:** Outstanding Teacher Award, University High School, Urbana, Illinois (1980) **Membership:** Urbana-Champaign Friends Meeting; Illinois State Historical Association; National Association of Victorian Studies; American Studies Association; Laborer's International Union; American Association of the History of Medicine; Organization of American Historians; Modernist Studies Association **Marquis Who's Who Honors:** Distinguished Humanitarian (2017) **Shipping Address:** 2906 Artesia Xing, Urbana, IL, 61802

Leslie P. Antalffy

Title: Mechanical Engineer **Industry:** Engineering **Company Name:** Fluor Enterprises **Date of Birth:** 10/31/1942 **Place of Birth:** Budapest **Country of Origin:** Hungary **Parents:** Vilmos Leslie Antalffy; Margo (Simay) Antalffy **Marital Status:** Married **Spouse Name:** Barbara Ann Clark (01/19/1970) **Children:** Julie; Michael; Nicole **Education:** MBA, Sam Houston State University (1980); Bachelor's Degree in Mechanical Engineering, University of Adelaide, Adelaide, South Australia, Australia (1970) **Certifications:** Registered Professional Engineer, State of Texas; Chartered Professional Engineer, Engineers Australia **Career:** Executive Director of Process Technology and Engineering, Fluor Enterprises, Houston, TX (2008-Present); Senior Fellow, Senior Mechanical Engineering Director, Fluor Enterprises, Houston, TX (1995-Present); Mechanical Engineering Director, Fluor Enterprises, Houston, TX (1989-1995); Supervising Mechanical Engineer, Fluor Enterprises, Houston, TX (1980-1989); Principal Engineer, Fluor Enterprises, Houston, TX (1975-1980); Senior Vessel Engineer, Fluor Enterprises, Houston, TX (1973-1975); Senior Vessel Engineer, Lummus Company, Toronto, Canada (1972-1973); Vessel Engineer, A.G. McKee & Company, Toronto, Canada (1972); Vessel Engineer, Lummus Company, Toronto, Canada (1970-1971); Mechanical Engineer, T. O'Connor & Sons, Adelaide, South Australia, Australia (1968-1969) **Creative Works:** Contributor, Articles, Professional Journals; Presenter, Technical Papers, International Conferences **Awards:** Lifetime Achievement Award, Hydrocarbon Processing Journal, Awards Banquet Dinner, Vienna, Austria (2017) **Membership:** Life Fellow, The American Society of Mechanical Engineers; Member, Numerous Code Committees, The American Society of Mechanical Engineers **Marquis Who's Who Honors:** Distinguished Humanitarian (2017) **Why did you become involved in your profession or industry:** As a child, he was always working on cars. His parents mandated that he get a proper education. **What do you consider to be the highlight of your career:** A highlight of his career is having 13 patents in his field, and receiving a Lifetime Achievement Award in Hydro Carbon Processing in 2017. **Where will you be in five years:** In five years, he will be retired. **Political Affiliations:** Republican **Religion:** Roman Catholic **Shipping Address:** 11946 Summerdale St, Houston, TX, 77077

Ronald Dean Archer

Title: Chemist, Educator **Industry:** Education/Educational Services **Date of Birth:** 07/22/1932 **Place of Birth:** Rochelle **State:** IL **Parents:** Don Adam Archer; Irma Cecil (Olson) Archer **Marital Status:** Widowed **Spouse Name:** Joyce Hildur Carlson (1954, Deceased 2004) **Children:** Paul Dean; Lynn Sue; Sharon Jean; Julie Ann **Education:** PhD, University of Illinois (1959); MS, Illinois State University (1954); BS, Illinois State University (1953) **Career:** Professor Emeritus, University of Massachusetts, Amherst (1999-Present); Head of Chemistry Department, University of Massachusetts, Amherst (1977-1983); Professor of Chemistry, University Massachusetts, Amherst (1970-1999); Associate Professor, University of Massachusetts, Amherst (1966-1970); Associate Professor, Tulane University (1965-1966); Assistant Professor, Tulane University (1963-1965); Assistant Professor, University California Riverside (1959-1963) **Career Related:** Consultant (1972-Present); Visiting Professor, University of Vienna (1987); Chief Chemistry Reader, Advanced Placement Program, Educational Testing Service (1985-1988); Research Scientist, U.S. Naval Research Laboratory (1980); Visiting Professor, Technical University of Denmark (1972); Consultant (1960-1970); Fellow, American Chemical Society **Civic:** Board of Trustees, Friends of the University of Massachusetts Libraries (2006-2016) **Military Service:** U.S. Army (1954-1956) **Creative Works:** Author, "Inorganic Organomet Polymers" (2001); Contributor, "Sputnik to Smartphones, A Half Century of Chemistry Education"; Contributor, Articles, Professional Journals **Awards:** Alumni Achievement Award, Illinois State University (1989); Grantee, Office of Naval Research; Grantee, American Chemical Society; Grantee, National Science Foundation; Grantee, Research Corporation for Science Advancement; Grantee, U.S. Air Force **Membership:** Treasurer, Melha Shrine Center (2016-Present); Senior Chemists Committee, American Chemical Society (2013-Present); Military Band Member, Melha Shrine Center (2005-Present); Senior Member, Chemical Committee, American Chemical Society (2013-2015); Board of Directors, Local Chapter, Rotary International (2013-2015); Treasurer, Melha Shrine Center (2009-2010); 32nd Degree Scottish Rite Mason (2008); Budget and Finance Committee, American Chemical Society (2007-2014); Board of Trustees, Friends of the University of Massachusetts Libraries (2006-2016); Board of Directors, Local Chapter, Rotary International (2005-2008); President, Retired Faculty Association, University of Massachusetts, Amherst (2003-2004); Committee on Committees, American Chemical Society (2001-2006); Science Committee, American Chemical Society (2001-2003); Chair, Committee for Economic Professional Affairs, American Chemical Society (2000); Committee for Economic Professional Affairs, American Chemical Society (1999-2000); Advisory Board Chair, General Chemical Curriculum Project, American Chemical Society (1997-2004); Chair, Chemical Education Division, American Chemical Society (1997); Council Policy Committee, American Chemical Society (1996-1998); Chair Emeritus, Chemical Education Division, American Chemical Society (1996-1998); Executive Committee, Chemical Education Division, American Chemical Society (1996-1998); Chair-Elect, Chemical Education Division, American Chemical Society (1996); Nominating and Election Committee, American Chemical Society (1990-1994); Chairman, Education Committee, American Chemical Society (1987-1989); Councilor, American Chemical Society (1981-2016); Chairman, Connecticut Valley Section, American Chemical Society (1979); American Association for the Advancement of Science; Massachusetts Freemasons; Shriners International; New England Association of Chemistry Teachers; New England Association of Chemistry Teachers; Sigma Xi, The Scientific Research Honor Society; Phi Lambda Upsilon **Marquis Who's Who Honors:** Albert Nelson Marquis Lifetime Achievement Award (2017) **Hobbies:** Tennis; Golf; Singing; Playing clarinet **Religion:** Lutheran **Shipping Address:** 3 Burgundy Lane, Amherst, MA, 01002

Emil Ardelean

Title: Mechanical Engineer, Researcher **Industry:** Engineering **Date of Birth:** 10/07/1966 **Place of Birth:** Ceanu Mare **Country of Origin:** Romania **Parents:** Valentin Ardelean; Ana Ardelean **Education:** PhD, Duke University, Durham, NC (2003); MS, University of Technology, Cluj-Napoca, Romania (1994); BS, University Technology, Cluj-Napoca, Romania (1992) **Career:** Co-owner, ACME Solutions, New Mexico (2016-Present); Senior Mechanical Engineer, SAIC, Albuquerque, NM (2003-Present); Graduate Research Assistant, Duke University, Durham, NC (1999-2003); Mapper, Drafter, ASI Landmark, Cary, NC (1998-1999); PC Manufacturing, Assembling, Configuration, Testing, IBM Corp., Research Triangle Park, NC (1997-1998); Engineer, Co-owner, Gimati SRL, Turda, Romania (1995-1997); Design Engineer, South Carolina Sinterom S.A., Cluj-Napoca, Romania (1993-1997); Co-owner, SAIC, New Mexico **Membership:** American Society of Mechanical Engineers; American Institute of Aeronautics and Astronautics; Romanian Engineering Society **Shipping Address:** 12529 Apache Court N.E., Alberquerque, NM, 87112

Kartik Balasubramanian Ariyur, PhD

Title: Control Systems Engineer, Researcher **Industry:** Engineering **Company Name:** Purdue University **Date of Birth:** 04/21/1974 **Place of Birth:** Hyderabad **Country of Origin:** India **Parents:** Balasubramanian M. Ariyur; Usha Baalasubramanian Ariyur **Education:** PhD, University of California, San Diego, CA (2002); Engineering Intern, Qualcomm Technologies, Inc., La Jolla, CA (2001-2002); MS, University of California, San Diego, CA (1999); Engineering Intern, United Technologies Research Center, East Hartford, CT (1998); BTech, Indian Institute of Technology, Madras, India (1996) **Career:** Visiting Assistant Professor, Purdue University (2015-Present); Assistant Professor, Purdue University (2008-2015); Instructor, Purdue University (2003-2014); Scientist, Honeywell Labs, Minneapolis, MN (2002-2008); Guest Lecturer, Purdue University (2001); Research Assistant, University of California, San Diego, CA (1997-2002); Research Assistant, University of Maryland, College Park, MD (1997); Teaching Assistant, University of Maryland, College Park, MD (1996) **Career Related:** Invited Lecturer, Autonomy, Coordinated Science Lab, University of Illinois at Urbana-Champaign (2016); Hot Topic Speaker, San Diego Venture Summit (2015); PI Mellon Foundation Grant, Equitable Water Policy Using Big Data (2014-2016); Invited Lecturer, Big Data from Sensors, Computational Engineering Series, Purdue University (2014); Program Committee, American Control Conference, Seattle, WA (2013-2016); Conference Editorial Board, Institute of Electrical and Electronics Engineers; Control Systems Society (2013); Program Committee, Institute of Electrical and Electronics Engineers MSC (2011-2012); Technical Communications Power Generation, Institute of Electrical and Electronics Engineers Control Systems Society (2011); Program Committee, International Conference on Intelligent Robotics and Applications (2011); Invited Lecturer, Energy Management, Mechanical and Aerospace Engineering, Lehigh University (2010); Invited Lecturer, Aerospace Engineering, Texas A&M University (2010); Guest Seminar, Varian Semiconductor (2009); Program Committee, American Control Conference, Seattle, WA (2008-2009); Program Committee, Hybrid Systems, Computation and Control Conference, Santa Barbara, CA (2005-2006); Student Mentor, Institute of Technology (Now College of Science and Engineering), University of Minnesota, Minneapolis, MN (2002-2005) **Creative Works:** Technical Editor, International Journal of Adaptive Control and Signal Processing (2005-Present); Editor, Hierarchical Innovation Algorithms (2007); Author, "Real-Time Optimization by Extremum Seeking Control" (2003); Contributor, Articles to Professional Journals, Chapters to Books, Numerous Publications; Author, 51 Conference Papers **Awards:** Outstanding Paper Award, Society of Automotive Engineers International (2004); Technological Achievement Award, Honeywell Labs (2003) **Membership:** Program Committee, Institute of Electrical and Electronics Engineers (2014, 2011); American Institute of Aeronautics and Astronautics; American Society of Mechanical Engineers; Society for Industrial and Applied Mathematics; Society of Automotive Engineers; Institute of Noetic Sciences; Society for Industrial and Applied Mathematics **Hobbies:** Philosophy; Law; Indian classical music; Drawing **Shipping Address:** 1918 Carlisle Rd, West Lafayette, IN, 47906

Peter H. Armacost

Title: President Emeritus **Industry:** Education/Educational Services **Company Name:** Forman Christian College **Date of Birth:** 07/12/1935 **Place of Birth:** New York City **State:** NY **Parents:** George Henry; Verda Gay (Hayden) Armacost **Marital Status:** Married **Spouse Name:** Mary-Linda Merriam (7/10/1993); Suzanne Lee Sadosky (6/22/1957, Deceased 2/1991) **Children:** Martha Hayden; David Keys; Sarah Jane; Rebecca Ann **Education:** Honorary LLD, Ottawa University (2011); PhD, University of Minnesota (1963); BA, Denison University (1957) **Career:** Consultant, North East Christian University (2016-Present); President Emeritus, Forman Christian College (2012-Present); President Emeritus, Eckerd College, St. Petersburg, FL (2000-Present); President, Principal, Forman Christian College (2002-2012); Senior Adviser, Council of Independent Colleges (2001-2003); President, Eckerd College, St. Petersburg, FL (1977-2000); President, Professor of Psychology, Ottawa University, Kansas (1967-1977); Program Director, Association of American Colleges, Washington (1965-1967); Dean of Students, Chairman, Department of Psychology, Augsburg College, Minneapolis (1959-1965) **Civic:** Board of Directors, United States Educational Foundation in Pakistan, Islamabad, Pakistan (2009-2011); Board of Trustees, Kinnaird College of Lahore, Pakistan (2005-2012); Board of Directors, United Way of Pinellas County (1995-2002); Southern University Conference (1977); President, American Baptist Churches of the United States (1974-1975); Chairman, Kansas City Regional Council for Higher Education, Missouri (1972-1974); Member, Higher Education Commission, Pakistan Task Force Goals **Creative Works:** Author, Materials in Field **Awards:** Named to Tampa Bay Business Hall of Fame (1999); Distinguished Alumnus Citation, Denison University; Woodrow Wilson Fellow; Danforth Fellow; Distinguished Service Award, National Association of Student Personnel Administrators **Membership:** Board of Directors, SunTrust Bank of Tampa Bay (1983-Present); Board of Directors, Florida Council of 100, St. Petersburg Chamber of Commerce (1995-2001); Board of Directors, National Association of Independent Colleges and Universities (1995-1998); Board of Directors, Council of Independent Colleges (1993-2000); Chairman, Independent Colleges and Universities of Florida (1991-1993); Vice Chairman, Independent Colleges and Universities of Florida (1990-1991); Board of Directors, Pinellas Economic Development Council (1989-2000); President, Florida Association of Colleges and Universities (1989-1990); Treasurer, Independent Colleges and Universities of Florida (1986-1988); Secretary, Independent Colleges and Universities of Florida (1984-1986); Chairman, Suncoast Chamber of Commerce (1984-1985); Chairman, Florida Chapter, Young President Organization (1983-1984); President, Association of Independent Colleges, Kansas (1970-1972); Board of Directors, Association of American Colleges; American Council of Education; Appeals Committee, Southern Association of Colleges and Schools; American Association of Higher Education; Society of Values in Higher Education; St. Petersburg Yacht Club; Suncoasters Club; Secretary, Executive Committee, Council of Independent Colleges; Rotary International; Blue Key; Phi Beta Kappa; Omicron Delta Kappa; Pi Gamma Mu; Psi Chi; Board of Directors, Division of Research and Publications, National Association of Student Personnel Administrators; Conference Chairman, National Association of Student Personnel Administrators **Marquis Who's Who Honors:** Albert Nelson Marquis Lifetime Achievement Award (2017) **To what do you attribute your success:** Dr. Armacost attributes his success to his strong faith, commitment to core values of integrity and respect for others, strong work ethic, and sense of social responsibility established early in life by his parents. He has also been blessed with very competent and caring professional colleagues as part of the leadership teams and faculty in his three college and university presidencies and within his field. **What do you consider to be the highlight of your career:** The highlight of Dr. Armacost's career has been his time at Forman Christian College in Pakistan. Over the course of a decade, his team succeeded in having the government denationalize the college and return it to the owners of the campus, the Presbyterian Church USA, gaining university status, and establishing the first liberal arts university in Pakistan. The school has had an enrollment growth of 95 percent, bringing it to a total of 6,084 students, and hiring a faculty of 296 members, with 50 percent of them holding a PhD. The average for this in the nation is 22 percent. A special accomplishment was providing a higher education opportunity to Christian students who had been denied such opportunities for 30 years. **Hobbies:** Travel **Political Affiliations:** Republican **Religion:** American Baptist **Shipping Address:** 555 5th Ave NE Ste 914, Saint Petersburg, FL, 33701

Geraldine Armendariz

Title: Lawyer **Industry:** Law and Legal Services **Date of Birth:** 03/09/1952 **Place of Birth:** El Paso **State:** TX **Parents:** Juan Sotelo Armendariz; Mary Marin Armendariz (Ybarra) **Education:** JD, John F. Kennedy University (1980); MA in Spanish Literature and Economics, University of California, Berkeley (1974) **Career:** Private Practice, San Francisco (1981-Present); Law Clerk Criminal Division, Superior Court California, San Francisco, CA (1979-1980); Public Defender, San Francisco, CA (1978); Law Clerk, City Attorney; Legal Assistant, San Francisco Lawyers' Committee on Urban Affairs (1974-1976); Legal Assistant, Heller, Ehrman, White & McAuliffe, San Francisco (1974-1976) **Awards:** Nominee, Woman of Distinction (2016) **Bar Admissions:** The State Bar of California (1981); United States District Court for the Central District of California (1981) **Business Address:** 870 Market Street, Suite 1175, San Francisco, CA, 94102 **Shipping Address:** 870 Market Street, Suite 1175, Geraldine Armendariz Attorney at Law, San Francisco, CA 94102

Frank Couchman Arnett Jr.

Title: Rheumatologist, Educator,Researcher **Industry:** Medicine & Health Care **Date of Birth:** 03/08/1942 **Place of Birth:** Salyersville **State:** KY **Parents:** Frank Couchman Arnett; Edna Carol Salyer Arnett **Marital Status:** Married **Spouse Name:** Lynne Anne Whetstone (8/29/1965) **Education:** MD, University of Cincinnati (1968); BA, University of Cincinnati (1964) **Certifications:** Certified in Diagnostic Immunology (1990); Certified in Rheumatology (1976); Certified in Internal Medicine, American Board of Internal Medicine (1972) **Career:** Professor Emeritus, The University of Texas Health Science Center at Houston (2012-Present); Chairman, Department of Internal Medicine, The University of Texas Health Science Center at Houston (2001-2004); Professor of Internal Medicine, The University of Texas Health Science Center at Houston (1984-2011); Director, Division of Rheumatology, The University of Texas Health Science Center at Houston (1984-2001); Assistant to Associate Professor of Medicine, Johns Hopkins Hospital (1975-1984); Instructor of Medicine, Johns Hopkins University, Baltimore, MD (1974-1975); Chief of Rheumatology, Wilford Hall Medical Facility, San Antonio, TX (1972-1974); Fellow, Rheumatology, Johns Hopkins Hospital (1970-1972); Resident, Medicine, Johns Hopkins Hospital, Baltimore, MD (1968-1970) **Career Related:** Member, PI-NIH CTSA Grant, Houston, TX (2006-2008); Researcher, Genetic Rheumatic Diseases **Civic:** Advisory Committee Member, Lupus Foundation; Advisory Committee Member, Scleroderma Foundation; Advisory Committee Member, Sjogrens Syndrome Foundation; Advisory Committee Member, Arthritis Foundation **Military Service:** US Airforce Medical Corp (1972-1974) **Creative Works:** Author, "Genome-Wide Scans"; Contributor, Chapters to Books; Contributor, More than 600 Articles to Professional Journals/Books **Awards:** Recipient, President's Scholar Teaching Award, The University of Texas Health Science Center at Houston (2009); Recipient, Distinguished Educator Award, TIAA-CREF (2006); Recipient, President's Scholar Teaching Award, The University of Texas Health Science Center at Houston (2005); Honoree, Best Doctors in America (2000-2010); Master, American College of Physicians; Master, American College of Rheumatology, Elected to Association of American Physicians **Membership:** Heritage Society, The University of Texas Health Science Center at Houston; Association of American Physicians; American Autoimmune Related Disease Association; American College of Physicians; American College of Rheumatology **Marquis Who's Who Honors:** Distinguished Humanitarian (2017) **To what do you attribute your success:** Dr. Arnett attributes his success to hard work, passion, interest and experience with autoimmune diseases. **Why did you become involved in your profession or industry:** Dr. Arnett entered his profession because he was influenced by his childhood medical doctor. **What do you consider to be the highlight of your career:** The highlight of Dr. Arnett's career was showing that autoimmune diseases happened largely due to genetics. **Where will you be in five years:** In the next five years, Dr. Arnett will be retired at his home in Texas. **Hobbies:** Gym; Movies; Books **Political Affiliations:** Democrat **Religion:** Christian **Business Address:** UT McGovern Medical School, Houston, TX, 77030 **Shipping Address:** 2345 Bering Dr Apt 506, Houston, TX, 77057

Robert Douglas Arnott

Title: Investment Company Executive **Industry:** Financial Services **Company Name:** Research Affiliates, LLC **Date of Birth:** 06/29/1954 **Place of Birth:** Chicago **State:** IL **Parents:** Robert James Arnott; Catherine (Bonnell) Cameron **Children:** Robert Lindsay; Sydney Allison; Richard James; Diana Haikova **Education:** BA, University of California, Santa Barbara (1977) **Career:** Founding Chairman, Research Affiliates, LLC (2002-Present); Chief Executive Officer, Research Affiliates, LLC (2002-Present); Chairman, First Quadrant (2002-2004); Managing Partner, First Quadrant (1988-2004); Vice President, Salomon Brothers Inc. (1987-1988); Global Equity Strategist, Salomon Brothers Inc. (1987-1988); President, TSA Capital Management (1984-1987); Chief Executive Officer, TSA Capital Management (1984-1987); Vice President, The Boston Company Asset Management, LLC (1977-1984) **Career Related:** Advisory Board, EDHEC Business School (2008-2010); Visiting Professor, University of California, Los Angeles, CA (2001-2003); Product Advisory Board, CME Group Inc. (1990-1996); Chairman's Advisory Council, CBOE (1989-1994); Board of Directors, International Faculty in Finance **Creative Works:** Editorial Board Member, The Journal of Wealth Management (1997-Present); Author, "The Fundamental Index" (2008); Editor-in-Chief, Financial Analysts Journal (2002-2006); Editor, "Handbook of Equity Style Management" (1997); Editor, "Active Asset Allocation" (1992); Editorial Board Member, The Journal of Investing (1990-1999); Editor, "Asset Allocation" (1988); Editorial Board Member, The Journal of Portfolio Management (1984-2002); Contributor, Articles, Professional Journals; Contributor, Chapters, Books **Awards:** Seven Graham and Dodd Scrolls and Awards, CFA Institute for the Top Financial Analysts Journal Articles of the Year; Lifetime Achievement Award, William F. Sharpe Indexing Achievement Awards; Lifetime Achievement Award, Several Organizations **Membership:** Advisory Council, Toronto Stock and Futures Exchange (1992-1999); Advisory Board, Institute for International Research (1990-1996); Association for Investment Management and Research; Institute for Quantitative Research in Finance (Now Q Group) **Marquis Who's Who Honors:** Albert Nelson Marquis Lifetime Achievement Award (2017) **What do you consider to be the highlight of your career:** Mr. Arnott is most proud of the fact that only three other people in history have earned more Graham and Dodd scrolls and awards than he has. **Hobbies:** Motorcycling; Astrophotography; Billiards; Wine making; Travel **Shipping Address:** 411 Avocado Avenue, Corona Del Mar, CA, 92625 **Website:** https://www.researchaffiliates.com/en_us/about-us/our-team/rob-arnott.html

Marie Matranga Ashdown

Title: Executive Director **Industry:** Business Management/Business Services **Company Name:** Musicians Emergency Fund **Place of Birth:** Mobile **State:** AL **Parents:** Dominic Matranga; Ave (Mallon) Matranga **Marital Status:** Married **Spouse Name:** Cecil Spanton Ashdown Jr. (5/12/1923) **Children:** Cecil Spanton III; Charles Coster; John Stephen Gartman; Vivian Gartman Silliman **Education:** Diplomate, Spring Hill College; Diplomate, Maryville University **Career:** Executive Director, Musicians Emergency Fund, New York, NY (1985-Present); Opera Instructor, In-Service Program, Marymount Manhattan College, New York, NY (1979-1985); President, The Opera Orchestra of New York (1971-1975); Opera Instructor, In-Service Program, Metropolitan Opera Guild, New York, NY (1970-1980); Vice President, Metropolitan Opera Guild, New York, NY; Feature Artist, Women's Program Director, Daily Program, Station WALA, WALA-TV, Mobile, AL **Career Related:** International Advisory Council, Van Cliburn Foundation (1998-Present); Consultant, College of Visual and Performing Arts, Northern Illinois University (1985-Present); Lecturer in Field **Civic:** Archivist, 87-Year History, "A Kaleidoscope of Classical Music," Musicians Emergency Fund; Member, Palm Beach Charities Advisory Board **Creative Works:** Author, "Opera Collectibles" (1979); Contributor, Articles to Professional Journals **Awards:** Recipient, Albanese-Puccini Award, Lincoln Center (2002); Recipient, Extraordinary Service Award, March of Dimes Foundation; Recipient, Medal of Appreciation Award, Harvard Business School Club of New York; Recipient, Certificate of Appreciation, Kiwanis International; Recipient, Arts Excellence Award, New Jersey State Opera; Recipient, Cipario Award **Membership:** The National Institute of Social Sciences; National Committee on United States-China Relations **To what do you attribute your success:** Ms. Ashdown attributes her success to adversity and opportunity. **Why did you become involved in your profession or industry:** Ms. Ashdown became involved in her profession due to a broad spectrum excellent education, hard work and study. **What do you consider to be the highlight of your career:** The highlight of Ms. Ashdown's career was being married to Cecil Ashdown. **Where will you be in five years:** In the next five years, Ms. Ashdown will be retired. **Shipping Address:** 25 Sutton Pl S Apt 16K, New York, NY, 10022 **Website:** http://musiciansemergencyfund.org

Stanley Edwin Asnis

Title: Orthopedic Surgeon **Industry:** Medicine & Health Care **Company Name:** University Orthopaedic Associates **Date of Birth:** 09/14/1943 **Place of Birth:** Newark **State:** NJ **Parents:** Gordon Asnis; Ruth Selma Asnis **Marital Status:** Married **Spouse Name:** Lisa Ann Langer (2/15/1997); Elaine Bluestein (6/18/1967, Deceased 1986) **Children:** Lauren Jill Ernberg; Peter David; Anna Ruth; Sarah Grace **Education:** Resident, Hospital for Special Surgery (1971-1975); Fellow in Orthopedic Surgery, Hospital for Special Surgery (1971-1975); Resident in Surgery, Weill Cornell Medicine, Cornell University (1968-1971); Intern, Weill Cornell Medicine, Cornell University (1968-1971); MD, Washington University in St. Louis (1968); Diploma, Franklin & Marshall College (1961-1964) **Certifications:** Board Certified in Orthopedic Surgery, American Board of Orthopedic Surgery, Inc. (1976) **Career:** Chairman, Department of Orthopedic Surgery, North Shore University Hospital (Now Northwell Health), Manhasset, NY (1999-Present); Chairman Emeritus, Northwell Health; Chief, Joint Replacement and Adult Reconstruction, Northwell Health; Chief, Adult Joint Reconstruction, North Shore University Hospital (Now Northwell Health), Manhasset, NY **Career Related:** Clinical Associate Professor of Orthopedic Surgery, Albert Einstein College of Medicine, Bronx, NY (1998-Present); Clinical Associate Professor, Donald and Barbara Zucker School of Medicine at Hofstra/Northwell, Hofstra University; Clinical Associate Professor of Orthopaedic Surgery, Weill Cornell Medicine, Cornell University **Creative Works:** Editor, "Cannulated Screw Fixation: Principles and Operative Techniques"; Contributor, Articles, Professional Journals **Awards:** Lewis Clark Wagner Research Award, Hospital for Special Surgery; The Frank E. Stinchfield National Hip Society Award **Membership:** Fellow, American College of Surgeons; Fellow, American Academy of Orthopaedic Surgeons; American Association of Hip and Knee Surgeons; The American Orthopaedic Association **Marquis Who's Who Honors:** Albert Nelson Marquis Lifetime Achievement Award (2017) **To what do you attribute your success:** Dr. Asnis attributes his success to his family and his love of learning. **Hobbies:** Cycling **Business Address:** 611 Northern Blvd Ste 200, Great Neck, NY, 11021 **Shipping Address:** 6 Hicks Ln, Sands Point, NY, 11050

Gus J. Athas

Title: Lawyer **Industry:** Law and Legal Services **Company Name:** Stamos & Trucco **Date of Birth:** 08/06/1936 **Place of Birth:** Chicago **State:** IL **Parents:** James G. Athas; Pauline (Parhas) Athas **Marital Status:** Married **Spouse Name:** Marilyn Carres (7/12/1964) **Children:** Paula C. Vlahakos; James G.; Christopher G. **Education:** JD, Loyola University, Chicago, IL, Cum Laude (1965); BS, University of Illinois (1958) **Career:** Lawyer, Stamos & Trucco, Chicago, IL (2000-Present); Senior Vice President, General Counsel, Great American Management and Investment, Inc. (1995-1997); Executive Vice President of Administration, General Counsel, Secretary, Falcon Building Products, Inc. (1994-1999); Senior Vice President, General Counsel, Secretary, Eagle Industries (1987-1997); Associate General Counsel, Itel Corporation, Chicago, IL (1987); Group General Counsel, Assistant Secretary, ITT (1969-1987); Lawyer, Isham, Lincoln & Beale, Chicago, IL (1965-1969) **Military Service:** First Lieutenant, U.S. Army (1958-1962) **Creative Works:** Contributor, Articles, Professional Journals **Membership:** American Bar Association; Chicago Bar Association **Bar Admissions:** State of Illinois (1965) **Marquis Who's Who Honors:** Albert Nelson Marquis Lifetime Achievement Award (2017) **To what do you attribute your success:** Mr. Athas is pleased and gratified of his time spent at Eagle Industries, Inc. and Falcon Building Products, Inc. **Religion:** Greek Orthodox **Shipping Address:** 1 E Wacker Drive, 3rd Floor, Stamos Trucco LLP, Chicago, IL, 60601

Robert G. Atnip

Title: Professor of Surgery and Radiology **Industry:** Medicine & Health Care **Company Name:** Division of Vascular Surgery, Milton S. Hershey Medical Center, Penn State Health **Marital Status:** Married **Children:** Lindsay; Elizabeth **Education:** Fellowship, Surgery, Vascular, Harvard Medical School, Massachusetts General Hospital (1985); Residency, Surgery, General, Harvard Medical School, Massachusetts General Hospital (1984); MD, School of Medicine, The University of Alabama at Birmingham (1978) **Awards:** Distinguished Reviewer Award, Editorial Board, Journal of Vascular Surgery (2015); Distinguished Reviewer Award, Editorial Board, Journal of Vascular Surgery (2013); Named Educator of the Year, PSHMC Department of Radiology (2013); Faculty Professionalism/Humanism in Surgery Award (2008); Teaching Award, Penn State College of Medicine (1997); Thomas Ballentine "Excellence in Surgical Education" Award, Department of Surgery, Milton S. Hershey Medical Center, Penn State Health (1992) **Membership:** President, Board of Directors, Alpha Omega Alpha (2016); Board of Directors, Harrisburg Symphony Orchestra; Alpha Omega Alpha; Medical Honor Society; Chapter Counselor, Milton S. Hershey Medical Center, Penn State Health; National Board of Directors; America's Top Doctors-Castle Connolly; American College of Surgeons **Shipping Address:** 46 Woodbine Dr, Hershey, PA, 17033

Stephen Neal Avery

Title: Playwright, Writer **Industry:** Writing and Editing **Date of Birth:** 03/20/1955 **Place of Birth:** Hot Springs **State:** AR **Parents:** Leo A. Avery; Dedette Carol (Miles) Sullivan **Marital Status:** Married **Spouse Name:** Kathleen Annette Twin (9/7/1979) **Career:** Freelance Reporter, The Sentinel-Record, Hot Springs, AR (1970-1973); Freelance Reporter, New Era, Hot Springs, AR (1970-1973) **Civic:** Founding Sponsor, National Museum of American Jewish History (2009-Present); Founding Sponsor, Flight 93 National Memorial (2006-Present); Founding Sponsor, Martin Luther King Jr. National Memorial (2005-Present); President's Council, World Jewish Congress (2005-Present); Scholarship Committee, American Indian Education Fund, Partnership with Native Americans (2005-Present); AmeriCares (2004-Present); Active Member, National Republican Congressional Committee (2004-Present); International Rescue Committee (2004-Present); Founders Circle, Vada Sheid Community Development Center, Arkansas State University, Mountain Home (2002-Present); Founding Member, The National Campaign for Tolerance (2002-Present); Active Member, United States Holocaust Memorial Museum (2001-Present); Delegate, Republican, Senatorial Election Platform Committee (2012); Friends of Sesame Workshop (2005-2008); Honorary Co-Chair, President's Dinner for George W. Bush (2004-2005); Active, Beit Hashoah Museum of Tolerance (2003-2006); Active Member, American Jewish Committee (2003-2005); Leadership Council, Southern Poverty Law Center (2002-2015); Active Member, Simon Wiesenthal Center (2002-2006) **Military Service:** U.S. Navy (1973-1977) **Creative Works:** Production Partner, "Viva La Causa," Southern Poverty Law Center Documentary (2008); Production Partner, "Ever Again," Moriah Films Documentary (2005); Author, "Burning Bridges" (1999); Author, "Insidious" (1992); Author, "Hungry: Three Plays" (1991); Author, "Because" (1991) **Awards:** World Jewish Congress Medallion of Commitment (2013); Gateway Award, Save Ellis Island, Inc. (2012); Leadership Award, World Jewish Congress Foundation (2011); Nahum Goldmann Leadership Award (2007); Republican Senatorial American Spirit Medal (2007); Congressional Order of Merit (2006-2007); Inclusion in Republican Presidential Honor Roll, Executive Committee, National Republican Congressional Committee (2005) **Membership:** Charter Member, George W. Bush Presidential Center; Drama League; Theatre Communications Group; Authors League of America (Now Authors Guild); Dramatists Guild of America, Inc.; Charter Member, World Trade Center Memorial Foundation (Now National September 11 Memorial & Museum); Americans for the Arts Action Fund; Save Ellis Island, Inc.; National Museum of the American Indian, Smithsonian Institution; National D-Day Museum (Now National WWII Museum); National Museum for Women in Arts; National Trust for Historic Preservation; Habitat for Humanity International; National Campaign Tolerance **Marquis Who's Who Honors:** Albert Nelson Marquis Lifetime Achievement Award (2017) **To what do you attribute your success:** Mr. Avery attributes his success to dedication, perseverance, the right luck, and a patient wife. **Why did you become involved in your profession or industry:** Mr. Avery became involved in his profession because of his desire to live a life of contribution and significance. **What do you consider to be the highlight of your career:** The one highlight of Mr. Avery's career was becoming an Albert Nelson Marquis Lifetime Achievement inductee. **Hobbies:** Museum and gallery exhibitions **Shipping Address:** 337 Del Mar Avenue, Chula Vista, CA, 91910

Hartman Axley

Title: Financial Planner **Industry:** Financial Services **Date of Birth:** 04/17/1931 **Place of Birth:** Madison **State:** WI **Parents:** Ralph Emerson Axley; Katharine Nella (Hartman) Axley **Marital Status:** Married **Spouse Name:** Marguerite Ann Thessin **Children:** Colleen Lynn Axley Patrick; Timothy Hartman Axley **Education:** MSFS, American College, Bryn Mawr, PA (1983); JD, University of Wisconsin (1956); BA, University of Wisconsin (1952) **Certifications:** Chartered Life Underwriter; Certified Financial Planner; Accredited Estate Planner; Chartered Financial Consultant; Registered Health Underwriter **Career:** Life Underwriter, Colorado Associates of Allmerica Financial, Denver, CO (1958-2003); Associate Attorney, Holland & Hart, Denver, CO (1956-1958) **Career Related:** Vice President, Colorado Ethics in Business Alliance Board (2001-Present); Colorado Ethics in Business Alliance Board (1995-Present); Coordinator, Badminton Rocky Mountain Senior Games (1987-Present); Founding Member, Boulder County Estate Planning Council (1976-Present); President, Denver Estate Planning Council (1968-1969); Board of Editorial Advisors, Financial Service Advisors, Lexington, KY **Civic:** Vice Chair, Colorado Ski Museum (2003-Present); National Ski Patrol Systems (1948-Present); Chair, Colorado Ski Hall of Fame (1996-1999); Board of Directors, Metropolitan Denver YMCA (1978-1981); Chairman, Southwest Denver Family YMCA (1978-1981) **Military Service:** Captain, Judge Advocate General's Corps, U.S. Army (1952-1960) **Creative Works:** Author, National Ski Patrol Awards Manual (1980); Author, National Ski Patrol Ski Lift Evacuation Manual (1975) **Awards:** Legend, Denver Athletic Club (2003); Senior Athlete of the Year, Denver Athletic Club (1997); Wesley Whitney Award, National Association of Insurance and Financial Advisors (1995); Colorado Ski Hall of Fame (1993); U.S. National Senior Games (1991, 1993, 1995, 1997, 1999, 2001, 2003, 2005); Minnie Dole Award (1988); U.S. Badminton Association Senior Championship (1988, 1992); Metropolitan Denver YMCA Hall of Fame (1987); Badminton Medal, Rocky Mountain Senior Games (1987); Leading Producers Roundtable, National Association of Health Underwriters (1981-1989); J. Stanley Edwards Award, Colorado and Denver Association Life Underwriters (1980); Spark Plug Award, University of Wisconsin Alumni Association (1977); Roll of Honor, Mile High American Red Cross (1974); Schobinger Outstanding Administrator Award (1973); Million Dollar Round Table, National Association of Insurance and Financial Advisors (1970-1985); Award of Merit (Lifesaving), American Red Cross (1959); National Quality Award, Colorado Association of Insurance and Financial Advisors; National Sales Achievement Award, Colorado Association of Insurance and Financial Advisors **Membership:** Accreditation Committee, National Association of Estate Planners and Council (1991-Present); Chairman, Colorado Insurance Commissioner's Advisory Council (1990-Present); Director Emeritus, National Association of Estate Planners and Councils (1989-Present); Charter Member, Colorado State Association of Health Underwriters (1986-Present); Patron Chair, National Association of Estate Planners and Council (1975-Present); Hartman Axley Award for Outstanding Service and Achievement, National Association of Estate Planners and Council (2004); Colorado Liaison, Association for Advanced Life Underwriting (1996-2000); Staff Volunteer, Olympic Games Atlanta, U.S. Badminton Association (1996); West Region Vice President, Society of Financial Service Professionals (1994-1995); Colorado-Wyoming Liaison, National Association of Estate Planners and Councils (1992-1997); Founder, Board Director, Estate Planning Law Specialists, Inc.; National Association of Insurance and Financial Advisors; Colorado Association of Insurance and Financial Advisors; National Association of Health Underwriters; Wisconsin Bar Association; National Honor Society of Scabbard and Blade; Provost Corps; Phi Delta Phi; Phi Mu Alpha; Real Property, Probate and Trust Section, American Bar Association **Hobbies:** Skiing; Badminton; Deltiology; Singing; Traveling **Religion:** Congregationalist **Shipping Address:** 1845 S. Jay Way, Lakewood, CO, 80226

Mary Ellen Ayres

Title: Federal Official **Industry:** Government Administration/Government Relations/Government Services **Date of Birth:** 06/23/1924 **Place of Birth:** Spokane **State:** WA **Parents:** Frank H. Ayres; Marion (Kellogg) Ayres **Education:** Postgraduate, American University (1960); BA, Stanford University (1946); Student, University of Washington (1942-1943) **Career:** Writer-Editor, Bureau of Labor Statistics (1975-2010); Public Information Specialist, Bureau of Indian Affairs, U.S. Department of Interior (1967-1975); Editor, Bureau of Labor Statistics, Manpower Administration, U.S. Department of Labor (1962-1967); Editor, Family Guide, Kiplinger Washington Editors (1958-1961); Editorial Staff, Changing Times (1952-1961); Reporter, Washington Post (1951-1952); U.S. Foreign Service, U.S. Department of the State (1950-1951); Reporter, Wenatchee Daily World, Washington, DC (1947-1950); Henry von Morpurgo, Advertising (1946-1947) **Career Related:** Editing Style and Technique Class (1987-1989); Teacher, Newsletter Class, Department of Agriculture, Graduate School (1975-1989); Past Treasurer, Government Information Organization **Civic:** Director, Wenatchee High School Scholarship Foundation (1988-1995); Publicity Committee, National Capitol YWCA (1982-1983) **Membership:** Founding Treasurer, Director, National Association of Government Communicators (1989-1991); National Capital Chapter Treasurer, National Association of Government Communicators (1989); Chairman, Blue Pencil Contest, National Association of Government Communicators (1987); Founding Treasurer, Director, National Association of Government Communicators (1975-1980); Stanford University Alumnae Association; Kappa Kappa Gamma **Religion:** Episcopalian **Shipping Address:** 900 University Street, Apartment 5R, Seattle, WA, 98101

Marianne Baird

Title: Corporate Director **Industry:** Medicine & Health Care **Company Name:** Emory Healthcare **Date of Birth:** 12/15/1953 **Place of Birth:** Chicago **State:** IL **Parents:** John Saunorus; Irene Saunorus **Marital Status:** Married **Spouse Name:** Thomas W. Baird (9/10/1983) **Children:** Rachel **Education:** MSN, Emory University (1982); BSN, Loyola University (1975) **Certifications:** Clinical Nurse Specialist in Adult Health; Certified Instructor, ACLS **Career:** Corporate Director, Magnet Recognition Program, Emory Health Care, Atlanta, GA (2016-Present); Clinical Nurse Specialist, Critical Care and Nursing, St. Joseph's Hospital, Atlanta, GA (2001-2012); Case Manager, Departments of Pulmonary and Nephrology, St. Joseph's Hospital (1996-2001); Clinical Associate Faculty Member, Emory University, Atlanta, GA (1990-1996); Clinical Nurse Specialist, Critical Care Unit, St. Joseph's Hospital (1982-1996); Supervisor, Surgical Nursing, Rush University Medical Center (1978-1980); Director of Medical-Surgical Unit, St. Joseph's Hospital; Staff Nurse, Intensive Care Unit, St. Joseph's Hospital **Career Related:** Vice-Chairperson, Georgia Hospital Association, Diabetes Special Interest Group (2003-2010); RN Preceptor, Educational Staff, Genentech, Inc. (1995-2002) **Civic:** Medical Supply Committee, Atlanta Committee, Olympic Games (1994-1996) **Creative Works:** Editor, "Manual of Critical Care, Seventh Edition"; Author, Several Nursing Textbooks; Contributor, Various Articles, Professional Journals **Awards:** Outstanding Young Women in America (1991); Federal Traineeship, Emory University (1980-1981) **Membership:** Board of Directors, Atlanta Chapter, American Association of Critical Care Nurses (1984-1986); Society of Critical Care Medicine; American Holistic Nurses Association; American Nurses Association; National Association of Clinical Nurse Specialists; American Organization of Nurse Executives; Blue Key; Kappa Gamma Pi; Sigma Theta Tau **Shipping Address:** 3788 Glengarry Way, Roswell, GA, 30075

Dina Gustin Baker

Title: Artist **Industry:** Fine Art **Place of Birth:** Philadelphia **State:** PA **Parents:** Albert Isadore Kevles Schwartz; Rose Schwartz **Marital Status:** Married **Spouse Name:** William Baker (1/5/1968); John Calvin Gustin (7/4/1964, Deceased) **Education:** Coursework, The Barnes Foundation (1942-1946); Coursework, Hayter Atelier 17 (1945); Coursework, The Art Students League (1945); Coursework, Tyler School of Art, Temple University (1943); Coursework, Pennsylvania Academy of the Fine Arts (1940) **Creative Works:** Exhibitor, Ezair Gallery (2006-Present); Exhibitor, Los Angeles Exhibiting Hall, Los Angeles (2018); Exhibitor, New York City (2018); Exhibitor, Jewish Community Center, West Palm Beach (2017); Group Exhibitor, Ora Sorensen Gallery (2005); Group Exhibitor, Ora Sorensen Gallery (2003); Group Exhibitor, Ora Sorensen Gallery (2002); Exhibitor, Ora Sorensen Gallery (2000-2002); Group Exhibitor, Ora Sorensen Gallery (2000); Group Exhibitor, Gracie Lawrence Gallery (2000); Exhibitor, Gracie Lawrence Gallery (2000); Group Exhibitor, Gracie Lawrence Gallery (1999); Group Exhibitor, Gracie Lawrence Gallery (1996); Exhibitor, Gracie Lawrence Gallery (1996); Group Exhibitor, Rutgers, The State University of New Jersey (1996); Group Exhibitor, Adlena Adlung Gallery (1991); Group Exhibitor, Ingber Gallery, ArtSlant, Inc. (1984); Group Exhibitor, Bergen Museum (1984); Exhibitor, Brigham Young University (1983); Exhibitor, Utah State University (1983); Exhibitor, Ingber Gallery, ArtSlant, Inc. (1982); Group Exhibitor, Parrish Art Museum (1981); Exhibitor, Ingber Gallery, ArtSlant, Inc. (1980); Exhibitor, Ingber Gallery, ArtSlant, Inc. (1978); Group Exhibitor, Montclair Art Museum (1978); Group Exhibitor, Lehigh University (1977); Exhibitor, Ingber Gallery, ArtSlant, Inc. (1976); Exhibitor, Regensburg Museum (1974); Exhibitor, Amerika House, Berlin Foundation (1974); Group Exhibitor, The National Academy (1968); Exhibitor, Angeleski Gallery (1965); Exhibitor, Roko Gallery (1963); Group Exhibitor, Pennsylvania Academy of the Fine Arts (1963); Group Exhibitor, Art USA (1955); Group Exhibitor, Guild Hall (1954); Permanent Exhibitor, Bergen Museum; Permanent Exhibitor, Rutgers, The State University of New Jersey; Permanent Exhibitor, New York University; Permanent Exhibitor, Gannett Foundation; Permanent Exhibitor, Columbia University; Permanent Exhibitor, Boca Raton Museum of Art **Membership:** Cultural Council of Palm Beach County; RoundTable **Marquis Who's Who Honors:** Albert Nelson Marquis Lifetime Achievement Award (2017) **Why did you become involved in your profession or industry:** Mrs. Baker became involved in her profession when she was 5 years old. It is something that she has done for her whole life, and she never questioned it. **What do you consider to be the highlight of your career:** Mrs. Baker is most proud of the grants and fellowships that she received, especially the graduate fellowship at the Barns Foundation. She has had shows regularly at the Walter Wickser Gallery. **Shipping Address:** 3487 SE Doubleton Dr., Stuart, FL, 34997 **Website:** http://www.dinagustinbaker.com

Robert Baker

Title: Lawyer **Industry:** Law and Legal Services **Date of Birth:** 12/15/1935 **Place of Birth:** Durham **State:** NC **Parents:** Lenox D. Baker; Virginia (Flowers) Baker **Marital Status:** Married **Spouse Name:** Barbara Downes; Billie Faye Edwards (Married, 6/12/1958, Deceased 5/27/1989) **Children:** William Lenox; Dial Baker Love; Robert Flowers **Education:** JD, Duke University (1961); BA, Davidson College (1958) **Certifications:** Certified Mediator and Arbitrator **Career:** Partner, Spears, Barnes, Baker, Wainio & Whaley, Durham, NC (1967-2000); Associate, Spears & Spears, Durham, NC (1963-1967) **Military Service:** Captain, US Army (1961-1963) **Membership:** The Order of Long Leaf Pine; Society of Cincinnati; President, Hope Valley Country Club (2004); Council Member, North Carolina State Bar (1990-1998); President, North Carolina Bar Association (1982-1983); Kiwanis Tobaccoland Club, Durham, NC (1975-1976); Fellow, American College of Trial Lawyers **Bar Admissions:** North Carolina (1961) **Hobbies:** Golf **Religion:** Episcopalian **Shipping Address:** 3126 Cornwall Rd, Durham, NC, 27707

William T. Baker

Title: Lawyer **Industry:** Law and Legal Services **Date of Birth:** 01/19/1944 **Place of Birth:** New York **State:** NY **Parents:** William Thompson; Elizabeth (Baird) Baker **Children:** Alice Whetherly; Richard Cass; Heather Thompson **Education:** JD, The University of Virginia (1968); BA, Yale University, Cum Laude (1965) **Career:** Of Counsel, Day Pitney LLC (2011-Present); Senior Counsel, Morgan Lewis & Bockius (2008-2011); Partner, Thelen (1975-2008); Chairman Executive Committee, Reid & Priest, Thelen (1990-1991); Member Executive Committee, Thelen (1986-1991); Managing Partner, Thelen (1986-1989); Member, Executive Committee, Thelen (1980-1982); Associate, Thelen (1968-1974) **Career Related:** Counsel, Day Pitey LLP (2011-Present); Senior Counsel, Morgan, Lewis & Bockius LLP (2008-2011); Chairman Emeritus, Legal Committee, Edison Electric Institute (2000-Present); Chairman, Legal Committee, Edison Electric Institute (1997-1999) **Membership:** Vice Chair of Infrastructure, Finance, Mergers and Acquisitions Committee, Section of Public Utility, Communications and Transportation Law, ABA (2005-Present); Board of Governors, Alumni Association, The Hotchkiss School (2003-2009); Secretary and Treasurer, Alumni Association, The Hotchkiss School (2005-2009); Subcommittee Chairman, Public Utility Holding Company Act, ABA (1990-2005); Yale Club New York City; New York Anglers Club **Bar Admissions:** United States Court of Appeals for the District of Columbia Circuit (1992); Supreme Court of the United States (1990); United States District Court Southern District of New York(1969); United States District Court for the Eastern District of New York (1969) **Marquis Who's Who Honors:** Albert Nelson Marquis Lifetime Achievement Award (2017) **Hobbies:** Fishing; Fly tying; Rod building; Wood working; Cosmology **Political Affiliations:** Republican **Religion:** Episcopalian **Shipping Address:** 49 E 86th St Apt 2C, New York, NY 10028

W. Scott Baldridge, PhD

Title: Geologist, Researcher **Industry:** Sciences **Company Name:** Los Alamos National Lab **Date of Birth:** 01/07/1945 **Place of Birth:** Lyons **State:** NY **Parents:** Warren Earl Baldridge; Virginia Alison (Stone) Baldridge **Marital Status:** Married **Spouse Name:** Helen Fabel (11/21/1974) **Children:** Gregory Scott **Education:** Postdoctoral Fellow, Los Alamos National Laboratory (1978-1980); PhD, California Institute of Technology (1978); MS, California Institute of Technology (1969); Coursework, University of Gottingen, Germany (1967-1968); AB, Hamilton College (1967) **Career:** Geologist, Los Alamos National Laboratory (1980-Present) **Career Related:** Adjunct Professor, University of New Mexico, Albuquerque, NM (1991-Present); Visiting Professor, Hebrew University, Jerusalem, Israel (1984-1985); Fulbright Fellow, Gottingen, Germany (1967-1968) **Creative Works:** Associate Editor, Geological Society of America Bulletin (1998-Present); Associate Editor, Journal of Geophysical Research (1993-1994); Contributor, Articles, Professional Journals; Author, "The Geology of the American Southwest: A Journey Through Two Billion Years" **Awards:** Special Commendation Award, Society of Exploration Geophysicists (2000); Excellence in Geophysical Education Award, American Geophysical Union (1998); Fulbright Senior Scholar, University of Oslo, Norway (1996-1997) **Membership:** Geological Society of America, Inc.; American Geophysical Union; Society of Exploration Geophysicists; New Mexico Geological Society **Marquis Who's Who Honors:** Albert Nelson Marquis Lifetime Achievement Award (2017) **Business Address:** PO Box 1663, Los Alamos, NM, 87545-0001

Lionel Vernon Baldwin, PhD

Title: University President, Academic Administrator **Industry:** Education/Educational Services **Company Name:** National Technological University **Date of Birth:** 05/30/1932 **Place of Birth:** Beaumont **State:** TX **Parents:** Eugene Baldwin, Wanda (Wiley) Baldwin **Marital Status:** Single **Spouse Name:** Kathleen Flanagan (9/3/1955, Deceased 2009) **Children:** Brian; Michael; Diane; Daniel **Education:** PhD, Case Institute of Technology (Now Case Western Reserve University) (1959); MSChemE, Massachusetts Institute of Technology (1955); BSChemE, University of Notre Dame, Magna Cum Laude (1954) **Certifications:** Registered Engineer, State of Colorado **Career:** President, National Technological University, Fort Collins, CO (1984-2000); Dean, Professor, College of Engineering, Colorado State University (1966-1984); Acting Dean, College of Engineering, Colorado State University (1964-1965); Associate Professor of Civil Engineering, Colorado State University (1961-1964); Unit Head, National Aeronautics and Space Administration (1959-1961); Research Engineer, National Advisory Committee for Aeroscience (1957-1959) **Career Related:** Director, Spherix (1975-2004); Fellow, American Society of Engineering Education **Civic:** Colorado Air Pollution Hearings Board; Longs Peak Science Foundation **Military Service:** Captain, U.S. Air Force (1955-1958) **Awards:** Innovator Award, Society of Satellite Professionals International (2000); Kenneth A. Roe Award, American Association of Engineering Societies (1996); Engineering Education Hall Of Fame (1993); Entrepreneur of the Year, Fort Collins Chamber of Commerce (1992); Engineering Manager of the Year, American Society of Engineering Management (1990); Centennial Professor, The American Society of Engineering Education (1987-1989); Chester F. Carlson Award for Innovation, American Society of Engineering Education (1987); Distinguished Service Award, University of Notre Dame (1984); Award for Plasma Research, National Aeronautics and Space Administration (1964) **Membership:** Centennial Professor, American Society of Engineering Education (1987-1989); Chairman, Engineering Deans Council, American Society of Engineering Education; American Society of Mechanical Engineers; IEEE; National Society of Professional Engineers; Sigma Xi; Tau Beta Pi; Sigma Pi Sigma **Marquis Who's Who Honors:** Distinguished Humanitarian (2017) **Shipping Address:** 1900 Sequoia Street, Fort Collins, CO, 80525

Elizabeth B. Baldwin-Gibbons

Title: Minister **Industry:** Religious **Date of Birth:** 06/16/1931 **Place of Birth:** Orange **State:** NJ **Parents:** Charles G. Baldwin; Kathrina C. Baldwin **Marital Status:** Married **Spouse Name:** David A. Gibbons (6/20/1953) **Children:** Laura Emily; Kenneth Charles; Phillip Baldwin; Alan Ray **Education:** MDiv, Methodist Theological School (1982); MA, University of Washington (1960); BA, Oberlin College (1953) **Certifications:** Ordained Minister, Methodist Church (1982) **Career:** Pastor, De Bows United Methodist Church, New Jersey (2004); Youth Pastor, Manasquan United Methodist Church, New Jersey (2001-2004); Minister, United Methodist Church, Browns Mills, NJ (1987-2001); Minister of Education, First Baptist Church, Hightstown, NJ (1983-1987); Director of Christian Education, First Baptist Church, Granville, OH (1965-1982) **Civic:** Habitat for Humanity **Awards:** Woman of the Year, Burlington County **Marquis Who's Who Honors:** Albert Nelson Marquis Lifetime Achievement Award (2017) **To what do you attribute your success:** Rev. Baldwin-Gibbons attributes her success to her strong family background. **Why did you become involved in your profession or industry:** Rev. Baldwin-Gibbons became involved in her profession because it was God's calling. **What do you consider to be the highlight of your career:** The highlight of Rev. Baldwin-Gibbons' career is her family. **Where will you be in five years:** In five years, Rev. Baldwin-Gibbons will remain living in Oakhurst, N.J. **Hobbies:** Going to the gym **Religion:** United Methodist **Shipping Address:** 14 Branch Road, Oakhurst, NJ, 07755

Royal Eugene Bales, PhD

Title: Philosophy Educator (Retired) **Industry:** Education/Educational Services **Date of Birth:** 09/23/1934 **Place of Birth:** Pratt **State:** KS **Parents:** Harold Thomas Bales; Gladys (German) Bales **Marital Status:** Married **Spouse Name:** Flossie Kathleen O'Reilly (4/16/1960) **Children:** David Scott; Elizabeth Laurel **Education:** PhD in Philosophy, Stanford University (1968); MA, Wichita State University (1960); BE in Music, Wichita State University, Cum Laude (1956) **Career:** Professor Emeritus, Menlo College (2000-Present); Adjunct Faculty, Menlo College (2000-2008); Professor, Menlo College (1970-2000); President of Faculty Senate (1997); Vice President, Faculty Senate, Menlo College (1996-1997); Provost, Menlo College (1979-1987); Dean of Liberal Arts, Menlo College (1974-1979); Standing Member, President's Advisory Council, Menlo College (1971-1987); Chairman of Social Sciences and Humanities, Menlo College (1971-1974); Adjunct Faculty, California State University, East Bay (1968-1970); Professor of Philosophy, Menlo College (1962-1969); Teaching Assistant, Stanford University (1966-1967); Teacher of Music, Kansas Public Schools (1959-1960, 1956-1957); Adjunct Faculty, Wichita State University (1959) **Career Related:** Wong Visiting Professor of Western Logic, Guangdong College of Law and Commerce, China (1999); Visiting Fellow, Harris Manchester College, University of Oxford (1998, 1994); Principal Investigator, Stanford University Consortium on Instructional Use of Computers, Menlo College (1971-1973) **Civic:** Honorary Governor, Harris Manchester College, University of Oxford (1994-Present); President, El Camino Youth Symphony (1985-1987) **Military Service:** U.S. Army (1955-1963) **Creative Works:** Author, "Grit Beneath My Nails," Abbott Press (2015); Author, "But Then My Voice Changed. From Fundamentalist to Nonbeliever: One Man's Story," Abbott Press (2012); Contributor, "About Philosophy, 9th Edition," Pearson Education, Inc. (2006); Commentator, "Moral Opinions Within Consequentialism: New Challenges," Pacific Division, American Philosophical Association Conference (1999); Author, "Utilitarianism: A Handbook for Students," Menlo College (1998); Author, "Utilitarianism and Alienation," Harris Manchester College, University of Oxford (1998); Commentator, "Promises and Promissory Obligations," Pacific Division, American Philosophical Association Conference (1998); Author, "On Formulating Rule-Utilitarianism," Harris Manchester College, University of Oxford (1994); Author, "Act-Utilitarianism: Account of Right-Making Characteristics or Decision-Making Procedure?" International Research Library of Philosophy (1994); Author, "Act-Utilitarianism: Account of Right-Making Characteristics or Decision-Making Procedure?" American Philosophical Quarterly (1994); Author, "Animals, Fetuses, and the Concept of a Person," University of Warsaw (1990); Author, "Utilitarianism, General Welfare, and Majority Rule," Honors Society, Utah State University (1977); Author, "Critical Review of Bergstrom" (1974); Author, "Utilitarianism, Overall Obligatoriness, and Deontic Logic," Analysis (1972); Author, "Is Act-Utilitarianism Self-Defeating?" Uppsala University (1970); "Act-Utilitarianism: Ethical Theory or Decision-Making Procedure?" Pacific Division, American Philosophical Association Conference (1969) **Awards:** Alumni News Profile, Wichita State University (1974); Recipient, Stipend, National Endowment for the Humanities (1973); Research Grantee, Stanford-Warsaw Exchange, University of Warsaw (1969-1970); Recipient, Scholarship, Stanford University (1966-1967); Recipient, Scholarship, Wichita State University (1952-1960) **Membership:** American Philosophical Association; Oregon Shakespeare Festival; Phi Mu Alpha Sinfonia Fraternity of America **Marquis Who's Who Honors:** Albert Nelson Marquis Lifetime Achievement Award (2017) **Hobbies:** Music **Political Affiliations:** Democrat **Shipping Address:** 1255 Sherman Ave, Menlo Park, CA, 94025

John Tilden Ballantine

Title: Lawyer **Industry:** Law and Legal Services **Company Name:** Stoll Keenon Ogden PLLC **Date of Birth:** 02/26/1931 **Place of Birth:** Louisville **State:** KY **Parents:** Thomas Austin Ballantine; Anna Marie (Pfeiffer) Ballantine **Marital Status:** Married **Spouse Name:** Beverley Jo Hackley; Mary January Strode (5/15/1954, Divorced 1964) **Children:** John T., Jr.; William Clayton; Douglas C.; Susan Marie **Education:** JD, Harvard University (1957); BA, University of Kentucky, with High Distinction (1952) **Certifications:** Admitted to Practice, Supreme Court of the United States (1982); Admitted to Practice, United States Court of Appeals for the Sixth Circuit (1968); Admitted to Practice, United States District Court Eastern District of Kentucky (1963); Admitted to Practice, United States District Court Western District of Kentucky (1957) **Career:** Counsel, Stoll Keenon Ogden PLLC (2014-Present); Partner, Member, General Counsel, Stoll Keenon Ogden PLLC (1958-2014); Law Clerk to Presiding Judge, United States District Court District of Western Kentucky (1957-1958) **Career Related:** Judicial Nominating Committee, Kentucky Supreme Court (2004-2012); Judicial Nominating Committee, Kentucky Court of Appeals (2004-2012); Member, Civil Rules Committee, Kentucky Supreme Court (1988-1996); Adjunct Professor, Brandeis School of Law, University of Louisville **Civic:** Honorary Director, Kentucky Derby Festival, Louisville, KY (1981-Present); Member, Kentucky Bar Association Ethics Committee (2003-2009); Member, Kentucky Bar Association Ethics Committee (1996); Chairman, Our Lady of Peace Hospital, Louisville, KY (1991-1993); Board of Directors, Our Lady of Peace Hospital, Louisville, KY (1988-1993); Member, Historical Landmarks and Preservation Districts Commission, Louisville, KY (1976-1988); Board of Directors, Metropolitan United Way, Louisville, KY (1975-1981); Board of Directors, Kentucky Derby Festival, Louisville, KY (1975-1981); Vice President, Kentucky Derby Festival, Louisville, KY (1975); President, Family and Children Agency, Louisville, KY (1971-1974); Board of Directors, Our Lady of Peace Hospital, Louisville, KY (1968-1973); Chairman, Our Lady of Peace Hospital, Louisville, KY (1968-1969); Board of Directors, Family and Children Agency, Louisville, KY (1965-1975) **Military Service:** First Lieutenant, US Air Force (1952-1954) **Awards:** Recipient, Sixth Circuit Professionalism Award, American Inns of Court (2012); Recipient, Judge Benjamin Shobe Civility and Professionalism Award (2005); Recipient, Outstanding Lawyer Award, Kentucky Bar Association (2003); Recipient, Outstanding Young Man in Field Of Law Award, Louisville Jaycees (1966); Recipient, Algernon Sydney Sullivan Award, University of Kentucky **Membership:** Ethics Committee, Kentucky Bar Association (1996-Present); President, Louis D. Brandeis American Inn of Court (2007-2009); Board of Directors, Louisville Bar Association (1996-2002); Board of Governors, Kentucky Bar Association (1996-2002); Kentucky Evidence Rules Review Commission, Kentucky Bar Association (1995-2002); Clients' Security Fund, Kentucky Bar Association (1993-1996); Board of Directors, Louisville Bar Association (1993); Board of Directors, Louisville Bar Association (1992); Chairman, Kentucky Bar Association (1989-1990); Board of Directors, Louisville Bar Association (1989); Professional Responsibility Committee, Louisville Bar Association (1988-1993); Board of Directors, Louisville Bar Association (1988); House of Delegates, Kentucky Bar Association (1985-1991); President, Kentucky Defense Counsel (1981-1982); President, Louisville Bar Association (1970); Board of Directors, Louisville Bar Association (1969-1971); Chairman, Physician-Attorney Committee, Louisville Bar Association; Life Member, United States Sixth Circuit Court of Appeals Judicial Conference; Kentucky Defense Counsel; American Inns of Court; Louis D. Brandeis American Inn of Court; Kentucky Character and Fitness Committee; The Law Club; Phi Beta Kappa; Fellow, American College of Trial Lawyers; ABA **Bar Admissions:** Kentucky (1957) **Marquis Who's Who Honors:** Albert Nelson Marquis Lifetime Achievement Award (2017) **Business Address:** 500 W Jefferson St Ste 2000, Louisville, KY, 40202 **Shipping Address:** 500 W Jefferson St Ste 2000, Stoll Keenon Ogden PLLC, Louisville, KY, 40202

Dawn Lois Balog

Title: Physical Therapist **Industry:** Health, Wellness and Fitness **Date of Birth:** 05/05/1940 **Place of Birth:** Lansing **State:** MI **Parents:** Harold James Gilpin; Edna Alice (Richmond) Gilpin **Marital Status:** Married **Spouse Name:** John Francis Balog (6/22/1963) **Children:** Monica Marie; Teresa Alice **Education:** PhD, Donsbach University (1983); MS, Donsbach University (1981); BA, Immaculate Heart College (1974) **Certifications:** Certified Biofeedback Therapist **Career:** Program Director, Co-Founder, Lifestyle Dynamics, Pasadena (1983-1994); Program Director, Life Fitness Center, Pasadena, CA (1980-1983); Founder, Awareness in Action, Kapalua, HI **Civic:** Board of Directors, Immaculate Heart College, Los Angeles, CA **Membership:** California Institute of Technology Associates, Pasadena, CA **Marquis Who's Who Honors:** Albert Nelson Marquis Lifetime Achievement Award (2017) **Why did you become involved in your profession or industry:** Dr. Balog became involved in her profession because she was always interested in making positive differences and helping people improve their lives and live without conflict. **What do you consider to be the highlight of your career:** Dr. Balog considers opening the Life Fitness Center, of which she was the founder and director, to be a professional highlight; she loves changing people's habits to be positive. **Shipping Address:** 143 Kualapa Place, Lahaina, HI, 96761 **Website:** http://www.awarenessinaction.net

Maria Lourdes Geraldine Banaad-Omiotek

Title: Medical Doctor **Industry:** Medicine & Health Care **Company Name:** Swedish Covenant Hospital **Education:** Chief Resident in Family Medicine, Swedish Covenant Hospital, Chicago, IL (2003-2004); Resident in Family Medicine, Swedish Covenant Hospital, Chicago, IL (2001-2003); Chief Resident, Cardinal Santos Medical Center (1997); Resident in Internal Medicine, Cardinal Santos Medical Center (1995-1997); Intern, Cardinal Santos Medical Center (1994); MD, UERMMMCI, Quezon City, Philippines (1993); BS in Biology, Ateneo de Manila University, Quezon City, Philippines (1989) **Certifications:** Certified in Family Medicine, The American Board of Family Medicine, Inc. (2004-Present); Diplomate, Philippine College of Physicians (1998-Present); Diplomate, Educational Commission for Foreign Medical Graduates (1995); Licensed to Practice Medicine, State of Illinois **Career:** Attending Physician, Family Doctor-Family Healthcare, Presence Health, Chicago, IL (2004-Present); Research Assistant, Department of Hepatology, Rush University Medical Center (1999-2001); Doctor, G.D. Banaad Clinic, Quezon City, Philippines (1998) **Career Related:** Director, Scholarship Program, Ateneo Alumni Association of North America, Inc. (2017-Present) **Civic:** Director, Scholarship Program, Ateneo de Manila University (2017-Present) **Creative Works:** Co-author, "Current liver biopsy practices for suspected parenchymal liver diseases in the United States: The evolving role of radiologists," American Journal of Gastroenterology (2002); Co-author, "Adult Living Donor Liver Transplantation: Preferences About Donation Outside the Medical Community," Liver Transplantation (2001); Co-author, "Patient's Values for Health States Associated With Hepatitis C and Physicians' Estimates of Those Values," American Journal of Gastroenterology (2001); Co-author, "Liver biopsy practices in the United States," American College of Gastroenterology (2001); Co-author, "Universal precaution practices of gastrointestinal endoscopy personnel," American College of Gatroenterology (2001); Co-author, "Differing attitudes towards virtual and conventional colonoscopy for colorectal cancer screening: Surveys among primary care physicians and potential patients," American Journal of Gastroenterology (2001) **Awards:** Honoree, Via Times Hall of Fame for Excellence in Medicine, CPRTV Channel, Via Times (2017); Honoree, Most Outstanding Resident, Swedish Covenant Hospital, Chicago, IL (2003-2004); **Membership:** Shodan, World Seido Karate Organization (2009-Present); American Academy of Family Physicians; American Board of Family Medicine; Chicago Medical Society; Illinois Academy of Family Physicians; Philippine College of Physicians **To what do you attribute your success:** Dr. Banaad-Omiotek attributes her success to encouragement that she received from her parents because she was good at science, so they encouraged her to go into the medical field. **Why did you become involved in your profession or industry:** Dr. Banaad-Omiotek became involved in her profession because it was something that was generally suggested by her parents. They didn't force it, but she knew that's what they wanted. Dr. Banaad-Omiotek's uncle was a physician, so she was exposed to it. She liked the sciences and did the residency program in Philippines in internal medicine. When she came to the states, Dr. Banaad-Omiotek applied to do internal medicine, which is family medicine. She was matched to a family practice residency, and she knew that she didn't want to do surgery. **Hobbies:** Family; Travel; Children's activities; Practicing martial arts **Business Address:** 6201 W Touhy Ave, Chicago, IL, 60646 **Shipping Address:** 1844 N Paulina St, Chicago, IL, 60622

Bruce Lord Bandurski

Title: Ecologist; Ecomanagement Advisor; Environmental Diplomat **Industry:** Environmental Services **Company Name:** International Joint Commission, U.S.A. and Canada **Date of Birth:** 06/28/1940 **Place of Birth:** Waterbury **State:** CT **Parents:** Stanley Alexander Bandurski; Virginia Ann (VanRensselaer) Bandurski Hinckley **Marital Status:** Married **Spouse Name:** Nancy Ann Spaulding (3/17/2007) **Education:** Graduate Coursework, The George Washington University, Washington, DC (1965-1966); BS, Honors College, Michigan State University, East Lansing, MI, with Honors (1962) **Career:** Senior Ecomanagement Adviser, International Joint Commission, Washington, DC (1985-2000); Ecologist, International Joint Commission (1985-2000); On Detail as Ecologist and Ecomanagement Adviser, International Joint Commission (1983-1985); Coordinator, U.S. Department of the Interior, Washington, DC (1974-1983); Branch Chief, U.S. Department of the Interior (1974-1983); National Environmental Policy Act Officer, U.S. Department of the Interior (1974-1983); Analyst Planner, U.S. Department of the Interior (1966-1974); Faculty Member, United States Department of Agriculture Graduate School (1966-1998); Science Reference Analyst, United States Division of Water Supply and Pollution Control, Washington, DC (1963-1965) **Career Related:** Binational Workshop on Indicators of Ecosystem Integrity/Diversity (1998); International Joint Commission Task Force on Indicators Implementation (1997-2000); Member, Lake Erie Task Force (1994-1997); Member, International Joint Commission Task Force on Indicators for Evaluation (1994-1996); Initiator, Multiyear Project, Ecological Committee, Great Lakes Science Advisory Board (1990-1994); Member, Executive Committee, Great Lakes Science Advisory Board (1986-1992); Member, Steering Group on Marine Environmental Monitoring, Commission on Engineering and Technical Studies, National Research Council (1986-1987); Binational Workshop on the Transboundary Monitoring Network, U.S. and Canada (1984); Chairman, Committee on Definitions, Special Committee on Environmental Protection, U.S. National Committee, World Energy Conference, Washington (1981-1985); Chairman, Conservation Roundtable of Washington (1970-1971); Watch Director, Deputy, Acting Mission Director, U.S. Man-in-Sea Program, St. John, Virgin Islands (1970); Faculty Member, United States Department of Agriculture Graduate School (1968-1996) **Civic:** Volunteer Patrol, Sabino Canyon, United States Forest Service (2010-Present); Lecturer, Earth Day, United States Department of the Interior (1970) **Military Service:** Sergeant, Military Police Platoon, Reserve Officers Training Corps (1960) **Creative Works:** Co-Author, "The Ecosystems Approach: Theory and Ecosystem Integrity (1993); Co-Author, "Perspectives on Ecosystems Management for the Great Lakes: A Reader" (1988); Co-Author, "Toward a Transboundary Monitoring Network" (1986); Author, "U.S. Bureau of Land Management Environmental Management Procedures" (1976-1984); Author, "Ecology and Economics: Partners for Productivity" (1973); Co-Author, "More Recreation: Implications for the Tropical Ecosystem" (1969); Writer, Planning and Recreation Impact Management Series (1967-1973); Author, "No Man is An Island" **Awards:** Fellow, International Biographical Association (2016-Present); The Sir Isaac Newton Legacy of Honour Award (2017); Recipient, The Tesla Award, International Biography Centre (2017); Five Stars of Excellence, International Biographical Center (2017); Decoration for Achievement in Science, International Biographical Center (2017); Honoree, World Leader of Sciences, Michigan State University (2017); Honoree, World Leader of Scientists (2017); Honoree, Outstanding Scientific Achievement, International Biographical Center, Cambridge, UK (2016); Honorary Director General, International Biographical Center (2016) **Membership:** Fellow, International Biographical Association (2016-Present); American Association for the Advancement of Science, Charter, Metropolitan Washington Chapter, Ecological Society of America; International Association for Ecology and Health (Now EcoHealth); American Society of Naturalists; The Wildlife Society; The American Society of Mammalogists; Federal Professional Association; Washington Society of Professional Engineers; Outdoor Ethics Guild; The Nature Conservancy; Maine Coast Heritage Trust; Island Institute; Earthwatch Institute; Association of Ecosystem Research Centers; Charter, International Society for Ecosystem Health; Charter, National Museum of Women in the Arts; Founder, National Campaign for Tolerance; Friesian Horse Association of North America; The Friesian Horse Society; Friends of Kentucky Educational Television; Friends of KUAT; Arizona Rangers; Founding Sponsor, The Memorial Foundation; Board Member, Bear Canyon Neighborhood Association, Albuquerque, NM; Alpha Zeta; Beta Beta Beta **Marquis Who's Who Honors:** Albert Nelson Marquis Lifetime Achievement Award (2017) **Hobbies:** Owning and managing three offshore islands registered in the state of Maine; Wildlife photography; **Shipping Address:** 7215 E Camino Valle Verde, Tucson, AZ, 85715

Robert J. Banis

Title: Pharmaceutical Company Executive, Educator, Publisher, Chief Executive Officer **Industry:** Pharmaceuticals **Company Name:** Science & Humanities Press **Date of Birth:** 10/26/1943 **Place of Birth:** New York **State:** NY **Parents:** Vincent Nicholas Banis; Roberta Irma (Shwedo) Banis **Marital Status:** Widowed **Spouse Name:** Lois Elaine Polson (1/25/1970, Deceased 9/30/2002) **Children:** Andrea Berit; Lauren Nicole **Education:** MBA in Marketing and Finance, University of Chicago, With Honors (1982); National Institutes of Health Postdoctoral Fellow, Harvard University, Cambridge, MA (1973-1975); PhD in Biochemistry, North Carolina State University (1973); MS in Animal Nutrition, Purdue University (1969); BS in Science Education, Cornell University (1967) **Certifications:** Certified Management Accountant **Career:** Instructor, St. Louis Community College, St. Louis, MO (1994-Present); Principal, Banis & Associates, St. Louis, MO (1994-Present); Adjunct Faculty, Webster University, St. Louis, MO (1995); President, 21st Century Stewardship Inc., St. Louis, MO (1994-2000); Adjunct Faculty, Vincennes University, St. Louis, MO (1994); Director, Operations and Finance, Monsanto Company, St. Louis, MO (1988-1994); Manager, Research Operations and Finance Planning, Searle R&D Division, Monsanto Company, St. Louis, MO (1986-1988); Manager, Research Operations and Finance Planning, Monsanto Company, St. Louis, MO (1985-1986); Research Group Leader, Health Care Division, Monsanto Company, St. Louis, MO (1983-1985); Manager, Biochemical and Pharmaceutical Development, Armour Pharmaceutical Co., Kankakee, IL (1981-1983); Technical Manager, Biochemicals and Parenterals, Armour Pharmaceutical Co., Kankakee, IL (1979-1981); Senior Research Scientist, Armour Pharmaceutical Co., Kankakee, IL (1975-1979) **Career Related:** Principal, Publisher, Chief Executive Officer, Science & Humanities Press (1995-Present); Adjunct Associate Professor, Full-time Lecturer, University of Missouri, St. Louis, MO (1992-Present); Founder, Science & Humanities Press, St. Louis, MO (1995); Adjunct Assistant Professor, Business, University of Missouri, St. Louis, MO (1987-1992) **Civic:** Management Consultant, United Way Management Assistance Center (1994-Present); General Chairman, World Burn Congress VII (1995); President, Chairman of the Board, Burns Recovered Support Group, Inc. (1993-1996); Torchlight Speaker, United Way (1993-1994); Regional Coordinator, The Phoenix Society (1993); Loaned Executive, Fundraisers, United Way (1993); Volunteer, St. John's Mercy Medical Center (1992-1998); Allocations Panel Volunteer, Greater St. Louis Area, United Way (1991-1995); Chairman, Campaign, United Way (1989-1990); Co-Chairman, Campaign, Searle-St. Louis Division, United Way (1988-1989) **Creative Works:** Editor, "Sexually Transmitted Diseases, A Practical Guide 2nd Edition" (2006); Editor, "Copyright Issues for Librarians, Teachers and Authors, 2nd Edition" (2001); Editor, "Inaugural Addresses–Presidents of the U.S. from George Washington to 2004" (1998); Editor, "Copyright Issues for Librarians, Teachers and Authors" (1998); Editor, "Copyright Issues for Teachers and Authors" (1997); Editor, "Sexually Transmitted Diseases, A Practical Guide" (1997); Contributing Author, "The Science of Meat and Meat Products, 3rd Edition" (1987); Contributing Author, "COMPUTE!'s Second Book of VIC" (1983) **Awards:** United Way Star Communicator Award (1993-1994); Volunteer of the Year Award, Trinity Lutheran Church (1991) **Membership:** Vice President, St. Louis Publishers Association (1999); President, INFORMS (1995-1996); Vice President, President-Elect, INFORMS (1994-1995); Associate Director, Certified Medical Assistant Review Course, Institute of Management Accountants, Inc. (1993-1995); Secretary, Gateway Chapter, INFORMS (1993-1994); Phi Lambda Upsilon; American Burn Association; American Association for the Advancement of Science; American Chemical Society; St. Louis Chapter Director, Civic Activities, Institute of Management Accountants, Inc.; Beta Gamma Sigma **Marquis Who's Who Honors:** Albert Nelson Marquis Lifetime Achievement Award (2017) **Shipping Address:** 63 Summit Pointe Court, Saint Charles, MO, 63301 **Website:** http://www.sciencehumanitiespress.com

Edward Bruce Barber

Title: Medical Products Executive **Industry:** Medicine & Health Care **Company Name:** Christiansen & Barber Associate Ltd. **Date of Birth:** 03/11/1937 **Place of Birth:** Chicago **State:** IL **Parents:** Edward Vanrennsaler Barber; Alice (Reinertsen) Barber **Marital Status:** Married **Spouse Name:** Louise Joy Griebler (5/23/1964) **Education:** JD, University of Chicago (1964); PhD, University of Chicago (1961); MBA, University of Chicago (1958); BS, Lake Forest College, Illinois (1957) **Career:** President, Christiansen & Barber Associate Ltd., Chicago, IL (1964-Present); Market Research Consultant, Container Corporation of America, Chicago, IL (1962-1964) **Career Related:** Partner, Wynne Medical/Statco Medical (1996-Present); Member, Board of Directors, Colts Necks Farms, Inc. (1990-Present); President, Colts Necks Farms, Inc. (1990-Present); Consultant, Laboratory Supply Company, Louisville (1990-Present); Scientific Supply Company, Schiller Park, IL (1990-President); Founder, M.E. Team, Inc., South Plainfield, NJ (1980-Present); Chairman, M.E. Team, Inc., South Plainfield, NJ (1980-Present); Chairman, Odyssey Travel Ltd., Chicago, IL (1974-Present); Chief Executive Officer, Odyssey Travel Ltd., Chicago, IL (1974-Present); Board of Directors, Golden Eagle Travel, Huntington Beach, CA; Advisory Board, North Park University School of Business **Membership:** AAONMS; Health Industries Distributor Association; International Association Travel Agencies; Freemasonry **Marquis Who's Who Honors:** Albert Nelson Marquis Lifetime Achievement Award (2017) **Why did you become involved in your profession or industry:** He became involved in his profession because he felt that there was a need for his services, and because he had a desire to help people. **Hobbies:** Traveling; Collecting coins **Political Affiliations:** Republican **Religion:** Lutheran **Shipping Address:** 22 Park Ln Unit 501, Park Ridge, IL, 60068

Jack David Barchas

Title: Psychiatrist, Chief **Industry:** Medicine & Health Care **Company Name:** Weill Cornell Medical College **Date of Birth:** 11/02/1935 **Place of Birth:** Los Angeles **State:** CA **Parents:** Samuel Isaac Barchas; Cecile Margaret (Pasarow) Barchas **Marital Status:** Married **Spouse Name:** Rosemary Anne Stevens (8/9/1994); Patricia Ruth Corbitt (2/9/1957, Deceased) **Children:** Isaac Doherty; Carey T. Stevens (Stepchild); Richard N. Stevens (Stepchild) **Education:** Resident in Psychiatry, Stanford Medical School, Palo Alto, CA (1964-1967); Medical Intern, Pritzker School of Medicine, Chicago, IL (1961-1962); MD, Yale Medical School (1961); BA, Pomona College (1956) **Certifications:** Licensed Psychiatrist, State of New York (1994) **Career:** Psychiatrist-in-Chief, NewYork-Presbyterian/Weill Cornell Medical Center, New York (1993-Present); Barklie McKee Henry Professor, Chair, Department of Psychiatry, NewYork-Presbyterian/Weill Cornell Medical Center, New York (1993-Present); Dean, Neuroscience and Research Development, University of California, Los Angeles School of Medicine (1990-1993); Professor, Psychiatry, University of California, Los Angeles School of Medicine (1990-1993); Associate Chair, Department of Psychiatry, Stanford Medical School (1982-1987); Nancy Friend Pritzker Professor, Psychiatry, Director, Nancy Pritzker Laboratory for Behavioral Neurochemistry, Stanford Medical School (1976-1989); Associate Professor, Stanford Medical School (1971-1976); Assistant Professor, Psychiatry, Stanford Medical School, Palo Alto, CA (1967-1971); Director, Laboratory for Behavioral Neurochemistry, Department of Psychiatry, Stanford Medical School (1964-1976); **Career Related:** Executive Director, Pritzker Network on Depression, New York (1996-2006); Founder, Co-Chair, Science Advisory Board, Member, Board of Directors, NEUREX Corp., Menlo Park, CA (1984-1990); Past Chair, Committee on Endowed Chairs, Stanford Medical School; Past Chair, Deanship Search Committee; Past Chair, Stanford Psychiatry Residency Program **Civic:** Chair, Pasarow Medical Research Awards Progressive, Los Angeles, CA (2000-Present); Chair, Board of Directors, Association for Research on Nervous and Mental Disorders, New York (1998-Present); Member, Board of Trustees, Hatos Foundation, Los Angeles, CA (1993-Present); Member, Science Advisory Board, National Alliance for Research on Schizophrenia and Depression (1987-Present); Chair, Board of Trustees, New York Academy of Medicine (2001-2010); President, Chair, Board of Directors, Robert J. and Claire Pasarow Foundation (2000-2016) **Military Service:** Lieutenant Commander, US Public Health Service (1962-1964) **Creative Works:** Associate Editor, Clinical Neuroscience Research, Elsevier, Amsterdam (2002-Present); Member, Editorial Board, Journal of the American Medical Association (1994-2001); Editor, "Archives of General Psychiatry," American Medical Association (1994-2001); Co-Editor, "Serotonin and Behavior, Psychopharmacology from Theory to Practice"; Co-Editor, "Neuroregulators and Psychiatric Disorders"; Co-Editor, "Biological Aspects of Substance Abuse"; Co-Editor, "Clinical Neuroscience of Depression"; Co-Editor, "Advances in Situ Hybridization Methodology"; Author, More than 300 Publications; Co-Editor, **Awards:** Recipient, Sarnat Prize in Mental Health, Institute of Medicine, National Academy of Sciences (2006); Recipient, Thomas William Salmon Medal, New York Academy of Medicine; Recipient, Lehmann Award For Psychiatric Research, New York State Office of Mental Health; Recipient, Sachar Award in Psychiatry, Columbia University; Recipient, Career Teacher Award; Recipient, Research Scientist Development Award; Recipient, National Institute of Mental Health; Recipient, Research Scientist Award, National Institute of Mental Health; Recipient, Efron Research Award, American College of Neuropsychopharmacology; Recipient, Bennett Research Award and Lifetime Achievement Award, Society of Biological Psychiatry; Grantee, National Science Foundation; Grantee, NASA **Membership:** Chair, Board of Biobehavioral Sciences and Mental Disorders, Institute of Medicine, National Academy of Sciences (1982-1994); Fellow, Lifetime Member, Honorary Member, American Psychiatric Association; American Medical Association; Advisory Board, University of California, Los Angeles Medical Center; Past Chair, Council on Research, American Psychiatric Association; Past Chair, Distinguished Service Awards Committee, American Psychiatric Association; American Behavioral Medical Research; American Association for the Advancement of Science; American Medical Association; American Society for Neurochemistry; American Psychopathological Association; **Marquis Who's Who Honors:** Distinguished Humanitarian (2017) **Hobbies:** Photography; High Haven music; Shenandoah Valley; Current events **Shipping Address:** 171 W 71st St Apt 3C, New York, NY 10023

Michael Harland Barcus

Industry: Writing and Editing **Date of Birth:** 03/24/1954 **Place of Birth:** Marietta **State:** GA **Parents:** Harland Deemar Barcus, Lorine Durham Barcus **Career:** Voucher Examiner, Department of Defense, Columbus, OH **Military Service:** Lance Corporal, U.S. Marine Corps (1972-1974) **Creative Works:** Author, Legend of the Phoenix (2000)

William P. Barlow Jr.

Title: Accountant **Industry:** Financial Services **Company Name:** Barlow & Hughan **Date of Birth:** 02/11/1934 **Place of Birth:** Oakland **State:** CA **Parents:** William P. Barlow; Muriel (Block) Barlow **Education:** AB in Economics, University of California, Berkeley (1956); Postgraduate Coursework, California Institute of Technology (1952-1954) **Certifications:** Certified Public Accountant, State of California **Career:** Partner, Barlow & Hughan (1990-Present); Accountant, Self-Employed (1978-1989); Partner, Touche, Ross & Company (1977-1978); Partner, J.K. Lasser & Company (Now John Wiley & Sons, Inc.) (1972-1977); Partner, Barlow, Davis & Wood (1964-1972); Accountant, Barlow, Davis & Wood (1960-1972) **Career Related:** Fellow, Gleeson Library Associates (1969) **Civic:** Chairman, Oakland Ballet Company (1995-1998); President, Oakland Ballet Company (1986-1989); Board of Directors, Oakland Ballet Company (1982-1999); Chairman, Friends of the Bancroft Library, University of California, Berkeley (1974-1979); Council Member, Friends of the Bancroft Library, University of California, Berkeley (1971-1998); President, Gleeson Library Associates (1971-1974) **Creative Works:** Editor, "Officially Sealed Notes" (1996-2004); Editor, "Book Catalogues: Their Varieties and Uses, Second Edition" (1986); Co-Author, "The Grolier Club, 1884-1984" (1984); Co-Author, "Collectible Books: Some New Paths" (1979); Contributor, Articles, Professional Journals **Awards:** Honoree, International Water Ski Hall Of Fame (2011); Herbert Howe Bancroft Award, Bancroft Library, University of California, Berkeley (2004); Honoree, Water Ski Hall of Fame (1993); Sir Thomas More Medal, Gleeson Library Associates (1989) **Membership:** Honorary Vice President, USA Water Ski (1969-Present); President, The International Machine Cancel Society (2003-2006); President, The Bibliographical Society of America (1992-1996); Council, The Bibliographical Society of America (1986-1992); Chairman, Board of Directors, USA Water Ski (1977-1979); Executive Board, IWWF (1975-1978); Treasurer, The Book Club of California (1971-1983); President, The Book Club of California (1968-1969); Chairman, Board of Directors, USA Water Ski (1966-1969); Board of Directors, The Book Club of California (1963-1976); President, USA Water Ski (1963-1966); Executive Board, IWWF (1961-1971); Regional Chairman, USA Water Ski (1959-1963); Board of Directors, USA Water Ski; The Grolier Club of New York; The Roxburghe Club **Marquis Who's Who Honors:** Albert Nelson Marquis Lifetime Achievement Award (2017) **Why did you become involved in your profession or industry:** Mr. Barlow became involved in his profession through a process of elimination from various fields. **What do you consider to be the highlight of your career:** Mr. Barlow is proud of establishing the Water Ski Hall of Fame and the International Hall of Fame. **Hobbies:** Collecting 16th-18th century books, mainly by John Baskerville; Collecting stamps **Business Address:** 1182 Market Street, Suite 400, San Francisco, CA, 94102

Milly Slater Barranger, PhD

Title: Theater Educator, Author **Industry:** Education/Educational Services **Date of Birth:** 02/12/1937 **Place of Birth:** Birmingham **State:** AL **Parents:** C. C. Slater Hinson; Mildred (Hilliard) Hinson **Marital Status:** Divorced **Spouse Name:** G. K. Barranger (1961, Divorced 1984) **Children:** Heather Dalton Barranger Case **Education:** Honorary Doctor of Humane Letters, University of Montevallo (2018); PhD, Tulane University (1964); MA, Tulane University (1959); BA, University of Montevallo (1958) **Career:** Alumni Distinguished Professor Emerita, College of Fellows of American Theatre (2003-Present); Dean, College of Fellows of American Theatre (2010-2012); Alumni Distinguished Professor, University of North Carolina, Chapel Hill (1997-2003); Professor, University of North Carolina, Chapel Hill (1982-2003); Producing Director, PlayMakers Repertory Co., Chapel Hill, NC (1982-1999); Chairman, Dramatic Art, University of North Carolina, Chapel Hill (1982-1999); Chairman, Theatre Department, Tulane University, New Orleans, LA (1971-1982); Assistant to Associate Professor, Tulane University, New Orleans, LA (1969-1982); Lecturer, Louisiana State University, New Orleans, LA (1964-1969) **Career Related:** Scholar-in-Residence, Yale School of Drama, New Haven, CT (1982); Visiting Young Professor in Humanities, University of Tennessee, Knoxville, TN (1981-1982); Distinguished, Visiting Associate Professor, University of Tulsa (1981); President, American Theatre Association (1978-1979) **Civic:** Trustee, The Paul Green Foundation (1982-2014) **Creative Works:** Author, "Theatre: A Way of Seeing" (2015, 2013); Co-Editor, "The Group Theatre: Passion, Politics, and Performance in the Depression Era" (2013); Author, "Audrey Wood and the Playwrights" (2013); Author, "A Gambler's Instinct: The Story of Broadway Producer Cheryl Crawford" (2010); Author, "Unfriendly Witnesses: Gender, Theater, and Film in the McCarthy Era" (2008); Author, "Theatre: A Way of Seeing" (2006); Author, "Understanding Plays" (2004); Author, "Margaret Webster: A Life in the Theater" (2004); Author, "Theatre: A Way of Seeing" (2002); Author, "Theatre: Past and Present," Revised Edition (2001); Author, "Theatre: A Way of Seeing" (1995); Author, "Understanding Plays" (1994); Author, "Margaret Webster" (1994); Author, "Jessica Tandy" (1991); Author, "Theatre: A Way of Seeing" (1991); Author, "Understanding Plays" (1990); Co-Editor, "Notable Women in American Theatre" (1989); Author, "Theatre: A Way of Seeing" (1986); Author, "Theatre: Past and Present" (1984); Author, "Theatre: A Way of Seeing" (1980); Co-Editor, "Generations: An Introduction to Drama" (1971); Contributor, Articles to Professional Journals; Editor, "The Selected Letters of Stella Adler" **Awards:** Tennessee Williams Distinguished Scholars Medallion Award, Tennessee Williams Tribute Festival (2015); New England Theatre Conference Award for American Theatre (2010); Outstanding Teacher of Theatre in Higher Education (2009); President's Award, University of Montevallo (1979); Award for Professional Achievement, Southwest Theatre Conference (1978); New Orleans Bicentennial Award for Achievement in the Arts (1976) **Membership:** Honorary Emeritus Partner, National Partners of the American Theatre (2015-Present); President, National Theatre Conference (2010-2013); Dean, College of Fellows of the America Theatre (2010-2012); Board of Directors, League of Professional Theatre Women (2007-2010); Board of Directors, College of Fellows of the America Theatre (1998-2001); President, National Theatre Conference (1991-1993); Theatre Library Association; Authors Guild **Marquis Who's Who Honors:** Albert Nelson Marquis Lifetime Achievement Award (2017) **Why did you become involved in your profession or industry:** Ms. Barranger was always interested in dramatic literature in college, although she was not an actress, producer or director. **What do you consider to be the highlight of your career:** Ms. Barranger is most proud of her role as president of both the American Theater Association and the National Theater Conference. **Hobbies:** Films; Travel **Shipping Address:** 245 W 107th St Apt 8F, New York, NY, 10025

Herbert Barry III, PhD

Title: Psychologist **Industry:** Medicine & Health Care **Date of Birth:** 06/02/1930 **Place of Birth:** New York **State:** NY **Parents:** Herbert Barry; Lucy Manning (Brown) Barry **Education:** PhD, Yale University (1957); MS, Yale University (1953); BA, Harvard University (1952) **Career:** Professor Emeritus, University of Pittsburgh (2001-Present); Professor of Pharmaceutical Sciences, University of Pittsburgh (1995-2001); Professor of Pharmacology and Physiology, School of Dental Medicine, University of Pittsburgh (1987-1994); Professor, University of Pittsburgh (1970-1987); Research Associate, School of Pharmacy, University of Pittsburgh (1963-1970); Professor of Pharmacology, School of Pharmacy, University of Pittsburgh (1963-1970); Assistant Professor of Psychology, University of Connecticut (1961-1963); Assistant Professor of Psychology, Yale University (1960-1961); USPHS-NIMH Research Fellow, Yale University (1957-1959) **Career Related:** Member, Sociobehavioral Subcommittee, AIDS Research Review Committee, National Institute on Drug Abuse (1988-1989); Member Alcohol, Research Review Committee, National Institute on Alcohol Abuse and Alcoholism (1972-1976); Principal Adviser for PhD Dissertations, School of Pharmacy, University of Pittsburgh **Civic:** Board of Directors, Center for Study of Economics (1988-Present); Board of Directors, Robert Schalkenbach Foundation (2005-2011); Board of Directors, Robert Schalkenbach Foundation (1996-2004); Member, Allegheny County Democratic Committee (1984-2010) **Creative Works:** Author, "Donald Trump and Other Presidents who Defeated Nominee of Rival Political Party" (2017); Co-Author, "Adolescence: An Anthropological Inquiry" (1991); Field Editor, "Journal of Psychopharmacology" (1974-1991); Co-Author, "Actions of Alcohol" (1970); Contributor, Over 250 Articles, Professional Journals **Awards:** Recipient, Research Scientist Development Award, National Institute of Mental Health (1967-1977) **Membership:** Executive Committee, American Name Society (2000-2003); President, Division of Psychopharmacology, American Psychological Association (1980-1981); Fellow, Council of Representatives, American Psychological Association (1975-1976); American Association for the Advancement of Science; American College of Neuropsychopharmacology; Psychonomic Society; Sigma Xi, The Scientific Research Society; Phi Beta Kappa Society **Marquis Who's Who Honors:** Distinguished Humanitarian (2017) **Hobbies:** Chess **Religion:** Unitarian Universalist **Shipping Address:** 552 N Neville St Apt 83, Pittsburgh, PA, 15213

David Barton

Title: Religious Studies Educator, Writer, Historian, Public Speaker, Researcher **Industry:** Religious **Company Name:** WallBuilders **Date of Birth:** 01/28/1954 **Place of Birth:** Austin **State:** TX **Parents:** Charles Grady Barton; Hilda Rose (Seely) Barton **Marital Status:** Married **Spouse Name:** Cheryl Edith Little (3/18/1978) **Children:** Damaris Ann; Timothy David; Stephen Daniel **Education:** PhD in Theology and American History, Life Christian University (2014); Honorary DLitt, Ecclesia College (2009); Honorary DLitt, Pensacola Christian College (1997); Bachelor of Religious Education, Oral Roberts University (1976) **Career:** Founder, President, Wallbuilders (1988-Present); Elder, Aledo Cornerstone Church, Aledo, TX (1987-Present); Vice-Chairman, Republican Party of Texas (1997-2006); Principal, Aledo Christian School, Aledo, TX (1981-1988); President, Owner, Maranatha Construction Company, Custom Homes, Aledo, TX (1978-1988); Director, Aledo Christian Center Bible School, Aledo, TX (1978-1982); Associate Pastor, Youth Director, Aledo Christian Center, Aledo, TX (1977-1988); Associate Pastor, Director, Christian Education, Youth Director, Sheridan Christian Center, Tulsa, OK (1976-1977) **Civic:** Advisory Board Member, Mighty Oaks Warriors Programs, Mighty Oaks Foundation (2015-Present); Advisory Board Member, Parental Rights (2014-Present); Advisory Board Member, Patriot Academy (2013-Present); Board of Reference, Christian Film and Television Commission (2013-present); President of Board, Mercury One (2012-Present); Board Member, United in Purpose (2011-Present); Board of Reference, Green Collection, Museum of the Bible (2011-Present); Board of Regents, Ecclesia College (2009-Present); Board of Reference, Oral Roberts University (2008-Present); Board of Directors, National Legal Foundation and Minuteman Institute (2008-Present); Board Member, Providence Foundation (2007-Present); Advisory Board, National Day of Prayer (2004-Present); Advisory Board Member, National Council on Bible Curriculum in Public Schools (2000-Present); President, Oral Roberts University Alumni Board (2004-2005); Board Member, Oral Roberts University Alumni Board (2001-2003) **Military Service:** Honorary Commission as an Admiral, U.S. Navy (2009) **Creative Works:** Signature Historian, "The Founders' Bible" (2012); Author, "The Jefferson Lies" (2012); Author, "Capitol Guidebook" (2009); Author, "The Bible, Voters & The 2008 Elections" (2008); Author, "Separation of Church and State" (2007); Author, "Freemasonry and the Founding Fathers" (2005); Author, "Restraining Judicial Activism" (2003); Author, "The Second Amendment" (2000); Author, "Benjamin Rush" (1999); Author, "Original Intent" (1995); Author, "The Bulletproof George Washington" (1990); Author, "America: To Pray or Not to Pray" (1987); Producer, "America's Godly Heritage"; Producer, "Keys to Good Government"; Producer, "Spirit of the American Revolution"; Producer, "Foundations of American Government"; Producer, "The Role of Pastors and Christians in Civil Government"; Producer, "The Spiritual Heritage Tour of the U.S. Capitol"; Producer, "Four Centuries of American Education"; Producer, "Setting the Record Straight: American History in Black & White"; Producer, "Influence of the Bible on America"; Producer, "The American Heritage Series"; Producer, "Building on the American Heritage Series"; Producer, "Science, the Bible, and Global Warming"; Producer, "America's War on Terror"; Producer, "Keeping Truth in History"; Producer, "Developing a Biblical Worldview"; Producer, "Eight Steps for Thinking Biblically"; Producer, "God in the Constitution, Principles of Limited Government" **Awards:** Issachara Award, Bott Radio Network (2017); Commendation, Resolution of Alabama State Senate (2016); Honoree, Person of the Year, Family PAC (2016); Military Certificate of Appreciation, First Stryker Brigade Combat Team "Arctic Wolves," Fort Wainwright (2015); Commendation, South Carolina State Senate (2014); Honoree, National Hero of the Faith, Vision America (2011); Commission as Kentucky Colonel, Governor of Kentucky (2009); Board of Directors Award, National Religious Broadcasters (2009); Champion Award, Torch of Freedom Foundation (2009); Military Certificate of Appreciation, Torch of Freedom Foundation (2008); Telly Award (2008, 2000-2001); Certificate of Honor, Harding University American Studies Institute (2008); Angel Award for Excellence in Media (2007, 1995-2000) **Marquis Who's Who Honors:** Albert Nelson Marquis Lifetime Achievement Award (2017) **Why did you become involved in your profession or industry:** Dr. Barton became involved in his profession after reading original documents from the Founding Fathers. He discovered that the information contained in those documents was very different from what he had been taught in school about those same documents. This discovery created a desire in him to look at other originals and see if they were also different from what he was taught. This started him on a path resulting in one of America's largest private collections of Founding Era documents and artifacts. **Shipping Address:** PO Box 397, c/o Misty Huddleston, Aledo, TX, 76008 **Website:** https://wallbuilders.com/bios/#tab-34c5fc6bd5eda685312

Aaron C. Bass Jr.

Title: School System Administrator **Industry:** Education/Educational Services **Company Name:** Pennsylvania State University, School District of Philadelphia **Date of Birth:** 05/26/1950 **Place of Birth:** Philadelphia **State:** PA **Marital Status:** Married **Spouse Name:** Jade King (7/3/1999) **Children:** Naja Killebrew; Clyde Killebrew; Aaron III; Jared; Sharita **Education:** Pursuing Doctorate, The United Lutheran Seminary; MDiv, The Lutheran Theological Seminary at Philadelphia (1998); AA in Data Processing, Community College of Philadelphia (1982); MA in Social Psychology, Temple University (1974); BA in Psychology, Lincoln University (1972); Coursework, Lutheran Theological Seminary at Gettysburg (Now Gettysburg Seminary); Intern, Oxford Presbyterian Church **Certifications:** Ableton Producer Certificate (2014) **Career:** Adjunct Professor, The Pennsylvania State University, School District of Philadelphia (2012-2014); Department Manager, Executive Sales, Joseph A. Bank (Now Jos. A. Bank Clothiers, Inc.), Plymouth Meeting, PA (2009-2011); Research and Assessment Specialist, William Penn School District (2005-2006); Analyst, Pupil Data, School District of Philadelphia (2000-2005); Research Assistant, School District of Philadelphia (1996-2000); Research Associate, School District of Philadelphia (1994-1996); Research Assistant, School District of Philadelphia (1974-1994); Learning Specialist, Urban Career Education Center, Philadelphia, PA (1974); Board Member, Urban Resources Development Corporation **Civic:** Elder, Member, Mount Airy Church of God in Christ (2001-2004); Elder, Eagle's Nest Christian Fellowship, Philadelphia, PA (1999-2001); Teacher, Germantown Community Photography Workshop, Philadelphia, PA (1972-1974); Philadelphia Interfaith Action; Church of Faith Hope and Love Noon Day Prayer (Now Interfaith Center of Greater Philadelphia); Elder, First Presbyterian Church in Germantown; Board Member, Urban Resources Development Corporation **Creative Works:** Author, Numerous Studies and Evaluations **Awards:** Award for Most Unique Reporting Technique for Career Education Accumulative Report, National Education Resource Information Center (1980); Outstanding Young Men in America Award (1979); Temple University Scholar (1972) **Membership:** Association for Supervision and Curriculum Development; W. Russell Johnson Music Guild; American Educational Research Association; Evangelical Training Association; Phi Delta Kappa; Omega Psi Phi; Phi Theta Kappa Honors Society **Marquis Who's Who Honors:** Albert Nelson Marquis Lifetime Achievement Award (2017) **Why did you become involved in your profession or industry:** He became involved in his profession because he wanted to help people. He enjoyed talking to people early on and assessing their needs. His father was an engineer in the sciences and his mother was an educator in the social sciences. He blended both disciplines. His father ended up as a systems analyst. The courses would eventually propel him into what he was doing. **What do you consider to be the highlight of your career:** A highlight of Mr. Bass's career was when students in the back of the classroom asked some other students to stop talking and listen to what Professor Bass had to say. He felt they were truly interested and that he had gotten through to them and was going to impact their career decisions. Another highlight was when he was running a report card system. He had to work with people from many different departments, clerks, data entry, computer systems analysts in data processing, etc., who were all working isolated from each other. He brought them all together in a conference and was able to motivate them to work together as a team. His management style is to not come across as being above people, but simply to work with them and assist them to do their jobs better. **Hobbies:** Running; Biking; Swimming; Reading; Travel; Photography; Music; Exercise; Working out at the gym **Shipping Address:** 6025 Morton St, Philadelphia, PA, 19144

Joe Ann Batcheller

Industry: Medicine & Health Care **Company Name:** Miami Heart Institute **Date of Birth:** 12/11/1932 **Place of Birth:** Jacksonville **State:** FL **Parents:** Osmer St. Clair Deming; Lorena (Jones) Deming **Marital Status:** Married **Spouse Name:** M. David Springsteen Batcheller (8/8/1957) **Children:** Elizabeth Batcheller-Whalen; Osmer Deming; John Alden **Education:** Bachelor's Degree, University of North Carolina (1955); AA, Stephens College, Columbia, MO (1952) **Career:** Vice President, Miami Heart Institute, Miami Beach, FL (1975-Present); Director, Miami Heart Institute, Miami Beach, FL (1973-Present); Chief Executive Officer, President, Miami Heart Institute, Miami Beach, FL (1989-1993); Executive Vice President, Miami Heart Institute, Miami Beach, FL (1986-1989); President, Chairman, Blue Water Mobile Home Sales, Inc., Tavernier, FL (1967-1976); President, Board of Directors, Seminole Oil Corporation, Miami, FL (1961-1965); Secretary, Seminole Oil Corporation, Miami, FL (1957-1961) **Career Related:** Board of Directors, Pan American Bank, Miami, FL (1984-1987); Board of Directors, Top Power Stations, Miami, FL (1961-1965); Vice President, Board of Directors, Pensacola Petroleum Company, Inc., Miami, FL (1961-1965); Secretary, Board of Directors, Bluegrass Plant Foods, Inc., Cynthiana, KY (1958-1972); Chairman, Superior Plant Foods, Inc., Lakeland, FL (1958-1960) **Civic:** Vice Chairman, Florida Heart Research Institute, Inc. (1993-Present); Board of Directors, Intercontinental Bank **Membership:** Vice Chairman, Surf Club on Miami Beach (1997-1999); President, Board of Governors, Surf Club on Miami Beach (1993-1997); President, Bay Point Property Owners Association (1991-1996); Board of Directors, American Heart Association, Miami, FL (1989-1991); Chairman, Debutante Committee, Surf Club on Miami Beach (1986-1987); Parents Advisory Board, Furman University, Greenville, SC (1979-1983); Chairman, Debutante Committee, Surf Club on Miami Beach (1976-1982); Advisory Board, Convent of Sacred Heart, Miami, FL (1973-1977); Young Patronesses of Opera; English Speaking Union; Daughters of the American Revolution **Marquis Who's Who Honors:** Albert Nelson Marquis Lifetime Achievement Award (2017) **Hobbies:** Travel; Reading; Boating; Beaux arts **Shipping Address:** 4595 Sabal Palm Road, Miami, FL, 33137

Bonnie W. Battey, PhD

Title: Nursing Educator **Industry:** Medicine & Health Care **Company Name:** Duldt & Associates, Inc. **Date of Birth:** 07/23/1933 **Place of Birth:** Stuttgart **State:** AR **Parents:** Merl D. Weaver; Louise C. (Schroeder) Weaver **Marital Status:** Married **Spouse Name:** Robert W. Battey (5/17/2003); John Duldt (10/15/1980, Deceased 1997) **Education:** Postgraduate Coursework, Quantitative Methodology Institute, National Center for Nursing Research, National Institutes of Health (1992); PhD in Speech Communication and Human Relations, The University of Kansas (1980); MS in Nursing Education, Vanderbilt University (1960); BSN, Wagner College (1955) **Certifications:** Registered Nurse, States of Arkansas, Registered Nurse, State of Tennessee; Registered Nurse, State of New York; Registered Nurse, State of Virginia; Registered Nurse, State of North Carolina; Registered Nurse, State of California **Career:** Private Practice (2006-Present); Adjunct Professor, School of Nursing, Samuel Merritt University, Oakland, CA (2003-2006); Adjunct Associate Professor, George Mason University, Fairfax, VA (1999-2003); Professor, School of Health Professions, Shenandoah University, Winchester, VA (1994-1997); Supplemental Nursing Pool Staff Nurse Progressive Care Unit, Pitt County Memorial Hospital (Now Vidant Medical Center) (1992); Professor of Adult Health Nursing, College of Nursing, East Carolina University, Greenville, NC (1984-1994); Assistant Dean of Graduate Program, College of Nursing, East Carolina University, Greenville, NC (1984-1986); Accreditation Site Visitor, National League for Nursing (1964-1990); Director of Graduate Studies, School of Nursing, University of North Dakota; Professor Chair, Department of Nursing, Memphis State University (Now University of Memphis); Instructor, Associate Director, Diploma Nursing Program, Little Rock, AK; Chairman, Department of Nursing, University of Arkansas at Little Rock; Chairman of Ad Hoc Committee, Arkansas State Board of Nursing; Site Visitor, Oklahoma State Board of Nursing; Professor, Chair, Memphis State **Career Related:** Research in Field **Civic:** Lay Chaplain, Mentor, Alexander, VA (1999-2003); Parish Nurse, Good Shepherd Evangelical Lutheran Church, Front Royal, VA; Volunteer Nurse, Secretary of Committee, Free Clinic for Local Unemployed Citizens, Lutheran Church **Creative Works:** Author, "Humanism, Nursing, Communication and Holistic Care: A Position Paper" Xlibris (2009); Co-Author, "Situational Leadership in Nursing" (1989); Author, Dissertation, "Anger, Group Cohesiveness, and Productivity in Small Task Groups"; Contributor, Articles to Professional Journals; Contributor, Chapters to Books; Contributor, Computer Assisted Introduction Programs; Contributor, Communication Research Tools **Awards:** Book of the Year, American Journal of Nursing, Wolters Kluwer Health, Inc. (1989); Nurse Scientist Scholarship, University of Kansas, Lawrence, KS **Membership:** American Nurses Association, Inc.; Sigma Theta Tau International; American Holistic Nursing Association **Marquis Who's Who Honors:** Albert Nelson Marquis Lifetime Achievement Award (2017); Distinguished Humanitarian (2017) **To what do you attribute your success:** Dr. Battey attributes her success to her mother who died at 98; she taught her to be polite and kind, as well as social skills which helped define her. **Why did you become involved in your profession or industry:** Dr. Battey wanted to be dancer at 4 or 5. However, her father and all 4 sisters were involved in healthcare in some way. **Shipping Address:** 2921 Bellflower Dr, Antioch, CA, 94531 **Website:** http://www.bwbatteyconsult.com

Nami Bayan

Title: Internist **Industry:** Medicine & Health Care **Company Name:** H and B Quality Medical Care LLC **Date of Birth:** 06/06/1968 **Place of Birth:** Tehran **Country of Origin:** Iran **Parents:** Nooshinraran Bayan; Villa S. Moghadam **Marital Status:** Married **Spouse Name:** Ladan Hamd **Education:** Internal Medicine Residency, St. Mary's Hospital, Health Sciences Center, University of Oklahoma; Fellow in Geriatric Medicine, University of Connecticut; Intern in Internal Medicine, Montefiore North Campus, New York Medical College; MD, Tehran University of Medical Science **Certifications:** Board Certified in Internal Medicine; Licensed to Practice Medicine, State of Connecticut; Licensed to Practice Medicine, State of Indiana; Licensed to Practice Medicine, State of Maine **Career:** Internist, H and B Quality Medical Care LLC (2013-Present); Doctor of Internal Medicine, Iran (2006-2013) **Creative Works:** Contributor, Articles, Professional Journals **Awards:** Expert in Medicine, Expert Network (2017); Vital's Patient Choice Award (2014); America's Top Physicians (2008-2017); Leaders of Healthcare's Doctors of Excellence; Peer Reviewed Professionals Physicians Award; Continental Who's Who Award **Membership:** American Medical Association; American College of Physicians; American Board of Internal Medicine; Saint Francis Hospital & Medical Center; Griffin Hospital **To what do you attribute your success:** He attributes his success to his dedication to patient care. **Why did you become involved in your profession or industry:** He became involved in his profession out of scientific curiosity, and because it was an intellectual challenge. But once he went into clinical work and started seeing patients, he found his passion in caring for humanity and trying to help people. **Where will you be in five years:** He is working on developing medical devices. He will continue giving to charity and solving complex medical issues. **Hobbies:** Swimming; Reading; Writing; Cooking; Soccer, Movies **Political Affiliations:** Independent **Religion:** Spiritual **Business Address:** 2 Ivy Brook Road Ste 120, Shelton, CT, 06484 **Shipping Address:** 100 Parrott Dr Unit 1207, Shelton, CT, 06484

Robert Lawrence Beal

Industry: Business Management/Business Services **Date of Birth:** 09/10/1941 **Place of Birth:** Boston **State:** MA **Parents:** Alexander Simpson; Leona M. (Rothstein) B. **Education:** MBA, Harvard University (1965); BS, Cum Laude, Harvard University (1963) **Career:** President, Beal and Co., Inc., Boston (1976-President); Partner, The Beal Companies; Vice President and Partner, Beacon Companies, Boston (1965-1976) **Career Related:** Director, Artery Business Committee (1989-Present); Chairman, Board of Directors, Massachusetts Development Financial Agency (1976-2004); Chairman, Artery Business Committee (1995-1999); Member, East Cambridge Rezoning Advisory Committee (1989-1996); Treasurer, Artery Business Committee (1989-1995); Corporator, Director, Executive Committee Member and Lending Committee President, Provident Institution Savings (1975-1986); Real Estate Instructor, Northeastern University (1969-1975) **Civic:** Chair, New Pentin (2000-Present); Board of Advisors, Old North Church (2009-Present); Tufts Medical Center Trust (2011-Present); Board of Directors, Boston Zoological Society (2011-Present) ; Overseer for Life, Museum of Fine Arts, Boston (2001-Present); Member, Visiting Committee, Harvard Divinity School (1989-Present); Advisory Committee, Taubman Center, John F. Kennedy School of Government, Harvard University (1989-President); New England Aquarium (1987-Present); Board of Governors, New England Aquarium (1993-1998, 2002-Present); Member, Executive Communications, New England Aquarium (2002-Present); Co-Chair, Campaign Steering Committee, New England Aquarium (2001-Present); Chair, Taubman Center, John F. Kennedy School of Government, Harvard University (2003-Present); Board of Directors, Boston Municipal Research Bureau (1978-Present); Campaign Board of Overseers, Massachusetts Society for the Prevention of Cruelty to Animals (1988-Present); Chair, School of Public Policy & Urban Affairs, Northeastern University (2007-Present); Co-Chairman, 25th Reunion, Co-Chairman, 35th and 40th Reunions, Class Gift, Class Secretary, Harvard College Fund Council (2000-President); Chair, Harvard Hillel (2007-2010); Chair, Council of Fellows, Angell Memorial Animal Hospital, Tufts (1999-2007); Co-Chair, Alexis de Tocqueville Society, United Way of Massachusetts Bay (2003); Co-Chair, Campaign Steering Committee, Taubman Center, John F. Kennedy School of Government, Harvard University (2001-2002); Overseer, Beth Israel Deaconess Medical Center (1981-2001); Board of Overseers, Museum of Fine Arts, Boston (1988-1997, 1998-2001); Co-Chair, Alexis de Tocqueville Society, United Way of Massachusetts Bay (2000); Cabinet Member, Alexis de Tocqueville Society, United Way of Massachusetts Bay (2000); Executive Board Member, Boston Chapter, American Jewish Committee (1987-1996); Chairman, Boston Municipal Research Bureau (1994-1996); Board of Directors, Metropolitan Boston Housing Partnership, Inc. (1983-1995); Overseer, Boys Club Boston (1975-1993); Vice Chairman, Boston Municipal Research Bureau (1990-1993); Member, Board of Governors, Boston Chapter, American Jewish Committee (1989-1992); Treasurer, Boston Municipal Research Bureau (1988-1989, 1992); Member, Building and Grounds Committee, Beth Israel Deaconess Medical Center (1976-1982, 1986-1990); Member, Visiting Committee School, Museum of Fine Arts, Boston (1974-1976, 1988-1989); Trustee, The Partnership, Inc. (1981-1989); Board of Directors, Boston Zoological Society (1972-1986); Honorary Chairman, Boston Zoological Society (1985); Capital Fund Director, Class of '63, Harvard College Fund Council (1979-1985); Chairman, Boston Zoological Society (1981-1984); Member, Advisory Task Force, John F. Kennedy Library (1982); President, Boston Zoological Society (1980) **Membership:** Director, Combined Jewish Philanthropies Greater Boston (2006-Present); Board of Directors, New Center for Arts and Culture (2003-Present); Executive Committee Member, Combined Jewish Philanthropies Greater Boston (1989-Present); Board of Directors, Greater Boston Chamber of Commerce (1992-Present); Primary Subscribing Member, International Association of Assessing Officers (1982-Present); Chairman, Combined Jewish Philanthropies Greater Boston (2004-2006); Chair, Community Capital Campaign, Combined Jewish Philanthropies Greater Boston (2002-2003); Chair, Development Committee, Combined Jewish Philanthropies Greater Boston (2001); Chairman, Committee on Endowment Fund, Combined Jewish Philanthropies Greater Boston (1999); Director, Former Secretary, Member, Executive Committee, National Realty Committee (1974-1999); Committee Coordinator, The Vault (1978-1997); Vice Chairman, Combined Jewish Philanthropies Greater Boston (1992-1993); Board of Directors, Greater Boston Real Estate Board (1970-1972, 1976-1990); Director, National Association Real Estate Appraiser, Massachusetts Taxpayers Foundation (1980-1986); National Governing Board, Ripon Society (1979-1985); Vice President, Vice Chairman, Director, Massachusetts Association of Realtors (1979-1981); President, Greater Boston Real Estate Board (1978-1979); Co-Founder, National Treasurer, Ripon Society (1968-1973) **Religion:** Jewish

Larry Alan Bear

Title: Lawyer, Educator (Retired) **Industry:** Law and Legal Services **Date of Birth:** 02/28/1928 **Place of Birth:** Melrose **State:** MA **Parents:** Joseph E. Bear; Pearl Florence Bear **Marital Status:** Married **Spouse Name:** Rita Maldonado (3/29/1975) **Children:** Peter; Jonathan; Steven **Education:** LLM, Columbia Law School, Columbia University (1967); JD, Harvard Law School, Harvard University (1953); BA, Duke University (1949) **Career:** Private Practice, New York City, NY (1970-1985); Public Affairs Radio Broadcaster, Moderator, "Conference Call," Station WABC, New York City, NY (1970-1982); Director, National Action Committee on Drug Education, University of Rochester, New York (1970-1977); Legal Counsel, Then Commissioner of Addiction Services, New York City, NY (1967-1970); Consultant on Legal Medicine, Puerto Rico Department of Justice and the Office of District Attorney of San Juan (1962-1966); Professor, University of Puerto Rico Law School (1962-1965); Trial Lawyer, Bear & Bear, Boston, MA (1953-1960) **Career Related:** Consultant, Substance Abuse Prevention and Education Programming (1978-Present); Visiting Professor of Business Ethics, Stern School of Business, New York University (1999-2003); Lecturer in Legislation and Ethics, Wharton School Executive Program, University of Pennsylvania (1996-2000); Visiting Professor, Legal, Social and Ethical Context of Business, Athens Laboratory of Business Administration (1996); Member, Attorney General's Medico-Legal Board on Drug Abuse, PA (1992); President, Foundation for a Drug Free Pennsylvania (1991-1992); Adjunct Professor of Markets Ethics and Law, Stern School of Business, New York University (1986-1999); Member, Alcohol and Drug Committee, National Safety Council (1972-1982); Lecturer in Legal Medicine, Rutgers Law School, Rutgers, The State University of New Jersey (1969) **Civic:** Chairman, Board of Ethics, Township of Mahwah, New Jersey (1990-1991); Alumni Admissions Advisory Committee, Duke University (1987-2003); Advisory Committee on Public Issues, Advertising Council (Now Ad Council) (1972-1995); Member-at-Large, National Council, Boy Scouts of America (1972-1985); Statewide Campaign Director for Governor Endicott, Peabody, MA (1961-1962) **Creative Works:** Author, "Descent into Danger" (2006); Author, "Free Markets, Finance, Ethics, and Law" (1994); Author, "The Glass House Revolution: Inner City War for Interdependence" (1990); Author, "Law, Medicine, Science and Justice" (1964); Contributor, Articles and Chapters, Legal and Economic/Financial Books and Professional Journals **Awards:** James Kent Doctoral Fellowship, Columbia University (1966-1967) **Membership:** ABA; Forensic Science Society of Great Britain; Academia Colombiana de Ciencias Medico-Forenses; Harvard Club of New York City; New York State Bar Association **Bar Admissions:** New York (1967); United States District Court for the District of Puerto Rico (1963); Massachusetts (1953) **Marquis Who's Who Honors:** Albert Nelson Marquis Lifetime Achievement Award (2017) **To what do you attribute your success:** Mr. Bear attributes his success to paying attention. **Why did you become involved in your profession or industry:** Mr. Bear became involved in his profession because of his admiration for his father's distinguished career as a practicing attorney. **What do you consider to be the highlight of your career:** A highlight of Mr. Bear's career was recognizing that full professionalism in law required, on his part, an interdisciplinary focus on understanding and utilizing key concepts of three legal system related areas: medicine, science, economics and finance. **Where will you be in five years:** In five years, Mr. Bear's intention remains to be seen. **Hobbies:** Writing; Reading; Music appreciation; Regular exercise **Shipping Address:** 210 Nahanton St Apt 111, Newton Center, MA, 02459

Roy L. Beavers

Title: Utilities Executive, Volunteer, Writer (Retired)
Industry: Business Management/Business Services
Date of Birth: 04/24/1930 **Place of Birth:** Joplin **State:** MO **Parents:** Roy L. Beavers, Sr.; Margarette Nellie (Loughlin) Beavers **Marital Status:** Single **Spouse Name:** Valerie Evelyn Gurney (Deceased 2005) **Children:** Leslie Anne; Brendan G. **Education:** MA in Political Science, University of Maryland (1970); BS in Business, University of Missouri (1952) **Certifications:** Program Intelligence Certification; Program Nuclear Weapons Certification **Career:** Manager, KAMO Power, Vinita, OK (1984-1993); Public Information and Legislation Liaison, Wholesale Power Cooperative, KAMO Power, Vinita, OK (1984-1993); Field Representative, National Rural Electric Cooperative Association, Washington, DC (1977-1984); Agent, Insurance Agency, Lebanon, MO (1972-1977); Broker, Insurance Agency, Lebanon, MO (1972-1977); With, Strategic Arms Limitation Talks I Strategic Arms Negotiations, United States Arms Control and Disarmament Agency, United States Department of State (1970-1972); Nuclear Weapons Officer-in-Charge on Aircraft Carrier; Assistant Naval Attachement, Tokyo, Japan **Civic:** Board Member, Missouri Community Betterment Education Fund Inc. (1990-1993); Board Member, Oklahoma Academy for State Goals (1990-1993); Activist, Against Ubiquitous Presence of Electromagnetic Radiation, Numerous Organizations (1989-2009); State Headquarters Director, Virginia Committee to Re-Elect Richard Nixon, Richmond, VA (1972) **Military Service:** Commander, US Navy (1966); Commissioned Ensign, US Navy (1952) **Creative Works:** Contributor, Articles to Professional Journals **Awards:** Decorated, Bronze Medal, United States Naval Institute; Decorated, Silver Medal, United States Naval Institute; Decorated, Gold Medal, United States Naval Institute; Decorated, President Merit Service Medal; Decorated, Navy Commendation Medal **Membership:** United States Naval Institute **Shipping Address:** 3600 William Penn Way Apt 220, Venice, FL, 34293

Charles Becker

Title: Adult Education Educator (Retired) **Industry:** Education/Educational Services **Company Name:** Pueblo Community College **Date of Birth:** 03/27/1944 **Place of Birth:** Spring Grove **State:** MN **Parents:** R.L. Becker; Cora T. Becker **Marital Status:** Married **Spouse Name:** Ann Buchanan (6/16/1983, Deceased 2009) **Education:** BS in Education, Winona State University, MN (1966) **Certifications:** Nationally Certified Exam Reviewer (2006-Present); Nationally Certified Exam Writer (2006-2014); Certified Food Management Professional (1997) **Career:** Faculty Member in Hospitality Studies and Culinary Arts, Pueblo Community College, CO (1985-2014); Manager, Greyhound Food Management, Rock Springs, WY (1977-1985) **Civic:** Volunteer, Local Democratic Party **Membership:** Committee for Examination Excellence, National Restaurant Association Educational Foundation (2006-Present) **Marquis Who's Who Honors:** Albert Nelson Marquis Lifetime Achievement Award (2017) **Why did you become involved in your profession or industry:** He attributes his success to strong family support. His mother and his two aunts were also teachers. **Hobbies:** Reading **Shipping Address:** 615 Tyler St, Pueblo, CO, 81004

Philip Scott Becker

Title: Neurologist **Industry:** Medicine & Health Care **Company Name:** Riverhills Neuroscience **Date of Birth:** 02/17/1959 **Parents:** Jerome Philip Becker; Norma Lillian Becker **Marital Status:** Married **Spouse Name:** Debra Morgan Becker (3/29/2008) **Children:** John Philip; Kathryn Anne; Jordan Daniel Flood; Jared Morgan Flood **Education:** Research Fellowship, Department of Pathology, Neuropathology Laboratory, School of Medicine, Johns Hopkins University, Baltimore, MD (1987-1989); Residency, Neurology, Northwestern Memorial Hospital, Chicago, IL (1983-1986); Internship, Internal Medicine, Northwestern Memorial Hospital, Chicago, IL (1982-1983); MD, Northwestern University Medical School (Now Northwestern University Feinberg School of Medicine), Chicago, IL (1982); BS, Northwestern University, Evanston, IL (1979) **Certifications:** Board Certified, American Society for Neurorehabilitation (1992-1998); Licensure, State of Kentucky (1990); Licensure, State of Ohio (1990); Board Certified, American Board of Psychiatry and Neurology (1990); Diplomate, American Board of Psychiatry and Neurology (1988) **Career:** Neurologist, Private Practice of Neuroscience, Riverhills Healthcare Inc., Cincinnati, OH (2015-Present); Neurologist, Private Practice of Neurology, Becker Neurological Institute, Inc., Crestview Hills, KY (2007-2015); Neurologist, Private Practice of Neurology, Riverhills Neuroscience, Riverhills Healthcare, Inc., Cincinnati, OH (1990-2007); Instructor, Department of Pathology, Neuropathology Laboratory, Johns Hopkins Hospital, Baltimore, MD (1988-1990); Consulting Neurologist, Jackson Park Hospital, Chicago, IL (1985-1986) **Career Related:** Medical Director, Gateway Rehabilitation Hospital, Florence, KY (2011-2012); Assistant Medical Director, Gateway Rehabilitation Hospital (2004-2011); Director, Traumatic Brain Injury Program, Health South Rehabilitation Hospital (Now HealthSouth Corporation), Edgewood, KY (1994-1996); Consulting Neurologist, Francis Scott Key Medical Center (Now Johns Hopkins Bayview Medical Center), Baltimore, MD (1987) **Creative Works:** Presenter, National Coalition of Physicians Against Family Violence (1994); Presenter, "Alzheimer's and Cognex: Parke Davis Treatment IND," Lecture Series, Cincinnati, Ohio (1993); Co-author, "Cytokine Expression of Macrophages in HIV-1-Associated Vacuolar Myelopathy," Neurology (1993); Co-author, "Multifocal Necrotizing Leukoencephalopathy with Pontine Predilection in Immunosuppressed Patients: A Clinicopathologic Review of 16 Cases," Human Pathology (1993); Co-author, "Cytokine Expression in the Brain During the Acquired Immunodefiency Syndrome," Annals of Neurology (1992); Co-author, "Epstein-Barr Virus in AIDS-Related Primary Central Nervous System Lymphoma," The Lancet (1991); Co-author, "Neuropathologic Changes with Experimental Spinal Instrumentation: Transpedicular Fixation," Journal of Spinal Disorders (1991); Co-author, "Correlation of Neuroimaging and Neuropathology in Acquired Immune Deficiency Syndrome," RadioGraphics (1990); Author, "Developmental Foix-Chavany-Marie Syndrome: Polymicrogyria or Macrogyras?" Annals of Neurology (1990); Presenter, "Cranial Nerves," Neurology Resident Noon Lecture Series, Johns Hopkins Hospital, Baltimore, MD (1989); Presenter, "Update on the Neuropathology of AIDS," Neurology Research Seminar, School of Medicine, Johns Hopkins University, Baltimore, MD (1989); Co-author, "Bilateral Opercular Polymicrogyria," Annals of Neurology (1989); Co-author, "Neuropathology with Spinal Instrumentation," Journal of Orthopaedic Research (1989); Co-author, "Pulfrich Stereo-Illusion Phenomenon" Poor Man's VEP?" Neuro-Ophthalmology (1989); Co-author, "Dural Scrofula," Neurology (1989); Co-author, "Neuropathological Changes in Early HIV-1 Dementia," Annals of Neurology (1989); Co-author, "Herapin-Induced Thrombocytopenia," Stroke (1989); Co-author, "Different Patterns of PNS Demyelination Occur in HIV Infection," Journal of Neuropathology & Experimental Neurology (1989); Co-author, "Vacuolar Myelopathy in Human Immunodeficiency Virus (HIV) Infection: Central Remyelination," Journal of Neuropathology (1989); Co-Author, "Multiple Types of Senile Plaques in Alzheimer's Disease: Assortment in Familial and Sporadic Cases," Journal of Neuropathology & Experimental Neurology (1988) **Membership:** Commonwealth Neurological Society (2008-Present); Board of Directors, Commonwealth Neurological Society (2007-Present); Kentucky Health Emergency Listing of Professionals for Surge Program, Kentucky Medical Reserve Corps (2007-Present); American Academy of Neurology (1982-Present); President, Commonwealth Neurological Society (2013-2014); Chair, Healthcare Reform Task Force, Northern Kentucky Chamber of Commerce (1995); American College of Physician Executives (Now American Association for Physician Leadership) (1995); Stroke Council, American Heart Association, Inc. (1995); American Medical Association (1990-2012) **Marquis Who's Who Honors:** Albert Nelson Marquis Lifetime Achievement Award (2017) **Hobbies:** Fishing; Traveling; Skiing; Golf **Business Address:** 320 Thomas More Parkway, Crestview Hills, KY, 41017

Angela O. Bedenbaugh

Title: Chemistry Educator **Industry:** Education/Educational Services **Company Name:** The University of Southern Mississippi **Date of Birth:** 10/06/1939 **Place of Birth:** Seguin **State:** TX **Parents:** Wintford Henry Owen; Nelia Melanie (Fischer) Owen **Marital Status:** Married **Spouse Name:** John Holcombe Bedenbaugh (12/27/1961, Deceased 2016) **Children:** Melanie **Education:** PhD in Organic Chemistry, University of South Carolina (1967); BS, The University of Texas at Austin, Cum Laude (1961) **Career:** Board Member, Women's Studies Program, The University of Southern Mississippi (2004-2007, 1996-1997); Research Associate Professor, Chemistry and Biochemistry, The University of Southern Mississippi, Hattiesburg, MS (1980-2011); Research Associate, Chemistry, The University of Southern Mississippi, Hattiesburg, MS (1966-1980); Instructor, Chemistry Laboratory, The University of Texas at Austin (1960-1961) **Career Related:** Co-principal Director, Grants from National Science Foundation (1984-1985, 1998-1996, 2000-2005); Project Director, Mathematics and Science Partner Program, U.S. Department of Education (2004); Director, Website, National Aeronautics and Space Administration Grant (1999-2001); Co-principal Investigator, Bell South Foundation Grant (1998-2000); Project Director, Grant from U.S. Department of Energy (1979-1980) **Civic:** Mississippi State Coordinator, Building a Presence for Science (2002-Present); Editor, U.S. Forum Connection, DKGSI (2000-Present); Member, Toastmasters International (1986-Present); National Women's Political Caucus (1976-Present); Member, Mathematics and Science Partnership, U.S. Department of Education (2007-2010, 2004-2006); Participant, US-Egypt Education Forum, Cairo, Egypt (2007); Member, Governor's Education Summit (2004); Administrator, Director, Teacher Mentoring Initiative through Bell South Foundation Grant (1998-2000); Area Governor, Toastmasters International (1994); Club President, Toastmasters International (1993); Women's Unit Treasurer, Parkway Heights United Methodist Church (1977); Board of Directors, Executive Committee, Forrest Stone Area Opportunity, Inc. (1972); Monitoring Committee, Office of Head Start, Administration for Children and Families (1971-1972); Committee to Rewrite Personnel Policies and Procedures, Forrest Stone Area Opportunity, Inc. (1971); Personnel Screening Committee, Office of Head Start, Administration for Children and Families (1971) **Creative Works:** Co-author, Program Manual, Mississippi Mathematics & Science Partnership, The University of Southern Mississippi Project (2007-Present); Co-author, "Teaching Physical Science, Volumes 1 and 2" (2003); Author, "Nomenplayture" (1998); Co-author, "Teaching First Year Chemistry, 4th Edition" (1993); Co-author, Handbook for High School Chemistry Teachers (1985); Author, "Teaching First Year Chemistry" (1983) **Awards:** John and Angela Bedenbaugh Award, Coastal Mississippi Association of High School Chemistry Teachers (1996-Present); Named Woman of Distinction, DKGSI (2013); Zeta State Achievement Award, DKGSI (2007); Research Grant, U.S. Department of Education Mathematics & Science Partnership Program (2004-2010); Johnnie Marie Whitfield Service Award, American Chemical Society (2004); Grantee, American Chemical Society (2002); Administrative Director Research Grant (2001-2004, 1993-1996, 1988-1991); Research Grant, National Science Foundation (2000-2005); Grantee, Mississippi-NASA Space Consortium (1999-2001); Distinguished Science Teacher Award, Mississippi Science Teachers Association (1994); Chemist of the Year Award, American Chemical Society (1991) **Membership:** Treasurer, DKGSI (2012-Present); State Legislative Liaison, Mississippi Science Teachers Association (2002-Present); State Coordinator, Building a Presence for Science Program, Mississippi Science Teachers Association (2001-Present); Resource Reviewer, National Science Teachers Association (1999-Present); Executive Board, Mississippi Science Teachers Association (1994-Present); Executive Board, American Chemical Society (1983-Present); Elected Chair, DKGSI (2010-2012); Elected Forum Chair, International U.S. Forum Committee (2010); Elected Southeast Regional Representative, International U.S. Forum Committee (2008); Elected Southeast Regional Representative, U.S. Forum Committee, DKGSI (2008); State President, Mississippi Science Teachers Association (2000-2002); Congress Member, National Science Teachers Association (2000-2002); President-Elect, Mississippi Science Teachers Association (1998-2000); Chairman, International Computer Share Fair, International Convention, DKGSI (1994); President, Mississippi Branch, DKGSI (1989-1991); Chairman, American Chemical Society (1984-1985); Program Chairman, American Chemical Society (1983-1984); Chairman, International Research Committee, DKGSI (1980-1982); The Nature Conservancy; Smithsonian; National Geographic Society; National Parks Conservation Association; The Humane Society of the United States **Marquis Who's Who Honors:** Albert Nelson Marquis Lifetime Achievement Award (2017); Distinguished Humanitarian (2017) **Political Affiliations:** Democrat **Religion:** Methodist **Shipping Address:** 63 Suggs Rd, Hattiesburg, MS, 39402

James R. Beer

Title: Circuit Judge **Industry:** Law and Legal Services **Company Name:** State of Wisconsin **Marital Status:** Married **Spouse Name:** Olga Beer (6/25/2004) **Children:** Tara; Crystal; Jennifer; Artem; Alexander **Education:** Coursework, National Prosecutors School, Pritzker School of Law, Northwestern University (1975); JD, Marquette University Law School (1972); BS, University of Wisconsin-Madison (1969) **Career:** Circuit Judge, State of Wisconsin **Membership:** Past President, Board of Directors, Genuine Indian Relic Society; Past Vice President, Badger State Archaeological Society **To what do you attribute your success:** Mr. Beer attributes his success to hard work. **Why did you become involved in your profession or industry:** Mr. Beer became involved in his career because his best friend's father was a judge who taught them how to play chess when he was about 5 years old. He was always curious about the court and used to stop in and watch it sometimes. As an undergraduate, Mr. Beers decided to apply to law school. Regarding becoming a judge, his predecessor was appointed to the Court of Appeals by Governor Thompson and he was one of four to apply to his former position, and Governor Thompson chose to appoint him. One year later, Mr. Beer ran for the office and won. **Hobbies:** Avocational archaeologist **Shipping Address:** 2841 6th St, Monroe, WI, 53566 **Website:** http://themonroetimes.com/main.asp?SectionID=2&SubSectionID=1352&ArticleID=46711

Craig Cano Beeson

Title: Pharmacologist **Industry:** Pharmaceuticals **Company Name:** Medical University of South Carolina **Date of Birth:** 12/20/1958 **Parents:** Ed O. Beeson; Esperanza C. Beeson **Marital Status:** Married **Spouse Name:** Gyda C. Grey **Education:** PhD, University of California, Irvine (1993) **Career:** Professor, Medical University of South Carolina (2016-Present); Associate Professor, Medical University of South Carolina, Charleston, SC (2002-2016); Assistant Professor, University of Washington, Seattle, WA (1996-2002); Postdoctoral Scholar, Stanford University (1993-1996) **Career Related:** Chief Executive Officer, MitoChem Therapeutics Inc., Charleston, SC (2011-Present); President, MitoChem Therapeutics Inc., Charleston, SC (2009-2014) **Awards:** Grantee, National Institutes of Health (1996-Present); Career Award, National Science Foundation (1996-2002); Research Award, The Hispanic Society of America (1997-2001); Postdoctoral Award, Cancer Research Institute (1993-1995) **Hobbies:** Cooking **Political Affiliations:** Independent **Shipping Address:** 825 Robert E Lee Blvd, Charleston, SC, 29412

Barbara Jeanne Belew

Title: Music Educator **Industry:** Education/ Educational Services **Company Name:** McNeese State University **Date of Birth:** 11/01/1929 **Place of Birth:** Plainview **State:** TX **Parents:** Horace Russell Belew; Mattilene Lloyd Belew **Education:** MusM, Indiana University, Bloomington, IN (1953); MusB, Hardin-Simmons University, Abilene, TX, Summa Cum Laude (1951) **Certifications:** Certified Teacher of Music, Music Teachers National Association (1980) **Career:** Associate Professor in Music, McNeese State University, Lake Charles, LA (1955) **Career Related:** Harpist, Lake Charles Symphony (1958-Present); Harpist, Rapides Symphony Orchestra, Alexandria, LA (1965-1999); Harpist, Baton Rouge Symphony Orchestra (1964-1968) **Civic:** Harp Camp (2000-Present); Sunday School Secretary, Trinity Baptist Church, Lake Charles, LA (1975-Present); National Board of Directors, Louisiana Chapter, American Harp Society, Inc. (1973-1979); Founder, Louisiana Chapter, American Harp Society, Inc.; Vice President, Louisiana Chapter, American Harp Society, Inc.; Advisor, Louisiana Chapter, American Harp Society, Inc.; Ensemble Coach, Louisiana Chapter, American Harp Society, Inc.; Leader, Alpha Gamma Chapter, DKGSI **Membership:** Recording Secretary, Lake Charles Piano Teachers Association; State Chairman, Baldwin Piano Competition, Louisiana Music Teachers Association **To what do you attribute your success:** Ms. Belew attributes her success to Christ and enjoying her work. **Why did you become involved in your profession or industry:** Ms. Belew became involved in her profession because of the love for music and piano she's had since the age of five. She started with the harp just for fun, and then she fell in love with it. **Hobbies:** Needlework; Reading; Crossword puzzles **Religion:** Baptist **Shipping Address:** 4022 Wooded Drive, Lake Charles, LA, 70605

Ann Marie J. Bellotti-Clark

Title: Chief Financial Officer **Industry:** Business Management/Business Services **Company Name:** Legacy Technologies, LLC **Marital Status:** Divorced **Children:** Lee Ann Viehouser **Education:** BS in Business Administration, Accounting, The University of Tulsa, Cum Laude, Tulsa, OK (1992); Graduate Coursework, Keller Graduate School of Management, Kansas City, MO **Certifications:** Certified Public Accountant, States of Kansas and Missouri; Chartered Global Management Accountant; Certified QuickBooks Pro Advisor **Career:** Chief Financial Officer, Executive Consultant, Legacy Technologies Inc., Mission, KS (2008-Present); Payroll Manager, Benefits Administrator, C. J. Foods, Inc., Pawnee City, NE (2012-2014); Consultant, Audit Manager, MDP Services, LLC, Overland Park, KS (2010-2012); Controller, Prosoco, Inc., Lawrence, KS (2005-2008); Accounting Manager, Central Salt, LLC, Overland Park, KS (2004-2005); Senior Executive Accountant, Deffenbaugh Industries, Inc., Shawnee, KS (2001-2004); Mentor, Coach, Leadership Team Development **Membership:** American Institute of Certified Public Accountants **Why did you become involved in your profession or industry:** Ms. Bellotti-Clark became involved in her profession because her father was a financial analyst with American Airlines, so she wanted to follow that. He died when she was young, and in college she took classes and it clicked. **What do you consider to be the highlight of your career:** A highlight of Ms. Bellotti-Clark's career was the support and mentoring she received early in her career. **Business Address:** 6700 W 47th Ter, Shawnee Mission, KS, 66203 **Shipping Address:** 4710 Roundtree Ct, Shawnee, KS, 66226 **Website:** http://www.legacytechnologies.com

Jenny Bencardino, MD

Title: Radiologist **Industry:** Medicine & Health Care **Company Name:** New York University School of Medicine **Date of Birth:** 08/06/1968 **Place of Birth:** Bogota **Country of Origin:** Colombia **Parents:** Libardo Bencardino; Teresa (Suarez) Bencardino **Marital Status:** Married **Spouse Name:** Alvand Hassankhani (4/20/2002) **Children:** Dario A. Hassankhani; Avan P. Hassankhani **Education:** Resident in Diagnostic Imaging, Albert Einstein College of Medicine, Bronx, NY (2000); MD, Pontifical Xavierian University (1991); Bachelor's Degree, Divine Savior School (1984) **Certifications:** Diplomate, American Board of Radiology (2000); Specialist in Diagnostic Imaging, Xaverian University, with Honors (1996) **Career:** Radiology Professor, New York University School of Medicine, New York (2014-Present); Director, Musculoskeletal MRI, Medical Arts Radiology (2003-2006); Assistant Radiology Professor, Harvard Medical School, Harvard University (2000-2003); Director, Musculoskeletal MRI, Massachusetts General Hospital (2000-2002) **Career Related:** Member-at-Large, Publications Committee, American Roentgen Ray Society (2012-Present); Publications Committee, ISMRM (2012-Present); International Outreach Committee, Global Partner Society Program, American Roentgen Ray Society (2011-Present); Musculoskeletal RadioGraphics Judging Panel, Radiological Society of North America (2010-Present); Chair Research Committee, SSR (2013-2015); International Skeleton Society (2012-2014); Committee Chair, SSR (2010-2014); Secretary, Musculoskeletal Study Group, ISMRM (2010-2012); Representative, Central and South America, SSR (2009-2012); Member Meeting Program Committee, SSR (2008-2014); Member-at-Large, Executive Committee, American Roentgen Ray Society **Creative Works:** Consulting Editorial Board Member, Skeletal Radiology, Springer Verlag (2005-Present); Editor, "The Shoulder: Imaging Diagnosis with Treatment Implications," Springer International Publishing (2015); Guest Editor, "Shoulder," Magnetic Resonance Imaging Clinics of North America, Elsevier, Inc. (2012); Co-Author, Magnetic Resonance Imaging in Orthopedic Sports Medicine, Springer Verlag (2007); Co-Editor, Topics in MRI (2003) **Awards:** Recipient, Honored Educator Award, Radiological Society North America (2014); Recipient, President's Medal, International Skeletal Society (2013); Recipient, Research Award, Radiological Society of North America (1999); Fellowship, New York University School of Medicine (1996-1997) **Membership:** Educational Exhibits Committee, Radiological Society North America (2012-Present); Vice Chair, American College of Radiology; SSR; Musculoskeletal Subcommittee, Radiological Society North America; International Skeletal Society; International Society for Magnetic Resonance in Medicine **Marquis Who's Who Honors:** Albert Nelson Marquis Lifetime Achievement Award (2017) **Hobbies:** Travel; Latin-American literature; Swimming **Shipping Address:** 19 Olde Hamlet Dr, Jericho, NY, 11753

J. Claude Bennett

Title: Professor Emeritus **Industry:** Education/Educational Services **Company Name:** University of Alabama at Birmingham **Date of Birth:** 12/12/1933 **Place of Birth:** Birmingham **State:** AL **Parents:** Claude Bennett; Clara Lucille (Clark) Bennett **Marital Status:** Married **Spouse Name:** Frances Caldwell Bennett (2002); Nancy Miller (6/17/1958, Deceased 2001) **Children:** Katherine Diane Miller; Clark Barton **Education:** Honorary MD, University of Zurich (2008); Honorary MD, University of Leipzig (1999); Honorary DSc, University of Alabama, With Honors (1992); Resident, UAB Health System, School of Medicine, University of Alabama at Birmingham (1959-1960); Intern, UAB Health System, School of Medicine, University of Alabama at Birmingham (1958-1959); MD, Harvard University (1958); BA, Samford University (1954) **Certifications:** Diplomate, American Board of Internal Medicine; Diplomate, American Board of Rheumatology; Diplomate, National Board of Medical Examiners **Career:** Medical Consultant, P&T Therapeutics (2017-Present); Medical Consultant, Bio-Cryst Pharmaceuticals, Inc (2008-Present); Spencer Professor of Medical Science, School of Medicine, University of Alabama at Birmingham (1992-Present); President, BioCryst Pharmaceuticals, Inc. (1996-2008); Chief Operating Officer, BioCryst Pharmaceuticals, Inc. (1996-2008); President, University of Alabama at Birmingham (1993-1996); Professor, School of Medicine, University of Alabama at Birmingham (1982-1992); Chairman, Department of Medicine, School of Medicine, University of Alabama at Birmingham (1982-1992); Distinguished Faculty Lecturer, School of Medicine, University of Alabama at Birmingham (1979); Multipurpose Arthritis Center Director, School of Medicine, University of Alabama at Birmingham (1977-1984); Director, Division of Clinical Immunology and Rheumatology, School of Medicine, University of Alabama at Birmingham (1970-1983); Professor, School of Medicine, University of Alabama at Birmingham (1970-1982); Chairman, Department of Microbiology, School of Medicine, University of Alabama at Birmingham (1970-1982); Assistant Professor, Department of Medicine, School of Medicine, University of Alabama at Birmingham (1965-1970); Associate Professor, Department of Microbiology, School of Medicine, University of Alabama at Birmingham (1965-1970); Assistant Director, Division of Clinical Immunology and Rheumatology, School of Medicine, University of Alabama at Birmingham (1965-1970) **Career Related:** Health Science Policies Board Member, National Academy of Sciences, NIH (1988-Present); Science Advisory Board Member, Gorgas Memorial Institute of Tropical and Preventive Medicine, School of Medicine, University of Alabama at Birmingham (1985-Present); Visiting Professor, Baylor College of Medicine (1989); Visiting Professor, Leiden University, Netherlands (1988); Science Advisory Board Member, Merck Sharp & Dohme Corporation (1987-1989); Visiting Professor, School of Medicine, University of Missouri (1987); Senior Research Fellow, Division of Biology, California Institute of Technology (1964-1965); Rheumatoid Arthritis Research Fellow, Harvard Medical School, Massachusetts General Hospital, Arthritis Foundation (1960-1962); Fellow, American Association for the Advancement of Science; Physician in Chief, UAB Health System, School of Medicine, University of Alabama at Birmingham **Civic:** Independent Committee for Research and Development, American Board of Internal Medicine (1988-Present); Governing Board, American Board of Internal Medicine (1987-Present); Certification Exam Committee, American Board of Internal Medicine (1989) **Creative Works:** Editorial Board Member, Current Opinion in Rheumatology (1988-Present); Co-Editor, "Cecil Textbook of Medicine" (1988-Present); Editorial Board Member, "Protein & Peptide Letters (1980-Present); Editor-in-Chief, American Journal of Medicine (1986-1997); Co-Editor, "Rheumatology and Immunology, Second Edition" (1986); Editor-in-Chief, Arthritis and Rheumatism (1975-1980); Editorial Board Member, Arthritis and Rheumatism (1969-1975) **Awards:** Alabama Academy of Honor Award (1987); Seale Harris Award, Southern Medical Association (1987); Research Career Development Award, NIH (1965-1975); Scholar in Academic Medicine, The Markle Foundation (1965-1970) **Membership:** Medical Science Secretary, Nominating Committee, American Association for the Advancement of Science (1989-Present); Executive Committee, American Board of Internal Medicine (1992); Advisory Panel on Biomedical Research, AAMC (1991-1992); Master, American College of Physicians (1990); Board of Directors Planning Group, American College of Rheumatology (1986-1987); President, American College of Rheumatology (1981-1982); The American Association of Immunologists, Inc.; Federated Council of International Medicine; Institute of Medicine, National Academy of Sciences; American Federation for Medical Research; American Society for Biochemistry and Molecular Biology; The American Society for Clinical Investigation **Marquis Who's Who Honors:** Albert Nelson Marquis Lifetime Achievement Award (2017); Distinguished Humanitarian (2017) **Shipping Address:** 2920 Redmont Park Circle, Apt. 401 E, Birmingham, AL, 35205

Reginald Wendell Bennett

Title: Senior Policy Analyst **Industry:** Sciences **Company Name:** U.S. Food and Drug Administration **Date of Birth:** 12/14/1933 **Place of Birth:** Bowling Green **State:** VA **Parents:** Commodore Nathenial Bennett; Burnley Muriel Bennett **Marital Status:** Married **Spouse Name:** Clara Francis Knight (6/4/1955) **Children:** Reinaldo; Regina; Ricardo **Education:** MS in Microbiology, University of Pittsburgh (1958) BS in Microbiology, University of Pittsburgh (1955) Coursework, NIH Graduate School, University of Virginia **Career:** Chief, Microbiological Methods, Development Branch, U.S. Food and Drug Administration (1997-2007); Acting Chief, Research Branch, U.S. Food and Drug Administration (1993-1997); Microbiologist, U.S. Food and Drug Administration (1960-1993); Assistant Professor, Benedict University (1959-1960); Bacteriologist, Children's General Hospital, UPMC (1959); Medical Technologist, Braddock General Hospital, UPMC (1957-1959); Bacteriologist, UPMC (1956-1958) **Career Related:** Chair, Food Division, American Society for Microbiology (1984); Research Coordinator, National Research Center, Cairo, Egypt (1978); Associate Official, Analytical Chemistry, Gaithersburg, MD (1971) **Civic:** Administrative Role, Boy Scouts of America, Washington D.C. (1970-1980); Volunteer, Scholarship Funds **Creative Works:** Author, "Gone Bad (Chinese Canned Mushrooms)," The Wall Street Journal (1989); Author, "Lesser Known Toxins," Food Chemical News (1989); Author, "Screening Bacillus Thuringiensis for Diarrheal Toxin Urged," Food Chemical News (1986); Contributor, Articles, Professional Journals; Contributor, Chapters, Books **Awards:** Humanitarian of the Year, International Association of Top Professionals (2018); Top Research Microbiologist of the Year, International Association of Top Professionals (2017); Nominee, Who's Who in Science and Engineering (2011-2012); Nominee, Who's Who in the World (2011); Nominee, Who's Who in America (2008); President's Lifetime Achievement Award, International Association for Food Protection (2004); Secretary's Award for Distinguished Service (2003); Group Recognition Award, Microbiology Rapid Methods Working Group, U.S. Food and Drug Administration (1997); In Superior Service Award for Public Health Service (1995); On the Spot and Excellence in Science Awards, U.S. Food and Drug Administration (1994); International's Harvey W. Wiley Award, AOAC International (1991); Group Recognition Award, U.S. Food and Drug Administration (1990); Distinguished Service Award, Division of Continuing Education, Kansas State University (1987-1997); Eponym, Reginald Bennett Garnet Wood Book Award **Membership:** Institute of Food Technologists; Fellow, American Academy of Microbiology; The American Society for Microbiology; International Association for Food Protection; Fellow, Association of Official Analytical Chemists International **Marquis Who's Who Honors:** Albert Nelson Marquis Lifetime Achievement Award (2017) **To what do you attribute your success:** Mr. Bennett attributes his success to his perseverance, creativity and multifaceted personality. **Why did you become involved in your profession or industry:** He became involved in his profession because he was always interested in science. **What do you consider to be the highlight of your career:** The highlight of his career is when he became a fellow of the American Academy of Microbiology. **Where will you be in five years:** In five years, Mr. Bennett hopes to work in government regulations. **Hobbies:** Baking Rum Cakes; Traveling; Photography; Cooking; Travel **Political Affiliations:** Democrat **Business Address:** 5100 Paint Branch Parkway, College Park, MD, 20740

Frank Stewart Berall

Title: Partner **Industry:** Law and Legal Services **Company Name:** Copp & Berall, LLP **Date of Birth:** 02/10/1929 **Place of Birth:** New York City **State:** NY **Parents:** Louis J. Berall; Jeannette F. Berall **Marital Status:** Married **Spouse Name:** Jenefer M. Carey (9/1/1980); Christiana Johnson (Married 7/5/1958, Deceased 7/1972) **Children:** Erik Dustin; Elissa Alexandra **Education:** LLM in Taxation, New York University (1959); JD, Yale University (1955); BS, Yale University (1950) **Certifications:** Accredited Estate Planner **Career:** Partner, Copp & Berall, LLP, Hartford, CT (1970-Present); Associate, Cooney & Scully, Hartford, CT (1968-1970); Attorney, Trust Department, Hartford National Bank & Trust Company, Hartford, CT (1965-1967); Attorney, Connecticut General Life Insurance Company, Bloomfield, CT (1960-1965); Associate, Firm, Townley, Updike, Carter & Rodgers, New York City, NY (1957-1960); Associate, Firm, Mudge, Stern, Baldwin & Todd, New York City, NY (1955-1957) **Career Related:** Chairman, Federal Tax Institute of New England (2010-2014); Counsel Committee on Tax Law Clarification (1984-1988); Adjunct Assistant Professor, Graduate Tax Program, University of Hartford (1973-1974); Counsel, State Tax Commissioner's Commission (1972-1975); Connecticut Governor's Commission on Tax Reform (1972-1973); Lecturer, University of Connecticut Law School (1972-1973); Counsel, Connecticut Governor's Strike Force for Full Employment (1971-1972); Vice President, Secretary, General Counsel, John M. Blewer, Inc., Essex, CT (1969-1986); Instructor, Estate Planning, American College of Life Insurance (1968-1969); Lecturer, University of Connecticut School of Insurance (1964-1967); Assistant in Instruction, Yale University Law School (1954-1955); Lecturer, Speaker in Field **Civic:** Co-chairman, Advisory Council, Hartford Tax Institute (1986-1994); Co-chairman, Notre Dame Estate Planning Institute (1977-2009); Advisory Council, University of Hartford Tax Institute (1970-1982); Board of Directors, Bloomfield Interfaith Homes (1967-1971) **Military Service:** First Lieutenant, Field Artillery, U.S. Army (1951-1952); Infantry, 45th Division, 160th Field Artillery Battalion, North Korea **Creative Works:** Member, Editorial Board, "Estate Planning magazine" (1973-Present); Senior Editor, Connecticut Bar Journal (1969-Present); Member, Editorial Board, "Estate Tax Planning Advisory" (2003); Co-Author, "The Migrant Client: Tax, Community Property, and Other Considerations" (1994); Member, Editorial Board, "Practical Tax Lawyer" (1988-2008); Member, Editorial Board, "Journal Taxation of Trusts and Estates" (1988-1992); Co-Author, "Revocable Inter Vivos Trusts" (1985); Editorial Board Member, Connecticut Chapter, American College Trust and Estate Counsel (1975-1987); Co-Author, A Practitioner's Guide to the Tax Reform Act of 1969" (1970); Co-author, Estate Planning and the Close Corporation (1970); Co-Author, Planning Large Estates (1970) **Awards:** Listed, Top 50 Super Lawyers, Connecticut Magazine; Nathan Hale Award, Yale Club, Hartford, CT **Membership:** Director, Yale Club of Hartford (1998-Present); Executive Committee, Estates and Probate Section, Connecticut Bar Association (1973-Present); Executive Committee, Connecticut Bar Association (1969-Present); Vice President, America, International Academy of Estate and Trust Law (2006-2010); President, Yale Club of Hartford (2005-2008); Executive Councilor, International Academy of Estate and Trust Law (2004-2006); President, Yale Club of Hartford (1999-2001); President, Culver Summer Schools Alumni Association (1997-1999); Trustee, Culver Educational Fund (1997-1999); Culver Club, Central New England (1996-1997); Board of Directors, Culver Summer Schools Alumni Association (1993-2001); Chairman, Connecticut Bar Association (1986-1988); Board of Directors, Culver Summer Schools Alumni Association (1985-1991); Vice Chairman, Connecticut Bar Association (1984-1986); Executive Councilor, International Academy of Estate and Trust Law (1980-1982); Fellow, Chairman, Connecticut Chapter, American College Trust and Estate Counsel (1975-1981); Regent, Connecticut Chapter, American College Trust and Estate Counsel (1977-1982); Vice President, Culver Summer Schools Alumni Association (1975-1985); Tax Club of Hartford (1975-1976); Bylaws Committee Charter, Hartford County Bar Association (1975); Chairman, Committee Liaison with IRS, Hartford County Bar Association (1972-1974); Chairman, Tax Section, Connecticut Bar Association (1969-1972); Lifetime Member, American Law Institute; American College Tax Counsel **Bar Admissions:** Connecticut (1960); New York (1955) **Marquis Who's Who Honors:** Albert Nelson Marquis Lifetime Achievement Award (2017) **Hobbies:** Photography; History; Stamp collecting **Political Affiliations:** Republican **Religion:** Episcopalian **Business Address:** 864 Wethersfield Ave Ste 8, Hartford, CT, 06114

Pat Berger

Title: Artist **Industry:** Fine Art **Date of Birth:** 03/17/1929 **Place of Birth:** New York **State:** NY **Parents:** Marion Sigmund Gardner; Florence (Hyman) Gardner **Marital Status:** Widowed **Spouse Name:** Merlin Clarence Czoschke (4/30/1978, Deceased 1995); Jack Berger (1/8/1948, Divorced 1971) **Children:** Kenneth Steven; Russell Howard **Education:** Coursework, University of California, Los Angeles (1974-1976); Coursework, University of California, Los Angeles (1963-1966); Coursework, University of California, Los Angeles (1955-1959); Student, Art Center College of Design (1947-1948) **Career Related:** Chairman of Art Unlimited, Downey Museum of Art (1975-1977); Painting and Drawing Instructor, Los Angeles Unified School District (1971-2003); Artist-in-Residence, Brandeis-Bardin Institute, American Jewish University (1970); Artist-in-Residence, Brandeis-Bardin Institute, American Jewish University (1951-1965) **Creative Works:** Exhibitor, Hebrew Union College Museum, New York, NY (2017); Exhibitor, Hebrew Union College Museum, New York, NY (2007); Exhibitor, West Valley Art Museum (2006); Exhibitor, Kitakyushu Municipal Museum (2005); Exhibitor, Finegood Art Gallery (2005); Exhibitor, Costello Childs Contemporary Fine Art (2004); Exhibitor, LA Artcore Center (2004); Exhibitor, LA Artcore Center (2002); Exhibitor, Fukuoka Prefectural Museum (2001); Exhibitor, Kitakyushu Municipal Museum (2001); Exhibitor, Karpeles Manuscript Library Museum (2000-2001); Exhibitor, University of Judaism (Now American Jewish University) (2000); Exhibitor, LA Artcore Center (1998); Exhibitor, The Jewish Museum (1993); Exhibitor, Museum of Biblical Art (1993); Exhibitor, University of Judaism (Now American Jewish University) (1991); Traveling Exhibitor, West 93 and the Law (1991); Exhibitor, The Jewish Museum (1991); Exhibitor, Finegood Art Gallery (1990); Exhibitor, Long Beach Museum of Art (1990); Exhibitor, West Los Angeles City Hall Gallery (1990); Exhibitor, Carson County Square House Museum (1990); Exhibitor, The Jewish Museum (1989); Exhibitor, Valerie Miller Gallery (1988-1993); Exhibitor, Jewish Federation Galleries (1988); Exhibitor, Bridge Gallery, City of Los Angeles (1986); Exhibitor, Moosart Gallery (1985); Traveling Exhibitor, West 93 and the Law (1983-1984); Exhibitor, Riverside Art Museum (1983); Exhibitor, Mendenhall Gallery, Whittier College (1982); Exhibitor, Metro Galleries; Exhibitor, Israeli Artist Exchange Show; Exhibitor, Jerusalem Binali Museum; Exhibitor, Jewish Artists Initiative; Exhibitor, Skirball Cultural Center; Exhibitor, School of Law, University of Minnesota; Exhibitor, Julia and David White Artists Colony; Exhibitor, The San Diego Museum of Art; Exhibitor, Springfield Museum of Art; Exhibitor, Polk County Bank; Exhibitor, Palm Springs Art Museum; Exhibitor, Sodertalje Konsthall; Exhibitor, City of La Mirada; Artist, Hallmark Licensing, LLC.; Exhibitor, The Marshall Gallery of Fine Art, Scottsdale, AZ **Awards:** Featured Artist, Cheviot Hills Art Crawl (2015-2018) **Membership:** Jewish Artists Initiative; Fine Arts Council; American Jewish University; President Emeritus, National Watercolor Society; Board of Directors Emeritus, Watercolor USA Honor Society **To what do you attribute your success:** Ms. Berger attributes her success to determination, love of what she does, and just keeping at it. **Why did you become involved in your profession or industry:** Ms. Berger became involved in her profession through a doctor friend who was staying with her family and took her to night art classes with him. She became entranced and submitted a portfolio to Art Center College of Design, and that was the start. **What do you consider to be the highlight of your career:** A highlight of Ms. Berger's career was her work with the homeless in the mid 80s. She became aware of their plight and decided to do a consciousness raising statement through art to raise people's awareness, and spent the next five years doing just that and still does. **Where will you be in five years:** Ms. Berger feels fortunate that at 89 years old, she is still healthy enough to keep on working and would like to be around those extra years if God is willing. **Hobbies:** Theatre; Traveling; Photography **Political Affiliations:** Democrat **Religion:** Jewish **Shipping Address:** 2648 Anchor Avenue, Los Angeles, CA, 90064

Eugene "Bert" Bertram Berkley

Title: Chairman of the Board **Industry:** Manufacturing **Company Name:** Tension Corporation **Date of Birth:** 05/08/1923 **Place of Birth:** Kansas City **State:** MO **Parents:** Eugene "Bert" Bertram Berkowitz; Caroline Newman (Newburger) Berkowitz **Marital Status:** Widowed **Spouse Name:** Joan Meinrath (9/1/1948) **Children:** Janet Lynn (Berkley) Dubrava; William "Bill" Spencer Berkley; Jane Ellen (Berkley) Levitt **Education:** Honorary LHD, Missouri Valley College, Marshall, MO (2010); MBA, Harvard Business School, Harvard University (1950); BA, Duke University (1948) **Career:** Chairman of the Board, Tension Envelope Corporation, Kansas City, MO (1967-Present); President, Tension Envelope Corporation, Kansas City, MO (1962-1988); Chief Executive Officer, Tension Envelope Corporation, Kansas City, MO (1962-1988) **Career Related:** Chairman, Global Envelope Alliance (2005-2011); President, Envelope Manufacturers Association (1983-1985); Executive Committee, Envelope Manufacturers Association (1981-1983); Vice Chairman, Executive Committee, Envelope Manufacturers Association (1981-1983); Executive Committee Envelope Manufacturers Association (1976-1979); Executive Committee, Envelope Manufacturers Association (1967-1970); Executive Committee, Envelope Manufacturers Association (1960-1963) **Civic:** Advisory Council, Smithsonian National Postal Museum (2016-Present); Director, Turn the Page KC (2012-Present); Board of Directors, Institute for Educational Leadership, Washington, DC (2000-Present); Founder, Chairman, and Board Member, Local Investment Commission, Investing in Children and Families (1992-Present); Council of Champions, National Grade Level Reading Effort (2018); Chair, Jewish Community Relations Bureau, American Jewish Committee (2009); Board of Directors, Centerpoint for Leaders, Washington, DC (2001-2004); Director, Missouri Family and Community Trust, State of Missouri (1999-2012); Board of Directors, National Youth Information Network (1997-2004); Director, Biodiversity Institute & Natural History Museum University of Kansas (1994-2000); Advisory Board, National Council for Economic Education (1993-1995); Chairman, Board of Directors, Center for Workforce Preparation, United States Chamber of Commerce (1991-2002); Board of Directors, Ewing Marion Kaussman Foundation Center for Entrepreneurial Leadership (1990-2002); Kitchen Cabinet, Kansas City Public Schools (1990-1992); Business Round Table, Department of Social Services, State of Missouri (1989-1999); Board of Directors, National Minority Supplier Development Council (1989-1998); Chairman, The Center for Business Innovation (1987-1989); Advisory Board, National Parks Conservation Association (1986-2006); Chairman, Board of Directors, National Minority Supplier Development Council (1986-1988); Chairman, Board of Directors, Human Services Testing and Retesting Council (1983-1990); Trustee, Chairman, University of Missouri-Kansas City Board of Trustees (1983-1985); Human Resources Committee, Heart of America United Way (1983); Board of Directors, Kansas City Area Health Planning Council, Inc. (1982-1983); Vice Chairman, University of Missouri-Kansas City (1981-1983); Director, Menorah Medical Center (1980-1994); Executive Committee, Center for Management Assistance (1980-1983); Chairman, National Alliance of Businessmen of Kansas City (1973) **Military Service:** First Lieutenant, Infantry, U.S. Army **Creative Works:** Co-Author, "Giving Back: Connecting You, Business and Community" (2009) **Awards:** Community Guardian Award, Ad Hoc Group Against Crime (2017); Lauriat, Jr. Achievement Business Hall of Fame (2016); Hugh J. Zimmer Award for Excellence in Urban Education, University of Missouri-Kansas City (2016); Adele Hall Spirit of Caring Award, United Way of Greater Kansas City (2015); Kansas City Globe Newspaper Lifetime Honoree, Society of Influentials Award (2015); Robert H. Meneilly Stand Up Speak Out Award from Mainstream Coalition (2014); Legacy Award, MidAmerica Minority Supplier Development Council, Kansas City, MO (2013); Award, The Pembroke Hill School (2011); Mayor of Independence, MO Award (2010); Harold L. Holliday Senior Civil Rights Award, NAACP (2009); Founder's Award, Envelope Manufacturer's Association (EMA) (2009); Proclamation from Mayor & City Council, Kansas City, MO (2008); Distinguished Service to State Government Award, National Governors Association (2000); Honorary Star, STOP Violence Coalition (1999); Human Relations Award, Jewish Community Relations Bureau, American Jewish Committee (1997); CEO Advocate of the Year Award, Mid-America Minority Supplier Development Council (1991); Bronze Star; Combat Infantry Badge **Membership:** Leadership Council, Graduate School of Education, Harvard University (2011-2014); Board of Directors, Flexographic Technology Association (1993-1997); Director, Council for Economic Education (1993-1995) **Marquis Who's Who Honors:** Albert Nelson Marquis Lifetime Achievement Award (2017) **Hobbies:** Fly fishing; Camping; Whitewater rafting **Shipping Address:** 819 East 19th Street, Kansas City, MO, 64108-1781 **Website:** www.tensioncorp.com

Martin Berkon

Title: Artist **Industry:** Fine Art **Date of Birth:** 01/30/1932 **Place of Birth:** Brooklyn **State:** NY **Parents:** Samuel F. Berkon; Sara (Hodes) Berkon **Marital Status:** Married **Spouse Name:** Eileen Phyllis Eichel (7/10/1960) **Education:** MA, New York University (1959); BA, Brooklyn College (1954); Coursework, Pratt Institute (1952) **Career:** Guest Lecturer, St. Thomas Aquinas College (1995); Guest Lecturer, Nassau Community College (1982); Guest Lecturer, Middlebury College (1977); Lecturer, City College of New York (1968-1969); Adjunct Faculty Member, Nassau Community College (1966-1967); Adjunct Faculty Member, Fairleigh Dickinson University (1966) **Career Related:** Teacher **Military Service:** U.S. Army **Creative Works:** Solo Exhibitor, Schering Plough Corporation Gallery, Madison, NJ (2001); Exhibitor, Group Show, Blue Hill Cultural Center, Pearl River, NY (1997-1998); Exhibitor, Group Show, Vero Beach Museum of Art, The Abstract Image, Florida (1996); Solo Exhibitor, Blue Hill Cultural Center, Pearl River, NY (1995); Exhibitor, Group Show, NASA Collection, Traveling Exhibition, Visions of Flight (1988-1991); Commissioned Artist, NASA (1987); Exhibitor, Group Show, Spaceport USA, Kennedy Space Center (1987); Featured Artist, Long Island Art Scene Television (1986); Exhibitor, Group Show, Spaceport USA, Kennedy Space Center (1985); Commissioned Artist, NASA (1984); Solo Exhibitor, Adelphi University, Garden City, NY (1983); Exhibitor, Group Show, Aldrich Museum of Contemporary Art, Ridgefield, CT (1982); Exhibitor, Group Show, Firehouse Gallery, Garden City, NY (1982); Exhibitor, Group Show, Barbara Walter Gallery, New York, NY (1982); Solo Exhibitor, Genesis Galleries, New York, NY (1978); Exhibitor, Group Show, American Federation Arts Traveling Show (1975-1977); Exhibitor, Group Show, Aldrich Museum of Contemporary Art, Ridgefield, CT (1975); Exhibitor, Group Show, Flint Institute of Art, Flint, MI (1974-1976); Exhibitor, Group Show, Aldrich Museum of Contemporary Art, Ridgefield, CT (1974); Exhibitor, Group Show, Soho Center for Visual Artists, New York, NY (1974); Exhibitor, Group Show, New Britain Museum, Connecticut (1974); Exhibitor, Group Show, Butler Institute of American Art (1969); Solo Exhibitor, 20th Century West Gallery, New York, NY (1967); Exhibitor, Group Show, Butler Institute of American Art (1967); Exhibitor, Group Show, Wesleyan College at Georgia (1965); Exhibitor, Group Show, Butler Institute of American Art (1965); Exhibitor, Group Show, Ball State University (1965); Exhibitor, Group Show, Ohio University Gallery (1964); Exhibitor, Group Show, Silvermine Guild Artists, Connecticut (1963); Solo Exhibitor, Smolin Gallery, New York, NY (1962); Exhibitor, Group Show, Brooklyn Museum (1958); Exhibitor, Permanent Collection, Aldrich Museum of Contemporary Art, Ridgefield, CT; Exhibitor, Permanent Collection, Texaco Inc., White Plains, NY; Exhibitor, Permanent Collection, PepsiCo Inc., Somers, NY; Exhibitor, Permanent Collection, Pfizer Inc., Rye Brook, NY; Exhibitor, Permanent Collection, NASA Gallery of Art, Kennedy Space Center; Exhibitor, Permanent Collection, Vero Beach Museum of Art; Exhibitor, Group Show, Meadowbrook Art Gallery, Oakland University, Rochester, MI **Marquis Who's Who Honors:** Albert Nelson Marquis Lifetime Achievement Award (2017) **Why did you become involved in your profession or industry:** Mr. Berkon was drawn to the field of arts because of his talent for drawing. **What do you consider to be the highlight of your career:** The highlight of Mr. Berkon's career was his commissions from NASA. **Shipping Address:** 503 Devries Court, Piermont, NY, 10968

Kenneth Ira Berns

Title: Physician **Industry:** Medicine & Health Care **Company Name:** Center for Disease Control and Prevention **Date of Birth:** 06/14/2017 **Place of Birth:** Cleveland **State:** OH **Parents:** Charles Berns; Delnet (Cohn) Berns **Marital Status:** Married **Spouse Name:** Laura Louise Lawless (6/26/1964) **Children:** Jonathan Charles; Deborah Louise **Education:** Intern, Johns Hopkins Hospital (1966-1967); MD, Johns Hopkins University (1966); PhD, Johns Hopkins University (1964); AB, Johns Hopkins University (1960); Coursework, Harvard University (1956-1959) **Career:** Advisory Committee Director, Centers for Disease Control and Prevention, U.S. Department of Health & Human Services (2014-Present); Distinguished Professor Emeritus, University of Florida Health (2012-Present); With, National Science Advisory Board for Biosecurity (2008-Present); Director, Genetics Institute, University of Florida (2003-Present); Distinguished Professor, University of Florida Health (2006-2012); President, Icahn School of Medicine at Mount Sinai (2002-2003); Chief Executive Officer, Icahn School of Medicine at Mount Sinai, (2002-2003); Vice President of Health Affairs, University of Florida Health (2000-2002); Dean, University of Florida Health (1997-2002); R.A. Rees Pritchett Professor, Weill Cornell Medicine (1984-1997); Chairman, Department of Microbiology, Weill Cornell Medicine (1984-1997); Professor, University of Florida Health (1976-1984); Chairman, Department of Immunology and Medical Microbiology, University of Florida Health (1976-1984); Professor of Pediatrics, University of Florida Health (1976-1984); Director, Year 1 Program, School of Medicine, The Johns Hopkins University (1973-1976); Associate Professor of Microbiology, School of Medicine, The Johns Hopkins University (1974-1976); Assistant Professor of Pediatrics, School of Medicine, The Johns Hopkins University (1970-1976); Assistant Professor of Microbiology, School of Medicine, The Johns Hopkins University (1970-1974) **Career Related:** National Advisory Council, National Center for Research Resources, NIH (1999-2003); Composite Committee Member, The United States Medical Licensing Examination, FSMB, NBME (1995-1998); Member, International Committee on Taxonomy of Viruses (1981-1998); Permanent Member, NIAID (1992-1996); Member, Executive Board, National Board of Medical Examiners (1986-1995); Member, Liaison Committee on Medical Education, American Cancer Society, Inc. (1989-1992); Member, Virology Study Section, NIH (1985-1989); Member, Virology and Microbiology Advisory Committee (1985-1989); Chairman, National Board of Medical Examiners (1983-1986); Member, Genetic Biology Panel, National Science Foundation (1981-1984); Chairman, NIH (1982-1983); Member, Recombinant DNA Advisory Committee, NIH (1980-1983); Delegate, U.S.-Japan Cooperative Program on Recombinant DNA (1981); Investigator, Howard Hughes Medical Institute (1970-1975) **Civic:** Board of Directors, Rosalind Franklin Society (2007-Present); Board of Trustees, Johns Hopkins University (2000-2006) **Military Service:** With, U.S. Public Health Service (1967-1970) **Awards:** Grantee, NIH (1970-1976, 1980-2005); Honoree, Distinguished Service Member, AAMC (2003); Distinguished Service Award, National Board of Medical Examiners (1995); Fogarty Senior International Fellow, Virology Department, Weizmann Institute of Science (1982-1983); Grantee, National Science Foundation (1973-1975, 1979-1980); Faculty Research Award, American Cancer Society, Inc. (1975-1976); Fellow, Shell Oil (1963-1964) **Membership:** Board of Governors, American Academy of Microbiology, ASM (2003-Present); President, ASM (1996-1997); Chair, Public and Scientific Affairs Board, ASM (1990-1996); Vice President, IUMS (1990-1994); President, ASV (1988-1989); President, AMSMIC (1985); Counselor, AMSMIC (1980-1983); Chairman, Committee on Public Policy, AMSMIC (1979); APS-SPR; Microbiology Society; National Academy of Sciences; Institute of Medicine, National Academy of Sciences; American Society for Biochemistry and Molecular Biology; Alpha Omega Alpha Honor Medical Society; Sigma Xi, The Scientific Research Honor Society; The Phi Beta Kappa Society **Marquis Who's Who Honors:** Albert Nelson Marquis Lifetime Achievement Award (2017) **Shipping Address:** 4321 SW 96th Dr, Gainsville, FL, 32608

John Anso Betti

Title: Federal Official, Automotive Executive (Retired) **Industry:** Business Management/Business Services **Date of Birth:** 01/06/1931 **Place of Birth:** Ottawa **State:** IL **Parents:** Louis Betti; Ida (Dallari) Betti **Marital Status:** Married **Spouse Name:** Joan Doyle (8/22/1953) **Children:** Diane; Denise; Donna (Deceased); Joan **Education:** MS in Automotive Engineering, Chrysler Institute of Engineering (1954); BS in Mechanical Engineering, Illinois Institute of Technology (1952) **Certifications:** Registered Professional Engineer, State of Michigan (1958) **Career:** Undersecretary of Defense, United States Department of Defense, Washington, DC (1989-1991); Acquisition and National Armaments Director, United States Department of Defense, Washington, DC (1989-1991); Executive Vice President, Diversified Products Operations, Ford Motor Company, Dearborn, MI (1988-1989); Member, Board of Directors, Finance and Executive Committees, Ford Motor Company, Dearborn, MI (1985-1989); Executive Vice President, Technical Affairs and Staff Operations, Ford Motor Company, Dearborn, MI (1984-1988); Vice President, Manufacturing and Business Development, Ford North American Automotive Operations, Dearborn, MI (1983-1984); Vice President, Powertrain and Chassis Operations, Ford North American Automotive Operations, Dearborn, MI (1979-1983); Vice President of Product Development, Ford of Europe, Warley, England (1976-1979); General Manager, Truck Operations, Ford Motor Company (1962-1976); Vice President, Ford Motor Company (1962-1976); Executive Engineer, Body Engineering, Ford Motor Company (1962-1976); Assistant Chief Engineer, FCA US LLC (1952-1962); Student Engineer, FCA US LLC (1952-1962); Director, Ford of Europe **Career Related:** Affiliate, Kaysor-Roth Corporation (1993-1994); Director, Compensation Committee, Breed Technologies, Inc. (Now Key Safety Systems) (1992-1994); Member, Compensation Committee, Breed Technologies, Inc. (Now Key Safety Systems) (1992-1994); Director, Collins & Aikman Corporation (1991-1994); Member, National Academy of Engineering (1989); Affiliate, Ford Electronics and Refrigeration Corporation (1988-1989); Affiliate, Ford Aerospace (1988-1989); Affiliate, Ensite Ltd. Can. (1979-1984); Affiliate, Caribbean Inc. (1979-1984); Instructor, Lawrence Institute of Engineering (Now Lawrence Technological University) (1953-1959); Instructor, Wayne State University, Detroit, MI (1953-1959); Director Park Ridge Corp (Hertz) **Civic:** Chairman, Board of Trustees, GMI Engineering and Management Institute (Now Kettering University) (1985-1989); Member, National Advisory Committee, Michigan Engineering, University of Michigan (1985-1989); Trustee, Detroit Institute for Children (1985-1989); Member, Board of Directors, Michigan Opera (1984-1987); President, Lost Tree Village Property Owners Association, North Palm Beach, FL; Vice President, Lost Tree Club, North Palm Beach, FL **Awards:** Honorary Citizen Award, Montese, Italy (2010); Inductee, Ottawa Township High School Hall of Fame (2008); Alumni Professional Achievement Award, Illinois Institute of Technology (1980); Named, John Morse Memorial Scholar **Membership:** Tau Beta Pi; Pi Tau Sigma; Alpha Sigma Phi; Beta Omega Nu **Marquis Who's Who Honors:** Albert Nelson Marquis Lifetime Achievement Award (2017) **Hobbies:** Golf; Spending time with family **Shipping Address:** 11964 Lost Tree Way, North Palm Beach, FL, 33408

Annette Beyer-Mears

Industry: Education/Educational Services **Company Name:** University of Medicine and Dentistry in New Jersey **Date of Birth:** 05/26/1941 **Place of Birth:** Madison **State:** WI **Parents:** Karl Beyer; Annette (Weiss) Beyer **Education:** PhD, College of Medicine and Dentistry in New Jersey (1977); MS, Fairleigh Dickinson University (1973); BA, Vassar College (1963) **Career:** Associate Professor, Department of Ophthalmology, University of Medicine and Dentistry in New Jersey, Rutgers, New Jersey Medical School (1986-2014); Associate Professor, Department of Physiology, University of Medicine and Dentistry in New Jersey, Rutgers, New Jersey Medical School (1986-2014); Assistant Professor, Department of Physiology, University of Medicine and Dentistry in New Jersey, Rutgers, New Jersey Medical School (1980-1985); Assistant Professor, Department of Ophthalmology, University of Medicine and Dentistry in New Jersey, Rutgers, New Jersey Medical School (1979-1985); Fellow, National Institutes of Health, Department of Ophthalmology, University of Medicine and Dentistry in New Jersey, Rutgers, New Jersey Medical School (1978-1980); Teaching Assistant, Department of Physiology, University of Medicine and Dentistry in New Jersey, Rutgers, New Jersey Medical School (1974-1977); Instructor of Physiology, Springside School (Now Springside Chestnut Hill Academy), Philadelphia, PA (1967-1971); Fellow, National Institutes of Health, Weill Cornell Medicine, Cornell University (1963-1965) **Career Related:** Visiting Associate Professor, Department of Ophthalmology and Vision Science, University of Wisconsin, Madison, WI (1995-2014); Consultant, Alcon Laboratories (Now Novartis AG) **Civic:** Vestry, Christ Church, Ridgewood, NJ (1994-1995); Long Range Planning Committee, Christ Church, Ridgewood, NJ (1985-1987); Fundraising Chairman, St. Bartholomew Episcopal Church (1978-1979); Minister Search Committee, St. Bartholomew Episcopal Church (1978); Delegate, Episcopalian Diocesan Convention (1977-1978); Chairman of Admissions, Vassar College (1974-1979); Trustee, National Foundation of Eye Research **Creative Works:** Contributor, Articles, Diabetic Lens & Kidney Therapy, Professional Journals **Awards:** Wright Spirit Award, Frank Lloyd Wright Building Conservancy (2007); Grant, Pfizer, Inc. (1993-2000); Grant, Pfizer, Inc. (1985-1989); Grant, Juvenile Diabetes Foundation (Now JDRF) (1985-1987); NEI Grantee, National Institutes of Health (1980-1995); Research Award, Foundation for The University of Medicine and Dentistry of New Jersey, Rutgers, New Jersey Medical School (1980); National Research Service Award, National Institutes of Health (1978-1980) **Membership:** The American Physiological Society; Association for Physiological Science; The American Society for Pharmacology and Experimental Therapeutics (ASPET); The Association for Research Vision & Ophthalmology; International Society for Eye Research; American Association for the Advancement of Science; Royal Society of Medicine; International Diabetes Federation; American Diabetes Association; Aircraft Owners and Pilots Association; Sigma Xi, The Scientific Research Honor Society; Aircraft Owners and Pilots Association (AOPA) **To what do you attribute your success:** Dr. Beyer-Mears attributes her success to passion for her work. **Shipping Address:** 120 Ely Place, Madison, WI, 53726 **Website:** http://www.drannettebyers.com

Peter Adolph Bien, PhD

Title: Language Educator, Writer **Industry:** Education/Educational Services **Company Name:** Dartmouth College **Date of Birth:** 05/28/1930 **Place of Birth:** New York City **State:** NY **Parents:** Adolph F. Bien; Harriet (Honigsberg) Bien **Marital Status:** Married **Spouse Name:** Chrysanthi Yiannakou (7/17/1955) **Children:** Leander; Alec; Daphne **Education:** Honorary PhD, Aristotle University of Thessaloniki (2007); Postgraduate Coursework, Woodbrooke College (1970-1971); PhD, Columbia University (1961); Postgraduate Coursework, University of Bristol (1958-1959); MA, Columbia University (1957); BA, Haverford College (1952); Coursework, Harvard University (1948-1950); Deerfield Academy (1947-1948) **Career:** Professor Emeritus, Dartmouth College (1997-Present); Frederick Sessions Beebe '35 Professor in the Art of Writing, Dartmouth College (1989-1997); Ted and Helen Geisel Third Century Professor in the Humanities, Dartmouth College; Professor, Dartmouth College (1969-1997); Professor, Dartmouth College (1974-1979); Associate Professor, Dartmouth College (1965-1968); Assistant Professor, Dartmouth College (1963-1965); Instructor in English, Dartmouth College (1961-1962); Lecturer, Columbia University (1957-1961) **Career Related:** Visiting Professor, University of Crete (2007); Visiting Professor, San Francisco State University (2005); Visiting Professor, Brown University (2005); Visiting Professor, Columbia University (2004); Visiting Professor, Princeton University (2001); Visiting Professor, Aristotle University of Thessaloniki (1996, 2000); Visiting Tutor, Woodbooke College (1995); Founder, Kendal Retirement Community at Hanover, New Hampshire (1991); Visiting Professor, The University of Melbourne (1983); Visiting Professor, Harvard University (1983); Founder, Peer Tutoring Program, Learning Center, Dartmouth College (1975); Founder, University Seminars for Faculty, Dartmouth College (1975) **Civic:** Chairman, Webster Performance Committee, Kendal at Hanover (2010-Present); President, Residents Council, Kendal at Hanover (2006-2007); Quaker in Residence, Pendle Hill (1998); Trustee, American Farm School (1998-2014); Treasurer, Hanover Friends Meeting (1998-2008); Chair, Board of Directors, Kendal at Hanover (1995-1996); Chair, Board of Overseers, Kendal at Hanover (1989-1995); Trustee, Pendle Hill (1977-2009); President, Board of Trustees, Hanover Friends Meeting (1979-1984, 1997); Clerk, Hanover Monthly Meeting of the Religious Society of Friends (1968-1970, 1976-1978); Corporation Member, Haverford College (1974-2001); Trustee, Kinhaven Music School (1973-1992) **Creative Works:** Author, "From 18 to 85: Chronicling a Fortunate Life" (2015); Author, "Kazantzakis and the Linguistic Revolution in Greek Literature" (1972, 2015); Translator, "Zorba the Greek by Nikos Kazantzakis" (2014); Translator, "Of Children and Adolescents by Stylianos Harkianakis" (2013); Author, "The Selected Letters of Nikos Kazantzakis" (2012); Author, "Yannis Ritsos: Collected Studies and Translations" (2011); Translator, "Greek Today" (2004); Translator, "Life in the Tomb by Stratis Myrivilis" (1977, 1987, 2004); Author, "Nikos Kazantzakis-Novelist" (1989); Author, "Kazantzakis: Politics of the Spirit," Volume I (1989); Author, "Three Generations of Greek Writers" (1983); Translator, "Demotic Greek 2" (1982); Translator, "Demotic Greek 1" (1972); Translator, "Report to Greco by Nikos Kazantzakis" (1965); Author, "L. P. Hartley" (1963); Translator, "Saint Francis by Nikos Kazantzakis" (1962); Translator, "The Last Temptation of Christ by Nikos Kazantzakis" (1960) **Awards:** Nikos Kazantzakis Prize, Municipality of Heraklion, Crete (2016); Translation Prize, Modern Greek Studies Association (2015); Honorary Doctorate from University of Thessaloniki (2007); Golden Cross, Greek Orthodox Archdiocese Australia (2000); Fulbright Fellowship, Institute of International Education, Inc. (1958, 1983, 1987); E. Harris Harbison Award For Distinguished Teaching, Danforth Foundation (1968) **Membership:** Yale Club, New York City (1979-Present); President, Modern Greek Studies Association (1982-1984, 2000-2002); Founding Member, Modern Greek Studies Association; Life Member, Modern Language Association of America; Honorary Member, Hellenic Authors' Society **Marquis Who's Who Honors:** Albert Nelson Marquis Lifetime Achievement Award (2017) **Hobbies:** Playing and performing piano; Working on an Adirondack farm in the summers **Political Affiliations:** Democrat **Religion:** Religious Society of Friends (Quaker) **Shipping Address:** 80 Lyme Rd Apt 171, Hanover, NH, 03755

Robert Alan Bildersee

Title: Lawyer **Industry:** Law and Legal Services **Company Name:** Bildersee & Silbert, LLP (Retired) **Date of Birth:** 01/22/1942 **Place of Birth:** Albany **State:** NY **Parents:** Max Ullman Bildersee; Hannah (Marks) Bildersee **Marital Status:** Married **Spouse Name:** Ellen Bernstein (06/09/1963) **Children:** Jennifer M. **Education:** LLB, Yale University (1967); MA, Columbia University (1964); BA, Columbia College, Columbia University (1962) **Career:** Founding Partner, Bildersee & Silbert LLP, Jenkintown, PA (1997-2018); Partner, Morgan, Lewis & Bockius LLP, Philadelphia, PA (1980-1997); Associate, then Partner, Fox Rothschild LLP, Philadelphia, PA (1973-1980); Sole Practice, Philadelphia, PA (1972-1973); Associate, Wolf, Block, Schorr and Solis-Cohen LLP, Philadelphia, PA (1967-1972) **Career Related:** Board of Directors, ASPPA Benefits Council of the Delaware Valley; Lecturer, Temple University Beasley School of Law, Philadelphia, PA (1978-1991); Assistant in Instruction, Yale Law School, New Haven, CT (1966) **Creative Works:** Editor, "Beyond the Fringes"; Contributor, Articles, Professional Journals; Author, "Pension Administrator's Forms and Checklists" (1987); Author, "Pension Regulation Manual" (1975); Contributing Author, "Employee Benefits Handbook" (1982-1998) **Awards:** Woodrow Wilson Fellow (1962) **Membership:** ABA; Pennsylvania Bar Association; Philadelphia Bar Association **Bar Admissions:** Pennsylvania **Hobbies:** Wildlife photography **Business Address:** P.O. Box 599, Abington, PA, 19001

Yaroslav Bilinsky

Title: Political Scientist **Industry:** Education/Educational Services **Company Name:** University of Delaware **Date of Birth:** 02/26/1932 **Place of Birth:** Lutsk **Country of Origin:** Ukraine **Parents:** Peter Bilinsky; Natalia (Balabaj) Bilinsky **Marital Status:** Married **Spouse Name:** Wira Rusaniwskyj (2/18/1962) **Children:** Peter Yaroslav; Sophia Vera Yaroslava; Nadia Yaroslava; Mark Paul Yaroslav **Education:** PhD, Princeton University (1958); Postgraduate Work in Soviet Affairs, Harvard University (1956-1957); AB, Harvard University, Magna Cum Laude (1954) **Career:** Professor Emeritus, University of Delaware (2002-Present); Professor, University of Delaware (1969-2002); Associate Professor, University of Delaware (1965-1969); Assistant Professor, University of Delaware (1961-1965); Instructor in Political Science, Douglass College, Rutgers, The State University of New Jersey (1958-1961); Associate, Russian Research Center, Harvard University (1956-1958) **Career Related:** Visiting Professor, Columbia University (1976); Visiting Instructor, University of Pennsylvania (1961) **Civic:** Trustee, Saints Peter and Paul UOC (1967-1971); Corresponding Secretary, Saints Peter and Paul UOC (1965-1966) **Creative Works:** Author, "Endgame in NATO's Enlargement: The Baltic States and Ukraine" (1999); Author, "The Second Soviet Republic: The Ukraine after World War II" (1964) **Membership:** President, Mid-Atlantic Slavic Conference, Association for Slavic, East European, and Eurasian Studies (1992-1993); President, Ukrainian Academy of Arts and Sciences in the U.S., Inc. (1987-1990) **Marquis Who's Who Honors:** Albert Nelson Marquis Lifetime Achievement Award (2017) **Why did you become involved in your profession or industry:** Dr. Bilinsky wanted to help his birth country of Ukraine. **What do you consider to be the highlight of your career:** A highlight of Dr. Bilinsky's career was being elected president of the Ukrainian Academy of Arts and Sciences in the United States in 1987. **Hobbies:** Writing; Being with his eight grandchildren **Shipping Address:** 2 Mimosa Drive, Newark, DE, 19711

Marian Bingham

Title: Artist, Printmaker **Industry:** Fine Art **Date of Birth:** 07/05/1940 **Place of Birth:** Oakland **State:** CA **Parents:** Woodbridge Bingham; Ursula Wolcott (Griswold) Bingham **Marital Status:** Married **Spouse Name:** Kenneth George McAdams (2/28/1998); William Bradford Hubbell, Jr. (Divorced 1990) **Children:** Drika B. Costantino; Jonathan Bradford Hubbell **Education:** MA in Liberal Studies, Wesleyan University, Middletown, CT (1995); BA, Connecticut College, New London, CT, Magna Cum Laude (1991) **Career Related:** Gallery Adviser, Greater Waterbury Arts Council (1991-1997); Teacher, Art Classes, Lyman Allyn Art Museum (1988-1991); Photographer's Representative; Office Manager; Assistant **Creative Works:** Exhibitor, Equestrian, Walter Wickiser Gallery, New York, NY (2015-2018); Exhibitor, Cooley Gallery, Old Lyme, CT (2015); Exhibitor, Center for Contemporary Printmaking, Norwalk, CT (2015); Exhibitor, Gallery Artists Part XI, Walter Wickiser Gallery, New York, NY (2014); Exhibitor, Fairleigh Dickinson University, Hackensack, NJ (2013); Exhibitor, Spiva Center for the Arts, Joplin, MO (2012); Exhibitor, Galerie Vieceli, Paris, France (2012); Exhibitor, Walter Wickiser Gallery, Inc., New York, NY (2012); Exhibitor, Simeza Gallery, Bucharest, Romania (2011); Exhibitor, Alex Galleries, Gallery A, Washington, DC (2010); Exhibitor, La Poelee, Revel, France (2010); Exhibitor, Bego Ezair Hotel Gallery, Southampton, Greenport, NY (2010); Exhibitor, Walter Wickiser Gallery, Inc., New York, NY (2010); Exhibitor, Museum of the Southwest, Midland, TX (2009); Exhibitor, Parkersburg Art Center, Parkersburg, WV (2008-2009); Exhibitor, Rankin Art Gallery, Ferris State University, Big Rapids, MI (2007); Exhibitor, Brassarie St. Martin, Sorenze, France (2006); Exhibitor, Bendheim Gallery, Greenwich, CT (2005-2006); Exhibitor, Moon Gallery, Berry College, Mount Berry, GA (2005-2006); Exhibitor, Opelousas Museum & Interpretive Center, Louisiana (2005); Exhibitor, Albany Museum of Art, Georgia (2004); Exhibitor, 4 Star Gallery, Indianapolis, IN (2004): Exhibitor, Alexey von Schlippe Gallery of Art, Groton, CT (2004); Exhibitor, Hotel Abbaye-Ecole de Soreze, France (2003); Exhibitor, So Hyun Gallery, New York, NY (2002); Exhibitor, Alexey von Schlippe Gallery of Art, Groton, CT (2002); Exhibitor, Connecticut Graphics Art Center, Norwalk, CT (2001-2006); Exhibitor, So Hyun Gallery, New York, NY (2000); Exhibitor, Greene Art Gallery, Guilford, CT (1998-2003); Exhibitor, Alexey von Schlippe Gallery of Art, Groton, CT (1998-2001); Exhibitor, Gallery Bai, Inc., New York, NY (1997-1999); Exhibitor, New Britain Museum of American Art, CT (1997-1999); Exhibitor, Silvermine Arts Center (1997-1999); Exhibitor, New Haven Council Small Gallery, New Haven, CT (1996); Exhibitor, Fernbank Museum of Natural History, Atlanta, GA (1996); Exhibitor, Gallery Bai, Inc., New York, NY (1995); Exhibitor, National Museum of Women in the Arts, Washington, DC (1995); Exhibitor, Garde Arts Center and Vangard Gallery, New London, CT (1994); Exhibitor, Mill Gallery (1994); Exhibitor, Paul Mellon Arts Center, Wallingford, CT (1994); Exhibitor, Slater Memorial Museum, Norwich, CT (1994); Exhibitor, She Luz Gallery, Manila, Philippines; Exhibitor, Fine Arts Fair, Houston, TX; Exhibitor, Art Busan Fair, Busan, Korea; Artist, Illustrations and Cover Art, "Bon Courage" by Kenneth McAdams; Solo, Group, and Private Collections, Various Exhibitions **Awards:** Art Department Award, Connecticut College **Membership:** Stamford Art Association; Greenwich Arts Council; Mystic Art Association League; Connecticut Academy of Fine Arts **Where will you be in five years:** In the next five years, Ms. Bingham sees herself as very alive and continuing with her art. The most exciting thing about art is that you can do it all your life. **Hobbies:** Walking; Hiking; Skiing; Traveling; Poetry; Meditating; Yoga **Shipping Address:** 2 Brighton Road, Old Lyme, CT, 06371 **Website:** http://www.theartofbing.com

Bruce Birch, PhD

Title: Theology Studies Educator **Industry:** Education/Educational Services **Date of Birth:** 12/03/1941 **Place of Birth:** Wichita **State:** KS **Education:** PhD, Yale University, New Haven, CT (1970); MPhil, Yale University, New Haven, CT (1968); MA, Yale University, New Haven, CT (1967); BD, Southern Methodist University, Dallas, TX (1965); BA, Southwestern College, Winfield, KS (1962) **Career:** Consultant, Wesley Theological Seminary, Washington, DC (2013-Present); Dean Emeritus, Wesley Theological Seminary, Washington, DC (2012-2013); Dean, Wesley Theological Seminary, Washington, DC (1998-2009); Professor, Old Testament, Biblical Theology, Wesley Theological Seminary, Washington, DC (1971-2010); Assistant Professor, Bible and Religion, Erskine College, Due West, SC (1970-1971); Assistant Professor, Bible and Religion, Iowa Wesleyan College, Mount Pleasant, IA (1968-1970) **Civic:** Faculty, Jerusalem Center for Biblical Studies (2015-Present); Board of Trustees, Moscow Theological Seminary of Methodist Church (2008-Present) **Membership:** Chair, Society of Biblical Literature (2008-2011); Council Chair, Society of Biblical Literature (2004-2001); Society of Biblical Literature **Hobbies:** Golfing; Photography **Religion:** Methodist **Shipping Address:** 3030 Mill Island Parkway, Apartment 313, Frederick, MD, 21701

Irwin Morton Birnbaum

Title: Educational Consultant, Lawyer **Industry:** Education/Educational Services **Company Name:** Yale School of Medicine **Date of Birth:** 07/15/1935 **Place of Birth:** Brooklyn **State:** NY **Parents:** Sol N. Birnbaum; Rose (Cohen) Birnbaum **Marital Status:** Married **Spouse Name:** Arlene R. Burrows (6/8/1957) **Children:** Bruce J.; Leslie R. Birnbaum Kline; Amy G. Birnbaum Heath **Education:** JD, New York University (1961); BS in Accounting, Brooklyn College (1956) **Career:** Senior Advisor, National Clinician Scholars Program, Yale School of Medicine (2005-Present); Senior Adviser to the Dean, Yale School of Medicine (2004-2005); Chief Operating Officer, Yale School of Medicine, New Haven, CT (1997-2004); Partner, Proskauer & Rose LLP, New York, NY (1989-1997); Counsel, Proskauer & Rose LLP, New York, NY (1986-1989); Vice President, Montefiore Medical Center (1970-1986); Chief Financial Officer, Montefiore Medical Center (1970-1986); Budget Officer, Montefiore Medical Center, Bronx, NY (1962-1970) **Career Related:** Mediator, Arbitrator, Alternative Dispute Resolution Service, American Health Lawyers Association (2008-Present); Chairman, Board of Directors, FOJP Service Corporation (2006-2011); Board of Directors, FFH Insurance Company (1998-2006); Member, Executive Committee, MCIC Vermont (1997-2005); Chair, Financial Committee, MCIC Vermont (1997-2005); Adjunct Professor, Yale School of Medicine; Lecturer, Public Health and Health Policy Administration, Yale School of Medicine **Civic:** Trustee, South County Health Systems, South Kingston, RI (2007-Present); Trustee, Hospital Association of Rhode Island, Cranston, RI (2007-Present); Trustee, Malmonides Medical Center, Brooklyn, NY (1988-Present); Treasurer, Malmonides Medical Center, Brooklyn, NY (1988-Present); Executive Committee, Malmonides Medical Center, Brooklyn, NY (1988-Present); Trustee, Cross Mills Public Library, Charlestown, RI (2011); Board of Directors, Jewish Home for the Aged, New Haven, CT (2003-2007); Secretary Treasurer, Hospital Trustees of New York State (1990-1997); Executive Committee, Hospital Trustees of New York State (1990-1997) **Creative Works:** Editor, "Health Care Law Treatise" (1990); Editor, "Montefiore Medical Center and the Loeb Center Experience: A Hospital's Fiscal Perspective"; Editor, "Medicare and Extended Care" **Awards:** Stevan Ryan Award, Metro New York Chapter, Hospital Financial Management Association **Membership:** Secretary, Health Law Committee, Association of the Bar of the City of New York (1995-1996); Secretary, Committee on Medicine and Law, Association of the Bar of the City of New York (1989-1990); Fellow, The New York Academy of Medicine; Special Committee on Healthcare Systems, American Academy of Hospital Attorneys (Now American Health Lawyers Association) **Bar Admissions:** New York (1962) **Marquis Who's Who Honors:** Albert Nelson Marquis Lifetime Achievement Award (2017) **To what do you attribute your success:** He attributes his success to the fact that he likes people. He is personable and can form special bonds. **What do you consider to be the highlight of your career:** The highlight of his career was teaching and being a faculty member at the Yale School of Medicine. **Where will you be in five years:** In five years he plans to keep doing what he is doing. He loves it, he loves mentoring. **Hobbies:** Sailing; Tennis; Reading; Travel **Political Affiliations:** Independent **Shipping Address:** PO Box 1493, Charlestown, RI, 02813

Charles Birnstiel

Title: Consultant Engineer **Industry:** Engineering **Date of Birth:** 12/06/1929 **Place of Birth:** New York **State:** NY **Parents:** Charles Conrad Birnstiel; Margarete (Heckel) Birnstiel **Marital Status:** Single **Education:** Doctor of Engineering Science, New York University (1962); MCE, New York University (1957); BCE, New York University (1954) **Career:** Consultant Engineer (1974-Present); Consultant on Structural and Mechanical Engineering, New York City; Professor of Civil Engineering, Polytechnic Institute of New York, Brooklyn (Now New York University Tandon School of Engineering), NY (1973-1974); Professor of Civil Engineering, New York University, Bronx (Now New York), NY (1968-1973); Faculty Member, New York University, Bronx (Now New York), NY (1954-1973) **Career Related:** Adjunct Professor of Civil Engineering, Columbia University, New York City, NY (1989-2000) **Creative Works:** Co-author "Moveable Bridge Design" (2015); Contributor, Chapters, Books; Contributor, Articles, Professional Journals **Awards:** Bridge Engineering Award, Bridge Engineering Association of New York (2017); Roebling Award, Metropolitan Section, American Society of Civil Engineers (2003); State-of-the-Art Paper Award, American Society of Civil Engineers **Membership:** Fellow, American Society of Civil Engineers; Fellow, The Institution of Civil Engineers, United Kingdom; American Railway Engineering and Maintenance-of-Way Association (AREMA); International Association for Bridge and Structural Engineering (IABSE) **Religion:** Lutheran **Business Address:** 626 Jacksonville Road, Suite 202, Warminster, PA, 18974-3392 **Shipping Address:** 35319 Anns Choice Way, Warminster, PA, 18974

Julia Bischoff

Industry: Business Management/Business Services **Education:** Master's Degree in Speech Pathology and Language Disorders, University of Central Florida (1997) **Civic:** Orlando Regional Medical Center; Big Brothers Big Sisters **Membership:** Association for Supervision and Curriculum Development **Hobbies:** Reading; Traveling; Computer software

Brad Bittenbender

Title: Safety Engineer **Industry:** Engineering **Company Name:** Jacobs Engineering Group Inc. **Date of Birth:** 12/04/1948 **Place of Birth:** Kalamazoo **State:** MI **Parents:** Don J. Bittenbender; Thelma Lula (Bacon) Bittenbender **Marital Status:** Married **Spouse Name:** Margaret Patricia Stahl Hubbell (6/1992) **Education:** Coursework, Environmental Auditing, California State University, Long Beach (1992); Post Graduate Certificate, Safety Engineering and Hazardous Materials Management, University of California, Irvine (1987); BS, Western Michigan University (1972) **Certifications:** Certified Safety Professional (CSP), National Board; Certified Hazardous Materials Manager (CHMM), National Board; Authorized Outreach Trainer and Special Government Employee (SGE), United States Department of Labor - OSHA; Class 3A Hoist Engineers License, Office of Public Safety and Inspections, Commonwealth of Massachusetts **Career:** Senior Safety Specialist, Jacobs Engineering Group / General Electric Aviation, Lynn, MA (2018-Present); Senior Safety Specialist, CH2M Hill Engineering / General Electric Aviation, Lynn, MA (2000-2017); Manager, Safety, Health and Environmental Department, Cytec Fiberite, California Division, Los Angeles, CA (1998-1999); Director, Environmental Safety and Health Department, Culver City Composites Corp, CA (1996-1998); Manager, Environmental Safety and Industrial Hygiene Department, Structural Polymer Systems, Inc., Montedison, CA (1991-1995); Manager, Environmental Safety and Industrial Hygiene Department, Composites Division, Ferro Corporation, Los Angeles, CA (1988-1991); Senior Environmental Engineer, Ferro Corporation, Los Angeles, CA (1980-1987); Environmental Administrator, Productol Chemical Division, Ferro Corporation, Santa Fe Springs, CA (1979-1980); Supervisor of Manufacturing, Productol Chemical Division, Ferro Corporation, Santa Fe Springs, CA (1977-1979); Supervisor of Manufacturing, American Cyanamid, Kalamazoo, MI (1971-1977) **Career Related:** Participant, SACMA Second Edition (1991); Participant, Conference on Occupational Health Aspects of Advance Composite Technology in the Aerospace Industry, United States Air Force, Dayton, Ohio (1989); Mediated Rule Making Advisory Committee for Workplace Exposure to Methylenedianiline, Federal Occupational Safety and Health Administration (1988); Member, Health & Safety Committee, Suppliers of Advance Composites Material Association (1985-1995); Member, Advisory Board, Extension Program for Industrial Health & Safety Education, University of California, Irvine (1985-1991); Participant, Pamphlet, "Safe Handling of Advanced Composite Materials" **Civic:** Member, People to People International (2010-Present); Delegate Member, American Society of Safety Engineers, India (2013); Delegate Member Education/Humanitarian, Cambodia and Vietnam (2012); Delegate Member, American Society of Safety Engineers, Brazil (2011); Delegate Member, American Society of Safety Engineers, China (2010); Community Right to Know, Culver City, CA (1987-1991); Member, Museum of Contemporary Art, Los Angeles, CA (1985-2000); Member, Advisory Committee for Hazardous Materials; Member, California Museum Foundation, Los Angeles, CA (1985-1990); Founding Sponsor, Challenger Center **Membership:** American Society of Safety Engineers; Alliance of Hazardous Materials Professionals; National Fire Protection Association (NFPA); Society of Fire Protection Engineers; TriBeta; Sons of the American Revolution **Hobbies:** Genealogy; Revolutionary War Re-enacter; Breeding Morgan Horses; Equestrian Carriage Driving **Political Affiliations:** Independent **Religion:** Congregational United Church of Christ **Shipping Address:** 215 Everett Street, Wrentham, MA, 02093

Michael A. Blakney

Title: Senior Manager, Operations Finance, KaVo North America **Industry:** Financial Services **Company Name:** KaVo Kerr **Place of Birth:** Windsor **Country of Origin:** ON/Canada **Education:** Bachelor of Commerce, University of Windsor (1995) **Certifications:** CMA Certification (2000) **Awards:** Outstanding Professional of the Year; VIP of the Year; Distinguished Humanitarian Award; Elite American Executives; Featured, Live 365 Radio Network; Featured, Front Cover of Pro-Files Magazine **To what do you attribute your success:** He attributes his success to hard work, and strong organizational skills. He is eager to learn, flexible, and a team player. **Why did you become involved in your profession or industry:** He became involved in his profession because he has always been good with numbers, and found that this was an appropriate position for someone with his personality and skills. **What do you consider to be the highlight of your career:** One highlight of his career was when he provided remediation of material weakness at the MCON technologies plant in Sparta, South Carolina. **Where will you be in five years:** In 5 years, Mr. Blakney hopes to continue to grow, take on more of a senior leadership position, and be more of a contributor to organizational strategy. **Hobbies:** Golfing; Music; Cars **Business Address:** 2800 Crystal Drive, Hatfield, PA, 19440 **Shipping Address:** 4235 Millennium Ave Apt 12114, Charlotte, NC, 28217 **Website:** www.michaelblakney.com

Bruce Blanchard

Title: Civil Engineer **Industry:** Engineering **Date of Birth:** 12/26/1932 **Place of Birth:** Fort Stotsenburg **Country of Origin:** Philippines **Parents:** Wendell Blanchard (Deceased); Marcella (Palmer) Blanchard (Deceased) **Marital Status:** Married **Spouse Name:** Mary Josie Cain (7/31/1992) **Children:** Wendell; Laura; Renee **Education:** Honorary Diploma, Commissioned General Staff Course, Fort Leavenworth, KS (1980); MS in Civil Engineering, Massachusetts Institute of Technology (1964); BS in Civil Engineering, Massachusetts Institute of Technology (1957) **Career:** Consultant, Natural Resources Management (2006-Present); Director of Planning and Policy Analysis, Indian Affairs Department Interior, Washington, DC (2005-2006); Assistant to Deputy Assistant Secretary of Management, Office of Indian Affairs, U.S. Department of the Interior, Washington, DC (2004-2005); Special Assistant for Tribal Self-Governance, Office of the Secretary of Interior (1997-2004); Deputy Director, U.S. Fish and Wildlife Service, U.S. Department of the Interior, Washington, DC (1989-1997); Director, Office of Environmental Project Review, Office of the Secretary of the Interior, Washington, DC (1971-1989); Environmental Specialist, Office of the Secretary of the Department of the Interior, Washington, DC (1970-1971); Senior Staff Specialist, Water Resources Council, Washington, DC (1966-1969); Water Resources Planning Engineer, Bureau of Reclamation, U.S. Department of the Interior, Phoenix, AZ (1961-1966); Assistant Lacrosse Coach, Massachusetts Institute of Technology (1958-1959, 1964); Hydraulic Engineer, Bureau of Reclamation, U.S. Department of the Interior, Denver, CO (1959-1960, 1960-1961); Teaching and Research Assistant, Massachusetts Institute of Technology (1957-1959) **Military Service:** Colonel, Maryland National Guard (1967-1985); Lieutenant, Arizona National Guard (1961-1966); Member, U.S. Army (1951-1953, 1960) **Creative Works:** Editor, "The Nation's Water Resources" (1968) **Awards:** Distinguished Service Medal (1999); Meritorious Service Medal, United States Department of the Interior (1985); Meritorious Service Medal, State of Maryland (1983); Commendation Medal, State of Maryland (1976, 1978-1979); Decorated Army Achievement Medal; Army Commendation Medal; Army Meritorious Service Medal; Distinguished Fiji Award **Membership:** Treasurer, Explorers Club (2015-Present); Washington Group Treasurer, Explorers Club (1997-Present); Board of Directors, Massachusetts Institute of Technology Club of Washington (1997-Present); Board of Directors, Massachusetts Institute of Technology Alumni Association (2001-2003); President, Massachusetts Institute of Technology Club of Washington (1999-2000); Vice President, Massachusetts Institute of Technology Club of Washington (1998-1999); Fellow, American Association for the Advancement of Science; American Society of Civil Engineers; Senior Executives Association; American Society of Public Administration; United States Armor Association; National Guard Association of the United States; American Water Resources Association American Geophysical Union; Phi Gamma Delta **Marquis Who's Who Honors:** Albert Nelson Marquis Lifetime Achievement Award (2017); Distinguished Humanitarian (2017) **Shipping Address:** 80 Observatory Cir NW, Washington, DC, 20008

John Robinson Block

Title: Newspaper Publisher **Industry:** Publishing **Date of Birth:** 10/01/1954 **Place of Birth:** Toledo **State:** OH **Parents:** Paul Block Jr.; Marjorie Jane (McNab) Block **Marital Status:** Divorced **Spouse Name:** Susan Lynn Jones (7/20/2002, Divorced 2017) **Children:** Caroline McNab Jones Block **Education:** DHL, Medical College of Ohio (Now The University of Toledo), Toledo, Ohio (2005); BA, Yale University, New Haven, CT (1977) **Career:** Publisher, Toledo Blade (2001-Present); Editor-in-chief, Toledo Blade (2001-Present); Publisher, Pittsburgh Post-Gazette (2001-Present); Editor-in-chief, Pittsburgh Post-Gazette (1993-Present); Co-publisher, Pittsburgh Post-Gazette (1989-2001); Co-publisher, Toledo Blade (1989-2001); Editor-in-chief, Toledo Blade (1989-2001); Executive Editor, Toledo Blade (1987-1989); Assistant Managing Editor, Toledo Blade (1985-1987); Sunday Editor, Toledo Blade (1983-1985); European Correspondent, Toledo Blade, London, England (1982-1983); Washington Correspondent, Toledo Blade (1980-1982); Reporter, Associated Press, New York City, NY (1978-1980); Reporter, Associated Press, Miami, FL (1977-1978); Chairman, Board of Directors, P.G. Pub. Company, Pittsburgh, PA **Career Related:** Vice Chairman, Board of Directors, Block Communications Inc. (1985-Present) **Civic:** Chairman, Airport Committee, Toledo-Lucas County Port Authority (1994-1997); Chairman, Historical Preservation Committee, Toledo, Ohio (1983-1985) **Awards:** Pulitzer Prize, Toledo Blade (2004) **Membership:** American Society of Newspaper Editors; Rowfant Club, Cleveland, Ohio; Toledo Club; Inverness Club, Toledo, OH; Yale Club; National Press Club **Marquis Who's Who Honors:** Albert Nelson Marquis Lifetime Achievement Award (2017) **Why did you become involved in your profession or industry:** Mr. Block became involved in his profession because his grandfather was involved with media and newspapers, so it was in his family. **What do you consider to be the highlight of your career:** A highlight of Mr. Block's career was when the Toledo Blade was awarded the Pulitzer Prize in 2004 under his leadership. **Hobbies:** Flying; Collecting Rare Books **Shipping Address:** 725 Devonshire St, Pittsburgh, PA, 15213 **Website:** http://www.wandtv.com

Cynthia Blodgett-Griffin, PhD

Title: President, Lead Educator **Industry:** Education/Educational Services **Company Name:** Blodgett Learning Systems **Place of Birth:** Minneapolis **State:** MN **Parents:** Helen White Blodgett (Deceased); Riley Blodgett (Deceased) **Marital Status:** Married **Spouse Name:** Charles Griffin **Education:** PhD in Education and Human Sciences, University of Nebraska-Lincoln; MA in Adult Education, University of Nebraska-Lincoln; BS in Graphic Communications and Advertising, Minnesota State University Moorhead **Career:** Online Adult Educator **Civic:** Current President, Lead Minister, Adult Education Coordinator, Prison Ministry for Religious Minority Prisoners, Nebraska **Awards:** Professional Woman of the Year, National Association of Professional Women (2010); Woman of Outstanding Leadership, IWLA; Outstanding Professionalism, Top Female Executive **Membership:** Association of Adult and Continuing Education; American Civil Liberties Union; Southern Poverty Law Center **Marquis Who's Who Honors:** Albert Nelson Marquis Lifetime Achievement Award (2017) **To what do you attribute your success:** Dr. Blodgett-Griffin attributes her success to her work ethic and value of education that she learned from her parents, both Army officers. The first in her family to earn a Ph.D., she applied that ethic throughout her postsecondary education. During her years in graduate school, she was inspired by her own professors who served as role models and shaped her understanding of what it means to be an educator. **Why did you become involved in your profession or industry:** Dr. Blodgett-Griffin's motto is "Teach the Mind, Inspire the Soul." She became involved in distance education as project manager for a grant designing the first pre-internet distance delivery of adult literacy teacher training via satellite in Nebraska. She learned first-hand the advantages and drawbacks of distance delivery in the early years of online education, from technical to time zone challenges. She was an Instructional Design Specialist on a grant-funded project to produce web-based high school curriculum for international distance delivery. During that experience, she began teaching for an internationally prestigious open and distance university where she has continued to teach graduate students for the past 15 years. Her experiences with online instructional design and postsecondary education for adults stemmed from her own experiences and witnessing professors whose teaching and mentoring skills ranged from excellent to absolutely abysmal. She is determined to facilitate educational experiences to support adults to achieve their educational goals. Her own advisers served as role models and shaped her understanding of what it means to be an educator. **What do you consider to be the highlight of your career:** Dr. Blodgett-Griffin considers the highlight of her career to be one that spans over 20 years. Having returned to postsecondary education while her children were still young, she dedicates her career in education to students like herself, midlife learners who return to school. Students are the heart of her work. Working with midlife adults has been the most rewarding part of her career. Each adult brings unique life experiences and perspective to graduate school. As a seasoned online educator, she is fully aware that attrition is a major problem in distance education, she encourages them to believe in themselves. She devotes her efforts to supporting her students to achieve their goals and dreams. Dr. Blodgett-Griffin believes that each student who successfully achieves their educational dream is a highlight of her career. **Where will you be in five years:** In five years, Dr. Blodgett-Griffin plans to continue to teach and expand into teaching teachers to transition into online education. **Hobbies:** Organic gardening; Writing; Patient advocacy for the elderly; Painting **Business Address:** 1001 S 36th St, Lincoln, NE, 68510 **Shipping Address:** 1001 S 36th St, Blodgett Learning Systems, Lincoln, NE, 68510 **Website:** http://cynthiablodgettgriffin.com

John Michael Boardman, PhD

Title: Mathematician, Professor Emeritus **Industry:** Education/Educational Services **Company Name:** Johns Hopkins University **Date of Birth:** 02/13/1938 **Place of Birth:** Manchester **Country of Origin:** England **Parents:** William Edgar Boardman; Carrie (Brown) Boardman **Marital Status:** Divorced **Spouse Name:** Jacqueline O'Brien Schulman (1967, Divorced 1977) **Children:** Susan; Andrew **Education:** PhD, Trinity College, University of Cambridge (1965); BA, Trinity College, University of Cambridge (1961) **Career:** Professor Emeritus, Johns Hopkins University (2010-Present); Professor, Johns Hopkins University, Baltimore, MD (1972-2010); Associate Professor, Johns Hopkins University, Baltimore, MD (1969-1972); Assistant Lecturer, University of Warwick, England (1967-1968); Visiting Lecturer, University of Chicago (1966-1967) **Career Related:** Fellow, Science Research Council (1964-1966); Fellow, American Mathematics Society **Military Service:** Royal Air Force (1956-1958) **Creative Works:** Author, "K(n)-torsion Free H-spaces and P(n)-Cohomology" (2007); Co-Author, "Conditionally Convergent Spectral Sequences" (1999); Author, "Unstable Operations on Generalized Cohomology" (1995); Co-Author, "Modular Representations on the Homology of Powers of Real Projective Space" (1993); Author, "Homotopy Invariant Algebraic Structures on Topological Spaces" (1973); Co-Author, "Singularities of Differentiable Maps" (1967) **Awards:** Grantee, National Science Foundation (1970-1988) **Marquis Who's Who Honors:** Albert Nelson Marquis Lifetime Achievement Award (2017) **Religion:** Quaker **Shipping Address:** 6217 Northwood Drive, Baltimore, MD, 21212

Danya Bogart

Title: Partner **Industry:** Real Estate **Company Name:** Sands Asset Advisors **Education:** BA in Spanish and Art History, Texas Christian University (1989) **Career:** Partner, Sands Asset Advisors **Civic:** Past President, Board Member, Volunteers Houston (2005-2015); Senior Warden, Associate Vestry Saint John the Divine; Hurricane Harvey Relief; Junior League of Houston, Inc.; Co-Chair, Texas Christian University Houston Business Network Breakfast **Awards:** Recognized as One of the 101 Houston's Best and Brightest Companies to Work For (2014-2015); Ranked #23 in Fastest Private Companies, Houston Business Journal (2013); Fastest Growing Woman-Owned Business, Houston Business Journal (2013); Fastest Growing Woman-Owned Business, Houston Business Journal (2012); Louisiana's Top Business List, DiversityBusiness.com (2011); Louisiana's Top Business List, DiversityBusiness.com (2008); Fastest Growing Woman-Owned Business, New Orleans City Business **Marquis Who's Who Honors:** Albert Nelson Marquis Lifetime Achievement Award (2017) **To what do you attribute your success:** Ms. Bogart attributes her success to her resilience, great attitude, and ability to push through roadblocks. **Why did you become involved in your profession or industry:** Ms. Bogart became involved in real estate because of the difference it makes to communities. While she was a student at Texas Christian University, she started a part-time job with Robert Half and found her passion. Ms. Bogart says she loves the industry because it is ever-changing and requires a lot of "outside the box" thinking. **What do you consider to be the highlight of your career:** A highlight of Ms. Bogart's career was starting a business and figuring it out. **Where will you be in five years:** In five years, Ms. Bogart intends to build a company with value that can be passed on to someone else. **Hobbies:** Spending time with her family; Being involved in her family farm and their horse program **Shipping Address:** 3702 Del Monte Drive, Houston, TX, 77019 **Website:** http://thesandsfarm.com

Bernard Saturnin Bonbon

Title: Associate Professor, Researcher, Specialist in Mathematical Problems of Visual Space **Industry:** Education/Educational Services **Company Name:** Ministere de l'Enseignement Superieur et de la Recherche **Date of Birth:** 11/29/1940 **Place of Birth:** Terre-de-Haut **Country of Origin:** France **Marital Status:** Married **Spouse Name:** Gwendal Bernard (Morgan) Bonbon **Children:** Maeva Claudie Melodie; Fabrice Yann Herve; Laurent Steve Wilhem **Education:** Doctorate Honoris Causa, International Academy for Contemporani Art (1992); DFA in Mathematics Arts, Universite Paris 8 (1981); DSc, Ecole des Hautes Etudes en Sciences Sociales (1976) **Career:** Associate Professor, Domaine Universitaire de Saint-Martin d'Heres; Lecturer, Domaine Universitaire de Saint-Martin d'Heres; Specialist in Mathematics of Visual Space, Domaine Universitaire de Saint-Martin d'Heres; Associate Professor, College Jean Jaures, Saint-Ouen; Professor of Technical Education, Lycee d'Enseignement Professionnel; Professor of Design, College d'Enseignement Technique de Dessin Industriel **Awards:** Reconnaissance Nationale Chevalier Dans L'Ordre National Du Merite **Hobbies:** Collecting books, paintings, and bronze sculptures; Oil painting; Visiting historical monuments **Religion:** Catholic **Business Address:** 204 Chagneux, Izeron, France, 38160

Joseph Bonfiglio

Title: Proprietor **Industry:** Financial Services **Company Name:** Joe Bonfiglio, CFP **Education:** MBA, Investments and Finance, University of Houston (1990); MS, Geology, University of Houston (1982); BS, Geology, City College of New York (1979) **Certifications:** Certified Financial Planner; Chartered Life Underwriter; Enrolled Agent; Security License, States of Florida, Massachusetts, Michigan, New Jersey, New York, Pennsylvania, and Texas; Investment Advisor Representative License, States of California, Connecticut, Florida, Massachusetts, Michigan, North Carolina, New Jersey, Pennsylvania, Texas, and Vermont **Career:** Independent Planning Firm (1997-2017) **Civic:** Chairman, Finance Committee, St. Catherine's Parish **Awards:** Listed, Top Wealth Managers of New Jersey, New Jersey Monthly Magazine (2017); Certified Financial Planner Certificate, Certified Financial Planner Board of Standards, Financial Planning Association of New Jersey **Membership:** National Association of Tax Professionals; National Association of Enrolled Agents **Shipping Address:** 36 Main Street, Joe Bonfiglio, CFP, Holmdel, NJ, 07733

David G. Borenstein

Title: Rheumatologist **Industry:** Medicine & Health Care **Company Name:** George Washington University **Date of Birth:** 07/15/1947 **Place of Birth:** Brooklyn **State:** NY **Parents:** Murray Borenstein; Mollie (Koren) Borenstein **Marital Status:** Married **Spouse Name:** Dorothy Regina Fait (8/6/1972) **Children:** Sylvia; Elizabeth; Rebecca **Education:** Fellow in Rheumatology, Johns Hopkins University (1976-1978); Resident in Medicine, Johns Hopkins Hospital (1974-1976); Intern in Medicine, Johns Hopkins Hospital (1973-1974); MD, Johns Hopkins University (1973); AB, Columbia University (1969) **Certifications:** Diplomate, American Board of Internal Medicine; Diplomate, American Board of Rheumatology **Career:** Clinical Professor of Medicine, George Washington University, Washington, DC (1997-Present); Clinical Professor of Neurosurgery, George Washington University, Washington, DC (1997-1998); Professor of Neurosurgery, George Washington University, Washington, DC (1991-1996); Professor of Medicine, George Washington University, Washington, DC (1989-1996); Associate Professor of Medicine, George Washington University, Washington, DC (1983-1989); Assistant Professor of Medicine, George Washington University, Washington, DC (1978-1983) **Career Related:** Consultant, Neurana (2017-Present); Consultant, AbbVie (2017-Present); Consultant, Medimergent, LLC (2014-Present); Consultant, Pfizer Inc. (2017); Consultant, Regeneron LLC (2017); Consultant, National Institutes of Health Research Task Force, Research Standards for Chronic Low Back Pain, National Institutes of Health Pain Consortium, Bethesda, MD (2015-2016); Consultant, Janssen Global Services, LLC (2015); Consultant, Iroko Pharmaceuticals, LLC (2015); Consultant, AbbVie Inc. (2014); Editor-in-Chief, inPractice Rheumatology (2013-2017); Consultant, Medtronic (2009); Consultant, Cephalon, Inc. (Now Teva Pharmaceuticals USA) (2009); Consultant, Biovail (Now Valeant) (2006); Consultant, Pfizer Inc. (2006); Consultant, EpiCept Corporation (Now Immune Pharmaceuticals Ltd.) (2004-2008); Consultant, Pfizer Inc. (2003-2004); Consultant, Merck Sharp & Dohme Corporation (1999-2004); Consultant, Department of Labor, OSHA (1998-1999); Consultant, G.D. Searle, LLC (Now Pfizer), Skokie, IL (1997-2002) **Civic:** Vice President, Arthritis Foundation, Washington, DC (2006-2008); Executive Board of Directors, Arthritis Foundation, Washington, DC (2006-2007); Board of Directors, Arthritis Foundation, Washington, DC (1999-2007); Medical Advisory Board, Lupus Foundation of America, Inc., Washington, DC (1992-2004); Appellate Judicial Nominating Commission, State of Maryland (1986-1994) **Creative Works:** Author, "Pain of Rheumatological Disease in Pain Medicine: An Interdisciplinary Case-Based Approach" (2015); Author, "Spine Pain," Conn's Current Therapy (2011-2018); Author, "Arthritic Disorders in the Spine" (2011); Author, "Heal Your Back: Your Complete Prescription for Preventing, Treating and Eliminating Back Pain" (2011); Contributing Author, "Low Back Pain in Rheumatology, Fourth Edition" (2008); Contributing Author, "Arthritis in Orthopaedic Knowledge Update, Ninth Edition" (2008); Contributing Author, "Approach To Patient with Neck Pain in Current Rheumatology, Second Edition" (2007); Author, "Low Back and Neck Pain: Comprehensive Diagnosis and Management, Third Edition" (2007); Contributing Author, "Inflammatory Arthritis and Psoriatic Arthritis in the Lumbar Spine, Third Edition" (2004); Contributing Author, "Approach to Patient with Neck Pain in Current Rheumatology" (2004); Contributing Author, "Low Back Pain in Rheumatology, Second Edition" (2003); Author, "Back in Control! A Conventional and Complementary Prescription for Eliminating Back Pain" (2001); Contributing Author, "Low Back Pain in Rheumatology" (1997) **Awards:** Marriott Lifetime Achievement Award (2011); President's Award, Arthritis Foundation, Metropolitan Washington Chapter **Membership:** Membership Committee, SPARTAN Spondyloarthritis Research and Treatment Network (2015-Present); Board of Directors, Patient Access Network Foundation (2012-2015); Nomination Committee, Association of Rheumatology Health Professionals (2012-2014); Chairman, Nomination Committee, Research & Education Foundation (2011-2012); President, Research & Education Foundation, American College of Rheumatology (2010-2011); Chairman, Pain Management Task Force (2009-2010); President-elect, Research & Education Foundation, American College of Rheumatology (2009-2010); Executive Committee, American College of Rheumatology (2007-2011); Treasurer, Research & Education Foundation, American College of Rheumatology (2007-2009); Executive Committee, Research & Education Foundation, American College of Rheumatology (2007-2009); Board of Directors, American College of Rheumatology (2005-2007); Chairman, Membership Committee, International Society for the Study of the Lumbar Spine (2002-2003) **Marquis Who's Who Honors:** Albert Nelson Marquis Lifetime Achievement Award (2017) **Religion:** Jewish **Business Address:** 2021 K Street NW, Washington, DC, 20006 **Shipping Address:** 10505 Scarboro Lane, Potomac, MD, 20854 **Website:** http://www.arapc.com

Jeffrey Stephen Borer

Title: Professor of Medicine, Cell Biology, Radiology, Surgery and Public Health **Industry:** Education/ Educational Services **Company Name:** SUNY Downstate Medical Center **Date of Birth:** 02/22/1945 **Place of Birth:** Deland **State:** FL **Parents:** Lee Norton Borer; Rita Doris (Feldt) Borer **Marital Status:** Married **Spouse Name:** Brondi Beth Topchik (9/16/1978) **Children:** Jon Andrew (9/5/1984); Justine Isolde (3/24/1981) **Education:** Visiting Fellow, Cardiac Department, Guy's Hospital, University of London, London, England (1974-1975); Glorney-Raisbeck Fellow in the Medical Sciences, New York Academy of Medicine (1974-1975); Senior Fulbright-Hays Scholar, Cardiac Department, Guy's Hospital, University of London, London, England (1974-1975); Cardiology Fellowship and Chief Resident Physician, National Heart, Lung and Blood Institute, National Institutes of Health, Bethesda, MD (1971-1974); Assistant Resident in Medicine, Massachusetts General Hospital (Now The General Hospital Corporation), Boston, MA (1970-1971); Clinical Fellow in Medicine, Harvard University, Cambridge and Boston, MA (1969-1971); Intern in Medicine, Massachusetts General Hospital (Now The General Hospital Corporation), Boston, MA (1969-1970); MD, Cornell Medical College (Now Weill Cornell Medicine), Cornell University (1969); BA in Government, Harvard College, Cum Laude (1965) **Certifications:** Diplomate, Certification Board of Nuclear Cardiology (1996); Diplomate, Subspecialty Board of Cardiovascular Disease (1975) Medical License, State of New York; Medical License, Washington, DC **Career:** Professor of Public Health, School of Public Health, SUNY Downstate Medical Center, Brooklyn, NY (2016-Present); Professor, Department of Academic Orthopedic Surgery, New York College of Podiatric Medicine, New York Citty, NY (2012-Present); Professor of Surgery, SUNY Downstate Medical Center, Brooklyn, NY (2009-Present); Professor of Cell Biology, SUNY Downstate Medical Center, Brooklyn, NY (2009-Present); Professor of Radiology, SUNY Downstate Medical Center, Brooklyn, NY (2009-Present); Professor of Medicine, SUNY Downstate Medical Center, Brooklyn, NY (2009-Present); Adjunct Professor of Cardiovascular Medicine in Cardiothoracic Surgery, Weill Medical College (Now Weill Cornell Medicine), Cornell University, New York, NY (2008-Present); Director, Schiavone Cardiovascular Translational Research Institute, SUNY Downstate Medical Center, Brooklyn, NY (2008-Present); Chairman, The Howard Gilman Institute for Heart Valve Disease, SUNY Downstate Medical Center, Brooklyn, NY (2008-Present); Chairman, Department of Medicine, SUNY Downstate Medical Center, Brooklyn, NY (2009-2013); Chief, Division of Cardiovascular Medicine SUNY Downstate Medical Center, Brooklyn, NY (2008-2015) **Career Related:** Chairman, Cardiovascular Devices Subcommittee of the International Standardization Organization (2016-Present); Chairman, Data and Safety Monitoring Board, National Institutes of Health GUIDE-IT Study, Heart Failure Management Trial (2013-2016); Ad Hoc Member, United States Food and Drug Administration (2009-Present); Member, United States Valve Experts Committee, Association for the Advancement of Medical Instrumentation (2007-Present) **Civic:** Board of Trustees, Committee to Reduce Infection Death (2016-Present); Chairman, Committee on Restoration, Brooklyn Jewish Center, Brooklyn, NY (2009-Present); Chairman, Building Preservation Committee, Brooklyn Jewish Center (2009-Present); President, Board of Trustees, Corlette Glorney Foundation, Inc. (2000-Present) **Military Service:** Senior Surgeon, United States Public Health Service **Creative Works:** Consulting Editor, Dialogues in Cardiovascular Medicine (2016-Present); Section Editor, Valve Disease, Journal of the American College of Cardiology (2014-Present); Editorial Board, European Heart Journal (2008-Present); Editor-in-Chief, Cardiology (2005-Present); Editor-in-Chief, Advances in Cardiology (2001-Present); Editorial Board, Journal of Heart Disease (1999-Present); Editorial Board, Journal of Clinical and Basic Cardiology (1998-Present); Editorial Board, The Journal of Heart Failure (1994-Present); Editorial Board, Cor et Vasa (Journal of the Czech Society of Cardiology) (1994-Present); Co-Contributor, Co-Editor, "Systemic Disease Manifestation in the Foot, Ankle and Lower Extremity," Wolters Kluwer, New York (2017) **Awards:** Recipient, Award for Lifetime Achievement in Heart Valve Diseases, Heart Valve Society of America (Now The Heart Valve Society International) and Society for Heart Valves Disease, London, England (2014); Recipient, Legend of Cardiology Award, 10th Annual Global Summit (C3) on Complex Cardiovascular Catheter Therapeutics: Advanced Endovascular and Coronary Intervention, Orlando, FL (2014); Recipient, Diversity in Cardiology Award, Association of Black Cardiologists (2013) **Membership:** Board of Trustees, The Heart Valve Society (2015-Present); Fellow, International Academy of Cardiovascular Sciences (2011-Present); Honorary Fellow, Argentine Heart Association (1985-Present); President, The Heart Valve Society of America (2004-2014) **Marquis Who's Who Honors:** Albert Nelson Marquis Lifetime Achievement Award (2017) **Religion:** Jewish **Shipping Address:** 47 E 88th St, New York, NY, 10128

Philip Borowsky

Title: Lawyer **Industry:** Law and Legal Services **Company Name:** Borowsky & Hayes LLP **Date of Birth:** 10/09/1946 **Place of Birth:** Philadephia **State:** PA **Parents:** Joshua Borowsky; Gertrude (Nicholson) Borowsky **Marital Status:** Married **Spouse Name:** Victoria Culko Smith (10/17/2004) **Children:** Miriam Isadora; Manuel; Nora Jo **Education:** JD, University of San Francisco (1973); BA, University of California, Los Angeles (1967) **Career:** Managing Partner, Borowsky & Hayes LLP, San Francisco, CA (2002-Present); President, Law Offices of Philip Borowsky, Inc., San Francisco, CA (1996-2002); President, Cartwright, Slobodin, Bokelman, Borowsky, Wartnick, Moore & Harris, Inc. (Now The Cartwright Law Firm), San Francisco, CA (1987-1995); Managing Partner, Cartwright, Slobodin, Bokelman, Borowsky, Wartnick, Moore & Harris, Inc. (Now The Cartwright Law Firm), San Francisco, CA (1987-1995) **Career Related:** American Arbitration Association (1982-Present); Faculty Member, Practising Law Institute, New York, NY (1983-1984); Adjunct Faculty Member, University of California, Hastings College of the Law, San Francisco, CA (1982-1983) **Military Service:** US Army, Vietnam (1968-1970) **Creative Works:** Consultant, Editorial Board, Bad Faith Law Update (1986-2004); Co-Author, "Unjust Dismissal and At-Will Employment" (1985) **Awards:** Northern California Super Lawyer (2004-2018); Fellow, Litigation Council of America **Bar Admissions:** California **Marquis Who's Who Honors:** Albert Nelson Marquis Lifetime Achievement Award (2017) **Political Affiliations:** Democrat **Business Address:** 101 Mission Street, Suite 1640, San Francisco, CA, 94105 **Shipping Address:** 101 Mission Street, Suite 1640, Borowsky & Hayes, San Francisco, CA, 94105

Douglas M. Borthwick

Title: Attorney **Industry:** Law and Legal Services **Company Name:** Law Offices of Douglas Borthwick **Place of Birth:** Cleveland **State:** OH **Marital Status:** Married **Children:** One Daughter **Education:** JD, Capital University Law School (1991); BA in Business, Muskingum University, Magna Cum Laude (1988); BA in Business, Economics, Religion, Muskingum University, Magna Cum Laude (1988); BA in Religion, Muskingum University, Magna Cum Laude (1988) **Certifications:** Licensed Attorney, State of California **Career:** President, Owner, Law Offices of Douglas Borthwick **Awards:** Preeminent 5.0 out of 5 Rating, Martindale-Hubbell (2017); Esteemed Lawyer of America (2017); Top 3 Personal Injury Lawyers in Rancho Cucamonga, CA (2017); Three Best Attorneys of America, Rue Ratings (2017); AV Preeminent Rating, Martindale-Hubbell; Dean's List, Capital University Law School Academic Scholarship, Capital University Law School; "Excellent" Rating, Avvo **Membership:** California DWI Lawyers Association (2016-Present); American Association for Justice (2016-Present); Lawyer's Den (2016-Present); AngelList (2015-Present); Vietnam Table Tennis Center (2015-Present); Orange County Real Estate Professionals (2014-Present); San Bernardino County Bar Association (2013-Present); Hispanic Bar Association (1995-Present); Orange County Bar Association (1992-Present); Association of Southern California Defense Counsel (1992-Present); Church of Jesus Christ of Latter Day Saints (1991-Present); Riverside Bar Association (2013-2017); Santa Ana Rotary Club (2012-2013); Growth Source Coaching Company (2011-2014); Consumer Attorneys Association of Los Angeles (2007-2009); Risk and Insurance Management Society (2007-2009); California Moving and Storage Association (2006-2008); Transportation Lawyers Association (2006-2008); San Bernardino County Bar Association (2005-2012); Orange County Celtic Bar Association (2002-2004); American Society for Testing and Materials (2001-2002); Western Fairs Association (2001-2002); National Association of Dealer Counsel (1999-2001); Outdoor Amusement Business Association (1999-2000); California Amusement Parks Association (1998-2001); National Recreational Park Association (1998-1999); World Waterpark Association (1996-2002); Roller Skating Association International (1995-2002); Defense Research Institute (1993-2003); International Association of Amusement Parks and Attractions (1992-2003); J. Reuben Clark Law Society (1992-2003); ABA (1992-2003); Amusement Industry Manufacturers & Suppliers International (1991-2006); Esteemed Lawyers of America; Best Attorneys of America **Bar Admissions:** United States Court of Appeals for the Sixth District (1999-Present); United State Court of Appeals for the Ninth Circuit (1999-Present); United States District Court for the Eastern District of California (1998-Present); United States District Court for the Northern District of California (1998-Present); United States District Court for the Southern District of California (1997-Present); United States District Court for the Central District of California (1997-Present); United Scottish Society of Southern California (1997-Present); Supreme Court of the United States (1997-Present); Arizona; Utah; Ohio; Arkansas; Minnesota; The District of Columbia; North Dakota **Why did you become involved in your profession or industry:** Mr. Borthwick had a choice between becoming an attorney or a minister, and chose to be an attorney. **Hobbies:** Travel **Shipping Address:** 1800 N Broadway Ste. 200, Law offices of Douglas Borthwick, Santa Ana, CA, 92706 **Website:** http://www.borthwicklawyer.com

Michael Jay Boskin

Industry: Education/Educational Services **Date of Birth:** 09/23/1945 **Place of Birth:** New York **State:** NY **Parents:** Irving Boskin; Jean Boskin **Marital Status:** Married **Spouse Name:** Chris Dornin (10/20/1981) **Education:** PhD in Economics, University of California, Berkeley (1971); MA in Economics, University of California, Berkeley (1968); AB, University of California, Berkeley, with Highest Honors (1967) **Career:** Board of Directors, Exxon Mobil Corp. (1996-Present); Board of Directors, Oracle Corp. (1994-Present); Senior Fellow, Hoover Institution, Stanford University (1993-Present); Scholar, American Enterprise Institute (1993-Present); President, Chief Executive Officer, Boskin & Co., Menlo Park, CA (1993-Present); Tully M. Friedman Professor of Economics, Professor Emeritus, Stanford University (1993-Present); Research Associate, National Bureau of Economic Research (1976-Present); Board of Directors, Vodafone Group PLC (1999-2008); Board of Directors, Airtouch Communications, Inc. (1996-1999); Chairman, Congressional Advisory Commission on the Consumer Price Index (1995-1997); Distinguished Faculty Fellow, Yale University (1993); Chairman, Council of Economic Advisors, Executive Office of the President, Washington, DC (1989-1993); Wohlford Professor of Economics, Stanford University (1987-1989); Director, Center for Economic Policy Research, Stanford University (1981-1988); Professor, Stanford University (1978-1986); Visiting Professor, Harvard University, Cambridge, MA (1977-1978); Associate Professor, Stanford University (1976-1978); Assistant Professor of Economics, Stanford University (1970-1975); President, Board of Directors, Koret Foundation; Advisor, Consultant, Numerous Government Agencies and Private Businesses **Civic:** Member, Board of Directors, Several Philanthropic Organiations **Creative Works:** Author, "Frontiers of Tax Reform" (1996); Author, "Capital Technology and Growth" (1996); Author, "Toward a More Accurate Measure of the Cost of Living" (1996); Author, "Reagan and the Economy: Successes, Failures Unfinished Agenda" (1987); Author, "Too Many Promises: The Uncertain Future of Social Security" (1986); Contributor, Articles to Professional Journals to Popular Media **Awards:** Recipient, Adam Smith Prize, National Association of Business Economists (1998); Recipient, Presidential Medal, Italian Republic (1998); Recipient, Distinguished Teaching Award, Stanford University (1998); Recipient, Distinguished Public Service Award, Stanford University (1993); Recipient, Medal of the President, Italian Republic (1991); Recipient, Public Servant of the Year Award, University o California Alumni Association (1990); Recipient, W.S. Johnson Award for Contributions to Free Enterprise, National Federation Independent Business (1990); Recipient, Dean's Award for Distinguished Teaching (1988); Recipient, Abramson Award for Outstanding Research, National Association of Business Economists (1987); Faculty Research Fellowship, Mellon Foundation (1973) **Membership:** Fellow, National Association of Business Economics **Hobbies:** Tennis; Skiing; Reading; Theater; Golf

Karen L. Bosley

Title: Professor of Humanities **Industry:** Education/Educational Services **Company Name:** Ocean County College **Date of Birth:** 09/23/1942 **Place of Birth:** Beech Grove **State:** IN **Parents:** Lowell Holmes; Kathryn Gertrude (Drake) Foley **Spouse Name:** Norman Keith Bosley (12/21/1964) **Children:** Mark Harold; Rachael Kathryn; Keith Lowell; Sidney Clark **Education:** MJ, Ball State University; MA, Northwestern University; AB, University of Indianapolis, Cum Laude **Career:** Retired (2008); Yearbook Adviser, Ocean County College, Toms River, NJ (1999-2004); Student Media Board Chairman, Ocean County College, Toms River, NJ (1983-2005); Student Newspaper Adviser, Ocean County College, Toms River, NJ (1971-2009); Professor of Humanities, Journalism, and English, Ocean County College, Toms River, NJ (1971-2008); English Teacher, Southern Regional High School, Manahawkin, NJ (1967-1968); English Teacher, Yearbook Adviser, Beech Grove Junior High School (1965-1966); Copy Editor, Reporter, Indianapolis News (1963-1965); English and Journalism Educator **Career Related:** Freelance Editor and Book Editor (2010-Present); Online Copy Editor, American Cinematographer (2008-2014); Part-Time Copy Editor, Daily Times-Observer, Toms River, NJ (1993); Part-Time Reporter (1972-1977) **Civic:** Advisory Council, Student Press Law Center (2002-Present); Democratic Committeeman, Long Beach Township District 2 (1985-Present); Charter Member, Correspondent Section, Southern Regional Jazz Band Parents Association (2001-2008); Secretary, Student Press Law Center (1998-2000); President, Southern Regional High School Band Parent Organization (1996-1997); Southern Regional High School Band Parent Organization (1995-1996); Board of Directors, Student Press Law Center (1987-2002); Friends of Island Library (1975-1979); Ocean County Family Planning, Inc. (1972-1978); Board of Directors, Ocean County Red Cross (1972-1978); Long Beach Township Recreation Commission (1972-1975); Democratic Committeeman, Long Beach Township District 2 (1971-1978); President, Long Beach I PTA Chairman, Long Beach Township Democratic Municipal Committee (1971-1978); Administrative Board, First United Methodist Church, Beach Haven Terrace, NJ; Island Democrats, Inc.; Founder, Board of Directors, Long Beach Island Historical Association; Chairman, Cub Scout Pack 32, Ocean County Council, Boy Scouts of America; Trustee, Long Beach Island Historical Association **Creative Works:** Contributor, Articles, Publications in Field **Awards:** First Amendment Award, Society for Collegiate Journalists (2009); Hall of Fame Award, College Media Association (2008); Hall of Fame, College Media Advisers, Inc. (2007); Louis E. Ingelhart First Amendment Award, College Media Advisers, Inc. (2006-2007); Louis E. Ingelhart Award, Society of Collegiate Journalists (2006); Beech Grove High School Wall of Fame (2005); Beech Grove High School Alumnus of the Year (1985) **Membership:** Founder, Southern Regional High School Alumni Association (2008-2011); Vice President, Faculty Association of Ocean County College (1984-1985); Distinguished Newspaper Adviser, U.S. Two-Year Colleges, College Media Advisers, Inc. (1978); Treasurer, Southern Regional High School Alumni Association; Beech Grove Alumni Association; Society of Professional Journalists; International Platform Association; Sigma Delta Chi; Society of Collegiate Journalists; Society of Professional Journalists; Director, Vice President, Community College Journalism Association; Association of Education in Journalism and Mass Communications; Secretary, Director, College Media Advisers, Inc.; Ocean County Education Association; National Education Association; New Jersey Education Association; President, Director, Barnegat Light Area Branch, American Association of University Women **To what do you attribute your success:** Ms. Bosley attributes her success to an excellent education and an ethical upbringing. **Why did you become involved in your profession or industry:** Ms. Bosley became involved in her profession because she had a talent for it. **What do you consider to be the highlight of your career:** The highlights of Ms. Bosley's career were winning the First Amendment Award, teaching young people to be ethical, responsible journalists, and advising the college newspaper. **Hobbies:** Reading; Knitting **Political Affiliations:** Democrat **Religion:** Protestant **Shipping Address:** 9 E Old Whaling Lane, Long Beach Township, NJ, 08008-2930

Thomas Lawrence Bosworth

Title: Architect, Educator (Retired) **Industry:** Architecture & Constrution **Company Name:** Bosworth Hoedemaker, Architecture and Planning **Date of Birth:** 06/15/1930 **Place of Birth:** Oberlin **State:** OH **Parents:** Edward Franklin Bosworth; Imogene (Rose) Bosworth **Marital Status:** Married **Spouse Name:** Elaine R. Pedigo (11/23/1974); Abigail Lumbard (11/6/1954, Divorced 11/1974) **Children:** Thomas Edward; Nathaniel David **Education:** Honorary PhD, Kobe University, Japan (2003); MArch, Yale University (1960); Postgraduate Coursework, Harvard University (1956-1957); MA, Oberlin College (Now Oberlin College and Conservatory) (1954); Postgraduate Coursework, Princeton University (1952-1953); BA, Oberlin College (Now Oberlin College and Conservatory) (1952) **Career:** Partner, Bosworth Hoedemaker (Now Hoedmaker Pfeiffer), Architecture and Planning, Seattle, WA (2004-Present); Professor Emeritus, University of Washington (1998-Present); Director, Multidisciplinary Program, University of Washington, Rome, Italy (1984-1986); Individual Practice, Architecture, Seattle, WA (1968-2004); Professor of Architecture, University of Washington, Seattle, WA (1968-1998); Department Chairman, University of Washington (1968-1972); Associate Professor, Head of Department, Rhode Island School of Design (1966-1968); Department Head, Rhode Island School of Design (1966-1968); Visiting Lecturer, Yale University (1965-1966); Chief of Architecture, Peace Corps Training Program, Tunisia, Brown University (1965-1966); Individual Practice, Architecture, Providence, RI (1964-1968); Assistant Professor, Rhode Island School of Design (1964-1966); Assistant Instructor of Architecture, Yale University (1962-1965); Designer, Field Supervisor, Eero Saarinen and Associates, Hamden, CT (1961-1964); Designer, Field Supervisor, Eero Saarinen and Associates, Birmingham, MI (1960-1961); Resident Planner, Tunnard & Harris Planning Consultant, Newport, RI (1959) **Career Related:** Professor, University of Washington, Rome, Italy (2003); Professor, University of Washington, Rome, Italy (2000); Visiting Lecturer, Kobe University, Japan (1998); Pietro Belluschi Distinguished Visiting Professor, University of Oregon (1996); Director of Architecture, Rome Program, University of Washington, Rome, Italy (1996); Visiting Lecturer, Kobe University, Japan (1995); Visiting Lecturer, Kobe University, Japan (1993); Visiting Lecturer, Kobe University, Japan (1990); **Civic:** Advisory Council, Pilchuck Glass School, Seattle, WA (1993-Present); Advisory Board, University of Washington, Rome, Italy (1999-2011); Board of Managers, YMCA Camping Services (1998-2002); Board of Directors, Arcade Magazine (1988-2002); President, Arcade Magazine (1988-2000); Board of Directors, The Civita Institute, The Northwest Institute for Architecture & Urban Studies in Italy (NIAUSI) (1983-1990); President, The Civita Institute - The Northwest Institute for Architecture & Urban Studies in Italy (NIAUSI) (1983-1985); Trustee, Pilchuck Glass School, Seattle, WA (1980-1991); Director, Pilchuck Glass School, Seattle, WA (1977-1980); King County Policy Development Commission, WA (1974-1977); Medina Planning Commission (1972-1974); Steering Advisory Committee, King County Stadium (1972-1974); Chairman, King County Environmental Development Commission, WA (1972-1974); Technical Committee, Site Selection, Washington Multi-Purpose Stadium (1970); Review Board, Seattle Model Cities Land Use (1969-1970) **Military Service:** United States Army (1954-1956) **Awards:** Associate Fellow, Ezra Stiles College, Yale University (1964-Present); Medal of Honor, Northwest Pacific Region, American Institute of Architects (AIA) (2013); Visiting Scholar, American Academy in Rome (2011); Visiting Scholar, American Academy in Rome (2007); Seattle Medalist, American Institute of Architects (AIA) (2003); Visiting Scholar, American Academy in Rome (1988); Mid-Career Fellow in Architecture, American Academy in Rome (1980-1981); Winchester Traveling Fellow, Yale University (1960); Recipient, 27 Design Awards **Membership:** Fellow, American Institute of Architects; Monday Club, Seattle, WA; Bohemian Club, San Francisco, CA; Tau Sigma Delta **Marquis Who's Who Honors:** Albert Nelson Marquis Lifetime Achievement Award (2017) **Shipping Address:** 2411 25th Ave E, Seattle, WA, 98112 **Website:** www.bosworthhoedemaker.com

Daniel B. Botkin

Title: Professor Emeritus of Biology **Industry:** Education/Educational Services **Company Name:** University of California, Santa Barbara **Date of Birth:** 08/19/1937 **Place of Birth:** Oklahoma City **State:** OK **Parents:** Benjamin Albert Botkin; Gertrude (Fritz) Botkin **Spouse Name:** Erene Victoria Youngberg (4/7/1978, Deceased 3/1994); Ellen Chase (12/22/1962, Divorced 1976) **Children:** Nancy; Jonathan **Education:** PhD, Rutgers, The State University of New Jersey (1968); MA, University of Wisconsin (1962); BA, University of Rochester (1959) **Career:** Adjunct Professor, Department of Biology, University of Miami, Coral Gables, FL (2013-Present); Emeritus Professor, University of California, Santa Barbara, CA (2004-Present); Research Professor of Biology, University of California, Santa Barbara (1999-2004); Professor of Biology, George Mason University, Fairfax, VA (1993-1999); Director, Program on Global Change, Biology Department, George Mason University, Fairfax, VA (1993-1997); President, Center for the Study of the Environment, United States Department of State (1992-2012); Professor of Biology, University of California, Santa Barbara (1978-1992); Chairman of Environmental Studies Program, University of California, Santa Barbara (1978-1985); Associate Scientist, Marine Biological Laboratory, Woods Hole, MA (1976-1978); Assistant Professor, Yale University, New Haven, CT (1968-1976); Associate Professor, Yale University, New Haven, CT (1968-1976) Faculty, Yale University School of Forestry & Environmental Studies; Chairman, Environmental Studies Program, Department of Ecology, Evolution, and Marine Biology, University of California; Research Scientist, The Marine Biological Laboratory, Woods Hole, MA; Director of Program on Global Change, George Mason University **Career Related:** Distinguished Visiting Scholar, Green Mountain College, Vermont (2008); Annual Distinguished Visiting Scientist, Long Beach Aquarium, California (2008); Astor Lecturer, University of Oxford (2007); Distinguished Visiting Professor, Michigan State University (2004); Visiting Professor, University of Notre Dame (2003-2004); Distinguished Visiting Professor, University of Montana; Distinguished Visiting Professor, Green Mountain College **Civic:** Science Advisor, Film, "Power to the People" (2014); Member, National Advisory Board, The Stetson Kennedy Trust, Jacksonville, FL (2006-2010); Trustee, The American Folklife Center, The Library of Congress (2004-2009); Board of Directors, The Environmental Literacy Council, Washington, DC (2003-2006); Commissioner, United States Department of State to United Nations Educational, Scientific and Cultural Organization (2002-2006) **Creative Works:** Co-Author, "What Makes Us One" (2016); Publisher, "Myths that are Destroying the Environment" (2016); Co-Author, "Environmental Science: Earth as a Living Planet, Ninth Edition" (2014); Author, "Discordant Harmonies Reconsidered" (2012); Author, "Powering the Future: A Scientist's Guide to Energy Independence" (2010); Co-Author, "Essential Environmental Science, First Edition" (2008); Author, "Beyond The Stony Mountains: Nature in the American West from Lewis and Clark to Today" (2004); Author, "JABOWA-4" (2004); Author, "Our Natural History: The Lessons of Lewis and Clark" (2004); Author, "Strange Encounters: Adventures of a Renegade Naturalist" (2003); Author, "No Man's Garden: Thoreau and a New Vision for Civilization and Nature" (2001); Co-Author, "Environmental Science: Earth as a Living Planet, Third Edition" (2000); Author, "JABOWA-3 for Windows" (1999); Co-Author, "The Blue Planet" (1999); Author, "Passage of Discovery: The American Rivers Guide to the Missouri River of Lewis and Clark" (1999); Author, "Our Natural History: The Lessons of Lewis and Clark" (1995); Author, "Forest Dynamics: An Ecological Model, First Edition" (1993); Author, "JABOWA-II: The Forest Growth Model" (1992); Author, "Discordant Harmonies: A New Ecology for the 21st Century, Paperback Edition" (1992); Author, "Discordant Harmonies: A New Ecology for the Twenty-First Century, Hardcover" (1990); Author, "Timber: Model of Forest Growth" (1987); Author, "Timber: Model of Forest Growth" (1983); Author, "Review Guide with Internet Companion to Accompany Environmental Science: Earth As a Living Planet, Second Edition"; Author, "An Introduction to Scientific Research Methods in Geography and Environmental Studies, Second Edition"; Author, "Precalculus: Graphical, Numerical, Algebraic, Eighth Edition"; Author, "Environmental Science Second Edition and Environmental Case Studies: Southeastern Region" **Awards:** Recipient, John C. Pritzlaff Conservation Award, Santa Barbara Botanic Garden (2012); Named, Green Mountain College Annual Distinguished Visiting Scientist (2008); Recipient, Astor Lectureship Award, University of Oxford (2007); Recipient, Texty Award for Best Biological Sciences Textbook, Textbook and Academic Authors Association (2004) **Marquis Who's Who Honors:** Albert Nelson Marquis Lifetime Achievement Award (2017); Distinguished Humanitarian (2017) **Business Address:** 245 8th Ave Unit 270, New York, NY, 10011 **Shipping Address:** 290 9th Ave Apt 20C, New York, NY, 10001 **Website:** http://www.drdanielbotkin.com

Marlene F. Bourke-Faustina

Title: Music Educator **Industry:** Education/Educational Services **Company Name:** Waianae Intermediate School **Date of Birth:** 03/10/1944 **Place of Birth:** Honolulu **State:** HI **Parents:** Francis Patrick Bourke; Violet Kahale Bourke **Marital Status:** Married **Spouse Name:** Manuel Edward Faustina (1/3/1990) **Children:** Aaron Faustina; Christian Faustina; Shane Faustina **Education:** Professional Diploma in Music Education, University of Hawai'i at Manoa (1973); Bachelor's Degree in Music Education, Walla Walla University (1970) **Career:** Chorus Teacher, Waianae Intermediate School (1992-Present); Music Teacher, Waianae Intermediate School (1992-Present); Chorus Teacher, Wahiawa Middle School (1988-1992); Music Teacher, Wahiawa Middle School (1988-1992); Chorus Teacher, Waianae Intermediate School (1977-1984); Chorus Teacher, Highlands Intermediate School (1984-1988); Music Teacher, Highlands Intermediate School (1984-1988); Music Teacher, Waianae Intermediate School (1977-1984); Chorus Teacher, Hawaiian Mission Elementary Academy (1974-1976); Music Teacher, Hawaiian Mission Elementary Academy (1974-1976); Chorus Coach, Hawaiian Mission Academy (1974-1976); Band Coach, Hawaiian Mission Academy (1974-1976); Vocal Coach, Hawaiian Mission Academy (1974-1976); Music Teacher, Umatilla County, Milton-Freewater, OR (1970-1972) **Career Related:** Vocalist, Kawaiahao Church and Mission Houses (2005-2006); Affiliate, Central Union Church (1977-1984); Affiliate, Royal Hawaiian Band (1972-1977) **Civic:** Director, Roses Waianae Charity WIS Campaign for Homeless; Coordinator, Roses Waianae Charity WIS Campaign for Homeless **Awards:** Named Hawaii Leeward State Teacher Of The Year (2003); Named Hawaii Leeward State Teacher Of The Year (1985); Outstanding Secondary Educators Of America Award (1978); Outstanding Alumni Award, Kamehameha Schools (1970) **Membership:** American Choral Directors Association; National Association for Music Education **Hobbies:** Designing Hawaiian floral arrangements; Gardening; Arranging music **Political Affiliations:** Democrat **Religion:** Seventh-Day Adventist **Business Address:** 85-626 Farrington Highway, Waianae, HI, 96792 **Shipping Address:** 85-223 Ala Akau St Apt C, Waianae, HI, 96792

Charles Percy Bourne

Title: Information Scientist, Educator **Industry:** Information Technology and Services **Company Name:** Dialog Information Services, Inc. **Date of Birth:** 09/02/1931 **Place of Birth:** San Francisco **State:** CA **Parents:** Frank Percy Bourne; Edith (Dunlap) Bourne **Marital Status:** Married **Spouse Name:** Elizabeth A. Scheidtmann (8/15/1953) **Children:** Glen Wade; Holly Ann **Education:** MS in Industrial Engineering, Stanford University (1963); BEE, University of California, Berkeley (1957) **Career:** President, Charles Bourne & Associates, Menlo Park, CA (1970-Present); Vice President, General Information Division, Dialog Information Services, Inc., Palo Alto, CA (1977-1992); Director, Institute of Library Research, University of California, Berkeley (1971-1977); Vice President, Information General Corporation, Palo Alto, CA (1966-1970); Senior Research Engineer, Stanford Research Institute, Menlo Park, CA (1957-1966); Professor in Residence, School of Library and Information Studies, University of California, Berkeley **Career Related:** Encyclopedia of Library and Information Sciences (1967-Present); Delegate-at-large, White House Conference Library and Information Services (1991); Network Advisory Committee, Library of Congress (1987-1992); Advisory Board, World Affairs Report (1987-1990); U.S. Delegate, United Nations Educational Intergovernmental Conference on Science and Technology Information for Development (1979); Sarada Ranganathan Lecturer, Bangalore, India (1978); U.S.-Egyptian Task Force on Technology Information Problems (1976); Consultant Correspondent, Committee on Science and Technology Information, National Academy of Sciences (1968-1970); Documentation Abstracts (1968-1969); U.S. Representative, International Federation for Documentation (1966-1976); Annual Review of Information Science and Technology (1966); Advisory Board, Chemical Abstracts (1965-1968); Guest Lecturer, University of California, Berkeley (1963-1966) **Military Service:** U.S. Marine Corps Reserve (1950-1951) **Creative Works:** Co-author, "A History of Online Information Services" (2003); Author, "Technology in Support of Library Science and Information Service" (1980); Author, "Methods of Information Handling" (1963); Contributor, Articles, Professional Journals **Awards:** Annual Award of Merit, America Documentation Institute (1965) **Membership:** Best Information Science Book Award, American Society of Information Science and Technology (2004); Board Directors, National Information Standards Organization (1987-1990); President, American Society of Information Science and Technology (1970); Director, Information Sciences and Automation Division, American Library Association (1966-1967) **Marquis Who's Who Honors:** Albert Nelson Marquis Lifetime Achievement Award (2017); Distinguished Humanitarian (2017) **Why did you become involved in your profession or industry:** Mr. Bourne became involved in his profession because the Marine Corps told him he should be in their electronics activity starting as a radio repairman, and they sent him to school to become an instructor at the Navy electronics school at the Naval Station Great Lakes. While doing that service he worked with Navy technicians, who were developing their own high tech audio system. That's what drove him to be an electrical engineer. That is how he got on to path of computer engineering and started a professional career at the SRI International, where he helped build developmental computers and worked on other computer related projects. **Shipping Address:** 1619 Santa Cruz Avenue, Menlo Park, CA, 94025

Michelle S. Bradbury, PhD

Title: Co-Director, Radiologist, Professor **Industry:** Medicine & Health Care **Company Name:** Memorial Sloan Kettering Cancer Center **Date of Birth:** 10/25/1960 **Place of Birth:** Washington **State:** DC **Parents:** Stanley Morton Neuder; Rosilyn Madeline Neuder **Marital Status:** Married **Spouse Name:** John Seferian Bradbury (5/10/1997) **Education:** Fellow in Molecular Imaging, Memorial Sloan Kettering Cancer Center (2003-2006); Fellow in Neuroradiology, Wake-Forest Baptist Medical Center, Wake Forest School of Medicine (2002-2003); Resident in Radiology, Wake-Forest Baptist Medical Center, Wake Forest School of Medicine (1998-2002); Intern in Surgery, Wake-Forest Baptist Medical Center, Wake Forest School of Medicine (1997-1998); MD, The George Washington University (1997); Postdoctoral Fellow, University of California, San Francisco (1992-1993); PhD, Massachusetts Institute of Technology (1991); MS, University of Maryland (1986); BA, University of Pennsylvania (1982) **Certifications:** Certified in Neuroradiology, American Board of Radiology (2013); Certification, Maintenance of Certification (2012); Certification, American Board of Radiology (2012); Licensed to Practice Medicine, State of New Jersey (2006); Licensed to Practice Medicine, State of New York (2003) **Career:** Attending Radiologist, Neuroradiology Service, Department of Radiology, Memorial Hospital for Cancer & Allied Diseases, Memorial Sloan Kettering Cancer Center (2016-Present); Memorial Sloan Kettering Cancer Center (2016-Present); Professor, Gerstner Sloan Kettering Graduate School, Memorial Sloan Kettering Cancer Center (2016-Present); Professor, Weill Cornell Medicine (2016-Present); Molecular Imaging and Therapy Service, Department of Radiology, Memorial Hospital for Cancer & Allied Diseases, Memorial Sloan Kettering Cancer Center (2015-Present); Co-Chair, Innovation and Technology Team, Memorial Hospital for Cancer & Allied Diseases, Memorial Sloan Kettering Cancer Center (2015-Present); Director of Intraoperative Imaging, Department of Radiology, Memorial Hospital for Cancer & Allied Diseases, Memorial Sloan Kettering Cancer Center (2014-Present); Associate Attending Radiologist, Neuroradiology Service, Department of Radiology, Memorial Hospital for Cancer & Allied Diseases, Memorial Sloan Kettering Cancer Center (2012-Present); Joint Appointee, Molecular Pharmacology and Chemistry Program, Sloan Kettering Institute, Memorial Sloan Kettering Cancer Center (2011-Present); Associate Professor of Radiology, Gerstner Sloan Kettering Graduate School, Memorial Sloan Kettering Cancer Center (2015-2016); Associate Professor of Radiology, Weill Cornell Medicine (2012-2016); Associate Member, Memorial Sloan Kettering Cancer Center (2012-2016); Assistant Professor of Radiology, Weill Cornell Medicine (2006-2012); Assistant Member, Memorial Sloan Kettering Cancer Center (2006-2012); Assistant Attending Radiologist, Neuroradiology Service, Department of Radiology, Memorial Hospital for Cancer & Allied Diseases, Memorial Sloan Kettering Cancer Center (2006-2012); Instructor of Neuroradiology Service, Department of Radiology, Memorial Hospital for Cancer & Allied Diseases, Memorial Sloan Kettering Cancer Center (2003-2006); Intramural Research Fellow, National Institutes of Health (1994); Research Assistant, National Institute of Standards & Technology (1985-1986); Research Assistant, National Institutes of Health (1983-1985) **Creative Works:** Senior Editor, "Journal of Interdisciplinary Nanomedicine" (2015-Present); Editorial Board Member, "Nanomedicine: Nanotechnology, Biology and Medicine" (2014-Present); Ad-Hoc Reviewer, "ACS Nano" (2009-Present); Ad-Hoc Reviewer, "Journal of Nuclear Medicine" (2009-Present); Ad-Hoc Reviewer, "Radiology Journal" (2008-Present); Ad-Hoc Reviewer, "Nano Letters" (2008-Present); Reviewer, "Molecular Imaging and Biology" (2008-Present); Ad-Hoc Reviewer, "Molecular Imaging" (2007-Present); Ad-Hoc Reviewer, "Cancer Research" (2007-Present) **Awards:** Research Grant, National Cancer Institute (2015); Bioaccelerate Phase II Award, Partnership for New York City (2014); BioAccelerate NYC Prize, Partnership for New York City (2011); Winner, Wharton Alumni Business Showcase, Wharton Alumni Club of New York (2011); Selectee, New York City Emerging Technologies Summit, Opportunities in Oncology, Memorial Sloan Kettering Cancer Center (2010); Early Career Women Faculty Development Leadership Training Award (2005); Young Investigator Travel Award, Society for Molecular Imaging (2005); Roentgen Resident/Fellow Research Award, Radiological Society of North America (2002); **Membership:** Founder, Molecular Imaging in Nanotechnology and Theranostics Interest Group, World Molecular Imaging Society (2015-Present); NANO Study Section Panel, National Institutes of Health (2015-Present); Founder, International Society of Image-Guided Surgery (2015-Present); Scientific Advisory Board for International Symposium on PolymerTherapeutics: From Laboratory to Clinical Practice (2014-Present); SPIE (2014-Present); **Marquis Who's Who Honors:** Albert Nelson Marquis Lifetime Achievement Award (2017) **Business Address:** 1275 York Avenue, New York, NY, 10065 **Shipping Address:** 1365 York Avenue, Apt. 33K, New York, NY, 10021

Everette Arnold Braden

Title: Attorney, Judge (Retired) **Industry:** Law and Legal Services **Company Name:** Everette A. Braden, Attorney at Law **Date of Birth:** 11/03/1932 **Place of Birth:** Chicago **State:** IL **Parents:** Zedrick Thomas Braden Sr., Bernice (Beckwith) Braden **Marital Status:** Widower **Children:** Marilynne **Education:** JD, The John Marshall Law School, Chicago, IL (1961); BS, Northwestern University, Evanston, IL (1954); LLB, The John Marshall Law School, Chicago, IL **Career:** Associate Judge, Office of the Clerk of the Circuit Court of Cook County, Chicago, IL (1977-1987); Supervising Trial Attorney, Law Office of the Cook County Public Defender, Chicago, IL (1976-1977); Trial Attorney, Law Office of the Cook County Public Defender, Chicago, IL (1969-1976); Property and Insurance Consultant, Cook County Sheriff's Office, Chicago, IL (1961-1969); Lawyer, Everette A. Braden Attorneys **Civic:** Board of Directors, LAF (1977); Vice President, Southeast CDC; President, South Shore Valley Community Organization; President, Board of Trustees, Illinois Bar Foundation; Secretary, Board of Trustees, St. Mark's United Methodist Church; NAACP; Illinois Congress of Parents and Teachers; Board of Directors, Alumni Coalition for Action, DuSable High School; Board of Commissioners, Cook County, Illinois; Supervising Judge, Child Support Enforcement Court, Cook County, Illinois; Justice, Illinois Appellate Court **Military Service:** U.S. Army (1955-1957) **Awards:** Chairman Emeritus and Lifetime Achievement Award, Illinois Judicial Foundation (2017); Man of the Year, St. Mark's United Methodist Church (2012); Court of Honor, Chicago Volunteer Legal Services (2000); Meritorious Service Award, Cook County Bar Association; Award of Merit, Illinois Judges Association; Distinguished Service Award, The John Marshall Law School; Community Service Award, MRT Scholarship Foundation; 33rd Degree Grand Inspector General, Prince Hall Mason; Award in Recognition of Outstanding Accomplishments and Dedicated Service to the Legal Community, The Black Law Students Association; Chairperson's Award for Outstanding Leadership, Illinois Judicial Council; Award for Outstanding Community Service, Geneva Scott Outreach Services; Inductee, Hall of Fame, Cook County Bar Association; Mary Merrick Lifetime Achievement Award; Action Award for Distinguished Achievement in the Legal and Judicial System and Continuing Dedication to DuSable High School and the Alumni Coalition; Honoree, Senior Counselor, Cook County Bar Association; Founder's Award, Illinois Judicial Council; Certificate of Excellence, Board of Directors, The Mary Herrik Scholarship Fund **Membership:** President, The John Marshall Law School Alumni Association (1990-1991); Second Vice President, The John Marshall Law School, Alumni Association (1988-1990); Board of Directors, Illinois Judges Association (1985-1991); Chairman, Illinois Judicial Council (1985-1986); Secretary, Illinois Judicial Council (1982-1984); Treasurer, Illinois Judges Association (1980-1981); Chairman, General Practice Section, Illinois State Bar Association (1979-1980); President, Cook County Bar Association (1975-1976); Illinois Bar Foundation; Lions Club International; The Chicago Assembly; Kappa Alpha Psi Fraternity, Inc.; Board of Directors, Phi Alpha Delta Law Fraternity; Northwestern University Alumni Association; Honorary Life Member, Prince Hall Masons; Board of Directors, Mary Merrick Scholarship Fund; National Bar Association; Illinois Judges Association; Cook County Judicial Advisory Council; Board of Directors, Cook County Bar Association Foundation; Privileged Member, Illinois State Bar Association; Board of Directors, The John Marshall Law School Alumni Association; Board of Visitors, The John Marshall Law School; The Chicago Bar Association; Illinois Judges Association Foundation; Charter Member, Illinois Bar Foundation; Fellow, Illinois Bar Foundation; Board of Directors, Illinois Judges Association Foundation; Founder, Illinois Judicial Council; Board of Directors, DuSable High School Alumni Association **Bar Admissions:** Supreme Court of the United States (1990); United States District Court for the Northern District of Illinois (1969); Illinois (1969) **Marquis Who's Who Honors:** Albert Nelson Marquis Lifetime Achievement Award (2017) **To what do you attribute your success:** Mr. Braden attributes his success to his helpful nature and passion for the work he does. **Why did you become involved in your profession or industry:** Mr. Braden became involved in his profession because of his father, who was also an attorney. He was additionally inspired by his brother, who was also an attorney. It was a natural progression given his family history. Another inspiration came from Col. Charles Cain. When Mr. Braden left the Army, he was interviewed by him, and he said, "the main purpose in life is to help someone else, beginning with your family." **What do you consider to be the highlight of your career:** Backed by a JD and LLB from John Marshall Law School, Mr. Braden has gathered countless accolades for his outstanding legal services over the last 50 years, including the honor of being appointed by the Supreme Court — a feat that he considers his greatest career accomplishment. **Business Address:** 8 S Michigan Ave. Suite 1401, Chicago, IL, 60603 **Shipping Address:** 8948 S Jeffery Blvd, Chicago, IL, 60617

Laurence Alan Bradley, PhD

Title: Psychologist **Industry:** Social Work **Company Name:** University of Alabama at Birmingham **Date of Birth:** 09/13/1949 **Place of Birth:** Cleveland **State:** OH **Parents:** Irving Bradley; Jeanne (Weil) Bradley **Marital Status:** Married **Spouse Name:** Virginia Wadley (3/26/2007); Elizabeth Wrenn (10/3/1981-1991); Gifford Weary (12/29/1974-1979) **Education:** PhD in Psychology, Vanderbilt University (1975); BA in Psychology, Vanderbilt University, Cum Laude With Honors (1971) **Career:** Professor, Division of Clinical Immunology, Rheumatology, MCRC, University of Alabama at Birmingham (2012-Present); Professor, Neuro-Behavioral Medicine Research, MCRC, University of Alabama at Birmingham (1999-2012); Director, Neuro-Behavioral Medicine Research, MCRC, University of Alabama at Birmingham (1999-2012); Professor, Education & Health Services Research, Comprehensive Arthritis, Musculoskeletal, Bone, and Autoimmunity Center, University of Alabama at Birmingham (1992-1999); Director of Epidemiology, Education & Health Services Research, Comprehensive Arthritis, Musculoskeletal, Bone, and Autoimmunity Center, University of Alabama at Birmingham (1992-1999); Associate Professor, Education and Health Services Research, Musculoskeletal, Bone, and Autoimmunity Center, University of Alabama at Birmingham (1989-1992); Director of Epidemiology, Education, and Health Services Research, Musculoskeletal, Bone, and Autoimmunity Center, University of Alabama at Birmingham (1989-1992); Associate Professor, Bowman Gray Center for Medical Education, Wake Forest School of Medicine (1982-1989); Administrative Head, Medical Psychology Section, Bowman Gray Center for Medical Education, Wake Forest School of Medicine (1981-1989); Assistant Professor, Bowman Gray Center for Medical Education, Wake Forest School of Medicine (1980-1982); Assistant Professor, Fordham University, Bronx, NY (1977-1980); Assistant Professor, The University of Tennessee at Chattanooga (1976-1977); Clinical Intern, Duke University and Duke University Health System, Durham, NC (1975-1976) **Career Related:** Visiting Behavioral Scientist, Orebro University Hospital (1986-1992); Adjunct Associate Professor, University of North Carolina at Greensboro (1983-1989); Fellow, American Psychological Association; Fellow, Society for Personality Assessment **Creative Works:** Co-Author, "The Complete Idiot's Guide to Fibromyalgia," Alpha (2009); Editorial Board, Journal of Back and Musculoskeletal Rehabilitation, IOS Press (1999-2010); Editorial Board, Health Psychology, American Psychological Association (1999-2001); Editorial Board, Arthritis Care & Research, Wiley Periodicals, Inc. (1995-2004); Associate Editor, Journal of Clinical Psychology, Wiley Periodicals, Inc. (1995-2000); Associate Editor, Journal of Clinical Pain, Lippincott Williams & Wilkins (1995-2000); Co-Author, "The Challenges of Pain in Arthritis," Arthritis Foundation (1993); Co-Author, "Health Psychology: Clinical Methods and Research," Macmillan Publishing Company (1991); Co-Editor, "Coping with Chronic Disease: Research and Applications," Academic Press (1983); Co-Editor, "Medical Psychology: Contributions To Behavioral Medicine," Elsevier Science (1981) **Awards:** Research Grantee, National Institutes of Health, U.S. Department of Health and Human Services (1989-Present); Research Grantee, The Fetzer Institute (2000-2005); Research Grantee, The American Fibromyalgia Syndrome Association, Inc. (1996); Distinguished Scholar, Arthritis Health Professions Association (1992); Research Grantee, The American-Scandinavian Foundation (1986); Research Grantee, Robert Wood Johnson Foundation (1982-1986) **Membership:** International Association for the Study of Pain; American Pain Society; Society of Behavioral Medicine; American College of Rheumatology; Osteoarthritis Research Society International; Arthritis Health Professions Association; Sigma Xi, The Scientific Research Honor Society; The Phi Beta Kappa Society **Marquis Who's Who Honors:** Albert Nelson Marquis Lifetime Achievement Award (2017) **Political Affiliations:** Democrat **Business Address:** 1825 University Boulevard, 177A Shelby Research Building, Birmingham, AL, 35294 **Shipping Address:** 3635 Dunbarton Drive, Birmingham, AL, 35223

Stephen Kalani Brady

Title: 1) Associate Professor 2) Physician **Industry:** Education/Educational Services **Company Name:** 1) John A. Burns School of Medicine, University of Hawaii at Manoa 2) Straub Medical Center, Hawaii Pacific Health **Date of Birth:** 10/13/1955 **Place of Birth:** New London **State:** CT **Parents:** Richard Harris Brady; Jeanne Margaret (Halpin) Brady **Marital Status:** Divorced **Spouse Name:** Elizabeth Ada Rewick (12/27/1994, Divorced 2006); Marsha Anne Erickson (6/18/1978, Divorced 1993) **Children:** Ericka Anuhea **Education:** Resident, Internal Medicine, University of Hawaii (1983-1985); Intern, University of Hawaii (1982-1983); MD, University of Pennsylvania, Philadelphia, PA (1982); Postgraduate Coursework, University of Hawaii (1979); MPH, University of Hawaii (1978); AB, Harvard University, Cum Laude, Cambridge, MA (1977) **Certifications:** Diplomate, American Board of Internal Medicine **Career:** Associate Professor, John A. Burns School of Medicine, University of Hawaii at Manoa (2003-Present); Physician, Straub Medical Center, Hawaii Pacific Health (1984-Present); Interim Chair, Department of Native Hawaiian Health, John A. Burns School of Medicine, University of Hawaii at Manoa (2009-2011); Vice Chair, Department of Native Hawaiian Health, John A. Burns School of Medicine, University of Hawaii at Manoa (2003-2006); Clinical Assistant Professor, John A. Burns School of Medicine, University of Hawaii at Manoa (1999-2003); Assistant Medical Director, Physician, American Hawaii Cruises, Honolulu, HI (1989-1995); Physician, Waianae Coast Comprehensive Health Center (1989-1994); Clinical Instructor, John A. Burns School of Medicine University of Hawaii at Manoa (1986-1999); Physician, Medical Director, Kokua Kalihi Valley, Honolulu, HI (1986-1989); Physician, Kaiser Permanente Honolulu Medical Office, Honolulu, HI (1985-1986); Director, Faculty Affairs, John A. Burns School of Medicine, University of Hawaii at Manoa **Career Related:** Founding Chair, Hawaii Consortium for Continuing Medical Education, John A. Burns School of Medicine, University of Hawaii at Manoa (1993-Present); Board of Directors, ACCME (2007-2009) **Civic:** Trustee, Saint Louis School (2006-Present); Cubmaster, Boy Scouts of America, Kailua, HI (1995-2000); Member, American Heart Association, Inc.; Member, Multicultural Initiative **Military Service:** Commander, U.S. Merchant Marine (1989-Present) **Creative Works:** Editor, Hawaii Journal of Medicine and Public Health (2005-Present); Co-Host, Ask the Doctor, KHON Morning News (1996-Present); Host, Television Series, UH on Call (2005-2006); Host, Television Series, Health in Paradise (2001-2003) **Awards:** Named, One of the Best Doctors in America (2001-Present); O'o Award, Native Hawaiian Chamber of Commerce (2015); Distinguished Achievers Award, Saint Louis School Gallery (2013); Guy Milnor Award (2010); Distinguished Eagle Scout Award, Boy Scouts of America (2008); Grand Marshall, Prince Kuhio Parade, Honolulu, HI (2008); Named, Physician of the Year, Hawaii Medical Association (2007); Named, Physician of the Year, Honolulu County Medical Society (2002); Cubmaster Award, Aloha Council, Boy Scouts of America (2000); Scot of the Year, State of Hawaii (1999); Cub Scouter Award, Boy Scouts of America (1999); Guy Milnor Award (1999); Po'okela Award (1999); Paul Harris Fellow (1995); Po'okela Award (1995, 1993, 1991); Research Grantee, Children's Hospital, Philadelphia, PA (1979); Research Grantee, Pacific Health Research Institute, Honolulu, HI (1972-1978); Research Grantee, Kuakini Medical Research Institute, Honolulu, HI (1971) **Membership:** Chair, Continuing Medical Education Committee, Hawaii Medical Association (1987-Present); Governor, Hawaii Chapter, American College of Physicians (2009-2013); President, Ahahui o na Kauka (2004-2006); President, Soroptimist International (1998-1999); The Rotary Club of Metropolitan Honolulu; Master, American College of Physicians; Laureate, Hawaii Chapter, American College of Physicians; Fellow, Internal Medicine, American College of Physicians; American Public Health Association; American Medical Association; Councillor, Hawaii Medical Association; BPO Elks; Delta Omega; Plaza Club **Marquis Who's Who Honors:** Albert Nelson Marquis Lifetime Achievement Award (2017) **To what do you attribute your success:** Dr. Brady attributes his success to listening to his patients and to taking advantage of the opportunities presented to him. **Why did you become involved in your profession or industry:** Since the age of three, Dr. Brady has been interested in helping people and going into the medical field. **What do you consider to be the highlight of your career:** The most rewarding part of Dr. Brady's career is taking care of Hensen's patients of Kalaupapa. **Where will you be in five years:** In five years, he hopes to be right where he is now. **Hobbies:** Singing; Scuba diving; Music **Religion:** Congregationalist **Shipping Address:** 4348 Waialae Ave PMB 534, Honolulu, HI, 96816

Ronald Lee Bramble

Title: President & CEO, Principal **Industry:** Business Management/Business Services **Company Name:** Benson Box, Inc., Bramble & Associates **Date of Birth:** 09/09/1937 **Place of Birth:** Pauls Valley **State:** OK **Parents:** Homer Lee Bramble; Ethyle Juanita (Stephens) Bramble **Marital Status:** Married **Spouse Name:** Kathryn Louise Seiler (7/2/1960) **Children:** Dr. Julia D. Quinlan; Kristin L. Koether-Walker **Education:** Diploma, Biblical Studies, Liberty Bible College and Seminary (2007); Honorary Doctor of Sacred Literature, Berean Christian College and Seminary (1975); JD, St. Mary's University (1975); DBA, Indiana Northern University (1973); MS, Trinity University (1964); BS, Trinity University (1959); AA, San Antonio College (1957) **Certifications:** Certified Leadership Coach, Faith-Based Counselor Training Institute (2006); Certified Member, American Society of Trial Consultants (2002); Certified Lay Speaker, United Methodist Church (1962) **Career:** President, Benson Box, Inc./Freight Mate, San Antonio, TX (2003-Present); Principal, Bramble & Associates (1995-Present); Director, Novatech LLC (1995-2012); Executive Vice President, MegaTronics International Corporation (1995-2003); Comptroller, Telstar Security Systems (1993-1995); Private Consulting Practice (1989-1993); Senior Staff, Ausburn, Astoria & Seale, San Antonio, TX (1984-1989); Vice President, Finance, Solar 21 (1983-1984); Vice President, PIA, Inc. (1982-1983); President, Administrative Research Associates, Inc. (1977-1982); Principal, Ron Bramble Associates, San Antonio, TX (1967-1977); Associate Professor, Department of Management, San Antonio College (1967-1973); Chairman, Department of Management, San Antonio College (1967-1973); Business Training Specialist, San Antonio Independent School District (1965-1967); Business Teacher, San Antonio Independent School District (1961-1965); Manager, FedMart, San Antonio, TX (1960-1961) **Career Related:** Consulting Editor, Prentice-Hall Publishing Co.; Officer/Director, SCP Foundation; President, Aldersgate United Methodist Church; Chairman, Board of Trustees, Aldersgate United Methodist Church; President, United Methodist Men, Aldersgate U.M.C.; Adult Bible Teacher, Aldersgate U.M.C.; Lecturer, Businesses and Church Groups **Civic:** San Antonio Manufacturer's Association; Past President, Administrative Management Society; Past President, Toastmasters International; Past President, Business Education Teacher's Association **Military Service:** U.S. Army Reserves (1960-1965); U.S. Army (1959-1960) **Creative Works:** Inventor, "Shock Resistant Box" (2007); Author, "Leadership Lessons from the Bible" (2005); Contributor, Articles to Professional Journals **Awards:** Life Achievement Award, Aldersgate United Methodist Church (2005); U.S. Law Week Award, St. Mary's University School of Law (1975); Outstanding Educators of America (1972); Merit Award, Administrative Management Society (1968); Distinguished Salesman Award, Sales and Marketing Executives, San Antonio, TX (1967); Outstanding Business Teacher, Administrative Management Society (1965); Honor Graduate, Ft. Sill Artillery School, U.S. Army (1960); Outstanding Soldier, 3rd Training Brigade, Fort Ord, U.S. Army (1959); Wall Street Journal Award, Trinity University (1959) **Membership:** Life Member, Phi Delta Phi; United Methodist Church; Independent Business Leaders; Christian Legal Society; Academy of Management; Toastmasters International **Marquis Who's Who Honors:** Albert Nelson Marquis Lifetime Achievement Award (2017) **To what do you attribute your success:** He attributes his success to hard work, perseverance, along with the love of God and his family. **Why did you become involved in your profession or industry:** Mr. Bramble became involved in his profession because he always sought knowledge and education. **Where will you be in five years:** In five years he will be retired. **Hobbies:** Church activities **Political Affiliations:** Republican **Religion:** Methodist **Business Address:** 5810 Business Park, San Antonio, TX, 78218 **Website:** http://www.rlbramble.com

David W. Brandes

Title: Neurologist, Educator, Multiple Sclerosis and Sleep Specialist **Industry:** Medicine & Health Care **Date of Birth:** 12/24/1943 **Place of Birth:** Elgin **State:** IL **Education:** MD, University of California, Los Angeles (1971); MS in Biochemistry, University of California, Los Angeles (1968); BA in Chemistry, Knox College, Galesburg, IL (1965); Coursework, David Geffen School of Medicine, University of California, Los Angeles Neurology Studies, VA of Greater Los Angeles, Greater Los Angeles Healthcare System; Intern in Medicine, VA Greater Los Angeles Healthcare System **Certifications:** Certification, American Board of Psychiatry and Neurology (1978); Certified Multiple Sclerosis Specialist, Consortium of Multiple Sclerosis Centers Certified in Neurology, American Board of Psychiatry and Neurology, Inc.; Licensed to Practice Medicine, State of California; Licensed to Practice Medicine, State of Tennessee; Diplomate, American Board of Psychiatry and Neurology, Inc.; Certified Specialist, The Consortium of Multiple Sclerosis Centers **Career:** Physician, Multiple Sclerosis Center, Hope Neurology (2009-Present); Clinical Instructor in Neurology, South College, Knoxville, Tennessee (2009-Present); Medical Director, Northridge Hospital Medical Center Sleep Evaluation Center (2009-Present); Medical Director, Rest Analysis (2005-Present); Medical Director, Northridge Multiple Sclerosis Center (Now The Neurology Center of Southern California) (2001-2008); Researcher in Neurology Studies, David Geffen School of Medicine, University of California, Los Angeles Neurology Studies (1990-2008); Assistant Clinical Professor, University of California, Los Angeles (1978-2008); Founder, Director, Northridge Neurological Center (1977-2008) **Creative Works:** Co-author, "Natalizumab Effects on Parameters of Sleep in Patients with Multiple Sclerosis," International Journal of Multiple Sclerosis Care (2016); Co-author, "Assessing risk to birds from industrial wind energy development via paired resource selection models," Conservative Biology (2014); Co-author, "Treatment selection and experience in multiple sclerosis: survey of neurologists," Patient Prefer Adherence (2014); Co-author, "Compliance to fingolimod and other disease modifying treatments in multiple sclerosis patients, a retrospective cohort study," BMC Neurology (2013); Co-author, "A cross-sectional survey of patient satisfaction and subjective experiences of treatment with fingolimod," Patient Prefer Adherence (2013); Co-author, "Implications of real-world adherence on cost-effectiveness analysis in multiple sclerosis," Journal of Medical Economics (2013); Co-author, "Implications of Real-world Adherence on Cost-effectiveness Analysis in Multiple Sclerosis," Journal of Medical Economics (2013); Co-author, "A Cross-sectional Survey of Patient Satisfaction and Subjective Experiences of Treatment With Fingolimod,"Patient Preference and Adherence (2013); Co-author, "Compliance to Fingolimod and Other Disease Modifying Treatments in Multiple Sclerosis Patients, A Retrospective Cohort Study," BMC Neurology (2013); Co-author, "Treatment Selection in Multiple Sclerosis: Results of a Physician Survey," The Consortium of Multiple Sclerosis Centers, Orlando, FL (2013); Co-author, "Impact of Real World Adherence on Effectiveness of First-line DMT's in Multiple Sclerosis," Annual Meeting, American Academy of Neurology (2013); Co-author, "Hidden Disabilities in Multiple Sclerosis-The Impact of Multiple Sclerosis on Patients and Their Caregivers," European Neurological Review (2012); Co-author, "The Manifold Economic Impact of Multiple Sclerosis–Indirect and Direct Costs of Managing Patients," European Neurological Review (2012); Co-author, "Comparison of Compliance to Fingolimod and Other First-Line Disease Modifying Treatments Among Patients with Multiple Sclerosis," Academy of Managed Care Pharmacy, Cincinnati, OH (2012); Co-author, "Quantifying the role of natalizumab in health and economic outcomes in multiple sclerosis," American Journal of Managed Care (2010); Co-author, "The role of glatiramer acetate in the early treatment of multiple sclerosis," Neuropsychiatric Disease Treatment (2010); Co-author, "Invited commentary. Efficacy and safety of mitoxantrone, as an initial therapy, in multiple sclerosis: experience in an Indian tertiary care setting," Neurology India (2009); Co-author, "A review of disease-modifying therapies for MS: maximizing adherence and minimizing adverse events," Current Medical Residents Opinion (2009); Co-author, "Factors that influence adherence with disease-modifying therapy in MS," Journal of Neurology (2009); Co-author, "Redefining functionality and treatment efficacy in multiple sclerosis," Neurology (2009); Co-author, "Managing adverse effects of disease-modifying agents used for treatment of multiple sclerosis," Current Medical Residents Opinion (2008) **Awards:** Honoree, Regional Top Doctor; Top Doctor Award, Castle Connolly Medical Ltd. **Membership:** Stroke Council, American Heart Association, Inc.; The Consortium of Multiple Sclerosis Centers **Marquis Who's Who Honors:** Albert Nelson Marquis Lifetime Achievement Award (2017) **Shipping Address:** 2060 Lakeside Centre Way, Knoxville, TN, 37922

Stephen Jon Brandow

Title: Catholic Priest, Diocesan Scout Chaplain **Industry:** Religious **Company Name:** The Diocese of Alexandria **Date of Birth:** 12/25/1960 **Place of Birth:** Olean **State:** NY **Parents:** David Arden Brandow; Jacqueline Delores (Johns) Brandow **Education:** MDiv, Notre Dame Seminary Graduate School of Theology (1996); BA in Social Work, Northwestern State University (1985); BA, Northwestern State University (1983) **Certifications:** Ordained to Ministry, Catholic Church (1996) **Career:** Staff Chaplain, Department of Veteran Affairs, Alexandria, LA (2000-Present); Associate Pastor, Immaculate Heart of Mary Parish, Tioga, LA (1997-2000); Associate Pastor, St. Rita Parish, Alexandria, LA (1996-1997); Medical Clerk, Alexandria VA Health Care System, U.S. Department of Veterans Affairs (1986-1991); Social Worker, Woodview Regional Hospital, Pineville, LA (1986) **Career Related:** Chaplain, Alexandria VA Health Care System, U.S. Department of Veterans Affairs (1998-Present); Committee Member, Continuing Formation of Clergy (1996-Present); James E. West Fellowship (2002); Chaplain, CHRISTUS St. Frances Cabrini Hospital, Alexandria, LA (1997-2001); Chaplain, Central Louisiana State Hospital, Louisiana State Department of Health (1997-2000); Secretary, Diocese of Alexandria, Louisiana (1996-1997) **Civic:** Community Advisory Board, Louisiana Purchase Council, Boy Scouts of America (2003-Present); National Catholic Committee on Scouting (1997-Present); Board of Directors, Council of Central Louisiana, Girl Scouts of the United States of America (2001-2002); Vice President, Louisiana Purchase Council, Boy Scouts of America **Awards:** Bronze Pelican, National Catholic Committee on Scouting (2003); Whitney M. Young Jr. Service Award, Boy Scouts of America (2002) **Membership:** Board of Directors, Louisiana Chaplains Association, Inc. (1999-2002); America Association of Christian Counselors; National Conference of Veterans Affairs Catholic Chaplains; Chairman of the Board, NAVAC; National Association of Catholic Chaplains **Marquis Who's Who Honors:** Albert Nelson Marquis Lifetime Achievement Award (2017); Distinguished Humanitarian (2017) **Hobbies:** Yoga **Shipping Address:** PO Box 39, Tioga, LA, 71477

William A. Brandt Jr.

Title: Executive Chairman **Industry:** Business Management/Business Services **Company Name:** Development Specialists Inc. **Date of Birth:** 09/05/1949 **Place of Birth:** Chicago **State:** IL **Parents:** William Arthur Brandt; Joan Virginia (Ashworth) Brandt **Marital Status:** Married **Spouse Name:** Patrice Bugelas (1/19/1980) **Children:** Katherine Ashworth; William George; Joan Patrice; John Peter **Education:** ABD in Sociology, The University of Chicago (1974); MA in Sociology, The University of Chicago (1972); BA in Sociology and Urban Affairs, Saint Louis University, with Honors (1971) **Career:** Executive Chairman, Development Specialists Inc., Chicago, IL (2017-Present); Consultant, Development Specialists Inc., Chicago, IL (1976-Present); Commentator, Station WBBM-AM, Chicago, IL (1977); President, Chief Executive Officer, Development Specialists Inc., Chicago, IL (1976-2017); Employee, Melaniphy & Associates, Inc., Chicago, IL (1975-1976); Assistant to President, Pyro Mining Company, Chicago, IL (1972-1974) **Career Related:** Member, Illinois Broadband Deployment Council (2010-2015); Chair, Illinois Finance Authority (2008-2015); Member, Advisory Board, Social Welfare, "Social Planning & Social Development: An International Database," Sociological Abstracts Inc., San Diego, CA (1979-1983); Visiting Research Associate, Department of Government, Harvard University (1972); Former Part-Time Member, Faculties, College of DuPage, Glen Ellyn, IL; Former Part-Time Member, Faculties, Thornton Community College, South Holland, IL; Speaker in Field; Panel Member, Numerous Conferences **Civic:** Chairman, National Advisory Council, Institute of Governmental Studies, University of California, Berkeley, CA (2016); Illinois Delegate, Democratic National Convention (2008); Board of Trustees, Loyola University, Chicago, IL (2007-2016); Board of Directors, Future Music Inc., San Francisco, CA (2006-2009); Board of Directors, Bay Area Bankrupt Forum (2003-2012); Member, Democratic Party Platform Committee (2000); Member, Florida Delegate, Democratic National Convention (1996); Life Trustee, Fenwick High School, Oak Park, IL; Lifetime Trustee, Commercial Law League of America; Lifetime Trustee, International Council of Shopping Centers; Lifetime Trustee, National Association of Bankruptcy Trustees; Lifetime Trustee, Illinois Sociological Association; Lifetime Trustee, Midwest Sociological Society; Lifetime Trustee, Urban Land Institute; Board of Trustees, Tina's Wish, The Honorable Tina Brozman Foundation; Governing Member, Chicago Symphony Orchestra Association **Awards:** The La Verne Noyes Scholarship for Graduate Training, The University of Chicago (1971-1974); Ford Foundation Research and Training Grant, Demography Population, Research Center, The University of Chicago (1971-1972); Nominee, Woodrow Wilson Scholarship, Saint Louis University (1971) **Membership:** Board of Directors, Bay Area Bankruptcy Forum (2003-2012); Commission to Study the Reform of Chapter 11, American Bankruptcy Institute; International Insolvency Institute; International Exchange of Experience on Insolvency Law; Los Angeles Bankruptcy Forum; Union League Club of Chicago; Clinton/Gore '96 National Finance Board; Lifetime Member, Zoo Miami Foundation; New York Institute of Credit; California Receivers Forum; Professional Association of Diving Instructors; Alpha Sigma Nu; Co-Commissioner, Labor and Benefits Advisory Committee, American Bankruptcy Institute; Co-Commissioner, Administrative Claims Advisory Committee, American Bankruptcy Institute; Board of Advisors, Annual Bankruptcy Battleground West Seminar, American Bankruptcy Institute; Former Member, Board of Directors, American Bankruptcy Institute; Central Florida Bankruptcy Law Association; Former Member, Bankruptcy Section Executive Council, Commercial Law League of America; Former Member, National Governmental Affairs Committee, Commercial Law League of America; Former Member, National Conference of Bankruptcy Judges Planning Committee, Commercial Law League of America; INSOL International **Political Affiliations:** Democrat **Religion:** Roman Catholic **Shipping Address:** 1134 Sheridan Rd, Winnetka, IL, 60093

Lewis Branscomb, LHD

Title: Physicist **Industry:** Sciences **Company Name:** University of California **Date of Birth:** 08/17/1926 **Place of Birth:** Asheville **State:** NC **Parents:** Bennett Harvie Branscomb; Margaret (Vaughan) Branscomb **Marital Status:** Married **Spouse Name:** Constance Mulli Branscomb; Margaret Anne Wells (Deceased 10/1997) **Children:** Harvie Hammond; Katharine C. Branscomb Kelley **Education:** DPP, Carnegie Mellon University (2000); Honorary DEng, Colorado School of Mines (1999); PhD, Harvard University (1949); MS, Harvard University (1947); AB, Duke University, Summa Cum Laude (1945); Honorary LHD, Pace University; Honorary DSc, State University of New York at Binghamton; Honorary DSc, University of Notre Dame; DSc, Lehigh University; Honorary DSc, Rutgers, The State University of New Jersey; Honorary DSc, Pratt Institute; Honorary DSc, University of Alabama; Honorary DSc, Lycoming College; Honorary DSc, Western Michigan University; Honorary DSc, University of Colorado; Honorary DSc, Rochester University; Honorary DSc, Clarkson College; Honorary DSc, Polytechnic Institute of New York; Honorary DSc, Duke University **Career:** Distinguished Research Fellow, Institute for Global Conflict and Cooperation, University of California (2007-Present); Adjunct Professor, School of Global Policy and Strategy, University of California, San Diego (2005-Present); Director, Belfer Center for Science and International Affairs (2001-Present); Professor Emeritus, Harvard University, Cambridge, MA (1996-Present); Aetna Professor, Public Policy and Corporate Management, Harvard University, Cambridge, MA (1994-1996); Albert Pratt Public Service Professor, Kennedy School of Government, Harvard University, Cambridge, MA (1988-1994); Director, Science and Technology Policy Program, Kennedy School of Government, Harvard University, Cambridge, MA (1986-1996); Member, Corporate Management Board, IBM, Armonk, NY (1983-1986); Chief Scientist, Vice President, IBM, Armonk, NY (1972-1986); Director, National Bureau of Standards (1969-1972); Chairman, Joint Institute Laboratory of Astrophysics, University of Colorado (1968-1969); Professor, Physics, University of Colorado (1962-1969); Chief, Laboratory of Astrophysics Division, National Bureau of Standards, Boulder, CO (1962-1969); Chairman, Joint Institute Laboratory of Astrophysics, University of Colorado (1962-1965); Chief, Atomic Physics Division, National Bureau of Standards (1960-1962); Visiting staff member, University College, London (1957-1958); Chief, Atomic Physics Section, National Bureau of Standards, Washington (1954-1960); Lecturer, Physics, University of Maryland (1952-1954); Instructor, Physics, Harvard University (1950-1951) **Career Related:** Director, Lord Corporation (1987-Present); Research Associate, Scripps Institution of Oceanography, University of California, San Diego (2005-Present); Laspau, Harvard University (2002-2003); Chairman, National Information Infrastructure (2000); Harvie Branscomb Distinguished Visiting Professor, Vanderbilt University (1999-2000); Woods Hole Oceanographic Institution (1993-1998); National Geographical Society (1984-2001); Trustee, Vanderbilt University (1980-2003); Trustee, Carnegie Institution (1973-1990) **Civic:** Founder, Lewis M. Branscomb Forum; Commission on Global Information Infrastructure (1995-Present) **Creative Works:** Author, "Seeds of Disaster, Roots of Response" (2006); Author, "Making America Safer" (2002); Author, "Taking Technical Risks" (2001); Author, "Industrializing Knowledge" (1999); Author, "Investing in Innovation" (1998); Author, "Korea at the Turning Point" (1996); Author, "Confessions of a Technophile" (1995); Author, "Empowering Technology" (1993); Editor, Reviews of Modern Physics (1968-1973) **Awards:** Recipient, Centennial Medal, Harvard University (2002); Recipient, Prize for Information And Telecommunications, Ohkawa Foundation (1998); Recipient, Vannevar Bush Award, National Science Board (2001); Recipient, William Procter Prize for Scientific Achievement, Research Society of America (1972); Recipient, Career Service Award, National Civil Service League (1968); Recipient, Samuel Wesley Stratton Award, Department of Commerce (1966); Recipient, Arthur Flemming Award, D.C. Junior Chamber of Commerce (1962); Recipient, Gold Medal for Exceptional Service, Department of Commerce (1961); Recipient, Rockefeller Public Service Award (1957-1958); Junior Fellow, Harvard Society of Fellows (1949-1951); Fellow, United States Public Health Service (1948-1949) **Membership:** Fellow, American Physical Society; American Association for the Advancement of Science; American Academy of Arts and Sciences; National Academy of Sciences, National Academy of Engineering; Engineering Academy of Japan; Russian Academy of Science; Washington Academy of Sciences; National Academy of Public Administration; American Philosophical Society; Phi Beta Kappa; Union of Concerned Scientists; Center for Science and Democracy; Sigma Xi; The Einstein Society **Marquis Who's Who Honors:** Albert Nelson Marquis Lifetime Achievement Award (2017) **Shipping Address:** 1600 Ludington Ln, La Jolla, CA, 92037

Rose M. Brault

Title: Advanced Registered Nurse Practitioner, Educator **Industry:** Medicine & Health Care **Date of Birth:** 04/20/1944 **Place of Birth:** Gadsden **State:** AL **Parents:** Dr. Clement Edmond Brault; Elizabeth Mary (McGuinn) Brault **Marital Status:** Widow **Spouse Name:** Dr. Stephen G. Gerzof (5/1974, Divorced 6/1979); Robert E. Lawrence (12/1992, Deceased 11/2001) **Children:** David G. Richard **Education:** EdD, Boston University, Boston, MA (1985); MSN, Boston University, Boston, MA (1977); BSN, Boston College, Chestnut Hill, MA (1966); Adult Nurse Practitioner, Post Master's Certificate, University of Florida, Gainesville, FL (1996) **Certifications:** Certified Adult Nurse Practitioner, American Academy of Nurse Practitioners Certification Board, Inc. **Career:** Advanced Registered Nurse Practitioner, Samaritan Touch Care Center (2015-Present); ARNP-Part Time, Ray H. Tangunan (2008-Present); Adjunct Associate Professor, American Sentinel University (2012-2015); Associate Professor, South University, Tampa, FL (2007-2015); Assistant Professor, Florida Southern College (2004-2007); Nurse Practitioner, Good Shepherd Hospice (2002-2004); Nurse Practitioner, Health Essentials Inc. (2002-2004); Nurse Practitioner, Heartland Internal Medicine Association (2000-2002); Nurse Practitioner, Florida Physicians Medical Group, Sebring, FL (1998-2000); Nurse Practitioner, Department of Veteran Affairs, Bay Pines, FL (1997-1998); Director, Health Education Services, Florida Institute for Neurologic Rehabilitation (1996-1997); Quality Improvement Practitioner, Volusia County Public Health Department, Daytona Beach, FL (1995-1996); Instructor, University of Central Florida (1994-1995); Consultant, Quality Assurance, HCA Grant Center and Charter Springs Hospital, Ocala, FL (1991); Instructor, Pediatric Nursing, Medical-Surgical Nursing, Central Florida Community College, Ocala, FL (1990-1994); Director, Professional Services Review, Massachusetts Eye and Ear Infirmary, Boston, MA (1981-1988); Director, Quality Assurance, St. Elizabeth's Hospital, Boston, MA (1979-1981); Medical Clinical Coordinator, University Hospital, Boston, MA (1973-1974); Staffing Coordinator, University Hospital, Boston, MA (1972-1973); Nursing Instructor, University Hospital, Boston, MA (1971-1972); Nursing Instructor, Whidden Memorial Hospital, Everett, MA (1968-1971); Nurse, Boston Floating Hospital (1967-1968); Nurse, Boston City Hospital (1964-1967) **Career Related:** Chairman, Annual Fundraising, Massachusetts Eye and Ear Infirmary, Boston, MA (1987); Adjunct Faculty, Boston College, Curry College, University of Massachusetts, Simmons College, Northeastern University (1979-1988) **Civic:** Board of Directors, Avon Park Lakes Association, Avon Park, FL (2015-Present); Choir Member, Lady of Grace Catholic Church, Avon Park, FL (2001-2016) **Creative Works:** Contributor, Articles, Professional Journals **Awards:** Fellow, American Association of Nurse Practitioners (2009); Outstanding Professor of the Quarter, South University, Tampa, FL. (2009) **Membership:** Founding President, Phi Beta Chapter, Sigma Theta Tau for South University, Tampa, FL. (2012); American Association of Nurse Practitioners; Florida Nurses Association; American Nurses Association **To what do you attribute your success:** Her success is directly related to her parents' love and support. They were both professionally educated and fully supported her public and private school education. Learning, education, and caring for people and animals have always been an important part of her interests and activism. **Why did you become involved in your profession or industry:** She became involved in her profession because of her drive to care for others. **What do you consider to be the highlight of your career:** She is most proud of having been elected as fellow of the American Academy of Nurse Practitioners. Another great source of pride for her is seeing very sick patients recover and return to their lives. **Hobbies:** Learning; Taking care of pets; Gardening-landscaping **Religion:** Catholic **Shipping Address:** 2120 N Shamrock Rd, Avon Park, FL, 33825

Fred James Brenner

Title: Biology Professor **Industry:** Education/Educational Services **Company Name:** Grove City College **Date of Birth:** 12/25/1936 **Place of Birth:** Warren **State:** OH **Parents:** Frederick James Brenner; Katherine Louise (Newberry) Brenner **Marital Status:** Married **Spouse Name:** Patricia Elaine Gavin (8/27/1967) **Children:** Elaine; Cheryl **Education:** PhD, The Pennsylvania State University (1964); MS, The Pennsylvania State University (1960); BS, Thiel College (1958) **Career:** Professor, Grove City College, Pennsylvania (1986-Present); Associate Professor, Grove City College (1970-1986); Assistant Professor of Biology, Grove City College (1969-1970); Assistant Professor of Biology, Thiel College (1965-1969); Teaching Intern, Denison University (1964-1965) **Career Related:** President, Brenner Ecological Service, Grove City College (1974-Present) **Civic:** Council President, French Creek Council (2007-Present); Secretary-Treasurer, The Mercer County Conservation District (1975-Present); Past Chairman, Mercer County Solid Waste Authority (1988-2015); Treasurer, Mercer County Regional Planning Commission (1989-1993); Vice-Chairman, Mercer County Regional Planning Commission (1989-1993); Chairman, Mercer County Regional Planning Commission (1989-1993); Mercer County Regional Planning Commission (1989-1993); Committee Chair, Mercer County Regional Planning Commission (1989-1993); Secretary, Mercer County Regional Planning Commission (1990); Director of Woodbadge Course, Boy Scouts of America (1973-1989) **Creative Works:** Editor, "Forests: A Global Perspective" (2005); Editor, "Wildlife Disease: Landscape Epidemiology Spatial Distribution and Utilization Remote Sensing Technology" (2005); Editor, "Biological Diversity: Problems and Consequences, Environmental Contaminants, Ecosystems and Human Health" (1995); Editor, "Wetlands Ecology and Conservation Emphasis in Pennsylvania" (1989); Editor, "Environmental Consequences of Energy Production" (1987); Editor, "Endangered and Threatened Species Program in Pennsylvania" (1986); Editor, "Species Special Concern Pennsylvania" (1985); Newsletter Editor, Pennsylvania Academy of Science (1966); Contributor, Articles Professional Journals **Awards:** Recipient, Distinguished Citizen Award, Boy Scouts of America (2004); Recipient, Distinguished Alumni Service Award, Alpha Phi Omega National Service Fraternity (1994, 2004); Recipient, Community Service Award, Grove City Area United Way (1993); Recipient, National Conservation Award, National Society Daughters of the American Revolution (1989); Recipient, District Award Merit, Boy Scouts of America (1976); Recipient, Silver Beaver Award, Boy Scouts of America (1973); Recipient, Lifetime Achievement Award, Pennsylvania Academy of Science; Recipient, Yokley Faculty Service Award, TriBeta **Membership:** District Governor, Rotary International (2007-Present); Vice President, TriBeta (1993-Present); Executive Council, Pennsylvania Academy of Science (1986-Present); President, National Association of Academies of Science (1999-2000); President-Elect, National Association of Academies of Science (1998-1999); Secretary, National Association of Academies of Science (1995-1998); President-Elect, Pennsylvania Academy of Science (1994-1996); President-Elect, Pennsylvania Academy of Science (1992-1994); Executive Council, Ecological Society of America (1978-1982); President, Pennsylvania Chapter, The Wildlife Society (1975-1977); Fellow, American Association for the Advancement of Science; Fellow, The Ohio Academy of Science **Hobbies:** Hunting; Fishing; Hiking; Camping **Political Affiliations:** Republican **Religion:** Episcopalian **Business Address:** 100 Campus Drive, Grove City, PA, 16127

Bonnie S. Briggs

Title: School Librarian, Minister **Industry:** Religious **Company Name:** Refuge Ministries & Outreach **Date of Birth:** 06/17/1947 **Place of Birth:** Paintsville **State:** KY **Parents:** Charles Baldwin; Joyce Baldwin **Marital Status:** Married **Spouse Name:** Ronald Briggs (1/26/1986) **Children:** Dawn Elaine Kauffman; Kristy Lynn Heath; Joy Ellen Hilderbrand; Mistie Sue Stephenson **Education:** AA, Liberty Bible College (Now Liberty Bible College & Seminary) (1989) **Certifications:** Certified in General Bible Studies, Liberty Bible College (1989); Licentiate, Refuge Ministerial Fellowship **Career:** Minister, Refuge Ministries (Now Refuge Ministries & Outreach), West Union, OH (1995-Present); Librarian, Ohio Valley Local Schools (Now Adams County Ohio Valley School District), West Union, OH (1994-2009) **Career Related:** Missionary, International Focus Ministries, Columbus, OH (2004-Present); Refuge Ministerial Fellowship **Civic:** Church Liaison, Christian Coalition of America, Washington, DC (2004-Present) **Creative Works:** Contributing Poet, "Anthology: Best 200 Poets of 2003" **Hobbies:** Traveling; Writing; Gardening **Political Affiliations:** Conservative **Religion:** Protestant **Shipping Address:** 1033 Tobe Lewis Road, Lynx, OH, 45650 **Website:** http://www.mercyministries.org

Allen Stephen Brings

Title: Musician, Educator, Professor Emeritus **Industry:** Education/Educational Services **Date of Birth:** 02/24/1934 **Place of Birth:** New York **State:** NY **Parents:** Adam Brings; Elfrieda (Kruse) Brings **Marital Status:** Married **Spouse Name:** Genevieve Chinn (8/29/1959) **Children:** Keira **Education:** DMA, Boston University, Boston, MA (1964); Postgraduate Work, Princeton University, Princeton, NJ (1963); Naumburg Fellow, Princeton University (1962); MA, Columbia University, New York, NY (1957); BA, Queens College, Magna Cum Laude (1955) **Career:** Professor Emeritus of Music, Aaron Copland School of Music, Queens College of the City University of New York (1963-Present); Teacher and Associate Director, Weston Music Center and School of the Performing Arts, Weston, CT (1960-Present); Teaching Fellow, Boston University (1960-1962); Instructor of Music, Bard College, Annandale-on-Hudson, NY (1959-1960); Coordinator, Theory and Ear Training Program **Career Related:** Composer; Pianist **Civic:** Catholic Commission on Intellectual and Cultural Affairs **Military Service:** US Army (1957-1959) **Creative Works:** Composer, "4 Revelations of Varying Intensities," Mira Music Associates (2017); Composer, "Duo for flute and piano" (2017); Composer, "3 Scintillae" (2017); Composer, "All Around and About" (2017); Composer, "A Poetic Reflection" (2018); Composer, Duologue 18b (2018); Composer, "To the Point" (2016); Composer, "Sonata for Two Violins" (2016); Composer, "Duologue 18" (2016); Composer, "Reverie" (2016); Composer, "Etchings" (2016); Composer, "A Linear Pursuit" (2016); Composer, "Four Differential Equations" (2016); Composer, "High and Low" (2015); Composer, "Notable Declamations" (2015); Composer, "Quartet" (2015); Composer, "Not So Serious" (2015); Composer, "Touch and Go" (2015); Composer, "Again and Again" (2015); Composer, "From Within and Without" (2014); Composer, "Duologue 17" (2014); Composer, "A Linear Engagement" (2014); Composer, "2 by 4" (2013); Composer, "Varied Intensities" (2013); Composer, "Duologue 15" (2013); Composer, "Projections All at Once" (2013); Composer, "Sinfonia da Camera" (1990); Composer, "Symphony" (1984); Composer, "Trio" (1984); Composer, "Five Pieces for Piano" (1980); Composer, "Tre Sonetti" (1975); Composer, "Music for Keyboard Instruments by Allen Brings," Parma Recordings, Navona; Composer, "Music for Voices by Allen Brings," Parma Recordings, Navona **Awards:** Grantee, Connecticut Commission on the Arts (1988); John Castellini Silver Jubilee Award, Choral Society, Queens College (1983) **Membership:** American Society of Composers (1975-Present); Chairman, Region II, Society of Composers, Inc. (1968-1971); National Association of Composers; Connecticut Alliance for Music, Inc.; The College Music Society; Connecticut Composers Inc.; Society for Catholic Liturgy; The Phi Beta Kappa Society **Marquis Who's Who Honors:** Albert Nelson Marquis Lifetime Achievement Award (2017) **Hobbies:** Tennis **Shipping Address:** 199 Mountain Rd, Wilton, CT, 06897 **Website:** http://www.library.newmusicusa.org/allenbrings

John Carrigan Britt

Title: History Professor (Retired), Academic Administrator (Retired) **Industry:** Education/Educational Services **Company Name:** Lee College **Date of Birth:** 03/21/1937 **Place of Birth:** Little Rock **State:** AR **Marital Status:** Married **Spouse Name:** Donna Lynn Montgomery (2/28/1985) **Children:** Wendy Carrigan; Elizabeth Hamilton Yollan **Education:** MA in History, Sam Houston State University, Huntsville, TX (1968); Graduate in History and Political Science, University of Houston, University Park, TX (1963); BS in History, Sam Houston State University, Huntsville, TX (1959); AA, Lee College (1957) **Career:** Honors Program Director, Lee College (1995-2013); History Professor, Lee College (1964-2013); History Teacher, Robert E. Lee High School, Baytown, TX (1959-1963); President, Monica Boyd Literacy Foundation, Baytown, TX **Career Related:** Teacher, Lee College Largest Prison Education Programs (2016-Present); Teacher, Sugarland Unit, Ellis 1 and Ellis 2, Ferguson, The Walls Unit, Huntsville, TX; Managing Editor, Touchston; Co-Founder, Second Chance Texas Department of Criminal Justice **Civic:** Board Member, Texas State Historic Association, Denton, TX (2004-Present); Board Member, Friends of Eddie Gray Wetlands Center, Baytown, TX (2003-Present); Member, Board of Directors, National Collegiate Honors Council, Lincoln, NE (2008-2009); Executive Committee, Chambers County Historic Commission, Anahuac, TX (2005); Treasurer, Monica Boyd Literacy Foundation, Baytown, TX; Commission, Chambers County Historical Commission; Historian, Texas House of Representatives **Creative Works:** Author, Historical Anthology, "From Humble Beginnings"; Editor, Historical Anthology, Baytown Vignettes; **Awards:** Recipient, Betty Trap Chapman Award, Houston History Alliance (2015); Grant, Summerlee Foundation (2015); Recognition for Work as an Historian, Texas House of Representatives (2013); Exemplary Service Award, Texas State Historical Association (2013); John

Britt Endowed Honors Chair, Lee College Board of Regents (2007); Humanities Texas Grant (2004); Grant, Summerlee Foundation (2003); Fifth Rockwell Foundation (2002); Association of Community College Trustees (2000); Texas State Historical Association (1999); Ima Hogg Achievement Award, Center of American History, University of Texas, Austin, TX (1997); Certificate of Commendation, American Association for State and Local History (1993); **Membership:** Education Committee,Texas State Historical Association (1995-2015); Elected Honorary Life Member, Great Plains Honors Council (2011); Lifetime Member, Board of Directors, Texas State Historical Association (2005-2010); Board of Directors, National Collegiate Honors Council (2008-2009); President, Elected Honorary Life Member, Great Plains Honors Council (2002-2003); Chambers County, Texas Historical Commission; President, Monica Boyd Literature Foundation, Baytown, TX; Texas Community College Teachers Association; Lifetime Member, American Studies Association; Lifetime Member, East Texas Historical Association; Lifetime Member, Bay Area Heritage Society; Community College Humanities Association; Chambers County Historic Commission **Marquis Who's Who Honors:** Albert Nelson Marquis Lifetime Achievement Award (2017) **Shipping Address:** 5130 Cotton Lake Rd, Cove, TX, 77523 **Website:** http://www.johncbritt.com

Stanley Heard Brobston

Title: Music Educator, Writer **Industry:** Education/Educational Services **Date of Birth:** 04/28/1937 **Place of Birth:** Jacksonville **State:** FL **Parents:** Stanley Prentiss Brobston; Elizabeth Lawrence Brobston **Marital Status:** Married **Spouse Name:** Sandra Holloway (8/22/1964) **Children:** Stanley Holloway; Stephen Henry **Education:** PhD, New York University (1977); MusM, University of Georgia, Athens, GA (1967); BS in Education, Georgia Southern University, Statesboro, GA (1958) **Career:** Music Educator, Syosset Public Schools (1969-1998) **Career Related:** Speaker, Field Zone 13; Representative, New York State School Music Association **Civic:** Chairman, Applying County Heritage Center, Baxley, GA **Military Service:** Lieutenant Jet Carrier Pilot, U.S. Naval Reserve, Vietnam (1959-1965) **Creative Works:** Author, "Daddy Sang Lead: The History and Performance Practice of White Southern Gospel Music" (2006) **Awards:** Community Service Award, Daughters of the American Revolution (2005); Builder Brotherhood Award, National Conference of Christians and Jews, Long Island, NY (1974); Decorated Vietnam Service Medal, U.S. Naval Reserve **Membership:** Retired Educators; Lions Club; Lifetime Member, Vietnam Veterans of America; Lifetime Member, Gospel Music Association; Kappa Phi Kappa; Phi Delta Kappa; Phi Mu Alpha Sinfonia **Marquis Who's Who Honors:** Albert Nelson Marquis Lifetime Achievement Award (2017) **Hobbies:** Flying; Church choir **Shipping Address:** 2598 Buck Head Rd, Baxley, GA, 31513

Arthur J. Brochu

Title: President **Industry:** Nonprofit & Philanthropy **Company Name:** Art Cycles Canada for Wishes **Education:** Associate's Degree, University of Alberta, Edmonton, Alberta, Canada (2005) **Career:** President, New Forces Ltd. (2015-Present); Chief Executive Officer, New Forces (2012-Present); Safety Specialist, Canadian Society of Safety Engineering (1992-Present); President, Art Cycles Canada for Wishes **Military Service:** Warrant Officer, Canadian Armed Forces **Awards:** Lions Club International; Society of Safety Engineers **Hobbies:** Long-distance cycling **Shipping Address:** PO Box 732, AB, Alberta Beach, Canada, T0E 0A0 **Website:** https://www.linkedin.com/in/art-brochu-28225211/?ppe=1

Robert Mark Brooks, PhD

Title: Associate Professor **Industry:** Education/Educational Services **Company Name:** Temple University **Parents:** Krishnamurthy Brooks; Vara Lakshmi (Kavaturu) Tangella Brooks **Education:** PhD, Indian Institute of Technology Kharagpur, Kharagpur, India (1990); Doctorate in Engineering, University of California, Berkeley (1989); MS in Civil Engineering, University of California, Berkeley (1988); Bachelor of Technology in Civil Engineering, Sri Venkateswara University (1979) **Certifications:** Registered Professional Engineer, State of Pennsylvania **Career:** Associate Professor of Civil Engineering, Temple University, Philadelphia, PA (1996-Present); Assistant Professor of Civil Engineering, Temple University, Philadelphia, PA (1991-1996); Assistant Research Engineer, Institute of Transportation Studies, University of California, Berkeley (1989-1990); Associate Professor, Department of Civil and Environmental Engineering, Temple University, Philadelphia, PA **Creative Works:** Co-Author, "Geotechnical Properties of Problem Soils Stabilized with Fly Ash and Limestone Dust in Philadelphia," American Society of Civil Engineers (2011); Co-Author, "Modeling Resilient Modulus Hysteretic Behavior with Moisture Variation," International Journal of Geomechanics, American Society of Civil Engineers (2011); Co-Author, "Removal of Mercury from Contaminated Water," Journal of Information Systems Technology & Planning (2011); Co-Author, "Effects of Fly Ash on Engineering Properties of Clays," International Journal of Applied Engineering Research (2011); Co-Author, "Properties of Palm Nut Fiber-Reinforced Cement Composite Containing Pulverized Kernel Shell as Supplementary Material," Journal of Materials in Civil Engineers, American Society of Civil Engineers (2011); Co-Author, "Assessment of Micro-Structural Development in a Cementiously Stabilized Aggregate Base Using Analytical Techniques," International Journal of Applied Engineering Research (2011); Author, "Soil Stabilization with Lime and RHA," International Journal of Applied Engineering (2010); Co-Author, "Imo Lateritic Soil As Sorbent For Heavy Metals in Contaminant Barrier," International Journal of Research & Reviews in Applied Sciences (2010); Co-Author, "Effect of Non-standard Curing Methods on the Compressive Strength of Laterized Concrete," ARPN Journal of Engineering and Applied Sciences (2010); Co-Author, "Properties of Alkali Activated Fly Ash: High Performance to Lightweight," International Journal of Sustainable Engineering, Taylor and Francis (2010); Co-Author, "Removal of Lead From Contaminated Water," International Journal of Soil, Sediment and Water (2010); Co-Author, "Early Prediction of Laterized Concrete Strength by Accelerating Testing," International Journal of Research & Reviews in Applied Sciences (2010); Author, "Influence of Vehicular Interaction on PCU Values," United Kingdom Institute of Civil Engineers, Transport Journal (2010); Author, "Influence of Roadway Width and Volume to Capacity Ratio on PCU Values," Transport Problems, Gliwice, Poland (2010); Co-Author, "Removal of Lead From Contaminated Water," International Journal of Soil, Sediment and Water (2010); Co-Author, "Stiffness and Drainage Characteristics of Unbound Aggregate Bases," International Journal of Geotechnical Engineering, J. Ross Publishing, Inc. (2010); Co-Author, "Performance of a Stabilized Aggregate Base Subject to Different Durability Procedures," Journal of Materials in Civil Engineering, American Society of Civil Engineers (2010); Co-Author, "Influence of Specimen Geometry on the Strengths of Laterized Concrete," International Journal of Research & Reviews in Applied Sciences (2010); Co-Author, "Residual Composition Strength of Laterized Concrete Subjected to Elevated Temperatures," Research Journal of Applied Sciences, Engineering and Technology, Maxwell Scientific (2010); Author, "Soil Stabilization with RHA and Flyash," International Journal of Research and Reviews in Applied Sciences (2009) **Awards:** Recipient, Commendation Letter for Excellent Service as an American Red Cross Volunteer, President Trump (2018); Recipient, Commendation Letter for Dedication, Commitment, Enrichment and Aspirations for New Generations of Scientists and Innovators, Former President Barack Obama (2016); Recipient, National Outstanding Teacher Award, American Society For Engineering Education (2015); Named, Teacher of the Year, College of Engineering, Temple University, Philadelphia, PA (2008) **Membership:** Vice Chairman, Committee on Dissemination of Failure Information, Council on Forensic Engineering, American Society of Civil Engineers (2007); College Promotion and Tenure Committee (2004-2011); Coordinator of Environment, Temple University (2004-2009); President, Philadelphia Chapter, Pennsylvania Society of Professional Engineers (2001-2002); Secretary, Committee on Dissemination of Failure Information, Council on Forensic Engineering, American Society of Civil Engineers (2000-2007) **Business Address:** 1217 W Jefferson St Rm 523, Philadelphia, PA, 19122

Charles K. Brown, PhD

Title: Chief of Surgery, Medical Director of Surgical Oncology **Industry:** Medicine & Health Care **Company Name:** Midwestern Regional Medical Center **Education:** MD, University of Florida (1992); PhD, Virology, University College of Medicine; BA, Interdisciplinary Studies in Biological Medicine **Certifications:** Pennsylvania State Medical License (1995-2018); Oklahoma State Medical License (2015-2018); Georgia State Medical License (2012-2017); Illinois State Medical License (2000-2017); American Board of Surgery; National Board of Medical Examiners **Career:** Medical Director, Surgery, Midwestern Regional Medical Center; Surgical Oncologist **Career Related:** Research Fellow, National Cancer Institute/National Institutes of Health, Bethesda, MD; Fellow, Biological Therapy, University of Pittsburgh Medical Center; Fellow, Surgical Oncology, University of Chicago Medical Center **Creative Works:** Co-Author, "Holland-Frei Manual of Cancer Medicine" (2005); Author, "Multicenter, Phase II Study of Axitinib, A Selective Second-Generation Inhibitor of Vascular Endothelial Growth Factor Receptors 1,2, and 3, in Patients with Metastatic Melanoma," Clinical Cancer Research; Author, "Phase I Study of Hyperthermic Isolated Hepatic Perfusion with Oxaliplatin in the Treatment of Unresectable Liver Metastases from Colorectal Cancer," Annals of Surgical Oncology **Awards:** Chicago Magazine Top Doctors, Surgery, Chicago Magazine (2017); Top Cancer Doctors, Newsweek (2016); Federal Executive Board's Excellence in Government Award for Research; Robert Baker Golden Apple Award for Excellence in Teaching, Department of Surgery, University of Chicago; Charles E. Huggins Research Award, Department of Surgery, University of Chicago; Top Doctors, Castle-Connolly **Membership:** American College of Surgeons; American Society of Clinical Oncology; Society of Surgical Oncology **Marquis Who's Who Honors:** Albert Nelson Marquis Lifetime Achievement Award (2017) **To what do you attribute your success:** Dr. Brown attributes his success to good mentors and a healthy work ethic. **Shipping Address:** N1460 Powers Lake Road, Genoa City, WI, 53128 **Website:** http://www.cancercenter.com/midwestern/doctors-and-clinicians/charles-komen-brown

Dean Naomi Brown

Title: Deputy State Forester (Retired) **Industry:** Government Administration/Government Relations/Government Services **Company Name:** State of Alaska **Date of Birth:** 03/09/1944 **Place of Birth:** Fairbanks **State:** AK **Parents:** James Heuston Alexander; Betty Jefford Alexander **Marital Status:** Single **Spouse Name:** Jim McCaslin Brown (9/1/1963, Divorced 1987) **Children:** Robin Wendy; Shelly Renee **Education:** BS in Geology, University of Wisconsin-Madison (1967) **Career:** Deputy State Forester, Division of Forestry, Department of Natural Resources, State of Alaska (2004-Present); Acting State Forester, Department of Natural Resources, State of Alaska (1990-Present); Acting Director of Agriculture, Department of Natural Resources, State of Alaska (2003-2004); Manager, Northern Region, Division of Land and Water Management, Department of Natural Resources, State of Alaska (1990-2003); Journeyman Carpenter, Enserch Alaska Construction, Inc., Bradley Lake, AK (1989); Geologist, Placer Dome United States Inc., Nome, AK (1989); Office Manager, Northwind Aviation, Anchorage, AK (1987-1988); Various Positions to Acting Director of Agriculture, Department of Natural Resources, State of Alaska (1978-1987); Environmental Geologist, Civil Engineer, Wasilla, AK (1977); Assistant Construction Engineer, Field Construction Engineer, Trans-Alaska Pipeline System, Fluor Corporation (1975-1976); Geologist, Amax Coal Company, Indianapolis, IN (1974); Geology Lecturer, Indiana University, Kokomo, IN (1971-1972) **Career Related:** Designated Alternate Member, Governor's Disaster Policy Cabinet (2009-Present); Designated Member, State Emergency Response Commission, United States Environmental Protection Agency (1997-Present); Co-Chair, Computer Group, Department of Natural Resources, State of Alaska (1996-Present); Member, Alaska Wildland Fire Coordinating Group, AICC- Alaska Fire Service (1996-Present); Chair, Alaska Wildland Fire Coordinating Group, AICC- Alaska Fire Service (2007-2008); Member, Governor's Disaster Policy Cabinet (2007-2008); Incident Commander, National Association of State Foresters' Annual Meeting, Anchorage, AK (2006); Member, Alaska-Taiwan Forestry Group (2006); Member, Governor's Transition Team (2002); Chair, Alaska Wildland Fire Coordinating Group, AICC- Alaska Fire Service (1999); Delegate, Alaska Forest Products Research and Marketing Program, Council of Western State Foresters (1994-1995); Delegate, National Association of State Foresters (1994); Adjunct Professor of Natural Resource Economics, Alaska Pacific University (1993); Vice-Chair, Alaskan-Chinese Timber Commission (1993); Adjunct Professor of Natural Resource Economics, Alaska Pacific University (1991) **Civic:** Alaska Delegate, Centennial, United States Forest Service, United States Department of Agriculture (2005); Volunteer, Iditarod Trail Committee **Creative Works:** Featured, USA Today **Awards:** Certificate of Appreciation, 4-H & Youth Development, Palmer, Alaska (1987); Outstanding Achievement Award, Department of Natural Resources, State of Alaska (1986); Certificate of Appreciation, Anchorage School District (1983); Certificate of Achievement, Susitna Council, Girl Scouts of the United States of America (1982); Certificate of Appreciation, City of Valdez, Alaska (1976); Medal, Department of State Foreign Service Institute **Membership:** Charter Member, Pacific Rim Arabian Horse Association (1997-Present); Interim Committee, National Association of State Foresters (2006); Board of Directors, Alaska Horse Breeders Association, Inc. (1984-1990); Aircraft Owners and Pilots Association; Alaska Airmen Association; The Ninety-Nines, Inc. **Marquis Who's Who Honors:** Albert Nelson Marquis Lifetime Achievement Award (2017) **Why did you become involved in your profession or industry:** Ms. Brown became involved in forestry because she was a natural resource manager. The state was in need of strong leadership, experience in Alaska, as well as experience in fire, so she was selected her for the position. **Where will you be in five years:** In five years, Ms. Brown may be in Antarctica. Wherever she is, she will be in the present. It will be interesting and challenging. **Hobbies:** Flying; Horse breeding and showing; Painting; Photography; Gold mining; Carpentry; Reading; Playing piano; Travelling **Business Address:** PO Box 870366, Wasilla, AK, 99687

Jerry M. Brown

Title: Health Products Executive **Industry:** Medicine & Health Care **Company Name:** Automated Medical Products Corporation **Date of Birth:** 04/30/1938 **Place of Birth:** Anderson **State:** SC **Marital Status:** Married **Spouse Name:** Janice Roleke Polites; Alice Alberta Thompson (7/30/1960, Divorced 11/2/2007) **Children:** John Milford; Allen Thompson **Education:** PhD in Physiology, University of Maryland School of Dentistry (1972); MA in Biology, Temple University (1967); MA in Biology, Wake Forest University (1963); BS, Furman University (1960) **Career:** Manager, Precision Medical Mfg LLC (2002-Present); Chief Executive Officer, Automated Medical Products Corp. (1997-Present); President, Automated Medical Products, Inc. (1990-Present); Vice President, M/D Frontiers (1990-Present); Chief Operating Officer, M/D Frontiers (1990-Present); President, Surgical Neurology International (1995-Present); Chief Operating Officer, Surgical Neurology International (1995-Present); Consultant and Special Assistant to the President, Bio Technology General Corporation (1991-1999); Medical Coordinator, Federal Emergency Management Agency, Department of Homeland Security (1987-1990); National Disaster Medical System Staff, Board of Governors, National Council for International Health (1980-1990); Chief of Plans Operations and Security, Landstuhl Regional Medical Center, U.S. Army (1984-1987); Director of International Health Affairs, United States Department of Defense (1980-1984); Deputy Director, United States Army Medical Intelligence and Information Agency (1976-1980); Instructor of Anatomy, University of Maryland School of Medicine (1970-1977); Section Leader, Experimental Medicine Division, U.S. Army Research Institute of Environmental Medicine (1973-1976); Section Leader, Experimental Medicine Division, Edgewood Chemical Biological Center (1967-1968); Research Instructor, Hahnemann University Hospital (1967-1968) **Civic:** Trustee, Spellman Museum of Stamps & Postal History (1980-1997); Commissioner, Explorer Scouts, The Scout Association (1975-1976) **Awards:** Gold Medal, Reserve Officers Association of the United States (1960); Decorated Legion of Merit, United States Armed Forces; Meritorious Service Medal with Oak Leaf Clusters **Membership:** President, Central Atlantic Region, National Stamp Dealers' Association (1977-1981); Electron Microscopy Society of America; ASDA; Research and Engineering Society of America; Baltimore Philatelic Society; Sigma Alpha Epsilon; Sigma Xi, The Scientific Research Honor Society **Marquis Who's Who Honors:** Albert Nelson Marquis Lifetime Achievement Award (2017) **Hobbies:** Stamp collecting; Writing books about the history of New Jersey, especially Sewaren, NJ, where he lives **Religion:** Baptist **Shipping Address:** 440 Cliff Rd, Sewaren, NJ, 07077

Michael D. Brown

Title: Founding Partner **Industry:** Law and Legal Services **Company Name:** Ohrenstein & Brown LLP **Marital Status:** Married **Children:** Four Daughters **Education:** JD, New York University School of Law (1970); BA, Beloit College **Career:** Founding Partner, Ohrenstein & Brown LLP (1983-Present); Attorney for Distinguished Program (1987-2012); Associate, Weil, Gothshal & Manges (1970-1973) **Civic:** Co-chairman, Corporate Committee, Nassau County Museum of Art; Member, American Heart Association, Inc.; Member, Children's Diabetes Foundation **Awards:** Honoree, One of New York's Best Law Firms, U.S. News & World Report L.P. (2016) **Membership:** Association of the Bar of the City of New York; New York County Lawyers Association **Bar Admissions:** New York State Bar Association **To what do you attribute your success:** Maurice Negeri, the former special prosecutor in New York, was a real mentor to him. He also had the great fortune of a few college professors, Warren Mills and Douglas Broome, who were very helpful to him. Douglas Broome was the first head of the Hubble Telescope. **Why did you become involved in your profession or industry:** He wanted to be a lawyer since he was in third grade. He used to come home from school and Jim McCay's television show, "The Verdict is Yours," was on and he would have his milk and cookies and watch the show. It was a cross between Judge Wapner and Perry Mason and it was very well done. He thought what the lawyers did was really neat, so he went from wanting to be a cowboy, to wanting to be a lawyer in the third grade. **Hobbies:** Baseball; Football; New York Mets; New York Jets; Golfing **Business Address:** 1305 Franklin Ave Ste 300, Garden City, NY, 11530 **Website:** http://www.OandB.com

Blanche Parisi Brownell

Title: Partner, Secondary School Educator **Industry:** Education/Educational Services **Company Name:** ERB Holdings Ltd. **Date of Birth:** 10/27/1934 **Place of Birth:** Waterbury **State:** CT **Parents:** Gustavo Mario Parisi; Philomena Marie (Santoro) Parisi **Marital Status:** Married **Spouse Name:** Edwin Rowland Brownell (12/26/1967) **Children:** Elizabeth R.; Elaine B. Dorrans; Evelyn B. Mika; Nancy Brownell Servat **Education:** BBA, University of Miami, Coral Gables, FL (1956) **Certifications:** Certified Teacher, University of Miami (1962) **Career:** Partner, ERB Holdings Ltd., Coral Gables, FL (1967-Present); Teacher, Business Education, Beautification Committee, City of Coral Gables, FL (1987-1997); Corporate Secretary, E.R. Brownell & Associate Inc., Miami, FL (1968-1992); Teacher, Business Education, Miami Jackson Senior High School (1962-1968); Classified, Display Ad Rep, Miami Herald Publishing Co. (1962); Secretary, Advertising Department, Burdines Department Store, Miami, FL (1961); Classified, Display Ad Rep, Miami Herald Publishing Co. (1953-1956); Secretary, Radio and Electronic Equipment Co., Miami, FL (1952) **Career Related:** Photographer (2009-2011) **Civic:** Founder, Ladies Auxiliary, Dade County Society Surveying and Mapping, Tallahassee, FL (1973); Founder, Ladies Auxiliary, Florida Society Surveying and Mapping, Tallahassee, FL (1973) **Awards:** Outstanding Service Award, American Congress of Surveying and Mapping, Washington, DC (1973); Sponsor of the Year, Future Business Leaders of America, Tallahassee, FL (1965-1966) **Membership:** Secretary, Steering Committee, UM Womens Guild (2005-2009); Corresponding Secretary, University of Miami Woman's Guild (2005-2007); Riviera Country Club; Country Club of Coral Gables; Coral Gables Garden Club; Coral Gables Woman's Club; Coral Cables Music Club; Gilded Lilies; Elkettes **Marquis Who's Who Honors:** Distinguished Humanitarian (2017) **What do you consider to be the highlight of your career:** The highlight of Ms. Brownell's career was her marriage and children. **Hobbies:** Crafts; Ballroom Dancing; Gardening; Travel; Computers; Sketching **Religion:** Roman Catholic **Shipping Address:** 1207 Sorolla Avenue, Coral Gables, FL, 33134

William Timothy Brox

Title: Orthopedic Surgeon **Industry:** Medicine & Health Care **Company Name:** Timothy Brox, MD **Place of Birth:** Aurora **State:** IL **Parents:** Rev. Howard Lewis Brox; Kathleen Anne Brox **Marital Status:** Married **Spouse Name:** Wendy **Education:** Orthopedic Surgery Residency, McMaster University, Hamilton, Ontario, Canada (1981-1985); Surgery Resident, University of Ottawa, Ottawa, Ontario, Canada (1980-1981); Mixed Internship, McMaster University, Hamilton, Ontario, Canada (1977-1978); MD, McMaster University, Hamilton, Ontario, Canada (1974-1977); BA, Systems Design Engineering, University of Waterloo, Waterloo, Ontario, Canada (1969-1974) **Certifications:** New York State Flex Exams (1982); Licensed Practitioner, Ontario (1978-1995); L.M.C.C. Exams Certificate (1978); Licensed Practitioner (1999-2003); State of Texas; Licensed Practitioner (1991-Present); State of California; Diplomate, American Board of Orthopedic Surgery Inc. **Career:** Appointed Independent Qualified Medical Examiner, California Worker Compensation (2015-Present); Medical Board, California Expert Medical Reviewer (1995-Present); Program Director, UCSF Fresno Orthopedic Surgical Residency Program (2010-2014); Permanente Medical Group, Department of Orthopedics, Fresno, CA (2003-2016); Orthopedic Surgery, Hanford Orthopedics/Visalia Clinic, Hanford, CA (2000-2003); Orthopedic Surgery, Dr. Allyn & Associates, Hanford, CA (2000); Orthopedic Surgery, Medical Arts Clinic, Corsicana, TX (1999-2000); Chief, Orthopedic Surgery, Permanente Medical Group, Fresno, CA (1991-1999); Assistant Clinical Professor, Department of Surgery, Faculty of Health Science, McMaster University, Hamilton, Ontario, Canada (1988-1991); Private Orthopedic Practice, Hamilton Civic Hospitals, Hamilton, Ontario, Canada (1987-1991); Private Orthopedic Practice, Scarborough Grace General Hospital, Scarborough, Ontario, Canada (1985-1987) **Civic:** Sequoia Council Executive Board (Fresno, CA), Boy Scouts of America (2005-Present) **Military Service:** Captain, Canadian Forces Medical Service (1974-1981) **Creative Works:** Co-Author, "Risk Factors for Reaching the Post-Operative Transfusion Trigger in a Community Primary Total Knee Arthroplasty Population" (2017); Co-Author, "Similar Mortality with General or Regional Anesthesia in Elderly Hip Fracture Patients" (2016); Co-Author, "Demographic Factors in Hip Fracture Incidence and Mortality Rates in California, 2000-2011" (2016); Co-Author, "Measuring Performance, Post-SGR: The Why , the What and the How" (2015); Co-Author, " What is AAOS Doing About Performance Measures?" (2015); Co-Author, "The American Academy of Orthopaedic Surgeons Evidence-Based Guideline on Management of Hip Fractures in the Elderly" (2015); Co-Author, "Management of Hip Fractures in the Elderly" (2015); Co-Author, "From Evidence to Application: AAOS Clinical Practice Guideline on Management of Hip Fractures in the Elderly" (2015); Co-Author, "Risk Factors for Total Knee Arthroplasty Aseptic Revision" (2013); Co-Author, "Total Joint Arthoplasty Aseptic Revision Risk Factors: Analysis of a US Registry with 72,000 Cases" (2011); Author, "Evidence-Based Practice Committee Scientific Exhibit" (2011); Co-Author, "Are Gender-Specific Knee Implants Necessary for Total Knee Replacements?" (2008); Co-Author, "Regarding a Cohort Study of Systemic and Local Complication Following Implantation of Testicular Prosthesis" (2003); Co-Author, "Defining the Relationship Between Obesity and Total Joint Arthoplasty" (2001); Author, "Implementation of Guidelines for Prevention of Deep Vein Thrombosis in a Managed Care Environment" (1996); Author, "Goodbye Ontario, Hello California: Leaving Medicare for the Kaiser Permanente System" (1992); Co-Author, "A Randomized Trial on the Efficiency of an Autologous Blood Drainage and Transfusion Device in Patients Undergoing Elective Knee Arthoplasty" (1992); Co-Author, "Surgical Palliation of Spinal Oncologic Disease: A Review and Analysis of Current Approaches" (1991); Co-Author, "Results in Scoliosis Fusion using Segmental Wires to Spinous Processes Combined with Distraction Rods" (1986); Co-Author, "The Use of Finite-Element Modeling for Custom Planning Corrective Scoliosis Surgery" (1986) **Awards:** James O. Johnson MD Award for Excellence in Orthopaedic Leadership, Research and Resident Training (2014) **Membership:** American Academy of Orthopaedic Surgeons Representative, Physician Consortium for Performance Improvement, American Medical Association; (2016-Present); Representative, Fragility Fracture Task Force, American Academy of Orthopaedic Surgeons (2016-Present); American Academy of Orthopaedic Surgeons Representative, American College of Surgeons Project, The Coalition for Quality in Geriatric Surgery (2015-2018); Performance Measures Committee, American Association of Orthopedic Surgeons (2014-2018); Oversight Chair, American Association of Orthopedic Surgeons, Hip Fracture Performance Work Group (2014-Present); **Business Address:** 1500 W Shaw Ave Ste 400, Fresno, CA, 93711 **Shipping Address:** 2259 W Magill Ave, Fresno, CA, 93711 **Website:** www.drbrox.com

Laura Adrienne Brozowski

Title: Principal Engineer **Industry:** Engineering **Company Name:** Aerojet Rocketdyne **Date of Birth:** 05/12/1960 **Place of Birth:** Yokohama **Country of Origin:** Japan **Parents:** John Brozowski; Muriel Sydney (Jackson) Brozowski **Education:** MBA, Pepperdine University (1988); MS in Mechanical Engineering, California State University (1987); BS in Mechanical Engineering, University of California, Berkeley (1982) **Certifications:** Registered Professional Engineer, State of California; Certified Professional Manager, Institute of Certified Professional Managers **Career:** Engineering Scientist, Aerojet Rocketdyne, Inc., Canoga Park, CA (1982); Mechanical Engineer, Pratt & Whitney Rocketdyne, Inc., United Technologies Corporation **Creative Works:** Contributor, Articles, Professional Journals; Author, Publications in Field **Awards:** Stellar Award (2003); National Award for Space Achievement, Rotary International (2003); Space Achievement Mid-Career Award, Rotary International **Membership:** Fellow, Institute for the Advancement of Engineering; National Society of Professional Engineers; American Society of Mechanical Engineers; Institute of Certified Managers; National Management Association, Inc. **Marquis Who's Who Honors:** Albert Nelson Marquis Lifetime Achievement Award (2017) **Hobbies:** Music; Continuing education; Dance **Business Address:** PO Box 7922 Mail Code LA-74, PO Box 7922 Mail Code LA-74, Canoga Park, CA, 91309 **Shipping Address:** 11507 Meleto Ln, Porter Ranch, CA, 91326

Erich Edward Brueschke

Title: Distinguished Professor of Medicine **Industry:** Education/Educational Services **Company Name:** Rush University **Date of Birth:** 07/17/1933 **Place of Birth:** Eagle Butte **State:** SD **Parents:** Erich Herman Brueschke; Eva Johanna (Joens) Brueschke **Marital Status:** Married **Spouse Name:** Frances Marie Bryan (3/25/1967) **Children:** Erich Raymond; Jason Douglas; Tina Marie; Patricia Frances; Susan Eva **Education:** Intern, Germantown Dispensary and Hospital (1965-1966); MD, Temple University (1965); Postgraduate Coursework, University of Southern California (1960-1961); BSEE, South Dakota School of Mines & Technology (1956) **Certifications:** Diplomate, The American Board of Family Medicine, Inc.; Certified in Geriatrics **Career:** Distinguished Professor of Medicine, Rush Medical College, Rush University (2002-Present); Distinguished Professor of Medicine, Rush-Presbyterian-St. Luke's Medical Center, Rush University (2002-Present); Vice President of University Affairs, Rush Medical College, Rush University (2000-2002); Dean, Rush Medical College, Rush University (1994-2000); Trustee, Synergon Health Systems (1993-1998); Acting Dean, Rush Medical College, Rush University (1993-1994); Vice-Dean, Rush Medical College, Rush University (1992-1993); Vice President of Medical and Academic Affairs, Anchor HMO (1981-2000); Program Director, Rush Christ Family Practice Residency, Rush Medical College, Rush University (1978-1993); Professor, Rush Medical College, Rush University (1976-1995); Chairman Department of Family Practice, Rush Medical College, Rush University (1976-1995); Trustee, Anchor HMO (1976-1981); Visiting Professor, Rush Medical College, Rush University (1974-1976); Member of Staff, Mercy Hospital and Medical Center, Rush University (1970-1976); Director of Research, Illinois Institute of Technology (1970-1976); Practice in General Medicine, Fullerton, CA (1968-1969); Research Assistant, Lewis Katz School of Medicine, Temple University (1965-1969); Professor, Lewis Katz School of Medicine, Temple University (1965-1969); Member, Technology Staff, Hughes Research and Development Laboratories (1956-1961); Vice Chairman, Board of Directors, Rush-Presbyterian-St. Luke's Medical Center, Rush University **Career Related:** Visiting Attendant, Rush University Hospital (2003-Present); Senior Attendant, Rush-Presbyterian-St. Luke's Medical Center, Rush University (1976-2003); Medical Director, Chicago Board of Health, Westside Hypertension Center, C-HCA, Inc. (1974-1978); Member, Board of Directors, Comprehensive Health Planning for Metropolitan Chicago (1971-1974); Member, Advisory Committee, Education to Careers, Health and Medicine, Chicago Board of Education; Member, Board of Directors, West Suburban Higher Education Consortium; Member, Board of Directors, Federation of Independent Illinois Colleges & Universities **Military Service:** Amateur Extra Class KC9ACE, U.S. Air Force (2001-Present); Medical Corps, U.S. Air Force (1966-1968) **Creative Works:** Contributor, Research Articles, American Wireless Review (2015); Editor-in-Chief, "Disease-a-Month" (1998-2003); Medical Editor, "World Book/Rush Presbyterian St. Lukes/Medical Encyclopedia," Rush University (1987-2003); Consulting Editor, "Hospital Medicine," Family Practice (1986-2003); Associate Editor, "Primary Cardiology" (1979-1985); Associate Editor, "American Wireless Association Review"; Contributor, Articles, Professional Journals **Awards:** Alumni of the Year, Lewis Katz School of Medicine, Temple University (1996); Physician Teacher of the Year, Illinois Academy of Family Physicians (1988); Physician's Recognition Award, American College of Occupational and Environmental Medicine (1975); Physician's Recognition Award, American College of Occupational and Environmental Medicine (1972); Physician's Recognition Award, American College of Occupational and Environmental Medicine (1969) **Membership:** Chairman, Chicago Section, Engineering in Medicine and Biology Group, IEEE (1974-1975); Master, Masons; Fellow, American Academy of Family Physicians; Fellow, Institute of Medicine of Chicago; ASAIO; American Fertility Society; American College of Occupational and Environmental Medicine; American Wireless Association; Chicago Medical Society; American Heart Association, Inc.; Association for the Advancement of Medical Instrumentation; The New York Academy of Sciences; Sigma Xi, The Scientific Research Honor Society; Phi Rho Sigma Medical Society; Eta Kappa Nu, IEEE; Alpha Omega Alpha Honor Medical Society; American Rocket Society (Now AIAA); Institute of Radio Engineers (Now IEEE); American Medical Association; National Association of Watch and Clock Collectors Inc; Radio Club of America **Marquis Who's Who Honors:** Albert Nelson Marquis Lifetime Achievement Award (2017) **What do you consider to be the highlight of your career:** He is most proud of his early work on the Surveyor Moon Lander for NASA in 1963, and combining his passion for science, technology and health in his work. **Shipping Address:** 319 N Lincoln St, Hinsdale, IL, 60521

Valerie Carson Bryan

Title: Professor, Charles Stewart Mott Eminent Scholar **Industry:** Education/Educational Services **Company Name:** Florida Atlantic University **Education:** EdD, Florida Atlantic University (1991); Master's Degree in Teaching, The Citadel, Charleston, SC (1973); BS, Clemson University (1970) **Career:** Charles Stewart Mott Eminent Scholar, Department of Educational Leadership, Florida Atlantic University (2011-Present); Chair of Adult and Community Education, Department of Educational Leadership, Florida Atlantic University (2009, 2011-Present); Professor, Department of Educational Leadership, Florida Atlantic University (2007-Present); Chief Executive Officer, Wild Horses Consulting, Inc. (1988-Present); Cohort Director for Masters Degree in Educational Leadership in the Adult Education Program, City of Delray Beach Police Department, Department of Educational Leadership, Florida Atlantic University (2006-2008); Associate Professor, Department of Educational Leadership, Boca Campus, Florida Atlantic University (2004-2007); Assistant Professor, Department of Educational Leadership, Florida Atlantic University (1995-2004); Visiting Professor, Department of Educational Leadership, Davie Campus, Florida Atlantic University (1994-1995); Adjunct Faculty, Department of Educational Leadership, Florida Atlantic University (1989-1994); Co-technical Support Institution Director, Region V Professional Development Councils, Florida Department of Education (1999-2007); Director, Florida Institute for the Development and Enhancement of Adult Learning (1994-2007); Adjunct Professor, Continuing Education Program, Palm Beach Atlantic University (1988-1992); Program Consultant, Division of Continuing Education, Florida Atlantic University (1987-1989); Assistant Professor, School of Health, Physical Education and Recreation, The University of North Carolina at Greensboro (1976-1986); Adjunct Faculty, The University of West Florida (1975-1976); Field Specialist, Center for Educational Improvement, University of Georgia (1974); Statistician, Center for Educational Improvement, University of Georgia (1974); Assistant Program Analyst, Center for Educational Improvement, University of Georgia (1974); Evaluator, Center for Educational Improvement, University of Georgia (1974); Head of Mathematics, John C. Calhoun Academy, Walterboro, SC (1971-1973); Instructor, John C. Calhoun Academy, Walterboro, SC (1971-1973); Coach, John C. Calhoun Academy, Walterboro, SC (1971-1973); Secondary School Teacher, Colleton County High School, Walterboro, SC (1971); Director of Environmental Education, Colleton County High School, Walterboro, SC (1971); **Career Related:** Committee Member, Florida Atlantic University **Civic:** President, Faculty Assembly, College of Education, Florida Atlantic University (2004-2005); Chair, Adult Practitioner's Task Force on Technology and Education, Division of Applied Technology and Adult and Community Education (1996-1997); Chair, Forest and Recreation Resources Advisory Committee, Clemson University (1993-1994); Vice President, North Carolina Recreation & Park Association (1983-1984); Co-chair, Governor's Outdoors Events, Department of Transportation, State of North Carolina (1983) **Creative Works:** Contributor, 63 Articles, Professional Journals; Contributor, 274 Presentations in Field; Contributor, 30 Book Chapters; Co-author, Four Books **Awards:** Honoree, Elite Women Worldwide (2016); Honoree, Legacymakers: 100 Women of Distinction, Florida Atlantic University (2016); Inductee, International Adult and Continuing Education Hall of Fame, ACE Worldwide (2015); Nominee, Exceptional Faculty Award, Florida Atlantic University (2015); Unsung Hero an Award, Florida Atlantic University (2013); Co-recipient, Outstanding Virtual Presentation Award, Association for the Advancement of Computing in Education (2012); Featured Listee, Faculty: Heart and Soul of FAU, Florida Atlantic University (2011); Honoree, Charles Stewart Mott Eminent Scholar in Community Education, Florida Atlantic University (2011); Graduate Mentor Award, Florida Atlantic University (2011); MACAWARD for The Outstanding Faculty, Florida Atlantic University (2009); Educational Leadership's Graduate Mentor Award (2009); Educational Leadership's Distinguished Teacher of the Year (2009); Honoree, President's Leadership Award Program, Florida Atlantic University (2006); Honoree, College of Education's Distinguished Teacher of the Year, Florida Atlantic University (2006); Grantee, ACENET (1999); Honoree, Best Educational Practices, Boca Raton Chamber of Commerce (1998); Honoree, Woman of Outstanding Leadership, The International Women's Leadership Association; Honoree, Pinnacle Lifetime Member, Continental Who's Who **Membership:** President, DKGSI (1987); American Association for Adult and Continuing Education; ISSDL; American Educational Research Association; The Phi Delta Kappa Society, University of Georgia Chapter **Marquis Who's Who Honors:** Albert Nelson Marquis Lifetime Achievement Award (2017) **Business Address:** 5353 Parkside Dr, Jupiter, FL, 33458 **Shipping Address:** 8907 S Indian River Dr, Fort Pierce, FL, 34982 **Website:** http://www.coe.fau.edu/faculty/bryan

Stanley Ira Buchin

Title: Marketing and Finance Educator, Management Consultant **Industry:** Business Management/Business Services **Date of Birth:** 09/07/1931 **Place of Birth:** New York **State:** NY **Parents:** K. Buchin; Bertha (Handman) Buchin **Marital Status:** Married **Spouse Name:** Jacqueline Thurber Chase (9/14/1957) **Children:** Linda C.; David L.; Gordon T. **Education:** DBA, Harvard University (1962); MBA, Harvard University (1956); SB, Massachusetts Institute of Technology (1952) **Career:** Adjunct Lecturer, Member of Hospitality Industry Advisory Board, Lasell College (2014-Present); Professor of Practice Emeritus, Boston University (2014-Present); Visiting Lecturer, University of Paris (2013-Present); Member, University Faculty Council Executive Committee, Boston University (2008-2012); Vice Chairman, University Student Life Committee, Boston University (2008-2012); Professor of Practice & Faculty Chair, Boston University (2012-2014); Associate Professor, Boston University (1997-2012); General Ship Cruising Corp. (1994-1997); Professor, Arthur D. Little School of Management (1992-2009); President, Boston-Bermuda Cruising Ltd. (1992-1997); Principal, Arthur D. Little School of Management (1991-1999); Visiting Lecturer, Templeton College, Oxford University (1991-1993); Senior Vice President, Temple, Barker & Sloane, Inc. (Now Oliver Wyman), Lexington, MA (1978-1990); Founder, President, Applied Decision Systems, Wellesley, MA (1969-1978); Associate Professor, Harvard Business School (1966-1969); Assistant Professor, Harvard Business School (1962-1966); Lecturer, Harvard Business School (1961-1962); Instructor, Harvard Business School (1960-1961); Research Associate, Harvard Business School (1959-1960); Research Assistant, Harvard Business School (1958-1959); Assistant to Treasurer, Bay State Abrasives (1956-1958) **Career Related:** Board of Directors, Electrolyzer Corp.; Board of Directors, Multicomp Computing Corp; Board of Directors, Diamond Machining Technology **Civic:** Member, Resident Advisory Council Executive Committee, Lasell Village; Chair, Finance Committee, Lasell Village; Trustee, Massachusetts School of Professional Psychology; Chairman, Long-Range Planning Committee, Massachusetts School of Professional Psychology; Treasurer, Human Relations Service of Wellesley and Weston; Member, Governor's Advisory Commission on Mental Health; Trustee Emeritus, Massachusetts School of Professional Psychology **Military Service:** Lieutenant, Chemical Corps, US Army (1952-1954) **Creative Works:** Author, "Hospitality Revenue Management Without Tears" (2016); Author, "Statistics Without Tears" (2014); Author, "E-Book about Marketing" (2001); Author, "E-Book about Business Strategy" (2000) **Awards:** IBM Fellow, Harvard University (1962-1963); Recipient, George F. Baker Scholarship (1956); Inductee, Tau Beta Pi (1951); Inductee, Kappa Kappa Sigma (1951) **Membership:** Class Secretary-Treasurer, Massachusetts Institute of Technology (1949-1957); American Marketing Association; Institute of Management Sciences; Financial Management Association; Harvard Club of Boston **Marquis Who's Who Honors:** Albert Nelson Marquis Lifetime Achievement Award (2017) **Political Affiliations:** Independent **Religion:** Congregationalist **Shipping Address:** 85B Seminary Ave Apt 145, Auburndale, MA, 02466

Fran Bull

Title: Artist, Owner **Industry:** Fine Art **Company Name:** Gallery in-the-Field **State:** NJ **Education:** BS in Textile Design, Fashion Institute of Technology, New York, NY (1984); MA in Fine Art and Education, New York University, New York, NY (1980); BA, Bennington College (1960); Private Study/Apprenticeship, Malcolm Morley, New York, NY **Career:** Director, Owner, Gallery in-the-Field (2004-Present); Resident, Taller 46 Printmaking Workshop, Barcelona, Spain (2001-Present); Artist, Professor of Art (1976-Present); Owner, Fran Bull Studio LLC (1974-Present) **Career Related:** Lecturer, Carving Studio and Sculpture Center, West Rutland, VT (2007-Present); Lecturer, Chaffee Art Center, Rutland, VT (2017); Presenter, Geo-Aesthetics Conference, Towson University (2015-2017); Panelist, "Entrepreneurship in the Arts," Bennington College, Bennington, VT (2013); Participant, "Seduction of the Sensuous," Fourth Annual Geo-Aesthetics Conference, International Association for the Study of Environment, Space and Place, Towson University, Towson, MD (2012); Visiting Artist, University of West Bohemia, Plzen, Czech Republic (2002-2003); Guest Lecturer, Painting Workshop, University of Wisconsin, La Crosse, WI (1988); Visiting Artist, Towson State University, Towson, MD (1986-1987); Adjunct Faculty, Painting, New York University, New York, NY (1980-1986) **Civic:** Juror, Ron Cubbison Memorial Exhibition, Towson University, Towson, MD (2012); Curator, SCULPTFEST, The Carving Studio (2009); Juror, Sculpture Center Gallery, The Carving Studio (2009) **Creative Works:** Solo Show, "In Flanders Fields: a meditation on War," Chaffee Arts Center, Rutland, VT (2016); Solo Show, "Master Printer and Paper maker: a collaboration," Museu-Moli y Paperer de Capellades, Barcelona, Spain (2016); Co-Author, "Artists=Poets" (2014); Author, "Transition" (2014); Solo Show, "STATIONS," Chaffee Art Center, Castleton Art Center, and Christine Price Gallery, Castleton College (2014); Group Show, "Impressions, etching," Vermont Metro Gallery (2014); Solo Show, "Land and Local," Burlington City Arts, Burlington and Shelburne, VT (2013); Group Show, "Barcelona!, Etching series," University of Massachusetts at Lowell (2013); Solo Show, "The Mysterious Mind," VTica, Chester, VT (2013); Solo Show, "Earth as Muse," Great Hall, Springfield, VT (2013); Solo Show, "Opera Portraits," Town Hall Theater, Middlebury, VT (2013); Solo Show, "HERoica," Soho20 Chelsea Gallery, New York, NY (2013); Solo Show, "Etchings," Barcelona, Spain and Shanghai, China (2013); Solo Show, "Drawings," Castleton College Downtown Gallery, Rutland, VT (2013); Group Show, "Home/Hogar: etching and sculpture," Soho20 Chelsea Gallery, New York, NY (2012); Solo Show, "8.15.11," Calvin Coolidge Library, Castleton College, VT (2011); Solo Show, "Prints, Proofs and Plates," Bennington College, Bennington, VT (2011); Solo Show, The Feick Gallery, Green Mountain College, Poultney, VT (2011); Solo Show, "In Flanders Fields," Christine W. Price Gallery, Castleton College, VT (2011); Author, "Grabado," Etching Retrospective (2010); Author, "Halleluiah Chorus, head sculptures" (2010); Solo Show, "In Flanders Fields," Woman Made Gallery, Chicago, IL (2010); Solo Show, "In Flanders Fields," The Carving Studio and Sculpture Center, Rutland, VT (2009); Solo Show, Amsterdam Whitney Gallery, New York, NY (2008); Solo Show, "Dark Matter," Gallery in the Field, Brandon, VT (2007); Solo Show, The Christine W. Price Gallery, Castleton College, VT (2007); Solo Show, Gallery Gora, Montreal, QC, Canada (2007); Co-Author, "Balm of My Dreams" (2003); Solo Show, Sheridan Russell Gallery, London, England (2003); Solo Show, The Old Fire Station Gallery, London, England (2003); Solo Show, "Paintings and Prints," Sotheby Auction, London, England (2003); Solo Show, "Night Passage," Printmaking Council of New Jersey, Somerville, NJ (2003); Solo Show, "The Magdalene Cycle," Flynn Center for the Performing Arts, Burlington, VT (2003); Solo Show, "World Wide Web and Barcelona Series," Gallerie Universitini, Plzen, Czech Republic (2003); Solo Show, "Art and Science," University of West Bohemia, Plzen, Czech Republic (2002); Solo Show, "Brava Diva!" Karpeles Manuscript Museum, Charleston, SC (2002); Solo Show, "Barcelona!" Trans Hudson Gallery, New York, NY (2001); Solo Show, "Plants and Prints," Dennis Morgan Gallery, Kansas City, MO (2001); Solo Show, City Without Walls, Newark, NJ (2000); Solo Show, "Feed the Body, Feed the Soul," Fitton Center for Creative Arts, Hamilton, OH (2000); Several Installations, Performances, and Theatrical Projects; Artist, Film and Video Work; **Awards:** Best in Show, "Food Chain," Printmaking Council of New Jersey (2002); Featured Artist, New Jersey State Council on the Arts (2002); Certificate of Merit, Seventh Annual "Feed the Body, Feed the Soul" Competition, Hamilton, OH (2000); American Institute of Graphic Arts Book Design Award, "Mordant Rhymes for Modern Times" (1992) **Membership:** Advisory Council, Chaffee Art Center, Rutland, VT (2014-Present); Board of Trustees, Carving Studio and Sculpture Center, West Rutland, VT (2005-Present); Board of Trustees, Opera Company of Middlebury, Middlebury, VT (2013); Soho20; The Carving Studio and Sculpture Center, Rutland, VT; Woman Made Gallery, Chicago, IL **Website:** http://www.franbull.com

George E. Bunnell

Title: Lawyer **Industry:** Law and Legal Services **Company Name:** Bunnell, Woulfe, Kirschbaum, Keller, McIntyre & Gregoire, PA **Date of Birth:** 04/28/1938 **Place of Birth:** Miami **State:** FL **Parents:** George A. Bunnell; Lillian E. (Hurley) Bunnell **Marital Status:** Married **Spouse Name:** Dianne Railton (12/1/1990) **Children:** Kelley; Courtney **Education:** LLB, University of Florida (1962); BA, University of Florida (1960) **Certifications:** Certified Mediator, Mediation Inc., Fort Lauderdale, FL (2009) **Career:** Civil Circuit Mediator, Bunnell, Woulfe, Kirschbaum, Keller, McIntyre & Gregoire, PA, Fort Lauderdale, FL (2009-2010); Counsel, Bunnell, Woulfe, Kirschbaum, Keller, McIntyre & Gregoire, PA, Fort Lauderdale, FL (2007-2010); President, Bunnell, Woulfe, Kirschbaum, Keller, McIntyre & Gregoire, PA, Fort Lauderdale, FL (1977-2004); Director, Bunnell, Woulfe, Kirschbaum, Keller, McIntyre & Gregoire, PA, Fort Lauderdale, FL (1977-2004); Officer, Huebner, Shaw & Bunnell, PA, Fort Lauderdale, FL (1972-1977); Director, Huebner, Shaw & Bunnell, PA, Fort Lauderdale, FL (1972-1977); Partner, Dean, Adams, George & Wood, Miami, FL (1968-1971); Associate, Dean, Adams, George & Wood, Miami, FL (1964-1967); Associate, Nicholson, Howard & Brawner, Miami, FL (1963-1964) **Civic:** Secretary, Board of Directors, Fort Lauderdale Museum of Art (Now NSU Art Museum) (1990-2005); Civil Service Board, City of Fort Lauderdale, Florida (1977-1979); Advance Staff, White House (1974-1976); Marine Advisory Board, City of Fort Lauderdale, Florida (1974-1976) **Awards:** A/V Preeminent Rating, Martindale-Hubbell **Bar Admissions:** 11th Circuit, U.S. Court of Appeals (1982); U.S. Supreme Court (1970); U.S. District Court, Southern District, State of Florida (1963); State of Florida (1963) **Marquis Who's Who Honors:** Albert Nelson Marquis Lifetime Achievement Award (2017) **Hobbies:** Hunting; Travel; Spending time with his dog **Shipping Address:** 7955 16th Manor, Apt. B311, Vero Beach, FL, 32966

Ada Puryear Burnette, PhD

Title: Director **Industry:** Education/Educational Services **Company Name:** Valdosta State University **Place of Birth:** Darlington **State:** SC **Parents:** Theodore Peoples; Floia (King) Peoples **Spouse Name:** Paul Lionel Puryear (3/27/1954, Divorced 1975) **Children:** Paul Lionel, Jr.; Paula Lynn **Education:** Postgraduate Coursework, University of Oxford (2005); Postgraduate Coursework, Florida Agricultural & Mechanical University (1994); PhD, Florida State University (1986); MA in Reading, The University of Chicago (1958); Postgraduate Coursework in Elementary Education, Chicago State University (1954-1956); BA in Mathematics, Talladega College (1953); Exchange Student Coursework, Cedar Crest College, Allentown, PA (1952); Valedictorian, Latin/Scientific Atkins High School, Winston-Salem, NC; Valedictorian, 14th Street Elementary School, Winston-Salem, NC **Certifications:** Certified in Secondary Mathematics, State of Florida (2009-2014); Certificate, Administration and Supervision K-12, State of Florida (2009-2014); Certified in Elementary Education, State of Florida (2009-2014); Certified in Early Childhood Education, State of Florida (2009-2014); Certified in Elementary and Secondary Reading, State of Florida (2009-2014); Certified in Educational Leadership Administrator Leadership and Principal Program, Florida Department of Education (2008); Approval for University and School District Program Approval, Florida Department of Education (2008); Continuing Education Certificate, Florida Society of Certified Public Managers (2005-2008) **Career:** Mentor, Mathematics and Reading, Sealy Elementary School, Tallahassee, FL (2012-Present); Teacher, Mathematics and Reading, Sealy Elementary School, Tallahassee, FL (2012-Present); Associate Professor, Valdosta State University (2005-Present); Coordinator, Off-Campus Programs, Valdosta State University (2005-Present); Professor Emeritus, Florida Agricultural & Mechanical University (2003-Present); Chairperson, Department of Educational Leadership, Florida Agricultural & Mechanical University (2007-2012); Coordinator, Masters Level Educational Leadership Program, Florida Agricultural & Mechanical University (2007-2012); Administrative Liaison, K-12 Developmental Research School District, College of Education, Florida Agricultural & Mechanical University (2007-2010); Teacher, Elementary Education and Leadership Courses, Florida Agricultural & Mechanical University (2003-2007); Advisor, Elementary Education and Leadership Courses, Florida Agricultural & Mechanical University (2003-2007); Provost, Florida Agricultural & Mechanical University (2003); Vice President, Academic Affairs, Florida Agricultural & Mechanical University (2003); Professor, Robert H. Anderson Educational Leadership Library, Florida Agricultural & Mechanical University (1998-2003); Director, Robert H. Anderson Educational Leadership Library, Florida Agricultural & Mechanical University (1998-2003); Coordinator, Florida Agricultural & Mechanical University (1998-2003); Professor, Educational Leadership Courses, Florida Agricultural & Mechanical University (1993-2003); Coordinator, Florida Agricultural & Mechanical University (1993-1998); Professor, Florida Agricultural & Mechanical University (1993-1998); Department Chairperson, Florida Agricultural & Mechanical University (1993-1998); Director, PhD Program Development, Florida Agricultural & Mechanical University (1993-1998); Director, Developmental Research School, Florida Agricultural & Mechanical University (1990-1993); Superintendent, Developmental Research School, Florida Agricultural & Mechanical University (1990-1993); Associate Professor, Bethune-Cookman University, Daytona Beach, FL (1988-1990); Kenan Pre-College Program Director, Bethune-Cookman University, Daytona Beach, FL (1988-1990); Director, Acting Education Division, Bethune-Cookman University, Daytona Beach, FL (1987-1990); **Career Related:** Job Corps Tutor, North Carolina Advancement School (1958-Present); Diagnostician, North Carolina Advancement School (1958-Present); Lecturer, North Carolina Advancement School (1958-Present); **Civic:** Secretary, Tallahassee Coalition for the Homeless (2004-Present); Grief Chairperson, African Methodist Episcopal Church, (2004-Present); Board of Directors, Tallahassee Coalition for the Homeless (2002-Present) **Creative Works:** Weekly Columnist, "Capital Outlook" (1991-1997) **Awards:** Trailblazer, The Oasis Center for Women & Girls (2013); C.K. Steele Honoree (2011); Speech Award, National Hook-Up of Black Women, Inc. (2010); Service Honoree, Phi Delta Kappa (2010); Honoree, Invited Speech, University of Oxford, Oxford, England (2010); Women's Month Honoree, Bethel Baptist Church (2010) **Membership:** President, Tallahassee Chapter, AAUW (2005-Present); Director, Florida Chapter, AAUW (2005-Present); Board of Directors, Florida Society of Certified Public Managers (2004-Present); President, North Florida Chapter, Florida Society of Certified Public Managers (2004-Present); State Board, Florida Society of Certified Public Managers (2004-Present); FAMU Advisor, Phi Delta Kappa International (2004-Present) **Business Address:** 2601 Cotuit Lane, Tallahassee, FL, 32309 **Website:** https://www.famu.edu/EduLeadership/CV%20Burnette.pdf

Boyd Edward Burnison

Title: Lawyer **Industry:** Law and Legal Services **Company Name:** Boyd E. Burnison, A Professional Law Corporation **Date of Birth:** 12/12/1934 **Place of Birth:** Arnolds Park **State:** IA **Parents:** Boyd William Burnison; Lucile (Harnden) Burnison **Marital Status:** Married **Spouse Name:** Mari Amaral **Children:** Erica Lafore; Alison Katherine **Education:** JD, University of California, Berkeley (1961); BS, Iowa State University (1951) **Career:** President, Boyd E. Burnison, A Professional Law Corporation, Diablo, CA (2005-2014); President, Boyd E. Burnison, A Professional Law Corporation, Walnut Creek, CA (2001-2005); Board of Directors, Crosby, Heafey, Roach & May, Professional Corporation, Oakland, CA (1975-2000); Vice President, Crosby, Heafey, Roach & May, Professional Corporation, Oakland, CA (1975-2000); Partner, St. Sure, Moore, Hoyt & Sizoo, Oakland and San Francisco, CA (1970-1975); Associate, St. Sure, Moore & Hoyt, Oakland, CA (1966-1970); Associate, Steel & Arostegui, Marysville, CA (1965-1966); Deputy Counsel, Yolo County, California (1962-1965) **Career Related:** Honoree, Lifetime Fellow, American Bar Association Foundation; Paul Harris Fellowship, National Conference of Bar Presidents, Rotary International **Civic:** Adviser, Berkeley YMCA, YMCA Central Bay Area (1971-Present); Diablo Advisory Committee (2009-2016); Diablo Municipal Advisory Council (2007-2009); President, Alameda County Law Library (2005-2007); Vice President, Alameda County Law Library (2003-2005); Trustee, Alameda County Law Library (2001-2017); Treasurer, East Bay Conservation Corps, Civicorps (2000); Board Director, East Bay Conservation Corps, Civicorps (1997-2000); Honorary Trustee, Easterseals (1979-2016); Trustee, Easterseals (1974-1979); Secretary, Easterseals (1974-1979); Legal Counsel, Easterseals (1974-1979); Board Director, Society for Crippled Children and Adults of Alameda County California, Easterseals (1972-1975); Board Director, Yolo County YMCA, YMCA of Superior California (1965); Adviser, Yolo County YMCA, YMCA of Superior California (1962-1965); Board Director, Moot Court Board, University of California (1960-1961) **Awards:** Honoree, Volunteer of the Year, Berkeley YMCA, YMCA Central Bay Area (1999); Distinguished Service Award, Alameda County Bar Association (1987) **Membership:** Labor and Employment Law Section, The State Bar of California (1982-Present); Board of Directors, Alameda County Bar Foundation (1993-1995); President, Alameda County Bar Association (1984); Chairman, Alameda County Bar Association (1984); Vice President, Alameda County Bar Association (1983); Vice Chairman, Bench Bar Liaison Committee, Alameda County Bar Association (1983); Director, Alameda County Bar Association (1981-1985); Special Labor Counsel, The State Bar of California (1981-1984); Chairman, Membership and Directory Committee, Alameda County Bar Association (1980); Chairman, Law Office of the Economics Committee, Alameda County Bar Association (1975-1977); Chairman, Membership and Directory Committee, Alameda County Bar Association (1973-1974); Equal Employment Law Committee, American Bar Association (1972-2004); Labor Relations, American Bar Association (1972-2004); Employment Law Section, American Bar Association (1972-2004); Secretary, Yolo County Bar Association (1965); Sproul Associate, University of California, Berkeley School of Law; Industrial Relations Research Association; Labor Law Section, Contra Costa County Bar Association; The Bar Association of San Francisco; Yuba Sutter Bar Association, The State Bar of California; Round Hill Country Club; Iowa State Alumni Association; Order Knoll; Phi Delta Phi; Pi Kappa Alpha **Bar Admissions:** U.S. District Court, Central District, State of California (1992); U.S. Supreme Court (1971); U.S. District Court, Eastern District, State of California (1970); U.S. District Court, Northern District, State of California (1962); Ninth Circuit, U.S. Court of Appeals (1962); State of California (1962) **Marquis Who's Who Honors:** Albert Nelson Marquis Lifetime Achievement Award (2017); Distinguished Humanitarian (2017) **Why did you become involved in your profession or industry:** Mr. Burnison first became involved in his profession when his undergraduate professor inspired his interest in employment law. **What do you consider to be the highlight of your career:** The highlight of Mr. Burnison's career has been his previous experience as the president of the Alameda County Bar Association. **Political Affiliations:** Democrat **Shipping Address:** PO Box 743, Diablo, CA, 94528

James W. Burns, EdD

Title: Academic Administrator, Researcher, Consultant **Industry:** Education/Educational Services **Company Name:** California State University Maritime Academy **Date of Birth:** 12/15/1957 **State:** IN **Parents:** Wesley Burns; Zelda Burns **Marital Status:** Married **Spouse Name:** Suzanne M. Barnell (8/15/1981) **Education:** Doctorate, Northern Arizona University (1990); Master's Degree, Northern Arizona University (1985) **Career:** Director, California State University Maritime Academy (2010-Present); Dean, Graduate School, California State University Maritime Academy (2004-Present); Director, Federal Research Center, University of California, Berkeley (2006-2010); Director, Graduate School, California State University (2002-2004); Director, Graduate Studies, MidAmerica Nazarene University, Olathe, KS (1995-2001) **Civic:** Member, Teacher of the Year Selection Committee, Kansas State Board of Education, Topeka, KS (1998-2001); Member, Policy and Procedures Committee, Kansas State Board of Education, Topeka, KS (1998-2001); Member, Executive Committee, Kansas Association of Colleges for Teacher Education, Topeka, KS (1998-2001); Moderator, Candidate Debates, Olathe Unified School Board (1996); Teacher, Education Reform Task Force, U.S. Department of Education, National Association of Colleges and Employers; Teacher, Education, Topeka, KS **Awards:** Development Grant, Alfred P. Sloan Foundation (2003-2005); Program Planning and Implementation Grant, Ford Foundation (2003-2005); International Program Development Grant, Henry Luce Foundation (2000); Named Alumnus of the Year, MidAmerica Nazarene University (1996) **Membership:** Council Member, Program Development Grants, Council of Graduate Schools (2003-2005); Secretary, Phi Kappa Phi (2004); Treasurer, The Honor Society of Phi Kappa Phi (2004); Life Member, The Honor Society of Phi Kappa Phi **Marquis Who's Who Honors:** Albert Nelson Marquis Lifetime Achievement Award (2017) **Hobbies:** Music; Art; Travel; Photography **Shipping Address:** 109 Chartmaster Pl, Vallejo, CA, 94591

Richard J. Burton

Title: Partner **Industry:** Law and Legal Services **Company Name:** The Burton Firm **Parents:** Melvin F. Burton; Shirley (Burton) Silber **Marital Status:** Married **Spouse Name:** Truly Demetra Dourdis (6/11/1972) **Children:** Marc Aaron **Education:** JD, University of Miami (1974); BA, The George Washington University (1971) **Career:** Lawyer, Sole Practice, Miami, FL (1982-Present); General Counsel, Rexall Sundown Inc. (1982-1990); Partner, Schoninger, Siegfried, Kipnis, Burton & Sussman PA, Miami, FL (1979-1982); Associate, Donald M. Murtha and Associates, Washington, DC (1978-1979); Associate, Pompan, Rumizen & Reynolds, Washington, DC (1978-1979); Attorney, Advisor, FAA, Washington, DC (1976-1977); Associate, Richard H.W. Maloy and Associates, Coral Gables, FL (1974-1976); Governor Affairs Liaison, Dade County Florida Legislature (1974); Administrative Aide, Florida Legislature (1973-1974); Founder, Medical Commission on Human Rights, Washington, DC (1969-1971) **Career Related:** Guest Lecturer, School of Law, University of Miami, Coral Gables (1982) **Civic:** Member, Construction Law Panel, American Arbitration Association (1974-Present); Member, Legislative Committee, Builders Association of South Florida (1980-Present); Member, Miami Iron Arrow Tappee (2009); Fire Commissioner, Metropolitan Dade County (1988, 1992); Vice Chairman, Fire Commission (1989-1990); Member, Builder Industry Political Action Committee **Awards:** Honoree, AV Rated Attorney, Martindale-Hubbell (2008-Present); Honoree, Elected to Iron Arrow Society (2008) **Membership:** Phi Alpha Delta Law Fraternity, International; Iron Arrow Honor Society at the University of Miami; ABA **Bar Admissions:** Supreme Court of the United States (1979); The District of Columbia Bar (1976); The Florida Bar (1974) **Marquis Who's Who Honors:** Albert Nelson Marquis Lifetime Achievement Award (2017) **Hobbies:** Skiing; Scuba diving; Tennis **Political Affiliations:** Democrat **Religion:** Jewish **Business Address:** 2875 NE 191st St Ste 403, Aventura, FL, 33180 **Shipping Address:** 4000 Island Blvd Apt 2602, Aventura, FL, 33160 **Website:** http://www.theburtonfirm.net/

Douglas Dale Busch

Title: Principal **Industry:** Law and Legal Services **Company Name:** Douglas Dale Busch, Attorney at Law **Place of Birth:** Oak Park **State:** IL **Parents:** Earl Busch; Evelyn Houlberg Busch **Marital Status:** Married **Spouse Name:** Beverly Wahl Busch **Children:** John; Eric **Education:** JD, University of San Diego School of Law, Cum Laude (1972); AB in Chemistry, Princeton University (1957) **Certifications:** Certified Licensing Professional, Licensing Executives Society (U.S.A. and Canada), Inc. (2008-2011); Registered Professional Engineer, Nuclear Engineering, State of California **Career:** Principal, Douglas Dale Busch, Attorney at Law (2000-Present); Vice President, General Counsel, Sidney Kimmel Cancer Center (2002-2003); Assistant to the President to General Counsel, First In-House Lawyer and Head of Technology Transfer, The Salk Institute for Biological Studies (1981-2000); Attorney, General Atomic, La Jolla, CA (1973-1981); High Temperature Gas-Cooled Reactor Project, Chemistry Department, General Atomic (1960-1972); Radiochemistry Group, Tracerlab, Inc. (1958-1960); Student Aide, Chemical Engineering, Argonne National Laboratory (1955-1957) **Career Related:** Consultant, Various Start-Up Companies **Membership:** San Diego County Bar Association (1973-Present); The State Bar of California (1972-Present); Association of Corporate Counsel (2002-2003); CONNECT, University of California, San Diego (1990-2003); Association of Corporate Counsel (1984-2000); President, Pacific Southwest Railway Museum Association, Inc. (1992); Director, Pacific Southwest Railway Museum Association, Inc. (1991-1996); Founder, Director, President, San Diego Chapter, Association of Corporate Counsel (1985-1987); Vice President, Director, Southern California Chapter, Association of Corporate Counsel (1984-1985); Chairman, Corporate Law Departments Section, San Diego County Bar Association (1978-1979); Vice Chairman, Corporate Law Departments Section, San Diego County Bar Association (1976-1978); Co-counsel, Member, San Diego Coalition for Economic and Environmental Balance (1974-1975); American Bar Association; Emeritus Member, AUTM; Licensing Executives Society (U.S.A. and Canada), Inc.; San Diego Biotechnology Lawyers Group; Biotechnology Innovation Organization; Biocom; American Nuclear Society; NACE International; American Chemical Society; USAEC Reactor Decontamination Information Exchange Group; Life Member, Pacific Southwest Railway Museum Association, Inc.; The San Diego Museum of Art **Bar Admissions:** The State Bar of California (1972) **To what do you attribute your success:** Mr. Busch attributes his success to a work ethic that he developed early. He enjoys his work, and he is grateful to have had caring parents and grandparents, very good teachers and mentors, a supportive and beautiful spouse and talented sons who turned out to be successful contributors to society. He also attributes his success to his interest in almost everything. **Hobbies:** Art; Architecture; Opera; Concert music; Travel; Theater; Railroads; Nineteenth-Century technology **Business Address:** PO Box 3067, Rancho Santa Fe, CA, 92067

Carolyn Elizabeth Buser

Title: Adult Education Educator **Industry:** Education/Educational Services **Company Name:** Correctional Education Association **Date of Birth:** 06/14/1946 **Place of Birth:** St. Paul **State:** MN **Parents:** Jerome Alfred Buser; Ella Caroline (Anderson) Buser **Marital Status:** Married **Spouse Name:** Richard John Ward (9/17/1977) **Children:** John Jerome Buser-Ward; Carl Alfred Buser-Ward **Education:** PhD in Educational Policy and Administration, University of Maryland (1996); MS in Special Education, University of Maryland (1985); BA in English, Carleton College (1968) **Career:** Consultant, Adult Correctional Education, Council of the State, Correctional Educated Association (2013-Present); Education Program Specialist Adult Education, U.S. Department of Education, Washington, DC (2006-2013); Director of Correctional Education, Maryland Department of Education (2001-2006); Field Coordinator, Correctional Education, Maryland Department of Education (1994-2001); Correctional Education Supervisor, Maryland Department of Education, Maryland Correctional Pre-Release Program, Maryland Correctional Institution for Women, Jessup, MD (1988-1994); Correctional Education Supervisor, Maryland Department of Education, Maryland Correctional Institution, Jessup, MD (1980-1988); Correctional Education Supervisor, Maryland Department of Education, Maryland Penitentiary, Baltimore, MD (1976-1980); Correctional Teacher, Maryland Division of Correction, Baltimore, MD (1974-1976); Correctional Teacher, Maryland Division of Correction, Hughesville, MD (1970-1974) **Career Related:** Maryland State Advisory Council on Adult Education (2004-2005); Maryland State Use Industrial Council (2001-2006); Maryland State Director, Region II Correctional Education Association, Laurel, MD (1988-1990); Exemplary Program Supervisor, Prison Literacy, National Institute Corrections, Washington, DC (1986); Fellow, Education Behaviorally Disordered Students, University of Maryland (1985); Maryland State Director, Region II Correctional Education Association, Laurel, MD (1972-1974) **Membership:** Editorial Board, Journal of Correctional Education (2002-Present); Phi Kappa Phi; Correctional Education Association **Marquis Who's Who Honors:** Distinguished Humanitarian (2017) **Shipping Address:** 601 Pennsylvania Avenue NW, Apt. 1108, Washington, DC, 20004

Arthur Buswell

Title: Physician, Surgeon **Industry:** Medicine & Health Care **Date of Birth:** 01/06/1926 **Place of Birth:** Oklahoma City **State:** OK **Parents:** Albert Currier Buswell; Enid May (Scott) Buswell **Marital Status:** Married **Spouse Name:** Jane Marie Fuksa (1969); Loleta JoAnn Sherrill (1950-1969) **Children:** Arthur Lee; Robert Joseph; Barbara JoAnn; Brian A.; Gayla; Richard **Education:** Postgraduate Studies, University of Southern California (1969); Student, Army Command and General Staff College (1966); Student, U.S. Army (1963); AA in Medical Services, U.S. Army (1963); MD, University of Oklahoma (1952); BS in Medicine, University of Oklahoma (1950) **Career:** Commander, Medical Department Activities, Alaska (1979-1983); Chief of Professional Services, Kenner Army Hospital, Fort Lee, VA (1977-1978); Commander, Medical Department Activities, Fort Stewart, GA (1973-1977); Chief of Professional Services, Reynolds Army Hospital, Fort Sill, OK (1972-1973); Medical Project Officer, U.S. Army Combat Developments Command, Experimentation Command, Fort Ord, CA (1968-1972); 1st Infantry Division, Vietnam (1967-1968); Division Surgeon, 1st Armored Division, Fort Hood, TX (1965-1967); Chief of Professional Service, Bassett Army Hospital (1963-1965); Deputy Surgeon, Fort Wainwright and Yukon Command (1963-1965); Superintendent of Health, Kingfisher County (1960-1961); Chief of Staff, Kingfisher Community Hospital (1956-1957); Practice Medicine and Surgery, Hennessey, OK (1955-1963); Surgical Resident, Wesley Hospital, Oklahoma City (1954-1955); Intern, Fitzsimons Army Hospital, Aurora, CO (1952-1953); Chief, Human Factors Division; Chief, Experimentation Division, Experimentation Command **Career Related:** Board of Directors, Friends of Libraries in Oklahoma (1987-Present); Board of Directors, Chisholm Trail Museum (1986-Present); Adjunct Assistant Professor of Medical Sciences, Baylor University (1973-Present); Fellow, Royal Society for Health **Civic:** Kingfisher Memorial Library; Board President, Friends of Library for Kingfisher County (1984-1988); Board of Directors, Fort Stewart Federal Credit Union (1977); President, Fort Stewart School Board (1977) **Military Service:** Major, Colonel, U.S. Army (1961-1983); First Lieutenant, U.S. Army (1952-1954); U.S. Army (1944-1946) **Awards:** Citizen of the Year, Kingfisher Chamber of Commerce (1988); Kingfisher High School Hall of Fame (1987); Armed Forces Honor Medal; Gallantry Cross with Palm; Army Commendation Medal; Air Medal with Three Oak Leaf Clusters; Meritorious Service Medal; Bronze Star Medal for Valor with Oak Leaf Cluster; Soldier's Medal; Legion of Merit with Two Oak Leaf Clusters **Membership:** American Medical Association; Garfield-Kingfisher County Medical Society; Association of Military Surgeons of the United States; Army Aviation Medicine Association; Aerospace Medical Association; Oklahoma State Medical Association **Shipping Address:** 1222 S 11th Street, Kingfisher, OK, 73750

William T. Butler

Title: Academic Administrator **Industry:** Education/Educational Services **Date of Birth:** 08/10/1932 **Place of Birth:** Boston **State:** MA **Parents:** Albert Quigg Butler; Elizabeth West (Viskniskki) Butler **Marital Status:** Married **Spouse Name:** Carol Ann Pike (1977); Marilou Beutel (4/36/1957) **Children:** Marilyn West; Thomas Charles; Robin Eileen **Education:** Coursework in Advanced Management Program, Harvard University (1979); Graduate Program for Health Systems Management, Harvard University (1974); Resident in Internal Medicine, Massachusetts General Hospital (1964-1965); Clinical Fellow in Medicine, Massachusetts General Hospital (1960-1961); Research Fellow in Bacteriology and Immunology, Harvard Medical School (1960-1961); Intern and Assistant Resident in Internal Medicine, Massachusetts General Hospital, Boston, MA (1958-1961); MD, Western Reserve University (1958); AB, Oberlin College (1954) **Career:** Chancellor Emeritus (2010-Present); Professor of Immunology and Internal Medicine, Baylor College of Medicine (2001-Present); Interim President, Chief Executive Officer, Baylor College of Medicine (2008-2010); Chancellor Emeritus, Baylor College of Medicine (2004-2008); Chancellor, Baylor College of Medicine (1996-2004); President, Baylor College of Medicine (1979-1996); Executive Vice President, Dean, Baylor College of Medicine (1977-1979); Acting Executive Vice President, Baylor College of Medicine (1976-1977); Dean of Admissions, Baylor College of Medicine (1974-1977); Associate Dean, Baylor College of Medicine (1973-1974); Professor of Microbiology and Immunology, Professor of Internal Medicine, Baylor College of Medicine (1971-2001); Associate Professor, Baylor College of Medicine (1968-1971); Assistant Professor, Baylor College of Medicine, Houston, TX (1966-1968); Acting Head, Clinical Immunology Section, Laboratory of Clinical Investigations, National Institute of Allergy and Infectious Diseases, National Institutes of Health (1965-1966); Clinical Investigator, Laboratory of Clinical Investigations, National Institute of Allergy and Infectious Diseases, National Institutes of Health (1963-1964); Chief Clinical Associate, Laboratory of Clinical Investigations, National Institute of Allergy and Infectious Diseases, National Institutes of Health (1962-1963) **Career Related:** Chairman of the Board, Lyondell Chemical Company (1997-2007); Executive Committee, Browning-Ferris, Inc. (1997-1999); Chairman, Southwest Chief Executive Officer Council, American Quality and Productivity Center (1997-1998); Member, American Quality and Productivity Center (1994-2004); Regulatory Compliance Committee, C.R. Bard, Inc. (1993-2003); Compensation Committee, Browning-Ferris, Inc.(1993-1999); Member, American Quality and Productivity Center (1991-2004); Chairman, Governance Committee, C.R. Bard, Inc. (1991-2003); Finance Committee, Browning-Ferris, Inc. (1991-1997); Study Commission on Medical Research and Education, The Cleveland Foundation, Ohio (1991-1992); Board of Directors, Browning-Ferris, Inc. (1990-1999); Pension Benefit Committee, Browning-Ferris, Inc. (1990-1993); Board of Directors, C.R. Bard, Inc. (1988-2003); Compensation Committee, C.R. Bard, Inc. (1988-2003); Finance Committee, C.R. Bard, Inc. (1988-1991); Visiting Committee, Case Western Reserve University School of Medicine (1987-2004); Board of Directors, First City Bancorporation of Texas, Inc. (1986-1995) **Civic:** Executive Committee, United Way of Texas, Gulf Coast (1998-1999); Board of Governors, The Houston Forum (1996-2004); National Board of Directors, Points of Light Foundation (1995-2004); Council of Advisors, South Main Center Association (1994-2004); United Way of Texas, Gulf Coast (1993-1999) **Membership:** Section 12, National Academy of Sciences (1992-Present); President, American Clinical and Climatological Association (1998-1999); Ad Hoc Committee on Distinguished Scholars Program, Chairman, W.M. Keck Foundation (1996-2008); Governmental Relations Advisory Committee, Greater Houston Partnership, Inc. (1995-1997); Chairman, National Academy of Sciences (1995-1996); Committee on the Prevention and Control of Sexually Transmitted Diseases, National Academy of Sciences (1995-1996); Business Issues Advisory Committee, Greater Houston Partnership, Inc. (1994-1999); Co-Chair, Healthcare Task Force, Greater Houston Partnership, Inc (1994-1997); Board of Directors, Greater Houston Partnership, Inc. (1992-1999); Membership Committee, National Academy of Sciences (1992-1996); Vice Chairman, National Academy of Sciences (1992-1994); Project 3000x2000 Implementation Committee Chairman, Association of American Medical Colleges (1991-2002); Chairman, Association of American Medical Colleges (1990-1991); Ex Officio, Houston Museum of National Science (1989-1994); Chairman-Elect, Association of American Medical Colleges (1989-1990); Chairman, Council of Deans, Association of American Medical Colleges (1987-1989); Management Education Programs Planning Committee, Association of American Medical Colleges (1986-1996) **Marquis Who's Who Honors:** Albert Nelson Marquis Lifetime Achievement Award (2017); Distinguished Humanitarian (2017) **Religion:** Methodist **Shipping Address:** 2121 Kirby Dr Unit 125, Houston, TX, 77019

Alexander Butterfield

Title: Aviation Executive (Retired), Former Military Officer, Presidential Appointee **Industry:** Military & Defense Services **Date of Birth:** 04/06/1926 **Place of Birth:** Pensacola **State:** FL **Parents:** Horace Bushnell Butterfield; Susan A. (Alexander) Butterfield **Marital Status:** Divorced **Spouse Name:** Charlotte Mary Maguire (September 9, 1949) (Divorced January 1985) **Children:** Leslie Carter (Deceased); Alexander Porter Junior; Susan Carter Hol **Education:** Doctoral Candidate in Clemency and Presidential Pardons, University of California (2005-Present); MA in American History, University of California (2005); Honorary PhD, Embry-Riddle University (Now Embry-Riddle Aeronautical University) (1973); MS in International Affairs, George Washington University (1967); Student, National War College (1966-1967); BS in Political Science, University of Maryland (1956); Graduate, St. Johns Military Academy, Cum Laude (1944) **Career:** Retired (1995); Founder, Consulting Firm, Armistead and Alexander, Inc., Los Angeles, CA (1983); President, Director, Chief Operating Officer, California Life Corporation (1979-1980); Director, Executive Vice President, Chief Operating Officer, International Air Service Company Ltd. (1977-1979); Lecturer, Ethics in Government, American Program Bureau (Now American Program Bureau, Inc.) (1975-1976); Administrator, FAA (Now Federal Aviation Administration) (1973-1975); Deputy Assistant to President Nixon, Secretary to Cabinet, The White House (1969-1973); Deputy Chief of Staff & Chief Administrative Officer, White House Staff (1969); Senior US Military Officer & Representative of the Commander-in-Chief, Pacific, Commonwealth of Australia (1967-1969); Military & Special Assistant for White House Matters, Immediate Office of the Secretary of Defense, United States Department of Defense (1965-1966); Tactical Air Warfare Policy Planner, United States Air Force Headquarters (1964-1965) **Career Related:** Vice President, Chairman, Board of Directors, Dr. Seuss Enterprises, LP (2014-Present); Guest Lecturer, British Library, Center for American Studies (Now Eccles Centre for American Studies) (2015); Guest Lecturer, University College of London (2015); Chairman & Chief Executive Officer, Armistead & Alexander, Inc. (1983-1994); Chairman, Global Networks, Inc. (1981-1982); Board of Directors, Aloha Airline; Chairman, GMA Corp.; Chairman, The Institute for Brain and Society **Civic:** Vice President, Board of Trustees, Dr. Seuss Foundation (2015-Present); Chairman, Dr. Seuss Foundation (2014-Present); Member, Board of Directors, Dr. Seuss Enterprises LP (2013-Present); Chairman, Board of Directors, The Institute for Brain and Society (2013-Present); Chairman, Chancellor's Associates, University of California, San Diego (2004-2006); Board of Directors, LA County Museum of Natural History (Now Natural History Museum of Los Angeles County) (1981-1985); Board of Directors, Aloha Airlines, Inc. (1979-1980); Board of Directors, International Flight Safety Foundation (Now Flight Safety Foundation) (1976-1981); Leader, United States Government and Industry Delegate to Moscow for Ministerial Level Talks on Technology and Trade (1973); Presidentially-Appointed Member, National Armed Forces Museum Advisory Board, Smithsonian Institution (1970-1976); Chairman, The Institute for Brain and Society; Watergate Committee **Military Service:** Colonel, United States Air Force (1966); Commander, Tactical Reconnaissance Task Forces, Southeast Asia (1963-1964); Commander, Fighter Squadron, Okinawa, Japan (1962-1964); Senior Aide to Commander-in-Chief, Pacific Air Forces (1959-1962); Assistant Professor, United States Air Force Academy (1957-1959); Operations Officer, Interceptor Squadron (1955-1956); Aide to Commander, Fourth Allied Tactical Air Force, NATO (1954-1955); Command Pilot, Parachutist, Member, Skyblazers, United States Air Force, NV (1949-1953); Commissioned Second Lieutenant, United States Air Force (1949); Colonel, United States Air Force (1948-1969) **Creative Works:** Subject, "The Last of the President's Men" by Bob Woodward, Simon and Schuster (2015); Consultant, Screenplay, Oliver Stone, "Nixon" (1995); Member, Editorial Board, LA County Museum of Natural History (Now Natural History Museum of Los Angeles County) Magazine Terra (1983-1986); Author, First 12th Air Force and United States Air Force, Europe "Fighter-Gunnery Training Manual"; **Awards:** Archibald Cox Uncommon Heroes of Watergate Award, Common Cause (2013); Decorated, Legion of Merit, Admiral John McCain, Commander in Chief of Pacific Command (1969); Winning Member, Six-Man Fighter-Gunnery Team, European Championship (1954); Presidential Appointment, 46th in the Country, United States Military Academy at West Point (1946); Honoree, Rutte Courtesy Medal, Class of 1944, St. Johns Military Academy (1944); Decorated, Air Medal with Three Bronze Oak Leaf Clusters; Decorated, Four Air Medals; Decorated, Bronze Star **Membership:** SAG-AFTRA; American Film Institute; Air Force Association; Tailhook Association; Thunderbird Alumni Association; Bel-Air Country Club, University Club, San Diego; Boy Scouts of America; Founding Member, American Air Museum, U.K.; **Marquis Who's Who Honors:** Albert Nelson Marquis Lifetime Achievement Award (2017) **Shipping Address:** 8040 El Paseo Grande, CA, La Jolla, CA, 92037

Stephen A. Butterfield, PhD

Title: Education Educator **Industry:** Education/Educational Services **Company Name:** University of Maine **Date of Birth:** 09/10/1948 **Place of Birth:** Middlebury **State:** VT **Parents:** Stewart Ellsworth Butterfield; Mary Elizabeth (Coursey) Butterfield **Marital Status:** Married **Spouse Name:** Jeanne Allison Zong (6/20/1970) **Children:** Sarah; Jason; Scott **Education:** PhD, Ohio State University (1984); MEd, Keene State College (1980); BS, Springfield College, Springfield, MA (1971) **Career:** Professor, Education, University of Maine, Orono, ME (1984-Present); Professor, Special Education, University of Maine, Orono, ME (1984-Present); Teacher, Physical Education, Austine School for the Deaf, Brattleboro, VT (1973-1981); Principal, Halifax School, West Halifax, VT (1972-1973); Teacher, Halifax School, West Halifax, VT (1972-1973); Fourth Grade Teacher, Whitingham Elementary School, Jacksonville, VT (1971-1972) **Career Related:** Project Director, National Youth Sports Program; State Coordinator, Maine Task Force on Adapted Physical Education, Chairman, Maine Task Force on Adapted Physical Education; Fellow, North American Society of Health, Physical Education, Recreation, Sports, and Dance Profiles; Fellow, American Alliance for Health, Physical Education, Recreation and Dance **Civic:** Revision Committee, Adapted Physical Education National Standards (APNES) (2017-Present); Governor's Council of Physical Fitness and Sports (2000-2012); Adapted Physical Education National Standards (2000-2002); Governor's Council of Physical Fitness and Sports (1996-1998); Board of Directors, The Banger Y, Bangor, ME (1990-1992) **Creative Works:** Editor, The Advocate (1994-1996); Editor, Maine Journal of Health, Physical Education, Recreation and Dance (1988-1996); Contributor, Articles, Professional Journals **Awards:** Honor Award, Alliance for Health (2012); High Praise Award, Maine Association of Health, Physical Education, Recreation and Dance (2008); Honor Award, Distinguished Leadership, Maine Association of Health, Physical Education, Recreation and Dance (1989); Eastern District Merit Award, Physical Education, Alliance for Health (1989); Meritorious Award for Exceptional Project Performance, National Youth Sports Program; Grantee, State, Federation Foundation **Membership:** Board of Directors, National Consortium for Physical Education and Recreation for Individuals with Disabilities (1997-1999); President, Maine Association of Health, Physical Education, Recreation and Dance (1986-1987); Alliance for Health; North America Society of Health, Physical Education, Recreation, Sports and Dance **Hobbies:** Military history **Political Affiliations:** Republican **Business Address:** 5740 Lengyel Hall, 5740 Lengyel Hall, Orono, ME, 04469 **Shipping Address:** 277 14th Street, Bangor, ME, 04401

Charlotte Grace Buzzelli

Title: Special Education Educator **Industry:** Education/Educational Services **Company Name:** Akron City School District and Project Learn of Summit County **Date of Birth:** 03/21/1947 **State:** OH **Parents:** Edmund Albert Buzzelli; Sarah Agnes (Russo) Buzzelli **Marital Status:** Single **Education:** MS in Education, The University of Akron, Ohio (1976); BS, The University of Akron, Ohio (1969) **Certifications:** Certifications in K-8 Elementary, Special Education K-12, Comprehensive Multi-specialization Areas and Levels, K-12 Reading Specialist, Ohio Department of Education **Career:** Training Coordinator, Northeast Regional and Program Educator Children Services, Ohio Department of Mental Health and Addiction Services (1999-2002); Developer, Job Training Partnership Grant Program and Special Needs Handicapped Grant Program, Fallsview Psychiatric Hospital, Ohio Department of Mental Health and Addiction Services, Cuyahoga Falls, Ohio (1992-1997); Director of Education, Fallsview Psychiatric Hospital, Ohio Department of Mental Health and Addiction Services, Cuyahoga Falls, Ohio (1977-1992); Program Coordinator, Continuing Education Program, Akron Montessori School, Eastwood Center, Akron, Ohio (1976-1977); Teacher, Continuing Education Program, Akron Montessori School, Eastwood Center, Akron, Ohio (1976-1977); Teacher, St. Anthony of Padua School, Akron, Ohio (1969-1976) **Career Related:** Project Learn of Summit County (2010-Present); Developer, Project RISE, Homeless Youth Family Learning Literacy Program, Akron Public Schools (2001-Present); College Education Alumni Board, The University of Akron (2004-2010); Special Education Services Developer and Educator, Community Services Division, Northcoast Behavioral Healthcare, Ohio Department of Mental Health and Addiction Services (1997-2002); Teacher, Adult Basic Literature, Education Program, Akron Public Schools (1992-2010); Participant, University of Hawaii Study Tours Research Projects, International Education and East Asia Pi Lambda Theta Orient Study Tour, Manoa Campus (1990) **Civic:** Choir Member, First Night Community, Akron, Ohio (2013-Present); Developer, Student Services Learners Program, Project RISE, Akron, Ohio (2000-Present); Developer, Literacy Evaluation Program, Project RISE, Akron, Ohio (2000-Present); Member, Progress Through Preservation of Greater Akron (1980-Present); Choir Member, Event Grand Finale Singing Stage Performance (2012-2013); Choir Member, Mass of Jubilee Gospel Choir (2000); Supervisor, Center for Literacy, The University of Akron; Supervisor, Programs, Homeless Shelters, Akron Public Schools; Choir Member, St. John's Cathedral; Choir Member, Diocese of Cleveland, Ohio; **Creative Works:** Author, Church Guides; Author, Proposals and Programs for ERIC Research Oriental Studies: Author, Education; Artist, Art and Photography Exhibits; Author, Grantsmanship Writing; Artist, Creative Projects; **Awards:** Women's Achievement Award, Akron Public Schools, Akron Homeless Shelter and OSIA Collaboration (2013); Outstanding Community Volunteer Award (2013); Outstanding Community Partnership Award (2010); Commendations Award, Governor's Council, Summit County (2009); Champion Partnership Award, The Ohio State University (2009); Distinguished Education Award, The University of Akron Alumni Association (2004); Community Collaboration Award, Summit County Housing Network (2003-2004); Urban Light Award for Outstanding Service, The University of Akron (2001); Ohio Teacher of the Year (1979) **Membership:** Council President, Council for Exceptional Children; Association for Supervision and Curriculum Development; International Reading Association (Now International Literacy Association); The University of Akron Alumni Association; University Club; Akron Woman's City Club; College Club of Akron; President, Pi Lambda Theta; Phi Delta Kappa International; President, Gamma Beta Chapter, The Delta Kappa Gamma Society International; Italian Sons and Daughters of America; The Society of St. Monica; Community Welfare Forum Garden Club **Marquis Who's Who Honors:** Albert Nelson Marquis Lifetime Achievement Award (2017); Distinguished Humanitarian (2017) **To what do you attribute your success:** Ms. Buzzelli's attributes her success to her family for encouraging her to learn in life. Her mentors, Dr. Ruth Clayton and Sister Mary Carmel, were influential role models and community leaders. **Why did you become involved in your profession or industry:** Ms. Buzzelli became involved in her profession because she wanted to help people improve their lives. She has always been active in school programs, working with the homeless and working to help young adults. **What do you consider to be the highlight of your career:** The highlight of Ms. Buzzelli's career was having a 16-year-old student and an 84-year-old student learn to read and write for the first time in their lives. It brought tears of joy to her eyes and smiles from the students and their families. **Hobbies:** Community Work; Pet Therapy to Children and Adults with Disabilities; Reading; Travel; Writing; Singing; Cultural Activities **Political Affiliations:** Conservative **Religion:** Christian **Shipping Address:** 662 Dayton St, Akron, OH, 44310

David A. Bythewood

Title: Attorney, Owner **Industry:** Law and Legal Services **Company Name:** David A. Bythewood, Esq. **Education:** JD, Hofstra University School of Law (1984) **Career:** Attorney, Owner, David A. Bythewood, Esq. (1984-Present) **Awards:** Trail Blazer Award, Amistad Bar Association (2016); Top Attorneys in North America, Who's Who Legal (2016); Top Attorneys in North America, Who's Who Legal (2015); Outstanding Trial Skills and Leadership, Hofstra Law School (2011); Client Rating, Martindale-Hubbell (2010) **Membership:** Board of Directors, Long Beach Lawyers Association (2009-Present) **Bar Admissions:** New York (1984); United States District Court for the District of Columbia; Supreme Court of the United States **To what do you attribute your success:** Mr. Bythewood attributes his success to honesty and hard work. **Why did you become involved in your profession or industry:** Mr. Bythewood was a funeral director at his grandparents' funeral home, but he wasn't getting along with them, so he had to choose another profession; it was between law, medicine, dentistry, acting, and psychology, and he picked law because it was a combination of all of them. **What do you consider to be the highlight of your career:** A highlight of Mr. Bythewood's career was his most famous case, the Joseph Gambino case. **Business Address:** 85 Willis Avenue, Suite J, NY, Mineola, 11501 **Shipping Address:** 459 Magnolia Blvd, Long Beach, NY, 11561 **Website:** http://www.attorneybythewood.lawyer/about.htm

S. Sammy Cacciatore

Title: Lawyer **Industry:** Law and Legal Services **Company Name:** Nance Cacciatore Law **Date of Birth:** 08/02/1942 **Place of Birth:** Tampa **State:** FL **Parents:** Sam Cacciatore; Margarita Cacciatore **Marital Status:** Married **Spouse Name:** Carolyn Michels (8/10/1963) **Children:** Elaine Michel; Sammy Michel **Education:** JD, Stetson University, DeLand, FL (1966); BA, Stetson University, DeLand, FL (1966); AA, Orlando Junior College (1962) **Certifications:** Board Certified in Medical Malpractice, American Board of Professional Liability Attorneys; Board Certified in Civil Trial Law, The Florida Bar; Board Certified in Civil Trial Advocacy, National Board of Trial Advocacy **Career:** Partner, Nance, Cacciatore, Hamilton, Barger, Nance & Cacciatore, Melbourne, FL (2003-Present); Private Practice, Melbourne, FL (1967-Present); Partner, Nance, Cacciatore & Hamilton (1999-2003); Partner, Nance, Cacciatore, Sisserson, Duryea & Hamilton (1991-1999); Partner, Nance, Cacciatore, Sisserson & Duryea (1983-1991); Partner, Nance, Cacciatore & Sisserson (1977-1983); Partner, Nance & Cacciatore (1970-1977); Law Offices of James H. Nance (1967-1970); Associate Firm, Billings, Frederick and Rumberger, Orlando, FL (1966-1967); Assistant Public Defender, Ninth Judicial Circuit Court, State of Florida (1966) **Career Related:** Trustee, Stetson University (2000-Present); Board of Overseers, Stetson University College of Law (1995-Present); Chairperson, Stetson University College of Law (2006-2008); Member, Supreme Court Jury Instruction Committee (2001-2010); Member, Florida Supreme Court Judicial Nominating Commission (1986-1990); Member, Florida Medical Malpractice Advisory Committee (1982); Member, Fifth District Court of Appeal Judicial Nominating Commission (1979-1983); Lecturer in Field **Civic:** Trustee, A. Max Brewer Memorial Law Library, Brevard County, FL (1972-1976); Chairman, A. Max Brewer Memorial Law Library, Brevard County, FL (1972-1975) **Creative Works:** Contributor, Articles, Professional Journals; Contributor, Chapters, Books **Awards:** Americas Top 100 Attorneys (2016); B. Masterson Professional Award, Florida Justice Association (2011); President's Award, Florida Justice Association (1983); President's Award, Brevard County Bar Association (1975); Trial Lawyer of the Year, Central Florida Chapter, American Board of Trial Advocates; Hall of Fame, Stetson University College of Law; Clarence T. Johnston Lifetime Achievement Award, Brevard County Bar Association; Named, Super Lawyer; A.V. Rated by Martindale-Hubble; Named, The Best Lawyers in America **Membership:** Chairman, Constitutional Revision Committee, The Florida Bar (1997-Present); Fellow, Board Director, Florida Justice Association (1970-Present); Jury Instruction Committee, Florida Supreme Court, The Florida Bar (2001-2010); Chairman, The Florida Bar (1998-1999); Chairman, The Florida Bar (1996); Legislative Committee, The Florida Bar (1995-1999); Executive Committee, The Florida Bar (1995-1999); Vice Chairman, Advertising Task Force, The Florida Bar (1995-1997); President, Stetson Lawyers Association (1995-1996); Board of Governors, The Florida Bar (1994-1999); Budget Committee, The Florida Bar (1994-1997); President-Elect, Stetson Lawyers Association (1994-1995); First Vice President, Stetson Lawyers Association (1992-1993); President, Florida Justice Association (1984-1985); Commodore, Eau Gallie Yacht Club (1983-1984); Governor, Vice Commodore, Eau Gallie Yacht Club (1981-1982); President's Award, Brevard County Bar Association (1975); Executive Committee, Trial Lawyer Section, The Florida Bar (1975); ABA; American Association for Justice; The American Law Institute; The International Academy of Trial Lawyers; American Board of Professional Liability Attorneys; American Board of Trial Advocates; National Board of Trial Advocacy; Southern Trial Lawyers Association; Board Director, Brevard County Bar Association; Emeritus Member, The Vassar B. Carlton American Inn of Court; Active Member, Holy Name of Jesus Catholic Church **Bar Admissions:** United States Court of Appeals for the District of Columbia Circuit (1982); United States Court of Appeals for the Eleventh Circuit (1981); Supreme Court of the United States (1971); United States Court of Appeals for the Fifth Circuit (1967); United States District Court Middle District of Florida (1966); Florida (1966) **To what do you attribute your success:** Mr. Cacciatore attributes his success to a love for the practice of law. **What do you consider to be the highlight of your career:** A highlight of Mr. Cacciatore's career were his pioneering efforts in the case, Jones v. Hoffman, established comparative negligence as the standard in Florida, which ultimately led the change to this standard throughout America. He stood off more than 400 corporations in America and changed the way in which injured people are compensated. **Hobbies:** Boating and fishing **Political Affiliations:** Democrat **Religion:** Roman Catholic **Shipping Address:** 525 N Harbor City Boulevard, Nance Cacciatore Law, Melbourne, FL, 32935 **Website:** http://www.nancelaw.com

Mary Josie Cain Blanchard

Title: Director **Industry:** Business Management/Business Services **Company Name:** Gulf of Mexico Restoration **Date of Birth:** 08/28/1947 **Place of Birth:** Texas City **State:** TX **Parents:** Joseph Thomas Cain; Mary Cain **Marital Status:** Married **Spouse Name:** Bruce Blanchard (7/31/1992) **Education:** Senior Executive Fellow, Harvard University, Cambridge, MA (1992); MA, The University of Texas at Austin, TX (1971); BA, The University of Texas at Austin, TX (1969); AA, Stephens College, Columbia, MO, With Honors (1967) **Career:** Director, Gulf of Mexico Restoration, Office of the Assistant Secretary, Fish and Wildlife and Parks, Department of the Interior (2017-Present); Deputy Director, Environmental Policy & Compliance, Office of the Secretary, United States Department of the Interior (2002-2017); Assistant Director, Office of Surface Mining, Reclamation and Enforcement, United States Department of the Interior (1995-2002); Special Assistant to the Director, Office of Surface Mining, Reclamation and Enforcement, United States Department of the Interior (1993-1995); Chief, Hazardous Materials Management Division, Environmental Policy & Compliance, Office of the Secretary (1990-1993); Chief, Minerals Resources Division, Environmental Policy & Compliance, Office of the Secretary (1987-1990); Branch Chief, Federal Regulatory Activities, Office of Surface Mining, United States Department of the Interior (1982-1987); Staff Assistant, Technical Services and Research, Office of Surface Mining, United States Department of the Interior (1979-1982); Program Specialist, Office of Surface Mining, United States Department of the Interior, Washington, DC (1978-1979); Chief, Permits and Research, Surface Mining Reclamation Division, Texas Railroad Commission, Austin, TX (1975-1978); Research Coordinator, Environmental Planning Division, Texas General Land Office, Austin, TX (1972-1975); Research Director, Prudhomme Corp., Austin, TX (1971-1972); Instructor, College of the Mainland, Texas City, TX (1970) **Awards:** Recipient, Hall of Honor Award, Texas City Independent School District (2012); Recipient, Woman of Distinction Award, Alpha Xi Delta (2009); Recipient, Stephens College Alumnae Achievement Award (2007); Recipient, Distinguished Service Medal, United States Department of the Interior (2000); Recipient, Interior Women's Distinguished Leadership Award (2000); Recipient, Stephens College Alumnae Service Award (2000); Recipient, Meritorious Service Medal, United States Department of the Interior (1995) **Membership:** Trustee, Cheetah Conservation Fund (2014-Present); Institute for Civility in Government Board of Directors (2015-Present); Capital Speakers Club (2012-Present); Executive Women in Government (2008-Present); D.C. Federation of Music Teachers (1979-Present); Stephens College Alumnae Club, Greater Washington, DC Chapter (1978-Present); Board of Directors, Executive Women in Government (2008-2012); President, Stephens College Alumnae Association Board (2004-2007); Board of Trustees, Stephens College (1988-1991); Washington, DC Chapter, Women in Mining (1987-1989); President, Washington, DC Chapter, Women in Mining (1986-1987); President, Stephens College Alumnae Club, Greater Washington (1984-1986); Secretary Research Committee, Interstate Mining Compact Commission (1976-1978); Lifetime Member, University of Texas Ex-Students Association; Lifetime Member, Texas City Heritage Association **Marquis Who's Who Honors:** Albert Nelson Marquis Lifetime Achievement Award (2017) **Hobbies:** Teaching and playing the flute; Gardening **Religion:** Church of the Pilgrims **Shipping Address:** 80 Observatory Circle NW, Washington, DC, 20008

Deborah J. Callender

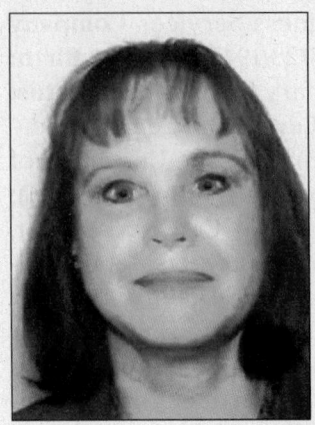

Title: Physical Scientist, Lieutenant Commander **Industry:** Sciences **Company Name:** Naval Oceanographic Office, U.S. Navy **Education:** MS in Computer Science, 3D Visualization and Animation, University of Southern Mississippi (2004); AA in Computer Systems Analysis, University of Maryland, University College of Europe (1991); MA in Management, University of Redlands (1988); BA in English, University of Utah (1985) **Certifications:** Geographic Information Science Certification, University of Southern Mississippi **Career:** Physical Scientist, Naval Oceanographic Office, John C. Stennis Space Center, Mississippi (2008-Present); Associate Software Engineer, General Dynamics Information Technology, John C. Stennis Space Center (2006-2008); Geographic Information Systems Programs Manager, Lincoln County, Libby, MT (2005-2006); Director, Spatial Information Management Services, Pearl River County, Poplarville, MS (2004) **Civic:** Regional Competition Moderator, National Ocean Science Bowl (2008-Present); Studio Staff, Dance Instructor Assistant, Maureen Bersuder Academy of Dance Arts (2007-Present); Judge, National SeaPerch Challenge (2014); Lifetime Member, DAV **Military Service:** Naval Intelligence Officer, U.S. Navy (1985-1998); Administrative Clerk, Personal Financial Records Clerk, MECEP Student, U.S. Marine Corps (1974-1985) **Membership:** American Association of Geographers; American Geophysical Union; American Meteorological Society **Marquis Who's Who Honors:** Albert Nelson Marquis Lifetime Achievement Award (2017); Distinguished Humanitarian (2017) **To what do you attribute your success:** Ms. Callender attributes her success to being tenacious and not giving up, as well as always looking to improve. **Why did you become involved in your profession or industry:** Ms. Callender is most inspired by the planet Earth. **What do you consider to be the highlight of your career:** The highlight of Ms. Callender's career is the work she is doing now, which is collecting ocean data. **Where will you be in five years:** In five years, Ms. Callender's goal is to develop a multi-million dollar specialized contract for her division. She would also like to return to school to pursue an education in marine biology. **Hobbies:** Spending time with her husband; Riding on her husband's Harley-Davidson motorcycle; Movies; Old movies; Reading; Puzzles **Shipping Address:** 39 Countryside Drive, Carriere, MS, 39426 **Website:** http://www.usno.navy.mil/NAVO

John William Camery

Title: Computer Engineer **Industry:** Engineering **Company Name:** Herbalife **Date of Birth:** 02/05/1951 **Place of Birth:** Cincinnati **State:** OH **Parents:** Donald Otis Camery; Mary Lynne Camery **Education:** MS, Carnegie Mellon University (1974); BA, University of Cincinnati (1972) **Certifications:** Certificate of Merit, Signal Processing Society, IEEE **Career:** Individual Distributor, Herbalife International of America, Inc. (2007-Present); Lead Application System Analyst, Battle Commissioned Training Center, General Dynamics Information Technology, Inc. (2001-2007); Software Engineer, RDA Logicon (1989-2001); Software Engineer, Automation Consultants Ltd (1988-1989); Software Engineer, Sygnetron Protection Systems (1987-1988); Programmer, General Scientific Corporation (1986-1987); Analyst, General Scientific Corporation (1986-1987); Mathematician, Defense Information Systems Agency (1983-1986); Computer Specialist, Management Systems Analysis Agency, U.S. Army (1983); Mathematician, Communications Electronics-Engineering Agency, U.S. Army (1975-1983); Student Assistant, Engineering Spectrum Analysis Task Force, Federal Communications Commission (1974); Mathematician, Material Systems Analysis Agency, U.S. Army (1973) **Career Related:** Consultant, Martin Marietta Ocean Systems Operations (1988-1989) **Awards:** Fellowship, Carnegie Mellon University (1972-1973) **Membership:** Chair, Hawaii Section, IEEE (2009-2013); Chair, Hawaii Chapter, IEEE Communications Society (2013); Chair, Signal Processing Society, Hawaii Chapter, IEEE (2013); Societe Mathematique de France; European Mathematical Society; Belgian Mathematical Society; The Imperial Hawaii Vacation Club; GCARA **Marquis Who's Who Honors:** Albert Nelson Marquis Lifetime Achievement Award (2017) **Hobbies:** Music; Dance; Swimming; Travel **Political Affiliations:** Republican **Religion:** Christian **Shipping Address:** 94-647 Kauakapuu Loop, Mililani, HI, 96789

Charles Henry Camp

Title: Lawyer **Industry:** Law and Legal Services **Company Name:** Law Offices of Charles H. Camp, P.C. **Date of Birth:** 06/30/1957 **Place of Birth:** Lake Charles **State:** LA **Parents:** John Clayton Camp; Frances Spencer Camp **Marital Status:** Married **Spouse Name:** Michelle Lebling **Education:** LLM, Taxation, GW Law, George Washington University (1983); JD, School of Law, Wake Forest University (1982); BS in Mathematics, Louisiana State University (1979) **Career:** President, Law Offices of Charles H. Camp, P.C., Washington, DC (2002-Present); Counsel, Cadwalader, Wickersham & Taft LLP, Washington, DC (2001-2002); Partner, Patton Boggs LLP, Washington, DC (1988-2001); Associate, Akin, Gump, Strauss, Hauer & Feld LLP, Washington, DC (1985-1988); Associate, Camp, Carmouche, Barsh, Hunter, Gray, Hoffman & Gill P.C., Lake Charles, LA (1983-1985) **Career Related:** Adjunct Professor, Negotiation, Persuasion and Influence, Flores MBA Program, E.J. Ourso College of Business, Louisiana State University (2014-Present); Adjunct Professor, International Negotiations, Law School, George Washington University (2005-Present) **Awards:** Honoree, Super Lawyers **Membership:** President, Washington Foreign Law Society; Board of Advisers, Washington Foreign Law Society; Congressional Country Club; Past Member, Board of Trustees, Meridian International Center; Chair, Governance and Nominating Committee, Meridian International Center; Audit Committee, Meridian International Center; Development and Compensation Committee, Meridian International Center; Past Chair, Tillar House Committee, The American Society of International Law; Former Chairman, Audit Committee, The American Society of International Law; Ex Officio Member, Executive Council, The American Society of International Law; Ex Officio Member, Executive Committee, The American Society of International Law; Past President, The Friends of the U.S. Law Library of Congress; International Bar Association; London Court of International Arbitration **Bar Admissions:** District of Columbia (1988); State of Louisiana (1982); U.S. Supreme Court; Second and District of Columbia Circuits, U.S. Court of Appeals; U.S. District Court, District of Columbia; U.S. District Court, Southern District, State of Texas; U.S. District Court, Western District, State of Louisiana; U.S. District Court, State of Colorado; U.S. District Court, Western District, State of Oklahoma **Marquis Who's Who Honors:** Albert Nelson Marquis Lifetime Achievement Award (2017) **Shipping Address:** 600 New Hampshire Avenue NW, Suite 640, Law Offices of Charles H. Camp, P.C., Washington, DC, 20037

William W. Campbell

Title: Medical Educator, Clinical Neurologist **Industry:** Medicine & Health Care **Company Name:** Uniformed Services University **Date of Birth:** 09/28/1944 **Place of Birth:** Macon **State:** GA **Parents:** William Wesley Campbell, Sr.; Lessie Rose Campbell **Marital Status:** Married **Spouse Name:** Rhonda Marie Pridgeon (5/2/1992) **Children:** William Wesley III; Matthew Ryan; Shannon Leigh Ward **Education:** MS in Health Administration, School of Medicine, Virginia Commonwealth University, Richmond, VA (1991); Resident in Neurology, Letterman Army Medical Center (1973-1976); Intern, Straight Medicine, Medical College of Georgia, Augusta University, Augusta, GA (1970-1971); MD, Medical College of Georgia, Augusta University, Augusta, GA (1970); BA, Emory University, Atlanta, GA (1966) **Certifications:** Certified Added Qualification in Neuromuscular Disease, American Board of Psychiatry and Neurology, Inc. (2009); Certified Added Qualification in Clinical Neurophysiology, American Board of Psychiatry and Neurology, Inc. (1996); Certification in Electrodiagnostic Medicine, American Board of Electrodiagnostic Medicine (1981); Certification in Neurology, American Board of Psychiatry and Neurology, Inc. (1978) **Career:** Semi-retired, Private Practice, Neurological Associates, Richmond, VA (2014-Present); Professor Emeritus, Department of Neurology, Uniformed Services University, Bethesda, MD (2011-Present); Consultant, Telemedicine & Advanced Technology Research Center, U.S. Army (2012-2013); Professor, Uniformed Services University, Bethesda, MD (2004-2010); Chairman, Department of Neurology, Uniformed Services University, Bethesda, MD (2004-2010); Professor of Neurology, Uniformed Services University, Bethesda, MD (2000-2010); Professor of Neurology, School of Medicine, Virginia Commonwealth University, Richmond, VA (1990-2000); Associate Professor of Neurology, School of Medicine, Virginia Commonwealth University, Richmond, VA (1986-1990); Assistant Professor of Neurology, School of Medicine, Virginia Commonwealth University, Richmond, VA (1981-1986); Private Practice, Anderson, SC (1980-1981); Neuromuscular Fellow, Medical College of Georgia, Augusta University, Augusta, GA (1979-1980); Staff Neurologist, Wilford Hall, United States Air Force Medical Center (1976-1979) **Civic:** American Board of Electrodiagnostic Medicine, Rochester, MN **Military Service:** Colonel, U.S. Army (2011); Active Duty, U.S. Army (2000-2011); U.S. Army Reserve (1983-2000); Active Duty, U.S. Air Force (1970-1979) **Creative Works:** Author, "DeJong's Neurologic Examination, Eighth Edition" (2019); Author, "Clinical Signs in Neurology: a Compendium" (2015); Author, "Essentials of Electrodiagnostic Medicine, Second Edition" (2014); Author, "DeJong's Neurologic Examination, Seventh Edition" (2013); Author, "Pocket Guide and Toolkit to DeJong's Neurologic Examination" (2008); Author, "DeJong's Neurologic Examination, Sixth Edition" (2005); Author, "Practical Primer of Clinical Neurology" (2002); Author, "Essentials of Electrodiagnostic Medicine" (1999); Contributor, Articles, Professional Journals **Awards:** Honoree, Best Doctors in America (2009-2016); Distinguished Physician Award, American Association of Neuromuscular and Electrodiagnostic Medicine (2011); Outstanding Teacher, Walter Reed Army Medical Center (2002); Honorable Mention Award, AMWA (1999); Named Outstanding Teacher, Medical College of Virginia (1988); Golseth Young Investigator Award, American Association of Electrodiagnostic Medicine (1981); Legion of Merit; Defense Meritorious Service Medal, Order of Military Medical Merit **Membership:** Fellow, American Association of Neuromuscular and Electrodiagnostic Medicine; American Academy of Neurology; Virginia Watercolor Society; Alpha Omega Alpha **Hobbies:** Clarinet; Piano; Watercolor; Golf; Exercise; Reading **Business Address:** 165 Wadsworth Drive, Richmond, VA, 23236 **Shipping Address:** 13800 Winterberry Ridge, Midlothian, VA, 23112 **Website:** http://nairichmond.com

Judy Canahuati

Title: Senior Nutrition, Maternal Child Health Advisor, Lactation Consultant **Industry:** Medicine & Health Care **Date of Birth:** 07/17/1941 **Place of Birth:** Philadelphia **State:** PA **Parents:** Max Weiner; Besse S. (Creshkoff) Weiner **Marital Status:** Married **Spouse Name:** Harry S. Glass (7/7/2015); Pedro Felipe Canahuati (9/6/1969, Deceased 2001) **Children:** Emilia; Pedro Cesar; Deborah Glass-Rosier **Education:** MPhil in Anthropology, Columbia University (1974); BA, University of Pennsylvania (1963) **Certifications:** La Leche League Leader (1973-Present); Certification, IBLCE (1985-2009) **Career:** Senior Nutrition Adviser, USAID Food for Peace, Washington, DC (2009-2016); Maternal Child Health, Nutrition, HIV Adviser, USAID Food for Peace, Washington, DC (2004-2009); Senior Nutrition Adviser, CARE, Atlanta, GA (2001-2003); Community Outreach Adviser, Wellstart International, Inc., Washington, DC (1991-1996); Project Director, La Leche League International, San Pedro Sula, Honduras (1989-1991); Technical Adviser, Management Sciences for Health, Boston, MA (1986-1988); Board of Directors, La Leche League International, Schaumburg, IL (1986); Technological Adviser, National Breastfeeding Program PROALMA, USAID, Tegucigalpa, Honduras (1982-1985); Import-Export Manager, Contessa Industrial, San Pedro Sula, Honduras (1978-1982); Instructor, Universidad Nacional Autonoma de Honduras, San Pedro Sula, Honduras (1970-1972); Community Organizer, Planned Parenthood, New York, NY (1966-1967) **Career Related:** Global Health Fellow, Public Health Institute (2006-2009); Health and Child Survival Fellow, Johns Hopkins University, USAID Food for Peace (2004-2006); Superintendent, Escuela Internacional Sampedrana, Honduras (1999-2001); Director, Project to Improve Basic Education, World Bank, Honduras (1998); Affiliate, UNICEF, China (1997); Affiliate, CARE, Honduras (1997); Affiliate, Academy for Educational Development (1997); Affiliate, Catholic Relief Services, San Salvador, El Salvador (1996); Affiliate, Project Hope, Managua, Nicaragua (1996); Consultant, Wellstart International, Washington, DC (1996); Affiliate, World Relief, Tegucigalpa, Honduras (1994); Researcher, Institute of Reproductive Health, Georgetown University, Washington, DC (1990-1992); Affiliate, UNICEF, New York, NY (1989); Affiliate, University of California, Davis (1989); Affiliate, Educational Development Center, Boston, MA (1985); Consultant, Centro de Apoyo a la Lactancia Materna, San Salvador, El Salvador (1981-1983); Fellow, NIMH (1968-1969) **Civic:** Action Committee, La Leche League International (2016-Present); Board of Directors, Sundays at Three, Columbia, MD (2008-Present); Board of Directors, Escuela Internacional Sampedrana, San Pedro Sula, Honduras (1980-1985); Board of Directors, Society Pro-Musica, San Pedro Sula, Honduras (1975-1976) **Creative Works:** Co-Author, "Community-based Breastfeeding Support: A Planning Manual" (1996); Co-Producer, "Investing in the Future: Women, Work, and Breastfeeding" (1995); Contributor, Articles, Professional Journals **Awards:** Dory Storms Child Survival Recognition Award (2017) **Membership:** Review Committee, History of Nutrition of USAID (2017-Present); ILCA (1985-Present); La Leche League International (1972-Present); Consumer's Education and Protective Association (1966-1989); World Alliance for Breastfeeding Action; Phi Beta Kappa **Marquis Who's Who Honors:** Albert Nelson Marquis Lifetime Achievement Award (2017); Distinguished Humanitarian (2017) **To what do you attribute your success:** Ms. Canahuati attributes her success to being in the right place at the right time. **Why did you become involved in your profession or industry:** Ms. Canahuati became involved in her profession after she had her first child, during which she discovered that breastfeeding was a learned skill. She received support from La Leche League in the in spite of the fact that she lived in Honduras. Once she learned the basics, she realized that other women had problems and needed support and started to offer help. She was able to take advantage of much of the training available at the time, almost all of it through La Leche League International, with support from her husband, who was behind what she did 100 percent. When USAID decided to support a national breastfeeding training program in Honduras, she was one of the only people in the country with breastfeeding counseling and support skills. The rest is history. **What do you consider to be the highlight of your career:** The highlight of Ms. Canahuati's career was learning and showing the tremendous importance of the breastfeeding relationship to children's development and the creativity and commitment of women to developing and preserving that relationship. **Where will you be in five years:** In five years, Ms. Canahuati plans to continue helping families give their babies the best start in life. **Hobbies:** Reading; Writing; Pilates; Aerobics; Cooking **Shipping Address:** 6258 Softshade Way, Columbia, MD, 21045

Mark Wilcox Cannon, PhD

Title: Federal Government Official (Retired), Venture Capitalist **Industry:** Financial Services **Place of Birth:** Salt Lake City **State:** UT **Parents:** Joseph J. Cannon; Ramona Wilcox Cannon **Marital Status:** Married **Spouse Name:** Betty S. Cannon (6/25/1993); Ruth D. Cannon (12/28/1956, Divorced 1992) **Children:** Lucile C. Critchley; Mark D. Cannon; Kristen C. Brown **Education:** PhD in Political Economy and Government, Harvard University (1961); MPA in Public Administration, Harvard University (1955); MA in Political Economy and Government, Harvard University (1954); BA in Political Science, Minor in Economics, University of Utah (1949) **Career:** Venture Capitalist, Broadly Varied Businesses (1989-Present); Executive Vice President, Cannon Industries (1989-1996); Executive Vice President, Geneva Development (1988-1989); Vice Chairman, Board of Directors, Geneva Steel (1988-1989); Staff Director, Commission on the Bicentennial of the United States Constitution (1985-1988); Counselor to the Chief Justice of the Warren E. Burger (1972-1985); Director, Institute of Public Administration, New York (1968-1972); Director, International Programs, Institute of Public Administration (1965-1968); Director, Venezuelan Urban Development Project, Institute of Public Administration, Ford Foundation (1964-1965); Part-Time Researcher, Unconventional Warfare Studies, China Lake Naval Station (1963-1964); Chairman, Political Science Department, Brigham Young University (1961-1964); Part-Time Legislative Assistant, United States Senator Wallace F. Bennett (1961-1963); Chief-of-Staff, United States Congressman Henry A. Dixon (1956-1961); Instructor, Political Science Department, Brigham Young University (1955); Secretary, Utah School Merit Study Committee (1954); Proctor and Freshman Advisor, Harvard University (1953-1955); Government Research Analyst, Utah Foundation (1953); Research Associate, Dan E. Clark Opinion Researchers (1952); Political Reporter, Deseret Evening News, Salt Lake City, UT (1948) **Career Related:** Lecturer, More than 70 Institutions in More than 18 Countries Including Argentina, Brazil, Chile, China, Egypt, Germany, Hungary, Japan, Uganda and Uruguay **Civic:** Board of Directors, Institute of Public Administration (1987-2004); Chairman, National Advisory Council, Marriott School of Management, Brigham Young University (1984-1986); Member, Commission on Public Understanding About the Law, ABA (1982-1986); Vice Chairman, National Advisory Council, Marriott School of Management, Brigham Young University (1982-1984); Harvard Overseers' Committee to Visit Harvard Law School (1979-1985); Chairman, Committee for the Selection of the Most Outstanding Dissertation in Public Administration, American Political Science Association (1977); Member, National Advisory Council, Marriott School of Management, Brigham Young University (1976-1989); Chairman, Committee on Court Administrations, ABA (1976-1978); Editorial Board, Judicature (1975-1976); Member, Inter-American Advisory Council, United States Department of State (1972-1974); Secretary, International Studies Association (1962-1963); Chairman, Littauer Graduate School of Public Administration Student Association, Harvard University (1954); Treasurer, Graduate Student Council, Harvard University (1953-1954); Missionary, The Church of Jesus Christ of Latter-day Saints, Argentina (1949-1952) **Creative Works:** Speaker, "Chief Justice Warren E. Burger," Memorial Service, Supreme Court of the United States (1996); Lecturer, "The Role of an Independent Judiciary in Undergirding Constitutional Democracy," Parliament and the Judiciary, Amman, Jordan (1995); Author, "The Constitution: The Real Thousand Points of Light," Phi Kappa Phi Journal (1990); Author, "The Constitution: The Real Thousand Points of Light," The Scottish Rite Journal (1990); Author, "A Tribute to Chief Justice Warren E. Burger," Harvard Law Review (1987); Author, "Judicial Administration to the 21st Century," Public Administration Review (1985); Author, "Stemming the Litigation Tide: An Interview," The Executive Letter Special Report, Insurance Information Institute (1985); Co-Author, "Bill of Responsibilities," Freedoms Foundation at Valley Forge (1985); Author, "The Spawning Ground for Better Federal Courts," ABA Journal (1983); Author, "Crime and Decline of Values" (1981-1982); Co-Author, "Interbranch Cooperation in Improving the Administration of Justice: A Major Innovation," Washington and Lee Law Review (1981) **Awards:** NESA Outstanding Eagle Scout Award, National Capital Area Council, Boy Scouts of America (2015); Eponym, Mark W. Cannon Endowed Scholarship, Romney Institute, Marriott School of Management, Brigham Young University (2014); Distinguished Service Award, Supreme Court Fellows Alumni Association (2004); American Eagle Award, Invest-in-America National Council (1988); Pi Sigma Alpha Award for Outstanding Political Scientist, National Capital Political Science Association (1986); Honorary Doctor of Law, Morris Brown College (1980); Eagle Scout, Boy Scouts of America (1943); **Membership:** National Academy of Public Administration (1973-Present); Beehive Honor Society, The University of Utah (1949-Present); Phi Kappa Phi (1949-Present); **Shipping Address:** 8360 Greensboro Dr Apt 917, McLean, VA, 22102

Anthony Joseph Capritto III

Title: Lawyer **Industry:** Law and Legal Services **Company Name:** AJ Capritto Law Offices **Date of Birth:** 07/11/1931 **Place of Birth:** New Orleans **State:** LA **Parents:** Philip Joseph Capritto; Marie Virginia (Longo) Capritto **Marital Status:** Married **Spouse Name:** Eileen Mary Frisbee (6/6/1964) **Children:** Ann; Jane; Michael; Margaret; Elizabeth; Alice; Judith; David; Mary **Education:** JD, Loyola University, New Orleans, LA (1959); BBA, Loyola University, New Orleans, LA (1953) **Career:** Lawyer, AJ Capritto Law Offices, New Orleans, LA (1959-Present); General Counsel, Bank of Louisiana, New Orleans, LA (1979-1990) **Civic:** President, New Orleans Opera Club (2016-Present); Member, Legal Committee, Board of Directors, New Orleans Opera Association (1975-Present); Member, President's Council, Loyola University, New Orleans, LA (1989-1993); President, Christian Brothers Foundation, New Orleans, LA (1985-1987); President, Catholic Charities, New Orleans, LA (1980); Vice Chairman, Louisiana Civil Service Commission, Baton Rouge, LA (1979-2000); Commissioner, Louisiana Civil Service Commission, Baton Rouge (1979-2000); President, Louisiana Cystic Fibrosis Foundation (1976-1978) **Military Service:** Captain, US Army (1953-1955); Adjutant, 21st Station Hospital, Republic of Korea **Awards:** Decorated, The Golden Palm of Jerusalem Award, Equestrian Order of the Holy Sepulchre of Jerusalem (2013); Recipient, Order of St. Louis Medallion (2006); Recipient, Monte M. Lemann Award (1988); Decorated, Designated Lieutenant of Honor, Equestrian Order of the Holy Sepulchre of Jerusalem **Membership:** Board of Directors, Semreh Club (1983-Present); President, New Orleans Opera Club (2016); President, St. Thomas More Catholic Lawyers Association (1980-1984); Louisiana Bar Association; Louisiana Trial Lawyers Association; American Judicature Society; American Association for Justice; Arbitrator, American Arbitrators Association; Southeastern Lieutenancy, Equestrian Order of the Holy Sepulchre of Jerusalem **Bar Admissions:** Supreme Court of the United States (1971); United State Court of Appeals for the Fifth Circuit (1965); United States District Court for the Eastern District of Louisiana (1959); Louisiana (1959) **To what do you attribute your success:** Mr. Capritto was always careful to do what he felt was the right thing to do; he wouldn't take a case if he didn't think he could win it. Additionally, Mr. Capritto's religious faith is important to him and he has always prayed and followed rules of the catholic church and has tried to do good. **What do you consider to be the highlight of your career:** Helping people is what he Mr. Capritto is most proud of. He always advised his clients to put the money he got them to good use. **Religion:** Roman Catholic **Business Address:** 1010 Common Street, Suite 2640, 1010 Common Street, Suite 2640, LA, New Orleans, 70112 **Shipping Address:** 600 Port of New Orleans Pl Apt 10H, New Orleans, LA, 70130

Ann M. Card

Title: Advocate **Industry:** Other **Career:** Advocate, Private Practice, Connecticut; Employee, Delta Air Lines, Inc. **Career Related:** Business Manager, Nagel Electric **Membership:** Business Enterprise Institute, Inc.; Delegate, The International Women's Leadership Association **Marquis Who's Who Honors:** Albert Nelson Marquis Lifetime Achievement Award (2017); Distinguished Humanitarian (2017) **To what do you attribute your success:** Ms. Card attributes her success to meeting a diverse range of people. **What do you consider to be the highlight of your career:** The highlight of Ms. Card's career was being instrumental in the HB600 Booster Seat Law passing in October of 2005. **Where will you be in five years:** In 5 years, Ms. Card will continue to be an advocate for children. **Hobbies:** Spending time with her son **Shipping Address:** 161 Teller Rd, Trumbull, CT, 06611

Christopher Blake Carlile

Title: Corporate Executive, Military Officer (Retired), Command Pilot **Industry:** Military & Defense Services **Company Name:** AECOM **Date of Birth:** 06/22/1962 **Place of Birth:** Paragould **State:** AR **Parents:** Donald Gene Carlile; Jo Ann (Dinwiddie) Carlile **Marital Status:** Married **Spouse Name:** Sandra F. Pickett (10/28/1989) **Children:** Chelsea Brook **Education:** Diplomate, Depot and Arsenal Executive Leader Program, Keenan-Flager Business School, The University of North Carolina at Chapel Hill (2010); MS in Strategic War Studies, United States Air War College (2009); MBA, Embry-Riddle College (1997); BS, Arkansas State University (1988) **Certifications:** Certified Test Pilot, Maintenance College, Fort Eustis, VA (1990); Certified Pilot, Fort Rucker, AL (1990); Diplomate, Aviation Officer Course, Fort Rucker, AL (1989) **Career:** Vice President, Business Operations, AECOM, Fort Rucker, AL (2014-Present); Commander, Chief Executive Officer, Corpus Christi Army Depot, United States Army (2010-2013); Director, Aviation Center of Excellence, US Army (2009-2010); Deputy Chief of Staff to Commanding General, US Army, Fort Rucker, AL (2007-2008); Commander, Aviation Flight Training Battalion, US Army, Fort Rucker, AL (2005-2007); Adviser, Nuclear Strikes, President George W. Bush (2003-2005); Commander, 101st Airborne Division, US Army (2000-2002); Lieutenant Commander, US Army (1999); Executive Officer, First Attack Training Battalion, US Army, Fort Knox, KY (1995-1999); Co-Commander, A-5-158th Aviation Regiment, US Army, Wiesbaden, Germany (1993-1995); Production Control Officer, 7-159th Aviation Regiment, US Army, Giebelstadt, Germany (1992-1993); Platoon Leader, 7-159th Aviation Regiment, US Army, Stuttgart, Germany (1990-1992); Executive Officer, 1-145th Aviation Regiment, US Army, Fort Rucker, AL (1989); Commissioned Second Lieutenant, US Army (1988); Colonel, US Army (1985-2014); Executive Officer 8-101 101st Avian Regiment, US Army; Executive Officer, 101st Airborne Division, US Army **Civic:** Member, Executive Board, United States Army Aviation Museum **Creative Works:** Author, "The Army Aviation Sustainment Strategy," US Army (2014); Author, "Business Reorganization at the Corpus Christi Army Depot," US Army (2011); Author, "U.S. Army Unmanned Systems Roadmap, 2010-2035," US Army (2010); Author, "Robot Revolution," Armed Forces Journal, Gannett Government Media (2010) **Awards:** Recipient, Distinguished Service Medal, United States Department of Defense (2014); Recipient, Robert T. Mason Award for Excellence in Organic Industrial Operations, Corpus Christi Army Depot, United States Department of Defense (2013); Recipient, Robert M. Leich Award for Significant Contributions, Army Aviation Association of America (2012); Recipient, John W. Macy Leadership Award, US Army (2012); Recipient, Ernest Young Logistics Executive Award, Materiel Command, US Army (2011); Recipient, General Douglas MacArthur Award, US Army (1994) **Membership:** Demonstrated Master Logistician, SOLE (2007-Present); Executive Board, Kentucky Board, Ducks Unlimited, Inc. (1996-1999); Chapter President, AAAA (1989-2014); Association of the United States Army (1989-2014); Treasurer, AAAA (1989-1996) **Marquis Who's Who Honors:** Albert Nelson Marquis Lifetime Achievement Award (2017) **Hobbies:** Golf; Hunting; Fishing; Trap shooting; Skeet shooting **Political Affiliations:** Conservative **Shipping Address:** 103 Saint Andrews Pl, Enterprise, AL, 36330

Herbert Christian Carlson Jr.

Title: Physicist, Consultant **Industry:** Sciences **Date of Birth:** 05/10/1937 **Place of Birth:** Brooklyn **State:** NY **Parents:** Herbert Christian Carlson; Mae (Jundel) Carlson **Marital Status:** Married **Spouse Name:** Ann Lagerquist Carlson (6/1/1986); Ritta Ilona Kaarela Carlson-Owens (1966, Divorced 1979) **Children:** Jennifer Mae Carlson-LaChance; Diane Maria Ilona **Education:** PhD, Cornell University (1965); MSc, Cornell University (1962); BEE, Cooper Union for the Advancement of Science and Art (1959) **Career:** Resident Professor, Center for Atmospheric and Space Sciences, Utah State University (2010-Present); Resident Professor, Space Weather Center, Utah State University (2010-Present); Senior Scientist, European Office of Aerospace Research and Development (2007-2010); Chief Scientist, ST-5, Air Force Office of Scientific Research, U.S. Air Force (1998-2006); Chief Scientist, Geophysics Laboratory, U.S. Air Force (1996-1998); Branch Chief, Department of Church Science, Geophysics Laboratory, U.S. Air Force (1981-1995); Program Director of Aeronomy, UAF National Science Foundation (1977-1981); Senior Research Associate, University of Texas at Dallas (1973-1977); Research Associate, Arecibo Observatory (1965-1973); Head of Ionospheric Department, Arecibo Observatory (1965-1973) **Career Related:** Consultant, AFRL Research Council, Research Laboratory, U.S. Air Force (1998-2006); Consultant in Field **Creative Works:** Contributor, Articles, Professional Journals; Contributor, Chapter, Books **Awards:** United States Presidential Rank Award (2003); Achievement Award, National Science Foundation; Achievement Award, National Aeronautics and Space Administration; Achievement Award, U.S. Air Force; Numerous Grants **Membership:** Technology Committee, AIAA (1984-Present); The Norwegian Academy of Science and Letters; Air Force Research Laboratory; RAS; American Association for the Advancement of Science; AIAA; USA Commission G.; International Science Radio Union; American Geophysical Union **Marquis Who's Who Honors:** Albert Nelson Marquis Lifetime Achievement Award (2017) **Religion:** Lutheran **Shipping Address:** 901 N Monroe Street, Apt. 1006, Arlington, VA, 22201

William D. Carmichael

Title: Consultant, Educator **Industry:** Education/Educational Services **Date of Birth:** 09/05/1929 **Place of Birth:** Denver **State:** CO **Parents:** Fitzhugh Lee Carmichael; Anna Devona (Sullivan) Carmichael **Marital Status:** Married **Spouse Name:** Faith Young (6/21/1958) **Children:** Amy; Philip Fitzhugh; Daniel Owen **Education:** Honorary LLD, University of Capetown, South Africa (2014); Honorary LLD, University of Wisconsin (1989); PhD, Princeton University (1959); BLitt, University of Oxford, England (1955); MPA, Princeton University (1952); AB, Yale University (1950) **Career:** Executive Director, Eastern European Programs, Institute of International Education, New York City, NY (1989-1993); Vice President, Developing Country Programs, Ford Foundation (1981-1989); Head, Ford Foundation, Middle East and Africa (1977-1981); Head, Ford Foundation, Latin America and Caribbean (1971-1977); Representative, Ford Foundation, Brazil (1968-1971); Professor, Economic Policy, Dean, Graduate School of Business and Public Administration, Cornell University (1962-1968); Assistant Professor, Princeton University (1960-1962); Director, Undergraduate Program, Woodrow Wilson School of Public and International Affairs (1958-1962); Lecturer, Economics and Public Affairs, Princeton University (1957-1960); Budget Analyst, United States Bureau of the Budget (1956-1957); Legislative Analyst, Bureau of Budget and Planning (1955-1956); Legislative Analyst, United States Bureau of the Budget (1955-1956) **Career Related:** Consultant on Education and Economic Development (1993-Present) **Civic:** Member Emeritus, Board of Directors, Human Rights Watch; Member, Board of Directors, Creative Vision Foundation; Member, Board of Directors, Southern Africa Legal Services Foundation **Membership:** Council on Foreign Relations; Association of American Rhodes Scholars; The Phi Beta Kappa Society **Shipping Address:** 603 W Lyon Farm Dr, Greenwich, CT, 06831

Caroline Carnahan

Title: Owner, Operator **Industry:** Other **Company Name:** Springfield Marine Company **Country of Origin:** Taiwan **Marital Status:** Married **Spouse Name:** Garnett **Education:** Bachelor of Foreign Languages, Soochow University **Career:** Owner, Springfield Marine Company **Civic:** Supporter, Various Charitable Organizations **To what do you attribute your success:** Ms. Carnahan attributes her success to her hard work. **Why did you become involved in your profession or industry:** Ms. Carnahan became involved in her profession after coming from Taiwan. She was able to help the company develop internationally. In 2001, she entered the world of sales and has been there ever since. **What do you consider to be the highlight of your career:** The highlight of her career thus far has been seeing her product all over the world. **Where will you be in five years:** In five years, Ms. Carnahan would like to continue thriving in her industry. **Hobbies:** Traveling for business and pleasure **Shipping Address:** 1093 N Cynthia Dr., Ste 1, Springfield Marine Company, Nixa, MO, 65714 **Website:** http://www.springfieldgrp.com

Denise Wilkinson Carson

Title: Gifted and Talented Educator (Retired) **Industry:** Education/Educational Services **Date of Birth:** 12/29/1946 **Place of Birth:** Providence **State:** RI **Parents:** Thaddeus Archiebald Wilkinson; Helen Gautier Wilkinson **Spouse Name:** Keith Robert Carson (9/9/1967) **Children:** Jeanne-Marie; Corwin Keith **Education:** MA in Education, College of William and Mary, Williamsburg, VA (1988-1989); BS in Mathematics and Government, Florida State University, Tallahassee, FL (1967-1969) **Certifications:** Gifted Certification, Shenandoah University (1998); Gifted Certification, American Montessori Society, Montessori Teacher Education Center, State of Michigan (1980) **Career:** Teacher, Gifted, South Morrison Elementary, Newport News, VA (2001-2006); Elementary Teacher, Armstrong Fundamental School, Hampton, VA (1990-2001); Teacher, St. Patrick's Catholic School, Tacoma, WA (1985-1987); Teacher, It's A Small World School, Tacoma, WA (1984-1985); Teacher, Troy Montessori/Montessori Teacher Education Center, West Bloomfield, MI (1978-1983); Budget Officer, Arlington School Systems, Virginia (1972-1974); Mathematician, RCA, Alexandria, VA (1971-1972); Statistician, Florida Board of Regents, Tallahassee, FL (1969-1970) **Career Related:** Chairman, Gifted Advisory Board, Tacoma, WA (1985-1986) **Awards:** P.A.C.E. Award, Beta Sigma Phi (2007-2008); Founder's Award, Beta Sigma Phi (2006-2008); Peninsula Woman of the Year, Beta Sigma Phi (2000-2002); Virginia Art Grant, Virginia Art Council (1992-1993); Chapter Woman of Year, Beta Sigma Phi (1991-1992, 1994-1995, 1999-2000, 2006-2008) **Membership:** Chapter Corresponding Secretary, Beta Sigma Phi (2015-Present); Yates Mill Chapter Treasurer, Daughters of the American Revolution (2014-Present); Delegate to Continental Congress, Daughters of the American Revolution (2008-Present); North Carolina State Conference, Daughters of the American Revolution (2015); Chapter Council Representative, Beta Sigma Phi (2014-2015); Vice President, Tidewater Daughters of the American Revolution Regents' Club (2013); Chapter Corresponding Secretary, Beta Sigma Phi (2012-2013); Chapter Corresponding Secretary, Beta Sigma Phi (2010-2011); Treasurer, Newport News Retired Teachers Association (2011-2013); Chapter Regent, Daughters of the American Revolution (2010-2013); State Vice President, Virginia Retired Teachers Association (2010-2012); Virginia State Conference, Daughters of the American Revolution (2008-2013); President, Newport News Retired Teachers Association (2008-2012); Chapter President, Beta Sigma Phi (2008-2009); Chapter Treasurer, Beta Sigma Phi (2007-2008); Chapter Recording Secretary, Beta Sigma Phi (2007-2008); Finance Chairman, Newport News Retired Teachers Association (2007-2008); Chapter Project Patriot Chair, Daughters of the American Revolution (2007-2013); District Press Book Chair, Daughters of the American Revolution (2007-2010); Chapter Press Book Chair, Daughters of the American Revolution (2007-2010); Virginia State Press Book Chair, Daughters of the American Revolution (2007-2010); Good Citizens Chair, Daughters of the American Revolution (2006-2010); Mentor, Preschool Partners (2006-2013); Chapter President, Beta Sigma Phi (2006-2007); Peninsula Council President, Beta Sigma Phi (2000-2002); Chapter President, Beta Sigma Phi (1999-2000); Newport News Retired Teachers Association; National Science Teachers Association; Virginia State Reading Association; National Mathematics Teachers Association; Beta Sigma Phi; Lifetime Member, Daughters of the American Revolution; Lifetime Member, General Society of Mayflower Descendants; The National Society Colonial Dames XVII Century **Hobbies:** Travel; Reading; Needle work **Religion:** Roman Catholic **Shipping Address:** 732 Blackfriars Loop, Cary, NC, 27519

Edward S. Cartlidge

Title: Professional Engineer **Industry:** Engineering **Date of Birth:** 02/05/1945 **Place of Birth:** Trenton **State:** NJ **Parents:** Leon James Cartlidge; Agnes Jean (Cinkay) Cartlidge **Marital Status:** Married **Spouse Name:** Maria C. Cartlidge (1/7/2017); Marilyn Spinuzza (7/21/1979, Deceased 7/1/2016) **Children:** One Daughter **Education:** MA, Biblical Theological Seminary (2001); MBA, Temple University (1982); MME, New Jersey Institute of Technology (1971); BS in Marine Engineering, U.S. Merchant Marine Academy (1968) **Certifications:** Certified Building Commissioning Professional, MEP Professional Engineer of Record, Princeton University (2013-2016); Registered Professional Engineer, States of Pennsylvania and Illinois; Registered Professional Engineer, States of Delaware; Registered Professional Engineer, States of Maryland; Registered Professional Engineer, States of New Jersey; Registered Professional Engineer, States of Virginia; Registered Professional Engineer, States of Wisconsin; Registered Professional Engineer, States of Florida; Registered Professional Engineer, States of New York; Registered Professional Engineer, States of Massachusetts; Registered Professional Engineer, Puerto Rico **Career:** Private Consultant (2013-Present); Senior Project Manager, Advanced Solar Products, Inc., Flemington, NJ (2010-2013); Solar Consultant, PSEG, Newark, NJ (2009); Associate Director, Program Management, Entech Solar, World Water & Solar Technologies, Inc., Ewing, NJ (2007-2009); Utilities Manager, All Star Services, FAA Technology Center, Pomona, NJ (2005-2007); Manufacturer's Representative, Tom Evans Environmental Water/Waste Water Products Inc., Lakeland, FL (2005); Manager Facilities Engineering, Cardinal Health, Inc., Softgel Pharmaceutical Manufacturing, St. Petersburg, FL (2000-2004); Senior Project Manager, Edward S. Cartlidge, PE and Associates, Blue Bell, PA (1993-2000); Senior Project Manager, Conmec, Inc., Bethlehem, PA (1992-1993); Senior Project Process Engineer, Power Utilities Supervisor, Merck & Co., Inc., West Point, PA (1982-1991); Senior Research and Development Engineer, Yarway Corp., Blue Bell, PA (1979-1982); Chief Engineer, Gimpel Corporation, Langhorne, PA (1976-1979); Consultant Engineer, Fluor, Sargent & Lundy, and Kuljian Corporation (1971-1975); Performance Engineer, Foster Wheeler Corporation, Livingston, NJ (1969-1971); Marine Engineer, Seatrain Lines (1968-1969); Executive Team Leader, Independent Business Owner, ACN **Career Related:** Consultant, Pharmaceutical; Consultant, Facilities Management; Consultant, Utilities; Consultant, Semiconductor, Solar Power Systems; Consultant, SteelFab; Consultant, Gideons International; Financial Counselor, Gideons International; Lecturer, Gideons International; Seminar Leader, Gideons International **Civic:** Board of Directors, Grand Old Gospel Fellowship; Past Chapter President, Gideons International; Past Chapter President, Pennsylvania Society of Professional Engineers **Military Service:** Served to Commander, U.S. Naval Reserve (1968-1991); Marine Engineer, Seatrain Lines (1968-1969) **Awards:** Young Engineer of the Year, Pennsylvania Society of Professional Engineers (1980) **Membership:** Chapter President, National Society of Professional Engineers; The American Society of Mechanical Engineers; ASHRAE; American Solar Energy Society; Pennsylvania Society of Professional Engineers; National Fire Protection Association; Camp President, Gideons International; National Eagle Scout Association **Marquis Who's Who Honors:** Albert Nelson Marquis Lifetime Achievement Award (2017) **Why did you become involved in your profession or industry:** Mr. Cartlidge became involved in engineering because his grandfather was a civil engineer in New Jersey. He liked to build things, so his dad suggested he go into mechanical engineering when he was in high school. His goal has always been to set a level of excellence, to give the best quality of service and design. He has been involved in developing patents that advanced knowledge in the field. **What do you consider to be the highlight of your career:** A highlight of Mr. Cartlidge's career was working on a 14-megawatt, 46-acre solar farm for McGraw Hill in New Jersey. It was the largest privately-owned solar project in the western hemisphere. **Where will you be in five years:** In five years, Mr. Cartlidge will be working with missionaries in developing countries to share the gospel. **Hobbies:** Golf; Running track **Religion:** Baptist **Business Address:** PO Box 304, Lake Harmony, PA, 18624

Hattie Virginia Carwell

Title: Health Physicist **Industry:** Medicine & Health Care **Date of Birth:** 07/17/1948 **Place of Birth:** Brooklyn **State:** NY **Parents:** George Carwell; Fannie (Tunstall) Carwell **Education:** Postgraduate Coursework, University of California, Berkeley (1973-1975); MS in Radiation Science, Rutgers, The State University of New Jersey (1971); BS in Chemistry and Biology, Bennett College, Greensboro, NC (1970) **Career:** Executive Director, Museum of African American Technology (2000-Present); Operations Branch Chief, U.S. Department of Energy, Berkeley, CA (1993-1994); Operations Team Head, U.S. Department of Energy, Berkeley, CA (1992-2008); Program Manager, U.S. Department of Energy, Berkeley, CA (1991-1993); Program Manager for High Energy and Nuclear Programs, U.S. Department of Energy, Oakland, CA (1990-1991); Health Physicist, U.S. Department of Energy, Oakland, CA (1985-1990); International Nuclear Safeguards Inspector, Group Leader, International Atomic Energy Agency, Vienna, Austria (1980-1985); Health Physicist, Energy Research Administration, Oakland, CA (1973-1980); Health Physicist, Atomic Energy Commission, Upton, NY (1972-1973); Research Assistant, Thomas Jefferson University Hospital, Philadelphia, PA (1970-1972) **Career Related:** Science Makers (2012); Board Member, History Makers, Science Makers (2011-2012); Assistant Environmental Survey Team Leader, Department of Energy, Washington, DC (1987); Lecturer, University of California, Berkeley, Stanford University, Cabrillo College, Canadian College, and Tougaloo College; Fellow, African Science Institute **Civic:** Co-Founder, Executive Director, Museum of African American Technology Science Village (2000-Present); Co-Founder, Chairman, Development Fund for Black Students in Science and Technology, Washington, DC (1983-Present); Treasurer, National Council of Black Scientists and Engineers (2001-2014); Board of Directors, National Inventors Hall of Fame Foundation (2001-2011); Fiscal Agent, International Network for Appropriate Technology; Coordinator, Coalition of Hispanic, African and Native Americans for the Next Generation of Engineers and Scientists **Creative Works:** Author, "African American Achievements in Air and Space" (2003); Exhibited, The African American Presence in Physics (1999); Author, "In Pursuit of Excellence: Dr. Warren Henry - World Class Scientist" (1998); Author, "Solar Cooker Design Training Guide" (1996); Author, "Blacks In Science: Astrophysicist to Zoologist" (1977); Contributor, Scientific Articles, Professional Journals **Awards:** History Makers-Science Makers, National Science Foundation (2012); Finalist, Benjamin Banneker Legacy Award (2007); One of 101 Outstanding Women in the Community, Black Business Listing (2006); Outstanding African American Women Award (2006); Inspiring Scientist Award, Junior Center of Art and Science of Oakland (2002); James C. Jones Humanitarian Award, National Technician Association (2000); Outstanding Woman Scientist Award, National Technician Association (1998); Outstanding Women in Science Award, National Technician Association (1998); Image Award, Bennett College (1997); Distinguished Alumni Award (1992); Inductee, Black College Hall of Fame (1991); Volunteer Recognition, Department of Energy (1990); Elijah McCoy Award (1989); Federal Community Service Award (1977) **Membership:** Board Member, National Technician Association (2008-Present); Past President, National Technician Association (2012); President, National Technician Association (2010-2011); Board Member, Northern California Council of Black Professional Engineers (2006-2012); President, Northern California Council of Black Professional Engineers (2000-2005); Secretary, Northern California Council of Black Professional Engineers (1996-1999); President, Northern California Council of Black Professional Engineers (1995); President, Northern California Council of Black Professional Engineers (1994); Secretary, Northern California Council of Black Professional Engineers (1988); President, Northern California Council of Black Professional Engineers (1986-1987); Treasurer, Vienna Chapter, Institute of Materials Management (1985); Lifetime Member, National Association for the Advancement of Colored People; Northern California Council of Black Professional Engineers; National Health Physics Society; National Technician Association **Marquis Who's Who Honors:** Albert Nelson Marquis Lifetime Achievement Award (2017) **Hobbies:** Writing; Travel; Gardening **Shipping Address:** 4622 Meldon Avenue, Oakland, CA, 94619

Betty Casbeer Carroll

Title: Application Developer (Retired) **Industry:** Financial Services **Date of Birth:** 12/05/1930 **Place of Birth:** San Antonio **State:** TX **Parents:** Jesse Irvin Casbeer; Nelda Martha Blum **Marital Status:** Divorced **Spouse Name:** John D. Kissack (10/5/1957, Divorced 10/1963); Richard Andrew Carroll (10/3/1946, Divorced 3/1954) **Children:** Peggy Jean Choka; Martha Ann Scott; Betty Jacquelyn; Richard Andrew; Michael Neil **Education:** BA in Liberal Arts, Wright State University, Dayton, OH (1976); AA, San Antonio College, Texas (1956) **Career:** Tax Services (2004-2013); Computer Programmer, STAR Financial Bank, Fort Wayne, IN (2000-2003); Office Manager, Accountant, Southern Ohio Growth Partnership (1995-1998); Computer Specialist/Programmer, Wright-Patterson Air Force Base, Dayton, OH (1970-1995); Cost Accountant, Air Flow Heating and Air Conditioning (1967-1970); Staff Accountant, Rignanese, Shannon & Horn CPA (1966-1967); Office Manager, Accountant, Civilian Building and Supply, Fort Wayne, IN (1963-1966) **Career Related:** President, American Federation of Government Employees (Local 1138), Wright-Patterson Air Force Base (1991-1995); Senior Vice President, Area A Vice President, and Union Rep, American Federation of Government Employees (Local 1138), Wright-Patterson Air Force Base (1971-1991) **Civic:** Secretary-Treasurer, Gingerbread House Day Care, Fort Wayne, IN (1999-2003); American Federation of Government Employees AFl-CIO Local 1138, Dayton, OH (1971-1995); Co-Chair, Women for Racial and Economic Equality (1987-1991); Charter Member, Coalition of Labor Union Women, Fairborn, OH (1985); Secretary-Treasurer, AFGE Council 214, Dayton, OH (1980-1982); Vice President, Miami Valley Freedom of Choice (1979-1980); Vice President, Women's International League for Peace and Freedom (1974-1975); Charter Member, Federally Employed Women, Fairborn, OH (1973); Member, Speaker's Collective and Women's Center Task Force, Dayton Women's Liberation, Ohio (1970-1975); Board Member, Midway Day Care Center (1969-1970) **Creative Works:** Author, "A Freethinker's Memoir of Bygone Days (Ruminations, Observations, and Insights)" (2018); Associate Editor, "Atheist in a Fox Hole: One Man's Quest for Meaning: the Reflections, Insights and Legacy of Richard Alan Langhinrichs" (2015); Author, "The Foothill Spirits-Book Two; Shawnees and Runaway Slaves" (2006); Mentioned in Book, "Feminists Who Changed America" (2006); Author, "The Foothill Spirits Book One: Frontier Life & the Shawnees" (2005); Author, "The Mystery of the Red-Brick House" (2002); Mentioned in Book, "Feminism in the Heartland" (2002) **Membership:** Racial Justice Study Group (2017-2018) **Marquis Who's Who Honors:** Distinguished Humanitarian (2017) **To what do you attribute your success:** Ms. Casbeer Carroll attributes her success to her positive attitude and ability to compartmentalize and remain focused on current tasks and goals. **Why did you become involved in your profession or industry:** Ms. Casbeer Carroll had five children when she started college, and chose business courses because she couldn't foresee a future that required a completed degree. She assumed, correctly, that she could begin working as an accountant without one. **What do you consider to be the highlight of your career:** Ms. Casbeer Carroll considers the highlight of her career to be getting hired and trained as a computer programmer at the Wright-Patterson Air Force Base in 1970. There, she was paid the same as men at the same grade level, a dream that came true after two decades of hoping and preparing for such. **Where will you be in five years:** Looking to the future, Ms. Casbeer Carroll hopes to have completed and published "The Foothill Spirits", a six-book historical fiction series for young adults, and her memoir. **Hobbies:** Reading; Book discussion groups; Writers' group; Collecting antique, first edition, and signed books; Writing historical novels and a memoir **Political Affiliations:** Democrat **Religion:** Unitarian-Universalist **Shipping Address:** 7109 Lower Huntington Rd, Fort Wayne, IN, 46809

Harrison Cavanagh, MD, PhD

Title: Ophthalmologist **Industry:** Medicine & Health Care **Company Name:** The University of Texas Southwestern Medical Center **Date of Birth:** 07/22/1940 **Place of Birth:** Atlanta **State:** GA **Parents:** William Edwards Cavanagh; Marie Corrine (Logue) Cavanagh **Marital Status:** Married **Spouse Name:** Lynn Ayres Gantt (12/27/1964) **Children:** Catherine DuVal **Education:** Fellow, Corneal Surgery, Massachusetts Eye and Ear Infirmary, Boston (1973-1975); Resident in Ophthalmology, The Johns Hopkins Hospital (1969-1973); PhD in Biology, Harvard University (1972); Intern, The Johns Hopkins Hospital (1965-1966); MD, The Johns Hopkins University (1965); AB, The Johns Hopkins University (1962) **Certifications:** Life Diplomate, American Board of Ophthalmology **Career:** W. Maxwell Thomas Chair Professor, The University of Texas Southwestern Medical Center (1995-Present); Medical Director, Associate Dean of Clinical Services, Zale Lipsky University Hospital, The University of Texas Southwestern Medical Center; Distinguished University Professor, The University of Texas Southwestern Medical Center (1991-1995); Vice Chairman, Department of Ophthalmology, The University of Texas Southwestern Medical Center (1991-1995); Professor, Georgetown University, Washington, DC (1987-1991); F. Phinizy Calhoun Professor of Ophthalmology, Emory University (1978-1987); Chairman, Department of Ophthalmology, Emory University (1978-1987); Member of Faculty, Emory University (1976-1987); Assistant Professor, Harvard University (1975-1976); Instructor in Ophthalmology, The Johns Hopkins Medical School (1969-1973) **Career Related:** Organizing Committee, Third-Fourth International Conference on Confocal Microscopy and Fourth-Fifth International Conference on 3D Image Processing in Microscopy (1991-Present); Member, Neurosciences Behavior Study Section, National Institutes of Health (1989-1993); Consultant, Bethesda Naval Hospital, U.S. Navy (1989-1991); Visiting Professor, Georgetown University (1986-1987); Knights Templar Foundation Civilian Consultant, U.S. Air Force (1983-1986); Consultant, Chairman, Visual Sciences Study Section, National Institutes of Health (1980-1984); Heed Foundation Scholar (1973-1974) **Creative Works:** Editor-in-chief, Eye and Contact Lens Journal (2002-2007); Editor-in-chief, Journal of Cornea (1989-1996); Member, Editorial Board, Journal of Scanning; Member, Editorial Board, Bioimaging Journal **Awards:** 35th Castroviejo Gold Medal (2009); Seventh Donald Korb Award, Contact Lens Society of America (2008); Hamano Gold Medal, 31st World Ophthalmology Congress, Contact Lens Society of America (2008); Named Top Doctor, Castle Connolly Medical Ltd. (2008); Texas Super Doctors (2008); Best Doctors in Dallas (2007); British Contact Lens Association Medal, International Society for Contact Lens Research (2007); Bausch and Lomb Visionaries Award, Eye Bank Association of America (2005); Montague Ruben Medal, International Society for Contact Lens Research (2005); Consumer Research Council Award (2002); Max Shapiro Award, American Academy of Optometry (2001); R. Townley Paton, M.D. Award, Eye Bank Association of America (2000); Senior Achievement Award, American Academy of Ophthalmology (1999); 21st James McDonald Lecturer, Loyola University Chicago (1998); George Nissal Lecturer, British Contact Lens Association (1997); Whitney Sampson Lecturer, American Academy of Ophthalmology (1997); Senior Scientist Investigators Award, Research to Prevent Blindness, Inc. (1996); Honor Recognition Award, Castroviejo Society for Corneal Surgeons (1987, 1996); Fifth Morton B. Server Lecturer, University of California, Berkeley (1991); 20th Conrad Behrens Medal Lecturer, Contact Lens Society of America (1989); Honor Recognition Award, Contact Lens Society of America (1988); 14th Waldert Lecturer, University of Rochester (1987); Honor Recognition Award, The Association for Research in Vision and Ophthalmology (1987); Honor Recognition Award, American Academy of Ophthalmology (1982); Heed Foundation Award (1981); Second Joseph Koplowitz Lecturer, Georgetown University (1983); Best Doctor in America (1979); Joseph Collins Scholarship, The Johns Hopkins University (1963-1965) **Membership:** Science Advisory Board, Singapore National Eye Center (2010-Present); President, International Society for Contact Lens Research (2009-2011); Lecturer, American Academy of Optometry (2005); Board of Directors, Eye Bank Association of America (1997-1999); President, South-Central Eyebank Association (1997); President, Castroviejo Society for Corneal Surgeons (1988-1990); Executive Secretary-treasurer, The Association for Research in Vision and Ophthalmology (1981-1986); Associate Section for Government Relations and Research, American Academy of Ophthalmology (1979-1983); Fellow, Royal Society of Medicine; Fellow, American Academy of Ophthalmology; Fellow, American College of Surgeons; Fellow, International College of Surgeons; Fellow, Royal Microscopy Society; Fellow, American Academy of Optometry; Board of Directors, Keratorefractive Society; Contact Lens Society of America; **Political Affiliations:** Republican **Religion:** Episcopalian **Business Address:** 5323 Harry Hines Blvd, Dallas, TX, 75390

William Cento

Title: Editor **Industry:** Writing and Editing **Date of Birth:** 03/20/1932 **Place of Birth:** St. Louis **State:** MO **Parents:** Frank Centro; Augusta A. (Albietz) Centro **Marital Status:** Single **Spouse Name:** Vera Ann Shaide (5/16/1964, Deceased 12/3/2006) **Education:** BS, Saint Louis University (1954) **Career:** Associate Editor, Pioneer Press, Digital First Media (1984-1990); Managing Editor, St. Paul Dispatch (Now Pioneer Press), Digital First Media (1977-1984); Graphics Editor, Pioneer Press & Dispatch (Now Pioneer Press), Digital First Media (1974-1977); Sunday Editor, Pioneer Press, Digital First Media (1967-1973); Wire Editor, Pioneer Press, Digital First Media (1965-1967); Make-Up Editor, Pioneer Press, Digital First Media (1962-1965); Copy Editor, St. Louis Post-Dispatch (1961-1962); Suburban Editor, St. Louis Globe-Democrat, LLC (1956-1961); General Assignment Reporter, East St. Louis Journal (1954-1956) **Career Related:** Owner, Give Me Rewrite (1990-2014); Editor, Letter from Minnesota (1999-2014); Publisher, Letter from Minnesota (1990-2014) **Civic:** Chairman, Newspaper Guild Unit, St. Louis Globe-Democrat (1959-1960) **Creative Works:** Editor, "Alone - For All Those Who Grieve" (2011); Editor, "Fifty and Feisty Associated Press Media Editors: 1933 to 1983" (1983); Producer, Monthly Newsletters, Twin Cities Unions; Producer, "AFL-CIO Newsletter," Minnesota AFL-CIO **Awards:** Award of Appreciation, Associated Press Managing Editors Association (1983); Makeup First Place Award (1969, 1971, 1974); Makeup Second Place Award (1971-1972); Page One Award, Twin Cities Newspaper Guild (Now Minnesota Newspaper and Communications Guild) **Membership:** Board of Directors, Associated Press Managing Editors Association (1982-1988); Society of Professional Journalists **Marquis Who's Who Honors:** Albert Nelson Marquis Lifetime Achievement Award (2017) **Why did you become involved in your profession or industry:** It all started when he would read the comics in the Sunday newspaper as a child. As he got older, he would read through the newspapers and always appreciated what the writers did. **Hobbies:** Painting; Graphic Design; Labor Unions **Religion:** Roman Catholic **Shipping Address:** 111 Imperial Dr W Apt 103, West Saint Paul, MN, 55118

Ronnie Chalif

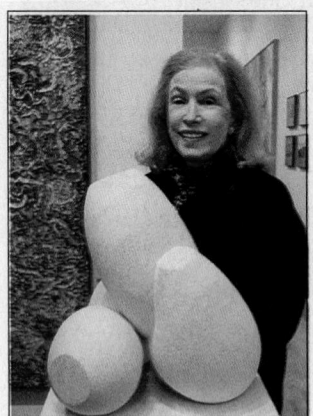

Title: Medical Association Co-Founder, Artist **Industry:** Fine Art **Date of Birth:** 04/14/1933 **Place of Birth:** New York City **State:** NY **Marital Status:** Married **Spouse Name:** Seymour Chalif (6/13/1954) **Children:** John Lewis; Peter Adley **Education:** BS in Art Education, New York University (1954); Graduate, Parsons School of Design, with Honors (1953) **Career:** Honorary President, Neuropathy Association (2009-Present); Artist, Sculptor, Painter (1968-Present); President, Neuropathy Association (2005-2009); Co-Founder, Director, Honorary President, Neuropathy Association (1995-2009); Buyer, I. Magnin & Co. (1954-1959) **Creative Works:** Exhibitor, Permanent Collection, Komas Hospice Center, Quiogue, NY (2017-2018); Exhibitor, Group Show, Southampton Cultural Center, NY (2012-2013); Solo Exhibitor, Arlene Bujese Gallery (2006, 1996); Solo Exhibitor, Gayle Willson Gallery (2003, 2000); Author, Illustrator, "Exercising with Neuropathy" (2001); Exhibitor, Group Show, Benson Gallery (2000-2002); Exhibitor, Group Show, Atelier 14, NY (2000); Exhibitor, Group Show, Arlene Bujese Gallery (1995-2006); Exhibitor, Group Show, Guild Hall Museum (1992-1993); Solo Exhibitor, Garrison Arts Center, NY (1989); Solo Exhibitor, Benton Gallery, Southampton, NY (1989); Exhibitor, Group Show, Ashwagh Hall, East Hampton, NY (1987-2008); Solo Exhibitor, Marymount Manhattan College Gallery (1986); Solo Exhibitor, Jackob K. Javits Federal Building (1986); Solo Exhibitor, Federal Court House, NY (1984-1985); Exhibitor, Group Show, GE Co., Fairfield, CT (1983); Solo Exhibitor, Benson Gallery, Bridghampton, NY (1975, 1972); Solo Exhibitor, Guild Hall Museum, East Hampton, NY; Exhibitor, Permanent Collection, Guild Hall Museum; Exhibitor, Permanent Collection, Continental Telephone Co., Washington; Exhibitor, Permanent Collection, McGraw-Hill, Inc.; Exhibitor, Permanent Collection, Cadillac-Fairview, Dallas, TX; Exhibitor, Permanent Collection, GE International Headquarters; Exhibitor, Permanent Collection, Grey Advertising Inc.; Exhibitor, Permanent Collection, US Home Corp., Houston, TX; Exhibitor, Permanent Collection, Zimmerli Art Museum, New Brunswick, NJ; Exhibitor, Permanent Collection, World Trade Center; Exhibitor, Permanent Collection, Sculpture Garden of the Gus & Judy Leiber Museum, East Hampton, NY **Membership:** Women's Caucus for Art; Women in Arts Foundation; National Association of Women Artists; New York Society Women Artists **What do you consider to be the highlight of your career:** A highlight of Ms. Chalif's Career was being featured in the World Trade Center. **Shipping Address:** 815 Park Ave Apt 8A, New York, NY, 10021

Johnnie Tucker Chambers

Title: Elementary School Educator **Industry:** Education/Educational Services **Company Name:** South Redford School District **Date of Birth:** 09/28/1929 **Place of Birth:** Crocket County **State:** TX **Parents:** Robert Leo; Lois K. (Slaughter) Tucker **Marital Status:** Married **Spouse Name:** R. Boyd Chambers **Children:** Theresa A.; Glyn Robert; Boyd James; John Trox **Education:** EdB, Sul Ross State University, Alpine, TX (1971) **Career:** Teacher, Fisher Elementary School, South Redford School District (2001-Present); With, Cactus Health Services; Teacher, Pre-K-6, Redford Elementary School, Texas (2001); Teacher, Pre-K, Kindergarten, 1st and 2nd Grades, Candelaria Elementary and Junior High (1996-1999); Head Teacher, Pre-K to 8th Grades, Candelaria Elementary and Junior High (1996-1998); Acting Principal, Candelaria Elementary and Junior High (1995-1998); Teacher, Pre-Kindergarten, Kindergarten and 1st grade, Candelaria Elementary School (1993-1998); Teacher, 2nd and 3rd Grades, Candelaria Elementary School (1991-1993); Head Teacher, K-8, Candelaria Elementary School (1977-1991); Head Teacher K-8, Ruidosa Elementary School, Texas (1973-1977); Teacher, 1st and 2nd grades, Candelaria Elementary School, Texas (1971-1973) **Career Related:** Board of Directors, Cactus Health Services Inc (2012-Present); President, Big Bend Retired Teachers Association (2014); Member, Sight-Based Decision Making, Presidio, Inc. (1991-1994); Member, Chihuahuan Desert Research Institute, Alpine (1982-1994); Member, Family Crisis Board **Civic:** Board of Directors, Big Bend Regional Hospital District (2001-Present); Family Crisis Center, Big Bend Inc. (2006); Chapter Member, Sheriffs Association of Texas, Austin (1980); Leader, Boy Scouts of America, Ruidoso and Candelaria (1973-1991); Cub Scout Leader (1973-1991); Member, Center for Big Bend Studies; Member, Cactus Health Services, Inc. **Awards:** Litter Gitter Award (1994-1995); Awards, Boy Scouts America (1969, 1983) **Membership:** Texas State Teachers Association; Texas Federation of Republican Women; Cactos Medical Services; The Archaeological Conservancy; Phi Alpha Theta; Daughters of the Texas Republic; Delta Kappa Gamma Society International; Beta Iota Chapter; President, Retired Teachers Association **Marquis Who's Who Honors:** Albert Nelson Marquis Lifetime Achievement Award (2017) **Hobbies:** Hiking; Camping; Anthropology; Cave exploring; Cooking **Shipping Address:** 707 E Hancock Ave, Alpine, TX, 79830

Paul Kukwon Chang, PhD

Title: Theology Studies Educator, Researcher, Pastor **Industry:** Religious **Date of Birth:** 04/15/1938 **Place of Birth:** Yesan **Country of Origin:** Chungnam/Korea **Parents:** Hyun Tae Chang; Dae Jae Lee **Marital Status:** Married **Spouse Name:** Yeon Sook Lee (5/15/1982) **Children:** Sang Eun; Sang Young **Education:** PhD, Muenster University (1980); AM, Duke University (1971); MA, Seoul National University (1967); BA, Seoul National University (1961) **Career:** Professor, Hansei University, Kunpo, Korea (1990-2001); President, Korean Society for Ancient Near Eastern Studies, Seoul, Korea (1983-2001); Director, Aram Institute for Ancient Studies, Anyang, Republic of Korea (1981-2001) **Career Related:** Director, Institute for Researchers on Metatheology, Chapel Hill, NC (2003-Present); Adviser to the Director of the General International Biographical Center, Cambridge, England (2001-Present); Secretary General, United Cultural Convention, Raleigh, NC (2001-Present); Senior Fellow, Institute for Interdisciplinary Studies, Pasadena, CA (1997-Present); Research Scholar, Duke University, Durham, NC (1999-2002); Visiting Scholar, Cornell University, Ithaca, NY (1985-1987); Visiting Scholar, University of Pennsylvania (1985-1987); Guest Lecturer, American Oriental Society, University of California, Los Angeles; Guest Lecturer, International Conference on the Tower of Babel and Ziggurats **Military Service:** First Lieutenant, Republic of Korea Army (1963-1967) **Creative Works:** Author, "Destiny Determinations in Ancient Mesopotamia, A Criterion for Culture Critique of the Ancient World"; Author, "Promotionsschrift"; Author, "Habilitationschrift"; Author, "Metatheology"; Contributor, "The Cardiomorphological Functions of the Sumerian SA for Heart," Journal of the Russian Academy of Sciences (Now Doklady Mathematics); Contributor, Articles, Professional Journals **Awards:** Honoree, One of the 500 Greatest Geniuses of the 21st Century, Board of Governors, American Biographical Institute (2007) **Marquis Who's Who Honors:** Albert Nelson Marquis Lifetime Achievement Award (2017) **Shipping Address:** 223 Forbush Mountain Drive, Chapel Hill, NC, 27514

James Min-Tzu Chao

Title: Architect **Industry:** Architecture & Construction **Company Name:** James M.T. Chao, Architect **Date of Birth:** 02/27/1940 **Place of Birth:** Dairen **Country of Origin:** China **Marital Status:** Married **Spouse Name:** Kirsti Helena Lehtonen (5/15/1968) **Education:** BArch, University of California, Berkeley (1965) **Certifications:** Certified Architect, National Council of Architectural Registration Boards (1998-Present); Registered Architect, State of California; Registered Architect, State of Arizona; Registered Architect, State of Colorado; Registered Architect, State of Illinois; Registered Architect, State of New Mexico; Registered Architect, State of Nevada; Certified Real Estate Instructor, State of California **Career:** Director of Real Estate, Papillon MDC Inc. (1998-Present); Architect, Private Practice, Berkeley, CA (1987-Present); Marketing Committee, Straw Hat Cooperative Corporation, San Francisco, CA (1988-1991); Senior Manager, The Straw Hat Restaurant Corporation, San Francisco, CA (1981-1987); Director of Real Estate and Construction, The Straw Hat Restaurant Corporation, San Francisco, CA (1981-1987); Construction Manager, The Straw Hat Restaurant Corporation, San Francisco, CA (1979-1981); Project Manager, B.A. Premises Corporation, San Francisco, CA (1971-1979); Job Captain, Hammaberg and Herman, Architects, Oakland, CA (1969-1971); Assistant to the President, Import Plus Inc., Santa Clara, CA (1967-1969); Intermediate Draftsman, Spencer, Lee & Busse, Architects, San Francisco, CA (1966-1967) **Career Related:** Chief Executive Officer, Nuts and Bolts Books (1997-Present); National Training Director, Excel Telecommunications, Inc. (Now Impact Telecom) (1995-1999); Vice President, Intersyn Industries California (1993-1999); Principal Architect, Alpha Consultant Group Inc. (1991-1998); President, Stratsac, Inc. (1987-1992); Chief Executive Officer, Stratsac, Inc. (1987-1992); President, Food Service Consultants Inc. (1987-1989); Lecturer on Commercial Real Estate Site Analysis; Lecturer on Site Selection for Professional Real Estate Seminars; Coordinator, Minority Vending Program, Bank of America Corporation; Coordinator, Solar Application Program, Bank of America Corporation; Guest Faculty Member, Northwest Center for Professional Education. **Civic:** Board of Directors, Berkeley City Ballet (2008-Present); Patron Charter Member, Asian Art Museum Chong-Moon Lee Center for Asian Art and Culture (2002-Present) **Creative Works:** Author, "Secrets from Macau" (2014); Author, "The Green Kayak" (2014); Author, "The Street-Smart Restaurant Development Handbook" (1996); Inventor, "Wheels for Luggage" (1972); Patentee, Tidal Electric Generating System; Author, First Comprehensive Consumer Orientated Performance Specification for Remote Banking Transaction **Membership:** Encinal Yacht Club (1974-Present); Board of Directors, Encinal Yacht Club (1977-1978); Gold Sponsor, Asian Pacific Islander American Public Affairs Association **Marquis Who's Who Honors:** Albert Nelson Marquis Lifetime Achievement Award (2017) **To what do you attribute your success:** Mr. Chao attributes his success to a positive attitude and strong determination to succeed. His father taught him self sufficiency at an early age. He put himself through college, and was originally designing furniture but switched to architecture to be able to have more of an impact on society. He bought his first house while attending college, and still lives in that house today. **Why did you become involved in your profession or industry:** Mr. Chao became involved in his profession to improve quality of life for society and the environment. **What do you consider to be the highlight of your career:** Mr. Chao is proud of being a problem solver through invention, taking risks, and not focusing on personal financial gains, but on how to be of service to society. He created many inventions, one of which was putting the wheels on luggage. He continues to serve on the board of Berkeley City Ballet, and was able to impart to them not just how to raise money, but how to make money which could be reinvested into the nonprofit. In other words, he imparted to them how to be self-sufficient and productive rather than asking for donations. He, for example, still lives in the house he purchased with the money he made while attending college. He has been caring for his wife throughout her illness and is continuing to do so; he has gone out of his way to give her the most pleasant experiences and taken her on trips to beautiful environments in Hawaii to keep her mentally positive, despite her illness. **Where will you be in five years:** In five years, Mr. Chao hopes to be in the same place, doing the same things. **Political Affiliations:** Republican **Shipping Address:** 1136 Keith Avenue, Berkeley, CA, 94708-1607

John M. Chaves

Industry: Medicine & Health Care **Company Name:** John Chaves, DDS **Education:** DDS, Loma Linda University (1990) **Career:** Dentist, Dr. John Chaves, DDS (1991-Present) **Career Related:** Fellow, World Congress of Micro-Invasive Dentistry; Fellow Associate, World Clinical Laser Institute; Fellow, American Association of Cosmetic Dentistry **Civic:** Charity Work, Women's Shelters **Membership:** Founding Member, ExperDent Centers of Dental Excellence; Co-Founder, World Congress of Minimally Invasive Dentistry; Co-Founder, World Clinical Laser Institute; Co-Founder, Academy of Clinical Sleep Disorders Dentistry; International College of Craniomandibular Orthopedics; International Congress of Oral Implantologists; American Academy of Pain Management; American Equilibration Society; American Academy of Cranial Facial Pain; American Academy of Implant Dentistry; American College of Oral Implantologists; Academy of General Dentistry; American Dental Association; California Dental Association; San Fernando Valley Dental Association; Academy of Laser Dentistry; Naturopathic Medical Association; Dental Organization of Conscious Sedation; Academy of Dental Sleep Medicine **Why did you become involved in your profession or industry:** Dr. Chaves became involved in his profession because he had an amazing dentist that he looked up to in South Africa. **Where will you be in five years:** In five years, Dr. Chaves intends to seek out the latest procedures in dentistry. **Hobbies:** Tennis; Cars **Shipping Address:** 5312 Comercio Lane, Suite A, Dr. John Chaves, DDS, Woodland Hills, CA, 91364 **Website:** http://www.woodlandhillsdentist.org

Kerry Cheesman

Title: Science Educator **Industry:** Education/Educational Services **Company Name:** Capital University **Date of Birth:** 09/28/1954 **Place of Birth:** Santa Barbara **State:** CA **Parents:** Theodore Richard Cheesman; Barbara Jean (Wyckoff) Cheesman **Marital Status:** Married **Spouse Name:** Maryann Cheesman (11/20/2010) **Children:** Ian Walling; Nathan Elisha **Education:** MS, Indiana University (1987); PhD, University of Illinois (1981); BA, UC Santa Barbara (1976) **Career:** Robert M. Geist Endowed Chair of Biological Sciences, Capital University (2012-Present); Professor, Capital University (1996-Present); Chair, Biology Department, Capital University (1994-2001); Associate Professor, Capital University (1993-1996); Associate Professor, St. Francis College (1991-1992); Assistant Professor, St. Francis College (1987-1990); Assistant Professor, Northwestern University (1983-1986); Research Associate, Feinberg School of Medicine, Northwestern University (1981-1982); Research Assistant, University of Illinois Hospital & Health Sciences System (1977-1980) **Career Related:** Director of Health Professors, Capital University (1993-Present); Director of Medical Technology Program, St. Francis College (1989-1992); Associate Director of Endocrine Laboratories, Feinberg School of Medicine, Northwestern University (1983-1986) **Civic:** Board of Directors, Building a Presence for Science in Ohio (2004-Present); Board of Directors, CAAHP (2002-Present); Board of Directors, National Council, Boy Scouts of America (1999-Present); Board of Directors, Native American Indian Center of Central Ohio (1996-Present); Board of Directors, Columbus Chapter, Boys Scouts of America (1994-Present); Board of Directors, NAAHP (2000-2012); Board of Directors, Ohio Scientific Education & Research Association (1997-2010); Board of Directors, Fort Wayne Habitat for Humanity (1985-1992); Board of Directors, Fort Wayne Chapter, Boy Scouts of America (1985-1992) **Creative Works:** Editor, Ohio Journal of Science (2004-2008); Author, "Photographic Guide to Species and Ecology of Camp Lazarus" (2006); Author, "Medical Terminology" (1999); Author, "Scientific Terminology" (1997) **Awards:** Scholarship, The University of California (1972) **Membership:** Fellow, The Ohio Academy of Science; American Association for the Advancement of Science; College Science Teaching Committee, National Science Teachers Association; Endocrine Society; Society for the Study of Reproduction; Board of Directors, The Society for College Science Teachers; Secretary Treasurer, The Society for College Science Teachers; The North American Association for Environmental Education; The New York Academy of Sciences; Board of Directors, The Ohio Academy of Science; Board of Directors, College and University Committee, National Association of Biology Teachers; Education Committee, Ohio Scientific Education & Research Association **Marquis Who's Who Honors:** Albert Nelson Marquis Lifetime Achievement Award (2017) **Hobbies:** Camping; Backpacking; Working with youth **Shipping Address:** 1 College and Main Dept Dr, Capital University - Biology Sciences, Columbus, OH, 43209

Chunduri Venkata Chelapati, PhD

Title: President **Industry:** Engineering **Company Name:** Irvine Institute of Technology **Date of Birth:** 03/11/1933 **Place of Birth:** Eluru **Country of Origin:** India **Parents:** Lakshminarayana Chunduri; Anjamma (Kanumuri) Chunduri **Education:** PhD, University of Illinois (1962); MS, University of Illinois (1959); Diploma in Civil Engineering and Hydraulics, Indian Institute of Science, Bangalore, India (1956); BE, Andhra University, with Honors (1954) **Career:** President, Irvine Institute of Technology (2002-Present); President, C.V. Chelapati & Associates, Inc., Huntington Beach, CA (1979-2001); Director, Research Center, The Center for Advanced Due Diligence Studies, California State University, Long Beach, CA (1986-1996); Director, Continuing Engineering Education, California State University, Long Beach, CA (1982-1996); Department Chairman, California State University, Long Beach, CA (1973-1979); Coordinator, Professional Engineering Review Programs, California State University, Long Beach, CA (1972-1981); Department Vice Chairman, California State University, Long Beach, CA (1971-1973); Professor, Civil Engineering, California State University, Long Beach, CA (1970-1996); Associate Professor, California State University, Long Beach, CA (1965-1970); Assistant Engineering Professor, California State University, Long Beach, CA (1962-1965); Research Assistant, Department of Civil Engineering, University of Illinois (1957-1962); Assistant Professor, Structural Engineering, Birla College of Engineering, Pilani, India (1956-1957); Junior Engineer, Office of Chief Engineer, State Of Andhra, India (1954-1955) **Career Related:** President, Continuing Professional Education Institute (2000-Present); President, Professional Engineering Development Publications (1988-Present); Consultant, Civil Engineering Laboratory, U.S. Navy (1975-1994); Consultant, Holmes & Narver, Inc., Anaheim, CA (1968-1973); Consultant, Civil Engineering Laboratory, U.S. Navy (1962-1968) **Creative Works:** Contributor, Articles, Professional Journals **Membership:** American Society of Civil Engineers; American Society for Engineering Education; Structural Engineers Association of Southern California; Earthquake Engineering Research Institute; Seismological Society of America; American Concrete Institute; American Institute of Steel Construction; Sigma Xi; Chi Epsilon; Tau Beta Pi; Phi Kappa Phi **Marquis Who's Who Honors:** Albert Nelson Marquis Lifetime Achievement Award (2017); Distinguished Humanitarian (2017) **Why did you become involved in your profession or industry:** Dr. Chelapati became involved in his profession because engineers are highly respected in his home country of India, and there were very few people in that field when he began in 1954. **What do you consider to be the highlight of your career:** While Dr. Chelapati does not have a singular highlight in his career, he is proud of his profession as a whole, as the world is becoming smaller and smaller. Yet with construction still needed throughout the world, there are more opportunities in the field of engineering to pursue. **Shipping Address:** 21 Shadowcast, Newport Coast, CA, 92657

Theresa Cheng

Title: Neurosurgeon **Industry:** Medicine & Health Care **Company Name:** Affinity Health Systems **Parents:** Wayne Cheng; Florence Cheng **Education:** Coursework, Johns Hopkins University (2016-Present); MD, Medical College of Wisconsin (1989); PhD, Medical College of Wisconsin (1989); Degree in Biomedical Engineering, Marquette University (1982) **Certifications:** Certified in Advanced Trauma Life Support, American College of Surgeons (1996); Certified in Advanced Cardiac Life Support, American Heart Association, Inc. (1989); Diplomate, American Board of Neurological Surgery; Ordained, Eucharistic Ministry of the Catholic Church (1980) **Career:** Director of Medical Operations, Affinity Health System (2007-2016); Chief of Neurosurgery, Affinity Health System (2002-2016); Chairman, Department of Neurosurgery, Luther Midelfort Campus, Mayo Clinic Health System (2000-2002); Consultant in Neurosurgery, Luther Midelfort Campus, Mayo Clinic Health System (1995-2002); Special Fellow in Neurosurgery, Mayo Foundation for Medical Education and Research (1998-1999); Postdoctoral Fellow in Molecular Genetics, Mayo Foundation for Medical Education and Research (1992-1993); Neurosurgery Resident, Mayo Foundation for Medical Education and Research (1989-1995); Adjunct Instructor of Medical Neuroanatomy, Department of Anatomy and Cellular Biology, Medical College of Wisconsin, (1987-1989); Teaching Assistant in Medical Neuroanatomy, Department of Anatomy and Cellular Biology, Medical College of Wisconsin (1984-1987); Research Assistant, Department of Neurology, Medical College of Wisconsin (1984); Research Assistant, Department of Medicine, Medical College of Wisconsin (1984); Research Assistant, Department of Endocrinology, Medical College of Wisconsin (1984); Teaching Assistant in Medical Gross Anatomy, Department of Anatomy and Cellular Biology, Medical College of Wisconsin (1983-1984); Teaching Assistant in Engineering-Level Mathematics and Physics, Marquette University (1979-1982) **Civic:** Board of Directors, Gold Cross Ambulance Service (2002-Present); Medical Executive Committee Member, Luther Midelfort Campus, Mayo Clinic Health System (2001-2007); Eucharistic Minister, Catholic Church (1980-2003); Medical Director, ThinkFirst (2000-2002); Co-Director of Neuro-Pediatrics-Trauma Intensive Care Unit, Luther Midelfort Campus, Mayo Clinic Health System (2001-2002); Board of Directors, Eau Claire Dunn Pepin Medical Society Fund, Eau Claire Community Foundation (1999-2002); President-Elect, Epilepsy Foundation Western Wisconsin (1999-2002); Board of Directors, Epilepsy Foundation Western Wisconsin (1999-2002); Professional Advisory Board, Epilepsy Foundation Western Wisconsin (1999-2002) **Creative Works:** Contributor, Articles, Professional Journals; Artist, Wax Paintings **Awards:** Recipient, Grant, Mayo Foundation for Medical Education and Research (1992); Recipient, Second Place Award, Wisconsin State Fair Park (1985); Recipient, Summer Research Fellowship, Medical College of Wisconsin (1983); Recipient, Scholarship, Park Nicollet (1979-1980); Recipient, College Scholarship, AAUW (1979) **Membership:** Honorary Master, Epilepsy Foundation Western Wisconsin; American Association for the Advancement of Science; American Association for Cancer Research; Wisconsin Medical Society; American Association of Neurological Surgeons; Caduceus Society, The City College of New York; Good Samaritan Club; Alpha Epsilon Delta The Health Preprofessional Honor Society; The Tau Beta Pi Association, Inc. **Marquis Who's Who Honors:** Albert Nelson Marquis Lifetime Achievement Award (2017) **Hobbies:** Outdoor activities; Sports and recreation; Music; Writing; Community volunteering **Shipping Address:** 3305A Walden Ln, Oshkosh, WI, 54904 **Website:** http://www.waxpaintings.com/

William Y. Chey

Title: Physician (Retired) **Industry:** Education/Educational Services **Date of Birth:** 01/21/1930 **Place of Birth:** Ki Jang **Country of Origin:** Republic of Korea **Parents:** Kee Bok Chey; Myungkwon (Lee) Chey **Marital Status:** Married **Spouse Name:** Fan K. Tang **Children:** William D.; Donna C.; Richard D.; Laura C. **Education:** DSc, University of Pennsylvania (1966); MSc, University of Pennsylvania (1962); Research Fellow in Gastroenterology, Samuel S. Fells Research Institute (1959-1960); Fellow in Hepatology, Seton Hall Medical College, Jersey City, NJ (1957-1958); Resident in Pathology, Mount Sinai Hospital, NY (1956-1957); Resident, New York City Hospital (1955-1956); Intern, New York City Hospital, New York City, NY (1954-1955); MD, Seoul National University, Korea (1953) **Career:** Professor of Medicine, University of Rochester, Rochester, NY (1995-2000); Founding Director, William B. and Sheila Konar Center for Digestive Liver Disease, Rochester, NY (1995-2000); Physician, Strong Memorial Hospital, Rochester, NY (1992-2000); Director, Division of Gastroenterology and Hepatology, School of Medicine and Dentistry, University of Rochester, Rochester, NY (1992-2000); Professor of Medicine, University of Rochester, Rochester, NY (1988-2000); Clinical Professor, University of Rochester, Rochester, NY (1977-1988); Senior Attending Physician, Founding Director, Isaac Gordon Center for Digestive Diseases and Nutrition, The Genesee Hospital, Rochester, NY (1971-1991); Professor of Medicine, University of Rochester, Rochester, NY (1971-1977); Associate Professor, Samuel S. Fels Research Institute, Yellow Springs, OH (1968-1971); Private Practice in Gastroenterology, Philadelphia, PA (1967-1971); Assistant Professor, Samuel S. Fells Research Institute (1965-1968); Associate, Samuel S. Fels Research Institute (1963); Attending Physician, Temple University Medical Center, Philadelphia, PA (1963-2014); Instructor of Medicine, Samuel S. Fels Research Institute (1961); Research Associate, Samuel S. Fells Research Institute (1961) **Career Related:** Visiting Professor, Korea University College of Medicine, Seoul, Republic of Korea (1991-Present); Hallym University College of Medicine, Choonchun, Republic of Korea (1986-Present); Peking Union Medical College, Chinese Academy Medical Sciences, Beijing, China (1985-Present); Honorary Professor, Catholic University Medical College, Seoul, Republic of Korea (1983-Present); Director, Rochester Institute of Digestive Diseases and Sciences, New York (2000-2011); Consultant, Gastroenterologist Canadaigua VA Hospital, Canandaigua, NY (1977-2000); Shanghai Medical University (1987); Member, Surgery and Bioengineering Study Section, National Institute of Diabetes, Digestive and Kidney Diseases, National Institutes of Health, Bethesda, MD (1982-1986); Clinical Professor of Medicine, Yunsei University School of Medicine (1984-1986) **Creative Works:** Editor-in-Chief, "Clinical Endoscopy" (2011-Present); Editorial Board, "The Pancreas, American Journal of Physiology"; Contributor, Articles, Professional and Scientific Journals and Textbooks **Awards:** Vay Liang and Frisca Go Award for Lifetime Achievement, American Pancreatic Association (2014); Distinguished Service Award, Rochester Academy of Medicine (2012); Mentors Research Award, American Gastroenterological Association (2007); American Gastroenterological Association Legacy Society (2007); Distinguished Clinician Award, American Gastroenterological Association (2004); Governor's Award for Excellence in Clinical Research, American College of Gastroenterology (2000) **Membership:** President, American Pancreatic Association (1999-2000); President, American Society of Acupuncturists (1991-1995); Fellow, American College of Gastroenterology; American Gastroenterological Association; American Association for the Advancement of Science; American Federation for Clinical Research; American Physiological Society; American Association for the Study of Liver Diseases; International Association of Pancreatology; American Motility Society; American Society for Gastrointestinal Endoscopy; American College of Acupuncture; Korean Society of Gastrointestinal Endoscopy; Rochester Academy of Medicine **Marquis Who's Who Honors:** Albert Nelson Marquis Lifetime Achievement Award (2017); Distinguished Humanitarian (2017) **Shipping Address:** 418 Stoutenbugh Ln, Pittsford, NY, 14534

Yung Frank Chiang

Title: Professor of Law **Industry:** Education/Educational Services **Company Name:** Fordham University **Date of Birth:** 01/02/1936 **Place of Birth:** Taichung **Country of Origin:** Taiwan **Parents:** Ruey-ting Chiang; Yueh-yin (Ho) Chiang **Marital Status:** Married **Spouse Name:** Quay-yin Lin **Children:** Amy P.; David H. **Education:** JD, The University of Chicago The Law School (1965); LLM, Northwestern University (1962); LLB, National Taiwan University (1958) **Career:** Professor, School of Law, Fordham University (1976-Present); Associate Professor, School of Law, Fordham University (1972-1976); Assistant Professor, School of Law, University of Georgia (1967-1972); Research Associate, Harvard Law School, Cambridge, MA (1965-1967); Editor, The Lawyers Cooperative Publishing Company, Rochester, NY (1965); Associate, Yen & Lai Law Office, Taipei, Taiwan (1960-1961) **Career Related:** Visiting Professor, Chuo University, Tokyo, Japan (2005); Visiting Professor, Institute of Comparative Law, Japan (2005); President, Law Faculty Union, Fordham University (1999-2010); Organizer, Five Russian Delegations to Ambassador Program, People to People International (1994-1995); Moderator, Five Russian Delegations to Ambassador Program, People to People International (1994-1995); Leader, New York Judge and Lawyers Delegation to China and Hong Kong, People to People International (1994); Legal Consultant, Asia Bank, N.A. (1983-1988); Vice-Chairman, Asia Bank, N.A. (1983-1988); Board of Directors, Asia Bank, N.A. (1983-1988); Board of Directors, New York Taiwan Center **Civic:** President, New York Chapter, FAPA (1991-1992); President, The Taiwan Merchants Association of New York (1980-1984); Organizer, Board of Directors, The Taiwan Merchants Association of New York (1976-1996) **Creative Works:** Author, "The One-China Policy: State, Sovereignty, and Taiwan's International Legal Status" (2017); Contributor, Articles, Professional Journals **Awards:** 20th Century Achievement Award, International Biographical Centre (1995) **Membership:** President, NATPA (1998-1999); Vice President, NATPA (1997-1998); Board of Directors, NATPA (1994-2000); Arbitrator, National Association of Securities Dealers (1976-1998); Order of the Coif **Bar Admissions:** New York State Bar Association (1974); Taiwan Bar Association (1960) **Why did you become involved in your profession or industry:** Mr. Chiang became involved in his profession because he believes that law is very important in society to keep everything peaceful and fair. **Where will you be in five years:** In five years, Mr. Chiang will continue doing what he has been doing, which is continuing to serve the people and grow in knowledge. **Hobbies:** Reading; Skiing; Archery; Swimming **Business Address:** 150 W 62nd Street, New York, NY, 10023 **Shipping Address:** 150 W 62nd Street, Fordham University Law School, New York, NY, 10023

Graciela Chichilnisky, PhD

Title: 1) Scientist, Mathematician, Economist, Educator, Writer 2) Chief Executive Officer **Industry:** Education/Educational Services **Company Name:** 1) Columbia University 2) Global Thermostat **Date of Birth:** 03/27/1946 **Place of Birth:** Buenos Aires **State:** Argentina **Parents:** Salomon Chichilnisky; Raquel Gavensky **Children:** Eduardo Jose; Natasha Sable; Artico Salomon Chichilnisky **Education:** PhD in Economics, University of California, Berkeley (1976); PhD in Mathematics, University of California, Berkeley (1971); MA, University of California, Berkeley (1970); Graduate Coursework, Special PhD Student in Mathematics, Massachusetts Institute of Technology (1967-1968) **Career:** Director, Columbia Center for Risk Management (Now Center for the Management of Systemic Risk), Columbia University, New York City, NY (1998-Present); Professor of Economics and Statistics, Columbia University, New York City, NY (1998-Present); Director, Program on Information and Resources, Columbia University, New York City, NY (1994-Present); Professor, Columbia University, New York City, NY (1980-Present); Sir Louis Matheson Distinguished Professor, Monash University, Australia (2008-2010); UNESCO Professor of Mathematics and Economics, Columbia University, New York City, NY (1995-2003); Keynes Salimbemi Chair in Economics, University of Siena, Italy (1994-1995); Keynes Chair in Economics, University of Essex, United Kingdom (1980-1983); Fellow, Harvard Institute for International Development, Harvard University (1978); Associate Professor, Columbia University, New York City, NY (1977-1979); Lecturer, Department of Economics, Harvard University (1975); Postdoctoral Fellow, Harvard University (1974); Distinguished Guest Professor, Nankai University; Distinguished Guest Professor, Beijing Normal University, China; Member, Board of Trustees, Capital Institute, New York, NY; Trustee, NRDC, New York **Career Related:** Co-founder, Chief Executive Officer, and Managing Director, Global Thermostat (2010-Present); Senior Adviser to the President, The University of Arizona (2004-Present); Department of Economics, Institute of International Studies (1993-Present); Visiting Professor, Stanford University (2015-2017); Consultant, The World Bank Group (2009); IUCN, International Union for Conservation of Nature (2009); European Economic Area (2009); Special Adviser to President Oscar Arias, Costa Rica (2007); Senior Research Fellow, International Monetary Fund, Washington, DC (2007); Consultant, International Monetary Fund (2007); Co-chairman, United Nations Latin American Economic Forum, NY (2007); Senior Adviser to the President, Costa Rica (2006-2007); Adviser, United Nations Association, United Nations Federation (2006); Co-chairman, United Nations Latin American Economic Forum, NY (2006); Special Adviser, WFUNA (2006); Chairman, Cross Border Exchange Corporation (Now Springboard Enterprises) (2003-2005); Representative, IPCC (2002-2006); University of Siena, Italy (2002); Chief Executive Officer, Cross Border Exchange Corporation (Now Springboard Enterprises) (1999-2003); Architect, Carbon Market, The Kyoto Protocol of the United Nations, United Nations Framework Convention on Climate Change (1997); US Lead Author, Working Group III, IPCC (1996-1998); United Nations Educational Chair in Mathematics and Economics, Columbia University (1995-2008) **Creative Works:** Author, "Handbook of the Economics of Climate Change" (2017); Author, "The Handbook of Economics of the Global Environment" (2017); Author, "The Economics of Climate Change" (2010); Author, "Saving Kyoto" (2009); Author, "Environmental Markets: Equity and Efficiency" (1999); Author, "Sustainability: Dynamics and Uncertainty" (1998); Author, "Mathematical Economics" (1998); Author, "Topology and Markets" (1998); Author, "Markets, Information and Uncertainty" (1998); Author, "Oil in the International Economy" (1991); Author, "The Evolving International Economy" (1986); Author, "Advances in Mathematics" (1985); Author, Journal of Development Economics (1976-1986); Associate Editor, Journal of Development Economics (1976-1986); Co-author, "Catastrophe or New Society? A Latin American World Model" (1976); Author, "Risk Decision and Policy"; Author, "Reversing Climate Change"; Patentee, 35 Patents, Direct Air Capture Technology and Trademark "Carbon Negative" **Awards:** 10 Most Influential Latinos in the U.S., Hispanic Business (2006-Present); Grantee, National Science Foundation (1974-Present); Great Immigrants, Great Americans Award, Carnegie Foundation (2017); Chief Executive Officer of the Year, Americas Renewable Energy Institute (2015); Global Leadership Award, Americas Renewable Energy Institute (2014); Speaking Out Prize, National Women's Studies Association (2007); Global Citizen, Athens, Greece (2007) **Membership:** AREI; Global Thermostat; National Women's Studies Association; American Chemical Society; The Royal Academy of Arts, London, United Kingdom; American Mathematical Society; American Economic Association **Marquis Who's Who Honors:** Albert Nelson Marquis Lifetime Achievement Award (2017) **Business Address:** 335 Riverside Drive, Global Thermostat, New York, NY, 10025

Nancy Childs-Kirkland

Title: Secondary School Educator, Consultant **Industry:** Education/Educational Services **Company Name:** Buchholz High School **Date of Birth:** 07/20/1937 **Place of Birth:** Ideal **State:** GA **Parents:** Millard Geddings Childs; Bessie Vioda (Forbes) Childs **Marital Status:** Widowed **Spouse Name:** Clarence Nathaniel Kirkland, Jr. (12/12/1987, Deceased 2/17/17); Allard Corley French, Jr. (4/22/1961, Divorced 12/7/1978) **Children:** Vianne Elizabeth French-Marchese; Alysia French-Joyce **Education:** EdD in School Management and Instructional Leadership, Nova University (1993); MS, Troy State University (1977); AB in Speech and Religious Education, LaGrange College (1959) **Certifications:** Certified Instructor of Professional Refinements in Developing Effectiveness; Certified Teacher of Effectiveness and Classroom Handling; Certified Teacher of English; Certified Teacher of Religion **Career:** English Teacher, Buchholz High School, Gainesville, FL (1982-2000); Director, Development Reading Laboratory, Chiefland High School (1979-1982); English Teacher, Marianna High School (1972-1977); English Teacher, Choctawhatchee High School, Fort Walton Beach, FL (1966-1968); English Teacher, Samson High School (1965); Teacher, Fifth Grade, Sheridan Elementary School, Bloomington, IL (1964-1965); English Teacher, Woodland Junior High School, Streater, IL (1963-1964); Social Studies Teacher, Woodland Junior High School, Streater, IL (1963-1964); English Teacher, Flanagan Junior-Senior High School (1962-1963); Director of Christian Education, First Methodist Church, Thomson, GA (1959) **Career Related:** Co-founder, KPS Leadership Specialists, Jonesboro, GA (1993-Present); Consultant, KPS Leadership Specialists, Jonesboro, GA (1993-Present); Chairperson, Buchholz Facilities Committee, Gainesville, FL (1993-Present); Adjunct Professor, English, Santa Fe Community College, Gainesville, FL (1996); Assistant Chairperson, Buchholz English Department, Gainesville, FL (1989-1992); English Instructor, Santa Fe Community College, Gainesville, FL (1982-1987) **Civic:** Secretary, Buchholz School Advisory Council, Gainesville, FL (1994-1995); Co-chairman, Buchholz School Advisory Council, Gainesville, FL (1994-1995); Buchholz School Advisory Council, Gainesville, FL (1994-1995); Coordinator, Gainesville Sister Cities Youth Correspondence Program (1991-1993); Teacher, Sunday School, State of Florida; Director, Sunday School, State of Florida; Teacher Trainer, Sunday School, State of Florida; Actress, Church Groups, Alabama; Actress, Church Groups, State of Georgia; Actress, Church Groups, State of Illinois; Director, Little Theaters, State of Illinois; Director, Little Theaters, State of Georgia; Director, Little Theaters, State of Alabama **Creative Works:** Contributor, Articles, Professional Journals; Author, Two Practicums **Membership:** Chair Person, Altrusa Evening Group, Altrusa House (2013-Present); President, Altrusa House (2011-Present); Chair Group, Altrusa International, Inc., Gainesville, FL (2013-2014); President, Gainesville Woman's Club (2010-2012); Board of Directors, Gainesville Woman's Club (2009-2010); President, Altrusa International, Inc., Gainesville, FL (2008-2009); Vice President, Altrusa International, Inc., Gainesville, FL (2007-2008); Board Member, Altrusa House (2006-2010); Second Vice President, Altrusa International, Inc., Gainesville, FL (2006-2007); Director, Altrusa International, Inc., Gainesville, FL (2003-2006); Secretary, Altrusa International, Inc., Gainesville, FL (2002); President, Alachua Council of Teachers of English (1992-1993); Grantee, Alachua Multicultural Council (1992); Vice President, Alachua Council of Teachers of English (1991-1992); American Association of University Women; Association for Supervision and Curriculum Development; NCTE; Gainesville Area Chamber of Commerce **Marquis Who's Who Honors:** Albert Nelson Marquis Lifetime Achievement Award (2017) **To what do you attribute your success:** Dr. Childs-Kirkland attributes her success to her nurture in solid Christian values and a positive work ethic. **Why did you become involved in your profession or industry:** Dr. Childs-Kirkland became involved in her profession because of her love of teaching and desire to use her talents to make a positive contribution to society. **What do you consider to be the highlight of your career:** A highlight of Dr. Childs-Kirkland's career was engaging school leadership to work with her school's students on poetry. **Hobbies:** Crafts; Sewing; Fishing; Travel; Bridge; Gem Mining; Stone Cutting **Religion:** Methodist **Business Address:** 210 NE 10th Avenue, Gainesville, FL, 32601 **Shipping Address:** 1728 NW 94th Street, Gainesville, FL, 32606

David Tak Wai Chiu

Title: Professor of Plastic Surgery and Neurosurgery **Industry:** Medicine & Health Care **Company Name:** NYU Langone Medical Center **Date of Birth:** 10/23/1945 **Place of Birth:** Kwangtung **State/Country of Origin:** China **Parents:** Bud Yick Chiu; Lai Kwai (Lum) Chiu **Marital Status:** Married **Spouse Name:** Lilian Wah-Ying Shen (6/19/1973) **Children:** Vincent; Edmund; Jerome; Miranda **Education:** Fellow, NYU Langone Medical Center, New York City, NY (1980); Resident of Plastic Surgery, Columbia Presbyterian Medical Center (1977-1979); Resident of General Surgery, Barnes Hospital, St. Louis, MO (1974-1977); Intern, Barnes Hospital, St. Louis, MO (1973-1974); MD, Columbia University (1973); BA, University of Missouri-St. Louis, MO (1969) **Certifications:** Diplomate, American Board of Plastic Surgery **Career:** Professor, Surgery, Plastic & Neurosurgery, New York University (2008-Present); Chief, Hand Services, New York University Medical Center (2006-Present); Director, Hand Surgery Fellowship, Wyss Department of Plastic Surgery, NYU Langone Medical Center, New York City, NY (2006-Present); Director, New York Nerve Center, NYU Langone Medical Center, New York City, NY (2003-Present); Director, Center of Restorative Surgery, New York City, NY (2000-Present); Clinical Professor, Surgery, New York University (2001-2006); Calvin F. Barber Professor, Columbia Presbyterian Medical Center, New York City, NY (2000-2001); Thomas S. Zimmer Professor, Columbia Presbyterian Medical Center, New York City, NY (1994-2000); Calvin F. Barber Professor of Clinical Surgery, Anatomy & Cell Biology, College of Physicians & Surgeons, Columbia University (2000-2001); Chief, Plastic Surgery Division, Department of Surgery, Columbia Presbyterian Medical Center, New York City, NY (1994-1997); Director, Microsurgery Center, Columbia Presbyterian Medical Center, New York City, NY (1993); Associate Director, Plastic Surgery, Columbia Presbyterian Medical Center, New York City, NY (1989-1994); Chief, Hand/Microsurgery and Replantation Surgery, Division of Plastic Surgery, Columbia Presbyterian Medical Center, New York City, NY (1989-1994); Supervisory Attending, Bellevue Hospital Hand Clinic, New York City, NY (1981-1989); Assistant Professor, NYU Langone Medical Center, New York City, NY (1981-1989); Instructor, Surgery, NYU Langone Medical Center, New York City, NY (1981) **Career Related:** Adjunct Professor, Anatomy and Cell Biology, College of Physicians and Surgeons, Columbia University, New York City, NY (2001-Present) **Creative Works:** Editorial Board Member, Journal of Reconstructive Microsurgery (1990-2008); Author, "Introduction to Microsurgery: A Lab Manual" (1985); Editorial Board Member, Plastic and Reconstructive Surgery Global Open **Awards:** Lifetime Achievement Award, New York Regional Society of Plastic Surgeon (2018); Chinese American Medical Society (2013); Sushruta Orator Award, Association of Plastic Surgeons of India (2013); Hanno Millesi Award, Vienna, Austria (2010); Scientific Award, Chinese American Medical Society (2001); Gold Medal, Federation of Alumni Associations of Columbia University (1997); Outstanding Achievement Award, Federation of Chinese American and Chinese Canadian Medical Societies (1996) **Membership:** Chairman, Board of Directors, World Association for Plastic Surgeons of Chinese Descent (2017); Vice President, New York Clinical Society (2015-Present); President, Sunderland Society (2008-Present); Founding President, Federation of Chinese American and Chinese Canadian Medical Societies (2002-Present); Emeritus President, Chinese American Medical Society (2001-Present); Director, Chinese American Medical Society (1983-Present); President, College Physicians and Surgeons Alumni Association (2001-2002); President, American Society of Peripheral Nerve Surgery (1999-2001); President, American Society of Reconstructive Microsurgery (1998-1999); New York Regional Society of Plastic and Reconstructive Plastic Surgery (1997-1998); Plastic Surgery Research Council, New York Society of Surgery of the Hand (1996-1997); Founding President, Federation of Chinese American and Chinese Canadian Medical Societies (1994-1996); Founder, Federation of Chinese American and Chinese Canadian Medical Societies (1994); Specialty Fellow, American Academy of Pediatrics (1992); President, Chinese American Medical Society (1986-1987); Director, College Physicians and Surgeons Alumni Association (1984); Fellow, American College of Surgeons; American Medical Association; Association of Plastic Surgeons of India; Chinese American Medical Society; Founding Member, World Society of Reconstructive Microsurgery; Tissue Engineering Society; International Society of Reconstructive Microsurgery; Northeast Society of Plastic Surgery; Royal Society of Medicine; Founding Member, American Society of Peripheral Nerve Surgery; American Association of Hand Surgery; American Society of Plastic and Reconstructive Surgeons; American Society of Surgery of the Hand; New York State Medical Society; New York County Medical Society; American Association of Plastic Surgeons; Chairman, Board of Directors, Federation of Chinese American and Chinese Canadian Medical Societies **Marquis Who's Who Honors:** Albert Nelson Marquis Lifetime Achievement Award (2017) **Shipping Address:** 900 Park Ave, David T.W. Chiu, MD, New York, NY, 10075

Jeong Hwan Choi

Title: Engineer **Industry:** Engineering **Company Name:** Korea Rail Network Authority **Date of Birth:** 10/30/1963 **Place of Birth:** Daejeon **State/Country of Origin:** South Korea **Parents:** Byeong Seok Choi; Young Nam Ju **Career:** Executive Director, Korea Rail Network Authority, Daejeon, Republic of Korea (2004-Present); Manager, Korea High Speed Rail Construction Authority, Seoul, Republic of Korea (1996-2003); Manager, Daewoo Cooperation, Seoul, Republic of Korea (1993-1996); Assistant Manager, Daewoo Engineering Co., Seoul, Republic of Korea (1988-1993) **Career Related:** Executive Director of Overseas Business Headquarter, Korea Rail Network Authority, Daejeon, Republic of Korea (2015-Present) **Civic:** Volunteer, Wonju City Soup Kitchen for the Homeless and Needy, Wonju, Republic of Korea (2015-2016); Supporter, National Assembly, Seoul, Republic of Korea (2004-2015) **Awards:** Achievement Award, Korea Tunnelling and Underground Space Association (2010) **Membership:** Director, Korea Tunnelling and Underground Space Association (2015-2016); Korea Tunnelling and Underground Space Association **Shipping Address:** F-2108 Tower Palace, 57 Eonju-ro 30-gil, Gangnam-gu, Seoul, South Korea 06293

Pritindra Chowdhuri

Title: Electrical Engineer (Retired), Professor (Retired) **Industry:** Engineering **Date of Birth:** 07/12/1927 **Place of Birth:** Kolkata **State/Country of Origin:** India **Parents:** Ahindra Chowdhuri; Sudhira Chowdhuri **Marital Status:** Married **Spouse Name:** Sharon **Children:** Naomi; Leshia; Robindro; Rajenho **Education:** Deng, Rensselaer Polytechnic Institute (1966); MSEE, Illinois Institute of Technology (1951); MSc in Physics, Calcutta University (1948); BSc in Physics, Calcutta University (1945) **Certifications:** Registered Professional Engineer, Commonwealth of Massachusetts **Career:** Staff Member, LANS, LLC (1975-1986); Engineer in Electrical Investigations, Transportation Systems Division, General Electric Company (1962-1975); Project Engineer, UTACV Project, General Electric (1962-1975); Electrical Engineer, Research and Development Center, General Electric (1959-1962); Laboratory Development Engineer, High Voltage Laboratory, General Electric (1956-1959); Research Engineer, High Voltage Research Commission of the Swiss Electrotechnical Society, Zurich, Switzerland (1953-1956); Electrical Engineer, Maschinenfabrik Oerlikon, Zurich, Switzerland (1952-1953); Junior Engineer, Westinghouse Electric Corporation (1951-1952); Junior Apprentice, Switchgear & Cowans Ltd. (1949); Student Apprentice, Calcutta Electric Supply Corporation (1948) **Career Related:** Professor Emeritus, Department of Electrical and Computer Engineering, Tennessee Technological University, Cookesville, TN (2005-Present); Professor of Electrical Engineering, Center for Electric Power, Tennessee Technological University, Cookeville, TN (1986-2005); Part-time Lecturer, Behrend College Graduate Center, The Pennsylvania State University (1969-1975); Graduate Assistant, Illinois Institute of Technology, Chicago, IL (1950-1951) **Civic:** Member, Utilities Board, Los Alamos County (1984-1986); President, Los Alamos Bus System, Inc. (1984-1985); Executive Secretary, New Mexico Association of Memorial Societies (1983-1984); President, Memorial Society of Northern New Mexico (1977-1978) **Creative Works:** Author, "Electromagnetic Transients in Power Systems, Second Edition," Research Studies Press (2004); Section Editor, Power System Transients, "Electric Power Engineering Handbook," CRC Press (2000); Author, "Electromagnetic Transients in Power Systems, First Edition," Research Studies Press (1996) **Awards:** Honoree, TVA Chair Professor in Electric Power (2000-2003); TBR Distance Education Committee Innovation Award (1999); Featured Listee, Men of Achievement, International Biographical Centre (1981-1982); Honorable Mention for Paper, Industry Applications Society Annual Meeting, IEEE (1974); First Prize in Paper Contest, Erie Section, IEEE (1964); First Prize in Tri-Sectional Paper Contest, American Institute of Electrical Engineers (1957); Invention Disclosure Award, Westinghouse Electric Corporation (1951) **Membership:** President, TTU Chapter, Sigma Xi (1999-2000, 2004-2005); President, Thanatopsis Society of Erie (1973-1974); Task Force 33.11-0.1 Lightning, International Conference on Large High Voltage Electric System; Committee C63 - Radioelectrical Coordination, American National Standards Institute; Industrial Control Systems Subcommittee, Industry Applications Society, IEEE; Insulated Conductors Committee, Power Engineering Society, IEEE; Standards Committee, Electromagnetic Compatibility Society, IEEE; Chairman, Standards Subcommittee, Power Semiconductor Committee, Industry Applications Society, IEEE; Lightning & Insulator Subcommittee, Transmission & Distribution Committee, Power Engineering Society, IEEE; Working Group on Lightning Performance of Distribution Lines, Power Engineering Society, IEEE; Working Group on Lightning Performance of Transmission Lines, Power Engineering Society, IEEE; Chairman, Task Force on Nonstandard Lightning Voltage Waves, Power Engineering Society, IEEE; Chairman, Task Force on Parameters of Lightning Strokes, Power Engineering Society, IEEE; Fellow, IEEE; Fellow, American Association for the Advancement of Science; Fellow, The New York Academy of Science; Fellow, Institution of Electrical Engineers; Tennessee Academy of Science; Eta Kappa Nu; The Tau Beta Pi Association, Inc. **Political Affiliations:** Democrat **Religion:** Hindu, Unitarian Universalist **Shipping Address:** 690 Valley Forge Rd, Cookeville, TN, 38501

Gordon A. Christenson

Title: Law Educator **Industry:** Law and Legal Services **Company Name:** University of Cincinnati **Date of Birth:** 06/22/1932 **Place of Birth:** Salt Lake City **State:** UT **Parents:** Gordon Brown Christenson; Ruth Arzella (Anderson) Christenson **Marital Status:** Single **Spouse Name:** Fabienne Fadeley (Deceased, October 2, 2016); Katherine Joy DeMik (November 2, 1951), Divorced (1977) **Children:** Gordon Scott; Marjorie Lynne (Deceased); Ruth; and Nanette **Education:** Doctor of Juridical Science, The George Washington University (1961); JD, The University of Utah (1956); BS in Law, The University of Utah (1955) **Career:** Professor Emeritus, College of Law, University of Cincinnati (1998-Present); Dean Emeritus, College of Law, University of Cincinnati (1998-Present); University Professor of Law, College of Law, University of Cincinnati (1985-1998); Dean, College of Law, University of Cincinnati (1979-1985); Nippert Law Professor, College of Law, University of Cincinnati (1979-1985); Charles H. Stockton International Law Professor, U.S. Naval War College, Newport, RI (1977-1979); Law Professor, American University Washington College of Law (1971-1979); Dean, American University Washington College of Law (1971-1977); University Dean for Educational Development, Central Administration, University at Albany (1970-1971); Executive Assistant to the President, The University of Oklahoma (1967-1970); Associate Law Professor, The University of Oklahoma (1967-1970); Chairman, Task Force on Telecommunications Missions and Organization, U.S. Department of Commerce (1967); Assistant General Counsel for Science and Technology, U.S. Department of Commerce (1962-1967); Counsel, Technical Advisory Board, U.S. Department of Commerce (1962-1967); Special Assistant to Undersecretary of Commerce, U.S. Department of Commerce (1967); Panel Counsel on Engineering and Commodity Standards, Technical Advisory Board, U.S. Department of Commerce (1963-1965); Attorney, Office of Legal Advisers, U.S. Department of State, Washington, DC (1958-1962); Acting Assistant Legal Adviser, Office of Legal Advisers, U.S. Department of State, Washington, DC (1958-1962); Attorney, National Guard Bureau, U.S. Army (1957-1958); Firm Associate, Christenson & Callister, Salt Lake City, UT (1956-1958); Law Clerk to Chief Justice, Utah Supreme Court (1956-1957) **Career Related:** Wallace S. Fujiyama Visiting Distinguished Law Professor, William S. Richardson School of Law, University of Hawai'i (1997); Visiting Scholar, University of Maine School of Law (1997); Visiting Scholar, Yale Law School (1985-1986); Visiting Scholar, Harvard Law School, Harvard University (1977-1978); Faculty Reporter, Seminars for Experienced Federal District Judges, The Federal Judicial Center, Washington, DC (1972-1977); International Law Consultant, U.S. Naval War College, Newport, CT (1969); Associate Professorial Lecturer in International Affairs, The George Washington University (1961-1967); Participant, Summer Conferences on International Law, Cornell University, Ithaca, NY (1962, 1964) **Civic:** Trustee, Glenn M. Weaver Institute of Law and Psychiatry Institute, University of Cincinnati (2006-Present); Trustee, Procedural Aspects of International Law Institute, New York, NY (1962-Present); Vice President, Procedural Aspects of International Law Institute (1962-2001); Consultant, Center for Policy Alternatives, Massachusetts Institute of Technology (1970-1981); Member, Intergovernmental Committee on International Policy and Weather Modification (1967) **Military Service:** Intelligence Section, U.S. Air Force, Japan (1951-1952) **Creative Works:** Co-Author, "The Future of the University" (1969); Co-Author, "International Claims: Their Preparation and Presentation" (1962); Contributor, Articles, Legal Journals **Awards:** Graduate School Fellow, University of Cincinnati **Membership:** The American Society of International Law; The Order of the Coif; The Literary Club; Cosmos Club; Kappa Sigma Fraternity; The International Legal Honor Society of Phi Delta; Cincinnati Bar Association **Bar Admissions:** The District of Columbia Bar (1978); Supreme Court of the United States of America (1971); The Utah State Bar (1956) **Marquis Who's Who Honors:** Albert Nelson Marquis Lifetime Achievement Award (2017) **Religion:** Episcopalian **Shipping Address:** 3465 Principio Ave, Cincinnati, OH, 45208

Jung G. Chung

Title: Aerospace Engineer **Industry:** Engineering **Date of Birth:** 04/12/1922 **Place of Birth:** Sun Wai **State/Country of Origin:** China **Parents:** Pak Wing Chung; Yow Fun (Dong) Chung **Marital Status:** Married **Spouse Name:** Fay Yung Ma (5/3/1951) **Children:** John Gingkeong **Education:** MA in Education, New York University (1951); BA in Education, New York University (1949) **Career:** T-46 Aeroperformance Engineer, Quality Control Flying Surfaces, Grumman F-14 (1986); A-10 Performance Maintenance Engineer, Grumman F-14 (1985); A-10 Capacity Accountant, Grumman F-14 (1985); A-10 Interface Manager, Grumman F-14 (1985); A-10 Aircraft Accident Analyst, Grumman F-14 (1985); ASW-340 Store Carriage and Separation, Grumman F-14 (1984); F-15 Dispenser Technology, Grumman F-14 (1984); Engineer of Advanced Medium-Range Air-to-Air Missile Ejection and Separation Dynamics, Grumman F-14 (1983); Aerial Refueling Tank Designer, Grumman E-2C, Grumman Aircraft (1982); Loads and Dynamics Engineer, Grumman E-2C, Grumman Aircraft (1981); Preliminary Design and Performance, FRC/SAAB Transport, Swearingen Aviation (1980); Air Loads Design Engineer, Boeing 757, Boeing (1979); NATO Fighter Design Specification Team Member (1969-1970); Air Loads and Performance Engineer, Mach-30 Aerospace Plane, Fairchild-Republic (1964-1966); Head of Transonic, Supersonic and Hypersonic Wind Tunnels, Fairchild-Republic (1963-1965); Air Loads and Performance Engineer, Fairchild Republic (1962-1964) **Career Related:** Nassau Library System (1995-2000); Instructor, SeniorNet Learning Center of Forest Hills, SeniorNet (1993-1995); Senior Connections Board Adviser, School of Social Work, Adelphi University (1991-1995); Instructor, Tax Preparer, Volunteer Income Tax Assistance (1986-1992); Faculty Member, New York Institute of Technology (1969) **Civic:** Instructor in 55-Alive Mature Driving, AARP (1998-2000); Advisory Council Member, Planning and Priorities Committee, Department of Human Services Office for the Aging, Nassau County (1996-2000); Technology Specialist, AARP (1996-1998); English Tutor, Nassau County Chapter, Literacy Volunteers of America (1993-2000); Membership Chair, Fairchild Republic Retirees (1986-1991); Tax Counseling Coordinator, AARP (1985-2000); Tax Counseling Instructor, AARP (1985-2000); Volunteer, American Federation of Arts **Awards:** Recipient, Tutor of the Year, Nassau County Chapter, Literacy Volunteers of America (1998) **Membership:** Long Island Section Council (1996-2000); Alternate Delegate, Biennial Convention (1994); Legislative Committee (1990-1994); President, Farmingdale Chapter, AARP (1992-1993); Vice President, Farmingdale Chapter, AARP (1988-1989); Civil Air Patrol; United States Naval Institute; American Association for the Advancement of Science; American Association of Independent Advisors; Mathematical Association of America; Metropolitan Museum of Art; American Museum of Natural History; United States Coast Guard Auxiliary; Air Force Association; National Defense Industrial Association; The New York Academy of Sciences **Marquis Who's Who Honors:** Distinguished Humanitarian (2017) **Political Affiliations:** Republican **Religion:** Presbyterian **Shipping Address:** 32 Mulberry Street, Apartment 5, New York, NY, 10013

Audrey Cielinski-Kessler

Title: Writer, Editor, Owner **Industry:** Writing and Editing **Company Name:** The Write Hand of Ohio **Date of Birth:** 09/10/1957 **Place of Birth:** Cleveland **State:** OH **Parents:** Joseph Cielinski; Dorothy Antoinette (Hanna) Cielinski **Education:** BJ, The University of Texas, with High Honors (1979) **Career:** Owner, Write Hand Ohio (1992-Present); Freelance Technical Writer (1992-Present); Freelance Writer and Editor (1984-Present); President, Geauga Astatebula Portage Partnership Inc. (2013); Technical Writer, Chevron Exploration and Production Services Company (1990-1992); Teacher, Technical Writing Class (1985-1989); Communications Specialist III, Wang System Administrator of Office Planning and Research, Houston Police Department; Procedures Analyst, Technical Writer, Technical Library, Harris County Data Processing Department (1981-1983); Secretary Department Psychiatry, Baylor College of Medicine (1980-1981); Editorial Assistant, Journal Health and Social Behavior, Houston, (1980-1981); Assistant Copy Chief, Medical World News Magazine (1983-1984); Reporter, Writer, Medical World News Magazine (1979) **Career Related:** Webmaster Kent Environmental Council **Civic:** Council Member, Portage County Ohio Housing Services (2013-Present); Board Member, Secretary, Portage County Ohio Housing Services (2007-Present); Board Member, Building Appeals, Mental Health & Recovery Board, Portage County (2007-Present); Member, Northeast Ohio Consortium Council Governments (Formerly Geauga Ashtabule Portage Partnership Area 19 Workforce Investment Board) (2005-Present); Member, Portage County (2005-Present); Member, Fair Housing Board, City of Kent (1998-Present); Member, Shade Tree Commission, City of Kent (1996-Present); Secretary, Northeast Ohio Consortium Council Governments (Formerly Geauga Ashtabule Portage Partnership Area 19 Workforce Investment Board) (2009); Vice Chair, Akron Metropolitan Area, Ohio (2008-2010); Chair, City of Kent (2007-2008); Recording Secretary, Catholic Charities Portage County (2007); Vice President, Catholic Charities Portage County (2005-2006); Vice Chair, City of Kent (2004-2005); President, Catholic Charities Portage County (2003-2004); Vice Chair, Keep Kent Beautiful (2002-2005); Vice President, Catholic Charities Portage County (2002); Chair, Akron Metropolitan Area (2001-2002); Vice Chair, Akron Metropolitan Area (2000); Chair, City of Kent (1999-2002); Chair, City of Kent (1999-2002); Board of Directors, Keep Kent Beautiful; Member, Leadership Portage County (1999); Member, Transportation Study Citizen Involvement Committee, Akron Metropolitan Area (1999); Member, Community Reinvestment Area Housing Council, City of Kent; Member, Environmental Commission, City of Kent (1999); Member, Assessment Equalization Board, City of Kent (1998-2003); Vice Chair, City of Kent (1998); Member, Board of Zoning Appeals, City of Kent (1996-2003); Volunteer Writer, Graphic Designer, Office of Religious Education, St. Ambrose Roman Catholic Church (1983-1992); Volunteer Editor, Newsletters, W. Knoll News; Volunteer Editor, Newsletters, VGS, Inc.; Volunteer Editor, Newsletters, Greater Houston Area; American Cancer Society; Trustee, Catholic Charities Portage County; Central Committee Member, Portage County Democratic Party; Member, Board of Building Appeals, Portage County; Council Member, Portage County Housing Services, Ohio; Newsletter Editor, Kent Environmental Council, Board of Directors, Kent Environmental Council; Member, Portage County Democratic Party Central Committee **Creative Works:** Editor, "At the Summut, Signals, CEPS Synergy, PCLIBtm Letter, Insights, Steps & Specs., The Voter, Kent Environmental Council, Kent Historian"; Contributor, Stories and Articles, Newspapers; Contributor, Stories and Articles, Magazines **Awards:** Distinguished Special Interest Group Service Award, Society of Technical Communications; Chief's Command Employee of the Month Award (1989); Commendation Award, Chief of Police, Houston, TX **Membership:** Board Member, Kent Historical Society (2008-Present); Manager, Policies and Procedures, Society of Technical Communications; Kent Area Chamber of Commerce; Alpha Lamda Delta; Phi Kappa Phi; Sigma Delta Chi; Board Member, Mental Health & Recovery Board of Portage County; Board Member, Kent Environmental Council **Marquis Who's Who Honors:** Albert Nelson Marquis Lifetime Achievement Award (2017) **Hobbies:** Oboe; Kent State University Communiversity Band; Stamp collecting; Hiking; Writing **Political Affiliations:** Democrat **Shipping Address:** 1638 S. Lincoln Street, Kent, OH, 44240

Jerry Clack

Title: Classics Educator **Industry:** Education/Educational Services **Date of Birth:** 07/22/1926 **Place of Birth:** New York **State:** NY **Parents:** Christopher Thrower Clack; Mildred Taylor (VanDyke) Clack **Education:** MA in Spanish, Duquesne University (1977); PhD in Classics, University of Pittsburgh (1962); MA in Classics, University of Pittsburgh (1958); AB in Classics, Princeton University (1946) **Career:** Professor, Duquesne University (1975-2011); Member, Core Curriculum Committee, Duquesne University (1979-1993); Member, Library Committee, Duquesne University (1979-1993); Member, Due Process Committee, Duquesne University (1988-1992); Member, Arts and Sciences Curriculum Committee, Duquesne University (1988-1990); Member, Promotion and Tenure Committee, Duquesne University (1988-1990); Chairman, Department of Classics, Duquesne University (1973-1975, 1980-1983); Member, Pre-Professional Health Committee, Duquesne University (1970-1976); Associate Professor, Duquesne University (1971-1975); Assistant Professor of Classics, Duquesne University (1968-1971); Executive Director, Allegheny County Chapter, The National Foundation (Now March of Dimes Foundation) (1952-1968); Documents Officer, United States Commission, UNESCO (1948-1951) **Civic:** Chairman, Board of Directors, Pittsburgh Festival Opera (2012-Present); Treasurer, Pittsburgh Festival Opera (2003-2010); Vice President, Western Pennsylvania Chapter, Citizens for Global Solutions (1965-2009); Treasurer. Western Pennsylvania Chapter, Citizens for Global Solutions (1987-2001); President, Western Pennsylvania Health Conference (1967); Member, General Conference, UNESCO, Paris (1950); Member, General Conference, UNESCO, Florence (1949) **Creative Works:** Author, "Dioscorides and Antipater of Sidon, The Poems" (2001); Author, "Asclepiades of Samos and Leonides of Tarentum, The Poems" (1999); Editorial Board Member, Duquesne University Press, Duquesne University (1991-1994); Author, "Meleager, The Poems" (1992); Author, "An Anthology of Hellenistic Poetry" (1982); Contributor, Articles; Contributor, Reviews **Awards:** Eponym, Annual Clack Lecture Series, Classical Association of the Atlantic States (2009-Present); National Trustee Award, OPERA America Inc. (2017); Norman Cousin's Award, Citizens for Global Solutions (2010) **Membership:** Treasurer, The Classical Association of Pittsburgh and Vicinity (1970-1978, 1988, 2006); Archivist, Classical Association of the Atlantic States (2001-2005); Executive Director, Classical Association of the Atlantic States (1993-2001); Treasurer, Pennsylvania Classical Association (1977-1999); Chairman, Committee on Regional Organizations, American Philological Association (1986-1995); Chairman, Working Group of Classical Editors, American Philological Association (1982-1993); President, Classical Association of the Atlantic States (1987); Trustee, The Vergilian Society, Inc. (1985-1987); Vice President, Classical Association of the Atlantic States (1975-1976); Phi Sigma Iota; Delta Phi Alpha; Alpha Epsilon Delta; Phi Alpha Theta **Marquis Who's Who Honors:** Albert Nelson Marquis Lifetime Achievement Award (2017) **Shipping Address:** 5850 Centre Ave Apt 512, Pittsburgh, PA, 15206

Daniel J. Claes

Title: Doctor **Industry:** Medicine & Health Care **Company Name:** Private Practice **Year of Passing:** 2018-06-20 **Parents:** John Claes; Claribel Claes **Marital Status:** Married **Spouse Name:** Gayla Christine Claes (1/19/1974) **Education:** Intern, University of California, Los Angeles (1957-1958); MD, Harvard University, Cum Laude (1957); AB, Harvard University, Magna Cum Laude (1953) **Career:** Physician, Private Practice Specializing in Diabetes (1962-Present); Research Fellow in Medicine, Bowyer Foundation (1958-1961) **Career Related:** Chief Executive Officer, Cavendish Associates (2008-Present); Chief Technology Officer, Cavendish Associates (2007-Present); President, Cavendish Associates (2002-Present); Chief Executive Officer, American Eye Bank Foundation (1995-Present); Chairman, Heuristic Group of Organizations (1981-Present) **Creative Works:** Contributor, Articles to Professional Journals **Membership:** American Association for the Advancement of Science; American Medical Association; Los Angeles Museum of Art; Phillips Gallery; National Museum; Metropolitan Museum; Cell Transplantation Society; Diabetes Technology Society; American Mathematics Society; International Pancreas and Islet Transplant Association; International Diabetes Federation; Professional Council on Immunology, Immunogenetics and Transplantation, American Diabetes Association; Los Angeles County Medical Association; California Medical Association; Royal Commonwealth Club; Harvard Club; Harvard Medical School of Southern California Club **Shipping Address:** 1336 Berea Pl, Pacific Palisades, CA, 90272

James F. Clawson Jr.

Title: Judge, Arbitrator, Mediator **Industry:** Law and Legal Services **Date of Birth:** 08/31/1923 **Place of Birth:** Coryell County **State:** TX **Parents:** James F. Clawson; Julia Josephine (Doolittle) Clawson **Marital Status:** Married **Spouse Name:** Mary Louise Forester (5/4/1945) **Children:** Marylou Bowen; Cathy Jo Young **Education:** JD, Baylor University (1948) **Career:** Senior Judge, 169th Judicial District of Texas, Belton, TX (1985-1990); Regional Administrative Judge, State of Texas (1985-1990); Presiding Judge, Third Administrative Judicial Region of Texas, Belton, TX (1985-1990); District Judge, 169th Judicial District of Texas, Belton, TX (1969-1985); County Judge, Commissioner's Court, State of Texas, Bell County, TX (1967-1969); Banker, First National Bank Texas, Temple, TX (1959-1967); Trust Officer, First National Bank Texas, Temple, TX (1959-1967); Attorney, Clawson, Jennings & Clawson, Houston, TX (1948-1959) **Career Related:** Chairman, Board, Regional Judges of Texas (1985-1990); Chairman, Central Texas Council of Governments, Belton, TX (1967-1969); Fellow, Texas Bar Foundation **Military Service:** Captain, U.S. Air Force (1951-1953); Captain, U.S. Air Force (1942-1946) **Awards:** Outstanding Citizen of the Year, Temple Jaycees, TX (1966) **Membership:** Chairman, Judicial Section, State Bar of Texas (1982-1983); Executive Committee, Judicial Section, State Bar of Texas (1972-1982) **Bar Admissions:** U.S. District Court, Southern District, State of Texas (1995); State of Texas (1948) **Marquis Who's Who Honors:** Albert Nelson Marquis Lifetime Achievement Award (2017) **Why did you become involved in your profession or industry:** Mr. Clawson became involved in his profession as a young child. As the middle child, he was always the peacemaker of his siblings. His older brother, who is 21 years older than him, practiced law in Houston, TX, and inspired him to also pursue law. **Shipping Address:** 3601 Victorian Drive, Temple, TX, 76502

Michael Craig Clements

Title: Health Services Consulting Executive, Renal Dialysis Technician (Retired) **Industry:** Consulting **Company Name:** Critical Care Services, Inc. **Date of Birth:** 09/17/1945 **Place of Birth:** Cincinnati **State:** OH **Parents:** Marvin Hubert Clements; Mildred Helen (Rabe) Clements **Marital Status:** Married **Spouse Name:** Minnie Faye Pospisil (12/1/1972) **Children:** Melissa Ayn; Michael Aaron **Education:** EMT/Paramedic, Good Samaritan Health Center (1980); Coursework, University of Cincinnati (1968-1970) **Certifications:** Certified Renal Dialysis Technician **Career:** President, Critical Care Services, Inc., Mason, OH (1987-Present); Technical Services Director, Dialysis Clinic, Inc., Cincinnati, OH (1980-1991); Hemodialysis Technician, Christ Hospital, Cincinnati, OH (1968-1979) **Career Related:** EMS Captain, Mason Volunteer Fire Company (1985); EMS Training Officer, Mason Volunteer Fire Company (1984); Firefighter/Paramedic, Mason Volunteer Fire Company (1978-1985); Co-op Employer, Environmental and Science Laboratory Technology Programs, Cincinnati State College **Civic:** Mason Environmental Advisory Commission (1990-Present); Vice Chairman, Mason Environmental Advisory Commission (1992-1993); Business and Parent Curriculum Review Committee, Mason City Schools (1992); Advisor, Cooperative Program, Cincinnati State Technical and Community College, Biomedical Engineering Technology (1986-1991); Disaster Responder, Mason Community Emergency Response Team **Military Service:** U.S. Naval Sea Cadet Corps (2002-Present); House Staff, U.S. Naval Sea Cadet Corps (2009-2012); Commanding Officer, Cincinnati Division, U.S. Naval Sea Cadet Corps (2006-2009); U.S. Navy (1964-1970) **Creative Works:** Contributor, Articles, Professional Journals **Awards:** Community Involvement Award, City of Mason (2016) **Membership:** National Association of Nephrology Technicians; Ohio Academy of Science; Association for the Advancement of Medical Instrumentation; Christ's Church at Mason **Marquis Who's Who Honors:** Albert Nelson Marquis Lifetime Achievement Award (2017) **Why did you become involved in your profession or industry:** Mr. Clements became involved in his profession when he developed a strong interest in dialysis after coming out of the Navy. **What do you consider to be the highlight of your career:** A career highlight that stands out the most to Mr. Clements is when he came to work one day, and the dialysis nurse noticed that the water looked strange. As it turned out, the water had copper in it. He then worked with the medical director and the hospital's water company to devise a solution. **Religion:** Church of Christ **Shipping Address:** 7577 Central Parke Boulevard, Suite 207, Critical Care Services., Inc., Mason, OH, 45040

David Click

Title: Lawyer **Industry:** Law and Legal Services **Date of Birth:** 12/17/1947 **Place of Birth:** Miami Beach **State:** FL **Parents:** David Gorman Click; Helen Margaret (McPhail) Click **Spouse Name:** Helaine London (6/2/1974) **Children:** Kenneth Randall; Adam Elliott **Education:** MA, Yale University (1974); JD, Yale University (1973); BA, Yale University (1969) **Certifications:** Board Certified in Wills, Trusts and Estates **Career:** Private Practice, Jupiter, FL (1986-Present); Associate, Nixon, Hargrave, Devans and Doyle, Jupiter, FL (1984-1986); Associate Professor, University of Maryland, Baltimore (1978-1984); Associate Professor, Indiana University (1977-1978); Assistant Professor, Western New England School of Law, Springfield, MA (1974-1977) **Career Related:** President, Click Capital Management, LLC **Civic:** Participant, Leadership Palm Beach County (1991-1992); President, Palm Beach County Estate Planning Council (1988-1989); Christmas Cove Improvement Association **Creative Works:** Contributor, Articles, Professional Journals **Awards:** Cultural Activities Award, Palm Beach County Bar Association (1992); Named, Florida Super Lawyer, Palm Beach County Bar Association **Membership:** ABA; The Florida Bar; Palm Beach County Bar Association; President, Yale Club Of The Palm Beaches; Chairman, Scholarship Committee, Kiwanis International **Bar Admissions:** Florida (1984); Maine (1984); Supreme Court of the United States (1983); Maryland (1983); Connecticut (1973) **Marquis Who's Who Honors:** Albert Nelson Marquis Lifetime Achievement Award (2017) **Religion:** Presbyterian **Business Address:** 810 Saturn Street, Ste 15, Jupiter, FL, 33477

Andrew Montgomery Coats

Industry: Law and Legal Services **Date of Birth:** 01/19/1935 **Place of Birth:** Oklahoma City **State:** OK **Parents:** Sanford Clarence Coats; Mary Ola (Young) Coats **Children:** Andrew; Michael; Jennifer; Sanford **Education:** JD, The University of Oklahoma (1963); BA, The University Oklahoma (1957) **Career:** Dean Emeritus, The University of Oklahoma College of Law (2010-Present); Dean, The University of Oklahoma College of Law (1996-2010); Mayor, City of Oklahoma City, Oklahoma (1983-1987); Senior Trial Partner, Crowe and Dunlevy, Oklahoma City, OK (1980-1996); District Attorney, Oklahoma County, Oklahoma City, OK (1976-1980); Partner, Crowe and Dunlevy, Oklahoma City, OK (1967-1976); Associate, Crowe and Dunlevy, Oklahoma City, OK (1963-1967); Samuel Roberts Nobel Foundation presidential professor, Arch B. & Joanne Gilbert professor law, University Oklahoma College Law; Fulltime Professor of Law, The University of Oklahoma College of Law **Career Related:** Director of International Bank of Congress, Oklahoma City, OK (2010-Present); Board of Directors, IBC Bank of Oklahoma (2004-Present) **Civic:** Democratic Nominee, United States Senate (1980); President, Oklahoma County Legal Aid Society (1972-1973) **Military Service:** Lieutenant, US Navy (1960-1963) **Awards:** Recipient, Professional Award, United States Tenth Circuit (2010); Inductee, Oklahoma Hall of Fame (2006); Eponym, Andrew M. Coats Building, University of Oklahoma College (2005); Named, Phi Beta Kappa of the Year (2003); Named, Outstanding Lawyer in Oklahoma, Oklahoma City University (1977); Recipient, AV Rating, Martindale Hubble **Membership:** President, American College of Trial Lawyers (1996-1997); President, Petroleum Club (1995); Board of Directors, Oklahoma City Golf and Country Club (1993-1996); Tenth Circuit Regent, American College of Trial Lawyers (1992-1996); President, Oklahoma Bar Association (1992-1993); Board of Directors, Oklahoma City Golf and Country Club (1977-1980); President, Oklahoma County Bar Association (1976-1977); President, Phi Beta Kappa (1975); Oklahoma City President, Oklahoma Young Lawyers Conference (1968-1969); President, Phi Delta Phi (1962); President, Pi Kappa Alpha (1956); Fellow, American College of Trial Lawyers; American Bar Foundation; International Academy of Trial Lawyers; ABA; Trustee, Supreme Court Historical Society; Charter President, Oklahoma Chapter, American Board of Trial Advisors; Order of Coif; Oklahoma City Golf and Country Petroleum **Achievements:** Broke up the NCAA football television monopoly **Hobbies:** Music; Golf **Political Affiliations:** Democrat **Religion:** Episcopalian

Donald George Cofrancesco

Title: Healthcare Administrator **Industry:** Medicine & Health Care **Date of Birth:** 05/29/1953 **Place of Birth:** New Haven **State:** CT **Parents:** George William Cofrancesco; Marie Teresa (Marra) Cofrancesco **Education:** MPH, Yale University (1992); MA in Gerontology, University of New Haven (1979); BS in Chemistry and Life Sciences, Worcester Polytechnic Institute, With Distinction (1975) **Certifications:** Licensed Nursing Home Administrator, State of Connecticut (1979-Present); Reiki Master (2008); Advanced Reiki Practitioner (2008); Second Reiki Practitioner (2008); First Reiki Practitioner (2007); General Class Amateur Radio License - Call Sign KB1FYK **Career:** President, Chief Financial Officer, Treasurer, All Around Town Home Care, Inc. (2013-Present); Chief Financial Officer, All Around Town Home Care, Inc. (2013-Present); Healthcare Consultant, Coe Enterprises LLC (2000-2013); Assistant Administrator, Lecturer, Clinical Practice Specialist, Yale School of Medicine (1990-2001); Financial Analyst, Yale School of Medicine (1990-2000); Hospice Consultant, Project Care, Inc. (1989-1990); Administrator, Hillside Manor (1987-1988); Administrator, Independence Manor (1986-1987); Administrator, West Haven Nursing Center (1981-1985); Administrator, Golden Manor Convalescent Home, Inc. (1980-1981); Director of Biostatistics and Health Planning, Department of Health, New Haven, CT (1980); Research Assistant, Yale School of Medicine (1975-1977) **Civic:** Weather Spotter, Skywarn, National Weather Service (2003-Present); Commissioner, Human Services Commission, Hamden, CT (1998-Present); Chair, Human Services Commission, Hamden, CT (2010-2016); Public Information Officer, Connecticut Amateur Radio Emergency Service Region 2 (2009-2017); Emergency Coordinator, Connecticut Amateur Radio Emergency Service Region 2 (2007-2017); Connecticut Amateur Radio Emergency Service Region 2 (2007-2017); Board Member, Connecticut Lifespan Respite Coalition, Inc. (2007-2016); Treasurer, Connecticut Lifespan Respite Coalition, Inc. (2007-2016); Board Member, Quinnipiack Valley Health District (2005-2017); Vice Chair, Human Services Commission, Hamden, CT (2002-2010); Secretary, Partnerships Adult Day Care Inc. (2001-2004); Board Treasurer, Partnerships Adult Day Care Inc. (1998-1999); President, Partnerships Adult Day Care Inc. (1997-1998); Board Member, Partnerships Adult Day Care Inc. (1991-2004) **Awards:** Outstanding Young Men of America (1983) **Membership:** Founding Member, Yale University Amateur Radio Club (2006-Present); Health Systems Agency of South Central Connecticut, Inc. (1982-1987); Association of Yale Alumni in Public Health, Yale School of Public Health; Life Member, American Radio Relay League **Marquis Who's Who Honors:** Albert Nelson Marquis Lifetime Achievement Award (2017); Distinguished Humanitarian (2017) **To what do you attribute your success:** Mr. Cofrancesco attributes his success to his own effort and determination. **Why did you become involved in your profession or industry:** Mr. Cofrancesco entered his profession because of his dedication to public service. **What do you consider to be the highlight of your career:** Mr. Cofrancesco considers his graduation from Yale University to be the highlight of his career. **Hobbies:** Amateur radio **Religion:** Roman Catholic **Shipping Address:** 104 Hillfield Road, Hamden, CT, 06518

William Thomas Coghill Jr.

Title: Trial Lawyer (Retired) **Industry:** Law and Legal Services **Date of Birth:** 07/20/1927 **Place of Birth:** St. Louis **State:** MO **Parents:** William Thomas Coghill; Mildred Mary (Crenshaw) Coghill **Marital Status:** Married **Spouse Name:** Patricia Lee Hughes (8/7/1948) **Children:** James Prentiss; Victoria Lynn; Cathryn Anne **Education:** JD, University of Missouri, Columbia, MO (1950); Undergraduate Coursework, University of Missouri, Columbia, MO (1944-1947) **Career:** Associate Managing Partner, Thompson Coburn (Formerly Thompson & Mitchell), Belleville, IL (1958-2001); Top Associate, Coburn & Croft, St. Louis, MO (1957-1958); Partner, Smith, Smith & Coghill, Farmington, MO (1952-1957); Special Agent, FBI, Boston, MA (1951-1952); Private Practice, Farmington, MO (1950-1951) **Career Related:** Chairman, Hearing Board, Illinois Attorney Registration and Disciplinary Commission; Senior Counselor, State of Missouri, State of Illinois **Military Service:** US Navy (1945-1946) **Creative Works:** Author, "Memoirs of a Trial Lawyer" (2018); Author, "Cavaliers" (1999); Co-Author, "Illinois Products Liability" (1991) **Awards:** Fellowship, American College of Trial Lawyers; Rated, AV Preeminent, Martindale-Hubble Peer Review **Membership:** Trial Attorneys of America; Sustaining Member, Product Liability Advisory Council; ABA; Fellow, Illinois State Bar Association; Missouri State Bar Association; Defense Research Institute; Illinois Association of Defense Council; National Association of Railroad Trial Council; The Bar Association of Metropolitan St. Louis; East St. Louis Bar Association; St. Clair County Bar Association **Bar Admissions:** Illinois (1958); Missouri (1950) **Marquis Who's Who Honors:** Albert Nelson Marquis Lifetime Achievement Award (2017) **Why did you become involved in your profession or industry:** Mr. Coghill became involved in his profession because he wanted to go into politics. He thought that political science and law would be an appropriate educational path. **Hobbies:** Writing letters and correspondence **Political Affiliations:** Conservative **Religion:** Christian **Shipping Address:** 715 W Moon Valley Dr, Phoenix, AZ, 85023

Irving David Cohen

Title: Chairman of the Board, Chief Executive Officer & President **Industry:** Environmental Services **Company Name:** ESI **Date of Birth:** 05/12/1945 **Place of Birth:** Brooklyn **State:** NY **Parents:** Harry Cohen; Fay (Minchenberg) Cohen **Marital Status:** Married **Spouse Name:** Dorothy Ann Joseph (8/21/1966) **Children:** Miriam Susan Cohen; Esther Heidi Cohen; Daniel Marc Cohen; Aaron Michael Cohen **Education:** Postgraduate Coursework in Environmental Safety and Health, New York University (1970-Present); MSChemE, New York University (1970); BSChemE, The City College of New York (1967) **Certifications:** Certified Environmental Professional, Academy of Board Certified Environmental Professionals; Board Member, National Association of Environmental Professionals; Diplomate, The Academy of Certified Consultants and Experts; Fellow, American College of Forensic Examiners; Licensed Subsurface Evaluation and Closure, State of New Jersey **Career:** Chief Executive Officer, Board Chairman, President, Enviro-Sciences of Delaware, Inc., Lake Hopatcong, NJ (1975-Present); Senior Project Manager, Woodward-Envicon, Inc., Clifton, NJ (1972-1975); Associate Chemical Engineer, Hoffmann-LaRoche, Nutley, NJ (1971-1972); Senior Process Engineer, Crawford & Russell, Inc., Stamford, CT (1967-1971) **Career Related:** Board Chairman, Art International Inc. (1988-2007), Board Chairman, ECRA Laboratories, Inc. (1986-1992); Board Chairman, Aero Instrumentation Resources, Inc. (1978-2006) **Creative Works:** Author, "Environmental Impact Reports for Energy Related Projects and Environmental Liability Audits"; Author, Numerous Due Diligence Reports on Property Acquisitions Worldwide; Author, Numerous Environmental & Property Condition Assessment Reports Worldwide. **Awards:** Recipient, Richard J. Kramer CEP Memorial Award For Environmental Excellence (2010); Recipient, Outstanding Leadership Award, National Association of Environmental Professionals (2006) **Membership:** American Institute of Chemical Engineers; American Industrial Hygiene Association; Worldwide Pollution Control Association; Scientists Committee for Publication Information; Air Pollution Control Association; National Association of Environmental Professionals; The New York Academy of Sciences; Academy of Board Certified Environmental Professionals; Board Member, Council of Engineering and Scientific Society Executives; Board Member, Pennsylvania Chapter and New Jersey Chapter, Air & Waste Management Association; Fellow, American College of Forensic Examiners Institute **Marquis Who's Who Honors:** Who's Who Lifetime Achievement (2018) **To what do you attribute your success:** Mr. Cohen attributes his success to hard work, listening to the needs of his clients and his capability of translating the requirements of environmental legislation to cost effective compliance; he also cites the spousal support that he receives in all that he does. **Why did you become involved in your profession or industry:** Mr. Cohen entered his profession out of his desire to keep and preserve the earth in an ever-changing world of progress. **What do you consider to be the highlight of your career:** The highlight of Mr. Cohen's career was being able to solve complex environmental problems in a cost-effective manner. **Where will you be in five years:** In the next five years, Mr. Cohen will be continuing to do what he is doing now. **Hobbies:** Gardening; Listening to music; Home repair **Political Affiliations:** Democrat **Religion:** Jewish **Shipping Address:** 781 State Route 15 S, Enviro-Sciences (of Delaware), Inc., Lake Hopatcong, NJ, 07849 **Website:** https://www.enviro-sciences.com

Robert Stephan Cohen

Title: Lawyer **Industry:** Law and Legal Services **Company Name:** Cohen Clair Lans Greifer Thorpe & Rottenstreich LLP **Date of Birth:** 01/14/1939 **Place of Birth:** New York **State:** NY **Parents:** Abraham Cohen; Florence Cohen **Marital Status:** Married **Spouse Name:** Stephanie J. Stiefel **Children:** Christopher; Ian; Joshua; Nicholas **Education:** LLB, Fordham University (1962); BA, Alfred University (1959) **Career:** Chairman of Judicial Screening Committee (2016-Present); Judicial Screening Committee, First Judicial Department (2011-2015); Senior Partner, Cohen Clair Lans Greifer Thorpe & Rottenstreich (1968) **Career Related:** Adjunct Professor of Law, University of Pennsylvania Law School (2003-Present) **Military Service:** First Lieutenant, Judge Advocate General, US Army Reserve (1965-1967) **Creative Works:** Author, "Reconcilable Differences," Simon & Schuster (2004); Editor, Law Review, New York State Bar Association (1963); Contributor, Various Articles to Legal Journals **Membership:** Fellow, American College of Family Trial Lawyers; ABA; New York State Bar Association; Association of the Bar of the City of New York; New York American Academy of Matrimonial Lawyers; International Academy of Matrimonial Lawyers **Bar Admissions:** United States Court of Appeals for the Second Circuit (1965); United States District Court of New York for the Southern District of New York (1964); United States District Court of New York for the Eastern District of New York (1964); New York **Hobbies:** Marathons **Shipping Address:** 885 Third Avenue, 32nd Floor, Cohen Clair Lans, New York, NY, 10022

Christopher C. Colenda III

Title: Consultant, Psychiatrist **Industry:** Medicine & Health Care **Date of Birth:** 02/14/1952 **Place of Birth:** Baltimore **State/Country of Origin:** MD **Parents:** Christopher Columbus Colenda, Jr.; Janet A. Colenda **Marital Status:** Married **Spouse Name:** Kathryn Wincklhofer Colenda (7/24/1976) **Children:** Meredith Lee; Stephanie Adair **Education:** MPH, Johns Hopkins University (1982); MD, School of Medicine, Virginia Commonwealth University (1977); BA, Wittenberg University (1973) **Certifications:** Certified in Geriatric Psychiatry, American Board of Psychiatry and Neurology (2010); Certified in Geriatric Psychiatry, American Board of Psychiatry and Neurology (2001); Certified in Geriatric Psychiatry, American Board of Psychiatry and Neurology (1991); Certified in Psychiatry, American Board of Psychiatry and Neurology (1986) **Career:** Chancellor of Health Sciences, Robert C. Byrd Health Sciences Center, West Virginia University (2009-Present); President Emeritus, Christopher C. Colenda, LLC (2016); Of Counsel, Witt/Kieffer (2016); President, University Health Systems (2014-2016); CEO, University Health Systems (2014-2016); Jean and Thomas McMullin Dean of Medicine, Health Science Center, College of Medicine, Texas A&M University (2003-2009); Acting Dean, College of Human Medicine, Michigan State University (2000-2001); Chairman, Department of Psychiatry, Michigan State University (1997-2002); Vice Chairman, Wake Forest School of Medicine (1990-1996); Section Head, Geriatric Psychiatry, Wake Forest School of Medicine (1990-1996); Director of Geriatric Psychiatry, School of Medicine, Virginia Commonwealth University, Richmond, VA (1985-1990) **Career Related:** Vice Chairman, Geriatric Psychiatry Test Writing Committee, American Board of Psychiatry and Neurology, Deerfield, IL (2000-Present); Faculty Fellow, Liaison Committee for Medical Education, Washington, DC (2001-2002) **Creative Works:** Author, Health Services and Policy Research, American Journal of Geriatric Psychiatry **Awards:** Honoree, Best Doctors in America, Woodward/White, Inc. (1994-Present); Grassroots Champion Award, West Virginia Hospital Association, American Hospital Association (2016); Becker's Hospital Review List of 100 Physician Leaders of Hospitals and Health Systems (2015); Edithe J. Levit Distinguished Service Award, National Board of Medical Examiners (2013); Article of the Year Award, AcademyHealth (2008); Presidential Award for Community Outreach, Health Science Center, College of Medicine, Texas A&M University (2006); Elected to Sigma Xi, Texas A&M University (2005); Jack Weinberg Award in Geriatric Psychiatry, American Psychiatric Association (2004); Honorable Mention, The Exemplary Psychiatrist Award, NAMI (2003); Alumni Star in Medicine, School of Medicine, Virginia Commonwealth University (2003); Outstanding Faculty Award, College of Human Medicine, Michigan State University (2002-2003); Special Commendation, Council of Aging, American Psychiatric Association (2000); Featured, Best Doctors in the Midwest, Woodward/White, Inc. (1998); Featured, Best Doctors in the Southeast, Woodward/White, Inc. (1995) **Membership:** Treasurer, American Association for Geriatric Psychiatry (2002-Present); Health Care Systems Council, American Hospital Association (2015-2016); Co-chair, Special Committee on Physician Executives and Continuing Maintenance of Certification, American Board of Medical Specialties (2015-2016); West Virginia State Innovation Model Grant: CMS, Better Value Workgroup, Health Care Delivery and Payment Model Task Force (2015-2016); West Virginia Political Action Committee (2014-2016); Executive Committee of the Board of Directors (2014-2016); Board of Directors, West Virginia Chamber of Commerce (2014-2016); Chancellor, Robert C. Byrd Health Sciences Center, West Virginia University (2014); Professor of Behavioral Medicine and Psychiatry, Robert C. Byrd Health Sciences Center, West Virginia University (2014); Board of Directors, American Board of Psychiatry and Neurology (2013-2016); Former Chair, International Collaborations Advisory Committee (2013-2014); Elected, Executive Board, National Board of Medical Examiners (2010-2013); President Emeritus, West Virginia University Health System (2009-2015); Finance Committee, National Board of Medical Examiners (2009-2015); Board of Directors, West Virginia University Health System (2009-2015); Chair, Council, LCME (2009-2013); Chair, Building Advisory Committee, American Board of Psychiatry and Neurology (2006-2013); West Virginia University Medical Corporation, University Health Associates (2006-2011); America Medical Association; Board of Directors, American Association for Geriatric Psychiatry (2000-2001); Chair, Council of Aging, American Psychiatric Association (1997-2000) **Marquis Who's Who Honors:** Albert Nelson Marquis Lifetime Achievement Award (2017) **Business Address:** 1959 N Peace Haven Road, Winston-Salem, NC, 27106 **Shipping Address:** 1959 N Peace Haven Road, #108, Winston-Salem, NC, 27106

Claudette A. Collier

Title: Senior Manager, Global Learning **Industry:** Other **Membership:** ATD; PMI; E-Learning Guild **Marquis Who's Who Honors:** Albert Nelson Marquis Lifetime Achievement Award (2017) **To what do you attribute your success:** As a woman in today's world, Ms. Collier attributes her success to perseverance and passion. Her commitment transfers to leadership and to others in the company; she has taken her passion for her work and the betterment of other women and has transferred it to her peers. Ms. Collier has nine years of experience in her profession and four years in her current position. She says she has been blessed with many great mentors. **Why did you become involved in your profession or industry:** She comes from a family with medical backgrounds and learned the power of research from them. **What do you consider to be the highlight of your career:** Ms. Collier started as a nursing student. She has worked with great people and has even brought some to her company so she can grow their skills. **Hobbies:** Traveling to see her children and grandchildren; Taking care of her mother and siblings **Shipping Address:** PO Box 491, Powers Lake, WI, 53159

Kevin S. Combs

Title: Emergency Room Physician **Industry:** Medicine & Health Care **Company Name:** Carilion Tazewell Virginia Medical Center **Date of Birth:** 05/01/1971 **Place of Birth:** Johnson City **State:** TN **Education:** Fellow, ACOI American College of Osteopathic Internists (2015); Resident, Norton Community Hospital, Mountain States Health Alliance (2008); DO, Kentucky College of Osteopathic Medicine, University of Pikeville (2004) **Certifications:** Board Certified in Internal Medicine (2014) **Career:** Emergency Room Physician, Carilion Tazewell Virginia Medical Center, Carilion Clinic (2014); Chair of Medicine, Russell County Medical Center, Mountain States Health Alliance (2009-2011); Vice Chief of Staff, Russell County Medical Center, Mountain States Health Alliance; Director of Respiratory Therapy, Russell County Medical Center, Mountain States Health Alliance; Associate Medical Director, Legacy Hospice; Assistant Professor, Clinical Faculty Member, Department of Internal Medicine, Edward Via College of Osteopathic Medicine **Awards:** National Dean's List **Membership:** American Medical Association; ACOA American College of Osteopathic Internists; American Osteopathic Association **To what do you attribute your success:** He attributes his success to his faith. **Why did you become involved in your profession or industry:** He became involved in his profession because his family members are physicians and it's a profession he has always been inspired to work in. **Where will you be in five years:** In five years, Dr. Combs wants to further educate his community on complications of diabetes. **Hobbies:** Martial arts **Business Address:** 445 Porterfield Highway, Suite A, Abingdon, VA, 24210 **Shipping Address:** 81 Gardenside Boulevard, Lebanon, VA, 24266

Billie Marie Connor-Dominguez

Title: Librarian (Retired) **Industry:** Library Management/Library Services **Date of Birth:** 10/04/1934 **Place of Birth:** Brighton **State:** MO **Parents:** Clifford Delmar Batten; Naomi Marie (Calhoun) Batten **Marital Status:** Married **Spouse Name:** Ramon Dominguez (9/10/1999); John Michael Connor (12/18/1968, Deceased 1978); Eugene Lee Struble (6/2/1962, Divorced 1968) **Education:** MLS, Rutgers, The State University of New Jersey (1959); Graduate Coursework, University of Guanajuato, Mexico (1956); BS, Southwest Missouri State University, Springfield, MO (1955) **Career:** Librarian (1996-2007); Manager, Business/Economics, Science/Technology/Patents, Water and Power Library, Los Angeles Public Library (1996-2007); Subject Department Manager, Science/Technology/Patents, Los Angeles Public Library (1979-1996); Subject Department Manager, Business/Economics, Los Angeles Public Library (1977-1979); Senior Librarian, Business/Economics, Los Angeles Public Library (1970-1977); Subject Specialist, SCAN, Los Angeles Public Library (1969-1970); Information Specialist, Business and Technology Service, Wichita Public Library (1962-1968); Extension Library, Southwest Regional Library, Bolivar, MO (1959-1962); Teacher, Auburn High School (1955-1958) **Civic:** Board of Directors, Community Career Development, Inc., Los Angeles, CA (2008-2010); Board of Directors, Community Career Development, Inc., Los Angeles, CA (1995-2002) **Creative Works:** Editor, Communicator (1995-2007); Co-Compiler, "Ottemiller's Index to Plays in Collections, Seventh Edition" (1988); Co-Compiler, "Ottemiller's Index to Plays in Collections, Sixth Edition" (1976); Editor, Communicator (1971-1974); Co-Compiler, "Ottemiller's Index to Plays in Collections, Fifth Edition" (1971); Contributor, Articles, Professional Journals **Awards:** Support Staff Award, Library Mosaics and Council Library/Media Technicians (2002); Rose Vormelker Award, Southern California Chapter, Special Libraries Association (2002); Eponym, Billie Connor Award for Outstanding Contributions, Southern California Chapter, Special Libraries Association (1994) **Membership:** Board of Directors, Business Economic Science and Technology Friends (2012-Present); Board of Directors, Bruckman Rare Books Friends (2012-Present); Co-Chair, Acquisitions, Board of Directors, Culinary Historians of Southern California (2007-Present); President, Southern California Chapter, Special Libraries Association (1998-1999); Library Liaison, Culinary Historians of Southern California (1995-2007); Board of Directors, Special Libraries Association (1992-1995); President, Southern California Chapter, Special Libraries Association (1991-1992); President, Patent and Trademark Depository Librarian Association (1988); Chairman, Business and Financial Division, Special Libraries Association (1977-1978); President, Heart America Chapter, Special Libraries Association (1967-1968); Lifetime Member, Librarians Guild; Lifetime Member, American Federation of State; American Association for the Advancement of Science **Marquis Who's Who Honors:** Albert Nelson Marquis Lifetime Achievement Award (2017) **To what do you attribute your success:** Mrs. Connor-Dominguez attributes her success to hard work. **Where will you be in five years:** Mrs. Connor-Dominguez will be retired in five years. **Hobbies:** Cooking; Creating menus; Reading; Traveling **Political Affiliations:** Democrat **Religion:** Catholic **Shipping Address:** 1707 Micheltorena Street, Apt. 312, Los Angeles, CA, 90026

Nancy R. Conrad

Title: Artist **Industry:** Fine Art **Company Name:** Nancy Conrad **Date of Birth:** 01/29/1940 **Place of Birth:** Houston **State:** TX **Marital Status:** Married **Education:** BFA in Painting, Randolph College; BFA in Art History, Randolph College **Career:** Oil Painting Workshop Instructor, Mountain Brook School Historical Foundation (2004); Digital Photography Workshop Instructor, Mountain Brook School Historical Foundation (2003); Art Teacher, Museum of Fine Arts, Houston, TX; Art Teacher, Contemporary Arts Museum Houston; Private Studio Art Teacher; Volunteer Art Consultant, Spring Branch Independent School District **Civic:** Volunteer Art Consultant, SBISD **Creative Works:** Illustrator, "Little Flower: A Journey of Caring" **Awards:** Listee, Art in America (2009-2010); Full Scholarship, Museum of Fine Arts, Houston, TX; Foley First Place Award, Dimension Houston V; Listee, Jacobson's Directory of American Artists **Membership:** American Fine Arts for Healthcare (2016-Present) **To what do you attribute your success:** Ms. Conrad attributes her success to her excellent gallery representation and great art consultants. **Why did you become involved in your profession or industry:** Ms. Conrad became involved in her profession because in the second grade, she won a full scholarship to the Museum of Fine Arts, and she followed through with art until high school. She then majored in art and art history in college. **What do you consider to be the highlight of your career:** The highlight of Ms. Conrad's career was winning the Purchase Award by the El Paso Museum of Fine Art and Randolph Macon College. **Where will you be in five years:** In five years, Ms. Conrad will continue painting. **Hobbies:** Silversmithing **Business Address:** 291 Conrad Point, 291 Conrad Point, MT, Lakeside, 59922 **Shipping Address:** 2202 Stanmore Drive, Houston, TX, 77019 **Website:** http://nancyconradartist.com

Hardy Merrill Cook III, PhD

Title: Literature and Language Professor **Industry:** Education/Educational Services **Date of Birth:** 07/21/1947 **Place of Birth:** Baltimore **State:** MD **Parents:** Hardy Merrill Cook, Jr.; Elizabeth (Frierson) Cook **Marital Status:** Widowed **Spouse Name:** Kathleen Mary Kelley (4/25/1975, Deceased 10/30/2004) **Children:** Melissa Lauren Cook-Ralph; Rebecca Mary Elizabeth **Education:** PhD in English, Theater, Radio, TV & Film, University of Maryland, College Park (1988); MA in English Language & Literature, University of Maryland, College Park (1972); BA in English Language & Literature, University of Maryland, College Park (1969) **Career:** Chair, Department of English and Modern Languages, Bowie State University (1996-2002); English Professor, Bowie State University, Maryland (1995-2009); Chair, Curriculum Committee, Bowie State University (1995-1996); Presidential Intern, Bowie State University (1995); Special Assistant to Provost, Bowie State University (1994-1995); Associate Professor of English, Bowie State University (1989-1995); Assistant Professor English, Bowie State University, Maryland (1979-1989); Professor Emeritus, Bowie State University **Creative Works:** Advisory Board, "Digital Renaissance Editions" (2006-Present); Editorial Board, "Multicultural Shakespeare: Translation, Appropriation and Performance" (2003-Present); Editorial Board, "Internet Shakespeare Editions" (1996-Present); Editorial Board, "Early Modern Literary Studies: An Electronic Journal of Sixteenth and Seventeenth Century English Literature" (1995); Contributing Editor, "Shakespeare Newsletter" (1990-1998); Co-Editor, "Shakespeare's Sonnets and Lovers Complaint 1609"; Editor, "Shaksper: The Global Electronic Shakespeare Conference, 28th Year of Service Academic Community"; Owner, "Shaksper: The Global Electronic Shakespeare Conference, 28th Year of Service Academic Community"; Moderator, "Shaksper: The Global Electronic Shakespeare Conference, 28th Year of Service Academic Community"; Contributor, Articles, Professional Journals **Awards:** Certificate of Achievement, University Systems of Maryland (1999); Regents' Faculty Excellence Award, University System of Maryland (1999); Nominee, Outstanding Educator of the Year, Maryland Association of Higher Education **Membership:** English Renaissance Text Society; Malone Society; International Shakespeare Association; Shakespeare Association of America **Marquis Who's Who Honors:** Albert Nelson Marquis Lifetime Achievement Award (2017) **Hobbies:** Studying Buddhism **Religion:** Buddhist **Shipping Address:** 7505 Citadel Drive, College Park, MD, 20740 **Website:** https://shaksper.net

Michael H. Cook

Title: Lawyer, Partner, and Co-chair, Health Care Group **Industry:** Law and Legal Services **Company Name:** Liles Parker PLLC **Date of Birth:** 06/09/1947 **Place of Birth:** Oshkosh **State:** WI **Parents:** Leonard James Cook; Ethel (Shapiro) Cook **Marital Status:** Married **Spouse Name:** Michele Anne Reday (4/21/1979) **Children:** Noah Reday; Megan Rose **Education:** JD, Charles Widger School of Law, Villanova University (1973); BA in Political Science, Temple University, Cum Laude (1969); Coursework, University of Wisconsin (1965-1966) **Career:** Strategic Healthcare Advisor, Impactwear International, LLLP, Washington, DC (2014-Present); Partner, Co-chair, Healthcare Practice, Liles Parker PLLC, Washington, DC (2010-Present); Partner and Contract Attorney, Blank Rome LLP, Washington, DC (2008-2010); Partner, Epstein Becker & Green, P.C., Washington, DC (2006-2007); Partner in Charge of DC Office Healthcare Practice, Baker & McKenzie, Washington, DC (2003-2006); Shareholder in Charge of DC Office Healthcare Group, Jenkens & Gilchrist, P.C., Washington, DC (1998-2003); Mintz, Levin, Cohn, Ferris, Glovsky and Popeo, P.C., Washington, DC (1997-1998); Partner in Charge of DC Office Healthcare Practice, Katten, Muchin & Zavis, Washington, DC (1991-1997); Partner and Associate, Wood, Lucksinger & Epstein (1985-1990); Associate, Wood, Lucksinger & Epstein, Washington, DC (1981-1985); Attorney, General Counsel's Office, U.S. Department of Health and Human Services, Washington, DC (1973-1980) **Career Related:** Guest Lecturer, Administrative Law Review, School of Law, American University; Guest Lecturer, Milken Institute School of Public Health, George Washington University; Guest Lecturer, Shenandoah University; Guest Lecturer, Bloomberg School of Public Health, Johns Hopkins University; Guest Lecturer, Washington College of Law, American University; Lecturer, Executive Education Course, Erickson School, University of Maryland, Baltimore County **Civic:** Board of Directors, First Star Inc. (2016-Present); Board of Directors, National Osteoporosis Foundation (2016-Present); Board of Medical Assistance Services, Commonwealth of Virginia (2014-Present); Advisory Board, Department of Political Science, Temple University (2013-Present); Executive Committee, Shenandoah University Center for Public Service and Scholarship (2012-Present); Advisory Board, Shenandoah University Center for Public Service and Scholarship (2009-Present); Board of Directors, Democratic Business Council of Northern Virginia (2008-Present) **Military Service:** Honorably Discharged, U.S. Army Reserves **Creative Works:** Author, "It's time for CMS and Congress to Review Outdated Medicare and Medicaid Provisions," Journal of Health & Life Science Law (2016); Author, "How Can Providers Challenge Medicaid Underpayments After Armstrong v. Exceptional Child Center?," Journal of Health & Life Science Law (2015); Co-author, "National Federation of Independent Businesses v. Sebelius - What Does It Mean for the Future of Medicaid and Health Care Reform?" Journal of Health and Life Science Law (2013); Author, "Independent Payment Advisory Board: Part of the Solution for Bending the Cost Curve?" Journal of Health & Life Science Law (2010); Author, "Key Changes in Health Care Law Policies - and Upcoming Responses," Inside the Minds (2009) **Awards:** Top Rated Lawyer, District of Columbia and Baltimore Legal Leaders (2015) **Membership:** District of Columbia Bar Association; Pennsylvania Bar Association; American Health Lawyers Association; American Bar Association; Nursing Home Advisory Group, Legal Committee, American Association of Homes and Services for the Aging (Now Leading Age); Reimbursement and Legal Subcommittees, National Subacute Care Association; Reimbursement and Legal Subcommittees, National Association for the Support of Long Term Care; OBRA Nursing Home Reform Implementation Task Force, American Health Care Association; Managed Care, Public Policy, and Legal Task Forces, Leadership and President's Councils, Assisted Living Federation of America (Now Argentum); National Advisory Task Force on Long Term Care, Healthcare Financial Management Association; Professional Certification Board, American College of Health Care Administrators **Bar Admissions:** Seventh Circuit, U.S. Court of Appeals (1984); Tenth Circuit, U.S. Court of Appeals (1984); Federal Circuit, U.S. Court of Appeals (1984); U.S. Court of Federal Claims (1982); Third Circuit, U.S. Court of Appeals (1982); District of Columbia Circuit, U.S. Court of Appeals (1981); 11th Circuit, U.S. Court of Appeals (1981); U.S. District Court, District of Columbia (1981); Ninth Circuit, U.S. Court of Appeals (1979); District of Columbia (1979); U.S. District Court, Northern District, State of Illinois (1977); U.S. Supreme Court (1976); Pennsylvania (1973) **Marquis Who's Who Honors:** Albert Nelson Marquis Lifetime Achievement Award (2017) **Political Affiliations:** Democrat **Religion:** Jewish **Business Address:** 2121 Wisconsin Avenue NW, Suite 200, Washington, DC, 20007 **Shipping Address:** 2724 King Street, Alexandria, VA, 22302 **Website:** http://www.lilesparker.com

Elaine Johnson Copeland, PhD

Title: Academic Administrator **Industry:** Education/Educational Services **Date of Birth:** 03/11/1943 **Place of Birth:** Catawba **State:** SC **Parents:** Aaron Jasper; Lucille Hawkins Johnson **Marital Status:** Widowed **Spouse Name:** Robert McDaniel Copeland (9/26/1964, Deceased) **Children:** Robert, Jr. **Education:** MBA, University of Illinois, Urbana-Champaign (1987); PhD, Oregon State University, Corvallis, OR (1974); MAT, Winthrop University, Rock Hill, SC (1971); BS, Livingstone College, Salisbury, NC (1964) **Certifications:** National Certified Counselor, Harvard Institute of Educational Management (Now Institute for Educational Management, Harvard Graduate School of Education) (2002); Licensed Professional Counselor, Harvard Institute of Educational Management (Now Institute for Educational Management, Harvard Graduate School of Education) (2002); Certificate, Harvard Institute of Educational Management (Now Institute for Educational Management, Harvard Graduate School of Education) (2002) **Career:** President Emeritus, Clinton College, Rock Hill, SC (2001-President); Vice President of Academic Affairs, Dean, Livingstone College, Salisbury, SC (2000-2001); Associate Dean, Associate Vice Chancellor for Academic Affairs, University of Illinois at Urbana-Champaign (1974-1998); Psychological Counselor, Instructor, Oregon State University, Corvallis, OR (1970-1974); Biology Teacher, York School District, South Carolina (1966-1970); Science Teacher, Florence School District, South Carolina (1964-1965) **Career Related:** President, National Association for Women in Education (1988-1999); Chair, Committee on Institutional Cooperation (Now Big Ten Academic Alliance) and Consortium of Big Ten Universities and the University of Chicago **Civic:** President, Girls Club Board, Champaign, IL (1982-1984); President, University of Illinois Chapter, YWCA USA (1980-1982); Rotary Club of Rock Hill, Rotary International **Creative Works:** Author, 30 Peer-Reviewed Articles; Author, Chapters, Books; Author, Book Reviews **Awards:** Order of the Silver Crescent Award for Leadership and Service in the Region and State, Given by Governor of South Carolina (2015); Lifetime Achievement Award, AME Zion Church (2012); Presidential Award, TRACS (2005); Citizen of the Year Award, Omega Psi Phi Fraternity Inc. (2004); Service Award, Committee for Institutional Cooperation (Now Big Ten Academic Alliance) (1999); Outstanding Black Faculty Award, National Black Graduate Student Association, University of Illinois at Urbana-Champaign (1989); Distinguished Alumni Award, National Association for Equal Opportunity in Higher Education (1986); Youth Motivation Task Force Award, National of Alliance Business, Business Money News (1981-1982); Outstanding Black Faculty Award, National Black Graduate Student Association (1981) **Membership:** President, National Association for Women in Education (1988-1989); Alumnae President, University of Illinois, Urbana-Champaign (1977-1983); Golden Life Member, Delta Sigma Theta Sorority, Inc., Rock Hill, SC; Lifetime Member, The Honor Society of Phi Kappa Phi; American Psychological Association; Phi Delta Kappa International **Marquis Who's Who Honors:** Albert Nelson Marquis Lifetime Achievement Award (2017) **To what do you attribute your success:** Dr. Copeland attributes her success to her parents, spouse, and mentors. **Why did you become involved in your profession or industry:** Dr. Copeland became involved in her profession because her parents and grandparents were educators. **What do you consider to be the highlight of your career:** The highlights of Dr. Copeland's career are becoming the first African-American woman to receive a MBA through the Executive MBA Program at Illinois, receiving the first Presidential Award from the Transnational Association of Christian Colleges and Schools in 2005, and becoming the first African-American woman to be elected President of the National Association for Women in Education in 1989. **Where will you be in five years:** In five years, Dr. Copeland plans to be traveling, volunteering, and consulting. **Political Affiliations:** Democrat **Religion:** African Methodist Episcopal Zion Church **Shipping Address:** 503 Birmingham Court, Rock Hill, SC, 29732 **Website:** http://www.elainejohnsoncopelandphd.com

John Barns Copenhaver

Title: Chief Executive Officer, Attorney **Industry:** Law and Legal Services **Company Name:** Contingency Management Group, Inc. **Date of Birth:** 08/18/1953 **Place of Birth:** Pearisburg **State:** VA **Parents:** William Pierce Copenhaver; Jane Farrier Copenhaver **Marital Status:** Married **Spouse Name:** Diana Lynn Thompson (12/10/1994) **Education:** JD in International Law and Legal Studies, University of Georgia School of Law, Athens, GA (1979); BSc in Planerary Geology, Brown University, Providence, RI (1975) **Certifications:** Certified Business Continuity Professional, DRI International, Inc. (1993-2009) **Career:** Chief Executive Officer, Contingency Management Group, Inc. (2009-Present); President, Chief Executive Officer, DRI International, Inc. (2005-2009); Senior Vice President, Marsh LLC (2001-2005); Regional Director, Region IV, FEMA, Atlanta, GA (1997-2001); Senior Director, Global Crisis Response Team (1996-1997); Director, Business Continuity Programs, BellSouth (Now AT&T Intellectual Property) (1996); Law Clerk, Court of Appeals of Georgia, Atlanta, GA (1980-1981); Geologist, Texasgulf Inc., Houston, TX (1975-1976) **Career Related:** Board of Directors, The Business Continuity Institute (2009-2012); Editorial Advisory Board, Journal of Emergency Management (2008-2010); Board of Directors, Canadian Center for Emergency Preparedness, Toronto, Ontario, Canada (2005-2010); Founder, Global Partnership for Preparedness Foundation, Washington, DC (2004-2007); President, Global Partnership for Preparedness Foundation, Washington, DC (2004-2007) **Civic:** Board of Directors, Angels Among Us (2017-Present); Business Advisory Council, Fulton Science Academy Private School (2016-Present); Board, Emergency Information Infrastructure Project (2011-Present); Private Sector Subcommittee, National Advisory Council, FEMA (2008-2010); Task Force, United States Chamber of Commerce National Security (2007-2010); Capital Campaign Committee, University of Georgia, Athens, GA (2005-2006); Board of Visitors, University of Georgia School of Law (2002-2005); Principal, Council for Excellence in Government **Creative Works:** Co-Author, "Homeland Security and Emergency Management: A Legal Guide for State and Local Governments" (2010); Editor, "Jane's Citizen's Safety Guide" (2004) **Membership:** Buckhead Club; Local Commerce Club; Capital City Club; Local Kiwanis Club (Now Kiwanis International) **Bar Admissions:** Georgia (1979-Present) **Marquis Who's Who Honors:** Albert Nelson Marquis Lifetime Achievement Award (2017) **To what do you attribute your success:** Mr. Copenhaver attributes his success to understanding what his particular profession can do for other people, as well as his ability to make connections with others to ensure what needs to be done can get done quickly. **Why did you become involved in your profession or industry:** Mr. Copenhaver became involved in his profession because he thought it would be good to have a law degree no matter his profession. Eventually, he settled on emergency management. **Where will you be in five years:** In five years, Mr. Copenhaver plans on being where he is now, while hopefully moving on to help other new technologies hit their stride. He hopes to work on technologies that make a difference in people's lives and he wants people to know about new technology that will help them with natural events. **Hobbies:** Golf; Traveling; Scuba diving **Religion:** Methodist **Shipping Address:** 8205 Overview Ct, Roswell, GA, 30076 **Website:** http://www.johnbcopenhaver.com

Patricia Corbett

Title: Social Worker **Industry:** Social Work **Education:** MSW, University of Calgary (2013); Master's Degree in Counseling, University of Calgary (2007); BE, University of Alberta (1976); Bachelor's Degree in Early Childhood Education, University of Alberta (1976) **Certifications:** Registered Social Worker (2013) **Career Related:** Adjunct Professor, Columbia University **Awards:** Honoree, Top Female Professional (2015) **Marquis Who's Who Honors:** Albert Nelson Marquis Lifetime Achievement Award (2017) **Why did you become involved in your profession or industry:** Ms. Corbett became involved in her profession because she wanted to work in the child care field for most of her life. She has two sons on the autism spectrum and saw the need to help the community. **Where will you be in five years:** In five years, Ms. Corbett intends to collaborate with her sons, who are artists, and create a parenting program using photographs as visuals. She also wants to continue writing poetry. **Hobbies:** Crochet; Reading; Gym **Shipping Address:** 4628 84 St NW, AB, Calgary, Canada, T3B 2R5 **Website:** http://www.reframingthebox.com

Carlos Cordon-Cardo, PhD

Title: Professor, Chair **Industry:** Education/Educational Services **Company Name:** Icahn School of Medicine at Mount Sinai **Date of Birth:** 02/25/1957 **Place of Birth:** Calella **State/Country of Origin:** Barcelona/Spain **Parents:** Juan Cordon; Montserrat (Cardo) Cordon **Marital Status:** Married **Spouse Name:** Alicia Bouzan (11/9/1990) **Children:** Carolina; Daniel **Education:** PhD in Cell Biology and Genetics, Cornell University (1985); Special Fellow, Immunopathology, Memorial Sloan Kettering Cancer Center, Cornell University, New York City, NY (1983-1987); MD, Universitat Autònoma de Barcelona (1980); BS in Biology, Santa Ana College, Mataro, Spain (1975); Honorary Doctorate, Universitat de Barcelona **Certifications:** Licensed Physician, Spain **Career:** Member, Professor, Attending Molecular Pathologist (1998-Present); Director, Division of Molecular Pathology, Memorial Sloan Kettering Cancer Center, Cornell University, New York City, NY (1995-Present); Associate Professor, Pathology, Weill Cornell Medicine, New York City, NY (1992-Present); Head, Laboratory Molecular Immunopathology, Memorial Sloan Kettering Cancer Center, Cornell University, New York City, NY (1988-Present); Associate Attending Molecular Pathologist, Memorial Sloan Kettering Cancer Center, Cornell University, New York City, NY (1992-1998); Associate Member, Professor, Memorial Sloan Kettering Cancer Center, Cornell University, New York City, NY (1992-1998); Acting Director, Experimental Pathology, Memorial Sloan Kettering Cancer Center, Cornell University, New York City, NY (1992-1994); Assistant Member, Professor, Memorial Sloan Kettering Cancer Center, Cornell University, New York City, NY (1987-1992) **Career Related:** Member, Roll of Honor, UICC (1996-Present); Member, Subcommittee C, National Cancer Institute (1995-Present); Member, Research Programs Review Committee, National Cancer Institute (1995-Present); Member, Bladder Cancer Advisory Network, National Cancer Institute (1988-Present); Chairman, Bladder Cancer Advisory Network, National Cancer Institute (1989-1992); Member, Committee on Immunodiagnosis, UICC, Geneva, Switzerland (1983-1987); Lecturer in Field; Conductor, Workshops in Field **Creative Works:** Contributor, Numerous Articles, Professional Journals; Contributor, Numerous Abstracts, Professional Journals; Contributor, Chapters, Books; Member, Editorial Board, The American Journal of Pathology; Member, Editorial Board, International Journal of Cancer; Member, Editorial Board, American Journal of Clinical Pathology; Member, Editorial Board, Clinical Cancer Research; Member, Editorial Board, Diagnostic Molecular Pathology; Member, Editorial Board, Applied Immunohistochemistry & Molecular Morphology; Member, Editorial Board, Urologic Oncology; Member, Editorial Board, Molecular Urology; Member, Editorial Board, Journal of Experimental and Clinical Cancer Research; Member, Editorial Board, Gaceta Mexicana de Oncología **Awards:** Research Grantee, National Institutes of Health (1993-Present); Research Grantee, National Cancer Institute (1988-Present); G.C. Ahlstrom Lecture and Medal, Swedish Society of Physicians (1996); Jaime Esperalba Award, Academia De Ciencias Mediques De Catalunya, Balears (1995); Annual Science Award, Academia Medico-Quirurgica Espanola (1995); Paul Harris Award, Rotary International (1994); Louise And Alliston Boyer Young Investigator Award, Memorial Sloan Kettering Cancer Center (1991); Featured Listee, List of 400 Most Highly Influential Biomedical Researchers Worldwide, European Journal of Clinical Investigation; Thought Leader Award, Agilent; Gold Medal, Swedish Medical Association; Gold Medal of Medical Sciences, Govierno de Galicia **Membership:** The Roll of Honour, UICC; Honorary Member, Spanish American Medical and Dental Society of New York; Honoree, Real Academia de Medicina de Catalunya; WHO Center for Urologic Tumors; Review Committee, Cancer Centers and Research Programs, National Cancer Institute; State Legislative Committee for New York, American Association for Cancer Research (1993-Present); President, Solid Tumor Chapter, Association for Molecular Pathology; Translational Chair, Genitourinary Section, SWOG; American Society for Investigative Pathology; United States & Canadian Academy of Pathology; International Society of Urological Pathology; ISIMM; Association for Molecular Pathology **Why did you become involved in your profession or industry:** Dr. Cordon-Cardo made a lab in his house at age ten and his grandmother bought him a microscope. He became very motivated to study science. He loves his work, which he is passionate about. **Hobbies:** Studying; Enjoying music; Soccer **Business Address:** One Gustave L. Levy Place, New York, NY, 10218 **Shipping Address:** 1235 Park Ave Apt 16A, New York, NY, 10128

Nancy Lee Latham Cornish

Title: Music Educator **Industry:** Education/Educational Services **Company Name:** Cranberry Coast Concert Chorale **Date of Birth:** 09/21/1946 **Place of Birth:** Providence **State:** RI **Parents:** Arthur Jeremiah Latham, Jr.; Doris Helen Salisbury Latham **Marital Status:** Divorced **Children:** Stephen James; Christopher Samuel **Education:** Coursework and Doctoral Recitals toward DMA, Choral Conducting, The University of Kansas (2000-2003); MME, The University of Kansas (1975); BME, The University of Kansas (1969); Coursework in Music Education, Graceland University, Lamoni, Iowa (1964-1966) **Career:** Director, Cranberry Coast Concert Chorale, Cape Cod, MA (2013-Present); Ordained Minister and Musician, Community of Christ, Warwick, RI (2012-Present); Instructor of Music, Laramie County Community College, Cheyenne, WY (2003-2016); Graduate Teaching Assistant, The University of Kansas, Lawrence, KS (2000-2003); Instructor of Music, Neosho County Community College, Chanute, KS (1991-2000); Instructor of Music, Allen County Community College, Iola, KS (1980-1986); Music Teacher, Chanute Senior High School and Royster Junior High School, Chanute, KS (1972-1974); Music Teacher, Leavenworth West Junior High School (1970-1971); Performer, Cheyenne Chamber Singers; Performer, Cheyenne Capital Chorale; Performer, Independence Messiah Choir; Performer, Trinity Vocal Trio; Performer, Chanute Community Theater; Performer, University of Kansas Chamber Choir and Collegium Musicum; Performer, St. Cecilia Choir and String Quartet; Performer, Graceland University Orchestra; Performer, All New England Youth Symphony **Career Related:** Director, Choir, Cathedral of St. Mary, Cheyenne, WY (2004-2012); Graduate Teaching Assistant Director, Women's Chorale, University Singers and Men's Glee Club, The University of Kansas, Lawrence, KS (2000-2003); Director, Performer, Voices of Light, Kansas City, MO (1988-1990); Director of Music, First United Methodist Church, Chanute, KS (1990-2000); Director, St. Cecilia Choir, Chanute, KS (1975-1990) **Civic:** Secretary, Historic Governor's Mansion Foundation, Cheyenne, WY (2003-2005); President, Neosho Valley Arts Council, Chanute, KS (1974-1976) **Creative Works:** Director, "Amahl and the Night Visitors"; Director, "Two by Two"; Music Director, "Brigadoon"; Music Director, "West Side Story"; Music Director, "Oliver"; Music Director, "The Fantastics"; Music Director, "Grease"; Music Director, "Bye Bye Birdie"; Music Director, "Paint Your Wagon"; Music Director, "Joseph and the Amazing Technicolor Dreamcoat"; Music Dircetor, "Baby"; Music Director, "Once Upon a Mattress" (Princess and the Pea); Performer, Contralto Soloist Handel's "Messiah", Erie, KS; Performer, Independence Messiah Choir, Independence, MO; Performer, Mother Superior in "The Sound of Music"; Performer, Catherine in "Pippin," Chanute Community Theater, Chanute, KS; Performer, Carole Bayer Sager in "They're Playing Our Song," Neosho County Community College, Chanute, KS; Premier Concert Performance, Marilyn Morales' "Always Remember", Onset, MA; Vocal Ensemble "Trinity"; Choral Director, Mozart's "Requiem" and Orff's "Carmina Burana", Cranberry Coast Concert Chorale, Cape Cod, MA; Choral Director, Bernstein's "Chichester Psalms" and Orff's "Carmina Burana", Whitbourne's "Luminosity", Karl Jenkins' "The Armed Man: A Mass for Peace", "Gloria" and "Stabat Mater", Laramie County Community College Choirs and Capital Chorale, Cheyenne, WY; Conductor and Transcriber, Guillaume Dufay's "Missa se la face ay Pale," Laramie County Community Choir and Capital Chorale, Cathedral of St. Mary, Cheyenne, WY; Doctoral Recital Conductor, Mozart's "Missa brevis in C, KV 220", Three Movements of Rachmaninoff's "All-Night Vigil", Corpus Christi Catholic Church, Lawrence, KS; Doctoral Recital Conductor, Britten's "A Ceremony of Carols", University of Kansas, Lawrence, KS; Presenter, Rhythmic Complexity in Guillaume Dufay's "Missa se la face ay pale" **Awards:** Faculty Teaching Excellence Award, Arts and Humanities Division, Laramie County Community College (2007-2008) **Membership:** Vice President of Higher Education, Wyoming Music Educators Association (2004-2006); National Association for Music Education; American Choral Directors Association; Kansas Music Educators Association **What do you consider to be the highlight of your career:** One set of highlights would be conducting the Rocky Mountain Region premiere performances of Karl Jenkins "The Armed Man; A Mass for Peace", "Stabat Mater" and "Gloria" performed by the Laramie County Community College Choirs and the Capital Chorale with full orchestra in Cheyenne, WY. Another would be the Cathedral of St. Mary's Choir Tours to Spain, France, Portugal, Austria, Poland, Czech Republic and Switzerland to sing Masses and concerts in many cathedrals. **Political Affiliations:** Conservative **Religion:** Community of Christ **Shipping Address:** 14 Hannah Drive, Warwick, RI, 02888 **Website:** https://www.linkedin.com/in/nancy-lee-latham-cornish-03610233

Richard G. Coss, PhD

Title: Psychology Professor **Industry:** Education/Educational Services **Company Name:** University of California, Davis **Date of Birth:** 01/03/1940 **Place of Birth:** Sanger **State:** CA **Parents:** Joe Glenn Coss; Cornelia Geraldine Coss **Children:** Craig Stewart; Diana Michelle Coss-Berti **Education:** PhD in Comparative Psychology, University of Reading, Reading, England (1973); MA in Design, University of California, Los Angeles (1966); BS in Architecture, University of Southern California, Los Angeles, CA (1962) **Career:** Faculty Member, Graduate Group in Animal Behavior, University of California, Davis (1979-Present); Emeritus Professor of Psychology, University of California, Davis (2014); Editorial Advisory Board Member, "Behavioral and Neural Biology" (1985-1991); Professor of Psychology, University of California, Davis (1984-2014); Associate Professor of Psychology, University of California, Davis (1978-1984); Faculty Member, Graduate Group in Ecology, University of California, Davis (1975-2009); Assistant Professor of Psychology, University of California, Davis (1974-1978); Design Lecturer, University of California, Los Angeles (1971-1974); Freelance Industrial Designer, Paris, France (1970-1971); Research Director, Compagnie de l'Esthetique Industrielle, Paris, France (1966-1970); Engineer-Scientist, Lunar Base Study, Douglas Aircraft Company, Santa Monica, CA (1962-1966) **Career Related:** Engineer Scientist, Douglas Aircraft Company, Santa Monica, CA (1962-1966) **Civic:** Public Service, Davis Arts Center (1990-1992) **Creative Works:** Editor, "Environmental Awareness: Evolutionary, Aesthetic & Social Perspectives" (2005); Contributor, Chapters, Books, Contributor, Chapters, Professional Journals **Awards:** Research Grant, United States Fish Wildlife Service (2010-Present); Fellow, Association for Psychological Science (2009); Chancellor's Award for Excellence in Mentoring Undergraduate Research, University of California (2008); Grantee, National Aeronautics and Space Administration (1987-1991); Fellowship, NASA Ames Research Center (1986-1987); Grantee, National Science Foundation (1984-1987); Grantee, National Science Foundation (1979-1981) **Membership:** Fellow, Association for Psychological Science; International Society for Ecological Psychology; International Society for the Arts, Sciences and Technology; Sigma Xi **Marquis Who's Who Honors:** Albert Nelson Marquis Lifetime Achievement Award (2017) **Hobbies:** Drawing; Travel; Hiking; Bicycling **Shipping Address:** 807 Falcon Ave, Davis, CA, 95616

Jim Cowles

Title: Lawyer **Industry:** Law and Legal Services **Company Name:** Cowles & Thompson **Date of Birth:** 03/03/1934 **Place of Birth:** Wichita Falls **State:** TX **Education:** LLB, University of Texas (1961); BBA, University of Texas (1958) **Career:** Shareholder, Founder, Cowles & Thompson (1978-Present) **Military Service:** Judge Advocate; General, U.S. Naval Reserve **Awards:** Honoree, True Texas Legend, State Bar of Texas (2010); Honoree, Top Ten Lawyers in Texas, Texas Monthly and Law & Politics Magazine (2005); Trial Lawyer of the Year Award, Dallas Bar Association (2005); Honoree, Top 100 Super Lawyers in Texas (2003-2013); Honoree, Best Lawyers in Dallas, D Magazine (1997-2013); Honoree, Best Lawyers in America, American Lawyer (1993-2013); President's Award, Texas Association Defense Council (1993); Honoree, Texas 25 Greatest Lawyers of the Last Quarter Century; Honoree, 500 Leading Lawyers in America, Lawdragon; Honoree, Top 15 Business Defense Lawyers in Dallas/Ft. Worth, Dallas Business Journal **Membership:** Patrick E. Higginbotham Inn of Court; American Board of Trial Advocates; Defense Research Institute; Texas Bar College; International Association of Defense Council; Texas Association of Defense Council; Dallas Association of Defense Council; Dallas Bar Association; American Bar Association **Bar Admissions:** U.S. District Court, Southern District, State of Texas (1979); U.S. Court of Appeals for the Fifth Circuit (1968); U.S. District Court, Eastern District, State of Texas (1964); U.S. District Court, Western District, State of Texas (1962); U.S. District Court, Northern District, State of Texas (1962); U.S. Supreme Court (1961) **Marquis Who's Who Honors:** Albert Nelson Marquis Lifetime Achievement Award (2017) **Why did you become involved in your profession or industry:** Mr. Cowles' father worked in the courthouse in his hometown; he worships his father and he spent a lot of time in his office, and was around the profession and was given permission as a teenager to listen to trials. **Hobbies:** Reading; Woodworking; Guitar **Business Address:** 901 Main Street, Suite 3900, Dallas, TX, 75202 **Shipping Address:** 901 Main Street, Suite 3900, Cowles & Thompson PC, Dallas, TX, 75202

Joyce Wellborn Cox

Title: Secondary School Educator **Industry:** Education/Educational Services **Date of Birth:** 04/16/1933 **Place of Birth:** Crossnore **State:** NC **Parents:** Joseph Marion Wellborn; Flossie Rebecca (Howard) Wellborn **Education:** MA, Appalachian State University (1957); BA, Emory & Henry College (1954) **Certifications:** Certified Teacher, State of Missouri **Career:** Operations Manager, Heartland Community Credit Union (2000-2007); English Teacher, Northwest University, Xian, China (1995-1996); Accountant Specialist, Heartland Community Credit Union (1994-2000); Social Studies Teacher, Center High School, Kansas City, MO (1992-1994); English Teacher, Fulbright Commission, Nove Mesto nad Vahom, Czech Republic (1991-1992); Social Studies Teacher, Center High School, Kansas City, MO (1962-1991); Social Studies Teacher, White Station High School, Memphis, TN (1958-1962); Sixth Grade Teacher, Edison Park, Fort Myers, FL (1957-1958); Seventh Grade Teacher, Harris Middle School, Spruce Pine, NC (1955-1957); Seventh Grade Teacher, Nebo Elementary School, Nebo, NC (1954-1955) **Career Related:** Director, Center School District Museum (2010-2013); Adjunct Faculty Member, Avila University, Kansas City, MO (1992-1993); Advisory Board Committee for Citizenship Education, Missouri Bar Association (1989-2003); Adjunct Faculty Member, Avila University, Kansas City, MO (1989-1991); Advisory Board, Cray Center for Economic Education, Kansas City, MO (1986-1993); Student Government Associate, Center High School (1985-1986); Political Science Club, Center High School (1976-1995); Leadership Conference, Center High School (1976-1985); Y-Teens, Kansas City, MO (1962-1968); Y-Teens, Memphis, TN (1958-1959); Editor, Graduate School News, Appalachian State University (1956); Sponsor, Brownie Scouts, Spruce Pine, NC (1955-1957); Co-President, Christian Student Movement, Emory & Henry College (1953-1954) **Civic:** Chairperson, Community Benefit, Aldersgate Retirement Community (2016-Present); Advisory Board Member, Kansas City Sister Cities Association (2006-2014); Vice President, Red Bridge Lioness Club, Kansas City, MO (2008-2013); Vice President, The Society for Friendship with China (2006-2013); President, Red Bridge Lioness Club, Kansas City, MO (2006-2008); Chair Member, The Society For Friendship With China, Inc. (2003-2006); President, Red Bridge Lioness Club, Kansas City, MO (1999-2001); Kansas City International Commission (1998-2009); Secretary, Kansas City-Xian Sister Cities Committee (1996-2009); Education Chairman, Kansas City Sister Cities Association (1996-2006); Leader, People to People International, Youth Summit (1994); Leader, People to People International, Youth Summit (1993); Board of Directors, South Kansas City Youth Court (1989-1995); Delegate, Missouri State Nominating Convention, St. Louis, MO (1988); Vice President, Red Bridge Lioness Club, Kansas City, MO (1987-1992); Board of Directors, Red Bridge Lioness Club, Kansas City, MO (1986-2013); Treasurer, Red Bridge Lioness Club, Kansas City, MO (1986-1987); Awards Chairman, Missouri Youth in Government, Jefferson City, MO (1979-1995); Legislative Director, Missouri Youth in Government, Jefferson City, MO (1978-1995); State Committee, Missouri Youth in Government, Jefferson City, MO (1976-1995); International Relations Council (1975-2014) **Awards:** Peace Builder Award, Global and Multicultural Education (2011); Volunteer of the Year Award, Kansas City Sister Cities Association (2006); Leadership Award, USCPFA (2005); Volunteer of the Year Award, YMCA of Greater Kansas City (1989); Teacher of the Year, Missouri Council for the Social Studies (1988); Achievement in Education Award, Optimist International (1988); Outstanding Teacher Award, Center School District, PTA (1984); Academy Leadership Award, International Relations Council (1984) **Membership:** Representative, SPARK, Aldersgate Residents' Council (2014-Present); Diplomat, Optimist Club (1983-Present); Associate, Missouri National Education Association (1974-Present); Aldersgate WNW President, SPARK, Aldersgate Residents' Council (2015); Delegate, International Conference, USCPFA (2014); National Convent Chairman, USCPFA (2011); Delegate, International Conference, USCPFA (2010); Union Station Volunteer, Women Vision International (2008-2013); Delegate, International Conference, USCPFA (2008); Midwest Region President, USCPFA (2006-2012); Great Decisions Coordinator, Speakers Bureau (2004-2013); Convention Chairman, USCPFA (2004); Delegate, International Conference, USCPFA (2004); Youth Mentor, Speakers Bureau (2003-2005); Vice President, Optimist Club (2000-2009); Program Chairman, USCPFA (2000-2006); Treasurer, Optimist Club (1999); Midwest Region Board of Directors, USCPFA (1998-2006); Program Committee, Women Vision International (1997-2001); President, USCPFA (1996-2013); Treasurer, Zonta International (1996-2000) **Marquis Who's Who Honors:** Albert Nelson Marquis Lifetime Achievement Award (2017); Distinguished Humanitarian (2017) **Shipping Address:** 3800 Shamrock Drive, Charlotte, NC, 28215

Nancy Alker Craigmyle

Title: Researcher **Industry:** Research **Date of Birth:** 01/08/1937 **Place of Birth:** New York **State:** NY **Parents:** Carroll Booth Alker; Vera Byrne (Kohler) Alker **Marital Status:** Married **Spouse Name:** Robert de Rochmont Craigmyle (10/28/1977) **Education:** Coursework, University of South Carolina, Columbia, SC (1984); Doctoral Coursework, Neuroscience Lab, Veterans Administration Hospital, Columbia, SC (1982-1984); BA in Psychology, Columbia University, New York, NY (1974) **Career:** Research Assistant, Neuroscience Lab, Veterans Administration Hospital, Columbia, SC (1982-1984); Research Assistant, Department of Physiological Psychology, Rockefeller University, New York, NY (1975-1979) **Marquis Who's Who Honors:** Albert Nelson Marquis Lifetime Achievement Award (2017) **Shipping Address:** 2135 Via Fuentes, Vero Beach, FL, 32963

John Sanderson Cramer

Title: Healthcare Executive **Industry:** Health, Wellness and Fitness **Date of Birth:** 02/22/1942 **Place of Birth:** Butte **State:** MT **Parents:** John Dale Cramer; Angela Rita (Sanderson) Cramer **Marital Status:** Married **Spouse Name:** Ellen E. McGrath (4/15/1968) **Children:** Jennifer; Jon **Education:** MBA in Hospital Administration, The George Washington University (1969); BBA in Small Business Administration, Adelphi University (1964) **Career:** President Emeritus, Pinnacle Health Systems (2001-Present); President, Chief Executive Officer, Pinnacle Health Systems, Harrisburg, PA (1996-2001); President, Chief Executive Officer, Capital Health System, Harrisburg, PA (1988-1995); Senior Vice President, Corporate Planning, Capital Health System, Harrisburg, PA (1984-1988); Vice President, Corporate Planning, Capital Health System, Harrisburg, PA (1978-1984); Director of Planning, Harrisburg Hospital, Harrisburg, PA (1973-1978); Assistant Director, Harrisburg Hospital, PA (1970-1973); Associate, John G. Steinle and Associates, Garden City, NY (1969-1970); Administrative Resident, Harrisburg Hospital, PA (1968-1969); Junior Associate, John G. Steinle and Associates, Garden City, NY (1964-1967); Assistant to Associates, John G. Steinle and Associates, Garden City, NY (1960-1964) **Civic:** Board of Directors, Vision Fund (2000-Present); Chair, Audit Committee (1998-1999); Board of Directors, Capital Region Economic Development Corporation (1996-1998); Ambassador, Capital Region Economic Development Corporation (1994-2000); Member, Greater Harrisburg YWCA Advisory Committee (1994-2000); Board of Directors, Governor's Fund (1994-1998); Member, Pennsylvania Health Care Cost Containment Council (1993-1997); Member, Advisory Committee, Harrisburg Academy (1992-1996); Board of Directors, Harrisburg Symphony Association (1992-1995); Member, Long Range Planning Committee (1992-1993); Member, Council for Public Education, Harrisburg, PA (1991-1997) **Creative Works:** Co-author, "Organizational Theory," Cases and Applications (1990) **Awards:** Senior Level Award, American College of Healthcare Executives (1998); Businessman of the Year Award, Harrisburg, PA (1992); Annual Creative Energy Award, Hospital and Health Systems Association of Pennsylvania (1981) **Membership:** Alternate Member, Regional Policy Board, American Hospital Association (2000-Present); Board of Directors, Institute of Healthy Communities (1998-Present); Blue Ribbon Vision Panel, Hospital and Health Systems Association of Pennsylvania (2000); Board of Directors, Susquehanna Alliance (1998-1999); Member, Executive Committee, Hospital and Health Systems Association of Pennsylvania (1998); Chairman, Strategic Planning Committee, Hospital and Health Systems Association of Pennsylvania (1998); Membership Committee, Volunteer Hospitals of Pennsylvania (1997-2001); Immediate Past Chairman, Hospital and Health Systems Association of Pennsylvania (1997); Judge, Marriott Service Excellence Award, Volunteer Hospitals of Pennsylvania (1997); Chairman, Board of Directors, Hospital and Health Systems Association of Pennsylvania (1996); Board of Directors, Health Alliance Pennsylvania (1995-2000); Pennsylvania Delegate Member, Regional Policy Board, American Hospital Association (1995-1998); Hospital Associate Trust Member, Hospital and Health Systems Association of Pennsylvania (1995); Chairman, Policy Review Group, Hospital and Health Systems Association of Pennsylvania (1995); Federal Board of Directors, Hospital and Health Systems Association of Pennsylvania (1994-1997); Member, Executive Committee, Hospital and Health Systems Association of Pennsylvania (1994); Chairman, Strategic Planning Committee, Hospital and Health Systems Association of Pennsylvania (1994); Board of Directors, Capital Area Chamber of Commerce (1993-1995); Member, Executive Committee, Hospital and Health Systems Association of Pennsylvania (1993); Chairman, Strategic Planning Committee, Hospital and Health Systems Association of Pennsylvania (1993); Officer, Executive Committee Member, Volunteer Hospitals of Pennsylvania (1992-2001); Board of Directors, Hospital and Health Systems Association of Pennsylvania (1991-1997); Secretary, Volunteer Hospitals of Pennsylvania (1991-1993); Charter Member, Society for Healthcare Planning and Marketing, Board of Directors, American Hospital Association (1990-1993); Statewide Medical Assistance Steering Committee, Hospital and Health Systems Association of Pennsylvania (1990-1991); Policy Review Group, Hospital and Health Systems Association of Pennsylvania (1990-1991); Nominating Committee Member, Hospital and Health Systems Association of Pennsylvania (1990); Panel, Hospital and Health Systems Association of Pennsylvania (1990); Board of Directors, Volunteer Hospitals of Pennsylvania (1988-2001); Colonial Country Club; Eclectic Club of Harrisburg; Fellow, American College of Healthcare Executives **Marquis Who's Who Honors:** Albert Nelson Marquis Lifetime Achievement Award (2017) **Where will you be in five years:** In five years Mr. Cramer looks forward to traveling more with his wife and keeping close to his grandchildren. **Shipping Address:** 2840 Oakwood Drive, Harrisburg, PA, 17110

Fred Crawford

Title: Public Information Officer **Industry:** Government Administration/Government Relations/Government Services **Company Name:** Social Security Administration **Date of Birth:** 08/30/1928 **Place of Birth:** Spartanburg County **State:** SC **Parents:** Fred Crawford; Missouri (Plemmons) Crawford **Education:** JD, University of South Carolina (1970); PhD, with Distinction (1965); MA, New York University (1958); BA, Furnam University (1957) **Career:** Social Security Administrator, Supplemental Security Income Planning Specialist, Social Security Administration, Baltimore, MD (1973-Present); Commission Administrator, South Carolina Commission for the Blind, Columbia, SC (1966-1973); Administrator, Professional Counseling Placement, Lighthouse International, New York, NY (1962-1966); Senior Advisor to Associate Commissioner for External Affairs, Social Security Administration, Baltimore, MD **Career Related:** Chairman, First President, The Alliance Inc., Baltimore County, MD (1979-1983) **Civic:** President, Lions Club International, Catonsville, MD (1977-1994) **Creative Works:** Author, "Career Planning for the Blind" (1965); Co-Author, "Counseling and Placement of Blind Persons in Professional Occupations, Practice and Research" (1965); Author, "A Study to Determine the Effect of Mobility Training on the Employment and Earnings of Blind Co-Workers" **Awards:** First Employee, First Executive Director, Commission of the Blind (1966-2005) **Bar Admissions:** South Carolina Bar **Marquis Who's Who Honors:** Albert Nelson Marquis Lifetime Achievement Award (2017) **Hobbies:** Ham radio operation; Reading; Volunteering in the community; Investments; Business **Religion:** Baptist **Shipping Address:** 3800 Capers Avenue, Columbia, SC, 29205

Arnie Creinin

Title: President, Chief Executive Officer **Industry:** Leisure, Travel & Tourism **Company Name:** Coastal Lifestyles Inc. **Date of Birth:** 02/28/1959 **Place of Birth:** Chicago **State:** IL **Parents:** Jerry Creinin; Marcia Creinin **Marital Status:** Married **Spouse Name:** Debbie Creinin **Children:** Jon; Brandon; Kristina **Education:** College Coursework; High School Diploma **Certifications:** Texas Realtor **Career:** President, CEO, Contracted Food Services Inc., South Padre Island, TX (2016-Present); Managing Partner, SPITOWN LLC, South Padre Island, TX (2016-Present); President, Meatball Entertainment Inc., South Padre Island, TX (2012-Present); President, CEO, Coastal Lifestyles, Inc., Creinin Enterprises, Inc. (2006-Present) **Career Related:** Texas Realtor; Board of Directors, South Padre Island Convention and Visitors Bureau; Owner, Operator, Gabriella's Italian Grill and Pizzeria **Civic:** Several City Committees **Awards:** Several culinary Awards; Senator Proclamations; Texas Small Business Award, Gov. Bill Abbott **Membership:** National Association of Realtors **Marquis Who's Who Honors:** Albert Nelson Marquis Lifetime Achievement Award (2017) **To what do you attribute your success:** Mr. Creinin attributes his success to his ability to be at the right place at the right time. He also utilizes resources and recognizes opportunities. **Why did you become involved in your profession or industry:** Mr. Creinin became involved in his profession after serving in the hotel industry for years. He saw a need for property management, and decided to make it available for his clients. **Hobbies:** Visiting luxury properties; Cooking **Shipping Address:** 5312 Padre Boulevard, Suite C, Coastal Lifestyles Inc., South Padre Island, TX, 78597 **Website:** http://www.vacationpadre.com

Mathew G. Crisci

Title: Author/Screenwriter, Social Commentator, Fortune 500 Executive **Industry:** Writing and Editing **Company Name:** AMRU Entertainment, MGC Consulting Company **Date of Birth:** 11/03/1941 **Place of Birth:** New York **State:** California **Parents:** Matthew Crisci; Frances (Coscia) Crisci **Marital Status:** Married **Spouse Name:** Mary Ann Crisci (11/14/1964) **Children:** Matthew; Mark; Mitchell **Education:** BA in English Literature, Iona College, New Rochelle, NY (1963) **Career:** President, AMRU Entertainment (2015-Present); President, MGC Consulting Company (2007-Present); Social Commentator (1999-Present); Executive Vice President, Board of Directors, Asset Marketing Systems, San Diego, CA (2001-2007); Executive Vice President, Board of Directors, Alton Entertainment, Los Angeles, CA (1997-2001); Executive Vice President, Managing Director, Interpublic Group of Companies (NYSE), New York, NY (1991-1997); Senior Vice President, General Manager, Board of Directors, Chiat/Day, San Francisco, CA (1986-1990); Executive Vice President, Board of Directors, Integrated Barter International (NASDAQ), New York, NY (1982-1985); Senior Vice President, Young & Rubicam (NYSE), New York, NY (1968-1982) **Career Related:** Best-Selling Author; Recognized Expert on Consumer Motivation and Behavior; Award-Winning Social Commentator; Internationally-Known Fortune 500 Senior Executive **Military Service:** Non-Commissioned Officer, E7, U.S. Army **Creative Works:** Author, "Project Zebra"; Author, "Salad Oil King"; Author, "Call Sign"; Author, "White Lily"; Author, "Papa Cado"; Author, "This Little Piggy"; Author, "Mary Jackson Peale"; Author, "Indiscretion"; Author, "Save the Last Dance"; Author, "Papa Cado's Book of Wisdom"; Author, "Seven Days in Russia"; Screenwriter, "The White Lily" **Awards:** Lifetime Achievement Award, The Eurasia Center, Washington, DC; Lifetime Achievement Award, American-Russian Cultural Cooperation Foundation, Washington, DC; Lifetime Achievement Award, Russian Cultural Center, Washington, DC; Lifetime Achievement Award, Albert Marcus Society, New York, NY; U.S. Defense Attack Award, Moscow, Russia; Excellence in Journalism, Rossiyskaya Gazeta, Moscow, Russia **Membership:** Board of Directors, Russian Cultural Center, Memphis, TN; Founder, Friends of Russia Society, Washington, DC; Board of Directors, Iona College, New Rochelle, NY **Marquis Who's Who Honors:** Albert Nelson Marquis Lifetime Achievement Award (2017) **To what do you attribute your success:** Mr. Crisci attributes his success to his ability to listen, motivate others to fulfill their hopes, dreams, and wishes, build international brands, and create critically-acclaimed literature. **Why did you become involved in your profession or industry:** Mr. Crisci's second career as an author, screenwriter, and speaker is about sharing universal truths based on the amazing experiences in his life, and leaving his family a rich cultural trail that he once passed through here with class and dignity. **What do you consider to be the highlight of your career:** The highlight of Mr. Crisci's career was having his books, "Call Sign" and "White Lily," become Amazon Best-Sellers. **Where will you be in five years:** In five years, Mr. Crisci will be building his legacy and writing books and screenplays. **Hobbies:** Collecting primitive art; Photography **Political Affiliations:** Republican **Religion:** Roman Catholic **Business Address:** 7113 Tatler Road, Carlsbad, CA, 92011 **Website:** http://www.mgcrisci.com

Richard D. Crites

Title: Lawyer, Deputy Sheriff **Industry:** Law and Legal Services **Date of Birth:** 09/03/1943 **Place of Birth:** Fort Worth **State:** TX **Parents:** Ewell Barnett Crites; Frances Loretta (Prichard) Castro Crites **Marital Status:** Divorced **Spouse Name:** Carrie M. Roat (5/2004, Divorced 2009); Judith Jean Gildig (5/30/1976, Divorced 1997); Annabel Shields Lee (6/1964, Divorced 5/5/1976) **Children:** Kimberly Ann Crites Garrett, LPC; Amy Lee Crites, JD; Detective Kevin John Crites; Jonathon Peter Crites, MD **Education:** Degree, Missouri Sheriff's Training Academy, Stone County, MO (2003); JD, University of Arizona (1968); BA, Arizona State University (1965) **Certifications:** Certified Hostage Negotiator (2008-Present); Licensed P.O.S.T. Specialist Instructor, Missouri Department of Public Safety (2004-Present); Licensed Peace Officer, Missouri Department of Public Safety (2003-Present); Advanced Specialist in the Behavioral Analysis of Force Encounters (2018); Certified Analyst of Use of Force, Force Science, Institute of Mankato, MN (2007); TASER Instructor, TASER, Inc. (2007); Licensed Attorney, Missouri Supreme Court (1978); Licensed Attorney, Arizona Supreme Court (1968) **Career:** Licensed P.O.S.T. Specialist Instructor, Missouri Department of Public Safety (2004-Present); Licensed Peace Officer, Missouri Department of Public Safety (2003-Present); Private Legal Practice, Springfield, MO (1979-Present); Chief Counsel, Board of Public Utilities, Springfield, MO (1978-1979); Partner, Law Firm of Knez, Glatz & Crites, Tucson, AZ (1973-1978); Associate, Law Firm of Knez & Glatz (1968-1973) **Career Related:** Sheriff's Office, Lawrence County, MO (2013-Present); Instructor, Missouri Sheriff's Training Academy (2004-Present); Deputy Sheriff, Christian County, MO (2012-2014); Deputy Sheriff, Stone County, MO (2003-2012); Deputy Sheriff, Pulaski County, MO (2003-2006); Juvenile Court Referee, Tucson, AZ (1972-1976); Superior Court, Pima County, AZ **Creative Works:** Author, "Wiretapping and Eavesdropping in Arizona: A Legislative and Constitutional Analysis"; Author, Law Review Article, "9 Arizona Law Review" **Awards:** Top Attorney for Law Enforcement Award, International Association of Top Professionals (2016); Bancroft-Whitney-Excellence in Criminal Law Award (1968); Excellence in Insurance Law Award (1967) **Membership:** Greene County Bar Association; Missouri Bar Association; Arizona Bar Association; Abou Ben Adhem Shrine; Montezuma Lodge #35 F&AM; Royal Order of Jesters **Bar Admissions:** Missouri Supreme Court; Arizona Supreme Court; United States Court of Appeals for the Ninth Circuit; United States Court of Appeals for the Eighth Circuit; United States District Court for the Western District of Missouri; United States District Court for the Northern District of Texas; United States District Court for the District of Arizona **Marquis Who's Who Honors:** Who's Who in America; Who's Who in the World **To what do you attribute your success:** Mr. Crites attributes his success to his love for fighting crime, bad guys, and bullies. **Why did you become involved in your profession or industry:** Mr. Crites became involved in his profession after following his father's footsteps in law enforcement. **What do you consider to be the highlight of your career:** Mr. Crites considers the highlights of his career to be helping clients and being one of the oldest SWAT team members. He was active until the age of 71. **Where will you be in five years:** Looking to the future, Mr. Crites hopes to be enjoying retirement. **Hobbies:** Shooting; Writing novels about police, law enforcement and the courts **Political Affiliations:** Republican **Religion:** Presbyterian **Shipping Address:** P.O. Box 14819, Richard D Crites Attorney, Springfield, MO, 65814

David S. Crosby, PhD

Title: Statistics Educator, Consultant **Industry:** Education/Educational Services **Date of Birth:** 06/04/1938 **Place of Birth:** St. George **State:** UT **Parents:** Samuel Wallace Crosby; Mae (Dodds) Crosby **Marital Status:** Widowed **Spouse Name:** Anna Jo Hovermale (4/15/1962, Deceased 3/2002) **Children:** Anna Danisha; Mae Melinda **Education:** PhD, University of Arizona (1966); MA, University of Arizona (1964); BS, American University (1962) **Career:** Statistics Professor Emeritus, American University, Washington, DC (2004-2007); Chair, Department of Mathematics, Statistics and Computer Science, American University, Washington, DC (1975-1977); Consulting Statistician, National Oceanographic and Atmospheric Administration, Washington, DC (1968-2003); Consulting Statistician, National Environmental Satellite Data Information Service, Washington, DC (1968-2001); Statistics Professor, American University, Washington, DC (1966-2003) **Career Related:** Visiting Scientist, National Institute of Water and Atmospheric Research, Wellington, New Zealand (1994); Visiting Scientist, Department of Atmospheric Physics, Hooke Institute for Atmospheric Research, University of Oxford (1987); Visiting Scientist, Department of Atmospheric Physics, University of Oxford, England (1972) **Civic:** Town Council Member, Berkeley Springs, WV **Creative Works:** Contributor, 24 Articles, Referred Scientific Journals; Co-Author, 94 Papers **Membership:** Phi Beta Kappa; Sigma Xi **Marquis Who's Who Honors:** Albert Nelson Marquis Lifetime Achievement Award (2017) **Why did you become involved in your profession or industry:** Dr. Crosby became involved in his profession because he is good at mathematics and it is something he enjoys doing. He entered the field of statistics accidentally and spent 30 years pursuing it, working with people all over the world. **What do you consider to be the highlight of your career:** A highlight of Dr. Crosby's career was the work he did with the beginning of remote sensing satellites, which acquires information about the earth's surface such as sea temperature. **Shipping Address:** 3498 Chiswick Court, Silver Springs, MD, 20906

Marena L. Crosby

Title: Academic Administrator **Industry:** Education/ Educational Services **Date of Birth:** 03/02/1948 **Place of Birth:** Shreveport **State:** LA **Parents:** John Joseph Lienhard; Clara Curtis (Lawton) Lienhard **Marital Status:** Widowed **Spouse Name:** John L. Crosby (11/23/1997, Deceased); H.W. Patrick O'Brien (9/23/1977) **Education:** JD, Loyola University, New Orleans, LA; MEd, University of New Orleans **Certifications:** Licensed Professional Counselor, State of Louisiana; Diplomate, American College of Professional Mental Health Practitioners **Career:** Assistant to Vice President, Student Affairs, Delgado Community College (1997-1998); Director, Degree Audit Program, Delgado Community College (1993-1997); Director, Counseling and Marketing, Delgado Community College (1990-1993); Director, Admissions, Delgado Community College (1988-1990); Testing Coordinator, Delgado Community College (1986-1988); Counselor, Delgado Community College (1980-1986); Instructor, Delgado Community College (1973-1980) **Membership:** American Psychological Association; National Society of the Daughters of the American Revolution; American Counseling Association; International Association for New Science; Edgar Cayce's Association for Research and Enlightenment; American Psychotherapy Association; American Mental Health Counselors Association; IONS; Theosophical Society of America; Louisiana Notary Association; Louisiana Chapter, ASERVIC; Womens Guild, New Orleans Opera; New Orleans Museum of Art; National Society of the Colonial Dames of America; National Society of Magna Carta Dames and Barons; Association of Family and Conciliation Courts; American College of Professional Mental Health Practitioners; American Counseling Association; LCA; Jefferson Bar Association **Bar Admissions:** State of Louisiana (1971) **Marquis Who's Who Honors:** Albert Nelson Marquis Lifetime Achievement Award (2017) **Hobbies:** Reading; Piano **Political Affiliations:** Republican **Shipping Address:** 811 Rue Royal, Metairie, LA, 70005

Frank Alphonso Crossley, PhD

Title: Metallurgical Engineer **Industry:** Engineering **Date of Birth:** 02/19/1925 **Place of Birth:** Chicago **State:** IL **Parents:** Joseph Buddie Crossley; Rosa Lee (Brefford) Crossley **Spouse Name:** Elaine J. Sherman (11/23/1950, Deceased 11/1996) **Children:** Desne Adrienne **Education:** PhD in Metallurgical Engineering, Illinois Institute of Technology, Chicago, IL (1950); MS in Metallurgical Engineering, Illinois Institute of Technology, Chicago, IL (1947); BSChemE, Illinois Institute of Technology, Chicago, IL (1945) **Career:** Retired (1991); Technology Principal, Aerojet Propulsion Division, GenCorp (Now Aerojet Rocketdyne Holdings), Rancho Cordova, CA (1990-1991); Research Director, Materials Applications, Aerojet Propulsion Research Institute, Rancho Cordova, CA (1987-1990); Director, Research Propulsion Materials, Aerojet Propulsion Research Institute, Rancho Cordova, CA (1986-1987); Consultant Engineer, Missile Systems Division, Lockheed Missiles & Space Company, Sunnyvale, CA (1979-1986); Manager, Department of Missile Body Mechanical Engineering, Lockheed Missiles & Space Company, Palo Alto, CA (1978-1979); Manager, Department of Producibility and Standards, Lockheed Missiles & Space Company, Palo Alto, CA (1974-1978); Senior Member, Research Laboratory, Lockheed Missiles & Space Company, Palo Alto, CA (1966-1974); Senior Scientist, Research Institute, Illinois Institute of Technology, Chicago, IL (1952-1966); Professor of Foundry Engineering, Tennessee Agricultural and Industrial College (Now Tennessee State University), Nashville, TN (1950-1952); Head of Department of Foundry Engineering, Tennessee Agricultural and Industrial College (Now Tennessee State University) Nashville, TN (1950-1952); Instructor, Illinois Institute of Technology, Chicago, IL (1948-1949) **Civic:** Volunteer, Math and Science Tutor (1998-2012); Member, Concerned Parents of Color, Greater Framingham Community Church, Framingham, MA (1997-2012) **Military Service:** Ensign (D)L, United States Naval Reserve (1944-1946); PTO, United States Naval Reserve **Awards:** Alumni Recognition Award, Mechanical, Materials and Aerospace Engineering Department (2010); Alumni Medal of Honor Award, Illinois Institute of Technology (2009); R.B. Young Technology Innovation Award, GenCorp (Now Aerojet Rocketdyne Holdings) (1990) **Membership:** Materials Technology Committee, American Institute of Aeronautics and Astronautics (1979-1981); Chairman, Titanium Committee, Minerals, Metals and Materials Society of the American Institute of Mining (1974-1975); Fellow, American Society for Metals International; Sigma Xi **Why did you become involved in your profession or industry:** Dr. Crossley became involved in his profession because it was always something that he wanted to do. He had been working since he was nine years old, and he knew what motivated him and what bored him to tears. **Religion:** Congregationalist **Shipping Address:** 369 Newport Ave, Attleboro, MA, 02703

Mary Lynn Crow, PhD

Title: Educator, Psychologist **Industry:** Education/Educational Services **Company Name:** University of Texas at Arlington **Date of Birth:** 08/30/1934 **Place of Birth:** Denton **State:** TX **Parents:** Herman G. Cox; Harriett (Copeland) Cox **Marital Status:** Widowed **Spouse Name:** Charles H. Farmer (Deceased 2017) **Children:** Karl F. **Education:** PhD, University of North Texas (1970); MEd, Texas Christian University (1967); BA, Texas Christian University (1956); Coursework, Monticello College, Alton, IL (1952-1953) **Certifications:** Certified Teacher, State of Texas; Licensed Psychologist, State of Texas; Licensed Psychologist, State of Massachusetts **Career:** Professor, University of Texas at Arlington (1978-Present); Private Practice, Fort Worth, TX (1971-Present); Director, University of Texas, Arlington (2011-2013); Distinguished Teaching Professor, University of Texas at Arlington (2004); Interim Director, Center for Professional Teacher Education (1995-1997); Director, Faculty Development Resource Center, University of Texas at Arlington (1973-1985); Associate Professor, University of Texas at Arlington (1973-1977); Adjunct Professor, Counselor Education, University of North Texas, Denton (1970-1976); Assistant Professor of Education, University of Texas at Arlington (1970-1972); Instructor, University of Texas at Arlington (1969-1970); Counselor, Hurst-Euless-Bedford Public Schools (1967-1968); Teacher, Romper Room International TV Kindergarten, Dallas, Fort Worth, TX (1961-1967); Teacher, Fort Worth and Tyler Public Schools (1956-1959) **Career Related:** Director of Teacher Education, University of Texas at Arlington (1995-1997) **Civic:** Board of Directors, Past President, Dispute Resolution Services of Tarrant County; Vice President, Board of Directors, Tarrant County Mental Health Association; Chairman, Scholarship Committee, Tarrant County Mental Health Association **Creative Works:** Author, "The Many Faces of Love" (2008); Author, "Teaching on Television" (1977); Co-Author, "Faculty Development in Southern Universities" (1976); Contributor, Articles, Professional Journals **Awards:** Academy of Distinguished Teachers (2004); Woman of the Year, Business and Professional Women's Club (1988-1989); Face of Arlington, Arlington Daily News (1976); Female Newsmaker of the Year, Arlington Citizen Journal (1975); Piper Professor of Texas (1975); Outstanding Teacher, Amoco Foundation (1972); AMOCO Outstanding Teacher Award, University of Texas at Arlington **Membership:** President, Professional and Organizational Development Network in Higher Education (1977-1978); American Psychological Association; Texas Psychological Association; Tarrant County Psychological Association **Marquis Who's Who Honors:** Albert Nelson Marquis Lifetime Achievement Award (2017) **Shipping Address:** 409 Green River Trl, Fort Worth, TX, 76103

John T. Crowe

Title: Lawyer **Industry:** Law and Legal Services **Date of Birth:** 08/14/1938 **Place of Birth:** Cabin Cove **State:** CA **Parents:** J. Thomas; Wanda (Walston) C. **Marital Status:** Married (12/12/1968) **Spouse Name:** Marina Protopapa **Children:** Erin Aleka Hayden **Education:** JD, University of Santa Clara (1962); BA, University of Santa Clara (1960) **Career:** Lawyer, Visalia, CA (1964-Present); General Counsel, Sierra Wine (1986-1996); Partner, Crowe, Mitchell & Crowe (1974-1985) **Career Related:** President, Willson Ranch Co. (1997-Present); Referee, State Bar Court (1976-1982); Board of Directors, Willson Ranch Co. **Civic:** Board of Directors, California Citrus Mutual (2016-Present), President, Mineral King District Association (2011-Present), Board of Directors, Mineral King District Association (2002-Present); Board of Directors, Tulare County Library Foundation (2000-2006); Chairman, Army Reserve Forces Policy Committee (1997-1999); Army Reserve Forces Policy Committee (1995-1999); Member, Visalia Airport Commission (1982-1990); President, Visalia Associated In-Group Donors (Now United Way Tulare County) (1978-1979); Board of Directors, Visalia Associated In-Group Donors (Now United Way Tulare County) (1973-1981); President, Mount Whitney Area Council, Boy Scouts of America (1972, 1971); Board of Directors, Mount Whitney Area Council, Boy Scouts of America (1966-1985) **Military Service:** Major General, US Army Reserve (1964-1999); First Lieutenant, US Army (1962-1964); Second Lieutenant, US ARmy Reserve (1960-1962) **Awards:** Named, Outstanding Eagle Scout, Boy Scouts of America (2015); Named, Senior Army Reserve Commanders Association Hall of Fame (2003); Recipient, Rudder Medal, Association of the United States Army (1999); Recipient, Silver Beaver Award, Boy Scouts of America (1983); Recipient, Young Man of the Year, Visalia, CA (1973); Named, Senator of the Junior Chamber International (1970); Decorated, Distinguished Service Medal with Oak Leaf Cluster; Decorated, Legion of Merit with Oak Leaf Cluster; Decorated, Meritorious Service Medal with 3 Oak Leaf Clusters; Decorated, Army Commendation Medal **Membership:** Sixth Region Vice President, Association of the United States Army (2008-Present); Northern California State President, Association of the United States Army (2001-2008); Board of Directors, Association of the United States Army (2000-2006); President, Visalia Rotary Club (1980-1981); President, Visalia Chamber of Commerce (1979-1980); ABA Tulare County Bar Association; State Bar of California; Visalia Country Club; Board of Directors, California Citrus Mutual **Bar Admissions:** United States District Court for the Eastern District of California (1967); California (1962) **Political Affiliations:** Republican **Religion:** Roman Catholic **Shipping Address:** 3939 W School Ave, Visalia, CA, 93291

Barbara Ann Croyle

Industry: Business Management/Business Services **Date of Birth:** 10/22/1949 **Place of Birth:** Knoxville **State:** TN **Parents:** Charles Evans Croyle; Myrtle Elizabeth (Kellam) Croyle **Marital Status:** Married **Spouse Name:** Jeffery Volpe **Education:** Master in Gerontology, St. Joseph University (2012); MBA, University of Denver (1983); Certificate in Program Management Development, Colorado Women's College (1980); JD, University of Colorado (1975); Certificate in Corporate Tax and Securities Law, Institute for Paralegal Training (1971); BA in Sociology, College of William and Mary, Cum Laude (1971) **Certifications:** Certified Nursing Home Administrator and Lecturer **Career:** Executive Director, Stratford House Retirement Community, Danville, VA (2014-Present); Executive Director, Jenner's Pond Retirement Community (2010-Present); Executive Director, Lutheran Senior Services of Southern Chester County (2010-2013); Executive Vice President, Peninsula United Methodist Homes, Inc., Hockessin, DE (2003-2010); Executive Director, Swedish American Center for Complementary Medicine, Rockford, IL (2000-2002); Vice President of Ambulatory Care Services, Compliance Officer, Franciscan Medical Center, Dayton Campus, Ohio (1994-2000); Chief Operating Officer, Vice President, D.T. Watson Rehabilitation Hospital (1992-1993); Managing Director, Benefit Resource Management Group Subsidiary, Blue Cross of Western Pennsylvania (1987-1992); Manager of Strategic Planning, Westinghouse, Transportation Division, Denver, CO (1985-1987); Manager of Acquisitions/ Lands, Petro-Lewis Corp., Denver, CO (1977-1985); Associate Firm, Shaw Spangler & Roth, Denver, CO (1976-1977); Law Clerk, Colorado Court of Appeals, Denver, CO (1976); Paralegal, Holland & Hart, Denver, CO (1972-1973) **Career Related:** Teacher, Oil and Gas Law, Colorado Paralegal Institute (1978-1979); Arbitrator, American Arbitration Association **Membership:** ABA **Bar Admissions:** Pennsylvania (1990); Colorado (1976) **Shipping Address:** 150 Mercer Mill Rd, Ladenberg, PA, 19350

Julius M. Cruse Jr.

Industry: Education/Educational Services **Date of Birth:** 02/15/1937 **Place of Birth:** New Albany **State:** MS **Parents:** Julius Major Cruse; Effie (Davis) Cruse **Education:** Honorary DD, General Theological Seminary, New York City, NY (1999); PhD in Pathology, U.S. Public Health Service Fellow, University of Tennessee (1966); U.S. Public Health Service Postdoctoral Fellow, University of Tennessee (1964-1967); MD, University of Tennessee (1964); DMS, University of Graz, Austria, with Honors (1960); BA, BS, University of Mississippi, with Honors (1958) **Career:** Guyton Disting Professor, University of Mississippi (2010-Present); Distinguished Professor of History of Medicine, Medical School, University of Mississippi (2003-Present); Associate Professor of Medicine, University of Mississippi (1989-Present); Director, Tissue Typing Laboratory, University of Mississippi (1980-Present); Director, Immunopathology Section, University of Mississippi (1978-Present); Director, Clinical Immunopathology, University of Mississippi (1978-Present); Director, Graduate Studies Program in Pathology, University of Mississippi (1974-Present); Associate Professor, Microbiology, University of Mississippi (1974-Present); Professor, Pathology, University of Mississippi (1974-Present); Professor, Microbiology, University of Mississippi (2010); Guyton Disting Professor, University of Mississippi (2004-2009); Professor, Immunology and Biology, Graduate School, University of Mississippi (1967-1974); Vice Chair, Pathology, Director, Anatomic Pathology, University of Mississippi; Professor, Medicine, University of Mississippi **Creative Works:** Member, Editorial Board, "Human Immunology" (2007-Present); Editor-in-Chief, "Experimental and Molecular Pathology" (1999-Present); Editor-in-Chief, "Experimental & Molecular Pathology" (1999- Present); Editor-in-Chief, "Transgenics: Biological Analysis Through DNA Transfer" (1992-Present); Editor-in-Chief, "Concepts in Immunopathology" (1985-Present); Editor-in-Chief, "The Year in Immunology" (1984-Present); Editor-in-Chief, "Immunologic Research" (1981-Present); Editor-in-Chief, "Pathobiology: Journal Immunopathology, Molecular and Cellular Biology" (1990-1998); Editor-in-Chief, "Pathology and Immunopathology Research" (1982-1990); Author, "Principles of Immuno-Pathology" (1979); Author, "Introduction to Immunology" (1977); Author, "Immunology Examination Review Book," Revised Edition (1975); Author, "Immunology Examination Review Book" (1971); Editor-in-Chief, "Immunology Cons.: Dorland's Illustrated Medical Dictionary" (1967-1994) **Awards:** Julius M. Cruse Collection of T.S. Eliot, Emory University, Woodruff Library, Atlanta, GA (2008); Julius M. Cruse Collection in History of Immunology Rowland Medical Library, University of Mississippi Medical Center (2004); Wilson Foundation Grantee (1999-2003); B.S. Guyton Lecturer on History of Medicine (1998); Wilson Foundation Grantee (1995-1998); Wilson Foundation Grantee (1993-1994); Julius M. Cruse Excellence in Pathology Award; Wilson Foundation Grantee (1990-1995); Julius M. Cruse Collection in Immunology Established in his Honor, Middleton Medical Library, University of Wisconsin, Madison, WI (1979); Pathologists Award in Continuing Education, College of American Pathologists-American Society of Clinical Pathologists (1976); Fulbright Scholar, University of Graz, Austria (1958-1960); Julius M. Cruse Collection of T.S. Eliot's Works, St. Mark's Library **Membership:** Historian, American Society for Histocompatibility and Immunogenetics (2000-Present); Historian, American Association of Immunologists (1990-Present); Councillor, American Society for Histocompatibility and Immunogenetics (1997-1999); Chairman, Publications Committee, American Society for Histocompatibility and Immunogenetics (1987-1995); Fellow, American Association for the Advancement of Science; Royal Society of Medicine; Royal Society of Promotion Health; American Academy of Microbiology; Intercontinental Biographical Association; American Medical Association; Clinical Immunology Society; American Institute of Biological Sciences; American Society of Clinical Pathologists; Canadian Society Microbiologists; New York Academy of Sciences; Experimental Biology and Medicine; American Diabetes Association; Society Francaise d'Immunologie; Reticuloendothelial Society; Transplantation Society; Electron Microscopy Society of America; American Association of History Medicine; The Paul Ehrlich Society; American Society of Investigative Pathology; American Association of Pathologists; American Chemical Society; British Society of Immunology; Canadian Society of Immunology; American Society of Microbiology; International Academy of Pathology; T.S. Eliot Society; Society of Mary; Mariological Society of America **Marquis Who's Who Honors:** Albert Nelson Marquis Lifetime Achievement Award (2017) **Religion:** Anglican Catholic **Shipping Address:** PO Box 16785, Jackson, MS, 39236

C. Barry Crutchfield

Title: Lawyer **Industry:** Law and Legal Services **Company Name:** Templeman and Crutchfield **Date of Birth:** 08/02/1946 **Place of Birth:** Eunice **State:** NM **Parents:** Carl Crutchfield; Estelle (Trimble) Crutchfield **Marital Status:** Married **Spouse Name:** Susan Elizabeth Davis (8/17/1968) **Children:** Jenna Leigh Adams; Kelli Elizabeth Gault **Education:** JD, The University of Texas at Austin (1971); BS, Eastern New Mexico University, Portales, NM (1968) **Career:** Attorney, Templeman and Crutchfield, Lovington (1977-Present); Partner, Sanders, Templeman & Crutchfield, Lovington, NM (1974-1977); Judge Advisor, Military Judge, U.S. Marine Corps (1971-1974); Deputy Counsel, Governor of Texas, Austin, TX (1971) **Career Related:** Member, New Mexico Board of Law Examiners, Santa Fe, NM (1982-Present) **Civic:** Member, Law School Board of Visitors, University of New Mexico, Albuquerque, NM (1981-1985) **Military Service:** Captain, U.S. Marine Corps (1971-1974) **Awards:** Outstanding Contribution Award, New Mexico State Bar (1993, 1990); Named One of the Top 100 Trial Lawyers; Named, Top Ten Trial Lawyers in New Mexico; Named, Top Ten Trial Lawyers in Criminal and Personal Injury Law **Membership:** Associate, American Board of Trial Advocates (1990-Present); Chairman, New Mexico Board of Bar Examiners, State Bar of New Mexico (1991-1993); Fellow, New Mexico Bar Foundation; New Mexico Bar Association; Texas Bar Association, Association of Trial Lawyers of America; National Criminal Defense Lawyers Association; American Board of Trial Advisors; New Mexico Trial Lawyers Association; New Mexico Criminal Defense Lawyers Association; Lea County Bar Association; State Bar of Texas; National Association of Criminal Defense Lawyers **Bar Admissions:** New Mexico (1974); United States District Court District of New Mexico (1974); United States Court of Appeals for the Tenth Circuit (1974); United States Court of Appeals for the Armed Forces (1972); Texas (1971) **Marquis Who's Who Honors:** Albert Nelson Marquis Lifetime Achievement Award (2017); Distinguished Humanitarian (2017) **Hobbies:** Golf **Political Affiliations:** Democrat **Religion:** Methodist **Shipping Address:** 113 E Washington Ave, Lovington, NM, 88260

William Gayle Crutchfield

Title: Retail Executive **Industry:** Technology **Company Name:** Crutchfield Corporation **Date of Birth:** 05/21/1905 **Place of Birth:** Charlottesville **State:** VA **Parents:** William Gayle Crutchfield; Theresa F. (Saltzsieder) Crutchfield **Marital Status:** Married **Spouse Name:** Scheline **Children:** Jennifer Crutchfield Worth; William G. Crutchfield III **Education:** BS in Commerce, University of Virginia (1965) **Career:** Chief Executive Officer, Crutchfield Corporation, Charlottesville, VA (1974-Present); Secretary-treasurer, Haight Engineering Co., Inc. (Now Haight Engineering, PLLC), Charlottesville, VA (1972-1975); Assistant to President, Ridge Electronics Corporation, Charlottesville, VA (1970-1972) **Career Related:** **Civic:** Visiting Lecturer, University of Virginia Darden School of Business (1988-Present); University of Virginia Health System Board (2018); University of Virginia Board of Visitors (1997-2005); Appointed by Four Virginia Governors of Both Political Parties to a Variety of State Boards, Councils and Commissions **Military Service:** Captain, United States Air Force (1966-1970) **Awards:** Patricia Rienzi Legacy Award, Anti-Defamation League (2016); Named One of Virginia's 25 Most Notable Entrepreneurs Over the Past 25 Years, Virginia Business Magazine (2011); Named to Consumer Electronics Association Hall of Fame (2007); Ernst & Young Master Entrepreneur of the Year for Virginia (1999); University of Virginia Raven Award (1997) **Membership:** Chief Executives Organization; Gold Member, Young Presidents Organization (YPO); The Raven Society; South Carolina Yacht Club; Farmington Country Club; Beta Gamma Sigma **Hobbies:** Aviation; Vintage Automobiles; Boating **Political Affiliations:** Republican **Shipping Address:** 1 Crutchfield Park, Charlottesville, VA, 22911

Nicholas Cummings, PhD

Title: Psychologist **Industry:** Medicine & Health Care **Company Name:** University of Nevada **Date of Birth:** 07/25/1924 **Place of Birth:** Salinas **State:** CA **Parents:** Andrew Cummings; Urania (Sims) Cummings **Marital Status:** Married **Spouse Name:** Dorothy Mills (2/5/1948) **Children:** Janet Lynn; Andrew Mark **Education:** PhD, Adelphi University (1958); MA, Claremont Graduate University (1954); AB, University of California, Berkeley, CA (1948) **Career:** Chairman, Chief Executive Officer, DynaMed Integrated Care, Inc. (1998-Present); Distinguished Professor, University of Nevada, Reno, NV (1997-Present); Chairman, The Nicholas & Dorothy Cummings Foundation, Reno, NV (1994-Present); President, Founder, Behavioral Health, San Francisco, CA (1976-Present); Founder, Cummings Institute (2015); Clinical Professor, Arizona State University (2009-2015); Chairman, President, U.K. Behavioural Health Limited, London, England (1996-1998); Chairman, Chief Executive Officer, Kendron International, Ltd., Reno, NV (1992-1995); Chairman, Chief Executive Officer, American Biodyne, Inc., San Francisco, CA (1985-1993); Chief Psychologist, Kaiser Permanente, San Francisco, CA (1959-1976) **Career Related:** President, National Academies of Practice (1981-1993); President, Institute For Psychosocial Interaction (1980-1984); Director, Mental Research Institute, Palo Alto, CA (1979-1980); Chairman, Board, California Community Mental Health Centers, Inc., Los Angeles, San Diego, San Francisco, CA (1975-1977); President, Chairman, Board, Psycho-Social Institute (1972-1980); President, Blue Psi, Inc., San Francisco, CA (1972-1980); President, California School of Professional Psychology, Los Angeles, CA (1969-1976); President, California School of Professional Psychology, San Francisco, CA (1969-1976); President, California School of Professional Psychology, San Diego, CA (1969-1976); President, California School of Professional Psychology, Fresno, CA (1969-1976); Member, Mental Health Advisory Board, City and County, San Francisco, CA (1968-1975); Board of Directors, Mental Health Association of San Francisco (1965-1975); Co-Director, South San Francisco Clinic (1959-1975) **Military Service:** U.S. Army (1944-1946) **Membership:** President, American Psychological Association (1979); Director, American Psychological Association (1975-1981); President, California Psychological Association (1968); Fellow, American Psychological Association **Marquis Who's Who Honors:** Albert Nelson Marquis Lifetime Achievement Award (2017) **Why did you become involved in your profession or industry:** Dr. Cummings was inspired to become a psychologist during recovery from a wound from World War II. While recovering, he met a psychologist in the field hospital, Dr. Frieda Fromm-Reichmann, who inspired him to become a psychologist. **What do you consider to be the highlight of your career:** One highlight that stands out the most is when his daughter followed in his footsteps and became a psychologist. **Business Address:** 4781 Caughlin Parkway, Reno, NV, 89519 **Shipping Address:** 4565 Mountaingate Dr, Reno, NV, 89519 **Website:** http://cummingsinstitute.com/nicholascummings/

Atlee Cunningham

Title: Aeronautical Engineer **Industry:** Engineering **Company Name:** Lockheed Martin **Education:** PhD in Mechanical Engineering, University of Texas at Austin (1966); MME, University of Texas at Austin (1963); BS in Mechanical Engineering, University of Texas at Austin (1961) **Career:** Senior Principal Research Engineer, Senior LM Fellow, Lockheed Martin, Fort Worth, TX (2002-Present); Lockheed Martin, Fort Worth, TX (1993-Present); Fort Worth Division, General Dynamics (1965-1969); Senior Research Engineer, Senior Technical Fellow, and Associate Fellow, American Institute of Aeronautics and Astronautics; Research Scientist, Defense Research Laboratory, Austin, TX; Engineering Staff Specialist, General Dynamics Corporation, Lockheed Corporation, and Lockheed Martin **Career Related:** Fellow, Welding Research Association (1961-1962); Guest Lecturer, Southern Methodist University, University of Texas, and National Cheng Kung University; Consultant, Aeroelastic and Vibration Issues for the F-16, C-130J, F-22, and F-35 Aircrafts, Lockheed Martin; Consultant, NASA, U.S. Air Force, U.S. Navy, and University of Texas; Technology Teams, International Technology Organizations **Military Service:** U.S.S. Saratoga, U.S. Navy (1962-1964) **Creative Works:** Contributor, Over 50 Technical Papers, Presentations, and Reports, Several Professional Journals, Symposia, and Books **Awards:** STO Air Vehicle Technical Panel Excellence Award (2014); Achievement Award, General Dynamics (1989); Achievement Award, General Dynamics (1983); Achievement Award, General Dynamics (1980); Certification of Recognition for Technical Publication, NASA (1980); Memorial Research Award, Foundation of Texas A&M University, International Technology Organization; Air and Space Friend, Smithsonian National Air and Space Museum Wall of Honor, Washington, DC **Membership:** Sigma Xi **Business Address:** P.O. Box 471552, Fort Worth, TX, 76114 **Website:** http://www.atleecunningham.com

Aneta Joan Cupp

Title: Music Educator **Industry:** Education/Educational Services **Company Name:** Memorial Hall School **Date of Birth:** 12/30/1940 **Place of Birth:** Bonham **State:** TX **Parents:** Emmett Morgan Northcutt; Hattie Faye (Taylor) Northcutt **Marital Status:** Married **Spouse Name:** Charles Daniel Cupp (3/8/1980) **Children:** Daniel Emmett (Deceased) **Education:** MEd, University of Houston (1983); MusB, University of North Texas (1963) **Certifications:** Lifetime Teaching Certificate **Career:** Substitute Teacher, Memorial Hall School (2000-Present); Substitute Teacher, Houston Independent School District (1996-2000); Secretary to Recreation Music Director, Houston Parks and Recreation Department (1968); Secretary to Recreation Music Director, Houston Parks and Recreation Department (1964-1966); Teacher, Elementary Itinerant Music, Houston Independent School District (1963-1996); Secretary, Health Workshop, University of North Texas (1963) **Career Related:** Leader, Elementary Classroom Teacher Music In-Service, Houston Independent School District (1974) **Creative Works:** Piano Lab System **Awards:** Certificate of Award, Burbank Elementary School (1993); Certificate of Appreciation, Burbank Elementary and Parent-Teacher Organization (1984); Inductee, Hall of Honor, Houston Independent School District (1982); Certificate of Appreciation, Houston Independent School District (1981); Semi-Finalist, Teacher of the Year Awards, Houston Independent School District (1978-1979); Semi-Finalist, Teacher of the Year Awards, Houston Independent School District (1977-1978); Certificate of Appreciation, Lucille Gregg Parent-Teacher Association, Houston Independent School District (1977); Teacher of the Year, Houston Independent School District (1976); Certificate of Recognition, Teacher of the Year Competition, Houston Independent School District (1975-1976); Certificate of Appreciation, AAU Bi-Centennial Project, Houston, TX (1975); Letters of Endorsement (1975); National Teacher of the Year (1975); Nominee, Teacher of the Year Award, Field Elementary School, Houston, TX (1975); Finalist, Teacher of the Year Competition, Field Elementary School, Houston, TX (1975); Featured in "Outstanding Elementary Teachers of America Book" (1974); Honoree, Outstanding Young Educator, Human Resources Committee, Houston Junior Chamber of Commerce (1970); Honoree, Jim Collins Scholar, Corsicana Senior High School (1959) **Membership:** Congress of Houston Teachers **To what do you attribute your success:** Ms. Cupp attributes her success to her determination, organizational skills, and faith in God. **Why did you become involved in your profession or industry:** Ms. Cupp comes from a musical family, and always had a love of music. **What do you consider to be the highlight of your career:** The highlight of Ms. Cupp's career was a piano lab she started with her own system of teaching. **Hobbies:** Travel **Political Affiliations:** Conservative **Religion:** Non-Denominational **Shipping Address:** 1237 Althea Drive, Houston, TX, 77018

Steven A. Curley

Title: Professor of Surgery **Industry:** Medicine & Health Care **Company Name:** Baylor College of Medicine **Education:** Fellow in Surgical Oncology, The University of Texas MD Anderson Cancer Center, Houston, Texas (1988-1990); Clinical Resident in Surgery, University of New Mexico Hospitals, Albuquerque, NM (1982-1988); MD, The University of Texas Health Science Center at Houston (1982); BS in Biology and Chemistry, The University of New Mexico, Albuquerque, NM (1978) **Certifications:** Certificate, American Board of Surgery, Inc. **Career:** Oncology Service Line Medical Director, CHI St. Luke's Health-Baylor St. Luke's Medical Center (2015-Present); Professor of Surgical Oncology, Chief of Surgical Oncology, Baylor College of Medicine (2014-Present); Adjunct Professor, Department of Mechanical Engineering and Materials Science, Rice University (2006-Present); Charles B. Barker Endowed Chair in Surgery, Division of Surgery, University of Texas MD Anderson Cancer Center (2006-2013); Professor of Surgical Oncology, The University of Texas MD Anderson Cancer Center (1990-2013); Professor of Surgical Oncology, The University of Texas MD Anderson Cancer Center (1988-2013) **Civic:** Surgeon, Helping Hands Medical Missions, Inc. (2012); Surgeon, Helping Hands International (2005); Coach, Local Soccer Team (1993-2004); Volunteer, The Women's Home, Rehab for Women with Drug and Alcohol Addiction; Operation Underground Railroad **Creative Works:** Author, "In My Hands: Compelling Stories from a Surgeon and His Patients Fighting Cancer" (2018) **Awards:** Featured Listee, America's Top Doctors for Cancer Database (2005-2017); Featured Listee, Best Doctor's of America Database (2002-2017); Patient's Choice Award, America's Most Compassionate Doctors (2001-2017); Named Top 1% of Physicians, U.S. News & World Report L.P. (2012-2015); Tribecca Disruptive Innovator Award (2012); Outstanding Teacher Award, Surgical Oncology Fellows, The University of Texas MD Anderson Cancer Center (2011); Patients' Choice Award, America's Most Compassionate Doctors (2010-2015); Outstanding Teacher Award, Surgical Oncology Fellows, The University of Texas MD Anderson Cancer Center (2001); Outstanding Teacher Award, Surgical Oncology Fellows, The University of Texas MD Anderson Cancer Center (1992); Named America's Top Doctors, Castle Connolly Medical Ltd. **Membership:** Society of Surgical Oncology (1990-Present); American College of Surgeons; American Society of Clinical Oncology; Society for Surgery of the Alimentary Tract; Southwest Oncology Group; Americas Hepato-Pancreato-Biliary Association; American Surgical Association; American Association of Cancer Research; Harris County Medical Society; Texas Medical Association **Why did you become involved in your profession or industry:** Dr. Curley became involved in his profession because when he was a surgical resident, he had an 18-year-old cousin who was diagnosed with stage-IV Ewing Sarcoma and he watched her die over the next ten months. Ever since then, he developed a very strong hatred for the disease and it still drives him today. **What do you consider to be the highlight of your career:** The highlights of Dr. Curley's career have been developing two FDA-approved devices for invasive radiofrequency ablation needles to treat unresectable liver cancers in 2001 and writing a paper in 1999, which, for the next three years, was the most surgically cited paper in the world. **Where will you be in five years:** In the next five years, Dr. Curley hopes to continue to help his patients and find less toxic ways to treat them. **Shipping Address:** 6620 Main St Ste 1350, Baylor College of Medicine, Houston, TX, 77030 **Website:** https://drstevencurley.blog/about

Peter William Curreri

Title: Health Facility Administrator **Industry:** Health, Wellness and Fitness **Company Name:** Strategem of Alabama Inc **Date of Birth:** 09/02/1936 **Place of Birth:** Milwaukee **State:** WI **Parents:** Anthony Rudolph Curreri; Dorothea Christiana (Heubsch) Curreri **Marital Status:** Divorced **Spouse Name:** Patricia Ann Egry (8/14/1958, Divorced 1975) **Children:** Charles Anthony; James Bradley; Regina Dawn **Education:** Resident of Surgery, Hospital of the University of Pennsylvania (1963-1968); Intern, Hospital of the University of Pennsylvania (1962-1963); MD, University of Pennsylvania (1962); BA, Swarthmore College (1958) **Certifications:** American Board of Surgery **Career:** Chairman, Strategem of Alabama, Inc. (1988-2016); Professor, University of South Alabama College of Medicine, USA Health (1981-1988); Chairman, Surgery, University of South Alabama College of Medicine, USA Health (1981-1988); Professor of Surgery, Weill Cornell Medical College, Cornell University (1977-1981); Associate Professor, Surgery, University of Washington School of Medicine (1974-1977); Assistant Professor, Surgery, The University of Texas Southwestern Medical Center (1971-1974) **Career Related:** Member, Medicare Payment Advisory Committee (1997-1999); Commissioner, Physician Payment Review Commission (1988-1997); Chairman of Surgery, Anesthesiology and Trauma Study Section, National Institutes of Health (1986-1988); Member, Surgery, Anesthesiology and Trauma Study Section, National Institutes of Health (1980-1984) **Military Service:** Lieutenant Colonel, US Army (1968-1971) **Creative Works:** Contributor, Articles to Professional Journals **Awards:** Recipient, Curtis P. Artz Award, American Trauma Society (1989); Recipient, Research Career Development Award, National Institutes Of Health (1972); Recipient, Meritorious Service Medal **Membership:** President, American Association for the Surgery of Trauma (1989-1990); President, The Halsted Society (1988-1989); Secretary, Board of Governors, American College of Surgeons (1987-1989); American Burn Association (1983-1984); President, Society of University Surgeons (1980-1981); Recorder, Association for Academic Surgery (1972-1974) **Marquis Who's Who Honors:** Albert Nelson Marquis Lifetime Achievement Award (2017) **To what do you attribute your success:** Dr. Curreri attributes his success to a devotion to medical education, provision of surgical care for all patients and clinical research. **Why did you become involved in your profession or industry:** Dr. Curreri entered his profession due to his desire to pursue his deep interest in science. **What do you consider to be the highlight of your career:** The highlight of Dr. Curreri's career was the respect given to him by national and international colleagues. **Where will you be in five years:** In the next five years, Dr. Curreri will be retired in Alabama. **Hobbies:** Golf; Walking **Shipping Address:** 30354 Middle Creek Cir, Spanish Fort, AL, 36527

Timothy J. Curry, PhD

Title: Economist **Industry:** Financial Services
Parents: Daniel James Curry; Joan Marie Curry
Devigili **Marital Status:** Married **Spouse Name:**
Mary Elizabeth Garver (5/29/1999) **Education:**
PhD, The George Washington University, Washington, DC (1979); MA, The Pennsylvania State
University, State College, PA (1968); BS, King's
College, Wilkes-Barre, PA (1966) **Career:** Senior
Financial Economist, Federal Deposit Insurance
Corporation, Washington, DC (1995-2012); Financial Economist, Resolution Trust Corporation,
Washington, DC (1989-1994); Financial Economist,
Federal Savings and Loan Insurance Corporation,
Washington, DC (1986-1988); Financial Economist, Federal Reserve Board, Washington D.C.
(1970-1985) **Career Related:** Visiting Professor,
George Mason University, Fairfax, VA (2008-2009); Adjunct Professor, The George Washington
University, Washington D.C. (1983-1994); Visiting
Professor, San Diego State University (1982-1983);
Professional Lecturer, DuBois Campus, The Pennsylvania State University (1968-1969) Researcher,
Teacher, Many International Conferences; Supervisor, Small Banks **Military Service:** US Army
Reserve (1968-1974) **Creative Works:** Contributor,
Articles to Professional Journals; Author, "History
of the 80s, Lessons for The Future, Two Volumes"
Marquis Who's Who Honors: Albert Nelson
Marquis Lifetime Achievement Award (2017) **Why
did you become involved in your profession
or industry:** Dr. Curry was always interested in
economics. He went straight to graduate school
and then got a job in the Federal Deposit Insurance Corporation in Washington, DC He taught
at more than five different Universities, then
decided to become a professional PhD. When Dr.
Curry was younger, he always wanted to go to
graduate school but wasn't sure where. He was
pretty good at it. **Hobbies:** Travel; Golf; Skiing;
Swimming; Visiting his second home in Naples,
Florida **Shipping Address:** 1406 Grady Randall Ct,
Mc Lean, VA, 22101

Joyce Mae Curtis

Title: Physical Education Educator (Retired) **Industry:** Education/Educational Services **Company Name:** Abilene Christian University **Date of Birth:** 08/27/1937 **Place of Birth:** Cleburne **State:** TX **Parents:** Robert Joyce Curtis; Maudie Mae Curtis **Marital Status:** Single **Education:** PED in Physical Education, Indiana University (1970); MS in Physical Education, North Texas State University (Now University of North Texas) (1960); BS, North Texas State University (Now University of North Texas) (1959) **Certifications:** Certification, United States Golf Teachers Federation (1995); Certification, National Bowling Council Education Service Center (1982) **Career:** Professor, Abilene Christian University, Abilene, TX (1959-2004); Graduate Assistant, Indiana University (1967-1970) **Career Related:** Treasurer, Association for Intercollegiate Athletics for Women, Texas (1971-1979) **Civic:** Volunteer, Hendrick Medical Center; Volunteer, Hope Fund Committee; Volunteer, Vera West Women's Center; Volunteer, Bunco for Breast Cancer Committee **Creative Works:** Author, "Pickle-Ball for Player and Teacher, Third Edition" (1999); Author, "Intermediate Bowling Notebook for Teacher," Abilene Christian University, Abilene, TX (1993); Author, "Manual for Badminton Teachers", Abilene Christian University, Abilene, TX (1985); Author, "Manual for Bowling Teachers," Abilene Christian University, Abilene, TX (1982); Co-Author, Bowling Section, "Bowling-Fencing Guide," (1975-1977); Co-Editor, "Physical Education Activities Handbook" (1971); Contributor, Articles to Professional Journals **Awards:** Recipient, Pathfinder Award, National Association for Girls and Women in Sports, American Alliance for Health, Physical Education, Recreation and Dance (Now SHAPEAmerica) (2009); Pathfinder Award, Texas Association for Health, Physical Education, Recreation & Dance (2008); Inductee, Sports Hall of Fame, Abilene Christian University Athletics (2003); Recipient, Volleyball Wildcat Award, Abilene Christian University (1997); Faculty Development Award, Abilene Christian University, Abilene, TX (1991); Recipient, Distinguished Service Award, Texas Association on Intercollegiate Athletics for Women (1982); Named, Outstanding Educator of America (1975); Named, Bowler of the Year, Abilene Women's Bowling Association (1967) **Membership:** Lifetime Member, Alliance for Health, AccentCare; Texas Association for Health, Physical Education, Recreation and Dance; Lifetime Member, Abilene Women's Bowling Association; Lifetime Member, Delta Psi Kappa; Phi Lambda Theta **Marquis Who's Who Honors:** Albert Nelson Marquis Lifetime Achievement Award (2017) **To what do you attribute your success:** Dr. Curtis attributes her success to her education, the timing of Title IX, personal dedication, and the influence of others in the field, particularly Dr. Dwain Hart. **Why did you become involved in your profession or industry:** Dr. Joyce M. Curtis has always loved learning and exploring a range of activities and sports. She knew from ninth grade that she wanted to be a physical education teacher. Dr. Curtis played the clarinet since elementary school and band ran a close second in what she wanted to do. Ultimately, physical education won out, though she was in her high school orchestra playing the clarinet. Dr. Curtis was an excellent student in both high school and college, beginning higher education at North Texas State College (Now University of North Texas) and pursuing graduate studies at Indiana University where she felt privileged to study under excellent teachers in her chosen field of physical education and health. Her first and only teaching position, lasting 45 years, was at Abilene Christian College (Now Abilene Christian University) in Abilene, Texas. Dr. Dwain Hart, a long-time department chairman, became an important mentor and friend while providing great teaching experiences and professional opportunities, including annual attendance for all departmental faculty members at the Texas Association of Physical Education, Recreation, and Dance conference. Dr. Curtis contends that the department grew to be outstanding under his leadership and encouragement to stay current in the profession. **What do you consider to be the highlight of your career:** One highlight of Dr. Curtis' career was having her book, "Pickle-Ball for Player and Teacher," published in 1985 and then having her brother, Bob Curtis, take the pictures for the third edition in 1998. Another highlight was starting the women's athletic program at Abilene Christian University. **Religion:** Church of Christ **Shipping Address:** 2501 Garfield Ave, Abilene, TX, 79601

Daniel J. D'Alesio Jr.

Title: Senior Litigation Attorney **Industry:** Law and Legal Services **Company Name:** University of Florida **Place of Birth:** Philadephia **State:** PA **Marital Status:** Married **Spouse Name:** Denise Mutter **Children:** Daniel; Cara; Amy Lyn; Joseph **Education:** JD, Villanova University (1973); BA in Psychology, La Salle University (1970) **Career:** Senior Litigation Attorney, J. Hillis Miller Health Center Self-Insurance Program, University of Florida (2001-Present); Associate Director, J. Hillis Miller Health Center Self-Insurance Program, University of Florida; Instructor, Columbia College of Missouri; Online Developer, Criminal Justice Evidence Course; Teen Court Magistrate Judge, Fourth Judicial Circuit, Duval County Teen Court Program **Civic:** Vocalist, St. Paul's Catholic Church, Jacksonville Beach, FL; Guitarist, St. Paul's Catholic Church, Jacksonville Beach, FL **Military Service:** U.S. Navy **Awards:** Leadership Award, Military Affairs Committee, The Florida Bar (2008-2009); Clayton B. Burton Award of Excellence, The Florida Bar (2008); Teen Court Magistrate Award, Fourth Judicial Circuit State Attorney (2007); Meritorious Community Service Award, Villanova University School of Law; Legion of Merit; Meritorious Service Medal; Navy-Marine Corps Commendation Medal; Navy Achievement Medal **Membership:** Psi Chi, National Honor Society in Psychology; Federal Bar Association; Former Chair, Military Affairs Committee, The Florida Bar; Jacksonville Bar Association; Catholic Lawyers Guild; Former President, School Board, St. Paul's Catholic School, Jacksonville Beach, FL; Board Member, Diocesan Advisory Board of Education, Diocese of St. Augustine **To what do you attribute your success:** He attributes his success to being goal-oriented, his positive attitude, and his time in the U.S. Navy. He comes to work and treats it as though it is his duty. **Why did you become involved in your profession or industry:** He was originally a pre-med student, but was advised to find another field. In eighth grade, Sister Leo Mary helped him to be a rebuttalist in a debate, and she helped him to look at a problem and become an advocate for it. He decided in his junior year to go to law school. He went into the U.S. Navy, and they deferred him so he could go. **Hobbies:** Songwriting; Playing guitar at local church **Business Address:** 580 W 8th St Fl 7, Jacksonville, FL, 32209 **Shipping Address:** 1408 Forest Marsh Dr, Neptune Beach, FL, 32266 **Website:** https://www.linkedin.com/in/daniel-j-d-alesio-jr-esq-2b702b21

Ida Jane Dalpino

Title: Retired Secondary Education Educator **Industry:** Education/Educational Services **Date of Birth:** 10/20/1936 **Place of Birth:** Newhall **State:** CA **Parents:** Bernhardt Arthur Melby; Wahneta May (Blyler) Melby **Marital Status:** Single **Spouse Name:** Gilbert Augustus (6/14/1963, Divorced 1976) **Children:** Nicolette Jane **Education:** MA, University of San Francisco (1978); Postgraduate Coursework, Sonoma State University (1970-1971); Postgraduate Coursework, Sacramento State University (1961-1965); BA, California State University, Chico (1960) **Certifications:** Community Counselor; Instructor for Learning Handicapped; Community College Instructor; Instructor for Exceptional Children; Pupil Personnel Specialist; Secondary Teacher; Resource Specialist **Career:** Retired (2000); Resource Specialist, Yuba City High School (1971-2000); ESL Teacher, Phoenix Independent High School (1968-1969); Counselor, Mira Loma High School, Sacramento, CA (1960-1966); Teacher, Chico High School (1959-1960) **Career Related:** English Teacher, Rough Rock Demonstration School (Now Rough Rock Community School) (1976); English Teacher, Rough Rock Demonstration School (Now Rough Rock Community School) (1975) **Civic:** Centerville Historical Association (Now Centerville Recreation And Historical Association Inc.) (1991-Present); Office Secretary, Job's Daughters (Now Job's Daughters International), North Bend, OR (1953-Present); Active Environmental Defense Fund **Membership:** National Education Association; California Teachers Association; Chico State Alumni Association; Sierra Club; The Nature Conservancy; Audubon (Now National Audubon Society); Greenpeace; Sigma Kappa Alumni Association **Marquis Who's Who Honors:** Albert Nelson Marquis Lifetime Achievement Award (2017) **Hobbies:** Reading; Ecology; Genealogy **Political Affiliations:** Democrat **Religion:** Science of the Mind Church **Shipping Address:** 6 Navajo Ln, Corte Madera, CA, 94925

James Michael Daly III

Title: President & Sr. Principle Infrastructure Architect **Industry:** Architecture & Constrution **Company Name:** Fitzergy Technology Consulting **Date of Birth:** 12/05/1958 **Place of Birth:** Evanston **State:** IL **Parents:** James Michael Daly II; Mary Helen (FitzGerald) Daly **Spouse Name:** Lisa Marie (Du Brock) Daly **Education:** Postgraduate Coursework, DePaul University (1990); BSBA, Marquette University (1981) **Career:** President, Fitzergy Technology Consultants (2014-Present); Senior Principle Infrastructure Architect, Fitzergy Technology Consultants (2014-Present); Facilities Management Specialist, IBM Global Services (Now IBM Services), Boulder, CO (2001-2013); Sr. Infrastructure Architect, IBM Global Services (Now IBM Services), Boulder, CO (2001-2013); Senior Network Engineer, IBM, Oakbrook, IL (1999-2001); Senior Consultant, Cardinal Health, McGraw Park, IL (1998-1999); Senior Consultant, Baxter, McGraw Park, IL (1997-1998); Senior Technical Consultant, Information Technology, Baxter, McGraw Park, IL (1993-1996); Senior Technology Consultant, Distribution Division, Baxter, McGraw Park, IL (1990-1993); Technology Consultant, Information Resources, Baxter, McGraw Park, IL (1987-1990); Senior Programmer Analyst, Travenol Laboratories, Baxter, McGraw Park, IL (1986-1987); Systems Analyst, American Hospital Supply Corporation, McGraw Park, IL (1985-1986); Senior Programmer Analyst, American Hospital Supply Corporation, McGraw Park, IL (1983-1984); Programmer Analyst, Information Services, American Hospital Supply Corporation, McGraw Park, IL (1981-1982) **Civic:** Member, Feral Friends Network, Alley Cat Allies, Bethesda, MD (2016-Present); Minister of Care, Prince of Peace Catholic Church (2007-Present); Lector, Prince of Peace Catholic Church (1984-Present); President, Lake Villa District Library (2005-2009); Founding Trustee, Lake Villa District Library Foundation (2004-2009); Trustee, Lake Villa District Library (2003-2009); Treasurer, Lake Villa District Library (2003-2005); District Commissioner, Northeast Illinois Council, Boy Scouts of America (1996-2000); Assistant Scoutmaster, Gurnee, Illinois Council, Boy Scouts of America (1989-1995); Eucharistic Minister, Prince of Peace Catholic Church (1988-1999); Catechist, Prince of Peace Lutheran Church (1987-2017); President, School Board, Prince of Peace Catholic School (1985-1987); Chairman, Alumni Admissions Recruiting Chapter, Marquette University (1982-1993) **Awards:** Catechetical Ministries Recognition Award, Archdiocese of Chicago (2005); Sherry Kalan Memorial Community Service Award, DBR Chamber of Commerce (1994); Reach Out Illinois Award, Office of the Governor (1994) **Membership:** Board of Directors, Marquette Club of Chicago, Marquette University (1983-1996); Vice President, Communications, North Shore Section, Data Processing Management Association (Now Association of Information Technology Professionals) (1982-1983); Director, Communications, Data Processing Management Association (Now Association of Information Technology Professionals) (1981-1982) **Marquis Who's Who Honors:** Albert Nelson Marquis Lifetime Achievement Award (2017) **Hobbies:** Scrapbooking; Feral Cat Care **Religion:** Roman Catholic **Business Address:** 38895 N Ashley Dr, Lake Villa, IL, 60046

Kenneth W. Dam

Title: Law Educator, Federal Agency Administrator (Retired) **Industry:** Law and Legal Services **Date of Birth:** 08/10/1932 **Place of Birth:** Marysville **State/Country of Origin:** KS **Parents:** Oliver W. Dam; Ida L. (Hueppelsheuser) Dam **Marital Status:** Married **Spouse Name:** Marcia Wachs (6/9/1962) **Children:** Eliot; Charlotte **Education:** Honorary LLD, New School of Social Research (1983); JD, University of Chicago (1957); BS, University of Kansas (1954) **Career:** Max Pam Professor Emeritus, University of Chicago Law School (2014-Present); Honorary Board Member, Brookings Institution (2006-Present); Senior Lecturer, University of Chicago Law School (2004-2014); Senior Fellow, Brookings Institution (2003-2012); Board Member, Brookings Institution (2003-2006); Max Pam Professor of American and Foreign Law, University of Chicago Law School (2003-2004); Deputy Secretary, United States Department of Treasury, Washington, DC (2001-2003); Max Pam Professor of American and Foreign Law, University of Chicago Law School (1992-2001); President, Chief Executive Officer, United Way of America (1992); Board Member, Brookings Institution (1986-2001); Vice President of Law and External Relations, IBM Corporation (1985-1992); Deputy Secretary, United States Department of State, Washington, DC (1982-1985); Provost, University of Chicago (1980-1982); Harold J. & Marion F. Green Professor, University of Chicago Law School (1976-1982); Professor, University of Chicago Law School (1974-1982, 1964-1971); Faculty, University of Chicago Law School (1960-1982); Associate, Cravath, Swaine & Moore, New York City, NY (1958-1960); Law Clerk to Justice Charles Whitaker, United States Supreme Court (1957-1958) **Career Related:** Advisory Board, BMW of North America (1990-1995); Board of Director, Alcoa, Inc. (1987-2001); Executive Director, Council Economic Policy (1973); Assistant Director, National Security and International Affairs, Office of Management and Budget, Executive Office of the President (1971-1973); Visiting Professor, University of Freiburg, Germany (1964) **Civic:** Honorary Trustee, Brookings Institution 11 (2009-Present); Lifetime Director, Atlantic Council (2006-Present); Board of Directors, Atlantic Council (2004-Present); Trustee, Brookings Institution 11 (2003-2009); Board of Directors, Chicago Council on Foreign Relations (1992-2001); Co-Chairman, Aspen Strategy Group (1991-2001); Trustee, Brookings Institution 11 (1989-2001); Board of Directors, America China Society (1989-1999); Board of Directors, American Council on Germany (1986-1995); Board of Directors, Atlantic Council (1985-1992) **Creative Works:** Co-Editor, Technology Policy Law and Ethics Regarding United States Acquisition and Use of Cyberattack Capabilities (2009); Author, "Law-Growth Nexus: The Rule of Law and Economic Development" (2006); Author, "The Rules of the Global Game: A New Look at United States International Economic Policymaking" (2001); Co-Author, "Economic Policy Beyond the Headlines, Second Edition" (1998); Chair, Board of Advisors, Foreign Affairs Journal (1997-2001); Co-Editor, "Cryptography's Role in Securing the Information Society" (1996); Author, "The Rules of the Game: Reform and Evolution in the International Monetary System" (1982); Co-Author, "Economic Policy Beyond the Headlines" (1977); Author, "Oil Resources: Who Gets What How?" (1976); Author, "The GATT: Law and International Economic Organization" (1970); Co-Author, "Federal Tax Treatment of Foreign Income" (1964) **Awards:** Recipient, Raimar Lust Award, Thyssen and Humboldt Foundation, Germany (2007) **Membership:** Shadow Committee (2015); Trustee, Committee on Economic Development (2006-2016); Board of Directors, Finance Services Volunteer Corps (2005-2016); Trustee, Munich Intellectual Property Law Center (2004-2008); Science, Technology and Law Panel, National Academy (2003-2008); American Academy of Arts and Sciences; American Academy of Diplomacy; American Law Institute; Shadow Financial Regulatory Committee, Munich Intellectual Property Law Center; Metropolitan Club, Washington; Quadrangle Club, Chicago, IL **Bar Admissions:** New York (1959) **Marquis Who's Who Honors:** Albert Nelson Marquis Lifetime Achievement Award (2017) **To what do you attribute your success:** Mr. Dam attributes his success to hard work, education and international experiences. **Where will you be in five years:** In five years from now, Mr. Dam will be retired. **Political Affiliations:** Republican **Shipping Address:** 5609 S Kenwood Ave, Chicago, IL, 60637

James Leonard Danielson

Title: Political Science Educator **Industry:** Education/Educational Services **Date of Birth:** 05/06/1938 **Place of Birth:** Hallock **State:** MN **Parents:** Silas Leonard; Alice (Hagen) Danielson **Children:** Silas; Cekiel; Monty; Tom; Micky; Jana; Meredith **Education:** PhD, University of Minnesota (1971); MA, University of Minnesota (1967); BA, Concordia College, Moorhead, MN (1960) **Career:** Professor of Political Science, Director of Public and Human Service Administration, Minnesota State University Moorhead (1987-1996); Professor of Political Science, University of North Texas, Denton (1967-1987) **Civic:** Moorhead City Council (2001-2005); Chair, Minnesota Political Science Association (1998-2002); Chair, Denton County Democratic Party (1980-1984); Denton County Democratic Campaign (1972) **Creative Works:** Author, "Achieving the American Dream, What We Should, Could and Would Become" (2015); Co-Author, "Monograph: Migration and Public Attitudes" (1982) **Membership:** American Political Science Association; Southern Political Science Association; Board of Directors, Minnesota Chapter, American Society for Public Administration (1988-2002); Grantee, National Endowment Humanities (1980) **Hobbies:** Fishing; Singing **Religion:** Unitarian-Universalist **Shipping Address:** 924 Belsly Blvd, Moorhead, MN, 56560

Kenneth Daugherty

Title: Research and Development Company Executive **Industry:** Research **Company Name:** TRAC Labs **Date of Birth:** 12/27/1938 **Place of Birth:** Pittsburgh **State:** PA **Parents:** Thomas Hill Daugherty; Laura Elizabeth (Schuda) Daugherty **Marital Status:** Married **Spouse Name:** Joan Kay (Ogrosky) Daugherty (12/22/1961) **Children:** Brian Earl; Kirsten Kay **Education:** Regents Professor, University of North Texas (1995); Director of National Defense, University of Dallas, Fort Worth Area; Master in Business Economics, Claremont Graduate School (1971); PhD in Analytical Chemistry, University of Washington (1964); BS in Chemistry, Carnegie-Mellon University (1960) **Career:** Owner, TRAC Laboratories, Denton, TX (1981-Present); Professor of Chemistry, North Texas State University (1979-2000); Chairman, Analytical Division, North Texas State University (1980-1995); Director of Energy and Materials Science, Institute of Applied Sciences, North Texas State University (1977-1979); Director of Research and Development, General Portland Inc., Dallas (1973-1977); Associate Professor of Chemistry, University of Pittsburgh (1971-1973); Group Leader, Senior Staff, Amcord (1966-1971); Research Chemist, Rohm and Haas Corporation (1964); Chemist, Marbon Chem.-Borg Warner (1960) **Career Related:** President, Chief Executive Officer, KEDS Inc., KD Consultant (1977-Present); Adjunct Professor of Chemistry, University of Pittsburgh (1973-2000); Adjunct Professor, North Texas State University, Denton (1974-2000); Adjunct Faculty, Army Command and General Staff College (1983-Present) **Military Service:** Colonel, U.S. Army Reserve (1966-1995); Colonel, U.S. Army (1964-1966) **Creative Works:** Author, Numerous Publications in Field; Recipient, Numerous Patents **Awards:** Achievement Award, Argonne National Laboratory (1987); Fellow, National Science Foundation (1964); Decorated Army Commendation Medal, U.S. Army; Army Achievement Medal, U.S. Army; Army Meritorious Service Medal, U.S. Army; Fellow, DuPont; Fellow, Shell Oil; Fellow, Standard Oil **Membership:** Program Chairman, American Ceramic Society (1986); Chapter President, American Chemical Society (1960); Fellow, American Institute of Chemists; Research Society of America; American Society for Testing and Materials; Transportation Research Board, Rilem; New York Academy of Sciences; Applied Spectroscopy Society; Society of Petroleum Engineers; Society of Plastics Engineers; Senior Army Commanders Association; Sigma Xi; Pi Kappa Alpha; Omicron Delta Epsilon; Phi Lambda Upsilon, Alpha Chi Sigma, Freemasonry; Shriners International; Rotary International **Political Affiliations:** Republican **Religion:** Methodist **Shipping Address:** 1912 Hunskor Road, Oak Harbor, WA, 98277

Judith A. Davidson, PhD

Title: Wealth Management Adviser, CFP **Industry:** Financial Services **Company Name:** Merrill Lynch **Date of Birth:** 11/07/1944 **Place of Birth:** New York City **State:** NY/US **Education:** PhD, University of Massachusetts (1983); MEd, Boston University (1974); BS, University of New Hampshire (1966) **Certifications:** Diploma, Chelsea College, Eastbourne, England (1967) **Career:** Director of Athletics, Central Connecticut State University, New Britain, CT (1988-Present); President's Council, Central Connecticut State University, New Britain, CT (1988); University Events Council, Central Connecticut State University, New Britain, CT (1988); Various Committees, Central Connecticut State University, New Britain, CT (1988); Advisory Board Member, Women's Sport Foundation (1985-1992); Owner, Manager, Atalanta Sports Ltd., Iowa City (1979-1982); Manager, Atalanta Sports Ltd., Iowa City (1979-1982); Assistant Professor, University of Iowa, Iowa City (1978-1988); Head Field Hockey Coach, University of Iowa, Iowa City (1976-1988); Teaching Associate, University of Massachusetts, Amherst, MA (1976-1978); Teacher, Newton Board of Education, MA (1968-1976); Teacher, North Rockland Board of Education, Haverstraw, NY (1967-1968) **Career Related:** Financial Adviser, Merrill Lynch, Roseville, CA **Civic:** Board of Directors, New Britain Teen Pregnancy Prevention Program (1994); Amateur Athletic Union Junior Olympics Committee, Iowa City (1985); Committee, Site Selection and Training Center, U.S. Olympic Games; Development Committee, International Hockey Federation; Chairman, Development Committee, Pan America Hockey Federation **Creative Works:** Contributor, Numerous Publications, Professional Journals **Awards:** New Agenda Award, Women's Hall Of Fame (1993); Women In Leadership Award, New Britain Young Women's Christian Association (1993); Service Award, Boston Four (1992); Recipient, Big 10 Field Hockey Champion (1980-1987.); National Champion in Field Hockey (1986); National Runner-Up, NCAA Final Four Field Hockey (1984); Coach Of Year, Big 10 Conference (1984); National Indoor Hockey Champion, NCAA Division I Field Hockey (1984); Field Hockey, Big 10 Conference, Chicago (1983) **Membership:** American Association for Health, Physical Education, and Recreation; East Coast Athletic Conference; East Coast Conference; North America Society of Sport History; US Field Hockey Association; National Association of Collegiate Women Athletic Administration; Popular Culture Association **Marquis Who's Who Honors:** Albert Nelson Marquis Lifetime Achievement Award (2017) **To what do you attribute your success:** Dr. Davidson attributes her success to always wanting to do her best as well as being fortunate to have an inquiring mind. **Why did you become involved in your profession or industry:** She was always involved in athletics competitions even as a young girl during an era when it was not as acceptable as it is today. Staying involved professionally was just a natural continuation of what she loved to do as a child and young woman. **What do you consider to be the highlight of your career:** There are particular events that she considers highlights: first, winning the 1986 NCAA Division One National Championship in Field Hockey while coaching at the University of Iowa; second, being the first woman selected from a national search to head a Division One Intercollegiate Athletics Program for both men and women sports including football; and third, being the first woman coach inducted into The University of Iowa Athletics Hall of Fame. **Where will you be in five years:** In five years, she will be retired. **Business Address:** 2998 Douglas Blvd Ste 290, Merrill Lynch, Roseville, CA, 95661

Bonnie Christell Davis

Title: Judge (Retired) **Industry:** Law and Legal Services **Date of Birth:** 07/13/1949 **Place of Birth:** Petersburg **State:** VA **Parents:** Robert Madison Davis; Margaret Elizabeth (Collier) Davis **Education:** JD, University of Richmond (1980); BA, Longwood University, Farmville, VA (1971) **Career:** Retired (2016); Judge, Juvenile and Domestic Relations Court for 12th Judicial District of Virginia (1993-2016); Assistant Commonwealth Attorney, Chesterfield County (1983-1993); Private Practice, Chesterfield, VA (1980-1983); Teacher, Chesterfield County Schools, Chesterfield, VA (1971-1977) **Career Related:** Board of Directors, Association of District Court Judges of Virginia (2014-Present); Board of Directors, Association of District Court Judges of Virginia (2013-Present); Chairman, Judicial Administration Committee, Judicial Conference of Virginia for District Courts (2001-2003); State Advisory Committee, CASA and Children's Justice Act (1998-2002); Chairman, Judicial Administration Committee, Judicial Conference of Virginia for District Courts (1995-1997); National Advisory Committee for Production on Missing and Runaway Children, Theatre IV Advisory Group to Set Standards and Training for Guardians Ad Litem, Supreme Court of Virginia (1994); Consultant, Step by Step Through the Juvenile Justice System in Virginia, Virginia Department of Children (1988); Adviser, Youth Services Commission, Chesterfield, VA (1983-1993); Consultant, Task Force on Child Abuse (1983-1993); Consultant, Metropolitan Richmond Multi-Discipline Team on Spouse Abuse (1983-1993) **Civic:** Member, Task Force on Core Values, Chesterfield County Public Schools (1999) **Creative Works:** Co-Author, "Juvenile Law and Practice in Virginia" (1994) **Awards:** Bravo Award, Chesterfield Public Education Foundation (2009); Thomas Jefferson Professional Achievement Alumni Award, Longwood University **Membership:** Board of Governors, General Practice Section, Virginia State Bar (2005-Present); Board of Directors, Association of District Court Judges of Virginia (2013-2017); Board of Governors, Senior Lawyers Conference, Virginia State Bar (2005-2009); Board of Governors, Family Law Section, Virginia State Bar (1997-2001); Chesterfield Public Education Foundation; Chesterfield-Colonial Heights Bar Association; Metropolitan Richmond Women's Bar Association; Virginia Trial Lawyers Association; Virginia Bar Association; State-Federal Judicial Council of Virginia **Bar Admissions:** United States Court of Appeals for the Fourth Circuit (1982); United States District Court Eastern District of Virginia (1980); Virginia (1980) **Marquis Who's Who Honors:** Albert Nelson Marquis Lifetime Achievement Award (2017) **Why did you become involved in your profession or industry:** Ms. Davis always wanted to become a lawyer, but when she was young there were very few opportunities for women in the profession. She went into teaching, but kept her focus on the goal of practicing law, and eventually she achieved that goal. **Hobbies:** Traveling; Photography **Religion:** Baptist **Shipping Address:** 3242 Jersey Ct, Colonial Heights, VA, 23834

Muller Davis

Title: Of Counsel, Partner **Industry:** Law and Legal Services **Company Name:** Davis | Friedman **Date of Birth:** 04/23/1935 **Place of Birth:** Chicago **State:** IL **Year of Passing:** 2018-02-21 **Parents:** Benjamin B.; Janice Muller D. **Marital Status:** Married **Spouse Name:** Lynn Straus **Children:** Melissa Davis Muller; Muller Junior; Joseph Jeffrey **Education:** JD, Harvard University (1960); BA, Yale University, Magna Cum Laude (1957) **Career:** Of Counsel, Davis, Friedman (2014-Present); Partner, Davis, Friedman (1967-Present); Lawyer, Chicago (1960-Present); Associate, Jenner & Block (1960-1967) **Career Related:** Member, State of Illinois Circuit Court of Cook County Domestic Relations Division Procedure and Policy Review Committee (2012-Present); Co-Chair, Committee to Study and Recommend a Comprehensive Rules Design for the Domestic Relations Division, Circuit Court of Cook County, IL (2003-2009); Lecturer, Continuing Legal Education, Matrimonial Law and Litigation Legal Adviser, Michael Reese Medical Research Institute Council (1967-1982) **Civic:** Board of Directors, Infant Welfare Society (1975-1996); Honorary, Board of Directors, Infant Welfare Society (1996-Present); President, Infant Welfare Society (1978-1982); Co-Chairman, General Gifts 40th and 45th Reunions, Phillips Exeter Academy; Chair, Class Capital Giving (1994-1998); 50th Reunion Gift Committee; 55th Reunion Gift Committee, Yale Class Council (2002-Present) **Military Service:** Captain, US Army, Illinois National Guard (1960-1967) **Creative Works:** Co-Author, "The Parental Couple in a Successful Divorce" (1984); Co-Author, "`Illinois Practice of Family Law' (1995); Co-Author, "The Illinois Practice of Family Law" (2014-2015); Co-Author, "Enforceable Civility: A Critical Part of the Judicial Process in Divorce Litigation" (2011); Contributing Author, "Marriage, Health and the Professions" (2002); Member, Editorial Board, Equitable Distribution Journal (1984-2007); Contributor, Articles, Law Journals **Awards:** Lawyer of the Year, Family Law, Chicago, Best Lawyers (2010); Samuel S. Berger Award, Illinois Chapter, American Academy of Matrimonial Lawyers (2009) **Membership:** Fellow, American Academy of Matrimonial Lawyers; Board of Managers, Illinois Chapter, American Academy of Matrimonial Lawyers (1996-1999); American Bar Association; Federal Bar Association; Illinois Bar Association; Matrimonial Committee, Chicago Bar Association (1968-1983); Secretary, Civil Practice Committee, Chicago Bar Association (1979-1980); Vice Chairman, Chicago Bar Association (1980-1981); Chairman, Chicago Bar Association (1981-1982); American Society of Writers on Legal Subjects; Vice Chairman, Matrimonial Bar, Legal Aid Society (1991-1995); Vice Chairman, Legal Aid Society (1995-1997); Chairman, Legal Aid Society (1997-1990); The Lawyers Club of Chicago; Lake Shore Country Club; Chicago Club **Bar Admissions:** Illinois (1960); U.S. District Court, Illinois (1961) **Political Affiliations:** Republican **Religion:** Jewish **Business Address:** 135 S. LaSalle Street, 36th Floor, Chicago, IL, 60603 **Shipping Address:** 135 S. LaSalle St, 36th Floor, Davis, Friedman, Chicago, IL, 60603 **Website:** www.davisfriedman.com

Paul J. Davis

Title: Endocrinologist **Industry:** Medicine & Health Care **Company Name:** Albany Medical Center **Date of Birth:** 10/28/1937 **Place of Birth:** Chicago **State:** IL **Parents:** Paul Albert Davis; Maxine Lydia (Mason) Davis **Spouse Name:** Faith Ainsworth Baker (12/8/1962-04/16/2017) **Children:** Matthew; John; Sarah **Education:** Resident in Medicine, Bronx Municipal Hospital Center (Now NYC Health + Hospitals/Jacobi, The City of New York) (1964-1967); Intern, Bronx Municipal Hospital Center (Now NYC Health + Hospitals/Jacobi, The City of New York) (1963-1964); MD, Harvard University, Cum Laude (1963); BA, Westminster College, Magna Cum Laude (1959) **Career:** Director, Ordway Research Institute, Albany, NY (2002-2010); Senior Associate Dean for Clinical Research, Albany Medical College, Albany Medical Center (1998-2008); Professor, Department of Medicine, Albany Medical College, Albany Medical Center (1990-1999); Chairman, Department of Medicine, Albany Medical College, Albany Medical Center (1990-1999); Chief Medical Service, VA Western New York Healthcare System, U.S. Department of Veterans Affairs (1980-1990); Professor of Medicine, University at Buffalo (1975-1990); Head, Endocrinology Division, University at Buffalo (1975-1990); Head, Endocrinology Division, Baltimore City Hospitals (1970-1975); Senior Staff Associate, National Institutes of Health (1969-1970); Clinical Associate, National Institutes of Health, Bethesda, MD (1967-1969); Vice Chairman, Department of Medicine, School of Medicine, University at Buffalo; Executive Vice President and Chief Scientific Officer, NanoPharmaceuticals LLC, Rensselaer, NY **Career Related:** Faculty of 1000 Medicine, Co-Head, Endocrinology Diabetes (2007-Present); External Reviewer Panel, Chernobyl Tissue Bank, European Union (2010-2015); Board of Directors, American Board of Internal Medicine; Board of Directors, Hauptman Woodward Medical Research Institute, Buffalo, NY (2009-2011); National Advisory Council, Health Sciences Center, West Virginia University (2008-2015); Director, Ordway Research Institute, Albany, NY (1999-2011); President, New York State Chapter, American College of Physicians (1999-2001); President, American Thyroid Association (1997-1998); Board of Scientific Counselors, National Institute on Aging, NIH (1977-1986); Merit Review Board, Endocrinology, U.S. Department of Veterans Affairs; Board of Directors, American Board of Internal Medicine; Merit Review Board of Oncology, American Board of Internal Medicine; Master, American College of Physicians; Co-Author, 300 Scientific Publications; Co-editor, Four Medical Textbooks **Civic:** Trustee, Westminster College, Fulton, MO (2000-Present) **Creative Works:** Editor-in-Chief, Immunology, Endocrine and Metabolic Agents in Medicinal Chemistry (2007-2011); Secretary Editor, "Current Opinion in Endocrinology, Diabetes, Obesity" (2004-2010); Editorial Board Member, Hormones & Cancer, Endocrine Research, Comprehensive Physiology, Medicine, and Biomedicines **Awards:** Distinguished Service Award, American Thyroid Association (2003); Laureate Award, New York Chapter, American College of Physicians **Membership:** American Thyroid Association; American College of Physicians; Gerontological Society of America; American Federation for Medical Research; American Society for Biochemistry and Molecular Biology; Endocrine Society **Shipping Address:** 35 Old South Road, West Sand Lake, NY, 12196

Richard L. Davis

Title: Reverend, Father, Academic Administrator **Industry:** Religious **Company Name:** Franciscan Friars, Third Order Regular, Loretto, PA **Date of Birth:** 06/02/1946 **Place of Birth:** Buffalo **State/Country of Origin:** NY **Marital Status:** Single **Education:** MA, LaSalle University, Philadelphia, PA (1979); MDiv, St. Francis Seminary, Loretto, PA (1979); BA in History, St. Francis University, Loretto, PA (1974) **Career:** Minister, Provincial, Province Most Sacred Heart of Jesus (2013-Present); Provincial Council, Province of Most Sacred Heart of Jesus (2000-Present); Vice President, Community Relations, Franciscan University (2004); Director, Vocations, Franciscan Friars, Province of Most Sacred Heart of Jesus, Loretto, PA (1996-2004); Executive Assistant to President, Franciscan University, Steubenville, OH (1992-2000); Teacher, Administrator, St. Francis Prep School, Spring Grove, PA (1981-1985); Teacher, Administrator, Bishop Egan High School, Fairless Hills, PA (1967-1992) **Career Related:** Paul Harris Fellowship, Rotary International (2006); Paul Harris Fellowship, Rotary International (1999); Chairman of the Board, St. Francis University, Loretto, PA; Chairman of the Board, Franciscan University of Steubenville, Ohio; Fellow, Rotary Club of Steubenville **Marquis Who's Who Honors:** Distinguished Humanitarian (2017) **To what do you attribute your success:** Rev. Davis attributes his success to the grace of God. **Why did you become involved in your profession or industry:** Rev. Davis became involved in his profession because he felt he was called to it. **What do you consider to be the highlight of your career:** The highlight of Rev. Davis' career has been being a Franciscan friar/priest. He entered the community in 1964. **Hobbies:** History; Classical music; Gardening **Political Affiliations:** Conservative **Religion:** Roman Catholic **Shipping Address:** PO Box 137, Loretto, PA, 15940-0137

Russell Haden Davis, PhD

Title: Professor, Rev. Robert B. Lantz Chairperson **Industry:** Education/Educational Services **Company Name:** Virginia Commonwealth University **Date of Birth:** 11/26/1940 **Place of Birth:** Washington **State:** DC **Parents:** Walter Haden Davis; Virginia (Russell) Edge **Marital Status:** Married **Spouse Name:** Iva Lee Crocker (1964) **Children:** Brandon Denise; Haden Arnold **Education:** PhD, Union Theological Seminary, New York, NY (1986); STM, Union Theological Seminary, New York, NY (1978); ThM, Southern Baptist Theological Seminary, Louisville, KY (1966); MDiv, Union Theological Seminary, New York, NY (1965); BA, University of Virginia (1962) **Certifications:** ACPE Certified Educator, Association for Clinical Pastoral Education (1964), Endorsed Chaplain, Alliance of Baptists in the USA (2000); Ordained Minister, Southern Baptist Church (1961) **Career:** Director of Pastoral Care, VCU Health (2015-Present); Professor and Rev. Robert B. Lantz Endowed Chair, Department of Patient Counseling, School of Allied Health Professions, Virginia Commonwealth University (2012-Present); President, Legacy Group International (1998-Present); Supervisor, Sentara Hospitals, Norfolk, VA (2001-2012); Executive Director, Association for Clinical Pastoral Education Inc., Decatur, GA (1995-1998); Associate Professor, University of Virginia (1994-1995); Assistant Professor, University of Virginia (1994); Director, Psy-Law, New York, NY (1989-1991); Faculty, Graduate Institute of Pastoral Psychotherapy, Blanton-Peale Institute and Counseling Center, New York, NY (1989-1991); Assistant Professor of Psychiatry and Religion, Union Theological Seminary, New York, NY (1986-1991); Associate Minister, The Riverside Church, New York, NY (1977-1986); Private Practice, Pastoral Psychotherapy (1974-1998); Clinical Chaplain, Central State Hospital, Milledgeville, GA (1971-1977); Clinical Chaplain, Kentucky State Reformatory, Lagrange, KY (1966-1971) **Career Related:** Adjunct Professor, John Leland Center for Theological Studies (2004-2006); Adjunct Professor, Virginia Commonwealth University (2001-2006); Adjunct Professor, Blanton Peale Graduate Institute, New York, NY (1989-1991); Adjunct Professor, New York Theological Seminary (1984-1990); Honoree, Fellowship, Oaklawn Foundation (1980); Honoree, Fellowship, Union Theological Seminary (1979-1981) **Civic:** Board of Directors, Virginia Council on Aging (2013-Present); Chair, COMISS Commission for the Accreditation Pastoral Service (2009); Board of Advisors, John Leland Center for Theological Studies, Hampton Roads (2002-2004); Board of Directors, Tidewater Pastoral Counseling Services, Norfolk, VA (2001-2009); Founding Member, National Interfaith Coalition for Spiritual Healthcare and Counseling (1997-1998); Clinical Pastoral Education Advisory Board, The Hospital Chaplaincy, New York, NY (1983-1985); Board of Directors, Institute for Relationship Therapy, New York, NY (1981-1988); Board of Directors, Counseling Center, The Riverside Church, New York, NY (1978-1982); Chairperson, Instructional Programs Committee, Baldwin County Education Study Team, Board of Education, Governor's Conference on Education (1976-1977); Secretary, Kentucky Chaplains Association (1970-1971) **Creative Works:** Author, "Freud's Concept of Passivity" (1993); Author, Contributor, Articles and Book Reviews **Awards:** Research Grantee, Rush University CPE Curriculum Development Grant, The John Templeton Foundation Transforming Chaplaincy: Promoting Research Literacy for Improved Patient Outcomes Grant (2017-2018); Honoree, Sentara Healthcare Key Contributor Award (2006); Research Grantee, Union Theological Seminary (1987-1990); Decorated, Kentucky Colonel, State of Kentucky (1970) **Membership:** President, COMISS Network on Ministry in Specialized Settings (2017-Present); President Elect, COMISS Network (2015-2017); Treasurer, COMISS Network (2013-2014); Member-At-Large, COMISS Network (2010-2013); Vice President, Racial, Ethnic, and Multicultural Network, Association for Clinical Pastoral Education (2006-2007); Board Certified Chaplain, Association of Professional Chaplains (1974-1999); American Association of Pastoral Counselors (1974-1999) **Marquis Who's Who Honors:** Albert Nelson Marquis Lifetime Achievement Award (2017) **Hobbies:** Collecting antique architectural photographs and postcards of the Morningside Heights area of New York **Shipping Address:** 3100 Earlysville Road, Earlysville, VA, 22936 **Website:** https://sahp.vcu.edu/departments/ptc

Trigg Thomas Davis

Title: Principal **Industry:** Law and Legal Services **Company Name:** Davis & Mathis PC **Date of Birth:** 07/28/1945 **Place of Birth:** Spokane **State:** WA **Marital Status:** Married **Education:** JD, Stanford Law School, Stanford University (1970); BA in Political Science, Washington State University, With Distinction (1967) **Career:** President, Davis & Mathis PC (1996-Present); Partner, Davis & Goerisa Professional Corporation (1978-1996); Attorney, Sole Practice, Anchorage, AK (1975); Partner, Owen, Davis, Bartlett, Anchorage, AK (1972-1975); Law Clerk to Chief Justice, Alaska Court System (1970-1972) **Career Related:** Probate Committee, Alaska Bar Association (1974-1984); Committee of Bar Examiners, Alaska Court System (1974-1976); Fellow, American College of Probate Counsel (Now The American College of Trust and Estate Counsel) **Civic:** Chairperson, Standing Advisory Committee on Rules, Alaska Supreme Court, Alaska Court System; Active Member, Board of Trustees, Alaska Pacific University; Chair, Board of Trustees, Alaska Pacific University **Creative Works:** Editor, "Journal of International Studies," Stanford Law School, Stanford University (1968-1969) **Awards:** RGS Sportsman Award (2012) **Membership:** American College of Probate Counsel (Now The American College of Trust and Estate Counsel) (1986-Present); State Chairman, American College of Probate Counsel (Now The American College of Trust and Estate Counsel); American Bar Association; Anchorage Bar Association **Bar Admissions:** State of Alaska; State of California **Marquis Who's Who Honors:** Albert Nelson Marquis Lifetime Achievement Award (2017) **Why did you become involved in your profession or industry:** Mr. Davis became involved in his profession because he really wanted the opportunity to choose where he lived, which meant to work for himself. He was also trying to help families. **What do you consider to be the highlight of your career:** One of the highlights of Mr. Davis' career has been the private foundation he started in 2000. "Gold 2002" trains skiers to get them on the Olympic team, and there were four from his squad in the next Olympic Games. Right now, they have eight people on the United States ski team, and it is unknown how many will shift over to the Olympic team this year. The ski team has moved over to Alaska Pacific University. **Hobbies:** Skiing **Shipping Address:** 405 W 36th Avenue, Suite 200, Davis and Mathis PC, Anchorage, AK, 99503 **Website:** http://www.davis2.com

Frederick De Armas

Title: Foreign Language Educator, Novelist **Industry:** Education/Educational Services **Company Name:** University of Chicago **Date of Birth:** 02/09/1945 **Place of Birth:** Havana **State/Country of Origin:** Cuba **Parents:** Alfredo De Armas; Ana Maria (Galdos) De Armas **Education:** PhD, University of North Carolina (1968); BA, Stetson University, Magna Cum Laude (1965) **Career:** Andrew W. Mellon Distinguished Service Professor, The University of Chicago (2010-Present); Chair, Department of Romance Languages and Literature, The University of Chicago (2005-2012); Andrew W. Mellon Distinguished Professor of Humanities, The University of Chicago (2001-2010); Professor of Spanish, The University of Chicago, (2000-2001); Fellow, Institute for Arts and Humanities, The Pennsylvania State University, (1989-2000); Edwin Erle Sparks, Professor of Spanish and Comparative Literature, The Pennsylvania State University, (1998-2000); Distinguished Professor of Spanish and Comparative Literature, The Pennsylvania State University, (1991-1998); Professor of Spanish and Comparative Literature, The Pennsylvania State University (1988-1991); Director of Graduate Studies, Louisiana State University (1980-1985); Acting Chair, Department, Louisiana State University (1979-1980); Professor of Spanish, Louisiana State University (1978-1988); Faculty Member, Louisiana State University (1968-1988) **Career Related:** Visiting Professor, Duke University (1994); Visiting Professor, University of Missouri, Columbia (1986); Visiting Associate Professor, University of Missouri, Columbia (1977) **Creative Works:** Editor, "IBERIC Series" (2011-Present); Editor, "Anales Cervantinos" (2011-Present); Editor, "Anuario Calderoniano" (2010-Present); Editor, "Modern Philology" (2006-Present); Editor, "Revue Romane" (2004-Present); Editor, "Hispanfila" (1981-1988, 2001-Present); Member, Editorial Board, Bulletin Comediantes, (1981-Present); Author, "El retorno de Astrea" (2016); Author, "El Abra Del Yumuri (2016); Author, "Objects Culture in the Literature of Imperial Spain" (2013); Author, "Don Quixote among the Saracens" (2011); Author, "Ovid in the Age of Cervantes" (2010); Author, "Quixotic Frescoes: Cervantes and Italian Renaissance Art" (2006); Author, "Ekphrasis in the Age of Cervantes" (2005); Author, "Writing for the Eyes in the Spanish Golden Age" (2004); Editor, "South Atlantic Review" (2003-2006); Author, "European Literary Careers" (2002); Author, "Cervantes, Raphael and the Classics" (1998); Author, "Star-Crossed Golden Age" (1998); Author, "Heavenly Bodies" (1996); Editor, "Journal of Interdisciplinary Literature Studies" (1993-2000); Editor, "Hispania" (1993-1995); Author, "The Prince in the Tower" (1993); Editor, "Pennsylvania State University Studies in Romance Literatures" (1991-2001); Editor, "Comparative Literature Studies" (1989-2001); Author, "The Return of Astraea" (1986); Author, "The Invisible Mistress" (1976); Author, "Paul Scarron" (1972); Author, "The Four Interpolated Stories in the Roman Comique" (1971) **Awards:** PROSE Award, American Publisher's Association (2011); Director, Summer Seminar (2003); Fellow, National Endowment of the Humanities (1985, 1995); Director, Summer Institute (1994) **Membership:** President, Asociacion Internacional Siglo de Oro (2014-2017); President, Cervantes Society of America (2007-2009); Modern Language Association; Renaissance Society of America; Association International Hispanistas; Hispanic Society of America **Shipping Address:** 5300 S Shore Dr Apt 98, Chicago, IL, 60615

David John de Harter

Title: Radiation Oncologist **Industry:** Medicine & Health Care **Company Name:** Mid-Florida Radiation Oncology Associates **Date of Birth:** 04/12/1942 **Place of Birth:** Milwaukee **State:** WI **Parents:** Herbert George de Harter; Marion Bertha (Kahl) de Harter **Marital Status:** Married **Spouse Name:** Diane Leigh (Kuebler) de Harter **Children:** Renee; Andrew; Susannah Lee **Education:** Fellowship in Radiotherapy, University of Texas MD Anderson Cancer Center (1975); Resident in Radiation Oncology, University of Texas MD Anderson Cancer Center (1972-1975); Rotating Internship, National Naval Medical Center, United States Navy, Bethesda, MD (1968-1969); MD, School of Medicine and Public Health, University of Wisconsin-Madison (1968); BA, College of Letters and Science, University of Wisconsin-Milwaukee (1965); Undergraduate Coursework, College of Arts and Sciences, Marquette University (1960-1962); Jesuit Novitiate (1959-1960) **Certifications:** License to Practice Medicine, State of Florida (1996); Certification, The Jesuit Order, Wisconsin Province (1960); Diplomate, American Board of Radiology; Certification, Preparatory Salvation Seminary, St. Nazianz, WI, Summa Cum Laude **Career:** Partner, Assistant Medical Director, Mid-Florida Radiation Oncology Associates (1999-2010); Head of Operations, Radiation Oncology, Treasure Coast Radiation Oncology, Port St. Lucie, FL (1996-2010); Director, Radiation Oncology, Flagstaff Medical Center (1994-1996); Director, Radiation Oncology, CHI Health Immanuel (1978-1994); Director, Radiation Oncology, Bishop Clarkson Memorial Hospital, Omaha, NE (1977-1980); Attending Radiation Oncologist, St. Joseph, Wheaton Franciscan Healthcare (1976-1977); Director, Radiation Oncology, Columbia St. Mary's Hospital (1976-1977); Attending Radiation Oncologist, Carilion Roanoke Memorial Hospital (1975-1976); Attending Radiation Oncologist, LewisGale Medical Center (1975-1976) **Career Related:** Director, Panasiatic Corp., Seattle, WA (1988-Present); President, Harter Land and Lumber Company, Greene County, VA (1986-Present); Middleton Fellow, School of Medicine and Public Health, University of Wisconsin (2012); Clinical Lecturer, Department of Radiation Oncology, University of Arizona College of Medicine (1994-2000); Consultant, W.L. Gore, Inc., Flagstaff, AZ (1994-1999); Assistant Clinical Radiology Professor, University of Nebraska Medical Center, Omaha, NE (1978-1995) **Civic:** Cancer Committee, St. Lucie Medical Center (1996-Present); Trustee, Omaha Public Library (1993-Present); Board of Directors, American Cancer Society (1980-Present); Ethics Committee, St. Lucie Medical Center (2006); Core Privileging Development Council, St. Lucie Medical Center (2002); Rotary Club of Port St. Lucie (2001); Chairman, Institutional Review Board, St. Lucie Medical Center (2000-2004); President, St. Lucie Unit, American Cancer Society, Inc. (1999-2001); Medical Advisor, Board of Directors, Students Working Against Tobacco (1998-2003); Medical Advisor, Board of Directors, Tobacco-Free Partnership of St. Lucie County (1998-2003); Research Committee, Florida Division, American Cancer Society, Inc. (1998-2002); Board of Directors, St. Lucie Unit, American Cancer Society, Inc. (1996-2004); Co-Chairman, Trustee Committee, Millicent Rogers Museum, Taos, NM (1989-1991) **Military Service:** Staff General Medical Officer, Orthopedics Department, Charleston Naval Hospital, U.S. Navy (1971-1972); Assistant Chief Medical Officer, Naval Dispensary, Charleston, SC (1970-1971); Staff Medical Officer, Atlantic Fleet, Destroyer Division 42, U.S. Navy, Charleston, SC (1969-1970) **Awards:** First Prize for Research, University of Texas MD Anderson Cancer Center and School of Medicine and Public Health (1974); Lewis E. and Edith Phillips Scholarship (1968); Alpha Omega Alpha, Honor Medical Society (1967); Evan S. and Marion Helfaer Scholarship (1967) **Membership:** The Chancellor's Club, University of Nebraska (1990-Present); American Medical Association; American College of Radiology; American Society for Therapeutic Radiologists (Now American Society for Radiation Oncology); American Radium Society; American Society of Clinical Oncology; The Gilbert H. Fletcher Society; Phi Kappa Phi; Lifetime Member, Alpha Omega Alpha; American Association for the Advancement of Science; Association of Radiology and Oncology; Omaha Mid-West Clinical Society; American Brachytherapy Society; Florida Medical Association; Lifetime Alumni Member, School of Medicine and Public Health, University of Wisconsin; Lifetime Alumni Member, University of Texas MD Anderson Cancer Center; Piper's Landing Yacht & Country Club; Central Arizona Masonic Lodge; The Jesuits; Rotary; Downtown Club; Omaha Country Club; Doctors Club of Houston **Marquis Who's Who Honors:** Albert Nelson Marquis Lifetime Achievement Award (2017) **Political Affiliations:** Republican **Religion:** Episcopalian **Shipping Address:** 4811 SW Thistle Terrace, Palm City, FL, 34990

Dorothea E. de Zafra-Atwell

Title: Director of Science Education, Senior Program Analyst (Retired) **Industry:** Sciences **Company Name:** United States Department of Health and Human Services **Date of Birth:** 04/08/1942 **Place of Birth:** Rochester **State:** NY **Parents:** Carlos de Zafra, Jr.; Dorothea Schwartz (Michelsen) de Zafra **Marital Status:** Widowed **Spouse Name:** Wilbur Munroe Atwell (8/11/2001, Deceased 2014) **Education:** Diploma in Information Resources Management, National Defense University, Washington, DC (1994); Management Intern, United States Public Health Service, Rockville, MD (1969-1970); Master of Public and International Affairs, University of Pittsburgh (1965); BA in Non-Western Civilizations, University of Rochester, Magna Cum Laude (1963) **Certifications:** Credentialed Long-Term Care Ombudsman (2010) **Career:** Senior Program Analyst, Science Education Program Director, National Institute on Alcohol Abuse and Alcoholism, National Institutes of Health, U.S. Department of Health & Human Services, Bethesda, MD (1996-2003); Information Systems Security Program Manager, U.S. Public Health Service, Rockville, MD (1984-1996); Privacy Act Officer and Health Agencies' Information Practices Program Coordinator, U.S. Public Health Service, Rockville, MD (1974-1984); Legislative, Program and Management Analyst, U.S. Public Health Service (1970-1974); Assistant to the Director, Study Abroad Program, The City University of New York (1967-1969); New England Regional Executive, World University Service, New York, NY (1965-1967) **Career Related:** Executive Board, Council of Former Federal Executives and Associates (2010-2016); Preparatory, Intergenerational Summit on Aging (2015); Commencement Speaker, "Life After GSPIA: Success is in Dealing with Plan B," Graduate School of Public and International Affairs, University of Pittsburgh (2006); Speaker, "Needs for the Nineties: Growing Professionalization of Security Training and Security Trainers," 16th National Computer Security Conference (1993); Equal Employment Opportunity Counselor, United States Public Health Service; Newsletter Editor, American Society of Access Professionals **Civic:** Chair, History Committee, Neighborhood Community Association, Rochester, NY (2018-Present); Lifelong Learning Advisory Council, University of Rochester (2011-Present); Montgomery County Long-Term Care Ombudsman Program, Maryland (2011); Point Person, Educational Programming for Seniors, Local Church (2004-2011); Election Operations Judge, County Board of Elections (2008-2010); Alumni Council, International Alumni Liaison, University of Pittsburgh Alumni Association (2004-2006); Volunteer Site Excavator, Arlington House, The Robert E. Lee Memorial, Alexandria, VA (1990-1991); Archaeology Consultant, Guest Instructor, Summer Enrichment Program for Gifted and Talented Elementary School Students, Alexandria City Schools, Alexandria, VA (1987-1988); Volunteer, Archaeological Field Teams, Earthwatch Institute, Honduras (1985-1986); Excavation Volunteer, Earthwatch, Nevada (1974); Adult Religious Education Committee and Small Group Discussion Facilitator, Local Unitarian Universalist Church **Creative Works:** Editor, "Personal Steps to a Healthy Choice: A Woman's Guide" (2000); Editor, "Identification of At-Risk Drinking and Intervention with Women of Child-Bearing Age: A Guide for Primary Care Providers," National Institutes of Health (1999); Editor, "Identification and Care of Fetal Alcohol-Exposed Children: A Guide for Primary Care Providers," National Institutes of Health (1999); Author, "A Management Model for the Implementation of Omnibus Legislation: A Case Study from the United States Public Health Service," Public Administration Review (1978) **Awards:** Volunteer Service Award, Commencement Speaker, Graduate School of Public and International Affairs, University of Pittsburgh (2006); Equal Employment Opportunity Special Achievement Award, National Institute on Alcohol Abuse and Alcoholism (1998); Educator of the Year, Federal Information Systems Security Educators' Association (1997); Federal 100 Award, Federal Computer Week Magazine (1995); Exemplary Service Award, Assistant Secretary for Health (1994) **Membership:** Career Workshop Panelist, University of Pittsburgh Alumni Association (2008); Leadership Council, University of Pittsburgh Alumni Association (2004-2006); Diversity Council, National Institutes of Health (1999-2002); Phi Beta Kappa Society; Mensa International Limited; Founding Member, President, Federal Information Systems Security Educators' Association; Executive Board Member, Federal Computer Security Program Managers Forum; Professional Standards and Ethics Committee, American Society for Public Administration **Marquis Who's Who Honors:** Albert Nelson Marquis Lifetime Achievement Award (2017) **Political Affiliations:** Democrat **Religion:** Unitarian Universalism **Shipping Address:** 16 Boulevard Parkway, Rochester, NY, 14612

Michael Thomas Dealy

Title: Headmaster **Industry:** Education/Educational Services **Company Name:** Bayridge Preparatory School **Date of Birth:** 03/27/1949 **Place of Birth:** Brooklyn **State:** NY **Parents:** John Edward Dealy; Marie Agnes Dealy **Education:** PhD in Psychology, Fordham University (1988); MS in School Psychology, Pace University (1978); MA in English Literature, Fordham University (1974); BA in English Literature, Fordham University, Bronx, NY (1970) **Career:** Psychologist, State Education Department (1990-Present); School Psychologist, New York City Board of Education (1978-Present); School Psychologist, State Education Department (1978-Present); Secondary School Teacher, State Education Department (1974-Present); Emergency Medical Technician, State Education Department (1975-1977) **Career Related:** Taekwondo Instructor; Adjunct Professor, Queens College; Adjunct Professor, Fordham University; Adjunct Professor, Pace University; Adjunct Professor, New York University; Headmaster, Bayridge Prep High School **Civic:** Headmaster, World Martial Arts Association, New York, NY (1975-Present); Founder, New York City Medical Reserve Corporation (1999); Instructor, Redeeman Church Montessori School Bayridge Preparatory; Founder, Universal Camping **Creative Works:** Publisher, "Angels in the Snow" (2017); Publisher, "Isabella and The Little Green Lantern" (2013); Author, "Martial Arts Therapy: The Groundbreaking Mix of Psychotherapy and Martial Arts"; Author, Numerous Books on Emotional Intelligence; Contributor, Articles, Professional Journal in Psychology Medicine **Awards:** Numerous Community Service Awards, New York City Board of Education **Membership:** American Psychological Association; International Dyslexia Association **Marquis Who's Who Honors:** Albert Nelson Marquis Lifetime Achievement Award (2017); Distinguished Humanitarian (2017) **Hobbies:** Running; Taekwondo; Music; Forensic psychology; Drama **Religion:** Roman Catholic **Shipping Address:** 7420 Fourth Avenue, Bay Ridge Preparatory School, Brooklyn, NY 11209

Marc Dean

Title: Surgeon **Industry:** Medicine & Health Care **Education:** Fellow, Otorhinology, LSU Health Shreveport, Shreveport, LA (2010-2011); Resident, Otolaryngology/Head & Neck Surgery, LSU Health Shreveport, Shreveport, LA (2006-2010); Internship, General Surgery, LSU Health Shreveport, Shreveport, LA (2005-2006); MD, Texas Tech University Health Science Center (2005); BS in Information in Bio Informatics, Baylor University (2001) **Certifications:** Certified in TORS (2011); Board Certified in Otolaryngology, American Board of Otolaryngology; Licensed Otolaryngologist, State of Texas; Licensed Otolaryngologist, State of Louisiana **Career:** Co-founder, This American Doc, San Jose, CA (2017-Present); Clinical Assistant Professor, Otolaryngology/ HNS, Texas Tech University Health Sciences Center, Lubbock, Texas (2015-Present); Professor, Otolaryngology/HNS, DHSC, Duhok, Iraq (2014-Present); Founder, Vitruvio Institute for Medical Advancement, Dallas, Texas (2013-Present); Chairman, Vitruvio Institute for Medical Advancement, Dallas, Texas (2013-Present); Founding Partner, International Medical Group, Dallas, Texas (2013-Present); Clinical Assistant Professor, Otolaryngology/HNS, LSU Health Shreveport, Shreveport, LA (2012-Present); Partner Otorhinologist, Texas Healthcare PLC, Fort Worth, Texas (2011-Present); Assistant Professor, Otolaryngology/HNS, LSU Health Shreveport, Shreveport, LA (2010-Present); Human Genome Project, Bioinformatics, Washington University in St. Louis (2000-2001) **Career Related:** Member, Medical Advisory Board, Hammes Company (2017-Present); Consultant, MDStart (2017-Present); R&D Consultant, BioInspire (2016-Present); Member, Medical Advisory Board, Employee Direct (2016-Present); R&D Consultant, Acclarent (J&J) (2014-Present); Medical Adviser, VSee (2014-Present); Medical Spokesman, GM Pharmaceuticals (2015-2016); Consultant, Biolase (2015-2016); R&D Consultant, Entellus (2013); Bioinformatics Consultant, St. John Mercy Hospital, St. Louis, MO (2005) **Civic:** Assistant Secretary, International College of Surgeons (2014-Present); Fellowship, International College of Surgeons (2014-Present); FICS Delegate to Young Physician Section, American Medical Association (2012-Present); Co-chair, State of the Art Surgical Symposium, Duhok, Iraq (2014); Chairman, Cancer Committee, LSU Health Shreveport (2012-2013); Director of Telemedicine, Department of Otolaryngology/HNS, LSU Health Shreveport (2012-2013); Vice Chairman, Cancer Committee, LSU Health Shreveport (2011-2012); President, Amarillo Campus Senate, Texas Tech University Health Sciences Center (2004-2005); Vice President, Amarillo Campus School of Medicine, Texas Tech University Health Sciences Center (2004-2005); Vice President, Amarillo Campus Student Body Senate, Texas Tech University Health Sciences Center (2003-2004) **Creative Works:** Author, "The Eustachian Tube Redefined," Otolaryngology Clinics of North American (2016); Author, "Transnasal Endoscopic Eustachian Tube Surgery," Otolaryngology Clinics of North American (2016); Author, "Eustachian Tube Dilation via a Transtympanic Approach in 6 Cadaver Heads: A Feasibility Study," Otolaryngology-Head and Neck Surgery (2016); Author, "Intraoperative Parathyroid Hormone Assay: A Necessary Tool for Multiglandular Disease," Otolaryngology-Head and Neck Surgery (2010); Author, "Intracerebral Metastasis of a Sinonasal Teratocarcinosarcoma: A Case Report," Skull Base (2010) **Awards:** Fellow, American College of Surgeons (2016); Top Ten Medical Doctor, Dallas-Fort Worth (2015); Rising Star, Texas Super Doctors (2015); America's Top Physicians (2014); Rising Star, Texas Super Doctors (2012-2013); Academic Bowl, American Academy of Otolaryngology-Head and Neck Surgery (2007); Honoree, Alpha Omega Alpha Honor Society, Texas Tech University Health Sciences Center (2004-2005) **Membership:** Fellow, Middle-East Academy of Otolaryngology-Head and Neck Surgery (2017-Present); Advisory Task Force, American Medical Association (2016-Present); Endoscopic Ear Surgery Study Group (2016-Present); Fellow, American College of Surgeons (2016-Present); Associate Fellow, American College of Surgeons (2015-Present); Fort Worth Surgical Society (2015-Present); American Rhinological Society (2015-Present); American Telemedicine Association (2014-Present); Eustachian Tube Study Group (2013-Present); Diplomate, American Board of Otolaryngology (2011-Present); Texas Medical Association (2011-Present); Tarrant County Medical Society (2011-Present); Fellow, International College of Surgeons (2010-Present); American Medical Association (2005-Present); Louisiana State Medical Society (2005-Present); Shreveport Medical Society (2005-Present); Cancer Committee, LSU Health Shreveport (2008-2013) **Business Address:** 901 Hemphill St, Fort Worth, TX, 76104 **Shipping Address:** 5639 Greenbriar Dr, Dallas, TX, 75209 **Website:** https://www.youtube.com/watch?v=Zd8kH6IMYkQ

Thomas Seymour Deans

Title: Lawyer **Industry:** Law and Legal Services **Company Name:** Knutson, Flynn & Deans P.A. **Date of Birth:** 03/21/1946 **Place of Birth:** St. Louis **State:** MO **Parents:** Thomas Ellison Deans; Eva May (Seymour) Deans **Marital Status:** Married **Spouse Name:** Barbara Jean Wilson (8/10/1974) **Children:** Katherine; Tyler **Education:** JD, University of Minnesota, Cum Laude (1973); BA, Northwestern University (1968) **Career:** President, Knutson, Flynn & Deans P.A., Mendota Heights, MN (2012-Present); Managing Partner, Knutson, Flynn & Deans P.A., Mendota Heights, MN (2007-2012); Vice President, Knutson, Flynn & Deans P.A., Mendota Heights, MN (1986-2007); Knutson & Flynn; Mendota Heights, MN (1978-1986); Attorney, Peterson, Popovich, Knutson & Flynn (1978-1986); Senate Counsel, Minnesota State Senate, St. Paul, MN (1973-1978); Board of Directors, Knutson, Flynn & Deans P.A., Mendota Heights, MN **Awards:** Associate Leaders Award, Minnesota Association of School Business Official (2014); Super Lawyer (2003) **Membership:** President, Council of School Attorneys, Minnesota School Boards Association (1994-1996); Vice President, Council of School Attorneys, Minnesota School Boards Association (1992-1994); American Bar Association; Minnesota State Bar Association; Dakota County Bar Association; National Association of Bond Lawyers; Council of School Attorneys, National School Boards Association **Bar Admissions:** U.S. District Court, State of Minnesota (1978); State of Minnesota (1973) **Marquis Who's Who Honors:** Albert Nelson Marquis Lifetime Achievement Award (2017) **Religion:** Lutheran **Shipping Address:** 1155 Centre Pointe Drive, Suite 10, Knutson, Flynn & Deans, Mendota Heights, MN, 55120

Ronald Gene DeBock

Title: Real Estate Company Executive **Industry:** Real Estate **Date of Birth:** 09/12/1928 **Place of Birth:** Buckley **State:** WA **Marital Status:** Married **Spouse Name:** Donna J. DeBock (9/24/1949) **Children:** Beverly J. DeBock Satter; Gary; Janice **Education:** PhD, California Graduate School of Theology, Glendale, CA (1979); AA, Tacoma Community College, Washington (1979); MDiv, Western Evangelical Seminary, Portland, OR (1960); BA, Northwest College, Kirkland, WA (1953) **Certifications:** Ordained Minister, Assemblies of God Church (1953-1996) **Career:** Founder, Fireball Publications, Puyallup, WA (1993-2009); Owner, Fireball Publications, Puyallup, WA (1993-2009); Founder, Rainier Rentals (Now Rainier Rentals & Sales), Puyallup, WA (1975-2011); Owner, Rainier Rentals (Now Rainier Rentals & Sales), Puyallup, WA (1975-2011); Director of Public Relations, North West University, Kirkland, WA (1972-1975) **Career Related:** Instructor, American Sign Language Community Educational Opportunity, Orting, WA (1995-1996) **Civic:** Vice President, Romanian Renewal International (1995-1996); Board of Directors, Romanian Renewal International (1993-1996); Active, Aloha Hotel Chapels Ministry, Honolulu, HI (1988-1996); Delegate, Pierce County Republican Convention; Charter Member, Republican Presidential Task Force; Patriotic Program Presenter, Republican Presidential Task Force **Military Service:** Lieutenant Commander, US Naval Reserve (1971); Chaplain, US Naval Reserve (1958-1971); Commissioned Ensign, US Naval Reserve (1957) **Creative Works:** Author, "Practice What You Preached" (1993) **Awards:** Recipient, Paul Harris Award, Rotary (1992); Recipient, Delta Epsilon Chi Award (1975); Named, First Alumnus of the Year, Northwest University (1967); Decorated, Vietnam Cross of Gallantry with Palm **Membership:** Washington Association of Realtors, Inc.; Puyallup Chamber of Commerce; Military Chaplains Association of the United States; Veterans of Foreign Wars; Disabled American Veterans; American Legion **Marquis Who's Who Honors:** Albert Nelson Marquis Lifetime Achievement Award (2017) **Hobbies:** Scrabble; Languages; Real estate investing **Shipping Address:** 422 W Main Ave, Puyallup, WA, 98371

Charles R. Debusk

Title: Vice President of Performance and Process Improvement **Industry:** Health, Wellness and Fitness **Company Name:** Universal Health Services **Date of Birth:** 05/08/1956 **Place of Birth:** Pikeville **Parents:** Charles Malcolm; Margaret DeBusk **Marital Status:** Married **Spouse Name:** Mary Elizabeth Roberts **Children:** Margaret Amelia Monroe; Amy Henderson (Stepchild); James Roberts (Stepchild) **Education:** MS in Industrial Engineering, University of Tennessee (1981-1987); BS in Industrial Engineering, Virginia Polytechnic Institute and State University (1974-1979) **Certifications:** Professional Engineer, State of Tennessee (1984); Certified Lean Six Sigma Master Black Belt GE (2001) **Career:** Vice President of Performance and Process Improvement, Universal Health Services (2007-Present); Master Black Belt, Senior Manager, GE Healthcare, Milwaukee (1991-2007); Corporate Director of Cost Accounting, The Health Central System, Minneapolis (1985-1986); Senior Manager, RSM McGladrey, Minneapolis (1985-1991); Management Systems Consultant, HCA, Nashville (1983-1985) **Career Related:** Instructor, St. Mary's University of Minnesota, Minneapolis, MN (1986-1992) **Membership:** Institute of Industrial Engineering; American Society for Quality; Alpha Pi Mu **Marquis Who's Who Honors:** Albert Nelson Marquis Lifetime Achievement Award (2017); Distinguished Humanitarian (2017) **Business Address:** 367 South Gulph Road, PA, King of Prussia, 19406 **Shipping Address:** PO Box 61558, Universal Health Services, Inc., King of Prussia, PA, 19406

Denise Kay DeGarmo, PhD

Title: Political Scientist, Professor **Industry:** Education/Educational Services **Company Name:** Southern Illinois University, Edwardsville **Date of Birth:** 02/16/1956 **Place of Birth:** Syracuse **State/Country of Origin:** NY **Parents:** Arthur V. DeGarmo; Billie L. DeGarmo **Children:** Carroll Lamar; Casey Johnsen **Education:** PhD in Political Science, University of Michigan (2001); BS, Political Science, University at Buffalo, Summa Cum Laude (1992); AS, Monroe Community College (1990) **Career:** Professor Emeritus (2017); Professor, Department of Political Science, SIUE (2016-Present); Research Associate, The Applied Research Institute - Jerusalem, Israel (2011-Present); Chair, Department of Political Science, SIUE (2009-2015); Associate Professor, Department of Political Science, SIUE (2007-2016); Assistant Professor of Political Science, SIUE (2001-2006); Instructor, University of Michigan (1992-2000); Fellow in Political Science, University of Michigan (1992-2000) **Career Related:** Facilitator, Foreign Policy's Great Decisions Program, SIUE (2001-Present) **Civic:** Active Member, CAN, World Wildlife Fund, Washington, DC (2000-2002); Vice President, Ann Arbor Artisan Association (1996-1998); Commissioner, Market Commission, City of Ann Arbor (1996-1998); Host, Slauson Middle School (1996); Active, Parent-Teacher Organization, Slauson Middle School (1992-1999); President, Activities Club, Monroe Community College (1989-1990); Facilitator, Foreign Policy Association **Creative Works:** Author, "The U.S.-Israeli Strategic Alliance: How the United States is Contributing to a 'Disappearing' Palestine," Open Journal of Political Science (2016); Author, "The Geneva Conventions of 1949 and Their Protocols: The Case of Israel," Lap Lambert Academic Press (2016); Contributor, "Liberation Hip-Hop: Palestinian Hip-Hop and Peaceful Resistance," The Organic Globalizer: Hip Hop, Political Development, and Movement Culture (2014); Author, "Approaching Democracy, Sixth Edition," Pearson (2012); Author, "Abode of Peace?" Center for Conflict Studies (2011); Author, "World Conflicts Since 1900," Excelsior College (2010); Author, "Approaching Democracy, Sixth Edition," Pearson (2009); Author, "MyPoliSciLab," Pearson (2009); Author, "Understanding American Politics and Government Instructor's Manual and Study Guide," Pearson (2008); Author, "Fermi and Pooh: A Strange Mix," Japanese Journal of Physics (2007); Author, "The U.S.-Israeli Strategic Alliance and the Disappearing Palestine" Lap Lambert Academic Press (2006); Author, "Fermi and Pooh: A Strange Mix," Physics Today (2006); Author, 'Conscientious Objection,' An Encyclopedia of Civil Rights and Liberties, Greenwood Press (2006); Author, 'Environmental Justice,' An Encyclopedia of Civil Rights and Liberties, Greenwood Press (2006); Author, 'Border Patrol,' An Encyclopedia of Civil Rights and Liberties, Greenwood Press (2006); Contributor, "2006 APSA Teaching and Learning Conference Track Summary - Internationalizing the Curriculum," PS: Political Science and Politics (2006); Author, "The Disposal of Radioactive Wastes in the Metropolitan St. Louis Area: The Environmental and Health Legacy of Mallinckrodt Chemical Works," Mellen Press (2005); Author, "International Environmental Treaties and State Behavior: Factors Influencing Cooperation," Routledge Press (2004); Author, Conference Proceedings; Author, Book Reviews; Contributor, Articles, Professional Journals **Awards:** Students First Award, Building Just Community, Southern Illinois University (2007); Honoree, Student Organization Adviser of the Year, Southern Illinois University (2004); Honoree, Faculty Member of the Year, Student Advisory Committee, Illinois Board of Higher Education (2002) **Membership:** International Studies Association; Women In International Security; APSA; Pi Sigma Alpha; Phi Theta Kappa; AWID; Bread for the World Institute; Conservation Action Network, World Wildlife Fund; Foreign Policy Association; The Association for Conflict Resolution; National Association of Professional Women; Nuclear Age Peace Foundation; Palestinian American Research Center; PCDN; The Honor Society of Phi Kappa Phi; Southern Political Science Association; World Pulse **Marquis Who's Who Honors:** Albert Nelson Marquis Lifetime Achievement Award (2017) **To what do you attribute your success:** Dr. DeGarmo's success is predicated upon the professors who mentored her throughout her educational pursuits. **Why did you become involved in your profession or industry:** Dr. DeGarmo loves to help others learn. **What do you consider to be the highlight of your career:** Since Dr. DeGarmo has had wonderful opportunities and access to education, her proudest achievements come from student recognition, giving back, and helping students excel. **Where will you be in five years:** In five years, Dr. DeGarmo wants to be doing research and more human rights work, looking at issues of social justice. **Political Affiliations:** Democrat **Shipping Address:** 279 Luis Lane, Debary, FL, 32713

James T. DeGroff

Title: Managing Partner **Industry:** Business Management/Business Services **Company Name:** Formulator Software LLC **Education:** Master's Degree in Research Management, Cornell University (1961) **Career:** Managing Partner, Formulator Software LLC (2004-Present) **Civic:** The Red Mill Museum Village Clinton, NJ; Sierra Club **Creative Works:** Paper Presenter, Seminars and Conferences, Clemson University; Paper Presenter, Seminars and Conferences, The University of Manchester; Paper Presenter, Seminars and Conferences, NC State University; Paper Presenter, Instrument Society of America; Paper Presenter, M.S. Chambers Wall Coverings Conference; Paper Presenter, Canadian Textile Seminar; Paper Presenter, Industry Panels **Awards:** Plaque for Contribution, Global Health & Beauty Conference, Society of Tribologists and Lubrication Engineers (1984-2012); Honoree, The Adhesive and Sealant Council; Honoree, FSCT-Federation of Societies for Coatings Technology; Honoree, Society of Petroleum Engineers; American Association of Textile Chemists and Colorists; The Gravure Association of the Americas, Inc.; Canadian Paint and Coating Association; Canadian Textile Industry Association; ASTM International **Membership:** IFCC **To what do you attribute your success:** Mr. DeGroff attributes his success to understanding his customers' laboratory requirements and multiple fields involved in his work. **Why did you become involved in your profession or industry:** Mr. DeGroff became involved in his profession because he had a chemical background and gradually got into software, first through color software and then through laboratory production when he was working for other people. He decided to start his own company in 1982. **Shipping Address:** 28 Center St Ste 4, Formulator Software, LLC, Clinton, NJ, 08809 **Website:** https://www.linkedin.com/in/james-degroff-4461254/

Dwighd Dubied Delgado

Title: Manufacturing Executive, Business Consultant **Industry:** Business Management/Business Services **Company Name:** Strategic Operations Solutions, LLC **Parents:** Ramon T. Delgado-Murphy; Rosalina (Ortez) Delgado **Marital Status:** Married **Spouse Name:** Laurel Lee Waters (1986) **Children:** Jennifer Leigh (Stepchild); Sarah Noel (Stepchild) **Education:** Master of Engineering Management, The George Washington University (1997); Bachelor of Industrial and Systems Engineering, Georgia Institute of Technology (1977) **Certifications:** Certified Leadership Coach and Trainer, Christian Business Men's Connection (2011); Private Pilot's License with Instrument Rating, Federal Aviation Administration (1998); Certified Quality Engineer, American Society for Quality (1986); Certified Engineer-in-Training, Georgia State Board of Professional Engineers (1977); US Sailing Certified in Basic Keelboat, Basic Cruising, and Bareboat Cruising; DISC Train the Trainer (SEPP6); Lean Facilitator Certification (MWCC); Jack Welch Management Institute Executive Certificates; Malcolm Baldrige National Quality Award Examiner (NIST); Project Management Body of Knowledge (PMI); Danaher Business System Leadership Boot Camp; Quality Function Deployment (QFDI); General Electric Management Development Institute **Career:** Founder, Sole Member, Strategic Operations Solutions, LLC, Gaithersburg MD (2000-Present); Account Manager, Maryland Manufacturing Extension Partnership, Columbia MD (2013-2016); Operations Manager, PremaTech Advanced Ceramics [General Carbide], Worcester MA (2011-2012); Vice President, Manufacturing, Clear Align LLC, Eagleville, PA (2009); Director, Manufacturing, Janos Technology [The Monroe Group, Danaher], Keene NH (2007-2008); Vice President, Operations, NDC Infrared Engineering [Spectris plc], Irwindale CA (2004-2005); Vice President, Operations, Fusion UV Systems [Spectris plc], Gaithersburg MD (2003-2004); Vice President, Manufacturing, Fusion UV Systems [Spectris plc], Gaithersburg MD (2001-2003); Director, Manufacturing, Fusion UV Systems [Spectris plc], Gaithersburg MD (1996-1999); Director, Manufacturing, Fusion UV Systems [Fusion Systems Corporation], Rockville MD (1994-1996); Director, Fabrication, Fusion Systems Corporation, Rockville MD (1991-1994); Technical Leader, GE Lighting Technology Division [General Electric Company], Mattoon IL (1990-1991); Resident Engineering Manager, GE Lighting Technology Division [General Electric Company], Mattoon IL (1987-1990); Senior Project Manager, GE Lighting Technology Division [General Electric Company], Mattoon IL (1987); Manager, New Processes and Equipment Programs, GE Lighting Production Division [General Electric Company], Cleveland OH (1987); Operations Manager, ECOM de Mexico, SA de CV, Ciudad Juarez, Chihuahua, Mexico [General Electric Technical Services Company, GE Ceramics] (1984-1986); Manager, Special Projects, GE Ceramics [General Electric Company], Pepper Pike OH (1984); Manager, Shop Operations, Euclid Lamp Plant, Specialty Division, Lighting Business Group [General Electric Company], Cleveland OH (1981-1984); Production Engineer, Miniature Lamp Engineering, Lighting Business Group [General Electric Company], East Cleveland OH (1979-1981); Specialist in Materials and Production Control, Miniature Lamp Engineering, Lighting Business Group [General Electric Company], East Cleveland OH (1977-1981) **Career Related:** Founding Member, Manufacturing Advancement Center Workforce Innovation Collaborative (MACWIC), Worcester MA (2012); Co-Founder, Strategic Path and Engineering, Inc., Burton OH (2001-2005); President, Strategic Path and Engineering, Inc., Gaithersburg MD (2001-2005); Board of Directors, Strategic Path and Engineering, Inc., Burton OH (2001-2005); President-Elect, AIIE Chapter 007, Cleveland OH (1984-1985); Vice President, Student and External Affairs, AIIE Chapter 007 (1983-1984); Senior Board of Directors, AIIE Chapter 007 (1980-1983) **Creative Works:** Author, "QFD Killed My Pet Project"; Author, "3D Printing Primer: What's the Buzz All About?"; Subject of numerous other published articles **Awards:** Albert Nelson Marquis Lifetime Achievement Award (2017); Citizens Bank & New Hampshire Business Review Award, Janos Technology (2007); Invention Disclosure, Fusion UV Systems (2001) **Membership:** The C12 Group; Mid-Atlantic Angels; IMC Club, Experimental Aircraft Association; Aircraft Owners and Pilots Association; United States Sailing Association; Lifetime Member, United States Chess Federation; Former Member AirLifeLine (Angel Flight); Former Member, Project Management Institute; Former Member, Sports Car Club of America; Former Senior Member, American Society for Quality Control; Former Senior Member, Society of Manufacturing Engineers; Former Member, Institute of Industrial Engineers **Marquis Who's Who Honors:** Albert Nelson Marquis Lifetime Achievement Award (2017) **Shipping Address:** 9443 Hickory View Pl, Gaithersburg, MD, 20886

Nicholas DelRaso, PhD

Title: Branch Technical Advisor **Industry:** Military & Defense Services **Company Name:** U.S. Air Force **Place of Birth:** Boston **State:** MA **Parents:** John DelRaso; Eleanor DelRaso **Children:** Christopher; Carissa; David **Education:** PhD in Biomedical Sciences, Wright State University (2001); MS in Microbiology and Immunology, Wright State University (1987); BA in Zoology, Ohio Wesleyan University (1981); BA in Microbiology, Ohio Wesleyan University (1981) **Career:** Technical Advisor, Molecular Bioeffects Branch, Wright Patterson AFB, OH (2014-Present); Associate Professor, Biomedical Sciences PhD Program, Wright State University, Dayton, OH (2013-Present); Adjunct Professor, Wright State University School of Graduate Studies, Dayton, OH (2008-Present); Research Microbiologist, Molecular Bioeffects Branch, Wright Patterson AFB, OH (1989-2014); Scientist, Toxic Hazards Research Unit, NSI Technology Services Corporation (1986-1989); Microbiological Aide, Universal Energy Systems (1985-1986); Microbiological Aide, Armstrong Medical Research Laboratory, Wright Patterson AFB (1984-1985) **Awards:** Civilian of the Year, U.S. Air Force (2014); Air Force Organizational Excellence Award, U.S. Air Force (2010); Midwest Region Partnership Award, Federal Laboratory Consortium for Technology Transfer, University of Cincinnati (2007); Civilian Employee of the Year, U.S. Air Force (1992); U.S. Air Force Distinguished Service (1984-1990) **Membership:** Ad Hoc Journal Reviewer, Joint Army-Navy-NASA-Air Force Journal of Propulsion and Energetics (2011); Molecular BioSystems (2011); Ad Hoc Journal Reviewer, Environmental Science & Technology (2007); Volunteer Coach, Kettering Youth Football (2004-2012); Ad Hoc Journal Reviewer, Toxicological Sciences (2003); Ad Hoc Journal Reviewer, Toxicology in Vitro (2003); Volunteer Coach, Dayton Youth Soccer (1997-2003); Our Common Heritage, Dayton, OH (1990-1991); Volunteer, Southeast Dayton Days (1990) **To what do you attribute your success:** Dr. DelRaso attributes his success to his family and moral values instilled in him by his parents, dedicated work ethics, and mentorship by his former football coaches, professors, and professional colleagues. **Why did you become involved in your profession or industry:** Dr. DelRaso became involved in his profession because of his love of science and desire to use molecular bioscience research to help service men and women perform their jobs optimally and safely to enhance their mission success. **What do you consider to be the highlight of your career:** A highlight of Dr. DelRaso's career was his research efforts that resulted in peer review publications, book chapters, and a patent concerning in-vitro methods that resulted in reduction of animal use and cost savings in performing toxicological research for the U.S. Air Force. **Where will you be in five years:** In five years, Dr. DelRaso will continue to serve the men and women who protect our country and defend our freedoms by providing the best science to help them perform their missions optimally and safely. He actively seeks opportunities for science and technology collaboration, innovation, and teaming with other U.S. Department of Defense laboratories, industry, and academia. He hopes to eventually move into more managerial role as an integration manager for development of innovative Air Force science technologies. **Hobbies:** Fishing; Hunting; Racquetball; Weightlifting; Canoeing; Hiking; History **Business Address:** 711 HPW/RHDJ, 2728 Q Street, Building 837, Area B, Wright-Patterson AFB, OH, 45433 **Shipping Address:** 421 Judith Drive, Dayton, OH, 45429 **Website:** ndelraso@att.net

John Joseph Deltuvia Jr.

Title: Systems and Operations Analyst, Information Technology Developer **Industry:** Information Technology and Services **Company Name:** Administrative Office of New Jersey Courts **Date of Birth:** 12/09/1962 **Place of Birth:** New Brunswick **State:** NJ **Parents:** John Joseph Deltuvia, Sr.; Margaret Helen Deltuvia **Education:** MS in Computer Information Systems and Information Technology Project Management, Boston University (2012); MA in Professional Studies, Thomas Edison State University, Trenton, NJ (2006); Diploma in Massage Therapy, Body, Mind, & Spirit Learning Alliance, Toms River, NJ (2002); BA in Computer Science, Thomas Edison State University, Trenton, NJ (1991); AAS in Computer Science, Ocean County College, Toms River, NJ (1987); BA in Political Science, Livingston College, Rutgers, The State University of New Jersey (1985); AA in Humanities and Mathematics, Ocean County College, Toms River, NJ (1982) **Certifications:** Licensed Massage Bodywork Therapist, State of New Jersey (2013-Present); Certified Master Reiki Practitioner (2005-Present); Certified Massage Practitioner, Associated Bodywork & Massage Professionals (2002-Present) **Career:** Systems and Operations Analyst, Information Technology Developer, Administrative Office of New Jersey Courts, Trenton, NJ (1999-Present); Programmer Lead, Dezine Healthcare Solutions, Inc., East Brunswick, NJ (1997-1999); Operations Analyst/Programmer, Monmouth County Probation Department, Freehold, NJ (1988-1997); Information Technology Operations Analyst, New Jersey Division of Public Welfare (Now Department of Human Services - Welfare Services), Trenton, NJ (1986-1988); Stand Manager, Six Flags Great Adventure, Jackson, NJ (1985-1987); Host, Six Flags Great Adventure, Jackson, NJ (1979-1985) **Civic:** Webmaster, IEEE New Jersey Coast Section (2018-Present); Media Chair, Board of Directors, SpiralHeart, Inc. (2011-2012); Religious Instructor, Wild Child WitchCamp, Chesterfield, VA (2009); Webmaster, Witchcamp.org (2003-2015); Media Chair, Board of Directors, Spiral-Heart, Inc. (2003-2006); Shop Steward, Local 54 Hotel Employees and Restaurant Employees International Union (1980-1985); Officer, Star Sea Junior Praesidium, Legion of Mary, Howell, NJ (1977-1984); Liturgy Committee Member, St. Veronica Church (Now Church of Saint Veronica) (1977-1983); Parish Organist, St. Veronica Church (Now Church of Saint Veronica), Howell, NJ (1975-1983) **Creative Works:** Author, Thesis, "Preservation of Organizational Knowledge Within a Volunteer Organization: A Contextual Explanation and Practical Example," Thomas Edison State University (2006) **Membership:** IEEE; Technology and Engineering Management Society, IEEE; New Jersey Coast Section, IEEE; Communications Society, IEEE; Technical Communications Society, IEEE; Project Management Institute, Inc.; Association for Transpersonal Psychology; Society for the Social Implications of Technology, IEEE; Associated Bodywork and Massage Professionals; Association of Humanistic Psychology; Association for Computing Machinery; Computer Society, IEEE **Marquis Who's Who Honors:** Albert Nelson Marquis Lifetime Achievement Award (2017) **To what do you attribute your success:** Mr. Deltuvia attributes his success to the way he interprets issues. His operating mode is taking problems, which most people aren't aware of, and looking at them in a completely different way to solve them. **Why did you become involved in your profession or industry:** Mr. Deltuvia became involved in his profession because his father was an MTS at Bell Telephone Laboratories, and at three, he punched his first Hollerith card. He followed in his father's footsteps. **What do you consider to be the highlight of your career:** One of the highlights of Mr. Deltuvia's career is when he developed an application, which aided in work production. The agency where he currently works coordinates enforcement of court-ordered payments on a state wide basis, which is sometimes enforced by arrest warrants. Approximately 25 field offices were manually generating each warrant. He wrote a desktop application for generating these documents, which was installed state wide, with options for each field office and the associated Sheriff's department. The application interfaced with a mainframe system reducing errors and increasing speed. Mr. Deltuvia estimates that the application reduced staff by about 30 people state-wide while increasing accuracy. All documents still have to be reviewed and signed by a judge in accordance with the Constitution, and the standard formatting aided the judges in reviewing the document before signing. **Political Affiliations:** Progressive **Religion:** Witchcraft **Shipping Address:** 1300 Violet Ln, Jackson, NJ, 08527

David B. Dempsey

Title: Founding Partner **Industry:** Law and Legal Services **Company Name:** Dempsey Fontana PLLC **Date of Birth:** 06/26/1949 **Place of Birth:** Washington **State:** DC **Parents:** James Raymon Dempsey; Dolores (Barnes) Dempsey **Marital Status:** Married **Spouse Name:** Elizabeth Carole Harwick Dempsey (10/9/1982) **Children:** Walker Harwick; Carole Elizabeth **Education:** JD, University of South Carolina School of Law (1977); MPA, The University of Tennessee Knoxville (1973); Bachelor's Degree in American Studies (Independent Scholar), Amherst College, Cum Laude (1972) **Career:** Partner, Dempsey Fontana PLLC (2012-Present); Partner, Blank Rome LLP (2011-2012); Partner, Holland & Knight LLP (2001-2010); Partner, Piper & Marbury (Now DLA Piper) (1996-2001); Partner, Akin Gump Strauss Hauer & Feld LLP (1987-1996); Partner, Gardner Carton & Douglas (1986-1987); Partner, Whitney, Dempsey & Greif (1984-1986); Private Practice, Washington, DC (1982-1984); Assistant Counsel, Defense Logistics Agency (1980-1982); Assistant Counsel, Defense Fuel Supply Center, Alexandria, VA (1979-1980); Attorney Advisor, Defense Logistics Agency, Alexandria, VA (1977-1979) **Career Related:** Chair, Operations Committee, Council of Defense & Space Industry Associations (1997-2000); Member, Council of Defense & Space Industry Associations (1994-2009); Member, Federal Advisory Committee, Section 807 Committee on Software and Technical Data Rights, Department of Defense (1992-1995); Chair, DAR Council Subcommittee on Foreign Purchases, DFARS Part 25, Foreign Acquisitions (Principal Author for the Implementation of the NATO MOUs and Trade Agreements Act of 1979 (1978-1980); Project Officer, FAR Part 15 Rewrite, Council of Defense & Space Industry Associations **Creative Works:** Author, "Be Aware: DCAA Audits Likely to Increase," Law360.com, Portfolio Media, Inc. (2013); Author, "So You Want to Get into FedBiz? - A Cautionary Dialogue," Federal Compass (2010); Author, "Liability for Health & Welfare: Cost Increases Experienced by Defined Benefit Plans," Professional Services Council (2005); Author, "Fraud: The 'F Word' in Government Contracting," Service Scope Issue Brief (2005); Author, "Computer Related Exemptions under the Service Contract Act," Boards of Contract Appeals Bar Association, Inc. (2002); Author, "Best Value Proposals Under OMB Circular A-76," Proposal Management (2001); Author, "Contracting Out Under OMB Circular A-76 / Best Value Selection," Outsourcing & Privatization Forum (2000); Author, "The FAR 15 Rewrite-Two Years Later," National Contract Management Association (1999); Author, "The Euro 11: Adopting a Single European Currency," National Contract Management Association (1999); Author, "Statutes & Regulations Governing Allowable Executive Compensation: An Overview," Thomson Reuters (1998); Author, "The Service Contract Act: A Look at Procurement and Labor Issues," National Contract Management Association (1997); Author, "Federal Agency Responsibilities Under the Electronic Freedom of Information Act Amendments of 1996," Thomson Reuters (1997); Author, "Contracting Out Under OMB Circular A-76 in the Department of Defense," National Contract Management Association (1982); Author, "Foreign Procurement Under Memoranda of Understanding and the Trade Agreements Act," ABA (1982) **Awards:** Named, Washington & Baltimore's Top-Rated Lawyers (2018); Listed, Virginia's Top-Rated Lawyers (2018); Named, AV-Preeminent Lawyer (2017-2018); Listed, Virginia's Top-Rated Lawyers (2016); Listed, Washington & Baltimore's Top-Rated Lawyers (2014-2015); Named, Washington & Baltimore's Top-Rated Lawyers (2014-2015); Listed, Virginia's Top-Rated Lawyers (2013); Listed, Top-Rated Lawyers in Technology (2013); Named, AV-Preeminent Lawyer, Martindale-Hubbell (1991-2016) **Bar Admissions:** Virginia (2001); United States Court of Appeals for the Federal Circuit (1982); United States Court of Federal Claims (1981); Supreme Court of the United States (1981); United States Court of Appeals for the Fourth Circuit (1980); United States Court of Appeals for the District of Columbia Circuit (1979); United States District Court for the District of Columbia (1978); Washington, DC (1978); South Carolina (1977); United States Tax Court **Marquis Who's Who Honors:** Albert Nelson Marquis Lifetime Achievement Award (2018); Who's Who in American Law (2015-2016); Who's Who in the World (2015-2016); Who's Who in American Law (2015-2016); Who's Who in America (2012-2018); Who's Who in America (2012-2018); Who's Who in American Law (2001); Who's Who in America (1994-1996); Who's Who in the East (1994); Who's Who in American Law (1993, 1991); Who's Who of Emerging Leaders in America (1987); Who's Who in the World (1986) **Business Address:** 8133 Leesburg Pike, Suite 500, Tysons Corner, VA, 22182 **Shipping Address:** 8509 White Post Ct, Potomac, MD, 20854 **Website:** http://www.deftlaw.com

Scott J. Denardo

Title: Cardiologist **Industry:** Medicine & Health Care **Company Name:** FirstHealth of the Carolinas, Inc. **Date of Birth:** 07/19/1958 **Place of Birth:** Palo Alto **State:** CA **Parents:** B. Pat Denardo; Arlene Denardo **Marital Status:** Married **Spouse Name:** Shirley Ann Cook (1/30/1988) **Children:** Stephanie Arlene; Sophia Dean; Sabrina Lynn **Education:** Fellow, Scripps Clinic and Research Foundation (1992-1993); Fellow, Cardiovascular Diseases, University of California San Francisco (1988-1992); Resident, University of California, Los Angeles (1986-1988); Intern, University of California, Los Angeles (1985-1986); MD, University of California San Francisco (1985); BA in Physics and Applied Mathematics, University of California, Berkeley, With Distinction (1981) **Certifications:** Re-certified, Cardiovascular Diseases, American Board of Internal Medicine (2014); Re-certified, Interventional Cardiology, American Board of Internal Medicine (2009); Re-certified, Cardiovascular Diseases, American Board of Internal Medicine (2004); Diplomate in Interventional Cardiology, American Board of Internal Medicine (1999); Diplomate, Cardiovascular Diseases, American Board of Internal Medicine (1993); Diplomate, American Board of Internal Medicine (1988); Diplomate, National Board of Medical Examiners (1986) **Career:** Staff Invasive/Interventional Cardiologist, FirstHealth of the Carolinas, Inc., Pinehurst, NC (2017-Present); Faculty Level B/Duke Clinical Research Institute, Durham, NC (2010-Present); Associate Professor of Medicine, Duke University Medical Center, Durham, NC (2010-2017); Staff Invasive/Interventional Cardiologist, Southeastern Regional Medical Center, Lumberton, NC (2010-2017); Assistant Professor of Medicine, University of Florida, Gainesville, FL (2007-2010); Director, Cardiac Catheterization Laboratory, North Florida, South Georgia Veterans Affairs, Gainesville, FL (2007-2010); Co-director, Cardiac Catheterization Laboratory, FirstHealth of the Carolinas, Inc., Moore Regional Hospital, Pinehurst, NC (1993-2006) **Creative Works:** Author, "Baseline Hemodynamics and Response to Contrast Media During Diagnostic Cardiac Catheterization Predicts Adverse Events in Heart Failure Patients," Circulation: Heart Failure (2016); Author, "Effects of Verapamil SR and Atenolol on 24 Hour Blood Pressure and Heart Rate in Hypertension Patients with Coronary Artery Disease: an International Verapamil SR-Trandolapril Ambulatory Monitoring Substudy," PLoS One (2015); Author, "Detailed Analysis of Polymer Response to Delivery Balloon Expansion of Drug Eluting Stents Versus Bare Metal Stents," EuroIntervention (2013); "Changes to Polymer Surface of Drug-Eluting Stents During Balloon Expansion," Journal of the American Medical Association (2012); "Effect of Phosphodiesterase Type 5 Inhibition on Coronary Microvascular Dysfunction in Women: A Women's Ischemia Syndrome Evaluation (WISE) Ancillary Study," Clinical Cardiology (2011); "Prior Coronary Revascularization Technique and Outcomes in Hypertensive Patients: an International Verapamil SR-Trandolapril Substudy," American Journal of Cardiology (2010); "Blood Pressure and Outcomes in Very Old Hypertensive Coronary Artery Disease Patients: an International Verapamil SR-Trandolapril (INVEST) Substudy," American Journal of Medicine (2010); "Pulse Wave Analysis of the Aortic Pressure Waveform in Severe Left Ventricular Systolic Dysfunction," Circulation: Heart Failure (2010); "Characteristics and Outcomes of Hypertensive Revascularized Patients in the International Verapamil SR-Trandolapril Study," Hypertension (2009); "Reduced-Dose Enoxaparin in Non-ST Segment Elevation Acute Coronary Syndrome, Followed by Antiplatelet Therapy Alone During Subsequent Percutaneous Coronary Intervention," American Journal of Cardiology (2007); "Elective Percutaneous Coronary Intervention Using Broad-Spectrum Antiplatelet Therapy (Eptifibatide, Clopidogrel, and Aspirin) Alone, without Scheduled Unfractionated Heparin or Other Anti-Thrombin Therapy," American Heart Journal (2005); "Efficacy and Safety of Minimal Dose (1000 Unit) Unfractionated Heparin with Abciximab in Percutaneous Coronary Intervention," American Journal of Cardiology (2003); "Minimal Dose Heparin with Abciximab in Coronary Intervention: Efficacy and Safety of a Novel Heparin Dosing Strategy," Advances in Coronary Artery Disease: Proceedings of the Fourth International Congress on Coronary Artery Disease (2001) **Awards:** Outstanding Teaching Award, University of Florida (2009-2010); UCSF Outstanding Clinical Preceptor Award, University of California, San Francisco (1989) **Business Address:** FirstHealth of Carolinas, Moore Regional Hospital, Pinehurst, NC, 28374 **Shipping Address:** 105 McKenzie Road W, Pinehurst, NC, 28374 **Website:** http://www.scottjdenardomd.com

Cyril Joseph Denn

Title: Financial Advisor (Retired) **Industry:** Financial Services **Date of Birth:** 01/23/1948 **Place of Birth:** Mankato **State/Country of Origin:** MN **Parents:** Bertram Denn; Hildegard (Drummer) Denn **Marital Status:** Divorced **Spouse Name:** Darlene Kay Wittrock (4/19/1974, Divorced 11/2014); Sandra Lee Jones (10/22/1966, Divorced 5/1970) **Children:** Darcy Ann Denn Bormann; Amanda Kay Denn Giuttari; Cassandra (Cassy) Jo Denn Stephanie **Education:** Honorary MBA, Minnesota State University, Mankato, MN (1982); BS in Finance, Political Science, Economics, Mankato State University, Mankato, MN (1977); Diploma, St. Clair High School (1966) **Certifications:** Life Underwriter Training Council Fellow, American College, Bryn Mawr, PA (1993); Chartered Financial Consultant, American College, Bryn Mawr, PA (1985); Chartered Life Underwriter, American College, Bryn Mawr, PA (1982) **Career:** Associate Financial Planner, MetLife Financial Services, Mankato, MN (1997-7/2000); Director, Prudential Financial Services, Aberdeen, SD (1992-1996); Director, Prudential Financial Services, Sioux Falls, SD (1989-1991); S.W. Regional Manager, Catholic Aid Association, St. Paul, MN (1986-1989); Associate Financial Planner, MetLife Financial Services, Sioux Falls, SD (7/1983-11/1986; Branch Manager, MetLife Financial Services, Sioux Falls, SD (7/1983-11/1986); Marketing Specialist, MetLife Financial Services, Aurora, IL (10/1982-7/1983); Financial Advisor, MetLife Financial Services, Mankato, MN (9/1974-10/1982); Factory Laborer, Kato Engineering Co., Mankato, MN (5/1971-9/1974); U.S. Army Security Agency (Military Intelligence) (5/1968-4/1971); Factory Laborer, Kato Engineering Co., Mankato, MN (5/1966-5/1968) **Civic:** Senator Tom Daschle Health Advisory Committee, Aberdeen, SD (1993-1995); Three Person Organization Committee, Diocese of Sioux Falls Foundation (1987-1991); Member, St. Clair Public School Board (1981-1983); Advocate for Veterans, Political, and Social Issues; Supporter, Minnesota State University, Mankato, MN; Supporter, Scholarship, Mayo Clinic Health Systems Foundation, Mankato, MN; Supporter, St. Thomas More Newman Center Campus Building Fund, Minnesota State University, Mankato, MN; Supporter, Minnesota State University Foundation, Mankato, MN; Supporter, Immaculate Conception Church, St. Clair, MN **Military Service:** Top-secret Crypto Clearance, U.S. Army Security Agency (MI) (5/1968-4/1971); Udorn, Thailand (1969-1970); Morse Code, Teletype Intercept, Non-Morse Communications Analyst and NSA "A538 Special Activities Analyst" **Awards:** Career Development Award, General Agency Managers Association (GAMA) (1992-1994); National Recognition "Rose Award" for Providing Broad Life Underwriter Training Council Educational Courses (1992); Regional Sales Manager Award, Catholic Aid Association (1987-1988); Leaders Conference Award, MetLife Financial Services (1975, 1978, 1980, 1985); U.S. Army: National Defense Medal, Vietnam Service Medal, Vietnam Campaign Medal and Expert Badge Rifle M14 **Membership:** AAA (2017-Present); Lifetime Member, Key Cities Conservation Club, Mankato, MN (2017-Present); Lifetime Member, Post 950, VFW, Mankato, MN (2010-Present); Lifetime Member, Chapter 10, Disabled American Veterans, Mankato, MN (2010-Present); National Corvette Museum (2005-Present); Minnesota Valley Corvette Club (2005-Present); AARP Minnesota Volunteer Advocate (2003-Present); AARP National Volunteer Advocate (2003-Present); FarmAmerica (2000-Present); Legislative Advocate, National Alliance for Mental Illness (1996-Present); Greater Mankato Growth Chamber (1996-Present); Lifetime Member, Post 475, The American Legion, St. Clair, MN (1982-Present); Legislative Committee, FarmAmerica (2011-2016); Development Committee, FarmAmerica (2003-2005); Programs Committee, FarmAmerica (2003-2005); Marketing Committee, FarmAmerica (2003-2005); Chairman, Business Development Committee (2000-2001); National Society of Financial Service Professionals; National Association of Insurance and Financial Advisors; National Society of Financial Service Professionals; Lifetime Member, AARP **Marquis Who's Who Honors:** Distinguished Humanitarian (2017); Lifetime Achievement Award (2017) **Hobbies:** Reading; Corvette cruises; Classic car shows; Guns: pistol/ rifle shooting; NASCAR; Rodeo shows, Professional Bull Rider shows; Dancing; Computers **Political Affiliations:** Independent **Religion:** Roman Catholic **Shipping Address:** 117 Cardinal Dr, Mankato, MN, 56001

Grace Dentino-Kelly

Title: Secondary School Educator **Industry:** Education/Educational Services **Date of Birth:** 03/30/1934 **Place of Birth:** Peoria **State:** IL **Parents:** Michael Dentino; Arnita Balagna (Barto) Dentino **Marital Status:** Married **Spouse Name:** Robert N. Kelly (8/31/1957) **Children:** Susan; James; Stephen; Patrick **Education:** MS, Bradley University, Peoria, IL (1973); BS, Bradley University, Peoria, IL (1971) **Certifications:** Certified Medical Technician, St. Francis School of Medical Technology, Peoria, IL (1955) **Career:** Instructor, Jo-Ann Fabrics (2010-2014); Reading Intervention Teacher, Thomas Jefferson School (2007-2010); Lead Teacher, Glen Oak Primary School, Peoria, IL (2002-2006); Principal, Trewyn Middle School, Peoria, IL (1998-2002); Principal, St. Mark School (1992-1998); Principal, Blessed Sacrament School, Morton, IL (1991-1992); Teacher, Biology and Chemistry, Woodruff High School Care Program, Peoria, IL (1989-1990); Principal, St. Thomas School, Peoria Heights, IL (1983-1989); Chairman, Junior High School Curriculum Committee for Drug Education, St. Thomas School, Peoria Heights, IL (1983-1989); Assistant Principal, St. Mark School (1980-1983); Mathematics Curriculum Committee, Trewyn Middle School, Peoria, IL; Teacher, Science, St. Mark School, Peoria, IL **Career Related:** Teacher, Aurora University, Illinois (2002-2010); Education Consultant, Two Rivers Professional Development Center (2002-2010); Presenter, Illinois Math Teacher Convention, Peoria, IL (1992) **Civic:** Board of Directors, Special Persons Encounter Christ (1997) **Creative Works:** Advisory Board, Peoria Journal Star Newspaper (1973-1980) **Awards:** Economics Educator Award, Joint Council on Economic Education, New York, NY (1982-Present); Teacher Who Makes a Difference, Positive Promotions (2006); Positive Promotions First Prize, Midwest Exceptional Teacher Award (2005); Teacher Who Makes a Difference, Positive Promotions (2004); Grantee, National City Bank (2003-2006); Dedication to Excellence in Education and to Justice and Equality Award, National Organization of Women (1998); Outstanding Community Service Award, AAUW (1998); Justice Education Award, AAUW (1998); Jean Tucker Award, Illinois Valley Mental Health Association (1994); Today's Catholic Teachers Project Sharing Award (1992); Administrator of the Year Award, Today's Catholic Teacher Magazine (1992); Those Who Excel Award, Illinois State Board (1989); PARC Award (1989); Esmark Foundation Award Illinois Council Economic Education (1984) **Membership:** AAUW; National Science Teachers Association; American Society of Clinical Pathologists; Director, Region III, Illinois Science Teachers Association; Presenter, Papers, Illinois Science Teachers Association; Director, Region I, Illinois Junior Academy of Science; Peoria Area Retired Teachers; Italian American Society; Mended Hearts; Phi Delta Kappa; BN Sigma Kappa **Marquis Who's Who Honors:** Albert Nelson Marquis Lifetime Achievement Award (2017) **Religion:** Roman Catholic **Shipping Address:** 1815 W High Street, Peoria, IL, 61606

Frederick Derr

Title: Chairman, Chief Executive Officer **Industry:** Architecture & Constrution **Company Name:** Frederick Derr & Co. Inc **Date of Birth:** 07/10/1932 **Place of Birth:** Plainfield **State:** NJ **Parents:** Ferdinand Earl Mueller Derr; Berenice (Yeager) Derr **Marital Status:** Married **Spouse Name:** Teresa Elbare (5/20/1988); Carol Membert (6/7/1957, Divorced 12/1987) **Children:** Elizabeth; Katherine; Charlotte **Education:** MCE, Tulane University (1964); BCE, Rensselaer Polytechnic Institute (1959); BS, U.S. Naval Academy (1957) **Certifications:** Registered Professional Engineer, States of New York, Louisiana, and Florida **Career:** Director, Secretary, Treasurer, Sarasota Military Academy (2002-Present); Chairman, CEO, Frederick Derr & Co., Sarasota, FL (1991-Present); Founder, Director, Shareholder, Flagship National Bank (1999); Executive Vice President, President, Wendel Kent & Co., Inc., Sarasota, FL (1967-1991); Director of Public Works, U.S. Naval Supply Center, Bayonne, NJ (1965-1967) **Career Related:** Director, Quality Aggregates, Sarasota, FL (1983-1999); Director, Gator Asphalt Co., Sarasota, FL (1983-1997) **Civic:** Chairman, La Musica International Music Festival (2013-Present); Chairman Emeritus, Mote Marine Laboratory, Sarasota, FL (2003-Present); Board of Trustees, Mote Marine Laboratory, Sarasota, FL (1982-Present); Chairman, Mote Marine Laboratory, Sarasota, FL (1999-2002); Vice Chairman, Board of Trustees, Mote Marine Laboratory, Sarasota, FL (1998); Director, La Musica International Music Festival, Sarasota, FL (1986-2013) **Military Service:** Lieutenant Commander, U.S. Navy Civil Engineer Corps (1957-1967); Captain, CEC, U.S. Naval Reserve **Awards:** Lifetime Achievement Award, Artist Foundation (2013); Outstanding Technology Achievement Award, Florida Engineering Society (1999); Engineer of the Year, Florida Engineering Society (1989) **Membership:** American Society of Civil Engineers; Society of American Military Engineers **Marquis Who's Who Honors:** Albert Nelson Marquis Lifetime Achievement Award (2017) **Business Address:** 3801 N Orange Avenue, Sarasota, FL, 34234 **Website:** http://www.frederickderrcompany.com

Maria DeSousa

Title: Adjunct Professor **Industry:** Education/ Educational Services **Company Name:** Cornell University **Date of Birth:** 10/17/1939 **Place of Birth:** Lisbon **State/Country of Origin:** Portugal **Parents:** Antonio DeSousa; Odete (Brito) DeSousa **Education:** PhD, Glasgow University (1971); MD, Lisbon University (1963) **Career:** Adjunct Professor, Cornell University Graduate School (1984-Present); Associate Professor, Cornell University Graduate School (1977-1984); Associate Member, Sloan Kettering Institute, New York, NY (1976-1984); Lecturer, Glasgow University (1967-1976); Research Assistant, Gulbenkian Science Institute, Oeiras, Portugal (1966-1967); Research Fellow, Imperial Cancer Research Fund (1964-1966) **Career Related:** President, Abel S. Foundation, New York, NY (1983-Present); Visiting Associate Professor, Harvard University Medical School, Boston, MA (1982-Present); Fellow, Royal College of Pathologists **Creative Works:** Author, "Lymphocyte Circulation" (1981) **Awards:** Portugal National Award, Portuguese Education Ministry **Membership:** President, Portuguese Society of Immunology (1982-Present); Royal College of Pathologists; British Society of Immunology; American Association of Pathologists; American Association of Immunologists; ASIP; AAI; EMBO **Marquis Who's Who Honors:** Distinguished Humanitarian (2017) **Hobbies:** Music; Poetry; Swimming **Shipping Address:** 35 E 85th Street, Apt. 14CN, New York, NY, 10028

Larry A. DeWerd, PhD

Title: Medical Physicist, Professor **Industry:** Medicine & Health Care **Company Name:** University of Wisconsin **Date of Birth:** 07/18/1941 **Place of Birth:** Milwaukee **State:** WI **Parents:** Anthony Lawrence DeWerd; Dorothy M. DeWerd **Marital Status:** Married **Spouse Name:** Veda Mary Anderson (9/14/1963) **Children:** Scott; Mark; Eric **Education:** PhD in Medical Physics, University of Wisconsin (1970); MS in Physics, University of Wisconsin (1965); BS in Mathematics and Physics, University of Wisconsin-Milwaukee (1963) **Career:** Tenured Professor, Medical Physics, University of Wisconsin (2014-Present); Professor, Medical Physics, University of Wisconsin (1997-2014); Clinical Professor, University of Wisconsin (1990-1997); Product Development Manager, Radiation Measurements Inc. (1986-1990); Clinical Associate Professor, University of Wisconsin (1979-1986); Clinical Assistant Professor, University of Wisconsin-Madison (1976-1979); Visiting Assistant Professor, University of Wisconsin-Madison (1975-1976); Research Assistant Professor, University of Washington, Seattle, WA (1972-1975); Research Associate, University of Washington, Seattle, WA (1970-1972) **Career Related:** Vice President, Standard Imaging, Madison, WI (1990-Present); Director, University of Wisconsin Accredited Radiation Calibration Laboratory, Madison, WI (1990-Present); Consultant, Instrumentarium, Milwaukee, WI (1990); Manager, Product Development, Radiation Measurements, Middleton, WI (1986-1990); Director, Radiation Calibration Laboratory, Madison, WI (1983-1986); Presenter in Field; Consultant, International Atomic Energy Agency **Civic:** Science Chairman, American Cancer Society, Wisconsin (1986-1990) **Creative Works:** Contributing Author, "Calibration Importance of Ionizing Radiation for Medical Applications in Radiation Therapy and Diagnostic Radiology," Proceedings of the National Conference of Standards Laboratories Symposium: Metrology, Why Not?!!, Albuquerque, NM (1998); Contributing Author, "Brachytherapy Dosimetric Assessment: Source Calibration, Categorical Course in Brachytherapy Physics Syllabus," RSNA Publications, Oak Brook, IL (1997); Contributing Author, "Entrance Skin Exposure and Mean Glandular Dose: Effect of Scatter and Field Gradient at Mammography" (1997); Contributing Author, "Comparison of Exposure Standards in the Mammography X-Ray Region" (1997); Contributing Author, "Radiation Dosimetry," Encyclopedia of Cancer, Academic Press, San Diego, CA, (1997); Contributing Author, "TLD Measurements of in Vivo Mammographic Exposures and the Calculated Mean Glandular Dose Across the United States" (1996); Contributing Author, "Quality Assurance Testing Service with Radiochromic Film" (1996); Contributing Author, "Calibration Services for Medical Applications of Radiation," Proceedings of the Workshop on Measurement Quality Assurance for Ionizing Radiation, Gaithersburg, MD (1993); Contributing Author, "QA Experience at the University of Wisconsin Accredited Dosimetry Calibration Laboratory," Proceedings of the Workshop on Measurement Quality Assurance for Ionizing Radiation, Gaithersburg, MD (1993); Contributing Author, "Brachytherapy, Ionization Chambers and Dosimetry"; Contributing Author, "Thermoluminescence and Mammography"; Contributor, Numerous Articles and Chapters, Books; Invited Speaker, XVII Course of Radiotherapy, Sao Paulo, Brazil; Author, "Metrology for Medical Physics" **Awards:** Quimby Lifetime Achievement Award, American Association of Physicists in Medicine (2015); Farrington Daniels Award, Best Paper in Medical Physics, American Association of Physicists in Medicine (2014, 2011, 2008); Randall S. Caswell Award, Council on Ionizing Radiation Measurements and Standards (2008); Larry Lanzel Honorary Award, American Association of Physicists in Medicine (2005); Grantee, National Cancer Institute (1994-1998); Grantee, National Cancer Institute (1979-1986); Lifetime Achievement Award, American Association of Physicists in Medicine **Membership:** President, Council on Ionizing Radiation Measurements and Standards (1995-1998); President, Fellow, American Association of Physicists in Medicine (1990-1992); Board of Directors, Sigma Xi (1984-1986); Health PHYSICS Society; Sigma Xi; American Physical Society **Marquis Who's Who Honors:** Albert Nelson Marquis Lifetime Achievement Award (2017) **Why did you become involved in your profession or industry:** He became involved in his profession because entered into medical physics in graduate school and found his passion in that field. **What do you consider to be the highlight of your career:** It's been fun all the way along. **Hobbies:** Golf; Fishing; Hunting; Backpacking **Business Address:** 1111 Highland Ave, B1002 WIMR, Madison, WI, 53705 **Shipping Address:** 13 Pilgrim Cir, Madison, WI, 53711 **Website:** http://www.larrydewerd.com

Joseph Alphonse Di Palma

Title: Investment Company Executive, Lawyer, Producer **Industry:** Financial Services **Company Name:** Di Palma Family Holdings **Date of Birth:** 01/17/1931 **Place of Birth:** New York **State:** NY **Parents:** Gaetano Di Palma; Michela May (Ambrosio) Di Palma **Marital Status:** Married **Spouse Name:** Joycelyn Ann Engle (4/18/1970) **Children:** Joycelyn Joan; Julianne Michelle **Education:** LLM in Taxation, New York University (1959); JD, Fordham University (1958); BA, Columbia University (1952) **Career:** Investor, Executive Director, Di Palma Family Holdings, Las Vegas, NV and New York, NY (1987-Present); Private Practice Law, New York, NY (1974-1987); Vice President, Tax Department, Trans World Airlines, New York, NY (1964-1974); Tax Attorney, CBS Interactive Inc., New York, NY (1960-1964) **Career Related:** Head, Study Group, Comprehensive Gaming Study, New York, NY and Washington, DC (1990-Present); Founder, Executive Director, Think Tank, The Di Palma Position Papers; Founder, The Di Palma Forum, UNLV; Founder, The Di Palma Center for the Study of Jewelry and Precious Metals, Cooper Hewitt Smithsonian Design Museum, New York, NY; Consultant in Field **Civic:** Chairman, Taxation Committee, Air Transport Association (1974); Board of Directors, Outdoor Cleanliness Association, New York, NY (1961-1965); Board of Directors, Friends of the Henry Street Settlement, New York, NY (1961-1963) **Military Service:** U.S. Army (1953-1954) **Creative Works:** Executive Producer, "Awakened" (2013); Executive Producer, "Shannon's Rainbow" (2009); Contributor, Articles, Professional Journals; Author, Weekly Column, Las Vegas Sun; Author, Tax and Legal Articles, Various Magazines and Publications **Awards:** Public Spirit Award, WNET/Channel 13 (2002); Tiffany Smithsonian Benefactors Circle Award (2001); Special Commendation, UNLV (1999); Special Commendation, New York City Mayor Rudolph Giuliani (1997); Distinguished Service and Valuable Counsel Commendation Award, Air Transport Association (1974) **Membership:** The International Platform Association; New York State Bar Association; New York Athletic Club **Bar Admissions:** State of New York (1959) **Marquis Who's Who Honors:** Albert Nelson Marquis Lifetime Achievement Award (2017) **Religion:** Roman Catholic **Shipping Address:** 930 5th Avenue, Apt. 4H, New York, NY, 10021

Stephen Earle Michael Diamond

Title: Investor, Consultant, Author, Inventor **Industry:** Consulting **Company Name:** The Dover Rd. Inn Group **Date of Birth:** 12/02/1944 **Place of Birth:** San Francisco **State/Country of Origin:** CA **Parents:** Earl Conrad Diamond; Sally (Gonzales) Diamond **Marital Status:** Single **Education:** Honorary LLD, London Institute of Applied Research (1996); Honorary DMS in Medical Science, London Institute of Applied Research (1995); Honorary PhD in Psychology, World Academy Association, Munich, Germany (1994); Continuing Education Coursework in Psychology, Stanford University (1989); Continuing Education Coursework in Drama, San Francisco State College (1966-1967); Graduate Coursework in Medicine, Fort Sam Houston Army Medical School, San Antonio, TX (1964); Continuing Education Coursework in Psychology, San Antonio College (1963-1964); Continuing Education Coursework in Criminology, San Francisco City College (1962); Private Music and Drama Studies, San Francisco, CA (1959-1967) **Certifications:** Certificate #1964 in Computer Science Programming, Elkins College, National Career Institute, San Francisco, CA (1969) **Career:** Owner, The Dover Rd. Inn Group (1990-Present); Owner, Stephen Earle Diamond Foundations (1990-Present); Owner, Stephen Earle Diamond Foundations (1985-1990); Chief Executive Officer, Global Competencies Inventory, San Francisco, CA (1978-1980); Executive Chairman, Gondia Corporation, San Francisco, CA (1976-1978); Owner, Stephen Earle Diamond Foundations, California (1974-1990); Executive Director, Gondia Corporation, San Francisco, CA (1973-1976) **Career Related:** Professor of Neurophysics, Life Fellow, Australian Institute for Coordinated Research (1994); Diagnostic Consultant, American Heart Association in Texas (1976); President, Olympic Touring Society, Sport Car Rally Club, Bay Area, California (1965); President, Junior Achievement Bay Area Corporation, San Francisco, CA (1961); Pharmacology Advisory Consultant, Purdue University; Law Advisory Consultant, Yale University, New Haven, CT; Economy-Business Standards Consultant, Harvard University, Boston, MA **Civic:** Smithsonian Air and Space National Museum (2004-Present); American Air Museum, Duxbury, England (1994-Present); Physician's National Advisory Board (1994-Present); Charter Member, Citizens Against Government Waste (1991-Present); Founding Charter Member, Normandy D-Day Museum, Caen, France (1990-Present); California Leader, Fifth-12th Congress Districts, Strategic Defense Initiative, Washington, DC (1989-Present); Honorary Charter Member, St. Mary's Hospital, San Francisco, CA (1988-Present); Charter Founder, Ronald Reagan Republican Center, Washington, DC (1987-Present); Challenger Space Center (1987-Present); Founding Member, American Space Frontier Committee, Falls Church, VA (1984-Present); Sponsor, Producer, Concerned Women for America (1984-Present); Active Member, American Institute for Cancer Research (1981-Present); Friend, San Francisco Symphony Orchestra (1980-Present); Team Leader, GOP (2004-2012); WWII Monument Memorial (2003); National Governor Board, United States Olympic Committee Shooting Team (1994); World Planning Council, WWII Victory 50th Anniversary Events (1992-1995); Chairman, Strategic Defense Initiative, High Frontier Defense Committee, United States Fifth-12th Congress Districts, West Region, California (1989-1995) **Military Service:** High Frontier Defense Committee West Chairman (1991-1996); Strategic Defense Initiative (1979-1992); U.S. Army (1962-1968) **Creative Works:** Author, "Architecture Engineering" (1976-Present); Online Miniseries, "The Epic Genealogy" (2007-2018); Co-Producer, Principal Narrator, Television Miniseries, "The Epic Genealogy" (1997); Associate Producer, National Empowerment Television (1992); Author, "Treatise on D.N.A./R.N.A.: Twenty Six Thousand Sequential Corporeal Movements" (1984-2018); Author, "Treatise on Cures and Treatments by Nationality," 70 Volumes (1971-1984); Artist, "Sixty Colors - Five Shapes" (1971-1976); Originator, Orator, Writer, "The Actual Human Vocabulary" (1970-2017); Author, "Beyond" (1970-2017); "The Evolution of Music in C"; Songwriter, "Here We Are," "Deed Dreams," "I Fly," "From Ashes to Dust"; Composer, "The Evolution of Music," "La Bala Du We," "AgathaDaemon," "Duisburg Somer," "Rurik (Ruthelois Byzantium)" **Awards:** Regent, North California San Francisco Chapter, National Society of Magna Carta Dames and Barons (2017); Nominee, Sovereign Colonial Society of Americans of Royal Descent (2016); Best Poet of 2,000 Poets (2003-2005); Golden Web Award (2001-2002); Poet of the Millennium (1999-2000); Baron, Somerset Charter, Magna Carta Society (1997); Knight Grand Cross, Order of Saints Peter and Paul (1996); Knights of Templar, STMOJ (1996); Captain, Legion De L'Aigle De Le Mer, The Netherlands (1995) **Membership:** Plantagenet Society (2017) **Political Affiliations:** Republican **Religion:** Roman Catholic **Shipping Address:** 439 Ala Wai Boulevard, Condominium 109, South Lake Tahoe, CA, 96150

Joe Gene Robert Dickhudt

Title: Electrical Engineer and Professor **Industry:** Education/Educational Services **Company Name:** McPherson College **Date of Birth:** 05/27/1944 **Place of Birth:** St. Paul **State:** MN **Parents:** John Rodney Dickhudt; Margaret Colleen Dickhudt **Children:** Beverly Ann MacKenzie; Kenneth Robert **Education:** AS in Auto Restoration, McPherson College, Kansas (2006); MBA, College of William & Mary, Williamsburg, VA (1991); BEE, California State Polytechnic University, Pomona, CA (1968); Engineering and Military Coursework, U.S. Military Academy, West Point, NY (1962-1964) **Certifications:** First Class Commercial Radio Telephone License, Federal Communications Commission (1976); Advanced and Extra Class Amateur License; Sport Pilot Private Aviation License; Certified Paraglider and Powered Parachute Ultra-Light Pilot; Certified, Open-Water SCUBA Diving, NAUI; Certified, Open-Water SCUBA Diving, PADI **Career:** Professor, McPherson College (2005-Present); Vice President, SI International, Colorado Springs, CO (2000-2004); Vice President, Computer Sciences Corporation, Falls Church, VA (1992-2000); Vice President, ROW Sciences, Rockville, MD (1990-1992); Director of Engineering, Computer Sciences Corporation, Santa Maria, CA (1981-1990); Engineering Project Manager, Systems Development Corporation, San Jose, CA (1971-1981); Lead Engineer, NASA General Electric (1965-1970) **Career Related:** Advisor, Technology Training, Colorado Springs, CO (2001-2003); Advisor, Leadership Training, Falls Church, VA (1992-1996); Owner, Classic Auto Electric, LLC; Principal, Classic Auto Electric, LLC **Civic:** Board of Directors, McPherson County Humane Society (2007); Guest Speaker/Lecturer, McPherson County Museum; Guest Speaker/Lecturer, Kiwanis; Guest Speaker/Lecturer, Rotary; Guest Speaker/Lecturer, McPherson Cedars **Awards:** Professor of the Year, McPherson College (2014); Inventions Award, National Aeronautics and Space Administration (1997); Federal Leadership Award (1992) **Membership:** The Humane Society of the United States; Society of Automotive Historians; SPCA; Ford Model Restorer Club; American Motorcycle Association; International Radio Museum; Ford Early V-8 Foundation; Beta Gamma Sigma; Experimental Aircraft Association; Aircraft Owners and Pilots Association; Harley-Davidson Owners Group **Marquis Who's Who Honors:** Albert Nelson Marquis Lifetime Achievement Award (2017) **To what do you attribute your success:** Mr. Dickhudt attributes his success to hard work, the support of his friends and family, and good fortune. **Why did you become involved in your profession or industry:** Mr. Dickhudt had the good fortune to be involved in the Apollo Lunar program, which inspired him for life. **What do you consider to be the highlight of your career:** Mr. Dickhudt is most proud of being named "Professor of the Year" at McPherson College in 2014. **Where will you be in five years:** In five years, Mr. Dickhudt hopes to still be flying airplanes, riding motorcycles, and restoring old cars. **Hobbies:** Antique and classic auto restoration; Motorcycling; Flying; Scuba diving; Parachuting and gliding; Antique radio restoration; Amateur radio **Shipping Address:** 401 N Carrie Street, McPherson, KS, 67460 **Website:** http://www.joedickhudt.com

Farrokh Avraham Dilmanian, PhD

Title: Professor of Research **Industry:** Education/Educational Services **Company Name:** Stony Brook University **State/Country of Origin:** Iran **Education:** Postdoctoral Research, University of Washington (1980-1983); PhD, Massachusetts Institute of Technology (1980); MSc in Physics, Technion – Israel Institute of Technology (1973); BSc in Physics, Technion – Israel Institute of Technology (1970) **Career:** Professor of Research, Department of Radiology (2014-Present); Professor of Research, Departments of Radiation Oncology and Neurology, Stony Brook Medicine (2013-Present); Employee, Stony Brook Medicine (1987-Present); Employee, Medical Department, Brookhaven National Laboratory, Upton, NY (1986-Present); Scientist, Brookhaven National Laboratory (1992-2011); Visiting Scientist, Nuclear Physics Department, The Weizmann Institute of Science, Rehovot, Israel (1986); Chief Physicist, Nuclear Medicine Division, Elscint Ltd., Haifa, Israel (1983-1986) **Awards:** Patent Award, Long Island Technology Hall of Fame (2008) **Membership:** Medical Advisory Board, Voices Against Brain Cancer (2010); Nuclear Medical and Imaging Sciences Council, IEEE (1996-1997); Radiation Research Society **To what do you attribute your success:** Dr. Dilmanian loves what he is doing and believes physics can contribute to medicine through radiation research. **Shipping Address:** 10 Adams Cmns, Yaphank, NY, 11980 **Website:** https://cancer.stonybrookmedicine.edu/diagnosis-treatment/radiation-oncology/dilmanian

Ann Monroe Dinger

Title: Private Interior Design Consultant **Industry:** Consulting **Date of Birth:** 01/28/1936 **Place of Birth:** Beckley **State:** WV **Parents:** Hoke Jefferson Monroe; Florence Parsons Monroe **Marital Status:** Married **Spouse Name:** Donald Brackett Dinger (8/13/1960) **Children:** Lynn Ann Dinger-Edmonds **Education:** EdB, University of Mary Washington, Fredericksburg, VA (1958); BA in Art, University of Mary Washington, Fredericksburg, VA (1958) **Certifications:** Certified Teacher, Commonwealth of Virginia **Career:** Private Interior Design Consultant, Alexandria, Charlottesville, and Great Falls, VA (1958-2012); Art Teacher, Alexandria City Public Schools (1958-1961) **Career Related:** Scottish Council, Clan Munro USA (1992-Present); President, Clan Munro USA (1992-Present); Advisory Board Member, Clan Munro USA (1992-1996); Director, Clan Munro USA (1988-1992); Hospitality Chairman, Great Falls Friends & Neighbors (1987-1988); Floral Chairman, James Monroe Highland (1982-1986); Chair, District of Columbia Embassy Tour, Alexandria Junior Woman's Club (1967-1968); Docent, Robert E. Lee Boyhood Home (Now Stratford Hall Plantation) (1967-1968); Participant, Activities, The George Washington University **Civic:** Fellowship Committee Chairman, Immanuel Presbyterian Church (1994-1998) **Membership:** Clan Munro USA; Great Falls Historical Society; Great Falls Citizens Association **Marquis Who's Who Honors:** Albert Nelson Marquis Lifetime Achievement Award (2017) **Why did you become involved in your profession or industry:** Ms. Dinger became involved in her profession because she always wanted to be an art teacher. **What do you consider to be the highlight of your career:** Ms. Dinger is most proud of having good friends, and her current home, a Williamsburg reproduction, which she and her husband have owned since 1986. **Hobbies:** Antiques; Gardening; Travel **Political Affiliations:** Republican **Religion:** Presbyterian **Shipping Address:** 9100 Potomac Woods Lane, Great Falls, VA, 22066

Gerald Francis Dionne

Title: Research Physicist, Educator, Consultant **Industry:** Research **Company Name:** Flex Time **Date of Birth:** 02/05/1935 **Place of Birth:** Montreal **State/Country of Origin:** Canada **Parents:** Louis Philip Dionne; Clare Isabel (Flood) Dionne **Marital Status:** Married **Spouse Name:** Claudette Leblanc (6/29/1963) **Children:** Stephen **Education:** PhD in Physics, McGill University, Montreal, Québec, Canada (1964); MS in Physics, Carnegie Mellon University (1959); Bachelor's Degree in Engineering Physics, McGill University, Magna Cum Laude, Montreal, Québec, Canada (1958); BS in Physics, Loyola College, Summa Cum Laude, Université de Montréal, Summa Cum Laude, Montreal, Québec, Canada (1956) **Career:** Research Staff, Lincoln Laboratory, Flex Time (2012-Present); Research Affiliate, Department of Materials Science and Engineering, Massachusetts Institute of Technology (2005-Present); Expert, Services Personnel, Lincoln Laboratory, Massachusetts Institute of Technology, Lexington, MA (1996-2012); Research Staff, Lincoln Laboratory, Massachusetts Institute of Technology, Lexington, MA (1966-1996); Senior Research Associate, Pratt & Whitney Aircraft (Now United Technologies Corporation), North Haven, CT (1964-1966); Research Assistant, Lecturer, McGill University, Montreal, Québec, Canada (1964); Fellow, National Research Council, National Academy of Sciences, Ottawa, Ontario, Canada (1961-1963); Senior Engineer, Sylvania Electric Products, Woburn, MA (1960-1961); Junior Engineer, IBM, Poughkeepsie, NY (1959-1960) **Career Related:** Research Advisor in Field; Consultant in Field **Creative Works:** Author, "Magnetic Oxides" (2009); Contributor, Articles to Scientific Journals; Contributor, Chapters to Books **Membership:** Senior Member, American Physical Society (2003-Present); Lifetime Member & Fellow, IEEE (1994-Present); Materials Research Society; Ordre des ingénieurs du Québec; Sigma Xi, The Scientific Research Honor Society **Marquis Who's Who Honors:** Albert Nelson Marquis Lifetime Achievement Award (2017) **Shipping Address:** 182 High St, Winchester, MA, 01890

Michael P. DiRaimondo

Title: Attorney **Industry:** Law and Legal Services **Company Name:** DiRaimondo & Masi, LLP **Date of Birth:** 06/02/1952 **Place of Birth:** Astoria, New York **Marital Status:** Married **Education:** JD, Antioch University School of Law (1980); MA, Stony Brook University (1976); BA, Stony Brook University (1974) **Career:** Lawyer, DiRaimondo & Masi, PC; Former Trial Attorney, Immigration & Naturalization Service; Former Special Assistant to United States Attorney, United States Attorney's Office for the Eastern District of New York **Awards:** Martindale-Hubbell AV Preeminent Peer Rated (2017); Super Lawyers (2007-2017); Named Best Lawyers in New York (2005-2017) **Bar Admissions:** New York; United States Court of Appeals for the Second Circuit; United States Court of Appeals for the Third Circuit; United States Court of Appeals for the Fifth Circuit; United States Court of Appeals for the Seventh Circuit; United States Court of Appeals for the Ninth Circuit; United States Court of Appeals for the Eleventh Circuit; United States District Court Southern District of New York; United States District Court for the Eastern District of New York **To what do you attribute your success:** Mr. DiRaimondo attributes his success to working seven years for the prior INS. It was great training and hard work. **Why did you become involved in your profession or industry:** He became involved in his profession because immigration is a people business and he loves to help people. **What do you consider to be the highlight of your career:** A highlight of his career is winning cases in the second and third Circuit Courts of Appeals and changing the law with respect to immigration. His biggest win is the case of Husic v. Holder (Second Circuit), changing the law with respect to section 212(h) waivers for lawful permanent resident aliens are now eligible for adjustment of status if they were granted adjustment of status in the U.S. **Business Address:** 120 Broadway, 18th floor, New York, NY, 10271 **Shipping Address:** 120 Broadway, 18th floor, DiRaimondo & Masi, LLP, New York, NY, 10271 **Website:** http://diraimondoandmasi.com

John James D'Luhy

Title: Investment Banker **Industry:** Financial Services **Date of Birth:** 09/18/1933 **Place of Birth:** Passaic **State:** NJ **Parents:** John George D'Luhy; Leonora (Fila) D'Luhy **Marital Status:** Married **Spouse Name:** Gale Rainsford (12/7/1968) **Children:** Amanda; Pamela **Education:** MBA, The Wharton School, University of Pennsylvania (1959); AB in Economics, Trinity College (1955) **Certifications:** Licensed Amateur Radio Operator, K2EXI; Licensed Commercial Pilot (Instrument-Rated) **Career:** Private Investor, Spring Lake, NJ (2002-Present); Financial Advisor, Robert Thomas Securities Division, Raymond James & Associates, Inc., New York City, NY (1990-2002); Dominick & Dominick, Wunderlich Industries, Inc., New York City, NY (1983-1986); Founder, President, United States Oil Company (1973-1983); Director of Money Management and Private Placements, Wood Walker & Co., New York City, NY (1972-1973); Senior Vice President, R.W. Pressprich & Co., New York City, NY (1968-1972); Director of Money Management, Venture Capital Division Partner, R.W. Pressprich & Co., New York City, NY (1968-1972); Associate, Syndicate Department, Investment Management, Investment Banking, Lazard Freres & Co. LLC, New York City, NY (1960-1968); Over-the-Counter Research Department, Merrill Lynch, New York City, NY (1959-1960); Junior Executive Trainee, Merrill Lynch, New York City, NY (1956-1958) **Career Related:** Business Council, Monmouth University, West Long Branch, NJ (1994-1998); Trustee, Collier Services Foundation, Marlboro, NJ (1986-1992); Senior Analyst, New York Society of Security Analysts; Speaker, Entrepreneurship and Economics, Symposium, Germany **Civic:** Trustee, Info-Age Museum, Wall, NJ (2015-Present); Member, Steering Committee, Wharton School Emeritus Society (2009-Present); Trustee, Newport, RI (2001-Present); Honorary Usher, St. Patrick's Catholic Church, New York City, NY (1969-Present); Director, Member, Scholarship Committee (2012-2013); Member, Finance Committee (2012-2013); Member, Investment Committee (2012-2013); Trustee, The Coast Guard Foundation (2011-2013); Trustee, Emeritus, United States Naval War College Foundation (2010); Member, Governance Committee (2008-2010); Chairman, Board of Trustees (2006-2008); Chairman, Finance Committee (2005-2006); Treasurer (2005-2006); Chairman, Audit Committee, Newport, RI (2004-2005); Vice Commander, United States Coast Guard Auxiliary (2003-2004); Member, Finance Committee, Newport, RI (2002-2006); Member, Strategic Planning Committee (2001-2003); First Pilot, Auxiliary Air Arm, United States Coast Guard Auxiliary (2001-2003); Flotilla Air Officer, United States Coast Guard Auxiliary (2001-2003); Member, Capital Campaign Committee (2001-2003); Member, Barbershop Chorus (2000-2005); Member, Business Council, Monmouth University, West Long Branch, NJ (1994-1998); Co-Chairman, Centennial Committee, Spring Lake, NJ (1990-1992); President, Spring Lake Chorus (1990-1992); Trustee, Collier Services Foundation, Marlboro, NJ (1986-1992); Chief Honorary Usher (1975-1976); Member, Friends of Frick Collection, New York City, NY (1970); Founding Member, United States Naval War College Foundation, Newport, RI (1969); Member, Bond Club, New York, NY (1965-1988); Treasurer, Executive Committee, Info-Age Museum Wall, New Jersey; Chorus of the Atlantic **Military Service:** Officer, Candidate School, U.S. Navy (1955) **Awards:** Special Award for Outstanding Service, Naval War College Foundation, Newport, RI (2008); Certificate of Achievement, The Institute of Chartered Financial Analysts; John J. D'Luhy Prize, Naval War College Foundation, Newport, RI **Membership:** Vero Beach Yacht Club, Vero Beach, FL (2017-Present); Blue Hill Troupe, New York City, NY (1965-Present); Senior Analyst, High Net Worth Investors Committee (2000-2002); Career Development Committee, New York Society Security Analysts (2000-2002); Chairman, Rules Committee, Jersey Aero Club (1992); Treasurer, Executive Committee, University Club, New York City, NY (1979-1983); Council, University Club, New York City, NY (1977-1983); Board of Directors, Investment Association of New York (1967); Chairman, Capital and Money Markets Committee, Investment Association of New York; Association for Investment Management and Research; CFA Society of New York; American Radio Relay League; Aircraft Owners and Pilots Association; Experimental Aircraft Association; Spring Lake Bath and Tennis Club; The Penn Club of New York; Clayton Yacht Club, New York **Religion:** Roman Catholic **Shipping Address:** 115 Ludlow Ave, Spring Lake, NJ, 07762

Randell C. Doane

Title: Attorney, Partner **Industry:** Law and Legal Services **Company Name:** Doane & Doane, P.A. **Marital Status:** Married **Spouse Name:** Rebecca Doane **Education:** LLM, University of Miami School of Law (1981); JD, Michigan State University College of Law (1975); BA, Michigan State University (1969) **Certifications:** Certification in Tax Law and Estate Planning, Bar Register of Preeminent Lawyers; Board Certification, Wills, Trusts and Estates, Florida Bar Board of Legal Specialization and Education **Civic:** Boy Scouts of America; Girl Scouts of Southeast Florida **Creative Works:** Co-author, "Death & Taxes: The Complete Guide to Family Inheritance Planning," Ohio University Press (1998); Author, Various Legal Articles **Awards:** Florida Super Lawyers (2010-2018); Award for Dedicated Service, Center for Abused Children (1995) **Membership:** The Florida Bar; Florida Institute of Certified Public Accountants; Past President, Palm Beach Chapter, East Coast Estate Planning Council; Palm Beach Tax Institute; Palm Beach County Estate Planning Council; American Bar Association (ABA); Former Member, Real Estate Tax Problems Committee; Past President, Loval Chapter, American Society of Chartered Life Underwriters **Bar Admissions:** United States Tax Court (1990); The Florida Bar (1981); State Bar of Michigan (1975); United States District Court for the Eastern District of Michigan (1975) **Marquis Who's Who Honors:** Albert Nelson Marquis Lifetime Achievement Award (2017) **Shipping Address:** 2000 PGA Blvd., Suite 4410, North Palm Beach, FL, 33408

Rebecca Doane

Title: Attorney **Industry:** Law and Legal Services **Company Name:** Doane & Doane, P.A. **Education:** JD, University of South Carolina School of Law (1985); BS in Accounting, San Jose State University (1981) **Certifications:** Certified Public Accountant (1988) **Awards:** Undergraduate of the Year (1982); Outstanding Business Student (1981); AV Preeminent Attorney, Martindale-Hubbell **Membership:** American Academy of Attorney-CPAs; Probate and Guardianship Law Committee, The Florida Bar; Florida Institute of CPAs; East Coast Estate Planning Council; Martin County Estate Planning Council; Palm Beach Tax Institute; Palm Beach County Estate Planning Council; Founder, Chairman, Guardianship Education Committee, Palm Beach County Bar Association; Probate Practice Committee, Palm Beach County Bar Association **Bar Admissions:** Florida (1986); Georgia (1985) **Shipping Address:** 2000 Pga Blvd Ste 4410, Doane & Doane, P.A., North Palm Beach, FL, 33408

Dennis W. Dobritt

Title: Assistant Clinical Professor of College Osteopathic Medicine **Industry:** Education/Educational Services **Company Name:** Michigan State University **Date of Birth:** 07/13/1953 **Place of Birth:** Detroit **State:** MI **Education:** Fellow, Providence Hospital, Southfield, MI (1985-1986); Resident Physician, Providence Hospital, Southfield, MI (1983-1985); Intern, Garden City Hospital, Michigan (1981-1982); DO, Philadelphia College of Osteopathic Medicine (1981); BS, Western Michigan University, Magna Cum Laude (1975) **Certifications:** Diplomate, American Board of Pain Medicine; Diplomate in Anesthesiology and Pain Management, American Board of Anesthesiology, National Board of Osteopathic Examiners **Career:** Assistant Clinical Professor of College Osteopathic Medicine, Michigan State University, East Lansing, MI (1987-Present); Attending Physician, Providence Hospital, Southfield, MI (1986-Present); Attending Physician, Botsford Hospital, Farmington Hills, MI (1986-1987); Chief Resident, Providence Hospital, Southfield, MI (1985); Emergency Physician, McPherson Hospital, Howell, MI (1983-1984); Emergency Physician, Garden City Hospital, Michigan (1982-1983) **Career Related:** Director, Pain Management Center (1996-2001); Chief of Pain Medicine, Providence Hospital (1994-1998); Director, Farmbrook Pain Control Center, Southfield, MI (1987-1996); Director, Botsford Center for Pain Control, Farmington Hills, MI (1986-1987) **Civic:** Advisory Committee on Pain and Symptom Management, State of Michigan; Chairman, Subcommittee on Professional Standards for Pain and Symptom Management **Creative Works:** Newsletter Editor, Osteopathic Pain Management News (1987-1988); Guest Editor, Michigan Osteopathic Journal (1987-1988); Contributor, Articles, Professional Journals **Membership:** American Medical Association; International Association for the Study of Pain; American Pain Society; International Anesthesiology Research Society; Executive Director, Michigan Society of Interventional Pain Physicians; American Society Anesthesiologists; American Osteopathic Association **Marquis Who's Who Honors:** Distinguished Humanitarian (2017) **Hobbies:** Computers; Reading; Basketball; Water skiing; Softball **Religion:** Roman Catholic **Shipping Address:** 6989 Locklin, West Bloomfield, MI, 48324

Robert Albertus Dobson III

Title: Lawyer, Executive, Volunteer **Industry:** Law and Legal Services **Date of Birth:** 11/27/1938 **Place of Birth:** Greenville **State:** SC **Parents:** Robert A. Dobson, Jr.; Dorothy (Leonard) Dobson **Marital Status:** Married **Spouse Name:** Elizabeth Cornmesser (09/17/1983); Linda Josephine Bryant (11/18/1956) **Children:** Robert (Deceased); William; Michael (Deceased); Daniel; Jonathan; Laura (Deceased); Andrew; Thomas; Annemarie **Education:** Doctor of Public Service, Limestone College (2002); JD, University South Carolina Law School, Magna Cum Laude (1962); BS in Accounting, University South Carolina, Summa Cum Laude (1960) **Certifications:** CPA (1964); Mentor for Education for Ministry in the Episcopal Church **Career:** Chairman, Board of Commissioners of the South Carolina School for the Deaf and Blind (2011-Present); Partner, Dobson & Dobson, Greenville, SC (1964-1993); Private Practice, Public Accounting, Greenville, SC (1962-1964); Assistant Dean of Students, University of South Carolina (1960-1962) **Career Related:** Trustee, The King's College (2003); Chairman, Board of Trustees, Limestone College (1987-1989); Founder, Dobson Volunteer Service Program, University of South Carolina; Founder, Christian Education and Leadership Program, Limestone College **Civic:** Chairman, South Carolina School for the Deaf and Blind (2011-Present); With, South Carolina School for the Deaf and Blind (2000); Senior Warden, St. Francis Episcopal Church, Greenville, SC; Board Chairman, Dobson Tape Ministry, Homeless Children International, Inc.; Board of Directors, A Child's Haven, Inc.; Chairman, Walker Foundation for the South Carolina School for the Deaf and Blind, Spartanburg, SC; Advisory Board, Salvation Army, Greenville, SC: Chairman, Board of School Ministries, Inc.; Active Member, History's Handful Campus Crusade for Christ; Founder, Supervisor, Dobson Volunteer Service Program, University of South Carolina; Board of Commissioners, South Carolina School for the Deaf and Blind; Board Member, ElderSource Senior Ministries; Board Member, Wisdom in Living Life Ministry, The Salvation Army of Greenville County, SC; Board Member, School Ministries; Board Member, National Released Time Bible Education Program; Founding Board Member, Acting Chairman, Greenville Connect; Board Member, Secretary-treasurer, South Carolina Christian Foundation; State of South Carolina Bipartisan Lottery Impact Study Commission; NCCAA Capital Campaign Steering Committee; United Way Endowment Committee; Alexis de Tocqueville Committee; Advisory Council, The Encouraging Word Ministry; Donor, Science and Religion Initiative, Educational Foundation, University of South Carolina; Vice Chairman, Jesus Video Project of South Carolina; National Board of Directors, Lift Up America; Mission Trips, China, Cambodia, Kenya; Chairman, Brotherhood of St. Andrew at St. Francis; Chairman, Diocesan Assembly of the Brotherhood; Elder, Worship Committee Member, St. Giles Presbyterian Church **Creative Works:** Associate Editor, South Carolina Law Quarterly; Featured, "Secrets of Success," Film Produced by Campus Crusade for Christ; Contributor, Articles to Professional Journals **Awards:** Distinguished National Service Award, National Released Time Bible Education Program (2011); Story of Character Award, University of South Carolina and the Southeastern Conference (2007); Algernon Sydney Sullivan Award for Distinguished Service as Alumnus, University of South Carolina (2005); John G. Tower Distinguished Alumni Award (2000); Stephen Alonzo Jackson Award (1998); Valedictorian, University South Carolina Law School (1962); Valedictorian, University South Carolina (1960); Valedictorian, Greenville Senior High School (1956); Distinguished Service Commendations, Supreme Executive Committee, Kappa Sigma; National Merit Scholarship; Interfraternity Man of the Year award, University of South Carolina **Membership:** John G. Tower Distinguished Alumni Award (2000); Stephen Alonzo Jackson Award (1998); Chairman, Legal Committee, Kappa Sigma (1989-1993); National District Grand Master of the Year (1986); District Grand Master, Kappa Sigma (1971-2002); American Bar Association; South Carolina Bar Association; American Institute of Certified Public Accountants; American Association of Attorneys and Certified Public Accountants; South Carolina Association of Public Accountants; Block C Association; The Group; Circuit Vice President, University of South Carolina Alumni Association; Phi Beta Kappa; President, Kappa Sigma Kappa; District Treasurer, Executive Sertoma Club; Gold Honor Club President, Greenville Club, Sertoma Sunrisers; Officer, Blue Key National Honor Fraternity; Officer, Literary Society; Officer, German Club; Founder, First Chief Justice, Interfraternity Council Tribunal **Bar Admissions:** South Carolina Bar; United States District Court for the Western District of South Carolina **Marquis Who's Who Honors:** Albert Nelson Marquis Lifetime Achievement Award (2017) **Religion:** Follower of Jesus Christ **Shipping Address:** 1207 Pelham Rd, Greenville, SC, 29615

Darlene Mae Dodd

Title: Nurse, Military Officer **Industry:** Military & Defense Services **Date of Birth:** 10/11/1935 **Place of Birth:** Dowagiac **State:** MI **Parents:** Charles B. Dodd; Lila H. Dodd **Education:** Postgraduate Coursework, Southern Oregon University (1987); BS in Psychology and General Studies, Southern Oregon University (1987); Diploma, United States Air Force Air Command and Staff College (1973); Diploma in Nursing, Borgess School of Nursing, Kalamazoo, MI (1957) **Career:** Employee, Bear Creek Corporation, Medford, OR (1986-2004); Clinical Nurse Coordinator, Obstetrics-Gynecology and Pediatric Services, U.S. Air Force Medical Center, Keesler Air Force Base, Biloxi, MS (1976-1979); Clinical Coordinator, Obstetrics-Gynecology, Flight Nurse, U.S. Air Force, Joint Base Elmendorf-Richardson, Anchorage, AK (1973-1976); Staff Nurse, U.S. Air Force Academy, Colorado Springs, CO (1971-1972); Flight Nurse, U.S. Air Force, Yokota Air Base, Japan (1969-1971); Chief Nurse, U.S. Air Force, Da Nang Air Base, Vietnam (1968); Staff Nurse, U.S. Air Force, Seymour Johnson Air Force Base, Goldsboro, NC (1967-1969); Staff Nurse, U.S. Air Force, Cam Ranh Air Base, Vietnam (1966-1967); Flight Nurse, 22nd Aeromedical Evacuation Squadron, Smyrna, TN (1963-1966); Staff Nurse, U.S. Air Force, Selfridge Air National Guard Base, Harrison Township, MI (1962-1963); Staff Nurse, U.S. Air Force, Ladd Air Force Base, Fairbanks, AK (1960-1962); Staff Nurse, U.S. Air Force, Randolph Air Force Base, Universal City, TX (1959-1960) **Military Service:** Lieutenant Colonel, U.S. Air Force (1975); Commissioned Second Lieutenant, U.S. Air Force (1959) **Awards:** Albert Nelson Marquis Lifetime Achievement Award (2017); Decorated Bronze Star **Membership:** DAV; VFW; Lifetime Member, The American Legion; Society of Air Force Nurses; Retired Officers Association (Now Military Officers Association of America); Vietnam Veterans of America; Uniformed Services Disabled Retirees, Vietnam War Commemoration; Air Force Association; Women of the Moose; Psi Chi; The Honor Society of Phi Kappa Phi **Marquis Who's Who Honors:** Albert Nelson Marquis Lifetime Achievement Award (2017) **To what do you attribute your success:** Ms. Dodd attributes her success to working hard and doing a good job. **Why did you become involved in your profession or industry:** Ms. Dodd became involved in her profession because all her life she wanted to be a nurse. **What do you consider to be the highlight of your career:** The highlight of Ms. Dodd's career was her time spent in Vietnam. **Shipping Address:** 712 W 1st St, Phoenix, OR, 97535

Timothy P. Doman

Title: Chairman of the Technology Education Department (Retired) **Industry:** Education/Educational Services **Company Name:** Sharon City School District **Education:** BS in Industrial Education, California University of Pennsylvania; Associate Degree in Agricultural Technology, The Pennsylvania State University; Graduate Coursework, The Pennsylvania State University; Coursework, Ohio Diesel Institute of Technology; Coursework, Community College of Allegheny County **Career:** Township Supervisor, Secretary/Treasurer of Buffalo Township, Washington County, PA (2014-Present); Secretary/Treasurer, Al's Water Services, Washington, PA (2014-Present) **Career Related:** Chairman, Technology Education Department; Court-Appointed Township Supervisor **Civic:** Member at Large, Planning Commission Acts; Temporary Acting Chairman, Planning Commission Acts **Membership:** Sharon Teachers Association; Planning Commission, Buffalo Township; Former Chairman, Anti-Park Committee; Former Chairman, Ordinance Committee; Life Member, Pennsylvania State Education Association; Life Member, National Education Association; Life Member, National Rifle Association of America **Marquis Who's Who Honors:** Albert Nelson Marquis Lifetime Achievement Award (2017); Distinguished Humanitarian (2017) **To what do you attribute your success:** He attributes his success to his ability to remain up-to-date and relate to his students, and his strong work ethic, which ensures the perpetual involvement of his students in their education. **Why did you become involved in your profession or industry:** He became involved in his profession because of his strong desire to help students achieve their career goals. **What do you consider to be the highlight of your career:** The highlight of his career was planning and implementing a $2.5 million-dollar renovation project for the technology education department on time and under budget to provide students with current skills. **Hobbies:** Hunting; Fishing; Bowling; Traveling **Business Address:** 1129 E State Street, 1129 E State Street, PA, Sharon, 16146 **Shipping Address:** 92 Doman Ln, Washington, PA, 15301 **Website:** http://www.sharon.k12.pa.us/site/default.aspx?PageID=1

Sharon (Stange) Domenigoni

Title: Science Educator (Retired), Artist, Writer **Industry:** Sciences **Company Name:** Heron Enterprises **Place of Birth:** Vallejo **State:** CA **Parents:** Edwin Lowry; Thelma Lowry **Marital Status:** Married **Spouse Name:** Donald Domenigoni **Children:** Brian Stange; Karla Sluis **Education:** Master's Degree in Education, University of La Verne (1996); Bachelor's of Science in Biology, University of California (1981); Associate of Science in Biology, Mt. San Jacinto College (1976) **Certifications:** Secondary Teaching Credential, California State University, San Bernardino (1982) **Career:** Founder, Heron Enterprises (2007-Present); Environmental Science Teacher, Mt. San Jacinto College (1989-1990); Science Teacher, San Jacinto Unified School District, California (1982-2007); Substitute Teacher, Hemet Unified School District, California (1979-1982); Biology Lab Assistant, Mt. San Jacinto College, San Jacinto, CA (1973-1982); Teaching Assistant, Kiddie Korners Preschool, Hemet, CA (1972-1974) **Career Related:** President, Mt. San Jacinto College Foundation (2016-2018); Diamond Valley Art Association Public Art Committee (2015-2017); Green Schools Coordinator, San Jacinto Unified School District (2004-2007); Scholarship Chair, Mt. San Jacinto College Foundation (2000-2016); Scholarship Chair, Hemet Valley Art Association, Hemet, CA (2000-2014); Eastern Municipal Bird Tour Leader, San Jacinto, CA (2000-2013); Science Department Chair, North Mountain Middle School, San Jacinto, CA (1999-2007); Science Fair Coordinator, North Mountain Middle School, San Jacinto, CA (1999-2007); Mentor Teacher, San Jacinto Unified School District (1998-2007); Junior Naturalist Teacher, Idyllwild Nature Center, California (1990-2018); Education Chair, San Bernardino Valley Audubon Society (1985-1998); Awards Presenter, Riverside Inland County Science Fair (1985-1998); Bird Tour Leader, San Jacinto Wildlife Area (1985-1998); Cheerleading Adviser, Monte Vista Middle School, San Jacinto, CA (1984-1992); Science Fair Coordinator, Science Department Chair, Monte Vista Middle School, San Jacinto, CA (1982-1999); Science Club Adviser, Monte Vista Middle School, San Jacinto, CA (1982-1999); Scholarship and Sunshine Chair, California Retired Teachers Association, Idyllwild, Diamond Valley Lake, CA; Audubon Christmas Bird Count Compiler, National Audubon Society **Civic:** Friends of the North San Jacinto Valley (1995-2005); Neighborhood Watch, Hemet/San Jacinto (1991-1998); Co-Founder, Valley Youth Task Force and Neighborhood Watch, Hemet/San Jacinto, CA (1991-1993); Friends of the San Jacinto Mountains (1985-2018); Member, National Audubon Society (1980-2018); Hemet/San Jacinto Parent Teacher Association (1973-2005); California Retired Teachers Association; Diamond Valley Art Association; Hemet/San Jacinto Genealogical Society, California Democratic Party; Hemet Valley Art Association **Creative Works:** Author, "The Lemon Lily Fairy"; Author, "The Creature Teacher"; Contributor, Book Readings and Programs, Hemet Library, Idyllwild Library, Idyllwild Lemon Lily Festival, Big Bear Fairy Festival; Author, "History of the San Jacinto Valley," Hemet/San Jacinto Genealogical Society **Awards:** California Senate Service Recognition Award (2013); Eastern Municipal Water District Service Award (2000-2013); Recipient, California Environmental Education Award, State of California (1995); Recipient, Audubon Naturalist Grant, Hemet Valley Women's Club (1995); Honoree, Inland Empire Environmental Educator of the Year, California State University, San Bernardino (1994); We Honor Ours Award, California Teachers Association (1994); We Honor Ours Award, California Teachers Association (1992); Recipient, Environmental Educator of the Year Award, National Audubon Society (1991); Honoree, Outstanding Biology Achievement, Mount San Jacinto College (1976); Recipient, Various Local Best of Show Awards and Ribbons; Recipient, Best of Show Awards, Hemet Valley Art Association; 25-Year Service Recognition Award, San Jacinto Unified School District **Membership:** Vice President, Member Scholarship and Art Committees, Gamma Theta Chapter, Delta Kappa Gamma (1999-Present); San Gorgonio Council Representative, San Jacinto Teachers Association (1983-2005); Idyllwild Christmas Bird Count Compiler, San Bernardino Valley Chapter, National Audubon Society (1980-2005); Living Desert Association (1975-2018); President, Foundation Board of Mt. San Jacinto College; National Science Teachers Association; California Teachers Association; National Education Association; Lifetime Member, Vice President, Mount San Jacinto College Alumni Association; Living Desert Association; National Audubon Society; Education Chair, San Bernardino Valley Chapter, National Audubon Society; Idyllwild Art Association; Diamond Valley Art Association; President, Vice President, Site Representative, San Jacinto Teachers' Association **Shipping Address:** 26637 Chad Ct, Hemet, CA, 92544 **Website:** http://heronenterprises.org

David Donaldson

Title: Consultant in Chemical Pathology (Retired) **Industry:** Sciences **Date of Birth:** 02/13/1936 **Place of Birth:** Birmingham **State/Country of Origin:** England **Parents:** Henry Donaldson; Esther Donaldson **Education:** MB, University of Birmingham (1959); Bachelor of Surgery, University of Birmingham (1959) **Career:** Consultant in Chemical Pathology, BUPA Gatwick Park Hospital, Spire Healthcare Group plc (1984-2006); Consultant in Chemical Pathology, Crawley Hospital, Crawley, Sussex Community NHS Foundation Trust (1970-2001); Consultant in Chemical Pathology, East Surrey Hospital, Redhill, Surrey and Sussex Healthcare NHS Trust (1970-2001); Clinical Director of Pathology, East Surrey Hospital, Redhill, Surrey and Sussex Healthcare NHS Trust (1991-1994); Lecturer, Institute for Neurology, National Hospital for Neurology and Neurosurgery, University College London Hospitals (1964-1970); Honorary Senior Registrar in Chemical Pathology, Institute for Neurology, National Hospital for Neurology and Neurosurgery, University College London Hospitals (1964-1970); Registrar in General Medicine, Victoria Hospital, Keighley, Yorkshire, England (1963-1964); Assistant Resident Medical Officer, General Infirmary, Leeds, England (1961-1962); Registrar in General Medicine, General Infirmary, Leeds, England (1961-1962); Senior House Officer in Clinical Pathology, Queen Elizabeth Hospital, Birmingham, England (1960-1961); House Surgeon, Birmingham Children's Hospital, Birmingham, England (1960); House Physician, Selly Oak Hospital, Birmingham, England (1959-1960) **Career Related:** Lecturer in Clinical Biochemistry, London South Bank University (1997-2011); Chairman, Southwest Thames Chemical Pathology Advisory Group, Southwest Thames Regional Health Authority (1995-2000); Vice Chairman, Medical Sub-Committee, Marie Curie Memorial Foundation (1978-1983); Lecturer in Chemical Pathology **Creative Works:** Author, "Psychiatric Disorders with a Biochemical Basis" (1998); Deputy Honorary Editor, "Journal Royal Society for the Promotion of Health" (1997-2004); Editorial Board Member, "Journal Royal Society for the Promotion of Health" (1997-2004); Co-Author, "Diagnostic Function Tests in Chemical Pathology" (1989); Co-Author, "Essential Diagnostic Tests in Biochemistry and Haematology" (1971); Contributor, Chapters, Books; Contributor, Articles, Professional Journals **Awards:** Five-year Voluntary Long Service Award for Piano Playing, Standen House, National Trust (2017); Mori Felicitation Award, International College of Human Nutrition and Functional Medicine (2002) **Membership:** The Guild of Freemen of the City of London (2002); Chairman, East Surrey Division, BMA (1992-1993); Fellow, The Hunterian Society; Fellow, The Medical Society of London; Life Fellow, International College of Human Nutrition and Functional Medicine; Royal Society of Medicine; Royal Society of Biology; Royal Society for Public Health; Royal Geographical Society; Royal Society of Chemistry; The Royal College of Pathologists; Royal College of Physicians; American Association for the Advancement of Science; The New York Academy of Sciences; British Association for the Advancement of Science (Now British Science Association); HEART UK; American Society for Clinical Pathology; The Association for Clinical Biochemistry and Laboratory Medicine; The Harveian Society of London; Faculty of History, London Division, The Worshipful Society of Apothecaries; Faculty of Philosophy of Medicine and Pharmacy, London Division, The Worshipful Society of Apothecaries **Marquis Who's Who Honors:** Albert Nelson Marquis Lifetime Achievement Award (2017); Distinguished Humanitarian Award (2017) **To what do you attribute your success:** Dr. Donaldson attributes his success to finding an interest in his work, as he believes that everything is interesting if you can find the interest in it. **Why did you become involved in your profession or industry:** Dr. Donaldson became involved in his profession when he went to King Edwards High School and became interested in chemistry. It was a subject that he really liked, and it was a turning point in his life since he knew from that point on that he wanted to go into chemistry, biology, and physics. His passion grew from there. **Hobbies:** Piano; Music; History of medicine **Shipping Address:** 5 Woodfield Way, Redhill, United Kingdom, RH1 2DP **Website:** http://www.david-donaldson.com

Ted A. Donner

Title: Attorney **Industry:** Law and Legal Services **Company Name:** Donner & Company Law Offices LLC **Date of Birth:** 11/22/1960 **Place of Birth:** New York City **State:** NY **Parents:** Robert A. Donner; Barbara (Wood) Donner **Children:** Alexandra Sofia; Samuel Joseph **Education:** JD, Loyola University (1990); BA, Roosevelt University (1987) **Career:** Manager, Donner & Co. Law Offices LLC (2002-Present); Of Counsel, Altheimer & Gray (1994-2000); Associate, Rock, Fusco, Reynolds & Garvey, Chicago, IL (1990-1994); Law Clerk, Corboy & Demetrio (1989-1990); Box Office Manager, The Second City (1978-1988) **Career Related:** Adjunct Professor, Loyola University, Chicago School of Law (1990-Present) **Civic:** President, Dupage County Bar Association; Co-founder, Public Interest in Education Commission, Chicago, IL **Creative Works:** Author, "Jury Selection Strategy & Science" (2000-2015); Author, "Jury Selection Handbook" (1999); Author, "Attorney's Practice Guide to Negotiations" (1995-2015) **Awards:** Lawyer of the Year Award, DuPage County Bar Association (2011); Director's Award, DuPage County Bar Association (2008); Best Oralist, Loyola University, Chicago School of Law (1999); Moot Court Board's Award, Loyola University, Chicago School of Law (1990) **Bar Admissions:** United States District Court for the Central District of Illinois (2009); United States Court of Appeals for the Seventh Circuit (2006); United States District Court for the Eastern District of Wisconsin (2002); Illinois (1990); United States District Court for the Northern District of Illinois (1990); United States District Court for the Central District of Indiana **Marquis Who's Who Honors:** Albert Nelson Marquis Lifetime Achievement Award (2017) **Why did you become involved in your profession or industry:** Mr. Donner always wanted to be a lawyer. His grandfather wanted to go to law school and never did, so his grandmother used to give him Supreme Court biographies to read for Christmas presents. He is the first lawyer in the family. **What do you consider to be the highlight of your career:** As a teacher at Loyola University, Mr. Donner had a few law students who were struggling and close to dropping out. He spent a significant time mentoring them. Two years later, one of them was listed under the "40 Under 40" category in the Chicago Law Bulletin as one of the brightest lawyers in the country. Another proud moment of his was authoring a book on jury selection published by Thomson Reuters, which is widely used and cited in many notable court cases. **Business Address:** 1125 Wheaton Oaks Ct, 1125 Wheaton Oaks Ct, IL, Wheaton, 60187 **Shipping Address:** 284 Spring Ave, Glen Ellyn, IL, 60137

Stephanie Anne Donoghue

Title: Senior Software Engineer (Retired) **Industry:** Information Technology and Services **Date of Birth:** 09/19/1950 **Place of Birth:** Oswego **State:** NY **Year of Passing:** 2018-05-14 **Parents:** Marian Louise (Farrell) Donoghue; James Charles Donoghue **Marital Status:** Divorced **Spouse Name:** Divorced (11/2013); Married (12/1969) **Children:** John Charles Donoghue II; Kelly Anne Donoghue **Education:** Postgraduate Coursework, Azusa Pacific University (1991-1993); Postgraduate Coursework, Western State University College (1988-1989); MA, University Redlands (1987); Postgraduate Coursework, University of California, Irvine, CA (1981-1982); BS in Electronic Technology, Chapman College (1981) **Certifications:** Certified, Biography Institute, Cambridge England for Outstanding People in the 20th Century (1999) **Career:** Freelance Photographer (2015); Lecturer, Speaking Engagements, Author, Conferences, Photographer (2015); Expert, Raytheon Certified Six Sigma (2001-2006); Senior Principal Software Engineer, Raytheon Missile Systems, Tuscon, AZ (1999-2011); Project Engineer, Northrop Corporation, Pico Rivera, CA (1985-1999); Manager, Lockheed Aircraft, Ontario, CA (1979-1985) **Career Related:** Member, Tucson Software Process Improvement Network (2000-Present); Member, Los Angeles Software Improvement Network, University of Southern California (1994-2000); Member, Capability Maturity Model Cooperative Group, Software Engineering Institute, Pittsburgh, PA (1993-1998); Member, Software Improvement Network, University of California, Irvine, CA (1988-2000); Member, Software Council Northrop Corporation, Hawthorne, CA (1987-1997); Consultant, Fontana, CA (1981-2001) Lecturer, Speaking Engagements, Conferences; Author **Civic:** Volunteer, PIMA Council on Ageing (2016-Present); Volunteer, VA Southern Arizona (2013-Present); South Arizona Gender Alliance (2000-Present); Volunteer, Veterans Administration, South Arizona Health System (2013); Volunteer, Full time, Wingspan (2012-2013); Wingspan (2004-2012); Volunteer, Part Time, Wingspan (2001-2012); Volunteer Consultant, Southwest Museum, Los Angeles, CA (1997-2000); Volunteer Consultant, Resource Conservation District, Rancho Cucamonga, CA (1996-2000); Volunteer Consultant, Southwest Anthropological Association, California State University, Los Angeles, CA (1996-1997); Parent to Parent Support Group (1982-1987); Block Parent Association Group (1981-1987); Active Member, PTA (1975-1985); Trainer, Project Visibility **Military Service:** Resigned, U.S. Air Force (1979); Staff Sergeant, U.S. Air Force (1977); Enlisted, U.S. Air Force (1969) **Creative Works:** Author, "Doctor's Guide Treating Transgender Intersex Patients" (2016); Author, "Transgender and Intersex Patience Guide, Understanding Treatment" (2014) **Awards:** The Torch Award, Community Help (2015-Present); Southern Arizona TORCH Award (2016); Named, Outstanding Young Men of America (1983); Tucson Aspiring and Professional Photographers; U.S. Air Force Commendation Medal **Membership:** IEEE Computer Society; IEEE; National Space Society; The New York Academy of Sciences **Hobbies:** Motorcycling; Snorkeling; Photography **Shipping Address:** 93 N Desert Stream Dr, Tucson, AZ, 85745

Ernest Joseph Dossin III

Title: Credit Manager (Retired) **Industry:** Business Management/Business Services **Date of Birth:** 05/24/1941 **Place of Birth:** Detroit **State:** MI **Parents:** Ernest Joseph Dossin; Jean (Dickson) Dossin **Marital Status:** Married **Spouse Name:** Mary Jane Mortimore (7/24/1965) **Children:** Ernest Joseph IV; Tobias Alfred **Education:** Postgraduate Coursework, Walden University (1995-1998); MBA in Finance, Fairleigh Dickinson University (1978); BA in Business, Valparaiso University (1963) **Career:** President, Dossin's Consulting Associates, Plattsburgh, NY (1993-2016); Executive Vice President, Global Collections Inc., Plattsburgh, NY (1985-1993); Vice President, Myers Group, Rouses Point, NY (1979-1992); Corporate Director of Credit, Americana Hotels, New York City, NY (1972-1979); Director of Casinos, Americana Hotels, New York City, NY (1970-1972); Assistant to Chairman, Americana Hotels, New York City, NY (1969); Director Accounting, American Express, Trenton, NJ (1968-1969); Assistant Store Manager, W.T. Grant, Norfolk, VA (1967-1968) **Career Related:** Adjunct Faculty, State University of New York at Plattsburgh (1993-Present); Adjunct Faculty, Community College of Vermont (1993-Present); Guest Lecturer, State University of New York at Plattsburgh (1995); Leader, Seminars in Improving Credit Practices (1985-1991) **Civic:** Corporate Board Member, Champlain Valley Physicians Hospital (1998-Present); Treasurer, New England Synod, Evangelical Lutheran Church of America (1997-Present); Member, Executive Committee, Boy Scouts of America, Clinton County (1994-Present); Board of Directors, Oratorio Society (1996-1998); President, Oratorio Society (1996-1998); Congregational Vice President, Redeemer Lutheran Church, Plattsburgh, NY (1990-1993); Board of Directors, Plattsburgh, NY (1986-1990); Congregational President, Redeemer Lutheran Church, Plattsburgh, NY (1985-1989); Treasurer, Lutheran College, Teaneck, NJ (1975-1979) **Creative Works:** Author, "Strictly Business" (1991) **Membership:** Vice President, Society for the Preservation of Barbershop Quartet Singing (1990-1993); Board of Directors, Management Club of Plattsburgh, NY (1987-1991); Cited, National Association Credit Managers (1985); Cited, National Association Credit Managers (1984); National Association Credit Managers; Executive Member, International Credit Association; Society of Certified Consumer Credit Executives; Plattsburgh Chamber of Commerce **What do you consider to be the highlight of your career:** Mr. Dossin is most proud of being a member of the executive board. **Where will you be in five years:** In five years Mr. Dossin will be enjoying his retirement. **Hobbies:** Boating; Barbershop quartet singing; Football **Political Affiliations:** Republican **Religion:** Lutheran **Shipping Address:** 175 First St S Apt 2801, Saint Petersburg, FL, 33701

Morgan Daniel Dowd

Title: Dean, Political Science Professor **Industry:** Education/Educational Services **Company Name:** State University of New York at Fredonia **Date of Birth:** 02/21/1933 **Place of Birth:** Boston **State:** MA **Parents:** Joseph Francis Dowd; Marion Caroline (Calcari) Dowd **Marital Status:** Married **Spouse Name:** Dianne May Robichaud (8/29/1959) **Children:** Megan Eileen; Sean Morgan; Colin Martin; Blaine Christopher; Roarke Terence **Education:** PhD, University of Massachusetts, Amherst (1964); MA, University of Massachusetts, Amherst (1962); JD, Catholic University of America, Washington, DC (1958); BA, Saint Michael's College, Winooski, VT, Cum Laude (1955) **Career:** Professor Emeritus, State University of New York at Fredonia (1998-Present); Senior Associate, Mendez England & Associates, Bethesda, MD (1998-Present); Distinguished Service Professor, State University of New York at Fredonia (1995-Present); Professor, State University of New York at Fredonia (1976-Present); Joint Professor, Business and Political Science, State University of New York at Fredonia (1984-1998); Dean, Faculty, Natural and Social Sciences, State University of New York at Fredonia (1978-1984); Dean, Graduate Studies and Research, State University of New York at Fredonia (1969-1978); Associate Professor, State University of New York at Fredonia (1967-1976); Assistant Professor, Political Science, State University of New York at Fredonia (1963-1967); Instructor, University of Massachusetts (1960-1961); Instructor, University of Maine (1959-1960) **Career Related:** Consultant, Middle States Commission on Higher Education (1977-Present); Project Director, Grant Division, United States Information Agency, Albania (1995-1996); Project Director, Grant Division, United States Information Agency, Albania (1992-1994); Associate Editor, The Catholic University Law Review (1956-1958) **Civic:** Convocation Speaker, West Chester University (1991); Executive Committee, Regional Member, New York State Commission on the Bicentennial of the United States Constitution (1987); Board of Directors, Committee, Health Systems Agency of Western New York, Inc. (1986-1987) **Creative Works:** Co-Editor, "World Dictionary of Environmental Research Centers," Second Edition (1974); Contributor, Articles, Law Journals (1956-1978) **Awards:** Extraordinary Service to Commission on Higher Education, University of Rochester (1994); President's Medallion Award, West Chester University, Pennsylvania (1991) **Membership:** Seminar on History of Legal and Political Theory, Columbia University; The Torch Club; Delta Epsilon Sigma; Pi Sigma Alpha; Delta Theta Phi; Phi Eta Sigma **Marquis Who's Who Honors:** Albert Nelson Marquis Lifetime Achievement Award (2017) **Political Affiliations:** Democrat **Religion:** Roman Catholic **Shipping Address:** 37 Central Avenue, Fredonia, NY, 14063

David R. Dowell

Title: Genetic Genealogist, Ethicist, Author, Lecturer, Librarian **Industry:** Education/Educational Services **Date of Birth:** 11/14/1942 **Place of Birth:** Trenton **State:** MO **Parents:** Clarence Ray Dowell; Ruth Lucille (Adams) Dowell **Marital Status:** Married **Spouse Name:** Denise Jaye Christie (8/19/1983); Arlene Grace Taylor (Divorced 1983) **Children:** Deborah Ruth; Jonathan Ray **Education:** PhD in Library Sciences, The University of North Carolina at Chapel Hill (1986); MLS in Library Sciences, University of Illinois at Urbana-Champaign (1972); AM in Latin American History, University of Illinois at Urbana-Champaign (1966); BA in History, Oklahoma Baptist University (1964) **Career:** Instructor, Cuesta College (1998-2011); Director of Library and Learning Resources and Distance Education, Cuesta College, San Luis Obispo, CA (1995-2007); Library Director, Assistant Dean, Pasadena City College (1991-1995); Director of Libraries, Illinois Institute of Technology, Chicago, IL (1981-1990); Assistant University Librarian, Duke University, Durham, NC (1975-1981); Head of Library Administrative Services, Iowa State University of Science and Technology (1972-1975); Teacher, Wilson Junior High School, Tulsa, OK (1964-1965) **Career Related:** Lecturer, Osher Lifelong Learning Institute, Vanderbilt University (2014-2015); Chair, Genealogy Committee (2008-2012); Library Support Staff, National Certification (2007-2010); Consultant, Governor's Conference on Libraries and Information Services, Raleigh, NC (1978); Consultant, Biblioteca do Centro Batista, Goiania, Brazil (1978); Consultant, County Commissioner's Library Planning Committee, Durham, NC (1976) **Civic:** Lecturer, Southern California Genealogical Society Jamboree (2012-Present); Visitor, DNA Project, American Council on Education (2012-Present); Board Member-at-Large, Middle Tennessee Genealogical Society (2015-2018); National Advisory Board, Future Libraries Workforce Study (2005-2008); Site Visiting Team Member, Western Association of Schools and Colleges (2000-2007); Board Member, Central Coast Natural History Association (1995-1999); Trustee, Glenwood-Lynwood Public Library District, Illnois (1985-1987); Treasurer, Chicago Academic Library Council (1982-1989); Administrator, Dowell Surname DNA Project, Smothers Tribe; Administrator, DNA Project, Dowell One-Name Study and Haplogroup R1b-S1026 **Military Service:** Captain, US Air Force Office of Special Investigations (1967-1971) **Creative Works:** Author, "NextGen Genealogy: The DNA Connection" (2015); Author, "Crash Course in Genealogy" (2011); Author, "Libraries in the Information Age" (2009); Author, "It's All About Student Learning" (2006); Author, "Libraries in the Information Age" (2002); Author, "Relationship of Sex to Salary in a Female Dominated Profession" (1986); Author, "Arturo Alessandri and the Widening of Political Participation in Chile (1966); Contributor, Articles to Professional Journals **Awards:** Recipient, Lifetime Service Award, Richland Place (2017); Recipient, Leadership Award, EBSCO Community College Learning Resources (2007) **Membership:** Scholarship Task Force, American Library Association (2004-2005); Education Committee, American Library Association (2003-2004); Library of Future Award Jury, American Library Association (2002-2003); Chairman, American Library Association (2002-2003); Awards Committee, American Library Association (2001-2005); Career Pathways Task Force, American Library Association (2000-2002); Professional Development Committee, Association of College & Research Libraries (1997-2001); Institutional Priorities and Faculty Rewards Task Force, Association of College & Research Libraries (1997); Academic Status Committee, Association of College & Research Libraries (1993-1997); Chair, Association of College & Research Libraries (1993-1995); Orientation Committee, Library Administration and Management Association (1985-1987); Alternative Finance Task Force, Library Administration and Management Association (1984-1985); Membership Committee and Governmental Affairs Task Force, Library Administration and Management Association (1983-1984); Chairman, Election Committee, American Library Association (1982-1983); Board of Directors, Library Administration and Management Association (1981-1983); Chairman, Library Personnel Advisory Committee, American Library Association (1979-1980); Nominating Committee, Association of College & Research Libraries (1979-1980); Library Technology Assistant Training Committee, Association of College & Research Libraries (1979-1980); Chairman, Professional Ethics Committee, American Library Association (1977-1978); International Society of Genetic Genealogy; National Genealogical Society; New England Historic Genealogical Society; Southern California Genealogical Society; Middle Tennessee Genealogical Society; Association of Professional Genealogists **Marquis Who's Who Honors:** Albert Nelson Marquis Lifetime Achievement Award (2017); Distinguished Humanitarian (2017) **Political Affiliations:** Democrat **Religion:** Baptist **Shipping Address:** 500 Elmington Ave Apt 509, Nashville, TN, 37205

Stephen E. Doyle

Title: Executive Vice President (Retired) **Industry:** Consulting **Company Name:** Clean Energy Systems, Inc. **Marital Status:** Married **Spouse Name:** Rosemary **Children:** Five Children **Education:** Postgraduate Coursework, Aerojet General Corporation, Advanced Management Program (1986); Postgraduate Coursework, Executive Program in Business Strategy, Graduate School of Business, Columbia University (1983); Postgraduate Coursework, National Security Management, Industrial College of the Armed Forces, Fort McNair, Washington D.C. (1968); JD, University of Massachusetts (1965); LLB, Duke University Law (1963); Postgraduate Coursework, Institute of Air and Space Law, McGill University, Montreal, Canada (1963-1965); Intern, Haley, Bader and Potts (1962-1964); BA in English and History, University of Massachusetts, Cum Laude with Departmental Honors (1960) **Career:** Consultant, Advisor, Clean Energy Systems, Inc. (2012-Present); Associate, International Space Services, Inc., McLean, VA (2008-Present); Independent Consultant (2007-Present); Executive Vice President, Clean Energy Systems, Inc. (2004-2012); Vice President, Administration, C2Associates, Phoenix, AZ (2005-2015); President, Board Member, Clean Energy Systems, Inc. (2001-2003); President, Chief Executive Officer, Board Member, Clean Energy Systems, Inc. (1999-2001); Incorporator, Vice President for Administration, Corporate Secretary, Board Member, Clean Energy Systems, Inc. (1996-1999); Director, Senior Manager, Manager, Aerojet-General Corporation (1981-1996); Program Manager, Telecommunication & Information Systems and Space Studies, Office of Technology Assessment, United States Congress, Washington D.C. (1981-1978); Deputy Director, Office of International Affairs, NASA Headquarters, Washington D.C. (1974-1978); Manager for International Organization Affairs, Office of Telecommunication Policy, Executive Office of the President, Washington D.C. (1972-1974); Attorney, International Affairs, Office of Telecommunication Policy, Executive Office of the President, Washington D.C. (1972); Special Assistant to the Director, Office of Telecommunication Policy, Executive Office of the President, Washington D.C. (1970-1971); Foreign Affairs Officer, Office of Telecommunication Policy, Bureau of Economic Affairs, U.S. Department of State, Washington D.C. (1967-1970); Attorney-Advisor, Satellite Communications Branch, International and Satellite Communication Division, Common Carrier Bureau, Federal Communications Commission, Washington D.C. (1965-1967); Associate, Haley, Bader and Potts (1965) **Career Related:** Consultant, SETI Institute, Mountain View, CA, (1991-1992); United Nations Consultant on Disarmament (1990-1993); Delegation Adviser, International Telecommunication Union (1988); Vice Chairman, United States Delegation, International Telecommunication Union (1985); Lecturer, Federal Office of Personnel Management; Lecturer, Visiting Lecturer, Several Colleges and Universities; Speaker, Civic Societies and Professional Organizations **Civic:** Delegate, International Astronautical Federation Observer, Committee on the Peaceful Uses of Outer Space and its Legal Subcommittee, Delegation to the United Nations (1998, 1995, 1991, 1989); Visiting Professor, International and Space Law, University of Western Sydney, Campbelltown, Australia (1998); Visiting Lecturer, Space Law, Space Policy, International Organizations and Policies Involved in Astronautics, Colleges and Universities (1971-1998) **Military Service:** Military Policeman, U.S. Army (1954-1957) **Creative Works:** Editorial Advisory Board, Journal of Telematics and Informatics (1984-1994); Author, Several Books; Author, Numerous Articles, Professional Journals; Author, Articles, Books; Presenter, Conferences and Symposia; Contributor, Chapters, Books **Awards:** Distinguished Service Award, International Institute of Space Law, International Astronautical Federation (1988); Co-winner, National Space Club Goddard Memorial Historical Essay Award (1981) **Membership:** Honorary Director, International Institute of Space Law (2001-Present); History Committee, American Astronautical Society (1990-Present); American Astronautical Society (1964-Present); Elected Fellow, American Astronautical Society (2008); American Institute of Aeronautics and Astronautics (2004-2010, 1966-1994); History Committee Chairman, American Astronautical Society (1996-2000); Director, International Institute of Space Law (1993-2001); Fellow, The British Interplanetary Society (1992-1996); The British Interplanetary Society (1986-1996); Phi Kappa Phi; Institute of Air and Space Law, McGill University; International Academy of Astronautics **Bar Admissions:** The District of Columbia (1964-1996); Supreme Court of the United States (1965-1996) **Business Address:** 3035 Prospect Park Dr, Rancho Cordova, NC, 95670 **Shipping Address:** 141 W Craftsman Way, Hampstead, NC, 28443 **Website:** http://oldinsulators.com/stephenedoyle/

George Albert Drake

Title: Academic Administrator **Industry:** Education/Educational Services **Company Name:** Grinnell College **Date of Birth:** 02/25/1934 **Place of Birth:** Springfield **State:** MO **Parents:** George Bryant Drake; Alberta (Stimson) Drake **Marital Status:** Married **Spouse Name:** Susan Martha Ratcliff (6/25/1960) **Children:** Christopher George; Cynthia May; Melanie Susan **Education:** Honorary LHD, Morningside College (1998); Honorary LHD, Doane University (1995); Honorary LHD, Ursinus College (1988); Honorary LHD, Illinois College (1985); Honorary LLD, Ripon College (1982); Honorary LLD, Colorado College (1980); PhD, University of Chicago (1965); MA, University of Chicago (1963); MA, University of Oxford (1963); BD, University of Chicago (1962); AB, University of Oxford (1959); Coursework, Universite Paris-Sorbonne (1956-1957); AB, Grinnell College (1956) **Career:** President Emeritus, Grinnell College (2006-Present); Professor Emeritus in History, Grinnell College (2004-Present); Professor, Grinnell College (1979-Present); President, Grinnell College (1979-1991); Instructor in History, Grinnell College (1960-1961) **Career Related:** Fellowship, National Endowment of the Humanities (1974); Dean, Colorado College (1969-1973); Acting Dean, Colorado College (1967-1968); Assistant Professor, Colorado College (1964-1979); Associate Professor, Colorado College (1964-1979); Professor in History, Colorado College (1964-1979); Rockefeller Fellowship **Civic:** President, Board of Trustees, Mayflower Homes, Inc. (2014-2017); Chair, FINE Foundation (2003-2005); Board of Directors, FINE Foundation (1998-2005); Commissioner, North Central Association of Colleges and Schools (1998-2001); Chair, Iowa Peace Institute (1996-1999); Trustee, Doane College (1995-2014); Board of Directors, Iowa Peace Institute (1994-2004); Volunteer, Peace Corps (1991-1993); Trustee, Grinnell Regional Medical Center (1980-1986); Trustee, Penrose Hospital (Now Penrose-St. Francis Health Services) (1976-1984); Trustee, Grinnell College (1970-1979) **Creative Works:** Author, "Our War: Stories of Poweshiek County's Greatest Generation"; Author, "No Ordinary Conference"; Author, "Algorithm Percy"; Author, "10th Earl of Northumberland Oxford Dictionary of National Biography"; Contributor, Chapters, Books **Awards:** Fulbright Scholarship (1956-1957); Rhodes Scholarship **Membership:** President of the Commission, National College Athletic Association (1984-1989); American Historical Association; American Society of Church History; National Merit Scholarship Corporation **Marquis Who's Who Honors:** Albert Nelson Marquis Lifetime Achievement Award (2017) **Shipping Address:** 531 May Flower Lane, Grinnell, IA, 50112

Cynthia Drew

Title: Principal **Industry:** Music Industry **Company Name:** EAST 84TH STREET ANALYTIC$ LLC **Date of Birth:** 04/14/1964 **Place of Birth:** Perthamboy **State:** NJ **Parents:** Roger Drew; Ardeth Drew **Marital Status:** Single **Education:** MBA Finance, Adelphi University (1994); BBA Finance, Hofstra University (1987); Pursuing, Professional Certificate Music Supervision, Berklee College of Music **Certifications:** Certified Level 10 USA Gymnastics Judge (2013-2017) **Career:** Financial Planning and Analysis Executive **Civic:** Student Mentor, FWA of New York, Inc. (2006-Present); Treasurer, 119-84 Corps. (2012-2017); President Board of Directors, 119-84 Corps. (2012-2017); Treasurer, National Association of Women's Gymnastics Judges (2014-2017); Community Outreach, Park Avenue United Methodist Church (2002-2017); Youth Advisor, Centerport United Methodist Church (1999-2004) **Awards:** Gold and Silver Medalist, Empire State Games Masters Gymnastics Competition (2001) **Membership:** Grammy Recording Academy (2018-Present); California Copyright Conference (2017-Present); AIMP (2016-Present); Songwriters of North America (2017-Present); NARIP (2017-Present); Financial Women's Association (2005-2017) **To what do you attribute your success:** Cynthia attributes her success to being raised with a very strong work ethic, and being taught to always operate from a place of integrity. She has boundless energy and drive, and a sharp analytical brain. She is also fortunate to have had wonderful mentors, and access to high quality education. **Why did you become involved in your profession or industry:** Ms. Drew has always been passionate about her profession. At the beginning of her career, she earned a Finance MBA and enjoyed many years working in strategic finance analytical roles in Capital Markets. In 2015, she began a major midlife career change. As a lifelong amateur musician and passionate lover of music, and with veteran experience driving P&L improvement in the trading technology space, an operating model remarkably similar to that of recorded music, she enrolled in the Berklee College of Music to pursue a Professional Certificate in Music Supervision, and a Masters Certificate in Music Business. She now has the wonderful opportunity to drive P&L success in the music industry, and to be a part of the solution to ensure an enduring legacy of rich musical creation. **What do you consider to be the highlight of your career:** The highlight of her career was the opportunity to be in a capital markets revenue generating role for the first time, after years in a finance analytical support role. In 2013, she was recruited to a startup electronic trading firm, Pico Quantitative Trading LLC. Two months into her role as the Head of Business Planning and Analysis, she was given the additional responsibility of managing the firm's Market Data business. **Where will you be in five years:** In 5 years, she will be at the heart of driving P&L growth in the recorded music industry, and promoting meaningful compensation and advocacy for music creators. **Hobbies:** Gymnastics; Concerts; Rock music; Political activism **Political Affiliations:** Democrat **Religion:** Methodist **Business Address:** 12504 Woodbridge St. Unit 201, Studio City, CA, 91604 **Website:** http://www.84analytics.com

Malcolm M. Drummond

Title: Electronics Engineer **Industry:** Engineering **Company Name:** ENI/MKS Instruments **Date of Birth:** 09/22/1937 **Place of Birth:** London **State/Country of Origin:** England **Parents:** George James Drummond; Winifred Ethel (Jaye) Drummond **Marital Status:** Married **Spouse Name:** Linda Jerome Banning (5/25/1968) **Children:** Heather Lynn **Education:** BSEE, City, University of London, with Honors **Certifications:** Registered Professional Electrical Engineer **Career:** Project Engineer, ENI/MKS, Emerson (2000-2008); Professor of Electronics, Principia College (2007); Project Engineer, Eastman Kodak Company (2000); Project Engineer, User Friendly Operating Systems, Inc. (1993-2000); Project Engineer, Hampshire Instruments Corporation (1985-1993); Project Engineer, Sybron Corporation, Taylor Precision Products Inc. (1972-1985); Technology Representative, Tymshare Inc. (1970-1972); Senior Engineer, General Dynamics Corporation (1966-1970); Engineer, Foreign & Commonwealth Office (1964-1966) **Career Related:** President, Care & Service Inc. (1986-1989); Director, Care & Service Inc. (1982-1990) **Civic:** President, First Church of Christ, Scientist (2013); First Reader, First Church of Christ, Scientist (2006-2009); Chairman, Board of Trustees, First Church of Christ, Scientist (1993-1994, 1998-1999); Christian Science Minister, Veteran's Affairs Hospital, U.S. Department of Veterans Affairs (1974-1980) **Membership:** Treasurer, Principle Foundation of Western New York (1994-Present); Chairman, American Society for Engineering Management (1990-2003); Ethics Committee, Monroe County Bar Association (1994-1995); Chairman, Application-Specific Integrated Circuit Seminar, IEEE (1987-1988); Chairman, Pension Task Force, IEEE (1983-1984); Vice Chairman, Engineers and Scientists Joint Committee on Pensions (1983-1984); Chairman, Area D, IEEE (1982-1985); Coordinator, Local Region, International Personnel Assessment Council, Inc. (1980-1982); Chairman, Rochester Section, IEEE (1979-1980); Life Senior Member, IEEE; New York State Society of Professional Engineers, Inc.; Former President, Computer Society, IEEE; Instrument Society (Now The International Society of Automation); Director Emeritus, Rochester Engineering Society; American Management Association; IEEE UK and Ireland Section **Marquis Who's Who Honors:** Albert Nelson Marquis Lifetime Achievement Award (2017); Distinguished Humanitarian (2017) **Shipping Address:** 60 Marberth Dr, Henrietta, NY, 14467

Jose Pinto Duarte, PhD

Title: Director **Industry:** Education/Educational Services **Company Name:** The Pennsylvania State University **Date of Birth:** 05/11/1964 **Place of Birth:** Lisboa **State/Country of Origin:** Portugal **Parents:** Jose Sousa Duarte; Delfina Pinto Duarte **Marital Status:** Married **Spouse Name:** Married Maria Rita Castro (5/25/2001); Married Sofia Assoreira Almendra (1/11/1992, Divorced) **Children:** Maria Pinto; Rita Celorico Palma (Stepchild); Joana Celorico Palma (Stepchild); Marta Celorico Palma (Stepchild) **Education:** Habilitation in Architecture, Technical University of Lisbon (Now University of Lisbon) (2008); PhD in Architecture, Design and Computation, Massachusetts Institute of Technology (2001); MS in Architecture Studies and Design Enquiry, Massachusetts Institute of Technology (1993); Licenciatura em Arquitectura, Technical University of Lisbon (Now University of Lisbon) (1987) **Certifications:** Certified Architect, Portuguese Architects Association **Career:** Director, Stuckeman Center for Design Computing, The Pennsylvania State University (2015-Present); Full Professor, Faculty of Architecture, Technical University of Lisbon (Now University of Lisbon) (2010-Present); Researcher, Research Center for Architecture, Urbanism and Design, CIAUD (2013-Present); Visiting Scientist, MIT Design Laboratory, Department of Architecture, Massachusetts Institute of Technology (2009-Present); Assistant Professor, Technical University of Lisbon (Now University of Lisbon) (2002-Present); Visiting Professor, School of Architecture, Technical University of Lisbon (Now University of Lisbon) (2001-Present); Lecturer, Department of Architecture and Civil Engineering, Institute of Superior Technology, Technical University of Lisbon (Now University of Lisbon) (2000-2002); Lecturer, Department of Architecture, Massachusetts Institute of Technology (1999-2000); Teaching Assistant, Department of Architecture, Massachusetts Institute of Technology (1997-1999); Research Assistant, Intelligent Engineering Systems Laboratory (IESL), Department of Civil Engineering, Massachusetts Institute of Technology (1992); Architect, Manuel Tainha Office, Lisbon, Portugal (1988-1991); Architect, Carlos S. Lameiro Office, Lisbon, Portugal (1990) **Career Related:** Member, Education and Research in Computer-Aided Architectural Design in Europe, Brussels, Belgium (2002-Present); Member, Governing Board for Program in Architecture, Council, Technical University of Lisbon (Now University of Lisbon) (2002-Present); Founder, Architecture Research Laboratories, ISTAR-IST (2001-Present); Head, Architecture Research Laboratories, ISTAR-IST (2001-Present); Co-Organizer, Second International Conference on Symbiotic Relationship between Engineering and Architecture, Lisbon, Portugal (2006); Advisor, Unit for Technical Planning, Ministry of Economy and Innovation, 18th Constitutional Government, Lisbon, Portugal (2005-2006); Coordinator, Unit for Technical Planning, Ministry of Economy and Innovation, 18th Constitutional Government, Lisbon, Portugal (2005-2006); Founder, FlexSystems (2004-2006); Chief Executive Officer, FlexSystems (2004-2006); Member, Senate Department of Architecture and Civil Engineering, Institute of Superior Technology, Technical University of Lisbon (Now University of Lisbon) (2003-2005); Coordinator, Architecture Division, Institute of Superior Technology, Technical University of Lisbon (Now University of Lisbon) (2003-2005); Freelance Architect (1990-2004) **Creative Works:** Author, "Customizing Mass Housing: A Discursive Grammar for Siza's Malagueira Houses" (2006); Author, "Type and Module: An Approach to the Housing Production Process" (1995) **Awards:** REcipient, Second Prize, Mars 3D-Printed Habitat Challenge, National Aeronautics and Space Administration (2017); First Prize, Scientific Award, Field of Architecture, Technical University of Lisbon (Now University of Lisbon) (2008); Honorable Mention, Scientific Award, Field of Architecture, Technical University of Lisbon (Now University of Lisbon) (2007); Best Paper Award, CAAD Futures Foundation Conference, Sydney, Australia (2007); Best PhD Thesis Publication Award, Competition for the Publication of Scientific Texts, Calouste Gulbenkian Foundation, Portugal (2004); Best PhD Thesis Publication Award, Competition for the Publication of Scientific Texts, The Foundation for Science and Technology, Portugal (2004); Named PhD Scholar, PRAXIS XXI Program, Foundation for Science and Technology, Lisbon, Portugal (1996-2000) **Membership:** Architecture Schools Accreditation Board, Portuguese Architects Association (2004-2005); Association for Promotion and Development of Information Society **Marquis Who's Who Honors:** Albert Nelson Marquis Lifetime Achievement Award (2017) **Business Address:** 121 Stuckeman Family Building, University Park, PA, 16802 **Website:** https://stuckeman.psu.edu/sites/default/files/facultycontent/jpduarte_resume_feb.pdf

Jimy Dudhia

Title: Research Scientist **Industry:** Research **Company Name:** National Center for Atmospheric Research **Date of Birth:** 09/20/1957 **Place of Birth:** London **State/Country of Origin:** England **Parents:** Maneklal Laxmanbhai Dudhia; Armi Sointu Haijele Dudhia **Education:** PhD, Imperial College London (1984); MSc in Atmospheric Physics and Dynamics, Imperial College London (1980); BSc, Imperial College, London University, with Honors (1979) **Career:** Project Scientist, National Center for Atmospheric Research, University Corporation for Atmospheric Research, Boulder, CO (1993-Present); Associate Scientist, National Center for Atmospheric Research, University Corporation for Atmospheric Research, Boulder, CO (1993); Visiting Scientist, National Center for Atmospheric Research, University Corporation for Atmospheric Research, Boulder, CO (1989-1993); Research Associate, The Pennsylvania State University (1985-1989); Research Assistant, Imperial College London (1984-1985) **Creative Works:** Editor, "Asia-Pacific Journal of Atmospheric Sciences" (2011-2016) **Membership:** Fellow, Royal Meteorological Society; American Meteorological Society **Shipping Address:** PO Box 3000, National Center for Atmospheric Research, Boulder, CO, 80307

Carol McCarthy Duhme

Title: Civic Worker (Retired) **Industry:** Civil Service **Date of Birth:** 04/13/1917 **Place of Birth:** St. Louis **State:** MO **Parents:** Eugene Ross McCarthy; Louise (Roblee) McCarthy **Marital Status:** Married **Spouse Name:** H. Richard Duhme, Jr. (4/9/1947); Sheldon Ware (6/12/1941, Deceased 1944) **Children:** David; Benton (Deceased) **Education:** Honorary DHL, Eden Theological Seminary (2002); AB, Vassar College (1939) **Career:** Board of Deacons, St. Louis Association Congressional Church (1992-1995); Member, Church Council, St. Louis Association Congressional Church (1987-1989); Chairman Board, Christian Education, St. Louis Association Congressional Church (1987-1988); Member, Church Council, St. Louis Association Congressional Church (1984-1985); Board of Deacons, St. Louis Association Congressional Church (1982-1985); Board of Deaconesses, St. Louis Association Congressional Church (1978-1981); Member, Church Council, St. Louis Association Congressional Church (1974-1975); Trustee, 1st Congressional Church (1964-1966); Moderator, St. Louis Association Congressional Churches (1959-1962); Teacher, Elementary School (1942-1944); Teacher, Elementary School (1939-1941) **Career Related:** Member, Advisory Council to the Board (1987-Present); Chairman, Annual Fund, YWCA, St. Louis, MO (1989-1990); Board of Directors, YWCA, St. Louis, MO (1973-1976); Board of Directors, Chautauqua Institution, NY (1971-1979); Board of Directors, North Side Team Ministry (1968-1984); Former Board of Directors, Community Music Schools, St. Louis, MO; Former Board of Directors, Community School; Former Board of Directors, Church Women United; Former Board of Directors, John Burroughs School; Former Board of Directors, St. Louis Bicentennial Women's Committee; President, St. Louis Junior League; President, St. Louis Vassar Club **Civic:** Member, National Council, School of Social Work, Washington University in St. Louis (1987-Present); Trustee, Joseph H. and Florence A. Roblee Foundation, St. Louis, MO (1984-Present); Board of Directors, President, Joseph H. and Florence A. Roblee Foundation, St. Louis, MO (2002); Chairman, 150th Annual Committee, Eden Theological Seminary (1996-2000); Member, UNA-USA National Council (1995-2001); National Council, United Nations Association, St. Louis, MO (1995-2001); Council of Advisors, United Nations Association, St. Louis, MO (1993-2010); Presidential Search Committee, Eden Theological Seminary (1992-1993); Vice President, Board of Directors, Eden Theological Seminary (1991); Presidential Search Committee, Eden Theological Seminary (1986-1987); President, Joseph H. and Florence A. Roblee Foundation, St. Louis, MO (1984-1990); Member, Executive Committee, Board of Directors, Eden Theological Seminary (1981-1995); Member, Chancellor's Long Range Planning Committee, Washington University in St. Louis (1980-1981); Member, Corporate Assembly, Blue Cross Hospital Service of Missouri (1978-1986); President, Board of Directors, Family and Children's Service of Greater St. Louis (1977-1979); Secretary, Board of Directors, United Nations Association, St. Louis, MO (1976-1984); Member, Advisory Council, Missouri Baptist Hospital (1973-1989); Chairman, Chautauqua Bell Tower Scholar Fund (1961-2014); Board of Directors, St. Louis Mercantile Library; Board of Directors, National Inland Waterways Library; Chairman, Benton Roblee Duhme Scholar Fund **Awards:** Dean's Medal, Washington University in St. Louis School of Social Work (2015); Lifetime Achievement Award, Women's Foundation, Greater St. Louis (2011); Humanitarian Award, Planned Parenthood, St. Louis, MO (2000); Outstanding Alumna Award, John Burroughs School (1992); Outstanding Lay Women Nomination, Missouri United Church Of Christ (1991); Woman of Achievement Award, St. Louis Globe Democrat (1980); Volunteer of the Year Award, YWCA (1976); Mary Alice Messerley Award For Volunteerism, Health And Welfare Council, St. Louis, MO (1971) **Marquis Who's Who Honors:** Albert Nelson Marquis Lifetime Achievement Award (2017); Distinguished Humanitarian (2017) **Shipping Address:** 1 McKnight Pl Apt 484, Saint Louis, MO, 63124

Donelson Edwin Dulany Jr., PhD

Title: Professor Emeritus **Industry:** Education/Educational Services **Company Name:** University of Illinois **Date of Birth:** 12/09/1928 **Place of Birth:** Shreveport **State:** LA **Parents:** Donelson Edwin Dulany; LaVera (Jackson) Dulany **Marital Status:** Married **Spouse Name:** Elizabeth Carolyn Gjelsness (3/19/1955) **Children:** Christopher Daniel **Education:** PhD, University of Michigan (1955); Rockefeller Research Fellow in Philosophy, University of Michigan, Ann Arbor, MI (1951-1952); AB, University of Tennessee (1948) **Career:** Professor Emeritus, University of Illinois at Urbana-Champaign (1998-Present); Professor of Psychology, University of Illinois at Urbana-Champaign (1964-1998); Associate Professor, University of Illinois at Urbana-Champaign (1959-1964); Visiting Faculty, Harvard University, Cambridge, MA (1958); Assistant Professor of Psychology, University of Illinois at Urbana-Champaign (1956-1959); Lecturer of Psychology, Florida State University Extension Overseas Military Personnel, Fort Brooke, Puerto Rico (1955-1956); Instructor of Psychology, University of Michigan, Ann Arbor, MI (1952-1954); Fellow, American Psychological Association; Fellow, Association for Psychological Science; Fellow, Psychonomic Society **Career Related:** Institute Affiliate, Beckman Institute, University of Illinois (1990-Present); Invited Speaker, Consciousness Focused Conferences With Book Chapter Publications, Purdue University (2011); Keynote Speaker, International Seminar on Mind, Brain and Consciousness, Joshi Bedekar, Thane College, Mumbai, India (2010); Commencement Address, Department of Psychology, University of Illinois (2006); Keynote Speaker, Science of Consciousness, University of Arizona (2000); Keynote Speaker, Conference on Consciousness and Cognition, Pennsylvania State University (1993); Invited Speaker, Consciousness Focused Conferences With Book Chapter Publications, Carnegie Mellon University (1993); Lecturer, WCB Psychology Videotape Library, W.H. Brown and Company (1983); Invited Speaker, Consciousness Focused Conferences With Book Chapter Publications, Penn State University (1973); Invited Speaker, Consciousness Focused Conferences With Book Chapter Publications, University of Kentucky (1966); Lecturer, WILL Radio and TV 1960s **Military Service:** U.S. Army, Fort Brooke, Puerto Rico (1954-1956); Liaison and Research Office, Pentagon (1954) **Creative Works:** International Editorial Advisory Board Member, Mens Sana Monographs (2010-Present); Presenter, "Scientific Study of Consciousness," Tucson, AZ (2016); Presenter, "Psychonomics," Chicago, IL (2015); Presenter, Online Nature Forum (2012); Editor, American Journal of Psychology (1988-2008) **Awards:** Prokasy Award for Distinguished Teaching in College of Liberal Arts and Sciences (1994); Hohenboken Award for Excellence in Teaching in Psychology (1992); Grantee, National Science Foundation, National Institutes of Health **Membership:** Chairman, Committee on Equal Opportunity and Conditions of Employment, American Psychological Association (1970) **Marquis Who's Who Honors:** Marquis Who's Who for Decades of University Experience (2017); Marquis Who's Who Top Educators (2017) **Business Address:** 603 E Daniel Street, Champaign, IL, 61820 **Shipping Address:** 73 Greencroft Drive, Champaign, IL, 61821

Christopher Michael Duma

Title: Neurosurgeon **Industry:** Medicine & Health Care **Company Name:** Brain and Spine Surgeons of Orange County **Date of Birth:** 05/19/1959 **Place of Birth:** New York City **State:** NY **Marital Status:** Married **Education:** Fellow, Stereotactic Neurosurgery and Gamma Knife, University of Pittsburgh, Presbyterian-University Hospital (Now UPMC), Pittsburgh, PA (1991-1992); Resident, Neurosurgery, Georgetown University Hospital (Now Medstar Georgetown University), Washington D.C. (1987-1991); Intern, General Surgery, Georgetown University Hospital (Now Medstar Georgetown University), Washington D.C. (1986-1987); MD, School of Medicine, Stony Brook University, Stony Brook Medicine (1986); Honorary BA in Neuroscience, Colgate University (1981) **Certifications:** Board Certified, American Association of Neurological Surgeons **Career:** Medical Director, Brain Tumor Program, Hoag Memorial Hospital, Newport Beach, CA 1997 to present; Chief Resident, Neurosurgery, Georgetown University Hospital (Now Medstar Georgetown University Hospital), Washington D.C. (1991-1993); Registrar, Neurosurgery, Atkinson Morleys Hospital, Wimbledon, England (1990); Pain Service Research Assistant, Department of Neurology, Memorial Sloan Kettering Cancer Center (1985); Research Assistant, Department of Neuropharmacology, Cornell University School of Medicine (Now Weill Cornell Medicine) (1981-1982) **Civic:** CEO and Founder, The Music-Heals Project **Membership:** Congress of Neurological Surgeons (2001-Present); American Association of Neurological Surgeons (2001-Present); International Stereotactic Radiosurgery Society (ISRS) (1990-Present) **Why did you become involved in your profession or industry:** Dr. Duma wanted to be a doctor since he was nine years old. His interest was piqued because of a family doctor. Dr. Duma loved science and math so he fell into this field naturally. He chose to study surgery in medical school because of the instant gratification of using his hands. **Shipping Address:** 3900 W Coast Hwy, Ste 300, Brain & Spine Surgeons of O.C., Newport Beach, CA, 92663 **Website:** www.cduma.com

Michael Godfrey Joseph Dumas

Title: Artist **Industry:** Fine Art **Company Name:** Lazare & Parker Studios **Date of Birth:** 09/20/1950 **Place of Birth:** Whitney **State/Country of Origin:** Canada **Parents:** Alphyr Adrian; Caroline Anna (Cenzura) D. **Marital Status:** Married **Spouse Name:** Ellen Kocsis (July 19, 1975) **Children:** Shae Shannon-Mae **Education:** Postgraduate Work, Cornell University (1984); Postgraduate Work, Humber College (1971); Diploma, Humber College (1970); Art Instruction School, Minneapolis, MN (1968) **Career:** Artist; Apprentice to Lewis Parker, Lazare & Parker Studios (1971-1972) **Career Related:** Member, Advisory Board, Buckhorn Fine Art Festival (2010-2015); Art Impressions Magazine (1993-1997) **Creative Works:** Exhibit, Leigh Yawkey Woodson Art Museum, WI (2016); Exhibit, National Wildlife Art Museum, WY (2016); Buckhorn Fine Art Festival Gallery Exhibition Mystique (2014); Curator, "Peterborough in Portrait," Community Living Art Exhibition (2013); Birds in Art, Woodson Art Museum (2014); Hamilton Center Arts Invitational (2011); Canadian Masters Exhibition Buckhorn Fine Art Festival (2010); The Lindsay Gallery, Ontario, Canada (2006-2008); Algonquin Art Center (2005-2015); Fukuyu Gallery, Hiroshima, Japan; Buckingham Gallery, Uxbridge, Ontario, Canada (2003-2008); Arai Gallery, Tokyo, Japan (2002-2004); Mitsukoshi Gallery, Sendai (1999-2004); Cedar Ridge Creative Center, Scarborough, Canada (1999); Save the Rhino Trust, Namibia (1998); Spanierman Gallery, New York, NY (1998); Matsuya Gallery, Tokyo, Japan (1997); Sogo Gallery, Osaka, Japan (1997); Yumehodaka Museum, Nagano, Japan (1997); Suntory Museum of Art, Tokyo, Japan (1996); Algonquin Gallery, Algonquin Park, Ontario, Canada (1995-2002); Suntory Museum of Art, Osaka, Japan (1995); Mitsukoshi Galleries, Tokyo (1994-2003); Designed Four Coins, Royal Canadian Mint (1994); Yamanaakako-Takamura Museum of Art (1991-2001); Author, "Nature in Art" (1991); Bird Preservation Fundraiser, Osaka, Japan (1990); Kenya Wild Elephant Fundraiser, Toronto, Canada (1987, 1991); Royal Botanical Gardens, Hamilton, Canada (1985); R.O.M. (1987-1988); The Spirit of the Wild Fundraiser and Exhibit (1982); McMichael Canadian Art Collection, Kleinburg, Ontario, Canada (1981); Exhibits, National Museum of Science and Technology, Ottawa, Ontario, Canada (1977); Theodore Roosevelt Inaugural National Historical Site, Buffalo, NY (1977); Columnist, "Angler & Hunter" (1976-1983); Masterworks Gallery; Permanent Collection, International Museum of Art Inspired by Nature, Gloucester, England; Permanent Collection, Yamanakaka-Takamura Museum of Art, Japan; Imaoka Collection, Japan; Ontario Provincial Collection, Queen's Park, Ontario Binghamton University Art Museum; Designed Canadian Commemorative Postage Stamps; The Simplest Act, The Artist's Magazine of Field Drawings, Arabella Magazine; "Strokes of Genius: The Best of Drawing: Cover Art and Interior Images, International Contemporary Masters" Volume 8; Contributor to Articles in Magazines **Awards:** President's Artistic Accomplishment Award, Society of Animal Artists (2016); Dual Category Award, Annual Art Renewal Centre's International Salon; Award of Excellence, National Oil and Acrylics Painters (2016); The President's Artistic Achievement Award for 2D, Annual Exhibition, Society of Animal Artists (2016); Volunteer Award, Festival and Events of Ontario (2016); One of the Top 60 Masters of Contemporary Art (2013, 2014); Dual Category Award (2014); American Red Cross International (2014); Kawartha Order of the Arts (2014); Artist of the Year, Ontario Federation of Anglers & Hunters (2013); Long Point Waterfowl Conservatory (2013); A Singular Creation Award, International Nature Art Competition (2013); First Place Award, Lights & Dark (2013); Artquence International Competition Category (2013); First Place, The Artist's Magazine Annual Competition (2012); First Place, A Singular Creation International Art Competition (2013); Medal of Excellence, Artist's Conservation (2012); Best Noctures Plein Air and Other Awards; Best of Show, Hamilton Center Arts Invitational (2011); Best of Show, Masterworks Gallery (2011); First Place, Artavita International Art Competition (2011); Master Palette Award, Masterworks in Miniature, Gallery One (2005, 2009, 2010); County Peterborough Award (2009); Peterborough Pathway to Fame Award (2004); Outdoor Card Program Award, Ontario Ministry of Natural Resources (1998); Artist of the Year, Ontario Federation of Anglers and Hunters (1993-2004); International Flyway Artist, Ducks Unlimited (1992); First Winner, Competition Wildlife of Habitat Canada (1990); Carling-O'Keefe Professional Conservation Award (1986); Waterfowl Art Award, Ducks Unlimited (1983-1984) **Membership:** Member, Society of Animal Artists; Society of Wildlife Art of the Nations **Hobbies:** Travel; Photography; Camping **Shipping Address:** 7 Grantsville Trail, Lakehurst, ON, Canada, K0L 1J0

Kathleen Marie Duyck

Title: Poet, Musician, Social Worker (Retired) **Industry:** Writing and Editing **Date of Birth:** 07/21/1933 **Place of Birth:** Portland **State:** OR **Parents:** Anthony Joseph Dwyer; Edna Elisabeth Hayes **Marital Status:** Married **Spouse Name:** Robert Duyck (2/3/1962) **Children:** Mary Kay Boeyen; Robert Patrick; Anthony Joseph **Education:** Honorary MA, IBC (2014); MSW, University of Washington (1956); BS, Oregon State University (1954) **Certifications:** Certified, National Association of Social Workers, State of Oregon **Career:** Member, World Cultural Council (2011-Present); Poet (1993-Present); Speaker, Cambridge & San Francisco World Forum, Boston, MA (2013); Speaker, Cambridge & San Francisco World Forum (2011-2012); Principal Cellist, Scottsdale Symphony (1974-1980); Principal Cellist, Phoenix College Orchestra (1968-1978); Musician, Tucson Symphony (1963-1965); Adoption Worker, Catholic Welfare, San Antonio, TX (1962); Adoption Worker, Catholic Services, Portland, OR (1956-1961) **Career Related:** Vice President, Phoenix Youth Symphony Board (2015-Present); Corresponding Secretary, Phoenix Youth Symphony Board (2013-2015); Chairman, Friends and Family Service (2013) **Civic:** President-elect, Friends Youth Symphony, NJAL (2012-Present); Member, Executive Board, Symphony Guild (2011-Present); Honorary Director, Gen IBC (2015); President, Phoenix Art Museum League (2013-2014); President-elect, NSAL (2012-2014); Chairman, Phoenix Art Museum League (2012-2013); Vice President, Phoenix Art Museum League (2012-2013); President-elect, Phoenix Art Museum League (2012-2013); Society of Arts Letters (2012); Vice President, Friends and Family Service (2011-2015); Secretary, Phoenix Art Museum League (2011-2012); Corresponding Secretary, Phoenix Art Museum League (2010-2012) **Creative Works:** Author, "Visions II" (1996); Author, "Visions" (1993); Author, Numerous Poems; Contributor, Compact Disc's **Awards:** Named, A Top Musician, IBC (2017); Listee, Dictionary of International Biography, IBC (2017); Named to Hall of Fame, International Biographical Convention (2015); Cambridge Ambassador Master of Fine Arts (2014); International Merit Award, Cambridge Ambassador of Arts and Science Committee (2013); Pinnacle of Achievement, American Biographical Institute (2013); Tesla Award, American Biographical Institute (2013); Scholar Ambassador, American Biographical Institute (2013); Olympic Achiever Award, American Biographical Institute (2012); Lifetime Award, International Biographical Convention (2012); Associate Member, American Biographical Institute (2012); Invitee, 500 Leaders, American Biographical Institute (2012); International Woman of the Year, American Biographical Institute (2012); International Merit Award, Cambridge Ambassador of Arts and Science Committee (2011); Attache Medal, American Biographical Institute (2011); Academician Award, American Biographical Institute (2011); Cambridge Medal, International Biographical Convention (2011); Mozart Award, International Biographical Convention (2010-2011); International Merit Award, Cambridge Ambassador of Arts and Science Committee (2010); Named to Inner Circle, American Biographical Institute (2010); Order of Distinction, American Biographical Institute (2010); Lifetime Award, American Biographical Institute (2009); Named Woman of the Year, American Biographical Institute (2009); International Merit Award, Cambridge Ambassador of Arts and Science Committee (2009); Outstanding Achievement Award in Poetry, International Society of Poets (2008); Excellence In Music Award, International Biographical Convention (2007); Outstanding Achievement Award in Poetry, International Society of Poets (2006); Outstanding Achievement Award in Poetry, International Society of Poets (2005); International Poet of Merit Award, International Society of Poets (2003) **Membership:** Board Secretary, Phoenix Youth Symphony (2013-Present); Vice President, Friends and Family Service (2008-Present); Honorary Director General, International Biographical Convention (2015); Master, International Biographical Convention; International Poetry Hall of Fame; Arizona Cello Society; National Library of Poetry; International Society of Poets; Phoenix Symphony Guild; National Museum of Women in the Arts; World War II Museum; St. Mary's Alumni Association; Oregon State University Alumni Association; University of Washington Alumni Association; Phoenix Symphony Allegro; Mental Health Guild; Phoenix Symphony Orchestra; International Biographical Center; World Cultural Convention; San Francisco World Forum; Boston World Forum; Corresponding Secretary, Philadelphia Art Museum League; Allegro General Board Member, Phoenix Youth Symphony **Marquis Who's Who Honors:** Albert Nelson Marquis Lifetime Achievement Award (2017); Distinguished Humanitarian (2017) **Political Affiliations:** Republican **Religion:** Roman Catholic **Shipping Address:** 4545 E Palomino Rd, Phoenix, AZ, 85018

Thomas Capper Eakin

Title: Sports Promotion Executive **Industry:** Advertising & Marketing **Company Name:** TCE Enterprises **Date of Birth:** 12/16/1933 **Place of Birth:** New Castle **State/Country of Origin:** PA **Parents:** Frederick William Eakin; Beatrice (Capper) Eakin **Marital Status:** Married **Spouse Name:** Brenda Lee Andrews (10/21/1961) **Children:** Thomas Andrews; Scott Frederick **Education:** BA in History, Denison University (1956) **Career:** Help Hospitalized Veterans, Friends Board (2008-Present); Founder, Ohio Baseball Associates (2005-Present); President, Ohio Baseball Associates (2005-Present); President, TCE Enterprises, Shaker Heights, Ohio (1973-Present); Founder and President, Golf International 100 Club, Shaker Heights, Ohio (1970-Present); Founder, President and Chairman, BainBridge Timeline Publication, BainBridge Township (2010); Founder, Summit Historical Society (2010); Founder and President, Community Publication, Eastlake, Ohio (2010); District Manager, Hitchcock Publishing Company, Cleveland, Ohio (1970-1972); District Manager, Hitchcock Publishing Company (1970); Regional Business Manager, Chilton Publishing Co., Cleveland, Ohio (1969-1970); District Manager, Putman Publishing Co., Cleveland, Ohio (1968-1969); Life Insurance Consultant, Northwestern Mutual Life Insurance Co., Cleveland, Ohio (1959-1967); Founder, Help Our New Americans; Chairman, Help Our New Americans; Founder, Summit County History Publication; President, Summit County History Publication **Career Related:** Ripley's Believe It or Not, Ripley Entertainment Inc. (2012-Present); President, Ashtabula County Sports Hall of Fame (2010-Present); Ohio Baseball Association (2005-Present); U.S. Humanitarian Hall of Fame (2004-Present); Ohio Pacesetters Hall of Fame (2004-Present); International Humanitarian Hall of Fame (2004-Present); Founder and President, Ohio Humanitarian Hall of Fame (2000-Present); Founder, Twinsburg Community Heritage Publications, Lecture Series "Catch the Spirit," Garrettsville Community Service Publication (2000-Present); Chairman, Twinsburg Community Heritage Publications, Garrettsville Community Service Publication (2000-Present); Ohio Promotions for Sports (2000-Present); Ohio Baseball Digest of Harrison County (1998-Present); Harrison County Baseball Digest (1998-Present); Belmont County Baseball League (1998-Present); Ohio Youth Sports Hall of Fame (1996-Present); National William "Dummy" Hoy Baseball Committee (1995-Present); Ohio Sports Logo Creations (1991-Present); Ohio Sports Stars Enterprises (1991-Present); Ohio Sports Licensing Enterprises (1991-Present); Ohio Sports Hall of Fame Promotional Enterprises (1990-Present); Summit County Sports Promotion Enterprises (1990-Present); Geauga County History and Sports Traditions Enterprises (1990-Present); Licking County Sports Stars Enterprises (1990-Present); Lake County Community Promotions Enterprises (1990-Present); Trumbull County Sports Stars Publications (1990-Present); Portage County History and Sports Publications (1990-Present); Cuyahoga County Promotion Co. (1990-Present); Ashtabula County History and Sports Publications (1990-Present); Ohio Pride in Community Publications (1990-Present); Mahoning County Sports Headlines Publications (1990-Present); Ohio Fire Department Promotional Publications (1990-Present); Ohio Law Enforcement Community Publications (1990-Present); Erie County Excellence in High School Sports Publications (1990-Present); D & D Sports Production and Marketing Creations (1990-Present); Advantage Sports Co. (1989-Present); Damascus Steel Casting Co. (1987-Present); M & M Publications (1987-Present); Tuscarawas County Sports Promotions Enterprises (1987-Present); Advisory Board, Sportsbeat (1985-Present) **Civic:** Founder and President, Ohio for History (2010-Present); Ohio Volunteer Hall of Fame (2009-Present); Ohio Philanthropist Society (2008-Present); Sports Highlights Publication, Fulton County, Ohio (2007-Present); History Speaks Publication, Ashland County, Ohio (2006-Present); Advisory Board, Cleveland Council on Corrections (2005-Present); Tuscarawas County American Revolution Bicentennial Commission, Sports Publication, Richland County, Ohio (2005-Present); Trustee, Great Expectations Ltd. (2004-Present); Ohio Baseball History Museum (2002-Present); Ohio Women's Baseball Hall of Fame (1998-Present); Ohio Minor League Baseball Hall of Fame Association (1992-Present); "Youth in Community Service" and "Volunteers are Winners" Lecture Series (1991-Present); Ohio Sports Legends Foundation (1991-Present); Ohio Negro Baseball Hall of Fame Veterans Council (1991-Present); Cleveland Baseball Old Timers Association, Ohio Sports Celebrity Golf Invitational (1991-Present); Ohio Sports Educational Council (1991-Present); Conneaut Community Promotional Fund (1991-Present); Ohio Founders League (1990-Present); Windham Community Service Foundation (1990-Present); Career Advisory Board, Denison University (1990-Present) **Military Service:** United States Army (1956-1958) **Shipping Address:** 245 Sandover Drive, Aurora, OH, 44202

William Eakins

Title: Lawyer **Industry:** Law and Legal Services **Company Name:** Patton, Eakins, Lipsett, Martin & Savage **Date of Birth:** 07/22/1951 **Place of Birth:** Glen Cove **State:** NY **Parents:** William Shannon; Jean (Pickup) E. **Children:** Amelia Moore **Education:** JD, Cornell University (1977); BA, Yale University (1974) **Career:** Partner, Chairman, Department of Trusts and Estates, Patton, Eakins, Lipsett, Martin & Savage, New York City, NY (1998-Present); Partner, Chairman, Department of Trusts and Estates, Olshan, Grundman, Frome & Rosenzweig, New York City, NYC (1993-1998); Partner, Phillips, Nizer, Benjamin, Krim & Ballon, New York City, NY (1989-1992); Associate, Phillips, Nizer, Benjamin, Krim & Ballon, New York City, NY (1984-1988); Associate, Gelberg & Abrams, New York City, NY (1981-1984); Counsel, Committee on Taxation, Investigations & Government Operations, New York State Senate, Albany, NY (1981-1984); In-house Lawyer, Trust Administrator, Portfolio Manager, J.P. Morgan Bank, New York City, NY (1977-1981) **Civic:** Commissioner, Historic Resources Commission, Asheville and Buncombe County, NC (2014-Present); Chief Judge, Board of Elections, Buncombe County, NC (2013-Present); Financial Committee Member, Church Gethsemane Brooklyn, NY (2006-Present); New York Foundation Senior Citizens (2006-Present); Director, Western North Carolina Historical Association, Asheville, NC (2015-2016); Delegate, Buncombe County North Carolina Republican County Convention (2013); North Carolina 10th Congressional District Republican Convention (2013); North Carolina State Republication Convention (2013); Member, Democratic Judicial Screening Panel 6th and 9th Districts, Manhattan and the Bronx (2009); Elder, Member Session Brick Presbyterian Church (2003-2006); Vice President, Board of Trustees (2006-2010); Member, New York Presbyterian-Jewish Dialogue Steering Committee; American Jewish Committee and Auburn Theology Seminary of Jewish-Presbyterian Relations (2005-2009); Overture Advocate, Presbyterian Church USA General Assembly (2006); Member, Steering Committee, Auburn Theologian Seminary Faith to Faith-Face to Face Program (2006-2009); Board of Directors, New York Theological Seminary (2007-2009); Board of Directors, Homecrest Community Services, Inc. (1999-2005); Representative, Manhattan Community Board 8, New York City, NY (1993-1997); Candidate, Ind. Neighbors and Conservative, New York State Assembly (1992); Vice-Chairman, New York Republican County Committee, New York City, NY (1985-1989); Executive Committee, New York Republican County Committee (1979-1987); District Leader, New York Republican County Committee (1979-1987); Director, Knickerbocker Republican Club (1979-1987); President, Ivy Republican Club (1980-1982); Vice-Chairman, Manhattan Community Board 8, New York City, NY (1980-1984) **Creative Works:** Contributor, Articles, Professional Journals **Membership:** Trusts, Estates and Surrogates Courts Committee, New York City Bar Association (2017-Present, 1990-1991); Income Tax Committee, New York City Bar Association (2017-Present); New York State Bar Association; New York City Bar Association; Yale Club; The Grolier; Metropolitan Club; University Club, St. Andrews Society **Marquis Who's Who Honors:** Albert Nelson Marquis Lifetime Achievement Award (2017) **Political Affiliations:** Republican **Religion:** Presbyterian **Shipping Address:** P.O. Box 890, Asheville, NC, 28802

Nancy R. Eaton

Title: Librarian **Industry:** Law and Legal Services **Company Name:** Pennsylvania State University **Date of Birth:** 05/02/1943 **Place of Birth:** Berkeley **State:** CA **Parents:** Don Thomas Linton; Lena Ruth (McClellan) Linton **Marital Status:** Divorced **Spouse Name:** Edward Arthur Eaton III (6/19/1965, Divorced 1980) **Education:** Postgraduate, University of Texas (1969); MLS, University of Texas (1968); AB, Stanford University (1965) **Career:** Dean Emerita, Pennsylvania State University (2010-Present); Dean, University Libraries, Pennsylvania State University, University Park, PA (1997-2010); Dean, Library Services, Iowa State University, Ames, IA (1989-1997); Director, Library, University of Vermont, Burlington, VT (1982-1989); Head, Technical Services, Atlanta Public Library (1976-1982); Automation Library, Stony Brook University (1974-1976); Cataloger, Assistant, Director, University of Texas Library, Austin, TX (1968-1974) **Career Related:** Member, Smithsonian Libraries. Advisory Board (2012-Present); Chair, Pennsylvania Humanities Council (2011-2013); Member, Pennsylvania Humanities Council (2008-2014); Co-Principal Investigator, Mellon Foundation Grant (2004-2008); Board of Directors, Research Libraries Group (2004-2006); Member, Advisory Board, National Digital Information Infrastructure and Preservation Program (2001-2002); Chair, Steering Committee, Digital Library Federation (2000-2002); Chair, Board of Trustees, Users Council, Member Executive Committee, Chair, Online Computer Library Center, Inc., Dublin, OH (1992-1996); Chair, Center for Research Library (1989-1990); Board of Directors, Center for Research Library (1988-1992); Trustee, Users Council, Member Executive Committee, Chair, Online Computer Library Center, Inc., Dublin, OH (1987-2002); Board of Directors, New England Library Network (1987-1989); Manager, National Agricultural Text Digitalizing Project (1986-1992); Delegate, Users Council, Member Executive Committee, Chair, Online Computer Library Center, Inc., Dublin, OH (1986-1988); Delegate, Users Council, Member Executive Committee, Chair, Online Computer Library Center, Inc., Dublin, OH (1980-1982) **Creative Works:** Co-Author, "Optical Information Systems: Implementation Issues for Libraries" (1988); Co-Editor, "Book Selection Policies in American Libraries" (1972); Co-Editor, "A Cataloging Sampler" (1971); Contributor, Articles to Professional Journals **Awards:** Title II-D Grantee, Department of Education (1992-1996); Title II-C Grantee, Department of Education (1987-1988); Title II-C Grantee, Department of Education (1985); Post-Master's Fellow, U.S. Office Of Education (1969); Mellon Foundation Grant **Membership:** Board of Directors, Research Libraries Group (2004-2006); Steering Committee, Coalition Networked Information (1999-2005); Executive Committee, Digital Library Federation (1997-2003); Board of Directors, Association of Research Libraries (1994-1997); President, Library and Information Technology Association (1984-1985); Board of Directors, Library and Information Technology Association (1980-1986); American Library Association; Friends Board, Schlow Center, Region Library **Hobbies:** Travel; Walking **Political Affiliations:** Democrat **Shipping Address:** 500 East Marylyn Avenue, Apartment I-135, Foxdale Village, State College, PA, 16801

Angela Beth Echeverria

Title: Vascular Surgeon **Industry:** Medicine & Health Care **Company Name:** Gulfcoast Vascular Surgeons **Education:** MD, American University of Antigua College of Medicine (2009); PharmD, Butler University, Indiana (2003); Resident in General Surgery, University of Arizona, Tucson, AZ **Certifications:** Certification in Surgery, American Board of Surgery; Medical License, States of Arizona and Florida **Career:** Vascular Surgeon, Gulfcoast Vascular Surgeons (2017-Present) **Career Related:** Keynote Speaker, Cape Coral Women's Leadership Conference **Creative Works:** Contributor, Articles, Professional Journals **Awards:** Fellowship, Vascular Surgery, Baylor College of Medicine (2017); Best General Surgery Video by a Resident Award, SLS-MIRA-SRS Joint Annual Meeting and Endo Expo (2012); Best Urology Video by a Resident Award, SLS-MIRA-SRS Joint Annual Meeting and Endo Expo (2012) **Membership:** American College of Surgeons; Society for Vascular Surgery; Association of Women Surgeons; Southern Association for Vascular Surgery; Society for Clinical Vascular Surgery **Why did you become involved in your profession or industry:** While Dr. Echeverria was in general surgery training, she became drawn to vascular surgery. She found fulfillment in allowing patients the quality of life. Vascular surgeons take care of problems from the skull to the toes, and she is able to see immediate improvements of a patient's well being. **Where will you be in five years:** In the coming years, Dr. Echeverria intends to experience the continued growth and success of her career. **Shipping Address:** 8010 Summerlin Lakes Drive, Suite 100, Gulfcoast Vascular Surgeons, Fort Myers, FL, 33907 **Website:** http://www.angelaecheverriamd.com

Heiner Eckert

Title: Vice President **Industry:** Sciences **Company Name:** BSAZ Biotech **Date of Birth:** 04/24/1946 **Place of Birth:** Muenchen **State/Country of Origin:** Germany **Parents:** Adam Christian Eckert; Irmengard Eckert **Education:** Privatdozent, Technology University Muenchen, Germany (2006); Habil, Technology University Muenchen, Germany (2005); Doctor Rerum Naturalium, Technology University Muenchen, Germany (1976); Diploma, Technology University Muenchen, Germany (1973) **Career:** Vice President, BSAZ Biotech, China (2013-Present); Academic Director, Technology University Muenchen (2002-Present); Chief Executive Officer, Dr. Eckert GmbH, Muenchen (1977-2002) **Civic:** Member, Bund Freunde Technology University Muenchen (2005) **Military Service:** With, Bundespolizei German Army (1965-1967) **Awards:** Qianjian Friendship Award (2015); Westlake Friendship Award (2015) **Membership:** American Chemical Society; Gesellschaft Deutscher Chemiker **Hobbies:** Mountain Climbing; History; Music; Chemistry Science **Shipping Address:** Helene-Mayer-Ring 10, Apartment 1303, Muenchen, Germany, 80809

Marlene R. Eckstein

Title: Vascular Radiologist (Retired) **Industry:** Medicine & Health Care **Date of Birth:** 09/06/1948 **Place of Birth:** Poughkeepsie **State:** NY **Parents:** Marc Eckstein; Lola (Charm) Eckstein **Education:** Resident in Diagnostic Radiology, Yale-New Haven Hospital (1974-1977); Intern in Internal Medicine, Yale-New Haven Hospital (1973-1974); MD, Albert Einstein College of Medicine (1973); AB, Vassar College (1970) **Certifications:** Diplomate, National Board of Medical Examiners; Certified, American Board of Radiology in Diagnostic Radiology **Career:** Retired (2013); Associate Radiologist, Massachusetts General Hospital, The General Hospital Corporation (1987-2013); Assistant Radiologist, Massachusetts General Hospital, The General Hospital Corporation (1983-1987); Assistant Director, Department of Radiology, Chief, Vascular Radiology Section, South Nassau Communities Hospital (1981-1983); Associate Radiologist, Chief, Vascular Radiology Section, South Nassau Communities Hospital (1978-1981); Assistant Radiologist, Chief, Vascular Radiology Section, South Nassau Communities Hospital (1977-1978)

Career Related: Assistant Professor of Radiology, Harvard Medical School (1984-2013); Instructor in Radiology, Harvard Medical School (1983-1984); Assistant Professor of Clinical Radiology, Stony Brook School of Medicine (1980-1983) **Civic:** Hospital Chairman, Executive Committee Member, UJA-Federation of Physicians and Dentists of Nassau County (1981-1983) **Creative Works:** Editor and Author, "Autobiography of Marc Eckstein" (2014); Poet, "Yearnings," in "Great Poems of the Western World Volume II," World of Poetry Press (1990); Co-author, "The Management of Massive Hemoptysis: Control by Angiographic Methods" (1986); Co-author, "Bifurcation of the Cervical Internal Carotid Artery: Case Report" (1986); Co-author, "Massive Arterial Hemorrhage in Patients with Pancreatitis: Complementary Roles of Surgery and Transcatheter Occlusive Techniques" (1986); Co-author, "The Normal Leg Venogram: Significance in Suspected Vein Thrombosis" (1985); Author, "Interventional Angiography in the Kidney" (1985); Co-author, "Gastrointestinal Bleeding: An Angiographic Perspective" (1984); Co-author, "Interventional Angiography of the Renal Fossa" (1984); Co-author, "Embolization in Gastrointestinal and Pelvic Bleeding" (1984); Co-author, "Aortofemoral Bypass Grafts: Safety of Percutaneous Puncture" (1984); Co-author, "Gastric Bleeding: Therapy with Intraarterial Vasopressin and Transcatheter Embolization" (1984); Co-author, "Digital Subtraction Angiography" (1983); Co-author, "Calcified Leiomyoma: An Unusual Cause of Large Soft Tissue Calcification of Calf in Childhood" (1983); Co-author, "Factors Affecting the Recognition of the Dilated Biliary Tree in the Jaundiced Patient" (1978); Co-author, "Amino Acide Oxidase of Leukocytes in Relation to H202-Mediated Bacterial Killing" (1971); Co-author, "Planning a Facility for Vascular Radiologic Procedures"; Co-author, "Small Bowel Hemorrhage: Angiographic Localization and Intervention"; Co-author, "Thrombolysis of Peripheral Arterial and Graft Occlusions: Results with Streptokinase and Urokinase"; Co-author, "Intraarterial DSA: Advantages Over Conventional Angiography"; Co-author, "Treatment of Pulmonary Arteriovenous Malformations"; Co-author, "Angiographic Evaluation of and Intervention in Hepatic and Splenic Artery Aneurysms"; Co-author, "Vascular Grafts: Evaluation with Intravenous DSA"; Contributor, Articles, Professional Journals; Lecturer, Various Conferences **Awards:** Love-of-a-Lifetime Award, Hadassah, The Women's Zionist Organization of America, Inc. (1997); Award, Poetry Contest **Membership:** Lifetime Member, Hadassah, The Women's Zionist Organization of America, Inc. (1973-Present); President, New England Society of Cardiovascular and Interventional Radiology (1985-1986); Fellow, American Society of Angiology; Associate Fellow, Society of Cardiovascular and Interventional Radiology; American Medical Association; American College of Radiology; American Institute of Ultrasound in Medicine; American Association of Women Radiologists; American Medical Women's Association; Massachusetts Radiological Society; Radiological Society of North America; Massachusetts Medical Society; The American Israel Public Affairs Committee; International Fellowship of Christians and Jews; Simon Wiesenthal Center; The Israel Project; Yad Vashem USA; Wounded Warrior Project, Inc.; Association of University Radiologists; Society of Thoracic Radiology; Radiology Council, American Heart Association, Inc.; International Union of Angiology **Marquis Who's Who Honors:** Albert Nelson Marquis Lifetime Achievement Award (2017); Marquis Top Doctor (2017) **Religion:** Jewish **Shipping Address:** 6 Merlot Dr Unit 640, Highland, NY, 12528

Athanassios Economou, PhD

Title: Professor of Architecture **Industry:** Education/Educational Services **Company Name:** Georgia Institute of Technology **Education:** PhD in Design Theory and Methods, School of Architecture, University of California, Los Angeles (1998); MArch, School of Architecture, University of Southern California (1992); Diploma in Architecture, Department of Architecture, National Technical University of Athens, Greece (1990) **Career:** Professor, Director, Shape Computation, PhD Program, Art & Architecture Study Abroad Program, School of Architecture, College of Design, Georgia Institute of Technology (2016-Present); Associate Professor, School of Architecture, Georgia Institute of Technology (2003-Present); Visiting Associate Professor, School of Architecture, Massachusetts Institute of Technology, Boston, MA (2001-2011); Assistant Professor, Architecture Program, Georgia Institute of Technology (1997-2003); Lecturer, School of Architecture, University of California, Los Angeles (1996-1997); Doctoral Researcher, School of Architecture, University of California, Los Angeles (1994-1996); Teaching Assistant, School of Architecture, University of Southern California (1990-1992) **Career Related:** Funded Research Projects which Include the Shape Grammar for Federal Courthouses and CourtsWeb; Presenter in Field **Creative Works:** Contributor, More than 40 Articles, Professional Journals; Contributor, Chapters, Books **Awards:** Course Release for Research Program Award, College of Design, Georgia Institute of Technology (2016); Outstanding Teacher Award, Center of Enhancement of Teaching and Learning, Georgia Institute of Technology (2011); Second Prize, Association of Collegiate Schools of Architecture International Competition (2005); Outstanding Teacher Award, College of Architecture, Georgia Institute of Technology (2002); Second Prize, Association of Collegiate Schools of Architecture International Competition (2001); Second Prize, Van Alen Awards, Public Architecture (1999); Chancellor's Dissertation Fellowship, University of California, Los Angeles (1996); Elaine Krown Klein Fine Arts Scholarship, University of California, Los Angeles (1996); Graduate Scholarship, University of California, Los Angles (1993-1995); Onassis Institution Scholarship, Athens, Greece (1991-1993); Alpha Association of Phi Beta Kappa Award, Los Angeles, CA (1991); Graduate Scholarship, University of Southern California (1990-1991) **Membership:** Association for Computer Aided Design in Architecture; Education and Research in Computer-Aided Architectural Design in Europe; Association for Computer-Aided Architectural Design Research in Asia; Iberoamerican Society of Digital Graphics; Computer Aided Architectural Design Futures; Scientific Committee of Mathematics and Design; Scientific Committee of Computational Aesthetics **Why did you become involved in your profession or industry:** Dr. Economou was studying architecture in Greece, but became inspired to become a professor while at the University of California, Los Angeles. **Where will you be in five years:** Dr. Economou intends to still be with Georgia Institute of Technology, but might be applying to other schools for a more prominent position. **Business Address:** 247 4th St Rm 407, Atlanta, GA, 30308 **Shipping Address:** 30 5th Street NE, Unit #602, Atlanta, GA, 30308 **Website:** http://shape.gatech.edu

Ake Edfeldt, PhD

Title: Professor Emeritus **Industry:** Education/Educational Services **Company Name:** Stockholm University **Date of Birth:** 02/24/1926 **Place of Birth:** Stockholm **State/Country of Origin:** Sweden **Year of Passing:** 2017-09-22 **Parents:** Johan Verner; Emy Elisabet (Fagerlund) Edfeldt **Marital Status:** Married **Spouse Name:** Maj Bildt (8/25/1957, Divorced 1965); Kerstin Anna Brita Joelson **Children:** Eric Johan Werner; Fredrik; Catti; Mikaela **Education:** EdD, Stockholm University (1960); PhD, Stockholm University (1954); MA, Stockholm University (1953) **Career:** Professor Emeritus, Stockholm University (1991-Present); Professor of Education, Stockholm University (1970-1990); Associate Professor, Stockholm University (1965-1968); Assistant Professor, Stockholm University (1960-1965) **Career Related:** Advisor, National Laws Against Family Violence Towards Children, New Zealand (2006); Advisor, National Laws Against Family Violence Towards Children, Germany (2002); Founder, Swedish Movement Education for Highly Gifted Children (2002); Inspector, RMI School of Advertising and Marketing, Sweden (1989-1997); Chairman, Informationskonsult Inc. (1986-2004); Advisor, National Laws Against Family Violence Towards Children, Sweden (1979); Professor of Education, Turku Academy, Finland (1968-1970); Managing Director, Informationskonsult Inc. (1965-1985) **Civic:** Board Member, Center for Distancebridging Media, Lulea Technology University (2000); Chairman, Swedish National Group of Jazz History (1998-2006); State Board of Film Censors (1967-1976); Expert, Several State Committees on Communications and Violence Towards Children **Creative Works:** Contributor, Articles, Professional Journals **Awards:** The Bass Player Mark of Distinction, The Swedish Jazz Federation (2000); Honorary Silver Plaque, Stockholm Community Board (1990) **Membership:** International Association of Reading and Learning Disabilities (1983-1984); President, Rotary **Marquis Who's Who Honors:** Distinguished Humanitarian (2017) **Hobbies:** Hunting; Vintage car motoring; Collecting vintage jazz records **Shipping Address:** Lasarettsvagen 1, Nacka, Sweden, 131 45

D.M. Edwards

Title: Vice President **Industry:** Real Estate **Company Name:** CountryMedic, Inc. **Date of Birth:** 04/12/1953 **Place of Birth:** Tyler **State:** TX **Parents:** Welby Clell Edwards; Davida (Mount) Edwards **Marital Status:** Divorced **Spouse Name:** Susan Alicia Pappas (1984, Divorced 1986) **Education:** Doctorate in Humanities, East Texas Baptist University (2016); BBA, Baylor University (1976); AA, Tyler Junior College, Cum Laude (1974) **Certifications:** Ordained Deacon, Baptist Church (2000-Present) **Career:** Development Board Chair, University of Texas at Tyler (2017-Present); Adviser, Baylor University Libraries (2016-Present); President, Owner, Shreveport Spring, Brake & Axle, Inc. (1998-Present); Board Chairman, Chief Executive Officer, Odessa Spring Brake & Axle, Inc. (1991-Present); Chief Executive Officer, Chairman, Board of Directors, Pruitt Co. Inc., Houston, TX (1988-Present); Vice President, CountryMedic, Inc., Fort Worth, TX (2001-2003); President, Owner, Edwards & Associates, Inc. (1984-1996); President, Owner, Walker Auto Spring, Inc., Shreveport, LA (1978-1988); Executive Vice President, W.C. Supply Co., Tyler, TX (1977-1983); Vice President, W.C. Square, Inc. (1976-1992); Corporate Coordinator, Dillard Department Stores, Inc., Fort Worth, TX (1976-1977) **Career Related:** General Partner, ESE Properties, Tyler, TX (1991-Present); Elected Member, Board of Directors, Texas Baptist Missions Foundation (2015); Vice President, Camp Fannin Associate (1992-2008); Managing General Partner, Heritage Drive Plaza Office Suites (1992-1995); Executive Committee Member, E.T. State Fair (1990-2009); Commercial Real Estate Investor, Shreveport, LA, Houston, Odessa, Tyler, TX **Civic:** Board of Directors, Timberline Baptist Camp & Conference Center (2010-Present); Vice President, Camp Fannin Association (2001-Present); Vice President, Camp Fannin Association, Tyler, TX (1992-Present); Board of Associates, East Texas Baptist University, Marshall, TX (1988-Present); Assistant District Governor Rotary District 5830 (2013-2015); Treasurer, Timberline Baptist Camp and Conference Center (2010-2012); Board President, E. T. Symphony Orchestra (2009-2015); Chairman, Board of Advisers, Baylor University Libraries (2004-2006, 2012-2013); Chairman, Board of Advisers, Baylor University Libraries (2004-2006); Chair, Board of Trustees, East Texas Baptist University, Marshall, TX (2003-2005); Treasurer, Timberline Baptist Camp and Conference Center (2002-2018); Trustee, Timberline Baptist Camp and Conference Center (2001-2004); Executive Committee Member, Board of Trustees, Vice Chairman, Board of Trustees, East Texas Baptist University, Marshall, TX (2001-2003); Long Range Planning Committee, First Baptist Church, Tyler, TX (1999-2007); Member, Finance Committee, First Baptist Church, Tyler, TX (1997-2001); Board of Trustees, East Texas Baptist University (1995-2018); Chairman, Stewardship Committee, First Baptist Church, Tyler, TX (1995-1996); Chairman, Merger Committee, Smith County Historical Society and Carnegie History Center Merger (1993-1994); Vice President, Camp Fannin Association (1992-1997); President, East Texas State Fair (1991-1994); Smith County Historical Commission (1991-1994); President, Board of Associates, East Texas Baptist University, Marshall, TX (1991-1993); Executive Committee, East Texas State Fair (1990-2009); Trustee, Timberline Baptist Camp and Conference Center (1987-2018) **Awards:** Founders Medal, East Texas Baptist University, Marshall, TX (2017); Distinguished Alumni Award, Baylor University Alumni Association (2009); Crystal Dove of Peace Award, Rotary International, Evanston, IL **Membership:** Board of Directors, East Texas Symphony Orchestra Foundation (2015-Present); President, East Texas Symphony Orchestra Foundation (2015-Present); President, Board of Directors, Camp Fannin Association Inc. (2011-Present); Board of Directors, Camp Ford Historical Association (1999-Present); Board of Directors, Rotary Club Tyler (1998-Present); Chair, Scholarship Committee, East Texas Baylor Club (1997-Present); Chairman, East Texas Symphony Orchestra Association (2014-2015); Chairman, East Texas Symphony Orchestra Association (2009-2011); President, Rotary Club Tyler (2009-2010); Committee Member, Nomination Boards of Affiliated Ministries, Baptist General Convention of Texas (2008-2011); President-elect, Rotary Club Tyler (2008-2009); President-elect, East Texas Symphony Orchestra Association (2008-2009); Vice President, East Texas Symphony Orchestra Association (2007-2008); President, Camp Ford Historical Association (2005-2010); President, Board of Directors, Camp Ford Historical Association (2005-2009); Board of Directors, Young Audiences of Northeast Texas (2002-2014); Foundation President, Rotary Club Tyler (2002-2005); President, East Texas Baylor Club (2001-2005); Vice President, Camp Ford Historical Association (2000) **Marquis Who's Who Honors:** Distinguished Humanitarian (2017) **Political Affiliations:** Republican **Religion:** Baptist **Shipping Address:** 3600 Jill Circle, Tyler, TX, 75701

Howard L. Edwards

Title: Mining, Oil and Gas Executive **Industry:** Mining & Metals **Company Name:** The Anaconda Company & Atlantic Richfield Company **Date of Birth:** 06/10/1931 **Place of Birth:** Baker City **State:** OR **Parents:** Elmer L. Edwards; Bernice (Stringham) Edwards **Marital Status:** Married **Spouse Name:** Carolyn Bagley (1954-2013, Deceased) **Children:** Bryant B. Edwards; H. McKay Edwards; Mitchell L. Edwards; Paul S. Edwards **Education:** JD, The George Washington University (1959); Postgraduate Coursework, University of Utah (1956-1957); Postgraduate Coursework, Stanford University (1955-1956); BS, Brigham Young University (1955) **Career:** Corporate Secretary, Atlantic Richfield Company, Los Angeles (1984-1995); General Attorney, ARCO Alaska Inc., Anchorage, AK (1982-1984); General Attorney, Anaconda Mining Company, Denver, CO (1977-1982); Vice President, The Anaconda Company, New York, NY (1970-1977); Assistant to the Chairman of the Board, The Anaconda Company, New York, NY (1969-1970); Partner, VanCott, Bagley, Cornwall and McCarthy, Salt Lake City, UT (1964-1969); VanCott, Bagley, Cornwall and McCarthy, Salt Lake City, UT (1961-1969); Attorney, U.S. Department of the Interior, Salt Lake City, UT (1960-1961); Legal Assistant, Mining US Bureau of Land Management, Washington, DC (1957-1960) **Civic:** National Advisory Council, Dixie State University, Saint George, UT (1987-Present); Trustee, Utah Valley University Foundation, Orem, UT (2005-2010); Director, Dynatronics Corporation, Electronic Medical Devices, Salt Lake City, UT (1996-2016); Chairman, National Advisory Council, Dixie State University, Saint George, UT (1994-1996); Board of Visitors, J. Reuben Clark Law School, Brigham Young University (1980-1983); President, Director, Provo, Brigham Young University Alumni Association (1972-1983); Director, Lerch, Bates and Associates, Inc., Consulting Engineers, Denver, CO (1970-1996) **Membership:** Sons of the Utah Pioneers (1995-Present); Rotary Club (1978-Present); Council on Foreign Relations (1970-Present) **Bar Admissions:** State of California (1987); State of Alaska (1982); State of Colorado (1981); State of Utah (1959) **Marquis Who's Who Honors:** Lifetime Achievement (2017) **To what do you attribute your success:** Mr. Edwards attributes his success to education and a supporting spouse and family. **Why did you become involved in your profession or industry:** He chose a legal education and concentration on studies relating to legal issues unique to mining and oil and gas industries. **Hobbies:** Biking; Skiing; Landscaping **Political Affiliations:** Republican **Religion:** The Church of Jesus Christ of Latter-Day Saints **Business Address:** P.O. Box 680934, Park City, UT, 84068

James B. Edwards, PhD

Title: Consultant **Industry:** Consulting **Date of Birth:** 04/27/1935 **Place of Birth:** Atlanta **State:** GA **Parents:** James T. Edwards; Frances L. (McEachern) Edwards **Marital Status:** Married **Spouse Name:** Virginia Ann Reagin (2/21/1958) **Children:** James Benjamin II; Chad Reagin; Calli Ann; Judy Clair **Education:** PhD in Business Administration, University of Georgia (1971); MBA, University of Georgia (1962); BBA in Finance, University of Georgia (1958) **Certifications:** Certified Cost Analyst; Certified Internal Auditor; Certified Management Accountant; Charted Global Management Accounting Designation, Association of International Certified Professional Accountants; Certified in Data Processing; Certified Public Accountant, State of Tennessee; Certified Public Accountant, Certified Public Accountant, State of South Carolina **Career:** Distinguished Professor Emeritus, Former William W. Bruner Distinguished Faculty Fellow, University of South Carolina, Columbia, SC; Vice President, Integrated Cost Management Systems Inc., Arlington, Texas (1990-1991); Internal Consultant, J.W. Hunt and Company, LLP, Columbia, SC (1983-1984); Professor, University of South Carolina, Columbia, SC (1977-2005); Fellow, Business Partnership Foundation, University of South Carolina, Columbia, SC (1977-1990); Associate Professor, University of South Carolina, Columbia, SC (1973-1977); Assistant Professor, University of South Carolina, Columbia, SC (1971-1973); Vice President, Chairman, Board of Directors, General Data Service Inc., Athens, GA (1970-1971); Partner, Q.F. Lester & Co., Athens, GA (1967-1968); Instructor, Accounting, University of Georgia, Athens, GA (1966-1971); Managing Partner, Wilson, Edwards and Swang, Accountants, Nashville, TN (1964-1966); Instructor, Nashville Center, The University of Tennessee (1964-1966); Instructor, Lipscomb University, Nashville, TN (1963-1966); Staff Accountant, Max M. Cuba & Co., Atlanta, GA (1962-1963); Controller, Better Maid Dairy Products, Inc., Athens, GA (1958-1962) **Career Related:** Served in a Variety of Professional Related Organizations **Civic:** Treasurer, Spring Valley Education Foundation (1985-1993); Board of Directors, Spring Valley Education Foundation (1983-1993); Vice President, Spring Valley Education Foundation (1983-1985); Coach, Little League Baseball, Columbia, SC (1972-1976); President, Georgia Christian Foundation, Inc. (1968-1969); Board of Directors, Atlanta Bible Camp, Inc.; Board of Directors, Georgia Christian Foundation, Inc. **Military Service:** United States Marine Core Reserve **Creative Works:** Editor, "Emerging Practices in Cost Management and Activity-Based Management," Handbook of Cost Management for Service Industries (1997-Present); Author, "The Final Word" (2016); Assistant Editor, National Magazine, Planning Executives Institute (1971-1977); Editor-in-Chief, Journal of Corporate Accounting and Finance; Editor, Annual Publications, Warren, Gorham & Lamont, Inc.; Contributor, Articles on Management Accounting, Professional Publications; Author, Editor-in-chief of Journal of Corporate Accounting and Finance **Awards:** Eight National Awards for Contributions to Accounting Literature **Membership:** National Education Committee, Institute of Management Accountants, Inc. (1977-1980, 1995-Present); National Vice President, Institute of Management Accountants, Inc. (1980-1981); President, Carolina's Council, Institute of Management Accountants, Inc. (1976); National Director, Institute of Management Accountants, Inc. (1975-1977); Vice President, Southeastern Section, Decision Sciences Institute (1975-1976); National Research Committee, Institute of Management Accountants, Inc. (1974-1975); President, Columbia Chapter, Institute of Management Accountants, Inc. (1973-1974); Founding President, South Carolina Association of Accounting Educators (1972-1973); American Accounting Association; Association of International Certified Professional Accountants; The Institute of Internal Auditors; Planning Executives Institute; South Carolina CPA's; Omicron Delta Epsilon; Beta Alpha Psi; Delta Sigma Pi; Sigma Chi Fraternity; Five Points **Marquis Who's Who Honors:** Albert Nelson Marquis Lifetime Achievement Award (2017) **To what do you attribute your success:** Dr. Edwards attributes his success to his commitment. **Why did you become involved in your profession or industry:** He became involved in his profession due to his interest in quantitative aspects of economics. **What do you consider to be the highlight of your career:** The highlight of Dr. Edwards career has been the success of his former students. **Hobbies:** Gardening; Golf **Religion:** Church of Christ **Shipping Address:** 38 Eastbranch Ct, Columbia, SC, 29223

Vicki Ann Edwards

Title: Director, Consultant **Industry:** Consulting **Date of Birth:** 12/19/1947 **Place of Birth:** Fremont **State:** NE **Parents:** Howard Carl Schneider; Donna Marie (Earleywine) Schneider **Marital Status:** Married **Spouse Name:** Charles Douglas Edwards (5/27/1977) **Children:** Janci **Education:** EdD in Curriculum and Instruction, Northern Arizona University (1988); MA in Education, Northern Arizona University (1986); MA in Education, Arizona State University (1979); BS in Education, Midland University, Fremont, NE (1972) **Career:** Student Teacher Supervisor, Arizona State University (2010-Present); Director of Assessment, Deer Valley School District (2004-2010); Principal, Reading Specialist, Deer Valley School District, Phoenix, AZ (1980-2004); Language Arts Teacher, Glendale Elementary School District (1977-1980); Language Arts Teacher, Arlington Public Schools (1972-1976) **Career Related:** Mentor, Midland University, Fremont, NE (2004); Teacher, Midland University, Fremont, NE (2004) **Civic:** President, Alumni Board, Midland University, Fremont, NE (2008-Present); Treasurer, Lutheran Church of the Master; Member, Alumni Board, Midland University, Fremont, NE **Creative Works:** Author, "Assessing Early Reading Skills with the Mountain Shadows Phonemic Awareness Scale," Journal of Psychoeducational Assessment (2004); Author, "One Year Stability of the Elementary Reading Attitude Survey," Mid-Western Educational Researcher (1995); Author, "Extracurricular Reading and Reading Achievement: The Rich Stay Rich and the Poor Don't Read," Reading Improvement (1992); Author, "The Search for the Ideal Teacher: Research on Teacher Characteristics, 1890-1950" (1988) **Awards:** Recipient, Mentor Award, Midland University, Fremont, NE (2004); Recipient, Outstanding Educator Award, Mountain Shadows PTSA (2001); Recipient, Award of Achievement, United States West Communications, Tuscon, AZ (1992); Named, Teacher of the Year, Deer Valley School District **Membership:** President, Alumni Board, Midland University, Fremont, NE (2006-2014); Life Member, Arizona State University Alumni Association; Lutheran Church of the Master; International Reading Association; Association for Supervision and Curriculum Development; National Council of Teachers of English; Arizona School Administrators **Marquis Who's Who Honors:** Albert Nelson Marquis Lifetime Achievement Award (2017) **Hobbies:** Reading; Needlecraft; Music; Playing piano **Political Affiliations:** Democrat **Shipping Address:** 2336 W Laurel Ln, Phoenix, AZ, 85029

Leif D. Eie

Title: Air Transportation Executive (Retired) **Industry:** Leisure, Travel & Tourism **Company Name:** Scandinavian Airline Systems **Date of Birth:** 07/12/1929 **Place of Birth:** Flekkefjord **State/Country of Origin:** Norway **Parents:** Lars Eie; Aagot Dagmar Eie **Marital Status:** Married **Spouse Name:** Patricia MacKean **Children:** Lisa Britt; Christian **Education:** Diplomate in Business, Heilbronn Army Education Center, with Distinction (1954); Diplomate in English, Heilbronn Army Education Center, with Distinction (1954); Coursework in Army Leadership, with Honors (1953); Coursework, University of Washington **Career:** Northwestern Area Manager, Scandinavian Airline Systems (1970-1991); District Sales Manager, Scandinavian Airline Systems, Seattle, WA (1965-1970); Ticket Counter Staff to Sales Manager, Scandinavian Airline Systems, New York City, NY (1952-1964) **Civic:** Honorary Vice-Consul, Royal Norwegian Consulate, Washington, DC (1990); Co-Founder, Seattle Sister Cities Program; Founder, Nordic Heritage Museum, Seattle, WA **Military Service:** Norwegian Air Force **Awards:** The Prestigious President of the United States Award (1990); Norwegian of The Year Award, His Majesty King Ovav V (1988); Honored Citizen, City Of Tacoma, Washington (1988); Eponym, Leif Eie Day, Mayor of Seattle (1988); Honoree, Man of the Decade, Norwegian American Chamber of Commerce (1985); First Citizen of Seattle Award, Mayor Wes Uhlman (1977); Distinguished Service Award, Pacific Lutheran University (1977); Boy Scouts of America Award (1976); Ski For Light Award (1976); Honoree, Decorated Knight Order of the Northern Star, Sweden; Honor Medal; St. Olav Medal; Honoree, Knight of the Royal Norwegian Order of Merit; Eponym, Leif Eie Scholarship, Norwegian American Chamber of Commerce; Eponym, Leif Eie Oral History Project, Nordic Heritage Museum; Distinguished Service Award, Builder of a New North Western Business, Pacific Lutheran University; J. Eldon Opheim Award, Norwegian American Chamber of Commerce; Norwegian War Veterans Association Award for Help and Support **Membership:** Sons of Norway; Norwegian Seamen War Veterans; Norwegian Singers Association; Rebuild National Park Society; Finnish American Chamber of Commerce; Honorary Board of Directors, Norwegian American Chamber of Commerce; Board of Directors, Swedish American Chamber of Commerce; Seattle Chamber of Commerce; Norwegian Commercial Club; Swedish Club; Danish Club; Washington State Codfish Club **Marquis Who's Who Honors:** Albert Nelson Marquis Lifetime Achievement Award (2017) **Why did you become involved in your profession or industry:** Mr. Eie wanted to work in travel so that he and his family could visit the world and meet new people. **What do you consider to be the highlight of your career:** Mr. Eie is most proud of creating the Sister Cities Program to bring people together. He always had an interest in helping people connect; he enjoys traveling and meeting people of different cultures. The Sister Cities Program brings the arts to other cities. For instance, they brought theater production to Bergen. **Hobbies:** Playing guitar; Painting; Salmon fishing; Composing music **Shipping Address:** 3203 NW 69th Street, Seattle, WA, 98117

Richard William Eiger

Title: Publisher (Retired) **Industry:** Publishing **Date of Birth:** 05/11/1933 **Place of Birth:** New York **State:** NY **Parents:** William Eiger; Hellen M. (Fetten) Eiger **Marital Status:** Married **Spouse Name:** Ruth B. Engelke **Children:** Keith R. **Education:** MBA, New York University (1960); BFA, Pratt Institute (1955) **Career:** Visiting Professor, School of Information, Pratt Institute (2000-2005); Publisher, The World Almanac (1993-1998); Vice President, K-III Reference Corporation (Now PRIMEDIA Reference Corporation) (1991-1993); Senior Vice President, MacMillan Publishing Company (1980-1991); President, MacMillan Educational Company (1980-1991); Vice President of Publications, Western Publishing Company (1975-1980); Publishing Director, Western Publishing Company (1968-1974); With, Western Publishing Company (1958-1980) **Career Related:** Professor, School of Information, Pratt Institute, New York, NY (2004-Present); Consultant, Langenscheidt Publishing Company (2002-Present); Consultant, VirtuelEd Inc. (2000-Present); Advisor, Bearport Publishing (2003-2009) **Civic:** Vice Chairman, Board of Trustees, Delaware College of Art and Design (2010-Present); Delaware College of Art and Design, Wilmington, DE (2004-Present); Historical Society, Princeton, NJ (2002-Present); Chairman, Development Committee, Pratt Institute, New York City, NY (1997-Present); Secretary, Pratt Institute, New York City, NY (1996-Present); Executive Committee, Pratt Institute, New York City, NY (1995-Present); Trustee, Pratt Institute, New York City, NY (1992-Present); Trustee Emeritus, Pratt Institute, New York City, NY (1986-Present); Board of Directors, Alumni Board, Pratt Institute, New York City, NY (1986-Present); Trustee, Katharine Gibbs School, New Jersey (1996-2001); Trustee, Katharine Gibbs School, Montclair, NJ (1995-2001); Public Committee, Brandeis University, Waltham, MA (1993-2000) **Military Service:** Lieutenant, U.S. Army (1956-1957) **Creative Works:** Author, "Booked for Life: An Uncommon Memoir, My Career in Publishing" (2020) **Membership:** Emeritus Member, The Old Guard of Princeton, NJ (2014-Present) **Marquis Who's Who Honors:** Albert Nelson Marquis Lifetime Achievement Award (2017) **Why did you become involved in your profession or industry:** He became involved in his industry at a young age, books were always around, and he thought of them as toys. He was interested and amused by childhood books like "Mother Goose" and "Aesops Fables." The two most important books in his life are the King James Bible and "Scotts International Book of Stamps." **What do you consider to be the highlight of your career:** One of the highlights of his career was working on books and projects as a collaborative team to produce books, both electronically and print, as he believes that books exist for long time and enrich and educate people's lives. **Religion:** Christian Scientist **Shipping Address:** 900 Hollinshead Spring Road, Apt. h-207, Skillman, NJ, 08558

Jeri A. Eimers

Title: Counselor **Industry:** Social Work **Company Name:** College Hospital **Date of Birth:** 01/20/1951 **Place of Birth:** Berkeley **State:** CA **Parents:** Alfred D. Wallace Stevens; Marjorie E. (Nordheim) Stevens **Marital Status:** Married **Spouse Name:** Richard A. Eimers (3/2/1996); Roy A. Neiman (1969-1977) **Children:** Lorien; Arwen **Education:** Postgraduate Coursework, Human Sexuality Program, University of California, Los Angeles (1991-1992); MA in Psychology, California State University, Long Beach, Long Beach, CA, With Distinction (1981); BA in Psychology, California State University, Long Beach, Long Beach, CA, With Distinction (1979); AA, Palomar College, San Marcos, CA (1977) **Certifications:** Certified Community College Instructor (1992); Licensed Marriage, Family and Child Therapist, State of California (1986); Certified Sex Therapist, State of California (1986); Certified Child Therapist, State of California (1986); Certified Marriage and Family Community College Instructor (1982); Certified Community College Counselor (1982); Certified Relationship Specialist **Career:** Group Chair, Leader, College Hospital, Cerritos, CA (1993-1995); Therapist, Private Practice, Cypress Mental Health, California (1988-1996); Senior Social Worker, Orange County Social Services Agency, Orange, CA (1988-1990); Social Worker, Los Angeles County Department of Children and Family Services, Long Beach, CA (1986-1988); Director, American Learning Corporation, Huntington Beach, CA (1983-1985); Teacher, ABC Unified School District, Cerritos, CA (1982-1983); Research Assistant, California State University (1978-1982) **Career Related:** Speaker and Presenter in Field **Civic:** Child Sexual Abuse Network, Orange, CA (1988); Legislative Committee, Child Abuse Prevention Council of Orange County (1988) **Awards:** Women's League Scholarships (1979-1982) **Membership:** American Psychological Association; American Association of University Women; Western Psychological Association; California Association of Marriage and Family Therapists; American Association for Marriage and Family Therapy; California American Professional Society on the Abuse of Children; American Professional Society on the Abuse of Children; American Group Psychotherapy Association; American Association of Integrative Therapy; National Association Professional Woman; Psi Chi; The Honor Society of Phi Kappa Phi **Marquis Who's Who Honors:** Albert Nelson Marquis Lifetime Achievement Award (2017) **Hobbies:** Writing; Theater; Classical music; Jazz music; Swimming; Dance **Political Affiliations:** Republican **Religion:** Methodist **Shipping Address:** 244 Via Tierra, Encinitas, CA, 92024

Howard Eisen

Title: Cardiologist **Industry:** Medicine & Health Care **Company Name:** Drexel University College of Medicine **Date of Birth:** 05/25/1956 **Place of Birth:** Forest Hills **State:** NY **Parents:** Ezra Michael Eisen; Gertrude M. (Schmidt) Eisen **Marital Status:** Married **Spouse Name:** Judith Ellen Wolf (6/26/1983) **Children:** Jonathan Ezra; Miriam Sarah **Education:** Fellow in Cardiology, Washington University School of Medicine-Barnes Hospital, St. Louis (1984-1987); Resident in Medicine, Hospital University of Pennsylvania (1982-1984); Medical Intern, Hospital University of Pennsylvania (1981-1982); MD, University Pennsylvania (1981); BA in Biology, Cornell University (1977) **Certifications:** Diplomate in Advanced Heart Failure and Transplantation, American Board of Internal Medicine; Certification, American Board of Cardiovascular Diseases; Certification, American Board of Internal Medicine; Certification, American Board of Medical Examiners **Career:** Thomas J. Vischer Professor of Medicine, Drexel University College of Medicine, Philadelphia, PA (2004-Present); Director of Advanced Heart Failure Center, Temple University (2002-2004); Medical Director, Advanced Heart Failure and Transplant Program, Temple University (1999-2002); Medical Director, Cardiomyopathy and Transplant Center, Temple University (1999-2002); Associate Director, General Clinical Research Center, Temple University (1995-2002); Medical Director, Cardiac Transplant Program, Temple University (1999-2004); Director, Heart Failure Care Unit, Temple University (1993-1999); Professor of Medicine and Physiology, Temple University (1997-2004); Associate Professor of Medicine and Physiology, Temple University (1993-1997); Assistant Professor of Medicine, University of Pennsylvania, Philadelphia (1990-1993); Family Professor of Cardiology, Joseph Di Palma; Chief, Division of Cardiology, Drexel University College of Medicine and Hahnemann University Hospital; Director, Center of Cardiovascular Disorders, Drexel University College of Medicine; Director, Center for Advanced Heart Failure Care at Hahnemann, Drexel University College of Medicine **Career Related:** Member, Study Section, National Institutes of Health (2002-Present); Member, Cryptosporidiosis Advisory Committee, Department of Public Health, Philadelphia (1995-2000) **Creative Works:** Author, Manuscript, New England Journal of Medicine (2003); Editorial Board Member, Journal of American College of Cardiology Heart Failure; Editorial Board Member, Journal of Cardiac Failure; Associate Editor, American Journal of Transplantation; Editorial Consultant, Journal of Heart & Lung Transplantation; Editorial Board, Journal of Heart & Lung Transplantation **Awards:** Honroee, Top Doctor, Philadelphia Magazine (1996-Present); Honoree, Castle & Connolly's Top Doctor in America (1996-Present); Alumni Service Award, American Federation of Clinical Research (2006); H. Christian Award, American Federation of Clinical Research (1993) **Membership:** Grants, Committee Member, Grants Executive Committee, American Society of Transplanation (2011-Present); Fellow, American Heart Association; Clinical Council, American Heart Association (1995-Present); Research Committee, American Heart Association (1995-Present); Chairman, Peer-Review Committee, American Heart Association (1996-Present); Chair, Program Chair, International and Inter-Social Coordinator Committee, International Society of Heart and Lung Transplanation (2014-2015); Transplantation; Chair, Thoracic Committee, American Society of Transplanation (2007-2008); Program Committee, International Society of Heart and Lung Transplanation (2004, 2007); President, Southeastern Pennsylvania American Heart Association Affiliate (2003-2005); Founder, Investigatorship Award, American Heart Association (1996-2001); National Council, American Federation of Clinical Research (1992-1995); American College of Cardiology; American College of Physicians; Member, American Society of Chair, Thoracic Committee, American Society of Transplanation; Phi Kappa Phi; Phi Beta Kappa; Alpha Omega Alpha **Marquis Who's Who Honors:** Albert Nelson Marquis Lifetime Achievement Award (2017) **Why did you become involved in your profession or industry:** He became involved in his profession because he had family members with heart disease and was interested in learning how to help them. **What do you consider to be the highlight of your career:** A highlight of his career happened in 2003 when he published a manuscript in the new england journal of medicine, about a new medication for heart transplant medication, he lead this. **Hobbies:** Reading; Rowing; Classical music; Running **Shipping Address:** 507 Shortridge Dr, Wynnewood, PA, 19096

Ronald Lee Eisenberg

Title: Radiologist **Industry:** Medicine & Health Care **Company Name:** Beth Israel Medical Center **Date of Birth:** 07/11/1945 **Place of Birth:** Philadelphia **State:** PA/US **Parents:** Milton Eisenberg; Betty (Klein) Eisenberg **Marital Status:** Married **Spouse Name:** Zina Leah Schiff **Children:** Avlana; Cherina **Education:** DSJS, Spertus Institute, Chicago (2010); JD, William Howard Taft University, Santa Ana, CA (1996); MD, University of Pennsylvania (1969); AB, University of Pennsylvania (1965) **Certifications:** Diplomate, American Board of Radiology **Career:** Staff Radiologist, Beth Israel Medical Center, Boston (2007-Present); Professor of Radiology, Harvard Medical School, Harvard University, Boston (2007-Present); Chairman, Department of Radiology, Highland Hospital, Oakland, CA (1991-2007); Professor and Chairman, Department of Radiology, Louisiana State University, Shreveport (1980-1991); Staff Radiologist, VA Medical Center, San Francisco (1975-1980) **Career Related:** Series Editor, Pattern of the Month, American Journal of Roentgenology (2009-2014); Editor, The Radiologist (1994-2004); Editor, Radiology Report (1988-1991) **Military Service:** Major, U.S. Army (1971-1973) **Creative Works:** Author, "Jews in Medicine: Contributions of Jewish Physicians to Health and Medicine" (2018); Author, "Comprehensive Radiographic Pathology," 6th Edition (2016); Author, "850 Intriguing Questions about Judaism" (2015); Author, "Trilogy of Essential Figures in the Bible, Talmud, and Jewish Scholarship" (2013-2014); Author, "What the Rabbis Said" (2010); Author, "Clinical Imaging: An Atlas of Differential Diagnosis, 5th Edition" (2010); Author, "Dictionary of Jewish Terms" (2008); Author, "The Streets of Jerusalem" (2006); Author, "The 613 Mitzvot" (2005); Author, "Radiology and the Law" (2005); Author, "The JPS Guide to Jewish Traditions" (2004); Author, "The Jewish World in Stamps" (2003); Author, "Gastrointestinal Radiology," Fourth Edition (2003); Author, "Radiology: An Illustrated History" (1992); Author, "Diagnostic Imaging in Surgery" (1986); Co-author, Newspaper Column, "Doctor/Doctor"; Contributor, Articles, Professional Journals **Awards:** Honored Educator Award, Radiological Society of North America (2012); Norman Jaffe Award, BIDMC Radiology (2009); Man of the Year, American Physicians Fellowship, Boston (1987); Outstanding Book in Health Sciences, Association of American Publishers (1986) **Membership:** Fellow, American College of Radiology; Radiological Society of North America; American Roentgen Ray Society; Association of University Radiologists; Society for Gastrointestinal Radiology **Bar Admissions:** The State Bar of California **Marquis Who's Who Honors:** Albert Nelson Marquis Lifetime Achievement Award (2017) **Hobbies:** Piano; Law; Stamp collecting/philately; Classical music; Theater; Ballet; Sunday New York Times crossword puzzles **Business Address:** 330 Brookline Ave, Boston, MA, 02215 **Shipping Address:** 1731 Beacon St Apt 717, Brookline, MA, 02445

Maurice Gray Eldridge

Title: Academic Administrator **Industry:** Education/Educational Services **Company Name:** Swarthmore College **Date of Birth:** 02/17/1940 **Place of Birth:** Washington **State:** DC **Parents:** Schuyler Thomas Eldridge; Thelma (Gray) Eldridge **Marital Status:** Married **Spouse Name:** Patricia Brooks (2016); Joan Alice Tibbs (6/21/1969, Deceased 2012); Susannah Stone (8/25/1962, Divorced 12/1968) **Children:** Maria Teresa (Deceased 5/11/2018); Jonathan Kenneth **Education:** MEd, University of Massachusetts (1976); BA, Swarthmore College (1962) **Certifications:** Certified Teacher, Commonwealth of Massachusetts; Certified Counselor, Commonwealth of Massachusetts; Certified Principal, Washington, DC **Career:** Executive Assistant to President, Vice President, College and Community Relations, Swarthmore College (1998-2016); Associate Vice President, Swarthmore College (1993-1998); Associate Director to Director, Development, Swarthmore College (1989-1993); Principal, Duke Ellington School of Arts, Washington, DC (1979-1989); Educational Specialist, Massachusetts Department of Education, Pittsfield, MA (1976-1979); Assistant Headmaster, Windsor Mountain School, Lenox, MA (1967-1975); Teacher, English and United States History, Windsor Mountain School, Lenox, MA (1965-1967); Teacher, English and Creative Writing, Pennsbury High School, Fallsington, PA (1962-1965) **Career Related:** Co-Founder, President, Board of Directors, Chester Charter School for the Arts (2005-Present); Independent Arts Consultant (1987-Present); President, International Network Schools of Arts (1987-1989); President, International Network Schools of Arts (1982); Educational Policy Fellow, Institute for Educational Leadership, Boston, MA (1978-1979) **Civic:** Vice Chair of the Board of Directors, Former Co-Founding Chair, Chester Fund for Education and the Arts (2006-Present); Co-Chairperson, Chester-Swarthmore College Community Coalition (1992-Present); School Board, Suburban Music School, Media, PA (1989-1995) **Creative Works:** Editor, "Network Bibliography: The Arts High School Library" (1991); Contributor, Articles, Professional Publications **Awards:** Distinguished Service Award, National Association of Presidential Assistants in Higher Education (2007); Whitney M. Young Junior Memorial Award, Urban League, Washington, DC (1982) **Membership:** Vice Chair, Board of Directors, The Chester Fund for Education and the Arts (2018-Present); Board of Directors, Greater Philadelphia Chapter, National Society of Fundraising Executives (1992-1994); National Society of Fundraising Executives; Council for Advancement and Support of Education; Board Member, Assistant Clerk of the Board, Pendle Hill; Board of Directors, The Chester Charter School for the Arts **Marquis Who's Who Honors:** Albert Nelson Marquis Lifetime Achievement Award (2017) **Why did you become involved in your profession or industry:** When Mr. Eldridge graduated college he knew he wanted to be a teacher, so he pursued a teaching career and has been in the field of education ever since. **What do you consider to be the highlight of your career:** The highlight of Mr. Eldridge's career was the ten years he spent at the Duke Ellington School of the Arts. He helped establish the school and its character while he was there. **Where will you be in five years:** In five years, Mr. Eldridge will be, all things being equal, continuing his present community service roles and enjoying the development of his grandchildren. **Hobbies:** Reading; Gardening; Tropical fish; Music; Stamp collecting; Writing **Shipping Address:** 605 N Chester Road, Swarthmore, PA, 19081 **Website:** http://www.chestercharterschoolforthearts.org

Angela V. Eleazar

Title: Consultant, Public Speaker, Writer-Poet, Photographer, Artist **Industry:** Other **Company Name:** Sand and Sky **Place of Birth:** Manila **State/Country of Origin:** Philippines **Children:** Gerard; Edward; Jemelle; Margaret **Education:** BA, Education and English, St. Theresa's College (1965); Postgraduate Coursework in Linguistics, University of the Philippines **Certifications:** Licensed in Real Estate; Certified Interpreter, U.S. Department of Justice **Civic:** Victims of Domestic Violence **Awards:** Ambassador Award **Marquis Who's Who Honors:** Albert Nelson Marquis Lifetime Achievement Award (2017) **To what do you attribute your success:** She attributes her success to her dedication to her work, knowledge of the field, public relations work, and public speaking engagements about the world stage, especially places in Southeast Asia. **Why did you become involved in your profession or industry:** She became involved in her profession because it was a very practical career choice for her. She is a single parent bringing up four children and thought this would be the best thing to do, as it is a flexible career. Previously, she worked as a teacher. **What do you consider to be the highlight of your career:** The highlight of her career was being a published poet and having her photography published. Another highlight was performing as a vocalist for a musical group at the Tabernacle in Martha's Vineyard. **Where will you be in five years:** In five years, Ms. Eleazar seeks to experience continued growth in her present field. **Hobbies:** Going to the beach; Being in the outdoors **Shipping Address:** PO Box 590405, Newton Centre, MA, 02459 **Website:** http://www.sand-sky.com

Michele Elia

Industry: Education/Educational Services **Date of Birth:** 01/02/1945 **Place of Birth:** Berzano, Asti-Piemonte **State/Country of Origin:** Italy **Parents:** Luigi Elia; Cristina (Fogliatti) Elia **Education:** Doctor in Engineering, Politecnico di Torino (1970) **Career:** Retired (2015); Professor, Politecnico di Torino (1990-2015); Associate professor, math., Politecnico di Torino (1977-1990); Researcher, Politecnico di Torino (1971-1977); Researcher, FIAT, Torino, Italy (1970-1971) **Career Related:** Vice Mayor (1999) **Creative Works:** Co-author, "The Information Theory Approach to Communications" (1977); Associate Editor, Mathematics Journals; Contributor, Articles, Professional Journals **Membership:** IEEE; New York Academy of Sciences; Fibonacci Association; Mathematics Association of America; American Mathematics Society; Unione Matematica Italiana **Religion:** Roman Catholic

Bruce Robert Ellig

Title: Personnel Director (Retired) **Industry:** Business Management/Business Services **Date of Birth:** 10/15/1936 **Place of Birth:** Manitowoc **State:** WI **Parents:** Robert Louis Ellig ; Lucille Marie (Westphal) Ellig **Marital Status:** Married **Spouse Name:** Janice Reals **Education:** MBA, University of Wisconsin (1960); BBA, University of Wisconsin (1959) **Career:** Vice President, Personnel, Pfizer, Inc., New York, NY (1985-1995); Vice President, Employee Relations, Pfizer, Inc., New York, NY (1983-1985); Vice President, Compensation and Benefits, Pfizer, Inc., New York, NY (1978-1983); Corporate Director, Compensation and Benefits, Pfizer, Inc., New York, NY (1970-1978); Manager, Compensation and Personnel Research, Pfizer, Inc., New York, NY (1968-1970); With, Pfizer, Inc., New York City, NY (1960-1996); Vice President, Employee Resources, Pfizer, Inc., New York, NY **Career Related:** Member, Advisory Panel, Career Central (2001-2003); Consultant, Organization Resources Counselors Inc. (1996-2001); Corporate Education, Corporate Advisory Council (1996-2001); Savings and Investment, Retirement Plan Assets, Retirement Plan, Employee Compensation & Management Development Standing Committees, Pfizer (1985-1996); Speaker in Field **Civic:** CalPERS Panel Discussion (2014); Dean's Advisory Board, School of Business, University of Wisconsin (2004-2008); Advisory Board, Global Remuneration Organization (1987-1990); Advisory Board, Kentucky Educational TV (1987-1990); Member, Center for Advanced Human Resource Studies, Cornell University (1985-1995); Chairman, Mayor's Advisory Pay Commission, New York, NY (1980); Sector Staff Member, Council for Wage and Price Stability (1979-1980); Merit Pay Task Force Member, United States Civil Service Commission (1979); Mayor's Advisory Pay Commission, New York, NY (1977-1978); Presidential Quadrennial Pay Commission (1976) **Creative Works:** Author, "American History Impact on Employee Pay and Benefits" (2015); Contributing Author, "Compensation Handbook" (2008); Author, "The Evolution of Employee Pay in the United States" (2005); Contributing Author, "The Future of Human Resource Management" (2005); Author, "The Complete Guide to Executive Compensation" (2002); Advisory Board, Executive Compensation Reports (1999-2002); Author, "Future Focus: Human Resources in the 21st Century" (1998); Contributing Author, "Tomorrow's Human Resources Management" (1997); Contributing Author, "Handbook for Professional Managers" (1985); Author, "Compensation and Benefits: Design and Analysis" (1985); Consultant Editor, Compensation and Benefits Review (1984-1996); Member, Advisory Board, Journal of Compensation and Benefits (1984-1996); Contributing Author, "Handbook of Business Administration" (1984); Author, "Executive Compensation, A Total Pay Perspective" (1982); Author, "Compensation and Benefits: Analytical Strategies" (1978); Contributing Author, "Encyclopedia of Professional Management" (1978); Contributor, More than 100 Articles to Professional Journals; Contributor, Mor ethan 400 Presentation, Radio and Television **Awards:** Distinguished Business Alumnus Award, University of Wisconsin School of Business (2007); Keystone Award, American Compensation's (1999); Lifetime Achievement Award, Society Human Resource Management (1999); Human Resources Executive of the Year, Human Resource Executive Magazine (1995); Person of the Year, University of Wisconsin Alumni Club of New York (1995); Aresty Fellow, Wharton Business School; Wall of Fame Award, American Management Association **Membership:** Faculty Staff, Society of Human Resource Management (1996-1999); Chairman, Board of Directors, Society Human Resource Management (1996); Fellow, Wharton's Aresty Institute; Fellow, Employer Benefits Research Institute; Fellow, National Academy of Human Resources; Metropolitan Club; Senior Executives Forum; Human Resources Roundtable Group; Advisory Council, Human Resource Management, Business Roundtable Conference Board; Lifetime Member, Personnel Round Table; American Compensation Association; Lifetime Member, Society of Human Resource Management; Past President, New York Personnel Management Association; American Management Association; New York Chamber of Commerce; Charter President, New York Association Compensation Administrators; Board of Directors Emeritus, University of Wisconsin Business School Alumni; Advisory Board Emeritus, University of Southern California Center for Effective Organizations; Past Partner, University of Illinois Center for Human Resource Management; Wharton/Spencer Stuart Director Institute; Phi Beta Kappa; Phi Eta Sigma; Beta Gamma Sigma **Political Affiliations:** Republican **Religion:** Roman Catholic **Shipping Address:** 10 Gracie Sq Apt 12G, New York, NY, 10028

James Ward Elliott

Title: Lawyer, Contracts Manager **Industry:** Law and Legal Services **Company Name:** Bechtel National, Inc **Date of Birth:** 03/04/1954 **Place of Birth:** Norwich **State:** NY **Parents:** George B. Elliott; Jayne Quinn Elliott **Marital Status:** Partnership **Spouse Name:** Nilda Aponte **Children:** Shawn; Chris **Education:** JD, Albany Law School [Union University](1979); BA & BS Education, SUNY Oneonta (1976) **Certifications:** Masters Certificate in Government Contracting, The George Washington University (2011); New York Teacher's Certificate **Career:** Prime Contracts Operation Manager, Bechtel National, Inc.(2004-Present); General Counsel, B&W Y12, LLC (now Consolidated Nuclear Security, LLC (2000-2004); Corporate Counsel, McDermott International, Inc. (1989-2000); Prime Contracts Counsel, Grumman Aerospace Corporation (now Northrop Grumman Corporation) (1986-1989) **Career Related:** Arbitrator, American Arbitration Association (1992-1997) **Military Service:** Lieutenant Colonel, U.S. Army Reserve (1986-2003); Judge Advocate, General Corps, U.S. Army (Active Duty: 1980-1986) **Awards:** Army Commendation Medal **Membership:** Virginia Bar Association; American Legion **Bar Admissions:** United States District Court Eastern District of Tennessee (2002); Tennessee (2002); Virginia (1991); New York (1980); United States Court of Appeals for the Armed Forces (1980); United States District Court Northern District of New York (1980) **Marquis Who's Who Honors:** Albert Nelson Marquis Lifetime Achievement Award (2017) **To what do you attribute your success:** He attributes his success to hard work, persistence, and attention to detail. **Why did you become involved in your profession or industry:** He became involved in his profession out of his thirst for knowledge: the law is diverse in its uses and applications. His father always taught him to pursue the truth, and that obvious solutions are not always the best. **What do you consider to be the highlight of your career:** The highlights of his career are working as General Counsel at the DOE Y12 National Security Complex, and his work on other national security projects. **Where will you be in five years:** In 5 years, he will be happily retired in Florida, but always willing to work special projects and offer his expertise either as an educator or project team member. **Hobbies:** Travel; Writing; Recording music **Political Affiliations:** Republican Leaning Independent **Business Address:** 12011 Sunset Hills Rd., Reston, VA, 20190-5919 **Shipping Address:** 43140 Huntsman Sq, Broadlands, VA, 20148

Jay D. Ellwanger

Title: Managing Partner **Industry:** Law and Legal Services **Company Name:** Ellwanger Law LLLP **Date of Birth:** 02/27/1976 **Place of Birth:** Chicago, IL **Parents:** J. David Ellwanger; Barbara Ellwanger **Marital Status:** Married **Spouse Name:** Christina Westfall **Children:** Jonas; Berit; Annika **Education:** JD, The University of Texas at Austin School of Law (2001); BA in English, The University of Texas at Austin, with Special Honors (1998) **Career:** Adjunct Professor, The Univ. of Texas School of Law (2003-Present); Managing Partner, DiNovo Price Ellwanger & Hardy LLP (2007-2017); Associate, Jenkens & Gilchrist (2001-2007) **Civic:** Chair of the Board, Wheat Ridge Ministries (2016-2017); Chair, Board of Urban Roots (2011-2016) **Creative Works:** Co-author, "Ten Patent Litigation Questions for Texas District Court Judges," Intellectual Property Legislation Committee, State Bar of Texas (2009); Speaker, "Current Trends in Employment Litigation," 43rd Annual DeWitty/Overton Freedom Fund Banquet, Austin Chapter, NAACP (2008); Speaker, "Discrimination in the Workplace," SummerFest Community Forum, KAZI (2008) **Awards:** Honoree, Super Lawyer (2013-2016); Austin Under 40 Award - Legal Category, Young Men's Business League and the Young Women's Alliance of Austin (2009); Honoree, Texas Rising Star in the Area of Commercial Litigation and Intellectual Property Litigation, Texas Super Lawyers, Texas Monthly Magazine (2007-2017); Leadership Austin Essential Class (2007-2008); Peregrinus Counsul Award, The University of Texas at Austin (2001); International Academy of Trial Lawyers Award (2001); Outstanding Advocate of the Graduating Class (2001); First Place, National Institute for Trial Advocacy Tournament of Champions (2000); Niemann Cup, School of Law, The University of Texas at Austin **Membership:** Texas International Law Journal (2001); Chair, Board of Advocates (2000-2001); The Order of Barristers; ABA; NELA; The State Bar of California; State Bar of Texas; Austin Bar Association; Former Member, Austin Young Lawyers Association; Barrister, Robert. W. Calvert Chapter, American Inns of Court; College of the State Bar of Texas **Bar Admissions:** Texas (2002); State of California (2001); United States District Court Northern District of Texas; United States District Court Western District of Texas; United States District Court Eastern District of Texas; United States District Court Southern District of Texas; United States District Court Northern District of California; United States District Court Eastern District of California; United States District Court Southern District of California; United States District Court Central District of California; United States Court of Appeals for the Federal Circuit **To what do you attribute your success:** Mr. Ellwanger attributes his success to hustle and believing in himself. **Why did you become involved in your profession or industry:** Mr. Ellwanger opened Ellwanger Law LLLP to fulfill a lifelong goal of honoring his family history by establishing a law firm dedicated to the eradication of discrimination and the defense of civil rights. **What do you consider to be the highlight of your career:** A highlight of his career is when he served as trial counsel to over 250 individual plaintiffs in one of the nation's largest employment discrimination cases, Taylor, et al v. Turner Industries. The case was covered by CNN and the Wall Street Journal and resulted in a $4.05 million verdict in the bellwether" trial of the first ten individual plaintiffs. This was the largest employment discrimination jury verdict in Texas in 2012. He also represented 74 Plaintiffs in Beaty, et al v. Hilshire Brands. The $4 million settlement was the largest in the history of the EEOC in Dallas involving a hostile work environment. He also represented sixteen plaintiffs in EEOC v. Allied Aviation, a class action racial discrimination lawsuit. This case resulted in what was also the largest settlement in the history of the Dallas office of the EEOC at the time. It garnered national media attention in the New York Times and the Los Angeles Times, as well as being featured on several national news broadcasts including Anderson Cooper's 360 on CNN. **Hobbies:** Family; Athletics; Cooking; Travel **Political Affiliations:** Democrat **Religion:** Evangelical Lutheran Church in America **Shipping Address:** 8310-1 N Capital of Texas Hwy Ste 190, Ellwanger Law, Austin, TX, 78731 **Website:** https://www.linkedin.com/in/jay-ellwanger-9006194/

Floyd Leroy English, PhD

Title: Telecommunications Industry Executive **Industry:** Telecommunications **Company Name:** Andrew Corporation **Date of Birth:** 06/10/1934 **Place of Birth:** Nicolaus **State:** CA **Year of Passing:** 2017-06-14 **Parents:** Elvan L. English; Louise (Corliss) English **Marital Status:** Married **Spouse Name:** Elaine Ewell (7/3/1981) **Children:** Christine; Roxane; Darryl **Education:** DSc, California State University, Honorary, Chico, CA (2005); PhD in Physics, Arizona State University (1965); MS in Physics, Arizona State University (1962); AB in Physics, California State University, Chico, CA (1959) **Career:** Board of Directors, Andrew Corporation, Orland Park, IL (1982-Present); Chairman Emeritus, Andrew Corporation, Orland Park, IL (2004); Chairman, Board of Directors, Andrew Corporation, Orland Park, IL (2002-2004); Chairman, Board of Directors, Andrew Corporation, Orland Park, IL (2001-2002); Board of Directors, Andrew Corporation, Orland Park, IL (1992-2001); President, Andrew Corporation, Orland Park, IL (1992-2001); Chief Executive Officer, Andrew Corporation, Orland Park, IL (1992-2001); Chief Executive Officer, Andrew Corporation, Orland Park, IL (1983-1992); Chief Operating Officer, Andrew Corporation, Orland Park, IL (1981-1982); President, Andrew Corporation, Orland Park, IL (1981-1982); Vice President, United States Operations, Andrew Corporation, Orland Park, IL (1981-1982); Consultant, Energy Management and Acquisitions, Albuquerque, NM (1980-1981); President, Darcom, Albuquerque, NM (1975-1979); General Manager, Integrated Circuits Division, Rockwell Collins, Newport Beach, CA (1973-1975); Division Supervisor, Sandia Laboratories, Albuquerque, NM (1965-1973) **Civic:** Creator, Floyd English Scholarship Fund for Students at University of California, Chico, CA **Military Service:** Captain, U.S. Army Reserve (1957-1969); 1st Lieutenant, U.S. Army (1954-1957) **Creative Works:** Contributor, Articles, Professional Journals **Membership:** Board of Directors, International Engineering Consortium (1984-2002); Executive Club Chicago (1983-2004); Institute of Electrical and Electronics Engineers; International Engineering Consortium **Marquis Who's Who Honors:** Albert Nelson Marquis Lifetime Achievement Award (2017) **Why did you become involved in your profession or industry:** Dr. English became involved in his profession because he always loved physics in high school. He had such a passion for it that he forewent a full football scholarship to Stanford because he could not pursue physics there, and instead attended California State University. **Political Affiliations:** Republican **Religion:** Presbyterian **Shipping Address:** 310A Padre Blvd Apt 2405, South Padre Island, TX, 78597

Carol Ennis

Title: Music Educator **Industry:** Education/Educational Services **Company Name:** American Guild **Date of Birth:** 07/05/1934 **Place of Birth:** Niagara Falls **State/Country of Origin:** ON/Canada **Parents:** George Burt Robbins; Mabel Marie Hallman **Marital Status:** Widowed **Spouse Name:** George Vernon Ennis (Deceased); Harold David Jamieson, Jr. (Deceased) **Children:** Stephen Jamieson (Deceased); Robin Jamieson; Glenn Jamieson **Education:** MEd, State University of New York, Buffalo (1971); BFA, State University of New York, Buffalo (1967) **Career:** Organist, American Guild (2010-Present); Music Director, Organist, Choir Director, Bacon Memorial Presbyterian Church, Niagara Falls, NY (1988-2010); Music Teacher, Tonawanda Public Schools, New York (1967-1996); Church Organist, Various Churches (1959-1988); Private Piano Teacher (1957-1967) **Civic:** Election Polling Inspector, Erie County Board of Elections, Amherst Town Board, New York (1998-Present); RSVP Volunteer, Ocala, FL (2007-2012); Reader, Radio Reading for the Blind, Cheektowaga, NY (1997-2005); Board Member, Treble Choral Ensemble, Niagara Falls, ON, Canada (1947-1952); Commemoration Committee for the War of 1812, Amherst, NY; Director, Readers Theatre, Cafe Improv, PBS Station; Director, Music Combo in Amherst, Cafe Improv, PBS Station **Creative Works:** Composer, "Patriotic Song" **Awards:** Voices of Tomorrow Winner, WBEN-TV, Buffalo, NY (1958); Scholar, Kiwanis Music Festival, Niagara Falls, ON, Canada (1952-1953) **Membership:** Daughters of the American Revolution; New York State United Teachers; University of Buffalo Women's Club; University of Buffalo Alumni Association **Hobbies:** Travel; Tennis; Current event discussion groups; Genealogy; Jazz **Shipping Address:** PO Box 152, 279 Brockmore Drive, East Amherst, NY, 14051

Karen Russell Entzi

Title: Music Educator **Industry:** Education/ Educational Services **Company Name:** Johnston County Schools **Date of Birth:** 08/17/1951 **Place of Birth:** Asheville **State:** NC **Parents:** John A. Russell; Angeline Noe Russell **Marital Status:** Married **Spouse Name:** John A. Entzi (01/04/1989) **Children:** Angeline Lorraine Bumgardner **Education:** MS in Teaching, Northwest Missouri State University (1995); MusB, University of North Carolina, Greensboro, NC (1973) **Career:** Orchestra Teacher, Johnston County Schools, Smithfield, NC (2002-Present); Orchestra Teacher, Cumberland County Schools, Fayetteville, NC; Teacher, Lancaster County School District, SC; Teacher, Lexington County School District Two, SC; Orchestra Teacher, Charlotte-Mecklenburg Schools, Charlotte, NC; Teacher, Richland School District One and Two, Columbia, SC **Career Related:** Adjunct Violin Teacher, University of North Carolina; Pembroke Conductor, Johnston County Youth Orchestra, Smithfield, NC (2003-Present) **Creative Works:** Musician, Various Professional Performances **Membership:** North Carolina Music Educators Association; American String Teachers Association; National String Orchestra Association **Marquis Who's Who Honors:** Albert Nelson Marquis Lifetime Achievement Award (2017) **Shipping Address:** 2 Cedarbrook Dr, Hendersonville, NC, 28739

Marc S. Ernstoff, MD

Title: Professor of Medicine **Industry:** Education/Educational Services **Company Name:** Roswell Park Cancer Institute **Date of Birth:** 09/04/1952 **Place of Birth:** Brooklyn **State:** NY **Marital Status:** Married **Spouse Name:** Linda Titus-Ernstoff **Children:** Five Children **Education:** Fellow in Medical Oncology, School of Medicine, Yale University, New Haven, CT (1981-1984); Resident in Internal Medicine, Bronx Municipal Hospital Center, Jack D. Weiler Hospital, Albert Einstein College of Medicine, Montefiore Medical Center, New York, NY (1979-1981); Intern in Internal Medicine, Bronx Municipal Hospital Center, Jack D. Weiler Hospital, Albert Einstein College of Medicine, Montefiore Medical Center, New York, NY (1978-1979); MD, School of Medicine, New York University (1978); BA in Art History, Emory University, Magna Cum Laude (1974) **Certifications:** Diplomate, American Board of Internal Medicine, Subspecialty in Medical Oncology (1989); Diplomate, American Board of Internal Medicine (1981); Diplomate, National Board of Medical Examiners (1979) **Career:** Professor of Medicine, Dartmouth-Hitchcock Medical Center, Lebanon, NH (1995-Present); Associate Director, Hematology/Oncology, Norris Cotton Cancer Center, Lebanon, NH (2000-2002); Section Chief, Hematology/Oncology, Dartmouth-Hitchcock Medical Center, Lebanon, NH (1996-2002); Deputy Director, Norris Cotton Cancer Center, Lebanon, NH (1995-2000); Director, Clinical Therapeutic Research Program, Norris Cotton Cancer Center, Lebanon, NH (1992-1995); Associate Professor, Dartmouth-Hitchcock Medical Center, Lebanon, NH (1991-1995); Associate Professor, University of Pittsburgh School Medicine (1990-1991); Medical Director, Genitourinary Tumors Study Group, University of Pittsburgh Cancer Institute (1986-1991); Director, Fellowship Program, Division of Medical Oncology and Hematology, University Pittsburgh (1986-1991); Assistant Professor of Medicine, University of Pittsburgh School of Medicine (1986-1990); Acting Director, Yale Melanoma Unit, Yale New Haven Hospital (1985-1986); Director, Clinical Research Office, Yale Comprehensive Cancer Center, New Haven, CT (1984-1986); Assistant Professor of Medicine, Yale University School of Medicine, New Haven, CT (1984-1986) **Career Related:** Fellow, American College of Physicians (1992) **Civic:** Board of Trustees, Hitchcock Foundation (1996-Present); Chairman, Hitchcock Foundation (1997-2001) **Awards:** New Hampshire Magazine Top Doctors Poll (2009-Present); Bernard Baruch Award, American College of Rehabilitation and Physical Medicine (1996-Present); Honoree, The Best Doctors in America (1996-Present); O. Ross McIntyre Professor of Medicine (2012); Best Educator, Hematology/Oncology Fellowship Program, Dartmouth Geisel School of Medicine (2012); Team Science Award, Society of Immunotherapy (2011); Team Science Award, Cancer Society of Immunotherapy for Cancer (2011); Distinguished Teacher Award for Residency Training, Department of Medicine, Dartmouth-Hitchcock Clinic (2000-2014); First Steven B. Currier Clinical Oncology Scholar (1997-2002) **Membership:** American Society of Clinical Oncology Program Committee (2000-Present); International Cytokine Society (1998-Present); Clinical Immunology Society (1988-Present); Society for Biological Therapy/Society of Immunotherapy of Cancer (SITC) (1988-Present); American Association for Cancer Research (1983-Present); American Society of Clinical Oncology (1983-Present); Melanoma Program Committee, International Society of Interferon Research (1983-Present); Melanoma Programme, World Health Organization (1997-2005); American Society of Clinical Oncology (1997); American College of Physicians (1993-1998); Affiliate Member, American Urological Association (1992-1996); American Federation of Clinical Research (1984-1991); Phi Beta Kappa; Sigma Xi; Omicron Delta Kappa; Alpha Epsilon Upsilon **Business Address:** Roswell Park Cancer Institute, Buffalo, NY, 14263 **Shipping Address:** 4 Stevens Road, Hanover, NH, 03755

Raymond M. Erwin

Title: Secondary School Educator **Industry:** Education/Educational Services **Date of Birth:** 12/08/1924 **Place of Birth:** Ames **State/Country of Origin:** IA **Parents:** Maurice Weir; Ruth (Martin) Erwin **Marital Status:** Married **Spouse Name:** Vivian Elaine Johnson (8/4/1995); Marion Emma Schwarting (10/14/1972); Gloria Yvonne Crews (6/18/1949) **Education:** MA (1971); BS, University of Minnesota (1954); BS, North Dakota State University (1948) **Certifications:** Certificate in Vocational Agriculture; Certified Agribusiness Teacher, State of Minnesota **Career:** Agriculture Advisor, Agency for International Development, Lam Don Province, South Vietnam (1966-1967); Freelance Commercial Photographer, Baytown Township Supervisor, Washington County, Minnesota (1963-1966); Vocational Agriculture Instructor, Stillwater High School, Minnesota (1954-1984); Veterans Institutional On-Farm Instructor, Minot State College, North Dakota (1948-1951); Audio-Visual Director, Minnesota **Career Related:** Sears College Scholar, North Dakota State University (1942) **Military Service:** Colonel, United States Marine Corps (1942-1984) **Creative Works:** Contributor, Articles, Professional Journals **Membership:** Sons of the American Revolution; Rotary International; Phi Delta Kappa; Alpha Phi Gamma; Alpha Tau Alpha; Alpha Zeta; Kappa Delta Pi; Reserve Officers Association; Marine Corps Reserve Officers Association; Marine Corps Association; Minnesota Vocational Association; American Vocational Association; Minnesota Vocational Agriculture Instructors Association; Minnesota Education Association; Future Farmers of America; National Education Association **Political Affiliations:** Republican **Religion:** Methodist **Shipping Address:** 5225 Northbrook Boulevard N, Stillwater, MN, 55082

Jane Erwin

Title: Board Member **Industry:** Education/Educational Services **Company Name:** Texas Woman's University **Awards:** Recipient, Outstanding Staff Award, Texas Woman's University; Lifetime Alumni, Texas Woman's University; Outstanding Young Women of America; Named, Above and Beyond Employee of the Year **To what do you attribute your success:** Ms. Erwin attributes her success to her relationship-building skills. **Why did you become involved in your profession or industry:** Ms. Erwin became involved in her profession because she firmly believes in Texas Woman's University, its mission and the strength and the leadership abilities it provides to women who attend and graduate. **What do you consider to be the highlight of your career:** The highlight of Ms. Erwin's career was when she first entered the development area and received an award for going above and beyond the call of duty. She has never been the kind of fundraiser that is pushy, but feels that if people trust her and she trusts them that it's a win all around. **Where will you be in five years:** In five years, Ms. Erwin plans to continue working with the aging population, as there are millions of baby boomers. She will also continue to better the lives of others by volunteering. Ms. Erwin enjoys ensuring that the donations received by the Texas Woman's University Foundation are properly used. **Hobbies:** Golfing; Reading; Music; Antiquing; Supporting the Dallas Mavericks **Shipping Address:** 8012 FM 2153, Aubrey, TX, 76227

Peter Quintus Eschweiler

Title: Planning Consultant (Retired) **Industry:** Civil Service **Date of Birth:** 11/02/1932 **Place of Birth:** Milwaukee **State:** WI **Parents:** Alexander Chadbourne Eschweiler, Jr.; Dorothy Quincy (Adams) Eschweiler **Marital Status:** Married **Spouse Name:** Mickie Pauline Symonds (8/13/1955) **Children:** Susan Marie; Steven Adams **Education:** Master of Regional Planning, Cornell University (1957); BA, Cornell University (1955) **Career:** Adviser, Nassau County Planning Commission, New York (1997-1998); Adviser, Greenway Community Council, Hudson River Valley, NY (1991-2000); Commissioner, Planning, Westchester County, White Plains, NY (1969-1991); Deputy Commissioner, Planning, Westchester County, White Plains, NY (1968-1969); Chief Planner, Westchester County, White Plains, NY (1967); Associate Planner, Frederick P. Clark & Associates, Rye, NY (1960-1966) **Civic:** Chairman, Mount Pleasant Public Library Lecture Group (2002-Present); Member, Mount Pleasant Public Library Lecture Group (1991-Present); Member, Advisory Board, Westchester County Storm Water (2012); Chairman, Westchester County Flood Action Task Force (2007-2011); Member, Pleasantville Business Support Council (2004-2012); Secretary, Pleasantville Housing Development Fund Co., Inc. (2003-2007); President, Pleasantville Community Housing Development Organization, Inc. (2003-2007); Member, Mission Planning Task Force, Presbytery of Hudson River (2002); Director, Westchester County Historical Society (2001-2007); Chairman, Westchester County Geographic Information Systems Task Force (1998-2009); President, Pleasantville, Housing Development Fund Co., Inc. (1997-2002); Chairman, Mission Planning Task Force, Presbytery of Hudson River (1997); Member, Mission Planning Task Force, Presbytery of Hudson River (1997); Member, Mission Planning Task Force, Presbytery of Hudson River (1994); Chairman, Westchester County Drought Management Task Force (1991-2002) **Military Service:** Lieutenant, U.S. Air Force (1957-1960) **Awards:** Top Honor Award, Westchester County Senior Citizens Hall of Fame (2005); Outstanding Community Service Award, Pleasantville Chamber of Commerce (2004); Lifetime Achievement Award, Westchester Municipal Planning Federation (2004); Meritorious Service Award, Board of Directors, North Atlantic Region, American Society for Photogrammetry and Remote Sensing (1997); Recognition Award, New York State Association of Counties (1991); Bausch and Lomb Photogrammetric Award, American Society for Photogrammetry and Remote Sensing (1957) **Membership:** Board of Directors, North Atlantic Region, American Society for Photogrammetry and Remote Sensing (1999-2009); Treasury Secretary, Board of Directors, North Atlantic Region, American Society for Photogrammetry and Remote Sensing (1988-1997); Board of Directors, National Association of Regional Councils (1988-1989); Board of Directors, North Atlantic Region, American Society for Photogrammetry and Remote Sensing (1987-1997); Board of Directors, National Association of Counties (1987-1989); President, Rotary Club of White Plains (1985-1986); President, National Association of County Planning Directors (1984-1985); President, New York State Association of Counties (1980-1981); President, New York Association of County Planning Directors (1970); Board of Directors, New York Association of County Planning Directors (1969-1991); American Institute of Certified Planners; Cornell Club, New York City, NY; Sigma Chi **Marquis Who's Who Honors:** Albert Nelson Marquis Lifetime Achievement Award (2017) **To what do you attribute your success:** Mr. Eschweiler attributes his success to the great support he had while working at Westchester County planning. He also had several great mentors who were able to help guide him, and help him understand the political process. **Why did you become involved in your profession or industry:** Mr. Eschweiler came from a family full of architects, but he wasn't able to get involved in architecture, so when he was attending Cornell University, he decided to pursue an education in city planning instead. **What do you consider to be the highlight of your career:** A career highlight that stands out the most to Mr. Eschweiler is creating a senior housing facility in Pleasantville, New York. **Hobbies:** Photography; Travel **Religion:** Presbyterian **Shipping Address:** 36 Wilton Rd, Pleasantville, NY, 10570

Harper Estes

Title: Lawyer **Industry:** Law and Legal Services **Company Name:** Lynch, Chappell & Alsup PC **Place of Birth:** Pecos **State:** TX **Parents:** Bobby Frank Estes; Gayle (Harper) Estes **Marital Status:** Married **Spouse Name:** Deidre Dement (3/19/1976) **Children:** Andrew Kimble; Jada Catherine **Education:** JD, Baylor University School of Law (1979); BA, Texas Tech University (1977) **Certifications:** Board Certified, Civil Trial Law, Texas Board of Legal Specialization **Career:** Shareholder, Lynch, Chappell & Alsup PC (1980-Present); Chair, Texas Bar Foundation (2014); President, Midland County Bar Association (1994-1995); Board of Directors, President Elect, President, State Bar of Texas (1987-2009); Partner, Lynch, Chappell & Alsup Professional Corporation, Midland, TX (1980) **Civic:** Member, Deacon, Elder, First Presbyterian Church, Midland; Big Brothers and Big Sisters Board of Ambassadors; Former Officer and Director, Midland Fair Havens, Inc.; Hearthstone Temporary Children's Shelter; Former Board Member and Big Brother of the Year, Big Brothers and Big Sisters of Midland; Former Member, Texas Book Festival Advisory Board **Creative Works:** Editorial Board, Texas Bar Journal **Awards:** Outstanding Pro Bono Lawyer, Legal Aid of Northwest Texas (2012); Outstanding Young Lawyer of Midland County, Midland County Young Lawyers Association (1992); Pro Bono Attorney Award, West Texas Legal Services (1991); Trimble Volunteer Service Award, Leadership Midland Alumni (1986); Big Brother of the Year Award, Big Brothers and Big Sisters of Midland (1985); AV Preeminent Rating, Martindale-Hubbell; Listed, Texas Super Lawyer, Texas Monthly Magazine **Membership:** Former Chair, Texas Bar Foundation (2013); Former President, State Bar of Texas (2008-2009); President, State Bar of Texas (2008-2009); Former President, Midland County Bar Association (2005); Former Member of the Board of Directors, Texas Young Lawyer's Association; Editorial Board, Texas Bar Journal; American Arbitration Association; International Centre for Dispute Resolution; Texas Board of Legal Specialization **Bar Admissions:** Supreme Court of the United States (1983); United States Courts of Appeal for Fifth Judicial Circuit (1982); United States District Court for the Western District of Texas (1981); Texas (1980); United States District Courts for the Northern District of Texas (1980) **Hobbies:** Singing; Songwriting **Religion:** Presbyterian **Business Address:** 300 N Marienfeld St Ste 700, Midland, TX, 79701 **Shipping Address:** 300 N Marienfeld Ave Ste 700, Chappell Lynch & Alsup Pc, Midland, TX, 79701 **Website:** http://lcalawfirm.com

Jack Charles Estes

Title: Oil Company Executive (Retired) **Industry:** Business Management/ Business Services **Date of Birth:** 04/07/1935 **Place of Birth:** Rogers **State:** AR **Parents:** Jack Russell Estes; Merle Clara (White) Estes **Marital Status:** Married **Spouse Name:** Sandra Jean Reeves (11/10/1961) **Children:** Michael Lynn; David Russell; Cristi Yvonne **Education:** Honorary Doctorate in Drilling Technology, Vice President of Amoco Research (1989); Postgraduate Coursework, Chemical Engineering, University of Tulsa (1965-1970); BS in Engineering Mathematics and Chemistry, College of Petroleum Sciences and Engineering, The University of Tulsa (1965) **Certifications:** Management Consultant **Career:** Retired (2011); President, Environmental Drilling Technology, Inc. (1990-2011); Principal, Estes Consulting Group, Inc. (1999-2010); Research Supervisor, Amoco Corporation (1976-1989); Research Engineer, Pan American Petroleum and Transport Company (Now Amoco Corporation) (1965-1976); Research Technician, Pan American Petroleum and Transport Company (Now Amoco Corporation) (1960-1965); Computer Engineer, UNIVAC, Remington Rand (1960) **Career Related:** Founder, Intechnology, LLC; Founder, Estes Consulting Group Inc.; Founder, Environmental Drilling Technology, Inc.; Doctoral Advisory Committee, Starkey Energy Institute, University of Oklahoma; Doctoral Advisory Committee, Tulsa University Drilling Research Projects; Doctoral Advisory Committee, Polymers and Coatings Department, North Dakota State University; Accreditation Committee, Petroleum College, University of Wyoming **Civic:** With, Republican Party (1980-Present); With, Democratic Party (1975-1979); Assistant Minister, Fundraising, Grace International Charitable Ministries, Inc.; Outreach Minister, United Methodist Church; Vice President, Evangelical Association **Military Service:** Four Years, Drill Instructor and Electronic Nuclear Weapons Fusing Systems Specialist, U.S. Air Force **Creative Works:** Technology Editor, "Journal of Petroleum Technology," Society of Petroleum Engineers (1977-1978); Contributor, Articles, Professional Journals; Author, Two Books, Seeking Publisher **Awards:** Inductee, Drilling Fluids Hall of Fame, American Association of Drilling Engineers (2010); Service Award, API (1991); Service Award, Society of Petroleum Engineers (1985); Service Award, American Chemical Society (1984); Citation for Service, American Petroleum Institute **Membership:** Task Group Chairman, API (1989-Present); Board of Directors, N.E.O.S.D.A. (1989-1992); Program Committee, Society of Petroleum Engineers (1989-1992); Vice Chairman, Committee 13, API (1986-1989); Chairman, International Subcommittee 13, API (1982-1985); Chairman, Drill Bit Standardization Task Group, International Drilling Contractors (1973-1980); American Society of Mechanical Engineers; AMA–American Management Association; American Chemical Society; International Science Fair Judge, Sigma Xi, The Scientific Research Honor Society; Masonic Lodge **Marquis Who's Who Honors:** Albert Nelson Marquis Lifetime Achievement Award (2017) **Hobbies:** Dance **Shipping Address:** 7404 S 2nd St, Broken Arrow, OK, 74011

John Thomas Evans

Title: Lawyer **Industry:** Law and Legal Services **Date of Birth:** 02/28/1948 **Place of Birth:** New York City **State:** NY **Parents:** John Arthur Evans; Dorothy (Reilly) Evans **Marital Status:** Married **Spouse Name:** Marie Tolnay Evans (6/2/1979) **Children:** Claire; Grace **Education:** JD, Fordham University (1973); BA, University of Wisconsin (1970) **Career:** Partner, Belair and Evans, New York City, NY (1991-Present); Partner, Belair, Klein, Groman & Evans, New York City, NY (1985-1988); Partner, Morris & Duffy, New York City, NY (1982-1985); Consultant, Hofstra University Law School Moot Court Program, Uniondale, NY (1982); Consultant, Lecturer, New York City Police Department Detectives Endowment Association (1981-1988); Consultant, Volunteer Lawyers for the Arts, New York City, NY (1979-1984); Associate, Blumenthal & Lynne, New York City, NY (1979-1981); Assistant District Attorney, New York City, NY (1973-1979) **Career Related:** President, North Ferry Company, Shelter Island, NY (1992-1998) **Creative Works:** Author, "Arguing Cases Before A Medical Malpractice Law & Strategy"; Contributor, Articles, Professional Journals **Awards:** Recipient, Highest Award, Manhattan Detective Area, New York City, NY (1979) **Membership:** New York Criminal Bar Association; Association of the Bar of the City of New York; New York State Bar Association; New York Athletic Club, New York City, NY **Bar Admissions:** New York (1974); United States Tax Court; United States District Court Southern District of New York; United States District Court Eastern District of New York **Marquis Who's Who Honors:** Albert Nelson Marquis Lifetime Achievement Award (2017) **Why did you become involved in your profession or industry:** Mr. Evans was interested in law since he was a child and watched trial law on television. **What do you consider to be the highlight of your career:** Mr. Evans is most proud of having a good number of successful cases. **Shipping Address:** 362 W Broadway Apt 4, New York, NY, 10013

Robert B. Evans III

Title: Attorney **Industry:** Law and Legal Services **Company Name:** Evans Law **Education:** JD, Loyola University; MBA, Loyola University **Career:** Attorney, Evans Law **Awards:** Distinguished Lawyer's Designation (2017); Honoree, Designated Trial Advocate, The National Institute of Trial Advocacy (2016); Honoree, AV-Rated Attorney, Martindale-Hubbell; Honoree, Top Attorney in Louisiana, Martindale-Hubbell; Honoree, Top Attorney, New Orleans Magazine **Marquis Who's Who Honors:** Albert Nelson Marquis Lifetime Achievement Award (2017); Distinguished Humanitarian (2017) **To what do you attribute your success:** He attributes his success to having a passion for what he does and top notch trial skills. **Why did you become involved in your profession or industry:** He became involved in his profession because he had a personal interest in securing justice. **What do you consider to be the highlight of your career:** The highlights of his career include winning rebates for gas customers as a result of fraudulent overcharges, and winning just compensation for the owners of Dixie Brewery against Louisiana State University. **Hobbies:** Spending time with his family **Shipping Address:** 3445 N Causeway Blvd Ste 707, Evans Law, Metairie, LA, 70002 **Website:** http://www.robertevanslaw.com

Otto George Everbach

Title: Lawyer (Retired) **Industry:** Law and Legal Services **Date of Birth:** 08/27/1938 **Place of Birth:** New Albany **State:** IN **Parents:** Otto G. Everbach; Zelda Marie (Hilt) Everbach **Marital Status:** Married **Spouse Name:** Nancy Lee Stern (6/3/1961) **Children:** Tracy Ellen; Stephen George **Education:** LLB, University of Virginia (1966); BS, United States Military Academy, West Point, NY (1960) **Career:** Senior Vice President, Law and Government Affairs, Kimberly-Clark Corporation, Dallas, TX (1988-2003); Senior Vice President, General Counsel, Kimberly-Clark Corporation (1986-1988); Vice President, Kimberly-Clark Corporation (1984-1986); Associate General Counsel, Warner-Lambert Corporation (Now Pfizer, Inc.), Morris Plains, NJ (1981-1983); Secretary, General Counsel, American Optical, Southbridge, MA (1976-1981); Corporate Counsel, ALZA Corporation, Palo Alto, CA (1974-1975); Corporate Counsel, Bristol-Meyers Company (Now Bristol-Myers Squibb Company), Evansville, IN (1967-1974); Counsel, Central Intelligence Agency, Langley, VA (1966-1967) **Military Service:** U.S. Army (1960-1963) **Membership:** Massachusetts Bar Association; Indiana Bar Association; California Bar Association **Bar Admissions:** Massachusetts State Bar (1978); California State Bar (1975); Virginia State Bar (1967); Indiana State Bar (1967) **Marquis Who's Who Honors:** Albert Nelson Marquis Lifetime Achievement Award (2017) **Shipping Address:** 5111 Meaders Ln, Dallas, TX, 75229

Pamela Binnings Ewen-Lott

Title: Lawyer, Author (Retired) **Industry:** Law and Legal Services **Date of Birth:** 03/22/1944 **Marital Status:** Married **Spouse Name:** James Craft Lott (12/27/2003); John Alexander Ewen (12/13/1974 Divorced, 2/2003); Jerome Francis Ayers (8/22/1965, Divorced, 7/1974) **Children:** Scott Dylan Ewen **Education:** JD, University of Houston, Cum Laude (1979); BA, Tulane University (1977) **Career:** Retired (2004); Partner, Baker Botts L.L.P., Houston, TX (1988-2004); Associate, Baker Botts L.L.P., Houston, TX (1980-1984); Attorney, Law Department, Gulf Oil Corporation, Houston, TX (1980-1984); Associate, Kleberg, Dyer, Redford and Weil, Corpus Christi, TX (1979-1980); Law Clerk, Harris, Cook, Browning and Barker, Corpus Christi, TX (1977-1979) **Awards:** Literary Artist of the Year, St. Tammany Parish, Louisiana (2009); Louisiana State Legislative Scholar, New Orleans, LA (1976-1977); Eudora Welty Memorial Award, National League of American Pen Women **Membership:** Founder, Northshore Literary Society (2008-Present); Board of Directors, Tennessee Williams Festival (2009-Present); Board of Directors, Inprint, Inc. (2002-2004); Board of Directors, Order of Barons, Junior Achievement Southeast Texas (1997-2001); Board of Directors, Texas Association of Bank Council, State Bar of Texas (1994-1997); Forum Committee on Franchising, ABA (1983-1985); Committee on Product Lability, Special Subcommittee to General Committee on Law, American Petroleum Institute (1982-1985); Member, Law Practice Management Section, Subcommittee, Women Rainmakers Association; Board of Directors, National League of American Pen Women; Board of Directors, Pirate's Alley Faulkner Society, New Orleans, LA **Shipping Address:** 715 Kiskatom Lane, Mandeville, LA, 70471 **Website:** pamelaewen.com

Michael J. Eyre

Title: Attorney **Industry:** Law and Legal Services **Company Name:** Law Offices of Michael J. Eyre **Date of Birth:** 04/10/1960 **Place of Birth:** Inglewood **State:** CA **Parents:** James Eyre; Jo-Ann Eyre **Marital Status:** Single **Children:** Joseph; Katherine **Education:** JD, Western State College of Law (1987); Postgraduate Studies in Political Science, California State University Long Beach (1983); BA in English Literature, University of California at Irvine (1982) **Career:** Principal/Owner, Law Offices of Michael J. Eyre, Long Beach and Lakewood, CA (2009-Present); Associate Attorney, Law Office of Rice & Rothenberg/The Law Firm of Marc S. Rothenberg, Long Beach, CA (2000-2009); Associate Attorney, Hollins, Schechter, Feinstein & Condas (1999-2000); Associate Attorney, Veatch, Carlson, Grogan & Nelson (Now Veatch Carlson Attorneys at Law), Los Angeles, CA (1997-1999); Associate Attorney, Cone, Chairez & Kassel/Law Offices of Joseph L. Chairez (1996-1997); Associate Attorney, Kaiser, DeBiaso, Palmer & Lopez (1988-1996) **Civic:** Community Volunteer, Shortstop Program, Long Beach Bar Foundation, Inc. (2010-Present); Instructor, Shortstop Program, Long Beach Bar Foundation, Inc. (2008-Present); Advisory Board, Paralegal Program of the Business Division, Mt. San Antonio College (2008-Present); Board Member, Long Beach Bar Foundation (2018); Volunteer Mock Trial Coach, Mt. San Antonio College (2009-2012); Boy Scouts of America **Awards:** Silver Client Champion Award, Martindale-Hubbell (2018, 2017); Instructor of the Year, SHORTSTOP (2018, 2017); 10.0 Superb Rating, Avvo Inc. (2014-2018); Honoree, One of the Top Temporary Judges in the Superior Court of California, County of Los Angeles (2014-2017); Featured, Southern California Top Attorneys (2013-2018); Client Distinction Award, Martindale-Hubbell (2013-2016); Honoree, PRR AV Preeminent Attorney, Lawyers.com (2011-2018); Honoree, AV Preeminent Attorney, Martindale-Hubbell (2011-2018); Honoree, PRR BV Distinguished Attorney, American Registry (2010) **Membership:** The State Bar of California; ABA; Consumer Attorneys Association of Los Angeles; Los Angeles County Bar Association; Orange County Bar Association; Long Beach Bar Association; Ball/Hunt/Schooley American Inn of Court **Bar Admissions:** California; United States District Court for the Central District of California; United States Court of Appeals for the Ninth Circuit; Supreme Court of the United States **Marquis Who's Who Honors:** Honoree, Humanitarian Award, Worldwide Branding (2016); Honoree, Professional of the Year, Worldwide Branding (2015); Industry Expert, "Top Lawyers: The Secrets to their Success," Worldwide Publishing (2014); Inductee, Lifetime Membership, Worldwide Registry (2014) **To what do you attribute your success:** He attributes his success to being passionate about the field, as well as to understanding the business of law and not just the practice of it. He also credits his focus on being productive and not just keeping busy. **Why did you become involved in your profession or industry:** Mr. Eyre became involved in his profession because he knew at the age of 14 that he wanted to be an attorney. His uncle, Donald M. Pach, was a lawyer and after watching him in court, he knew he wanted to be an attorney. **What do you consider to be the highlight of your career:** The highlights of Mr. Eyre's career include becoming an adjunct professor, working as a mock trial coach, and being accepted to the Temporary Judge Program for the Los Angeles Superior Court. **Where will you be in five years:** In five years, Mr. Eyre's goal is to become a judge. **Hobbies:** Camping; Hiking; Backpacking; Cycling; Water Sports **Business Address:** 4000 Long Beach Blvd Ste 218, Law Offices of Michael J. Eyre, Long Beach, CA, 90807 **Website:** http://www.eyrelaw.com

Nicola Fabbri

Title: Orthopedic Surgeon, Educator **Industry:** Medicine & Health Care **Company Name:** Memorial Sloan Kettering Cancer Center **Date of Birth:** 04/29/1962 **Place of Birth:** Bologna **State/Country of Origin:** Italy **Education:** Residency Fellowship, Mayo Clinic School of Graduate Medical Education, Rizzoli Orthopedic Institute, Hospital Rizzoli (1998-1993); MD, Medicine and Surgery, University of Bologna, Summa Cum Laude (1988) **Certifications:** United States Medical Licensing Examination (1995); Italian Board of Orthopedics (1993) **Career:** Attending Staff, Orthopaedic Service, Memorial Sloan Kettering Cancer Center (2012-Present); Professor of Surgery, Weill Cornell Medicine, Cornell University, New York, NY (2012-Present); Associate Professor of Orthopedics, Musculoskeletal Pathology, Rizzoli Orthopedic Institute, Hospital Rizzoli (1997-Present); Course Director, Musculoskeletal Pathology, Rizzoli Orthopedic Institute, Hospital Rizzoli (2009-2011); Visiting Professor, Department of Orthopedic Surgery, Mayo Clinic, Rochester, MN (2008); Attending Surgeon, Department of Musculoskeletal Oncology and Reconstructive Surgery, Rizzoli Orthopedic Institute, Hospital Rizzoli (1997-2012); Associate Professor of Orthopedic Surgery, Mayo Clinic, Rochester, MN (1995-1997); Research Fellow, Rizzoli Orthopedic Institute, Hospital Rizzoli (1993-1995) **Career Related:** Joe Miller Visiting Professor, Department of Orthopedic Surgery, McGill University (2008); Mark B. Coventry Adult Reconstruction Fellowship, Department of Orthopedic Surgery, Mayo Clinic, Mayo Clinic School of Graduate Medical Education (1996) **Awards:** Scholarship, Italian Ministry of Public Education **Membership:** International Society of Limb Salvage; Connective Tissue Oncology Society; EMSOS; Association of Bone and Joint Surgeons; Italian Society of Orthopedics and Traumatology; Chair, Local Speaker, Muscular Skeletal Tumor Society **To what do you attribute your success:** Dr. Fabbri attributes his success to hard work and receiving quality support and training. **Why did you become involved in your profession or industry:** Dr. Fabbri became involved in his profession to make a difference in the lives of his patients, as well as to help those afflicted with cancer. **Where will you be in five years:** In five years, Dr. Fabbri will be continuing to help make cancer beatable. **Hobbies:** History; Golf; Reading; Sports; Swimming; Movies **Shipping Address:** 515 E 72nd Street, Apt. 11K, New York, NY, 10021

Delmar McLean Fadden

Title: Electrical Engineer **Industry:** Engineering **Company Name:** Flight Advantage LLC **Date of Birth:** 11/10/1941 **Place of Birth:** Seattle **State:** WA **Parents:** Gene Scott Fadden; Alice Elizabeth (McLean) Fadden **Marital Status:** Married **Spouse Name:** Sandra Myrene Callahan (6/22/1963) **Children:** Donna McLean; Lawrence Gene **Education:** MEE, University of Washington, Seattle, WA (1975); BEE, University of Washington, Seattle, WA (1963) **Certifications:** Licensed Commercial Pilot, Single and Multi-Engine Land Airplanes, Instrument, State of Washington **Career:** Fadden Consulting, California (2012-Present); Owner, Flight Advantage LLC (2009-Present); Product Consultant, Sandel Avionics, Inc., Vista, CA (1999-Present); Owner, Delta Papa Ltd. (2000-2009); Retired (1999); Integration Manager, Airplane Services, Boeing, Seattle, WA (1999); Integration Manager, Cabin Systems, Boeing, Seattle, WA (1996-1998); Chief Engineer, 737/757 Avionics/Flight System, Boeing, Seattle, WA (1990-1996); Chief Engineer, Flight Deck, Boeing, Seattle, WA (1988-1990); Boeing, Seattle, WA (1969-1999); Consultant, Sandel Avionics, Inc. **Career Related:** Board of Directors, Sandel Avionics, Inc. (2011-2016); Consultant, Flight System Integration, Boeing P-8A (2009-2013); Consultant, Esterline Technologies Corporation, Bellevue, WA (2006-2011); Cirrus Design Corporation, Duluth, MN (2006-2008); Senior Consultant, SeaTec Consulting Inc., Bellevue, WA (2003-2013); Consultant, Connexion by Boeing, Seattle, WA (2002-2003); Chairman, Integration Task Group, Developed ARP 4754, SAE International (1990-1996) **Military Service:** Captain, U.S. Air Force (1963-1969) **Creative Works:** Contributor, Articles, Professional Journals **Awards:** Service Award, Mountaineers Club (1991) **Membership:** President, Mountaineers Foundation (1998-2001); President, Mountaineers Club (1984-1986); AIAA; IEEE; Human Factors and Ergonomics Society; The American Alpine Club **To what do you attribute your success:** Mr. Fadden attributes his success to curiosity. **Why did you become involved in your profession or industry:** Aviation and electronics were hobbies when Mr. Fadden was a child, and have captured his interest ever since. **What do you consider to be the highlight of your career:** Every step has had a highlight; what Mr. Fadden is doing now is for Sandel Avionics, bringing all of those things together. **Where will you be in five years:** In five years, Mr. Fadden will be officially retired and enjoying all the thing he hasn't had time for up to now. **Hobbies:** Flying; Hiking; Woodworking **Shipping Address:** PO Box 483, Preston, WA, 98050-0483

Bernice K. Faegenburg

Industry: Fine Art **Place of Birth:** Philadelphia **State:** PA **Parents:** Simon Faegenburg; Dora Kaufman (Rudnick) Faegenburg **Marital Status:** Married **Spouse Name:** David Faegenburg **Children:** Nancy; Glenn; Russell **Education:** MS in Art Education, LIU Post (1972); Postgraduate Studies, Art Students League, National Academy of Design; BS, Tyler School of Art, Temple University; Student, Leon Kroll, National Academy of Design, Tyler School of Art, Temple University **Career:** Teacher, Creative Arts Workshop (1977-Present); Silk Screen Printing Service (1975-Present); Teacher of Art to Emotionally Disturbed Children, Roslyn Junior High School (1972); Teacher of Art, Philadelphia Public Schools; Teacher of Children's Classes, First and Second Grade, Philadelphia Museum of Art; Student Teacher, Heritage House, Philadelphia, PA **Civic:** B.J. Spoke Gallery (1976-Present); Treasurer, Viridian Gallery (1981); Co-President, Long Island Artists Alliance (1975); President, East Hills PTA (1970) **Creative Works:** Permanent Collection, Rutgers Museum, Zimmerli Art Museum; Solo Show, Graphic Eye Gallery, Port Washington, NY (2017); Solo Show, Viridian Artists Inc, Chelsea, New York, NY (2017); Exhibition, Biennale, Florence, Italy (2015); Exhibition, Biennale, Florence, Italy (2007); Exhibition, Biennale, Florence, Italy (2005); Reviewed, Sheridan Sanseguendo, East Hampton Star (1999); Solo Show, The Chelsea Center, Nassau County Office of Cultural Development, Muttontown, NY (1996); Reviewed, Helen Harrison, New York Times (1992); Solo Show, Islip Museum, Islip, NY (1989); One-Man Show, St. Peter's Church, New York, NY (1986); Exhibition, Sarah Lawrence College (1985); One-Man Show, Frostburg State College (1985); Exhibition, Guild Hall (1985); One-Man Show, Isis Gallery (1985); Reviewed, Phyllis Brass, New York Times (1985); One-Man Show, Concordia College (1984); Exhibition, City Gallery (1982); One-Man Show, Country Art Gallery, Locust Valley, NY (1982); Reviewed, Malcolm Preston, Newsday (1982); Exhibition, Parrish Art Museum (1981); One-Man Show, Viridian Gallery (1980); Reviewed, L'Art a L'Etranger Article by La Review Moderne (1980); One-Man Show, Concordia College (1979); Exhibition, Silvermine Guild of Artists (1979); Exhibition, Gracie Square Art Show (1979); Exhibition, Avery Fisher Hall at Lincoln Center (1978); Exhibition, Huntington Township Art League (1977); Exhibition, National Society of Painters in Casein & Acrylic (1977); One-Man Show, B.J. Spoke Gallery (1977); One-Man Show, National Association of Women Artists (1976-1977); Exhibition, Group Shows, Locust Valley Art Show (1976-1977); Exhibition, Long Beach Art Association (1976); One-Man Show, Shelter Rock Library (1976); Exhibition, Firehouse Gallery, Nassau Community College (1975); One-Man Show, Syosset Library (1973); One-Man Show, Locust Valley Library (1973); One-Man Show, LIU Post (1972); Show, Onward Gallery, Tokyo, Japan; Exhibition, Ashawagh Hall, East Hampton, NY; Florence Biennale International, Florence, Italy; Fairleigh Dickenson University Exhibition; Exhibited, Parish Museum **Awards:** First Prize Peacock Showcase Award, Chelsea Center, Nassau County Office of Cultural Development (1996); Bell Kramer Memorial Award (1993); Owens Zlowe Award for Painting, Centennial Exhibition, National Association of Women Artists (1989); Henningsen Memorial Prize (1980); First Prize, Mixed Media, Manhasset Arts Association (1979); Grumbacher Award of Merit (1978); Award for Excellence, Long Beach Art Association (1976); Molly M. Kennedy Memorial Award for Painting, National Association of Women Artists **Membership:** Long Island Sumi-e Society (2014); Artist Alliance of East Hampton (2012); President, National Association of Women Artists (1993); Chairman, Program Committee, National Association of Women Artists (1986); Chairman, Viridian Artists Inc.; International Association of Art **Why did you become involved in your profession or industry:** Art has always been a part of Ms. Faegenburg's life. **Shipping Address:** 31 Canterbury Lane, Roslyn Heights, NY, 11577 **Website:** https://www.artslant.com/global/artists/show/74535-Bernice-Faegenburg

Federico Faggin, PhD

Title: President **Industry:** Technology **Company Name:** Federico and Elvia Faggin Foundation **Date of Birth:** 12/01/1941 **Place of Birth:** Vicenza **State/Country of Origin:** Italy **Parents:** Giuseppe Faggin; Emma Munari Faggin **Marital Status:** Married **Spouse Name:** Elvia Sardei (12/2/1967) **Children:** Marzia; Marc; Eric **Education:** PhD in Physics, Universita di Padova, Italy (1965); Istituto Tecnico Industriale Statale Alessandro Rossi, Vicenza, Italy (1960) **Career:** Chairman Emeritus, Synaptics, Inc. (2008-Present); President, Chief Executive Officer, Foveon, Inc. (2003-2008); Chairman, Synaptics, Inc. (1999-2008); Co-Founder, Chief Executive Officer, Synaptics, Inc., San Jose, CA (1986-1999); Co-Founder, President, Cygnet Techs., Inc., Sunnyvale, CA (1982-1986); Vice President, Computer Systems Group, Exxon Enterprises, New York (1981); Founder, President, Zilog Inc., Cupertino, CA (1974-1980); Department Manager, Intel Corporation, Santa Clara, CA (1970-1974); Section Head, Fairchild Camera & Instrument Company, Palo Alto, CA (1968-1970) **Career Related:** President, Federico and Elvia Faggin Foundation (2011-Present); Marconi Fellowship Award (1988) **Awards:** National Medal of Technology and Innovation, White House (2010); Lifetime Achievement Award, European Patent Office (2006); Kyoto Prize (1997); National Inventors Hall of Fame (1996); W. Wallace McDowell Award, IEEE Computer Society (1994) **Marquis Who's Who Honors:** Albert Nelson Marquis Lifetime Achievement Award (2017); Distinguished Humanitarian (2017) **Where will you be in five years:** In five years, Dr. Faggin hopes to be able to convey to people that are ready to hear that consciousness is an irreducible aspect of nature prior to matter, the opposite of what science is thinking today. This is his primary objective, and this takes a great amount of effort to convey to people to understand. **Shipping Address:** 27910 Roble Blanco Drive, Los Altos Hills, CA, 94022

Stanley Fahn, MD

Title: Neurologist, Educator **Industry:** Medicine & Health Care **Company Name:** Columbia University **Date of Birth:** 11/06/1933 **Place of Birth:** Sacramento **State:** CA **Parents:** Ernest Fahn; Sylvia Fahn **Marital Status:** Married **Spouse Name:** Charlotte (6/21/1958) **Children:** Paul N.; James D. **Education:** Resident, Neurology, The Neurological Institute of New York, New York, NY (1959-1962); MD, University of California, Berkeley (1958); BA, University of California, Berkeley (1955) **Certifications:** Diplomate, American Board of Psychiatry and Neurology, Inc. (1968) **Career:** H. Houston Merritt Professor, Columbia University, New York City, NY (1978-Present); Director, Morris K. Udall Parkinson Disease Research Center of Columbia University, New York City, NY (1999-2003); Professor, Neurology, Columbia University, New York City, NY (1973-1978); Faculty Member, University of Pennsylvania, Philadelphia, PA (1968-1973); Faculty Member, Columbia University, New York City, NY (1965-1968); Research Associate, National Institutes of Health (1962-1965); Director, Center for Parkinson's Disease and Other Movement Disorders, Columbia University, New York City, NY (1973-2013) **Career Related:** Board of Directors, Parkinson's Foundation (2016-Present); Board of Directors, Dystonia Medical Research Foundation (1998-Present); Organizer, Chairman, World Parkinson Coalition (2006-2013); Chairman, Advisory Committee, Peripheral and Nervous System Drugs, Food and Drug Administration (1991-1996); Chairman, Advisory Committee, Peripheral and Nervous System Drugs, Food and Drug Administration (1987-1989); Director, Dystonia Clinical Research Center (1981-1997); Scientific Director, Parkinson's Disease Foundation, Inc. (1979-2016) **Military Service:** U.S. Public Health Service (1962-1965) **Creative Works:** Co-author, "Principles and Practice of Movement Disorders, Second Edition" (2011); Co-author, "Principles and Practice of Movement Disorders, First Edition" (2007); Editor, Movement Disorders (1985-1995); Associate Editor, Neurology (1977-1987) **Awards:** Alfred Markowitz Clinical Service Award, Society of Practitioners, Columbia University Medical Center (2017); Jay Van Andel Award for Outstanding Achievement in Parkinson's Disease Research, Van Andel Research Institute (2016); James Parkinson Medal, Parkinson's Disease Foundation (2007); Honorary Lifetime Member, Board of Directors, Dystonia Medical Research Foundation (1998); Grantee, National Institutes of Health (1994-1997, 1984-1991, 1980-1982, 1974-1977); Springer Prize, American Parkinson Disease Association; Guthrie Family Humanitarian Award, Huntington Disease Society of America; Srinivasan Award, Chennai, India; Page and William Black Lifetime Achievement Award, Parkinson's Disease Foundation; Distinguished Service Award, Dystonia Medical Research Foundation; Donald Calne Award, Parkinson Society Canada; Bruce Ochsman Lifetime Achievement Award, Tourette Association of America; Hall of Fame, Benign Blepharospasm Research Foundation **Membership:** Board of Directors, Dystonia Medical Research Foundation (1998-Present); Chair, Meeting Management Committee, American Academy of Neurology (2009-2013); President, American Academy of Neurology (2001-2003); President-elect, American Academy of Neurology (1999-2001); Vice President, American Academy of Neurology (1993-1997); Chair, Education Committee, American Academy of Neurology (1986-1993); President, Movement Disorder Society (1988-1991); American Neurological Association; Member, Board of Directors, National Parkinson Foundation and Parkinson's Foundation; National Academy of Medicine **Marquis Who's Who Honors:** Albert Nelson Marquis Lifetime Achievement Award (2017) **Hobbies:** Baroque and Classical Music; Movies; Gardening **Shipping Address:** 155 Edgars Lane, Hastings On Hudson, NY, 10706

Joseph V. Fairchild Jr., PhD

Title: Finance Educator **Industry:** Education/Educational Services **Company Name:** Nicholls State University **Date of Birth:** 11/26/1933 **Place of Birth:** New Orleans **State:** LA **Parents:** Joseph Virgil Fairchild; Georgiana Malone (Bourgeois) Fairchild **Marital Status:** Married **Spouse Name:** Marion Peter (2/27/2009); Judith Champagne (8/12/1961, Deceased 2005) **Children:** Georgianna; Joseph; Benjamin **Education:** PhD, Louisiana State University (1975); MBA, Louisiana State University (1963); BS in Geology, Louisiana State University (1956) **Certifications:** Certified Public Accountant, State of Louisiana **Career:** Distinguished Professor Emeritus, Nicholls State University (2002-Present); Retired (2000); Assistant Dean, College of Business Administration, Nicholls State University (1985-1986); Distinguished Accounting Professor, Nicholls State University (1984-2000); Director, Graduate Business Studies, Nicholls State University (1982-1985); Professor, Nicholls State University (1976-1984); Associate Professor, Nicholls State University (1975-1976); Private Accounting Practice, Thibodaux, LA (1969-2000); Assistant Accounting Professor, Nicholls State University (1969-1975); Partner, L.A. Champagne & Co., LLP (1964-1969); Associate Accountant, Humble Oil & Refining Co. (Now Exxon Mobil Corporation) (1963-1964); Geologist, United Core, Inc., Houston, TX (1956-1957) **Career Related:** Visiting Professor, American University, Bulgaria (2004-Present); Visiting Professor, University of Indianapolis (2006-2009); Visiting Professor, Arkansas State University (2005-2006); Visiting Accounting Professor, Henderson State University (2000-2004); Consultant, Defense Systems Management College, Fort Belvoir, VA (1980-1981); Research Reviewer, Business Research Management Center, Wright-Patterson Air Force Base, U.S. Air Force (1974-1984); Faculty, Government Committee, Chairman Dean's Search Committee; Senate Vice President, Government Committee, Chairman Dean's Search Committee **Civic:** Choir, St. Genevieve Catholic Church (1989-Present); Lector, St. Genevieve Catholic Church (1975-Present); Chairman, Financial Committee, E.D. White Catholic High School (1985-1987); School Board Member, E.D. White Catholic High School (1985-1987); School Board Member, St. Genevieve Catholic Elementary School (1979-1983) **Military Service:** First Lieutenant, U.S. Air Force (1957-1960); Lieutenant Colonel, U.S. Air Force Reserve **Creative Works:** Actor, "Orleans," Columbia Broadcasting System (1997); Actor, "Kingfish: A Story of Huey P. Long," TNT (1995); Actor, "Dead Man Walking," Gramercy Pictures (1995); Co-author, "The Acquisition and Distribution of Commercial Products" (1985-1989); Co-author, "The Acquisition and Distribution of Commercial Products" (1980); Co-author, "Income Tax Guides for State Legislators"; Contributor, Articles, Professional Journals; Actor, "South Pacific"; Actor, "Arsenic and Old Lace"; Actor, "Brigadoon"; Actor, "Damn Yankees" **Awards:** Academy Excellence Award, Henderson State University (2003-2004); Honoree, Louisiana's Outstanding Accounting Educator, Society of Louisiana Certified Public Accountants (1994); Honoree, Case Educator of the Year, Nicholls State University Alumni Federation (1994); Honorary Alumnus Award, Nicholls State University Alumni Federation (1991); Honoree, Trueblood Professor, Touche Ross Foundation (Now Deloitte Touche Tohmatsu Limited) (1987) **Membership:** American Institute of CPAs; Lecturer, Seminars, Society of Louisiana Certified Public Accountants; American Accounting Association; National Society of Accountants; Nicholls State University Alumni Federation **Marquis Who's Who Honors:** Albert Nelson Marquis Lifetime Achievement Award (2017) **Religion:** Roman Catholic **Shipping Address:** 412 Plater Drive, Thibodaux, LA, 70301

Delvin Fanning

Title: Soil Scientist **Industry:** Sciences **Company Name:** University of Maryland **Date of Birth:** 07/13/1931 **Place of Birth:** Copenhagen **State:** NY **Parents:** C. Roscoe Fanning; Faye Theodora Hays Fanning **Marital Status:** Married **Spouse Name:** Emily Manning Fanning **Children:** Michael Christopher Fanning; Maurine Faye Fanning Maul; Christine Kay Fanning **Education:** PhD, University of Wisconsin (1964); MS, Cornell University (1959); BS, Cornell University (1954) **Career:** Emeritus Professor, University of Maryland, College Park (1999-Present); Assistant Professor, Department of Agronomy, Department of Natural Resource Sciences, University of Maryland, College Park (1964-1999); Graduate Research Assistant, Department of Soils, University of Wisconsin, Madison (1960-1964); Soil Scientist, Soil Conservation Service, U.S. Department of Agriculture (1954, 1959-1962) **Civic:** Bass Singer, Holy Redeemer Church Choir, College Park, MD (1968-Present) **Military Service:** U.S. Army (1954-1956) **Creative Works:** Senior Author, "Soil: Morphology, Genesis and Classification" (1989) **Awards:** Pons Medal, Acid Sulfate Soils Working Group, International Union of Soil Science (2016) **Membership:** Fellow, American Society of Agronomy; Soil Science Society of America, Lifetime member American Association for Advancement of Science **Marquis Who's Who Honors:** Albert Nelson Marquis Lifetime Achievement Award (2017) **To what do you attribute your success:** He attributes his success to good fortune. **What do you consider to be the highlight of your career:** His life has been a series of mostly fortunate accidents, the most important of which was meeting his first wife Mary Christine Falluff Fanning in 1958. She unfortunately passed in 1994. **Hobbies:** Writing **Political Affiliations:** Democrat **Religion:** Roman Catholic **Shipping Address:** 4809 Ravenswood Rd, Riverdale, MD, 20737

T. Brooke Farnsworth

Title: Attorney, Partner **Industry:** Law and Legal Services **Company Name:** Farnsworth & vonBerg **Date of Birth:** 03/16/1945 **Place of Birth:** Grand Rapids **State:** MI **Parents:** George Llelwyn Farnsworth; Gladys Fern Kennedy Farnsworth **Marital Status:** Married **Spouse Name:** Connie D. Farnsworth **Children:** Leslie Erin Farnsworth; T. Brooke Farnsworth, Jr. **Education:** JD, Robert H. McKinney School of Law, Indiana University (1971); BS in Business, Indiana University (1967) **Career:** Partner, Farnsworth & von Berg, LLP **Career Related:** Farnsworth & Associates (1979-1986); Assistant General Counsel, Damson Oil Corporation (1974-1978); Associate, Butler, Binion, Rice, Cook & Knapp (1971-1974); Administrative Assistant to the Indiana State Treasurer (1967-1970) **Creative Works:** Speaker, "Structuring Preferential Rights to Purchase," Strafford Publications, Inc.; Author, "Recent Developments Under RICO", Commercial Litigation Newsletter, Commercial Litigation Section, American Trial Lawyers of America; Author, Speaker, "Selected' Business Torts," Commercial Litigation Section, American Trial Lawyers Association Annual Meeting; Author, "Recent Developments in Take-or-Pay Litigation," The Natural Resources Law Newsletter, Natural Resources, Energy and Environmental Law Section, ABA; Author, Speaker, "Piercing the Corporate Veil," Advanced Creditors Rights Course, State Bar of Texas; Speaker in Field; Contributor, Articles, Professional Journals **Awards:** AV Preeminent Attorney, Martindale-Hubbell (2014-Present) **Membership:** Chair, Business Torts Subcommittee (1997-2000); Chair, Commercial Litigation Section, American Association for Justice (1996-1997); ABA; Houston Bar Association; State Bar of Texas; Sustaining Life Fellow, Texas Bar Foundation; Fellow, Texas Bar College **Bar Admissions:** Supreme Court of the United States; United States Court of Appeals for the Fifth Circuit; United States Court of Appeals for the Tenth Circuit; United States Court of Appeals for the Eleventh Circuit; United States Court of Appeals for the District of Columbia Circuit; United States District Court for the Southern District of Texas; United States District Court for the Western District of Texas; United States District Court for the Northern District of Texas **To what do you attribute your success:** He attributes his success to taking the effort to understand all aspects of a client's business in order to provide prompt, relevant and cost-effective advice. **Why did you become involved in your profession or industry:** Mr. Farnsworth decided to become involved in his profession after reading a biography of Clarence Darrow. **What do you consider to be the highlight of your career:** Arguments of two important cases to the Texas Supreme Court, one on implied easements and another on the voluntary payment rule. **Where will you be in five years:** In five years, Mr. Farnsworth intends to continue on the same road. **Hobbies:** Golf **Political Affiliations:** Republican **Religion:** Protestant **Shipping Address:** 333 N Sam Houston Pkwy E Ste 300, Farnsworth & vonBerg, Houston, TX, 77060 **Website:** http://www.fvllp.com/your-team/t-brooke-farnsworth

Herbert Fenster

Title: Lawyer **Industry:** Law and Legal Services **Company Name:** Covington & Burling **Date of Birth:** 03/29/1935 **Place of Birth:** New York **State:** NY **Parents:** Oscar Samuel Fenster; Bessie Estelle (Schafran) Fenster **Marital Status:** Married **Spouse Name:** Jane Porter Elam Allen (12/31/1993); Gail Frances Meier (4/18/1964, Divorced) **Children:** Christopher Lawrence; Jennifer Gail; Jonathan Adam **Education:** JD, University of Virginia (1961); MA, University of Pennsylvania (1958); AB, University of Pennsylvania (1957) **Career:** Senior Partner, McKenna, Long & Aldridge, Dentons (2002-Present); Senior Partner, McKenna & Cuneo (Now Dentons) (1990-2002); Senior Partner, McKenna, Conner & Cuneo (Now Dentons) (1980-1990); Senior Partner, Sellers, Conner & Cuneo (Now Dentons) (1978-1980); Partner, Sellers, Conner & Cuneo (Now Dentons) (1967-1978); Associate, Sellers, Conner & Cuneo (Now Dentons) (1961-1966) **Civic:** Member, President's Private Sector Survey on Cost Control, The Grace Commission (1982-Present); Litigation Counsel, Reagan-Bush Campaign Committee (1980-1983); Board of Directors, U.S. Chamber Litigation Center, U.S. Chamber of Commerce; Trustee, Keewaydin Foundation; Corporate Director, Keewaydin Foundation; Board of Directors, Keewaydin Foundation **Membership:** Fellow, American Association for Justice; ABA; The American Law Institute; Federal Bar Association; The University Club of New York; Metropolitan Club **Bar Admissions:** Colorado (1993); Supreme Court of the United States (1967); Washington, DC (1962); Virginia (1961) **Marquis Who's Who Honors:** Albert Nelson Marquis Lifetime Achievement Award (2017) **Political Affiliations:** Republican **Religion:** Episcopalian **Shipping Address:** 850 10th Street, Covington & Burling, Washington, DC, 20001

Joanne Fern

Industry: Business Management/Business Services **Date of Birth:** 01/01/1900 **Education:** High School Diplomate (1978) **Civic:** Member, Angels Against Hunger; Member, Various Charitable Organizations **Membership:** Council of Better Business Bureaus; Contractors Register, Inc; Air Resources Board **Hobbies:** Watching NASCAR

Olivia Ann Ferrante

Title: Consultant, Traveling Teacher, Teacher of the Visually Impaired (Retired) **Industry:** Education/Educational Services **Company Name:** Revere High School **Date of Birth:** 11/09/1948 **Place of Birth:** Revere **State:** MA **Parents:** Guy Ferrante; Mary Carmella (Prizio) Ferrante **Education:** Postgraduate Coursework, Lesley University (1982); Postgraduate Coursework, Boston College (1977-1981); Postgraduate Coursework, Middlebury College (1974); MEd, Boston College (1971); BA, Regis College (1970) **Certifications:** Certified History Teacher; Certified Teacher of the Blind **Career:** Traveling Teacher of the Visually Impaired, Special Needs Department, Revere High School and 50 Additional Schools (1974-1992); Chairman, Braille Department, National Braille Press, Boston, MA (1971-1974); Traveling Teacher, Revere High School and Five Other Schools **Career Related:** Steven J. Rich Scholarship Committee (1993-Present); Consultant, Revere PTA (1984-Present) **Civic:** Treasurer, Third Order of Mary (2010-Present); Parish Council, Third Order of Mary (2010-Present); Historic Massachusetts (1994-Present); Friend, Paul Revere House (1994-Present); Peregrine Fund (1994-Present); Teacher, Literacy Program, Revere Committee for Handicapped Affairs (1993-Present); Mentor, Vision Foundation (1993-Present); Advisory Board, Massachusetts Commission for the Blind (1988-Present); Volunteer, Morgan Memorial, Boston, MA (1983-Present); Publicist, Animal Umbrella Cat Shelter (2003); Cantor, Revere Commission on Disabilities (1997); Publicist, Next Door Theater Group (1996); Access Task Force, Revere Public Library (1996); Publicist, A Woman's Concern Inc. (1996); Publicist, Catholic Daughters, SHARE (1995-2000); Lecturer, Revere Commission on Disabilities (1995-2016); Mentor, Braille Institute of America (1995); Sponsor, Rite of Catholic Initiation for Adults (1995); The Catholic League (1994-2017); Mobility Advisory Board, Massachusetts Commission for the Blind (1994); Center for Marine Preservation (1994); Teacher, Braille, Revere Committee for Handicapped Affairs (1993-2015); Friend, Wang Center (1993); Friend, Boston Public Garden and Common (1993); Revere First Committee (1993); Mentor, National Braille Literacy Project (1992); Friends of the Sick Children's Trust (1992); Volunteer, Birthright International (1992); Volunteer, Pro-Life Office (1992); Active Member, Arts Council Coop (1992); Friend, Boston Pops (1992); Advisory Board, Radio Reading Service for the Blind (1989-2000); Adult Music Ministry (1989); Governing Board on Independent Living, Massachusetts Organization on Disability (1989); Access Monitor, Massachusetts Organization on Disability (1988-2008); Publicist, Revere Commission on Disabilities (1985-2017); Revere Committee for Handicapped Affairs (1985-2016); Partnership Committee, International Year of Disabled Persons (1980-1981); Publicist, Soloist, Revere Music Makers (1977-1979); Chorus Pro Musica (1974-1976); Everett Chorus, Massachusetts (1974-1976); Adult Choir, Immaculate Conception Church (1966-2008); Supporter, Church Railings, Immaculate Conception Church **Creative Works:** Contributor, Articles, Professional Journals **Membership:** Vice President, Lifetime Member, Publicist, Revere Society for Cultural and Historical Preservation (1998-Present); Chairman, Grants Committee, Revere Society for Cultural and Historical Preservation (2000); Chairman, Grants Committee, Revere Society for Cultural and Historical Preservation (1998); Committee, Revere Society for Cultural and Historical Preservation (1998); St. Kateri Tekakwitha Catholic Community, Inc. (1997); National Education Association; International Society for Endangered Cats; Massachusetts Teachers Association; Revere Teachers Association; National Space Society; National Catholic Association for Persons with Visual Impairment; Publicist, Catholic Daughters of the Americas; Friends of Revere Public Library; Friends of Libraries for the Blind; Friends of Boston Symphony Orchestra; National Writers Union; Amnesty International; Society for Creative Anachronism, Inc.; Women Affirming Life; Michael Crawford International Fan Association; Chelsea Area Historical Society & Museum; Massachusetts Aviation Historical Society; Brian Boitano Fan Club; Barry Manilow Fan Club; Michael Feinstein Fan Club; The Peregrine Fund; Paul Revere Memorial Association; Greater Lynn Arts and Crafts Society; Friends of the Longfellow House; Friends of the Old South Meeting House; Father Capodanno Guild **Marquis Who's Who Honors:** Albert Nelson Marquis Lifetime Achievement Award (2017); Distinguished Humanitarian (2017) **Hobbies:** Travel; Music; Swimming; Ice skating; Knitting for charity (veterans and sick babies); Crafts **Religion:** Roman Catholic **Business Address:** 101 School Street, Revere, MA, 02151 **Shipping Address:** 115 Reservoir Avenue, Revere, MA, 02151

Joan Evans Ferry

Title: Owner **Industry:** Business Management/Business Services **Company Name:** Capital Funding Solutions **Date of Birth:** 08/20/1941 **Place of Birth:** Summit **State/Country of Origin:** NJ **Parents:** John Stiger Ferry; Margaret Darling (Evans) Ferry **Education:** Postgraduate Studies, Villanova University (1981); Postgraduate Studies, University of Pittsburgh (1970); Postgraduate Studies, University of Hawaii (1968); EdM, Temple University (1967); BS, University of Pennsylvania (1964); Student, Lehigh University (1965); Student, Lansdale School of Business (1962) **Certifications:** Certified Cash Flow Consultant, The American Cash Flow Institute, Orlando, FL (2004); Certified Parent Effectiveness Therapist; Certified Youth Effectiveness Therapist; Certified Play Therapist; Certified School Counselor **Career:** Self-Employed, Cash Flow Consultant (2004-Present); Owner, Capital Funding Solutions (2003-Present); Editor, Princeton Publishing Group Inc., Princeton, NJ (2000-Present); Private Practice Counselor, Real Estate Partnership, Perkasie, PA (1981-Present); Chair Child Study Team, Perkasie Elementary School (Now Sellersville Elementary School) (1988-1994); Assistant Manager, Holiday House Pool & Recreation Center (1981-1987); Elementary School Counselor, Pennridge Schools, Perkasie, PA (1979-2001); Elementary School Teacher, Pennridge Schools, Perkasie, PA (1964-1977); Research Assistant, University of Pennsylvania (1963); Mathematics and German Tutor, St. Lawrence University (1959-1961); Industrial Photographer, Bucksco Manufacturing Company, Inc., Quakertown, PA (1958-1959) **Career Related:** Chairman, Board of Auditors (1990-Present); Municipal Auditor (1990-Present); Notary Public (1986-Present); Adjunct Faculty, Bucks County Community College (1983-Present); Instructor, The American Institute of Banking, American Bankers Association (1982-Present); Secretary, Board of Auditors (1984-1990); Supervisory Teacher, East Stroudsburg University (1971-1974); Director of First Aid, Harry Hopman International Tennis Camp, Amherst, MA (1970-1974); Tennis Instructor, Harry Hopman International Tennis Camp, Amherst, MA (1970-1974); Research Assistant, University of Pennsylvania, Philadelphia, PA (1963) **Civic:** President, Task Force on Small Business Issues, National Federation of Independent Business (2005-Present); Bucks County Crisis Response Team (2001-Present); Volunteer, Southeastern PA-Delaware Chapter, House Rabbit Society, Chadds Ford, PA (1998-Present); Member, Hilltown Civic Association (1992-Present); Chalfont Ambulance Squad (2000); Performer, Good Shepherd Episcopal Church Choir (2000); Volunteer Special Driver, Bush Family and Friends at the Republican National Convention, Philadelphia, PA (2000); Volunteer Marshal, The Wachovia US Pro Championship, Wachiova Cycling Series, Philadelphia, PA (1999-2006); Silverdale Quick Response Medical Service (1999-2001) **Creative Works:** Author, "Relationships of Selected Variables in a Fifth Grade Classroom" (1966); Author, "Learning Styles of Elementary School Children" (1963); Author, "Angola: A Nation in Ferment" (1963) **Awards:** World Lifetime Achievement Award, Raleigh, NC (2007, 2003); Decree of Excellence, St. Thomas' Place, UK (2006); Service Award, Spring Mountain Ski Patrol (2004, 1996); Service Recognition Award, National Ski Patrol (2004, 1994); Inductee, Women's International Hall of Fame (2003); Award for Outstanding Service to Education, Pennridge School District (1999); Certificate of Appreciation, Special Olympics World Summer Games (1999); Nancy Sugalski Outstanding Dedication Award (1999); Honor Award for Service to Education and Teaching Profession, Pennsylvania State Education Association (1999, 1996); Outstanding Auxiliary Award, Spring Mountain Ski Patrol (1999, 1993); Certificate of Appreciation, Atlanta Olympics Medical Team (1997); Certification of Recognition, International Olympic Committee (1997); Certificate of Appreciation, National Ski Patrol Systems (1997); Inductee, International Tennis Hall of Fame (1972) **Membership:** Chairman, Pennridge Community Republicans Club (1992-Present); Instructional Support Team, Pennridge Education Association (1992-Present); Executive Council, Pennridge Education Association (1986-Present); Chairman, Political Action Committee for Education, Pennsylvania State Education Association (1986-Present); American Association of University Women; National Education Association; National Association for Female Executives; Honorary Lifetime Member, United States Tennis Association; Women's Tennis Association; Professional Tennis Registry; Pennsylvania Elected Women's Association; Bucks County Association Township Officials; Bucks County School Counselors Association; American Society of Notaries; National Federation of Independent Business; Pennsylvania School Counselors Association; American Cash Flow Association, Inc.; Penn Club of Bucks County, University of Pennsylvania Alumni Association; Partner, ATP Tour, Inc.; Pennsylvania Association of School Retirees; Kappa Delta Pi **Marquis Who's Who Honors:** Albert Nelson Marquis Lifetime Achievement Award (2017); Distinguished Humanitarian (2017) **Shipping Address:** 834 Rickert Rd, Perkasie, PA, 18944

Bertram Fields

Title: Lawyer **Industry:** Law and Legal Services **Company Name:** Greenberg Glusker Fields Claman & Machtinger **Date of Birth:** 03/31/1929 **Place of Birth:** Los Angeles **State:** CA **Parents:** Maxwell Fields; Mildred Fields **Marital Status:** Married **Spouse Name:** Barbara Guggenheim Fields **Children:** James Fields **Education:** JD, Harvard Law School, Magna Cum Laude; BA University of California, Los Angeles **Career:** Instructor, Stanford Law School **Military Service:** 1st Lieutenant, U.S. Air Force, Korean War **Creative Works:** Author, "The Sunset Bomber"; Author, "The Lawyer's Tale"; Author, "Royal Blood"; Author, "Players"; Author, "Gloriana"; Author, "Destiny"; Author, "Shylock - His Own Story" **Membership:** Council on Foreign Relations **Bar Admissions:** California Bar; New York Bar; U.S. Supreme Court Bar **Marquis Who's Who Honors:** Albert Nelson Marquis Lifetime Achievement Award (2017); Distinguished Humanitarian (2017) **Shipping Address:** 1900 Avenue of the Stars, Suite 2100, Greenberg Glusker Fields Claman & Machtinger, Los Angeles, CA, 90067 **Website:** www.greenbergglusker.com

George Alvin Finley III

Title: President **Industry:** Business Management/Business Services **Company Name:** Fin, Inc. **Date of Birth:** 04/25/1938 **Place of Birth:** Aurora **State:** IL **Parents:** George Alvin Finley, II; Sally Ann (Lord) Finley **Marital Status:** Married **Spouse Name:** Phyllis Ann Finley (4/24/1999); Sue Sellors (6/20/1962, Deceased 1995) **Children:** Valerie; George Alvin IV (2005) **Education:** Postgraduate Coursework, College Graduate Program, Ford Motor Company (1963); BBA, Southern Methodist University (1962) **Career:** President, CC Distributors, Corpus Christi, TX (1967-2017); Chief Executive Officer, CC Distributors, Corpus Christi, Texas (1967-2017); Regional Manager, Behlen Mfg. Co. (1965-1967); Lease Manager, Sequoia Lincoln, International Cars & Motor Ltd., Oakland, CA (1965); Vice President of Marketing, International Cars & Motor Ltd., Oakland, CA (1963-1964); Trainee, Ford Motor Company, Dearborn, MI (1962-1963); Representative to Europe, Finco International **Career Related:** President, Nueces River Authority (1995-2000); Member, Nueces River Authority (1975-2001); President, Southern Methodist University (1956-1961); Guest Instructor, School of Business, Southern Methodist University; Member, Board of Directors, Contract Services Association of America (Now Professional Services Council); Board Secretary, The University of Texas MD Anderson Cancer Center; Member, CHRISTUS Spohn Health; Member, Executive Committee, McDonald Observatory, The University of Texas at Austin; Member, Foundation Executive Committee, Del Mar College **Civic:** Member, Board of Directors, Charlie's Coastal Bend Alcohol and Drug Rehabilitation Center (1974-2012); Member, President's Council, Texas A&M University **Membership:** Grievance Committee, State Bar of Texas (1995-2001); Board of Directors, National Association of Wholesaler-Distributors (1994-2012); President, Texas Hardware Associations (1991-1992); Chairman of the Board, Sandwich Illinois, Impact Industries Inc. (1986-1993); American Supply Association; North America Building Material Distribution Association; Rotary International; Phi Delta Theta **Marquis Who's Who Honors:** Albert Nelson Marquis Lifetime Achievement Award (2017) **To what do you attribute your success:** Mr. Finley attributes his success to his father, who was his mentor. **Why did you become involved in your profession or industry:** Mr. Finley became involved in his profession because he grew up with manufacturing and became proficient in distribution, his father was his mentor and his grandfather started the Rainbow Baking Company. **What do you consider to be the highlight of your career:** The highlight of Mr. Finley's career was that he was able to sell his company after 50 years to people who want to pursue the business, and they have kept every one of his employees. The company was also started by another family in 1906, making it more than 112 years old and still thriving in this time. **Hobbies:** Cars **Political Affiliations:** Democrat **Religion:** Episcopalian **Shipping Address:** 3360 Ocean Dr, Corpus Christi, TX, 78411

Wayne House Finley, PhD

Title: Medical Educator (Retired) **Industry:** Medicine & Health Care **Company Name:** University of Alabama School of Medicine **Date of Birth:** 04/07/1927 **Place of Birth:** Goodwater **State:** AL **Parents:** Byron Bruce Finley; Lucille (House) Finley **Marital Status:** Married, Widowed **Spouse Name:** Sara Will Crews (7/6/1952) **Children:** Randall Wayne; Sara Jane **Education:** Traineeship in Medical Genetics, Uppsala University, Sweden (1961-1962); Intern, University of Alabama Hospitals and Clinics (1960-1961); MD, University of Alabama (1960); PhD, University of Alabama (1958); MS, University of Alabama (1955); MA, University of Alabama (1950); BS, Jacksonville State University (1948) **Certifications:** Certified in Clinical Cytogenetics, American Board of Medical Genetics (1983) **Career:** Professor Emeritus, University of Alabama School Medicine (1996-Present); Director, Laboratory of Medical Genetics (1962-1996); Adjunct Professor of Biology, University of Alabama School Medicine (1960-1996); Professor of Epidemiology and Public Health, University of Alabama School of Medicine (1975-1996); Professor (Pediatrics), University of Alabama School of Medicine (1970-1996); Professor of Physiology and Biophysics, University of Alabama School of Medicine (1968-1975); Director, Faculty Council, University of Alabama School of Medicine (1966-1996); Chairman, Medical Student Research Day, University of Alabama School of Medicine (1965-1975); Professor of Pediatrics, University of Alabama School of Medicine (1962-1970); Science Teacher, High School, Tuscaloosa, AL (1949-1951) **Career Related:** Chairman, Alabama Healthcare Hall of Fame (2007-2018); Member, Advisory and Nominating Committee, Alabama Healthcare Hall of Fame (1998-2018); Chairman, Carey Phillips Travel Fellowship (1972-2018); Faculty Representative, University of Alabama Systems Board of Trustees (1995-1996); Senator, University of Alabama at Birmingham Faculty Senate (1995-1996); Carmichael Fund for Graduate Students (1989-2009); Committee on Future Needs in Medical Genetics, Genetics Service Branch, US Public Health Service (1987); Director, Medical Genetics Graduate Program, University of Alabama at Birmingham (1983-1996); Board of Directors, Southeastern Regional Genetics Group (1982-2000); Chairman, Steering Committee, Reynolds-Finley Historical Library Associates (1981-2007) **Military Service:** Officer, Chemical Corps, US Army (1951-1953); Lieutenant Colonel, US Army Reserve (1946-1974); Enlisted Man, Infantry, US Army, Germany (1945-1946) **Creative Works:** Editor, Newsletter (1997-2000); Author, University of Alabama Medical Alumni Association (1959-2003) **Awards:** Wayne H. Finley Endowed Student Travel Award in Genetics (2017); Plaque, Clay Co. Hospital in Ashland, AL in honor of Wayne H. and Sara C.Finley (2016); Wayne H. and Sara C. Finley Learning Community established by medical students. (2016); UAB President's Medal (2015); UAB Reynolds Historical Library and annual Lecture renamed Reynolds-Finley Historical Library and Lecture (2014); Martha Myers Role Model Award, University of Alabama School of Medicine Alumni Association (2008); Distinguished Service Award, University of Alabama School of Medicine Alumni Association (2005); Lifetime Achievement Award, Birmingham Business Journal (2003); Samuel Buford Word Award, Medical Association of the State of Alabama (2003); Gardner Award, Alabama Academy of Science (2002); Brother Bryan Humanitarian Award (2001); Induction, Alabama Healthcare Hall of Fame (2001); Finley-Compass Bank Genetics Conference Center with portrait established, University of Alabama at Birmingham (2001); Will Gaines Holmes Award, Children's Aid Society (1999); Physicians' Recognition Award, American Medical; Portrait, Reynolds Historical Library (1991); Association (1996); Physicians' Recognition Award, American Medical Association (1993); Physicians' Recognition Award, American Medical Association (1990); Alumnus of the Year Award, Jacksonville State University (1989); Physicians' Recognition Award, American Medical Association (1987); Wayne H. and Sara C. Finley Chair in Medical Genetics, University of Alabama at Birmingham (1986); Physicians' Recognition Award, American Medical Association (1984); Distinguished Faculty Lecturer Award, University of Alabama Medical Center (1983); Physicians' Recognition Award, American Medical Association (1983); Turlington Award (1982); Physicians' Recognition Award, American Medical Association (1981) **Membership:** Counselor, Medical Association of Alabama, (1990-Present); Gold Member, American Academy of Pediatrics Robbia Club (2008); Trustee, Alabama Academy of Science (1991-2001); Fellow, American College of Medical Genetics; Fellow, Royal Society of Medicine; American Medical Association **Marquis Who's Who Honors:** Albert Nelson Marquis Lifetime Achievement Award (2017); Distinguished Humanitarian (2017) **Religion:** Baptist **Shipping Address:** 3412 Brookwood Rd, Birmingham, AL, 35223

Edwin Brown Firmage

Title: Professor of Law Emeritus **Industry:** Education/Educational Services **Company Name:** University of Utah **Date of Birth:** 10/01/2017 **State:** UT **Parents:** Edwin Raddon Firmage; Mary Myrtice (Brown) Firmage **Children:** Edwin James; Miriam; Sarah; Zina; Joseph; Jonathan; David **Education:** LLM, University of Chicago (1964); SJD, University of Chicago (1964); JD, University of Chicago (1963); MS in Political Science and History, Brigham Young University, High Honors (1962); BS, Brigham Young University (1960); National Honors Scholar, School of Law, University of Chicago **Career:** Retired, Samuel D. Thurman Professor of Law Emeritus, S.J. Quinney College of Law, University of Utah, Salt Lake City, UT (2012-Present); Samuel D. Thurman Professor of Law, S.J. Quinney College of Law, University of Utah, Salt Lake City, UT (1990-2012); Professor of Law, University of Utah Law School (Now S.J. Quinney College of Law, University of Utah), Salt Lake City, UT (1970-2012); Associate Assistant Professor, University of Utah Law School (Now S.J. Quinney College of Law, University of Utah), Salt Lake City, UT (1966-1970); Staff Member, Vice President Hubert Humphrey, White House, Washington, DC (1965-1966) **Career Related:** Guest Speaker, "Beginnings," Native American and Tibetan Human Rights, United Nations (2001); Guest Speaker, "Toward the Creation of a Culture of Peace and Non-Violence Toward Children, 2000-2010," Sub-Commission on Human Rights, United Nations, Geneva, Switzerland (1999); Lecturer, Justice and Peace Representatives, International Congregation of Men and Women Religious, Rome (1993); Kellogg Lecturer, "The Human Being: War, Peace and Faith," Episcopal Divinity School, Cambridge, MA (1993); Lane Lecturer, Creighton University School of Law, Omaha, NE (1992); Visiting Professor, Constitutional Law, Bentham House, UCL, University of London (1992); Participant, Fulbright Seminar, Soviet Union (Now Russia) (1990); Guest Speaker, McDougall Lecture, "Reconciliation," Cathedral of the Madeleine, Salt Lake City, Utah (1989); Guest Speaker, Reynolds Lecture, "Ends and Means in Conflict," The University of Utah (1987); Senior Fellow, Keynes College, University of Kent, Canterbury, England (1987); Visiting Professor, Clark Law School (Now J. Reuben Clark Law School), Brigham Young University (1986); Visiting Professor, Clark Law School (Now J. Reuben Clark Law School), Brigham Young University (1983); Visiting Professor, University of Texas School of Law (Now Texas Law, The University of Texas at Austin), Austin, Texas (1979); Fellow, Law and Humanities, Harvard Law School (1974-1975); Visiting Scholar, United Nations, New York, NY (1970-1971); International Affairs Fellow, Council on Foreign Relations, Geneva, Switzerland (1970-1971); Editorial Board, The University of Chicago Law Review **Civic:** Utahns United Against the Nuclear Arms Race (1981-1984); Foundation President, Utah Opera Company (Now Utah Opera) (1976-1980) **Creative Works:** Author, "Three Chances to Avoid Four Years of Trump," The Salt Lake Tribune (2017); Editor, "The International Legal System, Fifth Edition," Foundation Press, NY (2001); Co-author, "To Chain the Dog of War: The War Power of Congress in History and Law," Revised Edition, University of Illinois Press (2001); Co-author, "Zion in the Courts: A Legal History of the Church of Jesus Christ of Latter-Day Saints," Revised Paperback Edition (2001); Editor, "The International Legal System: Cases and Materials" (1995); Co-author, "Religion and the Law: Biblical, Jewish & Islamic Perspectives," Eisenbrauns (1990); Co-author, "To Chain the Dog of War: The War Power of Congress in History and Law, Second Edition," University of Illinois Press (1989); Co-author, "Zion in the Courts: A Legal History of the Church of Jesus Christ of Latter-Day Saints" (1988) **Awards:** Lifetime Achievement Gold Medaille d' Excellence Laureates, Geneva, Switzerland (2001); Rosenblatt Prize for Excellence, University of Utah (1991); Turner-Fairbourn Award for Significant Contributions to Peace and Justice (1991); Honoree, Samuel D. Thurman Professor of Law, Utah Law School (Now S.J. Quinney College of Law, University of Utah) (1990); Alpha Sigma Nu Book Award for Best Book of the Year, Honor Society of the National Association of Jesuit Colleges & Universities in the United States (Now Association of Jesuit Colleges & Universities (AJCU) (1989); Governor's Award in the Humanities, Utah Endowment for the Humanities (1989); Charles Redd Prize for Outstanding Contributions in Humanities and Social Sciences, Utah Academy of Science, Arts and Letters (1988); Distinguished Achievement Award, Brigham Young University Alumni (1978) **Membership:** American Bar Association; Utah Bar Association; The American Society of International Law; Phi Alpha Delta; Phi Kappa Phi; Pi Sigma Alpha **Bar Admissions:** State of Utah; U.S. Supreme Court **Marquis Who's Who Honors:** Albert Nelson Marquis Lifetime Achievement Award (2017) **Shipping Address:** 1146 E Harvard Avenue, Salt Lake City, UT, 84105

Myrna Leah Fischman, PhD

Title: Accountant, Educator **Industry:** Education/Educational Services **Company Name:** Long Island University - Brooklyn **Date of Birth:** 07/29/1934 **Place of Birth:** New York City **State:** NY **Parents:** Isidore Fischman; Sally (Goldstein) Fischman **Marital Status:** Single **Education:** PhD, New York University (1976); MS, Baruch College, The City College of New York (1964); BS, Baruch College, The City College of New York (1960) **Certifications:** Certified Public Accountant, State of New York (1964) **Career:** Director, Center for Accounting & Tax Education, Long Island University - Brooklyn (1986-Present); Director, School of Professional Accountancy, Long Island University - Brooklyn (1984-Present); Professor of Accounting Taxation and Law, Long Island University (1979-Present); Self-Employed Accountant, NY (1960-Present); Coordinator, Graduate Capstone Courses, Long Island University (1982-1986); Adviser, Professor, Long Island University (1970-1979); Community Fellowship Coordinator, Queens District Attorney's Office (1970-1971); Chief Accountant, Investigator of Rackets, Queens District Attorney's Office (1969-1970); Instructor of Accounting, Borough of Manhattan Community College, The City University of New York (1963-1966); Vice Adviser, Center Commercial High School, NY (1963-1966); Teacher of Accounting, Center Commercial High School, NY (1960-1963); Chief Accountant Investigator, Queens District Attorney (1954-1970); Chairman, Department of Accounting, Long Island University; Assistant to Controller, Sam Goody, Inc., NY **Career Related:** Lecturer, Tax Seminar, 200 Licensed Certified Public Accountants (2017); Special Trustee, Professor Leo Schloss Excellence in Accounting Scholarship; Adviser, Accounting Society, Long Island University; Developer, BS/MS Accounting Program, Long Island University **Civic:** Business Education Advisory Council, Accounting Department Advisory Board, Borough of Manhattan Community College, The City University of New York (1997-Present); The New York City Department of Education (1992-2000); Subcommittee on Business Education, Economic Development and Marketing Committee, Brooklyn Chamber of Commerce (1984-2015); Chairman, Supervisory Committee, LOMTO FCU #1532, NY (1983-2016); Educational Task Force, AJC (1972-1995); Chairman, Consumer Council, Astoria Medical Center (1980-1992); Legislative Advisory Board, New York State Assemblyman Dennis Butler (1979-1997); Chancellor, Committee Against Discrimination in Education (1976-1997); Steering Committee, Youth Division, New York County Democratic Committee (1967-1968); Representative, Women's Activities Committee, YDA (1967); Delegate to National Convention, YDA (1967); Treasurer, Breakfree Inc., Lower East Side Preparatory School **Creative Works:** Editor, Eastern Business Educators Journal (1988) **Awards:** Special Award for 40 Years of Service to the Volunteer Income Tax Assistance Program, Internal Revenue Service (2014); Lifetime Achievement Award, Soroptimist International, Brooklyn, NY (1997); Dr. Emanuel Saxe Outstanding CPA in Education Award, New York State Society of Certified Public Accountants (1994-1995) **Membership:** Public Relations Committee, New York State Society of Certified Public Accountants (1992-Present); Director, Tax & Accounting Institute, Long Island University - Brooklyn (1984-Present); Chairman, Supervisory Committee 1532, Federal Credit Union (1983-Present); Director, New York Chapter, Institute of Management Accountants, Inc. (1983-Present); Board of Directors, New York State Society of Certified Public Accountants (2005-2010); President, Brooklyn Chapter, New York State Society of Certified Public Accountants (2001-2002) **To what do you attribute your success:** She attributes her success to her great parents. **Why did you become involved in your profession or industry:** She became involved in her profession because she loved the ambiance of the world of business. **What do you consider to be the highlight of your career:** The highlight of her career has been vicariously enjoying the success of her students. She was also proud to earn tenure and receive a promotion to full professor. **Where will you be in five years:** In five years, Dr. Fischman plans to continue doing what she loves. **Political Affiliations:** Democrat **Religion:** Jewish **Business Address:** 1 University Plaza, Room 700, Brooklyn, NY, 11201 **Shipping Address:** 370 E 76th St Apt A308, New York, NY, 10021

Charles John Fisk

Title: Meteorologist, Data Scientist, Consultant **Industry:** Sciences **Company Name:** Naval Base Ventura County **Date of Birth:** 09/02/1946 **Place of Birth:** Minneapolis **State:** MN **Parents:** Everett Vincent Fisk; Florence Linnea Carlson **Education:** MS in Meteorology, University of Wisconsin (1984) **Career:** Meteorologist, Naval Base Ventura County, Point Mugu, CA (1986-Present); Climatologist, Naval Base Ventura County, Point Mugu, CA (1986-Present) **Career Related:** Consultant, Certified Consulting Meteorologist (2017-Present); Consultant, Private Meteorologist (1996-2017) **Creative Works:** Author, "The First Fifty Years of Continuous Recorded Weather History In Minnesota (1820-1869): A Narrative Chronology"; Contributor, More Than 25 Conference Proceedings Presentations and Articles in Meteorology, Climatology, and Statistics **Membership:** American Statistical Association; American Meteorological Society **Hobbies:** Reading; Travel; Web publishing; Genealogy; Genetic genealogy; Research **Shipping Address:** 590 Gilbert St, Newbury Park, CA, 91320 **Website:** http://www.climatestations.com

Tom W. Fite

Title: Mathematics Educator, Farmer **Industry:** Education/Educational Services **Date of Birth:** 06/19/1937 **Place of Birth:** Bethel **State/Country of Origin:** OH **Parents:** Charles Lloyd Fite; Esther Iota Ogden **Marital Status:** Widowed **Spouse Name:** Mary Ann Lyons (7/27/1963, Deceased) **Children:** Lisa Teegarden; Michael **Education:** MS in Mathematics, University of Oklahoma, Norman, OK (1969); EdB, Wilmington College, Wilmington, OH (1959) **Career:** Math Instructor, Southern State Community College, Sardinia, OH (1998-2003); Math Instructor, Maysville Community College, Maysville, KY (1992-1997); Math Instructor, Northern Kentucky University, Alexandria, KY (1982-1983); Math Instructor, Southern State Community College, Sardinia, OH (1967-1977); Math Teacher, West Clermont High School, Glen Este, OH (1965-1990); Math Teacher, Western Brown High School, Mount Orab, OH (1960-1964) **Career Related:** Civic Leader, Boy Scouts of America (1958-1962); Leader, 4-H (1957-1960) **Marquis Who's Who Honors:** Albert Nelson Marquis Lifetime Achievement Award (2017) **Hobbies:** Hunting; Fishing; Gardening; Reading **Political Affiliations:** Republican **Religion:** Church of Christ **Shipping Address:** 4355 Sunshine Road, Georgetown, OH, 45121

Elayne Flamm

Title: President **Industry:** Nonprofit & Philanthropy **Company Name:** Friends of AKIM USA **Spouse Name:** Donald Flamm (Deceased) **Education:** Coursework, Manhattan School of Music **Career:** President, Friends of AKIM USA **Awards:** Fundraiser of the Year (2009); Honoree, Gala, Friends of AKIM; Named in Top Female Executives, Professionals & Entrepreneurs **Membership:** President, Advisory Board, Miracle Center; International Society of Palm Beach; Former Member, Friars Club; Honorary Chairman, Grandma's Place; Advisory Board, Jezreel International; Israel Bond; American Songbook **Hobbies:** Bible studies; Fundraising; Social events **Business Address:** 12 E 49th St Fl 11, New York, NY, 10017 **Shipping Address:** 400 S Ocean Blvd Apt 204, Palm Beach, FL, 33480 **Website:** https://www.akimusa.org

Thomas L. Flattery

Title: Lawyer, Administrator **Industry:** Law and Legal Services **Date of Birth:** 11/14/1922 **Place of Birth:** Detroit **State:** MI **Parents:** Thomas J. Flattery; Rosemary (Long) Flattery **Marital Status:** Widowed **Spouse Name:** Gloria M. Hughes (6/10/1947, Deceased) **Children:** Constance Marie; Carol Dianne Lee; Michael Patrick; Thomas Hughes; Dennis Jerome; Betsy Ann Sprec **Education:** LLM, University of California, Los Angeles (1965); JD, University of California, Los Angeles (1955); BS, U.S. Military Academy (1947) **Certifications:** State of New York (1984); State of Connecticut (1983); U.S. Supreme Court (1974); U.S. Customs Court (1968); U.S. Patent and Trademark Office (1957); State of California (1955) **Career:** Private Practice, Palisades, CA (1993-Present); Settlement Officer, Los Angeles Superior Court (1991-Present); Temporary Judge, Superior Court California, Los Angeles Judicial District and Santa Monica Unified Courts (1987-Present); Vice President, General Counsel, G&H Tech., Inc., Penn Central Corporation, Santa Monica, CA (1986-1993); Senior Vice President, Secretary, General Counsel, Automation Industries, Inc. (Now PCC Tech. Industries Inc., Penn Central Corporation), Greenwich, CT (1976-1986); Counsel, Assistant Secretary, C.F. Braun & Company, Alhambra, CA (1975-1976); Vice President, Secretary, General Counsel, Schick Inc., Los Angeles, CA (1972-1975); Vice President, Secretary and General Counsel, Amcord, Inc., Newport Beach, CA (1970-1972); Secretary, Corporate Counsel, Technicolor, Inc., Hollywood, CA (1964-1970); General Counsel, Assistant Secretary, McCulloch Corporation, Los Angeles, CA (1957-1964); Legal Staff, Assistant Contract Administrator, Radioplane Company, Van Nuys, CA (1955-1957); Bohn Aluminum & Brass Company, Hamtramck, MI (1952); Equitable Life Assurance Society, Detroit, MI (1951); Motor Products Corporation, Detroit, MI (1950) **Career Related:** Second Appellate District, California Court of Appeals (1999-Present); Alternative Dispute Resolution Committee, Los Angeles Superior Court (2001-2007); Judicial Arbitrator, Mediator, Alternative Dispute Resolution Programs, Los Angeles Superior Court (1993-2013); Panelist, American Arbitration Association (1991-2012) **Military Service:** First Lieutenant, U.S. Army (1942-1950) **Creative Works:** Contributor, Articles, Professional Journals **Awards:** Trumbull Award, Jonathan Club (2005) **Membership:** Arbitrator, Mediator, Beverly Hills Bar Association (2005-Present); Mandatory Fee Arbitrator, State Bar of California (2001-Present); Attorney-Client Fee Dispute Arbitrator and Mediator, Santa Monica Bar Association (2000-Present); Chairman, Alternate Dispute Resolution Section, Santa Monica Bar Association (2000-2007); Secretary, American Educational League (1998-2007); Board of Mediators, National Association of Securities Dealers (1997); Second Vice President, Jonathan Club (1997-1998); Director, Jonathan Club (1996-1999); Board of Arbitrators, National Association of Securities Dealers (1996); Dispute Resolution Services Attorney-Client Fee Dispute Arbitrator and Mediator (1993-2013); Trustee, American Educational League (1988-2010); Chairman, Corporate Law Department Committee, Century City Bar Association (1979-1980); Co-Chairman, Corporate Law Department Committee, State Bar of California (1978-1979); Los Angeles Regional Group President, American Society of Corporate Secretaries (1973-1974); Los Angeles Intellectual Property Law Association; Irish-American Bar Association of California; American Legion; West Point Alumni Association; Army Athletic Association; Friendly Sons of St. Patrick; Phi Alpha Delta Law Fraternity; American Bar Association; Lecturer, Continuing Legal Education Program, State Bar of California; Connecticut Bar Association; New York State Bar Association; Connecticut Bar Association; **Religion:** Roman Catholic **Shipping Address:** 439 Via De La Paz, Pacific Palisades, CA, 90272

Arthur C. Fleischer

Title: Medical Educator **Industry:** Medicine & Health Care **Company Name:** Vanderbilt University Medical Center **Date of Birth:** 05/15/1952 **Place of Birth:** Miami **State:** FL **Parents:** Eugene Fleischer; Lucille Fleischer **Marital Status:** Married **Spouse Name:** Leona Fleischer (05/25/1975) **Children:** Braden; Jared; Amy **Education:** MD, Medical College of Georgia, Augusta University (1976); BS in Biology, Emory University (1973) **Career:** Cornelius Vanderbilt Chair, Vanderbilt University Medical Center (2011); Professor of Obstetrics-Gynecology, Vanderbilt University Medical Center (1988-Present); Professor of Radiology, Vanderbilt University Medical Center, Nashville, TN (1987-Present) **Creative Works:** Author, "Sonography in Obstetrics & Gynecology: Principles and Practice" (2010); Author, 23 Books on Diagnostic Sonography **Awards:** Distinguished Alumnus Award, Medical College of Georgia, Augusta University (2007); Frank H. Boehm Award for Continuing Medical Education, Vanderbilt University Medical Center (2005); CANDLE Award for Medical Student Teaching, Vanderbilt University Medical Center (2005); Larry Mack Award, Society of Radiologists in Ultrasound (1999); William Fry Award, American Institute of Ultrasound in Medicine **Membership:** Fellow, American Institute of Ultrasound in Medicine; American College of Radiology; Society of Radiologists in Ultrasound; Board of Governors, American Institute of Ultrasound in Medicine (1989-1991) **Marquis Who's Who Honors:** Albert Nelson Marquis Lifetime Achievement Award (2017) **Why did you become involved in your profession or industry:** He became involved in his profession because since he was a young boy, he was interested in science and research. **Shipping Address:** 1161 21st Ave S, Vanderbilt University Medical Center, Nashville, TN, 37232

Jane Williams Fleming

Title: Teacher **Industry:** Education/Educational Services **Date of Birth:** 05/26/1926 **Place of Birth:** Bethlehem **State:** PA **Parents:** James Robert Groman; Marion Pauline (Melloy) Groman **Marital Status:** Single **Spouse Name:** Jerome Thomas Fleming (9/25/1980, Deceased 2002); George Elliott Williams (7/2/1955, Divorced 7/1/1965) **Children:** Rhett Dorman; Santee Stuart; Timothy Cooper **Education:** Coursework, Osher Lifelong Learning Institute (2013-Present); MA, California State University, Long Beach (1969); BS, University of California, Los Angeles (1951) **Career:** Teacher, Long Beach Unified School District (1962-1987); Teacher, Long Beach Unified School District, California (1956-1958); Teacher, Newport-Mesa Unified School District, California (1955-1956); Teacher, San Diego Unified School District (1951-1955) **Career Related:** Part-Time Teacher, Long Beach Unified School District (1990-1992); Speaker, Board of Education **Creative Works:** Author, "Why Janey Can't Teach" (2001); Contributor, Articles, Newspapers; Contributor, Short Stories, Popular Magazines **Membership:** The Honor Society of Phi Kappa Phi; Retired Teachers Association; UCLA Alumni; The Planetary Society; Red Hat Society; Museum of Tolerance, Simon Wiesenthal Center **Hobbies:** Theater; Travel **Shipping Address:** 420 Redondo Ave Unit 301, Long Beach, CA, 90814

Neil Floch

Title: General Surgeon **Industry:** Medicine & Health Care **Company Name:** Fairfield County Bariatrics & Surgical Specialists, P.C. **Marital Status:** Married **Spouse Name:** Robin **Children:** Jake; Sydney **Education:** Resident in General Surgery, Beth Israel Medical Center, New York City, NY; Fellow, Advanced Laparoscopic Surgery, Mayo Clinic, Jacksonville, FL; MD, Boston University School of Medicine (1992); Diplomate, Tufts University, Magna Cum Laude, Medford, MA **Career:** Surgeon, Fairfield County Bariatrics & Surgical Specialists, P.C. (1998-Present); Instructor in Surgery, Mayo Foundation for Medical Education and Research (1998); Director of Bariatric Surgery, Western Health Care Systems **Awards:** Presidential Award, ASMBS (2016); Named, Top Doctor in Bariatric Surgery, Connecticut Magazine (2011-2012); Best Physician, Consumers' Guide to Top Doctors (2009); Nominee, Melville G. Magida Award for Outstanding Young Physician, The Richard & Hinda Rosenthal Foundation and Fairfield County Medical Association (2004-2005); Scallen Award for Innovations in Antireflux Surgery, Norwalk Hospital **Membership:** Council for Advancement of Bariatrics, Lap-Band, Allergan Inc. and Apollo Endosurgery (2013); Connecticut State President, ASMBS; Connecticut State President, American Medical Association; Connecticut State President, Society of American Gastrointestinal and Endoscopic Surgeons; Fellow, American College of Surgeons **To what do you attribute your success:** Dr. Floch attributes his success to loving his work because he helps people lose weight, sometimes a tremendous amount of weight, and helps to resolve their medical issues. He finds it extremely rewarding. **Shipping Address:** 148 East Ave Ste 3A, FCB Bariatrics, Norwalk, CT, 06851

Marjorie Anne Flory

Title: Writer, Editor **Industry:** Writing and Editing **Date of Birth:** 04/01/1930 **Place of Birth:** London **State/Country of Origin:** England **Parents:** Harry Russell Flory; Florence Gilman Flory **Marital Status:** Single **Education:** Postgraduate Coursework, Columbia University, New York, NY (1952-1953); BA, Smith College, Northampton, MA (1951) **Career:** Freelance Writer, Freelance Editor, New York, NY (1985-Present); Senior Editor, Reader's Digest, New York, NY (1980-1985); Associate Editor, Reader's Digest, Pleasantville, NY (1960-1980); Researcher, Reader's Digest, New York, NY (1953-1960); Library Assistant, French Embassy Cultural Services, New York, NY (1951-1952) **Career Related:** Editor, Fourth Write Press, Shelburne, VT (1993-2010) **Civic:** Interpreter, New York Road Runners Club, New York, NY (1998-Present); Tutor, Volunteer Services for Children, New York, NY (1980-1985) **Creative Works:** Editor, "More Cooking with Pecans" (2003-2010); Copy Editor, "Made In Italy" (1988); Co-Author: "Reel Life/Real Life" **Membership:** Board Member, Smith College Club, New York, NY (2003-2005); Phi Beta Kappa Society **To what do you attribute your success:** Ms. Flory attributes her success to her interest in what she's done. She is a quick learner. **Why did you become involved in your profession or industry:** Ms. Flory's father was a journalist and she always had an interest in journalism, reading, and writing. **What do you consider to be the highlight of your career:** The highlight of Ms.Flory's career was working for the European editorial offices of Reader's Digest in Paris, France. **Where will you be in five years:** In the next five years, Ms. Flory hopes to be living in a retirement community in Vermont. **Hobbies:** Travel; Tennis; Language studies; Choral singing **Business Address:** 200 Wake Robin Drive, Apt. H108, Shelburne, VT, 05482 **Shipping Address:** 610 W End Avenue, Apt. 7E, New York, NY, 10024

Ann Florence Fogelman

Title: Nutrition Consultant, Educator, Researcher (Retired) **Industry:** Health, Wellness and Fitness **Company Name:** The University of Texas Medical Branch at Galveston **Date of Birth:** 10/12/1924 **Place of Birth:** Reading **State:** PA **Parents:** George Franklin Fogelman; Ruth Amelia Swartley Fogelman **Education:** MPH, University of California, Berkeley (1957); BS, University of Delaware (1950) **Certifications:** Licensed Dietitian, Texas; Registered Dietitian, American Dietetic Association **Career:** Nutritionist, Department of Obstetrics-Gynecology, The University of Texas Medical Branch at Galveston, Galveston, Texas (1963-1991); Nutrition Consultant, Maryland State Department of Health, Baltimore, MD (1960-1963); Nutritionist, Charlotte-Mecklenburg Health Department (1957-1960); Clinic and Teaching Dietitian, Vanderbilt University Hospital, Nashville, TN (1953-1956); Dietetic Intern, Frances Stern Food Clinic, Boston, MA (1952); Assistant Dietitian, Memorial Hospital, Wilmington, DE (1950-1951); Assistant Director, YWCA Camp Otonka, Dagsboro, DE (1949); Cook, Art Camp, Cragsmoor, NY (1948) **Career Related:** President, Various Offices and Committees, Texas State Nutrition Council (1976-1978); Texas Delegate, American Home Economics Association National Convention (1973); Texas Delegate, American Home Economics Association National Convention (1971); President, South Texas Dietetic Association (1969-1970); Executive Board, Texas Dietetic Association (1968-1969); Dietary Director, Texas Nutrition Survey (1968-1969); Recording Secretary, Houston Area Home Economics Association (1967-1968); Liaison, Texas Home Economics Association **Civic:** Volunteer, Senior Learning Center (1997-Present); Volunteer, Vitas Healthcare, Friendswood, Texas (1994-Present); Volunteer, Memorial Hermann Southeast Hospital, Houston, Texas (1994-Present); Active, Clear Lake Presbyterian Church (1992-Present); Stephen Minister, Clear Lake Presbyterian Church (2000); Deacon, Clear Lake Presbyterian Church (1996); Volunteer, Clear Lake Regional Medical Center, Webster, Texas (1992-1996) **Military Service:** WAVES (1944-1946) **Creative Works:** Contributor, Book Chapters; Contributor, Articles, Professional Publications; Writer, Memoir, Prose and Poetry **Awards:** Honoree, Ten Most Outstanding Students, School of Home Economics, University of Delaware (1962) **Membership:** President, Pasadena Chapter, Beta Sigma Phi (1974-1975); Girl of the Year, Beta Sigma Phi (1974-1975); Dickinson Chapter Girl of the Year, Beta Sigma Phi (1966-1967); President, Charlotte Chapter, Beta Sigma Phi (1959-1960); Charter Member, Gulf Coast Poets; Poetry Society of Texas; Waves National; Bay Area Writers League; Lifetime Member, Beta Sigma Phi; Clear Lake Chapter, Senior Friends; The Women's Memorial; UTMB Retirees Association, The University of Texas Medical Branch at Galveston **Marquis Who's Who Honors:** Albert Nelson Marquis Lifetime Achievement Award (2017) **Why did you become involved in your profession or industry:** Ms. Fogelman chose her profession because she grew up on a farm in a rural area. Her parents helped her to understand that it was important to be kind to people and to help others, and her mom taught her to be a nurturer. **Hobbies:** Travel; Dance; Reading **Shipping Address:** 16514 Barcelona Dr, Friendswood, TX, 77546-3304

Franco Fogliato

Industry: Apparel & Fashion **Education:** MBA in General Management, The Open University (2012) **Career:** Chief Executive Officer of a sporting goods retailer (2004-2013). **Marquis Who's Who Honors:** Albert Nelson Marquis Lifetime Achievement Award (2017); Distinguished Humanitarian (2017) **What prompted you to get involved in this profession or industry:** Mr. Fogliato became involved in his profession because he developed an interest in sports at an early age. **Where will you be in 5 years:** In five years, Mr. Fogliato plans for continued professional growth. **Hobbies:** Sports; Spending time with his family; Running **Shipping Address:** 2970 NW Circle A Dr., Portland OR 97229

Larry J. Forney

Title: Chemical Engineer, Educator **Industry:** Engineering **Date of Birth:** 11/01/1944 **Place of Birth:** Waterloo **State:** IA **Parents:** Loren John Forney; Ramona Leary Forney **Marital Status:** Married **Spouse Name:** Paula Hickey **Children:** Megan Catlin **Education:** PhD, Harvard University, Cambridge, MA (1974); ME, Massachusetts Institute of Technology, Boston (1969); MS, Massachusetts Institute of Technology, Boston (1968); BS, Case Institute of Technology (1966) **Career:** Emeritus Professor of Chemical Engineering, Georgia Institute of Technology (2009-Present); Associate Professor of Chemical Engineering, Georgia Institute of Technology, Atlanta (1979-2009); Assistant Professor, Department of Civil Engineering, University of Illinois at Urbana-Champaign (1974-1979); Research Engineer, Walden Research Division, Abcor, Inc., Cambridge, MA (1972-1974); Research Engineer, Norton Research Corporation, Cambridge, MA (1968) **Career Related:** Consultant, Crystal Clean Technologies (2006-Present); Consultant, Chemical Products Corporation (2004); Consultant, Dow Corning Corporation (1994-1996); Consultant, Leeds & Northrup (1991); Consultant, Dupont (1989-1991); Consultant, Sverdrup Technology, Inc. (1983-1987); Physical Scientist, Air Force Rocket Propulsion Laboratory, Edward Air Force Base, California (1983); Lockheed-Georgia Company (1982-1983); Consultant, Commercial Union Insurance Company (1977) **Civic:** Active Clean Air Council, Georgia Lung Association (1980-1982) **Military Service:** US Air Force (1983-1984, 1989-1995) **Creative Works:** Contributor, Articles to Professional Journals **Awards:** Food & Drink Processing Award, Institution of Chemical Engineers (2010); Water Award, Institution of Chemical Engineers (2008); Recipient, Award, Georgia FoodPAC (2002-2006); Fellow, NASA (1988); Fellow, Southeastern Center for Electrical Engineering (1982); Recipient, Award, United States Department of Energy (1977-1981); Recipient, Award, Environmental Protection Agency (1976-1978); Grantee, National Science Foundation (1975-1977) Fellow, National Institutes of Health (1968) **Membership:** Coordinator of Annual Meetings, American Institute of Chemical Engineers (2000, 1988, 1983); Harvard Society of Engineers and Scientists; North American Mixing Forum; Harvard Club; Massachusetts Institute of Technology Club **Marquis Who's Who Honors:** Albert Nelson Marquis Lifetime Achievement Award (2017); Distinguished Humanitarian (2017) **Shipping Address:** 4029 Menlo Way, Atlanta, GA, 30340

Bruce Alexander Forster, PhD

Title: John Becker Endowed Professor of Business Emeritus **Industry:** Education/Educational Services **Company Name:** The University of Nebraska at Kearney **Date of Birth:** 09/23/1948 **Place of Birth:** Toronto **State/Country of Origin:** Canada **Marital Status:** Divorced **Spouse Name:** Valerie Dale Pendock (12/8/1979, Divorced 10/2003); Margaret Jane Mackay (12/28/1968, Divorced 12/1979) **Children:** Kelli Elissa; Jeremy Bruce; Jessica Dale **Education:** PhD in Economics, Australian National University, Canberra, Australia (1974); BA in Mathematics and Economics, University of Guelph, Ontario, Canada (1970) **Career:** John Becker Endowed Professor Emeritus of Business, Professor Emeritus of Economics, The University of Nebraska at Kearney (2009-Present); Professor Emeritus, West Campus, Arizona State University (2005-Present); Dean, College of Business and Technology, John Becker Professor of Business, Professor of Economics, The University of Nebraska at Kearney (2005-2009); Dean of School of Management, West Campus, Professor of Economics, West Campus, Arizona State University (2000-2005); Dean, College of Business, University of Wyoming (1991-2000); Professor of Economics, University of Wyoming (1987-2000); Visiting Professor, University of Wyoming (1987); Professor, University of Guelph (1983-1987); Visiting Professor, University of Wyoming (1983-1984); Visiting Associate Fellow, University of Wyoming (1979-1980); Visiting Associate Professor of Economics, University of British Columbia, Vancouver, Canada (1979); Assistant Professor, University of Guelph, Guelph, Ontario, Canada (1973-1983); Teaching Assistant of Calculus, University of Guelph, Guelph, Ontario, Canada; Visiting Professor, NSW; Visiting Professor, Newcastle University; Adjunct Professor, International Studies, University of Wyoming **Career Related:** Visiting Professor, Professional Training Center, Ministry of Economic Affairs, Taiwan (1990-2002); Jayes-Qantas Visiting Scholar, UON (1983); Consultant, Acid Rain, United States Environmental Protection Agency and Several Canadian Government Agencies; Special Committee on Acid Rain, House of Commons of Canada; Interviewed on Acid Rain, TV Series "The Nature of Things," Radio and Print Media; Consultant in Field **Civic:** Member, Economic Development Advisory Board, City of Surprise (2002-2004); Economic Development Committee, Arizona Chamber (2002-2004); Trustee, Wyoming Retirement Systems (1995-2000); Trustee, Laramie Senior Housing, Inc. (1995-1996); Small Business Center, Kearney Area Chamber of Commerce; Chair, Investment Committee, Wyoming Retirement Systems **Creative Works:** Member, Editorial Advisory Board, National American Business Press (2012-Present); Member, Educated Advisory Board, North American Business Press (2012-Present); Member, Editorial Advisory Board, Journal of Applied Business Research (1987-Present); Co-author, "The Struggle for Human and Economic Development in Sub-Saharan Africa" (2012); Author, "The Acid Rain Debate: Science and Special Interest in Policy Formation" (1993); Associate Editor, Journal of Environmental Economics and Management (1989-1991); Member, Editorial Council, Journal of Environmental Economics and Management (1989); Associate Editor, Journal of Applied Business Research (1987); Co-author, "Economics in Canadian Society" (1986); Author, Article, Proceedings of a UNESCO Conference, Australia; Contributor, More than 50 Articles to Professional Journals **Membership:** President, Mid-West Association of Business Deans and Division Heads (1995-1996); President, Faculty Club, University of Guelph (1986-1987); Vice President, Faculty Club, University of Guelph, Guelph, Ontario, Canada (1985-1986); Vice President, Faculty Club, University of Guelph (1982-1983); Treasurer, Faculty Club, University of Guelph (1981-1982); National Association of Industrial Technology; Business Accreditation Committee, Association to Advance Collegiate Schools of Business; American Economic Association; Association of Environmental and Resource Economists **Marquis Who's Who Honors:** Albert Nelson Marquis Lifetime Achievement Award (2017) **Why did you become involved in your profession or industry:** Dr. Forster became involved in his profession during his junior and senior year at the University of Guelph in Canada. His main motivation was when he was an undergraduate and became a teacher's assistant in the mathematics department; it was during that time he realized that he loved teaching. **Hobbies:** Weightlifting; Swimming; Cooking **Shipping Address:** 2390 Peace Portal Dr PMB 97, Blaine, WA, 98230

David Lee Foster

Title: Lawyer **Industry:** Law and Legal Services **Date of Birth:** 12/13/1933 **Place of Birth:** Des Moines **State:** IA **Parents:** Carl Dewitt Foster; Dorothy Jo (Bell) Foster **Marital Status:** Married **Spouse Name:** Kathleen Walsh Foster (1979-Present); Marilyn Lee Bokemeier (8/12/1957, Divorced 6/1978) **Children:** Gwendolyn Foster Reed; Cynthia Foster Curry; David Lee Junior (Deceased); John Wickersham Foster **Education:** JD, University of Iowa (1957); BA, University of Iowa (1954); Coursework, Simpson College (1951-1952) **Career:** Partner, Willkie Farr & Gallagher, New York, NY (1972-2004); Counsel, Willkie Farr & Gallagher, New York, NY (2004-2006); From Associate to Partner, Jones, Day, Cockley & Reavis, Cleveland, Ohio (1963-1972); Associate, Cravath, Swaine & Moore, New York, NY (1957-1963) **Career Related:** Counsel, Trachtenberg Rodes & Friedberg, New York, NY (2007-2012); Member, Advisory Board, Civil RICO Report, LRP Publications (1988-2007); Board of Governors, New York Insurance Exchange (1987-1996); Practicing Law Institute, New York, NY (1984-1985); Lecturer, University of Pittsburgh (1984); Lecturer, Southern Methodist University (1979-1984); Board of Directors, Dowling Corp. **Civic:** Vice President, Cardigan Mountain School (2002-2003); Member, Board of Trustees, Cardigan Mountain School (1995-2004) **Military Service:** United States Naval Reserve (1952-1960) **Creative Works:** Contributor, Chapters, Books; Contributor, Articles, Legal Journals **Membership:** President, American Counsel Association (1994-1995); Board of Directors, American Counsel Association (1992-1998); Board Directors, International Academy of Trial Lawyers (1987-1992); Order of the Coif; Fellow, American College of Trial Lawyers; Phi Beta Kappa **Bar Admissions:** Supreme Court of the United States (1975); State of Ohio (1964); State of New York (1958); State of Iowa (1957) **Marquis Who's Who Honors:** Albert Nelson Marquis Lifetime Achievement Award (2017) **Why did you become involved in your profession or industry:** Mr. Foster was inspired to practice law by his father, who was also a lawyer. **What do you consider to be the highlight of your career:** Mr. Foster is most proud of never having lost a trial as a lawyer. **Shipping Address:** 1886 Brown Deer Rd, Coralville, IA, 52241

Elaine E. Foster

Title: Art Educator (Retired) **Industry:** Education/Educational Services **Date of Birth:** 01/13/1934 **Place of Birth:** Lawrence **State:** MA **Parents:** Ernest Webster Foster; Elizabeth Josephine (Dubuc) Foster **Marital Status:** Single **Education:** EdD, Columbia University (1970); Professional Diploma, Teacher's College, Columbia University (1965); MA, Clark University (1961); BA, Clark University (1957) **Certifications:** Certificate, School of the Worcester Art Museum (1955) **Career:** Retired (1999); Assistant, Associate, Professor of Art, Chairperson, Art Department, New Jersey City University (1966-1999); Supervisor, Teacher of Art, Elementary and Middle Public Schools, Auburn, MA (1959-1961); Supervisor, Teacher of Art, Senior High Schools (1961-1965) **Creative Works:** Lecturer, "The Brain and Art" (1975-Present); Author, "A Great School of Fine Arts in N.Y.C.: A Study of the Development of Art at Columbia University (1860-1914)" (1970); Author, "Collage Film Guide, Crayon Film Guide" (1966); Exhibitor, Group Shows, 25 Exhibitions in the Northeast **Awards:** Featured Listee, Who's Who of American Inventors **Membership:** President, University Council for Art Education (1980-1982); President, Local Chapter, American Association of University Professors (1978-1980); President, Auburn Teachers Association; Former Member, Society of North American Goldsmiths; American Craft Council, New York; Alumni Council, Teachers College, Columbia University; Board, Pen and Brush; National Art Education Association **Marquis Who's Who Honors:** Albert Nelson Marquis Lifetime Achievement Award (2017) **To what do you attribute your success:** Dr. Foster attributes her success to dedication and the support of others. **Why did you become involved in your profession or industry:** When she was in high school, she designed a hand-painted skirt, which gained a lot of recognition in magazines and newspapers and eventually led to a scholarship to art school. **What do you consider to be the highlight of your career:** When Dr. Foster was chairperson of the New Jersey City University art department, she guided it successfully through the accreditation process of the National Association of Schools of Art and Design, enabling it to offer accredited programs leading to a Master of Fine Arts degree. **Hobbies:** Art jewelry **Political Affiliations:** Independent **Shipping Address:** 35 E 9th St Apt 33, New York, NY, 10003

Maureen M. Fournier

Title: Freelance Consultant for Physical Education Programs **Industry:** Education/Educational Services **Date of Birth:** 02/27/1952 **Place of Birth:** Chicago **State:** IL **Parents:** George Joseph Lewis; Lauretta Marie (Tangney) Lewis **Marital Status:** Married **Spouse Name:** Thomas Joseph Fournier (9/21/1979) **Children:** Jennifer Lynn; Michele Marie **Education:** MS in Education, Chicago State University (1983); BS in Education, Northern Illinois University (1973) **Career:** Physical Education Teacher, School District 126, Alsip, IL (1974-2009); Recreation Leader, Alsip Park District, Illinois (1973-1975); Consultant, Physical Education Programs, Consultant for Illinois Public Health Institute; Member, Enhance Physical Education Task Force, Illinois State Board of Education **Career Related:** Member, Alsip Council, American Federation of Teachers Local 943, Illinois Federation of Teachers (1973-Present); President, Alsip Council, American Federation of Teachers Local 943, Illinois Federation of Teachers (2005-2008, 1992-1997, 1985-1987, 1977-1983) **Civic:** National Communication Association Committee Member, Booster Club, Harold L. Richards High School (2000-2006); Secretary, Booster Club, Harold L. Richards High School (2000-2006); Internal Review Committee, School District 126, Alsip, IL (1999-2006); Secretary, Girls Softball, Oak Lawn Baseball (1998); Secretary, Richards Area Swim Club (1997-1998); Manager, Girls Softball, Oak Lawn Baseball (1994-1998, 1990-1991); Volunteer, Advocate Children's Hospital, Oak Lawn, IL **Awards:** Service Award, Illinois Association for Health Physical Education, Recreation and Dance (2017); President's Achievement Award, Illinois Association for Health, Physical Education, Recreation and Dance (2013) **Membership:** Evaluator, Blue Ribbon Committee, Illinois Association for Health, Physical Education, Recreation and Dance (1999-Present); Alliance for Health; Task Force, Illinois State Board of Education; Illinois Association for Health, Physical Education, Recreation and Dance; Co-Chair, Blue Ribbon Committee, Illinois Association for Health, Physical Education, Recreation and Dance; Curriculum, Instruction, Assessments Committee, Illinois Association of Physical Education and Dance **Hobbies:** Bowling; Swimming; Reading **Shipping Address:** 5114 W 100th St, Oak Lawn, IL, 60453

Ronald Frank

Title: Equity Partner **Industry:** Law and Legal Services **Company Name:** Blank Rome, LLP **Date of Birth:** 03/11/1947 **Place of Birth:** Greensburg **State:** PA **Parents:** William John Frank; Louise (Mautino) Frank **Marital Status:** Married **Spouse Name:** Marsha Ann Kolesar (8/30/1969) **Education:** JD, Duke University (1972); BSChemE, Carnegie Mellon University (1969) **Career:** Equity Partner, Blank Rome, LLP (2016-Present); Partner, Reed Smith LLP, Pittsburgh (2000-2016); Partner, Babst, Calland, Clements & Zomnir, Professional Corporation, Pittsburgh (1993-1999); Partner, Buchanan Ingersoll Professional Corporation, Pittsburgh (1972-1993) **Career Related:** Board of Directors, SinterMet, LLC; Board of Directors, Meri Track, LLC **Civic:** Chairman, National Fundraising Committee, Carnegie Mellon University, Pittsburgh, PA (1983-1988); Board of Advisors, School of Engineering and Science, Carnegie Mellon University; Board of Visitors, School of Law, Duke University, Durham, NC; Board of Advisors, Center for International Legal Education **Creative Works:** Contributor, Articles, Professional Journals **Membership:** Chairman, International and Comparative Law Section, Pennsylvania Bar Association (1992-Present); American Bar Association; Allegheny County Bar Association; International Bar Association; Duquesne Club; Shannopin Country Club **Bar Admissions:** State of Pennsylvania (1972) **Hobbies:** Golf; Amateur radio; Computers **Political Affiliations:** Democrat **Religion:** Presbyterian **Shipping Address:** 1675 Gloucester Court, Sewickley, PA, 15143

William Emery Franklin

Title: International Business Educator **Industry:** Business Management/ Business Services **Company Name:** Franklin International Ltd. **Date of Birth:** 04/06/1933 **Place of Birth:** Sedalia **State:** MO **Parents:** Russell George Franklin; Edith Mae (Van Dyke) Franklin **Marital Status:** Single **Spouse Name:** Beverly Jean Feig (3/25/1933, Divorced 1963) **Children:** Stephen; Julia Connor; Angela Reese **Education:** Advanced Management Program, Harvard Business School (1982); BBA, University of Missouri (1954) **Career:** President, Franklin International, Ltd., Seattle, WA (1996-Present); President, Weyerhaeuser Far East Ltd., Hong Kong (1980-1997); Forestry Operations, Weyerhaeuser Company, Longview, WA (1954); Chairman, Kennedy Bay Timber Company (Malaysia); President, International Timber Company (Indonesia); Chairman, Weyerhaeuser China Ltd.; President, Weyerhaeuser Korea Ltd.; President, Weyerhaeuser Japan Ltd.; Chairman, Weyerhaeuser Taiwan; Advisory Board Member, Asia Foundation; Director, Pacific Basin Economic Council; Board Member, NCR Japan **Civic:** Director, Pacific Northwest Ballet; Trustee, Pacific Northwest Ballet; Chairman, Far East Council Friends of Scouting; Council on Foreign Relations; The Pacific Council on International Policy; The Japan Society; The Japan-America Society; The U.S.-Indonesia Society; The Asia Society; Seattle Rotary; World Affairs Council; Trustee, Seattle Repertory Theater; The Blakemore Foundation; Global Business Advisory Board, University of Washington; Former Chairman, Forestry Working Group, United Nations FAO Industry Cooperative Program; Advisory Committee on International Investment, Technology and Development, U.S. State Department; Industry Sector Advisory Committee on International Trade, U.S. Department of Commerce; Yomiuri International Economic Society; Director, NCR Japan **Creative Works:** Author, Several Vital Speeches of the Day; Commentator, NHKTV; Commentator, NBC; Commentator, PBS; Commentator, Japan Times; Fortune; Commentator, Yomiuri; Commentator, Japan Success **Awards:** Honoree, Order of the Rising Sun (2009); Outstanding Alumni Award, University of Missouri; Thomas S. Foley Leadership Award **Membership:** President, American Chamber of Commerce in Japan; Board of Directors, Yomiuri International Economic Society; Council of Foreign Relations; World Affairs Council; U.S.-Asian Business Council; Foreign Correspondents Club; Tokyo Lawn Tennis Club; Tokyo Club; Pacific Council on International Policy; The Japan-America Society; The U.S.-Indonesia Society; The Asia Society; Town Hall **Marquis Who's Who Honors:** Albert Nelson Marquis Lifetime Achievement Award (2017) **Hobbies:** Theater; Ballet; Music; Boating; Hiking; Spending time with grandchildren; Travel; Exploring; Learning **Shipping Address:** 1620 43rd Avenue E, Apt. 17A, Seattle, WA, 98112

Constantine T. Frantzides, PhD

Title: Medical Director **Industry:** Health, Wellness and Fitness **Company Name:** Chicago Institute of Minimally Invasive Surgery (CIMIS) **Date of Birth:** 11/06/1954 **Place of Birth:** Limassol **State/Country of Origin:** Cyprus **Parents:** Themistokles Frantzides; Christothea (Papageorgeou) Frantzides **Children:** Alexander; Marlena **Education:** PhD, Medical School, National and Kapodistrian University of Athens, Greece (1985); MD, National and Kapodistrian University of Athens, Greece (1976) **Certifications:** Board Certification in General Surgery, Licensed in Illinois, Wisconsin, Republic of Cyprus, Greece **Career:** Medical Director, Chicago Institute of Minimally Invasive Surgery (Now CIMIS) (Present); Director, Laparoscopic and Bariatric Fellowship Program, Chicago Institute of Minimally Invasive Surgery (Present); Professor of Surgery, University of Illinois, Chicago, IL (2009-Present); Professor of Surgery, Northwestern University (2004-2009); Director, Minimally Invasive Surgery Fellowship Program, NorthShore University HealthSystem (2003-2008); Director, Minimally Invasive Surgery, NorthShore University HealthSystem (2003-2006); Professor of Surgery, Rush University (2001); Director, Minimally Invasive Surgery, Rush-Presbyterian-St. Luke's Medical Center (Now Rush University Medical Center), Chicago, IL (2001); Chairman, Department of Surgery, Weiss Memorial Hospital (1998-2000); Director, Minimally Invasive Surgery Center, The University of Chicago (1997-2000); Professor of Surgery, The University of Chicago (1997-2000); Founding Director, Minimally Invasive Surgery Center, Medical College, WI (1995-1997); Associate Professor, Medical College of Wisconsin, Milwaukee (1993-1997); Staff Surgeon, Froedtert Memorial Hospital (Now Froedtert & the Medical College of Wisconsin), Milwaukee, WI (1989-1997); Staff Surgeon, Milwaukee Regional Medical Center (1989-1997); Assistant Professor, Medical College of Wisconsin, Milwaukee (1989-1993); Visiting Assistant Professor, Medical College of Wisconsin, Milwaukee (1986-1988); Assistant Clinical Professor, Medical College of Wisconsin, Milwaukee (1984-1985); Research Fellow, Medical College of Wisconsin, Milwaukee (1983-1984); Chief Resident, Athens University, Greece (1981-1982) **Creative Works:** Author, "Video Atlas of Advanced Minimally Invasive Surgery" with DVD Attachments of Surgical Procedures (2014); Author, "Atlas of Minimally Invasive Surgery," with DVD Attachments of Surgical Procedures (2008); Author, "Laparoscopic and Thoracoscopic Surgery" (1995); Author, Over 200 Articles, Professional Journals; Author, Three Books on Laparoscopic Surgery **Awards:** Honoree, Top Doctor, Castle Connolly Medical Ltd. (2017); Honoree, Top Doctor, Chicago Magazine (2012-2016); Recipient, Certificate of Excellence, US News & World Report (Now U.S. News & World Report L.P.) (2011-2013); Honoree, Most Compassionate Doctor, Consumers' Research Council of America (2010-2014); Honoree, America's Top Doctor, Castle Connolly Medical Ltd. (2009-2017); Honoree, America's Top Surgeon, Consumers' Research Council of America (2007-2008); Recipient, Physicians Recognition Award, American Medical Association, Chicago, IL (1998); Recipient, Physicians Recognition Award, American Medical Association, Chicago, IL (1990); Recipient, First Individual Research Award, National Institutes of Health (1986); Recipient, Shipley Medal, Southern Surgical Association, Hot Springs, VA (1985); Grantee, National Institutes of Health; Recipient, Achievement Award for Advanced Laparoscopic Surgery, American Society of General Surgeons **Membership:** American College of Surgeons; American Gastroenterology Association; Collegium International Chirurgiae Digestivae; The New York Academy of Sciences; Society for Surgery of the Alimentary Tract; Society of University Surgeons; Honorary Member, Brazilian Society of Surgery, Colegio Brasileiro de Cirurgia Digestiva; Society of Laparoscopic Surgeons; Honorary Member, Hellenic Surgical Association; Central Surgical Association (CSA); Western Surgical Association (WSA); Charter Member, United States Laparoscopic Founders Society **Marquis Who's Who Honors:** Albert Nelson Marquis Lifetime Achievement Award (2017) **Hobbies:** Tennis; Fast cars; Traveling; Artistic painting **Shipping Address:** 4905 Old Orchard Ctr Ste 409, Chicago Institute of Minimally Invasive Surgery, Skokie, IL, 60077-4738 **Website:** www.lapmd.com

Albert R. Frederick Jr.

Title: Ophthalmologist, Surgeon **Industry:** Medicine & Health Care **Date of Birth:** 05/17/1935 **Place of Birth:** St. Petersburg **State:** FL **Parents:** Albert R. Frederick **Marital Status:** Married **Spouse Name:** Suzanne Margareta Westerberg (5/3/1969) **Education:** Fellow, Massachusetts Eye and Ear, Boston, MA (1962-1965); Resident, Massachusetts Eye and Ear, Boston, MA (1962-1965); Intern, Boston City Hospital II & IV Medical Services (1961); MD, Harvard University (1961); SB, University of Florida (1957); Fellow, Massachusetts Medical Society **Certifications:** Diplomate, American Board of Ophthalmology **Career:** Retired (2013); Ophthalmic Surgeon, Ophthalmic Consultants of Boston (OCB) (1965-2013) **Career Related:** Class Agent, Medical School Class, Harvard Medical School **Civic:** Fundraiser, Harvard Medical School; Animal Conservation Organizations; Contributor, Land Trust Organizations **Military Service:** Captain, U.S. Air Force (1966-1968) **Awards:** Health Grades Honor Roll **Membership:** Harvard Medical Alumni Association; Class Agent, Class of 1961, Harvard Medical Alumni Association; Harvard Club of Boston **Marquis Who's Who Honors:** Albert Nelson Marquis Lifetime Achievement Award (2017) **Why did you become involved in your profession or industry:** Dr. Frederick, Jr. became involved in his profession because his father was a general practitioner. So, when he was five, he had a little black doctor bag and knew that he was going to be a doctor. He never considered anything else. As far as ophthalmology goes, he was mainly influenced by Frank West, his instructor in medical school. Dr. Frederick, Jr. does hobby work and machine work, and he likes gadgets. Surgery seemed to combine the fun and the intrigue of manipulation and modifying systems with the more intellectual aspects of deciphering the puzzle of a complex disease. **What do you consider to be the highlight of your career:** The highlight of Dr. Frederick, Jr.'s career has been his contact with very important people in medicine. He was taught parasitology by a Nobel Prize winner, and just being in the room with some of these professors who had fabled accomplishments was so honorific. **Hobbies:** Photography; Hunting; Beekeeping; Scuba diving; Coin collecting and numismatics; Paleography; Manuscript writing; Illumination; Calligraphy **Business Address:** 99 Florence St Unit 10-5B, Chestnut Hill, MA, 02467 **Shipping Address:** The Farm #10, Penthouse West, 99 Florence Street, Chestnut Hill, MA, 22467-1935 **Website:** https://www.healthgrades.com/physician/dr-albert-frederick-ydg89

William G.D. Frederick, PhD

Title: Research Scientist, Executive Manager **Industry:** Research **Company Name:** Raytheon Co., Photon Research Association **Date of Birth:** 06/23/1936 **Place of Birth:** Toledo **State:** OH **Parents:** Rolland Leslie Frederick; Ruth Matilda (Collins) Gates **Marital Status:** Married **Spouse Name:** Geralyn Goldman Middleton (8/14/1981); Nancy Lee Spalding (6/14/1958, Divorced 7/14/1981) **Children:** William George DeMott; Rebecca Ann Rudich; Frank Gibson Goldman **Education:** MS in Management, Massachusetts Institute of Technology (1980); PhD in Materials Science, University of Cincinnati (1973); MS in Physics, University of Dayton (1968); BS in Engineering Physics, University of Toledo (1958) **Career:** Executive Director, Photon Research Associates Inc., Raytheon Company (2004-2010); Corporate Vice President, Photon Research Associates, Inc., Raytheon Company (2001-2004); Deputy for Special Projects, Ballistic Missile Defense Organization (2000-2001); Chief Scientist, Ballistic Missile Defense Organization (1999-2000); Assistant Deputy for Technology, Ballistic Missile Defense Organization (1992-1999); Director of Sensor Technology, Strategic Defense Initiative Organization (1984-1992); Staff Specialist for Early Warning, Air Defense and Attack Assessment, Office of the Secretary of Defense (1983-1984); Physicist, Air Force Materials Laboratory, U.S. Air Force (1958-1983) **Career Related:** Fellowship, Military Sensing Symposium (2001) **Creative Works:** Editor, "Strategic Defense Initiative Launch Phenomenology" (1994-1997); Contributor, Articles, Professional Journals **Awards:** John A. Jamieson Memorial Award in Sensors, Environments And Algorithms, Military Sensing Symposium (2001); Strategic Defense Lifetime Achievement Award, AIAA (1995); Jerry L. Beard Award, Targets, Backgrounds, And Discrimination Group, IRIS (1995); Levinstein Award, Detector Speciality Group, Infrared Information Symposium (1989); Arthur S. Flemming Award, Downtown Jaycees, Washington, DC (1976); Decorated Pioneer Award, Ballistic Missile Defense Organization; Meritorious Medal, Department of Defense **Membership:** AIAA; National Space Society; Military Sensing Symposium **Marquis Who's Who Honors:** Albert Nelson Marquis Lifetime Achievement Award (2017) **What do you consider to be the highlight of your career:** The highlight of Dr. Frederick's career was working at the Air Force Materials Laboratory in Dayton, OH with the team who developed a permanent magnetic material that had applications in Air Force electronics. **Hobbies:** Travel **Business Address:** 1616 N Fort Myer Drive, VA, Arlington, 22209 **Shipping Address:** 2049 Castleway Lane NE, Atlanta, GA, 30345

Christine M. Frederickson

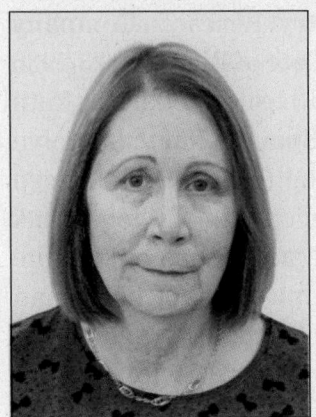

Title: Reporter, Researcher, Editor, Writer, Docent **Industry:** Writing and Editing **Date of Birth:** 01/24/1946 **Place of Birth:** Concord **State:** NH **Parents:** George Adolf Magnuson; Pauline Hazen Magnuson **Marital Status:** Widow **Spouse Name:** Arthur Robb Frederickson (6/6/1970, Deceased) **Children:** Timothy R.; Nathan B.; Julie H. **Education:** MEd, Boston College (1974); BA, University of New Hampshire, Cum Laude (1968); Coursework, Kalamazoo College (1964-1966) **Career:** Court Reporter, Los Angeles, CA (1999-2003); Independent Contractor, Los Angeles, CA (1999-2003); Radio Events Editor, Antique Radio Classified, Vintage Radio Publishing LLC, Carlisle, MA (1986-1997); Staff Writer, Computerworld Newsweekly, Newton, MA (1969-1971); College Board Member, Mademoiselle (1965-1966) **Career Related:** New Script Reader, The Fountain Theatre, Los Angeles, CA (1998-2003) **Civic:** Docent, San Gabriel Mission, San Gabriel, CA (2009-Present); Docent, Las Angelitas del Pueblo, Los Angeles, CA (2011-2013); Docent, San Gabriel Mission, San Gabriel, CA (1997-2006); Member, California Mission Studies Association **Creative Works:** Producer, Southwest Museum (1999-2000); Author, "Doña Victoria-First Lady of San Gabriel" (1998) **Awards:** History Award, San Gabriel Mission, San Gabriel, CA (2009); Critic Fellow, National Critics Institute, Waterford, CT (2000) **Membership:** Bulletin Editor, Caltech Women's Club (1998-2000); Association of LA Playwrights; California Mission Studies Association; Eugene O'Neill Society; International Bonhoeffer Society; Associate, Dramatists Guild (Now Dramatists Guild of America, Inc.) **To what do you attribute your success:** Ms. Frederickson attributes her success to her parents. **Why did you become involved in your profession or industry:** Ms. Frederickson became involved in her profession because she was inspired by playwrights like Eugene O'Neill and her love of learning, writing and reading. **What do you consider to be the highlight of your career:** The highlight of Ms. Frederickson's career was displaying her drama television show at the Southwest Museum. She also enjoyed researching the Cassini-Huygens mission while at archive library in Rome, Italy, as well as visiting other places in Europe, such as France and Holland. **Where will you be in five years:** In five years, Ms. Frederickson plans to be visiting family. **Hobbies:** Reading; Writing; Theatre; History; Traveling; Theology **Political Affiliations:** Democrat **Religion:** Christian **Shipping Address:** 2272 Norwic Pl, Altadena, CA, 91001

Algeania Warren Freeman

Title: Academic Administrator **Industry:** Education/Educational Services **Company Name:** Livingstone College **Place of Birth:** Benson **State:** NC **Marital Status:** Married **Spouse Name:** Ernest Freeman **Children:** Ernest Freeman III **Education:** Postgraduate Coursework, Harvard University (1998, 1983); PhD in Speech Communications, The Ohio State University (1977); MS in Speech Pathology and Audiology, Southern Illinois University (1972); BS in English, Fayetteville State University (1970); Postgraduate Coursework, Dartmouth College; Postgraduate Coursework, Northwestern University; Postgraduate Coursework, College of William & Mary **Certifications:** Ordained Minister, African Methodist Episcopal Zion Church **Career:** Instructor, Norfolk State University (1973); President, Livingstone College; Professor in Speech Communications, Norfolk State University; Vice President in Advancement and Program Development, Southern California College; Faculty, North Carolina A&T State University; Faculty, Orange Coast College; Faculty, East Tennessee State University; Assistant Vice President, Dean, Morgan State University; Acting Vice President of Advancement, Professor, Norfolk State University **Career Related:** Member, Virginia Board of Audiology and Speech-Language Pathology; Member, Deans' Task Force on Energy Security and Sustainability, Virginia Polytechnic Institute and State University; Founder, Science, Engineering, Mathematics and Aerospace Academies, National Aeronautics and Space Administration; International Consultant, W.K. Kellogg Foundation; Member, Institute of Medicine Study Committee on Allied Health, National Academy of Science **Civic:** Board of Directors, Association of California Community College Administrators; Board of Directors, Girl Scouts of Southern Appalachians; Board of Directors, Friends of the Norfolk Juvenile Court; Board of Directors, Maryland Easter Seals; Board of Directors, Montebello Rehabilitation Hospital, University of Maryland Medical System; Board of Directors, Kids Voting Virginia; Board of Directors, Foundation for the Carolinas; Executive Director, National Black Association for Speech-Language and Hearing; President, National Society of Allied Health **Creative Works:** Author, 25 Scholarly Publications; Author, "Step Up Sister"; Author, "Step Up Sister Music with Poetry Album"; Author, "Step Up Sister Poetry"; Author, "Black River" **Awards:** Pentagon Fellowship, U.S. Army Center of Military History (1999-2000); Honoree, Living Legion, Sable Journal; Harlem Renaissance Award; Finalist, White House Fellows Program **Membership:** Fellow, American Society of Allied Health; National Academy of Sciences, Institute of Medicine Committee; Founder, Greater Opportunity Development Center, Inc.; Institute of Hazardous Waste Management **Marquis Who's Who Honors:** Albert Nelson Marquis Lifetime Achievement Award (2017) **Shipping Address:** 221 City Central Ct, Virginia Beach, VA, 23452

Marion R. Fremont-Smith

Title: Lawyer (Retired) **Industry:** Law and Legal Services **Date of Birth:** 10/29/1926 **Place of Birth:** Boston **State:** MA **Parents:** Max Ritvo; Frances (Davis) Ritvo **Marital Status:** Single **Spouse Name:** Paul Fremont-Smith (Deceased); Joseph Miller (9/12/1948, Divorced) **Children:** Beth Miller Johnsey; Keith Lane Miller; E. Bradley Miller **Education:** LLB, Boston University, Cum Laude (1951); BA, Wellesley College, with Honors (1948) **Career:** Retired (2005); Of Senior Counsel, Choate Hall & Stewart LLP (Now Choate), Boston, MA (1997-2004); Partner, Choate Hall & Stewart LLP (Now Choate), Boston, MA (1971-1996); Associate, Choate Hall & Stewart LLP (Now Choate), Boston, MA (1964-1971); Project Director, Russell Sage Foundation, Boston, MA (1963-1965); Assistant Attorney General, Commonwealth of Massachusetts, Boston, MA (1961-1962); Instructor, Department of Political Science, Wellesley College (1958-1959) **Career Related:** Senior Research Fellow, Hauses Center for Nonprofit Organizations, Harvard University (1998-Present); Lecturer, Harvard Law School (2008-2011) **Civic:** Past Director, Independent Sector, Washington, MA; Honorary Trustee, Carnegie Endowment for International Peace, Washington, MA; Trustee, Massachusetts Environmental Trust, Commonwealth of Massachusetts **Creative Works:** Author, "Governing Nonprofit Organizations: Federal and State Law and Regulation," Belknap Press, Harvard University Press (2004); Author, "Philanthropy and the Business Corporation" (1972); Author, "Foundations and Government: State and Federal Law and Supervision" (1965); Co-reporter, American Law Institute's Restatement of Nonprofit Organizations; Contributor, Articles, Professional Journals; Publisher, Two Books; Publisher, Numerous Papers on Government Regulation and Taxation of Nonprofit Organizations **Membership:** Fellow, American Academy of Arts and Sciences; American Bar Foundation; American College of Tax Counsel; Past Chairman, Committee on Exempt Organizations, Tax Section, ABA; The American Law Institute **Bar Admissions:** Admitted to Practice, Supreme Court of the United States (1979); Admitted to Practice, Massachusetts Bar Association (1951) **Marquis Who's Who Honors:** Albert Nelson Marquis Lifetime Achievement Award (2017) **To what do you attribute your success:** Ms. Fremont-Smith attributes her second husband's support of her career as being integral to her continued success until his passing 17-years ago. **Why did you become involved in your profession or industry:** Ms. Fremont-Smith became involved in her profession because she believes that her education at Wellesley College was an excellent foundation, giving her the ability to be a pioneering woman in law. She is excited to see women's effective presence in the field grow through the years. **Shipping Address:** 50 Concord Ave, Cambridge, MA, 02138 **Website:** https://www.urban.org/author/marion-r-fremont-smith

Elizabeth Irene French

Title: Retired Biology Professor, Musician, Violin Teacher **Industry:** Education/Educational Services **Date of Birth:** 09/20/1938 **Place of Birth:** Knoxville **State:** TN **Parents:** Junius Butler French; Irene Rankin (Johnston) French **Education:** PhD, The University of Mississippi (1973); MS, The University of Tennessee (1962); MusB, The University of Tennessee (1959) **Career:** Retired (2008); Professor, Mobile College (Now University of Mobile) (1994-2008); Associate Professor, Mobile College (Now University of Mobile) (1983-1994); Assistant Professor, Mobile College (Now University of Mobile) (1973-1983); NASA Trainee in Biology, The University of Mississippi, Oxford, MS (1969-1973); Teacher of Music, Birmingham Public Schools (1964-1966); Teacher of Music, Kingsport Symphony Association (1962-1964) **Career Related:** Orchestra Contractor, American Federation of Musicians (1983-Present); Concertmaster, Riviera Symphony Orchestra and Chorus, AL (2005-2006); Mobile Symphony Players Committee (2001-2012); Mobile Symphony Orchestra (1974-2012); Memphis Symphony Orchestra (1970-1973); Knoxville Symphony Orchestra (1955-1962, 1966-1968); Birmingham Symphony Orchestra (1964-1966); First Violin, Kingsport Symphony Orchestra (1962-1964); Pensacola Symphony Orchestra; Gulf Coast Symphony Orchestra; Member, Piano Trio, Cardinal Trio; Freelance Violinist; Private Violin Teacher **Civic:** Member, Project Choctaw National Wildlife Refuge (1997-1998); Volunteer, Mercy Life of Alabama, Mercy Medical **Creative Works:** Faulkner State Community College Concert Series (Now Coastal Alabama Community College) (2016-Present); University South Alabama Opera Orchestra (2013); Fairhope Concert Series, AL (1998); Violin Recitalist, Alabama Artists Series (1978-1981); Performer, Violin, University of South Alabama Orchestra **Awards:** Named Career Woman of the Year, Gayfers, Inc. (1985) **Membership:** Advisory Board, Schumann Music Club (2005-Present); Board of Directors, Mobile Bay Audubon Society (1997-Present); Chairman, Annual State Convention, Alabama Federation of Music Clubs (2012); President, Schumann Music Club (1977-1979, 1985-1987, 1994-1997, 2000-2003, 2008-2012); National Committee to Construct Standardized Test on Anatomy and Physiology, Human Anatomy and Physiology Society (2008); Presenter, Alabama Academy of Science (1996-2008); Historian, Alabama Federation of Music Clubs (1991-1994); Chairman, Composition Contest, Alabama Federation of Music Clubs (1986-1990); National Association of Music Education; Daughters of Mary; Association Southeastern Biologists; The Wilderness Society; Alabama Ornithological Society; Coastal Birding Association; American Federation of Musicians **Hobbies:** Camping; Photography; Birdwatching **Political Affiliations:** Republican **Religion:** Roman Catholic

John French III

Title: Lawyer, Director **Industry:** Law and Legal Services **Company Name:** Tudor Associates LLC **Date of Birth:** 07/12/1932 **Place of Birth:** Boston **State:** MA **Parents:** John French; Rhoda (Walker) French **Marital Status:** Married (2011) **Spouse Name:** Marina Keller French (1987, Divorced 2011); Anne Hubbell (1/9/1965, Divorced 1983); Leslie Ten Eyck (1/11/1957, Divorced 1961); Carole Parsons Bailey **Children:** John B.; Lawrence C.; Daniel J.; Susann A. **Education:** JD, Harvard University, Cambridge, MA (1958); BA, Dartmouth College, Hanover, NH (1955) **Career:** Chairman, Tudor Associates LLC, New York, NY (1999-Present); Of Counsel, Beveridge & Diamond PC, New York, NY (1993-1999); Partner, Beveridge & Diamond PC, New York, NY (1985-1993); Partner, Appleton, Rice & Perrin, New York, NY (1982-1984); Vice President, General Counsel, Peabody International Corporation, Stamford, CT (1981-1982); Secretary, Peabody International Corporation, Stamford, CT (1981-1982); Assistant General Counsel, Continental Group, Inc., Stamford, CT (1973-1981); Associate, Satterlee Stephens LLP, New York, NY (1968-1973); Associate, Milbank, Tweed, Hadley & McCloy LLP, New York, NY (1961-1968) **Career Related:** Lecturer, Dartmouth Alumni, Dartmouth College (2010); Lecturer, Practising Law Institute (1979-1983); Lecturer, The American Law Institute (1978); Member, Board of Directors, Resorts Management, Inc.; Member, Board of Directors, Tudor Associates LLC, New York, NY; Member, Board of Directors, Philharmonic Society; Member, Board of Directors, The Smithsonian Institution; President, Salzburg Festival Society; Director, Salzburg Festival Society **Civic:** Board Member, Department of Environmental Conservation, New York State (1976-1988); Member, Planning Board, Westchester County (1974-1985); Founding Trustee, Hudson River Foundation for Science and Research; Trustee, Director, YMCA-YWCA Camping Services, Greater New York, Inc.; Member, Board of Directors, Third Street Music School Settlement, New York, NY; Member, Board of Directors, International House, New York, NY; Member, Board of Directors, The Metropolitan Opera Club; Member, Board of Directors, Young Concert Artists, Inc.; Member, Board of Directors, 33 East 70th Street Corp.; Member, Board of Directors, Teatro alla Scala Foundation; Bedford, NY, Republican Town Committee **Military Service:** Captain Judge, Advocate General Corps, U.S. Air Force Air Defense Command (1958-1961) **Creative Works:** Contributor, Articles, Professional Journals **Awards:** Lifetime Achievement Award, Young Concert Artists, Inc. (2017); Albert Nelson Marquis Lifetime Achievement Award (2017); Westchester County Distinguished Service Award (1980) **Membership:** VFW; ABA; Sharon Country Club; Holland Lodge No. 8; Society for Corporate Governance; Environmental Law Institute; Lecturer, Association of the Bar of the City of New York; New York State Bar Association; General Society of Mayflower Descendants; The Metropolitan Opera; The Century Association; The American Legion; Pilgrim John Howland Society; Knickerbocker Club; Harvard Club of New York City; The River Club of New York, Inc.; Class President, President, Dartmouth Class Presidents Association **Bar Admissions:** The District of Columbia (1988); New York (1959) **Marquis Who's Who Honors:** Albert Nelson Marquis Lifetime Achievement Award (2017) **Why did you become involved in your profession or industry:** Mr. French became involved in his profession because there have been lawyers in his family for generations, so it was something that he had always wanted to do. **What do you consider to be the highlight of your career:** A highlight of Mr. French's career was receiving an award from the New York State Bar Association, which recognized his accomplishments in the field of environmental law. **Political Affiliations:** Republican **Shipping Address:** 435 E 52nd St Apt 13G, New York, NY, 10022

Sybil Friedenthal-Roos

Title: Elementary School Educator **Industry:** Education/Educational Services **Company Name:** Houston Symphony **Date of Birth:** 01/29/1924 **Place of Birth:** Los Angeles **State:** CA **Parents:** Charles G. Friedenthal; Besse (Weixel) Friedenthal **Marital Status:** Widowed **Spouse Name:** Henry Kahn Roos (5/8/1949, Deceased 12/1989) **Children:** Catherine Alane Cook; Elizabeth Anne Garlinger; Virginia Ann Bertrand **Education:** MEd, Northwestern State University (1973); MusB, Centenary College (1948); ED, Shreveport, LA **Certifications:** Certified Elementary Education Teacher; Certified Special Education Teacher **Career:** Teacher, Spring Branch Independent Schools, Houston, Texas (1975-1985); Teacher, Caddo Parish Schools, Shreveport, LA (1968-1975) **Civic:** Volunteer, Houston Symphony (1997-Present); Volunteer, Houston Museum of Fine Arts/Guild (1990-Present); Volunteer, Houston Grand Opera/Guild (1979-Present); Coordinator, Special Olympics, Shreveport, LA (1974-1975); President, National Council of Jewish Women, Shreveport, LA (1958); Board of Directors, University of Houston Moore School of Music **Military Service:** Executive Board Member, United States Navy (1944-1946) **Awards:** Honorary Award, Houston Grand Opera (2014-2015); Mission Yahwah, Houston, Texas (2014); Houston Symphony (2013); Moore School of Music (2013) **Membership:** Secretary, Spring Branch, University of Women (2006-Present); President, Houston Grand Opera Guild (1989-1991); Treasurer, Delta Kappa Gamma (1987-1989); President, Spring Valley Houston Chapter, American Association of University Women (1985-1987); Houston Symphony League; Houston Ballet Guild; American Needlepoint Guild; The Women's Club of Houston; Board of Directors, Delta Kappa Gamma; Phi Mu **Marquis Who's Who Honors:** Albert Nelson Marquis Lifetime Achievement Award (2017) **To what do you attribute your success:** Mrs. Friedenthal-Roos attributes her success to an interest in what she does. **Why did you become involved in your profession or industry:** Mrs. Friedenthal-Roos became involved in her profession by chance. She was asked to participate in these areas. **What do you consider to be the highlight of your career:** The highlight of Mrs. Friedenthal-Roos' career was being Teacher of the Year. **Where will you be in five years:** In five years, Mrs. Friedenthal-Roos will hopefully still be participating in all that she does today. **Hobbies:** Music; Tennis; Needlepoint; Volunteering **Political Affiliations:** Republican **Religion:** Jewish **Shipping Address:** 5321 Fayette Street, Houston, TX, 77056

Richard Charles Friedman, MD

Title: 1) Psychiatrist 2) Adjunct Research Professor of Psychology 3) Clinical Professor **Industry:** Medicine & Health Care **Company Name:** 1) New York Hospital 2) Derner Institute of Advanced Psychological Studies, Adelphi University 3) Cornell University Medical College **Date of Birth:** 01/20/1941 **Place of Birth:** New York **State:** NY **Parents:** William Friedman; Henrietta Friedman **Marital Status:** Married **Spouse Name:** Susan Matorin (11/24/1979) **Children:** Jeremiah Simon **Education:** Graduate Studies, Columbia University (1978); MD, University of Rochester, NY (1966); BA, Bard College, Annandale-on-Hudson, NY (1961) **Certifications:** Diplomate, American Board of Psychiatry and Neurology, NY (1973) **Career:** Psychiatrist, New York Hospital (1996-Present); Adjunct Research Professor of Psychology, Derner Institute of Advanced Psychological Studies, Adelphi University, NY (1989-Present); Clinical Professor, Cornell University Medical College (1996-Present); Lecturer in Psychiatry, Columbia University (1994-Present); Associate Psychiatrist, New York Hospital-Cornell Medical Center, White Plains, NY (1981-1986); Associate Psychiatrist, St. Luke's-Roosevelt Hospital Center, NY, NY (1986-1994); Clinical Associate Professor of Psychiatry, Cornell University Medical College (1983-1986); Associate Professor of Clinical Psychiatry, Cornell University Medical College (1981-1983); Assistant Professor of Clinical Psychiatry, Cornell University Medical College, NY, NY (1977-1981); Assistant Professor, of Clinical Psychiatry, Columbia University (1977); Associate Clinical Professor of Psychiatry, Columbia University (1986-1994); Adjunct Assistant Professor, School of Public Health, Columbia University (1977-1979); Instructor of Clinical Psychiatry, College of Physicians and Surgeons, Columbia University (1973-1976); Associate Psychiatrist, Presbyterian Hospital (1976-1981); Assistant Psychiatrist, Presbyterian Hospital, NY, NY (1972-1976); Chief of In-Patient Psychiatry, William Beaumont General Hospital, El Paso, TX (1970-71); Chief Resident, New York State Psychiatric Institute (1969-1970); Resident in Psychiatry, New York State Psychiatric Institute (1967-1969); Resident in Psychiatry, Columbia Presbyterian Medical Center (1967-1969); Chief Resident, Department of Psychiatry, Columbia Presbyterian Medical Center, NY, NY (1969-1970) **Career Related:** Associate Editor (2003-Present); Consultant (1997-Present); Editorial Board Member, Archives of Sexual Behavior (1998-Present); Editor-in-Chief, Psychodynamic Psychiatry (2012); Co-Leader, Group for the Advancement of Psychiatry, Dallas, TX (2004); Assistant Editor, Journal of The American Academy of Psychoanalysis and Dynamic Psychiatry (1989-2002); President, American College of Psychoanalysts, Dallas, TX (1997-1998); International Journal of Sex Research; Psychodynamic Psychiatry: The Official Journal of the American Academy of Psychoanalysis and Dynamic Psychiatry; Member, Consultant, Joint Committee of the American Psychoanalytic Association, NY, NY; American Academy of Psychoanalysis and Dynamic Psychiatry **Military Service:** Major, Medical Corps, US Army (1970-1972); Major, William Beaumont General Hospital; Captain, US Army **Creative Works:** Author, "Male Homosexuality: A Contemporary Psychoanalytic Perspective"; Editor, "Behavior and the Menstrual Cycle"; Co-Author (with Downey), "Sexual Orientation and Psychoanalysis: Sexual Science and Clinical Practice"; Co-Editor, "Masculinity and Sexuality: Selected Topics in the Psychology of Men"; Co-Editor, "Sexuality: New Perspectives"; Co-Editor, "Sex Differences in Behavior"; Speaker, Invited Lecturer of Psychoanalysis, Psychotherapy and Sexual Orientation, Gender Role Behavior, Homosexuality: Historical Issues and Homophobia from a Psychoanalytic Perspective; Contributor, Articles to Numerous Professional Journals; Editor, "Psychonynamm Psychiatry Sturnol" (2012); Co-Leader, Human Sexuality Committee **Awards:** Recipient, Best Doctors in America Award, Castle Connolly Medical Ltd. (2006-Present); Recipient, John and Samuel Bard Award, Bard College (2011); Recipient, Presidential Award, Academy of Psychoanalysis and Dynamic Psychiatry (2009); Recipient, Mary S. Sigourney Award, International Psychoanalytic Association and The Sigourney Trust (2009); Recipient, American Henry and M. Page Laughlin Distinguished Teaching Award, American College of Psychoanalysts (2002); Recipient, Henry P. Laughlin Award (2002); Honoree, Teacher of the Year, Cornell University Medical College (1998); Recipient, Laughlin Award, Columbia University (1970) **Membership:** American Psychiatric Association; International Psychoanalytic Association, Group for the Advancement of Psychiatry; American Psychoanalytic Association; Association for Psychoanalytic Medicine; American Association for the Advancement of Science; International Academy of Sex Research **Shipping Address:** 225 Central Park W., Apartment 103, New York, NY, 10024

Robert Charles Friese

Title: Lawyer **Industry:** Law and Legal Services **Company Name:** Shartsis Friese LLP **Date of Birth:** 04/29/1943 **Place of Birth:** Chicago **State:** IL **Parents:** Earl Matthew Friese; Laura Barbara (Mayer) Friese **Marital Status:** Married **Spouse Name:** Chandra Ullom **Children:** Matthew Robert; Mark Earl; Laura Moore **Education:** JD, Northwestern University (1970); AB in International Relations, Stanford University (1964) **Career:** Partner, Shartsis Friese LLP, San Francisco, CA (1975-Present); Attorney, U.S. Securities and Exchange Commission, San Francisco, CA (1971-1975); Attorney, Shartsis Friese LLP, San Francisco, CA (1970-1971); Director, Tutor, Applied Linguistics Center, Geneva, Switzerland (1964-1966) **Career Related:** Chairman, NestWorth, Inc. (2011-Present); President, Custom Diversification Fund Management, Inc. (1993-Present); Board of Directors, Custom Diversification Fund Management, Inc. (1993-Present); Board of Directors, Presidio Graduate School (2011-2013); Director, International Plant Research Institute, Inc. (1978-1986); Co-Founder, International Plant Research Institute, Inc. (1978-1986) **Civic:** Vice Chairman, Nominating Committee, Worldwatch Institute (2008-Present); Director, Board of Directors, Worldwatch Institute (2008-Present); Chairman, SF Beautiful (2008-Present); Board of Directors, Presidio Heights Neighborhood Association (1993-Present); Board of Directors, SF Beautiful (1986-Present); Chairman, Nominating Committee, Worldwatch Institute (2006); Board of Directors, Worldwatch Institute (2005); President, Presidio Heights Neighborhood Association (1996-1998); Board of Directors, Palace of Fine Arts Theatre (1992-1994); Chairman, Citizens Advisory Committee for Embarcadero Project (1991-1998); Board of Directors, Institute of Range and the American Mustang (1990-2013); President, SF Beautiful (1988-2000); Chairman, San Franciscans for Cleaner City (1977); Board of Directors, Nob Hill Association (1976-1978); Executive Director, Nob Hill Neighborhood Association (1972-1981); Chairman, Board of Supervisors, Task Force on Noise Control (1972-1978); Major Gifts Committee, Stanford University **Membership:** Litigation Section, American Bar Association (2005-Present); Board of Directors, Association of Securities and Exchange Commission Alumni, Inc. (1995-Present); President, Association of Securities and Exchange Commission Alumni, Inc. (2005-2007); New Courthouse Committee, The Bar Association of San Francisco (1993-1995); Chairman, State Court Civil Litigation Committee, The Bar Association of San Francisco (1983-1990); Board of Directors, The Bar Association of San Francisco (1982-1985); Chairman, Business Litigation Committee, The Bar Association of San Francisco (1978-1979); Chairman, Swiss-American Friendship Society (1971-1979); Co-Chairman, American Bar Association; Secretary, Enforcement Subcommittee, American Bar Association; Board of Directors, Association of Business Trial Lawyers; The Lawyers' Club of San Francisco Inn of Court; Mensa International; California Historical Society; The Commonwealth Club **Bar Admissions:** State of California (1972) **Marquis Who's Who Honors:** Albert Nelson Marquis Lifetime Achievement Award (2017) **Shipping Address:** 3675 Clay Street, San Francisco, CA, 94118

Ralph Fuccillo

Title: Foundation Administrator, Consultant **Industry:** Medicine & Health Care **Company Name:** DentaQuest Foundation **Date of Birth:** 11/18/1951 **Place of Birth:** Somerville **State:** MA **Parents:** Ralph A. Fuccillo; Carmilla J. (D'Auria) Toner; Robert A. Toner (Stepfather) **Marital Status:** Life Partner **Spouse Name:** Paul Newman **Education:** MA, Fordham University, Bronx, NY (1977); BS, University of Massachusetts, Boston, MA (1973) **Career:** Senior Advisor, Dentaquest Corporation (2016-Present); Chief Mission Officer, Dentaquest Foundation (2013-2015); President, Dentaquest Foundation, Boston, MA (2006-2016); Executive Director, Harvard Pilgrim Health Care, Inc., Wellesley, MA (2000-2006); Community Service Director, Harvard Pilgrim Health Care, Inc., Boston, MA (1997-1999); Associate Director, Community Health, The Medical Foundation, Boston, MA (1986-1997); Teacher, Private Schools, State of Massachusetts (1975-1986) **Career Related:** Speaker, Public Health and Philanthropy, Harvard Divinity School, Cambridge, MA (1988-1992); Presenter, Public Health and Philanthropy, Harvard Divinity School, Cambridge, MA (1988-1992); Visiting Lecturer, Public Health and Philanthropy, Harvard Divinity School, Cambridge, MA (1988-1992) **Civic:** Trustee, Mount Ida College (2013-Present); Chair, Road Scholar (2013-Present); Board of Directors, Massachusetts Dental Society Foundation (2013-Present); Board Member, Massachusetts Dental Society Foundation (2006-Present); Chair, National Community Centers for Disease Control and Prevention (2006-Present); Board of Directors, Neighborhood Health Plan (2007-2012); Chair, National Community Committee, Centers for Disease Control and Prevention (2006-2010); President, Massachusetts Health Council (2005-2007); Vice President, Massachusetts Health Council, Boston, MA (2003-2004); Community Health Charities of Massachusetts, Dedham (2001-2007); President, AIDS Action Committee, Boston, MA (2001-2005); Albert Schweitzer Fellowship Program, Boston, MA (2000-2012); Treasurer, The Boston Coalition (2000-2004); Boston ASAP (1999-2006); Vice Chair, St. Clement Parish, Somerville, MA (1991-1992) **Creative Works:** Contributor, Articles, Professional Journals **Awards:** Medal of Honor for Community Service, Cambridge College (2007); Pride Award, Beth Israel Deaconess Medical Center (2006); Community Leadership Award with Special Recognition, Massachusetts Department of Public Health (2003) **Membership:** Board of Directors, Massachusetts Dental Society (2006-Present); Massachusetts Dental Society **Marquis Who's Who Honors:** Albert Nelson Marquis Lifetime Achievement Award (2017) **Hobbies:** Gardening **Shipping Address:** 46 Park Avenue, Stoneham, MA, 02180

Robert Kanji Fujimura, PhD

Title: Biochemist, Molecular Biologist **Industry:** Sciences **Date of Birth:** 07/28/1933 **Place of Birth:** Seattle **State:** WA **Parents:** Tatsuo Fujimura; Tamiko Ruth Fujimura **Marital Status:** Married **Spouse Name:** M. Shigeko Ichikawa (12/1/1962) **Children:** Dan; Tomi; Kei **Education:** PhD, University of Wisconsin-Madison (1961); MS, University of Wisconsin-Madison (1959); BS, University of Washington (1956) **Career:** Volunteer Professor, Geriatric Research Education and Clinical Center, VA Puget Sound Health Care System, Seattle, WA (2010-2012); Volunteer Professor, Geriatric Research Education and Clinical Center, Miami VA Healthcare System, Miami, FL (2001-2010); Professor, Leonard M. Miller School of Medicine, University of Miami, Miami, FL (1995-2000); Senior Resident Research Associate, Molecular Biology Branch, Center for Devices and Radiological Health, U.S. Food and Drug Administration (1992-1995); Biotechnology Consultant (1990-1995); Biotechnologist, Foreign Commercial Service Division, Embassy of the Tokyo, Japan (1985-1986); First Secretary, Embassy of the Tokyo, Japan (1985-1986); Adjunct Professor, Oak Ridge Graduate School of Biomedical Sciences, University of Tennessee, Knoxville, TN (1972-1992); Senior Staff Member, Biology Division, Oak Ridge National Laboratory, University of Tennessee, Knoxville, TN (1963-1990) **Career Related:** Adjunct Professor, University of Tennessee and Oak Ridge National Laboratory (1970-Present); Fellow, Japanese Society for the Promotion of Science (1981); Volunteer Researcher, Department of Pathology, University of Washington **Civic:** Volunteer, Post-Tsunami Disaster Relief, Ishinomaki, Tohoku, Japan (2012); Genetic Science Task Force, United Methodist Church (1989-1991); Foreign Commercial Service Officer in Biotechnology, American Embassy, Tokyo, Japan (1985-1986) **Creative Works:** Author, Memoir, "Current of My Life Fishing" (2013); Contributor, "DNA replication by bacteriophage T5 DNA polymerase"; Contributor, Articles, Professional Journals **Membership:** American Association for the Advancement of Science; Emeritus Member, American Society for Biochemistry and Molecular Biology **Marquis Who's Who Honors:** Albert Nelson Marquis Lifetime Achievement Award (2017) **To what do you attribute your success:** Dr. Fujimura attributes his success to being a self-motivated, curious, and driven hard worker. **Why did you become involved in your profession or industry:** The opportunities for Dr. Fujimura came at the right time that led to carrying out research in molecular biology. **What do you consider to be the highlight of your career:** The highlight of Dr. Fujimura's career was being the organizer and chairperson of the symposium by Oak Ridge National Laboratory on DNA-multiprotein interactions in transcription, replication, and repair in Gatlinburg in 1980. **Where will you be in five years:** In five years, Dr. Fujimura plans to be at University House Wallingford in Seattle, Wash. **Hobbies:** Tennis; Fishing; Hiking **Political Affiliations:** Democrat **Religion:** Methodist **Shipping Address:** 1325 N Allen Place, Apt. 134, Seattle, WA, 98103

Catherine Fulkerson

Title: CEO of Reston Association **Industry:** Business Management/Business Services **Date of Birth:** 06/14/1905 **Parents:** James Walter Lucas; Sara Stewart Lucas **Education:** MPA, George Mason University, Fairfax, VA (1997); BA in Political Science and American History, Washington College, Chestertown, MD (1989) **Certifications:** Certified Manager, Community Association Institute (2004) **Career:** CEO, Reston Association (2013-Present); Acting CEO, Reston Association (2013); Director, Administration, Member Services, IT, Reston Association, Reston, VA (2006-2013); Director, Administration and Member Services, Reston Association, Virginia (2004-2006); Executive Officer, Board and Legislative Affairs, Reston Association, Reston, VA (1998-2004) **Career Related:** Chair, Board of Directors, Leadership Fairfax, Inc. (2008-2009); Community Association Institute, Falls Church, VA (2002-2013); Chair, Reston Character Counts Coalition, Virginia (2000-2013) **Civic:** Treasurer, Community Association Institute, Legislative Action Committee, Falls Church, VA (2004-2007); Chair, Leadership Fairfax, Virginia (2002-2012); Chair, Character Counts, Reston Coalition, Reston, VA (2000-2013) **Awards:** Best of Reston Honoree, Individual Community Leader, Cornerstones of Reston (2014); Citizen of the Year, Reston Citizens Association (2012); Remarkable Resource Award, Leadership Fairfax, Inc. (2009); Community Service Award, Martin Luther King Day Planning Committee (2004); Virginia Legislative Action Committee, Spark-plug Award, Community Associations Institute (2003) **Membership:** Greater Reston Chamber of Commerce

Edwin Fuller

Title: Hotel Executive **Industry:** Leisure, Travel & Tourism **Company Name:** Laguna Strategic Advisors **Date of Birth:** 03/15/1945 **Place of Birth:** Richmond **State:** VA **Parents:** Ben Swint Fuller; Evelyn (Beal) Fuller **Marital Status:** Married **Spouse Name:** Michela Fuller **Children:** Elizabeth Dimond Allphin; Scott Dimond **Education:** Graduate, Advanced Management Course, Harvard Business School, Harvard University (1987); BSBA, Boston University (1968); Coursework, Wake Forest University (1965) **Career:** Chief Executive Officer, Laguna Strategic Advisors (2012-Present); President, Marriott International, Inc., Washington (1997-2012); Managing Director, Marriott International, Inc., Washington (1997-2012); Executive Vice President, Marriott International, Inc., Washington (1994-1997); Managing Director of International Lodging, Marriott International, Inc., Washington (1994-1997); Senior Vice President, Marriott International, Inc., Washington (1990-1993); Managing Director, Marriott International, Inc., Washington (1990-1993); Vice President of Operations, Western and Pacific Regions, Marriott International, Inc., Santa Ana, California (1989-1990); Vice President of Operations, Midwest Region, Marriott International, Inc., Rosemont, Illinois (1985-1989); General Manager, Marriott International, Inc., Copley Place, Boston, MA (1983-1985); General Manager, Marriott International, Inc., Hempstead, NY (1982-1983); Chief of Sales, Marriott International, Inc., Washington (1978-1982); Marketing Officer, Marriott International, Inc., Washington (1978-1982); Director of National and International Sales, Marriott International, Inc., Washington (1976-1978); National Sales Manager, Marriott International, Inc., New York City (1973-1976); Vice President, Marriott International, Inc., New York City (1973-1976); Sales Director, Twin Bridges Marriott Hotel, Marriott International, Inc., Arlington, Virginia (1972-1973); Security Officer, Pinkerton Consulting & Investigations, Inc., Boston, Massachusetts (1965-1968) **Career Related:** Adjunct Professor of Globalization, University of California, Irvine (2013-Present); Adjunct Professor of Leadership, San Diego State University (2012-Present); Adjunct Professor, California State University, Pomona (2012-Present); Board of Directors, Barnaby Books, Honolulu (1997-Present); Director of International Tourism, Partnership Environmental Organization (2001); Chairman, Board of Directors, SNR Reservation Systems, Zurich, Switzerland (1979-1981); Board Member, Concord Hotels; Member, Advisory Board, Merage Investment Group **Civic:** Director, San Marcos Foundation, California State University (2014-Present); Board Member, Mind Research Institute, Irvine, California (2014-Present); Director, United States Travel Association (2014-Present); Director, California Travel (2014-Present); President, Orange County Visitors Association (2013-Present); Chief Executive Officer, Orange County Visitors Association (2013-Present); Trustee, University Foundation, University of California, Irvine (2013-Present); Staff, Visit California (2013-Present); Board Member, Safe Kids Worldwide (2011-Present); Director, FBI National Academy Associates Foundation (2010-Present); Chairman, Advisory Board, Hospitality Management School, Boston University (2007-Present); Trustee, International Business Leadership Forum (2003-Present); Member, Advisory Board, School of Management Alumni Board, Boston University (1985-Present); Chairman, Advisory Board, Merage School of Business, University of California, Irvine (2010-2014); Chairman, Sigma Alpha Epsilon Foundation (2012); Commissioner of Travel & Tourism, State of California (2008-2012); Overseer, Boston University (2010); Executive Committee, Board of Trustees, Boston University (1994-1998); President, General Alumni Association, Boston University (1993-1996); Vice President, General Alumni Association, Boston University (1990-1993); Trustee, Boston University (1970-1989); Former Board Member, United Way International; Emeritus Member, Travel Industry Management School Advisory Board, University of Hawaii, Hawaii; Board Member, Althea Foundation; Member, Chancellor's Hospitality Management Education Board, California State University; Member, Chancellor's Chief Executive Officer Roundtable, University of California, Irvine; Past Vice Chair, Boston University; Chair, Governing Board, International Tourism Partnership; Trustee, Prince of Wales International Business Leaders Forum; Trustee, Sigma Alpha Epsilon Foundation; Former Board Member, Pacific Area Travel Association Foundation **Military Service:** Captain, U.S. Army (1968-1971) **Awards:** Hospitality Industry Leader of the Year Award, UNLV (2013); Lifetime Achievement Award, International Hotel Investment Forum (2012); Aatithya Award, Hotel Investment Forum, India (2010); Lifetime Achievement Award, China Hotel Investment Summit (2008); Chairman's Award, Marriott International, Inc. (1989); Decorated Commendation Medal U.S. Army; Recipient, Bronze Star, U.S. Army **Membership:** Vice President, Alumni Council, Boston University; Fund Agent, Advanced Management Program, Harvard Business School **Political Affiliations:** Republican **Shipping Address:** 25362 Derbyhill Dr, Laguna Hills, CA, 92653

William H. Funk

Title: Engineering Educator (Retired) **Industry:** Engineering **Date of Birth:** 06/10/1933 **Place of Birth:** Ephraim **State:** UT **Parents:** William George Funk; Henrietta (Hackwell) Funk **Marital Status:** Married **Spouse Name:** Lynn Bridget Robson (3/30/1996); Ruth Sherry Mellor (Deceased) **Children:** Cynthia Lynn **Education:** PhD in Limnology, University of Utah (1966); MS in Zoology, University of Utah (1963); BS in Biological Science, University of Utah (1955) **Career:** Director, State of Washington Water Research Center (1981-1999); Director, Environmental Research Center (1980-1983); Chairman, Environmental Science and Regional Planning Program, Washington State University (1979-1981); Professor, Washington State University (1975-1999); Associate Professor of Environmental Engineering, Washington State University (1971-1975); Faculty Member, Washington State University, Pullman, WA (1966-1999); Head of the Science Department, Northwest Junior High School, Salt Lake City, UT (1961-1963); Research Assistant, University of Utah, Salt Lake City, UT (1961-1963); Teacher of Science and Math, Salt Lake City Schools (1957-1960) **Career Related:** Member, Pure Water (2000); President, Terrene Institute, Washington, DC (1993-2002); High Level Nuclear Waste Board, Washington, DC (1986-1989); Consultant, United States Civil Service, Seattle, WA, Chicago, IL (1972-1974); Consultant, ORB Corp., Renton, WA (1972-1973); Consultant, Washington Department of Ecology, Olympia, WA (1971-1972); Consultant, Boise Cascade Corp., Seattle, WA (1971-1972); Consultant, Harstad Engineers, Seattle, WA (1971-1972); Consultant, United States Army C.E., Walla Walla, WA (1970-1974); Co-Director, Institute of Research Management **Civic:** Board Member, Manti-Ephraim Airport (2006-Present); Volunteer Area Coordinator, Central Utah AARP (2009-2013) **Military Service:** Captain, US Naval Reserve (1955-1976) **Creative Works:** Contributor, Articles to Professional Journals **Awards:** Grantee, United States Geological Survey (1999-2000); Recipient, Friend of Lakes Award, Washington Lakes Protection Association (1999); Grantee, United States Geological Survey (1997-1998); Grantee, United States Army C.E. (1997-1998); Grantee, United States Bureau of Reclamation (1995-1998); Grantee, Idaho Department of Environmental Quality (1995-1996); Grantee, United States Geological Survey (1995-1996); Grantee, EPA (1995-1996); Grantee, United States Army C.E. (1994-1996); Grantee, Environmental Protection Agency (1993-1994); Grantee, Washington Conservation Commission (1992-1995); Grantee, Nez Pierce Tribe (1992-1995); Grantee, Clearwater Co. (1992-1993); Grantee, Colville Confederated Tribes (1990-1992); Recipient, Secchi Disk Award, North America Lake Management Society (1988); Grantee, National Parks Service (1985-1987); Recipient, President's Distinguished Faculty Award, Washington State University (1984); Grantee, United States Geological Survey (1983-1994); Grantee, Environmental Protection Agency (1980-1983); Recipient, Arthur S. Bedell Award (1976); Grantee, Office of Water Resources Research (1973-1976); Grantee, Office of Water Resources Research (1971-1972); Grantee, United States Army C.E. (1970-1974); Fellow, United States Public Health Service (1963); Grantee, National Science Foundation Summer Institute (1961) **Membership:** Board of Directors, Research Foundation, Water Pollution Control Federation (1990-1992); Vice President, Washington Section, American Water Resources Association (1988); Board of Directors, University Council on Water Resources, National Association of Water Institute Directors (1986-1989); Co-Founder, Washington Lakes Protection Association (1986); Chair, National Association of Water Institute Directors (1985-1987); President, North American Lake Management Society (1984-1985); President, Pacific Northwest Pollution Control Association (1983-1984); President-elect, Pacific Northwest Pollution Control Association (1982-1983); National Board of Directors, Water Pollution Control Federation (1978-1981); Co-Founder, North America Lake Management Society (1972); Editor, Pacific Northwest Pollution Control Association (1969-1977); Chapter President, Naval Reserve Officers Association (1969); American Society of Limnology and Oceanography; Northwest Science Association; Sigma Xi; Phi Sigma **To what do you attribute your success:** Dr. Funk attributes his success to his excellent role models: parents, grandparents, teachers, professors, senior naval officers, colleagues and friends. **Why did you become involved in your profession or industry:** Dr. Funk became involved in his profession to make a contribution. **What do you consider to be the highlight of your career:** The highlights of Dr. Funk's career were the many successes of his colleagues, former students and friends –their expressions of thanks for what little boost he gave them along the way. **Shipping Address:** 202 W. 200 S., Manti, UT, 84642

David William Furnas

Industry: Education/Educational Services **Date of Birth:** 04/01/1931 **Place of Birth:** Caldwell **State:** ID **Parents:** John Doan Furnas; Esther Bradbury (Hare) Furnas **Marital Status:** Married **Spouse Name:** Mary Lou Heatherly (2/11/1956) **Children:** Heather Jean; Brent David; Craig Jonathan **Education:** MS, University of California, Berkeley (1957); MD, University of California, Berkeley (1955); AB, University of California, Berkeley (1952) **Certifications:** Diplomate, Royal College of Surgeons; Diplomate, American Board of Plastic Surgery **Career:** Emeritus Professor, Plastic Surgery, University of California, Irvine (2002-Present); Clinical Professor, Plastic Surgery, University of California, Irvine (1999-2002); Clinical Professor, Chief, Division of Plastic Surgery, University of California, Irvine (1980-1999); Professor, Chief of Division of Plastic Surgery, University of California, Irvine (1974-1980); Associate Professor of Surgery, Chief of Division of Plastic Surgery, University of California, Irvine (1969-1974); Associate Professor, University of Iowa (1968-1969); Assistant Professor in Surgery, University of Iowa (1966-1968); Senior Resident, Faculty Associate in Surgery, University of Iowa (1964-1965); Associate in Hand Surgery, University of Iowa (1964-1968); Registrar, Royal Infirmary and Affiliated Hospitals, Glasgow, Scotland (1963-1964); Chief Resident in Plastic Surgery, Cornell University Service, VA Hospital, Bronx, NY (1962-1963); Assistant Resident in Plastic Surgery, New York Hospital, Cornell Medical Center, New York, NY (1961-1962); Resident in General Surgery, Gorgas Hospital, Panama Canal Zone (1960-1961); Assistant Resident in Psychiatry, National Institute of Mental Health Fellow, Langley Porter Neuropsychiatric Institute, University of California, San Francisco (1959-1960); Assistant Resident in Surgery, University of California Hospital, San Francisco (1956-1957); Intern, University of California Hospital, San Francisco (1955-1956) **Career Related:** Godrej Visiting Professor, Association of Plastic Surgeons of India (2000); Keynote Speaker, Pan African Association of Plastic Surgeons (2000); Trustee, Royal College of Surgeons Foundation (1995-2002); Overseas Visiting Professor, Plastic Surgery, Educational Foundation (1994); Balakbayan Medical Mission, Mindanao and Sulu, The Philippines (1980-1982); Director, American Board of Plastic Surgeons (1979-1985); Surgeon, East Africa Flying Doctors Service, African Medical And Research Foundation, Nairobi, Kenya (1972-1973); Plastic Surgeon, Sri Lanka (1968); Plastic Surgeon, S.S. Hope, Nicaragua (1966); Fellow, American College of Surgeons; Fellow, Royal College of Surgeons of Canada; Fellow, Royal Society of Medicine; Fellow, Explorers Club; Fellow, Royal Geological Society; Fellow, American Association of Plastic Surgeons **Civic:** Board of Governors, Bowers Museum of Cultural Art (2000-2002); Expedition Leader, Flag 44, Skull Surgeons of the Marakwet Tribe, Explorer's Club (1987); Expedition Leader, Flag 171, Skull Surgeons of the Kisii Tribe, Explorer's Club, Kenya **Military Service:** Colonel, Medical Corps, U.S. Army Reserve (1989-1992); Captain, Medical Corps, U.S. Air Force (1957-1959) **Creative Works:** Contributor, Chapters to Textbooks, Articles to Professional Journals; Author, Editor, Five Textbooks; Editorial Board, Journal of Hand Surgery, Annals of Plastic Surgery, Journal of Craniofacial Surgery; Reviewer, Plastic and Reconstructive Surgery **Awards:** Alumnus of the Year, University of California, San Francisco Alumni Association (2005); (Distinguished Service Award, American Medical Association (2002); Physician of the Year, Orange County Medical Association (1998); Certificate of Special Recognition, U.S. Congress (1998) **Membership:** Chairman, Southern California Chapter, Explorers Club (2001-2002); Team Leader, Reconstruct! Mission for Victims of American Embassy Bombing, Nairobi, Kenya (1999); President, American Association of Plastic Surgeons (1995); President-Elect, American Association of Plastic Surgeons (1994); Vice President, American Association of Plastic Surgeons (1993-1994); Treasurer, American Association of Plastic Surgeons (1988-1991); Board of Directors, USA, African Medical and Research Foundation (1987-2002); American Medical Association; California Medical Association; Orange County Medical Association; American Society of Reconstructive Microsurgery; Society of Head and Neck Surgery; American Cleft Palate Association; American Society of Surgery of Hand; Society of University Surgeons; Honorary Member, British Association of Plastic Surgeons; American Society of Craniofacial Surgery; American Society of Aesthetic Plastic Surgery; American Society of Maxillofacial Surgeons; Association of Surgeons in East Africa; Honorary Member, Association of Plastic and Reconstructive Surgeons of Southern Africa; Pacific Coast Surgical Association; International Society of Aesthetic Plastic Surgery; International Society of Reconstructive Microsurgery; International Society of Craniomaxillofacial Surgery; Pan African Association of Neurological Science

John R. Furrer

Title: Manufacturing Executive (Retired) **Industry:** Manufacturing **Date of Birth:** 12/02/1927 **Place of Birth:** Milwaukee **State:** WI **Parents:** Rudolph Furrer; Leona (Peters) Furrer **Marital Status:** Married **Spouse Name:** Annie Louise Waldo (4/24/1954) **Children:** Blake Waldo; Kimberly Louise **Education:** BA in Economics, Harvard College (1946-1949) **Career:** Senior Vice President, FMC Corp., Chicago (1988-1990); Vice President of Corporate Development, FMC Corp., Chicago (1977-1988); Vice President, Material Handling Group, FMC Corp., Chicago (1971-1977); Vice President, Charge Planning Department, Central Engineering Laboratories and Engineered System Division, FMC Corp., Chicago (1970-1971); General Manager, Engineered Systems Division, FMC Corp., San Jose, CA (1968-1970); Director, Machinery and Systems Group, Central Engineering Laboratories, FMC Corp., San Jose, CA (1959-1968); Assistant Supervisor of Thermonuclear Development and Testing, Los Alamos (1952-1953); Director of Product Development, ACF Industries, New York City (1954-1959); Special Representative, ACF Industries, Madrid (1949-1951) **Civic:** Trustee, Grand Teton Music Festival (2002-2008); Trustee, Ravinia Festival (1986-1990); Chairman, San Jose Chapter, Children's Home Society, California (1964-1966) **Military Service:** With V-5 Pilot Training Program (1945-1946); With, U.S. Navy (1945-1946) **Membership:** American Society of Mechanical Engineers; Chairman, Conference Board, Council of Planning Executives (1986-1987) **Hobbies:** Boating; Skiing; Photography; Genealogy; Music **Political Affiliations:** Republican **Religion:** Episcopalian **Shipping Address:** 70 E. Cedar Street, Apt. 15E, Chicago, IL, 60611

Daniel Eric Furst

Title: Medical Educator **Industry:** Medicine & Health Care **Company Name:** University of California, Los Angeles **Education:** Medical Resident, Johns Hopkins University, Baltimore, MD (1969-1970); Medical Intern, Johns Hopkins University, Baltimore, MD (1968-1969) **Career:** Director, Clinical Research in Rheumatology, University of California, Los Angeles (2001-Present); Professor of Research, University of Florence, Italy (2015); Professor Emeritus of Rheumatology, University of California, Los Angeles (2014); Carl M. Pearson Professor of Rheumatology, David Geffen School of Medicine, University of California, Los Angeles (2001); Clinical Director, Virginia Mason Research Center (Now Benaroya Research Institute at Virginia Mason) (1993-2001); Clinical Professor of Medicine, University of Washington, Seattle, WA (1992-2001); Director, Clinical Research Programs, Virginia Mason Medical Center (Now Benaroya Research Institute at Virginia Mason), Seattle, WA (1992-1994); Director, Anti-inflammatory/Pulmonary Clinical Research, Ciba-Geigy Pharmaceuticals (Now Novartis AG), Summit, NJ (1987-1992); Clinical Professor of Medicine/Rheumatology, Robert Wood Johnson Medical School, Rutgers, The State University of New Jersey and University of Medicine & Dentistry of New Jersey, New Brunswick, NJ (1987-1992); Associate Professor of Medicine/Rheumatolgoy, The University of Iowa Carver College of Medicine, Iowa City, Iowa (1982-1987); Fellow, Clinical Pharmacology, University of California San Francisco Medical Center, San Francisco, CA (1975-1977); Assistant Professor, UCLA Medical Center (1977-1982); Fellow, Rheumatology, UCLA Medical Center (1973-1975) **Career Related:** Part-time, Private Practices; Arthritis Associates of Southern California; Visiting Professor **Civic:** Board of Directors, Arthritis Foundation, The Corrona Research Foundation, Scleroderma Foundation, Southern California Chapter; Founder, World Scleroderma Program; Vice President, Scleroderma Foundation, Southern California Chapter; Chair and Active Member, Medical Science Committee, Arthritis Foundation, Southern California Chapter **Military Service:** Captain, Medical Corps, United States Air Force (1970-1973) **Creative Works:** Co-editor, "Antirheumatic Therapy: Actions and Outcomes" (2004); Co-editor, "Rheumatology Trials Review" (2003); Co-editor, "Systemic Sclerosis" (2003); Co-editor, "Therapy of Systemic Rheumatic Disorders" (1998); Co-editor, "Scleroderma (1996); Co-editor, "Systemic Sclerosis" (1995); Co-editor, "Nonsteroidal Anti-Inflammatory Drugs, Secondary Edition" (1994); Co-editor, "Second Line Agents (DMARDS) in the Rheumatic Diseases" (1992); Co-editor, "Immunomodulators in the Rheumatic Diseases" (1990); Co-editor, "Drugs for Rheumatic Disease" (1987); Editorial Reviewer, Numerous Journals; Contributor, 400 Articles to Professional Journals; Contributor, Chapters to Books **Awards:** World Ranked in Scleroderma Research and Treatment, Expertscape (2014); Inducted, Rare Disease Research Hall of Fame (2013); James R. Klinenberg Research Award (2009); Named, Best Doctors in America (2007); Spirit of Hope Award, Scleroderma Foundation (2004); Distinguished Service Award, Arthritis Foundation **Membership:** Fellow, American College of Physicians; American Rheumatism Association; ASCPT; New York Academy of Sciences **Shipping Address:** 2114 Beech Knoll Road, Los Angeles, CA, 90046

Robert Elledy Gable

Title: Real Estate Company Executive **Industry:** Real Estate **Company Name:** The Stearns Co. Ltd. **Date of Birth:** 02/20/1934 **Place of Birth:** New York **State:** NY **Parents:** Gilbert Elledy Gable; Paulina (Stearns) Gable **Marital Status:** Widowed **Spouse Name:** Emily Brinton Thompson (7/5/1958, Deceased 4/11/2017) **Children:** James Stearns-Gable; Elizabeth Brinton-Gable; John Stearns-Gable **Education:** BS, Stanford University (1956) **Career:** Chairman of the Board, The Stearns Co. Ltd. (Formerly Stearns Coal & Lumber Co. Inc.), Lexington, KY (1970-2005); President, The Stearns Co. Ltd.; Director, The Stearns Co. Ltd.; Vice President, The Stearns Co. Ltd.; Treasurer, The Stearns Co. Ltd.; Secretary, The Stearns Co. Ltd. **Career Related:** Past Director, Audit Committee, Kuhn's Big K Stores Corporation, Nashville, TN (1979-1981); Past Chairman, Board of Directors, Kentucky & Tennessee Railway, Stearns, KY; Past Chairman, Board of Directors, Lumber King Inc., Stearns, KY; Director Emeritus, Blue Cross and Blue Shield, KY; Past Director, Bank of McCreary County; Kentucky Republican State Chairman; Trustee, George Peabody College for Teachers, Nashville, TN; Trustee, Vanderbilt University, Nashville, TN **Civic:** Kentucky State Board of Elections (2008-Present); Kentucky Republican Central Committee (2004-Present); Board of Directors, Executive Committee, Kentucky Center for the Arts (2004-2009); Chairman, Kentucky Arts Council (2004-2005); President, Chief Executive Officer, Kentuckians for Fair Redistricting, Inc. (2001-2003); President, Epworth Assembly, Ludington, MI (2000-2001); Board of Trustees, Epworth Assembly, Ludington, MI (1995-2001); Treasurer, Epworth Assembly, Ludington, MI (1995-2000); Candidate for Governor of Kentucky (1995); John F. Kennedy Center for Performing Arts, Washington, DC (1993-2004); President, Chief Executive Officer, John F. Kennedy Center for Performing Arts, Washington DC (1993-1997); Appointed, President, Advisory Committee of Arts (1992-1993); Budget Committee, Republican, National Committee (1989); Southern Association of Republican State Chairman (1987-1994); State Chairman, Republican Party, Kentucky (1986-1994); Republican, National Committee (1986-1994); Republican State Financial Chairman (1986); Board of Directors, Headley-Whitney Museum, Lexington, KY (1985-1990); Founding Board, Lexington Fund for the Arts (1984-1986); Board of Founders, National Council of Economic Education, New York City, NY (1982-2000); Board of Directors, Lexington Convention and Tourist Bureau (1982-1985); Board of Directors, Frazier Rehabilitation Foundation, Inc., Louisville, KY (1982-1984); Trustee, Vanderbilt University, Nashville, TN (1979-1987); Trustee, Kentucky State University Foundation (1979-1982); Chairman, Board, George Peabody College for Teachers, Nashville, TN (1979); Secretary, National Park Service (1977-1978); Vice Chairman, Kentucky Better Roads Council, Inc. (1976-1979); Executive Committee, George Peabody College for Teachers, Nashville, TN (1976-1979); Republican, Nominee for Governor of Kentucky (1975); Kentucky Republican State Central Committee (1974-1994); Vice President, Kentucky Mountain Laurel Festival Association (1974-1975); Southeast Regional Advisory Committee, National Park Service (1973-1978); Republican State Financial Chairman (1973-1975); Kentucky Co-Chairman, Financial Committee for Re-election of President (1972); Republican, Candidate for U.S. Senate from Kentucky (1972); Budget Committee, Republican National Financial Committee (1971-1976); Advisory Committee, Kentucky Educational TV (1971-1975); Trustee, George Peabody College for Teachers, Nashville, TN (1970-1979); Public Lands Committee, Interstate Oil Compact Commission (1968-1970); McCreary County Air Board (1967-1981); Commissioner, Kentucky Department of Parks (1967-1970); Advisory Board, University of Kentucky for Somerset Community College (1965-1973) **Military Service:** Lieutenant, Junior Grade, U.S. Naval Reserve (1956-1958) **Awards:** Kentucky Colonel, Mr. Coal of Kentucky (1970) **Membership:** Director, Lexington Chamber of Commerce (1984-1987); Director, Lexington Chamber of Commerce (1982); Secretary, Kentucky Coal Association (1979-1986); Financial Committee, Kentucky Chamber of Commerce (1978-1979); Executive Committee, Kentucky Chamber of Commerce (1976-1980); Regional Vice President, Kentucky Chamber of Commerce (1976-1980); Executive Committee, Kentucky Coal Association (1974-1978); Director, Kentucky Coal Association (1972-1986); Director, Kentucky Chamber of Commerce (1971-1980); Regional Vice President, Kentucky Chamber of Commerce (1971-1972); Executive Committee, Kentucky Chamber of Commerce (1971-1972) **Marquis Who's Who Honors:** Albert Nelson Marquis Lifetime Achievement Award (2017) **Political Affiliations:** Republican **Religion:** Episcopalian **Shipping Address:** 1715 Stonehaven Drive, Frankfort, KY, 40601

Robert William Gabrick

Title: Archival and Educational Consultant, Writer, Researcher, Teacher **Industry:** Education/ Educational Services **Company Name:** Legacy Preservation **Date of Birth:** 11/11/1940 **Place of Birth:** Minneapolis **State:** MN **Parents:** Michael Gabrick Jr.; Helen Marie (Lendt) Gabrick **Children:** Brad William; Ross Michael **Education:** Postgraduate Coursework, University of Massachusetts (1995); Postgraduate Coursework, University of California, Los Angeles (1990); Postgraduate Coursework, University of Minnesota (1989-1990); Postgraduate Coursework, University of Virginia (1988); Postgraduate Coursework, University of Wisconsin, River Falls, WI (1971); Postgraduate Coursework, University of Wisconsin, River Falls, WI (1984); MEd, Macalester College (1969); Postgraduate Coursework, University of Wisconsin, River Falls, WI (1968-1969); Postgraduate Coursework, University of Minnesota (1963); BS, University of Minnesota (1962) **Certifications:** Certified Social Studies Teacher **Career:** Archivist and Historian, The Four Wheel Drive Foundation and Museum, Clintonville, WI (2016-Present); Contributing Editor, "America in WWII" Magazine (2012-Present); President, Legacy Preservation, Somerset, WI (2008-Present); Visiting Instructor, Emory University (2016, 2018); Visiting Instructor, Emory University (2014); Teacher, Padua Academy, Wilmington, DE (2012-2016); Reviewer, National Endowment for the Humanities (2006-2008); President, Educational Growth, Inc. (2006); Vice President, EvaluMetrics, Inc. (2005-2006); Research, Evaluation, and Assessment Consultant, Los Angeles County Office Education (2002-2006); Social Studies Curriculum Leader, White Bear Lake Schools (1994-2004); Adjunct Faculty, History Department, University of Minnesota (1988-2004); Teacher, White Bear Lake Schools, Minnesota (1987-2004); Teacher, Blaine Senior High School, Minnesota (1984-1987); Consultant, Educational Growth (1974-2002); Teacher, White Bear Lake Schools, Minnesota (1970-1984); Teacher, River Falls, Wisconsin (1962-1970) **Career Related:** President, Consultant, Legacy Preservation, Establishing Corporation and Museum Archives, Somerset, WI (2008-Present); Curriculum Consultant, Padua Academy, Wilmington, DE (2007-Present); Vice President, EvaluMetrics, Inc. (2005-Present); Archival Consultant, The Four Wheel Drive Foundation and Museum, Clintonville, WI (2002-Present); Judge, National History Day (1996-Present); Adjunct Faculty, History, University of Minnesota (1989-Present); Consultant, Teaching Educational Growth (1974-Present); American History Grant, Assumption College, Worcester, MA (2007-2008); Curriculum Specialist, Consultant Presenter, Teaching American History Grant, Project Task, Topeka, KS (2005); Historical Channel, American History Colloquium, New York City, NY (2005); Chair, Evaluation Panel, Teaching American History Grant, University of Wisconsin - Eau Claire (2003-2005) **Creative Works:** Author, "FWD Railroad Equipment," Wheels of Time (2018); Author, "The Weight of History: Ford Motor Company in 1952," Collectible Automobile (2018); Author, "The Plymouth in the Barn," Vintage Truck (2018); Author, "Landings," America in WWII (2008-Present); Author, "Hug Trucks," Double Clutch (2016); Author, "1939-42 Crosley: The Car of Tomorrow Has Its Day," Collectible Automobile (2016); Author, "Traveling with Greyhound" (2014); Author, "An Illustrated History of American Delivery Trucks" (2014); Author, "Manufacturing Victory", America in WWII (2013); Curator, "Four-Wheeling in Wisconsin," America in WWII (2013); Author, "Lost Truck Legends" (2012); Author: "GIs Go Greyhound!" America in WWII (2011); Curator, "Greyhound: On the Road Through WWII and Beyond" (2011); Author, "Four Wheel Drive Automobiles" Hemmings Classic Car (2011); Author, "Going the Greyhound Way: The Romance of the Road" (2010); Author, "Sterling Trucks: A Photo Archive" (2009); Author, "Federal Trucks: A Photo Archive, 1910-1959" (2008); Author, "Grandpop's War," America in WWII (2007); Author, "Diamond T Trucks: A Photo Archive, 1911-1966" (2007); Author, "Reo Trucks: A Photo Archive, 1910-1966" (2006); Author, "First Wheel Drive Fire Trucks: A Photo Archive, 1914-1963" (2005); Author, "First Wheel Drive Trucks: A Photo Archive, 1910-1973" (2005); Author, "Autocar Trucks: A Photo Archive, 1899-1950" (2004); Author, "Freightliner Trucks: A Photo Archive, 1937-1981" (2003); Author, "Autocar Trucks: A Photo Archive, 1950-1987" (2002); Author, "Rutherford B. Hayes: Citizen, Soldier, President," Magazine of History (2000) **Awards:** Historian of the Industry Award, American Truck Historical Society (2016); Patricia Behring Teacher of the Year Award, Delaware Affiliate, National History Day (2016); Gilder Lehrman Institute of American History Seminar (2002); National Endowment for the Humanities, Humanities Teacher Leadership Grant (2002); National Endowment for the Humanities Summer Seminar, "Communism in American Life," Emory University (2000) **Shipping Address:** 424 165th Ave, Somerset, WI, 54025

Ugo Oscar Gagliardi

Title: Application Developer **Industry:** Education/Educational Services **Company Name:** Harvard University **Date of Birth:** 07/23/1931 **Place of Birth:** Naples **State/Country of Origin:** Italy **Parents:** Edgardo Gagliardi; Lina (Valenzuela) Gagliardi **Spouse Name:** Anna Josephine Italiano (1954-1972) **Children:** Oscar Marco; Alex Piero **Education:** DEng in Electrical Engineering, Università degli Studi di Napoli Federico II, Naples, Italy (1954); Diploma in Mathematics and Physics, Universitè degli Studi di Napoli Federico II, Naples, Italy (1951) **Career:** Visiting Professor, Harvard University Graduate School of Design (2000-Present); Gordon McKay Professor of the Practice of Computer Engineering, Harvard University, Cambridge, MA (1983-2000); Chairman, Software Technology, Inc. (1982-1999); President, General Systems Group, Salem, NH (1975-Present); Professor of Practice of Computer Engineering, Harvard University, Cambridge, MA (1974-1983); Director of Engineering, Honeywell Information Systems, Waltham, MA (1970-1975); Vice President of Tech. Operations, Interactive Sciences Corporation, Braintree, MA (1968-1970); Lecturer, Harvard University, Cambridge, MA (1967-1974); Research Fellow, Harvard University, Cambridge, MA (1966-1967) **Military Service:** Chief Scientist, U.S. Air Force, Hanscom Air Force Base, MA (1965-1966) **Awards:** Fulbright Scholar, Columbia University (1955-1956) **Business Address:** 48 Quincy Street, 335 Gund Hall, Cambridge, ME, 02138 **Shipping Address:** 280 Perry Oliver Road, Wells, ME, 04090

Deborah Lee Galesi

Title: Artist **Industry:** Fine Art **Place of Birth:** Paterson **State:** NJ **Parents:** John Michael Galesi; Ethel Marchitti **Marital Status:** Married **Spouse Name:** Samuel Peace Eagle Dolphin (10/3/1997) **Education:** MA, Villa Schifanoia/Florence Institute; BFA, University of Colorado **Career:** Artist **Career Related:** Studied with Benjamin Long, Florence, Italy; Studied with Raymond Whyte and Gene Scarpentoni, NY **Civic:** Volunteer, Natural Resource Defense Council; Pacific Whale Foundation; Center for Marine Conservation; WWF; Greenpeace **Creative Works:** Performer, One-Woman Show, Group Show Amsterdam Whitney Gallery, New York City, NY (2005-2006); Performer, One-Woman Show, Monteserrat Gallery, New York City, NY (2005); Featured Artist, Montserrat Gallery New York, NY (1997); Featured Artist, Palazzo Congressi, Salsomaggiore, Italy (1995); Featured Artist, Palazzo, Florence, Italy (1996); Featured Artist, Modigliani Gallery, Milan, Italy (1990); Featured Artist, Art Expo, Verona, Italy (1990); Performer, One-Woman Show, Lo Spirale, Prato, Italy (1988); Performer, One-Woman Show, Salaria Gallery, Spoleto, Italy (1987); Performer, One-Woman Show, Traghetto Gallery, Venice, Italy (1987); Performer, One-Woman Show, Benvenuti Gallery, Venice, Italy (1986); Performer, One-Woman Show, Spinetti Gallery, Florence, Italy (1985); Featured Artist, Cenacolo Gallery, Florence, Italy (1985); Featured Artist, Sieve Art Expo, Pontassieve, Italy (1984); Performer, One-Woman Show, Lo Sprone, Florence, Italy (1983); Featured Artist, New York Gallery, New York, NY (1981); Featured Artist, New Jersey Gallery (1981); Featured Artist, University of Avignon, France (1981); Featured Artist, University of Colorado, Boulder, CO (1980); Featured Artist, Montserrat Gallery Chelsea, New York, NY; Contributor, Various Articles and Professional Journals **Awards:** National Art Center Award, New York, NY (1978); Stewardess, Center of Light and Harmony Award, Sierra Club **Membership:** Partners of Destiny **Why did you become involved in your profession or industry:** As a small child, she discovered a great love for oil painting and was encouraged by her teacher to follow this strong passion. **Hobbies:** Scuba Diving; Rollerblading; Chinese Painting; Piano; Ballet; Snorkeling; Kayaking with Whales; Bow Shooting; Jazz Dance; Flamenco; Modern Dance **Shipping Address:** 1215 S. Kihei Road, Suite 523, Kihei, HI, 96753

Leo Galland

Title: Director, Researcher **Industry:** Medicine & Health Care **Company Name:** Foundation for Integrated Medicine **Date of Birth:** 03/07/1943 **Place of Birth:** Bombay **State/Country of Origin:** India **Parents:** H. William Galland; Rachel (Zakkai) Galland **Marital Status:** Married **Spouse Name:** Christine Oelz (9/29/1974) **Children:** Nicole; Jefferson; Jonathan; Christopher; Jordan **Education:** Fellow in Behavioral Medicine, University of Connecticut; Resident in Medicine, Bellevue Hospital Center, NYU School of Medicine, New York, NY (1968-1972); MD, New York University (1968); AB, Harvard University (1964) **Certifications:** Diplomate, American Board of Internal Medicine **Career:** Private Practice, New York City, NY (1985-Present); Director of Research, Gesell Institute, New Haven, CT (1982-1985); Private Practice, Winsted Hospital (Now Winsted Health Center), CT (1977-1982); Assistant Professor, State University of New York Medical Center (Now Stony Brook Medicine), Stony Brook, NY (1973-1977); Instructor, Albert Einstein College of Medicine, New York, NY (1972-1973); Director, Gesell Institute, New Haven, CT **Career Related:** Director, Foundation for Integrated Medicine, Dr. Leo Galland (1997-Present); Senior Research Consultant, Great Smokies Diagnostic Laboratory (Now Genova Diagnostics (GDX), Asheville, NC (1990-1997); Assistant Professor, University of Connecticut Health Center (Now UConn Health), Farmington, CT (1977-1985) **Creative Works:** Author, "Already Here: A Doctor Discovers the Truth about Heaven" (2018); Co-author, "The Allergy Solution: The Surprising Hidden Truth about Why You Are Sick and How to Get Well" (2016); Author, "The Gut Microbiome and the Brain," The Journal of Medicinal Food (2014); Author, "The Heartburn and Indigestion Solution" (2008); Author, "Gastrointestinal Dysregulation: Connection to Chronic Disease" (2008); Author, "The Fat Resistance Diet" (2005); Author, "Functional Foods," Encyclopedia of Human Nutrition (2005); Author, "The Four Pillars of Healing" (1997); Author, "Power Healing" (1997); Author, "Superimmunity for Kids" (1988); Author, Various Articles on Nutrition and Infectious Diseases; Creator, "The Allergy Solution"; Contributor, "Metabolic Medicine and Surgery"; Contributor, "Integrative Gastroenterology"; Contributor, "Textbook of Functional Medicine"; Contributor, "ACP Evidence-Based Guide to Complementary and Alternative Medicine" **Awards:** Seelig Magnesium Award, American College of Nutrition (2013); Clinician Award, National Nutritional Foods Association (Now Natural Products Association) (2004); America's Top Doctors Listing/The Leading Physicians of the World (2001-2002); Linus Pauling Award, The Institute for Functional Medicine (2000); Harold Harper Award, American College for Advancement in Medicine (1989); Honoree, Named to America's Top Doctors, Castle Connolly Medical Ltd.; Honoree, Leading Physicians in the World **Membership:** Fellow, American College of Physicians; Fellow, American College of Nutrition **Marquis Who's Who Honors:** Albert Nelson Marquis Lifetime Achievement Award (2017) **To what do you attribute your success:** He attributes his success to attempting to help patients solve difficult and complex problems by searching for root causes. **Why did you become involved in your profession or industry:** Dr. Galland became involved in his profession to help people using intellect and compassion. **What do you consider to be the highlight of your career:** One of the highlights of his career has been learning the value of careful listening. **Where will you be in five years:** In five years, Dr. Galland intends to continue his career. He feels that when one has spent their whole life being good at something, it is difficult to stop doing it. **Hobbies:** Traveling; Skiing; Surfing **Shipping Address:** 20 5th Ave Apt 1E, New York, NY, 10011 **Website:** http://drgalland.com

John Gardiner Gallup

Title: Paper Company Executive (Retired) **Industry:** Business Management/Business Services **Date of Birth:** 10/31/1927 **Place of Birth:** Bridgeport **State:** CT **Parents:** Prentiss Brownell Gallup; Evelyn (Crocker) Gallup **Marital Status:** Married **Spouse Name:** Paula Burgee (6/10/1951) **Children:** Susan; Paula; Bruce **Education:** Degree in Humanics, Springfield College (1998); AB, Dartmouth College (1949) **Career:** Division Manager, Corporate Fine Papers, International Paper Company (1989-1992); Director, American Pad & Paper Company, Holoyoke, MA (1981-1986); President, Division Manager, Strathmore Paper Company (1970-1992); Production Manager, Strathmore Paper Company (1968-1970); Employee, Strathmore Paper Company, Westfield, MA (1955-1992); Assistant Store Manager, A.T. Gallup, Inc., Holyoke, MA (1952-1955); Department Manager, Castner Knott Department Store, Nashville, TN (1951-1952); Department Manager, J.B. White Company, Greenville, SC (1951) Buyer, Mercantile Stores Company, Inc. (1950-1951) **Career Related:** With, Frank Stanley Beveridge Foundation (1984-1996); With, Bank of New England, Boston, MA (1981-1983); With, Springfield College (1979-1991); Director, Bank of New England-West, Springfield, MA (1971-1992); With, Economic Development Council; With, Reed's Landing Retirement Community; With, Friends of the Homeless; Senior Vice President, Greater Springfield Chamber of Commerce; With, Corporation for Business Work and Learnng; With, Community Music School; With, Economic Development Partners; Massachusetts Chairman, Massachusetts Ventures, Inc. **Civic:** Chairman, Baystate Health Systems, Inc. (1982-1983); Trustee, Springfield College (1979-1991); Chairman, Baystate Medical Center, Springfield, MA (1979-1982); Member, George Bush Campaign Committee (1979); Member, Board of Directors, Junior Achievement of Western Massachusetts (1979); Chairman, Valley 2000; Trustee, Community Foundation Western Massachusetts; With, Plan for Progress; With, Beveridge Found; Commissioner, Massachusetts Commission on Judicial Conduct; Trustee, St. Andrew's Church Longmeadow; Member, Economic Development Council of Western Massachusetts; Member, Board of Directors, Willie Ross School for the Deaf, Longmeadow, MA; Member, Board of Trustees, Glen Meadow (Retirement Community) **Military Service:** US Marine Corps (1945-1947) **Awards:** Recipient, William Pinchon Honorary Degree **Membership:** Chairman, Greater Springfield Chamber of Commerce (1988-1991); Vice Chairman, Greater Springfield Chamber of Commerce (1985-1988); Executive Committee, Cover and Text Paper Group, American Paper Institute (1979-1991); President, Boston Paper Trade Association (1979); Boston Paper Trade Association; American Paper Institute; Greater Springfield Chamber of Commerce; Volunteer for Economic Development, Greater Springfield Chamber of Commerce; Board of Directors, Visiting Nurses Association; Board of Directors, Corporation for Business, Work and Learning; Board of Directors, Community Service Learning; Board of Directors, World Affairs Council; Board of Directors, Friends of Homeless; President, Springfield Orchestra Association; Honorary Director, Associated Industries Massachusetts; Century Club; Colony Club, Springfield, MA **Marquis Who's Who Honors:** Albert Nelson Marquis Lifetime Achievement Award (2017) **Religion:** Episcopalian **Shipping Address:** 64 Cambridge Cir, Longmeadow, MA, 01106

Matthew Reppert Galvin

Title: Psychiatrist **Industry:** Medicine & Health Care **Company Name:** Indiana University Medical Center **Date of Birth:** 07/24/1950 **Place of Birth:** Seattle **State/Country of Origin:** WA **Parents:** Ralph Galvin; Virginia (Reppert) Galvin **Marital Status:** Married **Spouse Name:** Margaret Gaffney **Children:** Joseph; Sarah; Erin; Marella (Granddaughter) **Education:** MD, Indiana University (1979); AB, Indiana University, Cum Laude (1975) **Certifications:** Diplomate American Board of Adolescent Psychiatry; Diplomate, American Board of Psychiatry and Neurology, Inc. **Career:** Clinical Associate Professor, Indiana University of Health (1995-Present); Assistant Professor, Indiana University of Health (1984-1995) **Career Related:** Psychiatrist, Counseling Center, Christian Theological Seminary (2011-Present); Psychiatrist, Indiana School for the Blind & Visually Impaired, (2003-Present); Psychiatrist, Children's Bureau, Inc. (2001-2014); Psychiatrist, Damar Services Inc. (2007-2012); Psychiatrist, St. Vincent Stress Center, St. Vincent Indianapolis (2001-2006); Psychiatrist, Pleasant Run Children's Home (1998-2001); Child Psychiatrist, Riley Hospital for Children, Indiana University Health (1990-1998); Acting Director, Larue D. Carter Memorial Hospital, Indiana University (1988-1990); Associate Director, Youth Services, Larue D. Carter Memorial Hospital, Indiana University (1988); Staff Psychiatrist, Larue D. Carter Memorial Hospital, Indiana University (1984-1988); Volunteer Faculty, Riley Hospital for Children at Indiana University Health; Volunteer Faculty, Indiana University Center for Bioethics, Indiana University **Civic:** Board Member, Infancy Onward (2004-Present); Founding Member, Indiana University Conscience Project (1996-Present); President's Circle, Indiana University; Dean's Council Member, Arbutus Society, Indiana University; Member, J.O. Ritchey Society, Indiana University **Military Service:** Medical Corps, U.S. Army (1970-1973) **Creative Works:** Author, "Doubtless You Know" (2015); Author, "The Lyric of Lafracoth" (2008); Author, "Carlotta Learns About Her Medicine, Second Edition" (2007); Author, "Clouds and Clocks: A Story for Children Who Soil, Second Edition" (2007); Author, "Grandma Grady's Grade-A Gray Day" (2007); Co-Author, "A Guide to Conscience" (2007); Author, "The Otters of Conscience-Berg" (2005); Author, "Carlotta Learns About Her Medicine" (2005); Co-Author, "Rachel and the Seven Bridges of Conscience-Berg" (2002); Author, "Otto Learns About Medicine, Third Edition" (2001), Co-Author, "Right vs. Wrong: Raising a Child with a Conscience" (2000); Co-Author, "The Conscience Celebration" (1998); Co-Author, "Sometimes Y: A Story for Families with Gender Identity Issues" (1993); Author, "Clouds and Clocks: A Story for Children Who Soil" (1989); Author, "Robby Really Transforms: A Story About Grown-Ups Helping Children" (1988); Author, "Ignatius Finds Help: A Story about Psychotherapy" (1988); Author, "Otto Learns About Medicine" (1988); Editor, "Conscience Works"; Contributor, Articles, Professional Journals **Awards:** Named, Indianapolis Monthly Magazine Top Doctors (2016-2018); Fellow, American Psychotherapy Association (2016); Life Fellow, American Psychiatric Association (2013); Distinguished Fellow, American Psychiatric Association (2003); Department of Psychiatry Teaching Achievement Award, Indiana University (1997, 1999); Teaching Excellence Recognition Award, School of Medicine, Indiana University (1999); Psychiatry Residents' Teaching Excellence Award, Indiana University (1994); Sandoz Resident's Award (1983); Rader Resident's Award, Indiana University (1983) **Membership:** Alpha Omega Alpha Honor Medical Society (2009); President, Indianapolis Chapter, American Academy of Child & Adolescent Psychiatry (1990-1991); President Elect, Indianapolis Chapter, American Academy of Child & Adolescent Psychiatry (1989-1990); Treasurer, Indianapolis Chapter, American Academy of Child & Adolescent Psychiatry (1986-1989); American Psychiatric Association; American Academy of Child & Adolescent Psychiatry; American Society for Adolescent Psychiatry; American Psychotherapy Association **Why did you become involved in your profession or industry:** Dr. Galvin was a medic in the U.S. Army and he was encouraged by doctors and nurses with whom he worked to prepare for and seek admission to medical school. He did so, returning to school to complete an unfinished undergraduate degree, but also maintained a strong interest in philosophy in which he majored. Upon graduation from medical school, he chose child adolescent psychiatry. His research in moral psychological development in youth led to his involvement in the Indiana University Conscience Project from 1982 to the present. **What do you consider to be the highlight of your career:** A highlight of his career is the Indiana University Conscience Project. **Shipping Address:** 2113 W 42nd St, Indianapolis, IN, 46228

Frederick C. Gamst

Title: Professor Emeritus **Industry:** Education/Educational Services **Company Name:** University of Massachusetts Boston **Date of Birth:** 05/24/1936 **Place of Birth:** New York **State:** NY **Parents:** Rangvold Gamst; Edith Gamst **Marital Status:** Married **Spouse Name:** Marilou **Children:** Nicole **Education:** PhD, University of California, Berkeley; BA, University of California, Los Angeles; AA, Pasadena City College **Career:** Professor Emeritus, University of Massachusetts Boston (2001); Professor, University of Massachusetts Boston (1975-2001); Professor, Rice University (1966-1975) **Military Service:** Sergeant E-5, U.S. Army Reserve **Creative Works:** Contributor, Over 100 Articles, Book Chapters, Proceedings, Book Reviews; Contributor, Over 100 Consulting Reports and Technical Papers; Author, 12 Books; Editor 12 Books **Awards:** Honoree, Faculty Appreciation Day, University of Massachusetts Boston (1999); Outstanding Achievement Award, University of Massachusetts Boston (1994-1996); Conrad Arensberg Award, American Anthropological Association (1995); Distinguished Scholarship Address, University of Massachusetts Boston (1983, 1994); Award in Appreciation of His Contributions to Graduate Education, University of Massachusetts Boston (1988); Honoree for Service as Graduate Dean (1985); Outstanding Achievement Award for Pro Bono Service, University of Massachusetts Boston (1983-1984); Honoree, Moment of Silence, International Conference on Horn of Africa Studies **Membership:** Fellow, American Anthropological Association; Fellow, Society for Applied Anthropology; Fellow, American Association for the Advancement of Science; Associate in Railroad Transportation, Transportation Research Board, National Academy of Sciences; Society for the Anthropology of Work; Transportation Research Forum; National Association of Retired and Veteran Railway Employees; International Association of Railway Operating Officers; American Association of Railroad Superintendents; Railway and Locomotive Historical Society **To what do you attribute your success:** Dr. Gamst attributes his success to conduct research. **Why did you become involved in your profession or industry:** Dr. Gamst had a profound interest in his field, and chose to study it for his profession. **Hobbies:** Photography; Camping; Sailing **Shipping Address:** 2800 Rodman Drive, Los Osos, CA, 93402-4312

James Ganley

Title: Professor (Retired) **Industry:** Education/Educational Services **Company Name:** Louisiana State University Medical Center **Date of Birth:** 04/25/1937 **Place of Birth:** Altadena **State:** CA **Parents:** Joseph Harrington Ganley; Ruth Alice (Carr) Ganley **Marital Status:** Married **Spouse Name:** Anne Hay Hunter (8/7/1965) **Children:** Anne Hay; Susan Powell; Katherine Carr; Elizabeth Pearson **Education:** DPH, Johns Hopkins University (1972); Senior Staff Fellow, National Eye Institute, National Institutes of Health, Bethesda, MD (1971-1974); Resident in Preventive Medicine, Johns Hopkins University, Baltimore, MD (1969-1971); MPH, Johns Hopkins University (1969); Resident in Ophthalmology, SUNY Upstate Medical Center, Syracuse, NY (1965-1968); Intern, Washington Hospital Center (1963-1964); MD, Georgetown University (1963); BS in Biology, Mount St. Mary's University (1959) **Certifications:** Diplomate, American Board of Medical Examiners; Diplomate, American Board of Preventative Medicine; Diplomate, American Board of Ophthalmology **Career:** Professor, Louisiana State University Medical Center, Shreveport, LA (1998-2004); Professor, Department Head, Louisiana State University Medical Center, Shreveport, LA (1982-1997); Assistant Dean of Clinical Affairs, Louisiana State University Medical Center, Shreveport, LA (1981-1987); Associate Professor, Department Head, Louisiana State University Medical Center, Shreveport, LA (1980-1982); Assistant Professor of Ophthalmology, University of Arizona Medical Center, Tucson, AZ (1974-1980) **Career Related:** Chairman, International Eye Foundation, Bethesda, MD (2008-2009); Medical Director, International Eye Foundation, Bethesda, MD (2006-2007); Board of Directors, International Eye Foundation, Bethesda, MD (2004-2009); Epidemiological and Disease Control Study Section, National Institutes of Health (1982-1986); Ophthalmic Drugs Advisory Committee, Food and Drug Administration, Department of Health, Rockville, MD (1976-1982); Science Advisory Panel, Onchocerciasis Control Program, World Health Organization, Geneva, Switzerland (1974-1979); Medical Advisory Board, International Eye Foundation, Bethesda, MD (1974-1977); Class Representative, Mount St. Mary's University (1959-2014) **Civic:** Board of Directors, Northwest Lions Eye Bank, Shreveport, LA (1987) **Military Service:** Lieutenant, U.S. Navy (1964-1965) **Creative Works:** Emeritus Editor, Ophthalmic Epidemiology (2007-Present); Editorial Board, Evidence-Based Sight Care (1999-2004); Founding Editor, Ophthalmic Epidemiology (1993-2006); Editorial Board, Sightsaver, National Society to Prevent Blindness (1982-1986); Author, Book Chapters, Proceedings **Awards:** Promotion of Peace And Vision Award, International Eye Foundation **Membership:** Executive Board, International Society Geographical & Epidemiological Ophthalmology (1988-Present); First Vice Chairman, Secretary, Louisiana Association for the Blind (2014); Board of Directors, Gibson Island Corp. (2006-2008); International Members Committee, Association for Research in Vision and Ophthalmology (2001-2004); President, Shreveport Medical Society (1995); First Vice President, Shreveport Medical Society (1994); Program Planning Committee, Association for Research in Vision and Ophthalmology (1993-1996); Second Vice President, Shreveport Medical Society (1993); Chairman, Board, Louisiana for the Blind (1992-1993); Board of Directors, Shreveport Medical Society (1990-1996); Chairman, American Academy of Ophthalmology (1990-1991); Executive Board, Louisiana Association for the Blind (1989-1991); Treasurer, International Society Geographical & Epidemiological Ophthalmology (1988-2014); Committee for Research on Regulatory Agencies and Federal Systems, American Academy of Ophthalmology (1986-1991); President, International Society of Geographical & Epidemiological Ophthalmology (1982-1988); Board of Directors, Louisiana Association for the Blind (1980-1996); American College of Preventative Medicine; Monsignor Tierney Honor Society; Alpha Omega Alpha Medical Honor Society; American College of Epidemiology; Fellow, American Board of Preventative Medicine; Fellow, American Board of Ophthalmology; Chair, Pest Eradication Committee, Gibson Island Corp. **Hobbies:** Swimming; Sailing **Political Affiliations:** Democrat **Religion:** Roman Catholic **Shipping Address:** 644 Ayrlie Water Road, Gibson Island, MD, 21056

Mary Frances Gardner

Industry: Medicine & Health Care **Education:** Residency, Preventive Medicine, Obstetrics and Gynecology, Tulane University; Internship, Louisiana State University, New Orleans, LA; PhD in Obstetrics and Gynecology, School of Medicine, Louisiana State University, New Orleans, LA **Certifications:** Louisiana State Medical License (2018-Present); Certified in Obstetrics & Gynecology, American Board of Obstetrics and Gynecology; Certified in General Preventive Medicine, American Board of Preventive Medicine **Career Related:** ACOG Fellow **Marquis Who's Who Honors:** Distinguished Humanitarian (2017) **To what do you attribute your success:** Dr. Gardner attributes her success to her patients out there that say thank you and let her know that she's making a difference. **Why did you become involved in your profession or industry:** Dr. Gardner had no doctors in her family, but she was inspired by her mother's best friend, who was a female physician. **Business Address:** 927 Broadway Street, New Orleans, LA, 70118 **Shipping Address:** 17 Fontaine Bleau, New Orleans, LA, 70125 **Website:** https://health.usnews.com/doctors/mary-gardner-577897

Nancy Garfield-Woodbridge

Title: Children's Book Author **Industry:** Writing and Editing **Place of Birth:** New York **State:** NY **Parents:** Solomon Silbowitz; Betty Silbowitz **Marital Status:** Married **Spouse Name:** George Charles Woodbridge (4/20/1980) **Children:** Maurice; Joshua **Education:** Postgraduate Coursework, Hofstra University (1973); MS in Education, Hofstra University (1972); BA in Literature, Bennington College (1955) **Certifications:** Certified Teacher in Grades K-8, State of New York; Certified Teacher in English in Grades 7-9, State of New York **Career:** Author, Children's Books (2000-Present); Director of Special Projects, Girl Scouts of the United States of America, New York City, NY (1973-2000); Research Associate to Vice President and Editor, New York Institute of Technology, Westbury, NY (1972-1973); Vice President, Information Retrieval Systems, Great Neck, NY (1958-1972); Editor-in-Chief, The Gifted Child Magazine, New York City, NY (1957-1958); Picture Editor, Forbes Magazine, New York City, NY (1955-1956); Editorial Assistant, Wenner-Gren Foundation for Anthropological Research, New York City, NY (1952-1955) **Career Related:** Presenter, Education Commission for the States, Denver, CO (1979); Vice President's Task Force on Youth Employment, Little Rock, AR (1979); Speaker, Governor's Conference on Juvenile Justice, Baton Rouge, LA **Civic:** Volunteer, Biafran Refugee Campaign, New York to London (1967); Volunteer, Kennedy Kenya Airlift Program, New York City (1962); Fundraiser, Sara's Center Very Special Arts Festival, Long Island to Washington **Creative Works:** Author, "Suns of Darkness" (2018); Author, "Arctic Butterfly" (2016); Author, "The Islanders" (2016); Author, "Poems in Exile" (2012); Author, "A Bouquet of Fairy Tales" (2012); Author, "Hilary and the Secret Skulls" (2012); Author, "Journey" (2012); Author, "If I Had $1500 I Would Clean My Karma" (2012); Author, "Stories from Around the World" (2012); Author, "More Stories from Around the World" (2012); Author, "Juvenile Justice" (1981); Author, "The Dancing Monkey" (1970); Author, "The Tuesday Elephant" (1968); Contributor, "Directory of Anthropological Institutions," Wenner-Gren Foundation for Anthropological Research (1952-1955); Contributor, "Man's Role in Changing the Face of Earth," Wenner-Gren Foundation for Anthropological Research (1952-1955); Contributor, Articles in Professional Journals and Magazines **Awards:** Dr. John C. Sevier Award For Service to Youth With Disabilities, YMCA of the USA (1989); Scholarship, Breadloaf Writers Conference, Vermont (1967) **Membership:** Academy of American Poets; Authors Guild; Milford Fine Arts Council; Society of Children's Book Writers and Illustrators **Hobbies:** Travel; Reading; Opera; Painting; Photography; Sociology; Biography; Poetry **Business Address:** PO Box 9, Milford, CT, 06460 **Shipping Address:** 167 Cherry St Apt 193, Milford, CT, 06460 **Website:** http://www.nancygarfieldwoodbridge.com

B. John Garrick, PhD

Title: Research Scientist **Industry:** Government Administration/Government Relations/Government Services **Date of Birth:** 03/05/1930 **Place of Birth:** Eureka **State:** UT **Education:** PhD in Engineering and Applied Sciences, University of California, Los Angeles (1968); MS in Engineering, University of California, Los Angeles (1962); Postgraduate Coursework, Oak Ridge School Reactor Technology, U.S. Atomic Energy Commission (1954-1955); BS in Physics, Brigham Young University (1952) **Certifications:** Registered Professional Engineer, State of California **Career:** Appointed Chairman, U.S. Nuclear Waste Technology Review Board, President George W. Bush (2004-2012); President, Chief Executive Officer, PLG, Inc. (1975-1997) **Career Related:** Distinguished Adjunct Professor, Henry Samueli School of Engineering and Applied Sciences (2015-Present); Dean, Executive Board, School of Engineering, University of California, Los Angeles (2014-Present); Founder, Senior Advisor, B. John Garrick Institute for the Risk Sciences, University of California, Los Angeles (2014-Present); Member, Advisory Committee, Pacific Northwest National Laboratory, Energy and Environmental Directorate (2014-Present); Adjunct Professor, School of Engineering, Department of Civil and Environmental Engineering, Vanderbilt University, Nashville, TN (2006-Present); Member, Leadership Council of the School of Mathematical and Physical Sciences, Brigham Young University, Provo, UT (2006-Present); Member, Dean's Advisory Council, Henry Samueli School of Engineering and Applied Sciences, University of California, Los Angeles (2004-Present) **Creative Works:** Author, "Quantifying and Controlling Catastrophic Risks" (2008); Contributor, Numerous Articles, Professional Journals; Contributor, Chapters, Books; Contributor, Encyclopedias; Contributor, Refereed Papers, Technical Journals **Awards:** Alumnus of Year Award, School of Engineering and Applied Sciences, University of California, Los Angeles (2014); Distinguished Achievement Award, The Society for Risk Analysis (1994) **Membership:** President, The Society for Risk Analysis (1989-1990); Fellow, American Nuclear Society; Institute of Advancement Engineering; National Academy of Engineering; Chair, Numerous Committees, National Research Council; Commission on Geosciences, Environment, and Resources, National Research Council **Shipping Address:** 221 Crescent Bay Drive, Laguna Beach, CA, 92651 **Website:** https://www.risksciences.ucla.edu/

Gretchen Garrigues

Title: Global Chief Marketing Officer **Industry:** Advertising & Marketing **Company Name:** Manulife/John Hancock **Education:** MBA in Marketing, University of Wisconsin-Madison (1997); BA in Foreign Affairs, University of Virginia (1988) **Certifications:** Certification in Political Science, Institut d'Études Politiques de Paris (1989); Certified Six Sigma Quality Leader; Master Black Belt; Black Belt **Career:** Chief Marketing Officer, First Data (2014-Present); Senior Managing Director, Global Strategic Marketing, GE Capital (2012-2013); Senior Managing Director, Strategic Marketing, GE Capital-Americas (2009-2012); Global Business Program Leader, GE Capital Experience Commercial Leadership Program (2007-2011); Managing Director, Global Commercial Excellence Leader, GE Capital (2005-2009); Chief Marketing Officer and Quality Leader, GE Capital Corporate Lending Group (2002-2005); Senior Vice President, Strategic Partnerships, Access GE (1999-2002); Marketing Business Development and New Product Development Leader, GE Capital (1997-1999); Foreign Commercial Trade Officer, Department of Commerce, United States and Foreign Commercial Service (1992-1994) **Career Related:** Guest Lecturer in Marketing, MBA Program, University of Connecticut **Awards:** Top 50 Marketers to Watch for Excellence in Driving Transformation, Boardroom Insiders (2015); Capital Leadership Award for Outstanding Contributions to Diversity, GE (2013); Women's Network Award for Outstanding Leadership (2012); Best in Class Market Leader, Chief Marketing Officer of GE, Harvard Business Review (2011); Marketing Leader Award for Exceptional Performance Integrating and Leading Marketing Teams Across Profits and Losses, GE (2010); Capital Chairman's Award for Outstanding Leadership, GE (2009); Eight-Time Winner, Leadership Awards, GE (1998-2008); Outstanding Academic Award for Exceptional Academic Performance, University of Wisconsin-Madison (1997); Outstanding Performance Award, United States Department of Commerce (1994) **Membership:** Board of Directors, Education Committee Chair, Commercial Finance Association; Co-founder, Women in Financial Services; Chairperson, Stamford and Norwalk Hub, GE Women's Network; Board Member, National Council on Competitive Intelligence **To what do you attribute your success:** Ms. Garrigues attributes her success to her proven ability to set strategic direction, make decisions and inspire teams to deliver results above expectations. She is also recognized as having deep domain expertise in marketing and financial services. Additionally, she credits her finely honed communication skills built on expertise, credibility and unwavering integrity. Ms. Garrigues has experienced significant success developing and leveraging digital tools to improve sales (CRM, social media, apps, etc.), and utilizes strong analytical skills and a metric-driven approach. She has very high performance standards for herself and her teams coupled with a strong sense of accountability; excellence in execution is one of her trademarks. Ms. Garrigues is curious and always willing to take on new challenges. She has also worked to build considerable leadership agility. Ms. Garrigues is flexible and not only open to change, but actively seen as a change agent. Furthermore, she is a strong leader who has built multiple best-in-class marketing teams. She is passionate about building, empowering and promoting the best talent. **Why did you become involved in your profession or industry:** Ms. Garrigues became involved in marketing as a result of her passion to drive growth. She wanted to leverage her analytical skills and customer-centric mindset to define strategic direction and commercial actions. **Where will you be in five years:** In five years, Ms. Garrigues hopes to continue to take on roles of increasing responsibility in marketing, eventually leading to business management roles, such as a profit-and-loss leader. She enjoys working in high growth, fast-paced environments where the ability to drive change and deliver significant impact are the norm. **Business Address:** 601 Congress Street, Boston, MA, 02210 **Shipping Address:** 127 S. Lake Drive, Stamford, CT, 06903 **Website:** http://www.manulife.com

Milton McCormick Gatch

Title: Library Director, Clergyman, Educator **Industry:** Religious **Company Name:** Union Theological Seminary **Date of Birth:** 11/22/1932 **Place of Birth:** Cincinnati **State:** OH **Parents:** Milton McCormick; Mary (Curry) Gatch **Marital Status:** Widowed **Spouse Name:** Ione Georganna White (8/25/1956) **Children:** Ione Waite; Lucinda McCormick; George Crosby White **Education:** PhD, Yale University (1963); MA, Yale University (1961); BD, Episcopal Divinity School (1960); Coursework, College of Law, University of Cincinnati (1953-1955); AB, Haverford College (1953) **Certifications:** Ordained Priest, Episcopal Church (1961) **Career:** Emeritus, Union Theological Seminary in the City of New York (1998-Present); Priest-in-Charge, The Chapel of St. James the Fisherman (1976-2014); Director, Burke Library, Union Theological Seminary in the City of New York (1990-1998); Professor in Church History, Union Theological Seminary in the City of New York (1978-1998); Academic Dean, Union Theological Seminary in the City of New York (1978-1989); Provost, Union Theological Seminary in the City of New York (1978-1989); Department Chair, University of Missouri (1971-1974); Professor of English, University of Missouri (1968-1978); Associate Professor of English, Northern Illinois University (1967-1968); Chaplain, Chair of Humanities Department, Shimer College (1964-1967); Chaplain, Wooster School (1963-1964) **Career Related:** Bonhöffer Visiting Professor, Humboldt-Universität zu Berlin (1998); Council, College of Preachers (1992-1998); Visiting Fellow, Emmanuel College, University of Cambridge (1991) **Military Service:** U.S. Army (1955-1977) **Creative Works:** Author, "Till The Break of Day: Some Descendants of Philip Getch through Three Centuries" (2015); Co-Author, "A Little Dust: The Gatch Collection of Yeats" (2012); Author, "The Library of Leander van Ess and the Earliest American Collections of Reformation Pamphlets" (2007); Author, "The Yeats Family and the Book" (2000); Author, "Eschatology and Christian Nurture" (2000); Author, "So Precious a Foundation: The Library of Leander van Ess" (1996); Author, "Preaching and Theology in Anglo-Saxon England" (1977); Author, "Loyalties and Traditions: Man and His World in Old English Literature" (1971); Author, "Death: Meaning and Mortality in Christian Thought and Contemporary Culture" (1969); Contributor, Antiquarian Articles; Contributor, Bibliographical Articles; Contributor, Medieval Articles **Awards:** Senior Fellowship, National Endowment of the Humanities (1974-1975) **Membership:** Council Member, The Grolier Club of New York (2011-Present); Emeritus, The Medieval Academy of America (2014); Finance Committee, The Medieval Academy of America (2000-2010); Trustee, Yale Library Associates, Yale University Library (1999-2008); Fellow, The Medieval Academy of America (1998-2014); Trustee, American Printing History Association (1995-1999); Board of Directors, American Council of Learned Societies (1992-1993); Delegate to American Council of Learned Societies, The Medieval Academy of America (1981-1993); Founding Advisory Board Member, International Society of Anglo-Saxonists (1980-1985); Fellow, Society of Antiquaries of London; Early English Text Society; The Bibliographical Society; The Bibliographical Society of America; The Century Association **Marquis Who's Who Honors:** Distinguished Humanitarian (2017) **Hobbies:** Book collecting; Gardening; Photography **Political Affiliations:** Democrat **Religion:** Episcopalian **Shipping Address:** 575 W. End Avenue, Apartment 7C, New York, NY, 10024

Thomas Edward Gates

Title: Attorney, Civil Engineer **Industry:** Law and Legal Services **Company Name:** Gates Law, PLLC **Date of Birth:** 06/25/1953 **Place of Birth:** Tachikawa Air Force Base **State/Country of Origin:** Japan **Parents:** Harold Charles Gates; Masako (Endo) Gates **Education:** JD, Seattle University (2001); MS, Kansas State University, Manhattan, KS (1981); Graduate Research Assistant, Kansas State University, Manhattan, KS (1979-1981); BS, Kansas State University, Manhattan, KS (1979) **Certifications:** Registered Professional Engineer, State of Washington; Registered Professional Engineer, State of Kansas; Registered Professional Engineer, State of Alaska **Career:** Pro Team Judge, Federal Way, WA (2013-Present); Manager, Gates' Law, PLLC, Tukwila, WA (2004-Present); Consultant (1999-Present); Acting Program Manager, Support Projects, Basalt Waste Isolation Project, Battelle Pacific Northwest Laboratories, Richland, WA (1988-Present); Fellow, American Society of Civil Engineers (2010); Manager, PLG, Inc., Richland, WA (1994-1997); Manager, Technology Demonstration Program Operations, Westinghouse Hanford Company, Richland, WA (1991-1994); Manager, Technology Assessment and Application, Westinghouse Hanford Company, Richland, WA (1990-1991); Staff Manager, Engineering and Development Division, Westinghouse Hanford Company, Richland, WA (1990); Manager, Defense Programs, Westinghouse Hanford Company, Richland, WA (1988-1989); Manager, Waste Package Projects, BWIP, Battelle Pacific Northwest Laboratories, Richland, WA (1986-1988); Senior Research Engineer, Battelle Pacific Northwest Laboratories, Richland, WA (1983-1985); Engineer, Battelle Pacific Northwest Laboratories, Richland, WA (1981-1983); Consultant, Riley County Public Works, Manhattan, KS (1979); Field Supervisor, Riley County Public Works, Manhattan, KS (1978); State Inspector, Riley County Public Works, Manhattan, KS (1977-1978) **Career Related:** Chairman, Solid Waste Advisory Committee, State of Washington (1996-1998); Municipal Research and Service Center, Washington Department of Community Development (1991-1993); Advisory Committee, Washington Department of Community Development (1990-1993); Chairman, Washington State Air Transportation Commission (1993-1994); Lead Judge, Washington State Science Talent Search, Richland, WA (1985-1990); Consultant, Electrical Power Research Institute, Washington; Consultant, Atomic Energy of Canada, Limited; Consultant, Research Company, Ottawa, Canada **Civic:** Fourth Degree, Knights of Columbus (1989-Present); Third Degree, Knights of Columbus (1983-Present); Board of Directors, Richland Kiwanis Foundation (1997-1998); Board of Directors, Kamp Kiwanis Foundation (1996-1998); Eucharistic Minister, St. Vincent DePaul (1995-1997); President, Kiwanis Club, Richland, WA (1995-1996); Eucharistic Minister, Christ the King Church (1993-1998); Trustee, Knights of Columbus (1992-1995); Board of Directors, Association of Washington Cities (1990-1993); Energy Advisory Committee, Association of Washington Cities (1990-1993); Management Board, Risk Management and Service Agency, Association of Washington Cities (1990-1993); Chairman, Technology Advisory Committee, Hazardous Material Management, Columbia Basin College (1990-1996) **Awards:** Lifetime Achievement, American Top 100 Attorneys (2017); Top 10 Under 40 Award, National Academy of Personal Injury Attorneys (2016); Excellence in Legal Service, United States Commerce & Trade Research Institute (2015); Premier 100 Trial Attorneys, American Academy of Trial Attorneys (2015); Top 10 Under 40 Award, National Academy of Criminal Defense Attorneys (2014); Rising Star, Washington Super Lawyers (2012-2013); Volunteer Attorney of the Year, Volunteer Legal Services, KCBA (2004) **Membership:** Washington Attorneys Assisting Community Organizations (Now Wayfind) (2004-Present); Business Law Section, Washington State Bar Association (2004-Present); Real Property, Probate & Trust Section, Washington State Bar Association (2004-Present); Neighborhood Legal Clinic, King County Bar Association (2004-Present); Volunteer Legal Services, King County Bar Association (2004-Present); Real Property, Probate & Trust Section, King County Bar Association (2004-Present); King County Bar Association (2004-Present); Washington State Bar Association (2003-Present); Subcommittees 1 and 4, 349 – Nuclear Structures, American Concrete Institute (1996-2001); 227- Radioactive & Hazardous Waste, Technical Committee (1983-2001); 118 – Use of Computers, Technical Committee, American Concrete Institute (1983-2000); American Concrete Institute; American Society of Civil Engineers **Bar Admissions:** Washington State (2003); United States District Court Western District of Washington **Marquis Who's Who Honors:** Albert Nelson Marquis Lifetime Achievement Award (2017) **Religion:** Roman Catholic **Business Address:** 651 Strander Boulevard Ste 209, Tukwila, WA, 98188 **Shipping Address:** 33207 11th Ave SW, Federal Way, WA, 98023

Roger William Geiss

Title: Pathologist, Medical Educator **Industry:** Medicine & Health Care **Company Name:** University of Illinois College of Medicine **Date of Birth:** 09/13/1947 **Place of Birth:** Jersey City **State:** NJ **Parents:** Robert William Geiss; Eleanor Gladys Rich **Marital Status:** Married **Spouse Name:** Dianne Louise Welch (9/13/1980); Agnes Josephine Meadows (8/5/1972, Deceased) **Children:** Kevin James Easter; Kenneth David Geiss **Education:** MD, Cornell University Medical College (now Weill Cornell Medicine) (1975); BSc in Biology, Georgetown University (1969) **Certifications:** Certified in Cytopathology, American Board of Pathology (1996); Certified in Anatomic Pathology, American Board of Pathology (1980); Certified in Clinical Pathology, American Board of Pathology (1980); Medical License, State of Illinois **Career:** Professor Emeritus, University of Illinois College of Medicine at Peoria (UICOMP), Peoria, IL (2015-Present); Professor of Pathology, Chair of Pathology, UICOMP (2004-2015); Associate Professor of Pathology, University of Mississippi Medical Center, Jackson, MS (1995-2004); Assistant Professor of Pathology, Creighton University Medical Center (now CHI Health), Omaha, NE (1989-1995); Assistant Professor of Pathology, West Virginia University Medical Center, Morgantown, WV (1984-1989); Clinical Assistant Professor, West Virginia University Medical Center, Morgantown, WV (1982-1984); Associate Pathologist, Morgantown Pathology Consultants, West Virginia (1982-1984); Associate Pathologist, Clinical Pathologists, Inc., Colorado Springs, CO (1981-1982); Fellow in Anatomic Pathology, The University of Arizona Health Sciences Center, Tucson, AZ (1980-1981); Resident in Clinical Pathology, The University of Arizona Health Sciences Center, Tucson, AZ (1978-1980); Resident in Anatomic Pathology, The University of Chicago Hospitals and Clinics, Chicago, IL (1976-1978); Pathology Intern, Memorial Hospital Medical Center (now Long Beach Medical Center), Long Beach, CA (1975-1976) **Career Related:** Designated Forensic Pathologist in the State of Mississippi, Jackson, MS (2000-2004); Consulting Pathologist, Mercy Hospital (now CHI Health Mercy), Corning, IA (1989-1992); Deputy Medical Examiner, Monongalia County, WV (1984-1989); Deputy Coroner, El Paso County, CO (1981-1982) **Civic:** Member, Board of Directors, Tri-County Illinois Affiliate, National Alliance on Mental Illness (2008-2017) **Creative Works:** Contributor, Journal of Cancer Research (2008); Contributor, Archives of Pathology & Laboratory Medicine (2004); Contributor, Archives of Pathology & Laboratory Medicine (2002); Contributor, Pathology Education (2001); Contributor, Modern Pathology (1999); Contributor, Southern Medical Journal (1996); Contributor, Bulletin of Pathology Education (1994); Contributor, American Journal of Otolaryngology (1991); Contributor, Articles, Professional Journals **Awards:** Golden Apple Award, Creighton University School of Medicine, Omaha, NE (1993); Golden Apple Award, UICOMP (2015); Distinguished Service Award for Exceptional Lifetime Contributions to GRIPE (2016); Appreciation Award for Contributions and Dedication to Excellence in Medical Education, UICOMP (2015); Michele Raible Distinguished Teaching Award, Association of Pathology Chairs (2014); Alpha Omega Alpha Faculty Teaching Award, UICOMP (2012); Faculty Outstanding Service Award, UICOMP (2010-2011); Faculty Outstanding Teaching Award, UICOMP (2006-2007); Multiple Best Instructor Awards, UICOMP (2004-2015); Appreciation Award in Recognition of Dedication, Loyalty, and Expertise, Department of Pathology, Creighton University School of Medicine (1995); Alpha Omega Alpha (induction as Faculty), Creighton University School of Medicine (1994); Mahoney Medical for Excellence in Humanities Among Pre-Medical Students, Georgetown University (1969); Magna Cum Laude, Phi Beta Kappa, Georgetown University (1969); Rockland County (NY) Soroptimist Award (1965); National Honor Society, Pearl River (NY) High School (1964-1965) **Membership:** President, Group for Research in Pathology Education (GRIPE) (1999-2001); Chair, Learning Objectives Committee, GRIPE (1998-Present); Secretary/Treasurer, West Virginia Association of Pathologists (1988-1989); Fellow, College of American Pathologists; Fellow, American Society for Clinical Pathology; Senior Fellow, Association of Pathology Chairs; The International Academy of Pathology; International Association of Medical Science Educators (IAMSE); Pulmonary Pathology Society; Illinois Society of Pathologists; Illinois State Medical Society; Peoria Medical Society **Marquis Who's Who Honors:** Albert Nelson Marquis Lifetime Achievement Award (2017) **Political Affiliations:** Independent **Religion:** Roman Catholic **Business Address:** 1 Illini Drive, Peoria, IL, 61605 **Shipping Address:** 6637 N Toronado Ct, Peoria, IL, 61614

Myron Genel

Title: Pediatrician, Educator **Industry:** Education/Educational Services **Company Name:** Yale University **Date of Birth:** 01/06/1936 **Place of Birth:** York **State/Country of Origin:** PA **Parents:** Victor Genel; Florence (Mowitz) Genel **Marital Status:** Married **Spouse Name:** Phyllis Norma Berkman (8/25/1968) **Children:** Elizabeth; Jennifer; Abby **Education:** Honorary DSc, Moravian College, Bethlehem, PA (1995); Honorary MA, Yale University, New Haven, CT (1983); Resident in Pediatrics, Children's Hospital, Philadelphia, PA (1962-1964); Intern, Mount Sinai Hospital, New York, NY (1961-1962); MD, University of Pennsylvania (1961); BS, Moravian College, Bethlehem, PA (1957) **Certifications:** Diplomate, American Board of Pediatrics **Career:** Professor Emeritus, Senior Research Scientist, School of Medicine, Yale University, New Haven, CT (2004-Present); Faculty, School of Medicine, Yale University, New Haven, CT (1971-Present); Associate Dean, Director of Office of Government and Community Affairs, School of Medicine, Yale University, New Haven, CT (1985-2004); Robert Wood Johnson Health Policy Fellow, Institute of Medicine, National Academy of Sciences, Washington, DC (1982-1983); Professor, School of Medicine, Yale University, New Haven, CT (1981-2004); Attending Physician, Yale-New Haven Hospital (1971-2015); Program Director, Children's Clinical Research Center, School of Medicine, Yale University, New Haven, CT (1971-1986); Director of Pediatrics Endocrinology, School of Medicine, Yale University, New Haven, CT (1971-1985); Associate Physician, Children's Hospital, Philadelphia, PA (1969-1971); Associate in Pediatrics, School of Medicine, University of Pennsylvania (1969-1971); Trainee in Genetics, Inherited Metabolic Diseases, Children's Hospital of Philadelphia (1967-1969); Instructor of Pediatrics, School of Medicine, University of Pennsylvania (1967-1969); Trainee, Pediatrics Endocrinology, Johns Hopkins Hospital, Baltimore, MD (1966-1967) **Career Related:** Connecticut Commission on Women, Children and Seniors (2016-Present); Consultant, International Olympic Committee, Medical and Scientific Commission (2004-Present); C Genetic Advisory Board (1994-Present); Connecticut Commission on Children (2015-2016); Children's Mental Health Task Forces, Connecticut General Assembly (2013-2014); Secretary, Advisory Committee on Human Research Protections (2006-2009); Connecticut Stem Cell Advisory Committee, State of Connecticut (2005-2013); Federal Advisory Committee, National Children's Study, National Institute of Child Health and Development, National Institutes of Health (2005-2009); Clinical Research Round Table, Institute of Medicine, National Research Council (2000-2004); Consultant, Greenwich Hospital, Norwalk Hospital, Milford Hospital; Advisory Board, New England Congenital Hypothyroidism Collaborative **Civic:** Board of Directors, Stepping Stones Museum for Children (2017-Present); Children's Mental Health Task Force, Connecticut General Assembly (2013-2014) **Military Service:** Captain, U.S. Army Reserve (1964-1966) **Awards:** Distinguished Service Award, Connecticut Academy of Sciences and Engineering (2017); Stepping Up for Children Award, Stepping Stones Museum Children, Norwalk, CT (2012); President's Award, American Academy of Pediatrics (2011); Joseph W. St. Geme Leadership Award, Federation of Pediatrics Organizations (2004); Distinguished Service Award, Society of Pediatrics Research (2003) **Membership:** Medical Schools Secretary, Academic Physicians Section, American Medical Association (1985-Present); Executive Editor, Medicine, Bulletin of the Connecticut Academy of Science and Engineering (2016); President, Connecticut Academy of Science and Engineering (2008-2010); Vice President, President-Elect, Connecticut Academy of Science and Engineering (2006-2008); Distinguished Service Member, Association of American Medical Colleges (2005); Board of Governors, New Haven County of Medical Association (2004-2011); Chair, American Medical Association (2003-2004); Government Affairs Committee, Endocrine Society (2002-2005); Council, Connecticut Academy of Science and Engineering (2000); Advisory Panel on Research, Association of American Medical Colleges (1999-2003); Delegate, American Medical Association (1998-2002); American Pediatrics Society; American Federation of Medical Research; American Diabetes Association; American College of Preventative Medicine; American College of Nutrition; American Association of Clinical Endocrinologists; Task Force of Organ Transplants, American Academy of Pediatrics; Committee on Federal Government Affairs, American Academy of Pediatrics; American Association for the Advancement of Science; American College of Sports Medicine; American Public Health Association; Society of Clinical and Transnational Sciences; Association of Patient Oriented Research; New York Academy of Medicine **Marquis Who's Who Honors:** Albert Nelson Marquis Lifetime Achievement Award (2017) **Religion:** Jewish **Shipping Address:** 30 Richard Sweet Drive, Woodbridge, CT, 06525

Monica F. Gerard-Sharp

Title: President **Industry:** Media & Entertainment **Company Name:** Dandomar LLC **Date of Birth:** 10/04/1951 **Place of Birth:** London **State/Country of Origin:** England **Parents:** John Hugh Gerard-Sharp, Doreen May (Kearney) Dewhurst **Marital Status:** Married **Spouse Name:** Ali Edward Wambold (11/21/1981) **Children:** Marina; Daniela; Dominica **Education:** MBA in Finance, Marketing and International Business, Columbia University (1980); BA in Philosophy and Literature, The University of Warwick, With Honors (1973) **Career:** President, Dandomar Company, LLC (2010-Present); President, Wambold Farm (2008-Present); President, Monali Media, LLC (1991-Present); Publisher, Home Fashions Magazines (1988-1990); Director, Video Programming, Fairchild Publications, Inc., Capital Cities/ABC (1988-1989); Publisher, Travel Toda, Fairchild Publications, Inc. (1987-1988); Assistant Treasurer, Time Inc. (1985-1987); Officer, Time Inc. (1985-1987); Director of Strategy and Development, Home Box Office, Inc., ATC (Now Time Warner Inc.) (1984-1985); Vice President, T.V.I.S. (1982-1983); Financial Analysis Manager, Time Life (1981); Business Manager, Time Life (1980-1981); Press Officer, Editor, United Nations (1975-1978); Sub-Editor, TV Times (1974-1975); Editor, Institution of Chemical Engineers (1973-1974) **Career Related:** Consultant, Business Council for the United Nations, United Nations Foundation (1979); Board Representative, The USA Network, NBCUniversal, Inc. (1983-1985) **Civic:** Board Member, Executive Committee, Theatre for a New Audience (2007-Present); Board Member, Round Hill Development Corporation (2006-Present); American Associates of the National Theatre (2006-Present); Member, Advisory Board, American Museum of Natural History (1998-Present); Historic Royal Palaces (2005); President, Chances for Children-NY (2001-2003); Member, National Development Board, Chances for Children-NY (1995-2003); Founding President, Board Member, American Friends of Royal Court Theatre (1998-2002); Treasurer, Richmond Theatre (1992-1995); Treasurer, Help the Aged (Now Age UK Group) **Creative Works:** Editor, "Everyone's United Nations" (1977); Contributing Editor, Asia Pacific Forum (1976-1977); Article Contributor, Professional Journals and Magazines (1973-1978) **Awards:** Fellow, The Bronfman Fellowships (1979-1980) **Membership:** Beta Gamma Sigma, Inc. **Marquis Who's Who Honors:** Distinguished Humanitarian (2017) **Hobbies:** Theater; Conservation **Religion:** Roman Catholic **Business Address:** 128 Sunset Hill Rd, Pleasant Valley, NY, 12569 **Shipping Address:** 1 Sutton Pl S, New York, NY, 10022

Linda Ann Gerdner, PhD

Title: Consulting Assistant Professor **Industry:** Education/Educational Services **Company Name:** Stanford Geriatric Education Center **Date of Birth:** 09/17/1955 **Place of Birth:** Burlington **State/Country of Origin:** IA **Parents:** Richard Paul Gerdner; Edna Marie Gerdner **Education:** Mini-Fellowship, Ethnogeriatrics, Stanford Geriatric Education Center, Stanford University, Palo Alto, CA (2004-2006); Postdoctoral Fellow, Faculty, Department of Psychiatry, Veterans Affairs Medical Center, Division of Health Services Research and Development, Center for Mental Healthcare and Outcomes Research, University of Arkansas for Medical Sciences, Little Rock, AR (1998-2000); PhD in Nursing in Aging, University of Iowa (1998); Predoctoral Fellow, College of Nursing, University of Iowa (1996-1998); AARP Andrus Foundation Graduate Fellow in Gerontology, Association Gerontology in Higher Education (1996-1997); MSN, University of Iowa (1992); BSN, Iowa Wesleyan College (Now Iowa Wesleyan University) (1980); ADN, Southeastern Community College, Burlington, IA (1977); AA in Liberal Arts, Southeastern Community College, Burlington, IA (1975) **Certifications:** Registered Nurse, Iowa, Arkansas, and Minnesota **Career:** Assistant Director, Geriatric Education Center, Stanford University, Palo Alto, CA (2007-Present); Assistant Professor, Adjunct Faculty, College of Nursing, University of Iowa, Iowa City, IA (2006-2013); Assistant Professor, School of Nursing, University of Minnesota (2001-2007); Assistant Professor, Center for Spirituality and Healing, School of Nursing, University of Minnesota (2001-2007); Instructor, Department of Psychiatry and Behavioral Sciences, University of Arkansas for Medical Sciences, Little Rock, AR (1998-2000); Project Director, National Caregiver Training Project, College of Nursing, University of Iowa (1992-1997); Nursing Instructor, Division of Nursing, Grand View College (Now Grand View University), Des Moines, IA (1992-1993); Research Assistant, College of Nursing, University of Iowa, Iowa City, IA (1991-1993); Staff Nurse, College of Nursing, University of Iowa, Iowa City, IA (1990); Teaching Assistant, College of Nursing, University of Iowa, Iowa City, IA (1989-1992); Director of Nursing, Elm View Care Center, Burlington, IA (1988-1989); Staff Development Coordinator, Elm View Care Center, Burlington, IA (1985-1988); Clinical Instructor, Keokuk Campus, Southeastern Community College, Keokuk, IA (1983-1985); Clinical Instructor, Iowa Wesleyan College (Now Iowa Wesleyan University), Mount Pleasant, IA (1981-1983); Night Supervisor, Burlington Medical Center, Burlington, IA (1980-1981); Staff Nurse, Burlington Medical Center, Burlington, IA (1977-1979) **Career Related:** Visiting Professor, School of Medicine, University of California, Davis, Sacramento, CA (2017); Visiting Professor, Center for Gerontology Research and Partnerships and Center for Asian American Studies, University of Massachusetts, Lowell, MA (2016); Visiting Professor, Change the Conversation, Change the World Series, Framingham State University, Framingham, MA (2016); Visiting Professor, NURS 420 Nursing Theory, Framingham State University, Framingham, MA (2016) **Creative Works:** Nursing Research (2003-Present); Alzheimer's Disease and Related Disorders (2002-Present); International Psychogeriatrics (2002-Present); International Journal of Geriatric Psychiatry (2000-Present); Journal of Gerontological Nursing (1999-Present); Western Journal of Nursing Research (1998-Present); Referee Panel, Clinical Nursing Research (1997-Present) **Awards:** Albert Nelson Marquis Lifetime Achievement Award (2017); Distinguished Alumni Award at Iowa Wesleyan College (Now Iowa Wesleyan University), Mount Pleasant, IA (2013); Skipping Stones Honor Award, Multicultural & International Awareness Category (2009); CCBC Choices, Picture Books for School Age Children, "Grandfather's Story Cloth" (2009); Best-of-the-Year List of the Cooperative Children's Book Center, University of Wisconsin, Madison, WI (2009); Notable Children's Trade Book in the Field of Social Studies, National Council for Social Studies in Cooperation with the Children's Book Council (2009); Mom's Choice Award, Gold Medal, Children's Picture Book Category, Health and Safety (2009); ForeWord Magazine Book of the Year Award Winner (INDIEFAB Award), Gold Medal, Children's Picture Book Category (2008); Moonbeam Children's Book Award, Silver Medal, Health Issues Category (2008) **Membership:** Nurses Special Interest Group, International Psychogeriatric Association (2003-Present); Scientific Advisory Committee, International Psychogeriatric Association (2001-Present); Affiliate Member, American Association for Geriatric Psychiatry (2001-Present); Task Force on Behavioral and Psychological Symptoms of Dementia, International Psychogeriatric Association (1999-Present); Midwest Nursing Research Society (1993-Present); The American Nurses Association, Inc. (1992-Present) **Marquis Who's Who Honors:** Albert Nelson Marquis Lifetime Achievement Award (2017) **Shipping Address:** 1304 Lynnwood Drive, Burlington, IA, 52601

John Frederick Geweke, PhD

Title: Economics Professor **Industry:** Education/Educational Services **Company Name:** University of Iowa **Date of Birth:** 05/11/1948 **Place of Birth:** Washington **State:** DC **Parents:** Robert William Geweke; Winnifred Lois (Quies) Geweke **Marital Status:** Married **Spouse Name:** Lynne Marie Osborn (8/22/1970) **Children:** Andrew Robert **Education:** PhD, University of Minnesota (1975); BS, Michigan State University (1970) **Career:** Senior Principle Economist, Amazon (2016-Present); Distinguished Research Professor, University of Technology, Sydney, Australia (2009-2016); McGregor Chair in Economics & Statistics, University of Iowa (1999-2009); Professor, University of Minnesota, Minneapolis, MN (1990-1999); Director, Abel Rodriguez Institute of Statistics and Decision Sciences, Duke University, Durham, NC (1987-1990); William R. Kenan Junior Professor, Duke University, Durham, NC (1986-1990); Professor, Duke University, Durham, NC (1983-1986); Professor, University of Wisconsin-Madison (1982-1983); Associate Professor, University of Wisconsin-Madison (1979-1982); Assistant Professor, University of Wisconsin-Madison (1975-1979) **Career Related:** Research Fellow, Alfred P. Sloan Foundation, New York, NY (1982); Fellow, The Econometric Society **Creative Works:** Co-Editor, Journal of Econometrics, Elsevier B.V. (2003-Present); Associate Editor, Econometrica, The Econometric Society (1995-2002); Co-Editor, Journal of Applied Econometrics, John Wiley & Sons Ltd (1993-2002); Editor, Journal of Business & Economic Statistics, American Statistical Society (1989-1992); Associate Editor, Econometrica, The Econometric Society (1984-1988) **Membership:** President, International Society for Bayesian Analysis (1999); American Statistical Association; American Economic Association **Marquis Who's Who Honors:** Albert Nelson Marquis Lifetime Achievement Award (2017) **Hobbies:** International traveling; Hiking **Shipping Address:** 3027 Carriage Drive, Estes Park, CO, 80517

Corrado Anthony Giacona II

Title: President, Chief Executive Officer **Industry:** Business Management/Business Services **Company Name:** Giacona Container Company **Date of Birth:** 12/14/1942 **Place of Birth:** New Orleans **State:** LA **Parents:** Louis Joseph Giacona; Claire (LaRocca) Giacona **Marital Status:** Married **Spouse Name:** Patricia Ellen Nunez (7/25/1964) **Children:** Gina Lisa; Corrado Anthony; Louis **Education:** BA, University of New Orleans (1965) **Career:** President, Giacona Container Division, Giacona Group, New Orleans, LA (1972-Present); Territorial Manager, Ross Laboratories, New Orleans, LA (1964-1972); Plant Manager, Amos C. Harris Can Company, New Orleans, LA (1962-1964) **Civic:** Member, University of New Orleans Business and Higher Education Council; Board of Directors, President, Louisiana Maritime Museum; Board of Directors, Louisiana Science Center; Board of Directors, Family Services of Louisiana; Board of Directors, New Orleans Convention and Visiting Bureau; Officer, Krewe of Alla; Board of Directors, World Trade Center, New Orleans, LA; Chairman, International Business Committee; Advisory Board, Tulane Medical School **Awards:** Named, One of the 300 for the 300 "People & Moments that Inspire & Connect Us" for having created the Mardi Gras Throw Cups™ Times-Picayune **Membership:** Knights of Columbus; Board of Directors, New Orleans Convention and Visiting Bureau; Timberlane Country Club; Phi Kappa Theta; President, Louisiana Italian American Society **Marquis Who's Who Honors:** Albert Nelson Marquis Lifetime Achievement Award (2017) **Why did you become involved in your profession or industry:** Mr. Giacona became involved in the container industry when father purchased the Giacona Group in 1952. **Hobbies:** Spending time with his grandchildren **Political Affiliations:** Republican **Religion:** Roman Catholic **Business Address:** 121 Industrial Ave, New Orleans, LA, 70121 **Shipping Address:** 121 Industrial Ave, Louis Giacona Advertising LLC, New Orleans, LA, 70121

Steven L. Giannotta

Title: Neurosurgery Professor, Chairman of Neurological Surgery **Industry:** Education/Educational Services **Company Name:** University of Southern California **Date of Birth:** 04/04/1947 **Place of Birth:** Detroit **State:** MI **Parents:** Louis D. Giannotta; Betty Jane (Root) Giannotta **Marital Status:** Married **Spouse Name:** Sharon Danielak (6/13/1970) **Children:** Brent; Nicole; Robyn **Education:** Resident in Neurosurgery, University of Michigan, Ann Arbor, MI (1973-1978); Surgical Intern, University of Michigan, Ann Arbor, MI (1972-1973); MD, University of Michigan (1972); Coursework, University of Detroit Mercy (1965-1968) **Certifications:** Board Certified, American Board of Neurological Surgery (1980) **Career:** Chairman, Neurosurgery Department, University of Southern California (2004-Present); Professor of Neurosurgery, Keck School of Medicine, University of Southern California (1989-Present); Associate Professor of Neurosurgery, Keck School of Medicine, University of Southern California (1983-1989); Assistant Professor, Neurosurgery, Keck School of Medicine, University of Southern California (1980-1983); Assistant Professor of Neurosurgery, University of California, Los Angeles (1978-1980) **Career Related:** Chairman, American Board of Neurological Surgery (2000-2001); Secretary, American Board of Neurological Surgery (1999-2000); Board of Directors, American Board of Neurological Surgery (1995-2001) **Awards:** America's Top Doctors in Neurological Surgery, Castle Connolly (2015); America's Top Doctors for Cancer, Castle Connolly (2014-2015); America's Top Doctors, One of America's Leading Experts on Brain Cancer, Craniotomy, Intracranial Aneurysm, Meningioma, Radiosurgery and Transient Ischemic Attack, Castle Connolly (2011); Top Doctor, Pasadena Magazine (2011); America's Top Doctors, Castle Connolly (2010-2015); America's Top Doctors for Cancer, Castle Connolly (2009-2012); America's Top Doctors for Cancer, Castle Connolly (2005-2007); Distinguished Service Award, Joint Section on Cerebrovascular Surgery, AANS/CNS (2004); America's Top Doctors, Castle Connolly (2002-2008); Distinguished Service Award, Congress of Neurological Surgeons (1995); Research Grantee, American Heart Association (1984); Research Grantee, American Heart Association (1980); Fellow, American College of Surgeons; Alpha Epsilon Delta; Phi Chi Medical Fraternity **Membership:** Board of Directors, American Association of Neurological Surgeons (2001-Present); President, Southern California Neurological Society (1993-1994); Vice President, Congress of Neurological Surgeons (1993); President, Los Angeles Region, Society of Clinical Neurosciences (1992-1993); Secretary, Congress of Neurological Surgeons (1986-1989); American Heart Association; Fellow, American College of Surgeons **Marquis Who's Who Honors:** Albert Nelson Marquis Lifetime Achievement Award (2017); Distinguished Humanitarian (2017) **Why did you become involved in your profession or industry:** Dr. Giannotta became involved in his profession after originally deciding to become a mechanical and automotive engineer. After taking a class on the Freudian method of psychoanalysis, he changed his mind and decided he wanted to be a physician. **Where will you be in five years:** In five years, Dr. Giannotta intends to maintain and build the acoustic neuroma aspect of the practice and surgeries. Moving forward, he plans to focus on two sub-specialties. **Hobbies:** Golf; Skiing; Sports cars **Political Affiliations:** Democrat **Religion:** Roman Catholic **Business Address:** 1200 N. State Street, Room 3300, Los Angeles, CA, 90033 **Shipping Address:** 1520 San Pablo Street, Suite 3800, USC Neurological Surgery, Los Angeles, CA, 90033 **Website:** http://www.stevengiannottamd.com

Roberta C. Gibson Pevear

Title: State Legislator **Industry:** Civil Service **Date of Birth:** 07/04/1930 **Place of Birth:** Bethel **State/Country of Origin:** MA **Parents:** Frank Albert Gibson Sr.; Thirza Estella (Hickford) Gibson **Marital Status:** Widowed **Spouse Name:** Edward Gordon Pevear (8/21/1971) **Education:** Diploma in Commercial Art, Gould Academy (1947) **Career:** Retired (1988); Member, New Hampshire House of Representatives (1979-1988); Salesman, Avon Products, Hampton Falls, NH (1978-1986); Secretary and Administrative Assistant, Sears Brands, LLC, Exeter, NH (1971-1977); Secretary, Sears Brands, LLC, Overland Park, KS (1967-1970); Administrative Assistant, Sears Brands, LLC, Overland Park, KS (1967-1970); Legal Secretary, St. John, Ronder & Bell, Kingston, NY (1966); Legal Secretary, Johnson & Johnson, New Brunswick, NJ (1960-1965); Secretary, Anheuser-Busch Companies, LLC, Kansas City, MO (1957-1959); Secretary, Export Department, Whitaker Cable, North Kansas City, MO (1951-1956); Secretary, Wilner Wood Products, South Paris, ME (1947-1950) **Career Related:** Chairman, Rockingham County Nursing Home, Rockingham County, NH (1987-1988); Member, New Hampshire Planning Committee (1985-1988); Member, Executive Board, Rockingham County Home (1984-1988); Clerk, Environment and Agricultural Committee, New Hampshire House of Representatives (1983-1988); Member, Delegation, Rockingham County, NH (1979-1988); Commissioner, Rockingham Planning Commission, Rockingham County, NH (1979-1988); Member, Advisory Board, Vet. Family Pl. Island **Civic:** Director, Civil Defense, Hampton Falls, NH (1980-1988); Board of Directors, Lifewise Community Projects, Inc., Hampton, NH; Board of Directors, Transportation Assistance for Seacoast Citizens, Hampton, NH **Creative Works:** Co-Editor, "Write Quick: War And A Woman's Life in Letters, 1835-1867" **Awards:** Named Inspirational Woman of the Year, Women's Radio Network (2014); Woman of the Year Award, National Association of Professional Women (2013); Seacoast Retired Senior Service Award (1985); Community Citizen Award, Hampton Falls Grange (1982) **Membership:** Historical Secretary, Exeter Sportsman's Club (2012-Present); National Order of Women Legislators; New Hampshire Order of Women Legislators; Daughters of the American Revolution; Board of Directors, Exeter Sportsman's Club; National Association of Professional Women **Marquis Who's Who Honors:** Albert Nelson Marquis Lifetime Achievement Award (2017); Distinguished Humanitarian (2017) **What do you consider to be the highlight of your career:** The highlight of Ms. Gibson Pevear's career was being instrumental in crafting an evacuation plan for a nuclear power plant in New Hampshire and being featured in May's issue of American Legion Auxiliary Magazine. **Hobbies:** Writing; Portrait painting; Genealogy **Shipping Address:** 7 Riverwoods Dr Apt D125, Exeter, NH, 03833

Robert Gilkeson

Title: Vice Chairman of Radiology **Industry:** Medicine & Health Care **Company Name:** University Hospitals **Place of Birth:** Cleveland **State/Country of Origin:** OH **Marital Status:** Single **Children:** William; Katherine **Education:** Fellow in Throacic Imaging, Duke University Health System (1996); Resident in Diagnostic Radiology, Duke University Health System (1995); Resident in Diagnostic Radiology, University Hospitals, Cleveland, OH (1992); Intern, University Hospitals, Cleveland, OH (1990); MD, Case Western Reserve University (1989); BA in Art History, Princeton University (1981) **Certifications:** Medical License, State of Ohio (1998-Present); Medical License, State of North Carolina (1993-1996); Diplomate, American Board of Radiology (1985) **Career:** Professor of Radiology, Case Western Reserve University School of Medicine (2009-Present); Section Head, Thoracic Radiology, University Hospitals of Cleveland (1998-Present); Present Staff, Department of Radiology, University Hospitals of Cleveland (1996-Present); Research Assistant, Department of Neurosurgery, Massachusetts General Hospital, Boston, MA (1981-1984) **Career Related:** Visiting Professor, University of Colorado (2010); Visiting Professor, Pendergrass Lecturer, Vanderbilt University Medical Center (2010); Visiting Professor, Samedan Spital, St.Moritz, Switzerland (2010); Visiting Professor, University of Utah (2009); Visiting Professor, The Ohio State University (2006); Visiting Professor, University of New Mexico (2006); Visiting Professor, The University of Utah (2006); Visiting Professor, Ochsner Clinic (2004); Visiting Professor, University of Maryland (2003); Visiting Professor, University of South Carolina (2003); Visiting Professor, The University of Utah (2001); Fremantiz Visiting Professorship, Michigan State University (2000) **Creative Works:** Cardiac Section Editor, Radiographics (2014); Journal Reviewer, American Journal of Radiology; Journal Reviewer, Respiratory Care; Journal Reviewer, RadioGraphics; Associate Editor, RadioGraphics; Editorial Board, Journal of Thoracic Radiology; Journal Reviewer, Academic Radiology; Journal Reviewer, Society of Cardiac Computed Tomography; Contributor, Articles, Professional Journals **Awards:** Best Doctors (2002-Present); Teacher of the Year (2017); Best Doctors, Cleveland Magazine (2017); Honoree, Top Doctors, Castle Connolly Medical Ltd. (2016); Best Doctors, Cleveland Magazine (2016); Best Doctors, Cleveland Magazine (2015); Best Doctors, Cleveland Magazine (2014); America's Top Doctors, U.S. News and World Report (2013); Best Doctors, Cleveland Magazine (2013); America's Top Doctors, U.S. News and World Report (2012); Best Doctors (2012); America's Top Doctors, U.S. News and World Report (2011); Teacher of the Year (2001); Marconi Award for Technical Innovation (2000); Recipient, Marconi Award in Technical Innovation (1998); Honoree, Top Doctor, Cleveland Magazine; Honoree, Distinguished Doctor Expert Network; Alpha Omega Alpha Medical Honor Society; Noether Memorial Commencement Award in Clinical Therapies **Membership:** American Roentgen Ray Society; Radiological Society of North America; American College of Radiology; Senior Member, Society of Thoracic Radiology; Society of Cardiac Computed Tomography **To what do you attribute your success:** He attributes his success to identifying the importance of future discovery. **Why did you become involved in your profession or industry:** He has always been a visual learner, and his profession is a visual one. His ability to diagnose from a purely visual standpoint is what gives him an edge in the field. **Hobbies:** Golf; Working out; Art; Museums; Travel **Business Address:** 11100 Euclid Ave, Cleveland, OH, 44106 **Shipping Address:** 2520 Wellington Rd, Cleveland Heights, OH, 44118-4119 **Website:** https://www.uhhospitals.org/find-a-doctor/gilkeson-r-482-11#top

Anne Whalen Gill

Title: Lawyer **Industry:** Law and Legal Services **Company Name:** Gill & Ledbetter, LLP **Date of Birth:** 10/28/1948 **Place of Birth:** Greenwich **State/Country of Origin:** CT **Parents:** John James Whalen; Mary Jane (Stallcup) Whalen **Marital Status:** Married **Spouse Name:** David Masser Gill (5/27/1972) **Education:** JD, New York Law School (1979); Postgraduate Coursework, The City University of New York (1969-1971); BS, Dickinson College (1969) **Career:** Lawyer, Gill & Ledbetter LLP (2000-Present); Staff Attorney, Colorado Court of Appeals, Colorado Judicial Branch (1988-2000); Law Editor, Wiley Law Publications, John Wiley & Sons, Inc. (1986-1988); Senior Editor, Shepard's McGraw Hill (1985-1986); Attorney, Manville, Denver, CO (1984-1985); Attorney, New York Law Journal (1980-1984); Editor, New York Law Journal (1980-1984); Lawyer, Sole Practice, New York City, NY (1979-1980) **Career Related:** Member, Committee on the Colorado Appellate Rules, Colorado Supreme Court **Civic:** Assistant District Captain, Douglas County Republican Party (2004-Present); Chairman, Zoning Planning Committee, HOA-USA, Inc. (1987); Member, Citizens Budget Committee, Douglas County School District (1987); Founder, Jarre Canyon Protective Association, Sedalia, CO (1985-1988); Secretary, Bloomingdale Republican's Club (1983); Volunteer, TAPS; Speaker, Continued Education Seminars; Precinct Committeeman, Douglas County Republican Party **Creative Works:** Editor, "Colorado Shooting" (2002-Present); Co-Author, "Colorado Appellate Law and Practice" (1999); Contributing Author, "Wiley Employment Law Update, Bankruptcy and Divorce Law" (1992); Editor, "New York Law Journal Digest" (1981-1984); Contributor, Articles to Professional Journals; Contributor, "Practitioner's Guide to Domestic Relations" **Awards:** Honoree, Super Lawyers (2016-Present); Honoree, Top Lawyer in Appeals, 52 Magazine (2013-Present); Honoree, People's Choice Appellate Lawyer for the State, Colorado Law Week (2016); Rated 5.0/5, Martindale-Hubbell; Recipient, Tony David Volunteer of the Year Award **Membership:** Chair, Appellate Practice Subcommittee of Litigation Section, Colorado Bar Association (2000-2008); Executive Counsel, Colorado Bar Association; Denver Bar Association; Douglas Elbert Bar Association; Executive Counsel, Family Law Section **Bar Admissions:** United States Court of Appeals for the Tenth Circuit (2000); United States District Court for the District of Colorado (2000); Colorado (1985); United States District Court for the Southern District of New York (1981); New York (1980) **Marquis Who's Who Honors:** Albert Nelson Marquis Lifetime Achievement Award (2017) **Shipping Address:** 510 Wilcox Street, Suite C, Gill & Ledbetter, LLP, Castle Rock, CO, 80104 **Website:** https://coloradoappeals.com

Sid Gilman

Title: Neurologist **Industry:** Education/Educational Services **Company Name:** Hope Clinic **Date of Birth:** 10/19/1932 **Place of Birth:** Los Angeles **State/Country of Origin:** CA **Parents:** Morris Gilman; Sarah Rose (Cooper) Gilman **Marital Status:** Married **Spouse Name:** Carol G. Barbour **Education:** FRCP (2001); MD (1957); BA, University of California, Los Angeles (1954) **Career:** William J. Herdman Distinguished University Professor of Neurology, University of Michigan (2005-2012); William J. Herdman Professor of Neurology, University of Michigan (1997-2005); Professor, Chair, Department of Neurology, University of Michigan, Ann Arbor, MI (1977-2004); H. Houston Merritt Professor of Neurology, Columbia University, New York, NY (1976-1977); Assistant Professor, Professor of Neurology, Columbia University, New York, NY (1968-1976); Instructor, Associate in Neurology, Harvard Medical School (1965-1968); Resident in Neurology, Boston City Hospital (1960-1963); Intern, University of California, Los Angeles Hospital (1957-1958) **Career Related:** PPD Development (1999-Present); Consultant, VA Hospital, Ann Arbor, MI (1977-Present); Associate Director, Michigan Alzheimer's Disease Research Center (2011); Clinical Trials Subcommittee, National Advisory Neurological Disorders and Stroke Council (2001-2004); Henry Russel Lecturer, University of Michigan (2001); Research Advisory Committee, Dana Alliance; Science Advisory Board, Merck, Inc. (2000-2004); INC Research (2000); Consultant, Peripheral and Central Nervous System Drugs Advisory Committee, Food and Drug Administration (2000); Chairman, Peripheral and Central Nervous System Drugs Advisory Committee, Food and Drug Administration (1996-2000); National Advisory Neurological Disorders and Stroke Council (1994-1997); Director, Michigan Alzheimer's Disease Research Center (1991-2011); Peripheral and Central Nervous System Drugs Advisory Committee, Food and Drug Administration (1990-1994); Executive Board, National Coalition for Research (1989-1995); National Foundation for Brain Research (1989-1995); Detroit Member, Chronic Disease Advisory Committee, Michigan Department Public Health (1988-1994); Research Advisory Committee, National Multiple Sclerosis Society (1986-1990); Peripheral and Central Nervous System Drugs Advisory Committee, Food and Drug Administration (1983-1987); Science Programs Advisory Committee, National Institute Diseases, Communicative Disorders and Stroke (1982-1984); Project B Committee, Neurological Disorders Program (1976-1980); Neurological Science Research and Training Committee, National Institutes of Health (1971-1973); Adjunct Attending Neurologist, Henry Ford Hospital; Research Advisory Council, United Cerebral Palsy Foundation; Science Advisory Council, National Ataxia Foundation; National Amyotrophic Lateral Sclerosis Foundation, Inc.; Professional Advisory Board, Epilepsy Foundation of America **Civic:** U.S. Public Health Service (1958-1960) **Creative Works:** Experimental Neurology (2003-Present); Contemporary Neurology Series (1995-Present); "Oxford America Handbook of Neurology" (2010); Editor, "Neurobiology of Disease" (2007); Neurobiology of Disease (2005-2010); Co-Author, "Manter and Gatz's Essentials of Clinical Neuroanatomy and Neurophysiology," Tenth Edition (2003); Lancet Neurology Network (2000-2002); Author, "Clinical Examination of the Nervous System" (2000); Neurology Network Commentary (1996-2000); Co-Author, "Clinical Brain Imaging: Principles and Applications" (1992); Editor-in-Chief, MedLink Neurology (1992) **Awards:** A.B. Baker Award, American Academy of Neurology (2004); University of California, Los Angeles Alumni Professional Achievement Award (1992); University of California, Los Angeles Medical Alumni Professional Achievement Award (1992); Weinstein Goldenson Award, United Cerebral Palsy Association (1981); Lucy G. Moses Prize, Columbia University (1973) **Membership:** Vice Chairman, Geriatric Neurology Subcommittee, American Academy of Neurology (1992-1994); Chairman, Decade of Brain Committee, American Academy of Neurology (1990-1995); President, American Neurological Association (1988-1989); President-Elect, American Neurological Association (1987-1988); President, Michigan Neurological Association (1987-1988); First Vice President, American Neurological Association (1985-1986); Society of Clinical Investigation; American Physiological Society; American Association of Neuropathologists; Society of Neuroscientists; American Epilepsy Society; Association for Research in Nervous and Mental Diseases; Association of American Physicians; Institute of Medicine **Marquis Who's Who Honors:** Albert Nelson Marquis Lifetime Achievement Award (2017) **Business Address:** 518 Harriet Street, Ypsilanti, MI, 48197 **Shipping Address:** 3411 Geddes Road, Ann Arbor, MI, 48105

Nella Sue Girolo

Title: Voice Educator (Retired) **Industry:** Education/Educational Services **Company Name:** Cuesta College Foundation **Date of Birth:** 08/21/1938 **Place of Birth:** Newton **State/Country of Origin:** IA **Parents:** Dorman Daane; Clara Winifred Hundling **Marital Status:** Married **Spouse Name:** Patrick C. Murphy **Children:** Janella Wilimek Ingle; James Powell Wilimek II **Education:** Coursework, University of California, Irvine (1976); Coursework, Music Academy of the West (1973); Master, Drake University (1964); MusB, Drake University (1960) **Certifications:** Certified Elementary Teacher; Certified Secondary School Educator **Career:** Vice President, Cuesta College Foundation (2010-2015); Chairman, Performing Arts, Cuesta College (1996-2003); Drama, Music Coordinator, Cuesta College (1993-1996); Voice and Theater Instructor, Cuesta College, San Luis Obispo, CA (1972-2003); Assistant Voice Professor, Iowa State University (1966-1970); Music Instructor, Johnston High School (1960-1963) **Career Related:** Board Member, Women of Distinction (2013-Present); Board Member, Women's Legacy Fund (2006-Present); Alumni Advisory Board, Cuesta College (1986-Present); Advisory Board, Pacific Repertory Opera, San Luis Obispo, CA (1986-1989); President, Central Coast Music Teachers, San Luis Obispo (1975-1976) **Civic:** Special Events Coordinator, Cuesta College Foundation (1998-Present); Board Member, Cuesta College Foundation (1990-Present); Vice President, Cuesta College Foundation (2010-2015); Co-Chair, Grant Reviewer, Women's Legacy Fund (2007-2009); Co-Chair, Grant Reviewer, Women's Legacy Fund (2005); Board Member, Project Theatre Foundation, Paso Robles (2003-2006) **Creative Works:** Author, "Plain and Fancy" (1999); Author, "Grandma's Recipe Album" (1995); Author, "Uncommon Letters from a Common Man" (1993); Performer, Concerts, Operas and Musicals (1960-1987); Author, "The Wonderful Adventures of Rosie Posie and Kishkekosh" **Awards:** Volunteer of the Year, Cuesta College Foundation (2009); Layperson of the Year, Phi Delta Kappa (2006); Outstanding Volunteer, Board Member of the Year, Equal Opportunity Commission (2003); Outstanding Academy Employee, Cuesta College Foundation (1997); Outstanding Kappa of the Year, Drake University (1959-1960) **Membership:** Board Member, Woman's Legacy Fund (2006-Present); National Association of Teachers of Singing, Inc. (1967-Present); Secretary, Kappa Kappa Gamma (1990-2013); American Association of University Women **Marquis Who's Who Honors:** Albert Nelson Marquis Lifetime Achievement Award (2017) **Why did you become involved in your profession or industry:** She became involved in her profession because she comes from a legacy of performers. Her father played the clarinet and was a leader of his family orchestra. He played in silent films. Her uncle toured the country on the Big Band Circuit and played with Charlie Barnet. Nella played piano at the age of four, then played in the orchestra in high school, before moving on to voice in her college years. She toured the country, and participated in the theater. **What do you consider to be the highlight of your career:** One of her shining achievements was performing seven concerts for Aaron Copland. **Hobbies:** Gourmet Cooking; Writing; Swimming **Shipping Address:** 1374 Shane Ln, Templeton, CA, 93465

David L. Glass

Title: Division Director **Industry:** Law and Legal Services **Company Name:** Macquarie Group Ltd. **Date of Birth:** 09/22/1947 **Place of Birth:** Brooklyn **State/Country of Origin:** NY **Parents:** Benjamin Glass (Deceased 1991); Gertrude Glass (Deceased 2008) **Marital Status:** Married **Spouse Name:** Arlene Jackie Glass (nee Henkin) **Children:** Andrew L. Glass **Education:** JD, Fordham University Law School (1979); MBA, Stanford University (1972); BA, Amherst College (1968) **Career:** Division Director, Macquarie Group Ltd. (2009-Present); Head of Compliance for the Americas, Macquarie Group Ltd. (2006-2009); Counsel, Rogers & Wells/Clifford Chance (1997-2006); General Counsel, New York Bankers Association (1990-1997); Partner, Hawkins, Delafield & Wood (1988-1990); Associate, Debevoise & Plimpton (1983-1988); Attorney, Assistant to the President, Federal Reserve Bank of New York (1974-1983); Chief of Credit Analysis Division, Federal Reserve Bank of New York **Career Related:** Chair, New York State Bar Association Business Law Section (2007); Adjunct Professor of Law, New York Law School (1988-2014); Adjunct Professor of Law, Pace University School of Law; Special Advisor, New York State Banking Department; Chair, New York State Bar Association Banking Law Committee **Creative Works:** Editor-in-Chief, New York State Bar Association Business Law Journal (2006-Present); Co-Author, Banking Regulation in the United States (2011); Editor, "Savings Institutions: Mergers, Acquisitions and Conversions," Law Journal Press **Awards:** Ranked, Top Five Percent of Banking Lawyers in New York, New York Super Lawyers (2015-2016); Recipient, David Caplan Memorial Award for Distinguished Service to the Business Law Section, New York State Bar Association (2013); Recipient, AV Rating, Martindale-Hubbell **Membership:** Panel of Commercial Arbitrators, American Arbitration Association **Bar Admissions:** Supreme Court of the United States (1994); New York (1980) **Where will you be in five years:** In the next five years, Mr. Glass will be retired or working part time. **Business Address:** 125 W 55th St Fl 8, New York, NY, 10019 **Shipping Address:** 27 Barker Avenue, Apt. 1215, White Plains, NY, 10601

Milton Louis Glass

Title: Former Gillette Chief Financial Officer, Wall Street Spokesman, and Chief Investor Relations Officer (CIRO) **Industry:** Financial Services **Company Name:** The Gillette Company **Date of Birth:** 03/07/1929 **Place of Birth:** Burlington **State:** VT **Year of Passing:** 11/23/2017 **Parents:** Joseph Glass; Mary Lena (Smith) Glass **Marital Status:** Married **Spouse Name:** Renée Peritz (2/5/1950) **Children:** Jill Sharlene; Mikel Lewis **Grandchildren:** Zachary; Rebecca; Elias **Education:** Postgraduate Program for Management Development, Harvard University (1962); MBA, Northeastern University, with High Honors (1956); BBA, Northeastern University (1954); Graduate, Bentley College (1948) **Career:** Vice President of Finance, The Gillette Company (1952-1993); Chief Investor Relations Officer, The Gillette Company (1952-1993); Assistant Timekeeper, The Gillette Company (1952); Treasurer, The Gillette Company; Assistant Controller, The Gillette Company **Career Related:** Chairman and Chair Emeritus, Board of Directors, Blue Cross and Blue Shield of Massachusetts, Inc. (1988-Present); Chairman, Forsyth Dental Research Institute (1983-Present); Co-Founder and Co-President, Jaw Joints & Allied Musculo-Skeletal Disorders Foundation, Inc. (JJAMD), a 501(c)(3) Nonprofit Foundation (1982-Present); Board of Directors, Prevention Through Comprehensive Awareness by Medical and Dental Research to the Public, Blue Cross and Blue Shield of Massachusetts, Inc. (1968-1991) **Civic:** Board of Directors, International Catacomb Society (1987-1997); Director, Health Practice and Policy Institute, National Institutes of Health (1982-2014); Chairman, Mashpee School Committee, Mashpee Public Schools (1970-1976); Board of Directors, American Repertory Theater; Board of Directors, The Metropolitan Opera of Boston; Member, Board of Directors, Boston Lyric Opera; Founding Board Member, Boch Center for the Performing Arts; Director, Goldberg Wellness Center, Northeastern University; Adjunct Professor of Finance, Northeastern University; Board Member, New Seabury Peninsula Council, Inc.; Board Member, Friends of the Mashpee Indian Museum; Board Member, Arthur D. Little Educational Institute; Board Member, Mashpee Library Committee, The Town of Mashpee; Founding Board Member, Mashpee Music Festival; Board of Overseers, Harvard School of Medical and Dental Medicine; Director, Treasurer, United Way **Military Service:** U.S. Army (1948-1951); Q Clearance, U.S. Army; Officer, Executive Reserve Corps; Brigadier General, Executive Reserve Corps of FEMA **Awards:** Named, Best Investor Relations Contact (1992); Named, Best Investor Relations Contact (1991); Named, Best Investor Relations Contact (1990); Honoree, America's Most Admired Chief Financial Officer, Institutional Investor LLC (1989-1992); Honoree, Best Investor Relations Contact, Institutional Investor LLC (1989-1992); Named, Best Investor Relations Contact (1989); Honoree, America's Best Chief Finance Officer in Cosmetics Industry, Institutional Investor LLC (1986); Honoree, Lifetime Achievement Award for Community Service, B'nai B'rith International; Eponym, The Milton & Renée Glass Family Postdoctorate Fellowship in Jaw Joints & Allied Musculo-Skeletal Research, Dedicated to Children and Prevention, The Forsyth Dental Research Institute and the Harvard Medical School **Membership:** Board of Directors, National Investor Relations Institute (1990-Present); Founder, Mashpee Coalition for Negotiation of Wampanoag Indian Land Claim Suit (1976); U.S. Congress and Massachusetts Congressional Proclamation for "Jaw Joints-TMJ Awareness Month" in Perpetuity **Marquis Who's Who Honors:** Albert Nelson Marquis Lifetime Achievement Award (2017) **Shipping Address:** 5711 Hoback Glen Rd., Hidden Hills, CA, 91302

Renée Glass

Title: President, Co-Founder **Industry:** Nonprofit & Philanthropy **Company Name:** Jaw Joints & Allied Musculo-Skeletal Disorders Foundation, Inc. (JJAMD), a 501(c)(3) Nonprofit Foundation **Date of Birth:** 01/27/1928 **Place of Birth:** Elizabeth **State:** NJ **Parents:** Samuel Peritz; Helen Kirsch Peritz **Marital Status:** Widowed **Spouse Name:** Milton L. Glass (2/5/1950-11/23/2017) **Children:** Jill Sharlene; Mikel Lewis **Grandchildren:** Zachary; Rebecca; Elias **Education:** Coursework, University of Massachusetts, Boston (1984-1985); Coursework, Northeastern University (1954); Coursework, Tufts University (1952) **Career:** Co-Founder, Co-President, Prevention Through Comprehensive Awareness by Medical and Dental Research to the Public, Jaw Joints & Allied Musculo-Skeletal Disorders Foundation, Inc. (1982-Present); Board of Directors, Institute of Contemporary Art, Boston, MA (1979-1983); Executive Secretary to Lewis H. Weinstein, Foley, Hoag & Eliot; Executive Secretary, Deputy Director of Aeronautical Engineering, Dr. Walter Wrigley, Massachusetts Institute of Technology; Executive Secretary to Law Partners, Maged, Gold & Koenig; Executive Secretary to Robert G. Newman, Berkshire Athenaeum; Executive Secretary to Dr. Joseph A. Baer, National Foundation for Infantile Paralysis (Now March of Dimes Foundation) **Career Related:** Participant, Lecturer, Health Forums, National Institutes of Health (1982-Present); Executive-in-Residence, Northeastern University (1994-2000); Wellness Committee, Northeastern University (1994-2000); Director, Goldberg Wellness Center, Northeastern University (1993-2000); Board of Directors, Health Practice and Policy Institute, National Institutes of Health (1982-2014) **Civic:** Board Co-Director, International Catacomb Society (1987-1997); Board Member, Examining Committee, Boston Public Library (1983-1987); Board Director, Connoisseur Network (1981); Board of Directors, Institute of Contemporary Art, Boston, MA (1979-1983); Board of Directors, Boston Lyric Opera; Founding Board Member, Board of Directors, Boch Center for the Performing Arts, Cape Cod, MA; Board Member, Friends of the Mashpee Indian Museum; Board Member, Mashpee Library Committee, The Town of Mashpee; Founding Board Member, Mashpee Music Festival; Grand Jury, Barnstable County Court, Commonwealth of Massachusetts; Volunteer, Cotuit Library; Volunteer, Northampton Veterans Association **Military Service:** U.S. Army (1949-1951) **Creative Works:** Author, Pamphlets on Temporomandibular Joint Disorders (1982-Present); Author, Numerous Educational Booklets **Awards:** Honoree, Lifetime Achievement Award for Community Service, B'nai B'rith International; Eponym, The Milton & Renée Glass Family Postdoctorate Fellowship in Jaw Joints & Allied Musculo-Skeletal Research, Dedicated to Children and Prevention, The Forsyth Dental Research Institute and Harvard Medical School, Boston, MA **Membership:** Founder, Mashpee Coalition for Negotiation of Wampanoag Indian Land Claim Suit (1976); U. S. Congress and Massachusetts Congressional Proclamation for "Jaw Joints-TMJ Awareness Month" in Perpetuity **Marquis Who's Who Honors:** Albert Nelson Marquis Lifetime Achievement Award (2017) **Shipping Address:** 5711 Hoback Glen Rd., Hidden Hills, CA, 91302

Joseph Glasser

Title: Founder and President Emeritus **Industry:** Consulting **Company Name:** Eljen Corporation **Date of Birth:** 05/17/1925 **Place of Birth:** Philadelphia **State/Country of Origin:** PA **Education:** Graduate, Air War College, United States Air Force (1972); Graduate, U.S. Naval War College, United States Navy (1964); Graduate, Industrial College of the Armed Forces (1955); Graduate, Command and Staff Course (1954); Postgraduate Coursework, University of Pennsylvania, Philadelphia, PA (1948-1951); MBA, University of Pennsylvania, Philadelphia, PA (1948); BS in Economics, University of Pennsylvania, Philadelphia, PA (1947) **Career:** Chief Executive Officer, Eljen Corporation, East Hartford, CT (1970-Present); Founder, Eljen Corporation, East Hartford, CT (1970); Faculty, School of Business Administration, University of Connecticut (1955-1981); Professor Emeritus, School of Business Administration, University of Connecticut (1955-1981); Internal Management Consultant, National Industrial Laundries, Elizabeth, NJ (1953-1955); Labor Relations Neutral (1950); Member, National Labor Relations Board (1948-1951) **Career Related:** Presenter, Austrian Productivity Center, Linz, Austria (1976); Presenter, Association for Protection of Industrial Property, Budapest, Hungary (1976); Presenter, The Industrial Society, London, England (1974-1978); Presenter, National Association of Suggestion Systems (1974); Presenter, Seminars, American Management Association (1968-1969); Review Officer, Federal Aviation Administration; Speaker, Seminars; Member, Management Groups, England; Member, Management Groups, Austria; Member, Management Groups, Hungary **Civic:** Member, Panel of Arbitrators, Social Security Administration (1986-1995); Member, Panel of Arbitrators, U.S. Department of Veterans Affairs (1983-1995); Member, Panel of Fact-finders, Public Employee Labor Relations Board, State of New Hampshire (1983-1990); Member, Panel of Fact-finders, Board of Conciliation and Arbitration, Commonwealth of Massachusetts (1982-2006); Member, Panel of Arbitrators, National Mediation Board (1974-2012); Member, Panel of Fact-finders, Board of Mediation and Arbitration, State of Connecticut (1974-1990); Member, Panel of Mediators, Board of Education, State of Connecticut (1974-1983); National Defense Executive Reserve (1971-2008); Member, Panel of Arbitrators, Federal Mediation and Conciliation Service (1967-2013); Member, Panel of Arbitrators, American Arbitration Association (1951-2012); Member, National Labor Relations Board (1948-1951) **Military Service:** Lieutenant Colonel, Air Force, United States Army Reserve (1970-1973); Officer, Air Corps, United States Army Air Corps Reserve (1945-1970); Commissioned, Second Lieutenant, United States Army Reserve (1945); 34 Combat Missions, Germany, Air Corps, United States Army (1944-1945); Navigator Flight Officer, Air Corps, United States Army (1943); Aviation Cadet, Air Corps, United States Army (1943); Cadet, Air Corps, United States Army (1943) **Creative Works:** Patent, Wastewater Product (1990); Patent, Drainage Product (1984); Author, "A Philosophy of a Business Education," Improving College and University Teaching (1976); Author, Textbook, "Fundamentals of Applied Industrial Management" (1975); Author, Articles, "Success and Failure of Suggestion Systems" (1973); Author, "An Analysis of the Arbitration Procedure," Personnel Journal (1973); Author, "Profits: Surest Road to Labor Management Peace and Partnership-Partners," Journal of National Labor Management Foundation (1964); Author, "Results of a Suggestion Program Survey," National Association of Suggestion Systems (1963); Author, "Body Conditioning, An Integral Part of the Physical Education Picture," Connecticut Association for Health, Physical Education and Recreation (1961); Author, "Profits: Friend or Foe," Management (1961); Author, "The Human Relations of Management Techniques," Journal of Industrial Engineering (1960); Author, "It's the Little Things that Count," Connecticut Independent (1960); Author, "Management Techniques: Panacea or Problem?" Management (1960); Author, "Technical Perfection vs. Human Imperfection," Personnel Journal (1959); Author, "Mechanization - Society's Friend or Foe?" Personnel Administration (1959); Author, "Relearning - A Bad Word," Connecticut Independent (1959) **Awards:** Innovative Award in Management Education, National Association of Management Educators (1976); Best Entry Award, National Association of Suggestion Systems (1975); Air Force Commendation Medal (1973); Decorated Air Medal with Four Oak Leaf Clusters (1943-1944) **Membership:** Society of Professionals in Dispute Resolution; Industrial Relations Research Association (Now Labor and Employment Relations Association); National Associations of Management Educators (Now National Business Education Association); National Association of Suggestion Systems; Reserve Officers Association of the United States; Air Force Association **Shipping Address:** 160 Simsbury Rd Apt 124, West Hartford, CT, 06117

Guy C. Glenn

Title: Pathologist **Industry:** Medicine & Health Care **Date of Birth:** 05/13/1930 **Place of Birth:** Parma **State/Country of Origin:** OH **Parents:** Joseph Frank Glenn; Helen (Rupple) Glenn **Spouse Name:** Elizabeth McNamer (12/2015); Lucia Ann Howarth (6/13/1953, Deceased) **Children:** Kathryn Holly; Carolyn Helen; Cynthia Marie **Education:** Resident in Pathology, Fitzsimons Army Medical Center, Denver, CO (1959-1963); Intern, Walter Reed Army Medical Center, Washington, DC (1957-1958); MD, University of Cincinnati (1957); BS, Denison University (1953) **Certifications:** Diplomate, American Board of Radioisotopic Pathology; Diplomate, American Board of Pathology **Career:** Chief, Department of Pathology, Fitzsimons Army Medical Center, Denver, CO (1972-1977); Demonstrator, Pathology, Royal Army Medical College, London (1970-1972) **Career Related:** Chair, Department of Pathology, St. Vincent Hospital, Billings, MT (1977-2006); Past Member, Governing Board, Montana Health Systems Agency; Past President, Medical Staff, Montana Health Systems Agency **Military Service:** Colonel, U.S. Army (1972); Commissioned Second Lieutenant, U.S. Army (1956) **Creative Works:** Contributor, Articles, Professional Journals **Membership:** Fellow, College of American Pathologists; Chairman, Chemistry Resources Committee, College of American Pathologists Committee; Chairman, Commission of Science Resources, College of American Pathologists; Budget Committee, College of American Pathologists; Council on Quality Assurance, College of American Pathologists; Chairman, Practice Guidelines Committee, College of American Pathologists; Board of Governors, College of American Pathologists; Chairman, Nominating Committee, College of American Pathologists; Past President, Midland Empire Health Association; Society Medical Consultant to Armed Forces; Board of Directors, American Registry of Pathology; Executive Committee, American Registry of Pathology; Search Committee, American Registry of Pathology; Planning Committee, American Registry of Pathology; Board of Directors Emeritus, Local Chapter, American Society of Clinical Pathology, Rotary International **Marquis Who's Who Honors:** Albert Nelson Marquis Lifetime Achievement Award (2017) **Shipping Address:** 3225 Jack Burke Ln, Billings, MT, 59106

Jenny Glusker

Title: Professor Emeritus **Industry:** Sciences **Company Name:** The Institute for Cancer Research, Fox Chase Cancer Center **Date of Birth:** 06/28/1931 **Place of Birth:** Birmingham **State/Country of Origin:** England **Parents:** Frederick Alfred; Jane Wylie (Stocks) P. **Marital Status:** Married (12/18/1955) **Spouse Name:** Donald Leonard Glusker **Children:** Ann; Mark John; Katharine **Education:** DSc, College of Wooster, OH, Honorary (1985); DPhil in Chemistry, Oxford University, England (1957); MA in Chemistry, Oxford University, England (1957); BA in Chemistry, Oxford University, England (1953) **Career:** Professor Emeritus of Basic Science, The Institute for Cancer Research, Fox Chase Cancer Center (2003-Present); Senior Member Emeritus, The Institute for Cancer Research, Fox Chase Cancer Center (2003-Present); Senior Member, The Institute for Cancer Research, Fox Chase Cancer Center, Philadelphia (1979-2003); Associate Member, The Institute for Cancer Research, Fox Chase Cancer Center, Philadelphia (1967-1979); Assistant Member, The Institute for Cancer Research, Fox Chase Cancer Center, Philadelphia (1967); Research Associate, The Institute for Cancer Research, Fox Chase Cancer Center, Philadelphia (1957-1967); Research Fellow, The Institute for Cancer Research, Fox Chase Cancer Center, Philadelphia (1956); Postdoctoral Research Fellow, California Institute of Technology, Pasadena (1955-1956) **Career Related:** Visiting Professor, Turkey (2006); Visiting Professor, Egypt (1997); National Institutes of Health Research Resources Council (1995-1999); Chairman, Computer Graphics Laboratory Advisory Committee, University of California, (1988-Present); Member, Computer Graphics Laboratory Advisory Committee, University of California (1985-Present); Member, Advisory Committee, Center for History of Physics, American Institute of Physics (2003-2005); Vice Chairman, Cambridge Structural Database Center (1998-2001); Division of Research Grants Advisory Committee, National Institutes of Health (1989-1992); Visiting Fellow, Oriel College, Oxford, England (1994-1995); Member, Governor Board, England (1988-2001); Chairman, Teaching Committee, International Union of Crystallography (1987-1993); Chairman, Selection Committee, Rhodes Scholarship, Pennsylvania (1984-1989); Metallobiochemistry Study Section (1983-1987); Chairman, U.S. National Committee for Crystallography (1982-1984); Member, Study Secretary, National Institute of Health, Biophysics, And Biophysics Chemistry (1972-1976); Adjunct Professor, University of Pennsylvania (1969-2012) **Creative Works:** Co-Author, "Crystal Structure Analysis: A Primer," 3rd Edition, with K.N. Trueblood (2010); Co-Editor, "Aspects of Crystallography in Molecular Biology," with with S. Parthasarathy (1997); Co-Editor, "The Collected Works of Dorothy Crowfoot Hodgkin," with Dodson, Ramaseshan and Venkatesan (1994); Co-Author, "Crystal Structure Analysis for Chemists and Biologists," with M. Lewis, M. Rossi (1994); Editor, "Acta Crystallographica section D. Biological Crystallography" (1991-2003); Member, Advisory Board, "Molecular Structures in Biology" (1991); Co-Editor, "Patterson and Pattersons," with Patterson and Rossi (1987); Co-Author, "Crystal Structure Analysis: A Primer," 2nd Edition, with K.N. Trueblood (1985); Co-Editor, "Crystallography in North America," with McLachlan (1983); Editorial Advisory Board Member, Accounts Chemical Research (1982-1987); Member, Editorial Board, Biophysics Journal (1981-1986); Editor, "Structural Crystallography in Chemistry and Biology, Structures of Molecules of Biological Interest," with with Dodson and Sayre (1981); Co-Author, "Crystal Structure Analysis: A Primer," with K.N. Trueblood (1972); Contributor, Articles, Numerous Scientific Professional Publications **Awards:** William Proctor Prize, Royal Society of Chemistry (2014); International Year of Crystallography (2014); John Scott Award, Philadelphia, American Chemical Society (2011); Fankuchen Memorial Award, American Crystallography Award (1995); Public Service Award, American Crystallography Association (1991); Gold Medal, American Chemical Society (1979); Philadelphia Section Award, American Chemical Society (1978) **Membership:** Fellow, American Association for the Advancement of Science; Fellow, Royal Society of Chemistry; Fellow, American Crystallography Association; Fellow, American Society of Biochemistry and Molecular Biology; American Association for Cancer Research; The Chemical Society; American Society of Biological Chemists; Biophysics Society; American Chemical Society; American Physical Society; Sigma Xi; Protein Society **To what do you attribute your success:** Fellow, Royal Society of Chemistry **Shipping Address:** 1011 Anna Road, Huntingdon Valley, PA, 19006

Daryl Gold

Industry: Law and Legal Services **Date of Birth:** 08/15/1905 **Education:** JD, Louisiana State University (1971); Bachelor of Science in Business Administration, LSU (1966) **Certifications:** Certified in Capital Cases, State of Louisiana **Career Related:** Capital Assistance Project, Louisiana Death Penalty Cases (2009-2014) **Civic:** Elected Member, House of Delegates, Louisiana State Bar Association; Past President, Vernon Parish Bar Association **Membership:** Past Democratic State Central Committee

Peter Louis Goldman

Title: Writer **Industry:** Writing and Editing **Date of Birth:** 02/08/1933 **Place of Birth:** Philadelphia **State/Country of Origin:** PA **Parents:** Walter Goldman; Dorothy (Semple) Goldman **Marital Status:** Married **Spouse Name:** Helen Dudar (7/16/1961) **Education:** MS, Columbia University (1955); BA, Williams College (1954) **Career:** Contributing Editor, Newsweek (Now Newsweek LLC) (1988-2008); Field Director, Special Election Unit, Newsweek (Now Newsweek LLC) (1984-2008); Senior Editor, Newsweek (Now Newsweek LLC), New York, NY (1968-1988); General Editor, Newsweek (Now Newsweek LLC), New York, NY (1965-1968); Associate Editor, Newsweek (Now Newsweek LLC), New York, NY (1962-1964); Staff Writer, St. Louis Globe-Democrat (Now St. Louis Globe-Demcorat, LLC) (1955-1962) **Creative Works:** Author, "The Shape-Shifters" (2015); Author, "The Death and Life of Malcolm X, Revised Third Edition" (2013); Author, "The Last Minstrel Show" (2012); Editor, "The Attentive Eye: Selected Journalism by Helen Dudar" (2002); Author, "The Quest for the Presidency" (1994); Author, "The Quest for the Presidency" (1992); Author, "The Quest for the Presidency" (1989); Author, "The Quest for the Presidency" (1988); Author, "Brothers" (1988); Author, "The End of the World That Was" (1986); Author, "The Quest for the Presidency" (1985); Author, "The Quest for the Presidency" (1984); Co-Author, "Charlie Company: What Vietnam Did to Us" (1983); Author, "The Death and Life of Malcolm X, Revised Second Edition" (1979); Author, "The Death and Life of Malcolm X" (1973); Author, "Report from Black America" (1970); Author, "Civil Rights: The Challenge of the Fourteenth Amendment" (1965) **Awards:** Recipient, National Magazine Award (1992); Recipient, Page One Award, New York Newspaper Guild (1989); Recipient, Page One Award, New York Newspaper Guild (1988); Recipient, Page One Award, New York Newspaper Guild (1986); Recipient, New York Bar Media Award (1984); Recipient, National Magazine Award (1982); Recipient, Freedom Foundation Award (1982); Recipient, Fourth Estate Award, American Legion (1982); Recipient, Robert F. Kennedy Journalism Award (1972); Recipient, Silver Gavel Award, ABA (1972); Recipient, Page One Award, New York Newspaper Guild (1972); Recipient, Page One Award, New York Newspaper Guild (1967); Recipient, Sigma Delta Chi Award (1962); Nieman Fellow, Harvard University (1961) **Marquis Who's Who Honors:** Albert Nelson Marquis Lifetime Achievement Award (2017); Distinguished Humanitarian (2017) **Why did you become involved in your profession or industry:** Dr. Goldman became involved in his profession because his parents were avid readers when he was a child. He began writing short stories in grade school and knew at that point that he wanted to become a writer. **Shipping Address:** 36 Gramercy Park E Apt 3W, New York, NY, 10003

Jack C. Goldstein

Title: Attorney **Industry:** Law and Legal Services **Company Name:** Law Office of Jack C. Goldstein **Place of Birth:** Fort Worth **State/Country of Origin:** TX **Parents:** Bennie Harrison Goldstein; Rae (Shanblum) Goldstein **Marital Status:** Married **Spouse Name:** Leslie P. Silber (7/3/1965) **Children:** Jason Brent; Jill Paige **Education:** Honorary JD, The George Washington University (1968); BS in Mechanical Engineering, Purdue University (1964) **Certifications:** A.A. White Dispute Resolution, University of Houston Law Center (2015); Certificate in Advanced Arbitration Skills; Admitted to Practice, United States Patent and Trademark Office **Career:** Attorney, Law Office of Jack C. Goldstein, Houston, TX (1999-Present); Arbitrator, Law Office of Jack C. Goldstein, Houston, TX (1999-Present); Mediator, Law Office of Jack C. Goldstein, Houston, TX (1999-Present); Special Master, Law Office of Jack C. Goldstein, Houston, TX (1999-Present); Testifying Expert, Law Office of Jack C. Goldstein, Houston, TX (1999-Present); President, The Whitaker Corporation, Wilmington, DE (1998-1999); Late Acting President, The Whitaker Corporation, Wilmington, DE (1998-1999); Vice President, The Whitaker Corporation, Wilmington, DE (1998-1999); Attorney, Arnold, White & Durkee, Houston, TX (1969-1997); Adjunct Professor of Law, South Texas College of Law Houston (1974-1984); Law Clerk, United States Court of Customs and Patent Appeals, Washington, DC (1968-1969); Technical Advisor, United States Court of Customs and Patent Appeals, Washington, DC (1968-1969); Patent Agent, U.S. Naval Ordnance Laboratory (1967-1968); Attorney, United States Office of Naval Research, Patent Branch, Washington, DC (1967-1968); Civilian Patent Advisor, United States Naval Ordnance Laboratory, United States Office of Naval Research Patent Branch, Washington, DC (1964-1967); Patent Examiner, Patent Office (Now United States Patent and Trademark Office), Washington, DC **Creative Works:** Board Editor, "The Intellectual Property Law Strategist" (1994-Present); Contributor, Articles to Professional Publications **Awards:** Jacob Burns Award, The George Washington University (1996); Honoree, Named for 100 Most Influential Lawyers in America, "The National Law Journal" (1994); Chair's Award, Intellectual Property Law Section, State Bar of Texas (1992); President's Award, Houston Intellectual Property Law Association (1988); Gerald Rose Memorial Award, The John Marshall Law School (1986); Alumni Service Award, The George Washington University (1985); Journal Finalist Award, Texas Bar Foundation (1981); Superior Performance Award, Patent Office (Now United States Patent and Trademark Office (1965) **Membership:** Co-Chairman, Section of Dispute Resolution, ABA (2015-Present); Intellectual Property Committee, Section of Dispute Resolution, ABA (2015-Present); Parliamentarian, Section of Intellectual Property Law, ABA (2014-Present); Founding Member of the Bench, The Honorable Nancy F. Atlas Intellectual Property American Inn of Court (2012-Present); Section Delegate, House of Delegates (1999-2014); Intellectual Property Advisory Board, The George Washington University (2000-2011); President, AIPPI-US Division of the AIPLA (2001-2004); Board of Directors, George Washington Law Alumni Association (1993-2004); Advisory Board, Patent, Trademark and Copyright Journal (1978-2003); Treasurer, Gen'l, AIPPI, AIPLA (2000-2001); Board of Directors, Intellectual Property Owners Association (1998-2000); Board of Directors, The Intellectual Property Strategist (1994-1997); Intellectual Property Advisory Board, University of Houston Law Center (1991-1997); Board of Directors, Foundation for a Creative America (1989-1994); Chairman, Section of Intellectual Property Law, ABA (1992-1993); Advisory Committee, United States Court of Appeals for the Federal Circuit (1984-1992); President, AIPLA (1988-1989); Chairman, State Bar of Texas Intellectual Property Law Section (1988-1989); President, Federal Circuit Bar Association (1987-1988); Board of Directors, George Washington Law Alumni Association (1980-1984); Copyright Advisory Committee, Library of Congress (1981-1982); Board of Trustees, Copyright Society of the U.S.A. (1979-1982); President, Association of Former Federal Circuit Law Clerks and Technical Advisors (1979-1980); President, Houston Intellectual Property Law Association (1979-1980); Life Fellow, American Bar Foundation; Life Fellow, AIPLA; Life Fellow, Houston Bar Foundation; Life Fellow, Texas Bar Foundation **Bar Admissions:** Texas **Why did you become involved in your profession or industry:** Mr. Goldstein became involved in his profession while in engineering school, during which he stopped in St. Louis, Missouri, to visit his aunt, who knew an inventor who had more patents than most. She made an appointment for him to speak to the chief patent counsel at the firm where the inventor was employed. Mr. Goldstein received advice on ways to enter the field and the importance of getting experience. He then went to night law school in Washington, DC, where he also spent two years as a patent examiner during the day. Mr. Goldstein then received training at the Naval Ordnance Laboratory. **Shipping Address:** 16 Sugarberry Cir, Houston, TX, 77024

Bridgette L. Gomillion-Williams, PhD

Title: Senior Silicon Chemist **Industry:** Sciences **Company Name:** Quanex Building Products **Date of Birth:** 07/19/1966 **Place of Birth:** Augusta **State/Country of Origin:** GA **Marital Status:** Married **Spouse Name:** Robert **Children:** Catherine **Education:** PhD in Polymer Science, School of Material Science and Engineering, Clemson University (2000); BS in Polymer Chemistry, Georgia Institute of Technology (1990) **Civic:** United Way **Awards:** Professional of the Year (2017); Industry Expert Honoree (2017); Elite Women Worldwide (2016); Worldwide Lifetime Achievement (2015-2017); Inductee, Top Female Executives (2016-2017); Elite American Executives (2015-2016); Professional of the Year (2014-2015); Top Female Executives (2012-2014); Professional of the Year (2011-2012); Worldwide Lifetime Achievement (2011); Inductee, Elite American Executives (2011) **Membership:** Featured Member, Calendar Series (2017); Featured Member, Pro-Files Magazine (2016); Featured Member, Pro-Files Magazine (2012-2013); American Institute of Chemical Engineers; American Fiber Society; American Chemical Society; Society of Plastics Engineers **Marquis Who's Who Honors:** Albert Nelson Marquis Lifetime Achievement Award (2017) **To what do you attribute your success:** Dr. Gomillion-Williams attributes her success to her natural curiosity. **Why did you become involved in your profession or industry:** Dr. Gomillion-Williams became involved in her profession after majoring in chemical engineering and working with The Dow Chemical Company. **Where will you be in five years:** In five years, Dr. Gomillion-Williams hopes to continue to pursue new opportunities to broaden her expertise in material science. She also aims to teach at the college level. **Hobbies:** Golfing; Reading; Playing the piano; Playing the flute **Shipping Address:** 954 Wheeling Ave, General Delivery, Cambridge, OH, 43725 **Website:** http://www.quanex.com

Miguel González-Gerth, PhD

Title: Literature Educator, Language Educator **Industry:** Education/Educational Services **Company Name:** The University of Texas at Austin **Date of Birth:** 08/15/1926 **Place of Birth:** Mexico City **State/Country of Origin:** Mexico **Year of Passing:** 2017-07-18 **Parents:** Gen. Miguel Gonzalez-Cadena; Claire E. Gerth **Marital Status:** Married **Spouse Name:** Tita Valencia (10/9/1994); Betty Brumbalow (Deceased) **Education:** PhD, Princeton University (1970); MA, Princeton University (1960); MA, The University of Texas at Austin (1955); BA, The University of Texas at Austin (1950) **Career:** Professor Emeritus, The University of Texas at Austin (2001-2017); Professor in Spanish, The University of Texas at Austin (1995-2001); Professor in Comparative Literature, The University of Texas at Austin (1995-2001); Professor in Spanish, The University of Texas at Austin (1987-1995); Associate Professor in Spanish, The University of Texas at Austin (1973-1987); Assistant Professor in Spanish, The University of Texas at Austin (1965-1972); Instructor in Romance Languages, Bryn Mawr College (1960-1965); Master of Spanish, The Lawrenceville School (1956-1958); Master of French, The Lawrenceville School (1956-1958) **Career Related:** Consultant, Ransom Center, The University of Texas at Austin (1972-2017); Consultant, Educational Testing Service (1960-1975); Consultant, The College Board (1960-1970) **Civic:** Board of Directors, Humanities Texas (2007-2017) **Military Service:** Captain, U.S. Navy **Creative Works:** Author, "Looking For The Horse Latitudes" (2007); Author, "Nueve Musas Eroticas" (2005); Author, "The Brandywine in Winter" (2004); Author, "La Lengua Fracturads," Ediciones Calle de Cerezas, Mexico (2003); Author, "En Busca de las Calmas Ecuatoriales" (1996); Author, "T.E. Lawrence, Richard Aldington, and the Death of Heroes" (1994); Author, "The Musicians and Other Poems" (1991); Author, "Labyrinth of Imagery: Ramon Gomez de la Serna's Novelas de la Nebulosa" (1986); Editor, "Texas Quarterly" (1972-1978) **Awards:** Pro Bene Meritis Award, College of Liberal Arts, The University of Texas at Austin (2006) **Marquis Who's Who Honors:** Albert Nelson Marquis Lifetime Achievement Award (2017) **Hobbies:** Collecting antiques, art, and books; Nature watching **Shipping Address:** 303 E 42nd Street, c/o Tita Valencia, Austin, TX, 78751

Charles Thomas "Tom" Gooding

Title: Psychologist **Industry:** Education/Educational Services **Company Name:** State University of New York at Oswego **Date of Birth:** 11/18/1931 **Place of Birth:** Tampa **State/Country of Origin:** FL **Parents:** Charles T. Gooding; Gladys (Bingman) Gooding **Marital Status:** Married **Spouse Name:** Shirley Ann Puckett (6/7/1953) **Children:** Steven Thomas; Carol Ann; David Lee; Mark Charles **Education:** EdD, University of Florida (1964); EdM, University of Florida (1962); Postgraduate Studies, University of Tampa (1956-1958); BA, University of Florida (1954) **Career:** Emeritus, State University of New York at Oswego (1998-Present); Provost, State University of New York at Oswego (1995-1998); Vice President for Academic Affairs, State University of New York at Oswego (1995-1998); Dean of Graduate Studies and Research, State University of New York at Oswego (1989-1995); Associate Dean of Graduate Studies and Research, State University of New York at Oswego (1982-1989); Psychology Professor, State University of New York at Oswego (1980-1998); Associate Professor to Professor, State University of New York at Oswego (1964-1979); Instructor, University of Florida (1963-1964); Assistant Principal to Principal, St. Mary's School, Tampa, FL (1958-1962); Teacher, Memorial School, Tampa, FL (1956-1958) **Career Related:** Task Force on Teacher Education, State University of New York (1984); Visiting Professor, University of Liverpool (1979-1980); Graduate Fellow, University of Florida (1962-1963) **Civic:** Board of Directors, Bishop Gray Retirement Foundation (2008-Present); Trustee, University of the South (2002-2005); Board of Directors, Oswego College Foundation, Inc. (1996-2011); Lay Ministry, Episcopal Church **Military Service:** First Lieutenant, U.S. Army Reserve (1954-1956) **Creative Works:** Contributing Author, "Research Matters to the Science Teacher" (1992); Contributing Author "Questioning and Discussion: A Multidisciplinary Study" (1988); Co-Author, "Learning Theories in Educational Practice" (1971); Contributing Author, "Florida Studies in the Helping Professions" (1969); Contributor, Articles, Professional Journals **Awards:** Grantee, National Science Foundation (1990-1995); Grantee, New York State Education Department (1988-1994); Grantee, National Science Foundation (1985-1988); Grantee, National Science Foundation (1980-1981); Grantee, New York State Education Department (1971-1972); Grantee, The Research Foundation for the State University of New York (1969-1970); Grantee, The Research Foundation for the State University of New York (1966) **Membership:** Chair of Educational Enterprises, SIG, American Educational Research Association (1994-1996); Editorial Board, Eastern Educational Research Association (1991-2000); President, Eastern Educational Research Association (1989-1991); President-Elect, Eastern Educational Research Association (1987-1988); Director, Eastern Educational Research Association (1983-1985); Treasurer, Eastern Educational Research Association (1983-1985); Vice President, Eastern Educational Research Association (1979-1981); American Psychological Association **Marquis Who's Who Honors:** Albert Nelson Marquis Lifetime Achievement Award (2017) **Why did you become involved in your profession or industry:** Dr. Gooding has always loved learning and teaching, even in the beginning of his youth, and he did such activities as teaching model plane building during summer bible school when he was in junior high school. During the course of his career, among other things, he has conducted seminars and has conducted research on effective learning and teaching with a team that raised more than $1 million in grants. When he served as dean of graduate studies and research at the State University of New York at Oswego, he traveled the world creating faculty and student exchanges in Chinese, Japanese, British, European, and Australian universities. The turning point in his career was when he was a young principal at a parochial school, he enrolled in a master's program in educational administration. He enrolled in a psychology course with Dr. Arthur W. Combs. He later asked him if he would consider leaving his work in Tampa, Fla., moving his family, and relocating to become his doctoral student, assuring him that other opportunities would open for him. With the support of his family, they made the move, which turned out to be a pivotal one. **What do you consider to be the highlight of your career:** A highlight of Dr. Gooding's career is the work for the Bishop Gray Inns Foundation, whose mission is to assist people who are members of the Episcopal church who can no longer afford adequate senior housing. **Hobbies:** Sports cars, especially Jaguar **Shipping Address:** 3730 Cadbury Circle, Apt. 301, Venice, FL, 34293

Marcia Louisa Goodman, PhD

Title: Medical Resident (Retired) **Industry:** Medicine & Health Care **Company Name:** Knox Cardiology Practice **Education:** PhD, Yale University (2006); Honorary MD, Yale University; Registered Nurse **Career:** Social Security Administration (1967-1972); Nurse; Laboratory Technician, The American National Red Cross **Civic:** Donor, Toys to Children; Order of the White Shrine of Jerusalem; Order of the Eastern Star; American Red Cross; SPCA International; National Wildlife Federation **Membership:** Supreme Council Member, Order of the Amaranth; American Diabetes Association **Marquis Who's Who Honors:** Albert Nelson Marquis Lifetime Achievement Award (2017); Distinguished Humanitarian (2017) **Hobbies:** Bowling; Playing softball; Practicing archery; Sewing; Cooking **Shipping Address:** 165 Holland Ln, East Hartford, CT, 06118

Constance (Connie) Goodman-Milone

Title: Writer **Industry:** Writing and Editing **Company Name:** Mrs. **Date of Birth:** 09/03/1963 **Place of Birth:** Philadelphia **State/Country of Origin:** PA **Parents:** Marvin Joshua Goodman; Linda S. Goodman **Marital Status:** Married **Spouse Name:** David C. Milone (5/5/2002) **Education:** Social Work Intern, Miami Veterans Administration Medical Center, United States Department of Veterans Affairs, Miami, FL (1999); MSW, Barry University, Miami Shores, FL (1999); BA in Psychology, The George Washington University (1985) **Career:** Freelance Writer, Miami, FL (2001-Present); Case Manager in Skilled Nursing, Doctors Hospital (Baptist Health South Florida), HealthSouth Corporation, Coral Gables, FL (2000); Freelance Writer, New York City, NY (1989-1996); Freelance Writer, Philadelphia, PA (1987-1988); Editorial Assistant, Chelsea House Publishers, LLC, Edgemont, PA (1986-1987) **Civic:** World Jewish Congress, American Section, New York, NY (2017-Present); Supporter, USA for UNHCR, Washington, DC (2017-Present); Judging Coordinator, Creative Writing Competition, Miami Veterans Creative Arts Festival, Miami, FL (2017-Present); Amnesty International USA, New York, NY (2016-Present); Campaign Volunteer, Democratic Candidates, FL (2016-Present); Democratic Senatorial Campaign Committee (DSCC), Washington, DC (2016-Present); Field Partner, Doctors Without Borders, New York, NY (2015-Present); Leader's Club, National Wildlife Federation, Reston, VA (2015-Present); Supporter, Sandy Hook Promise, Newtown, CT (2015-Present); Wildlife Guardian, Defenders of Wildlife, Washington, DC (2014-Present); Wildlife Rescue Team, World Wildlife Fund, Washington, DC (2014-Present); Supporter, Americans for Responsible Solutions (Giffords PAC) (2014-Present); Sponsoring Member, USO, Inc. Washington, DC (2012-Present); Democrats of South Dade Club, Miami, FL (2012-Present); The Human Rights Campaign, Washington, DC (2009-Present); Creative Writing and Performing Arts Judge, Miami Veterans Creative Arts Festival, Miami, FL (2009-Present); Natural Resources Defense Council, New York, NY (2006-Present); Charter Member, United States Holocaust Memorial Museum, Washington, DC (1995-Present) **Creative Works:** Co-author, "Bereavement Poetry Project"; Poem, "Dark Wood" (2018); Letters To Editor, Sun Sentinel (2015-2017); Poems, "Florida State Poets Association Anthology" (2014-2017); Letters To Editor, San Antonio Express-News (2014); Poem, "Of Poets and Poetry" (2013); Poems, "Healthy Stories" (2010-2012); Poems, "Poet's Corner," Bridle Path Press (2010); Associate Editor, Author's Voice Newsletter, South Florida Writers Association (2009-2014); Poems, "Florida State Poets Association Anthology" (2008-2012); Article, "Vitas Vital Signs" (2008); Poems, "The Grief Observer" (2006-2007); Letters To Editor, Miami Herald (2002-2018); Poem, "Today's Caregiver" (2002); Articles, Poems, Photos, "Author's Voice," South Florida Writers Association (2001-2018); Poem, Articles, "New Directions/Social Work Advocate" (2001-2003); Poems, "Medicinal Purposes Literary Review" (1995-2003); Poem, "Poet's Market" (1995); Poems, "The New Press" (1991-1993); Author, "Walk a Giant Piano" (1991) **Awards:** Second Honorable Mention, Poetry Contest, Florida State Poets Association, Inc. (2017); Poetry Awards, Writing Contests, South Florida Writers Association (2013-2018); Exemplary Medal, Miami-Dade County School Board, District 9 (2013); Eleven Year Volunteer Award, Vitas Healthcare (2011); Bill Katzker Member of the Year Award, South Florida Writers Association (2003); Bereavement Volunteer of the Year, Vitas Dade Program, Vitas Healthcare (2001) **Membership:** Director of Community Relations, South Florida Writers Association (2017-Present); Secretary, South Florida Writers Association (2016); President, South Florida Writers Association (2015); Director, Creative Writing Committee, Junior Orange Bowl (2015-Present); Vice President, South Florida Writers Association (2014); Director-at-Large, South Florida Writers Association (2008-2013); Secretary, South Florida Writers Association (2006-2008); Board of Directors, Junior Orange Bowl (2006); Director of Community Relations, South Florida Writers Association (2005-2006); Chair, Creative Writing Committee, Junior Orange Bowl (2003-2014); Director of Marketing, South Florida Writers Association (2003-2005); Outreach Chair, South Florida Chapter, Association of Death Education and Counseling (2002-2006); Director, Creative Writing Committee, Junior Orange Bowl (2002); National Writers Union; Florida State Poets Association, Inc.; Miami Poets; Academy of American Poets; National Association of Social Workers; National Association for Poetry Therapy; Phi Eta Sigma; Psi Chi, The International Honor Society in Psychology; Delta Epsilon Sigma **Marquis Who's Who Honors:** Albert Nelson Marquis Lifetime Achievement Award (2017); Distinguished Humanitarian (2017) **Hobbies:** Photography; Tennis; Walking; Books **Political Affiliations:** Democrat **Religion:** Jewish **Shipping Address:** 12920 SW 95th Ave, Miami, FL, 33176 **Website:** www.conniegoodman-milone.com

Tricia D. Goostree

Title: Managing Partner **Industry:** Law and Legal Services **Company Name:** Goostree Law Group, P.C. **Marital Status:** Married **Education:** JD, John Marshall Law School (2002); Intern, Illinois Attorney General's Office; BA, Eastern Illinois University **Career:** Owner, Goostree Law Group, P.C.; Managing Partner, Goostree Law Group, P.C. **Career Related:** Clerk, Chicago Legal Clinic **Civic:** Board of Directors, Prairie State Legal Services; Volunteer, Northern Illinois Food Bank; Pro Bono Legal Service for Those in Need **Awards:** Super Lawyers (2016); Illinois Leading Lawyer (2016); Illinois Leading Lawyer (2015); Rising Star, Super Lawyers (2011-2015); Rising Star, Kane County Bar Association (2005) **Membership:** Kane County Bar Association (2005-Present); Chairman, Public Relations Committee, Kane County Bar Association (2010-2013); Chairman, Admissions and Membership Committee, Kane County Bar Association (2010-2011); Executive Board, John Marshall Moot Court **To what do you attribute your success:** Ms. Goostree attributes her success to a good work ethic. **Why did you become involved in your profession or industry:** She knew that she wanted to be a lawyer when she was four years old. **Hobbies:** Baseball; Travel; Running **Shipping Address:** 555 S Randall Rd Ste 200, Goostree Law Group, PC, St. Charles, IL, 60174

Ella Gordon

Title: Women's Health Nurse (Retired) **Industry:** Medicine & Health Care **Company Name:** Brooke Army Medical Center **Date of Birth:** 01/19/1947 **Place of Birth:** Chicago **State/Country of Origin:** IL **Parents:** Ed Hall; Mozelle (Jordan) Hall **Marital Status:** Married **Spouse Name:** Starling Alexander Gordon (8/2/1969) **Children:** Gerald Alexander; Dana Rolean **Education:** Master in Health Sciences, Armstrong State College (1983); BSN, Medical College of Georgia (1976); Coursework, Georgia State University (1969-1975); Diploma, Grady Memorial Hospital (1968) **Certifications:** Registered Nurse, States of Georgia, Texas **Career:** Head Nurse, Allergy/Immunology Service, Brooke Army Medical Center (2005-2007); Health-Nurse Educator, Health Promotion Center, Brooke Army Medical Center (2000-2005); Charge Nurse Orthopedics, Brooke Army Medical Center, Fort Sam, Houston, TX (1996-1999); Nurse, Labor and Delivery, Wilford Hall Air Force Medical Center, Lackland Air Force Base, Texas (1996); Charge Nurse Obstetrical, Brooke Army Medical Center, Fort Sam, Houston, TX (1990-1996); Charge Nurse, Oncology Days, Eisenhower Army Medical Center, Fort Gordon, Georgia (1989-1990); Clinical Nurse, Obstetrical, Gorgas Army Hospital, Republic of Panama (1987-1989); Instructor in Clinical Nursing, College of Nursing, Jacksonville State University (1984-1985); Staff Nurse, Obstetrical, Noble Army Hospital, Fort McClellan, Alabama (1984); Charge Nurse, Army Nurse Corps, Eisenhower Army Medical Center, Fort Gordon, Georgia (1976-1979); Nurse, Primary Care Medical ICU, VA Hospital, San Antonio, TX (1983); Staff Nurse, VA Hospital, Atlanta, GA (1972-1976); Charge Nurse, Pediatricians Office, Decatur, GA (1971-1972); Staff Nurse in Pediatrics, Doctor's Memorial Hospital, Atlanta, GA (1971); Charge Nurse of Pediatrics Evenings, Grady Memorial Hospital, Atlanta, GA (1968-1971) **Career Related:** Consultant, Health Education, ETOWAH County Clinics, Gadsden, AL (1985); Health Educator, Cardiovascular, Council of Savannah, GA (1983); Parent/Child Development Services, Savannah, GA (1982) **Civic:** Board Member, Volunteer Home Owners Association (2007-Present); Coordinator, National Night Out (2016); Co-coordinator, National Night Out (2015); Chairman, Fort McClellan Chapter, The American National Red Cross (1986-1987); Instructor, Fort McClellan Chapter, The American National Red Cross, Fort McClellan, AL (1985-1986); Artist Selection Committee, Joint City Commission, Elderly Affairs **Military Service:** Colonel, U.S. Army Reserve (1991); Captain, U.S. Army (1976-1979) **Creative Works:** Contributor, Articles, Professional Journals **Awards:** Honoree, One of the Outstanding Young Women in America (1979, 1983) **Membership:** Publicity Chairman, Officers Wives Club (1982-1983); Army Nurse Corps Association; Orthopaedic Nurses Association; Sigma Theta Tau **Marquis Who's Who Honors:** Albert Nelson Marquis Lifetime Achievement Award (2017) **Hobbies:** Travel; Cross-stitching; Bowling; Reading; Ceramics **Political Affiliations:** Democrat **Shipping Address:** 746 Best Way, San Antonio, TX, 78260

Helen H. Gordon

Title: Author, Game Publisher **Industry:** Education/Educational Services **Company Name:** Anacade Publishing Company, LLC **Date of Birth:** 09/07/1932 **Place of Birth:** Salt Lake City **State/Country of Origin:** UT **Parents:** Fred C. Heightsman; Florence Isabel Heightsman **Marital Status:** Single **Spouse Name:** Clifton B.Gordon (Deceased 2004); Norman C. Winn (8/10/1950, Divorced 9/1972) **Children:** Bruce Vernon Winn; Brent Terry Winn; Holly Winn Willer **Education:** EdD, Nova Southeastern University (1979); MA in English, Sacramento State (1967); BA in English, Sacramento State (1964); BA in Education, Sacramento State (1964); Coursework, The University of Utah (1959-1962) **Certifications:** Certified Teacher, State of California; Licensed Counselor, State of California **Career:** Publisher, Anacade Publishing Company (2006-Present); Editor, Department of Computer Engineering, University of California, Santa Barbara (1999-2006); Technology Writer, Department of Computer Engineering, University of California, Santa Barbara (1999-2006); Professor, Bakersfield College (1974-1995); Counselor, Bakersfield College (1974-1995); Associate Professor, Porterville College (1967-1974); Counselor, Porterville College (1967-1974); Teacher, Rio Americano High School, Sacramento, CA (1965-1966); Part-Time Instructor in Remedial English, The University of Utah (1960-1961); Stenographer, Associated Food Stores (1951-1959); Payroll Clerk, Associated Food Stores (1951-1959) **Career Related:** Articulation Coordinator, Bakersfield College (1992-1993); Director, Region V, English Council of California Two-Year Colleges (1990-1992); Administrative Intern (1982-1983); Coordinator of Women's Studies, Bakersfield College (1977-1978); Chair, Language Arts Division, Porterville College (1971-1974) **Civic:** Founding President, Writers of Kern (1993); Guest Member, Editorial Board, The Bakersfield Californian (1988); President, Unitarian Universalist Fellowship of Kern County (1976-1978) **Creative Works:** Author, "Malinalli of the Fifth Sun: The Slave Girl Who Changed the Fate of Mexico and Spain" (2011); Author, "The Secret Love Story in Shakespeare's Sonnets" (2008); Author, "Anagrams, Anagrabber and Other Word Games" (1999); Author, "Love Lyrics in Light and Shadow" (1999); Author, "Age is a Laughing Matter: How to Laugh Through the Second Half of Your Life" (1999); Author, "Life, Love and Laughter" (1998); Publisher, "Anagrabber, the Word Game for All Ages" (1998); Author, "Voice of the Vanquished: The Story of the Slave Marina and Hernan Cortes" (1995); Author, "First Captured, Last Freed: Memoirs of a P.O.W. in World War II Guam and Japan" (1995); Author, "Interplay: Sentence Skills in Context" (1991); Author, "Wordforms, Book I & II" (1990); Author, "Developing College Writing" (1989); Author, "From Copying to Creating" (1983) **Awards:** Faculty Colloquium Award, Levan Center For Humanities, Bakersfield College (2011); Grantee, California Fund For Instruction (1978); Scholarship, The University of Utah (1959-1962) **Membership:** President, Santa Barbara Chapter, Pi Lambda Theta (2008-2011); Columnist Academy Author, Textbook & Academic Authors Association (1996-Present); President, AAUW (1997-1998); Program Chair, Bakersfield Chapter, American Association Women in Community Colleges (1988-1991); President, Bakersfield Chapter, League of Women Voters (1981-1983, 1989-1990); National Education Association; Founder, Bakersfield Chapter, American Association of Women in Community Colleges; President, Bakersfield Chapter, American Association for Women in Community Colleges; NCTE; Faculty Association of California Community Colleges; Charter Member, Textbook & Academic Authors Association; National Writers Union; Shakespeare Authorship Roundtable **Marquis Who's Who Honors:** Albert Nelson Marquis Lifetime Achievement Award (2017) **To what do you attribute your success:** She attributes her success to excellent public school teachers, as well as her own work ethic, ambition, intelligence, and family support. **Why did you become involved in your profession or industry:** She always loved reading and writing, and her dream was to become a college professor. **What do you consider to be the highlight of your career:** She is most proud of having been able to publish five textbooks while teaching at Bakersfield College and raising three teenagers. **Where will you be in five years:** She is retired from the classroom now, but is actively volunteering. She is continuing to write, and publish her work. **Hobbies:** Poetry; Word games; Personal computer; Theater **Political Affiliations:** Democrat **Religion:** Unitarian Universalist **Shipping Address:** 5358 Calle Real Apt 2C, Santa Barbara, CA, 93111 **Website:** www.anacade.com

Sharon Ann Gordon

Title: Mathematics Educator (Retired), Preschool Educator (Retired) **Industry:** Education/Educational Services **Company Name:** Sparta High School **Date of Birth:** 08/08/1945 **Place of Birth:** Newton **State/Country of Origin:** NJ **Parents:** Kenneth William Gordon; Hazel Emma (Pascoe) Gordon **Marital Status:** Single **Education:** MEd, Montclair State University (1970); BA in Mathematics, Chemistry, and History, Drew University (1967); Coursework, Centenary College (1963-1964) **Certifications:** Certified Secondary School Mathematics Teacher, Grades 7-12, The State Board of Examiners, State of New Jersey (1969) **Career:** Preschool Teacher Aide, Circle of Friends Pre-School, Sparta Township, NJ (2000-2011); Mathematics Teacher, Sparta High School (1968-2000) **Civic:** Member, Sparta United Methodist Church (1956-Present); Member, Jack Russell Terrier Club of America **Awards:** Creative Writing Award, Centenary University (1963) **Membership:** National Education Association; Sussex County Retired Educators Association; New Jersey Education Association; Jack Russell Terrier Club of America; Phi Theta Kappa Honor Society **Marquis Who's Who Honors:** Albert Nelson Marquis Lifetime Achievement Award (2017) **To what do you attribute your success:** She attributes her success to perseverance, intelligence and a desire to not let her mother down, who always dreamed of her being a teacher. **Why did you become involved in your profession or industry:** She entered the field of education because her mother wanted her to become a teacher. **What do you consider to be the highlight of your career:** The highlight of her career was being able to sustain 32 years as a high school teacher with as much as the same enthusiasm as the teachers at the start of their career as well as working 11 years of preschool teacher aide service, following her high school retirement. **Where will you be in five years:** In five years, her hope is that she may be finally able to have some or all her original, uplifting poetry published. **Hobbies:** Writing poetry; Baking; Cooking; Counted cross stitch; Reading **Religion:** Methodist **Shipping Address:** 140 Woodport Rd, Sparta, NJ, 07871 **Website:** http://www.mww.com

Steven Lowell Gore

Title: Accountant **Industry:** Financial Services **Company Name:** Department of Commerce and Insurance **Date of Birth:** 06/22/1953 **Place of Birth:** Paducah **State/Country of Origin:** KY **Education:** BS in Accounting, Lipscomb University, Nashville, TN (1975) **Certifications:** CPA, State of Tennessee **Career:** Examiner, Tennessee Department of Commerce and Insurance, Nashville, TN (2005-Present); Freelance Consultant, Nashville, TN (2005-Present); Developing Officer, Genetics Associates Incorporated, Nashville, TN (2003-2005); Controller, Sumner Regional Medical Center, Gallatin, TN (1987-2003); Staff Auditor, HCA Management Services, L.P., Nashville, TN (1984-1987); Facility Accountant, American Retirement Corporation, Nashville, TN (1983); Analyst, Fiscal Services, King Faisal Hospital and Research Centre, Riyadh, Saudi Arabia (1976-1977) **Civic:** Poll Official, Metro-Davidson County Election Commission, Nashville, TN (1999); Volunteer, YMCA of Middle Tennessee, Nashville, TN (1997-2000) **Awards:** Appreciation Letter for Service, United Way of Sumner County (1997-2000) **Membership:** American Association for the Advancement of Science; New York Academy of Sciences; American Chemical Society; Church of Christ; Tennessee Society of Certified Public Accountants **Marquis Who's Who Honors:** Albert Nelson Marquis Lifetime Achievement Award (2017) **To what do you attribute your success:** Mr. Gore attributes his success to his family, friends, faith, good teachers, and schools. **What do you consider to be the highlight of your career:** One would be working overseas. It helped Mr. Gore to think globally. He met and made friends of people from different cultures. **Hobbies:** Fishing; Reading; Jogging **Religion:** Christian **Shipping Address:** 2540 Sharondale Drive, Apt. 7, Nashville, TN, 37215

Janet Marie Gorn

Title: Senior Foreign Affairs Officer **Industry:** International Affairs/International Business **Company Name:** U.S. Department of State **Date of Birth:** 09/29/1938 **Place of Birth:** Fond du Lac **State/Country of Origin:** WI **Parents:** A. Reinhold Walter Gorn; Glady Lucille (Schulze) Gorn **Marital Status:** Single **Spouse Name:** Ronald Lee Braun (6/20/1959, Divorced 3/20/1980) **Children:** Suzette Karen (Braun Batchelder Mitchell) Fulton; Gregory Reinhold William **Education:** Postgraduate Coursework, George Washington University (1984-1986); MA, San Jose State University, With Honors (1982); BA, Drew University (1973); Postgraduate Coursework, Special Studies, Harvard University; Two-Year Internship Program, U.S. Nuclear Regulatory Commission **Career:** Assistant Professor, Adjunct Staff, Northern Virginia Community College (2008-Present); United States Diplomat, Senior Foreign Affairs Officer, Civil Nuclear Energy and Non-Proliferation, Office of Nuclear Energy Safety and Security, Bureau of International Security and Non-Proliferation, U.S. Department of State (1999-Present); Senior International Relations Officer, U.S. Nuclear Regulatory Commission, Washington, DC (1988-1999); Congressional Affairs Officer, U.S. Nuclear Regulatory Commission, Washington, DC (1982-1987); Program Analyst in the Office of Radioactive Waste, U.S. Nuclear Regulatory Commission, Washington, DC (1980-1982); Research Analyst, Congressional Research Service, Washington, DC (1978-1979); Research Assistant to Senior Fellow, The Brookings Institution, Washington, DC (1978); Policy Analyst, City of San Jose, CA (1975-1976); Librarian, Library, Drew University Library (1969-1971); Librarian, Wisconsin University Library, WI (1963-1965); Librarian, Oshkosh Public Library, Oshkosh, WI (1961-1963); Special Assignments to the Chairman and Two Commissioners, U.S. Nuclear Regulatory Commission; Special Assignments in the State Department's Bureau of Oceans and International Environmental and Scientific Affairs; Senior Coordinator's Office for Russian and Eastern European Affairs; OES/Office of Nuclear Technology and Safeguards; ISN Deputy Assistant Secretary's Office; Special Assistant to Two Ambassadors **Career Related:** State Department Bureau Representative, Working Group, Intra-Department Regulatory Reform Task Force (2017-Present); Guest Lecturer, Foreign Service Institute (2008-Present); Co-Chairman, Interagency Steering Committee on the Joint Convention on Spent Fuel Management and Radioactive Waste (2003-Present); United States Representative and Head of Delegation, Joint Conventions on Spent Fuel Management and Radioactive Waste (2003-Present); United States Representative/Alternate Representative of Delegation, Steering Committee, Nuclear Energy Agency, Organisation for Economic Co-operation and Development (1991-Present) **Civic:** Vice President, Prince William Republican Women's Club (2008-2009); President, Prince William Public Library System Foundation (2005-2007); Board of Directors, Prince William Public Library System Foundation (2004-2007) **Creative Works:** Author, "The Joint Convention: Its Global Impact and U.S. Continuing Involvement" (2016); Author, "Setting the Stage for International Spent Fuel Storage" (2008); Author, "International Financing and Investment for Nuclear Power Projects" (2007); Author, "International Storage of Commercial Spent Fuel and High-Level Waste" (2004); Author, "Analysis of Low-Level Radioactive Waste Burial Site Capacity" (1981); Author, "National Security Counsel Interagency Policy Committee on Nuclear Energy"; Speaker, Domestic and International Conferences/Symposia **Awards:** Meritorious Honor Award, U.S. Department of State (2016); Meritorious Honor Award, U.S. Department of State (2015); Commendation, Assistant Secretary for Environmental Management, U.S. Department of Energy (2015) **Membership:** Bylaws Standing Committee, State Board of Directors, Virginia Federation of Republican Women (2017-Present); National Board of Directors Standing Membership Committee, National Federation of Republican Women (2016-Present); State Board of Directors Standing Membership Committee, Virginia Federation of Republican Women (2016-Present); Republican Women's Federal Forum (2016-Present); Executive Women at State Department (2015-Present); National Woman's Party, Belmont-Paul Women's Equality National Monument, (2014-Present); President, King's Highway Republican Women's E-Club (2013-Present); Prince William County Republican Committee (2012-Present); Vice Chairman, National Board of Directors, Standing Committee, Education & Literacy, National Federation of Republican Women (2012-Present); Prince William County Committee Of 100 Leaders (2008-Present); American Nuclear Society (2000-Present); Nuclear Women in Energy (2000-Present) **Marquis Who's Who Honors:** Albert Nelson Marquis Lifetime Achievement Award (2017) **Political Affiliations:** Republican **Religion:** Episcopalian **Shipping Address:** 15730 Cranberry Court, Montclair, VA, 22025

Walter R. Gove

Title: Sociology Educator **Industry:** Education/Educational Services **Date of Birth:** 06/08/1938 **Marital Status:** Married **Children:** Two Children **Education:** PhD in Sociology, University of Washington (1968); MA in Sociology, University of Washington (1967); BS in Forestry, State University of New York College of Environmental Science and Forestry (1960) **Career:** Professor, Vanderbilt University (1975-2003); Associate Professor, Vanderbilt University (1971-1975); Assistant Professor, Vanderbilt University (1968-1971) **Career Related:** Graduate Faculty Delegate Assembly Representative (1997-1998); Admissions Publications Advisory Committee (1988-1990); Chair, Institute Review Board, Protection of Human Subjects (1980); Committee on Women's Studies (1977-1984); Institute Review Board, Protection of Human Subjects (1977-1980); Institute Review Board, Protection of Human Subjects (1971-1974); Director, Graduate Training Program, National Institute of Mental Health (1972-1976) **Creative Works:** Associate Editor, Society and Mental Health (2012-Present); Advisory Editor, Social Science Research (1999-Present); Co-Author, "Age, Period, Cohort and Educational Attainment: The Importance of Considering Gender," Social Science Research (2011); Co-Author, "Depression in the United States and Japan: Gender, Marital Status and SES Patterns," Social Science and Medicine (2005); Author, "The Career of the Mentally Ill: An Integration of Psychiatric, Labeling/Social Construction, And Lay Perspectives," Journal of Health and Social Behavior (2004); Co-Author, "The Neurophysiology of Motivation and Habitual Criminal Behavior," Biosocial Criminology: Challenging Environmentalism's Supremacy (2003); Associate Editor, Journal of Health and Social Behavior (2001-2004); Author, "Gender Differences in Psychological Distress," Encyclopedia of Criminology and Deviant Behavior (2001); Author, "The Labeling Theory of Mental Illness," Encyclopedia of Criminology and Deviant Behavior (2001); Co-Author, "The Laws Regulating the Civil Commitment and Treatment of the Mentally Ill," Encyclopedia of Criminology and Deviant Behavior (2001); Co-Author, "The Neurophysiologic High that Would Appear to Positively Reinforce Criminal Behavior," Encyclopedia of Criminology and Deviant Behavior (2001); Reviewer, "Motivation and Delinquency Volume 44" Nebraska Symposium, Contemporary Sociology (1999); Co-Author, "The Age-Period Cohort Conundrum and Verbal Ability: Empirical Relationships and Their Interpretation," American Sociological Review (1999); Associate Editor, Journal of Health and Social Behavior (1997-2000); Editor, Symposium, "Is Sociology the Core Discipline in the Study of Human Behavior?" (1995); Author, "Is Sociology the Integrative Discipline in the Study of Human Behavior?," Social Forces (1995); Author, "Why We Do What We Do: A Biopsychosocial Theory of Human Motivation," Social Forces (1994); Author, "A Kayak Mountaineering Ascent of Mt. Abbe," The American Alpine Journal (1992); Author, "The Evidence Does Not Indicate that the Higher Rates of Physical Symptoms Among Homeless Women are Due to Reporting Bias: A Comment on Ritchey et al." Journal of Health and Social Behavior (1991); Author, "Sociobiology Misses the Mark: An Essay on Why Biology but Not Sociobiology is Very Relevant to Sociology," The American Sociologist (1987); Author, "Cerebral and Pulmonary Edema: The Verdict's in, Immunity Denied," Climbing (1987); Author, "From Despair to Freedom: The Power Within," The Climbing Art (1987) **Awards:** Vanderbilt's Outstanding Graduate Teacher Award (2001); Grantee, Kenan Venture Fund (1997); Grantee, University Research Council (1995-1996); Grantee, College of Arts and Science (1994-1995); Elected Fellow, American Association for the Advancement of Science (1992); Grantee, University Research Council (1990-1991); Recognition of Outstanding Scholarship and Service to the Psychiatric Sociology Award, Society for the Study of Social Problems (1989); Grantee, University Research Council (1988-1989); Grantee, University Research Council (1986-1987); Grantee, University Research Council (1984-1985); Grantee, Symposium on "The Effect of the Feminist Perspective on the Humanities and the Social Sciences," Ethel Mae Wilson Foundation (1980-1981); Leo Reader Award for Distinguished Contributions to Medical Sociology, Medical Sociology Section, American Sociological Association; Ranked First in the World in Cumulative Publications, American Sociological Association **Membership:** President, Southern Sociological Society (1993-1994); President-Elect, Southern Sociological Society (1992-1993); American Sociological Association Liaison Committee, American Association for the Advancement of Science (1990-1994); Executive Committee, Southern Sociological Society (1986-1997); Program Committee, Annual Meeting, Southern Sociological Society (1986); Sociology Research Association (1984); American Society of Criminology; Sociology Research Association **Marquis Who's Who Honors:** Albert Nelson Marquis Lifetime Achievement Award (2017) **Shipping Address:** PO Box 1399, Boulder, UT, 84716

Raghav Govindarajan, MD

Title: Neurologist **Industry:** Medicine & Health Care **Company Name:** University of Missouri **Date of Birth:** 03/23/1983 **Country of Origin:** India **Education:** Fellow, Washington University (2013-2014); Clinical Resident, Cleveland Clinic Florida (2009-2013); MD, Bangalore Medical College (2007) **Career:** Assistant Professor, University of Missouri (2014-Present) **Career Related:** Board Member, Florida Society of Neurology (2010) **Creative Works:** Contributor, 34 Peer Reviewed Articles, Professional Publications; Contributor, Chapters, Books; Presenter in Field **Awards:** Translational and Clinical Research Course (2016); Travel Award, American Neurological Association (2016); President's Research Award, American Association of Neuromuscular and Electrodiagnostic Medicine (2015); President's Research Award, American Association of Neuromuscular and Electrodiagnostic Medicine (2014); Annual Meet Travel Award, Florida Society of Neurology (2014); ACNS Travel Fellowship (2014); Best Abstract Runners-Up, American Association of Neuromuscular and Electrodiagnostic Medicine (2013); Florida Society of Neurology Travel Award (2013); Muscular Dystrophy Association Best Poster (2012); MGFA Newsom Davis Travel Award (2012); Muscle Study Group Travel Award, Arnold P. Gold Foundation (2012); Best Doctor Award, Arnold P. Gold Foundation (2012); Autonomic and Clinical Neurophysiology Highlights, 65th AAN Meeting (2012); Best Abstract, American Association of Neuromuscular and Electrodiagnostic Medicine (2011); Junior Member Recognition Award, American Association of Neuromuscular and Electrodiagnostic Medicine (2011-2013); Resident of the Year, Cleveland Clinic Florida (2010-2013) **Membership:** American Medical Association; American Association of Neuromuscular and Electrodiagnostic Medicine; American Academy of Neurology; Elected Member, Sigma Xi; Elected Member, Alpha Omega Alpha; Elected Member, Gold Humanism Honor Society **Hobbies:** Golf; Reading **Shipping Address:** 5012 Clark Ln Apt 204, Columbia, MO, 65202

Robert James Grammig

Title: Lawyer **Industry:** Law and Legal Services **Company Name:** Holland & Knight LLP **Date of Birth:** 06/15/1956 **Place of Birth:** Oceanside **State:** CA **Parents:** Richard Adolf Grammig; Mary Elizabeth (Spisak) Grammig **Marital Status:** Married **Spouse Name:** Laurel Jean Lenfestey (8/10/1996) **Children:** Clare Marie; James Richard; Grace Caroline; Julia Laurel **Education:** JD, Harvard University (1981); MA, University of Pennsylvania (1978); BA, University of Pennsylvania, Summa Cum Laude (1978) **Career:** Nationwide Practice for Corporate Mergers and Acquisitions and Securities, Holland & Knight LLP (2016-Present); Nationwide Practice Group Leader, Securities Law and Public Companies, Holland & Knight LLP (2005-Present); Chairman Elect, Florida Chamber of Commerce, Tampa Bay, FL (2016-2017); Regional Chair, Florida Chamber of Commerce, Tampa Bay, FL (2015-2016) **Career Related:** Board of Directors, Florida Chamber of Commerce (2011-Present) **Civic:** Florida Chamber of Commerce (2011-Present); Board of Governors, Crisis Center of Tampa Bay (2006-Present); Vice Chairman, Tampa Bay International Trade Council (1995); Leadership Tampa (1994-1995); Secretary, Tampa Bay International Trade Council (1994); Board of Directors, Child Abuse Council, Tampa, FL (1993-1997); Golden Triangle of Tampa Bay **Creative Works:** Contributor, Articles, Professional Journals **Membership:** Secretary, Florida Chapter, U.S. Austrian Chamber of Commerce (2012-Present); Hillsborough County Bar Association; Tampa Bay Area Committee on Foreign Relations; Florida Chapter, German American Chamber of Commerce; Phi Beta Kappa Society **Bar Admissions:** District of Columbia (1986); U.S. Supreme Court (1985); U.S. District Court, Middle District, State of Florida (1982); U.S. Court of Appeals for the 11th Circuit (1982); U.S. Court of Appeals for the Fifth Circuit (1982); State of Florida (1982) **Political Affiliations:** Republican **Religion:** Roman Catholic **Shipping Address:** 100 N Tampa Street, Suite 4100, Holland & Knight LLP, Tampa, FL, 33602

Irene H. Grant

Title: Physician **Industry:** Medicine & Health Care **Date of Birth:** 11/07/1953 **Place of Birth:** New York **State/Country of Origin:** NY **Parents:** Benton H. Grant, Irene A. Grant **Marital Status:** Divorced **Children:** Cedric Bluman; Sergei Bluman **Education:** Postgraduate Studies in Japanese Herbology, Kampo Internship with Nigel Dawes (2003); Postgraduate Studies in Asian Medicine, Pacific College of Oriental Medicine (1997-2003); Nutrition Fellowship, New York Academy of Medicine (1992); Fellow, Infectious Disease, Memorial Sloan-Kettering Cancer Center, New York City, NY (1985-1988); Internship, Residency, Montefiore Hospital, Bronx, NY (1982-1985); MD, Albert Einstein College of Medicine, Bronx, NY (1982); Pre-Medical Degree, Columbia University, New York, NY (1975-1978); BA, University of Pennsylvania, Cum Laude (1975) **Certifications:** Certification in Acupuncture, New York Medical College, Valhalla, NY (1997); Diplomate, American Board of Infectious Diseases; Diplomate, American Board of Internal Medicine **Career:** Clinical Assistant Professor of Medicine, New York Medical College (1997-Present); Clinical Preceptor, New York Medical College (1997-Present); Advisory Board, Pacific College of Oriental Medicine (2011-2016); Co-principal Investigator, Centers for Disease Control, Expanded Sentinel Hospital HIV Serosurvey (1992); Protocol Chief, Toxoplasmic Encephalitis Prevention Study, Community Programs for Clinical Research in AIDS, Bronx Lebanon Hospital Center (1990); Assistant Professor of Medicine, Albert Einstein College of Medicine (1988-1999) **Creative Works:** Presentation, "Immunodeficiencies associated with indoor mold exposures and persistent illness, and available immune therapies," The International Society for Human and Animal Mycoses Congress Symposium on Indoor Mold and Sick Building, Amsterdam, Netherlands (2018); Presentation, "Clinical Findings After Hazardous Indoor Microfungal Trichothecenes Mycotoxin Exposure: Disability outcomes risk analysis, immunosuppression and impaired genetic MTHFR detoxification status," The International Society for Human and Animal Mycoses Congress Symposium on Indoor Mold and Sick Building, Amsterdam, Netherlands (2018); Presentation, "Clinical Findings after Indoor Trichothecenes (DON, T-2) Exposure: Analysis of Outcomes, Immunosuppression and Impaired MTHFR Detoxification Status," The 10th Conference of The World Mycotoxin Forum: Strategies to Reduce the Impact of Mycotoxins, Amsterdam, Netherlands (2018); Presentation, "In Utero & Neonatal Complications with indoor Aspergillus, Penicillium, Chaetomium, Stachybotrys, Trichothecenes Environmental Exposure," The 5th Diagnosis and Therapy of Fungal Diseases Training Course for Fungal Infections in Neonates, Belgrade, Serbia (2017); Presentation, "Family of 7 simultaneously exposed to extremely high indoor Trichothecenes and multiple toxin-producing microfungi: analysis of exposure variables, clinical risks for toxic exposure fungal complications and clinical outcomes," The 8th Trends in Medical Mycology Congress, the European Confederation of Medical Mycology, Belgrade, Serbia (2017); Presentation, "Acute Myasthenia Gravis following extreme indoor hazardous environmental exposure: Mycotoxins documented in Thymoma and superior efficacy of antifungal therapy with Posaconazole. A case report," The 8th Trends in Medical Mycology Congress, the European Confederation of Medical Mycology, Belgrade, Serbia (2017); Presentation, "Scoring exposure hazard to indoor Trichothecenes and microfungi based on comparative analysis of clinical debility and disability outcomes, immunosuppression and impaired genetic MTHFR detoxification status," The 8th Trends in Medical Mycology Congress, the European Confederation of Medical Mycology, Belgrade, Serbia (2017) **Awards:** Convener and Chair for Symposium on Indoor Fungi and Sick Buildings, International Society for Human and Animal Mycoses Congress, Amsterdam, Netherlands (2018); Certificate of Achievement & Appreciation for Meritorious & Dedicated Service, State Board for Acupuncture, University of the State of New York Education Department (2013); Third Place Poster Competition, "The Effects of Acupuncture versus Wine on Cognitive Functions," 25th Anniversary Symposium American Academy of Medical Acupuncture, Baltimore, MD (2013); Leading Physician of the World, Doctors of Excellence, Top Internal Medicine and Infectious Disease Specialist, International Association of Healthcare Professionals (2012); Best Doctors of New York, New York Magazine (1st edition): Infectious Disease (1991) **Membership:** Infectious Diseases Society of America; American Society of Microbiology; International Society for Human and Animal Mycoses; American Society of Microbiology; International Society for Mycotoxicology **Marquis Who's Who Honors:** Albert Nelson Marquis Lifetime Achievement Award (2017) **Shipping Address:** 69 Church St, Tarrytown, NY, 10591

Murray Crossley Greason Jr.

Title: Lawyer (Retired) **Industry:** Law and Legal Services **Company Name:** Womble, Bond & Dickinson PLLC **Date of Birth:** 12/12/1936 **Place of Birth:** Wake Forest **State/Country of Origin:** NC **Parents:** Murray Crossley Greason; Evelyn Elizabeth (Hackney) Greason **Marital Status:** Married **Spouse Name:** Joan Millicent (Wilder) Greason **Children:** Murray C. Greason, III; Millicent Wilder Greason; Mary Elizabeth Greason **Education:** JD, Wake Forest University, Magna Cum Laude (1962); BS, Wake Forest University, Magna Cum Laude (1959) **Career:** Chairman, Firm Management Committee, Womble Carlyle Sandridge & Rice, LLP (Now Womble Bond Dickinson), NC (1987-1996); Firm Management Committee, Womble Carlyle Sandridge & Rice, LLP (Now Womble Bond Dickinson), NC (1978-2001); Partner, Womble Carlyle Sandridge & Rice, LLP (Now Womble Bond Dickinson), NC (1970-2002); Associate, Womble Carlyle Sandridge & Rice, LLP (Now Womble Bond Dickinson), NC (1965-1970) **Career Related:** Visiting Lecturer, Wake Forest University (1972-1974) **Civic:** Board of Directors, The Governor Morehead Forum for Economic Development (2015-Present); Board Member, Wake Forest College Birthplace Society, Inc. (2011-Present); Lifetime Member, Board of Trustees, Wake Forest University (2008-Present); Trustee, The James W. Denmark Loan Fund, Wake Forest University (1972-Present); President, Forsyth Tech Foundation, Forsyth Technical Community College (2010-2011); Board of Advisers, Brown Companies (2008-2012); Board of Directors, Forsyth Tech Foundation, Forsyth Technical Community College (2007-2012); Vice Chairman, Board of Directors, Wake Forest University Health Sciences (2007-2009); Board of Directors, Wake Forest Baptist Medical Center (2006-2010); Board of Directors, North Carolina Railroad Company (2003-2015); Board of Directors, Community Care Center (2003-2011); Chairman, Board of Advisers, Wachovia Bank (Now Wells Fargo), Forsyth County (2003-2006); Chairman, Wake Forest University (2003-2005); Advisory Board, Amarr Garage Doors, Entrematic Group AB (2002-2012); Board of Directors, Wake Forest University Health Sciences (2002-2010); Rail Advisory Council, NCDOT (2002-2006); Chairman, Board of Transportation (2002); Board of Visitors, School of Law, Wake Forest University (2001-2012); Board Member, Wake Forest College Birthplace Society, Inc. (2001-2008); Chairman, The Leadership Circle (2001); Chairman, Alexis de Tocqueville Division, General Campaign (2001); Board of Directors, Winston-Salem Alliance (2000-2005); Board of Directors, Idealliance (1999-2016); Board of Directors, Wake Forest Innovation Quarter (1999-2016); Executive Committee, Idealliance (1999-2016); Executive Committee, Wake Forest Innovation Quarter (1999-2016); Vice Chair for Transportation (1998-2001); Board of Directors, Forsyth Common Vision Council (1998-2000); Vice Chairman, Wake Forest University (1997-2002); Advisory Board, Health Care Division, The Kate B. Reynolds Charitable Trust (1997-2002); Board of Trustees, Wake Forest University (1996-2008); Board of Directors, Wake Forest Baptist Medical Center (1999-2003); Chairman, Board of Directors, Alexis de Tocqueville Division, General Campaign (1995-1996); Board of Directors, Forsyth Common Vision Council (1995); Chairman, Board of Visitors, School of Law, Wake Forest University (1994-1998); Chairman, General Campaign (1994); Board of Advisers, Wachovia Bank (Now Wells Fargo), Forsyth County (1993-2006) **Military Service:** Captain, Judge Advocate General's Corps, United States Army (1962-1965) **Awards:** Distinguished Service Award, Wake Forest College Birthplace Society, Inc. (2016); Norman Coan Hope Award for Volunteer of the Year, National Multiple Sclerosis Society, North Carolina Chapter (2012); The Order of the Long Leaf Pine, North Carolina Governor (2009); Medallion of Merit, Wake Forest University (2008); Named, North Carolina Super Lawyers (2005-2008); The Beverly Lake Public Service Award, North Carolina Bar Association (2005); Dean Carroll Weather's Award for Meritorious Service, School of Law, Wake Forest University (2005); Distinguished Citizen Award, Old Hickory Council, Boy Scouts of America (2004); Named, Legal Elite, Business North Carolina (2003-2008) **Membership:** Chairman, Winston-Salem Chamber of Commerce (2002); Vice Chairman, Winston-Salem Chamber of Commerce (2001); President, Rotary Club of Winston-Salem (1998-1999); Board of Directors, Winston-Salem Chamber of Commerce (1997-2012) **Bar Admissions:** North Carolina State Bar (1962) **Marquis Who's Who Honors:** Albert Nelson Marquis Lifetime Achievement Award (2017); Distinguished Humanitarian (2017) **Religion:** Episcopalian **Shipping Address:** 1 W 4th St Ste 100, Womble, Bond & Dickinson PLLC, Winston-Salem, NC, 27101

Steven M. Greenberg

Title: Lawyer **Industry:** Law and Legal Services **Company Name:** Greenberg & Lanz LLC **Date of Birth:** 04/09/1949 **Place of Birth:** Jersey City **State/Country of Origin:** NJ **Parents:** Joseph Greenberg; Rhoda (Weisenfeld) Greenberg **Education:** JD, University of Pennsylvania Law School, Philadelphia, PA (1974); AB in Political Science, Syracuse University, Cum Laude, Syracuse, NY (1971) **Career:** Senior Partner, Attorneys at Law, Greenberg & Lanz, LLC Hackensack, NJ (1997-Present); Attorney, Bergenfield Rent Leveling Board (1999); Senior Partner, Attorneys at Law, Greenberg & Marmorstein, Hackensack, NJ (1994-1997); Attorney, Bergenfield Planning Board (1993-1996); Attorney, Bergenfield Rent Leveling Board (1992-1993); Attorney, Bergenfield Rent Leveling Board (1985-1989); Sole Practitioner, Private Practice, Hackensack, NJ (1979-1994); Associate Attorney, Cole, Berman & Belsky, P.A., Rochelle Park, NJ (1977-1979); Associate Attorney, Carpenter, Bennett & Morrissey, Newark, NJ (1974-1977); Summer Associate, Carpenter, Bennett & Morrissey, Esqs., Newark, NJ (1973) **Civic:** Vice President, Jewish Home at Home, Inc. (2013-Present); Member, Board of Directors, Adler Aphasia Center (2012-Present); Member, Board of Directors, Jewish Home at Home, Inc. (2010-Present); Honorary Trustee, Jewish Association Development Disabilities (2008-Present); Board of Governors, Jewish Home for Assisted Living (2007-Present); Board of Governors, Jewish Home Family, Inc. (2007-Present); Jewish Family Service, Inc. (2005-Present); Governing Body Member, Jewish Home Foundation of North Jersey, Inc. (2003-Present); Vice President, Jewish Home (2003-Present); Committee Member, Jewish Home, Rockleigh, NJ (1999-Present); Board of Directors, Jewish Institute of Bioethics, New York City, NY (1998-Present); Member, New Jersey Regional Advisory Board, Anti-Defamation League (1989-Present); Jewish Home and Rehabilitation Center, Jersey City, NJ (1982-Present); Jewish Center Teaneck, NJ (1978-Present); President, Jewish Home Foundation of North Jersey, Inc. (2009-2012); Vice President, Jewish Family Service, Inc. (2007-2009); Trustee, American Society Protection of Nature in Israel (2006-2007); Secretary of Treasury, Jewish Home Foundation of North Jersey, Inc. (2005-2009); Vice President, Jewish Federation of Northern NJ (2005-2007); Board of Trustees, Jewish Federation of Northern New Jersey (2004-2013); Campaign Chair, Jewish Federation of Northern, NJ (2004-2005); Treasurer, Jewish Federation of Northern New Jersey (2004-2005); Executive Operations Committee, Association of Jewish Federations (2002-2003); Trustee, Association of Jewish Federations (2002-2003); Trustee, Bergen County High School Jewish Studies (2000-2005); New Jersey Leadership Think Tank, Allen and Joan Bildner Center to Study Jewish Life, Rutgers, The State University of New Jersey, New Brunswick, NJ (2001-2004); Trustee, Jewish Association of Developmental Disabilities (1999-2008); Jewish Community Relations Council of Northern New Jersey (1999-2007); Active, United Jewish Appeal Federation, Bergen County, NJ (1997-2004); President, Jewish Institute of Bioethics, New York City, NY (1998-2004); Director, Union Traditional Judaism (1993-1997); Jewish Family Service, Inc. (1986-1996); Jewish Community Relations Council of Northern New Jersey (1986-1993) **Awards:** Highest Rating in Legal Ability and Ethical Standards, Martindale-Hubbell (1980-Present); Bnos Menachem Yeshiva for Young Women Annual Gala Dinner - Guest of Honor (2016); Dr. Harry Brandeis Memorial Community Service Award, Community Resource Council (2010); Gates of Jerusalem Award, Boys Town Jerusalem (2004); Americanism Award, Anti-Defamation League (2003); Award, Ma'Ayanot Yeshiva High School Girls (2001); Jewish Theological Seminary of America - Second Century Award (1998); Award, Jewish Center of Teaneck (1997); Community Service Award, Friends of Lubavitch (1997) **Membership:** American Bar Association; New York State Bar Association; Bergen County Bar Association; New Jersey Bar Association; Pi Sigma Alpha; Phi Kappa Phi **Bar Admissions:** United States Court of Federal Claims (1989); United States Court of Appeals for the Third Circuit (1987); United States District Court for the Eastern District of New York (1986); United States District Court for the Southern District of New York (1986); New York (1980); United States District Court for the District of New Jersey (1974); New Jersey (1974) **Marquis Who's Who Honors:** Albert Nelson Marquis Lifetime Achievement Award (2017) **Shipping Address:** 2 University Plaza, Suite 300, Greenberg & Lanz, LLC, Hackensack, NJ, 07601 **Website:** http://www.greenberglanz.com

Kay C. Greene, PhD

Title: Founder, President **Industry:** Health, Wellness and Fitness **Company Name:** Bridge of Change **Date of Birth:** 07/10/1939 **Place of Birth:** Yankton **State/Country of Origin:** SD **Parents:** Fred Orin Green; Evelyn Irene (Sundy) Green **Marital Status:** Single **Education:** PhD in Clinical Psychology, The New School for Social Research (1983); MA in Psychology, The New School for Social Research (1980); BMus in Education, University of Nebraska (1962) **Certifications:** Licensed Psychologist, State of New York (1985-Present); Licensed Psychologist, State of Maryland (1987-2011); Licensed Psychologist, Washington, DC (1987-1997); Ordained Deacon, Fifth Avenue Presbyterian Church, NY (1997) **Career:** Clinical Psychologist, Private Practice, NY (1985-Present); Regional Trainer, HIV Office for Psychology Education (HOPE) Program, American Psychological Association (1992-1995) **Career Related:** Founder, President, Bridge of Change (1980-Present); Secretary General, International Council of Psychologists (2004-2005); Adjunct Associate Professor, John Jay College of Criminal Justice, NY (2002-2003); Chair, NGO/DPI Executive Committee, United Nations Headquarters (2000-2001); Adjunct Associate Professor, Pace University, NY (1999-2003); Vice Chair NGO/DPI Executive Committee, United Nations Headquarters (1998-2000); Adjunct Professor, Fordham University at Lincoln Center, NY (1998); Interim Executive Director, Millennium NGO Forum, United Nations Headquarters (1998); Adjunct Associate Professor, Fordham University at Lincoln Center, NY (1998); Secretary General, International Council of Psychologists (1997-2000); Adjunct Assistant Professor, St. Francis College, NY (1997-1998); Visiting Associate Professor, Fordham University at Lincoln Center, NY (1997-1998); Representative at the United Nations for the International Council of Psychologists (1996-2000); Keynote Speaker, World Friendship Week, VA (1995) **Civic:** Community Advisory Board of the Friendship Heights Village, Council of Chevy Chase, Maryland Council (2006-2010); FHV Council's Outstanding Community Service Certificate for Generous Donation of Time and Effort in Commitment to the Friendship Heights Village (2005) **Creative Works:** Contributor, Articles to Professional Journals **Awards:** Marie Curie Award for Significant Contributions to Psychology, International Biographical Centre (2006); Fellowship in Recognition of Outstanding and Unusual Contributions to the Science and Profession of Psychology, American Psychological Association (2000); Distinguished Leadership Award for Outstanding Service to the Health Field, International Directory of Distinguished Leadership (1996); Distinguished Leadership Award for Outstanding Service to the Health Field, International Directory of Distinguished Leadership (1994); International Woman of the Year in Recognition of Services to Mental Health, International Biographical Centre (1993-1994) **Membership:** Lifetime Fellow, International Division 52, American Psychological Association (1999-Life); Lifetime Member, Psi Chi, International Honor Society in Psychology (1997-Present); Lifetime Member, World Federation for Mental Health (1986-Present); Lifetime Member, American Psychological Association (1983-Present); Lifetime Member, Pi Kappa Lambda, American Honor Society for Undergraduate and Graduate Students and Professors of Music (1962-Present); Assistant Treasurer, International Division 52, American Psychological Association (2003); President, Academic Division, New York State Psychological Association (2001); President-elect, Academic Division, New York State Psychological Association (1999); Ambassador, International Council of Psychologists (1999); Representative, World Association for Psychosocial Rehabilitation, United Nations (1998-2000); Representative, International Council of Psychologists, United Nations (1996-2000) **Marquis Who's Who Honors:** Albert Nelson Marquis Lifetime Achievement Award (2017) **To what do you attribute your success:** In her careers involving psychology, Dr. Greene attributes her success to the training, advice, guidance, support, empathy and sympathy of her family, friends, teachers and colleagues. In addition, she cites her learned abilities to be focused, patient, tolerant and understanding. But these traits, Dr. Green believes, do not lead toward, determine, or create a sense of success. Her sense of success does not come from the things she does, rather it is a result of feeling inspired by what others do. She is inspired by her students, clients, and patients, as they proceed step after step, to move toward a meaningful goal. Dr. Green feels inspired by the inspiration others feel as they one day stop in awe, turn, reflect and realize they have reached a step toward their goal. **Hobbies:** Piano; Photography; Pets; Painting; Cooking **Political Affiliations:** Republican **Religion:** Presbyterian **Shipping Address:** 4701 Willard Ave Apt 1621, Chevy Chase, MD, 20815

George B. Greenfield

Title: Radiologist, Digital Photographer **Industry:** Health, Wellness and Fitness **Date of Birth:** 05/04/1928 **Place of Birth:** Brooklyn **State/Country of Origin:** NY **Parents:** Jacob Greenfield; Rose (Wolf) Greenfield **Marital Status:** Widowed **Spouse Name:** Barbara Anne O'Driscoll (3/3/1956, Deceased) **Children:** Edward James; Sheelagh Anne **Education:** MD, Utrecht University, Utrecht, Netherlands (1956); BA, New York University, New York, NY (1949) **Certifications:** Medical License, State of California (1984); Diplomate, American Board of Nuclear Medicine (1972); Medical License, States of Florida, New Jersey, and Wisconsin (1961); Diplomate, The American Board of Radiology (1961); Medical License, State of Illinois (1957) **Career:** Radiologist, Chicago, IL (1960-Present); Professor Emeritus, University of South Florida (2004); Professor of Radiology, University of South Florida, Tampa, FL (1989-2003); Vice Chairman, Department of Radiology, Chicago Medical School, Rosalind Franklin University of Medicine and Science (1988-1989); Professor of Radiology, Chicago Medical School, Rosalind Franklin University of Medicine and Science (1987-1989); President of Medical Staff, Mount Sinai Hospital (1983-1985); Professor of Diagnostic Radiology, Rush Medical College, Rush University (1976-1989); Professor, Department of Radiology, Mount Sinai Hospital (1969-1989); Chairman, Department of Radiology, Mount Sinai Hospital (1969-1989); Professor, Department of Radiology, Chicago Medical School, Rosalind Franklin University of Medicine and Science (1969-1974); Chairman, Department of Radiology, Chicago Medical School, Rosalind Franklin University of Medicine and Science (1969-1974); Associate Professor of Radiology, University of Illinois (1966-1969); Assistant Director, Diagnostic Radiology, John H. Stroger, Jr. Hospital of Cook County (1966-1969); Radiologist, John H. Stroger, Jr. Hospital of Cook County (1961-1966); Professor of Radiology, Cook County Graduate School of Medicine; Fellow, American College of Radiology **Military Service:** Honorable Discharge, U.S. Army (1951) **Creative Works:** Co-Author, "Imaging in Oncology: Radiologic abnormalities in the legs," Cancer Control Journal (2002); Senior Author, "Imaging of Arthritis" (2001); Co-Author, "Progression of bone disease in multiple myeloma patients treated with high dose and antologous stem cell Transplantation," Supplement to AJR (1997); Co-Author, "Evaluation of the child with a bone or soft tissue neoplasm," Orthopedic Clinics of North America (1996); Co-Author, "Osteochondromas: true, false, and malignant (ab.)," Program Book to American Roentgen Society, 95th Annual Meeting, Washington, DC (1995); Reviewer, "Imaging of Bone Tumors: A Multimodality Approach," Lippincott, Philadelphia, PA (1995); Co-Author, "Osteochondromas: true, false, and malignant (ab.)," Supplement to Radiology (1994); Author, "MRI of soft tissue tumors," Cancer Control: The Journal of Moffitt Cancer Center (1994); Co-Author, "MRI of soft tissue tumors," Skeletal Radiology (1993); Co-Author, "Cortical and periosteal changes as seen on MRI," Radio-graphics (1991); Co-Author, "Chondrosarcoma with avascular necrosis," Skeletal Radiology (1991); Author, "Radiology of Bone Diseases, Fifth Edition" (1990); Senior Author, "Computers in Radiology" (1985); Co-Author, "Diagnosis: Secondary hypertrophic osteoarthropathy associated with excavating pulmonary metastases from squamous carcinoma of the cervix," Skeletal Radiology (1980) **Awards:** Second Place, "Girl with Spaghetti Hair," T.I. Art Guild (2018); Honorable Mention, "Lily Pond," Suntan Art Center (2017); First Place, "Lurking," T.I. Art Guild (2015); First Place, "Spheres," T.I. Art Guild (2015); First Place, "Effect of Red Tide on a Wall Hanging Frog," T.I. Art Guild (2014); Second Place, "In Season," T.I. Art Guild (2014); Second Place, "Driftwood," T.I. Art Guild (2013); Honorable Mention, "Blue Salon," Suntan Art Center (2013); Exhibit, Morean Arts Center (2013); Second Place, "Tree of Gold," Suntan Art Center (2013); First Place, Third Place, Suntan Art Center (2011); Second Place, Suntan Art Center (2009); Exhibit, Treasure Island Art Guild Community Center (2008); First Place, Masters Category, APAA, Nashville, TN (2008); "How to Find the Best Doctors: Florida," First edition, Castle-Connolly (2000) **Membership:** American Medical Association; Chicago Medical Society; Chicago Radiological Society; American Roentgen Ray Society; Radiological Society of North America; Institute of Medicine of Chicago; International Skeletal Society; Society of Skeletal Radiology; Sigma Xi, The Scientific Research Honor Society; Treasure Island Art Guild; Suntan Art Center, Inc., St. Petersburg, FL; Guest Examiner and Surveyor of Residency Programs, American Board of Radiology **Marquis Who's Who Honors:** Albert Nelson Marquis Lifetime Achievement Award (2017) **To what do you attribute your success:** Dr. Greenfield attributes his success to his great interest in his work, as well as to being forward-thinking. **Shipping Address:** 12438 1st Street W, Treasure Island, FL, 33706

William Bates Greenough III

Title: Medical Educator **Industry:** Education/Educational Services **Company Name:** Johns Hopkins University **Date of Birth:** 01/03/1932 **Place of Birth:** Providence **State/Country of Origin:** RI **Parents:** William Bates Greenough, Jr.; Dorothy Garrison (Rand) Greenough **Marital Status:** Married **Spouse Name:** Quaneta Ahmed; Jane Cheney Woodruff (Deceased) **Children:** William Beckley; Kate; Thomas Clark; Elisabeth Bates **Education:** Senior Resident, Peter Bent Brigham Hospital, Boston, MA (1961-1962); Senior Research Fellow, Mary Imogene Bassett Hospital, Cooperstown, NY (1959-1961); Intern, College of Physicians and Surgeons, Columbia University, NY (1957-1959); MD, Harvard University, Cum Laude (1957); BA, Amherst College, Magna Cum Laude (1953) **Career:** Medical Director, Specialty Hospital, Bayview Medical Center, The Johns Hopkins Medical Center (2016-Present); Chairman, Independent Data Monitoring Committees, The Johns Hopkins Medical Center (2016-Present); Consultant, Cera Products Inc. (1993-Present); Member, Geriatric Medicine Division, Johns Hopkins University (1985-Present); Professor, Department of International Health, Bloomberg School of Public Health, Johns Hopkins University, Baltimore, MD (1985-Present); Professor of Medicine, School of Medicine, Johns Hopkins University, Baltimore, MD (1983-Present); Medical Director, Johns Hopkins Bayview Medical Center (2016); Director, International Centre for Diarrhoeal Disease Research, Dhaka, Bangladesh (1979-1985); Director, Robert Wood Johnson Clinical Scholars Program, School of Medicine, Johns Hopkins University, Baltimore, MD (1974-1977); Chief, Infectious Diseases Division, School of Medicine, Johns Hopkins University, Baltimore, MD (1970-1976); Staff Associate, Cholera Research Laboratory, National Heart Institute, Dhaka, Bangladesh (1962-1965) **Career Related:** Director, Scientific Advisory Board (2014-Present); Chairman, Scientific Advisory Board (2002-Present); Former Director, Chairman, Endowment Committee, International Centre for Diarrhoeal Disease Research, Bangladesh (1997-Present); Consultant, Cera Products Inc. (1993-Present); Former President, Chairman of the Board, Trustee, International Child Health Foundation, Columbia, MD (1985-1995); Ad Hoc Study Group on Enteric Disease, Walter Reed Army Institute of Research (1975-1977); Chairman, Bacteriology and Mycology Study Section, National Institutes of Health (1974-1976); Member, Bacteriology and Mycology Study Section, National Institutes of Health (1972-1976); Advisory Council, Bangladesh Foundation, Chicago, IL (1972) President, Bangladesh Information Center, Washington, DC (1971-1984); Governor's Commission on Physical Fitness and Sports (1971-1977) **Civic:** Senior Surgeon, U.S. Public Health Service (1962-1967) **Creative Works:** International Advisor, Kuwait Medical Journal, Journal of Health, Population and Nutrition (2000-Present); Editor, Topics in Infectious Disease (1976-Present); Contributor, Journal of General Internal Medicine (2016); Contributor, Journal of Critical Care Medicine (2015); Editor, Journal of Health & Population Research (1993-2000); Editor, Journal of Diarrhoeal Diseases Research (1983-1985); Editor, Infection and Immunity (1975-1978); Contributor, Articles, Professional Journals; Contributor, Book Chapters **Awards:** Arnold P. Gold Foundation Award, American Geriatric Society (2014); Friends of Liberation War Honor, Prime Minister Sheikh Hasina and President Mohammed Zillar Rahman (2012); Mary Betty Stevens Excellence in Clinical Investigation Prize, American College of Physicians (2012); Outstanding Service Award, Bangladesh American Foundation Inc. (2007); Paul G. Rogers Society for Global Health Research (2006); Howard Florey Memorial Lecturer, University of Adelaide (2001); Hajj (1989); International Prize in Medicine, King Faisal Foundation (1984); Maurice Pate Prize, UNICEF (1984); Recognized for Service to Children (1983) **Membership:** International Affairs Committee, Infectious Diseases Society of America (2000-2003); Fellow, American College of Physicians; Fellow, American Association for the Advancement of Science; Fellow, Infectious Diseases Society of America; Miller Coulson Academy of Clinical Excellence; Bangladesh Medical Society; American Society for Microbiology; Bangladesh Association for the Advancement of Science; American Geriatrics Society; American Society for Clinical Investigation; Association of American Physicians **Marquis Who's Who Honors:** Distinguished Humanitarian (2017) **Hobbies:** Long-distance Running **Political Affiliations:** Democrat **Religion:** Muslim **Shipping Address:** 1300 Hollins Ln, Baltimore, MD, 21209

Stephen T. Greer

Industry: Law and Legal Services **Education:** JD, University of Tennessee College of Law (1973); BS, Tennessee Tech University (1970) **Awards:** AV Preeminent Attorney, Martindale-Hubbell **Hobbies:** Traveling

John Patrick Gregan

Title: Finance Executive, Small Business Owner **Industry:** Financial Services **Company Name:** SMATAX **Date of Birth:** 11/24/1947 **Place of Birth:** Sigourney **State/Country of Origin:** IA **Parents:** Raymond Stephen Gregan; Ellen Mary (O'Brien) Gregan **Marital Status:** Married **Spouse Name:** Rhonda Mason Weissberg (11/19/1977) **Children:** Brien Geoffrey; Audrey Jane **Education:** BA in Accounting, St. Ambrose University, Davenport, IA (1970) **Career:** Tax Accountant, SMATAX, Waldorf, MD (1979-Present); Computer Audit Specialist, Office of International Operations (1974-1979); Revenue Agent, Office of International Operations, Washington, DC (1971-1973); Internal Revenue Agent, Internal Revenue Service, Davenport, IA (1970-1971) **Career Related:** Maryland Delegate, International Society of Public Accountants Convention (1992); Maryland Delegate, International Society of Public Accountants Convention (1987) **Civic:** Board of Directors, JP Home (2013-Present); Board of Directors, The Home Inc., Alexandria, VA (1992-1996); Diplomat, Rome, Italy (1973) **Membership:** National Society of Public Accountants; Maryland Society of Accounting & Tax Professionals; National Association of Enrolled Agents; Maryland Society of Enrolled Agents; National Society of Tax Professionals **Marquis Who's Who Honors:** Distinguished Humanitarian (2017) **Political Affiliations:** Democrat **Religion:** Roman Catholic **Shipping Address:** 13210 Breezy Court, Waldorf, MD, 20601

Lucius Perry Gregg Jr.

Title: Aerospace Executive (Retired) **Industry:** Business Management/Business Services **Company Name:** Hughes Electronics Products Corporation **Date of Birth:** 01/16/1933 **Place of Birth:** Henderson **State/Country of Origin:** NC **Parents:** Lucius Perry Gregg; Rachel (Jackson) Gregg **Marital Status:** Married **Spouse Name:** Beverly E.E. Ward (1/3/1994); Doris Marie Jefferson (5/30/1959, Deceased 11/1980) **Children:** Lucius Perry III; Essence Carmichael **Education:** AMP Program, Harvard Business School, Harvard College (1975); Honorary ScD, Grinnell College (1973); MS in Aero-and-Astronautics, Massachusetts Institute of Technology (1961); BSEE, United States Naval Academy, with Distinction (1955) **Career:** Vice President, Corporate Communications, Hughes Electronics Products Corporation (1989-1999); Vice President, Public Affairs, New York Daily News (1987-1989); Director, National Public Affairs, Citigroup Inc. (1983-1987); Vice President, Governor Relations, Citigroup Inc. (1983-1987); Vice President, Corporate Planning, Bristol-Myers Company (Now Bristol-Myers Squibb Company) (1979-1983); Vice President, First National Bank of Chicago (1972-1979); President, First Chicago Indemnity and Finance Corporation (1972-1979); Program Officer, Alfred P. Sloan Foundation, New York, NY (1969-1972); Director, Northwestern University, Evanston, IL (1965-1969); Research Coordinator, Northwestern University (1965-1969); Associate Dean, Northwestern University (1965-1969) **Career Related:** Co-Founder, Foundation for the Study of America's Technology Leadership (1999); Chairman, Board of Directors, Negro Ensemble Company, Inc. (1984-1989); Board of Trustees, WNET, New York, NY (1981-1989); Midwest Chairman, White House Fellows Selection Committee (1977-1979); Intelligence Review Committee, Chicago Police Department (1977-1979); Board of Directors, United States-South Africa Leadership Exchange Program (1975-1982); Vice Chairman, Board of Directors, Corporation for Public Broadcasting (1975-1981); Board of Directors, Chicago Council on Global Affairs (1975-1979); Visiting Committee on Physics, Harvard University (1973-1979); Chairman, Committee on Minorities in Science, National Academy of Sciences (1973-1978); Commission on Human Resources, National Academy of Sciences (1973-1978); Chairman, Board of Visitors, Tulane University (1972-1977); Visiting Committee on Aeronautics and Astronautics, Massachusetts Institute of Technology (1971-1979); Member, National Aeronautics and Space Administration University Research Center (1968-1972); Founding Trustee, Fermi National Accelerator Laboratory, United States Department of Energy (1968-1972) **Military Service:** Civilian Advisory Board, Chief of Naval Personnel, United States Naval Forces (1971-1981); Academy Advisory Board, United States Naval Academy, Annapolis, MD (1971-1981); Major, United States Air Force (1965-1985); Project Scientist, Office of Scientific Research, United States Air Force (1961-1965); Pilot, Military Air Command, United States Air Force (1956-1959); Aircraft Commander, Military Air Command, United States Air Force (1956-1959) **Awards:** Honoree, The History Makers of America Collection, Library of Congress (2014); Honoree, 10 Outstanding Young Men, Chicago Junior Association of Commerce & Industry (1966); Honoree, Engineer of the Year, Washington Academy of Sciences (1964) **Marquis Who's Who Honors:** Albert Nelson Marquis Lifetime Achievement Award (2017) **Shipping Address:** 4143 Via Marina PH 18, Marina Del Rey, CA, 90292

Carol Joseph Griesemer

Title: Owner, Counselor (Retired) **Industry:** Health, Wellness and Fitness **Company Name:** A Place for Healing **Date of Birth:** 02/26/1936 **Place of Birth:** Billings **State/Country of Origin:** MO **Parents:** Joseph John Griesemer; Margaret Catherine (Arend) Griesemer **Education:** MA in Counseling, University of Missouri (1984); MRE, Saint Meinrad Seminary and School of Theology (1974); BS in Education, Missouri State University (1957) **Certifications:** Former Licensed Professional Counselor **Career:** Owner and Counselor, A Place for Healing (2005-2011); Director, Midpoint Counseling Center, Joplin (1991-2004); Case Manager, Sexual Assault and Family Violence, Joplin, MO (1988-1990); Director, Koinonia House, Columbia, MO (1984-1988) **Career Related:** Chairman, Four-State Behavioral Health Network (2003) **Creative Works:** Author, Numerous Poems **Membership:** Trustee, American Counseling Association, MO (2006-2011); Former Member, American Counseling Association; Former Member, Association for Spirituality, Ethics, Religion and Values in Counseling; Former Member, International Association of Marriage and Family Counselors; Former Member, Amnesty International **Marquis Who's Who Honors:** Albert Nelson Marquis Lifetime Achievement Award (2017) **Why did you become involved in your profession or industry:** Both teaching and counseling came as a challenge to Ms. Griesemer. **What do you consider to be the highlight of your career:** The highlight of her career was having been a m/f counselor for over 20 years. **Where will you be in five years:** In five years, she will be retired and volunteering her time and service to those in need. **Hobbies:** Writing poetry; Writing fiction; Writing nonfiction; Reading **Political Affiliations:** Democrat **Religion:** Catholic **Shipping Address:** 1000 East Montclair Street, Apt 406, Springfield, MO, 65807

James Thomas Grimaldi

Title: Private Invester **Industry:** Financial Services **Date of Birth:** 12/08/1928 **Place of Birth:** Elizabeth **State/Country of Origin:** NJ **Parents:** Anthony Grimaldi; Helen (Bernatt) Grimaldi **Marital Status:** Widower **Spouse Name:** Norma Miriello (6/17/1951) **Children:** Patricia Ann Grimaldi; Pamela Gay Grimaldi; Donna Lynne Grimaldi **Education:** MBA, Columbia University (1955); BS in Economics, University of Pennsylvania (1951) **Certifications:** Chartered Life Underwriter (1964) **Career:** Engaged in Private Investments (1976-Present); Executive Vice President Sales, Keystone Custodian Funds, Inc., Boston, MA (1974-1976); President, Chief Executive Officer, Board of Directors, Cornerstone Financial Services, Inc., Boston, MA (1974-1976); President, Chief Executive Officer, Board of Directors, Keystone Company, Boston, MA (1974-1976); President, Chief Executive Officer, Board of Directors, Federal Life & Casualty Company (1971-1974); President, Chief Executive Officer, Director, Peoples Home Life Insurance Company of Indiana (1971-1974); Executive Vice President, Federal Life & Casualty Company, Battle Creek, MI (1970-1971); Executive Vice President, Peoples Home Life Insurance Company of Indiana (1969-1971); Vice President Marketing, Inland Life Insurance Company, Chicago, IL (1966-1969); Registered Agency Director, Assistant Vice President, American-Amicable Life Insurance Company, Fort Lauderdale, FL (1961-1966); Agent, Metropolitan Life Insurance Company (1956-1961); Senior Assistant District Manager, Metropolitan Life Insurance Company (1956-1961); Branch Accountant, Watson-Flagg Engineering Company, Paterson, NJ (1953-1956) **Career Related:** Member, Faculty, DePaul University, Chicago, IL (1969) **Civic:** Board of Directors, Michigan Chamber of Commerce (1972-1974); Trustee, Community Hospital Association, Battle Creek, MI (1971-1974) **Military Service:** First Lieutenant, U.S. Air Force (1951-1953) **Awards:** Special Tribute as Outstanding Citizen, State of Michigan (1974) **Membership:** President, Life Insurance Association of Michigan (1973); Sales Marketing Executives International; American Society of Chartered Life Underwriters; National Association of Life Underwriters; American Marketing Association; Association of Individual Investors; Executive Committee, Life Insurance Association of Michigan; National Association of Security Dealers; Academy of Political Science; University of Pennsylvania Alumni Association; Columbia University Alumni Association **Marquis Who's Who Honors:** Albert Nelson Marquis Lifetime Achievement Award (2017); Distinguished Humanitarian (2017) **Hobbies:** Golf **Shipping Address:** 4300 Sharon Rd Apt 528, Charlotte, NC, 28211

Jeanette A. Griver

Title: CEO **Industry:** Business Management/Business Services **Company Name:** Compsych Systems Inc. **Date of Birth:** 07/02/1932 **Place of Birth:** New York **State/Country of Origin:** NY **Parents:** Lawrence Maurice Rosenthal; Selma Demby-Rosenthal **Marital Status:** Widowed **Spouse Name:** David M. Griver (3/15/1951, Deceased 4/1991) **Education:** MA in Human Factors Psychology, University of Southern California (1964); BA in Psychology, University of California, Los Angeles (1961) **Career:** Chief Executive Officer, Compsych Systems, Inc., Los Angeles, CA (1962-Present); President, Jan Engineering Human Factors Division, Santa Monica, CA (1962-1989); Vice President, Jan Engineering Electronic Components, Santa Monica, CA (1955-1962) **Career Related:** Consultant, Several Organizations (1962-Present) **Civic:** Pacific Palisades Lions Club (2002-Present); Pacific Palisades Chamber of Commerce (1990-2003) **Creative Works:** Author, "Curio a Shetland Sheepdog Meets the Cat" (2009); Author, "Curio a Shetland Sheepdog and Her Pals" (2007); Author, "Curio a Shetland Sheepdog and Friends" (2005); Author, "Curio a Shetland Sheepdog Meets the Crow" (2004); Author, "Oh No! Not Another Problem" (2000); Author, "Applied Problem Analysis Plus" (1988); Author, "Curio, Journey of a Women Entrepreneur"; Contributor, Articles, Professional Journals **Membership:** Human Factors and Ergonomics Society (2003); President, Pacific Palisades Lions Club (1990); International Association of Nanotechnology **To what do you attribute your success:** Ms. Griver attributes her success to her persistence. She believes that one must have patience, a good idea, and put in time and due diligence in order to succeed. **What do you consider to be the highlight of your career:** A highlight of Ms. Griver's career is the dog books she has written, plus the design of motivational, theory-structured feedback. **Where will you be in five years:** Five years from now, Ms. Griver intends to write a book about a woman entrepreneur. **Hobbies:** Travel; Tennis **Shipping Address:** 417 26th Street, Compsych Systems Inc., Santa Monica, CA, 90402

Peter Z. Grossman, PhD

Title: Economics Professor **Industry:** Education/Educational Services **Company Name:** Butler University **Date of Birth:** 07/27/1948 **Place of Birth:** Waterbury **State:** CT **Parents:** Nicholas Grossman; Adlah Grossman **Marital Status:** Married **Spouse Name:** Pauline Spiegel (7/4/1983) **Children:** Nathan Spiegel-Grossman; Daniel Spiegel-Grossman **Education:** PhD, Washington University (1992); MFA, Columbia University (1972); AB, Columbia University (1970) **Career:** Research Associate, Hobby School of Public Affairs, University of Houston (2013-Present); Clarence Efroymson Professor of Economics, Butler University (1994-Present); Visiting Scholar, Energy Management and Policy, University of Houston (2012); Adjunct Professor, School of Law, Indiana University (2000-2005); Visiting Assistant Professor of Economics, Washington University (1993-1994); Affiliate Professor of Engineering, Washington University (1990-1993); Assistant Professor of Humanities, School of Engineering, New York University (1979-1985) **Career Related:** Director, Real Silk Investments (1998-1999); Consultant, Ralston Purina Inc. (1993-1994); Contributing Editor, "Financial World" (1980-1984) **Creative Works:** Author, "U.S. Energy Policy and the Pursuit of Failure"; Author, American Express: The History of the People Who Built the Great Financial Empire"; Co-Author, "Introduction to Energy: Resources, Technology & Society"; Co-Editor, "The End of a Natural Monopoly: Deregulation and Competition in the Electric Power Industry"; Editor, "How Cartels Endure and How They Fail: Studies of Industrial Collusion"; Co-Author, "Principles of Law and Economics"; Author, "V.D."; Contributor, Various Columns in Newspapers, Articles in Professional Journals and Chapters in Books **Membership:** American Economic Association; Association of Environmental and Resource Economists; International Society for New Institutional Economics; International Association for Energy Economics **Hobbies:** Bicycling **Business Address:** 4600 Sunset Avenue, Indianapolis, IN, 46208 **Shipping Address:** 4600 Sunset Avenue, Butler University, Indianapolis, IN, 46208

Richard David Grundy

Title: Engineer **Industry:** Engineering **Date of Birth:** 03/17/1937 **Place of Birth:** San Mateo **State:** CA **Parents:** John Richard Grundy; Violette Grundy **Marital Status:** Married **Spouse Name:** Jamei C. Haswell (1997); Claudia Copeland (1977, Divorced 1992) **Education:** Postgraduate Coursework, Harvard University (1980); Postgraduate Coursework, The George Washington University (1965-1967); Postgraduate Coursework, University of California (1964); MS, University of California (1963); BSEE, Stanford University (1958) **Certifications:** Certified in Water Quality Control, State of California **Career:** President, Alexandria Energy Associates Inc., Virginia (1995-2003); Member, Senior Professional Staff, Committee on Energy and Natural Resources, United States Senate, Washington, DC (1977-1994); Executive Secretary, National Fuels and Energy Policy Study, United States Senate, Washington, DC (1971-1976); Member, Senior Professional Staff, Committee on Environment and Public Works, United States Senate, Washington, DC (1967-1976); Sanitation Engineer, Bureau of Environmental Health, U.S. Public Health Service (1959-1967); Lieutenant Commander, Bureau of Environmental Health, U.S. Public Health Service (1959-1967); Commercial Engineer, Pacific Gas Electric Company, San Francisco, CA (1958-1959) **Career Related:** Alternate Board Member, Hearing Board, San Francisco Bay Area Air Quality Management District, EPA, California (2002-2011); Board Member, North Coast Regional Water Quality Control Board, EPA, California (2001-2005); Member, U.S. Delegation, UN Negotiations on Climate Change, Geneva, Switzerland (1994); Observer, White House Conference on Global Climate Change, Washington, DC (1993-1994); Member, U.S. Delegation, UN Negotiations on Climate Change, Geneva, Switzerland (1993); Participant, UN Conference on Clean Coal Technology in Developing Countries, Beijing, China (1991); Steering Committee, Aspen Institute Energy Forum (1985-1991); Observer, White House Conference on Global Climate Change, Washington, DC (1990); Chairman, Protocol Committee, Second International Clear Air Congress, International Union of Air Prevention Associations (1970) **Civic:** North coast Regional Director, Steve Westly for Governor (2005-2006); Executive Director, Eastern Orchid Congress (1997-2000); President, National Capital Orchid Society, Washington, DC (1989-1990); Member, Air Pollution Control Association (1967-1982); Member, National Planning Committee, National Youth Governors Conference, YMCA, Washington, DC (1975-1980); Member, National Planning Committee, National Youth Governors Conference, Readers Digest Foundation, Washington, DC (1975-1980); Chairman, Membership Commission, Foundry United Methodist Church, Washington, DC (1968-1970); Member, Council of Ministers, Foundry United Methodist Church, Washington, DC (1967-1970); Member, Administrative Board, Foundry United Methodist Church, Washington, DC (1966-1970); Commander, U.S. Public Health Service (1959-1967); SAN Engineer, U.S. Public Health Service (1959-1967); Member, Administrative Board, Foundry United Methodist Church, Washington, DC (1960-1962) **Creative Works:** Co-editor, "Consumer Health and Product Hazards" (1974); Co-author, "Air Pollution and Industry" (1972) **Awards:** Distinguished Service Award, United States Senate (1981); Young Engineer of the Year, District of Columbia Society of Professional Engineers (1970); California Water Quality Control Award **Membership:** Fellow, American Association for the Advancement of Science; IEEE; National Society of Professional Engineers; Association of Energy Engineers; District of Columbia Society of Professional Engineers; Conservation Committee, American Orchid Society; United States Energy Association **Marquis Who's Who Honors:** Albert Nelson Marquis Lifetime Achievement Award (2017) **Religion:** Methodist **Shipping Address:** 7201 Oakmont Dr, Santa Rosa, CA, 95409

Renee Gucciardo

Title: Lawyer **Industry:** Law and Legal Services **Company Name:** Law Offices Renee K. Gucciardo, PLLC **Date of Birth:** 08/22/1967 **Place of Birth:** East Lansing **State:** MI **Career:** Owner, Law Offices of Renee K. Gucciardo, PLLC (2002-Present); Associate, Law Offices of Raymond A. Cassar, P.L.C. (1999-2002); Lecturer, Polish Academy, Oakland County Prosecutor's Office (1995-1998); Assistant Prosecuting Attorney, Oakland County Prosecutor's Office (1993-1998); Intern, Jackson County Prosecutor's Office (1991-1993) **Membership:** State Bar of Michigan (SBM); Oakland County Bar Association **Shipping Address:** 30700 Telegraph Road, Suite 1580, Law Offices Renee K. Gucciardo, PLLC, Bingham Farms, MI, 48025

Raouf Albert Guirguis, PhD

Title: Health Science Executive **Industry:** Health, Wellness and Fitness **Date of Birth:** 08/25/1953 **Place of Birth:** Cairo **Country of Origin:** Egypt **Parents:** Albert Amin Guirguis; Georgette Dahabi **Marital Status:** Married **Spouse Name:** Loretta Elisabeth Moschetti (7/14/1989); Dana Lynn Lebo (8/26/1982, Divorced 6/1988) **Children:** Sandra Gene **Education:** PhD, Georgetown University (1988); MS, Georgetown University (1987); MS, University of Alexandria, Arab Republic of Egypt (1983); MD, University of Alexandria, Arab Republic of Egypt (1980); Intern, Alexandria University School of Medicine (1979-1980) **Career:** Owner, AiSimTech LLC (2005-Present); Owner, Global Preparedness International LLC (2005-Present); Owner, Learning Touch LLC (2005-Present); Owner, Operator, Fingerprint Biotech, LLC (2002-Present); Owner, Operator, Advanced Language Systems International LLC (2001-Present); Founder, President, Chief Executive Officer, Lamina Equities Corp. (2001-Present); Owner, Operator, Diplomatic Language Services LLC (2001-Present); Founder, President, Point of Care Techs., Inc. (1999-Present); Chairman, Cancer Diagnostics Holding Company, Fairfax, VA (1995-Present); Chairman, Comprehensive Cancer Care Centers. LLP (1994-Present); Owner, Operator, Biotech Pharma, LLC (1992-Present); Founder, President, Chief Executive Offoc, MonoGen, Inc. (1996-1999); Chairman, Board, Fingerprint Diagnostics, Inc., Rockville, MD (1989-1994); President, Chief Executive Officer, Cancer Diagnostics Inc., Rockville, MD (1989-1994); Chairman of the Board, Antibody Resources Inc., Gaithersburg, MD (1989-1993); Pathology Fellow, National Cancer Institute, National Institutes of Health, Bethesda, MD (1984-1989); Research Associate, Lombardi Cancer Center, Washington, DC (1983-1984); Navy Captain, Alexandria University School of Medicine (1980-1983) **Career Related:** Consultant, Nephrology Cancer Center, Mansura, Arab Republic of Egypt (1988-1994); Adjunct Professor, Department of Physiology and Biophysics, Georgetown University Medical School, Washington, DC (1988-1993) **Civic:** Associate, Smithsonian, Washington, DC (1990); Active, Kennedy Center, Washington, DC (1990); Georgetown Club, Washington D.C. (1989); Baltimore Council on Foreign Affairs; Board of Directors, United States-Israel Biotechnology Council **Creative Works:** Contributor, Articles to Professional Journals **Awards:** Named, Saudi Minister of Health Scholar (1986-1988); Grantee, National Council of Churches Research (1986); Research Grantee, Hoffmann-LaRoche Innovation (1986); Named, Georgetown University Scholar (1985-1988); Named, Scholar, Foreign Council, Maryland **Membership:** Chief, Executive Division, American Medical Association; American Association for the Advancement of Science; IEEE; American Mathematics Association; American Association for Clinical Chemistry; American Society for Microbiology; American Chemical Society; American Management Association; New York Academy of Science; Society for Computer Simulation; Presidential Roundtable, Sigma Xi **Marquis Who's Who Honors:** Albert Nelson Marquis Lifetime Achievement Award (2017); Distinguished Humanitarian (2017) **Why did you become involved in your profession or industry:** Dr. Guirguis entered his profession because his father had been a secretary of housing as a government job and he was a guide for him and his brother father in engineering. **Political Affiliations:** Republican **Religion:** Coptic Orthodox **Shipping Address:** 10202 Sherman Heights Pl, Columbia, MD, 21044

Wayne Campbell Gundersen

Title: Energy Executive, Consultant **Industry:** Consulting **Company Name:** Petroleum Synergy Group, Inc. **Date of Birth:** 05/27/1936 **Place of Birth:** Elgin **State:** IL **Parents:** LeRoy Arthur Gundersen; Jean Ellen (Campbell) Gundersen **Marital Status:** Married **Spouse Name:** Gail Andrews (3/21/1959) **Children:** Thomas Dexter; Lori Ann; Kathy Lee **Education:** MS, University of Nebraska (1961); BS, University of Nebraska (1959) **Career:** Founder, President, Chief Executive Officer, Chairman of Board of Directors, Petroleum Synergy Group, Inc. (1988-Present); Consultant, Oil and Gasoline (1987-Present); President, Kaiser Exploration and Mining Company, Oakland, CA (1985-1987); President, Kaiser Energy, Inc., Oakland, CA (1985-1987); Vice President, Kaiser Aluminum & Chemical Corporation, Oakland, CA (1983-1987); Vice President, General Manager, Kaiser Energy, Inc., Oakland, CA (1983-1985); Director, Oil and Gas, Kaiser Aluminum & Chemical Corporation, Oakland, CA (1980-1981); Assistant to Vice President, Chevron Overseas Petroleum, San Francisco, CA (1976-1980); Advisor, Foreign Operations, Standard Oil California, San Francisco, CA (1974-1976); President, Kaiser Aluminum Exploration Company, Oakland, CA **Career Related:** Member, Geology Advisory Board, University of Nebraska, Lincoln, NE (1984-1987); Manager, Western Geothermal Partners LLC **Civic:** President, Parents Club, Foothill School, Walnut Creek, CA (1978-1979) **Creative Works:** Contributor, Articles to Professional Journals **Awards:** Distinguished Alumni, Chancellor's Society, University of Nebraska Foundation (2015-Present); Distinguished Alumni, Burnett Society, University of Nebraska Foundation (2012-Present); Trustee, University of Nebraska Foundation (2010-Present); Distinguished Alumni, Department of Earth and Atmospheric Sciences (2011); Named, Man of the Year, New Orleans Jaycees (1973); Sinclair Fellow (1960-1961) **Membership:** American Association of Petroleum Geologists (1977-2017) **Political Affiliations:** Republican **Religion:** Methodist **Shipping Address:** 980 Caughlin Xing Ste 102, The Petroleum Synergy Group, Reno, NV, 89519

Caryl J. Guth

Title: Integrative Medicine Specialist and Anesthesiologist **Industry:** Medicine & Health Care **Company Name:** Wake Forest Baptist Medical Center **Place of Birth:** Peoria **State/Country of Origin:** IL **Parents:** Rev Walter; Helen Guth **Marital Status:** Widowed **Spouse Name:** John Falstad (1968, Deceased 2001) **Education:** Fellow, Anesthesiology, QVH, East Grinsted, Sussex, England (1966); Resident, Anesthesiology, Hospital of the University of Pennsylvania, Philadelphia, PA (1963-1965); Intern, The University of Kansas Medical Center, Kansas City, KS (1962-1963); MD, Wake Forest University (1962); BS, Wake Forest University (1957); AA, Mars Hill College (1955) **Certifications:** Diplomat, American Board of Anesthesiology **Career:** Retired (2000); Board of Directors, Mills-Peninsula Health Systems, Burlingame, CA (1996-2000); Member, Medical Staff, Mills-Peninsula Health Systems, Burlingame, CA (1996-2000); Chair, Department of Anesthesiology, Mills Memorial Hospital, San Mateo, CA (1992-1996); Board of Directors, Mills Memorial Hospital, San Mateo, CA (1992-1996); Chair, Initiate Non-Smoking Hospital Policy Task Force, Mills Memorial Hospital, San Mateo, CA (1994-1996); Member, Medical Staff, Mills Memorial Hospital, San Mateo, CA (1967-1996); Chair, Anesthesiology Department, Kaiser Permanente Hospital, Santa Clara, CA (1967); Visiting Instructor of Anesthesiology, Radboud University (Formerly the University of Nijmegen), Nijmegan, The Netherlands (1966); Instructor of Anesthesiology, Wake Forest Baptist Medical Center, Winston-Salem, NC (1965) **Career Related:** Advanced Holistic Concepts and Nutrition, Cultivated the Patient Clinic for Integrative Medicine, Wake Forest Baptist Medical Center (2017-Present); Nurtured Center for Integrative Medicine, WFBMC (2006-Present); Holistic and Integrative Medicine Physician, Bermuda Run, NC (2003-Present); Member, Board of Science and Policy Advisers, The American Council on Science and Health (1995-Present); Fostered Program for Integrative Medicine, WFBMC (2002-2006); Established Caryl J. Guth, MD Chair for Integrative Medicine, Wake Forest Baptist Medical Center (2002); Physician, Holistic and Integrative Medicine, San Mateo, CA (1998-2000) **Civic:** Board of Visitors, Wake Forest Baptist Medical Center (2004-Present); Advisory Committee for Establishing Life-Long Learning Courses, Winston-Salem Arts Council (2014-2015); Board of Directors, Deacon Booster Club, Wake Forest University (2008-2012) **Creative Works:** CSA Bulletin Editor, California Society of Anesthesiology (1976-1979); Associate Editor, ASA Newsletter, American Society of Anesthesiologists **Awards:** North Carolina Baptist Heritage Award, Wake Forest Baptist Medical Center (2013); Distinguished Alumna of the Year Award, Mars Hill College (2012); Deacon Club Member of the Year Award, Wake Forest University (2010); Distinguished Service Award, Wake Forest Medical Alumni Association (2010); Distinguished Service Award, California Society of Anesthesiology (2006) **Membership:** Back-Court Booster Club, WFU (2016-Present); President's Club, Wake Forest University (2007-Present); Dean's Leadership Council, Medical Alumni Association, Wake Forest University (2006-Present); Board of Directors, Medical Alumni Association, Wake Forest University (1999-Present); Half Century Class Representative, Medical Alumni Association, Wake Forest University (2012); Campaign Chair, Medical Alumni Reunion Class of 1962 Campaign, Wake Forest University (2011-2012); Board of Directors, Deacon Club, Wake Forest University (2008-2012); President, Board, Medical Alumni Association, Wake Forest University (2005-2006); President-elect, Board, Medical Alumni Association, Wake Forest University (2004-2005); Secretary, Board, Medical Alumni Association, Wake Forest University (2003-2004); Endowed Chair, Complementary and Integrative Medicine, Wake Forest School of Medicine (2002); Annual Meeting Program Organizer, American Society of Anesthesiologists (1997, 1994, 1987-1988, 1983-1984); Committee Chair, Professional Diversity, American Society of Anesthesiologists (1995-1997); Committee Chair, Communications, American Society of Anesthesiologists (1987-1990); Chair, Medical Staff Affairs Committee, San Mateo County Medical Association (1985-1986); Director, Board, San Mateo County Medical Association (1984-1986); Committee Chair, Section of Specialty Organizations, California Medical Association (1983-1984); President, California Society of Anesthesiologists (1982-1983); President-elect, California Society of Anesthesiologists (1981-1982); Assistant Treasurer, California Society of Anesthesiologists (1979-1981); Delegate, American Society of Anesthesiologists (1976-2000) **Marquis Who's Who Honors:** Albert Nelson Marquis Lifetime Achievement Award (2017) **Business Address:** Wake Forest Baptist Medical Center, Winston-Salem, NC, 27157 **Shipping Address:** 105 Willowbrook Pl, Bermuda Run, NC, 27006 **Website:** http://www.wakehealth.edu/Center-for-Integrative-Medicine/About-the-Center/History.htm

Joseph Gutheinz Jr.

Title: Law Educator **Industry:** Law and Legal Services **Company Name:** Gutheinz Law Firm LLP **Date of Birth:** 08/13/1955 **Place of Birth:** Camp Lejune **State/Country of Origin:** NC **Parents:** Lt. Col. Joseph Richard Gutheinz, Sr.; Rita O'Leary Gutheinz **Marital Status:** Married **Spouse Name:** Lori Ann Bentley (1/16/1976) **Children:** Joseph, IV; Christopher; Michael; Jim; Bill; Dave **Education:** JD, South Texas College of Law (1996); Distinguished Graduate, Office of the Inspector General, Federal Law Enforcement Training Centers (1989); Criminal Investigators Basic Course, Federal Law Enforcement Training Centers, With Honors (1988); MS in Systems Management, University of Southern California (1985); Postgraduate Studies, University of California, Davis (1979-1980); MA in Criminal Justice, California State University, Sacramento (1979); BA in Criminal Justice, California State University, Sacramento (1978); AA in Liberal Arts, Monterey Peninsula College (1975); AS in Administration of Justice, Monterey Peninsula College (1975); Teaching Credentials in Aeronautics, Sociology, Police Science, Public Services and Administration, Military Science, and Business and Industrial Management **Certifications:** Certified Fraud Examiner; Certified Commercial Pilot, Federal Aviation Administration; Board Member, Aviation Law Section, Texas State Bar Association; Pro Bono College, State Bar of Texas; Texas Bar College **Career:** Partner, Gutheinz Law Firm LLP (2010-Present); College Instructor, University of Phoenix (2002-2018); Commissioned Member, Texas Commission on Fire Protection (2013-2014); Adjunct Professor, Thurgood Marshall School of Law (2014); Commissioned Member, Texas Council on Sex Offender Treatment (2009-2012); College Instructor, Alvin Community College (2004-2012); Commissioned Member, Texas Department of Criminal Justice Advisory Committee on Offenders with Medical and Mental Impairments (2004-2008); Law Office of Joseph R. Gutheinz, Jr. (1997-2010); Senior Special Agent, Office of Inspector General, National Aeronautics and Space Administration (1990-2000); Senior Special Agent and Acting Senior Resident Agent-in-Charge, National Aeronautics and Space Administration (1990-2000); Special Agent, Office of Inspector General, U.S. Department of Transportation (1987-1990); Special Agent, Civil Aviation Security, Federal Aviation Administration (1986-1987); College Instructor, Central Texas College-Europe (1982-1983); Army Officer (Aviator and Intelligence) (1979-1986) **Creative Works:** Appearance, "NASA's Unexplained Files," Science Channel (2016); Author, "Lost History with Brad Meltzer," History Channel (2015); Author, "Missing Moon Rocks: A Documentary" (2014); Actor, "Unbelievable Mysteries Solved" (2013); Author, "Moon Rock Hunter," (2012); Author, "Case of the Missing Moon Rocks" (2012); Author, "NASA's Dirty Little Secrets About Moon Rocks" (2012); Actor, "Lunarcy" (2012); Author, "A Decade Plus Tracking Lunar Larceny" (2011); Co-Author, "Obama's Mission to an Asteroid" (2010); Co-Author, "Where Dinosaurs Were, Dreams Remain" (2010); Co-Author, "Confusing Science with Science Fiction: The Remarketing of an Asteroid Threat" (2010); Author, "Tarmac Delays Are Unlawful Restraint Of Passengers" (2009); Co-Author, "Sinkhole de Mayo Mystery of a Famous Texas Sinkhole" (2009); Co-Author, "Hubble Telescope Mankind's Spyglass On the Universe" (2008); Author, "Grand Jury System's a Bad Joke on Justice" (2008); Author, "A Home Away From Home: Settling the Moon" (2008); Author, "A Call for Compassion in the Gary McKinnon Case" (2008); Actor, "Moon for Sale" (2007); Author, "NASA is for Lovers, Psychos and Homicidal Maniacs" (2007); Author, "NASA's Fallen Star: The Investigation of Omniplan Corporation" (2006); Author, "NASA's Plutonium Gamble" (2006); Author, "Making Safety a Priority: NASA's Path to Mars" (2005); Author, "Cumbre Vieja: A Terrorist Time Bomb" (2005); Author, "Cover-up in Space" (2005); Author, "The Great Astronaut Impersonator" (2005) **Awards:** Award, National Association of Distinguished Counsel (2015-2016); Honoree, Top 100 Trial Lawyers, The National Trial Lawyer (2014-2016); Honoree, Top Lawyer in Houston, Houstonia Magazine (2014-2016); Exceptional Service Medal, National Aeronautics and Space Administration (2000); Career Achievement Award, President's Council on Integrity and Efficiency (2000) **Bar Admissions:** License, Texas State Supreme Court; U.S. Supreme Court; Fifth, Eighth, Tenth, 11th, and Federal Circuits, U.S. Court of Appeals; Circuits; U.S. Tax Court; U.S. Court of Appeals for the Armed Forces; U.S. Veterans Court of Appeals; U.S. District Court, Eastern District, State of Missouri; U.S. District Court, Southern District, State of Texas **Marquis Who's Who Honors:** Albert Nelson Marquis Lifetime Achievement Award (2017) **Political Affiliations:** Republican **Religion:** Roman Catholic **Business Address:** 307 S Friendswood Drive, Suite B3, Friendswood, TX, 77546

Mary "Dolly" Gwinn

Title: Business Developer, Organizational Theorist, Writer, Speaker, Lecturer **Industry:** Advertising & Marketing **Date of Birth:** 09/16/1946 **Place of Birth:** Oakland **State/Country of Origin:** CA **Parents:** Epifanio Cruz; Carolina (Lopez) Cruz **Marital Status:** Married **Spouse Name:** James Monroe Gwinn (10/23/1965) **Children:** Larry Allen **Education:** Coursework, Monterey Peninsula College (1965) **Career:** Founder, Gwinn Genius Institute (1998-Present); President, Gwinn Genius Institute (1998-Present); Founder, Strategic Integrations, Arizona's Innovative Business Development Center (1985-Present); President, Strategic Integrations, Arizona's Innovative Business Development Center (1985-Present); Executive Marketing Representative, KTAR New and Radio, Phoenix, AZ (1982-1983) Marketing Representative, Dale Carnegie & Associates, Inc. (1978-1979); Retail Store Manager, Consumer's Distributing Inc., Division, May Company (1973-1978) **Career Related:** Founder, International Institute for Conceptual Education (1993-Present); President, International Institute for Conceptual Education (1993-Present); Speaker, Willard InterContinental (2000); Speaker, Antelope Valley College (1998); Speaker, Inc. Magazine, Mansueto Ventures (1996); Speaker, Clemson University (1996); Speaker, St. John's College, University of Cambridge (1992) Speaker, Arizona Association for the Gifted and Talented **Civic:** Judge, Arizona International Pageants, Mrs. Arizona Organization, LLC (2018); Chairperson, Keble College, University of Oxford, United Kingdom (1997) **Creative Works:** Author, "Gwinn on Business," IMAGE Networker (1996); Author, "Genius Leadership Secrets from the Past for the 21st Century" (1995); Author, "Preparing for the 21st Century," Today's Arizona Woman (1993); Creator, "Whole Brain Business Theory" (1985); Founder, "New Fields of Study Genetics and NeuroBusiness"; Profiled, "The Thought Process of Genius"; Contributor, Articles, Professional Journals **Awards:** Inaugural Inductee, Lifetime Achievement Award, Arizona International Pageant (2018); World Intellectual (1993); Sales Person of the Month Award, Dale Carnegie (1978 -1979); Woman of the Decade **Marquis Who's Who Honors:** Albert Nelson Marquis Lifetime Achievement Award (2017) **To what do you attribute your success:** Mrs. Gwinn attributes her success to her God given ability and "natural talent" which unique and unusual circumstances revealed. She also credits focus, unrelenting determination, a great love of people and helping them get what they want. **Why did you become involved in your profession or industry:** Mrs. Gwinn became involved in her profession due to learning to be resourceful and inventive from her humble beginnings and growing up in Alaska. She learned to entertain herself, which inspired creativity. The time spent with her father taught her to think ahead. Her experience with Dale Carnegie also had a very positive impact on her, teaching her selling concepts and ideas. **What do you consider to be the highlight of your career:** A highlight in Mrs. Gwinn's career includes being a featured speaker at St. John's College, University of Cambridge, Cambridge, England in 1992. Her first speech in the world was "The Creative Quest of Whole Brain Business Theory: It's Development into Whole Brain Business." **Hobbies:** Show Dogs; Saluki; Cross Country Skiing; Mountain Climbing; Deep Sea Fishing; Croquet **Political Affiliations:** Republican **Shipping Address:** 5836 E Angela Dr, Scottsdale, AZ, 85254

Clovis Haden

Title: Academic Administrator **Industry:** Education/Educational Services **Date of Birth:** 04/10/1940 **Place of Birth:** Houston **State:** TX **Year of Passing:** 2017-01-25 **Parents:** Clovis Newton; Mary Aline (Baker) H. **Marital Status:** Married **Spouse Name:** Joyce Elaine Weathers (8/8/1956) **Children:** Cathy Rene Haden Fuchs; Kimberly Lynn Haden Jensen; Clovis Clay Haden **Education:** PhD, University of Texas (1965); MSEE, California Institute of Technology, Pasadena (1962); BSEE, University of Texas, Arlington (1961); Student, Navarro College, Corsicana, Texas (1958-1959) **Certifications:** Licensed Professional Engineer, State of Oklahoma, State of Texas **Career:** Vice Chancellor, Dean of Engineering, Director, Engineering Experiment Station, Texas Agricultural and Mechanical University (1993-2002); Vice Chancellor for Academy Affairs, Louisiana State University, Baton Rouge (1991-1993); Board of Directors, Arizona Transportation Research Center (1980-1991); President, Research Park Board, Arizona State University, Tempe (1983-1991); Provost West Campus, Arizona State University, Phoenix (1988-1989); Vice President for Academy Affairs, Arizona State University, Tempe (1987-1988); Dean, College of Engineering and Applied Sciences, Arizona State University, Tempe (1989-1991); Dean, College of Engineering and Applied Sciences, Arizona State University, Tempe (1978-1987); Director, Institute of Solid State Electronics, Texas Agricultural and Mechanical University (1969-1972); Professor, Texas Agricultural and Mechanical University, College Station (1971-1972); Associate Professor, Texas Agricultural and Mechanical University, College Station (1968-1971); Director, School of Electrical Engineering and Computing Sciences (1972-1978); Assistant Professor, University of Oklahoma (1965-1968) **Civic:** Reserve Valley Partnership (2004-2012); Star Rotor Inc. (2008-2012); Crosstex Energy (2002-2006); Inter-tel, Inc. (1983-2005); WAVO Corporation (1990-1999); E-System (1994-1995); Square D. Company (1985-1991); Board of Directors, Harrington Arthritis Research Center (1983-1987); Arizona Economic Development Board (1982-1985); Board of Managers, Tempe YMCA (1982-1984) **Military Service:** Admiral, Texas Navy (2011) **Creative Works:** Executive Editor, Electric Power Systems Research Journal (1978-Present) **Awards:** Lamme Award, IEEE (2007); Marlowe Award (1998); Engineer of the Year Award (1983); Oklahoma City Engineer of the Year Award, IEEE (1977) **Membership:** President, Vice President, Wingfield Family Society (2010-2013); Lamme Award Committee Member (2008-2011); Chair, Public Policy Committee, American Society of Engineering Education (1997-1999); Chairman, Council of Texas Engineering Deans (1995-1998); Board of Directors, Texas Society of Professional Engineers (1995-1998); Fellow, IEEE; National Society of Professional Engineers, Arizona Society of Professional Engineers; Arizona Association of Industrial Development; Society of Manufacturing Engineers, Sons of the American Revolution; Sons of Republic of Texas; Golden Key International Honor Society; Sigma Xi; Phi Kappa Phi; Eta Kappa Nu; Tau Beta Pi; Texas Navy **Marquis Who's Who Honors:** Albert Nelson Marquis Lifetime Achievement Award (2017) **Political Affiliations:** Republican **Religion:** Christian **Shipping Address:** 8412 Wildewood Circle, College Station, TX, 77845

Marilyn Geisler Haft

Title: Partner **Industry:** Law and Legal Services **Company Name:** Law Offices of Marilyn G. Haft, P.C. **Date of Birth:** 08/01/1943 **Place of Birth:** New York **State:** NY **Parents:** Frank Geisler; Sarah (Engelsohn) Geisler **Marital Status:** Married **Spouse Name:** Dr. Jay B. Adlersberg **Children:** Samantha Danielle Bowser **Education:** JD, School of Law, New York University (1968); BA, Brooklyn College (1965) **Career:** Entertainment Lawyer, Law Offices of Marilyn G. Haft P.C (2010-Present); Partner, Duval & Stachenfeld (2004-2010); Partner, Marshall Law Firm (1997-2004); Partner, Tanner, Propp and Farber, New York, NY (1993-1996); Partner, Fischbein, Badillo & Wagner, New York (1990-1993); Of Counsel, Summit, Rovins & Feldesman, New York, NY (1989-1990); Sole Practice, Entertainment Law, New York, NY (1981-1989); United States Representative, Mission to the United Nations, New York, NY (1980-1981); New York Primary Campaign Director, Re-Election for Jimmy Carter and Walter Mondale, New York, NY (1979-1980); Deputy Counsel to Vice President Walter Mondale, White House, Washington, DC (1978-1979); Associate Director, Office of Public Liaison, The White House, Washington, DC (1977-1978); Deputy Counsel, Government Operations Committee, United States Congress, Washington, DC (1976-1977); Full-Time News Consultant, NBC (1975-1976); Staff Counsel, National Office, ACLU, New York, NY (1970-1976); Adjunct Professor, Graduate Film Department, Tisch School of the Arts, New York University; Adjunct Professor, School of Law, New York University **Career Related:** Film Producer (1987-Present) **Civic:** Chair, Friends of the World Federation of United Nations Associations **Creative Works:** Producer, "Handsome Harry" (2010); Co-Producer, "Diminished Capacity" (2008); Co-Producer, "Birds of America" (2008); Producer, "Preston Sturges: The Rise and Fall of an American Dreamer" (1990); Producer, "In a Shallow Grave" (1988); Author, "Time Without Work" (1984); Author, "Rights of Gay People" (1973); Author, "The Rights of Prisoners: The Basic ACLU Guide to a Prisoner's Rights" (1973); Editor, "Rights of Gay People" (1973); Author, "Prisoner's Rights Sourcebook" (1972); Editor, "Prisoner's Rights Sourcebook" (1972) **Membership:** President, Friends of the World Federation of the United Nations Associations; Board, Foreign Press Association Foundation **Bar Admissions:** District of Columbia (1978); U.S. Supreme Court (1973); State of New York (1969); New York City Bar Association **Marquis Who's Who Honors:** Albert Nelson Marquis Lifetime Achievement Award (2017) **Why did you become involved in your profession or industry:** Ms. Haft became involved in her profession because of her desire to save the world. She saw a film about the Holocaust in school at the age of six, which motivated her to make sure nothing like that ever happens to anybody again. She was also inspired by visiting the United Nations on a school trip and after hearing a lawyer named Louis Nizer on the radio. **What do you consider to be the highlight of your career:** The highlight of Ms. Haft's career was starting the first gay rights litigation in the which included challenging sodomy laws and challenging visitation rights for gay people for their kids, as well as employment. **Hobbies:** Traveling; History **Political Affiliations:** Democrat **Religion:** Jewish **Shipping Address:** 140 Riverside Drive, Penthouse B, New York, NY, 10024 **Website:** http://www.mhaftlaw.com

Walter Albert Hairston

Title: School System Administrator **Industry:** Education/Educational Services **Company Name:** Baltimore City Department of Education **Date of Birth:** 09/14/1928 **Place of Birth:** Winston-Salem **State:** NC **Parents:** Harvey Hairston; Ethel (Marshall) Hairston **Marital Status:** Married **Spouse Name:** Jeanette Olivia (1/2/1979); Genell Rosella Bright (3/10/1951, Divorced 9/12/1972) **Children:** Jacqueline; Walter; Denice; Roslyn; Michael; Linda; Brenda; Telly **Education:** EdD, Morgan State University (2014); Graduate, National Defense University (1979); Graduate, United States Army Command and General Staff College (1974); MEd, Loyola College (1970); BS, Morgan State University (1959); Graduate, Air Transport Ability School, Fort Meade, MD (1950); Coursework, Non-Commissioned Officers Leadership School, Fort Dix, NJ (1948) **Certifications:** Number Four in Class of 80, Transportation Officers Career Course, Armed Forces Staff College, Norfolk, VA (1967); Training Course, Fort Indiantown Gap, PA; Coursework, Defense Advanced Traffic Management Course **Career:** Commander, Post 301, American Legion, Jacksonville, FL (2006); Teacher, Principal, Baltimore City Department of Education (1986-1997); Vice Chairman, Board of Directors, Progressive Horizon; Hand Trucker, Norfolk and Western Railroad, VA (1946) **Career Related:** Foreman of Mails, U.S. Postal Service (1955-1988); Liaison, Transportation Corp., U.S. Army, Fort Eustis, VA (1984); Instructor, Fundamentals of Postal Service Institute, Norman, OK (1975); Vice Chairman, Board of Directors, Shero Homeless Veterans, Tutties Place **Military Service:** Colonel, U.S. Army (1948-1988); Functional Area Assessment Team, Transportation Corps, U.S. Army, Fort Eustis, VA (1984); Chief Evaluator and Director, Command General Staff College (1979-1981); Commandant, 2071st U.S. Army School (1979); Chief Evaluator and Director, Command and General Staff College U.S. Army (1974) **Creative Works:** Author, "No Excuses" **Awards:** Inductee, Atkins High School Hall of Fame, Winston-Salem, NC (2009); Superior Recognition Certificate, U.S. Postal Service (1996); Honorary Recognition Certificate, U.S. Postal Service (1995); Honoree, Honor Graduate, Morgan State University (1959); Grantee, Athletic Scholarship, North Carolina College at Durham (Now North Carolina Central University) (1946); Inductee, National Thespian Honor Society (1945); Combat Infantry Badge, Korea, U.S. Army **Membership:** Masons; Baltimore Mules; International Thespian Society; Jacksonville Neighborhood Association; Life Member, Kappa Alpha Psi; Kappa Delta Pi; Committee X-71 **What do you consider to be the highlight of your career:** The highlight of Col. Dr. Hairston's career has been knowing that his involvement has had a true impact on those with similar backgrounds, such as veterans. **Hobbies:** Golf; Fishing; Boating; Woodworking **Political Affiliations:** Democrat **Religion:** Presbyterian **Shipping Address:** 14300 Robcaste Rd, Phoenix, MD, 21131

Nils Hemming Hakansson, PhD

Title: Economist, Educator **Industry:** Education/Educational Services **Date of Birth:** 06/02/1937 **Place of Birth:** Marby **Country of Origin:** Sweden **Parents:** Nils Hakansson; Anna (Nilsson) Hakansson **Marital Status:** Widowed **Spouse Name:** Joyce Beth Kates (Deceased) **Children:** Carolyn Ann Hakansson-Johnston; Nils Alexander **Education:** Honorary PhD in Economics, Stockholm School of Economics (1984); PhD, University of California, Los Angeles (1966); MBA, University of California, Los Angeles (1960); BS, University of Oregon, With Honors (1958) **Certifications:** Certified Public Accountant, State of California **Career:** Chairman, Department of Finance, University of California, Berkeley (1997-2000); Sylvan C. Coleman Professor of Finance and Accounting, University of California, Berkeley (1977-2003); Chairman, Department of Finance, University of California, Berkeley (1976-1979); Professor, University of California, Berkeley (1971-1977); Associate Professor, University of California, Berkeley (1969-1971); Assistant Professor, Yale University, New Haven, CT (1967-1969); Assistant Professor, University of California, Los Angeles (1966-1967); Staff Accountant, Consultant, Arthur Young & Company, Los Angeles, CA (1960-1963) **Career Related:** Board of Directors, Laudus Mutual Funds (1990-2009); Bell Laboratories, Murray Hill, NJ (1979-1981); Hoover Fellow, University of New South Wales (1975); Bell Laboratories, Murray Hill, NJ (1974); Consultant, Rand Corporation, Santa Monica, CA (1965-1971); Ford Foundation Fellow, University of California, Los Angeles (1963-1966); Chairman, Board of Directors, Anna och Nils Hakanssons Stiftelse; Fellow, Accounting Researchers International Association **Creative Works:** Author, "Social Security's Investment Shortfall: $8 Trillion Plus - and The Way Forward - Plus How the US Government's Financial Deficit Reporting = 64 Madoffs" (2013); Consultant Editor, Journal of Accounting and Economics (1978-1981); Editorial Consultant, Accounting Review (1977-1980); Contributor, Articles, Professional Journals **Awards:** Graham and Dodd Award, Financial Analysts Federation (1982); Graham and Dodd Award, Financial Analysts Federation (1976) **Membership:** Financial Economists Roundtable (1993-2003); President, Western Financial Association (1983-1984); American Economic Association; American Financial Association; Honorary Member, American Institute of Certified Public Accountants; American Accounting Association; Founding Member, Society for Financial Studies **Why did you become involved in your profession or industry:** Dr. Hakansson didn't intend to become involved in his profession. As he was studying for a PhD, he realized that economics is what he wanted to do. **What do you consider to be the highlight of your career:** A highlight of Dr. Hakansson's career was receiving an honorary doctorate in 1984. **Shipping Address:** 252 Clyde Drive, Walnut Creek, CA, 94598

Raymond M. Hakim, PhD

Title: Professor **Industry:** Medicine & Health Care **Company Name:** Vanderbilt University Medical Center **Marital Status:** Married **Education:** Research and Clinical Fellow in Medicine, Nephrology, Brigham and Women's Hospital, Harvard Medical School (1981); Internship and Resident in Internal Medicine, Royal Victoria Hospital, Montreal, Quebec, Canada (1976-1979); MD, McGill University, Montreal, Quebec, Canada (1976); PhD in Engineering, Massachusetts Institute of Technology, Cambridge, MA (1967); MS in Engineering, Rensselaer Polytechnic Institute, Troy, NY (1965) **Certifications:** Tennessee Medical Licensure (1987); Board Certified in Nephrology (1982); Diplomate, American Board of Internal Medicine (1980); Certification of Specialist in Internal Medicine, Quebec, Canada (1980); Massachusetts Medical Licensure (1979); Quebec Medical Licensure (1977) **Career:** Clinical Professor of Medicine, Nephrology, Vanderbilt University, Nashville, TN (2012-Present); Attending Physician, Vanderbilt University Medical Center, Nashville, TN (2012-Present); Co-founder, Renal Care Group (Now Fresenius Medical Care) (1995-2007); Professor of Medicine, Division of Nephrology, Vanderbilt University School of Medicine (19871995); Director, Clinical Services in Nephrology, Vanderbilt University School of Medicine (1987-1995); Chief Medical Officer, Clinical & Scientific Affairs, Fresenius Medical Care, Nashville, TN (2009-2012); Senior Executive Vice President, Clinical & Scientific Affairs, Fresenius Medical Care, Nashville, TN (2009-2012); Chief Medical Officer, Fresenius Medical Care, Nashville, TN (2009-2012); Adjunct Clinical Professor of Medicine, Vanderbilt University, Nashville, TN (1996-2011); Executive Vice President, University Division, Renal Care Group, Inc., Nashville, TN (1996-2006); Chief Medical Officer, University Division, Renal Care Group, Inc. (Now Fresenius Medical Care), Nashville, TN (1996-2006); Director, University Division, Renal Care Group, Inc. (Now Fresenius Medical Care), Nashville, TN (1996-2006); Chief Medical Officer, Renal Care Group (Now Fresenius Medical Care) (1995-2007); Professor of Medicine, Vanderbilt University, Nashville, TN (1991-1996); Medical Director, Inpatient and Outpatient Dialysis Services, Vanderbilt Dialysis Unit, Nashville, TN (1987-1999); Attending on the Renal Consult, Dialysis and Transplantation Services, Vanderbilt University Medical Center, Nashville, TN (1987-1996) **Career Related:** Visiting Professor, Nephrology Grand Rounds, University of West Virginia, Morgantown, WV (2012); Distinguished Visiting Professor, Nephrology Grand Rounds, Brigham and Women's Hospital, Beth Israel Hospital (Now Beth Israel Deaconess Medical Center), Harvard Medical School, Harvard University (2011); Visiting Professor, Nephrology Grand Rounds, Vanderbilt University, Nashville, TN (2005); Visiting Professor, University of Toronto, Toronto, Ontario, Canada (2000); Visiting Professor, Medicine Grand Rounds 3223 & Nephrology Grand Rounds, Anette Fitz Memorial Fellowship Lecture, The University of Iowa, Iowa City, IA (2000); Visiting Professor, University of Pennsylvania, Philadelphia, PA (1996); Visiting Professor, West Virginia University, Morgantown, WV (1996); Visiting Professor, University of Medicine and Dentistry of New Jersey, New Brunswick, NJ (1996); Robert and Elaine Collins Lecturer, University of Colorado, Denver, CO (1996); Visiting Professor, Mayo Clinic, (Now Mayo Foundation for Medical Education and Research, Rochester, MN (1996); John R. Richardson, Jr. Lecturer, University of Miami Miller School of Medicine, Miami, FL (1996); Visiting Professor, Hahnemann University Hospital, Philadelphia, PA (1995) **Creative Works:** Co-Editor, "Clinical Nephrology, Dialysis and Transplantation" (1999); Guest Co-editor, "25 Years of the ESRD Program, Part 1 & 2," Seminars in Nephrology (1997); Guest Editor, "Seminars in Nephrology" (1994); Author/Co-author, Articles to Professional Journals; Author, Chapters to Books; Editorial Board Member, American Journal of Kidney Diseases; Editorial Board Member, Seminars in Dialysis; Editorial Board, Kidney International **Awards:** Recipient, Belding H. Scribner Award, American Society of Nephrology (2017); Recipient, Medal of Excellence Award, American Association of Kidney Patients (2011); Recipient, Joel D. Kopple Award, National Kidney Foundation (2009); Named, America's Top Physicians (2007); Listee, "Best Doctors in America" (2005-2010); Listee, "Best Doctors in America" (2001-2002); Listee, "Nashville's Best Doctors" (1998); Listee, "Best Doctors in America" (1998) **Membership:** Public Policy Board, American Society of Nephrology (2012-Present); Renal Physicians Association (1994-Present); American Association of Kidney Patients (1998-Present); American Society of Nephrology (1982-Present); Massachusetts Medical Society (1982-Present); International Society of Nephrology (1981-Present); Board Member, American Association of Kidney Patients (2012-2015); Chairman, Medical Advisory Board, Prometic Life Sciences, Inc., Laval, Quebec, Canada (2012-2014); Chairman, Medical Advisory Committee (2012-2014) **Marquis Who's Who Honors:** Albert Nelson Marquis Lifetime Achievement Award (2017); Distinguished Humanitarian (2017) **Shipping Address:** 1119 Harpeth Ridge Rd, Franklin, TN, 37069

Arlie A. Hall

Industry: Education/Educational Services **Date of Birth:** 10/10/1935 **Place of Birth:** Curt **State/Country of Origin:** KY **Parents:** Alfred Hall; Janice Hall **Marital Status:** Married **Spouse Name:** June Adkins Hall **Children:** Gary; David; Robert; Ruth **Education:** EdD, Vanderbilt University (1991); BS, University of Kentucky (1967) **Career:** Assistant Professor, University of Kentucky (1994-2011) **Career Related:** IBM People Management Award, 25-Year Career **Military Service:** US Army (1957-1959) **Creative Works:** Author, Papers, Toyota Production System; Author, "Introduction to Sustainable Quality Systems Design: Integrated Approach from the Viewpoints of Dynamic Scientific Inquiry Learning and Toyota's Lean Principles & Practices" **Awards:** Fellow and Board Member, Lees Junior College (1984-1990); National Honor Society **Membership:** Gideons International **Achievements:** Patent in high vacuum insulating cell technology; Developed and published skills assessment instruments for the Malcolm Baldrige National Quality Award **Political Affiliations:** Republican **Religion:** Protestant Presbyterian **Shipping Address:** 4204 Rolling Hills Dr, Lexington, KY, 40516-9618

Blaine Hill Hall

Title: Librarian (Retired) **Industry:** Library Management/Library Services **Date of Birth:** 12/12/1932 **Place of Birth:** Wellsville **State/Country of Origin:** UT **Parents:** James Owen Hall; Agnes Effie (Hill) Hall **Marital Status:** Married **Spouse Name:** Carol Stokes (1959) **Children:** Suzanne; Cheryl; Derek **Education:** MLS, Brigham Young University (1971); MA, Brigham Young University (1965); BS, Brigham Young University (1960) **Career:** Humanities Librarian, Brigham Young University (1972-1996); English Instructor, Brigham Young University (1963-1972) **Career Related:** Book Reviewer, American Reference Book (1984-2000) **Civic:** Member, Orem Media Review Commission (1984-1986); Chairman, Utah Advisory Commission on Libraries (1983-1991); Board of Directors, Orem Public Library, Utah (1977-1984) **Military Service:** U.S. Army, Republic of Korea (1953-1954) **Creative Works:** Author, "Conversations with Grace Paley" (1997); Author, "Jewish American Fiction Writers Bibliography" (1991); Author, "Jerzy Kosinski Bibliography" (1991); Author, "Saul Bellow Bibliography" (1987); Author, "Collection Assessment Manual" (1985); Contributor, Book Reviews, American Reference Books Annual (1984-2000); Newsletter Editor, Mountain Plains Library Association (1978-1983); Editor, Utah Library Association (1972-1977); Author, Publisher, "The Roads I've Taken"; Contributor, Articles to Professional Journals **Awards:** Recipient, Distinguished Service Award, Mountain Plains Library Association (1991); Recipient, Distinguished Service Award, Utah Library Association (1989); Grantee, Mountain Plains Library Association (1979-1980); Recipient, Periodical Award, American Library Association (1977) **Membership:** President, Mountain Plains Library Association (1994-1996); Council Member, American Library Association (1988-1992); President, Utah Library Association (1980-1981); Board of Directors, Mountain Plains Library Association (1978-1983); The Honor Society of Phi Kappa Phi **Marquis Who's Who Honors:** Albert Nelson Marquis Lifetime Achievement Award (2017) **To what do you attribute your success:** Mr. Hall attributes his success to his very strong work ethic, which was instilled in him from his parents due to growing up on a sugar beet farm and having regular chores including milking the cows twice a day. These chores taught him about responsibility and accountability, traits which he has passed down to his own children. **Why did you become involved in your profession or industry:** Mr. Hall chose this career because he was always interested in reading as well as his education being interrupted by his service in the military during the Korean War. Following that experience, he served on a mission to Canada for two years for his church. While he was teaching, the University opened a library school; he took classes at night and over the summers and finally completed a Master of Library and Information Science degree. **What do you consider to be the highlight of your career:** Mr. Hall has always enjoyed writing and editing and he served an editor for many years for the official publication of the Utah Library Association. **Where will you be in five years:** In five years, Mr. Hall will be spending more time learning about his family's history. He recently traced one line back to the 1600s. **Hobbies:** Writing; Photography; Carpentry; Reading; Genealogy **Religion:** The Church of Jesus Christ of Latter-Day Saints **Shipping Address:** 230 E 1910 S, Orem, UT, 84058

Eric J. Hall

Title: Professor Emeritus **Industry:** Education/Educational Services **Company Name:** Columbia University **Date of Birth:** 07/05/1933 **Place of Birth:** Abertillery **Country of Origin:** Monmouthshire/Wales **Marital Status:** Married **Spouse Name:** Bernice Elizabeth Williams (7/27/1957) **Children:** Dr. Simon Hall **Education:** DSc Honoris Causa, Oxford University, United Kingdom (1977); MA Honoris Causa, Oxford University, United Kingdom (1966); DPhil in Radiobiology, Oxford University, United Kingdom (1962); BSc in Physics, UCL, with Honors (1953) **Career:** Higgins Professor Emeritus, Special Lecturer in Radiation Oncology, Special Research Scientist, Columbia University Medical Center (2008-Present); Operational Director, Kreitchman PET Center, Columbia University (2009-2010); FASTRO Fellow, American Society for Therapeutic Radiation & Oncology (2006); Honorary Fellow, The Society of Radiological Protection, Cardiff, United Kingdom (2005); Honorary Fellow, The Royal College of Radiologists, London, United Kingdom (1999); Higgins Professor of Radiation Biophysics, Columbia University Medical Center, (1993-2007); Professor of Radiation Oncology, Columbia University Medical Center, (1986-1993): Radiation Oncology and Radiology, Center for Radiological Research, New York, NY (1986-2007); Director, Center for Radiological Research, New York, NY (1984-2007); Radiation Biologist, Radiation Oncology Service, NewYork-Presbyterian Hospital (1983-2007); Honorary Fellow, American College of Radiology (1981); Professor, Radiology, Columbia University, New York, NY (1968-1986); Principal Physicist, Churchill Hospital, Oxford University Hospitals NHS Foundation Trust (1963-1968); Visiting Assistant Professor, Radiological Physics, University of Colorado (1962-1963); Senior Physicist, Churchill Hospital, Oxford University Hospitals NHS Foundation Trust (1957-1962); Assistant Physicist, Velindre Cancer Centre (1956-1957); Assistant Physicist, Churchill Hospital, Oxford University Hospitals NHS Foundation Trust (1955-1956) **Career Related:** Neuhauser Lecturer, The Society for Pediatric Radiology (2002); Keynote Speaker, American Society of Therapeutic Radiology and Oncology (ASTRO) (2001); John S. Laughlin Visiting Professor, Memorial Sloan Kettering Cancer Center (2000); 22nd Lauriston S. Taylor Lecturer, National Council on Radiation Protection and Measurements (1998); Fifth Lars Gunnar Larrsson Lecturer, UmeÃ¥ University, Sweden (1996); Sol Y. Eisenberg Lecturer, DMC Harper University Hospital, Wayne State University (1996); Friedell Lecturer, Case Western Reserve University (1996); Raymond S. Bush Visiting Professor, Ontario Cancer Institute, The Princess Margaret Cancer Centre, University Health Network, Canada (1995); Gilbert H. Fletcher Distinguished Professor, The University of Texas MD Anderson Cancer Center, Houston, TX (1995); Raymond S. Honoree, Leicester Atkinson Memorial Lecturer, COSA (1994); Chairman, Radioactive Drug Research Committee, Columbia Presbyterian Medical Center (1985-2007); Chairman, Joint Radiation Safety Committee, Columbia Presbyterian Medical Center, (1985-2007) **Creative Works:** Author," Radiobiology for the Radiologist" Chinese Mainland Edition (2015); Author, "Radiobiology for the Radiologist" Chinese Taiwan Edition (2013); Author, "Radiobiology for the Radiologist" Seventh Edition, With Amato Giaccia (2011); Author, "Radiobiology for the Radiologist" Sixth Edition with Amato Giaccia (2006); Author, "Principles and Practice of Brachytherapy: Using Afterloading Systems" (2001); Co-Author, "Principles of the Dose-rate Effect Derived from Clinical Data" (2001); Author, "Radiobiology for the Radiologist" Fifth Edition" (2000) **Awards:** The Gibbs Memorial Oration, American Academy of Oral and Maxillofacial Radiology (2013); Distinguished Service Award, Radiation Research Society (2012); Distinguished Service Award, Columbia University Medical Center (2009); Gold Medal, American College of Radiology (2008); Gold Medal, American Roentgen Ray Society (2008); Gray Medal, International Commission on Radiation Units & Measurements, Inc. (2007); Distinguished Scientific Achievement Award, Health Physics Society (2005); The Henry S. Kaplan Distinguished Scientist Award, 12th International Congress of Radiation Research, Brisbane, Australia (2003); Distinguished Service Award, American Board of Radiology (2002); John B. Little Award, Harvard T.H. Chan School of Public Health, Boston, MA (2000) **Membership:** Honorary Member, The Society for Pediatric Radiology, Philadelphia, PA (2002); President, International Association of Radiation Research (1999-2003); President, American Radium Society, Inc. (1999-2000) **Marquis Who's Who Honors:** Albert Nelson Marquis Lifetime Achievement Award (2017) **Hobbies:** Skiing; Sailing **Shipping Address:** 630 W 168th St, Room VC/11, 230, Columbia University Ctr. for Radiological Rsch, P&S 11-230, New York, NY, 10032

Henry L. Hall Jr.

Title: Lawyer **Industry:** Law and Legal Services **Company Name:** Ropes & Gray LLP **Date of Birth:** 07/23/1931 **Place of Birth:** Boston **State/Country of Origin:** MA **Parents:** Henry Lyon Hall; Edith Page (Blanchard) Hall **Marital Status:** Married **Spouse Name:** Jean Elizabeth Haring (9/13/1958) **Children:** Henry Lyon; George B. **Education:** JD, The George Washington University (1962); BA, University of Massachusetts (1953) **Career:** Counsel, Ropes & Gray LLP, Boston, MA (1998-Present); Partner, Ropes & Gray LLP, Boston, MA (1973-1997); Associate, Ropes & Gray LLP, Boston, MA (1963-1973) **Career Related:** Lecturer, Panelist Seminars **Civic:** Town Moderator, Belmont, MA (1991-2008); Chairman, Bylaw Review Committee, Belmont, MA (1983-1991); Chairman, Permanent Audit Committee, Belmont, MA (1982-1992); Member, Permanent Audit Committee, Belmont, MA (1979-2009); Chairman, Bylaw Revision Committee, Belmont, MA (1979-1983); Chairman, School Committee, Minuteman Regional Vocational Technical School District (1971-1985); Member, School Committee, Minuteman Regional Vocational Technical School District (1971-1983); Member, Massachusetts Governor's Commission on School District Organization (1971-1973); Corporator, Belmont Savings Bank; Trustee, Belmont Savings Bank **Military Service:** U.S. Army (1953-1956) **Membership:** President, Massachusetts Moderators Association (1998-1999); First Vice President, Massachusetts Moderators Association (1997-1998); Board of Directors, Massachusetts Moderators Association (1995-2005); National Association of Bond Lawyers; The Virginia Bar Association; Boston Bar Association; Massachusetts Taxpayers Foundation; Government Finance Officers Association of the United States and Canada; Massachusetts Charitable Society; Massachusetts Municipal Association; The George Washington Law Review; The Order of the Coif; The International Legal Honor Society of Phi Delta Phi; ABA; Massachusetts Bar Association **Bar Admissions:** Virginia (1963); Massachusetts (1963) **Marquis Who's Who Honors:** Albert Nelson Marquis Lifetime Achievement Award (2017) **Why did you become involved in your profession or industry:** After Mr. Hall graduated from college he immediately joined the U.S. Army. During his three years of service he attended language school and served as a Russian linguist for the federal government. When he left the U.S. Army he went right into law school and worked all his career at Ropes & Gray LLP. His area of expertise at Ropes & Gray LLP was public law and public finance. **Shipping Address:** 1010 Waltham St Apt 493, Lexington, MA, 02421

Wayne Bruce Hallard

Title: Economist/Manager (Retired) **Industry:** Financial Services **Date of Birth:** 12/28/1951 **Place of Birth:** Plainfield **State/Country of Origin:** NJ/USA **Parents:** Donald Jay Hallard; Patricia (Adelmann) Hallard **Marital Status:** Married **Spouse Name:** Deborah Jane Russo (8/16/1987); Grace Elizabeth Farrell (4/29/1972, Divorced) **Children:** Travis; Kayla (Grandchild); Connor (Grandchild) **Education:** Postgraduate Coursework, New York University (1984-1987); MBA in Economics, Fairleigh Dickinson University (1984); BS in Economics and Finance, Fairleigh Dickinson University (1980); AA in Business, Union College (1977); Coursework, Brown University (1970-1971) **Certifications:** Licensed Dog Show Superintendent, American Kennel Club (2008); Licensed Dog Show Judge, American Kennel Club (2000); Licensed Private Pilot (1993) **Career:** Superintendent, Rau Dog Shows, Reading, PA (2008-Present); Retired Economist (2003); Economist, Manager, Economic and Financial Analysis District, Bell Atlantic and New Jersey Bell Telephone, (Now Verizon), Newark, NJ (1983-2003); Assistant Staff Manager, Acronym Planning District, New Jersey Bell Telephone Company (Now Verizon) (1980-1983); Assistant Staff Manager, Network Management District, New Jersey Bell Telephone Company (Now Verizon) (1978-1980); Repair Technician, Summit-Elizabeth Central Office District, New Jersey Bell Telephone Company (Now Verizon) (1972-1978); Store Manager, Wine Art of New Jersey, Watchung, NJ (1972) **Career Related:** Consultant, F. A. Russo Associates, Scotch Plains, NJ (1989-2010); Consultant, New Jersey Council of Savings Institutions, West Orange, NJ (1987-1995); Session Chairman, Center for Research in Regulated Industries (1986-2003); Eastern Conference Organizer, Center for Research in Regulated Industries (1986-2003) **Civic:** Treasurer, Finance Committee, Men's Club, Choir, Gan Mazon Monmouth Reform Temple (2016-Present); Treasurer, Greenbriar Falls Condominium Association Board (2016-Present); Chairman, Central Jersey Blood Center Foundation (2015-Present); Board Secretary, Trustee, Central Jersey Blood Center (2014-Present); Emeritus, Fairleigh Dickinson University Alumni Association Board of Governors (2013-Present); Fairleigh Dickinson University Alumni Association Board of Governors (1997-Present); Vice President, Greenbriar Falls Condominium Association Board (2015-2016); Umpire, Scotch Plains-Fanwood Youth Baseball Association (1982-2012); Brotherhood Temple Sharey Tefilo-Israel, South Orange, NJ (1980-2016) **Military Service:** Sergeant First Class, NJ Army National Guard, 250th Signal Battalion, Westfield, NJ (1980-1981); Master Sergeant, U.S. Air Force Reserves, 514th Avionics Maintenance Squadron, McGuire Air Force Base (Now Joint Base McGuire-Dix-Lakehurst), New Jersey **Awards:** Inductee, Pinnacle Society, Fairleigh Dickinson University (2009); Distinguished Service Award, Scotch Plains-Fanwood Youth Baseball Association (1994); Honoree, Outstanding Young Men of America (1988, 1986, 1985, 1983, 1981); Inductee, Delta Mu Delta, National Honor Society in Business Administration (1984); Named NCO of the Year, 514th Avionics Maintenance Squadron, McGuire Air Force Base (Now Joint Base McGuire-Dix-Lakehurst) (1976) **Membership:** Monmouth Reform Temple (2016-Present); Babe Ruth League, National Umpires Association (2007-Present); Officer, Garden State Bailliage, The Confrerie de la Chaine des Rotisseurs (2005-Present); Societe Mondiale du Vin, The Chaine des Rotisseurs (2005-Present); Association of BellTel Retirees Inc. (2004-Present); Treasurer, Eastern Stewards Club, Inc. (2004-Present); AARP (2001-Present); American Dog Show Judges, Inc. (2000-Present); Senior Conformation Judges Association (2000-Present); ACLU (1998-Present); ARZA (1998-Present); Eastern Stewards Club, Inc. (1995-Present); Stewards Club of America (1995-Present); Aircraft Owners and Pilot Association (1994-Present); Telephone Pioneers of America (1992-Present); Garden State All Terrier Club (1990-Present); Fairleigh Dickinson University Alumni Association (1984-Present); Life Member, Mastiff Club of America (1983-Present); American Legion - Holmgren-Gurbisz Memorial Post 325 (2009-2017) **Marquis Who's Who Honors:** Albert Nelson Marquis Lifetime Achievement Award (2017) **Hobbies:** Cooking; Reading; Flying **Shipping Address:** 1 Majestic Dr, Tinton Falls, NJ, 07724

Diane Esther Halley

Title: Artist **Industry:** Fine Art **Date of Birth:** 05/14/1939 **Place of Birth:** Jasper **State/Country of Origin:** IN **Parents:** John Darden; Esther Margaret (Kruse) Darden **Marital Status:** Married **Spouse Name:** Norman B. Halley (5/21/1966) **Children:** William Tull **Education:** EdB in Elementary Education, Indiana State University, Terre Haute, IN (1961) **Career:** Portrait Artist, Arvada, CO (1979-Present); Teacher, Fourth Grade, Westminster, CO (1964-1968); Teacher, Fourth Grade, Seymour, IN (1962-1964); Teacher, Fourth Grade, New Albany, IN (1961) **Career Related:** Juror, Fall Exhibition, Colorado Watercolor Society (2002) **Civic:** President, Clear Creek Valley Medical Auxiliary, Lakewood, CO (1991-1992); President, Clear Creek Valley Medical Auxiliary, Lakewood, CO (1973-1974) **Creative Works:** Signature American Watercolor Exhibitions, Fallbrook Art Center (2017); Watercolor Missouri National, Central Library, St. Louis, MO (2016); NAWA, Portrait Exhibition, Arts Club, Washington, DC (2015); NAWA, 125 Years: Women of Vision, Armory Art Center, West Palm Beach, FL (2014); "Splash Retrospective, 20 Years of Contemporary Watercolor Excellence" (2013); Signature American Watercolor Exhibitions, Fallbrook Art Center (2012); CLWAC Members Show, Salmagundi Art Club (2012); Signature American Watercolor Exhibitions, Fallbrook Art Center (2010); Colorado Art Open, Foothills Art Center (2009); All Colorado Art Exhibition, Curtis Center for Arts and Humanities (2008); Western Federation Watercolors Societies Exhibition, Arvada Center for the Arts (2007); Watercolor Missouri National, Winston Churchill Memorial Library (2007); Brand Library and Art Center (2006); Great 8 Exhibition, Kansas Watercolor Society, Wichita Art Museum (2006); Karpeles Library Museum (2006); Ports of Call Gallery (2006); Small Works Exhibition, Attleboro Art Museum (2005); 50th Anniversary Member Exhibition, Colorado Watercolor Society (2004); "Artists Who Happen to be Women," Texas Agricultural and Mechanical University (2004); Great 8 Exhibition, Kansas Watercolor Society, Wichita Art Museum (2004); Watercolor Missouri National, Winston Churchill Memorial Library (2003-2004); Challenge of Champions Exhibition, Watercolor Art Society of Houston (2003); 53rd National Exhibition of Contemporary Realism in Art, Academy Artists Association (2003); 12th National Art Exhibition, Lincoln Center, Fort Collins, CO (2003); Solo Show, Lincoln Center, Fort Collins, CO (2003); Solo Exhibition Colorado Christian University (2000); Featured Paintings, "Splash Six-The Magic of Texture" (2000); Solo Exhibition, National Center for Atmospheric Research, Boulder (1991); Featured Paintings, "Best of Watercolor-Painting Textures," Denver Art Museum (1990); Solo Exhibition, Foothills Art Center (1984); Solo Exhibition, Denver National Bank (1983); 14th Annual Artists of Colorado Exhibition, Denver, CO; Featured Paintings, "Colorado 1990 Exhibition", Denver Art Museum **Awards:** Board of Directors Award, Watercolor Missouri National, Winston Churchill Memorial Library (2004); Best in Show Award, Colorado Watercolor Society 50th Annual Exhibition (2004); Westminster Community Artist Series Award (2003); Award of Distinction, Missouri National Watercolor Exhibition (2003); Cash Award, Lakewood Arts Council (2001); American Artist Cash Award, Kansas Watercolor Society (1999); Cecil Shapiro Memorial Award, National Association of Women Artists, Inc. (1998); Grumbacher Award, Pikes Peak Watercolor Society (1995); President's Award, Colorado Watercolor Society (1994); Founder's Award (1992); Cynthia Goodgal Award, Catharine Lorillard Wolfe Art Club (1986); Adriana Zahn Award, Catharine Lorillard Wolfe Art Club (1985); Del Mar College Award, National Watercolor Society (1981) **Membership:** Signature Member, Missouri Watercolor Society; Kansas Watercolor Society; Rocky Mountain National Watermedia Society; National Watercolor Society; National Association of Women Artists, Inc.; Catharine Lorillard Wolfe Art Club **Marquis Who's Who Honors:** Albert Nelson Marquis Lifetime Achievement Award (2017) **To what do you attribute your success:** Ms. Halley attributes all good things to the loving Father in heaven. **Why did you become involved in your profession or industry:** Ms. Halley did not begin painting full-time until she was 38. She had loved teaching art to her fourth grade students, finding art a great motivation in all the areas of a child's education. **Where will you be in five years:** In five years, Ms. Halley still has some paintings she would like to do. **Hobbies:** Bible study; Bridge; Gardening **Shipping Address:** 6631 Osceola Court, Arvada, CO, 80003

Mary Ann Hamburger

Title: Medical Management Consultant **Industry:** Consulting **Company Name:** Mary Ann Hamburger Associates **Date of Birth:** 08/25/1939 **Place of Birth:** Newark **State/Country of Origin:** NJ **Parents:** Herman Marcus; Sylvia (Strauss) Marcus **Marital Status:** Single **Children:** Bruce David; Marc Laurence **Education:** AA, University of Bridgeport (1960) **Career:** Practice Administrator for Hospitalist Group in Morris County, New Jersey (2012-Present); Medical Management Consultant, Mary Ann Hamburger Associates, Maplewood, NJ (1984-Present); Office Manager, Milburn, NJ (1970-1984) **Career Related:** Adult Education Teacher, South Orange Maplewood Board of Education (1975-1983); Professional Physician Recruiter, State of New York; Professional Physician Recruiter, State of New Jersey; Medical Practices Broker, State of New Jersey; Medical Practices Broker, State of New York **Membership:** National Association of Female Executives **Marquis Who's Who Honors:** Albert Nelson Marquis Lifetime Achievement Award (2017) **To what do you attribute your success:** Ms. Hamburger attributes her success to her professionalism, hard work, as well as being able to stay current with the constant cutting-edge changes in healthcare procedures and protocol. She has an ability to cut to the chase when there is an issue that has to be resolved. Currently, she manages 19 doctors. **Why did you become involved in your profession or industry:** Ms. Hamburger became involved in her profession upon realizing that medicine was a business and had to be run as such. She started her own consulting business in the medical management field. **What do you consider to be the highlight of your career:** Ms. Hamburger is most proud of being nominated for Marquis Who's Who. **Where will you be in five years:** In five years, Ms. Hamburger hopes to experience continued professional growth. **Hobbies:** Reading; Music; Needlepoint; Theater; Sports **Political Affiliations:** Democrat **Religion:** Jewish **Shipping Address:** 74 Hudson Avenue, Maplewood, NJ, 07040

Dale J. Hamilton

Title: Director **Industry:** Medicine & Health Care **Company Name:** Houston Methodist **Marital Status:** Married **Children:** Two Children **Education:** Resident, Baylor College of Medicine (1981-1983); MD, School of Medicine, St. Louis University (1978); BS, University of Washington (1974) **Certifications:** Board Certification in Internal Medicine (1978-1981); Specialty Training in Endocrinology and Diabetes, Baylor College of Medicine **Career:** Director, Center for Bioenergetics, Houston Methodist (2015-Present); Clinical Education, Center for Bioenergetics, Houston Methodist; Adjunct Research Professor, University of Houston **Military Service:** U.S. Army, Europe **Creative Works:** Contributor, Articles, Professional Journals **Awards:** Named Elaine and Marvy A. Finger Distinguished Chairman for Translational Research in Metabolic Disorders, Institute for Academic Medicine, Houston Methodist (2017); Physician of the Year Award (2012); Honoree, Alpha Omega Alpha **Membership:** Local President, American Diabetes Association; Endocrine Society; Fellow, American College of Physicians; Fellow, American College of Clinical Endocrinologists **To what do you attribute your success:** Dr. Hamilton attributes his success to following his heart, doing what he loves, and working towards a common goal with his team. **Why did you become involved in your profession or industry:** Dr. Hamilton became involved in his profession because after he got out of the military and back into college, he was working in an emergency room at night to help pay his way through. The experience of working in a hospital inspired him to become a doctor. **Hobbies:** German philosophy and literature; Traveling to France **Shipping Address:** 6670 Bertner Ave., MS R11-211, Houston Methodist, Houston, TX, 77030 **Website:** http://www.houstonmethodist.org/faculty/dale-hamilton

Joseph Hants Hamilton, PhD

Title: Garland Distinguished Professor of Physics, Researcher **Industry:** Education/Educational Services **Company Name:** Vanderbilt University **Date of Birth:** 08/14/1932 **Place of Birth:** Ferriday **State/Country of Origin:** LA **Parents:** Joseph Hants Hamilton; Letha (Gibson) Hamilton **Marital Status:** Married **Spouse Name:** Jannelle Landrum Hamilton (8/5/1960) **Children:** Melissa Claire; Christopher Landrum **Education:** PhD, Eastern Kentucky University, with Honors (2012); PhD, Berea College, with Honors (2007); PhD, Pt. Ravishankar Shukla University, with Honors (2006); PhD, Joint Institute for Nuclear Research, with Honors (2004); PhD, Saint Petersburg University, with Honors (2001); PhD, University of Bucharest, with Honors (1999); PhD, National University of Frankfurt, with Honors (1992); DSc, Mississippi College, Clinton, MS, with Honors (1982); PhD, Indiana University, Bloomington, IN (1958); MS, Indiana University, Bloomington, IN (1956); BS, Mississippi College, Clinton, MS (1954) **Career:** Landon C. Garland Distinguished Professor of Physics, Vanderbilt University, Nashville, TN (1992-Present); Adjunct Professor, Tsinghua University, People's Republic of China (1986-Present); Professor of Physics, Vanderbilt University, Nashville, TN (1966-Present); Faculty Member, Vanderbilt University, Nashville, TN (1958-Present); Visiting Distinguished Laboratory Fellow, Our Ridge National Laboratory (2000-2017); Landon C. Garland Professor of Physics, Vanderbilt University, Nashville, TN (1981-1992); **Career Related:** Honorary Advisory Professor, Fudan University, People's Republic of China (1988-Present); Organizer, The Joint Institute for Heavy Ion Research, Oak Ridge, TN (1980-Present); Consultant, Oak Ridge National Laboratory (1972-Present); Chairman, Fifth International Conference on Fission and Properties of Neutron Rich Nuclei (2012); Co-Chairman, Fourth International Conference on Fission and Properties of Neutron Rich Nuclei (2007); Chairman, Sixth International Conference on Fission and Properties (2006); Chairman, Third International Conference on Fission and Properties Neutron Rich Nuclei (2002); Co-Chairman, Second International Conference on Fission and Properties of Neutron Rich Nuclei (1999); Visiting Professor, University of Frankfurt (1998); Affiliate, International Symposium Perspectives in Nuclear Physics (1998); Affiliate, International Conference on Fission and Properties of Neutron Rich Nuclei (1997); Organizer, University Radioactive Ion Beam Consortium (1996); Board of Directors, Oak Ridge Associate University (1995-1997); Science and Technology Advisory Council for the State of Tennessee (1994-2001); Visiting Professor, University of Louis Pasteur, Strasbourg, France (1991); Chairman, International Symposium on Reflections and Directions in Low Energy Heavy Ion Physics (1991); Visiting Professor, University of Frankfurt (1990); Co-Chairman, International Workshop, Physics with a Recoil Mass Spectrometer (1986); International Conference of Directors, Nuclear Structure Research (1984); Director, The Joint Institute for Heavy Ion Research, Oak Ridge, TN (1980-2010); Visiting Professor, University of Frankfurt (1979-1980); Affiliate, International Conference, Future Directions in Studies Nuclei far from Stability (1979); National Policy Board Member, Holifield Heavy Ion Facility (1974-1984); Council Member, Oak Ridge Associate University (1974-1980) **Civic:** Historical Commission, Southern Baptist Convention (1983-1991); Board of Directors, Vineyard Conference Center, Louisville, KY (1972-1977) **Creative Works:** Editorial Board Member, "McGraw-Hill Encyclopedia of Science & Technology" (2010-Present); Associate Editor, "International Journal of Modern Physics" (2010-Present); Editorial Board Member, "McGraw-Hill Yearbook in Science & Technology" (2009-Present); Co-Author, "Fifth International Conference Fission and Properties of Neutron Rich Nuclei" (2013); Co-Author, "Modern Atomic and Nuclear Physics, Review Edition" (2010); Co-Author, "Fourth International Conference Fission and Properties of Neutron Rich Nuclei" (2008); Co-Author, "Third International Conference Fission and Properties of Neutron Rich Nuclei" (2003); Co-Author, "Fission and Properties of Neutron Rich Nuclei" (2000); Co-Author, "Perspectives in Nuclear Physics" (1999); Co-Author, "Fission and Properties of Neutron Rich Nuclei" (1998); Co-Author, "Structure of the Vacuum and Elementary Matter" (1997); Co-Author, "Modern Atomic and Nuclear Physics" (1996); **Awards:** Grantee, Department of Energy, Energy Research and Development Administration (1975-Present); Resolution for Leadership in Field, Tennessee General Assembly (2017); Mentoring Award, Division of Nuclear Physics, American Physical Society (2016); G. N. Flerov Prize, Russia (2003); D. Ilkovic Gold Medal, Slovak Academy of Science (2002) **Membership:** Governing Board, American Institute of Physics (2004-2007); Council Member, American Physical Society (1994-2004); Chairman, Southeastern Section, American Physical Society (1973-1974) **Marquis Who's Who Honors:** Albert Nelson Marquis Lifetime Achievement Award (2017) **Business Address:** 2301 Vanderbuilt Place, Nashville, TN 37235

Charles F. Hammer, PhD

Title: Chemistry Professor **Industry:** Education/Educational Services **Company Name:** Georgetown University **Date of Birth:** 07/22/1933 **Place of Birth:** Fremont **State/Country of Origin:** OH **Marital Status:** Married **Spouse Name:** Lois Reel (1957) **Children:** Laurence N. **Education:** PhD in Organic Chemistry, University of Minnesota, Minneapolis, MN (1959); BA, Bowling Green State University (1955) **Career:** Emeritus Professor, Georgetown University (1995-Present); Chemistry Professor, Georgetown University (1982-1995); Assistant Professor to Associate Professor, Georgetown University (1963-1982) **Career Related:** Director, Hoya New Mexico Schools, Santa Fe, NM (1995-Present); President of the Board, Academy for Technology and the Classics, Grades 7-12, Santa Fe County, New Mexico (2001-2011); Governing Council, Academy for Technology and the Classics, Charter School, Grades 7-12, Santa Fe County, New Mexico (2000-2011); Visiting Scholar, Nanjing University (1994); Visiting Scholar, National Institute of Chemistry, Ljubljana, Slovenia (1993); Visiting Scholar, National Institute of Diabetes and Digestive & Kidney Disease, National Institutes of Health (1986); Visiting Scholar, College of Chemistry, University of California, Berkeley (1978); Visiting Professor, Department of Energy and Hydrocarbon Chemical, Graduate School of Engineering, Kyoto University (1971-1972); NIHPD Fellow, Nuclear Magnetic Resonance and X-Ray Crystallography of Steroids, Brandeis University (1961-1963) **Civic:** Board Member, Training Center Corporation, Santa Fe Community (2005-2009); Board of Directors, Aiken Technical College Foundation (2004-2010); Founder, Aiken Technical College Foundation (2002); Founder, Academy for Technology and the Classics (2001) **Military Service:** Second Lieutenant-Captain, U.S. Air Force (1955-1964) **Creative Works:** ChemTec Writing Team, American Chemical Society (1970-1972) **Awards:** United States Navy & MWR Bronze Award, Academy for Technology and the Classics (2009); United States Navy & MWR Bronze Award, Academy for Technology and the Classics (2007); Newsweek Bronze Award (2007); Award for Creative Invention, American Chemical Society (1990); Alan Berman Research Publication Award, NRL Sigma Xi (1987) **Membership:** Academy for Technology and the Classics; American Association for the Advancement of Science; Society for Applied Spectroscopy; ASTM; Sigma Xi **To what do you attribute your success:** Dr. Hammer attributes his success to his good education. He earned a PhD at the University of Minnesota in chemistry and physics, and it was an excellent school. **Why did you become involved in your profession or industry:** Dr. Hammer was in the U.S. Air Force for two years, and received a commission and PhD. Prior to being called in to active duty, he worked in the research labs at Proctor and Gamble, and very much enjoyed his work. After getting out of active duty, he did postdoctoral research at Brandeis University and decided to work in academia after that. **Shipping Address:** 250 E Alameda Street, Apt. 222, Santa Fe, NM, 87501

William Michael Hammond, PhD

Industry: Education/Educational Services **Date of Birth:** 01/01/1943 **Place of Birth:** Pasadena **State/Country of Origin:** CA **Parents:** Paul Chester Hammond; Mary Ethel Champieux **Marital Status:** Married **Spouse Name:** Lillamaud Munsell Leike (4/28/1973) **Children:** Michael Anthony; Elizabeth Anne **Education:** PhD, The Catholic University of America (1973); MA, The Catholic University of America (1968); STB, The Catholic University of America (1967) **Career:** Chief, Retired, General Histories Branch, U.S. Army Center of Military History (2001-Present); Senior Lecturer in University Honors, University of Maryland (1991-2012) **Civic:** Editor, Civic Association, Strathmore Bel Pre (1986-Present); Web Master, Civic Association, Strathmore Bel Pre (1986-Present); Board of Directors, Civic Association, Strathmore Bel Pre (1986-Present) **Creative Works:** Author, "Reporting Vietnam, Military and Media at War" (1998); Author, "Black Soldier, White Army: The 24th Infantry in Korea" (1996); Author, "Public Affairs: The Military and the Media" (1968-1973, 1996); Author, "The Press in Vietnam as Agent of Defeat, a Critical Examination," Reviews in American History (1989); Author, "The U.S. Army in Vietnam: Public Affairs: The Military and the Media" (1962-1968, 1988); Author, "The Unknown Serviceman of the Vietnam Era" (1985); Author, "Who Were the Saigon Correspondents, and Does It Matter Today?" Shorenstein Center for the Press and Public Policy, Harvard University **Awards:** Honoree, Distinguished Lecturer, The Organization of American Historians (2002-Present); Recipient, Meritorious Civilian Service Award, U.S. Department of the Army (2010); Recipient, Richard W. Leopold Award, The Organization of American Historians (2000); Recipient, Research Fellowship, Joan Shorenstein Center For The Press And Public Policy, Harvard University (1999); Recipient, Honorary Membership, Alpha Lambda Delta (1999); Recipient, Commendation, University of Maryland (1998); Honoree, Book Listed in Notable Government Documents, American Library Association (1989); Recipient, Commander's Medal for Civilian Service, U.S. Army Center of Military History (1985) **Membership:** The Organization of American Historians; The Society for Military History **Marquis Who's Who Honors:** Albert Nelson Marquis Lifetime Achievement Award (2017) **Hobbies:** Photography; Watercolor painting; Travel **Religion:** Roman Catholic **Shipping Address:** 2604 Bainbridge Ln, Silver Spring, MD, 20906

Sam F. Hamra Jr.

Title: Lawyer, Entrepreneur **Industry:** Law and Legal Services **Company Name:** Hamra Enterprises **Date of Birth:** 01/21/1932 **Place of Birth:** Steele **State/Country of Origin:** MO **Parents:** Sam Farris Hamra, Sr.; Victoria (Homra) Hamra **Marital Status:** Married **Spouse Name:** June Samaha (4/1/1956) **Children:** Sam F., III; Karen E.; Michael K.; Jacqueline K. **Education:** LLB, University of Missouri (1959); BBA, University of Missouri (1954); Diploma, Gulf Coast Military Academy **Career:** Founder, Boston Bread, LLC, Hamra Enterprises (2001-Present); Chairman, Boston Bread, LLC, Hamra Enterprises (2001-Present); Founder, Chicago Bread, LLC, Hamra Enterprises (1998-Present); Chairman, Chicago Bread, LLC, Hamra Enterprises (1998-Present); Private Practice, The Law Offices of Sam F. Hamra, P.C., Springfield, MO (1976-Present); Founder, Wendy's of Missouri, Inc., Hamra Enterprises (1975-Present); Chairman, Wendy's of Missouri, Inc., Hamra Enterprises (1975-Present); Founder, Hamra Enterprises (1975-Present); Chairman, Hamra Enterprises (1975-Present); Organizer, Oak-Star Bank (2005); Founding Member, OakStar Bank (2005); Partner, Hamra & Crow, Springfield, MO (1971-1975); Private Practice, The Law Offices of Sam F. Hamra, P.C., Springfield, MO (1966-1971) **Career Related:** Board of Directors, Landmark Bancshares, Inc. (1980-1991); Landmark Bank, Springfield, MO (1980-1981); Chairman, Law Day, U.S.A. (1960) **Civic:** Emeritus Board Member, CoxHealth (2010-Present); Board of Directors, OTC Foundation, Ozarks Technical Community College (2008-Present); Advisory Board, Missouri Sports Hall of Fame (2005-Present); Board of Directors, ALSAC, St. Jude Children's Research Hospital, Memphis, TN (1985-Present); Lay Reader, St. James Episcopal Church (1959-Present); Board of Directors, Smith-Glynn-Callaway Medical Foundation (1997-2009); President, Missouri Sports Hall of Fame (1994-2005); Chairman, Jefferson Club Board of Trustees, University of Missouri (1988-1992); Chairman, Springfield Area Sports Hall of Fame Committee (1988-1989); Elected, Presidential Elector (1988); Board of Directors, CoxHealth (1986-2010); President, Board, CoxHealth (1986-1987); Elected, Delegate, Democratic National Convention (1984); Elected, Delegate, Democratic National Convention (1980); Elected, Delegate, Democratic National Convention (1972); Democratic Chairman, 7th District (1970-1972) **Military Service:** U.S. Civilian Aide to the Secretary of the U.S. Army, Missouri (1997-2003); First Lieutenant, U.S. Army (1956); Second Armored Cavalry Regiment, Fort Meade, MD (1955-1956); Second Armored Cavalry Regiment, Bamberg, Germany (1955); 70th U.S. Field Artillery Battalion, Nuremberg, Germany (1954-1955); Second Lieutenant, U.S. Army Field Artillery, University of Missouri (1954) **Awards:** Annual Springfieldian of the Year Award for Outstanding Community Service, Excellence in Field and Long-time Dedication to Improve the Quality of Life for Springfield and Its Citizens, Springfield Area Chamber of Commerce (2018); Hamra Enterprises, Philanthropic Business of the Year, Springfield Business Journal, Economic Impact Awards Dinner (2017); Recognized as a Legend, July 2017 Issue, Springfield Business Journal (2017); President's Award, Missouri Sports Hall of Fame (2014); President's Award, Springfield Missouri Bar Association (2013); Hall of Fame Award, Wendy's International, Inc. (2013); Distinguished Tiger Award, Greater Ozarks Chapter, University of Missouri Alumni Association (2012); Eponym, Sam F. Hamra Center for Justice (2012) **Membership:** Founder, Rotary Club of Springfield Southeast (1967-Present); Charter President, Rotary Club of Springfield Southeast (1967-Present); Hickory Hills Country Club (1961-Present); American Bar Association (1959-Present); The Missouri Bar (1959-Present); President, Bear's Paw Country Club, Naples, FL (2010); Board of Directors, Bear's Paw Country Club, Naples, FL (2009-2011); Board Member, Truman Library Institute (2003-2012); President, Southern Federation of Syrian Lebanese American Clubs, Inc. (1984-1985); Chairman, Board, Southern Federation of Syrian Lebanese American Clubs, Inc. (1981-1982) **Bar Admissions:** State of Missouri (1959) **Marquis Who's Who Honors:** Albert Nelson Marquis Lifetime Achievement Award (2017); Distinguished Humanitarian (2017) **Hobbies:** Golf; Spending time with family; Collecting and donating art **Political Affiliations:** Democrat **Shipping Address:** 1855 S Ingram Mill Road, Suite 100, Hamra Enterprises, Springfield, MO, 65804

Carin Gale Hanratty

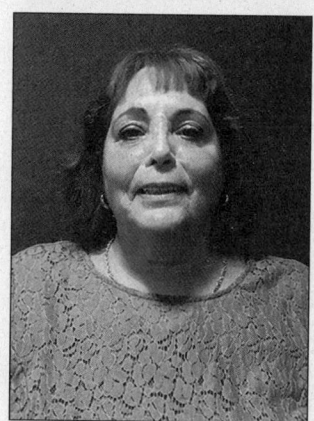

Title: Pediatric Nurse Practitioner **Industry:** Medicine & Health Care **Company Name:** Dr. Levy Pediatrics **Date of Birth:** 12/31/1953 **Place of Birth:** New York **State/Country of Origin:** NY **Parents:** Burton Aleskowitz; Lillian Aleskowitz **Marital Status:** Divorced **Children:** Tyler James; Alison Erin **Education:** Postgraduate Coursework, Pediatric Nurse Practitioner, St. Joseph's College (2002-2004); Postgraduate Coursework, Pediatric Nurse Practitioner, University of California, San Diego (1980); BSN, Russell Sage College (1975) **Certifications:** Certified Cardiopulmonary Resuscitation Instructor; Certified NALS; Certified Specialist, American Nurses Association **Career:** Pediatrics Nurse, Dr. Levy Pediatrics, Hurst, TX (2008-2012); Pediatrics Nurse, Home Health Care (2006-2008); Pediatrics Nurse, Healthcare Medical Associates (2004-2006); Pediatrics Nurse, Agape Clinics of Texas (2003-2004); Pediatrics Nurse, Sub School Nurse Practitioner, Carroll Independent School District, Southlake, TX (1998-2002); School Nurse Practitioner, Dallas Independent School District (1997-1998); Pediatric Drug Coordinator, Perinatal Intervention Team for Substance Abusing Women and Babies, Parkland Memorial Hospital, Dallas, TX (1990-1995); Clinical Manager of Pediatrics, Trinity Medical Center, Carrollton, TX (1985-1986); Pediatric Nurse Practitioner, Day Surgery Unit, Children's Medical Center, Dallas, TX (1981-1985) **Civic:** Chair, March of Dimes, Parkland Hospital (1992-1997); Blood Donor Chair, Parkland Hospital (1990-1997); Representative, United Way (1988-1997); Board of Directors, Medical Consultant, KIDNET Foundation **Creative Works:** Talk Show Guest, "Morning Coffee"; Guest, KPLX-FM Radio Station; Guest, Various Television Programs **Membership:** Vice President, Dallas Chapter, National Association of Pediatric Nurse Practitioners (1982-1983); Professional, Lifetime Member, American Red Cross; Texas Nurses Association **Marquis Who's Who Honors:** Albert Nelson Marquis Lifetime Achievement Award (2017) **Why did you become involved in your profession or industry:** Ms. Hanratty had a desire to help people. She was good in the sciences, and her roommate was a nurse who encouraged her to become a nurse as well. While she went through rotations in nursing, she wasn't interested in any of the specialties until she worked in pediatrics. A nine-year-old boy with a broken leg threw spit balls at everyone and it was the first time she smiled. She knew pediatrics was for her. **Hobbies:** Sewing; Swimming **Shipping Address:** 2021 Huntington Drive, Arlington, TX, 76010

Uwe J. Hansen

Title: Professor Emeritus of Physics **Industry:** Education/Educational Services **Company Name:** Indiana State University **Education:** NAS/NRC Postdoctoral Fellowship, U.S. Naval Research Laboratory, Washington, DC (1966-1968); PhD in Physics, Brigham Young University (1966); MA in Physics, Brigham Young University (1961); BS in Physics, Brigham Young University (1954) **Career:** Editor, Proceedings of the Indiana Academy of Science (2011-Present); Executive Director, Central States Universities, Inc (2002-Present); Physics Faculty, Indiana State University (1998); Visiting Professor, Northern Illinois University (1998); Professor Emeritus, Indiana State University (1998); Chairperson, Department of Physics, Indiana State University (1994-1997); Visiting Scientist, Physikalisch-Technische Bundesanstalt, Braunschweig, Germany (1992); Visiting Professor, Northern Illinois University (1991); Adjunct Professor of Physics, Rose Hulman Institute of Technology (1984); Visiting Professor, Northern Illinois University (1984); Interim Chairperson, Department of Physics, Indiana State University (1980-1983); Professor, Physics Faculty, Indiana State University (1978); Physics Faculty, Indiana State University (1968); Adjunct Professor of Mathematics, Indiana State University; Adjunct Professor of German, Indiana State University; Adjunct Professor of Physics, St. Mary of the Woods College **Career Related:** Consultant, Lockheed Research Laboratories; Consultant, TRW Research Laboratories; Consultant, U.S. Naval Research Laboratory **Civic:** The Church of Jesus Christ of Latter-day Saints, Intellectual Reserve, Inc. **Creative Works:** Translator, "Acoustics and the Performance of Music" (2009); Author, "Modeling Musical Instruments, Handbook of Signal Processing in Acoustics" (2008); Author, "Caribbean Steel Pans and Descendants," Proceedings of FA, Budapest, Hungary (2005); Author, "Vibrational mode shapes in Caribbean steelpans, Part II: Cello & Bass," Applied Acoustics (2004); Author, "Vibrational Mode Shapes in steelpans: Tenor & double second," Journal of the Acoustic Society of America (2000); Author, "Music from Oil Drums: The acoustics of the steelpan," Physics Today (1996) **Awards:** Distinguished Service Citation, Indiana Academy of Science (2014); Distinguished Service Citation, Acoustical Society of America (2011); Named Speaker of the Year, Indiana Academy of Science (1998-1999); Honoree, Outstanding Educators of America (1971); Named Fellow, Indiana Academy of Science; Named Fellow, Acoustical Society of America; Honoree, American Men and Women of Science **Membership:** Chairman, Wabash Valley Chapter, American Society for Metals (2010); President, Indiana Academy of Science (2005); President-Elect, Indiana Academy of Science (2004); Chairman, Wabash Valley Chapter, American Society for Metals (2004); Chairman, Wabash Valley Chapter, American Society for Metals (2003); Editor of Newsletter, Indiana Academy of Science (2000-2004); Chairman, ASA Committee on Online Education, Acoustical Society of America (1999-2002); Chairman, Amendments Committee, Indiana Academy of Science (1997-2000); General Chairman, Acoustical Society of America 132nd Meeting, Indianapolis Spring (1996); Chairman, Committee on Education in Acoustics, Acoustical Society of America (1996-2002); Chairman, Technical Committee on Musical Acoustics, Acoustical Society of America (1990-1996); Technical Council, Acoustical Society of America (1990-1996); Chairman, Research Grants Committee, Indiana Academy of Science; Chairman, Physics Section, Indiana Academy of Science; Chairman, History of Science Section, Indiana Academy of Science; Science & Society Committee, Indiana Academy of Science; Fellows Committee, Indiana Academy of Science; Proceedings Editorial Board, Indiana Academy of Science; Long-range Planning Committee, Indiana Academy of Science; Tutorial Committee, Acoustical Society of America; Education Committee, Acoustical Society of America; Committee on Meetings, Acoustical Society of America; Committee on Special Fellowships, Acoustical Society of America; Technical Committee on Musical Acoustics, Acoustical Society of America; Long-range Planning Committee, Acoustical Society of America; Membership Committee, Acoustical Society of America; Committee on Medals and Awards, Acoustical Society of America; Chairman, Wabash Valley Chapter, Sigma Xi **To what do you attribute your success:** Mr. Hansen attributes his success to consistent effort and having wonderful efforts. He also attributes it to his mentors and collaborators, Thomas D. Rossing. When he switched fields he worked with Dr. Rossing for a full year. They have become close friends and have collaborated for years. **Why did you become involved in your profession or industry:** Mr. Hansen became involved in his profession because he always enjoyed physics. Teaching gave him flexibility to do research, and he always enjoyed teaching. **What do you consider to be the highlight of your career:** The highlight of Mr. Hansen's career has been his research in musical acoustics. **Where will you be in five years:** In five years, he will continue to do research in musical acoustics of musical instruments. **Hobbies:** Serving in the church **Religion:** Mormon **Shipping Address:** 2137 E Cassidy Way, Eagle Mountain, UT, 84005

Arnold Harberger

Title: Economist **Industry:** Education/Educational Services **Date of Birth:** 07/27/1924 **Place of Birth:** Newark **State:** NJ **Parents:** Ferdinand C. Harberger; Martha (Bucher) Harberger **Spouse Name:** Ana Beatriz Valjalo (3/15/1958, Deceased 6/26,/2011) **Children:** Paul Vincent; Carl David **Education:** DHC Honorary Degree, Universidad del Defarrollo (2017); Honorary Doctor, University of Americana (2006); Honorary Doctor, Instituto Tecnolgico Autnomo de Mexico (2006); Honorary Doctor, University of Francisco Marroquin (2004); Honorary Doctor, Technical University of Central America (1989); Honorary Doctor, Catholic University of Chile (1988); Honorary Doctor, University of Tucuman (1979); PhD, University of Chicago (1950); MA, University of Chicago (1947); Student, Johns Hopkins University (1941-1943); Honorary Doctor, Universidad del Desarrollo (2017) **Career:** Professor Emeritus (2015-Present); Professor Emeritus, University of Chicago (1991-Present); Professor, University of Chicago (1959-Present); Professor, Economics, University of California, Los Angeles, CA (1984-1992); Distinguished Service Professor, Gustavus F. and Ann M. Swift, University of Chicago (1977-1991); Chairman Department, University of Chicago (1975-1980); Director, Center of Latin American Economic Studies, University of Chicago (1965-1992); Chairman Department, University of Chicago (1964-1971); Associate Professor, Economics, University of Chicago (1953-1959) **Career Related:** Professor, Economics, University of California, Los Angeles, CA (1984-Present); Consultant, Chilean Ministry of Social Development (2011-2013); Chief Economic Advisor, United States Agency for International Development (2006-2010); Consultant, Colombia (2006); Consultant, Panama Canal Authority (2005-2006); Consultant, International Monetary Fund (2002-2006); Consultant, Madagascar (2005); Consultant, Egypt (2002); Consultant, Colombia (2002); Vice President, Chairman, Advisory Council, Institute for Policy Reform Consultant Office of Economic Adviser to the President, Russia (2000-2004); Consultant, Indonesia (1997-2001); Consultant, Indonesian Ministry of Finance (1997-2000); Consultant, Dominican Republic (1997); Consultant, Dominican Republic (1996); Consultant, Ecuador (1996); Consultant, China (1995); Consultant, Economic Minister of Argentina (1994-2000); Consultant, Colombia (1994); Member, International Advisory Council, Institute of International Studies, Stanford University (1991-1999); Consultant, Canadian Department of Industry, Science and Technology (1991-1999); Consultant, Colombia (1991); Consultant, Nicaragua (1990); Consultant, Dominican Republic (1989); Consultant, Venezuela (1989); Consultant, International Monetary Fund (1989); Consultant, Ministry of Finance, Malawi (1988); Consultant, Indonesian Ministry of Finance (1986); Visiting Professor, University of Paris (1986); Visiting Professor, University of California, Los Angeles, CA (1984); Visiting Professor, University of California, Los Angeles, CA (1983); Consultant, Chinese Ministry of Finance (1983); Consultant, Canadian Department of Finance (1982-1988); Consultant, Indonesian Ministry of Finance (1981-1982); Consultant, Canadian Department of Employment and Migration (1980-1982); Consultant, USAID (1976-2010); Consultant, Mexico (1976-2005); Consultant, Financial Ministry, Bolivia (1976); Consultant, Canadian Department for Regional Economic Expansion (1975-1977); Consultant, Budget and Planning Office, Uruguay (1974-1975); Consultant, Planning Commission, El Salvador (1973-1975); Visiting Professor, Princeton University (1973-1974); Consultant, Planning Commission, India (1973); Visiting Professor, Harvard University (1971-1972); Consultant, Colombia (1969-1971); Consultant, Ford Foundation (1967-1977); Consultant, Central Bank, Chile (1965-1970); Visiting Professor, Economic Development Institute, International Bank for Reconstruction and Development (1965); Consultant, Planning Department, Panama (1963-1977); Consultant, Pan American Union (1962-1976); Consultant, Department of State (1962-1976); **Military Service:** U.S. Army (1943-1946) **Creative Works:** Editor, "On the Process of Growth and Economic Policy in Developing Countries" (2005); Editor with Glenn P. Jenkins, "Cost-Benefit Analysis" (2002); Editor, "World Economic Growth" (1985); Author, "Taxation and Welfare" (1974); Author, "Project Evaluation" (1972); Editor, "Key Problems of Economic Policy In Latin America" (1970); Editor, "The Taxation of Income from Capital" (1968); Editor, "Demand for Durable Goods" (1960) **Awards:** Recipient, Bradley Prize (2009); Royal Economic Society, National Tax Association, Holland Medal (2001); Faculty Research Fellow, Ford Foundation (1968-1969) **Membership:** President, Society for Benefit of Cost Analysis (2008-2009); Distinguished Fellow, American Economic Association (1999); President, American Economic Association (1997); President-Elect, American Economic Association (1996); Vice President, American Economic Association (1992); President, Western Economic Association (1989-1990); Vice President, Western Economic Association (1987-1988); American Economic Association (1970-1972) **Marquis Who's Who Honors:** Albert Nelson Marquis Lifetime Achievement Award (2017) **Business Address:** PO Box 91477, Los Angeles, CA, 90009-1477

Robert Morris Hardaway

Title: Surgeon **Industry:** Medicine & Health Care **Date of Birth:** 01/09/1916 **Place of Birth:** Camp John Hay **State/Country of Origin:** Philippines **Parents:** Robert Morris Hardaway; Olive (Gray) Hardaway **Children:** Robert Morris, IV; Elizabeth J.; Christopher L.; Thomas G., Jr. **Education:** MD, Washington University, St. Louis, MO (1939); AB, University of Denver (1936); Postgraduate Studies, University of Colorado Medical School (1935-1937) **Certifications:** Diplomate, American Board of Surgery **Career:** Commanding General, William Beaumont Army Medical Center, El Paso, TX (1970-1975); Professor of Surgery, Texas Tech University School Medicine, El Paso, TX (1976-2002); Staff, R.E. Thomason General Hospital, El Paso, TX (1975-2002); Commanding Officer, 97th General Hospital, Frankfurt, Germany (1967-1970); Director, Division of Surgery, Walter Reed Army Institute Research, Washington, DC (1960-1967); Surgical Service, Martin Army Hospital, Fort Benning, GA (1958-1960); Surgical Service, 97th General Hospital, Frankfurt, Germany (1954-1958); Chief, Surgical Service, Station Hospital, Fort Belvoir, VA (1950-1954); Resident of Surgery, Fitzsimons General Hospital, Denver, CO (1949-1950); Chief, Surgical Service, 34th General Hospital, Republic of Korea (1947-1949); Resident of Surgery, Madigan General Hospital, Tacoma, WA (1946-1947); Surgical Trainee, Nichols General Hospital, Louisville, KY (1945-1946); Teacher, Medical Field Service School, Carlysle Barracks, PA (1943-1945); Ward Officer, Surgical Service, North Sector, General Hospital, Hawaii (1941-1943); Ward Officer, Surgical Service, Fitzsimons General Hospital, Denver, CO (1940-1941) **Career Related:** Fellow, American College of Surgeons; Fellow, Microcirculation Association; Fellow, American Association for the Surgery of Trauma; Fellow, American College of Angiology **Military Service:** Advanced Through Grades to Brigadier General, U.S. Army (1970); Commissioned First Lieutenant, Medical Corps, U.S. Army (1939) **Creative Works:** Author, "Blood Problems in Critical Care" (1989); Author, "Treatment of Wounded in Vietnam" (1988); Author, "Shock - The Reversible Stage of Dying" (1988); Author, "Capillary Perfusion in Health and Disease" (1981); Author, "Clinical Management of Shock, Surgical and Medical" (1968); Author, "Syndromes of Disseminated Intravascular Coagulation" (1966) **Awards:** Certificate of Outstanding Achievement, U.S. Army Science Conference (1964); Silver Award Exhibit, American Society of Clinical Pathologists, College of American Pathologists (1964); Second Prize for Exhibition, American Medical Association (1964); Decorated Distinguished Service Medal; Legion of Merit with Oak Leaf Cluster **Membership:** American Medical Association; Association of Military Surgeons of the United States; Alpha Omega Alpha **What do you consider to be the highlight of your career:** The highlight of Dr. Hardaway's career was his observations while treating the wounded at Schofield Barracks on December 7th, 1941, the site of the first attack when Pearl Harbor was bombed. This led him to devote his future research to finding the most effective treatment of shock and trauma. **Religion:** Episcopalian **Shipping Address:** 10401 E Plumeria Road, Tucson, AZ, 85749

William Hardin

Title: 1) Pediatric Surgeon 2) Professor of Surgery 3) Associate Chief Medical Officer **Industry:** Medicine & Health Care **Company Name:** 1) LVPG Vascular Surgery 2) University of Colorado School of Medicine 3) Children's Colorado at Memorial Hospital and Southern Colorado **Education:** Resident in General Surgery, Charity Hospital, Louisiana State University, New Orleans (2007); Fellow in Pediatric Surgery, Children's Hospital Los Angeles, CA (1985); Resident in General Surgery, Tulane University, Charity Hospital, Louisiana State University (1981); Intern in General Surgery, Charity Hospital, Louisiana State University (1980); MD, School of Medicine, Tulane University (1979); BA in Biology, Harvard University (1975) **Certifications:** Certified Pediatric Surgeon, American Board of Surgery; Certified General Surgeon, American Board of Surgery **Civic:** Alumni Association, Harvard University; Alumni Association, Tulane University; Newark Academy **Awards:** Honoree, All American Shooter, National Sporting Clays Association (2017); Honoree, Best Doctors in America (2017); Honoree, Best Doctor, Colorado Springs (2016-2017); Recipient, Outstanding Teacher Awards **Membership:** American College of Surgeons; American Pediatric Surgical Association; Eastern Association for the Surgery of Trauma; American Trauma Society; Association for Academic Surgery; Society of Laparoendoscopic Surgeons; International Pediatric Endosurgery Group **Marquis Who's Who Honors:** Albert Nelson Marquis Lifetime Achievement Award (2017) **To what do you attribute your success:** He attributes his success to hard work, as well as his educational background and the support he receives from family and friends. **Why did you become involved in your profession or industry:** He became involved in his profession because he maintained an interest in the technical aspects of medicine. **What do you consider to be the highlight of your career:** The most gratifying aspect of his career is having the opportunity and the privilege to care for young children. **Where will you be in five years:** In five years, Dr. Hardin intends to grow within the medical field, and become a full-time professor with the department of surgery at the University of Colorado. **Hobbies:** Working on computers; Photography; Skiing; Traveling; Spending time with his daughter **Shipping Address:** 16692 Timber Meadow Dr, Colorado Springs, CO, 80908

Anne R. Hardin-Mason

Title: Teacher **Industry:** Education/Educational Services **Date of Birth:** 12/19/1931 **Place of Birth:** Hamlet **State/Country of Origin:** NC **Parents:** William Herbert Robertson; Catherine Holder Robertson **Marital Status:** Widowed **Spouse Name:** Robert L. Mason (3/29/1975, Deceased 3/1989); C. Dwight Hardin, Jr. (6/18/1955, Deceased 6/1972) **Children:** Charles David Hardin (Deceased 6/2016); Shelly Mason Ivey; Jennifer **Education:** BA, University of North Carolina at Greensboro (1954) **Career:** Teacher, College Park Middle School, Hickory, NC (1981-1992); Teacher, Southwest Elementary School (Now Southwest Primary School), Hickory, NC (1977-1981); Teacher, College Park Junior High School, Hickory, NC (1972-1977); Teacher, Oakwood Elementary School, Hickory, NC (1955-1959); Teacher, North School, Gastonia, NC (1954-1955) **Career Related:** Representative, Teacher of the Year Competition, Southwest Elementary School (Now Southwest Primary School) (1980) **Civic:** Chairperson, Transportation Committee, First Presbyterian Church (2005-Present); Congregational Care Committee, First Presbyterian Church (1997-Present); Chairperson, Christmas Gift Bag Committee, First Presbyterian Church (2005-2015); Chief Judge, Board of Elections, Newton, NC (1992-2003); Docent, Hickory Museum of Art, Hickory, NC; Docent, Harper House/Hickory History Center, Hickory, NC; Docent, Hickory Landmarks Society, Hickory, NC **Awards:** Representative, Teacher of the Year, Southwest Elementary School (1979) **Membership:** National Education Association; North Carolina Association of Educators **Marquis Who's Who Honors:** Albert Nelson Marquis Lifetime Achievement Award (2017); Distinguished Humanitarian (2017) **Why did you become involved in your profession or industry:** Ms. Hardin-Mason became involved in her profession because she always enjoyed working with students. While in college, she taught algebra and geometry at an orthopedic hospital, where she enjoyed the one on one interaction with the students. **What do you consider to be the highlight of your career:** Ms. Hardin-Mason is most proud of having a position in the Hickory Public School System. She has taught fifth grade in the best elementary school in the area, and was also asked by the principal to be a part of a tutoring center he was going to start. She was a private tutor for 12 years, and principals would call her when a student would need special help. She had many students needing special attention that have became successes. She considers this to be her most rewarding teaching experience. **Hobbies:** Bridge; Gardening **Political Affiliations:** Democrat **Religion:** Presbyterian **Shipping Address:** 771 9th Street NW, Hickory, NC, 28601

David Michael Hargis

Title: Lawyer **Industry:** Law and Legal Services **Company Name:** David M. Hargis, P.A., Attorney at Law **Date of Birth:** 02/10/1948 **Place of Birth:** Warren **State/Country of Origin:** AR **Parents:** Noma Lee (Anderson) Hargis Watkins; James Von Hargis **Marital Status:** Married **Spouse Name:** Linda Jane Huckelbury Hargis (1/8/1981); Carolyn Jane Sangster (Divorced 1981) **Children:** Michelle Leigh; Michael Bradley; Clayton Andrew Chisenhall; Christopher Key Hargis **Education:** Coursework, U.S. Department of Justice Trial Advocacy Institute (1974); JD, University of Arkansas (1973); Honorary BSBA in Economics and Finance, University of Arkansas (1970) **Career:** Trial Lawyer, Solo Private Practice (1973-Present); Special Counsel, Arkansas Insurance Department, Baldwin-United Bankruptcy (1984); Special Counsel, Office of Special Prosecutor, Pulaski County Grand Jury (1983-1984); Special Counsel, Pulaski County Judge, Arkansas (1980-1982); Partner, House, Holmes & Jewell, P.A., Little Rock, AR (1979-1985); Special Counsel, Legal Services Corporation, Little Rock, AR (1977); Associate, Partner, House, Holmes & Jewell, Little Rock, AR (1975-1985); Assistant Unites States Attorney, Eastern District of Arkansas, Little Rock, AR (1974-1975); Associate, Williamson Law Firm, Monticello, AR (1973-1974) **Career Related:** Trial Counsel, Numerous Trials (1973-Present); Special Justice, Arkansas Governor's Appointment, Muccio v. Hunt, Arkansas Supreme Court (2014); Lecturer, Abusive Litigation Tactics, National Business Institute (2010); Trial Counsel, Superior Federal Bank v. Mackey (2005); Trial Counsel, Stewart Title Company v. American Abstract, Arkansas Supreme Court (2005); Outstanding Trial Lawyer, Trial Counsel, Allstate Insurance Company v. Dodson, Arkansas Trial Lawyers Association, State of Arkansas (2001); Lecturer, Lender Liability in Arkansas, National Business Institute (1988); Faculty Member, College of American Pathologists (1987); Lecturer, Trial Practice, Arkansas Bar Association (1985); Lecturer, Trial Practice, Arkansas Institute for Continuing Legal Education (1982) **Military Service:** Captain, Military Police, Outstanding Graduate, Basic Training, U.S. Army, Fort Gordon, GA (1973) **Creative Works:** Co-Author, "Quality Assurance in Physician Testing," College of American Pathologists (1987); Co-Author, Quality Assurance in Health Test, American College of Pathologists (1986); Guest Columnist, Arkansas Gazette (1984); Author, "Electronic Banking," Arkansas Law Review (1978); Author, "Due Process and the Disciplinarian," Arkansas Law Review (1972); Editor-in-Chief, Arkansas Law Review (1972-1973); Editor's Forums, Arkansas Law Review (1972); Contributor, Articles to Legal Journals **Awards:** A/V Rated Attorney, Martindale-Hubbell (1981-Present); Best Trial Lawyer, Arkansas Trial Lawyers Association (2011); Honorary Scholastic Awards, Beta Gamma Sigma and Omicron Delta Kappa, University of Arkansas (1970) **Bar Admissions:** U.S. Supreme Court (1991); U.S. District Court, Western District, State of Arkansas (1974); U.S. District Court, Eastern District, State of Arkansas (1974); State of Arkansas (1973); Pro Hac Vice, State of Louisiana; Pro Hac Vice, State of Texas; Pro Hac Vice, State of Illinois **Marquis Who's Who Honors:** Albert Nelson Marquis Lifetime Achievement Award (2017) **Hobbies:** Painting **Political Affiliations:** Independent **Religion:** Methodist **Business Address:** 2207 Hidden Valley Drive, Little Rock, AR, 72212 **Shipping Address:** 40 Valley Club Circle, Little Rock, AR, 72212

Eugene C. Hargrove

Title: Professor Emeritus **Industry:** Education/Educational Services **Company Name:** University of North Texas **Parents:** Oren Keith Hargrove, Sr.; Eleanor Mae Lade Hargrove **Marital Status:** Divorced **Spouse Name:** Kathrine Paulette Cain Hargrove (Divorced) **Children:** David C. House Hargrove (Adopted); Jennifer C. House Hargrove (Adopted) **Education:** Fellowship in Environmental Affairs, Rockefeller Foundation (1976-1977); Postdoctoral Research, Wittgenstein, Philosophical Institute, University of Vienna (1974-1975); PhD in Philosophy, University of Missouri (1974); MA in Philosophy, University of Missouri, with Honors (1967); BA in Philosophy, University of Missouri, with Honors (1966) **Career:** Professor Emeritus, University of North Texas (2017-Present); Professor, University of North Texas (1997-2017); Chair, Professor, University of North Texas (1997-2004); Chair, Associate Professor, University of North Texas (1990-1997); Associate Professor, University of Georgia (1987-1990); Assistant Professor, University of Georgia (1981-1987); Adjunct Assistant Professor, The University of New Mexico (1978-1981) **Career Related:** Visiting Scholar, "The Evolution of Environmental Thought and Ethics," NEH Summer Institute (2001); Discussion Leader, Student Conference on National Affairs, Texas A&M, College Station, TX (1999); Chair, Philosophy Department, University of North Texas (1989); Song Writer; Music Publisher **Military Service:** First Lieutenant, U.S. Army Adjutant General's Corps, Stuttgart, Germany (1968-1970) **Creative Works:** Editor, "Environmental Ethics: An Interdisciplinary Journal Dedicated to the Philosophical Aspects of Environmental Problems, Volumes 38-39" (2016-2017); Co-Author, "Foundations of Environmental Ethics," Chongqing: Chongqing Publishing House (2007); Author, "Lying, Being Mistaken, and Not Knowing in Middle-Earth," Beyond Bree (2004); Author, "Invisibility in Middle-Earth: A Tentative Theory," Beyond Bree (2003); Author, "Choice and Providential Determinism in Middle-Earth," Beyond Bree (2003); Author, "Music of Middle-Earth, Volume 2: A Musical Journey from the Khazad-dum to Gondor," Old Forest Sounds (2002); Song Writer, "Music of Middle-Earth, Volume 2: A Musical Journey from the Khazad-dum to Gondor," Old Forest Sounds, Denton, TX (2002); Song Writer, "Music of Middle-Earth, Vol. 1: A Musical Journey from the Shire to Rivendell," Old Forest Sounds, Denton, TX (2001); Author, "Music of Middle-Earth: A Musical Journey from the Shire to Rivendell," Old Forest Sounds (2001); Author, "Music of Middle-Earth: A Musical Journey from Khazad-dum to Gondor," Old Forest Sounds (2001); Author, "Music of Middle-Earth, Vol. 1: A Musical Journey from the Shire to Rivendell," Old Forest Sounds (2001); Author, "Foundations of Environmental Ethics, Reprinted Edition," Environmental Ethics Books, Denton, TX (1996); Author, "Music in Middle-Earth," Beyond Bree (1995); Contributing Author, "Foundations of Environmental Ethics," Seoul: Chul-Hak-Kwa-Hyun-Sil-Sa (1994); Editor, "The Animal Rights/Environmental Ethics Debate: The Environmental Perspective," Albany: State University of New York Press (1992); Author, "Music of Middle-Earth," Old Forest Sounds (1991); Author, "Fondamenti di Etica Ambientale: Prospettive Filosofiche del Problema Ambientale," Padova: Muzzio (1990); Author, "Foundations of Environmental Ethics," Englewood Cliffs: Prentice-Hall (1989); Author, "Who is Tom Bombadil?" Mythlore 47 (1986); Editor, "Beyond Spaceship Earth: Environmental Ethics and the Solar System," San Francisco: Sierra Club Books (1986); Editor, "Religion and Environmental Crisis," Athens: University of Georgia Press (1986); Editor, "Environmental Ethics: An Interdisciplinary Journal Dedicated to the Philosophical Aspects of Environmental Problems, Volumes 1-37" (1979-2015); Guest Editor, Contributor, "Report of the Devils Icebox-Rockbridge Park Conservation Task Force," Missouri Speleology 13 (1973); Contributor, Numerous Chapters, Books; Presenter in Field **Awards:** National Speleological Society Fellowship (1981); Rockefeller Foundation Fellowship in Environmental Affairs (1976); U.S. Army Commendation Medal for Meritorious Service, Adjutant General's Corps, Seventh Corps, Stuttgart, Germany (1970) **Membership:** National Speleological Society; American Philosophical Society; Broadcast Music, Inc. **Hobbies:** Chess; Studying the works of J.R.R. Tolkien; Song writing **Religion:** Methodist **Business Address:** 1155 Union Cir, Box 310980, Denton, TX, 76203 **Shipping Address:** 2025 Houston Pl, Denton, TX, 76201 **Website:** http://www.cep.unt.edu/vech.html

Marilyn M. Harlin

Title: Marine Botany Educator, Researcher, Consultant **Industry:** Sciences **Company Name:** University of Rhode Island **Date of Birth:** 05/30/1934 **Place of Birth:** Oakland **State/Country of Origin:** CA **Parents:** George T.; Gertrude (Turula) Miler **Marital Status:** Widowed **Spouse Name:** John E. Harlin (10/25/1955, Deceased 1966) **Children:** John E. Harlin III; Andrea M. Cilento **Education:** PhD, University of Washington (1971); MA, Stanford University (1957); AB, Stanford University (1955) **Career:** Professor Emerita, University of Rhode Island, Kingston, RI (2000-Present); Chair, Botany Department, Biological Sciences, University of Rhode Island, Kingston, RI; Professor, University of Rhode Island, Kingston, RI (1983-2000); Associate Professor, University of Rhode Island, Kingston, RI (1975-1983); Assistant Professor of Marine Biology, University of Rhode Island, Kingston, RI (1971-1975); Assistant Professor, Pacific Marine Station, Dillon Beach, CA (1969); Instructor, American College of Switzerland (1964-1966) **Career Related:** Western Australia Water Authority, Perth (1994); Research Associate, University of California, Santa Cruz, CA (1993); Consultant, Applied Science Associates, Narragansett, RI (1988-1998); Honorary Visiting Professor, LaTrobe University, Bundoora, Victoria, Australia (1984); Resource Person, Rhode Island Coastal Resource Management Council (1980-2000); Rhode Island Department of Environmental Management (1980); Guest Scientist, Atlantic Regional Laboratory, Halifax, Nova Scotia, Canada (1973-1978) **Civic:** Board of Directors Westminster Unitarian Church, East Greenwich, RI (1987); Board of Governors Women's Center, Kingston, RI (1989-1990) **Creative Works:** Author, "Making Waves: Memoir of a Marine Botanist" (2014); Co-Editor, "Freshwater and Marine Plants of Rhode Island" (1988); Co-Editor, "Marine Ecology" (1976) **Awards:** Grantee, National Oceanographic and Atmospheric Administration (1975-1981); Department of Environmental Management EPA (1989-1991); U.S. Fish and Wildlife (1995) **Membership:** National Advancement Board, Union of Concerned Scientists (2004-2008); Editorial Board, Phycological Society of America (1988-1990); Member, International Phycological Society; Newsletter Editor, Psychological Society of America (1982-1984); Executive Committee, Northeast Algal Society; President, Secretary, Sigma Xi (1979-1982) **Marquis Who's Who Honors:** Albert Nelson Life Time Achievement Award **To what do you attribute your success:** She attributes her success to her upbringing, and following her heart. **Why did you become involved in your profession or industry:** She became involved in her profession because of her belief in the importance of science to society. **What do you consider to be the highlight of your career:** The highlight of her career has been bringing joy to young minds as a result of scientific investigations. **Where will you be in five years:** In the next five years, she plans to volunteer for environmental causes, and spend time outdoors. **Hobbies:** Yoga; Hiking; Reading; Writing; Gardening; Parks volunteer **Political Affiliations:** Democrat **Religion:** Unitarian **Shipping Address:** 255 SE 33rd Ave, Portland, OR, 97214 **Website:** http://www.marilynharlin.com

John Kevin Harms

Title: Lawyer **Industry:** Law and Legal Services **Company Name:** Marine Corps Recruiting Command **Date of Birth:** 10/19/1960 **Place of Birth:** Bittburg Air Base **State/Country of Origin:** Germany **Parents:** William Robert Harms; Catherine Dorothy (Heslin) Harms **Marital Status:** Married **Spouse Name:** Pamela Tinkham (1988) **Children:** William Cameron Harms; Wade Devlin Harms **Education:** Postgraduate Coursework, United States Naval War College, Navy Command and Staff Program (2009); Master of Strategic Studies, United States Army War College (2006); Coursework in Defense Strategy, United States Army War College (2003); Advanced Contract Attorney Coursework, The Judge Advocate General's Legal Center and School, U. S. Army (2002); Postgraduate Coursework, U. S. Air Force War College (1997); Postgraduate Coursework, United States Army Command and General Staff College (1997); Judge Advocate Officer Advanced Coursework, The Judge Advocate General's Legal Center and School, United States Army (1994); Contract Attorney Coursework, The Judge Advocate General's Legal Center and School, United States Army (1990); MBA, Western New England University (1989); Judge Advocate Officer Basic Coursework, The Judge Advocate General's Legal Center and School, United States Army (1986); JD, Northwestern University (1985); BPA, Loyola University, Magna Cum Laude, New Orleans, LA (1982); Coursework in Economic Policy, Loyola University, Washington, DC (1981); United States Army Airborne School (1980); United States Army Air Assault School (1979) **Career:** Associate Counsel, Quantico Area Counsel Office, Marine Corps Recruiting Command, Marine Corps Base Quantico, Virginia (2015-Present); Adjunct Professor of Business Administration, Northern Virginia Community College, Woodbridge, VA (2013-Present); Associate General Counsel, Office of the Assistant Secretary of the Navy, Financial Management and Comptroller, Washington, DC (2011-2015); Senior Reserve Component Judge Advocate, Office of the Staff Judge Advocate, Headquarters, U. S. Special Operations Command, MacDill Air Force Base, Florida (2010-2012); Program Attorney, Aegis Ballistic Missile Defense, Missile Defense Agency, Dahlgren, VA (2009-2011); Associate General Counsel, Environment, Installations, and Enterprise Support, Defense Logistics Agency (2005-2009); Commander, 151st Legal Support Organization, Commander, MG Albert Lieber U. S. Army Reserve Center, U. S. Army Reserve, Alexandria, VA (2005-2009); Joint Operations Law Attorney, United States Army Reserve, Joint Reserve Forces, Defense Logistics Agency (2004-2005); Associate General Counsel, Environment and Base Realignment and Closure, Defense Logistics Agency (2003-2005); Deputy Staff Judge Advocate, 94th Regional Support Command, U. S. Army Reserve (2000-2004); Attorney-Advisor of Government Contracts, Chief of Environmental Law, Electronic Systems Center, Hanscom Air Force Base, Massachusetts (1996-2003) **Career Related:** Member, Board of Correction for Naval Records (2013-Present); Deputy Counsel, Defense Federal Acquisition Regulation Supplement Information Technology Committee (2005-Present); Chief Counsel, Devens Reserve Forces Training Area, Massachusetts (1995-1996) **Civic:** Volunteer, Foster Parent, Homechecker, and Interviewer, Beagle Rescue, Education, and Welfare, Alexandria, VA (2015-Present); Alumni Admissions Interviewer, Northwestern Law School (2012-Present); President, Pentagon Chapter, Federal Bar Association (2011-Present); Treasurer, Prince William Committee of 100 (2016-2017); Program Chair, Prince William Committee of 100 (2016); Chair, Candidate Debate Questions Committee, Prince William Committee of 100 (2015); Treasurer, Chapter 007, National Active and Retired Federal Employees (2014-2015); Social Chair, Chapter 007, National Active and Retired Federal Employees (2013-2014); Federal Bar Association President's Award (2011) **Military Service:** Commander, United States Army Reserve (2005-2009); Aide-de-Camp to Commanding General, 33rd Infantry Brigade, Army National Guard, Illinois (1983-1985); Colonel, U. S. Army Reserve (1982-2012) **Awards:** Fellow, American Foundation (2017); Bronze Level Advanced Communicator, Toastmasters International (2013); Eastern Area Junior Officer of the Year, Military Traffic Management Command (1992); Named, Outstanding Young Man in America (1988); Defense Superior Service Medal; Meritorious Service Medal; Joint Service Commendation Medal; Army Commendation Medal; Joint Service Achievement Medal; Army Achievement Medal; National Defense Service Medal **Membership:** American Bar Association; Federal Bar Association; Association of the U. S. Army; U. S. Naval Institute; Marine Corp Association; National Contract Management Association; Toastmaster's International; Armed Forces Communications-Electronics Association; Navy League of the U. S.; National Society of Pershing Rifles **Bar Admissions:** Massachusetts (1994); U. S. Court of Appeals for the Armed Forces (1991); Illinois (1985) **Marquis Who's Who Honors:** Albert Nelson Marquis Lifetime Achievement Award (2017) **Hobbies:** Race walking; Rescuing beagles **Shipping Address:** 15707 Beacon Ct, Dumfries, VA, 22025

Sean Lalsingh Harribance

Title: Parapsychologist **Industry:** Social Work **Company Name:** Sean Harribance Institute for Parapsychology Research, Inc. **Date of Birth:** 11/11/1939 **Place of Birth:** Fyzabad **State/Country of Origin:** Trinidad and Tobago **Parents:** Harribance Singh; Sampatia Batchasingh **Marital Status:** Married **Spouse Name:** Christine Ann Comyn (2/28/1971) **Children:** Linnea Christine; Sean Lalsingh, Jr. **Career:** Honorary Director, Sean Harribance Institute for Parapsychology Research, Inc. (1995-Present); President, Sean Harribance Institute for Parapsychology, Inc (1980-Present); Visiting Professor, Part-Time Parapsychological Research Subject, Laurentian University (2009); Visiting Professor, Part-Time Parapsychological Research Subject, Laurentian University (2000); Parapsychology Research Subject, Foundation for Research on the Nature of Man, Rhine Research Center, Durham, NC (1997-1998); Visiting Professor, Part-Time Parapsychological Research Subject, Laurentian University (1996-1997); Research Subject, Psychical Research Foundation, Durham, NC (1980); Part-Time Research Subject, Mankind Research (1975-1976); Research Subject, Psychical Research Foundation, Durham, NC (1969-1973); Parapsychology Research Subject, Foundation for Research on the Nature of Man, Rhine Research Center, Durham, NC (1969-1973); Part-Time Parapsycholical Research Subject, Parapsychology Laboratory, Dr. Hamlyn Dukhan, Trinidad and Tobago (1966-1969); Cashier, Trinidad Bus Service, Public Transportation Service Corporation, San Fernando, Trinidad and Tobago (1959-1969) **Creative Works:** Co-author, "This Man Knows You" (1976); Contributor, Neuroquantology; Contributor, The Journal of Consciousness Exploration and Research; Contributor, International Journal of Psychophysiology; Contributor, International Journal of Neuroscience; Contributor, Perceptual and Motor Skills; Contributor, Journal of Parapsychology; Contributor, Journal of the American Society for Psychical Research; Contributor, Journal of Neuropsychiatry and Clinical Neuroscience; Contributor, Research in Parapsychology; Contributor, Australian Journal of Parapsychology; Contributor, Neuroscience Letters, International Journal of Yoga; Contributor, Theta; Contributor, New York Academy of Science; Contributor, Proceedings Parapsychology Association; Contributor, Symposium of the Parapsychological Association; Contributor, Symposium of the American Association for the Advancement of Science; Contributor, Chapter to "Extrasensory Perception," "Evidence for Psi," and "Psychic Phenomena and the Brain" **Awards:** Honorary Lieutenant Colonel, Aide-de-camp, Alabama State Militia (1975); Honorary Citizen, City of Baton Rouge/Parish of East Baton Rouge (1975); Key to the City, City of Baton Rouge/Parish of East Baton Rouge (1975) **Marquis Who's Who Honors:** Marquis Lifetime Achievement Award **To what do you attribute your success:** Mr. Harribance attributes his success to his Christian beliefs. **Why did you become involved in your profession or industry:** Mr. Harribance discovered as a young child that he could tell people things that would startle them. His friends and teacher would give him the name of "Mr. Accurate" in school. After doing fairs for charity, he received national fame. A newspaper manager and editor, Mr. Jackman, took him to the psychologist, Dr. Dukhan. He corresponded with Dr. J.B. Rhine in North Carolina, who invited him for research. He has continued in research with multiple labs and researchers for over 50 years. **What do you consider to be the highlight of your career:** The highlight of Mr. Harribance's career has been being able to document statistically that parapsychology is a solid science, and that other disciplines and scientists should further investigate the field. In addition, his biophotons can positively affect numerous animal systems and negatively affect cancer multiplication. **Religion:** Methodist **Business Address:** PO Box 908, Sugar Land, TX, 77487

George Harris

Title: Health Care Executive (Retired) **Industry:** Medicine & Health Care **Date of Birth:** 09/05/1938 **Place of Birth:** Gastonia **State/Country of Origin:** NC **Parents:** James A. Harris; Carolyn (Hord) Harris **Marital Status:** Married **Spouse Name:** Sondra Gilbert (3/29/1959) **Children:** Cynthia; Susan; David **Education:** BA in Mathematics, Duke University (1960) **Career:** President, Mariner Health Group (1994); Chief Operating Officer, Mariner Health Group (1994); Founder, Pinnacle Care Corp. (1985-1994); President, Pinnacle Care Corp. (1985-1994); Chief Executive Officer, Pinnacle Care Corp. (1985-1994); Chairman, Health Group Inc., Nashville, TN (1984-1985); Chief Executive Officer, Health Group Inc., Nashville, TN (1984-1985); Executive Vice President, American Hospital Supply Corp. (1978-1984); Corporate Vice President, American Hospital Supply Corp., Evanston, IL (1974-1978); President, Dietary Products Division, American Hospital Supply Corp., McGaw Park, IL (1971-1974); Vice President of Operations, American Hospital Supply Corp., Evanston, IL (1970-1971); President, American Hospital Supply Corp., Port Credit, Canada (1967-1970); Regional Manager, American Hospital Supply Corp., South San Francisco, CA (1964-1967); With, American Hospital Supply Corp. (1960-1984); Former Board of Directors, Mariner Health Group **Career Related:** Board of Directors, Union Special Corp.; Board of Directors, Monoclonal Antibodies, Inc., Mountain View, CA; Board of Directors, Electro Neucleonics Inc.; Board of Directors, Health Group; Board of Directors, Electro-Biology Inc.; Board of Directors, Dialogic Communications Corp. **Civic:** Board of Directors, Highland Park Hospital (1981-1984); Trustee, McCormick Seminary, Chicago, IL **Awards:** All American, High School Football; Football Scholarship, Duke University **Membership:** Board of Directors, Scientific Apparatus Manufacturers Association; Richland Country Club; SCORE Association; Christ Presbyterian Church, Nashville, TN **Marquis Who's Who Honors:** Albert Nelson Marquis Lifetime Achievement Award (2017) **To what do you attribute your success:** Mr. Harris attributes his success to a good education, hard work, good luck and God's blessing. **Why did you become involved in your profession or industry:** His grandfather was physician in Kings Mountain, North Carolina, but he passed away before Mr. Harris was born. Mr. Harris grew up with people telling him all about his grandfather, which made him think about becoming a doctor. When he went to a University, he realized that being a doctor wasn't what he really wanted, so he changed his major to math. In his senior year, he interviewed with a company called American Hospital Supply Corporation and got a job there. **What do you consider to be the highlight of your career:** A highlight of his career was managing the International Business at AHSC from 1974 until 1982. **Where will you be in five years:** In five years, he will still be spending a lot of time with his family, and traveling. **Hobbies:** Playing tennis; Reading; Travel; Plays; Movies **Political Affiliations:** Republican **Shipping Address:** 1204 Beddington Park, Nashville, TN, 37215

Ruth Hortense Coles Harris

Title: Accounting Educator **Industry:** Education/Educational Services **Date of Birth:** 09/26/1928 **Place of Birth:** Charlottesville **State/Country of Origin:** VA **Parents:** Bernard Albert Coles; Ruth Hortense (Wyatt) Coles **Marital Status:** Widowed **Spouse Name:** John Benjamin Harris (9/2/1950, Deceased 2014) **Children:** John Benjamin Harris, Jr.; Vita Michelle Harris **Education:** LHD, Virginia Union University (1998); EdD, College of William and Mary, VA (1977); CASE, College of William and Mary, VA (1977); MBA, New York University (1949); BSBA, Virginia State College (Now Virginia State University) (1948) **Certifications:** CPA, Commonwealth of Virginia **Career:** Distinguished Professor Emeritus, Virginia Union University (1997-Present); Chairman, Accounting Department, Virginia Union University (1987-1997); Professor, Accounting, Virginia Union University (1987-1997); Management Team, Sydney Lewis School of Business, Virginia Union University (1985-1987); Professor, Accounting, Virginia Union University (1981-1985); Director, Sydney Lewis School of Business, Virginia Union University (1973-1981); Professor, Virginia Union University (1969-1973); Director, Commerce Division, Virginia Union University (1969-1973); Associate Professor, Virginia Union University (1964-1969); Head of Accounting Department, Virginia Union University (1956-1969); Assistant Professor, Virginia Union University (1953-1964); Instructor, Commerce Department, Virginia Union University (1949-1953) **Career Related:** State Advisory Council, Community Service and Continuing Education (Title I) Agency, Charlottesville, VA (1977-1981); Board of Directors, American Assembly of Collegiate Schools of Business (AACSB), St. Louis, MO (1976-1979); Advisory Board, Intercollegiate Case Clearing House (1976-1979); **Civic:** Virginia Heroes, Inc., Richmond, VA (1996); Virginia Heroes, Inc., Richmond, VA (1991-1994); Chairman, Interdepartmental Committee on Rate-Setting for Children's Facilities, Richmond, VA (1983-1985); Appointed by Governor Robb to Interdepartmental Committee on Rate-Setting for Children's Facilities, Richmond, VA; Board of Directors, Richmond Urban League; Agency Evaluation Committee, United Way of Greater Richmond; Financial Secretary, Virginia Commonwealth Chapter, National Coalition of 100 Black Women; Agency Evaluation Committee, United Way **Awards:** Honoree, Virginia Women in History, Library of Virginia (2015); Business Leadership Award, Virginia Business and Professional Women's Foundation (2015); Community Service Award, Richmond North Chapter 5356, American Association of Retired Persons, Richmond, VA (2005); Award, Strong Men and Women: Excellence in Leadership, Dominion Power (1998); Tenneco Excellence in Teaching Award, UNCF (1995); Ebone Images Award, Northern Virginia Chapter, National Coalition of 100 Black Women (1993); Outstanding Faculty Award, Virginia Council for Higher Education (1992); Belle Ringer of Richmond, Richmond Branch, National Association of University Women (1992); Teaching Excellence Award, Sears-Roebuck Foundation (1990); Serwa Award, Virginia Commonwealth Chapter, National Coalition of 100 Black Women, Richmond, VA (1989); Outstanding Virginia Educator Award, Virginia Society of CPAs and the American Institute of CPAs; Distinguished Career in Accounting Education Award, Virginia Society of Certified Public Accountants **Membership:** American Institute of Certified Public Accountants; AARP; Virginia Society of Certified Public Accountants; Upsilon Omega Chapter, Alpha Kappa Alpha Sorority, Inc. **Marquis Who's Who Honors:** Albert Nelson Marquis Lifetime Achievement Award (2017) **Why did you become involved in your profession or industry:** Dr. Harris became involved in her profession because her older sister was her role model, and growing up she wanted to do everything she did. When her sister went to college, she majored in business administration. When she got to college, she told her parents that she was going to major in chemistry but decided that she didn't like biology or physics. On registration day at Virginia State University, Dr. Harris changed her major to business administration and especially loved accounting. She had a very inspiring accounting professor who told the class to be the best that they could be and reach for the top. **What do you consider to be the highlight of your career:** The highlight of Dr. Harris' career has been the success of her students. **Hobbies:** Handbells; Reading; Piano **Religion:** Baptist **Shipping Address:** 2816 Edgewood Ave, Richmond, VA, 23222

George Brooks Harrison

Title: Engineer, Researcher, Military Officer **Industry:** Military & Defense Services **Company Name:** Cable News Network **Date of Birth:** 07/30/1940 **Place of Birth:** Greenville **State/Country of Origin:** SC **Parents:** William Henry Harrison; Mary Carter (Ogburn) Harrison **Marital Status:** Married **Spouse Name:** Pennie Maria Jenkins (11/29/1963) **Children:** Taylor Leigh; Todd Henry; Tracy Elizabeth **Education:** Diplomate, Air War College, Montgomery, AL (1979); Diplomate, Armed Forces Staff College (Now Joint Forces Staff College), Norfolk, VA (1974); MBA, University of Pennsylvania (1970); BS in Engineering and Public Policy, U.S. Air Force Academy (1962) **Certifications:** Licensed Airline Transport Pilot; Certified Flight Instructor; Certified Multi-Engine Instrument Glider **Career:** Military Affairs Consultant, Cable News Network (1997-Present); Principal Research Engineer, Georgia Research Tech Institute (1997-Present); Associate Director, Georgia Research Tech Institute (1997-Present) **Career Related:** Science Advisory Board, U.S. Air Force, Washington, DC (1998-Present); Lecturer to Military, Technology and Civic Groups (1982-Present); United States Delegate, NATO Advisory Group, Aerospace Research and Development, Paris, France (1989-1991); Sponsor, MORS (1989-1991); Fellow, Beta Gamma Sigma, Inc. **Civic:** Board of Directors, Museum of Aviation (1998-Present); Executive Vice President, Air Warrior Courage Foundation (1998-Present); Board of Directors, Air Warrior Courage Foundation (1998-Present); Lieutenant Colonel, Civil Air Patrol, Georgia (1978-Present); Board of Directors, Georgia Aviation Hall of Fame (2005); Executive Council, Boy Scouts of America, New Mexico (1995-1997); Council Commissioner, Boy Scouts of America, Germany (1991-1992); District Commissioner, Boy Scouts of America, Germany (1986-1989); Atlanta Regional Airport Authority; Lieutenant Colonel, Civil Air Patrol, New Mexico; Lieutenant Colonel, Civil Air Patrol, South Carolina **Military Service:** Commander, Air Force Operational Test and Evaluation Center, Kirtland Air Force Base, New Mexico (1994-1997); Commander, Combined/Joint Task Force, U.S. Air Force, Southwest Asia (1993); Commander, Air Warfare Center, Eglin Air Force Base, Florida (1992-1993); Deputy Chief of Staff Operations, U.S. Air Force in Europe & Air Forces Africa, Ramstein Air Force Base, Germany (1991-1992); Assistant Chief of Staff, Studies and Analyses, Air Force District of Washington (1989-1991); Major General, U.S. Air Force (1989); Department Chief of Staff Plans, U.S. Air Force in Europe & Air Forces Africa, Ramstein Air Force Base, Germany (1986-1989); Chief, Joint Operations Division, Joint Chiefs of Staff, Washington, DC (1984-1986); Wing Commander, 479th Tactical Training Wing, Holloman Air Force Base, New Mexico (1982-1986); Commander, 4485th Test Squadron, Eglin Air Force Base, Florida (1975-1978); Operations Officer, 13th and 25th Tactical Fighter Squadron, Udorn, Thailand (1974-1975); Joint Exercise Planner, U.S. Readiness Command, MacDill Air Force Base, Florida (1971-1974); Fighter Pilot, 557th and 436th Tactical Fighter Squadron, Vietnam (1963-1969); Forward Air Controller, 557th and 436th Tactical Fighter Squadron, Vietnam (1963-1969); Instructor, 557th and 436th Tactical Fighter Squadron, Vietnam (1963-1969); Commissioned Second Lieutenant, U.S. Air Force (1962); Fighter Pilot, 557th and 436th Tactical Fighter Squadron, Florida; Forward Air Controller, 557th and 436th Tactical Fighter Squadron, Florida; Instructor, 557th and 436th Tactical Fighter Squadron, Florida **Creative Works:** Contributor, Articles, Military Journals **Awards:** Lieutenant General Glen Kent Leadership Award, U.S. Air Force (2005); Defense Superior Service Medal; Legion of Merit with One Oak Leaf Cluster; Air Medal with 11 Oak Leaf Clusters; Distinguished Flying Cross; Distinguished Service Medal with Oak Leaf Cluster; Gold Medal, Association of Old Crows **Membership:** Flight Captain, Order of Daedalians (2003-2005); Flight Captain, Order of Daedalians (1987-1989); Air Force Association; Quiet Birdmen **Marquis Who's Who Honors:** Albert Nelson Marquis Lifetime Achievement Award (2017) **Why did you become involved in your profession or industry:** Mr. Harrison's desire to fly lead him to this profession. **Hobbies:** Aviation **Religion:** Baptist **Shipping Address:** 109 Middleton Drive, Peachtree City, GA, 30269

Michael R. Harrison, MD

Title: Professor Emeritus **Industry:** Education/Educational Services **Company Name:** University of California San Francisco **Date of Birth:** 05/05/1944 **Place of Birth:** Portland **State/Country of Origin:** OR **Marital Status:** Married **Spouse Name:** Getchen Harrison **Education:** Fellow in Pediatric Surgery, Children's Hospital Los Angeles (1976-1978); Fellow in Pediatric Surgery, Rikshospitalet (1975-1976); Chief Resident in Surgery, Massachusetts General Hospital, The General Hospital Corporation, Boston, MA (1974-1975); Senior Resident in Surgery, Massachusetts General Hospital, The General Hospital Corporation, Boston, MA (1973-1974); Fellow, Laboratory of Immunology, National Institute of Allergy and Infectious Disease (1971-1973); Resident in Surgery, Massachusetts General Hospital, The General Hospital Corporation, Boston, MA (1970-1971); Intern, Massachusetts General Hospital, The General Hospital Corporation, Boston, MA (1969-1970); MD, Harvard Medical School, Harvard University, Magna Cum Laude (1969); BA, Yale University, Cum Laude (1965) **Certifications:** Diplomate in Surgical Critical Care, American Board of Surgery, Inc. (1991); Diplomate in Pediatric Surgery, American Board of Surgery, Inc. (1989); Diplomate, American Board of Surgery, Inc. (1988); Diplomate in Pediatric Surgery, American Board of Surgery, Inc. (1979); Diplomate, American Board of Surgery, Inc. (1978) **Career:** Affiliate, Kaiser Permanente, Kaiser Foundation Health Plan, Inc., San Francisco, CA (1983-Present); Professor, University of California San Francisco (1979-Present); Affiliate, California Pacific Medical Center (1979-Present); Affiliate, Moffitt-Long Medical Center, University of California San Francisco (1979); Professor Emeritus, University of California San Francisco **Creative Works:** Contributor, 453 Articles, Professional Journals **Membership:** AAPD; American College of Surgeons; APDSA; PCSA **Marquis Who's Who Honors:** Albert Nelson Marquis Lifetime Achievement Award (2017) **Why did you become involved in your profession or industry:** Dr. Harrison went into surgery, then pediatric surgery, and then fetal surgery. There were always people who wanted to learn new fields, so he naturally fell into teaching. **What do you consider to be the highlight of your career:** The highlight of Dr. Harrison's career was conducting the first fetal surgery, and essentially founding the field. **Hobbies:** Aerobic dancing; Making olive oil **Shipping Address:** 406 Pacheco St, San Francisco, CA, 94116 **Website:** https://pedsurg.ucsf.edu/faculty/pediatric-surgeons/michael-r-harrison,-md

Patrick W. Harrison

Title: Lawyer **Industry:** Law and Legal Services **Date of Birth:** 07/14/1946 **Place of Birth:** St. Louis **State/Country of Origin:** MO **Parents:** Charles William Harrison; Carolyn (Woods) Harrison **Education:** JD, Indiana University (1972); BS, Indiana University (1968) **Career:** Partner, Patrick W. Harrison Attorney at Law, Columbus, OH (1985-Present); Lawyer, Private Practice (2010); Partner, Cline, King, Beck and Harrison, Columbus, OH (1980-1985); Lawyer, Private Practice, Columbus, OH (1979-1980); Partner, Goltra & Harrison, Columbus, OH (1973-1978); Associate, Goltra, Cline, King & Beck, Columbus, IN (1972-1973); Sole Proprietor, Patrick W. Harrison Attorney at Law, Columbus, IN **Career Related:** Indiana Nominating Commission Nominee, Indiana Supreme Court (1984); Fellow, Indiana Trial Lawyers Association **Civic:** Board of Directors, Face to Face Ministries; Advisory Board, Bartholoma County, Salvation Army **Military Service:** U.S. Army (1968-1970) **Awards:** Co-Trial Lawyer of the Year, Indiana Trial Lawyers Association (1999) **Membership:** Emeritus Director, Indiana Trial Lawyers Association (1999); Board of Directors, Indiana Trial Lawyers Association (1984); American Association for Justice **Bar Admissions:** U.S. District Court, District of Nebraska (1982); U.S. Supreme Court (1977); U.S. District Court, Southern District, State of Indiana (1973); State of Indiana (1973) **To what do you attribute your success:** Mr. Harrison is very blessed; his wife really helps him as a sounding board. He grew up in southern Illinois, where the values are very different, had life changing experiences while in the military. He also attributes his success to really caring about his clients. **Why did you become involved in your profession or industry:** When in college, Mr. Harrison was drafted the day after he graduated. He went to Vietnam, and some of the guys suggested he look into going to law school, which he really had no desire to, but when he looked into it, he decided to apply and found he really enjoyed it. **What do you consider to be the highlight of your career:** The most important thing in Mr. Harrison's career was when he was nominated to be on the Indiana Supreme Court in 1984. In his career, his purpose and goal in life is to help people. Most of his clients are significantly injured and nowhere to turn, so he takes great pride in helping his clients and making a difference for them in their lives. **Where will you be in five years:** In five years, Mr. Harrison will be retired. **Hobbies:** Golf **Political Affiliations:** Republican **Religion:** Baptist **Shipping Address:** 14250 W Mount Healthy Road, Columbus, IN, 47201

John Clifton Hart

Title: Lawyer **Industry:** Law and Legal Services **Company Name:** Brown, Dean, Wiseman, Proctor, Hart & Howell LLP **Date of Birth:** 04/29/1945 **Place of Birth:** Chicago **State/Country of Origin:** IL **Parents:** Clifton Edwin Hart; Eleanor (Zielinski) Hart **Marital Status:** Married **Spouse Name:** Dianne Lynn Wenzel (1/18/1969) **Children:** David Clifton; Steven Philip; Kristin Dianne **Education:** JD, University of North Dakota (1972); Postgraduate Coursework, Northwestern University Pritzker School of Law (1967-1969); BS, Loyola University Chicago (1967) **Certifications:** United States District Court for the Northern District of Oklahoma (1999); Supreme Court of the United States (1997); United States District Court Eastern District of Texas (1984); United States District Court Western District of Texas (1981); United States District Court Eastern District of Oklahoma (1981); United States District Court Western District of Oklahoma (1981); United States Court of Appeals for the Fifth Circuit (1980); United States Court of Appeals for the Eighth Circuit (1980); United States District Court Southern District of Texas (1979); District Court Northern District of Texas (1979); United States District Court District of Minnesota (1973) **Career:** Partner, Brown, Dean, Proctor & Howell, LLP (1998-Present); Partner, Cantey Hanger LLP (1993-1998); Managing Partner, Southwest Regional Office, Robins, Kaplan, Miller & Ciresi (Now Robins Kaplan LLP) (1988-1993); President, Hart & Associates (1987-1988); President, Hart & Engen (1984-1987); Vice President, Gollaher & Hart (1981-1984); Partner, Robins, Zelle, Larson & Kaplan (Now Robins Kaplan LLP) (1973-1981) **Military Service:** Major, US Air Force (1969-1971) **Creative Works:** Contributor, Articles to Professional Journals **Membership:** ABA; American Bar Foundation; Texas Bar Foundatio; n Loss Executives Association; Federation Defense & Corporate Counsel, Inc.; Tarrant County Bar Association **Bar Admissions:** Texas **Political Affiliations:** Republican **Religion:** Lutheran **Shipping Address:** 306 W 7th St, Wiseman, Proctor, Hart & Howell LLP, Fort Worth, TX, 76102

Alan Charles Hartford, PhD

Title: Associate Professor **Industry:** Education/Educational Services **Company Name:** Dartmouth-Hitchcock Medical Center **Date of Birth:** 01/06/1962 **Place of Birth:** Berkeley **State/Country of Origin:** CA **Parents:** John Jewell Hartford; Heidi Marie (Froning) Hartford **Marital Status:** Divorced **Spouse Name:** Arianna Vora (Divorced) **Children:** Anya Hartford **Education:** Fellow in Radiation Oncology, Massachusetts General Hospital, Boston, MA (1998); PhD in Political Economy and Government, Harvard University (1997); Residency in Radiation Oncology, Massachusetts General Hospital, Boston, MA (1993-1998); Internship, Beth Israel Deaconess Hospital, Boston, MA (1992-1993); MD, Harvard Medical School (1992); MA in Philosophy, Stanford University (1983); BS in Biological Sciences, Stanford University, with Distinction (1983) **Certifications:** Medical License, State of Vermont (2007); Medical License, State of New Hampshire (2004); Medical License, Commonwealth of Massachusetts (1996); Diplomate, American Board of Radiology (1999) **Career:** Program Director, Radiation Oncology Residency, Dartmouth-Hitchcock Medical Center (2016-Present); Associate Professor of Medicine, Dartmouth Geisel School of Medicine (2010-Present); Interim Chief, Section of Radiation Oncology, Dartmouth-Hitchcock Medical Center (2004-2016); Assistant Professor of Medicine, Dartmouth Geisel School of Medicine (2004-2010) **Career Related:** Genitourinary Cancer Core Committee, NRG Oncology Clinical Trials Group (2016-Present); Commission on Cancer, American College of Surgeons (2015-Present); Chair of Cancer Clinical Research Quality Improvement Committee, Norris Cotton Cancer Center at Dartmouth-Hitchcock Medical Center (2015-Present); Committee on Practice Parameters and Technical Standards in Radiation Oncology, American College of Radiology (2007-present), Chair (2012-Present), Vice-Chair (2010-2012); Grand Rounds Course Director, Norris Cotton Cancer Center at Dartmouth-Hitchcock Medical Center (2009-Present); Principal Investigator, RTOG/NRG Oncology Clinical Trials Group at Dartmouth-Hitchcock Medical Center (2006-Present); More than 20 NIH-NCI Scientific Study Sections and Panels (2004-Present); Scores of Courses and Lectures for Medical Students, Residents and Fellows, Dartmouth Geisel School of Medicine (2004-Present); Executive Committee, Norris Cotton Cancer Center at Dartmouth-Hitchcock Medical Center (2006-2016); Scientific Program Committee for Radiation Oncology, Radiological Society of North America (2003-2009); Professionalism Committee, Radiological Society of North America (2003-2008); Scores of Courses and Lectures for Medical Students, Residents and Fellows, Harvard Medical School (1998-2004); Admissions Committee, Harvard Medical School (1996-2004); Council on Ethical & Judicial Affairs, American Medical Association (1995-1998); Council on Medical Service, American Medical Association (1990-1991); Board of Trustees, American Medical Association (1989-1990); Council on Long-Range Planning & Development, American Medical Association (1987-1989) **Civic:** Support through Financial Contributions and Organizational Activities, Christian Ministries, Educational Institutions and Charitable Groups **Creative Works:** Co-author, Dozens of Original Articles and Scientific Reviews in Medical Journals (1992-Present); Author, Pen Name Alan Froning, "First Days of August," Archway Publishing (2015) **Awards:** New Hampshire's Top Doctors, New Hampshire Magazine (2018, 2017); Fellow, American College of Radiology (2015); America's Top Cancer Doctors, Newsweek Magazine (2015); New Hampshire's Top Doctors, New Hampshire Magazine (2014); Excellence in Teaching Award, Department of Medicine, Dartmouth Geisel School of Medicine (2014); Continuing Medical Education Faculty Director Award, Dartmouth Geisel School of Medicine (2013); America's Top Doctors, Castle Connolly Medical Ltd. (2012-2018); New Hampshire's Top Doctors, New Hampshire Magazine (2012); AACR-AFLAC Scholar in Cancer Research Award (2000); Graduate Research Fellowship, MacArthur Foundation (1996); Graduate Fellowship, Program in Ethics and the Professions, Harvard University (1991); Nominee, Rhodes Scholarship, Stanford University (1983); The Phi Beta Kappa Society (1981) **Membership:** American Society for Radiation Oncology; American College of Radiology; American Medical Association; Radiological Society of North America; New Hampshire Medical Society; Vermont Medical Society; Massachusetts Medical Society **Marquis Who's Who Honors:** Albert Nelson Marquis Lifetime Achievement Award (2017) **Hobbies:** Jazz Piano; Creative Writing **Political Affiliations:** Independent **Religion:** Presbyterian **Shipping Address:** 99 Breck Hill Rd, Lyme, NH, 03768

Morris Lane Harvey

Title: Lawyer **Industry:** Law and Legal Services **Company Name:** Morris Lane Harvey Law Offices **Date of Birth:** 04/22/1950 **Place of Birth:** Madisonville **State/Country of Origin:** KY **Parents:** Morris Lee Harvey; Margie Lou (Wallace) Harvey **Marital Status:** Married **Spouse Name:** Mary Topel Harvey **Children:** Morris Lane, Jr.; John French; Laura Kathleen; Adam; Kim **Education:** JD, University of Kentucky (1974); BS, Murray State University (1972) **Certifications:** Diplomate, American Academy of Matrimonial Lawyers **Career:** Proprietor, Morris Lane Harvey Law Offices, Mount Vernon, IL (2007-Present); Partner, Harvey and Bradley, Mount Vernon, IL (2004-2007); Sole Practice, Mount Vernon, IL (1997-2003); Sole Practice, Fairfield, IL (1986-1997); Partner, Feiger, Quindry, Molt & Harvey and Successor Firms, Fairfield, IL (1977-1985); Associate, Hanagan & Dousman, Mount Vernon, IL (1975-1977) **Career Related:** Assistant Governor, District 6510, Rotary International (2011-Present); Alternate Delegate, Republican National Convention (2004); Alternate Delegate, Republican National Convention (1988); Instructor, Frontier Community College, Fairfield, IL (1977-1979); Special Assistant to Attorney General, State of Illinois, Fairfield, IL (1977-1982) **Civic:** Chairman-elect, United Way of Illinois (2009-Present); Board Member, United Way of Illinois (2009-Present); Board Member, United Way of Southern Central Illinois (2002-2009); President, Mount Vernon Rotary Club (2006-2007) **Creative Works:** Contributor, Articles, Professional Journals **Awards:** Named, Outstanding Young Men in America, U.S. Jaycees (1978, 1981, 1989) **Membership:** Family Law Section Committee, Association of Trial Lawyers of America (2010-Present); National Director, Woodmen of World Life Insurance Society (2005-2009); National Fraternal Committee, Woodmen of World Life Insurance Society (2000-2002); National Judicial Committee, Woodmen of World Life Insurance Society (1993-1997); National Legislative Committee, Woodmen of World Life Insurance Society (1989-1993); National Fraternal Committee, Woodmen of World Life Insurance Society (1987-1989); President, Illinois Chapter, Woodmen of World Life Insurance Society (1985-1987); ABA; Illinois Trial Lawyers Association **Bar Admissions:** United States District Court Southern District of Illinois (1979); State of Illinois (1975); United States Court of Appeals for the Seventh Circuit **Marquis Who's Who Honors:** Albert Nelson Marquis Lifetime Achievement Award (2017); Distinguished Humanitarian (2017) **Political Affiliations:** Republican **Shipping Address:** 2029 Broadway Street, Law Office of Morris Lane Harvey, Mount Vernon, IL, 62864

Hammam Adib Hasan, PhD

Title: Associate Professor, Faculty Senate President **Industry:** Education/ Educational Services **Company Name:** Spalding University **Parents:** Alfred Petty; Delores A. Petty **Spouse Name:** Vonda Henderson (4/14/1972, Divorced 4/20/1976) **Children:** Lawrence Donnell Petty **Education:** PhD, University of Washington, Seattle, WA (1997); MEd, University of Washington, Seattle, WA (1983); BA in Political Science, Washington State University, Pullman, WA (1971) **Certifications:** Certification in Teaching, Education Professional Standards Board, Commonwealth of Kentucky (2005); Certification in Teaching, Hawaii State Department of Education (2002) **Career:** Associate Professor of Special Education, Spalding University, Louisville, KY (2006-Present); Gang Intervention Specialist, Spalding University, Louisville, KY (2005-Present); President, Faculty Senate, Spalding University, Louisville, KY (2016-2017); College Education Curriculum Committee Chair, Spalding University, Louisville, KY (2005); Advisory Committee, Member, Quality Enhancement Plan, Spalding University, Louisville, KY (2004-2005); Dean, Daniel K. Inouye College of Pharmacy, University of Hawaii at Hilo, Kapolei, HI (2004-2005); Special Education Teacher, Waipahu High School, Hawaii (2002-2004); Assistant Professor of Special Education, Eastern Michigan University, Ypsilanti, MI (1998-2002); Lecturer, Western Washington University, Seattle, WA (1997-1998); Special Education Teacher, Seattle Public Schools (1985-1995) **Career Related:** Faculty Advisor, Council for Exceptional Children, Arlington, VA (2007); Reader, Education Professional Standards Board, Frankfort, KY (2006) **Civic:** Lay Officiator, Administrator Services Director, ECKANKAR, Louisville, KY (2009); Executive Board Member, Young Educators Society, Detroit, MI (1999-2002); Research Specialist, Self-Assessment Team, Lansing, MI (1999-2002); Board Member, Michigan Association of Teachers of Children with Emotional Impairments, East Lansing, MI (1999-2001); Co-Founder, Save Our County's Kids, Shelton, WA (1995-1998); Faculty Fellow, Academic Service-Learning, Eastern Michigan University, Ypsilanti, MI **Membership:** Association for Supervision and Curriculum Development; Phi Delta Kappa; Council for Exceptional Children; Phi Sigma Kappa **Marquis Who's Who Honors:** Albert Nelson Marquis Lifetime Achievement Award (2017); Distinguished Humanitarian (2017) **Why did you become involved in your profession or industry:** On Dr. Hasan's first day of kindergarten, his mother told him that he would go to college. Both his parents had masters degrees. His father took him to college campuses on weekends so he would know that it took hard work, and he often saw his dad studying in the middle of the night. Many people in his family were educated, so Dr. Hasan knew it would be his path as well. **What do you consider to be the highlight of your career:** Dr. Hasan is proud of creating the Hydroplane Racing Program, which was designed to encourage students of all ages and backgrounds to gain and maintain an interest in school and learning. **Hobbies:** Hydroplanes **Shipping Address:** 5207 Manor Dr, KY, Crestwood, 40014 **Website:** http://www.hahasanphd.com

John David Hatch

Title: John D. Hatch, P.C. **Industry:** Law and Legal Services **Company Name:** President **Date of Birth:** 08/26/1942 **Place of Birth:** Atlanta **State/Country of Origin:** GA **Parents:** Ernest Healey Hatch; Charlotte Blanchard (Chazal) Hatch **Marital Status:** Married **Spouse Name:** Pamela Faye Carr (6/13/1964) **Children:** Wendy H. Duncan; A. Candice Hatch; Teresa H. Caraker **Education:** JD, Georgetown University (1971); BS, Florida State University (1964); AA, College of Central Florida, Ocala, FL (1962) **Certifications:** United States District Court of the North District of Texas (1992); United States Tax Court (1979); Supreme Court of the United States (1979); United States District Court of Connecticut (1973); General Securities Licensee; General Principal Licensee **Career:** President, John D. Hatch, P.C. (1992-Present); President, Insurance Horizons, Inc., Ocala, FL (1992-2007); Senior Vice President, Resource Deployment, Inc., New York, NY (1988-1991); Senior Vice President, Resource Deployment, Inc., Fort Worth, TX (1988-1991); Vice President, Associated Madison Cos., Inc., New York, NY (1987-1988); Of General Counsel, Associated Madison Cos., Inc., New York, NY (1987-1988); Vice President, Special Operations, Commercial Life Insurance Co., Piscataway, NJ (1985-1987); Vice President, The Continental Corporation, New York, NY (1983-1985); Of General Counsel, The Continental Corporation, New York, NY (1983-1985); Of Counsel, Aetna Life & Casualty, Hartford, CT (1974-1983); Attorney, Aetna Life & Casualty, Hartford, CT (1971-1974) **Career Related:** Senior Counsel, American Health and Life Insurance Company, Fort Worth, TX (1995-Present); Member, Board of Directors, Public Service Mutual Insurance Company, New York, NY; Member, London and Midland General Insurance Company, London, England; London and Midland General Insurance Company, Ontario, Canada **Military Service:** Lieutenant, U.S. Naval Reserve (1964-1971) **Awards:** AV Preeminent Attorney, Martindale-Hubbell (1994-Present); Honoree, Best Corporate Consultancy Practice in the U.S., Acquisitions International Counsel on Supreme Court Case Tables-Norris (2016) **Membership:** TIPS Financial Services Committee, ABA (1992-1993); Chairman, TIPS Employee Benefits Committee, ABA (1983-1984); The Association of Life Insurance Counsel; Federal Bar Association; Association Internationale de Droit des Assurances **Bar Admissions:** State Bar of Texas (1992); Connecticut Bar Association (1972); The Florida Bar (1971) **Why did you become involved in your profession or industry:** Mr. Hatch became involved in his profession after he graduated from Georgetown, during which he was recruited by Hartford and Aetna. He thought that this would be temporary, but he enjoyed the in-house practice, and he stayed there until he went out on his own in 1992. **What do you consider to be the highlight of your career:** The highlight of Mr. Hatch's career was when he was counsel on a case in 1981 before the supreme court Norris vs. Arizona. He was still with Aetna, so he did not conduct the argument, but he did the research and sat at the table during the argument. It was a situation where Mr. Hatch feels that they lost the battle but won the war. This could have cost the insurance industry billions of dollars, and while they avoided that, they did lose the principle that they were sticking up for, which was using sex as a risk classification for underwriting annuities. In 1994, Mr. Hatch conducted all of the state compliance issues when Primerica acquired travelers insurance company. He handled all the state law compliance dealing with that transaction. **Hobbies:** Reading; Boating; Tennis **Political Affiliations:** Republican **Religion:** Roman Catholic **Shipping Address:** 1267 Berkshire Ln Ste 200, John D. Hatch, P.C., Tarpon Springs, FL, 34688 **Website:** http://jdhatchpc.com

Robert Dean Hatcher Jr., PhD

Title: Geologist, Educator, Research Scientist **Industry:** Education/Educational Services **Company Name:** The University of Tennessee, Knoxville **Date of Birth:** 10/22/1940 **Place of Birth:** Madison **State:** TN **Marital Status:** Married **Education:** PhD in Structural Geology, The University of Tennessee, Knoxville (1965); MS in Geology, Vanderbilt University (1962); BA in Geology, Vanderbilt University (1961); BA in Chemistry, Vanderbilt University (1961) **Certifications:** Registered Professional Geologist, State of Georgia; Registered Professional Geologist, State of Tennessee; Registered Professional Geologist, State of South Carolina **Career:** Faculty Member, Professor of Tectonics and Structural Geology, Distinguished Scientist, The University of Tennessee, Knoxville (1986-Present); Staff Member, Oak Ridge National Laboratory (1986-2000); Professor of Geology, University of South Carolina, Columbia, SC (1980-1986); Professor of Geology, Florida State University, Tallahassee, FL (1978-1980); Professor of Geology, Clemson University (1976-1978); Associate Professor of Geology, Clemson University (1970-1976); Assistant Professor of Geology, Clemson University (1966-1970); Staff Member, Humble Oil and Refining Company, New Orleans, LA (1965-1966); Teaching Assistant, The University of Tennessee, Knoxville, TN (1962-1965); Teaching Assistant, Vanderbilt University, Nashville, TN (1960-1962) **Career Related:** Member, Advisory Committee, National Cooperative Geologic Mapping Program (1996-Present); Member, Review Panel, National Science Foundation (1995); Member, Nuclear Reactor Safety Committee, National Research Council, National Academy of Sciences (1993-1995); Member, Board of Radioactive Waste Management, National Academy of Sciences (1990-1996); Member, Review Panel, National Science Foundation (1985); Member, Review Panel, National Science Foundation (1982); Member, Division of Mineral Resources, State of North Carolina (1974-1980); Member, Georgia Geological Survey (1970); Part-Time Geologic Mapper, Division of Geology, State of South Carolina (1966-1982); Part-Time Geologic Mapper, Division of Geology, State of Tennessee (1961-1964); Member, United States Geological Survey Advisory Committee **Creative Works:** Co-Editor, "Four-D Framework of Continental Crust" (2007); Co-Editor, "Variscan-Appalachian Dynamics: The Building of the Late Paleozoic Basement" (2002); Author, "Structural Geology: Principles, Concepts and Problems" (1995); Author, "Structural Geology: Principles, Concepts and Problems" (1990); Co-Author, "Laboratory Manual for Structural Geology" (1990); Co-Author, "U.S. Appalachian and Ouachita Orogens" (1990); Co-Editor, "Contributions to the Tectonics and Geophysics of Mountain Chains" (1983); Editor, "Geological Society American Bulletin" (1981-1988); Co-Author, "Physical Geology: Principles, Processes and Problems" (1976); Contributor, Scientific Papers; Contributor, Articles, Professional Journals **Awards:** Recipient, Marcus Milling Legendary Geoscientist Medal, American Geosciences Institute (2014); Recipient, Outstanding Education Award, Eastern Section, American Association of Petroleum Geologists (2011); Grantee, United States Geological Survey (2011); Grantee, United States Nuclear Regulatory Commission (2009-2011); Recipient, Appreciation Award (2007); Recipient, Penrose Medal, The Geological Society of America, Inc. (2006); Recipient, Ian Campbell Medal, American Geosciences Institute (2006); Grantee, National Science Foundation (2004); Grantee, United States Department of Energy (1993-2005); Recipient, John T. Galey Award, Eastern Section, American Association of Petroleum Geologists (2001); Grantee, Tennessee Valley Authority (1998); Honoree, Honorary Citizen Of West Virginia (1998); Grantee, United States Geological Survey (1997-2009); Grantee, Conoco-DuPont Foundation, Phillips 66 Company (1997-1998); Recipient, I.C. White Memorial Award, Eastern Section, American Association of Petroleum Geologists (1997); Grantee, National Science Foundation (1989-1992); Recipient, Distinguished Service Award, The Geological Society of America, Inc. (1988); Grantee, United States Nuclear Regulatory Commission (1978-1979); Grantee, National Science Foundation (1976-1987); Grantee, Duke Power Company (Now Duke Energy Corporation) (1974-1975); Grantee, Westinghouse Electric Corporation (1974-1975) **Membership:** Executive Committee, The Geological Society of America, Inc. (1999-2007); President, American Geosciences Institute (1996); President, The Geological Society of America, Inc. (1993); Chairman, Executive Committee, The Geological Society of America, Inc. (1991-1992); Fellow, Geological Association of Canada; Chair, Foundation Board of Trustees, The Geological Society of America, Inc.; American Association for the Advancement of Science; Georgia Geological Society; East. Tennessee Geological Society; Carolina Geological Society; American Geophysical Union; American Association of Petroleum Geologists; Sigma Xi, The Scientific Research Honor Society **Marquis Who's Who Honors:** Albert Nelson Marquis Lifetime Achievement Award (2017) **Shipping Address:** 107 Goldengate Ln, Oak Ridge, TN, 37830

Robert F. Hawke

Title: Dentist **Industry:** Health, Wellness and Fitness **Date of Birth:** 10/26/1946 **Place of Birth:** Pasadena **State/Country of Origin:** CA **Parents:** George Herbert Hawke; Mildred Estelle (Wood) Hawke **Marital Status:** Married **Spouse Name:** Emily Sue Wilkins (8/17/1973) **Children:** Kristen **Education:** DDS, Baylor University, Dallas, TX (1973); BA, University of Arizona (1969) **Career:** Private Practice, Tucson, AZ (1987-Present); Partner, Barber-Hawke, Professional Corporation, Tucson, AZ (1978-1987); Associate, B.J. Barber, Tucson, AZ (1976-1978) **Career Related:** Board of Directors, Delta Dental of Arizona, Phoenix, AZ (1985-1991); President, Delta Dental of Arizona, Phoenix, AZ (1985-1991) **Civic:** Tucson Business Alliance (1981-Present); President, Tucson Business Alliance (1994, 1983); Community Auto Immune Deficiency Syndrome Advisory Council, Tucson, AZ (1987-1990); Auto Immune Deficiency Syndrome Education Project, Tucson, AZ (1988-1990) **Military Service:** Major, U.S. Army **Awards:** Service Award, Arizona State Dental Association (2002); Pierre Faushad Award (1989) **Membership:** Southern Arizona Chairman, Give Kids a Smile Day (2003-2004); Chairman Council on Insurance, Arizona State Dental Association (1998-2003); Chairman Council on Constitution and Bylaws, Arizona State Dental Association (1996-1997); 14th District Chairman Political Action Committee, American Dental Association (1995-1998); Delegate, American Dental Association (1994-2000); Past President, Arizona State Dental Association (1994-1995); President, Arizona State Dental Association (1993-1994); Legal Liaison Committee, Arizona State Dental Association (1993-1994); President-Elect, Arizona State Dental Association (1992-1993); Chairman Council on Budget Planning, Arizona State Dental Association (1992-1993); Vice President, Arizona State Dental Association (1991); Alternate Delegate, American Dental Association (1988-1992); Trustee, Arizona State Dental Association (1988); President, Southern Arizona Dental Society (1987-1988); Board of Directors, Southern Arizona Dental Society (1983-1989); Pierre Fauchard Academy; Academy of Laser Dentistry; Academy of General Dentistry; Tucson Advanced Cosmetic & Restorative Study Club; World Clinical Laser Institute; Care Doctor, Cerec Club of Tucson; Paul Harris Fellow, Rotary; Beta Beta Beta; American College of Dentists; International College of Dentists **Why did you become involved in your profession or industry:** Dr. Hawke always wanted to be a dentist. His family are all physicians, and they encouraged him to pursue his dreams. **Hobbies:** Golf; Jogging; Tennis; Racquetball; Reading **Political Affiliations:** Republican **Religion:** Evangelical **Shipping Address:** 1575 N Swan Rd Ste 200, Robert Hawke, DDS, Tucson, AZ, 85712

Brett William Hawkins

Title: Political Science Professor (Retired) **Industry:** Education/Educational Services **Date of Birth:** 09/15/1937 **Place of Birth:** Buffalo **State/Country of Origin:** NY **Parents:** Ralph C. Hawkins; Irma A. (Rowley) Hawkins **Marital Status:** Married **Spouse Name:** Linda L. Knuth (10/31/1974) **Children:** Brett William **Education:** PhD, Vanderbilt University (1964); MA, Vanderbilt University (1962); BA, University of Rochester, with High Honors (1959) **Career:** Professor, University of Wisconsin, Milwaukee, WI (1971-1999); Associate Professor, University of Wisconsin, Milwaukee, WI (1970-1971); Associate Professor, University of Georgia (1968-1970); Assistant Professor, University of Georgia, Athens, GA (1965-1968); Assistant Professor, Washington and Lee University (1964-1965); Instructor, Political Science, Washington and Lee University (1963-1964); Instructor, Political Science, Vanderbilt University (1963) **Creative Works:** Author, "Professional Associations and Municipal Innovation" (1981); Author, "The Politics of Raising State and Local Revenue" (1978); Author, "Politics in the Metropolis, 2nd Edition" (1971); Author, "Politics and Urban Policies" (1971); Author, "The Ethnic Factor in American Politics" (1970); Author, "Nashville Metro" (1964); Contributor, Articles in Peer Reviewed Professional Journals **Awards:** New York State Scholarship for Competitive High School Exam **Membership:** Phi Beta Kappa, Iota, NY **Marquis Who's Who Honors:** Albert Nelson Marquis Lifetime Achievement Award (2017) **Hobbies:** Reading **Shipping Address:** 5318 N Kent Avenue, Whitefish Bay, WI, 53217

G. Austin Hay

Title: Actor, Artist, Pianist, Writer **Industry:** Fine Art **Date of Birth:** 12/25/1915 **Place of Birth:** Johnstown **State/Country of Origin:** PA **Parents:** George Hay; Mary Louise (Austin) Hay **Education:** MA, Columbia University (1948); MLitt, University of Pittsburgh (1948); Postgraduate Work, University of Rochester (1939); BS, University of Pittsburgh (1938) **Career Related:** Director, Hospital Shows, The Junior League of the City of New York (1948-1953) **Civic:** Museum Donor, Turn-of-Century Doctor's Office; Trustee, James Monroe Highland; Board of Governors, James Monroe Highland; President's Council, William & Mary **Military Service:** Pacific Theater of Operations, U.S. Army (1942-1946) **Creative Works:** Author, "The Arts Scene, Living on The Edge of Stardom" (2010); Illustrator, "The Arts Scene, Living on The Edge of Stardom" (2010); Producer-Director, U.S. Department of Transportation (1973-2010); Actor, "Head of State" (2003); Actor, "The Contender" (2000); Actor, "Air Force One" (1997); Actor, "Contact" (1997); Actor, "Guarding Tess" (1994); Producer-Director, Office of Presidential Personnel, The White House (1985-1993); Author, "The Moving Image, A Career in Pictures" (1990); Illustrator, "The Moving Image, A Career in Pictures" (1990); Actor, "Her Alibi" (1988); Actor, "No Way Out" (1986); Exhibitor, Le Salon des Nations a Paris (1983); Reference, "History of International Art" (1982); Exhibitor, Watergate Gallery and Frame Design (1981); Actor, "Being There" (1980); Exhibitor, Chevy Chase Gallery (1979); Actor, "Chekhov's The Bet" (1978); Exhibitor, "Bicentennial Exhibition of American Painters" (1976); Director, "Highways of History" (1976); Actor, "The Adams Chronicles" (1976); Exhibitor, Thomas Duncan Gallery (1973); Exhibitor, Carnegie Institute (1972); Director, "World Painting in Museum of Modern Art" (1972); Actor, "Love is a Many-Splendored Thing" (1972); Actor, "Child's Play" (1971); Casting Director, Films for the Department of Defense, Astoria Studios (Now Kaufman Astoria Studios) (1955-1970); Actor, "The Landlord" (1970); Exhibitor, Parrish Art Museum (1969); Actor, "As the World Turns" (1969); Actor, "Edge of Night" (1968); Exhibitor, Lincoln Center (1965); Writer, "National Council Churches" (1965); Actor, "Another World" (1965); Actor, "The United States Steel Hour" (1963); Actor, "Naked City" (1962); Actor, "Americans-A Portrait in Verses" (1962); Character Creator, "The Acrobats," The White Barn Theatre Foundation, Inc. (1961); Actor, "American Heritage" (1961); Actor, "Pretty Boy Floyd" (1960); Actor, "Murder, Inc." (1960); Actor, "North by Northwest" (1959); Actor, "Inherit the Wind" (1955-1957); Producer, Off-Broadway Productions (1953-1955); Director, Off-Broadway Productions (1953-1955); Actor, "What Every Woman Knows" (1954); Composer, "Rhapsody in E Flat for Piano and Strings" (1950); Author, "Seven Hops to Australia" (1945); Illustrator, "Seven Hops to Australia" (1945); Performer, Cruise Ship (1938); Pianist, Concerts (1937); Pianist, Recitals (1937); Represented Artist, The Metropolitan Museum of Art; Represented Artist, Library of Congress; Represented Artist, Private Collections; Contributor, Articles, Professional Journals; Contributor, Articles, Periodicals **Awards:** Federal Government Honor Award in Recognition of 55 Years of Dedicated Service (2010); Eponym, Austin Hay Film Festival (2010); Pictorial Award, The Smithsonian Institution (1982); Gold Medal, Accademia Italia (1980); St. Bartholomew's Silver Leadership Award (1966); Loyal Service Award, The Junior League of the City of New York (1953) **Membership:** American Federation of TV and Radio Artists (Now SAG-AFTRA); Screen Actors Guild (Now SAG-AFTRA); The American Artists Professional League; Allied Artists of America, Inc.; International Bach Society; The Rachmaninoff Network; Board of Directors, American Beethoven Society; Vice President, National Society of Arts and Letters; Music Library Association; National Symphony Orchestra Association (Now The Kennedy Center); Actors' Equity Association; National Trust for Historic Preservation; Sons of the American Revolution; National Parks Conservation Association; Shakespeare Oxford Society; The Saint Andrew's Society of the State of New York; Board of Directors, The Victorian Society; Cambria County Historical Society; American Philatelic Society; Museum of the Moving Image; The Jimmy Stewart Museum; Board of Directors, The English-Speaking Union; The National Arts Club; The Players; National Travel, Inc.; The Columbia University Club; The National Press Club; Arts Club of Washington; Cosmos Club; Classic Car Club of America; Sigma Chi Fraternity; Phi Mu Alpha Sinfonia Fraternity of America **Marquis Who's Who Honors:** Albert Nelson Marquis Lifetime Achievement Award (2017); Distinguished Humanitarian (2017) **Shipping Address:** 2022 Columbia Rd NW Apt 504, Washington, DC, 20009

A W. Hayes

Title: Adjunct Professor **Industry:** Education/Educational Services **Company Name:** University of South Florida College of Public Health **Date of Birth:** 08/21/1939 **Place of Birth:** Corning **State/Country of Origin:** AR **Parents:** Andrew Wallace Hayes; Helen (Latimer) Hayes **Spouse Name:** Sandra Smith Hayes (12/28/1963) **Children:** Andrew Wallace III; Helen Cathleen; Benjamin Bailey **Education:** PhD, Auburn University (1967); National Institutes of Health Postdoctoral Fellow, Research Associate, Division of Toxicology, Vanderbilt University School of Medical, Nashville, TN (1966-1968); MS, Auburn University (1964); AB, Emory University (1961) **Certifications:** Certified Medical Assistant, International Congress of Toxicology (1981-1984); Diplomate, American Board of Toxicology; Diplomate, American Board of Forensic Medicine; Diplomate, American Board of Forensic Professionals; Certified Nutrition Specialist; Eurotox Registered Toxicologist; Registered Toxicologist, European Union **Career:** Adjunct Professor, Michigan State University (2017-Present); Principal Consultant, Harvard School of Public Health (2005-2016); Principal Consultant, Sperix Corp. (2005-2015); Principal, Gradient Corp., Cambridge, MA (2002-2003); Vice President, Corporate Product Integrity, The Gillette Company, Boston, MA (1993-2002); Professor, Bowman Gray School of Medicine, Wake Forest University, Winston-Salem, NC (1992); Corporate Toxicologist, Vice President, Biochemistry and Biobehavioral Research, R.J. Reynolds Tobacco Company, Winston-Salem, NC (1987-1992); Corporate Toxicologist, Group Director, Biochemistry and Biobehavioral Research, R.J. Reynolds Tobacco Company, Winston-Salem, NC (1986-1987); Corporate Toxicologist, Director, Biochemistry and Biobehavioral Research, Bowman Gray Technology Center, R.J. Reynolds Tobacco Company, Winston-Salem, NC (1984-1986); Corporate Toxicologist, RJR Nabisco Inc., Winston-Salem, NC (1984); Director, Regulatory Affairs, Agricultural Chemistry (Worldwide), Rohm and Haas Company, Philadelphia, PA (1984); Director, Toxicology Research, Rohm and Haas Company, Spring House, PA (1980-1984); Program Director, NIEHS Training Program in Environmental Toxicology, University of Mississippi Medical Center, Jackson, MS (1977-1980) **Career Related:** Trustee, Food and Drug Administration Food Safety Committee (2014-Present); Board of Directors, Toxicology Education Foundation (1997-2001, 2005-Present); Secretary-general, IUTOX (2004-Present); Trustee, Scientists Center for Animal Welfare (2004-Present); Visiting Scientist, Harvard University School of Public Health, Boston, MA (2003-Present); Member, External Advisory Board, Louisiana Institute of Toxicology (1996-Present); Member, Nominating Committee, International Union of Toxicology (2013-2014); Member, Science Advisory Panel, EPA FIFRA (2004-2005); Board of Directors, Science Advisory Committee on Alternative Toxicology Methods, NIEHS (2002-2005); President, Toxicology Education Foundation (1998-2000); Member, Science Advisory Board, Institute of In-Vitro Sciences (1997-2002); Member, Commission on Strategic Development, IUTOX (1997); Member, Commission on Communications, International Union of Toxicology (1986-1989); Member, Program Committee, Toxicology Forum (1986-1987); Member, Selection Committee, Immunotoxicology Foundation (1986); Delegate, International Union of Toxicology (1984-1986); Member, Toxicology Advisory Board, Raven Press, New York City, NY (1982-1996); Member, Science Program Committee, International Congress of Toxicology (1982-1983); Alternate Delegate, International Union of Toxicology (1982-1983); Member, TDB/CIS User Assessment Panel, Life Sciences Research Office, FASEB, Bethesda, MD (1982); Member, Environmental Health Sciences Review Committee, NIEHS (1981-1985) **Civic:** Trustee, Scientists Center for Animal Welfare (2004-Present); Board of Directors, Florida College Academy (1998-Present); Board of Directors, IIVS, 2-15, Board of Trustees, Florida College Academy (2018) **Military Service:** Member, Science Expert Panel for Environmental Water Monitors, U.S. Army (2004-Present); Consultant, Walter Reed Army Institute of Research (1984-1986); Advisor, U.S. Army Medical Command (1982-1984) **Creative Works:** Member, Editorial Board, "Toxicology Research and Application" (2017-Present); Member, Editorial Board, "Food and Chemical Toxicology" (1987-Present); Associate Editor, "Regulatory Toxicology and Pharmacology" (1986-Present); Member, Editorial Board, Journal of Toxicology and Environmental Health (1979-Present) **Awards:** Fellow, American Association for the Advancement of Science (2014); Outstanding Leadership Award, International Dose-Response Society (2013); Distinguished Fellow, American College of Toxicology (2013); Ambassador Award, Mid-Atlantic Society of Toxicology (2006, 2012); Distinguished Scientist Award, American College of Toxicology (2012) **Membership:** Board Member, American Board of Toxicology (2008-Present); External Advisory Board, American Institute of Toxicology (1996-Present) **Hobbies:** Fishing **Religion:** Church of Christ **Shipping Address:** 318 Sleepy Hollow Ave, Temple Terrace, FL, 33617

Patricia Thornton Hayes

Title: Music Educator, Director **Industry:** Education/Educational Services **Company Name:** Campostella Elementary School **Date of Birth:** 07/16/1934 **Place of Birth:** Chesapeake **State/Country of Origin:** WV **Marital Status:** Married **Spouse Name:** Raymond S. Hayes, Jr. (11/28/1959) **Children:** Rhett S.; Amber Williams **Education:** MEd, Old Dominion University (1970); BA, West Virginia University Institute of Technology (1956) **Career:** Specialist of Music, Portsmouth Diagnostic Center (1993-2005); Director of Choral and Orchestra, Portsmouth City Schools, Virginia (1973-1996); Director of Music, Meadowbrook Elementary, Grades 1-7, Norfolk, VA (1972); Teacher of Music and Special Education, Mount Zion Elementary School, Suffolk, VA (1970-1971); Director of Music, Suburban Park Elementary School, Grades 1-8, Norfolk, VA (1958-1960); Director of Music, Shelton Park Elementary School, Grades 1-8, Virginia Beach, VA (1957-1958); Director of Music, Clendenin High School, Kanawha County Schools, Charleston, WV (1956-1957) **Career Related:** Fine Arts Commission, City of Chesapeake, VA (1981-1989); Judge, Doris Sahr Memorial Piano Competition, Chesapeake, VA; Director of Music Festivals, City of Portsmouth, VA; Director of School Theatre Productions; Organist for Churches, Weddings and Receptions; Music Education National Conference, National Association for Music Education; American String Teachers Association (ASTA); Tidewater Community Band **Civic:** Accompanist, Singing Beaz, Beazley Foundation, Inc., Portsmouth, VA (2007-Present); Historic St. Luke's Church (2006-Present); NEAT Summit, Portsmouth Police (1996-2001); Charleston Symphony Youth Orchestra (1957); All State College Chorus, Marshall University, Huntington, VA (1956); All State College Orchestra, West Virginia University Institute of Technology, Morgantown, VA (1956); Band, West Virginia University Institute of Technology (1952-1956); Glee Club, West Virginia University Institute of Technology (1952-1956); Senior Drama Director, West Virginia University Institute of Technology (1952-1956); The Charleston Light Opera Guild; Portsmouth Retired Teachers Association; Music Education National Conference, National Association for Music Education; Virginia Music Educators Association; Upper Kanawha Symphony Orchestra; Mayor's Breakfast, Portsmouth School System **Creative Works:** Choral Director, The Singing Beaz (2007-2011); Co-Composer, "We're Supporting You All The Way" (1991); Choral Director, Mayor's Breakfast; Choral Director, Seawall Festival; Orchestra Director, Manor High School Award Banquet; Choral Director, Programs, NAVSEA; Choral Director, Programs, U.S. Coast Guard; All-State Performer, Orchestra; All-State Performer, Chorus **Awards:** Outstanding Music Works Award, Portsmouth City School Board, Virginia (1992); Proclamation Award, Fine Arts Commission, Chesapeake, VA (1981-1989); Who's Who Amongst Students in American Universities and Colleges (1956); Order of the Eastern Star (1953); Grand Cross of Color, The International Order of the Rainbow for Girls (1951); Numerous Outstanding Music Works Awards, Portsmouth City School Board **Membership:** Virginia Music Education Association; Virginia Education Association; American String Teachers Association; Lifetime Member, Virginia PTSA; Virginia Retired Teachers Association; Alpha Psi Omega; Delta Sigma Lambda; Phi Mu Gamma; Alumni Association, West Virginia University Institute of Technology **Why did you become involved in your profession or industry:** Ms. Hayes started playing when she was a little girl between the ages of three and four, playing anything she wanted to and without sheet music. As she grew up, she wanted to continue with her music. She is thankful to have been able to share her music with children and adults. **What do you consider to be the highlight of your career:** Ms. Hayes most proud of the fact that her daughter and son are still alive, and that her granddaughters will be able to do what they want to with their lives. One is still in college working on a postgraduate degree, and the other recently graduated from a naval academy and is now located in Allen, TX. One of her granddaughters played violin all through high school, and the other one was in sports and went to nationals on her sporting abilities. They both excelled, and went on and worked hard to get where they are. She is very proud of all of her children and grandchildren. **Shipping Address:** 2841 Greenview Road, Chesapeake, VA, 23321

Winston Haythe

Title: Chief Counsel **Industry:** Law and Legal Services **Company Name:** National Enforcement Training Institute **Date of Birth:** 10/10/1940 **Place of Birth:** Reidsville **State:** NC **Parents:** McDonald Swann Haythe; Henrietta Elizabeth (East) Haythe **Marital Status:** Single **Spouse Name:** Glenann Leigh Rogers (8/17/1963, Divorced 1977) **Children:** Sheila Elaine; Rhonda Leigh; Kevin McDonald (Deceased) **Education:** Graduate Work, National Defense University (1984); Graduate Work, Command and General Staff School, Fort Leavenworth, KS (1982); LLM, The Judge Advocate General's Legal Center & School (1976); Postgraduate Work, University of Virginia (1968-1969); JD, College of William & Mary (1967); BS, Missouri State University (1963) **Career:** Chief Counsel, National Enforcement Training Institute (2005-2009); Senior Counsel, Office of Criminal Enforcement, Forensics and Training (2001-2005); Senior Legal Counsel, U.S. Environmental Protection Agency, Washington, DC (1996-2001); Assistant Director, U.S. Environmental Protection Agency, Washington, DC (1994-1996); Senior Attorney, National Enforcement Training Institute, U.S. Environmental Protection Agency, Washington, DC (1991-1994); Senior Attorney for Enforcement Policy, U.S. Environmental Protection Agency, Washington, DC (1985-1991); Staff Director, Legal Office, U.S. Environmental Protection Agency, Washington, DC (1982-1983); Assistant General Counsel, Senior Attorney, Consumer Produce Safety Commission, Washington, DC (1973-1982); Senior Trial Attorney, Atomic Energy Commission, Washington, DC (1972-1973); Associate, Rhyne & Rhyne, Washington, DC (1969-1972) **Career Related:** Advisory Board Member, George Washington Institute for Spirituality and Health (GWISH) (2015-Present); Board of Directors, Foundation of the Federal Bar Association (2011-Present); Adjunct Professor of Law, The George Washington University Law School (2002-Present); Consultant, Barrister Enterprises, Washington, DC (1978-Present); Federal Dispute Resolution Conference Advisory Board (2004-2009); Council Member, Foundation of the Federal Bar Association (2003-2012); Strayer University, Business Administrative Program Advisory Council (2003-2005); National Advocacy Center, U.S. Department of Justice, Columbia, SC (1999-2009); Guest Lecturer, The George Washington University Law School (1999-2002); Elected Member, Undergraduate Programs Advisory Council, University of Maryland (1993-1995); Legislative Fellow, United States Senate, Washington, DC (1983-1985); Advisory Council, Paralegal Studies, University of Maryland (1980-1995); Law Faculty, The Judge Advocate General's Legal Center & School, Charlottesville, VA (1969-1994) **Civic:** Clerk of Session, Georgetown Presbyterian Church (2003-2007); Elder, Member of Session, Georgetown Presbyterian Church (2000-2003); President of Trustees, Georgetown Presbyterian Church (1997-1998); Vice President of Trustees, Georgetown Presbyterian Church (1996); Trustee, Georgetown Presbyterian Church (1995-1998) **Military Service:** Colonel, Judge Advocate General's Corps, U.S. Army Reserve (1963-1994) **Awards:** Legion of Merit Award, U.S. Army (1994) **Membership:** Board of Directors Member, Foundation of the Federal Bar Association (2015-Present); Community Advisory Board Member, WETA (2000-Present); National Council, Federal Bar Association (1998-2012); Board of Directors, William & Mary Law School Association (1988-1995); Federal Career Services Division, Federal Bar Association (1974-1990); Lifetime Fellow, Foundation of the Federal Bar Association; WETA Leadership Circle; Advisory Board Member, George Washington Institute for Spirituality and Health (2015-Present); The Phillips Collection; Victorian Society, Washington, DC; St. Andrews Society, Washington, DC; Kappa Mu Epsilon; Cosmos Club; English Speaking Union; Knights Templar; The Social List of Washington **Bar Admissions:** District of Columbia (1969); State of Virginia (1967) **Marquis Who's Who Honors:** Distinguished Humanitarian (2017) **Hobbies:** Playing organ and piano; Theater; Concerts; Reading **Religion:** Presbyterian **Shipping Address:** 2141 P Street NW, Apt. 402, Washington, DC, 20037

Linda Ann Hazelip

Industry: Other **Date of Birth:** 10/20/1952 **Place of Birth:** El Campo **State:** TX **Parents:** Al Gareth Braswell; Annabelle (Black) Braswell **Marital Status:** Divorced **Spouse Name:** Richard Chris Hazelip (7/28/1972, Divorced 8/30/1984) **Education:** Diploma in Computer Programming and Data Processing, Massey Business College (1972) **Certifications:** Certified, Teacher Progressive Series, Intermediate-Level Piano, St. Louis Conservatory of Music (1971) **Career:** Teacher, Voice, Organ, and Piano (2000-Present); Business Owner, Organist/Choirmaster, Pianist, and Vocalist, Sacred Occasions, Select Secular Special Occasions, Metropolitan Area, Houston and Southeast Texas (1986-Present); Senior Administrative Assistant, M.D. Anderson Cancer Center (2016-2018); Secretary, Administrator, Management Assistant, Halliburton Energy Services, Houston, TX (1991-1996); Executive Secretary, InterFirst Bank Post Oak, Houston, TX (1986); Director, Executive Secretary, Exponet Trading Co., Houston, TX (1983-1986); Secretary, St. Andrew's United Methodist Church, Houston, TX (1975-1979); Bookkeeper, Millar Instruments, Houston, TX (1973-1974); Teacher, Basic Music and Piano (1971-1979) **Career Related:** Choir Director, Covenant United Methodist Church, Houston, TX (1985-1986); Choir Director, Vocalist, Reid Memorial United Methodist Church, Houston, TX (1985); Organist, Choir Director, Vocalist, Parker Memorial United Methodist Church, Houston, TX (1984-1985); Organist, Vocalist, St. Stephen's United Methodist Church, Houston, TX (1983-1985); Organist, Vocalist, Music Director, St. John's United Methodist Church, Baytown, TX (1980-1984); Organist, Vocalist, Children's Music Director, Old River Terrace United Methodist Church, Channelview, TX (1978-1980); Organist, Vocalist, Pianist, Children's Music Director, Faith United Methodist Church, South Houston, TX (1972-1977) **Civic:** First United Methodist Church, Houston, TX (1986-Present); Vocalist, Pianist, Open Door Mission, Houston, TX (1997-2014) **Awards:** Albert Nelson Marquis Lifetime Achievement Award (2017) **Membership:** National Mathematics Honor Society; National Honor Society; American Guild of Organists; American Business Women's Association; Choristers Guild; National Association of Female Executives **To what do you attribute your success:** Ms. Hazelip attributes her success to her Lord and savior, as well as to her many wonderful mentors and supportive friends. **Why did you become involved in your profession or industry:** Ms. Hazelip became involved in her profession because she enjoys providing administrative support to executives and upper level management in the business world. She also had a desire to use the musical talents God gave her. **What do you consider to be the highlight of your career:** In business, the highlight of Ms. Hazelip's career was writing 150 programs in dBase, totally automating the administrative work of a manufacturing facility and tripling the revenue. In music, the highlight of her career was serving and sharing her musical gifts with close to 300 churches, cross-pollinating liturgy, and music style amid denominations. **Where will you be in five years:** In five years, Ms. Hazelip will be wherever God chooses to use her as his instrument. **Hobbies:** Holy Land study tours **Political Affiliations:** Republican **Religion:** Methodist

Todd Christopher Xavier Headrick, PhD

Title: Professor of Quantitative Methods **Industry:** Education/Educational Services **Company Name:** Southern Illinois University **Date of Birth:** 02/04/1960 **Place of Birth:** Ann Arbor **State/Country of Origin:** MI **Parents:** Robert Frank Headrick; Sally Marie Wheeler **Education:** PhD, Wayne State University (1997); MA, Eastern Michigan University (1986); BS, Eastern Michigan University (1984) **Career:** Provost Faculty Fellow, SIUC Psychometric Team, Chair of AERA SIG/Educational Statisticians, Professor, Southern Illinois University, Carbondale, IL (2015-Present); Associate Dean of Research and Statistical Analysis, Chair of the Department of Counseling, Quantitative Methods, and Special Education, Professor, Southern Illinois University, Carbondale, IL (2012-2015); Professor, Coordinator, Southern Illinois University, Carbondale, IL (2011-2012); Associate Professor, Coordinator, Southern Illinois University, Carbondale, IL (2007-2011); Associate Professor, Coordinator, Southern Illinois University, Carbondale, IL (2004); Assistant Professor, Southern Illinois University, Carbondale, IL (1999-2004) **Creative Works:** Author, "Statistical Simulation: Power Method Polynomials and Other Transformations," Chatham Hall (2011); Contributor, Articles, Professional Journals; Author, Books **Awards:** Outstanding Scholar, Southern Illinois University, Carbondale, IL (2008) **Membership:** Program Chair, Educational Statisticians SIG, American Educational Research Association; The Psychometric Society; Mathematical Association of America; American Statistical Association; International Association for Statistical Computing; Institute of Mathematical Statistics **Hobbies:** Travel; Outdoor activities **Political Affiliations:** Conservative **Religion:** Roman Catholic **Shipping Address:** 625 Wham Drive, Office 222J, Carbondale, IL, 62901 **Website:** https://ehs.siu.edu/cqmse/_common/documents/vita/toddheadrick-cv.pdf

Douglas Geoffrey Hearle

Title: Public Relations Executive, Author, Lecturer **Industry:** Corporate Communications & Public Relations **Company Name:** Douglas G. Hearle & Co. **Date of Birth:** 04/07/1933 **Place of Birth:** New York **State/Country of Origin:** NY **Year of Passing:** 2018-09-07 **Parents:** Douglas G. Hearle; Regina Irene (Booth) Hearle **Marital Status:** Married **Spouse Name:** Mary Elizabeth Hogan (7/13/1957) **Children:** Douglas; Christopher; Matthew **Education:** MBA, Iona College (1971); BA, Iona College (1954) **Career:** Retired (1993); President, CEO, Carl Byoir and Associates (1990-1992); Vice Chairman, Hill and Knowlton Inc (Now Hill + Knowlton Strategies) (1989-1990); Founding President, Douglas G. Hearle & Associates, Inc. (1986-1989); Executive Vice President, Hill and Knowlton Inc (1980-1986); Senior Vice President, Hill+Knowlton Strategies (1973-1980); Vice President, Hill and Knowlton Inc (1970-1973); Account Executive, Hill and Knowlton Inc (1966-1970); Public Relations Manager, The Borden Company (Now Borden, Inc.) (1963-1966); Reporter-Editor, New York Journal-American (1954-1963); Board of Directors, Hill+Knowlton Strategies **Career Related:** Adjunct Professor, Fordham University (1998-1999); Adjunct Professor, The College of New Rochelle (1996-2008); Board of Directors, The Roper Center for Public Opinion Research, University of Connecticut (Now at Cornell University) (1990-2003); Association of Southeast Asian Nations, Jakarta, Indonesia (1988); Distinguished Lecturer, The University of Texas System (1984); Adjunct Professor, Iona College (1982-1984); Distinguished Lecturer, Ball State University (1981); President, John W. Hill Foundation (1980-1986); Author; Lecturer **Civic:** Board of Education, Pelham Public Schools (2009-2012); President, The Danny Fund (2003-2005); Vice Chairman, Board of Trustees, The College of New Rochelle (1989-1995); Board of Education, Pelham Public Schools (1972-1978); Executive Council, Westchester, Boy Scouts of America (1967-1969); Vice President, New York Newspaper Reporters Association (Now New York Press Association) (1961-1963) **Military Service:** Destroyer Force, United States Atlantic Fleet, U.S. Navy (1957-1959) **Creative Works:** Author, Historical Novel, "Outsource" **Awards:** All Star Award, Inside Public Relations Magazine, In Public Relations Media Group, Inc. (1992); Five Most Respected Award, Public Relations Week (1988); Distinguished Service Award, ASEAN Public Relations Congress (1981); Citizen of the Year Award, Pelham Men's Club (1978) **Membership:** Society of the Silurians; New York Newspaper Reporters Association (Now New York Press Association); Asia Society **Marquis Who's Who Honors:** Albert Nelson Marquis Lifetime Achievement Award (2017) **Why did you become involved in your profession or industry:** At first, Mr. Hearle wanted to become a teacher but that didn't work out. He took the police test because he came from a family of police officers. He took a job while he waited to hear about his police appointment, and ended up staying in journalism. **What do you consider to be the highlight of your career:** Mr. Hearle is most proud to have the opportunity to stay involved with many important people over the years, including presidents and world leaders. **Political Affiliations:** Republican **Religion:** Roman Catholic **Shipping Address:** 20 Maple Avenue, Pelham, NY, 10803

Larry Dean Hefti

Title: Materials and Processes Engineer, Educator **Industry:** Engineering **Company Name:** Boeing **Date of Birth:** 12/01/1959 **Place of Birth:** St. Louis **State/Country of Origin:** MO **Parents:** Norman Bruce Hefti; Patricia Ann Hefti **Marital Status:** Married **Spouse Name:** Diana Lynn Glennie (5/22/1982) **Children:** Michael Lawrence; Christopher Ryan **Education:** BSME, University of Missouri, Columbia, MO (1981) **Career:** Technology Fellow, Metallic Fabrication Forming Processes, Research & Technology (2010-Present); Technology Fellow, Superplastic Forming and Diffusion Bonding, Material & Process Technology (2007-2009); Associate Technology Fellow, Material & Process Technology, Auburn, WA (1999-2006); Engineering Scientist, Manufacturing Research and Development, Boeing, Auburn, WA (1995-1999); Engineering Scientist, Manufacturing Research and Development, Boeing, Kent, WA (1992-1995); Senior Engineer, Material and Process Development, St. Louis, MO (1985-1992); Engineer, Fatigue Test Laboratory, McDonnell Douglas, St. Louis, MO (1982-1985) **Creative Works:** Contributor, Articles, Professional Journals **Membership:** TMS; ASM International **To what do you attribute your success:** Mr. Hefti attributes his success to working hard in his field and working in the same manufacturing technology for most of his career. This has allowed him to work on numerous different projects that allowed him to gain a lot of experience. **Why did you become involved in your profession or industry:** He became involved in his profession because working on airplanes was fascinating so, he went into Engineering and then went to work for McDonnell Douglas. **What do you consider to be the highlight of your career:** A highlight of his career is developing processes that have been patented and used to manufacture products for aerospace. **Where will you be in five years:** In five years, he will probably be retired. **Business Address:** P.O. Box 3707, MC 5K-63, Seattle, WA, 98092 **Shipping Address:** 32323 107th Ave SE, Auburn, WA, 98092

Richard D. Heideman

Industry: Law and Legal Services **Company Name:** Heideman Nudelman & Kalik, PC **Date of Birth:** 04/04/1947 **Place of Birth:** Detroit **State:** MI **Parents:** Theodore Samuel Heideman; Marion (Yura) Heideman **Marital Status:** Married **Spouse Name:** Phyllis Greenberg Heideman **Children:** Stefanie Jo; Elana Yael; Ariana Michal **Education:** Graduate Coursework, National College of Criminal Defense Lawyers and Public Defenders (1974); JD, George Washington University (1972); Student, American University/Hebrew University, Jerusalem (1970-1972); BA, University of Michigan (1969) **Career:** Senior Counsel, Heideman Nudelman & Kalik, PC, Washington (1973) **Career Related:** Markham's Negligence Counsel (1989); Vice-Chairman, Legislative Committee, National Association of Criminal Defense Lawyers; Chair, Institute for Law and Policy, Hebre University Faculty of Law, Israel Forever Foundation; Lecturer in Field **Civic:** Delegate, NGO, UN World Conference Against Racism, Durban, South Africa (2001); Delegate-Prime Minister, Israel Solidarity Conference (1989); Non Governmental Organization Delegate, US Conference on Women, Nairobi, Kenya (1985); International President, B'nai B'rith Youth Organization (1964-1965); Former Chairman, Board of Directors, American Indoor Soccer Association; Former Mayor, Spring Valley, KY; Former General, Co-Chairman, State of Israel Bonds, Louisville; Former Member, Juvenile Delinquency Task Force, Kentucky Crime Commission; Former Member, Board of Directors, Health Care for America, Inc., Northern Virginia Family Services, Inc.; Former Chair, Herzliya Conference, International Advisory Board, US Holocaust Memorial; Museum Lawyers Committee, DCChairman Hebrew Faculty of Law Institute for Law and Policy, Jerusalem **Creative Works:** Author, "The Hague Odyssey: Israel's Struggle for Security on the Front Lines of Terrorism and Her Battle for Justice at the United Nations" (2013) **Awards:** Public Justice Trial Lawyer of the Year (2016); George Washington University Distinguished Alumni Achievement Award (2015); Joseph Papp Racial Harmony Award, Foundation for Ethic Understanding (2005); Merito de Mayo Decoration, President Duhalde of Argentina (2002); Sam Beber Distinguished Alumnus Award, B'nai B'rith Youth Organization (1999); Label A. Katz Young Leadership Award (1983); Heritage Award, State of Israel Bonds (1988); Designated People to Watch, Louisville Magazine (1986) **Membership:** President, B'nai Brith International (1998-Present); Executive Committee, Anti-Defamation League, (1998-2002); International Chairman, Center for Public Policy (1996-1998); Delegate, 50th World Jewish Congress (1986); International Family Award (1981); American Trial Lawyers Association; American Institute of Parliamentarians; Former Vice President, Main Street Association; Former President, University of Michigan Club; Former Resident Faculty Member, National College of Criminal Defense Lawyers; Former Chairman, Criminal Defense Committee, American Society of Criminology; Former Member, Board of Directors, International Association of Jewish Lawyers and Jurists; Former President, American-Israel Chamber of Commerce Inc. **Bar Admissions:** Fourth Circuit, US Court of Appeals (1993); US Court of Claims (1992); US Court of International Trade (1990); US District Court of Maryland (1989); US District Court of DC (1989); DC Circuit, US Court of Appeals (1984); US Supreme Court (1983); US District Court, Wyoming (1981); Eastern District, US District Court of Kentucky (1982); Southern District, US District Court of Indiana (1982); US Court of Military Appeals (1982); Wyoming Bar Association (1979); Indiana Bar Association (1979); Sixth Circuit, US Court of Appeals (1974); Maryland Bar Association (1972); Kentucky Bar Association (1972); Western District, US District Court of Kentucky (1972) **Shipping Address:** 1146 19th Street, NW, Fifth Floor, Washington, DC, 20036

Marvin Stewart Heiman

Industry: Financial Services **Company Name:** Sussex Financial Group, Inc. **Date of Birth:** 09/16/1945 **Place of Birth:** Chicago, September 16, 1945 **State/Country of Origin:** IL **Parents:** Samuel J. Heiman; Mildred (Miller) Heiman **Marital Status:** Married **Spouse Name:** Adrienne Joy Nathan (8/7/1966) **Children:** Scott; Michelle; Adam **Education:** Coursework, Roosevelt University (1963-1967) **Certifications:** Certified Personal Manager of Grammy Nominee Curtis Mayfield National Academy of Recording Arts & Sciences (1997) **Career:** Managing Member, "DASH" Minor League Baseball Team, Winston-Salem, NC (2015-Present); Partner, Spago Restaurant, Chicago, IL (1997-Present); President, Chairman of Board, Sussex Financial Group, Inc., Deerfield, IL (1986-Present); Investment Manager, Dash Baseball Team (2014); Managing Member, Partner, Spago Restaurant, Chicago, IL (1997-2003); Partner, Professional Real Estate Securities Company, Lincolnwood, IL (1982-1986); President, Gold Coast Entertainment, Chicago, IL (1980-1982); President, Curtom Record Company, Chicago, IL (1969-1980) **Career Related:** Bank Examining Committee, Cole Taylor Banks, Chicago, IL (1986-Present); Partner, Cole Taylor Banks, Chicago, IL (1984-Present); Partner, Chicago White Sox, American League Baseball Club (1981-Present); Sun Life of Canada (1993); Gore/Bronson Bancorp (1988-2005); Board of Directors, Skokie Bank, Drovers Bank, Metropolitan Health Care, Chicago, IL **Civic:** Member, Republican National Committee (1980-Present); Member, Simon Wiesenthal Center (1988) **Awards:** Recipient, World Series Champion Ring, Chicago White Society (2005); Recipient, National Quality Award, National Association of Life Underwriters (1992); Recipient, Humanitarian Award, American Jewish Committee (1978); Recipient, Men of Achievement Award, Cambridge, England **Membership:** American Funds Comittee, President's Club (1992); International Association of Financial Planners; Chicago Association of Life Underwriters; Real Estate Securities Syndication Association of America; Registered Republican, National Association Securities Dealers; American Jewish Committee; International Platform Association; Million Dollar Round Table **Hobbies:** Baseball; Tennis; Music **Shipping Address:** 1048 Saxony Dr, Highland Park, IL, 60035-4049

Charmaine Marie Heimes

Title: Elementary School Educator, Poet, Writer **Industry:** Education/Educational Services **Company Name:** Joaquin Cigarroa Middle School **Date of Birth:** 06/28/1960 **Place of Birth:** Detroit **State/Country of Origin:** MI **Parents:** Charles M. Heimes; Mary Patricia (Allen) Heimes **Education:** BA, Olivet College, Olivet, MI (1982) **Certifications:** Certified USA Track & Field Official (2005); National Certification, Abstinence Educator; Certified Teacher, State of Texas **Career:** Head, Physical Education Department, Joaquin Cigarroa Middle School, Laredo, TX (1988-Present); Teacher, Physical Education, Joaquin Cigarroa Middle School, Laredo, TX (1984-Present); Coach, Joaquin Cigarroa Middle School, Laredo, TX (1984-Present); Coach, Junior Varsity Softball, Charlotte High School (1984); Coach, Junior Varsity Volleyball, Charlotte High School (1983-1984); Substitute Teacher, Charlotte Public Schools (1982-1984) **Career Related:** Volleyball Official, Texas Association of Sports Officials (2009-Present); Texas Bess Mentor, Texas A&M International University (2004-Present); Quest Mentor, Texas A&M International University (2000-Present); Abstinence Master Teacher, Texas A&M International University (1999-2014); Assistant Field Hockey Coach, Olivet College, Olivet, MI (1982-1983) **Awards:** Nominee, Golden Apple, Joaquin Cigarroa Middle School (2007); Dean's Extra Miler Award, Texas A&M International University (2007) **Marquis Who's Who Honors:** Albert Nelson Marquis Lifetime Achievement Award (2017) **What do you consider to be the highlight of your career:** The most rewarding aspect of Ms. Heimes' entire career has been seeing her students and athletes grow. **Hobbies:** Numismatics; Plates; Poetry: Writing; Elvis memorabilia **Shipping Address:** 119 Washingtonia Drive, Laredo, TX, 78045

Stanley Dean Heisler

Title: Lawyer **Industry:** Law and Legal Services **Company Name:** Stanley D. Heisler, PC **Date of Birth:** 01/11/1946 **Place of Birth:** The Dalles **State/Country of Origin:** OR **Parents:** Donald Eugene Heisler; Roberta (Van Valkenburgh) Heisler **Education:** JD, Willamette University (1972); BA, Willamette University (1968) **Career:** Private Practice, Stanley D. Heisler, P.C., New York, NY (2001-Present); Managing Partner, Shays, Heisler & Rosenthal, LLP, New York, NY (2000-2001); Managing Partner, Shays, Rothman, & Heisler, LLP, New York, NY (1999-2000); Managing Partner, Shays & Kemper, LLP, New York, NY (1994-1998); Senior Associate, Squadron, Ellenoff, Plesent, Sheinfeld & Sorkin, New York, NY (1991-1994); Senior Associate, Phillips, Nizer, Benjamin, Krim & Ballon, New York, NY (1988-1991); Associate, Cohen & Shalleck, New York, NY (1985-1988); Partner, Heisler & Heisler, The Dalles, OR (1982-1984); Partner, Heisler, Van Valkenburgh & Coats, The Dalles, OR (1975-1981); Associate, Heisler & Van Valkenburgh, The Dalles, OR (1973-1974) **Civic:** Officer, The Most Venerable Order of the Hospital of Saint John of Jerusalem (2009); Vice Chairman, President's Air Quality Advisory Board, Washington, DC (1973-1976); Speechwriter, Legislative Assistant, United States Senator Bob Packwood, Washington, DC (1969-1973); Speechwriter, Governor Tom McCall, Salem, MA (1966-1968); Speechwriter, Secretary of State Tom McCall, Salem, MA (1965) **Awards:** Honoree, the Most Venerable Order of the Hospital of Saint John of Jerusalem, Her Majesty Queen Elizabeth II (2009); Honoree, the Most Venerable Order of the Hospital of Saint John of Jerusalem, Her Majesty Queen Elizabeth II (2005); Honoree, Knight of the Order of Saints Maurice and Lazarus, His Royal Highness Victor Emanuel, The Prince of Naples and Duke of Savoy **Membership:** Sons of the Revolution in the State of New York (2009-Present); Deputy Governor, General Society of Mayflower Descendants (2010-2014); Board of Directors, New England Society in the City of New York (2009-2011); Sons of the American Revolution (2009-2010); ABA (2009-2010); Director, Sons of the Revolution in the State of New York (2009-2010); Captain, Mayflower Descendants in the State of New York (2005-2010); Council Member, Society of Colonial Wars (2003-2006); Board of Directors, Mayflower Descendants in the State of New York (2001-2014); Edmund Rice (1638) Association, Inc.; Association of the Bar of the City of New York; New York State Bar Association; The Holland Society of New York; The Pilgrims of the United States; The Saint Andrew's Society of the State of New York; Society of the Descendants of Washington's Army of Valley Forge; Hellenic Society; St. George's Society of New York; Colonial Society of Pennsylvania (Now Historical Society of Pennsylvania); The Saint Nicholas Society of the City of New York; The Vancouver Club; The Yale Club of New York City; The Nassau Club of Princeton; The University Club of New York; University Club of Portland; Arlington Club **Bar Admissions:** Supreme Court of the United States (1985); New York (1985); United States Court of Appeals for the Armed Forces (1973); United States Court of Appeals for the Federal Circuit (1973); Washington, DC (1973); United States Courts for the Ninth Circuit (1972); United States Tax Court (1972); United States Court of Federal Claims (1972); Oregon (1972) **Marquis Who's Who Honors:** Albert Nelson Marquis Lifetime Achievement Award (2017) **Political Affiliations:** Republican **Religion:** Episcopalian **Business Address:** 330 Madison Ave 9th Fl, New York, NY, 10017 **Shipping Address:** 266 Ridgebury Rd, Ridgefield, CT, 06877

Stanley Heller

Title: Lawyer **Industry:** Law and Legal Services **Company Name:** Cirignani, Heller and Harman LLP **Date of Birth:** 05/10/1941 **Place of Birth:** Philadelphia **State/Country of Origin:** PA **Parents:** Albert Curtis Heller; Blanche (Solton) Heller **Marital Status:** Married **Spouse Name:** Brenda Anita West (12/29/1990); Martha Wright (Divorced, 1975) **Children:** Stephanie Gail; Michael Lawrence; Deborah Arlene **Education:** JD, Northwestern University (1988); MD, Johns Hopkins University (1965); BA, Johns Hopkins University (1962) **Certifications:** Diplomate, American Board of Cardiovascular Diseases, American Board of Internal Medicine **Career:** Partner, Cirignani, Heller & Harman, LLP (1988-Present); Clinical Associate Professor, Feinberg School of Medicine, Northwestern University (1980-1995); Associate Professor, Stritch School of Medicine, Loyola University Chicago (1971-1979); Assistant Professor, Rush University (1970-1971); Instructor, University of Illinois College of Medicine (1968-1970); Resident Physician in Medicine, Rush-Presbyterian St. Lukes Hospital (Now Rush University Medical Center) (1965-1968) **Career Related:** Attending Physician, Augustana Hospital (1973-1986); Attending Physician, Grant Hospital (1972-1985); Attending Physician, St. Joseph Hospital (Now Presence Health) (1971-1985); Consultant Physician, Columbus Hospital (1980-1984); President, Northside Cardiology (1973-1984); Director, Cardiac Diagnostic Laboratory (1971-1984) **Membership:** Fellow, American College of Legal Medicine (2002-Present); Cardiology Fellow, U.S. Public Health Service (1968-1970); Member Emeritus, American College of Physicians; Member Emeritus, Council of Clinical Cardiology, American Heart Association, Inc.; American College Cardiology Foundation; ABA; The Chicago Bar Association **Bar Admissions:** Illinois State Bar Association (1988) **Hobbies:** Hiking; Reading **Shipping Address:** 150 S. Wacker Drive, Suite 2600, Cirignani Heller & Harman, LLP, Chicago, IL, 60606

Richard Hellman

Title: President, Managing Partner, Endocrinologist **Industry:** Medicine & Health Care **Company Name:** Hellman and Rosen Endocrine Associates **Date of Birth:** 01/19/1943 **Place of Birth:** New York City **State:** NY **Parents:** Gabriel Michael Hellman; Rose Hellman **Marital Status:** Married **Spouse Name:** Julie Lynn Hellman (8/17/1997) **Children:** Leslie Gayle **Education:** Fellow in Endocrinology and Metabolism, University of Kansas (1972-1973); Resident in Internal Medicine, University of Kansas (1971-1972, 1967-1968); Intern in Straight Medicine, University of Kansas (1966-1967); MD, Chicago Medical School, Rosalind Franklin University of Medicine and Science (1966); BA in Mathematics, New York University (1962) **Certifications:** Diplomate, Endocrinology, Diabetes, & Metabolism Board, American Board of Internal Medicine; Diplomate, National Board of Medical Examiners; Diplomate, American Board of Internal Medicine **Career:** Associate Program Director of Endocrinology Practice, University of Missouri-Kansas City (1998-Present); Clinical Professor of Medicine, School of Medicine, University of Missouri-Kansas City (1998-Present); Physician, Private Practice, North Kansas City, MO (1981-Present); Clinical Associate Professor of Medicine, School of Medicine, University of Missouri-Kansas City (1981-1995); Associate Professor of Medicine, School of Medicine, University of Missouri-Kansas City (1975-1981) **Career Related:** Associate Director, Fellowship Program of Endocrinology and Metabolism, School of Medicine, University of Missouri-Kansas City (2016-Present); Member, Executive Committee, Physicians Consortium for Performance Improvement (2005-Present); Co-Chairman on Work Group Implementation, Physicians Consortium for Performance Improvement (2002-Present); Co-Chairman on Work Group Depression, Physicians Consortium for Performance Improvement (2001-Present); Member, Physicians Consortium for Performance Improvement (2000-Present); Founder, Medical Director, Heart of America Diabetes Research Foundation, North Kansas City, MO (1991-Present); Member, Board of Trustees, Endocrinology, Diabetes, & Metabolism Board, American Board of Internal Medicine (2008-2009); Member, Executive Committee, Physicians Consortium for Performance Improvement Foundation (2005); Medical Director, Diabetes Treatment Center, Trinity Lutheran Hospital, Kansas City, MO (1986-1994); Chairman, Advisory Board, Missouri Diabetes Control Program, Centers for Disease Control and Prevention (1981-1986); Medical Director, Midwest Diabetes Care Center, Kansas City, MO (1981-1986); Consultant in Field **Civic:** Member, Community Advisory Committee, Health Care Foundation of Greater Kansas City (2005-Present); Chair, Patient Safety Committee, Health Commission, Kansas City, MO (2005-Present); Member, Technology Advisory Panels, The National Quality Forum (2005-Present); Member, Mayor's Health Commission, City of Kansas City, Missouri (2001-Present); Member, Minority Health Committee, Kansas City, MO (2001-Present); Member, Improvement Committee, Kansas City, MO (2001-Present); Member, Missouri Foundation for Health (1999-Present); Active Member, Missouri Institute of Quality Health Care, Missouri Patient Care Review Foundation (1999-Present); Active Member, Center for Health Care Quality, University of Missouri **Military Service:** U.S. Air Force **Creative Works:** Editorial Board Member, "Diabetes Care" (2015-Present); Contributor, Articles, Professional Journals **Awards:** Lifetime Achievement Award, Kansas City Medical Society (2017); Honoree, Outstanding Clinical Endocrinologist Award, American Association of Clinical Endocrinologists (2016); Inaugural Innovation Award, Kansas City Medical Society (2015); Honoree, Distinguished Reviewer for Diabetes Care (2014-2016); Honoree, Recognition for Appreciation for Teaching, Inaugural Class, School of Medicine, University of Missouri-Kansas City (2011); Distinguished Alumnus Award, Chicago Medical School, Rosalind Franklin University of Medicine and Science (2008-2009); Honoree, Recognition for Leadership and Contributions, Physicians Consortium for Performance Improvement (2006); Meritorious Service Award, Metropolitan Medical Society of Greater Kansas City (2002) **Membership:** Chair, Patient and Safety Committee, American Association of Clinical Endocrinologists (2005-Present); Chairman, Task Force on Patient Safety, American Association of Clinical Endocrinologists (2003-Present); Board Director, American Association of Clinical Endocrinologists (1999-Present); Intimidate Past President, American Association of Clinical Endocrinologists (2008-2009); President, American Association of Clinical Endocrinologists (2007-2008) **Marquis Who's Who Honors:** Albert Nelson Marquis Lifetime Achievement Award (2017) **Hobbies:** Music; Theater; University of Kansas basketball team **Business Address:** 2790 Clay Edwards Dr Ste 1250, North Kansas City, MO, 64116 **Shipping Address:** 4900 W 112th Ter, Leawood, KS, 66211

Ronald G. Helms, PhD

Title: Director of Global Studies **Industry:** Education/Educational Services **Company Name:** Wright State University **Place of Birth:** Grafton **State:** WV **Parents:** Stanley Eugene Helms; Rosemary (Cockrell) Helms **Marital Status:** Married **Spouse Name:** Sharon Ann Verdigone (6/4/1966) **Children:** Scott Michael **Education:** PhD in Global and Cultural Studies, Ohio State University (1972); MA in Political Science and Government, University of Dayton (1968); EdB, Fairmont State College (Now Fairmont State University) (1966) **Certifications:** Certified in Gifted Education (K-12); Certified Secondary Principal; Certified Secondary Supervisor **Career:** Professor Emeritus, Wright State University, Dayton, OH (2016-Present); Professor, Wright State University, Dayton, OH (1995-2016); Adjunct Associate Professor, Wright State University, Dayton, OH (1972-1995); Adjunct Professor, University of Dayton, Dayton, OH (1972-1990) **Career Related:** Chair, Ohio Problem Solving Conference (1993); Academy Coach, International Gifted Conference, National and State Gifted Champions, Future Problem Solving Program (1988-1995); Five Season Sport Club; Marriott Vacation Clubs; Delta Elite Medallion Status, Delta Airlines; Marriott Platinum Elite Status, Marriott International, Inc.; National Council for the Social Studies, Board of Directors, Executive Committee; National Auditor, National and Regional Conference Planning, Social Education; Executive Committee, Board of Directors, Research Publications; National Council for Accreditation of Teacher Education; Board of Examiners, National Auditor, National Teaching American History Grant Program; Project Director and Consultant, National Teaching American History Grant Program; Kappa Delta Pi **Creative Works:** Author, "Current Issues: Global and Cultural Studies," Franklin Publishing, Arlington, TX (2016); Author, "Global and Cultural Studies," Franklin Publishing, Arlington, TX (2016); Author, "Social Studies for the Secondary School," XanEDU, Ann Arbor, MI (2012); Author, "Social Studies: Current Trends," XanEDU, Ann Arbor, MI (2012); Author, "Social Studies for the Middle School," XanEDU, Ann Arbor, MI (2012); Author, "Social Studies for the Elementary Teacher," XanEDU, Ann Arbor, MI (2011); Co-author, "Using Children's Literature to Teach the Ohio Social Studies Academic Content Standards," Ohio Council for the Social Studies, Columbus, OH (2011); Co-author, "History Success Kit," Curriculum Resource Materials, Computer Game and Website, ThinkTV, Dayton, OH (2006); Author, "Social Studies for the Early Childhood Educator," Anthology Pro., North Chelmsford, MA (2003); Author, "Social Studies for the Secondary School," Anthology Pro., North Chelmsford, MA (2002); Author, "Social Studies: Current Trends," Anthology Pro., North Chelmsford, MA (2002); Author, "Social Studies for the Middle School," Anthology Pro., North Chelmsford, MA (2002); Author, "Social Studies for the Elementary Teacher," Anthology Pro., North Chelmsford, MA (2002); Co-author, "On the Net: Multicultural Education," Allyn & Bacon, Needham Heights, MA (2002); Author, "Social Studies Ambassadors to People's Republic of China," People to People Ambassador Programs (2001); Co-author, "Quick Guide to the Internet for Multicultural Education," Allyn & Bacon, Needham Heights, MA (2000); Co-author, "The National Board Certified Teacher," Phi Delta Kappa International, Bloomington, IN (2000); Author, "Gifted and Talented Education: Curriculum, Methods, and Materials," Wright State University, Dayton, OH (1997); Author/Co-author, 17 Books; Contributor, Over 200 Educational Articles, Professional Journals **Awards:** Excellence in Research, Franklin Publishing Company (2014); President's Circle of Achievement, Fairmont Sate University (2011); Excellence in Scholarship Award, College of Education and Human Services, Wright State University (2010); Outstanding Faculty Member Award, College of Education and Human Services, Wright State University (2006); Excellence in Scholarship Award, College of Education and Human Services, Wright State University (2004); Excellence in Scholarship Award, College of Education and Human Services, Wright State University (2001); Excellence in Scholarship Award, College of Education and Human Services, Wright State University (1999) **Membership:** Five Season Sport Club; Sir Edmund Hillary Club, Overseas Adventure Travel; Marriott Vacation Club (Now Marriott Vacation Club International); Delta Elite Medallion Status; Marriott Platinum Elite Status; National Council for the Social Studies; National Social Science Association (NSSA); National Association for Gifted Children; Sister Cities International; People to People International; Kappa Delta Pi (Now Kappa Delta Pi, International Honor Society in Education) **Hobbies:** Outdoors; Tennis; Skiing; Travel: Expedition leadership; Well-being planning; Collecting Native American art, European and North American fine crystal art, Remington bronzes, fine art, plants, and men's fine watches; Writing; Cuisine; Fine and performing arts **Religion:** Metaphysics/Spirituality **Shipping Address:** 2179 Briggs Road, Dayton, OH, 45459 **Website:** http://www.wright.edu/~ronald.helms

Jane Knight Hence

Title: Architectural and Graphic Designer **Industry:** Graphic Design **Company Name:** JKH Design **Date of Birth:** 06/27/1937 **Place of Birth:** Pittsburgh **State/Country of Origin:** PA **Parents:** Luther Knight; Doris (Ayers) Knight **Marital Status:** Married **Spouse Name:** Carleton Campbell Hence (5/12/1962) **Children:** Kyle Fitz-Randolph Hence; Maxson Bentley Hence; Juliellen Hence Casey **Education:** Coursewoerk, Rhode Island School of Design (1988-1990); Coursework, Yale University (1986-1990); Diploma, Traphagen School of Design, New York, NY (1960); Coursework, Skidmore College, Saratoga Springs, NY (1955-1958); Diploma, Emma Willard School, Troy, NY (1955) **Career:** Principal Owner, JKH Design (1989-Present); Owner, Various Businesses including Bed and Breakfast, Catering Business, Freelance Interior Design (1982-Present); Designer, Consulting Associate, Michael McKinley & Associates, Stonington, CT (1993-2001) **Civic:** Alternate Newport Historic District Commission (2017-Present); Board of Directors, Nina Lynette Home, Newport, RI (2016-Present); First Vice President, The Point Association, Newport, Rhode Island (2011); Alternate, Westerly Zoning Board (2000-2002) **Creative Works:** Photographer, The Green Light, Newport, RI (2003-Present); Interviewer, The Green Light, Newport, RI (2003-Present); Interior Designer (1998-Present); Painter, Various Collectionsin the Midwest, the South and in New England; Designer, More than 55 Buildings, Renovations and Additions in New England; Co-Designer, More than 40 Buildings in Rhode Island and Connecticut **Membership:** Westerly School Facilities Committee, Westerly, RI (1993-1996); Westerly School Building Committee (1992-1993); Board Member, Southeast Museum, Brewster, NY (1970-1974) **Marquis Who's Who Honors:** Albert Nelson Marquis Lifetime Achievement Award (2017) **Why did you become involved in your profession or industry:** Ms. Knight entered her profession because of her intense fascination with houses from a very young age and being a voracious reader her whole life. **What do you consider to be the highlight of your career:** Ms. Knight is most proud of the fact that every client for whom she has designed or remodeled a house has asked her to design or remodel a second or third house, and while doing so, become a friend. **Where will you be in five years:** In the next five years, Ms. Knight hopes to still be alive and designing and being a joyous grandmother to her four grandchildren. **Hobbies:** Painting; Drawing; Gardening; Traveling; Reading; Opera; Theater **Political Affiliations:** Independent **Shipping Address:** 73 Washington Street, Newport, RI, 02840

Samuel Martin Herb

Title: Manufacturing Executive **Industry:** Manufacturing **Company Name:** JAOMAD Consultancy **Date of Birth:** 11/29/1938 **Place of Birth:** Yeadon **State/Country of Origin:** PA **Parents:** Samuel F. Herb; Mildred V. Herb **Marital Status:** Widower **Spouse Name:** Judith Anne Oesch (7/2/1966, Deceased) **Children:** Samuel S.; Corinne M.; David M.(Deceased); Elizabeth A. **Education:** BEE, Drexel University (1969) **Certifications:** Permanent Broadcaster's Licence (1963); Registered Professional Engineer, State of California; Certificate in Professional Selling Skills, Learning International; Certificate in Product Evaluation & Planning, Schrello Associates; Certificate in Problem Solving and Decision Making, Kepner-Tregoe **Career:** Owner, JAOMAD Consultancy (2002-Present); Director of Strategic Marketing, Invensys (Now Schneider Electric) (2003-2007); Market Analyst, Siemens Corporation (1996-2002); Director of Marketing, Procon Systems, Inc. (1994-1995); Market Manager of Control Applications, Leeds and Northrup (1993-1994); Product Manager, Leeds and Northrup (1979-1993); Product Application Specialist, Leeds and Northrup (1979-1993); Project Engineer, Honeywell International Inc. (1976-1979); Applications Engineer, Honeywell International Inc. (1973-1976); Technology Writer, Honeywell International Inc. (1964-1973); Technician, Honeywell International Inc. (1957-1964) **Career Related:** Contributor, Conduct Control Systems Seminars Worldwide (1970-Present) **Civic:** Display Curator, Reading Railroad Heritage Museum, Reading Company Technical & Historical Society, Inc. (2012-Present); Docent, Reading Railroad Heritage Museum, Reading Company Technical & Historical Society, Inc. (2012-Present); Judge, Philadelphia Future City Competition, The International Society of Automation (2011-Present); The International Society of Automation (1962-Present); Minister, Holy Communion of St. Jude Church; Lector; Religious Educator; Ecumenical Representative; Youth Minister; La Salle Academy; Volunteer, Nature Preserve Committee, New Britain Borough; Washington Crossing Council, Boy Scouts of America **Creative Works:** Author, Numerous Articles, Professional Journals; Author, Numerous Technical Papers, Professional Societies and Technical Magazines **Awards:** Eponym, Sam Herb/Jack McGrath Automation Award, Philadelphia Future City Competition, The International Society of Automation (2012-Present); Humanitarian Contribution Award, Boy Scouts of America (2015); Golden Eagle Award, The International Society of Automation (2001, 2007); Distinguished Society Service Award, The International Society of Automation (2004); Donald P. Eckman Education Award, The International Society of Automation (1999); Distinguished Commissioner Award (1990); Silver Beaver Award, Boy Scouts of America (1990); Wood Badge, Boy Scouts of America (1989); Honoree, Legion of Honor, Four Chaplains Memorial Foundation (1985); Recipient, Competent Toastmaster, Toastmasters International **Membership:** Commissioner, Boy Scouts of America (1961-Present); Senior Member, The International Society of Automation; Industrial Computing Society, INFORMS; Engineers Club of Philadelphia; Marketing Committee Council, Boy Scouts of America **Marquis Who's Who Honors:** Albert Nelson Marquis Lifetime Achievement Award (2017); Distinguished Humanitarian (2017) **Hobbies:** Travel; Swimming; Outdoors; Model railroading; House projects **Religion:** Roman Catholic **Shipping Address:** 117 Pawnee Rd, New Britain, PA, 18901 **Website:** joamad.com

LeRoy Alec Herbel

Industry: Engineering **Date of Birth:** 07/24/1954 **Place of Birth:** Fort Carson **State/Country of Origin:** CO **Parents:** LeRoy Alec Herbel; Mabel Bertha (Huffman) Herbel **Education:** MBA, Golden Gate University (1990); MS in Telecommunications, Golden Gate University (1987); MEd, Georgia Southern University (1978); BS, Southwest Missouri State University (1976) **Career:** Instructional System Specialist, Army Training Support Center, Fort Eustis, VA (2004-Present); Instructional System Specialist, Department of Defense, Fort Gordon, GA (1997-2004); Senior Network Analyst, Sprint PCS, Lenexa, KS (1996-1997); Switch Supervisor, Palmer Wireless (Cellularone), Fort Myers, FL (1995-1996); Field Engineer Manager, Western Wireless Corp., Bellevue, WA (1994-1995); Senior Engineer, Northern Telecom Inc., Raleigh, NC (1991-1993); Technology Instructor, Course Developer, Northern Telecom Inc., Raleigh, NC (1988-1991); Radio Operated, Army Military Auxiliary Radio Systems (MARS) (1988-1997); Assistant Professor of Military Science, Army ROTC, University of North Carolina, Durham, NC (1982-1985); Material Controller, GTE of the South, Durham, NC (1979-1980); Assistant Manager, Toy Department, Dillard's Department Store, Springfield, MO (1971-1976) **Career Related:** Adjunct Professor, North Carolina Wesleyan College, Rocky Mount, NC (1991); Adjunct Professor, DeKalb Community College (1978-1979) **Civic:** Assistant Council Commissioner, Georgia Carolina Council, Augusta, GA (2004-2005); Merit Badge Staff, National Jamboree, Boy Scouts of America (2001); District Commissioner, Kiokee District, Georgia Carolina Council, Augusta, GA (2000-2006); Troop 213 Committee, Boy Scouts of America (1993-2014); Merit Badge Staff, National Jamboree, Boy Scouts of America (1993); Assistant District Commissioner, Dan Beard District, Boy Scouts of America (1992-1996); Scoutmaster Troop 213, Boy Scouts of America, Cary, NC (1990-1993) **Military Service:** Major, U.S. Army Reserve (1988-2014); Captain, U.S. Army (1980-1988) **Awards:** Army Civilian Achievement Medal (2006); Bronze Leaf Meritorious Service Medal (2004); Distinguished Commissioner Service Award (2002); Silver Beaver Award, Boy Scouts of America (2002); Boy Scout Commissioner Key Award (1995); District Order of Merit, Boy Scouts of America (1994); Scoutmaster Key Award, Boy Scouts of America (1992); Scoutmaster Award of Merit, Boy Scouts of America (1991); Distinguished Leadership Citation, Boy Scouts of America (1991); Commanders Service Award; Korean Defense Medal **Membership:** Telephone Pioneers of America; Phi Delta Kappa; American Legion; Military Officers Association of America **Hobbies:** Golf; Running; Trains; Camping; Music

E. Patricia Herron

Title: Judge (Retired) **Industry:** Law and Legal Services **Date of Birth:** 07/30/1927 **Place of Birth:** Auburn NY **State/Country of Origin:** NY **Parents:** David Martin Herron; Grace Josephine (Berner) Herron **Marital Status:** Single **Education:** JD, University of California, Berkeley (1964); MA, The Catholic University of America (1954); AB, Trinity College (1949) **Career:** Private Judge, JAMS, Walnut Creek, California (1990-2005); Private Judge (1987-1990); Judge, Superior Court of California, County of Contra Costa (1977-1987); Partner, Knox, Herron and Masterson, Richmond, CA (1974-1977); Partner, Knox & Herron, Richmond, CA (1965-1974); Associate, Knox & Kretzmer, Richmond, CA (1964-1965); Director Row, Stanford, CA (1960-1961); Instructor of Psychology and American History, Contra Costa College, San Pablo, CA (1958-1960); Counselor, Contra Costa College, San Pablo, CA (1958-1960); Assistant Dean, Wells College, Aurora, NY (1957-1958); Instructor, East High School, Auburn, NY (1955-1957); Assistant Dean, The Catholic University of America (1952-1954) **Career Related:** Manager, The Barricia Vineyards (1978-2007); Owner, The Barricia Vineyards (1978-2007); Partner, Real Estate Syndicates, California (1967-1977) **Civic:** Active Member, Numerous Civic Organizations; Former Member, Numerous Foundation Boards; Former Member, Numerous Committees **Awards:** Citation Award, Law School, University of California, Berkeley (2011) **Bar Admissions:** State of California (1965) **Shipping Address:** 800 Oregon St Apt 220, Sonoma, CA, 95476

Daniel Leroy Hertz Jr.

Title: Entrepreneur **Industry:** Business Management/Business Services **Company Name:** Seals Eastern **Date of Birth:** 02/27/1930 **Place of Birth:** Montclair **State/Country of Origin:** NJ **Parents:** Daniel Leroy Hertz; Elizabeth Neilsen (Beet) Hertz **Marital Status:** Married **Spouse Name:** Isabel Waud Hurd (4/18/70); Valerie A. Smith (3/15/1956, Divorced 1962) **Children:** Valerie H. Boyle; Suzanne E.; Daniel L. **Education:** Honorary ME, Stevens Institute of Technology, Hoboken, NJ (1982) **Career:** Founder, Chief Executive Officer, Seals Eastern, Red Bank, NJ (1958-Present); Sales Engineer, C.E. Conover & Company, Fairfield, NJ (1953-1958) **Career Related:** Advisory Board Member, Polymer Technical Consultant, Texas A&M University, College Station, TX (1990-1994); Elastomerics, Atlanta, GA (1984-1992); CHEMTECH, Washington, DC (1983-1991) **Civic:** Visiting Committee Member, Mechanical Engineering Department, Stevens Institute of Technology (1992-1996); Secretary, Riverside Drive Association, Red Bank, NJ (1980-1985); Member, Vestry, Treasurer, All Saints Memorial Church **Military Service:** Corporal, US Army, Korean War (1950-1951) **Creative Works:** Contributor, Engineering with Rubber, Third Edition (2010); Contributor, Handbook of Elastomers, Third Edition (2010); Contributor, Vanderbilt Handbook, 15th Edition (2009): Contributor, Elastomer Technology- Special Topics (2003); Contributor, Rubber Technology (2001); Contributor, Handbook of Elastomers, Second Edition (2000); Contributor, Vanderbilt Handbook, 14th Edition (2000); Contributor, Engineering with Rubber, Second Edition (2000); Contributor, Rubber Products Manufacturing Technology (1993); Contributor, Engineering with Rubber (1992); Contributor, Vanderbilt Handbook (1990); Contributor, Handbook of Elastomers (1988); Contributor, Chapters to Intermediate Rubber Technology (1983); Contributor, Articles to Professional Journals **Awards:** Named, Rubber & Plastics/Rubber Industry Executive of the Year (2015); Recipient, Recognition, New Jersey Senate Resolution (2008); Named, Rubber & Plastics/Rubber Industry Executive of the Year (2007); Recipient, Distinguished Service Award, American Chemical Society (2000); Recipient, Leading Business Manufacturing Executive Technology Achievement Award; Recipient, Melvin Mooney Distinguished Technology Award **Membership:** Chairman, Rubber Division, American Chemical Society (1996); Treasurer, Rubber Division, American Chemical Society (1988-1990); Chairman, New York Rubber Group (1983); Rumson Country Club; Nassau Club; Seabright Tennis Club; Seabright Beach Club; Church Club, New York **To what do you attribute your success:** Mr. Hertz attributes his success to his continuous curiosity, attention to detail, education, hard work and being able to continually grow and innovate according to customers needs. He worked as a sales engineer in his early years for five years and then when the company was beginning to decline, he set up a distributorship and became a major competitor in the industry. When the Challenger disaster occurred, he was working on a chapter on sealant technology with university collaborators and was called to address the problem and determine a solution. His company determined the O-ring fault and created a design and formulation to serve as a solution from further issues. This became a turning point and Mr. Hertz became a lighting rod and noted change expert in the industry. This led to him becoming chairman of education in the rubber industry for the university and eventually attaining an honorary degree highly recommended by the university president. From then on, he maintained some of our nation's leading industry accounts. **Political Affiliations:** Republican **Religion:** Episcopalian **Business Address:** P.O. Box 520, Red Bank, NJ, 07701 **Shipping Address:** 8 Hasler Lane, Little Silver, NJ, 07739

Allan Duane Hess

Title: Medical Educator **Industry:** Education/Educational Services **Date of Birth:** 07/23/1948 **Place of Birth:** Chicago **State/Country of Origin:** IL **Parents:** Harry Joseph Hess; Sophia Hedwig (Bubacz) Hess **Marital Status:** Married **Spouse Name:** Mary Ellen Anne Storino (6/20/1970) **Children:** Joellyn Marie (Hess) Bowser **Education:** Postdoctoral Fellow, Duke University, Durham, NC (1976-1978); PhD, University of Illinois, Chicago, IL (1976); Graduate Fellowship, University of Illinois (1974-1976); BS in Biology, DePaul University, Chicago, IL (1970) **Career:** Professor Emeritus, Johns Hopkins University, Baltimore, MD (2014-Present); Professor, Johns Hopkins University, Baltimore, MD (1978-2014) **Career Related:** Director, Human Immunology Laboratory, Johns Hopkins University Cancer Center (2005-Present) **Civic:** Fundraiser, St. Joseph Catholic Church, Texas (1980-2007); Fundraiser, St. Joseph Catholic Church, Maryland (1980-2007) **Military Service:** Private Illinois National Guard, Fort Polk, LA (1971-1972) **Creative Works:** Contributor, Articles, Professional Journals **Awards:** Lectureship, Royal Society of Medicine (1987) **Membership:** American Society of Bone Marrow Transplantation; American Society of Hematology **Marquis Who's Who Honors:** Albert Nelson Marquis Lifetime Achievement Award (2017) **Hobbies:** Golf; Travel **Political Affiliations:** Democrat **Religion:** Catholic **Shipping Address:** 10392 Hedgeapple Bend, New Market, MD, 21774

John Warner Hetherington

Title: State Legislator, Attorney **Industry:** Law and Legal Services **Company Name:** Rucci Law Group, LLC **Date of Birth:** 08/15/1938 **Place of Birth:** New York **State/Country of Origin:** NY **Parents:** John Kells Hetherington; Susanna Louisa (Warner) Hetherington **Marital Status:** Married **Spouse Name:** Hope Luke (11/6/1976) **Children:** Kells; Jane **Education:** JD, Yale University (1963); BA, Yale University (1960) **Career:** Attorney, Rucci Law Group, LLC, Darien, CT (2007-Present); Assistant Minority Leader (2009-2013); State Representative, District 125, Connecticut State General Assembly (2003-2013); Attorney, Rucci, Burnham & Carta, LLP (2002-2011); Vice President, Westvaco Corporation, New York, NY (1987-2002); Secretary, Assistant General Counsel, Westvaco Corporation, New York, NY (1978-2002); Assistant Secretary, Assistant General Counsel, Westvaco Corporation, New York, NY (1977-1978); Attorney, Westvaco Corporation, New York, NY (1967-1977); Associate, Dickerson & Reilly, New York, NY (1965-1967); Attorney, Federal Reserve Bank of New York, New York, NY (1964-1965) **Career Related:** Advisory Committee on Shareholder Communications, U.S. Securities and Exchange Commission (1981-1982) **Civic:** Chairman, Assessment Appeals Board, New Canaan, CT (2000-2003); New Canaan Town Council (1989-1997); New Canaan Planning and Zoning, New Canaan, CT (1986-1989) **Military Service:** Captain, General Corps, U.S. Naval Reserve; Judge Advocate, General Corps, U.S. Naval Reserve **Membership:** Ranking Member, Judiciary Committee, Connecticut House of Representatives (2011-2013); Director, Society for Corporate Governance (1990-1993); Chairman, Tender Offers Committee, Society for Corporate Governance (1986-1989); Appropriations Committee, Connecticut House of Representatives; Ranking Member, Government Administration and Elections Committee, Connecticut House of Representatives; Sons of the Revolution; New York State Bar Association; Exchange Club of New Canaan; Kiwanis Club of New Canaan; The Country Club of New Canaan; Connecticut Bar Association; Fairfield County Bar Association; Past Director, United Way of New Canaan **Bar Admissions:** State of Connecticut (1987); U.S. Court of Appeals for the Armed Forces (1974); U.S. District Court, Eastern District, State of New York (1965); U.S. District Court, Southern District, State of New York (1965); State of New York (1964) **Why did you become involved in your profession or industry:** Mr. Hetherington became involved in his profession because his father and grandfather were both lawyers. **Where will you be in five years:** In five years, Mr. Hetherington plans to continue writing. **Hobbies:** Writing on Civil War subjects; Sailing **Political Affiliations:** Republican **Religion:** Congregationalist **Shipping Address:** 155 East Avenue, Unit 155, New Canaan, CT, 06840 **Website:** http://ruccilawgroup.com/your-team/john-w-hetherington

Ferol W. Hettick

Title: Director of Compliance **Industry:** Financial Services **Company Name:** Trustmark National Bank **Date of Birth:** 09/02/1950 **Place of Birth:** Jacksonville **State/Country of Origin:** IL **Parents:** Ralph Hettick; Margaret Hettick **Marital Status:** Married **Spouse Name:** Carol J. **Children:** Daryl W. Hettick; Gerald D. Hettick **Education:** EdB, Illinois State University, Normal, IL; Diploma, ABA Compliance and Graduate Compliance Schools **Certifications:** Certified Regulatory Compliance Manager, Institute of Certified Bankers **Career:** Director, Compliance, Trustmark National Bank (2005-Present); Director, Compliance, Synovus Financial Corporation (1997-2005); Compliance Manager, AT&T (1991-1997) **Civic:** President, Board of Directors, C.A.R.H.A.; Participant, Several Mission Trips, Haiti, England; Local Church **Membership:** Mississippi Regulatory Compliance Group; Open Compliance Committee, American Bankers Association; Chief Compliance Officer Group, Midsize Bank Coalition of America **Marquis Who's Who Honors:** Albert Nelson Marquis Lifetime Achievement Award (2017); Distinguished Humanitarian (2017) **To what do you attribute your success:** Mr. Hettick attributes his success to his dedication and hard work. He feels successful when his team is successful. **Why did you become involved in your profession or industry:** Mr. Hettick became involved in his profession after he worked in the financial services field for more than 10 years, and was approached for a compliance job opportunity. **What do you consider to be the highlight of your career:** The highlight of Mr. Hettick's career was going to work for Trustmark. The bank demonstrates a dedication to compliance and doing things right. **Where will you be in five years:** In the next five years, Mr. Hettick plans to be retired from the bank and will most likely be volunteering somewhere. He wants to be able to spend more time with C.A.R.H.A. **Hobbies:** Reading; College football **Business Address:** 248 East Capital, Suite 1302, Jackson, MS, 39201 **Shipping Address:** 532 Eastside Cove, Brandon, MS, 39047 **Website:** https://www.linkedin.com/in/ferol-hettick-1355776

Gary F. Hevel

Title: Research Collaborator **Industry:** Museums & Institutions **Company Name:** Smithsonian Institution **Date of Birth:** 11/30/1941 **Place of Birth:** Salida **State/Country of Origin:** CO **Parents:** Francis Marion Hevel; Doris Hevel **Marital Status:** Married **Spouse Name:** Julie Anne Fortin (7/18/1980); Susan Platkin (6/30/1970, Divorced 1980) **Children:** Amanda Simone; Derek Forrest **Education:** BS, Pittsburg State University (1969) **Career:** Public Information Officer, Department of Entomology, Smithsonian Institution (1995-2011); Collections Manager, Department of Entomology, Smithsonian Institution (1973-1995); Museum Specialist, Department of Entomology, Smithsonian Institution (1969-1973); Research Collaborator, Department of Entomology, Smithsonian Institution **Career Related:** Consultant, Andrew Stewart Publications (2005-2006); Consultant, IMAX (2003); Consultant, USA Weekend Magazine, USA TODAY (2003); Consultant, Orkin, LLC (2001); Consultant, U.S. Fish & Wildlife Service (2000-2002); Consultant, Dorling Kindersley Limited (2000-2001); Consultant, United States Military (1969-1970) **Creative Works:** Editor, "Insects and Spiders," United State Stamps; Co-Editor, "Animal"; Co-Creator "Bio-Blitz"; Co-Developer "BugFest"; Contributor, Articles, Professional Journals; Contributor, Insect Collecting Documentaries; Contributor, Museum Documentaries **Membership:** The Coleopterists Society; The New York Entomological Society, Inc.; The Entomological Society of Washington; Entomological Society of America; Kansas Entomological Society **Marquis Who's Who Honors:** Albert Nelson Marquis Lifetime Achievement Award (2017) **Hobbies:** Photography; Stamp collecting/philately; Birdwatching **Shipping Address:** PO Box 997, Washington, DC, 20044

Brett A. Hickey

Title: Founder, Chief Executive Officer **Industry:** Financial Services **Company Name:** Star Mountain Capital **Marital Status:** Married **Education:** MA, Owner/President Management Program, Harvard Business School, Harvard University (2011); BA in Finance, McGill University, Montreal, QC, Canada; Coursework in Business, Mount Royal University; Coursework in Entrepreneurship, Mount Royal University **Career:** Founder & Chief Executive Officer, Star Mountain Capital (2010-Present); Co-Founder & President, Aegis Capital Group LLC (2003-2010); Investment Banker, Citigroup Inc. (2002-2004); Investment Banker, Salomon Smith Barney (2002-2004) **Career Related:** Chairman, Maple Leaf Ball, Canadian Association of New York (2008); Board Member, New York Chapter, Harvard Alumni Entrepreneurs; Board of Governors, Small Business Investor Alliance; Former Chairman of Networks, New York City Chapter, YPO; Board Member, Quebec City Conference; Director, New York City Alumni Association, McGill University; Director, Canadian Association of New York; Tri-State Co-Chairman, Capital Campaign, McGill University; Speaker in Field **Civic:** Founder, Availor Philanthropy Corporation (Now Charitable Foundation, Star Mountain Capital) (2016-Present); Chairman, Availor Philanthropy Corporation (Now Charitable Foundation, Star Mountain Capital) (2016-Present) **Creative Works:** Author, "My Path To Prosperity: Create the Life You Really Want"; Contributor, Private Equity Interview on Star Mountain Capital, The Lead Left Interview; Contributor, "Importance of Strong Capabilities for Non-Sponsored Loans," The Lead Left Interview; Contributor, "Helping Business Owners Prepare for and think about Growth Capital," Eckfeldt and Associates; Featured Leader on Technology in the Workplace, Axial Forum; Contributor, "What makes an investment appealing," KITE Invest; Contributor, "Brett Hickey – Building Cultural Capital," INDVSTRVS; Contributor, "Star Mountain: Private Lending in the Lower Middle-Market," FINalternatives.com; Contributor, "Grit: A Key Determinant of Your Company's Success," SuperReturn 365; Contributor, "Developing a collaborative ecosystem is the path to success," SuperReturn 365; Contributor, "Finding uncorrelated returns through lower mid-market secondaries," Secondaries Investor **Awards:** Honoree, Crain's Best Place to Work in New York (2018); Pathfinders to Peace Award; President of the Year, McGill University; New York Chief Executive Officer of the Year Award, Smart CEO; Guiding Star Award, AYUDA for the Arts; Philanthropic Achievement Award, A Caring Hand, The Billy Esposito Foundation; Gold Medal in Speed Skating, Olympic Games **Membership:** YPO (2007-Present); Association for Corporate Growth (ACG); Harvard Club of New York City **Why did you become involved in your profession or industry:** Mr. Hickey likes building businesses and being entrepreneurial, but wanted to do this in a way that was low-risk. He finds it a very fulfilling and a purposeful life to help build companies with other passionate people. **Where will you be in five years:** Mr. Hickey will be continuing to grow his investor base, the size of his team, technology platform, and continue to be making high-quality investment returns. **Hobbies:** Family; Charity triathlons **Shipping Address:** 135 E 57th Street, Floor 25, Star Mountain Capital, New York, NY, 10022 **Website:** https://starmountaincapital.com/team/brett-hickey

Ruth A. Hickox Litchfield

Title: Reading and Early Literacy Specialist **Industry:** Education/Educational Services **Company Name:** Lexington Public Schools **Date of Birth:** 03/17/1945 **Place of Birth:** Cleveland **State:** OH **Parents:** Elizabeth Ann (Way) Hickox; Walter Alan Hickox **Children:** Mrs. Katherine Ann Litchfield Grote; Dr. C. Robert Litchfield **Education:** Certificate of Advanced Graduate Study, Boston University (1995); MEd in Reading, University of Hawaii (1974); BS in Elementary Education and French, University of Missouri (1969); AA, Columbia College, MO (1965) **Certifications:** Certified Consulting Teacher of Reading, State of Massachusetts; Certified French K-9 Teacher, State of Massachusetts; Certified K-12 Reading Teacher; Trained/Certified Orton Gillingham Project Read; Trained/Certified, Wilson Reading Systems & Foundations, Wilson Language Training Corporation; Trained/Certified, Lindamood-Bell Phoneme Sequencing Program, Lindamood-Bell Learning Processes, K-2, LIPS Reading Recovery; Trained/Certified, Teachers College Reading and Writing Project, Coach and Content Areas; Trained/Certified, Geselle Developmental Observation-Revised, Geselle Institute; Leveled Literacy Intervention Primary and Intermediate, Visualizing & Verbalizing, Geselle Institute; Certified Teacher, State of Ohio; Certified Teacher, State of Missouri; Certified Teacher, State of Hawaii **Career:** MELP METCO Extended Learning Program (2009-Present); Mission Teacher, AIDS Orphans, Vulnerable Children, Communities Without Borders, Lusaka Zambia, Africa (2008-Present); Critic's Corner, Continuing Group of Talented and Gifted Readers (2000-Present); Mission Teacher, North Dakota Lakota Indians, ND (1998-Present); Reading/Early Literacy Specialist, Bridge Elementary School (1997-Present); Private Tutor (1995-Present); Teacher, Lusaka Zambia Africa AIDS Orphans Vulnerable Children Program, Communities Without Borders (2008-2018); Teacher, Hurricane Katrina, New Orleans, LA (2006-2007); Teacher, Bombito, Dominican Republic (2003); Reading Recovery Teacher, Lt. Eleazer Davis Elementary, Bedford Public Schools, Bedford, MA (1994); Research Assistant, Harvard Graduate School of Education, Dr. Jeanne S. Chall (1993-2000); Reading Recovery Teacher, Bridge Elementary School, Lexington, MA (1992-1997); Church School Director, Pilgrim Congregational Church (1984-1995); Instructional Aide, Bridge Elementary School, Lexington, MA (1991-1992); Substitute Teacher, Lexington Public Schools, MA (1989-1991); Substitute Teacher, Community Nursery School, Lexington, MA (1985-1989); Private Tutor, United States Army, West Germany (1981-1984); National Consultant, The Economy Company/McGraw-Hill Division (Now McGraw-Hill Education), Oklahoma City, OK (1974-1981); Editor, The Economy Company/McGraw-Hill Division (Now McGraw-Hill Education), Oklahoma City, OK (1974-1975); Assistant Editor, The Economy Company/McGraw-Hill Division (Now McGraw-Hill Education), Oklahoma City, OK (1974-1975); Assistant to Managing Editor, The Economy Company/McGraw-Hill Division (Now McGraw-Hill Education), Oklahoma City, OK (1974-1975); Elementary Teacher, Punahou School, Honolulu, Hawaii (1971-1974); Teacher, Ecole Internationale Bilingue, Paris, France (1970-1971); Elementary Teacher, Claude O. Markoe Elementary School, Frederiksted, St. Croix, Virgin Islands (1969-1970); Teacher, Severance Millikin School, Cleveland Heights, Ohio (1969) **Civic:** Dyslexic Committee Parent Group; LEX Eat Together; Lexington Refugee Program, LexRap; Community Garden **Awards:** Community Service Award, Columbia College, Columbia, MO (April, 2013); Chiyembekezo Award for Outstanding Service to Vulnerable and Orphan Children in Zambia, their Teachers and Caregivers, Communities Without Borders (November, 2012); Appreciation Awards, Girl Scout of the United States of America; Appreciation Awards, Boy Scouts of America **Membership:** President, Local Board of Directors, International Reading Association (Now International Literacy Association) (1998-1999); Association for Supervision and Curriculum Development; MRA-National Reading Association; Massachusetts Reading Association; Ohio Reading Council (Now Ohio Council for the International Reading Association); New England Reading Association; Massachusetts Association for Bilingual Education; Reading Recovery Council of North America; International Dyslexia Association; Phi Delta Kappa International; Pi Lambda Theta; DKGSI **Marquis Who's Who Honors:** Albert Nelson Marquis Lifetime Achievement Award (2017) **Hobbies:** Reading; Swimming; Knitting; Cooking; Baking; Sewing; Crafts **Religion:** Christian (Pilgrim Congregational Church) **Shipping Address:** 6 Conestoga Rd, Lexington, MA, 02421

David G. Hicks

Title: Director of Surgical Pathology **Industry:** Education/Educational Services **Company Name:** University of Rochester Medical Center **Place of Birth:** Albion **State:** NY **Education:** Residency in Anatomic Pathology, Hospital of the University of Pennsylvania (1985-1989); Internship in Internal Medicine, Hospital of the University of Pennsylvania (1984-1985); MD, University of Rochester, With Honors (1984); Fellow, Department of Pathology, University of Rochester (1981-1982); BA, Canisius College (1979) **Certifications:** Diplomate in Anatomic Pathology, American Board of Pathology (1990); Licensed to Practice Medicine, Commonwealth of Pennsylvania; Licensed to Practice Medicine, State of New York; Licensed to Practice Medicine, State of Ohio **Career:** Professor of Pathology and Laboratory Medicine, School of Medicine, University of Rochester (2007-Present); Attending Staff, University of Rochester Medical Center (2007-Present); Staff Pathologist, Roswell Park Cancer Institute, Buffalo, NY (2006-2007); Professor of Oncology and Pathology, Roswell Park Cancer Institute, Buffalo, NY (2005-2007); Staff Pathologist, Cleveland Clinic (2001-2005); Senior Staff Pathologist, Rochester General Hospital, Rochester Regional Health (1999-2001); Associate Professor of Oncology School of Medicine, University of Rochester (1997-1999); Associate Professor, Department of Orthopaedics, School of Medicine, University of Rochester (1996-1999); Associate Professor, Department of Pathology, School of Medicine, University of Rochester (1996-1999); Associate Professor, Department of Laboratory Medicine, School of Medicine, University of Rochester (1996-1999); Attending Staff, University of Rochester Medical Center (1990-1999); Assistant Professor, Department of Orthopedics, School of Medicine, University of Rochester (1990-1996); Assistant Professor, Department of Pathology, School of Medicine, University of Rochester (1990-1996) **Creative Works:** Editorial Board Member, Archives of Pathology & Laboratory Medicine; Editorial Board Member, Biotechnic & Histochemistry; Editorial Board Member, Applied Immunohistochemistry & Molecular Morphology; Editorial Board Member, The Breast Journal; Ad Hoc Reviewer, Cancer; Ad Hoc Reviewer, The American Journal of Pathology; Ad Hoc Reviewer, Clinical Cancer Research; Ad Hoc Reviewer, Breast Cancer Research; Contributor, Articles, Professional Journals; Contributor, Book Chapters **Awards:** Eric A. Schenk Award for Excellence in Teaching, Department of Pathology and Laboratory Medicine, University of Rochester Medical Center (2012); Elected, The Best Doctors in America (2007-2012); Award for Mentoring Junior Faculty, University of Rochester Medical Center (2011); CAP Excellence in Education Award, Council on Education, College of American Pathologists (2011); Huaxia Pathology Teaching Award, China (2008); Dr. Edith E. Sproul Teaching Award, Department of Pathology and Laboratory Medicine, Roswell Park Cancer Institute, Buffalo, NY (2006); John Beach Hazard Distinguished Teaching Award, Department of Pathology and Laboratory Medicine, Cleveland Clinic (2002); Andrew W. Mellon Dean's Teaching Scholarship (1996-1999); Duthie-Evarts Resident Education Award, Department of Orthopaedics, University of Pennsylvania (1997); Kappa Delta Elizabeth Winston Lanier Award for Outstanding Orthopaedic Research, American Academy of Orthopaedic Surgeons (1995) **Membership:** Alpha Omega Alpha Honor Medical Society (1984); USCAP; Vice-Chairman, Self Assessment Module Committee, College of American Pathologists; Subject-Matter Expert, Breast Predictive Factor Advanced Practical Pathology Program, College of American Pathologists; Subject-Matter Expert, Multidisciplinary Breast Pathology, Advanced Practical Pathology Program Planning Committee, College of American Pathologists; Consensus Panel Expert, ASCO/CAP ER/PR Full Panel Guideline Meeting, College of American Pathologists; Pathology Co-Chairman, Testing in Breast Cancer Committee, College of American Pathologists; Scientific Steering Committee, Office of Biorespitories and Biospecimen Research, National Cancer Institute, NIH; Trustee, The Biological Stain Commission **Marquis Who's Who Honors:** Albert Nelson Marquis Lifetime Achievement Award (2017) **Hobbies:** Reading detective novels and murder mysteries; Golf; Drawing; Sketching; Watercolor painting **Business Address:** 601 Elmwood Avenue, Box 626, University of Rochester Medical Center, Rochester, NY, 14642

Pamela Leis Higdon

Title: Writer; Teacher; Editor; Copy Editor **Industry:** Writing and Editing **Date of Birth:** 09/02/1943 **Place of Birth:** San Bernardino **State/Country of Origin:** CA **Parents:** Stella Doss; Raymond Ellsworth Leis **Marital Status:** Married **Spouse Name:** Sherman Robert Higdon Junior (8/29/1964, Deceased) **Children:** Mary Katherine Christian **Education:** BS in Education, Texas Technological University, Lubbock, TX (1966) **Certifications:** Certified Teacher, State of Texas (1966) **Career:** Member, Organization Chapter, Recording Secretary, Alsatian Pioneers Chapter, The Daughters of the Republic of Texas (2013-Present); Freelance Writer, Editor, PLH Writing/Editing, Castroville, TX (1994-Present); Writer, Editor, Product Developer, Project Manager, Acquisitions Editor, Educational Insights, Carson, CA (1990-1994); Editor, Writer, Bird Talk Magazine and Birds USA, Fancy Publications, Irvine, CA (1987-1990); Teacher, Elementary School, Science Coordinator for Elementary School, District Language Arts Committee Member, After School Computer Instructor, Arabian American Oil Co., Ras Tanura, Saudi Arabia (1978-1986) **Civic:** Past Chair, Landmark Historical Preservation Commission (2011-Present); Past Chair, Landmark Historical Preservation Commission (2004-2005); Executive Board, Recording Secretary, Methodist Church, Castroville (2003-2004); Volunteer Writer, Designer, Public Town Newsletter, Castroville, TX (2001-2003); Volunteer Writer, Community Newsletter, Mills Branch Village Board Directors, Kingwood, TX (1996-2000); Commissioner, Planning and Zoning Commission, Castroville, TX; Member, Planning Zoning Committee, Castroville, TX; PPRC Member, Medina Valley Methodist Church, Castroville, TX; Advisor of Conservation, Wildlife & Land, Volunteer Copy Editor, National Wildlife Fund; Pastor, Parish Relations Committee, Medina Valley United Methodist Church; Past Chair, Missions Committee, Medina Valley United Methodist Church; Member, Historical Landmark Commission; Volunteer Writing Teacher, Castroville Library **Creative Works:** Former Copy Editor, Prehospital Medical Booklet (1995); Executive Producer, Writer, Former Copy Editor, Monthly Newsletter of Canadian Paramedics (1992-2008); Contributor, Journal of Emergency Medical Services, Fire Rescue Magazine (1992-2002); Co-Author, "Watching Backyard Birds"; Author, "Pattern Block"; Author, Project Manager, "Geosafari & Geosafari Junior"; Co-Author, "Third Grade Review"; Author, "National Wildlife Federation Insects, Exotic Animals, Sea Life, Wild Animals, Dinosaurs"; Co-Author, "Holistic Care for Birds: A Manual of Wellness and Healing"; Author, "Bird Care and Training, Happy Healthy Pets: The Quaker Parrot"; Author, Editor, "The Essential African Grey"; Copy Editor, "The Hospitalist"; Copy Editor, Volunteer, "Star Cactus" (2011); Author, "Science Notes: How Things Move"; Author, "The Life You Save: Community Defibrillation Programs & the Emergency Care Responder"; Contributor, EMS Best Practices, Caring for the Ages-for Long-Term Care Practitioners; Author, Editor, "The Essential Cockatiel, The Essential Zebra Finch"; Contributor, Columns in Newspapers, Articles and Professional Journals **Awards:** Community Service Award, Mills Branch Village Board of Directors (1997) **Membership:** Founding Member, First Recording Secretary Alsatian Pioneers Chapter (2012-Present); Freelance Writer, Association of Public Safety Communications Officials (2011-Present); Author of Restoration Column, Texas Historical Committee (2011-Present); Recording Secretary, Daughters Republic Texas (2002-2004); Alsatian Pioneers Chapter, TX (2013); United Daughters of the Confederacy; Daughters of the American Revolution; Historical Landmark Commission; Beautification Committee of Castorville Texas **Marquis Who's Who Honors:** Distinguished Humanitarian (2017) **Hobbies:** Mentoring children; Quilting; Reading; Swimming; Birdwatching **Political Affiliations:** Democrat **Shipping Address:** 514 Petersburg St, Castroville, TX, 78009

Ruth Ann Higgins

Title: Social Worker, Family Therapist **Industry:** Social Work **Date of Birth:** 09/23/1944 **Place of Birth:** Rock Valley **State/Country of Origin:** IA **Parents:** Neal Vonk; Tillie (Feekes) Vonk **Spouse Name:** (1972, Divorced 9/1986) **Children:** Ashlie Kay; Steven Grant **Education:** MSW, University of Denver (1983); MA, University of Colorado (1978); BA, Northwestern College (1966) **Certifications:** Certified Medical Social Worker, Exempla Lutheran Hospice Center (2007-Present); National Board Certified Diplomate in Clinical Social Work, National Association of Social Workers (2009-2010); Certified Medical Social Worker, Exempla Lutheran Hospital (2006); Licensed Clinical Social Worker, American Board of Examiners in Clinical Social Work (2004); Licensed Clinical Social Worker, University of Denver (1983); Certified Professional Teacher, State of Colorado; Advanced Certificate in Hospice and Palliative Care **Career:** Clinical Social Worker, Exempla Lutheran Hospice Care (2006-Present); Social Worker, Columbine Counseling Center, Broomfield, CO (1981-Present); School Social Worker, Adams 12 Five Star Schools, Northglenn, CO (1985-2005); Social Worker, Counseling Center & Outpatient Behavioral Health, Boulder Community Health (1979-1981); Social Worker, Mental Health Center of Boulder County, Colorado (1977); Teacher, Jeffco Public Schools, Lakewood, CO (1970-1975); Teacher, United States Department of Defense, Clark Air Force Base, Philippines (1969-1970); Teacher, Adams 12 Five Star Schools, Northglenn, CO (1967-1969) **Career Related:** Part-time Social Worker, Boulder Valley School District (1985); Part-time Social Worker, Lutheran Hospice, Wheatridge, CO (1985); Part-time Social Worker, The Denver Hospice (1984-1985); Board of Directors, Health and Human Services, City and County of Broomfield, Colorado **Civic:** Counselor, Trainer, Up with People (1998-2000) **Creative Works:** Author, Editor, "Nothing Could Stop the Rain" (1976) **Awards:** Finalist, Alteria M. Bryant Award, Metropolitan Denver Baha'i Center (1996); Honorary Mention Counselor of Year Award, Colorado School Counselors Association (1994) **Membership:** National Association of Social Workers **Marquis Who's Who Honors:** Albert Nelson Marquis Lifetime Achievement Award (2017) **To what do you attribute your success:** Ms. Higgins attributes her success to having determination, grit and goals. **Why did you become involved in your profession or industry:** Ms. Higgins entered her profession because she always had the belief that children love to learn new information. She promised herself she would make learning enjoyable so that children could meet their goals. **What do you consider to be the highlight of your career:** The highlight of Higgins' career was having the opportunity to help some people both in education and health care. She takes great pride in helping people. **Hobbies:** Stained glass; Hiking; Reading; Music **Political Affiliations:** Independent **Shipping Address:** 1350 Carmel Ct, Broomfield, CO, 80020

Patricia L. Highcove

Title: Vocational Consultant **Industry:** Consulting **Company Name:** Highcove Consulting **Education:** MS in Rehabilitation Counseling, Syracuse University (1982); BS in Rehabilitation Services, Syracuse University (1981) **Certifications:** Certified Ergonomic Assessment Specialist (2016); Certified Case Manager (1990); Certified Rehabilitation Counselor (1987); Certified Vocational Evaluator (1983) **Career:** Senior Executive, Guilford Group, LLC (1997-2001); Territory Director, Intracorp Companies (1996-1997); Field Service Manager, Intracorp Companies (1989-1996); Rehabilitation Specialist, Intracorp Companies (1986-1989); Rehabilitation Specialist IV, Division of Rehabilitation Services, Maryland Rehabilitation Center (1984-1986); Counselor, Alliance, Inc. (1983-1984); Evaluator, Alliance, Inc. (1983-1984); Vocational Evaluator, Merrimack Valley Rehabilitation Center (1982-1983); Student Assistant, Vocational Assessment and Career Center (1982); Independent Consultant, Highcove Consulting **Membership:** Board Member, Former President, Chesapeake Association of Rehabilitation Professionals in the Private Sector; Board of Directors, Kids' Chance of Maryland, Inc.; International Association of Rehabilitation Professionals **Marquis Who's Who Honors:** Albert Nelson Marquis Lifetime Achievement Award (2017); Distinguished Humanitarian (2017) **To what do you attribute your success:** Ms. Highcove attributes her success to her passion for her work. **Why did you become involved in your profession or industry:** She became involved in her profession after gaining experience working with developmentally-disabled children. **What do you consider to be the highlight of your career:** The most gratifying aspect of Ms. Highcove's career is being able to help others. **Where will you be in five years:** In the coming years, Ms. Highcove would like to expand her business. **Hobbies:** Spending Time with her Children; Reading; Traveling; Listening to Music **Shipping Address:** 303 Quaker Ridge Rd, Lutherville-Timonium, MD, 21093

Shadi B. Hijjawi

Title: Physician **Industry:** Medicine & Health Care **Company Name:** CaroMont Health **Place of Birth:** Nablus **State/Country of Origin:** Palestine **Education:** MD, Medical School, Jordan University of Science and Technology (2007); Residency, The University of Texas Medical Branch at Galveston; Residency, King Hussein Cancer Center; MBA, University of Massachusetts, Amherst **Certifications:** Medical License, State of North Carolina (2013-2018); Certificate, American Board of Internal Medicine; Certified in Health Care and Quality Management (CHCQM) **Career:** Hospitalist, Physician Advisor, Interim Chief Medical Information Officer, CaroMont Health **Awards:** Named Fellow, American College of Physicians (2016) **Membership:** Society of Hospital Medicine (SHM) **Shipping Address:** 300 W 5th St Apt 434, Charlotte, NC, 28202

H. Mark Hildebrandt

Title: Pediatrician (Retired) **Industry:** Medicine & Health Care **Date of Birth:** 10/23/1926 **Place of Birth:** Ann Arbor **State/Country of Origin:** MI **Parents:** Theophil Henry Hildebrandt; Dora (Ware) Hildebrandt **Marital Status:** Married **Spouse Name:** Emily Patterson (2006, Deceased 2017); Deborah Bush-B.; Linda Figen (Divorced, 1984); Jennie Parker (Divorced, 1974) **Children:** Marian; Carl; Janet; Jonathan; Lisabeth; Ursula **Education:** Resident in Pediatrics, Infectious Diseases Division, Cleveland City Hospital (1952-1955); Intern, Infectious Diseases Division, Cleveland City Hospital (1952-1955); MD, University of Michigan (1952); BA, University of Michigan (1948) **Career:** Clinical Associate Professor, University of Michigan, Ann Arbor, MI (1971-2006); Pediatrician, Private Practice, Ypsilanti, MI (1987-2005); Pediatrician, Private Practice, Ann Arbor, MI (1955-1987); Clinical Assistant Professor, University of Michigan, Ann Arbor, MI (1958-1971) **Career Related:** Affiliate Faculty, University of Michigan (1978-2006); Founder, Suspected Child Abuse and Neglect Team, University of Michigan Hospital (1971) **Civic:** Commissioner, Historical District Commission, Ann Arbor, MI (2000-2006) **Military Service:** United States Army (1944-1947) **Creative Works:** Author, "The Kaboodle Book, The Letters Between Theophil H. Hildebrandt and Dora E. Ware 1917-1921" (2017); Author, "A History of St. Andrews Episcopal Church, Ann Arbor, Michigan, Part II, 1900-2000" (2014); Co-author, "The Electric Trolleys of Washtenaw County" (2010); Author, "The Windows of St. Andrew's" (2006) **Membership:** The American Academy of Pediatrics; Ambulatory Pediatric Association; Academy of Breastfeeding Medicine **To what do you attribute your success:** He attributes his success to having good genes and putting in a lot of hard work. **Why did you become involved in your profession or industry:** When facing military service in 1943, Dr. Hildebrandt decided to save lives instead of shooting people. **What do you consider to be the highlight of your career:** The highlight of Dr. Hildebrandt's career was supporting one of the leading organizations through the development of the child abuse management program at University Hospital. **Where will you be in five years:** Dr. Hildebrandt plans to be plugging along in five years. **Hobbies:** Cello; History; Trains; Trolleys **Religion:** Episcopalian **Shipping Address:** 1930 Cambridge Road, Ann Arbor, MI, 48104 **Website:** http://www.drhildebrandt.com.html

David P. Hill, PhD

Title: Scientist Emeritus **Industry:** Sciences **Company Name:** U.S. Geological Survey **Date of Birth:** 06/18/1935 **Place of Birth:** Livingston **State/Country of Origin:** MT **Parents:** Sanford Hill; Gerda Hill **Marital Status:** Married **Spouse Name:** Ann Rivers (6/17/1961) **Children:** Peter Michael **Education:** PhD in Geophysics, California Institute of Technology (1971); MS in Geophysics, Colorado School of Mines (1961); BS in Geology, San Jose State University (1958) **Career:** Scientist Emeritus, Volcano Science Center, U.S. Geological Survey, Menlo Park, CA (2010-Present); Senior Research Geophysicist, Long Valley Observatory (2009-2010); Scientist-in-Charge, Long Valley Observatory, U.S. Geological Survey (1982-2009); Chief, Seismology Branch, U.S. Geological Survey, Menlo Park, CA (1978-1982); Geophysicist, U.S. Geological Survey, Menlo Park, CA (1971-1978); Geophysicist, U.S. Geological Survey, Pasadena, CA (1966-1971); Staff Seismologist, Hawaiian Volcano Observatory, U.S. Geological Survey (1964-1966); Geophysicist, U.S. Geological Survey, Denver, CO (1961-1964) **Career Related:** Fellowship, American Association for the Advancement of Science (2002); Task Group, Mammoth Mountain Interpretive Center (1999-2007); Guest Member, COMPLEX Panel, National Aeronautics and Space Administration (1998); Visiting Professor, Geophysics Institute, Eidgenossische Technische Hochschule, Zurich, Switzerland (1988); United States Chairman, United States-Japan Panel on Earthquake Prediction (1979-1982); Fellow, American Geophysical Union; Fellow, American Association for the Advancement of Science **Civic:** Review Panel, Basic Science Energy Program, United States Department of Energy (1996); Unified Command, Mono County (1984-2010) **Military Service:** Consultant, U.S. Navy (1984-1985) **Creative Works:** Associate Editor, "Journal of Volcanology and Geothermal Research" (2002-Present); Associate Editor, "Bulletin of the Seismological Society of America" (1996-1998); Associate Editor, "Journal of Geophysical Research" (1985-1988); Contributor, Articles, Professional Journals; Author, 82 Publications on Seismology, Volcanology, and Tectonics **Awards:** Distinguished Public Service Medal, Mineralogical Society of America (2002); Meritorious Service Award, U.S. Department of the Interior; Distinguished Service Award, U.S. Department of the Interior; Eugene Shoemaker Communications Award, U.S. Geological Survey; Public Service Recognition Award, U.S. Geological Survey **Membership:** Seismological Society of America **Marquis Who's Who Honors:** Albert Nelson Marquis Lifetime Achievement Award (2017) **To what do you attribute your success:** Dr. Hill attributes his success to curiosity about the natural world, integrity, and support from his family, friends, and colleagues. **Why did you become involved in your profession or industry:** Dr. Hill lived in Yellowstone as a child, and was infused with curiosity about nature and the outdoors. **What do you consider to be the highlight of your career:** The main highlight of Dr. Hill's career was leading the USGS effort to monitor and understand the volcanic unrest in Long Valley Caldera in eastern California, and explain the implication for volcanic hazards to the public and civil authorities. A second highlight of his career was his discovery that large earthquakes can trigger smaller earthquakes at global distances (now known as "remote dynamic triggering"). He is also proud of his mentor-ship role in the USGS. **Hobbies:** Bicycling; Hiking; Skiing; Drawing **Business Address:** 345 Middlefield Road, Menlo Park, CA, 94025 **Shipping Address:** 3794 Redwood Circle, Palo Alto, CA, 94306 **Website:** https://www.usgs.gov/staff-profiles/david-hill

George J. Hill

Title: Physician **Industry:** Medicine & Health Care **Date of Birth:** 10/07/1932 **Place of Birth:** Cedar Rapids **State:** IA **Parents:** Gerald Leslie Hill; Essie Mae (Thompson) Hill **Marital Status:** Married **Spouse Name:** Helene Zimmermann (7/16/1960) **Children:** James Warren; David Hedgcock; Sarah; Helena Rundall **Education:** DLitt, Drew University (2005); MA, Rutgers, The State University of New Jersey (1999); MD, Harvard University (1957); BA, Yale University (1953) **Career:** Professor Emeritus, New Jersey Medical School, Rutgers, The State University of New Jersey (1997-Present); Adjunct Professor of Surgery, Uniformed Services University (1989-Present); Deputy Governor General, Order of the First Families of New Hampshire (2014-2015); Chancellor General, Order of Descendants Colonials Physicians and Chirurgeons (2012-2015); Research Coordinator, Saint Barnabas Medical Center (1997-1999); Interim President, Sterling College (1996); President of Faculty, New Jersey Medical School, Rutgers, The State University of New Jersey (1991-1992); American Cancer Society Professor of Clinical Oncology, New Jersey Medical School, Rutgers, The State University of New Jersey (1989-1992); Professor of Surgical Oncology, New Jersey Medical School, Rutgers, The State University of New Jersey (1981-1996); Director of Surgical Oncology, New Jersey Medical School, Rutgers, The State University of New Jersey (1981-1996); Professor, Marshall University (1976-1981); Chairman, Marshall University (1976-1981); Professor, Washington University in St. Louis (1973-1976); Associate Professor, University of Colorado (1972-1973); Assistant Professor, University of Colorado (1967-1972); Instructor of Surgery, University of Colorado (1966-1967); Fellow, Peter Bent Brigham Hospital (1963-1966); Fellow, Harvard Medical School (1963-1966); Resident in Surgery, Peter Bent Brigham Hospital (1963-1966); Resident in Surgery, Harvard Medical School (1963-1966); Clinical Associate, National Institutes of Health (1961-1963); Fellow, Peter Bent Brigham Hospital (1958-1961); Resident in Surgery, Peter Bent Brigham Hospital (1958-1961); Fellow, Harvard Medical School (1958-1961); Resident in Surgery, Harvard Medical School (1958-1961) **Career Related:** Honorary Member of Medical School Staff, Saint Barnabas Medical Center (1999-Present); Clinical Professor of Surgery, Icahn School of Medicine at Mount Sinai (1999-Present); Adjunct Professor of History, Kean University (2000-2001); Visiting Fellow in Molecular Biology, Princeton University (1988); Chairman of Clinical Cancer Education Committee, National Cancer Institute (1978-1980); Damon Runyon Fellowship (1957-1958); Fellow, Royal Society of Medicine **Civic:** Advisory Council, Crossroads of the American Revolution (2014-Present); Dean's Advisory Council, Rutgers, The State University of New Jersey (2012-Present); Executive Board Member, Northern New Jersey Council, Boy Scouts of America (1998-Present); Honorary Life Member, American Cancer Society, Inc. (1996-Present); President, Hill Family Trust (1989-Present); Trustee, Frost Valley YMCA (1986-Present) **Military Service:** U.S. Navy (1968-1992); Active Duty (1961-1963); U.S. Public Health Service Reserve (1960-1968); Corporal, U.S. Marine Corps Reserve (1950-1952); Captain, Medical Corps, U.S. Naval Reserve **Creative Works:** Author, "Quakers and Puritans: The Shoemaker, Warren and Allied Families" (2015); Author, "Western Pilgrims: The Hill Stockwell and Allied Families" (2014); Author, "Liberia and the US, 1917-1947" (2014); Author, "Proceed to Peshawar" (2013); Author, "Hill: The Ferry Keeper's Family" (2011); Author, "John Saxe, Loyalist (1732-1808) and His Descendants for Five Generations" (2010); Author, "Edison's Environment, Revised Edition" (2010); Author, "Intimate Relationships Church and State US and Liberia" (2008); Author, "Edison's Environment" (2007); Author, "Outpatient Surgery, 3rd Edition" (1988); Author, "Leprosy in Five Young Men, Paperback Edition" (1979) **Awards:** Finalist's Medal, Indie Book Awards (2013); David L. Cowen Award, The Medical History Society of New Jersey (2013); Good Scout Award (2012); Russel C. Hill Award (2012); Delta Award, Essex County Medical Society (2010); Distinguished Eagle Award, Boy Scouts of America (2005); Vigil Honor (2005); Patriot Medal, Sons of the American Revolution (2003); New Jersey Distinguished Service Medal (2001); Silver Antelope Award (1998); National William Spurgeon, III Award (1994); Edwards Medal, American Association for Cancer Education (1994); Meritorious Service Medal, U.S. Navy (1993) **Membership:** Surgeon General, National Order of the Blue and Gray (2013-Present); Councilor General, The Order of the Founders and Patriots of America (2013-Present); Deputy Surgeon General, General Society of Colonial Wars (2009-Present); Historian, Essex County Medical Society (2009-Present); Surgeon General, Order of the Merovingian Dynasty (2007-Present); Trustee, New Jersey State Society, Sons of the American Revolution (2004-Present) **Marquis Who's Who Honors:** Albert Nelson Marquis Lifetime Achievement Award (2017); Distinguished Humanitarian (2017) **Hobbies:** Photography; Ballroom dancing; Writing books **Political Affiliations:** Independent **Religion:** Episcopal **Shipping Address:** 3900 N Charles Street, Apt. 901, Baltimore, MD, 21218

J. Robert Hillier

Title: Architect **Industry:** Architecture & Constrution **Company Name:** Studio Hillier **Date of Birth:** 07/24/1937 **Place of Birth:** Toronto **Country of Origin:** Ontario/Canada **Parents:** James Hillier; Florence (Bell) Hillier **Marital Status:** Married **Spouse Name:** Barbara Ann Feinberg (4/7/1986) **Children:** Jordan Rebecca Hillier; Kimberly (Deceased); James Baldwin Hillier **Education:** LHD, New Jersey Institute of Technology, Honoris Causa (2017); MBA, Bryant University, Honoris Causa, Smithfield, RI (1992); MFA, Princeton University (1961); BA, Princeton University (1959) **Career:** Principal, Studio Hillier, Princeton, NJ (2009-Present); President, Hillier Properties, LLC (2008-Present); Principal, RMJM Hillier (2007-2009); Deputy Chairman, RMJM Hillier (2007-2009); Chairman of the Board, Hillier Architecture (Now Studio Hillier), Princeton, NJ (2000-2007); Chairman of the Board, The Hillier Group (Now Studio Hillier), Princeton, NJ (1987-2000); President, The Hillier Group (Now Studio Hillier), Princeton, NJ (1972-1987); Principal, J. Robert Hillier (Now Studio Hillier), Princeton, NJ (1966-1972); Project Manager, Fulmer & Bowers, Princeton, NJ (1961-1966); Project Designer, J. Labatut, Princeton, NJ (1961-1962); Chairman, Obit-mag.com **Career Related:** Member, Core Faculty, School of Architecture, Princeton University; Founder, Publisher, Princeton Magazine **Civic:** Trustee, Peddie School, Hightstown, NJ (1981-Present); Chairman, Board of Directors, Princeton Regional Chamber of Commerce (2011-2012); Trustee, Edison College Foundation, Milton Hershey School (1997-2002); Chairman, Advisory Board, Albert Dorman Honors College, New Jersey Institute of Technology (1993-1999); Trustee, Bryant University, Smithfield, RI (1993-1996); Trustee, McCarter Theatre Center, Princeton, NJ (1983-1989); Trustee, Princeton University Art Museum; Member, Board of Overseers, New Jersey Institute of Technology; Treasurer, Board Member, Witherspoon Jackson of Cultural and History Society **Creative Works:** Principal Architect, Peddie Campus Buildings, Peddie School (1970-Present); Principal Architect, Copperwood, Princeton, NJ (2015); Principal Architect, University Medical Center (Now Princeton HealthCare System), Princeton, NJ (2008); Principal Architect, Irving Convention Center at Las Colinas (2006); Principal Architect, Los Colinas Live Master Plan, Urban Insertion, Princeton, NJ (2007); Principal Architect, The Waxwood, Princeton, NJ (2005); Principal Architect, Natirar Spa and Hotel, Peapack, NJ (2005); Principal Architect, Peddie Athletic Center, Peddie School (2004); Principal Architect, Princeton Public Library (2004); Principal Architect, Virginia State Capital Restoration and Preservation (2004); Principal Architect, Restoration Supreme Court Building, Washington, DC (2003); Principal Architect, Peddie Science Center (Now The Walter and Leonore Annenberg Science Center) (2002); Principal Architect, Capital One Corporate Headquarters (2002); Principal Architect, GlaxoSmithKline plc, London, United Kingdom (1998); Principal Architect, Sprint World Headquarters (1997); Principal Architect, GlaxoSmithKline plc, Harlowe, United Kingdom (1996); Principal Architect, American Home Products Corporate Headquarters (1992); Principal Architect, New Jersey Aquarium (Now Adventure Aquarium) (1991); Principal Architect, University of Pennsylvania, The Wharton School, Aresty Institute of Executive Education (1986); Principal Architect, Merritt Tower (1985); Principal Architect, New Jersey State Justice Complex (Now Richard J. Hughes Justice Complex), Trenton, NJ (1985); Principal Architect, Beneficial Corporation Complex (Now HSBC) (1982); Principal Architect, Harbor Island Design, Tampa, FL (1981); Principal Architect, Butler Hospital (Now Care New England Health System), Providence, RI (1978); Principal Architect, The Rutgers Athletic Center, Piscataway, NJ (1977); Principal Architect, Bryant College Campus, Smithfield, RI (1969) **Awards:** Recipient, More than 300 Design Awards, Architectural Associations (1966-Present); Recipient, 75th Anniversary Legacy Award, Urban Land Institute (2013); Recipient, President's Lifetime Achievement Medal, New Jersey Institute of Technology (2009); Recipient, Michael Graves Lifetime Achievement Medal, American Institute of Architects (2008); Named, Innovator of the Year, Princeton Regional Chamber of Commerce (2006); Recipient, Master of Infrastructure Medal, Penjendel Council (2005); Recipient, Da Vinci Award, Professional Service Management Association (2002); Recipient, Architect of the Year Award, New Jersey Contractors Association (1997); Recipient, Architect of the Year Award, New Jersey Contractors Association (1992); Recipient, Community Service Human Relations Award (1992); Named, New Jersey Entrepreneur of the Year (1989); Recipient, Distinguished Service Award, IACC (1988) **Membership:** Vice President, New Jersey Chapter, American Institute of Architects, Urban Land Institute (1974); Fellow, American Institute of Architects, Urban Land Institute; National Council of Architectural Registration Boards; Princeton Quadrangle Club **Marquis Who's Who Honors:** Albert Nelson Marquis Lifetime Achievement Award (2017) **Hobbies:** Bicycling; Swimming; Golf **Shipping Address:** 2846 River Rd, New Hope, PA, 18938

Muriel Ruth Nelson Hinkle

Title: President, Chief Executive Officer Emerita **Industry:** Information Technology and Services **Company Name:** Sonalysts Inc. **Date of Birth:** 03/17/1929 **Place of Birth:** Bayonne **State/Country of Origin:** NJ **Parents:** Andrew Nelson; Florence Martha Ida (Nuber) Nelson **Marital Status:** Widowed **Spouse Name:** David Randall Hinkle (6/5/1954, Deceased 7/27/2009) **Children:** Valerie Nelson; Janet Lee; Sally Ann **Education:** BA, University of Maryland (1951); Coursework, Maryland College for Women (1947-1949) **Career:** President Emerita, Sonalysts, Inc., Waterford, CT (2001-Present); Chief Executive Officer Emerita, Sonalysts, Inc. (2001-Present); President, Sonalysts, Inc. (1994-1998); President, Stonington Farms Inc. (Now Mystic Valley Hunt Club) (1983); Chief Executive Officer, Stonington Farms Inc. (Now Mystic Valley Hunt Club) (1983); Chairman, Stonington Farms Inc. (Now Mystic Valley Hunt Club) (1983); Chief Executive Officer, Sonalysts, Inc. (1973-2001); President, Sonalysts, Inc. (1973-1988); Illustrator, Naval Warfare Predictions/Computer Simulated Naval Engagements, Analysis & Technology, Inc., North Stonington, CT (1970-1973); Manager, Wildacres Thoroughbred Horse Farm, Waterford, CT (1960-1970); Ticket Agent, DCA & EWR, Eastern Air Lines (1951-1954); Founder, Command Engineering & Technical Services Company; Past Director, Command Engineering & Technical Services Company **Career Related:** Staten Island Economic Development Corporation (1989-2001); Chairman, Angiers Associates (1989-1996); Chief Executive Officer, Angiers Associates (1989-1996); Advisory Board, The Connecticut National Bank (1988-1992); Consultant, Tactical Nuclear Effects in Anti-Submarine Warfare, Defense Nuclear Agency (Now Defense Threat Reduction Agency) (1974-1975); Special Education Substitute Teacher, Waterford Public Schools (1968-1974); Board of Directors, Sonalysts, Inc. **Civic:** Board of Trustee, Thames Science Center, Inc. (1979-1982) **Creative Works:** Author, "Launching Sonalysts" (2013); Co-author, "Destroyer ASW Barrier" (1977); Co-author, "Naval Tactical Communications" (1975); Co-author, "Scope of Acoustic Communications Systems in Naval Tactical Warfare" (1974); Co-author, "Non-Acoustic Anti Submarine Warfare" (1974); Co-author, "Nuclear Weapons Effects in Anti Submarine Warfare" (1974); Co-author, "Measures of Effectiveness" **Awards:** William Crawford Distinguished Service Award, U.S. Chamber of Commerce (2002); Distinguished Community Service Award, Mitchell College, New London, CT (2001); Business Associate of the Year Award, U.S. Naval Institute (1999); New England Contractor of Year Award, U.S. Small Business Administration (1986); Administrator's Award for Excellence, U.S. Small Business Administration (1985-1986); Commendation for Services to Submarine Force, Commander of Submarine Squadron Ten (1973) **Membership:** President, Senesk Chapter, Sigma Kappa (1987-1989); President, Submarine Development Group Two Wives Club (1968); American Horse Shows Association (Now United States Equestrian Federation); National Audubon Society; Navy Wives Clubs of America **To what do you attribute your success:** Ms. Hinkle attributes her success to encouragement from her parents, husband, and children. **Why did you become involved in your profession or industry:** Ms. Hinkle became involved in her profession because her husband served in the Navy. **What do you consider to be the highlight of your career:** The highlight of Ms. Hinkle's career was founding Sonalysts with her husband. **Where will you be in five years:** In five years, Ms. Hinkle will be retired and living in Connecticut. **Hobbies:** Riding, raising, and racing horses **Political Affiliations:** Republican **Religion:** Baptist **Shipping Address:** PO Box 280, Waterford, CT, 06385

George W. Hinman

Title: Chair **Industry:** Sciences **Date of Birth:** 11/07/1927 **Place of Birth:** Evanston **State/Country of Origin:** IL **Year of Passing:** 2018-05-26 **Parents:** Norman Seymour Hinman; Bess Hinman **Marital Status:** Married **Spouse Name:** Mary Louise Cauffield (6/19/1952) **Children:** Norman Field; Lydia Seymour; Nancy Wheeler **Education:** DSc in Physics, Carnegie Mellon University, Pittsburgh, PA (1952); MS in Physics, Carnegie Mellon University, Pittsburgh, PA (1950); BS in Physics and Mathematics, Carnegie Mellon University, Pittsburgh, PA (1947) **Career:** Chair, Environmental Science and Regional Planning (1989-1997); Director, New Mexico Energy Research and Development Institute, Santa Fe, NM (1982-1983); Professor of Physics, Washington State University, Pullman, WA (1969-1997); Director, Applied Energy Studies, Washington State University, Pullman, WA (1969-1997); Chairman, Physics, General Atomics, San Diego, CA (1963-1969); Assistant Professor to Associate Professor of Physics, Carnegie Mellon University, Pittsburgh, PA (1952-1963) **Career Related:** Consultant, National Nuclear Accreditation Board (1992-1998); Consultant, General Accounting Office (1977-2010); Consultant, Los Alamos National Laboratory (1976-1990); Fellow, American Physical Society **Creative Works:** Author, "Nuclear Power at the Crossroads: Challenges and Prospects for the Twenty-First Century" (1994); Author, "Dictionary of Energy" (1983); Contributor, Articles, Professional Journals **Awards:** Grantee, National Science Foundation; Grantee, Various Foundations **Membership:** American Nuclear Society; American Association for the Advancement of Science; American Society for Engineering Education **Marquis Who's Who Honors:** Albert Nelson Marquis Lifetime Achievement Award (2017) **Hobbies:** Fly fishing **Political Affiliations:** Democrat **Shipping Address:** 6555 Gharrett Avenue, Missoula, MT, 59803

Bobbe Hirsh

Title: Lawyer **Industry:** Law and Legal Services **Company Name:** Skarzynski Black, LLC, Hirsh & Associates, LLC **Parents:** Bernard L. Hirsh; Regina Baker Hirsh **Children:** Jonathan William Benowitz; Robin Gayle Benowitz **Education:** JD, Harvard University, Cum Laude, Cambridge, MA (1980); MS in Business Administration, University of Denver (1975); BA, Brown University, Providence, RI (1973) **Certifications:** Certified Public Accountant, State of Illinois (1975) **Career:** Counsel, Skarzynski Black, LLC (2011-Present); Partner, Hirsh & Associates, LLC, Chicago, IL (2011-Present); Partner, Lipscomb, Brady & Eisenberg PL, Miami, FL (2010-2011); Partner, K & L Gates LLP, Chicago, IL (2006-2010); Partner, Lord, Bissell & Brook LLP, Chicago, IL (1993-2006); National Director, International Tax Service, McGladrey & Pullen, Chicago, IL (1988-1993); Associate, Cadwalader, Wickersham & Taft, New York (1985-1988); Manager, Tax Planning, PepsiCo, Purchase, NY (1984-1985); Associate, Baker & McKenzie, New York (1980-1984); Senior Accountant, Peat, Marwick, Mitchell, Chicago, IL (1975-1977) **Career Related:** Board Adviser, Journal of Taxation of Financial Products, Chicago, IL (2002-Present); Board of Advisers, Journal of International Taxation, New York **Civic:** Committee Member, Anti-Defamation League (2016); Chairman, Board of Directors, Ballet Theater, Chicago, IL (1997); Board of Directors, Chicago Jaycees (1976-1977); President, Board of Directors, Litsky Foundation, Chicago, IL; Former Treasurer, Board of Directors, Litsky Foundation, Chicago, IL **Creative Works:** Co-Author, "The NAFTA Guide" (1995); Contributor, Articles, Professional Journals; Articles Editor, "Harvard International Law Review" **Awards:** Williston Prize, Harvard Law School (1978); Silver Medal, COCPA (1975); Elijah Watts Sells Award, American Institute of CPAs (1975); Honoree, Leading Lawyer in Tax Law and International Business and Trade Law; Honoree, Illinois Super Lawyer; Honoree, 100 Leading Women Lawyers in Illinois; Honoree, AV Rated Attorney, Martindale-Hubbell **Membership:** Former Member, Board of Directors, International Tax Policy Forum; ABA; American Society of Attorney-CPAs; Former Member, International Tax Planning Association; Beta Gamma Sigma; Beta Alpha Psi **Bar Admissions:** Illinois (1991); United States Tax Court (1982); United States District Court Southern District of New York (1981); United States District Court Eastern District of New York (1981); New York (1981) **Marquis Who's Who Honors:** Albert Nelson Marquis Lifetime Achievement Award (2017) **Shipping Address:** 310 Whytegate Ct, Hirsh & Assoc. LLC, Lake Forest, IL, 60045

James A. Hixon

Title: Lawyer, Rail Transportation Executive **Industry:** Law and Legal Services **Company Name:** Northfolk Southern Corporation **Education:** Master of Law in Taxation, College of William & Mary (1980); JD, College of William & Mary (1979); BS, Virginia Polytechnic Institute (1976) **Career:** Executive Vice President of Law and Corporate Relations, Norfolk Southern Corp. (2005-2016); Executive Vice President of Financial and Public Affairs, Norfolk Southern Corp. (2004-2005); Senior Vice President of Legal and Government Affairs, Norfolk Southern Corporation (2003-2004); Senior Vice President of Administration, Norfolk Southern Corporation (2000-2003); Senior Vice President of Employee Relations, Norfolk Southern Corporation (1999-2000); Vice President of Taxation, Norfolk Southern Corporation (1993-1999); Assistant Vice President, Tax Counsel, Norfolk Southern Corporation (1991-1993); General Tax Attorney, Norfolk Southern Corporation (1987-1991); Assistant Tax Counsel, Norfolk Southern Corporation (1985-1986) **Civic:** Board of Visitors, College of William and Mary (2015-Present); Board Member, Virginia Arts Festival (2008-Present); Board of Visitors, Old Dominion University (2002-2010) **Marquis Who's Who Honors:** Albert Nelson Marquis Lifetime Achievement Award (2017); Distinguished Humanitarian (2017) **Why did you become involved in your profession or industry:** Mr. Hixon entered his field because one of his teachers suggested it to him. **Shipping Address:** 3329 Kline Dr, Virginia Beach, VA, 23452 **Website:** http://www.wm.edu/about/administration/bov/members/hixon

John Hochstein, PhD

Title: Professor, Mechanical Engineering **Industry:** Education/Educational Services **Company Name:** University of Memphis **Place of Birth:** Brooklyn **State:** NY **Parents:** Harry S. Hochstein; Ruth K. Hochstein **Marital Status:** Married **Spouse Name:** Deborah Hochstein (1976) **Children:** David; Ann; Marie; Daniel **Education:** PhD, Mechanical Engineering, The University of Akron (1984); MSME, The Pennsylvania State University (1979); BE, Stevens Institute of Technology (1973) **Career:** Professor, The University of Memphis (1996-Present); Department Chair, The University of Memphis (1996-2015); Associate Professor, The University of Memphis (1991-1996); Associate Professor, Washington University in St. Louis (1989-1991); Assistant Professor, Washington University in St. Louis (1984-1989); Special Lecturer, The University of Akron, Ohio (1979-1984); Engineer, Babcock & Wilcox Co., Barberton, Ohio (1977-1979); Engineer, Electric Boat Division, General Dynamics (Now General Dynamics Electric Boat), Groton, CT (1975-1977) **Career Related:** Organizer, 9th and 10th AIAA Space Processing Symposia (1995, 1996) **Civic:** Shelby County Sustainability (2007-Present); Germantown Youth Athletic Association, TN (1991); Coach of Little League, Creve Couer Athletic Association, MO (1988-1990) **Creative Works:** Contributor, Articles to AIAA Journals & Conferences (1990-Present); Co-author, "Fundamentals of Fluid Mechanics, Eighth Edition," John Wiley & Sons, Inc. (2016); Co-author, "Fundamentals of Fluid Mechanics, Second Edition," Addison-Wesley (1991) **Awards:** Grantee, U.S. Department of Energy (2012-Present); Grantee, NASA (1984-Present); NASA Summer Faculty Fellow (1994, 1995); Professor of the Year, School of Engineering, Washington University in St. Louis (1991) **Membership:** Co-founder, Center for Biofuel Energy and Sustainable Technologies, The University of Memphis (2007); Chair, Space Processing Technical Committee, American Institute of Aeronautics and Astronautics (AIAA) (1997-1998); Associate Fellow, American Institute of Aeronautics and Astronautics (AIAA); Several Offices, Different Chapters, American Institute of Aeronautics and Astronautics (AIAA); The American Society of Mechanical Engineers; American Society for Engineering Education (ASEE) **Marquis Who's Who Honors:** Albert Nelson Marquis Lifetime Achievement Award (2017) **To what do you attribute your success:** Dr. Hochstein attributes his success to a supportive wife, great parents, great children and an excellent PhD adviser. **Why did you become involved in your profession or industry:** Dr. Hochstein likes to teach. He likes to understand how things work; he like to make and break things. **Hobbies:** Woodworking; Camping; Travel; Old Cars **Shipping Address:** University of Memphis, Mechanical Engineering/ES312, Memphis, TN, 38152

Robert J. Holland

Title: Lawyer **Industry:** Law and Legal Services **Date of Birth:** 01/08/1936 **Place of Birth:** Dayton **State/Country of Origin:** OH **Parents:** John Edward Holland; Alma Naomi (Himes) Holland **Marital Status:** Married **Spouse Name:** Barbara Jane Drake (1960) **Children:** Robert, Jr.; Duncan; Wendolyn; Justin **Education:** JD, Ohio State University (1963); BA, Yale University (1958) **Certifications:** U.S. Supreme Court (1972) **Career:** General Counsel, Board of Directors, Servinat, Inc. (1976-2001); Attorney, Upper Arlington, OH (1976-1986); General Counsel, Mid-Ohio Regional Planning Commission, Columbus, OH (1971-1985); Partner, Bodiker & Holland, Columbus, OH (1971-1997); Partner, Mid-Ohio Regional Planning Commission (1970-1971); General Counsel, BancOhio Financial (1967-1971); Associate, Chester & Rose (1963-1967); General Counsel, Central Regional Automated Funds Transfer System **Career Related:** Board of Directors, First Community Bank **Civic:** Founder, Board of Directors, Wellington School, Columbus, OH (1979-1989); President, Board of Directors, Central Ohio Transit Authority, Columbus, OH (1971-1974) **Military Service:** Lieutenant, U.S. Navy Reserve (1958-1960) **Creative Works:** Co-Author, "Ohio Taxation: Truth in Lending" (1969) **Awards:** Honoree, Ten Outstanding Men, Columbus Jaycees (1970) **Membership:** International Food and Wine Society; Union League Club of Chicago; Scioto Country Club, Athletic Club; President's Club, Ohio State University; Life Member, Trout Unlimited **Bar Admissions:** Ethics Committee, Columbus Bar Association (1973-1977); Chairman, Unauthorized Practice, Columbus Bar Association (1973-1974); Chairman, Law Institutes Committee, Columbus Bar Association (1968-1970); Ohio State Bar Association (1963); American Bar Association **Marquis Who's Who Honors:** Albert Nelson Marquis Lifetime Achievement Award (2017); Distinguished Humanitarian (2017) **Hobbies:** Fly fishing **Shipping Address:** 4837 Slate Run Court, Columbus, OH, 43220

Susan Tower Hollis, PhD

Title: History Professor, Cultural Studies Professor **Industry:** Education/Educational Services **Company Name:** Empire State College **Date of Birth:** 03/17/1939 **Place of Birth:** Boston **State:** MA **Parents:** James Wilson Tower; Dorothy Parsons (Moore) Tower **Marital Status:** Single **Spouse Name:** Allen Hollis (11/10/1962, Divorced 1975, Deceased 2017) **Children:** Deborah Durfee; Harrison **Education:** PhD, Harvard University (1982); AB, Smith College, Cum Laude (1962) **Certifications:** Lifetime Certified Instructor in History and Humanities, Community College, State of California **Career:** Professor Emerita, Empire State College (2017-Present); Adjunct Professor, San Diego Mesa College (1990-Present); Acting Chairperson, Master of Arts in Liberal Studies Program, Empire State College (2014-2016); Professor, Empire State College (2007-2017); Seminar Facilitator, University of Rochester Medical Center (2003-2004); Regional Coordinator, Master of Arts in Liberal Studies Program West, Empire State College (2000-2007); Associate Professor, Empire State College (1996-2007); Center Director, Empire State College (1996-1999); Associate Dean, Empire State College (1996-1999); Professor of Humanities, Sierra Nevada College (1993-1995); Dean, Sierra Nevada College (1993-1995); Adjunct Professor, Graduate School, Union Institute & University (1992-1994); Professor, College of Undergraduate Studies, Union Institute & University (1991-1993); Core Faculty, College of Undergraduate Studies, Union Institute & University (1991-1993); Director of Humanities Internship Program, Scripps College (1988-1991); Assistant Professor of Humanities, Scripps College (1988-1991); Consultant, Ramesses II Exhibit, Museum of Science, Boston, MA (1987-1988); Coordinator, Meet the Scientist Course, Museum of Science, Boston (1987); Program Coordinator, Radcliffe Summer Program in Science, Radcliffe College (Now Radcliffe Institute for Advanced Study, Harvard University) (1984-1987); Teaching Assistant, Harvard University (1983-1988) **Career Related:** Visiting Scholar, Institute for Antiquity and Christianity, Claremont Graduate University (1991-Present); GVC Chairperson, Employee Giving Campaign (2011); Associate Dean Search Committee, Niagara Frontier Center, Empire State College (2011); Chairperson, Academic Personnel Committee, Empire State College (2010-2011); Chairperson, Research Committee, Center for Graduate Programs, Empire State College (2009-2016); Presenter, New Mentor Workshop, Saratoga Springs, New York (2009-2011); Member, Task Force on Academic Programs, Genesee Valley Center, Empire State College (2009); Chairperson, Academic Personnel Committee, Empire State College (2008-2009); Middle State Reaccreditation Reviewer, Niagara Frontier Center, Empire State College (2008-2009); Member, Middle States Subcommittee on Academic Programs, Empire State College (2008); Chairperson, Center Task Force, Middle States Review, Empire State College (2008); Core Faculty, Master of Arts in Liberal Studies Program, Empire State College (2007-2017) **Creative Works:** Advisory Board Member, "KMT, A Modern Journal of Ancient Egypt" (1991-2014); Author, "The Ancient Egyptian: Tale of Two Brothers, Revised Edition," Bannerstone Press (2008); Editor, "Ancient Egyptian Hymns, Prayers, and Songs: An Anthology of Ancient Egyptian Lyric Poetry," Scholars' Press (1995); Co-Editor and Contributor, "Feminist Theory and the Study of Folklore," University of Illinois Press (1993); Author, "The Ancient Egyptian 'Tale of Two Brothers': The Oldest Fairy Tale in the World," University of Oklahoma Press (1990); Assistant Editor, "Working With No Data: Semitic and Egyptian Studies Presented to Thomas O. Lambdin," Eisenbrauns (1987); Author, "Egyptian Goddesses: Their Beginnings, Actions, and Relationships in the Third Millennium BCE," Bloomsbury Press, Ltd.; Contributor, Book Chapters; Contributor, Articles to Professional Journals; Contributor, Reviews; Contributor, "Oxford Handbook of Ancient Egypt and the Hebrew Bible," Oxford University Press; Editor, "Oxford Handbook of Ancient Egypt and the Hebrew Bible," Oxford University Press **Awards:** Honoree, Scholar Across the College, Empire State College (2013-2014); Recipient, Susan H. Turben Award for Excellence in Scholarship, Empire State College (2006); Recipient, Award for Outstanding Service in Mentoring and Status of Women in the Profession, Society of Biblical Literature (2003) **Membership:** Rochester Chapter, American Recorder Society (2004-Present); American Recorder Society (2014-Present); Professional Association of Dive Instructors, Professional Association of Diving Instructors (2006-Present); Oceanic Society (2006-Present); Convener, Ancient Near Eastern Studies Sections and Groups, Society of Biblical Literature (1998-Present); Adirondack Mountain Club (1996-Present); Volunteer, Sierra Club (1988-Present); Appalachian Mountain Club (1978-Present); Board of Directors, New York State ACE Women's Network (1997-2006) **Marquis Who's Who Honors:** Albert Nelson Marquis Lifetime Achievement Award (2017) **Hobbies:** Playing the recorder; Reading; Scuba diving; Snorkeling; Kayaking; Canoeing **Political Affiliations:** Democrat **Shipping Address:** 7 New Wickham Dr, Penfield, NY, 14526

Dallas Scott Holmes

Title: Judge **Industry:** Law and Legal Services **Company Name:** State of California **Date of Birth:** 12/02/1940 **Place of Birth:** Los Angeles **State:** CA **Parents:** Donald Cherry Holmes; Hazel N. (Scott) Holmes **Marital Status:** Married **Spouse Name:** Patricia McMichael (8/21/1965) **Children:** Mark Scott; Tobin John **Education:** JD, University of California, Berkeley (1967); MS, LSE (1964); AB, Pomona College, Cum Laude (1962) **Career:** Judge on Assignment by the Chief Justice, State of California (2009-Present); Lecturer in Environmental Law, Pomona College (2008) (2015); Superior Court Judge (1996-2007); Partner, Best Best & Krieger LLP, Riverside, CA (1974-1996); Associate, Best Best & Krieger, Riverside, CA (1968-1974) **Career Related:** Chairman, Jury Committee, Superior Court of California, County of Riverside (1997-2003, 2005-2007); Chairman, Task Force Jury System Improvements, California Judicial Council (1998-2003); Lecturer, Judicial, Local Government and University Extension Groups, University of California, Los Angeles (1987-2002); Member, California Judicial Council (1995-1996); Vice President, The State Bar of California (1992-1993); Member, Board of Governors, The State Bar of California (1990-1993); Adjunct Professor, University of California Hastings College of the Law, San Francisco (1990); Assistant Adjunct Professor, The A. Gary Anderson Graduate School of Management, University of California, Riverside (1977-1988); Executive Assistant, Assembly Majority Floor Leader, California State Legislature, Sacramento, CA (1969-1970) **Civic:** Elder, Calvary Presbyterian Church (2008-2011); Member, Board of Trustees, University of California, Riverside Foundation (1983-2006); President, Torchbearers, Pomona College (1995-1996); City Attorney, Corona, CA (1976-1996); Chairman, Legal Affairs Committee, Association of California Water Agencies (1985-1991); President, Downtown Riverside Association (1987-1988); President, Citizens University Committee (1983-1985); President, Century Club, Riverside, CA (1974-1976); President, Alumni Council, Pomona College (1973-1974) **Creative Works:** Contributor, Articles on Mass Transit, Professional Journals; Contributor, Articles on Assessment of Farmland in California, Professional Journals; Contributor, Articles on Exclusionary Zoning and Environmental Law, Professional Journals; Author, Proposed Tort Reform Initiative for California Physicians **Awards:** Named Young Man of Year, Riverside Junior Chamber of Commerce (1972); Named Man of the Year, "The Press-Enterprise" (1962) **Membership:** Board Member, Feeding America Riverside and San Bernardino Counties (2008-Present); Chairman, Jury Center Advisory Committee, American Judicature Society(2000-2012); Executive Committee, Public Law Section, The State Bar of California (1983-1986); President, Riverside County Bar Association (1982); Rotary Club of Riverside **Bar Admissions:** The State Bar of California (1968) **Marquis Who's Who Honors:** Albert Nelson Marquis Lifetime Achievement Award (2017) **Why did you become involved in your profession or industry:** Mr. Holmes became involved in his profession because he always wanted to be a teacher as a child. One day, his eighth-grade science teacher called him over and asked, "I understand you want to be a teacher?" Mr. Holmes said "yes," and the teacher said, "Oh, no. You won't make any money." So, he thought that he had better do something besides teaching, so the teacher diverted him into law, and it was pretty clear to him that this was where he belonged. **What do you consider to be the highlight of your career:** Mr. Holmes is most proud of his involvement with jury reform. Being the chairman of the task force on jury system improvements for the state of California was a wonderful task, and he got a lot done and enjoyed it a lot. Mr. Holmes enjoys working with jurors more than any other aspect of the job. **Political Affiliations:** Republican **Shipping Address:** 604 Via La Paloma, Riverside, CA, 92507 **Website:** https://www.martindale.com/riverside/california/dallas-scott-holmes-p-c-194724-a/

Jean L. Holmes

Title: Museum Director, Preservationist, Humanities Educator **Industry:** Museums & Institutions **Date of Birth:** 12/09/1943 **Place of Birth:** Butler **State/Country of Origin:** MO **Parents:** Victor Julius Witte; Helen Emilia (Knapheide) Witte **Marital Status:** Married **Spouse Name:** Reed M. Holmes (1/26/1993); Eugene Philmore Carter, Jr. (8/21/1965, Divorced 8/1992) **Children:** Kristen; Lance **Education:** Postgraduate Coursework, Yad Vashem, Poland (1998); Postgraduate Coursework, Ratisbonne Center of Judaic Studies, Jerusalem, Israel (1993-1995); Postgraduate Coursework, Hebrew University, Yad Vashem, Israel (1992-1995); MA in Judaic Studies, Hebrew College, Brookline, MA, Magna Cum Laude (1989); Postgraduate Coursework, Tufts University (1973); Postgraduate Coursework, University of Paris (1965); BA, Iowa State University of Science and Technology (1965); AA, Graceland College, Lamoni, IA (1963) **Certifications:** Licensed Building Construction Supervisor, Commonwealth of Massachusetts **Career:** Director, Maine Friendship House Museum, Jaffa American Colony, Tel Aviv-Yafo, Israel (2004-Present); President, Keshet Hashalom, Jerusalem, Israel (1989-Present); Educational Tour Organizer (1983-Present); President, Manager, Viewpax Mondiale, Independence, MO (1982-Present); Real Estate Broker, Carter Realty, Pepperell, MA (1975-Present); Teacher, French, Iowa and Massachusetts (1966-1969); Teacher, English Language and Literature, Iowa (1966-1967) **Career Related:** Director, Adjunct Professor, Student Intercultural Travel to Israel, Jordan, and Egypt, Park University, Graceland University (1982-Present); International Holocaust Scholars Conference, Minneapolis, MN (1996); Lecturer, Remembering for the Future II, Berlin, Germany (1994); President, Central Middlesex Multiple Listing Service, Concord, MA (1983); Vice President, Central Middlesex Multiple Listing Service, Concord, MA (1982); Clerk, Central Middlesex Multiple Listing Service, Concord, MA (1980-1981) **Civic:** Director, Maine Friendship House (2003-Present); Executive Committee, National Christian Leadership Conference for Israel (2001-2008); Interfaith Relations Committee, Community of Christ, Independence, MO (2000-2004); Advisory Board, Peace Center, Independence, MO (1989-1991) **Creative Works:** Co-Author, "HaNachshonim" (2003); Co-Author, "The Forerunners" (2003); Co-Author, "Israel and Post-Holocaust Christianity in Dialogue, Theology Six: Interfaith Ministry" (1998) **Awards:** Maine Preservation Award, 1866 Maine Friendship House, Jaffa American Colony (2004); Friendship Award, Israel Ministry of Tourism, Jerusalem, Israel (1992) **Membership:** Christians and Jews United for Israel **Hobbies:** Photography; Archaeology; Literature; Travel **Business Address:** PO Box 763, Pepperell, MA, 01463

Stephen Paul Holowenzak, PhD

Title: Professor Emeritus **Industry:** Education/Educational Services **Company Name:** University of Maryland University College **Date of Birth:** 11/30/1944 **Place of Birth:** Newark **State:** NJ **Parents:** Stephen Holowenzak; Helen Holowenzak **Marital Status:** Single **Children:** Amy Katherine **Education:** PhD in Educational Psychology and Technology, Statistics and Measurement, Catholic University of America (1974); MA in Counseling, Guidance and Personnel Management, Catholic University of America (1971); BA in Philosophy and English, Mount St. Paul College, Waukesha, WI (1967) **Career:** Honorary Professor Emeritus, University of Maryland University College, Adelphi, MD (2010-Present); Senior Trainer, University of Maryland University College, Adelphi, MD (2006-2010); Adjunct Professor of Psychology, University of Maryland University College, Adelphi, MD (2006-2010); Senior Program Manager, Faculty Services and Communication, University of Maryland University College, Largo, MD (2006-2010); Evaluator, University of Maryland University College, Adelphi, MD (2006); Candidate Selection Committee, Fulbright Program, Japan-U.S. Education Committee, Tokyo, Japan (2000-2001); Academic Director, Education and Student Teaching Services, University of Maryland University College Asia, Tokyo, Japan (1998-2006); Collegiate Professor, University of Maryland University College, Adelphi: USA, Europe, Middle East, Asia (1989-2010); Distance Educator, University of Maryland University College, Adelphi: USA, Europe, Middle East, Asia (1988-2006); Senior Trainer and Evaluator, Defense Contractor, Ford Aerospace Corporation, Hanover, MD (1985-1988); Lecturer, Education, Computer Studies and Mathematics, University of Maryland University College Europe, Heidelberg, Germany (1984-1985); Health Computer Education Coordinator, University of Maryland, Baltimore, Health Professional Schools, and Cumberland Area Health Education Center, Cumberland, MD (1983-1984) **Military Service:** U.S. Air Force; U.S. Navy; U.S. Marine Corps; Operation Desert Shield and Desert Storm; Operation Provide Comfort; Operation Northern Watch; Multi-National Force & Observers; IFOR; Operation Joint Endeavor; UMUC Operation Appreciation; Walter Reed Army Medical Center (Now Walter Reed National Military Medical Center); Malone House, Washington, DC **Creative Works:** Featured, "Over There: The Adventures of Maryland's Traveling Faculty," 70th Anniversary 1947-2017, Documentary by Maryland Public Television, University System of Maryland (2018); Editor, The Patriot (2016-2017); Featured, "The Achiever," University of Maryland University College (2014-2015); Editor, Archangel Calling Publications (2010-2015); Featured, "The Achiever," University of Maryland University College (2009-2010); Featured, "The Achiever," University of Maryland University College (1996); Featured, "A Maryland State of Mind Special: Bullets, Books and Bosnia," Documentary by Maryland Public Television, University System of Maryland (1996); Featured, "The Achiever," University of Maryland University College (1989); Principal, "9/11: We Will Never Forget"; Principal, "Stars and Stripes Forever" **Awards:** Star Assembly Award, Knights of Columbus (2017); Distinguished Worldwide Humanitarian Award (2017); Sir Knight of the Year Title Award, Master of the Fourth Degree - Patriotism, Archdiocese of Washington District (2017); Past Faithful Navigators Award (2016-2017); Recognition, Knights of Columbus Council 15084 (2015); Excellence Awards, Church, Council, Family, Community, Culture of Life, Youth Services and General Programs, Knights of Columbus, Maryland State Council (2014-2015); Past Grand Knight Award (2014-2015); Award, Commitment and Dedicated Service for More than 20 Years to Military Personnel Around the Globe, University of Maryland University College (2009); American Educational Research Association (1980); General Programs of Excellence Award, Knights of Columbus Council 15084 **Membership:** Past Faithful Navigator, Knights of Columbus Fourth Degree Assembly 386, New Haven, CT (2017-Present); Chief Executive Officer, Knights of Columbus Fourth Degree Assembly 386, New Haven, CT (2017-Present); Contributor to Works, Franciscan Monastery of the Holy Land in America (2016-Present); Past Grand Knight, Knights of Columbus Council 15084 (2014-Present); Faithful Admiral, Knights of Columbus Fourth Degree Assembly 386, New Haven, CT (2017-2018); Faithful Navigator, Knights of Columbus Fourth Degree Assembly 386, Patriotically Promoting Our Faith, Walking Humbly with God, New Haven, CT (2016-2017); Grand Knight, Knights of Columbus Council 15084 (2014-2015); Chief Executive Officer, Knights of Columbus Council 15084 (2014-2015); Ministry Member, Apostleship of the Sea, Archdiocese of Baltimore (2012-2015); Overseas Marylanders of University of Maryland University College, European and Asian Division Association - "Global Academic Professors without Boundaries (Now USA-UMUC Academic Foreign Legion); Charter Member, 9/11 Memorial **Marquis Who's Who Honors:** Distinguished Humanitarian (2017) **Hobbies:** Travel; Photography; Hiking **Religion:** Roman Catholic **Business Address:** 3501 University Boulevard E, Adelphi, MD, 20783-8003 **Shipping Address:** 1110 Fidler Lane, Apt. 403, Silver Spring, MD, 20910

Ole Rudolf Holsti

Title: Political Scientist, Educator **Industry:** Education/Educational Services **Date of Birth:** 08/07/1933 **Place of Birth:** Geneva **Country of Origin:** Switzerland **Parents:** Rudolf Waldemar Holsti; Liisa (Franssila) Holsti **Spouse Name:** Ann Wood (9/20/1953, Deceased 2006) **Children:** Eric Lynn; Maija **Education:** PhD in Political Science, Stanford University (1962); MA in Teaching, Wesleyan University, Middletown, CT (1956); BA, Stanford University, with Highest Honors (1954) **Career:** Emeritus Professor, Duke University (2010-Present); Professor, Department of Political Science, University of California, Davis (1978-1979); Chairman, Department of Political Science, Duke University (1977-1983); George V. Allen Professor, Political Science, Duke University (1974-2010); Professor, The University of British Columbia, Vancouver, Canada (1971-1974); Associate Professor, The University of British Columbia, Vancouver, Canada (1967-1971); Instructor, Assistant Professor, Political Science, Stanford University (1962-1967); Research Coordinator, Stanford University (1962-1967) **Career Related:** Co-Director, Triangle University Security Seminar, Duke University (1983-1998); Member, Advisory Committee, Historic Diplomatic Documentation, United States Department of State (1983-1986); Member, Oversight Committee, National Science Foundation (1981-1984) **Military Service:** Fourth Infantry Division, US Army (1956-1958) **Creative Works:** Editor, Board of Editors, International Studies Perspectives (1999-Present); Advisory Board, University Press of America (1976-Present); Author, "When Great Powers Invade Small Countries: The Issue of War Crimes" (2015); Author, "Public Participation in Foreign Policy" (2012); Author, "Public Opinion and International Intervention" (2012); Author, "American Public Opinion on the Iraq War" (2011); Author, "To See Ourselves as Others See Us: How Publics Abroad View the US Since 9/11" (2009); Author, "Making American Foreign Policy" (2006); Co-Author, "On The Cutting Edge of Globalization" (2005); Author, "Public Opinion and American Foreign Policy" (2004); Co-Author, "Explaining the History of American Foreign Relations, Second Edition" (2004); Co-Author, "Millennial Reflections on International Studies" (2002); Co-Producer, "Eagle Rules: Foreign Policy and American Primacy in the 21st Century" (2001); Co-Author, "Soldiers and Civilians: The Civil-Military Gap and American National Security" (2001); Co-Producer, American Democracy Promotion (2000); Co-Author, "Pondering Postinternationalism" (2000); Co-Author, "The New International Studies Classroom" (2000); Co-Author, "Encyclopedia of United States Foreign Relations" (1997); Author, "Public Opinion and American Foreign Policy" (1996); Co-Author, "Diplomacy, Force and Leadership" (1993); Editor, Board of Editors, Journal of Politics (1991-2000); Co-Author, "Explaining the History of American Foreign Relations" (1991); Co-Author, "Psychological Dimensions of War" (1991); Co-Author, "Soviet-American Relations After the Cold War" (1991); Co-Author, "Behavior, Society and Nuclear War" (1989); Co-Author, "Containment" (1986); Corresponding Editor, Running Journal (1984-2010); Author, "American Leadership in World Affairs: The Vietnam and Breakdown of Consensus" (1984); Correspondent, Racing South (1983-1987); Author, "Change in the International System" (1980); Co-Author, "Challenges to America" (1979); Co-Author, "Diplomacy" (1979); Co-Author, "The Behavior of Nations" (1976); Co-Author, "World Politics" (1976); Co-Author, "Political Science Annual" (1975); Co-Author, "Thought and Action in Foreign Policy" (1975); Board of Editors, American Journal of Political Science (1975-1980); Author, "Unity and Disintegration in International Alliances: Comparative Studies" (1973); Author, "Crisis Escalation War" (1972); Co-Author, "International Crises" (1972); Associate Editor, Western Political Quarterly (1970-1979); **Awards:** Eponym, Ole R. Holsti Distinguished Scholar Award, International Studies Association (2014); Recipient, Dave Smith Award, Carolina Godiva Track Club (2007); Recipient, Best Foreign Policy Paper Award, American Political Science Association (2004); Recipient, All-American Award, USATF Masters (2002); Recipient, All-American Award, USATF Masters (2000); Recipient, Teacher Scholar Award, International Studies Association (2000); Recipient, Distinguished Lifetime Achievement Award, American Political Science Association (1999); Grantee, National Science Foundation (1996-1998); Recipient, Alumni Distinguished Undergraduate Teaching Award (1995); Grantee, National Science Foundation (1992-1995); Champion, Triple Crown Race (1992-1993); Pew Faculty Fellow, Harvard University (1990); Distinguished Teachers Award, Howard Johnson (1990); Grantee, National Science Foundation (1988-1990); Recipient, Nevitt H. Sanford Award, International Society of Political Psychology (1988); Champion, Men 50-59, National Champion Cross Country Team (1988); Champion, Tar Heel Running Tour (1987); Runner of the Year Award, Carolina Godiva Track Club (1985); Grantee, National Science Foundation (1983-1985); Guggenheim Fellow (1981-1982) **Marquis Who's Who Honors:** Albert Nelson Marquis Lifetime Achievement Award (2017) **Hobbies:** Running; Competitive race walking **Shipping Address:** 1878 Harvard Ave, Salt Lake City, UT, 84108

Robert Neil Nehemiah Holtzman

Title: Neurosurgeon **Industry:** Medicine & Health Care **Company Name:** Neurological Surgery, P.C. **Date of Birth:** 08/11/1941 **Place of Birth:** Brooklyn **State:** NY **Parents:** Sidney Holtzman; Filia Esther (Ravitz/Ravicher) Holtzman **Marital Status:** Married **Spouse Name:** Li Li Holtzman **Children:** Maia Merav; Jonathan Nisson; Matthew Isaac; Sidney Isaiah **Education:** Resident in Neurosurgery, Neurological Institute of New York, Columbia University (1973-1977); Resident in General Surgery, Harbor UCLA Medical Center (1972-1973); Resident in Neurology, Neurological Institute of New York, Columbia University (1970-1972); Rotating Intern, Harlem Hospital Center, City of New York (1969-1970); MD, Columbia University College of Physicians and Surgeons (1969); AB, Harvard College (1964) **Certifications:** Diplomate, American Board of Neurological Surgery (1980); Diplomate, American Board of Psychiatry and Neurology, Inc. (1978) **Career:** Attendant, St. Francis Hospital, Catholic Health Services of Long Island (2012-Present); Attendant, South Nassau Communities Hospital (2011-Present); Attendant, Mercy Medical Center, Catholic Health Services of Long Island (2011-Present); Attendant, NYU Winthrop Hospital (2011-Present); Attendant, St. Joseph Hospital, Catholic Health Services of Long Island (2011-Present); Attending Neurosurgeon, Lincoln Hospital, City of New York (2001-2012); Attendant in Neurosurgery, Lenox Hill Hospital, Northwell Health (2000-2012); Attending Neurosurgeon, Metropolitan Hospital, City of New York (2000-2009); Attending Neurosurgeon, Harlem Hospital, City of New York (1999-2010); Attending Neurosurgeon, Cabrini Medical Center (1999-2008); Chief of Neurosurgery, Cabrini Medical Center (1999-2007); Assistant in Neurosurgery, Harlem Hospital, City of New York (1997-1983); Associate Attendant in Neurosurgery, NewYork-Presbyterian Hospital (1996-2010); Associate Clinical Professor of Neurological Surgery, Columbia University (1996-2010); Associate Attending Neurosurgeon, Cabrini Medical Center (1996-1999); Assistant Neurosurgeon, Cabrini Medical Center (1994-1996); Associate Attendant in Neurosurgery, Lenox Hill Hospital, Northwell Health (1992-1999); Attending Staff, Astoria General Hospital (1991-1992); Assistant Attendant in Neurosurgery, NewYork-Presbyterian Hospital (1990-1996); Assistant Clinical Professor of Neurological Surgery, Columbia University (1990-1996); Assistant Attendant, Mary Immaculate Hospital (1987-1992); Neurosurgical Adjunct, Lenox Hill Hospital, Northwell Health (1987-1992); Assistant Attendant, Jamaica Hospital (1987-1992); Assistant Attendant, St. John's Medical Center (1985-1992); Associate Attending Neurosurgeon, Harlem Hospital, City of New York (1984-1998); Clinical Assistant Professor of Neurosurgery, SUNY Downstate Medical Center (1983-1991); Assistant Attending Neurosurgeon, Harlem Hospital, City of New York (1983-1984); Assistant Attending Neurosurgeon, Mount Sinai Beth Israel, Icahn School of Medicine at Mount Sinai (1982-2002); Lecturer in Neurosurgery, Icahn School of Medicine at Mount Sinai (1980-2002); Instructor in Clinical Neurosurgery, Columbia University (1980-1990); Assistant Attendant, Maimonides Medical Center (1978-1993); Assistant in Neurosurgery, Caledonian Hospital (1978-1988); Assistant in Neurosurgery, Victory Memorial Hospital (1978-1987); Assistant Attendant, Coney Island Hospital (1977-1988); Assistant in Neurosurgery, Maimonides Medical Center (1977-1980); Clinical Assistant in Neurosurgery, Mount Sinai Medical Center, Icahn School of Medicine at Mount Sinai (1977-1980); Lecturer in Neurosurgery, Harlem Hospital, City of New York (1977-1980); Instructor in Neurosurgery, Icahn School of Medicine at Mount Sinai (1977-1980) **Career Related:** Co-Chairman, New York Chapter of the National Council, Jackson Laboratory, Bar Harbor, ME (2008); Co-Founder, Ronald H. Winston Travelling Fellowship (1986); Co-Director, Stonwin Medical Conference (1984-1991); Co-Founder, Stonwin Medical Conference (1983-1991) **Civic:** Board of Directors, World Jewish Congress Foundation (2009-2013) **Creative Works:** Author, "Carcinoembryonic Antigen Immunostaining in Benign Multicystic Mesothelioma of the Peritoneum," Archives of Pathology & Laboratory Medicine (2001); Author, "Lobular Capillary Hemangioma of the Cauda Equina," Journal of Neurosurgery" (1999); Editor, "Endovascular Interventional Neuroradiology" (1995); Editor, Contributor, "Spinal Instability" (1993); Editor, Contributor, "Surgery of the Spinal Cord: The Potential for Regeneration and Recovery" (1991); Editor, "Surgery of the Diencephalon" (1989); Editor, Contributor, "The Tethered Spinal Cord" (1985) **Membership:** New York Society for Neurosurgery; New York State Neurosurgical Society; American Association of Neurological Surgeons; The Medical Society of the State of New York; Nassau County Medical Society **Marquis Who's Who Honors:** Albert Nelson Marquis Lifetime Achievement Award (2017) **Hobbies:** Commercial piloting; Acrobatics in a decathalon taildragger; Snap roll acrobatics; Linked hammerhead stall acrobatics; Skiing; Squash; Scuba diving **Political Affiliations:** Democrat **Religion:** Jewish **Shipping Address:** 1815 Ditmas Avenue, Brooklyn, NY, 11226 **Website:** https://nspc.com/physician/robert-holtzman

James C. Hopkins III

Title: Trial Attorney and Owner **Industry:** Law and Legal Services **Company Name:** James Hopkins Law Firm **Parents:** J. Clancy Hopkins, Jr.; Margaret O'Connor Hopkins **Marital Status:** Married **Spouse Name:** Rosanne Pennisi Hopkins **Children:** Heather; Courtney; J. Conor **Education:** JD, Syracuse University College of Law (1978); Bachelor of Arts in Government, St. Lawrence University (1975) **Career:** Owner and Trial Attorney, James Hopkins Law Firm (1988-Present); Onondaga County Assistant District Attorney (1981-1987); Trial Attorney, Hopkins Law Firm (1979-1981) **Career Related:** Franciscan Legal Clinic Pro Bono Lawyer; Legal Counsel for Syracuse Citizen Review Board of Police Misconduct **Civic:** President, Most Holy Rosary School PTO; South Side American League Coach; Christian Brothers Academy Wrestling Coach; Syracuse University Alumni Association, SLU Alumni Association; CBA Alumni Association **Awards:** Named to National Trial Lawyers Top 100, The National Trial Lawyers (2014-2017); Top 10 Lawyers for Client Satisfaction, The American Institute of Criminal Law Attorneys; New York State Youth Courts Certificate; Varsity Letter Recipient, St. Lawrence University; Coach of the Year, South Side American League **Membership:** American Bar Association; New York State Bar Association; Onondaga County Bar Association; National Trial Lawyers; American Institute of Criminal Law Attorneys; American Trial Lawyers Association; International Narcotics Enforcement Officers Association; Beta Theta Pi Fraternity **Bar Admissions:** New York; United States District Court, Northern District of New York **To what do you attribute your success:** He attributes his success to his insight, tenacity and experience, which he gained over decades practicing law, and to his ability to craft novel solutions to complicated issues. He loves the challenge of the courtroom, and in preparation for trial. **Why did you become involved in your profession or industry:** He became involved in his profession because family members had been stymied in their quest for justice. He has an affinity for research and writing, and eclectic interests, which had led him to try novel approaches to problem solving. Moreover, the competitive nature of trial law continues to hold an appeal for him. **Where will you be in five years:** In five years, Mr. Hopkins hopes to still be an effective litigator and confidante. **Shipping Address:** 217 Montgomery St., Ste 1200, James Hopkins Law Firm, Syracuse, NY, 13202 **Website:** http://jameshopkinslawfirm.com

William K. Hoskins

Title: President **Industry:** Law and Legal Services **Company Name:** Hoskins & Associates **Date of Birth:** 02/22/1935 **Place of Birth:** Cincinnati **State/Country of Origin:** OH **Parents:** John Hobart Hoskins; Gertrude Louise (Keller) Hoskins **Marital Status:** Married **Spouse Name:** Elizabeth Ann Grimm (8/5/1961) **Children:** Bruce; Andrew; John; Elizabeth; Allison **Education:** LLB, Harvard University (1962); BA, Yale University (1956) **Career:** Partner, Resolution Strategies LLP, Portland, OR (2008-Present); President, Hoskins & Associates, Boston, MA (1998-Present); Special Counsel, Bristol Myers and Company (Now Bristol-Meyers Squibb) New York, NY (1982-Present); Managing Partner, Resolution Counsel LLP, Portland, OR (2002-2007); Co-general Counsel, Hoechst Marion Roussel (1995-1997); Vice President, General Counsel, Marion Merrell Dow (1982-1995); Associate General Counsel, Bristol Myers and Company (1981-1982); Vice President, General Counsel, The Drackett Company, Cincinnati, OH (1971-1981); General Counsel, The Drackett Company (1968-1971); Associate, Frost & Jacobs, Cincinnati, OH (1962-1968) **Career Related:** Board of Directors, Ferrellgas Inc., Kansas City, MO (2003-2011); Chairman, J.C. Nichols, Inc., Kansas City, MO (1997-1999); Chairman, Chemical Specialties Manufacturing Association, Washington (1982); Chairman, Household Division, Soap and Detergent Association, New York, NY (1978-1979) **Civic:** Vice Chairman, Landmark Legal Foundation, Kansas City, MO (2001-2003); Board of Directors Landmark Legal Foundation (1995-2003); Secretary-Treasurer, Marion Laboratories Political Action Committee (1982-1989); Secretary-Treasurer, Political Action Committee, Mid-American Committee for Sound Government, Lake Quivira, KS (1982-1986); Member, Hamilton County Republican Central Committee (1970-1981) **Military Service:** Lieutenant Junior Grade, U.S. Navy (1956-1959) **Membership:** Board of Directors, Harvard Law School Alumni Association (1991-1995); Harvard Law School Alumni Association; The Missouri Bar; Ohio State Bar Association; New York State Bar Association; Cincinnati Bar Association **Bar Admissions:** Missouri Board Of Law Examiners (1983); The New York State Board Of Law Examiners (1982); United States Court Appeals for the Sixth Circuit (1964); United States District Court Southern District of Ohio (1963); United States Tax Court (1963); The Supreme Court Of Ohio (1962) **Marquis Who's Who Honors:** Albert Nelson Marquis Lifetime Achievement Award (2017) **Religion:** Roman Catholic **Business Address:** 27 Harvest Cir, Lincoln, MA, 01773 **Shipping Address:** 79 Rachels Way, Vineyard Haven, MA, 02568 **Website:** http://resolutionstrategies.com/index.html

Gilbert J. Houseaux

Title: Associate Broker **Industry:** Real Estate **Company Name:** Russ Lyon Sotheby's International Realty **State/Country of Origin:** France **Marital Status:** Married **Spouse Name:** Virginia Gee **Children:** Angelique **Education:** Degree in Mathematics, University of Bordeaux, France (1968) **Certifications:** Real Estate License; Martial Arts Grand Master; Licensed Private Eye **Career:** Associate Broker, Russ Lyon Sotheby's International Realty (2012-Present); Associate Broker, Coldwell Banker Residential Brokerage (1984-2012) **Career Related:** Affiliate, Merrill Lynch; Math Teacher, France; Private Investigator; Manager, Nightclub/Restaurant **Civic:** Community Emergency Response Team **Military Service:** French Armed Forces **Creative Works:** Actor, Producer, "A Dozen Ways to Die!!" (1990); Producer, Actor, Films **Awards:** Inductee, Karate & Kickboxing Hall of Fame, Ohio Judo and Karate Association (2015); Top Realtor Award **Membership:** Leading Edge Society; National Association of Realtors; SAG-AFTRA; DKI; Service Corporation International **Marquis Who's Who Honors:** Albert Nelson Marquis Lifetime Achievement Award (2017) **To what do you attribute your success:** Mr. Houseaux attributes his success to hard work, enjoying interactions with others, and his worldly experience. **What do you consider to be the highlight of your career:** The highlight of Mr. Houseaux's career was being recognized as the top realtor in the state. **Where will you be in five years:** In five years, Mr. Houseaux thinks he will be retired. **Hobbies:** Martial arts; Outdoors; Reading; Training; Acting **Religion:** Christian **Shipping Address:** 6900 E Camelback Road, Suite 110, Russ Lyon Sotheby's, Scottsdale, AZ, 85251

C. Stuart Houston

Title: Radiologist **Industry:** Medicine & Health Care **Company Name:** University of Saskatchewan **Date of Birth:** 09/26/1927 **Place of Birth:** Williston **State:** ND **Parents:** Clarence Joseph Houston; Sigridur (Christianson) Houston **Marital Status:** Married **Spouse Name:** Mary Isabel Belcher (8/12/1951) **Children:** Stanley; Margaret; David; Donald **Education:** DLitt, University of Saskatchewan, Saskatoon, Canada (1987); Teaching Fellow, Radiology, University of Saskatchewan (1963-1964); MD, University of Manitoba, Winnipeg, Canada (1951) **Career:** Professor Emeritus, University of Saskatchewan (1995-Present); Head, Department of Medical Imaging, University of Saskatchewan (1982-1987); Professor, University of Saskatchewan (1969-1995); Associate Professor, University of Saskatchewan (1967-1969); Assistant Professor, University of Saskatchewan (1965-1967); Lecturer, University of Saskatchewan (1964-1965); Demonstrator in Anatomy, University of Saskatchewan (1960-1961) **Creative Works:** Co-Author with Alan R. Smith and J. Frank Roy, "Birds of Saskatchewan. Regina: Nature Saskatchewan" (2018); Co-Author with Merle Massie, "36 Steps on the Road to Medicare: How Saskatchewan Led," University Press, McGill-Queen's University (2013); Co-Author with Bill Waiser, "Tommy's Team: The People Behind the Douglas Years" (2010); Co-Author with T. Ball and M. Houston, "Eighteenth-Century Naturalists of Hudson Bay" (2003); Co-Author with W. Anakam, "Birds of Yorkton-Duck Mountain" (2003); Co-Author with A.L. Leighton, J. Hay, J.F. Roy and S.J. Shadick, "Birds of the Saskatoon Area. Regina: Saskatchewan Natural History Society, Special Publication" (2002); Author, "Steps on the Road to Medicare: Why Saskatchewan Led the Way" (2002); Author, "Arctic Artist, the Journal and Paintings of George Back, Midshipman with Franklin, 1819-1822" (1994); Author, R.G. Ferguson: Crusader Against Tuberculosis," Hannah Institute & Dundurn Press (1991); Author, "Arctic Ordeal, The Journal of John Richardson, Surgeon-Naturalist with Franklin, 1820-1822" (1984); Editor, Journal, Canadian Association of Radiologists (1976-1981); Co-Author with C. J. Houston, "Pioneer of Vision. The Memoirs of Dr. T.A. Patrick," Western Producer Prairie Books (1980); Author, "Nature Saskatoon, an Account of the Saskatoon Natural History Society, 1955-1980" (1980) **Awards:** Queen's Diamond Jubilee Medal (2012); Shortlist, Canadian History Award, Canadian Author's Association (2011); Stuart Houston Award for Medical Imaging Research, University of Saskatchewan (2011); Honoree, National Philanthropy Day Luncheon, University of Saskatchewan Library (2010); Champion of Owls Award, World Owl Hall of Fame, Center for Biological Diversity (2008); Guest Speaker, Fifth Annual Golden Heart Dinner, McClure Place Foundation (2007); Keynote Speaker, White Coat Ceremony, Convocation Hall, University of Saskatchewan (2006); Centennial Leadership Award, Honorable David Forbes, Saskatchewan Minister of the Environment, Regina (2005); Honorary Member, Canadian Society for the History of Medicine (2005); Honorary Member, Saskatoon Nature Society (2005); Invitee, Royal Centennial Luncheon (2005); Commemorative Medal for the Centennial of Saskatchewan, Lieutenant Governor Lynda Haverstock (2005); Marion Jenkinson Service Award, American Ornithologists' Union (2004); Frances Hamerstrom Award, Raptor Research Foundation (2003); Queen's Golden Jubilee Medal and Certificate (2002); Honorary Doctor of Canon Law, College of Emmanuel and St. Chad (2002); Gold Medal, Canadian Association of Radiologists (1997); Regional History Certificate of Merit, Canadian Historical Association (1995); Honorary President, Student Medical Society, University of Saskatchewan (1973-1974, 1987-1988, 1994-1995); John B. Neilson Award, Associated Medical Services, Inc./Hannah Institute for the History of Medicine (1993); Officer, Order of Canada (1993); Canada 125 Medal, Premier Roy Romanow (1993); Honorary President, Saskatchewan Natural History Society (1993-1997); Invested, Saskatchewan Order of Merit, Lieutenant Governor Sylvia Fedoruk (1992); Initiated, Walter Murray Society, University of Saskatchewan (1992); Ken More Award, Saskatchewan Lung Association (1992); Eugene Eisenmann Medal, New York Linnean Society (1990); Doris Huestis Speris Award, Canadian Society of Ornithologists, Pittsburgh, PA (1989); Elected Fellow, American Ornithologists' Union, Pittsburgh, PA (1989); Prairie Conservation Award, World Wildlife Fund (1989); Douglas H. Pimlott Conservation Award, Canadian Nature Federation (1988); Fellow, Saskatchewan Natural History Society (1987); Sigma Xi Lecturer, Great Horned Owls, Mayo Clinic, Rochester, MN (1986); Roland Michener Conservation Award, Canadian Wildlife Federation (1986); Research Award, North American Bluebird Society (1985); Chairman, Memorials Committee, American Ornithologists' Union (1984-2004); Member, Council, Royal College of Physicians and Surgeons of Canada (1984-1990) **Marquis Who's Who Honors:** Distinguished Humanitarian (2017) **Hobbies:** Bird banding **Political Affiliations:** New Democratic Party (NDP) **Business Address:** 607-1223 Temperance St, SK, Saskatoon, Canada, S7N 0P2

Yiwu Huang

Industry: Medicine & Health Care **Company Name:** Maimonides Cancer Center **Date of Birth:** 10/28/1963 **Place of Birth:** Quanzhou **Country of Origin:** Fujian/China **Parents:** Rongsheng Huang; Lan C. Huang **Education:** Hematology-Oncology Fellowship, Cancer Institute of New Jersey, Robert Wood Johnson Medical School, University of Medicine and Dentistry of New Jersey, New Brunswick, NJ (2000-2003); Internal Medicine Residency, Staten Island University Hospital, New York (1997-2000); MD in Cancer Immunology, Graduate School of Peking, Union Medical College and Chinese Academy of Medical Sciences, Beijing, China (1989); Resident Physician, Peking Union Medical College Hospital, Chinese Academy of Medical Science, Beijing, China (1984-1989); MB, Fujian Medical University, China (1984) **Certifications:** Certificate of Qualification as a Laboratory Director for Hematology, New York State Department of Health (2004-Present); New York State Medical License (2003-Present); Certified, Hematology Board (2003-Present); Certified, Medical Oncology Board (2003-Present); New Jersey State Medical License (2001-Present); Certified, Internal Medicine Board (2000-Present); Permanent ECFMG Certificate **Career:** Adjunct Associate Professor of Medicine, SUNY Downstate Medical Center (2016-Present); Program Director, Hematology/Oncology Fellowship Program, Maimonides Medical Center, Brooklyn, NY (2016-Present); Associate Professor of Clinical Medicine, Department of Medicine, Albert Einstein College of Medicine (2013-Present); Medical Director, Asian Community Outreach, Maimonides Medical Center (2013-Present); Attending Physician, Division of Hematology and Medical Oncology, Department of Medicine, Maimonides Medical Center, Brooklyn, NY (2003-Present); Assistant Professor of Medicine, Department of Medicine, SUNY Downstate Medical Center (2009-2013); Associate Program Director, Hematology/Oncology Fellowship Program, Maimonides Medical Center, Brooklyn, NY (2006-2016); Assistant Professor of Medicine, Department of Medicine, Mount Sinai School of Medicine, New York, NY (2005-2013); Director of Clinical Research, Division of Hematology and Medical Oncology, Department of Medicine, Maimonides Medical Center, Brooklyn, NY (2004-2006); Assistant Program Director, Hematology/Oncology Fellowship Program, Department of Medicine, Maimonides Medical Center, Brooklyn, NY (2004-2005); Instructor, Cancer Immunobiology Center, Department of Microbiology, University of Texas Southwestern Medical School (1992-1997); Assistant Instructor, Cancer Immunobiology Center, Department of Microbiology, University of Texas Southwestern Medical School, Dallas, TX (1990-1992) **Career Related:** Guest Professor, Second Affiliated Hospital of Fujian Medical University, Quanzhou City, China (2013-Present); Guest Professor, Fujian Medical University, China (2000-Present) **Civic:** Vice President, American Association, Fujian Medical University Alumni (2004-Present) **Creative Works:** Editorial Board, Annals of Carcinogenesis, New Jersey (2016-Present); Editorial Board, Austin Hematology, Austin Publishing Group, New Jersey (2016-Present); Editorial Board, Journal, Austin Medical Sciences, New Jersey (2015-Present); Media Expert Interview on New Treatment for Lung Cancer, British Broadcasting Cooperation (2006); Media Expert Interview on New Advances for Colon Cancer, British Broadcasting Cooperation (2005); Media Expert Interview on Colon Cancer, Voices of America (VOA), Washington, DC (2005); Media Expert Interview on New Advances for Breast Cancer, British Broadcasting Cooperation (2005); Media Expert Interview on New Treatment for Cancer, British Broadcasting Cooperation, London, UK (2004); Media Expert Interview on Colon Cancer, AM1489 Radio Broadcasting, New York (2003) **Awards:** Honorary Associate Director, Fujian Institute of Hematology, Fujin Medical University, China (2005-Present); Excellence in Community Service Award, Chinese-American Planning Council of New York (2014); Honoree, Doctor of the Year, Maimonides Cancer Center (2010); Honoree, Outstanding Alumni, 70th Anniversary of Fujian Medical University, China (2007); Honoree, Outstanding Alumni, American Association of Fujian Medical University Alumni (2006); First Place in Clinical Vignette Division, Associates Abstract Competition, American College of Physicians-American Society of Internal Medicine (ACP-ASIM), New York Chapter (2000); Honoree, Finalist in Associates Research Competition, American College of Physicians-American Society of Internal Medicine (ACP-ASIM), Philadelphia (2000); Resident Physician Dedicated to Research Award, Staten Island University Hospital (2000) **Membership:** American Society of Clinical Oncology; American Society of Hematology; Lifetime Member, Chinese American Hematologist/Oncologist Network **Marquis Who's Who Honors:** Albert Nelson Marquis Lifetime Achievement Award (2017); Distinguished Humanitarian (2017) **Business Address:** 6300 8th Avenue, Brooklyn, NY, 11220 **Shipping Address:** 367 Ramona Avenue, Staten Island, NY, 10312

Marianne J. Huber

Title: Art Dealer **Industry:** Fine Art **Company Name:** New World Art Services **Date of Birth:** 06/09/1936 **State/Country of Origin:** IL **Parents:** John Francis Faivre; Jeannette Marie (Wurth) Faivre **Marital Status:** Married **Spouse Name:** Robert L. Huber (10/3/1959) **Children:** Michael Robert; Stephan Louis; Edward Francis **Education:** BA, Cardinal Stritch University, Milwaukee, WI (1958) **Certifications:** Certified, Appraisers Association of America **Career:** Expert, Heritage Auctions (2010-Present); Founder, President, New World Art Services, New York, NY (1993-Present); Founder, President, New World Art Services, Dixon, IL (1993-Present); Art Dealer, Consultant, Appraiser, Huber Primitive Art, New York, NY (1963-Present); Art Dealer, Consultant, Appraiser, Huber Primitive Art, Dixon, IL (1963-Present); Teacher, The Garside School, Mexico City, Mexico (1959-1961); Teacher, Sixth Grade, St. Andrew Catholic Grade School (1958-1959) **Career Related:** Participant, Maya Meetings, Austin, TX (1985-Present); Affiliate, Naprstek Museum, Prague, Czech Republic (1995); Affiliate, Indianapolis Museum of Art (1994); Affiliate, Freeport Art Museum, Freeport, IL (1993); Lecturer, Primitive Art Society, Chicago, IL (1987); Consultant, Primitive Art Society, Chicago, IL (1987) **Civic:** Committeewoman, Democratic Precinct (2002-Present); Election Judge, Ogle County, IL (1993-Present) **Creative Works:** Translator, "The Frida Kahlo Papers" (2007); Author, "The Maya Calendar" (2003-2009); Co-Producer, "The Maya Calendar" (2003-2009); Co-Producer, "Nebaj, Cotzal and Chajul" (1987); Author, "Nebaj, Cotzal and Chajul" (1987); Author, "Echoes of a Distant Flute" (1984); Contributor, "The Cuna" (1980); Author, Numerous Exhibitions; Co-Producer, Numerous Exhibitions **Membership:** Library Board, National Museum of Women in the Arts (2005-Present); Governor, International Platform Association (1993-2001); League of Women Voters; AAUW, National Women's History Museum; Appraisers Association of America; American Society of Appraisers; Phidian Society; Illinois Democratic Women; The Metropolitan Museum of Art; Delta Epsilon Sigma **To what do you attribute your success:** Ms. Huber attributes her success to Linda Schele and a lot of other people at The University of Texas who helped her and taught her how to read hieroglyphics. **Why did you become involved in your profession or industry:** She became involved in her profession because she married a man who loved Mexico and Mexican art, and they decided to move there so he could go to school at Mexico City College. **What do you consider to be the highlight of your career:** The highlight of her career was giving someone an appraisal of something that was worth much more than they thought it was worth. **Where will you be in five years:** In five years, she plans to continue acting as an art dealer, appraiser, consultant and lecturer. **Hobbies:** Hiking; Wilderness camping; Painting; Piano; Travel **Political Affiliations:** Democrat **Shipping Address:** 1012 Timber Trail Dr, Dixon, IL, 61021 **Website:** https://www.linkedin.com/in/mariannehuber

David M. Hudiak

Title: Partner **Industry:** Law and Legal Services **Company Name:** DD&E Group,. LLC **Date of Birth:** 06/27/1953 **Place of Birth:** Darby **State/Country of Origin:** PA **Parents:** Michael Paul Hudiak; Sophie Marie (Glowaski) Hudiak **Marital Status:** Married **Spouse Name:** Veronica Ann Barbone (8/28/1982) **Children:** David Michael; Christopher Andrew; Jonathan Joseph **Education:** JD, University of Pennsylvania (1978); BA, Haverford College (1975) **Career:** Consultant, Dalucci Design Co. LLC (2012-Present); Partner, DD and E. Group LLC (2011-Present); Special Assistant, Office of the President, Prism Education Group (2008-2011); Regional Vice President, Prism Education Group (2007-2008); Campus President, PJA School, Upper Darby, PA (2006-2007); Vice President, Secretary-Treasurer, Board of Directors, 7900 West Chester Pike Corporation (1994-2012); Vice President, PJA School, Upper Darby, PA (1989-2006); Director, PJA School, Upper Darby, PA (1989-2006); Acting Director, PJA School, Upper Darby, PA (1983-1989); Director, Training Paralegal Program, PJA School, Upper Darby, PA (1982-2005); Private Practice, Aldan, PA (1980-1981); Associate, Berson, Fineman & Bernstein, Philadelphia, PA (1979-1980); Associate, Jerome H. Ellis, Philadelphia, PA (1978-1979); Board of Directors, PJA School, Upper Darby, PA (1989-2006) **Career Related:** Instructor, Law and American History, Osher Lifelong Learning Institute, Widener University (2017-Present); Instructor, Villanova University, Pennsylvania (1985); Member, Staff, National Center for Educational Testing, Philadelphia, PA (1982-1987) **Civic:** Member, Tenth Synod for the Archdiocese of Philadelphia (2002); Member, The University of Pennsylvania's Light Opera Company (1977-1984); Active Member, Havertown Choristers; Active Member, Financial Committee, Saint Eugene Church; Active Member, Parish Council, Saint Eugene Church; Lector, Saint Eugene Church; Cantor, Saint Eugene Church **Membership:** Dean Clinton Society, University of Pennsylvania Law School; Delco Property Investors; Sharpless Society, Haverford College; Founders Club, Haverford College **Bar Admissions:** United States District Court District of New Jersey (1981); New Jersey (1981); United States District Court Eastern District of Pennsylvania (1979); Pennsylvania (1979) **Religion:** Roman Catholic **Shipping Address:** 909 Broadway Ave, Secane, PA, 19018

Jeffry Huffman

Title: Urologist **Industry:** Medicine & Health Care **Company Name:** University of Southern California **Marital Status:** Married **Spouse Name:** Therese Huffman **Children:** Three Children **Education:** Resident in Urology, University of Chicago; Resident in General Surgery, OSF Healthcare System; Resident in Urology, Memorial Sloan Kettering Cancer Center; Intern, OSF Healthcare System; MD, Loyola University, Chicago, IL; Diplomate, Indiana University; MD, Health Sciences Division, Loyola University, Chicago, IL; Undergraduate Coursework, Indiana University **Certifications:** Diplomate, American Board of Urology **Career:** Director, Institute of Urology, University of Southern California (2007-Present); Professor, Urology, University of Southern California (1987-2007); Chief Executive Officer, USC Care Medical Group, University of Southern California; Founding President, USC Care Medical Group, University of Southern California; Senior Associate Dean, Clinical Affairs, Keck Medicine of USC **Career Related:** da Vinci Robotic Program, Memorial Sloan Kettering Cancer Center; Urological Oncologist **Military Service:** Trauma Surgeon, U.S. Air Force (2007); Urologist, Trauma Surgeon, U.S. Air Force (2007); Air Force Reserve; Colonel, 349th Medical Squadron, Travis Air Force Base; Chief of Staff, 349th Medical Squadron, Travis Air Force Base **Awards:** Best Doctors in America, Castle-Connolly Medical Ltd. (2017); Air Force Expeditionary Medal with Gold Border (2009); Air Force Expeditionary Medal with Gold Border (2007); Operation Iraqi Freedom Campaign Medal; Two Meritorious Service Medals **Membership:** American Urology Association; American Board of Urology **Marquis Who's Who Honors:** Albert Nelson Marquis Lifetime Achievement Award (2017) **Business Address:** 6001B Truxtun Avenue, Bakersfield, CA, 93307 **Shipping Address:** 702 Jasmine Parke Drive, Apt. 4, Bakersfield, CA, 93312

Robert Joe Hull

Title: Lawyer **Industry:** Law and Legal Services **Company Name:** Bracewell, LLC **Date of Birth:** 12/16/1944 **Place of Birth:** Fort Momouth **State/ Country of Origin:** NJ **Parents:** Thurman Beuford Hull; Helen Louise (Bracey) Hull **Marital Status:** Married **Spouse Name:** Susan Diane Hull (3/12/1966) **Children:** Robert Steven; L Courtney (Grandchild); Justin (Grandchild) **Education:** JD, The University of Texas at Austin (1969); BA, The University of Texas at Austin (1966) **Career:** Counsel, Bracewell, LLP (2016-Present); Partner, Bracewell LLP (1998-2016); Partner, Sheppard, Mullin, Richter & Hampton LLP (1976-1998); Associate, Sheppard, Mullin, Richter & Hampton LLP (1969-1976) **Creative Works:** Editorial Board Member, "Journal for Multistate Taxation" (1991-Present); Contributor, "Journal for Multistate Taxation" (1991-Present); Co-Author, "Representing Start-Up Companies" (1992) **Membership:** Escondido Golf & Lake Club; President, State & Local Tax Committee, ABA **Bar Admissions:** Supreme Court of the United States (1992); United States Tax Court (1971); United States District Court Central District of California (1970); United States Court of Appeals for the Ninth Circuit (1970; State of California (1970); State of Texas (1969) **Marquis Who's Who Honors:** Albert Nelson Marquis Lifetime Achievement Award (2017) **What do you consider to be the highlight of your career:** The highlight of Mr. Hull's life has been having and raising his son. **Hobbies:** Golf; Walking his Havanese dogs **Political Affiliations:** Republican **Religion:** Episcopalian **Shipping Address:** 111 Congress Ave, Ste 2300, Bracewell, LLP, Austin, TX, 78701

Marian L. Hummel

Title: Art Educator, Fine Arts Photographer, Coordinator of Gifted Education **Industry:** Education/Educational Services **Date of Birth:** 05/12/1943 **Place of Birth:** Bethlehem **State:** PA **Parents:** Donald Clare Conner; Helen Florence (Harman) Conner **Marital Status:** Widowed **Spouse Name:** Gerard G. Hummel (6/29/1998, Deceased) **Education:** Master's Degree, William Paterson University, Wayne, NJ (1991); Certificate in Photojournalism, Germain School of Photography, New York (1972); MA in Visual Arts, William Paterson University, Wayne, NJ (1971); Certificate in Commercial Photography, Germain School of Photography, New York (1971); BA in Fine Arts, Fairleigh Dickinson University (1966) **Certifications:** Certified Art Teacher, State of New Jersey; Certified Supervisor, State of New Jersey; Certified Principal, State of New Jersey **Career:** Gifted/Talented Coordinator, Boonton Township School Systems, New Jersey (1989-1999); Art Instructor, Boonton Township School Systems, New Jersey (1968-1999); Art Instructor, American Academy for Girls, Istanbul, Turkey (1967-1968); Art Teacher, Hopatcong School Systems, Lake Hopatcong, NJ (1966-1967) **Civic:** Board of Directors, Lehigh County Humane Society **Creative Works:** Photographer, Group Shows and Solo Shows, Pennsylvania and New Jersey; Artist, Photo Exhbit, Harrison Street Gallery in Frenchtown, Straub Center, Gallery of Fine Photography in Frenchtown; Artist, InVision Photo Festival, Banana Factory Gallery, Bethlehem, PA **Awards:** Grade Teacher's Award for Teaching Excellence; Outstanding Elementary Teacher of America Award; Certificate from New Jersey Department of Education for Contribution to Performance Evaluation Project **Membership:** Vice President, Negotiations Chair, Boonton Township Education Association (1989-1999); Association for Supervision and Curriculum Development; Art Educators of New Jersey; Order of the Eastern Star **Marquis Who's Who Honors:** Marquis Who's Who Lifetime Achievement Award (2017); Who's Who in America; Who's Who in American Education; Who's Who in the World; Who's Who in American Women **To what do you attribute your success:** Ms. Hummel attributes her success to her ability to focus intently on whatever she was working on at the time, which led her to research and investigate all aspects of a topic. This focus allowed her to become intimately familiar with that topic and led her to pursue her passion for knowledge. **Why did you become involved in your profession or industry:** Ms. Hummel's mother was trained as a teacher and bought her art books and encouraged her to paint. She began in the arts from a very young age. Ms. Hummel had such a great response while teaching in Turkey that it made her want to continue. **What do you consider to be the highlight of your career:** For Ms. Hummel, the highlight of her career was traveling to Turkey to teach foreign students and to experience their culture, and to see, in person, some of the things that she had studied in her art history classes. As she photographed the people of the country while she was there, Ms. Hummel developed her passion for photojournalism, which inspired her to study photography when she returned to the U.S. **Hobbies:** Landscape photography; Travel photography **Political Affiliations:** Republican **Religion:** Presbyterian **Shipping Address:** 234 Buckingham Dr, Bethelem, PA, 18017

Scott Alfred Hundahl

Title: Chief of Surgery, Professor of Surgery **Industry:** Medicine & Health Care **Company Name:** Department of Veterans Affairs, University of California, Davis **Date of Birth:** 02/01/1956 **Parents:** Robert E. Hundahl; Mariann Berg (Appley) Hundahl **Marital Status:** Married **Spouse Name:** Christine Ung (8/2/1997); Conchita Leilani Siri (5/13/1986, Divorced 1992) **Education:** Fellowship, Surgical Oncology, Memorial Sloan Kettering Cancer Center, New York, NY (1986-1988); General Surgical Resident, Hawaii Residency Programs, University of Hawaii, Honolulu, HI (1981-1986); MD, Yale School of Medicine, New Haven, CT, Cum Laude (1981); BA in Chemistry, Harvard University, Cambridge, MA, Magna Cum Laude (1977) **Certifications:** Re-Certified, American Board of Surgery, Inc. (2017); Certified, American Board of Medical Specialties (2006); Certified, American Board of Surgery, Inc. (1988) **Career:** Chief, Surgery, Department of Veteran Affairs, VA Northern California Health Care System (2002-Present); Professor, Clinical Surgery, University of California, Davis (2002-Present); Lifetime Director, Comprehensive Home Services Hawaii (Now CareResource Hawaii) (1996-Present); Chair, Commission on Cancer, American College of Surgeons, Chicago, IL (1998-2000); Chief, Surgery, The Queen's Medical Center, Honolulu, HI (1994-2000); Associate Chief, Surgery, Queen's Medical Center, Honolulu, HI (1993-1995); Private Practice, Surgical Oncology, Honolulu, HI (1988-2002); Co-Founder, Comprehensive Home Services Hawaii (Now CareResource Hawaii) (1986) **Career Related:** Lifetime Board Member, Comprehensive Home Services Hawaii (Now CareResource Hawaii) (1996-Present); Medical Director, Queen's Cancer Institute (2000-2002); Board of Governors, American College of Surgeons (1998-2002); Chair, American College of Surgeons Commission on Cancer, Chicago, IL (1998-2000); Associate Clinical Professor, Surgery, John A. Burns School of Medicine, University of Hawaii at Manoa (1996-2002); International Cancer Data Base Committee, Union Internationale Countra Le Cancer (1995-1998); Vice Chair, American College of Surgeons Commission on Cancer (1994-1998); Vice Chair, National Cancer Data Committee (1994-1996); Assistant Research Professor and Research Staff, Cancer Research Center Hawaii, Honolulu, HI (1993-2002); Assistant Professor in Surgery (1988-1993); Board of Directors, Comprehensive Home Services Hawaii (Now CareResource Hawaii) (1986-2002); Fellow, American College of Surgeons; Fellow, Society of Surgical Oncology; Fellow, American Association for the Advancement of Science; Fellow, Pacific Coast Surgical Association; Fellow, International Gastric Cancer Association; Fellow, American Head and Neck Society **Civic:** Vice Chair, Division Board of Directors, American Cancer Society, Inc. (2001-2002); Clinical Trials Working Group, American Cancer Society, Inc. (1995-2000); Governing Council, National Cancer Database (1994-2000); Vice President, Hawaii-Pacific Division, American Cancer Society, Inc. (1993-1996); President, Honolulu Unit, American Cancer Society, Inc. (1992-1993); Ad Hoc, National Task Force on Privacy of Medical Records, National Cancer Database; Division Level (Now Hi-Tex Division), American Cancer Society, Inc. **Creative Works:** Medical Editor, Journal of Registry Management (2000-2008); Author, Over 60 Journal Articles; Author, 18 Chapters; Reviewer, Multiple Professional Journals **Awards:** Best Doctors in America (1995-Present); Honorary Commander, 60th Medical Group, Travis Air Force Base (2014-2016); Joan Oettinger Memorial Award, School of Medicine, University of California, Davis (2009); Nishi Award, Best Paper in Gastric Cancer, International Gastric Cancer Association (2008); Distinguished Service Award, American College of Surgeons (2000); Best Presentation Award, WHO (1994); State Chairman of the Year, Commission on Cancer (1994); Hobart Keese Award for Best Thesis, Yale School of Medicine (1981); Top Surgeons, Consumers' Research Council of America; Distinguished Service Award as Chair of Commission on Cancer, American College of Surgeons **Membership:** Governor's Committee on Fiscal Affairs, American College of Surgeons (2001-2002); Chair Elect, Pan-Pacific Surgical Association (2000-2002); Board of Governors, American College of Surgeons (1998-2002); Congress Planning Committee, Pan-Pacific Surgical Association (1996-2002); Committee on Applicants, Hawaii Chapter, American College of Surgeons (1996-2000); Trustee, Pan-Pacific Surgical Association (1994-2004); Program Chair, General Surgery, Pan-Pacific Surgical Association (1994-2002); Executive Committee, Hawaii Chapter, American College of Surgeons (1991-2002); State Cancer Liaison Chairman for Hawaii, American College of Surgeons (1991-1998); Past President, Sacramento Surgical Society; The Pacific Club, Honolulu, HI; St. Botolph Club, Boston, MA; Nantucket Yacht Club, Nantucket, MA; UICC **Marquis Who's Who Honors:** Albert Nelson Marquis Lifetime Achievement Award (2017) **Hobbies:** Sailing **Political Affiliations:** Independent **Religion:** Episcopalian **Shipping Address:** VA Northern California HCS - Sacramento VAMC, 10535 Hospital Way, Surgical Services 112, Mather, CA, 95655

Raymond Breedlove Hunkins

Title: Lawyer, Rancher **Industry:** Law and Legal Services **Company Name:** Hunkins Newton Law **Date of Birth:** 03/19/1939 **Place of Birth:** Culver City **State/Country of Origin:** CA **Parents:** Charles F. Hunkins; Louise (Breedlove) Hunkins **Marital Status:** Married **Spouse Name:** Mary Deborah McBride (12/22/1967) **Children:** Amanda; Blake; Ashley **Education:** JD, University of Wyoming (1968); BA, University of Wyoming (1966) **Career:** Of Counsel, Hunkins Newton Law (2010-Present); Partner, Jones, Jones, Vines & Hunkins, Wheatland, WY (1968-2010) **Career Related:** Cheyenne Faculty, College of Law, Trial Institute University of Wyoming (2011-2016); Vice Chairman, Board of Directors, BH Inc. Brttz & Company (2005-2014); Founder, President, Wyoming Chapter, Federalist Society for Law and Public Policy Studies (2003-2004); Wyoming Member, Faculty, Wyoming Supreme Court Commission on Judicial Salary and Benefits (1996-1998); Western Trial Advisory Institute (1993-1995); Special Counsel, Local Rules Committee, United States District Court (1990-2012); Special Assistant, Attorney General, Wyoming General Partner, Split Rock Land & Cattle Company; Owner, Thunderhead Ranches, Albany and Platte Counties; Special Counsel, State of Wyoming **Civic:** Wyoming Delegate, Republican National Convention, Cleveland, OH (2016); President, Board of Trustees, Wyoming Stock Growers Association Land Trust (2011-2014); Chairman, Louisa Swain Foundation (2009-2010); Republican Nominee, Governor of Wyoming (2006); Wyoming Delegate, Republican National Convention, New York, NY (2004); Board of Directors, Louisa Swain Foundation (2002-2014); Republican Candidate, Governor of Wyoming (2002); Board of Directors, University of Wyoming Foundation (1996-2002); Board of Advisers, American Heritage Center (1995-1999); Board of Directors, Laramie Peak Museum (1989-2004); Commissioner, Wyoming Aeronautics Commission (1987-1998); Chairman, Advisory Council, College Commerce and Industry, University of Wyoming (1978-1979); President, Wyoming University Alumni Association (1973-1974); Representatives, Wheatland, WY (1972-1974); Member, Governor's Crime Commission (1970-1978); Chairman, Platte County **Military Service:** US Marine Corps Reserve (1956-1962); Active Duty, Marine Corps Reserve (1956-1957) **Creative Works:** Author, "Article on Henry Poling, Henry's Indomitable Spirit" (2017); Featured, Rancher in Wyoming, Range Magazine **Awards:** Recipient, Special Service Award, United States District Court (2012); Wyoming State Bar Achievement Award, Wyoming Bar Association (2008); Wyoming State Bar Leadership Award (2008); Distinguished Alumnus Award, University of Wyoming (2005); Big Horn Mountain Roundup Pax Irvine Award (1989); Outstanding Adviser Award, Phi Delta Theta (1968) **Membership:** Forum Committee, Construction Industry Litigation Section, Committee on Ethics and Professionalism, ABA (2012-Present); National Ethics Committee, American College of Trial Lawyers (2000-2004); Member Committee, Civil Pattern Jury Instructions, Wyoming Bar Association (1999-2002); Wyoming State Chairman, Fellow, American College of Trial Lawyers (1998-2000); Past President, Wyoming Trial Lawyers Association (1981-1982); Aviation Committee, ABA (1980-1986); Chairman, Grievance Committee, Wyoming Bar Association (1980-1986); Wyoming Stock Growers Association; State Bar-Law School Committee, Wyoming Bar Association; Bench-Bar Relations Committee, Wyoming Bar Association; Unauthorized Law Practice Committee Member, Wyoming Bar Association; Dean's Advisory Board, Wyoming College of Law, Wyoming Bar Association; International Society of Barristers; American Board of Trial Advisers **Shipping Address:** PO Box 4597, Tubac, AZ, 85646

Leslie G. Hunter

Title: Historian **Industry:** Education/Educational Services **Company Name:** Texas A&M University, Kingsville **Date of Birth:** 09/26/1941 **Place of Birth:** Meadville **State/Country of Origin:** PA **Parents:** George Harper Hunter; Gladys Laverne (Bowland) Hunter **Marital Status:** Married **Spouse Name:** Cecilia Aros Hunter (8/15/1969) **Children:** Louis; Raquel; Daniel; Joseph **Education:** PhD in History, University of Arizona (1971); MA in History, University of Arizona (1966); BA in History, University of Arizona (1964) **Career:** Regents Professor Emeritus, Texas A&M University, Kingsville (2009-Present); Regents Professor, Texas A&M University, Kingsville (1998-2009); Chairman, Department of History, Texas A&M University, Kingsville (1986-1996); Professor, Texas A&M University, Kingsville (1981-2006); Associate Professor, Texas A&M University, Kingsville (1974-1981); Assistant Professor, Texas A&M University, Kingsville (1969-1974) **Career Related:** Faculty Exchange, Kiev Policy Institute, Ukraine (1991) **Civic:** Chair, History Review Board, Kingsville, TX (1987-1990) **Creative Works:** Author, "The 75th Anniversary History of Texas A&M University-Kingsville" (2000); Editor, Journal of South Texas (1997-2007); Editor, "Historic Kingsville, Texas" (1994); Editorial Board, Journal of South Texas (1989-2007); Editorial Board, Social Studies Texan (1989-2007); Author, "Missions in Spanish Texas" (1987); Contributor, Articles, Professional Journals **Membership:** Board of Directors, Southern Arizona Chapter, Arizona Historical Society (2015-Present); American Association of University Professors; Texas Council for the Social Studies; Texas Computer Education Association; South Texas Historical Association; Vice President, Phi Alpha Theta **Marquis Who's Who Honors:** Albert Nelson Marquis Lifetime Achievement Award (2017) **Hobbies:** Computers **Political Affiliations:** Democrat **Religion:** Episcopalian **Shipping Address:** 4418 E 14th Street, Tucson, AZ, 85711

Rachel Irene Huot

Title: Family Medical Physician **Industry:** Health, Wellness and Fitness **Company Name:** Caroline Family Practice **Date of Birth:** 10/16/1950 **Place of Birth:** Manchester **State/Country of Origin:** NH **Parents:** Omer Joseph Huot; Irene Alice (Girard) Huot **Marital Status:** Single **Education:** Resident, Family Practice, Eastern Virginia Medical School/Ghent Family Practice Residency (2005-2007); Resident, Family Practice, University of Minnesota Rural Family Practice-Waseca/Mayo Clinic School of Health Sciences, Mayo Foundation for Medical Education and Research (2002-2005); Resident, Family Practice, Aultman Health Foundation (2001-2002); MD, LSU Health Shreveport (2000); Postdoctoral Fellow, Southwest Foundation for Biomedical Research (Now Texas Biomedical Research Institute) (1982-1985); PhD in Biology, The Catholic University of America (1980); MS in Biology, The Catholic University of America (1976); BA in Biology, Rivier University, Cum Laude (1972) **Certifications:** Certificate, American Board of Family Medicine, Inc. (2008); Certified to Practice Family Medicine (2008); License, Commonwealth of Virginia (2007) **Career:** Family Medicine Physician, Caroline Family Practice (2014-Present); Family Practice Physician, Lunenberg Medical Center Kencare, Southern Dominion Health System, Inc. (2012-2014); Medical Director, Health Care Square, Boydton Medical Center (2011-2012); Family Medicine Physician, Health Care Square, Boydton Medical Center (2008-2012); Assistant Professor, LSU Health New Orleans (1990-1996); Director, Basic Urologic Research, LSU Health New Orleans (1990-1996); Instructor, The University of Texas Health Science Center at Houston (1988-1989); Staff Scientist, Southwest Foundation for Biomedical Research (Now Texas Biomedical Research Institute) (1987-1988); Assistant Scientist, Southwest Foundation for Biomedical Research (Now Texas Biomedical Research Institute) (1985-1987); Biologist, National Cancer Institute, National Institutes of Health (1979-1982); Chemist, Uniformed Services University (1977-1979); Senior Technician, Microbiology Associates (1974-1977) **Career Related:** Judge, Senior Division, Alamo Regional Academy of Science and Engineering, San Antonio, TX (1989-1990) **Civic:** Volunteer Patient Educator, Martin Luther King Health Center & Pharmacy (1996-2000); Volunteer, CHRISTUS Health Shreveport-Bossier; Volunteer, The American National Red Cross; Choir Member, Good Shepherd Church; Parish Council Financial Committee, Good Shepherd Church **Awards:** Young Investigator Award (1994); Grantee, National Institutes of Health (1983-1986); Grantee, National Science Foundation (1972-1974) **Membership:** American Medical Association; Sierra Club; Sigma Xi, The Scientific Research Honor Society; Delta AAUW; League of Women Voters; American Association for the Advancement of Science; Virginia Academy of Family Physicians; Medical Society of Virginia; American Academy of Family Physicians; Federation of American Societies for Experimental Biology; National Council of the United States SVdP; The New York Academy of Sciences; The Society for In Vitro Biology; Federation of American Scientists; The American Society for Cell Biology; American Association for Cancer Research; American Society For Microbiology; Delta Epsilon Sigma; Iota Sigma Pi **Marquis Who's Who Honors:** Albert Nelson Marquis Lifetime Achievement Award (2017) **To what do you attribute your success:** Dr. Huot attributes her success to her perseverance and to her love of science and medicine. **Why did you become involved in your profession or industry:** Dr. Huot's main goal has always been to help others. As a teen, she watched a dear aunt slowly and painfully die from metastatic cancer, which greatly influenced her to pursue a career in cancer research. Later in life, she strongly desired to care for patients directly, so she earned an MD a few months shy of the age of 50. **What do you consider to be the highlight of your career:** Dr. Huot doesn't have any particular highlights. She enjoyed the years that she was involved in basic research and finds great satisfaction in her current work as a physician in a community health center because she serves patients that would otherwise be without medical care. **Where will you be in five years:** Dr. Huot will likely be retired or semi-retired. She would like to continue being active in the medical or even biomedical field at least part time as long as her health allows, however. **Hobbies:** Drawing; Painting; Reading; Cooking; Stamp collecting/philately **Political Affiliations:** Democrat **Religion:** Roman Catholic **Business Address:** 102 W Broaddus Ave suite 102, Bowling Green, VA, 22427 **Shipping Address:** 375 Roper Dr, Bowling Green, VA, 22427

Dennis Jay Hurwitz

Title: Plastic Surgeon, Director **Industry:** Medicine & Health Care **Company Name:** The Hurwitz Center for Plastic Surgery **Date of Birth:** 06/08/1946 **Place of Birth:** Baltimore **State/Country of Origin:** MD/USA **Parents:** Howard C. Hurwitz; Minna S. Posner Hurwitz **Marital Status:** Married **Spouse Name:** Linda F. Furst (6/8/1969) **Children:** Jeffrey; Julia; Karen **Education:** Fellowship, Craniofacial Surgery, General Hospital of Mexico City (1977); Resident, Plastic Surgery, UPMC (1975-1977); Resident, General Surgery, Mary Hitchcock Hospital, New Hampshire Hospital Association (1972-1975); Resident, Surgery, Yale New Haven Hospital, Yale New Haven Health (1971-1972); Intern, Yale New Haven Hospital, Yale New Haven Health (1970-1971); MD, University of Maryland, Baltimore, MD (1970); BA, University of Maryland, Baltimore, MD (1966) **Certifications:** Certified, State Board of Medicine, Commonwealth of Pennsylvania (1976-Present); Voluntary Maintenance of Certification Re-Certification, American Board of Plastic Surgery (2015); Certified, The Medical Board of California, State of California (2007-2012); Voluntary Maintenance of Certification Re-Certification, American Board of Plastic Surgery (2005); Diplomate, American Board of Plastic Surgery (1979); Certified, American Board of Surgery (1976-1987) **Career:** President, The Hurwitz Center for Plastic Surgery, Pittsburgh, PA (1984-Present); Clinical Professor, Plastic Surgery, School of Medicine, University of Pittsburgh (2000-2012); Medical Director, Cleft Palate Craniofacial Center, School of Medicine, University of Pittsburgh (1996-2004); Professor, Plastic Surgery, School of Medicine, University of Pittsburgh (1996-2000); Visiting Professor, Surgery, School of Medicine, University of Pittsburgh (1994-1996); Clinical Associate Professor, School of Medicine, University of Pittsburgh (1983-1984); Assistant Professor of Surgery, School of Medicine, University of Pittsburgh (1977-1983); Attending Surgeon, Magee-Women's Hospital, UPMC; Attending Surgeon, Children's Hospital of Pittsburgh, UPMC **Career Related:** Founder, Aesthetic Plastic Surgery Center, University of Pittsburgh (1995); Founder, Craniofacial Surgery Program, University of Pittsburgh (1978); Visiting Speaker, Royal College of Physicians and Surgeons of Canada **Civic:** Director, Maimonides Division, Jewish Federation of Greater Pittsburgh (2016-Present); Director, Physician Division, Jewish Federation of Greater Pittsburgh (2000-2001); Director, Medical Division, Israel Bonds, Development Corporation for Israel (1997-1998); Vice President, Zionist Organization of America (1995); Board Member, Jewish Education Institute (1993-1995); Treasurer, Zionist Organization of America (1992-1995); Vice President, Zionist Organization of America (1988-1992); Board Member, Jewish Federation of Greater Pittsburgh (1987-1990); President, Young Leadership, Israel Bonds, Development Corporation for Israel (1986-1987); Board Member, Community Day School (1982-1986) **Military Service:** Captain, U.S. Army Reserves (1972-1980); Lieutenant, U.S. Army National Guard (1970-1972) **Creative Works:** Author, "Comprehensive Body Contouring: Theory and Practice" (2016); Clinical Editor, "Aesthetic Surgery Journal" (2007-2014); Author, "Total Body Lift" (2005); Author, More than 170 Scientific Papers, Professional Journals; Contributor, Book Chapters; Section Editor, Body Contouring Surgery, "Aesthetic Plastic Surgery Journal" **Awards:** Best Attending Presentation, 34th Annual Meeting of the Northeaster Society of Plastic Surgeons (2017); Faculty Teaching Award, Department of Plastic Surgery, University of Pittsburgh (2005); Top Doctor Award, Castle Connolly (2001-2017); Walter Scott Brown Lectureship, College of Medicine, University of Illinois **Membership:** American Association of Plastic Surgeons; Alpha Omega Alpha; Charter Member, American Alpine Workshop in Plastic Surgery; Charter Member, Royal and Ancient Society of American Plastic Surgeons; Omicron Kappa Upsilon; President, Allegheny County Medical Society; President, Greater Pittsburgh Plastic Surgery Society; President, Ohio Valley Society of Plastic Surgeons (OVSPS); President, Robert H. Ivy Pennsylvania Plastic Surgery Society; American Cleft Palate Association; Greater Pittsburgh Plastic Surgery Society; The Robert H. Ivy Society of Plastic and Reconstructive Surgeons; American College of Surgeons; Lipoplasty Society of North America; Founding Member, Northeastern Society of Plastic Surgeons **Marquis Who's Who Honors:** Albert Nelson Marquis Lifetime Achievement Award (2017) **Hobbies:** Golf; Skiing **Religion:** Jewish **Business Address:** 3109 Forbes Avenue, Pittsburgh, PA, 15213 **Shipping Address:** 1450 Wightman Street, Pittsburgh, PA, 15217

B. Paul Husband

Title: Attorney **Industry:** Law and Legal Services **Company Name:** Husband Law **Date of Birth:** 08/15/1950 **Place of Birth:** Los Angeles **State/Country of Origin:** CA **Parents:** Bertram Perry Husband; Ruth (Eatough) Husband **Marital Status:** Married **Spouse Name:** Evelyn Concepcion Ferrer (4/20/06); Beverly Ruth Hyams (5/1/1987, Divorced 3/6/2003) **Children:** Joseph Bertram; Daniel James; David Paul **Education:** JD, University of California, Los Angeles (1977); BA, Occidental College (1972) **Career:** Private Practice, Burbank, CA (1997-2002, 2014-Present); Attorney, Private Practice, Universal City, CA (2002-2014); Attorney, Private Practice, Valencia, CA (1994-1997); Attorney, Private Practice, Encino, CA (1991-1994); Partner, Husband & Roberts, Los Angeles and Encino, CA (1989-1991); Partner, Husband & Morris, Los Angeles, CA (1984-1989); Private Practice, Los Angeles, CA (1981-1984); Associate, Cooper, Epstein & Hurewitz, Beverly Hills, CA (1979-1981); Associate, Coskey, Coskey & Boxer, Los Angeles, CA (1978-1979) **Career Related:** Director, American College of Equine Attorneys (2012-Present); Vice President, American College of Equine Attorneys (2016-present); Speaker Sections Internal Revenue Code Sections183 and 469, USC Tax Institute (2017); Speaker, Equine Industries: Tax Issues, Commerce Clearing House (2017); Speaker, Equine Industries: Tax Issues, Commerce Clearing House (2016); Adjunct Professor of Law, Pepperdine University, Malibu, CA (1978-1979); Lecturer in Law, Tax Section, The State Bar of California; Lecturer in Law, California Tax Policy Conference, Los Angeles County Bar Association; Lecturer in Law, Beverly Hills Bar Association; Lecturer in Law, Tax Section, ABA; Lecturer in Law, American Horse Council; Lecturer in Law, University of Kentucky; Lecturer in Law, National Equine Law Conference **Civic:** General Counsel, International Animated Film Society, ASIFA-Hollywood (1997-Present); Director, General Counsel, Burbank International Children's Film Festival (2000-2003); Recommended Judge, Equestrian Trials Inc. (1988-1994); Registered Judge, American Horse Shows Association (1975-1994) **Creative Works:** Editorial Advisory Board, American Horse Council Tax Bulletin (1994-Present); Co-Author, "Tax Planning for Horse Owners and Breeders" (2008); Writer, Producer, "Fighting Back: Successfully Representing Your Horse Business to the IRS" (1991); Author, Equine Law Column, Journal of Agricultural Taxation and Law (1987-1993); Contributor, Industry Articles, The National Law Journal; Contributor, Industry Articles, The ABA Entertainment & Sports Lawyer; Contributor, Industry Articles, Entertainment Law & Finance; Contributor, Industry Articles, The American Horse Council Business Quarterly; Contributor, Industry Articles, California Tax Lawyer; Contributor, Horse and Breeders Tax Handbook **Awards:** Honoree, Named Super Lawyer, Thomson Reuters (2018); Certificate of Merit (1998); ASIFA-Hollywood ANNIE Awards **Membership:** Association Internationale du Film d'Animation ASIFA-Hollywood (1997-Present); Fellow, American College of Equine Attorneys (2005); Tax Section Committee, The State Bar of California (2003); Seminar Lecturer, The State Bar of California (2003); Director, Association Internationale du Film d'Animation (1997-2003); Chair, Los Angeles County Bar Association (1995-1996); Officer, Entertainment Tax Committee, Tax Section, Los Angeles County Bar Association (1993-1996); Executive Committee, Entertainment Section, Beverly Hills Bar Association (1992-1996); Chair, Tax Section, San Fernando Valley Bar Association (1993-1994); Vice Chair, Federal Tax Study Committee, Arabian Horse Association (1979-1992); Seminar Lecturer, The State Bar of California (1988); Chairman, Pro Bono Oversight Committee, Tax Section, Los Angeles County Bar Association (1987-1988); ABA; World Arabian Horse Organization; Hollywood Chapter, Association Internationale du Film d'Animation; American Horse Council Tax Bulletin; Graded Stakes Committee, Arabian Jockey Club; Board of Advisers, The American Horse Council Tax Bulletin **Bar Admissions:** United States Court of Appeals for the Fourth Circuit (2017); United States Court of Appeals for the Third Circuit (2015); United States Supreme Court (2010); United States District Court Northern District of California (1988); United States Tax Court (1987); United States District Court Southern District of California (1980); United States Court of Appeals for the Ninth Circuit (1979); United States District Court Central District of California (1978); State of California (1977) **Marquis Who's Who Honors:** Albert Nelson Marquis Lifetime Achievement Award (2017) **Hobbies:** Speculative fiction **Religion:** Christian **Shipping Address:** 2600 W Olive Ave Fl 5, Law Offices of B. Paul Husband, Burbank, CA, 91505 **Website:** http://www.husbandlaw.com

Ronald Lee Huston, PhD

Title: Professor Emeritus **Industry:** Education/ Educational Services **Company Name:** University of Cincinnati **Date of Birth:** 08/05/1937 **Place of Birth:** Somerset **State:** PA **Parents:** Charles Virgil Huston; Pauline Alda (Brubaker) Huston **Marital Status:** Single **Spouse Name:** Barbara Ann Howe (7/30/1956, Deceased) **Children:** Thomas R.; Dryver R.; Suzanne H. Phillips **Education:** PhD, University of Pennsylvania (1962); MS, University of Pennsylvania (1961); BS, University of Pennsylvania (1959) **Career:** Director, Institute for Applied International Research, University of Cincinnati (1989-Present); Professor of Mechanics, University of Cincinnati (1970-Present); Affiliate, University of Cincinnati (1962-Present); Director, Division of Civil and Mechanical Engineering, National Science Foundation, Washington, DC (1979-1980) **Career Related:** Life Fellow, American Society of Mechanical Engineers (2007); Fellow, American Society of Mechanical Engineers; Fellow, AIAA; Consultant in Field **Creative Works:** Editor, "Dynamics of Mechanical Systems" (2002); Editor, "Formulas for Dynamic Analysis" (2001); Author, "Multibody Dynamics" (1989); Editor, "Ergonomics and Human Factors" (1988); Author, "Finite Element Methods" (1984); Editor, "Aircraft Crashworthiness" (1975) **Awards:** Distinguished Research Professor in Numerous Areas, University of Cincinnati **Membership:** Board of Directors, Tri State Human Factors (1984-1990); SAE International **Marquis Who's Who Honors:** Albert Nelson Marquis Lifetime Achievement Award (2017) **Hobbies:** Weightlifting; Running; Reading; Travel **Political Affiliations:** Democrat **Religion:** Presbyterian; Pentecostal **Shipping Address:** 6242 Savannah Avenue, Cincinnati, OH, 45224

Jane Campbell Hutchison

Industry: Museums & Institutions **Date of Birth:** 07/20/1932 **Place of Birth:** Washington **State:** D.C. **Parents:** James Paul Hutchison; Leone Bailey (Warrick) Hutchison **Education:** PhD in Art History, University of Wisconsin (1964); MA in Art History, Oberlin College (1958); BA in Fine Arts, Western Maryland College (1954) **Career:** Professor, University of Wisconsin-Madison (1975-Present); From Instructor to Associate Professor, University of Wisconsin-Madison (1964-Present); Department Chairman, University of Wisconsin-Madison (1992-1993); Department Chairman, University of Wisconsin-Madison (1977-1980); Teaching Assistant, University of Wisconsin-Madison (1959-1963); Research Librarian, Toledo Museum of Art (1957-59); Technical Illustrator, Department of Model Basin, US Navy, Washington, DC (1954-1956) **Career Related:** Expert Witness, United States District Court for the Southern District of New York (2000); Visiting Assistant Professor, Temple University, Philadelphia, PA (1968); Consultant in field **Civic:** Secretary, Midwest Art History Society (2004-Present); President, St. Andrew's Society Madison, WI (1995-Present); Treasurer, Midwest Art History Society (2001-2004); Member, Special Committee on Arts Funding, Wisconsin State Legislation Council (2000-2001); Secretary-Treasurer, Historians of Netherlandish Art (1995-1999); Midwest Art History Society (1983-1985); President, Madison Chapter, American Association of University Professors (1979-1981) **Creative Works:** Member of Editorial Board, Studies in Iconography (1997-Present); Author, "Sixteenth Century Journal" (2003-2008); Author, "Source" (2003); Author, "Albrecht Durer: A Guide to Research" (2000); Author, "Early German Artists, Volume Eight, Part Six" (1996); Author, "Albrecht Durer: A Biography, German Edition" (1994); Author, "Early German Artists, Volume Nine, Part Two" (1991); Author, "Albrecht Durer: A Biography" (1990); Author, "Early German Artists, Volume Nine" (1981); Author, "Early German Artists, Volume Eight" (1980); Author, "Master of the Housebook" (1972) **Awards:** Grantee, German Academy Exchange Service, Germany (1989); Recipient, Alumni Award, Western Maryland College of Trustees (1987); Grantee, American Council on Learned Society, Amsterdam (1984); Research Grantee, National Endowment of the Humanities, Germany (1982); Fellow, University of Wisconsin (1961-1963); Recipient, Fulbright Fellow, Rijksuniversiteit Utrecht, Netherlands (1960-1961); Fellow, University of Wisconsin (1959-1960); Recipient, Graduate Fellowship, Oberlin College (1955-1957) **Membership:** Board Member, Midwest Art History Society (2008-Present); University Club, University of Wisconsin (2005-Present); Secretary, Midwest Art History Society (2004-2008); Treasurer, Midwest Art History Society (2001-2003); Treasurer, Historians of Netherlandish Art (1995-1999); Vice President, Madison Chapter, Wisconsin Association of Scholars (1990-1995); President, Midwest Art History Society (1983-1985); President, University Club, University of Wisconsin (1980); President, Madison Chapter, American Association of University Professors (1979-1981); Board of Directors, University Club, University of Wisconsin (1976-1980); Print Council of America; Wisconsin Academy of Sciences, Arts and Letters; Minerva Society; International Council Museum; American Association Museum; Medieval Academy of America; College Art Association

Martha Strawn Iley

Title: Music Educator **Industry:** Education/Educational Services **Company Name:** Metropolitan Music Ministries **Date of Birth:** 06/01/1925 **Place of Birth:** Marshville **State/Country of Origin:** NC **Parents:** Dr. Stephen Hasty Strawn; Lila Faircloth Strawn **Marital Status:** Widowed **Spouse Name:** Bryce Baxter Iley (8/7/1948, Deceased 2009) **Children:** Deborah Iley-Hodde; Sheila Iley-McLean; Cheryl Iley-Lindstrom (Deceased 2005); Stephanie Iley-Salb **Education:** ThM, Gordon-Conwell Theological Seminary (1998); EdD, Nova Southeastern University (1979); EdM, UNC Charlotte (1974); MusM, Winthrop University (1973); MA, Western Kentucky University (1947); BA, East Carolina Teachers College (Now East Carolina University) (1946) **Certifications:** Certification, Music Teachers National Association; Certification, North Carolina Music Teachers Association (1950) **Career:** Founder, Metropolitan Music Ministries, Charlotte, NC (1984-Present); Chairman, Board of Directors, Metropolitan Music Ministries, Charlotte, NC (1984-Present); Teacher, Piano and Theory (1952-Present); Minister of Music, Carmel Baptist Church, Charlotte, NC (1975-1976); Project Director, Music Education, Central Piedmont Community College, Charlotte, NC (1974-1983); Minister of Music, Carmel Baptist Church, Charlotte, NC (1968-1970); Music Teacher, Charlotte Country Day School (1955-1959); Minister of Music, Providence Baptist Church, Charlotte, NC (1954-1957); Music Teacher, Alexander Graham Junior High School, Charlotte, NC (1948-1952); Music Teacher, Lincoln County Schools (1947-1948); Mezzo Soprano Soloist **Career Related:** Ordained, Gospel Ministry in Music and Social Service, Providence Baptist Church, Charlotte, NC (1985) **Civic:** Adjudicator, Piano and Voice, Various Organizations, North Carolina (1980-Present); Board of Directors, Charlotte Community Concert Association (1980-1993); Secretary, Charlotte Community Concert Association (1980-1993); Director, Recital Series, Shepherd Center of Charlotte, NC (1980-1983) **Creative Works:** Editor, Newsletter, "Arty-Facts" (1983) **Awards:** Marquis Who's Who Lifetime Achievement Award (2017); Woman of the Year, Charlotte Observer (2010); Woman of the Year, International Biographical Centre of Cambridge, England (2004); Distinguished Music Alumni Award, East Carolina University (2002); Martha Strawn Iley Church Music Scholarship in Voice; Scholarship, Metropolitan Music Ministries, Charlotte, NC; Bryce and Martha Iley Scholarship, Gordon-Conwell Theological Seminary **Membership:** Board of Directors, Metropolitan Music Ministries, Charlotte, NC (1984-Present); Chaplain, Charlotte Piano Teachers Forum (1987-2017); Certification Chairman, North Carolina Music Teachers Association (1981-1983); Vice President, North Carolina Music Teachers Association (1981-1983); Board of Directors, Charlotte Piano Teachers Forum (1979-2016); President, Charlotte Piano Teachers Forum (1979-1981); Charlotte Clergy Association; Board of Directors, Charlotte Music Club; National Guild of Piano Teachers; American College of Musicians; Providence Baptist Church, Charlotte, NC **Marquis Who's Who Honors:** Albert Nelson Marquis Lifetime Achievement Award (2017) **What do you consider to be the highlight of your career:** The highlight of Dr. Iley's career was her call to ministry in July of 1976. **Hobbies:** Writing; Painting **Political Affiliations:** Republican **Religion:** Baptist **Shipping Address:** 10151 Robinson Church Road, Harrisburg, NC, 28075

Sumant Inamdar

Title: Interventional Gastroenterologist **Industry:** Medicine & Health Care **Company Name:** University of Arkansas **Education:** Fellow, Hofstra University; Resident, Hofstra University; Master's Degree, School of Public Health, University at Albany; Coursework, Medical School, Jawaharlal Institute of Postgraduate Medical Education and Research **Certifications:** Certified in Gastroenterology, American Board of Internal Medicine **Career:** Interventional Gastroenterologist, Medical Sciences, University of Arkansas; Physician, Donald and Barbara Zucker School of Medicine, Hofstra University **Membership:** American Society for Gastrointestinal Endoscopy; American College of Gastroenterology; American Gastroenterology Association; American College of Physicians **Why did you become involved in your profession or industry:** Dr. Inamdar became involved in his profession because he was always interested in human physiology and always felt a need to help people. He obtained an MD in India, and then moved to the United States to further pursue his career. **Where will you be in five years:** In five years, Dr. Inamdar hopes to set up his program at the University of Arkansas. He also hopes to expand it to the national and international levels. **Shipping Address:** 424 Chenal Woods Drive, Little Rock, AR, 72223 **Website:** http://doctors.uamshealth.com/profile/?pid=3326

Alec Ingraham

Title: Mathematics Professor **Industry:** Education/Educational Services **Date of Birth:** 10/17/1946 **Place of Birth:** North Billerica **State/Country of Origin:** MA **Parents:** Chester Doane Ingraham; Margaret Helen Blakely Ingraham **Education:** MA in Mathematics, University of Massachusetts, Boston, MA (1975); BA in History, University of Massachusetts, Boston, MA (1970) **Career:** Chairman, Mathematics Department, Southern New Hampshire University, Manchester, NH (1982-2012); Professor, Mathematics, Southern New Hampshire University, Manchester, NH (1976-2011); Lecturer, Mathematics, Newbury College, Boston, MA (1975-1978) **Civic:** Town Historian, Billerica, MA (2015-Present); Chairman, Middlesex Canal Commission, Billerica Section (2011-Present); Chairman, Billerica Historical Commission, Massachusetts (2000-Present); Treasurer, Middlesex Canal Commission, Billerica Section, Massachusetts (1997-Present); Chairman, Middlesex Canal Commission, Billerica Section, Massachusetts (1997-Present); Co-Chairman, SNHU Mathematics Department (2011); Board Member, New England Association of Two-Year Colleges at Warge (1998-2002); State Delegate, American Mathematics Association of Two-Year Colleges, Memphis, TN (1993-2001) **Awards:** Preservationist of the Year Award, Billerica Historical Society (2001) **Membership:** Conference Co-Chairman, New England Mathematics Association of Two-Year Colleges (2009); Conference Co-Chairman, New England Mathematics Association of Two-Year Colleges (2006); Department Liaison, Mathematics Association of America (2002-2012); Board Member, New England Mathematics Association of Two-Year Colleges (1998-2002); President, Billerica Historical Society (1997-2000); Early American Industries Association; New Hampshire Teachers of Mathematics **Marquis Who's Who Honors:** Albert Nelson Marquis Lifetime Achievement Award (2017) **To what do you attribute your success:** Prof. Ingraham attributes his success to hard work, honesty, and fairness. **Why did you become involved in your profession or industry:** Prof. Ingraham became involved in this profession after he took calculus as an elective, and was advised to change from history to mathematics as a course of study. **What do you consider to be the highlight of your career:** The highlights of Prof. Ingraham's career include chairing the curriculum committee in 1994 when the university established its first general education core, being appointed to full-time professor in 1994, writing and receiving a historical preservation grant helping to establish the Middlesex Canal Museum, and hitting a home run for the faculty's women's softball team. **Hobbies:** Sports; Collecting old tools **Business Address:** 2500 N River Road, Manchester, NH, 03106 **Shipping Address:** 48 Mount Pleasant Street, North Billerica, MA, 01862

Margaret-Anne Irvine

Title: Human Resource Manager **Industry:** Human Resources **Company Name:** Puresource-NOW Health Group Canada **Education:** BBA in Human Resources Management/Personnel Administration, Sheridan College (1966); Student, Ontario Ladies College **Career:** Human Resource Manager, Puresource-NOW Health Group Canada, Guelph, ON, Canada (2009-Present); Human Resource Manager, Hitachi Construction Truck, Guelph, ON, Canada (2004-2009) **Civic:** Dedicated Supporter, Autism Speaks Canada, Guelph Wellington Women in Crisis, Ontario Special Olympics, All Saints Anglican Church-Whitby **Shipping Address:** 5-5068 Whitelaw Road, Puresource-NOW Health Group Canada, ON, Guelph, Canada, N1H 6J3 **Website:** https://www.linkedin.com/in/maggie-irvine-73b58b57

Lesley Lowe Israel

Title: Political Consultant (Retired) **Industry:** Government Administration/ Government Relations/Government Services **Date of Birth:** 07/21/1938 **Place of Birth:** Philadelphia **State/Country of Origin:** PA **Parents:** Herman Albert Lowe; Florence (Segal) Lowe **Marital Status:** Married **Spouse Name:** Fred Israel (12/18/1960) **Children:** Herman Allen; Sanford Lawrence **Education:** BA, Smith College (1959) **Career:** President, Politics, Inc., Washington, DC (1987-1995); Chief Executive Officer, Politics, Inc. (1987-1995); Senior Vice President, The Kamber Group (1981-1987); Coordinator, National Labor, Kennedy for President (1979-1980); Special Assistant, Jackson for President (1975-1976); Director, Political Intelligence, Humphrey for President (1972); Director, Scheduling, Bayh for President (1971); Director, Media Advance, Humphrey for President (1967-1968) **Civic:** Board, Temple B'nai Israel, Easton MD, Chair, Avalon Coordination Centre (2009-2013); International Election Expert, U.S. Department of State (1997-Present); Director, IFES (1997-21016); Chair, Bender JCC of Greater Washington (1995-1998); Member, National Executive Commission, Anti-Defamation League (1994-Present); Member, National Commission, Anti-Defamation League (1991-2016); Member, Democratic Site Selection Committee (1989-Present); President, NCSEJ (2008-2009); Treasurer, IFES (2006-2017); Senior Election Officer, OSCE (1996-present); Chairman, Washington Regional Board, Anti-Defamation League (1991-1994); Member, Democratic Delegate Selection Commission (1983-1984); Member, Democratic Charter Commission (1982-1983); International Election Coordinator, Bender JCC of Greater Washington (1981-1983); President, Bender JCC of Greater Washington (1981-1983); Board of Managers, Adas Israel Congregation (1981-1983); Former Chairman, Washington Board, American Friends of Tel Aviv University **Awards:** Presidential Appointment, President Barack Obama, U.S. Commission for the Preservation of America's Heritage Abroad (2016); Named, 100 Most Powerful Women, Washington Magazine (1990); Special Service Award, Jewish Community Center (1984) **Membership:** Member, U.S. Commission for the Preservation of America's Heritage Abroad (2016-Present) **Marquis Who's Who Honors:** Albert Nelson Marquis Lifetime Achievement Award (2017) **To what do you attribute your success:** Ms. Israel attributes her success to great parents, husband and very good luck. **Why did you become involved in your profession or industry:** She became involved in her profession because her parents were journalists. She entered that field and moved into politics. **What do you consider to be the highlight of your career:** A highlight of her career are her days as an "insider" at the DNC and Democratic politics. **Where will you be in five years:** In five years she hope to be right here. **Political Affiliations:** Democrat **Religion:** Jewish **Shipping Address:** PO Box 69, 6433 Cedar Cove Road, Royal Oak, MD, 21662

Yoichiro Ito

Title: Pathologist, Senior Investigator **Industry:** Medicine & Health Care **Company Name:** National Institutes of Health **Date of Birth:** 12/22/1928 **Place of Birth:** Osaka **State/Country of Origin:** Japan **Parents:** Taichi Ito; Ai (Kubota) Ito **Marital Status:** Married **Spouse Name:** Ryoko Tanioka (12/23/1963) **Children:** Koichi; Shin **Education:** Resident in Pathology, Michael Reese Hospital, Chicago, IL (1961-1963); Resident in Pathology, Cleveland Metropolitan General Hospital (Now The MetroHealth System) (1959-1961); Intern, United States Naval Hospital Yokosuka, Japan (1958-1959); MD, Osaka City University (1958) **Career:** Medical Officer, National Institutes of Health (1978-Present); Visiting Scientist, National Heart, Lung and Blood Institute, National Institutes of Health, Bethesda, MD (1968-1978); Instructor of Physiology, Graduate School of Medicine, Osaka City University (1963-1968) **Creative Works:** Contributor, More than 600 Articles, Professional Journals **Awards:** FLC Mid-Atlantic Region's Award for Excellence in Technology Transfer for High-speed Countercurrent Chromatography (2010); Technology Excellence Award (1979); Research Travel Grant, WHO (1968); First Place Award in Annual Science Research Presentation, Cleveland Metropolitan General Hospital (Now The MetroHealth System) (1960); Fulbright Exchange Scholarship (1959-1963) **Membership:** American Chemical Society **Marquis Who's Who Honors:** Distinguished Humanitarian (2017) **Hobbies:** Gardening **Religion:** Kenshinkai **Business Address:** 10 Center Drive, Building 10, Bethesda, MD, 20814 **Shipping Address:** 18 Lake Court, Rockville, MD, 20853 **Website:** http://www.nhlbi.nih.gov/research/intramural/researchers/pi/ito-yoichiro

Aura Lee Jabs

Title: Minister **Industry:** Religious **Date of Birth:** 04/21/1932 **Place of Birth:** Lewistown **State/Country of Origin:** MT **Parents:** Stephen Ellias Sande; Mabel Harriet Sande **Marital Status:** Married **Spouse Name:** Edward Henry Jabs (6/20/1954) **Children:** Mark Allan; Mary Kay; David Stephen **Education:** MA in Religion, Iliff School of Theology (1983); MDiv, Iliff School of Theology (1982); BS, Montana State University (1954) **Certifications:** Ordained to Ministry, United Presbyterian Church (1984) **Career:** Co-Pastor, Camas Valley United Methodist Church (2008-2014); Pastor, Sutherlin/Wilbur United Methodist Churches (1993-2002); Pastor, Nampa Southside United Methodist Church (1990-1993); Pastor, Vale United Methodist Church (1984-1990); Teacher, English, American Dependents School, Molesworth Air Force Base, England (1959-1960); Teacher, English, Williams Bay High School, Williams Bay School District (1957-1958); Teacher, French, Williams Bay High School, Williams Bay School District (1957-1958); Teacher, English, Box Elder High School (1954-1955); Teacher, Spanish, Gallatin County High School (1953-1954) **Career Related:** Conference Board of Elders Task Force, City of Portland, OR (2004-2008); Southern District Leadership Team, Eugene, OR (2002-2004); Central District Committee Superintendence, Bend, OR (1989-1990); Board of Trustees, Oregon-Idaho Conference (1988-1990) **Civic:** Board Member, Sutherlin/Oakland Emergency Food Pantry (1993-2002); Volunteer, Suicide Crisis Hotline (1983-1984); Senior Deaconess, United Church of Christ (1976-1979); Volunteer Driver, Silver Key (1976-1978) **Awards:** Iliff Preaching Prize, Iliff School of Theology (1982) **Membership:** Mensa; Society of St. Luke **Marquis Who's Who Honors:** Albert Nelson Marquis Lifetime Achievement Award (2017) **To what do you attribute your success:** Rev. Jabs attributes her success to her love of teaching, preaching, and the students and adults she worked with. **Why did you become involved in your profession or industry:** Rev. Jabs wanted to teach and travel, so she graduated college with teaching majors in English and modern languages. She gave up her dreams of travel to marry a Montana rancher, who happened to have a three-year ROTC commitment in the U.S. Air Force. 20 years later, they had traveled all over the United States and Europe, been stationed in England and Turkey, and visited Egypt, Greece, and the Holy Land. After her husband's retirement, they settled in Colorado Springs, Colo. Several new Bible translations were being published, and she had no tools to evaluate them. She enrolled in the Iliff School of Theology in Denver, Colo. to study Greek and prepare for a job in Christian education. After her first year at Iliff, she took part in a program that required her to prepare and deliver a Sunday morning sermon at a very large church in Denver, Colo. Preaching that sermon and the response she got from members of the congregation persuaded her to accept her call to ministry. **Where will you be in five years:** Rev. Jabs hopes she will be in her beautiful home on the South Umpqua River, where she can stand on her deck and watch the salmon spawning in the crystal clear water. **Hobbies:** Reading; Travel; Photography; Computers **Religion:** Methodist **Shipping Address:** 3960 Hitchman Lane, Roseburg, OR, 97471

Deborah C. Jackson, PhD

Title: Mathematician **Industry:** Education/Educational Services **Company Name:** Mathematical Reviews **Date of Birth:** 02/02/1955 **Place of Birth:** Melbourne **State/Country of Origin:** VIC/Australia **Parents:** Frederick Arthur; Beryl Victoria (Potter) Trueman **Marital Status:** Married **Spouse Name:** Clive Warwick Jackson (1/6/1990) **Education:** AA in Music, Australian Music Examination Board (1986); PhD, Monash University, Clayton, VIC, Australia (1981); BA, Monash University, Clayton, VIC, Australia, Double Honors (1978) **Career:** Tutor, Monash University (2007-Present); Reviewer, Mathematical Reviews, Ann Arbor, MI (1983-Present); Lecturer, Swinburne University of Technology, Hawthorn, VIC, Australia (1986-1998); Senior Tutor, Monash University (1984-1985); Tutor, Monash University (1981-1983) **Civic:** Chair, Victorian Algebra Group (1996-2003) **Creative Works:** Contributor, Articles, Professional Literature; Co-Author, Textbooks **Awards:** College Citation for Outstanding Contribution to Student Learning, Trobe University (2015); Commonwealth Postgraduate Research Award (1979-1981); Scholar, Australian Commonwealth University Scholar, Monash University (1973) **Membership:** Mathematics Association of America; Victorian Algebra Group; Australasian Association for Engineering Education; Australian Statistics Society; Institute of Mathematical Statistics; American Mathematics Society; Australian Mathematics Society **Religion:** Anglican **Shipping Address:** 26 Clyde Street, Oakleigh, VIC, Australia, 3166

William Richard Jackson, PhD

Title: Co-founder, Chairman of the Board **Industry:** Environmental Services **Company Name:** Environmental Care & Share, Inc. & Jackson International, Inc. **Date of Birth:** 08/23/1936 **Place of Birth:** Nampa **State/Country of Origin:** ID **Parents:** Richard W. Jackson; Josie P. (Mulder) Jackson **Marital Status:** Divorced **Children:** James Lee; Robbi Jo; Jolynn Kay **Education:** ScD, Northwest Nazarene University (2014); Postdoctoral Coursework, Stanford University Advanced Management College (1991); PhD in Higher Education Administration and Research, University of Denver (1991); EdM, University of Denver (1964); MA in Secondary Education Administration, University of Northern Colorado (1961); BA in Secondary Education, Northwest Nazarene University (1957) **Certifications:** Certification in Toxic Waste Remediation and Hyperbaric Oxygenation Medicine **Career:** Co-founder and Chairman of the Board, Environmental Care & Share, Inc (2001-Present); Founder and President, Enviro Consultant Service (1989-2003); President, Jackson International, Inc. (1984-Present); President, Jackson Brothers Industries (1984-Present); Co-Owner and President, International Bell Museum, Inc. (1978-1986); Co-Owner, Operator, Jackson Brothers Investments (1970-1984); Director of Student Council, Brook Forest Leadership Institute, Evergreen, CO (1961-1964); Teacher in Psychology, Englewood School District (1961-1964); Teacher in Economics, Englewood Schools (1961-1964); School Teacher in Humanities, Speech and Art, Caldwell, ID (1958-1960); Football Coach, Caldwell, ID (1958-1960); Executive Insurance Director of Education Services, Idaho School of Employment, Boise, ID (1957-1958); Account Manager, Collection Contractor, Montgomery Ward, Inc., Walla Walla, WA (1953-1957); Owner, Operator, Janitorial Service (1950-1954) **Career Related:** Chairman of Board, Petro Silver, Inc., Denver, CO (1979-1983); Research Consultant in Agriculture; Research Consultant in Toxic Waste Remediation and Hyperbaric Oxygenation Medicine; Senior Consultant, Environmental Health Foundation 501c3; San Francisco Member of Staff, Southwest Research Institute, San Antonio, TX; Speaker on Organic Soil **Civic:** Co-Founder, Benevolent Brotherhood Foundation (1971-Present) **Creative Works:** Author, "Humic, Fulvic and Microbial Balance: Volume III - Hyperbaric Oxygen and Beyond" (2018); Author, "Humic, Fulvic and Microbial Balance: Volume II - Life: More Abundant" (2016); Author, "Blueprints for Positive Living" (2014); Author, "Hello God It's Me" (2013); Author, "Weathered Wisdom" (2004); Co-Author, "From Humic Substances in Academia To The Needs Of International Commerce", International Humic Substances 20th Anniversary Conference (2001); Author, Environmental Care & Share" (1995); Author, "Fabulous Fulvic Electrolyte" (1995); Author, "The Arthritis, Osteoporosis and Silica Link" (1995); Author, "The Calcium Deception" (1995); Author, "Silver For Human Health", for the Environmental Health Foundation (1995); Author, "Humic, Fulvic and Microbial Balance: Volume I - Organic Soil Conditioning" (1993); Author, "Hyperbaric Oxygenation Effects on the Cognitive Function of Memory" (1991); Co-Author, "Disciplining Curriculum" (1978); Co-Author, "Brook Forest Leadership Curriculum" (1964); Author, "Barter, The History, Mystery and Mastery of Mutual Exchange" **Awards:** First Place, National Self-Publishing Award, Writer's Digest, F+W (1993); Grant, Denver Presbyterian Medical Center (Now Presbyterian/St. Luke's Medical Center), C-HCA, Inc. (1991); Grant, San Diego Center for Hyperbaric Therapy (1991); Award, Undersea & Hyperbaric Medical Society **Membership:** Research Consultant, Undersea & Hyperbaric Medical Society (1990-Present); International Hyperbaric Medical Foundation; Alumni Association, Stanford University; Phi Delta Kappa International **Marquis Who's Who Honors:** Albert Nelson Marquis: Lifetime Achievement Award (2017) **To what do you attribute your success:** Dr. Jackson attributes his success to his love for his fellow man and his desire to take actions every day to help them have a better life. **Why did you become involved in your profession or industry:** Dr. Jackson originally wanted and trained to be a minister, but was turned down. So he broadened his love of God and humanity to encompass the Earth and help provide safe, non-toxic and non-hazardous environments for all creatures, and to help in the production of abundant, healthy food. He found out about 10 years ago that the reason he was turned down as a minister was that they felt he was an entrepreneur, not a shepherd. **Where will you be in five years:** In the next five years, Dr. Jackson's goal is to continue helping the world. One way he plans to do this is to work on water purification methods that will remove toxic substances from water sources. He is excited with the prospect of improving life around the world and will continue to help feed the world with abundant and nutritiously grown food. **Hobbies:** Bartering; Writing; Reading; Travel; Artwork; Oil painting; Tesla science **Political Affiliations:** Republican **Religion:** Christian **Business Address:** Environmental Care & Share, Inc., Golden, CO, 80401 **Shipping Address:** 655 McIntyre Street, Golden, CO, 80401 **Website:** http://www.ecands.bio

William Jerome Jacoby Jr.

Title: Military Officer, Associate Clinical Professor (Retired) **Industry:** Medicine & Health Care **Date of Birth:** 08/09/1925 **Place of Birth:** Mount Carmel **State/Country of Origin:** PA **Parents:** William Jerome Jacoby; Florence Marie Jacoby **Marital Status:** Married **Spouse Name:** Joeann J. Powroznick (5/5/1956) **Children:** William Jerome III; Teresa Marie **Education:** Resident in Internal Medicine, Jefferson Medical College Hospital, Philadelphia, PA (1955-1956); Resident in Internal Medicine, Jefferson Medical College Hospital, Philadelphia, PA (1951-1952); Intern, Jefferson Medical College Hospital, Philadelphia, PA (1950-1951); MD, Jefferson Medical College (1950); AB, Emory University (1946) **Certifications:** Diplomate, American Board of Internal Medicine (1960) **Career:** Deputy Chief, Medical Director, VA Central Office, Washington, DC (1980-1983); Director of Medical Services, VA Central Office, Washington, DC (1978-1980); Commanding Officer, Naval Regional Medical Center, Portsmouth, VA (1975-1978); Chairman, Department of Medicine, Walter Reed National Naval Medical Center, Bethesda, MD (1972-1975); Director, Education and Research, Walter Reed National Naval Medical Center, Bethesda, MD (1972-1975); Chairman, Department of Medicine, Naval Hospital Philadelphia, Philadelphia, PA (1969-1972); Chairman, Department of Medicine, U.S. Naval Hospitals, Great Lakes, IL (1964-1969); Fellow, American Heart Association, Inc. (1956-1957); Fellow, American College of Physicians **Career Related:** Associate Clinical Professor, Jefferson Medical College, Philadelphia, PA (1969-Present); Affiliate, Eastern Virginia School of Medicine, Norfolk, VA (1976-1978); Advisory Council, National Heart, Lung, and Blood Institute, National Institutes of Health (1972-1975); Professor of Medicine, The School of Medicine & Health Sciences, The George Washington University (1972) **Military Service:** Rear Admiral, Medical Corps, U.S. Navy (1972); Junior Grade Commissioned Lieutenant, Medical Corps, U.S. Navy (1950) **Creative Works:** Contributor, Articles, Professional Journals **Awards:** Laureate Award, American College of Physicians (1996); Veterans Administration Exceptional Service Award (1983); Decorated Legion of Merit (1978); Founders Medal, AMSUS The Society of Federal Health Professionals (1974); Meritorious Service Medal **Membership:** AMSUS The Society of Federal Health Professionals; Alpha Omega Alpha Honor Medical Society; Phi Beta Pi **Marquis Who's Who Honors:** Who's Who in America; Who's Who in Medicine; Who's Who in the World; Albert Nelson Marquis Lifetime Achievement Award **To what do you attribute your success:** Dr. Jacoby attributes his success to his father and mother. **Why did you become involved in your profession or industry:** Dr. Jacoby became involved in his profession because his father was a dedicated internist. **What do you consider to be the highlight of your career:** Over the years, Dr. Jacoby has experienced a number of highlights. Some of them include graduating from medical school, serving as a governor in the American College of Physicians, being selected as a rear admiral in the U.S. Navy, joining the Alpha Omega Alpha Honor Medical Society, and earning a fellowship in cardiology. He is also proud of his marriage and family. **Hobbies:** Golf; Reading; Gardening **Political Affiliations:** Republican **Religion:** Roman Catholic **Shipping Address:** 737 E Tazewells Way, Williamsburg, VA, 23185

Muhammad Shah Jahan, PhD

Title: Professor **Industry:** Education/Educational Services **Company Name:** University of Memphis **Date of Birth:** 12/21/1943 **Place of Birth:** Rajshahi **State/Country of Origin:** Bangladesh **Parents:** Muhammad Jamir Jahan; Saratun (Nesa) Uddin Jahan **Marital Status:** Married **Spouse Name:** Kaniz Jahan (3/26/1967) **Children:** Muhammad Ashif; Ishrat Shampa **Education:** PhD, The University of Alabama (1977); MSc, University of Rajshahi (1965) **Career:** Professor, Physics, University of Memphis (1988-Present); Chairman, Department of Physics, University of Memphis (1999-2014); Associate Professor, University of Memphis (1985-1988); Assistant Professor, University of Memphis (1980-1985); Research Associate, The University of Alabama (1980); Lecturer, University of Khartoum (1977-1980); Senior Lecturer, University of Rajshahi (1967-1972); Lecturer, Rajshahi College (1966-1967); Lecturer, Ayub Cadet College (Now Rajshahi Cadet College) (1965-1966); Lecturer, Government Saadat College (1964-1965) **Career Related:** Consultant, RTI International, NC (1989-Present); Visiting Staff Member, Los Alamos National Laboratory, NM (1989-1990); Consultant, Los Alamos National Laboratory, NM (1988-1990); Consultant, Schering Plough, Memphis, TN (1982-1988) **Civic:** Member, Board of Trustees, House of Mannan Charitable Trust; Member, Past Board of Directors, Pleasant View School; Past Master Auditor, Academic Audit, Tennessee Board of Regents **Creative Works:** Contributor, Articles, Professional Journals, Contributor, Book Chapters **Awards:** Travel Enrichment Award, College of Arts and Sciences, University of Memphis (2015); Professional Development Assignment Award, University of Memphis (2014-2015); Award, Industry/University Center for Biosurfaces, The National Science Foundation (2003); Meritorious Faculty Award, University of Memphis (2000); Spur Award, University of Memphis (1994); Spur Award, University of Memphis (1992); Recognition of Achievement Award, LANS, LLC (1990); Professional Development Assignment Award, University of Memphis (1989-1990); Spur Award, University of Memphis (1987-1989); Faculty Research Grant, University of Memphis (1989); Research Grant, Naval Surface Weapon Center (1986); Faculty Research Grant, University of Memphis (1984); Research Grant, Naval Surface Weapon Center (1982); Faculty Research Grant, University of Memphis (1981); Dutch-Sudanese Education Exchange Fellow (1978); Fulbright-Hayes Fellowship (1972-1977); U.S. Agency For International Development Fellowship (1968); Residential Merit Scholarship (1958-1964) **Membership:** President, Local Chapter, Sigma Xi, The Scientific Research Honor Society (1989-1992); American Physical Society; American Chemical Society; Materials Research Society; Society for Biomaterials; International EPR (ESR) Society; Founding Fellow, FedEx Institute of Technology, University of Memphis **Marquis Who's Who Honors:** Albert Nelson Marquis Lifetime Achievement Award (2017) **Why did you become involved in your profession or industry:** Dr. Jahan became involved in his profession because he enjoyed the study of physics from an early age. Although he was encouraged to try chemistry, and he was open to it, he knew that he was meant to follow his passions and returned to physics, where he has been able to make significant contributions. **Hobbies:** Gardening; Visiting Sites of Natural Beauty **Religion:** Islam **Business Address:** 3720 Alumni Ave, Memphis, TN, 38152 **Shipping Address:** 8082 Cambury Cove W, Germantown, TN, 38138

Veronica James

Title: Physics Professor **Industry:** Education/Educational Services **Company Name:** Australian National University **Date of Birth:** 03/24/1935 **Place of Birth:** Crows Nest **State/Country of Origin:** QLD/Australia **Parents:** Perch William Stark; Veronica Battaglini **Education:** PhD in Physics, University of New South Wales, Sydney, Australia (1969); BS, University of Queensland, Brisbane, Australia (1966); BA, University of Queensland, Brisbane, Australia (1955) **Certifications:** Certified Member, Royal Society of Australia (1998); Certified Member, New York Academy of Science (1990); Certified Member, Australian Crystallographic Association (1967); Certified Member, Australian Institute of Physics (1967); Certified Member, Order of Australia Canberra Governor General (1967) **Career:** Adjunct Professor research school chemistry, Australian National University, Canberra, Australia (2003-Present); Visiting Fellow, Department of Pathology, University of Western Australia, Perth, Australia (2001); Visiting Fellow, Australian National University, Canberra, Australia (1998-2002); Visiting Associate Professor, School of Physics, Sydney University (1997-2003); Associate Professor, University of New South Wales (1985-1997); Head, Rex Vowels Low Angle Diffraction Laboratory, University of New South Wales (1979-1997); Senior Lecturer, University of New South Wales (1978-1985); Lecturer, School of Physics, University of New South Wales (1973-1978); Senior Tutor of Physics, University of New South Wales, Sydney, Australia (1971-1973); Senior Mathematics Mistress, Edgecliff, Sydney, Australia (1964-1966); Senior Mathematics Mistress, Loreto Convent, Brisbane, Australia (1963); Senior Ma thematic Mistress, Girls' Grammar School, Australia (1956-1962) **Career Related:** Director, Fiberscan Pty Ltd, Sydney, Australia (1999-2005); Authorised Proprietor, Selected Courses for Gifted & Talented Students, Sydney, Australia (1996-2000); Assessor, Victorian Cancer Council, Melbourne, Australia (1994-1999); Founder, Director, Phones Deaf (1985-1999); Executive, Australian Neutron Beam Users' Group, Sydney, Australia (1980-1982) **Civic:** Quota International, Gold Coast, Australia (2007-2008) **Creative Works:** Contributor, Articles to Professional Journals **Awards:** International Scientist of the Year Award (2011); International Scientist of the Year Medal (2004); Barry Preston Award (2001); Scientist of the Year Award (1999); University Teaching Fellow, Commonwealth of Australia (1995); Sydney Electricity Community Spirit Award (1995); Award, Australian Deafness Awareness Council (1992); Breast Cancer Research Award, Quota South Pacific (1992); Alumni Award, University of New South Wales (1991); Vice Chancellor's Teaching Award (1990) **Marquis Who's Who Honors:** Albert Nelson Marquis Lifetime Achievement Award (2017) **Hobbies:** Travelling; Music; Gardening **Political Affiliations:** Conservative **Religion:** Roman Catholic **Business Address:** 4 Mountain Ash Circuit, Robina, Australia, 4226

Alexis Jarrett

Title: Insurance Agent **Industry:** Insurance **Date of Birth:** 07/02/1948 **Place of Birth:** Independence **State/Country of Origin:** KS **Parents:** Robert Patterson; Betty June (Johnson) Jarrett **Education:** JD, The John Marshall Law School (2001); Postgraduate Studies, University of Missouri (1974-1977); BS, The University of Minnesota (1970) **Certifications:** Life Underwriting Training Council; Licensed in Life and Health Insurance, State of Indiana; License in Property and Casualty Insurance, State of Indiana; Coach, Minnesota **Career:** Insurance Agent, Private Practice (1984-Present); Assistant Director of Athletics, University of Missouri (1974-1977); Head Coach of Basketball, University of Missouri (1974-1977); Head Coach of Softball, University of Missouri (1974-1977); Head Coach of Track, University of Missouri (1974-1977); Teacher, Esko Public Schools (1970-1974) **Career Related:** Judicial Extern, Circuit Court of Cook County (1999); Member, Moot Court Council, The John Marshall Law School Moot Court Council (1999); Women's Basketball and Softball Color Analyst, Regional Radio Sports Network (1992-1994); Coordinator, Women's Sports Information Department, University of Missouri (1974-1977) **Civic:** Board of Directors, Boys & Girls Clubs of Northwest Indiana (1999-Present); Member, Board of Advisors, The Naismith Memorial Basketball Hall of Fame (1999-2003); Sponsor, Lake County HS Girls Basketball Banquet (1989-1999); Member, Advisory Board, Industrial Research Liaison Program, Indiana University (1990-1996); Secretary-treasurer, Board of Directors, VNA Foundation (1994); President, Board of Directors, Samaritan Counseling Center (1994); Vice President, Southwest Lake Division, American Heart Association, Inc. (1992-1994) **Creative Works:** Contributor, Sports Articles to Newspapers **Awards:** Individual with Vision Award, Indiana High School Athletic Association, Inc. (1996); Woman of the Year, ABWA Management, LLC (1983) **Membership:** Committee Member, Labor and Employment Law, The Chicago Bar Association (1996-2010); Committee Member, Immigration Law, The Chicago Bar Association (1996-2010); Committee Member, Health Law, The Chicago Bar Association (1996-2010); The Sports Lawyers Association (1996-2006); Board of Directors, Indiana Chapter, National Life Underwriters (1995-1997); Media Relations Chair, Indiana State Medical Association (1993-1994); President, Lakecountymedicalsociety.net (1992-1994); Treasurer, Indiana State Medical Association (1992-1993); Media Relations Chair, Indiana State Medical Association (1990-1991); President, New Image Chapter, ABWA Management, LLC (1983); Forum Member, Entertainment and Sports Law, ABA; Committee Member, Labor and Law, ABA; Committee Member, Insurance Law, ABA; Subcommittee Member, Sports Law, ABA **Marquis Who's Who Honors:** Distinguished Humanitarian (2017) **Business Address:** 2330 Wicker Boulevard, Schererville, IN, 46375

Richard W. Jenkins

Title: Sergeant First Class E-7, 25Z Visual Information Chief (Retired) **Industry:** Military & Defense Services **Company Name:** U.S. Army **Education:** AS in Applied Science in Electrical Engineering Technology, Erie Community College **Military Service:** Combat Photographer, Vietnam War, U.S. Army (1967-1968); U.S. Army (1966-1990); Sergeant First Class E-7, 25Z Visual Information Chief, U.S. Army **Awards:** Two-Time Recipient, Meritorious Service Medal; Three-Time Recipient, Commendation Medal, U.S. Army; Achievement Medal, U.S. Army; Recipient, Vietnam Service Medal with Three Stars; Recipient, Republic of Vietnam Campaign Medal with 1970 Device; Recipient, Meritorious Unit Commendation; Recipient, Republic of Vietnam Gallantry Cross Unit Citation; Recipient, Korea Defense Service Medal; Recipient, Cold War Recognition Certificate; Recipient, New York State Conspicuous Service Cross with Silver Device; Recipient, New York State Conspicuous Service Star with Silver Device; Recipient, German Army Bronze and Silver Shooting Awards; Recipient, The German Army Reserve Silver Honor Pin **Membership:** Lifetime Member, Dallas Safari Club; Lifetime Member, Boone and Crockett Club; Lifetime Member, DAV; Lifetime Member, Vietnam Veterans of America; Lifetime Member, The National Rifle Association of America; Lifetime Member, Safari Club International; Lifetime Member, Former Commander, Post 264, The American Legion **Marquis Who's Who Honors:** Albert Nelson Marquis Lifetime Achievement Award (2017); Distinguished Humanitarian (2017) **To what do you attribute your success:** He attributes his success to self motivation. **Why did you become involved in your profession or industry:** He became involved in this profession because of his family's background in the military. He is a third-generation army serviceman with a legacy dating back to the Civil War and the Battle of Mobile Bay. **What do you consider to be the highlight of your career:** His greatest career achievement was running the Korean and Panama television and radio services as chief of maintenance for both networks. **Where will you be in five years:** In five years, Mr. Jenkins hopes to teach at the Pulmonary Rehabilitation Center and continue assisting other veterans. **Hobbies:** Computers **Religion:** Baptist **Shipping Address:** 3959 Forest Park Way Apt 216, North Tonawanda, NY, 14120

Alice B. Jennings

Title: Partner **Industry:** Law and Legal Services **Company Name:** Edwards & Jennings, PC **Marital Status:** Married **Education:** JD, Wayne State University Law School (1978); BA in Social Work, Michigan State University (1971); MA in Social Work, Michigan State University **Career:** Founder, Partner, Edwards & Jennings PC (1982-Present); Legal Apprentice, Philo, Atkinson, Darling, Steinberg, Harper and Edward, Michigan; Teacher, Detroit Board of Education; Social Worker, Detroit Board of Education **Career Related:** Member, People to People Delegation (1988) **Civic:** Chairperson, Civil Liberties Section, Michigan State Bar Association (1996-1998); Founding Member, Detroiters Working for Environmental Justice (1995-1996); Founding Member, Black Women's Lawyers Association; Lead Counsel, Sugar Law Center; Mentor for Young Lawyers; Co-Coordinator, Michigan Coalition to Overturn the Bakke Decision **Awards:** Spirit of Detroit Award **Membership:** National Bar Association; Wolverine Bar Association; Michigan Trial Lawyers Association; American Trial Lawyers Association; Trial Lawyers for Public Justice **Bar Admissions:** Michigan **Why did you become involved in your profession or industry:** While going for a master's degree in social work, Ms. Jennings was watching the impeachment proceedings of President Nixon and saw an elegant congresswoman on television. It made her want to become a lawyer. She felt that social work wouldn't provide as good of a platform for making a difference and that she would still been able to do a lot of social work as a lawyer. **Shipping Address:** 495 Lodge Dr, Detroit, MI, 48214 **Website:** http://thewright. org/lfs/jennings.biography.pdf

Karen Jez

Title: Superintendent, School System Administrator **Industry:** Education/Educational Services **Company Name:** Titusville Area School District **Date of Birth:** 01/19/1964 **Place of Birth:** Oil City **State/Country of Origin:** PA **Parents:** Byron A. Enos; Eleanor Loveless Enos **Education:** MS in Education and Letter of Eligibility, Westminster College, New Wilmington, PA (1998); BS in Art Education, Edinboro University, Pennsylvania (1986) **Career:** Superintendent, Titusville Area School District (2006-Present); Assistant Superintendent, Titusville Area School District (2004-2006); Middle School Principal, Titusville Area School District (1998-2004); Teacher, Titusville Area School District, Pennsylvania (1996-1998); Secondary Art Teacher, Valley Grove School District, Franklin, PA (1988-1996) **Career Related:** President, Pennsylvania Rural and Small Schools Association (2016-Present); Board Member, University of Pittsburgh at Titusville (2013); Board Member, Pennsylvania Rural and Small Schools Association (2012); Member, FORUM of Western Pennsylvania Superintendents, Pittsburgh, PA (2009); Pennsylvania Association of School Administrators, Harrisburg, PA (2006); President, Pennsylvania Middle School Association, Harrisburg, PA (2002-2003) **Civic:** Member, Titusville Rotary; Member, United Way of Titusville Regional Literacy Council; President, Titusville Regional Literacy Council **Political Affiliations:** Democrat **Religion:** Espicopalian **Business Address:** 221 N Washington Street, PA, Titusville, 16354 **Shipping Address:** 301 E Spruce Street, Titusville Area School District, Titusville, PA, 16354

Earl Johnson Jr.

Title: Judge (Retired), Professor, Author **Industry:** Law and Legal Services **Company Name:** USC Gould School of Law **Date of Birth:** 06/10/1933 **Place of Birth:** Watertown **State:** SD **Parents:** Earl Jerome Johnson; Doris Melissa (Schwartz) Johnson **Marital Status:** Married **Spouse Name:** Barbara Claire Yanow (10/11/1970) **Children:** Kelly Ann; Earl Eric; Agaarn Yanovitch **Education:** LLM, Northwestern University (1961); JD, The University of Chicago (1960); BA in Economics, Northwestern University (1955) **Career:** Visiting Scholar, USC Gould School of Law (2013-Present); Associate Justice, California Courts of Appeal, Judicial Council of California (1982-2007); Professor of Law, USC Gould School of Law (1976-1982); Program Director, Study on Dispute Resolution Policy, Social Science Research Institute, USC Gould School of Law (1975-1982); Co-Director, Access to Justice Project, European University Institute (1975-1979); Associate Professor, USC Gould School of Law (1969-1975); Director of Clinical Programs, USC Gould School of Law (1970-1973); Visiting Scholar Center for Study of Law and Society, University of California, Berkeley (1968-1969); Director, Legal Service Program, Office of Economic Opportunity (1966-1968); Deputy Director, Legal Service Program, Office of Economic Opportunity (1965-1966); Deputy Director, NLSP (1964-1965); Trial Attorney, Organized Crime Section, The United States Department of Justice (1961-1964) **Career Related:** Scholar-in-Residence, Western Center on Law & Poverty, Inc. (2008-Present); Member, Commission on Access to Justice, State of California (1997-2004); Co-Chairman, Commission on Access to Justice, State of California (2002-2003); Board Director, Consortium for National Equal Justice Library, Georgetown Law (1995); Chair, Access to Justice Working Group, State of California (1993-1996); President, Consortium for National Equal Justice Library, Georgetown Law (1992-1995); Chair, National Equal Justice Library, Georgetown Law (1989-1992); Executive Committee, National Senior Citizens Law Center (Now Justice in Aging) (1980-1982); Robert H. Jackson Lecturer, The National Judicial College (1980); Legislative Impact Panel, National Academy of Sciences (1977-1980); Advisory Panel, Legal Services Corporation (1976-1980); Trustee, Western Center on Law & Poverty, Inc. (1976-1980); President, Western Center on Law & Poverty, Inc. (1976-1980); Visiting Scholar, Institute Comparative Law, Université degli Studi di Firenze (1975); Secretary, National Consumer Law Center, Inc. (1974-1982); Faculty. Asian Workshop on Legal Services to Poor (1974); Vice President, CRLA (1973-1974); Chairman, Executive Committee, CRLA (1973-1974) **Military Service:** U.S. Naval Reserve (1955-1958) **Creative Works:** Author, "Justice for All: The Past and Future of Civil Legal Aid in the United States, Three Volumes" (2014); Author, "The Firenze Faction" (2004); Author, "Murder on Appeal" (2001); Author, "California Criminal Trial Guide, Three Volumes" (1994); Author, "North Carolina Civil Trial Guide, Five Volumes" (1993); Author, "Michigan Trial Guide, Five Volumes" (1993); Author, "Pennsylvania Civil Trial Guide, Five Volumes" (1992); Author, "California Family Law Trial Guide, Five Volumes" (1992); Author, "Indiana Civil Trial Guide, Five Volumes" (1992); Author, "Federal Trial Guide, Five Volumes" (1992); Author, "Illinois Civil Trial Guide, Five Volumes" (1991); Author, "Florida Civil Trial Guide, Five Volumes" (1990); Author, "New York Trial Guide, Five Volumes" (1990); Author, "Texas Trial Guide, Six Volumes" (1989); Editorial Board Member, "Journal of Law and Social Inquiry" (1987-2001) **Awards:** Outstanding Jurist Award, Los Angeles County Bar Association (2007); Appellate Justice Of Year Award, Consumer Attorneys Association of Los Angeles (2007); Beacon Of Justice Award LA Law Library (2006); Aranda Access To Justice Award, Judicial Council, California Judges Association, The State Bar of California (2004); Appellate Judge of the Year Award, Consumer Attorneys of California (2003); Outstanding Judicial Achievement Award, Legal Aid Foundation of Los Angeles (1999) **Membership:** Civil Right to Counsel Working Group, ABA (2009-Present); Standing Committee on Legal Aid and Indignant Defendants, ABA (2007-2010); Special Adviser, Presidential Commission to the Access of Justice, ABA (2005-2006); Chair, American Bar Foundation (1999-2002); Fellow, American Bar Foundation; Appellate Courts Committee, The American Academy of Political and Social Science (1998-1999); Research Advisory Committee, American Bar Foundation (1996-2014); Consortium on Legal Service and the Public, ABA (1991-1994); Council, Section of Individual Rights and Responsibilities, ABA (1990-1991); Board Director, National Legal Aid & Defender Association (1988-1992); Ethics Committee, The American Academy of Political and Social Science (1985-1989); Fellow, American Bar Foundation; Appellate Courts Committee, The American Academy of Political and Social Science (1983-1987) **Bar Admissions:** State of California (1972); Supreme Court of the United States (1966); The District of Columbia (1965); United States Court of Appeals for the Ninth Circuit (1964); Illinois (1960) **Marquis Who's Who Honors:** Albert Nelson Marquis Lifetime Achievement Award (2017) **Political Affiliations:** Democrat **Shipping Address:** 1525 Ocean Dr, Oxnard, CA, 93035

Knut S. Johnson

Title: Attorney **Industry:** Law and Legal Services **Company Name:** Law Office of Knut S. Johnson **Date of Birth:** 09/20/1957 **Place of Birth:** Chicago **State/Country of Origin:** IL **Education:** JD, School of Law, University of San Diego, Cum Laude (1986); BS in Earth Science, Tulane University, New Orleans, LA, With Honors (1980) **Certifications:** Certified Specialist in Criminal Law, Board of Legal Specialization, State Board of California (2002) **Career:** Attorney, Private Practice, San Diego, CA (1996-Present); Trial Attorney, Federal Defenders of San Diego, Inc. (1988-1994); Associate Attorney, Jenkins & Perry, San Diego, CA (1986-1988); Geologist, Gulf Oil L.P., New Orleans, LA (1980-1983); Associate Attorney, McKenna & Cuneo, LLP, San Diego, CA **Career Related:** Criminal Justice Act Panel Representative, U.S. District Court of South Dakota (2006); Criminal Justice Act Panel Representative, U.S. District Court, Southern District of California (2006); Lawyer, U.S. Court of Appeals for the Ninth Circuit (2003-2005); Representative, U.S. Court of Appeals for the Ninth Circuit (2003-2005); President, CDBA-CDLC (2001-2002); Solo Committee, Criminal Justice Section, American Bar Association (2000-2006); Small Firm Committee, Criminal Justice Section, American Bar Association (2000-2006); Board of Directors, CDBA-CDLC (1996-2001); Fellow, American Bar Foundation **Civic:** Volunteer, Rugby Coach (2015-Present); Law Alumni Board of Directors, School of Law, University of San Diego (2008); Board of Directors, Unitarian University Fellowship, San Diego, CA (2000-2003) **Awards:** Best Lawyers in America, White Collar and Non-White Collar Criminal Defense (2000-Present); Lawyer of the Year, Criminal Defense, White Collar, Best Lawyers (2017); Top 50 Attorneys, Southern California Super Lawyers (2017); E. Stanley Conant Award, Federal Defenders of San Diego, Inc. (2014); Honoree, Top Ten Attorneys of San Diego, United States Magistrate Judge Selection Committee (2013); Honoree, Best Attorneys of California, San Francisco Chronicle, Hearst Corporation (2012); Honoree, Southern California Super Lawyers (2010-2011); Top Ten Attorneys, California Super Lawyers (2010-2011); Top 50 Attorneys, Southern California Super Lawyers (2009-2012); E. Stanley Conant Award, Defenders Organization of San Diego (2006); Certificate of Commendation, U.S. Marine Corps (2001); A/V Rated Attorney, Martindale-Hubbell; Honoree, Bar Register of Preeminent Lawyers; Honoree, San Diego County Top Attorneys **Membership:** The State Bar of California; San Diego County Bar Association; San Diego Criminal Defense Lawyers Club **Marquis Who's Who Honors:** Albert Nelson Marquis Lifetime Achievement Award (2017) **Why did you become involved in your profession or industry:** Mr. Johnson became involved in his profession because he has lawyers in the family, but he was originally working in geology before he realized that he wanted to pursue law. **Political Affiliations:** Democrat **Shipping Address:** 550 W C Street, Suite 790, Law Office of Knut S. Johnson, San Diego, CA, 92101

Matilee Howard Johnson

Title: Headmistress (Retired) **Industry:** Education/Educational Services **Date of Birth:** 12/09/1934 **Place of Birth:** Palmetto **State/Country of Origin:** GA **Parents:** Amplus Dilworth Howard; Mattie (King) Howard **Marital Status:** Married **Spouse Name:** Andrew Emerson Johnson III (12/27/1977) **Education:** Postgraduate Work, Oxford University, United Kingdom (1980); MA in Administration, Georgia State University (1970); Postgraduate Coursework, Emory University (1966-1967); Postgraduate Coursework, Colgate University (1963); Postgraduate Cousrwork in Mathematics, Stanford University (1962); Postgraduate Coursework, Colgate University (1960); BS, University of Georgia (1957) **Certifications:** Certificate in Educational Administration, State of Georgia **Career:** Headmistress, Westminster Girls' School, Atlanta, GA (1972-1977); Dean of Students, Westminster Girls' School, Atlanta, GA (1966-1972); Teacher, Dean of Students, Westminster Girls' School, Atlanta, GA (1961-1966); Teacher, The Hamlin School, San Francisco, CA (1960-1961); Teacher, Everglades School for Girls, Miami, FL (1957-1961) **Career Related:** Substitute Teacher, Dana Hall School, Wellesley, MA (1990); Conference Chairman, MISBO, Atlanta, GA (1973); Educational Consultant, Pingry School (1972); Educational Consultant, Kent Place School, Elizabeth, NJ (1972); Convention Committee, National Association of Principals of Schools for Girls **Civic:** Volunteer, Disney Family Museum, San Francisco, CA (2009-Present); Volunteer, The Presidio of San Francisco, San Francisco, CA (2009-Present); Member, Special Acquisition Committee, Montgomery Museum of Fine Arts, Montgomery, AL (1997-1999); Member, Community Council of Montgomery, Montgomery, AL (1997-1998); Board of Directors, Landmarks Foundation, Montgomery, AL (1996-1999); Montgomery Chorale (1994-1998); Member, Women's Committee, Carnegie Museum, Pittsburgh, PA (1983-1998); Advisory Board, Convocation Chairman, March of Dimes, Atlanta, GA (1974) **Marquis Who's Who Honors:** Albert Nelson Marquis Lifetime Achievement Award (2017) **Why did you become involved in your profession or industry:** Ms. Johnson became involved in her profession because she was inspired by all the wonderful teachers she had in high school. **Where will you be in five years:** In the next five years, Ms. Johnson will be in Aiken, South Carolina. **Hobbies:** Creating jewelry; Art; Swimming; Skiing; Decorating; Flower arranging **Religion:** Methodist **Shipping Address:** 3093 Wise Creek Ln, Cumberland Village, Aiken, SC, 29801

Richard Dean Johnson, PhD

Title: Pharmaceutical Executive **Industry:** Pharmaceuticals **Company Name:** K.C. BioPharma, LLC **Date of Birth:** 07/08/1936 **Place of Birth:** DeKalb **State:** IL **Parents:** Arthur Dean Johnson; Evelyn Alice (Telford) Williams **Spouse Name:** Paula Marcellus Jennings (1942-2015, Deceased) **Children:** Janet Telford Bijur; Julie Johnson McVeigh; Richard Dean, Jr.; Jennings Brodie (Deceased) **Education:** PharmD, University of California, San Francisco (1961); PhD, University of California, San Francisco (1965); MS, University of California, San Francisco (1962); MBA, Rockhurst University (1984); BS, University of California, Berkeley (1960) **Certifications:** Licensed Pharmacist, State of California; Certified Teacher, California State Board of Pharmacy **Career:** Principal, K.C. BioPharma, LLC, Kansas City, MO (1991-Present); Owner, K.C. BioPharma, LLC, Kansas City, MO (1991-Present); Retired, Marion Merrell Dow, Inc., Kansas City, MO (1991); Corporate Vice President, Marion Merrell Dow, Inc., Kansas City, MO (1989-1991); Vice President, Business Alliances, Marion Laboratories, Inc., Kansas City, MO (1987-1988); Vice President, Corporate Development, Marion Laboratories, Inc., Kansas City, MO (1983-1987); Vice President of Licensing, Marion Laboratories, Inc., Kansas City, MO (1980-1982); Managing Director of Licensing, Marion Laboratories, Inc., Kansas City, MO (1973-1979); Director of Regulatory Affairs, Syntex Laboratories, Inc., Palo Alto, CA (1967-1973); Section Head, Research and Development, Allergan, Irvine, CA (1965-1967) **Career Related:** Medical Analyst, Reynders, McVeigh Capital Management LLC, Boston, MA (2005-Present); Adjunct Graduate Professor, School of Pharmacy, University of Missouri-Kansas City (1995-Present); Research and Development Council, School of Pharmacy, University of Missouri-Kansas City (1993-Present); Medical Analyst, NanoCell Biotech, LLC, San Francisco, CA (2008-2010); Pharmaceutical Analyst, Cottonwood Capital Management, LLC (2002-2004); Pharmaceutical Analyst, SunTrust Robinson Humphrey (2002); Adjunct Professor, School of Pharmacy, University of Missouri-Kansas City (1991-1995); Guest Lecturer, Darla Moore School of Business, University of South Carolina, Columbia, SC (1975-1979); Board of Directors, Dey Laboratories, Inc., Concord, CA; Board of Directors, Tanabe-Marion Laboratories, Kansas City, MO; Board of Directors, U.S. Bioscience Inc., Blue Bell, PA; Board of Directors, ImmunoPharmaceutics, Inc., San Diego, CA; Board of Directors, LRRI, Albuquerque, NM; Board of Directors, Micrologix Biotech Inc., Vancouver, British Columbia, Canada; Compensation Committee, AusAm Biotechnologies, Inc., Santa Monica, CA; Audit Committee, AusAm Biotechnologies, Inc., Santa Monica, CA **Civic:** Dean's Resident Council, School of Pharmacy, University of Missouri, Kansas City, MO (2010-Present); President Emeritus, Pharmacy Foundation, University of Missouri-Kansas City (1998-Present); Dean's Advisory Board, Pharmacy Foundation, University of Missouri-Kansas City (1995-Present); Trustee, Johnson Family Fund, Kansas City Community Foundation (1993-Present); Dean's Development Committee, School of Pharmacy, University of California, San Francisco (2010-2012); Development Committee, Life Sciences Initiative, Kansas City, MO (2010-2012); Undergraduate Research Committee, Life Sciences Initiative, Kansas City, MO (2001-2010); Real Estate Committee, University of Missouri, Kansas City, MO (1998-2010); Life Sciences Committee, University of Missouri, Kansas City, MO (1998-2010); Science Research Board, Jefferson City, MO (2005-2008); Active International Relations Council, Kansas City, MO (1998-2008); Trustee, Pharmacy Foundation, University of Missouri-Kansas City (1993-2007); Life St. Luke's Hospital Stroke Committee (1993-2006); Executive Roundtable, Henry W. Bloch School of Business and Public Administration, University of Missouri, Kansas City, MO (1998-2003); Trustee, Conservatory of Music, University of Missouri, Kansas City, MO (1998-2002); Committee of Review, U.S. Pharmacopeia (1999-2001); Finance Committee, University of Missouri, Kansas City, MO (1998-2001); Vet. Drug Committee, U.S. Pharmacopeia (1998-2001) **Creative Works:** Author, Doctoral Thesis, "A study of physical and chemical properties of solutions by thermal electric methods" (1965) **Awards:** FBI Citizens' Academy, Kansas City, MO (2007-Present); Taft Union Hall of Fame (2016); Fellow, American Institute of Chemists (1965-1970); Fellow, American Foundation for Pharmaceutical Education (1962-1965); Grantee, National Institutes of Health and Public Health Service Training (1962-1965); Sir Henry S. Wellcome Memorial Fellow (1962-1963); 50 Years Emeritus Award, American Chemical Society; 50 Years Recognition Award, California State Board of Pharmacy; Graduate Award, Borden Co. **Membership:** American Chemical Society; American Association of Pharmaceutical Sciences; American Foundation for Pharmaceutical Education; Kirkwood Society, American Red Cross; Kansas City Country Club, Shawnee Mission, KS; River Club, Kansas City, MO; Carriage Club, Kansas City, MO; La Jolla Beach & Tennis Club, La Jolla, CA; La Jolla Country Club; Sigma Xi; Theta Delta Chi; Phi Lambda Sigma; The Rho Chi Society **Shipping Address:** 5330 Ward Pkwy, Kansas City, MO, 64112

Samuel Paul Johnson

Industry: Business Management/Business Services **Education:** BA, Auburn University (1969) **Certifications:** Accredited Investment Fiduciary **Career:** Chairman, Co-Chief Executive Officer, Johnson Sterling, Inc. (1997-Present) **Awards:** Named, Best Financial Adviser, Birmingham Magazine (2017)

Waine C. Johnson

Title: Dermatologist, Educator **Industry:** Medicine & Health Care **Company Name:** University of Pennsylvania **Date of Birth:** 09/30/1928 **Place of Birth:** Mount Vernon **State/Country of Origin:** TX **Parents:** Tulley Bell Johnson; Lizzie Johnson **Marital Status:** Married **Spouse Name:** Deanna Glutz (12/1973) **Children:** Susan Lynn; Carol Ann; Sandra Kay **Education:** Fellow in Dermal Pathology, Armed Forces Institute of Pathology (1960-1961); Resident in Dermatology, Walter Reed Army Hospital (1955-1958); Intern, Brooke Army Hospital (1953-1954); MD, University of Texas (1953); BS, East Texas State University (1949) **Career:** Department of Dermatology, University of Pennsylvania, Philadelphia, PA (2006-Present); Clinical Professor, University of Pennsylvania Medical School (1978-Present); Co-Managing Director, Delaware Valley Dermatopathology Division, Institute for Dermatopathology, Conshohocken, PA (2001-2005); Managing Partner, Delaware Valley Dermatopathology LLP (1998-2000); Chairman, Department of Dermatology, Graduate Hospital, University of Pennsylvania (1978-1998); Professor of Dermatology, Temple University Medical School (1970-1978); Director, Skin and Cancer Hospital (1970-1978); Faculty Member, Temple University Medical School, Philadelphia, PA (1962-1978); Staff Member, Skin and Cancer Hospital, Philadelphia, PA (1962-1978); Assistant Laboratory Director, Skin and Cancer Hospital (1962) **Military Service:** Major, Medical Corps, U.S. Army Reserve (1953-1962) **Creative Works:** Co-Editor, Dermal Pathology (1974); Author, Numerous Papers in Field **Awards:** Gold Medal Science Exhibit, American Society for Clinical Pathologists, College of American Pathologists (1962) **Membership:** American Registry of Pathology (2003-2005); Chairman, Dermatology Section, College of Physicians of Philadelphia (1994-1997); American Society of Dermatopathology (1988); President, Atlantic Dermatological Conference (1979-1980); Philadelphia Dermatological Society (1979-1980); Chairman, Pathology Committee, American Academy of Dermatology (1976-1980); International Academy of Pathology; American Dermatological Association; American College of Physicians; American Medical Association; Histochemical Society; Society for Investigative Dermatology **Marquis Who's Who Honors:** Albert Nelson Marquis Lifetime Achievement Award (2017) **Why did you become involved in your profession or industry:** Dr. Johnson wanted to become a doctor to help people. He knew other dermatologists. **Shipping Address:** 744 Crosswicks Road, Rydal, PA, 19046

Walter Earl Johnson

Title: President **Industry:** Engineering **Company Name:** Exploration GeoCons., Inc. **Date of Birth:** 12/16/1942 **Place of Birth:** Denver **State/Country of Origin:** CO **Parents:** Earl S. Johnson; Helen F. (Llewellyn) Johnson **Marital Status:** Married **Spouse Name:** Ramey Kandice Kayes (8/6/1967) **Children:** Gretchen; Roger; Aniela **Education:** Graduate in Geophysical Engineering, Colorado School of Mines (1966) **Certifications:** Registered Professional Engineer, State of Colorado; Certified Geologist, State of Colorado **Career:** President, Exploration GeoCons., Inc., Denver, CO (2000-Present); Geophysical Manager, ANR Production Co., Denver, CO (1985-1999); Exploration Manager, Rocky Mountain and Gulf Coast Division, Denver, CO (1982-1984); Chief Geophysicist, Husky Oil Co., Denver, CO (1981-1982); Geophysical Supervisor, Northern Thrust Belt, Denver, CO (1979-1980); Division of Processing Consultant, Amoco Production Co., Denver, CO (1976-1979); Marine Technology Supervisor, Amoco Production Co., Denver, CO (1974-1976); Seismic Processing Supervisor, Amoco Production Co., Denver, CO (1973-1974); Geophysicist, Pan American Petroleum Corp. (1966-1973) **Career Related:** President, School Lateral Ditch Company; Consultant Engineer **Civic:** Board of Directors, Rocky Mountain Residence **Membership:** Denver Geophysical Society; Society of Exploration Geophysicists **Political Affiliations:** Republican **Religion:** Baptist **Shipping Address:** 675 Estes Street, Lakewood, CO, 80215

Sara C. Johnston, PhD

Title: Research Microbiologist **Industry:** Sciences **Company Name:** GDIT, U.S. Army Medical Research Institute of Infectious Diseases **Education:** PhD in Microbiology and Immunology, University of Rochester Medical Center, Rochester, NY (2009); MS in Microbiology and Immunology, University of Rochester Medical Center, Rochester, NY (2007); BS in Biology, Utica College, Summa Cum Laude, Utica, NY (2004) **Certifications:** Certified in CPR (2013); Certified in Hazardous Materials Operations (2013); Certified Rescue Technician (2013); Positive Pressure Certified (2009); Biological Personal Reliability Program Certified (2009); BSL-3 Certified (2009); BSL-4 Certified (2009); HIPAA Certified (2009) **Career:** Instructor, Tae Kwon Do and Women's Self-Defense, Kyobum, Han Mi Martial Arts (2015-Present); BSL-4 Mentor, U.S. Army Medical Research Institute of Infectious Diseases (2013-Present); Research Microbiologist, U.S. Army Medical Research Institute of Infectious Diseases (2009-Present); Master's Thesis Mentor, U.S. Army Medical Research Institute of Infectious Diseases (2011-2012) **Career Related:** Subject Matter Expert, Deviations SOP CAPA Working Group, U.S. Army Medical Research Institute of Infectious Diseases (2017-Present); Subject Matter Expert, GLP Management Meeting Working Group, U.S. Army Medical Research Institute of Infectious Diseases (2016-Present); Subject Matter Expert, Well-Documented Non-Clinical Studies, U.S. Army Medical Research Institute of Infectious Diseases (2016-Present); Research Microbiologist, U.S. Army Medical Research Institute of Infectious Diseases (2012-Present); Subject Matter Expert-RT-PCR IPT, U.S. Army Medical Research Institute of Infectious Diseases (2012-Present); GLP Study Director, Virology Division, U.S. Army Medical Research Institute of Infectious Diseases (2012-Present); Henipavirus Subject Matter Expert, Institute-Wide, U.S. Army Medical Research Institute of Infectious Diseases (2011-Present); Annual GLP Training Working Group Member, U.S. Army Medical Research Institute of Infectious Diseases (2017); Team Member, FDA Euthanasia Criteria Discussion, U.S. Army Medical Research Institute of Infectious Diseases (2016); Team Member, FDA Aerosol Exposure in Primates Discussion, U.S. Army Medical Research Institute of Infectious Diseases (2016); Molecular Core Co-Chief, Virology Division, Viral Therapeutics Department, U.S. Army Medical Research Institute of Infectious Diseases (2011-2012); Postdoctoral Fellowship, United States Nuclear Regulatory Commission (2009-2012) **Civic:** Member, Advanced Technical Rescue, Frederick, MD (2015-Present); With, EMT, Frederick, MD (2014-Present); Fire Fighter, Frederick, MD (2014-Present); With, Recreation Co-Ed Softball League, Frederick, MD (2010-Present); Participant, Tae Kwon Do, University of Rochester, Rochester, NY (2007-2009) **Military Service:** Employee, U.S. Army Medical Research Institute of Infectious Diseases **Creative Works:** Author, "Iteration 5: Efficacy Testing of Filovirus Vaccines in Non-human Primates," National Institute of Allergy and Infectious Diseases, NIH (2017); Author, "Detection of Ebola Virus RNA through Aerosol Sampling of ABSL-4 Rooms Housing Challenged Nonhuman Primates," The Journal of Infectious Diseases (2017); Author, "Iteration 4: Efficacy Testing of Filovirus Vaccines in Non-human Primates," National Institute of Allergy and Infectious Diseases, (NIH) (2016); Author, "Iteration 3: Efficacy Testing of Filovirus Vaccines in Non-human Primates," National Institute of Allergy and Infectious Diseases, (NIH) (2016); Author, "Iteration 2: Efficacy Testing of Filovirus Vaccines in Non-human Primates," National Institute of Allergy and Infectious Diseases, (NIH) (2016); Author, "Iteration 1: Efficacy Testing of Filovirus Vaccines in Non-human Primates," National Institute of Allergy and Infectious Diseases (NIH) (2016); Author, "Two and Three Dose VRP EBOV-GP Challenge Studies to Assess the Ability to Provide Protection against Zaire 7U: Study 1b (Three Dose Study)," Medical Countermeasure Systems (MCS)-Joint Vaccine Acquisition Program (JVAP) and Bioscavenger (2016); Author, "Study 1a of B.27: Two Dose VRP EBOV-GP Challenge Studies to Assess the Ability to Provide Protection against Zaire 7U," Medical Countermeasure Systems (MCS)-Joint Vaccine Acquisition Program (JVAP) and Bioscavenger (2016); Author, "B.25: Efficacy of Filovirus Sudan VRP-GP Construct via Intramuscular and Aerosol Challenge," Medical Countermeasure Systems (MCS)-Joint Vaccine Acquisition Program (JVAP) and Bioscavenger (2016) **Awards:** Recognition Award for Involvement in EBOV Outbreak Response, U.S. Army Medical Research Institute of Infectious Diseases (2015); President's Scholarship, Utica College, Utica, NY (2000-2004); Ralph F. Strebel Scholarship, Utica College, Utica, NY (2002-2004); Empire 8 President's List, Utica College, Utica, NY (2002-2004); Ralph F. Strebel Prize, Utica College, Utica, NY (2002) **Membership:** Ice Hockey Club, University of Rochester, Rochester, NY (2004-2009); Asa Gray Biological Society, Utica College, Utica, NY (2001-2004) **Hobbies:** Playing drum and guitar; Playing soccer and lacrosse **Business Address:** 1425 Porter St, Fort Detrick, MD, 21702 **Shipping Address:** 1449 Ramblewood Dr, Emmitsburg, MD, 21727

Daniel E. Jolly

Title: Dental Educator and Practitioner **Industry:** Health, Wellness and Fitness **Company Name:** Daniel E. Jolly, DDS **Date of Birth:** 08/25/1952 **Place of Birth:** St. Louis **State/Country of Origin:** MO **Parents:** Melvin Joseph Jolly; Betty Ehs (Koehler) Jolly **Children:** Farrell **Education:** DDS, University of Missouri-Kansas City (1977); BA in Biology and Chemistry, University of Missouri-Kansas City (1974) **Certifications:** Diplomate, American Board of Special Care Dentistry (2004) **Career:** Private General Dentistry Practice, Herrick Family Dental and Beechcroft Family Dental, Columbus, OH; Part-time Dental Director, Insurance Company (2013-Present); President, Immediadent of Ohio (2008-2013); Professor, Director, General Practice Residency Program, Ohio State University, Columbus, OH (1993-2008); Associate Professor, Director, General Practice Residency Program, Ohio State University, Columbus (1987-2008); Director of Dental Oncology, Trinity Lutheran Hospital (1982-1987); Chief of Restorative Dentistry, Truman Medical Center, Kansas City, MO (1979-1987); Assistant Professor, University of Missouri-Kansas City (1979-1987); Private Practice, Newcastle, WY (1978-1979); Resident in Hospital Dentistry, VA Medical Center, Leavenworth, KS (1977-1978) **Career Related:** Director, Honduras Clinic Project (1992-Present); President, Combined Hospital Dental Staff, Columbus, OH (1991-1992); Vice President, Combined Hospital Dental Staff, Columbus, OH (1990-1991); Secretary, Combined Hospital Dental Staff, Columbus, OH (1989-1990); Consultant, Longview Nursing Center, Grandview, MO (1986-1987); Board of Directors, Rinehart Foundation, School of Dentistry, University of Missouri-Kansas City (1985-1987); Consultant, Lee's Summit Care Center, Missouri (1984-1987) **Civic:** Secretary, Board of Directors, Easter Seal Rehabilitation Center, Easter Seal Society, Columbus, OH (1990-1993); Member, Professional Advisory Council, Easter Seal Society (1986-1992); Member, Regional Council, Easter Seal Society, Kansas City (1985-1987); President, Health Professionals Serving Humanity **Creative Works:** Author, "OSU Manual Hospital Dentistry" (1989-Present); Author, "Nursing Home Dentistry" (1986); Author, "Dental Oncology" (1986); Author, "Hospital Dentistry" (1985); Author, "Hospital Dental Hygiene" (1984) **Awards:** Honduras Project, Alumni Achievement Award in Dentistry, University Missouri-Kansas City (1998, 1994-1995); Humanitarian Award, Ohio Dental Association (1998); Alumni Achievement Award in Dentistry, University of Missouri-Kansas City (1995) **Membership:** ImmediaDent, Ohio (2008-Present); President, American Board of Special Care Dentistry (2004-Present); President, American Association of Hospital Dentists (2003-Present); Regional Vice President, American Association of Hospital Dentists (1993-Present) ; Secretary, President-Elect, American Association of Hospital Dentists (2002-2003); President, International Association of Dentistry for the Handicapped (1994-1996); Chairman, Federation of Special Care Dentistry Association (1992-1993); President, Academy of Dentistry for the Handicapped (1992); Fellow, Pierre Fauchard Academy; Fellow, American College of Dentistry; Fellow, Academy of Dentistry for the Handicapped; Fellow, American Society of Geriatric Dentistry; Fellow, American Dentistry International; Fellow, American Association of Hospital Dentists; Fellow, Academy of General Dentistry; American Dental Association; Ohio Dental Association; International Society of Oral Oncology; Southwest Oncology Group; Greater Kansas City Dental Society; Magna Charta Barons Club **Marquis Who's Who Honors:** Albert Nelson Marquis Lifetime Achievement Award (2017) **To what do you attribute your success:** Dr. Jolly attributes his success to hard work, commitment, and stamina, as well as to his life philosophy. **Why did you become involved in your profession or industry:** Dr. Jolly became involved in this profession to be of service to others. **What do you consider to be the highlight of your career:** Dr. Jolly's legacy is the commitment he instilled in his students and residents to be dedicated to quality and compassionate oral health care for people with disabilities, medically complex conditions, and the aged. **Where will you be in five years:** In five years, Dr. Jolly will be devoting more time to education. **Hobbies:** Photography; Scuba diving; Swimming; Horses **Shipping Address:** 5991 Outville Rd SW, Pataskala, OH, 43062

Bruce H. Jones

Title: Physician **Industry:** Medicine & Health Care **Company Name:** U.S. Army **Education:** MPH, Harvard University (1986); MD, Kansas University, Kansas City, KS (1977); MA in Biology, Kansas University (1974); BA in History and Science, Harvard University, Cum Laude (1970) **Career:** Division Chief, U.S. Army Center for Health Promotion and Preventive Medicine (Now Injury Prevention Division, Army Public Health Center), Aberdeen Proving Ground, MD (2002-Present); Team Leader, Motor Vehicle Injury Prevention, National Center for Injury Prevention and Control, CDC, Atlanta, GA (1998-2002); Retired, Active Duty (1998); Director, Epidemiology and Disease Surveillance, U.S. Army Center Health for Promotion and Preventive Medicine (Now Army Public Health Center) (1996-1998); Program Manager, Injury and Occupational Illness, U.S. Army Center for Health Promotion and Preventive Medicine (1994-1996); Chief, Occupational Medicine Research Division, U.S. Army Research Institute of Environmental Medicine, Natick, MA (1989-1994); Medical Officer, U.S. Army Research Institute of Environmental Medicine, Natick, MA (1986-1989); Resident in Preventive Medicine, Walter Reed Army Institute of Research (1986); Medical Officer, U.S. Army Research Institute of Environmental Medicine, Natick, MA (1980-1984); Intern, Winter General VA Hospital, Stormont Vail Hospital, Topeka, KS (1979-1980) **Career Related:** Department of Defense Representative, DHHS, CDC Advisory Committee on Injury Prevention and Control; Chairman, DOD Work Group on Injury Surveillance and Prevention; DOD Military, Training Task Force; Co-Chair, DOD Military Injury Work Group **Military Service:** Advanced Through Grades to Colonel, U.S. Army (1995); General Medical Officer, U.S. Army, Fort Jackson, SC (1977-1979); Commissioned Captain, U.S. Army (1977) **Creative Works:** Editor, Contributor, Supplements, American Journal of Preventative Medicine (2010); Editor, Contributor, Supplements, American Journal of Preventative Medicine (2000); Editor, Author, "The Atlas of Injuries in Military Medicine" (1999); Author/Co-Author, More Than 130 Peer-Reviewed Articles **Membership:** Fellow, American College of Preventive Medicine; Fellow, American College of Sports Medicine **Business Address:** 5158 Blackhawk Road, Aberdeen Proving Ground, MD, 21010 **Shipping Address:** 4902 Wilmslow Road, Baltimore, MD, 21210

Gregory Jones

Title: Lawyer, Owner **Industry:** Law and Legal Services **Company Name:** Greg Jones Law, P.A. **Education:** JD, University of North Carolina at Chapel Hill (1985); BA in Communications, Wingate University (1982); AA, Wingate University (1980) **Career:** Owner, Lawyer, Greg Jones Law, P.A. (1998-Present); Partner, Baker & Jones, P.A., Wilmington, NC (1992-1998); Associate, Parker, Pollard & Brown, P.C., Charlotte, NC (1987-1992); Associate, Haynes, Baucom, Chandler, Claytor & Benton, Charlotte, NC (1985-1987) **Career Related:** Speaker, Winter Convention, Ethical Considerations with Social Networking (2010); Speaker, Annual Convention, Face-to-Face Marketing: Gain Client Referral the Old Fashioned Way (2010); Speaker, Annual Convention, Marketing for Your Practice: The Art of Face to Face Marketing (2009); Speaker, Winter Convention, Viagra, Levitra, and Cialis (2006); Speaker, Teleseminar Ethics in Lawyer Advertising (2003) **Creative Works:** AAJ Press, Ethical Considerations with Social Networking (2010); AAJ Press, Face to Face Marketing: Gain Client Referrals the Old Fashioned Way (2010); AAJ Press, Marketing for Your Practice: The Art of Face to Face Marketing (2009); AAJ Press, Viagra, Levitra, and Cialis (2006); PESI Publication, Settling With the Liability Insurance Carrier and Living To Tell About It, Insurance Law Update (1998); Lorman Education Services, Publication Wage Loss Claims, Workers Compensation In North Carolina (1991) **Awards:** Top 100 Trial Lawyers, National Trial Lawyers Association (2018); Distinguished, Martindale-Hubbell (2017); North Carolina's Most Influential Law Firm, Corporate Vision (2016); Ten Best in Client Satisfaction, American Institute of Personal Injury Attorneys (2015); Super Lawyers (2009); Nation's Top One Percent, National Association of Distinguished Counsel Client Distinction Award, Martindale-Hubbell **Bar Admissions:** Texas (2015); U.S. District Court, Northern District, State of Georgia (2006); Georgia (2002); South Carolina (2001); U.S. District Court, Eastern District, State of North Carolina (2000); U.S. District Court, Middle District, State of North Carolina (2000); U.S. District Court, District of South Carolina (2000); U.S. District Court, Western District, State of North Carolina (1985); North Carolina (1985) **Business Address:** 3015 Market Street, Wilmington, NC, 28403 **Shipping Address:** 1319 Military Cutoff Road, Suite CC138, Wilmington, NC, 28405

H (Harold) Gilbert Jones Jr.

Title: Lawyer **Industry:** Law and Legal Services **Company Name:** Lewis, Brisbois, Bisgaard & Smith **Date of Birth:** 11/02/1927 **Place of Birth:** Fargo **State/Country of Origin:** ND **Parents:** Harold Gilbert Jones; Charlotte Viola (Chambers) Jones **Marital Status:** Widower **Spouse Name:** Julie Squier (2/15/1964, Deceased 3/10/2014) **Children:** Lettice Jones Carroll; Thomas Squier Jones; Christopher Lee Jones **Education:** JD, University of California, Los Angeles (1956); Postgraduate Coursework, Michigan University (1948-1949); BS, Yale University (1947) **Career:** Of Counsel, Lewis, Brisbois, Bisgaard & Smith (1990-Present); Private Practice (1959-Present); Of Counsel, Bonne, Jones, Bridges, Mueller & O'Keefe, Los Angeles, CA (1990-1992); Founding Partner, Bonne, Jones, Bridges, Mueller & O'Keefe, Los Angeles, CA (1961-1990); Partner, Overton, Lyman & Prince, Los Angeles (1960-1961); Member, Overton, Lyman & Prince, Los Angeles, CA (1956-1961) **Civic:** Board of Directors, Wilshire YMCA (1969-1975) **Military Service:** US Army (1950-1952) **Awards:** Best Lawyers in America (1997-Present); Who's Who Defendants Trial Lawyer of the Year, Orange County, CA (2014); Lifetime Achievement Award, American Board of Trial Advocates (2007); California Trial Lawyer of the Year, American Board of Trial Advocates (1999); Blue Water Cruising Award, L.A. Yacht Club (1986) **Membership:** Diplomat, American Board of Trial Advocates (1963-Present); Center Club; Commodore, Newport Harbor Yacht Club (1998); Commodore Transpacific Yacht (1996-1998); National Executive Committee, American Board of Trial Advocates (1990-1996); National President, American Board of Trial Advocates (1989); President, Los Angeles Chapter, American Board of Trial Advocates (1980); Fellow, American College of Trial Lawyers (1974); Fellow, International Academy of Trial Lawyers (1973); ABA (1958); California Bar Association (1957); Fellow, American College of Trial Lawyers; Fellow, International Academy of Trial Lawyers; Former Chairman, Legal-Medical Relations Committee, Los Angeles County Bar Association; Orange County Bar Association; Southern California Association Defense Counsel; Jonathan Club; Cruising Club of America **Bar Admissions:** California (1957); Supreme Court of the United States; Supreme Court of California **Marquis Who's Who Honors:** Albert Nelson Marquis Lifetime Achievement Award (2017) **Hobbies:** Sailing **Business Address:** 650 Town Center Dr Suite 1400, Costa Mesa, CA, 92626 **Shipping Address:** 818 Harbor Island Dr, Newport Beach, CA, 92660

Robert G. Jones, Esq.

Title: Lawyer, Mayor **Industry:** Law and Legal Services **Company Name:** Jones, Walker & Lake, P.C. **Date of Birth:** 03/25/1936 **Place of Birth:** State College **State/Country of Origin:** PA **Parents:** Edward H. Jones; Dorothy (Griffiths) Jones **Marital Status:** Married **Spouse Name:** Carolyn E. Hazard (8/29/1959) **Children:** Robert Griffith, Jr.; Chester H. **Education:** JD, The University of Virginia (1974); PhD, Duke University (1966); MDiv, Yale University (1961); AB, Davidson College (1958) **Career:** Chairman, Jones, Walker & Lake (1991-Present); Mayor, City of Virginia Beach (1986-1988); Professor, The University of Virginia (1971-1974); Associate Professor, Lehigh University (1965-1971); Assistant Professor, Davidson College (1964-1965); Assistant to the President, Lehigh University **Career Related:** Member, Advisory Board, Southern Bank & Trust (1997-2005) **Civic:** Chairman, Virginia Beach Economic Development, City of Virginia Beach (2001-2005); Chairman, Tidewater Transportation District Commission (1988); Vice-Chairman, Tidewater Transportation District Commission (1987-1988); Councilman, City Council, City of Virginia Beach (1982-1988) **Bar Admissions:** Supreme Court of the United States (1977); Virginia (1974) **Marquis Who's Who Honors:** Albert Nelson Marquis Lifetime Achievement Award (2017) **To what do you attribute your success:** Dr. Jones attributes his success to supportive colleagues and staff. **Why did you become involved in your profession or industry:** He became involved in his profession to help people. **What do you consider to be the highlight of your career:** A highlight of his career has been leading a successful law firm and severing the City of Virginia Beach. **Where will you be in five years:** In five years, he will be enjoying full retirement. **Political Affiliations:** Democrat **Religion:** Presbyterian **Shipping Address:** Robert G. Jones, Esq., 128 S. Lynnhaven Rd., Virginia Beach, VA, 23452

Louise Herron Jordan

Title: Signature Artist **Industry:** Fine Art **Date of Birth:** 12/25/1938 **Place of Birth:** Shanghai **State/Country of Origin:** China **Parents:** Edwin Warren Herron; Marie Standley Herron **Marital Status:** Married **Spouse Name:** John Patrick Jordan (6/24/1995); Michael Dean Salmon (6/21/1958, Divorced 1976) **Children:** Catherine Louise Boggess; Michael Dean Salmon; Richard Dean Salmon; Marianne Salmon Lynch **Education:** Coursework, New Orleans Academy of Art (1996-2012); Coursework, Smith College (1956-1958) **Career:** Professional Artist (1996-Present); Executive Assistant to the President, Lawrence Technological University, Southfield, MI (1993-1995); Member, Director, Meetings, American Institute of Biological Sciences, Washington, DC (1985-1993); Parish Secretary, St. Lawrence Catholic Church, Alexandria, VA (1977-1980); Signature Artist, Louisiana Watercolor Society **Civic:** Member, Dominican Institute for the Arts, Adrian, MI (2001-Present); Professed Lay Member, Dominican Order, New Orleans, LA (1997-Present); Board Member, International Dominican Foundation (2007-2014) **Creative Works:** Exhibitor, Dominican Institute Arts Group Show, Sparkill, NY (2003); Solo Exhibitor, The Long Gallery, Ochsner Medical Center, New Orleans, LA (2002); Exhibitor, Group Shows, River Road Juried Exhibit, Baton Rouge, LA (2002); Solo Exhibitor, Café Dégas, New Orleans, LA (2002); Solo Exhibitor, St. Tammany Art Association, Holiday Inn, Covington, LA (2001); Solo Exhibitor, The Upstairs Gallery (2001); Solo Exhibitor, The Long Gallery, Ochsner Medical Center, New Orleans, LA (2000); Exhibitor, Group Shows, Juried Show, Masur Museum (1997); Exhibitor, Group Shows, Fest for All, Baton Rouge, LA (1997); Exhibitor, Group Shows, National Exhibit, New Orleans Art Association (1997) **Membership:** Board, International Dominican Foundation (2008-Present); Workshop Director, Louisiana Watercolor Society (1999-Present); President, Louisiana Watercolor Society (1998-2000); Signature Member, President, Louisiana Watercolor Society (1998-2000); Chairman, International Exhibition, Louisiana Watercolor Society (1997-1999); Associate, St. Tammany Art Association; Associate, New Orleans Art Association; Lifetime Member, Louisiana Watercolor Society; Honorary Member, Xavier University Alumni Association; Associate, Smith College Alumni Association; Awards Committee, The National World War II Museum; Lady with Star, Papal Order, Equestrian Order of the Holy Sepulchre of Jerusalem **Marquis Who's Who Honors:** Albert Nelson Marquis Lifetime Achievement Award (2017) **Hobbies:** Reading; Painting; Gardening; Spending time with her grandchildren and great-grandchildren **Religion:** Roman Catholic **Shipping Address:** 4644 Bancroft Dr, New Orleans, LA, 70122

Paul Christopher Joss

Title: Professor Emeritus of Physics, Astrophysicist, Atmospheric Physicist, Educator **Industry:** Sciences **Company Name:** Massachusetts Institute of Technology **Date of Birth:** 05/07/1945 **Place of Birth:** Brooklyn **State/Country of Origin:** NY **Parents:** Everett Henry Joss; Magda Anna (Hohorst) Joss **Marital Status:** Married **Spouse Name:** Rhoda Kupferberg J. (11/14/2010); Karen Elizabeth Murray (7/3/1992, Divorced); Marjorie Jean Axton (1/24/1970, Divorced) **Children:** Susan Elizabeth; Matthew Albert Henry **Education:** PhD, Cornell University (1971); BA, Cornell University, Magna Cum Laude (1966) **Career:** Founder and Chief Technology Officer, Tropical Weather Analytics, Inc., Burlington, MA (2016-Present); Senior Vice President for Research, Visidyne, Inc., Burlington, MA (2015-Present); Professor of Physics Emeritus, Massachusetts Institute of Technology, Cambridge, MA (2014-Present); Kavli Institute for Astrophysics and Space Research, Massachusetts Institute of Technology (2005-Present); President, Joss Consulting Associates, Dracut, MA (1992-Present); Center for Theoretical Physics, Massachusetts Institute of Technology (1973-Present); Astrophysics Division, Massachusetts Institute of Technology (1973-Present); Consultant, SEAC, Inc., Burlington, MA (2008-2015); Senior Scientist and Special Assistant to the President, Visidyne, Inc. (1993-2015); Consultant, Visidyne, Inc. (1992-1993); Associate Head, Astrophysics Division, Massachusetts Institute of Technology (1986-1988); Acting Head, Astrophysics Division, Massachusetts Institute of Technology (1985-1986); Professor, Massachusetts Institute of Technology (1983-2014); Associate Head, Astrophysics Division, Massachusetts Institute of Technology (1983-1985); Consultant, Visidyne, Inc. (1979-1982); Associate Professor, Massachusetts Institute of Technology (1978-1983); Institute for Advanced Study, Princeton, NJ (1976); Center for Space Research, Massachusetts Institute of Technology (1973-2005); Assistant Professor, Massachusetts Institute of Technology (1973-1978); Institute for Advanced Study, Princeton, NJ (1971-1973) **Career Related:** Principal Scientist, Tropical Cyclone Project, International Space Station, NASA (2013-Present); Visiting Scientist, Aspen Center for Physics, Aspen, CO (1972-Present); Visiting Scientist, Institute of Astronomy, University of Cambridge, England (1993); Institute for Theoretical Physics, University of California, Santa Barbara (1991); Astronomy and Space Physics Science Council, Universities Space Research Association (1988-1992); High Energy Astrophysics Management Operations Working Group, NASA (1988-1991); Advisory Committee, Institute of Geophysics and Planetary Physics, Los Alamos National Laboratory, NM (1987-1992); Executive Committee, High Energy Astrophysics Division, American Astronomical Society (1983-1985); Consultant, Los Alamos National Laboratory (1980-1992); Visiting Staff Member, Los Alamos Scientific Laboratory (1979-1980); Visiting Scientist, Weizmann Institute Science, Rehovot, Israel (1978); Visiting Scientist, Institute of Astronomy, University of Cambridge, England (1977); Fellow, Alfred P. Sloan Foundation (1976); Visiting Scientist, Weizmann Institute Science, Rehovot, Israel (1974-1975); Fellow, National Science Foundation (1970); Fellow, Woodrow Wilson Foundation (1966) **Creative Works:** Editor, "High Energy Astrophysics in the 21st Century," American Institute of Physics, New York (1989); Contributor, 203 Articles, Professional Journals **Awards:** Award for Innovation in Earth Science and Remote Sensing on the International Space Station, American Astronautical Society (2017); Helen B. Warner Prize, American Astronomical Society (1980) **Membership:** American Astronomical Society; American Physical Society; International Astronomical Union; Phi Beta Kappa **Marquis Who's Who Honors:** Albert Nelson Marquis Lifetime Achievement Award (2017) **Hobbies:** Classical music; Chess **Religion:** Unitarian Universalist **Business Address:** MIT Kavli Institute for Astrophysics and Space Research, Cambridge, MA, 02139 **Shipping Address:** 810 Concord Street, Carlisle, MA, 01741 **Website:** http://web.mit.edu/physics/people/faculty/joss_paul.html

Marc W. Judice

Title: Lawyer **Industry:** Law and Legal Services **Company Name:** Judice & Adley, PLC **Date of Birth:** 10/22/1946 **Place of Birth:** Lafayette **State:** LA **Parents:** Marc Judice; Gladys B. Judice **Marital Status:** Married **Spouse Name:** Michelle Regan **Children:** Renee; Saint-Marie Judice **Education:** JD, Louisiana State University Paul M. Hebert Law Center, Louisiana State University (1977); MBA in Management and Finance, The University of Utah (1974); BS in Accounting, University of Louisiana (1969) **Certifications:** Certified in Civil Trial Law, National Board of Trial Advocacy (2015); Certified in Civil Trial Law, National Board of Trial Advocacy (1995, 2000, 2005, 2010) **Career:** President, Judice & Adley, PLC (1993-Present); Partner, Juneau, Judice, Hill & Adley (1985-1993); Partner, Voorhies & Labbe (1977-1985) **Civic:** Board of Directors, Home Savings Bank, F.S.B., Lafayette, LA (1996-Present); Chairman, Board of Trustees, Medical Center of Southwest Louisiana (1999-2002); Board of Trustees, Medical Center of Southwest Louisiana (1998-2001); Board of Trustees, Women's & Children's Hospital, Lafayette, LA (1992-1994); Chairman, Board of Directors, University Medical Center (1990-1991); President, Our Lady of Fatima School Foundation, Lafayette, LA (1986-1987) **Military Service:** U.S. Air Force (1969-1974) **Creative Works:** Annual Meeting, Louisiana Podiatric Medical Association Speaker, "Reflection on DPM Cases" (2017); Seminar Speaker, "Expert Witness Trial Preparation & Testimony," 33rd Annual Defense Counsel Seminar, Louisiana Medical Mutual Insurance Company (2016); Seminar Co-Speaker, "DPM Practice -Statute & Regulations and Louisiana State Board Medical Examiners Issues," Meeting and Seminar, Louisiana Podiatric Medical Association (2015); Seminar Speaker, "Expert Medical Testimony Viewed from the Witness Stand. Co-Presentation with Dr. Weston P. Miller, III," 32nd Annual Defense Counsel Seminar, Louisiana Medical Mutual Insurance Company (2015); Seminar Speaker, "Charting Role in Defense of DPM," Meeting and Seminar, Louisiana Podiatric Medical Association (2015); Seminar Speaker, Panel Presentation, "Loss of Chance - Is There a Chance for Defense?," 29th Annual Defense Counsel Seminar, Louisiana Medical Mutual Insurance Company (2012); Seminar Speaker, "PCF and Malpractice Cap: How Medical Malpractice Has Changed in Last 30 Years," Annual Meeting, Louisiana Orthopaedic Association (2011); Seminar Speaker, "Potpourri of Medical Malpractice Legal Issues/Court Developments in Case Law," 25th Annual Defense Counsel Seminar, Louisiana Medical Mutual Insurance Company (2008); Seminar Speaker, "Direct and Re-Direct of Defendant's Expert," Masters In Trial Seminar, Louisiana Chapter, American Board of Trial Advocates (2008); Seminar Co-Speaker, "Winning at the Beginning: The Importance of Jury Selection and Opening Statements, 24th Annual Defense Counsel Seminar, Louisiana Medical Mutual Insurance Company (2007); Contributing Author, "The Defendant Physician at Trial," LAMMICO, the Letter (1994, 2007); Seminar Speaker, "Medical Malpractice Update," Annual Scientific and Educational Meeting, Louisiana Orthopaedic Association (2006); Seminar Speaker, "Charting - How? Why? When?," Seminar, Louisiana Society for Healthcare Risk Management (LASHRM) (2006) **Awards:** Honoree, Super Lawyers: Business Edition (2011-2017); Honoree, Super Lawyers: Business Edition (2016); Senior Fellow, The Trial Lawyer Honorary Society, Litigation Counsel of America (2016); Honoree, Top Lawyers, Acadiana Profile (2015-2016); Honoree, Louisiana Super Lawyers (2007-2015); Honoree, AV Preeminent Attorney, Martindale-Hubbell (1994-2015); Honoree, Top Rated Lawyers, Louisiana's Legal Leaders (2013); Honoree, Top Lawyers, Acadiana Profile (2012); Fellow, The Trial Lawyer Honorary Society, Litigation Counsel of America (2008-2012); Honoree, Super Lawyers: Corporate Counsel Edition (2009-2011); Honoree, Best of Acadiana, Time of Acadiana (2008-2009); Honoree, Outstanding Lawyers of America (2003); Recipient, Outstanding Accounting Alumni Award, College of Business Administration, University of Louisiana at Lafayette (1996); Honoree, First Place, Flory Trial Competition, Louisiana State University Paul M. Hebert Law Center, Louisiana State University (1976); Recipient, Commendation Medal, U.S. Air Force (1974); Recipient, Meritorious Service Medal, U.S. Air Force (1973) **Membership:** Louisiana Chapter, American Board of Trial Advocates (2016); State Board of Certified Public Accountants of Louisiana (1976-2012); Association of Attorney-Certified Public Accountants (1995-2000); American Society of Law, Medicine & Ethics (1987-2000); Inactive Member, Society of Louisiana Certified Public Accountants; Inactive Member, American Institute of Certified Public Accountants; American Board of Trial Advocates **Bar Admissions:** ABA (1977-2017); Louisiana State Bar Association (1977); Lafayette Parish Bar Association **Marquis Who's Who Honors:** Albert Nelson Marquis Lifetime Achievement Award (2017) **Political Affiliations:** Republican **Shipping Address:** 926 Coolidge Blvd, Judice & Adley, PLC, Lafayette, LA, 70503

Diana Juettner

Title: Lawyer, Department Chair **Industry:** Law and Legal Services **Place of Birth:** New York **State/Country of Origin:** NY **Marital Status:** Married **Spouse Name:** Paul J. Juettner (6/29/1963) **Children:** John; Laura; Amber (Grandchild); Jake (Grandchild); Falyn (Grandchild) **Education:** JD, Touro College Jacob D. Fuchsberg Law Center, Cum Laude (1983); Postgraduate Work, American University (1963); BA, Hunter College (1961) **Certifications:** Certified in Mediation, Institute Mediation and Conflict Resolution (2003) **Career:** Chair of Legal & Justice Studies, Mercy College (2008-Present); Co-Chair, Social and Behavioral Sciences Division, Mercy College (2002-Present); Private Practice (1984-Present); President, Faculty Senate, Mercy College (2000-2002); President, Faculty Senate, Mercy College (1996-1998); Assistant Chair, Department of Law, Mercy College (1994-1998); Professor of Law, Mercy College (1985-2008); Program Director for Legal Studies, Mercy College (1985-2008); District Manager for Westchester County, United States Census Bureau (1979-1980); Office Manager, Westchester County Democratic Committee (1976-1979) **Civic:** Councilwoman, Town of Greenburgh, NY (1992-Present); Chair, Citizens Consumer Advisory Council, Westchester County (1991); Vice-Chair, Law Committee, Westchester County Democratic Committee (1987-1991); Corresponding Secretary, Greenburgh Democratic Committee (1986-1991); Member, Citizens Consumer Advisory Council, Westchester County (1975-1991); Chair, Consumer Advisory Commission, Village of Ardsley (1974-1979) **Membership:** Chair, Paralegal Subcommittee, Westchester County Bar Association (1990-Present); Co-Chair, Technology Committee, Westchester Women's Bar Association (1996-2000); Chair, Professional Ethics Committee, Women's Bar Association of the State of New York (1997-1998); Chair, Legislative Committee, American Association for Paralegal Education (1995-1997); Director, Westchester Women's Bar Association (1994-1996); Model Syllabus Task Force, American Association for Paralegal Education (1992-1995); Elder Law Section Committee on Public Agency Liaison and Legislation, New York State Bar Association (1992-1995); Vice President, Westchester Women's Bar Association (1989-1991); Chair, Bicentennial United States Constitution Committee, Westchester County Bar Association (1987-1991); President, Local Group, Rotary International **Bar Admissions:** Supreme Court of the United States (1987); United States District Court Southern District of New York (1984) **Marquis Who's Who Honors:** Albert Nelson Marquis Lifetime Achievement Award (2017); Distinguished Humanitarian (2017) **Why did you become involved in your profession or industry:** She raised her children and was very active in the schools and the community. She was elected as a councilwoman for the Town of Greenburgh since 1982. She saw a need for helping others and enrolled in law school. She has been aiding the less fortunate and giving a voice to those that do not have one. **Hobbies:** Sailing; Walking **Shipping Address:** 598 Ashford Ave, Ardsley, NY, 10502

Barbara J. Justice

Title: Forensic Psychiatrist **Industry:** Medicine & Health Care **Company Name:** Barbara J. Justice, MD **Education:** MD, Howard University (1977); Bachelor's, The City University of New York; Fellowship in Surgical Oncology; Fellowship in Endoscopy, Columbia University Medical Center; Coursework in Psychodynamic Psychotherapy, New York University Psychoanalytic School; Coursework in Forensic Psychiatry, University of California, Los Angeles; Training in Surgery, Columbia University Medical Center; Training in Surgical Oncology, Howard University Cancer Center **Certifications:** Certification, American Board of Forensic Psychiatry; Certification, American Board of Psychiatry and Neurology, Inc. **To what do you attribute your success:** Dr. Justice attributes her success to her faith and effort to constantly improve. **Why did you become involved in your profession or industry:** Dr. Justice became involved in her profession because she feels blessed with intellectual and personality skills that could be best used in the healing art of helping people. **Hobbies:** Reading; Pets; Traveling **Shipping Address:** 2211 E Orangewood Ave, Apt 412, Anaheim, CA, 92806

Robert J. Kabel

Title: Co-founder **Industry:** Law and Legal Services **Company Name:** Consejo-Sano **Date of Birth:** 11/30/1946 **Place of Birth:** Burbank **State/Country of Origin:** CA **Parents:** Herman J. Kabel; Margaret E. Kabel **Education:** LLM in Taxation, Georgetown Law (1979); JD, Vanderbilt University (1972); BA, Denison University (1969) **Career:** Co-founder, ConsejoSano (2013-Present); National Committee-man, District of Columbia Republican Party (2012-Present); Co-founder, Work-place Wellness Council-Mexico (2009-Present); Chairman, District of Columbia Republican Party (2005-2012); Senior Adviser, Faegre Baker Daniels Consulting (Now Faegre Baker Daniels LLP) (2002-2016); Of Counsel, Faegre Baker Daniels LLP (2002-2016); Vice Chairman, District of Columbia Republican Party (2000-2004); Partner, Manatt, Phelps & Phillips, LLP (1985-2002); Special Assistant for Legislative Affairs to President Ronald Reagan (1982-1984); Legislative Director to Senator Richard G. Lugar (1977-1982); Legislative Assistant to Senator Paul Fannin (1975-1977); Administrative Assistant to Governor Winfield Dunn (1972-1975) **Civic:** Member, Presidential Advisory Council on HIV-AIDS (2006-2009); Board of Trustees, Denison University (2005-2010); Chairman, Liberty Education Forum (1999-2005); Chairman, Liberty Education Forum (1999-2004); Dean's Council Member, Vanderbilt Law School, Vanderbilt University (1998-2001); Chairman, Log Cabin Republicans (1993-1999); Member, Foreign Claims Settlement Com-mission of the United States (1988-1989) **Military Service:** First Lieutenant (Retired), United States Army **Awards:** Lincoln Award for Service to the District of Columbia Republican Committee (2016); Certification of Appreciation from the Secretary of HHS for Service on Presidential Advisory Council on HIV-AIDS (2009); Ronald Reagan Award, Log Cabin Republicans (2007); Alumni Citation, Denison University (2004) **Membership:** Alumni Society, Denison University; Republican National Lawyers Association; The Federalist Society; The Metro-politan Club of the City of Washington **Bar Admissions:** Admitted to Practice, Supreme Court of the United States (1998); The District of Columbia Bar; Ohio State Bar Association; Tennessee Bar Association **Marquis Who's Who Honors:** Albert Nelson Marquis Lifetime Achievement Award (2017) **To what do you attri-bute your success:** Mr. Kabel attributes his success to his supportive family, his education, and his willingness to take advantage of opportunities that arose. He also credits his passion for politics and policy. **Why did you become involved in your profession or industry:** Mr. Kabel became involved in his profession because of his childhood hero, Perry Mason. He looked up to Mr. Mason because of his knowledge, even his tempered demeanor and hard work. He has also had an interest in politics for the majority of his life. **What do you consider to be the highlight of your career:** One of the highlights of his career was working in the White House during President Reagan's first term. **Where will you be in five years:** In five years, Mr. Kabel hopes to be continuing to engage in activities and endeavors that he didn't have time for until after retiring from his full-time practice. **Hobbies:** Reading; Traveling; Gardening; Sports; The Arts **Religion:** Presbyterian **Shipping Address:** 1401 S St NW Apt 721, Washington, DC, 20009

J. Michael Kabo

Title: Professor of Mechanical Engineering **Industry:** Education/Educational Services **Company Name:** California State University **Date of Birth:** 11/18/1951 **Place of Birth:** Newark **State:** NJ **Parents:** Myron Philimon; Julia Kabo **Spouse Name:** Brooks Westcott **Children:** Kirstin; Sean **Education:** PhD in Applied Mechanics, University of California, Berkeley (1980); MS in Mechanical Engineering, University of California Berkeley (1975); AB in Economics, Rutgers, the State University of New Jersey (1974); BS in Mechanical Engineering, Rutgers, the State University of New Jersey (1974) **Career:** Professor, Mechanical Engineering Department, California State University, Northridge (2007-Present); Associate Dean, College of Engineering and Computer Science, California State University, Northridge (2004-Present); Co-director of Injury Biomechanics, Executive Committee, Southern California Injury Prevention Research Center (2001-Present); Co-chair of Biomechanics, Biomaterials, Tissue Engineering Field of Study, Biomedical Engineering Interdisciplinary Program, Henry Samueli School of Engineering and Applied Science, UCLA (1998-2003); Professor in Residence, Department of Orthopaedic Surgery, UCLA School of Medicine (1996-2003); Research Bioengineer, Orthopaedic Surgery Section, Research Service, Wadsworth Veterans Administration Medical Center (1980-1997); Adjunct Professor, Department of Orthopaedic Surgery, UCLA School of Medicine (1993-1996); Adjunct Associate Professor of Surgery, Orthopaedics and Biomechanics, UCLA School of Medicine (1987-1993); Visiting Lecturer, Civil Engineering Department, UCLA School of Engineering (1988-1991); Adjunct Assistant Professor of Surgery, Orthopaedics and Biomechanics, UCLA School of Medicine (1980-1987); Visiting Lecturer, Mechanical, Aerospace and Nuclear Engineering Department, UCLA School of Engineering (1983-1985) **Civic:** CSUN Student Veteran Advisory Committee (2016-Present); CSUN Mechanical Engineering Department Assessment Coordinator (2014-Present); CSUN Mechanical Engineering Department Graduate Coordinator (2008-Present); Parliamentarian, North Hills West Neighborhood Council (2012-Present); Parliamentarian, Granada Hills South Neighborhood Council (2007-Present); Director, Granada Hills Chamber of Commerce (2005-Present); Former Commander, Valley Ho Power Squadron, US Power Squadrons, Granada Hills, California (1990-Present); Post-tenure Review Committee, CSUN ME Department (2016-2017); Search and Screen Committee, CSUN ME Department (2016-2017); CSUN Mechanical Engineering Department Personnel Committee (2016-2017); Search and Screen Committee, Material Science Cluster, CECS/CSM (2016); CSUN Personnel Planning and Review Committee (2011-2016); Post Tenure Review Committee, CSUN ME Department (2016); Search and Screen Committee, CSUN Dean, College of Health and Human Development (2015-2016); Search and Screen Committee, CSUN ME Department Chair, Committee Chair (2015); Search and Screen Committee, CSUN Vice President of Facilities (2013-2014); Search and Screen Committee, CSUN Provost (2005-2006) **Creative Works:** Co-author, "Metabolic Measurement Techniques to Assess Bone Fracture Healing: A Preliminary Study," Clinical Orthopaedics and Related Research (2004); Co-author, "Mathematical Modeling of Human Secondary Osteons," Scanning (2004); Co-author, "Determination of Mechanical Stiffness of Bone by pQCT Measurements: Correlation with Non-Destructive Mechanical Four-Point Bending Test Data," Journal of Biomechanics (2004); Co-author, "Endoprosthetic Reconstructions for Bone Metastases," Clinical Orthopaedics and Related Research (2003); Co-author, "Custom Cross-Pin Fixation of 32 Tumor Endoprostheses Stems," Clinical Orthopaedics and Related Research (2003); Co-author, "Pressure and Temperature Distribution in Biologic Materials by Focused Ultrasound," Smart Nondestructive Evaluation and Health Monitoring of Structural and Biological Systems II (2003); Co-author, "Interaction of Focused Ultrasound with Biological Materials," Proceedings of SPIE - The International Society for Optical Engineering (2002) **Awards:** Recipient, Gil Benjamin Citizen of the Year Award, Granada Hills Chamber of Commerce (2015); Honoree, Outstanding Board Member of the Year, Granada Hills Chamber of Commerce (2008, 2013); Recipient, Distinguished Engineering Educator Award, San Fernando Valley Engineers Council (2011); Honoree, "Third Place – Best NDE Paper" (2002); Recipient, Dean's Prize for Undergraduate Research (2001); Recipient, Rookie of the Year Award, NASA Ames Research Center, USFIRST Robotics Regional Competition (2000); Recipient, Certificate of Recognition, Transcutaneous Spine Trauma and Disorders Treatment using Ultrasonically Induced Confined Heat (ULICH) Zone, NASA (2000); Recipient, Frank Stinchfield Award, Hip Society, American Academy of Orthopaedic Surgeons (2000) **Membership:** American Academy for the Advancement of Science; National Computer Graphics Association; Association for Computing Machinery **Marquis Who's Who Honors:** Albert Nelson Marquis Lifetime Achievement Award (2017) **Shipping Address:** 17048 Jeanine Pl, Granada Hills, CA, 91344

Witold Kaczanowski

Title: Painter, Sculptor **Industry:** Fine Art **Company Name:** Self-Employed **Date of Birth:** 05/15/1932 **Place of Birth:** Warsaw **Country of Origin:** Poland **Parents:** Feliks Kaczanowski; Zofia Kaczanowski **Marital Status:** Divorced **Children:** Paul; Paulina; Wit **Education:** Graduate, Academy of Fine Arts (Akademia Sztuk Pieknych w Warszawie), Warsaw, Poland (1956) **Career:** Set Designer, Cleo Parker Robinson Dance Theatre, Denver, CO (2001); Set Designer, "Cite Sans Sommeil," L'Alliance Francaise, University of Colorado (2001); Architectural Designer, Oswiecim Cultural Center, Auschwitz Jewish Cultural Center (1959) **Creative Works:** Author, Zycie Kolorado (2011-Present); Artist, Retrospective Exhibition, L'Alliance Francaise de Denver (2016); Artist, Solo Exhibition, The National Museum in Krakow (2013); Artist, Solo Exhibition, Sotheby's (2007); Artist, Solo Exhibition, Royal Lazienki Museum (2004); Artist, Private Commission, Colorado Symphony Orchestra (2004); Artist, Private Commission, Aspen Music Festival (1992); Artist, Exhibition, Otis College of Art and Design (1973); Artist, Exhibition, Graphics By Masters (1968); Muralist, Oswiecim Cultural Center, Aushwitz Jewish Cultural Center (1961); Artist, Permanent Collection, Conoco Oil Company (Now ConocoPhillips Company), Houston, TX; Artist, Permanent Collection, United California Bank, Beverly Hills, CA **Awards:** Honoree, Outstanding Polishman in the Government of Poland (2015); Medal for Merit to Culture-Gloria Artis, Minister of Culture, Government of Poland (2013); Honoree, Accomplishment Celebration, American Consulate, City of Krakow, Poland (2011); Nominee, Denver Mayor's Award for Excellence in Arts & Culture, Denver Office of Cultural Affairs (2007); Honoree, "Witold-K Day," Mayor of Denver, Colorado (1995) **Marquis Who's Who Honors:** Albert Nelson Marquis Lifetime Achievement Award (2017) **Shipping Address:** 329 Detroit Street, Denver, CO, 80206

Joseph L. Kagle

Title: Artist **Industry:** Fine Art **Date of Birth:** 05/02/1932 **Place of Birth:** Pittsburgh **State/Country of Origin:** PA **Parents:** Joseph Louis Kagle; Edith (Marcellus) Kagle **Marital Status:** Married **Spouse Name:** Anne Cornelia (Schiller) Kagle (1/19/1957) **Children:** Samantha Anne; Christopher Yung Wook **Education:** MEd in Gifted and Talented Education, University of Arkansas, Little Rock, AR (1984); MFA in Art and Art History, University of Colorado (1958); BA in English, Dartmouth College, Hanover, NH (1955); Student, Carnegie Museum School of Art (1938-1951) **Certifications:** Certified Teacher, K-12, Bridgewater State University **Career:** Professor, Art and History, Lone Star College, Kingwood, TX (2005-2016); Visiting Scholar, Mongolian State University (2004); Honorary Professor, Tbilisi Academy of Fine Arts (2001-2003); Professor of Art, McLennan Community College (1987-2005); Director, The Art Center, Waco, TX (1987-2000); Director, Bridgewater State College (1986-1987); Director, Brockton Art Museum (1984-1986); Executive Director, Southeast Arkansas Arts and Science Center, Pine Bluff, AR (1978-1984); Professor of Art, Community College of the Finger Lakes (1976-1978); Professor, Head, Department of Fine Arts, Visual Arts, Dance, Music, and Theatre, University of Guam (1970-1976); Artist in Residence, Chapman College, World Campus Afloat (1968-1969); Head, Department of Art, Associate Professor, Keuka College (1964-1968); Head, Department of Art, Assistant Professor, Washington and Jefferson College, Pennsylvania (1960-1964); Instructor, Wisconsin State University, Whitewater, WI (1958-1960) **Career Related:** Artist in Residence, International Plenary of Artists, Kutaisi, GA (2001); Artist in Residence, Naples Mill School (1976-2001); Lecture, USIS, Taiwan (1970-1976); Artist in Residence, Washington State University, Spokane, WA (1965-1966); Critic, Pine Bluff, AR; Board of Contributors, Waco Tribune-Herald Opinion Editorials **Civic:** Board of Directors, Greater Waco Council on the Arts (1989-Present); Chairman, Board of Directors, Association for Retarded Citizens (1990-1994); Advisory Board, Station KCTF (1989-1992); Planning Board, Pine Bluff Committee of the Gifted and Talented (1979-1980); **Creative Works:** Exhibited, Upstream People Gallery (2009-Present); Curator, "My Peace Journey by Ryofu Pussel," Japan (2007-Present); Contributor, Articles, Professional Publications (2010-2013); Author, 100 Essays and Two Major Works on Peace, Rotary Global History Fellowship (2006-2007); Author, "Death Is All the Time" (1976); Exhibited, Over 950 National and International Exhibitions, National Gallery, Washington, DC, National Museum, Tbilisi, GA; Director, 50 TV Shows on Art; Muralist, Hafa Adai Theatre, Bank of Guam, Fine Arts Building, University of Guam; Curator, "Open the Door"; Author, 118 Books of Works **Awards:** One of 12 American Artists, Houston, TX (2013); Systems Public Award, Lone Star Systems (2009); Outstanding Alumni, Dartmouth College (2006); Dartmouth College Alumni Award for Outstanding Service, Class of 1955 (2006); Fulbright Specialist, Mongolia (2004); Fulbright Specialist, Mongolia (2003); Fulbright Scholar, Georgia (2001-2003); National Volunteer of the Year, Arc (1993); Project Scholar, Smithsonian Institution Kellogg Foundation (1983); Artist of the Year, Pacific Chapter, American Institute of Architects (1976-1977); Artist of the Year, American Institute of Architects (1975); Fulbright Scholar, Taiwan (1965) **Membership:** President, E-Club Southwest USA (2010-2011); President, Rotary Global History Fellowship (2007-2010); Chairman, Board of Directors, Waco Association of Museums (1995-1997); Board of Directors, Waco Chamber of Commerce (1994-1997); American Museum Association; College Art Association; Texas Association of Museums; College Art Association; American Association of Museums; Rotary; Rotarians on the Internet **To what do you attribute your success:** Mr. Kagle attributes his success to starting early in art, having excellent teachers and mentors, and a passion for art, plus world travel to see Western, Eastern, and global masters in the arts. **Why did you become involved in your profession or industry:** Mr. Kagle was bedridden for two years between six and eight years old with rheumatic heart disease, so he drew and painted what he saw. He was selected in grade school through high school as a student artist at Carnegie Museum of Fine Arts. He taught college art classes for over 50 years, and has had and still has a passion for seeing and creating art worldwide. **What do you consider to be the highlight of your career:** The highlights of Mr. Kagle's career were being selected as an art student at Carnegie Museum of Fine Arts for 20 years, studying poetry by Robert Frost in his four years at Dartmouth College, winning international awards from the Upstream Peoples Gallery since the 1970s, and having work in private, national, and international sources since the 1950s. **Hobbies:** Travel; Art; Writing **Political Affiliations:** Democrat **Shipping Address:** 3767 Glade Forest Drive, Kingwood, TX, 77339

Fran Kaiser

Title: Endocrinologist, Gerontologist **Industry:** Medicine & Health Care **Company Name:** Kaiser and Associates Consulting **Date of Birth:** 12/06/1949 **Place of Birth:** New York **State/Country of Origin:** NY **Parents:** Philip Francis Kaiser; Bronia (Weiss) Kaiser **Education:** Resident to Chief Resident, Beth Israel Medical Center, New York, NY (1975-1978); Intern, Beth Israel Medical Center, New York, NY (1974-1975); MD, New York Medical College, New York, NY (1974); BS, City College of New York (1970) **Certifications:** Diplomate, American Board of Internal Medicine; Diplomate, American Board of Geriatric Medicine **Career:** CEO, Kaiser and Associates Consulting (2016-Present); Consultant, Kaiser and Associates Consulting (2004-Present); Medical Director, Health Systems, Medical Affairs, Merck & Co. Inc. (2014-2016); Executive Medical Director, Merck & Co., Inc., Irving, TX (2005-2013); Executive Medical Director, Merck & Co., Inc., Irving, TX (2003); Senior Regional Medical Director, Merck & Co., Inc., Irving, TX (1997-2003); Professor, St. Louis University (1994-1997); Associate Director, Division of Geriatric Medicine, St. Louis University (1989-1997); Associate Professor of Medicine, St. Louis University (1989-1994); Assistant Professor in Residence, University of California, Los Angeles, School of Medicine (1986-1989); Assistant Professor, University of Minnesota, Minneapolis, MN (1981-1986); Instructor, Department of Medicine, University of Minnesota, Minneapolis, MN (1980-1981); Fellow in Endocrinology and Metabolism, University of Minnesota, Minneapolis, MN (1978-1981) **Career Related:** Adjunct Professor of Medicine, St. Louis University (1997-Present); Clinical Professor of Medicine, University of Texas Southwestern Medical School, Dallas, TX (1999-2008); Chief, Geriatric Medicine, Olive View Medical Center, University of California, Sylmar, CA (1987-1989); Medical Director, Hospital Based Home Care, VA Medical Center, Sepulveda, CA (1987-1989); John A. Hartford Geriatric Faculty Development Award Scholar, Hartford Foundation, School of Medicine, University of California, Los Angeles, CA (1986-1987); Chief, Section of Endocrinology and Metabolism, Department of Internal Medicine, St. Paul Ramsey Medical Center, University of Minnesota Hospitals, St. Paul, MN (1981-1986); Fellow, American Geriatrics Society **Civic:** Volunteer, North Texas Veteran Affairs Medical Center (2016-Present) **Creative Works:** Editorial Board, Journal of Clinical Endocrinology and Metabolism; Ad Hoc Reviewer, Endocrinology; Ad Hoc Reviewer, Journal of the American Medical Association; Ad Hoc Reviewer, Journal of American Geriatrics Society; Editorial Board, American Geriatric Society; Editorial Board, International Medicine Bulletin; Consultant Editor, American Health Magazine; Contributor, Articles, Professional Journals; Contributor, Geriatrics Review Syllabus; Editorial Board, Internal Medicine Bulletin, Journal of Geriatric Nephrology & Urology **Awards:** Grantee, National Institutes of Health (1997); Grantee, Upjohn (1995-1997); Grantee, Merck (1994-1997); Grantee, VIVUS (1993-1997); Grantee, Hoechst-Roussel (1992-1994); Grantee, Bureau of Health Professions (1991-1997); Grantee, Syntex Corporation (1990-1992); Grantee, Genetech (1987-1989); Grantee, National Institutes of Health (1980-1981) **Membership:** Gerontological Society of America; American Association for the Advancement of Science; American Association of Home Care Physicians; New York Academy of Science; American Federation for Clinical Research; Endocrine Society; American Diabetes Association; Alpha Omega Alpha **Shipping Address:** 3510 Edgewater Drive, Dallas, TX, 75205

Jean Kalin

Title: Artist, Educator **Industry:** Fine Art **Company Name:** Portraits of Life **Date of Birth:** 02/11/1932 **Place of Birth:** Kansas City **State:** MO **Parents:** William Warner Johnson; Esther Dorothy (Peterson) Johnson **Marital Status:** Married **Spouse Name:** John Baptist Kalin, Jr. (1/5/1952) **Children:** Jean Loraine; Debra Ann; Diana Yvonne **Education:** Coursework, Kansas City Art Institute (1951-1952); AA, St. Joseph's Junior College (Now Missouri Western State University) (1951); Coursework, Pastel Artist Daniel E. Greene; Coursework, Oil Painter Gregg Kreutz **Career:** Art Teacher, Portraits of Life, Kansas City, MO (1988-Present); Owner, Portraits of Life, Kansas City, MO (1986-Present); Senior Process Artist, Graphic Division, Hallmark Licensing, LLC, Kansas City, MO (1973-1993); Freelance Artist, Kansas City, MO (1953-1972); Artist, Hallmark Licensing, LLC, Kansas City, MO (1952-1953) **Creative Works:** Featured Artist, "Acrilicworks 5" (2018); Featured Artist, "Art Journey Animals" (2017); Featured Artist, "Artistic Touch 6" (2014); Featured Artist, "Splash 14" (2012); Featured Artist, "Artistic Touch 5" (2012); Featured Artist, "Best of Worldwide Watermedia, Volume II" (2012); Featured Artist, "Splash 12" (2011); Featured Artist, "Watercolor Magazine" (2005); Featured Artist, "Acrylic Highlights Magazine" (2004); Featured Artist, "Midwest Art" (2003); Featured Artist, "The Artists' Magazine" (2003); Featured Artist, "Best of Collected Watercolor" (2002); Featured Artist, "American Artist Magazine" (2000); Featured Artist, "American Artist Magazine" (1998); Featured Artist, "Splash 5" (1998); Featured Artist, "Rockport Publications Best of Watercolor 2" (1997); Featured Artist, "Painting Light and Shadow" (1997); Illustrator, "Article Directory of American Portrait Artists" (1985); Featured Artist, "Art Journey Animals," Artists's Magazine; Exhibitor, American Watercolor International, New York; Exhibitor, Rockies West National Exhibition, Colorado; Exhibitor, Governor's Mansion Special Exhibition, Jefferson City, MO; Exhibitor, San Diego Watercolor Society; Exhibitor, Audubon Artists; Exhibitor, National Society of Painters in Casein and Acrylic; Exhibitor, Red River Watercolor Society, Fargo, ND; Featured Artist, Winston Churchill Museum, Fulton, MO **Awards:** Finalist, Summer Cover Competition, Watercolor Magazine (2005); Full Merit Scholarship, Kansas City Art Institute (1951-1952) **Membership:** Signature Member, National Oil and Acrylic Painters' Society; Signature Member, National Acrylic Painters' Association; Signature Member, The International Society of Acrylic Painters; Signature Member, Kansas Watercolor Society; Signature Member, Women Artists of the West; Associate, American Watercolor Society, Inc.; Associate, National Watercolor Society; Signature Member, Transparent Watercolor Society of America; Charter Member, National Museum of Women in the Arts; Signature Member, Missouri Watercolor Society; Board of Directors, Missouri Watercolor Society; Master Signature Member, Western Colorado Watercolor Society; Signature Member, Red River Watercolor Society; International Platform Association; Signature Member, National Acrylic Painters' Association; Signature Member, Illinois Watercolor Society; Signature Member, Audubon Artists **Marquis Who's Who Honors:** Albert Nelson Marquis Lifetime Achievement Award (2017) **Hobbies:** Gardening; Traveling **Shipping Address:** 20650 371 Hwy, Platte City, MO, 64079 **Website:** http://mowsart.com/page-18087

Ikar J. Kalogjera

Title: Psychiatrist, Educator **Industry:** Medicine & Health Care **Company Name:** Ikar J. Kalogjera, MD, SC **Date of Birth:** 08/30/1945 **Place of Birth:** Zagreb **State/Country of Origin:** Croatia **Parents:** Jaksa Jakov Kalogjera; Biserka Erak Kalogjera **Marital Status:** Married **Spouse Name:** Araceli Colina Cabaron **Children:** Liliana Marie **Education:** Fellow in Child and Adolescent Psychiatry, University of Cincinnati (1974-1976); Resident in Psychiatry, Medical College of Wisconsin, Wauwatosa, WI (1972-1974); Intern, University of Zagreb (1970-1971); MD, University of Zagreb, Croatia (1970) **Certifications:** Certified in Psychiatry, American Board of Psychiatry and Neurology, Inc.; Certified in Child Psychiatry, American Board of Psychiatry and Neurology, Inc.; Certification, American Board of Addiction Medicine **Career:** Psychiatrist, Private Practice, Adult, Child and Adolescent Psychiatry, Wauwatosa, WI (1981-Present) Clinical Professor, Medical College of Wisconsin (2001) Director of Adolescent In-Patient Service, Medical College of Wisconsin (1980-1981) Director of Adolescent In-Patient Unit, Medical College of Wisconsin (1979-1980) Psychiatrist, Private Practice, Rockford, IL (1976-1979) **Career Related:** Clinical Professor of Psychiatry, Medical College of Wisconsin (2001-Present); Honorary Staff Member, Aurora Psychiatric Hospital, Wauwatosa, WI (1999-Present); Founder, Leader, Milwaukee Group for the Advancement of Self-Psychology (1991-Present); Associate Clinical Professor of Psychiatry, Medical College of Wisconsin (1987-2001); Assistant Clinical Professor of Psychiatry, Medical College of Wisconsin (1981-1987) **Civic:** Contributor, Croatian Community, Milwaukee, WI (1979-Present); Consultant, Jewish Family Service, Milwaukee, WI (1979-Present); Consultant, Lutheran Social Services, Milwaukee, WI (1984-1990); Consultant, Family Service, Milwaukee, WI (1982-1989) **Creative Works:** Contributor, Book Chapter, "Disordered Couple" (1998); Author, "Hospital and Community Psychiatry" (1989); Co-author, "American Journal of Psychotherapy" (1988) **Awards:** America's Most Honored Professionals - Top 1%, American Registry (2017); Compassionate Doctor Award, Vitals (2012-2018); On-time Doctor Award, Vitals (2014, 2016-2018); Patients' Choice Award, Vitals (2014, 2016-2018); Featured Listee, One of America's Best Physicians, National Consumer Advisory Board (2016-2018); America's Most Honored Professionals - Top 5%, American Registry (2016); Honoree, Trademark's Top Doctor's Honors Edition, American Registry of Most Honored Professionals (2014-2017); Featured Listee, Top Ten Doctors in Wisconsin - Psychiatrists, Vitals (2014); Distinguished Service Award, Medical College of Wisconsin (2014); Community Service Honor, Jewish Family Services, Milwaukee, WI (2003, 2010); Excellence Award, Child & Adolescent Psychiatry Training Program (2010); Irma Bland Award, American Psychiatric Association (2006); Give a Damn Award, Medical College of Wisconsin (1991, 2003); America's Top Psychiatrists, Consumers Research Council of America (2002-2012); Featured Listee, Top Psychiatrists, Psychotherapists, Milwaukee Magazine (1994, 1996, 2001); Golden Apple Teaching Award (1996, 2000); Marvin Wagner Clinical Preceptor Award (1999); Award for Excellence in Teaching, Department of Psychiatry and Behavioral Medicine, Medical College of Wisconsin (1992); Featured Listee, Outstanding Therapists, Town and Country Magazine (1988); Distinguished Life Fellow, American Psychiatric Association; Distinguished Life Fellow, American Academy of Child Psychiatry; Founding Fellow, Academy of Cognitive Therapy **Membership:** Distinguished Fellow, Academy of Cognitive Therapy; Founding Fellow, Academy of Cognitive Therapy; Lifetime Fellow, American Academy of Child Psychiatry; Wisconsin Council of Child and Adolescent Psychiatry, International Association of Psychoanalytic Self Psychology; Special Member, Wisconsin Psychoanalytic Society; Medical Society of Milwaukee County; Alumni Association of Family, Institute of Northwestern University; American Society of Addiction Medicine; American Group Psychotherapy Association; Wisconsin Psychiatric Association; American Medical Association; Wisconsin State Medical Society **Marquis Who's Who Honors:** Albert Nelson Marquis Lifetime Achievement Award (2017); Distinguished Humanitarian (2017) **To what do you attribute your success:** Dr. Kalogjera attributes his success to his wonderful mother, wonderful wife and wonderful daughter, as well as her wonderful husband and wonderful granddaughters. **Why did you become involved in your profession or industry:** Dr. Kalogjera became involved in his profession because he always wanted to be a psychiatrist since age of 15. **What do you consider to be the highlight of your career:** The highlight of his career has been becoming a Clinical Professor of Psychiatry at the Medical College of Wisconsin. **Where will you be in five years:** In five years, Dr. Kalogjera will hopefully still be practicing and teaching. **Hobbies:** Boating; Photography; Movies; Theater; Travel **Shipping Address:** 1220 Dewey Ave, Aurora Psychiatric Hospital, Wauwatosa, WI, 53213

Angelo John Kaltsos

Title: Ethnology Executive **Industry:** Research **Date of Birth:** 08/19/1930 **Place of Birth:** Boston **State/Country of Origin:** MA **Parents:** John Angelo Kaltsos; Rita Thomas (Goudas) Kaltsos **Marital Status:** Widowed **Spouse Name:** Verna Kay Wilson (6/30/1952, Deceased 1/1973) **Children:** Pamela; Elaine; Gregory; Stephanie; Lenora; Demetra; Dana **Education:** Coursework, Fitchburg State University (1977); Coursework, University of New Mexico (1976); Coursework, Boston State College (Now University of Massachusetts, Boston) (1965-1967); Coursework, Harvard Extension School, Harvard University (1964); Coursework, Massachusetts Radio and TV School (1955-1957) **Certifications:** Certified Teacher, Commonwealth of Massachusetts **Career:** Independent Ethnology Researcher, New Mexico (1969-Present); Manager, Pampas Inc. (1987-1990); Educator, Cambridge Public Schools (1961-1981); Electronic Research Production Technician, Raytheon Company (1957-1963); Electronic Research Technician, Avco Division, Crosley (1957); Clerk, USPS (1954-1957) **Career Related:** Consultant, Five P.I.E., Albuquerque, NM (1976-Present); Lecturer on Southwest Indian Culture, Boston, MA (1990-1997); Lecturer on Southwest Indian Culture, Cambridge, MA (1990-1997); Manager, Cambalache Restaurant, Boston, MA (1987); President, Spartan Enterprises, Inc. (1965-1969); Treasurer, Spartan Enterprises, Inc. (1965-1969); Board of Directors, Expansion Dance Company **Civic:** Coordinator, Amateur Photo Contest, Town of Andover (2001-2011); Judge, Amateur Photo Contest, Town of Andover (2001-2011); Project Director, HYT S.A. (2001-2008); Treasurer, HYT S.A. (2001-2008); Judge, Amateur Photo Contest, Town of Andover (1996-1999); Project Director, Northeast Alliance to Protect James Bay (1995-2001); Coordinator, Dryden, Maine (1991-2001); Executive Board, Northeast Alliance to Protect James Bay (1991-2001); Treasurer, Advisory Board, Northeast Alliance to Protect James Bay (1991-2001); The Paulist Center (1991-1992); Educator, The Cambridge Center for Adult Education (1990-1997); Regional Media Coordinator, Northeast Alliance to Protect James Bay (1990-1991); Chairman, No Thank Q Hydro Quebec (1988-1991); Senate Faculty, Cambridge Public Schools (1980-1981); Secretary, New England Model Car Association of Raceways (1966-1969) **Military Service:** U.S. Army (1948-1952) **Creative Works:** Author, "Hello Officer" (2017); Author, "Music You Will Never True Crime Revision" (2015); Exhibitor, One-Man Show, Oil Paintings Proctors and Sunnyview (2014); Author, "The Boy Who Was Shanghaied" (2014); Author, "Life in A Troubled Land" (2012); Exhibitor, One-Man Show, Maine Bookhouse (2012); Author, "Of Bears, Mice and Nails" (2009); Author, "Too Good Cooking" (2008); Author, "Music You Will Never Hear, True Crime" (2005); Author, "Unfurling Leaves of the Mind" (2005); Exhibitor, One-Man Show, Andover Public Library (1997-1998); Exhibitor, One-Man Show, The Fourth Street Photo Gallery (1990); Exhibitor, One-Man Show, Cambalache Gallery (1986-1987); Exhibitor, One-Man Show, Town Hall, Town of Andover (1986); Author, "Southwest Indian" (1986); Exhibitor, One-Man Show, Piedmont Art (1985-1986); Exhibitor, One-Man Show, Town Hall, Town of Andover (1984); Exhibitor, One-Man Show, Here Today Gallery (1984); Exhibitor, One-Man Show, Jay's, Cambridge, Massachusetts (1983); Exhibitor, One-Man Show, Cambridge Rindge and Latin School, Cambridge Public Schools (1981); Exhibitor, One-Man Show, The Fourth Street Photo Gallery (1980); Exhibitor, One-Man Show, Christmas Tree Gallery (1977); Contributing Journalist in Field **Awards:** Honoree, Teacher of the Year, Rindge Alumni Association (2008); Robert Sweeney Award, Rindge Alumni Association (1996) **Membership:** Appalachian Mountain Club **To what do you attribute your success:** Mr. Kaltsos attributes his success to hard work. **Why did you become involved in your profession or industry:** Mr. Kaltsos became involved in his profession to be productive and to contribute to society. **Hobbies:** Cooking; Gardening; Hiking **Religion:** Greek Orthodox **Business Address:** PO Box 33, ME, Andover, 04216 **Shipping Address:** PO Box 33, Andover, ME, 04216

Robert Hilary Kane, PhD

Title: Philosophy Educator **Industry:** Education/Educational Services **Date of Birth:** 11/25/1938 **Place of Birth:** Boston **State/Country of Origin:** MA **Parents:** Hilary Thomas Kane; Vivian Lenzi Kane **Marital Status:** Married **Spouse Name:** Claudette Marcile Drennan (1/23/1965) **Children:** Russell Hilary; Nathan Robert **Education:** PhD, Yale University (1964); MA, Yale University (1962); BA, Holy Cross College (1960) **Career:** University Distinguished Professor Emeritus of Philosophy and Law, University of Texas at Austin (2008-Present); University Distinguished Teaching Professor of Philosophy, University of Texas at Austin (1995-2008); Professor of Philosophy, University of Texas at Austin (1985-1995); Associate Professor, University of Texas at Austin (1974-1985); Alfred E. Sloan Assistant Professor of Philosophy, Haverford College (1967-1970); Assistant Professor of Philosophy, Fordham University, New York, NY (1964-1967) **Career Related:** Honorary Fellow, Phi Kappa Phi National Honor Society (1996); Woodrow Wilson Fellow, Yale University, Woodrow Wilson Foundation (1961-1964); Advisor, Graduate Students **Creative Works:** Editor, "Libertarian Free Will: Contemporary Debates" (2014); Editor, "The Oxford Handbook of Free Will, Second Edition" (2011); Author, "Ethics and the Quest For Wisdom" (2010); Author, "A Contemporary Introduction to Free Will" (2005); Editor, "The Oxford Handbook of Free Will" (2002); Lecturer, "Great Minds of the Western Tradition," The Great Courses on Tape Series, The Teaching Company, Chantilly, VA (2000); Lecturer, "The Quest for Meaning: Values, Ethics and the Modern Experience," The Teaching Company, Chantilly, VA (1999); Author, "The Significance of Free Will" (1996); Author, "Through the Moral Maze" (1994); Author, "Free Will and Values" (1985) **Awards:** R.W. Hamilton Faculty Book Award, "The Significance of Free Will" (1997); Quality of Life Award, Alliance for the Mentally Ill, Texas (1993); Teaching Excellence Award, Liberal Arts Council (1993); Teaching Excellence Award, Friar Society (1989); President's Associates Teaching Excellence Award (1987); 12 Teaching Excellence Awards (1973-2008) **Membership:** Inaugural Member, Academy of Distinguished Teachers, University of Texas at Austin (1995) **Marquis Who's Who Honors:** Albert Nelson Marquis Lifetime Achievement Award (2017) **Shipping Address:** 2501 Bettis Boulevard, Austin, TX, 78746

Lambert Houssou Ble Kanga

Industry: Agriculture **Education:** Doctorate, Texas A&M University (1994) **Awards:** Honoree, Outstanding Researcher of the Year, Florida Agricultural & Mechanical University (2011)

Henry Jerrold Kaplan

Title: Ophthalmologist, Educator **Industry:** Education/Educational Services **Company Name:** University of Louisville School of Medicine **Date of Birth:** 12/29/1942 **Place of Birth:** New York **State:** NY **Parents:** Ralph Kaplan; Henrietta (Davis) Kaplan **Marital Status:** Married **Spouse Name:** Adele Lotner (6/26/1966) **Children:** Wendi Suzanne; Todd Daniel; Ariane Dev **Education:** Retina-Vitreous Fellow, Department of Ophthalmology, Medical College of Wisconsin, Milwaukee, WI (1978-1979); Resident in Ophthalmology, University of Iowa Hospitals and Clinics, Iowa City, IA (1975-1978); National Institutes of Health Research Fellow in Immunology, University of Texas Southwestern Medical School, Dallas, TX (1972-1974); Surgical Resident, Bellevue Hospital, New York University Medical Center (1969-1970); Intern in Medicine, Lakeside Hospital, University Hospitals of Cleveland, Case-Western Reserve University (1968-1969); MD, Cornell University (1968); AB, Columbia University (1964) **Certifications:** Diplomate, American Board of Ophthalmology **Career:** William H. and Blondina F. Evans Professor of Ophthalmology, School of Medicine, University of Louisville, Kentucky (2000-Present); Professor, Chairman, Department of Opthalmology and Visual Sciences, School of Medicine, University of Louisville, Kentucky (2000-Present); Professor, Department of Ophthalmology and Visual Sciences, School of Medicine, Washington University, St. Louis, MO (1988-2000); Chairman, Department of Ophthalmology and Visual Sciences, School of Medicine, Washington University, St. Louis, MO (1988-1998); Associate Professor, Department of Microbiology, School of Medicine, Emory University, Atlanta, GA (1985-1988); Professor, Director of Research, School of Medicine, Emory University, Atlanta, GA (1984-1988); Associate Professor, Department of Ophthalmology, School of Medicine, Emory University, Atlanta, GA (1979-1984) **Career Related:** President, Eye Specialists, University of Louisville (2000-Present); Director, Kentucky Lions Eye Center, University of Louisville (2000-Present); Adjunct Professor, Department of Small Animal Medicine, University of Georgia, Athens, GA (1985-Present); Affiliate Scientist in Pathology and Immunology, Yerkes Regional Primate Research Center, Atlanta, GA (1981-Present); President, University of Louisville Medical School Fund (2015-2018); Treasurer, University of Louisville Physicians (2013-2018); Board of Directors, Executive Committee, Financial Committee, University of Louisville Physicians (2011-2018); Board of Directors, Chair, Executive Compensation Committee, University of Louisville Physicians (2011-2013); Gold Fellow, Association for Research in Vision and Ophthalmology (2010); Silver Fellow, Association for Research in Vision and Ophthalmology (2009); Board of Directors, Executive Committee, University Physical Associates, University of Louisville (2004-2011); Chairman, University of Physician Associates, University of Louisville (2004-2006); President, Barnes Eye Care Network (1994-1998); Ophthalmologist in Chief, Barnes-Jewish Hospital, Washington University Medical Center (1988-1998); Chairman, Visual Sciences Study Section, A-1 National Institutes of Health, Bethesda, MD (1987-1989); Visual Sciences Study Section, A-1 National Institutes of Health, Bethesda, MD (1985-1989) **Civic:** Major, Medical Corps, U.S. Air Force (1970-1972) **Military Service:** Major, U.S. Air Force, Sheppard Air Force Base, Wichita Falls, TX (1970-1972) **Creative Works:** Associate Editor and Editorial Board Member, Translational Vision Science & Technology (2012-Present); Scientific Journal Review Board, Current Eye Research (1986-Present); Scientific Journal Review Board, Experimental Eye Research (1986-Present); Scientific Review Board, Investigative Ophthalmology and Visual Science (1983-Present); Scientific Journal Review Board, American Journal of Ophthalmology (1983-Present); Scientific Journal Review Board, Ophthalmology (1983-Present); Scientific Journal Review Board, Retina (1982-Present); Scientific Journal Review Board, Archives of Ophthalmology (1978-Present); Author, Co-Author, Editor, Co-Editor, More than 300 Medical Textbooks, Chapters and Articles on Uveitis and Macular Degeneration and Retinal Degeneration, Referred Science and Medical Journals, (1974-Present); Editor, "Ocular Immunology and Inflammation" (1999-2009) **Awards:** Lifetime Achievement Award, American Academy of Ophthalmology (2014); Senior Honor Award, American Academy of Ophthalmology (1994); Science Award, Alcon Research Institute (1987); Honor Award, American Academy of Ophthalmology (1984); Olga Keith Weiss Research Scholar to Prevent Blindness, New York, NY (1984) **Membership:** President, American Uveitis Society (1997-1999); American Academy of Ophthalmology; American Medical Association; Association for Research in Vision and Ophthalmology; American Association of Immunologists; Macula Society; Retina Society; American Society of Retina Specialists; Louisville Ophthalmology Society; Kentucky Academy of Eye Physicians and Surgeons **Marquis Who's Who Honors:** Albert Nelson Marquis Lifetime Achievement Award (2017) **Political Affiliations:** Democrat/Independent **Religion:** Jewish **Shipping Address:** 1400 Willow Avenue, Apt. 901, Louisville, KY, 40204 **Website:** http://www.louisvilleeyedocs.com

Philip Spangler Kappes

Title: Lawyer **Industry:** Law and Legal Services **Date of Birth:** 12/24/1925 **Place of Birth:** Detroit **State:** MI **Parents:** Philip Alexander Kappes; Wilma Fern (Spangler) Kappes **Marital Status:** Married **Spouse Name:** Glendora Galena Miles **Children:** Susan Lea; Philip Miles; Mark William **Education:** LLD, University of Michigan; JD, University of Michigan (1948); BA, Butler University, Cum Laude (1945) **Certifications:** Indiana (1948) **Career:** Active, Law Practice (1948-Present); Partner, Lewis Kappes PC, Indianapolis, (1993-Present); Manager, Labeco Properties, LLC, Indianapolis (1985-Present); President, Director, K&K Realty, Inc., Indianapolis (1983-Present); Partner, Creston Group, Indianapolis (1989-1998); Partner, Lewis & Kappes, Indianapolis (1989-1992); Partner, Lewis Kappes Fuller & Eads, Indianapolis, (1985-1989); Of Counsel, Dutton, Kappes & Overman (1983-1985); Partner, Dutton, Kappes & Overman (1952-1985); Associate, C.B. Dutton (1950-1951); Associate, Armstrong and Gause (1948-1949) **Career Related:** Board of Trustees (1987-1990); First Chairman, Ovid Butler Society (1982-1983); Secretary, Board Member, Laboratory Equipment Corp., Mooresville, IN (1952-2000) **Civic:** Ruling Elder, First Presbyterian Church, Indianapolis, IN (2015-Present); Chairman, Buildings and Grounds Committee, First Presbyterian Church, Indianapolis, IN (2015-Present); Chairman, Board of Trustees, First Meridian Heights Presbyterian Church (2014-Present); Vice Chairman, Indianapolis 32-Degree Masonic Learning Center for Children (2002-Present); Honorary Trustee (2001-Present); Director, Indianapolis 32-Degree Masonic Learning Center for Children (1998-Present); Life Director Emeritus (1994-Present); Trustee, Boy Scouts of America (1987-Present); Life Member, Board of Directors, Crossroads of America Council, Boy Scouts of America (1965-Present); Chairman of the Board, Indianapolis 32-Degree Masonic Learning Center for Children (2002); Chairman, Gathering of Eagles Dinner (2000); Planning Committee, Indianapolis 32-Degree Masonic Learning Center for Children (1997-1998); Audit and Finance Committee (1992-1994); Chairman, Nominating Committee (1991); Board of Distinguished Advisors (1990-2001); Chairman of the Board (1988-1991); Chairman, Trustees Endowment Fund, Boy Scouts of America (1987-1992); Executive Committee (1987-1994); Board of Directors, Fairbanks Hospital, Indianapolis (1986-1994); President, Board of Trustees (1984-1985); Vice President of Finance, Executive Committee Member, President, Boy Scouts of America (1977-1979); First Meridian Heights Presbyterian Church (1933-Present); Chairman, Board of Trustees, First Meridian Heights Presbyterian Church (1958-1961, 1969-1972); Ruling Elder, First Meridian Heights Presbyterian Church (1994-1999, 1982-1985) **Awards:** James E. West Fellow, Crossroads Council, Boy Scouts of America (2014); Professionalism Award (2014); Butler Medal, Butler University Alumni Association (2010); Legion of Merit (2010); Distinguished Barrister, Indiana Business Journal (2008); Distinguished Barrister, American Judicature Society (2008); Legendary Lawyers of Year, Indiana State Bar Association (2006); Distinguished Eagle Scout Award, National Council, Boy Scouts of America (2004); Board Managers Award for Judicial System Improvement (1995); Golden Legion (1993); Silver Beaver Award, Crossroads Council, Boy Scouts of America (1978) **Membership:** American Judicature Society (2008); Chairman, Subcommittee on Merit Selection of Trial Court Judges (2005-2008); Chairman, Judicial Selection and Retention Subcommittee on Improvement in the Judicial System, Standing Committee, Indiana State Bar Association (2005); Director, Chairman, Indianapolis Scottish Rite Foundation (2001-2010); Chairman, Senior Lawyers Division, Indianapolis Bar Association (1999-2000); Chairman, Board of Trustees, Indianapolis Valley Scottish Rite (1998-1999); Trustee, Indianapolis Valley Scottish Rite (1996-1999); Past First Vice President, Director, Court Unification Implementation Committee, Chairman, Indianapolis Legal Aid Society (1995-1998); Indiana State Bar Association (1959-Present); Chairman, Most Wise Master, Indianapolis Valley Scottish Rite (1982-1984); Secretary, Indiana State Bar Association (1973-1974); Board of Managers, Indiana State Bar Association (1975-1977); Committee, Board of Managers, Indianapolis Bar Association (1994-1996); Executive Counsel, Board of Managers, Indianapolis Bar Association (1994); Family Law Implementation Committee, Indianapolis Bar Association (1993-1997); Committee, Indianapolis Bar Association (1992-1993); Chairman, Law Day Committee, Indianapolis Bar Association (1991-1992); Chairman, Law Practice Management Committee, Indiana State Bar Association (1991-1992); Indiana Bar Foundation of Indiana State Bar Association; Settlement Week Committee, Indianapolis Bar Association (1989-1995); Board of Managers, Indianapolis Bar Association (1968-1971, 1975-1977) **Marquis Who's Who Honors:** Distinguished Humanitarian (2017) **Political Affiliations:** Republican **Religion:** Presbyterian **Business Address:** 9229 Tamarack Dr, Indianapolis, IN, 46282 **Shipping Address:** 1 American Square, Suite 2500, Lewis & Kappes, Indianapolis, IN, 46282

Michael Kashgarian

Title: Pathologist, Educator **Industry:** Medicine & Health Care **Date of Birth:** 09/20/1933 **Place of Birth:** New York City **State:** NY **Parents:** Toros Kashgarian; Arax Kashgarian **Marital Status:** Married **Spouse Name:** Jean Gaylor Caldwell (7/2/1960) **Children:** Michaele; Thea **Education:** Resident in Pathology, Yale New Haven Medical Center (1962-1963); Research Fellow in Renal Physiology, University of Goettingen, Germany (1961-1962); Assistant Resident in Pathology, Yale New Haven Medical Center (1959-1961); Intern, Barnes Hospital, St. Louis, MO (1958-1959); MD, Yale University (1958); MBA, New York University (1954) **Certifications:** Diplomate, American Board of Pathology (1967) **Career:** Pathologist, Private Practice, New Haven, CT (1962-Present); Assistant in Medicine, Washington University in St. Louis (1958-1959) **Career Related:** Attending Pathologist, Yale New Haven Hospital (1969-Present); Consultant, Pathology, Yale New Haven Hospital (1962-Present); Professor Emeritus, Yale University (2008); Interim Chairman, Yale University (1989-1990); President, Medical Staff, Yale New Haven Hospital (1983-1984); Vice Chairman, Department, Yale University (1976-1989); Professor, Yale University (1974-2008); Associate Professor, Yale University (1967-1974); Assistant Attending Pathologist, Yale New Haven Hospital (1966-1969); Assistant Professor, Yale University (1964-1967); Associate Pathologist, Yale New Haven Hospital (1964-1966); Instructor, Yale University (1962-1964) **Civic:** Chairman, Educational Advisory Council, North Haven Board of Education (1971); Chairman, Christian Education Committee, Church of Christ, Yale University (1970); Board of Directors, New Haven Symphony Orchestra (1988-1997); Vice President, Connecticut Fund for the Environment **Military Service:** First Lieutenant, Medical Corps, U.S. Army Reserve (1954-1965) **Creative Works:** Editorial Board, American Journal of Pathology (1975-Present); Editorial Board, "Nephron" (1970-Present); Author, "Diagnostic Atlas of Renal Pathology, 2nd Edition" (2012); Author, "Diagnostic Atlas of Renal Pathology, Third Edition" (2016); Co-Author, "Diagnostic Atlas of Renal Pathology" (2005); Co-Author, "Renal Disease" (1974); Co-Author, "The Endocrine Glands"; Editorial Board, American Journal on Kidney Diseases; Contributor, Articles, Medical Journals; Editor, "Yearbook of Nephrology," Yale Medicine, Current Opinion in Nephrology **Awards:** Research Career Development Awardee (1965-1975); U.S. Public Health Service Fellow (1963-1965); Jacob Churg Award, Renal Pathology Society; Distinguished Achievement Award, National Kidney Foundation **Membership:** President, Connecticut Society of Pathologists (1975); Fellow, American Association for the Advancement of Science; American Society for Clinical Pathologists; College of American Pathologists; American Society of Nephrology; American Heart Association; American Medical Association; International Academy of Pathology; Chairman, Committee on Organ and Tissue Transfer, Connecticut State Medical Society; President, Board of Governors, New Haven County Medical Association; American Society of Investigative Pathologists; American Physiological Society; Honorary Member, Gesellshaft Nephrologie; Renal Pathology Society; National Kidney Foundation; Sigma Xi; Alpha Omega Alpha; Alpha Kappa Kappa **Marquis Who's Who Honors:** Albert Nelson Marquis Lifetime Achievement Award (2017) **Hobbies:** Fly fishing **Shipping Address:** 200 Leeder Hill Dr Apt 2602, Hamden, CT, 06517 **Website:** http://www.michaelkashgarian.com

Joel Abraham Katz

Title: Chairman **Industry:** Law and Legal Services **Company Name:** Greenberg Traurig, LLP **Date of Birth:** 05/27/1944 **Place of Birth:** Bronx **State/Country of Origin:** NY **Parents:** Harry Katz; Hilda (Weezenthal) Katz **Marital Status:** Married **Spouse Name:** Kane Swims (1994) **Children:** Leslie Helaine; Jeni Michelle **Education:** Honorary PhD, University System of Georgia, Kennesaw State University (2014); Honorary PhD, City University of New York at Hunter College (2008); JD, University of Tennessee, Knoxville (1969); BA in Economics, City University of New York at Hunter College (1966) **Career:** Founder, Katz, Smith & Cohen (1981-1998); Senior Partner, Galkin, Katz & Tye (1971-1981); Lawyer, Department of Housing and Urban Development (1969-1971); Law Professor, Georgia State University, (1969-1971); Law Clerk, Medium-Sized Atlanta Law Firm (1969-1971); Chairman, Global Entertainment and Media Practice, Greenberg Traurig, LLP; Founding Shareholder, Greenberg Traurig, LLP, Atlanta, GA; Co-Managing Shareholder Emeritus, Greenberg Traurig, LLP; Member, Music Advisory Board, Hunter College; Founding Partner, Katz, Smith & Cohen **Career Related:** General Counsel, Farm Aid; Member, Board of Directors, Farm Aid; Special Counsel, CMA County Music Association, Inc; Former Vice Chairman, Gibson Foundation; Affiliate, Gibson Brands, Inc.; Former Vice Chairman, Baldwin; State Music Industry Representative, State of Georgia; Chairman, Entertainment Advisory Council, United Service Organizations; Presenter in Field **Civic:** Member, Board T.J. Martell Foundation for Leukemia Research, New York City, NY; Board of Directors, Very Special Arts; Board of Directors, TouchTunes Music Corporation; Board of Directors, Kiz Toys Inc.; Board of Directors, Luxure Media Group; Board of Directors, MultiplyLive; Board of Directors, Charity Partners LLC; Board of Governors, Buckhead Club; Special Council, Rock and Roll Hall Fame; Member, Board of Representatives, Sony/ATV Music Publishing **Awards:** Named, 100 Power Lawyers in Entertainment, The Hollywood Reporter (2007-2012); Recipient, "Outstanding Georgia Citizen," Secretary of State, The Mexican American Business Chamber (2007); Recipient, "Spirit of Excellence Award," T.J. Martell Foundation for Leukemia, Cancer and AIDS Research (2007); Listed, Lawdragon 500, "Leading Lawyers in America" (2005); Inductee, Hunter College Hall of Fame (2003); Recipient, "Spirit of Music Award," UJA Federation of New York and The Music for Youth Foundation (2003); Recipient, "Heroes Award," Atlanta Chapter of the Recording Academy (2002); Named, 100 Most Influential Georgians, Georgia Trend Magazine (2002); Recipient, "University of Tennessee Founder's Day Medal" (1999); Inductee, Georgia Music Hall of Fame (1995); Named, Number One Entertainment Attorney, "Power 100," Billboard Magazine; Rated, AV Preeminent, Martindale-Hubbel **Membership:** Advisory Board Member, Atlanta Songwriters Association (1992); Advisory Board, Atlanta Committee for the Olympic Games (1991); Fellow, Royal Society for Encouragement Arts, Manufacturers, and Commerce; General Counsel, Past Vice President, Recording Academy, Past National Trustee, Director of Foundation Board, National Chairman, Chairman Emeritus, Board of Trustees, Recording Academy; Trustee, Atlanta Chapter, Recording Academy; ABA; State Bar Of Georgia; Tennessee Bar Association **Bar Admissions:** Georgia (1971); United States Court of Appeals for the Eleventh Circuit (1971); United States District Court Eastern District of Tennessee (1970); Tennessee (1969) **Marquis Who's Who Honors:** Albert Nelson Marquis Lifetime Achievement Award (2017) **Shipping Address:** 3333 Piedmont Rd NE Ste 2500, Greenberg Traurig, LLP, Atlanta, GA, 30305

Michael J. Katz

Title: Orthopedic Surgeon **Industry:** Medicine & Health Care **Company Name:** Michael J. Katz MDPC **Date of Birth:** 03/07/1956 **Place of Birth:** New York City **State:** NY **Parents:** Walter Katz; Thea Katz **Marital Status:** Married **Spouse Name:** Sherry Falk (7/4/1979) **Children:** Jonathan; Judith; Ezra; Daniel **Education:** Intern, Hospital of the University of Pennsylvania (1980-1981); MD, Albert Einstein College of Medicine, with Honors, New York City, NY (1980); BA, Queens College, with Honors, New York City, NY (1976) **Certifications:** Diplomate, American Board of Forensic Medicine; Diplomate, American Board of Orthopaedic Surgery; Diplomate, National Board of Medical Examiners **Career:** Orthopedic Surgeon, Michael J. Katz MDPC (2015-Present); Chief, Orthopedic Surgery, Department of Veterans Affairs New York Harbor Medical Center, Brooklyn, NY (2014-2015); Chief, Orthopaedic Surgery, Department of Veterans Affairs New York Harbor Medical Center (2014); President, Michael J. Katz MDPC, Flushing, NY (1985-2013); Resident, Orthopedic Surgery, Hospital of the University of Pennsylvania, Philadelphia, PA (1981-1985) **Career Related:** Visiting Clinical Associate Professor, Orthopedic Surgery, SUNY Downstate School of Medicine (2015-Present); Consultant, United States Federal Courts, NY (1994-Present) **Civic:** Member, International Congress on Joint Reconstruction (2014-Present); Active Alumni Advisement, Albert Einstein College of Medicine (2001-Present); Volunteer, Albert Einstein College of Medicine Alumni (2016); Committee Member, Class of 1980 Reunion, Albert Einstein College of Medicine (2014); Member, American Physician Fellowship for Israel (2001) **Awards:** United Healthcare Heart Award, United Health Foundation (2017); America's Top Orthopaedist, Top Docs (2013); Leading Physicians of the World, Leading Physicians (2013); Faculty Fellow, University of Pennsylvania (1981); Jonas Salk Scholar (1976); Named, Best Doctors, New York Magazine; Named Best Doctors, Castle and Connolly **Membership:** Elected Member, DeForest Willard Society, University of Pennsylvania (2011-Present); Fellow, American Academy of Orthopaedic Surgeons; Fellow, American Board of Forensic Medicine; American Medical Association; Nassau County Medical Society; American Fracture Association; New York State Society of Orthopaedic Surgeons; Fellow, J. Robert Gladden Society; Association of Military Surgeons of the United States; Federal Physicians Association; Eastern Orthopaedic Association; International Association of Privacy Professionals **Marquis Who's Who Honors:** Albert Nelson Marquis Lifetime Achievement Award (2017) **To what do you attribute your success:** Dr. Katz attributes his success to hard work and never giving up. He has a very supportive spouse who is a strong motivator and coach! He also really likes people. He finds people very fascinating. **Why did you become involved in your profession or industry:** Dr. Katz became involved in his profession because it was a ticket out of South Queens. They were middle class and the middle class was getting crushed. **What do you consider to be the highlight of your career:** One of the highlights of his career was reforming a broken Orthopedic Department at NY Harbor VA as Chief of Orthopedic Surgery and having the courage to act strictly on behalf of those who served. Another highlight was walking down the surgery corridor for the last time and having everyone stand at attention. **Where will you be in five years:** In five years, Dr. Katz will be a husband, a father of four, and a grandfather of seven. He will also be a writer, mentor, student of life, a voracious reader, traveler, and world citizen at large. **Hobbies:** Vintage Car Restoration, Long Distance Bicycling, Beach Walking, Photography (Learning), Chess **Political Affiliations:** Independent **Religion:** Jewish **Shipping Address:** 170 Pond Xing, Lawrence, NY, 11559

Charles A. Kaufmann

Title: Clinical Professor of Psychiatry **Industry:** Education/Educational Services **Company Name:** Charles A. Kaufmann, MD, DLFAPA, Columbia University **Education:** Post Baccalaureate Pre-Medical Program, College of Physicians and Surgeons, Columbia University (1977); BS, Massachusetts Institute of Technology (1973); Columbia Resident, New York Hospital **Career:** Associate Professor of Clinical Psychiatry, Columbia University Medical Center **Awards:** New York Metro Area's Top Doctors, Castle-Connolly; Best Doctors in America **To what do you attribute your success:** Dr. Kaufmann attributes his success to his passion for his work in psychogenetics and psychopharmacology. **Why did you become involved in your profession or industry:** Dr. Kaufmann became involved in his profession after making a later life decision following college. He was a New York school teacher for many years. At the urging of his family doctor, Dr. Norman Weiselberg, he was pushed to apply for medical school. **Where will you be in five years:** In the coming years, Dr. Kaufmann will finish up a couple of research projects that he has a been working on that he'd like to pursue in psychiatric genetics. **Business Address:** 16 Dakin Avenue, Mount Kisco, NY, 10549 **Shipping Address:** 9 North Lane, Chappaqua, NY, 10514 **Website:** http://www.cnsgenes.com

William Michael Kearns Jr.

Title: Investment Banker **Industry:** Financial Services **Company Name:** Keefe Ventures LLC **Date of Birth:** 06/26/1935 **Place of Birth:** Newark **State:** NJ **Parents:** William Michael Kerns; Doris Mae (Hodgkinson) Kearns **Marital Status:** Single **Spouse Name:** Patricia Anne Wright (8/17/1957,Deceased 2016) **Children:** William Michael III; Susan Elizabeth Hubbard; Kathleen Anne; Michael Patrick **Education:** Honorary LLD, Gonzaga University (1988); Postgraduate Studies, New York University (1960-1964); AM, New York University (1960); Postgraduate Studies, Boston College Law School (1957-1958); AB, University of Maine (1957) **Career:** Chairman, Keefe Ventures LLC, (2008-Present); Managing Principal, Keefe Ventures LLC, (2008-Present); President, W. M. Kearns & Co. Inc., Morristown, NJ (1994-Present); Chairman, Keefe Managers, LLC (Now Keefe Ventures, LLC) (2002-2007); Co-Chief Executive Officer, Keefe Managers, LLC (Now Keefe Ventures, LLC) (2002-2007); Vice Chairman, Keefe Managers, LLC (Now Keefe Ventures, LLC) (1998-2002); Managing Director, Shearson Lehman Brothers Inc. (1984-1993); Managing Director, Lehman Brothers Kuhn Loeb Inc. (1977-1984); Managing Director, Kuhn, Loeb & Co. (1976-1977); General Partner, Kuhn, Loeb & Co. (1970-1975); Sales Manager, Kuhn, Loeb & Co. (1968-1969); Vice President, Kuhn, Loeb & Co. (1966-1968); Assistant Vice President, Kuhn, Loeb & Co. (1964-1966); Associate, Institutional Sales and Syndicate Department, Kuhn, Loeb & Co. (1962-1964); Security Analyst, Hayden, Stone & Co., Inc. (1960-1962) **Career Related:** Trustee, EQ Advisors Trust, AXA Equitable Life Insurance Company, New York, NY (1997-Present); Board of Directors, TDI Power (1991-2014); Advisory Director, Gridley & Company LLC, New York, NY (2001-2011); Senior Adviser, Management Consulting Group PLC (1997-2010); Advisory Director, Private Client Resources, LLC (2005); Senior Consultant, Ing Baring Furman Selz LLC, New York, NY (1994-1998); Investment Adviser, Young Nichols Gilstrap, Inc. (1982-1992); Adjunct Professor, Leonard N. Stern School of Business, New York University (1971-1972); Chairman, New York Finance Forum, Columbia University (1971); Faculty Member, Samuel J. Silberman College of Business Administration, Fairleigh Dickinson University (1959-1968); Security Analysis Instructor, New York Institute of Finance (1961-1967); Lecturer, Columbia University; Lecturer, Fairleigh Dickinson University; Lecturer, University of Rochester; Lecturer, New York University **Civic:** Director, Palm Beach Polo Homeowners Association (2016-Present); Co-chair, New Jersey Marine Corps Scholarship Foundation (2008-Present); Advisory Board Member, Greater New York Council, Boy Scouts of America (2008-Present); Chairman, New Vernon Cemetery Association (2008-Present); Trustee, New Vernon Cemetery Association (2006-Present); Advisory Board Member, Morris Museum (1987-Present); President Emeritus, Tri-County Scholarship Fund (1990-Present); Trustee, Tri-County Scholarship Fund (1982-Present); Vice President, FHRD (2007-2010); Chairman, Immune Disease Institute, Inc., Harvard University (2007); Board of Trustees, Immune Disease Institute, Inc., Harvard University, Boston (2006-2007); Trustee, Oncology Philanthropy Council (2005-2012); Director, FHRD (2004-2011); Member, 1910 Society, Boy Scouts of America (2000); Trustee, Morristown Medical Center, Atlantic Health System (1999-2005); International Council Member, International Tennis Hall of Fame (1995-1997); Advisory Board Member, Templeton Prize, John Templeton Foundation (1990-1999); Development Committee, University of Maine (1990-1996); Vice President, Greater New York Council, Boy Scouts of America (1990-2007); Board of Directors The American Friends of Covent Garden, Royal Opera House (1989-1999); President, Tri-County Scholarship Fund (1987-1989); Board of Directors, International Tennis Hall of Fame (1986-1995); Board of Directors, Greater New York Council, Boy Scouts of America (1986-2008); Executive Committee, Simon Business School, University of Rochester (1986-2006); Diocesan Investment Committee, Diocese of Paterson (1986-2003); Vice President, Tri-County Scholarship Fund (1985-1986); Trustee, Drumthwacket Foundation, Inc. (1985-1995) **Military Service:** U.S. Marine Corps (1955-1961) **Awards:** Augusta Stone Award, Foundation for Morristown Medical Center (1999); Leadership Award, Morristown Medical Center, Atlantic Health Systems (1998); Leadership Award, Tri-County Scholarship Fund (1990); Silver Beaver Award, Boy Scouts of America (1989); Honoree, Decorated Master Knight, Sovereign Military Order of Malta, American Association; Honoree, Pontifical Equestrian Order of St. Gregory the Great **Membership:** Founder, Hot Springs, Virginia Chapter, Green Jacket Club (1991-Present); Minority Capital Committee, Security Industry Association (1978-1986); Trustee, The University Club of New York (1978-1981); Corporate Finance Committee, National Association Security Dealers (Now FINRA) (1976-1980); Chairman, Security Industry Association (1974) **Marquis Who's Who Honors:** Albert Nelson Marquis Lifetime Achievement Award (2017) **Shipping Address:** 310 South St Ste 2, W M Kearns & Co. Inc., Morristown, NJ, 07960

Philip Earl Keen

Title: Physician, Laboratory Administrator, Pathologist **Industry:** Medicine & Health Care **Date of Birth:** 12/11/1942 **Place of Birth:** Berryville **State:** IL **Parents:** Budd Keen; Ruby Virgina (Doty) Keen **Marital Status:** Married **Spouse Name:** Lois Marie Anderson (6/6/1966) **Children:** Marilynn; Sharilynn; Harvey; April **Education:** MD, University of New Mexico (1969); BS in Chemistry, University of New Mexico (1965) **Certifications:** Diplomate, American Board of Pathology **Career:** Medical Examiner, Yavapai County Government (1995-2009); Deputy Medical Examiner, Maricopa County, Arizona (1986-1992); Chief of Staff, Yavapai Regional Medical Center (1984-1985); Medical Examiner, Yavapai County Government (1975-1992); Laboratory Director, Yavapai Regional Medical Center (1975-1992); Fellow in Forensic Pathology, Office of the Chief Medical Examiner, State of Oklahoma (1973-1974); Fellowship in Forensic Pathology; Fellow, College of American Pathologists **Civic:** Lay Minister, Church of Christ; Prescott Unified School District; Board of Directors, Arizona Medical Association; Treasurer, Organ and Tissue Agency, State of Arizona; Chairman, Board of Directors, Arizona Medical Board **Creative Works:** Author, "Overruled"; Author, "Objection Sustained"; Author, "Objection, He is Still Alive" **Membership:** Yavapai County Medical Society (1975-1992); American Society for Clinical Pathology; American Medical Association; Director, Northwest District, Arizona Medical Association; President, Arizona Medical Association **Marquis Who's Who Honors:** Albert Nelson Marquis Lifetime Achievement Award (2017) **Why did you become involved in your profession or industry:** Despite the fact that Dr. Keen was the top of his class in high school, he didn't want to go into engineering and wanted to do something significant. He was also strong in math and science. **Hobbies:** Playing stringed instruments; Singing **Political Affiliations:** Republican **Shipping Address:** 4060 W Grandview Road, Phoenix, AZ, 85053

Ruth Keene-Burgess

Title: Military Official **Industry:** Military & Defense Services **Company Name:** United States Army Signal Command **Date of Birth:** 10/07/1948 **Place of Birth:** South Bend **State:** IN **Parents:** Seymour; Sally (Morris) Keene **Marital Status:** Married **Spouse Name:** Leslie University Burgess (10/1/1983) **Children:** Michael Leslie; David William; Elizabeth Sue; Rachael Lee **Education:** Graduate Work, United States Army Command and General Staff College (1986); MS, Fairleigh Dickinson University (1978); BS, Arizona State University (1970) **Career:** Specialist, Logistics Management, United States Army Signal Command, Fort Huachuca, AZ (1989-Present); Analyst, Supply System, U.S. Armament, Munitions & Chemical Command, Rock Island, IL (1988-1989); Inventory Management Specialist, 200th Theater Army Materiel Management Center, Zweibruecken, Germany (1985-1988); Chief Control Division, Crane Army Ammunition Activity (1985); Chief Inventory Management Division, Crane Army Ammunition Activity (1983-1985); Supply Systems Analyst, Headquarters 60th Ordnance Group, Zweibruecken, Germany (1980-1983); Chief Inventory Management Division, Crane Army Ammunition Activity (1979-1980); Inventory Management Specialist, US Army Communications-Electronics Materiel Readiness Command, Fort Monmouth, NJ (1974-1979); Inventory Management Specialist, U.S. Army Electronics Command, Philadelphia, PA (1970-1974) **Civic:** Troop Leader, Girl Scouts of the Unites States of America **Membership:** American Association of University Women (AAUW); Association for Computing Machinery (ACM, Inc.); Society of Logistics Engineers (SOLE); Federally Employed Women (FEW) **Political Affiliations:** Democrat **Shipping Address:** 822 N. Central Avenue, Sierra Vista, AZ, 85635

James Edgar Keesling, PhD

Title: Professor **Industry:** Education/Educational Services **Company Name:** University of Florida **Date of Birth:** 06/26/1942 **Place of Birth:** Indianapolis **State:** IN **Parents:** Fred Edgar Keesling; Martha Belle (Grimes) Keesling **Marital Status:** Married **Spouse Name:** Marian Ellen Calley (1/26/1963) **Children:** James Jr.; Marian Esther; Timothy Carl; Ruth Emily **Education:** PhD in Mathematics, University of Miami (1968); MS in Mathematics, University of Miami (1966); BS in Industrial Engineering, University of Miami (1964) **Career:** Chairman, Faculty Assembly, College of Liberal Arts and Sciences, University of Florida (2010-Present); Professor, Mathematics, University of Florida (1975-Present); Colonel Allen R. and Margaret G. Crow Term Professor, University of Florida (2016-2017); Chair, Department of Mathematics, University of Florida (2008-2013); Parliamentarian, College of Liberal Arts and Sciences, University of Florida (2006-2011); President Pro-Tempore, College of Liberal Arts and Sciences, University of Florida (1989-1990); Associate Professor, Mathematics, University of Florida (1971-1975); Assistant Professor, Mathematics, University of Florida, Gainesville (1967-1971) **Career Related:** Visiting Lecturer, Society of Industrial and Applied Mathematics (1992-Present); Lecturer, Numerous National and International Conferences in Mathematics (1969-Present); Visiting Faculty, University of Utah (1991-1992); Visiting Faculty, University of Georgia (1976-1977) **Civic:** Clerk of Session, First Presbyterian Church (2014-Present); Kappa Phi Epsilon (2014-Present); Elder, First Presbyterian Church (2013-Present); Bridges (2013-2015); Member, First Presbyterian Church (2012-Present); Member, Christian Fraternity, University of Florida (2012-Present); Faculty Advisor, The Navigators (2001-Present); President, Christian Faculty Fellowship, University of Florida (2000-2004); Elder, Church Chairman, Creekside Community Church, Evangelical Free Church of America, Gainesville, FL (2001-2003); Elder, Church Chairman, Creekside Community Church, Evangelical Free Church of America, Gainesville, FL (1994-1997); President, Christian Faculty Fellowship, University of Florida (1995-1996); President, Christian Faculty Fellowship, University of Florida (1993-1994); Faculty Advisor, The Navigators (1983-1991); President, Christian Faculty Fellowship, University of Florida (1989-1990); Elder, Church Chairman, Creekside Community Church, Evangelical Free Church of America, Gainesville, FL (1987-1990); Heritage Advisory Board, Kappa Phi Epsilon **Creative Works:** Editor, Revista Matematica Complutense (2006-2012); Board of Advisors, Topology and Its Applications (2009-Present); Patient Simulation Code, University of Florida Research Foundation (2017); Managing Editor, Topology and Its Applications (2000-2009); Contributor, Articles, Professional Journals **Awards:** Grantee, Co-PD USDS-NIFA, University of Florida (2017-2020); Grantee, Co-PI USDA-NIFA, University of California Davis and University of Florida (2015-2020); Grantee, PI Citrus Research and Development Foundation (2014-2016); Fellow, Australian National University (2011, 2008); Grantee, Co-PI National Science Foundation Grant (2008, 2001); TIP Award for Teaching, University of Florida (1998, 1994); Grantee, Applied and Computational Mathematics Program, Defense Advanced Research Projects Agency (1989-1990); Grantee, CBMS Travel, Conference on Combinatorial Theory and Linear Programming (1975); Grantee, International Travel Grant to Yugoslavia, National Science Foundation (1974); Grantee, Topology, National Science Foundation (1970-1973) **Membership:** American Mathematics Society; Mathematics Association of America; Society of Industrial and Applied Mathematics; Tau Beta Pi; Phi Kappa Phi; American Association for the Advancement of Science; The New York Academy of Sciences; Society for Mathematical Biology **Marquis Who's Who Honors:** Albert Nelson Marquis Lifetime Achievement Award (2017) **Hobbies:** Tennis **Political Affiliations:** Republican **Religion:** Christian, Presbyterian Church (USA) **Shipping Address:** 710 NE 6th St, FL, Gainesville, 32601 **Website:** http://www.math.ufl.edu/~kees

Philip C. Keevil

Title: Investment Banker **Industry:** Financial Services **Company Name:** Compass Partners Advisors, LLP **Date of Birth:** 10/19/1946 **Place of Birth:** London **Country of Origin:** England **Parents:** Ambrose Clement Arthur Keevil; Olwen Marjorie Enid (Gibbins) Keevil **Marital Status:** Married **Spouse Name:** Augusta Day McGrail (6/10/1972) **Children:** Adrian Ambrose Clement; Augusta Hall; Peter Larimer **Education:** MBA, Harvard University (1975); MA, University of Oxford, England (1972); BA, University of Oxford, England (1968) **Career:** Senior Partner, Compass Partners (2005-Present); Managing Director, Salomon Brothers Inc. (Now Citigroup Global Markets), New York, NY (1995-2005); Head, Mergers and Acquisitions, Schroder Salomon Smith Barney, London, England (2000-2002); Head, European Mergers and Acquisitions, Salomon Smith Barney, London, England (1997-2000); Head, International Mergers and Acquisitions, Salomon Brothers Inc. (Now Citigroup Global Markets), New York, NY (1995-1997); Head, Investment Banking, S.G. Warburg and Co. Inc. (Now UBS), New York, NY (1991-1995); Managing Director, Head, Mergers and Acquisitions, S.G. Warburg and Co. Inc. (Now UBS), New York, NY (1987-1991); General Partner, Lazard "Frères & Co. LLC, New York, NY (1983-1987); Vice President, Lazard Frères & Co. LLC, New York, NY (1981-1982); Associate, Lazard Frères & Co. LLC, New York, NY (1979-1980); Associate, Morgan Stanley, New York, NY (1975-1978); Manager, Unilever, England (1968-1973) **Career Related:** Chairman, The Risk Advisory Group (2007-2014); Board of Directors, The Risk Advisory Group (2006-2014); Advisory Board, NBD Sana Capital Limited, Dubai, United Arab Emirates (2007-2009); Board of Directors, S.G. Warburg and Co. Inc., London, England (1987-1995) **Civic:** Trustee, American London Symphony Orchestra Foundation (2011-Present); Member, Choir, The Episcopal Church of Heavenly Rest (2010-Present); Patron, Said Business School, University of Oxford (2009-Present); Liveryman, The Worshipful Company of International Bankers, London, England (2006-Present); Member, Advisory Council, London Symphony Orchestra (2004-Present); Liveryman Worshipful Company of Poulters, London, England (1968-Present); Member, Court, Worshipful Company of Poulters (1992-2013); Board of Governors, City of London School for Girls (2002-2009); Business Advisory Forum, Said Business School, University of Oxford (1999-2009); Board of Directors, Americans for Oxford, Inc. (1995-2002); Trustee, St. Andrew's School, DE (1993-2001); Master, Worshipful Company of Poulters (2000-2001); Upper Warden, Worshipful Company of Poulters (1999-2000); Renter Warden, Worshipful Company of Poulters (1998-1999); Trustee, St. Bernard's School, NY (1991-1997); Vestryman, St. John's of Lattingtown, Locust Valley, NY (1986-1989); Freeman, City of London (1968) **Awards:** Baker Scholar, Harvard Business School, Boston, MA (1975); Major Scholarship in Mathematics, Trinity College, Oxford University (1963) **Membership:** Director, BritishAmerican Business (2004-2015); Deputy Chairman, BritishAmerican Business (1999-2001); Director, BritishAmerican Business (1993-2000); Fellow, RSA; Pilgrims of Great Britain; Pilgrims of the United States; Knickerbocker Club; London Rowing Club; Cavalry & Guards; Leander Club; The Brook **Why did you become involved in your profession or industry:** He became involved in his profession because he was always interested in mergers since his time in business school. He was also very interested in cross-border mergers as a Brit in the states, and he wanted a career where he could visit Europe regularly. When he had come back to the states to continue his education, he was intrigued to know more about investment banking. He enjoys advising companies from different countries and different cultures, and bridging the gap between different cultures. **What do you consider to be the highlight of your career:** Becoming a partner at Lazard Frères & Co. LLC was the highlight of his career. He was the first in his business class to become a partner at a Wall Street firm. He is also proud of building a merger & acquisitions team for what is now UBS in the US and then repeating that for what is now CitiGroup in Europe. Overall, he believes advisory work is very satisfying because he helps people achieve their goals and solve problems, which there always are. **Religion:** Episcopalian **Business Address:** 825 Third Avenue, 32nd Floor, New York, NY, 10022 **Shipping Address:** 460 Sea Oak Drive, Vero Beach, FL, 32963

Deborah Keirstead Bublitz

Title: Pediatrician **Industry:** Medicine & Health Care **Company Name:** University of Colorado Health Sciences Center, The Children's Hospital **Date of Birth:** 02/28/1933 **Place of Birth:** Boston **State/Country of Origin:** MA **Parents:** George Keirstead; Dorothy (Kingsbury) Keirstead **Marital Status:** Married **Spouse Name:** Clark Bublitz (6/1/1958) **Children:** Nancy B. Dyer; Susan B. Schooleman; Philip K. Bublitz; Caroline D. Bublitz; Elizabeth E. Bublitz **Education:** Resident, Department of Public Health and Hospitals, University of Colorado Health Sciences Center, Denver, CO (1968-1974); Resident, St. Louis Children's Hospital (1959-1960); MD, Johns Hopkins University (1959); BS, Bates College (1955) **Career:** Associate Clinical Professor of Pediatrics, University of Colorado Health Sciences Center, The Children's Hospital (1987-Present); Private Practice, Littleton, CO (1974-Present); Assistant Clinical Professor of Pediatrics, University of Colorado Health Sciences Center, The Children's Hospital (1975-1987) **Career Related:** Advisor, Medical Associate, La Leche League International (1975-Present); Credentials Committee, Swedish Medical Center and Porter Adventist Hospital, Englewood, CO (1985-1987); Chief of the Department of Pediatrics, La Leche League International (1985-1987); Fellowship, American Academy of Pediatrics **Creative Works:** Co-Author, "Clinical Pediatric Otolaryngology" (1986) **Membership:** Chair, Colorado Medical Society (1994-1995); Assistant Chair, Woman's Governing Council, Colorado Medical Society (1993-1994); Women's Governing Council, Colorado Medical Society (1990-1996); Arapahoe-Douglas-Elbert Medical Society; American Medical Association; American Medical Women's Association **Marquis Who's Who Honors:** Albert Nelson Marquis Lifetime Achievement Award (2017); Distinguished Humanitarian (2017) **Hobbies:** Painting; Gardening; Bird watching **Religion:** Episcopalian **Shipping Address:** 206 W County Line Road, Suite 110, Littleton Pediatric Medical Center, Highlands Ranch, CO, 80129

Lucille Knight Kelley

Title: Minister **Industry:** Religious **Company Name:** Genesee Baptist Church **Date of Birth:** 09/29/1929 **Place of Birth:** Tallahassee **State:** FL **Parents:** Godfrey Knight; Harriet Davis Knight **Marital Status:** Widowed **Spouse Name:** Clarence Kelley (Deceased 1964) **Children:** David; Foster Children **Education:** Diplomate in Ministry, Colgate Crozer Divinity School (2002); BA in Religion, Family and Society, Empire State College, Rochester, NY (2001); Postgraduate Coursework, Colgate Crozer Divinity School (1970); AS in Nursing, Rochester Community College (Now Monroe Community College) (1970) **Certifications:** Ordained to Ministry, Genesee Baptist Church, Rochester, NY (2003); Licensed Minister, Genesee Baptist Church (2002); Registered Nurse, County Hospital, Rochester, NY **Career:** Supporting Minister, Genesee Baptist Church, Rochester, NY (2003-Present); Foster Care Staff Member, Monroe Community Hospital, Rochester, NY (1991-2001); Registered Nurse, Monroe Community Hospital, Rochester, NY (1970-1985); Licensed Practical Nurse, Monroe Community Hospital, Rochester, NY (1960-1968) **Civic:** Genesee Baptist Church (2000-Present); Director of Social Functions, Mount Olivet Baptist Church (1996-2000); Treasurer, Mount Olivet Baptist Church (1995-1996); Choir Member, Mount Olivet Baptist Church (1980-2000); Mount Olivet Baptist Church (1951-1954); New Salem Baptist Church, Sanford, FL (1942-1950) **Marquis Who's Who Honors:** Albert Nelson Marquis Lifetime Achievement Award (2017) **To what do you attribute your success:** Ms. Kelley attributes her success to changing herself in order to adapt to situations. **Why did you become involved in your profession or industry:** Ms. Kelley entered his profession because she works best in collection. She did the job because of the needs of people. **Hobbies:** Family reunions; Visiting the sick in homes and hospitals **Religion:** Baptist **Shipping Address:** 35 Bobbie Drive, Rochester, NY, 14606

Mark Allen Kellner

Title: Chief Content Officer **Industry:** Writing and Editing **Company Name:** Mark A. Kellner, LLC **Date of Birth:** 07/17/1957 **Place of Birth:** New York **State:** NY **Parents:** Jacques Kellner; Arlene Kellner **Marital Status:** Married **Spouse Name:** Jean Ann Viechec **Education:** Coursework, Boston University (1975-1977) **Career:** Chief Content Officer, Mark A. Kellner LLC (1998-Present); National Reporter, Deseret News, Deseret Digital Media (2014-2015); Assistant Editor, Adventist Review (2007-2014); Reporter, Defense News, Sightline Media Group Site (2006-2007); Assistant Director of News & Information, General Conference of Seventh-day Adventists (2003-2006); Contributor, Los Angeles Times (2000-2002); Contributing Writer, Government Computer News, 1105 Media, Inc. (1998-2005); Editor-in-Chief, PC Portables Magazine, Larry Flynt Publications (1996-1998); Senior Editor, Government Computer News, 1105 Media, Inc. (1996); Columnist/Contributor, The Washington Times, LLC (1991-2014); Editor, Report on AT&T, Capitol Publications (1988-1993) **Career Related:** Lecturer, World Journalism Institute (2002); Team Member, Y2K Lecture Team, USIS (1999) **Creative Works:** Author, "Y2K: Apocalypse or Opportunity" (1999); Author, "God on the Internet" (1996); Editor, "Philatelic Communicator" (1995-1996); Author, "WordPerfect 3.5 for Macs For Dummies" (1995) **Awards:** Finalist, Religion Newswriters Association Awards (2015); Finalist, Society of Professional Journalists (2014-2015); Finalist, Rocky Mountain Chapter (2014-2015); Finalist, Associated Church Press (2014); Finalist, Associated Church Press (2013); Cahners Editorial Merit Award, Cahners Publishing Inc. (1996); Linn's Literature Award, Linn's Stamp News (Now Amos Media) (1974) **Membership:** Religious News Association; American Philatelic Society; National Writer's Union **Marquis Who's Who Honors:** Albert Nelson Marquis Lifetime Achievement Award (2017) **Hobbies:** Philately **Shipping Address:** 5036 S Oban Ct, Salt Lake City, UT, 84117

Martin William Kendig, PhD

Title: President **Industry:** Sciences **Company Name:** Kendig Research Associates LLC **Date of Birth:** 10/20/1945 **Place of Birth:** Danville **State:** PA **Parents:** Paul Miller Kendig; Adelaide Anna Augusta (Hagerty) Kendig **Marital Status:** Married **Spouse Name:** Michele Lynne Mulligan (2/19/1969) **Children:** Rebecca; Jamie **Education:** PhD in Physical Chemistry, Brown University, Providence, RI (1974); AB in Chemistry, Franklin & Marshall College, Lancaster, PA (1967) **Career:** President, Kendig Research Associates LLC (2008-Present); Manpower Professional Consultant, Teledyne Scientific (2008-Present); Technical Staff Member, Senior Scientist, Rockwell Science Center, Thousand Oaks, CA (1980-2008); Associate Chemist, Department of Nuclear Energy, Brookhaven National Laboratory, Upton, NY (1976-1980); Post-Doctoral Research Associate, Lehigh University, Bethlehem, PA (1974-1976) **Career Related:** Project Manager **Civic:** Member, Rotary Club of Thousand Oaks **Creative Works:** Editorial Staff, "Corrosion Journal," NACE International (1989-Present); Editor, "Electrochemical Impedance: Analysis and Interpretation" (1993); Contributor, Articles, Professional Journals **Awards:** Fellow, National Association of Corrosion Engineers (2009); Fellow, Electrochemical Society (2002); Selected, Rockwell Chairman's Team of the Year (1997); Corrosion Committee Publication Award, Federation of Societies for Coatings Technology (1997); Selected, Rockwell Chairman's Team of the Year (1994); Melvin Romanoff Award - Best First Paper in Corrosion (1976) **Membership:** President, Sigma Xi, The Scientific Research Honor Society (1989-1995); Chairman, Corrosion Aerospace Structural Materials, National Association of Corrosion Engineers (1989-1990); Vice President, Rockwell Chapter, Sigma Xi, The Scientific Research Honor Society (1988-1989); Executive Committee, Corrosion Division, The Electrochemical Society (1987-2000); Chairman, Task Group, NACE International (1986-1989); Former Member, American Society for Testing and Materials; Fellow, The Electrochemical Society; Fellow, NACE International **Marquis Who's Who Honors:** Albert Nelson Marquis Lifetime Achievement Award (2017) **Why did you become involved in your profession or industry:** Dr. Kendig became involved in his profession because he was always a good chemistry student. When he graduated with a PhD, he was interested in some sort of industrial application of chemistry so he went into corrosion studies. He did a post-doctoral at Lehigh University under Dr. Henry Leidheiser, and he worked on corrosion protection by organic coatings. **What do you consider to be the highlight of your career:** A highlight of Dr. Kendig's career is his work involving the aspects of electrochemical process in wetting and wear, which was one thing that he was very interested in and is not highly recognized. He is also interested in mechanisms that are related to that and mechanisms of the disbonding of paint coating from corroding metal. Dr. Kendig has also worked on corrosion protective coatings for aircraft which may have some applications. Another highlight was receiving an award for life prediction of materials and corrosion protective coatings and paints presented by Federation of Societies for Coatings Technology. **Where will you be in five years:** In five years, he is going to do what he is doing, and he may retire for good. **Hobbies:** Hiking; Outdoors **Shipping Address:** 496 Hillsborough St, Thousand Oaks, CA, 91361 **Website:** http://martinkendig.com/1852.html

Lynn T. Kenison

Title: Chemist (Retired) **Industry:** Sciences **Date of Birth:** 02/20/1943 **Place of Birth:** Provo **State:** UT **Parents:** John Silves Kenison; Grace (Thacker) Kenison **Marital Status:** Married **Spouse Name:** Daralyn Wold **Children:** Marlene; Mark; Evan; Guy; Amy; Suzanne **Education:** MS in Chemistry, Brigham Young University (1971); BS in Chemistry, Brigham Young University (1968) **Certifications:** Certified High School Teacher **Career:** Senior Chemist, OSHA Salt Lake Technology Center, United States Department of Labor (1984-2009); Chemist, OSHA Salt Lake Technology Center, United States Department of Labor (1974-2009); Supervisor, Branch Chief, Bench Chemist, OSHA Salt Lake Technology Center, United States Department of Labor (1974-1977); Bench Chemist, Salt Lake City Health Department (1971-1974); Teacher, Weber County School District, Ogden, UT (1968-1969) **Career Related:** Safety Officer, OSHA Technology Center (2002-2009); Technical Writer, Occupational Safety and Health Administration **Civic:** Second Mission, Church History Library, The Church of Jesus Christ of Latter-Day Saints (2014-2015); Wolf Leader, Boy Scouts of America (2013-2015); Volunteer, Family History Library, The Church of Jesus Christ of Latter-Day Saints, Salt Lake City, UT (2009-2010); Cubmaster, Local Pack, Boy Scouts of America (2005-2010); Unit Commissioner, Scouting, Boy Scouts of America (1995-1997); Cubmaster, Local Pack, Boy Scouts of America (1990-1994); Volunteer Speaker, Chemist, Local Public Schools (1988-2003); Webelos Den Leader, Boy Scouts of America (1985-1990); Councilman, City of West Bountiful, UT (1985-1989); Councilman, City of West Bountiful, UT (1980-1983); Full-Time Missionary, The Church of Jesus Christ of Latter-Day Saints (1962-1964) **Creative Works:** Editor, Review Methods, Analytical Papers (1984-2009) **Awards:** Recipient, Junior Award for Outstanding Federal and Community Service, Federal Executive Association (1980); Distinguished Service Award, Federal Executive Association **Membership:** Treasurer, Salt Lake City Chapter, Toastmasters International (1987-1991); Federal Executive Association; American Industrial Hygiene Association **Marquis Who's Who Honors:** Albert Nelson Marquis Lifetime Achievement Award (2017) **Why did you become involved in your profession or industry:** Ms. Kenison entered her profession because she had polio when she was six months old. Over the years, she has had 27 major surgeries to correct effects of polio in her legs. Ms. Kenison needed a profession that did not require the use of her legs. She enjoyed chemistry, so she earned a bachelor's degree and a master's degree in the subject. **Where will you be in five years:** In the next five years, Ms. Kenison will be enjoying retirement and serving in her church. **Hobbies:** Woodworking **Political Affiliations:** Republican **Religion:** The Church of Jesus Christ of Latter-Day Saints **Shipping Address:** 784 Aspen St, Tooele, UT, 84074

John Wayne Kennedy

Title: President **Industry:** Consulting **Company Name:** John W. Kennedy Consultants **Children:** Six Children **Education:** BS in Botany and Natural Science, University of Wisconsin-Madison (1962); Coursework in Advanced Biological Studies **Career:** Staff Officer, Animal and Plant Health Inspection Service, U.S. Department of Agriculture **Career Related:** Founder, Zero Gravity Solutions, Inc.; Chief Science Officer, Ion Biotechnologies, Inc. **Creative Works:** Author, "To Slay A Demon," Galde Press, Inc. (2001) **Awards:** Presenter, Eagle Scout Award (2016); "Chesapeake Business Ledger" (2010); Distinguished Alumni Award, D.C. Everest Senior High School (2002); A&E and Discovery Channel, For Finding the Lost Pyramid in Rock Lake, WI (1998); Skin-Diver Magazine, For Finding the Lost Pyramid in Rock Lake, WI (1969); Two-Time Winner, NASA Space Act Agreement **Membership:** National Eagle Scout Association (1954-Present); Lifetime Member, Laurel Volunteer Rescue Squad, Inc.; Entomological Society of America; The American Legion; BPO Elks **Marquis Who's Who Honors:** Albert Nelson Marquis Lifetime Achievement Award (2017) **To what do you attribute your success:** Mr. Kennedy attributes his success to his hard work, education, and the inspiration he receives from his mother and colleagues. **What do you consider to be the highlight of your career:** The highlights of Mr. Kennedy's career was representing 90 companies from 19 countries and being awarded the NASA Space Act Agreement twice. **Hobbies:** Scuba diving **Shipping Address:** 101 Beachside Drive, Stevensville, MD, 21666 **Website:** http://www.zerogsi.com/corporate/management-team

Thomas Patrick Kennedy

Title: Financial Executive (Retired) **Industry:** Financial Services **Company Name:** Effie Technologies, Inc. **Date of Birth:** 10/13/1932 **Place of Birth:** New York **State:** NY **Parents:** Andrew Francis Kennedy; Marie P. (Scullen) Kennedy **Marital Status:** Married **Spouse Name:** Mary P. Drennan (1/14/1956, Deceased); Elizabeth Ryan Kennedy **Children:** Thomas Patrick Kennedy; Kevin M. Kennedy (Deceased); Michael J. Kennedy; Mary P. Kennedy Handsman; Deborah A. Kennedy **Education:** Postgraduate Coursework, Seton Hall University (1959); BS, Saint Peter's University (1958) **Career:** Chairman of the Board, Effie Techs., Inc. (1984-2010); Chief Executive Officer, Effie Techs., Inc. (1984-2010); Chairman of the Board, Tomken Management, Ltd. (1983-2010); President, Tomken Management, Ltd. (1980-2010); Senior Vice President, Children's Television Workshop (Now Sesame Workshop) (1978-1980); With, Children's Television Workshop (Now Sesame Workshop) (1969-1980); Treasurer, Chief Financial Officer, Vice President of Finance and Administration, Children's Television Workshop (Now Sesame Workshop) (1969-1978); Director of Finance, Public Broadcasting Laboratory (1967-1969); With, Ford Foundation, New York, NY (1967); Various Executive Positions, CBS (1958-1967); Staff, Emerson Radio & TV (1957-1958); Accountant, Deloitte Haskins & Sells CPAs (1955-1957); Accountant, Deloitte Haskins & Sells CPAs (1953-1954) **Career Related:** Vice President, Vantage Securities, Inc. (1991-1994); Chief Executive Officer, Chairman of the Board, Corporate Strategies Group, Inc. (1988-1989); Vice President of Corporate Finance, Jersey Capital Markets Group, Inc. (1987-1988); Consultant in Field, Board of Directors, Executive Director, Center for Non-Broadcast Television (1980-1985) **Military Service:** Korea, US Army (1954-1955) **Membership:** Finance Executives Institute; American Association of Individual Investors; The American Legion; Korean War Veteran's Association; Veterans of Foreign Wars; New York Athletic Club; Knights of Columbus Fourth Degree **Marquis Who's Who Honors:** Albert Nelson Marquis Lifetime Achievement Award (2017) **To what do you attribute your success:** Mr. Kennedy attributes his success to being ambitious. He always asked what he could do next. **Why did you become involved in your profession or industry:** Mr. Kennedy became involved in his profession because he was very intrigued with finance. He started going to college at night. **Political Affiliations:** Republican **Religion:** Roman Catholic **Shipping Address:** 215 E 68th St Apt 20X, New York, NY, 10065

Patricia Clark Kenschaft, PhD

Title: Mathematics Professor (Retired) **Industry:** Education/Educational Services **Company Name:** Montclair State University **Date of Birth:** 03/25/1940 **Place of Birth:** Philadelphia **State/Country of Origin:** PA **Parents:** John Randolph Clark; Bertha Francis Clark **Marital Status:** Married **Spouse Name:** Frederick Donald Chichester (12/27/1975); Roland Paul Kenschaft (6/13/1959, Divorced 12/1971)) **Children:** Lori; Edward **Education:** PhD, University of Pennsylvania (1973); MA, University of Pennsylvania (1963); AB, Swarthmore College (1961) **Career:** Lecturer, Bloomfield College (2006-2008); Part-Time Teacher, Bloomfield College (2005-2007); Professor, Montclair State University (1987-2005); Assistant Professor, Associate Professor, Professor, Montclair State University, New Jersey (1973-2005); Lecturer, Bloomfield College, New Jersey (1971-1973); Mathematics Teacher, Ridley Township High School, Pennsylvania (1961-1962) **Career Related:** First National Chair, Committee for Participation of Women, Mathematical Association of America (1989-1995); Director, Project for the Resourceful Instruction of Mathematics in Elementary School (1988-1995); Founder, New Jersey Faculty Forum (1988-1990); President, New Jersey Faculty Forum (1988-1990); President, American Association of University Professors of New Jersey (1987-1991); Consultant Editor, National Academy of Sciences (1986); President, New Jersey Chapter, Association of Women in Mathematics (1981-1987) **Civic:** Secretary, Cornucopia Network Of New Jersey (2009-Present); President, United Nations Association of Montclair (1990-1996); Secretary, Cornucopia Network Of New Jersey (1988-1991); President, Zero Population Growth Essex County (Now Population Connection), Montclair, NJ (1972-1973); Founder, First President, Milldam Nursery School, Concord, MA (1969-1970) **Creative Works:** Author, "Math Power: How To Help Your Child Love Math Even If You Don't, Revised Edition" (2014); Author, "Linear Mathematics, A Practical Approach, Republished" (2013); Author, "Math Power: How To Help Your Child Love Math Even If You Don't, Republished" (2006); Author, "Change Is Possible: Stories of Women and Minorities in Mathematics" (2005); Author, "Racial Equity Requires Teaching Elementary School Teachers More Mathematics in the Notices of the American Mathematical Society" (2005); Co-Editor, "Environmental Mathematics in the Classroom" (2003); Author, "Mathematics for Human Survival" (2000); Radio Talk Show Host, "Math Medley" (1998-2004); Author, "Math Power: How To Help Your Child Love Math Even If You Don't" (1997); Newsletter Editor, Cornucopia Network Of New Jersey (1992-2009); Co-Author, Editor, "Winning Women Into Mathematics" (1991); Co-Author, "Winning Women Into Mathematics" (1991); Co-Author, "Mathematics, A Practical Approach" (1978); Author, "Linear Mathematics, A Practical Approach" (1978); Author, "Childbirth, Cooperative Style: Family Experience with Prepared Childbirth and Prenatal Classes" (1977); Co-Author, "Calculus, A Practical Approach" (1975); Contributor, Articles to Professional Journals **Awards:** Louise Hay Award in Recognition of a Long Career of Dedicated Services to Mathematics and Mathematics Education, Association for Women in Mathematics (2016); Sr. Stephanie Sloyan Distinguished Service Award, Mathematical Association of America, New Jersey Section (2012); Grantee, 14 Grants for the Project for Resourceful Instruction of Mathematics in the Elementary School; Award, Association for Women in Mathematics **Membership:** Governor, New Jersey Section, Mathematical Association of America (2006-2009); Chair, Task Force on Integration and Diversity, National Council of Teachers of Mathematics (2003); Chairman, Environmental Committee, Mathematical Association of America (1998-2004); Vice Chair, Environmental Committee, Mathematical Association of America (1995-1998); Chair, Committee on Participation of Women, Mathematical Association of America (1987-1993); National Association of Mathematicians; American Mathematical Society; United Nations Association; Peace Action; Interfaith Environmental Coalition of Montclair Area; Brookdale Park Conservancy; Cornucopia Network of New Jersey; National Council of Teachers of Mathematics; Association of Women in Mathematics; Mathematical Association of America **Marquis Who's Who Honors:** Albert Nelson Marquis Lifetime Achievement Award (2017) **Hobbies:** Gardening year-round with no poisons and no power machinery; Ecumenical evangelizing; Writing **Religion:** Society of Friends **Shipping Address:** 56 Gordonhurst Ave, Montclair, NJ, 07043 **Website:** http://www.pkenschaft.com

Tom Kenyon

Title: Researcher, Composer, Author, Psychotherapist, Teacher **Industry:** Health, Wellness and Fitness **Date of Birth:** 01/27/1949 **Place of Birth:** Norfolk **State/Country of Origin:** VA **Marital Status:** Married **Spouse Name:** Judi Sion Kenyon **Education:** Postgraduate Studies, Ericksonian Medical Hypnosis, Southeast Institute, Chapel Hill, NC (1984); MA in Psychological Counseling, Columbia Pacific University (1983); Humanistic Counseling and Breath Work (1980); BA in Communications, Drama and Speech, The University of North Carolina at Greensboro (1976) **Certifications:** Certified in Whole Brain Learning, John David Learning Institute, Carlsbad, CA (1983) **Career:** Psycho-acoustic Immersion Seminars (1993-Present); Psychotherapist (1983-Present); Director, Acoustic Brain Research (1983-1993) **Civic:** Co-Founder, Sound Healing Foundation **Creative Works:** Author, "Brain States"; Author, "Mind Thieves"; Co-Author, "The Magdalen Manuscript"; Co-Author, "The Arcturian Anthology"; Creator, More than 60 Psychoacoustic Recordings under the Auspices of Acoustic Brain Research; Producer, Documentary, "Song of the New Earth: Tom Kenyon and the Power of Sound" **Awards:** Raymond Taylor Award for Excellence in the Performing Arts, The University of North Carolina at Greensboro (1970) **Marquis Who's Who Honors:** Albert Nelson Marquis Lifetime Achievement Award (2017); Distinguished Humanitarian (2017) **Where will you be in five years:** In five years, Mr. Kenyon will be continuing to travel the world and educate. **Business Address:** PO Box 98, Orcas, WA, 98280 **Website:** http://tomkenyon.com/

Carolyn L. Kessler, PhD

Title: Professor Emerita **Industry:** Education/Educational Services **Company Name:** University of Texas at San Antonio **Place of Birth:** Evansville **State/Country of Origin:** IN **Parents:** Frank Kessler; Genevieve Kessler **Education:** PhD, Georgetown University; MS, Georgetown University; BA, Saint Mary-of-the-Woods College **Certifications:** Certified, Sisters of Providence; Certificate in French, University of Grenoble, France **Career:** Professor Emeritus, Bicultural-Bilingual Studies, College of Human Development and Education, The University of Texas at San Antonio; Professor, Linguistics, Second Language Teaching and Learning, The University of Texas at San Antonio; Associate Professor, Immaculata College of Washington D.C.; Assistant Professor, Saint Mary-of-the-Woods College; Lecturer, ESL, Stanford University; Research Associate, San Francisco Hearing and Speech Center; Project Officer, Ford Foundation/NCEA Project for San Francisco Unified School District and Archdiocesan Catholic School System, Joint Planning Council of San Francisco; Fulbright Lecturer, University of Rome; Secondary School Teacher, French, Chemistry, Marywood School, Evanston, IL; Secondary School Teacher, French, Chemistry, Memorial High School, Evansville, IN **Career Related:** Consultant, Bilingual/ESL Education, School Districts, Texas; Consultant, Bilingual/ESL Education, School Districts, New York; Consultant, Bilingual/ESL Education, School Districts, Nebraska; Consultant, Bilingual/ESL Education, School Districts, Florida; Conference Presenter, Second Language Acquisition, Language Teaching and Learning, Regionally, Nationally, Internationally **Civic:** Member, Sisters of Providence, Saint Mary-of-the-Woods College (1954-Present) **Creative Works:** Co-author, "Literacy con Carino: A Story of Migrant Children's Success"; Co-author, "The Acquisition of Syntax in Bilingual Children"; Editor, "Cooperative Language Learning: A Teacher's Resource Book"; Co-author, "Scott Foresman ESL: Accelerating English Language Learning," Three Editions; Co-author, "Making Connections: An Integrated Approach to Learning English," Two Editions; Co-author, "Reading 2004 Pupil Edition," Three Editions; Co-author, Parade, New Parade," Two Editions; Co-author, "Home-School Partnerships in Building Learning Communities for Culturally Diverse Children"; Co-author, "Teaching Science to English Learners, Grades 4-8"; Author, Multiple Monographs; Contributor, Articles, Professional Journals; Contributor, Chapters, Books **Awards:** National Science Foundation Grant in Physics, Illinois Institute of Technology; University Fellow, Georgetown University; Million Dollar Scholar Award; President's Distinguished Achievement Award in Recognition of Teaching Excellence, The University of Texas at San Antonio; Dean's Outstanding Teacher Award Graduate Level, The University of Texas at San Antonio; National Association for Research in Science Teaching Award for Presentation of Outstanding Paper at a National Conference; The University of Texas at San Antonio College of Social and Behavioral Sciences Grant Awards **Membership:** The International Women's Leadership Association; International Teachers of English to Speakers of Other Languages; Linguistic Society of America; International Association of Applied Linguistics; American Association for the Advancement of Science; National Science Teachers Association; Founder, Affiliate, TexTESOLTwo **Marquis Who's Who Honors:** Distinguished Humanitarian (2017) **To what do you attribute your success:** Dr. Kessler attributes her success to the strong support of her parents, her superb foundation at Villa Maria Elementary and Villa Maria Academy, and the guidance of God's Providence in her life. **Why did you become involved in your profession or industry:** She became involved in her profession because she grew up wanting to help others. After a number of years planning to become a doctor, she developed a passion for teaching. Linguistics, the science of language, found her. It was a discipline that combined her interests in language, learning, and science. **What do you consider to be the highlight of your career:** A highlight of her career is observing the growth in students as they too became captured by the joy of learning. Also watching it lead many on to positions of leadership in diverse educational settings impacting a broad range of English language learners from the United States to Japan, Taiwan, Saudi Arabia, United Arab Emirates and many places in between. Having a role to play in the development of outstanding educators leaves her filled with awe and wonder. **Where will you be in five years:** In five years, if it is God's will, after celebrating the 300th anniversary of San Antonio in 2018 and The University of Texas' 50th anniversary in 2019, she looks forward to discovering in greater depth the joys and wonders of life. **Hobbies:** Reading; Movies; Symphony; Theater; Time with friends locally and nationally, including former students **Religion:** Catholic **Shipping Address:** 8103 North Holw Apt 307, San Antonio, TX, 78240

Beatrice Card Kettlewood

Title: Artist, Retired Educator **Industry:** Fine Art **Date of Birth:** 06/07/1929 **Place of Birth:** Pompton Plains **State:** NJ **Parents:** James Whitfield Card; Florence B. (Payne) Card **Marital Status:** Widowed **Spouse Name:** James Kettlewood (6/28/1952, Deceased) **Education:** EdD in Creative Arts, New York University (1972); MA, New York University (1955); BS, Newark State College (Now Kean University) (1951); Diploma, Butler High School, Butler, NJ (1947) **Certifications:** Certified Teacher, State of New Jersey **Career:** Freelance Painter (1959-Present); Chairman, Home Economics Department, High School, New Milford School District (1981-1984); Chairman, Language Department, High School, New Milford School District (1981-1984); Part-Time Instructor in Art, Extension Division, William Paterson University, Wayne, NJ (1963-1967); Chairman, Art Department, New Milford High School (1959-1984); Art Teacher, Junior-Senior High School, New Milford School District (1951-1984) **Career Related:** Freelance Illustrator; Lecturer in Art History; Lecturer in Art; Home Economics and Language Teacher **Civic:** Elder on Consistory, The First Reformed Church of Pompton Plains (1992-1995); Elder on Consistory, The First Reformed Church of Pompton Plains (1987-1990) **Creative Works:** Designer, Stained Glass Windows, Chilton Medical Center; Designer, Stained Glass Windows, Morristown Medical Center, Atlantic Health System; Designer, Stained Glass Windows, Rehabilitation Institute, Atlantic Health System; Designer, Stained Glass Windows, The First Reformed Church of Pompton Plains; Designer, Stained Glass Windows, Hackettstown Medical Center, Atlantic Health System; Exhibitor, Solo Shows, Over Ten States; Exhibitor, "Retrospective: 50 Years of Painting"; Gallery Director, FRC PP Art Gallery, Pompton Plains, NJ **Awards:** Butler High School Hall of Fame (2016) **Membership:** Co-President, Northern Jersey Interbranch, AAUW (2009-2011); Co-President, Northern Jersey Interbranch, AAUW (1991-1993); Gallery Committee, Orange County Arts Council (1985-1995); Chapter President, DKGSI (1978-1980); Secretary, AAUW; Representative, AAUW; President, Northern Jersey Interbranch, AAUW; Maine Art; Ringwood Manor Association of the Arts **Marquis Who's Who Honors:** Albert Nelson Marquis Lifetime Achievement Award (2017) **To what do you attribute your success:** Dr. Kettlewood attributes her success to her love of extensive work. She was interested in doing artwork from childhood. **Why did you become involved in your profession or industry:** Dr. Kettlewood became involved in her profession because she sees being an educator as a beloved career. **What do you consider to be the highlight of your career:** Dr. Kettlewood is most proud of the number of former students who are successful in art careers and/or teaching who still keep contact with her. She is also proud of her induction into the Butler High School Hall of Fame in honor of her career achievements, and her shows at galleries, university galleries, and art organizations. **Hobbies:** Writing; Architecture history; History **Shipping Address:** 45 Wilrue Parkway, Pompton Plains, NJ, 07444

Nilesh Vijay Khambekar, PhD

Title: President & Chief Executive Officer **Industry:** Technology **Company Name:** SpectrumFi, Inc. **Parents:** Vijay Shriram Khambekar; Ranjana Vijay Khambekar **Marital Status:** Married **Spouse Name:** Snehal Gurunath Joshi **Children:** Poorva Khambekar **Education:** PhD in Computer Science and Engineering, University at Buffalo (2015); MS in Computer Science, Wayne State University (2006); BS in Computer Engineering, University of Pune, India (2001) **Career:** President, Chief Executive Officer, SpectrumFi, Inc. (2015-Present); Senior Technical Leader, Juniper Networks (2007-2014) **Career Related:** Panel Moderator, IEEE MILCOM (2016); Technical Editor, IEEE 802.22.3 Spectrum Characterization and Occupancy Sensing (2016); Technical Reviewer, Conferences, Journals, Book-Chapter Publications **Creative Works:** Author, Springer Publications (2016-Present); Contributor, More Than 10 Research Papers; Contributor, More Than 10 Invention Disclosures; Contributor, Several White Papers **Awards:** Invited Paper, "Spectrum Sensing for Cognitive Radio: A Signal-Processing Perspective on Signal-Statistics Exploitation," IEEE ICNC (2012); Thomas Rumble Fellowship, Wayne State University (2004); National Merit Scholarship, India (1997) **Membership:** 5G Wireless Standardization, IEEE (2016-Present); Working Group, Interference, National Public Safety Telecommunications Council (2016-Present); Working Group, Spectrum Management Committee, National Public Safety Telecommunications Council (2016-Present); IEEE Communications Society (2016-Present); Working Group, IEEE 802.22 Wireless Regional Area Networks (2016-Present); Working Group, IEEE 1918.1 Tactical Internet (2016-Present); National Spectrum Consortium (2015-Present); SA Voting Member, IEEE (2015-Present); Working Group, IEEE 1900.5 Dynamic Spectrum Access Networks (2014-Present); IEEE (2008-Present); Wireless Innovation Forum (2015) **To what do you attribute your success:** Dr. Khambekar attributes his success to his family, including his mom, dad, his brother Jaynat and his wife, Snehal. **Why did you become involved in your profession or industry:** Dr. Khambekar became involved in his profession because at the time he was completing a PhD, one of the top defense companies approached him for collaboration and that's where his journey began. He always wanted to start his own venture; this was a great opportunity and his dear wife provided wholehearted support in this decision. **What do you consider to be the highlight of your career:** A highlight of Dr. Khambekar's career was after he earned a PhD and dared to start a company based on his 10 years of research. This research was highly appreciated by top-defense companies and his company started collaborations with them for applying this technology. **Where will you be in five years:** In five years, Dr. Khambekar sees himself continuing his passion for betterment of wireless technology and growing the business. There is tremendous demand for wireless spectrum and it is ever-increasing, but there is only a limited wireless spectrum. **Hobbies:** Hiking; Drawing; Painting; Teaching mathematics and science; Following scientific discoveries and technology inventions **Shipping Address:** 1247 Manet Dr, Sunnyvale, CA, 94087 **Website:** https://www.cse.buffalo.edu/~nvk3

Sanjay V. Khare, PhD

Title: Chair, Professor **Industry:** Education/Educational Services **Company Name:** The University of Toledo **Education:** PhD in Theoretical Condensed Matter Physics, University of Maryland (1996); MSc in Physics, Indian Institute of Technology Bombay (1989); BSc in Physics, University of Bombay (Now University of Mumbai) (1987) **Career:** Chair, Department of Physics and Astronomy, The University of Toledo (2016-Present); Professor, Department of Physics and Astronomy, The University of Toledo (2015-Present); Director, Professional Science Masters Program in Photovoltaics, Department of Physics and Astronomy, The University of Toledo (2010-Present), Director, Minor in Renewable Energy Program, Department of Physics and Astronomy, The University of Toledo (2009-Present); Associate Professor, Department of Physics and Astronomy, The University of Toledo (2009-2015); Assistant Professor, Department of Physics and Astronomy, The University of Toledo (2004-2009); Research Scientist, Department of Materials Science and Engineering, University of Illinois (1999-2004); Postdoctoral Researcher, Department of Physics, The Ohio State University (1996-1999); Graduate Research Assistant, Department of Physics, University of Maryland (1989-1996) **Career Related:** Directed Research of and Graduated More than 10 PhD Students; Served on PhD Committees of More than 25 Students; Directed Research and Graduated 17 MS Students; Directed Research of Eight Undergraduate Students **Civic:** Grant Reviewer, Various U.S. Federal and International Agencies **Creative Works:** Reviewer, "Materials Science," Lincoln Library Press (2011); Author, More than 65 Scientific Papers, Book Chapters, Invited Reviews; Referee, Peer-reviewed Journals **Awards:** Graduate Research Award, American Vacuum Society (1996); Institute Medal, Indian Institute of Technology Bombay (1989); Recipient, Federal, State and Private Industrial Research Grants; Recipient, Travel Grants **Membership:** American Ceramic Society **To what do you attribute your success:** Dr. Khare attributes his success to how his parents raised him with good Hindu spiritual and moral values, work ethic and hard work. He also credits his intrinsic scientific curiosity and inspiration by his early science teachers. **Why did you become involved in your profession or industry:** At the age of 12, Dr. Khare went to a special science program for bright young middle-school students in India and grew so enamored with science, by the time he reached 13, that he decided he wanted to be a scientist. By 16, he had determined to be a physicist. **Religion:** Hinduism **Business Address:** University of Toledo, University of Toledo, OH, Toledo, 43606 **Shipping Address:** 2801 West Bancroft Street, Toledo, OH, 43606 **Website:** http://www.utoledo.edu/nsm/physast/facstaff/_People/_Facpages/faKhare.html

Natalia S. Khvost-Vostrikova

Industry: Education/Educational Services **Date of Birth:** 05/24/1905 **Parents:** Serg I Khvostionkov; Maya Jacob Khvostionkova **Education:** BD Arts, Technological Institute, Moscow (1981) **Certifications:** Certified in Fashion Design, Russian Ministry of Fashion Industry (1981) **Creative Works:** Various Exhibitions and Performances **Achievements:** Achievements include Participation Biennale Internationale Firenze(Italy)

Assumpta Kiang

Title: Brokerage House Executive **Industry:** Financial Services **Company Name:** Merrill Lynch, Bank of America Corporation **Date of Birth:** 08/15/1939 **Place of Birth:** Beijing **Country of Origin:** People's Republic of China **Parents:** Pei-yu Chao; Yu-Jean (Liu) Chao **Marital Status:** Married **Spouse Name:** Wan-lin Kiang (8/14/1965) **Children:** Eliot Y. **Education:** MBA, California State University, Long Beach (1977); MS, Marywood University (1964); BA, National Taiwan University (1960) **Certifications:** Certified Financial Manager **Career:** Vice President, Merrill Lynch, Bank of America Corporation, Costa Mesa, CA (1996-Present); Senior Financial Consultant, Merrill Lynch, Bank of America Corporation, Costa Mesa, CA (1996-Present); Wealth Management Advisor, Merrill Lynch, Bank of America Corporation, Costa Mesa, CA (1996-Present); Vice President, Merrill Lynch, Bank of America Corporation, Santa Ana, CA (1977-Present); Senior Financial Advisor, Merrill Lynch, Bank of America Corporation, Santa Ana, CA (1977-Present); Reference Librarian, U.S. Information Service, Taipei, Taiwan (1971-1974); Lecturer, National Taiwan University (1971-1973); Librarian, ECPL (1964-1968); Data Programmer, IBM World Trade Corporation, IBM, New York, NY (1963) **Career Related:** Chairperson, Wan Lin Kiang International Financial Research Center, Zhejiang University (2004-Present); Director, WLK PhD Foundation, Institute of Finance & Banking, Chinese Academy of Social Sciences (2004-Present); Committee Member, Dean's Council, School of Social Sciences, University of California, Irvine (2002-Present) **Civic:** Founder, Pan Pacific Performing Arts Incorporated (1987); President, Women's League, California State University, Long Beach (1980-1982) **Creative Works:** Seminar Speaker, European Business Leaders in People's Republic of China (2010); Conference Speaker, Gold Industry Leaders in People's Republic of China (2008); Author, Numerous Research Reports in Field **Membership:** Board of Directors, Executive Women's Council, Center Club Orange County (1998-Present); President, Chinese-American Professional Women's League (1997-Present); Treasurer, Newport-Costa Mesa Branch, AAUW (1996-Present); Chairman, Chinese Business Association Society of California (1987-Present); Vice Chair, Pacific Rim Investment and Trade Association (1994-1996); Treasurer, Chinese-American Professional Women's League (1993); Vice President, Chinese Business Association Society of California (1986-1987); Chancellor's Club, University of California, Irvine; Old Ranch Country Club **Marquis Who's Who Honors:** Albert Nelson Marquis Lifetime Achievement Award (2017) **Why did you become involved in your profession or industry:** Ms. Kiang always had a passion for economics and finance. **What do you consider to be the highlight of your career:** Ms. Kiang is most proud of helping people, and helping her clients over the course of her career. **Political Affiliations:** Democrat **Religion:** Roman Catholic **Shipping Address:** 8 Stargazer, Newport Coast, CA, 92657

Ray Edward Kidder

Title: Consultant, Physicist **Industry:** Consulting **Date of Birth:** 11/12/1923 **Place of Birth:** New York **State:** NY **Parents:** Harry Alvin Kidder; Laura Augusta (Wagner) Kidder **Spouse Name:** Marcia Loring Sprague (6/12/1947, Divorced 1975, Deceased 2016) **Children:** Sandra Laura; David Ray (Deceased 2016); Matthew Sprague **Education:** PhD, Ohio State University (1950); MS, Ohio State University (1948); BS, Ohio State University (1947) **Career:** Physicist, Lawrence Livermore National Laboratory, Livermore, CA (1956-2014); Physicist, California Research Corporation, La Habra, CA (1950-1956) **Career Related:** Honorary Member, Advisory Board, Institute for Advanced Physics Studies, La Jolla, CA (1991-Present); Consultant, SAIC, San Diego, CA (1991-1994); Board of Editors, International Atomic Energy Agency, Vienna, Austria (1979-1984); Advisory Board, Max Planck Institute for Quantum Optics, Garching, Germany (1976-1990) **Military Service:** U.S. Navy (1944-1946) **Creative Works:** Contributor, Book Chapters **Awards:** Leo Szilard Award, American Physical Society (1993); Humboldt Award, Alexander Von Humboldt Foundation (1988) **Membership:** American Physical Society; American Association for the Advancement of Science; Sigma Xi **Marquis Who's Who Honors:** Albert Nelson Marquis Lifetime Achievement Award (2017); Distinguished Humanitarian (2017) **Why did you become involved in your profession or industry:** Dr. Kidder was inspired most by his father, Harry Kidder. **What do you consider to be the highlight of your career:** The highlight that stood out most during Dr. Kidder's career was winning the Leo Szilard Award. **Shipping Address:** 637 E Angela Street, Pleasanton, CA, 94566

P. Douglas Kiester

Title: Professor of Orthopedics **Industry:** Medicine & Health Care **Company Name:** University of California, Irvine **Children:** Six Children **Education:** Fellow, Rush-Presbyterian St. Luke's, Chicago, IL (1988); Resident, Orthopedic Surgery, Bronx-Lebanon Hospital Center (1987); Fellow, Pathokinesiology, Rancho Los Amigos National Rehabilitation Center (1983); Surgical Intern, University of Southern California (1982); MD, Indiana University (1981); PhD Coursework, Biophysics and Computing, University of Utah; Degree, University of Utah **Certifications:** Certified in Orthopedic Surgery, American Board of Orthopedic Surgery, Inc.; License to Practice Medicine, State of California **Career:** Professor, Department of Orthopedic Surgery, University of California, Irvine; Spinal Reconstruction Surgeon, University of California, Irvine **Creative Works:** Co-author, "Surgical Techniques for Spinopelvic Reconstruction Following Total Sacrectomy: A Systematic Review" (2013); Co-author, "Fixation Techniques for Complex Traumatic Transverse Sacral Fractures: A Systematic Review" (2013); Co-author, "Lumbar Disk Replacement Failures: Review of 29 Patients and Rationale for Revision" (2009); Co-author, "Is it Malingering, or is it 'Real'? Eight Signs that Point to Nonorganic Back Pain" (1999); Co-author, "Femoral Stem Failures in Total Hip Arthroplasty: An Unusual Causal Mechanism" (1982); Co-author, "Fibular Head Dislocation—Another Differential in the Diagnosis of Knee Injury" (1985) **Awards:** Named, Top Doctors in the San Diego Area (2013); Named, Top Doctors in the Los Angeles Area (2013); Named, America's Top Doctors in Minimally Invasive Spine Surgery, Neck Surgery, Scoliosis, Spinal Tumors, Spine Reconstruction, Castle Connolly Medical Ltd. (2013); Named, Top Doctors in Southern California (2012); Resident Faculty Teaching Award, Department of Orthopedic Surgery, University of California, Irvine (2004) **Membership:** California Orthopaedic Association **To what do you attribute your success:** Dr. Kiester attributes his success in his field to his need to know how things work. **Why did you become involved in your profession or industry:** Dr. Kiester became involved in his profession because his father was a surgeon. He followed in his footsteps. **Business Address:** 101 the City Dr S, Orange, CA, 92868 **Shipping Address:** 19 Rippling Strm, Irvine, CA, 92603 **Website:** http://www.orthopaedicsurgery.uci.edu/faculty-kiester.html

Sun-Hae Kim

Title: Medical/Surgical Nurse **Industry:** Medicine & Health Care **Date of Birth:** 07/16/1941 **Place of Birth:** Jinju **Parents:** Sampil Kim; Bok-Sun Lee **Education:** BA in England Literature, Youngnam University (1966) **Career:** Retired, Elmhurst Hospital (1997); Staff Nurse, Elmhurst Hospital, New York (1990-1997); Staff Nurse, Queens Hospital Center, Jamaica, NY (1973-1990); Staff Nurse, Harper Hospital, Detroit, MI (1972-1973); Staff Nurse, Cook County Hospital, Chicago, IL (1971-1972); Chief Nurse, Swedish Saved Children Federation, Pusan, Republic of Korea (1966-1970) **Creative Works:** Author, "Among Hibiscus and Roses, English Edition" (2013); Author, "Among Hibiscus and Roses, Korean Edition" (2004) **Hobbies:** Reading, walking **Shipping Address:** 152-18 Union Tpke Apt 12F, Flushing, NY, 11367

Yoon Berm Kim, PhD

Title: Immunologist, Educator, Professor Emeritus **Industry:** Education/Educational Services **Company Name:** Rosalind Franklin University of Medicine and Science, Chicago Medical School **Date of Birth:** 04/25/1929 **Place of Birth:** Pyongnam **Country of Origin:** Republic of Korea **Parents:** Sang Sun; Yang Rang (Lee) Kim **Marital Status:** Married **Spouse Name:** Soon Cha Kim (2/23/1959) **Children:** John, MD; Jean, Esq.; Paul, MD **Education:** PhD, University of Minnesota (1965); MD, Seoul National University (1958) **Career:** Professor Emeritus, Microbiology, Immunology & Medicine, Rosalind Franklin University of Medicine and Science, Chicago Medical School (2006-Present); Distinguished Professor, Institute of Biomedical Science & Technology, Konkuk University, Seoul, Republic of Korea (2006-2012); Acting Dean, School Graduate and Postdoctoral Studies, Rosalind Franklin University of Medicine and Science, Chicago Medical School (1994-1995); Professor of Microbiology, Immunology & Medicine, Rosalind Franklin University of Medicine and Science, Chicago Medical School (1983-2006); Chairman, Department of Microbiology and Immunology, Rosalind Franklin University of Medicine and Science, Chicago Medical School (1983-2004); Chairman, Immunology Unit, Cornell University Graduate School of Medical Sciences (Now Weill Cornell Medicine Graduate School of Medical Sciences), New York, NY (1980-1982); Professor, Immunology, Cornell University Graduate School of Medical Sciences (Now Weill Cornell Medicine Graduate School of Medical Sciences), New York, NY (1973-1983); Head, Laboratory of Ontogeny of Immune System, Sloan Kettering Institute, Memorial Sloan Kettering Cancer Center, New York, NY (1973-1983); Sloan Kettering Institute, Memorial Sloan Kettering Cancer Center, New York, NY (1973-1983); Associate Professor, Microbiology, School of Medicine, University of Minnesota, MN (1970-1973); Assistant Professor, Microbiology, School of Medicine, University of Minnesota, MN (1965-1970); Intern, Seoul National University Hospital (1958-1959) **Career Related:** Elected Fellow, American Academy of Microbiology (1995-Present); Lobund Advisory Board, University of Notre Dame (1977-1988); Fellow, American Academy of Microbiology **Creative Works:** Contributor, Numerous Articles, 122 Research Papers, 270 Abstracts on Immunology, Professional Journals **Awards:** Who's Who in American Education (2004-Present); Elected Member, The Korean Academy of Science and Technology (1998-Present); Who's Who in Medicine and Healthcare (1997-Present); Who's Who in the Midwest (1995-Present); Who's Who in Science and Engineering (1992-Present); Elected Member, Alpha Omega Alpha Honor Medical Society (1985-Present); Who's Who in Frontier Science and Technology (1984-Present); Who's Who in America (1982-Present); Who's Who in the World (1982-Present); American Men and Women of Science (1978-Present); Distinguished Professor Award, Institute of Biomedical Science & Technology, Konkuk University, Seoul, Republic Of Korea (2006-2012); Distinguished Alumni Award in Recognition of Life-Long Achievements and Leadership in the Field of Medical Science, Seoul National University (2004); Ham Choon Distinction in Medical Research Grand Prize, Seoul National University College of Medicine Alumni Association (2003); Secretary/Treasurer, Alpha Omega Alpha Honor Medical Society, Delta Chapter (1996-2006); Korean Abroad Who Illuminated Homeland Country by Prominent Achievement in the Field of Biomedical Sciences and Honorary Citizens of Seoul Award, 50th Anniversary of Liberation Day (1995); Morris Parker Meritorious Research Award, University of Health Sciences, Rosalind Franklin University of Medicine and Science, Chicago Medical School (1984); Research Career Development Award, U.S. Public Health Service (1968-1973) **Membership:** Sigma Xi; Alpha Omega Alpha Honor Medical Society; Charter Member, Society of Natural Immunity; Charter Member, International Endotoxin Society (Now International Endotoxin and Innate Immune Society); American Association for the Advancement of Science; Korean Academy of Science and Technology; President, Association of Gnotobiotics; Founding Member, International Association for Gnotobiology; American Association of Immunologists; American Society for Microbiology; American Association of Pathologists; Korean-American Medical Association; New York Academy of Sciences; Society for Leucocyte Biology; International Society for Developmental and Comparative Immunology (Now ISCDI); The Harvey Society; International Cytokine & Interferon Society; President, Chicago Association of Immunologists; Association of Medical School Microbiology and Immunology Chairs (Now AMSMIC); Advisory Member, Xenotransplantation Research Center; Advisory Member, Seoul National University College of Medicine; Advisory Member, Sigma Xi; Advisory Member, Alpha Omega Alpha Honor Medical Society **Shipping Address:** 5434 Belarus Street, Danville, CA, 94506

John K. King

Title: Lawyer **Industry:** Law and Legal Services **Company Name:** Lewis Thomason **Parents:** Dale G. King; Ann E. King **Marital Status:** Married **Spouse Name:** Elaine G. King (6/3/1962) **Children:** Shannon **Education:** JD, The University of Tennessee Knoxville (1965); BS, The University of Memphis (1962) **Certifications:** Admitted to Practice, Supreme Court of the United States (1970); Admitted to Practice, United States Court of Appeals for the Sixth Circuit (1970); Admitted to Practice, United States District Court Northern District of Tennessee (1965) **Career:** Attorney, Lewis Thomason (1981-Present); Chairman, Board Member, Tennessee Housing Development Agency (1981-1989); Commissioner of Revenue, State of Tennessee, Nashville, TN (1979-1981); Attorney, Lewis Thomason (1965-1979) **Membership:** Nashville Bar Association; Knoxville Bar Association **Bar Admissions:** Tennessee (1965) **Marquis Who's Who Honors:** Albert Nelson Marquis Lifetime Achievement Award (2017) **What do you consider to be the highlight of your career:** Mr. King is most proud of successfully representing minority shareholders against Busch Brothers Beans Company and also representing the claimant National Geographic Society. **Where will you be in five years:** In five years, Mr. King will be continuing his profession. **Hobbies:** Hunting; Fishing **Political Affiliations:** Republican **Religion:** Methodist **Business Address:** 620 Market Street, One Centre Sq 5th Fl, Knoxville, TN, 37902 **Shipping Address:** PO Box 2425, Lewis, Thomason King, Krieg & Waldrop, Knoxville, TN, 37901

Ordie H. King

Title: Oral Pathologist (Retired) **Industry:** Medicine & Health Care **Date of Birth:** 08/11/1933 **Place of Birth:** Memphis **State/Country of Origin:** TN **Parents:** Ordie Herbert; Hazel (Eaton) King **Marital Status:** Married **Spouse Name:** Violette Papagianis (3/21/1974, Deceased) **Children:** Anna LaVelle; Ordie Herbert III; Catherine Ann; Alexander Carlos **Education:** PhD, University of Tennessee (1965); Resident, Oral Pathology, City of Memphis Hospitals, University of Tennessee (1962-1963); U.S. Public Health Service Postdoctoral Fellow, University of Tennessee (1960-1962); DDS, University of Tennessee (1959); BS, Memphis State University (1957) **Certifications:** Diplomate, American Board of Oral and Maxillofacial Pathology **Career:** Chairman, Department of Diagnostic Specialties School of Dental Medicine, Southern Illinois University, Alton (1979-1992); Clinical Professor of Pathology, School of Dental Medicine, Washington University, St. Louis (1979-1980); Professor, Pathology, School of Dental Medicine, Southern Illinois University, Alton (1974-1997); Director, Cytopathology Laboratory, Medical Center, West Virginia University, Morgantown (1971-1974); Professor of Pathology, School of Medicine, West Virginia University, Morgantown (1974); Professor of Oral Pathology, School of Dentistry, West Virginia University, Morgantown (1970-1974); Acting Chairman, Visiting Associate Professor, Oral Pathology, Washington University, St. Louis (1969-1970); Chairman, Department of Dentistry, University hospitals, St. Louis University (1967-1970); Department Chairman, St. Louis University (1967-1970); Professor, St. Louis University (1969-1970); Associate Professor, Oral Pathology, St. Louis University (1967-1969); Assistant Professor of Pathology, Northwestern University (1966); Assistant Professor of Pathology, University of Tennessee (1965); Research Associate, Department of Pathology, University of Tennessee (1963-1965) **Career Related:** Member, Medical/Dental Staff, Department of Pathology, Alton Memorial Hospital (1986); Missouri Board of Dental Specialty Examiners (1982-1984); Director, Southern Illinois Pathology Laboratory, Ltd. (1977-2015); Member, Medical Staff, West Virginia University Hospital (1970-1974); Consultant, VA Hospital, Clarksville, WV (1973-1974); Dental Consultant, St. Louis County Medical Examiner (1968-1970); Consultant, Cancer Control Program, National Center Chronic Disease Control, U.S. Public Health Service (1967-1970); Member, Executive Committee, St. Louis University Hospitals (1967-1970); Dental Consultant to Chief Medical Examiner, State of Tennessee (1963-1965); West Tennessee Cancer Clinic (1962-1965) **Creative Works:** Contributor, Articles, Professional Publications **Awards:** Outstanding Teacher Award, West Virginia University (1972-1973) **Membership:** Vice President, Illinois Walking Horse Association (2009); Board of Directors, Illinois Walking Horse Association (2000-2008); Board of Directors, West Virginia Division, American Cancer Society (1972-1974); Fellow, American Academy of Oral Pathology; American Dental Association; American Cancer Society; American Society of Cytopathology; Illinois Walking Horse Association; Spotted Saddle Horse Association of Illinois; Tennessee Walking Horse Breeders and Exhibitors Association; Spotted Saddle Horse Breeders and Exhibitors Association; Omicron Kappa Upsilon; Phi Rho Sigma; Kappa Alpha Order; Delta Sigma Delta **Hobbies:** Horseback riding; Fishing; Hunting **Shipping Address:** 6111 Vollmer Ln, Godfrey, IL, 62035

Carolyn Ann Kingsbury

Title: Aerospace Engineer, Craftsman, Writer **Industry:** Engineering **Date of Birth:** 08/04/1938 **Place of Birth:** Newark **State/Country of Origin:** OH **Parents:** Cecil C. Layman; Orpha Edith (Hisey) Layman Dick **Marital Status:** Married **Spouse Name:** L.C. James Kingsbury (4/25/1959) **Children:** Donald Lynn; Kenneth James **Education:** Postgraduate Coursework, West Coast University (1982-1984); BS in Mathematics, University of California, Irvine (1979); BS in Information and Computer Science, University of California, Irvine (1979) **Career:** Writer (2001-Present); Systems and Research Engineer, Hughes Aircraft Co., Fullerton, CA (1990-1991); Systems and Research Engineer, Hughes Aircraft Co., Long Beach, CA (1989-1990); System and Software Engineer, Northrop Corporation, Pico Rivera, CA (1984-1989); Systems Engineer Analyst, Rockwell International, Downey, CA (1979-1984) **Career Related:** Speaking Engagements, Getting Women Interested in Science; Presenter in Field; Speaker, High Schools; Science Workshops **Civic:** Blue Ridge Literacy Council (2002-2003); Henderson County Public Library (2000-2002); Head Start Program, Blue Ridge Literacy Council (1998-1999); Blue Ridge Literacy Council (1998); Volunteer Computer Consultant, Henderson County Assessor's Office (1997-1998); Radio Reader, Regional Audio Information Service Enterprises (1997-1998); Cub Scout Den Mother, Boy Scouts of America, Manhattan Beach, CA (1972-1973); President, PTA, Manhattan Beach, CA (1971-1973) **Creative Works:** Author, "I'm in Good Shape for the Shape I'm In" (2001) **Awards:** Leadership Achievement Award, YWCA, Los Angeles, CA (1984); Continuing Award, Rockwell International (1983); Achievement Award, NASA (1983); Leadership Achievement Award, YWCA, Los Angeles, CA (1980); Service Award, California Congress of Parents and Teachers (1973) **Membership:** Newtowners Club (1962); National Association of Female Executives; American Association of University Women; National Management Association; Newtowners Club **Marquis Who's Who Honors:** Albert Nelson Marquis Lifetime Achievement Award (2017) **Hobbies:** Stamp collecting; Reading; Needlework **Shipping Address:** 319 Mockingbird Drive, Hendersonville, NC, 28792

Nancy M. Kingsbury Smyrski

Title: Dean (Retired) **Industry:** Education/Educational Services **Company Name:** Ball State University **Place of Birth:** Wilmington **State:** NC **Parents:** James Pruette Morgan; Frances Juanita Cornwell **Spouse Name:** William E. Kingsbury (7/15/1972, Divorced 2000) **Children:** Monica Folken; Mark Jordan; Heather Carlson; Charles **Education:** Postgraduate Coursework, Harvard University (2004, 1995); PhD, University of North Carolina, Greensboro (1983); MEd, University of North Carolina, Greensboro (1976) **Certifications:** Certified Family Life Educator **Career:** Dean, Applied Sciences and Technology, Ball State University, Muncie, IN (2002-2007); Chairman, Professor, Georgia Southern University, Statesboro, GA (1997-2002); Chairman, Professor, Texas Women's University, Denton, TX (1992-1997); Associate Professor, University of Manitoba, Winnipeg, Canada (1983-1992) **Civic:** Family Resource Center, Denton, TX (1995-1997) **Creative Works:** Co-author, "Sourcebook of Family Theory and Methods" (1993); Contributor, Articles, Science Journals **Awards:** Harvard Scholar (1995) **Membership:** American Association of Family and Consumer Science; Junior League; Kappa Omicron Nu; Groves Conference on Families; National Council on Family Relations **Marquis Who's Who Honors:** Distinguished Humanitarian (2017) **Hobbies:** Writing; Real estate investing; Reading **Political Affiliations:** Democrat **Religion:** Methodist **Shipping Address:** 232 Bloomington Lane, Wilmington, NC, 28411

E.C. Deeno Kitchen

Title: Lawyer **Industry:** Law and Legal Services **Company Name:** Ervin, Kitchen & Ervin **Date of Birth:** 05/01/1942 **Place of Birth:** Tallahassee **State/Country of Origin:** TN **Parents:** Oscar Edward Kitchen; Rose (Deeb) Kitchen **Marital Status:** Single **Spouse Name:** Married Patricia Gautier (6/22/1968) **Children:** Anne-Elizabeth K. Williams; Kimberly Gautier K. Robson; William Gautier; Deeb-Paul II **Education:** JD, Cum Laude, University of Florida (1967) **Career:** Partner, Ervin, Kitchen & Ervin (2006-Present); Partner, Dobson, Kitchen & Smith (2004-2006); Partner, Kitchen, Judkins, Simpson & High (1993-2004); Partner, Kitchen & High (1988-1993); Partner, Ervin, Varn, Jacobs, Odom & Kitchen (1971-1988); Associate, Ervin, Pennington, Varn & Jacobs (1969-1971); Associate, Gautier & Chisholm, New Smyrna Beach (1968-1969) **Career Related:** Former Chairman, Trial Bar Performance Review Committee, Northern District, US District Court, Florida **Civic:** Board of Trustees, University Florida Law Center Association (2001-Present); Chairman, Executive Committee, Leon County Democratic Party (1971-1973); Member, State Executive Committee, Democratic Party (1971-1975) **Creative Works:** Former Member, Editorial Board, University of Florida Law Review; Contributor, Articles, Professional Publications **Awards:** AV Preeminent Attorney, Martindale-Hubbell (1981-Present); Black Belt, Cuong Nhu Oriental Martial Arts; Black Belt, Isshin-Ryu Karate **Membership:** Charter Member, Master Tallahassee American Inn of Court; Fellow, American College of Trial Lawyers; International Society of Barristers; American Bar Foundation; Florida Bar Foundation; American Bar Association; Board of Regents, National College of Criminal Defense (1981-1984); American Board of Trial Advocates; Association of Trial Lawyers of America; National Association of Criminal Defense Lawyers; Academy Florida Trial Lawyers; Board of Directors, Florida Bar; Second Judicial Circuit Court, Florida; Order of the Coif; Phi Kappa Phi; Phi Alpha Delta; Sigma Chi; Chairman, Steering Committee, Trial Lawyers Section, Second Judicial Circuit Court, Florida; Chairman, Trial Advocacy Program, Second Judicial Circuit Court, Florida (1982, 1988); Executive Council, Criminal Law Section, Second Judicial Circuit Court, Florida (1976-1985) **Hobbies:** Karate **Political Affiliations:** Democrat **Religion:** Roman Catholic **Shipping Address:** 223 S Gadsden Street, Ervin, Kitchen & Ervin, Tallahassee, FL, 32302 **Website:** www.ervinkitchenlaw.net

Karel Kithier

Title: Pathologist (Retired) **Industry:** Medicine & Health Care **Date of Birth:** 12/06/1930 **Place of Birth:** Prague **Country of Origin:** Czech Republic **Parents:** Karel Kithier; Marie (Bohackova) Kithier **Marital Status:** Married **Spouse Name:** Viktorie Svecova (5/6/1961) **Children:** Karel Kithier **Education:** PhD, Charles University (1967); Resident in Pediatrics, Czechoslovakia (1962-1964); MD, Charles University (1962) **Certifications:** FLEX (1976); ECFMG (1975) **Career:** Medical Director, Special Chemistry, Detroit Receiving Hospital and University Health Center (1989-1996); Associate Professor of Pathology, Wayne State University School of Medicine (1978-1995); Associate Head of Clinical Chemistry, Detroit Receiving Hospital and University Health Center (1978-1989); Chief of Clinical Immunology, Detroit Receiving Hospital and University Health Center (1978-1989); Staff Pathologist, VA Medical Center, Allen Park, MI (1976-2001); Assistant Professor of Pathology, Wayne State University School of Medicine, Detroit, MI (1974-1978); Research Scientist, Michigan Cancer Foundation, Detroit, MI (1972-1974); Research Scientist, Child Research Center of Michigan (1968-1971); Research Scientist, Research Institute for Child Development, Prague, Czechoslovakia (1967-1968) **Career Related:** Visiting Scientist, Hokkaido University, Sapporo, Japan (1988-1989) **Creative Works:** Contributor, Articles, Professional Journals **Awards:** Fellow, National Academy of Clinical Biochemistry **Membership:** Czechoslovak Society of Arts & Sciences (1978-1992); Founding Member, International Society for Oncodevelopmental Biology and Medicine; American Association for Clinical Chemistry; The American Association of Immunologists, Inc.; American Association for Cancer Research; The New York Academy of Sciences; Czechoslovak National Council of America **Marquis Who's Who Honors:** Albert Nelson Marquis Lifetime Achievement Award (2017) **Why did you become involved in your profession or industry:** Dr. Kithier chose this career because his grandfather was a doctor who did many important things yet died before he was born. One day as a boy, he found some of the papers that his grandfather had published and, at that point, he was so moved and impressed that he decided to follow in his footsteps. **Where will you be in five years:** His grandfather, who had the same name, Karel Kithier, had a profound influence on his life. For that reason, he hopes that his own son and grandson will be inspired by his story to make a difference in the world and to help others. He hopes that others will do the same as well. **Hobbies:** Fishing; Outdoor Living; Fencing; Photography of Military Aircraft from WWI and WWII; Reading **Shipping Address:** 5022 Temple Dr, Sterling Heights, MI, 48310

Howard Klebanoff

Title: Attorney (Retired) **Industry:** Law and Legal Services **Company Name:** McGuigan, Hoberman, Sabanosh & Klebanoff, P.C. **Date of Birth:** 05/17/1937 **Place of Birth:** New Haven **State:** CT **Parents:** Max Edward Klebanoff; Sayre (Witten) Klebanoff **Marital Status:** Married **Spouse Name:** Sandra Fleischner (6/14/1959) **Children:** Marcie; Amy; Betsy **Education:** JD, University of Connecticut (1962); BA, Yale University (1959) **Certifications:** Certified Individualized Education Program Facilitator, State of Connecticut **Career:** Retired (2017); Partner, Rome, McGuigan, Hoberman, Sabanosh & Klebanoff, P.C. (1995-2017); Partner, Rome, Case, Kennelly & Klebanoff, P.C., Hartford, CT (1983-1994); Partner, Cohen, Wolf, Rome & Klebanoff, Hartford, CT (1982-1983); Partner, Rome, Case, Donnelly, Kennelly & Klebanoff, Hartford, CT (1979-1982); Partner, Kennelly & Klebanoff, Hartford, CT (1978-1979); Attorney, Private Practice (1977-2017); Partner, Kennelly, Klebanoff & Ellis, Hartford, CT (1973-1978); State Representative, United States Department of Labor (1969-1977); Partner, Novick, Klebanoff & Ellis, Hartford, CT (1969-1973); Partner, Ritter, Berman and Klebanoff, Hartford, CT (1963-1969); Attorney, United States Department of Labor, Washington D.C. (1962-1963) **Career Related:** Board of Directors, Newington Children's Hospital (1993-1994); First Chairman, Connecticut Board of Higher Education, Greater Hartford Convention and Visitors Bureau (1990-1992); Visiting Professor, Education, Trinity College (1978); Adjunct Professor, Education, Southern Connecticut State University (1977-1978); Chief Consultant, Connecticut General Assembly, House and Senate Majority (1977-1978); Lecturer, Trinity-Rensselaer Institute Community Education (1975-1976); Adjunct Professor, Educational Law, University of Connecticut; Adjunct Professor, Many of Connecticut's Private and Public Colleges and Universities **Civic:** Member, Rehabilitation Advisory Council, State of Connecticut (1993-Present); Founder, Commission on Developmental Disabilities (2016-2017); Founder, MORE Commission for Special Education (2014-2015); Member, Advisory Board, Connecticut Judiciary Task Force for Children (1993-1994); Member, Advisory Board, Learning Disability Association, Connecticut (1993-1994); Independent State Mediator, State Department of Education **Creative Works:** Lecturer, Special Education Law, University of Connecticut; Lecturer, Special Education Law, State Universities; Lecturer, Numerous Conferences **Awards:** Named, Super Lawyers, New England Super Lawyers (2014); President's Award for Excellence, Hartford County Bar Association (2004); Eponym, Klebanoff Institute of Special Education, University of Connecticut (1997); Special Citation, West Hartford Education Association (1980); National Leadership Award, The George Washington University (1979); Outstanding Legislator, House of Representatives, Eagleton Institute of Politics, Carnegie Foundation (1972); The Hall of Fame Award, Connecticut Association for Children with Learning Disabilities; A Friend of Education Award, Connecticut Education Association; Outstanding Public Service Award, Connecticut Association for Retarded Citizens; Honoree, Best Lawyers in America; Honoree, Connecticut Super Lawyers, Connecticut Magazine; Honoree, America's Most Top-Honored Professionals, American Registry; Outstanding Legislator, House of Representatives, Eagleton Institute of Politics; Named, Best Lawyers and Best Law Firms in Education Law, The U.S. News & World Report; Lexis/Nexis Martindale-Hubbell Registry of Preeminent Lawyers; AV Peer Review Rated, Martindale-Hubbell **Membership:** Commission on Developmental Disabilities (2016-2017); MORE, Commission for Special Education (2014-2015); Caucus Of Connecticut Democrats (1975); Fellow, The Connecticut Bar Foundation; Fellow, Hartford County Bar Association; Co-Chair, Force on Mentoring, Connecticut Bar Association; ABA **Bar Admissions:** United States Court of Appeals for the Second Circuit (1980); United States District Court District of Connecticut (1970); Connecticut (1962) **Marquis Who's Who Honors:** Albert Nelson Marquis Lifetime Achievement Award (2017) **Political Affiliations:** Democrat **Religion:** Jewish **Shipping Address:** 76 High Farms Rd, West Hartford, CT, 06107 **Website:** http://www.howardklebanoff.com/default.htm

Herbert David Kleber

Title: Professor of Psychiatry, Founder and Director Emeritus, Division on Substance Use Disorders **Industry:** Education/Educational Services **Company Name:** Columbia University Medical Center **Date of Birth:** 06/19/1934 **Place of Birth:** Pittsburgh **State:** PA **Parents:** Max J. Kleber; Dorothea (Schulman) Kleber **Spouse Name:** Marian W. Fischman (1989, Deceased 10/2001); Joan Louise Fox (9/9/1956, Divorced 1/1988); Anne B. Lawver **Children:** Elizabeth; Marc; Pamela **Education:** Honorary PhD, New York Medical College (1990); Honorary MA, Yale University, New Haven, CT (1975); Resident in Psychiatry, Yale University, New Haven, CT (1961-1964); Rotating Intern, Health Center Hospitals, University of Pittsburgh (1960-1961); MD, Jefferson Medical College (1960); Lederle Research Fellow, Jefferson Medical College (Now Sidney Kimmel Medical College, Thomas Jefferson University) (1959-1960); BA in Psychology, Dartmouth College, Cum Laude (1956) **Career:** Attending Psychiatrist, Columbia-Presbyterian Medical Center (Now NewYork-Presbyterian/Columbia University Medical Center, NewYork-Presbyterian Hospital) (1992-Present); Professor of Psychiatry, The College of Physicians and Surgeons (Now Vagelos College of Physicians and Surgeons), Columbia University, New York, NY (1991-Present); Professor, New York State Psychiatric Institute (1991-Present); Director, Division of Substance Abuse, New York State Psychiatric Institute (1991-Present); Executive Vice President, National Center on Addiction and Substance Abuse, Columbia University (1992-2001); Medical Director, National Center on Addiction and Substance Abuse, Columbia University (1992-2001); Professor, Yale University (1975-1991); Director, Substance Abuse Treatment Unit, Connecticut Mental Health Center, Yale School of Medicine (1975-1989); Executive Director of Psychiatric Emergency Room Service, Yale-New Haven Hospital, Yale New Haven Health (1967-1968); Director, Drug Dependence Unit, Connecticut Mental Health Center, Yale School of Medicine (1968-1975); Founder, Drug Dependence Unit, Connecticut Mental Health Center, Yale School of Medicine (1968-1975); Outpatient and Admissions Coordinator, Connecticut Mental Health Center, Yale School of Medicine (1967-1968); From Assistant Professor to Associate Professor, Yale School of Medicine, New Haven, CT (1966-1975); Assistant Chief, Hill-West Haven Division, Connecticut Mental Health Center, Yale School of Medicine (1966-1967) **Career Related:** Director, National Institute of Drug Abuse Medication Development Center (1994-Present); Research Training Fellowship Program, Columbia University (1993-Present); Deputy Director, Office of National Drug Control Policy (ONDCP) (1989-1992); Director, Research Training Fellowship in Substance Abuse, Yale University (1988-1989); Drug Abuse Advisory Committee, Food and Drug Administration (1987-1990); Director, NIDA Clinical Research Center for Treatment of Opioid and Cocaine Abuse, Yale University (1986-1989); Nolan D.C. Lewis Visiting Professor, Carrier Foundation (Now Carrier Clinic) (1985); Chief Executive Officer, APT Foundation, Inc. (1982-1989); Board of Science Counselors, Addiction Research Center, National Institute on Drug Abuse (1982-1985); National Institute of Mental Health (1977-1979); National Advisory Council, National Institute of Drug Abuse (1975-1979); Founder, APT Foundation (1970); Board of Directors, College on Problems of Drug Dependence; Board of Directors, Partnership for a Drug-Free America (Now Partnership for Drug-Free Kids); Board of Directors, Phoenix House Foundation (Now Phoenix House); Board of Directors, Betty Ford Institute (Now Hazelden Betty Ford Foundation) **Civic:** National Advisory Council, National Institute for Drug Abuse (2003-Present) **Creative Works:** Contributor, "Cocaine: Scientific and Social Dimensions" (1992); Editor, "Clinician's Guide to Cocaine Addiction: Theory, Research, and Treatment" (1992); Contributor, "Clinical Psychiatric Medicine" (1981); Contributor, "Treatment Aspect of Drug Dependence" (1978); Contributor, Chapters, "Opiate Addiction: Origins and Treatment" (1973) **Awards:** Distinguished Alumni Award, Yale School of Medicine (2017); Distinguished Scientist Award, American Society of Addiction Medicine (2005); Charles Burlingame Award, Institute of Living, Hartford HealthCare (2005); Albert Biele Memorial Award, Jefferson Medical College (Now Sidney Kimmel Medical College, Thomas Jefferson University) (2000); Distinguished Alumni Award, Yale University (2000); Jellinek Sward, Yale University (1994); Families in Action Drug Prevention Award (1990) **Membership:** Chair, Practice of Guidelines for Treatment of Substance Use Disorders, American Psychiatric Association (2002-2006); American Psychiatric Association; Consultant, Joint Commission on Public Affairs, American Psychiatric Association; Task Force on Benzodiazepine Dependency, American Psychiatric Association; American College of Neuropsychopharmacology; The New York Academy of Medicine; American Academy of Psychiatrists in Alcoholism and Addictions; Institute of Medicine **Political Affiliations:** Independent **Religion:** Jewish **Shipping Address:** 10 W 66th Street, Apt. 19F, New York, NY, 10023 **Website:** https://en.wikipedia.org/wiki/Herbert_Kleber

A. Bernhard Kliefoth III

Title: Neurosurgeon **Industry:** Medicine & Health Care **Place of Birth:** San Antonio **State/Country of Origin:** TX **Parents:** S. Arthur Bernhard Kliefoth, Jr.; Pauline G. Kliefoth **Children:** Karena; Tanya **Education:** Chief Resident, Washington University in St. Louis (1976-1977); Resident, General Surgery, NMCSD (1972-1973); Intern, Naval Hospital Oakland (1970-1971); MD, The University of Texas Medical Branch at Galveston (1970); AB in Chemistry, Princeton University (1965) **Certifications:** Diplomate, American Board of Neurological Surgery (1980) **Career:** Neurosurgery Specialist, Private Practice (1981-Present); Chairman, Institutional Review Board, St. Mary's Hospital (1984-2008); Secretary Medical Staff, St. Mary's Hospital (1990); Chairman, Surgery Department, Tennova Healthcare (1989-1990); Neurosurgeon, Washington University in St. Louis (1973-1978); Teacher, Washington University in St. Louis (1976-1978); Research Fellow, Department of Radiation Oncology, Washington University in St. Louis (1977-1978); Neurosurgery Instructor, Washington University in St. Louis (1976-1978); Associate Professor of Clinical Surgery, The University of Tennessee, Knoxville, TN; Member of Staff, The University of Tennessee Medical Center; Member of Staff, Physicians Regional Medical Center, Tennova Heathcare **Career Related:** Board of Directors, Tennessee Donor Services; Cole Neuroscience Foundation, University of Tennessee Medical Center; Knoxville Donor Services; Epilepsy Foundation; Visiting Professor, Walter Reed National Military Medical Center **Civic:** President, Knoxville & Eastern Tennessee Chapter, Alumni Association of Princeton University; Treasurer, Knoxville & Eastern Tennessee Chapter, Alumni Association of Princeton University; Member, Executive Committee, West Hills Association; President, Westborough Association **Military Service:** Retired Captain, U.S. Navy (2002); Captain, U.S. Navy Reserve (1985); Medical Officer, U.S. Marines (1981-1996); Medical Officer, U.S. Navy Reserve (1981-1996); Staff Neurosurgeon, Naval Hospital Oakland (1978-1981); Commander, U.S. Navy (1977); Commissioned Ensign, U.S. Navy (1969); Medical Officer, USS Bainbridge, and Radiation Safety Officer, USS Bainbridge, DLG(N)-25, U.S. Navy; Officer-in-Charge, PRIMUS Group of Physicians and Nurses, Knoxville, TN **Awards:** Distinguished Southern Neurosurgeon Award, Southern Neurosurgery Society (2003) **Membership:** Fellow, American College of Surgeons; Fellow, Stroke Council, American Heart Association, Inc.; American Medical Association; American Association of Neurological Surgeons; American Society Stereotactic and Functional Neurosurgery; Tennessee Neurosurgery Society; World Society Stereotactic and Functional Neurosurgery; Congress of Neurological Surgeons; Southern Neurosurgery Society; Southern Medical Association; Tennessee Medical Association; Knoxville Academy of Medicine; San Francisco Neurological Society; Society of Medical Consultant to the Armed Forces; AMSUS; Society for Neuroscience; North American Neuromodulation Society; International Neuromodulation Society; American Nuclear Society **Hobbies:** Photography; Coin collecting/numismatics; Stamp collecting/philately; Computers; Traveling; Scuba diving **Business Address:** PMB 264, UPS Store, Knoxville, TN, 37923 **Shipping Address:** P.O. Box 51648, Knoxville, TN, 37950

Kenneth Alan Kline, PhD

Title: Mechanical Engineering Educator Emeritus **Industry:** Education/ Educational Services **Company Name:** Wayne State University **Date of Birth:** 07/11/1939 **Place of Birth:** Chicago **State:** IL **Parents:** George Lester Kline; Beverly Gretchen (Hanson) Kline **Marital Status:** Married **Spouse Name:** Nancy Ann Bixler (6/25/1960) **Children:** Lisa Kline Richman; John Kenneth Kline; Jeffery Eastbury Kline; Gretchen Kline King **Education:** PhD, University of Minnesota (1965); Research Fellow, University of Minnesota, Minneapolis, MN (1962-1965); BS, University of Minnesota (1961) **Career:** Director, Kline Family Tree Farm (2005-Present); Chair, Mechanical Engineering, Wayne State University, Detroit, MI (1997-Present); Interim Dean, Engineering, Wayne State University, Detroit, MI (1996-Present); Owner, Kline Family Tree Farm (1975-Present); Professor, Mechanical Engineering, Wayne State University, Detroit, MI (1973-Present); Chair, Wayne State University, Detroit, MI (1987-1995); Interim Chair, Department of Mechanical Engineering, Wayne State University, Detroit, MI (1986-1987); Associate Professor, Wayne State University, Detroit, MI (1966-1973); Senior Research Engineer, Esso Production Research Company, Houston, TX (1965-1966); Research Assistant, University of Minnesota, Minneapolis, MN (1961-1962) **Career Related:** Consultant, Ford Motor Company, Detroit, MI (1976-Present); Visiting Scientist, Ford Motor Company, Detroit, MI (1984-1985); Visiting Professor, Ludwig-Maximilian University of Munich (1972-1973) **Civic:** Representative, Grosse Pointe Park, Michigan (1982-1984); Precinct Delegate, Grosse Pointe Park, Michigan (1982-1984); Volunteer, Grosee Pointe Neighborhood Club (1973-1982) **Creative Works:** Editor, "Proceedings on the Sixth International Conference Vehicle Structures" (1986); Contributor, Articles to Professional Journals **Awards:** Named, Principal Investigator, Research Experiences for Undergraduate Sites, National Science Foundation (1995-Present); Recipient, Dedicated Service Award, The American Society of Mechanical Engineers (1996); Recipient, Forest R. McFarland Award, Society of Automotive Engineers (1993); Recipient, Senior United States Science Award, Alexander Von Humboldt-Stiftung, Federal Republic of Germany (1972); Fellow, National Aeronautics and Space Administration (1964-1965); Fellow, National Science Foundation (1961-1964); Named, A.P. Sloan Foundation National Scholar (1959-1961) **Membership:** Chair, National Department Heads Committee, The American Society of Mechanical Engineers (1998-Present); National Nominating Committee, The American Society of Mechanical Engineers (1997-Present); Vice Chair, The Engineering Society of Detroit (1988-Present); General Chair, International Mechanical Engineering Congress & Expo, The American Society of Mechanical Engineers (1994); Program Chair, Winter Annual Meeting, The American Society of Mechanical Engineers (1993); Chair, The American Society of Mechanical Engineers (1989-1991); Chair, SAE International (1984-1986); Fellow, The American Society of Mechanical Engineers (1974-1975); AIAA; The Society of Rheology **Marquis Who's Who Honors:** Albert Nelson Marquis Lifetime Achievement Award (2017) **Why did you become involved in your profession or industry:** Dr. Kline became involved in his profession because his high school mathematics teacher saw that engineering gave the promise of thinking for a living. **Hobbies:** Bird-watching; Tree farming; Reading, Swimming; Hiking **Shipping Address:** 1645 Marion Hills Dr, Charlevoix, MI, 49720

Lewis M. Kling

Title: Manufacturing Executive (Retired) **Industry:** Manufacturing **Date of Birth:** 02/28/1945 **Place of Birth:** Brooklyn **State:** NY **Parents:** William Kling; Evelyn Kling (Deceased) **Marital Status:** Married **Spouse Name:** Rebecca **Children:** Cheryl Roesch; Carrie West; Chris Brecher **Education:** MBA, Stetson University; BSEE, Rensselaer Polytechnic Institute **Career:** Vice Chairman, Flowserve Corp., Irving, Texas (2009-2010); Chief Executive Office, President, Flowserve Corp., Irving, Texas (2005-2009); Chief Operating Officer, Flowserve Corp., Irving, Texas (2004-2005); Corporation Vice President, Officer, SPX Corp. (1999-2004); President Dielectric Communications, Gen Signal (Merged with SPX Corp.), Raymond, ME (1997); Senior Vice President, General Manager Commercial Avionics Systems, AlliedSignal Aerospace, Fort Lauderdale, FL (1995-1997); Vice President, General Manager, Electronic Systems Division, Harris Corp., Melbourne, FL (1990-1995); Computer Engineer to Several Managerial Positions, Apollo Division (Later Simulation and Control Systems), General Electric Co. (1966-1990); Board Chairman, American Russian Integrated Avionics JV, AlliedSignal Aerospace **Shipping Address:** 3 Elk Pointe Ln, Castle Rock, CO, 80108

Rex Carter Klopfenstein

Title: Electrical Engineer (Retired) **Industry:** Engineering **Date of Birth:** 03/03/1938 **Place of Birth:** Pittsfield **State:** MA **Parents:** Glenn A. Klopfenstein; Jasmine V. (Carter) Klopfenstein **Marital Status:** Married **Spouse Name:** Linda Gilgore (10/6/1962) **Children:** Mark W.; Eric G. **Education:** MEE, Syracuse University (1963); BSEE, University of Connecticut (1959) **Career:** Retired (2009); Lead Engineer, Noblis, Inc., McLean, VA (1996-2009); Lead Engineer, The MITRE Corporation, McLean, VA (1982-1996); Technology Staff, The MITRE Corporation, McLean, VA (1970-1977); Engineering Manager, AMF Electronic Research Laboratory, Sterling, VA (1981-1982); Software and Test Manager, Acuity Systems (1978-1981); Hardware Engineering Manager, Logicon Inc. (Now Northrop Grumman Corporation) (1977-1978); Laboratory Manager, Division E Systems, Melpar (1963-1970); Engineer, General Electric (1959-1963) **Career Related:** Secretary, Technology Committee X3K5, American National Standards Institute (ANSI) (1992-1994) **Civic:** Chairman, Honor Roll, Republican National Committee (1997) **Creative Works:** Associate Editor, "Third Millennium Medal" (2000); Editor, IEEE (1998-1999); Co-author, "Microcomputer Design and Application" (1977); Contributor, Articles, Professional Journals **Awards:** Honoree, Engineer of Year, District of Columbia Council of Engineering and Architectural Societies (2000) **Membership:** Web Site Manager, IEEE (1997-Present); Vice President of Administration, Washington Academy of Sciences (2004-2007); Board of Directors, IEEE (2002-2005); President, Washington Academy of Sciences (1999-2000); President-Elect, Washington Academy of Sciences (1999-2000); Board of Managers, Washington Academy of Sciences (1996-1998); Chairman, National Area Council, IEEE (1995-1996); Vice-Chairman, National Area Council, IEEE (1994-1995); Chairman, Northern Virginia Section, IEEE (1993-1994); Vice-Chairman, Northern Virginia Section, IEEE (1992-1993); Treasurer, Northern Virginia Section, IEEE (1992-1993); Secretary, Northern Virginia Section, IEEE (1991-1992); Fellow, Washington Academy of Sciences; Senior Life Member, IEEE; Chi Phi, OmegaFi; The Tau Beta Pi Association, Inc. **Marquis Who's Who Honors:** Albert Nelson Marquis Lifetime Achievement Award (2017) **Hobbies:** Photography **Shipping Address:** 4224 Worcester Dr, Fairfax, VA, 22032

Mark Paul Klutho

Title: Landscape Architect **Industry:** Architecture & Constrution **Date of Birth:** 02/20/1949 **Place of Birth:** St. Louis **State:** MO **Parents:** Paul Ralph Klutho; Mary Lee Klutho **Marital Status:** Married **Spouse Name:** Barbara Ellen Klutho **Education:** Coursework, University of Missouri, St. Louis, MO **Career:** Landscape Architect **Civic:** Active Member, Community and School Board, Largo, FL **Military Service:** Sergeant, U.S. Army, Vietnam (1968-1971) **Why did you become involved in your profession or industry:** Mr. Klutho became involved in his career because of his great love of plants and waterfalls. **What do you consider to be the highlight of your career:** Out of the many highlights of Mr. Klutho's career, he is most proud of his involvement in the battle stopping the nuke plank at the Levy Company. **Where will you be in five years:** In five years, Mr. Klutho will be continuing his efforts arguing for high-performance works in passive solar design. **Political Affiliations:** Democrat **Shipping Address:** 14496 120th Avenue N, Largo, FL, 33774

Peter C. Knudson

Title: State Legislator **Industry:** Civil Service **Date of Birth:** 10/26/1937 **Place of Birth:** Brigham City **State/Country of Origin:** UT **Marital Status:** Married **Spouse Name:** Georgianna White (1963) **Certifications:** Diplomate, American Board of Orthodontics **Career:** Associate Professor, School of Dentistry, University of Utah (2013-Present); Majority Assistant Whip, State Senate District 17, State of Utah (2003-Present); State Senator, District 24, State of Utah (1999-2002); State Representative, District Two, State of Utah (1995-1998); Chairman, State Job Training Coordinator Council (1992-1994); Mayor, Brigham City, Utah (1978-1990); City Councilman, Brigham City Corp (1974-1978); Private Practice in Orthodontics (1967-2010); Co-Chairman, Ethics Committee, State of Utah; Member, Economic Develop Committee, State of Utah; House Representative, State of Utah; Former Chairman, Labor & Economic Development Standing Committee; Former Member, Environmental Quality Appropriations Committees; Former Member, Transportation Standing Committee **Military Service:** Colonel, U.S. Army Reserve **Awards:** Most Outstanding Elected Public Official, Utah League of Cities and Towns; Distinguished Service Award, UDA; Honorary Colonel, Utah Highway Patrol; Honorary Colonel Corporal, Utah National Guard **Membership:** Rotary International; Utah Association of Orthodontists, UDA; Pierre Fauchard Academy; American Dental Association; American Association of Orthodontists; Fellow, International College of Dentists; Fellow, American College of Dentists; Rocky Mountain Association of Orthodontists; Executive Committee, Western Division, The Council of State Governments; CDABO; Board of Directors, National League of Cities; Advisory Council, National League of Cities; Past President, Utah League of Cities **Marquis Who's Who Honors:** Albert Nelson Marquis Lifetime Achievement Award (2017) **Hobbies:** Hunting; Skiing **Political Affiliations:** Republican **Shipping Address:** 1209 Michelle Dr, Brigham City, UT, 84302

Gerd Hermann Koch

Title: Artist, Educator **Industry:** Education/Educational Services **Date of Birth:** 01/30/1929 **Place of Birth:** Detroit **State:** MI **Parents:** Hermann Koch; Margaret Koch **Marital Status:** Life Partnership **Spouse Name:** Carole Milton **Children:** Keari **Education:** MFA in Painting, University of California, Santa Barbara (1967); Postgraduate Coursework, University of California, Los Angeles (1956); BFA, Wayne State University, Detroit, MI (1951); Postgraduate Coursework, University of California, Los Angeles (1950) **Career:** Art Instructor, Self-workshops, Southern California (1952-Present); Art Professor, Ventura College (1966-1998); Art Instructor, Upper Division, University of California Extension, Santa Barbara/Ventura (1966-1974); Art Instructor, Santa Barbara Community College Center for Lifelong Learning (1965-1968); Art Professor, Ventura College (1960) **Career Related:** Co-Founder, Board of Directors, Studio Channel Islands Art Center, Camarillo, CA (1997-Present); Curator, Exhibits on National and Internally Known Artists (1999-2007); Co-founder, Channel Islands Art Center Campus, California State University (1987); Curator, Numerous Exhibitions (1973-2009); Curator, Exhibits, Ventua College (1973-1996); Teaching Assistant to Kurt Kranz, Master of Fine Art, University of California, Santa Barbara (1967); Original Member, Ferus Gallery (1957); Summer Film Workshop, Graduate School, University of California, Los Angeles (1955); Founder, Artists' Commune, Ojai, CA (1952); Curator, Tenth Anniversary Invitational Exhibit, Channel Islands Art Center Campus, California State University Channel Islands; Leading Organizer, Partner Carole Milton, 20 International Art Tours; Leading Organizer, Partner Carole Milton, Van Gogh 100th Anniversary of His Death, Fiji and New Zealand; Leading Organizer, Partner Carole Milton, Berlin After the Fall of the Berlin Wall **Civic:** Board of Directors, Focus on the Masters (1998-Present); Juror, Art Exhibits (1975-Present); Chairman, Municipal Art Collection Acquisition Committee (2004-2005); Public Art Commissioner, City of Ventura, CA (2003-2006); Founder, Ventura Beautiful (2001-2005) **Creative Works:** Curator, Studio Channel Islands Art Center, California State University, Camarillo, CA (1997-Present); Exhibitor, Creative Photography (1953-Present); Exhibitor, "Then and Now," Studio Channel Islands Art Center (2018); Curator, "20th Anniversary Show," Channel Islands Art Center (2018); Exhibitor, Paintings for Professors of Ventura College, Museum of Ventura County (2014); Composer, International Composers Micuel Del Aguila, Ventura, CA (2013); Exhibition, "Our Journey Together," Studio Channel Islands Art Center, Camarillo, CA (2013); Four Masters-Four Legends, Museum of Ventura County, CA (2011); One-Person Show, Annual Exhibition, Studio Channel Islands Art Center, California State University, Channel Islands (2010); Retrospective Exhibition, The Artful Couples with Partner Carole Milton, County Government Center (2010); Exhibitor, Cochineal Red A Glorious Experience Lecturer, Studio Channel Islands Art Center (2010); Retrospective Exhibition, The Founders Exhibition, Studio Channel Islands Art Center (2009); Curator, One-Person Show, 60-Year Respective and 80th Birthday, Studio Channel Islands Art Center, California State University, Channel Islands (2009); International Recognized Artists, Walter Askin & Roland Reiss (2007-2008); Retrospective Exhibition, Rembrandt Exhibition Gallery, Talks, The J. Paul Getty Museum, Los Angeles, CA (2005); Exhibitor, "Memento Many," SciArt Center (2003); Retrospective Exhibition, Studio Channel Islands Art Center (2003); Exhibitor, "Visions and Encounters," Studio Channel Islands Art Center, California State University, Camarillo, CA (2000); One-Person Show, Ventura Music Festival (1998); Retrospective Exhibition, The Ojai Art Center (1998); Exhibitor, Paintings, Thousand Oaks Performing Art Center (1996); Retrospective Exhibition, Carnegie Art Museum, Oxnard, CA (1988); One-person Show, Santa Barbara Museum of Art (1968); One-Person Show, Esther Bear Gallery, Santa Barbara, CA (1965-1967); One-Person Show, Esther-Robles Gallery, Los Angeles, CA (1965, 1963, 1961); One-Person Show, Long Beach Museum of Art (1961); Exhibitor, Group Show, La Jolla Museum of Art (1961); Exhibitor, Three-person Travelling Exhibition, Western Association of Art Museums (1960-1963) **Awards:** Studio Channel Islands Art Center, Studio Channel Islands Art Center (2013); Recipient, Special Certificate for Art Recognition, Ventura County Board of Supervisors (2009); Eponym, Gerd Koch Gallery, Studio Channel Islands Art Center (2007); Recipient, Artist of Distinction Exhibit Award, Recipient, Mayor's Award, Artist in the City, Ventura, CA (2006); Recipient, Southern California Intercollegiate Science and Art Conference, California State University Channel Islands, Camarillo, CA (2005); Recipient, Special Certificate for Art Recognition, Ventura County Board of Supervisors (2004); Recipient, Purchase Awards, National Watercolor Society (1976); Recipient, First Purchase Award, Professional Competition, California State Fair (1963); Recipient, Purchase Awards, Grumbacher, Inc. (1962, 1960); Recipient, Morrison Medal, Oakland Art Museum (1960) **Business Address:** 444 Aliso Street, Ventura, CA, 93001 **Shipping Address:** 809 Via Cielito, Ventura, CA, 93003

Edward J. Kollar, PhD

Title: Professor Emeritus **Industry:** Education/Educational Services **Company Name:** University of Connecticut **Date of Birth:** 03/03/1934 **Place of Birth:** Forest City **State:** PA **Parents:** I.J. Kollar; Mary (Zaverl) Kollar **Marital Status:** Married **Spouse Name:** Catherine Ann Tobin (2/23/1963) **Children:** Michelle; Elizabeth; Rachael; Brian; Rebecca **Education:** PhD, Syracuse University (1963); MS, Syracuse University (1959); BS, University of Scranton (1955) **Career:** Professor Emeritus, School of Dental Medicine, University of Connecticut Health Center (1998-Present); Acting Head, Department of Oral Biology, University of Connecticut Health Center (1996-1998); Program Director, Dental Science Award Program, University of Connecticut Health Center (1990-1997); Associate Dean, Academic Affairs, University of Connecticut Health Center (1988-1998); Acting Head, Department of Oral Biology, University of Connecticut Health Center (1985-1986); Oral Biology Graduate Program Director, University of Connecticut Health Center (1983-1988); Professor, Oral Biology, University of Connecticut Health Center (1976-1997); Associate Professor, Oral Biology, University of Connecticut Health Center (1971-1976); Assistant Professor, Anatomy, University of Chicago (1969-1971); Assistant Professor, Anatomy, Biology, University of Chicago (1967-1969); Assistant Professor, Biology, University of Chicago (1966-1967); Research Associate, Zoology, University of Chicago (1966-1967); Instructor, Zoology, University of Chicago (1963-1966); Research Associate, University of Chicago (1963-1966) **Career Related:** Visiting Professor, Guy's Hospital, School of Medicine, King's College London (1978); Professor, Department of Molecular Biology, Universitat Salzburg, Austria (1971-1990); Presenter in Field **Civic:** Numerous Executive Positions, Various Educational Committees **Creative Works:** Editor-in-Chief, Archives of Oral Biology (1978-1997); Editorial Board, Saudi Dental Journal of Epithelial Cell Biology **Awards:** Frank J. O'Hara Recognition of Distinguished Achievement in Science and Technology, Alumni Society, University of Scranton (2000); Bronze Echelon Medal of the City of Paris, Recognition of the Contribution to Dental Science (1986); Isaac Shour Outstanding Research in the Field of Anatomical Sciences, International Association for Dental Research (1981); Isaac Shour Memorial Basic Science Award (1981); Quantrell Award, University of Chicago (1968); Excellence in Teaching (1968); Grantee, National Institutes of Health **Membership:** President, Craniofacial Biology Group, International Association for Dental Research (1983); Secretary, Sigma Xi (1970); Treasurer, Chicago Chapter, Sigma Xi (1969); American Society of Zoologists; International Society of Developmental Biologists; ISD; Developmental Biology; Tissue Culture Association; Bone and Tooth Society **Marquis Who's Who Honors:** Albert Nelson Marquis Lifetime Achievement Award (2017) **Why did you become involved in your profession or industry:** Curiosity drove Dr. Kollar to become involved in his field. He was interested in biological sciences, tooth development, and wanted to advance medicine. He also wanted to advance dental medicine with a design and research program. **What do you consider to be the highlight of your career:** The highlights that stood out the most for Dr. Kollar are teaching at the University of Chicago, producing a tooth using chicken tissue and mouse tissues called a chicken tooth in 1980, and making the cover of the Science Magazine. **Political Affiliations:** Democrat **Religion:** Roman Catholic **Shipping Address:** 17 Gloucester Lane, West Hartford, CT, 06107

Philip Peter Kovinick

Title: Writer **Industry:** Writing and Editing **Date of Birth:** 07/04/1924 **Place of Birth:** Detroit **State:** MI **Parents:** Philip Peter Kovinick; Christine (Selesan) Kovinick **Marital Status:** Married **Spouse Name:** Marian Tsugie Yoshiki (6/17/1973) **Education:** MA, CSU, Chico (1955); AB, CSU, Chico (1954) **Career:** Writer, Los Angeles, CA (1968-Present); Researcher, Los Angeles, CA (1968-Present); Lecturer, Los Angeles, CA (1976-Present); Curator, Art Exhibits, Los Angeles, CA (1976-1986); Social Studies Teacher, Lennox High School (1957-1981); Department Head, Lennox High School (1957-1981) **Creative Works:** Contributor, "Emerging from the Shadows: A Survey of Women Artists Working in California, 1860-1960," Schiffer Publishing, Atglen, PA (2016); Contributor, "The Beach" (2015); Contributor, "California and Western Paintings and Sculptures" (2015); Author, "John Frost: A Quiet Mastery," The Irvine Museum, California (2013); Contributor, "Love Never Fails: The Art of Edouard and Luvena Vysekal," Pasadena Museum of California Art (2011); Co-Author, "The Art and Life of Edwin Roscoe Shrader," George Stern Fine Arts, Los Angeles, CA (2010); Contributor, "Alfredo Ramos Martinez and Modernismo," The Alfredo Ramos Martinez Research Project (2009); Contributor, "A Seed of Modernism: The Art Students League of Los Angeles," Pasadena Museum of California Art (2008); Contributor, "An American Impressionist: Alson Skinner Clark," Hudson Hills Press LLC, Manchester, VT (2005); Contributor, "Scenic View Ahead: The Westways Cover Art Program, 1928-1981," Automobile Club of Southern California (2004); Contributor, "Grove's Encyclopedia of American Art to 1914," Grove's Dictionaries Inc, New York, NY (1999); Co-Author, "Publications in Southern California Art," Dustin Publications, Los Angeles, CA (1999); Contributor, "California Art: 450 Years of Painting and Other Media," Dustin Publications, Los Angeles, CA (1998); Co-Author, "An Encyclopedia of Women Artists of the American West, 1840-1980," University of Texas Press, Austin, TX (1998); Contributor, "Guy Rose: American Impressionist," The Irvine Museum, California (1995); Contributor, "California Light, 1900-1930," Laguna Art Museum, California (1990); Contributor, "The Rocky Mountains: A Vision form Artists in the Nineteenth Century," University of Oklahoma Press, Norman, OK (1983); Co-Curator, "The Woman Artist in the American West, 1860-1960," The Muckenthaler Cultural Center, Fullerton, CA (1976); Author, "The Woman Artist in the American West, 1860-1960," The Muckenthaler Cultural Center, Fullerton, CA (1976); Contributor, "Solon Borglum: A Man who Stands Alone," Globe Pequot, Chester, CT (1974); Author, "South Dakota's "'Other' Borglum," South Dakota Historical Society Quarterly (1971); Co-Author, "Contemporary International Problems: A Comparative Political, Economic, and Cultural Analysis," Centinela Valley Union High School District, Lawndale, CA (1962); Contributor, Articles, Professional Journals; Contributor, Chapters, Books **Awards:** Western Heritage Award For Outstanding Art Book (1998) **Membership:** LA Westerners; Huntington Westerners; Archives of American Art; Huntington Library Reader **Marquis Who's Who Honors:** Albert Nelson Marquis Lifetime Achievement Award (2017) **Hobbies:** High repetition exercises **Political Affiliations:** Democrat **Shipping Address:** 4735 Don Ricardo Dr, Los Angeles, CA, 90008

Gene Harry Koziara

Title: Aerospace Engineer, Operations Research Analyst Economist, Systems Analyst (Retired) **Industry:** Engineering **Company Name:** EHK, LLC **Date of Birth:** 12/20/1929 **Place of Birth:** Hamtramck **State/Country of Origin:** MI **Parents:** Frank Joseph Koziara; Angela (Zur) Koziara **Marital Status:** Married **Spouse Name:** Laura Ann Bomarito (6/21/1958) **Children:** Eugene H. Junior; Ann E. Castro; Frank J. II; Linda M. Frassrand **Education:** PhD in Operations Research, The Ohio State University, Columbus, OH (1969); PhD in Economics and Operations Research, Wayne State University, Detroit, MI (1965); MBA in Management and Economics, Wayne State University, Detroit, MI (1964); PhD in Physics and Electronics, University of Michigan, Ann Arbor, MI (1954); MS in Physics and Electronics, Wayne State University, Detroit, MI (1954); BS in Physics and Mathematics, University of Michigan, Ann Arbor, MI (1951) **Career:** Team Leader, Central Air Defense Command, Hughes Aircraft Company; Manager, EHK, LLC, MI (1999-Present); General Partner, Koziara Family Limited Partnership (1999-Present); Investment Analyst, Koziara Family Limited Partnership (1977); Manager, Koziara Family Limited Partnership (1977); Senior System Analyst, World Headquarters, Ford Motor Company, Mount Clemens, MI (1972-1977); Engineering System Analyst, Continental Motors Group, Teledyne Technologies (1970-1971); Member, Technical Staff V, North American Rockwell Corporation, Columbus, OH (1965-1970); Engineering Specialist, Assistant Department Head, Michigan Division, Ling-Temco-Vought (Now LTV Corporation), Warren, MI (1963-1965); Staff Engineer, Benedix Systems Division, Bendix Corporation, Ann Arbor, MI (1960-1963); Staff Engineer, Sparton, Jackson, MI (1959-1960); Group Engineer, Martin Co., Baltimore, MD (1958-1959); Staff Engineer, Martin Co., Baltimore, MD (1958-1959); Fire Control System Engineer, Chrysler Missile Division, Chrysler Corporation, Sterling Heights, MI (1956-1958); System Engineer, Chrysler Missile Division, Chrysler Corporation, Sterling Heights, MI (1956-1958); Unity Supervisor, Chrysler Missile Division, Chrysler Corporation, Sterling Heights, MI (1956-1958); Project Engineer, Chrysler Missile Division, Chrysler Corporation, Sterling Heights, MI (1956-1958); Electronics Engineer, Hughes Aircraft Company, Culver City, CA (1954-1956); Graduate-in-Training, GM Research, Detroit, MI (1954); Physics Fellow, Wayne State University, Detroit, MI (1953-1954); Research Analyst, University of Michigan, Ypsilanti, MI (1951-1953); Senior System Analyst, World Headquarters, Ford Motor Company, Dearborn, MI **Creative Works:** Author, "Linear Programming and Economic Analysis" (1964); Lecturer in Field **Membership:** American Association for the Advancement of Science; Materials Research Society; The Electrochemical Society; Council for Chemical Research, American Institute of Chemical Engineers; AVS; American Physical Society; American Chemical Society; Sigma Xi, The Scientific Research Honor Society; Sigma Pi Sigma, American Institute of Physics **Marquis Who's Who Honors:** Albert Nelson Marquis Lifetime Achievement Award (2017) **Why did you become involved in your profession or industry:** Dr. Koziara became involved in his industry through a series of very fortunate events in his early career years. His father had a farm, but he did not want to pursue farming, so he instead followed his love of reading and research to the University of Michigan, Wayne State University, and a number of impressive positions at companies like General Motors, Howard Hughes and Chrysler. **What do you consider to be the highlight of your career:** One of the highlights of Dr. Koziara's career was being able to make the lance missile viable to combat the Russian threat. He was able to help create a guided missile at Texas Instruments by developing a silicone transistor and launching the lance missile over Europe to disable Russia. **Shipping Address:** 11406 Savage Dr, Sterling Heights, MI, 48312

Keith Allan Kramer

Title: Music Educator, Composer **Industry:** Fine Art **Date of Birth:** 03/19/1968 **Place of Birth:** Baltimore **State:** MD **Education:** Pursuing Master of Music Education, University of Massachusetts Lowell; DMA, University of Miami (1999); MusM, University of Maryland, College Park, MD (1994); BA, University of Maryland, Baltimore County, MD (1991); Composition/Theoretical Studies, Thomas DeLio; Composition/Theoretical Studies, John Van der Slice; Composition/Theoretical Studies, Stuart Saunders Smith; Composition/Theoretical Studies, Ladislav Kubik; Composition/Theoretical Studies, Paul Wilson; Composition/Theoretical Studies, John Patrick Welsh; Jazz Studies, Walt Namuth; Jazz Studies, Scott McGill; Jazz Studies, Carl Filipiak; Jazz Studies, Chris Vadala; Jazz Studies, Paul Wingo; Jazz Studies, Derek Day **Career:** Private Lesson Instructor, Boston, MA (2010-Present); Assistant Professor, Central Connecticut State University (2012-2016); Visiting Professor, Harford Community College, Bel Air, MD (1998-2009); Private Lesson Instructor, Miami, FL (1996-1998); Graduate Assistant, University of Miami, Coral Gables, FL (1995-1998); Private Lesson Instructor, Baltimore, MD (1992-2010) **Career Related:** Chief Executive Officer, Chen Li Music (2015-Present); Board of Directors, Baltimore Composers Forum (2010-2017); President, Baltimore Composers Forum (2008-2010) **Civic:** Board of Directors, Baltimore Composers Forum (2010-2017); Beta Beta Chapter, Pi Kappa Lambda (1998) **Creative Works:** Composer, String Quartet Piece, "La Tranquillita" (2016); Composer, iPad Ensemble, Orator and Various Found Objects, "The Lorax" (2016); Composer, Trumpet and Electronics Piece, "Electronic and Electroacoustic: Sedia Vuota" (2016); Composer, Brass Quintet Piece, "Pale Blue Dot" (2015); Composer, Horn and Marimba Piece, "Equanimity," (2015); Composer, Piano and Percussion Piece, "Rinnovo" (2014); Composer, Trumpet and Electronics Piece, "Frozen in that Fatal Climb," (2014); Composer, Soprano and Piano Piece, "Jasmine" (2013); Composer, Dancer and Live Electronics Piece, "Shattered Skies" (2013); Composer, Piano Trio Piece, "Suspension of Disbelief" (2012); Composer, Violin, Clarinet, and Piano Piece, "For Us, No Limits" (2011); Composer, Electronic Media Piece, "Before and Beyond" (2011); Composer, Electronic Media Piece, "Amalgam," CD, "Emerge," Navona Records (2011); Composer, Mid-Sized Ensemble, Flute, Piano, and String Quartet Piece, "Equilibrium" (2011); Composer, Solo Violoncello and String Quartet Piece, "Indelible," DVD, "Beyond Sonic Boundaries, Live!" (2010); Composer, Mid-Sized Ensemble, Flute, Soprano Saxophone, Bass Trombone, Piano, and String Quartet Piece, "In Double Quadruplicate," DVD, "Beyond Sonic Boundaries, Live!," and CD, "Emerge," Navona Records (2010); Composer, Mid-Sized Ensemble, Flute, Piano, and String Quartet Piece, "Cathartic," DVD, "Beyond Sonic Boundaries, Live!," and CD, "Emerge," Navona Records (2010); Composer, Symphony Orchestra Piece, "Emerge," CDs, "Emerge" and "Mementos," Navona Records (2008); Composer, Tenor Saxophone, Violoncello, and Piano, "Planned Disarrangement" (2008); Composer, Mid-Sized Ensemble, Soprano Saxophone, Bass Trombone, and String Quartet Piece, "Duality," CD, "Casual Dualism," Navona Records (2006); Composer, Flute and Piano Piece, "Moment" (2006); Composer, Mid-Sized Ensemble, Flute, Soprano Saxophone, and String Quintet Piece, "Compact Disparity," CD, "Emerge," Navona Records (2005); Composer, Flute, Oboe, and Piano Piece, "Fallen" (2004); Composer, Electronic Media Piece, "Snow," CD, "Emerge," Navona Records (2003); Composer, Sting Orchestra, Percussion, and Piano Piece, "Casualty," CD, "Casual Dualism," Navona Records (1999); Composer, Electric Bass Piece, "Childhood's End" (1999); Composer, Revised Solo Violin and Oration Piece, "Quagmire" (1997); Composer, String Quartet Piece, "Gaia" (1997); Composer, Revised Solo Violin and Oration Piece, "Query" (1997); Composer, Clarinet Quintet or Clarinet and String Quartet, "The Axis and The Rim" (1997); Composer, Soprano Orchestra and String Orchestra Piece, "Limits of Reason," University of Miami Society of Composers Series (1996); Composer, Flute Piece, "Crystalline," University of Miami Society of Composers Series (1996); Composer, Soprano Sax Piece, "Flame of Attention," University of Miami Society of Composers Series (1996); Composer, Marimba Piece, "Freedom from the Known" (1996); Composer, Electric Bass Piece, "Being is the Great Explainer" (1996) **Awards:** Member, Beta Beta Chapter, National Music Honor Society of Pi Kappa Lambda (1998-Present); Winner, College Music Society Mid-Atlantic Student Composer Competition (1999); Finalist, Morton Gould Young Composer Awards, ACSAP Foundation (1998); Winner, University of Miami Symphony Orchestra Composition Competition (1998) **Membership:** BMI; College Music Society; American Composers Forum; Baltimore Composers Forum; Society of Composers, Inc.; The Society for Music Theory, Inc.; Audio Engineering Society **Marquis Who's Who Honors:** Albert Nelson Marquis Lifetime Achievement Award (2017) **Shipping Address:** 461 Parmenter Road, Marlborough, MA, 01752 **Website:** http://keithkramer.org

Philipp Kronberg, PhD

Title: Physicist **Industry:** Education/Educational Services **Company Name:** University of Toronto **Date of Birth:** 09/16/1939 **Place of Birth:** Toronto **State/Country of Origin:** ON/Canada **Parents:** Philipp Kronberg; Jean Stewart (Davidson) Kronberg **Children:** Paul Andrew; Martin Thomas; Michael Philipp **Education:** DSc, University of Manchester, England (1995); PhD in Physics, Manchester University, England (1967); MSc in Physics, Queen's University, Canada (1963); BSc in Engineering Physics, Queen's University, Canada (1961) **Career:** Visiting Scholar, Los Alamos National Laboratory (LANS, LLC) (2003-Present); Professor Emeritus, Department of Physics, University of Toronto (1999-Present); Distinguished Orson Anderson Scholar, Los Alamos National Laboratory (LANS, LLC), NM (2002-2003); Fellow, Killam Foundation (1990); Assistant to Full Professor of Physical Sciences and Astronomy, University of Toronto (1968-1999); Lecturer, University of Manchester, England (1966-1968); Fellow, American Physical Society **Career Related:** Distinguished Visiting Fellow, University of Sydney (2009); Distinguished Visiting Fellow, Commonwealth Scientific and Industrial Research Organization (CSIRO) (2009); Distinguished Visiting Fellow, Australia (2007); Co-organizer, Workshop on Astrophysical Dynamos, Aspen Institute for Physics (Now Aspen Center for Physics) (2000); Canadian Representative, Scientific Review Committee, Very Long Baseline Interferometry Satellite, Japan Institute of Space and Astronautical Sciences (Now Japan Aerospace Exploration Agency)/Canadian Space Agency (2000); Scientific Organizing Committee, Workshop on Cosmological Magnetic Fields, CO (1996); Project Leader, Millimetre Astronomy, Proposed Collaboration with California Institute of Technology and University of Toronto (1990-1992); Management Board, James Clerk Maxwell Submillimetre Telescope (1990-1991); Management Board, IsoTrace Laboratory, University of Toronto (1990); Review Board, Design and Construction, Green Bank Telescope, National Science Foundation (1989-1990); Co-chairman, Reorganization Committee, Physics Division, National Research Council of Canada (1988-2002); Assessment Committee, National Research Council of Canada and United States Department of Energy (1988-1990); Chairman, International Astronomical Union Symposium No. 140, Heidelberg, Germany (1988-1990); Chairman, Scientific and Technological Review Committee, Sudbury Neutrino Observatory, National Research Council of Canada and United States Department of Energy (1988); Task Force to Assess US Radio Astronomy Facilities (1988); Presidents' Committee, Innovations Foundation (1988); NRC Governing Council, Canada (1987-1990); Governing Council, National Research Council of Canada (1987-1990); Ontario Inter-University Advisory Board, Ontario Center for Large Scale Computation Modeling (1986-1990); Atlantic Council (Now NAOC), Toronto, Canada (1985-1990); Chairman, Steering Committee, Algonquin Radio Observatory Millimetre Telescope (1983-1986); Chairman, Connaught Physical Sciences and Engineering Review Panel (1982-1985); Chairman, Visiting Committee, Associated Universities, Inc. (AUI) (1981-1982); Management Board, Mont Magantic Observatory, University of Montreal and University of Laval (1980-1984); VLA Advisory Committee, National Radio Astronomy Observatory, United States (1978-1980); Chairman, Multi-Decade Plan for Space and Astronomy Research in Canada, NRC (1974); Chairman, Supercomputer User's Group, Canada (1968-1988); Federal Task Force to Recommend a Major Astronomy Facility in Quebec **Civic:** Adviser, Management and Future Development, Arecibo Observatory, National Science Foundation (2008); President, Reserve Condo Association, Santa Fe, NM (2005-2009) **Creative Works:** Author, "Cosmic Magnetic Fields," Cambridge University Press **Awards:** Humboldt Award, Max Planck Institute, Max Planck Society (2007); Humboldt Award, Max Planck Institute, Max Planck Society (1998); Humboldt Award, Max Planck Institute, Max Planck Society (1990); Guggenheim Foundation (1985); Humboldt Award, Max Planck Institute (1980); Humboldt Award, Max Planck Institute (1975-1977) **Membership:** President, Toronto Chapter, Sigma Xi, The Scientific Research Honor Society (1999-2001); Commodore, The Boulevard Club, Toronto, Canada (1998-2000); American Astronomical Society **Hobbies:** Sailing; Tennis; History; International affairs **Shipping Address:** 60 St. George Street, Physics Department, University of Toronto, Toronto, ON Canada, M5S 1A7

Harry Elno Krug

Industry: Fine Art **Date of Birth:** 08/20/1930 **Place of Birth:** Oshkosh **State/Country of Origin:** WI **Marital Status:** Married **Education:** Postgraduate Coursework, University of New Mexico (1979); Postgraduate Coursework, Pittsburg State University (1975-1977); MS, University of Wisconsin-Madison (1956); BFA, University of Wisconsin-Milwaukee (1954) **Career:** Professor Emeritus, Pittsburg State University (1996-Present); Chairman, Art Department, Pittsburg State University (1981-1995); Special Services, Stuttgart, Germany (1969-1971); Professor, Printmaking, Drawing, Painting, Design, and Photography, Pittsburg State University, Kansas (1958-1996) **Career Related:** Artist-in-Residence, Anderson Ranch Arts Center, Colorado; Artist-in-Residence, Centrum, Port Townsend, WA **Civic:** Commissioner, Kansas Creative Arts Industries Commission **Military Service:** U.S. Army (1956-1958) **Creative Works:** Contributor, Textbooks; Exhibitor, The Nelson-Atkins Museum of Art; Exhibitor, The New York Public Library; Exhibitor, Springfield Art Museum, Missouri; Exhibitor, Wichita Art Museum; Exhibitor, Museum of Fine Arts, Boston; Exhibitor, Muskogee Art Show, Oklahoma; Exhibitor, National Exhibition of Contemporary American Art; Exhibitor, National Print Exhibition; Exhibitor, Painters and Sculptors Society of New York; Exhibitor, Northwest Printmakers, Seattle, WA; Exhibitor, Galerie Van De Loo Projekte, Munich, Germany; Exhibitor, Moderne Galerie Otto Stangl; Exhibitor, American Graphic Arts and Drawing Exhibition, Wichita, KS; Exhibitor, Nebraska Wesleyan University; Exhibitor, 26th Annual Color Print Exhibition, Philadelphia, PA; Exhibitor, SAGA NYC; Exhibitor, Fifth Annual Mercyhurst National Exhibition, Erie, PA; Exhibitor, Invitational Art Works, Joplin, MO; Exhibitor, Permanent Collections, Library of Congress; Exhibitor, Mercyhurst University; Exhibitor, Numerous Regional, National and Private Gallery Exhibitions **Awards:** Eponym, Harry Krug Art Gallery, Pittsburg State University; Purchase Award, The Nelson-Atkins Museum of Art; Purchase Award, Springfield Art Museum; Gropper Gallery Purchase Prize, Museum of Fine Arts, Boston; First Prize in Graphics, Muskogee Art Show, Oklahoma; Purchase Award, National Exhibition of Contemporary American Art; Purchase Award, National Print Exhibition; Purchase Award, Painters and Sculptors Society of New York; Honorable Mention, Northwest Printmakers; Purchase Award, Nebraska Wesleyan University; Sonia Watter Award, 26th Annual Color Print Exhibition **Marquis Who's Who Honors:** Albert Nelson Marquis Lifetime Achievement Award (2017) **Hobbies:** Painting **Shipping Address:** 512 N Lynn Street, Frontanac, KS, 66762

Patricia Kubistal

Title: Educational Consultant **Industry:** Education/Educational Services **Company Name:** Lake View Evening School **Date of Birth:** 01/19/1938 **Place of Birth:** Chicago **State:** IL **Parents:** Edward John Kubistal; Bernice Mildred (Lenz) Kubistal **Education:** Postgraduate Coursework, National College of Education (1974-1975); PhD, Loyola University (1968); AM, Loyola University (1965); AM, Loyola University (1964); Postgraduate Coursework, Iowa State Universityof Science and Technology (1963); Postgraduate Coursework, Illinois Institute of Technology (1963); Postgraduate Coursework, Chicago State University (1962); AB, Loyola University, Cum Laude (1959) **Certifications:** Certified Chief School Business Official; Certified Superintendent; Certified K-12 Administrator; Certified Supervisor for K-14; Certification in Guidance; Certified in Special K-12 Learning Disabilities and Social Emotional Disorders; Certification in High School 6-12 Political Science, Social Science, U.S. History and World History **Career:** Educational Consultant, Lake View Evening School (1993-Present); Educational Consultant, Lenz & Associates (1996); With, Chicago Board of Education (1959-1993); Supervisor, Lake View Evening School (1982-1992); Administrator, Department of Special Education, Jones Metropolitan High School Business and Commerce (1990-1993); Principal, Cook County Juvenile Temporary Detention Center School, Jones Metropolitan High School Business and Commerce (1989-1990); Principal, Haugan School (1989); Principal, Roosevelt High School (1987); Principal, Brentano School (1975-1987); Principal, Simpson School (1975-1976); Principal, Special Education School, Chicago Board of Education (1969-1975); Assistant to District Superintendent, Chicago Board of Education (1966-1969); Administrative Intern, Chicago Board of Education (1965-1966); Counselor, Chicago Board of Education (1963-1965); Teacher, Chicago Board of Education (1959-1963) **Career Related:** Lecturer, DePaul University (1998-1999); Lecturer, National College of Education Graduate School, Mundelein College (1982-1991); Coordinator, Upper Bound Program, University of Illinois Circle Campus (1966-1968); Lecturer, Loyola University School of Education **Civic:** President, St. Matthews Parish Council (1995-1998); Governor, Loyola University (1961-1987); Educational Advisor, North Side Chicago PTA Region (1975); Member, Education Committee, Field Museum (1971); Member, Citizens School Committee (1969-1971); Member, Committee Illinois Constitutional Convention (1967-1969); Active Crusade of Mercy **Creative Works:** General Editor, Chicago Principals Journal (1982-1990); Author, "Centennial History of St. Matthias Parish, 1887-1987" (1988); Co-Author, "Apples to Share" (1986); Book Review Editor, Chicago Principals Journal (1970-1976) **Awards:** Nominee, Community Women's Award, Cook County Commissioners (2017); Commissioned Kentucky Colonel, Governor of the Commonwealth of Kentucky (2012); Faith and Service Recognition Award, Kappa Gamma Pi (2009); International Lambda State Achievement Award (2000); Research Grant Award, Delta Kappa Gamma Society International (1993); First Place Recognition, Photographic Juried Exhibit, Delta Kappa Gamma Society International (1991); Management Award, Delta Kappa Gamma Society International (1990); Nominee, Whitman Award for Outstanding Principal (1989-1990); Outstanding Principal Award, Citizen's School Committee of Chicago (1986); Administrative Fellow, The University of Chicago (1984); Honoree, St. Luke's Logan Square Community Person of Year (1977); Drug Education Grantee, Department of Health Region 5 (1974); Outstanding Illinois Educator (1970), Honoree, One of the Outstanding Women of Illinois (1970); Outstanding Intern Award, National Association of Secondary School Principals (1966); Grantee, National Science Foundation (1965); Grantee, National Defense Education Act (1963); Honoree, Outstanding History Teacher, Chicago Public Schools (1963); Grantee, Chicago Board of Education Principals **Membership:** Chairman, Lambda State Communications Committee, The Lambda State Organization of The Delta Kappa Gamma Society International (1992); Editor, The Lambda State Organization of The Delta Kappa Gamma Society International (1982-1992); President, Kappa Chapter, Delta Kappa Gamma (1988-1990); Parliamentarian, Delta Kappa Gamma (1979-1980); Member, Illinois Personnel and Guidance Association; National Education Association; Illinois Education Association; Chicago Education Association; American Academy of Political and Social Sciences; President Auxiliary, Chicago Principals and Administrators Association; National Council of Administrative Women; Chicago Council of Exceptional Children; Loyal Christian Benevolent Association; Kappa Gamma Pi; Pi Gamma Mu; Phi Delta Kappa; Delta Sigma Rho; Phi Sigma Tau **Marquis Who's Who Honors:** Albert Nelson Marquis Lifetime Achievement Award (2017) **Shipping Address:** 5111 N. Oakley Avenue, Chicago, IL, 60625

Subodh Kumar

Title: Investment Banker **Industry:** Financial Services **Date of Birth:** 01/01/1953 **Place of Birth:** New Delhi **Country of Origin:** India **Parents:** Satyaindar Kumar; Savitri Devi Kumar **Education:** MBA, University of Toronto (1976); BSc in Engineering, University of Toronto (1973); BA, University of Toronto (1973); Postgraduate Work, University of St Michael's College (1969); Coursework, Comboni College (1968) **Certifications:** Chartered Financial Analyst (1980) **Career:** Chief Investment Strategist, Subodh Kumar & Associates (2006-Present); Managing Director, CIBC (1988-2006); Research Analyst, CIBC (1976-2006); Chemical Design Engineer, Imperial Oil Limited (1973-1974) **Career Related:** President, StrategeInvest, Inc. **Civic:** Board Member, Islington Seniors' Center **Awards:** Masters Fellowship, University of Toronto (1974); J.P. Bickell Foundation Scholarship, University of Toronto (1969) **Membership:** Fellow, CFA Society Toronto; Fellow, CFA Society New York; Fellow, CFA Institute **Marquis Who's Who Honors:** Albert Nelson Marquis Lifetime Achievement Award (2017) **To what do you attribute your success:** Mr. Kumar attributes his success to listening to others and assessing hard and soft factors globally to then make a clear decision. **Why did you become involved in your profession or industry:** As an immigrant, Mr. Kumar took advantage of the opportunities presented to him and this is how he chose his profession. He went from being offered an engineering career with a top firm, to being exposed to finance, to being offered an opportunity with a top investment bank to gaining global opportunities. **What do you consider to be the highlight of your career:** A highlight that stood out during his career was visiting with small and large institutions, private and sovereign funds in some 95 cities around the world including New York, London, Tokyo and Toronto. Another highlight was having the ability demonstrated in 1987, 1999-2000 and 2006-2007 to warn about risk and then after the event to avail of opportunity in investments. **Where will you be in five years:** In five years Mr. Kumar expects to be identifying and distilling key global factors, both quantitative and qualitative factors, affecting investments to then communicating them. He expects more focus on quantity of management execution and strength more likely to be crucial for companies and countries than seen during massive quantitative ease by central banks. **Hobbies:** Cycling; Reading; Walking **Shipping Address:** 1464 Islington Ave, Etobicoke, ON, Canada, M9A 3L3

Steven Jay Kumble

Title: Founder, Chairman **Industry:** Financial Services **Company Name:** Corinthian Capital Group, LLC **Date of Birth:** 07/03/1933 **Spouse Name:** Angela Marie Giguere; Peggy Basten Vandervoort (Divorced); Barbara Kumble (Divorced) **Children:** Charles Todd; Roger Glenn **Education:** Honorary LLD, Long Island University (1990); JD, Harvard University (1959); BA, Yale University (1954) **Career:** Chairman, Board of Directors, Corinthian Capital Group, LLC (2005-Present); Chairman, Board of Directors, Lincolnshire Management, New York City, NY (1985-2004); Counsel, Summit Rovins & Feldesman, New York City, NY (1988-1990); Partner, Finley, Kumble, Wagner, Underberg, Manley & Casey, New York City, NY (1968-1987) **Career Related:** Member, Dean's Advisory Board, Harvard Law School (2006-Present); Member, Advisory Board, RAND Institute for Civil Justice (1999-2005) **Civic:** Vice Chairman, Board of Directors, LIU Post, Greenvale, NY (1984-Present); Trustee, Board, Governor's Committee for Scholastic Achievement, New York City, NY (1981-Present); Chairman, LIU Post, Greenvale, NY (1982-1994) **Military Service:** First Lieutenant, U.S. Army (1955-1957) **Membership:** Association of the Bar of the City of New York; Harvard Club; Wanumetonomy Golf & Country Club, Newport, RI; The Yale Club of New York City; The Breakers Palm Beach, FL; Phi Beta Kappa **Bar Admissions:** New York (1960) **Marquis Who's Who Honors:** Distinguished Humanitarian (2017) **Hobbies:** Skiing; Golf **Business Address:** 366 Madison Avenue, Ninth floor, 366 Madison Avenue, Ninth floor, NY, New York, 10017 **Shipping Address:** 9 Via Los Incas, Palm Beach, FL, 33480

Judy A. Kundert

Title: Writer **Industry:** Writing and Editing **Company Name:** Cypress Production LLC **Date of Birth:** 09/19/1944 **Place of Birth:** Denver **State/Country of Origin:** CO **Marital Status:** Married **Spouse Name:** Donald P. Kundert **Children:** Gail Venus (Stepchild); Mike Kundert (Stepchild) **Education:** MA, DePaul University, Chicago, IL (1984); BA, Loyola University Chicago (1976); MA in Public Relations and Marketing, University of Denver **Career:** Legal Administrator, Williams Production RMT CO, Denver, CO (2007-Present); President, Cypress Production LLC, Denver, CO (1997); Award-Winning Author, Children's Books; Award-Winning Author, Women's Fiction Novels **Career Related:** Secretary, Chicago Women in Government Relations (1993-1995) **Civic:** Board of Directors, Broomfield Public Library, Colorado (2004-2007); Publicity Chair, Rocky Mountain Fiction Writers (2004-2007) **Creative Works:** Author, "Hanging Cloud" (2019) **Awards:** Winner, USA Best Books, "Tressi's Magical Chest Series" (2015); Finalist, Mom's Choice Award, "Samantha and the Legend of the Whispering Trees"; Finalist, USA Best Books, "Samantha and the Legend of the Whispering Trees" **Membership:** Rocky Mountain Fiction Writers ; Society of Children's Book Writers and Illustrators; Women's Fiction Writers Association; Toastmasters International **To what do you attribute your success:** Ms. Kundert attributes her success to the support she has received from fellow writers and to her creative inspiration. **Why did you become involved in your profession or industry:** Books and nature influenced Ms. Kundert's desire to become a writer. She wanted to inspire both the young and the old to read a lot and to explore their world and the outside world with new eyes. **Hobbies:** Hiking; Biking; Reading; Needlepoint design; Tennis; Movies **Business Address:** P.O. Box 1205, Broomfield, CO, 80023 **Shipping Address:** 14184 Waterside Lane, Broomfield, CO, 80023 **Website:** http://www.judykundert.com

Judith Ann Kutchi

Title: Elementary School Educator (Retired) **Industry:** Education/Educational Services **Date of Birth:** 10/20/1942 **Place of Birth:** Hazleton **State/Country of Origin:** PA **Parents:** Nicholas I. Bachman; Elizabeth Bachman **Marital Status:** Married **Spouse Name:** Robert John Kutchi (8/10/1963, Deceased 1/23/2016) **Children:** Robert S.; Steven N.; Nicholas A.; Elizabeth A. (Deceased) **Education:** MEd, Bloomsburg State University (1967); BE, Bloomsburg State University (1963) **Career:** Reading Specialist, Prince George's County Public Schools, Upper Marlboro, MD (2001-2009); Mentor, Prince George's County Public Schools, Upper Marlboro, MD (2001-2009); Test Coordinator, Prince George's County Public Schools, Upper Marlboro, MD (2001-2009); Teacher, St. Mary Star of the Sea, Indian Head, MD (1992-2001); Resource Teacher, Prince George's County Public Schools, Upper Marlboro, MD (1967-1969); Language Arts Teacher for Grades 6-8, Prince George's County Public Schools, Upper Marlboro, MD (1963-1992); Teacher, Prince George's County Public Schools, Upper Marlboro, MD (1963-1967) **Membership:** International Reading Association; Former President, Alpha Epsilon Chapter, Delta Kappa Gamma Society; National Education Association; MSTA; Prince Georges County Educators' Association **Marquis Who's Who Honors:** Albert Nelson Marquis Lifetime Achievement Award (2017) **Why did you become involved in your profession or industry:** Ms. Kutchi was inspired to pursue teaching after having a young home economics teacher in high school. **What do you consider to be the highlight of your career:** Ms. Kutchi is most proud of having created her own curriculum for a pre-first grade program for underprepared students. She received support from her school and the program was very successful. **Hobbies:** Reading; Quilting; Sewing **Shipping Address:** 2951 Bannock St, Bryans Road, MD, 20616

Ronald Kutscher

Title: Federal Agency Administrator **Industry:** Government Administration/Government Relations/Government Services **Date of Birth:** 04/18/1932 **Place of Birth:** Hebron **State:** NE **Parents:** Earl Harvey Kutscher; Doris Lillian (Zong) Kutscher **Marital Status:** Married **Spouse Name:** Elizabeth Elin Granholm (12/28/1963) **Children:** Laura Ingrid; Steven Ronald **Education:** Postgraduate Coursework, University of Illinois (1955-1956); BA, Doane University (1955) **Career:** Associate Commissioner, U.S. Bureau of Labor Statistics, Washington, DC (1982-1996); Assistant Commissioner, U.S. Bureau of Labor Statistics, Washington, DC (1976-1982); Assistant Chief, Research Division of Economic Growth, U.S. Bureau of Labor Statistics, Washington, DC (1968-1976); Economist, U.S. Bureau of Labor Statistics, Washington, DC (1957-1968) **Career Related:** Fellow, American Statistical Association (1996) **Military Service:** U.S. Army (1952-1954) **Creative Works:** Contributor, Articles, Professional Journals **Awards:** Prize Best Economic Forecast, American Statistical Association (1973) **Membership:** Chair, Committee on Committees, American Statistical Association (1989-1991); Chair, Program Committee, American Statistical Association (1985) **Marquis Who's Who Honors:** Albert Nelson Marquis Lifetime Achievement Award (2017) **Hobbies:** Photography; Golf; Softball **Religion:** Lutheran **Shipping Address:** 21045 Cardinal Pond Terrace, Apt. 419, Asburn, VA, 20147

Benjamin Ching Kee Kwan

Title: Clinical Professor **Industry:** Education/Educational Services **Company Name:** University of California, Los Angeles **Date of Birth:** 07/12/1940 **Place of Birth:** Hong Kong **Country of Origin:** China **Parents:** Shun Ming Kwan; Lurk Ming (Lai) Kwan **Marital Status:** Married **Spouse Name:** Catherine Ning (8/29/1964) **Children:** Susan San; David Daiwai **Education:** MD, Washington University in St. Louis (1967) **Certifications:** Diplomate, American Board of Ophthalmology **Career:** Clinical Professor, Department of Ophthalmology, University of California, Los Angeles (1995-Present); Partner, Southern California Permanente Medical Center, Harbor City, CA (1976-2003); Chief of Service, Ophthalmology, Southern California Permanente Medical Center, Harbor City, CA (1976-1988) **Civic:** Member, Board of Directors, Asian American Senior Citizens Service Center (1993-Present); Chairman, Winter Blossom Ball, Chinese American Debutante's Guild (1993) **Military Service:** Captain, U.S. Army (1969-1971) **Awards:** Pioneer Award, Chinese American Ophthalmological Society (2015); Service Award, Chinese American Ophthalmological Society (2006, 1994); Service Award, East L.A. Chinese Everspring Senior Association (1994); Service Award, Asian American Senior Citizens Service Center (1993); Proclamation Award, California Secretary of State (1993); Service Award, Chinese Physician's Society of Southern California (1989); Service Award, Chinese Physician's Society of Southern California (1983) **Membership:** Executive Vice President, Chinese American Ophthalmological Society (2011-Present); President, Chinese American Ophthalmological Society (1999-2000); President Elect, Chinese American Ophthalmological Society (1997-1999); President, Los Angeles Chapter, Organization of Chinese Americans (1986-1987); President, Chinese Physician's Society of Southern California (1983); Fellow, American Academy of Ophthalmology; President, Board of Directors, Chinese Physician's Society of Southern California **Hobbies:** Ballroom dancing; Singing; Skiing **Religion:** Roman Catholic **Shipping Address:** 6327 Tarragon Rd, Rancho Palos Verdes, CA, 90275

Roselia I. Labbe

Title: Medical Branch Chief for the Air Reserves Component **Industry:** Military & Defense Services **Company Name:** U.S. Air Force **Education:** Residency, Wright State University; MD; BA in Biology, Midwestern State University; AS in Electronics, Air University **Civic:** Local Breast Cancer Organizations **Military Service:** Military Physician, U.S. Air Force **Awards:** Bronze Star Medal **Marquis Who's Who Honors:** Albert Nelson Marquis Lifetime Achievement Award (2017) **To what do you attribute your success:** Dr. Labbe attributes her success to doors opening at the right time and staying aware of opportunities while never being afraid to take risks. **Why did you become involved in your profession or industry:** Dr. Labbe became involved in her profession after joining the U.S. Air Force in order to receive an education. **What do you consider to be the highlight of your career:** The highlight of Dr. Labbe's career was all the different opportunities with the U.S. Air Force she has had over the last 29 years as a military physician. **Where will you be in five years:** In five years, Dr. Labbe intends to organize a non-profit in Central America to help set up surgical centers a teaching hospital for the local medical community with the help of medical volunteers. **Hobbies:** Cooking; Traveling **Shipping Address:** 214 Oak Park Dr, San Antonio, TX, 78209 **Website:** http://www.af.mil

Jeanne Margaret Ladewig Goodman

Title: Artist **Industry:** Fine Art **Date of Birth:** 06/26/1923 **Place of Birth:** Grand Rapids **State:** MI **Parents:** Roland Adolph Ladewig; Margaret (Palmer) Ladewig **Marital Status:** Divorced **Education:** MS in Design, Illinois Institute of Technology (1970); Postgraduate Coursework, Chicago Art Institute (1959-1968); BEd in Art Education, Concordia College (1945) **Career:** Art Coordinator, Park Ridge Public School District 64 (1974-1988); Art Teacher, Park Ridge Public School District 64, Park Ridge, IL (1962-1974); Teacher, Lutheran Schools, Chicago, IL (1952-1962) **Career Related:** Chair of Art Board, Biannual Art Show, National American Pen Women, Denver, CO (2005-2006); Chicago Hiring Consultant, Evanston Schools, Illinois (1985); Guest Lecturer, University of Illinois (1971-1972); Member Advisory Board, Contemporary Art Workshop; Workshop Presenter, NAEA-IAEA **Civic:** Volunteer, Free Meals, Lutheran Church, Chicago, IL (1990-1995); Volunteer, Terra Museum of Art, Chicago, IL (1989-1995); Member, Studio Owner, Method Art Gallery, Scottsdale, AZ **Creative Works:** Group Show, Wilde Meyer Gallery, Methods Art Gallery, Scottsdale, AZ (2012); Solo Exhibit, Art Space on 6th Gallery, Scottsdale, AZ (2010); Group Show, Golden Celebration Art Show, Concordia University, Chicago, IL (2010-2012); Group Show, San Bernardino Annual Arizona Watercolor Art Show (2009); Group Show, The Faber Biovren Color Award Show, Stamford, CT (2008); Group Exhibit, "Barewalls," Chicago Art Institute (2007-2008); Solo Exhibit, Arizona State University (2007); Solo Exhibit, Meyers Art Gallery (2006); Solo Exhibit, "Artistic Expressions," Scottsdale, AZ (2005); Solo Exhibit, Wilde Meyer Gallery, Scottsdale, AZ (2005); Solo Exhibit, Gallery Z, Providence, RI (2005); Group Show, Arizona State University Downtown (2004); Group Show, San Bernardino Annual Arizona Watercolor Art Show (2003); Solo Exhibit, Arizona State University Downtown(2001); Group Show, San Bernardino Annual Arizona Watercolor Art Show (2001); Designer, Life-sized Horse for Scottsdale Parade of Horses (2001); Group Show, San Bernardino Annual Arizona Watercolor Art Show (1999); Group Show, Arizona State University, Gammage Auditorium (1998); Solo Exhibit, Arizona State University Downtown (1998); Group Show, World Fine Art, New York (1997-2003); Group Show, Concordia University (1996); Group Show, Abney Galleries (1973); Author, "Adventures in Art" (1973); Group Show, Ditmar Gallery Northwestern (1972); Artist, 2 Murals, Illinois Research Hospital (1964); Contributor, Articles to Professional Journals **Awards:** Vista Show Merit Award (2002); Vista Show Merit Award (2001); Best of Show Award (1999); First Prize, Water Color Show, Artist Guild of Chicago (1986); Grantee, Helene Wurlitzer Foundation (1972) **Membership:** Art Board Chair, President of Scottsdale Branch, National League of American Pen Women (2004-Present); American Association of University Women; Class of '62 Half Century Club, School of the Art Institute of Chicago; Scottsdale Artists League; Arizona Artists League; Chicago Artists Coalition; Chicago Society of Artists **Marquis Who's Who Honors:** Albert Nelson Marquis Lifetime Achievement Award (2017) **Why did you become involved in your profession or industry:** Ms. Ladewig Goodman was always involved in creating and making something out of anything around; she constructs her thoughts and memories into art. **What do you consider to be the highlight of your career:** Ms. Ladewig Goodman is still looking to the highlight of her career. She feels each adventure in art is the best each time she does it. **Where will you be in five years:** In five years, Ms. Ladewig Goodman intends to be in her studio. **Hobbies:** Travel; Writing **Religion:** Lutheran **Shipping Address:** 7319 E Northland Dr Unit 5, Scottsdale, AZ, 85251 **Website:** http://www.jeanneladewiggoodman.com

Feng-Qi Lai, PhD

Title: Professor Emerita **Industry:** Education/Educational Services **Date of Birth:** 03/25/1948 **Place of Birth:** Shanghai **Country of Origin:** China **Parents:** Zheng-Zhong Lai; Yao-Zhang Zhu **Marital Status:** Married **Spouse Name:** Qun Zhang (10/22/1984) **Children:** Yi-Ming Lai **Education:** PhD, Purdue University (1997); MS, Purdue University (1994); BA, Changsha Railway Institute (1982) **Career:** Professor Emerita, Indiana State University (2017-Present); Vice President of Academic Affairs, Xian International University, Xian, China (2017); Professor, Indiana State University (2012-2016); Associate Professor, Indiana State University, Terre Haute, IN (2008-2012); Assistant Professor, Indiana State University, Terre Haute, IN (2002-2008); Senior Instructional Designer, Cognitive Concepts, Inc., Evanston, IL (2000-2002); Project Manager, Cognitive Concepts, Inc., Evanston, IL (2000-2002); Senior Instructor, Advanced Technical Support, Inc., Schaumburg, IL (1998-2000); Training Director, Advanced Technical Support, Inc., Schaumburg, IL (1998-2000); Instructional Designer, National Education Training Group, Naperville, IL (1998); Lecturer, Shanghai Tiedao University (1986-1991); Associate Director, Shanghai Tiedao University (1986-1991); Assistant Lecturer, Shanghai Tiedao University (1982-1986) **Career Related:** Guest Professor, Xian International University (2016); Supervisor, Research Affairs of SOLE, East China Normal University (2015); Guest Professor, Henan Normal University (2014); Guest Professor, Henan University (2013); Foreign Languages Educational Technology Expert Committee, Association of Shandong Higher Education (2007); Guest Professor, Shanghai Normal University (2006) **Creative Works:** First-Editor, Learning and Knowledge Analytics in Open Education: Selected Readings from the AECT-LKAOE 2015 Summer International Research Symposium (2017); Translator-in-Chief, Learning and Instructional Technologies for the 21st Century: Visions of the Future (2017); Translator-in-Chief, Design in Educational Technology: Design Thinking, Design Process, and Design Studio (2017); Translator-in-Chief, Encyclopedia of Terminology for Educational Communications and Technology (2017); First-Author, Mastering Computer Skills through Experiential Learning (2009, 2012); First-Author, Fundamental Computer Skills (2004); Co-Author, Applied Cryptography (1999); Sole-Translator, Writing Scientific Papers in English (1983) **Awards:** Excellence in Global Education Faculty Award, Indiana State University (2-15-2016); Award for Contributions to International Education, Indiana State University (2016); Presidential Award, Association for Educational Communications and Technology (2014); Award of Special Recognition, Society of International Chinese in Educational Technology (2013); Reitzel Faculty Research Award for 2012-2013, Bayh College of Education, Indiana State University (2013); Employee of the Year, Advanced Technical Support, Inc. (1999); Best Contributor to the University Teaching and Research Award, Shanghai TieDao University (1991); Excellent Teaching Award, Shanghai TieDao University (1997-1990); Scientific English Translation Award, The Second Scientific Translation National Competition in China (1983) **Membership:** The Honor Society of Phi Kappa Phi; Association for Educational Communications and Technology **Marquis Who's Who Honors:** Albert Nelson Marquis Lifetime Achievement Award (2017) **To what do you attribute your success:** Professor Feng-Qi Lai attributes her success to her integrity as a person and as a scholar, as well as to her belief and practice as a life-long learner. **Why did you become involved in your profession or industry:** Professor Feng-Qi Lai became involved in her profession because she believes education makes a difference. **What do you consider to be the highlight of your career:** The highlight of Professor Feng-Qi Lai's career was her contribution to global education. She taught in China and the United States from kindergarten, elementary school, middle school, high school, undergraduate, up to the graduate school. She also did training in the U.S. business. **Where will you be in five years:** Professor Feng-Qi Lai retired from Indiana State University at the end of the year of 2016. In five years, she will continue her contribution to global education. She has been invited to many universities in China to do academic presentations. She also does academic services for Association for Educational Communications and Technology in planning and organizing international research symposiums. **Hobbies:** Music; Reading; Chinese poetry; Photography; Crafts **Shipping Address:** 617 S Dobbsdell St, Terre Haute, IN, 47803

Irene Lamb

Title: Medical Researcher **Industry:** Medicine & Health Care **Date of Birth:** 05/09/1940 **Place of Birth:** Kentucky **State/Country of Origin:** KY **Parents:** Daily P. Lamb; Bertha (Hendricks) Lamb **Marital Status:** Widow **Spouse Name:** Edward B. Meadows (Deceased) **Education:** Coursework, California State University, Los Angeles; Coursework, Berea College; Diploma in Nursing, Kentucky Baptist Hospital; RN, States of Kentucky and California **Career:** Senior Community Health Nurse, Madison County Health Department, Berea, KY (2003-2015, 1993-1997); Senior Clinical Research Manager, Stroke Program, University of Kentucky College of Medicine, Lexington, KY (1997-2002); Director, Clinical Research, San Diego Cardiac Center (1989-1992); Senior Research Nurse, Cardiology, Stanford University School of Medicine, California (1974-1985); Nurse Manager, Clinical Research Center, University of Southern California, Los Angeles County Medical Center (1969-1974); Staff Nurse, Research CCU, University of Southern California, Los Angeles County Medical Center (1968); Head Nurse, Acute Medicine, Medical ICU, Surgical ICU, Various Medical Centers (1963-1967); Research Coordinator, Private Clinic, San Diego, CA **Civic:** Board of Directors, Kentucky Stroke Association (1998-2000) **Creative Works:** Contributor, Articles, Professional Journals; Contributor, Chapters to Books **Marquis Who's Who Honors:** Albert Nelson Marquis Lifetime Achievement Award (2017) **To what do you attribute your success:** She found success because of the professors of medicine at the University of Southern California and Stanford University who mentored, encouraged, and trusted her to assist with their medical research when she was a nurse. **What do you consider to be the highlight of your career:** The highlight of her career was working with John Speer Schroeder MD, who was Professor of Medicine and Cardiology at Stanford University School of Medicine. **Hobbies:** Hand weaving; Photography **Political Affiliations:** Democrats **Shipping Address:** 107 Lorraine Ct, Berea, KY, 40403

Ronald William Lamont-Havers

Title: Physician (Retired), Medical Association Administrator **Industry:** Medicine & Health Care **Date of Birth:** 03/06/1920 **Place of Birth:** Norfolk **Country of Origin:** United Kingdom **Marital Status:** Married **Spouse Name:** Gabrielson (10/16/1965) **Children:** Wendy; Melinda; Ian **Education:** Diploma in Internal Medicine, McGill University (1953); Canadian Arthritis and Rheumatism Society Fellow, Columbia Presbyterian Hospital, College Physicians and Surgeons, Columbia University, New York City, NY (1951-1953); Resident in Internal Medicine, Queen Mary Veterans Hospital, Montreal, Canada (1949-1951); Intern, Vancouver General Hospital, Canada (1946-1948); MD, University of Toronto (1946); BA, University of British Columbia (1942) **Career:** Senior Adviser, Massachusetts General Hospital and Harvard University (1999-2005); Deputy Director, Cutaneous Biology Research Center, Massachusetts General Hospital (1990-1999); Deputy Director, Cutaneous Biology Research Center, Harvard University (1990-1999); Senior Consultant for Research, Massachusetts General Hospital, Boston, MA (1990-1999); Vice President for Research and Technical Affairs, Massachusetts General Hospital, Boston, MA (1987-1990); Deputy to General Director for Research Policy and Administration, Massachusetts General Hospital, Boston, MA (1976-1987); Acting Director, National Institutes of Health, Bethesda, MD (1975); Deputy Director, National Institutes of Health, Bethesda, MD (1974-1976); Acting Director, Deputy Director, National Institutes of Health, Bethesda, MD (1974-1976); Deputy Director, NIAMD, Bethesda, MD (1972-1974); Associate Director of Extramural Programs, National Institutes of Health, Bethesda, MD (1968-1972); Associate Director, Extramural Programs, NIAMD, Bethesda, MD (1964-1968); Instructor in Medicine, College Physicians and Surgeons, Columbia University (1955-1964); Medical Director, Arthritis and Rheumatism Foundation, New York City, NY (1955-1964); Medical Director, Canadian Arthritis and Rheumatism Society, British Columbia Division, Vancouver, Canada (1953-1955) **Career Related:** United States Coordinator, U.S.-USSR Cooperative Program in Arthritis (1973-1975); Delegate, USSR-Arthritis Exchange Program (1964) **Awards:** Special Citation, Secretary of Department of Health (1975); Superior Service Award, Department of Health (1973) **Membership:** President, Massachusetts Chapter, Arthritis Foundation (1987-1989); Director, Governing Member, Arthritis Foundation (1966-1980); Director, Metropolitan Washington Section, American College of Rheumatology (1964-1966); President, New York Rheumatism Association (1960); Alpha Omega Alpha Honor Medical Society; Fellow, Royal College of Physicians, Canada **Marquis Who's Who Honors:** Albert Nelson Marquis Lifetime Achievement Award (2017); Distinguished Humanitarian (2017) **Shipping Address:** 173 Morse Rd, Sudbury, MA, 01776

Lois E. Landis Shenk

Title: Freelance Writer **Industry:** Writing and Editing **Date of Birth:** 05/30/1944 **Place of Birth:** Ephrata **State:** PA **Parents:** Raymond E. Landis; Esther M. Landis **Marital Status:** Single **Spouse Name:** John Barge Shenk (6/12/1965, Divorced 10/22/2010) **Children:** Philip Jon Shenk; Matthew Alan Shenk; Harrison Hayson Shenk (Grandson) **Education:** MSc in Education, Temple University (1984); BA in English, Eastern Mennonite University (1966) **Career:** Freelance Writer (1978-Present); Religious News Correspondent, Gospel Herald, Scottdale, PA (1978-1982); English Teacher, Kraybill Campus, Lancaster Mennonite School Mount Joy, Lancaster, PA (1976-1977); English Mistress, Githumu Secondary School, Thika, Kenya (1966-1968) **Career Related:** Observer, Correspondent, United States Senate, Washington, DC (2006-Present) Observer, Correspondent, United States Senate, Washington, DC (1987-2001) **Civic:** Lancaster Church of the Brethren Membership (2004-present); Secretary, Leadership Search Committee for Lancaster Church of the Brethren (2014-2017); Choir, Concert Tour to Germany (2014); United States Ambassador, World Forum, Inc. (2007); Member, Chancel Choir, Lancaster Church of the Brethren (2004-2014); Tutor, English as a Second Language (2004); Community Living Advisor, Friendship Community, Lititz, PA (1997-1999) Sunday School Teacher, Alive Church Ephrata (1997-1999) **Creative Works:** Author, "The Story of Ephrata Mennonite School" (1996) Author, "Hebrews: A Study Guide for Christian Education" (1988) Author, "Swords into Plowshares: An Anthology" (1983) Playwright, One-Act "Play House for David", Published in "Swords into Plowshares: An Anthology" (1983) Author, "Out of Mighty Waters" (1982) Editorial Assistant, Mennonite Central Committee, Akron, PA (1977) Contributor, Poems, Professional Journals; Contributor, Articles, Professional Journals; Contributor, Features, Professional Journals **Awards:** World Leader of the Humanities, International Biographical Center, Cambridge, England (2017); Honorary Director General, IBC, England (2009); Ambassadorship of U.S. Certificate, World Forum, Washington, DC (2007); Global Fellowship Certificate (2007); Lifetime Achievement Award, International Biographical Center, England (2007); Senatorial Medal of Freedom, U.S. Senate; Order of International Fellowship, Cambridge, England; Lifetime Order of Distinction for Writing **Membership:** Lifetime Member, Lancaster County Conservancy; Lifetime Member, International Biographical Centre **Marquis Who's Who Honors:** Albert Nelson Marquis Lifetime Achievement Award (2017) **Why did you become involved in your profession or industry:** Ms. Shenk became involved in her profession because she has always had an interest in writing. **What do you consider to be the highlight of your career:** The highlight of Ms. Shenk's career has been becoming a well-known writer. **Hobbies:** Reading; Writing; Music; Homemaking **Religion:** Christian **Shipping Address:** 821 Hershey Ave, Lancaster, PA, 17603

Gordon Lang Jr.

Title: Lawyer (Retired) **Industry:** Law and Legal Services **Company Name:** Drinker, Biddle & Reath LLP **Date of Birth:** 07/27/1933 **Place of Birth:** Evanston **State:** IL **Parents:** Gordon Lang; Harriet (Kendig) Lang **Marital Status:** Married **Spouse Name:** Clara Bates Van Derzee (9/26/1970) **Children:** Elizabeth K.; Gordon, III; Harriet B. **Education:** LLB, Harvard University (1960); MA in History, The University of Arizona (1958); BA, Yale University (1954) **Career:** Partner, Gardner Carton & Douglas (1967-1998); Associate, Gardner Carton & Douglas (1960-1967) **Career Related:** Consultant in Field **Civic:** Director, Chicago Youth Centers (1967-Present); Appointed Bush/Cheney Elector, State of Illinois (2000); Member, United Way/Crusade of Mercy (Metropolitan Chicago) (1989-1995); Director, United Way of Chicago (1984-1990); Trustee, Groton School (1982-1993); President, Chicago Youth Centers (1982-1984); Trustee, Chicago Latin School Foundation (1978-2016); Member, Associates of Northwestern University (1970-2005); President, Yale Scholarship Trust of Illinois (1967); Director, Yale Scholarship Trust of Illinois (1966-1969); Member, Associates of Rush-Presbyterian-St. Luke's Medical Center (Now Rush University Medical Center) (1962-2003); Director, North Side Boys' Clubs (1961-1967) **Military Service:** First Lieutenant, U.S. Air Force (1955-1957) **Awards:** Spirit of Youth Award, Chicago Youth Centers **Membership:** Financial Institutions Committee, The Chicago Bar Association (1985-1998); Corporation Law Committee, The Chicago Bar Association (1975-1998); Illinois State Bar Association; Business Law Section, American Bar Association; Director Emeritus, The Chicago Club; Secretary Emeritus, The Chicago Club; Director Emeritus, The Economic Club of Chicago; Secretary Emeritus, The Economic Club of Chicago; Onwentsia Club; The Racquet Club of Chicago; Commonwealth Club of Chicago; Director Emeritus, Yale Chicago; President Emeritus, Yale Chicago **Bar Admissions:** State Bar of Illinois (1960) **Marquis Who's Who Honors:** Albert Nelson Marquis Lifetime Achievement Award (2017) **Why did you become involved in your profession or industry:** Mr. Lang became involved in his profession because he was always interested in government, politics and law. By extension of this interest, Mr. Lang was inspired to help people and corporations solve corporate and legal problems. **What do you consider to be the highlight of your career:** The highlight of Mr. Lang's career was working with the William Wrigley, Jr., Company on general corporate matters and the Illinois National Bank and Trust Company, where he helped with financial transactions and various corporate matters. **Hobbies:** Golf; Skiing; Hiking **Political Affiliations:** Republican **Religion:** Episcopalian **Shipping Address:** 1440 N State Pkwy Apt 16D, Chicago, IL, 60610

Robert M. Lang Jr.

Title: Manufacturing Executive **Industry:** Manufacturing **Company Name:** Fabrique Cosmetique, Inc. **Place of Birth:** Oceanside **State/Country of Origin:** NY **Parents:** Robert Mays Lang; Mary Elizabeth Davis Lang Mannweiler; Gordon Banatynne Mannweiler (Stepfather) **Marital Status:** Married **Spouse Name:** Janice Ruth Mooney (1978); Sarah N. McIntyre (1965, Divorced 1974) **Education:** BA in Economics, Miami University, Oxford, Ohio (1965); Graduate Coursework in Economics and English **Career:** Chief Executive Officer, Next Level Analysis LLC (2016-Present); Chief Executive Officer, Endless Sky L3C, Granite Springs, NY (2010-Present); Chief Executive Officer, L3C Advisors L3C, Granite Springs, NY (2008-Present); Chief Executive Officer, Americans for Community Development LLC, Granite Springs, NY (2007-Present); Chief Executive Officer, Mary Elizabeth & Gordon B. Mannweiler Foundation, Inc., Cross River, NY (2005-Present); Private Practice and Investments (1972-Present); Chief Executive Officer, Fabrique Cosmetique, Inc., Cross River, NY (1992-2010); President, Imagination Group, Ltd., Cross River, NY (1990-2000); Partner, Symphonic Teamwork, LLC, Cross River, NY; President, Reach for the Stars Inc., Cross River, NY (1982-1994); Representative, Arkay Packaging Inc. (1968-1972); Representative, Creative Packaging Inc. (1965-1968) **Career Related:** Strategic Advisor, First Miami Student & Alumni FCU (2015-Present); Creator, L3C; Founder, Americans for Community Development; Creator, First L3C in the World, L3C Advisors L3C; Creator, Endless Opportunities L3C; Advisory Board, Mission Center L3C, The Mission Center; Creator and Leader, ACD Taskforce, Education & The Workforce; Next Level Analysis; Consultant; Advisor **Civic:** Board Member, The Alliance for Charitable Reform (2006-2009); Board of Directors, Naumburg Orchestral Concerts (2005-2014); Finance Committee, Katonah United Methodist Church (1997-1999); Treasurer, Pound Ridge Community Church, Pound Ridge, NY (1984-1987); Participant, Numerous Other Charitable Organizations; Advisor, Significant Number of L3Cs; Other Various Activities **Military Service:** U.S. Air Force ROTC **Creative Works:** Lecturer in Field; Participant, Seminars and Panels, Worldwide; Consultant, Issues Related to Saving Newspapers, United States; Author, White Papers, Popular Magazines, Websites and Newspapers; Contributor, Articles to Professional Journals; Contributor, Articles to Trade Magazines **Awards:** Cosmetic Innovator of the Year Award, Independent Cosmetic Manufacturers and Distributors (2004) **Membership:** Chapter President, National Association of Watch & Clock Collectors Inc. (2001-2008); American Chemical Society; Independent Cosmetic Manufacturers and Distributors Association; National Association of Watch & Clock Collectors Inc.; Various Square Dance Clubs **Hobbies:** Collecting Books; Collecting and Repairing Antique Clocks; Gardening; Woodworking; Square Dancing **Political Affiliations:** Independent **Religion:** Protestant **Business Address:** PO Box 362, Cross River, NY, 10518 **Website:** http://americansforcommunitydevelopment.org

Genevieve Krause LaRobardier

Title: Lawyer **Industry:** Law and Legal Services **Company Name:** Bressler, Amery & Ross, P.C. **Parents:** Allan Joseph Krause; Genevieve Ferington Krause **Marital Status:** Married **Spouse Name:** Lamont Marcell LaRobardier (Deceased 6/14/2008) **Children:** Lamont Jr.; Allan Lamont; Suzanne; Marie Bernadette; Genevieve **Education:** Degree in International Law, Columbia Law School (1983); JD, Rutgers, the State University of New Jersey (1983); MA in Teaching, Fairleigh Dickenson University, Summa Cum Laude, Teaneck, NJ (1966); BA, Barnard College **Career:** Lawyer, Bressler, Amery & Ross, P.C., Florham Park, NJ (1993-Present); Special Counsel, Hannoch Weisman Law Firm, Roseland, NJ (1990-1993); Legal Intern, Associate, Partner, Margolis Law Firm, Verona, NJ (1983-1990); Assistant to Director, Latin American Affairs, National Foreign Trade Council, New York City, NY **Career Related:** Adjunct Faculty Member, Language Department, Fairleigh-Dickinson University, Teaneck, NJ **Civic:** Member, International Moot Court Team **Creative Works:** Contributing Author, "New Jersey Federal Civil Procedure" (1999-Present); Contributing Author, "New Jersey Federal Civil Practice Handbook"; Contributor, Articles, Professional Journals; Author, "Doing Business in National Guard for Foreign Entities"; Editor, Judicial Board, Rutgers Law Review, Newark, NJ **Awards:** International Allegiance Award (2014); Distinguished Legislative Service Award, New Jersey State Bar Association (1997) **Membership:** Legal Counsel, Women's Automotive Association International (2012-Present, 2004-2007); Board Member, Trans-Atlantic Business Council (2006-Present); Chair, New Jersey State Bar Association (2006-2008); Legal Council, Trans-Atlantic Business Council; First Vice Chair, International Litigation and Arbitration Committee, New Jersey State Bar Association; Member, International Law Organizations Section, New Jersey State Bar Association; International Law Section, ABA; Franchise Law Section, ABA; Litigation Section, ABA; National Association of Dealer Counsel **Bar Admissions:** Supreme Court of the United States (1989); United States District Court, Southern District of New York (1987); United States District Court, Eastern District of New York (1987); United States Court of Appeals for the Second Circuit (1987); United States Court of Appeals for the Third Circuit (1985); New York (1985); New Jersey (1983); United States District Court, District of New Jersey (1983) **To what do you attribute your success:** Ms. LaRobardier attributes her success to the opening up of opportunities in her lifetime. In high school people found it unbelievable that she wanted to be an attorney, so few women had achieved it, and there were so many obstacles that she had to overcome. She was very fortunate and had a lot of encouragement. **Why did you become involved in your profession or industry:** She became involved in her profession because she had opportunities to read about it. She read books about attorneys and it drove her to want to do it. She found the legal background interesting and intriguing. **Shipping Address:** 852 Huron Rd, Franklin Lakes, NJ, 07417

Claire Mary Lathers

Title: Pharmacologist **Industry:** Pharmaceuticals **Parents:** Schuyler Wilson Lathers; Carol Gretchen Fraker Lathers **Education:** Postdoctoral Fellowship, National Institute of General Medical Sciences, Medical College, Pennsylvania (1973-1975); PhD, State University of New York, University at Buffalo (1973); Pre-Doctoral Training, National Institutes of Health, SUNY Medical School, Department of Pharmacology, Buffalo, NY (1969-1973); BS in Pharmacy, Union University, Albany, NY (1969) **Certifications:** Licensed Pharmacist **Career:** Consultant in Clinical Pharmacology (2003-Present); Senior Adviser for Science, Food and Drug Administration (2002-2003); Lead Scientist, Post-911 Biomedical Countermeasures, Former President George W. Bush (2002-2003); Lead Scientist, Post-911 Biomedical Countermeasures, Food and Drug Administration (2002-2003); Lead Scientist, Post-911 Biomedical Countermeasures, National Institutes of Health (2002-2003); Lead Scientist, Post-911 Biomedical Countermeasures, National Aeronautics and Space Administration (2002-2003); Director, Office of New Animal Drug Evaluation, Food and Drug Administration (1999-2002); Food Safety Officer, Former President Bill Clinton (1999-2002); Food Safety Officer, Food and Drug Administration (1999-2002); Pharmacology Reviewer, Cardiovascular Renal Drugs, Food and Drug Administration (1989-1994) **Career Related:** LLC President, Clinical Pharmacology (2014-Present); Appellate Law Clerk (2010-2013); Representative, United States Pharmacopoeia Quinquennial Anniversary Celebration, Food and Drug Administration (2000); Presenter, International Academy for Astronauts Meetings (1989-2000); Chief Scientific Officer, Barr Pharmaceuticals, Pomona, NY (1996-1999); Lecturer, Annual Edward William Hawthorne Memorial Lecture, Howard University (1996); Presenter, Community Health Plan, "The Future of Pharmacy in Light of the Health Care Reform Revolution" Pharmacy Week Lecture, Albany, NY (1995); President, Albany College of Pharmacy, Union College (1994-1996); Dean, Albany College of Pharmacy, Union College (1994-1996); Keynote Speaker, Sudden Death in Epilepsy, Third International Cleveland Clinic-Bethel Epilepsy Symposium, Intraosseous Administration of Anticonvulsant Drugs, Cleveland Clinic (1992); Co-chair, Frontiers Symposia, American College of Clinical Pharmacology (1990, 1992); Visiting Scientist, National Aeronautics and Space Administration, Houston, TX (1988); Invited Keynote Speaker, Sudden Death Epilepsy, Fifteenth International Symposium, American Epilepsy Society (1983) **Civic:** Restoration Volunteer, Federal and New York State Historic Registry 1802 Beecher House and Barn (2015-Present); Advisory Board, Joint Initiative on Food Safety & Nutrition, Food and Drug Administration, University Maryland (1999-2003); Board Member, Annapolis Center, Maryland (1994-1998); Member, Board Albany-Tula Alliance (1994-1996); Co-organizer, Review Courses, ABCP (1991-1992); Chair, Liaison Committee, American College Clinical Pharmacology (1989-1990); Chair, Liaison Committee, American Society for Clinical Pharmacology and Therapeutics (1989-1990); Chair, Liaison Committee, The American Society for Pharmacology and Experimental Therapeutics (1989-1990) **Military Service:** U.S. Coast Guard Auxiliary, Pennsylvania (1980-1982) **Creative Works:** Contributor, Articles, Various Publications (1973-Present); Editor, Educational Section, "Innovative Teaching Methods for Clinical Pharmacology," The Journal of Clinical Pharmacology (1988-2005); Co-editor, The Journal of Clinical Pharmacology (1991, 1994); Author, The Journal of Clinical Pharmacology (1991, 1994); Author, "Sudden Death in Epilepsy: Forensic and Clinical Issues"; Co-editor, "Sudden Death in Epilepsy: Forensic and Clinical Issues"; Author, Co-editor, "Epilepsy and Sudden Death"; Author, "Cardiovascular Therapeutics in Clinical Practice" **Awards:** Honoree, Citation for Service to the Nation, President Bill Clinton and President Barack Obama (2012); Recipient, Nathan Quick Distinguished Service Award, Profession of Clinical Pharmacology, American College of Clinical Pharmacology (1997); Recipient, President's Award, Grateful Recognition of Outstanding Leadership and Service to the College as its President, American College of Clinical Pharmacology (1996); Honoree, Best Scientific Exhibit, Intraosseous Route, American College of Emergency Physicians (1985) **Membership:** Federal Executive Institute Leadership for a Democratic Society (1999); FDA Commissioner's Senior Science Council (1999-2002); President, American College of Clinical Pharmacology, Ashburn, VA (1994-1996); President-elect, American College of Clinical Pharmacology, Ashburn, VA (1992-1994); Treasurer, American College of Clinical Pharmacology, Ashburn, VA (1992-1994) **Marquis Who's Who Honors:** Albert Nelson Marquis Lifetime Achievement Award (2017) **Political Affiliations:** Independent **Religion:** Protestant **Shipping Address:** 115 S Manning Blvd, Albany, NY, 12203

Mitchell Lee Lathrop

Title: Arbitrator/Mediator/Lawyer **Industry:** Law and Legal Services **Company Name:** Law Office of Mitchell L. Lathrop **Date of Birth:** 12/15/1937 **Place of Birth:** Los Angeles **State:** CA **Parents:** Alfred Lee Lathrop; Barbara (Mitchell) Lathrop **Marital Status:** Married **Spouse Name:** Lynn Mara (Dalton) Lathrop **Children:** Christin Lorraine Newlon; Alexander Mitchell Lathrop **Education:** JD, University of Southern California (1966); BSc, United States Naval Academy (1959) **Certifications:** Diplomate, International Arbitration Law, The College Law of Law of England and Wales (2005); Certified Arbitrator, ARIAS-US; Certified London Court of International Arbitration; Chartered Arbitrator **Career:** Independent Consultant and Practitioner, Law Office of Mitchell L. Lathrop (2012-Present); Independent Arbitrator Mediator, Mintz, Levin, Cohn, Ferris, Glovsky & Popeo, P.C. (2012); Member, Mintz, Levin, Cohn, Ferris, Glovsky & Popeo, P.C. (2009-2012); Counsel, Duane Morris LLP, San Diego, CA (2003-2009); Senior Partner, Luce, Forward, Hamilton & Scripps, San Diego and New York City (1994-2003); Firm Chairman, Adams, Duque & Hazeltine, Los Angeles, San Francisco, New York City, San Diego (1992-1994); Senior Partner, Executive Committee, Adams, Duque & Hazeltine, Los Angeles, San Francisco, New York City, San Diego (1986-1994); Senior Partner, Rogers & Wells, New York City, San Diego (1980-1986); Partner, Macdonald, Halsted & Laybourne, Los Angeles and San Diego (1971-1980); Partner, Brill, Hunt, DeBuys and Burby, Los Angeles, CA (1968-1971); Deputy Counsel, Los Angeles, CA (1966-1968); Partner, Duane Morris LLP, New York, NY **Career Related:** Presiding Referee, The State Bar Court of California (1984-1986); Member, Executive Committee, The State Bar Court of California (1981-1988); Lecturer of Law, California Judges Association; Lecturer of Law, Practicing Law Institute; Lecturer of Law, CEB; Lecturer of Law, The State Bar of California; Lecturer of Law, ABA **Civic:** President, Metropolitan Opera National Council (2010-2018); President, San Diego Opera Association (1994-1996); President-elect, San Diego Opera Association (1993); Vice President, San Diego Opera Association (1985-1989); Board of Directors, Metropolitan Opera Association, New York, NY (1982-2018); Board of Directors, San Diego Opera Association (1980-2003); Secretary, Music Center Opera Association (1974-1980); Board of Directors, Music Center Opera Association, Los Angeles, CA (1973-1980); Trustee, Honnold Mudd Library, The Claremont Colleges (1972-1980); Vice President, Executive Committee Member, Metropolitan Opera National Council (1971-2018); Western Regional Chairman, Metropolitan Opera National Council (1971-1981) **Military Service:** Retired Captain, Judge Advocate General's Corps, US Naval Reserve **Creative Works:** Member, Editorial Board, Defense Counsel Journal (1997-Present); Author, "Insurance Coverage for Environmental Claims" (1992); Contributor, Journal Insurance Coverage **Membership:** Vice President, San Diego County Bar Association (1985); Board of Directors, San Diego County Bar Association (1982-1985); Chairman, Ethics Committee, San Diego County Bar Association (1980-1982); President, Friends of The Claremont Colleges (1978-1979); President, S.R. (1977-1979); President, Southern California Chapter, Judge Advocates Association (1977-1978); Director, Friends of The Claremont Colleges (1975-1981); Director, Los Angeles Chapter, Judge Advocates Association (1974-1980); Director, British United Services Club, Los Angeles, CA (1973-1975); Governor, Society of Colonial Wars in the State of California (1970-1972); President, Los Angeles Opera Associates (1970-1972); The District of Columbia Bar; The State Bar of California; Federal Bar Council; Federal Bar Association; New York State Bar Association; Mensa International; The Naval Club, London, United Kingdom; Metropolitan Club, New York, NY; California Club, Los Angeles, CA; Phi Delta Phi; Order of Saint Lazarus of Jerusalem; Center for International Legal Studies; Chartered Institute of Arbitrators, London, United Kingdom; ABA; International Association of Defense Counsel; American Board of Trial Advocates; Association of Southern California Defense Counsel; Association of Business Trial Lawyers **Bar Admissions:** New York (1981); Supreme Court of the United States (1969); Washington, DC (1966); California (1966) **Marquis Who's Who Honors:** Albert Nelson Marquis Lifetime Achievement Award (2017) **Political Affiliations:** Republican **Religion:** Catholic **Shipping Address:** 600 W Broadway Ste 500, Law Office of Mitchell L. Lathrop, San Diego, CA, 92101 **Website:** http://www.mlathroplaw.com

Clarene Law

Title: Small Business Owner **Industry:** Business Management/Business Services **Company Name:** Elk Country Motels, Inc. **Date of Birth:** 07/22/1933 **Place of Birth:** Thornton **State:** ID **Parents:** Clarence Riley Webb; Alta (Simmons) Webb **Education:** Coursework, Idaho State College (1953) **Career:** Innkeeper, Chief Executive Officer, Elk Country Motels, Inc., Jackson, WY (1962-Present); Representative, Wyoming House of Representatives, Cheyenne, WY (1991-2004); Auditor, Wort Hotel, Jackson, WY (1960-1962); Secretary, Substitute Teacher, Grand County Schools, Cedar City, UT (1954-1957); United Press International Representative, Newspaper Agency, Moab, UT; United Press International Representative, Regional Papers, Salt Lake City, UT; United Press International Representative, Regional Papers, Denver, CO **Career Related:** Chairman, Minerals and Economic Development Committee, Wyoming State House of Representatives (2001-2004); Chairman, Travel Committee, Wyoming State House of Representatives (1993-2000); Member, Bank Board, Wyoming State House of Representatives (1991-1998); Board of Directors, Jackson State Bank, Snow King Resort **Civic:** Board of Directors, Wyoming Taxpayers Association, Business Council (1998-2004); Chairman, School Board of Directors, Teton County Schools, Jackson, WY (1983-1986) **Awards:** Named to the Business Hall of Fame (2013); Named, Citizen of the Year, Jackson Chamber of Commerce (1976, 1999); Named, Business Person of the Year, Jackson Hole Realtors (1987); Big Wyoming Award, Wyoming Lodging & Restaurant Association (1987); Named, Wyoming Small Business Person, Small Business Administration (1977); Named, Woman of the Year, National Women's Business Council (1975) **Membership:** Heritage Steering Committee, National Women's Business Council (1996-Present); President, Chairman, Board of Directors, Wyoming Lodging & Restaurant Association (1988-1989); Government's 15-Member Business Council; Charter Member, Soroptimist International **Hobbies:** Travel; Study **Political Affiliations:** Republican **Shipping Address:** P.O. Box 575, Jackson, WY, 83001

Richard Dean Lawrence

Title: Lawyer **Industry:** Law and Legal Services **Company Name:** Lawrence Firm, PSC **Date of Birth:** 09/20/1944 **Place of Birth:** Jefferson City **State:** MO **Parents:** Charles Eugene Lawrence; Edith Lucille (Moore) Lawrence **Marital Status:** Widowed **Spouse Name:** Diana H. McIntyre (8/13/1967, Deceased) **Children:** Jennifer; Daniel; Michael; David; Lindsay **Education:** AA, University of Cincinnati, Cincinnati, OH (1974); JD, Salmon P. Chase College of Law, Cum Laude, Highland Heights, KY (1971); BA, University of Cincinnati, Cincinnati, OH (1967) **Career:** Partner, President, Lawrence, Linder & McGrath, Cincinnati, OH (1991-Present); Founder, Partner, President, Gustin & Lawrence (1971); President, Lawrence Firm, PSC **Career Related:** Founder, The Lawrence Firm (1991); Guest Lecturer, Chase College of Law (1983-1987); Guest Lecturer, Ohio Trial Practice Institute, Cincinnati, OH (1975-1977); Co-Founder, Law Firm of Gustin and Lawrence (1972); Speaker, Medical Malpractice, Kentucky Bar Association, Cincinnati Bar Association, and Ohio Academy of Trial Lawyers; Fellow, International Society of Barristers **Civic:** President, Washington Hills Association, Cincinnati, OH (1977-1978); Past Member, Administrative Board, United Methodist Church of Milford; Past Deacon, Pleasant Ridge Presbyterian Church; Board of Directors, Hamilton Mutual Insurance Co.; Past President, Salmon P. Chase American Court Chapter **Awards:** Best Lawyers in America (1995-Present); Pre-Eminent Lawyer, Martindale-Hubbell (1970-Present); Trial Lawyer of the Year for the Southern Ohio Region in Medical Malpractice Law (2013); Cincinnati Area Personal Injury Litigation Lawyer of the Year, Best Lawyers (2010); Trial Lawyer of the Year, Southern Ohio Region for Personal Injury Litigation (2010); Outstanding Personal Injury Lawyer in the Southern Ohio Region, Best Lawyers in America (2009); Presidential Recognition for Outstanding Contributions to the Organization (2009); Lifetime Achievement Award, Salmon P. Chase College of Law (2008); Dan Cullan Memorial Award, Birth Trauma Litigation Group (2008); Key to the City of Covington, KY for Outstanding Contributions to the Historical Value of the City (2005); Northern Kentucky Lifetime Achievement Award (2005); Two Wiedemann & Wysocki Awards, Association of Trial Lawyers of America (2004); Northern Kentucky Bar Association Lifetime Achievement Award (2004); Excellence in Medical Malpractice Litigation, Cincinnati Magazine (2004); Top Ten Lawyers in Ohio, National Law Journal (2000); One of Three American Lawyers Chosen to Speak, First National Convention, Australian Plaintiff Association (1998); Weiderman and Wysocki Medal for Outstanding Contributions for Civil Justice, Association of Trial Lawyers (1998); Top Ten Trial Attorneys, National Law Journal of Ohio; Distinguished Lawyer Award, Northern Kentucky Bar Association (1996); Weiderman and Wysocki Medal for Outstanding Contributions for Civil Justice, Association of Trial Lawyers (1996); Trial Lawyer of the Year, Kentucky Academy of Trial Lawyers (1996); Statewide Traveler of the Year Award, Kentucky Academy of Travelers (1996); Lifetime Achievement Award, Northern Kentucky Bar Association (1996); Excellence in Medical Malpractice Litigation, Cincinnati Magazine (1995); Top 100 Lawyers in Ohio; Top 50 Lawyers in Kentucky; Super Lawyer, Ohio; Super Lawyer, Kentucky; Proclamation, House of Representative, State of Kentucky for Lifetime Achievement and Contributions; Kentucky Colonel **Membership:** Stalward Member for Outstanding Service for 25 Years (1996); Board Member, Ohio Attorneys for Justice (1995-1996); American Bar Association; Kentucky Academy of Trial Attorneys; Ohio Academy of Trial Lawyers; Hamilton County Trial Lawyers Association; Northern Kentucky Bar Association; Kentucky Bar Association; Association of Trial Lawyers of America; Cincinnati Bar Association; Ohio Bar Association; Former Board Member, Association of Trial Lawyers of America (Now American Association for Justice); Former National Co-Chairman, Birth Trauma Litigation Section, Association of Trial Lawyers of America (Now American Association for Justice); Former Chairman, Professional Negligence Section, Association of Trial Lawyers of America (Now American Association for Justice); Former Co-Chairman, International Law Section, Association of Trial Lawyers of America (Now American Association for Justice); Inner Circle Emeritus; Past National Chair of Birth Trauma Litigation Group, American Association for Justice; Past National Co-Chair, Medical Negligence Group, American Association for Justice; Past National Chair, Professional Negligence Section, American Association for Justice; President Past Treasurer, Secretary, Kentucky Justice Association; Ohio Academy of Trial Lawyers; Inner Circle of Advocates; Melvin M. Belli Society, Former Co-Chair, Medical Negligence, American Association for Justice **Bar Admissions:** State of Kentucky (1989); State of Ohio (1971); U.S. Court of Appeals; U.S. District Court, State of Ohio **Marquis Who's Who Honors:** Albert Nelson Marquis Lifetime Achievement Award (2017) **Religion:** Christian **Business Address:** 606 Philadelphia Street, Covington, OH, 41011

Donald Harvey Layton

Title: CEO **Industry:** Financial Services **Company Name:** Freddie Mac **Date of Birth:** 05/09/1950 **Parents:** Irving Layton; Charlotte (Bell) Layton **Marital Status:** Married **Spouse Name:** Sandra Lynn Lazo (6/1/1974) **Children:** Todd Samuel (1990); Ross Charles (1994) **Education:** MBA, Harvard University (1974); MS in Economics, Massachusetts Institute of Technology (1972); BS in Economics, Massachusetts Institute of Technology (1972) **Career Related:** Board of Directors, Freddie Mac, Federal Home Loan Mortgage Corporation (2012-Present); American International Group, Inc. (2010-2012); Senior Adviser, Securities Industry and Financial Markets Association (2006-2008); Assured Guaranty Ltd. (2005-2012) **Civic:** Chair Emeritus, Partnership for Homeless, New York City, NY (2015-Present); Chairman, Board of Directors, Partnership for Homeless, New York City, NY (2005-2015); Board of Directors, Foreign Policy Association (1998-2006) **Awards:** George F. Baker Scholar, Harvard Business School (1974) **Membership:** Chair Emeritus, Harbor Club, New York City, NY; Harvard Club, New York City, NY **Marquis Who's Who Honors:** Albert Nelson Marquis Lifetime Achievement Award (2017) **Business Address:** Freddle Mac Headquarters, Mclean, VA, 22102 **Shipping Address:** 885 Park Ave Apt 5A, New York, NY, 10075

Robert Eldon Leamer

Title: Health Care Lawyer, Executive **Industry:** Law and Legal Services **Company Name:** Metropolitan Jewish Health Systems **Date of Birth:** 01/04/1950 **Place of Birth:** Chicago **State:** IL **Parents:** Laurence Eugene Leamer; Helen Mae (Burkey) Leamer **Marital Status:** Married **Spouse Name:** Mary Frances Leamer **Children:** Stephen; Christina; Grechen O'Shea (Stepdaughter) **Education:** JD, Albany University (1976); AB, Colgate University (1972) **Career:** Executive Vice President, General Counsel, Chief Administrative Officer, Metropolitan Jewish Health System, Brooklyn, NY (2016-Present); Senior Vice President, General Counsel, Metropolitan Jewish Health System, Brooklyn, NY (2011-2016); Vice President, General Counsel, Metropolitan Jewish Health System, Brooklyn, NY (1998-2011); General Counsel, United Health Services, Binghamton, NY (1988-1998); Private Law Practice, Binghamton, NY (1979-1988); Counsel, New York State Assembly Committee on Health, Albany, NY (1979-1986); Assistant Counsel, New York State Assembly, Albany, NY (1976-1979) **Career Related:** Adjunct Professor, School of Management, Binghamton University and the New School for Social Research; Fellow, American College of Healthcare Executives **Civic:** LeadingAge New York (2013-Present); Medical Trust Board Member, Church Pension Group (2001-2010); Center for Adolescent Services (1993-1998); Good Shepard Fairview Home, Inc. (1989-1996); Broome County Council on the Arts (1988-1994); Board of Directors, Broome Legal Assistance Corporation (1985-1993); Partnership 2000 **Membership:** American College of Healthcare Executives; American Bar Association; New York State Bar Association; Broome County Bar Association; American Health Lawyers Association **Bar Admissions:** State of New York (1977); U.S. District Court, Northern District, State of New York (1977) **Marquis Who's Who Honors:** Albert Nelson Marquis Lifetime Achievement Award (2017) **To what do you attribute your success:** Mr. Leamer believes his success can be attributed to a commitment to a lifetime of learning, a sense of humor, and the belief that every individual has value and offers an opportunity for growth, insight, and fellowship. **Why did you become involved in your profession or industry:** Mr. Leamer's parents were interested in justice issues, so he gravitated towards law. Early in his career, he was able to pursue his interest in healthcare law, a growing specialty that gave him opportunities to work in a industry that addresses vital human needs. **What do you consider to be the highlight of your career:** Mr. Leamer is most proud of his ability to adapt and his openness to change that led him to move from the private practice of law to corporate health care law and ultimately to healthcare leadership. **Where will you be in five years:** Mr. Leamer will continue to promote the mission of Metropolitan Jewish Health Systems, seeking better health care for the frail and elderly of the New York region. **Hobbies:** Golf; European travel; History **Political Affiliations:** Democrat **Religion:** Episcopalian **Shipping Address:** 207 Noe Avenue, Chatham, NJ, 07928

Rachel L. Lebon, PhD

Title: Professor Emeritus **Industry:** Education/Educational Services **Company Name:** Women in Higher Education, People to People Ambassadorship Program **Date of Birth:** 11/27/1951 **Place of Birth:** Woonsocket **State:** RI **Parents:** Raymond Joseph Lebon; Georgette Lebon (Deceased) **Marital Status:** Single **Education:** PhD, University of Miami (1986); Master of Music, University of North Texas (1979); Bachelor of Music, University of North Texas (1977) **Career:** Professor, Coordinator of Jazz Voice, University of Miami, Coral Gables, FL (1986-Present); Delegate, People to People Ambassadorship Program, Women in Higher Education (2010); Visiting Professor, Leeds College of Music, England (2009-2010); Performer, Air Force Tops in Blue, Randolph Air Force Base, Texas (1973); Assistant Professor, Belmont College, Nashville, TN (1979-1983); Academic Instructor, United States Air Force; Academic Instructor, United States Air Force, Sheppard Air Force Base, Texas; Associate Professor to Full Professor to Professor Emeritus, University of Miami **Career Related:** Reviewer in Fields, Voice Specialist, Professional Voice Institute, Hallandale Beach, FL (1985) **Civic:** External Reviewer of Manuscripts, Journal of Voice (2012); Child Advocate, Guardian Ad Litem, Miami, FL (1990-2006) **Military Service:** Academic Instructor of Air Force Accounting, United States Air Force; Tops in Blue Tour, 100 Shows in 100 Days; Continental State of Alaska, Aleutian Islands, Southeast Asia (Thailand, Taiwan, Philippines, Guam, Okinawa, Japan, Korea) **Creative Works:** Vocal Coach in Residency, Voice Council Magazine (2011) ; Author, "The Versatile Vocalist: Singing Authentically in Contrasting Styles and Idioms (2006); Author, "The Professional Vocalist: A Handbook for Commercial Singers and Teachers" (1999); Singer, CD, "Voicings"; Contributor, Articles, Chapters to Books **Awards:** Award, Frost School of Music Tribute Concert (2018) **Membership:** International Association for Jazz Education; National Association of Teachers of Singing; Alpha Delta Kappa; Pi Kappa Lambda **Marquis Who's Who Honors:** Distinguished Humanitarian (2017); Who's Who in America, Who's Who in the South and Southeast; Who's who of American Women; Who's Who in the World **To what do you attribute your success:** Dr. Lebon has been very blessed with role models, teachers and professors, supervisors and colleagues that have been first rate! The students have also been of good character. **Why did you become involved in your profession or industry:** She has always loved singing and has been well-received as a vocalist. She also likes to teach and work with young people who display a thirst for knowledge and growth in their fields. She has been very fortunate to have wonderful colleagues! **What do you consider to be the highlight of your career:** The highlight of Dr. Lebon's career has been her time in the Air Force teaching and with Tops in Blue. She also cherishes her years at North Texas, supporting herself with singing gigs and recording sessions in Dallas/Ft. Worth. She has enjoyed teaching at Belmont College in Nashville and doing recording sessions in Miami. Another standout was earning her PhD and joining the faculty at the University of Miami. **Hobbies:** Writing; Travel **Political Affiliations:** Democrat **Religion:** Christian (Catholic) **Shipping Address:** 245 Old Village Center Circle, Unit 7112, St. Augustine, FL, 32084

David J. Leciston

Title: Computer Engineer, Computer Scientist **Industry:** Sciences **Company Name:** U.S. Army **Date of Birth:** 12/25/1958 **Place of Birth:** Passaic **State:** NJ **Parents:** Alex Leciston; Rose (Kozmoski) Leciston **Marital Status:** Married **Spouse Name:** Deborah Ann Owens (12/30/1999); Wendie Sue Orr (2/3/1987, Divorced 10/1998); Diane Carol Hirth (6/19/1981, Divorced 4/1985) **Children:** Jennifer Ann; David Jonathan; Mary Rose **Education:** BS in Computer Science, Seton Hall University (1982) **Career:** Program Executive Officer, Intelligence and Electronic Ware and Sensors, Project Manager Distributed Common Ground System, U.S. Army, Computer Engineer, Aberdeen Proving Ground, MD (2010-Present); Project Manager, Distributed Common Ground Systems, U.S. Army (2005-2010); Computer Engineer, Communications-Electronics Command, Software Engineering Center, U.S. Army, Fort Monmouth, NJ (2001-2005); Computer Scientist, Communications-Electronics Command, Research and Development Engineering Center, Software Engineering Directorate, Fort Monmouth, NJ (1989-2001); Computer Scientist, Communications-Electronics Command, Research and Development Engineering Center, Software Engineering Directorate, Fort Huachuca, AZ (1987-1989) **Military Service:** First Lieutenant, U.S. Army (1983-1987) **Awards:** Secretary of the Army Award for Outstanding Achievement in Materiel Acquisition (1997, 1991) **Membership:** Initiative on Software Engineering as a Profession (1994-Present); Life and Senior Member, Association for Computing Machinery; Life Member, Armed Forces Communications-Electronics Association; Senior Member, IEEE **To what do you attribute your success:** He attributes his success to parents that supported his interests. **Why did you become involved in your profession or industry:** He became involved in his profession because of his interest in mathematics, science, and history. **What do you consider to be the highlight of your career:** He is most proud of continuing to field improvements to system concepts he started over 30 years ago. **Hobbies:** Tabletop role-playing games; Tabletop historical wargames; Computers **Religion:** Catholic **Shipping Address:** 105 Deerfield Rd Apt F, Elkton, MD, 21921

Tahk Guhn Lee

Industry: Technology **Date of Birth:** 08/04/1984 **Place of Birth:** Ulsan **Country of Origin:** Republic of Korea **Education:** MME, Sogang University, Seoul, Republic of Korea (2012); Bachelor in Electronics and Communications Engineering, Kwangwoon University, Seoul, Republic of Korea (2010) **Career:** Chief Strategy and Technology Officer, Pastel Laboratory, Seongnam-si, Republic of Korea (2015); Software Engineer, Samsung Electronics, Suwon-si, Republic of Korea (2012-2015); Chief Executive and Technology Officer, Nearpia, Seoul, Republic of Korea (2010-2012) **Military Service:** Sergeant, Korean Army (2004-2006) **Achievements:** Achievements include development of automatic stock trading system with algorithm store; development of created word and location based social media service; development of lane detection and departure warning system for people driving on highways using Android smartphone platform

William Gentry Lee

Title: Lawyer **Industry:** Law and Legal Services **Company Name:** Vinson & Elkins LLP **Date of Birth:** 04/02/1944 **Place of Birth:** St. Louis **State/Country of Origin:** MO **Parents:** Gentry Lee; Wilma (Elliott) Lee **Marital Status:** Married **Spouse Name:** Carter Kerr (8/9/1969) **Children:** William Gentry, Jr.; Kathryn Carter **Education:** JD, University of Oklahoma (1969); BA, Harvard University, Cum Laude (1966) **Career:** Of Counsel, Vinson & Elkins LLP, Houston, TX (2007-Present); Partner, Vinson & Elkins LLP, Houston, TX (1981-2006); Associate, Vinson & Elkins, Houston, TX (1973-1981) **Career Related:** Committee on Revision of Corporate Laws, Business Law Section, State Bar of Texas (1975-2000) **Civic:** Board Member, First Presbyterian School, Houston, TX (2012-Present); Administrative Board Member, Cho-Yeh Camp and Conference Center, Livingston, TX (1990-1994); Elder, First Presbyterian, Houston, TX (1984-2009); Deacon, First Presbyterian Church of Houston (1979-1983) **Military Service:** Captain, Judge Advocate General's Corps, U.S. Army (1969-1973) **Creative Works:** Editor, Oklahoma Law Review (1967-1969); Contributor, Articles, Professional Journals **Awards:** Order of the Coif, University of Oklahoma (1969) **Membership:** Treasurer, Kiwanis Foundation, Houston, TX (2018-Present); Secretary, Kiwanis International (2011-2012); Board of Directors, Kiwanis International (1993-1995); Allegro Club; Houston Center Club; River Oaks Country Club **Bar Admissions:** State of Texas (1972); State of Oklahoma (1969) **Religion:** Presbyterian **Shipping Address:** 3665 Overbrook Lane, Houston, TX, 77027

Yeu-Tsu Margaret Lee

Industry: Medicine & Health Care **Date of Birth:** 03/18/1936 **Place of Birth:** Xian, Shensi **Country of Origin:** China **Spouse Name:** Thomas V. Lee, December 29, 1962 (Divorced 1987) **Children:** Maxwell M. **Education:** MD, Harvard University (1961); AB in Microbiology, University South Dakota (1957) **Certifications:** Diplomate, American Board of Surgery **Career:** Clinical Professor of Surgery, Medical School, University of Hawaii, Honolulu (1992-Present); Associate Clinical Professor of Surgery, Medical School, University of Hawaii, Honolulu (1984-1992); Associate Professor of Surgery, Medical School, University of Southern California, LA, 1973-1983) **Civic:** Member, Hawaii Chapter, U.S.-China Friendship Association (1991-Present); President, Organization of Chinese-American Women, L.A. (1981) **Military Service:** Retired, U.S. Army (1999); Chief Surgical Oncology, Tripler Army Medical Center, Honolulu (1983-1998); Colonel, U.S. Army Medical Corps (1989); Commissioned Lieutenant Colonel, U.S. Army Medical Corps (1983) **Creative Works:** Author, "Malignant Lymphoma" (1974); Author, Chapters, Various Books; Contributor, Articles, Professional Journals **Awards:** Honoree, Chinese-American Engineers and Sciences Association (1987); Science Woman Warrior, Asian-Pacific Womens Network (1983); Decorated National Defense Service Medal; Army Commendation Medal; Army Meritorious Service Medal; Army Humanitarian Service Medal **Membership:** American College of Surgeons; Society Surgical Oncology; Association of Women Surgeons **Hobbies:** Classical music; Movies; Hiking; Ballroom dancing

Muriel Kauimaeole Lee Stevens

Title: Elementary School Educator **Industry:** Education/Educational Services **Date of Birth:** 05/29/1942 **Place of Birth:** Hana **State:** HI **Parents:** Charles Pohaku Lee; Violet Leimamo (Wahihako) Lee **Marital Status:** Single **Spouse Name:** James Gary Stevens (1964, Divorced 1976) **Children:** James Todd (Deceased) **Education:** Postgraduate Coursework, University of Hawaii (1974-Present); Postgraduate Coursework, University of Utah (1969); EdB, Brigham Young University (1964); AS, Church College of Hawaii (1962) **Certifications:** Certified and Licensed Elementary Teacher, State of Hawaii **Career:** Teacher, Hana Elem High School (1999-2006); Teacher, Honowai Elementary School, Waipahu, HI (1978-1999); Kindergarten to First Grade Team Teacher, Ewa Elementary School (1971-1978); First Grade Teacher, Woodstock Elementary School, Salt Lake City, UT (1965-1969) **Career Related:** Aerospace Teacher, Coordinator of After-school Improvement Program, Honowai Elementary School (1995); Aerospace Teacher, Coordinator of After-school Improvement Program, Honowai Elementary School (1991); Citizen Ambassador Program, Spokane, WA (1987-1995); Participant, Teacher in Space Program, National Aeronautics and Space Administration (1985-1986); Teacher, Space Program, National Aeronautics and Space Administration (1985-1986) **Civic:** Teacher, Music Leader, Latter-Day Saints Primary, Hana Branch (1999-2001); Seminary Teacher, Single Adult Representative, Waipahu II Ward (1996); Spiritual Living Teacher, Latter-Day Saints Church, Kaneohe, HI (1994); Choir Member, Latter-Day Saints Church, Kaneohe, HI (1992-1994); Ambassador, People to People International, Spokane, WA (1987-1995) **Military Service:** Civil Air Patrol, U.S. Air Force (1985-1995) **Awards:** Aerospace Education Achievement Award, Civil Air Patrol, Auxiliary U.S. Air Force (1985) **Membership:** ASCD; Hawaii State Parent Teacher Student Association; National Education Association; Hawaii State Teachers Association; Wilson Center Associates; Academy of Political Science; World Aerospace Education Organization **Marquis Who's Who Honors:** Albert Nelson Marquis Lifetime Achievement Award (2017) **Why did you become involved in your profession or industry:** Ms. Stevens student taught in Payson, UT. An elderly teacher heavily influenced her, who had an unconventional ways of teaching. **Hobbies:** Hula dancing; Swimming; Sewing; Baking; Arts and crafts **Political Affiliations:** Republican **Shipping Address:** PO Box 879, Hana, HI, 96713

Albert Meyer Lefkovits

Title: Dermatologist **Industry:** Medicine & Health Care **Company Name:** Icahn School of Medicine at Mount Sinai **Date of Birth:** 06/30/1937 **Place of Birth:** New York City **State/Country of Origin:** NY **Year of Passing:** 2018-05-11 **Parents:** Aaron Melchoir Lefkovits; Muriel (Mark) Lefkovits **Marital Status:** Married **Spouse Name:** Cheryl Beth Kornberg (4/25/1971) **Children:** Ari Nathan; Lauren Blair **Education:** Resident in Dermatology, Kings County Hospital Center, State University of New York, Downstate Medical Center, Brooklyn, NY (1963-1965); Intern, Newark Beth Israel Hospital (1962-1963); MD, New York Medical College (1962); AB, Cornell University (1958) **Career:** Associate Clinical Professor, Icahn School of Medicine at Mount Sinai (2006-Present); Co-director, Cosmetic Dermatologic New York Surgery Training Program, Icahn School of Medicine at Mount Sinai (2003-Present); Assistant Attending Physician, Icahn School of Medicine at Mount Sinai (1982-Present); Assistant Professor, Icahn School of Medicine at Mount Sinai (1982-Present); Medical Practice Specializing in Dermatology, New York City, NY (1966-Present); Clinical Instructor, New York Medical College (1966-Present); Senior Clinical Instructor, Icahn School of Medicine at Mount Sinai (1970-1982); Senior Clinical Assistant, Mount Sinai Hospital (1970-1982); Instructor of Dermatology, Icahn School of Medicine at Mount Sinai (1966-1970); Clinical Assistant, Mount Sinai Hospital, New York City, NY (1966-1970); Research Fellow in Dermatology, Mount Sinai Hospital, New York City, NY (1966-1967); Chief Resident of Dermatology, Mount Sinai Hospital, New York City, NY (1965-1966) **Civic:** President, Mount Sinai Alumni (1995-1997); Vice President, Mount Sinai Alumni (1993-1995); Secretary, Mount Sinai Alumni (1991-1993); Treasurer, Mount Sinai Alumni (1988-1990); Alumni Fundraising Chairman, Horace Mann School (1976-1978) **Military Service:** Served to Major, Army Medical Corps Reserve (1969-1971) **Awards:** Maimonides Award, Keren Or Foundation for Handicapped Blind Children (1994); Torch of Liberty Award, Anti-Defamation League (1987); Fredrick Wise Dermatology Award, New York Academy of Medicine (1965); Lederle Research Fellow, New York Medical College **Membership:** Medical Advisory Board, Skin Cancer Foundation (1986-Present); Commodore, Lawrence Yacht Club (1987); Treasurer, Lawrence Yacht Club (1985); Secretary, Lawrence Yacht Club (1984); Fleet Surgeon, Lawrence Yacht Club (1982-1983); Board of Governors, Cornell Alumni Association of New York (1974-1976); Harvey Society; Society for Investigative Dermatology; Dermatology Foundation; Society for Tropical Dermatology; American Academy of Dermatology; Task Force on Therapeutics, American Academy of Dermatology; Food and Drug Administration Liaison Committee, American Academy of Dermatology; Communications Council, American Academy of Dermatology; Physicians Practice Committee, American Academy of Dermatology; American Medical Association; International Society of Human and Animal Mycology; New York Academy of Sciences; American Physicians Federation; Trustee, Executive Committee, American Physicians Federation; Life Member, Jewish Chautauqua Society; Dermatology Society of Greater New York; President, Dermatology Society of Greater New York; New York State Medical Society; Harmonie Club; Cornell Club; Friar's Club; Lawrence Yacht Club **Marquis Who's Who Honors:** Albert Nelson Marquis Lifetime Achievement Award (2017) **Religion:** Jewish **Business Address:** 1040 Park Ave, New York, NY, 10028 **Shipping Address:** 945 5th Ave Apt 3G, New York, NY, 10021 **Website:** http://dralbertlefkovits.com

Jennifer Lendl

Title: Psychologist **Industry:** Medicine & Health Care **Company Name:** Performance Enhancement Unlimited **Date of Birth:** 07/29/1951 **Place of Birth:** Santa Monica **State:** CA **Parents:** Gerald Lyle Lendl; Joyce Lucille (Devine) Lendl **Education:** PhD in Psychology, International College, Los Angeles (1984); MS in Psychology, San Jose State University (1982); MA in History, Stanford University (1975); AB in History, Stanford University (1973) **Certifications:** Diplomate, National Institute of Sports (2003); Diplomate, American Academy of Experts in Traumatic Stress (1999); Certified Therapist and Approved Consultant in Eye Movement Desensitization and Reprocessing (1999); Licensed Psychologist, State of California (1990); History Credential, California Chamber of Commerce (1976) **Career:** Private Practice, San Jose (1988-Present); Psychologist, Mare Island Nuclear Submarine Base, Vallejo, CA (1992); Psychologist, Family Service Center; Psychological Assistant, San Jose, CA (1982-1988); Lecturer, Department of Sociology, San Jose State University (1978-1984); Head Coordinator, Women's Center, San Jose State University (1978-1979) **Civic:** Member, Santa Clara County Sheriff's Advisory Committee for Women (1983); Assistant to Campaign Manager, Mayor Janet Gray Hayes Campaign for Reelection (1978); Student Member, California Community for Drug Rehabilitation (1969) **Awards:** Francine Shapiro Award for Outstanding Service and Contribution, Eye Movement Desensitization and Reprocessing International Association (2006); Woman of Achievement, San Jose Mercury News and Santa Clara County Women's Fund (1994); Scholar, National Institute of Mental Health (1979-1981); Kathryn Uhl Carr Scholar, California State University and College Board of Trustees (1979-1980); California State Scholar (1969-1973); Governor's Scholar, State of California (1969) **Membership:** Public Information Committee, California Psychological Association; Associate, American Psychological Association; California Association of Marriage and Family Therapists; Milton H. Erickson Foundation; Association for the Advancement of Applied Sport Psychology; National Institute of Sports; Lifetime Member, Stanford University Alumni Association; National Association of Professional Women; Lifetime Member, Stanford University Varsity Block S Association; Founding Member, Convention Committee, Eye Movement Desensitization and Reprocessing International Association (2001-Present); Government Relations Chair, Santa Clara County Psychological Association (1991-1992); Secretary of the Treasury, Division of Media Relations, California Psychological Association (1991-1992); Member-at-Large, Division of Media Relations, California Psychological Association (1990); Trauma Response Committee, Santa Clara Psychological Association (1989-1991) **Marquis Who's Who Honors:** Albert Nelson Marquis Lifetime Achievement Award (2017) **Hobbies:** Swimming; Great Danes; Home renovation; Dowsing **Shipping Address:** 1142 Mckendrie Street, San Jose, CA, 95126

Arthur Sol Leon

Title: Research Cardiologist, Exercise Physiologist **Industry:** Medicine & Health Care **Company Name:** University of Minnesota **Date of Birth:** 04/26/1931 **Place of Birth:** Brooklyn **State:** NY **Parents:** Alex Leon; Anne (Schrek) Leon **Marital Status:** Married **Spouse Name:** Gloria Rakita (12/23/1956) **Children:** Denise; Harmon; Michelle **Education:** Intern, Henry Ford Hospital (1957-1958); MD, University of Wisconsin (1957); MS in Biochemistry, University of Wisconsin (1954); BS in Chemistry, University of Florida, with High Honors (1952) **Career:** H.L. Taylor Professor of Exercise Science and Health Enhancement, University of Minnesota, Minneapolis, MN (1991-Present); Emeritus Director of Laboratory Physiological Hygiene and Exercise Science, Division of Kinesiology, University of Minnesota, Minneapolis, MN (1991-Present); Professor, Division of Epidemiology, University of Minnesota, Minneapolis, MN (1973-Present); Director of Applied Physiology and Nutrition, University of Minnesota, Minneapolis, MN (1973-1991); Director of Clinical Pharmacology Research Unit, Hoffmann-La Roche Inc., Newark Beth Israel Medical Center (1969-1973); Associate Professor of Medicine, College of Medicine and Dentistry, New Jersey (1967-1973); Fellow in Cardiology, Jackson Memorial Hospital, University of Miami Medical School, Florida (1960-1961); Fellow in Internal Medicine, Lahey Clinic (1958-1960) **Career Related:** Member, Medical Evaluation Team, Gemini Projects, NASA (1964-1967) **Civic:** Trustee, Vinland National Sports Health Center for Disabled (1978-Present); Member, Governor's Council of Physical Fitness and Sports (1979-1990) **Military Service:** Officer, Medical Corps, U.S. Army (1990-1991); Reserve Colonel, U.S. Army (1978-1992); Officer, Medical Corps, U.S. Army (1961-1967) **Creative Works:** Editor, "Proceedings of the National Institutes of Health Consensus Conference on Physical Activity and Cardiovascular Health" (1997); Associate Editor, "Surgeon General's Report on the Health Benefits of Exercise" (1996); Contributor, Articles, Professional Publications **Awards:** Presidential Award for Exercise Science Research, International Olympic Committee (1999); Award, American College of Sports Medicine (1995); Meritorious Service Medal, U.S. Army (1993); Citation Anderson Award, AAHPER (1981); Fellow, American Heart Association (1960-1961) **Membership:** Trustee, American Association of Cardiovascular and Pulmonary Rehabilitation (1989-1990); President, Hennepin County Division, American Heart Association (1982-1983); Trustee, American College of Sports Medicine (1982-1983); Vice President, Hennepin County Division, American Heart Association (1980-1981); Trustee, Minnesota Lung Association (1978-1981); Vice President, American College of Sports Medicine (1977-1979); Trustee, American College of Sports Medicine (1976-1978); President, Northland Chapter, American College of Sports Medicine (1975-1976); American Institute of Nutrition; Fellow, American College of Cardiology; American College of Chest Physicians; American College of Clinical Pharmacology; New York Academy of Sciences; American College of Nutrition; American Federation of Clinical Research; American Academy of Kinesiology and Physical Education; American Physiological Society; American Society of Pharmacology and Experimental Therapeutics; Phi Beta Kappa; Phi Kappa Phi **Marquis Who's Who Honors:** Albert Nelson Marquis Lifetime Achievement Award (2017) **Religion:** Jewish **Shipping Address:** 5628 Glen Ave, Minnetonka, MN, 55345

Thomas A. Leonard

Title: Lawyer **Industry:** Law and Legal Services **Company Name:** Obermayer Rebmann Maxwell & Hippel LLP **Date of Birth:** 09/05/1946 **Place of Birth:** Philadelphia **State:** PA **Parents:** Thomas Aloysius Leonard; Mary Teresa (Kelly) Leonard **Marital Status:** Married **Spouse Name:** Kathleen Mary Duffy **Children:** Sarah; Mary Kate; Tom **Education:** JD, Temple University (1971); BS, Drexel University (1968) **Career:** Chairman, Litigation Department, Obermayer Rebmann Maxwell & Hippel LLP, Philadelphia, PA (1991-Present); Senior Partner, Obermayer Rebmann Maxwell & Hippel LLP, Philadelphia, PA (1991-Present); Permanent Member, Management Committee, Obermayer Rebmann Maxwell & Hippel LLP, Philadelphia, PA (1991-Present); Controller, City of Philadelphia (1991-Present); Partner, Dilworth, Paxson, Kalish & Kauffman, Philadelphia, PA (1983-1991); Senior Partner, Dilworth, Paxson, Kalish & Kauffman, Philadelphia, PA (1979-1983); Member, Executive Committee, Dilworth, Paxson, Kalish & Kauffman, Philadelphia, PA (1979-1983); Partner, Dilworth, Paxson, Kalish & Kauffman, Philadelphia, PA (1976-1979); Associate, Dilworth, Paxson, Kalish & Kauffman, Philadelphia, PA (1972-1976) **Career Related:** Chairman, Delaware Valley Real Estate Investment Fund; Chairman, Crowley Chemical; Chairman, Permalith Plastics; Chairman, Hahnemann Hospital; Board Directors, Hahnemann Hospital; Board of Directors, U.S. Facilities, PRWT Services, Inc.; Board of Directors, World Affair Council of Philadelphia; Member, Board of Directors, Independence Blue Cross; Member, Board of Directors, Federal National Mortgage Association **Civic:** Board of Directors, World Trade Center of Greater Philadelphia (2003-Present); Chairman, Supreme Court of Pennsylvania (1996-Present); Vice-Chair of Finance, Democratic National Committee, Washington, DC (1993-Present); Chairman, Casey Senate Campaign (2012); Chairman, Casey Senate Campaign (2006); Board of Directors, TelAmerica LLC (2001-2008); Chairman, Pennsylvania Finance Committee, Clinton for President (1996); Delegate, Democratic National Convention (1996); Vice Chairman, Supreme Court of Pennsylvania (1995-1996); Co-Chairman, Rendell for Mayor (1995); Delegate, Democratic National Convention (1992); Co-Chairman, Rendell for Mayor (1991); Board of Directors, Democratic National Committee (1993-2000); Pennsylvania Finance Chair, Democratic National Committee (1993-2000); Chairman, Pennsylvania Finance Committee, Clinton for President (1992); Member, Disciplinary Board, Supreme Court of Pennsylvania (1991-1995); Member, Finance Committee, Democratic National Committee, Washington, DC (1988); Member, Council, Philadelphia Orchestra (1981-1986); Board of Directors, Academy of Sciences, Philadelphia, PA (1981-1985); Delegate, Democratic National Convention (1980); Member, Sinking Fund Commission, City of Philadelphia (1979-1983); Vice Chairman, Philadelphia Gas Commission (1979-1983); Register of Wills, City of Philadelphia (1976-1979); Member, Democratic National Committee, Washington, DC (1976-1983); Delegate, Democratic National Convention (1976); Board of Directors, PIDC (1975-1980); President, Pennsylvania Chapter, The Irish American Partnership **Military Service:** Captain, U.S. Army (1971-1977) **Creative Works:** Editorial Board Member, Amran's Pennsylvania Practice (1972); Contributor, Articles, Professional Journals **Awards:** Greater Philadelphia Area Leadership Award (2013); Learned Hand Award, American Jewish Committee (2010); Merit Award, Chapel of Four Chaplains (1983); Man of the Year Award, Korean-American Friendship Society (1982); Carmel Humanitarian Award, Haifa University (1981); Honoree, Emerald Society (1979) **Membership:** Board of Governors, Philadelphia Bar Association (1979-1982); ABA; Past President, Sierra Club; Racquet Club; Union League **Bar Admissions:** United States District Court, Southern District of New York; United States District Court of Utah; United States District Court Southern District of New Jersey; United States District Court, Eastern District of Pennsylvania; United States District Court, Middle District of Pennsylvania; United States District Court, Western District of Pennsylvania; United States Court of Appeals for the Third Circuit; Supreme Court of the United States; Pennsylvania Bar Association **Marquis Who's Who Honors:** Albert Nelson Marquis Lifetime Achievement Award (2017) **Religion:** Roman Catholic **Shipping Address:** 1500 Market St., Ste. 3400, Obermayer Rebmann Maxwell & Hippel LLP, Philadelphia, PA 19102

Brian Reid Lessing

Title: Senior Director and Actuary **Industry:** Insurance **Company Name:** AXA Equitable Life Insurance Company **Date of Birth:** 02/02/1954 **Place of Birth:** Miami **State:** FL **Parents:** Kenneth Oliver Ralph Lessing; Margaret (Takash) Lessing **Marital Status:** Single **Education:** MS, New York University (1979); AB, Princeton University, Magna Cum Laude (1976) **Certifications:** Certified Fellow of the Society of Actuaries (1989); Chartered Life Underwriter, American College (1992) **Career:** Senior Director and Actuary, AXA Equitable Life Insurance Co. (2012-Present); Vice President and Actuary, AXA Equitable Life Insurance Co. (1998-2012); From Actuarial Assistant to Vice President and Actuary, AXA Equitable Life Insurance Co. (1984-1998); Technical Assistant, Mutual of New York (1980-1984) **Career Related:** Adjunct Professor, Department of Finance and Risk Engineering, New York University Tandon School of Engineering (2011-Present); Adjunct Assistant Professor, The College of Insurance (1989-1991); Adjunct Instructor, New York Institute of Technology (1979); Adjunct Instructor, Pace University (1979-1980); Research Assistant, New York University (1976-1980) **Civic:** Church Council, Executive Committee, Community Church of New York (1984-1987); Financial Committee, Community Church of New York (1989-1999) **Awards:** Finalist AXA Innovation Award (2013); Phi Beta Kappa **Membership:** Member, American Academy of Actuaries, Society of Financial Service Professionals **To what do you attribute your success:** Mr. Lessing attributes his success to trying to understand things in his own terms and being able to help other people accomplish their goals. **Why did you become involved in your profession or industry:** He started out studying theoretical mathematics and gradually moved to applications of math to real-world financial problems. **Where will you be in five years:** Mr. Lessing hopes to experience continued professional growth, contribute to the actuarial field by actively participating on committees and work groups addressing industry issues, and continue teaching actuarial science at the university level. **Hobbies:** Reading; Physical Activity; Traveling; Arts and Music **Religion:** Unitarian Universalist **Shipping Address:** 405 Main St Apt 8R, New York, NY, 10044

Harold Powrie LeVander Jr.

Marquis Who's Who 18 98 Biographee

Title: Lawyer (Retired) **Industry:** Law and Legal Services **Date of Birth:** 08/28/1940 **Place of Birth:** St. Paul **State/Country of Origin:** MN **Parents:** Harold LeVander (Deceased); Iantha (Powrie) LeVander (Deceased) **Marital Status:** Married **Spouse Name:** Carla Ann Augst (11/15/1969) **Children:** Eric; Wade; Laura **Education:** JD, Harvard Law School (1965); BA in Political Science, Gustavus Adolphus College, Magna Cum Laude (1962); Coursework, Exchange Student, University of Minnesota, Soviet Union (Now Russia) (1961); Coursework, Exchange Student, American Field Service-United States of America Intercultural Program (Now AFS-USA), Germany (1957) **Career:** Retired (2015); Partner, Felhaber, Larson, Fenlon & Vogt (Now Felhaber Larson), St. Paul, MN (2000-2015); Partner, Maun & Simon, St. Paul, MN (1989-2000); Partner, LeVander Gillen Miller Anderson & Kuntz, South St. Paul, MN (1965-1988) **Civic:** Member, Governor's Council, Red River Valley Flood Control (1997); President, Svenska Sallskapet (Swedish Society) (1993-1994); Member, Board of Governors, The American National Red Cross (1988-1994); President, South St. Paul Rotary (Now Rotary Club of South St. Paul/Inver Grove Heights), Rotary International (1986-1987); Board Member, Minnesota Church Foundation (1985-2013); Chairman, St. Paul Area, The American National Red Cross (1985-1987); Board Member, Greater Gustavus Foundation (1978-1994); Delegate, Republican National Convention, Kansas City, MO (1976); Minnesota Chairman, President Ford Campaign (1976) **Awards:** Regional Award for Outstanding Service, National Rural Electric Cooperative Association (2006); WCCO-TV Good Neighbor Award (1995); Harriman Award, The American National Red Cross (1995); Honoree, Named One of the Outstanding Young Men of America, JCI Inc. (1972); Honoree, Named Super Lawyer, Minnesota Law and Politics **Membership:** Former Vice President, Board of Advisers, Electric Cooperative Bar Association (Now National Rural Electric Cooperative Association) (2000-2012); Former Representative, Lawyers Committee, Region Six, National Rural Electric Cooperative Association (1993-1996); Former Representative, Lawyers Committee, Region Six, National Rural Electric Cooperative Association (1986-1988); Former President, Dakota County Bar Association (1983-1986); Former Member, ABA; Former Member, Minnesota State Bar Association **Bar Admissions:** United States District Court for the District of Minnesota (1967); Minnesota State Bar Association (1965) **Marquis Who's Who Honors:** Albert Nelson Marquis Lifetime Achievement Award (2017) **To what do you attribute your success:** Mr. LeVander attributes his success to guidance from his parents and the support of his family. **Why did you become involved in your profession or industry:** Mr. LeVander once listened to his father deliver a final argument to a jury, and he knew without a doubt that he wanted to do that someday as well. **What do you consider to be the highlight of your career:** The highlight of Mr. LeVander's career was handling the regulatory work for the acquisition of Alliant Energy's Minnesota operations by twelve electric cooperatives from 2013-2015. It was the last project of his legal career. **Where will you be in five years:** In five years, Mr. LeVander will be playing squash, helping in the community and enjoying his family. **Hobbies:** Public Speaking; Tennis; Squash; Hunting; Politics **Political Affiliations:** Republican **Religion:** Lutheran **Shipping Address:** 1431 Palisade Path, Woodbury, MN, 55129

Bruce H. Levin

Title: Certified Pain Management Specialist **Industry:** Medicine & Health Care **Company Name:** Pennsylvania Spine and Headache Center **Education:** Residency in Anesthesiology, Albert Einstein College of Medicine, Bronx, NY (1985-1987); Internship, Internal Medicine, Stamford Hospital, Stamford, CT (1984-1985); MD, Albert Einstein College of Medicine at Yeshiva University (Now Albert Einstein College of Medicine) (1984); Diploma, Howard University (1980) **Certifications:** American Board of Addiction Medicine (2015); Recertification in Pain Medicine (2014); Subspecialty Certification in Pain Medicine, Certificate #15948 (2003); American Board of Anesthesiology (1988); Board Certified Pain Management Specialist; Medical License, Commonwealth of Pennsylvania; Medical License, State of New York; Medical License, State of Maryland; Medical License, State of Michigan **Career:** Pain Management Specialist, Pennsylvania Spine and Headache Center (2004-Present); Interventional Pain Management, Haverford Anesthesia (2002-2007); Interventional Pain Management, Private Practice Interventional Pain Management (2002-2004); Fellowship, Pain Management, New York University (2001-2002); Clinical Anesthesiologist, Albert Einstein Medical Center (1988-2001); Fellowship in Trauma and Obstetrical Anesthesiology, University of Miami Jackson Memorial Medical Center, Miami, FL (1987-1988) **Career Related:** MLS Physician Reviewer (2016-Present); Advisor of New Product Design, Martech Medical Products Inc. (2015-Present); Physician Reviewer, First Choice Evaluations (2015-Present); Consultant, New Project Development, Specialty Pharma Medical Components Inc. (2015-Present); Chief Medical Officer, IPMed Inc. (2014-Present); Consultant, Advanced Medical Reviews (2013-Present); Consultant, Physician Case Reviewer, MES Group (2010-Present); Consultant, Autonomic Technologies (2009-Present); Assistant Professor of Anesthesiology, School of Medicine, Thomas Jefferson University (2001); Consultant, Ausmedics, Marsam Pharmaceuticals, AstraZeneca (1988-2002); Assistant Professor of Anesthesiology, Lewis Katz School of Medicine, Temple University (1988-2000); Affiliated, Mercy Suburban Hospital, Norristown, PA; Affiliated, Sunbury Community Hospital, Sunbury, PA; Affiliated, Towanda Guthrie Memorial Hospital, Towanda, PA; Affiliated, Evangelical Community Hospital, Lewisburg, PA; Affiliated, Brandywine Hospital, Coatesville, PA **Awards:** Honoree, Top Doctor of North America, Who's Who Directories (2017); Honoree, Most Honored Top 5% Professionals, American Registry America's (2017); Honoree, Top 3% of Physicians Nationwide, Expert Network Distinguished Doctor (2015); Honoree, Leading Physicians in the World, Top Doctor (2015); Honoree, Top 10 Anesthesia Subspecialist (2014); Honoree, Pain Physician of the Year, American Registry (2014); Patients' Choice Award, Top 5% of Physicians Nationwide (2011-2014); Compassionate Doctor Recognition Award (2011-2014); AstraZeneca Pain Fellowship (1999); Distinguished Fellow Commendation, Albert Einstein College of Medicine (1987); Alaine Locke Award, Phi Beta Kappa; American Chemical Rubber Co. Award; Science Achievement Award, Herricks High School; Bausch & Lomb Science Medal, Herricks High School **Membership:** North American Spine Society; Pennsylvania Medical Society **Marquis Who's Who Honors:** Albert Nelson Marquis Lifetime Achievement Award (2017) **Shipping Address:** 3 N 2nd St., Ste 3, Bruce H Levin, MD, Philadelphia, PA, 19106 **Website:** https://drbrucelevin.wordpress.com/author/drbrucelevin/

I. Richard Levy

Title: Lawyer **Industry:** Law and Legal Services **Company Name:** I. Richard Levy PC **Date of Birth:** 04/19/1959 **Place of Birth:** Albuquerque **State/Country of Origin:** NM **Parents:** Joseph Leon Levy; Paula Maxine (Block) Levy **Marital Status:** Married **Spouse Name:** Kathryn Hasson (1997) **Children:** Steven Randall; Daniel Lawrence; Simon Michelle; Dena Raquel **Education:** JD, The University of Texas at Austin, with Honors (1986); BA in Political Science, Yale University, Cum Laude (1981); BA in Economics, Yale University, Cum Laude (1981) **Certifications:** Board Certified, American Board of Certification (2005); Board Certified in Business Bankruptcy Law, Texas Board of Legal Specialization (2005); Certified Preeminent Lawyers Bar Registry (1996) **Career:** Shareholder, I. Richard Levy PC (2003-2010, 2014-Present); Partner, Block & Garden, LLP (Now Block Garden & McNeill, LLP) (2011-2013); Shareholder, Gerard, Singer & Levick, Professional Corporation (1999-2003); Senior Associate, Gibson, Dunn & Crutcher LLP (1992-1999); Associate, Akin, Gump, Strauss, Hauer & Feld LLP (1986-1992); Teaching Quizmaster in Legal Research, The University of Texas at Austin (1985-1986); Writing Instructor, The University of Texas at Austin (1985-1986); Freshman Counselor, Timothy Dwight College, Yale University (1980-1981) **Civic:** Religious Educator, Temple Emanu-El (2000-2003, 2008-2012); Member, Board of Trustees, Temple Emanu-El (2005-2007); Chairman, Religious School Committee, Temple Emanu-El (2003-2006); Chairman, National School Public Relations Association (2003-2006); Vice President, The Yale Club of Dallas (2003-2005); Chairman, Alumni Schools Committee, Yale Club of Dallas (1992-2005); Den Leader, Pack 1077, Boy Scouts of America (1993-2000); Pack Committee Member, Pack 1077, Boy Scouts of America (1993-2000); Cubmaster, Pack 1077, Circle 10 District, Boy Scouts of America (1994-1998) **Awards:** Honoree, Texas Super Lawyer (2012-Present); Honoree, Bar Register of Preeminent Lawyers (1996-Present); Honoree, Outstanding Young Men in America (1989); Henry N. Mallon Scholarship, Yale University (1977-1981); Edward McGuire Gordon Cup Prize, Timothy Dwight College, Yale University (1981) **Membership:** Berzelius Senior Honor Society (1980-1981); ABA; American Bankruptcy Institute; Yale Alumni Association; Yale Alumni Schools Committee, Yale University; Temple Emanu-El **Bar Admissions:** United States Court of Appeals for the Fifth Circuit (1992); United States District Court Eastern District of Texas (1986); United States District Court Northern District of Texas (1986); United States District Court Southern District of Texas (1986); State Bar of Texas (1986) **Marquis Who's Who Honors:** Albert Nelson Marquis Lifetime Achievement Award (2017) **Why did you become involved in your profession or industry:** Mr. Levy became involved in his profession because as a child, he became very interested in law. He wanted to do something important to help people, also wanted to be creative and use his intellect. In high school, he was very lucky and went to Dallas magnet school. He ended up in the program of advanced social sciences. By his senior year, he was able to work as an assistant to a well known executive attorney in Dallas. This deepened his passion to get into the field. At Yale University, he studied political philosophies and majored in economics and learned about distribution of scarce resource. He wrote a paper on distribution systems. His passion is practices with creativity and knowledge. His profession compliments his love for art. **What do you consider to be the highlight of your career:** A highlight of his career are his 30+ years of interviewing students who have applied to Yale University and finding people who wouldn't have had an opportunity unless they got a good report from a Yale University alumni. **Hobbies:** Politics; History; Art; Golf; Physics; Cosmology; Furniture refinishing; Home improvement **Shipping Address:** 16314 Shadybank Dr, Dallas, TX, 75248

Leslie A. Levy

Title: President, Secretary **Industry:** Business Management/Business Services **Company Name:** Directors Data, Inc. **Date of Birth:** 12/25/1941 **Place of Birth:** New York **State:** NY **Parents:** Paul Bauman; Ruth Candace (Tachna) Bauman **Marital Status:** Single **Spouse Name:** Marc Gersan Gerard Levy (10/1962, Divorced) **Children:** Benjamin Gerard Levy; Remy Marcel Gerard Levy **Education:** DBA, Harvard University, Boston, MA (1980); MBA, Harvard University, Boston, MA (1976); Coursework in Philosophy, University of California, Los Angeles (1962-1963); BA in Philosophy and History, Smith College, Summa Cum Laude, Northampton, MA (1962) **Career:** President, Director, Treasurer, Secretary, Directors, Data, Inc. (1998-Present); President, Secretary, Life Choices and Death Wishes (1990-Present); President, Chief Executive Officer, Academy for Corporate Governance, Fordham University Graduate School of Business (1990-1991); Assistant Professor of Management Policy and Industry Analysis, Board of Directors, Case Western Reserve University, Cleveland, OH (1981-1984); Senior Research Associate, Harvard School of Business Administration, Boston, MA (1979-1981); President, Commonwealth Collaborative, Inc., Cambridge, FL, Sarasota, FL (1976-1999); Teaching Assistant in Philosophy, University of California, Los Angeles (1962-1963) **Career Related:** Senior Advisor, President, Director, Institute Research on Board Directors (1998-Present); Product Announcement Team Member, Honeywell Information Systems (1975); Acting Department Manager, Document Control Department, Honeywell Information Systems (1974); Supervisor, Release Control, Document Control Department, Honeywell Information Systems (1974); Project Manager, Publications Documentation Interface Project, Honeywell Information Systems (1972-1974); Staff Member, Document Control Department, Honeywell Information Systems (1973); Senior Technical Writer, Engineering Publications Department, Honeywell Information Systems (1972-1973); Associate Engineer, Design Automation Department, Honeywell Information Systems (1971-1972); Programmer-Analyst, Administrative Computing Group, Stanford University (1969-1971); Contract Programmer (1968-1969) **Creative Works:** Columnist, "Directors and Boards" (1996-1997); Author, "Director Motivation: Incentives and Disincentives to Board Service" (1996); Author, "Significant Issues Facing Directors" (1996); Host, Session Presentation to ASCS Essentials of the Corporate Secretary Function (1994); Author, "Forecasting the Future of Corporate Governance" (1994); Corporate Governance Advisor, The Debate Over Corporate Governance (Insights) Performance (1993); Author, "Separate Chairmen of the Board: Their Roles, Legal Liabilities, and Compensation" (1982); Contributor, More than 100 Articles to Professional Journals; Co-Author, "Life Choices and Death Wishes"; Author, "Blow Up in the Boardroom (A) and (B)"; Author, "Legal Shields Still Leave Directors Vulnerable"; Contributor, Numerous Letters to the Editor, New York Times; Author, "Special Report: Separate Chairmen of the Board: Their Roles, Legal Liabilities, and Compensation"; Author, "Recruiting Directors for Small Company Boards"; Author, "Surveying Directors' Views is a Bad Idea"; Author, "Will Investor Pressure on Boards Improve the Corporate Bottom-Line?"; Creator, Honeywell: The RTL System (and Leveraged Leasing Program); Author, "Board Secrets: Should They Be Told?"; Author, "Corporate Governance Annotated Bibliography"; Author, "Serving More than One Master"; Author, "Helping the CEO to Retire Gracefully"; Host, "Directors Data: The Gold Standard for Board and Governance Information & Practice," Presentation to Bob Kirby and Other Senior Managers at Capital Group; Author, "Course Design: The Board of Directors of the Large, Publicly Held Company (Policy 434)"; Author, "Course Description for Teachers"; Author, "Director Monitoring Has its Limits"; Author, "How to Evaluate a Conceptual Framework"; Author, "Corporate Strategy and the Board"; Author, "Deciding on the Role of the Corporate Secretary"; Author, "Marcel (A) through (E)" **Membership:** Business Law Division, American Bar Association; American Bar Association; ACLU; Society for Corporate Governance; Affiliate, National Association of Corporate Directors; Academy Management (Article Reviewer); National Association of Corporate Directors; National Investor Relations Institute; Affiliate, Central Florida Chapter, Institute of Directors; Former Member, Society for Corporate Compliance & Ethics; Former Member, Yale Governance Forum; Institutional Corporate Governance Network; Federalist Society; Harvard Club of Sarasota; American Jewish Committee; Former Member, American Jewish Congress; Tampa Bay Committee of Foreign Relations **Marquis Who's Who Honors:** Marquis Who's Who Lifetime Achievement Award (2017) **Political Affiliations:** Center **Religion:** Jewish, Unitarian, Zen, Christian **Shipping Address:** 6754 W. Country Club Lane, Sarasota, FL, 34243

Jonathan Lewis, PhD

Title: Surgeon, Biomedical Researcher, Oncologist, Entrepreneur **Industry:** Medicine & Health Care **Company Name:** Molecular Ninja, Samus Therapeutics **Date of Birth:** 05/23/1958 **Place of Birth:** Johannesburg **Country of Origin:** South Africa **Parents:** Myer Philip Lewis; Maisie (Bagg) Lewis **Marital Status:** Married **Education:** PhD, Yale University (1990); BMBS, University of the Witwatersrand, Johannesburg, South Africa (1982) **Career:** Chief Executive Officer, Chairman, Samus (2016-Present); Chief Executive Officer, Chairman, Molecular Ninja (2015-Present); Attending Surgeon, Memorial Sloan Kettering Cancer Center, New York, NY (1994-Present); Chairman, Chief Executive Officer, President, Ziopharm, New York, NY (2004-2015); Chairman, Joint Committee, Ziopharm-Intrexon (2004-2015); Fellow, Department of Surgery, Memorial Sloan Kettering Cancer Center, New York, NY (1992-1994); Chief Resident of Surgery, Yale School of Medicine, New Haven, CT (1990-1992); Postdoctoral Associate, Yale School of Medicine, New Haven, CT (1987-1990); Registrar of Surgery, School of Medicine, University of the Witwatersrand, Johannesburg, South Africa (1982-1987) **Career Related:** Chief Medical Officer, Antigenics Inc., New York, NY (2000-2003); Professor, Weill Cornell Medical College (Now Weill Cornell Medicine) (1999-2001); Medicine Memorial Sloan Kettering Cancer Center, New York, NY (1999-2001); Surgery Memorial Sloan Kettering Cancer Center, New York, NY (1994-1999); Professor of Surgery, Weill Cornell Medical College (1994-1999); Fellow, American College of Surgeons; Fellow, Royal Society of Medicine; Fellow, Royal College of Surgeons **Civic:** Board Member, Combat Wound Initiative and Limb Salvage Program, HJF; Chairman, Science Advisory Council, Hope Funds for Cancer Research; Chairman, Board of Trustees, Hope Funds for Cancer Research; Board Member, POPPA (NYPD) **Creative Works:** Contributor, Articles, Professional Journals; Contributor, Book Chapters, Books **Awards:** Brennan Award, KACR (2010); Vision of Hope Award, Sarcoma Foundation of America (2009); Outstanding Teacher Award, Memorial Sloan Kettering Cancer Center (1997); Winston Fellowship, Sloan Kettering Institute, Memorial Sloan Kettering Cancer Center (1994-1995); Traveling Fellowship Award, Association for Cancer Research (1994); Young Investigator Award, the American Society of Clinical Oncology (1994); Ohse Award, Yale University (1989); Trubshaw Medal, College of Surgeons, the Colleges of Medicine of South Africa, Johannesburg, South Africa (1984); Abelheim Medal, South African Medical Research Council (1982); Sulliman Medal in Physiology (1979) **Membership:** Board Member, Yale Biotechnology Society; Chairman, Sweet Rexies LLC; American Society of Hematology; The New York Academy of Sciences; Society of Surgical Oncology; Association of Academy Surgeons; American Society of Clinical Oncology; American Association for Cancer Research; American Society for Cell Biology **Marquis Who's Who Honors:** Albert Nelson Marquis Lifetime Achievement Award (2017); Distinguished Humanitarian (2017) **Why did you become involved in your profession or industry:** Dr. Lewis was inspired by a love of people, biology, and mathematics. **What do you consider to be the highlight of your career:** Dr. Lewis' shining achievement was convincing a hospital and associated lawyers to allow him to perform an eight-hour operation on a woman who had been left to die at another hospital. She was an immigrant and had no insurance. He successfully saved her life, and she came back to thank him 22 years later. He passed on those values to his children and was able to show them the right thing to do and what is worth fighting for. **Where will you be in five years:** Dr. Lewis wants to be an outstanding role model and inspiration for his children and all children. **Religion:** Jewish **Shipping Address:** 125 Hillandale Road, Westport, CT, 06880

Genyuan Li, PhD

Title: Research Chemist **Industry:** Sciences **Company Name:** Princeton University **Date of Birth:** 09/21/1938 **Place of Birth:** Chengdu **Country of Origin:** China **Marital Status:** Married **Spouse Name:** Shugui Zhang **Children:** Chuan Li **Education:** PhD, Princeton University (1990) **Career:** Research Chemist, Princeton University (1999-Present); Researcher, Princeton University (1993-1999); Research Associate, Princeton University (1990-1993); Instructor, Beijing University of Chemical Technology (1980-1985); Researcher, Beijing Research Institute of Chemical Technology (1959-1980) **Creative Works:** Author, "Model Reduction: Lumping of Chemical Kinetic Equations" **Marquis Who's Who Honors:** Albert Nelson Marquis Lifetime Achievement Award (2017) **Business Address:** Princeton University, Frick Laboratory, Princeton University, Frick Laboratory, Princeton, NJ, 08544 **Shipping Address:** 7 Monmouth Street, Plainsboro, NJ, 08536

Arthur F. Licata

Title: Lawyer **Industry:** Law and Legal Services **Company Name:** Arthur F. Licata, PC **Date of Birth:** 06/16/1947 **Place of Birth:** New York **State:** NY **Education:** JD, Suffolk University, Cum Laude (1976); Postgraduate, State University of New York, Binghamton (1969-1971); BA in English, Le Moyne College (1969) **Career:** Principal, Arthur F. Licata Professional Corporation, Boston, MA (1982-Present); Associate, Parker, Coulter, Daley & White, Boston, MA (1977-1982) **Career Related:** Guest, WGBH-Ch 2 TV, Greater Boston with Emily Rooney (2012); WCRNAM Radio Guest Lecturer, Massachusetts Institute of Technology (2011); Guest Lecturer, Ethics and Robotics, Massachusetts Institute of Technology (2011); Congress Fellow, Center for International Legal Studies, Salzburg, Austria (2004); Guest, WGBH-Ch 2 TV, Greater Boston with Emily Rooney (2001); Chair, Seminar, Massachusetts Continuing Legal Education (2000); Guest, WGBH-Ch 2 TV, Greater Boston with Emily Rooney (1999); Speaker, Harvard University, Conference on Proposed Tobacco Settlement and Tort Law (1997); Delegate, White House Conference on Trade and Investment in Central Europe (1995); Russian Children's Fun (1992-1994); Estonia Academy for Public Safety (1992-1994); Co-Sponsor, Estonian Legal Delegate Visit to Massachusetts and New Hampshire Correctional Institutions (1990); Legal Advisor, Czech Anglo-American Business Institute (1989-2005); Principle, Eastern and Central Europe and Russia, Ardlee International Trading Company (1989-1999); Host, Former Soviet Legal Delegate Visit (1989); Speaker, Convention on National Federation of Paralegal Associations (1987); Delegate, US-China Joint Session on Trade, Investment and Economic Law (1987); Working Group on Drinking and Drunk Driving, Harvard School of Public Health Center for Health Communications (1986); Trial Advisory Committee (1984-1988); Lecturer, Massachusetts Continuing Legal Education (1982-2001); Participant, U.S.-Russian Investment Symposium **Civic:** Participant, Harvard Law School Seminar Program on Negotiation and Mediation (2000-2001); Board of Directors, Boston Center for the Arts (1990-1994); U.S. Delegate, Sixth People to People Juvenile Justice Program to USSR, Moscow, Russia (1989); Professional Advisory Board, Massachusetts Epilepsy Association (1986-1993); State Advisory Committee, Medical Malpractice, Boston, MA (1985); Legal Advisor, Massachusetts Chapter, MADD, Plymouth County (1984-1987); Counsel, State Coordinator Commission, MADD (1984-1986) **Creative Works:** Panel Member, Station WBZ-TV, Boston, MA; Contributor, Articles, Professional Journals **Awards:** Super Lawyer, Boston Magazine (2010-Present); ACQ Global Award (2016); Boston Top Rated Lawyers (2014); Superlawyers.com, Massachusetts (2009-2013); Super Lawyer, Boston Magazine (2006); Sacred Angelic Imperial Constantinian Order of Saint George, Duke of Parma, Italy (2000); Outstanding Citizen Award, MADD (1986); Top Ten Attorney Award, National Academy Personal Injury Attorneys Inc. **Membership:** Executive Committee, Board of Directors (2009-2013); Board Certified Civil Trial Advisor, National Board of Trial Advocacy (1992-2012); Board of Directors, Massachusetts Academy of Trial Attorneys (1991-1999); Massachusetts Bar Foundation; American Association of Justice **Bar Admissions:** Frank B. Murray, Junior Inns of Court (1990-1992); State of New York (1985); State of Massachusetts (1977); First Circuit, U.S. Court of Appeals (1977); U.S. District Court, State of Massachusetts (1977) **To what do you attribute your success:** Mr. Licata attributes his success to perseverance. **Hobbies:** Aviation **Shipping Address:** 12 Post Office Square, Floor 2, Arthur F. Licata, P.C., Boston, MA, 02109 **Website:** https://aboutthelaw.wordpress.com

Alfred R. Light

Title: Law Educator **Industry:** Law and Legal Services **Company Name:** St. Thomas University School of Law **Date of Birth:** 12/14/1949 **Parents:** Alfred M. Light, Jr.; Margaret Francis (Asbury) Light **Marital Status:** Married **Spouse Name:** Mollie Sue Hall (5/28/1977) **Children:** Joseph Robert; Gregory Andrew **Education:** JD, Harvard University, Cum Laude (1981); PhD, University of North Carolina (1976); BA, Johns Hopkins University, with Highest Honors (1971); Coursework, Georgia Institute of Technology (1967-1969) **Career:** Professor, St. Thomas University School of Law, Miami, FL (1993-Present); Of Counsel (1995-1996); Associate Professor, St. Thomas University School of Law, Miami, FL (1989-1993); Of Counsel (1989-1993); Hunton & Williams, Richmond, VA (1981-1989); Associate, Bracewell & Patterson, Washington, DC (1980); Associate, Butler, Binion, Rice, Cook & Knapp, Houston, TX (1980); Research Assistant, Graduate School of Education, Harvard University (1978-1979); Assistant Professor in Political Science, Research Scientist, Center for Energy Research, Texas Tech University, Lubbock, TX (1977-1978); Research Assistant, Institute of Research in Social Science (1975-1977); Program Analyst, Office of Secretary Defense (1974); Research and Teaching Assistant, Department of Political Science, University of North Carolina, Chapel Hill (1971-1974); Clerk, Typist Systems Management Division, Defense Contract Administrative, Defense Supply Agency, Atlanta, GA (1971); Warehouse Assistant, State of Georgia Mines, Mining and Geology (1970); Lab Technician, Custom Farm Services Soils Testing Lab (1968); Tax Clerk, IRS (1967) **Career Related:** Director, LLM Program in Environmental Sustainability (2010-Present); Board of Advisors, Toxics Law Reporter, Bureau of National Affairs, Washington, DC (1987-Present); Adjunct Professor, University of Miami School of Law (2008); Interim Dean (1993-1994) **Civic:** Charter Member, West Broward Community; Church Member, First Baptist Church, Weston, CT **Military Service:** Captain, US Army Reserve (1971-1985) **Creative Works:** Contributor, Articles to Professional Journals **Awards:** Certificate Award, Corporate Sustainability (2012-Present); Award, United States Environmental Protection Agency (2003-2006); Award, Center of Energy Research, Texas Tech University (1977-1978); William Anderson Award, American Political Science Association (1977); Grantee, National Science Foundation; Institute of Evaluation Research, University of Massachusetts **Membership:** Vice Chair, Committee on Smart Growth and Green Building (2011-2013); Board of Directors, Association of Climate Change Officers (2010-2014); Chairman, ABA (1995-2000); National Resource and Environmental Section, ABA (1993-1995); Tort and Insurance Practice Section, ABA (1988-1997); LEED Green Associate; Federal Bar Association; Phi Beta Kappa; Phi Eta Sigma; Vice Chairman, ABA; First Baptist Church of Weston **Bar Admissions:** Virginia (1982); Washington, DC (1981) **Hobbies:** Baseball **Political Affiliations:** Republican **Shipping Address:** 1042 Woodfall Court, Weston, FL, 33326

Dorothy Lincoln-Smith

Title: Vocalist, Professor **Industry:** Fine Art **Date of Birth:** 05/03/1936 **Place of Birth:** Lansing **State:** IA **Parents:** Harold J. Ashbacher; Louise Scharping Ashbacher **Marital Status:** Single **Spouse Name:** Harvey K. Smith (3/5/1976, Deceased 2012); Joseph C. Lincoln (7/25/1970, Deceased 1975) **Children:** Kerstan Louise Lincoln; Lisa Marianne Lincoln; Camille Lincoln Paulin (Stepchild); John C. Lincoln (Stepchild); Gregory Lincoln (Stepchild); Bruce Lincoln (Stepchild); Harvey K. Smith, II (Stepchild); Mark Russell Smith (Stepchild) **Education:** EdD, Arizona State University (1973); MusM, Arizona State University (1964); BS in Music Education, Cornell College (1958) **Certifications:** Certified Advanced Scuba Diver, PADI; Certified Iron Driver **Career:** Soloist, Christian Science First Church, Phoenix, AZ (1994-Present); Tour Coordinator, Phoenix Boys Choir (1976-1999); Vocal Coach, Phoenix Boys Choir (1976-1999); Soloist, Phoenix Boys Choir (1976-1999); Professor, Phoenix College (1973-2003); Singer, Roger Wagner Chorale (1966-1969); Teacher, Maryvale High School (1964-1968); Singer, Soloist, Arizona Opera and Bach Society (1959-1967); Professor, Singer, Glendale Community College **Career Related:** Board Member, Arizona District, The Metropolitan Opera National Council (1999-Present); Associate Director, Arizona District, The Metropolitan Opera National Council (1999-Present); Board Member, Scottsdale Arts (1999-Present); Member, Advisory Board, Phoenix Boys Choir (1985-Present); President, Board of Trustees, National Society of Arts and Letters (2016-2018); National President, National Society of Arts and Letters (2014-2016); Board Member, National Association of Teachers of Singing, Inc. (1999-2003); Trustee, San Francisco Theological School (1980-1985) **Civic:** Board of Directors, Scottsdale Arts (2005-Present); Episcopalian Lay Eucharistic Minister (1995-Present); Vestry, Saint Barnabas on the Desert (2004-2006) **Creative Works:** Co-Author, "Singing and Growing" (1984); Co-Author, "Singing and Growing" (1981); Dorothy Lincoln-Smith Voice Competition **Awards:** Distinguished Achievement Award, Cornell College Alumni Association (2018); Longtime Service Honor, Scottsdale Arts (2017); Philanthropy Award, State of Arizona (2016); Rose Of Honor, Sigma Alpha Iota (2000) **Membership:** Chapter President, National Society of Arts and Letters (2005-Present); Executive Board, National Society of Arts and Letters (1973-Present); National Music Chairman, National Society of Arts and Letters (2004); Auditions Chairman, National Association of Teachers of Singing, Inc. (1976-2003); Phoenix Art Museum; Scottsdale Museum of Contemporary Art; Ballet Arizona; Heard Museum **Marquis Who's Who Honors:** Albert Nelson Marquis Lifetime Achievement Award (2017) **To what do you attribute your success:** Dr. Lincoln-Smith attributes her success to working hard on the farm in Iowa where she grew up, and attending Cornell College. **Why did you become involved in your profession or industry:** Becoming involved in her profession was a "no-brainer" for Dr. Lincoln-Smith. She sang to the pigs and cows when she was three years old. **What do you consider to be the highlight of your career:** Several highlights stand out in Dr. Lincoln-Smith's career, including being a soprano soloist with the Phoenix Boys Choir, being a guest soloist for Sir David Willcocks in 1998, singing a faculty recital with Roger Wagner and singing with a chamber orchestra in 1969, and being a soprano soloist for the Phoenix Symphony Chorale. **Where will you be in five years:** In five years, Dr. Lincoln-Smith plans to continue promoting young singers through the DLS Classical Voice Competition through the National Society of Arts and Letters and lecturing in modern art collections. Another goal is to achieve 1,000 scuba dives and she is currenly at 849. **Hobbies:** Scuba diving **Political Affiliations:** Republican **Religion:** Episcopalian **Shipping Address:** 3228 E San Miguel Place, Paradise Valley, AZ, 85253

Eric Everett Lindstrom

Title: Ophthalmologist **Industry:** Medicine & Health Care **Company Name:** Lindstrom Eye and Laser Center **Date of Birth:** 11/28/1936 **Place of Birth:** Helena **State:** MT **Parents:** Everett Harry Lindstrom; Nan Augusta (Johnson) Lindstrom **Marital Status:** Married **Spouse Name:** Nancy Jo Alexander (7/24/1960) **Children:** Laura Ann; Eric Everett **Education:** MPH, Harvard University (1966); Intern, Madigan Army Medical Center, Tacoma, WA (1963-1964); MD, University of Maryland (1963); BS, Wheaton College (1958) **Certifications:** Diplomate, American Board of Preventive Medicine; Diplomate, American Board of Ophthalmology **Career:** Lindstrom Eye Clinic (1987-Present); Assistant Chief, Ophthalmology Clinic, Madigan Army Medical Center, Tacoma, WA (1975-1976); Medical Director, Palo Pinto County Mental Health Clinic (1970-1972); Chief, Professional Services and Aviation Medicine, Beach Army Hospital, Fort Wolters, TX (1969-1972) **Career Related:** Chairman, Board of Trustees, South Central Regional Medical Center (1982-2001); Consultant, Texas State Rehabilitation Committee (1971-1972); Fellow, American College of Surgeons; Associate Fellow, Aerospace Medical Association; Fellow, American Academy of Ophthalmology **Civic:** Deacon First Baptist Church, Laurel, MS (1978-Present); Board of Directors, Laurel Salvation Army; Board of Directors, Good Shepherd Medical and Dental Clinic; Board of Trustees, William Carey University, Hattiesburg, MS **Military Service:** Surgeon, 12th Combat Aviation Group, U.S. Army, Vietnam (1968-1969); Senior Aviation Medical Examiner; FAA Flight Surgeon, Mississippi Air National Guard **Awards:** Decorated Bronze Star; Air Medal With Two Oak Leaf Clusters; Meritorious Service Medal **Membership:** American College of Physician Executives; American College of Preventive Medicine; American Medical Association; American Academy of Cataract and Refractive Surgery; New Orleans Academy of Ophthalmology; President, Mississippi Medical Association; South Mississippi Medical Society; President, Southern Medical Association; Flying Physicians Association; Society of Military Ophthalmologists; Society of the U.S. Air Force and U.S. Army Flight Surgeons; Alliance of Air National Guard Flight Surgeons; Military Officers Association of America; Aircraft Owners and Pilots Association; Kiwanis; Nu Sigma Nu **Marquis Who's Who Honors:** Albert Nelson Marquis Lifetime Achievement Award (2017) **Religion:** Protestant **Shipping Address:** 809 Cherry Lane, Laurel, MS, 39440

Marcella E. Lingham

Title: Chief Executive Officer **Industry:** Medicine & Health Care **Company Name:** Quality Community Health Care, Inc. **Date of Birth:** 01/15/1942 **Place of Birth:** Philadelphia **State:** PA **Parents:** Harry Boyd Lawson; Gladys Marcella Lawson **Education:** PhD in Education and Sociology, Rutgers, The State University of New Jersey (1980); MS in Education, Temple University (1970); BS in Secondary Education and History, Cheyney University (1965); Coursework, Temple University (1960-1962) **Career:** Executive Director, 2501 Primary Community Health Care Center, Inc. (1986-Present); Learning Specialist, Rutgers School of Nursing (1985-1986); Project Director, Mantua Community Development Corporation (1984-1985); Executive Director, Primary Community Health Center of Mantua, Inc. (1983-1984); Assistant Professor, Rutgers University Newark College of Arts and Sciences (1980-1983); Project Director, Curriculum Developer, Educational Consultant, Research for Better Schools, Inc., Philadelphia, PA (1972-1979); Curriculum Development Specialist, Reading Specialist, RCA Service Company, Cherry Hill, NJ (1970-1972); Teacher, School District of Philadelphia (1965-1970) **Career Related:** Vice Chairperson, Board of Directors, 2501 Health Care Corporation, Philadelphia, PA (1980-1983); Board of Directors, Black Family Services; Panel, American Education Research Association Annual Conference **Awards:** Recipient, Recognition Award **Membership:** Association of Supervision and Curriculum Development; American Public Health Association; American Association of University Women; International Reading Association; American Educational Research Association; Alpha Kappa Alpha Sorority, Inc.; Association of Fundraising Professional **To what do you attribute your success:** Dr. Lingham attributes her success to her hard work and having a sense of what she likes to do. **Why did you become involved in your profession or industry:** Dr. Lingham became involved in her profession because she was a board member and educator when this community health center started. She was finishing undergraduate school when people were marching for younger blacks to have their rights. Her parents told her she could do that as soon as she finished school, and she promised herself that she would give back to her community. She started giving back by being on the family board for her organization and has been there ever since. Part of the responsibility is helping people be able to grow and utilize the skill they have acquired so that you have the option of having a career. **Where will you be in five years:** In five years, Dr. Lingham aspires to keep the organization up-to-date with all the new changes likely to come up. **Hobbies:** Spending time with her family and friends; Reading; Theater **Political Affiliations:** Democrat **Religion:** Baptist **Shipping Address:** 8446 Suffolk Pl, Philadelphia, PA, 19153

Richard G. Linowes

Title: Management Educator **Industry:** Business Management/Business Services **Company Name:** American University **Date of Birth:** 01/29/1951 **Place of Birth:** Washington **State:** DC **Parents:** David Francis Linowes; Dorothy Lee (Wolf) Linowes **Marital Status:** Married **Spouse Name:** Elisa M. Gropper (4/8/2000) **Children:** Selia Josephine Marie; Jeremiah Robinson Camille; Dahlia Hannah; Nathaniel Joseph **Education:** DBA, Harvard University (1984); MS in Computer and Communication Sciences, University of Michigan (1975); AB in Cybernetics, Princeton University (1973) **Certifications:** Baldrige National Quality Award Examiner (1994) **Career:** Founding Professor, Clarewood University, Reston, VA (2016-Present); Kogod Outstanding Professor, Undergraduate Programs, Kogod School of Business, American University, Washington, DC (1986-Present); Visiting Professor, Tel Aviv University, Tel Aviv, Israel (2016); Visiting Professor, Ritsumeikan University, Kyoto, Japan (2010); Professor, Israel School for Enterprise Management and Innovation (1999-2008), Consulting Services, Goldman Sachs, New York, NY (1983-1986); Research Assistant, Harvard Business School, Boston, MA (1978-1982); Senior Systems Analyst, Arthur Andersen & Co., Washington, DC (1975-1977); Management kenshusei, Matsushita Electric Industrial Company, Ltd., Osaka, Japan (1974) **Career Related:** Educator, Foreign Services Institute, United States Department of State (2003-Present); Adjunct Professor, New York University (1985-1986); Consultant, Baldrige National Quality Award Programs, Education Pilot Team **Civic:** Member, Greater Washington Area Board of Trade (1987-Present); Volunteer, Local Schools; Organizer, Sustainability Management Program, American University, Washington, DC; Member, Shaare Torah, Germantown, MD; Vice President, Homeowners Association **Creative Works:** Co-Author, "Enablers of Knowledge Creation in Japanese and United States-Based Firms" (2011); Editor, "Portraits of Small Business from the Developing World, Management Casebooks, Volumes One through Five" (1994-2010); Contributing Author, "Emerging Trends in Japanese Business" (1994); Host, "The Japanese Manager's Traumatic Entry into the United States", Academy of Management Executive (1993); Featured, PBS Program, "Writing Across the Curriculum" (1993); Host, "Getting Down to Business," Voice of America (1992-1994); Contributing Author, "Japanese Direct Investment in the United States" (1992); Contributing Author, "Catching Up with the Computer Revolution," Harvard Business Review (1983); Contributing Author, With R.F. Vancil, "Decentralization" (1979); Contributor, Articles to Professional Journals; Creator, Experiential Exercises Offering New Approaches to Management Education, Conceptual Frameworks for Managing Five Layers of Complexity of International Business, Globalization of American and Japanese Firms; Author, "Design of American and Japanese Bicultural Work Teams" **Awards:** Fulbright Fellowship for Pedagogical Innovation, New Zealand (1989) **Membership:** Academy of Management, International Personnel Association; International Public Management for Human Resources; Association of Japanese Business Studies; Fulbright Association; Princeton Club; Harvard Club **Marquis Who's Who Honors:** Albert Nelson Marquis Lifetime Achievement Award (2017) **To what do you attribute your success:** Dr. Linowes attributes his success, in part, to his Ivy League education, which he spent studying mathematics, philosophy, engineering, computer science and psychology. **Why did you become involved in your profession or industry:** Dr. Linowes became involved in his profession because he excelled at mathematical and conceptual work and yearned to find connections between disciplines. He was inspired by the older generation of his family, which included very successful men that held prominent positions in business, law, medicine and diplomacy. Their high integrity and accomplishment set the standard for him to follow in their footsteps. Dr. Linowes endeavors to help prevent unethical behavior in the business world. His mission statement is to "build enlightened leaders." One of his most important lessons he gives to students is to strive to maintain unquestioned integrity. **What do you consider to be the highlight of your career:** The highlight of Dr. Linowes' career was the inaugural meeting of the Kogod Alumni Network of Greater New York, where 30 former students gathered around him at a huge dinner table. He also values the extensive traveling trips that he took to visit American and Japanese companies and meeting with former students around the globe during these excursions. **Where will you be in five years:** In five years, Dr. Linowes plans to be president of Clarewood University. **Hobbies:** Public speaking; Landscaping; Photography; Singing; Travel; Stamp collecting; Cross-cultural encounters **Religion:** Jewish **Business Address:** 4400 Massachusetts Ave NW, Washington, DC, 20016 **Shipping Address:** 17505 Carlson Farm Ct, Germantown, MD, 20874 **Website:** https://www.american.edu/kogod/faculty/linowes.cfm

Verna May Linzey

Title: Minister **Industry:** Religious **Company Name:** Holy Spirit Evangelism **Date of Birth:** 05/19/1919 **Place of Birth:** Coffeyville **State:** KS **Year of Passing:** 2017-05-17 **Parents:** Carey Franklin Hall, Jr.; Alice May (Hart) Hall-Doyle **Spouse Name:** Stanford Eugene Linzey, Jr. (7/13/1941, Deceased) **Children:** Gena May English; Janice Ellen Mathis; Stanford Eugene III; Virginia Darnelle Lemons; Sharon Faye Ackerman; George **Education:** Honorary DD, Kingsway University (2001); Coursework, Fuller Theological Seminary (1978-1980); Coursework, Southwestern Assembly of God University (1938-1939) **Certifications:** Licensed Minister, The General Council of the Assemblies of God (1945) **Career:** Co-Founder, Holy Spirit Evangelism (1976-Present); Co-Pastor, First Assembly Of God Church, Baldwin Park, CA (1953-1954) **Career Related:** Consultant, Holy Spirit Evangelism (1976-Present); Featured Guest, Prime Time Christian Broadcasting Network (2004); Featured Guest, Public Broadcasting Service (2004); Leader, Pentecostal Movement Worldwide (1945-2016); Founding Pastor, El Cajon Evangelistic Tabernacle, El Cajon, CA **Civic:** Member, Advisory Board, Operation Freedom, LLC (2003-Present); Member, Republican National Committee (1946-Present); Leader, Azusa Street Revival (2012); Bonnie Brae Street Revival (2012); Member, Democratic National Committee (1943-1945) **Creative Works:** Author, "The Gifts of the Spirit" (2014); Author, "The Leadership Bible" (2013); Author, "Baptism in the Spirit" (2012); Host, "Holy Spirit Today" (2012); Translator, "King James Version" (2011); Producer, "Iniquity" (2010); Chief Editor, "New Tyndale Translation New Testament" (2009); Chief Editor, "New Tyndale Version Host Holy Spirit Today" (2007-2012); Host, "Holy Spirit Today" (2007); Author, "Spirit Baptism" (2007); Songwriter, "Oh Blessed Jesus" (2007); Radio Broadcaster, "Lectures on Pneumatology" (2007); Author, "The Baptism with the Holy Spirit" (2004); Translator, "Modern English Version" **Awards:** Recipient, Leader Of The Year Award, The Heritage Foundation (2011); Honoree, Evangelist Of Year (2010); Eponym, Congressional Proclamation Reverend Dr. Verna May Linzey Day (2001); Recipient, Certificate Of Recognition, Mayor Lori Holt Pfeiler (2001) **Membership:** Co-Founder, Military Bible Association Vice President, Military Bible Association **Marquis Who's Who Honors:** Albert Nelson Marquis Lifetime Achievement Award (2017) **To what do you attribute your success:** Ms. Linzey credits her parents and being brought up in such a Godly home. She comes from a ministry-orientated family and everyone learned to play instruments. **Why did you become involved in your profession or industry:** Ms. Linzey entered her profession because after her father passed away, her mother got remarried to a minister with several connections; this opened many doors for her at a very young age. **What do you consider to be the highlight of your career:** A highlight of Ms. Linzey's career traveling, which she really enjoyed even though it was more apart of her work as a minister to speak and sing. She also enjoyed gardening and looking at photo albums - she loved to keep track of her lineage. Ms. Linzey is most proud of her television work; she loved speaking on television, her personality was so sweet and big and perfect for television. **Hobbies:** Gardening; Piano; Photography; Genealogy; Singing **Political Affiliations:** Republican **Religion:** Southern Baptist **Shipping Address:** 1641 Kenora Drive, Escondido, CA, 92027

Philip Edward Lippincott

Title: Paper Company Executive **Industry:** Other **Date of Birth:** 11/28/1935 **Place of Birth:** Camden **State:** NJ **Parents:** J. Edward Lippincott; Marjorie Nix (Spooner) Lippincott **Marital Status:** Married **Spouse Name:** Naomi Catherine Prindle (8/22/1959) **Children:** Grant; Kevin; Kerry **Education:** Honorary MBA, Michigan State University (1964); BA, Dartmouth College (1957) **Career:** Chairman, Scott Paper Company, Philadelphia, PA (1983-1994); Chief Executive Officer, Scott Paper Company, Philadelphia, PA (1982-1994); President, Scott Paper Company, Philadelphia, PA (1980-1994); Chief Operating Officer, Scott Paper Company, Philadelphia, PA (1980-1994); Director, Scott Paper Company, Philadelphia, PA (1978-1994); Vice President, Group Executive, Packaged Products Division, Scott Paper Company, Philadelphia, PA (1977-1979); Senior Vice President, Marketing, Scott Paper Company, Philadelphia, PA (1975-1977); Corporate Vice President, Marketing, Scott Paper Company, Philadelphia, PA (1972-1975); Division Vice President, Consumer Products Marketing, Scott Paper Company, Philadelphia, PA (1971-1972); Staff Vice President, Corporate Planning, Scott Paper Company, Philadelphia, PA (1971); Employee, Scott Paper Company, Philadelphia, PA (1959-1994) **Career Related:** Chairman, Board, Campbell Soup Company Brands (1999-2001); Board of Directors, Exxon Mobil Corporation (1985-2008); Board of Directors, Campbell Soup Company Brands, L.P. (1984-2008); Trustee, Penn Mutual Life Insurance Company (1983-2008) **Civic:** Vice Chairman, Moorestown Friends School (2011-Present); School Committee, Moorestown Friends School (2010-Present); Director, Linear Signal (2008-Present); Independent School Committee (2002-Present); Fox Chase Cancer Center, Philadelphia, PA (2002-Present); Lifetime Trustee, Fox Chase Cancer Center, Philadelphia, PA (1981-Present); Chairman, Board of Trustees, Fox Chase Cancer Center, Philadelphia, PA (1995-2003) **Military Service:** Captain, U.S. Army (1957-1959) **Membership:** Pine Valley Golf Club; Quail West Foundation; Kappa Kappa Kappa; Pi Sigma Epsilon; Beta Gamma Sigma; Sunnybrook Golf Club; Bonita Bay Club **Marquis Who's Who Honors:** Albert Nelson Marquis Lifetime Achievement Award (2017) **Religion:** Quaker **Shipping Address:** 4731 Bonita Bay Boulevard, Unit 1204, Bonita Springs, FL, 34134

Pauline (Polly) Roush Liss

Title: Editor (Retired), Education Advocate (Retired) **Industry:** Education/Educational Services **Date of Birth:** 10/18/1927 **Place of Birth:** Winston-Salem **State/Country of Origin:** NC **Parents:** Rose Likoff Roush; Louis Roush **Marital Status:** Widow **Spouse Name:** Merwin Edgar Liss (4/20/1958-11/22/2017, Deceased) **Children:** Sharon; David; Leslie **Education:** Master's Degree in Social Foundations of Education, University of Virginia (1983); BA, The University of Alabama (1948) **Career:** Secretary-Treasurer, American Association for Career Education, Hermosa Beach, CA (1982-Present); Editor-in-Chief, National Curriculum Audit Center, American Association of School Administrators, Arlington, VA (1983-1995); Editor, Pan American Union, Organization of American States Inter American Statistical Institute (1948-1960) **Career Related:** Member, Science, Technology, Engineering and Mathematics Group, United States Department of Education (2013); Former Board Member, Y-ME National Breast Cancer Organization, Mid-Atlantic Affiliate, Herndon, VA (1990-2012); Match Peer Counselor, Y-ME National Breast Cancer Organization, Mid-Atlantic Affiliate, Herndon, VA (1990-2012); Chairman, Virginia State Career Education Advisory Committee, Richmond, VA (1980-2005); Founder, Arlington County Coalition Career Education (1978-1999); President, Arlington County Coalition Career Education (1978-1999) **Civic:** Member, Advisory Committee on Career, Technology, & Adult Education, Arlington County, Virginia (1979-2016); Past Chairman, Advisory Committee on Career, Technology, & Adult Education, Arlington County, Virginia (1979-Present); Lifetime Member, Local Chapter, ORT America (1961-Present); Education Committee Chairman, League of Women Voters of Arlington, VA (2005-2006); Representative, ORT America (1995-2012); Representative, Advisory Council, Arlilngton County Public Schools (1985-1995); Secretary-Treasurer, American Association for Career Education, Arlington, VA, Ashburn, VA, (1982-2018); Ad Hoc Member, Advisory Committee on Career, Technology, & Adult Education, Arlington County, Virginia (1979-2008); Former Board Member, League of Women Voters of Arlington, Virginia (1974-2012); Past President, Local Chapter, ORT America (1961-1965) **Creative Works:** Contributor, Articles to Professional Journals **Awards:** Recipient, Gina Award, Y-ME National Breast Cancer Organization (2007); Recipient, Civic Award, Arlington School Administrators (2004); Recipient, Citation in Career Education Initiatives Award, American Association for Career Education (2001); Recipient, Golden Rule Volunteer Finalist Award, J.C. Penney (2000); Recipient, Various Other Recognitions **Membership:** Secretary, Citizens for the Classics (1975-2012); Past President, Citizens for the Classics; Associate, Citizens for the Classics; Founder and Past President, Arlington County Coalition for Career Education, Arlington County Public Schools; ORT America; American Association for Career Education; various advisory committees of the Arlington County Public Schools; STEM Group, Ashby Ponds Retirement Community; League of Women Voters **Marquis Who's Who Honors:** Albert Nelson Marquis Lifetime Achievement Award (2017) **To what do you attribute your success:** Ms. Liss attributes her success to her curiosity, the rewards of her research and her many models of success. **Why did you become involved in your profession or industry:** Ms. Liss became involved in her profession as a result of her interest in how, what, and when people learn and where help is when needed. **What do you consider to be the highlight of your career:** The highlight of Ms. Liss' career has been the three programs that she has developed and presented on science, technology, engineering and mathematics. The first, in 2013, was a panel of six K-12 education professionals from four school divisions in Northern Virginia, representing 280,467 students, who talked about health and STEM programs in their schools. The second, in 2014, was a panel of four of Virginia's esteemed institutions of higher education who talked about health, the arts, STEM and their links to K-12 students and their preparation for a United States workforce that is capable and flexible and needed to compete globally. The last program, in 2015, brought together a panel of a high school student with three young university graduates of STEM, health, and the arts programs who are currently employed in those fields. **Where will you be in five years:** In five years, Ms. Liss will still be retired and she will look into ways that she can give a voice to people with unmet needs. **Hobbies:** Writing **Political Affiliations:** Liberal **Religion:** Jewish **Shipping Address:** 21145 Cardinal Pond Ter Apt 302, Ashburn, VA, 20147

Jacqueline R. Livesay

Title: Music Educator, Church Musician **Industry:** Education/Educational Services **Company Name:** First United Methodist Church **Date of Birth:** 02/13/1949 **Place of Birth:** Charlottesville **State/Country of Origin:** VA **Parents:** Eldridge G. Ryder; Elizabeth Row Ryder **Marital Status:** Married **Spouse Name:** Charles Jackson Livesay (6/30/1973) **Children:** Jennifer Livesay Pereira; Jean Livesay Subramanian; Ellen (Deceased) **Education:** MA in Education, Spring Arbor University, Spring Arbor, MI (2001); MusM, University of Michigan, Ann Arbor, MI (1977); MusB, Westminster Choir College, Princeton, NJ (1973) **Certifications:** Orff-Schulwerk Certification, Level I; Orff-Schulwerk Certification, Level II; Orff-Schulwerk Certification, Level III **Career:** Instructor of Early Childhood Education, Jackson Symphony Community Music School (2013-Present); Director, Jackson Chorale Children's Choir (2008-Present); Director, Orff Music, First Presbyterian Church, Jackson, MS (2005-Present); Director, Children's Music, Organist, First United Methodist Church, Jackson, MS (2003-Present); Teacher, Elementary Music, Jackson Public Schools (1998-2012); Teacher, Elementary Music, Vandercook Lake Public Schools (1989-1998); Organist, Trinity United Methodist Church, Jackson, MI (1977-2003); Minister of Music, Trinity United Methodist Church, Jackson, MI (1977-2003) **Career Related:** Adjunct Instructor of Music, Spring Arbor University, Spring Arbor, MI (2008-Present); Adjunct Instructor of Music, Albion College, Albion, MI (2003-Present); Guest Organ Soloist, Jackson Symphony Orchestra (2013); Magnet Committee, Jackson Public Schools (2007-2012); Planning Committee Member, Jackson Symphony Orchestra Family Concert (2003-2006); Human Resources Committee, Jackson Public Schools (2003-2005); Adjunct Instructor of Music, Spring Arbor University (1975-1986) **Civic:** Board Member, President (2017-Present); Member, Vice President, P.E.O. Sisterhood (2016-Present); Worship Design Committee, First United Methodist Church (2015-Present); Tuesday Musical Association (2013-Present); Member, Woman's Club of Jackson (2012-Present); Member, Jackson Symphony Guild (1999-Present); Education Committee, First United Methodist Church (2012-2014); Member, Academic Boosters, Western High School, Jackson, MS (1995-2004) **Awards:** Named Outstanding Elementary Educator, Jackson Public Schools (2001) **Marquis Who's Who Honors:** Albert Nelson Marquis Lifetime Achievement Award (2017); Distinguished Humanitarian (2017) **Why did you become involved in your profession or industry:** Mrs. Livesay became involved in her profession because she loves music and the field worked for her. **Hobbies:** Reading; Travel; Walking; Gardening **Shipping Address:** 4897 Indian Creek Dr, Jackson, MI, 49201

Lee Franklin Livingston

Title: Real Estate Consultant **Industry:** Real Estate **Company Name:** Anasarca Corporation **Date of Birth:** 02/20/1942 **Place of Birth:** Boston **State:** MA **Parents:** William Livingston; Frances (Turner) Livingston **Marital Status:** Married **Spouse Name:** Elaine Wiesenfeld (6/9/1968) **Children:** Eli; Jed **Education:** Student, School of Visual Arts, New York, NY (1959-1962) **Career:** Managing Director, Secretary, Treasurer, Anasarca Corporation, North Brunswick, NJ (1971-Present); Staff, Public Relations and Promotion Department, Newsweek, New York, NY (1965-1970) **Career Related:** Consultant, Charitable Fund Raising, Various Charities (1971-Present); President, Imperial Consultant, Inc. **Civic:** Treasurer, Jewish Social Services Vice Chair, United Way of Central New Jersey (2011); Jewish Federation of Greater Middlesex County, New Jersey (2007-2010); President, Anshe Emeth Memorial Temple (1995-1997); Treasurer, Robert Wood Johnson Hospital Foundation; State of New Jersey Fee Arbitration Panel **Military Service:** Corps Engineers, U.S. Army (1962-1964) **Awards:** United Way Community Hero (2010); New Jersey Person of the Year Award (1992); Service Award in Special Education (1991); Service Award in Special Education (1989); American Service Award, Girl Scouts of America; Bronze Service Award, Special Olympics **Membership:** Greenacres Country Club **Marquis Who's Who Honors:** Albert Nelson Marquis Lifetime Achievement Award (2017) **Political Affiliations:** Democrat **Business Address:** 850 Carolier Lane, North Brunswick, NJ, 08902 **Shipping Address:** 12 Derby Lane, North Brunswick, NJ, 08902

Virginia LiVolsi

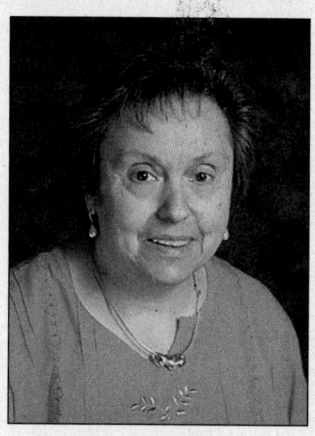

Title: Professor **Industry:** Education/Educational Services **Company Name:** University of Pennsylvania **Date of Birth:** 07/29/1943 **Place of Birth:** New York **State/Country of Origin:** NY **Parents:** Epifanio LiVolsi; Mary Ann (LaPorta) LiVolsi **Education:** MA, University of Pennsylvania, Honoris Causa (1983); Chief Resident in Pathology, Columbia Presbyterian Medical Center, New York, NY (1973-1974); National Cancer Institute Traineeship, Surgical Pathology, Columbia Presbyterian Medical Center, New York, NY (1970-1974); Intern, Pathology, Columbia Presbyterian Medical Center (1969-1970); MD, Columbia University (1969); BS, College of Mount Saint Vincent, Cum Laude, New York, NY (1965) **Certifications:** Certified, American Board of Pathology (2014); Certified in Anatomic Pathology, American Board of Pathology (1974); Diplomate, National Board Of Medical Examiners (1970) **Career:** Professor, Pathology and Laboratory Medicine, Hospital of the University of Pennsylvania, Philadelphia, PA (1983-Present); Vice Chair, Anatomical Pathology, Hospital of the University of Pennsylvania, Philadelphia, PA (1994-1999); Director of Surgical Pathology, Hospital of the University of Pennsylvania, Philadelphia, PA (1983-1994); Associate Professor, Yale School of Medicine, Yale University (1979-1983); Director of Cytology, Yale University (1975-1977); Attending Pathologist, Yale-New Haven Hospital (1974-1983); Assistant Professor, Yale School of Medicine, Yale University (1974-1979); Instructor of Pathology, Columbia University, New York, NY (1973-1974) **Creative Works:** Contributor, Articles to Professional Journals **Awards:** Recipient, Mentoring Award, American Society of Clinical Pathology (2012); Recipient, Harvey Goldman Teaching Award, United States and Canadian Academy of Pathology (2012); President's Medal (2009); James E. Wheeler, MD Award for Teaching, Department of Pathology and Laboratory Medicine (2008); Named, Master Pathologist, American Society of Clinical Pathologists (2007); Named, Best Doctors in America (2005-2013); Recipient, Mostofi Award for Service, United States and Canadian Academy of Pathology (2001); Recipient, Scanno Prize in Medicine, Scanno, Italy (1997); Recipient, Distinguished Service Award, American Society of Clinical Pathologists (1995); Recipient, Merit Award, American Society of Clinical Pathologists (1995); Recipient, Medal of Honor, The University of Tokyo, Tokyo, Japan (1992) **Membership:** Association of Clinical Scientists (1998-Present); President, Association of Directors of Anatomic and Surgical Pathology (1997-Present); President, Arthur Purdy Stout Society (1997-Present); International Society for Biological and Environmental Repositories (1995-Present); American Association for Bone and Mineral Research (1993-Present); American Association of Clinical Endocrinologists (1992-Present); Abstract Review Committee, American Society of Clinical Pathologists (1991-Present); Association of Directors of Anatomic and Surgical Pathology (1989-Present); Pathology Society of Philadelphia (1988-Present); The College of Physicians of Philadelphia (1984-Present); American Thyroid Association (1975-Present); President-elect, Arthur Purdy Stout Society (1995-1997); Vice President, Association of Directors of Anatomic and Surgical Pathology (1995-1996); Practice Parameters Committee, American Society of Clinical Pathologists (1993-1995); Secretary, Arthur Purdy Stout Society (1987-1993); United States and Canadian Academy of Pathology; College of American Pathologists; Pennsylvania Association of Pathologists; International Society of Neuropathology; American Association for the Advancement of Science **Marquis Who's Who Honors:** Albert Nelson Marquis Lifetime Achievement Award (2017) **Why did you become involved in your profession or industry:** Dr. LiVolsi became interested in her profession as a child while watching relatives go through issues with opthamalogical problems. She became interested in pathology when she got to medical school. **What do you consider to be the highlight of your career:** A highlight of Dr. LiVolsi's career was when she was involved with the pathology review of thyroid tumors that arose in children after the Chernobyl accident. She was the American representative to that international panel. In 2006, the 20-year anniversary of the accident, there was an event at the United Nations and she was invited to give a presentation. Dr. LiVolsi is also proud of her time as president of the United States and Canadian Academy of Pathology in 2003-2004; this is the premiere academic Pathology society in North America. **Shipping Address:** 3400 Spruce St, Hospital of the University of PA, Founders Building, Rm 6040, Philadelphia, PA, 19104

Shui-Yin Lo, PhD

Title: Director **Industry:** Medicine & Health Care **Company Name:** Institute for Integrative Health **Date of Birth:** 10/20/1941 **Place of Birth:** Canton **Parents:** Long Tin Lo; Ty-Fong Lo **Marital Status:** Married **Spouse Name:** May Chen **Children:** Alpha Wei-Min; Fiona Al-Ming; Hao-Min **Education:** PhD, University of Chicago (1966); BS, University of Illinois at Urbana-Champaign (1962) **Career:** Director, Institute for Integrative Health (2015-Present); Director, Quantum Health Research Institute (2005-Present); Chairman, America East Asia Education & Culture Foundation (2005-Present); Professor, Research in Chinese Medicine, American University of Complementary Medicine, Beverly Hills, CA (2003-Present); President, Institute for Boson Studies, Pasadena, CA (1986-1992); Senior Lecturer, University of Melbourne (1972-1989); Research Associate, University of Glasgow (1969-1972); Research Associate, Rutherford Appleton Laboratory, Chilton, United Kingdom (1966-1969) **Career Related:** Professor, Science Advisory Board, ACIM (2012); Visiting Faculty, California Institute of Technology (1994-1998); Fellow, Australian Institute of Physics **Civic:** Principal, Chinese School of the Chinese Fellowship of Victoria, VIC, Australia (1977-1984) **Creative Works:** Editor, "Meridians and Stable Water Clusters" (2013); Editor, "Autism and Stable Water Clusters" (2013); Editor, "Biophysics Basis for Acupuncture and Health" (2004); Editor, "Physical, Chemical and Biological Properties of Stable Water Clusters" (1998); Author, "Scientific Studies of Chinese Characters" (1986); Author, "Geometrical Picture of Hadron Scattering" (1986); Editor, "Geometrical Picture of Hadron Scattering" (1986); Author, "Double Helix Water"; Editor, "Double Helix Water"; Columnist, "Acupuncture Today"; Contributor, Articles, Professional Journals **Membership:** Director, Rosemead Chamber of Commerce (2007); American Physical Society **Marquis Who's Who Honors:** Albert Nelson Marquis Lifetime Achievement Award (2017) **Shipping Address:** 3579 E Foothill Boulevard, Suite 654, Pasadena, CA, 91107 **Website:** http://solidwaterparticles.com

Gerald Ivan Locklin, PhD

Title: Language Educator, Poet, Writer **Industry:** Education/Educational Services **Company Name:** California State University, Long Beach **Date of Birth:** 02/17/1941 **Place of Birth:** Rochester **State/Country of Origin:** NY **Parents:** Ivan Locklin; Esther Locklin **Marital Status:** Married **Spouse Name:** Barbara Locklin **Children:** Seven Children **Education:** PhD, The University of Arizona (1964); MA, The University of Arizona (1963); BA, St. John Fisher College (1961) **Certifications:** Certified in University Teaching **Career:** Professor Emeritus, California State University, Long Beach (2007-Present); Professor of English, California State University, Long Beach (1965-2007); Associate Instructor, California State University, Los Angeles (1964-1965); Senior Poetry Editor, Chiron Review **Civic:** Founder, Endowment for Student Writing Competition, California State University, Long Beach **Creative Works:** Co-Author, "The Toad Poems" (2007); Author, "New Orleans, Chicago and Points Elsewhere" (2006); Author, "The Pocket Book: A Novella and Nineteen Short Fictions" (2003); Author, "The Life Force Poems" (2002); Author, "A Simpler Time A Simpler Place: Three Mid-Century Stories" (2000); Author, "Candy Bars: Selected Stories" (2000); Author, "Down and Out" (1999); Author, "Go West, Young Toad: Selected Writings" (1999); Author, Annual Jazz Poem Chapbooks (1997-2007); Contributor, "The Oxford Companion to Twentieth Century Literature in English" (1996); Author, "Charles Bukowski: A Sure Bet" (1995); Co-Editor, "A New Geography of Poets" (1992); Author, "The Gold Rush" (1989); Author, "The Case of the Missing Blue Volkswagen" (1984); Author, Numerous Poems; Author, Short Stories; Author, 13E Note Editions; Contributor, Ambit Magazine; Contributor, BlazeVox Books; Contributor, Bottle of Smoke Press; Contributor, Burning Shore Press; Contributor, Chiron Review; Contributor, Chuckwagon Press; Contributor, Coagula; Contributor, Connotation Press; Contributor, Iconoclast Literary Magazine; Contributor, Kamini Press; Contributor, Leconte Editore; Contributor, Lummox Press; Contributor, Mark Weber Jazz for Mostly; Contributor, Narrative Magazine; Contributor, Outlaw Poetry Network; Contributor, Pearl Magazine; Contributor, Presa Press; Contributor, Rattle; Contributor, Ravenna Press; Contributor, Slipstream Press; Contributor, Spout Hill Press; Contributor, Tears in the Fence; Contributor, The Spot Lit Magazine; Contributor, Verdant Press; Contributor, Water Row Books; Contributor, Wormwood Review; Contributor, Yossarian Universal News Service **Membership:** Western Literature Association; Associate Writing Programs; Hemingway Society; E.E. Cummings Society; PEN Center USA; Beyond Baroque Literary Arts Center; Los Angeles County Museum of Arts; Norton Simon Museum; Huntington Library and Museum **Marquis Who's Who Honors:** Albert Nelson Marquis Lifetime Achievement Award (2017) **To what do you attribute your success:** Dr. Locklin attributes his success to his lifelong career activity. **Why did you become involved in your profession or industry:** Dr. Locklin entered his profession because his talent was literacy. **What do you consider to be the highlight of your career:** The highlight of Dr. Locklin's career was being nominated and listed in Marquis Who's Who. **Where will you be in five years:** In the next five years, Dr. Locklin hopes to still be literary. **Hobbies:** Swimming; Jazz; Travel; Watching the New York Yankees and the Los Angeles Lakers **Shipping Address:** 2835 Albury Ave, Long Beach, CA, 90815

Molly Ann Lockwood

Title: President, Chief Executive Officer **Industry:** Advertising & Marketing **Company Name:** Conceptual Marketing Inc. **Date of Birth:** 09/19/1936 **Place of Birth:** London **State/Country of Origin:** England **Parents:** Warren Sewell Lockwood; Ann Frances (Gleason) Lockwood **Education:** BS, Pennsylvania State University (1958) **Career:** Patient Care Coordinator, Beltone Five Star Hearing (2016-Present); President, Conceptual Marketing Inc. (1997-Present); Chief Executive Officer, Conceptual Marketing Inc. (1997-Present); Senior Vice President, Marketing, Health Expo, Inc. (1997-2005); Marketing Director, Going Bonkers Magazine (1996-1997); Executive Training Program, Lord & Taylor (1994-2007); President, National Advantage, Crane Media Services (1992-1997); Secretary, Board 244, Madison Realty Corporation (1984-1993); Marketing and Sales Director, Museum Magazine (1979-1983); President, Catalyst Communications Inc., New York, NY (1977-1997); Chief Executive Officer, Catalyst Communications Inc., New York, NY (1977-1997); Partner, Catalyst Communications Inc., New York, NY (1977-1997); Marketing Director, East-West Network Magazine, New York, NY (1974-1977); Associate Publisher, East-West Network Magazine, New York, NY (1974-1977); Advisory Director, Girl Talk Magazine (1972-1974); Account Manager, Ladies' Home Journal Magazine, New York, NY (1970-1972); Merchandising Director, Holiday Magazine, New York, NY (1970); Advertising Director, Status Magazine, New York, NY (1965-1970); Associate Merchandising Editor, House & Garden Magazine, New York, NY (1960-1965); Executive Training Program, Lord & Taylor, New York, NY (1958-1960) **Membership:** Probus Club, Naples (2012-2015); Pennsylvania State University Alumni Association; New York Women in Communications, Inc.; American Society of Travel Agents; Advertising Women of New York; Kappa Kappa Gamma Alumnae Association **Marquis Who's Who Honors:** Albert Nelson Marquis Lifetime Achievement Award (2017) **Hobbies:** Swimming; Theater **Shipping Address:** 445 Cove Tower Drive, Apt. 304, Naples, FL, 34110

Howard Lonsdale

Title: Physician **Industry:** Medicine & Health Care **Date of Birth:** 09/24/1933 **Place of Birth:** Berlin **Country of Origin:** Germany **Year of Passing:** 2017-08-16 **Parents:** Henry Lonsdale; Hilda M. Lonsdale **Children:** Lauren; Elizabeth; Henry; Geraldine **Education:** MD, University of Arkansas (1960); BA, Princeton University (1955) **Career:** Board Director, Broadway Hospital (1972-1974); Board Director, Village General Hospital (1971-1974); Staff, Broadway Hospital (1971); Chairman, California Medical Society (1970); Chief Physician, Ear Nose & Throat Clinical (1966-1999); President, Broadway Hospital **Career Related:** Medical Director, 30 Martial Arts Tournaments, World Martial Art Association (1997-2001); Co-Founder, Solano County Hospice (1978); President, Solano County Medical Association (1977); Vice President, Bay Area Comprehensive Health Pharmacy (1976); Comprehensive Health Planning Association (1966-1974); Aero Engineering (Now Weatherford International) (1966) **Civic:** President, Vallejo Symphony (1969-1970) **Military Service:** Captain, U.S. Air Force (1964-1966) **Awards:** Who's Who of American Politics (1970); Man of the Year, Junior Chamber of Commerce of Vallejo (1968) **Membership:** California Medical Society (1972); American Academy of Laryngology **Hobbies:** History; Music; Sports; Reading **Shipping Address:** 589 Highline Drive, Suite 34, Hearthstone Cottage, East Wenatchee, WA, 98802

Cornelis Albertus Los, PhD

Title: Economist, Finance Educator, Financial Engineer, Risk Analyst **Industry:** Financial Services **Company Name:** University of California **Date of Birth:** 12/14/1951 **Place of Birth:** Purmerend **Country of Origin:** Netherlands **Parents:** Klaas Los; Adriaantje (Nieuwland) Los **Marital Status:** Married **Spouse Name:** Elvira R. Los (8/25/2006); Rose Lee Haubenstock (5/5/1994, Divorced 2006); Elizabeth M. Ten Houten (6/18/1986, Divorced 1991); Diane Nichols (6/10/1979, Divorced 1984) **Children:** Arman K.R. Los; Francesca R. E. Nichols; Marguerita E. A. Ten Houten **Education:** PhD, Columbia University (1984); MPhil, Columbia University (1980); Diploma, International Institute of Social Studies, The Hague (1977); Doctorandus (MPhil), Groningen University (1976); Candidatus Cum Laude (Honorary BA), Groningen University (1974) **Certifications:** Bloomberg Market Concepts, Bloomberg Institute (2016); Firearms Safety, California Department of Justice (2015); Chief Firearms Officer, Alberta, Canada (2010); Conservationist & Hunter, Alberta, Canada (2009); CFA Institute (2003); Portfolio Management, New York Institute of Finance (1993); Interest Rate Risk, New York Institute of Finance (1993); Asset/Liability Management, Euromoney Institute (1993); Russian, Ostakademie Eisenstadt (1974) **Career:** Professor, Finance, University of California, Irvine, CA (2018-present); Professor, Finance, Alliant International University, San Diego, CA (2011-2017); Professor, Finance, University of Lethbridge, Lethbridge, Alberta, Canada (2008-2011); Visiting Professor, Financial Management, Peter F. Drucker and Masatoshi Ito Graduate School of Management, Claremont Graduate University, Claremont, CA (2007-2008); Professor, Finance and Accounting, Kazakh-British Technical University, Kazakhstan (2005-2006); Associate Professor, Finance, Kent State University (2001-2005); Visiting Associate Professor, Finance, Deakin University, Australia (2001); Associate Professor, Finance, The University of Adelaide, Australia (2000); Associate Professor, Banking and Finance, Nanyang Technological University, Singapore (1995-1999); Chief U.S. Economist, ING Group, New York City, NY (1991-1993); Senior Economist, Nomura Research Institute America, Inc. (1987-1990); Senior Economist, Federal Reserve Bank New York, New York City, NY (1985-1987); Economist, Federal Reserve Bank New York, New York City, NY (1981-1985); Instructor, Columbia University, New York City, NY (1980-1981); Preceptor, Columbia University, New York City, NY (1979); Teaching Assistant, Columbia University, New York City, NY (1978-1980) **Career Related:** Instructor, Executive Education, Advanced Derivatives, University of California, Irvine, CA (2014-2017); Instructor, Advanced Derivates and Financial Engineering, Stevens Institute of Technology (2013-2014); Chief Executive Officer, EMEPS Associates Inc. (1986-Present); Consultant, Asian Development Bank (1996-1999); Consultant, Asian Development Bank (1996-1999) **Civic:** Member, Institutional Review Board, California school of Psychology, Alliant International University (2016-2017) **Creative Works:** Author, "Solutions Manual: Computational Finance: A Scientific Perspective" (2004); Author, "Solutions Manual: Financial Market Risk: Measurement and Analysis" (2004); Author, "Financial Market Risk: Measurement and Analysis" (2003); Author, "Computational Finance: A Scientific Perspective" (2000); Author, "Econometrics of Models with Evolutionary Parameter Structures" (1984); Editorial Board Member, Journal of Financial Risk Management (2006-Present); Editorial Board Member, European Journal of Scientific Research; Editorial Board Member, European Journal of Social Sciences; Editorial Board Member, European Journal Economics, Finance and Administrative Sciences **Awards:** Outstanding Paper Award, Asia-Pacific Risk and Insurance Association (1998); Scholar, Fulbright-Hays Program (1977-1978); M.A.O.C. Countess van Bylandt Foundation Award (1976); Scholten Cordes Foundation Award (1976-1977); Lady van Renswoude of The Hague Foundation Award (1974-1975) **Membership:** Fellow, Society of Senior Scholars, Columbia University; Fellow, Australian Institute of Banking and Finance (Now Finsia); Lifetime Fellow, American College of Forensic Examiners Institute; CFA Institute; Senior Life Member; IEEE; Executive Member, Front Sight Firearms Training Institute; The New York Academy of Sciences; European Financial Management Association; The Bachelier Finance Society; American Mathematical Society; American Finance Association; American Economic Association; American Statistical Association; International Association for Mathematical and Computer Modelling; International Association of Financial Engineers; The Econometric Society; Mathematical Association of America; Executive Member, Friends of New Netherland Project (Now New Netherland Institute); London Goodenough Trust (Now Goodenough College); World Council of Alumni, International House, New York City, NY **Marquis Who's Who Honors:** Albert Nelson Marquis Lifetime Achievement Award (2017) **Political Affiliations:** Republican **Religion:** Christian **Shipping Address:** 2444 Bobcat Glen, Escondido, CA, 92029 **Website:** https://merage.uci.edu/research-faculty/faculty-directory/Cornelis-Los.html

Lewis David Lowenfels

Title: Partner **Industry:** Law and Legal Services **Company Name:** Law Offices of Lewis D. Lowenfels, Esq. **Date of Birth:** 06/09/1935 **Place of Birth:** New York City **State:** NY **Parents:** Seymour Lowenfels; Jane (Phillips) Lowenfels **Marital Status:** Married **Spouse Name:** Fern Gelford (8/15/1965) **Children:** Joshua; Jacqueline **Education:** LLB, Harvard University (1961); BA, Harvard University, Magna Cum Laude (1957) **Career:** Partner, Tolins & Lowenfels, New York City, NY (1967) **Career Related:** Public Governor, American Stock Exchange (Now Intercontinental Exchange, Inc.) (1993-1996); Federal Bar Association (1972); Adjunct Professor, Seton Hall University School of Law; Lecturer, Practicing Law Institute (Now PLI Practising Law Institute); Lecturer, Southwestern Legal Foundation, University of Minnesota **Military Service:** United States Army Reserve (1957-1963) **Creative Works:** Co-author, "Bromberg and Lowenfels on Securities Fraud and Commodities Fraud," 8 Volumes (2011); Contributor, Articles, Professional Journals **Membership:** Federal Regulation of Securities Committee, American Bar Association (Now ABA) (1978-Present); Securities and Exchanges Committee, New York County Lawyers Association (1974-Present); Lecturer, American Bar Association (Now ABA); Phi Beta Kappa (Now The Phi Beta Kappa Society); Harvard Club (Now Harvard Club of New York City) **Bar Admissions:** Licensed Corporations and Securities Attorney, New York (1961) **Marquis Who's Who Honors:** Albert Nelson Marquis Lifetime Achievement Award (2017) **Why did you become involved in your profession or industry:** He became involved in his profession because he was always interested in capital markets and securities. He finds it challenging; capital markets are at the center of our economic system and are essential to the property and welfare or our citizens. **What do you consider to be the highlight of your career:** One of his proudest moments is when he received front page coverage from the New York Times with an article written by the well-known columnist Bill Pennington, which covered the basketball team at Harvard, for which he played. He turned down an opportunity to play in New Orleans because they insisted on separate facilities for the African American player on the Harvard team. It was an important stance to take especially because of the Harvard name. **Hobbies:** Reading; Writing; Athletics; Travel **Business Address:** 25 Sutton Place South Suite 6F, New York, NY, 10022 **Shipping Address:** 97 Montebello Rd, Suffern, NY, 10901

Josè L. Lozano

Title: Nephrologist **Industry:** Medicine & Health Care **Company Name:** Kidney Center **Date of Birth:** 02/11/1941 **Place of Birth:** San Vicente **Country of Origin:** El Salvador **Parents:** Josè E. Lozano; Transito Maria (Mendez) Lizabi **Marital Status:** Married **Spouse Name:** Hilda Berganza (1/27/1965) **Children:** Josè E.; Claudia Maria **Education:** Fellow in Nephrology, Baylor University Affiliated Hospitals, Houston, TX (1973-1974); Fellow in Nephrology, Baylor University Affiliated Hospitals, Houston, TX (1970-1971); Resident in Internal Medicine, Baylor University Affiliated Hospitals, Houston, TX (1968-1970); Resident in Internal Medicine, Rosales Hospital, San Salvador (1966-1967); Assistant Resident in Internal Medicine, Rosales Hospital, San Salvador (1965-1966); MD, University of El Salvador (1965); Rotating Intern, National Medical Center, San Salvador, El Salvador (1963-1964) **Career:** Medical Director, Kidney Center, Jasper, TX (2001-Present); Medical Director, Kidney Center, Beaumont, TX (2001-Present); Medical Director, BMA Orange, Orange, TX (1987-1990); Medical Director, BMA Jasper, Jasper, TX (1986-1998); Medical Director, Golden Triangle Dialysis Center, Beaumont, TX (1977-1998); Clinical Assistant, Professor of Medicine, Baylor College of Medicine, Houston, TX (1976-1980); Staff Member, Internal Medicine, St. Elizabeth Hospital, Beaumont Medical/Surgical Hospital, Baptist Hospital, Beaumont, TX (1976); Assistant Professor, Medicine in Nephrology, Baylor College of Medicine, Houston, TX (1975-1976); Instructor in Medicine, Baylor College Medicine, Houston, TX (1974-1975); Internist, Nephrologist, Social Security Hospital, San Salvador (1971-1972); Assistant Professor of Medicine, University of El Salvador (1971-1972); Chief Resident in Internal Medicine, Rosales Hospital, San Salvador (1967-1968) **Career Related:** Kidney Center of Jasper (2001-Present); Beaumont Kidney Center (2001-Present); Medical Director, Jasper Dialysis Center (1986-1998); Member, Kidney Health Care Advisory Committee (1981-1982); Presenter in Field **Creative Works:** Contributor, Articles to Professional Publications, Editorials in Local Papers **Awards:** Best Doctors List; Top Doctors, Consumer Reports **Membership:** Fellow, American College of Physicians; American Society of Nephrology; Member, American Medical Association; International Society of Nephrology; Texas Medical Association; Harris County Medical Society; Jefferson County Medical Society; Physicians for a National Health Plan **Shipping Address:** 2422 S. Mystic Meadows, Houston, TX, 77021

Arthur M. Luby

Title: Assistant Director **Industry:** Law and Legal Services **Company Name:** Air Line Pilots Association International **Education:** JD, University of Michigan (1979); Coursework, Brown University, Cum Laude **Career:** Assistant Director of Representation, Air Line Pilots Association International (2006-Present); With Senior Labor Relations Counsel, Air Line Pilots Association International (2005-2006) **Career Related:** Affiliate, Private Practice, Labor Law, TWU; Affiliate, Private Practice, Collective Bargaining Issues, TWU; Affiliate, Private Practice, Labor Law, APWU; Affiliate, Private Practice, Collective Bargaining Issues, APWU **Awards:** Award, Air Line Pilots Association International (2015) **Why did you become involved in your profession or industry:** Mr. Luby became involved in his profession when he was inspired as a young boy to pursue a profession where he could help working people. He saw from an early age that one of the most effective ways to make a meaningful impact would be through the practice of law. There were a number of figures in Mr. Luby's childhood who he greatly admired who practiced law on behalf of unions and working people. **Business Address:** 535 Herndon Parkway, 535 Herndon Parkway, VA, Herndon, 20170 **Shipping Address:** 8706 Middleford Dr, Springfield, VA, 22153 **Website:** https://expertnetwork.co/members/arthur-m-luby/15d0997f38da4624

Willis Bernard Lukenbill, PhD

Title: Adult Education Educator **Industry:** Education/Educational Services **Company Name:** The University of Texas at Austin **Date of Birth:** 03/27/1939 **Place of Birth:** Mount Sylvan **State:** TX **Parents:** Lee Roy Clayton Lukenbill; Tommie Lee McCorkle **Marital Status:** Married **Spouse Name:** Shirley Ann Hebert (6/1/1968) **Children:** James Frederick **Education:** PhD, Indiana University (1973); MLS, The University of Oklahoma (1963); BS in Education, University of North Texas (1961) **Certifications:** Certified Teacher, State of Texas **Career:** Professor Emeritus, The University of Texas at Austin (2010); Professor, The University of Texas at Austin (1996-2010); Assistant Professor, University of Texas, Austin (1976-1996); Assistant Professor, University of Maryland, College Park (1973-1975); Instructor, Louisiana Polytechnic, Ruston (1964-1969); Reference Librarian, Austin College, Sherman, TX (1963) **Career Related:** Archivist Consultant, MCC Austin (1994-Present); Board of Directors, MCC Austin (1987-1990); Community Resource, Media Center, School Library; Consultant for Public Libraries, Schools, Nonprofits and Churches; Conducts Geographical Research for Local Communities and Libraries; Updates and Promotes Archives **Civic:** Mt. Sylvan (Texas) Cemetery Foundation **Creative Works:** Author, "Writing about Islam for Youth" (2017); Author, "Broadway Musicals and the Christian Sermon" (2017); Author, "Research Information Studies" (2012); Author, "Health Information for Youth" (2004-2008); Author, "Biography in the Lives of Youth: Culture, Society and Information" (2006); Author, "Collection Development for the School Library Media Center: New Directions for a New Century" (2002); Presentations at Numerous International Professional and Academic Conferences (2000-2017); Author, "AIDS-HIV Information Services and Programs in Libraries" (1994-2000); Author, "Youth Literature: An Interdisciplinary, Annotated Guide to North American Dissertation Research, 1930-1985" (1988); Contributor, Articles, Professional Journals **Awards:** Grant for Recruiting And Educating Librarians for the 21st Century, Institute of Museum and Library Studies (2004-2006); Temple Teaching Fellowship, University of Texas at Austin (1987-1988, 1996-1997); Library Education for At-Risk Youth Award, U.S. Department of Education (1993-1994); International Research Grant (1990); Policy Research Grant, Policy Research Institute, The University of Texas at Austin (1988); Whitney Carnegie Grant, American Library Association (1986) **Membership:** Commons Teaching Fellow, School of Information, The University of Texas at Austin (2001-2003); Doctoral Fellow, U.S. Department of Education (1970-1973); American Library Association; Texas Library Association; The Honor Society of Phi Kappa Phi; UT Retired Faculty-Staff Association **Marquis Who's Who Honors:** Albert Nelson Marquis Lifetime Achievement Award (2017) **To what do you attribute your success:** He attributes his success to hard work and working well with others. **Why did you become involved in your profession or industry:** He became involved in his industry out of his interest in libraries. His father encouraged him to go to the public library when he was a child. **What do you consider to be the highlight of your career:** He is most proud of having been given tenure, and being promoted to professor at a well-known research university. **Where will you be in five years:** In 5 years, he will be enjoying his life, and contributing to society as best he can. **Hobbies:** Travel; Theater; Art; Music; Reading; History; Genealogy **Political Affiliations:** Democrat **Religion:** Christian **Shipping Address:** 1205 Spearson Ln, Austin, TX, 78745

Jon Lum

Title: Physician Assistant, Consultant **Industry:** Medicine & Health Care **Company Name:** Waterbury Hospital **Date of Birth:** 10/03/1954 **Place of Birth:** Hong Kong **Country of Origin:** China **Parents:** So Hong Lum; Shok Hing Yuen Lum **Marital Status:** Married **Spouse Name:** Nancy Virginia Caron (5/13/1995) **Education:** BA in Physician Assistant, Trevecca Nazarene University (1986) **Certifications:** Certification in Surgical Technology, Bridgeport Hospital School of Nursing, Connecticut (2001); Certification in Respiratory Therapy, Bay City College (1978) **Career:** Physician Assistant, Waterbury Hospital, Connecticut (2004-Present); Physician Assistant, Danbury Internal Medicine Associates (2003-Present); Physician Assistant, Arthritis Center of Connecticut, Waterbury, CT (1997-2003); Physician Assistant, The Vein Treatment Center, New York City, NY (1996-1997); Physician Assistant, Beth Israel Medical Center, New York City, NY (1992-1996); Physician Assistant, Correctional Medical Systems, Inc., Reidsville, GA (1987-1992); Physician Assistant, Baptist Medical Center, Jacksonville, FL (1986-1987) **Career Related:** Lead Project Designer, World Trade Center Site Memorial Competition Lower Manhattan, Development Corporation, New York City, NY (2003-Present); Consultant, Pfizer, Miami, FL (2003-Present) **Civic:** Volunteer, Pet Shelter **Membership:** Society of Physician Assistants in Rheumatology; Connecticut Academy of Physician Assistants; American Academy of Physician Assistants **Why did you become involved in your profession or industry:** Mr. Lum entered his profession because he wanted to help people, because he is a caring and devoted person. **Where will you be in five years:** In five years, Mr. Lum hopes to continue his career in healthcare. **Hobbies:** Photography; Running Marathons **Shipping Address:** 4-6 Union Ave Apt 20, Norwalk, CT, 06851 **Website:** http://www.jon-lum.com

Rami E. Lutfi

Title: Clinical Associate Professor of Surgery **Industry:** Education/Educational Services **Company Name:** Chicago Institute of Advanced Surgery **Education:** Fellow in Laparoscopic Surgery, Vanderbilt University (2003-2005); Resident in General Surgery, University of Illinois College of Medicine (1998-2003); MD, School of Medicine, Damascus University (1997) **Certifications:** Diplomate, American Board of Surgery, Inc. **Career:** Chief of Surgery, Mercy Hospital & Medical Center (2014-Present); Vice President, Illinois Association of Bariatric Surgeons, Inc. (2010-Present); Medical Director, The Chicago Institute of Advanced Bariatrics, Saint Joseph Hospital, Presence Health (2008-Present); Founder, The Chicago Institute of Advanced Bariatrics, Saint Joseph Hospital, Presence Health (2008-Present); Past President, Illinois Association of Bariatric Surgeons, Inc. (2012-2014) **Career Related:** Skills Lab Director, Saint Joseph Hospital, Presence Health (2013-2015); Clinical Associate Professor, University of Illinois at Chicago **Awards:** Honoree, Teacher of the Year, Saint Joseph Hospital Residency Program, Presence Health (2014); Recipient, Research Grant Award, Society of American Gastrointestinal and Endoscopic Surgeons (2005); Honoree, Best Laparoscopic Fellows Oral Presentation, Society of American Gastrointestinal and Endoscopic Surgeons (2004); Recipient, Scholarship Award, Society of Laparoendoscopic Surgeons (2004); Recipient, Scholarship Award, Society of Laparoendoscopic Surgeons (2003); Recipient, Resident Achievement Award, University of Illinois at Chicago (2003); Honoree, Healthgrades Honor Roll **Membership:** Executive Medical Board, Mercy Hospital & Medical Center (2009-Present); Council, Illinois Chapter, American College of Surgeons (2009-Present); Advisory Board, West Central Region, Allergan Council for the Advancement of Bariatrics (2009-Present); Member-at-Large, American Society of Metabolic and Bariatric Surgery; Fellow, American College of Surgeons Society of American Gastrointestinal and Endoscopic Surgeons; Society of Laparoenodscopic Surgeons; American Society of Gastrointestinal Endoscopy; American Society of Healthcare Executives; Honorary Fellow, Brazilian College of Digestive Surgeons **Shipping Address:** 331 W Surf St., Ste 5100, Chicago Institute of Advanced Surgery, Chicago, IL, 60657

Charles Lynch

Title: Investment Company Executive **Industry:** Financial Services **Company Name:** Market Value Partners Company **Date of Birth:** 09/07/1927 **Place of Birth:** Denver **State:** CO **Parents:** Laurence J. Lynch; Louanna (Robertson) Lynch **Marital Status:** Married **Spouse Name:** Justine Bailey (12/27/1992) **Children:** Charles A.; Tara O'Hara; Casey Alexander **Education:** BS, Yale University (1950); Honorary LLD, Golden Gate University **Career:** Chairman, Market Value Partners Company (1999-Present); Chairman, Market Value Partners Company (1990-1995); Chairman, Executive Committee, Board of Directors, Levolor, Inc. (1989-1990); President, Levolor, Inc. (1988-1989); Chief Executive Officer, Levolor, Inc. (1988-1989); Chairman, DHL Airways, Inc. (1986-1988); Chief Executive Officer, DHL Airways, Inc. (1986-1988); Chairman of the Board, Saga Corporation (1978-1986); Chief Executive Officer, Saga Corporation (1978-1986); Executive Vice President, W. R. Grace & Company (1972-1978); Rotating Board Director, W. R. Grace & Company (1972-1978); Vice President of Manufacturing, SCOA Industries (1969-1972); Director of Marketing, DuPont (1965-1969); Employee, DuPont (1950-1969); Chairman, Fresh Choice, Inc.; Chairman, Arrowhead Mills, Inc., The Hain Celestial Group, Inc.; Chairman, Mauna Loa Macadamia Nut Corporation; Chief Executive Officer, Mauna Loa Macadamia Nut Corporation; Chairman, nSpired Natural Foods, Inc, Hain Celestial; Chief Executive Officer, nSpired Natural Foods, Inc, Hain Celestial **Career Related:** Chairman, Board of Directors, Corazonas Foods, Inc.; Adviser, Bain & Company; Adviser, Sienna Ventures; Adviser, Roscko Technologies; Adviser, VIVOtech Inc.; Chairman, Age Wave, Inc.; Chairman, Authentic Specialty Foods, Inc.; Chairman, Bojangles, BJ Acquisitions, Corporation; Web Designer, CloudSource, Inc.; Director, Consolidated Freightways, Inc.; Director, Crocker National Corporation; Director, Crocker National Bank; Director, Cucina Holdings, Inc.; Chairman, Dakin, Inc.; Chairman, Fresh Choice, Inc.; Chairman, Greyhound Lines, Inc.; Director, Hexcel Corporation; Director, Industrial Indemnity Company; Director, Josh Blair and Company; Director, KaiserTech, Ltd.; Director, Kaiser Aluminum and Chemical Corporation; Chairman, LaSalsa Holding Company; Director, Madge Networks; Director, Mid-Peninsula Bank; Director, MiFund.com; Director, Nordstrom, Inc.; Director, Pacific Mutual Holding Company; Director, PST Vans, Inc.; Chairman, Audit Committee, Secure Data Motion; Director, Shari's Management Corporation; Director, Southern Pacific Transportation Company; Director, Spectrum Organic Products, Inc.; Director, SRI International, Inc.; Director, Syntex Corporation; Director, Tradepoint Solutions; Director, Vocent; Joslin Diabetes Center, Inc.; Founder, Lincoln Club of Northern California; Project Interdependence; Adviser, Big Tray.com; Adviser, Decibel; Adviser, Demeter Group; Adviser, EnviroSystems, Inc.; Adviser, iHello; Adviser, Mercanti; Adviser, Senior Surfers.com; Adviser, Shoppingtheworld.com; Adviser, Team-Tooz.com; Adviser, WiseConnect; Adviser, WishClick; Adviser, Zingdata **Civic:** Chairman, Board of Directors, United Way of the Bay Area (1990-1992); Past Chairman, Bay Area Campaign (1987); Vice Chairman, Bay Area Council; Director Bay Area Council; Past Chairman, California Business Roundtable; Past Chairman, Board of Trustees Palo Alto Medical Foundation; California Chamber of Commerce; The Conference Board; World Affairs Council; Advisory Council, Graduate School of Business, Stanford University; Governance Board, University of Notre Dame; Industry Education Council of California; Board of Trustees, Occidental College; Trustee, The Hill School; Trustee, Haas School of Business, University of California, Berkeley; Founding Director, American Institute of Wine & Food; Business Advisory Committee, Northern California Chapter, Economic Literacy Council; Adviser, Girl's Club of America; Trustee, YMCA of America; Board of Trustees, San Francisco Ballet; Board of Directors, YMCA of San Francisco **Membership:** Yale Club of New York City; International Lawn Tennis Club, IC Council; Menlo Country Club; Pacific-Union Club; Coral Beach & Tennis Club; The Vintage Club; Menlo Circus Club **Marquis Who's Who Honors:** Albert Nelson Marquis Lifetime Achievement Award (2017) **To what do you attribute your success:** Mr. Lynch attributes his success to hiring very accomplished and smart individuals. **Why did you become involved in your profession or industry:** Mr. Lynch became involved in his profession when he started out in the Navy, and learned very quickly that he needed to create a good team in order to succeed. **Hobbies:** Golf **Political Affiliations:** Republican **Religion:** Catholic **Shipping Address:** 24 Susan Gale Court, Menlo Park, CA, 94025

Ralph Mabey

Title: Lawyer, Shareholder **Industry:** Law and Legal Services **Company Name:** Kirton McConkie PC **Date of Birth:** 05/20/1944 **Place of Birth:** Salt Lake City **State:** UT **Parents:** Rendell Noel Mabey; Rachel (Wilson) Mabey **Marital Status:** Married **Spouse Name:** Sylvia States (6/5/1968) **Children:** Kathryn; Rachel; Elizabeth; Emily; Sara **Education:** JD, Columbia University (1972); BA, University of Utah (1968) **Career:** Partner, Kirton-McConkie (2014-Present); Senior of Counsel, Stutman Treister & Glatt, LA (2006-2014); Partner, Mabey & Murray LC (2005-2006); Partner, LeBoeuf, Lamb, Greene & MacRae LLP (1983-2005); Bankruptcy Judge, U.S. Court, Salt Lake City, UT (1979-1983); Partner, Irvine, Smith & Mabey (1973-1979); Law Clerk, U.S. District Court, Salt Lake City, UT (1972-1973); Law Clerk, Attorney General, Salt Lake City, UT (1970) **Career Related:** Professor of Law, S.J. Quinney College of Law, The University of Utah (2007-Present); Senior Lecturer, BYU Law, Brigham Young University (1983-2005) **Military Service:** With, U.S. Army Reserve (1968-1974) **Creative Works:** Managing Editor, Norton Bankruptcy Law Adviser (1983-1985) **Membership:** Business Bankruptcy Committee, ABA; National Bankruptcy Conference; American Law Institute; American Bankruptcy Institute; American College of Bankruptcy; Director, International Insolvency Institute **Bar Admissions:** United States Court of Appeals for the Third Circuit (1993); Supreme Court of the United States (1988); United States Court of Appeals for the Fourth Circuit (1988); United States Court of Appeals for the Second Circuit (1985); United States Court of Appeals for the Tenth Circuit (1976); United States District Court for the District of Utah (1972); Utah (1972) **Hobbies:** Running; Fly fishing **Political Affiliations:** Republican **Religion:** Mormon **Shipping Address:** Kirton Mcconkie Building, 50 E South Temple, Ste. 400, Salt Lake City, UT, 84111

Diana T. MacArthur

Title: Advanced Technology Executive **Industry:** Technology **Date of Birth:** 07/07/1933 **Place of Birth:** Santa Fe **State:** NM **Marital Status:** Widowed **Children:** Elizabeth Tschursin; Alexander Tschursin **Education:** BA, Vassar College, Poughkeepsie, NY (1955) **Career:** Chairman, President, CEO, Dynamac International Inc. (1988-2010); Chairman, CEO, Research Analysis and Management Corporation (1988-1992); Vice President, Director, Dynamac International Inc. (1980-1988); President, Consumer Dynamics (1977-1980); Program Manager, Aerospace Division, General Electrical Company (1974-1976); Private Consultant (1966-1974); Director, Division of Private and International Organizations, Peace Corps (1965-1966); Registered Program Officer, North Africa, Near East, South Asia, Peace Corps (1964); Deputy Chief, West Africa, Peace Corps (1963); Vice President, Director, Thomas J. Deegan Company (1961-1962); Consultant, Economist, Checchi & Company (1957-1961) **Career Related:** President, Foreign Traders, Inc. (1980-1986) **Civic:** Lady Bird Johnson Wildflower Center (1985-Present); Trustee, Santa Fe Institute (2005-2012); Board of Directors, Science and Technology Corporation, University of New Mexico (2004-2012); Board Visitors, Menninger-Baylor College of Medicine, Methodist Hospital Foundation (2004-2006); Center Strategic & International Studies: Senior Policy on National Challenges (1996); President's Committee of Advisors on Science and Technology (1994-2001); National Benefits from National Laboratory Committee (1993); CSIS Strengthening of America Committee (1992); Trustee, Menninger Foundation, Topeka, KS (1972-2004); Citizens Advisory Board to the President Council on Youth Opportunity (1966-1970); The Chancellor's Advisory Council; University Systems of Maryland; Board Visitors, University of Maryland Biotechnology Institute; Advanced Committee, Center for Strategic and International Studies; Board of Directors, Atlantic Council; USA Business Advisory Council, Center for China-United States Cooperative, University of Denver; Geopolitics of Energy **Membership:** Council on Competitiveness; Executive Committee, Business-Higher Education Forum; Executive Committee, Technology Council of Maryland; President, Board of Directors, Los Alamos National Laboratory Foundation; National Hispanic Cultural Center Foundation; The Santa Fe Opera; Phi Beta Kappa **Marquis Who's Who Honors:** Albert Nelson Marquis Lifetime Achievement Award (2017) **Shipping Address:** 3101 Old Pecos Trail, Unit 624, Santa Fe, NM, 87505

Ilone M. Macduff

Title: Music Educator **Industry:** Education/Educational Services **Company Name:** Private Music Studio **Date of Birth:** 01/30/1938 **Place of Birth:** Berwyn **State:** IL **Parents:** Albert Kenneth Hinckle; Dorothy Lydia Ardina Lange **Marital Status:** Married **Spouse Name:** James Donald Macduff Jr. (4/2/1959) **Children:** Gordon Scott; James Alexander; Charles Colin **Education:** MusB, University of Idaho (1976) **Career:** Private Voice and Piano Teacher (1964-Present) **Career Related:** 25-year Volunteer, Boy Scouts of America **Civic:** Member, Thurston County Historic Commission (1984-1998); Boy Scouts of America, Tumwater, Washington (1968-1993); International Representative, Boy Scouts of America (1983-1993); Council Member, Eagle Board, Boy Scouts of America (1985-1990); Chairman, Scout-O-Rama (1979-1981); Council Member, Pow Wow Staff, Boy Scouts of America (1973-1976); District Cub Scout Program Chairman, Boy Scouts of America (1973-1975); Director, Monthly Musicales, State Capitol Museum (1970-1974); Founder, Cub Scout Day Camp, Tumwater Area Council (1973) **Awards:** Lamb Award (1987); District Commissioner Award, Boy Scouts of America (1981); Silver Beaver Award, Boy Scouts of America (1981); Single and Double Awards, National Federation of Music Clubs (1969, 1977) **Membership:** Former Member, American College Musicians; Student Recitals Chair, Olympia Music Teachers Association (2005); President, Olympia Music Teachers Association (2003-2004); Voice Auditions Chair, Olympia Chapter, MTNA (2001, 2004); Show Chairman, Puget Sound Gordon Setter Club (2003-2004); Chairman, National Dog Show, Gordon Setter Club of America, Inc. (2003); Treasurer, Puget Sound Gordon Setter Club (1998-2000) **Marquis Who's Who Honors:** Albert Nelson Marquis Lifetime Achievement Award (2017) **To what do you attribute your success:** Ms. Macduff attributes her success to her voice teacher and adviser at the University of Idaho, the late Professor Norman Logan. **Why did you become involved in your profession or industry:** Ms. Macduff became involved in music and music education because of her admiration for Professor Logan. **What do you consider to be the highlight of your career:** Ms. Macduff considers the knowledge that one of her students not only has a degree in music, but has become a private music teacher to be the highlight of her career. **Where will you be in five years:** Since she is currently 80 years old, she will probably be dead. **Hobbies:** Photography **Political Affiliations:** Independent **Religion:** Lutheran **Shipping Address:** 8524 Delphi Road S.W., Olympia, WA, 98512

Richard P. Mackessy

Title: Surgeon **Industry:** Media & Entertainment **Company Name:** Union County Orthopedic Group **Place of Birth:** Elizabeth **State:** NJ **Marital Status:** Married **Spouse Name:** Karen **Children:** Andrew; Patrick; Timothy; Danielle **Education:** Fellow in Hand Microsurgery, Jefferson Medical College (1983-1984); Resident in Orthopedic Surgery, St. Luke's Hospital (1980-1983); Resident in General Surgery, St. Vincent's Hospital (1978-1980); MD, University of Medicine and Dentistry of New Jersey (Now Rutgers School of Biomedical and Health Sciences) (1978); Diploma, College of the Holy Cross (1972) **Certifications:** Diplomate in Surgery of the Hand, The American Board of Orthopaedic Surgery (1990, 1997, 2007); Diplomate, The American Board of Orthopaedic Surgery (1986) **Career:** Owner, Union County Orthopaedic Group, P.A.; Chief of Orthopedics, Trinitas Regional Medical Center (2001-Present); Director of Hand Service, University Hospital, Newark, New Jersey (1986-1999); Director of Pediatric Hand Service, United Hospitals, Newark, New Jersey (1986-1991); Chairman, Department of Orthopedics, Trinitas Regional Medical Center, Elizabeth, New Jersey; Attending Orthopedic Surgeon, Trinitas Regional Medical Center, Elizabeth, New Jersey; Attending Orthopedic Surgeon, Rahway Hospital, New Jersey; Attending Orthopedic Surgeon, Overlook Hospital, Summit, New Jersey **Career Related:** Instructor, Synthes Courses (1995, 2007); Lecturer, Hand Review Course, New York (1988-1990); Presenter in Field **Awards:** Recipient, Outstanding Medical Educator Award, Medical Society of New Jersey (2015); Recipient, Distinguished Trustee Award, United Hospital Fund (2013); Honoree, Top 100 Doctors in New Jersey (2010); Recipient, Sergio Award (1999); Honoree, Teacher of the Year, Department of Orthopedics, University of Medicine and Dentistry of New Jersey (Now Rutgers, The State University of New Jersey) (1993, 1998); Healing the Children Award for Treating Poor Children from Underdeveloped Countries; Top Doctor, Castle Connolly Medical Ltd; Honoree, Named Top Doctors for Seven Years, Inside New Jersey Magazine **Membership:** Board of Trustees, Elizabeth General Medical Center (1999-Present); Board of Councilors, Trinitas Regional Medical Center (2002); President, New Jersey Orthopedic Society (2001-2002); Board of Trustees, Trinitas Regional Medical Center (2001); President, Jefferson Alumni Association (1999-2001); American Association of Orthopaedic Surgeons; American Medical Association; Medical Society of New Jersey; Union County Medical Society; Past President, Jefferson Hand Society; American Society for Surgery of the Hand; New York Society for Surgery of the Hand; Irish Orthopaedic Association; Eastern Orthopaedic Association; International College of Surgeons; Medical Staff President, Elizabeth General Medical Center; New Jersey State Representative, American Academy of Orthopaedic Surgeons; Board of Councilors, American Academy of Orthopaedic Surgeons **Hobbies:** Skiing; Sailing; Golf; Hiking national parks; Traveling **Business Address:** 210 W Saint Georges Ave., Ste 301, Linden, NJ, 07036 **Shipping Address:** 17 Hickory Rd, Short Hills, NJ, 07078

Cherie K. MacQueen

Title: Interior Designer, Radio and TV Broadcaster **Industry:** Media & Entertainment **Date of Birth:** 03/20/1952 **Place of Birth:** Kansas City **State:** MO **Parents:** Ira Raymond Milks; Margaret Estelle (Turner) Milks; Ward L. Cruce (Stepfather) **Education:** Postgraduate Work, California State University, San Bernardino (1998); BS in Liberal Studies, Excelsior College (1993); AA in Liberal Arts, Los Angeles Valley College (1982) **Certifications:** Certified in Interior Design, University of California, Riverside (2002) **Career:** Owner, Ladysmythe Handcrafts (2003-2007); Owner, The Keilani Company (2003-2007); News and Sports Specialist, Armed Forces Radio and TV (Now American Forces Network) (1994-1999); Internal Information Manager, Armed Forces Radio and TV (Now American Forces Network) (1991-1994); Broadcast Support Manager, Armed Forces Radio and TV (Now American Forces Network) (1990-1991); Supervisor Broadcast Support Specialist, Armed Forces Radio and TV (Now American Forces Network) (1986-1990); Radio Production Specialist, Armed Forces Radio and TV (Now American Forces Network) (1984-1986); Radio Traffic Specialist, Armed Forces Radio and TV (Now American Forces Network) (1980-1984) **Civic:** Author, "Sweet Pea Teddy Bear," National Library of Poetry (1995) **Military Service:** Broadcast Journalist, U.S. Army (1977-1980); Administrative Specialist, U.S. Army (1975-1977); Personnel Specialist, U.S. Army (1973-1975) **Awards:** Army Commendation Medal, U.S. Army (1980); National Defense Service Medal, U.S. Army (1973); Good Conduct Medal, U.S. Army **Membership:** Women in Military Service for America (1997-Present); Allied Member, Pasadena Chapter, American Society of Interior Designers (2004-2008); Board of Directors, Inland-Palm Springs Chapter, American Society of Interior Designers (2003-2004); Allied Member, American Society of Interior Designers (2002-2004); Student Member, Inland-Palm Springs Chapter, American Society of Interior Designers (1999-2002); Vice President, Los Angeles Chapter, Armed Forces Broadcasters Association (1991-1993); Association of the United States Army (1975-1980); Pacific Pioneer Broadcasters; Life Member, DAV **Marquis Who's Who Honors:** Albert Nelson Marquis Lifetime Achievement Award (2017) **To what do you attribute your success:** She attributes her success to her education and her professional experience. **Why did you become involved in your profession or industry:** She became involved in her industry because of her interest in radio and TV production, as well as her interest in art, handcrafts, and drafting. **What do you consider to be the highlight of your career:** The highlight of her career was her Army assignment in Vicenza, Italy, and the work she did there in radio and TV broadcasting. **Hobbies:** Crafts; Crocheting **Shipping Address:** 2887 Indian Canyon Ct, Highland, CA, 92346

Jamshid Maddahi

Title: Cardiologist, Nuclear Medicine Physician, Professor **Industry:** Medicine & Health Care **Date of Birth:** 08/28/1950 **Place of Birth:** Tehran **State/Country of Origin:** Iran **Marital Status:** Married **Education:** Resident in Nuclear Medicine, Cedars-Sinai Medical Center, University of California, Los Angeles School of Medicine (1980-1982); Fellow in Cardiology, Cedars-Sinai Medical Center, University of California, Los Angeles School of Medicine (1977-1979); Resident in Internal Medicine, University of Illinois Affiliated Hospitals (1975-1977); MD Degree, University of Tehran, with Distinction (1975) **Career:** Professor of Molecular and Medical Pharmacology (Nuclear Medicine) and Medicine (Cardiology), David Geffen School of Medicine at University of California, Los Angeles (1996-Present); Director of Biomedical Imaging Institute (1992-Present) **Career Related:** Presenter, More than 1,300 Invited Lectures throughout the World **Civic:** Chairman, Advanced Cardiac Imaging Committee, American Heart Association, Inc. **Creative Works:** Author, More than 200 Research Manuscripts and Abstracts in Peer-Reviewed Scientific Journals **Awards:** Named, Best Doctors in America (1992-Present); Named, Professional of the Year (2014-2015); Recipient, Award, American College of Cardiology Foundation (2005); Recipient, Faculty Teaching Award, University of California, Los Angeles Division of Cardiology (2004); Recipient, Herman Blumgart Award of the Cardiovascular Council, Society of Nuclear Medicine (2004); Recipient, Tree of Life Award, 100th Anniversary of Jewish National Fund (2002); Recipient, Faculty Teaching Award, University of California, Los Angeles Division of Cardiology (2000); Recipient, Homi Bhabha Award for Outstanding Contributions to Nuclear Cardiology, Nuclear Cardiological Soceity of India (1999); Named, Best Doctors in Los Angeles, Los Angeles Magazine (1998); Recipient, Distinguished Scientist Award for Distinguished Contributions to Nuclear Medicine, Western Regional Society of Nuclear Medicine (1998); Named, Taplin Memorial Lecturer, Western Chapter, Society of Nuclear Medicine (1997); Named, Winfield Evan Memorial Lecturer, Southwestern Chapter, Society of Nuclear Medicine (1995); Recipient, Distinguished Ted Block Memorial Lecturer Award, Southwestern Chapter of the Society of Nuclear Medicine (1992); Certificate of Honor for Humanitarian Achievements and Dedication to Hadassah Medical Center (1991); Recipient, Norman D. Poe Scholarship Award, Society of Nuclear Medicine (1981); Honoree, Best Doctors in America; Recipient, Numerous Grants and Awards **Membership:** American Heart Association; American College of Cardiology; Former President, Pacific Southwest Chapter, Society of Nuclear Medicine and Molecular Imaging; Institute for Clinical PET; Founding Member, Chair, Southern California Working Group, American Society of Nuclear Cardiology **To what do you attribute your success:** Dr. Maddahi attributes his success to staying on the cutting edge of the industry. **Why did you become involved in your profession or industry:** Dr. Maddahi became involved in his profession because of his passion for medicine. He had an intuition at the very young age of 12; it was at the time of the first heart transplant that was done by Dr. Barnard, a south African physician, in December of 1967. It memorized Dr. Maddahi and he got very interested in the field of cardiology. His interest in nuclear medicine happened when he was in elementary school there was an event at their university honoring Albert Einstein, who passed in 1965. It was an anniversary of his death, the event was about the peaceful use of nuclear energy and it was organized to bring the attention to people. This event got Dr. Maddahi very much interested in nuclear medicine. **Where will you be in five years:** In five years, Dr. Maddahi intends to continue on the same path. **Hobbies:** Skiing; Biking; Wine making **Business Address:** 100 UCLA Medical Plz, Ste 410, Los Angeles, CA, 90095 **Website:** http://www.drjamshidmaddahi.com

Naeem H. Mady

Title: Vice President of Regulatory Services **Industry:** Consumer Goods and Services **Company Name:** Intertek Group PLC **Children:** Two Children **Education:** Master's Degree, Fairleigh Dickinson University (1973); Bachelor's Degree, Alexandria, Egypt (1966) **Certifications:** Business Certificate, Management and Marketing, Long Island University (1985) **Career:** Vice President of Regulatory Services, Intertek Group PLC (2010-Present); Vice President of Regulatory Services, Ciba Expert Chemicals (1996-2003); Chief Executive Officer, Mthree Productions (1983-2011); Manager, Analytical Research, Cibi-Geigy Corporation (1983-1996); Vice President of Regulatory Services, Ciba Expert Services (1980-2010) **Civic:** President, Board of Directors, The Ocean Club, Inc. (2013-Present) **Membership:** American Chemical Society; Society of Petroleum Engineers; Society of Plastic Industry; Board Member, Plastics Industry Association **To what do you attribute your success:** Mr. Mady attributes his success to the passion that he has for his work. **Why did you become involved in your profession or industry:** Mr. Mady became involved in his profession because he is a chemist, so he had to find a job within the chemistry industry. **Shipping Address:** 1060 Holland Drive, Suite G, Intertek Group PLC, Boca Raton, FL, 33487 **Website:** https://www.linkedin.com/in/naeem-mady-30303112

Subhash Mahajan

Title: Distinguished Professor **Industry:** Education/Educational Services **Company Name:** University of California, Davis **Place of Birth:** Gurdaspur **Country of Origin:** India **Marital Status:** Married **Spouse Name:** Sushma Sondhi (9/3/1965) **Children:** Sanjoy; Sunit; Ashish **Education:** PhD in Materials Science and Engineering, University of California (1965); BE in Metallurgy, Indian Institute of Science, Bengaluru, Honors (1961); BS, Panjab University, Highest Honors, Chandigarh, India (1959) **Career:** Distinguished Professor, Department of Chemical Engineering and Materials Science, University of California, Davis (2011-Present); Professor, Electronic Materials, Arizona State University, Tempe, AZ (1997-Present); Special Advisor to the Chancellor, University of California, Davis (2011-2016); Professor of Electronic Materials, Arizona State University, Tempe, AZ (1997-2011); Fulton Technology Fellow, Ira A. Fulton Schools of Engineering, Arizona State University, Tempe, AZ (2009-2010); Fulton Technology Fellow, Ira A. Fulton School of Engineering, Arizona State University, Tempe, AZ (2009-2010); Director, School Materials, Arizona State University, Tempe, AZ (2006-2009); Regents Professor, Arizona State University, Tempe, AZ (2007); Interim Chairman, Chemical and Materials Engineering, Arizona State University, Tempe, AZ (2000-2006); Department Chairman, Chemical and Materials Engineering, Arizona State University, Tempe, AZ (2000-2006); Associate Chairman, Arizona State University, Tempe, AZ (1999); Professor, Material Science and Engineering, Electronic Materials Department, Carnegie Mellon University, Pittsburgh, PA (1983-1997); Research Manager, AT&T Bell Laboratories, Murray Hill, NJ (1981-1983); Member, Technology Staff, AT&T Bell Laboratories, Murray Hill, NJ (1971-1983); Harwell Fellow, Atomic Energy Research Establishment, Harwell, England (1968-1971); Research Metallurgist, University of Denver (1965-1968); Research Assistant, University of California, Berkeley (1961-1965) **Career Related:** Visiting Professor, Ecole Centrale de Lyon, Ecully, France (1993); Member, Site Panel, Materials Research Laboratory (1993); Visiting Professor, University of Antwerp, Antwerpen, Belgium (1991); Lecturer in Field; Speaker in Field; Patentee in Field; Consultant in Field **Civic:** Member, Materials Research Advisory Committee, Division of Materials Research, National Science Foundation (1989-1992) **Creative Works:** Coordinating Editor, "The Acta Journals" (2004); Editor, "Acta Materialia" (2001); Co-Editor, "Encyclopedia of Materials: Science and Technology" (2001); Editor, "Handbook on Semiconductors, Volume 3" (1994); Co-Editor, "The Encyclopedia of Advanced Materials" (1994); Co-Editor, "The Concise Encyclopedia of Semiconducting Materials and Related Technologies" (1992); Co-Editor, "Electrochemical Society Symposium Volume" (1983); Contributor, Articles, Professional Journals **Awards:** Albert Sauveur Achievement Award, ASM International; Gold Medal, ASM International; John Bardeen Award, The Minerals, Metals & Materials Society; The Educator Award, The Minerals, Metals & Materials Society; Albert Easton White Distinguished Teacher Award; Distinguished Alumnus Award, IISc Alumni Association, Bangalore, India **Membership:** Electronic Materials Committee, The Minerals, Metals & Materials Society (1990-1994); Chairman, Electronic, Magnetic and Photonic Materials Committee (1984-1986); Divisional Editor, The Electrochemical Society (1976-1986); Electronics Division, The Electrochemical Society (1973-1986); Physical Metallurgy Committee, The Minerals, Metals & Materials Society (1976-1983); The Minerals, Metals & Materials Society (1975-1980); Vice Chairman, Mechanical Metallurgy Committee, The Minerals, Metals & Materials Society (1978-1979); Fellow, The Minerals, Metals & Materials Society; Fellow, Materials Research Society; Fellow, ASM International; Trustee Board, ASM International; Campbell Memorial Lecturer, ASM International; Organizer, Symposium, American Association for Crystal Growth; Fellow, Indian National Academy of Engineering; Technical Director Board, The Minerals, Metals & Materials Society **Marquis Who's Who Honors:** Albert Nelson Marquis Lifetime Achievement Award (2017) **Why did you become involved in your profession or industry:** Dr. Mahajan became involved in his profession because he loved science and mathematics, and he wanted to study engineering to work in research. **What do you consider to be the highlight of your career:** The highlight of Dr. Mahajan's career was working at Bell Laboratories in New Jersey and Harwell Fellowship in Atomic Research in England. These experiences exposed him to a kind of work that was way ahead of most organizations. **Shipping Address:** 44218 Lakeview Dr, El Macero, CA, 95618

Michael E. Mahla

Title: Professor of Anesthesiology, Chairman, Department of Anesthesiology **Industry:** Medicine & Health Care **Company Name:** Sidney Kimmel Medical College, Thomas Jefferson University **Date of Birth:** 03/08/1953 **Place of Birth:** Wilmington **State/Country of Origin:** DE **Parents:** Elbert Myron Mahla; Mary Pauline (Tice) Mahla **Marital Status:** Married **Spouse Name:** Sno Ellen White (6/9/1979) **Children:** Melody Joy **Education:** Fellow, Neuroanesthesia, Johns Hopkins Medical Center, Baltimore, MD (1982); Resident, Walter Reed National Military Medical Center (1980-1983); Intern, Walter Reed National Military Medical Center (1979-1980); MD, Sidney Kimmel Medical College, Thomas Jefferson University (1979); BS in Chemistry, Davidson College, Magna Cum Laude (1975) **Certifications:** Diplomate, American Board of Anesthesiology (1984-Present); Certification, National Board of Medical Examiners (1980); Medical License, Commonwealth of Pennsylvania; Medical License, State of New York **Career:** Professor, Department of Anesthesiology, Sidney Kimmel Medical College, Thomas Jefferson University (2015-Present); Chair, Department of Anesthesiology, Sidney Kimmel Medical College, Thomas Jefferson University (2018); Professor, Department of Anesthesiology and Neurosurgery, College of Medicine, University of Florida Health (2001-2015) **Career Related:** Chair, Department of Anesthesiology, Sidney Kimmel Medical College (2018-Present); Chief of Anesthesiology, Jefferson Hospital for Neuroscience, Thomas Jefferson University Hospitals (2015-Present); Chief, Division of Neuroanesthesia, Department of Anesthesiology, Sidney Kimmel Medical College, Thomas Jefferson University (2015-Present); Attending Anesthesiologist, Thomas Jefferson University Hospitals (2015-Present) **Military Service:** Active Duty, US Army Medical Corps (1979-1988) **Creative Works:** Ad-Hoc Consultant, Anesthesiology (1995-Present); Ad-Hoc Consultant, Anesthesia and Analgesia (1995-Present); Contributing Author, "Miller's Anesthesia" (2015); Contributing Author, "Anesthesiology" (2012); Contributing Author, Journal of Neurosurgery (2011); Contributing Author, "Critical Care" (2009) **Awards:** Recipient, Teacher of the Year Award, Department of Anesthesiology, Sidney Kimmel Medical College, Thomas Jefferson University (2016); Recipient, Teacher of the Year Award, Society for Neuroscience in Anesthesiology and Critical Care (2012); Recipient, Outstanding Poster by a Professional Medical Educator Award, Southern Group on Educational Affairs (2010) **Membership:** Enterprise Pharmacy and Therapeutics Committee, Jefferson Health, Thomas Jefferson University (2017-Present); Pharmacy and Therapeutics Committee, Thomas Jefferson University Hospitals (2016-Present); Clinical Competence Committee, Department of Anesthesiology, Sidney Kimmel Medical College, Thomas Jefferson University (2015-Present) **Marquis Who's Who Honors:** Albert Nelson Marquis Lifetime Achievement Award (2017) **Hobbies:** Classically trained pianist and tenor; Church **Political Affiliations:** Moderate **Religion:** Mormon **Shipping Address:** 111 S 11th St Gibbon 8490, Sidney Kimmel Medical College of Thomas Jefferson University, Philadelphia, PA, 19107

Ursula Mahlendorf, PhD

Title: Literature Educator **Industry:** Education/Educational Services **Company Name:** University of California, Santa Barbara **Date of Birth:** 10/24/1929 **Place of Birth:** Strehlen **Country of Origin:** Silesia, Germany **Education:** Graduate, New Directions in Psychoanalysis, Washington, DC (2002); PhD in German Literature, Brown University, Providence, RI (1958); MA in English Literature, Brown University, Providence, RI (1956); Student, Brown University, Providence, RI (1953-1957); Student, Bonn University, Federal Republic of Germany (1953); Student, University of Tubingen, Federal Republic of Germany (1950-1952); Student, Oberschule an der Hamburger Straße, Bremen, Federal Republic of Germany (1950); Student, London University **Career:** Emerita, University of California, Santa Barbara (1993-Present); Professor, Women's Studies, University of California, Santa Barbara (1988-1993); Associate Dean, College of Letters and Science, University of California, Santa Barbara (1986-1989); Chairman, Department of Germanic and Slavic Languages and Literature, University of California, Santa Barbara (1980-1983); Associate Director, Campus Coordinator, Education Abroad Program, University of California, Santa Barbara (1967-1969); Acting Instructor to Professor of German, University of California, Santa Barbara (1957-1993); Teaching Assistant, Brown University, Providence, RI (1953-1957) **Career Related:** Co-Chair, Nietzsche Symposium, Department of Germanic and Slavic Languages and Literature, University of California, Santa Barbara (1981); Chairman, Symposium in Honor of Harry Slochower (1977); Fulbright Fellow (1951-1952) **Creative Works:** Author, "The Wellsprings of Literary Creation," Second Edition (2010); Editor, "The Shame of Survival: Working Through a Nazi Childhood" (2009); Editor, "Life Guidance through Literature" (1992); Author, "The Wellsprings of Literary Creation" (1985); Co-Editor, "Dimensions of Social Psychiatry" (1979); Co-Editor, "Man for Man: A Multi-Disciplinary Workshop Affecting Man's Social and Psychological Nature through Community Action" (1973); Editor, "Fuhrers Begeisterte Toechter," German Edition; Editor, American Journal of Social Psychiatry and Journal of Evolutionary Psychology; Contributor, More Than 90 Articles, Professional Journals **Awards:** Dickson Emeriti Professorship, University of California, Santa Barbara (2009-2010); Named in Honor, Festschrift, California (2004); Alumni Teaching Award (1981); Research Grantee, University of California, Santa Barbara (1974-1990) **Membership:** Modern Language Association; Professional Member, Association for Applied Psychoanalysis; General Services Administration; Women in German **To what do you attribute your success:** Dr. Mahlendorf attributes her success to her love of reading. **Why did you become involved in your profession or industry:** Dr. Mahlendorf wishes to communicate her love of literature. **What do you consider to be the highlight of your career:** A highlight of Dr. Mahlendorf's career was receiving teaching prizes in 1980 and 2009. **Hobbies:** Sculpting; Woodcarving **Political Affiliations:** Democrat **Shipping Address:** 1505 Portesuello Avenue, Santa Barbara, CA, 93105

Maurice Jeremiah Mahoney

Title: Professor Emeritus in Genetics **Industry:** Medicine & Health Care **Company Name:** Yale University **Date of Birth:** 08/04/1935 **Place of Birth:** Washington **State/Country of Origin:** DC **Parents:** Maurice Mahoney; Julia Johnson Mahoney **Marital Status:** Married **Spouse Name:** Blanche Katz (5/23/2004) **Children:** Tatyana Renner; Karen; Cydney; Matthew; Allison; Linnea **Education:** JD, University of Connecticut (1994); MD, University of Pittsburgh (1962); AB, Cornell University (1957); Fellow, Children's Hospital Of Pittsburgh, UPMC; Fellow, Yale School of Medicine **Certifications:** Medical License, State of Connecticut (1994); Certified in Clinical Biochemical Genetics, American Board of Medical Genetics and Genomics (1982); Diplomate, American Board of Pediatrics (1967); Certified in Clinical Genetics; Certified in Pediatrics **Career:** Executive Director, Human Investigation Committee, Yale School of Medicine, Yale University (2000-2017); Professor of Genetics, Yale University, New Haven, CT (1970) **Career Related:** Fellow, American College of Medical Genetics and Genomics, Bethesda, MD (1993-Present); Affiliate, Fetal Diagnosis and Therapy, Basel, Switzerland (1984-Present); Affiliate, APS-SPR, The Woodlands, TX (1983-Present); Member, Board of Directors, Society for Inherited Metabolic Disorders (1984-1987); Member, The American Society of Human Genetics, Bethesda, MD (1981-1984) **Military Service:** Captain, US Army, Fort McClellan, Alabama (1966-1968) **Creative Works:** Member, Editorial Board, "The Journal of BioLaw & Business," Denville, NJ (1997-Present); Contributor, "American Journal of Medical Genetics," John Wiley & Sons, Inc., New York, NY (1977-1994); Editor, "Medicine of the Fetus & Mother" **Awards:** CMS Meaningful Use Stage 1 Certification, EpicCare Ambulatory EMR, Epic Systems Corporation (2014); Named, America's Top Doctors (2003-2014); Named, Top Doctors in New York Metropolitan Area (2002-2014); Listee, Top Doctors, New York Magazine, New York Media LLC (2002-2008) **Membership:** Fellow, American Association for the Advancement of Science (1998-2005); Women's Reproductive Health Research Career Development Center, National Institutes of Health; Office of Cooperative Research, Yale University **Bar Admissions:** Connecticut (1994) **Marquis Who's Who Honors:** Albert Nelson Marquis Lifetime Achievement Award (2017) **Where will you be in five years:** In the next five years, Dr. Mahoney will continue with limited research on medical genetics. **Hobbies:** Kayacking; Opera **Business Address:** PO Box 208005, New Haven, CT, 06520 **Shipping Address:** 526 Riverdale Dr, Stratford, CT, 06615

Patricia Davison Mail, PhD

Title: Public Health Service Officer (Retired) **Industry:** Government Administration/ Government Relations/Government Services **Date of Birth:** 12/10/1940 **Place of Birth:** Kamloops **State/Country of Origin:** Canada **Parents:** George Allen Mail; Constance (Davison) Mail **Marital Status:** Widow **Education:** PhD, University of Maryland (1996); Postgraduate Coursework, Seattle University, Seattle, WA (1974); MA, The University of Arizona, Tucson, AZ (1970); MPH, Yale University, New Haven, CT (1967); MS, Smith College, Northampton, MA (1965); BS, The University of Arizona, Tucson, AZ (1963) **Certifications:** Certified Health Education Specialist **Career:** Franke Tobey Jones Board of Directors (2018-2020); Board President, American Public Health Association (2005-2007); Faculty, Medicine Creek Tribal College (1998-1999); Extramural Science Administrator, National Institute on Alcohol Abuse and Alcoholism (1993-1997); Staff Member, Clinical and Prevention Research Division, National Institute on Alcohol Abuse and Alcoholism (1991-1993); Officer, Substance Abuse and Mental Health Services Administration (1990-1992); Officer Personnel Specialist, Alcohol, Drug Abuse and Mental Health Administration (1990-1992); Deputy Staff Director, Office of Public Health Service Surgeon General (1989); Branch Chief, Health Resources and Services Administration, National Health Service Corps. (1988); Deputy Clinical Chief, Professor of Activities Board, National Health Service Corps., Health Resources and Services Administration (1987-1988); Deputy Chief of Field Operations, National Health Service Corps., Health Resources and Services Administration (1986-1987); Chief, Health Educational Branch, Portland Area Indian Health Service (1979-1986); Commissioned Officer, United States Public Health Service (1970-1997) **Career Related:** Research Scientist, Addictive Behaviors Research Center, University of Washington (1999-Present); President, Dragon-Archer Consultant (1997-Present); Accreditation Site Visitor, Council on Education for Public Health (1996-Present); Visiting Scientist, Addictive Behaviors Research Center, University of Washington (1998-1999); Assistant Professor, Oregon Health & Science University (1998-1999); Chairman, Commissioner, National Commission for Health Education Credentialing, Inc. (1993-1994); Faculty Member, Seattle University, Seattle, WA (1974-1978) **Creative Works:** Co-Editor, With Heurtin-Roberts, Martin and Howard, "American Indian Alcoholism: Multiple Perspectives on a Complex Problem" (2002); Co-Author, With D.R. McDonald, "Tulapai to Tokay: A Bibliography of Alcohol Use and Abuse Among Native Americans of North America" (1980); Editor, "Society for Public Health Education Sounds" (1976-1986); Associate Editor, "Health Promotion Practice," American Journal of Health Behavior; Contributor, Chapters to Books, Articles to Professional Journals **Awards:** Honoree, Luther Terry Lecturer, Commissioned Officers Association (2008); Tom Drummey Award, Washington State Public Health Association (2002); Executive Director's Citation, American Public Health Association (1999); Judith Miller Award, American Public Health Association (1998); Meritorious Service Award, Uniformed Services University of the Health Sciences (1991); Early Career Award, Public Health Education Section, American Public Health Association (1979); Grantee, National Defense Education Act (1968-1970); United States Public Health Services Traineeship (1965-1967) **Membership:** President, American Public Health Association (2006); President-elect, American Public Health Association (2005); Executive Board, American Public Health Association (2001-2004); Board of Directors, American Academy of Health Behavior (2001); Chairman, Continuing Professional Education Committee, American Public Health Association (1997-1998); Chairman, Public Health Education Section, American Public Health Association (1995-1996); Fellow, American School Health Association; Society for Applied Anthropology; Lifetime Member, American Association for the Advancement of Science; Washington State Public Health Association; Lifetime Member, Military Officers Association of America; Commissioned Officers Association; Lifetime Member, United States Public Health Services; Lifetime Member, American Association for Health Education; Society for Public Health Education; Society for Medical Anthropology; Lifetime Member, Association of Military Surgeons of the United States; Lifetime Member, Reserve Officers Association of the United States; Smith College Alumnae Relations; Lifetime Member, University of Arizona Alumni Association; Delta Psi Kappa; Eta Sigma Gamma **Marquis Who's Who Honors:** Albert Nelson Marquis Lifetime Achievement Award (2017) **Religion:** Methodist **Shipping Address:** 6250 N Park Ave., Apt. A05, Tacoma, WA, 98407

Andrew G. Malis

Title: Telecommunications Industry Executive **Industry:** Telecommunications **Company Name:** Futurewei Technologies **Marital Status:** Married **Spouse Name:** Leslie Seaton Malis **Children:** Jonathan D. Malis **Education:** MSc in Applied Mathematics, Harvard University, Cambridge, MA (1979); BSc in Computer Science, Brown University, Providence, RI (1975) **Career:** Distinguished Engineer, FutureWei Technologies (2013-Present); Verizon Fellow, Verizon, Waltham, MA (2006-2013); Chief Technologist, Tellabs, San Jose, CA (2003-2006); Chief Technologist, Vivace Networks, Inc. (Now Tellabs), San Jose, CA (2000-2003); Senior Consulting Engineer, Cascade Communications/Ascend Communications/Lucent Technologies, Westford, MA (1996-2000); Consulting Engineer, Ascom Nexion, Acton, MA (1993-1996); Division Engineer, Bolt Beranek and Newman (Now Raytheon), Cambridge, MA (1979-1993); Member of Technical Staff, The MITRE Corporation, Bedford, MA (1975-1978) **Career Related:** Scientific Committee, Upperside MPLS, Ethernet, SDN, and NFV World Congress (1999-Present); Technical Committee Member, Past Co-Chair, Isocore MPLS/SDN International Conference (1998-Present); Speaker, Chairman, Numerous Telecommunications-Related Conferences (1995-Present); Working Group Chair, Internet Engineering Task Force (1993-Present); Services Area Director, Open Networking Foundation (2014-2017); Rapporteur, Chair for Architectural Framework, European Telecommunications Standards Institute, Network Functions Virtualization, Industry Standards Group (2012-2013); Vice President, Broadband Forum (2009-2013); Member of the Board, Broadband Forum (2009-2013); Distinguished Fellow, Broadband Forum (2009-2013); President & Chairman, MPLS, Frame Relay, and ATM (MFA) Forum (2002-2009); Advisory Board, Business Briefing: Global Optical Communications (2002); Board of Broadband Executives, ZAP Ventures (2001-2006); Council of Technology Advisors, Gerson Lehrman Group (Now Gerson Lehrman Group, Inc.) (2000-2006) **Civic:** Board of Directors, Temple Emanuel, Andover, MA (1997-Present); President, Temple Emanuel, Andover, MA (1995-1997) **Creative Works:** Contributor, Articles to Scientific Journals Including Proceedings of the IEEE and IEEE Communications; Author, Technical Standards Documents Including 40 Internet Engineering Task Force Requests for Comment and Numerous Other Telecommunications Standards **Awards:** Recipient, Leadership Award, Open Networking Foundation (2016); Recipient, Broadband Forum Leadership Award (2014); Recipient, MPLS Conference Recognition Award (2012); Recipient, Broadband Forum Distinguished Fellow Award (2012); Recipient, MFA Forum Special Recognition Award (2005); Recipient, State of California Commendation (2002); ATM Forum Spotlight Award (2000); Frame Relay Forum Distinguished Service Award (1999) **Membership:** Senior Member, IEEE Communications Society (1997-Present); Sigma Xi, The Scientific Research Honor Society (1975-Present); Internet Society **Marquis Who's Who Honors:** Albert Nelson Marquis Lifetime Achievement Award (2017) **Why did you become involved in your profession or industry:** Mr. Malis initially entered the fields of engineering and computer science in college. Through his first job, he entered the communications industry. He enjoyed his profession, so he continued with it. **What do you consider to be the highlight of your career:** A highlight of Mr. Malis' career has been his many contributions to the telecommunications standardization community. **Hobbies:** Traveling; Reading; Consuming art **Political Affiliations:** Democrat **Religion:** Jewish **Shipping Address:** 30 Kirkland Dr, Andover, MA, 01810

Milford Charles Maloney

Title: Internal Medicine Educator (Retired) **Industry:** Education/Educational Services **Company Name:** Historic Port Anne Homeowner's Association **Date of Birth:** 03/15/1927 **Place of Birth:** Buffalo **State:** NY **Year of Passing:** 2018-02-22 **Parents:** John Angelus Maloney; Winifred Hill Maloney **Marital Status:** Married **Spouse Name:** Dione Ethyl Sheppard **Children:** Kevin Maloney; Michael Maloney; Diane Enriquez; John Maloney; Rosemary Calame; Brian Maloney; Caroline Mintz; Mark Maloney; Patricia Maloney **Education:** Medical Resident, Buffalo Vetearans Affairs Medical Center, United States Department of Veterans Affairs (1954-1956); Intern, Mercy Hospital, Georgetown University (1953-1954); MD, University at Buffalo (1953); Postgraduate Coursework, Canisius College (1949); BS in Chemistry & Premedical Science, Canisius College (1947) **Certifications:** Diplomate, American Board of Internal Medicine **Career:** President, Historic Port Anne Homeowner's Association, Williamsburg, VA (1997-2018); Faculty Instructor, Christopher Wren Association, William & Mary, Williamsburg, VA (1997-2008); Education Leader, Southern American Seminar, American Society of Internal Medicine (1988); Education Leader, European Seminar, American Society of Internal Medicine (1987); Trustee, American Society of Internal Medicine (1984-1990); Clinical Professor of Medicine, University at Buffalo (1981-1994); Council Member, Association of Program Directors in Internal Medicine (1977-1980); Steering Committee, Association of Program Directors in Internal Medicine (1976); Program Director, Internal Medicine Residency, Mercy Hospital, Buffalo, NY (1972-1989); Chairman, Department Medicine, Mercy Hospital (1969-1994); Cardiology Fellow, Buffalo General Hospital (1956-1957); Research Chemist, Buffalo Electrochemical Company (1947-1949) **Career Related:** Faculty Instructor, Member, Curriculum Committee, Christopher Wren Association, College of William & Mary, Williamsburg, VA (1997-1999); Member, Internal Medicine Liaison Committee, New York State (1980-1990); Board of Directors, Heart Association of Western New York, Buffalo, NY (1969); Senior Cancer Research Physician, Roswell Park Memorial Cancer Institute (1959-1962); Board of Directors, Internal Medicine Center for Advancement and Research Education, Center of Excellence in Aging and Geriatric Health, Williamsburg, VA **Civic:** Member, Board of Regents, Canisius College, Buffalo, NY (1987-Present); Board of Directors, Williamsburg Center for Excellence in Aging and Geriatric Health (2004); Director of Development, Williamsburg Center for Excellence in Aging and Geriatric Health (2004); Board of Directors, Virginia Symphony, Norfolk, VA (2001); Founding Member, Virginia Symphony Society, Greater Williamsburg, Virginia (1998); Member of Executive Committee, Board of Directors, Blue Cross, Western New York, Buffalo, NY (1987-1994); **Military Service:** Captain, Medical Corps, US Army (1957-1959) **Creative Works:** Editor, Newsletter, New York State Society for Internal Medicine (1972-1978) **Awards:** Recipient, Heritage Award, Mercy Hospital Foundation, Buffalo, NY (2005); Recipient, Lifetime Career Achievement Award, Medical Alumni Association, University at Buffalo (2005); Recipient, Outstanding Medical Teaching Attending Award, Mercy Hospital, SUNY Medical Residents (1994); Recipient, Berkson Excellence Award in Teaching and Art of Medicine, University at Buffalo (1992); Recipient, Distinguished Alumni Award, Canisius College (1991); Recipient, Scroll of Honor, Benefactor for Internal Medicine, Center for the Advancement of Research and Education (1991); Recipient, Upstate Physician Recognition Award, American College of Physicians (1989); Recipient, Annual Honoree Award, Trocaire College (1986); Recipient, Man of the Year Award, Heart Association of Western New York (1982); Recipient, Award of Merit, New York State Society for Internal Medicine (1980); Inductee, Sports Hall of Fame, Canisius College (1978) **Membership:** Editor, Newsletter, Williamsburg Virginia Symphony Society (1998-2003); Founding Member, Greater Williamsburg Virginia Symphony Society (1998); President, Erie County Medical Society (1991-1992); Chairman, Section on Internal Medicine, American Medical Association (1990-1991); Chairman, Long-Range Planning Committee, Representative to Federated Council on Internal Medicine, American Society of Internal Medicine (1990-1991); President, American Society of Internal Medicine (1990-1991); Representative, National Practice Parameters and Guidelines Committee, American Society of Internal Medicine (1989-1991); Board of Directors, Internal Medicine Center for the Advancement of Research Education, American Society of Internal Medicine (1988-1991); State University of New York Representative, American Medical Association (1986-1994); Representative to Section Medical Schools at Annual Meetings, American Medical Association (1984-1994); Trustee, American Society of Internal Medicine (1984-1990) **Marquis Who's Who Honors:** Albert Nelson Marquis Lifetime Achievement Award (2017); Distinguished Humanitarian (2017) **Shipping Address:** 3000 Earls Ct Unit 1211, Williamsburg, VA, 23185

Paul B. Manchester

Title: Economist **Industry:** Financial Services **Company Name:** Federal Housing Finance Agency **Date of Birth:** 10/07/1942 **Place of Birth:** Winsted **State:** CT **Parents:** Elbert Grant Manchester; Eleanor Elizabeth (Jones) Manchester **Marital Status:** Married **Spouse Name:** Ruth Elaine Garbisch (10/25/1969) **Children:** Sarah H.; Daniel P. **Education:** PhD, University of Minnesota (1973); BA, Yale University (1964) **Career:** Manager, Federal Housing Finance Agency, Washington, DC (2009-Present); Director, Financial Institutions Regulation Division, U.S. Department of Housing and Urban Development, Washington, DC (2007-2008); Financial Economist, U.S. Department of Housing and Urban Development, Washington, DC (1991-2007); Economist, Office of Thrift Supervision, Washington, DC (1990-1991); Senior Economist, U.S. League of Savings Institutions, Washington, DC (1989-1990); Economic Adviser to Tennessee State Senator, U.S. Senate, Washington, DC (1988); Economist, Joint Economic Committee, United States Congress, Washington, DC (1978-1989); Consultant, Robert R. Nathan Associates, Washington, DC (1975-1978); Assistant Professor, The Catholic University of America, Washington, DC (1974-1978); Consultant, U.S. Department of Treasury, Washington, DC (1974-1975); Assistant Professor, University of Mary Washington, Fredericksburg, VA (1971-1974); Teaching Associate, University of Minnesota, Minneapolis, MN (1966-1969) **Civic:** Volunteer, Peace Corps, Colombia (1964-1966); President, Woodmoor-Pinecrest Citizens' Association, Silver Spring, MD **Creative Works:** Contributor, Articles, Professional Journals **Membership:** Vice President, The Yale Club, Washington, DC (2004-2007); Board of Directors, National Economists Club (1989-1992); Vice President, National Economists Club (1987); Vice President, National Economists Club (1985); American Economic Association; The Society of Government Economists; Board of Directors, The Yale Club, Washington, DC **Hobbies:** Tennis; Bowling **Religion:** Lutheran **Shipping Address:** 105 Lexington Drive, Silver Spring, MD, 20901

Robert Mandl

Title: Application Developer **Industry:** Technology **Country of Origin:** Romania **Parents:** Paul Mandl; Eva Mandl **Education:** PhD in Engineering, Massachusetts Institute of Technology, Cambridge, MA (1970); MSEE, Massachusetts Institute of Technology, Cambridge, MA (1969); MSc in Mathematics, Hebrew University (1965); BSc in Mathematics, Physics, and Linguistics, Hebrew University (1963) **Career:** Independent Researcher, Cambridge, MA (2001-Present); Principal Engineer, Digital Equipment Corporation, Littleton, MA (1996-2001); Consultant, AT&T Bell Laboratories, North Andover, MA (1991-1995); Senior Software Engineer, Information Engineering, Bedford, MA (1990); Manager Software Engineering, Analogic Corporation, Peabody, MA (1983-1989); Senior Software Engineer, Softech, Waltham, MA (1980-1983) **Career Related:** Presenter in Field **Creative Works:** Compiler, Editor, "Massachusetts Institute of Technology Folk Dance Club Song Book" (1975); Contributor, Articles, Professional Journals **Membership:** IEEE; New York Academy of Sciences; IEEE Computer Society; Linguistic Society of America; Mathematical Association of America; Sigma Xi; American Mathematical Society **Marquis Who's Who Honors:** Distinguished Humanitarian (2017) **Hobbies:** Languages; Running; Hambo; Dance **Shipping Address:** PO Box 397199, Cambridge, MA, 02139 **Website:** http://www.robertmandl.com

James Horace Manges

Title: Investment Banker (Retired) **Industry:** Financial Services **Date of Birth:** 10/08/1927 **Place of Birth:** New York City **State:** NY **Year of Passing:** 2018-08-22 **Parents:** Horace S. Manges; Natalie (Bloch) Manges **Marital Status:** Single **Spouse Name:** Mary T. Seymour (3/28/1974, Divorced 2000); Joan Brownell (1969, Divorced) **Children:** Alison Manges Nogueira; James H. Manges, Jr. (Jamie); Zoe Manges (Grandchild); Kaia Manges (Grandchild); Olivia Nogueira (Grandchild); Marina Nogueira (Grandchild); Gerard H. Manges (Brother, Deceased 3/6/1983); Kirsten Manges Hamm (Niece); Van Trang Manges (Daughter-in-Law); Dr John F. Nogueira, Jr. (Son-in-Law) **Education:** MBA, Harvard Business School (1953); BA, Yale University (1950); Diploma, Phillips Exeter Academy (1945) **Career:** Retired (1996); Advisory Director, Lehman Brothers, New York City, NY (1990-1996); Managing Director, Shearson Lehman Brothers, Inc., New York City, NY (1984-1990); Managing Director, Lehman Brothers, Kuhn, Loeb Inc., New York City, NY (1977-1984); Partner, Kuhn, Loeb & Co., New York City, NY (1967-1977); Associate, Kuhn, Loeb & Co., New York, NY (1954-1967) **Career Related:** Director, Proudfoot (1996-1998); Member, Executive Committee, Proudfoot (1996-1998); Director, Metromedia, Inc. (1970-1986); Member, Executive Committee, Metromedia, Inc. (1970-1986); Director, Baker Industries Inc. (1967-1977); Member, Executive Committee, Baker Industries Inc. (1967-1977) **Civic:** Member, Executive Committee, Class of 1950, Yale University (2010-Present); Member, Center for Strategic & International Studies, Washington, DC (1988-Present); Trustee, Phillips Exeter Academy (1985-1989); Member, Trustee Council, Phillips Exeter Academy (1989-1995); Trustee, St. Bernard's School, New York City, NY (1985-2000); Trustee, Episcopal School, New York City, NY (1978-1992) **Military Service:** U.S. Army Counter Intelligence Corps, Italy and Austria (1946-1947) **Membership:** The Yale Club of New York; Harvard Club of New York City; Century Country Club, Purchase, NY; The Bond Club of New York, Inc. **Marquis Who's Who Honors:** Albert Nelson Marquis Lifetime Achievement Award (2017) **Why did you become involved in your profession or industry:** Mr. Manges became involved in his profession because his father and mother were outstanding and encouraged him to make his own decisions. In 1943, during the middle of World War II, he went away to school at Phillips Exeter Academy and found that experience to be a real maturing process. With the war over and opportunities in investment banking increasing, he plunged in. **Business Address:** 45 Rockefeller Plaza, 20th Fl, New York, NY, 10111 **Shipping Address:** 888 Park Ave., Apt 7A, New York, NY, 10075

W. Steve George Mann

Title: Visiting Full Professor **Industry:** Education/Educational Services **Company Name:** Stanford University **Education:** Doctorate, Massachusetts Institute of Technology (1997) **Awards:** Honoree, Mannlabs, Wearable Computing Association (2017) **Why did you become involved in your profession or industry:** Dr. Mann was interested quite early on in seeing things on top of the real world. His grandfather taught him how to weld and he set about building glasses to help others see better. He experimented with old television to see radio waves. **Business Address:** 350 Serra Mall, Mail Code 9505, Rm 216, Stanford, CA, 94305 **Shipping Address:** 350 Serra Mall, Mail Code 9505, Rm 216, Stanford University, Dept of Electrical Engineering, Stanford, CA, 94305

Greta Craig Manville

Title: Writer **Industry:** Writing and Editing **Date of Birth:** 06/12/1932 **Place of Birth:** Clarinda **State:** IA **Parents:** William Donald Craig; Eunice Catherine Nolan **Marital Status:** Widowed **Spouse Name:** Wallace Carruthers Manville Jr. (2/1/1953, Deceased) **Education:** MA, San Jose State University (1978); BA, San Jose State University (1975) **Career:** Freelance Writer, Sun City West, AZ (1991-Present); Executive Manager, Quality Control, Consolidated Freightways, Menlo Park, CA (1977-1991); Assistant Treasurer, Argonaut Insurance Co., Menlo Park, CA (1962-1975) **Career Related:** Treasurer (2009-2010); Member, Board of Directors, Arizona Authors' Association (2006-2008); Literary Contest Coordinator, Arizona Authors' Association (2006-2008) **Creative Works:** Author, "Flight into Reality" (2012); Transitions Editor (2011); Author, "Murder Online" (2009); Author, "Death Key" (2002); Co-Author, "The Purgatory Trail" (2001); Author, "Passage" (1999); Former Bibliographer **Awards:** Steinbeck Fellowship, Martha H. Cox Center for Steinbeck Studies, San Jose State University (2002-2003); First Place in Mystery/Suspense Category, Authorlink Website, New Authors Awards Competition (2000); Grand Prize, Sparrowgrass Poetry Forum (1999); First Prize Southwest Writers Workshop (1993) **To what do you attribute your success:** She attributes her success to her parents, teachers, and employers, all of whom encouraged the pursuit of her dream to become a writer. **Why did you become involved in your profession or industry:** She has had a lifelong fascination with reading and writing fiction. **What do you consider to be the highlight of your career:** The highlight of her career was receiving the John Steinbeck Fellowship at San Jose State University, which sparked her interest in literary research and writing. **Where will you be in five years:** In 5 years, she will be writing another mystery novel. **Hobbies:** Duplicate bridge; Reading; Movies **Shipping Address:** 20819 N 148th Dr, Sun City West, AZ, 85375 **Website:** http://www.gretamanville.com

John M. Marion

Title: Educational Technology Educator (Retired) **Industry:** Education/Educational Services **Date of Birth:** 01/11/1947 **Place of Birth:** Fitchburg **State:** MA **Parents:** Don Louis; Violet Pearl Marion **Marital Status:** Married **Spouse Name:** Joann Elizabeth Marion (8/8/1970) **Children:** Benjamin Andrew; Jessica Noelle **Education:** EdD in Educational Technology, Pepperdine University (2011); MEd, Fitchburg State University (1971); BS in Education, Fitchburg State University (1969) **Career:** Technology Education Teacher/Administrative Software Trainer, Jefferson County Public Schools, Colorado (2003-2012); Media Technology Specialist, Dracut Public Schools, Massachusetts (2000-2003); Director of Technology, Reading Public Schools, Massachusetts (1998-2000); Associate Dean of Academic Computing, Endicott College, Beverly, MA (1990-1998); Computer Coordinator, Newburyport Public Schools, Massachusetts (1986-1990); Computer Teacher, Littleton Public Schools, Massachusetts (1985-1986); Teacher, Groton-Dunstable Regional Schools, Massachusetts (1969-1984) **Career Related:** Master-Teacher, Intel-Teach to the Future Program and Information Literacy Advisory Committee, Jefferson County Public Schools, CO (2004-2005); Board of Directors, Massachusetts Computer Using Educator (1989-1990); Teacher Trainer, Lego-Decta, Lego Systems, Inc., Enfield, CT (1987-1990); Trainer, Consultant, Logo Computer Systems, Inc., New York, NY (1984-1990); Instructor, Merrimack Education Center, Chelmsford, MA (1980-1990); Advisory Board, Claris Software Co. **Civic:** Board of Directors, Reading Community TV, Inc., Reading, MA (1998-1999) **Awards:** Fulbright Scholar, Teacher Exchange Program, Southampton, England (1973-1974) **Shipping Address:** 205 Autumn Ridge Dr., Ayer, MA, 01432

Steve J. Mariotti

Title: President **Industry:** Business Management/Business Services **Company Name:** Network for Teaching Entrepreneurship **Date of Birth:** 08/14/1953 **Place of Birth:** Ann Arbor **State:** MI **Parents:** John Mariotti; Nancy Gilbert (Mason) Mariotti **Education:** Honorary PhD in Business and Entrepreneurship, Johnson & Wales University (1990); MBA, University of Michigan (1977); BBA, University of Michigan (1975); Coursework, Harvard University; Coursework, Stanford University; Coursework, Brooklyn College; Coursework, Babson College **Career:** Fellow for Entrepreneurship Education, Philadelphia University Center for Entrepreneurship, Philadelphia University (2016-Present); Blogger, The Huffington Post (2015-Present); Founder, Atlas Learning (2014-Present); President, Network for Teaching Entrepreneurship (1988-Present); Special Education Teacher, New York City Public Schools, New York City Department of Education (1982-1987); President, Mason Import/Export (1979-1982); Founder, Mason Import/Export (1979-1982); Financial Analyst, Ford Motor Company (1977-1979); Assistant to Senior Vice President of Finance, Ford Motor Company (1975-1979) **Career Related:** Co-Founder, Inmates Teaching Entrepreneurship and Mentoring (2004); Featured Speaker in Field **Creative Works:** Author, "An Entrepreneur's Manifesto, Templeton Press (2016); Author, "Entrepreneurship and Small Business Management," Pearson (2011); Author, "Entrepreneurship: Starting and Operating a Small Business," Pearson (2011); Author, "Entrepreneurship: Owning Your Future," Prentice Hall (2009); Author, "Entrepreneurs in Profile: How 20 of the World's Greatest Entrepreneurs Built Their Business Empires...and How You Can Too," Career Press (2002); Author, "The Young Entrepreneur's Guide to Starting and Running a Business: Turn Your Ideas into Money," Penguin Random House (2000); Author, "The Very, Very Rich, How They Got That Way, and How You Can, Too," Career Press (2000); Co-Author, "The Young Entrepreneurs Guide to Starting and Running a Business" (1996); Co-Author, "Entrepreneurship: How to Start and Operate a Small Business" (1995); Author, "Homeboys: Diary of an Inner-City Teacher" (1990); Co-Author, "Educating the Next Wave of Entrepreneurs"; Contributor, Articles, Professional Journals **Awards:** Golden Lamp Award, The Association of American Publishers (2010); Bernard A. Goldhirsh Social Entrepreneur of the Year Award (2005); Entrepreneur of the Year Award, Ernst & Young Global Limited (2004); Golden Lamp Award, The Association of American Publishers (2002); National Director's Entrepreneurship Award, Minority Business Development Agency, U.S. Department of Commerce (2002); Appel Award, Price Institute For Entrepreneurial Studies (1994); Entrepreneur of the Year Award, New York State in Support of Entrepreneurship, Inc. Magazine (1992); Humanitarian Venture Award, ACE/Currie Foundation (1990); Best Business Teacher of the Year, National Federation of Independent Business (1988); Leavey Award For Outstanding Achievement in the Field of Free Enterprise Education (1985) **Membership:** Council on Foreign Relations; Speaker, World Economic Forum **Marquis Who's Who Honors:** Albert Nelson Marquis Lifetime Achievement Award (2017) **Hobbies:** Collecting rare books; Giving historical walking tours; Chess **Shipping Address:** 231 Victoria Mews, Princeton, NJ, 08542

Joan Markessini

Title: Healthcare Research Scientist, Psychologist **Industry:** Medicine & Health Care **Company Name:** WELLTrek International, LLC. **Date of Birth:** 08/14/1942 **Place of Birth:** New York **State:** NY **Parents:** John Demetrius Markessini; Diana (Vlahos) Markessini **Marital Status:** Married **Spouse Name:** Kenneth W. Lucas (8/14/1999) **Education:** PhD in Psychology, University of Delaware (1978); MA in Instructional Technology, University of Washington (1978); MA in Psycholinguistics, University of Washington (1966); BA in English, French, Science and Music, University of Delaware (1964) **Career:** Founder, WELLTrek International, LLC. (1995-Present); President, WELLTrek International, LLC (1995-Present); Affiliate, LINK Simulation and Training, New York, NY (1995-2002); Psychologist, Allen Corporation of America, Inc., Alexandria, VA (1990-1995); Director of Publications and Communications, Maxwell Communication Corporation, McLean, VA (1987-1990); Senior Staff Psychologist, BDM International, Inc., McLean, VA (1985-1987); Assistant Director, Resources Development, National Trust for Historic Preservation (1984-1985); Director of Corporation and Foundation Relations, The Catholic University of America (1978-1984); Educational Psychologist, University of Delaware, Newark, DE (1972-1978); Writer, Edcom Systems, Inc., Princeton, NJ (1970-1972); Editor-in-Chief, Edcom Systems Ltd, Princeton, NJ (1970-1972); Training Psychologist, U.S. Department of State, Washington, DC (1967-1970); Inventor, WELLTrek Electronic Medical Record & Information Management; Patent Holder, WELLTrek Electronic Medical Record & Information Management; Director of Research and Development, L-3 Communications, Inc. (Now L3 Technologies, Inc.); Deputy Director of Medical Systems and Distance Learning, L-3 Communications, Inc. (Now L3 Technologies, Inc.) **Military Service:** Contractor, Adult Professional Development, U.S. Army Research Institute for the Behavioral and Social Sciences **Creative Works:** Author, "A Letter to the Earth: Defining the Middle East and Its Levels of Warfare" (2018); Author, "Is This What's Really Out There? Opening Engagements" (2016); Author, "Up from Grief: A Widow's Tale" (2015); Author, "Around the World of Orthodox Christianity" (2012); Producer, "Dream Work" (2009); Producer, "Meeting the Challenge" (2000); Author, "TeleMedicine Art and Practice: An Instructional Program Series" (1995); Editor, "Perspectives on Leadership, Volumes 1-5" (1994); Author, "A Taxonomy of Cognitive Capabilities for Executives" (1991); Author, "Effects of Listener Familiarity and Topic Knowledge on Speech Communication" (1979); Author, "The First Twelve Months of Life" (1973); Author, "The First Year of Life" (1971); Producer, "Death of a Giant" (1967); Contributor, Articles, Professional Journals; Contributor, Film Reviews **Awards:** Fellow, University of Delaware (1977-1979); Graduate Fellow, University of Washington (1965-1966); Fellow, University of Michigan (1965) **Membership:** American Psychological Association; General, Association for Psychological Type International; The New York Academy of Sciences; Charter Member, National Museum of Women in the Arts; American Film Institute **To what do you attribute your success:** Dr. Markessini attributes her success to her discipline, hard work, devotion to her field, intellectual curiosity, professional achievement, and the support that she received from her parents and teachers who encouraged excellence. **Why did you become involved in your profession or industry:** Dr. Markessini became involved in her profession because of her interest in human behavior from the time of her first scientific experiment at nine years old. **What do you consider to be the highlight of your career:** The highlight of Dr. Markessini's career was creating an entire body of research work focused on executive excellence, which includes a five-volume published series of structured interviews with U.S. Army high command on the ingredients of professional and executive leadership. **Where will you be in five years:** In five years, Dr. Markessini expects to be in an international executive position working overseas for the United States government. **Hobbies:** Historic property restoration, captured in a full-color illustrated book distributed by Ocean Atlantic Sotheby's; Antiques and art collection; Historic property restoration; Opera; Theater; Gardening; Landscaping **Political Affiliations:** Independent **Religion:** Orthodox Catholic Christian **Business Address:** 211 N Union St., Ste 141, Alexandria, VA, 22314 **Shipping Address:** 1410 S Monroe St, Arlington, VA, 22204 **Website:** http://www.welltrekintl.com

Andrei Steven Markovits, PhD

Title: Political Science Professor **Industry:** Education/Educational Services **Company Name:** University of Michigan **Date of Birth:** 10/06/1948 **Place of Birth:** Timisoara **Country of Origin:** Romania **Parents:** Ludwig Markovits; Ida (Ritter) Markovits **Education:** Honorary PhD, Leuphana University of Luneburg, Germany (2007); PhD, Columbia University, New York City, NY (1976); MPhil, Columbia University, New York City, NY (1974); MA, Columbia University, New York City, NY (1973); MBA, Columbia University, New York City, NY (1971); BA, Columbia University, New York City, NY (1969) **Career:** Arthur F. Thurnau Professor, University of Michigan (2009-Present); Karl W. Deutsch Collegiate Professor of Comparative Politics and German Studies, University of Michigan, Ann Arbor, MI (2003-Present); Professor, Department of Germanic Languages and Literature, Department of Political Science, Department of Sociology, University of Michigan, Ann Arbor, MI (1999-2003); Professor, Department of Politics, University of California, Santa Cruz, CA (1995-1999); Chair, Department of Politics, University of California, Santa Cruz, CA (1992-1995); Associate Professor, Political Science, Boston University (1983-1992); Assistant Professor of Government, Wesleyan University, Middletown, CT (1977-1983); Member, Adjunct Faculty, Columbia University (1975); Member, Adjunct Faculty, John Jay College of Criminal Justice (1974); Member, Adjunct Faculty, New York University (1974) **Career Related:** Sir Peter Ustinov Professor, University of Vienna (2010-2011); Visiting Professor, Webster Vienna Private University (2008); Visiting Professor, TU Dortmund University (2006); Visiting Professor, Hebrew University of Jerusalem (2005); Visiting Professor, University of St. Gallen, Switzerland (2004); Visiting Professor, Harvard University (2002-2003); Visiting Professor, Ruhr University, Bochum (1991); Visiting Professor, Osnabruck University (1987); Visiting Professor, Tel Aviv University (1986); Fulbright Professor, University of Innsbruck, Austria (1996); Research Associate, International Institute of Comparative Social Research, Science Center of Berlin (1980); Research Associate, Institute of German Trade University Federation, Dusseldorf, Germany (1979); Senior Research Associate, Central European Studies, Harvard University (1975-1999); Research Associate, Institute of Advanced Studies, Vienna, Austria (1973-1974); Fellow, Institute for Advanced Study Berlin; Fellow, Center for Advanced Study in Behavioral Sciences at Stanford University **Creative Works:** Author, Books and Papers in Field; Editor, Books and Papers in Field; Television and Radio Commentator; Author, "The German Left: Red, Green, and Beyond"; Author, "The German Predicament: Memory & Power in the New Europe"; Author, "The Politics of the West German Trade Unions: Strategies of Class and Interest Representation in Growth and Crisis"; Author, "From Bundesrepublik to Deutschland: German Politics After Unification"; Author, "Gaming the World: How Sports are Reshaping Global Politics and Culture"; Author, "Offside: Soccer and American Exceptionalism"; Author, "Sportista: Female Fandom in the United States"; Author, "Uncouth Nation: Why Europe Dislikes America"; Author, "From Property to Family: American Dog Rescue and the Discourse of Compassion"; Author, "Hillel at Michigan 1926/27-1945: Struggles of Jewish Identity in a Pivotal Era" **Awards:** Tronstein Award (2016); Cross of the Order of Merit First Class, Bestowed by the Federal Republic of Germany (2012); Year-Long Fellowship, Center for Advanced Study in the Behavioral Sciences, Stanford University (2008-2009); Tronstein Award (2007); Golden Apple Award for Best Teacher, University of Michigan (2007); Year-Long Fellowship, Institute for Advanced Study, Berlin, Germany (1998-1999); Excellence in Teaching Award, The University of California, Santa Cruz (1997); Fellow, Hans Boeckler Foundation (1982); Fellow, Ford Foundation (1979); Fellow, B'nai B'rith Foundation (1976-1977); Fellow, Kalmus Foundation (1976-1977); University President's Fellow, Columbia University (1969); New York State Scholar, Columbia University (1969) **Membership:** New York Academy of Sciences; American Political Science Association; International Political Science Association; American Association of University Professors; American Sociological Association; American Historical Association **Marquis Who's Who Honors:** Albert Nelson Marquis Lifetime Achievement Award (2017) **Shipping Address:** 718 Onondaga St, Ann Arbor, MI, 48104

Theodore Lee Marks

Title: Lawyer **Industry:** Law and Legal Services **Company Name:** Morrison Cohen LLP **Date of Birth:** 10/18/1935 **Place of Birth:** New York City **State/Country of Origin:** NY **Parents:** Irving Edward Marks; Isabel (Goodman) Marks **Marital Status:** Married **Spouse Name:** Benita Cooper (7/13/1958) **Children:** Eric; Robert; Jennifer **Education:** LLB, New York University (1958); BS, New York University (1956) **Career:** Counsel, Morrison Cohen LLP, New York City, NY (2004-Present); Partner, Morrison Cohen Singer & Weinstein (1987-2004); Partner, Gelberg & Abrams (1986-1987); Partner, Epstein Becker Borsody & Green, P.C., New York City, NY (1985-1986); Partner, Bromberg, Gloger, Lifschultz & Marks, New York City, NY (1979-1985); Partner, Vogel, Marks & Rosenberg, New York City, NY (1976-1979); Partner, Lee, Cash & Marks, New York City, NY (1970-1976); Private Practice, New York City, NY (1965-1970); Associate, Silver, Bernstein, Seawell & Kaplan, New York City, NY (1959-1965) **Career Related:** Presenter in Field; Lecturer in Field; Speaking Engagements **Civic:** Multiple School Boards; Citizens Committee, Representing Over 1000 Families **Military Service:** Army National Guard (1958-1961) **Creative Works:** Contributor, Articles, Professional Journals **Awards:** AV Preeminent Rating, Martindale-Hubbell; Super Lawyer, Multiple Times **Membership:** New York State Bar Association; Real Property Law Section, New York State Bar Association; Banking Law Section, New York State Bar Association; Corporate and Business Law Sections, New York State Bar Association; New York County Lawyers Association; T&M **Bar Admissions:** United States District Court for the Eastern District of New York (1978); United States Court of Appeals for the Second Circuit (1975); Supreme Court of the United States (1964); United States District Court for the Southern District of New York (1963); New York State Bar Association (1959) **Marquis Who's Who Honors:** Albert Nelson Marquis Lifetime Achievement Award (2017) **Hobbies:** Golf; Reading **Shipping Address:** 909 Third Ave., Fl 27, Morris Cohen LLP, New York, NY, 10022

Lawrence Markus, PhD

Title: Regents Professor **Industry:** Education/Educational Services **Company Name:** University of Minnesota **Date of Birth:** 10/13/1922 **Place of Birth:** Hibbing **State:** MN **Parents:** Benjamin Markus; Ruby (Friedman) Markus **Marital Status:** Married **Spouse Name:** Lois Shoemaker (12/9/1950) **Children:** Sylvia; Andrew **Education:** PhD, Harvard University, Cambridge, MA (1951); MSc in Meteorology, University of Chicago (1946); Honorary BSc in Mathematics and Physics, University of Chicago (1942) **Career:** Regents' Professor Emeritus, University of Minnesota, Minneapolis, MN (1993-Present); Regents' Professor of Mathematics, University of Minnesota, Minneapolis, MN (1980-1993); Director of Control Science and Dynamical Systems Center, University of Minnesota, Minneapolis, MN (1980-1989); Director of Control Science and Dynamical Systems Center, University of Minnesota, Minneapolis, MN (1964-1973); Associate Chairman, Department of Mathematics, University of Minnesota, Minneapolis, MN (1961-1963); Professor of Mathematics, University of Minnesota, Minneapolis, MN (1960-1993); Associate Professor, University of Minnesota, Minneapolis, MN (1958-1960); Assistant Professor, University of Minnesota, Minneapolis, MN (1957-1958); Lecturer, Princeton University and the Institute for Advanced Study (1955-1957); Instructor, Yale University (1952-1955); Instructor of Mathematics, Harvard University (1951-1952); Research Meteorologist, Atomic Project, Hanford, WA (1944); Instructor of Meteorology, University of Chicago (1942-1944) **Career Related:** Honorary Professor, University of Warwick (1985-Present); Chairman, Conference Markus-80 (2002); Honorary Fellow, Royal Society of Edinburgh (2000); Tate Lecturer, University of Cincinnati (1998); Principal Lecturer, Symposium in Honor of His 75th Birthday (1997); Director, National Science Foundation Workshop (1989); Principal Lecturer, Symposium, University of Minnesota (1988); Neustadt Memorial Lecturer, University of Southern California (1985); Visiting Professor, Technical Institute of Zurich (1983); Beer-Sheeva, Ben-Gurion University of the Negev, Israel (1983); Visiting Professor, Peking University (1983); Visiting Professor, Science and Engineering Research Council, University of Warwick, England (1982-1990); Plenary Lecturer, The Institute of Electrical and Electronics Engineers, Orlando, FL (1982); The Royal Institution, London, England (1982); United Nations Educational Science Advisory Committee Control Symposium, University of Strasbourg, France (1980); Visiting Professor, University of Warsaw (1980); Technical University of Denmark (1979); Panel Member, International Congress of Mathematicians, Helsinki, Finland (1978); Senior Visiting Fellow, Science Research Council, Imperial College, London, England (1978); British Mathematical Society (1976); Japan Society for the Promotion of Science (1976); Professor, University of Tokyo (1976); Iranian Mathematical Society (1975); Director, Conference of International Center of Mathematics, Trieste (1974); Lecturer, International Mathematics Congress (1974); Nuffield Professor of Mathematics, University of Warwick (1970-1985); Leverhulme Professor, Control Theory, Director, Control Theory Center, University of Warwick, England (1970-1973); Regional Conference Lecturer, National Science Foundation (1969); Guggenheim Fellow, Lausanne, Switzerland (1963); Fulbright Fellow, Paris, France (1950) **Civic:** Military Record, Documents, World War II Permanent Collection; Veterans History Project, Library of Congress (2016) **Military Service:** Lieutenant, Junior Grade, U.S. Naval Reserve (1944-1946); North Atlantic Anti-Submarine Patrol and Weather Analysis on Frigate, USS Peoria **Creative Works:** Editorial Board, Proceedings of the Georgian Academy of Sciences (1993-Present); Author, "History of Mathematics: Duplicate the Cube" (2018); Author, "Oral History of the Military Experience of Lieutenant Lawrence Markus in World War II", Library of Congress (2016); Author, "Complex Symplectic Spaces and Boundary Value Problems" (2006); Author, "Infinite Dimensional Complex Symplectic Spaces" (2004); Author, "Elliptic Partial Differential Operators and Symplectic Algebra" (2003); Author, "Multi-Interval Linear Ordinary Boundary Value Problems and Complex Symplectic Algebra" (2001); Author, "Boundary Value Problems and Symplectic Algebra for Ordinary Differential and Quasi-Differential Operators" (1998); Author, "Distributed Parameter Control Systems" (1991); Author, Review Edition, "Foundations of Optimal Control Theory" (1985) **Awards:** Festschrift Volume (1993); Itinerant Lecturer, Japanese Society for Promotion of Science (1976); Research Prize, International Conference on Nonlinear Oscillations, Ukrainian Academy of Science, Kiev, Ukraine (1969); War Department Certificate for Research Service on Atomic Bomb project and Naval Recognition for Radar Research (1946) **Membership:** Speaker Committee, International Mathematical Union (1976); National Council, American Mathematical Society; American Geophysical Society; National Lecturer, Society of Industrial and Applied Mathematics **Marquis Who's Who Honors:** Albert Nelson Marquis Lifetime Achievement Award (2017) **Shipping Address:** 1235 Yale Place, Apt. 1010, Minneapolis, MN, 55403

Lawrence W. Marquess

Title: Lawyer (retired) **Industry:** Law and Legal Services **Date of Birth:** 03/02/1950 **Place of Birth:** Bloomington **State:** IN **Parents:** Earl Lawrence Marquess; Mary Louise (Coberly) Marquess **Marital Status:** Married **Spouse Name:** Barbara Ann Bailey Marquess **Children:** Alexander Lawrence Marquess (Deceased); Michael Wade Marquess **Education:** JD, West Virginia University College of Law (1977); BS in Electrical Engineering, Purdue University (1973) **Career:** Retired (2017); Special Counsel, Littler Mendelson, P.C., Denver, CO (2016); Managing Shareholder, Denver Office, Littler Mendelson, P.C. (2001-2009); Shareholder, Littler Mendelson, P.C., Denver, CO (2001-2015); Shareholder, Otten, Johnson, Robinson, Neff & Ragonetti, P.C., Denver, CO (1994-2001); Shareholder, Harding & Ogborn, P.C., Denver, CO (1990-1994); Shareholder, Heron, Burchette, Ruckert & Rothwell, Denver, CO (1989-1990); Shareholder, Nelson & Harding, P.C., Denver, CO (1987-1988); Shareholder, Stettner, Miller & Cohn P.C., Denver, CO (1985-1987); Associate, Stettner, Miller & Cohn, P.C., Denver, CO (1984-1985); Partner, Bradley, Campbell & Carney, Golden, CO (1983-1984); Associate, Bradley, Campbell & Carney, Golden, CO (1979-1982); Associate, Johnson, Bromberg, Leeds & Riggs, Dallas, TX (1977-1979) **Career Related:** Member, Faculty American Law Institute, American Bar Association Advanced Labor and Employment Law Course (1986-1987) **Civic:** Chair, Board of Directors, Denver Urban Debate League (2016-Present); Founding Member, Board of Directors, Denver Urban Debate League (2007-Present); Volunteer, Wild Animal Sanctuary; Volunteer, Friends of the Cumbres & Toltec Scenic Railroad, Inc. **Awards:** Named, Colorado Super Lawyer (2007-2016); Fellow, College of Labor and Employment Lawyers; Named, Best Lawyers in America **Membership:** Chairman, Associated General Contractors Labor and Employment Law Committee (2016-2017); Board of Directors, Rocky Mountain Chapter, Labor and Employment Relations Association (2012-2013); Co-chairman, Labor Law Committee, Colorado Bar Association (1989-1992); First Judicial District Bar Association (1979-2016); Denver Bar Association (1979-2016); ABA (1978-2016); Colorado Bar Association (1978-2016); American Civil Liberties Union; Founding Member, Historical Society of the 10th Judicial Circuit; American Bar Foundation; Colorado Bar Foundation; National Railway Historical Society; National Model Railroaders Association; Railway & Locomotive Historical Society, Inc.; Sierra Club; The Nature Conservancy; Colorado Mountain Club; SkiMeisters; Trout Unlimited **Bar Admissions:** Colorado (1980); State of Texas (1977); West Virginia (1977); Supreme Court of the United States; United States Court of Appeals District of Columbia Circuit; United States Court of Appeals for the Tenth Circuit; United States District Court Southern District of West Virginia; United States District Court Northern District of Texas; United States District Court District of Colorado; United States District Court Northern District of Ohio; United States District Court District of Nebraska **To what do you attribute your success:** Mr. Marquess attributes his success to his desire and effort to be as good as his talents allowed in whatever he chose to do, personal and professional. He also attributes his success to a lifelong dedication to honesty and integrity in everything he undertook, having a sense of his own limits and fallibility and appreciation of the merits of others, the help and support of his family, friends, colleagues, and often, strangers and a lifelong desire to continue to learn. He also has an empathy for those less fortunate. **Why did you become involved in your profession or industry:** He became involved in his profession because the law was a challenging and interesting field that, he felt, would force him to step outside of his comfort zone and strive for steady improvement, if he was to succeed. **What do you consider to be the highlight of your career:** The highlights of his career were working with clients who stayed with him for many years and became, in a sense, part of a family that trusted him to represent and protect their best interests, also working with many excellent lawyers including colleagues, adversaries, and members of the judiciary. Another highlight was mentoring many fine young lawyers. **Where will you be in five years:** In five years, he hopes he is still volunteering for a number of worthy causes, pursuing his leisure interests both indoor and out, and spending lots of time with family and friends. **Hobbies:** Hiking; Biking; Fly fishing; Skiing; Reading; Athletics; Model railroading **Political Affiliations:** Democrat **Religion:** Methodist **Shipping Address:** 2615 Oak Drive, No. 32, Lakewood, CO, 80215

Milton Marsh

Title: Composer **Industry:** Media & Entertainment **Date of Birth:** 09/29/1945 **Place of Birth:** Hamilton **Country of Origin:** Bermuda **Parents:** Milton Murray; Gwendolyn Isadora Marsh **Children:** Tanya; Jonathan Milton; Milton Andre **Education:** MusM, New England Conservatory, Boston, MA (1971); MusB, Berklee College of Music, Boston, MA (1969) **Certifications:** Certificate in Education, London University (1964) **Career:** Professor, Director, Afro-American Music Studies, State University of New York, Buffalo (1973-1977); Visiting Professor, State University of New York, Oneonta (1972-1973); Music Consultant, National Center for Afro-American Artists, Boston, MA (1970-1971) **Career Related:** Consultant, National Center for Afro-American Artists, Boston, MA (1970-1971) **Creative Works:** Author, "We Are Not Separate" (2003); Author, "Continuum" (1985); Author, "Monism" (1975) **Shipping Address:** 192 Kennedy Drive, Apt. 302, Malden, MA, 02148

David Martin, PhD

Title: Education Educator **Industry:** Education/Educational Services **Company Name:** Gallaudet University **Date of Birth:** 08/24/1937 **Place of Birth:** New Bedford **State:** MA **Parents:** Theodore Tripp Martin; Elinor Louise (Raymond) Martin **Marital Status:** Married **Spouse Name:** Susan Katherine Orowan (6/30/1962) **Education:** PhD, Boston College (1971); Certificate of Advanced Study, Harvard University (1968); MEd, Harvard University (1961); BA, Yale University (1959) **Certifications:** Certified Teacher; Certified Principal; Certified Professional Trainer for Instrumental Enrichment; Certified Professional Trainer for Feuerstein Instrumental Enrichment **Career:** Professor, Gallaudet University (2002-Present); Dean Emeritus, Gallaudet University (2002-Present); Professor of Education, Gallaudet University (1995-2001); Dean of School Education and Human Services, Gallaudet University (1985-1995); Undergraduate Teacher Education Coordinator, Gallaudet University (1980-1985); Chairman, Education Department, Dominican College (1978-1980); Curriculum Director, Mill Valley School District (1975-1980); Principal, Mill Valley School District (1973-1975); Curriculum Director, Beverly Public Schools (1970-1973); Assistant Principal, Newton Public Schools (1969-1970); Teaching Assistant, Boston College (1968-1969); Teacher, Newton Public Schools (1961-1968) **Career Related:** Fulbright Fellow, The Open University (2005); Fulbright Fellow, University of the Witwatersrand, Johannesburg (2003-2004); Consultant Curriculum Development Associates (1975-2001); Board of Examiners, National Council Accreditation Teacher Education; Board of Directors, US-SINO Teacher Education Consortium; Board of Directors, Western Pennsylvania School for the Deaf; Visiting Research Professor **Creative Works:** Editor, "Advances in Cognition Education and Deafness" (1991); Author, "Case Studies in Curriculum" (1989); Editor, "Cognition, Education and Deafness" (1985); Co-Editor, "Assessing Deaf Adults, Curriculum for Deaf Learners"; Author, "Assessing Deaf Adults, Curriculum for Deaf Learners"; Contributor, Articles, Professional Journals **Awards:** Outstanding Genealogical Volunteer, New England Regional Genealogical Consortium (2015); Lifetime Achievement Award, ACE-DHH (2006); Grantee, Knight Foundation (1995-2001); Grantee, Ford Foundation (1998-2001); Grantee, U.S. Department of Education (1985); Grantee, U.S. Department of Education (1970) **Membership:** President, Marston's Mills Historical Society (2014-Present); Co-President, Cape Cod Genealogical Society (2006-Present); Dean Emeritus, Educational Consulting for Schools and Universities (2002-Present); President, Cape Cod Genealogical Society (2011-2015); President, DC Chapter, DC Association for Teacher Education (1989-1992); ASCD; National Council for the Social Studies; American Educational Research Association; Board of Directors, AACTE; Council for Exceptional Children; Phi Delta Kappa International; Publication Chair, Kappa Delta Pi, International Honor Society in Education; Professor, Educational Consulting for Schools and Universities; Co-Chair of Steering Committee, NAFA **Hobbies:** Genealogy; Sailing; Classical organ; Astronomy **Political Affiliations:** Democrat **Religion:** Unitarian Universalist **Shipping Address:** 10 Colonial Farm Circle, Marstons Mills, MA, 02648

Joseph P. Martino, PhD

Title: Research Scientist **Industry:** Sciences **Date of Birth:** 07/16/1931 **Place of Birth:** Warren **State:** OH **Parents:** Joseph Martino; Anna Elizabeth (Kubina) Martino **Marital Status:** Married **Spouse Name:** Nancy McCoy (12/28/2000); Mary Lou Bouquot (5/18/1957, Deceased 1/1988) **Children:** Theresa; Anthony; Michael **Education:** Diploma, United States Air Force Air War College (1972); PhD in Mathematics and Statistics, The Ohio State University (1960); MSEE in Electrical Engineering, Purdue University (1955); AB in Physics, Miami University (1953) **Career:** Senior Scientist, Research Institute, University of Dayton (1975-1993) **Military Service:** Director of Engineering Standardization, Defense Electronics Supply Center, US Air Force (1973-1975); Colonel, US Air Force (1973); Staff Scientist, Avionics Laboratory, US Air Force (1972-1973); Mathematician, Office of Science Research, US Air Force (1961-1962); Project Engineer, Armament Laboratory, US Air Force (1955-1958); Commissioned Second Lieutenant, US Air Force (1953) **Creative Works:** Author, "Resistance to Tyranny" (2010); Author, "The Justice Cooperative" (2004); Author, "Research and Development Project Selection" (1995); Author, "Science Funding: Politics and Porkbarrel" (1992); Author, "Technological Forecasting for Decision Making, Third Edition" (1992); Author, "A Fighting Chance-The Moral Use of Nuclear Weapons" (1988); Associate Editor, "Technology Forecasting and Social Change Journal" (1968-2016); Author, "Technological Forecasting for Decision Making, Revised Edition" (1983); Author, "Technological Forecasting for Decision Making" (1972) **Awards:** Recipient, Centennial Medal, IEEE (1984) **Membership:** International Conference on Mechanical and Electrical Technology; Institute for Operations Research and the Management Sciences; American Society for Engineering Management; Engineers Club of Dayton; Associate Fellow, American Association for the Advancement Science; Associate Fellow, American Institute of Aeronautics and Astronautics; Fellow, Portland International Center for Management of Engineering and Technology **Marquis Who's Who Honors:** Distinguished Humanitarian (2017) **Hobbies:** Target shooting; Bicycling **Religion:** Roman Catholic **Shipping Address:** 905 S Main Avenue, Sidney, OH, 45365

William C. Martucci

Title: Executive Partner, American Litigator, Strategist **Industry:** Law and Legal Services **Company Name:** Shook, Hardy & Bacon L.L.P. **Date of Birth:** 03/10/1952 **Place of Birth:** Asbury Park **State:** NJ **Parents:** Frank Martucci; Evelyn (Gerrity) Martucci **Marital Status:** Married **Spouse Name:** Kelly **Children:** Daniel Robert; William Sessions; John Andrew; James Christopher; Andrew Michael; Matthew Peter; Caroline Kenney **Education:** Executive Education Diploma, Harvard Business School (1997); LLM, Georgetown University, With Honors (1981); JD, University of Arkansas, With Honors (1977); AB, Rutgers College (Now Rutgers, The State University of New Jersey), Magna Cum Laude (1974) **Career:** Executive Partner, Shook, Hardy & Bacon L.L.P., Kansas City (2000-Present); Leader, National Employment Litigation & Policy Group, Shook, Hardy & Bacon L.L.P., Kansas City; Executive Partner, Shook, Hardy & Bacon L.L.P., Washington; Partner, Spencer, Fane, Britt & Browne, Kansas City (1987-1999); Associate, Spencer, Fane, Britt & Browne, Kansas City (1981-1986); Law Clerk to Presiding Justice, Missouri Court of Appeals, Kansas City (1977-1978) **Career Related:** Professor of Multinational Business Policy & The Global Workplace, Georgetown University (2008-Present); Charter Member, American Employment Council (1993-Present); Chair, Minority Affairs Committee (1992-2002); Guest Lecturer, Georgetown University (2007-2008); Adjunct Professor of Employment Law, University of Missouri Law School, Kansas City (1988-1995); Practice Leader, Shook Global Employment Litigation & Policy Practice, Shook, Hardy & Bacon L.L.P.; Model Federal Civil Jury Instructions Subcommittee, Shook, Hardy & Bacon L.L.P. **Civic:** Chairman, Mentor Program, Georgetown University Law Center (1988-2005); Member, Kansas City Tomorrow Leadership Program (1992-1993); Chairman, Minority Affairs Committee, Georgetown University Law Center; Member, Kansas City Civic Council; Member, Advisory Board, Boys and Girls Club of Kansas City; Member, Reviving Baseball in the Inner City; Chairman, Advisory Council, Urban League of Greater Kansas City Training Center; Human Resources Advisory Policy Board, Commerce Clearing House; Active Member, Retail Industry Litigation Center **Military Service:** Lieutenant, Judge Advocate General Corps, US Navy (1978-1981) **Creative Works:** Contributor, Global Legal Group (2010-Present); Contributor, The International Comparative Legal Guide to Employment & Labor Law (2010-Present); Contributor, USA Employment Law (2010-Present); Contributor, Global Employment Standards & Corporate Social Responsibility (2010-Present); Contributor, Global Diversity & Inclusion (2010-Present); Global Employment, Employment Laws (2010-Present); Editor-in-Chief, Arkansas Law Review (1976-1977); Contributor, Articles, Professional Journals **Awards:** Lawyer of the Year, Employment Litigation, Global 100 Lawyers (2015); Leadership Award, ABA (2010); President's Award, Missouri Bar Association (1992, 1997); The Best Lawyers in America, Business Litigation and Employment Litigation, Guide to the World's Leading Labour & Employment Lawyers; Who's Who Legal: The International Who's Who of Business Lawyers; Navy Achievement Medal; Navy Commendation Medal; National Honoree, Chambers USA **Membership:** Employment Law Committee, The Association of the Bar of the City of New York (2009-Present); Employment and Labor Relations Committee ABA (1987-Present); Equal Employment Opportunity Litigation Committee, ABA (1987-Present); Executive Committee, Continuing Legal Education, ABA (1987-Present); Chair, Executive Committee, Continuing Legal Education, ABA (1993-2000); Member, Executive Committee, Missouri Bar Association (1985-1998); Chairman, Labor and Employment Law Committee, Missouri Bar Association (1988-1990); Chairman, Continuing Legal Education, Kansas City Bar Association (1984-1986); Executive Committee, Young Lawyers Section, Lawyers Association of Kansas City (1981-1982); The District of Columbia Bar; International Bar Association; Los Angeles County Bar Association; San Francisco Bar Association, Kansas City Club; Indian Hills Country Club; Rotary International; Princeton Club of New York **Bar Admissions:** District of Columbia (2010); New York (2009); Missouri (1977) **To what do you attribute your success:** He attributes his success to hard work, respect for others and gratitude. **Why did you become involved in your profession or industry:** He has a deep interest in people and in business. He found the courtroom to be a fulfilling dimension of the practice since he tried cases as a Navy Judge Advocate General in the Third Marine Corps Division in Okinawa, Japan. **Hobbies:** Coaching; Youth sports **Political Affiliations:** Republican **Religion:** Roman Catholic **Business Address:** 155th Street NW, Washington, DC, 20004 **Shipping Address:** 3216 West 69th Street, Mission Hills, KS, 66208

Joseph Richard Masci

Title: Physician **Industry:** Medicine & Health Care **Company Name:** Elmhurst Hospital Center **Date of Birth:** 11/27/1950 **Place of Birth:** New Brunswick **State:** NJ **Parents:** Joseph Nicholas Masci; Delfina (Musa) Masci **Marital Status:** Married **Spouse Name:** Elizabeth Bass (5/21/1993) **Children:** Jonathan Samuel **Education:** MD, New York University (1976); BA, Cornell University (1972) **Certifications:** Diplomate, American Board of Internal Medicine; Diplomate, American Board of Infectious Disease **Career:** Chairman of Global Health (2018-Present); Board of Directors, Hope for a Healthier Humanity (2012-Present); Professor, Preventive Medicine, Mount Sinai School of Medicine (2006-Present); Professor of Medicine, Mount Sinai School of Medicine (2003-Present); Director of Medicine, Elmhurst Hospital Center (2002-2017); Chief, Infectious Diseases, Elmhurst Hospital Center (1999-2002); Associate Professor of Medicine, Mount Sinai School Medicine (1990-2003); Assistant Professor of Medicine, Mount Sinai School Medicine (1988-1990); Associate Director of Medicine, Elmhurst Hospital Center, New York (1987-2002); Assistant Professor, Clinical Medicine, Mount Sinai School of Medicine (1984-1988); Instructor of Medicine, Mount Sinai School Medicine, New York, NY (1982-1984); Instructor of Medicine, Boston University School of Medicine (1979-1980) **Career Related:** Peer Reviewer, National Institutes of Health (1994-Present) **Creative Works:** Author, "Ebola: Clinical Patterns, Pubic Health Concerns" (2017); Author, "Outpatient Management of HIV-Infection" (2011); Author, "Bioterrorism: A Guide for Hospital Preparedness" (2005); Author, "Outpatient Management of HIV-Infection" (2001, 1996); Author, "Primary and Ambulatory Care of the HIV-Infected Adult" (1992) **Awards:** Recipient, Jacobi Medallion, Icahn School of Medicine at Mount Sinai (2018); Recipient, Faculty Council Academic Excellence Award, Mount Sinai School of Medicine (2008); Recipient, Ruth Abrams Award, New York State Aids Institute (2006); Dr. Linda Laubenstein Award (2002); Recipient, Presidential Voluntary Service Gold Award **Membership:** Fellow, New York Academy of Medicine; Royal Society Medicine; American College of Physicians; American Society Microbiology; Association of Program Directors in Internal Medicine; Association of Professors of Medicine; United States Agency for International Development **Marquis Who's Who Honors:** Albert Nelson Marquis Lifetime Achievement Award (2017) **Shipping Address:** 75 Papermill Rd, Manhasset, NY, 11030

Keith E. Maskus

Title: Arts & Sciences Professor of Distinction **Industry:** Education/Educational Services **Company Name:** University of Colorado, Boulder **Date of Birth:** 09/16/1954 **Place of Birth:** Dodge City **State:** KS **Parents:** Jack Lawrence Maskus; Dorothy Louise (Leighty) Maskus **Marital Status:** Married **Spouse Name:** Susan Emily Rehak (12/30/1978) **Children:** Carol Lillian **Education:** Fellow, Kiel Institute for the World Economy (2005-Present); Non-Resident Research Fellow, Peterson Institute for International Economics (1998-Present); PhD in Economics, University of Michigan (1981); MA in Economics, University of Michigan (1979); BA, Knox College (1976) **Career:** Director, Program on International Development, Institute of Behavioral Science, University of Colorado, Boulder (2015-Present); Senior Program Associate, Robert Schuman Centre, European University Institute (2014-Present); College of Arts and Sciences Professor of Distinction, University of Colorado, Boulder (2012-Present); Research Affiliate, CESifo Institute, Ludwig-Maximilians-Universitat Munchen (2007-Present); Adjunct Professor, Economics, University of Adelaide (2001-Present); Professor, Economics, University of Colorado, Boulder (1995-Present); Associate Dean, Social Sciences, University of Colorado, Boulder (2007-2013); Stanford Calderwood Professor, Economics, University of Colorado, Boulder (2004-2007); Chairman, Economics Department, University of Colorado, Boulder (2002-2006); Director, Carl McGuire Center for International Studies, University of Colorado, Boulder (1996); Associate Professor, Economics, University of Colorado, Boulder (1989-1995); Assistant Professor, Economics, University of Colorado, Boulder (1981-1989) **Career Related:** Chief Economist, U.S. Department of State (2016-2017); Lead Economist, The World Bank Group (2001-2002); Visiting Professor, School of Economics, University of Adelaide (1997); Visiting Research Scholar, Federal Reserve Bank of Kansas City (1992); Visiting Senior International Economist, Planning and Economic Analysis Staff, U.S. Department of State (1986-1987); Visiting Research Scholar, Federal Reserve Bank of Kansas City (1983-1985); Visiting Professor, Various Universities; Speaker in Field; Consultant in Field **Civic:** Co-Chair, Task Force on Intellectual Property, Initiative for Policy Dialogue (2005-Present); Project Leader, Environmental Program Panel on Innovation and Intellectual Property Rights in Green Technologies, United Nations (2011-2012); Global Agenda Council on Intellectual Property Rights, World Economic Forum (2009-2012); Shadow Committee on U.S. Trade Policy, United States Trade Representative (2009-2012); Expert Advisory Committee, China: The Balance Sheet, Center for Strategic International Studies and Peterson Institute for International Economics (2005-2006) **Creative Works:** Editor, World Scientific Publishing Series in International Economics (2015-Present); Editorial Board Member, Journal of International Trade Law and Policy (2014-Present); Associate Editor, "Economic Inquiry" (2013-Present); Advisory Board Member, Law, Policy and Economics of Technical Standards (2013-Present); Editorial Board Member, International Review of Economics and Finance (2010-Present); Editorial Board Member, The WIPO Journal: Analysis and Debate of Intellectual Property Issues (2009-Present); Editorial Board Member, Forum for Research on Empirical International Trade (2006-Present); Editorial Board Member, Review of International Economics (2006-Present); Advisory Board, "SCRIPT-Ed," AHRB Research Centre for Studies in Intellectual Property and Technology, University of Edinburgh (2004-Present); Guest Editor, China Economic Review, Special Issue (2012); Author, "Private Right and Public Problems: The Global Economics of Intellectual Property in the 21st Century" (2012); Co-Editor, Journal of International Economic Law, Symposium Issue (2004); Editorial Board Member, North American Journal of Economics and Finance (2002-2013) **Awards:** Stanford Calderwood Award for Teaching Excellence, Department of Economics, University of Colorado, Boulder (2016); Friend of the Law School, University of Colorado, Boulder (2015); Outstanding Member, Chinese Economist Society (2010); Alumni Achievement Award, Knox College (2010); Stanford Calderwood Award for Teaching Excellence, Department of Economics, University of Colorado, Boulder (2006); Faculty Assembly Award for Excellence in Research, Scholarly, and Creative Work, University of Colorado, Boulder (2003) **Membership:** Board of Distinguished Advisers, DIW DC (2009-Present); Advisory Council, Intellectual Property Watch (2004-Present); International Council on Intellectual Property Rights (2004-Present); Chair, Panel on International Technical Standards and Patent Policy, National Academy of Sciences (2011-2013); Board of Directors, Chinese Economist Society (2010-2012); President, IEFS (2008-2010); Working Group on Commission on Macroeconomics and Health, World Health Organization (2001-2002) **Marquis Who's Who Honors:** Albert Nelson Marquis Lifetime Achievement Award (2017) **Business Address:** 256, University of Colorado, Boulder, CO, 80309 **Shipping Address:** 64 Illini Court, Boulder, CO, 80303

Dean Towle Mason

Title: Cardiologist, Coronary Thrombolysis **Industry:** Medicine & Health Care **Company Name:** St. Mary's Medical Center - San Francisco, CA **Date of Birth:** 09/20/1932 **Place of Birth:** Berkeley **State:** CA **Parents:** Ira Jenckes Mason; Florence Mabel (Towle) Mason **Marital Status:** Married **Spouse Name:** Maureen O'Brien (6/22/1957) **Children:** Kathleen; Alison **Education:** Resident, Medicine, The Johns Hopkins Hospital (1960-1961); Resident, Medicine, Duke University Medical Center (1959-1960); Intern, Medicine, The Johns Hopkins Hospital (1958-1959); MD, Duke University (1958); BA in Chemistry, Duke University (1954) **Certifications:** Diplomate, National Board of Medical Examiners; Diplomate, American Board of Cardiovascular Diseases; Diplomate, American Board of Internal Medicine **Career:** Honorary Medical Staff, St. Mary's Medical Center (2000-Present); Chairman, Department of Cardiovascular Medicine, St. Mary's Medical Center (1986-2000); Physician-in-Chief, Western Heart Institute, St. Mary's Medical Center (1983-2000); Director, Cardiac Center, Cedars Medical Center, Miami, FL (1982-1983); Professor, Medicine, UC Davis Medical Center (1968-1982); Professor, Physiology, UC Davis Medical School (1968-1982); Chief, Cardiovascular Medicine, UC Davis Medical Center (1968-1982); Assistant Section Director, Cardiovascular Diagnosis, NHLBI (1963-1968); Attending Physician, NHLBI (1963-1968); Senior Investigator, Cardiology Branch, NHLBI (1963-1968); Clinical Associate, Cardiology Branch, NHLBI (1961-1963); Senior Assistant Surgeon, NHLBI (1961-1968) **Career Related:** Honorary Professor, Medicine, Peking University Health Science Center (1987); Co-Chairman, Cardiovascular-Renal Drugs, United States Pharmacopeia Committee Revision (1970-1975); Medical Research Review Board, National Institutes of Health; Member, Life Sciences Committee, National Aeronautics and Space Administration; Field Consultant; Visiting Professor, Universities **Creative Works:** Editor-in-Chief, "American Heart Journal," Elsevier-Mosby, Inc. (1980-1996); Contributor, Chapters, Books; Contributor, Articles, Professional Journals **Awards:** Lifetime Achievement Award, University of California, Davis, CA (2008); Norman Vincent Peale Healing Power of Prayer Award (2005); Newton Kugelmass Children's Cardiology Crusader Award (2004); Paul Dudley White Award for Distinguished Service in Cardiovascular Medicine (2004); Will Durant Philosopher-Physician Award (2004); Ernest Hemingway Award for Major Contributions to Medical Literature (2003); John Wayne Pioneer of America Award (2003); Albert Einstein Science Research Award (2003); Jonas Salk Award for Medical Research (2003); Albert Schweitzer World Humanitarian of Wisdom Award (2002); Cardiologist of the Century Wisdom Award (2001); Dean Towle Mason, M.D. Medal of Wisdom Award (2001); Dean Towle Mason Eminent Physician of Wisdom Award (1998); Blessed Lord's Prayer Award (1998); Eternal Jesus Christ Award (1998); Dwight D. Eisenhower Admirable American of Achievement Award (1998); Armand Hammer Creative Genius Award (1998); Medal of Honor, The International Churchill Society (1998); Award of Honor, Wisdom Society (1997); Distinguished Alumnus Award, School of Medicine, Duke University (1979); Symbol of Excellence, Texas Heart Institute (1979); Theodore and Susan B. Cummings Humanitarian Award, American College of Cardiology Foundation (1972, 1973, 1975, 1978); Faculty Research Award, University of California, Davis, CA (1978); Skylab Achievement Award, National Aeronautics and Space Administration (1974); Experimental Therapeutics Award, The American Society for Pharmacology and Experimental Therapeutics (1973); Research Award, American Therapeutic Society (1965) **Membership:** President, American College of Cardiology (1977-1978); Fellow, American College of Physicians; Fellow, American Heart Association, Inc.; Fellow, American College of Chest Physicians; Fellow, Royal Society of Medicine; American Society for Clinical Investigation; The American Physiological Society; The American Society for Pharmacology and Experimental Therapeutics; American Federation for Clinical Research; The New York Academy of Sciences; Association of University Cardiologists; American Society for Clinical Pharmacology and Therapeutics; Western Association of Physicians; American Association of University Professors; President Emeritus, Western Society for Clinical Research; The Phi Beta Kappa Society; Alpha Omega Alpha Honor Medical Society **Marquis Who's Who Honors:** Albert Nelson Marquis Lifetime Achievement Award (2017); Distinguished Humanitarian (2017) **Political Affiliations:** Republican **Religion:** Presbyterian **Shipping Address:** 44725 Country Club Dr, El Macero, CA, 95618

Patrick E. Matoole

Title: Physician, Neurologist **Industry:** Medicine & Health Care **Company Name:** Josephson-Wallack-Munshower Neurology **Education:** Fellowship in Clinical Neurophysiology, Indiana University (2001); Residency in Neurology, Creighton University (2000); Internship in Internal Medicine, Medical College of Wisconsin Affiliated Hospitals (1997); MD, University of Nebraska (1996); BA, Chemistry, University of Denver (1991) **Certifications:** Medical License, State of Indiana (2001-2015); Certified, American Board of Psychiatry and Neurology **Research:** Sub-Investigator, Clinical Study Of Droxidopa In Patients With Neurogenic Orthostatic Hypotension; EDSS Rater, Comparison Of Alemtuzumab And Rebif Efficacy In Multiple Sclerosis, Study Two; Sub-Investigator, Randomized Evaluation Of Recurrent Stroke Comparing PFO Closure to Established Current Standard of Care Treatment; Sub-Investigator, Safety of New Formulation of Glatiramer Acetate; Sub-Investigator, A Clinical Study of The Efficacy of Natalizumab on Reducing Disability Progression in Participants with Secondary Progressive Multiple Sclerosis; Sub-Investigator, Conversion to Embeda with Rescue Trial **Membership:** Community Hospital East; Community Hospital North; Community Hospital South; St. Vincent Hospital Indianapolis; St. Vincent Heart Hospital; St. Vincent Hospital Carmel; Johnson County Memorial Hospital; St. Francis Hospital Mooresville; Community Heart And Vascular Center; St. Francis Hospital Indianapolis; Indianapolis Medical Society; Indiana State Medical Association; AANEM; American Academy of Neurology; American Medical Association; American Association of Neuromuscular and Electrodiagnostic Medicine; National Multiple Sclerosis Society; Phi Gamma Delta **Marquis Who's Who Honors:** Albert Nelson Marquis Lifetime Achievement Award (2017); Distinguished Humanitarian (2017) **To what do you attribute your success:** Mr. Matoole attributes his success to hard work and dedication. **Why did you become involved in your profession or industry:** Mr. Matoole became involved in his profession after being inspired by his father and developing an interest in neurology at an early age. Before diving into the field of neurology, Dr. Matoole first concentrated on higher education, building an extensive base of knowledge on which to develop his career. He graduated from the University of Denver with a Bachelor of Arts in Chemistry in 1991. Five years later he completed an MD from the University of Nebraska, the same institution which his father attended. Following an internship in internal medicine with the Medical College of Wisconsin Affiliated Hospitals in 1997, a residency in neurology at Creighton University in 2000, and the completion of a fellowship in clinical neurophysiology at Indiana University in 2001, Dr. Matoole began his career at Josephson-Wallack-Munshower Neurology (JWM), one of the largest neurology practices in Indiana. JWM currently has 11 locations across the United States. Dr. Matoole is also certified by the American Board of Psychiatry

Patrick E. Matoole (continued)

and Neurology. **If you could solve problem in the world today, what would it be:** He would solve the problem of inadequate access to health care. **If you could have lunch with anyone, dead or alive, who would it be and why:** He would have lunch with Saint Patrick, the original one, who lives by his original views and values. **What lessons have you learned as an expert in your field:** "Compassion is necessary, and when you are dealing with patients you must be thorough." Dr. Matoole shared that his concern for the well-being of his patients derives from a genuine and innate desire to help others. Success, as he describes it, "is nothing if only a monetary gain; it needs to come from a place of happiness." His reliability and love of the field have earned him recognition and accolades alike by a wide range of organizations. **What is the most significant issue facing your profession today:** Recruitment of doctors in the field. When medical students are trained, they are geared towards primary care and not specialties. Also, the transition into the electronic record keeping. **What do you find to be the most rewarding aspect of your profession:** Doing what he loves and doing it to the best of his ability seeing how pleased patient's families are with the outcome of success for the patient. **On what topics do you consider yourself to be an expert:** Neurological health care, specializing in Alzheimer's disease, epilepsy, stroke patients, head injuries and neuromuscular diseases. **What characteristics help to separate you from your peers:** The fact that he is fellowship trained in epilepsy. **What motivates you:** He enjoys his profession and loves helping his patients. **What has been the most difficult obstacle or challenge you've faced in pursuit of your goals:** The mountain of information you have to learn and boil down. **What advice can you offer fellow members or others aspiring to work in your industry:** "To work hard. Even though it is difficult most of the time, it is extremely rewarding. You get out of it what you put into it." **Where will you be in five years:** In five years, Dr. Matoole hopes to expand his current practice. **How would you like to be remembered by your peers:** He would like to be remembered as knowledgeable and compassionate. **Hobbies:** Walking; Swimming; Travel **Shipping Address:** 8051 S Emerson Ave., Ste 350, Josephson-Wallack-Munshower Neurology, Indianapolis, IN, 46237 **Website:** http://www.jwmneuro.com

Susan Matorin

Title: Senior Lecturer of Social Work in Psychiatry **Industry:** Education/Educational Services **Company Name:** Weill Cornell Medicine **Date of Birth:** 01/09/1943 **Place of Birth:** Boston **State:** MA **Parents:** Mervyn Donald Matorin; Eleanor (Marinoff) Matorin **Marital Status:** Married **Spouse Name:** Richard Charles Friedman (11/24/1978) **Children:** Jeremiah Simon **Education:** Postgraduate Coursework, Columbia School of Social Work (1966); AB, Vassar College (1964) **Certifications:** Certified Social Worker, State of New York **Career:** Treatment Coordinator, Affective Disorder Team, Cornell Psychiatry Intensive Outpatient Program (2000-Present); Program Director, Cornell Psychiatry Intensive Outpatient Program (1997-2000); Director of Social Work, The Payne Whitney Clinic NewYork-Presbyterian/Weill Cornell Medical Center (1981-1997); Chief Ambulatory Social Work in Psychiatry, New York-Presbyterian/Columbia University Medical Center (1978-1981); Chief of Social Work, Washington Heights Community Service, New York State Psychiatric Institute (1966-1978) **Career Related:** Member, Advanced Council, Columbia School of Social Work (1994-Present); 2nd Vice Chair, Columbia School of Social Work (1994-Present); Panel Presentation, "Getting Better Health Care For Your Mind and Body," Fountainhouse (2016); Adjunct Associate Professor, Columbia School of Social Work (1977); Board of Trustees, Martha K. Selig Educational Institute, The Jewish Board; Member, Pastoral Education and Research Committee, HealthCare Chaplaincy Network; Speaker in Field **Creative Works:** Author, "Letters, Science, The New York Times Company" (2016); Author, "Programs Offer people with Schizophrenia a Greater Role in their Own Care"; Letters, Science, The New York Times Company (2016); Author, "Social Workers: Finding Solutions For Real Problems," The Helen Rehr Center for Social Work Practice (2015); Author, "Clutter Is In The Eye of The Beholder"; Author, "Still Stressed About My Grades"; Author, "An Interdisciplinary Team to Inform Patient Decisions"; Author, "Finding Joy in Social Work"; Author, "Finding Joy in Social Work"; Author, "Thriving at 70 and Beyond"; Contributor, Chapter, "Clinical Social Work with Troubled Couples"; Contributor, Articles, Professional Journals **Awards:** Hyman J. Weiner Award, Society for Social Work Leaders in HealthCare (2006); Centennial Award (1998); Nominated, Social Work Director of the Year, Society for Social Work Leadership in Health Care (1995); Distinguished Service Medal, Columbia University (1989) **Membership:** New York Chapter Program Co-chair, Society for Social Work Leadership in Health Care (1994); Fellow, American Orthopsychiatry Association; Metropolitan Chapter Licensing Task Force, National Association of Social Workers; National Association of Social Workers; Academy of Certified Social Workers **Marquis Who's Who Honors:** Albert Nelson Marquis Lifetime Achievement Award (2017); Distinguished Humanitarian (2017) **Hobbies:** Spending time with family; Playing piano; Reading; Walking; Ballet; Art **Political Affiliations:** Democrat **Religion:** Jewish **Shipping Address:** 27 W 86th St., Apt 9C, New York, NY, 10024

Raymond Frank Mawson

Title: Food Scientist **Industry:** Sciences **Date of Birth:** 12/31/1945 **Place of Birth:** Wellington **Country of Origin:** New Zealand **Education:** PhD in Animal Science, Colorado State University, Fort Collins, CO (1982); Master of Technology in Food Processing, Massey University, Palmerston North, New Zealand (1969); Bachelor of Technology in Food Science, Massey University, Palmerston North, New Zealand (1967) **Career:** Senior Scientist, CSIRO Food and Nutritional Sciences, Werribee, Australia (2004); Senior Scientist, Australian Food Industry Science Center, Werribee, Australia (1991-2003); Research and Development Manager, Huttons Kiwi Ltd., Hamilton, New Zealand (1985-1988); Research Scientist, Meat Industry Research Institute of New Zealand, Hamilton, New Zealand (1972-1984); Manager, Department of Agriculture, Food Research Center, Apia, Western Samoa (1970-1971) **Civic:** Donor, World Wildlife Fund and New Zealand Forest and Bird Society, New Zealand (1982-1990); Volunteer First Aider, St. John's Ambulance, Hamilton, New Zealand (1976-1979) **Membership:** American Association for the Advancement of Science; American Chemical Society; Institute of Food Technologists **Marquis Who's Who Honors:** Albert Nelson Marquis Lifetime Achievement Award (2017) **Hobbies:** Gardening; Painting; Music; Photography **Religion:** Unitarian Universalist **Shipping Address:** 8 Carapooka Avenue, Clifton Springs, VIC, Australia, 3222

Marie Lois Maxwell

Industry: Medicine & Health Care **Education:** MSN, Boston College (1975) **Career:** Clinical Nurse Specialist, Greene County Mental Health Clinic (1993-2015) **Achievements:** Plaque of Appreciation

Anne Russell Mayeaux, PhD

Title: Education Educator **Industry:** Education/Educational Services **Company Name:** Candler School of Theology **Date of Birth:** 08/27/1943 **Place of Birth:** Meridian **State:** MS **Parents:** Constant Hyacinth Mayeaux; Laura Archer Mayeaux **Education:** PhD, Emory University (1975); BA, St. Xavier University (1965) **Career:** Postdoctoral Fellow, Candler School of Theology, Atlanta, GA (1975-1981); Adjunct Faculty, Candler School of Theology, Atlanta, GA (1975-1981); Director, World Peace Center, Chicago, IL (1967-1968) **Career Related:** Adjunct Faculty, Hinds Community College, Jackson, MI (2000-Present); Chair, Theology Department, Saint Joseph Catholic School, Madison, MS (1999-Present); Researcher, Institute for Social Research, University of Michigan (1996-1999); Associate Professor, Siena Heights University, Adrian, MI (1991-1996); Visiting Scholar in Ethics and Society, Harvard Divinity School, Cambridge, MA (1990-1991); President, Faculty, Aquinas Center of Theology, Emory University, Atlanta, GA (1983-1990); Executive Director, Georgia Endowment for the Humanities (1979-1981) **Civic:** Board of Directors, National Assembly of Religious Women, Chicago, IL (1991-1994); President, Las Casas, National Ministry Among the Native Americans, Clinton, OK (1989-1993); Secretary-treasurer, International Foundation for Scholarly Exchange, Atlanta, GA (1988-1994); Jackson Federation of Teachers; Cheshire Abbey **Creative Works:** Contributor, Articles, Journals **Awards:** Conservation Prize, Department of Agriculture (2015); Grant, Junior League of Jackson (2014); Nominated, Teacher of the Year Award, Jackson Mississippi Jackson Federation of Teachers **Membership:** Vice President, Siena Heights University Chapter, American Association of University Professors (1995); Chair, Program Section, Southeast Region, American Academy of Religion (1975-1991); American Association of University Professors; American Academy of Religion **Marquis Who's Who Honors:** Distinguished Humanitarian (2017) **Why did you become involved in your profession or industry:** She was inspired to study philosophy at 15 years old after she learned about the life of Socrates from her Ancient History professor. **What do you consider to be the highlight of your career:** The highlight of her career was when she went to Iraq in 1991 while working with the Harvard Divinity School. While there she worked as an activist, learning about the plight of hospitalized children in the country, and risked her life by walking through minefields. **Hobbies:** Horseback riding; Creative writing; Conservation **Political Affiliations:** Democrat **Religion:** Roman Catholic **Shipping Address:** 550 Post Rd., Apt 105, Ridgeland, MS, 39157

Arlene Mazak

Title: Principal, Owner **Industry:** Consulting **Company Name:** Mazak Global Management; Innercall: Personal and Transpersonal Development **Date of Birth:** 03/17/1946 **Place of Birth:** Bayonne **State:** NJ **Parents:** John Andrew Mazak; Irene Kraszewski Mazak **Marital Status:** Widow **Spouse Name:** Mark Benninghofen II (2009, Deceased 2010); Pierre Breuinin (1970, Divorced 1991, Deceased 2014) **Education:** Coursework in Transpersonal Hypnotherapy and Past Life Regression, Institute of Thought (2007); Coursework for Certificate in Gerontology, Coastline Community College (2003); Coursework for Certificate in Spiritual Direction (2008-2010); PhD in South Asian Languages and Civilizations, The University of Chicago (1994); MA in South Asian Studies University of Chicago (1994); Master's Degree in Counseling, School of Education, University of San Francisco (1992); BA in Liberal Arts, Sarah Lawrence College **Certifications:** Certification in Intercultural Foundations and Intercultural Practitioner, Intercultural Communication Institute, Portland, OR (2018); Certificate in Ethno-Religious Mediation, International Center for Ethno-Religious Mediation (2016); Certification and Ordination in Interfaith Ministry, One Spirit Interfaith Seminary (2016); Certifications in Global Leadership and Transnational Management Training, Assessments and Simulations, The Summer Institute for Intercultural Communication (2013-2015); Licensed Marriage and Family Therapist, State of California (2001-2012); Graduate Certificate in Organizational Development and Transformation, California Institute of Integral Studies (1993); Certified in Foreign Languages, University and Private Institutions (1970); Licensed Past Life Regressionist, International Association Regression Research and Therapy; Licensed Marriage and Family Therapist, Board of Behavioral Sciences **Career:** Intercultural Trainer, Executive Coach, Organization Development Consultant, Mazak Global Management, Orange and Norwalk, CA (2013-Present); Transformational Speaker, Trainer, Coach, Orange and Norwalk, CA (2013-Present); Interfaith/Interspiritual Minister (2016-2018); Marriage and Family Therapist, Life Coach and Spiritual Director, Innercall: Transpersonal Healing and Developmental Services, Fountain Valley, Encinitas, CA (2001-2010); Associate Director, Acting Director, MA Program, Associate Professor, Core Faculty, MA and PhD Programs, Institute of Transpersonal Psychology (1993-2000); Training Director, Spiritual Emergence Network, Menlo Park, CA (1990-1991); Associate Director, Associate Professor, Core Faculty, East-West Psychology, California Institute of Integral Studies, San Francisco, CA (1986-1993) **Career Related:** Adjunct Faculty, School of Light, Unity of Tustin (2003-2014); Adjunct Faculty, Transpersonal Psychology, San Diego University for Integrative Studies (2001-2004); Faculty Sabbatical, Tibetan Buddhist Community, Kathmandu Valley, Nepal (1998); Intercultural Research Director, International Management Trainer, Sunrock, Inc., Woodside, CA (1991-1993); Training Director, Spiritual Emergence Network, Palo Alto, CA (1990-1991); Curriculum Advisory Committee on Gerontology, Coastline Community College; Adjunct Faculty, Gerontology (2001-2006). Faculty Member, Campus Diversification Committee, Institute of Transpersonal Psychology **Civic:** Staff Member, Member, Board of Trustees, Spiritual Emergence Network; Faculty Representative, Board of Trustees, California Institute of Integral Studies **Creative Works:** Professional Conference Presentations, Professional Journals; Contributor, Articles, Professional Journals; Contributor, Article to Navonmesha, a Festschrift honoring the contributions of Pandit Gopinath Kaviraj **Awards:** Partial Tuition Scholarships, One Spirit Interfaith Seminary (2013-2015); Partial Tuition Scholarships, Summer Institute of Intercultural Communication (2013-2015); Grant for Developing Online Course, California Virtual Campus, Coastline Community College (2002); Dean's Prize for Faculty Research, California Institute of Integral Studies (1993); Fulbright-Hays Fellowship for Research Abroad in India, U.S. Department of Education (1971-1972); NDFL Title VI Fellowship, U.S. Dept. of Education, The University of Chicago (1970-1971); National Defense Education Act Title IV Fellowship (1967-1970); Scholarship, Sarah Lawrence College (1963-1967); Scholarship, Holy Family Academy (1959-1963) **Membership:** Affiliate Minister, One Spirit Interfaith Seminary; A World Alliance of Interfaith Clergy; United Religions Initiative; California Association of Marriage and Family Therapists; Academy of Management; The Jung Club; Institute of Noetic Sciences; Society for the Anthropology of Consciousness; Sri Aurobindo Society; Unity of Tustin; Vajrayana Foundation; Fellowship of Reconciliation; Spiritual Directors International; International Association for Regression Research & Therapies, Inc.; Orange County Interfaith Network; Theosophical Society **Political Affiliations:** Independent, leaning progressive **Religion:** Interspiritual - Tibetan Buddhist, Hindu, esoteric **Business Address:** 12073 Highdale St., Norwalk, CA, 90650 **Website:** http://www.mazakglobalmgmt.com/

Roger Geoffrey Mazlen

Title: Pharmacologist **Industry:** Pharmaceuticals **Date of Birth:** 11/23/1937 **Place of Birth:** Brooklyn **State:** NY **Parents:** Henry Gershwin Mazlen; Ann Kurland (Shapero) Mazlen **Marital Status:** Married **Spouse Name:** Sandra Phyllis Kuritzky (8/7/1960) **Children:** James Edward; Vivien Gayle **Education:** Resident in Medical Ophthalmology, Mount Sinai Medical Center, New York City, NY (1967-1969); Resident in Medicine, Maimonides Medical Center, Brooklyn, NY (1964-1965); Intern, Maimonides Medical Center, Brooklyn, NY (1963-1964); MD, State University of New York, Brooklyn (1963); BS in Biology, Rensselaer Polytechnic Institute (1959) **Career:** Associate Director for Clinical Research, Schering Corp., Bloomfield, NJ (1975-1978); Senior Attendant, Division of Endocrinology and Metabolism, Mount Sinai Medical Center (1972-2008); Senior Faculty, Assistant Director of Clinical Research, Ayerst Laboratories, New York City, NY (1971-1975); Associate Medical Director, Pfizer Inc., New York City, NY (1970-1971); Postdoctoral Fellow, Harvard Medical School, Peter Bent Brigham Hospital, Boston, MA (1967-1968); Research Associate, National Institutes of Health, Bethesda, MD (1965-1968); Senior Clinical Assistant Professor, Mount Sinai School of Medicine; Adjunct Assistant Professor of Medicine, New York Medical College **Career Related:** Speaker, Breast Cancer Conference, Sass Medical Research Foundation **Civic:** Chief Science Officer, Biomolecular Sciences Inc. (2000-2007); Nutritional Director, Cernitin American Nutritional (1983-1988); Vice Chairman for New York State, Queens County Common Cause (1974-1975); Founder, Chairman, Queens County Common Cause, New York City, NY (1972-1975); Board of Directors, Bayside Hills Civic Association (1970-1980); Member, Board of Directors, U.S.A., Inc. (1970-1972); Consultant, Expert Medical Lecturer, The SASS Foundation for Medical Research, Inc.; Former Director, Clinical Research North America Immunotec Ltd, Montreal, Canada; Former Chairman, Hyperalimentation Committee, Astoria General Hospital, New York City, NY; With, United States Public Health Service; Consultant, Clinical Nutrition and Metabolism, South Oaks Hospital, Long Island Home; Consultant, Professional Children's School **Creative Works:** Author, "A New Manifesto for Middle America" (1972); Co-Author, "Nutrition and Health Care"; Contributor, Chapter, "Quick Reference to Clinical Nutrition" **Awards:** Honoree, Top Doctor Award for Internal Medicine, New York Magazine, New York Media LLC (2017); Recipient, Good Doctors List Award, American Society for Clinical Pharmacology and Therapeutics (ASCPT); Honoree, Named a Top Doctor USA **Membership:** Chairman, Council on Nutrition and Cardiovascular Diseases, American College of Nutrition (1976-1985); American Chemistry Society; Society for Natural Immunity; Constituent Member, New York State Chapter, American College of Cardiology; American Society for Clinical Pharmacology and Therapeutics; Fellow, American College of Nutrition **Marquis Who's Who Honors:** Albert Nelson Marquis Lifetime Achievement Award (2017) **Why did you become involved in your profession or industry:** Dr. Mazlen became involved in his career for the advancement of public health. **Where will you be in five years:** In the next five years, Dr. Mazlen will be semi-retired. **Hobbies:** Civil rights advocacy **Political Affiliations:** Republican **Business Address:** 58-32 212th Street, Flushing, NY, 11364 **Shipping Address:** 30 Middleneck Rd., Ste 1F, Roslyn Chiropractic Ctr, Roslyn, NY, 11576 **Website:** http://www.drmazlen.com

Angela Barron McBride

Title: Distinguished Professor, University Dean Emeritus **Industry:** Education/Educational Services **Company Name:** Indiana University **Date of Birth:** 01/16/1941 **Place of Birth:** Baltimore **State:** MD **Parents:** Mary Barron; John Barron (Deceased) **Marital Status:** Married **Spouse Name:** William Leon McBride **Children:** Catherine Alexandra McBride; Kara Angela McBride **Education:** Honorary DSc, Indiana University (2014); Honorary LittD, Purdue University (1998); Honorary LHD, University of Akron (1997); Honorary DSc, Medical College of Ohio (1995); Honorary LHD, Georgetown University (1993); Honorary LLD, Eastern Kentucky University (1991); Honorary Doctorate of Public Service, University of Cincinnati (1983); PhD, Purdue University, West Lafayette, IN (1978); MSN in Psychiatric-Mental Health Nursing, Yale University, New Haven, CT (1964); BSN, Georgetown University, Washington, DC (1962) **Certifications:** Diplomate, Institute for Educational Management, Harvard University (1992) **Career:** Distinguished Professor Emeritus, School of Nursing, Indiana University (2006-Present); University Dean Emeritus, School of Nursing, Indiana University (2003-Present); Consulting Professor, School of Nursing, Duke University (2008-2010); Scholar-in-Residence, Institute of Medicine, The National Academies (2003-2004); Senior Vice President for Academic Affairs, Nursing/Patient Services Clarian Health Partners, Inc. (1997-2003); Adjunct Professor, Philanthropic Studies School of Liberal Arts, Indiana University, - Purdue University Indianapolis (1995-2005); Distinguished Professor of Nursing, School of Nursing, Indiana University (1992-2005); University Dean, Indiana University (1992-2005); Associate Director for Academic Affairs, Department of Nursing Services, Indiana University Medical Center (1992-1996); Interim Dean, School of Nursing, Indiana University (1990-1991); Adjunct Professor of Women's Studies, Indiana University, Purdue University Indianapolis (1988-2005); Associate Dean for Research, School of Nursing, Indiana University (1985-1990); Adjunct Professor, Department of Psychiatry, Indiana University (1981-2005); Professor, Department of Psychiatric/Mental Health Nursing, Indiana University (1981-1992); Chairperson, Department of Psychiatric/Mental Health Nursing, Indiana University (1980-1984); Adjunct Associate Professor, Department of Psychology, School of Science, Purdue University (1980-1981); Adjunct Associate Professor, Department of Psychiatry, Indiana University (1980-1981); Assistant Chairperson, Department of Psychiatric/Mental Health Nursing, Indiana University (1979-1980); National Institute of Mental Health Trainee, Purdue University (1976-1978); Acting Instructor, Department of Philosophy, Purdue University (1974); Assistant Professor, School of Nursing, Yale University (1972-1973); Research Assistant, School of Nursing, Yale University (1969-1971); Lecturer, School of Nursing, Yale University (1967-1968); Coordinator of Clinical Experience, Psychiatric Nursing, School of Nursing, Yale University (1965-1967); Director, Psychiatric Work-Study Program, Connecticut Valley State Hospital (1964); Evening Charge Nurse, Phipps Clinic of Johns Hopkins Hospital (1963); Professional Nurse Trainee, Yale University School of Nursing (1962-1964) **Career Related:** Adviser, Hong Kong Academy of Nursing (2014-Present); Member, Advisory Board, School of Nursing, Purdue University (2009-Present); Adviser, Hong Kong Society for Nursing Education (2004-Present); Member, Advisory Board, School of Nursing & Health Sciences, Georgetown University (2012-2017); Old Master Program (2007); Board Member, Indiana University Health (2004-2016); Adviser, University of Hong Kong (2004-2006); Advisory Committee, Research on Sex and Gender Factors, Office of Women's Health Research Specialized Centers, National Institutes of Health (2003-2006); Adviser, School of Nursing, Hong Kong Polytechnic University (2000-2006) **Creative Works:** Author, "The Growth and Development of Nurse Leaders" (2011); Compiler, "Nursing and Philanthropy" (2000); Editor, "Psychiatric-Mental Health Nursing: Integrating the Behavioral and Biological Sciences" (1996); Author, "How to Enjoy a Good Life with Your Teenager" (1987); Author, "Living with Contradictions: A Married Feminist" (1976) **Awards:** Distinguished Woman Scholar, Purdue University (2016); Honorary Fellow, NLN Academy of Nursing Education (2015); Recipient, Presidential Medal, Indiana University (2012); Recipient, President's Award, National League of Nursing (2012); Recipient, Prose Award, Nursing and Allied Health Division (2011); Honoree, Named to Hall of Fame, Yale School Nursing (2008); Recipient, Harold Burdette Award, Behavioral Cooperative Oncology Group (2007); Recipient, Melva Jo Hendrix Leadership Award, International Society of Psychiatric-Mental Health Nurses (2006) **Membership:** Founding Co-Chair, National Advisory Committee, Institute for Nursing Leadership (2014-Present); Reviewer of Reports, Epilepsy Across the Spectrum: Promoting Health and Understanding (2012); Reviewer of Reports, Better Care, Lower Costs: Building A Continuously Learning Health Care System (2012); Chair, Task Force on Living Legends, American Academy of Nursing (2010); Founding Trustee, MNRS Foundation (2007-2009) **Shipping Address:** 744 Cherokee Ave, Lafayette, IN, 47905

William Leon McBride, PhD

Title: Philosopher **Industry:** Education/Educational Services **Company Name:** Purdue University **Date of Birth:** 01/19/1938 **Place of Birth:** New York **State/Country of Origin:** NY **Parents:** William Joseph McBride; Irene May (Choffin) McBride **Marital Status:** Married **Spouse Name:** Angela Barron (6/12/1965) **Children:** Catherine; Kara **Education:** PhD, Yale University, New Haven, CT (1964); MA, Yale University, New Haven, CT (1962); Postgraduate Studies, University of Lille (1959-1960); AB, Georgetown University, Washington, DC (1959) **Career:** Arthur G. Hansen Distinguished Professor, Purdue University, West Lafayette, IN (2001-Present); Professor, Purdue University, West Lafayette, IN (1976-2001); Associate Professor, Purdue University, West Lafayette, IN (1973-1976); Lecturer, Northwestern University, Evanston, IL (1972); Associate Professor, Yale University, New Haven, CT (1970-1973); Assistant Professor, Yale University, New Haven, CT (1966-1970); Instructor of Philosophy, Yale University, New Haven, CT (1964-1966) **Career Related:** Senate Chairman, Purdue University (2004-2005); Fulbright Lecturer, Sofia University, Bulgaria (1997); Lecturer, Korcula Summer School, Yugoslavia (1973); Lecturer, Korcula Summer School, Yugoslavia (1971) **Creative Works:** Editor, "Social and Political Philosophy" (2006); Author, "The Idea of Values" (2003); Co-editor, "Calvin O. Schrag and the Task of Philosophy after Postmodernity" (2002); Author, "From Yugoslav Praxis to Global Pathos" (2001); Author, "Philosophical Reflections on the Changes in Eastern Europe" (1999); Editor, "Sartre and Existentialism, Eight Volumes" (1997); Author, "Social and Political Philosophy" (1994); Author, "Sartre's Political Theory" (1991); Co-editor, "Phenomenology in a Pluralistic Context" (1983); Co-author, "Demokrati og Autoritet" (1980); Author, "Social Theory at a Crossroads" (1980); Author, "The Philosophy of Marx" (1977); Author, "Fundamental Change in Law and Society" (1970) **Awards:** Decorated Chevalier, Ordre des Palmes Académiques; Silver Medal, Institute of Philosophy, Russian Academy of Sciences **Membership:** Bureau, International Council Philosophy and Human Sciences (2014-Present); Past President, Fédération Internationale des Sociétés de Philosophie (2013-Present); Steering Committee, Fédération Internationale des Sociétés de Philosophie (1998-Present); President, Fédération Internationale des Sociétés de Philosophie (2008-2013); Secretary General, Fédération Internationale des Sociétés de Philosophie (2003-2008); President, North American Society for Social Philosophy (2000-2005); Vice President, North American Society for Social Philosophy (1997-2000); President, American Society of Philosophy in the French Language (1994-1996); Board of Directors, Chairman, Committee on International Cooperation, American Philosophical Association (1992-1995); Chairman, Board of Directors, Sartre Society of North America (1991-1993); President, Indiana Conference, American Association of University Professors (1988-1989); Chairman, Board of Directors, Sartre Society of North America (1985-1988); President, Purdue Chapter, American Association of University Professors (1983-1986); Executive Co-Secretary, Society for Phenomenology and Existential Philosophy (1977-1980); American Society for Political and Legal Philosophy **Marquis Who's Who Honors:** Albert Nelson Marquis Lifetime Achievement Award (2017); Distinguished Humanitarian (2017) **Shipping Address:** 744 Cherokee Avenue, Lafayette, IN, 47905

Edward J. McCambridge

Title: Senior Shareholder **Industry:** Law and Legal Services **Company Name:** Segal McCambridge Singer and Mahoney Ltd. **Date of Birth:** 12/06/1949 **Place of Birth:** Evergreen Park **State/Country of Origin:** IL **Parents:** Edward Joseph McCambridge; Irene (Kimmerling) McCambridge **Marital Status:** Married **Spouse Name:** Joann Randall (2/5/1974) **Children:** Christopher; Michael **Education:** JD, The John Marshall Law School (1975); BA, University of St. Thomas, Minnesota (1971) **Career:** Attorney, Segal McCambridge Singer and Mahoney Ltd. (1986-Present); Founding Partner, Corporate Secretary, Segal McCambridge Singer and Mahoney Ltd. (1986-Present); Partner, Lurie, Sklar & Simon (1984-1986); Attorney, Lurie, Sklar & Simon (1984-1986); Partner, Epton, Mullen, Segal & Druth (1980-1984); Attorney, Epton, Mullen, Segal & Druth (1980-1984); Corporate Secretary, Epton, Mullen, Segal & Druth (1980-1984); Attorney, Epton, Mullen, Segal & Druth (1975-1980) **Career Related:** Board of Directors, Asbestos Property Damage Group (1983-Present); President, Asbestos Defense Group, City of Chicago (1978-1983); Chairman of the Board, Asbestos Defense Group, City of Chicago (1978-1983); Executive Committee, Segal McCambridge Singer & Mahoney **Civic:** Trustee, Village of Brookfield, Illinois (1980-1982) **Creative Works:** Contributor, Chapters, Books **Awards:** Fellowship, Litigation Counsel of America (2013); Honoree, Top Attorney's in Illinois **Membership:** Defense Research Institute; Illinois Defense Counsel; Union League Club; Litigation Counsel of America; American Law Registry; Lawyers Club of Chicago; Illinois State Bar Association; SBM **Bar Admissions:** Michigan (1992); United States Court of Appeals for the Seventh Circuit (1987); United States District Court Eastern District of Wisconsin (1987); Illinois (1975); United States District Court Northern District of Illinois (1975) **Marquis Who's Who Honors:** Albert Nelson Marquis Lifetime Achievement Award (2017) **Hobbies:** Fishing; Handball; Boating **Shipping Address:** 233 S Wacker Dr Ste 5500, Segal McCambridge Singer and Mahoney Ltd., Chicago, IL, 60606

Eugene H. McCarthy

Title: Professor **Industry:** Education/Educational Services **Company Name:** Middlesex Community College **Place of Birth:** Los Angeles **State:** CA **Education:** Master's Degree in Comparative Literature, San Francisco State University; BA in Classical Greek Language and Literature, Boston University (1965); Degree, MassBay Community College (1963) **Career:** Professor, Middlesex Community College (1991-Present); Professor, English and Humanities, European Division, University of Maryland; Professor, English and Humanities, The Cambridge Center for Adult Education, MA; Professor, English and Humanities, MassBay Community College; Professor, Latin and Greek, San Francisco State University; Teacher, Latin, Math and English, Boston Area High Schools **Career Related:** Media Relations Officer, White House Conference on Small Business, The White House; Public Information Officer, Disaster Relief Program, U.S. Small Business Administration; Regional Public Relations Director, New York Region, U.S. Small Business Administration **Civic:** Coach, Women's Softball, Massachusetts Institute of Technology; Coach, Women's Softball, Emmanuel College **Awards:** Professional of the Year, Biltmore Publishing (2008); Inductee, Charter Member, Leading Educators of the World, International Biographical Centre, London, England (2006); Numerous Awards in Men's Basketball, Baseball, Football and Softball; Honorary Citizenship, New Orleans, LA; Honorary Citizenship, Detroit, MI; Recognition, Top Softball Pitcher, Organizer and Umpire, Boston Area **Membership:** Former Member, National Association for Public and Continuing Adult Education; Co-founder, Student Organization, San Francisco State University **Why did you become involved in your profession or industry:** Mr. McCarthy knew when he was 12 that he wanted to be a teacher, so it was a natural progression. When he was in high school, he had to take four years of Latin and three years of Greek. He got immersed in language early on and loved it. **Where will you be in five years:** In five years, he will be continuing to teach. **Hobbies:** Competitive Men's Softball, Humorous Columns **Shipping Address:** 31 Governor Rd, Arlington, MA, 02474

Doran C. McCarty, PhD

Title: Executive Director **Industry:** Religious **Company Name:** Seminary Extension **Date of Birth:** 02/03/1931 **Place of Birth:** Bolivar **State:** MS **Parents:** Bartie Lee; Donta Marian (Russell) McCarty **Marital Status:** Married **Spouse Name:** Catherine Hearne McCaty (12/30/2017); Gloria Jean Laffoon (6/14/1952, Deceased) **Children:** Gaye; Rise; Marletta; Leslie **Education:** PhD, Southern Baptist Theological Seminary (1963); BD, Southern Baptist Theological Seminary (1956); AB, William Jewell College (1952); AA, Southwest Baptist College (1950) **Career:** Executive Director, Seminary Extension, Nashville; TN (1988-1994); Coordinator, Northeastern Baptist School Ministry, New York City, NY (1987-1994); Professor, Golden Gate Baptist Theological Seminary, Mill Valley, CA (1981-1987); Professor, Midwestern Baptist Theological Seminary, Kansas City, MS (1967-1981); Pastor, Susquehanna Baptist Church, Independence, MS (1965-1967); Pastor, 1st Baptist Church, Pleasant Hill, MA (1962-1965); Pastor, 1st Baptist Church, Switz City, IN (1956-1962) **Career Related:** Consultant, Baptist Home Mission Board (1981-Present); Director, Doctorate Program, Hong Kong Baptist Theological Seminary (2007); President, McCarty Services (1994-2005); Associate Dean, Southern Baptist Theological Seminary, Louisville, KY (1989) **Creative Works:** Author, "The Oasis for the Soul" (2018); Author, "Hallowed Be Thy Name" (2002); Author, "Making the Most of Pastoral Leadership" (2002); Author, "Making the Most of Coping" (2000); Author, "Making the Most of Empowerment" (1999); Author, "Making the Most of Change" (1998); Author, "Making the Most of Conflict" (1997); Author, "Making the Most of Your Time" (1996); Author, "Supervision: Developing and Directing People on a Mission" (1994); Author, "Leading the Small Church" (1991); Author, "Working With People" (1987); Author, "The Inner Heart of Ministry" (1985); Author, "The Supervision of Mission Personnel" (1983); "The Supervision of Ministry Students" (1978); "Author, "Teilhard de Chardin (1976); Author, "Rightly Dividing the Word" (1973) **Awards:** William Jewell College Achievement Citation (1987); Life Service Award, Southwest Baptist University, Bolivar (1973) **Membership:** Association for Theological Field Education; Institute of Theological Reflection; Fellowship In Service Guidance Directors **Marquis Who's Who Honors:** Albert Nelson Marquis Lifetime Achievement Award (2017); Distinguished Humanitarian (2017) **To what do you attribute your success:** He attributes his success to seeing a cause and meeting the need of the cause. He says to his family: always live with the character they grew up with. **Why did you become involved in your profession or industry:** Ministry was a goal from a young age; theology and philosophy fields answered questions he had. He always felt like this was the direction he should go in. This led him to be a religious organization administrator. **Shipping Address:** 116 Village Del Lago Ln, Saint Augustine, FL, 32080

James D. McChesney

Title: Chairman, CEO **Industry:** Medicine & Health Care **Company Name:** Cloaked Therapeutics, LLC **Marital Status:** Married **Spouse Name:** Sally Ann McChesney **Children:** Daniel; Lisa; Thomas; Elizabeth; Margaret; Amy; Matthew **Education:** PhD in Organic Chemistry, Indiana University, Bloomington, IN (1965) MA in Botany, Indiana University, Bloomington, IN; BSc in Chemical Technology, Iowa State University, Ames, IA **Career:** Founder, Cloaked Therapeutics, LLC, Etta, MS (2014-Present); Chairman, Cloaked Therapeutics, LLC, Etta, MS (2014-Present); CEO, Cloaked Therapeutics, LLC, Etta, MS (2014-Present); Founder, Arbor Therapeutics, LLC, Etta, MS (2010-Present); Managing Director, Arbor Therapeutics, LLC, Etta, MS (2010-Present); Founder, Ironstone Separations Inc., Oxford, MS (2009-2017); Principal, Ironstone Separations Inc., Oxford, MS (2009-2017); Chief Scientific Officer, ChromDex Inc., Boulder, CO (2003-2011); Chief Scientific Officer, Tapestry Pharmaceuticals, Boulder, CO (2003-2008); Vice President, Development, Napro Biotherapeutics, Boulder, CO (1996-2003); Director, Research Institute of Pharmaceutical Sciences, University of Mississippi, Oxford, MS (1986-1995); Faculty, University of Mississippi, Oxford, MS (1978-1996); Faculty, University of Kansas, Lawrence, KS (1965-1978) **Career Related:** Fellow, American Society of Pharmacognosy (2016); Fellow, AAAS; Fellow, ASP **Creative Works:** Contributor, 200 Peer Reviewed Articles, Scientific Publications; 45 Patents **Awards:** International Conference on the Science of Botanicals (2014); F.A.P. Barnard Professor, University of Mississippi **Membership:** American Society of Pharmacologists; American Chemical Society; American Association for the Advancement of Science; American Society of Pharmacognosy **To what do you attribute your success:** Dr. McChesney attributes his success to hard work and good fortune. **Why did you become involved in your profession or industry:** Dr. McChesney became involved in his profession because of his lifelong interest in nature. **Hobbies:** Farming **Religion:** Catholic **Shipping Address:** 147 County Road, 245, Etta, MS, 38627

Marion Andrus McCollam

Title: Owner **Industry:** Consulting **Company Name:** McCollam Consulting, LLC **Date of Birth:** 02/08/1931 **Place of Birth:** New Orleans **State:** LA **Parents:** Gerald Louis; Lucile Gordon (Isacks) Andrus **Marital Status:** Divorced **Spouse Name:** Andrew McCollam, Jr. (Married 1/29/1955, Divorced 1978) **Children:** Andrew III; Gerald Andrus; Marion Cage **Education:** Master of Urban and Regulation Planning, University of New Orleans (1978); BS in Engineering, Tulane University (1952) **Career:** President, McCollam Consultant, LLC (1998-Present); Executive Director, Cultural Arts Council of Houston and Harris County (1991-1998); Executive Director, Arts Council of New Orleans (1981-1990); President, Andrus and Roberts Inc., Phoenix, AZ, New Orleans, LA (1980-1984); Director of Planning, Downtown Development District, New Orleans, LA (1980-1981); Director of Planning, Principal Consultant, Duncan Plaza Design Project, New Orleans, LA (1978-1980); Arts Coordinator, Office of the Mayor, City of New Orleans, Louisiana (1978-1980); Human Affairs Coordinator, Office of the Mayor, City of New Orleans, Louisiana (1978) **Career Related:** Directors Council, New Orleans Museum of Art (2013-Present); Member, National Advisory Committee, Goucher College Master's Program in Arts Administration (2004-Present); Consultant in Field, Vice Chair, Newcomb Art Gallery (2009-2012); National Advisory Board, Tulane University (2005-2012); Adjunct Instructor (1999-2004) **Civic:** National Advisory Committee, Working Capital Fund, Minneapolis (1995-1999); Member, Community Assessment Committee, United Way of the Texas Gulf Coast (1995-1999); Advisory Panel, Design, National Endowment for the Arts, Washington (1995); Board of Directors, Senior Fellow, American Leadership Forum, Houston (1994-1997); Board of Directors, Urban League of New Orleans (1984-1989); President, Junior League of New Orleans (1969-1970) **Awards:** Chairman's Award, Americans for the Arts (formerly National Assembly of Local Arts Agencies) (1992); Award for Sustained Management Excellence, Greater New Orleans Foundation (1989); Arts Administrator of the Year Award, Arts Management Institute, National News Service (1987) **Membership:** Collaboration Public Education Committee, American Leadership Forum (2012-Present); American Institute of Certified Planners (1978-Present); Curriculum Committee, American Leadership Forum (2006-2012); Vice Chairman, Board of Directors, Americans for the Arts (Previously National Assembly of Local Arts Agencies) (1988-1994); President, United States Urban Arts Federation (1988); Phi Kappa Phi Honor Society; Honorary Member, American Institute of Architects **Hobbies:** Music; Art; Reading; Travel; Photography **Shipping Address:** 121 N Post Oak Ln, Apt., 602, Houston, TX, 77024

Homer L. McCormick Jr.

Title: Lawyer **Industry:** Law and Legal Services **Date of Birth:** 11/11/1928 **Place of Birth:** Frederick **State:** MD **Parents:** Homer Lee McCormick; Rosebelle Irene Biser **Marital Status:** Married **Spouse Name:** Jacquelyn R. **Children:** Deidre Ann; Thomas Lee **Education:** JD, University of California, San Francisco (1961); AB, San Jose State University (1951); Coursework, The George Washington University (1946-1948) **Certifications:** United States Tax Court (1977); United States Court of Federal Claims (1977); Supreme Court of the United States (1977); United States District Court for the Southern District of California (1976); United States District Court for the Central District of California (1972); United States District Court for the Northern District of California (1961); United States District Court of Appeals for the Ninth Circuit (1961) **Career:** Owner, McCormick Mediation Services, Orange County, CA (2006-Present); Founding Partner, Senior Partner, McCormick, Kidman & Behrens, Costa Mesa, CA (1988-Present); Managing Partner, Rutan & Tucker, Costa Mesa, CA (1984-1988); Department Head, Public Law, Rutan & Tucker, Costa Mesa, CA (1974-1988); Attorney, Senior Partner, Rutan & Tucker, Costa Mesa, CA (1970-1988); Attorney Partner, Rutan & Tucker, Santa Ana, CA (1966-1970); Attorney Associate, Rutan & Tucker, Santa Ana, CA (1963-1966); Attorney, Holiway Jones State of California (1961-1963) **Career Related:** Member, California Condemnation Lawyers (1994-Present); Judge Pro Tempore, Orange County Superior Court (1984, 1981, 1975); Arbitrator, American Arbitration Association (1966-1988); Professional Designation, International Right of Way Association; Speaker, Lecturer in Field **Military Service:** Lieutenant, US Marine Corps Reserve (1951-1956); Pilot, Republic of Korea **Creative Works:** Contributing Author, "Real Property Remedies" (1982); Contributor, Articles, Professional Journals **Awards:** Honoree, Named Alumnus of the Year, Hastings Law School (1992) **Bar Admissions:** California (1961) **Marquis Who's Who Honors:** Albert Nelson Marquis Lifetime Achievement Award (2017) **Hobbies:** Boating; Fishing; Flying; Golfing; Foreign traveling **Political Affiliations:** Republican **Religion:** Episcopalian **Shipping Address:** 13101 Saint Marks Dr, Law Office of H.L. McCormick, Santa Ana, CA, 92705 **Website:** http://mccormickmediations.com

Caron F. McCracken

Industry: Information Technology and Services **Date of Birth:** 01/12/1951 **Place of Birth:** Detroit **State:** MI **Parents:** William Joseph McCracken; Constance Irene (Kramer) McCracken (Deceased) **Education:** Mandarin Coursework, Wayne State University and Oakland University (2005); MBA in Finance, Wayne State University, with High Honors (2003); Spanish-language Coursework, Wayne State University (1994-1996); Computer Science Coursework, Wayne State University (1994); Pre-med Coursework, Wayne State University (1979-1981): MA, University of Michigan (1978); BS, Central Michigan University, with High Honors (1973); AS, Mott Community College (1971) **Career:** Senior Consultant, PwC (1992-1993); Senior Corporate Manager, Technology Specialists Inc. (1990-1991); Account Manager, Sprint (1987-1990); Senior Telecommunications Analyst, Fruehauf Corp. (1985-1987); Administrative Systems Manager, Wayne County Community College, Systems & Computer Technology Corporation (1984-1985); Academic Systems Manager, Systems & Computer Technology Corporation (1983-1984); Academic Specialist, Systems & Computer Technology Corporation (1982-1983); Satellite Site Laboratory Coordinator, Systems & Computer Technology Corporation (1981-1982); Planning and Research Specialist, Police Department, City of Flint (1977-1979); Adjunct Instructor, Mott Community College (1974-1978); Teacher, Davison Middle School (1974-1975); Teacher, Laker School District (1973-1974) **Career Related:** Speaker in Field (2006-2008) **Civic:** Volunteer Writer for a Congressional Campaign (2003-2014); Volunteer Researcher for a Congressional Bill and for a Congressional Campaign (2003-2008); Workshops Presenter, Creator, SCORE (2008-2013); Business Consultant to Local Entrepreneurs, SCORE (2008-2013) Precinct Delegate, Fourth Precinct, Bloomfield Township (2002, 2004, 2006, 2008-10); Volunteer, Congressional Re-Election Campaigns (2002-2009); Volunteer, AARP Tax Preparer for Senior Citizens, Bloomfield Township (2008-2009); Volunteer, Congressional Campaign (2002-2008); Researcher in International Intellectual Piracy Policy (China), Background/Support for Local Congressman's IP Bill (2004-2005); Volunteer Computer Lab Consultant, Business School, Wayne State University (1997-1998); President, Bloomfield Courts Condominium Association (1996-1998); Board Chair, Bloomfield Courts Condominium Association (1996-1998); Student Manager, Computer Science Lab, Wayne State University (1993-1995); Volunteer, Core Cities (1991-1994); Volunteer, Paint the Town (1991-1994); Volunteer, Coalition on Temporary Shelter (1991) **Creative Works:** Contributor, Articles, Professional Journals **Awards:** Professional Achievement Awards, Sprint Corporation; Professional Achievement Award, Systems & Computer Technology **Membership:** Daughters of the Union, 1861-1865 (2018); Daughters of the American Revolution (2018); Beta Gamma Sigma **Marquis Who's Who Honors:** Albert Nelson Marquis Lifetime Achievement Award (2017) **To what do you attribute your success:** She attributes her success to parental and family influences in her formative years, an Intrinsic need to learn everything and being a self-starter in the extreme. Once she is involved in any project, the time spent on it was as required. Her involvement knew no bounds until "delivery", whatever the project was, from childhood to date. **Why did you become involved in your profession or industry:** She became involved in her profession because information technology was where the coolest things were going on. Her learning curve was on steroids in IT. She had to be a part of that. She wishes she could be out there still as high tech expands exponentially in every possible direction. In retirement, she is involved to the best extent she can be, which includes tech-based volunteer efforts. During this interim, she will continue to seek her next career. **What do you consider to be the highlight of your career:** A highlight of her career was the discovery of a technical application for a client that resulted in moving up to that calendar year, a significant hardware project (multi-million dollar tech-forward installation) by 6-8 years, as it had been originally planned. **Hobbies:** Distance bicycling; Cross country skiing; Hiking; Reading, especially economics, China, general business, and technology **Religion:** Roman Catholic **Shipping Address:** 100 W Hickory Grove Rd., Unit H4, Bloomfield Hills, MI, 48304

Kilmer Serjus McCully

Title: Pathologist **Industry:** Medicine & Health Care **Company Name:** VA Boston Health Care System **Date of Birth:** 12/23/1933 **Place of Birth:** Daykin **State:** NE **Parents:** Cyrus Harold McCully; Lulu Viola (Litwinenco) McCully **Marital Status:** Married **Spouse Name:** Annina Elena Jacobs (8/14/1955) **Children:** Michael Kilmer; Martha Elizabeth **Education:** MD, State of Rhode Island and Providence Plantations (1988); Honorary MA Ad Eundem, Brown University (1983); Resident, Massachusetts General Hospital, Boston, MA (1965-1968); Research Fellow, Biology, Harvard University, Cambridge, MA (1964-1965); Research Associate, Genetics, Glasgow University, Scotland (1963-1964); Research Fellow in Medicine, Massachusetts General Hospital, Boston, MA (1962-1963); Associate in Biochemistry, National Institutes of Health, Bethesda, MD (1960-1962); Intern, Massachusetts General Hospital, Boston, MA (1959-1960); MD, Harvard Medical School, Cum Laude (1959); AB, Harvard College, Magna Cum Laude (1955) **Certifications:** Physician, Commonwealth of Massachusetts (1965-Present); Diplomate, Anatomic and Clinical Pathology, American Board of Pathology (1968); Diplomate, National Board of Medical Examiners (1959) **Career:** Consultant; Medical Director, New England VA Labs (2005-2015); Director, Boston Area VA Laboratories (2001-2015); Chief Pathologist, VA Medical Center, Providence, RI (1981-2001); Visiting Professor, Laboratory of Medicine, University of Connecticut, Farmington, CT (1980-1981); Pathologist, Massachusetts General Hospital, Boston, MA (1968-1979); Biochemist, National Institutes of Health, Bethesda, MD (1960-1962) **Career Related:** Fellow, Association of Clinical Scientists (2010-Present); Annals of Clinical Laboratory Science, Editorial Board (2001-Present); Associate Clinical Professor, Pathology, Harvard Medical School, Boston, MA (2001-Present); Editorial Board, Research Communications in Chemical Pathology and Pharmacology, (1983-Present); Associate Professor, Pathology, Brown University, Providence, RI (1997-2001); Associate Professor, Pathology, Brown University, Providence, RI (1981-1988); Assistant Professor, Pathology, Harvard Medical School, Boston, MA (1970-1979) **Civic:** Harvard Pierian Foundation, Cambridge, MA (1983-1986); Violinist, First Congregational Church, Winchester, MA (1965-2002); Senior Assistant Surgeon, U.S. Public Health Service (1960-1962) **Military Service:** Senior Assistant Surgeon, U.S. Public Health Service (1960-1962) **Creative Works:** Author, "Melatonin, Hyperhomocysteinemia, Thioretinaco Ozonide, Adenosyl Methionine and Mitochondrial Dysfunction in Aging and Dementia," Annals of Clinical & Laboratory Science (2018); Author, "Homocysteine, Infections, Polyamines, Oxidative Metabolism and the Pathogenesis of Dementia and Atherosclerosis," Handbook of Infection and Journal of Alzheimer's Disease, IOS Press (2017); Author, "Altered Homocysteine Metabolism and Oxidative Metabolism Caused by Microbial Infection in Alzheimer's Dementia and Atherosclerosis: A Strategy for Prevention," Journal of Alzheimer's Disease (2017); Author, "Homocysteine, Thioretinaco Ozonide and Oxidative Phosphorylation: A Proposed Clinical Trial Protocol, " Methionine Dependence of Cancer and Aging: Methods and Protocols, Springer Science (2017); Author, "Infections, Hyperhomocysteinemia, Suppressed Immunity and Alteration of Oxidative Metabolism by Pathogenic Microbes in Atherosclerosis and Dementia," Frontiers in Aging Neuroscience (2017); Author, "Homocysteine, Thioretinaco Ozonide, Oxidative Phosphorylation, Biosynthesis of Phosphoadenosine Phosphosulfate and the Pathogenesis of Atherosclerosis," Annals of Clinical & Laboratory Science (2016); Author, "Lack of Association or an Inverse Association Between Low-density Lipoprotein Cholesterol and Mortality in the Elderly: A Systematic Review," BMJ Open (2016); Author, "The Role of Infections, Lipoproteins and Hyperhomocysteinemia in the Pathogenesis of Vulnerable Atherosclerotic Plaques," Columbus Publishing Company Press (2016); Author, "Homocysteine, Infections, Polyamines, Oxidative Metabolism and the Pathogenesis of Dementia and Atherosclerosis," Journal of Alzheimer's Disease (2016); Author, "The Active Site of Oxidative Phosphorylation and the Origin of Hyperhomocysteinemia in Aging and Dementia," Annals of Clinical & Laboratory Science (2015); Author, "Homocysteine Metabolism in Atherosclerosis and Diseases of Aging, Comprehensive Physiology (2-16); Author, "The Heart Revolution" (1999); Author, "The Homocysteine Revolution" (1997); Author, "Chemical Pathology of Homocysteine" (1994-2018); Author, "Homocysteine Theory of Arteriosclerosis" (1983) **Awards:** F. William Sunderman Diploma of Honor, Association of Clinical Scientists (2015); Career Development Award, National Institutes Of Health (1971-1976); Faculty Research Award, American Cancer Society (1963-1968) **Membership:** President, Association of Clinical Scientists (2014); President, Harvard Musical Association (1994-1997); American Society of Investigative Pathology **Marquis Who's Who Honors:** Albert Nelson Marquis Lifetime Achievement Award (2017) **Political Affiliations:** Democrat **Religion:** Protestant **Business Address:** 1400 VFW Parkway, West Roxbury, MA, 02132

George E. McDavid

Title: Publishing Executive **Industry:** Publishing **Company Name:** Houston Chronicle **Date of Birth:** 06/30/1930 **Place of Birth:** McComb **State:** MI **Parents:** O.C. McDavid; Inez S. McDavid **Marital Status:** Married **Spouse Name:** Betty Ernestine Tinsley (9/24/1949) **Children:** Carol; Martha Gene Newman **Education:** BBA, University of Houston, Cum Laude (1965) **Career:** Member Emeritus, Houston Chronicle, Hearst Newspapers, LLC (1958-Present); President, Houston Chronicle, Hearst Newspapers, LLC (1990-1998); Vice President, Houston Chronicle, Hearst Newspapers, LLC (1985-1990); General Manager, Houston Chronicle, Hearst Newspapers, LLC (1985-1990); Vice President Operations, Houston Chronicle, Hearst Newspapers, LLC (1974-1985); Production Manager, Houston Chronicle, Hearst Newspapers, LLC (1967-1974); Owner, Wilk-Amite Record, LLC (1949-1958); Publisher, Wilk-Amite Record, LLC (1949-1958) **Career Related:** Past President, Southwest Precision Printers, L.P.; Board of Directors, Southwest Precision Printers, L.P.; Member, Advisory Board, American Press Institute **Civic:** Chairman, Board of Regents, American Cancer Society, Inc. (1997-Present); Chair, Board of Regents, University of Houston (2003); Chairman, Houston Region, American Cancer Society, Inc.; Chairman, Houston Forum; Vice-Chairman, YMCA of the USA; Vice Chairman, Asia Society Goodwill Industries; Vice Chairman, UNCF; Vice Chairman, Sam Houston Area Council, Boy Scouts of America; Member, President's Counsel, Houston Baptist University; First Vice Chairman, Greater Houston Chapter, The American National Red Cross; Chairman, National Board, The American National Red Cross; Special Deacon, Second Baptist Church; Board of Directors, National Conference of Christians and Jews (Now National Conference for Community Justice); Member, Board of Directors, University of Houston Foundation; Secretary, University of Houston Foundation; Vice Chairman of Development Board, University of Houston; Board of Directors, Books of the World; Vice President, Books of the World; Board of Directors, Houston Symphony; President, Houston Symphony; Board of Directors, Greater Houston Partnership **Awards:** Honoree, Hall Of Fame, Mississippi Journal (2002); Honoree, Houston Cultural Leader of the Year, Houston Metropolitan Chamber of Commerce (1998); Recipient, Man of the Year Award, National Conference of Christians and Jews (Now National Recipient, Distinguished Alumnus Award, University of Houston (1990, 1997); Honoree, Houston Father of the Year (1996); Conference for Community Justice (1993); Recipient, Houston Citizen's Community Service Award, Houston Metropolitan Chamber of Commerce (1993); Recipient, Taggart Award, Texas Daily Newspaper Association (Now Texas Press Association) (1992); Honoree, Outstanding Ex-Citizen of Gloster (1973); Recipient, Franklin Award (1961) **Membership:** President, Southern Newspaper Publishers Association; Chairman, Technology Committee, American Newspaper Publishers Association; Pine Forest Country Club; Houston Metropolitan Chamber of Commerce; President, Texas Daily Newspaper Association (Now Texas Press Association); Beta Gamma Sigma, Inc.; The Honor Society of Phi Kappa Phi **Marquis Who's Who Honors:** Distinguished Humanitarian (2017) **Shipping Address:** 403 Hunters Park Ln, Houston, TX, 77024

Samantha M. McDermitt

Title: Educator and Lawyer **Industry:** Law and Legal Services **Date of Birth:** 11/29/1953 **Place of Birth:** Hagerstown **State:** MD **Parents:** Edward Bernard McDermitt; Genevieve Natalie (Gallo) McDermitt **Children:** Edward S.; Maureen K. **Education:** Postgraduate Coursework, Harvard Law School (1989-2005); LLM, University of Pennsylvania (1984); JD, Santa Clara Law, Santa Clara University (1980); MA, Georgetown University (1978); Congressional Intern to Representative Pat Schroeder (1975); BA, Georgetown University (1975) **Certifications:** Admitted to Practice, Supreme Court of the United States (2011); Admitted to Practice, United States District Court for the District of Columbia (1981) **Career:** Part-time Full Professor, University of Maryland University College (2016-Present); Adjunct Professor, University of Baltimore (2003-Present); Lawyer, Private Practice, Washington D.C. (1984-Present); Collegiate Full Professor, University of Maryland (2003-2016); Research Assistant, University of Pennsylvania (1983-1984); Associate Trial Attorney, Law Offices of Miller, Loewinger & Associates (1982); Research Assistant, Santa Clara Law, Santa Clara University (1980); Founder, Law Theater Project; Executive Director, Law Theater Project **Career Related:** Adjunct Professor, Yale Gordon College of Arts and Sciences, University of Baltimore (1991-Present); Professor, Special and Memorable Merchandise (1985-Present); Judge, American University Mock Trials (2013-2017); Adjunct Professor, Montgomery College (2003-2009); Lecturer in Law, The Catholic University of America Columbus School of Law (1999); Adjunct Associate Professor, University of Maryland (1998-2003); Visiting Assistant Professor, University of Baltimore (1996); Writing Lecturer, The Writer's Center (1987-1990); Managing Partner, JLS Services (1985-2005); Volunteer Attorney, National Capital Area, ACLU (1982-2000); Basketball Referee, Washington, DC (1976-1979); Speaker/Presenter, Law Conferences **Civic:** Judge, Mock Trial Tournaments, Georgetown University (2013-Present); Judge, Mock Trial Tournaments, American University (2013-Present); Judge, National Mock Trial Tournaments (2013); Sarbanes Re-election Campaign (1982); Urban Coalition Basketball League (1977-1978); United Farm Workers (1973-1977) **Creative Works:** Executive Producer, "Myra Bradwell: American Portia" (2017); Executive Producer, "The IMHO Series" (2016); Playwright, "In Re Yamashita" (2016); Playwright, "IMHO Series 1 Trilogy" (2016); Playwright, "Frontiero v. Richardson"; Playwright, "Cohen v. California"; Playwright, "Katz v. The United States" (2016); Playwright, "Justice Disordered" (2016); Playwright, "New York Times v. United States" (2015); Playwright, "Schenck v. United States" (2015); Playwright, "Buck v. Bell" (2015); Playwright, "Erie Railroad v. Tompkins" (2015); Playwright, "International Shoe Co. v. The State of Washington" (2015); Playwright, "Santa Clara County v. Southern Pacific Rail Company" (2015); Playwright, "29 May 1787" (2015); Playwright, "Chunnel Vision" (2015); Artist, "Epiphany III" (2014); Playwright, "Bradwell v. State of Illinois" (2014); Playwright, "Chunnel Vision" (2013); Author, "Speech: Gender, Gender Variance and the Law" (2013); Author, "Pilgrims' Product" (2013); Artist, Diplomacy (2013); Artist, "Epiphanies and Other Revelations" (2013); Author, "Creatures/Creators of Language, Creatures or Creations of Languages" (2012); Artist, "Masterson v. United States" (2010, 2012); Author, "North American Ideologies in Conflict: Political Theory as Socio-Economic Wants - We Are Not an Empire or If It Walks Like a Duck" (2007); Author, "Return to Berlin" (2006); Author, "International Human Rights: Final Bulwarks Against the War on Terrorism's Imperial Overreach at Home and Abroad, or, For What the Hell Are We Fighting??!!" (2003); Author, "The Good and the Bad News on Enlightenment Thought in Modern Euro-Social Theory: More Than Good Works-Human Subjectivity in the Era of Exploitative Corporate Objectification" (2003); Author, "Human Rights, Humiliation, Externalization/Objectification, and Guilt: More Than Good Works-Human Subjectivity in the Era of Exploitative Corporate Externalization" (2003); Author, "Gender, Social Identity, and the LGBT Community in a Globalised World: Do We Still Live in a Bi-Gendered World? Did We Ever??" (2003); Author, "John Marshall: Farmer Extraordinaire and the Seeds of Corporate Capitalism" (2001); Author, "Toward a New Social (Democratic) Contract" (2000); Author, "Is it Ethical to Teach Ethics on the Web" (2000); Author, "Return to Berlin" (1996); Author, "Overruled, Mr./ Ms. Writer: An Argument in Favor of Accuracy in Depiction" (1990); Playwright, "Marbury v. Madison" **Awards:** Invitee, Plays, The John F. Kennedy Center for the Performing Arts (2016); Professional Achievement Award, University of Maryland (2016); Honoree, Outstanding Teacher of the Year, University of Baltimore (2008-2009) **Membership:** Superior Court Trial Lawyers' Association; Washington Writing Group; Association for Practical and Professional Ethics, Indiana University; Pi Sigma Alpha **Bar Admissions:** The District of Columbia Bar (1981) **Political Affiliations:** Democrat **Shipping Address:** PO Box 15192, Chevy Chase, MD, 20825

Marianne McDonald, PhD

Title: Classicist, Educator, Scholar, Philanthropist, Addiction Facilitator **Industry:** Education/Educational Services **Date of Birth:** 01/02/1937 **Place of Birth:** Chicago **State:** IL **Parents:** Eugene Francis McDonald; Inez (Riddle) McDonald **Children:** Eugene; James; Bryan; Bridget; Kirstie (Deceased); Hiroshi **Education:** Honorary DLitt, National University of Ireland (2001); Honorary DLitt, Aristotle University of Thessaloniki (1997); Honorary DLitt, University of Dublin (1994); Honorary DLitt, National and Kapodistrian University of Athens (1994); Honorary Diploma, Society for American Archaeology; Honorary Doctorate, The American College of Greece (1988); PhD, University of California, Irvine (1975); MA, University of Chicago (1960); BA, Bryn Mawr College, Magna Cum Laude (1958) **Certifications:** Licensed Facilitator **Career:** Founder, Thesaurus Linguae Graecae Project, University of California, Irvine (1975-1997); Research Fellow, Thesaurus Linguae Graecae Project, University of California, Irvine (1975-1997); Instructor, Greek, Latin, English, Mythology, Cinema, University of California, Irvine (1975-1979) **Career Related:** Facilitator to Addicts, Sharp McDonald Center; Board of Directors, Centrum; Visiting Professor, University College Cork (1999-Present); Professor, Theatre and Classics (1994-Present); Visiting Professor, University of Dublin (1990-Present); Visiting Professor, University College Dublin (1999, 2002); Visiting Professor, Ulster University, Ireland (1997); Adjunct Professor, Theatre, University of California, San Diego (1992-1994); Teaching Assistant, University of California, Irvine (1972-1974) **Civic:** Founder, Thesaurus Linguarum Hiberniae (1991-Present); President, Society for the Preservation of the Greek Heritage (1990-Present); Board of Directors, American School of Classical Studies at Athens (1986-Present); Board of Overseers, University of California, San Diego (1985-Present); National Board of Advisors, American Biographical Institute (1982-Present); President, Asian American Repertory Theatre (2003); Founder, Hajime Mori Chair for Japanese Studies, University of California, San Diego (1985); Founder, Substance Abuse Treatment, Sharp Vista Pacifica Hospital (Renamed Sharp McDonald Center for her Generosity) (1984) **Creative Works:** Author, Play, "And Then He Met a Woodcutter" (2005); Translator, "Euripides' Hecuba" (2005); Translator, "Euripides' Electra" (2004); Author, "The Living Art of Greek Tragedy" (2003); Co-editor, with Michael Walton, "Six Greek Tragedies" (2002); Co-editor, with Michael Walton, "Amid Our Troubles: Irish Versions of Greek Tragedy" (2002); Editor, "Canta la tua Pena" (2002); Translator, "Sing Sorrow: Classics, History, Heroines in Opera" (2001); Co-translator, with Michael Walton, "Euripides Andromache" (2001); Translator, "Mythology of the Zodiac: Tales of the Constellations" (2000); Translator, "Antigone by Sophocles" (2000); Translator, "Mythology of the Zodiac" (2000); Translator, "Sole Antico Luce Moderna" (1999); Translator, "Star Myths: Tales of the Constellations" (1996); Translator, "Modern Critical Theory and Classical Literature" (1994); Translator, "A Challenge to Democracy" (1994); Translator, "Views of Clytemnestra, Ancient and Modern" (1990); Translator, "Classics and Cinema" (1990); Translator, "Ancient Sun/Modern Light: Greek Drama on the Modern Stage" (1990); Author, "Trojan Women" (1988); Author, "Iphigenia in Taurus" (1988); Translator, "The Cost of Kindness and Other Fabulous Tales" by Shinichi Hoshi (1986); Author, "Ion" (1985); Author, "Hecuba" (1984); Author, "Hercules Furens" (1984); Author, "Electra" (1984); Author, "Euripides in Cinema: The Heart Made Visible" (1983); Author, "Heraclidae, Hippolytus" (1979); Author, "Semilemmatized Concordance to Euripides Cyclops" (1978); Author, "Terms for Happiness in Euripides" (1978) **Awards:** Distinguished Professor of Theatre and Classics, Theatre Department, Classics Program, University of California, San Diego (2013); Award for Best Play, San Diego Critics Circle (2005); Egeria Award, Women's International Center (2004); Billie Award (2004); Patté Award (2004); Laud and Laurels, University of California Distinguished Alumni Award, Hellenic Cultural Society, San Diego, CA (2003); Sledgehammer Theatre Award (2003); New Path Award (2003); Distinguished Service Award, University of California, Irvine (1982, 2001); Theatre Excellence Award, KPBS Patte (2001); Council Award, Hellenic Cultural Society (2000); Fulbright Award (1999); Ellis Island Award (1999); Spirit of Scripps Award (1999); Distinguished Service Award, American Philological Association (1999); Golden Aeschylus Award, National Institute of Ancient Drama, Siracusa Institute (1998); Women Who Mean Business, Fine Arts Award, San Diego Business Journal (1998); Gold Star Award, San Diego Arts League (1997); Volunteer of the Decade, Women's International Center (1994, 1996); Alexander the Great Award; Hellenic Cultural Society (1995); Conference for Community and Justice) (1986); Philanthropist of the Year (1985); Headliner, San Diego Press Club (1985); Citations, U.S. Congress and California Senate **Marquis Who's Who Honors:** Albert Nelson Marquis Lifetime Achievement Award (2017) **Shipping Address:** P.O. Box 929, Rancho Santa Fe, CA, 92067 **Website:** http://www.mariannemcdonald.org

Ann Louise McFarland

Title: Music Educator **Industry:** Education/Educational Services **Date of Birth:** 08/03/1953 **Place of Birth:** Danville **State:** PA **Parents:** Robert E. Montague; Jane F. Montague **Marital Status:** Married **Spouse Name:** James R. McFarland (6/3/1972) **Children:** Ailie; Herr; Kevin; Jennie; Grant **Education:** PhD in Music Education, Temple University (2006); MusM, Temple University, Philadelphia, PA (1978); MusB, Susquehanna University, Selinsgrove, PA (1975) **Certifications:** Certified Movement Teacher, High Scope (2005); Music and Movement Teacher Level III, American Orff Schulwerk Association (1999) **Career:** Associate Professor of Music Education, West Chester University (2010-2015); Assistant Professor of Music Education, West Chester University (1999-2010); Teacher, Conestoga Valley School District (1992-1999); Teacher, Hempfield School District, Lancaster, PA (1991-1992) **Career Related:** Presenter in Field, International Music Educators Conference; Presenter in Field, Music Educators National Conference **Civic:** Key West Education Board; South Florida Symphony **Creative Works:** Contributor, Articles, Professional Journals; Pianist, McFarland Piano Trio **Membership:** International Society of Music Education; Society for Ethnomusicology; American Orff-Schulwerk Association; Music Educators National Conference **Marquis Who's Who Honors:** Distinguished Humanitarian (2017) **To what do you attribute your success:** Dr. McFarland attributes her success to her perseverance and to her desire to meet her goal of earning a doctorate in music. After receiving a master's degree and being a mother of four children, she was able to do it. **Hobbies:** Gardening; Swimming; Reading; Piano **Shipping Address:** 1314 William St, Key West, FL, 33040

Barbara Ann McFarlin-Kosiec, PhD

Title: Elementary School Educator **Industry:** Education/Educational Services **Company Name:** Info-Connect **Date of Birth:** 10/04/1937 **Place of Birth:** Lamesa **State:** TX **Parents:** Roy W. McFarlin; Laura Corine (Daniel) McFarlin **Marital Status:** Widowed **Spouse Name:** Leonard E. Kosiec (Deceased) **Children:** James Daniel **Education:** Coursework, Eastern Washington University (1963, 1972, 1974, 1977. 1989); Coursework, Central Washington University (1971, 1973, 1976-1977, 1987-1988); PhD in Leadership in Education, Gonzaga University (1985); Coursework, Universidad de San Carlos de Guatemala (1967); Coursework, Universidad de las Américas, Asociación Civil (1966); MA in Spanish, Texas Christian University (1964); Coursework, Pan American College (Now The University of Texas Rio Grande Valley), Edinburgh, Texas (1962); Coursework, Instituto Tecnológico y de Estudios Superiores de Monterrey (1961-1962); BA in Spanish, Texas Christian University (1960) **Career:** President, Info Connect (2012-Present); President, McFarlin-Kosiec Enterprises (1986-Present); Teacher, Mount Baker Secondary School, Southeast Kootenay School District Five, Cranbrook, Canada (1997-2004); Spanish Teacher, Grades 1-8, St. Joseph's Catholic School, Kennewick, WA (1995-1996); Teacher, Texas-Washington Migrant Education Program, Pasco School District (1973-1982, 1993-1995); Teacher in Bilingual Education, Othello Public Schools, Washington (1985-1993); Substitute Teacher, Fernie Public Schools (1982-1985, 1990-1992); Spanish Teacher, Columbia Basin Community College (1973-1980); Teacher, Grades 4-12, Burbank Public Schools (Now Columbia School District) (1968-1973) **Career Related:** Member, Fernie Arts Theatre Ensemble Society (2009-2018); President, Elk Valley and South Country Health Care Coalition (2005-2011); Researcher, Maternity Care Experiences, Elk Valley and South Country Health Care Coalition (2004-2006); Vice President, Elk Valley and South Country Health Care Coalition (2004-2005); Delegate, Annual General Meeting, BC Teacher's Association (2002); Representative, Labour Affiliation, Cranbrook District Teachers' Association (2001-2002); Activist, State Committee, Washington (1995-1996); Member, Facilities Committee, Kennewick School District (1990-1996); Member, Growth Management Act Committee, Kennewick (1990-1996); Instructor, Columbia Basin Community College, Pasco, Washington (1973-1980, 1987-1989); Member, Tri-Cities Higher Education Organization (1987-1988); Instructor in Spanish, Big Bend Community College, Moses Lake, WA (1986-1987); Instructor, Seattle Pacific University (1986); Adjunct Professor in Second Language and Culture, Seattle Pacific University (1980) **Civic:** Active Member, Washington Recreation and Park Association (1993-Present); Founder, Lutacaga Modern Dance Troupe (1991-Present); Member, Precinct Committee, Benton County, Washington (1991-Present); Member, Center Committee, Benton County, Washington (1991-Present); Member, Negotiations Committee, Othello School District (1990-Present); Member, Fernie Community Choir (2013-2018); Director, Society for the Restoration of Fernie Heritage Cemetery (2009-2018); Volunteer, Canadian Cancer Society (2005-2018); Member, Branch 36, Royal Canadian Legion (2004-2018); Director, Fernie Arts Cooperative (2005-2007); Precinct Committeewoman, Democratic Party (1988-2006); Secretary, Kootenay East Constituency Executive Committee, New Democratic Party (2002-2006); Delegate, Benton County Democratic Convention (1988, 1992, 1994, 1996, 2004); Delegate, Washington State Democratic Convention (1988, 1992, 1994, 1996, 2004); Delegate, Kootenay East Constituency Executive Committee, New Democratic Party (2003) **Creative Works:** Director, "How He Lied to her Husband," British Columbia Community Theatre (2011); Writer, "Windows on Women," Fernie, British Columbia (2007); Producer, "Windows on Women," Fernie, British Columbia (2007); Actor, "Windows on Women," Fernie, British Columbia (2007); Choreographer, "Meet Me in St. Louis" (1993); Exhibitor, City Hall, Othello (1993); Exhibitor, Mark Twain Elementary School, Pasco, Washington (1993); Exhibitor, The US Bank, Othello (1992); Artistic Director, "Desert Storm Charity Show," Pasco, Washington (1991); Director, "Hook" (1992); Choreographer, "Phantom of the Opera Ballet," Lutacoga Modern Dance Troup" (1991); Director, "Phantom of the Opera Ballet," Lutacoga Modern Dance Troup" (1991); Choreographer, "Desert"; Choreographer, "Art of Noise"; Choreographer, "Water"; Choreographer, "Fire" **Awards:** Award, Rainbow Rockers to Lutacaga Dance Troupe (1992); Award, Association Quality Participation (1989-1992); Scholarship, Legislative Conference, AAUW (1977) **Membership:** Executive Board, Washington Education Association (1992-Present); Vice President, Association for Quality and Participation (1996-1997); Chairman, Education Committee, Association for Quality and Participation (1991); Board of Directors, Tri Cities Higher Education Organization (1987); Chairman, Unemployed Teachers of Fernie District, Teachers' Federation and College of Teachers (1984-1985); Building Representative, Pasco Association of Educators (1980); Grievance Representatives, Pasco Association of Educators (1975-1977) **Shipping Address:** PO Box 1275, BC, Fernie, Canada, V0B 1M0

Jere McGaffey

Title: Retired Partner **Industry:** Law and Legal Services **Company Name:** Foley & Lardner LLP **Date of Birth:** 10/06/1935 **Place of Birth:** Lincoln **State:** NE **Marital Status:** Widowed **Spouse Name:** Ruth S. Michelsen (8/19/1956, Deceased) **Children:** Beth; Karen **Education:** LLB, Harvard University, Magna Cum Laude (1961); BA, BSc, University of Nebraska, with High Distinction (1957) **Career:** Partner, Foley & Lardner LLP, Milwaukee, WI (1968-2004); Foley & Lardner LLP, Milwaukee, WI (1961-2004) **Civic:** Chairman, Board of Directors, Bader Philanthropies (1992-Present); Investment & Finance Committee, Aurora Health Care (2013-2018); Chairman, Investment Committee, Aurora Health Care (2010-2018); Secretary Treasurer, Wisconsin Taxpayers Alliance (1994-2016); Board of Directors, Aurora Health Care (1986-2013); Chairman, Aurora Health Care (1986-1990); Former Vice Chairman of Legislature, Milwaukee Metropolitan Association of Commerce (1984-2003); Former Chairman, Wisconsin Taxpayers Alliance; Chairman, Board of Advisors, University of Wisconsin School of Nursing, Milwaukee, WI **Awards:** Alumni Achievement Award, University of Nebraska (2016); Lifetime Achievement Award, Leaders in the Bar in Wisconsin (2015); Section Taxation Distinguished Service Award, American Bar Association (2005) **Membership:** Regent, American College of Trust and Estate Counsel (2000-2006); Chairman, American College of Tax Counsel (1996-1998); Honorary Delegates, American Bar Association (1995-2000); Chairman, Business Planning Committee, American College of Trust and Estate Counsel (1994-1997); Chairman, Tax Section, American Bar Association (1990-1991); American Institute of Certified Public Accountants; Wisconsin Bar Association; Wisconsin Institute of CPAs; American Law Institute; University Club; Milwaukee Country Club; Harvard Club; Phi Beta Kappa; Beta Gamma Sigma; Delta Sigma Rho **Marquis Who's Who Honors:** Albert Nelson Marquis Lifetime Achievement Award (2017) **To what do you attribute your success:** He attributes much of his success to his college debate coach, Donald Olsen. **Shipping Address:** 12852 NW Shoreland Drive, Mequon, WI, 53097 **Website:** https://www.foley.com

Charlotte McGowan

Title: Anthropologist, Archaeologist (Retired) **Industry:** Education/Educational Services **Company Name:** Southwestern College **Date of Birth:** 02/19/1930 **Place of Birth:** Ridgefarm **State:** IL **Parents:** Ira Patrick Acord; Edythe Mae Minerva (Lewis) Acord **Marital Status:** Married **Spouse Name:** James Patrick McGowan Jr. (6/4/1949) **Children:** James Patrick McGowan III; Lauren Louise **Education:** MA, San Diego State University, with Honors (1969); BA, San Diego State University, with Honors (1967) **Career:** Professor of Anthropology, Southwestern College, Chula Vista, CA (1971-1999); Professor of Anthropology, San Diego Evening College (1969-1971); Teaching Assistant, Director of Physical Anthropology Laboratory, Professor of Anthropology, San Diego State University (1967-1969) **Career Related:** Director, Liaison, National American Interface (1995-Present); Consultant, Campo Band of Mission Indians, Campo, CA (1995-Present); Native American Groups, San Diego, CA (1994-Present); California Department of Transportation (1995-1998); Professor of Anthropology, Universidad De Las Americas, Puebla, Mexico (1978); Environmental Impact Studies, San Diego (1975-2000); Patrick Henry Adult School, San Diego (1970-1971); North Shores Adult School, San Diego (1968-1971); San Diego Adult School (1967-1969) **Creative Works:** Author, Final Report on Excavation (1997); Author, Inventory of Artifacts from Archaeological Excavation (1995); Contributor, Chapters in Books; Contributor, Articles to Professional Journals **Awards:** Fulbright Scholar, Taiwan (1996); Fulbright Scholar, Peru (1982) **Membership:** Congress of History of San Diego and Imperial Counties; San Diego Natural History Museum; San Diego Museum of Man; Southwestern Missions Research Center; Southwestern Anthropological Association; Archaeological Institute of America **Marquis Who's Who Honors:** Albert Nelson Marquis Lifetime Achievement Award (2017) **Why did you become involved in your profession or industry:** She always wanted to ve a teacher. When she took a course in anthropology at San Diego State, she knew that was what she wanted to do. **Hobbies:** Practicing tai chi; Spending time with her five grandchildren and three great-grandchildren; Traveling; Reading; Writing; Embroidery **Shipping Address:** 10101 Sierra Vista Ave, La Mesa, CA, 91941

Irvin McKlenshaw

Title: Small Business Owner **Industry:** Business Management/Business Services **Date of Birth:** 06/12/1945 **Place of Birth:** Waco **State:** TX **Parents:** Irvin Nicholas McClendon, Jr.; Evelyn Lucile (Maycumber) McClendon **Marital Status:** Married **Spouse Name:** James William Kershaw, Jr. (7/1/2008, Deceased 2016) **Children:** Michael Boyd; Irvin Lee Jr.; Laura Ann; Paul Nichola; Richard Lester **Education:** Postgraduate Coursework, Claremont School of Theology, Lay Ministry Academy, CA (2010-2012); Postgraduate Coursework in Religion, School of Theology, Summit University, Denver, CO (1982-1984); Postgraduate Coursework in Business Administration, California State University, Fullerton, CA (1976); BA in Mathematics, California State University, Fullerton, CA (1970); Coursework, University of Southern California (1962-1966); Coursework, El Camino College (1961-1963) **Certifications:** Certified in National Security Management, Industrial College of Armed Forces, (Now Dwight D. Eisenhower School for National Security and Resource Strategy), Washington D.C. (1974) **Career:** Information Processing Technician, Orange County Health Care Agency (2013-Present); Proofreader, Olympic Staffing Services, Covina, CA (2010-2011); Film Crew Associate, AMC Orange 30, CA (2006-2010); Assistant Project Manager, Social Science Research Center, California State University, Fullerton, CA (2005-2006); Owner, McClendon Professional Services, Garden Grove, CA (2004-2006); General Manager, McClendon Professional Services, Garden Grove, CA (2004-2006); Writer, McClendon Professional Services, Garden Grove, CA (2004-2006); Editor, McClendon Professional Services, Garden Grove, CA (2004-2006); Proofreader, McClendon Professional Services, Garden Grove, CA (2004-2006); Tutor, McClendon Professional Services, Garden Grove, CA (2004-2006); Tutor, English and Mathematics, Disability Support Services, Fullerton College (2004-2005); Copy Editor, Orange County and Long Beach Blade, Laguna Beach, CA (2003-2004); Information Processing Technician, Orange County Health Care Agency, Santa Ana, CA (1998-2002); Owner, Berkeley Group, LLC, Denver, CO (1997-1999); General Manager, Berkeley Group, LLC, Denver, CO (1997-1999); Writer, Berkeley Group, LLC, Denver, CO (1997-1999); Chief Editor, Berkeley Group, LLC, Denver, CO (1997-1999); Writer, American Resume Center, Northglenn, CO (1997-1998); Senior Multimedia Developer, TTS Inc., Aurora, CO (1996-1997); Senior Technical/Instructional Writer, Editor, TTS Inc., Aurora, CO (1990-1996); Staff Consultant, Civil Air Patrol, Gemini America, Englewood, CA (1989); Senior Technical Writer, CDI Corporation, Arvada, CO (1987-1988); Engineering Writer III, CalComp Inc., Lockheed Corporation, Hudson, NH (1987); Senior Technical Writer, Editor, Colorado Data Systems, Inc., Englewood, CO (1984-1987); Senior Technical Editor, Auto-Trol (1982-1984); Systems Programmer, Auto-Trol, Denver, CO (1981-1982); Member, Technical Staff, Rockwell International, Anaheim, CA (1970-1982); Test Data Analyst, Rockwell International, Anaheim, CA (1968-1970); Engineering Laboratory Assistant, Rockwell International, Anaheim, CA (1967-1968) **Civic:** Member, The California-Pacific Conference, The Justice and Compassion Essential Ministry Team, The United Methodist Church (2011-Present); Convener, Orange County Community Reconciling United Methodists (2010-Present); Member, Community United Methodist Church, Huntington Beach, CA (2005-Present); Member, Soulforce, Orange County, CA (2004-Present); Secretary, Board of Directors, Friendly Center (2005-2006); Member, MenAlive, Orange County Gay Men's Chorus (2004-2006); Volunteer, The Center OC, David Bohnett Foundation, Garden Grove, CA (2002-2004); Technical Support Adviser to Chairman, Colorado Republicans (1997-1998); Member, Denver County Republican Central Committee (1992-1995); Member, Adams County Republican Central Committee (1984-1990); Treasurer, Church Of God Seventh Day, Bloomington, CA (1980-1981); Trustee, Church Of God Seventh Day, Bloomington, CA (1979-1981); Secretary, Governing Board, Yorba Linda Library District (1973-1978); President, Orange County Chapter, California Special Districts Association (1977); Member, CSU Statewide Alumni Council (1976-1977); Second Vice President, Orange County Chapter, California Special Districts Association (1976) **Military Service:** U.S. Air Force Reserve (1964-1970) **Awards:** National Merit Scholarship, U.S. Air Force (1963-1967) **Membership:** Orange County and Long Beach Speakers Bureau Panelist, PFLAG (2001-Present); Volunteer, Orange County Chapter, PFLAG (1988-Present); Executive Board, Southern California Republicans, California Association of Library Trustees and Commissioners (1976-1978); Director, Alumni Association, California State University, Fullerton, CA (1975-1977); Lifetime Member, The National Eagle Scout Association; Lifetime Member, The Bible Sabbath Association; Reconciling Ministries Network **Marquis Who's Who Honors:** Albert Nelson Marquis Lifetime Achievement Award (2017) **Political Affiliations:** Republican **Shipping Address:** 12410 Woodbridge Dr, Garden Grove, CA, 92843

Christine E. McLaren, PhD

Title: Professor, Statistician **Industry:** Education/Educational Services **Company Name:** University of California, Irvine **Date of Birth:** 02/12/1947 **Place of Birth:** Higginsville **State:** MO **Parents:** Harold Irby Owens; Olene (Bolstad) Owens **Marital Status:** Married **Spouse Name:** Gordon Douglas McLaren (6/14/1969) **Children:** Graham Douglas **Education:** PhD in Biostatistics, Case Western Reserve University (1983); MS in Mathematical Statistics, Case Western Reserve University (1976); AM in Mathematics Education, Stanford University (1970); BS in Mathematics, San Jose State University, With Distinction (1969) **Career:** Professor, Department of Mathematics, Minnesota State University, Moorhead, MN (1992-Present); Associate Professor, Department of Mathematics, Minnesota State University, Moorhead, MN (1987-1992); Assistant Professor, Department of Mathematics, Minnesota State University, Moorhead, MN (1986-1987); Assistant Professor, Department of Epidemiology and Biostatistics, Department of Medicine, Case Western Reserve University, Cleveland Metropolitan General Hospital (1984-1986); Senior Instructor, Department of Biometry, Department of Medicine, Case Western Reserve University, Cleveland Metropolitan General Hospital (1983-1984); Research Biostatistician, Department of Biometry, Case Western Reserve University, Cleveland, OH (1980-1983); Research Biostatistician, Department of Biometry, Case Western Reserve University, Cleveland, OH (1976-1979) **Career Related:** Subcommittee on Blood Count (1995-Present); Statistical Consultant, International Committee for Standardization in Hematology (1986-Present); Senior International Fellow, National Institutes of Health Fogarty International Center (1995); Raybould Visiting Fellow, The University of Queensland, Australia (1994-1995); Outside Statistical Reviewer, Hematology Study Section, NIH (1994); University of Glasgow Senior Honor Research Fellow (1991); Grant Review Panel, Division of Mathematical Sciences, National Science Foundation (1990); Statistical Consultant, Area Committee on Hematology Subcommittee on Qualitative Cellular Hematology, National Committee for Clinical Laboratory Standardization (1989-1995); Secretary, Fellow, Red River Valley Chapter, American Statistical Association (1989-1990); American Heart Association Research Fellow (1983-1984); Case Western Reserve University Tuition Fellow (1974-1976); Stanford University Prospective Teacher Fellowship (1969-1970); Presenter in Field; Co-Director, Cancer Center Program, Cancer Prevention Outcome Survivorship; Interim Director of Biostatistical Shared Resource, University of California, Irvine Cancer Center (Now Chao Family Comprehensive Cancer Center), University of California, Irvine Health **Creative Works:** Contributor, Articles, Professional Journals **Awards:** Clinical and Translational Science Award, Clinical and Translational Science (2013); Minnesota College Science Teacher of the Year, Minnesota Academy of Science, The Minnesota Science Teachers Association (1996); Grantee, Case Western University Graduate Alumni Fund (1983) **Membership:** Editor, Stats Magazine for Students of Stats, American Statistical Association (1996-Present); Science Committee, Biometric Society (Now The International Biometric Society) (1998); Governing Board Council of Chapters, American Statistical Association (1995-1997); Subcommittee on Undergraduate Research in Mathematics, Mathematical Association of America (1994-1997); Executive Committee, Section on Statistical Education, American Statistical Association (1994-1996); Program Committee, Joint Statistics Meetings, American Statistical Association (1994); Associate Editor, Stats Magazine for Students of Stats, American Statistical Association (1993-1996); Councilor, Mathematics and Computer Sciences Council, The Council on Undergraduate Research (1992-1995); Chair, Committee on Data and Statistics, The Council on Undergraduate Research (1992-1995); Chapter Representative, American Statistical Association (1992-1995); President, American Statistical Association (1990-1991); Phi Theta Kappa Honor Society; The Honor Society of Phi Kappa Phi; The Royal Statistical Society/Institute of Statisticians; International Biometric Conference, Biometric Society (Now The International Biometric Society) **Marquis Who's Who Honors:** Albert Nelson Marquis Lifetime Achievement Award (2017) **Business Address:** 214 Irvine Hall, Irvine, CA, 92697 **Shipping Address:** 66 Whitman Court, Irvine, CA, 92617

Shirley Ann McManigal

Title: University Educator, Dean Emerita (Retired) **Industry:** Health, Wellness and Fitness **Date of Birth:** 05/04/1938 **Place of Birth:** Deering **State:** MO **Parents:** Jadie C. Naile; Willie B. (Groves) Naile **Education:** PhD in Medical Microbiology, University of Oklahoma (1979); MS, University of Oklahoma (1976); BS, Arkansas State University (1971) **Career:** Dean, School of Allied Health, Health Sciences Center, School of Medicine, Texas Tech University, Lubbock, TX (1987-1997); Chair, Department of Medical Technology, Health Sciences Center, School of Medicine, Texas Tech University, Lubbock, TX (1983-1987); Chair, Department of Medical Technology, University of Southern Mississippi, Hattiesburg, MS (1979-1983); Medical Technologist (1958-1975) **Career Related:** Governor's Appointee, Statewide Health Coordinator Council (1994-1997) **Civic:** Lieutenant Alumnae Regional Director (1994-1997); Leadership Texas (1992) **Awards:** Woman of the Year, Texas Division, American Association of University Women (1990); Educator of the Year, Texas Society of Medical Technology (1990); Woman of Excellence in Education, Young Women's Christian Association, Lubbock, TX (1990); Citation, State of Texas (1988) **Membership:** Chair, American Association of University Women (1998-2001); Educational Foundation International Fellows Panel, American Association of University Women (1994-1998); Chair, Education Committee, Clinical Laboratory Management Association (1991); Texas Board of Directors, American Association of University Women (1990-1994); President, Texas Society of Allied Health Professions (1990-1991); Chair, Education Committee, Clinical Laboratory Management Association (1989); American Association of University Women; Texas Society of Medical Technology; Texas Society of Allied Health Professions; Southern Association of Allied Health Deans at Academy Health Centers; National Association of Women in Education; American Society of Medical Technology; Clinical Laboratory Management Association; Phi Beta Delta; Alpha Eta **Marquis Who's Who Honors:** Albert Nelson Marquis Lifetime Achievement Award (2017) **Shipping Address:** 612 S 72nd St., Broken Arrow, OK, 74014

Brenda N. McNamara

Title: Secondary Education Educator (Retired) **Industry:** Education/Educational Services **Date of Birth:** 08/08/1945 **Place of Birth:** Blackpool **Country of Origin:** Lancashire/England **Parents:** Milford Hampson Jones; Nola (Welsby) Jones **Marital Status:** Married **Spouse Name:** Michael James McNamara (7/19/1969) **Education:** Post-graduate Coursework, California State University Campuses (1967); BA in History, California State University, Long Beach (1967) **Certifications:** Certified Secondary Teacher, State of California; Certified Language Development Specialist, State of California **Career:** Department Chair, West High School, Torrance, CA (2000-2004); Department Chair, West High School, Torrance, CA (1989-2004); History Teacher, West High School, Torrance, CA (1968-2004) **Career Related:** Local Delegate, Annual Meeting, National Education Association (2003-2004); State Delegate, Annual Meeting, National Education Association (2002, 2000); Consultant in History, Golden State Exam, California State Department of Education (1998); Consultant in Field **Creative Works:** Co-Author, "World History" (1988) **Awards:** Grantee, Western International Studies Consortium (1988) **Membership:** President, National Education Association, California Teachers Association, Bay Valley, CA (2009-Present); Secretary, Treasurer, National Education Association, California Teachers Association, Bay Valley, CA (2006-2009); California Teachers Association (2004); Board of Directors, Torrance Teachers Association (1992-2004); American Historical Association; National Council for the Social Studies; California Council for the Social Studies **Hobbies:** Travel; Theater; Mystery reading; Gourmet cooking **Shipping Address:** 5402 Bayridge Road, Rancho Palos Verdes, CA, 90275

Lyle Glen McNeal, PhD

Title: Carnegie Professor **Industry:** Education/Educational Services **Company Name:** Utah State University **Date of Birth:** 05/16/1942 **Place of Birth:** Glendale **State:** CA **Parents:** Darrell Glenn McNeal; Elizabeth Bessie McNeal **Marital Status:** Married **Spouse Name:** Nancy Coles Wilkie (8/10/1962) **Children:** Tamara A.; Sean E.; Joshua M.; Travis G.; Susannah R.; Jenny L.; Ian B.; Ilene L. **Education:** PhD, Physiology of Reproduction & Range Science, Utah State University (1978); MS in Animal Breeding & Range Management, University of Nevada, Reno, NV (1966); BS in Animal Husbandry, California State Polytechnic University, Pomona, CA (1964) **Certifications:** Certified OFDA Australian Wool Tester, American Sheep Industry Association (2010-Present); Certified in Radiological Monitoring, U.S. Department of Education and U.S. Department of Defense (1966) **Career:** Technical Consultant, Navajo Sheep Project (2002-Present); Professor, Department of Animal, Dairy & Veterinary Science, Utah State University, Logan, Utah (1979-Present); Co-Founder, American Polypay Sheep Association (1980); Administrator, Animal and Equine Science Internship Program (1979-2017); Associate Staff Scientist, International Sheep and Goat Institute, Utah State University (1979-1989); Founding Director, Navajo Sheep Project, Utah State University, Logan, UT (1977-2002); Seasonal Staff Scientist, United States Sheep Experiment Station, U.S. Department of Agriculture (1972-1977); Professor, Animal Science Department, California Polytechnic State University, San Luis Obispo, CA (1969-1979); Extension Agent, University of Nevada Cooperative Extension (1966-1969); Co-Owner, Quaking Aspen Ranch (1964-1972); Manager, Quaking Aspen Ranch (1964-1972); Graduate Research Assistant, University of Nevada, Reno, NV (1964-1966); Shepherd, Animal Husbandry Department, California State Polytechnic University, Pomona, CA (1962-1964); Horse Handler, Animal Husbandry Department, California State Polytechnic University, Pomona, CA (1961-1964); Swine Herdsman, Animal Husbandry Department, California State Polytechnic University, Pomona, CA (1961-1964); Assistant Ranch Manager, Hidden Trails, Ltd, Agoura, CA (1960-1961); Ranch Hand, Bar Lazy B Ranch, Ronan, MT (1958-1961); State Educational Program Leader, Sheep and Wool Program, Utah State University; Member-in-Charge, Animal Fiber Laboratory, Utah State University; Horse and Sheep Specialist, University of Nevada Cooperative Extension; Veterinarian's Assistant to Dr. Kurt A. Schilling, DVM, P.C.; Stud and Broodmare Manager, Asil Arabian Horse Ranch; General Horse Management, Gimple Training Stables; Resident Live-In, Gimple Training Stables; Groom and Show Handler, McCoy Arabians; Veterinarian's Assistant, Broodmare Breeding Program, Ellsworth Thoroughbred Ranch; Cattle Feeder, Feed Mill Operations, Ellsworth Feedyard; Feeder, Liggett Farms; Candler, Liggett Farms; Brooders, Liggett Farms; Egg Collector, Liggett Farms; Sanitation, Liggett Farms; Packaging, Liggett Farms; Babcock Butter-Fat Tester, Adohr Farms Creamery; Ice Cream and Cheese Maker, Adohr Farms Creamery; Sheep/Goat and Fiber Specialist **Career Related:** Director, Nevada Range Camps for Boys (Now Youth Range Camp, Nevada Section, Society for Range Management) (1966-1968); Counselor, Society for Range Management (1966-1968) **Civic:** Faculty Adviser, Sheep & Goat Club, Utah State University (2003-Present); Charter Member, National WWII Museum (2009-Present) **Military Service:** First Lieutenant, U.S. Air Force, Norton Air Force Base (1959-1961); Pilot, 2848th Air Base Wing, U.S. Air Force (1958-1962); Operations Officer, 125th Composite Squadron, U.S. Air Force (1958-1962) **Creative Works:** Author, "Wool Grading and Fleece Evaluation Training Manual," USDA-IIRD Program (2005-Present); Author, "Small Ruminant Production Medicine and Management," Animal Health Publications (2002-Present) **Awards:** Undergraduate Faculty Mentor of the Year Robbins Award, Utah State University (2018); Undergraduate Faculty Mentor of the Year Award, College of Agriculture & Applied Sciences, Utah State University (2017); Animal Science Professor of the Year Award, Utah State University (2013); Foreign Agricultural Service Award, U.S. Department of Agriculture, Iraq (2013) **Membership:** Founding Board Member, American Sheep Center (1999-Present); Honorary Lifetime Board Member, Dine' Be'iina, The Navajo Lifeway (1991-Present); Life Member, Navajo-Churro Sheep Association (1986-Present); Alpha Zeta, National Honorary Agricultural Fraternity (1964-Present) **Hobbies:** Horseback riding; Fly fishing; Piloting aircrafts; History; Reading; Collecting historical memorabilia **Shipping Address:** 85 Quarter Circle Drive, Logan, UT, 84321 **Website:** https://www.navajosheepproject.com

Scott Douglas McPhee

Title: Executive Director for Strategy and Program Development **Industry:** Education/Educational Services **Company Name:** Bay Path University **Date of Birth:** 05/02/1950 **Place of Birth:** Tacoma **State:** WA **Parents:** William Archibald McPhee; Georgia Mae (Lynch) McPhee **Marital Status:** Married **Spouse Name:** Hope Marie **Children:** Sarah (McPhee) Heckmann; Jennifer (McPhee) Hudson; Carter McPhee; Anthony McPhee; William Chambers **Education:** DPH, The University of Texas Health Science Center at Houston, Texas (1990); MPA, Western Kentucky University, Bowling Green, KY (1987); Diploma, Command and General Staff College, Fort Leavenworth, KS (1987); MS, Virginia Commonwealth University, Richmond, VA (1983); BS in Occupational Therapy, University of Puget Sound, Tacoma, WA (1974); BA in Psychology, University of Washington, Seattle, WA (1972) **Certifications:** Registered Occupational Therapist, State of Indiana **Career:** Executive Director for Strategy and Program Development, Bay Path University, Longmeadow, MA (2017-Present); Dean, College of Health Professions, South University (2015-2017); Dean, School of Health Sciences, Indiana Wesleyan University (2013-2015); Chairman, Department of Occupational Therapy, College of Health Sciences and Nursing, Belmont University, Nashville, TN (1996-2013); Associate Dean, College of Health Sciences and Nursing, Belmont University, Nashville, TN (1996-2013); Chairman, Department of Occupational Therapy, Misericordia University, Dallas, PA (1994-1996); Director, School of Occupational Therapy Specialists, Academy of Health Sciences, Fort Sam Houston, Texas (1990-1994); Director, Occupational Therapy, Ireland Army Community Hospital, Fort Knox, KY (1983-1986); Occupational Therapist, Walter Reed Army Medical Center, Washington, D.C. (1978-1981); Occupational Therapist, Womack Army Hospital, Fayetteville, NC (1974-1978) **Career Related:** Executive Director, PAMPCA (2004-Present); Chairman, Occupational Therapy Studies Committee, International Commission on Health Professions (2000-2007); Chairman, Tennessee Education Council for Health Science Professions (2000-2002); President, Board of Directors, Technology Access Center of Middle Tennessee, Nashville, TN (1996-2003); Consultant, National Institute of Health Statistics, Washington, D.C. (1994-1996); Consultant, World Health Organization, Washington, D.C. (1987-1992) **Military Service:** Lieutenant Colonel, United States Army (1986-1994); First Lieutenant, United States Army (1974); Enlisted, Private First Class, United States Army (1973) **Creative Works:** Member, Editorial Board, Family and Community Health Journal (2002-Present); Manuscript Reviewer, American Journal of Occupational Therapy (1990-Present); Member, Editorial Board, Innovations in Occupational Therapy Education (1998-2000); Member, Editorial Board, Occupational Therapy in Health Care (1994-2008); Member, Editorial Board, Military Medicine (1990-1994); Contributor, Over 30 Articles, Professional Peer-Reviewed Journals **Awards:** Service Award, American Occupational Therapy Association (1992-1993, 1995-1996, 2001, 2003, 2005); Award of Excellence in Research, Tennessee Occupational Therapy Association (2000); Myra McDaniel's Writer's Award (1992, 1994); Decorated Legion of Merit; Inductee, Order of Military Medical Merit (1993); Meritorious Service Medal; Army Commendations **Membership:** Founding Member, American Occupational Therapy Foundation's Leaders and Legacies Society (2015); Ethics Chairman, Tennessee Occupational Therapy Association (1997-2001); Roster of Accreditation Evaluators, American Occupational Therapy Association (1997); Fellow, American Occupational Therapy Association (1993) **Marquis Who's Who Honors:** Albert Nelson Marquis Lifetime Achievement Award (2017) **To what do you attribute your success:** Dr. McPhee attributes his success to luck. His father once told him that he was the luckiest man in the world and that the harder he worked, the luckier he became. He does not attribute his successes to himself but to the team members who surround him as they collectively work toward goals either set by the organization or by the team. **Why did you become involved in your profession or industry:** He became involved in his profession because the country was involved in a war in Vietnam. Although he personally did not support it, he felt that those soldiers who were putting themselves in harm's way deserved the best rehabilitation that could be offered to them. He felt that he should provide that service. **What do you consider to be the highlight of your career:** Throughout his career, one highlight that stood out was his ability to grow graduate programs. Being able to have a vision of what could be and sharing it with administration in a way that they could readily come on board to support that vision was very rewarding. This happened at Belmont University, Indiana Wesleyan University and Bay Path University. **Where will you be in five years:** In five years he hopes to be retired. **Hobbies:** Cooking; Baking; Playing with his Grandchildren; Reading **Religion:** Methodist **Shipping Address:** 4010 Ivy Dr., Nashville, TN, 37216 **Website:** www.baypath.edu

Hobart Amory McWhorter Jr.

Title: Lawyer (Retired) **Industry:** Law and Legal Services **Company Name:** Bradley Arant Rose & White **Date of Birth:** 12/24/1931 **Place of Birth:** Birmingham **State:** AL **Parents:** Hobart Amory McWhorter; Marjorie (Westgate) McWhorter **Marital Status:** Married **Spouse Name:** (2/1/1997) **Children:** Margaret G.; Marjorie W. **Education:** LLB, University of Virginia (1958); BA, Yale University (1953) **Career:** Partner, Bradley Arant Rose & White, Birmingham, AL (1958) **Military Service:** First Lieutenant, US Army (1953-1955) **Awards:** Listed, B-Metro "Top Lawyers" (2016-2017); Listed, BHM BIZ "Top Lawyers" (2016); Listed, Mid-South Super Lawyers, Business Litigation (2016); Listed. Personal Injury Litigation-Defendants (2011-2017); Listed, Alabama Super Lawyers, Business Litigation (2009-2015); Listed, Benchmark Litigation, "Litigation Star," Alabama (2008-2017); Listed, Bet-the-Company Litigation (2006-2017); Listed, Commercial Litigation (2006-2017); Listed, Chambers USA, Litigation: General Commercial (2003-2012); Listed, Personal Injury Litigation (1987-2010); Listed, Business Litigation (1987-2005); Student Legal Research Prize, University of Virginia School of Law (1957); Dean Hudnut Memorial Award, Yale University (1953); Listed, The Best Lawyers in America **Membership:** Fellow, American College of Trial Lawyers; International Association of Defense Counsel; National Association of Railroad Trial Counsel; Former Member, International Association of Insurance Counsel; Yale Legacy Partners; National Association of Railroad Counsel; ABA; Alabama State Bar Association; Birmingham Bar Association **Bar Admissions:** Alabama (1958) **Marquis Who's Who Honors:** Albert Nelson Marquis Lifetime Achievement Award (2017) **Why did you become involved in your profession or industry:** When Mr. McWhorter was in the army, he realized that he couldn't make a living unless he used his mind. So he became a lawyer. **Political Affiliations:** Republican **Religion:** Presbyterian **Shipping Address:** 2828 Cherokee Rd, Mountain Brook, AL, 35223 **Website:** https://www.bradley.com/people/m/mcwhorter-hobart-a

Margaret A. Mead

Title: Criminal Defense Attorney **Industry:** Law and Legal Services **Company Name:** MeadLaw, P.A. **Marital Status:** Married **Children:** Two Sons; One Daughter **Education:** JD, School of Law, University of Baltimore (1989); MA in Criminal Justice, Troy State University, Troy, AL (1980); BS in Criminal Justice, Troy State University, Troy, AL (1979) **Career:** Founder, Managing Partner, Mead-Law, P.A., Baltimore, MD (2016-Present); Private Practice Attorney; Judicial Law Clerk, Court of Special Appeals; Judicial Law Clerk, Circuit Court for Baltimore City **Awards:** Margaret Brent-Juanita Mitchell Award (2011); Maryland Super Lawyer, Super Lawyers Magazine (2007-2017); Top 100 Attorneys, America's Top 100; Leadership in Law Award **Membership:** Maryland State Bar Association; Bar Association of Baltimore City; Co-Chair, Criminal Law Committee, Bar Association of Baltimore City; Baltimore County Bar Association; Secretary/Treasurer, Character Committee, Maryland State Board of Law Examiners; Board of Trustees, Office of the Public Defender; Nominating Committee Member, Baltimore County Judicial Commission **Bar Admissions:** State of Maryland; Maryland Court of Appeals; U.S. District Court, District of Maryland; Fourth Circuit, U.S. Court of Appeals; U.S. Supreme Court **Why did you become involved in your profession or industry:** Ms. Mead read Nancy Drew and watched Perry Mason and Ellery Queen as a child, which led her to study criminal justice. She didn't believe she was capable of going to law school. When she was 30, however, she took an evaluation test which told her she should go into law so she decided to pursue a doctorate. **Shipping Address:** 1 N Charles Street, Suite 2470, Mead Law, P.A., Baltimore, MD, 21201 **Website:** https://meadlaw.com/attorney-profilesmargaretmeadbrandonmead

Brian D. Meagher

Title: Diagnostic Radiologist **Industry:** Health, Wellness and Fitness **Date of Birth:** 08/17/1956 **Place of Birth:** Bronx **State:** NY **Marital Status:** Separated **Education:** MD, Georgetown University (1982); BA in Neurobiology and Behavior, Cornell University (1978); Internship, David Grant USAF Medical Center, Travis Air Force Base, CA; Diagnostic Radiology Residency, University of Massachusetts Medical Center, Worcester, MA **Certifications:** Board Certification, American Board of Radiology (1995) **Career:** Contract Diagnostic Radiologist, Chautauqua Radiologists, Brooks Memorial Hospital, Dunkirk, NY **Membership:** Chautauqua Medical Society; Medical Society of the State of New York; American College of Radiology; American Medical Association; American Roentgen Ray Society; Radiological Society of North America, Inc. **Marquis Who's Who Honors:** Albert Nelson Marquis Lifetime Achievement Award (2017); Distinguished Humanitarian (2017) **To what do you attribute your success:** He had great teachers at the University of Massachusetts who helped develop his skill set in radiology, starting him out with a great background knowledge of imaging. **Why did you become involved in your profession or industry:** He became involved in his profession after running his own family practice. He wanted to venture into another field of medicine and expand his knowledge of the health care industry. **Where will you be in five years:** In five years, Dr. Meagher intends to be fully retired from medicine. **Hobbies:** Skiing **Religion:** Roman Catholic **Shipping Address:** 204 Sanbury Rd, Jamestown, NY, 14701 **Website:** http://www.jamrads.com

Robert T. Means Jr.

Title: 1) Dean of Quillen Medical College 2) Professor of Internal Medicine **Industry:** Education/ Educational Services **Company Name:** 1) East Tennessee State University 2) Medical Education Assistance Corporation **Date of Birth:** 07/14/1957 **Place of Birth:** Midland **State:** TX **Parents:** Robert Taylor Means; Anna Therese (Cassidy) Means **Marital Status:** Married **Spouse Name:** Stacey W. McKenzie (5/23/1992) **Children:** Anna; Robert III; Patrick **Education:** Postdoctoral Fellow, Division of Hematology, Vanderbilt University School of Medicine (1986-1988); Resident in Medicine, Baylor College of Medicine (1983-1986); Intern in Medicine, Baylor College of Medicine (1983-1984); MD, Vanderbilt University (1983); BA in Biochemistry, Rice University, Magna Cum Laude (1979) **Certifications:** Diplomate in Hematology (2016, 1988); Diplomate, American Board of Internal Medicine (1986) **Career:** Dean, Quillen College of Medicine, East Tennessee State University, Johnson City, TN (2014-Present); Professor of Internal Medicine, East Tennessee State University (2014-Present); President, Medical Education Assistance Corporation, Quillen College of Medicine, East Tennessee State University (2014-Present); Executive Dean, University of Kentucky College of Medicine (2012-2014); Executive Vice Dean, University of Kentucky College of Medicine (2011-2012); Senior Associate Chair, University of Kentucky (2007-2011); Professor of Internal Medicine, University of Kentucky (2004-2014); Associate Research Chair, Internal Medicine, University of Kentucky (2004-2007); Interim Associate Dean, University of Kentucky (2004-2006); Chief Medical Service, Veterans Affairs Medical Center (Now Lexington Veterans Affairs Medical Center), United States Department of Veterans Affairs, Lexington, KY (2004-2006); Director, Division of Hematology-Oncology, Medical University of South Carolina (2000-2004); Chief of Hematology/Oncology, Veterans Affairs Medical Center (Now Ralph H. Johnson Veterans Affairs Medical Center), United States Department of Veterans Affairs, Charleston, SC (1998-2004); Professor, Head of Hematology, Medical University of South Carolina (1998-2000); Associate Division Chief, Medical University of South Carolina (1998-2000); Associate Professor, Hematology Division, University of Cincinnati (1992-1998); Assistant Chief of Hematology/Oncology, Veterans Affairs Medical Center, United States Department of Veterans Affairs, Cincinnati, OH (1992-1998); Assistant Professor of Medicine, Vanderbilt University (1990-1992); Associate Investigator, Veterans Affairs Medical Center, United States Department of Veterans Affairs (1988-1991); Instructor of Medicine, Vanderbilt University (1988-1990) **Career Related:** Interim Director, Kentucky Neurosciences Institute (2013-2014); Associate Dean for Veterans Affairs, Markey Cancer Center, University of Kentucky (2011-2012); Associate Dean for Veterans Affairs, University of Kentucky College of Medicine (2011-2012); Medical Director/Clinical Service Chief, Department of Internal Medicine, University of Kentucky (2010-2011); Senior Associate Chair, Department of Internal Medicine, University of Kentucky (2007-2011); Interim Director, Markey Cancer Center, University of Kentucky (2006-2009); Acting Chief, Medical Service, Veterans Affairs Medical Center (Now Lexington Veterans Affairs Medical Center), United States Department of Veterans Affairs, Lexington, KY (2006-2007); Interim Director, Markey Cancer Center, University of Kentucky (2006-2007); Interim Associate Dean for Veterans Affairs, University of Kentucky College of Medicine, Lexington, KY (2004-2007); Associate Chair for Research, Department of Internal Medicine, University of Kentucky College of Medicine, Lexington, KY (2004-2007); Chief, Medical Service, Veterans Affairs Medical Center, United States Department of Veterans Affairs, Lexington, KY (2004-2006) **Creative Works:** Deputy Editor, Journal of Investigative Medicine (2015-Present); Editorial Board, Blood Research (Formerly Korean J. Hematology) (2010-Present); Editorial Board, American Journal of the Medical Sciences (2006-Present); International Editorial Board Member, International Journal of Hematology (1999-Present); Editor, "Topics in Nutritional Anemia" (2017); Editor, "Wintrobe's Clinical Hematology, 13th Edition" (2013); Editorial Board, Academic Internal Medicine Insight (Now Alliance for Academic Internal Medicine) (2010-2014); Editor, "Wintrobe's Clinical Hematology, 12th Edition" (2008); Associate Editor, Journal of Investigative Medicine (1998-2015) **Awards:** Recipient, Founder's Medal, The Southern Society for Clinical Investigation (2016); Inductee, Alpha Omega Alpha (Now Alpha Omega Alpha Honor Medical Society) (2016); Inductee, Honorable Order of Kentucky Colonels (2013); Recipient, Chief Resident's Faculty of the Year Award, University of Kentucky (2006); Recipient, Ralph H. Johnson Merit Award, Ralph H. Johnson Veterans Affairs Medical Center, United State Department of Veteran Affairs (2002) **Marquis Who's Who Honors:** Albert Nelson Marquis Lifetime Achievement Award (2017) **Shipping Address:** 3 Straw Flower Pl, Johnson City, TN, 37604 **Website:** http://www.etsu.edu/com/dean/aboutthedean.php

Richard J. Medalie

Title: Lawyer **Industry:** Law and Legal Services **Company Name:** The Medalie Law Office **Date of Birth:** 07/21/1929 **Place of Birth:** Duluth **State:** MN **Parents:** William Louis Medalie; Mona (Kolad) Medalie **Marital Status:** Married **Spouse Name:** Susan Diane Abrams (6/5/1960) **Children:** Samuel David; Daniel Alexander **Education:** JD, Harvard University, Cum Laude (1958); AM, Harvard University (1955); BA, University of Minnesota, Summa Cum Laude (1952) **Certifications:** Certificate, University of London (1953) **Career:** Lawyer, Private Practice, Hull, MA (2006-Present); Chairman Emeritus, Appleseed, Washington, DC (2003-Present); Lawyer, Private Practice, Washington, DC (1998-2006); President, Appleseed, Washington, DC (1995-1998); Board Chairman, Appleseed, Washington, DC (1993-2002); Executive Director, Appleseed, Washington D.C. (1993-1994); Founding Member, Appleseed, Washington, DC (1993); President, Pegasus International, Washington, DC (1970-2010); Partner, Friedman & Medalie and Predecessors, Washington, DC (1968-1998); Deputy Director, Ford Foundation Institute, Criminal Law and Procedure, Georgetown University Law Center (1965-1968); Associate, Kaye, Scholer, Fierman, Hays & Handler, New York City, NY (1962-1965); Assistant Solicitor General, United States (1960-1962); Law Clerk to Honorable George T. Washington, United States Court of Appeals for the District of Columbia Circuit (1958-1959) **Career Related:** Vice President, Board of Directors, Trial Lawyers for Public Justice, Washington, DC (1998-2006); Chairman, Harvard Law School Annual Fund (1987-1989); Deputy Chairman, Harvard Law School Annual Fund (1986-1987); Chairman, National Major Gifts, Harvard Law School Annual Fund (1984-1986); Vice Chairman, Harvard Law School Annual Fund (1981-1984); Executive Committee, Criminal Law Task Force (1978-1982); Chairman, Member, District of Columbia Law Revision Commission (1975-1987); Adjunct Professor, Administrative and Criminal Law, Georgetown University Law Center (1967-1970); Vice President for Educational Affairs, United States National Student Association (1949-1950) **Civic:** President, Alumni Association Experiment in International Living, Brattleboro, VT (1962-1963); Board of Directors, Alumni Association Experiment in International Living, Brattleboro, VT (1961-1964) **Creative Works:** Co-Author, Co-Editor, "American Students Organize: Founding the National Student Association After World War II" (2006); Co-Author, Editor, "Commercial Arbitration for the 1990s" (1991); Author, "The Libyan Producers' Agreement Arbitration: Developing Innovative Procedures in a Complex Multiparty Arbitration," Journal of International Arbitration (1990); Co-Author, "Federal Consumer Safety Legislation" (1970); Co-Author, "Custodial Police Interrogation in Our Nation's Capital: The Attempt to Implement Miranda," Michigan Law Review (1968); Co-Editor, "Crime: A Community Responds" (1967); Author, "From Escobedo to Miranda: The Anatomy of a Supreme Court Decision" (1966); Author, "The Communist Theory of State," The American Slavic and East European Review (1959); Author, "Observations on East West Exchange," I.I.E. News Bulletin (1958); Case Editor, Harvard Law Review (1957-1958); Staff, Harvard Law Review (1956-1958); Author, "The Policy of Take-Over: The Stages of Totalitarian Development in Eastern Europe," in C.J. Friedrich & S.E. Harris, Public Policy (1956); Contributor, Articles, Legal Journals **Awards:** Ford Fellow (1954-1955); Fulbright Scholar (1952-1953); Phi Beta Kappa (1952); Phi Alpha Theta (1952) **Membership:** Panelist, Commercial Arbitrators, National Arbitration Forum (2004-2010); Co-Chair, National Conference on Critical Issues in Arbitration, ABA (1993); Law School Director, Harvard Alumni Association (1991-1995); Vice Chairman, ABA (1991-1994); National Conference on Emerging Alternative Dispute Resolution Issues in State and Federal Courts, ABA (1991); Program Chair, ABA (1990); Chair, Legislative Subcommittee, ABA (1986-1989); Program Chair, ABA (1984); National Vice President, Harvard Law School Association of Washington, DC (1977-1978); President, Harvard Law School Association of Washington, DC (1976-1977); Panelist, Commercial Arbitrators, American Arbitration Association (1964-2006); Fellow, American Bar Foundation; Lifetime Member, American Law Institute; Alternative Dispute Resolution/Arbitration Committee, ABA; Representative on Advisory Committee, ABA; Arbitration Committee, Litigation Section, ABA; The District of Columbia Bar; Association of the Bar of the City of New York; Cosmos Club of Washington D.C. **Bar Admissions:** New York (1963); Supreme Court of the United States (1961); The District of Columbia (1958) **Marquis Who's Who Honors:** Albert Nelson Marquis Lifetime Achievement Award (2017) **Shipping Address:** 46 P Street, Hull, MA, 02045 **Website:** http://www.appleseednetwork.org

Violet Meek

Title: Dean, Pastor **Industry:** Education/Educational Services **Company Name:** The Ohio State University at Lima **Date of Birth:** 06/12/1939 **Place of Birth:** Geneva **State:** IL **Parents:** John Imhof; Violet (Krepel) Imhof **Marital Status:** Married **Spouse Name:** Don M. Dell (1/4/1992); Devon W. Meek (8/21/1965, Deceased 1988) **Children:** Brian; Karen; Michael Dell (Stepson); Amy Dell (Stepdaughter); Kathryn Dell-Frickel (Stepdaughter) **Education:** ChD, University of Illinois (1964); MS, University of Illinois (1962); BA, St. Olaf College, Summa Cum Laude (1960) **Certifications:** Ordained Pastor, Evangelical Lutheran Church of America (2004) **Career:** Pastor Emerita, Emanuel Lutheran Church, Logan, OH (2014-Present); Pastor, Emanuel Lutheran Church, Logan, OH (2003-2014); Dean, Director, The Ohio State University at Lima (1992-2003); Associate Director of Sponsored Program Development, Research Foundation, The Ohio State University, Columbus, OH (1986-1991); Director of Annual Programs, Council of Independent Colleges, Washington, DC (1984-1986); Dean for Educational Services, Ohio Wesleyan University, Delaware, OH (1980-1984); Assistant Professor to Professor, Ohio Wesleyan University, Delaware, OH (1965-1984); Instructor of Chemistry, Mount Holyoke College, South Hadley, MA (1964-1965); Woodrow Wilson Fellowship (1960); Graduate Fellowship (1960) **Career Related:** Reviewer, Goldwater National Fellowships, Princeton, NJ (1990-1998); Reviewer, GTE Science and Technology Program, Princeton, NJ (1986-1992); Visiting Dean, Stanford University, Palo Alto, CA (1982); Visiting Dean, University of California, Berkeley (1982) **Civic:** Board, Columbus Rotary Foundation (2012-Present); Chair, Board of Directors, Allen County Chamber of Commerce (1999); President, Board of Directors, Lima Symphony Orchestra (1997-2002); Chair, Board of Trustees, Trinity Lutheran Seminary, Columbus, OH (1996-2004); Chairman, Board of Directors, Allen County Chamber of Commerce (1995-2001); Board of Directors, Lima Symphony Orchestra (1993-2002); Board, Art Space, Lima, OH (1993-2000); Chair, Allen Lima Leadership (1993-1999); Lima Veterans Memorial Civic Center Foundation (1992-2001); American House (1992-1998); Board of Directors, Americom Bank, Lima, OH (1992-1998); Board of Directors, Lutheran Campus Ministries, Columbus, OH (1988-1991); Lutheran Social Services (1988-1991); Chairman, Synodical Committees, Evangelical Lutheran Church of America, Columbus, OH (1982) **Creative Works:** Co-Author, "Experimental General Chemistry" (1984); Contributor, Articles, Professional Journals **Awards:** Athena Award, Lima/Allen County Chamber of Commerce (2001); Woman of Distinction, Golden Paradigm Award, Appleseed Ridge Girl Scout Council (1995); Honoree, Outstanding New Professional, Midwest Region, National Council of Research Administrators (1990) **Membership:** Chair, Board of Directors, Deaconess Community for the Evangelical Lutheran Church of America; Rotary International; American Association of Higher Education; National Council of University Research Administrators; The Phi Beta Kappa Society; Sigma XI **Marquis Who's Who Honors:** Albert Nelson Marquis Lifetime Achievement Award (2017) **Hobbies:** Music; Skiing; Woodworking; Civil War history; Travel **Shipping Address:** 209 W Beechwold Boulevard, Columbus, OH, 43214

Cynthia A. Mehary

Title: School System Administrator **Industry:** Education/Educational Services **Date of Birth:** 06/24/1942 **State/Country of Origin:** GA **Parents:** Frank Ellison; Jewell (Ogletree) Ellison **Children:** Elsabeth B. **Education:** MA, Western Michigan University (1971); BEd, University at Buffalo (1965); AAS, University at Buffalo (1963) **Certifications:** Certified in Administration, State of New York (1991); Certified Secondary Teacher, State of New York **Career:** Part-Time Teacher, Buffalo Public Schools (2016-Present); Adjunct Professor, Buffalo State College (1989-1992); Business Teacher, Buffalo Public Schools (1986-2008); Computer Teacher, Buffalo Public Schools (1986-2008); Part-time Teacher, Erie Community College (1978-1990); Lecturer, Bryant and Stratton Business Institute (Now Bryant & Stratton College) (1978-1986); Teacher, Niagara Falls City School District; Teacher, Peace Corps, Ethiopia **Career Related:** Adjunct Professor, Buffalo State The State University of New York (1989-1992); Part-Time Lecturer, ECC (1978-1990); Business Education Supervisor in Workforce Development, Buffalo Public Schools **Creative Works:** Author, "Cynthia's Insights" (2015-Present); Author, "Electronic Typewriters, Dedicated Word Processors, Computer Word Processing Packages-Where is the Similarity?" (1988-1989); Author, "Teaching Records Management at the Post-Secondary Independent Business Schools and Colleges" (1986); Author, "Suggestions to Improve Business Education Programs" (1980); Contributor, Articles, Professional Journals **Awards:** Apple for the Teacher Award, Buffalo Chapter of IOTA Phi Lamda Sorority **Membership:** Board Member, Buffalo Retired Teachers Association, Buffalo, NY (2010-Present); Co-President, AAUW (2008-Present); Vice President, Recruitment, AAUW (2009-2013); ACSD; National Business Education Association; Business Teachers Association New York State; Corresponding Secretary, Local Chapter, Iota Phi Lambda; Returned Peace Corps Volunteers, Buffalo, NY; New York State United Teachers; Western Zone **Why did you become involved in your profession or industry:** Ms. Mehary became involved in her profession because she always wanted to be a teacher. She goes above and beyond for her students to help them grow academically, and has tried helping in their personal lives as well. Even after she retired, she returned to a part time teaching job so she can still be active with students and helping them succeed. **Hobbies:** Reading; Traveling to foreign countries **Shipping Address:** 227 Dartmouth Ave, Buffalo, NY, 14215

Leonard Evert Mellberg

Title: Physicist **Industry:** Medicine & Health Care **Company Name:** Ocean Physics Associates **Date of Birth:** 12/18/1935 **Place of Birth:** Springfield **State:** MA **Parents:** Evert Mellberg; Dorothy (Baker) Mellberg **Marital Status:** Married **Spouse Name:** Pamela Narbeth **Education:** MS in Physics, Trinity College (1968); Postgraduate Coursework, University of Connecticut (1961-1966); BS in Physics, University of Massachusetts Amherst (1961) **Career:** Chief Scientist, Ocean Physics Associates, South Dartmouth, MA (2000-Present); Chief Scientist, SAIC, La Jolla, CA (1994-2000); Senior Scientist, Marine Acoustics, Inc., Newport, RI (1991-1994); Research Physicist, Underwater Systems Center, U.S. Navy, Newport, RI (1972-1991); Research Physicist, Office of Naval Research, London, England (1968-1972); Research Physicist, Undersea Research Center (Now Centre for Maritime Research & Experimentation, Science & Technology Organization), NATO, LaSpezia, Italy (1968-1972); Research Physicist, Underwater Sound Laboratory, U.S. Navy, New London, CT (1961-1968) **Career Related:** Fellow, Acoustical Society of America (1990); Government and Professional Technical Advisory Boards and Committees **Civic:** President, Eastern Division, Veterans Chorus (2001-2008); Board of Directors, Verdandi Chorus, American Union of Swedish Singers, Providence, RI (1992-2010); President, Verdandi Swedish Cultural Foundation, Providence, RI (1992-1997) **Military Service:** Research Physicist, Naval Undersea Warfare Center, U.S. Navy (1972-1991); Research Physicist, Office of Naval Research, U.S. Navy (1968-1972); Research Physicist, Underwater Sound Laboratory, U.S. Navy (1961-1968); Occupational Forces, U.S. Army, Berlin and Esslingen am Neckar, Germany (1955-1956) **Creative Works:** Contributor, Over 70 Articles, Professional Journals **Awards:** Navy Meritorious Civilian Service Medal, U.S. Department of the Navy (1991); Decorated Civilian Navy Meritorious Arctic Commendation, U.S. Department of the Navy (1985); Excellence in Science Award, Naval Underwater Systems Center, U.S. Navy (1984); Service Award, American Institute of Aeronautics and Astronautics (1977); Special Achievement Award for Excellence in the Area of Science, Naval Underwater Systems Center (1977); Commendation, Commander Seventh Fleet, U.S. Navy (1975); Commendation, Commander, Task Force 77 (1974); Supreme Allied Commander Atlantic Service Award, NATO (1972) **Membership:** Technical Committee for Air Transportation Services, American Institute of Aeronautics and Astronautics (1975-1977); Emeritus Fellow Member, Acoustical Society of America; Lifetime Member, IEEE; Senior Member, IEEE; American Geophysical Union; American Institute of Physics **Marquis Who's Who Honors:** Albert Nelson Marquis Lifetime Achievement Award (2017) **To what do you attribute your success:** Mr. Mellberg attributes his success to looking at what needs to be learned in ocean physics, realizing what's necessary, networking, and remaining current in advances in ocean physics and related fields. **Why did you become involved in your profession or industry:** Mr. Mellberg submitted to the study of physics. He always enjoyed science even as a young man, and it has been his passion. **What do you consider to be the highlight of your career:** A highlight of Mr. Mellberg's career was being the recipient of the Excellence in Science Award by the Naval Underwater Systems Center in 1977. **Where will you be in five years:** In five years, Mr. Mellberg will be helping others to achieve successful enjoyable lives in science. **Hobbies:** Outdoor hiking; Mountains; Cross-country skiing; Snowshoeing **Shipping Address:** 109 Wilson Street, South Dartmouth, MA, 02748

Dunstana Rabelo Melo, PhD

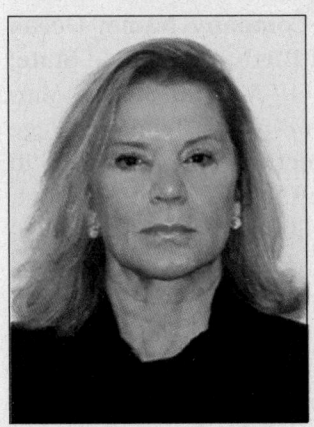

Title: President, Chief Scientist **Industry:** Sciences **Company Name:** Melohill Technology LLC **Education:** PhD in Biophysics, Federal University of Rio de Janeiro, Rio de Janeiro, Brazil (1995); MS in Biophysics, Federal University of Rio de Janeiro, Rio de Janeiro, Brazil; BS in Biology, Federal University of Rio de Janeiro, Rio de Janeiro, Brazil; Postdoctoral Coursework, Radiation Dosimetry, National Cancer Institute, NIH **Career:** Director, Center for Countermeasures Against Radiation, LRRI (2013); Designated Director, Center for Countermeasures Against Radiation, LRRI (2011); Head, Internal Dosimetry Division, Institute of Radiation Protection and Dosimetry, Brazilian Nuclear Energy Commission; President, Melohill Technology LLC **Awards:** Research NIH (2016); Merit Honor Diploma, National Atomic Energy Commission, Brazil (2002) **Membership:** ICRP; Brazilian Radiological Protection Society; Dosimetry Group, Radiation Epidemiology Branch, National Cancer Institute, NIH; National Council on Radiation Protection and Measurements **Business Address:** 1 Research Ct., Ste 450, Rockville, MD, 20850 **Shipping Address:** 4620 N Park Ave., Apt 805E, Chevy Chase, MD, 20815 **Website:** http://www.melohilltech.com

Jose Mena

Title: Physician **Industry:** Medicine & Health Care **Company Name:** Miami Orthopedics and Sports Medicine Institute **Place of Birth:** San Juan **State/Country of Origin:** Puerto Rico **Parents:** Luis Mena; Agnes Mercado **Children:** Adrian Jose; Julian Jose **Education:** Fellow in Pain Medicine, Department of Anesthesiology and Perioperative Medicine, University of Louisville Health Science Center, Louisville, KY (2007-2008); Chief Resident, Department of Physical Medicine and Rehabilitation, Boston University Medical Center, Boston, MA (2004-2007); Internship in Internal Medicine, Veterans Affairs Medical Center, San Juan, Puerto Rico (2003-2004); MD, University of Puerto Rico School of Medicine, Magna Cum Laude (2003); BS in General Science, University of Puerto Rico School of Medicine, Summa Cum Laude (1999) **Certifications:** License to Practice Medicine, State of Florida (2008-Present); License to Practice Medicine, Puerto Rico (2006-Present); Diplomate, American Board of Physical Medicine & Rehabilitation (2008); Pain Medicine Sub-Specialty Certification, American Board of Physical Medicine & Rehabilitation (2008); License to Practice Medicine, State of Kentucky (2007-2008) **Career:** Physician at Miami Orthopedics and Sports Medicine Institute; Team Physician for Florida International University Athletics (2015-Present); Assistant Professor, Florida International University (2015-Present); Assistant Professor, Department of Physical Medicine & Rehabilitation, University of Miami (2008-2015); Associate Residency Program Director, Department of Physical Medicine & Rehabilitation, University of Miami (2008-2015); Co-medical Director, UHealth Advanced Institute for Pain Management, University of Miami (2008-2015); Medical Director, UHealth Clinic at Hialeah, Miami Lakes, FL (2008-2015); Medical Director of Clinical Affairs, Department of Physical Medicine & Rehabilitation, University of Miami (2008-2015); Chemistry Tutor, Rio Piedras Campus, University of Puerto Rico (1999) **Civic:** Medical Student Mentorship Program, American Academy of Physical Medicine & Rehabilitation (2005-Present); Staff Physician, 5th Annual Boston Athletic Association Half Marathon (2005); Staff Physician, Liga Atletica Interuniversitaria **Creative Works:** Editorial Board Member, "PM&R Knowledge NOW Essentials of Rehabilitation Practice and Science" (2012-Present); Contributor, Numerous Articles to Scientific Journals **Awards:** Named, America's Top Physicians, Consumers' Research Council of America (2009-Present); On-Time Doctor Award (2014-2016); Named, Top 10 Doctor, Florida (2014); Named, Top 10 Doctor, Miami Metro Area (2014); Compassionate Doctor Recognition Award (2013-2016); Patients' Choice Award (2013-2016); Compassionate Doctor Recognition Award (2010-2011); Patients' Choice Award (2010-2011); Educator of the Year, Department of Physical Medicine & Rehabilitation, University of Miami Leonard M. Miller School of Medicine (2010); Outstanding Student, Recognition by President of the University of Puerto Rico (1999); Academic Excellence Award, Natural Science College, University of Puerto Rico Rio Piedras Campus (1999); Highest GPA in General Science Major, Natural Science College, University of Puerto Rico Rio Piedras Campus (1999); USAA All-American Scholar Collegiate Program (1997-1999); USAA National Science Award (1997-1999) **Membership:** American Society of Interventional Pain Physicians (2008-Present); American Academy of Physical Medicine and Rehabilitation (2004-Present); American Medical Association (2000-Present); Golden Key International Honour Society (1996-Present); Musculoskeletal Practicing Curriculum Workgroup, American Academy of Physical Medicine and Rehabilitation (2010); Association of Academic Physiatrists; North American Spine Society; Spine Intervention Society; American Association of Neuromuscular & Electrodiagnostic Medicine **Business Address:** 1150 Campo Sano Ave., Suite 200, Coral Gables, FL, 33146 **Shipping Address:** 4401 NW 87th Ave., Unit 512, Doral, FL, 33178 **Website:** https://baptisthealth.net/en/health-services/orthopedics-and-sports-medicine-services/our-doctors/pages/jose-mena-md.aspx

Linda K. Menard Post

Title: State Legislator **Industry:** Government Administration/Government Relations/Government Services **Company Name:** Alaska State Senate, District G **Date of Birth:** 12/21/1943 **Place of Birth:** Cheboygan **State:** MI **Marital Status:** Married **Spouse Name:** Michael Post (6/21/2014); Sen. Curtis D. Menard (Deceased 2009) **Children:** Robert; Curtis; Steven; Dirk; McKenzy **Education:** EdB in Elementary Education, University of Alaska (1975) **Career:** Alaska State Senate District G (2009-2013); School Board, Matanuska-Susitna Borough (1996-2007); Substitute Teacher, Alaska Job Corps; Founder, Owner, All I Saw Cookware; Owner, Mrs. Alaska Franchise; Chief Financial Officer, Wasilla Dental Center; Chief Financial Officer, Palmer Dental Centers; Teacher, Mat-Su Borough School District **Civic:** Founder, Matanuska Susitna Schools Foundation; Charter Member, Mat-Su Convention & Visitors Bureau; Vice Chairman, Mat-Su Health Foundation; Interim Director, Mat-Su Health Foundation **Awards:** Champion for Children (2007); Citizen of the Year, Wasilla Chamber of Commerce (1999); First Lady's Volunteer Award, Ermilee Kickel, State of Alaska (1994); Henry Jall Fellowship Award; First Lady of Matanuska-Susitna College **Membership:** The Salvation Army; Wasilla Chamber of Commerce; President, Alaska Chapter, American Cancer Society, Inc.; Alaska Antique Tractor Club **Marquis Who's Who Honors:** Albert Nelson Marquis Lifetime Achievement Award (2017) **To what do you attribute your success:** Ms. Post attributes her success to a strong work ethic and ability to follow through on commitments. **Why did you become involved in your profession or industry:** Ms. Post was inspired to leadership by being a school board member for 12 years, assisting with her first husband's successful dental practice, and being elected to the Alaska State Senate in 2009. Her first husband was also a senator, and they were the first husband and wife team to be elected. **What do you consider to be the highlight of your career:** The highlights of Ms. Post's career were being able to represent the fabulous state of Alaska, raising her children, and giving back to her community. **Hobbies:** Bridge; Scrabble **Political Affiliations:** Republican **Religion:** Catholic **Shipping Address:** 3060 N Lazy Eight Court, Suite 2, PMB 777, Wasilla, AK, 99654

Howard Shigeharu Mende

Title: Mechanical Engineer **Industry:** Engineering **Company Name:** Defense Contracts Management West **Date of Birth:** 11/19/1947 **Place of Birth:** Hilo **State:** HI **Parents:** Tsutomu Mende; Harue (Kubomitsu) Mende **Marital Status:** Single **Education:** MS in Mechanical Engineering, University of Southern California (1975); BS in Mechanical Engineering, University of Hawaii (1969) **Certifications:** Registered Professional Engineer, State of California **Career:** Electronics Engineer, Defense Contracts Management West, Santa Ana, CA (1994-Present); Mechanical Engineer, Defense Contracts Management West, Santa Ana, CA (1987-1994); Member, Technical Staff IV, Rockwell International, LA (1984-1986); Development Engineer, AiRsch. Manufacturing Company, Torrance, CA (1977-1983); Member, Technical Staff II, Rockwell International, Los Angeles, CA (1973-1977); Member, Technical Staff I, Rockwell International, Los Angeles, CA (1971-1973); Member, Technical Staff I, Rockwell International, Anaheim, CA (1970-1971) **Career Related:** Lecturer, Pacific States University, Los Angeles, CA (1974-1975) **Membership:** The American Society of Mechanical Engineers **Marquis Who's Who Honors:** Albert Nelson Marquis Lifetime Achievement Award (2017); Distinguished Humanitarian (2017) **To what do you attribute your success:** Mr. Mende would like to think that he tried to fully realize why things happen the way they do. **Why did you become involved in your profession or industry:** He became involved in his profession because his father, a mechanic, pushed him toward a profession in engineering at an early age. **Where will you be in five years:** He is at the tale end of his career and in five years, he would like to continue to work for the government. **Hobbies:** Gardening; Home improvements **Political Affiliations:** Democrat **Religion:** Buddhist **Shipping Address:** 1946 W 180th Pl, Torrance, CA, 90504

M. Alan Menter

Title: Dermatologist **Industry:** Medicine & Health Care **Company Name:** Texas Dermatology Associates **Date of Birth:** 10/30/1941 **Place of Birth:** Doncaster, England **Country of Origin:** England **Parents:** Harry Menter; Esme (Green) Behr **Marital Status:** Married **Spouse Name:** Pamela Mary Williams (12/4/1966) **Children:** Keith; Colin; Kerith **Education:** Fellow, The University of Texas Southwestern Medical Center, Dallas, TX (1975-1977), Tutor in Dermatology, St. John's Hospital for Disease of Skin, London, England (1972-1973); Senior Resident in Dermatology, Guy's Hospital, London, England (1972); Master of Medicine in Dermatology, University of Pretoria (1971); Resident in Dermatology, University of Pretoria, Pretoria General Hospital (1968-1971); Senior Intern in Medicine and Dermatology, Johannesburg General Hospital (1968); Intern, Department of Medicine, Department of Surgery, Johannesburg General Hospital (1967); Bachelor of Medicine, Bachelor of Surgery, University of Witwatersrand, South Africa (1966) **Career:** Principal Faculty, Texas A&M Health Science Center, College of Medicine, Dallas, TX (2012-Present); Chair, Dermatology Residency Program, Baylor University Medical Center (2010-Present); Director, Baylor Psoriasis Research Center (2007-Present); Clinical Professor of Dermatology, The University of Texas Southwestern Medical Center (1996-Present); Chairman, Dermatology Division, Baylor University Medical Center (1992-Present); Dermatologist, Baylor University Medical Center, Dallas, TX (1975-Present); Medical Director, National Psoriasis Foundation Tissue Bank, Dallas, TX (1993-1999) **Career Related:** Chairman, Residency Program, Baylor University Medical Center, Dallas, TX (2010-Present); Clinical Associate Professor, Department of Periodontics, Baylor College of Dentistry, Dallas, TX (1985-Present); Medical Director, Psoriasis Center, Baylor University Medical Center, Dallas, TX (1979-Present); Associate Clinical Professor of Dermatology, University of Texas Southwestern Medical School, Dallas, TX (1977-1995); Fellow, Department of Dermatology, University of Texas Southwestern Medical School, Dallas, TX (1977-1979); Presenter in Field **Civic:** Coach, Commissioner, Boys Under 12 Classic League Soccer, Dallas, TX (1978-1982); Coach, Rugby Football Team, University of Pretoria (1974); Captain, Rugby Team, University of Pretoria (1969); Represented, South Africa National Rugby Football Team (1968); Captain, University of Witwatersrand, Rugby Team (1961-1968); Represented, Cricket Team, South African Universities (1961); Active, Various Local Civic Organizations and Committees; Texas State Chairman, Dermatology Foundation; Research Chairman, National Psoriasis Foundation; Medical Advisory Board Executive Committee **Creative Works:** Editorial Board Member, Journal of American Academy of Dermatology (1993-2003); Co-Author, "The First Gene Discovery for Psoriasis" (1994); Author, 4 Books; Contributor, 385 Articles to Professional Journals, 21 Chapters to Books **Awards:** Top Doctor, Castle Connolly Medical Ltd. (2004-Present); Best Doctors in America (1994-Present); Presidential Citation Award, American Academy of Dermatology (2015, 2018); Annual Clark W. Finnerud Award, Dermatology Foundation (2015); Presidential Citation Award, Stars of the Academy (2015); Clark Finerud Award Dermatology Foundation (2014); London Life Time Achievement Award, National Psoriasis Foundation (2013); Texas Super Doctors (2004-2012) **Membership:** Director, Psoriasis Symposium, American Academy of Dermatology (2010-2013); President, Third-World Congress Psoriasis & Psoratic Arthritic Conference, Stockholm, Sweden (2012); President, International Psoriasis Council (2005-2010); Chairman, Committee on Standards Care for Psoriasis, American Academy of Dermatology (2007-2009); Committee on Standards Care for Psoriasis, American Academy of Dermatology (2007); Board of Directors, Psoriasis Symposium, American Academy of Dermatology (1995-1997); President, Texas Dermatological Society (1995-1996); Subcommittee Member on Joint Sponsorship, Texas Medical Association (1992-1995); Chairman, American Academy of Dermatology (1990-1993); Director, Psoriasis Symposium, American Academy of Dermatology (1990-1993); Committee on Psoriasis, American Academy of Dermatology (1988-1993); Chairman, Committee on Standards Care for Psoriasis, American Academy of Dermatology (1989-1992); Committee on Standards Care for Psoriasis, American Academy of Dermatology (1988-1992); Representative to Advisory Council, American Academy of Dermatology (1987-1989); President, Dermatological Therapy Association (1985); President, Dallas Dermatological Society (1980); Secretary-Treasurer, Dallas Dermatological Society (1979); American Dermatological Association; American Medical Association; American Society for Laser Medicine & Surgery; American Society of Dermatologic Surgery; British Association of Dermatology; **Marquis Who's Who Honors:** Albert Nelson Marquis Lifetime Achievement Award (2017); Distinguished Humanitarian (2017) **Shipping Address:** 3900 Junius St Ste 145, Baylor Medical Pavilion, Dallas, TX, 75246

Roland S. Merchant Sr.

Title: Health Facility Administrator **Industry:** Health, Wellness and Fitness **Company Name:** Roland Merchant & Associates **Date of Birth:** 04/18/1929 **Place of Birth:** New York **State/Country of Origin:** NY **Parents:** Samuel Merchant; Eleta (McLymont) Merchant **Marital Status:** Married **Spouse Name:** Audrey Bartley (6/6/1970) **Children:** Orelia Eleta; Roland Samuel; Huey Bartley **Education:** Master's Degree, Health Services Administration, Columbia University (1974); MS, Columbia University (1963); MA, New York University (1960); BA, New York University (1957) **Career:** Consultant, Roland Merchant & Associates (1994-Present); Vice President of Strategic Planning, Cedars-Sinai (1990-1994); Director of Management Planning, Stanford Health Care (1986-1990); Director of Management and Strategic Planning, Stanford Health Care (1982-1985); Special Assistant to the Associate Vice President for Medical Affairs, Stanford Health Care (1977-1982); Administrator, West Adams Community Hospital (1976); Assistant Administrator, West Adams Community Hospital (1976); Director of Health and Hospital Management, Department of Health and Mental Hygiene, City of New York (1974-1976); Resident in Administration, Roosevelt Hospital (Now Mount Sinai West), Icahn School of Medicine at Mount Sinai (1973-1974); Biostatistician, Institute of Surgical Studies, Montefiore Medical Center (1965-1972); Administrative Coordinator, Institute of Surgical Studies, Montefiore Medical Center (1965-1972); Statistician, New York Tuberculosis and Health Association (1963-1965); Statistician, Department of Health and Mental Hygiene, City of New York (1960-1963); Assistant Statistician, Department of Health and Mental Hygiene, City of New York (1957-1960) **Career Related:** Department of Health Research and Policy, Stanford Health Care (1988-1990); Clinical Associate Professor, Department of Family, Community and Preventive Medicine, Stanford University (1986-1988) **Military Service:** United States Army (1951-1953) **Creative Works:** Author, "Passion-Sustained Commitment to Excellence: Family-Oriented Parenting and Training" (2004); Contributor, Scientific Papers **Membership:** Fellow, Commissioned Corps of the U.S. Public Health Service, U.S. Department of Health and Human Services; Fellow, American Public Health Association; American College of Healthcare Executives; The New York Academy of Sciences **Why did you become involved in your profession or industry:** He went to Colombia University and listened to the advice of his professor John Fertig; he wanted to emulate him. He followed in his footsteps and there was a surgeon he worked for at the time that he learned a lot from. He was then able to make a choice for himself. **Shipping Address:** 4445 Arcola Ave, Toluca Lake, CA, 91602

Frederick B. Merk

Title: Medical Educator **Industry:** Education/Educational Services **Company Name:** Tufts University School of Medicine **Date of Birth:** 02/21/1936 **Place of Birth:** Cambridge **State:** MA **Parents:** Frederick Merk; Lois Bannister Merk **Marital Status:** Married **Spouse Name:** Elizabeth Johnson **Children:** John F. Merk; R.Daniel Merk; Letty B. London **Education:** PhD, Boston University (1971); AB, Harvard College (1958) **Career:** Emeritus Professor, Pathology and Anatomy, Tufts University School of Medicine, Boston, MA (2002-Present); Director, Electron Microscopy Facility, Tufts University School of Medicine, Boston, MA (1975-1985); Part-time Teacher, Anatomy and Pathology, Tufts University School of Medicine, Boston, MA (2002-2013); Associate Professor, Department of Anatomy, Tufts University School of Medicine, Boston, MA (1973-2002); Associate Professor, Departments of Pathology and of Anatomy, Tufts University School of Medicine, Boston, MA (1973-2002); Assistant Professor, Pathology, Boston University School of Medicine (1972-1973) **Civic:** Trustee, Annual New England Conference, Grace United Methodist Church, Lynn, MA (2010-Present); Trustee, Frederick and Paula Anna Markus Foundation, Audubon Society, Moultonboro, NH (2005-Present); Lay Representative, Annual New England Conference, Grace United Methodist Church, Lynn, MA (2000-2010); Trustee, Broadway United Methodist Church, Lynn, MA (1994-2000); Chairman, Broadway United Methodist Church, Lynn, MA (1994-2000) **Awards:** Distinguished Career in Teaching Award, Tufts University (2002); Grantee, National Institutes of Health (1994-1998) **Membership:** The American Society for Cell Biology; Federation of American Societies for Experimental Biology; American Association of Anatomists; Microscopy Society of America; Boston Cancer Research Association; Sigma Xi **Marquis Who's Who Honors:** Albert Nelson Marquis Lifetime Achievement Award (2017) **Hobbies:** Gardening; Photography; Swimming; Scuba Diving **Business Address:** 338 Cowpond Brook Rd, Groton, MA, 01450

Jesse Howard Merrell

Title: Writer, Realtor **Industry:** Writing and Editing **Company Name:** Merrell Enterprises **Date of Birth:** 12/09/1938 **Place of Birth:** Shelby **State:** AL **Parents:** James Walton Merrell; Emma Thelma (Davis) Merrell **Marital Status:** Divorced **Spouse Name:** Betsy Lee Davis (1/11/1964, Divorced 1979) **Children:** Sandra; Mark; Brad; Carolyn; Gwen **Career:** President, Merrell Enterprises, Washington, DC (1977-Present); Editor, Transport Topics, Washington, DC (1976-1977); Special Assistant to President, American Trucking Association, Washington, DC (1975-1976); Associate Editor, Transport Topics, Washington, DC (1968-1975); Public Information Officer, Kettering Medical Center, Kettering, OH (1968); State Editor, Daily Progress, Charlottesville, VA (1965-1968); Writer, Editor, Hopewell News (1963-1965); Reporter, News Director, WHAP Radio, Hopewell, VA (1963); Pitcher, Cincinnati Redlegs (1958-1962) **Career Related:** Speechwriter, Interstate Commerce Commission Chairman, Washington, DC (1982); Consultant, Middle Atlantic Conference, Riverdale, MD (1981-1982); First President, Dale Carnegie Courses, Washington, DC (1980-1981); Contract Carrier Conference, Middle Atlantic Conference, Riverdale, MD (1977-1982); Instructor, Dale Carnegie Courses, Washington, DC (1974-1981); Public Relations Committee, American Movers Conference, Washington, DC (1969-1972) **Civic:** National Trust for Historic Preservation; Association for the Preservation of Virginia Antiquities; Volunteer, John Hopkins Medicine, Sibley Memorial Hospital **Military Service:** U.S. Army (1960-1962) **Creative Works:** Author, "Talking Tombstones" (2017); Author, "Reflections of an Ole Alabama Country Boy" (2016); Author, "My Name is America! I Was Born at Jamestown! (2002); Author, "The Merrells of Alabama (1995); Author, "A Christmas Gift" (1979); Syndicated Columnist, Religion and the Times, "Washington Welter" **Awards:** George Washington Honor Medal, Freedoms Foundation (2002); Honor Certificate, Freedoms Foundation (1972); Liberty Award, Congress of Freedom, Jackson, MS (1971); Liberty Award, Congress of Freedom, Jackson, MS (1970); Local Column Writing Award, Virginia Press Association (1968); Runner Up, Series of Articles, Virginia Press Association (1967); Runner-Up, Local Column Writing, Virginia Press Association (1966); First Place, News Writing, Virginia Press Association (1965); Runner-Up, First Place, Editorial Writing, Virginia Press Association (1964) **Membership:** Jamestown Speakers Bureau (2007); National Press Club; Association for the Preservation of Virginia Antiquities; Charter Member, General Washington's Council of the 1607 Society; Regent's Circle of Mount Vernon; Jamestown-Yorktown Foundation; Colonial Williamsburg Raleigh Tavern Society **Marquis Who's Who Honors:** Albert Nelson Marquis Lifetime Achievement Award (2017) **To what do you attribute your success:** Mr. Merrell attributes his success to hard work, persistence, and determination. **Why did you become involved in your profession or industry:** After an arm injury forced the end of a promising career with the Cincinnati Reds, Mr. Merrell decided to go into writing. **Hobbies:** Photography **Political Affiliations:** Conservative **Religion:** Protestant **Shipping Address:** 3542 East Street, Route 73, Waynesville, OH, 45068

Donald H. Messinger

Title: Lawyer **Industry:** Law and Legal Services **Company Name:** Thompson Hine LLP **Date of Birth:** 07/01/1943 **Place of Birth:** Lyons **State/Country of Origin:** NY **Parents:** Donald H. Messinger; Thelma (Hubbard) Messinger **Marital Status:** Married **Spouse Name:** Sara L. Stock (6/3/1967) **Children:** Michael David; Robert Stephen; Daniel Mark **Education:** JD, Duke University (1968); BA, Colgate University (1965) **Career:** Partner, Thompson Hine, Cleveland, Ohio (1976-Present); Executive Committee, Thompson Hine, Cleveland, Ohio (1996-2000); Partner-in-Charge, Cleveland Office, Thompson Hine, Cleveland, Ohio (1991-1996); Vice Chairman, Corporate Practice Group, Thompson Hine, Cleveland, Ohio (1989-1992); Associate, Thompson Hine, Cleveland, Ohio (1968-1976) **Career Related:** Board of Directors, Cedar Fair Management Company (1993-2002); Secretary, Lee Wilson Engineering Company, Inc. (1989-1994); Board of Directors, Lee Wilson Engineering Company, Inc. (1989-1994); Secretary, American Steel & Wire Corporation (1986-1993); Board of Directors, American Steel & Wire Corporation (1986-1993) **Civic:** Chairman of the Board, Cleveland Pops Orchestra (2015-Present); Class Vice President, Leadership Cleveland (2007-Present); Advisory Board, Greater Cleveland New Stadium Corporation; Director, Cleveland Pops Orchestra (2006-Present); Court Nisi Prius (1990-Present); Cleveland Leadership Center Corporation (1984-Present); Trustee, Cleveland Hearing and Speech Center (1980-Present); President, Free Medical Clinic of Greater Cleveland, Ohio (2002-2004); President, Cleveland Hearing and Speech Center (1998-2000); Vice President, Free Medical Clinic of Greater Cleveland (1996-2002); Secretary, Business Volunteers Unlimited (1992-2012); Trustee, Business Volunteers Unlimited (1992-2012); Vice President, Cleveland Hearing and Speech Center (1992-1993); Chairman, University for Young Americans (1991-1995); President, University for Young Americans (1986-1988); President, Cleveland Hearing and Speech Center (1986-1988); Vice President, Cleveland Hearing and Speech Center (1984-1986); Executive Board, Boy Scouts of America (1983-1988); Trustee, University for Young Americans (1982-1995); Secretary, University for Young Americans (1982-1986); Vice President, Free Medical Clinic of Greater Cleveland (1982-1986); Trustee, Community Information Volunteer Action Center (1981-1988); President, Community Information Volunteer Action Center (1981-1984); Director, Colgate University Alumni Corp. (1979-1983); Trustee, Free Medical Clinic of Greater Cleveland (1970-2017); Secretary, Buckeye Area Development Corp. (1970-1990); Secretary, Free Medical Clinic of Greater Cleveland (1970-1982) **Awards:** Daniel D. Dauby Award, Cleveland Hearing & Speech Center (2017); Lawyer of the Year, Securities/Capital Markets Law (2017); Lawyer of the Year, Securities/Capital Markets Law (2015); Malvin E. Bank Client Service Award (2011); Jurisprudence Award, ORT America (2011); Daniel D. Dauby Award, Cleveland Hearing & Speech Center (2007); Client Service All Star, BTI (2006); Community Service Award, Federation for Community Planning (1981-1982); One of the Outstanding Young Citizens of Greater Cleveland (1971-1975); One of the Best Lawyers in America; Ohio Super Lawyers; Legal 500 **Membership:** Chairman, Securities Law Institute, Cleveland Metropolitan Bar Association (1983); Trustee, Cleveland Metropolitan Bar Association (1975-1979); ABA; Ohio State Bar Association **Bar Admissions:** Ohio (1968) **Marquis Who's Who Honors:** Albert Nelson Marquis Lifetime Achievement Award (2017); Distinguished Humanitarian (2017) **Shipping Address:** 127 Public Square, Suite 3900, Cleveland, OH, 44114

Marilyn Baird Mets

Title: Division Head **Industry:** Medicine & Health Care **Company Name:** Ann & Robert H. Lurie Children's Hospital of Chicago **Date of Birth:** 01/01/1948 **Place of Birth:** Providence **State:** RI **Parents:** Russell James Baird; Beatrice (Wentworth) Baird **Marital Status:** Married **Spouse Name:** Laurens Jan Mets, PhD (6/12/1971) **Children:** Rebecca Mets-Halgrimson, MD; David Mets, PhD; Catherine Mets Darbyshire, RN **Education:** Fellow in Ophthalmic Genetics, Irene Maumenee, MD (1980-1981); Fellow in Ophthalmology and Strabismus, Marshall Parks, MD (1980-1981); Pediatric Resident, Cleveland Clinic (1977-1980); Intern, Cleveland Clinic (1977); MD, George Washington University (1976); MS, School of Public Health, Harvard University (1972); BA, Wheaton College (1969) **Certifications:** Diplomate, American Board of Ophthalmology; Licensed to Practice Medicine, State of Illinois **Career:** Lillian Sherman Cowen Reiger and Harold L.S. Cowen Reiger Research Professor in Pediatric Ophthalmology, Northwestern University (2011-Present); Head, Division of Ophthalmology, Lurie Childrens' Hospital, Chicago, IL (2000-Present); Director, Ophthalmology Laboratory, Lurie Children's Hospital, Chicago, IL (1993-Present); Director, Retinal Electrophysiology Laboratory, Department of Ophthalmology, Northwestern University (1990-Present); Professor, Department of Ophthalmology, Northwestern University (1990-Present); Clinician-investigator, Northwestern University (1990-Present); Associate Professor of Ophthalmology and Visual Science, University of Chicago (1989-1990); Seeberger Fellow, University of Chicago (1987-1990); Assistant Professor of Ophthalmology and Pediatrics, University of Chicago (1983-1989); Wheaton Eye Clinic, Wheaton, IL (1981-1983); Instructor in Ophthalmology and Pediatrics, Rush Medical College, Rush University, Chicago, IL (1981-1983) **Career Related:** Lecturer, Rush Presbyterian-St Luke's, Rush University Medical Center, Chicago, IL (1993-Present); Staff Ophthalmologist, NorthShore University HealthSystem-Glenbrook Hospital, NorthShore University HealthSystem, Glenview, IL (1993-Present); Associate Professor, Ann & Robert H. Lurie Children's Hospital of Chicago (1990-Present); Director, Retinal Physiological Laboratory, Feinberg School of Medicine, Northwestern University (1990-Present); Adviser, Spark Pediatric Ophthalmologist Advisory Board (2017); Staff Ophthalmologist, Michael Reese Hospital, Chicago, IL (1994-1997) **Civic:** Professional Advisory Council, The Chicago Lighthouse for the Blind (2004-Present); Board of Directors, Illinois Society for the Prevention of Blindness, Chicago, IL (2004-Present); Volunteer, Surgical Missions, Healing the Children Foundation (2003); Board of Directors, Illinois Society for the Prevention of Blindness, Chicago, IL (1986-1994) **Creative Works:** Editorial Board Member, "Pediatric Ophthalmology" (1996-1997); Editor-in-Chief, "Focal Points," American Academy of Ophthalmology (1993-1997); Editorial Board Member, Pediatric Section, "Focal Points," American Academy of Ophthalmology (1987-1997); Editorial Board Member, "Investigative Ophthalmology and Visual Science" (1987-1990); Ad Hoc Reviewer, Professional Journals; **Awards:** Honoree, Exceptional Women in Medicine, Castle Connolly Medical Ltd. (2017); Nominee, Americas Best Physicians (2016); Honoree, Americas Most Honored Professionals (2016); Honoree, Top Doctor, Chicago Magazine (2016); Best Doctors in America, U.S. News and World Report (2013); Honoree, Sutton Who's Who in Healthcare (2011-2013); America's Top Doctors, Castle Connolly Medical Ltd. (2008-2017); Honoree, Top Doctor, Chicago Magazine (2006-2013); Honoree, Best Doctors in America (2005-2012); The David S. Friendly Honor Award, Costenbader Society (2005); Honoree, Women of Vision, Prevent Blindness America (2003); Senior Achievement Award, American Academy of Ophthalmology (2003); Honoree, America's Top Ophthalmologists, Consumer's Research of America (2002-2003); Featured Listee, Guide to Top Doctors (2002); Honor Award, AAPOS (1998); Honoree, First Distinguished Alumni Lecturer, Cleveland Clinic (1997) **Membership:** Chair, Finance Committee, Childrens' Surgical Foundation (2015-Present); Emeritus Director, American Board of Ophthalmology (2012-Present); Illinois Registered Agent, Pan American Association of Ophthalmology (2012-Present); Associate, American Ophthalmological Society (1999-Present); Secretary-Treasurer, AAAPOS (1998-Present); American Orthoptic Council (2016-2018); Past President, American Ophthalmological Society (2016); Chair, Patient Safety Cross Committee, American Board of Medical Specialties (2011-2012); Chair, Committee on Oversight and Monitoring of Maintenance of Certification, American Board of Medical Specialties (2010-2012); Council Chair, American Ophthalmology Society (2010); Chair, Finance Committee, American Board of Ophthalmology (2009-2012); Nominating/Governing Committee, American Board of Ophthalmology (2008-2012); Treasurer, Childrens' Surgical Foundation (2007-2015); Board of Directors, Childrens' Surgical Foundation (2007-2012) **Business Address:** 225 E Chicago Avenue, Box 70, Chicago, IL, 60611 **Shipping Address:** 417 N Canal Street, Chicago, IL, 60654

Gerald Meyer

Title: Chemistry Professor **Industry:** Education/Educational Services **Date of Birth:** 11/02/1919 **Place of Birth:** Albuquerque **State/:** NM **Parents:** Leopold Meyer; Beatrice (Ilfeld) Meyer **Marital Status:** Single **Spouse Name:** Betty F. Knobloch (7/4/1941, Deceased) **Children:** Lee Gordon; Terry Gene; David Gary **Education:** PhD, The University of New Mexico (1950); MS, Carnegie Mellon University (1942); BS in Chemistry, Carnegie Mellon University (1940) **Career:** Professor Emeritus, University of Wyoming (1990-Present); Dean Emeritus, University of Wyoming (1990-Present); Professor of Chemistry, University of Wyoming (1980-1990); Professor of Energy, University of Wyoming (1980-1990); Vice President for Research, University of Wyoming (1975-1980); Vice President for Research, University of Wyoming (1975-1980); Professor, University of Wyoming (1963-1975); Dean, College of Arts and Sciences, University of Wyoming (1963-1975); Professor of Chemistry, New Mexico Highlands University (1953-1963); Graduate Dean, New Mexico Highlands University (1953-1963); Director, Research Division, New Mexico Highlands University (1953-1963; Professor of Chemistry, University of Albuquerque (1950-1953); Head, Department of Science, University of Albuquerque (1950-1953); Instructor, The University of New Mexico (1947-1950); Chemist, New Mexico Technology (1945-1947) **Career Related:** President, Coal Technology Corporation (1990-Present); Managing Partner, Advanced Coal to Chemicals Technologies, LLC (1990-Present); Senior Negotiator, Department of Energy (1984-1985); Senior Consultant, Diamond Shamrock (1980-1981); Science Adviser, State of Wyoming (1967-1980); Member, Industrial Sitting Committee, State of Wyoming (1968-1972); Fulbright Exchange Professor, Chile (1959-1960); Consultant, Exxon Mobil Corporation; Consultant, LANS, LLC; Consultant, U.S. Department of the Interior **Civic:** Board Member, Laramie Regional Airport (1989-2014); Vice Mayor, Laramie, Wyoming (1998-2001); City Council, Laramie, Wyoming (1997-2001); Board Chair, Laramie Regional Airport (1992-1997); Treasurer, Board, Laramie Regional Airport (1989-1992); President Laramie Chamber of Commerce (1984); Board Member, Laramie Plains Museum; Board Member, Wyoming Territorial Prison State Historic Site; Arts & Science College Visitors, University of Wyoming **Military Service:** U.S. Navy (1943-1945); Lieutenant Commander, U.S. Naval Reserve **Creative Works:** Co-author, "Industrial Research & Development Management" (1982); Co-author, "Legal Rights of Chemists and Engineers" (1977); Co-author, "Chemistry-Survey of Principles" (1963); Contributor, Articles, Professional Journals; Patentee in Field **Awards:** Distinguished Faculty Award, University of Wyoming (2009); Honorable Recognition, New Mexico Highlands University (2009); Volunteer Service Award, Mountain Region, American Chemical Society (2008); Volunteer Service Award, American Chemical Society (2006); Research Fellowship, The University of New Mexico (1948-1950); Distinguished Service Award, U.S. Jaycees **Membership:** Chairman, Rocky Mountain Region, American Chemical Society (2009-Present); Chairman, Wyoming Section, American Chemical Society (2002); Chairman, Rocky Mountain Region, American Chemical Society (2000); Chairman, Wyoming Section, American Chemical Society (1997); Chairman, American Institute of Chemists (1994-1995); President, American Institute of Chemists (1992-1993); Councilor, American Chemical Society (1962-1990); Chairman, Rocky Mountain Region, American Chemical Society (1972-1988); Secretary-treasurer, Council of Colleges of Arts & Sciences (1972-1975); Chairman, Association of Western Universities (1972-1974); Director, Washington Office, Council of Colleges of Arts & Sciences (1973); President, Council of Colleges of Arts & Sciences (1971); Fellow, American College of Surgeons; Fellow, American Association for the Advancement of Science; Senior, American Institute of Chemical Engineers; American International College; Biophysical Society **Hobbies:** Art **Shipping Address:** 1058 Colina Drive, Laramie, WY, 82072

Wayne M. Meyers

Title: Microbiologist (Retired), Physician (Retired) **Industry:** Sciences **Date of Birth:** 08/28/1924 **Place of Birth:** Huntingdon **State:** PA **Parents:** John William Meyers; Carrie Venca (Weaver) Meyers **Marital Status:** Married **Spouse Name:** Esther Louise Kleinschmidt (8/26/1953) **Children:** Amy; George; Daniel; Sara **Education:** Honorary DSc, Juniata College, Huntingdon, PA (1986); Intern, Conemaugh Valley Memorial Hospital, Johnstown, PA (1959-1960); MD, Baylor College of Medicine (1959); PhD in Medical Microbiology, University of Wisconsin (1955); MS in Medical Microbiology, University of Wisconsin (1953); Diploma, Moody Bible Institute (1950); BS in Chemistry, Juniata College (1947) **Career:** Visiting Scientist, Armed Forces Institute of Pathology, Washington, DC (2005-2011); Assistant to Registrar, Leprosy Registry, Armed Forces Institute of Pathology, Washington, DC (2005-2011); Visiting Scientist, American Red Cross (2005-2011); Chief, Myco-bacteriology Division, Armed Forces Institute of Pathology, Washington, DC (1989-2005); Research Affiliate, Tulane University (1981-2005); Registrar, Leprosy Registry, Armed Forces Institute of Pathology, Washington, DC (1975-2005); Consultant, Leonard Wood Memorial (1990-2004); Science Director, Leonard Wood Memorial (1987-1990); Chief, Microbiology Division, Armed Forces Institute of Pathology, Washington, DC (1975-1989); Science Consultant Director, Leonard Wood Memorial (1985-1987); Member, Science Advisory Board, Leonard Wood Memorial (1981-1985); Member, Leprosy Panel, United States-Japan Cooperative Medical Science Program (1976-1983); Professor of Pathology, School of Medicine, University of Hawaii, Honolulu, HI (1973-1975); Missionary Physician, American Leprosy Missions, Congo-Zaire, Burundi (1961-1973); Staff Physician, Berrien General Hospital (1960-1961); Instructor, Baylor College of Medicine (1955-1959) **Career Related:** Member, Board of Directors, Leonard Wood Memorial; Member, Board of Directors, Gorgas Memorial Institute of Tropical and Preventive Medicine **Civic:** Corporate Board of Directors, Damien-Dutton Society Leprosy Aid, Inc. (1996-Present); Member, Board of References, American Leprosy Missions (1988-Present); Member, Buruli Ulcer Task Force, World Health Organization (1998-2004); Program Consultant to Board of Directors, American Leprosy Missions (1988-2003); Advisory Board, Damien-Dutton Society Leprosy Aid, Inc. (1983-1996); Chairman, Gillis W. Long Hansen's Disease Center, Carville, LA (1985-1992); Member, Hansen's Disease Research Advisory Committee, Gillis W. Long Hansen's Disease Center, Carville, LA (1985-1992); Chairman, Board of Directors, American Leprosy Missions (1985-1988); Member, Advisory Board, American Leprosy Missions (1979-1988) **Military Service:** U.S. Army (1944-1946) **Creative Works:** Board of Directors, Journal of Leprosy (1978-1993); Contributor, Book Chapters; Contributor, Articles, Professional Journals **Awards:** Life Achievement Award, Alumni Association, Baylor College of Medicine (2009); Research Grantee, World Health Organization (1978-1987); Fellow, Allergy Foundation of America (1957-1958) **Membership:** President, Binford-Dammin Society of Infectious Disease Pathologists (1995-1996); President, International Leprosy Association (1988-1993); Secretary-Treasurer, Binford-Dammin Society of Infectious Disease Pathologists (1988-1991); Councillor, International Leprosy Association (1978-1988); Sigma Xi; International Society of Travel Medicine; American Society of Microbiology; American Society of Tropical Medicine and Hygiene; International Society of Tropical Dermatology; International Academy Pathology **Achievements:** Testing **Hobbies:** Photography; Genealogy **Political Affiliations:** Independent **Religion:** Protestant **Business Address:** 6825 16th St NW #54, Washington, DC, 20306 **Shipping Address:** 12202 Brittany Pl, Laurel, MD, 20708

Anthony Wayne Middleton Jr.

Title: Urologist, Educator **Industry:** Medicine & Health Care **Company Name:** The University of Utah **Date of Birth:** 05/06/1939 **Place of Birth:** Salt Lake City **State:** UT **Parents:** Anthony Wayne Middleton; Dolores Caravena (Lowry) Middleton **Marital Status:** Married **Spouse Name:** Carol Samuelson (10/23/1970) **Children:** Anthony Wayne; Suzanne; Kathryn; Jane; Michelle **Education:** Resident in Urology, Massachusetts General Hospital, The General Hospital Corporation, Boston, MA (1970-1974); Intern, University of Utah Hospital, University of Utah Health, Salt Lake City, UT (1966-1967); MD, Cornell University (1966); BS, The University of Utah (1963) **Certifications:** Medical License, State of Utah (1969-Present); Certified, American Board of Urology **Career:** Physician, The Church of Jesus Christ of Latter-day Saints, Intellectual Reserve, Inc. (2008-Present); President, Emeritus Alumnus Board, The University of Utah (2014-2015); Member, Emeritus Alumnus Board, The University of Utah (2012-2014); Practice in Urology, Middleton Urological Associates, Salt Lake City, UT (1974-2005) **Career Related:** Staff Member, Division of Urology, School of Medicine, The University of Utah (2009-Present); Member, Admissions Committee, School of Medicine, The University of Utah (2009-Present); Staff Member, Mission Medical, The Church of Jesus Christ of Latter-day Saints, Intellectual Reserve, Inc. (2008-Present); Associate Clinical Professor of Surgery, School of Medicine, The University of Utah (1977-Present); Delegate, Salt Lake County GOP Convention (2012-2013); Vice Chairman, Board of Governors, Utah Medical Self-Insured Association (1996-2005); Affiliate, Utah Division Rocky Mountain Prostate (2001-2004); Staff Member, Intercontinental Health Care (1974-2005); Medical Director, Utah-Idaho Lithotripsy (2001-2003); Affiliate, Uromed, Prostate Microwave Co. (1999-2000); Chairman, Medical Advisory Board, UroQuest Medical Corp. (1996-1999); Chairman, Utah Medical Self-Insured Association (1985-1987); Chairman, Division of Urology Salt Lake Regional Medical Center (1984-1986) **Civic:** Admissions Committee, School of Medicine, The University of Utah (2010-Present); Utah Symphony Honorary Board Member, Utah Symphony (2009-Present); Member, Collegium Aesculapium of The Church of Jesus Christ of Latter-day Saints, Intellectual Reserve, Inc. (2008-Present); Group Leader, The Church of Jesus Christ of Latter-day Saints, Intellectual Reserve, Inc. (2011-2018); President-elect, Collegium Aesculapium (2011-2012); Chapter Advisor, School of Medicine, The University Utah (2009); Mission President, Canada Vancouver Mission (2005-2008); President, Collegium Aesculapium of The Church of Jesus Christ of Latter-day Saints, Intellectual Reserve, Inc. (2004-2005); President, Timpanogos Club (2002-2005); Delegate, Utah State Republican Convention (2000-2001); Member, Board of Directors, Primary Children's Hospital Foundation (1989-1996); Member, Board of Directors, Utah Symphony (1985-2005); High Priest, The Church of Jesus Christ of Latter-day Saints, Intellectual Reserve, Inc. (1983-2018); Chairman, Utah Physicians for Reagan (1983-1984); Staff President, Primary Children's Hospital, Intermountain Healthcare (1982) **Military Service:** Captain, US Air Force (1968-1970) **Creative Works:** Co-Author, "Vancouver Mission Memories, 2005-2008" (2017); Editor: AACU-FAX (1992-2005); Associate Editor, Millennial Star Brit. Latter Day Saints Magazine (1960-1961) **Awards:** Recipient, Distinguished Service Award, American Urologic Association (2011); Recipient, Outstanding Service Award, Western Section, American Urological Association, Inc. (2005); Recipient, President's Distinguished Service Award, American Association of Clinical Urologists, Inc. (2000); Recipient, Distinguished Service Award, Utah Medical Association (1993) **Membership:** Beta Rising Reorganization Committee, Beta Theta Pi (2010-2012); Governing Council, American Medical Association (2002-2005); Chairman, Referred Committee I, American Medical Association (2001); President, Western Section, American Urologic Association (2000-2001); Delegate to House of Delegates, American Medical Association (1998-2005); Board of Directors, Utah Medical Association (1998-2005); Chairman, Western Section, Health Policy Committee, American Urologic Association (1990-2002); President-elect, Western Section, Health Policy Committee, American Urologic Association (1999-2000); Alternate Delegate, AMA House of Delegates (1996-1998) National Board Chairman, Urologic Political Action Committee, American Association of Clinical Urologists, Inc. (1992-1998); President, American Association of Clinical Urologists, Inc. (1991-1992); National President-Elect, American Association of Clinical Urologists, Inc. (1990-1991); Alternate Delegate, House of Delegates (1989-1992); Board of Directors, American Association of Clinical Urologists, Inc. (1989-1990); Chairman, Western Section, Socioeconomics Committee, American Urologic Association (1989-1990); President, Utah Medical Association (1987-1988); President, Salt Lake County Medical Association (1984); **Marquis Who's Who Honors:** Albert Nelson Marquis Lifetime Achievement Award (2017) **Political Affiliations:** Republican **Religion:** Mormon **Shipping Address:** 2798 E Chancellor Pl, Salt Lake City, UT, 84108

Martin C. Mihm Jr.

Title: Director of Melanoma **Industry:** Medicine & Health Care **Company Name:** Brigham & Women's Hospital **Date of Birth:** 03/15/1934 **Place of Birth:** Pittsburgh **State:** PA **Parents:** Martin Charles Mihm; Cecilia Matilda (Hepp) Mihm **Education:** Honorary DSc, Duquesne University (2009); Honorary MA, Harvard University (1990); MD, School of Medicine, University of Pittsburgh (1961); Coursework in Premedical Sciences, Duquesne University (1956-1957); Coursework, School of Law, University of Pittsburgh (1955-1956); AB, Duquesne University, Summa Cum Laude (1955) **Certifications:** Puerto Rico Registration (2005); Tennessee License (1999); Diplomate in Dermapathology, ABD (1975); Diplomate, The American Board of Pathology (1974); New York License Registration (1971); Certified, ABD (1969); Diplomate, ABD (1969); Massachusetts License Registration (1964); Pennsylvania License Registration (1962); California License Registration (1962) **Career:** Professor of Dermatology, Harvard University (2014-Present); Honorary Clinical Professor of Pathology, Albany Medical Center (2013-Present); Active Staff, Massachusetts Eye and Ear (2010-Present); Director of Melanoma Program, Brigham and Women's Hospital (2010-Present); Associate Director of Melanoma Program, Dana Farber Brigham and Women's Cancer Center, Brigham and Women's Hospital (2010-Present); Associate Physician in Dermatology, Brigham and Women's Hospital (2005-Present); Dermatology Staff Member, Beth Israel Deaconess Medical Center (2001-Present); Adjunct Professor of Pathology, Microbiology & Immunology, Vanderbilt University School of Medicine (1989-Present); Clinical Professor of Dermatology, Harvard University (2012-2014); Adjunct Professor of Dermatology, School of Medicine, University of Puerto Rico (2006-2011); Clinical Professor of Pathology and Dermatology, Harvard University (2004-2012); Professor, Department of Otolaryngology, Children's Hospital, School of Medical Sciences (2002-2003); Professor of Pathology, Jefferson Medical School (2000-2006); Clinical Professor of Pathology, Albany Medical Center (1996-2013); Clinical Professor of Pathology, Harvard Medical School (1995-2004); Director, Division of Dermatology and Dermatopathology, Albany Medical Center (1993-1996); Professor of Pathology and Laboratory Medicine, Albany Medical Center (1993-1996); Chief, Dermatopathology Division, Harvard Medical School (1988-1993); Chief, Dermatopathology Unit, Harvard Medical School (1982-1987); Professor of Pathology, Harvard Medical School (1980-1993); Pathologist, Massachusetts General Hospital, The General Hospital Corporation (1980-1990); Associate Staff, Brigham and Women's Hospital (1975-1993); Associate Professor of Pathology, Harvard Medical School (1975-1980); Associate Pathologist, Massachusetts General Hospital, The General Hospital Corporation (1975-1980); Chief, Dermatopathology Unit, Massachusetts General Hospital, The General Hospital Corporation (1974-1993); Assistant Professor of Pathology, Harvard Medical School (1972-1975) **Career Related:** Professor of Otolaryngology, University of Arkansas for Medical Sciences (2002-Present); Adjunct Professor, Sidney Kimmel Medical College, Thomas Jefferson University (2000-Present); Senior Dermatopathologist, Massachusetts General Hospital, The General Hospital Corporation (1996-Present); Pathologist, Massachusetts General Hospital, The General Hospital Corporation (1996-Present); Clinical Professor of Pathology, Harvard Medical School (1996-Present); Chairman, Pathology Standing Committee (1991-Present); Fellow, College of American Pathologists (1991-Present); Adjunct Professor of Pathology, Vanderbilt University (1989-Present); Fellow, Royal Academy of Medicine in Ireland (1989-Present); First American Co-Director, Melanoma Pathology Group, European Organization of the Research and Treatment of Cancer (2008); Chief Senior Administrator, Wellman Laboratories, Massachusetts General Hospital, The General Hospital Corporation (1985-1993); Chairman of Pathology Committee, Intergroup Melanoma Study (1983-1988); Pathologist, Malignant Melanoma Cooperative Group (1972-1977) **Civic:** Board, Boston Symphony Orchestra (2001-Present); Chairman, Harvard Dermatopathology Residency Selection Committee, Harvard Medical School (1977-Present) **Creative Works:** Associate Editor, Journal of Cutaneous Pathology, John Wiley & Sons, Inc. (1985-Present) **Awards:** Master of Immunology Title, American Association for Cancer Research (2015); Research Director of the Year, Vascular Birthmarks Foundation (2014); Certificate of Appreciation, ILDS (2014); Founder, Martin C. Mihm, Jr. Scholarship in Recognition for Outstanding Work in the Research of Vascular Birthmarks (2013) **Membership:** Commission on Melanoma and Other Skin Diseases, American Academy of Dermatology (1993-Present); Cancer Center, Massachusetts General Hospital, The General Hospital Corporation (1985-Present) **Political Affiliations:** Independent **Religion:** Roman Catholic **Shipping Address:** 41 Avenue Louis Pasteur, Room 317, Boston, MA, 02115

George Eugene Mikhailovsky, PhD

Title: Principal Systems Analyst **Industry:** Information Technology and Services **Company Name:** CALIBRE **Date of Birth:** 01/03/1945 **Place of Birth:** Moscow **Country of Origin:** Russia **Parents:** Eugene Mikhailovsky; Larissa Mikhailovsky **Marital Status:** Married **Spouse Name:** Alla **Children:** Yaroslav; Maria; Anton; Katerina **Education:** DSc, P.P. Shirshov Institute of Oceanology, USSR Academy of Science (1983); PhD in Biophysics, Lomonosov Moscow State University (1969); MS in Biophysics and Physiology, Lomonosov Moscow State University (1966) **Certifications:** Certified Service-Oriented Architecture Associate (2008); Certified Professional Oracle 10g Administrator (2004); Certified Professional Oracle 9i Administrator (2003); Certified Project Manager (2003); Certified Oracle 8i Database Administrator (2002); Certified Oracle 8 Database Administrator (2001); Certified Master PowerBuilder Programmer (1999) **Career:** President, Chief Executive Officer, Global Mind Share, Norfolk, VA (2012-Present); Editor-in-chief, Journal of Evolutionary Science(2018-Present); Principal Systems Analyst, CALIBRE, Alexandria, VA (1998-Present); Professor, Software Quality Learning, Inc., Rockville, MD (1997-1999); Senior Programmer, ISSI, Silver Spring, MD (1996-1998); Professor, System Ecology Department, People's Friendship University of Russia, Moscow, Russia (1992-1995); Principal Scientist, P.P. Shirshov Institute of Oceanology, Russian Academy of Sciences, Moscow, Russia (1981-1995); Professor, Irkutsk State University, Russia (1978-1981); Senior Scientist, Lomonosov Moscow State University (1969-1978); Junior Scientist, Lomonosov Moscow State University (1969-1978); Laboratory Assistant, Lomonosov Moscow State University (1969-1978) **Creative Works:** Author, "Life and Its Organization in the Pelagial of the World Ocean" (1992); Editor, "A View of the Biosphere" by R.Margalef (1992); Author, "Biological Monitoring in Coastal Waters of the White Sea" (1990); Author, "Description and Assessment of Plankton Communities' Condition" (1988); Author, "Elements of Biological Thermodynamics," Irkutsk State University Publishers; Co-Author, Chapter, "HUBE: Habitability of the Universe before Earth"; Contributor, 80 Articles, Professional Journals **Awards:** Certificate of Achievement, CALIBRE (2014); Certificate of Excellence, Washington Metropolitan Area Transit Authority (2006); Named to 5000 Outstanding Scientists of Russia, The Government of the Russian Federation (1995) **Membership:** Moderator from PowerBuilder.NET/PFC Developer's Group (2008); Gold Benefits Member, International Sybase User Group (1999) **Hobbies:** Sailing **Shipping Address:** 878 W Ocean View Ave, Norfolk, VA, 23503 **Website:** https://www.linkedin.com/in/george-mikhailovsky-b3a5a885/

George H. Miley, PhD

Title: Engineering Educator, Researcher **Industry:** Education/Educational Services **Company Name:** University of Illinois **Date of Birth:** 08/06/1933 **Place of Birth:** Shreveport **State/Country of Origin:** LA **Parents:** George Hunter Miley; Norma Angeline (Dowling) Miley **Marital Status:** Married **Spouse Name:** Elizabeth Burroughs (11/22/1958) **Children:** Susan Miley-Hibbs; Hunter Robert **Education:** PhD in Chemical and Nuclear Engineering, University of Michigan (1959); MS, University of Michigan (1956); BSChemE, Carnegie Mellon University (1955) **Career:** Emeritus Professor, University of Illinois (2010-Present); President, NPL Associates Inc. (1994-Present); Director of Research, NPL Associates Inc. (1994-Present); Director of the Fusion Studies Laboratory, University of Illinois (1976-Present); Professor, University of Illinois (1967-Present); Chief Scientist, Lattice Energy, LLC (2001-2003); Director of Research, Rockford Technology Associates Inc. (1990-1994); Chairman, Nuclear Engineering Program, University of Illinois (1975-1986); Faculty Member, University of Illinois (1961-2010); Nuclear Engineer, Knolls Atomic Power Laboratory, General Electric Company, Schenectady, NY (1959-1961) **Career Related:** Manager, Lenuco LLC (2013); Fellow, Japanese Society for the Promotion of Science (1994); Chairman, Technology Advisory Committee, Illinois Low Level Radioactive Waste Site (1990-1996); Chairman, Committee on Industrial Uses of Radiation, Illinois Department of Nuclear Safety (1989-2000); Visiting Professor, Imperial College of London (1987); Visiting Professor, University of New South Wales (1986); Fellow, The Solomon R. Guggenheim Foundation (1985-1986); Associate Fellow, Center for Advanced Studies, University of Illinois (1985-1986); Fellow, North Atlantic Treaty Organization (1975-1976); Visiting Professor, Cornell University (1969-1970); Visiting Professor, University of Colorado (1967); Fellow, IEEE; Fellow, ANS; Fellow, APS; Associate Fellow, AIAA **Civic:** U.S. Army Corps of Engineers (1960) **Creative Works:** Co-Author, "Lasers with Nuclear Pumping," Springer Press (2015); Co-Author, "Inertial Electrostatic Confinement Fusion," Springer Press (2014); Author, "Life at the Center of the Energy Crisis: A Technologist's Search for a Black Swan," World Scientific Publishing Company (2013); Co-Author, "Edward Teller Lectures: Lasers and Inertial Fusion Energy," Imperial College Press (2005); Co-Author, "Principles of Fusion Energy: An Introduction to Fusion Energy for Students of Science and Engineering," World Scientific Publishing Company (2000); U.S. Editor, Journal of Plasma Physics (1995-2003); Editor-in-Chief, Laser and Particle Beams (1991-2002); Managing Editor, Laser and Particle Beams (1987-1991); Associate Editor, Laser and Particle Beams (1982-1986); Editor, Journal of Fusion Technology (1980-2001); Author, "Direct Conversion of Nuclear Radiation Energy," American Nuclear Society (1971); Author, "Fusion Energy Conversion," American Nuclear Society **Awards:** Seaborg Medal, American Nuclear Society (2016); Integrity in Research Award (2006); Preparata Medal, College of Computer, Mathematical & Natural Sciences (2006); Fusion, Engineering and Science Award, IEEE (2004); Radiation Science and Technology Award, American Nuclear Society (2004); Recognition Award, National Aeronautics and Space Administration (2003); Scientist of the Year Award, The Institute For New Energy (1996); Edward Teller Medal (1995); Outstanding Achievement Award, Fusion Energy Division, American Nuclear Society (1992); Engineering Education Leadership Award, Halliburton (1990); Distinguished Service Award, American Nuclear Society (1980); Technology-Research Award, Western Electric Export Corporation (1977); Senior Science Outstanding Teacher Award, American Society for Engineering Education (1973) **Membership:** Illinois Radiation Protection Board (1988-Present); Air Force Studies Board (1990-1994); Director, American Nuclear Society (1980-1983); Chairman, Nuclear Division, American Society for Engineering Education (1975-1976); President, University of Illinois Chapter, American Society for Engineering Education (1973-1974); Chairman, Energy Conversion Committee, American Society for Engineering Education (1967-1970); American Physical Society; Associate, American Institute of Aeronautics and Astronautics; Sigma Xi; Tau Beta Pi **Marquis Who's Who Honors:** Albert Nelson Marquis Lifetime Achievement Award (2017) **Hobbies:** Tennis; Hiking **Religion:** Presbyterian **Shipping Address:** 104 S Wright Street, Room 216, Talbot Lab, Urbana, IL, 61801

Thomas Herrick Milhorat

Title: Neurosurgeon **Industry:** Medicine & Health Care **Company Name:** American Association of Neurological Surgeons **Date of Birth:** 04/05/1936 **Place of Birth:** New York **State:** NY **Parents:** Ade Thomas Milhorat; Edith Caulkins (Herrick) Milhorat **Marital Status:** Married **Spouse Name:** Edith Mostile (1961) **Children:** John Thomas; Robert Herrick **Education:** Intern, New York-Presbyterian Hospital, Weill Cornell Medical Center (1961-1963); MD, Cornell University (1961); BA, Cornell University (1957) **Career:** Neuroscience Scholar in Residence, Feinstein Institute for Medical Research, Northwell Health (2009-Present); Emeritus Professor of Neurosurgery, Hofstra Northwell School of Medicine at Hofstra University (2009-Present); Emeritus Chairman, Department of Neurosurgery, North Shore-LIJ Health System (Now Northwell Health) (2009-Present); Founder, Harvey Cushing Institutes of Neuroscience, North Shore-LIJ Health System (Now Northwell Health) (2001-Present); Director, Harvey Cushing Institutes of Neuroscience, North Shore-LIJ Health System (Now Northwell Health) (2001-Present); Founder, Chiari Institute of the Neuroscience Institute, North Shore University Hospital, Northwell Health (2001-Present); Director, Chiari Institute of the Neuroscience Institute, North Shore University Hospital, Northwell Health (2001-Present); Founding Chairman, Department of Neurosurgery, North Shore-LIJ Health System (Now Northwell Health) (2001-Present); Professor of Neurological Surgery, NYU School of Medicine (2002-2007); Professor of Neurological Surgery, Health Science Center, SUNY Downstate Medical Center, College of Medicine, Brooklyn, NY (1982-2001); Department Chairman, Health Science Center, SUNY Downstate Medical Center, College of Medicine, Brooklyn, NY (1982-2001); Founder, Department of Neurosurgery, Children's National Health System, Washington, DC (1971-1981); Chairman, Department of Neurosurgery, Children's National Health System, Washington, DC (1971-1981); Professor of Neurological Surgery, School of Medicine & Health Sciences, George Washington University, Washington, DC (1974-1981); Professor of Child Health and Development, School of Medicine & Health Sciences, George Washington University, Washington, DC (1974-1981); Associate Professor of Neurological Surgery, School of Medicine & Health Sciences, George Washington University, Washington, DC (1971-1974); Associate Professor of Child Health and Development, School of Medicine & Health Sciences, George Washington University, Washington, DC (1971-1974); Assistant Neurosurgeon, NIH, New York-Presbyterian Hospital, Weill Cornell Medical Center (1968-1971); Chief Resident in Neurosurgery, New York-Presbyterian Hospital, Weill Cornell Medical Center (1965-1968); Assistant Resident, New York-Presbyterian Hospital, Weill Cornell Medical Center (1965-1968) **Career Related:** Fellow, American Association of Neurological Surgeons (1972-Present); Director, Harvey Cushing Institutes of Neuroscience, North Shore-LIJ Health System (Now Northwell Health), NY (2001-2009); Examiner, American Board of Neurological Surgery (1990-1994); Regional Chairman of Neurological Surgery, Long Island College Hospital (1986-2001); Program Director, Neurosurgery Research Training Program (1982-2001); Neurosurgeon-in-Chief, Kings County Hospital Center (1982-2001); National Council of Scientists, National Institutes of Health (1969-1982) **Military Service:** Lieutenant Commander, U.S. Public Health Service (1963-1965) **Creative Works:** Editorial Board, "Neurosurgical Focus: Syringomyelia" (2000-Present); Editorial Board, Neurosurgery (1997-Present); Author, "Melia in Foreverland" (2017); Author, "The Devil's Dance" (2016); Author, "Cerebrospinal Fluid and The Brain Edemas" (1987); Co-Author, "Cranial Computed Tomography in Infancy and Childhood" (1981); Author, "Pediatric Neurosurgery" (1978); Author, "Hydrocephalus and the Cerebrospinal Fluid" (1972) **Awards:** Neurosurgery and Neuroscience Man of the Year, American Biographical Institute (2012); White House Recognition Lifetime Achievement Award (2008); Arthur A. Kaplan Award for Excellence in Neurosurgery (1999); E. Jefferson Browder Award for Excellence in Neurosurgery (1996); Robert H. Pudenz Award for Excellence in Cerebrospinal Fluid Physiology (1994); Best Paper Award, Annual Combined Meeting, The New York Academy of Medicine/ New York State Neurosurgical Society (1965); Charles L. Horn Prize for Leadership, Weill Cornell Medical College (1961) **Membership:** Chairman, Medical Advisory Board, American Syringomyelia & Chiari Alliance Project (1996-2007); Board of Directors, American Syringomyelia & Chiari Alliance Project (1996-2007); President, Brooklyn Neurologic Society (1988-1995); President, New York State Neurosurgical Society (1988-1990); American Association for the Advancement of Science; The International Society for Pediatric Neurosurgery; Surgical Section, American Academy of Pediatrics; APS-SPR; The New York Academy of Medicine; Society of Neuroscience; The Society of Neurological Surgeons **Marquis Who's Who Honors:** Albert Nelson Marquis Lifetime Achievement Award (2017) **Shipping Address:** 146 Hickory Kingdom Road, Bedford, NY, 10506

Lynn Millane

Title: Municipal Official **Industry:** Government Administration/Government Relations/Government Services **Date of Birth:** 10/14/1928 **Place of Birth:** Buffalo **State:** NY **Parents:** Robert P. Schermerhorn; Justine A. Schermerhorn **Career:** Supervisor, Amherst Town Board (1996); Chairperson, Aging Services, Advisory Committee, New York State Office of the Aging (1995-2005); Deputy Town Supervisor, Amherst Town Board (1990-1996); Council Member, Amherst Town Board, New York (1982-1996); First Women Deputy Supervisor, Amherst Town Board **Career Related:** Commissioner, New York State Ethics Commission (1999-2007); Chair, Advisory Board, New York State Office of Aging (1997-2005); Legislative Liaison, State University of New York Family Violence Clinical School of Law, Buffalo, NY (1997-1998); Advisory Board, New York State Office of Aging (1996-2005); First Records Management Advisory Board, Liaison Ethics Board, Town of Amherst (1994-1996); Liaison, Amherst Chamber of Commerce (1993-1996); Liaison, Ad Hoc Cable TV Committee (1992-1996); Founder, Liaison, First Adult Day Services Advisory Board (1988); President, E.J. Meyer Hospital Junior Board (1962-1964); Speaker in Field **Civic:** Board of Directors, Friendship Foundation Inc. (2015-Present); Chair, Membership Enrollment Committee, Daemen College (2009-Present); Advisory Board, Amherst Symphony Orchestra (2003-Present); Founding Member, Lunch and Issues, Amherst, NY (1981-Present); Emeriti, Board of Trustees, Daemen College (2015); Service to Older Adults Committee (2002-2005); Volunteer, Life Project, Greater Buffalo Chapter, American Red Cross (2002-2005); Daemen College of Trustees (1998-2015); Aging Services, Erie County Industrial Development Agency, Erie County Regional Development Corporation (1996-1997); White House Conference on Aging (1995); Delegate, New York State Governors Conference on Aging (1995); Liaison, Alternate Fuel and Clean Cities Committee (1994-1996); Board of Directors, Operating Board, Millard Fillmore Suburban Hospital (1992-1998); Director, Eighth Judicial District, New York State Association of Large Towns (1989-1991); Board of Overseers, Buffalo Philharmonic Orchestra Society, Inc. (1987-1992); Housing Committee, Network in Aging of Western New York, Inc. (1987-1989); Liaison, Code of Ethics Committee, Amherst Branch, American Red Cross (1987-1989); By-Laws Committee, Amherst Branch, American Red Cross (1984); Co-Associate Chair, Major Gift Division, Capital Campaign, Daemen College (1983-1984); Board of Directors, Amherst Elderly Transportation Corporation (1982-1999); Chair, Senior Concerns Committee, Amherst Branch, American Red Cross (1982-1991); Board of Directors, Amherst Branch, American Red Cross (1982-1991); Liaison, Amherst Town Board (1982-1996); Board of Directors, Education Committee, Network in Aging of Western New York, Inc. (1982-1989); Second Vice President, Longview Protestant Home for Children (1982-1985); Director-at-Large Community Advisory Council, State University of New York, Buffalo (1981-1991); By-Laws Committee, Amherst Branch, American Red Cross (1981); Friends of Baird Hall, State University of New York, Buffalo (1980-1982); First Vice President, Fans for 17 (1980-1982); Secretary, Amherst Senior Citizens Advisory Board (1980-1981); Treasurer, Town and Country Republican Club (1980-1981); Nominating Committee, Federation of Republican Womens Clubs of Erie County (1980); Council Member, Trustee, Buffalo Philharmonic Orchestra Society, Inc. (1979-1987); Longview Protestant Home for Children (1979-1985); Chair, Advisory Board, Buffalo Philharmonic Orchestra (1979-1982); National Music Committee, Womens Association for Symphony Orchestras in America and Canada (1977-1979); Vice President, Buffalo Philharmonic Orchestra Society, Inc. (1976-1978); Womens Committee, Buffalo Philharmonic Orchestra (1976-1978); Vice President of Administration, Buffalo Philharmonic Orchestra (1975-1976); Vice President, Public Affairs, Buffalo Philharmonic Orchestra (1974-1975); Co-Chair, Women United Against Drugs Campaign (1970-1972); Executive Board, Erie County Republican Committee, Womens Executive Council (1969-1971) **Awards:** Zontian of the Year, Zonta (1992) **Membership:** Parliamentarian, Twentieth Century Club, Buffalo, NY (2014-Present); Trustee, Amherst Symphony Orchestra Association (2003-Present); Parliamentarian, Twentieth Century Club, Buffalo, NY (2010-2013); President, Twentieth Century Club, Buffalo, NY (2009-2010); First Vice President, Twentieth Century Club, Buffalo, NY (2008-2009); Board of Directors, Amherst Republican Womens Club (1999); Vice Chair, 50th Annual Committee, Amherst Symphony Orchestra Association (1994-1996); President, Amherst Chapter, Zonta (1986-1988); Nominating Chair, Amherst Symphony Orchestra Association (1985-1986); Board of Directors, Amherst Symphony Orchestra Association (1981-1987); Honorary Member, Pi Lambda Theta; Niagara Connect; League of Women Voters; Communications Division, Women's 20th Century Club **Shipping Address:** 94 Surrey Run, Williamsville, NY, 14221

Alan M. Miller

Title: Writer, Educator, Television Host **Industry:** Writing and Editing **Date of Birth:** 07/24/1934 **Place of Birth:** New York **State:** NY **Parents:** Philip Miller; Sylvia (Lubash) Miller **Marital Status:** Married **Spouse Name:** Sharon A. Tanenbaum (8/29/1996) **Children:** Peter; Stephanie Handlin; Douglas; Holly Harouche (Stepdaughter); Becky Theodoratos (Stepdaughter) **Education:** JD, Syracuse University (1968); LLB, Syracuse University (1958); AB, Syracuse University (1955) **Career:** Principal Attorney Editor, Thomson/West, Eagan, MN (1985-2004); Counsel to Minority, Nassau County Board of Supervisors (1974-1975); Assistant Counsel, Three Joint Legislation Committees, New York State Legislature (1968-1970) **Career Related:** Board Member, Inver Hills Foundation (2005-2011); Humanities Faculty, Inver Hills Community College (2004-2012); Faculty, Cinema Division, Minneapolis College (1999-2015); Faculty, Cinema Division, Hofstra University (1990-1997); Faculty, Cinema Division, Discovery Center (1990-1994); Faculty, Cinema Division, New York Institute of Technology, Old Westbury, NY (1987-1989) **Civic:** Coordinator, Human Rights and Social Justice Seminar (2009); Presenter, Holocaust and Genocide Seminar, Metropolitan State University (2006); Vice-Chairman, Eagan, MN (2003); Vice-Chairman, Minnesota Association of Cable TV Administrators (2002-2003); Chairman, Eagan, MN (2002); Citizens Advocacy Committee, Minnesota Twins (2000-2002); Telecommunications Committee, Eagan, MN (1999-2005); Commissioner, Woodsburgh, NY (1980); Assembly District Leader, New York State Democratic Committee (1965-1976) **Creative Works:** Guest, Radio Host, AM950, Progressive Voice of Minnesota (2005-Present); Host, Producer, TwinsTalk (2003-Present); Host, Producer, Access to Democracy, Cable TV (1999-Present); Author, "Holding Court" (2018); Author, "My Name Was Toby" (2012); Author, "You Can Make A Difference" (2011); Editor, "Beyond the Bar," Thomson West Group (2005); Editor, "Beyond the Bar," Thomson West Group (2000-2002); Writer, Editor, USCAdvantage (1995-1999); Columnist, New York Bowler (1991-1993); Columnist, Single-Minded (1991-1992); Columnist, Nostalgia Magazine (1990-1991); Columnist, Another Viewpoint (1985-1999); Contributor, Articles to Publications Including New York Times, Newsday, Newsday Magazine, Minneapolis Star-Tribune, St. Paul Pioneer Press, Humanistic Judaism; Motion Picture Credit, "Into Temptation"; Columnist, South Shore Record, Woodmere, NY; Producer, Cable TV, "Behind the Game" **Awards:** Century Club Award (2005); Millennium Club Award (2004); Citizens Impact Award, Burnsville/Eagan Telecommunications (2003-2004); IMMY Award (1996-1997); New York Press Association Award (1994); Best Column Award, New York Press Association (1992); Multiple Awards, Coverage of Persian Gulf War from Israel (1991); Bowling Magazine Award (1990-1993); New York Press Association Award (1989); New York Press Association Award (1988) **Membership:** Dakota County Historical Society; The Loft Literary Center **Marquis Who's Who Honors:** Albert Nelson Marquis Lifetime Achievement Award (2017) **Religion:** Jewish **Shipping Address:** 4316 Aries Court, Eagan, MN, 55123

Albert Miller

Title: Director **Industry:** Medicine & Health Care **Company Name:** Mount Sinai Beth Israel **Date of Birth:** 07/28/1936 **Place of Birth:** New York **State:** NY **Parents:** Israel Miller; Mollie Miller **Marital Status:** Married **Spouse Name:** Elaine Grant (6/6/1959) **Children:** Dina; Jeffrey; Neil; Michele **Education:** MD, University of Wisconsin (1959); BA, University of Wisconsin (1955) **Certifications:** Diplomate, American Board of Internal Medicine; Diplomate, American Board of Pulmonary Medicine; Certified Expert in Pneumoconiosis, American College of Radiology; Certified Expert in Pneumoconiosis, National Institute for Occupational Safety and Health **Career:** Clinical Professor of Medicine, Icahn School of Medicine at Mount Sinai (2014-Present); Director of Pulmonary Function Laboratory, Mount Sinai Beth Israel, New York, NY (2009-Present); Clinical Professor of Medicine, Albert Einstein College of Medicine (2011-2014); Professor of Clinical Medicine, New York Medical College (2003-2011); Director, Pulmonary Division, Saint Vincent Catholic Medical Centers, Brooklyn, Queens, NY (1994-2009); Professor of Medicine, Albert Einstein College of Medicine (1994-2003); Clinical Professor of Community Medicine, Icahn School of Medicine at Mount Sinai, New York, NY (1981-1994); Associate Clinical Professor of Community Medicine, Icahn School of Medicine at Mount Sinai, New York, NY (1981-1994); Associate Clinical Professor to Clinical Professor, Medicine, Icahn School of Medicine at Mount Sinai, New York, NY (1981-1994) **Civic:** Board of Trustees, University of Wisconsin Hillel Foundation (2002-2015); Scientific Adviser, Ovarian Cancer Research Foundation **Military Service:** Commander, US Public Health Service (1962-1964) **Creative Works:** Editor, Chief Author, "Pulmonary Function Tests: A Guide for the Student and House Officer" (1987); Editor, Chief Author, "Pulmonary Function Tests in Clinical and Occupational Lung Disease" (1986); Contributor, More than 120 Articles to Professional Journals **Awards:** Named, Outstanding Physician, New York Magazine, New York Media LLC (1998-2012); Listee, Castle Connolly Guide to Best Physicians, Castle Connolly Medical Ltd. (1998-2006); Recipient, Globus Award for Outstanding Article in Mount Sinai Journal of Medicine, Icahn School of Medicine at Mount Sinai (1998) **Membership:** Fellow, American College of Physicians; Fellow, American College of Chest Physicians; American Thoracic Society; American Public Health Association; The Phi Beta Kappa Society; Alpha Omega Alpha Honor Medical Society **To what do you attribute your success:** Dr. Miller attributes his success to his recognition that medicine is a unique profession based on science, yet is primarily about serving people. **Why did you become involved in your profession or industry:** Dr. Miller was inspired to go to medical school by the opportunity afforded to him by the Ford Foundation to attend the University of Wisconsin and then go on to medical school after. **What do you consider to be the highlight of your career:** The highlight of Dr. Miller's career has been working with inspirational leaders within his specialties of pulmonary and occupational medicine. **Where will you be in five years:** In five years, Dr. Miller hopes to still be productively engaged in training and publishing. **Shipping Address:** 179 West Shore Rd, Great Neck, NY, 11024

Dorothy Eloise Miller

Title: Education Educator **Industry:** Education/Educational Services **Company Name:** Harford Community College **Date of Birth:** 04/13/1944 **Place of Birth:** Fort Pierce **State:** FL **Parents:** Robert Foy Wilkes; Aline (Mahon) Wilkes **Education:** EdD, Teachers College, Columbia University (1991); MEd, Bloomsburg University of Pennsylvania (1969); BS in Education, Bloomsburg University of Pennsylvania (1966) **Career:** Assistant Dean, Harford Community College (1969-Present); Professor, Harford Community College (1969-Present); Teacher, Aberdeen High School (1968-1969); Teacher, Central Dauphin East High School (1966-1968) **Career Related:** Member, Workgroups in English, PARCC Assessment (2011-Present); Member, English Alignment Committee, Maryland Higher Education Commission (2002-Present); Adjunct Professor, University of Baltimore (2001-Present); English Composition Committee, Maryland Higher Education Commission (1997-Present); Member, Accreditation Team, Middle States Commission (1995-Present); Owner, Ideas by Design (1995-2010); Member, Statewide Writing Skills Assessment Committee, Maryland Higher Education Commission (1997-2001); Member, Statewide English Standards Committee, Maryland Higher Education Commission (1997-2001); English and Teacher Education Center of Maryland; Chairperson, Statewide Standards for College English Committee **Civic:** Member, People's Advisory Council, Harford County Council, Harford County Government (1994-2003); Member, Maryland International Division, St. Petersburg Sister State Committee (1993-2001); Faculty Member, Advisory Committee, Maryland Higher Education Commission (1993-1996); President, Harlan Square Condominium Unit Owners Association (1990-1996); Education Liaison, AAUW (1982-1992); President, Harlan Square Condominium Unit Owners Association (1982); Crusade Co-Chairperson, American Cancer Society, Inc. (1976-1978); Member, Republican Party Centennial Committee, Harford County Government (1974-1978) **Creative Works:** Editor, "Renewing the American Community Colleges" (1984); Contributor, Articles, Professional Journals **Awards:** Woman of the Year, National Association of Professional Women (2014-2015); Woman of the Year, Continental Who's Who (2004-Present); Woman of the Year, National Association of Professional Women (2004); National Teaching Excellence Award, NISOD (1992) **Membership:** Charter Member, National Museum of Women in the Arts; Modern Language Association; National Association of Professional Women **Marquis Who's Who Honors:** Albert Nelson Marquis Lifetime Achievement Award (2017) **Why did you become involved in your profession or industry:** When she was in graduate school, she took a typing class. Women were taught shorthand typing while the men were taught medicine and law. She knew she wanted more knowledge. The dean of her university then helped her realize her profession. He asked her: "What do you like to do in your free time?" She said, "Read books," and he responded with, "Maybe you should become an English major." She took his advice. **Where will you be in five years:** In five years, she will be doing consulting work. **Hobbies:** Skiing; Swimming; Golf; Reading; Image consulting **Political Affiliations:** Republican **Religion:** Methodist **Shipping Address:** 206 Patriots Way, Elkton, MD, 21921

Linda Karen Miller

Title: Educator **Industry:** Education/Educational Services **Date of Birth:** 01/22/1948 **Place of Birth:** Kansas City **State:** KS **Parents:** Bennie Chris Miller; Thelma Jane (Richey) Miller **Marital Status:** Single **Education:** EdD, University of Virginia (1991); MEd in Secondary Education, University of Virginia (1978); EdB in Secondary Education, University of Kansas (1970) **Certifications:** Certified in Education, Environment and Interpretation, University of Nevada, Las Vegas (2009) **Career:** Teacher, Instructor, Department of Education, College of Southern Nevada (2003-2010); Social Studies Teacher, Fairfax High School (1978-2002) Social Studies Teacher, Herndon Intermediate (Now Herndon Middle School) (1975-1978); Social Studies Teacher, Mark Twain Intermediate (Now Mark Twain Middle School) (1974-1975); Reading Aide, Lake Braddock Secondary School, Fairfax County Public Schools (1973-1974); Substitute Reacher, Fairfax County Public Schools (1972-1973); Social Studies Teacher, Pierson Junior High School (1970-1972); Teacher, Turner Unified Schools, Kansas City, KS **Career Related:** Delegate to Turkey People to People International (2010); Delegate to Egypt People to People International (2007); Delegate to China People to People International (2005); Fellow, The Korea Society (2004); American Revolution Fellow, New York Historical Society (2001); Fellow, The Korea Society (2000); Delegated Consultant in Field **Civic:** Various Board of Directors; East-West Center Development Committee, University of Hawaii (2016-Present); Historical Interpreter, Helen J. Stewart First Lady of Las Vegas (2004-Present); President, Southern Nevada Peace Corps Association (2009-2010); President, Nevada Women's History Project (2008-2009); Nevada Coordinator, NCHE (2005-2010); Various Offices, Genealogical Societies **Creative Works:** Author, "USS Nevada BB36" (2017); Author, "Early Las Vegas," Arcadia Publishing (2013); Author, "Put a Little Acting Into Your Teaching," National Social Science Association (2006) **Awards:** U.S. Daughters of 1812 History Award (2017); Historic Preservation Medal, National Society Daughters of American Revolution (2016); Diversity Award, College of Southern Nevada (2009); Woman of Excellence Award College of Southern Nevada (2009); Outstanding Leadership, People to People International (2009); Asia-Pacific Islander Award, College of Southern Nevada (2008); National Peace Educator, National Peace Corps Association (2002); World History Teaching Prize, The World History Association (2002); Teacher of the Year, Global Teachnet (1999); Teacher of the Year, Virginia Geographical Society (1999); Excellence in Teaching Award, School of Education, The University of Kansas (1999); Celebrating Teaching Excellence Award, The American Council of Teachers of Russian (1998); Honoree, Outstanding Secondary Teacher, Virginia Historical Society (1998); George Washington Medal, Freedoms Foundation at Valley Forge (1998); Secondary Teacher of the Year, University of Virginia (1997); Secondary Teacher of the Year, National Council for the Social Studies (1996); Pre-Collegiate Teacher of the Year, The Organization of American Historians (1996); Teacher Historian, U.S. Capitol Historical Association (1986) **Membership:** University of Virginia Alumni Association; University of Kansas Alumni Association; National Society Daughters of the American Revolution; U.S. Daughters of 1812; National Society of Colonial Dames of the 17th Century; Daughters of Union Veterans of the Civil War; Ladies of the Grand Army of the Republic; National Society of Magna Carta Dames and Barons; Continental Society of the Daughters of Indian Wars; National Society of the Daughters of Colonial Wars; Dames of the Court of Honor; Daughters of American Colonists; League of Women Voters of Las Vegas Valley; East West Center, University of Hawaii CTAPS Alumni **To what do you attribute your success:** Dr. Miller attributes her success to her parents and a high school teacher. As a child, her parents took her to historical places and her high school history teacher, Mrs. Zimmerman, was the one who got her to love history. **Why did you become involved in your profession or industry:** Mr. Toothaker and Mrs. Zimmerman instilled her love of history into her. **What do you consider to be the highlight of your career:** The highlight of Dr. Miller's career was when she took four World War II veterans, who served on the USS Nevada, to the 75th Anniversary of Pearl Harbor. She was able to relive some of those moments with them, as well as honor them at other events. **Where will you be in five years:** In five years, Dr. Miller will be working at the East West Center in Hawaii. **Hobbies:** Collecting dolls **Political Affiliations:** Republican **Religion:** Episcopalian **Shipping Address:** 2319 Great Elk Drive, Henderson, NV, 89052

Richard Miller

Title: Law Educator **Industry:** Education/Educational Services **Company Name:** University of Hawaii **Date of Birth:** 12/11/1930 **Place of Birth:** Boston **State:** MA **Parents:** Max Miller; Mollie Miller **Marital Status:** Life Partner **Spouse Name:** Betty L. Sugarman; Doris Sheila Lunchick (5/24/1956, Deceased 4/23/2005) **Children:** Andrea Jayne Armitage; Matthew Harlan **Education:** LLM, Yale University, New Haven, CT (1959); JD, Boston University, Magna Cum Laude (1956); BBA, Boston University (1951) **Certifications:** State of Hawaii (1977); State of Michigan (1961); State of Massachusetts (1956) **Career:** Professor Emeritus, University of Hawaii, Honolulu, HI (1995-Present); Director, Summer Externship Program, University of Hawaii, Honolulu, HI (2006-2010); Dean, University of Hawaii, Honolulu, HI (1981-1984); Professor, University of Hawaii, Honolulu, HI (1973-1995); Director, Clinical and Interdisciplinary Programs, Ohio State University, Columbus, OH (1972-1973); Professor of Law, Ohio State University, Columbus, OH (1965-1973); Professor, Wayne State University, Detroit, MI (1962-1965); Associate Professor of Law, Wayne State University, Detroit, MI (1959-1962); Private Practice in Law, Boston, MA (1956-1958) **Career Related:** Delegate, Hawaii State Judicial Conference (1989-1992); Visiting Professor in Law, Victoria University, Wellington, New Zealand (1987); Visiting Professor in Law, USIA/University of Hawaii-Hiroshima University Affiliation Program, Japan (1986) **Civic:** Kokua Council (2007-Present); Citizens Against Gasoline Price Gouging (2003-Present); Consultant, Hawaii Coalition for Health (1997-Present); Board of Directors, Drug Policy Forum, Hawaii (1996-Present); Hawaii Patients Rights Task Force (2005-2006); Citizens for Competitive Air Travel (2002); Save Our Star-Bulletin Committee (1999-2001); Hawaii Substance Abuse Task Force (1994-1995) **Military Service:** First Lieutenant, U.S. Air Force (1951-1953) **Creative Works:** Author, "Courts and the Law: An Introduction to our Legal System" (1980); Co-Editor, "Essays on Expropriations" (1967); Editor-in-Chief, Boston University Law Review (1955-1956); Contributor, Articles, Professional Journals **Awards:** Community Service Award, Hawaii Medical Association Alliance (1999); Lawyer of the Year, Japan-Hawaii Lawyers Association (1990); Sterling-Ford Fellow, Yale University (1958-1959) **Membership:** American Humanist Association (2007-Present); Board of Directors, Media Council of Hawaii (1994-Present); Chair, Media Council of Hawaii (1989-1994); ACLU, Hawaii; Board Member, Kokua Council **Marquis Who's Who Honors:** Albert Nelson Marquis Lifetime Achievement Award (2017) **Political Affiliations:** Democrat **Shipping Address:** 45-090 Namoku Street, Apartment 1202, Kaneohe, HI, 96744

Ronald H. Miller, PhD

Title: President **Industry:** Business Management/ Business Services **Company Name:** Ronald H. Miller, PhD, LLC **Date of Birth:** 03/13/1948 **Place of Birth:** St. Louis **State:** MO **Parents:** Ilion Louis Miller (Deceased); Joyce Gloria Rimerman (Deceased) **Marital Status:** Divorced **Children:** Nathan Joel; Samuel Miller **Education:** MA in Teaching, Lindenwood University, Saint Charles, MO (2007); PhD in Public Administration, New York University (1990); Master of Public Policy Studies, University of Michigan (1978); Master of City Planning, The Ohio State University (1972); BA in Journalism, Indiana University (1970) **Certifications:** Certified Teacher in K-12 Vocal Music Education, State of Missouri; Certified Teacher in 9th-12th Grade Social Sciences, State of Missouri **Career:** President, Ronald H. Miller, PhD, LLC **Civic:** Advisory Board, Walbridge Elementary School; Children's Policy Forum Website, Vision for Children at Risk; Treasurer, Lilian Circle Neighborhood Development Association **Creative Works:** Contributor, Articles to 40 Publications; Presenter, More than 35 Events **Awards:** Recipient, Newcomer Award, MAACCE (1997) **Membership:** Phi Eta Sigma (1967) **Marquis Who's Who Honors:** Albert Nelson Marquis Lifetime Achievement Award (2017) **To what do you attribute your success:** Dr. Miller attributes his success to his knowledge in the sectors of the education field. **Why did you become involved in your profession or industry:** Dr. Miller became involved in his profession because of his interest and background in education. **What do you consider to be the highlight of your career:** The highlight of Dr. Miller's career was being recruited by a task force for the National Center for Higher Education Management Systems that expanded the Program Classification System to include adult learning programs in post-secondary education in 1978. That expansion still exists today. **Where will you be in five years:** In five years, Dr. Miller intends to expand his research and update the statistics used for previous articles for comparisons. **Hobbies:** Singing in church choirs and Jewish temples; Watching major league baseball; Watching college football **Shipping Address:** 2841 Adie Rd Apt., 9, Saint Ann, MO, 63074

James Michael Millis

Title: Professor **Industry:** Education/Educational Services **Company Name:** The University of Chicago **Date of Birth:** 02/22/1959 **Place of Birth:** Nashville **State:** TN **Parents:** James Brown Millis; Mary Vonda Millis **Marital Status:** Married **Spouse Name:** Janet Kassel Millis (1/15/1985) **Children:** Michael Andrew; Mary Katherine **Education:** Fellow, Organ Transplants, UCLA Health, Los Angeles, CA (1992-1994); Resident, General Surgery, UCLA Health, Los Angeles, CA (1986-1992); Intern, UCLA Health, Los Angeles, CA (1985-1986); MD, The University of Tennessee Health Science Center, Memphis, TN (1985) **Certifications:** Diplomate, American Board of Surgery; Diplomate, American Board of Surgical Critical Care **Career:** Medical Director, Transplantation Services, The University of Chicago Medicine (2001-Present); Chief, Section of Transplantation, The University of Chicago Medicine (2001-Present); Associate Professor to Professor of Surgery, The University of Chicago (1997-Present); Assistant Professor of Surgery, The University of Chicago (1994-1997) **Creative Works:** Author, "Voluntary Organ Donation System Adapted to Chinese Cultural Values and Social Reality," Scientific Publishing **Awards:** Honoree, Global Citizen Hero, The American National Red Cross (2017); Award for the Publication of an Article Announcing the End of the Use of Organs from Executed Prisoners (2015) **Membership:** American College of Surgeons; American Society of Transplant Surgeons; American Society of Transplant Physicians; Association for Academic Surgery; American Association for the Study of Liver Diseases; International Pediatric Transplant Association; Society of University Surgeons **Marquis Who's Who Honors:** Albert Nelson Marquis Lifetime Achievement Award (2017) **Shipping Address:** 751 The Pines, Hinsdale, IL, 60521 **Website:** https://www.washingtonpost.com/world/asia_pacific/in-the-face-of-criticism-china-has-been-cleaning-u

Micol Mion

Title: Partner **Industry:** Medicine & Health Care **Company Name:** Immigration Solutions LLC, EB5 Global Ventures **Date of Birth:** 09/19/1978 **Place of Birth:** Padova **Country of Origin:** Italy **Parents:** Sergio Mion; Mirella Busacca Mion **Marital Status:** Married **Spouse Name:** Andrew A. Gordon (2/23/2008) **Children:** Alexander Sergio Gordon **Education:** JD, School of Law, Boston University (2006); BA, Harvard University; MS, Brandeis University; MA, Northeastern University; LLM, City University of New York **Certifications:** Supreme Court of the United States (2017); United States District Court District of Massachusetts (2014); United States Court of Appeals for the First Circuit (2014) **Career:** Immigration Attorney, Immigration Solutions LLC, EB5 Global Ventures, Boston, MA (2009-Present); Partner, Immigration Solutions LLC, EB5 Global Ventures, Boston, MA (2009-Present); Law Clerk, Craig & Macauley, Boston, MA (2009); Immigration Attorney, Law Offices of Ara H. Margosian II, Watertown, MA (2006-2009); Law Clerk, Ropes & Gray, Boston, MA (2005); Law Clerk, Simmons & Simmons (2004) **Creative Works:** Author, "The Past, Present and Future of EC Bankruptcy Regulation 1346/2000," New England Journal of International and Comparative Law (2006); Author, "European Union and Solvency Laws"; Author, "Repatriation: An Assessment of Its Historical, Cultural, Ethical and Scientific Dimensions," Journal of Museum Management and Curatorship; Editor, "New England Journal of International and Comparative Law" **Awards:** Honoree, Top Woman Attorney in Immigration Law, Super Lawyers (2017); Honoree, US Immigration Attorney of the Year, Finance Monthly (2017); Honoree, US Immigration Lawyer of the Year, ACQ Global Awards (2016-2017); Featured Listee, Best Client Satisfaction, Immigration Division, American Institute of Legal Counsel (2016-2017); Honoree, Top Immigration Attorney, Three Best Rated (2016-2017); Best Immigration Attorney and Excellence Award for Employment-Based Immigration Visas, Acquisition International–The Voice of Corporate Finance (2016); Honoree, Best Immigration Lawyer, Expertise (2016-2017); Honoree, Best Immigration Law Firm, Legal Elite (2016-2017); Honoree, Top Contributor for Pro Bono Work, Avvo (2016-2017); Honoree, US Independent Immigration Law Firm of the Year, ACQ Global Awards (2015-2017); Recipient, Client's Choice Award, Avvo (2015-2017); Honoree, Best for Immigration Law, Corporate America Legal Elite (2015-2016); Honoree, Game Changer of the Year for Immigration Law, ACQ Global Awards (2015-2016); Recipient, CALI Award for Future Excellence for Securities Regulation; Honoree, Associate Editor of the Year; Honoree, Northeastern Scholar, National Honor Criminology Society; Honoree, Rising Star in Immigration Law, Super Lawyers **Membership:** American Immigration Lawyers Association; Boston Bar Association; Harvard Alumni Association; Brandeis Alumni Association; Committee for Jewish Families and Children Services **Bar Admissions:** Massachusetts (2006) **To what do you attribute your success:** She attributes her success to relating well to people, and having traveled extensively and observed different cultures. She feels that people are comfortable speaking with her because they know it is a safe space, and she will follow through and always reply to their questions. **Why did you become involved in your profession or industry:** She is an immigrant from Italy, and came here as a student after finishing high school in London. Her plan was always to go back to Italy, as her family owned a Textile business, but unfortunately her father passed away when she was in college. She didn't want to go back to Italy because it was too painful. She decided to pursue an English degree instead of Economics. Then she got a masters in criminology, and attended law school after that. As a student, she had visa troubles because of poor guidance from her immigration attorney. She couldn't believe that people might be barred from living in the U.S. simply because of bad advice from a lawyer, so she decided to become involved in the process, because she understood how it felt, and speaks five languages. **What do you consider to be the highlight of your career:** A highlight of her career is that sometimes she has the privilege of seeing the entire immigration process through, from a school visa to a work visa, then to a green card, and then finally naturalization. It feels good because she almost feels like a part of their family. **Where will you be in five years:** In five years, she hopes to be doing the same thing that she is now, because she loves her work. She hopes to petition the government and lift the current travel ban that exists. She hopes that in the future, she will be able to make a difference. Whether it's becoming an immigration judge or work in the foreign service. **Hobbies:** Reading; Archeology; Traveling around the world; Public speaking; Visiting museums **Religion:** Jewish **Shipping Address:** 585 Boylston St., Fl 4, Immigration Solutions LLC, Boston, MA, 02116 **Website:** http://www.immsolutionsllc.com

Ferenc Mark Miskolczi, PhD

Industry: Sciences **Date of Birth:** 04/20/1947 **Place of Birth:** Budapest **Country of Origin:** Hungary **Education:** PhD in Earth Sciences, Hungarian Academy of Sciences, Budapest, Hungary (1981); PhD in Physics, Eotvos Lorand University, Budapest, Hungary (1975); MS in Physics, Eotvos Lorand University, Budapest, Hungary (1971) **Career:** Senior Principal Scientist, Analytical Services & Materials Inc., Hampton, VA (2001-2006) **Creative Works:** Contributor, Articles, Professional Scientific Journals

Edward John Mitchell

Title: Economist, Educator (Retired) **Industry:** Education/Educational Services **Company Name:** University of Michigan **Date of Birth:** 08/15/1937 **Place of Birth:** Newark **State:** NJ **Parents:** Edward Charles Mitchell; Gladys (Werner) Mitchell **Marital Status:** Married **Spouse Name:** Mary Josephine Osborne (6/14/1958) **Children:** Susan; Edward **Education:** PhD in Economics, University of Pennsylvania (1966); Postgraduate Work, University of Oxford (1963-1964); BA, Bowling Green State University (1960) **Career:** Professor Emeritus in Business Economics and Public Policy, University of Michigan (1988-Present); Professor, University of Michigan (1975-1988); Associate Professor in Business Economics, University of Michigan (1973-1975); Visiting Associate Professor in Economics, Cornell University (1972-1973); Senior Economist, President's Council of Economic Advisers (1969-1972); Member, Institute for Advanced Study (1968-1969); Economist, RAND Corporation (1965-1968); Lecturer in Economics, The Wharton School, The University of Pennsylvania (1964-1965) **Career Related:** Director of National Energy Project, American Enterprise Institute (1974-1976) **Creative Works:** Author, "The Deregulation of Natural Gas" (1983); Author, "Vertical Integration of the Oil Industry" (1976); Author, "Financing the Energy Industry" (1975); Author, "U.S. Energy Policy: A Primer" (1974); Author, "Dialogue on World Oil" (1974); Contributor, Articles, Professional Journals **Marquis Who's Who Honors:** Albert Nelson Marquis Lifetime Achievement Award (2017) **Shipping Address:** 310 Penny Ln, Santa Barbara, CA, 93108

Jere Holloway Mitchell

Title: Physiologist **Industry:** Health, Wellness and Fitness **Company Name:** Zale Lipshy University Hospital **Date of Birth:** 10/17/1928 **Place of Birth:** Longview **State:** TX **Parents:** William Holloway Mitchell; Dorothea (Turner) Mitchell **Marital Status:** Married **Spouse Name:** Pamela Battey (10/1/1960, Deceased 2010) **Children:** Wendy Mitchell O'Sullivan; Laurie Mitchell Woods; Amy Mitchell Poeppel **Education:** Honorary PhD, University of Copenhagen (2000); Cardiology Fellow, The University of Texas Southwestern Medical Center (1956-1958); Resident, Internal Medicine (1955-1956); Intern, Parkland Health & Hospital System, Dallas, TX (1954-1955); MD, The University of Texas Southwestern Medical School (1954); BS, Virginia Military Institute, with Honors (1950) **Career:** Courtesy Staff, Zale Lipshy University Hospital (1990-Present); Holder, Carolyn P. and S. Roger Horchow Chair, Cardiac Research (1989-Present); Attending Physician, VA Medical Center, Dallas, TX (1969-Present); Professor (1969-Present); Attending Physician, Saint Paul Family Medical Center (1966-Present); Attending Physician, Parkland Health & Hospital System (1963-Present); Holder Frank M. Ryburn Junior Chair, Heart Research (1982-2000); Director, Harry S. Moss Heart Center (1976-2000); Director, Weinberger Laboratory for Cardiopulmonary Research (1966-1999); Associate Professor, The University of Texas Southwestern Medical Center, Dallas, TX (1966-1969); Assistant Professor, Medicine and Physiology, The University of Texas Southwestern Medical Center, Dallas, TX (1962-1966); Public Health Service, Laboratory of Cardiac Energetics, National Heart, Lung, and Blood Institute, Bethesda, MD (1958-1962); Fellow, American College of Cardiology Foundation **Career Related:** Research Review Committee A, National Heart, Lung and Blood Institute (1992-1997); Percy Russo Lecturer, Professor, Cumberland College of Health Sciences, The University of Sydney (1991); Pfizer Visiting Professor, The Pennsylvania State University (1990); Science Advisory Board, United States Air Force (1988-1990); Respiratory & Applied Physiology Study Section, National Institutes of Health (1981-1982); Applied Physiological Orthopedic Study Section, National Institutes of Health (1979-1981); Established Investigator, American Heart Association, Inc. (1962-1967) **Creative Works:** Editorial Board, "Clinical Physiology and Functional Imaging" (1981-Present); Editorial Board, "Circulation" (1993-2004); Associate Editor, "Experimental Physiology" (1993-2000); Associate Editor, Journal of Applied Physiology (1984-1993); Editorial Board, American Journal of Cardiology (1982-1984); Editorial Board, Journal of Cardiopulmonary Rehabilitation and Prevention (1981-1991); Editorial Board, "Cardiovascular Research" (1979-1987); Associate Editor, Journal of Applied Physiology (1978-1982); Editorial Board, "Circulation" (1978-1981); Editorial Board, American Journal of Physiology (1972-1976); Editorial Board, American Journal of Cardiology (1965-1974) **Awards:** Recipient, Paton Prize, The Physiological Society (2012); Recipient, Honor Award, The American Physiological Society (2007); Named, Edward Adolph Distinguished Lecturer, Environmental and Exercise Physiology Section, The American Physiological Society (2003); Recipient, Distinguished Scientist Award, American College of Cardiology Foundation (1999); Recipient, Carl J. Wiggers Award, Cardiovascular Section, The American Physiological Society (1992); Recipient, Honor Award, American College of Sports Medicine (1988); Recipient, Award of Merit, American Heart Association, Inc. (1984); Recipient, Citation Award, American College of Sports Medicine (1983); Recipient, Donald W. Seldin Research Award, The University of Texas Southwestern Medical Center (1978); Recipient, Career Development Award, United States Public Health Service (1968-1973); Recipient, Young Investigators Award, American College of Cardiology Foundation (1961) **Membership:** Medical Science Committee, American Association for the Advancement of Science (1988-Present); Council, Cardiac Rehabilitation, International Society for Heart Research (1981-Present); Commission on Cardiovascular Physiology, International Union of Physiological Sciences (1977-Present); National Vice President, American Heart Association, Inc. (1990-1991); Joseph B. Wolffe Lecturer, American College of Sports Medicine (1989); President, Texas Affiliate, American Heart Association, Inc. (1983-1984); President, Dallas Division, American Heart Association, Inc. (1977-1978); Emeritus Member, American Federation for Clinical Research; Emeritus Member, The American Society for Clinical Investigation; Association of American Physicians; The American Physiological Society; Association of University Cardiologists; The Physiological Society; Alpha Omega Alpha **Marquis Who's Who Honors:** Albert Nelson Marquis Lifetime Achievement Award (2017); Distinguished Humanitarian (2017) **Shipping Address:** 11211 Leachman Cir, Dallas, TX, 75229

Luke Mo, PhD

Title: Physicist **Industry:** Education/Educational Services **Company Name:** Virginia Polytechnic Institute and State University **Date of Birth:** 06/03/1934 **Place of Birth:** Shandong **Country of Origin:** China **Parents:** Si-leng Mo; Shu-feng (Lo) Mo **Spouse Name:** Doris Chang (12/31/1960) **Children:** Curtis L.; Alice **Education:** PhD, Columbia University (1963); MS in Physics, National Tsinghua University (1959); BEE, National Taiwan University (1955) **Career:** Professor Emeritus of Physics, Virginia Polytechnic Institute and State University (2003-Present); Professor of Physics, Virginia Polytechnic Institute and State University (1976-2003); Assistant Professor of Physics, University of Chicago (1969-1976); Research Physicist, Stanford Linear Accelerator (1965-1969); Research Associate, Columbia University (1963-1964) **Career Related:** Fellow, American Physical Society **Civic:** Taiwan Air Force (1955-1956) **Creative Works:** Contributor, Various Articles, Professional Journals **Shipping Address:** 1387 Caminito Diadema, La Jolla, CA, 92037

Paul Lawrence Modrich, PhD

Title: Biochemist **Industry:** Sciences **Company Name:** Howard Hughes Medical Institute, Duke University **Place of Birth:** Raton **State:** NM **Education:** Postgraduate Coursework, Harvard University (1973-1974); PhD in Biochemistry, Stanford University (1973); BS in Biology, Massachusetts Institute of Technology (1968) **Career:** Investigator, Howard Hughes Medical Institute, Duke University (1994-Present); Director, Program in Genetics, Duke University (1989-1992); Professor of Biochemistry, Duke University (1984); Associate Professor of Biochemistry, Duke University (1980); Assistant Professor of Biochemistry, Duke University (1976); Assistant Professor of Chemistry, University of California, Berkeley (1974); James B. Duke Professor of Biochemistry, Duke University **Career Related:** Fellow, American Academy of Arts & Sciences **Creative Works:** Editorial Committee, Annual Review of Biochemistry (2004-Present); Editorial Board, Proceedings of the National Academy of Sciences (2000-2008); Associate Editor, Biochemistry (1992-1994); Editorial Advisory Board (1986-1991); Editorial Board, Journal of Biological Chemistry (1982-1983); Editorial Board, Nucleic Acids Research (1980-1982); Contributor, Articles, Professional Journals **Awards:** Nobel Prize in Chemistry, Nobel Foundation, Nobel Media AB (2015); Medal of Honor for Basic Research, American Cancer Society, Inc. (2005); Robert J. and Claire Pasarow Foundation Medical Research Award in Cancer Research (1998); Charles S. Mott Prize in Cancer Research, General Motors (1996); NIGMS MERIT Award, National Institutes of Health (1986); Pfizer Award in Enzyme Chemistry, American Chemical Society (1983) **Membership:** Publications Committee, American Society for Biochemistry and Molecular Biology (1995-1997); Councillor, American Society for Biochemistry and Molecular Biology (1989-1992); National Academy of Sciences; Institute of Medicine (Now National Academy of Medicine); National Academy of Sciences **Marquis Who's Who Honors:** Albert Nelson Marquis Lifetime Achievement Award (2017) **Why did you become involved in your profession or industry:** Dr. Modrich became interested in science as a child. His interests were primarily in chemistry and biology. **Hobbies:** Reading; Photography; Traveling **Business Address:** PO Box 3711, Durham, NC, 27514 **Shipping Address:** 5820 Brisbane Drive, Chapel Hill, NC, 27514 **Website:** https://en.wikipedia.org/wiki/Paul_L._Modrich

Charles Gerard Moerdler

Title: Lawyer **Industry:** Law and Legal Services **Company Name:** Stroock & Stroock & Lavan LLP **Date of Birth:** 11/15/1934 **Place of Birth:** Paris **Country of Origin:** France **Parents:** Herman Moerdler; Erna Anna (Brandwein) Moerdler **Marital Status:** Married **Spouse Name:** Pearl G. Hecht (12/26/1955) **Children:** Jeffrey Alan; Mark Laurence; Sharon Michele **Education:** JD, Fordham University (1956); BA, Long Island University (1953) **Career:** Senior Partner, Chairman Litigation Department, Stroock & Stroock & Lavan LLP (1967-Present); Commissioner of Buildings, City of New York (1966-1967); Special Counsel of Committees, City of New York, Judiciary New York State Assembly (1960-1961); Associate, Cravath, Swaine & Moore (1956-1965) **Career Related:** Metropolitan Transportation Authority (2010-Present); New York City Board of Collective Bargaining (2000-Present); Vice Chairman, Character and Fitness of Applicants for Admission to Bar, Appellate Division First Department, New York, NY (1998-Present); New York City Housing Development Corporation (1997-Present); Board of Directors, New York City Residential Mortgage Insurance Corporation (1997-Present); Member Committee, Character and Fitness of Applicants for Admission to Bar, Appellate Division First Department, New York, NY (1977-Present); New York State Dormitory Authority (2010-2012); Disciplinary Committee, Appellate Division, First Department, New York, NY (2006-2012); Chairman, Board of Directors, Bank Austria Creditanstalt American LLC (1999-2001); Disciplinary Committee, Appellate Division, First Department, New York, NY (1998-2004); Chairman, New York State Insurance Fund (1995-1997); Mayor's Committee on Judiciary (1994-2001); Board of Directors, General Counsel, Director, New York Post Company, Inc. (1987-1992); Vice Chairman, New York State Insurance Fund (1986-1994); Commissioner, New York State Insurance Fund (1978-1997); Consultant, Housing, Urban Development and Real Estate to Mayor of New York City (1967-1973) **Civic:** Senior Vice President, Executive Committee Member, American Jewish Congress (2005-Present); Trustee, St. Barnabas Hospital, Bronx, NY (1985-Present); Board of Overseers, Jewish Theological Seminary of America (1993-1995); Trustee, Long Island University (1985-1991); Advisory Board, School of International Affairs, Columbia University (1977-1980); Chairman, Community Planning Boards 8 and 14, Bronx County, NY (1977-1978); Board of Governors, Long Island University (1966); Assistant Director, Rockefeller National Presidential Campaign Committee (1964) **Awards:** Castle Award, Manhattanville College (2005); Walker Metcalf Award, Long Island University (1966) **Membership:** American Bar Association; New York State Bar Association; New York County Lawyers Association; International Bar Association; Association of the Bar of the City of New York; Metropolitan Club **Bar Admissions:** U.S. Supreme Court (1962); State of New York (1956) **Marquis Who's Who Honors:** Albert Nelson Marquis Lifetime Achievement Award (2017); Distinguished Humanitarian (2017) **Shipping Address:** 7 Rivercrest Road, Bronx, NY, 10471

Stanley F. Moeschl

Title: Electronics Engineer, Vice President, President **Industry:** Engineering **Company Name:** Honeywell Avionics Division, Sundstrand Data Control **Date of Birth:** 03/14/1931 **Place of Birth:** Cincinnati **State:** OH **Parents:** Stanley F. Moeschl; Matilda F. (Trenkamp) Mosechl **Marital Status:** Married **Spouse Name:** Kathleen K. Koebel (8/21/1954) **Children:** Stanley; Melissa; Deborah; Karen **Education:** BSEE, Purdue University (1957) **Career:** President, Sundstrand Data Control, Redmond, Washington, DC (1988-1992); Vice President, General Manager, Honeywell Avionics Division, Minneapolis, MN (1982-1988); Vice President, General Manager, Honeywell Space Division (1980-1982); Director of Engineering, Honeywell Avionics Division, Minneapolis, MN (1977-1980); Program Manager, Honeywell Space Division (1969-1977); Engineering Manager, Honeywell Space Division (1960-1969); Engineer, Honeywell Space Division (1957-1960) **Career Related:** Board Member, Committee of 100, St. Petersburg (1980-1982); Washington Round Table, Seattle, WA (1989-1992) **Civic:** Board of Directors, Junior Achievement, Minneapolis, MN (1983-1986); Junior Achievement, Seattle, WA (1989-1992) **Military Service:** U.S. Coast Guard, Korea (1951-1954) **Membership:** IEEE; American Association of Individual Investors; Tau Beta Pi; Eta Kappa Nu **To what do you attribute your success:** Mr. Moeschl attributes his success to treating people the way you like to be treated. **Why did you become involved in your profession or industry:** He became involved in his profession because of U.S. Coast Guard Electronic School. **Where will you be in five years:** In five years, he will be enjoying retirement. **Hobbies:** Boating; Golf; Tennis **Shipping Address:** 3110 Van Ave #5, Alexandria, MN, 56308

Tungesh Nath Mohan

Industry: Media & Entertainment **Company Name:** L.I.F.E. Inc. **Date of Birth:** 10/30/1949 **Place of Birth:** Lucknow **Country of Origin:** India **Parents:** Bhola Shambu Nath; Saraswati P. (Devi) **Education:** MA, Andrews University (1980); Diploma in Cinema, Film and TV Institute India, Poona (1972); BS, Kalyani University, India (1969) **Career:** Producer, Director, Protestant Reformation, Quo Vadis (2013-Present); Producer, Director, Enterplexx, Woodland Hills, California (2012-2013); Academy Director, Filmmaking and Animation, Art Institute Ohio, Cincinnati (2009-2012); Director, Digital Video Center, Samford University, Birmingham, AL (2005-2009); President, TriAngel Media Corp., Thousand Oaks, CA (1992-1994); Manager, Adventist Communications Network, Silver Spring, MD (1992-1993); Director, International NorthStar Entertainment Group, LA (1989-1992); Director, International CBN Producers Group (1987-1989); Producer, Special Projects, Christian Broadcasting Network Cable Productions, Inc., Virginia Beach (1986-1987); Producer, Special Projects, Christian Broadcasting Network, Virginia Beach (1982-1986); TV Producer, 700 Club, Virginia Beach, VA (1980-1982); Assistant professor, Film and TV Institute India, Poona (1975-1977); Producer, Bombay TV (1972-1975, 1977-1979) **Career Related:** Consultant, Global TV Syndication (1998-Present); Producers Unit One, Virginia Beach (1982-Present); President, L.I.F.E. Inc. (1993-Present); Director, Telecommunications Center, Huntsville, AL (1998-2000); Adjunct Professor, Hampton University, Virginia (1980-1992); Global Communications Associates, Virginia Beach (1987-1988); Spicer College, Poona (1975-1979); Film and TV Institute, India, Poona (1975-1979) **Creative Works:** Producer, Director, Writer, "The Very German Protest" (2017); Producer, Director, "This Changed Everything" (2016); Producer, Director, "The 51st State" (2014); Producer, Director, "Faith Matters" (2012); Producer, Director, "What Poor Child is This?" (2011); Producer, Director, "The Faith We Confess" (2010); Producer, Director, "O For A Thousand to Sing" (2010); Producer, Director, "Apostles Creed" (2009); Producer, Director, "Faith of Our Fathers, Hymns of Our Fathers" (2009); Producer, Director, "Truth Matters" (2008); Producer, Director, "A Heart Set Free" (2008); Producer, Director, A Heart Set Free! (2007); Producer, Director, "Life is Calling" (2007); Producer, Director, "Called" (2007); Producer, Director, "The 51st State" (2006); Producer, Director, "Born With a Wooden Spoon" (2006); Producer, Director, "Christianity & Islam: A Dialogue" (2004); Producer, Director, "Thank You, Mr. Hodges" (2003); Producer, Director, "The Invitation" (2003); Producer, Director, "Truth to Tell" (2003); Producer, Director, "The Hymnmaker" (2002); Producer, Director, "For One English Officer" (2002); Producer, Director, "The Dawning" (2002); Producer, Director, "Realizing the Vision" (2001); Executive Producer, A Father of Preachers (2001); Producer, Director, Revolution of Conscience (2001); Producer, Director, Here I Stand (2001); Producer, Director, In the Footsteps of Martin Luther (2001); Producer, Director, Afghanistan: Under the Iron Claw (1982); Producer, Director, Raktajeevee (1977); Producer, Director, Dishantar (1975); Producer, Director, Writer, "U-Turn" (1973); Producer, Director, Even So (1972); Producer, "The Invitation" (1997); Producer, "The Gift" (1997); Producer, "Bought at a Price" (1996); Producer, "Hanged on a Twisted Cross" (1996); Producer, "Inn Keeper" (1996) **Awards:** Silver Remi: World Fest Houston (2016); Honoree, Columbus International Film Festival (2008); Silver Telly Award (2008); Bronze Telly Award (2008); Participant: Columbus International Film Festival (2007); Silver Remi: World Fest Houston (2005); Gold Award: Aurora Awards (2003); Silver Award: Aurora Awards (2003); Silver Award: Aurora Awards (2003); Silver Axiom Award (2003); Bronze Axiom Award (2003); Silver Telly Award (2003); Silver Telly Award (2003); Honoree: Columbus International Film Festival (2003); Movie Guide Templeton Foundation Peace Prize Nomination for Best Inspirational Program (2002); Best of Show Platinum Award, Aurora Awards: Best TV documentary Film (1999); Bronze World Medal: New York Festivals (1999); Bronze Plaque: Second Prize: Columbus International Film and TV Festival (1998); Chris Award for Best TV documentary Film, Columbus International Film and TV Festival (1996); Bronze Plaque: Screenplay, Columbus International Film and TV Festival (1996); Honorable Mention, Columbus International Film and TV Festival, The Midnight Cry (1995); Silver Telly, International Telly Awards: Strange Encounters (1993); Gold Medal: Prime Time Special, New York International Film & TV Festival (1984); Special Mention & Certificate of Proficiency, Prague International Film Festival, Dishaantar (1975) **Membership:** National Academy of Television Arts and Sciences; Directors Guild of America; Writers Guild of America; University Film & Video Association, Lions **Religion:** Seventh-Day Adventist Christian **Shipping Address:** P O Box 19843, Birmingham, AL, 35219

Sunil K. Mohanty, PhD

Title: Department of Finance Chair **Industry:** Education/Educational Services **Company Name:** Brooklyn College **Date of Birth:** 10/28/1958 **Place of Birth:** Cuttack **Country of Origin:** India **Parents:** Biswanath Mohanty; Khyana Prava Mohanty **Marital Status:** Married **Spouse Name:** Tamera Lyn Mohanty **Children:** Rani; Raj **Education:** PhD in Business Administration, Cleveland State University (1995); MBA, Minnesota State University (1989); Bachelor of Technology, Indian Institute of Technology, Kharagpur, India (1981) **Career:** Chair, Department of Finance, Koppelman School of Business, Brooklyn College (2015-Present); Professor of Finance, Brooklyn College (2014-Present); Professor of Finance, University of Saint Thomas, Minneapolis, MN (2012-2014); Associate Professor of Finance, University of Saint Thomas, Minneapolis, MN (2004-2012); Assistant Professor of Finance, University of Saint Thomas, Minneapolis, MN (2001-2004); Assistant Professor of Finance, Hofstra University, Hempstead, NY (1995-2001); Visiting Assistant Professor of Finance, Hofstra University, Hempstead, NY (1994-1995); Instructor, Department of Marketing, Minnesota State University, Mankato, MN (1988-1989); Business Consultant, Small Business Development Center, Mankato, MN (1986-1987); Assistant Engineer, Engineers India Ltd., New Delhi, India (1983-1985); Junior Engineer, Engineers India Ltd., New Delhi, India (1981-1983) **Creative Works:** Editorial Board, Academy of Commercial Banking and Finance (2004-2012); Editorial Board, Academy of Financial Studies (2000-2007); Associate Editor, Contributor, Articles, Professional Journals **Awards:** Outstanding Research Award, Academy of Accounting and Financial Studies (2002); ANBAR Citation of Highest Quality Rating (1997) **Membership:** Associate, Financial Management Association International; Associate, Eastern Finance Association; Associate, American Finance Association; Beta Gamma Sigma; Phi Kappa Phi **Marquis Who's Who Honors:** Albert Nelson Marquis Lifetime Achievement Award (2017) **To what do you attribute your success:** Dr. Mohanty attributes his success to being a problem solver, leader, negotiator, and moderator. **Why did you become involved in your profession or industry:** Competitiveness in India is India's equivalent to getting into Harvard University among elite groups. **Where will you be in five years:** In five years, Dr. Mohanty will still be remaining as chair and helping people maximize their potential at Brooklyn College and see their possibilities. **Hobbies:** Tennis; Swimming; Travel **Shipping Address:** 1111 Ocean Avenue, Apt. #515, Brooklyn, NY, 11230

Jay P. Mohr

Title: Neurologist, Educator **Industry:** Education/Educational Services **Company Name:** Columbia University **Date of Birth:** 03/05/1937 **Place of Birth:** Philadelphia **State:** PA **Parents:** John G. Mohr; Marguerite F. Mohr **Marital Status:** Married **Spouse Name:** Joan L. Seal (3/10/1962) **Children:** Thea; Gregory **Education:** MS, University of Virginia (1963); AB, Haverford College (1958); MD, University of Virginia **Certifications:** Diplomate, American Board of Psychiatry and Neurology, Inc. **Career:** Daniel Sciarra Neurology Professor, Columbia University (1983-Present); Chairman, Department of Neurology, University of South Alabama (1978-1983); Associate Neurology Professor, Harvard Medical School, Harvard College (1971-1978) **Career Related:** Director, Doris and Stanley Tananbaum Stroke Center (2003-Present); Director, Cerebrovascular Research, Neurological Institute of New York, Columbia University (1983-Present); Neurology Fellow, General Hospital Corporation, Boston, MA (1966-1969); Fellow, American Academy of Neurology **Creative Works:** Contributor, Medical Corps. Magazine, U.S. Army (1969-1972); Contributor, Articles, Medical Journals **Awards:** Founders Award for Lifetime Achievement, New York Chapter, American Heart Association, Inc. (2016); Johann Josef Wepfer Award, ESO-STROKE (2009); Honoree, Distinguished Scientist, American Heart Association, Inc. (2006) **Membership:** American Neurological Association; Stroke Council, American Heart Association; Sigma Xi **Marquis Who's Who Honors:** Albert Nelson Marquis Lifetime Achievement Award (2017) **Why did you become involved in your profession or industry:** As a college student, Dr. Mohr was interested in brain function, which led to him going to medical school and then becoming a neurologist. **Where will you be in five years:** In five years, Dr. Mohr will be continuing his career. **Hobbies:** Trapshooting; Sailing **Political Affiliations:** Democrat **Religion:** Quaker **Shipping Address:** 710 W 168th Street, Columbia University, Neurological Institute, New York, NY, 10032

Lawrence Charles Mohr

Title: Professor, Physician **Industry:** Medicine & Health Care **Company Name:** Medical University of South Carolina **Date of Birth:** 07/08/1947 **Place of Birth:** Staten Island **State/Country of Origin:** NY **Parents:** Lawrence Charles Mohr, Sr.; Mary Estelle (Dawsey) Mohr **Marital Status:** Married **Spouse Name:** Linda Johnson (6/14/1970) **Children:** Andrea Marie **Education:** Chief Resident, Walter Reed Army Medical Center, Washington, D.C. (1982-1983); Resident in Medicine, Walter Reed Army Medical Center, Washington, D.C. (1980-1982); Medical Intern, Walter Reed Army Medical Center, Washington, D.C. (1979-1980); MD, The University of North Carolina (1979); Honorary AB, The University of North Carolina (1975) **Certifications:** Diplomate, American Board of Internal Medicine **Career:** Director, Environmental Bioscience Program, Medical University of South Carolina, Charleston, SC (1995-Present); Professor, Medicine, Medical University of South Carolina, Charleston, SC (1994-Present); Associate Professor, Medicine, Uniformed Services University Health Sciences, Bethesda, MD (1991-1994); Associate Clinical Professor, Medicine, The George Washington University, Washington, D.C. (1990-1994); White House Physician, Washington, D.C. (1987-1993); Assistant Professor, Medicine, Uniformed Services University of the Health Sciences, Bethesda, MD (1984-1991); Pulmonary Fellow, Walter Reed Army Medical Center, Washington, D.C. (1986-1987); Attending Physician, Walter Reed Army Medical Center, Washington, D.C. (1984-1986); Medical Consultant, Madigan Army Medical Center, Tacoma, WA (1983-1984); Commander Surgeon, Ninth Infantry Division, Fort Lewis, WA (1983-1984) **Career Related:** Member, Working Group on Disability in United States Presidents (1995-Present); Attending Physician, Medical University Hospital, Charleston, SC (1994-Present); Attending Physician, Charleston Memorial Hospital (1994-Present); Board of Governors, Nebraska Wesleyan University, Lincoln, NE; Board of Directors, Harry and Reba Huge Foundation, Charleston, SC **Civic:** Board of Directors, International Lung Foundation; Advisory Board, National Museum of Health and Medicine; Member, Scientific Advisory Board, Consortium in Environmental Risk Evaluation; Principal Investigator, Consortium in Molecular Epidemiology and Biomarker Research **Military Service:** Colonel, United States Army (1989); Commissioned Second Lieutenant, United States Army (1967) **Creative Works:** Editor, "Biomarkers: Medical and Workplace Applications" (1998); Editor, "International Case Studies in Risk Assessment and Management" (1997); Contributor, Articles, Professional Journals and Books **Awards:** Erskine Award, Walter Reed Army Medical Center (1982); Named, Outstanding Medical Resident (1982); Silver Star; Bronze Star with 2 V Devices and 3 Oak Leaf Clusters; Purple Heart; Meritorious Service Medal with Oak Leaf Cluster; Air Medal; Army Commendation Medal with Oak Leaf Cluster; Distinguished Service Medal; Awarded, Doctor of Science, Nebraska Wesleyan University **Membership:** Board of Regents, Uniformed Services University, Bethesda, MD (2003-2009); Fellow, American College of Physicians; American College of Chest Physicians; American Medical Association; Army and Navy Club; Order of Military Medical Merit; Harbour Club; Phi Beta Kappa **Marquis Who's Who Honors:** Albert Nelson Marquis Lifetime Achievement Award (2017); Distinguished Humanitarian (2017) **To what do you attribute your success:** Dr. Mohr attributes his success to hard work and persistence. **Hobbies:** Mountain Climbing; Skiing **Religion:** Episcopalian **Shipping Address:** 673 Lake Francis Dr, Charleston, SC, 29412 **Website:** http://www.lawrencecharlesmohr.com

Ronald "Rob" Brown Moir Jr., PhD

Title: Executive Director **Industry:** Business Management/Business Services **Company Name:** Ocean River Institute **Date of Birth:** 12/18/1953 **Place of Birth:** Romulus **State:** NY **Parents:** Ronald Brown Moir; Tia Dangler Andrew Moir **Marital Status:** Married **Spouse Name:** Toni Czekanski **Children:** Jesse; Ryan; Brady **Education:** PhD in Environmental Studies, Antioch University New England (2002); MS in Teaching, Antioch University (1979); BA in Natural Science, Hampshire College (1977) **Certifications:** Certification in Environmental and Climate Sciences, USC Wrigley Institute, Catalina Island (2003); Certification in Ecology, The Marine Biological Laboratory, Woods Hole, MA (1979) **Awards:** Recipient, Switzer Environmental Fellowship, Robert and Patricia Switzer Foundation (1996); Recipient, James Centorino Award for Distinguished Performance in Marine Education, National Marine Educators Association (1988); Recipient, Rockefeller Brothers Fund Award for the Development of a College Course on Cetacean Biology, Ecology and Conservation (1976) **Membership:** Partner, Representing Advisory Council, Boston Harbor Islands National Park Area; Advisory Council, Stellwagen Bank National Marine Sanctuary; President, National Marine Educators Association; President, Gulf of Maine Marine Education Association; President, Essex County Ornithological Club **Marquis Who's Who Honors:** Albert Nelson Marquis Lifetime Achievement Award (2017); Distinguished Humanitarian (2017) **To what do you attribute your success:** Dr. Moir attributes his success to his organizational skills, management expertise and listening and communication skills. He also credits his success to his ability to learn, both from others and from his own experiences. **Why did you become involved in your profession or industry:** Dr. Moir became involved in his profession because of his desire to protect clean water, wildlife, landscapes and seascapes through education, compassionate stewardship (no poverty) and no pollution. **What do you consider to be the highlight of your career:** The highlight of Dr. Moir's career was organizing individuals from fifty states to speak out in their own voices, work with the New England Congressional Delegation in Washington, DC, the president's Center for Environmental Quality and with many other organizations to create the Northeast Canyons and Seamounts Marine National Monument co-directed by departments of interior and commerce with collaborative management by eleven federal agencies in communication with state agencies from five states and ten tribal nations. **Where will you be in five years:** Dr. Moir intends to further engage citizens, families, and governments to further compassionate stewardship for clean water, healthy environments and to continue attaining a better quality of life without poverty for humans and wildlife. **Hobbies:** Networking; Field biology; Natural history; Admiring wildlife; Sailing; Whale watching; Canoeing; Kayaking; Skiing; Hiking; Snorkeling; Scuba diving; Pub sings **Shipping Address:** 12 Eliot Street, Cambridge, MA, 02138 **Website:** http://www.robmoirphd.com

Ann Moliver Ruben, PhD

Title: Therapist, Psychologist **Industry:** Medicine & Health Care **Date of Birth:** 01/09/1925 **Place of Birth:** Pittsburgh **State:** PA **Parents:** Max Moliver; Fannie (Landy) Moliver **Marital Status:** Married **Spouse Name:** Gershon Ruben (6/26/1943) **Children:** Stephen; Richard; David **Education:** PhD, University of Pittsburgh (1969); MEd, University of Pittsburgh (1965); BS, University of Pittsburgh (1961) **Certifications:** Licensed Psychologist, States of Florida and Pennsylvania **Career:** Private Practice, North Miami Beach, FL (1974-Present); Associate Professor, Barry University, Miami Shores, FL (1972-1976); Mental Health Consultant, University of Pittsburgh (1966-1971); School and Community Agent, Pittsburgh Public Schools (1964-1966); Elementary School Teacher, Pittsburgh Public Schools (1961-1964) **Career Related:** Adjunct Professor, St. Thomas University (1994-Present); President, Women are Wonderful, Inc. (1993-Present); Developer, Marriage Enrichment Program (CAMM) (1980) **Civic:** President, B'nai B'rith Women's Association, Miami, FL (1950-Present); Board of Directors, Alliance for Aging (1999); Jewish Vocational Services (1998) **Creative Works:** Author, "The Memoirs of a Happy Psychologist" (2005); Author, "How I Grew Up Feeling Some Day I Could Be President of the United States of America" (1993); Developer, "Making Marriage Into an Equal Partnership" (1992); Author, "How I Grew to be a Happy Child" (1985); Author, "Our Teachers are Crying" (1975); Designer, Margaret T-shirt **Awards:** Recipient, Unsung Heroine Award (1996); Recipient, Woman of Distinction Award, American Association of University Women (1995); Recipient, Award, Dropout Advisory Commission (1988); Recipient, Special Recognition Award, Association for Couples in Marriage Enrichment (1988); Fellow, Marital and Family Therapy (1982); Fellow, Maurice Falk Medical Foundation (1968); Recipient, Outstanding Service Award, Virginia (1955) **Membership:** President, Florida Association for Marriage and Family Therapy (1985); Citadel Chapter, B'nai B'rith Women (1955); American Counseling Association; Association for Couples in Marriage Enrichment; American Association for Marriage and Family Therapy **Marquis Who's Who Honors:** Albert Nelson Marquis Lifetime Achievement Award (2017) **Hobbies:** Writing; Golf; Playing bridge **Political Affiliations:** Democrat **Shipping Address:** 52 Garetta St Apt., 607B, Pittsburgh, PA, 15217

Matthew Eli Moloshok

Title: Lawyer **Industry:** Law and Legal Services **Company Name:** Hellring Lindeman Goldstein & Siegal LLP **Date of Birth:** 11/14/1952 **Place of Birth:** New York **State:** NY **Parents:** Norman Moloshok; Rita Moloshok **Marital Status:** Married **Spouse Name:** Judith Ann Hudson (7/4/1976) **Children:** Rachel E.; Jared S.; Hannah F. **Education:** JD, George Washington University (1977); BA, Trinity College, Hartford, CT (1974) **Career:** Partner, Hellring Lindeman Goldstein & Siegal LLP (1993-Present); Associate, Hellring Lindeman Goldstein & Siegal LLP (1990-1993); Associate, Taub & Fasciana PC, New York, NY (1987-1990); Associate, Helm Shapiro Anito & Aldrich PC, Albany, NY (1984-1987); Associate, Delson & Gordon, New York, NY (1978-1984); Assistant Clerk, Superior Court Connecticut, Hartford, CT (1977-1978) **Civic:** Fee Arbitration Committee, Supreme Court of New Jersey, Newark, NJ (2010-2014) **Creative Works:** Associate Editor, The Antitrust Source (2002-Present); Author, "Free Speech Versus Fair Markets: Will Credit-Card Surcharge Cases Supercharge the First Amendment?" The Antitrust Source (2017); Author, "Resale Price Maintenance-The New Frontier in Franchising?" Global Competition Review Special Report (2008); Author, "Dr. Miles-A Rock of Ages," The Antitrust Source (2007); Author, "Antitrust Review of the Americas" (2007); Author, "Constraints Against Termination of Dealers and Franchisees," The Antitrust Source (2006); Author, "Franchise and Dealership Arrangements-in the Antitrust Cross-Hairs," Global Competition Review Special Report (2007); Author, "Antitrust Review of the Americas" (2006); Contributor, "The Franchise and Dealership Termination Handbook," ABA Section of Antitrust Law (2003); Co-Author, with Jonathan L. Goldstein, "Antitrust in IP Licensing: Concerns and Considerations," ALA-ABA Course Intellectual Property Licensing in Today's Economy (2002-2003); Program Chair, Moderator, "The Antitrust Injury Doctrine," ABA Antitrust Section Spring Meeting (2002); Co-Moderator, "Redistribution of Power - Antitrust Implications of Internet Distribution of Goods and Services," ABA Antitrust Section Annual Meeting (2000); Contributor, "State Antitrust Practice and Statutes, Second Edition," ABA Section of Antitrust Law, New Jersey Chapter (1999); Co-Author, With Michael J. Lockerby, Diane Green Smith, Ellen R. Lokker and Wayne A. Mack, "Antitrust Class Actions," ABA Antitrust Section Spring Meeting (1999); Co-Author, with Stuart Hershman and Richard J. Wolf, "Problems in Supplying the System," 20th Annual Forum, ABA Forum on Franchising (1997); Author, "Practical Approaches to Termination - From the Dealer/Franchisee Perspective," ABA Antitrust Section Annual Meeting (1995); Author, "Summary Disposition of Material Misstatement Issues in 10b-5 Claims" ABA Litigation Section, Committee on Securities, Securities News (1993); Contributor, "Franchise Protection: Laws Against Termination and the Establishment of Additional Franchises," ABA Section of Antitrust Law, Monograph 17 (1990); Author, "11th Annual Forum, ABA Forum on Franchising" (1988); Author, "Business Opportunity Litigation: Issues & Strategies" **Membership:** Chairman, Franchise and Dealership Committee, Antitrust Section, American Bar Association (1999-2002); New Jersey State Bar Association; New York City Bar Association **Bar Admissions:** United States Court of International Trade (2017); Supreme Court of the United States (2008); United States Tax Court (2007); United States Court of Appeals for the Third Circuit (1991); United States Court of Appeals for the District of Columbia Circuit (1991); United States District Court of New Jersey (1989); United States Court of Appeals for the Second Circuit (1986); United States District Court of New York for the North District (1984); United States District Court of New York for the Eastern District (1980); United States District Court of New York for the Southern Circuit (1980); United States District Court of Connecticut (1978) **Why did you become involved in your profession or industry:** Mr. Moloshok was inspired to go into this law profession by such lawyers as Thurgood Marshall, William Kunstler and Paul Rheingold. His father, lawyer Norman Moloshok and attorney Jacob Stein have also been his mentors. **Where will you be in five years:** In five years, Mr. Moloshok will still be practicing law; it's hard work, but he loves it. **Hobbies:** Triathalons **Business Address:** One Gateway Center, 8th Floor, Newark, NJ, 07102 **Shipping Address:** 1006 Prospect Street, Westfield, NJ, 07090

Frederick Monroe

Title: Geologist, Oceanographer (Retired) **Industry:** Environmental Services **Company Name:** Henderson Unlimited Company **Date of Birth:** 05/03/1936 **Place of Birth:** Washington **Parents:** Sheldon McKinley; Fredericka Fales Monroe **Marital Status:** Married **Spouse Name:** Lori Rose Farquaharson (Married, June 11, 1988); Patricia Ann Lynch (July 11, 1971) (Deceased); Sue Ellen Reeves (Married, October 7, 1963) (Divorced, October 7, 1970) **Children:** Patricia Alexis (Deceased) **Education:** PhD, The American University (1989); MA, University of Miami (1977); MS, The American University (1970); BA, Amherst College (1958) **Certifications:** Professional Geologist, Virginia (1983) **Career:** Faculty, Molecular & Microbiology Department George Mason University; Associate LLC, PRO-telligent, LLC (2007-2011); Defense Trade Analyst, PRO-telligent, LLC (2010-2015); Defense Trade Analyst, US Department State (2006-2010); Coordinator Political Military Action Team, US Department State (2002-2006); Foreign Affairs Officer, US Department State, Washington, DC (1975-2001); Oceanographer Consultant, Arthur Strock, Inc. (1971-1975); Assistant Professor, Ocean Engineering, Florida Atlantic University, Boca Raton, FL (1967-1971); Oceanographer, US Army Corps Engineers, Washington, DC (1962-1967); Physical Science Aide, US Geological Survey, Denver, CO (1962); Geologist, King & Gavaris, Consultant Engineers, New York City, NY (1960-1962) **Career Related:** Adjunct Assistant Professor, Northern Virginia Community College, Alexandria, VA (2002-2005); Professorial Lecturer, The American University, Washington, DC (1989-1993) **Creative Works:** Author, "Stand Up! Hook Up! Shuffle to the Door! The Guide to Choosing the Right Job"; Author, "Score the Right Job! You've Got to Work Anyway-You Might As Well Like It!" (2014) **Awards:** Career Achievement Medal, US Department of State (2001); Meritorious Honor Award (1983) **Membership:** Fellow, The Explorers Club; American Institute of Professional Geologists; Founder, Marine Technology Society **Shipping Address:** 6205 18th St N, Arlington, VA, 22205

Sarah Mook

Title: Chemist (Retired) **Industry:** Sciences **Date of Birth:** 10/29/1929 **Place of Birth:** Brooklyn **State:** NY **Parents:** Wong Mook; Lie Won (Woo) Mook **Education:** Postgraduate Work, Columbia University (1962-1965); Postgraduate Work, University of Hartford (1958-1959); Postgraduate Work, Columbia University (1954-1957); BA, Hunter College (1952) **Certifications:** Diplomate, Citizens Police Academy Program, The City of New York (2001) **Career:** Principal Chemist, Bellevue Hospital Center, The City of New York (1989-1995); Associate Chemist, Bellevue Hospital Center, The City of New York (1984-1989); Community Board, Coney Island Hospital, The City of New York (1978-1980); Clinical Chemist, Coney Island Hospital, The City of New York (1974-1984); Senior Chemist, Nuclear Research Associates, Inc., National Rifle Association of America (1964-1975); Chemist, Marks Polarized Corporation (1962-1964); Research Scientist, Radiations Applications Inc. (1959-1962); Analytical Chemist, Nuclear Division, Combustion Engineering, Inc. (Now ALSTOM) (1957-1959); Research Assistant, Mineral Beneficiation Laboratory, Columbia University (1954-1957); Cartographic Aide, United States Geological Survey, U.S. Department of the Interior (1952-1954) **Career Related:** Member, Patient Safety Committee, Coney Island Hospital, The City of New York (2007-Present); Instructor in English as a Second Language, Jay-Harama Senior Center, The City of New York (2006-Present); Staff, Homecrest Community Services (1999-2005) **Civic:** Member, By-Laws Committee, Coney Island Hospital, The City of New York (2009-Present); Member, Community Advisory Board, Coney Island Hospital, The City of New York (2004-Present); Member, Neighborhood Advisory Board, Department of Youth & Community Development, The City of New York (1996-Present); Elder, Women's Christian Fellowship (1982-Present); Chair, Legislative Committee, Coney Island Hospital, The City of New York (2011-2013); Member, Membership Committee, Coney Island Hospital, The City of New York (2011-2012); Member, Community Board, Department of Youth & Community Development, The City of New York (2002-2004); Chair, Neighborhood Advisory Board, Department of Youth & Community Development, The City of New York (2000-2002); Secretary, Neighborhood Advisory Board, Department of Youth & Community Development, The City of New York (1996-1999); Chair, Board of Trustees, Park Avenue Christian Church (1981-1982); Trustee, Park Avenue Christian Church (1973-1982); Vice-Chair, Park Avenue Christian Church (1980-1981); Secretary, Park Avenue Christian Church (1973-1980); Member, Advisory Committee to State Assemblyman, State of New York (1970-1972); President, Women's Christian Fellowship (1962-1965) **Creative Works:** Contributor, Articles, Professional Journals **Awards:** Certificate of Recognition, Coney Island Hospital, The City of New York (2012); Marjorie Matthews Community Advocate Recognition Award, Health & Hospital Committee, The New York City Council (2008); Woman of Year Humanitarian Award, The New York State Senate (2004); Honoree, Woman Of Year, New York City Council (2004); Margaret M. McCord Woman of the Year Memorial Award, Brooklyn Historical Society (2004); Distinguished Leadership in Community Award, Office Of the New York City Comptroller **Membership:** Publicity Committee, National Citizens Police Academy Association (2004-Present); Secretary, New York Metropolitan Section, American Association for Clinical Chemistry (1999-2008); American Association for the Advancement of Science; American Chemical Society; The New York Academy of Sciences; Van Slyke Society **Marquis Who's Who Honors:** Albert Nelson Marquis Lifetime Achievement Award (2017); Distinguished Humanitarian (2017) **Why did you become involved in your profession or industry:** She always wanted to be in medicine. When she realized it was not in her best interest, she switched to chemistry. **What do you consider to be the highlight of your career:** Being published in analytical chemistry journals, and being cited in chemistry abstracts. **Political Affiliations:** Republican **Shipping Address:** 2042 E. 14th St., Brooklyn, NY, 11229

Charles Loyd Moore

Title: Chancellor, Lawyer **Industry:** Law and Legal Services **Company Name:** New Mexico United Methodist Church **Date of Birth:** 08/14/1944 **Place of Birth:** El Paso **State:** TX **Parents:** Charles McKinney Moore; Alice Adeline (Loyd) Moore **Marital Status:** Married **Spouse Name:** Peggy Jo Ball (12/20/1969) **Children:** Kirk; Julie **Education:** JD, Southern Methodist University, Dallas, TX, Summa Cum Laude (1975); MME, California Institute of Technology (1968); BS in Military Engineering, U.S. Military Academy, West Point, NY (1966) **Career:** Associate General Counsel, PNM Resources (2005-2016); Keleher & McLeod, P.A., Albuquerque, NM (1979-2005); Associate, Keleher & McLeod, P.A., Albuquerque, NM (1975-1979) **Civic:** Emeritus Trustee, The Hatton W. Sumners Foundation, Dallas, TX (2017-Present); Vice Chairman, The Hatton W. Summers Foundation, Dallas, TX (2006-2016); Director, Foundation Board, Robert O. Anderson School of Management, University of New Mexico (2003-2005); Co-Chairman, New Mexico Lawyers for General Wesley Clark for President Campaign (2003-2004); Trustee, The Hatton W. Sumners Foundation, Dallas, TX (1999-2016); Trustee, McMurry University, Abilene, TX (1989-1992); District Co-Chairman, Annual Fund Campaign, McMurry University, Abilene, TX (1988); Chancellor, New Mexico United Methodist Church **Military Service:** Resigned, U.S. Army (1972); Captain, U.S. Army (1968); Commissioned Second Lieutenant, U.S. Army (1966) **Creative Works:** Contributor, Articles, Professional Journals **Awards:** Honoree, New Mexico Business Lawyer of the Year (2005); One of the Best Lawyers of America (1989-2006); Honoree, International Graduate of the Year Biennial Convention, The International Legal Honor Society of Phi Delta Phi (1975); Decorated Joint Service Commendation Medal; Bronze Star; Vietnam Campaign Medal; Vietnam Service Medal **Membership:** Chairman, Business Law Section, State Bar of New Mexico (2001); Vice President, Young Lawyers Division, State Bar of New Mexico (1977-1978); American Bar Association; Albuquerque Bar Association; The International Legal Honor Society of Phi Delta Phi; The Honor Society of Phi Kappa Phi; West Point Association of Graduates; Society for Military History **Bar Admissions:** State Bar of New Mexico (1975); U.S. District Court (1975) **Marquis Who's Who Honors:** Albert Nelson Marquis Lifetime Achievement Award (2017); Distinguished Humanitarian (2017) **Hobbies:** Running; Reading **Political Affiliations:** Democrat **Religion:** Methodist **Shipping Address:** 5901J Wyoming Boulevard NE, 154, Albuquerque, NM, 87109

James Conklin Moore

Title: Lawyer **Industry:** Law and Legal Services **Company Name:** Law Offices of James Moore **Date of Birth:** 12/20/1939 **Place of Birth:** Albany **State:** NY **Parents:** James Alexander Moore; Doris Virginia (Conklin) Moore **Marital Status:** Married **Spouse Name:** Shirley Jean Mitchell (6/17/1961, Deceased) **Children:** James; Jennifer; David; Eliza **Education:** LLB, Cornell University (1964); BS, Cornell University (1961) **Career:** Independent Mediator, Harter, Secrest & Emery LLP (2011-Present); Arbitrator, Harter, Secrest & Emery LLP (2011-Present); Senior Counsel, Harter, Secrest & Emery LLP (2004-2010); Partner, Harter, Secrest & Emery LLP (1974-2003); Associate, Wiser, Shaw, Freeman, VanGraafeiland, Harter & Secrest (Now Harter Secrest & Emery LLP) (1966-1974) **Career Related:** Board of Directors, Arts & Cultural Council for Greater Rochester (2009-Present); Chairman, Empire Justice Center (2007-2009); Fellow, American Bar Association **Civic:** Board of Governors, Memorial Art Gallery (2015-Present); Director, Highlands Pittsford Entities, Strong Partners Inc. (2012-Present); Director, Hillside Family of Agencies (2011-2014); Trustee, National Equal Justice Library, Georgetown Law (2006-2008); Board of Directors, Geva Theater Center (2002-2009); Board of Directors, Monroe County Bar Foundation (2002-2004); President, The Legal Connection Inc. (2002-2004); Chairman, Board of Trustees, New York Lawyer Assistance Trust (2001-2004); Council Member, Cornell University (1997-2002); Trustee, Friends & Foundation of the Rochester Public Library (1993-1998); President, Friends & Foundation of the Rochester Public Library (1993-1998) **Military Service:** Captain, U.S. Army, Vietnam (1964-1966) **Creative Works:** Board of Editors, "Warren's Negligence in the New York Courts" (2001-2013) **Awards:** Elder, Third Presbyterian Church, Rochester, NY; Trustee, Third Presbyterian Church, Rochester, NY **Membership:** Executive Committee, Union International Advocate (2007-Present); Chairman, Committee on Judicial Nominations, New York State Bar Association (2006-Present); House of Delegates, New York State Bar Association (1993-Present); Chairman, Committee for Lawyer Advertising, Monroe County Bar Association (2006-2012); Chairman, Committee on ADR, New York State Bar Association (2006-2008); United States President, Union International Advocate (2005-2007); Trustee, Monroe County Bar Association (2004-2006); Chairman, Nominating Committee, New York State Bar Association (2001); Executive Committee, National Conference Bar President (1999-2002); President, New York State Bar Association (1998-1999); House of Delegates, American Bar Association (1998-2006); Board of Directors, The New York Bar Foundation (1997-2000); Vice President, New York State Bar Association (1994-1997); Executive Committee, New York State Bar Association (1992-2000); Chairman, Committee for Insurance Programs, New York State Bar Association (1988-1994); Chairman, Task Force on Liability Insurance, New York State Bar Association (1986-1987); Chairman, Task Force on Liability Insurance, New York State Bar Association (1986-1987); Chairman, Insurance Section, New York State Bar Association (1984-1985); Chairman, Judiciary Committee, Monroe County Bar Association (1982-1985); Advisory Board, Rochester Area Educational TV (1981-1987); Standing Communications on Legal Assistance to Indigent Defendants, American Bar Association; Commercial Panel Neutral, American Arbitration Association; American Law Institute **Bar Admissions:** U.S. District Court, Middle District, State of Pennsylvania (1981); U.S. District Court, Northern District, State of New York (1980); U.S. District Court, Western District, State of New York (1966); U.S. Court of Military Appeals (1965); State of New York (1964) **Hobbies:** History; Restoring old furniture; Art **Religion:** Presbyterian **Shipping Address:** 19 Oakfield Way, Pittsford, NY, 14534

Wesley Sanford Moore

Title: Vascular Surgeon **Industry:** Medicine & Health Care **Company Name:** David Geffen School of Medicine at UCLA **Date of Birth:** 08/01/1935 **Place of Birth:** San Bernardino **State:** CA **Parents:** Louis Moore; Anna Moore **Marital Status:** Married **Spouse Name:** Patricia Lorenz (10/25/1960) **Children:** Edward Lorenz; Michael Robertson **Education:** Assistant Resident in General Surgery, UCSF Medical Center (1960-1963); Intern, University of California San Francisco (1959-1960); MD, UCSF School of Medicine (1959); BS, University of Southern California (1955) **Certifications:** Medical License, State of California at UCLA (2005); Certified in General Vascular Surgery, American Board of Surgery, Inc. (2003); Certified X-ray Supervisor and Operator, State of California (2000); Certified in General Vascular Surgery, American Board of Surgery, Inc. (1992); Certified in General Vascular Surgery, American Board of Surgery, Inc. (1983); Medical License, State of Arizona (1977); Certified in Surgery, American Board of Surgery, Inc. (1966); Medical License, State of California at UCLA (1960) **Career:** Professor Emeritus, David Geffen School of Medicine, UCLA (2004-Present); Chief Emeritus, David Geffen School of Medicine, UCLA (2004-Present); Attending Vascular Surgeon, David Geffen School of Medicine, UCLA (2004-Present); Professor of Surgery, David Geffen School of Medicine, UCLA (1980-2004); Staff Surgeon, VA West Los Angeles Medical Center, U.S. Department of Veterans Affairs (1980-1984); Chief, Vascular Surgery Section, Center for the Health Sciences, UCLA (1980-1996); Program Director, General Vascular Surgery Residency, Center for the Health Sciences, UCLA (1980-1996); Staff Surgeon, VA Sepulveda Ambulatory Care Center, U.S. Department of Veterans Affairs (1984-1993); Chief, Vascular Surgery Section, Southern Arizona VA Health Care System, U.S. Department of Veterans Affairs (1977-1980); Professor of Surgery, College of Medicine, University of Arizona (1977-1980); Assistant Chief of Surgery Service, San Francisco VA Health Care System, U.S. Department of Veterans Affairs (1975-1977); Associate Professor of Surgery, UCSF School of Medicine (1973-1977); Assistant Professor of Surgery, UCSF School of Medicine (1968-1973); Clinical Instructor in Surgery, UCSF School of Medicine (1966-1968); Chief, Vascular Surgery Section, San Francisco VA Health Care System, U.S. Department of Veterans Affairs (1966-1967); National Institutes of Health Research Fellow in Cerebrovascular Insufficiency, San Francisco VA Health Care System, U.S. Department of Veterans Affairs (1966-1967); Chief Resident in General Surgery, UCSF Medical Center (1963-1964) **Career Related:** Consultant, Medical Policy Committee, Blue Cross of California (1987-1996) **Civic:** Member, College of Applied Anatomy Advisory Council, Center for the Health Sciences, UCLA (2000-Present); Appointee, Volunteer Clinical Appointments and Promotions Committee, Center for the Health Sciences, UCLA (1996-Present); Member, Executive Council for Investigative Study, Center for the Health Sciences, UCLA (1991-Present) **Creative Works:** Editorial Board Member, Vascular (2003-Present); Member, Editorial Panel, Indian Journal of Vascular and Endovascular Surgery (1999-Present); Senior Editor, EndoCardioVascular Multimedia Magazine (1998-Present); Editorial Board Member, International Vascular Surgery (1991-Present); Editor, "Vascular and Endovascular Surgery. A Comprehensive Review, Eighth Edition," Elsevier (2012); Co-Editor, "A Handbook of Vascular Disease Management," Word Scientific (2011); Co-Editor, "Endovascular Surgery, Fourth Edition," Elsevier (2010); Editor, "Vascular and Endovascular Surgery: A Comprehensive Review, Seventh Edition," Elsevier (2006) **Awards:** Lifetime Achievement Award, Institute of Vascular Diseases (2014); Recipient, Dickson Emeriti Faculty Award, UCLA Health (2012); Recipient, Lifetime Achievement Award, Society of Vascular Surgery (2011); Recipient, Leonard Tow Humanism in Medicine Award, The Arnold P. Gold Foundation (2007); Recipient, America's Top Doctor Award, Castle Connolly Medical Ltd. (2001); Honoree, Best Doctors in America (1996); Recipient, Paulo Samual Santos Medal, International Symposium in Vasuclar Surgery (1988); Recipient, Golden Scalpel Award for Excellence in Teaching, (1984-1985); David Geffen School of Medicine, UCLA (1984-1985); Recipient, Research Fellowship, National Institutes of Health (1966) **Membership:** Gold Humanism Honor Society, Gold Foundation (2007-Present); Honorary Member, New England Society for Vascular Surgery (2003-Present); Honorary Member, Canadian Society for Vascular Surgery (2003-Present); Board of Technology and Clinical Studies, Society for Vascular Surgery (2001-Present); European Society for Vascular Surgery (1996-Present); Society of University Surgeons (1975-Present); International Union of Angiology (1994-Present); Longmire Surgical Society, UCLA Health (1993-Present); Founder, Western Vascular Society (1985-Present); Founder, Southern California Vascular Surgical Society (1982-Present); Fellow, American Surgical Association (1980-Present) **Marquis Who's Who Honors:** Albert Nelson Marquis Lifetime Achievement Award (2017) **Shipping Address:** 11467 W Sunset Blvd, Los Angeles, CA, 90049

Dennis Richard Morgan

Title: Lawyer **Industry:** Law and Legal Services **Date of Birth:** 01/03/1942 **Place of Birth:** Lexington **State:** VA **Parents:** Benjamin Richard Morgan; Gladys Belle (Brown) Morgan **Marital Status:** Single **Education:** LLM in Labor Law, New York University (1971); JD, University of Virginia (1967); BA, Washington and Lee University (1964) **Career:** Private Practice, Columbus, Ohio (1978-1992); Associate, Clemans, Nelson & Associates, Columbus, Ohio (1981); Director, Ohio Legislative Reference Bureau, Columbus, Ohio (1979-1981); Assistant City Attorney, Columbus, Ohio (1975-1977); Director, Labor Relations, Ohio Department of Administrative Services (1972-1975); Member, Marshman, Snyder & Seeley, Cleveland, Ohio (1971-1972); Law Clerk to Chief Judge, United State District Court for the Eastern District of Virginia (1967-1968) **Career Related:** Assistant Attorney General, State of Ohio (1991-2003); Personnel Director, Public Utilities Commission, Ohio (1989-1991); Judge, Moot Court (1983); Legal Counsel, District IV, Communications Workers of America (1982-1988); Judge, Moot Court (1981); Graduate Division, The Ohio State University Moritz College of Law (1976); Guest Lecturer, Central Michigan University (1975); Graduate Division, The Ohio State University Moritz College of Law (1973-1974); Guest Lecturer, Baldwin-Wallace University (1973); Lecturer in Field **Civic:** Vice President, Woodbrook Village Condominium Association (2005-2009); Board of Directors, Hilltop Civic Council, Inc. (1997-1999); Member, Greater Hilltop Area Commission (1989-2006); President, Woodbrook Village Condominium Association (1985-2005); Negotiator, Franklin County United Way (1977-1981); Regional Chairman, Annual Alumni Fundraising Program, University of Virginia School of Law (1976-2007); Vice-chairman, Franklin County Democratic Party (1976-1982); Co-founder, Greater West Side Democratic Club (1974); Trustee, Greater West Side Democratic Club (1974); Chairman, Rules Committee, Ohio State Democratic Convention (1974); Democratic Committee Person, Ward 58, Columbus, Ohio (1973-2006) **Military Service:** Captain, United States Army (1968-1970) **Awards:** American Jurisprudence Award (1967); Scholar, Robert E. Lee Research (1965) **Membership:** Federal Bar Association; Pi Sigma Alpha **Bar Admissions:** Supreme Court of the United States (1972); United States Court of Appeals for the Sixth Circuit (1971); United States Court of Appeals for the Fourth Circuit (1968); Virginia State Bar (1967); Ohio State Bar (1967) **Marquis Who's Who Honors:** Albert Nelson Marquis Lifetime Achievement Award (2017) **Why did you become involved in your profession or industry:** He became involved in his profession because he loves working with people. Working as a lawyer is very exciting, as every case and situation are different, and it allows a freedom that other professions do not. **Where will you be in five years:** In five years he will continue to do what he is doing now, as he loves his work. **Political Affiliations:** Democrat **Religion:** Roman Catholic **Shipping Address:** 21320 Lancaster Run Unit 1116, Estero, FL, 33928

Paula S. Morgan

Title: Engineer **Industry:** Engineering **Company Name:** California Institute of Technology **Education:** BS in Aerospace Engineering, California State Polytechnic University, Pomona, CA (1980) **Career:** Section 349 Technical Leader, Jet Propulsion Laboratory, California Institute of Technology, National Aeronautics and Space Administration (2013-Present); Lead Engineer, Cassini Spacecraft Command & Data System Fault Protection Team, Jet Propulsion Laboratory, California Institute of Technology, National Aeronautics and Space Administration (1997-Present); Flight Software Engineer, Jet Propulsion Laboratory, California Institute of Technology (1997-Present); Group Supervisor, Multimission Operations, Flight Avionics Section, Jet Propulsion Laboratory, California Institute of Technology (2009-2011); Team Member, Constellation Level 2 Program, Jet Propulsion Laboratory, California Institute of Technology (2009-2010); Mars Reconnaissance Orbitor, Anomaly Investigation Team, Jet Propulsion Laboratory, California Institute of Technology (2008-2009); EPOXI Lead Engineer, Jet Propulsion Laboratory, California Institute of Technology (2007-2009); Kepler Fault Protection Engineer, Jet Propulsion Laboratory, California Institute of Technology (2005-2007); CloudSat Spacecraft Fault Protection Review, CJet Propulsion Laboratory, California Institute of Technology (2000); Command & Data Subsystem Test Engineer, Madentech Engineering (1997); Loads Analyst, Kenetch Wind Power (1994-1995); Senior Engineer Specialist, Rockwell International Space Systems Division (1980-1994); Separation Systems Team Leader, Rockwell International Space Systems Division (1980-1994) **Career Related:** Board Member, Stardust Spacecraft, Cal Tech/ Jet Propulsion Laboratory (1997) **Creative Works:** Author, "Cassini Mission-to-Saturn Spacecraft Overview & CDS Preparations for End-of-Mission Proximal Orbits," IEEE Conference (2015); Author, "Cassini Spacecraft In-Flight Fault Protection Redesign for Unexpected Regulator Malfunction"; Author, 'Resolving the Difficulties Encountered by JPL Interplanetary Robotic Spacecraft in Flight,' "Spacecraft," InTech Open Access Publishers; Author, 'Robotic Spacecraft Health Management,' "Systems Health Management," Wiley Publishers; Author, "Protecting Against Faults in JPL Spacecraft"; Author, "Fault Protection Techniques in JPL Spacecraft" **Awards:** Certificate of Recognition, National Aeronautics and Space Administration (2006) **To what do you attribute your success:** Ms. Morgan attributes her success to self-learning and learning about every aspect of what she does. Every spacecraft is different, so it forces you to learn. **Why did you become involved in your profession or industry:** Ms. Morgan became involved in her profession because she always wanted to be an astronaut, but it is a very risky profession and she decided against it. Because of her interest in astronomy, satellites, and robotics, she naturally came to become a spacecraft engineer. **Where will you be in five years:** In five years, Ms. Morgan hopes to be working on the new spacecraft project. For now, she is finishing up on the Cassini project. **Hobbies:** Guitar **Shipping Address:** 23484 Thornewood Drive, Newhall, CA, 91321

Alisa M. Morgenthaler

Title: Lawyer **Industry:** Law and Legal Services **Date of Birth:** 06/03/1960 **Place of Birth:** St. Louis **State:** MO **Parents:** Gerald Thomas Morgenthaler; Mary Louise (Neece) Morgenthaler **Education:** JD, Cornell University (1985); BA, Missouri State University (1982) **Career:** Founding Partner, Morgenthaler Law Group, Los Angeles, CA (2011-Present); Of Counsel, Frandzel Robins Bloom & Csato, L.C., Los Angeles, CA (2011-2014); Partner, Glaser Weil Fink Howard Avchen & Shapiro LLP, Los Angeles, CA (1989-2011); Associate, Stroock & Stroock & Lavan LLP, Washington, DC (1988-1989); Associate, K&L Gates LLP, Washington, DC (1986-1988); Attorney, Board of Governors, Federal Reserve System, Washington, DC (1985-1986); Attorney, Board of Governors, Federal Reserve System, Washington, DC (1984); Law Clerk, Springfield, MO (1981) **Civic:** Member, Board of Directors, South Brentwood Residents Association (2015-Present); Member, Brentwood Community Council (2018-Present), Member, Board of Directors, L.A. Retarded Citizens Foundation (2000-Present); President, Board of Directors, Mayfield Gardens Townhomes Association (2011-Present); Member, Board of Directors, Malibu Riviera 3 Homeowners Association, Inc. (2000-2004); Member, Board of Directors, 3019 Third Street Owner's Association (1991-2002) **Awards:** Named to Southern California Super Lawyers (2006-Present); Named One of Top 50 Women Lawyers of Southern California (2009-2010); Named One of Top 50 Women Lawyers of Southern California (2007) **Membership:** Judicial Appointments Committee, Los Angeles County Bar Association (1999-2007); ABA; Committee on Administration of Justice, The State Bar of California; The District of Columbia Bar; New York Bar Association; Beverly Hills Bar Association; Member, Board of Directors, Century City Bar Association; Board of Directors, Women Lawyers Association of Los Angeles; Order of Omega; Phi Alpha Delta; Rho Lambda; Phi Kappa Phi; Pi Sigma Alpha; Gamma Phi Beta **Bar Admissions:** State of California (1990); The District of Columbia (1988); New York (1986) **Marquis Who's Who Honors:** Albert Nelson Marquis Lifetime Achievement Award (2017) **Shipping Address:** 11974 Mayfield Ave Unit 7, Los Angeles, CA, 90049 **Website:** http://morgenthalerlawgroup.com/

James Morphy

Title: Lawyer **Industry:** Law and Legal Services **Company Name:** Sullivan & Cromwell LLP **Date of Birth:** 01/16/1954 **Place of Birth:** Pittsburgh **State:** PA **Parents:** Robert Samson Morphy; Autumn (Phillips) Morphy **Marital Status:** Married **Spouse Name:** Priscilla Winslow Plimpton (7/11/1981) **Children:** Calvin; Katherine; Victoria **Education:** JD, Harvard University, Cambridge, MA (1979); BA, Harvard University, Cambridge, MA (1976) **Career:** Firm Managing Partner, Sullivan & Cromwell LLP (2007-Present); Partner, Sullivan & Cromwell LLP, New York, NY (1986-Present); Managing Partner, Mergers and Acquisitions Group, Sullivan & Cromwell LLP, New York, NY (1995-2007); Managing Partner, Committee, Sullivan & Cromwell LLP, New York, NY (1992-1995); Associate, Sullivan & Cromwell LLP, New York, NY (1979-1986) **Career Related:** Advisory Board of Governors, Harvard Corporate Governance Program; Guest Lecturer, Harvard Law School; Former Co-Chairman, Tulane University Law School **Civic:** Former Trustee, Greenwich Academy **Creative Works:** Contributor, "Treatise Transactional Lawyer's Deskbook" (2001); Contributor, "Treatise New York and Delaware Business Entities: Choice Formation, Operation, Financing, and Acquisition" (1997) **Awards:** New York Merger and Acquisitions Lawyer of the Year (2010); American Lawyer Dealmaker of the Year (2007); Ten Most Highly Regarded Lawyers in the World; One of Lawdragon's 500 Leading Lawyers in America; Best Lawyer's Award **Membership:** Committee, Corporate Law, American Bar Association (2009-Present); Committee, Federal Securities Law, American Bar Association (1992-Present); Association for the Bar of the City of New York; Board of Governors, Wianno Club; Greenwich Country Club; Wianno Yacht Club; Phi Beta Kappa; Farmington County Club; The Sanctuary Golf Club **Bar Admissions:** State of New York (1980) **Marquis Who's Who Honors:** Albert Nelson Marquis Lifetime Achievement Award (2017) **Shipping Address:** 4 Lindsay Drive, Greenwich, CT, 06830

Joseph Constantino Morreale

Industry: Education/Educational Services **Date of Birth:** 10/26/1944 **Place of Birth:** Bronx **State:** NY **Parents:** Joseph Vincent Morreale; Grace (Soricelli) Morreale **Marital Status:** Married **Spouse Name:** Barbara McAdorey **Children:** Gwenn F.; Margaret I.; Adam J.; Neil J. (Stepchild); Michael D. (Stepchild); John D. (Stepchild) **Education:** MS in Higher Educational Administration, University at Albany (1989); PhD in Economics, University at Buffalo (1972); MA, University at Buffalo (1969); BA, Queens College, The City College of New York (1967) **Career:** Chair, Economics Department, Pace University (2014-Present); Visiting Professor, University of Shanghai for Science and Technology (2009-2016); Provost, Pace University (2003-2007); Chief Academic Officer, Pace University (2003-2007); Vice President, Planning, Assessment, Research and Academy Support, Pace University (1998-2003); Vice-Provost, Planning Assessment and Institutional Research, Pace University (1996-1998); Professor, Graduate School, Pace University (1989-1996); Chairman, Department of Public Administration, Graduate School, Pace University (1989-1996); Visiting Research Fellow, Higher Education Administration, Graduate School of Education, University at Albany (1988-1989); Professor, Economics, Bard College (1979-1988); Professor, Environmental Studies, Bard College (1979-1988); Associate Professor, Economics, Bard College (1979-1988); Associate Professor, Environmental Studies, Bard College (1979-1988); Associate Professor, Health Services Administration, Graduate School of Public Health, University of Pittsburgh (1975-1979); Associate Professor, Economics, Graduate School of Public Health, University of Pittsburgh (1975-1979); Assistant Professor, Health Services Administration, Graduate School of Public Health, University of Pittsburgh (1975-1979); Assistant Professor, Economics, Graduate School of Public Health, University of Pittsburgh (1975-1979); Research Associate, University of Wisconsin-Madison (1974-1975); Assistant Professor, Economics, Western Michigan University (1970-1974) **Career Related:** Health Care and Government Finance Consultant, Federal Agencies (1979-Present); Health Care and Government Finance Consultant, State and Local Governments (1979-Present); Health Care and Government Finance Consultant, Private Firms (1979-Present); Adjunct Professor, Law, Pace University (1990-1996); Adjunct Professor, Public Administration, Graduate School of Public Affairs, University at Albany (1990-1996); Visiting Professor, Lancaster University (1984-1985); Research Associate, Hudsonia Ltd. (1985-1995); Board of Directors, Hudsonia Ltd. (1985-1995); Financial Planner, Prudential Financial, Inc. (1987-1989); Founder, Chinese Economics Studies Program, Pace University **Civic:** Appointed Public Representative, Westchester County Deferred Compensation Board; Appointed Public Representative, Planning Board, Village/Town of Mount Kisco **Creative Works:** Author, "Post Tenure Review and Renewal: Experienced Voices" (2002); Editor, "Post-tenure Review: Policies, Practices, Precautions" (1997); Author, "Health Care Economics" (1977); Editor, "The U.S. Medical Care Industry" (1974); Contributor, Articles, Professional Journals **Awards:** Senior Research Fellowship, Institute for Educational Management, Graduate School of Education, Harvard University (2000); American Council on Education Fellowship, UNC Charlotte (1995-1996); Research Fellowship, Graduate School of Education, University at Albany (1988-1989); Post-Doctoral Fellowship, Health Economic Research Center, University of Wisconsin (1974-1975); National Defense Education Act Fellowship (1967-1970); Pharmaceutical Manufacturing Association Fellowship (1969-1970) **Membership:** The American Society for Public Administration; American Economic Association; American Educational Financial Association; Association for Institutional Research; AAHEA; American Council on Education; Executive Board, International Atlantic Economic Society **Marquis Who's Who Honors:** Albert Nelson Marquis Lifetime Achievement Award (2017) **Why did you become involved in your profession or industry:** Dr. Morreale was always very curious about everything and enjoying the whole idea of transferring what he was learning to students who were just being exposed to the field. He really enjoys researching as well. **Hobbies:** Photography; Tennis; Music **Religion:** The Religious Society of Friends **Shipping Address:** 7 Rolling Ridge Ct, Mount Kisco, NY, 10549

James Winston Morris, PhD

Title: Professor **Industry:** Education/Educational Services **Company Name:** Boston College **Date of Birth:** 03/18/1949 **Place of Birth:** Mendota **State:** IL **Parents:** Fred Morris; Mildred Morris **Marital Status:** Married **Spouse Name:** Corinna Fernald Merriman-Morris **Children:** Gabriel E.; Michael J.; Julia E.; Jacob S. **Education:** PhD in Near Eastern Languages and Civilizations, Harvard University, Cambridge, MA (1980); BA, University of Chicago, Chicago, IL, Summa Cum Laude (1971) **Career:** Professor in Islamic Studies, Department of Theology, Boston College, Chestnut Hill, MA (2006-Present); Professor, Sharjah Chair of Islamic Studies, Institute of Arab and Islamic Studies, University of Exeter, Exeter, United Kingdom (1999-2006); Associate Professor, Department of Religion, Oberlin College, Oberlin, OH (1989-1999); Visiting Professor, Department of Religion/NES, Princeton University, Princeton, NJ (1988-1989); Professor in Islamic Studies, Institute of Ismaili Studies, Paris, France (1981-1987) **Career Related:** Leverhulme Fellowship (2005); Arts and Humanities Research Board Fellow (2003); Powers Traveling Fellowship (1998); Life Fellow, Muhyiddin Ibn 'Arabi Society (1992-2010); Fellow, Rumi Institute **Awards:** Tercuman Prize for Contributions to Ibn Arabi Studies, Ibn Arabi Latina, Murcia (2014); Research Grant, Nour Foundation (2012); Research Grant, British Academy and British Institute for Persian Studies (2007); International Book Prize for Islamic Philosophy and Spirituality, Iran (2007); Research Grant, National Endowment for the Humanities **Membership:** Head, International Advisory Committee, Rumi Institute (2005-2007); UK Board Member, BRISMES (2002-2006); Society for Iranian Studies; Middle East Studies Association; American Academy of Religion; American Oriental Society; Societe Asiatique; Muhyiddin Ibn 'Arabi Society **Marquis Who's Who Honors:** Albert Nelson Marquis Lifetime Achievement Award (2017) **Business Address:** 140 Commonwealth Avenue, 140 Commonwealth Avenue, MA, Chestnut Hill, 02467 **Shipping Address:** 140 Commonwealth Avenue, Boston College Department of Theology, Chestnut Hill, MA, 02467

Kenneth Wayne Morris

Title: Dentist **Industry:** Health, Wellness and Fitness **Company Name:** VCU Health **Date of Birth:** 03/12/1939 **Place of Birth:** Lynchburg **State:** VA **Parents:** Ulysses Bernice Morris; Elvira (Adams) Morris **Marital Status:** Married **Spouse Name:** Robin C. Morris (6/19/1977); Judy A. Morris (Deceased 12/1976) **Education:** DDS, School of Dentistry, Virginia Commonwealth University (1965); BA, University of Virginia (1961) **Career:** Staff, Community Memorial Hospital, VCU Health (1967-Present); Specialist in General Dentistry, Private Practice (1967) **Civic:** Chairman, Foundation Board, Mid-Atlantic Christian University; Chairman, Board of Elders, Pleasant Hill Christian Church; Member, Deacon's Board, Pleasant Hill Christian Church **Creative Works:** Recording Artist, Gospel Records (1978) **Membership:** American Dental Association; State Chaplain, The Gideons International; State Faith Fund Coordinator, The Gideons International; State Vice President, The Gideons International; State President, The Gideons International; Virginia Dental Association; Southside Component, South Hill Chamber of Commerce; Tanglewood Shores Association; Lake Gaston Golf Club **Marquis Who's Who Honors:** Albert Nelson Marquis Lifetime Achievement Award (2017) **Hobbies:** Fishing; Skiing; Golf; Tennis; Baseball **Political Affiliations:** Republican **Shipping Address:** PO Box 598, Gasburg, VA, 23857

James William Morrison Jr.

Title: Government Agency Administrator **Industry:** Government Administration/Government Relations/Government Services **Date of Birth:** 01/14/1936 **Place of Birth:** Bluefield **State:** WV **Parents:** James William Morrison; Winnie Ella (Hendricks) Morrison **Marital Status:** Married **Spouse Name:** Jean Murray Barber (5/15/2001); Marva Elizabeth Tillman (8/8/1957, Divorced 1984) **Children:** Traquita Renee; James William, III; Susannah Claire (Stepdaughter) **Education:** MPA, University of Dayton, Dayton, Ohio (1970); BA, West Virginia State College (Now West Virginia State University) (1957) **Career:** President, Morrison Associates (1988-2013); Senior Management, CNA Insurance Company (Now CNA Financial Corporation) (1987-1988); Associate Director of Compensation, United States Office of Personnel Management (1981-1987); Director of Congressional Relations, United States Office of Personnel Management (1979-1981); Assistant Director of Economic and Government, United States Office of Personnel Management (1979); Senior Management Associate, Executive Office of the President, Office of Management and Budget (1974-1979); Executive Assistant to Director of Management System, NASA, Washington, DC (1972-1974); Management Specialist, Air Force Logistics Command (Now Air Force Material Command), Dayton, Ohio (1963-1972); Inventory Manager, Dayton Air Force Depot/Defense Electronics Supply Center (1959-1963) **Career Related:** Visiting Lecturer, Public Executive Project, University at Albany, State University of New York, Albany, NY (1974-1976) **Civic:** Advisory Committee, Dayton Board of Education (Now Dayton Public Schools) (1971) **Military Service:** Lieutenant, United States Army (1957-1959) **Creative Works:** Contributor, Articles to Professional Journals **Awards:** Presidential Rank Award of Distinguished Executive (1985); Presidential Award for Meritis (1981) **Membership:** Alpha Phi Alpha; Pi Delta Phi; Pi Alpha Alpha **Marquis Who's Who Honors:** Albert Nelson Marquis Lifetime Achievement Award (2017) **What do you consider to be the highlight of your career:** The highlight of Mr. Morrison's career was successfully starting and managing his own company. **Hobbies:** Jazz **Political Affiliations:** Independent **Religion:** Presbyterian **Shipping Address:** 7078 E Chipmunk Ct, Tucson, AZ, 85750

Linda June Morton

Title: Academic Administrator **Industry:** Education/Educational Services **Date of Birth:** 01/21/1943 **Place of Birth:** Nashville **State:** TN **Parents:** William Taylor Morton; Ruby Grayson (Maiden name-Page) Morton **Education:** PhD, Vanderbilt University (1981); MS, Peabody College (1976); BA, Peabody College (1964) **Certifications:** Certified Career Ladder III Teacher, State of Tennessee (1985); Certified Educational Administrator, State of Tennessee (1981); Certified Music Teacher, Grades K-12, State of Tennessee (1964); Certified English Teacher, Grades 7-12, State of Tennessee (1964) **Career:** Assistant Principal, Metro Nashville Public Schools (1989-2000); Middle School Music Teacher, Metro Nashville Public Schools (1967-1989); High School English Teacher, Metro Nashville Public Schools (1964-1967); High School Music Teacher, Metro Nashville Public Schools (1964-1967) **Career Related:** Member, Special Education Principals Advisory Committee, Metro Nashville Public Schools (1992-1994); Chairman, Curriculum Committee, Sacs Evaluation, McGavock High School (1992); Chairman, McGavock Cluster Principals (1990-1991) **Civic:** Vice Chairman, Board of Trustees, Memphis Theological Seminary (1998-2003); Member, Established Ruby Page Morton Endowment, Memphis Theological Seminary (2001); Member, Established William Taylor Morton Endowment, West Nashville Cumberland Presbyterian Church (1998); Member, Board of Directors, Tennessee Kidney Foundation (1981-1983); Director, Junior Department, The Woman's Club of Nashville (1972-1974); Member, West Nashville Cumberland Presbyterian Church; Former Trustee, West Nashville Cumberland Presbyterian Church; Elder, West Nashville Cumberland Presbyterian Church; Deacon, West Nashville Cumberland Presbyterian Church; Pianist, West Nashville Cumberland Presbyterian Church; Choir Director, West Nashville Cumberland Presbyterian Church **Creative Works:** Author, Seventh Grade Music Curriculum Outline **Membership:** People-to-People; Florida Oceanographic Society; Aerospace Education; International Society for Music Education; The University Club of Nashville; Life Member, The Woman's Club of Nashville; Phi Delta Kappa; Alpha Delta Kappa; Delta Kappa Gamma; National Society Daughters of the American Revolution; Oak Leaf Society; West End High Alumni Association **Hobbies:** Photography; Swimming; Travel; Music; Scuba diving **Religion:** Presbyterian **Shipping Address:** 6740 Currywood Drive, Nashville, TN, 37205

Sally Mosher

Title: Lawyer, Musician **Industry:** Law and Legal Services **Date of Birth:** 07/26/1934 **Place of Birth:** New York **State:** NY **Parents:** Leslie Joseph Ekenberg; Frances Josephine (McArdle) Ekenberg **Marital Status:** Married **Spouse Name:** James Kimberly Mosher (8/13/1960, Deceased 8/1982) **Education:** JD, University of Southern California (1981); Postgraduate Coursework, University of Southern California (1973-1974); Postgraduate Coursework, Hofstra University (1960-1961); MusB, Manhattanville College (1956) **Career:** President, Oakhill Enterprises, Pasadena, CA (1984-Present); Real Estate Broker (1984-1996); Associate, White-Howell, Inc., Pasadena, CA (1984-1994); President, James K. Mosher Company, Pasadena, CA (1982-1984); Representative, Occidental Life Insurance Company, Pasadena, CA (1975-1978); Manager, Contrasts Concerts, Pasadena Art Museum (1971-1972); Music Critic, Pasadena Star-News (1967-1972); Vice President, James K. Mosher Company, Pasadena, CA (1961-1982); Musician, Pianist, and Teacher (1957-1974) **Career Related:** Harpsichordist, Lecturer, Composer (1994-Present); Publisher, Silver Wheels Publishing, American Society of Composers **Civic:** Board of Directors, Los Angeles Philanthropic Committee for the Arts (2011-Present); Corporate Counsel, Los Angeles Philanthropic Committee for the Arts (2012-2014); Los Angeles Philanthropic Committee for the Arts (2010-2014); Southern California Baroque Association (2004-2014); President, Board of Directors, Piano Spheres Concerts (2002-2012); Secretary, Board of Directors, Piano Spheres Concerts (2001-2002); Chair, Foothill Area Community Services (1994-1995); Vice Chair, Foothill Area Community Services (1992-1994); Chair of Advisory Board, Pasadena Arts Council (1992-1993); Treasurer, Foothill Area Community Services (1991); Board of Directors, Foothill Area Community Services (1990-1995); President, Pasadena Arts Council (1989-1992); I Cantori (1989-1991); Pasadena Historical Society (1989-1991); California Music Theatre (1988-1990); Endowment Advisory Commission, Pasadena, CA (1988-1990); California 200 Council for Bicentennial of United States Constitution (1987-1990); President, Pasadena Chamber Orchestra (1987-1988); Board of Directors, Pasadena Arts Council (1986-1992); Vice President, Board of Directors, Pasadena Chamber Orchestra (1986-1988); University of Southern California Friends of Music, Los Angeles, CA (1973-1976); Encounters Concerts, Pasadena, CA (1966-1972); Board of Directors, Junior League of Pasadena (1966-1967) **Creative Works:** Musician, with Patrick Lindley and Scott Fraser, "Soundings" (2015); Musician, "Explorations" (2010); Musician, with Patrick Lindley, Scott Frasier, Justin Weaver, "Towards the Light" (2006); Musician, "Images and Moods Improvisations" (2004); Musician, "Sally Mosher Plays English Renaissance Harpsichord Music" (2004); Musician, "From Now On: New Directions For Harpsichord" (1998); Musician, "William Byrd: Songs, Dances, Battles, Games" (1995); Author, "People and Their Contexts: A Chronology of the 16th Century World"; Contributor, Articles, Various Publications **Awards:** Vero Nihil Verius Award for Artistic Excellence for People and Their Contexts, Concordia University (2011); Dom Mocquereau Honor Scholar, Manhattanville College (1952-1956) **Membership:** Board of Directors, Southern California Baroque Association (2004-Present); Associates of the California Institute of Technology; Athenaeum at the California Institute of Technology; Kappa Gamma Pi; Mu Phi Epsilon; Phi Alpha Delta; ABA; California Bar Association **Bar Admissions:** California (1982) **Shipping Address:** 1260 Rancheros Rd, Pasadena, CA, 91103

Eberhard Mueller-Heubach

Title: Professor Emeritus **Industry:** Education/Educational Services **Company Name:** Wake Forest University **Date of Birth:** 02/24/1942 **Place of Birth:** Berlin **Country of Origin:** Germany **Parents:** Heinrich Gustav Mueller; Elisabeth (Heubach) Mueller **Spouse Name:** Cornelia Rosemarie Uffmann (9/6/1941, Deceased) **Children:** Oliver Maximilian **Education:** Chief Resident in Obstetrics and Gynecology, Columbia, Presbyterian Medical Center, Columbia University, New York, NY (1974-1975); Resident in Obstetrics and Gynecology, NewYork-Presbyterian/Columbia University Medical Center, Columbia University, New York, NY (1971-1974); Research Fellow in Reproductive Physiology, Department of Obstetrics and Gynecology, Columbia University, New York, NY (1969-1971); Intern, Robert Wood Johnson University Hospital, New Brunswick, NJ (1968-1969); Intern, Women's Hospital, University of Köln (1967-1968); MD, University of Köln (1966) **Certifications:** Certified in Maternal-Fetal Medicine, American Board of Obstetrics and Gynecology, Inc.; Certified in Obstetrics and Gynecology, American Board of Obstetrics and Gynecology, Inc. **Career:** Professor Emeritus, Wake Forest University, Winston-Salem, NC (2007-Present); Professor of Obstetrics-Gynecology, Wake Forest University, Winston-Salem, NC (2002-2007); Professor of Obstetrics-Gynecology, School of Medicine, Wake Forest University, Winston-Salem, NC (1989-2002); Chairman, Obstetrics-Gynecology, School of Medicine, Wake Forest University, Winston-Salem, NC (1989-2002); Associate Professor of Obstetrics and Gynecology, Magee-Women's Hospital, University of Pittsburgh (1981-1989); Assistant Professor of Obstetrics and Gynecology, Magee-Women's Hospital, University of Pittsburgh (1975-1981) **Career Related:** President, American Gynecological and Obstetrical Society (2005-2006); President, Council of University Chairs of Obstetrics and Gynecology (1998-2000) **Creative Works:** Member, Editorial Board, Obstetrics and Gynecology (1999-2002) **Membership:** President, American Gynecological and Obstetrical Society (2005-2006); Secretary, American Gynecological and Obstetrical Society (2002-2004); Assistant Secretary, American Gynecological and Obstetrical Society (1999-2001); President, Society of Reproductive Investigation, Council of University Chairs in Obstetrics and Gynecology (1998-2000); Perinatal Research Society **Marquis Who's Who Honors:** Distinguished Humanitarian (2017) **Hobbies:** Travel; Art; Opera; Theater; Classical music; Horses **Shipping Address:** PO Box 1335, Clemmons, NC, 27012

Jimmy Kun Mui

Title: Architect **Industry:** Architecture & Constrution **Company Name:** NYC Administration for Children's Services **Date of Birth:** 09/01/1958 **Place of Birth:** Hong Kong **Country of Origin:** China **Parents:** Yuk-on Mui; Kum-Ngor (Yuen) Mui **Marital Status:** Married **Spouse Name:** Susan Mui **Children:** Deborah Yoke-Kit; Peter Wai-Loon **Education:** Postgraduate Coursework, University at Buffalo (1982-1984); Bachelor of Professional Studies in Architecture, University at Buffalo (1982) **Certifications:** Registered Architect, State of New York **Career:** Architect, NYC Administration for Children's Services (2016-Present); Inter-agency Liaison-Architect, NYC Department of Parks & Recreation (2014-2016); Housing Inspector, NYC Department of Housing Preservation and Development (2013-2014); Transaction Services Project Manager, Global Realty Services Group (2012-2013); Principal Architect, J.K. Mui Design (2010-2012); Supervising Architect, MTA Bridges & Tunnels Authority (2007-2010); Associate Project Manager, Level 2/Plan Examiner, NYC Buildings Department (2007); Senior Manager, IVI Due Diligence Services, Inc., CBRE (2004-2007); President, Mui Enterprises, Incorporated (2001-2005); CCM & Associates LLC (2001-2003); Construction Manager, Fedayeen Construction Company, LLC (1998-2000); Senior Manager, NYC Division of School Facilities (1991-1998); Principal Architect, J.K. Mui Design (1989-2004); Assistant Architect, NYC Department of Education (1987-1991); Assistant Architect, NYC Department of Housing Preservation and Development (1985-1987); Architect, Bradley Corporate Park, Blauvelt, NY (1984-1985); Drafter, Bradley Corporate Park, Blauvelt, NY (1984-1985); Intern Architect, Niagara Frontier Transportation Authority (1983); Architecture Aide, Department of Health, City of New York (1978) **Civic:** Steering Committee Member, Chinatown Partnership Local Development Corporation (2004); Incorporated Member, Founding Director, and Corporation Secretary, Create in Chinatown, Inc. (2003-2004); Steering Committee Member, Rebuild Chinatown Initiative (2002-2004); Board Member, Chinese Consolidated Benevolent Association (2001-2002) **Awards:** Regent Scholarship Award, New York State (1977-1981); Husted Eward Scholarship, State University of New York (1980) **Membership:** President, Moy Shee Family Association, New York, NY (2005-2006); Adviser, Moy Shee Family Association, New York, NY (2003-2004); Board Director, Moy's Clan Association (Now Moy's Family Association) (2002-2006); President, Moy Shee Family Association, New York, NY (2001-2002); Secretary, Moy Shee Family Association, New York, NY (1999-2000); Vice-Chairman, Board of Directors, Hong Kong Students Association of New York (1989-1991); Chairman, Board of Directors, Hong Kong Students Association of New York (1987-1989); President, Hong Kong Students Association of New York (1986) **Marquis Who's Who Honors:** Albert Nelson Marquis Lifetime Achievement Award (2017) **To what do you attribute your success:** Mr. Mui attributes his success to keeping up with changes and really enjoying what he does. **Why did you become involved in your profession or industry:** Mr. Mui became involved in his profession after initially being in engineering. He realized after a year that he didn't want to pursue that. He liked architecture and drawing and believed that they were good fits, so he is doing something that he likes to do. **Where will you be in five years:** In five years, Mr. Mui plans to continue doing what he is doing now. **Religion:** Tibetan Buddhism **Business Address:** 150 William Street, New York, NY, 10038 **Shipping Address:** 3129 Wissman Avenue, Bronx, NY, 10465

Rod G. Mullen

Title: Not-for-Profit Executive **Industry:** Nonprofit & Philanthropy **Company Name:** Amity Foundation **Date of Birth:** 08/02/1943 **Place of Birth:** Puyallup **State:** WA **Parents:** Charles Rodney Mullen; Grace Violet (Fritsch) Mullen **Marital Status:** Married **Spouse Name:** Naya Arbiter (10/17/1977); Lois Fern Tobiska (5/3/1963, Divorced 1977) **Children:** Cristina; Charles; Moneka; Angelo **Education:** Coursework, Eller Executive Leadership Program, University of Arizona (1991); Postgraduate Coursework, San Francisco Art Institute (1968); AB in Political Science, University of California, Berkeley (1966); Coursework, University of Idaho, Moscow, ID (1961-1963); Coursework, University of Maryland (1960-1961) **Career:** President, Amity Foundation (2018); Co-Founder, President, Chief Executive Officer, Amity Foundation, Tucson, AZ (1995-2018); Executive Director, Amity, Inc., Tucson, AZ (1984-1995); Director, Resources and Development, Amity, Inc., Tucson, AZ (1982-1984); Treatment Director, National Programs, Vision Quest, Inc., Tucson, AZ (1981-1982); Director, Tomales Bay Facility, Synanon Foundation, Inc. (1976-1978); Director, Synanon Education Programs, Synanon Foundation, Inc. (1973-1976); Director, San Francisco Facility, Synanon Foundation, Inc. (1972-1973); Director, Oakland Facility, Synanon Foundation, Inc. (1971-1972) **Career Related:** Board of Directors, Amity Foundation (1995-Present); Board of Directors, Amity Works Foundation-Dragonfly Village, Arizona (2006-2011); President, California Therapeutic Committee (2004-2006); Editorial Advisory Board, Offender Substance Abuse Report (2000-2004); Consultant, California Office for Criminal Justice Planning, Sacramento, CA (1993); Advisory Board, Center Therapeutic Community Research, National Development and Research Institutes, New York, NY (1991-2002); Member, National Advisory Committee, Substance Abuse Prevention (1990-1996); Principal Investigator, Program, National Institute on Drug Abuse (1990-1993) **Creative Works:** Director, "Native Voices" (2013); Exhibitor, Dragonfly Gallery, Tucson, AZ (2011-2017); Director, "Native Voices" (2011); Director, "Tell Me About It" (2008); Director, "Improving TC Encounter Groups" (2006); Director, "History of Therapeutic Communities in Corrections" (2006); Director, "Essential Elements of the Therapeutic Community" (2005); Director, "TC Pioneers" (2003); Director, "Prodigal Daughters" (2002); Contributor, Chapters to Books; Contributor, Articles to Professional Journals; Speaker, Local, National and International Conferences **Membership:** European Federation of Therapeutic Communities (2009-Present); Treasurer, Therapeutic Committees of America (2006-2008); President, California Therapetic Center (2004-2006) **Marquis Who's Who Honors:** Albert Nelson Marquis Lifetime Achievement Award (2017); Distinguished Humanitarian (2017) **Why did you become involved in your profession or industry:** Mr. Mullen entered his profession because he was interested in the model of an integrated society. **Where will you be in five years:** In the next five years, Mr. Mullen will remain as president of Amity and focus on leadership development and staff training. **Hobbies:** Hiking; Photography; Videography **Shipping Address:** 120 S Houghton Rd., Ste 138-321, Amity Foundation, Tucson, AZ, 85748 **Website:** http://amityfdn.org

Gerard E. Munera

Title: Mining and Finance Executive **Industry:** Mining & Metals **Company Name:** Synergex **Date of Birth:** 12/02/1935 **Place of Birth:** Algiers **Country of Origin:** Algeria **Parents:** Gabriel Munera; Laure (Labrousse) Munera **Marital Status:** Married (7/28/1959) **Spouse Name:** Paule A. Ramos **Children:** Catherine; Philippe; Emmanuelle; Jean-Marie **Education:** CE, Ecole des Ponts ParisTech, Paris, France (1959); Master's Degree, Ecole Polytechnique, Paris, France (1956) **Career:** Chairman, Arcadia Inc., Vernon, CA (1997-Present); Managing Director, Synergex, Greenwich, CT (1997-Present); Chairman, Latin American Gold Inc, Greenwich, CT (1994-1997); Chief Executive Officer, Latin American Gold Inc, Greenwich, CT (1994-1997); Member, Board of Directors, Minorco USA, Englewood, CO (1991-1994); President, Minorco USA, Englewood, CO (1991-1994); Chief Executive Officer, Minorco USA, Englewood, CO (1991-1994); Senior Vice President, Corporate Planning and Development, RTZ, London, UK (1989-1991); Head of Corporate Planning and Development, RTZ, London, UK (1989-1991); Vice Chairman, Union Miniere, Brussels, Belgium (1984-1989); Chief Executive Officer, Union Miniere, Brussels, Belgium (1984-1989); Senior Vice President of Nuclear Fuels, Pechiney, Brussels, Belgium (1983-1985); President, Howmet Aluminum Corp., Greenwich, CT (1980-1983); Chief Executive Officer, Howmet Aluminum Corp., Greenwich, CT (1980-1983); President, Howmet Aluminum Corp., Greenwich, CT (1977-1981); Chief Operating Officer, Howmet Aluminum Corp., Greenwich, CT (1975-1977); Executive Vice President, Howmet Aluminum Corp., Greenwich, CT (1975-1977); Chief Executive Officer, Camea Group Pechiney Ugine Kuhlmann, Buenos Aires, Argentina (1976-1975); Senior Vice President of Finance, Camea Group Pechiney Ugine Kuhlmann, Buenos Aires, Argentina (1966-1968); Consultant, French Ministry of Foreign Affairs, Argentina (1962-1966); Chief County Engineer, Department of Roads. and Bridges, South Algiers (1959-1962) **Career Related:** Member, Board of Directors, Chairman, Dynamic Materials Corp., Inc.; Executive Chairman, Arcadia Inc.; Managing Partner, Synergex **Military Service:** Lieutenant, French Air Force (1956-1957) **Creative Works:** Patentee, Low-Income Housing System **Awards:** Decorated Officer, Legion of Honor, France; French Veterans Medal **Religion:** Roman Catholic **Shipping Address:** 19 Cobb Island Dr, Synergex, Greenwich, CT, 06830

John Francis Murphy

Title: Law Educator **Industry:** Education/Educational Services **Company Name:** Villanova University **Date of Birth:** 04/25/1937 **Place of Birth:** Portchester **State:** NY **Parents:** Francis John Murphy; Emilie (Tourtellot) Murphy **Marital Status:** Married **Spouse Name:** Laura S. Murphy **Children:** Andrew; Robert; Dan; Jessie; Gabriel **Education:** LLB in International Affairs, Cornell University (1962); BA, Cornell University (1959) **Career:** Professor Emeritus, Villanova University (2014-Present); Professor of Law, School of Law, Villanova University (1984-2014); Visiting Professor of Law, Villanova University, Pennsylvania (1983-1984); Associate Dean, School of Law, University of Kansas, Lawrence, KS (1975-1977); Professor of Law, University of Kansas, Lawrence, KS (1972-1984); Associate Professor of Law, University of Kansas, Lawrence, KS (1969-1972); Associate, Kirkland, Ellis, Hodson, Chaffetz & Masters, Washington, DC (1967-1969); Attorney, Office of the Legal Adviser, Department of State, Washington, DC (1964-1967); Associate, Winthrop, Stimson, Putnam & Roberts, New York, NY (1963-1964); Africa-Asia Public Service Fellow, India (1962-1963) **Career Related:** Visiting Professor of Law, Haifa University (1997); Visiting Professor of Law, San Diego University, Paris, France (1995); Visiting Professor of Law, Louisiana State University, Aix-en-Provence, France (1990); Visiting Professor of Law, San Diego University, London, England (1989); Visiting Professor of Law, San Diego University, Mexico City, Mexico (1988); Visiting Professor of Law, San Diego University (1986); Visiting Professor of Law, Georgetown University (1982); Charles H. Stockton Professor of International Law, Naval War College (1980-1981); Visiting Professor of Law, Cornell University, Ithaca, NY (1979) **Creative Works:** Editorial Board, International Law Studies, Naval War College (2003-Present); Board of Editors, The International Lawyer (1998-Present); Author, "Luck of the Irish: A Memoir" (2015); Author, "The Evolving Dimensions of International Law: Hard Choices for the World Community" (2010); Author, "The United States and The Rule of Law in International Affairs" (2004); Board of Editors, Transnational Publishers (1999-2006); Author, "The Constitutional Law of the European Union" (1996); Board of Editors, Terrorism and Political Violence (1993-2003); Author, "The Regulation of International Business and Economic Relations" (1991); Author, "State Support of International Terrorism: Legal, Political and Economic Dimensions" (1989); Author, "Punishing International Terrorists" (1985); Author, "The United Nations and the Control of International Violence" (1982); Board of Editors, Terrorism: An International Journal (1981-1992); Author, "Legal Aspects of International Terrorism: Summary Report of an International Conference" (1980); Editor, Legal Aspects of International Terrorism (1978); Contributing Author, Legal Aspects of International Terrorism (1978); Board of Editors, Cornell Law Quarterly (1962); Board of Editors, Cornell Law Quarterly (1961); Contributor, Articles, Comments, Book Reviews, Professional and Popular Journals **Awards:** Louis B. Sohn Award for Distinguished Long-standing Contributions to the Field of Public International Law, American Bar Association (2011); Certificate of Merit, American Society of International Law (1992) **Membership:** Patron, International Law Association (2009-Present); Honorary Vice President, American Branch, International Law Association (2005-Present); Alternate Representative, U.S. Mission to United Nations, American Bar Association (2006-2007); American Society of International Law **Bar Admissions:** State of Pennsylvania (1987); State of Kansas (1970); District of Columbia (1963) **Marquis Who's Who Honors:** Albert Nelson Marquis Lifetime Achievement Award (2017); Distinguished Humanitarian (2017) **Hobbies:** Tennis; Theater; Writing; Travel **Religion:** Episcopalian **Shipping Address:** 1191 Telegraph Road, West Chester, PA, 19380

Marilyn Musacchio, PhD

Title: Administrator, Educator, Nurse Midwife **Industry:** Medicine & Health Care **Date of Birth:** 12/07/1938 **Place of Birth:** Louisville **State:** KY **Parents:** Robert William Poulter; Loretta C. (Liebert) Poulter **Marital Status:** Married (5/13/1961) **Spouse Name:** David Edward Musacchio **Children:** Richard Peter; Michelle Marie **Education:** PhD, Case Western Reserve University (1993); MSN, University of Kentucky (1972); BSN, Spalding College, Cum Laude (1968); Diploma, St. Joseph Infirmary School of Nursing (1959) **Certifications:** Nurse-Midwifery Certification, University of Kentucky (1976); Advanced Registered Nurse Practitioner Certification **Career:** Dean, Professor of Nursing Education, Sullivan University, (Now Spencerian College), Louisville, KY 2009-Present); Director, RN to BSN Program, Aquinas College, Nashville, TN (2008-2009); Professor, Spalding University, Louisville, KY (2005-2009); Dean, Professor, Tennessee Technological University, Cookeville, TN (1998-2005); Associate Professor, The University of Alabama at Birmingham (1997-1998); Associate Professor, Director of Nurse-Midwifery, University of Alabama at Birmingham (1992-1996); Coordinator for Nurse-Midwifery, University of Kentucky College of Nursing, Lexington, KY (1987-1992); Acting Coordinator for Nurse-Midwifery, University of Kentucky College of Nursing, Lexington, KY (1982-1984); Associate Professor, Coordinator, University of Kentucky College of Nursing, Lexington, KY (1979-1992); Assistant Professor, University of Kentucky College of Nursing, Lexington, KY (1976-1979); From Assistant Professor to Associate Professor, Director, Department of Nursing Education, Kentucky State University, Frankfort, KY (1972-1975); Instructor, St. Joseph Infirmary School of Nursing, Louisville, KY (1960-1971); Staff Nurse, Male General Surgery Unit, St. Joseph Infirmary (1960); Staff Nurse, Gynecological Unit, St. Joseph Infirmary (1959-1960); Chairman, Spalding University **Career Related:** Consultant in Field **Civic:** Brigadier General, Army Nurse Corps, US Army Reserve (1992-1995); Louisville Safety Council (1973-1980) **Creative Works:** Editorial Board Member, Journal of Obstetric, Gynecologic, & Neonatal Nursing (1976-1982); Author, Pamphlet; Contributor, Articles to Professional Journals **Awards:** Hall of Distinguished Alumni, University of Kentucky (1995); Outstanding Alumna, Mercy Academy (1993); Jefferson Cup Award, Jefferson County, Kentucky (1991); Distinguished Citizen Award, City of Louisville (1977); Recipient, Scholarships, Fellowships, Other Awards **Membership:** Charter Member, National Secretary, Nurses Association of the American College of Obstetrics and Gynecology (1970-1972); Chairman, District V, Nurses Association of the American College of Obstetrics and Gynecology (1969); American College of Nurse-Midwives; Reserve Officers Association; Association of Military Surgeons of the United States; Senior Army Reserve Commander Association; Association of the United States Army; Army Nurse Corps Association; Lifetime Member, Army War College Alumni Association; Association of Women's Health, Obstetric and Neonatal Nurses; American Nurses Association **Hobbies:** Reading; Candy making; Cake decorating; Cooking, Sewing **Religion:** Roman Catholic **Business Address:** P.O. Box 4907, Louisville, KY, 40204

Katherine Leigh Myers

Title: Assistant Technology Specialist **Industry:** Technology **Company Name:** Wright State University **Education:** Master's Degree in Rehabilitation Counseling, Wright State University; BS in Rehabilitation Services, Wright State University **Career:** Assistant Technology Specialist, Wright State University **Civic:** Volunteer, Patterson Park Church; Choir Member, Patterson Park Church **Membership:** AHEAD; RESNA **Marquis Who's Who Honors:** Albert Nelson Marquis Lifetime Achievement Award (2017); Distinguished Humanitarian (2017) **Why did you become involved in your profession or industry:** Ms. Myers chose this path because she and her son, Rob, fell in love with technology. **What do you consider to be the highlight of your career:** Ms. Myers' greatest accomplishment is keeping the department together during difficult times. **Where will you be in five years:** Ms. Myers' professional goal is to continue working in her profession for the next five years and then to retire to do volunteer work. **Hobbies:** Quilting; Crocheting; Listening to music; Playing the piano; Playing the organ **Shipping Address:** 3802 Greenbriar Dr., Fairborn, OH, 45324 **Website:** http://www.wright.edu

Trygve Edward Myhren

Title: Communications Executive **Industry:** Media & Entertainment **Company Name:** Myhren Media Inc. **Date of Birth:** 01/03/1937 **Place of Birth:** Palmerton **State:** PA **Parents:** Arne Johannes Myhren; Anita (Blatz) Myhren **Marital Status:** Married **Spouse Name:** Victoria Hamilton (11/14/1981); Carol Jane Enman (8/8/1964, Divorced) **Children:** Erik; Kirsten; Tor; Paige (Stepchild) **Education:** MBA, Tuck School of Business, Dartmouth College (1959); BA in Philosophy and Political Science, Dartmouth College (1958) **Career:** President, Myhren Media Inc., Denver, CO (1990-Present); Myhren Media Inc., Denver, CO (1988-Present); President, The Providence Journal Company (1990-1997); Board Chairman, American Television and Communications Corporation, Englewood, CO (1980-1988); Chief Executive Officer, American Television and Communications Corporation (1980-1988); From Vice President of Marketing to President, American Television and Communications Corporation (1975-1980); Vice President, Communications, Research Machines, Inc. (1973-1974); President, Communications, Research Machines, Inc. (1973-1975); President, Auberge Vintners, Inc. (1970-1973); Executive Vice President, Marketing Continental (1969-1973); Senior Consultant, Glendinning Cos., Westport, CT (1965-1969); Unit Manager, Procter & Gamble (1963-1965); Sales Manager, Procter & Gamble (1963) **Career Related:** President, King Broadcasting Company (1991-1996); Chief Executive Officer, King Broadcasting Company (1991-1996); President, The Providence Journal, RI (1990); Member, Advisory Committee on HDTV, Federal Communications Commission (1987-1989); Executive Committee Member, National Cable TV Association (Now NCTA), Washington, DC (1982-1991); Treasurer, National Cable TV Association (Now NCTA) (1982-1991); Vice Chairman to Chairman, Board of Directors, National Cable TV Association (Now NCTA) (1982-1991); Vice President to Executive Vice President, Time Inc., New York, NY (1981-1988); President, Cable TV Administration and Marketing Society (1978-1979); Board of Directors, Advanced Marketing Services, Inc.; Board of Directors, Dreyfus Founders Funds Corporation; Board of Directors, J.D. Edwards World Solution Company (Now Oracle); Board of Directors, Verio; Board of Directors, The Cable Center, Denver, CO; Board of Directors, CableLabs, Boulder, CO; Board of Directors, Peapod, Inc., Skokie, IL; Contributor, New York Times; Contributor, Associated Press; Founder, The Food Network (Now Scripps Networks, LLC); Founder, Northwest Cable News; Co-founder, E! Entertainment (Now E! Entertainment Television, LLC); Co-founder, Four Cable Networks **Civic:** Chairman Emeritus, University of Denver (2014-Present); Trustee, University of Denver (1997-Present); Executive Committee, University of Denver (1997-Present); Board of Directors, Denver Art Museum (1996-Present); Trustee, National Jewish Health (1989-Present); Member, Colorado Forum (1984-Present); Chairman, Board of Trustees, University of Denver (2009-2014); Chairman of the Board, University of Denver (2009-2014); Foundation Trustee, U.S. Ski and Snowboard Association (1998-2003); Chairman, Local Organizing Commission, Men's Ice Hockey Championship, NCAA (1995); Trustee, Lifespan (1994-1997); Trustee, Rhode Island Hospital; Member, Colorado Baseball Commission, State of Colorado (1989-1991); Executive Council Member, Foundation for Commemoration of the U.S. Constitution (1987-1990); Member, National GED Task Force (1987-1990); Chairman, Higher Education Committee, Colorado Forum (1986); Board of Directors, Colorado Business Committee for the Arts (1985-1991); Co-founder, Colorado Business Committee for the Arts (1985-1991); Co-founder, Adaptive Spirit; Principal Supporter, U.S. Paralympic Ski Team, United States Olympic Committee **Military Service:** Junior Grade Lieutenant, U.S. Navy (1959-1963) **Awards:** Humanitarian Award, Josef Korbel School of International Studies, University of Denver (2014); Inductee, Hall of Fame, Colorado Ski Museum (2010); Lifetime Achievement Award, AJC (2010); Chef de Mission, U.S. Paralympic Team, Torino, Italy (2006); Inductee, Cable TV Hall of Fame, The Cable Center (2004); Humanitarian Award, National Jewish Health (1996); One of A Kind Award, CTAM: Cable & Telecommunications Association for Marketing (1994); Distinguished Leader Award, National Cable TV Association (Now NCTA) (1988); Grand Tam Award, CTAM: Cable & Telecommunications Association for Marketing (1985) **Membership:** President, CTAM: Cable & Telecommunications Association for Marketing (1978-1979); Co-founder, Cable Advertising Bureau (1978); Cable TV Pioneers **Marquis Who's Who Honors:** Albert Nelson Marquis Lifetime Achievement Award (2017) **Religion:** Episcopalian **Shipping Address:** 3033 E 1st Ave., Ste 720, Myhren Media Inc., Denver, CO, 80206

Irwin David Nahinsky, PhD

Title: Professor Emeritus **Industry:** Education/Educational Services **Company Name:** University of Louisville **Date of Birth:** 04/04/1931 **Place of Birth:** St. Paul **State:** MN **Parents:** Anna Nahinsky; David Nahinsky **Marital Status:** Married **Spouse Name:** Gertrude Nahinsky **Children:** Joanna Nahinsky; Beth Nahinsky **Education:** PhD in Psychology, University of Minnesota (1955); BA in Psychology, University of Minnesota (1952) **Career:** Professor Emeritus of Psychology, University of Louisville (1993-Present); Professor of Psychology, University of Louisville (1970-1993); Associate Professor of Psychology, University of Missouri, Columbia, MO (1965-1970); Assistant Professor of Psychology, Saint Louis University (1963-1965); Assistant Professor of Psychology, University of Kansas City (1960-1963); Research Psychologist, Oregon State Hospital (1957-1960); Research Psychologist, United States Naval Personnel Research Field Activity, San Diego, CA (1956-1957) **Military Service:** Captain, Medical Service Corps, US Army Reserves (1948-1968) **Creative Works:** Author, "Parallel Interactive Processing as a Way to Understand Complex Information Processing: The Conjunction Fallacy and Other Examples," American Journal of Psychology (2017); Co-Author, "The Interaction Between Specific and General Information in Category Learning and Representation; Unitization and Parallel Interactive Processing," American Journal of Psychology (2011); Co-Author, "How Learning One Category Influences the Learning of Another," American Journal of Psychology (2004); Co-Author, "What is Learned from Experience in a Probabilistic Environment?" Journal of Behavioral Decision Making (2004); Co-Author, "Case Study: Melatonin in Severe Obesity," Journal of The American Academy of Child and Adolescent Psychiatry (1997); Co-Author, "Instances and Category Structure in Intercategory Relationships," Perceptual and Motor Skills (1997); Co-Author, "Nocturnal Serum Melatonin Profile in Major Depression in Children and Adolescents," Archives of General Psychiatry (1996); Author, "'Bouncing Back' from a Loss: No Statistical Artifact," Perceptual and Motor Skills (1994); Author, "Episodic Components of Concept Learning and Representation," Percepts, Concepts and Categories (1992); Author, "Belief that Experiments Work and Equal Distribution of Ignorance: What Happens When These Tendencies Compete?" The Journal of General Psychology (1991); Author, "Bouncing Back in the World Series," Psychonomic Society (1991); Author, "Anomalies in the Judgment of Statistical Association: Fallacies Based on Unidirectional Independence, Shifting Dependence and Conjunction," Perceptual and Motor Skills (1990); Co-Author, "The Conjunction Fallacy: Judgmental Heuristics or Faulty Extensional Reasoning?" Psychonomic Society (1986); Co-Author, "Unidirectional Independence and Judgmental Heuristics," Psychonomic Society (1985); Co-Author, "Episodic Components of Concept Representation Indicated in Concept Acquisition," Psychological Reports (1983); Co-Author, "Strategy Choice and the Effect of Field Independence on Abstraction, Storage and Retrieval," Psychonomic Society (1980); Author, "Notes on a Theory of Concept Representation in Semantic Memory," University of Louisville (1979); Co-Author, "Cognitive Strategies, Field Dependence and the Abstraction Process," Journal of Research in Personality (1979); Co-Author, "Stimulus Memory and Contextual Cues in the Abstraction Process," Canadian Journal of Psychology (1977); Co-Author, "Interaction of Rule and Attribute Learning in Identification of Concepts Involving Binary Rules," Psychonomic Society (1976); Co-Author, "The Influence of Specific Stimulus Information on the Concept Learning Process," Journal of Experimental Psychology (1975); Co-Author, "Resampling of Hypotheses After Negative Instances," Psychonomic Society (1975); Author, "Going by Rules," PsycCRITIQUES (1974); Co-Author, "The Concreteness of Attributes in Concept Learning Strategies," Memory and Cognition (1973); Author, "Identifiability of a Class of Theories with States Not Directly Observed Over Trials," Journal of Mathematical Psychology (1973); Co-Author, "Relationship of Component Cues to Hypotheses in Conjunctive Concept Learning," Journal of Experimental Psychology (1970); Co-Author, "Conjunctive Hypothesis Sampling: A Reconsideration," Psychonomic Science (1970); Author, "A Hypothesis Sampling Model for Conjunctive Concept Identification," Journal of Mathematical Psychology (1970); Co-Author, "The Effect of Number of Attribute-Values in Conjunctive Concept Identification," Psychonomic Science (1969); Co-Author, "Sampling Without Replacement and Information Following Correct Responses, in Concept Identification," Journal of Experimental Psychology (1969); Co-Author, "Language Patterns in Conjunctive Concept Identification," Psychonomic Science (1969) **Membership:** Former Member, American Psychological Association and Psychonomic Society; Present Member, Society for American Baseball Research **Marquis Who's Who Honors:** Albert Nelson Marquis Lifetime Achievement Award (2017) **Shipping Address:** 3805 Old Brownsboro Hills Rd, Louisville, KY, 40241

Louis M. Naidorf

Title: Principal **Industry:** Architecture & Constrution **Company Name:** Allen/Naidorf Design Consultants **Parents:** Jack Naidorf; Meriam (Abbott) Naidorf **Marital Status:** Married **Spouse Name:** Sandy Chronis; Patricia Ruth Allen (Deceased); Patricia Ann Shea (Divorced); Dorise D. Roberts (Divorced) **Children:** Victoria Beth **Education:** Honorary Doctorate, Woodbury University (2000); MA, University of California, Berkeley (1950); BA, University of California, Berkeley (1949); Fellow, American Institute of Architects **Certifications:** Registered Architect, California **Career:** Principal, Allen/Naidorf Design Consultant (1995-Present); Dean, School of Architecture and Design, Woodbury University (1990-2000); Senior Vice President, Design Principal, Ellerbe Becket Associates (1988-1993); Senior Vice President, Director Design, Welton Becket Associates (1973-1988); Senior Vice President, Director of Research, Welton Becket Associates (1970-1973); Vice President Assistant, Director of Design, Welton Becket Associates (1959-1970); Senior Project Designer, Welton Becket Associates (1955-1959); Project Designer, Welton Becket Associates (1952-1955); Designer, Pereira and Luckman (1951-1952); Designer, Welton Becket Associates (1950-1951) **Career Related:** Peer Review Panel, National Endowment for the Arts (1995-Present); Otis-Parsons (1986-1992); Instructor, School of Architecture, University of California, Los Angeles (1985); Landscape Architectural Program, University of California, Los Angeles (1980-1985); Visiting Lecturer, California Polytechnic School of Architecture (1975-1982) **Civic:** Board of Directors, Institute for Garden Studies (1986-Present); American National Red Cross (2000); Trustee, Woodbury University (2000) **Creative Works:** Capitol Records Building, Century City, Los Angeles, CA; Hyatt Regency, Dallas, TX; Restoration, California State Capitol Building; Naval Medical Center, San Diego, CA **Awards:** Educator of the Year, American Institute of Architects (1997); National Honor Award, American Institute of Architects (1985); Honor Award, National Trust for Historical Preservation (1985); Silver Medal, American Institute of Architects (1950) **Membership:** Board of Directors, Los Angeles Chapter, American Institute of Architects (1977-1979) **Shipping Address:** 668 Wild Oak Drive, Santa Rosa, CA, 95409

H. Gregory Nasky

Title: Lawyer **Industry:** Law and Legal Services **Date of Birth:** 06/09/1942 **Place of Birth:** Titusville **State:** PA **Year of Passing:** 2017-09-29 **Parents:** Harold G. Nasky; Majella Marie (Beck) Nasky **Marital Status:** Married **Spouse Name:** Rosanne Guson (7/22/1967) **Education:** JD, University of Notre Dame (1967); AB, St. Bonaventure University (1964) **Career:** Partner, Goodsill Anderson, Quinn & Stifel (2006-Present); Principal, Resort Development Consultant (1998-2008); Counsel, Kummer, Kaempfer, Bonner & Renshaw (1994-2006); Managing Partner, Vargas & Bartlett (1981-1991); Partner, Vargas & Bartlett (1974-1994); Associate, Vargas, Bartlett & Dixon (1972-1973); Associate, Eaton Hill Textile Works (1967-1968) **Career Related:** Executive Vice President, Showboat, Inc. (1995-1998); Chairman, Board of Directors, University of Nevada, Reno School of Medicine (1993); Member, Board of Directors, Notre Dame Law Association, Notre Dame Law Association (1990-2000); Member, Board of Directors, Showboat, Inc. (1983-1998); Corporate Secretary, Showboat, Inc. (1978-1998); Advisory Board, University of Nevada, Reno School of Medicine **Civic:** Delegate, Citizen Ambassador Program, People to People International, Russia (1992); Delegate, Citizen Ambassador Program, People to People International, Estonia (1992); Member, Legal Committee, Nevada Resort Association (1990-1993); Member, Gaming Regulations Committee, Nevada Resort Association (1990-1993); Delegate, Citizen Ambassador Program, People to People International, Hungary (1990); Delegate, Citizen Ambassador Program, People to People International, Czech Republic (1990); Delegate, Citizen Ambassador Program, People to People International, Poland (1990); Member, Board of Directors, Nevada Ballet Theatre (1988-2000); Delegate, Citizen Ambassador Program, People to People International, New Zealand (1987); Delegate, Citizen Ambassador Program, People to People International, Australia (1987); Member, Board of Directors, Boulder Dam Council, Boy Scouts of America (1986-1993); Delegate, Citizen Ambassador Program, People to People International, People's Republic China (1985); Legal Adviser, Nevada Ballet Theatre (1977-1994) **Military Service:** Judge Advocate, U.S. Army (1968-1972) **Creative Works:** Author, "A Glimpse of China" (1986); Contributor, Real Property, Probate & Trust Law Journal, Disposition of Rents (1981); Author, Inter Alia Journal of State Bar of Nevada **Awards:** Oak Leaf Cluster (1972); Decorated Bronze Star (1970); Army Commendation Medal (1969) **Membership:** Board Member, HiBEAM (2006-Present); Task Force Conflicts Interest Committee, Business Section, ABA (1993-1995); Chairman, President's Associates, UNLV Foundation, UNLV (1993); Executive Committee, Gaming Law Section, State Bar of Nevada (1985-1993); Chairman, Fee Dispute Committee, State Bar of Nevada (1983-1989); President, Notre Dame Club Las Vegas, University of Notre Dame Notre Dame Alumni Association (1978-1979); American Society of Corporate Secretaries (Now Society for Corporate Governance); International Association of Gaming Advisors **Bar Admissions:** Hawaii State Bar Association (2003); State Bar of Nevada (1972); Pennsylvania Bar Association (1967) **Marquis Who's Who Honors:** Albert Nelson Marquis Lifetime Achievement Award (2017) **To what do you attribute your success:** He attributes his success to being honest and above board. **Why did you become involved in your profession or industry:** He was inspired in eighth grade when his mother pulled him form class and sent him to the courthouse to watch a murder trial (State of PA vs. Lydia Dean). It turned out she was the victim of domestic violence and was acquitted. It was at that moment that he realized he had to become a lawyer. **Shipping Address:** 999 Bishop St., Ste 1600, Goodsill Anderson Quinn & Stifel, Honolulu, HI, 96813

Rosalia Josephine Nastasi-Scripa, PhD

Title: Engineering Professor (Retired), Distinguished Professor Emerita **Industry:** Education/Educational Services **Company Name:** University of Alabama at Birmingham School of Engineering **Date of Birth:** 07/01/1948 **Place of Birth:** New York City **State:** NY **Parents:** Rosario Nastasi; Bridget Nastasi **Marital Status:** Married **Spouse Name:** Louis Scripa **Education:** PhD in Materials Science and Engineering, University of Florida, Gainesville, FL (1976); MS in Materials Science and Engineering, University of Florida, Gainesville, FL (1975); MS in Ceramic Science, The Pennsylvania State University, State College, PA (1972); BS in Ceramic Science, Alfred University, Alfred, NY (1970) **Certifications:** Licensed Professional Engineer, State of Alabama Board of Licensure (1982-Present) **Career:** Distinguished Service Professor Emerita of Engineering, School of Engineering, University of Alabama at Birmingham (2016-Present); Distinguished Service Professor, University of Alabama at Birmingham (2015-Present); Associate Provost, Faculty Development and Faculty Affairs, Provost Office, University of Alabama at Birmingham (2005-2006); Associate Provost, Undergraduate Programs and Faculty Affairs, Provost Office, University of Alabama at Birmingham (2001-2005); Associate Provost, Provost Office, University of Alabama at Birmingham (2000-2006); Associate Provost, Undergraduate Programs, Provost Office, University of Alabama at Birmingham (2000-2001); Associate Dean, Academic and Student Affairs, School of Engineering, University of Alabama at Birmingham (1996-2000); Program Scientist, Materials Science, Microgravity Science and Applications Division, NASA Headquarters (1995-1996) **Career Related:** Licensed Professional Engineer, State of Alabama (1982-Present); Editor, Peer-Reviewed Proceedings of the ACCGE-11, Crystal Growth Conference, Journal of Crystal Growth (2011); Nationally Elected, American Association of Crystal Growth Executive Board (2009-2013); Chair, NCAA Postgraduate Scholarship Committee (1998-1999); Principal Investigator, Co-Investigator, Numerous Research Grants, NASA, NSF Industry; Director, Co-Director, Numerous PhD Dissertation Students, MS Thesis Students and Postdoctoral Fellows **Civic:** Volunteer, Veterans Administration Hospital, Birmingham, AL (2014-Present); Volunteer Tutor, Science and Mathematics for University Students, High School Students (Grades 9-12) (1976-Present) **Creative Works:** Contributor, Book Chapter, "Theory for Thermal Conductivity Measurement Based on the Laser Flash Method" (2006); Chair, Editorial Board, Ingenuity Magazine, University of Alabama at Birmingham School of Engineering (1997-2000); Contributor, More than 100 Peer-Reviewed Research Papers; Contributor, Articles, Professional Journals **Awards:** University of Alabama at Birmingham Faculty Senate Outstanding Committee Member Award (2014); International Woman of the Year, General Assembly of the United Cultural Convention for Exceptional Character and Accomplishments (2012); Top 100 Educators in Materials Science and Engineering, International Biographical Centre (2012); Woman of the Year, American Biographical Institute (2009); Distinguished Alumna Award, Department of Materials Science and Engineering at the University of Florida (2009); Ellen Gregg Ingalls/University of Alabama at Birmingham National Alumni Society Award, Lifetime Achievement in Teaching (2007); Faculty Senate Resolution in Recognition of Service, Hard Work, Dedication, and Many Contributions to the University of Alabama at Birmingham and to the University's Faculty Senate (2006); National Science Foundation/ADVANCE Grant for the Advancement of Women in Science and Engineering (2005-2006); Lifetime Achievement Award, World Congress of Arts, Sciences and Communications (2005) **Membership:** School of Engineering Tenure and Promotion Committee (2011-Present); American Society for Engineering Education (1977-Present); Women in Engineering Division, Mara H. Wasburn Early Engineering Educator Grants (2014); Chair, University of Alabama at Birmingham Faculty Senate Governance and Operations Committee (2013-2014); Reviewer, Technical Papers, Malaysian International Tribology Conference (2013) **Marquis Who's Who Honors:** Albert Nelson Marquis Lifetime Achievement Award (2017) **Hobbies:** Reading; Spending time with family; Traveling **Shipping Address:** 2200 Tanglewood Rd, Vestavia, AL, 35216

Nickolas E. Nasuta

Title: Sole Proprietor **Industry:** Law and Legal Services **Company Name:** Nickolas E Nasuta, Attorney At Law **Marital Status:** Divorced **Children:** Nancy; Kim **Education:** JD, American University (1967); BS in Economics, St. Peter's College, Jersey City, NJ (1962) **Career:** Attorney at Law, Law Office of Nickolas E. Nasuta, Esq. (1972-Present); Owner, Law Office of Nickolas E. Nasuta, Esq. (1972-Present); Associate Counsel, Robert Inglima, Esq. Law Firm (1972); Trust Officer, United Jersey Bank (1968-1972); Senior Trust Officer, Peoples Trust Company, Hackensack, NJ (1969); Personal Judicial Clerk to Honorable Charles Paulis, Chief Presiding Judge, Warren County, NJ (1968); Chief of Counsel's Office, Internal Revenue Service (1966); Interpretative, Internal Revenue Service (1966); Editorial & Research Staff, International Chiefs of Police Association (1965) **Awards:** Featured Listee, Top 10% of America's Most Honored Professionals, American Registry (2017); Certificate of Appreciation for Services Rendered in Connection with the Settlement Conference Committee, State of New Jersey (1992); High Rating in Legal and Ethical Standards, Martindale-Hubbell **Membership:** New Jersey State Bar Association (1972); Bergen County Bar Association (1972); ABA; International Association of Chiefs of Police **Bar Admissions:** New Jersey State Bar Association (1972); United States Tax Court (1972) **To what do you attribute your success:** He attributes his success to an ingrained work ethic attributed to his parents, who taught him that success or failure in life is due to actions or inaction attributable solely to himself; never to third parties. **What do you consider to be the highlight of your career:** Mr. Nasuta feels there are too many highlights to mention, other than to say his ability to aid, resolve, and eliminate the fears, concerns, and apprehensions of his clients over the years. **Where will you be in five years:** In five years, Mr. Nasuta will most probably still be in his office. His goal is motivated by his favorite saying, "the only question about my retirement is whether they carry me out of my office feet first or head first." **Hobbies:** Watching the History Channel **Shipping Address:** 475 Kinderkamack Rd., Ste 2, Nickolas E. Nasuta, Esq., Oradell, NJ, 07649 **Website:** http://www.nasutalaw.com

Kirmach Natani, PhD

Industry: Consulting **Company Name:** Private Practice **Date of Birth:** 06/05/1935 **Place of Birth:** Milwaukee **State:** WI **Education:** Postdoctoral Resident, St. Mary's Hospital, East St, Louis, Illinois (1992-1997); Postgraduate Coursework, United States Air Force School of Aerospace Medicine, San Antonio, TX (1977-1979); PhD in Biopsychology, The University of Oklahoma Health Sciences Center (1977); MS in Clinical Psychology, The University of Oklahoma Health Sciences Center (1970); Honorary BS, Personnel Board of Action, University of California, Berkeley (1962); Coursework, University of Nevada, Reno (1953-1957) **Certifications:** Certified Divorce Mediator; Certified, Senior Disability Analyst; Certified Forensic Neuropsychologist; Licensed Clinical Psychologist; Licensed Health Service Provider **Career:** Evaluations Consultant, Disability Service (2012-Present); Private Practice, Clinical Neuropsychologist, Consultant, Bi-State Neurometric Services, Various Cities (1998-Present); Self-Employed Mental Health Consultant (1992-Present); Human Factors Engineer, McDonnell Douglas, St. Louis, MO (1980-1992); Clinical Researcher, Oklahoma City Veterans Affairs Health Care System, United States Department of Veterans Affairs (1966-1977); Physics Technician, Lawrence Berkeley Laboratory, University of California, Berkeley (1958-1963) **Career Related:** Senior Care Manager, Magellan Health, Inc., St. Louis, MO (2001-2002); Clinical Manager, Missouri Department of Corrections, Farmington, MO (1999-2001); Applicant Evaluator, Biological Sciences Panel, Ford Foundation Doctoral Fellowship for Minorities Program, Fellowship Program Section, National Research Council (1986); Applicant Evaluator, Biomedical Sciences, NATO Postdoctoral Fellowship Panel, Graduate and Postdoctoral Programs, Division of Scientific Personnel Improvement, National Science Foundation (1979-1983); Applicant and Proposal Evaluator, Neurosciences & Ergonomics Section, NAS/NRC Scientist Exchange Program, Commission on International Relations, National Research Council (1978-1983); Exchange Researcher, Union of Soviet Socialist Republics, National Academy of Sciences (1974) **Military Service:** Consultant, Cruise Missiles Upgrade, U.S. Naval Forces, Crystal City, VA (1990-1992); Consultant, Operational Psychiatry Division, United States Naval Health Center, San Diego, CA (1966-1983); Consultant, Operational Psychiatry Division, United States Naval Health Center (1966); U.S. Air Force Reserve (1954-1963); Air National Guard (1954-1963) **Creative Works:** Ad-Hoc Peer Reviewer, "Professional Psychology: Research and Practice," American Psychological Association (2001-Present); Featured Subject, "American Men and Women of Science," The Social and Behavioral Sciences (2003); Featured Listee, "Directory of Resident Research Associates, 1959-1995," National Academy Press (1996); Contributing Author, "From Antarctica to Outer Space: Life in Isolation and Confinement," Springer-Verlag (1991); Contributing Author, "Human Factors in Outer Space Production," Westview Press (1980); Contributing Author, "Proceedings of the Sixth Symposium on Psychology in the Department of Defense" (1978); Co-Author, "Space Manufacturing Facilities (Space Colonies) II," American Institute of Aeronautics and Astronautics (1977); Writer, Dissertation, "Laterality Effects in a Tachistoscopic Optional Shift task in Young Adults," Dissertation Abstracts International (1977); Co-Author, "Self-regulation of the Sleep Processes," Biological Psychology Bulletin (1975); Author, "Experiences as a Science Exchange Visitor to the USSR" (1975) **Awards:** Grantee, Nature Publishing Group (2006); Honoree, 2000 Outstanding Scientists of the 20th Century, International Biographical Center, Cambridge, United Kingdom (2001); Fellow, American College of Forensic Examiners Institute (1998); Postdoctoral Fellow, United States Air Force School of Aerospace Medicine (1978-1979); Honoree, The 36th Meeting of the MIT Neuroscience Research Program Associates, Boston, MA (1978); Roche Neuroscience Award for Excellence in Research, 14th Annual SAMA-UTMB National Student Research Forum (1973); Scholar, Group Relations Conference and Group Therapy Workshop, A.K. Rice Institute, Northfield, MN (1973); Travel Grantee, National Science Foundation (1972); Travel Grantee, Graduate College, University of Oklahoma (1969) **Membership:** PTSD Counselor, American Psychotherapy Association (2015-Present); American College of Forensic Examiners Institute (1995-Present); International Organization for Psychophysiology (2002-2005); Missouri State Psychological Association (1993-2008); Human Factors Society (1980-1992); Society for Neuroscience (1977-1982); Society for Psychophysiological Research (1970-1990); Association for the Psychophysiological Study of Sleep (1966-1976); Lifetime Member, American Psychological Association; American Association for the Advancement of Science; New York Academy of Sciences; Lifetime Member, American Board of Disability Analysts **Marquis Who's Who Honors:** Who's Who in America and the World **Shipping Address:** 2838 Gainsboro Ct, Saint Louis, MO, 63121

Ronald Clinton Naugle, PhD

Title: Historian, Professor Emeritus **Industry:** Education/Educational Services **Company Name:** Nebraska Wesleyan University **Date of Birth:** 09/18/1942 **Place of Birth:** Mitchell **State:** IN **Parents:** Durward Clinton Naugle; Martha May Naugle **Marital Status:** Married **Spouse Name:** Gretchen Rohn (6/2/1963) **Children:** Meredith; Heilig **Education:** PhD in American Studies, The University of Kansas (1976) MA in American History, Purdue University (1966) BA in American Government and Politics, Purdue University (1964) **Career:** Professor Emeritus, Nebraska Wesleyan University (2004-Present); Director, Historical Studies Graduate Program, Nebraska Wesleyan University (2004-2006); Chairman, Graduate Program, Nebraska Wesleyan University (2002-2005); Director, Wesleyan Honors Academy, Nebraska Wesleyan University (2001-2003); Huge-Kinne Professor of History, Nebraska Wesleyan University (1985-2004); Department Chairman, Nebraska Wesleyan University (1985-2004); Associate Professor, Nebraska Wesleyan University (1980-1985); Huge-Kinne Endowed Chairman of History, Nebraska Wesleyan University (1980-1984); Assistant Professor, Nebraska Wesleyan University, Lincoln (1971-1980); Instructor of History, Nebraska Wesleyan University (1966-1971) **Career Related:** Director, Nebraska Summer Institute for High School History and Social Studies Teachers (1991-2006); Representative, Mountain-Plains States Coordinators, Executive Committee of State Coordinators (1997-2005); State Coordinator, National History Day (NHD), NE (1985-2005); Co-coordinator, "We the People" Program for High School History and Social Studies Students, NE (1990-2003) **Civic:** Chairman, Nebraska Hall of Fame Commission (2015-Present); Director, Honors Academy Dual Credit, Nebraska Wesleyan University (2006-Present); Member Emeritus, Four-Year Private College and Universities, National Board (2006-Present); Member, Nebraska Hall of Fame Commission (2003-Present); Member, National Alliance of Concurrent Enrollment Partnerships (2001-Present); Representative, Four-Year Private College and Universities, National Board (2003-2006); Founder, Nebraska Foundation for the Preservation of Oral History (2001-2006); Treasurer, Nebraska Foundation for the Preservation of Oral History (2001-2006); Creator, Two-Week Educational Program for Social Studies Teachers, Fort Robinson, NE (1992-2003); Affiliate, Seven Denominational-Sponsored Ministries for Inner-City Omaha National Americans (1996-2001); Chairman, Native-American Strategy and Action Team of Interchurch Ministries of Nebraska (1985-2000); Member, Multi-Cultural Education Training Team (1990-1993); Member, Planning Committee, Healing the Hoop (1992); Head, One-Week Immersion Experiences for College Juniors, Omaha and Winnebago Indian Reservations (1991); Member, Congregational Council, First Lutheran Church, Lincoln, NE (1981-1984); Chairman, Property Committee, UNL Lutheran Student Center, Lincoln, NE (1974-1976); President, University Lutheran Church, The University of Kansas, Lawrence, KS (1971-1972); Member, Multicultural Ministries Commission, Nebraska Synod ELCA **Creative Works:** Author, "Short History of Nebraska" (2018); Co-author, "History of Nebraska" (2015); Co-author, "Nebraska Quilts and Quiltmakers" (2003); Editor, "Life, Liberty and the Pursuit of Happiness: Volume II" (2003); Editor, "Ham, Eggs and Corncakes: A Nebraska Territorial Diary" (2001); Co-author, "History of Nebraska (1997); Co-author, "In the White Man's Image" (1992); Co-author, "Nebraska Quilts and Quiltmakers" (1991); Co-author, "White Man's Way" (1986) **Awards:** Award, "History of Nebraska, Fourth Edition," Nebraska Center for the Book (2015); Named Paul Beck Social Studies Teacher of the Year, Nebraska State Council of Social Studies (2003); Nebraska Sower Award, Nebraska Humanities Council (2003); Addison E. Sheldon Award, Nebraska Historical Society (1998); Frost Award for the Book, "Nebraska Quilts and Quiltmakers," Smithsonian Institution (1993); Clarion Award for the Film, "White Man's Way," Women In Communications (1987) **Membership:** Chairman, Nebraska Hall of Fame Commission (2015-Present) President, Nebraska State Council History Education (2005-2008) Associate Fellow, Center for Great Plains Studies; Associate, International Quilt Study Center; Nebraska Historical Society; Lifetime Member, Phi Kappa Phi; Phi Alpha Theta International History Honor Society **Marquis Who's Who Honors:** Albert Nelson Marquis Lifetime Achievement Award (2017); Distinguished Humanitarian (2017) **Hobbies:** Carpentry; Cooking **Political Affiliations:** Democrat **Religion:** Episcopalian **Shipping Address:** 6325 O St Apt 615, Lincoln, NE, 68510

St. Elmo Nauman Jr.

Title: Minister, University Professor (Retired) **Industry:** Education/Educational Services **Date of Birth:** 03/11/1935 **Place of Birth:** Phoenix **State:** AZ **Parents:** St. Elmo Harry Nauman; Frances Irma Wolf **Marital Status:** Married **Spouse Name:** Meijijati Supoto (2011); June Johanna Anderson (1954) **Children:** Constance Ann Busch; April Diana **Education:** PhD, Boston University (1969); Degree, Andover-Newton Theological School, Newton Centre, MA (1959); MDiv, Berkeley Baptist Divinity School (Now American Baptist Seminary of the West, Berkeley), California (1957); BA, University of Chicago, Illinois (1954) **Certifications:** Certified Ordained Minister, First Baptist Church, St. Paul, MN (1957) **Career:** Asylum Officer, United States Immigration & Naturalization Service, Anaheim, CA (1992-2001); Professor, Baylor University, Waco, TX (1985-1986); Faculty, George Washington University, Hampton, VA (1972-1980); Faculty, College William and Mary, Newport, RI (1971-1980); Faculty, Rutgers, The State University of New Jersey, New Brunswick (1968-1971) **Career Related:** Expert Witness, Immigration Court, Immigration Specialists, Arcadia, CA (2001-2004); Board Member, Inter-Church Child Care Center, Philadelphia, PA (1968-1969) **Civic:** Minister, Alpine Community Church, California (1990-1991); Minister, Newport Congregational Church, Rhode Island (1982-1983); Minister, Congregational Church, Berea, OH; Minister, Chelesford St. Baptist Church, Lowell, MA **Military Service:** Commander, Naval Air Station, Lemore, CA (1992); Commander, Third Marine Air Wing, El Toro Marine Corps Air Station, California (1991); Commander, U.S. Naval Reserve, Washington, DC (1973-1995) **Creative Works:** Author, "Treasury of Philosophy"; Author, "Fallacies and Logic-the Secret World of Evil Arguments"; Author, "Dictionary of Asian Philosophies"; Author, "Exorcism Through the Ages"; Author, "Dictionary of American Philosophy"; Author, "New Dictionary of Existentialism" **Awards:** Teacher of the Year, College of William & Mary (1980); Civic Award, Iota Pi Chapter, Alpha Kappa Psi (1978); National Chaplain, Association of the United States Navy **Hobbies:** Music; Art **Political Affiliations:** Republican **Shipping Address:** 3053 W Craig Rd., Ste E, Postal Connections, North Las Vegas, NV, 89032

Jens Naumann, RSSW

Title: Administrator **Industry:** Education/Educational Services **Company Name:** Gems Field Private School **Parents:** Dietrich Franz-Otto Naumann; Erika Regina Naumann **Marital Status:** Married **Spouse Name:** Ndeyapo Yolanda Naumann **Children:** Danielle Nicole Naumann; Ryan Jens Naumann; Leah Rene Naumann; Kyle Richard Naumann; Brandon Cole Naumann; Joel Lee Naumann; Jordan Grant Naumann; Aaron Alden Naumann; Ilta Shangalao Naumann **Education:** Associate, University of Toronto (1989); Diploma in Social Work, Loyalist College **Certifications:** RSSW, Ontario College of Social Workers and Social Services Workers **Career:** Entrepreneur; Artificial Vision Consultant, Renewable Energy, Green-First Technologies and Dezman Investments, Solar-Electric and Wind Energy; International Development Education Sector, Gems Field Private School, Namibia, Mozambique **Career Related:** Motivational Speaker, Self-Empowerment of People Living with Disabilities **Creative Works:** Author, "Search for Paradise: A Patient's Account of the Artificial Vision Experiment," Xlibris **Awards:** Fellowship, Best Social Worker Student Award, United Way of Quinte (2012); Honorary Diploma, Community Leadership and Outstanding Achievements in Renewable Energy Advocacy, St. Lawrence College (2005) **Marquis Who's Who Honors:** Albert Nelson Marquis Lifetime Achievement Award (2017) **To what do you attribute your success:** Mr. Naumann attributes his success to his parents for emphasizing the importance of self-motivation and his spouse and children for their support. **Why did you become involved in your profession or industry:** Mr. Naumann entered his profession because in 1981, at age 17, he lost his left eye in an industrial accident, then the other one by bad luck in 1983. At age 20, he was then suddenly totally blind, learning quickly the difficulty of life in total blindness including the social disparity and labor force restrictions of this community despite being very successful at rehabilitation. Mr. Naumann had a young family with a child and wife to support and quickly realized that getting into his own business circumvents the employment challenges as clients are apt to judge the product, not the one who delivers it. He began a piano tuning and repair shop, trained as piano player via Toronto Royal Conservatory of Music, bought a farm in 1989 where he worked on his own agriculture operation milking cows, driving his own haying and cultivation machinery and building the demo solar-wind electrical station. Mr. Naumann dreamt of being able to see again via computer vision and when the chance came in 2002, he was the first patient accepted at Dobelle Institute in New York and through his computer programming skill, electronics knowledge and language diversity, he gained employment with Dobelle Institute as patient representative. This led him to collect enough information to write the book, "Search for Paradise." Mr. Naumann now works with the Netherlands Institute of Neurology as a consultant for their new Roelfsema vision project in Amsterdam. **What do you consider to be the highlight of your career:** The highlight of Mr. Naumann's was in 2002 when he drove a car at a American Society of Artificial Internal Organs meeting using the first artificial vision brain computer implant. This moment was captured by CNN and the cameras of other media giants. **Where will you be in five years:** In the next five years, Mr. Naumann is planning to sail around the world alone by a boat powered with a self-built solar electricity system. As a totally blind person, he will use available technology such as GPS, talking/Braille magnetic compass and sensory substitution technology as his aids. This will lead him to write a comprehensive book on discovering the world's beauty on its seas seen through the eyes of a blind person. **Hobbies:** Electronic circuit design; Computer programming; Classical piano and guitar playing and composition; Traveling internationally to new cultures; Wilderness adventure trips; Astronomy **Shipping Address:** PO Box 3772, Gems Field Private School, Ongwediva, Namibia, 9000 **Website:** http://www.jensnaumann.green-first.com

Janet Neal Siamis

Industry: Fine Art **Place of Birth:** Cleveland **State/Country of Origin:** OH **Education:** Coursework, Antelope Valley College (1978-1981); Coursework, Rollins College (1956-1957); Coursework, Ralph Love **Creative Works:** Artist, Exhibition, Florida Watercolor Annual, Saint Petersburg, Russia (1996, 1991); Artist Exhibition, Tallahassee City Hall (1988-1989); Marriott Hotel Presidential Suites Artist Exhibition, Lancaster Museum (1985) Artist, Showcased Home Savings America, Fluor Corporation, Irvine CA; Artist, Security Pac Bank Embassy Suites Hotel **Awards:** Judge's Choice Award, Florida Watercolor Annual, Saint Petersburg, Russia (1991)

Belverd Earl Needles Jr., PhD

Title: Distinguished Professor at DePaul University School of Accountancy, Educator **Industry:** Education/Educational Services **Company Name:** DePaul University **Date of Birth:** 09/16/1942 **Place of Birth:** Lubbock **State:** TX **Parents:** Belverd Earl Needles; Billie (Anderson) Needles **Marital Status:** Married **Spouse Name:** Marian Powers (5/23/1976) **Children:** Jennifer Helen; Jeffrey Scott; Annabelle Marian; Abigail Marian **Education:** PhD in Accounting, University of Illinois (1969); MBA, Texas Tech University (1965); BBA, Texas Tech University (1964); MBA, Texas Tech University **Certifications:** Certified Public Accountant, State of Illinois; Certified Management Accountant **Career:** Member, Intergovernmental Working Group of Experts on International Standards of Accounting and Reporting, United Nations Conference on Trade and Development (2009-Present); Ernst & Young Distinguished Distinguished Professor at DePaul University School of Accountancy (2003-Present); Principal, Needles & Powers, Inc. (1994-Present); Arthur Andersen & Co. Alumni Distinguished Professor of Accounting, DePaul University (1988-2002); Professor of Accounting, DePaul University (1976-1988); Director, School of Accountancy & MIS, DePaul University (1976-1986); Professor of Accounting, University of Illinois at Urbana-Champaign (1976-1978); Dean, Chicago State University College of Business (1972-1976); Associate Professor of Accounting, Texas Tech University, Lubbock, TX (1968-1972); Assistant Professor of Accounting, Texas Tech University, Lubbock, TX (1968-1972) **Creative Works:** Editor, "Accounting Instructors' Report: A Journal for Accounting Educators" (1981-Present); Co-Author, "Principles of Accounting, 12th Edition," Houghton Mifflin Harcourt (2013); Co-Author, "Financial and Managerial Accounting, 11th Edition" (2013); Co-Author, "International Financial Reporting Standards: An Introduction, Third Edition," Cengage Learning (Now Cengage) (2012); Co-Author, "Financial Accounting (with IFRS), 11th Edition," South Western College Publishing (2011); Contributing Author, "Financial and Managerial Accounting," South Western College Publishing (2010-2013); Co-Author, "Financial Accounting: A Global Approach," Russian Edition, South Western College Publishing (2006); Co-Author, "International Financial Reporting Standards: An Introduction," Cengage Learning (Now Cengage) (2003); Co-Author, "Financial Accounting: A Global Approach," South Western College Publishing (1999); Co-Author, "Accounting Education for the 21st Century," Pergamon Press, Elsevier (1994); Contributing Author, "Educational Standards" (1990); Contributing Author, "Comparative International Accounting" (1990); Author, "A Profession in Transition: The Ethical and Responsibilities of Accountants" (1989) **Awards:** Lifetime Achievement Award, American Institute of CPAs (Now Association of International Certified Professional Accountants) (2013); Lifetime Service Award, American Accounting Association (2013); Lifetime Achievement Award, Accounting Today (Now SourceMedia) (2013); Wicklander Fellow, Institute for Business & Professional Ethics, DePaul University (2010-2011); William Holmes McGuffey Longevity Award, "Principles of Accounting," Textbook & Academic Authors Association (2008); Lifetime Achievement Award, Illinois CPA Society (2008); 100 Most Influential Accountants, Accounting Today (Now SourceMedia) (2001); Excellence in Teaching Award, DePaul University (1998); Outstanding International Accounting Educator, American Accounting Association (1996); Accountant of the Year for Education, Beta Alpha Psi (1992); Outstanding Educator, American Institute of CPAs (Now Association of International Certified Professional Accountants) (1992); Outstanding Accounting Educator, Illinois CPA Society (1990); Faculty Award of Merit, Federation of Schools of Accountancy (1990); Honoree, Distinguished Alumnus, Texas Tech University (1986); Award of Merit, DePaul University (1986) **Membership:** Vice President, American Accounting Association (2011-Present); Vice President of Education, American Accounting Association (2008-2011); Council Member, American Institute of CPAs (Now Association of International Certified Professional Accountants) (2003-2005); Chairman, Illinois CPA Society (2003-2004); Senior Vice Chair, Illinois CPA Society (2002-2003); Vice Chair, Illinois CPA Society (2001-2002); President, IAAER (1997-2002); Board of Directors, Illinois CPA Society (1994-1996); Secretary Treasurer, IAAER (1992-1997); Vice President, IAAER (1989-1992); Chairman, American Accounting Association (1987-1988); Executive Committee, European Accounting Association (1986-1989); Vice Chairman, American Accounting Association (1986-1987); President, Federation of Schools of Accountancy (1986); Secretary, International Section, American Accounting Association (1984-1986); Board of Directors, Federation of Schools of Accountancy (1980-1987); Academy of International Business; Phi Delta Kappa **Marquis Who's Who Honors:** Albert Nelson Marquis Lifetime Achievement Award (2017) **Shipping Address:** 1600 Barton Springs Rd Unit 4601, Austin, TX, 78704

Thomas Neff

Title: Executive Recruiter **Industry:** Staffing and Recruiting **Company Name:** Spencer Stuart **Date of Birth:** 10/02/1937 **Place of Birth:** Easton **State:** PA **Parents:** John Wallace; Elizabeth Ann (Dougherty) N. **Marital Status:** Married **Spouse Name:** Susan Culver Paull (11/26/1971, Deceased); Sarah Brown Hallingby **Children:** David Andrew; Mark Gregory; Scott Dougherty **Education:** MBA, Lehigh University (1961); BS in Industrial Engineering, Lafayette College (1959) **Career:** Chairman, Spencer Stuart & Associates US (Now Spencer Stuart), New York City, NY (1996-Present); Board of Directors, Spencer Stuart & Associates (Now Spencer Stuart), New York City, NY (1996-Present); President, Managing Partner, Spencer Stuart & Associates (Now Spencer Stuart), New York City, NY (1979-1996); Regional Partner, Spencer Stuart, Inc. (Now Spencer Stuart), New York City, NY (1976-1979); Principal, Booz Allen & Hamilton Inc., New York City, NY (1974-1976); President, Hospital Data Sciences, Inc., New York City, NY (1969-1974); Director of Marketing Planning, Trans-World Airlines, New York City, NY (1966-1969); Associate, McKinsey & Company, New York City, NY and Australia (1963-1966) **Career Related:** Former Board of Directors, Lord Abbett Mutual Funds (Now Lord, Abbett & Co. LLC); Former Board of Directors, Ace Ltd. (Now Chubb); Former Board of Directors, Hewitt Associates, Inc. (Now Aon plc); Former Board of Directors, McMillan Inc., Former Board Member, Exult, Inc. **Civic:** Trustee Emeritus, Lafayette College (2004-Present); Chairman, Brunswick School (1991-1995) **Military Service:** First Lieutenant, United States Army (1961-1963) **Creative Works:** Co-author, "Lessons From the Top" (1999); Author, "You're in Charge–Now What: The 8-Point Plan" (2005) **Membership:** Links Club; Blind Brook Club, Quogue, NY; Beach Club; Quogue Field Club; Round Hill Club; Quantuck Beach Club; National Golf Links; Lost Tree Club; McArthur Golf Club; Everglades Club; Nantucket Golf Clubs **Marquis Who's Who Honors:** Albert Nelson Marquis Lifetime Achievement Award (2017) **Political Affiliations:** Republican **Religion:** Roman Catholic **Shipping Address:** 277 Park Ave., Fl 32, Spencer Stuart & Assocs, New York, NY, 10172

Ei-ichi Negishi, PhD

Title: Chemistry Professor **Industry:** Education/Educational Services **Company Name:** Purdue University **Date of Birth:** 07/14/1935 **Education:** PhD in Organic Chemistry, University of Pennsylvania (1963); BS in Organic Chemistry, University of Tokyo (1958) **Career:** Herbert C. Brown Distinguished Professor in Organic Chemistry, Director of the Negishi-Brown Institute, Purdue University **Career Related:** Consultant in Field, National University of Singapore (2000); Lecturer in Field, National University of Singapore (2000); Visiting Professor, National University of Singapore (2000); Fellow, John Simon Guggenheim Memorial Foundation (1987); Consultant in Field, University of California, Santa Cruz (1980); Lecturer in Field, University of California, Santa Cruz (1980); Visiting Professor, University of California, Santa Cruz (1980); Harrison Fellow (1962-1963) **Creative Works:** Author, "Handbook of Organopalladium Chemistry for Organic Synthesis," Wiley-Interscience (2002); Contributor, Several Articles, Publications **Awards:** Co-Recipient, Nobel Prize in Chemistry, The Nobel Foundation (2010); ACS Award for Creative Work in Synthetic Organic Chemistry (2010); Yamada-Koga Prize, Japan Research Foundation of Optically Active Compounds (2007); Gold Medal, Charles University, Prague, Czech Republic (2007); Professional/Scholarly Publishing Division Award, Chemistry, Association of American Publishers (2003); Sir Edward Frankland Prize Lectureship, Royal Society of Chemistry (2000); Humboldt Researcher Award, Alexander von Humboldt-Stiftung Foundation (1998-2001); Organometallic Chemistry Award, American Chemical Society (1998); Award, Chemical Society of Japan (1996-1997); A.R. Day Award (1996); Fulbright Scholar (1960-1963) **Membership:** American Association for the Advancement of Science; Royal Society of Chemistry; Chemical Society of Japan; American Chemical Society; Sigma Xi; Phi Lambda Epsilon **Marquis Who's Who Honors:** Albert Nelson Marquis Lifetime Achievement Award (2017); Distinguished Humanitarian (2017) **What do you consider to be the highlight of your career:** The highlight of Dr. Negishi's career was winning the Nobel Prize in Chemistry in 2010. **Shipping Address:** 560 Oval Drive, Purdue University, Chemistry Department, West Lafayette, IN, 47907 **Website:** https://www.chem.purdue.edu/activity/public/profile/chem/negishi

Patricia Joanne Nellor Wickwire, PhD

Title: Psychologist, Educator **Industry:** Education/Educational Services **Company Name:** The Nellor Wickwire Group **State:** IA **Parents:** William McKinley Nellor; Clara Rose (Pautsch) Nellor **Marital Status:** Married **Spouse Name:** Robert James Wickwire (9/7/1957) **Children:** William James **Education:** PhD in Educational Psychology, The University of Texas at Austin (1971); MA in Special Education, Guidance, Counseling, The University of Iowa, Iowa City, IA (1959); BA in English, Journalism, Music, Education, University of Northern Iowa, Cum Laude, Cedar Falls, IA (1951); Postgraduate Coursework, California State University, Long Beach; Postgraduate Coursework, University of California, Los Angeles **Certifications:** Licensed Educational Psychologist, State of California; Licensed Marriage and Family Therapist, State of California; National Certified Counselor; California Credentials for Community College and Public School Administrative Services, Student Personnel and Pupil Services; Iowa Permanent Professional Credentials **Career:** Teacher, School Psychologist, Administrator, South Bay Union School District, Redondo Beach, CA (1962-1982); Reading Consultant, Head Dormitory Counselor, The University of Iowa, Iowa City, IA (1955-1957); Teacher, Counselor, Waverly-Shell Rock Community School District, Iowa (1951-1955); Teacher, Ricketts Independent School District, Iowa (1946-1948); **Career Related:** Consultant, Management and Education President, Nellor Wickwire Group (1981-Present); Chairman, Friends of Dominguez Hills, California (1981-1985); Member Executive Board, Beach Cities Symphony Association (1970-1982); Member, Executive Board, California Mental Health Planning Council (1968-1972) **Civic:** President, California Women's Caucus (2003-2006); President, California Women's Caucus (1993-1995) **Creative Works:** Editor, American Association for Career Education (1991-Present); Journal Editor, California Counseling Association (1990-2002); Editor, Association for Measurement and Evaluation in Guidance (1987-1990); Western Regional Editor, Association for Measurement and Evaluation in Guidance (1985-1987); Newsletter Editor, Association for Assessment in Counseling and Education; Consulting Editor, Association for Assessment in Counseling and Education; Editor-Elect, Association for Assessment in Counseling and Education; Western Regional Editor, Association for Assessment in Counseling and Education; Author, "Handbook on Convention Coordination," Association for Assessment in Counseling and Education; Committee to Revise "Responsibilities of Users of Standardized Tests," Association for Assessment in Counseling and Education; Chair, Publications Group, National Career Development Association; Advisory Board, "The Family Journal," International Association of Marriage and Family Counselors; Editor, CACD Journal, California Association for Counseling and Development **Awards:** Inductee, H.B. McDaniel Hall of Fame for Exceptional Contributions, Stanford University (2016); Kenneth Hoyt Lifetime Career Education Achievement Award (2014); International Women's Review Board (2014); CACD Clarion Modell Award (1997); Honoree, Woman of the Year, American Biographical Institute (1990-2010); CACD Distinguished Service Award; California Women's Caucus Extraordinary Leadership Award; AMCD President's Award; NCDA Merit Award; NCDA President's Award; AACE President's Special Merit Award; Honoree, AACE Distinguished Member Recognition; Honoree, South Bay Woman of the Year Recognition; California Governor's Special Citation for Achievement and Contributions in Education; Inductee, "Dictionary of International Biography"; National Distinguished Service Registry for Counseling and Development **Membership:** Representative to Joint Committee on Testing Practices, American Counseling Association (2001-2007); President, California Association for Measurement and Evaluation in Guidance (2004-2005); Chairman, Bylaws Committee, American Counseling Association (1998-2001); President, California Association for Measurement and Evaluation in Guidance (1998-2000); Media Chair, National Career Development Association (1992-1998); Member Committee on Women, American Counseling Association (1989-1992); Executive Board of Directors, Association of Measurement and Evaluation in Guidance (1987-1991); Editor, Association of Measurement and Evaluation in Guidance (1987-1990); President, California Association for Counseling and Development (1988-1989); Convention Chair, Association of Measurement and Evaluation in Guidance (1986); Western Regional Editor, Association of Measurement and Evaluation in Guidance (1985-1987); President, California Association for Measurement and Evaluation in Guidance (1984-1985) **Marquis Who's Who Honors:** Albert Nelson Marquis Lifetime Achievement Award (2017); Who's Who in America; Who's Who in American Education; Who's Who of American Women; Who's Who in Finance and Business; Who's Who Among Human Services Professionals; Who's Who in Medicine and Healthcare; Who's Who in Science and Engineering; Who's Who in the World **Shipping Address:** 2900 Amby Pl, Hermosa Beach, CA, 90254

Amanda Nelson Pittman

Title: Music Educator **Industry:** Education/Educational Services **Company Name:** Los Angeles City Schools **Parents:** General Lee Nelson; Amanda Hopkins Nelson **Marital Status:** Married **Spouse Name:** Marvin Benjamin Pittman (1964) **Children:** Marvin Benjamin Pittman, Jr. **Education:** MusD, University of Southern California, Los Angeles, CA (2003); MusM, University of Southern California, Los Angeles, CA (1961); MusB, University of Southern California, Los Angeles, CA (1948) **Certifications:** General Teaching Credential, Elementary Education, State of California **Career:** Elementary School Music Teacher, Los Angeles City Schools (1999-Present); Elementary School Music Teacher, Clark County School District, Las Vegas, NV (1992-1998); Elementary School Music Teacher, Los Angeles City Schools (1990-1991); Elementary School Music Teacher, Beverly Hills Unified Schools, California (1975-1990); Elementary School Music Teacher, Los Angeles City Schools (1966-1975); Elementary School Music Teacher, Montgomery County Schools, Rockville, MD (1964-1966); Elementary School Music Teacher, Los Angeles City Schools (1957-1964); Elementary School Teacher, Fort Worth Schools (1949-1951) **Career Related:** Ambassador, University of Southern California (2017-Present); Instructor, Music Education, California State University, Los Angeles, CA (2002-2003); Instructor, Music Education, University of Southern California (1975-1977); Instructor, Music Education, Pepperdine University, Los Angeles, CA (1967-1970) **Military Service:** Administrative Officer, U.S. Air Force Reserve, March Air Force Base, California (1959-1964); Captain, U.S. Air Force (1951-1956) **Membership:** National Women's History Museum (2017-Present); Military Officers Association of America (2014); Vice President, Los Angeles City Elementary School Music Association (2004-2006); Presenter, Music Educators National Conference (1960-2006); California Music Educators Association; International Association for Jazz Education; Charter Member, Women in Military Service for America Memorial Foundation **Marquis Who's Who Honors:** Albert Nelson Marquis Lifetime Achievement Award (2017) **Why did you become involved in your profession or industry:** When Dr. Nelson Pittman became a teacher, she wanted to teach music but that wasn't available. One day she saw a woman in uniform walking down the street and decided she was going to enlist to get a commission. Dr. Nelson Pittman joined the U.S. Air Force and after she left with her commission she decided she wasn't going to move back to Texas. She moved in with her brother in California for a while and went to school to get her music degree. She moved into her own apartment and finally was able to become a music teacher to fulfill her dream. **Shipping Address:** 8957 Haas Ave, Los Angeles, CA, 90047

Michael Lee Nemec

Title: Lawyer **Industry:** Law and Legal Services **Company Name:** Hall, Estill, Hardwick, Gable, Golden & Nelson, PC **Date of Birth:** 08/01/1949 **Place of Birth:** Tulsa **State:** OK **Parents:** Milton L. Nemec; Betty D. (Lawrence) Nemec **Marital Status:** Married **Spouse Name:** Vivian Strobel (12/26/1970) **Children:** Adam; Jennifer; David **Education:** JD, The University of Tulsa (1976); BA in Political Science, The University of Tulsa (1971) **Career:** Counsel, Hall, Estill, Hardwick, Gable, Golden & Nelson, PC, Tulsa, OK (2015-Present); Shareholder, Hall, Estill, Hardwick, Gable, Golden & Nelson, PC, Tulsa, OK (1993-2014); Associate, Hall, Estill, Hardwick, Gable, Golden & Nelson, PC, Tulsa, OK (1989-1993); Private Practice Law, Tulsa, OK (1985-1989); Vice President, Trust Officer, Bank of Commerce and Trust Company, Tulsa, OK (1980-1985); Assistant Vice President, Trust Officer, The Bank N.A., Tulsa, OK (1980); Associate Director, Deferred Giving, Oklahoma State University Foundation, Stillwater, OK (1978-1980); Private Practice, Law, Tulsa, OK (1976-1978) **Civic:** Member, Long-Range Planning Committee, TU College of Law (2005-2008); Member, Major Gifts Council, American Heart Association, Inc. (1998-1999); Volunteer, Boy Scouts of America, Tulsa, OK (1997-2001); Volunteer, Boy Scouts of America, Tulsa, OK (1984-1986); Participant, U.S. Naval Academy Foreign Affairs Conference (1971) **Awards:** Outstanding Senior Alumnus, TU College of Law (2013); Golden Rule Award, Tulsa Bar Association (2006); Named Family of the Year, Church of Jesus Christ of Latter Day Saints, Tulsa, OK (1985); Albert Nelson Marquis Lifetime Achievement Award **Membership:** Board of Directors, TU College of Law Alumni Association (2002-Present); Tulsa Title and Probate Lawyers (2001-Present); President, TU College of Law Alumni Association (2011); President-Elect, TU College of Law Alumni Association (2010); Vice President, TU College of Law Alumni Association (2009); Treasurer, TU College of Law Alumni Association (2008); Secretary, TU College of Law Alumni Association (2007); President, Tulsa Title and Probate Lawyers (2005); Vice President, Tulsa Title and Probate Lawyers (2004); Secretary, Tulsa Title and Probate Lawyers (2003); Board of Directors, Tulsa Estate Planning Forum (2000-2003); President, Tulsa Tax Forum (1994-1995); Secretary Tax Section, Tulsa Bar Association (1988); ABA **Bar Admissions:** State of Oklahoma (1976) **Marquis Who's Who Honors:** Albert Nelson Marquis Lifetime Achievement Award (2017); Distinguished Humanitarian (2017) **Why did you become involved in your profession or industry:** Mr. Nemec was influenced to get involved in his profession by his grandfather, who was a bailiff, and by watching Perry Mason. He was always interested in the law, and he always wanted to help people. **What do you consider to be the highlight of your career:** The highlight of Mr. Nemec's career is having met all of the people he has during his life. **Religion:** Roman Catholic **Shipping Address:** 2651 E 22nd St, Tulsa, OK, 74114

Rachel N. Newman

Title: Editor (Retired) **Industry:** Writing and Editing **Company Name:** Hearst Communications Inc. **Date of Birth:** 05/01/1938 **Place of Birth:** Malden **State:** MA **Parents:** Maurice Newman; Edythe Brenda (Tichell) Newman **Marital Status:** Married **Spouse Name:** Michael Lucas (2004) **Education:** Coursework, Grand Central Atlier, New York (2011-Present); BA, The Pennsylvania State University, University Park, PA (1960) **Certifications:** Certificate, New York School Interior Design, New York City, NY (1963) **Career:** Founding Editor, Healthy Living Magazine (1996-2000); Founding Editor, Country Living Gardener Magazine (1993-2000); Founding Editor, Country Kitchens Magazine (1990-1993); Founding Editor, Dream Homes Magazine (1989-2000); Founding Editor, Country Cooking Magazine (1985-1990); Editor-in-Chief, Country Living Magazine, New York City, NY (1978-1998); Home Building and Decorating Director, Good Housekeeping Magazine, New York City, NY (1978-1982); Fashion Director, Good Housekeeping Magazine, New York City, NY (1977-1978); Editor-in-Chief, American Home Crafts Magazine, New York City, NY (1972-1977); Managing Editor, Ladies Home Journal Needle and Craft Magazine, New York City, NY (1970-1972); Managing Editor, McCall's You-Do-It Home Decorating (1968-1970); Associate Editor, McCall's Sportswear and Dress Merchandiser Magazine, New York City, NY (1967); Designer, Publicist, Grandoe Glove Corporation, New York City, NY (1965-1967); Accessories Editor, Women's Wear Daily, New York City, NY (1964-1965) **Civic:** Former Board of Directors, Mothers and Others for a Livable Planet **Creative Works:** Painter, Commission Landscapes, Still Life and Portraits, Phyllis Lucas Gallery, New York **Awards:** Named to the YMCA Hall of Fame (1992); Circle of Excellence Award, International Furnishings and Design Association (1992); Named, Distinguished Alumna, The Pennsylvania State University (1988); The Pennsylvania State University Alumni Fellow (1986) **Membership:** American Society of Magazine Editors; American Society of Interior Designers; National Home Fashions League; New York Fashion Group **Hobbies:** Travel; Painting **Shipping Address:** 301 E. 52nd Street, Apartment 3B, New York, NY, 10022

San Duy Nguyen

Title: Psychiatrist, Educator **Industry:** Medicine & Health Care **Date of Birth:** 09/25/1932 **Place of Birth:** Langson **Country of Origin:** Vietnam **Parents:** Nguyen Duy; Tran Tuyet; Quyen (Trang) San **Marital Status:** Married **Spouse Name:** Eddie Jean Ciesielski (8/24/1971) **Children:** Thuan Le San; Megan Thu-loan San; Muriel Mylinh San; Claire Kimlan San; Robin Xuanlan San; Baodan Edward San **Education:** Resident, The Clarke Institute of Psychiatry, Toronto, Canada (1971-1972); Resident, Lafayette Clinic, Detroit, MI (1970-1971); Postgraduate Coursework, University of Michigan (1970); Resident, University Hospital, University of Michigan, Ann Arbor, MI (1968-1970); MD, Saigon University (1960); Intern, Cho Ray Hospital, Ho Chi Minh City, Vietnam (1957-1958) **Career:** Chairman, Board of Directors, Access Alliance Multicultural Health Center, Toronto, Canada (1988-Present); Consultant, United Nations High Commissioner for Refugees (1987-Present); Director, East-West Mental Health Center, Toronto, Canada (1987-Present); Board of Directors, Hong Fook Mental Health Association, Toronto, Canada (1987-Present); Associate Professor, Psychiatry, University of Ottawa Faculty of Medicine (1985-1987); Director, Psychiatric Rehabilitation Program, Royal Ottawa Hospital (1985-1987); Associate Professor, Psychiatry, University of Ottawa Faculty of Medicine (1980-1985); Unit Director, Inpatient Service, Royal Ottawa Hospital, Canada (1980-1984); Medical Practice Specializing in Psychiatry, Guelph, Canada (1974-1980); Consultant Psychiatrist, Guelph General Hospital, Guelph, Canada (1974-1980); Unit Director, Homewood Sanitarium, Guelph, Canada (1974-1980); Senior Psychiatrist, Centre for Addiction and Mental Health, Toronto, Canada (1972-1974); Chief of Psychiatry, South Vietnamese Army (1964-1968); Consultant Psychiatrist, St. Joseph's Hospital, Guelph, Canada **Military Service:** Army of the Republic of Vietnam (1953-1968) **Creative Works:** Author, "Refugee Resettlement and Well-Being" (1989); Author, "Ten Years Later: Indochinese Communities in Canada" (1988); Author, "Southeast Asian Mental Health" (1985); Author, "Uprooting, Loss and Adaptation" (1984-1987); Author, "Psycholsomatic Medicine: Theoretical, Clinical, and Transcultural Aspects" (1983); Co-author, "The Psychology and Physiology of Stress" (1969); Author, "Etude du Tetanos au Vietnam" (1960) **Awards:** Commemorative Medal for the 125th Anniversary of the Confederation of Canada, Governor General of Canada (1993); Outstanding Achievement Award, Ontario Government (1992) **Membership:** The New York Academy of Sciences; The International Society of Hypnosis; American Society of Clinical Hypnosis; American Psychiatric Association; Canadian Psychiatric Association; CMA **Marquis Who's Who Honors:** Albert Nelson Marquis Lifetime Achievement Award (2017); Distinguished Humanitarian (2017) **Why did you become involved in your profession or industry:** Dr. Nguyen became involved in his profession when he was in the Vietnamese army. During the Vietnamese War, he served as an American doctor. The Vietnamese army didn't have much in the way of psychiatric services, and he felt a need to help. He was chief of psychiatry in the Army during the war, as well as chief consultant in neuropsychiatry to the surgeon general. **Hobbies:** Spending time with family **Religion:** Buddhist **Shipping Address:** 87 Golfwood Heights, ON, Etobicoke, Canada, M9P 3L8

Ashutosh Niraj

Title: Cardiologist **Industry:** Medicine & Health Care **Company Name:** Heart & Brain Center of Texas **Parents:** Ram Narayan Singh **Marital Status:** Married **Spouse Name:** Ranjeeta Mani (6/24/2006) **Education:** Fellowship in Cardiology, DMC Main (2008-Present); Fellowship in Cardiology, Wayne State University (2008-Present); Resident in Internal Medicine, DMC Main (2005-2008); Resident in Internal Medicine, Wayne State University (2005-2008); MS in Basic Medical Sciences, The University of Alabama at Birmingham (2004); Bachelor of Medicine, Bachelor of Surgery, Savitribai Phule Pune University (2001); BS in Intermediate Science Patna Science College (1994) **Certifications:** Certified in Internal Medicine, American Board of Internal Medicine (2008); Licensed Cardiologist, Educational Commission for Foreign Medical Graduates (2003); Certified in Computerized Tomography Coronary Angiogram, Certification Board of Cardiovascular Computed Tomography, Inteleos Inc.; Certified in Nuclear Cardiology, Certification Board of Nuclear Cardiology, Inteleos Inc.; Certified in Echocardiography, National Board of Echocardiography, Inc.; Certified in Cardiology, American Board of Internal Medicine **Career:** Member, Heart and Brain Center/Family Care Clinic of Texas (2016-Present); Research Assistant in Cell Biology, The University of Alabama (2001-2004); Member, West Houston Medical Center, C-HCA, Inc.; Founder, Heart and Brain Center/Family Care Clinic of Texas; Medical Director, Heart and Brain Center/Family Care Clinic of Texas **Creative Works:** Author, "Two-dimensional strain profiles in patients with physiological and pathological hypertrophy and preserved left ventricular systolic function: a comparative analyses" (2012); Author, "Association of novel biomarkers with future cardiovascular events is influenced by ethnicity: Results from a multi-ethnic cohort," International Journal of Cardiology" (2012); Author, "Predictors of residual cardiovascular risk in patients on statin therapy for primary prevention" (2011); Author, "Relationship between red cell distribution width and microalbuminuria: a population-based study of multiethnic representative US adults" (2011); Author, "Red cell distribution width and mortality: effect of left ventricular hypertrophy" (2011); Author, "Homocysteine and reclassification of cardiovascular disease risk" (2011); Author, "Glycosylated hemoglobin and prevalent metabolic syndrome in nondiabetic multiethnic U.S. adults" (2011); Author, "Coronary revascularization strategy for ST elevation myocardial infarction with multivessel disease: experience and results at 1-year follow-up" (2011); Author, "Usefulness of intravenously administered fluid replenishment for detection of patent foramen ovale by transesophageal echocardiography" (2010); Author, "Red cell distribution width and risk of coronary heart disease events" (2010); Author, "Traditional cardiovascular risk factors and severity of angiographic coronary artery disease in the elderly" (2010); Author, "Gender difference in novel biomarkers for predicting future cardiovascular and coronary events" (2010); Author, "Prognostic implications of atherogenic/anti-atherogenic lipid ratios in an ethnically diverse population" (2010); Author, "Gender and ethnic differences in cardiovascular events and mortality in patients with depressive symptoms" (2010); Author, "Effect of lipid subclasses on the risk of cardiovascular outcomes in an ethnically diverse asymptomatic population" (2010); Author, "Is there a gender disparity in risk association of inflammatory biomarkers with new onset diabetes in healthy adult population?" (2010); Author, "Microalbuminuria in non-diabetic patients with metabolic syndrome is a strong predictor of subclinical atherosclerosis: a multi-ethnic perspective" (2010); Author, "Waist hip ratio, not body mass index predicted cardiovascular risk in a multi ethnic cohort of healthy adults" (2010); Author, "Global and regional left ventricular contractile impairment in patients with wolff-Parkinson-white syndrome" (2009); Author, "Spectrum of electrocardiographic and angiographic coronary artery disease findings in patients with cocaine-associated myocardial infarction" (2009); Author, "Correlation of Lipid Profile with Angiographic Coronary Artery Disease Burden and All-Cause Mortality Among Elderly Patients Undergoing Coronary Angiography" (2009); Author, "Detectable Troponin In Non-Acute Coronary Syndrome Patients In The Intensive Care Unit setting. Long Term Prognosis?" (2009); Author, "Coronary Artery Bypass grafting vs Percutaneous Coronary Intervention in Octogenarians: Impact on clinical outcomes" (2009) **Membership:** Community of Science; Society of General Internal Medicine; American College of Cardiology Foundation; American Geriatrics Society; International Society for Heart Research; American Society for Biochemistry and Molecular Biology; The American Society for Cell Biology; Associate, American College of Physicians **Shipping Address:** 7810 Bellaire Blvd, Houston, TX, 77036 **Website:** http://www.hbctx.com

William A. Nitze

Title: Entrepreneur, Not-for-Profit Developer, Government Official, Lawyer **Industry:** Business Management/Business Services **Company Name:** Oceana Energy Company **Date of Birth:** 09/27/1942 **Place of Birth:** New York **State:** NY **Parents:** Paul Henry Nitze; Phyllis (Pratt) Nitze **Marital Status:** Married **Spouse Name:** Ann Kendall Richards (6/5/1971) **Children:** Paul Kendall; Charles Richards **Education:** JD, Harvard University (1969); BA, University of Oxford (1966); BA, Harvard University (1964) **Career:** Vice Chairman, Senseye, Inc., Austin, TX (2015-Present); Chairman, Clear Path Technologies, LLC, Corona, CA (2007-Present); Chairman, GridPoint, Washington, DC (2003-2007); President, Gemstar Group, Washington, DC (2001-2005); Assistant Administrator for International Activities, United States Environmental Protection Agency, Washington, DC (1994-2001); President, Alliance to Save Energy, Washington, DC (1990-1994); Department Assistant Secretary for Environment, Health and Natural Resources, United States Department of State, Washington, DC (1987-1990); Assistant, General Counsel, Exploration and Producing Division, Exxon Mobil Corporation, New York, NY (1980-1987); Of General Counsel, Mobil Oil Japan, Tokyo, Japan (1976-1980); Counsel, Mobil South, Inc., New York, NY (1974-1976); Vice President, London Arts, Inc., New York, NY (1972-1973); Associate, Sullivan and Cromwell, New York, NY (1970-1972) **Career Related:** Chairman, Oceana Energy Company, Washington, DC (2006-Present); Professorial Lecturer, Paul H. Nitze School of Advanced International Studies (2001-Present); Adjunct Faculty, George Mason University (2016); Professorial Lecturer, Paul H. Nitze School of Advanced International Studies (1993-1994); Visiting Scholar, Environmental Law Institute, Washington, DC (1990); Advisory Committee, Professorial Lecturer, Paul H. Nitze School of Advanced International Studies (1982-1995); Chairman, Advisory Board, Krasnow Institute, George Mason University **Civic:** Chairman, Advisory Board, Krasnow Institute (2004-Present); Trustee, The Aspen Institute, Queenstown, MD (1988-Present); Chairman, Galapagos Conservancy (2003-2009); Board of Directors, Atlantic Council, Washington, DC (2002-2010); Chairman, Climate Institute (2002-2009); Vice Chairman, Galapagos Conservancy (2002-2003); Chairman, Alliance to Save Energy (2001-2012); Board of Directors, Galapagos Conservancy, Falls Church, VA (2001-2009); Board of Directors, Climate Institute, Washington, DC (2001-2009); Vice Chairman, Climate Institute (2001-2002); Trustee, Krasnow Institute, Fairfax, VA (1996-2001); Board of Directors, National Symphony Orchestra Association, Washington, DC (1990-2002); Board of Directors, Charles A. Lindbergh Fund, Minneapolis, MN (1990-1994) **Membership:** National Advisory Council, Redwood Library & Athenaeum; Council on Foreign Relations; Association of the Bar of the City of New York; Chevy Chase Club; Knickerbocker Club; The Links Club; Cosmos Club; Metropolitan Club **Bar Admissions:** U.S. Supreme Court (1987); State of New York (1970) **Marquis Who's Who Honors:** Distinguished Humanitarian (2017) **Hobbies:** Jogging; Piano; Collecting art **Political Affiliations:** Republican **Religion:** Episcopalian **Shipping Address:** 1537 28th Street NW, Washington, DC, 20007

Daniel Walker Nixon

Title: Adjunct Professor of Medicine **Industry:** Education/Educational Services **Company Name:** Morehouse School of Medicine **Date of Birth:** 09/08/1943 **Place of Birth:** Brunswick **State:** GA **Parents:** Marvin Elesberry; Mildred Anita (Whitehead) Nixon **Marital Status:** Married **Spouse Name:** Sandra Gayle Brakefield (7/18/1970) **Children:** William B.; Marvin A **Education:** MD, University of Georgia (1969); BS, University of Georgia (1965) **Certifications:** Diplomate, American Board of Internal Medicine; Diplomate, American Board of Medical Oncology; Licensed Physician, States of South Carolina, New York, Georgia **Career:** Research Professor, Department of Biological Sciences, Clemson University (2008-2009); President, Institute for Cancer Prevention, New York, NY (1999-2004); Folk Professor, Hollings Cancer Center, Medical University of South Carolina, Charleston, SC (1994-1999); Associate Director of Prevention and Control, Hollings Cancer Center, Medical University of South Carolina, Charleston, SC (1994-1999); Vice President of Professional Education, American Cancer Society, Atlanta, GA (1989-1994); Associate Director, Division of Cancer Prevention and Control, National Cancer Institute, National Institutes of Health, Bethesda, MD (1987-1989); From Associate Professor to Professor, Emory University, Atlanta, GA (1975-1987); Assistant Professor, Medical College of Georgia, Augusta, GA (1973-1975); Adjunct Professor of Medicine, Department of Medicine, Morehouse School of Medicine **Career Related:** Chairman, Board of Science Counselors (1999-2008); Member, Science Board, Cancer Treatment Research Foundation **Military Service:** Captain, US Naval Reserve **Creative Works:** Editor-in-Chief, Preventive Medicine (1999-2004); Editor, "Cancer Chemoprevention" (1994); Author, "Cancer Recovery Eating Plan" (1994); Contributor, More Than 100 Articles to Medical Journals **Awards:** Grantee, National Institutes of Health (1975-2004); Recipient, Several Foundation Awards **Membership:** Army and Navy Club; Fripp Island Golf Club **Marquis Who's Who Honors:** Albert Nelson Marquis Lifetime Achievement Award (2017) **Religion:** Protestant **Shipping Address:** 1611 Atlantic Ave, Sullivans Island, SC, 29482

Peter Nolan, PhD

Title: Physics Professor **Industry:** Education/ Educational Services **Company Name:** State University of New York at Farmingdale **Date of Birth:** 03/25/1934 **Place of Birth:** New York **State:** NY **Parents:** Peter John Nolan; Nora (Gleeson) Nolan **Marital Status:** Married **Spouse Name:** Barbara Nolan **Children:** Thomas; James; John; Kevin **Education:** PhD in Physics, Adelphi University (1974); MS in Physics, Adelphi University (1966); BS in Physics, Manhattan College (1956) **Certifications:** Certification in Meteorology, University of California, Los Angeles (1958) **Career:** Professor of Physics, State University of New York at Farmingdale (1971-2015); Associate Professor of Physics, State University of New York at Farmingdale (1968-1971); Assistant Professor of Physics, State University of New York at Farmingdale (1966-1968); Systems Analysis Engineer on Lunar Module, Gruman Aircraft Engineering Corporation (1963-1966); Engineer, Various Corporations (1956-1963) **Career Related:** Chairman, Physics Department, State University of New York at Farmingdale (1970-1977) **Creative Works:** Author, "Physics for Students of Science and Engineering, Fundamentals of the Theory of Relativity" (2013); Author, Fundamentals of the Theory of Modern Physics (2013); Author, "Fundementi Di Fisica" (1996); Author, "Experiments in Physics," Second Edition (1995); Author, "Electromagnetic Theory for Electrical Technology Students" (1995); Author, "Fundamentals of College Physics" (1993); Author, "Experiments in Physics" (1982) **Awards:** Teaching Recognition, State University of New York at Farmingdale (2015); Chancellor's Award for Excellence in Teaching (1995) **Membership:** American Association of Physics Teachers **Marquis Who's Who Honors:** Distinguished Humanitarian (2017) **Shipping Address:** 59 Parnell Drive, Smithtown, NY, 11787

Richard Thomas Nolan

Title: Episcopal Minister, Professor, Writer (Retired) **Industry:** Education/Educational Services **Date of Birth:** 05/30/1937 **Place of Birth:** Waltham **State:** MA **Parents:** Thomas Michael; Elizabeth Louise (Leishman) Nolan **Marital Status:** Married **Spouse Name:** Robert C. Pingpank (6/4/2009) **Education:** Research Fellow in Biomedical Ethics, Harvard University (1991); PhD in Religion and Philosophy, New York University (1973); MA in Religion, Yale University (1967); Postgraduate Studies in Religious Education, Union Theological Seminary (1963); MDiv in Theological Studies, Hartford Seminary Foundation (1963); Diploma in Theological Studies, Berkeley Baptist Divinity School (1960); BA, Trinity College (1960) **Certifications:** Certification in Career Assessment, Center for Career Development and Ministry, Massachusetts (1987); Certification in Death, Dying and Bereavement, Waterbury Hospital Health Center, Connecticut (1977); Certified Priest (1965); Ordained Deacon, Episcopal Church (1963); Certification in Clinical Pastoral Education, Connecticut Valley Hospital (1962); Certification in Classical Piano **Career:** Professor Emeritus, Mattatuck Community College, Waterbury, CT (1992-Present); Pastor Emeritus, St. Paul's Parish, Bantam (1988-Present); Adjunct Lecturer in Philosophy, Palm Beach Chamber of Commerce, Florida (2000-2002); President, Litchfield Institute, Connecticut and Florida (1984-1996); Professor of Philosophy and Social Science, Mattatuck Community College, Waterbury, CT (1978-1992); Part-Time Vicar, St. Paul's Parish, Bantam, CT (1974-1988); Associate Professor, Mattatuck Community College, Waterbury, CT (1974-1978); Assistant Professor of Philosophy and History, Mattatuck Community College, Waterbury, CT (1970-1974); Instructor, Mattatuck Community College, Waterbury, CT (1969-1970); Assistant Academy Dean, Lecturer of Philosophy and Education, Hartford Seminary Foundation (1968-1970); Instructor of Philosophy & Education, Hartford Seminary Foundation, Connecticut (1967-1968) **Career Related:** Society of Regents, Cathedral Church, St. John the Divine (2002-Present); Retired Priest-in-Residence, St. Andrew's Church, Lake Worth, FL (2002-Present); Retired Honorary Canon, Christ Church Cathedral, Hartford, CT (1991-Present); Lecturer in Philosophy and Religious Studies, John Knox Village, Florida (2012); Guest Speaker, Trinity College Chapel (2012); Adjunct Professor, The Union Institute, FL (1999); Adjunct Professor of Philosophy, Florida Atlantic University (1998-1999); Lecturer of Philosophy and Theology, Barry University (1997-1998); Supply Priest, Episcopal Diocese of Southeast Florida (1994-2002); Visiting College, College of Preachers, Washington National Cathedral (1994); Faculty of Consultant Examiners, Charter Oak State College, Connecticut (1990-1993); Consultant, Department of Defense Activity, Non-Traditional Educational Support, Educational Testing Service, Princeton, NJ (1990); Lecturer of Philosophy and Theology, Barry University (1989-1992); Associate for Education, Connecticut (1988-1994); Rabbi Harry Halpern Memorial Lecturer, Southbury, CT (1987); Ethics Committee, Waterbury Hospital Health Center (1984-1988); Research Fellow, Medical Ethics, Yale University (1978); Lecturer in Philosophy and Theology, Florida (1973); Visiting and Adjunct Professor of Philosophy, Theology and Religious Studies, Broward Community College, Florida (1964-1995); Visiting and Adjunct Professor of Philosophy, Theology and Religious Studies, Central Connecticut State University (1964-1995) **Creative Works:** Author, "Living Issues in Ethics," Second Edition (2000); Co-author, "Living Issues in Philosophy," Ninth Edition (1995); TV Host, "Conversations With..." (1987-1989); Co-author, "Living Issues in Philosophy," Eighth Edition (1986); Co-author, "Living Issues in Philosophy," Indonesian Edition (1984); Co-author, "Living Issues in Ethics" (1982); Co-author, "Living Issues in Philosophy," Seventh Edition (1979); Contributing Editor, "Diaconate Now" (1968) **Awards:** Co-recipient, Award for Exceptional Leadership and Community Service, Palm Beach Chapter, ACLU (2008); Co-recipient, Marital Recognition, Cathedral St. John Divine (2005); Honored Author for Books Exceeding 100,000 Copies Award, Wadsworth Publishing Co. (1986); Founder's Day Award, New York University (1973) **Membership:** American Academy of Religion; American Philosophical Association; Authors Guild; Interfaith Alliance; Integrity; 1635 Society, Boston Latin School Alumni Association; Elizabeth S. Taber Society; Tabor Academy Alumni Association; ELMS Society, Trinity College; Yale Legacy Partners; Harwood Society, Cheshire Academy; Society of The Torch of New York University; Founders Society of the Washington National Cathedral; ACLU; GLAAD; Pride Center, Fort Lauderdale, Fl; Equality Florida; Human Rights Campaign; Friends of St. Patrick's Cathedral, Dublin; Phi Delta Kappa **Marquis Who's Who Honors:** Albert Nelson Marquis Lifetime Achievement Award (2017) **Hobbies:** Piano **Political Affiliations:** Independent **Religion:** Episcopalian **Shipping Address:** 451 Heritage Dr, Apt 1014, Pompano Beach, FL, 33060-7777 **Website:** www.richardthomasnolan.com

Stanton Peelle Nolan

Title: Surgeon, Educator **Industry:** Education/Educational Services **Company Name:** University of Virginia Medical Center **Date of Birth:** 05/29/1933 **Place of Birth:** Washington **State:** DC **Parents:** James Parker Nolan; Ellen Dubose (Peelle) Nolan **Marital Status:** Widowed **Spouse Name:** Ruth Marion Nolan (6/16/1955, Deceased 8/22/2011) **Children:** Stanton Peelle Jr.; Tiphanie Ravenel Clarke **Education:** MS, University of Virginia, Charlottesville, VA (1962); Assistant Resident in General Surgery, University of Virginia Medical Center, Charlottesville, VA (1960-1961); Intern, University of Virginia Medical Center, Charlottesville, VA (1959-1960); MD, University of Virginia, Charlottesville, VA (1959); BA, Princeton University, New Jersey (1955) **Certifications:** Diplomate, American Board of Thoracic Surgery; Diplomate, American Board of Surgery **Career:** Professor Emeritus of Surgery, University of Virginia Medical Center (2005-Present); Clinical Professor, Surgery, University of Virginia Medical Center, Charlottesville, VA (1998-2005); Medical Director, Thoracic Cardiovascular Post-Operative Unit, University of Virginia Medical Center, Charlottesville, VA (1989-1993); Claude A. Jessup Professor of Surgery, University of Virginia Medical Center, Charlottesville, VA (1981-1998); Professor of Surgery, University of Virginia Medical Center, Charlottesville, VA (1974-1981); Surgeon-in-Charge, Thoracic Cardiovascular Surgery, University of Virginia Medical Center, Charlottesville, VA (1970-1993); Associate Professor of Surgery, University of Virginia Medical Center, Charlottesville, VA (1970-1974); Assistant Professor of Surgery, University of Virginia Medical Center, Charlottesville, VA (1968-1970); Senior Research Associate Clinic of Surgery, National Heart Institute, National Institutes of Health, Bethesda, MD (1966-1968); Chief Resident of Thoracic Cardiovascular Surgery, University of Virginia Medical Center, Charlottesville, VA (1965-1966); Chief Resident of General Surgery, University of Virginia Medical Center, Charlottesville, VA (1964-1965); Senior Assistant, Resident of General Surgery, University of Virginia Medical Center, Charlottesville, VA (1962-1964) **Career Related:** Keynote Speaker, American Association of Surgical Physician Assistants (2000); Consultant, Southern Petrochemical Industries Corporation, Chennai, India (2000); Visiting Consultant, Voluntary Health Services, Madras, India (1997); Visiting Consultant, Cardiothoracic Surgery, Aga Khan University, Karachi, Pakistan (1995); Visiting Professor, Cardiac Surgery, University of Wisconsin (1992); Visiting Professor, University of Hanover, Germany (1990); American Board of Surgery Consultant to Qualifying Examination Committee (1988-1991); Chairman, American Heart Association (1985-1987); Surgery and Bioengineering Study Section, American Heart Association (1984-1987); Established Investigator, American Heart Association (1969-1974) **Civic:** Emeritus Member, Piedmont Liability Trust (2007-Present); Board Chairman, Westminster Canterbury of the Blue Ridge (2010-2013); Foundation Board, Westminster Canterbury of the Blue Ridge (2007-2013); Chairman Residents' Association, Westminster Canterbury Blue Ridge (2004-2006); Board of Managers, Central Virginia Health Network (2000-2005); Claims Committee, Piedmont Liability Trust (1991-2006) **Military Service:** Senior Surgeon, Commander, United States Public Health Service (1966-1968); Captain, US Army Reserve, Medical Corps (1961-1966) **Creative Works:** Co-Editor, "Comprehensive Thoracic Surgery Curriculum," TSDA (1995); Science Advisory Board, Journal for Heart Valve Disease (1993-2006); Editorial Advisory Board, ECRI Operating Room Risk Management (1992-2006); Member, Annals of Thoracic Surgery (1979-1988); Member, Editorial Board, Journal of Surgical Research (1973-1979) **Awards:** REcipient, Award for Exceptional Service, Commission on Accreditation Allied Health Education Programs (2007); Eponym, Stanton P. Nolan Professorship for Thoracic and Cardiovascular Surgery, University of Virginia Board of Visitors (2006); Recipient, Clyde Watson Distinguished Service Award, Pastoral Care and Education (2006); Grantee, Medtronic Corporation (1975-1981); Grantee, American Heart Association (1970-1973) **Membership:** Standards and Ethics Committee, Society for Thoracic Surgeons (1998-2001); Chair, Association for the Advancement of Medical Instrumentation (1998-2000); Executive Committee, American College of Surgeons (1997-2000); Chair, New Century Society Committee, Thoracic Surgery Foundation for Research and Education (1997-2000); Fellow, Committee of Allied Health Personnel, American College of Surgeons (1996-2004); Executive Committee, Association for the Advancement of Medical Instrumentation (1996-2000); Government Relations Committee, Association for the Advancement of Medical Instrumentation (1996-2000); Nominating Committee, Association for the Advancement of Medical Instrumentation (1996-2000); Education and Resources Committee, Society for Thoracic Surgeons (1996-1997); Science Committee, International Association for Cardiac Biological Implants (1994) **Shipping Address:** 250 Pantops Mountain Rd Apt 5204, Charlottesville, VA, 22911

James Jackson Nora

Title: Physician, Writer, Educator **Industry:** Education/Educational Services **Company Name:** University of Colorado **Date of Birth:** 06/26/1928 **Place of Birth:** Chicago **State:** IL **Parents:** Joseph James Nora; Mae Henrietta (Jackson) Nora **Marital Status:** Married **Spouse Name:** Audrey Faye Hart; Barbara June Fluhrer (9/7/1949, Divorced 1963) **Children:** Wendy Alison; Penelope Welbon; Marianne Leslie; James Jackson, Jr.; Elizabeth **Education:** MPH, University of California, Berkeley (1978); Fellow, Genetics, Montreal Children's Hospital, Montreal, QC, Canada (1964-1965); Fellow, Cardiology, University of Wisconsin Hospitals and Clinics, Madison, WI (1962-1964); Resident, Pediatrics, University of Wisconsin Hospitals and Clinics, Madison, WI (1959-1961); Intern, DMC Detroit Receiving Hospital (1954-1955); MD, Yale University (1954); AB, Harvard University (1950) **Certifications:** Diplomate, American Board of Pediatrics; Diplomate, American Board of Medical Genetics; Diplomate, American Board of Cardiology **Career:** Professor Emeritus, School of Medicine, University of Colorado, Denver, CO (1993-Present); Professor, Genetics, Preventive Medicine and Pediatrics, School of Medicine, University of Colorado, Denver, CO (1971-1993); Associate Professor, Pediatrics, Baylor College of Medicine, Houston, TX (1965-1971) **Career Related:** Consultant, WHO, Geneva, Switzerland (1983-2011); U.S.-U.S.S.R. Health Exchange Program in Cardiovascular Diseases, Moscow and Leningrad, Russia (1975); Task Force, National Heart and Lung Program, Bethesda, MD (1973); Director, Pediatric Cardiology and Cardiovascular Training, University of Colorado School of Medicine (1971-1978); Fellow, American College of Medical Genetics and Genomics; Fellow, American College of Cardiology **Military Service:** Second Lieutenant, U.S. Army Air Corps (1945-1947) **Creative Works:** Author, "Fire and Flood" (2014); Author, "Beyond Sixty-Third Street" (2014); Author, "Searching" (2013); Author, "By a Truthful Storyteller, Second Edition" (2012); Author, "Later" (2011); Author, "Homeless" (2010); Author, "War Crimes" (2009); Author, "By a Truthful Storyteller" (2009); Author, "Rules of the Game" (2008); Author, "Climate" (2008); Author, "The 9/11 Dialogues" (2006); Author, "Half-Open Windows" (2005); Author, "Progress Notes" (2005); Author, "What Every Senior Needs to Know About Health Care" (2004); Author, "Panacea" (2002); Author, "Songs from a Brazen Bull" (2001); Author, "The Hemingway Sabbatical" (1996); Co-Author, "Medical Genetics, Fourth Revised Edition" (1994); Author, "Cardiovascular Diseases: Genetics, Epidemiology and Prevention" (1991); Author, "The Whole Heart Book, Second Revised Edition" (1989); Author, "The Upstart Spring" (1989); Author, "The Psi Delegation" (1989); Author, "Genetics of Man, Second Revised Edition" (1986); Author, "The Whole Heart Book" (1980) **Awards:** Grantee, National Heart, Lung and Blood Institute; Grantee, National Institute of Child Health and Human Development; Grantee, American Heart Association, Inc.; Grantee, National Institutes of Health; Virginia Apgar Memorial Award **Membership:** Poets & Writers, Inc.; Academy of American Poets; Mystery Writers of America; League of American Writers; Authors Guild **Marquis Who's Who Honors:** Albert Nelson Marquis Lifetime Achievement Award (2017) **Why did you become involved in your profession or industry:** Dr. Nora became involved in his profession because it seems like being a physician was a good idea. He enjoyed helping people and saving lives. **Hobbies:** Writing fiction; Poetry; Textbooks **Political Affiliations:** Democrat **Religion:** Presbyterian **Shipping Address:** 1973 S Kenton Court, Aurora, CO, 80014

Eugene Jorgen Nordby

Title: Orthopedic Surgeon **Industry:** Medicine & Health Care **Date of Birth:** 04/30/1918 **Place of Birth:** Abbotsford **State:** WI **Parents:** Herman Preus Nordby (Deceased); Lucille Violet (Korsrud) Nordby (Deceased) **Marital Status:** Married **Spouse Name:** Olive Marie Jensen (6/21/1941, Deceased) **Children:** Jon Jorgen Nordby **Education:** Intern, Madison General Hospital, Madison, WI (1943-1944); MD, University of Wisconsin (1943); BA, Luther College, Decorah, IA (1939) **Certifications:** Diplomate, American Board of Orthopaedic Surgery, Inc. (1950) **Career:** Practice Medicine, Specializing in Orthopedic Surgery, Madison, WI (1948-1981); Assistant in Orthopedic Surgery, Madison General Hospital, Madison, WI (1944-1948) **Career Related:** Chairman Emeritus, Wisconsin Physicians Service Insurance Corporation (2009-Present); Chairman, Executive Committee, WPS Community Bank (2008-Present); Chairman, Wisconsin Physicians Service Insurance Corporation (1979-Present); Associate Clinical Professor, University of Wisconsin School of Medicine and Public Health (1961-Present); Board of Directors, WPS Community Bank (2008-2013); Board of Directors, Wisconsin Physicians Service Insurance Corporation (1958-2013); Chairman, Board of Directors, Wisconsin Physicians Service Insurance Corporation (1929-2009); Board of Attorneys, Professional Responsibility, Wisconsin Supreme Court (1992-1995); President, Bone & Joint Surgery Associates, S.C. (1969-1991); Chief of Staff, Madison General Hospital (1957-1963); Chairman, Trustees, SMS Realty Corporation; Board of Governors, Wisconsin Health Care Liability Insurance Plan; Director, Wisconsin Regional Medical Program, Chicago, Madison and No R.R.; Board of Directors, Norwegian American Genealogical Center and Naeseth Library **Civic:** President Emeritus, Vesterheim: The National Norwegian-American Museum & Heritage Center, Decorah, IA (1997-Present); President, WPS Charitable Foundation (2010); President, Vesterheim: The National Norwegian-American Museum & Heritage Center, Decorah, IA (1968-1997) **Military Service:** Served to Medical Corps Captain, U.S. Army (1944-1946) **Creative Works:** Editorial Board, Clinical Orthopaedics and Related Research (1964-Present); Editorial Board, Spine (1994-2000); Author, "Sections on Chemonuclysis" **Awards:** Distinguished Eagle Scout Award, Boy Scouts of America (2010); First World Congress of Minimally Invasive Spine Surgery and Techniques (2008); Lifetime Achievement Award, IITS (2006); Eponym, Lyman Smith, MD and Eugene J. Nordby, MD Award for Minimally Invasive Spine Surgery, North American Spine Society (1998); Designated, Nordby Building, Wisconsin Physicians Service Insurance Corporation (1998); Notable Norwegian Dane, County Norwegian-American Fest (1995); Den Hoyeste Aere Award (1993); Eponym, Eugene J. Nordby Research Award, IITS (1993); Distinguished Service Award, Rotary International (1987); Decorated, Knight First Class, Royal Norwegian Order of Merit, St. Olav, Norway (1979); Council Award, Wisconsin Medical Vesterheim: The National Norwegian-American Museum & Heritage CenterSociety (1976) **Membership:** Executive Director Emeritus, WPS Community Bank (2006-Present); President Emeritus, Madison Torske Klubben (1998-Present); Chairman, Executive Committee, WPS Community Bank (2009-2013); Board Member, Norwegian American Genealogical Center and Naeseth Library (2006-2008); Executive Director, IITS (1996-2006); Secretary, IITS (1987-1999); President, Madison Torske Klubben (1978-1998); Treasurer, Wisconsin Medical Society (1976-1997); President, The Association of Bone and Joint Surgeons (1973); Board of Directors, American Academy of Orthopaedic Surgeons (1972-1973); First Chairman, Board of Councilors, American Academy of Orthopaedic Surgeons (1972); Chairman, Wisconsin Medical Society (1968-1976); President, Dane County Medical Society (1957); Fellow, Wisdom Hall of Fame, The Clinical Orthopaedic Society; The International Society for the Study of the Lumbar Spine; The American Orthopaedic Association; North American Spine Society; Wisconsin Orthopaedic Society; National Exchange Club; Founder, Madison Torske Klubben; The Nordic Orthopaedic Federation; The American-Scandinavian Foundation; Phi Chi **Marquis Who's Who Honors:** Albert Nelson Marquis Lifetime Achievement Award (2017) **To what do you attribute your success:** He attributes his success to hard work and friendships. **Why did you become involved in your profession or industry:** Dr. Nordby became interested in his profession when a local doctor removed his appendix in 1928. **What do you consider to be the highlight of your career:** A highlight of his career was passing certifying examinations for the American Board of Orthopedic Surgery in 1950. **Where will you be in five years:** In five years, he will be celebrating his 104th birthday. **Hobbies:** Woodworking; Watch and clock repair; Fishing **Political Affiliations:** Republican **Religion:** Lutheran **Shipping Address:** 7707 N. Brookline Drive, Apartment 207, Madison, WI, 53719

Mary Beth Norton, PhD

Title: History Professor, Writer **Industry:** Education/Educational Services **Company Name:** Cornell University **Date of Birth:** 03/25/1943 **Place of Birth:** Ann Arbor **State:** MI **Parents:** Clark Frederic Norton; Mary Elizabeth (Lunny) Norton **Education:** Honorary DLitt, Illinois Wesleyan University (1992); Honorary DHL, DePauw University (1989); Honorary DHL, Marymount Manhattan College (1984); Honorary DHL, Siena College (1983); PhD, Harvard University (1969); MA, Harvard University (1965); BA, University of Michigan (1964) **Career:** Mary Donlon Alger American History Professor, Cornell University (1987-Present); From Assistant Professor to Professor, Cornell University (1971-1987); Assistant History Professor, University of Connecticut, Storrs, CT (1969-1971) **Career Related:** President Elect of American Historical Association (2017-Present); Pitt Professor of American History and Institutions, University of Cambridge (2005-2006) **Civic:** Trustee, Cornell University (1983-1988); Member, National Council on the Humanities, National Endowment for the Humanities (1979-1984); Trustee, Cornell University (1973-1975) **Creative Works:** Author, "1774: Year of Revolution," Alfred A. Knopf, Inc. (2019); Co-Editor, "Major Problems in American Women's History" (2014); Co-Author, "A People and A Nation" (2014); Co-Author, "Separated by Their Sex: Women in Public and Private in The Colonial Atlantic World" (2011); Author, "In the Devil's Snare: The Salem Witchcraft Crisis of 1692" (2002); Author, "Founding Mothers and Fathers: Gendered Power and the Forming of American Society" (1996); Editor, "The AHA Guide to Historical Literature" (1995); Co-Editor, "Major Problems in American Women's History" (1989); Co-Editor, "To Toil the Livelong Day: America's Women at Work, 1790-1980" (1987); Co-Author, "A People and A Nation" (1982); Author, "Liberty's Daughters: The Revolutionary Experience of American Women, 1750-1800" (1980); Co-Editor, "Women of America: A History" (1979); Author, "The British-Americans: The Loyalist Exiles in England, 1774-1789" (1972); Contributor, Articles, Professional Journals **Awards:** Distinguished Fellow, Los Angeles Times (2008-2009); Recipient, Ambassador Book Award, The English-Speaking Union (2003); Mellon Postdoctoral Fellow, The Huntington Library, Art Collections, and Botanical Gardens (2001); Starr Foundation Fellow, Lady Margaret Hall, Oxford University (2000); Honoree, Pulitzer Prize Finalist in History, The Pulitzer Prizes, Columbia University (1997); Fellow, John Simon Guggenheim Memorial Foundation (1993-1994); Society for the Humanities Fellow, Cornell University (1989-1990); Fellow, The Rockefeller Foundation (1986-1987); Recipient, Best Book Prize, Berkshire Conference of Women Historians (1980); Shelby Cullom Davis Center Fellow, Princeton University (1977-1978); Fellow, National Endowment for the Humanities (1974-1975); Recipient, Allan Nevins Prize, Society of American Historians, Columbia University (1970); Fellow, Woodrow Wilson Foundation (1964-1965); Fellow, Society of American Historians, Columbia University **Membership:** Executive Board, Society of American Historians, Columbia University (2003-Present); President, Society of American Historians, Columbia University (2008-2009); Vice President, Society of American Historians, Columbia University (2007); Vice President for Research, American Historical Association (1985-1987); Executive Board, The Organization of American Historians; President, Berkshire Conference of Women Historians (1983-1985); Executive Board, Society of American Historians, Columbia University (1974-1987); The American Philosophical Society; American Academy of Arts & Sciences; President-Elect, American Historical Association **Marquis Who's Who Honors:** Albert Nelson Marquis Lifetime Achievement Award (2017) **Why did you become involved in your profession or industry:** Dr. Norton always wanted to be a teacher, and in graduate school, she got very interested in studying early American history. **Political Affiliations:** Democrat **Religion:** Methodist **Shipping Address:** PO Box 722, West Tisbury, MA, 02575

H. Scott Norville, PhD

Title: Professor of Civil Engineering **Industry:** Education/Educational Services **Company Name:** Texas Tech University **Date of Birth:** 10/21/1948 **Place of Birth:** Toledo **State/Country of Origin:** OH **Parents:** Horace Norville; Norma Norville **Marital Status:** Married **Spouse Name:** Heather J. Norville **Children:** Julie E. Norville; Kristin N. Nolan; Sean A. Norville **Education:** PhD in Structural Reliability, Purdue University (1981); MS in Civil/Structural Engineering, Purdue University (1976); BS in Civil Engineering, The University of Toledo (1974) **Certifications:** Licensed Professional Engineer, State of Texas (1984) **Career:** Professor of Civil and Environmental Engineering, Texas Tech University (1990-Present); Faculty Member, Texas Tech University (1981-Present); Department Chairman, Texas Tech University (2004-2014) **Civic:** Supporter, United Way; Co-chairman, ASTM International Task Group on Glass Strength (ASTM); Vice Chairman, Committee on Building Security, ASTM International (ASTM); Donates to Local Charities **Military Service:** United States Marine Corps, Vietnam **Creative Works:** Contributor, Articles, Journal of Architectural Engineering, American Society of Civil Engineers (ASCE) (2018); Co-author, Computer Design Software, "WGD Mobile," Standards Design Group, Lubbock, Texas (2018); Author, "Engineering Mechanics: Statics," Great River Technologies, Dubuque, Iowa (2014); Co-author, Computer Design Software, "Window Glass Design 2005," Standards Design Group, Lubbock, Texas (2010); Co-author, Computer Design Software, "Blast Resistant Glazing Design - 2003," Standards Design Group, Lubbock, Texas (2003); Co-author, Computer Design Software, "Wind Loads on Structures-2002," Standards Design Group, Lubbock, Texas (2003); Contributor, Articles, Journal of Performance of Constructed Facilities, American Society of Civil Engineers (ASCE) (1999); Contributor, Articles, American Ceramic Society Bulletin, The American Ceramic Society (1985); Co-author, "Glass-Related Injuries in the Oklahoma City Bombing"; Co-author, "The Strength of Weathered Window Glass"; Co-author, "Selection of Architectural Glazing Construction Without Calculations" **Awards:** Award of Merit, ASTM International (ASTM) (2016); Award of Appreciation, ASTM International (ASTM) (2014); President's Excellence in Teaching Award, Texas Tech University (2006) **Membership:** Fellow, American Society of Civil Engineers (2016); Fellow, ASTM International (ASTM) (2014); Fellow, Facade Tectonics Institute (Facade Tectonics) **To what do you attribute your success:** Dr. Norville attributes his success to long hours of hard work, and a lot of luck. **Why did you become involved in your profession or industry:** Dr. Norville became involved in his profession because his father was a civil engineer. After high school, Dr. Norville joined the Marine Corps and fought in the Vietnam War. Upon separation from the Marines, he pursued his civil/structural engineering education. He went into academia because he found university teaching and research exhilarating. **What do you consider to be the highlight of your career:** One of the highlights of his career is seeing many of his findings actually being put into practice in the glazing industry. **Where will you be in five years:** Dr. Norville feels that only fools try to predict the future, but in five years he plans to be getting close to retirement, and hopes to be traveling extensively, and spending time with his grandchildren. **Hobbies:** Bicycling; Competitive Bridge; Piano **Political Affiliations:** Republican **Business Address:** 911 Boston Ave, Lubbock, TX, 79409 **Shipping Address:** 3123 19th St., Lubbock, TX, 79410

Patarica Dian Nunn

Title: Poet **Industry:** Writing and Editing **Date of Birth:** 08/10/1951 **Place of Birth:** Arkadelphia **State:** AR **Parents:** LeRoy Hunter; Louise Hunter **Marital Status:** Married **Spouse Name:** Freddie Lee Nunn (3/16/1979) **Children:** Katarica Lakisha; Roshonda Lanae; Ophelia Lorraine Morgan; Opal Laverne Clark **Education:** Student, Ouachita Baptist University (1971-1972) **Certifications:** Registered, U.S. America **Career:** Retired (2002); Directory Assistance Operator, Southwestern Bell Telephone Company, Hot Springs, AR (1978-2003) **Civic:** Board of Directors, National Library of Poetry; Advisory, Committee, National Library of Poetry **Awards:** Hall of Fame Museum, International Poetry Hall of Fame (1997) **Membership:** Poetry Guild; The Authors Registry **Marquis Who's Who Honors:** Albert Nelson Marquis Lifetime Achievement Award (2017) **To what do you attribute your success:** Ms. Nunn's family and her surroundings helped her to speak out and express herself through poems and songs. **Why did you become involved in your profession or industry:** This is how Ms. Nunn began to speak out and express herself on how she felt, whether it was good or bad in her life. **What do you consider to be the highlight of your career:** A highlight of Ms. Nunn's career would be the Marquis Who's Who and being recognized through them and the others for her work with thesis honors. **Where will you be in five years:** In five years, Ms. Nunn will be enjoying her family and continuing to making her voice heard with the love of her poems. **Hobbies:** Writing poems and songs; Reading; Enjoying spending time with family and love ones **Political Affiliations:** Democrat **Religion:** Methodist **Shipping Address:** 3003 Vancouver Drive, Little Rock, AR, 72204

Geoffrey D. Nusbaum

Title: Psychotherapist **Industry:** Medicine & Health Care **Company Name:** MedPsych Associates **Date of Birth:** 04/01/1946 **Place of Birth:** Berkeley, CA **State/Country of Origin:** CA **Parents:** Wayne Nusbaum; Jeanne Nusbaum **Marital Status:** Married **Spouse Name:** Barbara **Children:** Michael; Doris (Granddaughter) **Education:** PhD, Hartford Seminary Foundation (1978); MA, Hartford Seminary Foundation (1971); AB, Washington University in St. Louis (1967) **Certifications:** Fellow, Diplomate, American Board of Medical Psychotherapy; Certified Therapist, American Association for Marriage and Family Therapy; Licensed Therapist, State of New Jersey **Career:** Private Practice (1972-Present); Consultant, Bancroft School, Haddonfield, NJ (1983-1987); Consultant, New York Fertility Research Foundation, New York City, NY (1978-1983) **Career Related:** International Council of Sex Education and Parenthood; Fellow, The American University **Civic:** Board of Directors, Calcutta House AIDS Hospice **Creative Works:** Author, "The Country Place: An Intentional Therapeutic Community" (1978); Peer Reviewer, American Journal for Obstetrics and Gynecology **Membership:** The North American Menopause Society (1991); Charter Member, Jacobs Institute of Women's Health (1990); International Psychosomatic Institute (1985); American Academy of Psychotherapists (1981); Founding Member, Psychological Issues Section, American Society for Reproductive Medicine; North American Society for Psychosocial Obstetrics & Gynecology; New York Academy of Science; American Board of Medical Psychotherapists; World Federation for Mental Health; Fallopius International Society; Mensa International **Marquis Who's Who Honors:** Albert Nelson Marquis Lifetime Achievement Award (2017) **To what do you attribute your success:** Dr. Nusbaum attributes his success to a strong sense of intuition, compassion and empathy while attempting to help those who are suffering. **Why did you become involved in your profession or industry:** He is a product of his generation. Dr. Martin Luther King was his hero and he wanted to be like him and uplift people from hopelessness and pain. **What do you consider to be the highlight of your career:** The highlight of his career would be the ongoing process of realization that he was able to learn as much from his patients as they hopefully learned from him. **Where will you be in five years:** Dr. Nusbaum hopes to be in good health and still be able to help those around him. He also wants to continue traveling. **Hobbies:** Quantum Cosmology; Dark and absurd humor; Clowning; Psycholinguistics; Science fiction; Dogs; Opera **Religion:** Judaeo-Christian **Shipping Address:** 663 S Rancho Santa Fe Rd., Ste 224, San Marcos, CA, 92078

Jeffrey M. Nuskind

Title: Senior Medical Physicist **Industry:** Sciences **Company Name:** Keesler Air Force Base **Education:** MS in Health Physics, Georgia Institute of Technology (1980) **Certifications:** Licensed Medical Physicist, State of Florida (2014-Present); Board Certified in Therapeutic Radiologic Physics, American College of Radiology (1984-Present); Principles and Practice of Gamma Knife Radiosurgery; Commercial Pilot's License **Career:** Senior Medical Physicist, U.S. Air Force, Keesler Air Force Base **Awards:** Honoree, Pinnacle Professional of the Year, Continental Who's Who (2016) **Membership:** American Cancer Society; American College of Radiology; American Society for Radiation Oncology; Radiosurgery Society **Marquis Who's Who Honors:** Albert Nelson Marquis Lifetime Achievement Award (2017); Distinguished Humanitarian (2017) **To what do you attribute your success:** Mr. Nuskind attributes his success to the fact that he has been a chief physicist for most of his professional career, and that he has the ability to get the job done, give patients the best care possible, and help departments achieve expectations regarding implementing and acquiring new technologies. **Why did you become involved in your profession or industry:** Mr. Nuskind became involved in his profession because, while he was a student at the Georgia Institute of Technology, he took an introduction to medical physics course and fell in love with it. For him, being able to apply his passion for physics to eradicating tumors and helping patients is a win-win situation. **Where will you be in five years:** In five years, Mr. Nuskind plans to continue in his profession and deliver the best treatment to his patients. **Hobbies:** Owning and flying a plane; Shooting pool; Bowling **Shipping Address:** 2668 Beach Blvd Unit 406A, Biloxi, MS, 39531 **Website:** http://www.linkedin.com/pub/jeffrey-nuskind/3b/aa8/526

David George Nutter

Title: Principal **Industry:** Infrastructure **Company Name:** Nutter Associates **Date of Birth:** 11/25/1939 **Place of Birth:** Manchester **State:** CT **Parents:** George Nutter; Catherine Nutter **Marital Status:** Married **Spouse Name:** Ellen Nutter **Children:** Susan Bailey; Amelia Nutter **Education:** Postgraduate Work in Real Estate Law and Construction Management, Johns Hopkins University, Baltimore, MD (1974); Postgraduate Work, Columbia University, New York City, NY (1974); MS in Urban Planning, Columbia University (1967); BA in English and Philosophy, Tufts University, Cum Laude (1961); Coursework in Ancient Greek and Modern Drama, Brandeis University (1960) **Certifications:** Certified, Form-Based Codes Institute (2013); Certified in Real Estate Market Analysis, Urban Land Institute (1986); Certified, American Institute of Certified Planners (1978); Certified Real Estate Appraiser, American Institute of Real Estate Appraisers (1977) **Career:** Principal, Nutter Associates (1987-Present); Project Manager, University of Maryland, Baltimore (2000-2002); Project Manager, Downtown Social Security Officer Center (2000-2002); Director, Salisbury-Wicomico Planning and Zoning Commission, Maryland (2000-2002); Principal Community and Regional Planner, New York State Canal Recreation Way Plan (1997-1999); Executive Director, Rochester Downtown Development Corp., New York, NY (1985-1987); Director, 16th Street Transitway Mall, Downtown Mall Management District, Denver Partnership, Inc. (1983-1985); Urban Renewal Plan Project Director, Lexington Market Station Transit Joint Development Project (1975); Principal Author, Retail District Urban Renewal Plan (1974); Project Director, Planning, Site Selection, and Design, Baltimore Convention Center (1973); Vice President, Charles Center - Inner Harbor Management, Inc. (1972-1976); Director of Planning, Charles Center - Inner Harbor Management, Inc. (1969-1972); City Planner, Baltimore City Planning Commission (1967-1969); Active in City Planning, City Point of View **Civic:** Preservation Society of Asheville-Buncombe County, North Carolina (2016-Present); Member, Preservation, City of Asheville-Buncombe County Historic Resources Commission (2010-2016); Lower Eastern Shore Heritage Commission (2000-2002); Nabb Research center for Delmarva History and Culture, Salisbury University, Maryland (1998-2003); Chairman, Town of Brighton Conservation Board, New York, NY (1992-1995); Arts for Greater Rochester (1986-1990); Board of Directors, Society for the Preservation of Federal Hill, Fells Point, and Montgomery Street, Baltimore, MD (1969-1973) **Membership:** City Member, Greenway Committee, City of Asheville (2016-Present); Thomas Wolfe Memorial Advisory Committee (2015-Present); Board of Directors, Asheville Design Center, Basilica St. Lawrence Preservation Fund (2014-Present); City Council Appointee, Haywood/Page Redevelopment Advisory Team (2016); Founding Member, Gentlemen of Asheville History Book Club (2016); Board Member, Preservation Society of Asheville and Buncombe County (2016); Board of Directors, Eagle Market Streets Development Corporation (2011-2015); Downtown Management Committee, Asheville Downtown Master Plan (2010-2012); American Institute of Certified Planners; American Planning Association; Chesapeake Bay Foundation; Canal Society of New York State; Manchester Historical Society, Connecticut; Sierra Club; City of Asheville Multimodal Transportation Commission **Marquis Who's Who Honors:** Albert Nelson Marquis Lifetime Achievement Award (2017) **Hobbies:** Urban Hiking; Walking; Swimming; History; Traveling **Religion:** Roman Catholic **Shipping Address:** 169 Flint St., Asheville, NC, 28801

Rick D. Nydegger

Title: Lawyer **Industry:** Law and Legal Services **Company Name:** Workman Nydegger **Date of Birth:** 04/24/1949 **Place of Birth:** Salt Lake City **State:** UT **Parents:** A. Don Nydegger; Jean Virginia (Hansen) Nydegger **Marital Status:** Married **Spouse Name:** Denise Winegar (10/22/1970) **Children:** Dan L.; Chad E.; Kurt D.; Brittney Smith; Trent R. **Education:** JD, Brigham Young University Law School, Cum Laude (1977); BEE, Brigham Young University, Cum Laude (1974) **Career:** Founding Shareholder, Workman Nydegger, Salt Lake City, UT (1984-Present); Director, Workman Nydegger, Salt Lake City, UT (1984-Present); Officer, Workman Nydegger, Salt Lake City, UT (1984-Present); Shareholder, Fox, Edwards, & Gardiner (1981-1984); Director, Fox, Edwards, & Gardiner (1981-1984); Associate, Fox, Edwards, & Gardiner (1977-1981) **Career Related:** Adjunct Professor, J. Reuben Clark Law School, Brigham Young University (1998-2002); Adjunct Professor, S.J. Quinney College of Law, University of Utah (1988-1999); Fellow, American Intellectual Property Law Association **Civic:** Chair, Patent Publishing Advisory Committee, United States Patent and Trademark Office (2003-2006); President, National Inventors Hall of Fame (2003-2005); Honorary Member, Charter of Order of the Conference, J. Reuben Clark Law School (2002); President, American Intellectual Property Law Education Foundation (2001-2003); Trustee, American Intellectual Property Law Education Foundation (2001-2003); Board of Directors, Invent Now Inc. (Formerly NIHF Foundation) (1998-2011); Chair, Lawyers Centennial Committee, Utah State Centennial Commission (1996-1997); Eagle Scout, Boy Scouts of America (1953) **Creative Works:** Contributor, Articles, Professional Journals; Author, "U.S. and International Intellectual Property Professional Programs" **Awards:** Honoree, Chambers USA Band I Ranking (2008-Present); Honoree, One of the Best Lawyers in America (1990-Present); Honoree, Alumnus of the Year, J. Reuber Clark Law School, Brigham Young University (2005); Honoree, Honorary Alumnus of the Year, S.J. Quinney College of Law, University of Utah (2004) **Membership:** Trustee, U.S. Supreme Court Historical Society (2005-Present); Chairman, Nominations Committee, American Intellectual Property Law Association (2005); President, American Intellectual Property Law Association (2003-2004); President-elect, American Intellectual Property Law Association (2002-2003); First Vice President, American Intellectual Property Law Association (2001-2002); Chairman, National Council Intellectual Property Law Association (2000-2001); Second Vice President, Planning Committee, American Intellectual Property Law Association (2000-2001); Chairman, Mid-winter Institute, American Intellectual Property Law Association (2000); Vice Chairman, Ad Hoc Committee, PCT Practice, American Intellectual Property Law Association (1994-1998); Board of Directors, American Intellectual Property Law Association (1993-1996); Board of Directors, U.S. Supreme Court Historical Society (1993-1994); Chairman, Electronic Computer Law Committee, American Intellectual Property Law Association (1990-1993); Chairman, Patent, Trademark, Copyright Section, Utah State Bar (1985-1987); Founding Member, American Intellectual Property Law Association; Editorial Board, Quarterly Journal, American Intellectual Property Law Association; American Bar Association; Federal Circuit Bar Association; Honorary Member, J. Reuben Clark Law School Chapter, Order of the Coif; Eta Kappa Nu **Bar Admissions:** Federal Circuit, U.S. Court of Appeals (1994); U.S. Supreme Court (1990); Fifth Circuit, U.S. Court of Appeals (1980); Tenth Circuit, U.S. Court of Appeals (1980); State of Utah (1977); U.S. District Court, Central District, State of Utah (1977); U.S. Patent and Trademark Office (1977) **Marquis Who's Who Honors:** Albert Nelson Marquis Lifetime Achievement Award (2017) **Hobbies:** Fishing; Tennis; Reading **Shipping Address:** 60 E South Temple, Suite 1000, Workman Nydegger, Salt Lake City, UT, 84111

Molly Oberbillig

Title: Utilities Executive **Industry:** Utilities **Date of Birth:** 02/11/1934 **Country of Origin:** Gibraltar **Parents:** William Ferguson Castleman; Mary Castleman (Davis) Cavenaugh **Marital Status:** Married **Spouse Name:** Gary Joel Oberbillig (11/8/1961) **Children:** Andrew Ferguson; Julie Anne **Education:** Coursework, San Jose State University (1963-1964); Coursework, University of Washington, Seattle, WA (1954-1955); Coursework, Reed College, Portland, OR (1951-1953) **Career:** Conservation Manager, Mason County Public Utility District No. 1 (1975-1990) **Civic:** Charter Member, Wellstone Action Leadership Council (2012-Present); Board Treasurer, All Souls Unitarian Universalist Church (2010-Present); Founding Sponsor, Martin Luther King, Jr. National Memorial, Washington, DC (2005-Present); Charter Member, National Women's History Museum (2003-Present); Sustainer, Rural Advancement Fund International (1995-Present); Founder and Chairman, Youth Diversity Award, Thurston Council Cultural Diversity and Human Rights (1995-Present); Leadership Council, Southern Poverty Law Center (1992-Present); Vice Chairman, Democratic Central Committee, Shelton, WA (1991-1992); Founding Trustee, Anne Williston Scholarship, Seattle, WA (1988-2007); Secretary, Mason Council Fire District, Lilliwaup, WA (1979-1981); Founding Member, Progressive Patriots Club; Nordiska Folkdance Exhibition Team (1953-1961); Charter Member, National Museum of African-American History and Culture; Charter Member, Food and Water Watch Leader's Circle **Creative Works:** Contributor, Articles, Professional Journals **Awards:** Woman of the Year, National Association of Professional Women (2012-2013) **Membership:** American Association of University Women; National Association of Professional Women; Thurston Diversity Council **Marquis Who's Who Honors:** Distinguished Humanitarian (2017) **Hobbies:** Gardening **Shipping Address:** 1907 Parkwood Drive SE, Olympia, WA, 98501

Robert L. O'Block

Title: Executive Director **Industry:** Education/Educational Services **Company Name:** American College of Forensic Examiners Institute **Date of Birth:** 07/15/1951 **Place of Birth:** Pittsburg **State:** KS **Education:** Honorary STD, Hellenic College Holy Cross (2003); Doctor of Ministry, Trinity College (2003); MDiv, Trinity College (2001); Education Specialist Degree, Pittsburg State University, Kansas (2001); Doctor of Psychology, Christopher Newport University (2000); MA in Psychology, Christopher Newport University (1998); PhD, Kansas State University (1976); MS in Sociology, Pittsburg State University, Kansas (1973); BS in Sociology, Pittsburg State University, Kansas (1972) **Certifications:** Ordained Priest, Southern Episcopal Church (2002); Ordained Deacon, Southern Episcopal Church (1999) **Career:** Chief Executive Officer, President, Center for National Threat Assessment (2008-Present); Executive Director, American College of Forensic Examiners Institute, Springfield, MO (1994-Present); Professor and Chair, Department of Administration Justice, College of the Ozarks, Point Lookout, MO (1989-1993); Associate Professor, Department of Government and Justice Studies, Appalachian State University, Boone, NC (1979-1989); Assistant Professor, Department of Administrative Justice, Wichita State University (1977-1979); Director, Night School, Marymount Manhattan College (1976); Administrative Assistant to Dean, Student Affairs, Community Service, Labette Community College (1976); Supervisor, Children's Court Center (1974); Probation Officer, Crawford County Juvenile Court (1973-1974); Patrolman, Frontenac Police Department (1971-1973) **Career Related:** Founder, American Board of Forensic Medicine; Founder, American College of Forensic Examiners Institute; Founder, American Board of Forensic Psychology, Inc.; Lecturer in Field; Consultant in Field **Civic:** Advisory Board, Larned State Hospital **Creative Works:** Author, "The 7 Steps to the Cure of Souls" (2005); Author, "Criminal Justice Research Sources," 4th Edition (1992); Co-Author, "Security and Crime Prevention," 2nd Edition (1990); Author, "Criminal Justice Research Sources" (1983); Founder, Publisher, The Forensic Examiner; Founder, Publisher, Annals of Psychotherapy & Integrative Health; Contributor, Articles, Professional Journals **Awards:** Knight of Chevalier, Sovereign Military Order of the Temple of Jerusalem (2001); Grantee, Governor's Commission on Criminal Administration (1976-1977) **Membership:** Co-Founder, Chief Executive Officer, American Association of Integrative Medicine; Founder, American College of Forensic Examiners Institute; Founder, Chairman, Chief Executive Officer, American Psychotherapy Association **Shipping Address:** 2750 E Sunshine St., Springfied, MO, 65804

Robert Paul O'Block

Title: Management Consultant **Industry:** Business Management/Business Services **Company Name:** Freeport Center **Date of Birth:** 03/09/1943 **Place of Birth:** Pittsburgh **State:** PA **Parents:** Paul Joseph O'Block; Mary Elizabeth (Galicic) O'Block **Marital Status:** Married **Spouse Name:** Megan Marie Silletti **Education:** MBA, Harvard University (1967); BS in Mechanical Engineering, Purdue University (1965) **Career:** Director Emeritus, McKinsey & Company, Boston, MA (1998-Present); General Partner, Freeport Center Associates, Clearfield, UT (1971-Present); Managing Partner, Freeport Center Associates, Clearfield, UT (1971-Present); Director, McKinsey & Company, Boston, MA (1984-1998); Principal, McKinsey & Company, Boston, MA (1979-1984); Principal, McKinsey & Company, New York, NY (1979-1984); Associate in Real Estate Management and Finances, McKinsey & Company, New York, NY (1969-1978); Research and Teaching Fellow in Finance, Harvard University (1967-1970); Research and Teaching Fellow in Economics, Harvard University (1967-1970); Research and Teaching Fellow in Urban Management, Harvard University (1967-1970) **Career Related:** Chairman, Management Committee, Snowbird Lodge, Utah (1974-1986); Consultant of Massachusetts Housing Financial Agencies (1968-1976); Consultant of New Jersey Housing Financial Agencies (1968-1976); Consultant, Rockefeller Association (1968-1976); Consultant of U.S. Department of Housing and Urban Development (1968-1976); Visiting Lecturer, Urban Economics, Yale Law School; Visiting Lecturer, Urban Economics, Princeton University **Civic:** Vice Chairman, Board of Trustees, Beth Israel Deaconess Medical Center (2012-Present); Co-Chair, Board of Trustees, Boston Symphony Orchestra (2009-2011); Vice Chairman, Board of Trustees, Boston Symphony Orchestra (2002-2009); Trustee, Boston Symphony Orchestra (2000-2014); Trustee, Park School (1997-2003); Chairman, Boston Symphony Orchestra (1995-2000); Vice Chairman, Board of Overseers, Boston Symphony Orchestra (1992-1995); Trustee, USSA (1989-2001); Board of Directors, International Tennis Hall of Fame (1989-1995); Board of Overseers, Boston Symphony Orchestra (1988-2000); Advisory Board, International Tennis Hall of Fame (1986-1989); National Advisory Board, Snowbird Arts Institute (1977-1983); Budget Committee, The New York Public Library (1977-1979); Board of Directors, Bankrate, LLC **Membership:** Devon Yacht Club; Maidstone Club; National Golf Links of America; The Country Club **Marquis Who's Who Honors:** Albert Nelson Marquis Lifetime Achievement Award (2017) **Shipping Address:** 60 Cramond Rd., Chestnut Hill, MA, 02467

Leonard G. Obloy

Title: Reverend **Industry:** Religious **Date of Birth:** 09/01/1951 **Place of Birth:** Cleveland **State:** OH **Parents:** Henry Joseph Obloy; Ruth Elsie (Walter) Obloy **Marital Status:** Single **Education:** Postgraduate Studies, Pontifical Biblical Institute (1984); SSL, Pontifical Biblical Institute (1983); MDiv, St. Mary's Graduate School of Theology (1977); AB, Borromeo College of Ohio (1973) **Certifications:** Ordained Priest, Roman Catholic Church (1977) **Career:** Academic Dean, St. Cyril and Methodius Seminary (2012-2018); Faculty, St. Cyril and Methodius Seminary (2010-2018); Pastor, Parochial Vicar Cathedral of St. John the Evangelist (2010); Pastor, St. William Parish (2002-2009); Associate Pastor, St. Francis of Assisi Parish (1999-2002); Director of Auxiliary Services, Mount St. Mary's Seminary (1997-1999); Assistant Professor of Sacred Scripture and Computer Science, Mount St. Mary's Seminary (1988-1999); Vice-Rector, Mount St. Mary's Seminary (1988-1997); Associate Pastor, St. Rose of Lima Parish, Cleveland, OH (1984-1988); Associate Pastor, St. Helen Parish (1977-1980) **Career Related:** Dean Emeritus, Catholic Distance University (2003-Present); Adjunct Professor, St. Mary's Graduate School of Theology (1999-2009); Lecturer in Field; Guest Lecturer, Our Lady of Holy Cross College (1998-2003); Dean, Graduate Division (1995-2003); Adjunct Professor, St. Mary's Graduate School of Theology (1984-1988) **Creative Works:** Author and Lecturer, "And God Said; Witness, a Journey through the Passion Narratives"; Author and Lecturer, "The Psalms; The Book of Job"; Author and Lecturer, "The Book of Revelation"; Author, Various Pamphlets, Audio Cassettes, Catholic Distance University, Television Series, "Introduction to the Bible, The Passion Narrative for WLEA," New Orleans, LA **Awards:** Chaplain of the Year, Knights of Columbus; Knight of the Year, Knights of Columbus **Membership:** IEEE Computer Society; Alumni Association, Pontifical Biblical Institute; Vatican Radio; Sacred Congregation for Doctrine of Faith; National Catholic Education Association; Corporation for Public Broadcasting; Catholic Biblical Federation; New York Academy of Sciences; Association of Computing Machinery; GTO Association of America **Hobbies:** Audio recording: Automotive drag racing; Computers **Political Affiliations:** Independent **Religion:** Roman Catholic **Shipping Address:** 3535 Commerce Road, St. Cyril & Methodius Seminary, Orchard Lake, MI, 48324

Mary Ellen Christina O'Brien

Title: Artist, Educator **Industry:** Fine Art **Date of Birth:** 11/15/1928 **Place of Birth:** Caribou **State:** ME **Parents:** Richard Stephen; Caroline Elizabeth (McGuire) Sullivan **Marital Status:** Married **Spouse Name:** John Michael O'Brien (5/15/1965) **Children:** Maureen-Caroline; Kathleen **Education:** Coursework, Penland School of Crafts (1994); Coursework, Paul Puzinas Art Studio (1959); Coursework, Crafts Students League (1958); Certificate in Arts, Cambridge School of Design **Career:** Art Teacher, Academy of Holy Names, Tampa, FL (1986-1994); Art Specialist, Tampa, FL (1979-1981); Art Teacher, Most Holy Redeemer School, Tampa, FL (1971-1978); Arts and Crafts Director, Special Services, U.S. Army, Europe (1961-1964); Arts and Crafts Director, Special Services, U.S. Army, Fort Totten, NY (1957-1961); Arts and Crafts Director, Special Services, U.S. Army, Fort Devens, MA (1956-1957); Freelance Commercial Artist, Jordon March, Boston, MA (1955-1956); Art Teacher, Red Feather Agencies, Boston, MA (1955-1956); Arts and Crafts Director, Cambridge Council, Girl Scouts of America (1955); Freelance Designer, Massachusetts Institute of Technology, Cambridge, MA (1954-1955); Freelance Designer, Harvard University, Cambridge, MA (1954-1955) **Career Related:** Private Teacher (1981-1986); Creative Art Director, Political Campaign, Democratic Party, Tampa, FL **Civic:** Docent, Museum of Art (1994-Present); Delegate to Japan to Observe Art in Schools, People to People Delegation (1995); Docent, Museum of Art (1974-1985); Volunteer, Performing Arts Center **Creative Works:** Albuquerque Balloon Museum (2008-2009); Exhibitor, Juried Show, Sandy Springs Museum; Exhibitor, Juried Show, Kohler Gallery, Tampa, FL (2008); Exhibitor, Juried Show, Carollwood Cultural Center Gallery (2008); Exhibitor, Eustis Museum, FL (2008); Exhibitor, Kotler Art Gallery, Tampa, FL (2008); Exhibitor, Lacy Gallery, Tampa, FL (2008); Exhibitor, Deltona Art Center, FL (2008); Exhibitor, Brandon Art Center, FL (2007-2008); Exhibitor, St. Joseph's Art Gallery, FL (1978); Exhibitor, Rental Gallery of Tampa Bay Art Center, FL (1973); Cover Design Artist, The Patron Saints (1959); Exhibitor, Busch-Reisinger Museum, Cambridge, MA (1955); Exhibitor, One-Woman Show, Methodist Administration Building; Exhibitor, One-Woman Show, Realistic Artist Gallery; Exhibitor, One-Woman Show, Federal Bank Building; Exhibitor, Portland Art Museum; Exhibitor, Gallery Puzinas Studio, Art League of Long Island, Great Neck, NY; Exhibitor, Living Design Studio, Manchester, NH; Exhibitor, Bayside Branch, New York Public Library Systems; Exhibitor, First Presbyterian Church Temple Terrace; Stewart Art Show; Exhibitor, Gasparilla Outdoor Art Show; Exhibitor, Lowry Park Outdoor Art Show; Exhibitor, Veterans Administration Hospital, FL; Exhibitor, Museum of Art, FL; Exhibitor, Performing Art Center, FL; Exhibitor, Florida Craftsmen Gallery, St. Petersburg, FL; Exhibitor, Juried Show, Ratner Museum, Bethesda, MD **Awards:** One Woman Show Award, County Library (2015) **Membership:** President, National League of American Pen Women (1984-1985); Chair, National Art Competition, National League of American Pen Women; Sick Painters; Alpha Delta Kappa **Marquis Who's Who Honors:** Albert Nelson Marquis Lifetime Achievement Award (2017) **To what do you attribute your success:** Ms. O'Brien attributes her success to her mentors. This includes her high school art teacher, Miss Robinson, who got her going in the whole field. She defines success as being "happy with what you are doing yourself, and bringing people upward." That is what she strives to do. **Why did you become involved in your profession or industry:** Ms. O'Brien wasn't one of those kids that drew all the time, but when they got a new art teacher in her high school, that teacher was the one that completely changed her. She is the one that really made her want to go into the field of art. **What do you consider to be the highlight of your career:** Ms. O'Brien was very proud of working for the military and bringing the arts to the guys, something uplifting other than military type things. **Where will you be in five years:** In five years, Ms. O'Brien wants to keep going and show some more art, and maybe do a lecture series. **Hobbies:** Sewing; Reading; Arts **Religion:** Roman Catholic **Shipping Address:** 10801 N Edison Avenue, Tampa, FL, 33612

Charles Edward O'Connor

Title: State Government Official, Lawyer **Industry:** Government Administration/Government Relations/Government Services **Date of Birth:** 02/21/1960 **Place of Birth:** Philadelphia **State:** PA **Parents:** Charles Edward O'Connor; Ruth Pauline Cardamone-O'Connor **Education:** JD, Widener University, Wilmington, DE (1988); BA, LaSalle College, Philadelphia, PA (1982) **Career:** 45th Ward Republican Committeeman; Head Legislator, Reapportion Commission; Executive Director, Legislative Reapportionment Commission, (2011-2012); Executive Director, Legislative Reapportionment Commission, Harrisburg, PA (2001-2002); Deputy Prothonotary for Eastern District of Pennsylvania, Superior Court of Pennsylvania, Philadelphia, PA (1997-2014); Chief Law Clerk to Hon. John T.J Kelly, Jr., Superior Court of Pennsylvania, Philadelphia, PA (1992-1997); Law Clerk to Hon. John T.J Kelly, Jr., Superior Court of Pennsylvania, Philadelphia, PA (1989-1992); Bail Interview Supervisor, Common Pleas Court of Philadelphia (1985-1989); Letter Carrier, U.S. Postal Service, Abington, PA (1983-1985); Parcel Post Machine Clerk, U.S. Postal Service, Philadelphia, PA (1982-1983); Election Clerk, County Commissioners Office, Philadelphia, PA (1978-1981) **Career Related:** Counsel Summerdale Boys Club, Philadelphia, PA (1993-1997); Member, 24th District Police Advisory Council (1989-1992); Member, 2nd District Police Advisory Council, Philadelphia, PA (1998-2004) **Civic:** President, Friends of Summerdale Civic Association, Philadelphia, PA (1999-2004); Member, 25th Ward Republican Executive Committee, Philadelphia, PA (1988-1989); Member, 53rd Ward Republican Executive Committee, Philadelphia, PA (1978-1982); Member, Calvin Coolidge Foundation; Volunteer, Philadelphia, PA; President, Bernard Samuel Society **Creative Works:** Co-author, "Criminal Appellate Practice in the Pa Superior Court" (2010); Co-author, "Winning Your Case on Appeal" (2007); Co-author, "Practical Tips for Navigating Appellate Courts" (2006) **Awards:** First Degree, Ancient Order of Hiberians (2000) **Membership:** Bernard Samuel Society; United Republican Society; Master, Emmet Dalton Society; Wynnewood Institute; General George Meade Society; Holmesburg Fish & Rifle Club; National Association Appellate Court Clerks; Brehon Law Society; 69th Pennsylvania Irish Volunteers; Order Sons of Italy in America; Grand Army of The Republic Museum; Custodes Pacis Lodge; Ancient Order of Hiberians **Hobbies:** Pennsylvania history; Neighborhood clean-up/graffiti removal; Old car repair and restoration; Urban affairs **Religion:** Roman Catholic **Shipping Address:** 3628 E Thompson St., Philadelphia, PA, 19134

Michael E. O'Connor

Title: Lawyer **Industry:** Law and Legal Services **Company Name:** Costello, Cooney & Fearon, PLLC **Date of Birth:** 09/15/1948 **Place of Birth:** Syracuse **State:** NY **Parents:** Leo T. O'Connor; Geraldine (Hager) O'Connor **Marital Status:** Married **Spouse Name:** Margaret A. Soplop (6/3/1972) **Children:** Michael E., Jr.; Kelly R.; Bradley J. **Education:** JD, Syracuse University (1974); BA, University at Buffalo (1970) **Career:** Counsel, Costello, Cooney & Fearon, PLLC (2016-Present); Partner, DeLaney & O'Connor LLP (1994-Present); Partner, Hancock Estabrook, LLP (1990-1994); Partner, Coulter, Fraser, Bolton, Bird & Ventre (1981-1990) **Career Related:** Adjunct Professor, Cornell University (2016-Present); Chair, Trusts and Estates Section, New York State Bar Association (2005); Chair, Elder Law Section, New York State Bar Association (1999-2000); State Chair, The American College of Trust and Estate Counsel (1997-2002); Board of Directors, Onondaga County Bar Association (1984-1986); House of Delegates, New York State Bar Association (1982-1985); Chairman, Estate and Surrogates Court Committee, Onondaga County Bar Association (1981-1987); President, Estate Planning Council of Central New York, National Association of Estate Planners & Councils, NAEPC (1981); Onondaga Title Association (1979); Adjunct Professor of Law, College of Law, Syracuse University **Civic:** President, Aurora of Central New York Inc. (2007-2008); President, Most Holy Rosary Home School Association (1985-1986); President, Citizens Foundation, Inc. (1983-1985); Chairman of the Board, Community Foundation of Central New York; Board of Directors, Symphony Syracuse **Membership:** President, Syracuse Lions Club (1984-1985); The Century Club, Syracuse, NY **Bar Admissions:** U.S. Supreme Court (1983); State of New York (1975) **Marquis Who's Who Honors:** Albert Nelson Marquis Lifetime Achievement Award (2017) **Why did you become involved in your profession or industry:** As long as Mr. O'Connor could remember, this is always something that he wanted to do. He did plenty of reading about what a lawyer did on a typical day, including all kinds of different lawyers, so he thought it was something he could get into. **Where will you be in five years:** Mr. O'Connor plans on still practicing law. **Political Affiliations:** Republican **Religion:** Roman Catholic **Shipping Address:** 500 Plum Street, Suite 300, Costello, Cooney & Fearon PLLC, Syracuse, NY, 13204 **Website:** http://www.ccf-law.com

Jean Phifer Oden

Title: Special Education Educator **Industry:** Education/Educational Services **Date of Birth:** 05/02/1936 **Place of Birth:** Chicago **State:** IL **Parents:** Dillard James Phifer; Lena (Conner) Phifer **Marital Status:** Married **Spouse Name:** James Edward Oden (4/26/1959) **Children:** Eric James **Education:** EdD, National Louis University (1995); Postgraduate Coursework, National College of Education, National Louis University, Evanston, IL (1986); MEd in Learning Disabilities, Chicago State University (1973); BE, Chicago Teachers College (1958) **Certifications:** Certified Research Professor in Education/Social Policy, International Biographical Centre, Cambridge, England (2015); Certified in Advance Studies, National College of Education, National Louis University, Evanston, IL (1987) **Career:** Learning Disability Specialist, Harold Washington Elementary School, Chicago, IL (1994-1998); Learning Disability Specialist, Englewood High School, Chicago, IL (1987-1994); Co-Chair, Englewood High School, Chicago, IL (1987-1994); Learning Disability Specialist, Phillips Academy High School, Chicago, IL (1982-1987); Co-Chair, Phillips Academy High School, Chicago, IL (1982-1987); Special Education Consultant, Chicago Board of Education (1981); Independent Education Program Facilitator, City of Chicago, Illinois (1981); Learning Disabilities Teacher, Elementary Schools, City of Chicago (1973-1981); Elementary School Teacher, City of Chicago, Illinois (1958-1973) **Career Related:** Member, Committee to Develop State Test for Learning Disabilities Teachers, Springfield, IL (1986-Present); Secretary, Chicago Southside Chapter, National Association for the Advancement of Colored People (2003); Worldwide Conference, People to People International (2002); Member, Delegate to South Africa (2001); Chair, Education Committee, Chicago Southside Chapter, National Association for the Advancement of Colored People (2000); African Affairs Advisory Council, Commission on Human Relations, City of Chicago (1999-2012); Member, Delegate to Oxford University (1997); Member, Delegate to China (1994); Member, Delegate to Vietnam (1993); Speaker, Who's Who Congress, Cambridge, England (1992); State Advisor, United States Congressional Advisory Board (1985); Member, Illinois Guidelines for Learning Disabilities Development Committee (1981-1982); Speaker, Education Seminar, 19th Congress on Arts and Communication, Cambridge, England **Civic:** Secretary, Chicago Southside Branch, National Urban League (1999-Present); State Chair, African American Economic Development Task Force, Illinois Legislative Black Caucus, National Association for the Advancement of Colored People (1992-Present); Member, Coalition of Black Trade Unionists (1991-Present); Consultant Pool, National Juvenile Justice Resource Center (1991-Present); Charter Board Member, America's National Museum of African American History and Culture (2014); Board of Directors, African Scientific Research Museum Institute (2003); Charter Member, Center for the Study of the Presidency & Congress (1998); Charter Member, Republican Inner Circle (1991); Charter Member, Republican Presidential Advisory Task Force (1989); Member, Parent-Community Council on Educational Reform, Mayoral Summit (1988); Congressional Member, Gay & Lesbian Victory Fund (1985); Secretary, New York City Conference, National Urban League (1980-2005); Southern Christian Leadership Congress, City of Chicago (1979-1981); Carter Temple Christian Methodist Episcopal Church **Awards:** Named, Research Professor, International Biographical Centre, Cambridge, England (2015); Grantee, Chicago Board of Education (1986); Citizenship Award, Mayor of Chicago (1984); Certificate of Merit, Chicago Southside Branch, National Association for the Advancement of Colored People (1978) **Membership:** Liaison, State Board of Illinois, Division for Citizens with Learning Disabilities, Council for Exceptional Children (1980); Association for Supervision and Curriculum Development; Learning Disabilities Association of America; League of Women Voters; Minority Mainstream; Founder, United Neighborhoods Intertwined for Total Equality; Executive Director, United Neighborhoods Intertwined for Total Equality; Researcher, United Neighborhoods Intertwined for Total Equality; Association for Citizens with Learning Disabilities; Founder, National Association of Special Education Teachers; First President, National Association of Special Education Teachers; Founder, Black Parents United for Education and Related Services; Kappa Delta Pi, International Honor Society in Education; Policy Research/Think Tank, Heartland Institute; Lehigh Country Club, Florida; Thousand Trails Club, Ottawa, IL **Marquis Who's Who Honors:** Albert Nelson Marquis Lifetime Achievement Award (2017) **Hobbies:** Hiking; Racquetball; Travel; Camping **Religion:** Methodist Episcopal **Shipping Address:** 10848 S Parnell Ave, Chicago, IL, 60628

Waldo Talmage Oden Jr.

Title: Lawyer **Industry:** Law and Legal Services **Date of Birth:** 05/17/1929 **Place of Birth:** Altus **State:** OK **Marital Status:** Married **Spouse Name:** Rebecca Jane Hazlitt (3/25/1951) **Children:** Waldo Talmage Oden III; Timothy Patrick Oden; Amy G.; Jonathon Andrew **Education:** Honorary Doctorate of Juris Prudence, Oklahoma City University (1999); Coursework, Oklahoma City University (1995); Paul Harris Fellowship (1993); JD, University of Oklahoma (1970); Doctorate in Law, University of Oklahoma (1952); BA in Political Economics, University of Oklahoma (1950) **Career:** Farmers and Merchants Bank (1960-Present); Lawyer, Sole Practice, Altus (1952-Present); Professor, Master's Degree Program, Webster University, Altus Air Force Base (1975-2002); Faculty Coordinator, Master's Degree Program, Webster University, Altus Air Force Base (1975-2002); Oklahoma Judicial Nominating Commission (1967-1971); County Director of Civil Defense, Jackson County Detention Center (1959-1998); Instructor of Criminology, Altus Air Force Base, Altus (1958); Instructor of Business Law, Western Oklahoma State College (1956-1959); Oden & Oden (1954-1981); Assistant Attorney, Jackson County (1953-1954); Member Robinson & Oden (1952-1953); Robinson, Oden & Oden; Lecturer Agricultural Law; United States Court of Appeals for the Tenth Circuit **Career Related:** Board Member, Area Agency on Aging; Chair, Adult Council RSVP **Civic:** Boy Scouts of America; Board Member, Salvation Army; United Methodist Church; Halfway Houses; Board Member, Community Action Elder Services; Headstart; Meals on Wheels America; American Red Cross; Habitat for Humanity International; Jackson County Free Health Clinic **Awards:** Named, ProBono Attorney of the Year Award, Oklahoma Bar Association (1999, 1998); Recipient, Silver Beaver Award, Last Frontier Council **Membership:** President, Western Trails Historical Society (2003-Present); Chairman, Oklahoma Bar Association Task Force on Farm Crisis (1985-Present); Chairman, Boy Scouts of America, Kicking Bird District (1982-2003); Board of Directors, General Board of Global Ministries, United Methodist Church (1984-1996); Lay Leader, Oklahoma Conference of United Methodist Church (1982-1996); Chair, General Practice Section Council (1982-1983); United Methodist General Board of Higher Education and Ministry (1980-1984); Chairman, Agricultural Law Committee, General Practice Section, ABA (1976-1984); Oklahoma Humanities (1976-1980); Chairman, Boy Scouts of America, Kicking Bird District (1969-1978); Secretary, Executive Committee United Methodist Series of Protestant Hour (1968-1972); Trustee, Altus Library Board (1965-1982); President, Rotary Club (Now Rotary International), Altus (1959-1960); Staff Member, Oklahoma Law Review (1950-1952); Delegate, United Methodist Church Jurisdictional and General Conferences; Chairman, General Practice Section, Oklahoma Bar Association; Jackson County Bar Association; Phi Delta Phi; Masons; President, Altus Library Board; Chair, Museum of the Western Prairie; Board, Southwest Enterprises **Marquis Who's Who Honors:** Albert Nelson Marquis Lifetime Achievement Award (2017) **Why did you become involved in your profession or industry:** Dr. Oden became involved in his profession because he has family members in the clergy and medical industries, but his natural disposition was more attuned to law. He wanted to provide a service to his community, as his father had. **Hobbies:** Writing; Performing comedy; Musical entertainment; Jazz pianist; Piano vocalist **Shipping Address:** 913 E Elm St., Altus, OK, 73521

William James O'Donnell

Title: Engineering Executive **Industry:** Engineering **Company Name:** O'Donnell Consulting Engineers **Date of Birth:** 06/19/1935 **Place of Birth:** Pittsburgh **State:** PA **Parents:** William James O'Donnell; Elizabeth (Rau) O'Donnell **Marital Status:** Married **Spouse Name:** Joanne Mary Kusen (1/31/1959) **Children:** Suzanne; Janice; William John; Thomas Paul; Kerry; Amy Meghan **Education:** PhD, University of Pittsburgh (1962); MS in Mechanical Engineering, University of Pittsburgh (1959); BS in Mechanical Engineering, Carnegie Institute of Technology, Carnegie Mellon University (1957) **Career:** President, O'Donnell Consulting Engineers, Inc. (1970-Present); Chairman of the Board, O'Donnell Consulting Engineers, Inc. (1970-Present); Advisory Engineer, Bettis Atomic Power Laboratory, Naval Nuclear Laboratory (1966-1970); Staff, Bettis Atomic Power Laboratory, Naval Nuclear Laboratory (1961-1970); Associate Engineer, Westinghouse Research Laboratory, Westinghouse Electric Corporation (1958); Junior Engineer, Westinghouse Research Laboratory, Westinghouse Electric Corporation (1957-1958) **Civic:** Civil Engineer, US Army (1963-1964) **Creative Works:** Contributor, Articles on Engineering and Mechanics to Professional Journals; Holder, Patents on Processes; Holder, Patents on Devices; Author, "Handbook of Lessons Learned in Engineering, Design, Manufacturing, and Construction from 50 Years of Failure Experience" **Awards:** Recipient, Distinguished Achievement Award, Carnegie Mellon University (2004); Recipient, Distinguished Alumni Award, School of Mechanical Engineering, University of Pittsburgh (1996); Recipient, Pressure Vessel and Piping Award, American Society of Mechanical Engineers (1994); Recipient, Engineer of the Year Award, American Society of Mechanical Engineers (1988); Recipient, International Award for Best Publication in Pressure Vessels and Piping, American Society of Mechanical Engineers (1988); Recipient, National Award for Outstanding Contribution to Engineering Profession (1973); Recipient, Gold Medal for Achievements in Engineering, Pi Tau Sigma (1967); Recipient, Machinery's Achievement Award as an Outstanding Mechanical Designer (1957) **Membership:** FESI, United Kingdom Forum for Engineering Structural Integrity (2014-Present); Fellow, American Society of Mechanical Engineers; Boiler and Pressure Vessel Code, American Society of Mechanical Engineers; National Society of Professional Engineers; American Association for the Advancement of Science; American Society for Testing and Materials; Society for Experimental Mechanics; American Nuclear Society; Advanced Semiconductor Materials International; The Minerals, Metals & Materials Society; Sigma Xi, The Scientific Research Honor Society **Business Address:** 2940 S Park Road, Bethel Park, PA, 15102 **Shipping Address:** 121 Sunrise Lane, Venetia, PA, 15367 **Website:** http://www.odonnellconsulting.com

Nils Oeijord

Industry: Education/Educational Services **Place of Birth:** Mo i Rana **State/Country of Origin:** Norway **Education:** Coursework in Agriculture, Agricultural University of Norway (1973) **Career:** Lecturer on Mathematics, Tromso College (1998-2000); Researcher, Agriculture Experimental Station (1973-1976) **Creative Works:** Author, "The General Genetic Catastrophe"; Contributor, Articles, Professional Journals **Achievements:** Achievements include discovery of the general genetic catastrophe

Frederick James Olk

Title: County Official, Paralegal **Industry:** Law and Legal Services **Company Name:** Independent Practice **Date of Birth:** 04/30/1952 **Place of Birth:** Clintonville **State:** WI **Parents:** James Howard Olk; Bernice Helen (Durben) Olk **Education:** BS in Liberal Arts, University of Wisconsin-River Falls (1976); BS in Social Science, University of Wisconsin-River Falls (1976); BS in Library Science, University of Wisconsin-River Falls (1976); Degree, Institute on Comparative Political & Economic Systems (1973) **Certifications:** Certified Notary Public, State of Illinois (1982-Present); Certified School Real Estate Agent, State of Wisconsin (1980) **Career:** Tax Examiner/Clerk, Cook County Clerk's Office (1990-2016); Assistant Reference Librarian, Cicero Public Library (1989); Patrolman, Glenbrook Security Services, Inc., Wheeling, IL (1988-2009); Vice President, New World Credit Union, Chicago, IL (1981-1986); Editorial Librarian, Chicago Catholic, New World Publications (1980-1988); Library Assistant, Polk Library, University of Wisconsin Oshkosh (1980); Contract Librarian, U.S. Department of Justice, Oxford, WI (1980); Library Assistant, FCI Oxford (1980); Sales Representative, Waupaca Publishing Company, Waupaca, WI (1978-1979); Library Assistant, University of Wisconsin-Stevens Point (1977-1978); Intern, Office of Representative Wendell Wyatt (R-Oregon), U.S. House of Representatives (1973); Summer Worker, Wisconsin Youth Conservation Camp (1970); Subscription Salesman, Wisconsin State Farmer; Subscription Salesman, Wisconsin Horsemen's News **Career Related:** Freelance Paralegal, Chicago (1988-Present); Security Guard, Glenbrook Security Services (1988-Present); Account Manager, Glenbrook Security Services (1988-Present); Assistant Reference Librarian, Cicero Public Library (1989); Vice President, New World Credit Union (1981-1986); Genealogy Researcher, Lineage Search Associates (1980-1999); Sales Representative, Wisconsin Public Company, Waupaca, WI (1978-1979); Congressional Intern, U.S. House of Representatives (1973) **Civic:** President, Founder, Catholic Diabetes Foundation (2017-Present); Republican National Committee Presidential Advisory Board (2017-Present); Coordinator, American Friends of the Vatican Library (1995-Present); Judge of Election, Cook County, IL (1980-Present); Judge of Election, Cook County, IL (1980-Present); Precinct Captain, Wisconsin Republican Committees (1973-Present); Precinct Captain, Illinois Republican Committees (1973-Present); Union Steward, SEIU Local 73 (2012-2016); Executive Board Member, Customer Advisory Council, USPS (2001-2003); Choir Member, St. Peter's Basilica Performance, Parish Resurrection Choir, St. John Cantius Church (2001); Choir Member, Rome Tour, Parish Resurrection Choir, St. John Cantius Church (2001); Vice President, Customer Advisory Council, USPS (1999-2001); Cicero Representative for Illinois, 43rd District, Anti-Crime Advisory Board (1999-2001); Secretary, Customer Advisory Council, USPS (1997-1999); Tutor, Mercy Home for Boys & Girls (1987-1988) **Creative Works:** Columnist, Looking Back, Chicago Catholic (1985-1989) **Awards:** Honoree, Selected for Choir Performance, St. Peter's Basilica (2016); Honoree, Selected for Choir Performance, St. Peter's Basilica (2013); Honoree, Selected for Choir Performance, St. Peter's Basilica (2001); Recipient, Legion of Merit, Republican National Committee (1997); Honoree, International Citizen of the Year, Principality of Hutt River, AU (1995); Honoree, Colonel, State of Alabama (1988); Honoree, Admiral, Nebraska Admirals Association, State of Nebraska (1982); Inductee, Order of the Arrow, Boy Scouts of America (1971); Honoree, Employee of the Month, Tax Examiner, Cook County Clerk's Office **Membership:** Correspondent, 20th Century Railroad Club (2001-Present); Assistant Archivist, Amtrak Historical Society (1996-Present); Grand Knight, Cardinal Council, Knights of Columbus (2001-2003); Director, 20th Century Railroad Club, Chicago, IL (1998-2000); Secretary, 20th Century Railroad Club (1994-1998); Board of Directors, Chicago Genealogical Society (1988-1990); Director, Chicago Genealogical Society (1986-1988); Delegate, Archdiocesan Pastoral Council, Knights of Columbus (1986-1988); Chairman, Government Relations, American Society of Notaries (1984-1985); Lifetime Member, American Society of Notaries; NAIS; Lifetime Member, The American Legion; Lifetime Member, Chicago Genealogical Society **Marquis Who's Who Honors:** Albert Nelson Marquis Lifetime Achievement Award (2017) **Hobbies:** Rail travel; Genealogy; Reading; Music; Philately **Shipping Address:** 1041 Stockton Avenue, Des Plaines, IL, 60018

John Olson

Title: Power Industry Electrician **Industry:** Facility Management **Company Name:** IBEW **Date of Birth:** 09/06/1956 **Place of Birth:** St. Paul **State:** MN **Parents:** Arthur Norman; Viola Ann Olson **Marital Status:** Married (7/21/89) **Spouse Name:** Diane Evelyn Steen-Hinderlie **Children:** Peder Donald Hinderlie (Stepchild); Erik Steen Hinderlie (Stepchild) **Education:** Electrical Degree, Dunwoody Industrial Institute, Minneapolis, MN (1977) **Career:** Journeyman Wireman, Occasional Job Steward, Foreman, Member, International Brotherhood of Electrical Workers, Minneapolis, MN (1977-Present); Properties Manager, First Lutheran Church, St. Louis Park, MN (1984-1986) **Career Related:** Editor, Viking Age Club Newsletters (2001-2007) **Civic:** Trustee, St. Louis Park Historical Society (2014-Present); Treasurer, Joint Committee, Sons of Norway Lodges (2002-Present); President, St. Louis Park Historical Society (2002-2014); President, Syttende Mai Lodge (2000-2002); President, Joint Committee, Sons of Norway Lodges, Twin Cities, MN (2000-2002); Coach, Baseball Association, St. Louis Park, MN (1992-1998) **Awards:** Recipient, Coach's Hall of Fame Award, Baseball Association, St. Louis Park, MN (1998) **Membership:** Coordinator, Thrivent Financial Grants, Trinity Congregation (2005-Present); Chicago Northwestern Historical Society; National Railroad Passenger Association; National Model Railroad Association; Soo Line Historical & Technical Society **Hobbies:** Building models; Photography; Bowling **Religion:** Lutheran **Shipping Address:** 2829 Yosemite Ave. S, Minneapolis, MN, 55416

Richard G. Olsen

Title: Biomedical Engineer **Industry:** Sciences **Date of Birth:** 08/10/1945 **Place of Birth:** Colorado Springs **State:** CO **Parents:** Floyd Edwin Olsen; Ruth Elizabeth (Robinson) Olsen **Marital Status:** Married **Spouse Name:** Karen Fidler Brubaker (June 17, 1973) **Children:** Kathryn Elizabeth; Nickolas Robert **Education:** PhD, The University of Utah (1975); MS, The University of Utah (1970); BSEE, University of Missouri (1968) **Career:** Consultant, Bioelectromagnetics (2001-Present); Head of Bioengineering Department, Naval Health Research Center (1994-2000); Head of Bioengineering Division, Naval Aerospace Medical Research Laboratory (1982-1994); Chief of Engineering Systems Division, Naval Aerospace Medical Research Laboratory (1979-1982); Electrical Engineer, Naval Aerospace Medical Research Laboratory (1975-1979); Engineer, Bendix Commercial Vehicles Systems LLC (1968-1969) **Career Related:** Technology Consultant, Selicor, Inc. (2001-2004); Naval Command, Control and Ocean Surveillance Command (1996-1997); Armstrong Laboratory US Air Force (Now Air Force Research Laboratory) (1991-1999); Naval Surface Warfare Center (1989-1995); Naval Sea Systems Command (1989-1991) **Military Service:** US Army (1970-1972) **Creative Works:** Contributor, Articles, Professional Journals; Contributor, Articles, Books. **Awards:** Recipient, Fred A. Hitchcock Award Aerospace Physiologist, Aerospace Medical Association (1987); Recipient, Award For Excellence In Technology Transfer, Federal Laboratory Consortium for Technology Transfer (2004); Recipient, Engineer Of The Year, Northwest Florida Engineers Council (1991) **Membership:** Chairman, SCC-28 Committee, IEEE (1982-2000); Chairman, SCC-34 Committee, IEEE (1982-2000); Editorial Board Member, The Bioelectromagnetics Society (1990-1996); Chairman, Pensacola Section, IEEE (1982-1983); Chartering Member, The Bioelectromagnetics Society; Sigma Xi, The Scientific Research Honor Society; Eta Kappa Nu, IEEE; The Tau Beta Pi Association, Inc.; The Honor Society of Phi Kappa Phi **Marquis Who's Who Honors:** Distinguished Humanitarian (2017) **Shipping Address:** 1503 N Baylen Street, Pensacola, FL, 32501

Yoshiaki Omura

Title: Medical Educator **Industry:** Education/Educational Services **Date of Birth:** 03/28/1934 **Place of Birth:** Tomari **Country of Origin:** Japan **Parents:** Tsunejiro Omura; Minako (Uozu) Omura **Marital Status:** Single **Spouse Name:** Rose Ninon Alexander (9/8/1962, Separated 1983) **Children:** Alexander Kenji; Vivienne Midori; Richard Itsuma **Education:** ScD, College of Physicians and Surgeons, Columbia University (1965); Resident Physician in Surgery, Francis Delafield Hospital, Cancer Institute, Columbia University (1961-1965); Postgraduate Coursework in Experimental Physics, Columbia University (1960-1963); Research Fellow, Cardiovascular Surgery, Columbia University, New York City, NY (1960); Rotating Intern, Norwalk Hospital, Connecticut (1959); Rotating Intern, Tokyo University Hospital (1958); MD, Yokohama City University (1958); BSc in Applied Physics, Waseda University (1957) **Certifications:** Diplomate, American Academy of Experts in Traumatic Stress; Diplomate, American Board of Forensic Medicine; Diplomate, American Academy of Pain Management; Diplomate, International College of Acupuncture and Electro-Therapeutics **Career:** Adjunct Professor of Family and Community Medicine, New York Medical College (2016); Maitre de Eecherche, Distinguished Foreign Scientist Program, French National Institute of Health and Medical Research, Government of France (1977); Visiting Summer Professor, University of Paris (1973-1977); Assistant Professor of Pharmacology, Instructor of Surgery, New York Medical College (1966-1972) **Career Related:** Adjunct Professor of Preventive Medicine, New York Medical College (1997-Present); Professor, Department of Non-Orthodox Medicine, Ukrainian National Medical University, Kiev, Ukraine (1993-Present); Member, Alumni Council, College of Physicians and Surgeons, Columbia University (1986-Present); Director, Medical Research, Heart Disease Research Foundation, Brooklyn, NY (1972-Present); Keynote Speaker, Medical Congress, Tokyo University, Tokyo, Japan (2017); Keynote Speaker, First World Congress on Integrated Medicine, Sao Paolo, Brazil (2017); Speaker, Anti-Cancer Committee Meeting, European Parliament (2017); Keynote Speaker, Preventive Oncology Congress, Chicago, IL (2017); Keynote Speaker, Annual Congress of Forensic Research & Technology, Houston, TX (2017); Keynote Speaker, International Congress on Cancer, Cardiology and Forensic Medicine (2016); Vice Chair, American Board of Forensic Medicine (2002-2007); Visiting Professor, Institute of Anesthesiology and Reanimation, University of Padua, Italy (1999); Visiting Research Professor, Department of Electrical Engineering, Manhattan College (1960-1999); Consultant, Research Grant Evaluation, National Institutes of Health (1994-1996); Visiting Professor of Physiology, Medical School, Showa University, Tokyo, Japan (1988-1996); Member, New York State Board of Medicine (1984-1994); Vice President, International Kirlian Research Association (1981-1994); Adjunct Professor, Department of Pharmacology, Chicago Medical School (1982-1993); New York Pain Center (1988-1992); Chairman, Science Division, Children's Art & Science Workshops, New York City, NY (1971-1992); Attending Physician, Department of Neuroscience, Long Island College Hospital (1980-1988); Chairman, Columbia University Affiliation and Community Medicine Committee, Community Board, Francis Delafield Hospital (1974-1975); Co-Founder, Consultant, Lincoln Hospital Acupuncture Drug Detoxification Program (1974-1975) **Creative Works:** Editorial Consultant, American Journal of Traditional Chinese Medicine (2006-Present); Editorial Board Member, Scandinavian Journal of Acupuncture and Electrotherapy (1987-Present); Editor-in-Chief, "Acupuncture & Electro-Therapeutics Research, the International Journal" (1975-Present); Editorial Board Member, Functional Neurology (1988-2002); Editorial Board Member, Alternative Medicine (1985-1993) **Awards:** Grantee, Heart Disease Research Foundation (1972-2015); World First Qi Gong Scientist of the Year Award, International Congress of Chinese Medicine & Qi Gong (1990); Acupuncture Scientist of the Year Award, International Congress of Chinese Medicine (1989); Grantee, National Institutes of Health (1967-1972); Grantee, John Polacek Foundation (1966-1972); Grantee, American Cancer Society, Inc. (1961-1963); Fellow, Columbia University (1960) **Membership:** Lifetime Fellow, Royal Society of Medicine (2016-Present); International Congress of Forensic Medicine (2016-Present); International Symposium on Cancer (2016-Present); Japan Bi-Digital O-Ring Test Medical Society (1990-Present); Japan Bi-Digital O-Ring Test Association (1986-Present); President, International College of Acupuncture and Electro-Therapeutics (1980-Present); Founding Member, International Association for the Study of Pain (1975-Present); Vice Chairman, American Association of Integrative Medicine (2002-2007); New York Japanese Medical Society (1963-1973); Fellow, International College of Angiology; Fellow, New York Cardiology Society; Fellow, American College of Angiology; Life Fellow **Shipping Address:** 800 Riverside Dr Apt 8I, New York, NY, 10032

Thomas F. O'Neil

Title: Lawyer **Industry:** Law and Legal Services **Date of Birth:** 04/08/1957 **Place of Birth:** Fairfield **State/Country of Origin:** CT **Parents:** Thomas F. O'Neil, Jr.; Carmen A. (Therrien) O'Neil **Marital Status:** Married **Spouse Name:** Nancy D. (8/14/1982) **Children:** Caley Elizabeth; P. McGee. **Education:** JD, Georgetown University (1982); AB, Dartmouth College, Magna Cum Laude (1979) **Career:** Global Compliance Officer, Cigna (2017-Present); Director, TRLG Holdings, LLC (2013-Present); Independent Trustee, Brown Advisory Funds (2012-Present); Director, BevMo Holdings, LLC (2011-Present); President, The Saranac Group LLC (2010-2016); Vice Chairman, WellCare Health Plans, Inc., Tampa, FL (2009-2010); Senior Vice President, General Counsel, Secretary, WellCare Health Plans, Inc., Tampa, FL (2008-2009); Joint Global Leader, Legislative and Regulatory Group, DLA Piper, Washington D.C. (2005-2008); Chairman, Government Affairs Practice Group, DLA Piper, Washington D.C. (2005-2008); Co-Chairman, Government Controversies Practice Group, DLA Piper, Washington D.C. (2005-2008); Partner, Piper Rudnick LLP (2002-2004); Senior Vice President, General Counsel, MCI Global (2001-2002); Senior Vice President, Chief Legal Counsel, MCI Global (1999-2001); Chief Litigation Counsel, MCI Communications Corp., Washington D.C. (1995-1998); Partner, Hogan & Hartson, Baltimore, MD (1992-1995); Associate, Hogan & Hartson, Baltimore, MD (1990-1991); Assistant United States Attorney, U.S. Department of Justice, Baltimore, MD (1986-1989); Associate, Venable, Baetjer & Howard, Baltimore, MD (1984-1986); Legislative Assistant, Congressman Stewart B. McKinney, Washington D.C. (1980-1982); Law Clerk, Honorable Alexander Harvey II, United States District Court District of Maryland **Career Related:** Board of Regents Member, Georgetown University (2005-2011); President, Board of Trustees, The Contemporary, Baltimore, MD (2005-2007); Member, Advisory Board, Marbury Institute (2000-2002); Member, Board of Visitors, Georgetown University Law Center (1999-2011); Trustee, The Walters Art Museum (1997-2002); Ex-Officio Trustee, The Walters Art Museum (1995-1996); Board of Governors, Federal Bar Association, Baltimore, MD (1992); Member, Co-Chairman, Advisory Board, Corporate Counsel Institute, Georgetown Law **Creative Works:** Contributor, Articles, Professional Journals **Awards:** Paul R. Dean Award, Georgetown University Law Center (2007); Letter of Commendation Award, Bureau of Investigation, Washington D.C. (1989); Special Achievement Award, U.S. Department of Justice (1989); Chief Postal Inspectors Special Award, USPS, Washington D.C (1988) **Membership:** International Bar Association; Serjeants' Inn Law Club **Bar Admissions:** The Dirstict of Columbia Bar (1992); United States District Court District of Maryland (1983); United States Court of Appeals for the Fourth Circuit (1983); Maryland (1982); New York **Religion:** Roman Catholic **Shipping Address:** 100 Light Street, Suite 1350, The Saranac Group LLC, Baltimore, MD, 21202

John Arthur Orcutt, PhD

Title: Geophysicist **Industry:** Sciences **Company Name:** Scripps Institution of Oceanography, UC San Diego **Date of Birth:** 08/29/1943 **Place of Birth:** Holyoke **State:** CO **Marital Status:** Married **Spouse Name:** (1967) **Children:** Two Children **Education:** PhD in Earth Sciences, University of California, San Diego, CA (1976); MSc, University of Liverpool, England, U.K. (1968); BS, U.S. Naval Academy, Annapolis, MD (1966) **Career:** Distinguished Professor, Cecil H. and Ida M. Green Institute of Geophysics and Planetary Physics, Scripps Institution of Oceanography, La Jolla, CA (2015-Present); Distinguished Professor, Geophysics, Scripps Institution of Oceanography (2005-Present); Research Geophysicist, Scripps Institution of Oceanography, La Jolla, CA (1977-Present); Associate Vice Chancellor, Government Relations, University of California, San Diego, CA (2006-2008); Associate Vice Chancellor, Deputy Director, Scripps Institution of Oceanography, University of California, San Diego, CA (2002-2006); Director, Cecil H. and Ida M. Green Institute of Geophysics and Planetary Physics, Scripps Institution of Oceanography, La Jolla, CA (1984-2015); Professor, Geophysics, Scripps Institution of Oceanography, La Jolla, CA (1984-1985); Associate Professor, Scripps Institution of Oceanography, La Jolla, CA (1982-1984) **Career Related:** Distinguished Researcher, San Diego Supercomputer Center (2008-Present); Secretary, Chief of Naval Operations Oceanography Chair (1996-Present) **Military Service:** Commander, U.S. Navy (1966-1978) **Creative Works:** Contributor, More Than 179 Peer-Reviewed Science Papers; Contributor, Numerous Chapters, Books **Awards:** Honorary Fellow, RAS (2005-Present); Lockheed Martin Award, Marine Technology Society (2007); Outstanding Alumnus Of The Year, University of California, San Diego, CA (1997); Maurice Ewing Medal, American Geophysical Union (1994); Newcomb Cleveland Prize, American Association for the Advancement of Science (1980); Scholar, Fulbright, U.K. (1966-1967); University of California, San Diego's Top 100 Influential Alumni **Membership:** National Academy of Engineering (2011-Present); The American Philosophical Society (2002-Present); President, American Geophysical Union (2004-2006); Secretary General, American Geophysical Union (1998-2002); Fellow, American Geophysical Union; Society of Exploration Geophysicists; Seismological Society of America **Shipping Address:** 9500 Gilman Drive, Mail Code 0225, Scripps Institution of Oceanography, La Jolla, CA, 92093

Nora Orphanides

Title: Performing Arts Educator **Industry:** Education/Educational Services **Company Name:** Princeton Ballet School **Date of Birth:** 06/04/1951 **Place of Birth:** New York **State:** NY **Parents:** M.T. Feffer; Mary Elsie (Tilly) Feffer **Marital Status:** Married **Spouse Name:** James Mark Orphanides (7/1/1972) **Children:** Mark; Elaine Orphanides-Mastrosimone; Jennine **Education:** Postgraduate Studies, Princeton Ballet School (1976-1986); BA, City University of New York (1973); Student, Joffrey Ballet School, New York, NY (1970-1975) **Certifications:** Certification, Speech and Hearing Handicapped Teacher **Career:** President, CEO, Orphanides and Associates LLC (2012-Present); Faculty Emeritus, Princeton Ballet School (2012-Present); Trustee Emeritus, Princeton Ballet School (1992-Present); Membership Department, MMA, New York, NY (1987-2002); Faculty, Princeton Ballet School (1983-2012) **Career Related:** Master Teacher, Ballroom Dance **Civic:** Foundation Board of Directors, University Medical Center of Princeton (2004-Present); Trustee, Princeton Medical Center Auxiliary Board (1995-Present); Chairman, Nutcracker Benefit, Princeton Ballet School (1990-Present); Chairman, Special Events, Princeton Ballet School (1987-Present); Trustee, Princeton Ballet School (1986-Present); Judge, Princeton's Breakfast for Dancing Classrooms (2012-2013); Honorary Chairman, Benefit Chairman, Dancing Classrooms, American Ballroom Theatre Company (2010); Sponsor, Co-Chair, American Ballet Theatre Spring Gala, New York, NY (2007); Art First to Benefit University Medical Center (2006); Board of Directors, University Medical Center of Princeton (2004-2010); Choreographer, Stuart Country Day School, Princeton, NJ (2001); Past President, Princeton Medical Center Auxiliary Board (2000-2002); Chairman, Benefit Dinner, Eden Institute (2000); Department Chairman, June Fete to Benefit Princeton Hospital, Princeton Ballet School (2000); Honoree, Princeton Ballet School (1999); President, Princeton Medical Center Auxiliary Board (1997-1999); Choreographer, Stuart Country Day School, Princeton, NJ (1996-1999); Department Chairman, June Fete to Benefit Princeton Hospital, Princeton Ballet School (1996); Trustee, Princeton Ballet School (1995-1999); Chairman, Christmas Boutique, Princeton Medical Center (1993); Honorary Chairman, Princeton Ballet Gala (1993); Princeton Chamber Symphony (1993); Handel Festival, Nassau Church (1993); Trustee, Princeton Medical Center Auxiliary Board (1992-2002); Dinner Chairman, Nassau Church Music Festival (1992); Volunteer, National Headquarters of Recording for the Blind (1991-1993); Fundraising Gala Chairman, Princeton Ballet School (1991-1992); Dracula Benefit, Princeton Ballet School (1991); Department Chairman, June Fete to Benefit Princeton Hospital, Princeton Ballet School (1990-1992); Department Chairman, June Fete to Benefit Princeton Hospital, Princeton Ballet School (1988); Fundraising Gala Chairman, Princeton Ballet School (1986); Fundraising Gala Chairman, Princeton Ballet School (1985); Founder, Pierre Dulaine **Creative Works:** Cast Member, Princeton Ballet (Now American Repertory Ballet Company) (1993-Present); Appearance, "Romeo & Juliet" (2000); Appearance, "Romeo & Juliet" (1995-1996); Cast Member, Princeton Ballet Annual Nutcracker (1985-1990) **Awards:** Eden Dreams Visionary Award (2013); Edward R. And Irene D. Farley Community Stewardship Award, Eden Institute Foundation (2003); Honoree, Princeton Ballet (1999) **Marquis Who's Who Honors:** Albert Nelson Marquis Lifetime Achievement Award (2017); Distinguished Humanitarian (2017) **Hobbies:** Piano; Golf **Shipping Address:** 35 Brearly Road, Princeton, NJ, 08540

Charles D. Orth, PhD

Title: Physicist **Industry:** Sciences **Company Name:** Lawrence Livermore National Security, LLC **Date of Birth:** 06/01/1942 **Place of Birth:** Seattle **State:** WA **Parents:** William Harold Orth; Lois Janet (Sims) Orth **Marital Status:** Divorced **Spouse Name:** Teresa Ann Stout (8/30/1992, Divorced 2018); Shirley Lee Crouse (6/14/1964, Divorced 5/20/1992) **Children:** Kenneth James; Michael Douglas **Education:** PhD, California Institute of Technology, Pasadena, CA (1970); BS, University of Washington, Seattle, WA (1964) **Career:** Physicist, Lawrence Livermore National Laboratory, Livermore, CA (1978-Present); Physicist, University of California, Berkeley, CA (1972-1978); Research Associate, Manned Spacecraft Center (Now Johnson Space Center), National Aeronautics and Space Administration, Houston, Texas (1970-1972) **Creative Works:** Author, "Spallation as a Dominant Source of Pusher-Fuel and Hot-Spot Mix in Inertial Confinement Fusion Capsules," AIP Physics of Plasmas 23, 022706 (2016); Author, "VISTA - A Vehicle for Interplanetary Space Transport Application Powered by Inertial Confinement Fusion," LLNL Report UCRL-TR-110500 (2003); Lead Co-author, "A Diode Pumped Solid State Laser Driver For Inertial Fusion Energy," Nuclear Fusion (1996) **Awards:** Award, National Ignition Facility Advanced Radiographic Capability (ARC), Lawrence Livermore National Laboratory Director (2016) **Membership:** Sigma Xi; Phi Beta Kappa Society; American Physical Society **Marquis Who's Who Honors:** Albert Nelson Marquis Lifetime Achievement Award (2017) **To what do you attribute your success:** Dr. Orth attributes his success to his close relationship with God. **Why did you become involved in your profession or industry:** Dr. Orth became involved in his profession because he wanted to understand lightning after seeing it hit the top of a flagpole a few hundred yards away from where he was sleeping as a young child. **What do you consider to be the highlight of your career:** A highlight of Dr. Orth's career was the understanding that spallation of shocked target materials inhibited the National Ignition Facility (NIF) from achieving fusion "ignition." **Where will you be in five years:** In five years, God only knows where Dr. Orth will be. **Hobbies:** Pianist **Religion:** Christian **Shipping Address:** PO Box 808, Lawrence Livermore National Lab, L-462, Livermore, CA, 94551-0808 **Website:** http://www.charlesdorth.com

LaDonna Carol Osborn

Title: Minister **Industry:** Religious **Company Name:** 1) Women International Network 2) OSBORN Ministries **Date of Birth:** 03/13/1947 **Place of Birth:** Portland **State:** OR **Parents:** T.L. Osborn; Daisy (Washburn) Osborn **Marital Status:** Married **Spouse Name:** Cory A. Nickerson (12/11/1981) **Children:** Tommy O'Dell; LaVona Thomas; Daneesa O'Dell; Donald O'Dell **Education:** DD, Zoe University (2001); Doctor in Ministry, American Christian College and Seminary (2001); MA, Oral Roberts University (2000); Honorary LHD, Wesley Synod (1998); DD, Bethel College (1995); BA, Oklahoma City University (1994); Coursework, Assemblies of God College (1963) **Career:** President, OSBORN Ministries (2009-Present); Founder, President, Women International Network (2003-Present); Overseer, International Gospel Center (1997-Present); President, International Gospel Fellowship (2013); Vice President, CEO, OSBORN Ministries (1998-2009); Founder, Presiding Bishop, International Gospel Fellowship, Tulsa, OK (1997-2013); Senior Pastor, International Gospel Center, Tulsa, OK (1994-1997); Senior Pastor, International Gospel Center, Tulsa, OK (1989-1994); Associate Pastor, International Gospel Center, Tulsa, OK (1986-1989); Corporate President, Osborn Foundation, Tulsa, OK (1986-1993); International Editor-in-Chief, Osborn Foundation, Tulsa, OK (1981-1986); International General Manager, Osborn Foundation, Tulsa, OK (1976-1981); Executive Assistant, Osborn Foundation, Tulsa, OK (1975-76); Foreign Mission Correspondent, Purchaser, Personnel Agent, Osborn Foundation, Tulsa, OK (1969-1975) **Career Related:** International Minister, Religious Teacher, and Motivational Speaker in Nigeria, Kenya, Uganda, Colombia, Papua New Guinea, France, Russia, Belarus, Kazakhstan, Kyrgyzstan, Ukraine, Sweden, England, Brazil, Holland, Canada, India, Zambia, Ecuador, China, Mizoram, Guatemala, Mexico, Myanmar, Indonesia, Angola, Congo, Togo, Benin, Democratic Republic of Congo, South Africa, Malawi, Cote d'Ivoire, Madagascar; International Spiritual Advisor, Christian Women's Fellowship International, Nigeria; Founder Believers' Network International **Creative Works:** Author, "Jesus is Touching Soshanguve" (2012); Author, "Unknown But Not Forgotten" (2012); Author, "Give Thanks" (2012); Author, "Chaos of Miracles" (2011); Author, "10 Gospel Basics" (2008); Author, "Peace is a Lifestyle" (2005); Author, "New Miracle Life Now" (2004); Author, "Cross-Cultural Communication in a Multicultural Church" (2002); Author, "God's Big Picture" (2001); Author, "Jesus & Women" (2000); Author/Editor, Bible Training Courses **Marquis Who's Who Honors:** Albert Nelson Marquis Lifetime Achievement Award (2017); Distinguished Humanitarian (2017) **Political Affiliations:** Independent **Shipping Address:** 6246 S. Utica Avenue, Tulsa, OK, 74136

Edwin Dean Overton

Title: Educator, Campus Minister **Industry:** Education/Educational Services **Date of Birth:** 12/02/1939 **Place of Birth:** Elmwood **State:** OK **Parents:** William Edward Overton; Georgia Beryl (Fronk) Overton **Marital Status:** Single **Education:** Postgraduate Coursework, Fuller Theological Seminary (1980); EdS, Eastern New Mexico University (1978); MA in Religion, Eastern New Mexico University (1969); BTh, Midwest Christian College (1963) **Certifications:** Ordained to Ministry, Christian Church (1978) **Career:** Acting Chairman, Religion Department, Eastern New Mexico University, Portales, NM (2000); Teacher, Religion, Philosophy, Counseling, Eastern New Mexico University, Portales, NM (1970-2005); Campus Minister, Christian Campus House, Portales, NM (1968-2005); Campus Minister, Central Christian Church, Portales, NM (1967-1968); Youth Minister, 1st Christian Church, Beaver, OK (1963-1967); Minister, Christian Church, Englewood, KS (1962-1963) **Career Related:** Power-of-Attorney, Older Sister (2009-Present); Professor Emeritus, Eastern New Mexico Council, Council of Professors Emeriti (2008-Present); Farm and Ranch Partner, Beaver, OK (1963-Present); Guide, Beaver High School, Class of 1957 Bus Tour (2008); Director, Christian Campus House (1980-2005) **Civic:** Neighborhood Chairman, Portales March of Dimes (1997); Elder, Central Christian Church, Portales, NM (1990-1993); Elder, Central Christian Church, Portales, NM (1985-1988); President, Portales Tennis Association (1977-1978); Chairman, Beaver County March of Dimes (1966); State Director, Beaver Junior Chamber of Commerce (1964-1965); President, Beaver High School Alumni Association (1964-1965) **Military Service:** U.S. Army Reserve (1957-1960) **Creative Works:** Editor, "The Christian Campus House at Eastern New Mexico University: 1968-2005" (2008) **Awards:** Mr. Midwest, Midwest Christian College; Junior Master Farmers Award **Membership:** U.S. Tennis Association; American Association of Christian Counselors; Faith in Life Committee, Eastern New Mexico University; Lions International **Marquis Who's Who Honors:** Albert Nelson Marquis Lifetime Achievement Award (2017) **Hobbies:** Golf; Tennis; Table tennis; Traveling **Political Affiliations:** Republican **Religion:** Christian **Shipping Address:** 1129 Libra Drive, Portales, NM, 88130

John Arthur Owens

Title: Senior Partner **Industry:** Law and Legal Services **Company Name:** Owens & Millsaps, LLP **Date of Birth:** 07/07/1939 **Place of Birth:** Birmingham **State:** AL **Parents:** James King Owens; Beatrice (Geer) Owens **Marital Status:** Married **Spouse Name:** Dorothy Terry (7/7/1962) **Children:** Apsilah (Appie) Geer Owens Millsaps; Terry Owens Alvarez **Education:** LLB, University of Alabama (1967); BS in Commerce and Business Administration, University of Alabama (1961) **Career:** Senior Partner, Owens & Millsaps, LLP, Tuscaloosa, AL (2003-Present); Partner, Owens and Almond, Tuscaloosa, AL (1997-2002); Founder, Owens and Carver, Tuscaloosa, AL (1994-1996); Partner, Phelps, Jenkins, Gibson & Fowler, Tuscaloosa, AL (1969-1994); Associate, Sam M. Phelps, Tuscaloosa, AL (1968-1969); Associate, Spiro & Phelps, Tuscaloosa, AL (1967-1968) **Career Related:** Fellow, American Bar Foundation; Fellow, Alabama Bar Foundation; Fellow, Tuscaloosa County Bar Association **Civic:** Board of Directors, Tuscaloosa Symphony Orchestra (1989-Present); Chairman, Board of Trustees, First United Methodist Church Tuscaloosa (1967-Present); Board of Directors, Professional Division, United Way of West Alabama (1997-2003); President, Tuscaloosa Symphony Orchestra (1997-1999); Chair, Professional Division, United Way of West Alabama (1997); President, The Arts and Humanities Council of Tuscaloosa County, Inc. (1993-1994); Board of Directors, Children's Hands-On Museum of Tuscaloosa, Tuscaloosa, AL (1985-1989); President, The Arts and Humanities Council of Tuscaloosa County, Inc. (1981-1982); The Arts and Humanities Council of Tuscaloosa County, Inc. (1980-2002); Advisory Committee Member, The Junior League of Tuscaloosa, Inc; Officer, Tuscaloosa County Solid Waste Authority; Chairman, Jemison-Van de Graaff Mansion Foundation **Military Service:** Lieutenant, U.S. Naval Reserve (1964-1975); U.S. Navy (1961-1964) **Awards:** Distinguished Alumnus Award, University of Alabama (2012); Honoree, Alumni of the Year, University of Alabama (2012); Pillar of the Bar Award, Tuscaloosa County Bar Association (2010); Distinguished Service Award, The Arts and Humanities Council of Tuscaloosa County, Inc. (1995); Patron of the Arts Award, The Arts and Humanities Council of Tuscaloosa County, Inc. (1985); Honoree, A/V Preeminent Rating, Martindale-Hubbell; Honoree, 50-Year Recognition, Alabama State Bar Association **Membership:** Tuscaloosa Rotary Club (1969-Present); President, Alabama Law Foundation (2005-2007); Vice President, Alabama Law Foundation (2003-2005); Vice President, Alabama Law Foundation (2003-2005); President, Alabama State Bar Association (1995-1996); Board of Directors, Alabama Law Foundation (1994-1997); Board of Directors, Alabama Law Foundation (1994-1997); President-elect, Alabama State Bar Association (1994-1995); President, Farrah Order, Order of the Coif (1994-1995); Vice President, Alabama State Bar Association (1990-1991); Commissioner, Alabama State Bar Association (1987-1994); Director, Alabama Defense Lawyers Association (1984-1987); President, Tuscaloosa Rotary Club (1983-1984); Alabama State Bar Association; Alabama Defense Lawyers Association; International Association of Defense Counsel; Omicron Delta Kappa **Bar Admissions:** U.S. Supreme Court (1990); U.S. District Court, Northern District, State of Alabama (1975); State of Alabama (1967); Fifth and 11th Circuits, U.S. Court of Appeals **Marquis Who's Who Honors:** Albert Nelson Marquis Lifetime Achievement Award (2017) **Why did you become involved in your profession or industry:** Mr. Owens became involved in his profession after taking some business law courses in commerce school. He developed a liking to it, and friends in school were involved in it. **Religion:** Methodist **Shipping Address:** 1303 Indian Hills Circle, Tuscaloosa, AL, 35406 **Website:** http://theowensfirm.com/#s2

Sally Jacquelyn Page

Title: Lecturer in Management **Industry:** Education/Educational Services **Company Name:** University of North Dakota **Place of Birth:** Saingra **State:** MI **Year of Passing:** 2018-04-18 **Education:** MBA, Southern Illinois University (1973); BA, The University of Iowa (1965) **Career:** Lecturer in Management, University of North Dakota (1978-2010); Officer of Institution, University of North Dakota (1977-2013); Assistant to the President, Southern Illinois University (1974-1977); Affirmative Action Officer, Southern Illinois University (1974-1977); Research Administrator, Southern Illinois University (1970-1974); Editorial Consultant, Editorial Associates (1969-1970); Copy Editor, C.V. Mosby Company (Now Elsevier) (1965-1969) **Civic:** Member, Foundation Board, Valley Memorial Homes (2005-Present); Vice Chair, Valley Memorial Homes (2007); Member, Mayor's Advisory Cabinet, City of Grand Forks (1998-2000); President, Grand Forks Homes (1996-2001); Chairman, Civil Service Commission (1996, 1992); Chairman, North Dakota Equal Opportunity Affirmative Action Officers (1987-2003); Chairman, Civil Service Commission (1986); Board of Directors, Grand Forks Homes (1985-2003); Chairman, Civil Service Commission (1984); Civil Service Commissioner, City of Grand Forks (1983-1998); Member, Civil Service Review Task Force, City of Grand Forks (1982); President, Pine to Prairie Council, Girl Scouts of the United States of America (1980-1985); Employment Committee Member, Commission on the Status of Women, State of Illinois (1976-1977); Member, Bicentennial Committee, City of Edwardsville (1976); Member, Bikeway Task Force, City of Edwardsville (1975-1977); Member, Greater Grand Forks Business Leadership Network; Chairman, Diversity Council, North Dakota University System **Membership:** Member of Research and Publications Board, CUPA-HR (1982-1984); Director, Illinois Chapter, American Association of University Women (1975-1977); P.E.O. Sisterhood; Society for Human Resource Management; American Association for Access, Equity and Diversity; American Dental Association **Marquis Who's Who Honors:** Albert Nelson Marquis Lifetime Achievement Award (2017) **Religion:** Presbyterian **Shipping Address:** 3121 Cherry Street, Grand Forks, ND, 58201

Matthew Palumbo

Title: Marketing Executive, Management Consultant **Industry:** Advertising & Marketing **Company Name:** Palumbo Consultants **Date of Birth:** 09/17/1961 **Place of Birth:** Queens **State:** NY **Parents:** John Christopher Palumbo; Seiko (Murakami) Palumbo **Education:** MBA in Marketing Management, St. John's University (1990); BS, Cornell University (1986) **Career:** President, Palumbo Consultants, Kent, CT (2000-Present); Director, Product Marketing, Cyberian Outpost, Kent, CT (1997-2000); Special Projects Manager, Group Product Manager, Global Computer Supplies, Port Washington, NY (1993-1997); Marketing Director, Copy Director, Flaghouse Inc., Mount Vernon, NY (1990-1993); Adjunct Professor, St. John's University, Staten Island, NY (1990); Director Marketing Consultant, Palumbo Associates, Staten Island, NY (1989-1990); Copywriter, Pierce Associates, New York City, NY (1988-1990); Mutual Fund Administrator, Bank of New York Co., Inc., New York City, NY (1986-1988); Mortgage Clerk, Salomon Brothers, Inc., New York City, NY (1986) **Career Related:** Ambassador Committee, Cornell University Council (2016-Present); Administrative Board, Cornell University Council (2015-Present); At-Large Member, Cornell University Council (2014-Present); Guest Lecturer, Designed and Acquired Funding, Cornell University (1992-Present); U.S. Delegate, Cornell University, Asia-Pacific Leadership Conference (2013); Board of Directors, Park Ave. (2010-2012); Guest Lecturer, American Direct Marketing Techniques, Sheffield Halleron University, England (1993); Chair, Vice Chair, Ambassador Committee, Cornell University Council; Monsignor Farrell High School **Awards:** Annette Brodsky Scholar (1988); New York State Regents Scholar (1979); Direct Marketing Club of New York Award; ECHO Academy of Direct Marketing Arts & Sciences-Award **Membership:** Vice President, Alumni Affairs, Cornell Asian Alumni Association (1993-1995); Advisory Board, Cornell Asian Alumni Association; Vice President, Cornell Class of 1983; Cornell ILR Alumni Association; Monsignor Farrell; High School; Direct Marketing Club of New York; Co-Chair, Speakers Committee, Cornell Club of New York; Cornell University Quadrangle Club; Lifetime Member, New York City Chapter, Beta Gamma Sigma; Kent Connecticut Sewer Commission; National Honor Society Collegiate Schools of Business **Shipping Address:** 6 Meadow Street, Kent, CT, 06757

Clifton W. Pannell, PhD

Title: Geography Educator, Writer **Industry:** Education/Educational Services **Company Name:** The University of Hong Kong **Date of Birth:** 03/24/1939 **Place of Birth:** Tuscaloosa **State:** AL **Parents:** Henry Clifton Pannell; Anne Thomas (Gary) Pannell **Marital Status:** Married **Spouse Name:** Sylvia Hillyard (1994); Laurie Preston DeBuys (2/14/1964, Deceased 1992) **Children:** Alexander; Richard; Charles; Thomas **Education:** PhD, The University of Chicago (1971); Postgraduate Coursework, Inter-University Program for Chinese Language Studies, Taipei, Taiwan (1969); MA, University of Virginia (1962); AB, University of North Carolina at Chapel Hill (1961) **Career:** External Examiner, Department of Geography, The University of Hong Kong (2008-Present); Professor, University of Georgia, Athens, GA (1980-Present); Associate Dean, Franklin College of Arts and Sciences, University of Georgia, Athens, GA (1994-2005); Department Head, University of Georgia, Athens, GA (1992-1993); Director, Center for Asian Studies, University of Georgia, Athens, GA (1987-1992); Associate Professor, University of Georgia, Athens, GA (1975-1980); Assistant Professor of Geography, University of Georgia, Athens, GA (1971-1975); Lecturer, University of Maryland University College Asia (1970-1971) **Career Related:** Visiting Professor, The University of Hong Kong (2014); Visiting Professor, The University of Hong Kong (2011); Visiting Professor, Geography and Urban Studies, University of Oregon (2010); Visiting Professor, The University of Hong Kong (2009); Visiting Professor, The University of Hong Kong (2002); Visiting Professor, The University of Hong Kong (1992); Member, Advisory Board, Department of Revenue, Georgia (1982-1986); Visiting Professor, United States Military Academy Preparatory School (1984) **Military Service:** Commander, United States Naval Reserve (1962-1966); With, United States Navy (1962-1966) **Creative Works:** Member, Editorial Advisory Board, "Eurasian Geography & Economics" (2013-Present); Asian Geographer, "Eurasian Geography & Economics" (2013-Present); Editorial Board Member, "Eurasian Geography & Economics" (2013-Present); Co-author, "China's Geography, Third Edition" (2016); Co-author, "China's Geography, Second Edition" (2011); Co-author, "China's Geography" (2007); Co-editor, "Eurasian Geography and Economics" (2005-2012); Author, "China: The Geography of Development and Modernization" (1983); Author: "East Asia: Geographical and Historical Approaches to Foreign Area Studies" (1983); Contributor, Articles, Professional Journals; Contributor, Reviews, Professional Journals; Contributor, Articles, Magazines; Contributor, Reviews, Magazines; Contributor, Textbook Chapters **Awards:** Outstanding Service Award, China Specialty Group, American Association of Geographers (2004); Research Grantee, National Science Foundation (1979-1982); Medal for Creative Research, University of Georgia Research Foundation (1981) **Membership:** Council, American Geographical Society (2001-Present); American Association of Geographers **Marquis Who's Who Honors:** Albert Nelson Marquis Lifetime Achievement Award (2017) **Why did you become involved in your profession or industry:** Dr. Pannell became involved in his profession after getting started in undergraduate school. He had a strong interest in Mainland China and pursued that as an undergraduate student. He then served in the U.S. Navy and was on the China desk, so he has been working on China for his whole life. It is Dr. Pannell's passion and obsession. **Business Address:** Department of Geography, University of Georgia, Athens, GA, 30602 **Shipping Address:** 520 W Cloverhurst Ave., Athens, GA, 30606

Jean William Pape

Title: Professor of Medicine, Director **Industry:** Engineering **Company Name:** Center for Global Health, Weill Cornell Medicine, Cornell University, GHESKIO **Date of Birth:** 06/24/1946 **Place of Birth:** Port-au-Prince **Country of Origin:** Haiti **Parents:** William Pape; Marie (Laraque) Pape **Marital Status:** Married **Spouse Name:** Dominique Pape (3/30/1964) **Children:** Douglas; Clifford; Alain; Vincent **Education:** Rockefeller's Foundation Fellow in Infectious Diseases, New York Hospital-Cornell Medical Center (Now New York-Presbyterian/Weill Cornell Medical Center) (1978-1980); Resident, North Shore University Hospital, New York (1976-1978); Intern, Cornell University Affiliated Hospitals (1975-1978); Resident, Cornell University Affiliated Hospitals (1975-1978); Intern, North Shore University Hospital, Northwell Health, New York, NY (1975-1976); MD, Weill Cornell Medicine, Cornell University (1975); BS, Columbia University (1971) **Certifications:** Licensed to Practice Medicine, Haiti (1980); Licensed to Practice Medicine, State of New York (1977) **Career:** Howard and Carol Holzman Professor of Clinical Medicine, Division for Infectious Diseases, Center for Global Health, Weill Cornell Medicine, Cornell University (2014-Present); Professor of Medicine, Division of International Medicine & Infectious Diseases, Weill Cornell Medicine, Cornell University (1995-Present); Professor of Medicine, State University Hospital School of Medicine, Port-au-Prince, Haiti (1983-Present); Associate Professor of Medicine, Division of International Medicine & Infectious Diseases, Weill Cornell Medicine, Cornell University (1989-1994); Assistant Professor of Medicine, Division of International Medicine & Infectious Diseases, Weill Cornell Medicine, Cornell University (1983-1989); Instructor in Medicine, Division of International Medicine & Infectious Diseases, Weill Cornell Medicine, Cornell University (1980-1983) **Career Related:** Founder, Master's Public Health Program, Weill Cornell Medicine, Cornell University (2009-Present); Founder, Nurse Practitioner Program, Weill Cornell Medicine, Cornell University (2009-Present); Lecturer, More than 30 Presentations (2006-Present); Founder, Groupe Haitien d'Etude du Sarcome de Kaposi et des Infections Opportunistes (GHESKIO) (1982) **Civic:** Member, National Task Force Against Cholera, Ministry of Heath, Haiti (2017-Present); Member, Expert Panel, UNAIDS, United Nations (2014-Present); Board Member, Doctoral College of Haiti (2013-Present); Member, National Red Cross Blood Bank Commission, Port-au-Prince, Haiti (1989-Present) **Creative Works:** Reviewer, AIDS (1988-Present) **Awards:** Honorary ScD, State University of New York (2018); Recipient, Joan and Sanford I. Weill Exemplary Achievement Award, Weill Cornell Medical College (2018); Recipient, National AIDS Program of Haiti Award for Significant Contribution to the Fight Against HIV/AIDS (2017); Recipient, National AIDS Program of Haiti Award for significant contribution to the fight against HIV/AIDS (2017); Recipient, 30-Year Recognition Award, International Association of Providers of AIDS Care (2016); Named, Distinguished Global Faculty Member, University of Toledo, College of Medicine & Life Sciences (2016); Honoree, Distinguished Faculty Member, The University of Toledo and the College of Medicine and Life Sciences (2016); Honneur et Mérite, Grade Commandeur, Haitian Government, United Nations Secretary-General Kofi A. Annan (2015); Named, Distinguished Global Faculty Member, College of Medicine and Life Sciences, University of Toledo (2015); Featured Listee, 12 Personalities in Haiti, Le Nouvelliste (2015); Recipient, Rotary Club Award, Rotary International, Port-au-Prince, Haiti (2015); Recipient, Haiti Cherie Award, New York, NY (2015); Honneur et Mérite, Grade Commandeur, President Martelly, Port-au-Prince, Haiti (2014); Recipient, Kochon Award for Tuberculosis, WHO (2014); Recipient, Prix, Fondation Lucienne Deschamps (2014); Leadership Award, GRAHN-Monde (2012); Overseas Special Recognition Award, Haitian Medical Association (2012) **Membership:** Haut Conseil, Université Quisqueya (2017-Present); Chairman, National Immunization Technical Advisory Group (2017-Present); Co-Chairman, External Working Group of TB/HIV of the PEPFAR Scientific Advisory Board (2015-Present); Honorary Board Member, Institut des Sciences, des Technologies et des études Avancée d'Haiti (2015-Present); Technical Group on HIV/AIDS, Pan American Health Organization (2015-Present); Board Member, Institut Pasteur, France (2014-Present); Board Member, Mérieux Foundation (2014-Present); Scientific Committee, French Conference On AIDS (2013-Present); Scientific Committee, HIV in the Americas (2013-Present); Executive Committee, Adult AIDS Clinical Trials Group (2013-Present); Board Member, MACAIDS (2012-Present); Honorary Life Member, Medical Mission Hall of Fame (2009-Present); Board Member, Gabriel Network, Mérieux Foundation (2008-Present) **Marquis Who's Who Honors:** Albert Nelson Marquis Lifetime Achievement Award (2017) **Religion:** Catholic **Business Address:** 402 E 67th St, 402 E. 67th St., New York, NY, 10065 **Shipping Address:** 139 St Andrews Ln, Glen Cove, NY, 11542 **Website:** http://vivo.med.cornell.edu/display/cwid-jwp2001

Alceste Thetis Pappas, PhD

Title: Management Consultant **Industry:** Consulting **Company Name:** Pappas Consulting Group Inc. **Date of Birth:** 05/05/1945 **Place of Birth:** Dix Hills **State:** NY **Parents:** Costas Ernest Pappas; Thetis (Hero) Pappas **Marital Status:** Married **Spouse Name:** Sylvan V. Endich (9/13/1987) **Education:** PhD, University of California, Berkeley, CA (1978); EdM, Harvard University (1969); Bachelor of Arts, University of California, Berkeley, CA (1967) **Certifications:** Certified Guidance Counselor, State of Massachusetts; Certified Secondary School Teacher, State of Massachusetts **Career:** President, Chief Executive Officer, Pappas Consultant Group, Inc., Palm Beach Gardens, FL (1992-Present); Partner in Charge of Education, Other Institutions, KPMG, New York, NY (1984-1993); Senior Manager, Peat, Marwick, Mitchell & Co., New York, NY (1982-1984); Senior Consultant Manager, Peat, Marwick, Mitchell & Co., New York, NY (1980-1982); Senior Consultant Manager, Peat, Marwick, Mitchell & Co., New York, NY (1979-1980); Director, Housing and Childcare, University of California, Berkeley (1973-1979); Director, Residential Programs, University of California, Berkeley (1971-1973); Director, Students, Young Alumni Affairs, California Alumni Association, Berkeley (1969-1971) **Career Related:** Speaker in field **Civic:** Member, Advisory Board, Graduate School Education, University of California, Berkeley, CA (2005-Present); Board of Directors, National Council for Research on Women (1996-1998); Trustee, University of California Foundation (1993-1999); Trustee, Clark University (1993-1995); Catalyst, Member Executive Committee YWCA, New York City, NY (1988-1990); Board of Directors, New York Chiropractic College (1986-1988); Committee on Economic Development (1986-1988); Board of Directors, Member, Executive Committee, YWCA, New York City, NY (1985-1990); Greek Orthodox Archdiocese Council, New York City, NY (1985-1989); Board of Overseers, Regents College (1986-1989); Seabury Western Theological Seminary, Evanston, IL (1983-1989); Board of Directors, Vice Chairman, St. Basil Academy (1983-1987); Board of Directors, Member, Financial Committee, Hellenic College and Holy Cross School of Theology, Brookline, MA (1983-1987); Member, Merola Opera Board, San Francisco, CA (1978-1980); Member, California Alumni Council (1976-1979); Chairperson, Capital Campaign Committee, University of California, Berkeley, CA; Executive Vice President, Executive Council, College of Letters and Science, University of California, Berkeley, CA; Active, Development and Fundraising, Maltz Jupiter Theatre, FL **Creative Works:** Author, "Reengineering Your Non-Profit Organization: A Guide to Strategic Transformation" (1996); Contributor, Articles to Professional Journals; Author, Monographs **Awards:** Recipient, Award, National Management Association (1997); Named, Member, Academy of Women Achievers, YWCA, New York, NY (1984) **Membership:** Planning Committee, Middle States Association of Colleges and Schools (1988-1989); Board of Directors, Financial Committee, Middle States Association of Colleges and Schools (1984-1989); Mortar Board; Order of the Kentucky Colonels; Pi Lambda Theta; Prytanean Women's Honor Society **Marquis Who's Who Honors:** Albert Nelson Marquis Lifetime Achievement Award (2017) **Hobbies:** Travel; Photography; Gourmet cooking **Shipping Address:** 117 Island Cove Way, Palm Beach Gardens, FL, 33418

Linda Lee Paralez, PhD

Title: President, CEO **Industry:** Consulting **Company Name:** Demarche Consulting Group **Date of Birth:** 10/29/1955 **Place of Birth:** Raton **State/Country of Origin:** NM **Education:** MBA, Minor in Economics, Century University, Beverly Hills, CA (1987); BBA, Century University, Beverly Hills, CA (1984); Coursework, West Texas State University (1975-1977); AS, Amarillo College (1975); PhD in Business Administration, Century University, Beverly Hills, CA **Career:** President, Treefarm Center Inc. (1999-Present); Professor of Technology Management, University of Phoenix, Murray, UT (1995-1996); President, Rose Enterprises, Inc. (1986-1999); Drafting Supervisor, Engineering Services, Supervisor, Director of Speakers Bureau, Thunder Basin Coal Company, Atlantic Richfield Company, Wright, WY (1977-1986); Senior Drafter, Exploration Division, Amarillo Oil Company (1976-1977); Drafter, Natural Gas Division, Pioneer Corporation, Amarillo, TX (1975-1976); Teaching Assistant, Amarillo College, Amarillo, TX (1974-1975); Chief Executive Officer, REZ Global, Poulsbo, WA; Owner, Treefarm Center Consultant, Poulsbo, WA; President, Treefarm Center Consultant, Poulsbo, WA; Chief Executive Officer, Treefarm Center Consultant, Poulsbo, WA; President, CEO Demarche Consulting Group, Seattle, WA **Career Related:** Consultant, Process Redesign Benchmarking Group, City of Seattle (1995-Present); Research Benchmarking Specialist, Western Regional Water Utilities Benchmarking Group (1996-1999); Research Specialist, Child Abuse Prevention Center (1994-1999); Manager, Total Quality Management, Space Operations Center (1990-1998); Design Specialist, Space Operations (1989-1990); Technical Writer, Publishing Consultant, Thiokol Corporation, Brigham City, UT (1987-1989); Consultant, State of Wyoming Office on Family Violence and Sexual Assault, Cheyenne, WY (1986-1989); Technical Writer, Eaton Corporation, Riverton, WY (1986-1988); Diamond L. Industries, Inc., Gillette, WY (1986-1988); Adjunct Professor, Weber State University, Ogden, UT; Consultant, Organizational Effectiveness and Quality Management Principles, Consultant Incident Investigation Team, NASA Space Shuttle, Solid Rocket Booster Program, Huntsville, AL; Consultant, Process Improvement, Puget Power, Seattle, WA; Public Service Company of Colorado; W.R. White Consultant, Process Design, Microsoft Corporation; Seattle Management Consultant, Consulting Director, Western Regional Water Utilities; CEO, Demarche Consulting Group **Civic:** Volunteer, Advisory Committee, NASA Young Astronauts Program (1991-Present); Board of Directors, Campbell County Drafting Advisory Council (1984-1985); Secretary, Board of Directors, Executive Committee, American Institute of Design and Drafting, (1984-1985); Technology Publication Chairperson (1984-1985); Volunteer Educator, Data Specialist, Child Abuse Prevention Council, Ogden, UT; Executive Board Member, West Sound Technology Council; State of Washington Ferry Advisory Council; The Shaken Baby Syndrome Board **Creative Works:** Contributing Author, "The Changing Water Utility" (1999); Author, "Gift of Wings" (1980); Author, "God Was Here, But He Left Early" (1976); Columnist, "Wytech Digest"; Contributor, Numerous Articles, Professional Journals **Awards:** Most Outstanding Woman, Beta Sigma Phi (1981); Woman in the Industry Recognition, International Reprographics Association (1980); Most Outstanding Woman, Beta Sigma Phi (1980); Grand Prize Winner, "Energy" Painting, Wyoming Art Show (1976) **Membership:** Grant Proposal Writer, Ocean Research Education Society, Gloucester, MA (1984); American Association of University Women; National Association of Female Executives; National Organization of Women; American Society for Quality Control; American Productivity and Quality Council; American Legion Auxiliary; Society for Technical Communications; 4-H Club **Marquis Who's Who Honors:** Albert Nelson Marquis Lifetime Achievement Award (2017) **Business Address:** 600 1st Avenue, Seattle, WA, 98104 **Shipping Address:** 22259 Treefarm Lane NE, Poulsbo, WA, 98370 **Website:** http://www.demarcheconsulting.com

Roy H. Park Jr.

Title: Director, President, Chief Executive Officer **Industry:** Advertising & Marketing **Company Name:** Park Outdoor Advertising of New York Inc. **State:** NC **Parents:** Roy Hampton; Dorothy Goodwin (Dent) Park **Marital Status:** Married **Spouse Name:** Elizabeth P. Park **Children:** Elizabeth P. Fowler; Roy H. Park, III **Education:** MBA, Cornell University, Ithaca, NY (1963); BA in Journalism, The University of North Carolina at Chapel Hill (1961); Degree, Lawrenceville School (1956) **Career:** President, Chief Executive Officer, Director, Park Outdoor Advertising of New York Inc. (1984-Present); President, Chairman, Triad Foundation, Inc. (2003 - Present); Director, Senior Vice President, RHP Properties Inc. (1994-1996); Director, Senior Vice President, RHP Inc. (1994-1996); Chairman, Director, Outdoor Advertising Council of New York Inc. (1992-1995); President, Outdoor Advertising Council of New York Inc. (1986-1991); Vice President, General Manager, Park Outdoor Advertising (1981-1984); Managing Director, Agricultural Research Advertising Agency, Ithaca (1976-1981); Managing Editor, Park Communications Newsletter, Ithaca, (1976-1981); Vice President of Advertising and Promotion, Park Broadcasting Inc., Ithaca (1976-1981); Vice President, Park Outdoor Advertising, Ithaca (1971-1975); Vice President, Marketing and Account Management, Kincaid Advertising Agency Division, First Union National Bank Corp., Charlotte, NC (1970-1971); Senior Accountant Executive, Review Board Executive, Advertising Planning Director, J. Walter Thompson Co., New York City and Miami (1963-1970) **Career Related:** Member, Region I Planning Board, Institute for Outdoor Advertising (1984-1986) **Civic:** Leadership Council, Cornell SC Johnson College of Business (2017); Trustees, Boca Grande Health Clinic Foundation, Inc. (2008-Present); Trustee Emeritus, Presidential Councillor, Cornell University (2007-Present); Member, Advisory Council, Johnson Graduate School of Management (1996-Present); Director, Boyce Thompson Institute for Plant Research Inc. (1995-Present); Board of Advisors, University of North Carolina School of Media and Journalism (1994-Present); Trustee, Cornell University (1999-2007); Trustee, Vice President, Park Foundation Inc. (1995-2002); Founding Member, Alumni Executive Committee, Cornell University (1984-1988); Director of Public Relations, Tompkins County Conference and Tourist Council (1976); Chairman, Public Relations Committee, United Way of Tompkins County (1973-1974); Board Chairman, Publicity Director, Junior Olympics (1973-1974); Director of Public Relations, United Fund, Raleigh, NC (1971) **Creative Works:** Author, "Sons In The Shadow: Surviving in the Family Business as an SOB (Son of the Boss)" (2016) **Awards:** Order of the Long Leaf Pine, conferred by the Governor of North Carolina (2017); Inductee, North Carolina Media and Journalism Hall of Fame (2017); William Richardson Davie Award, University of North Carolina (2015); Inductee, North Carolina Advertising Hall of Fame (2011), Distinguished Alumnus Award, University of North Carolina (2005); Inductee, Johnson Hall of Honor, Johnson Graduate School of Management (2004); Project of the Year Award, Tompkins County Chamber of Commerce **Membership:** Public Relations Council, Chairman, Legislative Action Committee, Acting Chairman, Nominating Committee, Tompkins County Chamber of Commerce (1976); Chairman, Sign Ordinance Committee, Tompkins County Chamber of Commerce (1975-1976); Ithaca Country Club; Boca Bay Pass Club; Gasparilla Inn and Club **Shipping Address:** 11 Ascot Place, Ithaca, NY, 14850

Ronald Dean Parker

Title: Senior Environmental Engineer **Industry:** Engineering **Company Name:** United States Environmental Protection Agency **Date of Birth:** 02/07/1948 **Place of Birth:** Waterloo **State:** IA **Parents:** Lyle Robert Parker; Ruth Eitemiller Parker **Marital Status:** Married **Spouse Name:** Renee Marie Smith Parker (5/20/1995) **Children:** Benjamin William Nitti; Priya Narayan-Parker; Lauren Nadine Nitti **Education:** PhD in Watershed Hydrology, University of Arizona, Tucson, AZ (1991); MCE in Civil & Environmental Engineering, Iowa State University, Ames, IA (1978); BS in Biology, Iowa State University, Ames, IA (1971); BS in Engineering Operations, Iowa State University, Ames, IA (1971) **Career:** Senior Environmental Engineer, United States Environmental Protection Agency, Washington, DC (2002-Present); Environmental Engineer, FAO, Rome, Italy (2001-2002); Environmental Engineer, United States Environmental Protection Agency, Washington, DC (1991-2002); Environmental Engineer, WHO, United Nations, Jakarta, Indonesia (1985-1986); Environmental Engineer, WHO, United Nations, Male, Maldives (1983-1985); Environmental Engineer, Trans-Century Resources, Gaborone, Botswana (1980-1982); Environmental Engineer, Peace Corps, Yaounde, Cameroon (1972-1974) **Career Related:** Trainer in Ministries of Environment, Agriculture, and Health in Pesticide Risk Assessment Methods, Latin America, Asia, and Africa; Assistant in Drought Recovery, Southern African Governments, U.S. Office of Foreign Disaster Assistance **Civic:** Coach, Youth Sports Teams, Vienna, VA; Co-Director, Marriage Mentoring Program, McLean Bible Church, Vienna, VA **Creative Works:** Speaker, "Exploring Approaches to Pesticide Aquatic Ecological Exposure Assessment: Issues in Evaluating Risk Across the National Landscape," American Chemical Society (2011); Speaker, "Overview of Activities in Aquatic Exposure Modeling in the United States Environmental Protection Agency Office of Pesticide Programs, Environmental Fate and Effects Division," American Chemical Society Symposium (2011); Co-Author, "Evaluation of Three Watershed-Scale Pesticide Environmental Transport and Fate Models," Journal of the American Water Resources Association (2007); Author, "Development of Simplified Methods and Tools for Ecological Risk Assessment of Pesticides," Proceedings: International Workshop on Crop Protection Chemistry in Latin America: Harmonized Approaches for Environmental Assessment and Regulation, International Union of Pure and Applied Chemistry Conference, San Jose, Costa Rica (2005); Co-Author, "FAO Simplified Pesticide Ecological Risk Assessment Methodology," Harmonization of Data Requirements and Evaluation: Environmental Chemistry, Toxicology/Ecotoxicology, Risk Assessment, and Regulation, International Union of Pure and Applied Chemistry (2004); Author, "Use of EXPRESS Pesticide Simulation Shell for Pesticide Aquatic Exposure Assessment," Universita Cattolica del Sacro Cuore, Piacenza, Italy (2002); Author, "Mathematical Modeling of Aquatic Pesticide Exposure," Simposio De Toxicologia, Agricultura E Preservacao Da Qualidade Da Aqua, Ribeirao Preto, Sao Paolo, Brazil (1999); Co-Author, "Development of GENEEC for Estimation of Pesticide Exposure," Society of Environmental Toxicology and Chemistry (1996); Co-Author, "GENEEC: A Screening Model for Pesticide Environmental Exposure Assessment," Water Quality Modeling Proceedings, American Society of Agricultural Engineers (1995); Author, "Computer Models for Pesticide Risk Assessment: An International Progress Report - United States Environmental Protection Agency Perspective," International Union of Pure and Applied Chemistry (1994); Co-Author, "Recommendations for Developing Risk Mitigation Strategies for High Risk Pesticides"; Contributor, International Articles to Professional Journals **Awards:** Silver Medal, U.S. Environmental Protection Agency; Multiple Bronze Medals, U.S. Environmental Protection Agency; Peer Award for Excellence, U.S. Environmental Protection Agency **Membership:** American Chemical Society; Division of Chemistry & Environment, International Union of Pure and Applied Chemistry; Chi Epsilon, The Civil Engineering Honorary Society **Marquis Who's Who Honors:** Albert Nelson Marquis Lifetime Achievement Award (2017) **Hobbies:** Traveling; Hitchhiking across the Sahara desert through a dozen countries in western and northern Africa **Business Address:** 1200 Pennsylvania Avenue NW, Washington, DC, 20460 **Shipping Address:** 3925 Stoney Point Place, Indian Head, MD, 20640

John E. Parks

Title: Chief of Party **Industry:** Environmental Services **Company Name:** Tetra Tech **State:** HI **Marital Status:** Married **Children:** Two Sons **Education:** Master's Degree in Marine Affairs and Policy, Rosenstiel School of Marine and Atmospheric Science, University of Miami (1995); Bachelor's Degree in Behavioral Science and Marine Biology, University of Miami (1992) **Certifications:** Certified in Wilderness and Remote First Aid, American National Red Cross (2004-Present); Certified in Automated External Defibrillators, American National Red Cross (1998-Present); Certified in Adult First Aid, American National Red Cross (1998-Present); Certified in Cardiopulmonary Resuscitation (1998-Present); Certified Open Water Diver, National Association of Underwater Instructors (1990-Present) **Career:** Founder, Exo Scientific LLC (2017-Present); Founder, Executive Member, Marine Management Solutions LLC, Honolulu, HI (2010-Present); Senior Advisor, The Nature Conservancy, Honolulu, HI (2008-2010); Federal Officer, National Oceanic and Atmospheric Administration, Honolulu, HI (2004-2008); Marine Research Associate, Community Conservation Network, Honolulu, HI (2002-2004); Research Associate, World Resources Institute, Washington, DC (1999-2002); Program Officer, World Wildlife Fund, Washington, DC (1995-1999); Project Assistant, World Wide Fund for Nature, Western Province, Solomon Islands (1994-1995) **Career Related:** Fellowship, Environmental Leadership Program (2002-2004); Fellowship, Rosenstiel School of Marine and Atmospheric Science, University of Miami (1993-1995); Presenter in Field **Awards:** Award, Marine Policy (2016); Invited Expeditionary Member, Papahanaumokuakea Marine National Monument, Holo i Moana Research Cruise, National Oceanic and Atmospheric Administration (2010); Official Delegate, United States of America, APEC Ocean and Fisheries Working Group (2000); World of Difference Award, World Wildlife Fund (1998); Award of Academic Excellence, Rosenstiel School of Marine and Atmospheric Science, University of Miami (1995); Outstanding Employee Award for Significant Contributions Toward World Wildlife Fund's Mission, Board of Directors of World Wildlife Fund **Membership:** American Association for the Advancement of Science; Society for Conservation Biology; Pacific Science Association; Chamber of Commerce in Hawaii; International Union for Conservation of Nature's World Commission on Protected Areas **Marquis Who's Who Honors:** Albert Nelson Marquis Lifetime Achievement Award (2017) **Shipping Address:** 2047 Wilhelmina Rise, Honolulu, HI, 96816 **Website:** www.seafdec-oceanspartnership.org

Francis William Parnell Jr.

Title: Chairman & C.E.O. **Industry:** Pharmaceuticals **Company Name:** Parnell Pharmaceuticals, Inc. **Date of Birth:** 05/22/1940 **Place of Birth:** Woonsocket **State:** RI **Parents:** Francis W. Parnell; Dorothy V. (Lalor) Parnell **Marital Status:** Married **Spouse Name:** Diana DeAngelis, M.D. (2/27/1965) **Children:** Cheryl Lynn; John Francis; Kathleen Diana; Alison Anne; Thomas William **Education:** Resident in Otolaryngology, University of Wisconsin Hospitals (1967-1970); Resident in General Surgery, University of Wisconsin Hospitals (1966-1967); Intern, University of Wisconsin Hospitals (1965-1966); MD, Georgetown University (1965); AB, Clark University (1961) **Certifications:** Diplomate, National Board of Medical Examiners; Diplomate, American Board of Otolaryngology **Career:** Chairman, San Rafael, California (1982-Present); President, San Rafael, California (1982-2010); Chief Executive Officer, Parnell Pharmaceuticals, Inc., San Rafael, California (1982-Present); Private Practice in Otolaryngology, Greenbrae, California (1978-2001); Private Practice in Otolaryngology, San Rafael, California (1972-1975) **Career Related:** Consultant, Corporate Medical Affairs (1978-1982); Corporate Medical Director Becton, Dickinson & Company, Rutherford, New Jersey (1976-1978); Assistant Clinical Professor, University of California San Francisco (1975-1976); Clinical Instructor, University of California San Francisco (1972-1975); Alternate Delegate, United States Delegation, 27th World Health Assembly, WHO, Geneva, Switzerland (1974) **Civic:** President, College Marin Foundation (2006-2010); Director, College Marin Foundation (2004-2010); President, Governing Board, Marin Community College District (1999-2000, 2002-2003); Member, Governing Board, Marin Community College District (1995-2003); Board of Directors, Marin Coalition (1980-2001); Trustee, Ross School District (1981-1989); Candidate, California State Assembly (1988) **Military Service:** Lieutenant Colonel, Medical Corps, U.S. Army Reserve (1986-1993); Major, Medical Corps, U.S. Army (1970-1972) **Creative Works:** Contributor, Articles, Professional Journals; Six Patents **Membership:** House of Delegates, California Medical Association (1995-2005); Board of Governors, American College of Surgeons (1988-1994); Fellow, American College of Surgeons; American Academy of Otolaryngology-Head and Neck Surgery; AMA; San Francisco Marin Medical Society **Marquis Who's Who Honors:** Albert Nelson Marquis Lifetime Achievement Award (2017) **Why did you become involved in your profession or industry:** He always wanted to be a doctor and be in medicine. **What do you consider to be the highlight of your career:** While working in practice, Dr. Parnell was asked to attend the 27th conference on behalf of the United States in Geneva. He was introduced to many new faces in public health. He saw the relationship between business, diplomacy and medicine and began to see the needs of people who had issues that could be addressed by products, so he began product development, including products to solve the issue of extremely dry mouth caused by medications, cancer and aging. **Shipping Address:** 3070 Kerner Blvd., Ste A, Parnell Pharmaceuticals, Inc., San Rafael, CA, 94901 **Website:** parnellpharm.com

Frank R. Parth

Title: Chief Executive Officer **Industry:** Business Management/Business Services **Company Name:** Project Auditors LLC **Date of Birth:** 08/26/1949 **Place of Birth:** Eichendorf **Country of Origin:** Germany **Parents:** Frank Parth; Erna (Framelsberger) Parth **Marital Status:** Divorced **Spouse Name:** Jane Hoppe (1974, Divorced 1985) **Children:** Katherine; Frank **Education:** MBA, Drucker Institute (2000); MS in Systems Management, University of Southern California, Los Angeles, CA (1986); MS in Physics, University of Wyoming (1978); BS in Physics, Creighton University (1972) **Certifications:** PMP **Career:** Chief Executive Officer, Project Auditors LLC (2001-Present); President, Project Auditors LLC (2003-Present); Chief Technology Officer, E-commerce, Overstock Market (2000-2001); Director, System Engineering, Experian Information Solutions, Inc., Orange, CA (1995-1997); President, Intervolve, Mission Viejo, CA (1994-2004); Assistant Technology Director, Martin-Marietta Space Systems, Long Beach, CA (1981-1992); Design Engineer, Texas Instruments, Dallas, TX (1978-1981) **Career Related:** Faculty, Claremont Graduate University (2000-2004); Faculty, University of California, Irvine (1996-Present); Faculty, University of Southern California (1993-1997); Visiting Professor, University of Sharjah, United Arab Emirates; Speaker in Field; Director, Experian **Civic:** Board of Directors, Project Management Institute Educational Foundation (2016-Present); PMI Orange County (1996-Present); Board of Directors, Project Management Institute, Inc. (2010-2012); Vice President of Professional Development, PMI Orange County (2004); Vice President of Membership, PMI Orange County (2003); Constitutional Review Officer, Mensa International Limited (1993-2011); Board of Directors, Search and Rescue, Orange County, CA (1989-2002) **Creative Works:** Author, "Successful Strategy Implementation" (2018); Contributing Author, "Project Portfolio Management Strategies for Effective Organizational Operations" (2017); Contributing Author, "Project Management Body of Knowledge, 6th Edition" (2017); Author, "Successful Program Delivery Begins Long Before the Program Does," PMWorld Library (2016); Author, "The Effect of Organization Unwritten Rules on PMO Success," PMWorld Library (2015); Author, "Failures in Construction Due to Ineffective Project Management Information Systems," PMWorld Library (2014); Author, "Critical Decision Skills in Project Managers," Proceedings – 2013 EMEA Project Management Congress, PMI (2013); Contributing Author, "Business Driven PMO Success Stories" (2013); Project Lead, "Standard for Program Management, 2nd Edition" (2012); Contributing Author, "77 Deadly Sins of Project Management" (2011); Author, "Managing Scope in International Projects," Proceedings 2008 EMEA Project Management Congress, PMI (2008); Author, "Process Improvement Projects that Will Change Your Company," Proceedings of PMI's Europe/Africa/ Middle East (EMEA) Congress (2006); Co-Author, "Introduction to IT Project Management" (2006); Author, "Managing Multiple Projects," Projects and Profits (2005); Author, "Systems Engineering in An Outsourcing Environment," Proceedings – 2004 International Systems Engineering Conference, International Council on Systems Engineering (2004); Author, "Managing IT Projects in a Multi-tasking Environment," Proceedings – 2004 European Project Management Convention, PMI (2004); Author, "The Largest Peoplesoft Implementation Ever – Implications," Proceedings – 2004 International Systems Engineering Conference, International Council on Systems Engineering (2004); Interviewed, Institute of Chartered Financial Accountants of India, Projects and Profits (2003); Author, "Trends in Software Development," Projects and Profits (2003); Author, "Categorization of Small Projects," Projects and Profilts (2003); Author, "Implementing a Program Management Office at Toyota Financial Services," Proceedings – International Conference on Project Management, ProMAC (2002); Author, "The Roles of The User in Project Planning an ERP Implementation," PM Network (2003) Author, "Trends in Software Development – A Project Management Perspective," United Nations Economic & Social Commission for Western Asia (1999); Author, "Year 2000 Project Management," United Nations Economic & Social Commission for Western Asia (1999); Author, "The Need for Project Management in Solving Y2K Problems," Y2K Advisor (1999); Author, "Business Continuity Planning," PM Network (1999); Author, "Categorization of Small Projects," Proceedings: 1998 International Project Management Symposium (1998) **Awards:** Distinguished Contribution Award, Project Management Institute, Inc. (2009); Speaker's Award, PMI Orange County (1998); International Service Award, Mensa International (2000) **Membership:** Fellow, PMI Orange County; International Council on Systems Engineering; President, Orange County Chapter, Mensa International Limited; Association for the Advancement of Cost Engineering **Business Address:** P.O. Box 80688, Rancho Santa Margarita, CA, 92688 **Shipping Address:** 21901 Palanca, Mission Viejo, CA, 92692 **Website:** http://www.projectauditors.com/

Saundra Paschal

Title: Mathematics Teacher **Industry:** Education/Educational Services **Company Name:** San Angelo Independent School District **Education:** BS in Mathematics, Minor in Biology, Angelo State University (1980) **Career:** Teacher, Honors Algebra II and Precalculus, Lake View High School, San Angelo Independent School District **Career Related:** Coach, Mathematics Team, Lake View High School; Coordinator, University Interscholastic League, Lake View High School **Civic:** Local Church; Local Charitable Organizations **Creative Works:** Advisor, Books for Publication **Awards:** Listee, Top 12 Educators of the Year Calendar, IAOTP Top Professional in Education (2017); Teacher of the Year Award (2014); VIP of the Year Award (2011-2012); Teacher of the Year Award (2000) **Membership:** Curriculum Writing Team, San Angelo Independent School District; Texas Math and Science Coaches Association; Association for Supervision and Curriculum Development **Marquis Who's Who Honors:** Albert Nelson Marquis Lifetime Achievement Award (2017); Distinguished Humanitarian (2017) **To what do you attribute your success:** Ms. Paschal attributes her success to her ability to teach students and the support she has received from her high school teachers. **Why did you become involved in your profession or industry:** Ms. Paschal became involved in her profession after starting her career as a teacher's aide. **What do you consider to be the highlight of your career:** A highlight of Ms. Paschal's career is that her former students are now teaching alongside her at the school they attended. In 2008, the football coach and his staff were all her former students. **Where will you be in five years:** In five years, Ms. Paschal intends to continue teaching at the school, sharing her knowledge with students and mentoring other teachers. **Hobbies:** Playing the organ at church; Photographing high school sports teams and natural landscapes; Reading **Business Address:** 900 E 43rd St, San Angelo, TX, 76903 **Shipping Address:** 900 E 43rd St, Lake View High School, San Angelo, TX, 76903

Jeanette Passty

Title: Literature and Language Professor **Industry:** Education/Educational Services **Company Name:** St. Philip's College **Date of Birth:** 01/19/1947 **Place of Birth:** Los Angeles **State:** CA **Parents:** Walter Isaac Nyda; Mollie Sarah Nyda **Marital Status:** Married **Spouse Name:** Gregory Bohdan Passty (6/18/1976) **Children:** Benjamin; Jocelyn **Education:** PhD, University of Southern California (1982); MA, University of Southern California (1974); BA, UCLA (1968); AA, L.A. Valley College (1966) **Certifications:** Certified Community College Instructor, State of California **Career:** Associate Professor, St. Philip's College, San Antonio, TX (1992-Present); Assistant Professor, St. Philip's College (1988-1992); Visiting Assistant Professor and Adjunct Associate Professor, Texas Lutheran University, Seguin, TX (1983, 1985-1987); Lecturer, English Department, University of Texas, Austin (1983-1985); Visiting Scholar, English Department, Texas State University, San Marcos (1982-1983); Teaching Assistant, Lecturer and Associate Director, Freshman English Program, University of Southern California (1971-1978) **Career Related:** Manuscript Reviewer, Fairleigh Dickinson University Press (1991-Present); Lecturer, University of California, Berkeley (2012); College English Consultant, Scholar Strategies Korean Program (2008-2011); Editorial Consultant, CONNECTIONS: Online Distance Learning Faculty Forum (2002-2010); Humanities Book Reviewer, CHOICE (1985-1986); Lecturer, University of London; Lecturer, UCLA; Lecturer, University of Texas, Austin; Lecturer, Western Michigan University; Lecturer, University of Louisville; Lecturer, Salisbury State University; Lecturer, Morehead State University; Lecturer, Texas Tech University; Lecturer, University of Wales, Bangor **Civic:** Organizer, International Conference on the Holocaust, San Antonio (2000); Member, National Abortion Rights Action League; Audubon Society; Environment Texas; Environmental Defense Fund; Greenpeace; Handgun Control; The Nature Conservancy; National Organization of Women; Sierra Club; World Wildlife Fund; Member, Gilbert & Sullivan Society; Austin Opera; Zach Scott Theatre **Creative Works:** Author, "Conquering Diabetes" (2012); Author, "The Music of the Spheres" (2011); Author, "Hard Times and Great Expectations" (2010); Author, "Creating the Spark" (2009); Author, "Bringing Denis Home: The Hero from Hope, Kansas" (2001); Guest, "Roadside" (2000); Guest, Channel 12 Morehead, KY (1998); Guest, CNN (1998); Author, "The Lion Tells Her Story: A Biography of the Honorable N.P. Brooks Hinton" (1998); Annotator, "Alice Crawford's Paradise Pursued" (1995); Guest, Station KENS-TV (1992); Guest, Station KSPL Radio (1989); Author, "Eros and Androgyny: The Legacy of Rose Macaulay" (1988); Contributor, Articles, Various Encyclopedia, Professional and Literary Journals; Contributor, Book Chapters **Awards:** Recipient, Albert Nelson Marquis Lifetime Achievement Award (2017); P.I., William C. Davis Biography Project, (2016); Nominee, Minnie Stevens Piper Professor (2012); Inductee, Alamo Colleges Women's Hall of Fame (2009); Recipient, St. Philip's College Teaching Excellence Award (2003-2004); Recipient, NISOD International Conference on Teaching and Leadership Excellence Award (2003); Recipient, Katherine Anne Porter Literature Prize (1999); Recipient, Women Honoring Women Award, American Association of Women in Community Colleges (1997); Recipient, Letters of Appreciation, HRH Princess Margaret (1989-1990); Recipient, Outstanding Academic Book Award, American Library Association (1989); Recipient, Letters of Appreciation, Lord Bonham-Carter (1987); Recipient, Elizabeth K. Pleasants Teaching Award, University of Southern California (1974) **Membership:** American Association of University Women; Modern Language Association; NCTE; Texas College English Association; South Central Society 18th Century Studies; Victorian Studies Institute; Virginia Woolf Society; HistoryMakers **Marquis Who's Who Honors:** Albert Nelson Marquis Lifetime Achievement Award (2017) **Hobbies:** Tae Kwon Do; Traveling **Shipping Address:** 2028 Ramona Cir, San Marcos, TX, 78666-2224

Dorothy Pathak

Title: Epidemiologist **Industry:** Health, Wellness and Fitness **Company Name:** Michigan State University **Date of Birth:** 11/26/1947 **Place of Birth:** Dlugosiodlo **Country of Origin:** Warsaw, Poland **Parents:** Henryk M. Rybaczyk; Anna Bobowska Rybaczyk **Marital Status:** Married (12/6/1969) **Spouse Name:** Pramod K. Pathak **Children:** Bogdan A.; Leszek A.; Anna D. **Education:** PhD, University of New Mexico (1975); MS, Harvard School of Public Health (1983) **Career:** Professor, Michigan State University, E. Lansing (1998-Present); Visiting Scholar, Harvard School of Public Health, Boston, MA (2001-2002); Associate Professor, Michigan State University, East Lansing (1995-1998); Visiting Scholar, Stanford University, California (1988); Associate Professor, University of New Mexico, Albuquerque, NM (1986-1994); Visiting Assistant Professor, Harvard Medical School, Boston, MA (1982-1983); Assistant Professor, University of New Mexico, Albuquerque, NM (1975-1986) **Civic:** Zdrowie Plus Inc.; NFP-Breast Cancer Survivors Club, Chicago, IL **Creative Works:** Contributor, "Cancer Causes and Control"; Contributor, American Journal of Epidemiology, International Journal of Cancer **Awards:** Grantee, Breast Cancer, Gene-Diet Interactions in Polish Women, National Cancer Institute (2002-Present); Breast Cancer in Women of Polish Ancestry, National Cancer Institute (1997-Present); Improved Follow-up of Breast Abnormalities through Comprehensive Breast Care in Women 40 Years and Older, Department of Defense (1998-2001) **Membership:** American Statistical Association; Society for Epidemiologic Research **Marquis Who's Who Honors:** Albert Nelson Marquis Lifetime Achievement Award (2017) **Shipping Address:** 3947 Belding Court, Okemos, MI, 48864 **Website:** http://www.epi.msu.edu/zdrowieplus

Mark W. Patnode

Title: Artist, Teaching Artist **Industry:** Fine Art **Date of Birth:** 04/29/1956 **Parents:** Edward M. Patnode; Arlene D. (Bull) Smith Patnode **Marital Status:** Divorced **Spouse Name:** Judith R. Abrams (6/21/1980, Divorced) **Children:** Rebekah; Benjamin **Education:** BFA, School of Art and Design, Purchase College State University of New York (1978) **Certifications:** Certified Arts in Education Teaching Artist, State of Connecticut **Career:** Graphic Designer, Sonalysts, Inc., Waterford, CT (1986-1997); Graphic Designer, Illustrator, Sonalysts, Inc., Waterford, CT (1984-1986); Analyst, Senior Graphic Designer, Sonalysts, Inc., Waterford, CT (Retired) **Career Related:** Master Teaching Artist, Connecticut Commission on Culture and Tourism; Adjunct Professor, Mitchell College, New London, CT **Creative Works:** Author, "Cultivating Illusions" (2017); Solo Exhibition, Reflecting Illuminations: Israel, Selected Works, "Then & Now," Norwich Arts Center Gallery, Norwich, CT (2016); Group Exhibition, New England Landscape Invitational, Lyme Art Association (2016); Group Exhibition, "Celebrating Lyme's Beauty: Paintings of Hamburg Bridge District," Lyme Art Association, Lyme, CT (2016); Group Exhibition, "Color and Light," Hygienic Art, Inc., New London, CT (2016); Group Exhibition, "Meadow Light," Slater Memorial Museum, Norwich, CT (2016); Group Exhibition, Annual Summer Members Exhibition, Salmagundi Club, New York, NY (2015); Artist, Catalog Cover Annual Summer Members Exhibition, Salmagundi Club, New York, NY (2015); Group Exhibition, Tenth Crossing Annual Juried Exhibition, Hygienic Art, Inc., New London, CT (2015); Group Exhibition, Landscape Exhibit, Salmagundi Club, New York, NY (2015); Group Exhibition, Urban Exhibit, Salmagundi Club, New York, NY (2015); Group Exhibition, Home Exhibition, Mystic Museum of Art, Mystic, CT (2015); Group Exhibition, New Members Show, Salmagundi Club, New York, NY (2015); Freedom Trail Panelist, Amistad (2015); Presenter, "Inventory: It's Your Story," Artists Academy at Hygienic Art (2015); Juror, 104th Annual Exhibition, Connecticut Academy of Fine Arts (2015); Contributor, Article, INK Magazine, Ink Publishing, LLC (2015) **Awards:** Recipient, Silver Rose, Lyubomir Levchev (2005-Present); Recipient, Third Place Prize, Juried Invitational, Ninth Crossing Annual Juried Exhibition, Hygienic Art, Inc., New London, CT (2014); Named, Best in Show, Group Exhibition, Slater Memorial Museum, Norwich, CT (2013); Recipient, Honorable Mention, Group Exhibition, "Elected Artists," Mystic Museum of Art, Mystic, CT (2012); Recipient, Honorable Mention, Group Exhibition, Juried Invitational, The Sixth Crossing Annual Juried Exhibition (2011); Recipent, Grant, State of Connecticut Arts in Education Teaching Artist Mentor Program, Henry Whitfield State Museum, Guilford, CT (2011); Recipient, Essex Art Association Award, Group Exhibition, "Open Art Show: Anything Goes," Essex Art Association (2010); Recipient, Grant, Fisher Foundation Funding for Salvation Army Pilot Arts in Education Program, The Right Place, Hartford, CT (2009); Nominee, Education Achievement Award, Guilford Art Center (2006); Recipient, Honorable Mention, Group Exhibition, "Fragment," Mystic Museum of Art, Mystic, CT (2004); Recipient, Six Non-Matching Grants, National Endowment for the Arts, Connecticut Commission on Culture and Tourism in Partnership with Institute for Community Research (2003-2005); Recipient, Grant, Urban Artists Initiative (2002); Recipient, Honorable Mention, Group Exhibition, "The Colors Freedom," Mystic Art Museum, Mystic, CT (2002); Recipent, President's Grant, Purchase College (1978) **Membership:** Mentor, Teaching Artist, Arts in Education, Office of the Arts, Department of Economic and Community Development, State of Connecticut (2009-Present); Rotary International (2008-Present); Programming Committee, Hygienic Art, Inc., New London, CT (2006-Present); Griffis Foundation, Bulgarian-American Creative Society (2006-Present); Orpheus Foundation, Bulgarian-American Creative Society (2006-Present); Elected Artist, Norwich Arts Center Gallery (2006-Present); Elected Artist, Mystic Museum of Art (2006-Present); Teaching Artist, Arts in Education, Office of the Arts, Department of Economic and Community Development, State of Connecticut (2005-Present); Fellow, Urban Artists Initiative, Connecticut Commission on the Arts (2005-Present); Official Member, United States Coast Guard Art Program (2016); Elected Artist, Salmagundi Club, New York, NY (2014); Arts Council, Department of Economic and Community Development, State of Connecticut (2012-2013); Director, Purchase College Alumni Association; Board of Directors, Purchase College Alumni Association; Designer, Purchase College Alumni Association; Gideons International New London Camp; Member, Connecticut Trust for Historic Preservation **Marquis Who's Who Honors:** Albert Nelson Marquis Lifetime Achievement Award (2017) **Shipping Address:** 33 Granite St Apt 303, New London, CT, 06320 **Website:** https://www.amazon.com/Cultivating-Illuminations-Paintings-Mark-Patnode/dp/0998543691/ref=sr_1_1?ie=

Thomas Earl Patton

Title: Lawyer **Industry:** Law and Legal Services **Company Name:** Butzel Long **Date of Birth:** 11/25/1940 **Parents:** Thomas E. Patton; Alice F. (Rodarmel) Patton **Marital Status:** Married **Spouse Name:** Yogi Yogan (2006); Barbara Wood (9/21/1974, Divorced 2005); Patricia Mann (Deceased 8/12/1965) **Children:** David Earl **Education:** JD, Catholic University of America, Summa Cum Laude (1965); AB, Catholic University of America (1962) **Career:** Partner, Schnader, Harrison, Segal & Lewis, Washington, DC (1979-1994); Assistant General Counsel, US Department of Energy, Washington, DC (1977-1978); Member, Williams Connolly & Califano, Washington, DC (1970-1975); Associate, Sullivan & Cromwell, New York City, NY (1965-1969) **Career Related:** Distinguished Lecturer, Catholic University of America (1995-Present); Distinguished Lecturer, Catholic University of America (1970-1990); Board of Regents, National Arbitrator, American Arbitration Association; Board of Directors, Elcotel, Inc.; Board of Directors, IXI, Inc.; Board Directors, Vanguard Foundation **Civic:** Member, Washington World Affairs Council (1980-Present); Board of Directors, PCIX Inc (2009); Director, General Counsel for Faces & Voices of Recovery **Creative Works:** Author," Federal Procedure Casebook" (1990); Author, "Securities Litigation" (1989); Contributor, Articles, Professional Journals; Editor-in-Chief, Catholic University of America Law Review **Awards:** AV Preeminent, Martindale Hubbell **Membership:** ABA Representative for Model Codes, ABA; Founder, Chair Litigation Section, The District of Columbia Bar; Cosmos Club **Bar Admissions:** Virginia (1982); New York(1966); The District of Columbia (1966) **Marquis Who's Who Honors:** Albert Nelson Marquis Lifetime Achievement Award (2017) **Religion:** Roman Catholic **Shipping Address:** 1909 K Street NW, Ste 500, Butzel Long, Washington, DC, 20006

Jonathan Patz

Title: Affiliate Scientist **Industry:** Sciences **Company Name:** UCAR **Marital Status:** Married **Spouse Name:** Jean Patz **Children:** Evan **Education:** Resident, Environmental and Occupational Medicine, Bloomberg School of Public Health, Johns Hopkins University (1993-1994); MPH, Bloomberg School of Public Health, Johns Hopkins University (1992); MD, Case Western Reserve University (1987); BA, Colorado College, Colorado Springs, CO (1980) **Certifications:** Medical Board Certification, Occupational/Environmental Medicine; Medical Board Certification, Family Medicine **Career:** Affiliate Scientist, UCAR (2004-Present); Associate Professor, Department of Population Health Science, Nelson Institute for Environmental Studies, University of Wisconsin-Madison (2004-2008); Assistant Professor, Department of Environmental Health Sciences, Bloomberg School of Public Health, Johns Hopkins University (1999-2003); Assistant Scientist, Department of Environmental Health Sciences, Bloomberg School of Public Health, Johns Hopkins University (1997-1999); Research Associate, Department of Molecular Microbiology, Bloomberg School of Public Health, Johns Hopkins University (1994-1996); Research Associate, Department of Immunology, Bloomberg School of Public Health, Johns Hopkins University (1994-1996); Consultant, WHO (1993-1995); Task Force Member, WHO (1993-1995); Clinician, Family Medicine, Misoula, MT (1990-1993); Professor, Department of Population Health Science, Nelson Institute for Environmental Studies, University of Wisconsin-Madison; John P. Holton Chairman, Department of Population Health Science, Nelson Institute for Environmental Studies, University of Wisconsin-Madison; Director, Global Health Institute, University of Wisconsin-Madison **Career Related:** Board Member, Center for Disease Control and Prevention, U.S. Department of Health & Human Services (2006-Present); President, International Association for Ecology and Health, EcoHealth (2006-Present); Member, Steering Committee, Environment Tracking Program, Wisconsin Department of Health Services (2005-Present); Member, Executive Board, Consortium for Conservation Medicine (2003-Present); Founding President, International Association for Ecology and Health, EcoHealth (2010); Panel Member, Decision to Support Climate Change, National Academy of Sciences (2006-2009); Member, Task Force for Environmental Sustainability, Millennium Development Goals, United Nations (2003-2005); Co-Chairman, Health Expert Panel, National Assessment on Climate Variability & Change (1998-2001); Teacher, Massive Open Online Course, "Climate Change Policy and Public Health"; Scientific Advisor, Conference on Climate Change, American Public Health Association **Creative Works:** Co-Editor, "Climate Change and Public Health" (2015); Co-Editor, "Encyclopedia of Environmental Health," Five Volumes (2011); Principal Lead Author, Intergovernmental Panel on Climate Change (1994-2006); Convening Lead Author, Millennium Ecosystem Assessment (2002-2005); Lead Author, WHO (1993-1995); Lead Author, United Nations Intergovernmental Panel on Climate Change; Contributor, Over 90 Scientific Papers; Co-Editor, Two Textbooks; Author, Encyclopedias; Contributor, Articles, Professional Journals **Awards:** Alumni Special Recognition Award, School of Medicine, Case Western Reserve University (2017); Homer N. Calver Award, American Public Health Association (2015); Fulbright Scholar Award (2014); H.I. Romnes Faculty Fellowship Award, University of Wisconsin-Madison (2009); Nobel Peace Prize (2007); Zayed International Prize (2006); Grantee, University of Wisconsin-Madison (2005); Aldo Leopold Leadership Fellowship (2005); Family Medicine Teaching Award, Medical University of South Carolina (1989) **Membership:** Advisory Board, United States Environmental Protection Agency (2007-Present); Committee Member, National Association of County and City Health Official (2007-Present); Scientific Committees, National Academy of Sciences; Founding President, International Association for Ecology and Health, EcoHealth **Marquis Who's Who Honors:** Albert Nelson Marquis Lifetime Achievement Award (2017) **What do you consider to be the highlight of your career:** The highlight that stood out the most in Dr. Patz's career was winning the Homer N. Calver Award in 2015. **Shipping Address:** 1710 University Ave, Nelson Institute for Environmental Studies, University of Wisconsin-Madison, Madison, WI, 53726

Edward Mark Paul

Title: Psychiatrist, Educator **Industry:** Education/Educational Services **Parents:** Bernard Paul; Gertrude Paul **Marital Status:** Married **Spouse Name:** Caryl Oris **Children:** Sarah; Harry **Education:** Fellowship in Substance Abuse Disorders, New York Hospital (Now NewYork-Presbyterian Hospital)(1986-1987); MD, College of Physicians and Surgeons, Columbia University, New York, NY (1982); AB, Harvard University, Cambridge, MA (1978); Residency in Psychiatry **Certifications:** Certified in Level Two Training, Internal Family Systems Therapy (2017); Certified in Level One Training, Internal Family Systems Therapy (2016); Certified Psychiatrist, American Board of Psychiatry and Neurology (1987); Board Certified in Addiction Psychiatry **Career:** Lecturer (2008-Present); Specialist in Addiction Psychiatry, Manhattan and Nassau County, New York (2003-Present); Psychiatrist, Private Practice, Alcoholism Unit, Bellevue Hospital Center (1986-2008); Psychiatrist, Private Practice, Manhattan and Nassau County, New York **Career Related:** Clinical Associate Professor, Department of Psychiatry, NYU Langone Health (1991-2008) **Civic:** The Foundation of Orthopedics and Complex Spine; American Cancer Society, Inc.; Ronald McDonald House; Environmental Defense Fund; National Wildlife Federation; Sierra Club; Rails to Trails (Now Rails-to-Trails Conservancy); Supporter, Reading is Fundamental; Supporter, CARE; Supporter, Meals on Wheels **Awards:** Featured Listee, Top Doctors, New York Media, LLC (2002-Present); Honoree, Top 1%, America's Most Honored Professionals (2017); Recipient, Compassionate Doctor Award (2016); Named, Top 10% of America's Most Honored Businesses (2016); Named, Top 1% of America's Most Honored Professionals (2016); Featured Listee, New York Metro Area's Top Doctors (2016); Recipient, On-Time Physician Award (2015-2016); Featured Listee, Top Doctors, Castle Connolly Medical Ltd. (2012-2013); Featured Listee, New York Metro Area's Top Doctors (2010-2012); Recipient, Compassionate Doctor Award (2010-2011); Recipient, Patients' Choice Award (2010); Recipient, Patients' Choice Award (2009); Featured Listee, New York Metro Area's Top Doctors (2008); Featured Listee, New York Metro Area's Top Doctors (1999-2006); Featured Listee, Top Doctors, New York Media, LLC (1999-2000); Named, Vitals Top Ten Doctor by State; Honoree, Father of the Year, Port Washington, NY; Featured Listee, Top 50 Addiction Psychiatrists, U.S. News and World Report L.P. **Membership:** American Psychiatric Association; American Psychological Association; American Academy of Addiction Psychiatry; American Society of Addiction Medicine; American Medical Association; Alpha Chapter, The Phi Beta Kappa Society **Hobbies:** Swing dancing; Writing; Improv acting **Shipping Address:** 155 E 31st St., Apt 25J, New York, NY, 10016 **Website:** http://www.edwardmpaul.com

Donald Pearce

Title: Librarian **Industry:** Library Management/ Library Services **Date of Birth:** 05/31/1924 **Place of Birth:** Southampton **Country of Origin:** England **Parents:** Alfred Ernest Pearce; Constance May (Jeffrey) Pearce **Spouse Name:** June Inez Bond (12/7/1946) **Children:** Kristin; Kim **Education:** MLS, Catholic University of America (1954); AB, George Washington University (1953); Student, School of Oriental and African Studies, University of London (1942-1943) **Career:** Library Director, Assistant Professor of Philosophy, University of Minnesota, Duluth, MN (1975-1988); Assistant Director of Libraries, University of North Dakota (1973-1975); Assistant Professor, Oriental Philosophy, University of North Dakota (1969-1975); Chief Bibliographer, University of North Dakota (1969-1973); Head Librarian, Assistant Professor, University of North Dakota (1959-1969); Assistant Acquisition Librarian, Ohio State University Library (1958-1959); Staff, Ohio State University Library (1956-1959); Circulation Librarian, Denison University (1954-1956); Student Assistant, George Washington University Library (1950-1953); Part-Time Library Assistant, U.S. Department of Agriculture (1949-1954) **Career Related:** Chairman, Staff Organization Roundtable, Ohio Library Association (1958-1959) **Civic:** British Army (1943-1947) **Membership:** President, Minnesota Library Association (1986); Vice President, Minnesota Library Association (1985); Secretary, Minnesota Library Association (1978-1980); Vice President, Mountain Plains Library Association (1968-1969); President, North Dakota Library Association (1965-1967); American Library Association; Association of College Reference Librarians; Buddhist Association; Phi Beta Kappa; Beta Phi Mu **Shipping Address:** 1700 Norton Avenue NW, Apartment 118, Bemidji, MN, 56601

Raymond Charles Peck Sr.

Title: President, Behavior Research Specialist, Consultant **Industry:** Business Management/Business Services **Company Name:** R.C. Peck & Associates **Date of Birth:** 11/18/1937 **Place of Birth:** Sacramento **State:** CA **Parents:** Emory Earl Peck; Margaret Helen (Fiebiger) Peck **Marital Status:** Single **Spouse Name:** Ellie Ruth Enriquez (9/5/1957, Deceased 7/30/2013) **Children:** Teresa M. Peck-Montijo; Linda M. Peck-Heisler; Margaret V. Peck-Henley; Raymond C., Jr.; Christina **Education:** MA in Psychology, California State University, Sacramento(1968); BA in Psychology, California State University, Sacramento (1961) **Career:** President, R.C. Peck & Associates, Folsom, CA (2000-Present); Senior Statistical Advisor, PIRE, Calverton, MD (2006-2010); Senior Research Scientist, PIRE, Calverton, MD (2004-2006); Chief of Research, Department of Motor Vehicles, State of California, Sacramento, CA (1984-2000); Research Program Specialist II, Department of Motor Vehicles, State of California, Sacramento, CA (1980-1984); Acting Chief of Research, Department of Motor Vehicles, State of California, Sacramento, CA (1980-1981); Senior Research Analyst, Department of Motor Vehicles, State of California, Sacramento, CA (1971-1980); Program Manager, Department of Motor Vehicles, State of California, Sacramento, CA (1971-1980); Research Analyst, Department of Motor Vehicles, State of California, Sacramento, CA (1962-1971) **Career Related:** Session Co-chairman, Annual Workshops on Human Factors in Transportation, Human Factor Society, Washington, DC (1996); Session Co-chairman, Annual Workshops on Human Factors in Transportation, Human Factor Society, Washington, DC (1990); Chairman, Committee on Operator Regulation, Transportation Research Board, National Academy of Sciences (1976-1982); Session Co-chairman, Annual Workshops on Human Factors in Transportation, Human Factor Society, Washington, DC (1972); Statistical Consultant in Field; Lecturer in Field **Creative Works:** Co-Author, "Evaluation of the safety benefits of the risk awareness and perception training program for novice teen drivers," National Highway Traffic Safety Administration (2016); Co-Author, "Meta-analysis of graduated driver licensing laws," National Highway Traffic Safety Administration (2015); Co-Author, "Review of driver sanction and remediation programs," Ministry of Transportation, Ontario, Canada (2012); Author, "Do driver training programs reduce crashes and traffic violations? — A critical examination of the literature, "IATSS RESEARCH (2011); Co-Author, "The Long Beach/Fort Lauderdale relative risk study," Journal of Safety Research (2009); Co-Author, "Validity of surrogate measures of alcohol moderation when applied to non-fatal crashes," AAP (2009); Co-Author, "Evaluation of high visibility enforcement project focused on passenger vehicles interacting with commercial vehicles," Journal of Safety Research (2008); Co-Author, "The relationship between blood alcohol concentration (BAC), age and crash risk," Journal of Safety Research (2008); Co-Author, "Improved methods for estimating relative crash risk in a case-control study of blood alcohol levels," International Council on Alcohol, Drugs and Traffic Safety (ICADTS) (2007); Co-Author, "Validity of the passive alcohol sensor for estimating BACs in DWI-enforcement operations," Journal of Studies on Alcohol (2006); Co-Author, "Problem driver remediation: A meta-analysis of the driver improvement literature" Journal of Safety Research (2004); Co-Author, "A Guide to Reducing Collisions Involving Heavy Trucks," NCHRP Report 500-Vol. 13, Transportation Research Board (2004); Co-Author, "Safety Data and Analysis in Developing Emphasis Area Plans," NCHRP Report 500-Vol. 21, Transportation Research Board (2004); Co-Author, "Use of traffic conviction correlates to identify high-risk drivers," Accident Analysis & Prevention (2003); Co-Author, "Graduated driver licensing & safer driving," Journal of Safety Research (2003) **Membership:** Member Emeritus, TRB Committee, Operator Education & Regulation (2002); American Public Health Association; American Association for the Advancement of Science; American Statistical Association; Committee on Professional Ethics, American Statistical Association; Association for the Advancement of Automotive Medicine; ICADTS; Human Factors and Ergonomics Society; Society for Epidemiologic Research; Emeritus Member, Transportation Research Board, National Academy of Sciences; Committee on Alcohol **Marquis Who's Who Honors:** Albert Nelson Marquis Lifetime Achievement Award (2017) **Political Affiliations:** Democrat **Shipping Address:** 101 Simmons Way, Folsom, CA, 95630

James A. Peden Jr.

Title: Attorney **Industry:** Law and Legal Services **Company Name:** Stennett Wilkinson & Peden, P.A. **Date of Birth:** 04/24/1944 **Place of Birth:** Gainesville **State:** FL **Parents:** James Alton Peden; Frances Merle (Wilson) Peden **Education:** JD, University of Mississippi School of Law (1970); Ford Foundation Law Fellowship, University of Mississippi School of Law (1967-1970); Fulbright Scholar, Postgraduate Coursework, British Government and Politics, University of Bristol, England (1966-1967); BA in History, Political Science, and Latin, University of Mississippi, Summa Cum Laude (1966); Diplomate, Air War College **Career:** Adjunct Professor, Mississippi College School of Law (2009-Present); Shareholder, Stennett Wilkinson & Peden, P.A. (Formerly Stennett, Wilkinson & Ward), Jackson, MS (1973-Present); Services Officer, Parliamentarian and Reading Clerk, Mississippi State Senate, Staff Assistant to Lieutenant Governor William F. Winter (1972-1974); Associate, Stennett Wilkinson & Peden, P.A. (Formerly Stennett, Wilkinson & Ward) (1970-1973); Mississippi Air National Guard (1968-1999); Staff Judge Advocate, 172nd Airlift Wing (1974-1988); Staff Judge Advocate, Mississippi Air National Guard State Headquarters (1988-1999); Staff Assistant/Intern, Senator John C. Stennis, United States Senate (1964-1965); Driver and Campaign Aide, William F. Winter's Campaign for State Treasurer (1963); Fellow, American Bar Foundation; Fellow, Mississippi Bar Foundation; Fellow, Young Lawyers Division, ABA; Fellow, Young Lawyers Division, The Mississippi Bar **Career Related:** Judge, Mississippi Court of Military Appeals (2004-Present); Judicial Nominating Committee, Governor of Mississippi (1980-1983); Adjunct Faculty, Air Force Judge Advocate General's School **Civic:** Co-President, Millsaps Arts & Lecture Series, Millsaps College (2004-2005); Board of Directors, Millsaps Arts & Lecture Series, Millsaps College (1995-2005); Leadership Jackson (1991-1992) **Military Service:** Staff Judge Advocate, State Headquarters, Mississippi Air National Guard (1988-1999); Staff Judge Advocate, 172nd Airlift Wing, Mississippi Air National Guard (1974-1988); Mississippi Air National Guard (1968-1999); Upon Retirement, Promoted from Colonel to Brigadier General **Awards:** Honoree, Best Lawyers in America in Fields of Land Use and Zoning (2008-Present); Distinguished Civilian Service Medal, State of Mississippi (2017); Top Ten in Mississippi Business Journal's First Leadership in Law Class (2010); Legion of Merit, United States Air Force (1999); Honoree, Outstanding Air National Guard Judge Advocate in United States (1991); Mississippi Law Journal Award for Best Comment (1970); Full Colours in Basketball, University of Bristol (1966-1967); Omicron Delta National Scholarship (1966); Phi Eta Sigma Founders Fund Scholarship (1966); Taylor Medal in Political Science and Latin, University of Mississippi (1965); James George Smith Memorial Scholarship, Beta Theta Pi (1965); Carrier Scholarship, University of Mississippi (1962-1966); National Guard Bureau Minuteman Award; Meritorious Service Medal, United States Air Force; Air Force Commendation Medal, United States Air Force; Mississippi Magnolia Cross, Mississippi Air National Guard **Membership:** President, Fellows of the Young Lawyers Division, The Mississippi Bar (1989-1990); Board of Bar Commissioners of The Mississippi Bar (1981-1983); Second Vice President, The Mississippi Bar (1979-1980); Chairman, Mississippi Law Institute (1979); President, Young Lawyers Division, The Mississippi Bar (1978-1979); Co-Chairman, Law Day USA Committee, Young Lawyers Division, ABA (1977-1978); Editorial Board, Mississippi Law Journal (1969-1970); University Scholars, University of Mississippi (1963-1966); Capital Area Bar Association (Formerly Hinds County Bar Association); The Supreme Court Historical Society; Omicron Delta Kappa; President, Local Chapter, Pi Sigma Alpha; Beta Theta Pi; The Honor Society of Phi Kappa Phi; Phi Eta Sigma; Eta Sigma Phi; Phi Alpha Theta; The International Legal Honor Society of Phi Delta Phi; Life Member, University of Mississippi Alumni Association; Life Member, Air Force Association; Life Member, National Guard Association of the United States; Life Member, National Guard Association of Mississippi; Life Member, Military Officers Association of America; Charter Member, National World War II Museum; American Air Museum in Britain; Military Order of the World Wars; Civil War Trust; The English-Speaking Union; Academy of Political Science; United States Naval Institute; Society for American Baseball Research; Institute of Politics, Mississippi **Bar Admissions:** Supreme Court of the United States (1973); United States Court of Appeals for the Fifth Circuit (1970); Supreme Court of Mississippi (1970); United States District Court for the Southern District of Mississippi (1970); United States District Court for the Northern District of Mississippi (1970) **Marquis Who's Who Honors:** Albert Nelson Marquis Lifetime Achievement Award (2017) **Hobbies:** American history; Military history; Baseball; Basketball **Religion:** Baptist **Shipping Address:** PO Box 13308, Jackson, MS, 39236 **Website:** http://www.swplaw.net/peden

Brandy A. Peeples

Title: Attorney **Industry:** Law and Legal Services **Company Name:** Law Office of Brandy A. Peeples, PC **Marital Status:** Married **Spouse Name:** Jennifer Kirkman (9/2/2004) **Education:** JD, University of Baltimore School of Law (1998); BA, Towson University (1993) **Career:** Attorney, Law Office of Brandy A. Peeples, PC (2011-Present); Associate, Hodes, Pessin, and Katz (2008-2011); Associate, Weinberg and Miller (2004-2008); Associate, McCarter and English (2000-2004) **Career Related:** Adjunct Faculty, Notre Dame University, MD (2016-Present); Fellow, Maryland State Bar Leadership Academy (2009-2010); Judicial Law Clerk, Honorable Thomas E. Noel, Circuit Court for Baltimore City (1998-2000) **Civic:** Board Member, Fredrick Maryland Chapter of Habitat for Humanity; Pro Bono Work, Maryland Legal Aide **Creative Works:** Author, Numerous Appellate Briefs **Awards:** Honoree, Lawyer of Distinction (2017); Honoree, Expert Arbitrator (2017); Honoree, Superb Attorney, AVVO (2017); Honoree, Named Maryland's Super Lawyer Rising Star (2011) **Membership:** Board Member, Maryland State Bar Association Leadership Academy (2010-2011); Board Member, National Lesbian and Gay Law Association (2003-2004); Fredrick County Bar Association; Maryland Bar Association; ABA **Bar Admissions:** United States Court of Appeals for the Fourth Circuit (2017); Maryland (1998) **Why did you become involved in your profession or industry:** Mrs. Peeples entered law because she wants to help people. **Hobbies:** Playing Tennis; Cycling; Martial Arts **Shipping Address:** 47 E. All Saints St., Law Office of Brandy A Peeples, PC, Frederick, MD, 21701-5633 **Website:** http://www.peeples-law.com

Margaret Miller Pelton

Title: Art Educator (Retired) **Industry:** Education/Educational Services **Date of Birth:** 11/05/1934 **Place of Birth:** Charlotte **State:** NC **Parents:** William Andrew Miller; Helen Cook Miller Margolin **Marital Status:** Married **Spouse Name:** Donald Wesley Pelton Jr. **Children:** Charles F.; Donald W. III **Education:** EdD in College Administration, Nova Southeastern University (1979); MS, Florida State University (1957); BS, University of Miami (1956) **Career:** Founder, New World School of the Arts (1987-1996); Vice Provost, New World School of the Arts (1987-1996); Associate Dean of Humanities, Kendall Campus, Miami Dade College, Miami, FL (1979-1986); Rank Professor, Kendall Campus, Miami Dade College, Miami, FL (1979-1986); Chairman, Art Department Kendall Campus, Miami Dade College, Miami, FL (1971-1979); Art Instructor, Kendall Campus, Miami Dade College, Miami, FL (1970-1979); Teacher, Miami Dade Public School, Miami, FL (1957-1970) **Career Related:** Vice President, Lynn and Louis Wolfson II Florida Moving Image Archives, Miami Dade College, Miami, FL (1996-Present); President, Lynn and Louis Wolfson II Florida Moving Image Archives, Miami Dade College, Miami, FL (1986-Present); Founder, Lynn and Louis Wolfson II Florida Moving Image Archives, Miami Dade College, Miami, FL (1986-1996); Board Member, VSA Florida (1986-1996); Board Member, Vice President, International Network Performing and Visual Arts Schools (1986-1996); President, Florida Art Education Association Inc. (1970-1972); Florida Representative, Southeastern Board (1960-1980); Member, Florida Art Education Association Inc. (1957-1980) **Civic:** Board Member, Dade Heritage Trust, Florida (1995-2001); Dade Commission on the Status of Women, Florida (1983-1986); Chairman, American Crafts Council, Southeast Florida (1974-1977) **Creative Works:** Exhibitor, One-Woman Show, Complete Choice Gallery (2012); Exhibitor, Art Guild Orange Park (2010); Exhibitor, Art Guild of Orange Park, Spring Exhibition (2010); Exhibitor, Jacksonville Watercolor Society (2009); Exhibitor, Florida Watercolor Society (2009); Exhibitor, One-Woman Show, Jacksonville Water Color Society Show (2009); Exhibitor, One-Woman Show, Florida Water Color Society Show (2009); Exhibitor, One-Woman Show, Richmond Cottage Deering Estate, Miami, FL (2006); Exhibitor, Watercolor Society of North Carolina, New Bern, NC (2003); Exhibitor, Florida Professional Art Guild (2003); Exhibitor, Bascom Gallery Exhibitor, Highlands, NC (2003); Exhibitor, Highlands Art League (2003); Exhibitor, Bet Breira Gallery (2002); Exhibitor, One-Woman Show, Kendall Campus Gallery, Miami Dade College, Miami, FL (2002); Exhibitor, "Spring Exhibition," Miami Water Color Society (2001-2003); Exhibitor, "Fall Exhibition," Miami Water Color Society (2001); Exhibitor, "Western Regional Show," Watercolor Society North Carolina, Asheville, NC (2001); Exhibitor, Macon County Fair, Franklin, NC (2001); Exhibitor, Macon County Fair, Franklin, NC (2000); Exhibitor, "Spring Exhibition," Miami Water Color Society (1999); Exhibitor, St. Augustine Art Association Tactile Show; Two-Person Exhibitor **Awards:** Named, Best in Show, St. Augustine Art Association Tactile Show (2014); Recipient, Best Show Award, Florida Watercolor Society Exhibition, Bradentor, FL (2011); Recipient, Best Show Award, Washington, DC National Competition, National Society of Daughters of the American Revolution (2011); Recipient, Lifetime Achievement Award, Dade Art Education Associate Dr. Clem Pennington (2011); Three-Time Recipient, Iris First Place Awards, Art Guild of Orange Park (2010); Recipient, Azaleas & Monarcks Honorable Mention Award, Jacksonville Water Color Society Show (2009); Recipient, Sweet Magnolias Gallery Directors Award, Jacksonville Watercolor Society (2009); Recipient, Second Place Award, Florida Professional Art Guild (2003); Recipient, First Award, Bet Breira Gallery (2002); Recipient, People's Choice Award, Miami Water Color Society (2001); Named, Florida Art Educator of the Year Award, Florida Art Education Association Inc (1989); Recipient, Award, Florida Endowment Humanities Board (1984-1989); Recipient, Outstanding Award, Miami Water Color Society **Membership:** Hanna Dustin Chapter, National Society of Colonial Dames XVII Century, Jacksonville, FL (2005-Present); Patriots Chapter, United Daughters of 1812, Jacksonville, FL (2008); Regent, Coral Gables Chapter, Daughters of the American Revolution (2006-2008); Trustee, Miami Water Color Society; Signature Member, Miami Water Color Society; Art Guild of Orange Park; Signature Member, Florida Watercolor Society; Jacksonville Fine Arts Forum; Jacksonville Watercolor Society; Macon County Art Association; Watercolor Society of North Carolina; United Daughters of the Confederacy **Political Affiliations:** Republican **Religion:** Presbyterian **Shipping Address:** 1326 Riverplace Drive, Jacksonville, FL, 32223

Syd S. Peng

Title: Professor, Chair **Industry:** Education/Educational Services **Company Name:** West Virginia University **Date of Birth:** 01/27/1939 **Country of Origin:** Taiwan **Parents:** Wangxing Peng; Ianmei Xie **Marital Status:** Married **Spouse Name:** Felicia **Children:** Stanford; Wildon **Education:** PhD in Mining Engineering, Stanford University, CA (1970); Master's Degree, South Dakota School of Mines & Technology (1967); Diplomate in Mining Engineering, Taiwan (1959) **Career:** Professor, China University of Mining and Technology, Xuzhou, China (2013-Present); Emeritus Professor, Mining Engineering, West Virginia University, Morgantown, WV (2013-Present); Professor, Henan Polytechnic University, Henan, China (2009-Present); Charles E. Lawall Chair, Mining Engineering, West Virginia University, Morgantown, WV (2006-2013), Charles T. Holland Distinguished Professor, West Virginia University (1987-2006); Director, Longwall Mining and Ground Control Research Center, West Virginia University (1985-2013); Professor and Chairman, Department of Mining Engineering, West Virginia University (1978-2006); Associate Professor, West Virginia University (1976-1978); Assistant Professor, West Virginia University (1974-1976); Head of Rock Physics Lab, Twin Cities Research Center, United States Bureau of Mines (1972-1974); Mining Engineer, Twin Cities Research Center, U.S. Bureau of Mines (1970-1972) **Creative Works:** Author, "Coal Mine Ground Control, 3rd Edition" (2008); Author, "Ground Control Failure" (2007); Author, "Longwall Mining, 2nd Edition" (2006); Author, "Surface Subsidence Engineering" (1992); Author, "Coal Mine Ground Control, 2nd Edition" (1986); Author, "Longwall Mining" (1984); Author, "Coal Mine Ground Control" (1978); Contributor, Articles, Science Journals; Editor, "Advance in Coal Mine Ground Control" **Awards:** 100 Distinguished Alumni, National Taipei University of Technology (2009); Named to 100 Most Influential, The Dominion Post (2008); Featured in Coal's People Magazine (2008); Research and Development 100 Award, R&D Magazine (2006); Research and Development 100 Award, R&D Magazine (2005); Research and Development 100 Award, R&D Magazine (2004); Medal for Excellence, Institute of Materials, Minerals and Mining, United Kingdom (2004); Erskine Ramsey Medal Award, American Institute of Mining, Metallurgical, and Petroleum Engineers (2002); Donald S. Kingery Memorial Award, Pittsburgh Coal Mining Institute of America (2001); Howard N. Eavenson Award, SME (1999); Institution Overseas Medal Award, Institution of Mining Engineers, United Kingdom (1992); Rock Mechanics Award, SME (1986) **Membership:** National Academy of Engineering **Why did you become involved in your profession or industry:** After graduation from the National Taipei University of Technology, Dr. Peng went to work in coal mining in Taiwan. He found that it was a very dangerous industry, and realized that he needed to find a way to make it safer. Thus, he found his lifelong passion: making coal mining (an industry upon which the world depends for much of its energy) safer for the men and women who go underground. **What do you consider to be the highlight of your career:** He is most proud of being elected to the National Academy of Engineering in 2007. It is the highest honor one can achieve in engineering, and he was the first person from West Virginia University to be elected since its founding 150 years ago. **Where will you be in five years:** In five years he will continue to serve as an Emeritus Professor of Mining Engineering. **Hobbies:** Reading; Swimming **Business Address:** PO Box 6070, Morgantown, WV, 26506 **Shipping Address:** 490 Rebecca St., Morgantown, WV, 26505

Walter Penk, PhD

Title: Psychologist **Industry:** Medicine & Health Care **Company Name:** U.S. Department of Veterans Affairs, The University of Texas at Austin, UT Health San Antonio **Date of Birth:** 08/22/1933 **Place of Birth:** Houston **State:** TX **Parents:** Walter Erich Penk; Elsie Pearl (Teinert) Penk **Marital Status:** Married **Spouse Name:** Dolores Mae Kraijek Little (1/8/1985) **Children:** Mark; David **Education:** PhD in Clinical Psychology, University of Houston (1965); MA in Clinical Psychology, University of Houston (1964); Intern in Clinical Psychology, Dallas VA Medical Center, U.S. Department of Veterans Affairs (1963-1965); Pre-Internship Practicum, Michael E. DeBakey VA Medical Center, U.S. Department of Veterans Affairs (1962-1963); BA in History and German, University of Houston (1954); AA in Concordia University Texas (1953) **Certifications:** Diplomate, Board of Registration of Psychologists, Commonwealth of Massachusetts (1984-Present); Diplomate, Board of Examiners of Psychologists, State of Texas (1968-Present); Diplomate in Clinical Psychology, American Board of Professional Psychology (1980) **Career:** Consultant, Career Development Award, Durham VA Medical Center, U.S. Department of Veterans Affairs (2015-Present); Member, Advisory Board, VISN 17 Center of Excellence, Doris Miller VA Medical Center, U.S. Department of Veterans Affairs (2014-Present); Consultant, Dean of Students, The University of Texas at Austin (2010-Present); Consultant, STRONG STAR Data and Statistics Core, UT Health San Antonio (2008-Present); Consultant, Central Texas Veterans Health Care System, U.S. Department of Veterans Affairs (2003-Present); Consultant, Rehabilitation Research & Development Service, U.S. Department of Veterans Affairs (1993-Present); Psychological Rehabilitation Training, Edith Nourse Rogers Memorial Veterans Hospital, U.S. Department of Veterans Affairs (1999-2003); Clinical Psychology Training, Edith Nourse Rogers Memorial Veterans Hospital, U.S. Department of Veterans Affairs (1999-2003); Associate Director, Bedford Division, VISN 1 New England MIRECC, U.S. Department of Veterans Affairs (1998-2003); Chief, Psychology Service, Edith Nourse Rogers Memorial Veterans Hospital, U.S. Department of Veterans Affairs (1993-2003) **Career Related:** Consultant, Rehabilitation R&D Service, Edith Nourse Rogers Memorial Veterans Hospital, U.S. Department of Veterans Affairs (2015-Present); Consultant, Improving Employment Outcomes, National Institute of Disabilities and Rehabilitation Research (2015-Present); Graduate Fellowship Reviewer, National Science Foundation (2013-Present); Lecturer, Warriors Resiliency Program, U.S. Department of Defense (2012-Present); Professor in Psychiatry/Behavioral Sciences, Texas A&M College of Medicine (2004-Present); Researcher on Compensated Work Therapy vs. Job Placement, MIRECC (1999-Present); Developer, Continuing Education Program, Edith Nourse Rogers Memorial Veterans Hospital, U.S. Department of Veterans Affairs (1993-Present); Supervisor, Fellowship for Minority Students, Boston University (1990-Present); Clinical Psychology Training Supervisor, School of Medicine, Tufts University (1984-Present); Lecturer, Various Regional VA Medical Education Centers, U.S. Department of Veterans Affairs (1981-Present); Presenter, MMPI Continuing Education Workshops, University of Minnesota (1981-Present) **Civic:** Consultant, Clinical Research Centers **Creative Works:** Academic Editor, Journal of Rehabilitation Research and Development (2016-Present); Academic Editor, PLOS-ONE (2016-Present); Editorial Board, Journal of Rehabilitation Research and Development (2015-Present); Editorial Board, Psychiatric Rehabilitation Journal (2007-Present); Ad-hoc Reviewer, Journal of Rehabilitation Research and Development (2006-Present); Editorial Board, Psychological Services (2004-Present); Ad-hoc Reviewer, Journal of Consulting and Clinical Psychology (1970-Present); Ad-hoc Reviewer, Journal of Abnormal Psychology (1970-Present); Ad-hoc Reviewer, Clinical Psychology Review (1970-Present) **Awards:** PTSD Research Grantee, Veterans Health Administration, U.S. Department of Veterans Affairs (2005-Present); Psychosocial Rehabilitation Training Grantee, Veterans Health Administration, U.S. Department of Veterans Affairs (2003-Present); Grantee, Federal Emergency Management Agency, U.S. Department of Homeland Security (1994-Present); Fellow, American Psychological Society (1988-Present); Fellow, American Psychological Association (1980-Present); Charles S. Gersoni Award, Division 19, American Psychological Association (2017); Exceptional Achievement Commendation, The Senate of the State of Texas (2017); Gold Medal in Life Achievement for Practice of Psychology, American Psychological Foundation (2015) **Membership:** Founding Member, Association of Retired VA Psychology Leader Auxiliary (2016-Present); PTSD Mentor/Mentee Committee, Veterans Integrated Service Network 17, U.S. Department of Veterans Affairs (2004-Present); Texas Psychological Association (2003-Present); **Marquis Who's Who Honors:** Albert Nelson Marquis Lifetime Achievement Award (2017) **Shipping Address:** 1936 Oak Glen, New Braunfels, 7TX, 8132 **Website:** https://www.researchgate.net/profile/Walter_Penk2

John Arthur Peoples Jr., PhD

Title: President Emeritus **Industry:** Education/ Educational Services **Company Name:** Jackson State University **Date of Birth:** 08/26/1926 **Place of Birth:** Starkville **State:** MS **Parents:** John Arthur Peoples; Maggie Rose Peoples **Marital Status:** Married **Spouse Name:** Mary E. Galloway (7/13/1951) **Children:** Mark Adam; Kathleen **Education:** PhD, University of Chicago (1961); MA, University of Chicago (1951); BA, Jackson State University (1950) **Career:** Consultant in Higher Education (1985-Present); Distinguished Professor, University Center of Jackson (1984-1985); President, University of Jackson (1967-1984); Assistant President, University at Binghamton (1965-1966); Vice President, Jackson State University (1964-1967) **Career Related:** Summer Lecturer, Universities **Civic:** Active, Boy Scouts of America; Board of Governors, Southern Regional Education Board; Board of Visitors, Air University; Advisory Committee, U.S. Army Command and General Staff College; Commission for Excellence, American Association of State Colleges and Universities **Military Service:** U.S. Marine Corps (1944-1947) **Creative Works:** Author, "How We Got Over" (2008); Author, "To Survive and Thrive" (1985); Contributor, Articles, Professional Journals **Awards:** Miss Netel of Service, Governor Haley Barber (2009); Presidential Citation, National Black College Alumni Foundation (1993); Lifetime Achievement Award, National Black College Alumni Foundation (1993); Distinguished American Award, National Football Foundation; Congressional Gold Medal **Membership:** Chairman Director, American Counsel of Education (1975); American Association of Higher Education (1971-1974); National Education Association; Miss Teachers Association; Jackson Chamber of Commerce; Alpha Kappa Mu; The Honor Society of Phi Kappa Phi; Phi Delta Kappa; Sigma Phi Phi **Marquis Who's Who Honors:** Albert Nelson Marquis Lifetime Achievement Award (2017) **Hobbies:** Golf; Computers **Political Affiliations:** Independent **Religion:** Baptist **Shipping Address:** 386 Heritage Place, Jackson, MS, 39212

Camillo Peracchia, MD

Title: Professor Emeritus **Industry:** Education/Educational Services **Company Name:** University of Rochester **Date of Birth:** 03/31/1938 **Place of Birth:** Milan **Country of Origin:** Italy **Parents:** Luigi Peracchia; Ida Magnocavallo; **Marital Status:** Married **Spouse Name:** Lillian Mae Leverone **Children:** Luigi Francesco; Carla Maria; Tanya Elena **Education:** MD, University of Milan, Cum Laude (1962) **Certifications:** Certificate, Educational Council Foreign Medical Graduates **Career:** Professor Emeritus, Pharmacology and Physiology, University of Rochester Medical Center (2007-Present); Professor, Pharmacology and Physiology, University of Rochester Medical Center (1996-2007); Acting Chair, Department of Physiology, University of Rochester Medical Center (1995); Professor, Physiology, University of Rochester Medical Center (1983-1996); Tenured Associate Professor, Physiology, University of Rochester Medical Center (1979-1983); Associate Professor, Physiology, University of Rochester Medical Center (1975-1979); Assistant Professor, Physiology, University of Rochester Medical Center, New York (1970-1975) **Career Related:** National Reviewers Respondent, National Institutes of Health (1994-Present); Member, Cell Biology and Physiology Study Section, Maryland (1991-1994); Visiting Associate Professor, Anatomy, Harvard University Medical Center, Boston, MA (1978) **Creative Works:** Author, "Gap Junction Structure and Chemical Regulation - Direct Role of Calmodulin in Cell-to-Cell Channel Gating," Elsevier (2018); Co-author, "Lung Function in Health and Disease Basic Concepts of Respiratory Physiology and Pathophysiology," Bentham Science Editors (2014); Editor, "Gap Junctions - Molecular Basis of Cell Communication in Health and Disease," Academic Press (2000); Editor, "Handbook of Membrane Channels - Molecular and Cellular Physiology," Academic Press (1994); Editor, "Biophysics of Gap Junction Channels," CRC Press (1991) **Awards:** Elected Honorary Member, Società di Medicina e Scienze Naturali di Parma, Università di Parma, Italy (1994-Present); Commendation for Excellence in First Year Medical School Teaching (1995, 1996, 1999, 2002, 2005); Edward F. Adolph Medal Award for Excellence in Physiology (2004); Manuel D. Goldman Prize for Excellence in First-Year Medical School Teaching (1998) **Membership:** Biophysical Society; The American Society for Cell Biology **Marquis Who's Who Honors:** Albert Nelson Marquis Lifetime Achievement Award (2017) **To what do you attribute your success:** Dr. Peracchia attributes his success to great education, hard work and wonderful scientific collaborators, especially the invaluable scientific collaboration of his wife Lillian for almost half a century. **Why did you become involved in your profession or industry:** He became involved in his profession because of the great example of his father, a renowned physician specialized in Dermatology and Venereology, inspired him to pursue academic medicine. **What do you consider to be the highlight of your career:** A highlight of his career happened in 1981 when he pioneered the direct role of calmodulin in chemical gating of gap junction channels for direct cell-to-cell communication. **Hobbies:** Skiing; Windsurfing; Travel; Collecting antique tribal rugs and carpets **Political Affiliations:** Independent **Religion:** Roman Catholic **Shipping Address:** 111 Penfield Crescent, Rochester, NY, 14625 **Website:** http://www.urmc.rochester.edu/profiles/display/137188

Betty Jolly Perkinson, PhD

Title: Literature Professor, Language Professor **Industry:** Education/Educational Services **Date of Birth:** 10/05/1947 **Place of Birth:** Roanoke Rapids **State:** NC **Parents:** Joseph Heber Jolly; Ethel Mae Kennedy-Jolly **Marital Status:** Married **Spouse Name:** James Earl Perkinson (4/6/1968) **Children:** Rebecca Caroline Day Lewis; Christina Elizabeth Thornburg; James Earl III **Education:** PhD in Arts, George Mason University, Fairfax, VA (2009); MS in Reading, Old Dominion University, Norfolk, VA (1981); BS in English, East Carolina University, Greenville, NC (1970) **Certifications:** Certified Education Specialist, Developmental Studies, Appalachian State University (1999) **Career:** Faculty Member, Tidewater Community College, Portsmouth, VA (1979-Present); Faculty Member, Frederick Military Academy, Portsmouth, VA (1973-1979); Eighth Grade Developer, Frederick Military Academy, Portsmouth, VA (1973-1979); Implementer, Frederick Military Academy, Portsmouth, VA (1973-1979); Leader, Frederick Military Academy, Portsmouth, VA (1973-1979) **Career Related:** Consultant, Magna Carta Consultant, LLC, Gainsville, VA (2008-Present); Chancellors Fellow, Virginia Community College Systems (2004-2005); Chairperson, Media Board Tidewater Community College, Norfolk, VA (2001-2004); Visiting Professor, University of Bialystok, Poland (1999); Exchange Professor, Charles University, Prague, Czech Republic (1996-1997); Visiting Faculty, Anglo-American College, Prague, Czech Republic (1995); Faculty, Portsmouth City Public Schools (1970-1971); Chairperson, Faculty, Senate, Portsmouth Campus **Civic:** Youth Group Leader, St. Andrew Presbyterian Church, Suffolk, VA (1974-1978) **Creative Works:** Columnist, "Suffolk Magazine"; Author, "Chocolates"; Contributor, Columns, Newspapers; Contributor, Textbooks; Co-author, "Reading, Thinking, Writing" **Awards:** Sabbatical Award, Tidewater Community College (2004-2005); Student Choice Award (1998); Appreciation Award (1995); Outstanding Advisor Award, Government Association, Tidewater Community College (1993); Return-to-Industry Grantee, Tidewater Community College (1984); First Instructional Leadership Class Award, Virginia Community College **Membership:** State Chairman, Delta Kappa Gamma (1998-2000); President, Delta Kappa Gamma (1989-1990); President, National PTA (1985-1986); Rotary International **Marquis Who's Who Honors:** Albert Nelson Marquis Lifetime Achievement Award (2017) **Why did you become involved in your profession or industry:** Dr. Perkinson became involved in her profession because of her teacher, Mrs. Hill, who was a great influence on her. **What do you consider to be the highlight of your career:** Dr. Perkinson is very proud of the Student Newspaper. **Hobbies:** Reading; Writing; Travel **Religion:** Presbyterian **Business Address:** PO Box 5066, Suffolk, VA, 23435

Sharon A. Perlis

Title: Lawyer **Industry:** Law and Legal Services **Company Name:** DBA Perlis & Associates **Place of Birth:** New Orleans **State:** LA **Education:** JD, Tulane University (1970); BA in French, Principia College (1967) **Career:** President, SILREP International Company (1984-Present); President, DBA Perlis & Associates (1981-Present); Officer, Director, Perlis (1973-Present); Director, Officer, International Advisory Services, Inc. (1985-1989) **Career Related:** Commission to Reorganize City Government, Leadership Louisiana, Council for a Better Louisiana (2001); New Orleans Regional Leadership Institute; Fellow, Institute of Politics, Loyola University New Orleans; Government Leadership Institute, University of New Orleans **Civic:** Member, Human Relations Commission, The City of New Orleans, Louisiana (1992-1993); Director, Metropolitan YMCA of the Oranges (1990-1997); Executive Committee Member, Agency Relations, United Way (1987-1990); Executive Committee Member, Project Business, Junior Achievement USA (1987); Member, Private Enterprise Education Foundation, Scholarship America (1986-1989); Member, Executive Board, Louisiana Council for Economic Education (1986-1989); Louisiana Representative on International Trade Issues (1986); State Delegate, White House Conference on Small Business; Vice Chairman, Louisiana District Export Council; Board of Directors, Bureau of Governmental Research; Board of Directors, Louisiana International Trade Commission; Advisory Board Member, International Program for Nonprofit Leadership; Member, Economic Development Commission, State of Louisiana; Vice Chairman, Business-Higher Education Council, The University of New Orleans, Louisiana; Chairman, New Orleans Public TV Foundation, WLAE-TV; Member, Jefferson Economic Development Commission; Former Commissioner, New Orleans Public Belt Railroad; Board of Directors, Louisiana Children's Museum; Executive Committee, Louisiana Children's Museum; Board Member, Former Chairperson, YES-Public Broadcasting Station **Awards:** Distinguished Alumni Award, Principia College (2006); Honoree, Role Model, Young Leadership Council (2001); Woman of the Year Award, New Orleans Public Group (2000); Patty Strong Award, Jefferson-25 (2000); Iberville Award, New Orleans Public Group (1996); Achiever's Award, National Association of Women Business Owners (1994); Jefferson Economic Development Commission Award, Jefferson Economic Development Commission (1994); Advocacy of the Year Award, United States Small Business Administration (1988-1989) **Membership:** Board of Directors, New Orleans Chamber of Commerce (1990-2001); Institute for Women in Government, Nicholls State University; International Advisory Board, College of Business, Loyola University New Orleans; Jefferson Bar Association; New Orleans Bar Association; ABA; American Bankers Association; Arbitrator, American Arbitration Association; Mediator, American Arbitration Association; Federal Bar Association; Former Advisory Council Member, The Federalist Society; Governor's Commission on International Trade Development; President, New Orleans Area Political Action Council; Greater New Orleans Foundation; National Association of Estate Planners & Council; Board of Executives Committee Member, McFarland Institute Advisory Council; Baptist Community Ministries; Executive Board Committee, The Data Center, Nonprofit Knowledge Works; New Orleans Estate Planning Council **Marquis Who's Who Honors:** Albert Nelson Marquis Lifetime Achievement Award (2017) **Why did you become involved in your profession or industry:** Originally Ms. Perlis wanted to be a teacher, but she became involved in her profession after making the decision on a study abroad program with her college. She wanted to do international work and help people. **Hobbies:** Reading; Sailing; Tennis **Shipping Address:** 1211 Henry Clay Ave, New Orleans, LA, 70118

Ralph B. Perry III

Title: Lawyer **Industry:** Law and Legal Services **Company Name:** Perry & Grossman **Date of Birth:** 03/17/1936 **Place of Birth:** New York **State/Country of Origin:** NY **Parents:** Ralph Barton Perry, Jr.; Harriet Armington (Seelye) Perry **Marital Status:** Married **Spouse Name:** Mary Elizabeth Colburn (9/2/1961) **Children:** Katherine Suzanne; Daniel Berenson **Education:** LLB, Stanford University (1963); AB, Harvard University (1958) **Career:** Perry & Grossman, Los Angeles, CA (2006-Present); Graven, Perry, Block, Brody & Qualls, Los Angeles, CA (1968-2006); Associate Member, Keatinge & Sterling, Los Angeles, CA (1963-1968) **Civic:** Board of Directors, PLC Foundation (2005-Present); President, CCA, Inc. (1985-1988); President, CCA, Inc. (1972-1980); Board of Directors, CCA, Inc. (1970-2007); Board of Directors, Planning and Conservation League (1968-2005) **Military Service:** U.S. Army (1956-1958) **Awards:** Lifetime Achievement Award, Coalition for Clean Air **Membership:** House of Delegates, American Bar Association (1975-1995); Governor, Lawyers Club of Los Angeles County (1968-1982); Los Angeles County Bar Association; International Wildlife Conservation, National Wildlife Federation; Sierra Club; Los Angeles Athletic Club **Bar Admissions:** State of California (1964) **Marquis Who's Who Honors:** Albert Nelson Marquis Lifetime Achievement Award (2017) **To what do you attribute your success:** Mr. Perry attributes his success to hard work and persistence. **Why did you become involved in your profession or industry:** Mr. Perry became involved in his industry because everyone in his family was either a teacher or doctor, but law appealed to him most when he was in college. **What do you consider to be the highlight of your career:** Mr. Perry is most proud of the fact that he has put all of his grandchildren through college. **Hobbies:** Singing; Playing guitar; Handball; Hiking **Shipping Address:** 2212 El Molino Avenue, Unit M401, Altadena, CA, 91001

Frederick Peters

Title: Lawyer **Industry:** Law and Legal Services **Company Name:** Williams & Connolly LLP **Date of Birth:** 08/20/1946 **Place of Birth:** Omaha **State:** NE **Parents:** Jordan Holt Peters; Elizabeth (O'Bryant) Peters **Children:** Mary Irvin; Elizabeth Holt; Margaret Etheridge; Finian O'Bryant; Fiona Whitten **Education:** JD, Harvard University, Magna Cum Laude (1976); MS, London School of Economics, With Distinction (1973); BA, Harvard University, Magna Cum Laude (1968) **Career:** Partner, Williams & Connolly LLP, Washington, DC (2001-Present); Secretary, U.S. Air Force, Department of Defense (1999-2001); Undersecretary, U.S. Air Force, Department of Defense (1997-1999); Acting Secretary U.S. Air Force, Department of Defense (1997-1999); Principal Deputy General Counsel, Department of Defense (1995-1997); Partner, Williams & Connolly LLP, Washington, DC (1984-1995); Associate, Williams & Connolly LLP, Washington, DC (1978-1984); Law Clerk, Justice William J. Brennan, U.S. Supreme Court, Washington, DC (1977-1978); Law Clerk, Honorably J. Skelly Wright, U.S. Court Appeals for the District of Columbia Circuit, Washington, DC (1976-1977) **Career Related:** Rules Committee, U.S. Court of Military Appeals (1993-1995); Chairman, Rules Review Committee (1991-1996); Legal Ethics Committee, District of Columbia Bar (1988-1994) **Civic:** Chair, Air Force Association (2016-Present); Air Force Association (2009-Present); Defense Science Board (2009-2013); Chair, Department of Defense Advisory Committee on Roles of Civilian and Military Attorneys in the Military Services (2005); Air Force Aid Society (2002-2014); Air Force Enlisted Village (2001-2006); Board of Directors, Cleveland Park Historical Society (2001-2002); Vice Chairman, Advisory Committee on the Future of U.S. Aerospace Industry, Department of Defense (2001-2002); Advisory Committee on Streamlining Procurement Laws, Department of Defense (1991-1993); WALA (1987-1989); Board of Directors, Cleveland Park Historical Society (1986-1991) **Military Service:** Lieutenant, U.S. Navy Reserve (1969-1972) **Creative Works:** President, Harvard Law Review (1975-1976) **Membership:** American Bar Foundation; American Bar Association **Bar Admissions:** U.S. District Court, State of Maryland (1994); U.S. Court of Military Appeals (1993); 11th Circuit, U.S. Court of Appeals (1986); U.S. Court of Claims (1981); District of Columbia Circuit, U.S. Court of Appeals (1979); District of Columbia (1978); U.S District Court, District of Columbia (1978); Third Circuit, U.S. Court of Appeals **Hobbies:** Sailing; Computer science; Golf **Political Affiliations:** Democrat **Religion:** Episcopalian **Shipping Address:** 3615 Newark Street NW, Washington, DC, 20016

Parker Petit

Title: Investment Company Executive **Industry:** Financial Services **Company Name:** The Petit Group **Date of Birth:** 08/04/1939 **Place of Birth:** Decatur **State:** GA **Parents:** James Percival Petit; Ethel (Holmes) Petit **Marital Status:** Married **Spouse Name:** Janet Lewis **Children:** William Wright; Patricia Monique; Meredith Katherine **Education:** MBA, Georgia State University (1973); MME, Georgia Institute of Technology (1964); BS in Mechanical Engineering, Georgia Institute of Technology (1962) **Career:** Founder, MiMedx Group, Inc. (2009-Present); Chairman, MiMedx Group, Inc. (2009-Present); President, MiMedx Group, Inc. (2009-Present); Chief Executive Officer, MiMedx Group, Inc. (2009-Present); Founder, The Petit Group, Roswell, GA (2008-Present); President, The Petit Group, Roswell, GA (2008-Present); President, Healthdyne, Inc., Marietta, GA (1971-2008); Founder, Healthdyne, Inc., Marietta, GA (1971-2008); Chief Executive Officer, Healthdyne, Inc., Marietta, GA (1971-2008); Engineering Project Manager, Lockheed Martin Corporation, Marietta, GA (1967-1971); Engineer, General Dynamics Corporation, Fort Worth, TX (1966-1967) **Career Related:** Member, Board of Trustees, National Health Museum (2009-Present); Member, Board of Directors, Atlantic Southeast Airlines, Atlanta, GA; Member, Board of Directors, Healthdyne Technologies, Inc., Atlanta, GA; Member, Board of Directors, Healthdyne Information Enterprises, Inc., Marietta, GA; Member, Board of Directors, Matria Healthcare, Inc., Marietta, GA; Member, Board of Directors, Logility, Atlanta, GA; Member, Board of Directors, Intelligent Systems, Norcross, GA **Civic:** Member, Board of Directors, Georgia Research Alliance (1995); Chairman, Board of Directors, Sudden Infant Death Syndrome Alliance, Washington D.C. (1986); Active Member, National Advisory Council, Council Fellows for the Emory, The Wallace H. Coulter Department of Biomedical Engineering at Georgia Institute of Technology & Emory University School of Medicine **Military Service:** First Lieutenant, U.S. Army (1964-1967) **Creative Works:** Author, "Primer on Composite Materials" (1968); Patentee in Field **Awards:** Honoree, Georgia State Business School Hall of Fame (2007); Honoree, Academy of Distinguished Alumni, Georgia Institute of Technology (1994); Honoree, Named to Georgia Institute of Technology Hall of Fame (1994); International Business Fellowship (1986); Humanitarian Award, La Societe Francaise De Bienfaisance (1981) **Membership:** Board of Directors, Atlanta Chamber of Commerce (1997-Present); Board of Directors, Cobb County Chamber of Commerce (1980-1982); National Academy of Engineering; Health Industry Manufacturers Association; Pi Kappa Phi **Marquis Who's Who Honors:** Albert Nelson Marquis Lifetime Achievement Award (2017); Distinguished Humanitarian (2017) **Hobbies:** Flying; Painting; Golf; Tennis **Political Affiliations:** Republican **Religion:** Methodist **Shipping Address:** 1650 Cox Rd, Roswell, GA, 30075 **Website:** http://www.petepetit.com/pete-petit-personal.html

Elizabeth D. Petty, PhD

Title: Numeracy Coach, Data Coach **Industry:** Education/Educational Services **Company Name:** Meigs Middle Magnet School **Date of Birth:** 05/25/1969 **Place of Birth:** Nashville **State:** TN **Parents:** Donald Bruce Petty; Martha Jane (Morrissey) Petty **Marital Status:** Single **Education:** PhD (ABD) in Mathematics Education, Vanderbilt University (1998); MEd, Belmont University (1995); BS in Mathematics, Belmont College, Summa Cum Laude (1991) **Certifications:** National Board Certified Teacher, Adolescent and Young Adulthood Mathematics; Licensed Professional Teacher, State of Tennessee **Career:** Numeracy/Data Coach, Meigs Middle Magnet School (2016-Present); Consulting Teacher, Martin Luther King Jr. Magnet School (2005-2016); Instructional Coach, Martin Luther King Jr. Magnet School (2005-2016); Data Coach, Martin Luther King Jr. Magnet School (2005-2016); Mathematics Teacher, Martin Luther King Jr. Magnet School (2005-2016); Curriculum Supervisor, Mathematics, Davidson Academy (1998-2005); Adjunct Instructor, Cumberland University (1998); Mathematics Teacher, Davidson Academy (1998-2005); Research Assistant, Vanderbilt University (1994-1998); Teaching Assistant, Vanderbilt University (1994-1998); Mathematics Teacher, Davidson Academy (1992-1994); Mathematics Teacher, Bellevue Middle School (1991-1992) **Career Related:** Discussion Leader, Various Workshops and Presentations; Mentor, Teachers Seeking National Board Certification; Accreditation Site Visit Team Member, Council for the Accreditation of Educator Preparation **Civic:** Assistant Treasurer, Grace Baptist Church, Nashville, TN; Stewardship Committee Member, Grace Baptist Church, Nashville, TN; Stewardship Committee Chairman, Grace Baptist Church, Nashville, TN; Teller Committee Member, Grace Baptist Church, Nashville, TN; Teller Committee Chairman, Grace Baptist Church, Nashville, TN; Wilson Scholarship Committee Chairman, Grace Baptist Church, Nashville, TN; Future Planning/Vision Team Member, Grace Baptist Church, Nashville, TN; Sunday School Teacher, Grace Baptist Church, Nashville, TN; Substitute Sunday School Teacher, Grace Baptist Church, Nashville, TN; Member, Friends of Monroe Carell Jr. Children's Hospital at Vanderbilt **Creative Works:** Co-author, "Activities for Mathematics for Elementary Teachers," Vanderbilt University (1996); Presentations, Numerous Workshops **Awards:** Byrn Bible Award, Belmont University (1991); Richard Bryan Award, Belmont University (1988) **Membership:** Leadership Development Committee, DKGSI (2017-Present); Finance Committee Chairman, DKGSI (2016-2018); Metropolitan Nashville Public Schools Workshop Designer, Tennessee Mathematics Standards Revision Teacher Training (2017); Nominations Committee Chairman, DKGSI (2014-2016); Achievement Award Committee, DKGSI (2011-2015); Tennessee State Department of Education Workshop Designer, Dual Credit College Algebra Teacher Training (2013-2014); Consultant, HUMRRO (2014); Tennessee State Department of Education Committee, Development of Standards for Dual Credit College Algebra (2012-2014); President, DKGSI (2012-2014); Battelle for Tennessee Grant Reviewer (2011-2012); Tennessee State Department of Education Committee, Review and Revision of Mathematics Teaching Standards (2011-2012); Educational Support Staff Committee, Tennessee Education Association (2011-2012); PACE Representative, Metropolitan Nashville Education Association (2011-2012); School-Level Representative, Metropolitan Nashville Education Association (2009-2012); First Vice President, DKGSI (2008-2010); Second Vice President, DKGSI (2006-2008); Legislative Committee Chairman, DKGSI (2007-2009); Communications Chairman, DKGSI (2004-2006); Communication Committee, DKGSI (2003-2007); National Council of Teachers of Mathematics; National Council of Supervisors of Mathematics; Tennessee Mathematics Teachers Association; Middle Tennessee Mathematics Teachers Association; ASCD; National Education Association **Marquis Who's Who Honors:** Albert Nelson Marquis Lifetime Achievement Award (2017) **Hobbies:** Reading; Watching Sports; Walking; Hiking **Shipping Address:** 2430 Brittany Dr, Nashville, TN, 37206

Alfred Karl Pfister

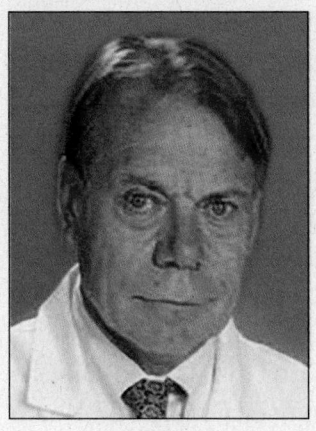

Title: Educator, Internist **Industry:** Education/Educational Services **Place of Birth:** Wheeling **State:** WV **Year of Passing:** 2017-07-31 **Parents:** Alfred Pfister; Anna Seeger Pfister **Marital Status:** Married **Spouse Name:** Nancy Ann Taylor (6/24/1989) **Children:** Alfred; Constance; Philip **Education:** MD, George Washington University, Washington, DC (1962); BA, Washington & Jefferson College, Pennsylvania (1958) **Certifications:** American Board of Geriatrics (2005); International Society for Clinical Densitometry (2000); Diplomate, American Board of Internal Medicine (1969-1978); National Board of Medical Examiners (1964) **Career:** Clinical Professor, Medicine, West Virginia School of Osteopathic Medicine, Lewisburg, VW (2006-Present); Director of Bone and Mineral Clinic, Charleston Area Medical Center (1995-Present); Attending, Rheumatology Clinic, Charleston Area Medical Center (1968-Present); Professor, School of Medicine, West Virginia University (2003); Clinical Professor, Robert C. Byrd Health Sciences, School of Medicine, West Virginia University (1976-2003); Clinical Associate Professor, Medicine, Robert C. Byrd Health Services, School of Medicine, West Virginia University (1974-1976); Director, Ambulatory Care, Charleston Area Medical Center (1972-1992) **Civic:** Volunteer, Health Rights Clinic (1978-Present); Board Member, West Virginia Senior Olympics (1995-2009); Medical Advisory Board, Lawrence Frankel Foundation (1980-1991); Charleston Distance Run Committee, Sternwheel Regatta (1979-2002); Board of Directors, Kanawha Valley Road Runners (1979-1982); Conference Director, Sports Medicine Conference for the Runner (1979-1982); Physician, Charleston Charlies Baseball Team (1971-1981) **Military Service:** Lieutenant Commander, U.S. Public Health Service (1966-1968) **Creative Works:** Author, "Changes in Nonosteoporotic Bone Density and Subsequent Fractures in Women" (2016); Author, "Significance of High and Low Energy Distal Forearm Fractures" (2013); Author, "Significance of Distal Forearm Fractures" (2013), Author, "Fracture Prediction in Early Postmenopausal Women (2013); Author, "An Approach to Identify Rural Women Age 60-64 for Osteoporosis Treatment" (2012); Author, "Bisphosphonate Use and Femoral Fractures in Older Women" (2011); Author, "Screening for Osteoporosis: U.S. Preventive Services Task Force" (2011); Author, "A Controversy: Linking Atypical Fractures to Bisphosphonate Therapy (2011); Author, "The Economics of Fragility Fractures in West Virginia" (2009); Author, "An Assessment of Postmenopausal Women's Adherence to Calcium with Vitamin D Supplements (2008); Author, "OST Risk Index With Forearm Densitometry" (2008); Author, "Cost-Effective Strategies to Treat Osteoporosis in Elderly Women" (2006); Author, "Porphyroa Cutanea Tarda in a Patient with HIV Infection" (2005); Author, "Implantable Cardioverter-Defibrillator Infection Caused By Tsukamurella" (2003); Author, "The Use of Calcaneal Ultrasound for Determining Bone Mass of the Hip" (2003); Author, "A Single Determination of a Urinary Biochemical Marker of Bone Turnover for Detecting Bone Material Density in the Hip" (2002); Author, "Another Study Finds Low Calcium Intakes in Southern West Virginia" (2002); Author, "The Clinical Entity of Remitting Seronegative Symmetrical Synovitis with Pitting Edema" (2001); Author, "Factors Determining Foodstuff Calcium Intake in Elderly Women of Appalachia" (2001), Author, "Cyclooxygenase-2I Inhibition and Renal Function" (2001); Author, "A Pilot Study of the Use of Smokeless Tobacco" (1999); Author, "Hip Fractures in Kanawha County and Their Prevention" (1999); Author, "Vertebral Erosion, Paraplegia and Spinal Gout" (1998); Author, "An Implication for Bone Posterity: Dietary Calcium Intake in Southern West Virginia" (1992) **Awards:** Dean's Award, School of Medicine, West Virginia University, Morgantown, WV (2008); Faculty Attending of the Year Award (2006-2007); Clinical Faculty of the Year, Robert C. Byrd Health Science Center, Charleston Division, School of Medicine, West Virginia University (2001-2002); Award, Special Recognition Award for Unsurpassed Approach to Medicine and Exceptional Capabilities as a Teacher, Department of Internal Medicine, Robert C. Byrd Health Science Center, Charleston Division, School of Medicine, West Virginia University (1997-1998); Physician of the Year, Charleston Division, School of Medicine, West Virginia University (1992-1994); Laureate Award, West Virginia American College of Physicians (1990); John Smallridge Memorial Award, Charleston Distance Run Committee (1990); Distinguished Service Award as a Role Model, Educator and Physician, Charleston Division, School of Medicine, West Virginia University (1988-1989); Outstanding Clinician Teaching Award, Charleston Area Medical Center (1977); Jacobs Award, Proficiency in Pediatrics, School of Medicine, George Washington University (1961) **Membership:** Integrated Healthcare (1997-2002); Charleston Medical Group, West Virginia (1969-1996); Smith-Reed-Russel Honor Society (1961) **Marquis Who's Who Honors:** Albert Nelson Marquis Lifetime Achievement Award (2017) **Political Affiliations:** Republican **Religion:** Unitarian **Shipping Address:** 1 Beta Lane, Charleston, WV, 25304

George J. Phocas

Title: International Lawyer **Industry:** Law and Legal Services **Date of Birth:** 12/01/1927 **Place of Birth:** New York City **State:** NY **Marital Status:** Married **Spouse Name:** Katrin Gorny **Children:** George Alexander Phocas, Esq. **Education:** JD, The University of Chicago Law School (1953); AB, The University of Chicago (1950) **Career:** Private International Practice, London, England (1972-2000); Counsel, Casey, Lane & Mittendorf, London, England (1972-1973); Senior Partner, Casey, Lane & Mittendor, London, England (1963-1972); International Negotiator, Standard Oil Company of New Jersey (Now Exxon Mobil Corporation), Argentina, Saudi Arabia, United Arab Emirates, East Asia, and Philippines (1960-1963); Mediator, North Sea Oil-Gas Settlement, The Hague, Netherlands (1960-1963); Counsel, Creole Petroleum Corporation (Subsidiary of Exxon), Caracas, Venezuela (1956-1960); Associate, Sullivan & Cromwell, LLP, New York, NY (1953-1956); Board of Directors, Several Clients; Chairman, Numerous Boards of Shareholders, Various Nations **Career Related:** Executive Vice President, Occidental Petroleum Corporation, Los Angeles, CA (1972-1974); United States Delegate Adviser, Economic Commission for Asia and the Far East, United Nations, Tehran, Iran (1963) **Civic:** Trustee, Association of Naval Aviation (ANA), Washington, DC; Trustee Emeritus, Owls Head Transportation Museum, Maine; Board of Visitors, University of Chicago Law School **Military Service:** Captain, Special Forces, U.S. Army Reserve; Active Duty in Berlin, Germany, U.S. Army; Private First Class Infantry & Paratrooper, Airborne Forces **Membership:** ABA; Law Society, London, England; British Institute of International and Comparative Law; The American Society of International Law; Association of the Bar of the City of New York; Boodle's, London, England; Metropolitan Club, New York City, NY; New York Athletic Club; Air Line Pilots Association International; Aircraft Owners and Pilots Association **Bar Admissions:** Supreme Court of the United States (1962); New York (1955) **Marquis Who's Who Honors:** Albert Nelson Marquis Lifetime Achievement Award (2017) **Business Address:** PO Box 1513, Sanibel, FL, 33957 **Shipping Address:** 5020 Goodridge Avenue, Riverdale, NY, 10471

Grover Lee Pickel

Title: Immunochemist **Industry:** Sciences **Company Name:** Ozark Environmental Awareness **Date of Birth:** 01/01/1950 **Place of Birth:** Wooster **State:** OH **Parents:** Wilton Edgar Pickel; Josie Marie (Axe) Pickel **Marital Status:** Single **Spouse Name:** May Ann Cosgrove (1/17/1982, Divorced 10/1991); Vicki Lynn Rector (8/18/1975, Divorced 7/9/1981) **Children:** Peter A.; John J.; Gabriel L.; Brandon C. **Education:** MS in Biochemistry and Molecular Biology, University of Georgia (1990); BS in Organic Chemistry and Compound Identification, University of Arkansas (1983); BS in Organic Chemistry, University of Massachusetts, Dartmouth (1976-1980); BS in Chemistry, Southwest Missouri State University (1976); Instructor's Certification, Troy State University (1968) **Certifications:** Certified Pesticide Applicator, Missouri Department of Agriculture (2012); Certified Official Analytical Chemist, Member of the AOAC, Associate Referee (1984-1993); Certified Instructor, Troy State University (1968) **Career:** President, Board of Directors, Branson Aquaponics and Technology Center (2012-Present); President, Board of Directors, Ozark Environmental Awareness (1995- Present); Master Gold/Silver Smith, The Itinerary (1972-Present); Master Gold/Silversmith and Diamond Setter, Breit's Jewelry (2000-2004); Board of Directors, Southwest Missouri Indian Center (1995-2004); Associate Referee, AOAC, Internal Cooking Temperature (1987-1993); Special Projects Chemist, Eastern Laboratory, Food Safety and Inspection Service, U.S. Department of Agriculture, Athens, GA (1984-1993); Engineer, White Lightnin' Racing, Fayetteville, AR (1978-1981); Race Car Driver/Pit Crew, White Lightnin' Racing, Fayetteville, AR (1978-2003); Master Gold/Silversmith and Diamond Setter, Breit's Jewelry (1978-1979); Master Goldsmith, Dieges and Clust Fine Jewelers (1976-1977); Electrician, R.G. Carrignan & Sons, South Weymouth, MA (1971-1972) **Career Related:** Silversmith, Pickel's Works, Branson, MO (1972-Present); Goldsmith, Pickel's Works, Branson, MO (1972-Present); Diamond Setter, Pickel's Works, Branson, MO (1972-Present); Judge, Gamma Sigma Delta Awards (1985-1993); Judge, Georgia State Science and Engineering Fair, Athens, GA (1985-1992); Master Goldsmith, Dieges & Clust, Providence, RI (1975-1976) **Civic:** Board of Directors, Southwest Missouri Indian Center (1995-2004); President, Board of Directors, Ozark Environmental Awareness **Military Service:** Aviation Instructor, U.S. Army (1968-1971) **Creative Works:** Craftsman, LeMaster's Collection, Alice Walton's Crystal Bridges Museum (1974-Present); Developer, Hardwood Stacking and Storage System (2005); Developer, Solar Operated Lake Water Purification Module (1997); Developer, 32 Methods in Chemical Analysis (1987-1993); Lead Chemist, New Animal Drug Analysis, U.S. Food and Drug Administration (1987); Craftsman, Native American Jewelry, Margaret Meade Collection (1974) **Awards:** Albert Nelson Marquis Lifetime Achievement Award, Marquis Who's Who (2018); Honoree, Stanford Who's Who, Stanford University (2008); Featured Listee, Who's Who in America, Stanford University (2005); Honoree, Outstanding College Students in America (1989-1990); Honoree, Three Times Distinguished Graduate, Aviation School, U.S. Army (1968-1969); Honoree, Best Science Project, Loren Andrews Junior High School (1963) **Membership:** Sons of the American Revolution; American Chemical Society; AOAC International Association of Analytical Chemists; American Association for the Advancement of Science; Bioresearch Separations Forum; Atlanta Chromatography Discussion Group; Lifetime Member, 101st Division, U.S. Army; Lifetime Member, A Company 101st Aviation Battalion Association **Marquis Who's Who Honors:** Albert Nelson Marquis Lifetime Achievement Award (2017) **To what do you attribute your success:** Mr. Pickel attributes his success to challenging himself. He was the first in his family to go to college. A professor at Dartmouth College challenged him to try his hand at chemistry. **Why did you become involved in your profession or industry:** Mr. Pickel already liked chemistry because in his seventh-grade science and engineering contest, he built a nuclear reactor and won the first place award. That started his love of chemistry. He started college as pre-law, but took a course "Chemistry for Artists and Lovers C-100" and every day he learned something he had wondered about. **Hobbies:** Race car driving; Making fashion and Native American jewelry; Making Indian artifact reproductions; Robotics; Electronics; Goldsmithing; Silversmithing; Diamond setting; Lapidary; Aquaponics using the symbiotic relationship of live fish creating the food for plant; Numismatics; Engineering **Shipping Address:** 98 Streamside Drive, Branson, MO, 65616 **Website:** www.bransonaquaponics.com

Marc H. Pillinger

Title: Partner **Industry:** Law and Legal Services **Company Name:** Pillinger Miller Tarallo LLP **Date of Birth:** 11/06/1951 **Place of Birth:** Bronx **State:** NY **Marital Status:** Married **Spouse Name:** Ava Pillinger **Education:** JD, Brooklyn Law School (1979); University of Paris Medical School; Diplomate, Pace University **Career:** Executive Partner, PMT Law Firm (2002-Present); Lecturer, New York State Bar Association; Lecturer, Numerous Insurance Carriers; Lecturers, Insurance Society of Philadelphia; Lecturer, Bronx County Bar Association; Lecturer, New York State Academy of Trial Lawyers **Awards:** Honoree, Super Lawyers (2017); AV Rated Martindale-Hubbell **Membership:** American Association for Justice; ABA; Association of Trial Lawyers of America; CLM; The New York County District Attorney's Office; National Fire Protection Association; New York State Trial Lawyers Association; Platinum Member, DRI; RIMS; CLM; New York State Academy of Trial Lawyers **Bar Admissions:** New York; United States District Court Southern District of New York; United States District Court Eastern District of New York **Shipping Address:** 555 Taxter Rd., Ste 5, Pillinger Miller Tarallo LLP, Elmsford, NY, 10523

Sandra May Pillsbury-Gredzens

Title: Sole Proprietor, Art Educator **Industry:** Fine Art **Company Name:** North Shore Serenity **Date of Birth:** 09/30/1949 **Place of Birth:** Minneapolis **State:** MN **Parents:** Robert Kinsey Pillsbury; Elizabeth Anne (Massie) Pillsbury **Marital Status:** Married **Spouse Name:** David Inesis Gredzens (11/25/1989) **Children:** Tabatha (Stepdaughter); Alex (Stepson) **Education:** MEd, Hamline University (1995); BFA, University of California, Santa Cruz (1980); AA, Stephens College (1971) **Certifications:** Certified in Elementary Education; Certified in Secondary Education **Career:** Art Teacher, Community Educator, Lake Superior School District #381, Two Harbors, MN (1997-2008); Elementary School Art Teacher, Art Consultant, Anoka-Hennepin Schools (1987-1997); Elementary School Teacher, Woods Academy, Maple Plain, MN (1986-1987); Art Educator, Shattuck-St. Mary's School, Faribault, MN (1982-1984); Teacher's Aide for Special Education, Substitute Teacher, Pacific Grove Unified School District (1978-1982); Layout Artist, Monterey County Herald, California (1973-1975) **Career Related:** Curator, Guest Artist, Lake Superior 20/20 Studio Art Tour (2017); Grand Marais Plein Air Competition; Artist-in-Residence, Silver Bay; Artists' Roster, Minnesota State Arts Board, Artists-in-Residency Programs **Civic:** Volunteer, Third Grade Classroom, "Masterpiece Art Program"; Teacher, Community Education Art Classes, Grand Marais Art Colony **Creative Works:** Exhibitor, Members Show, Duluth Art Institute, Duluth, MN (2018); Exhibitor, Group Show, Expressive Realism, Aitkin, MN (2018); Exhibitor, Members Show, Grant Marais Art Colony (2018); Exhibitor, Vanilla Bean Bakery and Cafe (2008); Exhibitor, "Itasca Art Association Exhibition" (2007); Exhibitor, Johnson Heritage Post, Grand Marais, MN (2006); Exhibitor, Cross River Heritage Center, Schroeder Area Historical Society, Minnesota (2004-2007); Exhibitor, Johnson Heritage Post, Grand Marais, MN (2004); Exhibitor, "Itasca Art Association Exhibition" (2003-2004); Exhibitor, Vanilla Bean Bakery and Cafe (2003); Exhibitor, Duluth Art Institute, Duluth, MN (2002-2008); Exhibitor, Lake County Courthouse Atrium (2002); Exhibitor, Group Shows, Grant Marais Art Colony (2001-2008); Exhibitor, "Itasca Art Association Exhibition" (2001); Exhibitor, Union Street Gallery, Chicago Heights, IL (2000); Exhibitor, "Itasca Art Association Exhibition" (1999); Exhibitor, "Itasca Art Association Exhibition" (1996); Exhibitor, "Sally Brown Collaborative Art Exhibition" (1995); Exhibitor, Group Shows, Grant Marais Art Colony (1986-1998) **Membership:** Secretary, Voyageur Artists; Board Member, Northern Lake County Arts Board; National Art Education Association; Art Educators of Minnesota; Delta Phi Delta Dance Fraternity, Inc.; President, Voyager Artist Outdoor Painters of Minnesota; Chair, Grand Marais Art Colony Board **To what do you attribute your success:** Ms. Pillsbury-Gredzens attributes her success to her mentors, including the late George Morrison, Hazel Belvo, Elizabeth Erickson, and Mary Pettis. **What do you consider to be the highlight of your career:** Mrs. Pillsbury-Gredzens is a native Minnesotan who has been coming up to the North Shore of Lake Superior since she was a baby. In 1995, she made a dream come true and purchased a year-round home in Castle Danger on the Big Lake. Lake Superior and its environment has been a long-time inspiration for her work. **Where will you be in five years:** In recent years, Mrs. Pillsbury-Gredzens has rediscovered the joys and challenges of painting "en plein air," which is French for "painting in the outdoors." Whenever possible, she likes to paint directly from nature, taking her paints and easel out on the shores of Lake Superior and capturing the various moods of this magnificent lake. As David Thoreau once said, "Life consists with wildness; the most alive is the wildest." She feels most alive when she is painting directly from nature, whether it is in the forest, on the lake shore, or in her garden. In upcoming years, she intends to continue painting in the outdoors. **Hobbies:** Painting; Hiking; Church activities; Photography; Gardening **Political Affiliations:** Democrat **Religion:** Lutheran **Shipping Address:** 2880 Highway 61, Two Harbors, MN, 55616 **Website:** http://www.lakesuperior2020.com

Anthony Michael Pisani

Title: Architect **Industry:** Architecture & Constrution **Company Name:** Anthony M. Pisani & Associates, Architects **Date of Birth:** 05/18/1943 **Place of Birth:** Cambridge **State:** MA **Parents:** Anthony Joseph Pisani; Josephine Ann (Tortorella) Pisani **Marital Status:** Married **Spouse Name:** Emilia D'Agostino (8/27/1967) **Children:** Emiliabianca; Giancarlo **Education:** MArch, Harvard University (1971); BFA, Tufts University (1966); Diploma, Museum School (1966) **Certifications:** Registered Architect, States of Massachusetts, California, Maine, Michigan, New York, New Hampshire, Texas, and Vermont **Career:** President, Anthony M. Pisani & Associates, Architects, Boston, MA (1978-Present); Project Architect, Desmond & Lord, Architects, Boston, MA (1974-1977); Project Architect, Charles G. Hilgenhurst & Associates, Boston, MA (1973-1974); Project Architect, Kallmann & McKinell, Architects, Boston, MA (1971-1973) **Career Related:** Vice-Chairman, Boston Landmarks Commission (1987-1995); Instructor of Design, Boston Architectural Center (1971-1974) **Civic:** Member, Boston Zoning Board of Appeals (1998-Present) **Creative Works:** Major Works in Eastern U.S., Ireland, Canada, Mexico, Puerto Rico, and Japan; Contributor, Articles, Professional Journals **Membership:** American Institute of Architects; Boston Society of Architects; Construction Specifications Institute; Urban Land Institute; National Council of Architectural Registration Boards; Society of Architectural Historians **Marquis Who's Who Honors:** Distinguished Humanitarian (2017) **Shipping Address:** 374 Congress St Ste. 301, Pisani and Associates Architects, Boston, MA, 02210-1807

Chris Dimitrios Platsoucas

Title: Immunologist **Industry:** Medicine & Health Care **Company Name:** Old Dominion University **Date of Birth:** 04/17/1951 **Place of Birth:** Athens **Country of Origin:** Greece **Parents:** Dimitrios Evagelos Platsoucas; Maria (Tsonidis) Platsoucas **Marital Status:** Married **Spouse Name:** Emilia L. Oleszak (10/18/1985) **Education:** PhD (Honorary), University of Patras School of Science, Greece (2011); PhD (Honorary), University of Thrace School of Medicine, Greece (2009); PhD, Massachusetts Institute of Technology (1978); Postgraduate Coursework, Purdue University (1974); BS, Patras University, Greece (1973) **Career:** Dean, College of Science and Technology, Old Dominion University, Norfolk, VA (2007-Present); Dean, College of Science and Technology, Temple University, Philadelphia, PA (2000-2004); Acting Dean, College of Science and Technology, Temple University, Philadelphia, PA (1998-2000); Chairman, Department of Microbiology and Immunology, Temple University School of Medicine, Philadelphia, PA (1993-2006); L.H. Carnell Professor, Department of Microbiology and Immunology, Temple University School of Medicine, Philadelphia, PA (1993-2007); H.L. and O. Stringer Professorship in Cancer Research, M.D. Anderson Cancer Center, Houston, TX (1992-1993); Ashbel Smith Professorship, M.D. Anderson Cancer Center, Houston, TX (1991-1992); Professor, M.D. Anderson Cancer Center, Houston, TX (1989-1993); Deputy Chairman, M.D. Anderson Cancer Center, Houston, TX (1989-1993); Associate Professor, Department of Immunology, M.D. Anderson Cancer Center, Houston, TX (1985-1989); Assistant Member, Memorial Sloan-Kettering Cancer Center, New York City, NY (1982-1985); Head, Laboratory Biological Response Modifiers, Memorial Sloan-Kettering Cancer Center, New York City, NY (1981-1985); Assistant Professor, Memorial Sloan-Kettering Cancer Center, New York City, NY (1981-1985); Research Fellow, Memorial Sloan-Kettering Cancer Center, New York City, NY (1978-1981); Professor, Biological Science, Old Dominion University, Norfolk, VA; Director, Center for Molecular Medicine, Old Dominion University, Norfolk, VA; Dean, College of Science, Old Dominion University, Norfolk, VA **Career Related:** Biotechnology Consultant, National Institutes of Health, Bethesda, MD (1982-Present); Science Reviewer, Study Sections, National Institutes of Health, Bethesda, MD (1982-Present) **Creative Works:** Contributor, Articles, Professional Journals **Awards:** National Research Service Award, National Institutes of Health (1978-1979); Grantee, National Institutes of Health; American Cancer Society, Texas **Membership:** American Association of Immunologists; American Association of Biochemistry and Molecular Biology; Society of Investigative Pathology; American Association of Cancer Research **Religion:** Greek Orthodox **Shipping Address:** 4600 Elkhorn Ave., OCNPS Room 143, Old Dominion University, Norfolk, VA, 23529

Jeanine Parisier Plottel, PhD

Title: Foreign Language Educator **Industry:** Education/Educational Services **Company Name:** Hunter College **Date of Birth:** 09/21/1934 **Place of Birth:** Paris **Country of Origin:** France **Marital Status:** Married **Spouse Name:** Roland Plottel (1956) **Children:** Claudia S.; Michael E.; Philip B. **Education:** PhD, Columbia University, with Distinction (1959); MA, Columbia University (1955); BA, Barnard College, with Honors (1954); Baccalauréat Lettres, Lycée Français de New York (1952) **Career:** Professor Emeritus, Hunter College (2000-Present); Professor, French Doctoral Program, Graduate School, University Center, Hunter College (1981-2000); Professor, Department of Romance Languages, Hunter College (1981-2000); Associate Professor, French Doctoral Program, Graduate School, University Center, Hunter College (1980-1981); Associate Professor, Department of Romance Languages, Hunter College (1969-1981); Assistant Professor, Department of Romance Languages, Hunter College (1965-1969); Director, Language Laboratories, Hunter College (1965-1969); Assistant Professor, Humanities Division, Julliard School of Music, New York City, NY (1960-1965); Lecturer, Department of Romance Languages, City University of New York, New York City, NY (1960); Research Associate, Foreign Language Program, Modern Language Association of America, New York City, NY (1959-1960); Lecturer, Department of French and Romance Philology, Columbia University, New York City, NY (1955-1959) **Career Related:** Board of Trustees, President's Advisory Council, Barnard College (2006-Present); Executive Director, American Association of University Professors (2002-2007); Executive Committee, New York Chapter, American Association of Teachers of French (1960-1970); Chair, Department of Romance Languages, Hunter College **Civic:** Board of Trustees, Barnard College (2007-2011); Association du Mécénat de Institute de France (2007-2009); Chair, Education Committee, League of Women Voters, New York City, NY (2004-2007) **Creative Works:** Co-author, "Alain," The Columbia History of Twentieth-Century French Thought" (2006); Guest Editor, "Culture and Daily Life in Occupied France" (1999); Author, "A Tomb for Stéphane Mallarmé," A Painter's Poet (1999); Co-author, "Rodin's Monument to Victor Hugo" (1998); Author, "The Politics of Marguerite Duras" (1998); Author, "Jewish Identity in Raymond Aron, Emmanuel Berl, & Claude Lévi-Strauss" (1995); Author, "Raymond Roussel: Traditions Ésotériques et Traditions Populaires" (1994); Author, "Colette's Love Triangles," L'Esprit Créateur XXXIV, No. 3 (1994); Author, "La Presse Française à New York," France-Amérique (1992); Author, "Le Culte des morts: Barrés et Lacan," in Barrés. Une Tradition dans la Modernité (1991); Author, "Alain Robbe-Grillet," European Writers: The Twentieth Century (1990); Author, "Memory, Fiction and History," L'Esprit Créateur XXX, 1 (1990); Author, "Intertextuality in Albert Camus," Critical Essays on Albert Camus (1988); Author, "Raymond Roussel, Les Ecrivains et les Livres," Europe (1988); Author, "The Legacy of Jacques Lacan," Beyond Freud: A Study of Modern Psychoanalytic Theorists (1985); Author, "Three French Novelists: Antoine-François Prévost, Choderlos de Laclos, Benjamin Constant," European Writers. Vol. 4, The Age of Reason and the Enlightenment (1984); Author, "La Psychanalyse des Parenthéses dans les Nouvelles Impressions d'Afrique," Recherches Surréalistes (1984); Author, "Surrealist Archives of Anxiety," The Anxiety of Anticipation, Yale French Studies 66 (1984); Author, "Styles of Naming in Honoré de Balzac and Marcel Proust," Writing in a Modern Temper. Essays on French Literature and Thought in Honor of Henri Peyre (1984); Author, "The Battle of Charles Baudelaire's 'Les Chats," Romanic Review, LXXIV, 1 (1983); Author, "Poeticity of Critical and Creative Texts," Cream City Review, 8 (1983); Author, "Raymond Roussel: Flotsam and Jetsam," Dada Surrealism, 10 11 (1982) **Awards:** Officer, Des Palmes Academy (1999); Florence J. Gould Foundation (1988); Grantee, New York Council for the Humanities (1986); Helena Rubenstein Foundation (1986); Florence J. Gould Foundation (1986); New York Times Foundation (1986); National Endowment of the Humanities Fellowship (1979) **Membership:** Executive Director, New York State Conference, American Association of University Professors (2002-2006); Board of Directors, Columbia University, Maison Française; Chair, Executive Committee, Maison Française; Board of Directors, Peyre Institute, City University of New York; Society for French American Cultural Services & Educational Aid; Executive Committee, Board of Trustees, French American Cultural Exchange; Board of Directors, Florence Gould Advisory Committee, The Merc Library, Board of Directors, New York Society Library Visitor's Committee; Board of Directors, Small Press Center Benefit Board, Center for Independent Publishing; Board of Directors, Société Raymond Roussel; Board of Directors, Amis de la Bibliothèque Nationale; Board of Directors, Amis de la Bibliothèque Jacques Doucet; Honorary Life Member, Modern Language Association of America; Life Member, American Association of University Professors; Panel Member, Fulbright Hays Fellowship Committee for France **Shipping Address:** 50 E 77th St Apt 14A, New York, NY, 10075

Richard Welch Pogue

Title: Lawyer **Industry:** Law and Legal Services **Company Name:** Jones Day **Date of Birth:** 04/26/1928 **Place of Birth:** Cambridge **State:** MA **Parents:** Lloyd Welch Pogue; Mary Ellen (Edgarton) Pogue **Marital Status:** Married **Spouse Name:** Patricia Ruth Raney (7/10/1954) **Children:** Mark; Tracy; David **Education:** Honorary Degree, Cleveland State University (2017); Honorary Degree, Cleveland Institute of Music (2006); Honorary Degree, University of Akrom (2004); JD, University of Michigan Law School (1953); BA, Cornell University (1950) **Career:** Consultant, Jones Day (2004-Present); Senior Adviser, Dix & Eaton, Cleveland, OH (1994-2003); Senior Partner, Jones, Day, Reavis & Pogue (Now Jones Day) (1993-1994); Managing Partner, Jones, Day, Reavis & Pogue (Now Jones Day) (1984-1992); Partner, Jones, Day, Cockley & Reavis (1961-1994); Associate, Jones, Day, Cockley & Reavis (1957-1960) **Career Related:** Commencement Co-Speaker, Michigan Law, University of Michigan (2017); Visiting Professor, University of Michigan Law School (1993-1995); Board of Directors, Rotek Inc., Aurora, OH **Civic:** Chairman, Dean's Advisory Council, Michigan Law, University of Michigan (2006-Present); Kulas Foundation (1998-Present); Active, Council on Foreign Relations (1989-Present); Trustee, The University of Akron (2004-2015); Governor's Commission on Higher Education and the Economy (2003-2004); Newcomen Society of the United States (2000-2005); Chairman, Business Volunteers Unlimited (1998-2001); Member, National Inventors Hall of Fame (1996-2006); Co-Chairman, Rock & Roll Hall of Fame (1996); Director, TRW (Now ZF Friedrichshafen AG) (1994-2001); Chairman, University Hospitals (1994-1999); Interim Chairman, Cleveland Institute of Music (1994); Chairman, Continental Airlines (1993-2003); Chairman, Greater Cleveland Growth Association (Now Greater Cleveland Partnership) (1991-1993); Trustee, Case Western Reserve University (1989-2003); Campaign Chairman, United Way of Greater Cleveland (1989); Vice Chairman, Cleveland Tomorrow (1988-1993); Business Advisory Council, AMEC (1988-1993); Chairman, Greater Cleveland Roundtable (1986-1989); Chairman, The Cleveland Foundation (1985-1989); Director, KeyCorp (1975-2003); Member, Administrative Conference of the United States (1974-1980); Co-Chairman, Cleveland Bicentennial Commission; Director, Redland Ltd.; Founding Trustee, Ohio Legal Assistance Foundation **Military Service:** Captain, US Army (1954-1957) **Creative Works:** Author, "Oppenheim, Cases on Federal Antitrust Laws" (1959) **Awards:** Honoree, Cleveland State University (2017); Recipient, Ohio Bar Medal (2015); Recipient, Outstanding Alumnus Award, University of Michigan (2008); Honoree, Volunteer of the Year, United Way of Greater Cleveland (2002); Honoree, Named Cleveland Business Executive of the Year (2000); Recipient, First Economic Development Workshop Award, National Council on Urban Economic Development (1992); Recipient, Humanitarian Award, National Conference Christians and Jews (Now National Conference for Community and Justice) (1992); Recipient, Leadership Cleveland Volunteer of the Year Award, Cleveland Leadership Center (1990); Recipient, Torch Of Liberty Award, Anti-Defamation League (1989) **Membership:** Chairman, Antitrust Section, ABA (1983-1984); Chairman, Antitrust Section, Ohio State Bar Association (1969-1973); Union Club of Cleveland; Pepper Pike Club **Bar Admissions:** United States Court of Appeals for the District of Columbia (1979); United States Court of Appeals for the Ninth Circuit (1979); United States Court of Appeals for the Sixth Circuit (1972); United States District Court for the Northern District of Ohio (1960); Ohio (1957); Maryland (1953) **Marquis Who's Who Honors:** Albert Nelson Marquis Lifetime Achievement Award (2017) **To what do you attribute your success:** Mr. Pogue attributes his success to hard work and good education. **Why did you become involved in your profession or industry:** Mr. Pogue entered a career in law for the opportunity to affect society. **What do you consider to be the highlight of your career:** The highlight of Mr. Pogue's career was taking a position at Jones Day International. **Where will you be in five years:** In five years, Mr. Pogue will still be plugging away in his profession. **Hobbies:** Tennis; Golf **Political Affiliations:** Republican **Religion:** United Church of Christ **Shipping Address:** 901 Lakeside Ave E, Jones Day, Cleveland, OH, 44114

Joanne Pollara

Title: Elementary School Principal **Industry:** Education/Educational Services **Company Name:** Kelly Elementary School **Date of Birth:** 04/18/1954 **Place of Birth:** Hoboken **State/Country of Origin:** NJ **Parents:** Ralph Frank Pollara; Katharine Stark (Cunningham) Pollara **Children:** Angela; Joshua (Deceased) **Education:** EdD, College of Saint Elizabeth (2012); MA, Montclair State University (1994); BA, St. Joseph's College (1976) **Certifications:** Certified Elementary School Special Education Teacher, State of New Jersey; Certified Learning Disabilities Teacher-Consultant, State of New Jersey; Certified Education Supervisor, State of New Jersey; Professionally Recognized Special Educator, Educational Diagnosis, State of New Jersey **Career:** Elementary School Principal, Kelly Elementary School (2009-Present); Special Education Supervisor, West Orange Public Schools (2005-2009); Learning-Disabled Teacher Consultant, West Orange Public Schools (1997-2005); Special Education Teacher, Redwood Elementary School, West Orange, NJ (1988-1997); Special Education Institute Aide, West Orange Board of Education (1986-1988); Special Education Teacher, Kessler Institute for Rehabilitation, West Orange, NJ (1978-1986); Bedside Instructor, West Orange Board of Education (1976-1986); Fourth Grade Teacher, Holy Trinity Elementary School, Hackensack, NJ (1976-1977) **Career Related:** Parent-Teacher Association Faculty Representative, Redwood Elementary School (1994-1995); Building Management Committee Member, Township of West Orange, NJ (1991-1992); Special Education Representative, Reading Curriculum Committee, Township of West Orange, NJ (1990); Special Education Curriculum Committee Member, Township of West Orange, NJ (1989) **Civic:** Religious Educator, Notre Dame Church, North Caldwell, NJ (1991-1992); Girl Scout Leader, Girl Scouts of the United States of America, West Orange, NJ (1986-1987); Religious Educator, Our Lady of Lourdes RC Church, West Orange, NJ (1984-1985); Girl Scout Leader, Girl Scouts of the United States of America, West Orange, NJ (1983-1984) **Creative Works:** Interviewer, Video Conference, Scott Kelly, International Space Station **Membership:** Kappa Gamma Pi, National Catholic College Graduate Honor Society (2012); Learning Disabilities Division, Council for Exceptional Children (CEC); Council for Educational Diagnostic Services, Council for Exceptional Children (CEC); New Jersey Association of Learning Consultants (NJALC); The Honor Society of Phi Kappa Phi **Marquis Who's Who Honors:** Albert Nelson Marquis Lifetime Achievement Award (2017) **Why did you become involved in your profession or industry:** Dr. Pollara became involved in her profession because she always had a love of learning, and she had teachers whom inspired her. She wanted to facilitate success for all students. **What do you consider to be the highlight of your career:** One of the highlights from her career that stands out was when one of Dr. Pollara's special education students transitioned into general education classes, and then invited her to her high school and college graduations. She learned a lot from this student and was proud to be her teacher. Another highlight in her career was when she facilitated a video conference for the school with Scott Kelly, the astronaut for whom the elementary school is named after, while he was on the International Space Station. She enjoyed being able to communicate with an astronaut while he was in space. **Where will you be in five years:** In five years, Dr. Pollara intends to continue in education. **Hobbies:** Reading; Piano; Guitar; Swimming **Business Address:** 555 Pleasant Valley Way, NJ, West Orange, 07052 **Shipping Address:** 23 Espy Road, Apt. B5, NJ, Caldwell, 07006

Wayne Porter, PhD

Title: Executive Director **Industry:** Education/Educational Services **Company Name:** Naval Postgraduate School **Parents:** William Henry Porter; Eve Porter **Marital Status:** Married **Spouse Name:** Kathleen Louise Conroy (2/14/1985) **Children:** Shannon Maureen Sullivan-Hanson; Matthew Keegan; Ryan Kathleen **Education:** PhD in Information Sciences, Naval Postgraduate School (2014); MS in C4I Systems Technology, Naval Postgraduate School (1999); MS in Computer Science, Naval Postgraduate School (1999); BA in Humanities, Cinematography, University of Southern California **Career:** Executive Director, CORE Lab, Naval Postgraduate School (2015-Present); Director, Littoral Operations Center, Naval Postgraduate School (2015-Present); Senior Lecturer, Defense Analysis Department, Naval Postgraduate School (2015-Present); Chairman, Systemic Strategy and Complexity, Naval Postgraduate School (2011-Present) **Career Related:** Special Assistant, Chairman of Strategy, Office of the Chairman of the Joint Chiefs of Staff (2008-2011); Deputy Political Advisor, The Balkans, NATO (2001-2004); Senior Advisory Committee Corporation; Freelance Consultant, System Science and Systemic Strategy; Walton Fellow, Global Institute of Sustainability, Arizona State University **Military Service:** Captain, U.S. Navy (2007-2014); Assistant Chief of Staff, Intelligence, Fifth Fleet Commander, U.S. Naval Forces Central Command (2007-2008); Deputy Operations Officer, Maritime Operations Center, U.S. Navy (2007-2008); Director, Strategic Actions Group, U.S. Chief of Naval Operations (2005-2007); Operational Net Assessment Supervisor, Sixth Fleet Commander, U.S. Naval Forces Europe-Africa (2004-2005); Commander, U.S. Navy (2001-2007); Deputy Operations Officer, USNIC (1999-2001); Lieutenant Commander, U.S. Navy (1994-2001); Officer-in-Charge, Reserve Intelligence Program Office, JWICS, CONUS (1994-1997); Intelligence Division Officer, U.S.S. Blue Ridge, U.S. Navy (1992-1994); Surface Warfare Officer, Steam Engineer, U.S. Navy (1992-1994); Desk Officer, Soviet Northern Fleet Submarine, U.S. Navy (1989-1992); FOSIC Watch Officer, U.S. Navy (1989-1992); Lieutenant, U.S. Navy (1986-1994) **Creative Works:** Contributing Author, Chapter, "The Value of System Dynamics Modeling in Policy Analytics and Planning, Policy Analytics, Modeling, and Informatics: Innovative Tools for Solving Complex Social Problems," Springer Publishing (2017); Co-Author, "A National Strategic Narrative," Woodrow Wilson International Center for Scholars; Contributing Author, Harvard Business Review; Contributing Author, "American Foreign Policy Interests"; Contributing Author, The Hot Spring Quarterly; Contributing Author, The Washington Times, LLC; Contributing Author, "White Papers", Office of the Secretary of Defense & Joint Staff; Contributing Author, Proceedings Magazine, United States Naval Institute; Contributing Author, "Eighth Euromicro Workshop on Parallel and Distributed Processing"; Contributor, Articles to Professional Journals **Awards:** Ellis Island Medal of Honor, National Ethnic Coalition of Organizations (2012); Defense Superior Service Medal, U.S. Department of Defense; Four Legions of Merit, U.S. Department of Defense; Meritorious Service Medal, NATO; Vice Admiral Rufus B. Taylor Award for Professional Excellence in Intelligence, U.S. Navy **Membership:** Vulcan Philanthropic Advisory Committee of Experts; Global Institute of Sustainability, Arizona State University **Marquis Who's Who Honors:** Albert Nelson Marquis Lifetime Achievement Award (2017) **To what do you attribute your success:** Dr. Porter attributes his success to being blessed with a wonderful family, which include great parents and a sister, a wonderfully supportive and intelligent wife, three incredible and inspiring children, and a great-granddaughter. He is also grateful for the opportunity to live in and serve the United States of America. **Why did you become involved in your profession or industry:** Dr. Porter became involved in his profession because his father served in the Navy during the World War II as a SEABEE Chief Petty Officer, and he had always dreamed of serving in the Navy. Having worked in the entertainment industry and as a senior contracts administrator for a defense company after leaving the University of Southern California, he decided to pursue that dream by seeking a commission as a Naval Intelligence Officer. **What do you consider to be the highlight of your career:** The highlight of Dr. Porter's career was having the opportunity to serve his country as a Naval Officer, meet incredible people in a variety of roles worldwide, and to share that experience with his family. He was also fortunate to serve on the personal staff of ADM Mike Mullen when he was Chief of Naval Operations and when he was Chairman of the Joint Chiefs of Staff. **Hobbies:** Motorcycling; Surfing; Fitness; Swimming; Fishing **Religion:** Roman Catholic **Business Address:** 589 Dyer Road, Room 214, Monterey, CA, 93943 **Shipping Address:** 1 Surf Way, Apt. 206, Monterey, CA, 93940

Patrick Stephen Portway

Title: Founder, President, Executive, Educator **Industry:** Consulting **Company Name:** 1) Applied Business Telecommunications, 2)Telecon 3) United States Distance Learning Association **Date of Birth:** 06/18/1939 **Place of Birth:** Chicago **State:** IL **Parents:** Christopher Leo Portway; Cecelia (King) Portway **Marital Status:** Married **Spouse Name:** Malle Mai Portway **Children:** Shawn Patrick Portway; Pamela Ann Eilts; Victoria Ann Portway **Education:** MA, University of Maryland (1973); BA, University of Cincinnati (1963); Postgraduate Coursework in Publishing, Columbia University; Intern in Federal Management, United States General Services Administration **Career:** Consultant (1998-Present); Professor of Graduate Studies, Golden Gate University (1983-2016); Lecturer, Graduate Studies, Golden Gate University (1983-2016); Founder, TeleCon (Now Advanstar Communications Inc.) (1981-1998); Professorial Lecturer, Communications Department, Golden Gate University (1981-1993); Founder, Applied Business Telecommunications (1980-1998); Western Regional Manager, American Satellite Company (1980-1981); Financial Industrial Marketing Executive, Satellite Business Systems (1978-1980); Manager of Plans and Programs, SDC (1974-1978); Federal Government Marketing Office, Boeing, Washington, DC (1974); Manager of Strategic Marketing Planning, Xerox Corporation (1969-1974); Marketing Manager, USPS, Xerox Corporation (1969); Regional Automatic Data Processing Coordinator, United States General Services Administration (1963-1968); Educator, Applied Business Telecommunications; Instructor, California State University, Hayward, CA; Manager of Automated Data and Communications, United States General Services Administration; Consultant, United States Social Security Administration; Consultant, Polycom, Inc.; Consultant, Various Universities **Career Related:** Chief Executive Officer, ET3 Internet Education Company (1998-Present); Producer, Telecon Europe, Telecon & Idlcon Conferences (1981-1998); Chief Executive Officer, Applied Business Telecommunications (1980-1998) **Civic:** Board Member, Corporate Secretary, George C. Marshall Center - European Center for Security Studies, Leesburg, VA (2003-2006); Chairman, Discovery Bay Municipal Advisory Council (1992-1996); Discovery Bay Municipal Advisory Council (1992-1996); Presidential Elector, Commonwealth of Virginia (1976); Candidate, Nineteenth District, Virginia General Assembly (1971); Advisory Committee, Congressional Internet Caucus **Military Service:** First Lieutenant, Army Intelligence, Disabled Vietnam-Era Veteran, US Army (1963-1965); US Army Reserve, Washington, DC **Creative Works:** Co-Author, "The Guide to Teleconferencing and Distance Learning, Third Edition" (1997); Co-Author, "The Guide to Teleconferencing and Distance Learning, Second Edition" (1994); Co-Author, "The Guide to Teleconferencing and Distance Learning" (1992); Publisher, "Teleconference Magazine" (1981-1998); Publisher, "Delta Clipper Newspaper," Discovery Bay, CA **Awards:** Recipient, Award for Higher Education, International Rotary Clubs of India (Now Rotary International), Bombay, India (1999); Recipient, Distinguished Service Award, Dale City, Virginia Chapter, JCI, Inc.; Named, Outstanding Young Man of America, United States Jaycees Foundation of Dale City **Membership:** President, International Internet Association (2001-Present); Founder, Old Farts Foundation (2012); Chief Operating Officer, Global Distance Learning Association (1998-1999); Founder, Global Distance Learning Association (1998-1999); Executive Director, Global Distance Learning Association (1998-1999); Executive Director, Founder, United States Distance Learning Association (1987-1999); Board of Directors, Advisory Board, National University Technology Network (1986-1989); Board of Directors, Founder, International Teleconferencing Association (1983-1988); Board of Directors, Founder, EFTA (1980); International Higher Education Academy of Science; Charter President, Chantilly, Virginia Chapter, JCI, Inc.; Satellite Professionals; Honorary Lifetime Member, United States Distance Learning Association **Marquis Who's Who Honors:** Albert Nelson Marquis Lifetime Achievement Award (2017) **Religion:** Roman Catholic **Shipping Address:** 40869 Hannah Dr, Waterford, VA, 20197

Robert J. Poulson Jr.

Title: Attorney **Industry:** Law and Legal Services **Company Name:** Law Office of Robert J. Poulson Jr. **Date of Birth:** 08/12/1937 **Place of Birth:** New York **State:** NY **Parents:** Robert J. Poulson, Sr.; Louise Poulson nee Hauser **Marital Status:** Married **Spouse Name:** Peggy Ann Poulson **Children:** Eric; Sharon; Joanne; Susanna; Jill Ann **Education:** JD, New York University (1970); BA, University of Florida (1963) **Career:** Owner, Law Offices of Robert J. Poulson Jr.; General Counsel for Major Brokerage Firm **Career Related:** Representative, Broker Dealers, Investment Professionals, and Private Investors; Special Litigation Counsel for Bankruptcy Trustees; Special Litigation Counsel for Debtors-in-Possession; Special Litigation Counsel for Securities Investor Protection Corporation Trustees; Special Litigation Counsel for Voluntary Corporate Liquidations **Military Service:** US Marine Corp Reserve **Awards:** Recipient, Award, Preservation League of New York State (2000) **Membership:** ABA; American Bankruptcy Institute; National Association of Bankruptcy Trustees **Bar Admissions:** New York State (1970); Various Federal District and Circuit Courts **To what do you attribute your success:** Mr. Poulson attributes his success to his tenacity and independence while taking cases that caught the attention of the financial services community. **Why did you become involved in your profession or industry:** Mr. Poulson became involved in his profession because he wanted to understand the law and legal process. He remains fascinated by the study of law. **What do you consider to be the highlight of your career:** The highlights of Mr. Poulson's career are many and mostly involved solving a problem that a client perceived as insurmountable. **Hobbies:** Traveling; Tennis; Puttering on his historic property in Cooperstown, NY **Shipping Address:** 29 Pioneer St Ste. 301, Law Office of Robert J. Poulson Jr., Cooperstown, NY, 13326 **Website:** http://poulsonlaw.com/Home.html

Jonathan Patrick Powell

Title: Owner, President **Industry:** Medicine & Health Care **Company Name:** Clockworks Dental Associates, LLC **Marital Status:** Married **Spouse Name:** Ruth **Children:** Alexander; Devon; Joseph (Stepchild); Deanna (Stepchild); Brandi (Stepchild); Angela (Stepchild); Samantha (Stepchild) **Education:** DMD, School of Dental Medicine, University of Pennsylvania (1992); BA in Biology **Career:** Owner, Clockworks Dental Associates, LLC (1996-Present); General Dentist **Military Service:** Commissioned First Lieutenant, United States Army (1986); Enlisted, United States Marine Corps (1982-1984) **Awards:** AAA Rating, Council of Better Business Bureaus, Inc. **Membership:** PAAGD; American Medical Association **To what do you attribute your success:** Dr. Powell attributes his success to being conscientious and honest with everything that he does, as well as his abilities to fix things. **Why did you become involved in your profession or industry:** Dr. Powell became involved in his profession because he was originally going for a degree in biology, but he didn't want to teach or work in a lab. **What do you consider to be the highlight of your career:** The highlight of Dr. Powell's career has been being fair and honest throughout its duration. **Hobbies:** Woodworking; Electronics; Building PCs; Dentistry; Jewelry Making and Repair; Making and Repairing Time Pieces; Working on Motorcycles; Riding Motorcycles **Religion:** Catholic **Shipping Address:** 1590 Medical Dr Ste D, Clock Works Dental Associates, LLC, Pottstown, PA, 19464 **Website:** http://www.clockworksdental.com

Robert Pringle

Title: Lawyer **Industry:** Law and Legal Services **Company Name:** Winston & Strawn LLP **Education:** JD, School of Law, Duke University (1969); BBA in Business and Managerial Economics, University of North Carolina at Chapel Hill (1966) **Career:** Partner, Winston & Strawn, LLP **Career Related:** Clerkship, Ninth Circuit, U.S. Court of Appeals **Awards:** Antitrust/Competition Practice, GCR 100 (2018); Best Lawyers in America (2016-2018); Chambers USA (2016-2018); The Legal 500 (2015-2016); Cartel Defense Team of the Year, The Legal 500 (2015); Antitrust Lawyer of the Year, Antitrust and Unfair Competition Section, State Bar of California (2010); Super Lawyers, San Francisco Magazine; Litigation Stars, Benchmark Litigation; U.S. News & World Report **Membership:** Unfair Competition and Antitrust Section, State Bar of California; Section of Public Utility, Communications, and Transportation Law, Litigation Section, American Bar Association; Board of Visitors, Duke University Law School **Bar Admissions:** State of California; Ninth Circuit, U.S. Court of Appeals; U.S. Supreme Court; Federal Circuit, U.S. Court of Appeals **Shipping Address:** 101 California Street, 35th Floor, Winston & Strawn LLP, San Francisco, CA, 94111 **Website:** https://www.linkedin.com/in/robert-pringle-89607016

Ronald Probstein, PhD

Title: Engineering Educator **Industry:** Engineering **Date of Birth:** 03/11/1928 **Place of Birth:** New York **State:** NY **Parents:** Sidney; Sally (Rosenstein) P. **Marital Status:** Married **Spouse Name:** Irene Weindling (7/30/1950) **Children:** Sidney **Education:** Honorary ScD, Brown University (1997); PhD, Princeton University (1952); AM, Princeton University (1951); MSE, Princeton University (1950); BME, New York University (1948) **Career:** Ford Professor of Engineering Emeritus, Massachusetts Institute of Technology (1996-Present); Professor of Mechanical Engineering, Massachusetts Institute of Technology (1996-2001); Ford Professor of Engineering, Massachusetts Institute of Technology (1989-1996); Senior Corp. Technical Advisor, Foster-Miller, Inc. (1983-1991); Chairman of the Board, Water General Corp. (1982-1983); Senior Partner, Water Purification Associate (1974-1982); Distinguished Professor Engineering, University of Utah (1973); Professor of Mechanical Engineering, Massachusetts Institute of Technology (1962-1989); Professor, Brown University (1959-1962); Associate Professor, Brown University (1955-1959); Assistant Professor, Division of Engineering, Applied Mathematics, Brown University (1954-1955); Assistant Professor, Princeton University (1953-1954); Research Associate, Princeton University (1952-1953); Research Assistant, Department of Aeronautical Engineering, Princeton University (1948-1952); Instructor of Engineering Mechanics, New York University (1947-1948); Research Assistant of Physics, New York University (1946-1948) **Career Related:** Member, Space Studies Board (2004-2007); Science Advisor to Board, Corrpro Companies, Inc. (1993-2001); Commissioner, Commission on Engineering and Technical Systems, National Research Council (1980-1983) **Creative Works:** Author, Audiobook (2015); Author, "Honest Sid, Memoirs of a Gambling Man" (2013); Author, "Honest Sid, Memoirs of a Gambling Man" (2009); Author, "Synthetic Fuels" (2006); Author, "Physicochemical Hydrodynamics" (2003); Author, "Hypersonic Flow Inviscid Flows" (2003); Editor, "Physics of Shock Waves" (2002); Author, "Physicochemical Hydrodynamics" (1989); Editor, "Journal of PhysicoChemical Hydrodynamics" (1987-1989); Author, "Synthetic Fuels" (1982); Author, "Water in Synthetic Fuel Production" (1978); Editor, "Physics of Shock Waves" (1966); Author, "Hypersonic Flow Inviscid Flows" (1966); Editor, "Introduction to Hypersonic Flow" (1961); Author, "Hypersonic Flow Theory" (1959); Contributor, Articles to Professional Journals; Patentee in field **Awards:** Recipient, Pendray Aerospace Literary Award, American Institute of Aeronautics and Astronautics (2013); Recipient, R.F. Probstein Lecture Series in Engineering Science, Massachusetts Institute of Technology (1999); Recipient, Freeman Award, American Society of Mechanical Engineers (1971)**Membership:** American Institute of Chemical Engineers; Chairman, Engineering Science Section, National Academy of Sciences (2005-2008); Chairman, National Academy of Engineering (2005); Committee Membership, National Academy of Engineering (2001-2005); Councilor, American Academy of Arts and Sciences (1975-1979); Fellow, American Association for the Advancement of Science; American Institute of Aeronautics and Astronautics; American Physical Society; American Society of Mechanical Engineers; International Academy of Astronautics **Shipping Address:** 5 Seaver St, Brookline, MA, 02445

Charles Prochaska

Title: Aerospace Engineer **Industry:** Engineering **Date of Birth:** 12/08/1941 **Place of Birth:** Nampa **Career:** Deputy Master, Washington State Grange (2015-Present); Master, Washington State Grange (2015-Present); Treasurer, Whidstar Consultant (2015-Present); Member, Whidbey Island Arer Fair Association (2014-Present); President, CAMR Ltd. (2013-Present); Sales Representative, Engrav Systems (2013-Present); Member, Holmes Harbor Activity Club (2012-Present); President, Sound ICF Products (Formerly Polysteel Island County) (2006-Present); Steward, Deer Lagoon Grange, Langley, WA (2011-2014); Overseer Member, Washington State Grange (2007-2014); Deputy Master, Washington State Grange (2006-2011); President, Whidstar Consultant, Greenbank, WA (2002-2006); Master, Deer Lagoon Grange, Langley, WA (2000-2006); Assistant Steward, Island County Grange, Washington (2000-2010); Principal Engineer, Payload Concept Center (1999-2002); Principal Engineer of Emergency Equipment, 767 Plane Cabin Interiors, Payloads, Boeing Co. Emergency Equipment-Narrow Bodies, Everett, WA (1999); Manager, Payloads, Boeing Co. Emergency Equipment-Narrow Bodies, Everett, WA (1998-1999); Option Management, Boeing Co., Everett, MA (1997-1998); Manager, Payloads, Boeing Co. Insulation-New Process, Everett, WA (1995-1997); Manager, 777 Division Boeing Co. Insulation, Everett, WA (1994-1995); Manager, 777 Division, Boeing Co. Cargo Furnishings, Everett, WA (1991-1995); Principal Engineer, 777 Divison, Boeing Co. Cargo Systems, Renton, WA (1990-1991); Principal Engineer, Sea Lance, Boeing Aerospace & Electronics, Kent, WA (1987-1990); Senior Specialist Engineer, Boeing Marine Systems, Renton, WA (1982-1987); Senior Specialist Engineer, 767 Divison, Boeing Co., Everett, WA (1979-1982); Specialist Engineer, BCAC/BMS/BAC, Renton, WA (1965-1979) **Civic:** Advisor, South Whidbey Chapter, National FFA Organization (2015-Present); Scoutmaster, Troop 478, Boy Scouts of America, Auburn, WA (1983-1991); Round Table Commissioner, Green River District, Seattle, WA (1981-1984); Cubmaster, Pack 478 (1980-1983) **Membership:** Councilman, Seattle Professional Engineering Employees Association (1967-1972) **Marquis Who's Who Honors:** Albert Nelson Marquis Lifetime Achievement Award (2017) **Religion:** Methodist **Shipping Address:** 3499 Smugglers Cove Rd, Greenbank, WA, 98253

David Thomas Prosser Jr.

Title: State Supreme Court Justice, State Legislator **Industry:** Law and Legal Services **Date of Birth:** 12/24/1942 **Place of Birth:** Chicago **State:** IL **Parents:** David Thomas Prosser, Sr.; Elizabeth Averell (Patterson) Prosser **Education:** JD, University of Wisconsin (1968); BA, DePauw University (1965) **Career:** Justice, Judicial Council (2002-2006); Justice, Supreme Court of Wisconsin (1998-2016); Commissioner, Tax Appeals Commission (1997-1998); State Representative, State of Wisconsin, Madison, WI (1979-1996); District Attorney, Outagamie County Wisconsin, Appleton,WI (1977-1978); Private Practice, Appleton, WI (1976); Private Practice, Washington, DC (1975); Administrative Assistant to U.S. Representative, Harold V. Froehlich, Washington, DC (1973-1974); Adviser, U.S. Department of Justice, Washington, DC (1969-1972); Lecturer, School of Law, Indiana University, Indianapolis, IN (1968-1969) **Career Related:** Commissioner, National Conference of Commissioners on Uniform State Laws (2012-Present); Commissioner, National Conference of Commissioners on Uniform State Laws (2005-2007); Speaker, Wisconsin Assembly (1995-1996); Wisconsin Sesquicentennial Commission, Madison, WI (1993-1999); Minority Leader, Wisconsin Assembly (1989-1994); Commissioner, National Conference of Commissioners on Uniform State Laws (1982-1996) **Membership:** Outagamie Bar Association; Wisconsin Bar Association **Bar Admissions:** State of Wisconsin (1968) **Marquis Who's Who Honors:** Albert Nelson Marquis Lifetime Achievement Award (2017) **To what do you attribute your success:** Mr. Prosser attributes his success to persevering through adversity in his career, especially when he was involved in a statewide recount while running for re-election to the Wisconsin Supreme Court. He won the primary with 55 percent of the vote, and went on to win the general election by 7,000 votes. **Why did you become involved in your profession or industry:** Mr. Prosser became involved in his profession because he had been interested in politics since the age of nine. **Hobbies:** Collecting and researching American prints **Religion:** Presbyterian **Shipping Address:** 57 Golf Course Road, Unit F, Madison, WI, 53704

Thomas Leffingwell Pulling

Title: Investment Advisor (Retired) **Industry:** Financial Services **Date of Birth:** 05/01/1939 **Place of Birth:** New York City **State:** NY **Parents:** T.J. Edward Pulling; Lucy (Leffingwell) Pulling **Marital Status:** Married to Eileen KS Pulling (since 1989) **Spouse Name:** Sheila Sonne (3/12/1970, Divorced 1980); Lisa Canby (9/14/1962, Divorced 1968) **Children:** Elizabeth; Edward L.; Victoria D.; Diana; Christopher **Education:** BA, Princeton University, Cum Laude (1961) **Career:** Managing Director, Citigroup Asset Management, New York City, NY (1976-2007); Managing Director, Citigroup Asset Management, New York City, NY (1976-2007); Vice President, L.M. Rosenthal & Company, New York City, NY (1971-1976); Vice President, New York Securities Company, New York City, NY (1968-1971); Assistant Treasurer, J.P. Morgan & Co. Inc., New York City, NY (1962-1968) **Civic:** Trustee Emeritus, Long Island University (1995-Present); Board of Directors, Henry Luce Foundation (1988-Present); Woodlawn Cemetery (1980-Present) **Military Service:** U.S. Marine Corps (1962-1967) **Membership:** Council on Foreign Relations; Pilgrims of the New York City, NY; The Bohemian Club, San Francisco, CA; The Brook Club, New York City, NY; The University Club of New York City, NY; Piping Rock Club, Locust Valley, NY **Marquis Who's Who Honors:** Albert Nelson Marquis Lifetime Achievement Award (2017) **Why did you become involved in your profession or industry:** Mr. Pulling says investment has always been in his blood. He has always been interested in Wall Street and was offered a job out of the U.S. Marine Corps. Mr. Pulling has grown his business over time, which has always been rewarding for all his hard work. **Political Affiliations:** Republican **Religion:** Episcopalian **Shipping Address:** 34 Yellow Cote Rd., Oyster Bay, NY, 11771

William Richard Purdy

Title: Lawyer **Industry:** Law and Legal Services **Company Name:** Bradley Arant Boult Cummings LLP **Date of Birth:** 05/03/1946 **Place of Birth:** Statesville **State:** NC **Parents:** Frank Kerr Purdy; Catherine Ritchie Purdy **Marital Status:** Married **Spouse Name:** Susan Clark Smith (8/18/1968) **Children:** Kathryn Blythe Purdy-Barton; Susanna Grey **Education:** JD, University of North Carolina at Chapel Hill (1975); BA, University of North Carolina at Chapel Hill (1972) **Career:** Partner, Bradley Arant Rose & White LLP (Now Bradley Arant Boult Cummings LLP), Jackson, MS (2008-Present); Partner, Purdy & Germany PLLC (2003-2008); Founding Partner, Ott & Purdy, P.A., Jackson, MS (1980-2003); Principal, Ott & Purdy, P.A., Jackson, MS (1980-2003); Vice President, Southeastern Services, Inc., Jackson, MS (1977-1980); Associate, Smith, Currie and Hancock LLP, Atlanta, GA (1975-1977) **Career Related:** General Counsel, Mississippi Asphalt Pavement Association, Jackson, MS (1998-Present); Associate, General Controllers of Mississippi, Jackson, MS (1995-Present); Associate, MS Road Builders Association, Jackson, MS (1993-Present); State Chair, American Bar Association (1980-1983); Fellow, Mississippi Bar Foundation; Fellow, International Society Barristers; Fellow, The American College of Construction Lawyers **Military Service:** First Lieutenant, U.S. Marine Corps (1968-1972) **Creative Works:** Author, "Contractor's Desk Book on Mississippi Construction Law" (1996); Editor, "Contractor's Desk Book on Mississippi Construction Law" (1996); Lecturer in Field **Awards:** Master of the Bench, Charles Clark Inn of the American Inns of Court (1994-Present); Best Lawyer in America (2003); Commendation for Distinguished Professional Achievement, Joint Resolution of Mississippi Senate and House Of Representatives (2000); Bronze Star Medal **Membership:** Forum Committee on Construction Law, American Bar Association (1980-Present); Public Contract Law Section, American Bar Association (1980-1983); Best Lawyers **Marquis Who's Who Honors:** Albert Nelson Marquis Lifetime Achievement Award (2017) **To what do you attribute your success:** Mr. Purdy attributes his success to his focus and drive to satisfy his clients' needs and comply with his professional responsibility. **Why did you become involved in your profession or industry:** Mr. Purdy graduated with a history degree and always thought of law as an appropriate profession to use his talents. **Where will you be in five years:** In five years, Mr. Purdy will stop the actual day-to-day work as a lawyer. Instead, he plans to take on a supervisory role to mentor and help young lawyers. **Hobbies:** Jogging; Rock and roll; College sports **Shipping Address:** PO Box 1789, Bradley Arant Boult Cummings LLP, Jackson, MS, 39215

Cecilia Pursel Williams

Title: Optometrist **Industry:** Medicine & Health Care **Date of Birth:** 11/15/1948 **Place of Birth:** Lewisburg **State:** PA **Parents:** Lee LaVerne Pursel; Geraldine May (Steininger) Pursel **Marital Status:** Divorced **Spouse Name:** Richard Lee Williams (5/17/1975, Divorced 2007) **Children:** Kent Lee **Education:** OD, Salus University Pennsylvania College of Optometry (1972); BS, Salus University Pennsylvania College of Optometry (1970); Coursework, Lycoming College (1966-1968) **Certifications:** Licensed Optometrist, The District of Columbia; Licensed Optometrist, Commonwealth of Pennsylvania; Licensed Optometrist, State of New York; Licensed Optometrist, State of New Jersey; Licensed Optometrist, Commonwealth of Virginia **Career:** Private Practice, Optometry, Springfield, VA (1980-Present); Optometrist, Sterling Optical Contact Lens Center (Now Sterling Optical), Washington D.C. (1974-1979); Research Optometrist, Soft Lens Materials, Gumpelmayer Optik, Vienna, Austria (1973) **Awards:** Clinical Efficiency Award, Salus University Pennsylvania College of Optometry (1972); Optometrists Scholarship, Women's Auxiliary of Pennsylvania (1970-1972); Grantee, Commonwealth of Pennsylvania (1970-1972); Optometrists Scholarship, Women's Auxiliary of Pennsylvania (1968-1970); Grantee, Commonwealth of Pennsylvania (1968-1970) **Membership:** Director, Optometric Center of the Nation's Capital (1977-1980); American Optometric Association; Virginia Optometric Association (VOA); Northern Virginia Optometric Society; Beta Sigma Kappa; Omega Delta **Marquis Who's Who Honors:** Albert Nelson Marquis Lifetime Achievement Award (2017) **To what do you attribute your success:** Dr. Williams attributes her success to her love of talking and helping people. **Why did you become involved in your profession or industry:** She became involved in her profession because when she was in high school, the optometrist suggested she look into this as a career, so she did and hasn't looked back. **Shipping Address:** 3600 Wilton Hall Ct, Alexandria, VA, 22310

John Brewton Rabun Jr.

Title: Criminal Justice Agency Administrator **Industry:** Nonprofit & Philanthropy **Company Name:** National Center for Missing & Exploited Children **Date of Birth:** 11/16/1946 **Place of Birth:** Augusta **State:** GA **Parents:** John Brewton Rabun; Alsie Imor (Bateman) Rabun **Marital Status:** Married **Spouse Name:** Anna Betsy Park (12/27/1967) **Children:** Kerry Kristin; John Candler **Education:** MSW, University of Louisville (1971); Postgraduate Coursework, Southern Baptist Theological Seminary (1970); BA, Mercer University (1967) **Certifications:** Certified Social Worker, Academy of Certified Social Workers, Commonwealth of Kentucky; Certified Social Worker, Academy of Certified Social Workers, Washington, DC **Career:** Director, Infant Abduction, National Center for Missing & Exploited Children, Savannah, GA (2012-Present); Executive Vice President, National Center for Missing & Exploited Children (2006-2012); Chief Operating Officer, National Center for Missing & Exploited Children, Washington, DC (1984-2012); Executive Vice President, National Center for Missing and Exploited Children, Washington, DC (1984-2012); Program Manager, National Center for Exploited & Missing Child Unit, Louisville, KY (1980-1984); Program Manager, Field Services, Louisville, KY (1978-1980); Director, Community Residential Treatment Services, Louisville, KY (1973-1978); Executive Director, American Civil Liberties Union, Louisville, KY (1971-1972) **Career Related:** Alumni Fellow, University of Louisville (1999); Mayor's City Youth Commission, Louisville, KY (1983-1984); Alderman's Task Force on Social Services, Louisville, KY (1982); Trainer, Numerous Agencies; Consultant, Numerous Agencies **Creative Works:** Author, "Healthcare Guidelines on Infant Abduction" (2014); Contributor, Articles, Professional Journals; Contributor, Chapters, Books **Awards:** Distinguished Alumnus Award, University of Louisville (2003); Russell L. Colling Literary Award, International Association for Healthcare Security and Safety (1991); Distinguished Alumnus Award, University of Louisville (1985); Keys to the City, Louisville, KY (1983); Honorable Chief of Police, City of Louisville (1982) **Membership:** ACLU; National Association of Social Workers; National Sheriff's Association; International Juvenile Officers Association, Inc.; Academy of Certified Social Workers; International Association for Healthcare Safety and Security; American Society for Industrial Security; International Association of Chiefs of Police **Marquis Who's Who Honors:** Albert Nelson Marquis Lifetime Achievement Award (2017); Distinguished Humanitarian (2017) **Hobbies:** Photography; Hunting; Fishing; Computers **Religion:** Baptist **Business Address:** 699 Prince Street, Alexandria, VA, 22314 **Shipping Address:** PO Box 2210, Tybee Island, GA, 31328

Rubin Rachamim

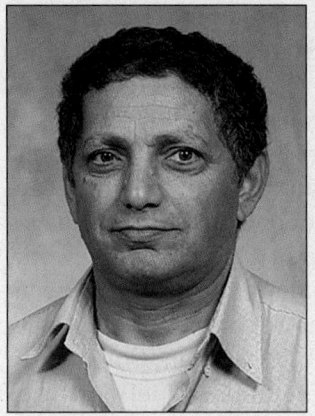

Industry: Sciences **Date of Birth:** 03/17/1952 **Place of Birth:** Beer Ya'akov **Country of Origin:** Israel **Parents:** Rubin Gavriel; Rubin Bracha **Education:** MSc in Physical Chemistry, Bar-Ilan University, Ramat-Gan (1980); BS in Chemistry, Bar-Ilan University, Ramat-Gan (1977) **Career:** Researcher, Weizmann Institute of Science, Rehovot, Israel (1987-Present); Researcher, Israel Desalination Engineering, Hertzeliya (1984-1987); Researcher, Bar-Ilan University (1980-1984) **Achievements:** Achievements include innovation of a direct irradiated annular pressurized receiver for solar energy uses; innovation of high temperature solar receiver; innovation of sea water treatment to inhibit corrosion and solids precipitation in desalination units; breakthroughs in solar energy storage by a chemical heat pipe system; breakthroughs in measuring the kinetics of reactions type Atom and di-atoms molecule, mainly chlorine atom reaction

Dick Elliot Ragsdale

Title: Health Company Executive (Retired) **Industry:** Medicine & Health Care **Date of Birth:** 12/20/1943 **Place of Birth:** St. Louis **State:** MO **Parents:** Billie Oscar Ragsdale; Isabelle (Roques) Ragsdale **Marital Status:** Married **Spouse Name:** Ping Xu Ragsdale (10/11/2013); Anne Elizabeth Ward (8/20/1968, Deceased 6/30/2008) **Children:** Richard; Kevin; Bethany Corrieri **Education:** MS in International Commerce, Thunderbird School of Global Management, Arizona State University (1968); Bachelor's Degree, Thunderbird School of Global Management, Arizona State University (1968); BBA, Ohio University (1965); Coursework, University of Vienna (1964) **Career:** Co-Chairman, Community Health Systems Inc., Brentwood, TN (1996-1998); Retired (1996); Chairman, Great Northern Health Management, Ltd., London, England (1986-1989); Chairman, Community Health Systems Inc., Brentwood, TN (1985-1996); Co-Founder, Chief Financial Officer, Senior Executive Vice President, Director, Republic Health Corporation, Dallas, TX (1981-1985); Senior Vice President, Republic Health Corporation, Dallas, TX (1981-1983); Chief Financial Officer, Republic Health Corporation, Dallas, TX (1981-1983); Vice President, INA Healthcare Group, Dallas, TX (1980-1981); Treasurer, INA Healthcare Group, Dallas, TX (1980-1981); Chief Financial Officer, INA Healthcare Group, Dallas, TX (1980-1981); Vice President, Hospital-Affiliates-International, Nashville, TN (1973-1980); Treasurer, Hospital-Affiliates-International, Nashville, TN (1973-1980); Assistant Treasurer, Chase Bank, New York, NY (1968-1973) **Career Related:** Director, American Addiction Centers, Brentwood, TN (2012-Present); Co-Founder, BreatheAmerica, Franklin, TN (2016); Director, HealthMont, Inc. (2000-2003); Chairman, HealthMont, Inc. (2002-2003); Co-Founder, New Life Treatment Centers Inc., Laguna Beach, CA (1988-1994); Co-Founder, American Transitional Hospitals Inc., Franklin, TN (1987-1994); Co-Founder, Advanced Rehabilitation Resources Inc., St. Louis, MO (1990-1993); Co-Founder, Synergos, Inc., Santa Ana, CA (1987-1992); Co-Founder, Samissa Psychiatric, Inc., Los Angeles, CA (1987-1990) **Civic:** Director, Nashville Zoo at Grassmere (2000-Present); Trustee, Maryville College (1990-Present); Trustee, Benton Hall Academy (1988-Present); Chairman, Board of Trustees, The Hospital Authority of Metropolitan Nashville and Davidson County, Nashville, TN (1999-2008); Chair, Trustee, Maryville College (1992-2004); Director, Vanderbilt University Technology Company (2001-2003); Chair, Trustee, Benton Hall Academy (1991-2002); Trustee, Watkins College of Art, Design, and Film (1988-1994); Coach, Spring Valley Athletic Association (1985) **Military Service:** U.S. Army Reserve, New Jersey (1968-1970); U.S. Army Reserve, Arizona (1967) **Awards:** Sage Award, Council on Aging of Middle Tennessee (2011); Honoree, Benton Hall Academy Hall of Fame (2010); Honoree, 100 Black Men of Middle Tennessee (2001); Maryville College Medallion (1999); Jonas Meyer Distinguished Alumni Award, Thunderbird School of Global Management (1993); Thunderbird Distinguished Alumni Award for Entrepreneurship, Thunderbird School of Global Management (1990) **Membership:** Legislative Commission, Federation of American Hospitals (1984-1995); Advisory Board, Nashville Zoo at Grassmere; Advisory Board, Nashville Opera; Advisory Board, The Salvation Army of Nashville, Nashville, TN **Marquis Who's Who Honors:** Albert Nelson Marquis Lifetime Achievement Award (2017) **Hobbies:** Scuba diving; Video editing, Drag racing **Political Affiliations:** Republican **Shipping Address:** 124 Taggart Ave., Nashville, TN, 37205

Fernando O. Raineri, PhD

Title: Senior Lecturer **Industry:** Education/ Educational Services **Company Name:** Stony Brook University **Education:** PhD, Universidad de Buenos Aires (1987); Postdoctoral Coursework, Stony Brook University **Career:** Lecturer, Physical and General Chemistry, Stony Book University **Awards:** Provost's Outstanding Lecturer Award, Stony Brook University (2013) **Why did you become involved in your profession or industry:** Dr. Raineri became involved in his career because he was always interested in how chemical reactions occur. **Business Address:** 100 Nicolls Rd, 100 Nicolls Rd, NY, Stony Brook, 11794 **Shipping Address:** 100 Nicolls Rd, Stonybrook University, Dept Of Chemistry, Stony Brook, NY, 11794

Edgar Frank Raines Jr.

Title: Contract Historian **Industry:** Government Administration/Government Relations/Government Services **Company Name:** Department of Defense **Date of Birth:** 08/17/1944 **Place of Birth:** Murphysboro **State:** IL **Parents:** Edgar F. Raines; Mary B. (Mohlenbrock) Raines **Marital Status:** Married **Spouse Name:** Rebecca Celia Robbins (6/20/1987); Gretchen Rose Beuscher (8/9/1975, Divorced 12/1982) **Children:** Edgar Jacob **Education:** PhD in History, University of Wisconsin-Madison (1976); MA in History, Southern Illinois University (1968); BA in History, Southern Illinois University (1966) **Career:** Contract Historian, Joint History Office (2015-Present); Senior Historian, U.S. Army Center of Military History (2003-2011); Historian, U.S. Army Center of Military History (1980-2003); Historian, Office of Air Force History (1979-1980); Assistant Academic Dean, Silver Lake College (1976-1979) **Career Related:** Historical Support, Chief of Staff, U.S. Army Transition Team (2007); Headquarters, Department of the Army Realignment Task Force, Office of the Secretary of the Army (2001-2002); Directorate of Roles and Missions, Office of the Deputy Chief of Staff for Operations and Plans, Army Staff (1994-1995); U.S. Army Special Review Committee, Department of Defense Reform (Goldwater-Nichols Bill) (1985); Historian, Army Operations Center, Operation URGENT FURY (1983) **Civic:** Volunteer, U.S. Army Center of Military History (2011-Present); Volunteer, U.S. Army Center of Military History (1980); Civilian Employee, U.S. Air Force (1979) **Creative Works:** Author, "Contingency Operations Series," U.S. Army Center of Military History, Washington, DC (2010); Author, "Eyes of Artillery: The Origins of Modern U.S. Army Aviation during World War II, Army Historical Series," U.S. Army Center of Military History, Washington, DC (2000); Co-Author, "The Army and the Joint Chiefs of Staff: Evolution of Army Ideas on the Command, Control, and Coordination of the U. S. Armed Forces, 1942-1985, Historical Analysis Series," U.S. Army Center of Military History, Washington, DC (1986); Author, "The Rucksack War: U.S. Army Operational Logistics in Grenada" (1983) **Awards:** Meritorious Civilian Service Award, U.S. Army (2011); Army History Foundation Award, History of the U.S. Army (2002); Secretary of the Army Fellowship, U.S. Army (1987); Harry E. Pratt Award (1985) **Membership:** American Historical Association; Organization of American Historians; Society for Military History; Society for History in the Federal Government; Society for Historians of American Foreign Relations; Air Force Historical Foundation **To what do you attribute your success:** Dr. Raines attributes his success to the love and support of his family, some outstanding teachers and colleagues, hard work, and a good deal of luck. **Why did you become involved in your profession or industry:** Dr. Raines developed an early love of history sparked by the stories his grandfather, Mohlenbrock, and his grandmother, Raines, told him about growing up in the 19th century. He also had excellent history teachers in junior high school, high school, college, and graduate school that took that initial interest and kept it alive. **What do you consider to be the highlight of your career:** The publication of "The Rucksack War: U.S. Army Operational Logistics in Grenada in 1983" on the last day of December of 2010 was the highlight of Dr. Raines' career, 27 years after he was first dispatched to the Army Operations Center in the midst of the Grenada operation to collect documents and conduct interviews with members of the Army Staff. He completed an initial draft in July of 1989, but the manuscript did not survive declassification review. He was able to resume work on it in 1999, when much more material had become available. Although he was frequently diverted to other tasks, he was able to keep coming back to the Grenada project and eventually the manuscript passed through all the required historical and classification reviews. He was encouraged to keep at it by friends on the Army Staff, who argued that they needed a detailed post-Vietnam study of an Army operation. It was a long, hard slog, but at last the effort was capped by success. As of 2012, at least two Army schools were using it as a text. **Where will you be in five years:** Dr. Raines hopes to have completed work on his current project for the Joint History Office and be fully retired, able to travel with his wife, and to research and write on historical topics of interest to him. **Political Affiliations:** Independent **Religion:** Methodist **Business Address:** The Pentagon, Washington, DC, 20318-5000 **Shipping Address:** 2307 Candlewood Drive, Alexandria, VA, 22308 **Website:** http://www.edgarfrankraines.com

Vikram Rajadhyaksha

Title: Civil Engineering Consultant, Engineering Company Executive **Industry:** Engineering **Company Name:** DLZ Corporation **Date of Birth:** 05/04/1946 **Education:** MS in Geotechnical Engineering, University of Cincinnati (1986); BS in Civil Engineering, Indian Institute of Technology Delhi; Coursework, Administrative and Financial Management, The Ohio State University **Career:** Chief Executive Officer, Dodson-Lindblom Associate, Columbus, OH (1979-Present); President, DLZ Corporation, Columbus, OH; Chief Executive Officer, DLZ Corporation, Columbus, OH; Chairman, Board of Directors, DLZ Corporation, Columbus, OH **Membership:** American Society of Civil Engineers; Society of American Military Engineers; Fellow, National Society of Professional Engineers **Marquis Who's Who Honors:** Albert Nelson Marquis Lifetime Achievement Award (2017) **To what do you attribute your success:** Rajadhyaksha attributes his success to being very driven and having great mentors. **Why did you become involved in your profession or industry:** Rajadhyaksha became involved in his industry due to his family's business. **Shipping Address:** 6121 Huntely Rd., DLZ Corporation, Columbus, OH, 43229 **Website:** http://www.dlz.com

NancyJo Ralph

Title: Music Educator (Retired) **Industry:** Education/Educational Services **Parents:** Alfred M. Niles; Phyllis L. Niles **Marital Status:** Married **Spouse Name:** Dwight G. Ralph (3/28/1970) **Children:** Victoria L.; Erik C. **Education:** Postgraduate Work in Music Education, Kent State University (1989); Master's Degree in Elementary Education, Edinboro University (1974); MusB in Education, Grove City College (1969) **Certifications:** Registered Music Educator **Career:** Elementary School Music Teacher, Penncrest School District (2000-2005); Music Teacher, Cambridge Springs High School, Penncrest School District (1970-2000); Elementary School Music Teacher, Lakeview School District (1969); Private Piano Teacher **Career Related:** With, Red Door Ringers (2013); Member, Tool City Bell Ringers (2005-2014); Volunteer Music Teacher, Cornerstone Day Care Center (2005-2007); Penncrest Day Care Center (2005-2007) **Civic:** Director, Chancel Choir, Sagertown United Methodist Church (2014-Present); Director, Justified By Faith (2002-Present); Choir Member, Saegertown United Methodist Church (1970-Present); Pianist, Saegertown United Methodist Church (1970-Present); Committee Member, Saegertown United Methodist Church (1970-Present) **Awards:** Honoree, National Honor Roll for American Outstanding Teachers (2005-2006) **Membership:** Alternate Professional Rights and Responsibilities Commission, Pennsylvania State Education Association (2001-2005); President, Penncrest Area Education Association (2001-2003); Vice President, Penncrest Area Education Association (2001-2002); Negotiator, Penncrest Area Education Association (2000-2001); Curriculum and Instruction Chair, District Two, Pennsylvania Music Educators Association (1993-2003); President, Penncrest Area Education Association (1984-1986); Negotiator, Penncrest Area Education Association (1982-1986); Vice President, Penncrest Area Education Association (1982-1984); Associate, Penncrest Area Education Association; Red Door Ringers; Tool City Ringers **Marquis Who's Who Honors:** Albert Nelson Marquis Lifetime Achievement Award (2017) **Hobbies:** Music; Reading; Painting; Knitting; Quilting **Religion:** Methodist **Shipping Address:** 17768 Grange Center Rd, Saegertown, PA, 16433

James Byrne Ranck Jr.

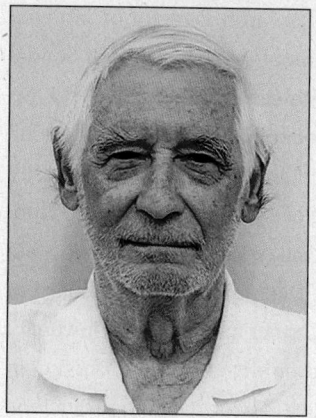

Title: Neuroscience Researcher, Educator **Industry:** Education/Educational Services **Company Name:** SUNY Downstate Medical Center **Date of Birth:** 08/17/1930 **Place of Birth:** Frederick **State:** MD **Parents:** James Byrne Ranck; Dorothy Irene (Schwieger) Ranck **Marital Status:** Married **Spouse Name:** Helen Haukeness (6/9/1961) **Children:** Mary Ranck Bolieu **Education:** Honorary Doctorate, SUNY Downstate Medical Center (2017); Postdoctoral Fellow, Laboratory of Walter Woodbury, University of Washington, Seattle, WA (1959-1961); Intern, The University of Chicago Medicine (1955-1956); MD, Columbia University (1955); BA, Haverford College (1952) **Career:** Distinguished Teaching Professor in Physiology, SUNY Downstate Medical Center (2005-2014); Professor, Department of Physiology, SUNY Downstate Medical Center, Brooklyn, NY (1975-2005); Professor, Department of Physiology, University of Michigan, Ann Arbor, MI (1962-1975); Assistant Professor, Department of Physiology, University of Michigan, Ann Arbor, MI (1962-1975); Instructor of Biophysics, Department of Physiology, University of Washington, Seattle, WA (1960-1961); Scientist, Laboratory of Neuroanatomy, National Institutes of Health, Bethesda, MD (1956-1958) **Creative Works:** Co-author, "Head-Direction Cells Recorded from the Postsubiculum in Freely Moving Rats. I. Description and Quantitative Analysis" (1990); Co-author, "Spatial Firing Patterns of Hippocampal Complex-Spike Cells in a Fixed Environment" (1987); Author, "Head Direction Cells in the Deep Layer of Dorsal Presubiculum in Freely Moving Rats" (1984); Co-author, "Sensory-Behavioral Correlates of Individual Hippocampal Neurons in Three Situations: Space and Context," Neurobiology of the Hippocampus (1983); Author, "Which Elements are Excited in Electrical Stimulation of Mammalian Central Nervous System: A Review" (1975); Author, "Studies on Single Neurons in Dorsal Hippocampal Formation and Septum in Unrestrained Rats. I. Behavioral Correlates and Firing Repertoires" (1973); Co-author, "Studies on Single Neurons in Dorsal Hippocampal Formation and Septum in Unrestrained Rats. II. Hippocampal Slow Waves and Theta Cell Firing During Bar Pressing and Other Behaviors" (1973); Author, "Electrical Impedance in the Subicular Area of Rats During Paradoxical Sleep" (1966); Contributor, Book Chapters; Contributor, Articles, Professional Journals **Marquis Who's Who Honors:** Albert Nelson Marquis Lifetime Achievement Award (2017) **Why did you become involved in your profession or industry:** Dr. Ranck was inspired to enter his profession during the doctors' draft of 1955. He was recruited by the National Institutes of Health to perform research. He enjoyed research and decided to stay with it. **What do you consider to be the highlight of your career:** Dr. Ranck is noted and most proud of his achievement in discovering Head-Direction cells. This was an important discovery in his field, and led to further research. **Shipping Address:** 100 Bank St Apt. 4D, New York, NY, 10014

R. Lor Randall

Title: LB & OLIVE S. Young Presidential Endowed Chair in Cancer Research, Director of Sarcoma Services **Industry:** Education/Educational Services **Company Name:** University of Utah School of Medicine **Date of Birth:** 01/11/1966 **Place of Birth:** Washington **State:** DC **Parents:** Robert Lawrence Randall; Mary (Hartley) Randall **Marital Status:** Married **Spouse Name:** Susannah Randall **Education:** MD, Yale University (1992); BA in Human Biology/Molecular Biology, Brown University (1988) **Certifications:** Licensed Fluoroscopy X-ray Supervisor, State of Washington; Licensed Fluoroscopy X-ray Supervisor, State of Utah; Certified Operating Physician Assistant Supervisor, State of California; Certified, American Board of Orthopedic Surgeons; Diplomate, National Board of Medical Examiners **Career:** Director, Sarcoma Service, Huntsman Cancer Institute, The University of Utah (1998-Present); Director, Sarcoma Service, Primary Children's Hospital, Intermountain Healthcare (1998-Present) **Career Related:** President, Connective Tissue Oncology Society; President Elect, Musculoskeletal Tumor Society, MSTS; President Elect, Association of Bone and Joint Surgeons; Chairman of Orthopoaedics, The Children's Oncology Group; Vice-Chairman, Bone Committee, The Children's Oncology Group **Civic:** Second Vice President, Association of Bone and Joint Surgeons (2017-Present); Member, Career Enhancement Program Committee, Sarcoma Alliance for Research through Collaboration (2016-Present); Member, HCI Melanoma SPORE Campaign Developmental Research Program, Huntsman Cancer Institute, The University of Utah (2016-Present); Member, Health Care Safety Committee, The University of Utah (2015-Present); Member, Medical Advisory Council for Sarcoma Research, Alan B. Slifka Foundation (2014-Present); Member, Scientific Program Advisory Committee, International Society of Paediatric Oncology (2014-Present); Advisory Council Member, Focus on Rhabdomyosarcoma (2014-Present); Member, Adolescent & Young Adult Steering Committee, The Children's Oncology Group (2014-Present); Affiliate, Ontario Cancer Care, Program in Evidence-Based Care, Sarcoma Disease Site Group (2013-Present); Vice Chairman, Soft Tissue Sarcoma Committee, National Comprehensive Cancer Network (2013-Present); Member, Medical Advisory Board, Sarcoma Foundation of America (2013-Present); Member, Soft Tissue Sarcoma Steering Committee, The Children's Oncology Group (2013-Present); Chairman, Membership Committee, Utah Chapter, American College of Surgeons (2013-Present); Chairman, Lean Time Out Program, University of Utah Health (2013-Present); Chairman, Steering Committee HCI/PCH Adolescent Young Adult Oncology Program (2013-Present); Member, Surgical Quality Committee, The University of Utah (2013-Present); Member, Osteosarcoma Biospecimen Committee, The Children's Oncology Group (2012-Present); Vice Chairman, Bone Cancer Committee, The Children's Oncology Group (2012-Present); Chairman, Bone Cancer Surgery Committee, The Children's Oncology Group (2012-Present); Member, PDQ Pediatric Treatment Editorial Advisory Board, NCI, Content Management Office (2012-Present); Member, Peer Case Sarcoma Advisory Board (2011-Present); Member, Scientific and Medical Advisory Board, The MHE Research Foundation (2011-Present); Chairman, Surgical Specimen Tracking Committee, University of Utah Heath (2011-Present); Member, Ad hoc RPT Committee, University of Utah School of Medicine (2010-Present); North American Surgery Chairman, European and American OS Study Group (2009-Present); Member, Scientific Advisory Board, Quad W Sarcoma Biostatistics Office (2009-Present); Member, CME Advisory Board, The University of Utah School of Medicine (2009-Present); Member, Faculty Advancement Committee, Department of Orthopaedics, The University of Utah (2009-Present); Abstract Reviewer, Annual Meeting, Orthopaedic Research Society (2008-Present) Chairman, OR Committee, Huntsman Cancer Institute, The University of Utah (2008-Present) **Awards:** Named Among America's Top Doctors for Cancer, Castle Connolly Medical Ltd., (2009-Present); Named Among America's Top Doctors, Castle Connolly Medical Ltd. (2008-Present); Achievement Award, American Academy of Orthopaedic Surgeons (2010-2014); Named Among Top 13 United States Orthopaedic Oncologists, "Orthopedics This Week" (2013) **Membership:** Surgery Chairman, Risk-Based Treatment for Pediatric NRSTS, The Children's Oncology Group (2007-Present); Ewing's Sarcoma Committee, The Children's Oncology Group (2005-Present); Euramos Osteosarcoma Protocol, Surgery Committee, The Children's Oncology Group (2002-Present); Euro-Ewing 99 Surgery Committee, The Children's Oncology Group (2002-Present); Orthopaedic Committee, The Children's Oncology Group (1999-Present) **Marquis Who's Who Honors:** Albert Nelson Marquis Lifetime Achievement Award (2017) **Business Address:** 2000 Circle of Hope Ste. 4260, Salt Lake City, UT, 84112 **Shipping Address:** 1765 E Fort Douglas Cir, Salt Lake City, UT, 84103

Leonard McElroy Randolph Jr.

Title: Military Officer **Industry:** Military & Defense Services **Date of Birth:** 09/22/1943 **Place of Birth:** Washington **State:** DC **Marital Status:** Married **Spouse Name:** Linda Fleming Raney (8/1/1987) **Children:** Nathaniel; Brion; Holly Tocknell; Chad Muterspaw; Judd Muterspaw **Education:** Honorary LHD, Meharry Medical College (2001); MD, Meharry Medical College (1972); MS in Microbiology, Howard University (1967); BS in Biology, Marietta College (1965) **Certifications:** Board Certified General Surgeon **Career:** President, Phoenix Caduceus Leadership Consulting (2013-Present); Chief Medical Officer, Mercy Health (2005-2012); U.S. Medical Operations, Catholic Healthcare West (2003-2005); Command Surgeon, U.S. Transportation Command (1997-1999); Chief Executive Officer, U.S. Transportation Command (1997-1999); Command Surgeon, U.S. Central Command (1991-1994); Chief Executive Officer, U.S. Central Command (1991-1994); Assistant Professor of Surgery, Boonshoft School of Medicine, Wright State University (1983-1988); Chemistry Teacher, Frank W. Ballou High School, Washington, DC (1967-1968); Research Microbiologist, Georgetown University (1966-1967); Graduate Teaching Assistant, Howard University (1966-1967) **Civic:** Chairman of the Board, YMCA of Greater Cincinnati (2017-Present); Board Vice-Chair, Tri-State Veterans Community Alliance (2015-Present); Health Policy Institute of Ohio (2012-Present); Vice-Chair, Mercy Health (2005-Present); Board Chair, Tri-State Veterans Community Alliance (2014-2017); Board Member, Mercy Health (2013-2016); Board Vice-Chair, YMCA of Greater Cincinnati (2012-2017); Board of Directors, Cincinnati Symphony Orchestra (2009-2015); Board of Directors, HealthEast Care System (2008-2016); Board of Trustees, Cincinnati Hills Christian Academy (2008-2014); Board of Directors, Health Foundation Greater Cincinnati (Now Interact for Health) (2006-2012); Board of Directors, Tri-State Trauma Coalition (2006-2009); Board of Trustees, Marietta College (2001-2015) **Military Service:** Major General, U.S. Air Force (1998); Medical Center Commander, Travis Air Force Base, U.S. Air Force (1994-1997); Chief Executive Officer, Travis Air Force Base, U.S. Air Force (1994-1997); Forward Command Surgeon, Operation Desert Storm, U.S. Air Force (1990-1991); Deputy Command Surgeon, Tactical Air Command, U.S. Air Force (1990-1991); Chief Operating Officer, Tactical Air Command, U.S. Air Force (1990-1991); Hospital Commander, George Air Force Base, U.S. Air Force (1988-1990); Chief Executive Officer, George Air Force Base, U.S. Air Force (1988-1990); Chief Medical Officer, Minot Air Force Base, U.S. Air Force (1985-1986); Director of Medical Education, Wright-Patterson Air Force Base, U.S. Air Force (1984-1985); Attending Surgeon, Wright-Patterson Air Force Base, U.S. Air Force (1983-1984); Chief of Surgical Services, Bergstrom Air Force Base, U.S. Air Force (1980-1983); Chief of General Surgery, Bergstrom Air Force Base, U.S. Air Force (1978-1980); Commissioned Second Lieutenant, U.S. Air Force, (1978); General Surgeon, Bergstrom Air Force Base, U.S. Air Force (1977-1978); Resident, Kessler Air Force Base, U.S. Air Force (1972-1977) **Awards:** Inductee, Marietta College Hall of Honor (2016); Mister Mac Award, Marietta College (2012); Honoree, Hall of Excellence, Ohio Foundation of Independent Colleges (2003); Exceptional Service Award, Uniformed Services University (2003); Distinguished Alumnus Award, Alumni Association, Marietta College (2000); Distinguished Alumni of the Year Award, National Association for Equal Opportunity in Higher Education (1999); Excellence Award, American College of Healthcare Executives (1997); Decorated Defense Superior Service Medal, Operation Restore Hope, U.S. Air Force; Legion Of Merit Operation Desert Storm, U.S. Air Force; Distinguished Service Medal, U.S. Air Force; Boys State, Georgetown University **Membership:** Distinguished President, American College of Healthcare Executives (2000-2001); Board of Governors, American College of Surgeons (1996-2002); Board of Governors, Society of Air Force Clinical Surgeons (1996-2002); Honorary Member, American Academy of Medical Administrators; Society of Medical Administrators; Society of Medical Consultants to Armed Forces; AMSUS; Air Force Association; Christian Medical & Dental Associations; Aerospace Medical Association; The Cincinnatus Association; Alpha Omega Alpha Honor Medical Society; Beta Kappa Chi National Honor Society; TriBeta **Marquis Who's Who Honors:** Albert Nelson Marquis Lifetime Achievement Award (2017) **Hobbies:** Reading; Sports; Writing **Religion:** Protestant **Shipping Address:** 13 Woodcreek Drive, Blue Ash, OH, 45241

Rama K. Rao

Title: Pharmaceutical Executive, BlockChain Entrepreneur **Industry:** Pharmaceuticals **Company Name:** BloqCube Inc. **Date of Birth:** 11/20/1955 **Place of Birth:** Tanuku **Country of Origin:** Andhra Province, India **Parents:** Rayavarapu Ramachandra Rao; Rayavarapu Satyavani Rao **Marital Status:** Married **Spouse Name:** Kavitha Advikolanu Rao, PhD **Children:** Trishna **Education:** MBA, INSEAD, Fontainebleu, France (1989); Postgraduate Diploma in Management, Indian Institute of Management, Calcutta, India (1981); BS in Technology, Indian Institute of Technology, Delhi, India (1977) **Career:** CFO, Novartis Pharma, Russia (2013-Present); CFO/COO, Cytovia Oncology (2017-2018); Executive Director, Head, U.S. Research and Development Finance, U.S. Global Development (2010-2013); Executive Director, Head of Finance, Oncology Global Development Unit, Novartis (2006-2009); CFO, Vice President of Finance, Novartis Canada, Dorval, QC, Canada (2004-2006); Financial Director, Intercontinental Region, Novartis Oncology Business Unit, East Hanover, NJ (2001-2004); CFO, Financial Manager, PC/NS Lilly USA, Indianapolis, IN (1999-2001); Financial Advisor, Corporate Finance and Investment Banking, Lilly Corporate Center, Indianapolis, IN (1998-1999); Manager, Global Treasury, Gems Eli Lilly, Brussels, Belgium (1995-1997); Financial Manager for Africa, Eli Lilly, Geneva, Switzerland (1994-1995); Credit and Customer Service Manager, Eli Lilly, Geneva, Switzerland (1993-1994); Executive Assistant to General Manager, Bank of Bahrain & Kuwait, Bahrain (1985-1988); Assistant Manager, Metal Box India, Calcutta, India (1977-1984); Financial Associate, Eli Lilly, Geneva, Switzerland; CEO, BloqCube Inc. **Civic:** Volunteer, Samaritans/Befrienders, Bahrain (1987-1988); Blood Donor, Red Cross/Crescent, India, Belgium, and Bahrain (1974-1997) **Awards:** Brain of IIT; Global Systems Award, Eli Lilly; President's Award, Novartis Oncology for Operational Excellence **Membership:** American Medical Association; Association of Investment Management and Research; Institute of Management Accountants **Marquis Who's Who Honors:** Albert Nelson Marquis Lifetime Achievement Award (2017); Distinguished Humanitarian (2017) **To what do you attribute your success:** Mr. Rao attributes his success to his parents, Rev. Brother Fitzpatrick, and the teaching staff at St. Columba's High School in New Delhi, India. **Why did you become involved in your profession or industry:** Mr. Rao became involved in his profession in order to use his skills to make a difference to patients who need treatment. **What do you consider to be the highlight of your career:** The highlights of Mr. Rao's career were developing an innovative Leukemia patients assistance program in emerging countries for Novartis, setting up a global center of FX/Tax excellence for Lilly, and training almost 150 associates in R&D Finance. **Where will you be in five years:** In five years, Mr. Rao will be building his company, BloqCube. **Hobbies:** Travel; Military history; Foreign policy **Political Affiliations:** Independent **Religion:** Hindu **Shipping Address:** 5 Muirfield Lane, Bridgewater, NJ, 08807

R. Ronald Rau

Title: Physicist (Retired) **Industry:** Sciences **Date of Birth:** 09/01/1920 **Place of Birth:** Tacoma **Parents:** Ralph Campbell Rau; Ida (Montgall) Rau **Marital Status:** Married (6/2/1944) **Spouse Name:** Maryjane Uhrlaub **Children:** Whitney Leslie; Littie Elise **Education:** Honorary LHD, University of Puget Sound (2002); PhD in Physics, California Institute of Technology (1948); MS in Physics, California Institute of Technology (1943); BS in Physics, University of Puget Sound (1941) **Career:** Associate Director for High Energy Physics, Brookhaven National Laboratory (1970-1981); Chairman, Department of Physics, Brookhaven National Laboratory (1966-1970); Physicist, Brookhaven National Laboratory, Upton, NY (1956-1966); Fulbright Research Professor of Physics, Ecole Polytechnique, Paris, France (1954-1955); Assistant Professor of Physics, Princeton University (1947-1956) **Career Related:** Visiting Professor, Massachusetts Institute of Technology (1984-1988); Staff Scientist, Desy Laboratory, Hamburg, Federal Republic of Germany (1984-1985); Research Scientist, CERN, Geneva, Switzerland (1962-1963) **Civic:** Trustee, University of Puget Sound (1978-1984); Member, Steilacoom Tribe, Steilacoom, WA **Membership:** American Association for the Advancement of Science; American Physical Society **Marquis Who's Who Honors:** Distinguished Humanitarian (2017) **Shipping Address:** 6 Peathole Lane, Bellport, NY, 11713

Marilyn A. Ray

Title: Professor Emeritus **Industry:** Education/Educational Services **Company Name:** Florida Atlantic University **Date of Birth:** 01/24/1938 **Place of Birth:** Hamilton **Country of Origin:** Ontario/Canada **Parents:** Arthur William Anthony Ray; Elvera Caroline (Montag) Ray **Spouse Name:** James L. Droesbeke (8/18/1979, Deceased 2001) **Education:** Honorary Degree, Nevada State College (2005); PhD in Nursing, University of Utah (1981); MA in Anthropology, McMaster University (1978); MSN, University of Colorado Denver (1969); BSN, University of Colorado Denver (1968); Diploma, St. Joseph's Hospital School Nursing, Hamilton, Canada (1958) **Certifications:** Certified, Transcultural Nurse; Certified, Registered Nurse, State of Florida **Career:** Professor Emeritus, Florida Atlantic University (2006-Present); Adjunct Professor, Florida Atlantic University (2004-2005); Professor, College of Nursing, Florida Atlantic University (1995-2004); Christine E. Lynn Eminent Scholar, College of Nursing, Florida Atlantic University (1989-1994); Assistant Professor, University of Colorado (1984-1989); Assistant Professor, School of Nursing, McMaster University (1973-1976); Instructor, School of Nursing, University of San Francisco (1970-1972) **Career Related:** Visiting Professor, Alberta Heritage Foundation, University of Alberta (2005); Yingling Visiting Scholar, Virginia Commonwealth University, Richmond, VA (1994-1995); Visiting Professor, University of Colorado (1989-2004) **Military Service:** Colonel, United States Air Force (1967-1999) **Creative Works:** Author and Co-editor, "A Hand Book for Caring Science: Expanding the Paradigm" (2018); Author, "Nursing, Caring & Completely Science: For Human Environment Wellbeing" (2011); Author, "A Study of Caring Within an Institutional Culture: The Discovery of the Theory of Bureaucratic Caring" (2010); Author, "Transcultural Caring Dynamics in Nursing & Healthcare"; Author, "Phenomenology of Caring"; Contributor, Articles to Professional Journals **Awards:** Lifetime Achievement Award, University of Colorado College of Nursing Alumni Association (2017); Honorary Distinguished Fellow of the European Society for Person Centered Healthcare (2016); Book of the Year Award (2011); Distinguished Alumni Award, University of Utah College of Nursing (2007); Transcultural Nursing Scholarship (2005); Leininger Award (1989) **Membership:** Fellow, American Academy of Nursing; Fellow, Society of Applied Anthropology; American Nurses Association; Charter Member, International Association of Human Caring; Board Member, International Association of Human Caring; Charter, Space Nursing Society; Charter, Aerospace Human Factors Association; Editorial Board Journal, College Nurses of Ontario, Transcultural Nursing Society; Board Member, Qualitative Health Research, College Nurses of Ontario, Transcultural Nursing Society; Sigma Theta Tau **Marquis Who's Who Honors:** Albert Nelson Marquis Lifetime Achievement Award (2017); Distinguished Humanitarian (2017) **Hobbies:** Travel; Music **Shipping Address:** 8487 Via D Oro, Boca Raton, FL, 33433 **Website:** https://www.marilynray.com

Constantin Anis Rebeiz

Title: Biochemist **Industry:** Research **Company Name:** Rebeiz Foundation for Basic Research **Date of Birth:** 07/11/1936 **Place of Birth:** Beirut **Country of Origin:** Lebanon **Parents:** Anis C. Rebeiz; Valentine A. (Choueyri) Rebeiz **Marital Status:** Married **Spouse Name:** Conness Carole Louise (8/18/1962) **Children:** Paul A.; Natalie; Mark J. **Education:** PhD, University of California, Davis (1965); MS, University of California, Davis (1960); BS, American University, Beirut, Lebanon (1959) **Career:** President, Rebeiz Foundation for Basic Research, Champaign, IL (2005-Present); Professor Emeritus, University of Illinois, Urbana-Champaign (2005-Present); Professor, University of Illinois, Urbana-Champaign (1976-2005); Director, Laboratory Plant, Biochemistry and Photobiology, University of Illinois, Urbana-Champaign (1973-2005); Associate Professor, Biochemistry, Plant Physiology, University of Illinois, Urbana-Champaign (1972-1976); Research Associate of Biology, University of California, Davis (1969-1971); Director, Department of Biological Sciences, Agricultural Research Institute, Beirut, Lebanon (1965-1969) **Awards:** Recipient, Outstanding Scientific Achievement Award, Faculty of Agricultural and Food Sciences, American University, Beirut, Lebanon (2002); Grantee, C.A. and C.C. Rebeiz Endowment for Basic Research (2000); Recipient, Presidential Green Chemistry Challenge Award (1999); Recipient, Senior Research Award, University of Illinois (1994); Recipient, John P. Trebellas Research Endowment Award (1986); Recipient, Beckman Research Award (1985); Recipient, Funk Award (1985); Listed, One of 100 Outstanding Innovators, Scientific Digest (1984-1985); Recipient, Beckman Research Award (1982) **Membership:** Executive Committee, Lebanese Association for the Advancement of Sciences (1967-1969); American Association for the Advancement of Science **Marquis Who's Who Honors:** Albert Nelson Marquis Lifetime Achievement Award (2017) **Why did you become involved in your profession or industry:** Dr. Rebeiz entered his profession because when he was in Lebanon, in the backyard of the National Research Institute, he looked around and saw all the trees with green leaves and he thought chlorophyll was important. **Shipping Address:** 2209 Edgewater Pl, Champaign, IL, 61822 **Website:** http://www.vlpbp.org

Avelino Luis Rebuelta

Title: Public Administration Educator **Industry:** Education/Educational Services **Date of Birth:** 06/22/1944 **Education:** Master's Degree in Educational Administration, University of Texas, Edinburg (Now the University of Texas Rio Grande Valley) (1999); MPA, American University, Washington, DC (1982) **Career:** Professor, Universidad Pedagogica Nacional, Mexico City, Mexico (1982-Present); Professor, Instituto Politecnico Nacional, Mexico City, Mexico (1962-Present); Professor, Universidad Nacional Autonoma De Mexico, Mexico City, Mexico (1962); Manager, Ram Apartments **Marquis Who's Who Honors:** Albert Nelson Marquis Lifetime Achievement Award (2017) **Shipping Address:** 701 Hibiscus Avenue, Apt. 5, McAllen, TX, 78501

Robert R. Recker

Title: Medical Educator, Internist **Industry:** Education/Educational Services **Company Name:** Creighton University **Date of Birth:** 04/05/1939 **Place of Birth:** St. Libory **State:** NE **Parents:** Robert Libory Recker; Dorothy E. Evers **Marital Status:** Married **Spouse Name:** Susan Marie Cody **Children:** Katherine; Sarah; Robert; Michael **Education:** MD, Creighton University, Omaha, NE (1963) **Certifications:** Diplomate, American Board of Internal Medicine (1971) **Career:** O'Brien Endowed Chair, Creighton University, Omaha, NE (2016-Present); Associate Dean of Research, Creighton University, Omaha, NE (2006-Present); Division Chief of Endocrinology, Creighton University, Omaha, NE (1974-Present); Professor of Medicine, Creighton University, Omaha, NE (1971-Present); Director, Osteoporosis Research Center, Creighton University, Omaha, NE (1974); Fellow, Creighton University (1970) **Career Related:** Vice President, National Osteoporosis Foundation (2006) **Military Service:** Flight Surgeon, U.S. Air Force (1964-1967) **Awards:** Endowed O'Brien Chair (2016); Outstanding Performance as Faculty Member, Creighton University **Membership:** American Association of Endocrinology; American Medical Associate **Marquis Who's Who Honors:** Albert Nelson Marquis Lifetime Achievement Award (2017) **Why did you become involved in your profession or industry:** He grew up on a farm, and when he was younger he wanted to be a veterinarian. However, while attending Creighton University, he was persuaded by his mentor, Dr. Robert Heaney, to study endocrinology. **Business Address:** 6829 N 72nd St. Ste. 7400, Omaha, NE, 68122 **Shipping Address:** 3309 S 116th St, Omaha, NE, 68144

Robert R. Reed III

Title: Professor **Industry:** Education/Educational Services **Company Name:** University of Alabama **Education:** PhD, Pennsylvania State University (1998) **Career:** Professor, University of Alabama (2015-Present); Morrow Faculty Excellence Fellow, University of Alabama (2011-Present); Professor of Economics, The University of Alabama, Tuscaloosa, AL (2007-Present); Associate Professor, University of Alabama (2010-2015); Assistant Professor, University of Alabama (2007-2010); Visiting Scholar, Center for European Integration Studies, University of Bonn (2003); Assistant Professor of Economics, University of Kentucky, Lexington, KY (2000-2007); Assistant Professor of Economics, Iowa State University, Ames, IA (1998-2000) **Career Related:** Visiting Scholar, Federal Reserve Bank of Atlanta (2007-Present); Lecturer, Pennsylvania State University (1998); Research Assistant, Professor Ping Wang (1998); Teaching Assistant, Pennsylvania State University (1995-1997) **Business Address:** 200 Alston Hall University of Alabama, AL, Tuscaloosa, 35487 **Shipping Address:** 200 Alston Hall, University of Alabama, AL, Tuscaloosa, 35487 **Website:** https://robertrreed.wordpress.com

Robert H. Reeder

Title: Lawyer (Retired) **Industry:** Law and Legal Services **Date of Birth:** 12/03/1930 **Place of Birth:** Topeka **State:** KS **Parents:** William Harry Reeder; Florence Mae (Cochran) Reeder **Education:** JD, Washburn University (1960); AB, Washburn University (1952) **Career:** Executive Director, National Committee for Uniform Traffic Laws and Ordinances, Evanston, IL (1982-1990); General Counsel, Traffic Institute, Northwestern University (1967-1992); Assistant Counsel, Traffic Institute, Northwestern University (1960-1967); Research Assistant, Kansas Legislative Research Department (1955-1960) **Civic:** Pro Bono Work, American Bar Association Traffic Court Committee (1992-2006) **Military Service:** US Army (1952-1954) **Creative Works:** Co-Author, "Vehicle Traffic Law" (1974); Author, "Interpretation of Implied Consent by the Courts" (1972) **Membership:** Chairman, Committee on Alcohol & Other Drugs (1973-1975); Kansas Bar Association **Bar Admissions:** Supreme Court of the United States (1968); Kansas (1960); United States District Court for the District of Kansas (1960) **Marquis Who's Who Honors:** Albert Nelson Marquis Lifetime Achievement Award (2017) **To what do you attribute your success:** Mr. Reeder attributes his success to his work ethic and hard work. **Why did you become involved in your profession or industry:** Mr. Reeder entered his profession because ever since he was a child he was interested in political science and history. Law was a natural progression. **Hobbies:** Family history; Genealogy **Political Affiliations:** Republican **Religion:** Methodist **Shipping Address:** 1407 SW Summit Woods Dr., Apt 3, Topeka, KS, 66615

Edward Reid

Title: Senior Counsel **Industry:** Law and Legal Services **Company Name:** Davis, Polk & Wardwell **Date of Birth:** 03/24/1930 **Place of Birth:** Detroit **State:** MI **Parents:** Edward S. Reid Jr.; Margaret (Overington) Reid **Education:** LLB, Harvard University, Magna Cum Laude (1956); BA, Yale University (1951) **Career:** Senior Counsel, Davis, Polk & Wardwell (1996-Present); Director, General Mills, Inc. (1974-1989); Partner, Davis, Polk & Wardwell (1964-1995); Associate, Davis, Polk & Wardwell, New York City, NY (1957-1964) **Civic:** Board of Directors, Brooklyn Botanical Garden Corp. (1996-2010); Trustee, Brooklyn Museum of Art (1994-2010); Board of Directors, Bargemusic Ltd. (1990-1993); Board of Directors, Brooklyn Botanical Garden Corp. (1977-1992); Chairman, Brooklyn Institute of Arts and Sciences (1974-1979); Trustee, Brooklyn Museum of Art (1973-1993); Member, New York City Board of Higher Education (1971-1973); Trustee, Brooklyn Institute of Arts and Sciences (1966-1993) **Membership:** American Bar Association; New York State Bar Association; Association of Bar of City of New York; American Law Institute; Heights Casino Club; Rembrandt Club; Century Association Club; Yale Club; Quoque Beach Club; Shinnecock Yacht Club; Quoque Field Club **Marquis Who's Who Honors:** Albert Nelson Marquis Lifetime Achievement Award (2017) **Business Address:** PO Box 39, Quogue, NY, 11959 **Shipping Address:** 450 Lexington Avenue, Davis Polk & Wardwell, New York, NY, 10017

Daniel Jay Reidenberg

Title: Executive Director **Industry:** Business Management/Business Services **Company Name:** Suicide Awareness Voices of Education **Date of Birth:** 08/05/1966 **Place of Birth:** St. Paul **State:** MN **Parents:** Louis M. Reidenberg; Loni Schnitzer Reidenberg **Marital Status:** Single **Education:** Doctor of Clinical Psychology, Minnesota School of Professional Psychology, Argosy University, Twin Cities, Eagan, MN (1994); BA in Psychology and Child Psychology, University of Minnesota Twin Cities, Minnesota (1989) **Certifications:** Certified Psychological Autopsy Investigator; Board Certified Professional Counselor; Certified Master Therapist; Certified Relationship Specialist; Certified Crisis Debriefer and Aviation Disaster Responder **Career:** Executive Director, SAVE; Clinical and Forensic Psychologist **Career Related:** National Presentation, The Pentagon (2017); National Presentation, The White House (2015-2016); National Presentation, The Pentagon (2014); National Presentation, The White House (2011); International Presentation, Rome, Italy; International Presentation, London, England; International Presentation, Oslo, Norway; International Presentation, Tokyo, Japan; International Presentation, Alberta, Canada; International Presentation, Montreal, Canada; International Presentation, Trinidad and Tobago; International Presentation, Dublin, Ireland; Two-Time Featured Guest, Larry King; Three-Time Featured Guest, "CNN Newsmakers" **Civic:** Advisory Board, Crisis Text Line (2015-present); Advisory Board, TalkLife.com (2016-Present); Editorial Board, The Journal of Clinical Psychiatry (2013-Present); Advisory Board, Reachout.com (2009-Present); Advisory Board, Your Life Counts, California (2009-Present); Editorial Advisory Board, Esperanza (2007-Present); Board of Directors, Open Door Support Group (2005-Present); Editorial Advisory Board, American Psychiatric Association (2005-Present); Chair, Certified Relationship Specialist Program, American Psychotherapy Association (2006-2017); Advisory Board of Directors and Chair, Certified Relationship Specialist Program, American Psychotherapy Association (2006-2017); Advisory Council, Camp Hope Heartland (2005-2012); Event Coordinator, Camp Hope Heartland (2002-2015); Thanksgiving Meals on Wheels, Inc. (2001-2014); The Salvation Army USA (2000-2014); Board of Directors, Camp Heartland-Heart & Soul (1996-2001); Lead Event Coordinator, Camp Heartland-Heart and Soul (1996-2001); Board Member, American Psychotherapy Association (1995-2017) **Creative Works:** Author, "Changing the Direction of Suicide Prevention in the United States" (2017); Author, Book Forward, "Cracked Not Broken: Surviving and Thriving After a Suicide Attempt" (2013); Author, Book Forward, "The Power of Acceptance: Finding Peace from Panic and Anxiety Attacks" (2008); Author, Book Chapters, Media and Suicide; Author, Book Chapters, Adolescent Suicide; Author, Book Chapters, Suicide Risk Assessment and Management; Author, Book Chapters, Sports Talk; Contributor, More than Articles to Professional Journals Including American Journal of Preventive Medicine; Lead Author, Recommendations for Media Reporting on Suicide; Contributor and Special Expert, Recommendations for Media Reporting on Bullying; Lead Author, Recommendations for Bloggers and Social Media; Lead Author, National Strategy for Suicide Prevention **Awards:** Recipient, Award for Applied Contributions to the Field of Suicidology and Crisis Intervention, American Association of Suicidology (2018); Recipient, Best Doctor's Award (2013-2017); Recipient, Best Women's, Children's, and Families Charities (2012-2016); Recipient, Healthy Mind/Healthy Body Award (2012); Recipient, "Champion of Change from the Obama Administration, The White House (2011); Named, Non-Profit Professional of the Year (2010); Listee, Who's Who of Prevention Leaders in Florida (2008); Named, Ten Outstanding Young Minnesotans (2006); Recipient, B. Warren Hart Award for Service to Humanity (2006); Recipient, Outstanding Leadership Award, American Psychotherapy Association (2004); Recipient, Distinguished Service Award, American Psychotherapy Association (2002); Listee, International Biography of Distinguished Leaders (2001); Recipient, KDWB and Variety Children's Hospital Dedicated Service Award (1997); Recipient, Certificate of Commendation, Minnesota Governor (1995); Recipient, Certificate of Commendation, Minnesota Governor (1993) **Membership:** Steering Committee, National Suicide Prevention Lifeline; Steering Committee, National Suicide Prevention Resource Center; Executive Committee and General Secretary, International Association for Suicide Prevention; United States Representative, International Association for Suicide Prevention; Co-Chair, International Association for Suicide Prevention's Media and Internet Task Force; Advisory Board Chair, American Psychotherapy Association; Co-Chair, National Strategy for Suicide Prevention; Multiple Task Forces, National Action Alliance for Suicide Prevention; Mental Health/Suicide Expert, Entertainment Resource Professionals Association **Marquis Who's Who Honors:** Who's Who in America; Who's Who in the World **Shipping Address:** 8120 Penn Ave. S, Ste 470, Suicide Awareness Voices of Education, Bloomington, MN, 55431 **Website:** https://save.org

Norman Reinertsen

Title: Air Transportation Executive (Retired) **Industry:** Aviation **Date of Birth:** 03/27/1934 **Place of Birth:** Brooklyn **State:** NY **Parents:** Berthin Reinertsen; Malene Katherine (Dahl) Reinertsen **Marital Status:** Life Partner **Spouse Name:** Joan Hayes; Elizabeth T. O'Shea (8/30/1958, Deceased 2003) **Children:** Michael; Christopher; Katherine **Education:** Postgraduate Work, Harvard University (1982); BEE, The City College of New York (1960) **Certifications:** Registered, Professional Engineer, State of California **Career:** Retired (1994); Vice President, Quality Operations, Grumman Aircraft Systems Division, Northrop Grumman (1987-1994); Senior Vice President, Vehicle Division, Grumman Allied (1985-1987); Senior Vice President, Vehicle Division, Grumman Allied Industries (1983-1994); President, Grumman Olson, Melville, NY (1983-1985); Executive Vice President, Grumman Flexible, Delaware, Ohio (1979-1982); Vice President, Automotive, Grumman Allied Industries, Melville, NY (1977-1983); Senior Vice President, Olson Bodies, Inc. (1977-1979); General Manager, Great River Operations, Grumman Aerospace Corporation (1975-1977); Various Positions, Grumman Aerospace Corporation (1960-1975) **Military Service:** United States Army (1955-1957) **Membership:** Past Member, Air Force Association; Northport Yacht Club; Indian Hills Country Club **Marquis Who's Who Honors:** Albert Nelson Marquis Lifetime Achievement Award (2017) **Hobbies:** Traveling with Partner Joan Hayes **Shipping Address:** 7 Oleander Drive, Northport, NY, 11768

Richard Thomas Reminger

Title: Lawyer, Artist **Industry:** Law and Legal Services **Date of Birth:** 04/03/1931 **Place of Birth:** Cleveland **State:** OH **Parents:** Edwin Carl Reminger; Theresa Henrietta (Bookmyer) Reminger **Marital Status:** Married **Spouse Name:** Billie Carmen Greer (6/26/1954) **Children:** Susan Greer; Patricia Allison; Richard Thomas, Jr. **Education:** JD, Cleveland State University (1957); AB, Case Western Reserve University (1953) **Career:** Managing Partner, Reminger Co, L.P.A., Cleveland, OH (1958-1992); Personnel and Safety Director, Motor Express, In., Cleveland, OH (1954-1958); Founder, Reminger Co, L.P.A., Cleveland, OH **Career Related:** Faculty Member, National Institute for Trial Advocacy (1992); Lecturer, Products Liability, University of Wirtschaft at Schloss Gracht, Erftstadt-Liblar, Germany (1990-1991); Lecturer, Products Liability, Bar Association, City of Hamburg, Germany (1990); Advisory Board, National Claims Council, Commercial Union Assurance Company (1980-1990); Lecturer, Business Law, Case Western Reserve University (1962-1964); Lecturer, Transportation Law, Fenn College (Now Cleveland State University) (1960-1962) **Civic:** Trustee, Intracoastal Health Systems, Palm Beach, FL (1992-2000); Trustee, Cleveland School for the Blind (1987-1988); Trustee, Andrew School (1984-1996); Trustee, Cerebral Palsy Association (1984-1987); Vice President, Cleveland Zoological Society (1984-1987); Trustee, Meridia Huron Hospital, Cleveland, OH (1978-1996); Joint Committee, Cleveland Academy Medicine-Greater Cleveland Bar Association **Military Service:** Air Corps, US Naval Reserve (1950-1958) **Creative Works:** Landscape, Seascape and Portrait Artist, Representative Works in Oil (1965-Present) **Awards:** Recipient, President's Award for Excellence, Case Western Reserve University (2018); Named, Hall of Fame, Cleveland-Marshall College of Law, Cleveland State University (2018); Nominee, Distinguished Alumni Award, Case Western Reserve University (2017); Man of the Year, Cleveland-Marshall College of Law, Cleveland State University (1989) **Membership:** Honorary Trustee, Cleveland-Marshall Law Alumni Association (1980-Present); Bohemian Club, San Francisco, CA (1992-1999); Board of Governors, Lost Tree Club, FL (1991-1994); International Law Committee, Ohio State Bar Association (1990-1991); Council of Delegates, Ohio State Bar Association (1987-1990); President, Mayfield Country Club, Cleveland, OH (1980-1982); Chairman, Medical Legal Committee, Cleveland Metropolitan Bar Association (1978-1979); Professional Responsibility Committee, ABA (1977-1990); Professor, Liability Committee, Cleveland Metropolitan Bar Association (1977-1990); President, Hermit Club, Cleveland, OH (1973-1975); Federal Bar Association; Committee of Law and Medicine, ABA; Palm Beach County Bar Association; International Insurance Law Society; American College of Legal Medicine; Maritime Law Association of the United States; DRI; American Judicature Society; Ohio Association of Civil Trial Attorneys; Society for Ohio Health Care Attorneys; American Health Lawyers Association; Cleveland Association of Civil Trial Attorneys; Transportation Lawyers Association; Pennsylvania Bar Association; International Bar Association; Federation of Insurance and Corporate Counsel; Lifetime Member, Eighth Judicial Circuit Bar Association; Vice President, International Society of Marine Painters; Oil Painters of America; Portrait Society of America; The Society of the Four Arts; Edgcomb Tennis Club, Maine; Kennebunk River Club, Maine; Salmagundi Club, New York, NY; Rolling Rock Club, The Kirtland Country Club, Cleveland, OH; Everglades Club, Florida; Lifetime Member, Varsity Football, Case Reserve Athletic Club **Bar Admissions:** Pennsylvania (1978); Supreme Court of the United States (1961); Ohio (1957) **Marquis Who's Who Honors:** Albert Nelson Marquis Lifetime Achievement Award (2017) **Hobbies:** Tennis **Political Affiliations:** Republican **Shipping Address:** 400 N Flagler Drive, Apt. 1204, West Palm Beach, FL, 33401

Roberta I. Rempfer-Smith

Title: Educator (Retired) **Industry:** Education/Educational Services **Date of Birth:** 08/12/1926 **State:** IL **Marital Status:** Married **Spouse Name:** Robert **Children:** AnnMarie; David; Michael **Education:** BS in Elementary Education, Northern Illinois University (1984); College Coursework **Certifications:** Certification in Special Education (1996); Certification in the Rehabilitation of Blind Adults, Northern Illinois University (1986) **Career:** Child Care Program Director, Chanute Air Force Base, Rantoul, IL (1980-1981); Resource Development Person, DCFS (1975-1976) **Awards:** Human Relations Commissions Award, DeKalb and Sycamore, IL (1973); Nominee, DeKalb County Citizen of the Year (1971) **Marquis Who's Who Honors:** Distinguished Humanitarian (2017) **To what do you attribute your success:** Ms. Rempfer-Smith attributes her success to her faith in Jesus Christ and to the lessons she learned from her mentor, Robert Earl Price. **Why did you become involved in your profession or industry:** She became involved in her profession because of her lifelong desire to become a teacher. **What do you consider to be the highlight of your career:** The highlight of her career was teaching Kenny Battle, who later became a first-pick in the NBA Draft. Another highlight was when she met Carol Owens while studying at Northern Illinois University. **Hobbies:** Attending church services; Mentoring; Basketball; Attending concerts and plays; Scrapbooking; Entertaining; Reading **Shipping Address:** 736 Carlson St, Sycamore, IL, 60178

Elaine Resnick

Title: Psychotherapist **Industry:** Social Work **Company Name:** Psychiatry & Family Therapy **Date of Birth:** 04/02/1944 **Place of Birth:** Orlando **State:** FL **Parents:** Julius Milton Bernstein; Annette (Chusid) Bernstein **Marital Status:** Married **Spouse Name:** Richard B. Resnick (5/21/1975); Peter Schuyten (Divorced 1973) **Children:** Demian; Jesse; Nora; Deborah (Stepchild) **Education:** Postgraduate Studies, New York University (1992-Present); MSW, The City University of New York (1971); BA, New York University, Cum Laude (1966) **Certifications:** Chronically and Terminally Ill Patients (2002); Certification, Institute for Study Psychotherapy (1979); Certification in Hypnosis Training and Supervision, Columbia University (1978); Comprehensive Training Program with Licensed Clinical Social Worker, State of New York; Board Certification in Clinical Social Work; Diplomate in Clinical Social Work **Career:** Psychotherapist, Private Practice (1973-Present); Fieldwork Supervisor, Wurzweiler School of Social Work, Yeshiva University (1991-1992); Clinical Director, Psychiatry & Family Therapy, New York, NY (1986-2016); Clinical Instructor, New York Medical College (1982-1983); Clinical Director, Division of Drug Abuse Research and Treatment, New York Medical College (1977-1983); Research Associate, New York Medical College (1973-1982); Fieldwork Supervisor, New York University (1973-1982); Fieldwork Supervisor, York College/ City University of New York (1976-1977); Lecturer, Marymount Manhattan College (1974-1975); Copy Editor, McGraw-Hill Education **Career Related:** Adjunct Assistant Professor, Silver School of Social Work, New York University (1977-1982); Psychiatric Social Worker, Biological Psychiatric Division, Metropolitan Hospital (1971-1973); New York State Psychiatric Institute (1970-1971); Psychiatric Social Worker, St. Vincent's Catholic Medical Center (1970); Social Worker, Intensive Family Counseling Unit, New York City Department of Social Services, City of New York (1969-1970); Columbia University Medical Center; Fellow, Society of Clinical Social Work Psychotherapists **Creative Works:** Contributor, Professional Journals; Presenter, Field Presentations **Membership:** National Association of Social Workers; National Registry Health Care Providers in Clinical Social Work **Shipping Address:** 43 W 94th Street, Psychiatry & Family Therapy, New York, NY, 10025

William D. Reynolds

Title: Unit Director, Director of Dialysis and Hemodialysis **Industry:** Medicine & Health Care **Company Name:** St. Francis Hospital **Education:** Registered Nurse, University of Phoenix (1996); AS in Nursing, Southern Union State Community College (1995); BSN, Troy University **Certifications:** Certification in Basic Life Support; Certification in Advanced Cardiovascular Life Support, American Stroke Association; Certification in Water Treatment in Nephrology; Certification in Medical-Surgical Nursing **Career:** Unit Director, St. Francis Hospital; Director of Dialysis and Hemodialysis, St. Francis Hospital **Military Service:** National Guard (1998-Present); Deployed, Operation Iraqi Freedom, Kuwait (2005); Chief Warrant Officer III, U.S. Army, Alabama; Active Duty Human Resources Technician, U.S. Army; Sergeant, U.S. Army **Awards:** Meritorious Service Medal **To what do you attribute your success:** Mr. Reynolds attributes his success to the work ethic he learned from his father. **Why did you become involved in your profession or industry:** Mr. Reynolds became involved in his profession because while he was in the military. He took master fitness and combat lifesavers courses and gained an interest in health care. **Where will you be in five years:** In five years, Mr. Reynolds hopes to earn a master of science in nursing, particularly in administration, and obtain a promotion. **Hobbies:** Running **Business Address:** 2122 Manchester Expressway, Columbus, GA, 31904 **Shipping Address:** 4448 Desoto Drive, Columbus, GA, 31909

David Reznik

Title: Dental Medicine Chief **Industry:** Medicine & Health Care **Company Name:** Grady Health System **Place of Birth:** Atlanta **State:** GA **Education:** DDS, Emory University (1984); BA in Political Science, Emory University (1980) **Career:** Chief, Grady Health System's Dental Service, Atlanta, GA (2000-Present); Director, Founder, Oral Health Center, Grady's Health System Infectious Disease Program, Grady Health System's Dental Service, Atlanta, GA (1991-Present); President, HIVdent.org (1997); Founder, HIVdent.org (1997); Assistant Clinical Professor, Emory University; Director, Southeast AIDS Education & Training Center; Director, The Mountain Plains AIDS Education and Training Center; Associate Director, AEGD Program, Lutheran Medical Center, Georgia **Civic:** Researcher, Oral Manifestations of HIV Disease; Researcher, Dental Treatment Considerations for People with HIV Disease; Affiliate, United States Domestic and International HIV/AIDS Policy **Creative Works:** Contributor, "Oral Health In Communities and Neighborhoods" **Awards:** Award, Robert Wood Johnson Foundation (2016); Distinguished Dentist Award, Expert Network (2015); Honoree, Atlanta's Healthcare Heroes, Atlanta Business Chronicle (2014); Associate Administrators Award, Ryan White All Grantees Meeting (2008); Award of Merit, National Dental Association (2004); John Cappers Community Service Award (2001) **Membership:** Elected Board Member, Organization of Safety, Asepsis and Prevention (OSAP) in Dentistry (2017); American Dental Association; Georgia Dental Association; International Association for Dental Research; Board of Directors, The AIDS Institute, Inc.; The Presidential Advisory Council on HIV/AIDS; The Secretary's Minority AIDS Initiative Fund **Business Address:** 341 Ponce De Leon Avenue NE, Atlanta, GA, 30308 **Shipping Address:** 2132 Wood Glen Lane SE, Marietta, GA, 30067 **Website:** https://www.colgateoralhealthnetwork.com/dental-expert/david-reznik

Stephen Headley Rhinesmith

Title: Senior Partner, Global Leadership Consultant **Industry:** Consulting **Company Name:** Stephen Rhinesmith, Inc. **Date of Birth:** 12/13/1942 **Place of Birth:** Mineola **State:** NY **Parents:** Homer Kern Rhinesmith; Winifred Headley Rhinesmith **Marital Status:** Married **Spouse Name:** Kathleen Alys Law (8/28/1965) **Children:** Christopher Law; Colin Headley **Education:** PhD, University of Pittsburgh (1972); MS in Public and International Affairs, University of Pittsburgh (1966); BA, Wesleyan University (1965) **Career:** Senior Partner, Stephen Rhinesmith, Inc. (2010-Present); Senior Partner, Mercer Leadership Development (2004-2010); Partner, CDR International (1998-2004); President, AFS Intercultural Programs, New York City, NY (1987-1989); President, Rhinesmith & Associates Inc., Chatham, MA (1984-2009); President, Moran, Stahl, Boyer, New York City, NY (1982-1984); President, Holland American Cruises, New York City, NY (1980-1982); President, AFS Intercultural Programs, New York City, NY (1972-1980); Director, International Services, McBer and Company, Cambridge, MA (1969-1971) **Career Related:** China Chairman, Department of Organizational Sociology, Moscow State University (1991-1996); Named Ambassador, Coordinator, President's United States-Soviet Exchange Initiative (1986-1987); Director, Naisbitt China Institute; Professor, School of Business; Professor, Finance and Economics, Tianjin University **Creative Works:** Co-Author, "Leading in Times of Crisis: Navigating Through Complexity, Diversity and Uncertainty to Save Your Business" (2009); Co-Author, "Head Heart and Guts: How the World's Best Companies Develop Complete Leaders" (2006); Author, "A Manager's Guide to Globalization: Six Skills for Success in a Changing World, Second Edition" (1996); Author, "Bring Home the World: A Management Guide to Community Leaders of International Programs" (1985); Author, "Bring Home the World: A Management Guide to Community Leaders of International Programs" (1975) **Awards:** Distinguished Alumnus Award, University of Pittsburgh; Bliss Award, American Society for Training and Development; National Defense Education Act Fellowship; Heinz Fellowship; Baker Scholarship **Membership:** Chair, American Society for Training and Development (1994); Council on Foreign Relations **Marquis Who's Who Honors:** Albert Nelson Marquis Lifetime Achievement Award (2017) **Political Affiliations:** Republican **Religion:** Congregationalist **Business Address:** 2630 Grey Oaks Dr. N, Apt 19, Naples, FL, 34105 **Shipping Address:** 105 Lower Moulton Ln, Stowe, VT, 05672

Stephen Gary Rice, PhD

Title: Pediatrician, Sports Medicine Physician, Educator **Industry:** Medicine & Health Care **Date of Birth:** 12/21/1945 **Place of Birth:** Brooklyn **State:** NY **Parents:** Abraham S. Rice; Anne (Shelling) Rice-Brown **Marital Status:** Married **Spouse Name:** Hilary Jo Turett (5/10/1987) **Children:** Adam; Bryan **Education:** MPH, University of Washington (1983); Intern, Children's Hospital, University of Washington, Seattle, WA (1974-1977); Resident, Children's Hospital, University of Washington, Seattle, WA (1974-1977); PhD, NYU School of Medicine (1974); MD, School of Medicine, New York University (1974); AB, Columbia College (1967) **Certifications:** Diplomate in Pediatrics, American Board of Pediatrics; Diplomate in Sports Medicine, American Board of Pediatrics **Career:** Clinical Professor, Pediatrics, Robert Wood Johnson Medical School, Rutgers, The State University of New Jersey (2011-Present); Director, Primary Care Sports Medicine Fellowship Program, Jersey Shore University Medical Center, Neptune, NJ (1996-Present); Associate Clinical Professor, Pediatrics, Robert Wood Johnson Medical School, Rutgers, The State University of New Jersey (1999-2011); Faculty Member, Sports Medicine, University of Washington, Seattle, WA (1977-1996) **Career Related:** Board of Directors, New Jersey Pediatric Council on Research and Education (2008-Present); Team Physician, Georgian Court University (1997-Present); Director, Jersey Shore Sports Medicine (1997-Present); Developer, Athletic Health Care Systems (1978-Present); Director, Athletic Health Care Systems (1978-Present); Chairman, New Jersey Student Athlete Cardiac Screening Task Force (2010-2015); Medical Consultant, New Jersey Youth Soccer Olympic Development Program (2002-2015); Team Physician, University of Washington (1977-1981); Consultant in Field; Fellow, ACSM **Civic:** Concussion in Sports Steering Committee, Brain Injury Alliance of New Jersey (2005-Present); Alumni Representative Committee, Columbia College (1974-Present) **Creative Works:** Section Editor, New Jersey Chapter, American Academy of Pediatrics (2002-2004); Author, "Athletic Health Care System" (1988) **Awards:** Citation Award, ACSM (2017); Silvio O. Conte Award, Brain Injury Alliance of New Jersey (2015); Top Doctors in Sports Medicine, New Jersey Magazine (2010-2011); Top Doctors in Sports Medicine, New Jersey Magazine (2005); Top Doctors in Sports Medicine, New Jersey Magazine (2003); One of the Top Doctors in Greater New York Metropolitan Area, Castle Connelly (2002-2013); Top Doctors in Sports Medicine, New Jersey Magazine (2001); Volunteer Faculty Teaching Award, Robert Wood Johnson Medical School, Rutgers, The State University of New Jersey (2000); Commendation Award, Washington State Interscholastic Activities Association (1995); Commendation Award, Washington State Interscholastic Activities Association (1981) **Membership:** President, New Jersey Chapter, American Academy of Pediatrics (2010-2012); Vice President, New Jersey Chapter, American Academy of Pediatrics (2008-2010); Board of Trustees, ACSM (2007-2010); Vice President-Elect, New Jersey Chapter, American Academy of Pediatrics (2006-2008); Treasurer, New Jersey Chapter, American Academy of Pediatrics (2004-2006); Executive Committee, Sports Medicine and Fitness Council, American Academy of Pediatrics (2003-2009); Chairman, Health and Science Policy Committee, ACSM (2000-2013); Chairman, Government Affairs Committee, New Jersey Chapter, American Academy of Pediatrics (2000-2006); Chairman, Sports Medicine Committee, New Jersey Chapter, American Academy of Pediatrics (1999-2012); Alliance for Health; Medical Society of New Jersey; The American Medical Society for Sports Medicine; National Strength and Conditioning Association **Marquis Who's Who Honors:** Albert Nelson Marquis Lifetime Achievement Award (2017); Distinguished Humanitarian (2017) **Why did you become involved in your profession or industry:** Dr. Rice became involved in sports medicine serendipitously. He was always interested in sports, and even did some sports broadcasting. He always enjoyed being a keen observer. He never put sports and medicine together. During his internship at Columbia University, he was exposed to Dr. James Garrick, the team physician at the University of Washington, and did some injury surveillance and gave talks. During his second year of residency, he spent three months at Harvard Medical Center. He took one afternoon a week to work to help a team physician at local high school. This prompted him to begin doing an injury surveillance study, and he became instrumental in gaining continued grants in injury preparedness. He had a spark that it was not knowledge, but organization to be systematized in being prepared. He then had an opportunity to continue in this field. **Business Address:** 51-02 Davis Avenue, Neptune, NJ, 07753 **Shipping Address:** 6 Wildflower Court, Manalapan, NJ, 07726

David A. Richards

Title: Lawyer **Industry:** Law and Legal Services **Company Name:** Steptoe & Johnson LLP **Date of Birth:** 09/21/1945 **Education:** JD, School of Law, Yale University (1972); MA, Cambridge University (1971); BA, Cambridge University, With First Class Honors (1969); BA, Yale College (1967) **Creative Works:** Author, "Skulls and Keys: Yale's Secret Societies and Their Hidden Role in American History" (2017); Contributor, Real Property, Probate & Trust Journal, American Bar Association (1986); Contributor, Real Estate Law Journal (1973); Author, "Development Rights Transfer in New York City," Yale Law Journal (1972); Author, "Development Rights Transfer Documentation: From Proposal to Partnership," Practising Law Institute; Presenter, International Bar Association, American Bar Association, Association of the Bar of the City of New York, American Law Institute, Practising Law Institute, and New York Law Journal Seminars-Press; Co-Author, "The Commercial Office Lease Handbook — New York Model Clauses and Commentary," American Bar Association Press; Contributor, Articles, Yale Law Journal, Real Property, Probate, & Trust Journal, Taxes International, Real Estate Law Journal, New York Law Journal, and International Property Investment Journal **Awards:** New York Super Lawyers (2015-2017); Best of The Best (2011); Featured Real Estate Lawyer, Super Lawyers, New York (2011); Super Lawyers, New York (2006-2017); Best Lawyers in America; Who's Who in American Law, Euromoney's Guide to the World's Leading Real Estate Lawyers **Membership:** Chair, Anglo-American Real Property Institute (1993); Chair, Real Property, Probate & Trust Section, American Bar Association (1991-1992); Board, American College of Real Estate Lawyers (1987-1993); Chair, Yale Library Associates; American Bar Association; Association of the Bar of the City of New York **Bar Admissions:** U.S. Supreme Court; State of New York **What do you consider to be the highlight of your career:** Mr. Richards represented Conrail and CSX Transportation in the disposition of the one and a-half mile High Line elevated rail viaduct on New York City's west side (now a city park) to the City of New York, for a public-private project, in negotiation with the city, the Metropolitan Transit Authority, the Javits Center, 26 underlying property owners, the Federal Surface Transportation Board, and the New York State Department of Transportation. It took 14 years. **Business Address:** Steptoe & Johnson LLP, New York, NY, 10036 **Shipping Address:** 77 Havemeyer Lane, Unit 412, Stamford, CT, 06902

William Chase Richardson, PhD

Title: Executive (Retired) **Industry:** Cosmetics **Company Name:** Johns Hopkins University **Date of Birth:** 05/11/1940 **Place of Birth:** Passaic **State:** NJ **Parents:** Henry Burtt Richardson; Frances Chase Richardson **Marital Status:** Married **Spouse Name:** Nancy Freeland (6/18/1966) **Children:** Elizabeth; Jennifer **Education:** Honorary PhD, University of Michigan (2006); PhD, University of Chicago (1964); MBA, University of Chicago (1964); BA, Trinity College (1962) **Career:** Professor of Policy, Kalamazoo College (2005-Present); President Emeritus, Johns Hopkins University, Baltimore, MD (1995-Present); President, Chief Executive Officer, W.K. Kellogg Foundation, Battle Creek, MI (1995-2005); President, Johns Hopkins University, Baltimore, MD (1990-1995); Professor, Department of Health Policy and Management, Johns Hopkins University, Baltimore, MD (1990-1995); Executive Vice President, Provost, Professor, Department of Family and Community Medicine, Pennsylvania State University (1984-1990); Dean of Graduate School and Vice Provost, Research, University of Washington (1981-1984); Acting Dean, University of Washington (1977-1978); Professor, University of Washington (1976-1984); Associate Dean, School of Public Health, University of Washington (1976-1981); Chairman, Department of Health Services, University of Washington (1973-1976); Associate Professor, University of Washington (1973-1976); Assistant Professor of Health Services, University of Washington (1971-1973); Research Associate, Instructor, University of Chicago (1967-1970) **Career Related:** Board Member, Exelon Corporation (2005-2016); Board Member, Bank of New York (1998-2007); Chairman, Kellogg Trust (1996-2007); Board Member, CSX Corporation (1992-2008); Chairman, Kaiser Family Foundation (1985-1998); Chairman, Pew Charitable Trust (1984-1990); Board Member, Mercantile Bankshares; Consultant in Field; Chairman, Board of Directors, Council on Foundations **Civic:** Member, Advisory Committee, RAND Corporation **Creative Works:** Author, "Health Program Evaluation" (1978); Author, "Ambulatory Use of Physicians Services" (1971); Contributor, Articles to Professional Journals; Author, "To Err is Human: Building a Safer Health System"; Author, "Crossing the Quality Chasm: A New Health System for the 21st Century" **Awards:** Kellogg College Fellow, Oxford University (1995-Present); David Rall Medal, Institute of Medicine (2007) **Membership:** National Academy of Sciences (1981); American Academy of Arts and Sciences; Institute of Medicine **Where will you be in five years:** In five years, Dr. Richardson will still be retired and engaged in volunteer work. **Shipping Address:** 4392 E Gull Lake Dr, Hickory Corners, MI, 49060

Ronald LeRoy Richmond

Title: Aerospace Engineer **Industry:** Engineering **Date of Birth:** 08/16/1931 **Place of Birth:** Los Angeles **State:** CA **Parents:** William Paul Richmond; Martha Emelia (Anderson) Richmond **Marital Status:** Married **Spouse Name:** Mary Louise Gates (1/2/1955) **Children:** Pandora Deanne Richmond Whitson; Steven Lee **Education:** PhD in Aeronautical Engineering, California Institute of Technology (1957); MS in Aeronautical Engineering, California Institute of Technology (1953); BSME, University of California, Berkeley (1952) **Career:** Director of Engineering, Brunswick Defense, Costa Mesa, CA (1988-1994); Adjunct Associate Professor, School of Engineering, University of California, Irvine (1987-1988); Director of Engineering, Advanced Development, Ford Aerospace, Newport Beach, CA (1959-1987); Assistant Group Leader, Aeronautical Performance, Douglas Aircraft Company, Long Beach, CA (1957-1959); Teaching/Research Assistant, California Institute of Technology, Pasadena, CA (1952-1957); Aerodynamicist, Lockheed Aircraft Company (Now Lockheed Martin Corporation), Burbank, CA (1952-1954) **Career Related:** Subgroup Leader, NATO Industrial Advisory Group #16, Brussels, Belgium (1984-1986); Shelby American Automobiles, Los Angeles, CA (1960-1962); Aerodynamics Consultant, Douglas Aircraft (1956-1957) **Civic:** Reserve Lieutenant, Orange County Sheriff's Department (1976-2012); Flight Instructor, Young Eagles Program **Creative Works:** Author, Thesis, California Institute of Technology **Awards:** Teaching Assistantship, California Institute of Technology Research (1955-1957); Grantee, California Institute of Technology Research (1955-1957); Research Assistantship, California Institute of Technology (1953-1957) **Membership:** Chairman, Orange County Section, Associate Fellow, American Institute of Aeronautics and Astronautics (1989-1990); Commander, Western States Association of Sheriff's Air Squadrons (1987-1988); President, Board Chairman, Skylarks of Southern California (1987-1988) **To what do you attribute your success:** Dr. Richmond attributes his success to his interest in the technology involved in his projects and his tenacity to stick with difficult projects to a successful conclusion. **Why did you become involved in your profession or industry:** Since a very young age, he was interested in airplanes, so aerospace engineering was a natural fit. **What do you consider to be the highlight of your career:** Dr. Richmond believes that his greatest professional achievement/highlight was his thesis at California Institute of Technology. Proving that skin friction forces on a long slender cylinder are much greater than on a flat plate. **Where will you be in five years:** In five years, Dr. Richmond will still fly planes, and will do maintenance on his own aircraft. **Hobbies:** Flying; Maintenance of planes **Political Affiliations:** Republican **Religion:** Protestant **Shipping Address:** 1307 Seacrest Dr, Corona Del Mar, CA, 92625

Daniel Lyman Ridout III

Title: Gastroenterologist **Industry:** Medicine & Health Care **Date of Birth:** 06/13/1953 **Place of Birth:** Salisbury **State:** MD **Parents:** Dr. Daniel L Ridout, Jr.; Lois M. Ridout **Marital Status:** Married **Spouse Name:** Maria C. Go, MD **Education:** Resident, Graduate Hospital of the University of Pennsylvania (Now Penn Medicine at Rittenhouse) (1979-1982); Internship in Internal Medicine and Gastroenterology, Graduate Hospital of the University of Pennsylvania (Now Penn Medicine at Rittenhouse) (1979-1982); MD, University of Cincinnati (1979); BA in Music Composition and Orchestration, Dartmouth College (1975) **Certifications:** Diplomate, National Board of Medical Examiners, American Board of Internal Medicine; Diplomate, Gastrointestinal Board, American Board of Internal Medicine; Licensed Physician, Commonwealth of Pennsylvania; Licensed Physician, State of Delaware; Certified in Advanced Cardiac and Life Support; Certified in Advanced Trauma and Life Support; Certified in Endoscopic Laser Therapy; Certified in Endoscopic Ultrasonography Training; American Medical Association Certificate of Continuing Medical Education; Sub-Specialty Board Certification in Gastroenterology, American Board of Internal Medicine; Licensed to Practice, States of Pennsylvania, Delaware, California, Virginia, and New Mexico; Certified Chief Medical Resident; Board Certification in Internal Medicine, American Board of Internal Medicine **Career:** Attending Physician, Riverside Shore Memorial Hospital, Nassawadox, VA (2005-Present); Attending Physician, Hospital of the University of Pennsylvania, University of Pennsylvania (1986-Present); Teaching Staff, Hospital of the University of Pennsylvania, University of Pennsylvania (1986-Present); Assistant Professor of Medicine, Burrell Osteopathic Medical School, Las Cruces, NM (2018); Riverside Shore Gastroenterology (2009-2015); Partner, Eastern Shore Physicians and Surgeons, Inc., Riverside Health System (2005-2009); Assistant Clinical Instructor of Medicine, Temple University School of Medicine (2001-2005); Gastroenterology Associates of Delaware County, Inc. (1996-2005); Attending Physician, Crozer-Chester Medical Center, Crozer-Keystone Health System (1988-2005); Private Practice (1987-1996); Clinical Instructor, Hospital of the University of Pennsylvania, University of Pennsylvania (1983-1984); Attending Physician, Emergency Medicine Graduate Hospital (1982-1986); Chief Medical Resident, Clinical Instructor of Internal Medicine, University of Pennsylvania, Graduate Hospital (1982-1983) **Career Related:** Private Practice (1986-Present); Elected Fellow, American Society for Gastrointestinal Endoscopy (2017); Inducted Fellow, American Gastroenterological Association (2015); Honored Speaker, Commencement Address, Tidewater Community College Registered Nursing School at Eastern Shore Community College (2014); Chief Medical Advisor, Principal Speaker for Educational Program to Increase Colorectal Cancer Screening, Morehouse School of Medicine, NBLIC Virginia Coalition Region EPICS (2014); Honored Speaker, Commencement Address, Tidewater Community College Registered Nursing School at Eastern Shore Community College (2011); Honored Speaker of Community Service Awards, Murphy African Methodist Episcopal Church of Chester, Pennsylvania (2002); Chief of Gastrointestinal Division, Coatesville Veterans Affairs Medical Center (1987-1989); Fellow, American College of Physicians **Creative Works:** Contributor, Articles, Professional Journals **Awards:** Highest Patient Satisfaction/Quality Care Assessment, 90th Percentile, Riverside Medical Group (2014); Top 101 Industry Experts (2012); Inducted Fellow, American College of Physicians (2005); Inducted, Hall of Fame, African American Museum and Historical Society of Delaware (2003); Outstanding Man of the 20th Century in Recognition for Contribution to Humanity through Medicine Award, International Biographical Centre Cambridge, England (1999); Community Service Award, Delaware County (1998); Achievement and Service in Medicine Award, Afro-American Historical Society of Delaware (1989); Numerous Civic Awards for Contributions to Community-Based Medicine and Preservation of the Arts; Academic Awards **Membership:** American Medical Association; American Professional Practice Association; American Society for Gastrointestinal Endoscopy; Pennsylvania Medical Society; Board of Directors, Delaware County Medical Society; American Society of Internal Medicine; Medical Society of Eastern Pennsylvania; Philadelphia County Medical Society; The College of Physicians of Philadelphia; New Castle County Medical Society **Marquis Who's Who Honors:** Albert Nelson Marquis Lifetime Achievement Award (2017); Distinguished Humanitarian (2017) **Hobbies:** Listening to music; Boating; Choral singing; Conducting a choir **Business Address:** 405 W Country Club Road, Roswell, NM, 88201 **Shipping Address:** 350 W Country Club Road, Suite 105, Eastern NM Gastroenterology, Roswell, NM, 88201

C. Alan Riedesel

Title: Professor Emeritus **Industry:** Education/Educational Services **Company Name:** State University of New York at Buffalo **Date of Birth:** 07/21/1930 **Place of Birth:** Davenport **State:** IA **Parents:** F. Clark Riedesel; Dorothy H. (Franco) Riedesel **Marital Status:** Widowed **Spouse Name:** Ardeth Scott (1951) **Children:** Christine; Mark; Claudia; Matthew; Craig **Education:** PhD, University of Iowa (1962); MA, University of Iowa (1956); BA, Cornell College (1951) **Career:** Library of Westfield, New York (2016-Present); Professor Emeritus, State University of New York, Buffalo (1995-Present); Professor, Education Department Director, Software Laboratory Director, State University of New York, Buffalo (1972-1995); Professor of Education, Georgia State University (1970-1972); Professor of Education, Kansas State University (1962-1963); Professor of Education, State University of New York, Plattsburgh (1953-1956); Teacher, Lisbon Schools **Creative Works:** Author, "Buddy Goes to Heaven" (2016); Series Developer, "Essentials in Teaching" (2000); Author, "Teaching Elementary School Math" (1998); Series Developer, "Essentials in Teaching" (1994); Author, "Teaching Elementary School Math" (1990); Software Author, "Sunburst" (1989-1990); Author, "Teaching Elementary School Math" (1985); Author, "Teaching Elementary School Math" (1980); Author, "Teaching Elementary School Math" (1975); Author, "Handbook: Elementary School Math" (1975); Author, "Mathematics for Elementary Teachers" (1975); Author, "Teaching Elementary School Math" (1967); Contributor, Articles, Professional Journals **Awards:** Distinguished Professor Award (1995); Grantee, National Science Foundation (1974); Grantee, National Science Foundation (1968); Grantee, National Science Foundation (1966); Grantee, National Science Foundation (1962) **Membership:** Editor, "The Arithmetic Teacher," National Council on Teachers of Math (1967-1972); Association for Supervision and Curriculum Development; National Council of Social Studies Teachers Anglican **Hobbies:** Nature; Bird carving; Woodworking **Religion:** Episcopalian **Shipping Address:** 6983 Munson Lane, Mayville, NY, 14757

Mark Joseph Riedy, PhD

Title: Finance Educator **Industry:** Education/Educational Services **Company Name:** Riedy Advisors **Date of Birth:** 07/09/1942 **Place of Birth:** Aurora **State:** IL **Parents:** Paul Bernard Riedy; Kathryn Veronica Riedy **Marital Status:** Married **Spouse Name:** Erin Jeanne Lynch (8/29/1964) **Children:** Jennifer Riedy-Salamon; John Mark **Education:** PhD, University of Michigan (1971); MBA, Washington University in St. Louis (1966); BA in Economics, Loras College, Maxima Cum Laude (1964) **Career:** Principal, Riedy Advisors (2015-Present); Executive Director Emeritus, Burnham-Moores Center for Real Estate, University of San Diego (2015-Present); Executive Director, Burnham Moores Center for Real Estate, University of San Diego (2004-2015); Professor of Real Estate Finance, University of San Diego (1993-2015); Ernest W. Hahn Chair in Real Estate Finance (1993-2015); President, National Council of Community Bankers (1988-1992); President, Chief Operating Officer, JER Partners (1987-1988); President, Chief Operating Officer, Director, Federal National Mortgage Association (Now Fannie Mae) (1985-1986); Executive Vice President, Chief Operating Officer, Mortgage Bankers Association (1978-1984); Vice President, Chief Economist, Federal Home Loan Bank of San Francisco (1973-1977); Vice President, Director of Research, PMI Mortgage Insurance Company (1973); Director of Research, PMI Mortgage Insurance Company (1973); Special Assistant to Chairman, Federal Home Loan Bank Board (1972); Senior Staff Economist, Council of Economic Advisers (1971-1972); Assistant Professor of Business Administration, University of Colorado, Boulder (1969-1971) **Career Related:** Advisory Council Member, Credit Research Center, Purdue University (1981-1982); Earhart Foundation Fellowship (1968-1969); Fellow, Robert G. Rodkey Foundation (1966-1969); Fellow, United States Steel Foundation, United States Steel (1966-1968); Board of Directors, Federal National Mortgage Association (Now Fannie Mae); Continental Savings Bank (Now HomeStreet, Inc.); AccuBanc Mortgage Corporation; Pan Pacific Retail Properties, Inc.; American Residential Mortgage Corporation; American Mortgage Network, Inc.; Bio-Med Realty; Noble Broadcast Group, Inc.; Drayton Insurance Services; Perpetual Federal Savings Bank; Neighborhood Bancorp; Lead Director, Advisory Board, Southwest Properties; Chair of Audit Committee, Board of Trustees, Multi Strategy Growth and Income Fund **Civic:** Board of Directors, Lambda Alpha International; Chairman, Board of Directors, St. Vincent de Paul Village; San Diego Mayor's Renaissance Commission, City of San Diego; Scripps Mercy Hospital Foundation Board **Awards:** Eponym, The Mark J. Riedy Legacy Scholarship (2016); Top Influential Award, San Diego Source (2014); Crystal Globe Career Achievement Award, Lambda Alpha International (2009); National Defense Scholarship (1964-1966); Woodrow Wilson Scholarship (1964) **Membership:** Honorary Life Member, Mortgage Bankers Legion, Mortgage Banker Association (1986); American Economic Association; American Finance Association; National Association for Business Economists; ASAE; NAIOP; Urban Land Institute **Marquis Who's Who Honors:** Albert Nelson Marquis Lifetime Achievement Award (2017); Distinguished Humanitarian (2017) **To what do you attribute your success:** Dr. Riedy attributes his success to having outstanding mentors and gifts from God. **Why did you become involved in your profession or industry:** Dr. Riedy became inspired by his mentor, Dr. Paul W. McCracken at the University of Michigan. **What do you consider to be the highlight of your career:** A highlight of Dr. Riedy's career is the achievements of his students. **Hobbies:** International travel; Golf; Writing; Being a grandfather, father, and husband **Political Affiliations:** Independent **Religion:** Roman Catholic **Shipping Address:** 14084 Rue Saint Tropez, Del Mar, CA, 92014

Robert Bartlett Riley

Title: Professor of Architecture and Landscape Architecture **Industry:** Architecture & Constrution **Company Name:** University of Illinois **Date of Birth:** 01/28/1931 **Place of Birth:** Chicago **State:** IL **Parents:** Robert James Riley; Ruth (Collins) Riley **Marital Status:** Divorced **Spouse Name:** Nancy Rebecca Mills **Children:** Rebecca Hill; Kimber Bartlett **Education:** BArch, Massachusetts Institute of Technology (1954); PhB, University of Chicago (1949) **Career:** Director, PhD Program, University of Illinois at Urbana-Champaign (1999-Present); Professor Emeritus, Director, Joint PhD Program, University of Illinois (1997-Present); Professor of Landscape Architecture and Architecture, University of Illinois at Urbana-Champaign (1970-Present); Visiting Professor, Harvard University (1996-1997); Head, Department of Landscape Architecture, University of Illinois at Urbana-Champaign (1970-1985); Director, Center for Environmental Research and Development, University of New Mexico (1966-1970); Principal Partner, Robert B. Riley (A.I.A.), Albuquerque, NM (1964-1970); Chief Designer, Kea, Shaw, Grimm & Crichton, Hyattsville, MD (1959-1964); Campus Planner, Associate Professor of Architecture, Center for Environmental Research and Development, University of New Mexico **Career Related:** Senior Fellow, Landscape Architecture Studies, Dumbarton Oaks, Harvard University (1992-Present); Chairman Fellows (1996-Present); Review Panel Member, Landscape Architects, Federal Civil Service, National Endowment for the Arts **Military Service:** US Air Force (1954-1958) **Creative Works:** Editor, Landscape Journal (1987-Present); Chairman, Editorial Advisory Board, Landscape Architecture (1996-1999); Associate Editor, Landscape Magazine (1967-1970); Author, "The Camaro in the Pasture," The University of Virginia Press **Awards:** Recipient, Career Award, Environmental Design Research Association (2003); Recipient, President's Award, Council of Educators in Landscape Architecture (1994); Recipient, Outstanding Educator Award, Council of Educators in Landscape Architecture (1992); Recipient, National Honor Award, American Society of Landscape Architects (1979); Recipient, Environmental Service Award, AIA New Mexico (1970); Recipient, Design Award, AIA New Mexico (1968); Recipient, Design Award, AIA Maryland (1962) **Membership:** Chairman of Board, Environmental Design Research Association (1990-1991); Chairman, Board of Directors, Council of Educators in Landscape Architecture (1985-1986); Project Fellow, National Endowment for the Arts (1985); President, Council of Educators in Landscape Architecture (1984-1985); Nell Norris Fellow, University of Melbourne, Australia (1977); Fellow, American Society of Landscape Architects; Council of Educators in Landscape Architecture; American Institute of Architects; Phi Beta Epsilon **Marquis Who's Who Honors:** Albert Nelson Marquis Lifetime Achievement Award (2017) **Religion:** Unitarian Universalist **Shipping Address:** 407 E George Huff Dr., Urbana, IL, 61801 **Website:** http://www.upress.virginia.edu/title/4702

James Franklin Rill

Title: Senior Counsel **Industry:** Law and Legal Services **Company Name:** Baker Botts L.L.P. **Date of Birth:** 03/04/1933 **Place of Birth:** Evanston **State:** IL **Parents:** John Columbus Rill; Frances Eleanor (Hill) Rill **Marital Status:** Married **Spouse Name:** Mary Elizabeth Laws (6/14/1957, Deceased 5/11/2017) **Children:** James Franklin, Jr.; Roderick M. **Education:** LLB, Harvard University (1959); AB, Dartmouth College, Cum Laude (1954) **Career:** Senior Counsel, Baker Botts L.L.P., Washington, DC (2012-Present); Partner, Howrey Simon Arnold & White LLP, Washington, DC (2000-2011); Co-Chair, International Competition, Policy Advisory Committee, U.S. Department of Justice (1997-2000); Partner, Collier, Shannon, Rill & Scott, (Now Kelley Drye & Warren LLP), Washington, DC (1992-2000); Assistant Attorney General, Antitrust Division, U.S. Department of Justice, Washington, DC (1989-1992); Partner, Collier, Shannon, Rill & Scott, (Now Kelley Drye & Warren LLP), Washington, DC (1969-1989); Partner, Collier, Shannon & Rill (Now Kelley Drye & Warren LLP), Washington, DC (1963-1969); Associate, Steadman, Collier & Shannon, Washington, DC (1959-1963); Legislative Assistant, Congressman James P. S. Devereux, Washington, DC (1952) **Career Related:** Co-Chair, International Competition Policy Working Group, U.S. Chamber of Commerce (2005-Present); Non-Governmental Advisor, International Competition Network (2001-Present); Chairman, Business and Industry Advisory Committee, Competition Committee, Organisation for Economic Co-operation and Development (2005-2007); Vice-Chair, Business and Industry Advisory Committee, Competition Committee, Organisation for Economic Co-operation and Development (1993-2005); Public Member, Administrative Conference of the United States (1992-1994); Chairman, Anti-Trust Law Section, ABA (1987-1988); Of Principal Council, Council for Excellence in Government; Member, Advisory Panel, Office of Technology, Assessment of Multinational Firms and United States Technology Base **Civic:** Trustee Emeritus, Bullis School, Potomac, MD **Military Service:** First Lieutenant of Artillery, U.S. Army (1954-1956) **Creative Works:** Contributor, Numerous Articles, Professional Journals **Awards:** John S. Sherman Award, U.S. Department of Justice (2012); Lifetime Achievement Award, Global Competition Review (2011); Lifetime Achievement Award, ABA, Section of Antitrust Law (2011); Hall of Fame, Business and Industry Advisory Committee **Membership:** Past Chairman, Anti-Trust Law Section, ABA (1987-1988); Tri-National NAFTA Task Force, ABA; Fellow, American Bar Foundation; The District of Columbia Bar; International Bar Association; Loudoun Golf & Country Club, Inc.; Metropolitan Club; Phi Delta Theta Fraternity **Bar Admissions:** The District of Columbia (1959); Supreme Court of the United States; United States Court of Appeals for the District of Columbia Circuit **Marquis Who's Who Honors:** Albert Nelson Marquis Lifetime Achievement Award (2017) **Why did you become involved in your profession or industry:** Mr. Rill became involved in his profession because his father was in the railroad industry, and this led to him becoming interested in competition policy. In addition to this, he always had an interest in the law, economics and public policy. **What do you consider to be the highlight of your career:** The highlight of Mr. Rill's career was having seen the young lawyers that he has mentored, grow and become successful on their own. He is also proud of his involvement in anti-trust policies going international. When Mr. Rill was assistant attorney general and chairman of the International Competition Policy Advisory Committee, his influence helped spread anti-trust policies throughout the world. **Hobbies:** History; Military Strategy; Baseball **Business Address:** 1299 Pennsylvania Ave NW Ste 12002, 1299 Pennsylvania Ave NW Ste 12002, DC, Washington, 20004 **Shipping Address:** 1299 Pennsylvania Ave NW Ste 12002, Baker Botts L.L.P., DC, Washington, 20004 **Website:** http://www.bakerbotts.com/people/r/rill-james-f

Ann Leslie Ringler Vasey

Title: Psychotherapist, Educator **Industry:** Cosmetics **Company Name:** Private Practice **Date of Birth:** 05/03/1949 **Place of Birth:** Cleveland **State:** OH **Parents:** Albert Ringler; Dr. Norma M. Ringler **Marital Status:** Married **Spouse Name:** Graham C. Vasey (2/20/1972) **Children:** Rachel N. Vasey; Corinne E. Vasey Breed **Education:** MEd in Counseling Psychology, Northeastern University, Boston, MA (1974); BS in Elementary Education and Early Childhood, Boston University, Boston, MA (1972); Group Leadership Training, Adult Education and Administration, Boston University, Boston, MA (1972); Postgraduate Coursework **Certifications:** Certification in Teaching Specialty Children's Yoga (2011-Present); Certification in Trauma Sensitive Yoga, The Trauma Center at Justice Resource Institute, Brookline, MA (2008); Registered Yoga Teacher, 200 Hours (2004-Present); Validator, National Association for the Education of Young Children (1995-2004); Licensed Mental Health Counselor, State of Massachusetts; Licensed Marriage and Family Therapist, State of Massachusetts; National Certified Clinical Mental Health Counselor, National Board for Certified Counselors, Inc.; National Certified Counselor; Certified Clinical Supervisor, Massachusetts Mental Health Counselors Association, Inc. **Career:** Psychotherapist, Private Practice, Hudson, MA (2006-Present); Trainer, Together for Kids, CSEFEL, Worcester, MA (2007); Psychological Consultant, Together for Kids, CSEFEL, Worcester, MA (2007); Founding Supervisor, Southbridge Family Resource Center, Southbridge, MA (2000-2006); Project Director, Parent-Child Home Program, Southbridge, MA (2000-2002); Established and Chaired, Family Literacy Coalition, Southbridge, MA (1998-2006); Therapist, YOU Inc. Family Services, Southbridge, MA (1995-2015); Grants Manager, Southbridge Community Partnerships for Children, Massachusetts Department of Education Early Learning (Now Massachusetts Department of Early Education and Care), Malden, MA (1993-2006); Director, Helping Hands Preschool, Southbridge Public Schools (1993-2006); Project Director, Parent-Child Home Program, Southbridge, MA (1993); Mental Health Referral Coordinator, MACIPA, Mount Auburn Hospital, Tufts Health Plan, Cambridge, MA (1992); Mental Health Reviewer Administrator, MACIPA, Mount Auburn Hospital, Tufts Health Plan, Cambridge, MA (1991-1992); Academic Advisor, Quinsigamond Community College, Worcester, MA (1990-1993); Psychological Consultant, Child Study Center, Quinsigamond Community College Childcare, Worcester, MA (1989-1991); Chairperson, Part-Time Faculty, Professional Development Committee, Quinsigamond Community College, Worcester, MA (1988-1992); Member, Childcare Advisory Group, Campus Childcare Center, Quinsigamond Community College, Worcester, MA (1986-1990); Founder, The Learning Experience Elementary School, Marlborough, MA (1981-1988); Director, The Learning Experience Elementary School, Marlborough, MA (1981-1988); Psychology Instructor, Social Sciences Department, Quinsigamond Community College, Worcester, MA (1978-1992) **Career Related:** Trauma Sensitive Yoga Instructor, YOU, Inc. Wetzel Center, Worcester, MA (2009-2017); Consultations on National Association for the Education of Young Children Accreditation Preparation (1996-2006) **Civic:** Team Member, Site Reviews, Community Partnerships for Children, Massachusetts Department of Education Early Learning (Now Massachusetts Department of Early Education and Care), Malden, MA (2005); Team Member, Site Review, Community Partnerships for Children, Massachusetts Department of Education Early Learning (Now Massachusetts Department of Early Education and Care), Malden, MA (2004); Member, Youth Advisory Board, Southbridge, MA (2002-2003); Member, Steering Committee, Community Connections, Southbridge, MA (1998-2007) **Creative Works:** Presenter, "Psychotherapy and Yoga & Mindfulness Interventions," MAMHCA, Foxboro, MA (2014); Presenter, "Psychotherapy, Yoga & Mindfulness: An Integrated Approach," Massachusetts Mental Health, Newton, MA (2012); Presenter, "Mindfulness and Body-Based Interventions," YOU Inc., Worcester, MA (2010); Presenter, Early Childhood Director's Association (2002); Workshop Presenter, "Growing Up Female," Inter-District Conference-Diversity on Common Ground, Fitchburg State College (Now Fitchburg State University), Fitchburg, MA (1996) **Awards:** Recognition for Many Years of Leadership and Dedication to Southbridge Community Connections and the Southbridge Community (2007); Grantee, Massachusetts Department of Early Care and Education and Care (Now Department of Early Education and Care) (1993-2006) **Membership:** Massachusetts Mental Health Counselors Association, Inc.; American Association for Marriage and Family Therapy; National Board for Certified Counselors, Inc.; Yoga Alliance; International Association of Yoga Therapists **Marquis Who's Who Honors:** Albert Nelson Marquis Lifetime Achievement Award (2017) **Business Address:** 34 Pope St Ste. 5, Hudson, MA, 01749 **Shipping Address:** 83 Woodland Rd, Ashland, MA, 01721

James Quentin Riordan

Title: Oil Industry Executive, Lawyer **Industry:** Law and Legal Services **Company Name:** Quentin Partners Co. **Date of Birth:** 06/17/1927 **Place of Birth:** Brooklyn **State:** NY **Parents:** James A. Riordan; Ruth M. (Boomer) Riordan **Marital Status:** Married **Spouse Name:** Gloria H. Carlson (6/23/1951) **Children:** Harris; Susan; James; Ruth **Education:** LLB, Columbia University (1949); BA, Brooklyn College (1945) **Career:** Chairman, Quentin Partners Co. (1996-Present); President, Bekaert (1989-1992); Vice Chairman, Mobil Corporation (1957-1989); Chief Finance Officer, Mobil Corporation (1957-1989); Attorney, Chadbourne, Parke, Whiteside, Wolff & Brophy (Now Chadbourne & Parke LLP) (1955-1957); Attorney, Tax Division, U.S. Department of Justice (1952-1955); Staff, Ways and Means Sub-Committee (1951-1952); Attorney, Winthrop, Stimson, Putnam & Roberts (1949-1951) **Civic:** Board of Directors, Tax Foundation, Inc.; Committee on Economic Development, Tax Foundation; Trustee, Brooklyn Museum **Military Service:** U.S. Navy (1945-1946) **Membership:** Rembrandt Club, Brooklyn, NY; The Blind Brook Club; Sailfish Point Golf Club, Florida; Stockbridge Golf Club **Bar Admissions:** U.S. Supreme Court (1954); State of New York (1951) **Marquis Who's Who Honors:** Albert Nelson Marquis Lifetime Achievement Award (2017) **Shipping Address:** 851 SE Johnson Avenue, Suite 100, Quentin Partners Co., Stuart, FL, 34994 **Website:** http://www.quentinpartnersco.com

Hildegard Rissel, PhD

Title: Associate Professor **Industry:** Education/ Educational Services **Company Name:** Virginia State University **Date of Birth:** 05/21/1956 **Place of Birth:** Westerholt **State/Country of Origin:** Germany **Year of Passing:** 2018-07-27 **Parents:** Herbert Joseph Rissel; Hannelore Halsband Rissel **Education:** PhD, Georgetown University (1990); PhD in Golden Age Spanish Literature, Georgetown University (1990); MS, Georgetown University (1983); BS, Georgetown University (1981) **Career:** Associate Professor of Languages and Literature, Virginia State University (1996-Present); Assistant Professor, University of Wisconsin-Washington County (1991-1996) **Civic:** Regent, Regina Caeli, Inc., Colonial Heiths, VA (2001-2004) **Creative Works:** Contributor, Articles, Professional Journals **Membership:** The Phi Beta Kappa Society **Marquis Who's Who Honors:** Albert Nelson Marquis Lifetime Achievement Award (2017) **Why did you become involved in your profession or industry:** Dr. Rissel became involved in her profession due to an interest in foreign languages and a love of reading. **What do you consider to be the highlight of your career:** The highlight of her career was when her thesis was published. **Where will you be in five years:** In five years, Dr. Rissel hopes to be teaching and advising students. **Hobbies:** Travel; Reading **Religion:** Roman Catholic **Shipping Address:** 107 New Castle Dr. Apt A, Colonial Heights, VA, 23834

Harry A. Rissetto

Title: Lawyer **Industry:** Law and Legal Services **Company Name:** Morgan, Lewis & Bockius LLP **Date of Birth:** 12/01/1943 **Education:** AB, Fairfield University (1965); JD, Georgetown University (1958) **Career:** Senior Counsel, Morgan, Lewis & Bockius, Washington, DC (2010); Partner, Morgan, Lewis & Bockius, Washington, DC (1975-2010); Associate, Morgan, Lewis & Bockius LLP, Washington, DC (1970-1975); Law Clerk to Chief Justice Warren E. Burger, U.S. Supreme Court (1969-1970); Law Clerk to Honorable John J. Sirica, United States District Court, District of Columbia (1968-1969) **Career Related:** Adjunct Professor, Law Center, Georgetown University (1986-1989) **Civic:** Chair, American Horticulture Society **Creative Works:** Author, "History of the American Dahlia Society 1965-2015" **Awards:** Gold Medal, American Dahlia Society **Membership:** Co-Chairman, Railway Labor Act Committee, Section of Labor and Employment Law, American Bar Association (1987-1989); The College of Labor and Employment Lawyers Inc. **Bar Admissions:** District of Columbia (1970); State of New York (1969); U.S. Supreme Court **Marquis Who's Who Honors:** Albert Nelson Marquis Lifetime Achievement Award (2017) **Why did you become involved in your profession or industry:** Originally, Mr. Rissetto worked on discrimination work and began to do some collective bargaining and then continued to focus on that field. **What do you consider to be the highlight of your career:** In retrospect, Mr. Rissetto is most proud of the work he did on the Conrail to help reform the collective bargaining agreement. **Hobbies:** Gardening **Religion:** Roman Catholic **Shipping Address:** 502 W Broad Street, Apt. 508, Falls Church, VA, 22046

Nancy Ann Roberson

Title: President, Attorney at Law **Industry:** Law and Legal Services **Company Name:** Roberson Law **Place of Birth:** Batesville **State:** IN **Parents:** Edward Mosmeier; Helen Mosmeier **Marital Status:** Married **Spouse Name:** Bob Roberson (10/12/1984); David Phillips (Deceased 1977) **Children:** Amy Cary **Education:** JD, School of Law, University of Dayton (1982); BA in English, Indiana University, Bloomington, IN (1971) **Certifications:** Board Certified Specialist in Estate Planning, Ohio State Bar Association (2003-Present); Board Certified Specialist in Probate, Ohio State Bar Association (2003-Present); Board Certified Specialist in Trust Law, Ohio State Bar Association (2003-Present) **Career:** Estate Planning Lawyer (1986-Present); Probate Lawyer (1986-Present); Trust Lawyer (1986-Present); Affiliate, Nancy A. Roberson Co., L.P.A. **Career Related:** Chairperson, Estate Planning, Probate, and Trust Law Group, Dayton Bar Association; President, Dayton Trust and Estate Planning Group **Civic:** Co-Founder, Two Support Groups for Widows; Co-Facilitator, Two Support Groups for Widows; Active Member, Church; Development Committee Member, Dayton Foundation **Creative Works:** Co-Author, "Solutions" (1994); Author, "You Don't Know What You Don't Know," Living With Loss Magazine; Seminar Presenter, "Are You Prepared?"; Editorial Board Member, Law Review, School of Law, University of Dayton **Awards:** Finalist, Eclipse Integrity Award, Council of Better Business Bureaus, Inc. (2017); Leadership Excellence Award, Ohio Diversity Council (2013); Distinguished Communication and Leadership Award, District 41, Toastmaster's International (2012); Featured Listee, Ten Top Women in Dayton, Dayton Daily News (2012); Finalist, Eclipse Integrity Award, Council of Better Business Bureaus, Inc. (2010); Winner, Lloyd O'Hara Public Interest Law Award, Greater Dayton Volunteer Lawyers Project, Legal Aid of Western Ohio, Inc., Advocates for Basic Legal Equality, Inc. **Membership:** American Bar Association; Dayton Bar Association; Christian Legal Society; NAELA **Bar Admissions:** State of Ohio **To what do you attribute your success:** Ms. Roberson attributes her success to God, who has called, equipped, enabled, and blessed her. She has pursued excellence and integrity in carrying out her mission and educating the community about planning for death and disability, as well as providing estate planning and probate services to her clients. **Why did you become involved in your profession or industry:** Ms. Roberson's interest in the fields of estate planning and probate law grew out of her experience of being widowed at the age of 27, when her daughter Amy was two years old. **What do you consider to be the highlight of your career:** The highlight of Ms. Roberson's career was becoming one of the first 100 attorneys in Ohio to become certified in her area of practice. She is also proud of being board certified by the Ohio State Bar Association as a specialist in the areas of estate planning, probate, and trust Law, which became possible only about 15 years ago. **Where will you be in five years:** In five years, Ms. Roberson will be practicing law and enjoying her family. **Hobbies:** Indiana University basketball **Religion:** Christian **Shipping Address:** 1225 E David Road, Nancy A. Roberson Co., L.P.A., Kettering, OH, 45429 **Website:** http://roberson-lawdayton.com/content/nancy-roberson

Victor Lawrence Roberts

Title: President, Chief Executive Officer **Industry:** Medicine & Health Care **Company Name:** Endocrine Associates of Florida, P.A. **Date of Birth:** 06/02/1952 **Place of Birth:** New York **State:** NY **Parents:** Allan Roberts; Arlene Roberts **Marital Status:** Married **Spouse Name:** Lucy Duque-Roberts **Children:** Mara Isabelle; Allan Joshua; Daniel Alexander **Education:** MBA, Crummer Graduate School of Business, Rollins College, Winter Park, FL (1995); Fellowship, Endocrinology, Diabetes Metabolism, University of Miami (1985); Resident, Internal Medicine, Upstate Medical University, Syracuse, NY (1983); MD, Autonomous University, Guadalajara, Mexico (1979); BS in Biology, Hobart College, Geneva, NY (1974) **Certifications:** Certified in Endocrinology, Diabetes and Metabolism, American Board of Internal Medicine (1987); Certified in Internal Medicine, American Board of Internal Medicine (1984); Certified Physician Executive, American Association of Physician Leadership; Endocrine Coder, AACE-CEC; Healthcare Quality Manager, ABQAURP; CHCQM; American Board of Quality Assurance and Utilization Review Physicians; Fellow, American College of Physicians; Fellow, American College of Endocrinology; Affiliate Member, American College of Cardiology **Career:** Professor, Internal Medicine, University of Central Florida College of Medicine, Orlando, FL (2008-Present); President, Endocrine Associates of Florida, PA, Lake Mary, FL (1988-Present); Chief Executive Officer, Endocrine Associates of Florida, PA, Lake Mary, FL (1988-Present); Consulting Endocrinologist, Endocrine Associates of Florida, PA, Lake Mary, FL (1988-Present); Consulting Endocrinologist, Endocrine and Diabetes Associates of Texas (Now Texas Associates of Endocrinology & Diabetes, P.A.) (1985-1988) **Career Related:** Professor of Internal Medicine, University of Central Florida College of Medicine, Orlando, FL (2008-Present); Clinical Professor of Clinical Sciences, Florida State University College of Medicine, Tallahassee, FL (2006-Present); Clinical Professor, Pharmacy Practice, University of Florida College of Pharmacy (2006-Present); Clinical Professor, Medicine, University of Florida College of Medicine, Gainesville, FL (2001-Present); Dean's Society, University of Central Florida College of Medicine **Civic:** Central Florida Medical Reserve Corps, Florida Department of Health (2008-Present); President, Seminole County Medical Society (SCMS) (2015); President, Orange County Medical Society (2001) **Creative Works:** Editor-in-Chief, Journal of Diabetes Research and Therapy (2017-Present); Editor, First Messenger -The American Association of Clinical Endocrinologists Publication (2017-Present); Editorial Board, Internal Medicine News; Contributor, Articles, Professional Medical Publications in English and Spanish **Awards:** Named, Top Doctors, Castle Connolly Medical Ltd. (2002-Present); Elected by Peers for Inclusion in Best Doctors in America (2015-2018); Practice Medicine Preceptor Award, University of Central Florida College of Medicine (2014); Practice Medicine Preceptor Award, University of Central Florida College of Medicine (2012); Governor's Appointment Diabetes Advisor Council Award, Florida Governor's Office (2000-2004); Elected by Peers for Inclusion in Best Doctors in America (1998-2012); Academic and Leadership Achievement Award, National Honor Society (1970); Named, Top 5% of Healthcare Professionals in the Country, Top Doctors, Castle Connolly Medical Ltd. **Membership:** National Board Member, AACE The American Association of Clinical Endocrinologists (1997-2000); National Board of Directors, American Diabetes Association (1997-2000); Fellow, ABQAURP; American Institute of Healthcare Quality; Fellow, American College of Endocrinology; Fellow, American College of Physicians **Marquis Who's Who Honors:** Albert Nelson Marquis Lifetime Achievement Award (2017); Distinguished Humanitarian (2017) **To what do you attribute your success:** Dr. Roberts attributes his success to the support of his family and great mentors in training. **Why did you become involved in your profession or industry:** Dr. Roberts became involved in his profession because he wanted to make a difference, and there were patients who were in need of help. **What do you consider to be the highlight of your career:** The highlight of his career was the appreciation of his patients for the care they receive. **Where will you be in five years:** In five years, Dr. Roberts will be practicing clinical endocrinology. **Hobbies:** Travel; Reading; History; Golf **Business Address:** 766 N Sun Dr., Ste 2060, Lake Mary, FL, 32746 **Shipping Address:** 1809 Alaqua Dr., Longwood, FL, 32779 **Website:** http://victorlrobertsmd.com

Ned Robertson

Title: Dentist **Industry:** Medicine & Health Care **Company Name:** Penobscot Nation Health Department **Date of Birth:** 03/03/1950 **Place of Birth:** Rumford **State:** ME **Parents:** Edward Norris Robertson; Edith Louise (Kirk) Robertson **Children:** Christie Portia; Juliet Melissa (Deceased); Jenni Celia; Edward Noah; Jessica Edith **Education:** DMD, Case Western Reserve University (2004); DDS, Case Western Reserve University (1983); MS in Epidemiology, The Ohio State University (1977); BS in Biology, Antioch College, Yellow Springs, OH (1973) **Career:** Assistant Clinical Professor, Department of General Practice Dentistry, School of Dental Medicine, Case Western Reserve University (1997-1999); Private Practice, Lyndhurst, OH (1995-2000); Assistant Professor, School of Dental Medicine, Case Western Reserve University (1991-1997); Professor, Dental Lab Technician Program, Cuyahoga Community College (1984-1986); Private Practice, Cleveland Heights, OH (1983-1994); Medic, Jones and Laughlin Steel Corporation, Cleveland, OH (1979-1984); Epidemiologic and Statistics Consultant, Los Angeles, CA (1977); Research Associate, University of California, Los Angeles (1977); Research Consultant, Ohio Department of Health, Columbus, OH (1976-1977); Faculty Advisor to Medical Students, The Ohio State University, Columbus, OH (1975-1977); Director, Dental Department, Penobscot Nation Health Department, Indian Island, ME **Career Related:** Overseer, Case Western Reserve University Dental Students at Care Alliance, Cleveland, OH (2011-2012); Clinical Instructor, Department of Community Dentistry, School of Dental Medicine, Case Western Reserve University (2011-2012); Assistant Professor, Department of General Practice Dentistry, School of Dental Medicine, Case Western Reserve University (2010); Facilitator, School of Dental Medicine, Case Western Reserve University (2009, 2006); Private Contractor, Indian Health Service Dental Clinic, Pine Ridge, SD (1999-2000); Clinical Instructor, University of Maryland School of Dentistry (1999-2000); Assistant Professor, School of Dental Medicine, Case Western Reserve University, Cleveland, OH (1997-2003); Associate Professor, School of Dental Medicine, Case Western Reserve University (1991-1996); Member, Adjunct Faculty, Cuyahoga Community College, Cleveland, OH (1986-1988) **Civic:** President, Robertson Family Association of North America (1986-1988) **Awards:** Named, One of the Best Dentists in America, Northern Ohio Live (2007); Recipient, Numerous Research Grants **Membership:** American Dental Association; ICOI; American Academy of Craniofacial Pain; International Association for the Study of Pain; Greater Cleveland Dental Association; Ohio Dental Association; Academy of General Dentistry; Midwest Pain Society; American Society for Laser Medicine and Surgery, Inc.; United States Dental Institute; American Chronic Pain Association; Ohio Academy of General Dentistry; American Pain Society; Academy of Integrative Pain Management **Marquis Who's Who Honors:** Albert Nelson Marquis Lifetime Achievement Award (2017) **Why did you become involved in your profession or industry:** Dr. Robertson was told all throughout his life that he would become a physician. He ended up going to dental school at The Ohio State University after seeing how excited the students were about their job. Dr. Robertson has since done everything in general dentistry. **Hobbies:** Hiking; Canoeing; Bicycling; Genealogy **Shipping Address:** 23 Wabanaki Way, Indian Island, ME, 04468

Joseph Allen Robinette

Title: Playwright **Industry:** Media & Entertainment **Date of Birth:** 02/08/1939 **Place of Birth:** Rockwood **State:** IL **Parents:** Paul Henry Robinette; Willie Merle (Ghormley) Robinette **Marital Status:** Married **Spouse Name:** Helen Marie Seitz **Children:** John; Anne; Michael; Christopher; Andrew **Education:** PhD, Southern Illinois University (1972); MA, Southern Illinois University (1966); BA, Carson-Newman College (1960) **Career:** Professor of Theater Arts, Rowan University, Glassboro, NJ (1971-2005); Instructor, University of Hawaii, Hilo (1968-1969); Instructor, Southern Illinois University, Carbondale, IL (1965-1971); Instructor, Arkansas City Junior College (1963-1964); Teacher, Bearden High School, Knoxville, TN (1962-1963) **Civic:** Founding Member, Opera for Youth (1978-Present) **Creative Works:** Playwright, 54 Plays and Musicals; Authorized Dramatizer, "Charlotte's Web"; Authorized Dramatizer, "Stuart Little"; Authorized Dramatizer, "The Lion, The Witch and the Wardrobe"; Authorized Dramatizer, "The Paper Chase"; Authorized Dramatizer, "A Rose for Emily"; Authorized Dramatizer, "A Christmas Story The Musical"; Authorized Dramatizer, "A Gift to Remember"; Authorized Dramatizer, "The Inn at Rose Harbor" **Awards:** Nominee, Tony Award (2012) **Membership:** American Alliance for Theatre and Education **Shipping Address:** PO Box 11, Richwood, NJ, 08074

Nicholas Adams Robinson

Title: Professor Emeritus **Industry:** Education/Educational Services **Company Name:** Elisabeth Haub School of Law at Pace University **Date of Birth:** 01/20/1945 **Place of Birth:** New York City **State:** NY **Parents:** Albert Lewis Robinson; Agnes Claflin (Adams) Robinson **Marital Status:** Married **Spouse Name:** Shelley Miner (1/5/1969) **Children:** Cynthia M.; Lucy A. **Education:** JD, Columbia University, Cum Laude (1970); BA, Brown University, Cum Laude (1967) **Career:** Kerlin Professor Emeritus, University Professor for the Environment, Pace University (2013-Present); Adjunct Professor, School of Forestry & Environmental Studies, Yale University (2005-Present); Gilbert and Sarah Kerlin Distinguished Professor of Environmental Law, Elisabeth Haub School of Law, Pace University, White Plains, NY (1999-2013); Legal Adviser, Observer Mission to the United Nations, Asian-African Legal Consultative Organization (2005-2009); Chair, Academy of Environmental Law, International Union for Conservation of Nature (2004-2008); Legal Adviser, Observer Mission to the United Nations, International Union for Conservation of Nature (2002-2005); Legal Adviser, International Union for Conservation of Nature (1996-2004); Professor, Elisabeth Haub School of Law, Pace University, White Plains, NY (1981-1999); Counsel, Sidley & Austin (Now Sidley Austin LLP) (1992-1996); Counsel, Sive, Paget & Riesel (Now Sive, Paget & Riesel P.C.) (1985-1992); Deputy Commissioner, Department of Environmental Conservation, New York State, Albany (1983-1985); General Counsel, Department of Environmental Conservation, New York State, Albany (1983-1985); Counsel, Winer, Neuburger & Sive, New York (1982-1983); Counsel, Marshall, Bratter, Greene, Allison & Tucker, New York City (1978-1982); Associate Professor, School of Law, Pace University, White Plains, NY (1978-1981); Associate, Marshall, Bratter, Greene, Allison & Tucker, New York City, NY (1972-1978); Law Clerk, United States District Court for the Southern District of New York (1970-1972) **Career Related:** Member, Environmental Social Advisory Council, European Bank for Reconstruction and Development (2005-Present); Co-director, Global Center for Environmental Legal Studies, Elisabeth Haub School of Law, Pace University (1982-Present); Chairman, Environmental Advisory Board to Governor Mario Cuomo (1985-1994); Delegate, US-USSR Environmental Law Meetings (1974-1992); Founder, Environmental Law Program, Center for Environmental Studies (Now Global Center for Environmental Studies), Elisabeth Haub School of Law, Pace University; Founder, Environmental Law Review; Founder, Doctor of Juridical Sciences Program, Pace University; Founder, Master of Laws Degree in Environmental Law, Pace University; Founder, Feldschuh LLM Fellowship, Pace University; Founder, JD Certification in Environmental Law, Pace University; **Civic:** Chairman, Planning Board, Village of Sleepy Hollow, NY (1999-2008); Member, World Environment Center (1981-2006); Chairman, World Environment Center (1993-1996) **Creative Works:** Author, "Capacity Building for Environmental Law in the Asia and Pacific Region," Asian Development Bank; Author, "Agenda 21 and the UNCED Proceedings," Oceana Publications; Author, "Environmental Regulation of Real Property," Law Journal Press; Contributor, Articles to Professional Journals **Awards:** John J. Medal of Service, Jay Heritage Center (2016); Inductee, American College of Environmental Lawyers (2012); National Environment Quality Award, Natural Resources Council of America (2002); Honoree, Gilbert & Sarah Kerlin Distinguished Professor of Environmental Law, Elisabeth Haub School of Law, Pace University (1999); Elizabeth Haub Prize in Environmental Law, Universite Libre du Bruxelles (1992); Honoree, James D. Hopkins Professor, Pace University (1991-1992); Raymond J. Sherwin Award, Sierra Club (1984) **Membership:** Honorary Member, International Union for Conservation of Nature (IUCN) (2012-Present); Fellow, American College of Environmental Lawyers (2012-Present); Honorary Vice President, Sierra Club (2004-Present); Governor, International Council of Environmental Law (ICEL) (1993-Present); Chair, Section on Postgraduate Legal Education, Association of American Law Schools (1999-2009); Chairman, Commission on Environmental Law (Now World Commission on Environmental Law) (1996-2004); Russian Law Committee, Association of the Bar of the City of New York (1992-1995); International Environmental Law Committee, Association of the Bar of the City of New York (1990-1992); Chair, Section on Environmental Law, Association of American Law Schools (1987-1988); International Law Committee, Association of the Bar of the City of New York (1985-1988) **Bar Admissions:** Supreme Court of the United States (1974); United States District Court for the Southern District of New York (1972); United States District Court for the Eastern District of New York (1972); United States Court of Appeals for the Second Circuit (1972); United States District Court for the Seventh Circuit (1972) **Marquis Who's Who Honors:** Albert Nelson Marquis Lifetime Achievement Award (2017) **Hobbies:** Violist **Political Affiliations:** Democrat **Religion:** Unitarian Universalist **Shipping Address:** 258 Kelbourne Avenue, Sleepy Hollow, NY, 10591 **Website:** http://www.law.pace.edu

Ronald Michael Robinson

Title: Corporate Financial Executive **Industry:** Financial Services **Company Name:** Robinson Properties **Date of Birth:** 05/01/1942 **Place of Birth:** New York **State:** NY **Parents:** Arthur John Robinson; Matilda (Siegel) Robinson **Marital Status:** Married **Spouse Name:** Mary Jane Reemelin (2/25/1972) **Children:** Scott Edward; Elizabeth Drew **Education:** MBA, University of Pennsylvania (1966); BS, The Ohio State University (1964) **Certifications:** Certified Public Accountant, State of Pennsylvania **Career:** Robinson Properties, Pennsylvania (1999-Present); Director of Finance and Administration, Presbyterian Senior Services (1982-1999); Chief Financial Officer, Presbyterian Senior Services (1982-1999); President, Robinson & Associates, Inc., Paoli, PA (1975-1981); Management Consultant, Coopers & Lybrand (1973-1975); Financial Manager, American Airlines, Inc., New York, NY (1969-1972); Principal, Robinson Properties **Career Related:** Board of Directors, Geneva House; Board of Directors, Continuing Care RX; Board of Directors, Members 1st Federal Credit Union; Board of Directors, HealthAssurance (Now Coventry Health Care); Board of Directors, HealthAmerica (Now Coventry Health Care) **Civic:** Member, Carlisle Borough Council (1988-1992); Member, Marine Corp League; Director, Rotary of Carlisle; Trustee, Shriners International **Membership:** Rotary International; Shriners International; Grand Lodge of Pennsylvania **Marquis Who's Who Honors:** Albert Nelson Marquis Lifetime Achievement Award (2017) **Why did you become involved in your profession or industry:** Mr. Robinson was inspired by his father who was in business and he was supported throughout his career by incredible mentors and networks. **Hobbies:** Running; Working out; Golf; Tennis **Political Affiliations:** Republican **Religion:** Presbyterian **Shipping Address:** PO Box 908, Carlisle, PA, 17013

Mary Columbro Rodgers

Title: English Language and Literature Educator, Writer, Academic Administrator **Industry:** Writing and Editing **Date of Birth:** 04/17/1925 **Place of Birth:** Aurora **State:** OH **Parents:** Nicola Columbro; Nancy (DeNicola) Columbro **Marital Status:** Widowed **Spouse Name:** Daniel Richard Rodgers (7/24/1965) **Children:** Robert; Patricia; Kristine **Education:** DLitt, California National Open University (1978); EdD, California National Open University (1975); Postgraduate Coursework, Sapienza University of Rome (1964-1965); PhD, The Ohio State University (1964); MA, Case Western Reserve University (1962); AB, Notre Dame College (1957) **Career:** Independent Researcher, Writer (2000-Present); President, Maryland National University (1972-2006); Professor, English, District of Columbia Teachers College, University of the District of Columbia (1968-2000); Associate Professor, Trinity College (1967-1968); Founder, Chancellor, AOU (1965-2007); Assistant Professor, English, University of Maryland (1965-1966); Supervisor English, Student Teachers, The Ohio State University (1962-1964); Teacher, English, Cleveland Secondary Schools (1952-1962); Teacher, English, Cleveland Elementary Schools (1945-1952); Dean, AOU **Creative Works:** Author, "Jezu My Beloved: Jezu Ufam Tobie, Autobiography, First Edition" (2009); Author, "A Family Book for Benjamin: Poems and Vignettes" (2008); Author, "Catholic Faith Poems" (2007); Author, "Catholic Open University of America System Poems 1962-2005" (2005); Author, "Fifth and Final Access List to the Mary Columbro Rodgers Literary Trust with Annotations" (2004); Author, "Fourth Access List to the Mary Columbro Rodgers Literary Trust for K-PhD Open Learning-Open University Methods with Data Batches Delineated" (2002); Author, "Third Access List to the Mary Columbro Rodgers Literary Trust by Subject" (1996); Author, "Second Access List to the Mary Columbro Rodgers Literary Trust by Alphabet" (1995); Author, "Fables and Farm Stories for Fiction Analysis" (1995); Author, "Biographical Sourcebook I: Mary Columbro Rodgers 1969-1995" (1995); Author, "Catholic Teacher Poems 1945-1995" (1995); Author, "Catholic Widow with Children Poems 1979-1993" (1994); Author, "First Access List to the Mary Columbro Rodgers Trust by Year" (1994); Author, "Nicola Columbro: A Brief Biography, Third Edition" (1994); Author, "Catholic Marriage Poems 1962-1979" (1993); Author, Journals Reflections and Resolves (1992-2013); Author, "Catalogue for the Mary Columbro Rodgers Literary Trust" (1992); Author, "A Chapbook of Poetry and Drama Analysis" (1992); Author, "Convent Poems 1943-1961" (1992); Author, "Convent Poems" (1992); Author, "Analyzing Fact and Fiction" (1991); Author, "Analyzing Poetry and Drama" (1991); Author, "Some Successful Literary Research Papers: An Inventory of Titles and Theses" (1991); Author, "Twelve Lectures in Literary Analysis" (1990); Author, "Ten Lectures in Literary Production" (1990); Author, "Poet and Pedagogue in Moscow and Leningrad: A Travel Report" (1989); Author, "Foundations of English Scholarship in the American Open University" (1989); Author, "The American Open University and Other Open Universities: A Comparative Study Report" (1988); Author, "New Design II: English Pedagogy in the American Open University" (1987); Author, "A Research Report" (1987); Author, "Claims and Counterclaims Regarding Instruction Given in Personalized Degree Residency Programs Completed by Graduates of California National Open University" (1986); Author, "History and Sourcebook" (1986); Author, "Conceptual History and Rationale" (1985); Author, "Design for Personalized English Graduate Degrees in the Urban University" (1984); Author, "English Pedagogy in the American Open University" (1983); Author, Papers in Applied English Linguistics (1982); Author, "Twelve Lectures on the American Open University" (1982); Author, "Open University Structures and Adult Learning" (1982); Author, "Modes and Models: Four Lessons for Young Writers" (1981); Author, "Essays and Poems on Life and Literature" (1979); Author, Comprehensive Catalogue, "The Open University of America System" (1978-1980); Author, "Open University of America System Source Book, V, VI, VII" (1978); Author, "Chapbook of Children's Literature" (1977); Author, "A Short Course in English Composition" (1976); Author, "Open University English Teaching 1945-1985"; Author, "The American Open University 1965 to 1985"; Contributor, Articles to Professional Journals **Awards:** Fulbright Scholar, Sapienza University of Rome (1964-1965) **Membership:** Fellow, The Fellowship of Catholic Scholars; United States Distance Learning Association; Poetry Society of America; National Council of Teachers of English; American Educational Research Association; Academy of American Poets; Pi Lambda Theta **Marquis Who's Who Honors:** Albert Nelson Marquis Lifetime Achievement Award (2017) **Shipping Address:** 1 Meadowgate Cir, Gaithersburg, MD, 20877

Richard Malcolm Rodgers

Marquis Who's Who
18 98
Biographee

Title: Management Accountant **Industry:** Financial Services **Date of Birth:** 06/23/1949 **Place of Birth:** Montgomery **State:** AL **Parents:** Charles Malcolm Rodgers; Betty Jean (Gilbert) Rodgers **Marital Status:** Married **Spouse Name:** Sharon Lynn Thomas (5/10/1992); Linda Joyce Meeks (12/9/1966-1970) **Children:** Angela Christina Rodgers Bolin **Education:** BBA, Georgia State University, Magna Cum Laude (1988); Coursework, Emory University (1967-1969) **Certifications:** Novice, Grey Robe Monks of St. Benedict, Southern Cross Abbey, Acworth, GA (2009-Present); Ordained Deacon, Ecumenical Catholic Church (1999); Certified Management Accountant **Career:** Controller, Hudson Everett Simonson Mullis & Associates, Inc., Atlanta, GA (1990-1996); Accounting Manager, W.L. Thompson Consultant Engineers, Inc., Atlanta, GA (1988-1990); Internal Audit Manager, Waffle House, Inc., Norcross, GA (1980-1987); Chief Cost Accountant, General Assembly Mission Board, Presbyterian Church U.S., Atlanta, GA (1974-1980); Justice of Peace, Justice's Court District 531, Decatur, GA (1973-1976); Controller, Royal Arts & Crafts, Inc., Atlanta, GA (1972-1973); Staff Accountant, Charter Enterprises, Inc., College Park, GA (1971-1972) **Career Related:** Freelance Consultant and Writer (1995-Present); Instructor, Gwinnett College Business, Lilburn, GA (1997-1999) **Civic:** Vice President, Emory Garden Condominium Association, Decatur, GA (2014-2018); President, Emory Garden Condominium Association, Decatur, GA (2006-2010); Judge, Chapbook Award (1998, 1996, 1991); Secretary, Chapbook Award (1986); Founding Director, Treasurer, Georgia Business Committee for Arts, Inc., Atlanta, GA (1981-1986); Executive Committee Member, DeKalb County Republican Party, Decatur, GA (1969-1976); Vice President, Georgia Association Justices of the Peace and Constables, Inc., Warner Robins, GA (1973-1974); Georgia State Poetry Society, Inc., Atlanta, GA; **Creative Works:** Playwright, Musical Play, "Take the Money and Run" (1991, 1979); Composer, Musical Play, "Take the Money and Run" (1991, 1979); Lyricist, Musical Play, "Take the Money and Run" (1991, 1979); Composer, Musical Play, "Many a Glorious Morning" (1971); Lyricist, Musical Play, "Many a Glorious Morning" (1971); Poet, Archon Magazine (1968-1970); Contributing Editor, Archon Magazine (1968-1970); Contributor, Articles, Heritage of Chambers County, AL; Contributor, Heritage of Fayette County, GA **Awards:** Anthology Award (1970); Stipe Scholar, Emory University (1968) **Membership:** Institute of Management Accountants, Inc.; ACLU; Corporate Accountability International; Union of Concerned Scientists; Amnesty International; Pi Delta Epsilon Journalism Honor Society; Charter Member, Golden Key International Honour Society; Mortar Board; Beta Gamma Sigma, Inc.; Phi Kappa Phi **Marquis Who's Who Honors:** Albert Nelson Marquis Lifetime Achievement **To what do you attribute your success:** Mr. Rodgers attributes his success to a combination of high ethical standards, well-developed analytical and communication skills, and old-fashioned hard work. **Why did you become involved in your profession or industry:** He became involved in his profession by the convergence of interest, aptitude, and opportunity. **What do you consider to be the highlight of your career:** A highlight of his career was becoming a Certified Management Accountant. **Hobbies:** Archeology; Geophysical research; Genealogy; American history; Playing jazz on the trumpet **Political Affiliations:** Democrat **Religion:** Ecumenical Catholic Church **Shipping Address:** 1111 Clairemont Ave., Apt K2, Decatur, GA, 30030-1216

Judith A. Rogala

Title: Chief Executive Officer **Industry:** Business Management/Business Services **Company Name:** The Catapult Factor **Education:** MBA, University of New Mexico (1982); BS, Roosevelt University (1976) **Career:** President, The Catapult Factor, Murrieta, CA (2003-Present); Chief Executive Officer, The Catapult Factor, Murrieta, CA (2002-Present); Chief Executive Officer, President, La Petite Academy, Inc. (1999-2003); President, Aramark Uniform Services (1997-1999); Executive Vice President, Office Depot, Inc., Delray Beach, FL (1994-1997); Chief Executive Officer, EQ - The Environmental Quality Company (1992-1994); President, EQ - The Environmental Quality Company (1992-1994); Chief Executive Officer, Flagship Express, Inc. (1990-1992); President, Flagship Express, Inc. (1990-1992); Senior Vice President, Central Support Services, Federal Express Corporation, Memphis, TN (1987-1990); Regional Vice President, Federal Express Corporation (1980-1987); General Manager, Pacific Northwest, Canada, Alaska, Trans World Airlines, Inc. (1962-1980) **Career Related:** Senior Executive, National Women's Fitness Network, Inc.; Adjunct Professor, Business Management, University of California **Creative Works:** Contributor, "The Golden Flame: The Heart and Soul of Remarkable Leadership" (2008); Author, "Winds of Change" (1991); Author, "TRUST, INC."; Co-Author, "The Briefcase," Various Journals; Author, "The Leadership Guide" **Awards:** James Zimmerman Award, University of New Mexico (2007); Inductee, Hall of Fame, University of New Mexico (1996); Honoree, Magazine Profile, "CEO Material: Who's on the Short List to Head a Major Corporation," Working Woman (1996); Women Who Make a Difference Award, International Women's Forum (1995); Honoree, Book Profile, "America's Competitive Secret" (1995); Honoree, Distinguished Executive, University of Kansas (1992); Honoree, Newspaper Profile, "The New Wave Director," The New York Times (1990); Honoree, Top 100 Women in Corporate America, Business Monthly (1989); Honoree, Most Powerful Women in Corporate America, Savvy (1989); Honoree, Leadership, Memphis Class of 1989; Honoree, Top Fifty Corporate Women, Business Week (1987); Professional Achievement Award, Roosevelt University (1987); Honoree, Academy of Women Achievers, Young Women's Christian Association (1987); Chief Executive Officer Award, Federal Express (1985-1986); Honoree, Outstanding Achievement, Business Leader, Young Women's Christian Association (1985) **Membership:** Founding Member, National Advisory Board, National Museum of Women in the Arts (1991-Present); The Committee of 200 (1988-Present); The California Trusteeship (1984-Present); The Chicago Network (1984-Present); International Women's Forum (1984-Present); Advisory Board, PCL Construction, Orlando, FL (2007-2010); Director, La Petite Academy, Inc., Chicago, IL (1999-2003); Harvard Women's Leadership Board (1999-2003); Board of Directors, The University of New Mexico Alumni Association (1997-2010); Director, Red Roof Inns, Inc., Hilliard, OH (1997-1999); Vice President, Strategic Planning, The Committee of 200 (1995-1998); The Conference Board (1993-2002); Advisory Board, DSC Logistics, Inc. (1993-2002); The Chicago Club (1993-2002); Director, Leadership Foundations (1993-1995); Board of Directors, Michigan Chamber of Commerce (1993-1994); Director, EQ - The Environmental Quality Company, United States Ecology, Inc. (1992-1994); Director, Flagship Express (1990-1992); National Research Council (1990-1991); Director, Butler Manufacturing, BlueScope Buildings North America, Inc. (1989-1999); Advisory Board, Catalyst Foundation (1989-1994); Board, Dixon Gallery and Gardens (1987-1990); The Mental Health Board of Chilton and Shelby Counties, Inc. (1987-1990); Board of Governors, Chicago Association of Commerce and Industry (1987-1988); President's Club and Alumni Advisory Council, Roosevelt University (1986-1988); Board of Governors, Illinois Council for Economic Education (1986-1987); The Economic Club of Chicago (1985-2002); Board of Trustees, College of St. Francis (1985-1989) **Marquis Who's Who Honors:** Albert Nelson Marquis Lifetime Achievement Award (2017); Distinguished Humanitarian (2017) **Hobbies:** Golf; Tennis; Sports; Horses **Shipping Address:** 37626 Avenida La Cresta, Murrieta, CA, United States, 92562

Charles R. Rogers

Title: Minister **Industry:** Religious **Company Name:** Evangelism in Action **Date of Birth:** 11/26/1935 **Place of Birth:** Grapevine **State:** TX **Parents:** Arlin Avery Rogers; Bessie Lorene Rogers **Marital Status:** Widowed **Spouse Name:** Oma Fay Hines (8/21/1954, Deceased) **Children:** Sheree Gay Rogers (Deceased); Charles Denne Ray Rogers; Robin Celeste Rogers-Eddins **Education:** ThM, Central American Theological Seminary (2000); BTh, Central American Theological Seminary (2000); Honorary Doctorate of Ministry in Humanities, Seminary of Theological Missions (1992); Honorary DD in Humanities, Faith Bible College (1981); MS in Christian Education, Faith Bible College (1980); ThD, Faith Theological Seminary **Career:** President, Evangelism in Action (1969-Present); Pastor, Interdenominational Churches (1965-1969); Pastor, Baptist Churches (1960-1964) **Career Related:** Leader, Humanitarian Trips Evangelism in Action (1976-Present) **Creative Works:** Author, "Transforming Power of a Godly Mind" (2016); Author, "The Beautiful Body of Christ" (2009); Author, "Tithe and Grow Rich" (2008); Author, How to Develop Christian Love (1981); Vocalist, "Charlie" (1981); Author, "Handbook for Victorious Living" (1980); Author, "Joy" (1979); Contributor, Articles, Numerous Publications **Hobbies:** Golf; Tennis; Swimming; Running; Computers **Political Affiliations:** Republican **Shipping Address:** 6417 Rogers Drive, Fort Worth, TX, 76182

Jose Alejandro Rojas Ramirez

Title: Alternate Executive Director **Industry:** Financial Services **Company Name:** International Monetary Fund **Date of Birth:** 09/03/1959 **Place of Birth:** Caracas **Country of Origin:** Venezuela **Children:** Jose Alejandro Rojas Rojas **Education:** PhD in Econometrics Mathematics Economics, Universite Paris II Pantheon-Assas (1993); MS in Mathematics Economics and Econometrics, Universit Paris II Pantheon-Assas (1988); Coursework in Energy Economics, IFP School (1987); Coursework in Senior Company Management, IFP School (1987); Coursework in Energy Models, IFP School (1987); BS in Mathematics, Universidad Central de Venezuela (1983); BS in Mathematics Statistics, Universidad Central de Venezuela (1983) **Career:** Executive Director, The World Bank Group (2006-Present); Executive Director, International Monetary Fund (2006-2010); Adviser to President, Banco Central De Venezuela (2005-2006); Executive Director, Inter-American Investment Corporation (2001); Executive Director, Inter-American Developmental Bank (2001); Minister of Finance, Republic of Venezuela (1999-2001); Deputy Minister, Ministry of Hacienda (1997-1999); Senior Economist, Ministry of Hacienda (1997-1999); Vice President of Finance and Planning, Petrleos de Venezuela, PDVSA **Awards:** Tres Honor Award, Universit Paris II Pantheon-Assas **Marquis Who's Who Honors:** Albert Nelson Marquis Lifetime Achievement Award (2017) **To what do you attribute your success:** Dr. Rojas Ramirez attributes his success to perseverance, attention to detail, work ethic and hard work. **Hobbies:** Hiking; Yoga **Shipping Address:** 7911 Quarry Ridge Way, Bethesda, MD, 20817

Signe Alice Rooth, PhD

Title: Editor **Industry:** Writing and Editing **Date of Birth:** 08/14/1924 **Place of Birth:** New York **State:** NY **Parents:** Gerhard Teodor Rooth; Florence Elizabeth (Miner) Rooth **Marital Status:** Single **Education:** PhD, University of Chicago (1953); MA, University of Southern California (1945); BA, University of Miami, Summa Cum Laude (1944) **Career:** Consultant Editor, Department of Trusteeship, Public Information, General Assembly, Conference Management, United Nations Secretariat, New York, NY (1993-2016); Consultant Editor, United Nations Development Program, United Nations Secretariat (1985-1992); Senior Editor, Division of General Assembly Affairs, United Nations Secretariat (1969-1984); Interpreter, Mission to Congo, United Nations (1962-1963); Translator and Editor, United Nations Secretariat (1956-2016); Translator, International Monetary Fund, Washington, DC (1954-1956) **Career Related:** Board Member, Association Culturelle Francophone, United Nations **Creative Works:** Editor, United Nations ESCAP (1999); Editor, "Proceedings of United Nations Congress on Public International Law: International Law as a Language for International Relations" (1995); Author, "Seeress of the Northland: Fredrika Bremer's American Journey, 1849-1851," American Swedish Historical Foundation (1955); Contributor, Articles, Professional Journals **Awards:** American Swedish Woman of the Year, Woman's Auxiliary, American Swedish Historical Museum (1984) **Membership:** French Institute Alliance Francaise; Swedish Women's Educational Association International, Inc.; The American Scandinavian Society; The American-Scandinavian Foundation; Lifetime Member, American Swedish Historical Museum; Southampton Historical Museum; Rogers Memorial Library; Paris American Club **Marquis Who's Who Honors:** Albert Nelson Marquis Lifetime Achievement Award (2017) **Why did you become involved in your profession or industry:** Dr. Rooth became involved in her profession because she always loved languages. **What do you consider to be the highlight of your career:** The highlight of Dr. Rooth's career was when she was recognized by the Deputy Secretary-General as the longest-serving retiree after 60 years of working at the United Nations. **Hobbies:** Reading; Travel; Art; Music **Shipping Address:** 12 Beekman Place, Apt. 1CD, New York, NY, 10022-8059

William C. Rorick

Title: Artist, Librarian (Retired) **Industry:** Fine Art **Company Name:** Queens College, CUNY **Date of Birth:** 06/23/1941 **Place of Birth:** Elyria **State:** OH **Parents:** Harold Rorick; Edythe E. (Harris) Rorick **Marital Status:** Married **Spouse Name:** Anne L. Sherbondy (8/21/1971) **Education:** MA in Musicology, New York University (1982); MLS, Pratt Institute (1974); MusM in Music History and Literature, Northwestern University (1970); MusB in Music History and Literature, The University of Utah (1968); BA in Economics and Business Administration, Ohio Wesleyan University (1963); Coursework in Portraiture, Various Art Schools and Workshops **Certifications:** Certified Leader, Portrait Clubs of America (2003-Present) **Career:** Assistant Professor Emeritus, Music Library, Queens College, CUNY, Flushing, NY (1996-Present); Member, Senate Nominating Committee, Delegate-at-Large, Arts Division, Music Library, Queens College, CUNY, Flushing, NY (1984-1986); Assistant Professor, Music Library, Queens College, CUNY, Flushing, NY (1979-1996); Music Reference Librarian, Music Library, Queens College, CUNY, Flushing, NY (1974-1996); Instructor, Music Library, Queens College, CUNY, Flushing, NY (1974-1979); Office Manager, Manhattan School Music Library, New York City, NY (1970-1974); Reference Assistant, Manhattan School Music Library, New York City, NY (1970-1974); Orchestral-Choral Librarian, Manhattan School Music Library, New York City, NY (1970-1974); Curator, Manhattan School Music Library, New York City, NY (1970-1974) **Career Related:** Portrait Painting Instructor; Portrait Painting Demonstrator; Show Chairman, Various Art Organizations; Juror, Various Art Organizations **Civic:** Historian, South Britain Congregational Church (2002); Board of Deacons, South Britain Congregational Church (1998-2001) **Military Service:** Untied States Army (1964-1966) **Creative Works:** Commission Artist, Corporate Institutions; Commission Artist, Public Institutions; Commission Artist, Private Institutions; Historians, Oil Portrait Series; Composer, Oil Portrait Series; Contributor, Articles, Professional Journals; Contributor, Reviews, Professional Journals; Exhibitor, Kent Art Association, Kent, CT **Awards:** Award, Allied Art Association (2013); Grantee, Research Foundation of CUNY (1981-1984); Local, Regional and National Art Awards; Best in Show, Connecticut Classic Arts Association **Membership:** Instructor, Portrait Clubs of America (2003-Present); Founding Member, CSOPA (2002-Present); The American Legion (2015); Secretary, CSOPA (2008-2010); Board of Directors, Kent Art Association (2003-2007); Leadership Team, New York Society of Portrait Artists (2001-2002); Corresponding Secretary, Society of Creative Artists of Newtown (1999-2002); Publicity Chairman, Connecticut Classic Arts (1996-1999); Joint Committee, Music Public Association, Music Library Association (1986-1988); Chapter Chairman, Music Library Association (1983-1985); Delegate, Library Association, The City University of New York (1983-1985); Editor, Directory, Library Association, The City University of New York (1980-1981); Chairman, National Membership Committee, Music Library Association (1979-1982); Publication Committee, Library Association, The City University of New York (1979-1981); Secretary, Treasure Chapter, Music Library Association (1979-1981); Chairman, Grants Committee, Library Association, The City University of New York (1978-1980); National Subcommittee on Basic Music Collection, Music Library Association (1977-1979); Program Chairman, Greater New York Chapter, Music Library Association (1977-1979); Elected Artist, Kent Art Association; Exhibition Committee, Kent Art Association; National Honor Society; Hudson Valley Art Association; Allied Artists of America; American Artists Professional League; Audubon Artists; Connecticut Pastel Society; Artist Member, Academy Artists Association; The Portrait Society of Atlanta; Portrait Society of America; American Society of Portrait Artists; International Association of Music Libraries; ARSC; American Printing History Association; American; The American Musicological Society; Sonneck Society (Now Society for American Music); Greater Southbury Chapter, Portrait Clubs of America; Beta Phi Mu, Phi Mu Alpha Sinfonia **Marquis Who's Who Honors:** Albert Nelson Marquis Lifetime Achievement Award (2017) **Where will you be in five years:** In five years, Mr. Rorick plans to be painting oil portraits of composers and other famous historical figures. **Hobbies:** Playing the Oboe **Shipping Address:** 63 Beacon Hill Dr, Southbury, CT, 06488

Daniel Rose

Title: Chairman, Board Member **Industry:** Financial Services **Company Name:** Rose Associates, 22 Dreyfus Funds **Date of Birth:** 10/31/1929 **Place of Birth:** New York City **State:** NY **Parents:** Samuel B. Rose; Belle (Bernstein) Rose **Marital Status:** Married **Spouse Name:** Joanna Semel (9/16/1956) **Children:** David Semel; Joseph Benedict; Emily; Gideon Gregory **Education:** Honorary ScD, Technion - Israel Institute of Technology, Haifa, Israel; Honorary PhD in Humane Letters, Long Island University; Honorary PhD in Engineering, Polytechnic Institute of New York University; Postgraduate Work, University of Paris; Bachelor of Arts, Syracuse University (1952); Certification of Proficiency in Russian Language; Student, Yale University (1947-1950) **Career:** Board Member, 22 Dreyfus Funds (1992-Present); Chairman, Rose Associates, Inc., New York City, NY (1999-Present); Vice-Chairman, Baltic American Enterprise Fund, New York City, NY (1994-Present); President, Rose Associates, Inc., New York City, NY (1980-1999); Chief Executive Officer, Rose Associates, Inc., New York City, NY (1980-1999); Director, Dreyfus Money Market Fund, Inc. (1980-1982); Director, Dreyfus Tax Exempt Bond Fund Inc. (1976-1982) **Career Related:** Associate Fellow, Pierson College, Yale University (1974-Present); Governor (1993-Present); Trustee, Urban Development/Mixed-Use Council, Urban Land Institute (1986-1993); Vice-Chairman, Urban Development/Mixed-Use Council, Urban Land Institute (1986-1993); Trustee, Compensation and Benefits Committees, U.S. Trust Company of New York (1982-1992); Executive Member, Compensation and Benefits Committees, U.S. Trust Company of New York (1982-1992); Vice-Chairman, Lionel Trilling Seminars, Columbia University; Executive Committee, Urban Land Foundation; Board of Governors, Technion - Israel Institute of Technology; Honorary Life Member, Technion - Israel Institute of Technology **Civic:** Board of Trustees, MBA of New York Scholarship Foundation, Inc., NY (1996-Present); Board of Advisors, National Convention, Democratic Leadership Council (1992-Present); Partner, New York City Partnership (1990-Present); Honorary Trustee, Horace Mann-Barnard School (1989-Present); Director, New York Council for the Humanities (1980-Present); Honorary President, Jewish Community Centers (1978-Present); Treasurer, Citizens Housing and Planning Council of New York (1972-Present); Board of Directors, Citizens Housing and Planning Council of New York (1972-Present); Board of Directors, Jewish Community Center Association (1970-Present); Social Research Overseers Committee, Center for International Affairs, Harvard University (1992-1998); Director, Get Ahead Foundation (1989-1998); Director, Fifth Avenue Association (1989-1998); Progressive Policy Institute Trustee, Democratic National Committee (1988); Trustee, Museum of City of New York (1984-1990); Consultant, Housing and Urban Development Panel (1984-1986); Chairman, Democratic Platform Advisory Committee (1984); Director, New York Convention Center Development Corporation (1980-1990); Board of Directors, New York Landmarks Conservancy (1977-1990); Vice President, World Confederation of Jewish Community Centers (1977-1983); Municipal Broadcasting System (1977-1978); Task Force on Taxation, Municipal Assistance Corporation (1976-1977); Member, Governor's Task Force on Housing (1975); President, Jewish Community Centers (1974-1978) **Military Service:** U.S. Air Force Program (1951-1954) **Awards:** King David Award, Jewish Heritage Commission and Aish International (2017); Outstanding Individual Philanthropist of the Year, Association of Fundraising Professionals (2013); Entrepreneur of the Year in Real Estate, Ernst & Young (2003); Harlem Renaissance Award, Abyssinian Development Corporation; Joseph Papp Racial Harmony Award, Foundation for Ethnic Understanding; Man of the Year Award, Realty Foundation; Award for Excellence for Large Scale Mixed Use Development, Urban Land Institute; Community Service Award, Building Owners and Managers Association; Cicero Speechwriting Awards; James E. Landauer Award, American Society of Real Estate Counselors; Rudin Award, New York Building Congress; Mayor's Award of Honor for Arts and Culture, The City of New York; W.E.B. DuBois Award, W.E.B. DuBois Institute, Harvard University **Membership:** Board Directors, East-West Institute (1982-Present), Treasurer, East-West Institute (1988-Present); Co-Chairman, Finance Committee, East-West Institute (1990-Present); Chairman, Executive Committee, East-West Institute (2000-Present); Chairman, Housing Committee, Real Estate Board of New York Inc. (1975-Present); Member, Board Governors, Real Estate Board of New York Inc. (1977-1980, 1990-Present); Fellow, American Academy of Arts and Sciences; Member, International Institute of Strategic Studies (1987-Present); Director Advisory Committee, International Institute of Strategic Studies (1987-Present); Board Directors, Council on Foreign Relations (1971-Present); Board Directors, Foreign Policy Association (1971-Present); Member, Real Estate Board of New York Inc. Foundation; Class of 1951, Delaware (1986-1989) **Shipping Address:** 200 Madison Ave Fl 5, Rose Associates, NY, New York, 10016

Susan Porter Rose

Title: Effecter: White House; Education **Industry:** Government Administration/Government Relations/Government Services **Date of Birth:** 09/20/1941 **Place of Birth:** Cincinnati **State:** OH **Parents:** Elmer Johnson Porter; Dorothy (Wurst) Porter **Marital Status:** Married **Spouse Name:** Jonathan Chapman Rose (1/26/1980) **Children:** Benjamin Chapman Rose (5/25/1982) **Education:** Honorary HDL, Rose-Hulman Institute of Technology (2002); MS, Indiana State University (1970); BA, Earlham College (1963) **Career:** Deputy Assistant to the President, George H.W. Bush (1989-1993); Chief of Staff to First Lady, Barbara Bush (1989-1993); Assistant to the Vice President, George H.W. Bush (1981-1989); Chief of Staff to Barbara Bush (1981-1989); Special Assistant to Deputy Assistant Attorney General, Justice Management Division, United States Department of Justice (1978-1981); Special Assistant to Assistant Attorney General, Office for Improvements in the Administration of Justice, United States Department of Justice (1977-1979); Director of Scheduling and Projects, First Lady Betty Ford (1974-1977); Director of Scheduling and Projects, First Lady Pat Nixon (1972-1974); Assistant Director of Correspondence to First Lady Pat Nixon (1971-1972); Assistant Director of Admissions, Mount Holyoke College (1966-1971); Assistant Dean, George School (1964-1966); Staff Assistant to Congressman Richard L. Roudebush (1963-1964) **Civic:** Spouse Participant, Yale Global Alumni Leadership Exchange (Yale/GALE) (2008-2017); Participant, Renaissance Weekend (1986-2014); Member, Board of Directors, Barbara Bush Foundation for Family Literacy (1993-2002); Effecter (1992); Commissioner, United States Commission of Fine Arts (1993-1998); President, Alumni Association, Earlham College (1978-1981); Member, Alumni Council, Earlham College (1975-1978); Trustee, George H.W. Bush Presidential Library and Museum **Awards:** Distinguished Alumni Award, Earlham College (1992); Distinguished Alumni Award, Indiana State University (1991) **Membership:** The Indiana Academy **Marquis Who's Who Honors:** Distinguished Humanitarian (2017) **To what do you attribute your success:** She attributes her success to her wonderful, creative, hard working parents, a fine liberal arts education and having worked hard in each position, as did everyone around her. **What do you consider to be the highlight of your career:** Discussing a dilemma with the First Lady, Mrs. Rose offered a solution, which she loved, but she felt that she needed to run it by her husband to get his thoughts. She called the next morning and said, "He says it's brilliant." **Where will you be in five years:** In five years, Ms. Rose hopes to be healthy, involved with family and friends, and doing some good every day. **Hobbies:** Worldwide Political Scene; Travel; Books; Family; Pets; Golf-to-be **Religion:** Quaker, Congregational, Episcopalian **Shipping Address:** 5955 Ranleigh Manor Dr, McLean, VA, 22101

Elizabeth Ann Roseberry

Title: Neonatologist **Industry:** Medicine & Health Care **Company Name:** Marion General Hospital **Date of Birth:** 01/26/1947 **Place of Birth:** Athens **State:** OH **Parents:** Horace Hewell Roseberry; Margaret Elizabeth (Ross) Roseberry **Marital Status:** Divorced **Spouse Name:** Matthew Martin Hine (6/14/1986, Divorced 10/15/1989); Massimo Costa (6/15/1974, Divorced 9/9/1982) **Education:** Fellow in Neonatology, The University of Texas Medical Branch at Galveston (1988-1990); Resident in Pediatrics, The University of Texas Medical Branch at Galveston (1985-1988); MD, The University of Texas Health Science Center at Houston (1985); Postgraduate Coursework, University of Arizona (1974-1976); MS in Zoology, Oregon State University (1970); BS in Biology, Wake Forest University, Cum Laude (1968) **Certifications:** Medical License, State of Ohio (2018); Medical License, State of West Virginia (2017); Medical License, State of Colorado (2017); Medical License, State of North Dakota (2017); Medical License, State of Indiana (2017); Medical License, State of Virginia (2016); Medical License, State of Idaho (2016); Medical License, State of Texas (2016); Diplomate, Pediatrics and Neonatal-Perinatal Medicine, American Board of Pediatrics; Certification in Pediatrics, American Board of Pediatrics; Certification in Neonatal-Perinatal Medicine, American Board of Pediatrics **Career:** Independent Contractor, Consultant to Ohioans with Disabilities (2015-Present); Independent Contractor, Neonatologist, Marion General Hospital (2001-2015); Associate Neonatologist, Marion General Hospital, Marion, OH (2005-2007); Associate Neonatologist, Central Ohio Newborn Medicine, Inc., Columbus, OH (2001-2005); Principal, NeoHealth, Port Arthur, TX (1998-2001); Associate Neonatologist, Pediatrix Medical Group, Charleston, WV (1992-1998); Affiliate Neonatologist, Fairfax Neonatal Associates, PC, Falls Church, VA (1990-1992); Research Associate, Department of Surgery, Division of Immunology and Organ Transplantation, University of Texas, Houston (1980-1981); Technician I, Forest Science Laboratory, Texas Agricultural and Mechanical University, College Station, TX (1979-1980); Research Assistant II, Department of Laboratory Medicine, Biological Sciences Group, University of Connecticut, Farmington, CT (1977-1978); Research Assistant, Department of Anesthesiology, University of Arizona Medical Center, Tucson, AZ (1975-1976); Laboratory Technician II, Departments of Pharmacology and Anesthesiology, University of Arizona Medical Center, Tucson, AZ (1974-1975); Laboratory Technician III, Litton-Bionetics, Inc., Bethesda, MD (1971-1974) **Career Related:** Director, NICU Texas Health Presbyterian Hospital, Flower Mound, TX (2010-Present); Director, Cypress-Fairbanks Medical Center (2009-Present); Director, Wadley Regioanl Medical Center, Texarkana, TX (2010); Trinity Hospital, Minot, ND (2007-2009); Thomas Memorial Hospital, South Charleston, WV (2007-2009); Eastern Idaho Regional Medical Center, Idaho Falls, ID (2006-2008); Odessa Regional Hospital, Texas (2002); Marion General Hospital (2001-2007); Abiline Regional Medical Center, Texas (2001); Orange Baptist Hospital (1998-2001); St. Mary Hospital (1998-2001); Med-Jefferson Hospital, Nederland, TX (1998-2001); Park Place Medical Center, Port Arthur, TX (1998-2001); Staff Neonatologist, Park Plaza Hospital, Houston, TX (1997-1998); St. Joseph Hospital, Houston, TX (1997-1998); Virginia Beach General Hospital (1994-1998); Alexandria Hospital (1993-1998); Mary Washington Hospital, Fredericksburg, VA (1993-1998); Clinical Assistant Professor of Pediatrics, West Virginia University School of Medicine (1993-1994); Women and Children's Hospital, Charleston Area Medical Centers (1992-1998); Potomac Hospital, Woodbridge, VA (1990-1992); Fairfax Hospital, Falls Church, VA (1990-1992) **Creative Works:** Contributor, Articles, Professional Journals **Awards:** Physician Recognition Award, American Medical Association (1992-Present); Minnie L. Maffett Award (1989-1990); Physician Recognition Award, American Medical Association (1988-1991) **Membership:** Fellow, American Academy of Pediatrics; American Medical Association; Texas Medical Association; Medical Society of Virginia; Marion Academy of Medicine; Ohio State Medical Association **Marquis Who's Who Honors:** Albert Nelson Marquis Lifetime Achievement Award (2017) **To what do you attribute your success:** Dr. Roseberry attributes her success to Dr. Joan Richardson, her mentor, and Dr. Bahtia of the Athens Campus of Georgia Medical School. **Why did you become involved in your profession or industry:** While Dr. Roseberry was in training, she had to work a lot of hours in a neonatal clinic, and she has stayed in the field ever since. **Hobbies:** Gardening; Theater; Bridge; Foreign travel; Small adventures with friends **Shipping Address:** 1446 Eagle Pass Dr., Marion, OH, 43302

Edwin Harold Rosenberg

Title: Senior Programmer Analyst (Retired) **Industry:** Medicine & Health Care **Company Name:** Johns Hopkins Health System **Date of Birth:** 06/17/1949 **Place of Birth:** Baltimore **State:** MD **Parents:** Mervin Rosenberg; Helen Rosenberg **Education:** BS in Psychology and Computer Science, Towson University (1984); BS in Physics and Mathematics, Towson University (1976) **Certifications:** Certifications of Achievements, MITx, Massachusetts Institute of Technology (2016-Present) **Career:** Senior Programmer Analyst, Johns Hopkins Health Systems, Baltimore, MD (1993-2015); Research Psychologist, Gerontology Research Center, National Institute on Aging, National Institutes of Health, Baltimore, MD (1983-1992) **Career Related:** Amateur Violinist, Baltimore Symphony Orchestra (2013-Present) **Creative Works:** Contributor, Articles to Professional Journals **Awards:** Sustained Superior Performance, National Institutes of Health (1984) **Membership:** Baltimore Symphony Orchestra Academy (2013-Present); President, Junior Chapter, American Physical Society, Towson University (1975-1976) **Marquis Who's Who Honors:** Albert Nelson Marquis Lifetime Achievement Award (2017) **What do you consider to be the highlight of your career:** The highlight of Mr. Rosenberg's career has been generating data for a presidential candidate, the United States Senate, the United States House of Representatives and the Library of Congress. This data analyzed the status of healthcare from the perspective of Johns Hopkins Hospital and Johns Hopkins Bayview Medical Center in 2008. **Hobbies:** Online academic learning; Playing violin; Science; Science fiction; Crossword puzzles; Number puzzles **Shipping Address:** 4501 Dunton Ter Apt. A, Perry Hall, MD, 21128

Lucille Glicklich Rosenberg

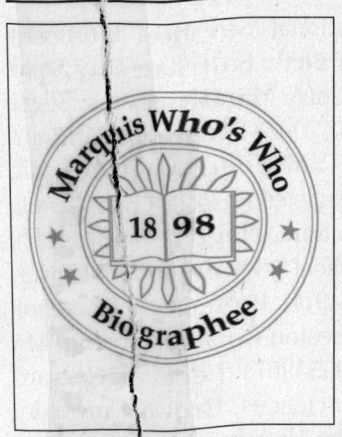

Industry: Medicine & Health Care **Date of Birth:** 01/10/1926 **Place of Birth:** Fond du Lac **State:** WI **Parents:** Peter Barash, Freda (Pevnick) Barash **Education:** MD, University of Wisconsin (1950); BA, University of Wisconsin (1947) **Certifications:** Diplomate, American Board of Child Psychiatry; Diplomate, American Board of Psychiatry and Neurology; Diplomate, American Board of Pediatrics **Career:** Professor of Psychiatry, Medical College, University of Wisconsin (1995-Present); Medical Director, Child and Adolescent Psychiatric Clinic, Sinai Samaritan (1985-Present); Associate Professor, Vice Chairman, Department of Psychiatry, University of Wisconsin Medical School, Milwaukee Clinical Campus (1985-Present); Clinical Professor, Medical College, University of Wisconsin (1985-Present); Director, Liaison Psychiatry, Milwaukee Children's Hospital (1975-1985); Professor of Psychiatry, Medical College, University of Wisconsin (1971-1985); Child Psychiatry Fellow, Marquette and Milwaukee Children's Hospital (1969-1971); Physician, Medicine, Psychiatry, Marquette Medical School Associated, Wisconsin (1967-1969); Assistant Professor of Pediatrics, Medical College, University of Wisconsin, Milwaukee, WI (1965-1985); Chief Medical Consultant, Milwaukee Public Schools (1964-1967); Medical Director, Children's Division, Easterseals Child Development Program (1963-1967); Medical Director, Children's Division, Curative Workshop, Milwaukee, WI (1959-1963); Intern, Pediatrics, Milwaukee Children's Hospital (1951-1953); Intern, Youngstown Hospital Association, Ohio (1950-1951); Lecturer, Various Colleges and Universities; Director, Child-Family Psychiatry Program; Hospital Staff Appointments, Milwaukee County Medical Complex, Mount Sinai Medical Center, Milwaukee Psychiatric Hospital, Milwaukee Children's Hospital **Career Related:** Consultant in Field; Fellow, Wisconsin Branch, American Academy of Pediatrics; Fellow, American Psychiatric Association; Fellow, American Academy of Child And Adolescent Psychiatry **Civic:** Board of Directors, Milwaukee Jewish Council on Community Relations (1997-Present); Board of Directors, Wisconsin State Medical Society Foundation (1996-Present); Volunteer, Social Justice Tutoring; Board of Directors, Congregation Shir Hadash (2010-2012); President, Congressional Shir Hadash (2010); Education Committee, Congregation Shir Hadash (2010); Task Force on Teen Pregnancies, Planned Parenthood (1984); Marquette University Panel on Survivors of the Holocaust (1984); Congressional Emmanuel Yom Hashoah (1982); Active Member, N'Shei Group, Milwaukee Children's Hospital Junior Auxiliary Target MD Program, University of Wisconsin (1981); President, Milwaukee Jewish Federation (1977-1984); Board of Trustees, Congressional Beth Israel (1975-1977); President, Milwaukee Board, Jewish Education Board (1974-1976); Board Director, Milwaukee Board, Jewish Education Board (1971-1978); Board of Trustees, Youth Commission (1971-1977); Kesher Jewish Woman's Network; Congressional Milwaukee Neonatal Nursing Consortium; Active Member, N'Shei Group, Jewish Federation of Women's Division; Active Member, N'Shei Group, Jewish Parenting, Communication 80's **Creative Works:** Contributor, Articles, Professional Publications **Awards:** Women Influence Award, American Society of Adolescent Psychiatry (2013); Distinguished Service, Lifetime Achievement Award, Wisconsin Council on Child & Adolescent Psychiatry (2009) **Membership:** Art At Large (2008-Present); Legislative Council Committee, Strengthening Wisconsin Families (2008-Present); Council Member, Wisconsin Psychiatric Association (1989-Present); Alternate Regional Assembly Delegate, American Academy of Child and Adolescent Psychology (1989-Present); Committee, American Academy of Child And Adolescent Psychiatry (1988-Present); Board of Directors, Wisconsin State Medical Society (1985-Present); Reference Committee, Wisconsin State Medical Society (1982-Present); Delegate, Wisconsin State Medical Society (1978-Present); President, Wisconsin Psychiatric Association (1995-1997); President-Elect, Wisconsin Psychiatric Association (1993-1995); President, Milwaukee County Medical Society (1985); President-Elect, Milwaukee County Medical Society (1984); President, Wisconsin Council on Child and Adolescent Psychiatry (1983-1986); President-Elect, Wisconsin Council on Child and Adolescent Psychiatry (1982-1983); Secretary, Wisconsin Council on Child and Adolescent Psychiatry (1981-1982); Secretary-Treasurer, Milwaukee County Medical Society (1981); Board of Directors, Women in Medicine of Wisconsin (1979-1982); President, Women in Medicine of Wisconsin (1979-1980); Southeastern Wisconsin Chapter Vice-Director, American Medical Women's Association (1977-1979); Society of Adolescent Medicine; Milwaukee Pediatrics Society; American Orthopsychiatric Association; Wisconsin Council on Adolescent and Child Psychiatry; American Society of Adolescent Psychiatry; American Medical Association; Advisory Board, Wisconsin Society of Jewish Learning **Hobbies:** Travel; Bicycling; Poetry; Tennis; Walking; Reading **Religion:** Jewish

Judy Francis Rosenblith, PhD

Title: Psychology Professor **Industry:** Education/Educational Services **Company Name:** Wheaton College **Date of Birth:** 03/20/1921 **Place of Birth:** Salt Lake City **State:** UT **Parents:** John Edward Francis; Mary Louise (Slack) Francis **Marital Status:** Single **Spouse Name:** Walter A. Rosenblith (9/27/1941, Deceased 5/1/2002) **Children:** Sandra Y. (Deceased); Ronald F. **Education:** PhD, Harvard University, Cambridge, MA (1958); MA, Radcliffe College (1950); AB, University of California, Los Angeles (1942); Coursework, Occidental College (1940) **Career:** Professor Emerita, Wheaton College (1984-Present); Senior Research Investigator, Division of Biological and Medical Science, Brown University (1975-1977); Meneely Professor, Wheaton College (1972-1974); Professor of Psychology, Wheaton College (1968-1984); Associate Professor, Wheaton College, Norton, MA (1965-1968); Clinical Associate, Harvard Medical School (1965-1967); Lecturer, Harvard University (1962-1963); Assistant Member, Institute of Life Sciences, Brown University (1961-1975); Associate Psychology, Department of Psychiatry, Harvard Medical School (1961-1964); Assistant Professor of Psychology, Brown University (1957-1961); Instructor, Harvard University (1956-1957); New England Supervisor, National Opinion Research Center (1953-1967); Teaching Fellow, Graduate School of Education, Harvard University (1953-1956); Assistant Professor of Psychology, Simmons College (1951-1952); Teaching Fellow, Social Relations, Harvard University (1948-1950) **Career Related:** Visiting Committee, Buswell Memorial Library (1997-2000); Visiting Professor, Florida International University (1992); Maternal and Child Health Research Advisory Committee, National Institute of Child Health and Human Development (1974-1978); Fellow, American Psychological Association **Creative Works:** Co-Author, "Portraits of Pioneers in Psychology" (2003); Co-Author, "A Century of Developmental Psychology" (1994); Author, "In the Beginning: Development from Conception to Age Two, Second Edition" (1992); Co-Author, "Student Manual for In the Beginning" (1992); Co-Author, "In the Beginning: Development in the First Two Years" (1985); Advisory Editor, "Contemporary Psychology" (1979-1980); Senior Editor, "The Causes of Behavior: Readings in Child Development and Educational Psychology, Third Edition" (1972); Senior Editor, "The Causes of Behavior: Readings in Child Development and Educational Psychology, Second Edition" (1966); Senior Editor, "The Causes of Behavior: Readings in Child Development and Educational Psychology" (1962); Contributor, Chapters, Books **Awards:** Fellow, New York Academy of Sciences (1976); Grantee, Grant Foundation (1971-1977); Grantee, Child Health and Human Development (1966-1970); Grantee, Neurological Diseases and Blindness (1961-1964); Grantee, National Institute of Mental Health (1958-1960) **Membership:** Chairman, History Committee, Society for Research in Child Development (1993-1995); Public Information Committee, American Psychological Association (1981-1984); Chairman, Convention Arrangements, Society for Research in Child Development (1979-1981); Board of Social and Ethical Responsibility for Psychology, American Psychological Association (1977-1981); Secretary, Society for Research in Child Development (1965-1969); Society for Research in Child Development; American Psychological Society; Psychonomic Society **Marquis Who's Who Honors:** Albert Nelson Marquis Lifetime Achievement Award (2017) **To what do you attribute your success:** Dr. Rosenblith attributes her success to the support she received from her parents. **Why did you become involved in your profession or industry:** Dr. Rosenblith became interested in physiological psychology, but after being exposed to prejudice, she changed her focus to social psychology. She then earned a PhD in child development. **What do you consider to be the highlight of your career:** The highlight of Dr. Rosenblith's career was the new courses she introduced at Wheaton College, and her textbook, "In the Beginning Development from Conception to Age Two, Second Edition." **Shipping Address:** 555 NE 34th Street, Apt. 908, Miami, FL, 33137

William A. Rosoff

Title: Counsel **Industry:** Law and Legal Services **Company Name:** Dechert LLP **Date of Birth:** 06/21/1943 **Place of Birth:** Philadelphia **State:** PA **Parents:** Herbert Rosoff; Estelle (Finkel) Rosoff **Marital Status:** Married **Spouse Name:** Beverly Rae Rifkin (2/7/1970) **Children:** Catherine D.; Andrew M. **Education:** LLB, University of Pennsylvania, Magna Cum Laude (1967); BS, Temple University, with High Honors (1964) **Career:** Counsel, Dechert LLP (2011-Present); President, Advanta Corp. (1999-2011); Vice Chairman, Board of Directors, Advanta Corp. (1996-2011); Chairman, Executive Committee, Wolf, Block, Schorr & Solis-Cohen (1987-1988); Partner, Wolf, Block, Schorr & Solis-Cohen (1975-1996); Associate, Wolf, Block, Schorr & Solis-Cohen (1969-1975); Instructor, University of Pennsylvania Law School (1968-1969); Law Clerk to Honorable Abraham L. Freedman, United States Court of Appeals for the Third Circuit (1967-1968) **Career Related:** Chairman, Board of Directors, RMH Teleservices, Inc. (1997-1999); Trustee, Atlantic Realty Trust (1996-2006); Tax Advisory Board Member, Little, Brown and Company, Hachette Book Group, Inc. (1994-1996); Trustee, RPS Realty Trust (1990-1996); Member, Tax Advisory Board, CCH Incorporated (1983-1994); Member, Legal Activities Policy Board of Tax Analysts (1978-1995); Outside Adviser to United States Treasury Department (1977-1980); Speaker, Tax Matters, National Office of the Internal Revenue Service, Harvard Law School's Tax Policy Institute **Civic:** Dean's Counsel, Fox School of Business, Temple University (2012-Present); Board of Directors, Rothman Institute (2011-Present); Board of Visitors, Fox School of Business, Temple University (2005-2012) **Creative Works:** Editorial Board Member, Journal of Partnership Taxation (1983-2000); Editor, University of Pennsylvania Law Review (1965-1967); Contributor, Articles to Professional Journals **Awards:** Co-Recipient, with Beverly Rosoff, Martin D. Ginsburg Award, Cedille Chicago, NFP (2017) **Membership:** Advisory Group, Federal Income Tax Project, The American Law Institute (1982-Present); Consultant for Taxation of Pass-through Entities, The American Law Institute (1995-2000); Associate Reporter for Taxation of Partnerships, The American Law Institute (1978-1982); Consultant for Taxation of Partnerships, The American Law Institute (1976-1978); Fellow, American College of Tax Counsel; Order of the Coif; Beta Gamma Sigma , Inc.; Beta Alpha Psi; Lifetime Member, The American Law Institute **Bar Admissions:** New York (2017); United States District Court for the Eastern District of Pennsylvania (1968); Pennsylvania (1968) **Marquis Who's Who Honors:** Who's Who Life Time Achiever Award; Who's Who in the World, Who's Who in American Law, Who's Who Top Lawyers **Shipping Address:** 721 Bryn Mawr Ave, Penn Valley, PA, 19072

Carl E. Rosow, PhD

Title: Anesthesiologist, Educator **Industry:** Education/Educational Services **Parents:** William Arthur Rosow; Emma Rosow **Marital Status:** Married **Spouse Name:** Anna Laura Strow (7/21/1973) **Children:** David Edward; Laura Katherine **Education:** Honorary MA, Harvard University, Boston, MA (2003); PhD, Boston University (1979); Honorary MD, Boston University **Certifications:** Certified American Board of Anesthesiologists (1979); Certified Physician, Medical Board of California (1974); Massachusetts Board of Registration in Medicine (1974) **Career:** Course Director, Pharmacology, Harvard Medical School (2007-Present); Professor, Anesthesiology, Harvard Medical School (2003-Present); Anesthetist, Massachusetts General Hospital, Boston, MA (1994-Present); Course Director, Principal, Pharmacology, Harvard-MIT Division of Health Science and Technology (1994-Present); Adjunct Associate Professor, Anesthesia, Harvard-MIT Division of Health Science and Technology (1986-Present); Adjunct Associate Professor, Pharmacology, Boston University School of Medicine (1984) **Career Related:** Editorial Board Member, International Anesthesia Research Society (2007-Present); Associate Examiner, American Board of Anesthesiologists (1986-Present); Chairman, Anesthesiology Expert Committee, United States Pharmacopaeia, Rockville, MD (2000-2005); Elected Member, Joint Committee on Training Examiners (1991-2001); American Society of Pharmacology and Experimental Therapeutics (1983-1987); Chairman, Community Drugs and Therapeutics, Massachusetts Medical Society (1979-1984) **Creative Works:** Contributor, Articles, Professional Journals **Awards:** Paul Janssen Lifetime Achievement Award, International Society for Anesthetic Pharmacology (2009); Michael Dykes Distinguished Lectureship Award, Northwestern University School of Medicine (1998); Robertazzi Memorial Lecturer Award, New York State Society of Anesthesiologists (1997); Irving London Teaching Award, Harvard-MIT Division of Health Science and Technology (1987) **Marquis Who's Who Honors:** Albert Nelson Marquis Lifetime Achievement Award (2017) **Why did you become involved in your profession or industry:** Dr. Rosow was attracted to anesthesiology by the fact that it is the application of pharmacology to people. **Shipping Address:** 15 Marshall Ter, Wayland, MA, 01778

Marilyn J. Ross, PhD

Title: Professor of Higher Education **Industry:** Education/Educational Services **Company Name:** Florida Memorial University **Children:** Sharyn (Thal); Andrew **Education:** PhD in Higher Education Leadership, University of Miami (1995); MA in American Studies, University of Miami (1971); BA in American Studies, University of Miami (1969) **Career:** Professor of Higher Education, Florida Memorial University (1995-Present); Associate Professor of English, Florida Memorial College (1985-1994); Associate Professor of Mass Communication Arts, Florida Memorial College (1985-1994); Assistant Professor of English, Florida Memorial College (1971-1984) **Career Related:** Coordinator, Modern Languages (1999-Present); Scholarly Presenter, Round Table, "African American Women's Steadfast Resolve to Overcome Obstacles and Pursue Success," Oxford University (2005); Founder, Mass Communications Arts Program, Florida Memorial College (1980); President, International Program Channel 77, Village of Key Biscayne; Historian, Rotary Club of Key Biscayne, Village of Key Biscayne; Chairman, English Majors Division, Humanities Scholarship Banquet; Scholarly Presenter, "Continuing Relevance of the Black College to Individuals who Might not have the Opportunity to Gain Access to College," Faculty Senate, Florida Memorial University; Scholarly Presenter, "Black Males Plight/Black Women's Plight in American Society," NAAAS and Ethnic Studies Conference, College of Charleston, SC; Scholarly Presenter, University of South Carolina; Chairman, Division of the Humanities, Scholarship Banquet **Creative Works:** Producer, Rotary On-Air Television Programming, Channel 77, Key Biscayne, FL (2016-Present); Author, "Voices of the Inner City" Chapter, "HBCUs Models for Success, Supporting Achievement and Retention of Black Males," Thurgood Marshall Scholarship Publication (2006); Author, "Success Factors of Young African American Women at a Historically Black College" (2002); Author, "Success Factors of Young African American Males at a Historically Black College" (1998); Producer, Florida Memorial University/Multi-Ethnic Community Cable Programming, Florida Memorial University, Miami, FL (1980); Producer, "Historical Prospective," Channel 77, Key Biscayne, FL **Awards:** Award, The Black Archives (1999); Award, Florida Memorial College (1999); Outstanding and Dedicated Service in Behalf Of FMC Award, Miami-Dade County (1987); Outstanding Service Award, Veterans Club (1979); Recognition for Dedication, Loyalty and Service to the President, Florida Memorial University **Membership:** Chapter 6990, Rotary International, Key Biscayne, FL (2016-Present); Modern Language Association; AAUW; Association Educational Leadership; NCTE; National Association of African American Studies & Affiliates; American Studies Association; Epsilon Tau Lambda; Kappa Delta Pi, International Honor Society in Education; Phi Lambda Pi; Delta Theta Mu; Honor Society of Phi Kappa Phi; Phi Alpha Theta History Honor Society; Faculty Advisor, Sigma Tau Delta; On-campus Advisor, Alpha Lambda Gamma **Marquis Who's Who Honors:** Distinguished Humanitarian (2017) **Shipping Address:** 1121 Crandon Boulevard, Apt. F602, Key Biscayne, FL, 33149

Michael Aaron Ross

Title: Consultant **Industry:** Law and Legal Services **Company Name:** Blaqwell, Inc. **Date of Birth:** 09/15/1941 **Place of Birth:** Newark **State:** NJ **Parents:** Alexander Ash Ross; Matilda (Blumenthal) Ross **Marital Status:** Married **Spouse Name:** Leslie Gordon (6/26/1976) **Children:** Christopher Gordon; Alan Gordon; Jessica Siegel (Daughter-in-Law) **Education:** MSc in International Law, LSE (1967); JD, Columbia University (1966); BA, Franklin & Marshall College (1963) **Career:** Advisory Board, Clutch Group, Morae Global Corporation (2007-Present); Consultant, Blaqwell Legal Consulting (Now Blaqwell, Inc.), New York, NY (2006-Present); Counsel, Wilmer Cutler Pickering Hale and Dorr LLP, New York, NY (2004-2005); General Counsel, Citigroup International (Now Citigroup Inc.) (2002-2003); General Counsel, Citibank (Now Citigroup Inc.) New York, NY (1998-2003); Deputy General Counsel, Citicorp (Now Citigroup Inc.), New York, NY (1993-2001); Associate to Partner, Shearman & Sterling, New York, NY (1967-1993) **Civic:** Board of Directors, Board Finance Committee, Greater New York Councils, Boy Scouts of America (2000-Present); Board of Directors, AIESEC United States Inc. (2009-2017), Board of Directors, AIESEC United States Inc. (1979-1992) **Membership:** The American Law Institute; ABA; New York County Lawyers Association; Association of the Bar of the City of New York; The University Club of New York **Bar Admissions:** New York (1968) **Marquis Who's Who Honors:** Albert Nelson Marquis Lifetime Achievement Award (2017) **Why did you become involved in your profession or industry:** Mr. Ross became involved in his profession at a young age. He watched his parents live through the Great Depression, which inspired him to pursue a career that would allow him to help people. Mr. Ross also wanted a broad education in college and a profession that challenged him personally, so he decided to study law. **Hobbies:** Exercise and fitness; Theatre; Movies; Art exhibitions; Travel **Shipping Address:** 262 Central Park W., Apt 12A, New York, NY, 10024

Eugene Roth

Title: Lawyer **Industry:** Law and Legal Services **Company Name:** Rosenn, Jenkins & Greenwald, LLP **Date of Birth:** 06/28/1935 **Place of Birth:** Wilkes-Barre **State:** PA **Parents:** Max Roth; Rae (Klein) Roth **Marital Status:** Married **Spouse Name:** Constance D. Smulyan (6/16/1957) **Children:** Joan Roth Kleinman; Steven P.; Jeffrey H.; Lawrence W. (Deceased) **Education:** LLB, Pennsylvania State University (1960); BS, Wilkes University (1957) **Career:** Partner, Rosenn, Jenkins & Greenwald, LLP, Wilkes-Barre, PA (1964-Present); Associate, Rosenn, Jenkins & Greenwald, LLP, Wilkes-Barre, PA (1960-1964) **Career Related:** Director, Joint Urban Studies Center (Now The Institute for Public Policy & Economic Development at Wilkes University) (2006-Present); Chairman, Wyoming Valley Retirement Community, Inc. (2004-2007); Chairman, Greater Wilkes-Barre Partnership, Inc. (1991-1993) **Civic:** Trustee, Wilkes University, (1979-Present); Chairman, Eastern Pennsylvania Regional Board of Directors, Geisinger Wyoming Valley Medical Center (2004); Chairman, Wilkes-Barre City Transition Committee (2004); Annual Campaign Chairman, Osterhout Free Library (1999); Chairman, Wilkes University (1993-1998); Chairman, United Way of Wyoming Valley (1983) **Awards:** Recipient, Lifetime Achievement Award, Wilkes University Ancestral Cornels (2009); Recipient, Eugene S. Farley Memorial Achievement Award, John Wilkes Society, Wilkes University (2009); Listee, Pennsylvania Super Lawyers (2006); Recipient, Shofar Award, United Hebrew Institute (2001); Distinguished Citizen Award, Northeastern Pennsylvania Council, Boy Scouts of America (1998); Recipient, Community Service Award, B'nai B'rith (1994); Named, Outstanding Volunteer Fund Raiser, Association of Fundraising Professionals (1993); Named, Distinguished Pennsylvania Award, Philadelphia Chamber of Commerce (1980) **Membership:** Chairman, Wyoming Valley United Jewish Campaign (1993); Chairman, Greater Wilkes-Barre Chamber of Commerce (1980); Chairman, Wyoming Valley United Jewish Campaign (1978); ABA; Pennsylvania Bar Association; Luzerne County Bar Association, Wilkes-Barre Law & Library Association; Vice Committee for Economic Growth, Greater Wilkes-Barre Chamber of Commerce; B'nai B'rith **Bar Admissions:** United States District Court for the Middle District of Pennsylvania (1961); Pennsylvania (1960) **Marquis Who's Who Honors:** Albert Nelson Marquis Lifetime Achievement Award (2017) **Hobbies:** Reading; Community service **Political Affiliations:** Republican **Religion:** Jewish **Shipping Address:** 15 S Franklin St., Ste 1000, Rosenn Jenkins & Greenwald LLP, Wilkes Barre, PA, 18711

John Reece Roth, PhD

Title: Electrical Engineer, Educator, Researcher, Inventor **Industry:** Engineering **Company Name:** University of Electronic Science and Technology of China **Date of Birth:** 09/19/1937 **Place of Birth:** Washington **State:** PA **Parents:** John Meyer Roth; Ruth Evangeline (Iams) Roth **Marital Status:** Married **Spouse Name:** Helen Marie DeCrane (1/14/1972) **Children:** Nancy Ann; John Alexander **Education:** PhD, Cornell University (1963); BS in Physics, Massachusetts Institute of Technology (1959) **Career:** Honorary Professor, University of Electronic Science and Technology of China, Chengdu, China (1992-Present); Professor Emeritus, The University of Tennessee, Knoxville (2004-2006); Principal Investigator, National Science Foundation (2002-2003); Principal Investigator, Langley Research Center, NASA, Hampton, VA (2001-2003); Principal Investigator, Air Force Office of Scientific Research, Washington, DC (2001-2003); Principal Investigator, March Instruments, Inc., Concord, CA (1996-1998); Principal Investigator, Langley Research Center, NASA, Hampton, VA (1995-1998); Principal Investigator, Army Research Office (1988-1993); Principal Investigator, Air Force Office of Scientific Research, Washington, DC (1981-1995); Principal Investigator, Office of Naval Research, Arlington, VA (1980-1989); Professor, The University of Tennessee, Knoxville (1978-2004); Principal Investigator, Lewis Research Center, NASA, Cleveland, OH (1963-1978); Aerospace Engineer, North American Aviation, Canoga Park, CA (1959); Engineering Aide, Aerojet Rocketdyne Holdings, Inc., Azusa, CA (1958); Engineering Aide, Aerojet Rocketdyne Holdings, Inc., Azusa, CA (1957); Civilian Consulting, Industrial Plasma Engineering **Career Related:** Honorary Guest Professor, Tsinghua University, Shenzhen Campus (2006-2008); Consultant, Harrick Plasma (2006); Consultant, YTC-Am., Inc. (2005); Consultant, Procter & Gamble (2000); Consultant, Atmospheric Glow Technologies Inc. (1999-2005); Consultant, Tetra Pak International S.A. (1998-2000); Consultant, Environmental Elements Corporation (1997-2000); Consultant, Eco Science Solutions, Inc. (1997-1998); Consultant, Procter & Gamble (1996); Consultant, March Instruments, Inc. (1995-1998); Consultant, Eastman Chemical Company, Kingsport, TN (1989-1990); Consultant, BDM Corporation (1987-1988); NAS-NRC Committee on Aneutronic Fusion (1986-1987); Consultant, Tennessee Valley Authority, Chattanooga, TN (1982-1984); Ford Fellow (1961-1962); Speaker at Professional Meetings; Lifetime Fellow, IEEE; Associate Fellow, American Institute of Aeronautics and Astronautics **Creative Works:** Author, "Applications to Nonthermal Plasma Processive Volume Two" (2001); Author, "Industrial Plasma Engineering: Principles Volume One" (1995); Author, "Introduction to Fusion Energy"; Contributor, Articles to Professional Journals **Awards:** Gonzalez Family Lifetime Achievement Award (2006); Inventor's Award, NASA (2004); B. Otto and Katherine Wheeley Award for Excellence in Technology Transfer (1999); Sloan Scholar (1955-1959) **Membership:** President, University of Tennessee Chapter, Sigma Xi (1985-1986); Executive Committee, North Ohio Section, American Nuclear Society (1975-1978); American Chemical Society; American Nuclear Society; Lifetime Member, Sigma Xi, The Scientific Research Honor Society; Lifetime Member, American Nuclear Society; Lifetime Member, American Society for Engineering Education; American Physical Society; Lifetime Member, American Association for the Advancement of Science; Knoxville Museum of Art; East Tennessee Society, Knoxville, TN; Archaeological Institute of America; Associate, Nuclear and Plasma Sciences Society **Marquis Who's Who Honors:** Albert Nelson Marquis Lifetime Achievement Award (2017) **Why did you become involved in your profession or industry:** Dr. Reece became involved in his profession because of his interest in hands-on research and development. **Where will you be in five years:** The highlight of Dr. Reece's career was the development of the DNA atmosphere uniform glow discharge plasma and the aerodynamic plasma actuator. **Shipping Address:** 9511 Hoyle Beals Drive, Knoxville, TN, 37931

Pamela Roth

Title: Attorney at Law **Industry:** Law and Legal Services **Company Name:** The Law Offices of Pamela S Roth, Esq., P.C. **Education:** JD in International Law and Legal Studies, Pace University (1990); MBA in International Business, Banking, and Finance, Adelphi University (1986); BS in Biology and Pre-Med, Adelphi University (1984) **Career:** Legal Advisor, Village Connection Network, Huntington, NY (2017-Present); Attorney at Law, The Law Office of Pamela S. Roth (1995-Present); Associate Attorney, Law Office of R.E. Chips Portales, P.C., Denver, CO (1993-1995); Assistant District Attorney, Kings County District Attorneys Office, Brooklyn, NY (1991-1993); Assistant General Counsel, New York City Department of Probations, Brooklyn, NY (1990-1991); Currency Trader, Solomon Brothers, New York, NY (1986-1987); Sales Representative, Bloomingdale's, Garden City, NY (1984-1985) **Awards:** Brooklyn Power Women in Business Award (2017); Top Women Attorneys in Metro New York, Super Lawyers (2015-2016); Top Attorneys in Metro New York, Super Lawyers (2014-2015); Top Attorney in New York, Super Lawyers (2014) **Membership:** Associate, WomenInBusiness.org (2014); Vice President, Brooklyn Women's Bar Association (2004-2005) **To what do you attribute your success:** Ms. Roth attributes her success to her drive and tenacity. **Why did you become involved in your profession or industry:** Ms. Roth became involved in her profession because she wanted to help others and have a sustainable job for herself. She wanted to be recognized and appreciated as a successful woman, as she previously worked in a male-dominated industry. She started college at age 16, and finished her undergraduate degree by age 20. **Where will you be in five years:** Looking forward, Ms. Roth intends expand her practice in Manhattan. **Hobbies:** Spending time with her family; Visiting museums; Traveling **Shipping Address:** 20 Vesey Street, Suite 701, The Law Offices of Pamela S. Roth, New York, NY, 10007

Jacques Rottembourg

Title: Medical Educator **Industry:** Medicine & Health Care **Company Name:** Centre Suzanne Levy **Date of Birth:** 05/19/1942 **Place of Birth:** Lyon **Country of Origin:** France **Parents:** Georges Rottembourg; Monique Rottembourg **Marital Status:** Married **Spouse Name:** Chantal Babronski **Children:** Segolene Brueziare; Aude Lafond; Mathilde; Mathieu Mattei **Education:** BS, Lycée Charlemagne, St. Antoine, Paris, France (1959) **Career:** Medical Director, Dialysis Unit, Suzanne LEVY Center, Paris, France (1992-Present); Professor of Nephrology, Hôpital de la Pitié, Paris, France (1988) **Career Related:** Medical Consultant, Ministry of Health, Paris, France (1995-1997) **Civic:** Counselor, Society de Nephrologie, Paris, France (1974-2008) **Military Service:** Medical Captain, Service de Santé (1971-1972) **Creative Works:** Producer, Dialysis Ultrafiltration Processing Unit **Membership:** American Society of Nephrology; Society International de Néphrologie; Association Européenne de Dialyse et Transplantation **Marquis Who's Who Honors:** Albert Nelson Marquis Lifetime Achievement Award (2017) **Religion:** Roman Catholic **Shipping Address:** 35 Rue de Ponthieu, 8E Arrondissement, Paris, France, 75008

Jack A. Rounick

Title: Lawyer **Industry:** Law and Legal Services **Company Name:** Law Offices of Jack A. Rounick LLC **Date of Birth:** 06/05/1935 **Place of Birth:** Philadelphia **State:** PA **Parents:** Philip Rounick; Nettie (Brownstein) Rounick **Marital Status:** Married **Spouse Name:** Noreen A. Garrigan **Children:** Ellen; Eric; Amy; Michelle **Education:** JD, University of Pennsylvania, Philadelphia, PA (1959); BBA, University of Michigan, Ann Arbor, MI (1956) **Certifications:** Diplomate, American College of Family Trial Lawyers **Career:** Of Counsel, Law Offices of Jack A. Rounick LLC (2012-Present); Of Counsel, Flamm Walton PC (2010-2012); Of Counsel, Flamm, Boroff & Bacine, Professional Corporation, Blue Bell, PA (2006-2010); Counsel to Firm, Wolf, Block, Schorr & Solis-Cohen LLP (1997-2006); Vice President, General Counsel, Martin Lawrence Limited Editions, Inc. (1987-1993); Director, Martin Lawrence Limited Editions, Inc. (1984-1995); Director, Deb Shops, Inc. (1974-2007); Assistant Secretary, Deb Shops, Inc. (1974-2007); Partner, Pechner, Dorfman, Wolffe, Rounick and Cabot, Norristown, PA (1973-1987); Partner, Moss & Rounick, Norristown, PA (1972-1973); Partner, Moss, Rounick & Hurowitz, Norristown, PA (1969-1972); Partner, Moss & Rounick (1968-1969); Special Assistant, Attorney General (1963-1971); Partner, Israelit & Rounick (1960-1967) **Career Related:** Fellow, American Academy of Matrimonial Lawyers; Fellow, IAFL **Civic:** Chairman, American Friends of the Hebrew University (1970); Chairman, Pennsylvania Young Republicans (1968-1970); Treasurer, Pennsylvania Young Republicans (1966-1968); Finance Chairman, Pennsylvania Young Republicans (1964-1966) **Creative Works:** Author, "Pennsylvania Matrimonial Practice," Six Volumes (1982); Editor, "Pennsylvania Family Lawyer" (1980-1987); Board of Editors, Family Advocate **Awards:** Eric Turner Award, Family Law Section, Pennsylvania Bar Association (2009); One of Top 100 Attorneys, Worth Magazine (2005); Certificate of Appreciation, Pennsylvania Bar Institute (1980); Special Achievement Award, Pennsylvania Bar Association (1979-1980); Boss of Year Award, Montgomery County Legal Secretaries Association (1970) **Membership:** Chairman, Scope and Correlation Committee (2005-2006); Council, ABA (2000-2003); Chairman, Board Review, American Academy of Matrimonial Lawyers (1997-1998); Vice President, American Friends of the Hebrew University (1990-1991); President, Philadelphia Chapter, American Friends of the Hebrew University (1988-1991); Board of Trustees, American Friends of the Hebrew University (1987-2006); National Council of Trustees, American Friends of the Hebrew University (1987-1993); Board of Directors, American Friends of the Hebrew University (1987-1993); Vice President, American Academy of Matrimonial Lawyers (1985-1987); Governor, American Academy of Matrimonial Lawyers (1983-1985); Council, Family Law Section, ABA (1982-1987); President, Pennsylvania Chapter, American Academy of Matrimonial Lawyers (1982-1984); Past Chairman, Family Law Section, Pennsylvania Bar Association (1978-1980); FLS; Montgomery Bar Association **Bar Admissions:** U.S. District Court, Eastern District, State of Pennsylvania (1960); State of Pennsylvania (1960) **Marquis Who's Who Honors:** Albert Nelson Marquis Lifetime Achievement Award (2017); Distinguished Humanitarian (2017) **Political Affiliations:** Republican **Religion:** Jewish **Shipping Address:** 25 E Marshall Street, Jack A. Rounick LLC, Norristown, PA, 19401 **Website:** http://www.rounicklaw.com

Mary-Julia Campbell Royall

Title: Musician, Historian, Accompanist, Church Organist, Author **Industry:** Religious **Company Name:** Several Charleston Churches **Date of Birth:** 12/30/1925 **Place of Birth:** Donalds **State:** SC **Parents:** John McCants Campbell; Cordelia Bearden Campbell **Marital Status:** Married **Spouse Name:** Jervey DuPrE Royall (9/18/1949) **Children:** Julia C.; Anne DuPre **Education:** Coursework, Salem College Organ Academy (1979-1987); MA, University of South Carolina (1948); BA, Erskine College (1945) **Certifications:** Performers Certification in Organ, University of South Carolina (1953); Certification in Musical Instrument Supervision, Erskine College (1945) **Career:** Director, Glee Club, College Preparatory School, Charleston, SC (1972-1974); Erskine Alumni Board of Visitors (1964-1966); Organist, Charleston Churches (1950-Present); Director, Glee Club, Moultrie High School (1962-1964); Director, Glee Club, Moultrie High School, Mount Pleasant, SC (1960-1962); Private Piano Teacher (1953-1966); Music Teacher, Montreat High School and College, North Carolina (1946-1947); Counselor, Accompanist, Brevard Music Center (1946) **Career Related:** Accompanist, Trio, Weddings **Civic:** Historian, Town of Mount Pleasant (1996-Present); President, Christ Church Parish Preservation Society, Mount Pleasant, SC (1994-Present); President, Confederate Memorial Association, Mount Pleasant, SC (1984-Present); Member, Mount Pleasant Presbyterian Church (1950-Present); Committee Member, Charleston County South Carolina National Heritage Corridor (1995-1998); Registered Charleston Tour Guide (1968-1978) **Creative Works:** Musician, St. Lukes Chapel (1994-Present); Author, "Mount Pleasant, South Carolina: The Friendly Town" (2001); Author, "Mount Pleasant, South Carolina: The Victorian Village" (1997); Organist, Huguenot Church Tricenternial (1980); Musician, Spoleto Festival (1977-1978) **Awards:** Sons of Confederate Veterans (2003); Recipient, Parish Nurses Institute (1998-2008); Robert N. Pryor Service Award, Confederation of Local Historical Societies, South Carolina (1997); Named, Order of the Gavel, Town of Mount Pleasant (1996); Named, Tree Farmer of the Year, South Carolina (1982-1983); Recipient, Outstanding Southern Citizen Award, Town of Mount Pleasant; Recipient, Cresco Historical Stewardness Award **Membership:** South Carolina State Chairman, Charleston Chapter, American Guild Organists (1950-Present); Newsletter Editor, Organ Historical Society (1979-1984); Charleston Events Reporter, Musical America; Competitions Chairman, Charleston Preservation Society; Poetry Society of South Carolina; South Carolina Historical Society; South Carolina Forestry Association **Marquis Who's Who Honors:** Distinguished Humanitarian (2017) **To what do you attribute your success:** Ms. Campbell attributes her success to her interest. **Shipping Address:** 349 Bayview Dr, Mount Pleasant, SC, 29464

Sharon V. Rudacille

Title: Technologist (Retired) **Industry:** Technology **Date of Birth:** 09/11/1950 **Place of Birth:** Ranson **State:** WV **Parents:** Albert William Rudacille; Roberta Mae (Anderson) Rudacille **Education:** BS, Shepherd University, Cum Laude (1972) **Certifications:** Registered Medical Technologist, American Society for Clinical Pathology (1972) **Career:** Medical Technologist, Martinsburg Veterans Affairs Medical Center, West Virginia (1972-2006) **Career Related:** Senior Medical Technologist, School of Medical Technology (1995-Present); Supervisory Medical Technologist, School of Medical Technology (1994-1995); Staff Medical Technologist, School of Medical Technology (1986-1994); Clinical Chemistry Section Leader, School of Medical Technology (1984-1986); Laboratory Service Quality Assurance and Education Officer, School of Medical Technology (1980-1984); Quality Assurance Officer, Clinical Chemistry, School of Medical Technology (1978-1980); Adjunct Faculty Member, Shepherd University (1977-1978); Adjunct Faculty Member, Shippensburg University (1977-1978); Education Coordinator, School of Medical Technology (1977-1978); Associate Coordinator, Education, School of Medical Technology (1976-1977); Instructor, School of Medical Technology (1972-1976) **Membership:** Shepherd University Alumni Association; West Virginia Society of Radiologic Technologist; American Society for Clinical Pathology; American Society of Medical Technicians; Sigma Pi Epsilon **Marquis Who's Who Honors:** Albert Nelson Marquis Lifetime Achievement Award (2017) **Religion:** Southern Baptist **Shipping Address:** PO Box 14, Ranson, WV, 25438

Kal Solomon Rudman

Title: Humanitarian/Philanthropist, Media Executive and Educator **Industry:** Media & Entertainment **Company Name:** Kal and Lucille Rudman Foundation **Date of Birth:** 03/06/1930 **Place of Birth:** Philadelphia **State:** PA **Parents:** Benjamin Rudman; Lena (Holtzman) Rudman **Marital Status:** Married **Spouse Name:** Lucille Steinhauer (6/29/1958) **Children:** Mitchell **Education:** Honorary PhD, University of the Arts, Philadelphia, PA (2006); Honorary LHD, University of the Arts, Philadelphia, PA (2005, 2003); Honorary LHD, Holy Family University, Philadelphia, PA (2002); Honorary HHD, Drexel University, Philadelphia, PA (1970); Postgraduate Coursework, Temple University, Philadelphia, PA (1958); MS in Education, Temple University, Plus 30, Philadelphia, PA (1957); BS in Education, University of Pennsylvania, Philadelphia, PA (1951) **Certifications:** Certified in Special Education **Career:** Publisher and Editor-in-Chief, Premier Record, Radio Trade, "Friday Morning Quarterback," Cherry Hill, NJ (1968-Present); Chairman, Department of Special Education, Franklin D. Roosevelt School, Bristol Township, PA (1960-1968); Chairman, Founder, Department of Special Education, Upper Darby High School, Upper Darby, PA (1952-1953) **Career Related:** Co-Host, "The Merv Griffin Show" (1981-1982); Music Expert, "The Today Show" (1981-1982); Music Expert and Co-Host, "Tom Snyder Tomorrow Show" (Following the Johnny Carson Show) (1981-1982); Board of Directors, Famous National Variety Club for Handicapped Children; Board of Directors, The Recording Academy; Board of Directors, Citizen's Crime Commission, Philadelphia, PA, Camden, NY and Delaware; Host, Mobile Science Programs, The Franklin Institute of Science Museum and Fels Planetarium; Host, Entertainment Shows, Philadelphia Senior Citizens; Host, Entertainment Shows, New Jersey Senior Citizens' Homes; Host, Entertainment Shows, Children's Hospitals; Host, Entertainment Shows, VA Hospitals; Co-Host, Talent Booker, Easter Seals Telethon; Creator, High School Jazz Piano Competition, University of the Arts, Philadelphia, PA; Eponym, Kal and Lucille Rudman Institute, Drexel University; Financial Supporter, National Academy of Television Arts & Sciences; Founder, Media Center and Financial Digital TV Station, Temple University; Author, Money Music Column, Hollywood Reporter **Civic:** Founder, Kal and Lucille Rudman Institute for Entertainment Studies, Westphal College of Media Arts & Designs, Drexel University, Philadelphia, PA (1974); Board of Directors, Philadelphia Broadcast Pioneers; Elected Vice President, Philadelphia Broadcast Pioneers; Sponsor, Carillon Bells, Avenue of the Arts Inc., Philadelphia, PA; Sponsor, TV Cameras, Temple University School of Communications; Sponsor, The Huge Franklin Institute Travelling Science Show, Philadelphia Elementary Schools; Sponsor, First Annual Classical Piano High School Competition, Citizens' Crime Commission, Chestnut Hill College; Sponsor, 100th Anniversary, Jewish Federation of Greater Philadelphia; Sponsor, The Franklin Institute Time Capsule, Philadelphia, PA; Sponsor, Jewish Federation Atrium Headquarters .5 mil, Philadelphia, PA; Co-Sponsor, Purchase and Distribution of Dictionaries, Philadelphia Elementary School; Co-Sponsor, Robotics Competition, Philadelphia High Schools; Active Co-Sponsor, Succeeding By Reading Program, Philadelphia Middle Schools; Graduate, FBI Community Outreach; Founder, Creche, Christmas at City Hall, etc. Philadelphia, PA; Co-Donor, $1.5 Million, Temple University; Sponsor, Time Box, Fire Department, Philadelphia, PA; Sponsor, Music Industry Conventions, Boulder, CO; Sponsor, Philadelphia Eagles Games, Philadelphia Police Department **Creative Works:** Publisher, "Modern Music Quarterback"; Founder "Pro QB" Music Trade Magazine; Founder, Q-Beatl; Creator, 50 Billboards, Mothers In Charge; Quoted in 38

Kal Solomon Rudman (continued)

Celebrity Biographies, including Bruce Springsteen's **Awards:** Marquis Who's Who Humanitarian of the Year (2018); Person of the Year, Philadelphia Art Community College (1970); Lifetime Achievement Award, Philadelphia Music Conference; Lifetime Music Achievement Award, Delaware Valley Music Poll; Presidential Citation, Citizens Crime Commission; Plaque on Walk of Fame, Avenue of the Arts Inc.; Enforcement Award, U.S. Marine Corps; Radio Milestone Award to Philadelphia Radio Legends, March of Dimes Foundation; T. Seddon Duke Award; Bennell Award; Top Civilian Award, Philadelphia Fire Department; Marshall Award, Citizens Crime Commission; Award, National Academy of Television Arts & Sciences; Top Civilian Award, Citizens Crime Commission of Delaware Valley; Top Award, Citizens Crime Commission, Philadelphia, PA; Named Penndelphia Humanitarian of the Year; Humanitarian of the Year, National Sunshine Federation; Honorary Deputy Commissioner (by Police Commissioner Sylvester Johnson), Philadelphia Police Department; Honorary Fire Commissioner, (Lloyd Ayers) Philadelphia, PA; Person of the Year, The Broadcast Pioneers of Philadelphia; Community Philanthropist of the Year; Named to The Broadcast Pioneers Hall of Fame, Philadelphia, PA; Honoree, Hall of Fame, Klein College of Media and Communication, Temple University; Golden Gavel Award, Community College of Philadelphia; Scholar, Hahnemann Medical School, Drexel University, Philadelphia, PA; Donor, Mini-Medical Scholarships, Hahnemann Medical School, Drexel University; 20th Year Scholarship, Olney High School; 20th Year Scholarship, Program, St. Christopher's Hospital for Children; College Communication Grants, Temple University, Holy Family University, Community College of Philadelphia **Membership:** Board of Directors, Philadelphia Music Alliance; Board of Directors, National Arthritis Foundation; Board of Directors, The Recording Academy; Grand Master, Freemasons; Honorary Deputy Police Commissioner, Police Athletic League of Philadelphia **Why did you become involved in your profession or industry:** When his voice changed during puberty, his dream was to be on radio and television. This led immediately to working on the air with contemporary popular music recordings. He quickly learned he had the gift of picking songs that would become commercial hits. As a result, he became known as "The Man with the Golden Ears." **What do you consider to be the highlight of your career:** Having the ability to help others to change their lives through the Kal and Lucille Rudman Foundation is the highlight of his career. **Where will you be in five years:** In five years, Mr. Rudman hopes to continue to help others change their lives. **Shipping Address:** 56 Southwood Dr, Cherry Hill, NJ, 08003

Caroline Rule

Title: Partner **Industry:** Law and Legal Services **Company Name:** Kostelanetz & Fink, LLP **Place of Birth:** Harare **Country of Origin:** Zimbabwe **Parents:** Mark Rule; June Rule **Marital Status:** Married **Spouse Name:** William Finnegan **Children:** Mollie Rule Finnegan **Education:** JD, Yale Law School (1989); MFA, San Francisco Art Institute, Cum Laude (1984); BFA, University of Cape Town, With Honors, South Africa (1981) **Career:** Partner, Kostelanetz & Fink, LLP (1996-Present); Associate, Rabinowitz, Boudin, Standard, Krinsky & Lieberman, PC (1992-1996); Staff Attorney, Office of the Appellate Defender (1990-1992); Associate, Cahill Gordon & Reindel, LLP (1990); Summer Associate, Cahill Gordon & Reindel, LLP (1988-1989); Law Clerk to the Honorable John J. Gibbons, Chief Judge, United States Court of Appeals for the Third Circuit (1989-1990) **Creative Works:** Author, "United States v. Greenfield: A Triumph of the Fifth Amendment's Act of Production Privilege; or Confirmation that the Privilege Can Be Entirely Abrogated by Any Act of Congress, or Even by a Treasury Regulation?" (2018); Author, "A Long Overdue Check on Prosecutorial Power in Tax Cases" (2018); Author, "Statutory Maximum/Minimum Sentences And Application Of Offense Levels" (2017); Author, "IRS Form 3520, Penalties, And Whether To Make A Protective Filing" (2017); Author, "How Not to Waive Privilege When Consulting Non-Attorney Experts or Professionals" (2016); Author, "Applying Civil Penalties for Willful Violations of FBAR Requirements" (2016); Author, "An Update on the IRS's War Against Midco Transactions: Some Courts Hold That Taxpayer Knowledge is Irrelevant when the IRS Uses State Constructive Fraud Theories to Prove Transferee Liability" (2016); Author, "The Key to Transferee Liability in Midco Cases: Did the Taxpayers Know Or Have Reason to Know of the Unpaid Taxes?" (2015); Author, "The IRS LB&I's New Document Request Process, 18 Months Later: How it Works, and How to Make it Work" (2015); Author, "BNA Tax Management Portfolio, IRS Procedures: Examinations and Appeals, No. 623-3rd" (2013); Senior Editor, "Yale Law Review" (1988-1989) **Awards:** Honoree, New York Super Lawyers (2011-Present) **Membership:** Chair, Subcommittee on Tax Crimes, Criminal Law Committee, ABA Section of Litigation; Member, Administrative Practice Committee, ABA Section of Taxation; New York Council of Defense Lawyers; Federal Bar Council, Committee on Sentencing Reform and Alternatives to Incarceration; Criminal Advocacy Committee, and Mass Incarceration Task Force, New York City Bar Association; Master, Federal Bar Council Inn of Court; National Association of Women Lawyers **Bar Admissions:** Supreme Court of the United States (2014); United States Court of Appeals for the Fourth Circuit (2013); United States Court of Appeals for the Second Circuit (2007); United States Court of Appeals for the Third Circuit (1990); United States Tax Court (1998); United States District Court for the Southern District of New York (1990); United States District Court for the Eastern District of New York (1998); New York (1990); New Jersey (1989) **To what do you attribute your success:** Ms. Rule attributes her success to a great deal of hard work, a modicum of luck, congenial colleagues, and a supportive family. **Why did you become involved in your profession or industry:** Ms. Rule studied fine art both as an undergraduate and at graduate school, and imagined that she would spend her life as a struggling artist. She worked various jobs to make ends meet, including assisting a private detective who worked for lawyers, which made her curious about the lawyers' work. She applied to law school on a whim, to see if she could do it, but it grew from a whim to a calling, and she is still practicing as a lawyer decades later. **What do you consider to be the highlight of your career:** Ms. Rule recalls more than one highlight, but a standout is having persuaded a federal judge to dismiss an indictment against multiple defendants, in a case that was then termed the largest tax fraud prosecution in United States history, because of prosecutorial misconduct. Other highlights are managing, on numerous occasions, to persuade a judge not to sentence a client-defendant to prison, particularly when Ms. Rule has come to care about the client on a personal level. **Where will you be in five years:** Ms. Rule hopes to be just where she is now, having helped many more clients in what can be the most difficult time of their lives, with a few more trials under her belt, and having published more legal writing. **Hobbies:** Printmaking; Etching; Reading **Shipping Address:** Kostelanetz & Fink, LLP, 7 World Trade Center, 34th Floor, New York, NY, 10007 **Website:** http://www.kflaw.com/caroline_rule

Inge Juliana Sackmann Christy

Title: Research Associate **Industry:** Research **Date of Birth:** 02/08/1942 **Place of Birth:** Schoenau **Country of Origin:** Prussia **Marital Status:** Widowed **Spouse Name:** Robert Fredrick Christy (8/4/1973, Deceased) **Education:** PhD in Astrophysics, University of Toronto (1968); MA in Astronomy, University of Toronto (1965); BA in Physics, University of Toronto (1963) **Career:** Faculty Associate, California Institute of Technology (1981-Present); Senior Research Fellow, California Institute of Technology (1976-1981); Research Associate, NASA Jet Propulsion Laboratory (1974-1976); Research Fellow, California Institute of Technology (1971-1974); Research Associate, Hamburger Sternwarte (1971); Postdoctoral Fellow, Max-Planck Institute for Physics and Astrophysics, Max-Planck-Gesellschaft (1969-1971); Postdoctoral Fellow, Georg-August-Universität Göttingen (1968-1969) **Creative Works:** Author, "Achieving the Rare - Robert F. Christy's Journey in Physics and Beyond" (2013); Contributor, Articles to Publications **Awards:** Named, Outstanding Scientist of the 20th Century, Personalities of America (2000); Named, American Men and Women of Science (1986); Recipient, Alexander Von-Humbolt Award (1970-1971); Recipient, Postdoctoral Fellowship, National Research Council Canada (1968-1970) **Marquis Who's Who Honors:** Distinguished Humanitarian (2017) **Hobbies:** Children; Flower arranging; Growing organic gardens; Horseback riding; Hiking **Shipping Address:** 1230 Arden Road, Pasadena, CA, 91106

Michel Sadelain

Title: Director **Industry:** Medicine & Health Care **Company Name:** Memorial Sloan Kettering Cancer Center **Education:** PhD, University of Alberta (1989); MD, University of Paris; Resident, Centre Hospitalier Universitaire Saint-Antoine, Paris, France; Fellowship, Massachusetts Institute of Technology **Career:** Director, Center for Cell Engineering, Memorial Sloan Kettering Cancer Center (2008-Present); Professor of Medicine and Immunology, Memorial Sloan Kettering Medical School (2004-Present); Head of the Gene Transfer and Gene Expression, Laboratory at Memorial Sloan-Kettering Cancer Center **Career Related:** Board of Directors, American Society of Gene Therapy (2004-2007); Stephen and Barbara Friedman Chair, Founding Director, Center for Cell Engineering, Memorial Sloan Kettering Cancer Center **Creative Works:** Editorial Board Member, Molecular Therapy, Human Gene Therapy, Gene Therapy **Awards:** Sultan Bin Khalifa International Award (2013); Award for CAR Therapy, Cancer Research Institute (2012) **Membership:** Past President, American Society of Gene Cell Therapy (2015) **What do you consider to be the highlight of your career:** A highlight of Dr. Sadelain's was being one of the first wave of physicians to explore using genetic engineering to cure diseases. He is best known for the design of "Car Therapy," which involves chimeric antigen receptors. **Shipping Address:** 15 W 84th Street, Apt. 2C, New York, NY, 10024 **Website:** https://www.mskcc. org/announcements/mskcc-researcher-recognized-stem-cell-therapy-trial-thalassemia-

Guy Saint-Pierre

Title: Engineering Executive **Industry:** Engineering **Date of Birth:** 08/03/1934 **Place of Birth:** Windsor Mills **Country of Origin:** QC/Canada **Parents:** Armand Saint-Pierre; Alice (Perra) Saint-Pierre **Marital Status:** Married **Spouse Name:** Francine Garneau (5/4/1957) **Children:** Marc; Guylaine; Nathalie **Education:** Honorary Degree, University of Ottawa (2002); Honorary Degree in Applied Science, Universite de Sherbrooke (1994); Honorary Degree, College Militaire Royal de Saint-Jean (1993); Honorary LLD, Concordia University (1992); Honorary DSc, Universite Laval (1992); MSc, University of London (1959); Diploma, Imperial College London (1958); Bachelor of Applied Science in Civil Engineering, Universite Laval (1957); Honorary DSc, Universite de Montreal **Certifications:** Registrar, Corporation Engineers, Quebec, Canada (1964-1966) **Career:** Board Chairman, Royal Bank of Canada (2001-2004); Board Chairman, SNC-Lavalin (1996-2002); Director, Royal Bank of Canada (1990-2004); President, SNC-Lavalin (1989-1996); Chief Executive Officer, SNC-Lavalin (1989-1996); Board of Directors, SNC-Lavalin (1989-1996); President, Ogilvie Flour Mills Ltd., Montreal, QC, Canada (1977-1988); Chief Operating Officer, Ogilvie Flour Mills Ltd., Montreal, QC, Canada (1977-1988); Senior Vice President, John Labatt Limited, Montreal, QC, Canada (1977-1988); Assistant to the President, John Labatt Limited, Montreal, QC, Canada (1977-1988); Employee, Industry and Commerce, Government of Quebec (1972-1976); Minister, Education, Government of Quebec (1970-1972); Vice President, Acres Quebec (1967-1970) **Career Related:** Director, Institute for Research on Public Policy (2003-2011); Director, Alcan Inc. (1995-2007); Director, General Motors of Canada (1995-2004); Chairman, Business Council on National Issues (1995-1997); Director, BCE Inc. (1994-2003) **Civic:** Governor, Conseil du Patronat du Quebec **Military Service:** Officer, Corps of Engineers, Canadian Army (1959-1964) **Awards:** Inductee, Canadian Business Hall of Fame (2001); Canadian Engineers Gold Medal Award, Canadian Council of Professional Engineers (1996); Canada's International Executive of the Year (1996); Canada's Chief Executive Officer of the Year (1994); Sir John Kennedy Medal (1993); Decorated Companion, Order of Canada; Grand Officer, L'Ordre National du Quebec **Membership:** President, Canadian Manufacturers and Exporters (1987); Ordre des Ingenieurs du Quebec; Chairman to Board, Canadian Manufacturers and Exporters; The Engineering Institute of Canada; Montreal Chamber of Commerce; Vice President, Canadian Unity Council; The Mount Royal Club **Marquis Who's Who Honors:** Albert Nelson Marquis Lifetime Achievement Award (2017) **Political Affiliations:** Liberal **Religion:** Roman Catholic **Shipping Address:** 11-1485 Rue Sherbrooke W, QC, Montreal, Canada, H3G 0A3

Dorothy Myers Sampas, PhD

Title: Government Official (Retired) **Industry:** Government Administration/Government Relations/Government Services **Date of Birth:** 08/24/1933 **Place of Birth:** Washington, DC **State:** DC **Parents:** Lawrence Myers; Anna Cornelia (Henkel) Myers **Marital Status:** Married **Spouse Name:** James George Sampas (12/8/1962) **Children:** George; Lawrence James **Education:** PhD, Georgetown University (1970); Postgraduate Coursework, University of Paris (1955-1956); AB, University of Michigan (1955) **Certifications:** Certificate, Defense Resource Management Institute, Naval Postgraduate School (1993); Certificate, National War College, Washington D.C. (1987) **Career:** Retired (1998); American Ambassador, Islamic Republic of Mauritania (1994-1997); Minister-Counselor, U.S. Mission to the United Nations, New York City, NY (1991-1994); Embassy Minister-Counselor, Embassy of the Beijing, China (1987-1990); Director, Office of Management, U.S. State Department, Washington, DC (1984-1986); Division Chief, Office of Management, U.S. State Department, Washington, DC (1983-1984); Division Chief, Deputy Chief, Office of Position and Pay Management, U.S. State Department, Washington, DC (1979-1983); General Services Officer, U.S. Embassy in Belgium (1975-1979); Analyst, Bureau of Administration, U.S. State Department, Washington, DC (1973-1975); Consultant, Transcentury Corporation, Washington, DC (1972); Vice-Consul, U.S. Consulate General Hamburg, Federal Republic of Germany (1960-1962); Member, Bureau of Public Affairs, U.S. State Department, Washington, DC (1958-1960); Registered Lobbyist, The Michigan Legislature (1954-1955) **Civic:** Volunteer, Sibley Memorial Hospital, Johns Hopkins Health System (1999-2013) **Membership:** Cosmos Club **Marquis Who's Who Honors:** Albert Nelson Marquis Lifetime Achievement Award (2017); Distinguished Humanitarian (2017) **Why did you become involved in your profession or industry:** She became involved in her profession because her father did similar work. **Hobbies:** Reading; Theatre **Religion:** Presbyterian **Shipping Address:** 9707 Old Georgetown Rd., Apt 1401, Bethesda, MD, 20814

Ramiro Sanchez Jr.

Title: Senior Vice President **Industry:** Pharmaceuticals **Company Name:** Otsuka America Pharmaceutical, Inc. **Parents:** Ramiro Montesino-Sanchez; Maria Julia Suarez-Sanchez **Education:** Instructor, Yale School of Medicine, Department of Psychiatry (1999-2000); Fellow in Psychiatry, Yale School of Medicine (1998-1999); Chief Resident in Psychiatry, Yale School of Medicine (1997-1998); Resident in Psychiatry, Yale School of Medicine (1995-1997); Intern in Medicine, Neurology and Psychiatry, Yale School of Medicine (1994-1995); MD, Northwestern University Feinberg School of Medicine (1994); Intern, National Institutes of Mental Health Research (1987); Post-Baccalaureate in Sleep Disorders Medicine, Harvard Medical School, Boston, MA (1984-1986); AB, Northwestern University Weinberg College (1984) **Career:** Senior Vice President, Global Clinical Development, Otsuka America Pharmaceutical, Inc. (2013-Present); Vice President, Global Clinical Development, Otsuka America Pharmaceutical, Inc. (2010-2013); Senior Director, Global Clinical Development, Otsuka America Pharmaceutical, Inc. (2007-2010); Group Medical Director, Neurosciences, Bristol-Myers Squibb Company (2005-2007); Group Medical Director, Neuroscience Global Clinical Research, Bristol-Myers Squibb Company, France (2004-2005); Medical Director, Bristol-Myers Squibb Company, Wallingford, CT (2000-2004); Associate Medical Director, Purdue Pharma, L.P., Stamford, CT (2000-2002); Instructor in Psychiatry, Yale School of Medicine, New Haven, CT (1999-2000) **Career Related:** Trustee, Board of Directors, Connecticut Mental Health Foundation, Yale University, New Haven, CT (1999-Present); Consultant, Connecticut Science Fair Association, Inc., Hartford, CT (1996-Present) **Creative Works:** Member, Executive Board, Journal of Sleep Disorders and Management (2017-Present); Editorial Board Member, Austin Psychiatry (2016-Present); Contributor, Articles, Professional Journals **Awards:** Leadership Award, International Society for CNS Drug Development (2016); Otsuka President's Award for Rexulti Dual-Indication Approval (2015); Otsuka President's Award for Abilify Maintena Program Leadership (2010); Grant Award for Outstanding Performance and Leadership, Bristol-Myers Squibb Company (2006); STAR Award, Bristol-Myers Squibb Company (2004); Triumph Development Operating Committee Award, Bristol-Myers Squibb Company (2003); STAR Award, Bristol-Myers Squibb Company (2003); STAR Award, Bristol-Myers Squibb Company (2002); Yale Psychiatry Residents' Association Award for Outstanding Scholarship and Service (1998); Charter Fellow Leadership Award, American Academy of Child & Adolescent Psychiatry (1996); Grant Research Award, American Medical Association Education and Research Foundation (1994-1997); Rock Sleyster Scholar in Psychiatry, American Medical Association, Chicago, IL (1994); Research Grant, National Institutes Of Health (1987); Elliot Weitzman Award, Harvard Medical School (1986); Lincoln Laureate, Illinois Lincoln Academy (1983); Richter Scholar, R. Gene and Nancy D. Richter Foundation (1983); Silver Knight Award in Science, Miami Herald (1979) **Membership:** Executive Chairman, International Society for CNS Drug Development (2017-Present); Overseas Fellow, The Royal Society of Medicine, England (2017-Present); Advisory Board, Founders Bay Technologies (2017-Present); Board Member, Jewels for Justice Organization (Now Jewels4Justice) (2016-Present); Executive Advisory Council, National Alliance of Mental Illness (2016-Present); Alumni Society, Hispanic Leadership Society (Now United Way Tarrant County) (2015-Present); Biomedical Advisory Council, PhRMA (2014-Present); Founding Member, International Society for CNS Drug Development (2012-Present); American Society of Clinical Psychopharmacology (2012-Present); Founding Member, CNS Summit (2012-Present); The New York Academy of Sciences (2004-Present); Trustee, Board of Trustees, Connecticut Mental Health Center Foundation, Yale School of Medicine, New Haven, CT (2000-Present); American Psychiatric Association (1998-Present); American Medical Association (1998-Present); BMAC Working Group, PhRMA (2012-2014); Representative, Yale University Resident Association (1995-1998); Fellow in Addiction Psychiatry, Betty Ford Center (Now Hazelden Betty Ford Foundation), Rancho Mirage, CA (1990); Eisenhower Professional in Residence, Betty Ford Center (Now Hazelden Betty Ford Foundation), Rancho Mirage, CA (1990); American Academy of Pharmaceutical Physicians Connecticut Psychiatric Society, American Psychiatric Association; The Society for Light Treatment and Biological Rhythms; Sigma Xi, The Scientific Research Honor Society; Sleep Research Society; The Phi Beta Kappa Society **Marquis Who's Who Honors:** Albert Nelson Marquis Lifetime Achievement Award (2017) **Hobbies:** History; Traveling; Community service; Art **Business Address:** 508 Carnegie Center, 4th floor, Princeton, NJ, 08540 **Shipping Address:** 323 Field Stone Dr, New Hope, PA, 18938

Georgia Elizabeth Sanders

Title: Mathematics Teacher **Industry:** Education/ Educational Services **Date of Birth:** 07/14/1933 **Place of Birth:** Holmwood **State/Country of Origin:** LA **Parents:** Frederick Rudolph Sanders; Susie W. (Hackett) Sanders **Education:** MS in Mathematics, University of Southern Mississippi, Hattiesburg, MS (1983); MS in Microbiology, University of Southwestern Louisiana, Lafayette, LA (1970); BS in Microbiology, University of Southwestern Louisiana, Lafayette, LA (1970); Coursework, Louisiana State University, Baton Rouge, LA (1959-1960); Coursework, Louisiana College, Pineville, LA (1951-1953) **Certifications:** Certification in Special Education (1990) **Career:** Adjunct Professor, Delgado Community College (2003-2016); Tutor, Sylvan Learning, LLC (1996-2003); Mathematics Teacher, St. Tammany Parish, Louisiana (1990-1998); Teacher, East Baton Rouge Parish Schools (1988-1989); Instructor, Department of Mathematics, University New of Orleans (1983-1986); Instructor, Department of Biology, University New Orleans (1976-1979) **Membership:** National Education Association; American Mathematics Society; Mathematics Association of America; National Council of Teachers of Mathematics **Marquis Who's Who Honors:** Albert Nelson Marquis Lifetime Achievement Award (2017) **Shipping Address:** PO Box 968, Slidell, LA, 70459

Warren S. Satterlee II

Title: Retail Management Professional (Retired), Writer **Industry:** Retail/Sales **Date of Birth:** 12/08/1946 **Place of Birth:** Harlingen **State:** TX **Parents:** Ralph Pickard Satterlee; Diane (Royall-Mann) Satterlee **Spouse Name:** Virginia Lou Schumacher (7/17/1971, Deceased 5/24/2011) **Children:** Heather Irene **Education:** BA, St. Cloud State University (1974); AA, Cayuga Community College (1972) **Certifications:** Graduate Certificate in Theological Studies, Texas Christian University (1991) **Career:** Retired (2006); Retail Management Staff, Ross Dress For Less (2000-2006); Member, Supervisory Training Program, Eckerd Drug (1999); Member, Management Training Program Retail Management Practices, Eckerd Drug (1999); Member, Customer Service Staff, Office Depot (1998); Retail Management, Eckerd Drug (1995-2000); Supervisor and Bakery Support Staff, Schlotzsky's Deli Sandwich Shop (1993-1996); Supervisor and Bakery Support Staff, Schlotzsky's Deli Sandwich Shop (1989-1993); Retail Management Staff, Southwest Chapter, AARP **Civic:** Member, Rite I, Choir (2012-Present); Member, St. Timothy's Church Choir, Fort Worth, TX; Member, Rite I, Church of Saints Peter and Paul Anglican Church Choir (1999-2006); Member, Church Choir (1999-2001); Volunteer, Cowtown Marathon (1991-2011); Former Member, Fort Worth Genealogical Society; Former Member, Crowley Art Guild; Member, St. Timothy's Church, Fort Worth, TX **Military Service:** U.S. Air Force, E4 (1966-1970) **Creative Works:** Author, "Meditation" (1997); Author, "Meditation III" (1997); Author, Numerous Poems; Contributor, Articles, Professional Journals **Membership:** International Order of St. Luke the Physician **Hobbies:** Creative writing; Making church worship banners and visuals; Music; Crafts **Religion:** Anglican **Shipping Address:** 4004 Bradley Ln., Arlington, TX, 76017

George Satterthwaite II

Title: Security Firm Executive, Colonel (Retired) **Industry:** Business Management/Business Services **Company Name:** SSI Inc., United States Army **Date of Birth:** 04/18/1935 **Place of Birth:** San Jose **Country of Origin:** Costa Rica **Parents:** Livingston Lord Satterthwaite; Adelaide (Bristol) Satterthwaite **Marital Status:** Widower **Spouse Name:** Deanna Marie Kelliher (4/30/1983, Deceased 2012); Helen Marie McCann (6/28/1958, Divorced 7/1982) **Children:** Patricia Ann; Livingston Lord; Frank Lord; Kelley Elizabeth **Education:** MA in History, Johns Hopkins University (1965); BA in International Relations, University of Pennsylvania (1957) **Career:** Photography and Security Consultant, SSI Inc. (2000-Present); Chairman, Sidwell Friends Alumni Fund (2011-2015); Member, Sidwell Friends Alumni Executive Board (2010-2016); Quality Assurance Officer, Dale Photo and Imaging Company (Now Dale Photo Imaging and Copy Center), Alexandria, VA (2006-2009); Assistant Manager, Radio Shack, Alexandria, VA (2000-2006); Consultant, Contracts Officer, SSI Inc., McLean, VA (1998-2000); Consultant (1996-1998); Corporate Director of Security, PRC Inc., McLean, VA (1989-1996); Chief of Industrial Security, Planning Research Corp., McLean, VA (1987-1989) **Career Related:** President, Citizens Association (2017-Present); Chapter Secretary, Sons of the American Revolution (2009-Present); Location Leader, Veteran Cemetery, Wreaths Across America Program (2006-Present) **Civic:** Member, Admissions Council, University of Pennsylvania (2002-Present); Member, County Board Elections, Prince George County (2003-2010) **Military Service:** US Army (1987); Colonel, US Army (1979); Commissioned Second Lieutenant, US Army (1957) **Awards:** Recipient, Patriot Medal, Sons of the American Revolution (2016); Recipient, Nemayer Alumni Award, Sidwell Friends (2015); Recipient, Meritorious Service Medal, Sons of the American Revolution (2009); Recipient, Military Awards Including Legion of Merit, Defense Superior Service Medal, Meritorious Service, Bronze Star, Three Army Commendations (1959-1987) **Membership:** Vice President, Piscataway Hills Citizens Association (2015-Present); Board of Directors, Piscataway Hills Citizens Association (2010-Present); State Chairman, ROTC Committee, Chaplain, Sons of the American Revolution (2010-Present); Chapter Secretary, Sons of the American Revolution (2007-Present); Lifetime Member, Military Officers Association of America **Marquis Who's Who Honors:** Albert Nelson Marquis Lifetime Achievement Award (2017) **To what do you attribute your success:** Mr. Satterthwaite attributes his success to a devotion to duty on the tasks at hand and an understanding of a good work ethic, being fair, just and honest in his dealings with employees and management. **Why did you become involved in your profession or industry:** Mr. Satterthwaite became involved in his military profession to serve his country. His civilian professions enhance his knowledge of the industrial security field. He decided to explore what it is like to be involved in a store like Radio Shack because he is a hobbyist, and then a photography store, where he could use his photo skills to improve other people's pictures and images. In his semi-retirement life, Mr. Satterthwaite enjoys the volunteer work in the Sons of the American Revolution, Wreaths Across America and local citizens association. **What do you consider to be the highlight of your career:** The highlight of Mr. Satterthwaite's career was developing a sense of pride in his accomplishments, which increased his faith and helped to produce a remarkable family. **Where will you be in five years:** In five years, Mr. Satterthwaite will be continuing his semi-retired lifestyle in good health and enjoying it to the fullest alongside his children, grandchildren and maybe some great-grandchildren. **Hobbies:** Photography; Music; Volksmarching; Travel **Political Affiliations:** Independent **Religion:** Roman Catholic **Shipping Address:** 513 Holly Rd, Fort Washington, MD, 20744

Joyce Anne Sattler Howard

Title: Elementary School Educator **Industry:** Education/Educational Services **Company Name:** North Bellmore School District **Date of Birth:** 10/24/1940 **Place of Birth:** New York City **State/Country of Origin:** NY **Parents:** Theodore Sattler; Jessie Lillian Sattler **Marital Status:** Married **Spouse Name:** Philip Laurance Howard (8/14/1959) **Children:** Robert; Douglas **Education:** MA, Adelphi University (1976) BA in Elementary Education, Adelphi University; AA, Nassau Community College **Certifications:** Certified Teacher, K-6, New York City, NY; Certified Police/Community Relations Mediator, National Conference of Christians and Jews **Career:** Executive Board, North Bellmore Teachers Association (1997-Present); Retirement Representative, North Bellmore School District (1997-Present); Teacher, North Bellmore School District **Career Related:** Consultant, Learn City, San Ronson, CA (1990-2000); Consultant, Nassau County Health Center, New York (1990-2000); Trainer, Growing Healthy Teacher Training Workshop; Instructor, North Bellmore Teacher Center; Space and Enrollment Committee, Shared Decision Making Committee, North Bellmore School District; Mentor, North Bellmore School District Mentor Program; Contact Person, Park Avenue Elementary School, Mepham High School Community Service Program; Talent Show Coordinator, Park Avenue Elementary School; Presenter, Various Conferences and Workshops **Creative Works:** Author, "Windows" (2000); Producer, "Stranger Danger" **Awards:** Distinguished Service Award, North Bellmore Teachers Association (2005); Lifetime Award, North Bellmore Teachers Association (2000); Educator of the Week Award, WLNY-55, New York State Lottery; Honorary Life Member, New York State Congress of Parents and Teachers; Grantee, "Stranger Danger" **Membership:** President, Retired Teachers Association (2008-Present); Building Representative, North Bellmore Teachers Association (2001-2004); Staff Development Committee, North Bellmore School District **Marquis Who's Who Honors:** Albert Nelson Marquis Lifetime Achievement Award (2017) **To what do you attribute your success:** Ms. Howard believes you should do things that you enjoy. If you are doing what you enjoy doing, you don't look at the clock, you're more creative, and you share with other people. **Why did you become involved in your profession or industry:** Ms. Howard married her high school teacher. After having children, she wanted to help them with their education and that's how she became interested in teaching. **What do you consider to be the highlight of your career:** One highlight of Ms. Howard's career is a video she recorded with a group of second graders and their parents called "Stranger Danger." It is still viewed by all children in her district to this day. **Political Affiliations:** Republican **Shipping Address:** 14 Prade Ln, Massapequa Park, NY, 11762

Dahleen Emi Sawai

Title: Language Educator (Retired) **Industry:** Education/Educational Services **Company Name:** W. R. Farrington High School **Date of Birth:** 03/13/1954 **Place of Birth:** Honolulu **State:** HI **Parents:** Kiyoto Sawai; Aiko Sawai **Education:** MEd, University of Hawaii at Manoa (1984); Diploma in Secondary Education, University of Hawaii at Manoa (1981); Diploma in Elementary Education, University of Hawaii at Manoa (1977); BA, University of Hawaii at Manoa (1975) **Certifications:** Certified Teacher, State of Hawaii **Career:** Mentor Teacher (1995-2012); Educator, Consortium for Teaching Asia and the Pacific in the Schools, Honolulu, HI (1989-1995); Japanese Teacher, W. R. Farrington High School, Honolulu, HI (1985-2015); English Teacher, Family Court Probation Officer Training School, Tokyo, Japan (1983-1984); Japanese Teacher, Kailua High School, Honolulu, HI (1978-1980); English Teacher, Tokyo Family Court (1977-1978) **Career Related:** Chairman, Department of World Languages, W.R. Farrington High School (2001-Present); Lead Instructor, International Studies Academy, W.R. Farrington High School (2008-2013); Instructor, School for Community Based Management, Honolulu, HI (2000-2004); Interpreter, Star Tanjo (1976) **Civic:** Ad Hoc Committee Member, School for Community Council (2005); Secretary, Moanalua Gardens Community Association, Honolulu, HI (1978-1980); Director, Moanalua Gardens Community Association, Honolulu, HI (1976-1977) **Awards:** Scholar, Keio Gijuku Daigaku (1982-1984) **Membership:** The Hawaii Association of Teachers of Japanese; Hawai'i State Teachers Association; Hawaii Association of Language Teachers; American Association of Teachers of Japanese; Farrington Alumni and Community Foundation; Japanese Cultural Center of Hawai'i; Temari Center Asian & Pacific Arts; Alliance for Drama Education; Pi Lambda Theta **Marquis Who's Who Honors:** Albert Nelson Marquis Lifetime Achievement Award (2017); Distinguished Humanitarian (2017) **Hobbies:** Travelling; Walking **Shipping Address:** 1519 Mahiole St., Honolulu, HI, 96819

Mildred Clementina Sawyer

Title: Real Estate Agent in Sold Mutual Funds, Life Insurance, and Annuities **Industry:** Real Estate **Company Name:** Home Realty **Date of Birth:** 08/16/1929 **Place of Birth:** Boston **State:** MA **Parents:** Joseph Felix Volpe; Assunta (Malone) Volpe **Marital Status:** Widowed **Spouse Name:** Frederick Myles Sawyer (7/15/1957, Deceased 1/1995) **Children:** Frederick G.; Bernard G. **Education:** High School Diploma, Brockton, MA (1946) **Career:** Retired (1995); Security Sales Representative, First American National Securities Inc., Cranston, RI (1986-1989); Real Estate Sales Representative, JLC and Home Realty, Chepachet, RI, North Scituate, MA (1984-1997); Insurance Sales Agent, Massachusetts Indemnity Life Insurance Company, Cranston, RI (1984-1989); Typist, Rhode Island (1958-1987); Typist, New Jersey (1958-1987); Clerk, Clark Brothers, Olean, NY (1957-1958); Clerk, Prudential Insurance Company, Brockton, MA (1947-1957) **Civic:** Secretary, Students for a Democratic Society, Warwick, RI (1970-1972); Secretary, Save All Foster's Environmental, Foster, RI (1969-1987); Secretary, Cold Spring Harbor Civic Association, Huntington, NY (1961-1963); Rhode Island Council for the Humanities **Creative Works:** Author, "Letter to the Editor," Providence Journal (2017); Unpublished Author, "Remnants of a Marriage" (2014); Unpublished Author, "A Lifetime of Hints for Everyday Living" (1996); Author, "Remembering Sunday, Journey to Infinity," The International Library of Poetry; Author, Numerous Poems and Children's Stories **Membership:** Society of Children's Book Writers and Illustrators; Union of Concerned Scientists; Institute of Noetic Sciences **Marquis Who's Who Honors:** Albert Nelson Marquis Lifetime Achievement Award (2017) **To what do you attribute your success:** Ms. Sawyer attributes her success to her professional life. **Why did you become involved in your profession or industry:** Ms. Sawyer felt the urge to write, and copyrighted her manuscripts to help others. The "Lifetime of Hints for Everyday Living" was recognized by Marquis Who's Who. **Where will you be in five years:** Ms. Sawyer does not know where she'll be in five years, but she has copyrighted an additional story, "An American Look at Vietnam." **Hobbies:** Reading; Gardening; Cooking; Sewing; Exercise **Religion:** Quaker **Shipping Address:** 49A Mount Hygeia Road, Foster, RI, 02825

Joseph Benedict Scerno

Title: Managing Director **Industry:** Business Management/Business Services **Company Name:** Joseph B. Scerno, International Management Consultancy **Date of Birth:** 12/25/1936 **Place of Birth:** Brooklyn **State:** NY **Parents:** Benedict Scerno; Mary (DeMartini) Scerno **Marital Status:** Single **Spouse Name:** Susan (9/10/2001, Divorced 2005); Patricia Ann (6/11/1960, Divorced 1997) **Children:** Joseph B. III; George P. **Education:** MA in Counseling, Marywood University, Scranton, PA (1977); BS in Personnel Management, New York University (1962) **Certifications:** Certified Senior Practitioner, Human Resource Management, HR Certification Institute, Washington, DC (1975) **Career:** President, SJM Holdings Limited, Clarks Summit, Pennsylvania (2002-Present); Managing Director, Joseph B. Scerno Associates, International Management Consultancy, Clarks Summit, Pennysylvania (1997-Present); Commissioner, FMCS, Washington, DC (1988-1997); Vice President, Human Resources, Coastal Corporation, Brooklyn, NY (1984-1988); Vice President, Human Resources, GBP Industries, Buffalo, NY (1979-1984); Vice President, Employee, Government, and Community Relations, Intext, Inc., Scranton, PA (1974-1979); Director, Employee Government Community Relations, Intext, Inc., Scranton, PA (1974-1979); Vice President, Personnel, Hospital for Joint Diseases and Medical Center, New York, NY (1972-1974); Vice President, Industrial Relations, Occidental Petroleum Corporation, Los Angeles, CA (1966-1972); Assistant Vice President, Industrial Relations, Technical Material Corporation, Mamaroneck, NY (1962-1966); Vice President, General Manager, Express Haulage Corporation, New York, NY (1959-1962) **Career Related:** Arbitrator, Joseph B. Scerno Arbitrator, Clarks Summit, PA (1997-Present); Arbitrator, New York State Panel of Arbitrators, New York, NY (1966-Present); Consultant, City of Scranton, PA (1976-1979) **Military Service:** US Air Force, Korea (1954-1957) **Creative Works:** Author, "Managing from the 21st Century and Beyond: Human Centered Facilitative Management" (1997) **Awards:** Honorary Kentucky Colonel; Honorary Tennessee Squire; Mu Gamma Tau Management Honorary Society; Pi Sigma Epsilon Marketing Honorary Society **Membership:** Regional Director, Society for Human Resource Management (1979-1982); Veterans Club, New York University (1958-1962); Chapter President, Zeta Beta Tau (1960); Benevolent and Protective Order of Elks; Lehigh Country Club; Nyack Boat Club; Mensa International Limited; The Pennsylvania Society; The New York Academy of Sciences; Air Force Association; Academy of American Poets; The American Academy of Political and Social Science; Academy of American Writers; The American Legion; Veterans of Foreign Wars; Nyack Boat Club; Poets House **To what do you attribute your success:** Mr. Scerno attributes his success to his father and mother serving as good examples, having caring mentors, hard work, and having the ability to bring people to together and developing creative solutions to complex problems. **Why did you become involved in your profession or industry:** Mr. Scerno entered his profession because Helen Kinchlow, who was personnel manager at Gimbels' Department Store, in Yonkers, New York, asked him to work in her department and transfer from his sales position during his summer employment. At the time, he was attending New York University. She inspired him to select personnel management as his career field. **What do you consider to be the highlight of your career:** The highlight of Mr. Scerno's career was not having a union contract ending in a strike when he was the chief negotiator for his company. **Where will you be in five years:** In five years, Mr. Scerno plans to still be living, with God's help. **Hobbies:** Golf; Travel; Sailing; Writing **Political Affiliations:** Independent **Religion:** Roman Catholic **Business Address:** 508 Carnation Dr, PA, Clarks Summit, 18411 **Shipping Address:** 508 Carnation Dr, Clarks Summit, PA, 18411

Charlene Joanne Schade

Title: Adult and Early Childhood Education Educator **Industry:** Education/ Educational Services **Date of Birth:** 06/26/1935 **Place of Birth:** San Bernardino **State:** CA **Parents:** Clarence George Linde; Helen Anita (Sunny) Hardesty **Marital Status:** Widowed **Spouse Name:** Thomas Byron Killens (9/25/1983, Deceased 10/21/2009); William Joseph, Jr. (4/12/1958, Divorced 1978, Deceased 9/23/2013) **Children:** Sabrina; Eric (Deceased); Camela; Cyndie **Education:** BS, University of California, Los Angeles (1959) **Certifications:** Certification, Arthritis Foundation Exercise Program; Stability Ball Certification **Career:** Associate Professor of Continuing Education, San Diego Community Colleges (1997-Present); Instructor, Older Adults, San Diego Community Colleges (1977-Present); Artist-in-Residence, Wolf Trap/Headstart (1984-1985); Senior Instructor, California Aerobic Dance Company (1976-1978); Director, Instructor, Kindergym, La Jolla YMCA, California (1972-1976); Teacher, Dance and Physical Education, Los Angeles Unified School District, California (1959-1963) **Career Related:** Emeritus Assistant Program Chair, San Diego Continuing Education (2008-Present); Instructor, Trainer, Aging and Independence Services, Feeling Fit Club (2007-Present); Workshop Leader, Southwest Dance, Movement and Acro-Sports Workshop, Performances Activities Coordinator (2004-Present); Associate Professor, Continuing Education, San Diego Community College (1997-Present); Presenter, Southwest Dance, Movement and Acro-Sports Workshop (1984-Present); Instructor, San Diego Continuing Education (1976-Present); Presenter, Fall Prevention Task Force (2012); Presenter, Professional Dance Network (2005-2006); Presenter, California Dance and Movement Workshop for Educators (2004); Presenter, National Pediatric Support Services (1999); Presenter, California Dance Educators (Now California Dance Education Association) (1999); Special Advisor, San Diego Council on Physical Fitness and Sports (1998-2002); Presenter, Southern California Kindergarten Association (1997); Speaker, Fourth International Congress on Physical Activity, Aging and Sports (1996); Consultant, California Governor's Council on Physical Fitness and Sports (1993-2002); Professional Presenter, IDEA International Association for Fitness Professionals (1984-1985); Feature Guest, Station KFMB, KPBS-TV, San Diego, CA (1980-1988) **Civic:** Instructor, National Arthritis Foundation (1995-2013); Trainer, Arthritis Foundation Exercise Program (1995-2013); Chairman, People with Arthritis Can Exercise Committee, San Diego Chapter, Arthritis Foundation (1994-1995); Meet the Author Programs, San Diego County Schools (1988-2007); Administrator, Vice President, ODEM Chapter, Toastmasters, San Diego, CA (1982); Founder, SOLO, San Diego, CA (1981-1983); Board of Directors, We Care Foundation, San Diego, CA (1977-1979) **Creative Works:** Co-Author, "Handbook for Instructors of Older Adults" (1994); Co-Author, "Muevete Conmigo, Uno, Dos, Tres" (1990); Co-Author, "Guide for Physical Fitness Instructors of Older Adults," Grant Project (1990); Co-Author, "The Empowering Teacher" (1990); Author, "Move With Me, One, Two, Three (1988); Author, "Move With Me From A to Z" (1982); Co-Author, "Prime Time Aerobics" (1982) **Awards:** Recipient, Faculty Appreciation Award (2018); Recipient, Live Well San Diego Public Health Champion Award, Aging and Independence Services (2017); Grantee, Video Showcase of Exercises for Older Adults (1992-1993); Recipient, San Diego Continuing Education Empowering Teacher Award (1990) **Membership:** IDEA Health & Fitness Association; California Association for Health, Physical Education, Recreation and Dance **Marquis Who's Who Honors:** Albert Nelson Marquis Lifetime Achievement Award (2017) **To what do you attribute your success:** Ms. Schade attributes her success to her passion for teaching and dancing, as well as the influence and guidance of her mother, who was a dancer and an educator. **Why did you become involved in your profession or industry:** Ms. Schade became involved in her profession by following in her mother's footsteps. **What do you consider to be the highlight of your career:** A highlight of Ms. Schade's career was being recognized as a leader in her field by her colleagues and community organizations. **Where will you be in five years:** Ms. Schade plans to continue teaching health, wellness and fitness classes to those over 55. She will also be dancing and directing with the Prime Time Steppers Dance Troupe. **Hobbies:** Dancing; Traveling; Walking **Shipping Address:** 3077B Clairemont Dr, Box 130, San Diego, CA, 92117

Susan O. Schall, PhD

Title: Founder & Operations Leader **Industry:** Consulting **Company Name:** SOS Consulting, LLC **Date of Birth:** 05/26/1959 **Place of Birth:** Buffalo **State:** NY **Parents:** William Edward Schall; Carol Ruth Schall **Marital Status:** Married **Spouse Name:** Gary Lyle Morrison (5/8/1999) **Education:** PhD in Industrial Engineering, The Pennsylvania State University (1988); MS in Industrial Engineering, The Pennsylvania State University (1986); BS in Industrial Engineering, The Pennsylvania State University (1982); BS in Mathematics, State University of New York at Fredonia (1981) **Certifications:** ASQ Certified Manager of Quality/Organizational Excellence (2016); Certified Lay Servant, Front Royal United Methodist Church, VA (2008-2014); ASQ Certified Quality Engineer (1989); Six Sigma Master Black Belt **Career:** Authorized Partner, Everything Disc, John Wiley & Sons, Inc. (2017-Present); Authorized Partner, Five Behaviors of a Cohesive Team, John Wiley & Sons, Inc. (2017-Present); Founder, Operations Leader, SOS Consulting, LLC (2004-Present); Methodology Director, RR Donnelley & Sons Company Inc., Downer's Grove, IL (2002-2004); President, Susan O. Schall Process Improvement Consulting, Front Royal, VA (1999-2002); Technical Superintendent, Control System Engineering, DuPont Engineering Polymers, Parkersburg, WV (1997-1998) **Career Related:** Consultant, ABET Foundation, Inc. (2014-Present); Adjunct Training Director, ABET Foundation, Inc. (2008-2011); Board of Directors, ABET Foundation, Inc. (2005-2008); Engineering Accreditation Commission Commissioner, ABET Foundation, Inc. (1997-2003); President, Engineering Alumni Society, The Pennsylvania State University (1996-1998); Member, Industrial and Professional Advisory Council, Harold and Inge Marcus Department of Industrial and Manufacturing Engineering, The Pennsylvania State University (1993-2014) **Civic:** Project Lead the Way, Warren County Public Schools, Front Royal (2010-2017); Lay Leader, Front Royal United Methodist Church (2010-2012); Board of Examiners, Malcolm Baldrige National Quality Award (2008); Board of Examiners, Malcolm Baldrige National Quality Award (2006) **Creative Works:** Contributor, "Is Your Organization Healthy Enough for Six Sigma?" ASQ Six Sigma Forum Magazine (2015); Contributor, "Variability Reduction: A Statistical Engineering Approach to Engage Operations Teams in Process Improvement," Quality Engineering (2012); Contributor, Articles, Professional Journals **Awards:** Medallion Award, Institute of industrial & System Engineers (2018); Outstanding Engineering Alumna Award, College of Engineering, The Pennsylvania State University (2009); Distinguished Service Award, Engineering Alumni Society, The Pennsylvania State University (1999); Engineering Excellence Silver Award, DuPont Engineering (1992); Engineering Excellence Bronze Award, DuPont Engineering (1990) **Membership:** Chair, Freund-Marquarat Medal Committee, ASQ (2014-Present); Internet Liaison, Northern Shenandoah Valley Section ASQ (2004-Present); Awards Board Member, Northern Shenandoah Valley Section ASQ (2008-2013); Chair, Northern Shenandoah Valley Section ASQ (2001-2003); Fellow, ABET FOundation, Inc.; American Society of Engineering Education; Senior Member, American Society of Quality; Senior Member, Institute of Industrial and Systems Engineers; Treasurer, Northern Shenandoah Valley Section ASQ **To what do you attribute your success:** Dr. Schall attributes her success to her education, support of family and her persistence. **Why did you become involved in your profession or industry:** While Dr. Schall was in High School, she thought she wanted to be a patent lawyer. She kept visiting schools and learning about pre-law programs. They sounded boring to her because they didn't require mathematics and science, which is what she enjoyed. Her dad was at a Lions' meeting and asked a Lawyer what he studied as an undergraduate and the lawyer said engineering and told him that the field requires critical thinking skills. Her dad came home and told Dr. Schall that she needs to look into engineering. When she read about industrial engineering, she knew that it was what she was supposed to do. Once she got into it, she never thought about law again. Her father taught her to love Math. He was encouraging of women in the sciences. Her grandfather was a carpenter and helped with her love of building. She pays it forward by helping mentor young women. **What do you consider to be the highlight of your career:** Dr. Schall is proud of the work that she did with her first client, which involved bringing some data tools together. They were so excited about making a difference in their own work and organizations. She wants to make a difference in organizations and for people who work in the organizations. Dr. Schall enjoys mentoring to help others have the tools and mindset to always make a difference. **Political Affiliations:** Democrat **Religion:** Methodist **Shipping Address:** 160 Boulder View Ln, Front Royal, VA, 22630 **Website:** http://www.execute2compete.com

Debbie M. Schaum

Title: Associate Chair of Applied Aviation Sciences **Industry:** Education/Educational Services **Company Name:** Embry-Riddle Aeronautical University **Education:** MA in Management, Webster University; BS in Atmospheric Sciences, University of Missouri System, Columbia, MO **Career:** Associate Professor, Applied Aviation Sciences, Embry-Riddle Aeronautical University **Military Service:** Major, United States Air Force **Membership:** University Aviation Association **Marquis Who's Who Honors:** Albert Nelson Marquis Lifetime Achievement Award (2017) **To what do you attribute your success:** Ms. Schaum attributes her success to her prior experiences. Before joining the United States Air Force, she was a member of the ROTC and created a scholarship program for students. She has an innate understanding of students' needs and reaches out to the middle school students to explain the real-world benefits of mathematics and science, always keeping in mind the importance of pursuing endeavors related to aviation and meteorology. **Why did you become involved in your profession or industry:** Ms. Schaum became involved in her profession because she is a retired major in the United States Air Force whose primary responsibility was working as a meteorologist. She has tried to open the doors of aviation and meteorology for women, who are traditionally under-represented in this field, by acting as a role model and reaching out to middle school children to give them an introduction into the field. **Where will you be in five years:** In five years, Ms. Schaum plans on continuing her career with Embry-Riddle Aeronautical University. **Hobbies:** Hosting International Exchange Students; Benefiting from the Lasting Friendships She Has Made with Students **Shipping Address:** PO Box 731085, Ormond Beach, FL, 32173

Frederic Michael Scherer

Title: Professor Emeritus **Industry:** Education/Educational Services **Company Name:** Harvard University **Date of Birth:** 08/01/1932 **Place of Birth:** Ottawa **State:** IL **Parents:** Walter King Scherer; Margaret (Lucey) Scherer **Marital Status:** Married **Spouse Name:** Barbara A. (Silbermann) Scherer (8/17/1957) **Children:** Thomas; Karen; Christina **Education:** Honorary Doctorate, University of Hohenheim, Germany (1996); PhD, Harvard University (1963); MBA, Harvard University, With High Distinction (1958); AB, University of Michigan, With Honors (1954) **Career:** Aetna Professor Emeritus, Harvard Kennedy School, John F. Kennedy School of Government, Harvard University, Cambridge, MA (2000-Present); Aetna Professor of Public Policy and Management, Harvard University, Cambridge, MA (1989-2000); Joseph Wharton Professor of Political Economy, Swarthmore College, Pennsylvania (1982-1989); Professor of Economics, Northwestern University, Evanston, IL (1976-1982); Chief Economist, Federal Trade Commission, Washington, DC (1974-1976); Senior Research Fellow, Science Center Berlin (1972-1974); Professor of Economics, University of Michigan, Ann Arbor, MI (1966-1972); Assistant Professor, Princeton University, NJ (1963-1966); Research Associate, Harvard Business School (1958-1963); Research Assistant, Harvard Business School (1958-1963) **Career Related:** Interviewee, Oral History Project, Antitrust Section, American Bar Association (2009); Amici Curiae Brief with William S. Comanor to the Supreme Court of the United States in Leegin Creative Leather Products v. PSKS Inc. (2007); Amicus Curiae Brief to the Supreme Court of the United States in the Independent Ink v. Illinois Tool Case (2005); American Bar Association Visiting Professor, Haverford College (2004-2006); Lecturer, Princeton University (2000-2005); Ludwig Erhard Visiting Professor, University of Bayreuth (2000); Distinguished Fellow, Mossavar-Rahmani Center for Business and Government, John F. Kennedy School of Government, Harvard Kennedy School (2000); Amici Curiae Brief with Robert Litan, William Nordhaus, and Roger Noll in the U.S. v. Microsoft Case (2000); Distinguished Fellow, Industrial Organization Society (1999); Arthur Andersen Distinguished Visitor, University of Cambridge (1997); Visiting Professor, Central European University, Prague, Czech Republic (1993-1994); Economic Adviser to Judge Hubert Will in the Glass Bottles Litigation (1991); Census Fellow, American Statistical Association (1989-1990); Economic Adviser to Federal Judges Charles Robson and Hubert Will in the Folding Carton Litigation (1979-1981); Provided Advisory Memorandum to Attorney General Griffin Bell on Proposed Merger of LTV and Lykes-Youngstown (1978); Principal Economic Adviser, Committee on Government Patent Policy (1966-1969); Consultant, U.S. Arms Control and Disarmament Agency (1966-1968); Predoctoral Fellow, Harvard University, Ford Foundation (1959-1962) **Civic:** Co-Chair, U.S. Census Bureau Professional Advisory Committee, U.S. Bureau of Census, U.S. Department of Commerce (1999); Advisory Panel, U.S. Bureau of Census, U.S. Department of Commerce (1997-2000); Advisory Panel, U.S. Office of Technology Assessment (1989-1993); Advisory Panel, National Science Foundation, Washington, DC (1980-1983) **Military Service:** Counter Intelligence Corps, U.S. Army, West German Border Town (1954-1956) **Creative Works:** Author, "Quarter Notes and Bank Notes: The Economics of Music Composition in the 18th and 19th Centuries," Princeton University Press (2004); Author, "New Perspectives on Economic Growth and Technological Innovation," Brookings Institution (1999); Author, "Industry Structure, Strategy and Public Policy," Harper Collins (1996); Author, "Competition Policies for an Integrated World Economy," Brookings Institution (1994); Author, "International High-Technology Competition," Harvard University Press (1992); Co-author, "Industrial Market Structure and Economic Performance, Third Edition," Houghton Mifflin (1990); Co-author, "Mergers, Sell-Offs and Economic Efficiency," Brookings Institution (1987); Author, "Innovation and Growth: Schumpeterian Perspectives," MIT Press (1984); Author, "Industrial Market Structure and Economic Performance, Second Edition," (1980) **Awards:** Co-Founder's Award, European Association for Research and Industrial Economics (2014); Lifetime Achievement Award, American Antitrust Institute (2002); Grantee, Alfred P. Sloan Foundation (1996); Centennial Research Grantee, O'Melveny & Myers LLP (1989); Grantee, National Science Foundation (1982); Grantee, National Science Foundation (1979) **Membership:** President, Industrial Organization Society (1992-1993); British-North American Committee (1990-2000); Chair, Advisory Panel, Study of Pharmaceutical R&D: Costs, Risks, and Rewards, U.S. Office of Technology Assessment (1990-1993); Vice President, Southern Economic Association (1990); President, International J.A. Schumpeter Society (1988-1990) **Marquis Who's Who Honors:** Albert Nelson Marquis Lifetime Achievement Award (2017) **Religion:** Roman Catholic **Shipping Address:** 53 Standish Street, Unit 2, Cambridge, MA, 02138

David T. Schiff

Title: Investment Banker **Industry:** Financial Services **Company Name:** Kuhn, Loeb & Co. **Date of Birth:** 09/03/1936 **Place of Birth:** New York **State:** NY **Parents:** John Mortimer Schiff; Edith Brevoort (Baker) Schiff **Marital Status:** Married **Spouse Name:** Martha Elisabeth Lawler (5/11/1963) **Children:** Andrew Newman; David Baker; Ashley Reynolds **Education:** Bachelor of English, Yale University (1958); Brooks School (1954) **Career:** Managing Partner, Kuhn, Loeb & Co. (1993-Present); Managing Partner, KLS Enterprises (1984-1993); Managing Director, Lehman Brothers Kuhn Loeb Inc. (1977-1983); Vice Chairman, Kuhn Loeb & Co. Inc. (1977); General Partner, Kuhn, Loeb & Co. (1967-1977); Associate, Kuhn, Loeb & Co. (1963-1966); Analyst, Madison Fund Inc. (1962); Trainee, Chemical Bank New York Trust Company (Now JP Morgan Chase & Co.) (1959-1962) **Career Related:** Member of Advisory Board, Yale Center Environmental Law & Policy (2006-Present); Member, Advisory Board, Venture Capital Fund of America (1999-Present); Board of Advisors, VCFA Group (1996-Present); Partner, Rabbit Hollow Partners (1981-Present); Member, Leadership Council, Yale School of Forestry & Environmental Studies (2000-2008); Director, Distribix Inc., St. Louis, MO (1985-1990); Director, Crown Life Canada (1981-1995); Vice Chairman, Crown Life Canada (1981-1995); Member, Lower Manhattan Advisory Board, Chemical Bank New York Trust Company (Now JP Morgan Chase & Co.) (1977-1985); Director, Distribix Inc., St. Louis (1977-1983); Board of Directors, Crown Life Canada (1971-1992); Board of Directors, Kuhn, Loeb & Co. **Civic:** Chairman Emeritus, Wildlife Conservation Society (2013-Present); Trustee Emeritus, Citizens Budget Commission (2009-Present); Trustee Emeritus, The Metropolitan Museum of Art (2008-Present); Board of Governors, Federal Hall Memorial Association (1970-Present); Member, The Provident Loan Society of New York (1968-Present); Director, Vice Chairman, The Schiff Foundation (1964-Present); Life Trustee, Wildlife Conservation Society (1965-2013); Trustee, Citizens Budget Commission (1973-2009); Trustee, The Metropolitan Museum of Art (1971-2008); Chairman, Wildlife Conservation Society (1996-2007); Board of Directors, The American Hospital of Paris Foundation (1987-2006); Member, Advisory Board of Directors, Outward Bound (1983-1999) Board of Governors, The Yale University Art Gallery (1973-1997); Trustee, Greater New York Council, Boy Scouts of America (1965-1991); Treasurer, Brooks School (1987-1990); Trustee, Brooks School (1972-1990); Chairman, Beekman Downtown Hospital (Now Lower Manhattan Hospital), New York-Presbyterian Hospital (1975-1979); Trustee, Beekman Downtown Hospital (Now Lower Manhattan Hospital), New York-Presbyterian Hospital (1966-1982) **Military Service:** U.S. Army (1959) **Membership:** Life Member, Executive Committee Member, The Pilgrims of the US (1992-Present); Life Fellow, The Morgan Library & Museum (1973-Present); Governor, Federal Hall Memorial Associates (1970-Present); The Century Association; The Yale Club New York City; Mill Reef Club, Antigua; Maroon Creek Club, Aspen, CO; Brook Club **Marquis Who's Who Honors:** Albert Nelson Marquis Lifetime Achievement Award (2017); Distinguished Humanitarian (2017) **Why did you become involved in your profession or industry:** Mr. Schiff became involved in his profession because his family was always in investment banking. **Hobbies:** Tennis; Biking; Conservation & environment; Art **Religion:** Episcopalian **Shipping Address:** 1177 Avenue of the Americas, Fl. 42, Kuhn, Loeb & Co., New York, NY, 10036 **Website:** kuhnloebco.com

Sanford Joel Schlesinger

Title: Lawyer **Industry:** Law and Legal Services **Company Name:** Schlesinger Lazetera & Auchincloss LLP **Date of Birth:** 02/08/1943 **Place of Birth:** New York **State:** NY **Parents:** Irving Schlesinger; Ruth (Rubin) Schlesinger **Marital Status:** Married **Spouse Name:** Lianne Lazetera **Children:** Merideth; Jarrod; Alexandra **Education:** JD, Fordham University (1966); Honorary BS in Government, Columbia University, with Honors (1963) **Career:** Founding Partner, Schlesinger Lazetera & Auchincloss LLP (2018-Present); Schlesinger Gannon & Lazetera LLP, New York, NY (2004-2018); Kaye Scholer LLP (Now Arnold & Porter Kaye Scholer LLP), New York, NY (1993-2004); Partner & Chair, Trusts and Estates Department, Kaye Scholer LLP (Now Arnold & Porter Kaye Scholer LLP), New York, NY (1993-2004); Partner & Head, Trusts and Estates Department, Shea & Gould, New York, NY (1985-1993); Partner, Goldschmidt, Oshatz, Powsner & Saft, New York, NY (1981-1985); Partner, Rose & Schlesinger, New York, NY (1969-1981); Assistant Attorney, General Trusts and Estates Bureau, Charitable Foundations Division, State of New York, New York, NY (1967-1969); Associate, Frankenthaler & Kohn (Now Frankenthaler, Kohn, Schneider & Katz), New York, NY (1966-1967) **Career Related:** Co-Chair, Institute of Federal Taxation, New York University School of Professional Studies (2010-Present); Emeritus, New York State Bar Journal (Now New York State Bar Association Journal) (2005-Present); Journal Board of Editors, New York State Bar Association (1995-Present); Columnist & Member, Editorial Board, Estate Planning Magazine (1995-Present); Practising Law Institute (1990-Present); Member, Financial and Estate Planning Advisory Board, Commerce Clearing House, Wolters Kluwer (1988-Present); Chair, 76th Institute on Federal Taxation Conference-Trusts and Estates, New York University School of Professional Studies (2017); Chair, 48th Annual Estate Planning Institute (2017); Practising Law Institute (2017); Chair, "Trusts and Estates 75th New York University Institute on Federal Taxation, New York University School of Professional Studies (2016); Chair, 47th Annual Estate Planning Institute, Practising Law Institute (2016); Co-Chair, Summer Institute in Taxation, New York University School of Professional Studies (2016); Chair, Trusts and Estates 74th New York University Institute on Federal Taxation, New York University School of Professional Studies (2015); Chair, 46th Annual Estate Planning Institute, Practising Law Institute (2015); Chair, 46th Annual Estate Planning Institute, Practising Law Institute (2015); Chair, 45th Annual Estate Planning Institute, Practising Law Institute (2014); 73rd Institute on Federal Taxation, New York University School of Professional Studies (2014); Member, Trusts, Estates and Surrogate's Courts Committee, New York City Bar Association (Now Association of the Bar of the City of New York) (2013-2016); Chair, Institute on Federal Taxation, New York University School of Professional Studies, Estate Planning Day (2013-2014); Director, The New York State Bar Foundation (Now The New York Bar Foundation) (2004-2013); New York State Bar Journal (Now New York State Bar Association Journal) (1995-2005); University of Miami Graduate School of Law (Now University of Miami School of Law) (1995-2003); Chairman, Institute on Federal Taxation, New York University School of Professional Studies (1993-1994); Board of Advisors and Contributors, The Journal of Corporate Taxation (1989-1996); Adjunct Faculty, Columbia University Law School (Now Columbia Law School) (1989-1994); Member, Advisory Board, Institute on Federal Taxation, New York University School of Professional Studies (1988-1996) **Membership:** Academician, The International Academy Estate and Trust Law (1992-Present); Chairman & Fellow, The American College Trust and Estate Counsel, Downstate New York (2001-2007); Chairman, Trusts and Estates Section, New York State Bar Association (1994-1995); Chairman, Probate and Trust Committee Estate Planning, ABA (1992-1994); Charitable Giving Committees, ABA (1992-1994); Secretary, Trusts and Estates Section, New York State Bar Association (1992-1993); Treasurer, Trusts and Estates Section, New York State Bar Association (1991-1992); Chairman, Social Security and Other Government Entitlements Committee, ABA (1990-1991); Chairman, Executive Committee, First Judicial District, New York State Bar Association (1987-1991); Estate Planners Hall of Fame, National Association of Estate Planners & Councils; National Academy of Family Law Attorneys; Brooklyn Bar Association; Association of the Bar of the City of New York **Bar Admissions:** United States Tax Court (1993); Supreme Court of the United States (1978); United States Court for International Trade (1969); United States Court of Appeals for the Second Circuit (1968) **Marquis Who's Who Honors:** Albert Nelson Marquis Lifetime Achievement Award (2017) **Hobbies:** Baseball; Writing **Shipping Address:** 535 Madison Ave 5th Floor, Schlesinger Lazetera & Auchincloss LLP, New York, NY, 10022

Herbert S. Schlosser

Title: Senior Advisor to Communications Group **Industry:** Financial Services **Company Name:** Citigroup, Inc. **Date of Birth:** 04/21/1926 **Place of Birth:** Atlantic City **State:** NJ **Parents:** Abraham Schlosser; Anna (Olesker) Schlosser **Marital Status:** Married **Spouse Name:** Judith P. Gassner (7/8/1951) **Children:** Lynn C.; Eric M. **Education:** JD, Yale University (1951); AB, Princeton University, Summa Cum Laude (1948) **Career:** Senior Adviser, Independent Consultant Communications and Investment Banking, Citigroup Global Markets Inc. (2000-2012); Senior Adviser for Broadcasting and Entertainment, Schroder & Co., Inc. (1986-2000); Executive Vice President, RCA (1978-1985); Chief Executive Officer, NBC, Inc. (1977-1978); President, NBC, Inc. (1974-1978); Board of Directors, NBC-TV Network (1973-1978); President, NBC-TV Network (1973-1974); Executive Vice President, NBC-TV Network (1972-1973); Vice President of Programs, West Coast NBC (1966-1972); Vice President of Talent and Program Administration, California National Productions, Inc., NBC (1962-1966); Director of Talent and Program Administration, California National Productions, Inc. (1961-1962); Vice President, California National Productions, Inc. (1960-1961); General Manager, California National Productions, Inc. (1960-1961); Associate, Phillips, Nizer, Benjamin, Krim & Ballon (1954-1957); Associate, Wickes, Riddell, Bloomer, Jacobi & McGuire (1951-1954); Board of Directors, Hubbard Broadcasting **Career Related:** Partner, Arts and Entertainment Cable Network; Partner, RCA; Partner, Columbia Home Video **Civic:** Chairman Emeritus, Museum of the Moving Image (2015-Present); Chairman, Board of Directors, Museum of the Moving Image (1988-2014); Trustee, IRTS Foundation (1972-1974); Board of Trustees, Ford's Theatre Society; Former Trustee, National Urban League; Board of Directors, The Chamber Music Society of Lincoln Center **Military Service:** U.S. Naval Reserve (1944-1946) **Creative Works:** Interviewee, Carson Podcast (2016); Reviewer, Scripts; Producer, Various Television Programs **Awards:** Inductee, Broadcasting & Cable Hall of Fame (2000) **Membership:** President, Alumni Association of Southern California, The Phi Beta Kappa Society (1970-1972); Trustee, HRTS (1970-1972); Council on Foreign Relations; Academy of Television Arts & Sciences; Ad Council; The Century Association; Princeton Club of New York; Yale Law School Association; Chairman Emeritus, Martha Graham Center for Contemporary Dance; American Bar Association; Association of the Bar of the City of New York **Bar Admissions:** State of New York (1952) **Marquis Who's Who Honors:** Distinguished Humanitarian (2017) **Shipping Address:** 784 Park Avenue, Apt. 2B, New York, NY, 10021

Michael David Schlosser

Title: Director **Industry:** Education/Educational Services **Company Name:** University of Illinois **Parents:** David Schlosser; Judith Schlosser **Marital Status:** Married **Spouse Name:** Kimberly Schlosser (10/10/1980) **Children:** Chad; Drew; Kristina **Education:** MA in Legal Studies, University of Illinois, Springfield (2017); EdD, University of Illinois, Urbana-Champaign (2011); MPA, Governors State University (2000); BA, Eastern Illinois University (1988); AAS in Criminal Justice, Parkland College (1983) **Career:** Director, Police Training Institute, University of Illinois, Champaign, IL (2012-Present); Associate Director, Police Training Institute, University of Illinois, Champaign, IL (2011-2012); Police Training Specialist, Police Training Institute, University of Illinois, Champaign, IL (2004-2011); Owner, Schlosser's Martial Arts & Conditioning, Rantoul, IL (1998-2007); Lead Instructor, Schlosser's Martial Arts & Conditioning, Rantoul, IL (1998-2007); Adjunct Instructor, Police Training Institute, University of Illinois, Champaign, IL (1998-2004); Part-Time Fitness Instructor, Police Training Institute, University of Illinois, Champaign, IL (1998-2004); Lead Instructor, BW Karate Studio, Rantoul, IL (1990-1998); Lieutenant, Rantoul Police Department, Rantoul, IL (1984-2004); Field Training Officer, Rantoul Police Department, Rantoul, IL (1984-2004); Field Training Supervisor, Rantoul Police Department, Rantoul, IL (1984-2004); Investigator, Rantoul Police Department, Rantoul, IL (1984-2004); Wellness Officer, Rantoul Police Department, Rantoul, IL (1984-2004); Training Coordinator, Rantoul Police Department, Rantoul, IL (1984-2004) **Creative Works:** Author, "Escaping from Standing Choke Holds," Police Magazine (2017); Author, "Using Force Scenarios for Training," Police Magazine (2017); Author, "Getting the Gun," Police Magazine (2017); Author, "Don't Forget About Your Baton," Police Magazine (2016); Author, "In Praise of Pepper Spray," Police Magazine (2016); Co-author, "Gaining Compliance with Targeted Pressure," Police Magazine (2016); Co-author, "Police Endorse Color-Blind Racial Beliefs More Than Laypersons," Race and Social Problems (2016); Author, "Instinct and Knife Attack," Police Magazine (2015); Co-author, "Strength in Numbers: the Best Way to Make an Arrest with at Least Two Officers for Each Arrestee," Police Magazine (2015); Co-author, "Police Use of Force: A Descriptive Analysis of Illinois Police Officers," Law Enforcement Executive Forum (2015); Co-author, "Improving Policing in a Multiracial Society in the United States: A New Approach," International Journal of Criminal Justice Sciences (2015); Co-author, "Reacting to Gun Grabs: There's More to Stopping this Extremely Deadly Type of Attack Than Just Holding onto Your Weapon," Police Magazine (2015); Author, "Pepper Spray Remains a Viable Option for Today's Police Officers," Illinois Cops (2015); Author, "Getting Proactive About Gaining Citizens' Trust," Illinois Cops (2015); Author, "Responding to Domestic Disturbances," Illinois Cops (2014); Co-author, "Rear Wrist Lock: Used Correctly This Technique Can Help You Gain Control of Resisting Suspects and Keep You on Your Feet," Police Magazine (2014); Author, "Keeping Police Report Writing Simple," Illinois Cops (2014); Author, "Some Tips to Making Control Tactics Training Realistic and Safe," Illinois Cops (2014); Author, "Making the "Known Risk" Vehicle Stop," Illinois Cops (2014); Co-author, "Two Simple Submissions That Could Save Your Life," Police Magazine (2014); Author, "Multiple Roles and Potential Role Conflict of a School Resource Officer: A Case Study of the Midwest Police Department's School Resource Officer Program in the United States," International Journal of Criminal Justice Science (2014); Author, "Making the Unknown Risk Vehicle Stop," Illinois Cops (2014); Author, "Tactical Communications," Illinois Cops (2014); Co-author, "Animal Abuse and Cruelty: Canine Behavior and Police Response," Illinois Cops (2014); Co-author, "University of Illinois Police Training Institute Rejuvenated," Illinois Cops (2014); Co-author, "Suspect Contact and Control," Police Magazine (2014); Co-author, "Defending Against the Choke on the Ground," Police Magazine (2014); Co-author, "Concealed Carry Law Will Change Tactics: But Not Mindset," Illinois Cops (2014) **Awards:** Defenders of the Innocent Award, Illinois Innocence Project (2017); Inductee, LeRoy High School Hall of Fame (Now LeRoy Oatka Knights Sports Hall of Fame) (2016); Model Administrator Award, The American Society for Public Administration (2013); Governor's Award for Excellence in Law Enforcement Training (2004); Volunteer of the Year, Village of Rantoul, IL (2003); Inductee, Universal Martial Arts Hall of Fame (UMAHOF) (2001); Commendation for Community Involvement, Rantoul Police Department (2000); Officer of the Year, Rantoul Police Department (1986) **Membership:** International Association of Chiefs of Police; Midwest Criminal Justice Association; IADLEST; The National Organization of Black Law Enforcement Executives; Illinois Police Association, Illinois State Police; PBPA; ILEETA; Board Member, Law Enforcement Foundation of Illinois (LEFI); Board Member, Illinois Law Enforcement Training and Standards Board **Shipping Address:** 1004 S 4th Street, University of Illinois Police Training Institute, Champaign, IL, 61820

Christopher Eric Schmidt

Title: Managing Partner **Industry:** Law and Legal Services **Company Name:** C. E. Schmidt & Associates, Attorneys at Law **Date of Birth:** 08/26/1950 **Place of Birth:** Atlanta **State:** GA **Parents:** Norbert Schmidt; Laurie Schmidt **Marital Status:** Married **Spouse Name:** L. Michelle Schmidt **Children:** Anna Schmidt; Laura Schmidt; Jonathan Schmidt **Education:** JD, Maurice A. Deane School of Law, Hofstra University (1978); Bachelor of Economics, Brigham Young University (1974) **Career:** Managing Partner, C.E. Schmidt & Associates, Attorneys at Law (2012-Present); Partner, Schmidt & Rothenberg (1985-1995); Solo Practice (1983-1985); Real Estate Associate Attorney, Coppock & Teltschick, PLLC (1980-1982) **Civic:** Volunteer, LDS Church Mission in Norway (1971-1973); Scoutmaster, Sam Houston Area Council, Boy Scouts of America; Level Four Certified and Sanctioned Youth Ice Hockey Coach, USA Hockey Association **Membership:** Fellow, Texas Bar College (2001); New York Bar Association; Texas Bar Association; Harris County Bar Association; American Bar Association **Bar Admissions:** U.S. District Court- Western District of Texas (1995); State Bar of Texas (1980); U.S. District Court- Southern District of Texas (1980); State Bar of New York (1979) **Marquis Who's Who Honors:** Who's Who in American Law (1990-1991) **To what do you attribute your success:** He attributes his success to the education that he gained locally and abroad, as well as the values taught by his parents and local church leaders. **Why did you become involved in your profession or industry:** Mr. Schmidt joined the profession to assist others in resolving their disputes and dedicated to seek justice on their behalf. With 37 years of handling litigation involving real estate, personal injury, medical malpractice, criminal defense and family law matters, Mr. Schmidt is well versed in representing clients in complicated divorce actions. **What do you consider to be the highlight of your career:** The highlight of his career was becoming a member of the College of the State Bar of Texas. **Where will you be in five years:** In five years, Mr. Schmidt plans to continue as senior and managing partner of C. E. Schmidt & Associates, Attorneys at Law. **Hobbies:** Ice hockey; Skiing; Art; Architecture; Camping; Cooking **Political Affiliations:** Republican **Religion:** Christian-Mormonism **Shipping Address:** 14780 Memorial Dr., Ste 103, C E Schmidt & Associates, Houston, TX, 77079 **Website:** http://www.westhoustonattorney.com/

Daniel Edward Schmidt IV

Title: Lawyer, Arbitrator **Industry:** Law and Legal Services **Date of Birth:** 12/17/1946 **Place of Birth:** New York **State:** NY **Parents:** Daniel Edward Schmidt, III; Mary (Mannion) Schmidt **Marital Status:** Married **Spouse Name:** Gail Kennedy (9/5/1980) **Children:** Kathryn Kennedy; Michael Kennedy **Education:** JD, St. John's University (1975); Postgraduate Coursework, The New School (1972); BA, St. Lawrence University (1971) **Certifications:** Certified Arbitrator; Certified Umpire **Career:** Consultant, Sorema NA Group (2000-2003); Director, Executive Committee, Sorema N.A. Group, New York, NY (1999-2000); Group Executive Vice President, Sorema N.A. Group, New York, NY (1999-2000); Chief Legal Officer, Sorema N.A. Group, New York, NY (1999-2000); U.S. Counsel, Groupama, France (1996-2000); Director, Executive Committee, Sorema N.A. Group, New York, NY (1995-1999); Executive Vice President, Sorema N.A. Group, New York, NY (1995-1999); Group General Counsel, Sorema N.A. Group, New York, NY (1995-1999); Deputy General Manager, Sorema International Holding, N.V., Netherlands (1993-1996); General Counsel, Sorema International Holding, N.V., Netherlands (1993-1996); Corporate Secretary, Sorema International Holding, N.V., Netherlands (1993-1996); Director, Executive Committee, Sorema N.A. Group, New York, NY (1989-1994); Senior Vice President, Sorema N.A. Group, New York, NY (1989-1994); General Counsel, Sorema N.A. Group, New York, NY (1989-1994); Corporate Secretary, Sorema N.A. Group, New York, NY (1989-1994); Director, Senior Vice President, Scor U.S. Group, New York, NY (1986-1989); General Counsel, Scor U.S. Group, New York, NY (1986-1989); Corporate Secretary, Scor U.S. Group, New York, NY (1986-1989); Director, Scor U.S. Group, New York, NY (1984-1986); Vice President, Scor U.S. Group, New York, NY (1984-1986); General Counsel, Scor U.S. Group, New York, NY (1984-1986); Corporate Secretary, Scor U.S. Group, New York, NY (1984-1986); Vice President, Prudential Reins Co., Newark, NJ (1982-1984); Associate General Counsel, Prudential Reins Company, Newark, NJ (1982-1984); Assistant Secretary, Prudential Reins Co., Newark, NJ (1982-1984); Associate General Counsel, Prudential Property & Casualty, Holmdel, NJ (1981-1982); Division Head, Prudential Property & Casualty, Holmdel, NJ (1981-1982); From Assistant Counsel to Associate General Counsel, Prudential Property & Casualty, Holmdel, NJ (1975-1981) **Career Related:** Private Practice, Little Silver, NJ (1987-Present); Commercial Arbitrator, Little Silver, NJ (1987-Present); Umpire, Little Silver, NJ (1987-Present); Reins. Lecturer, ARIAS, New York, NY (1984-Present); Chairman, ARIAS, New York, NY (2002-2003); President, ARIAS, New York, NY (1999-2002); Founding Director, ARIAS, New York, NY (1994-2003); Board of Directors, ARIAS-U.S., New York, NY **Civic:** Board of Directors, Marine Corps Scholarship Foundation, New Jersey (2007-Present); Judge, Ecclesiastical Trial Court (1997-2000); Associate Presiding Judge, Episcopal Diocese of New Jersey (1997-2000); Board of Directors, American Red Cross, Monmouth County, Shrewsbury, NJ (1981-1984); Executive Committee, American Red Cross, Monmouth County, Shrewsbury, NJ (1981-1984); Listed Arbitrator, ARIAS, England **Military Service:** Senior Interrogation Advisor, II Corps Interrogation Center, U.S. Army, Pleiku, Vietnam (1967-1970) **Creative Works:** Associate Editor, Arias-U.S. Quarterly **Membership:** American Bar Association; Panel of Commercial Arbitrators, American Arbitration Association; Roster of Umpires, American Arbitration Association; Panel of International Arbitrators, American Arbitration Association; U.S. Chapter, Association International Droit des Assureurs; Beacon Hill Country Club; Desert Mountain Club; Sands Beach Club **Bar Admissions:** State Bar of New York (1976) **Marquis Who's Who Honors:** Albert Nelson Marquis Lifetime Achievement Award (2017) **Hobbies:** Bicycling; Golfing; Hiking **Religion:** Episcopalian **Shipping Address:** 13 Country Lane, Dispute Resolution Services International, Little Silver, NJ, 07739

Robert Allen Schmitz

Title: Managing Director **Industry:** Business Management/Business Services **Company Name:** Quest Turnaround Advisors **Date of Birth:** 01/19/1941 **Place of Birth:** Chicago **State:** IL **Parents:** John Schmitz; Lee (Zeal) Schmitz **Marital Status:** Married **Spouse Name:** Judith Mair Grey (10/25/1997); Jenny Ann Quest (8/23/1969, Divorced) **Children:** Alexander; Nicholas; Lara; Maximilian **Education:** MS in Management, MIT Sloan School of Management (1965); BA, University of Michigan, with Distinction (1963) **Career:** Managing Director, Founder, Quest Turnaround Advisors (1999-Present); President, Founder, Quest Capital Ltd. (1989-Present); Chief Restructuring Officer, World Space Inc. (2008-2012); Chief Operating Officer, PTV Inc. (2003-2007); Chairman, Founder, Headline Media Group (2001-2004); Management Director, The TCW Group, Inc. (1993-1997); Senior Partner, TCW Capital, The TCW Group, Inc. (1993-1997); Investment Consultant, Soros Fund Management (1990-1992); Chairman, President, Chief Executive Officer, Richard D. Irwin, Inc., Homewood, IL (1983-1989); Vice President, Books, Dow Jones & Company, New York City,NY (1982-1988); Principal, McKinsey & Company, Inc., New York City, NY (1970-1982); Assistant to Chairman, Northwest Industries, New York City, NY (1969-1970); Acquisition Analyst, W.R. Grace and Company, New York City, NY (1967-1969); Assistant to President, Lima Light and Power Company, Peru (1965-1967); Chief Restructuring Officer Fontainebleau Hotel-Miami **Career Related:** Advisory Board Member, College Commerce, DePaul University, Chicago, IL (1985-1992); Chairman, Board, Dune Energy (2012-2015) Board of Directors, Houghton Mifflin Harcourt Publishing Company, Boston, MA; Board of Directors, Sun-Times Media Group, Chicago, IL; Board of Directors, Two Way Media, London, United Kingdom; Board of Directors, Premium TV LLC, London, United Kingdom; Board of Directors, Cablecom GmBH, Zurich, Switzerland; Board of Directors, Adams Rite Sabre, Inc., Glendale, CA; Board of Directors, Superior Fireplace Company, Fullerton, CA; Houston Foods Company, Chicago, IL; Board of Directors, Archibald Candy Company, Chicago, IL; Board of Directors, U.S. Media Group, Inc., Crystal City, MO; Board of Directors, Central Valley Publication, Merced, CA; Board of Directors, Hobby Products Co., Inc., Penrose, CO; Board of Directors, Automated Bar Controls, Vacaville, CA; Board of Directors, SpecTran Technologies, Inc., Sturbridge, MA; Non-Executive Chairman, PTV Ltd., London, United Kingdom; Non-Executive Chairman, Two Way Media Ltd., London, United Kingdom **Civic:** President, Cultural Arts Center Foundation, Homewood, IL (1984-1989) **Membership:** Chairman, Higher Education Division, Association of American Publishers (1989); Trustee, New York State Chapter, The Nature Conservancy **Marquis Who's Who Honors:** Albert Nelson Marquis Lifetime Achievement Award (2017) **To what do you attribute your success:** Mr. Schmitz attributes his success to hard work and creativity. **Why did you become involved in your profession or industry:** Prior to founding Quest Turnaround Adviors, Mr. Schmitz led the turnarounds of media, manufacturing and consumer goods businesses as a partner in a private equity firm and an international management consulting firm. He served as the Chief Restructuring Officer of WorldSpace, Inc., a global satellite radio business that operated in Europe, Asia, Africa and Latin America from 2008 to 2012. **Hobbies:** Ballroom dancing **Business Address:** 800 Westchester Avenue, NY, Rye Brook, 10573 **Shipping Address:** 34 Seville Ave., Rye, NY, 10580 **Website:** http://www.qtadvisors.com/robert-a.-schmitz.html

Shirley Schmitz

Title: Marketing Professional **Industry:** Advertising & Marketing **Date of Birth:** 12/19/1927 **Place of Birth:** Brackenridge **State:** PA **Parents:** Wienand Gerard Schmitz; Florence Marie (Grimm) Schmitz **Career:** Senior Vice President of Marketing and Sales, Entertainment Publication Corp., Troy, MI (1989-1992); Executive Vice President, Sales and Market Development, Entertainment Publication Corp., Birmingham, MI (1983-1989); Vice President of Sales, Midwest Telephone Company Inc., Indianapolis, IN (1982-1983); General Manager, Bobbs-Merrill Company, Inc., Indianapolis, IN (1976-1982); President, CHB Port-A-Book Store, Inc. (1973-1976); Executive Vice President, Director of Sales, F.E. Compton Co. Division, Encyclopedia Britannica, Chicago, IL (1971-1973); Vice President, General Sales Manager, F.E. Compton Co. Division, Encyclopedia Britannica, Chicago, IL (1970-1971); National Sales Manager, Field Enterprises Educational Corp., Chicago, IL (1965-1970); Assistant Sales Manager, Field Enterprises Educational Corp., Chicago, IL (1963-1965); National Supervisor, Field Enterprises Educational Corp., Chicago, IL (1961-1963); Branch Manager, Field Enterprises Educational Corp., Montreal, QC, Canada (1955-1961); Regional Manager, Field Enterprises Educational Corp., Phoenix, AZ (1953-1955); District Manager, Field Enterprises Educational Corp., Phoenix, AZ (1952); Area Manager, Field Enterprises Educational Corp., Phoenix, AZ (1951-1952); Teacher, Guidance Counselor, Mesa High School, Mesa, AZ (1949-1951) **Career Related:** Principal, Innovators-Changemakers LLC, Arizona (2005-Present); Principal, S.G. Schmitz and Associates, Chicago, IL (1992-Present); President's Cabinet Capital Fund Raising Campaign, Arizona State University; Board of Advisors, Founder, Center for the Advancement of Small Business (now Spirit of Enterprise Center), W.P. Carey School of Business, Arizona State University **Civic:** Founder, Managing Partner, Innovators-Changemakers, LLC (2005-Present); Board Director, Founder, President, Shirley G. Schmitz Foundation, Inc. **Creative Works:** Author, "Guts Imagination Vision Conversations with Innovators-Changemakers" (2008) **Marquis Who's Who Honors:** Distinguished Humanitarian (2017) **Shipping Address:** 11899 N 135th Way, Scottsdale, AZ, 85259

Anne Schnoebelen

Title: Musicologist, Educator **Industry:** Education/Educational Services **Company Name:** Rice University **Date of Birth:** 08/04/1933 **Place of Birth:** Tomahawk **State:** WI **Parents:** Herman Sabas Schnoebelen; Katherine Alma (Yenor) Schnoebelen **Marital Status:** Married **Spouse Name:** John Albert Meixner (5/7/1980) **Education:** PhD, University of Illinois (1966); MusM, University of Illinois (1960); BA, Rosary College (1958) **Career:** Professor Emerita, Shepherd School of Music, Rice University (2004-Present); Independent Musicology Researcher (2016); Interim Dean, Rice University (2002-2003); Interim Dean, Rice University (1981); Chairman, Department of Musicology, Shepherd School of Music, Rice University (1974-2004) **Career Related:** Fellow, Fulbright (1964) **Creative Works:** Co-Editor, "Journal of Seventeenth-Century Music Instrumenta: A Catalogue of Mass, Office and Holy Week Music Printed in Italy 1516-1770" (2014); Contributor, "Barocco Padano e Musici Francescani" (2014); Contributor, "Carlo Donato Cossoni nella Milano spagnola" (2007); Contributor, "Seventeenth Century Italian Sacred Music, 10 vols" (1995-1999); Contributor, "Solo Motets from the Seventeenth Century, 10 vols" (1987-1989); Editor, "Cantatas by Maurizio Cazzati in the Italian Cantata in the Seventeenth Century" (1985); Author, "Padre Martini's Collection of Letters in the Civico Museo Bibliografico Musicale: An Annotated Index" (1979); Contributor, Articles, Professional Journals; Contributor, Book Chapters **Awards:** Travel Grant, American Council of Learned Societies (1984); Grantee, National Endowment of the Humanities (1983); Grantee, National Endowment of the Humanities (1969) **Membership:** Council Secretary, American Musicology Society (1986-1988); American Association of University Women; Society of 17th-Century Music **Shipping Address:** 2001 Holcombe Boulevard, Unit 702, Houston, TX, 77030

Jonathan Schochor

Title: Lawyer, Law Educator **Industry:** Law and Legal Services **Company Name:** Schochor, Federico & Staton, P.A. **Date of Birth:** 09/09/1946 **Place of Birth:** Suffern **State:** NY **Parents:** Abraham Schochor; Betty (Hechtor) Schochor **Marital Status:** Married **Spouse Name:** Joan Elaine Brown (5/31/1970) **Children:** Lauren Aimee; Daniel Ross **Education:** JD, American University School of Law (1971); BA, Pennsylvania State University (1968) **Career:** Senior Managing Partner, Schochor, Federico & Staton, Baltimore, MD (1984-Present); Associate, Ellin & Baker, Baltimore, MD (1974-1984); Associate, McKenna, Wilkinson & Kittner, Washington, DC (1971-1974) **Career Related:** Guest Expert, Numerous Radio and TV Programs, including the Dr. Oz Show; Testified before State Legislature on Issues Involving Medical Malpractice and Tort Reform; Lecturer in Law, MedStar, Johns Hopkins Hospital, Johns Hopkins School of Medicine; National Association of Dosimetrists **Civic:** Multiple Scholarship Endowments, The Pennsylvania State University; Scholarship Endowment, The University of Maryland Francis King Carey School of Law; Scholarship Endowment, The University of Baltimore School of Law **Creative Works:** Associate Editor-in-Chief, American University Law School Review (1971) **Awards:** Top 100 Litigation Lawyer, American Society of Legal Advocates (2018); Best Law Firms in Maryland, US News and World Report (2018); American Top 100 High Stakes Litigators, Maryland (2018); Member, Best Law Firms of America (2018); 10 Best Attorneys, American Institute of Personal Injury Attorneys (2017-2018); Medical Malpractice Top 25 Trial Lawyers, National Trial Lawyers and the Medical Malpractice Trial Lawyers Association (2017); Mass Tort Top 26 Trial Lawyers, National Trial Lawyers Mass Tort Trial Lawyers Association (2017); Best Lawyers in America (2016-2017); Best Lawyers in America, Maryland Super Lawyers; Baltimore Medical Malpractice Law Plaintiffs Lawyer of the Year, Best Lawyers (2016); Best Lawyers Lawyer of the Year, Baltimore, MD (2016); Co-recipient, Trial Lawyer of Year, Maryland Association for Justice (2015); Cornerstone Award, SmartCEO Magazine (2015); Influential Marylander, Daily Record (2015); Top One Percent, National Association of Distinguished Counsel (2015); Top 100 Litigation Lawyers in the State of Maryland, The American Society of Legal Advocates (2013); Outstanding Liberal Arts Alumni Award, Pennsylvania State University (2006); Top 100 Lawyers, American Trial Lawyers Association; Maryland Super Lawyers; Baltimore and Washington, DC's Best Lawyers; Bar Register of Pre-Eminent Lawyers; AV Rating, Martindale-Hubbell; Million Dollar Advocates Forum; Multi-Million Dollar Advocates Forum; America's Top 100 Attorneys Lifetime Achievement Award; Rue Ratings Best Attorneys of America Lifetime Charter Member; Strathmore's Who's Who Lifetime Member **Membership:** American Board of Trial Advocates (1994-Present); Circuit Court for Baltimore City Task Force, Civil Document Management System, Baltimore City Bar Association (1994-1995); Governor, Association of Trial Lawyers of America (1992-1995); Maryland State Delegate, Association of Trial Lawyers of America (1991); President, Maryland Trial Lawyers Association (1990-1991); Medicolegal Committee, Baltimore City Bar Association (1989-1990); President-elect, Maryland Trial Lawyers Association (1989); Executive Committee, Maryland Trial Lawyers Association (1987-1992); Vice President, Maryland Trial Lawyers Association (1987-1988); Secretary, Maryland Trial Lawyers Association (1987-1988); Chairman, Legislative Committee, Maryland Trial Lawyers Association (1986-1987); Board of Governors, Maryland Trial Lawyers Association (1986-1987); Legislative Committee, Baltimore City Bar Association (1986-1987); Special Committee on Tort Reform, Baltimore City Bar Association (1986); Legislative Committee, Maryland Trial Lawyers Association (1985-1988); Special Committee on Health Claims Arbitration, Maryland State Bar Association (1983) **Bar Admissions:** Supreme Court of the United States (1986); United States District Court for the District of Maryland (1974); Maryland State Bar (1974); District of Columbia Bar (1971); United States District Court for the District of Columbia (1971); United States Court of Appeals for the District of Columbia Circuit (1971); Baltimore City Bar Association; American Bar Association **Marquis Who's Who Honors:** Distinguished Humanitarian (2017); Who's Who Lifetime Achievement Award (2017); Who's Who in the East (2015-2016, 1997-1998); Who's Who in Finance and Business (2004-2007); Who's Who in American Education (2004-2007, 1992-1993); Who's Who In Finance and Industry (2001-2003); Who's Who in America (1997-2016); Who's Who of Emerging Leaders in America (1993-1994, 1987-1988); Who's Who in the World (1987-2018); Who's Who in American Law (1985-2016) **Hobbies:** Traveling; Reading; Golf; Fishing **Shipping Address:** 1211 Saint Paul St, Schochor, Federico & Staton, P.A., Baltimore, MD, 21202 **Website:** https://www.sfspa.com/attorney/jonathan-schochor

Edison E. Scholes

Title: Military Officer **Industry:** Military & Defense Services **Date of Birth:** 08/16/1939 **Place of Birth:** McCaysville **State:** GA **Parents:** Alvin L. Scholes; Marie (Plemmons) Scholes **Marital Status:** Married **Spouse Name:** Elva E. (Bussey) Scholes (6/4/1961) **Children:** Juana Kimberly; Tracy Michele Scholes-Heller; Brigadier Gen. Michael Lee **Education:** Postgraduate Coursework, Harvard Defense Policy Seminar (1991); Postgraduate Coursework, Army War College (1980); MS in Operations Research, Naval Postgraduate School (1970); BS in Physics, University of North Georgia, Cum Laude (1961) **Career:** Private Contractor, Support of Military Activities in Middle East (2002-Present); Program General Manager, Saudi Arabia National Guard Modernization Program, Vinnell, Arabia (1996-2002); Deputy Commander, Allied Land Forces, Southeast Europe, North Atlantic Treaty Organization (1993-1995) **Civic:** Speaker, Daughters of the American Revolution, Various Veteran Organizations **Military Service:** Deputy Commanding General, XVIII Airborne Corps, U.S. Army, Fort Bragg, NC (1991-1993); Major General, U.S. Army (1991); Deputy Commanding General, XVIII Airborne Corps, Operation Desert Shield/Desert Storm, U.S. Army, Saudi Arabia, Iraq (1990-1991); Chief of Staff, Joint Task Force-South, Operation Just Cause, U.S. Army (1989-1990); Chief of Staff, XVIII Airborne Corps, U.S. Army, Fort Bragg, NC (1989-1990); Assistant Division Commander, 82nd Airborne Division, U.S. Army, Fort Bragg, NC (1988-1989); Deputy Commanding General Chief of Staff, Third U.S. Army/U.S. Army Central Command, U.S. Army, Fort McPherson, GA (1986-1988); Commander, First Infantry Training Brigade, U.S. Army Infantry Training Center, United States Army, Fort Benning, GA (1983-1985); Commander, Second Training Battalion, School Brigade, U.S. Army Infantry School, U.S. Army, Fort Benning, GA (1978-1979); Commander, First Battalion, Twenty-Third Infantry, Second Infantry Division, U.S. Army, Republic of Korea (1976-1977); Senior Adviser, I Corps., Ranger, U.S. Army, Vietnam (1970-1971); Commander, Company D, Second Battalion, Eighth Cavalry, First Cavalry Division, U.S. Army, Republic of Vietnam (1967-1968); Detachment Commander, 10th Special Forces Group, U.S. Army, Europe (1963-1966); Commissioned Second Lieutenant, U.S. Army (1961) **Creative Works:** Reading; Camping; Fishing **Awards:** Georgia Military Veterans' Hall of Fame (2015); Certificate of Honor for Service in Vietnam, Governor Nathan Deal, Commissioner of Veteran's Services (2015); Proclamation Certificate, Outstanding Georgia Citizen, Georgia Secretary of State (2015); Medal of Honor, Daughters of the American Revolution (2009); Inducted, Army Ranger Hall of Fame (2007); Inducted, University of North Georgia Hall of Fame (2003); Decorated, Department of Defense Distinguished Service Medal; Army Distinguished Service Medal with Oak Leaf Cluster; Silver Star; Legion Of Merit with Oak Leaf Cluster; Bronze Star with V Device and Four Oak Leaf Clusters; Purple Heart with Oak Leaf Cluster; 6 Air Medals; Army Commendation Medal with V Device and Oak Leaf Cluster; Armed Forces Expeditionary Medal; Combat Infantryman Badge; Expert Infantry Badge; Cross of Gallantry with Silver and Bronze Stars and Palm, Republic Of Vietnam; Various National and International Awards **Membership:** 82nd Airborne Division Association; Special Forces Association; U.S. Army Ranger Association; Special Operations Association; XVIII Airborne Corps Association **Marquis Who's Who Honors:** Albert Nelson Marquis Lifetime Achievement Award (2017) **What do you consider to be the highlight of your career:** A highlight of Maj. Gen. Scholes' career was his biggest mission, which involved positioning and preparing 300,000 troops in Saudi Arabia for Operation Desert Shield/Storm. **Hobbies:** Reading; Camping; Fishing **Religion:** Baptist **Shipping Address:** 1909 Townsend Boulevard, Franklin, TN, 37064

Joyce K. Schroeder

Title: Mathematician (Retired) **Industry:** Business Management/Business Services **Date of Birth:** 04/01/1951 **Place of Birth:** Moline **State:** IL **Parents:** Reinhold J. Schroeder; Miriam May Schroeder **Education:** MA in Operations Research, University of Illinois Springfield (1978); BS in Mathematics, University of Illinois Urbana-Champaign (1973) **Career:** Manager, Crash Information Section, Illinois Department of Transportation (2010-2012); Manager of Crash Studies and Investigation, Illinois Department of Transportation (1992-2010); Manager, Safety Project Evaluation, Illinois Department of Transportation (1983-1992); Team Leader, Fatality Analysis Reporting System, Illinois Department of Transportation (1980-1983); Data Analyst, Illinois Department of Transportation (1978-1980); Operations Research Analyst, Illinois Department of Transportation (1976-1978); Computer Programmer, Springfield, IL (1974-1975); Underwriter, Springfield, IL (1973-1976) **Career Related:** Member, Safety Engineering Technical Advisory Group, Illinois Center for Transportation (2005-2012); Member, Illinois Traffic Records Coordinating Committee, State of Illinois (2004-2012); Member, Illinois Construction/Work Zone Safety Committee, State of Illinois (2003-2012); Member, Illinois Traffic Safety Information Systems Council, State of Illinois (1993-1996); Staff Member, Illinois Driving Under the Influence Advisory Council, State of Illinois (1989-1992); Staff Member, Governor's Task Force on Occupant Protection, State of Illinois (1988-1990); Systems Engineering Delegate to the People's Republic of China, China Association for Science and Technology (1986); Staff Member, Driving While Intoxicated Task Force, State of Illinois (1983-1986); Member, Illinois Traffic Safety Leaders; Member, Illinois Association of Highway Engineers **Civic:** Manager, Usher Corps, Sangamon Auditorium Volunteer Association, University of Illinois Springfield (2009-Present); Member, Sangamon Auditorium Volunteer Association, University of Illinois Springfield (2007-Present); Recording Secretary, Sangamon Auditorium Volunteer Association, University of Illinois Springfield (2009-2013); Member, Board of Directors, Sangamon Auditorium Volunteer Association, University of Illinois Springfield (2009-2013); News Editor, Springfield Lincoln Land Lions Club (1995-2014); Leaderboard Co-Chair, Rail Classic, Ladies Professional Golf Association (1983-1987); Volunteer, Animal Protective League, Springfield, IL **Awards:** Named, Manager of the Year, Sangamon Auditorium Volunteer Association, University of Illinois Springfield (2015); Inductee, William W. Root Society, University of Illinois College of Medicine (2014); Recipient, Safety Champion Award, National Highway Traffic Safety Administration, United States Department of Transportation (2012); Recipient, President's Volunteer Service Award, United States White House (2011); Recipient, Lifetime Service Award, Lions of Illinois Foundation (2011); Inductee, President's Council, University of Illinois (2004); Distinguished Service Award, Lions of Illinois Foundation (2003); Foundation Fellow Laureate, Lions of Illinois Foundation (2002); Foundation Fellow, Lions of Illinois Foundation (1995); 100% District Governor's Award, Lions Clubs International (1993); Melvin Jones Fellow, Lions Clubs International (1993); Honoree, Ambassador of Goodwill, Lions of Illinois Foundation (1993); Listed Among Top 30 District Governors in World for Membership Growth, Lions Clubs International (1993); Achievement Award, Lions Clubs International Foundation (1993) **Membership:** Board of Directors, Rochester Lions Club (2015-Present); Rochester Lions Club (2014-Present); Past District Governors of Illinois, Lions Club (1993-Present); Trustee, Lions of Illinois Endowment Fund (2013-2015); Trustee, Lions of Illinois Foundation (2013-2015); Lifetime Member, Lions Clubs International (2009); Secretary-Treasurer, Springfield Lincoln Land Lions Club (2008-2014); Lifetime Charter Member, Abraham Lincoln Presidential Library Foundation (2007); Treasurer, North American Conference of Lions Foundations, Inc. (2005-2013); Board of Directors, North American Conference of Lions Foundations, Inc. (2004-2013); Chairman, Policy Ad Hoc Committee, Lions of Illinois Foundation (2002-2015); Treasurer, Springfield Lincoln Land Lions Club (2002-2008); Annual Conference Steering Committee, North American Conference of Lions Foundations, Inc. (2001-2003); Policy Ad Hoc Committee, Lions of Illinois Foundation (1999-2015); District Coordinator, Memorials and Endowments, Lions of Illinois Endowment Fund (1999-2013); Trustee, Lions of Illinois Endowment Fund (1998-1999); President, Lions of Illinois Foundation (1998-1999); Chairman, Long Range Planning Committee, Lions of Illinois Foundation (1997-2015) **Marquis Who's Who Honors:** Worldwide Lifetime Achievement Award (2016) **Hobbies:** Traveling; Music; Sports **Shipping Address:** 3704 Buckeye Drive, Springfield, IL, 62712-8948

John Nielsen Schulian

Title: Sports Columnist, Screenwriter, Author **Industry:** Writing and Editing **Date of Birth:** 01/31/1945 **Place of Birth:** Los Angeles **State:** CA **Parents:** John Schulian; Estella Katherine (Nielsen) Schulian **Marital Status:** Divorced **Spouse Name:** Paula Lynn Ellis (8/20/1977, Divorced 10/1984) **Education:** MS, Northwestern University (1968); BA, University of Utah (1967) **Career:** Author, Novel, "A Better Goodbye" (2015); Editor, Nonfiction Anthology, "Football" (2014); Co-Editor, Nonfiction Anthology, "At the Fights" (2011); Co-Editor, Anthology, "The Fighter Still Remains" (2011); Author, Nonfiction Collection, "Sometimes They Even Shook Your Hand" (2011); Editor, Nonfiction Anthology, "The John Lardner Reader" (2010); Author, Nonfiction Collection, "Twilight of the Long-ball Gods" (2005); Co-Executive Producer, TV Series, "Tremors," Universal City, CA (2002-2003); Culture Columnist, MSNBC.com, NBC Universal (2001-2002); Writer Producer, TV Series, "The Outer Limits," Vancouver, Canada (2000-2001); Consulting Producer, TV Series, JAG, Universal City, CA (1999-2000); Co-Executive Producer, TV Series, "Lawless," Culver City, CA (1996-1997); Associate Producer, Documentary, "Ben Johnson: Third Cowboy on the Right" (1996); Co-Creator, "Xena: Warrior Princess," Universal City, CA (1995); Co-Executive Producer, TV Series, "Hercules," Universal City, CA (1994-2000); Creative Consultant, TV Series, "The Untouchables," Los Angeles, CA (1992-1993); Co-Executive Producer, TV Series, "Reasonable Doubts," Burbank, CA (1991-1992); Supervising Producer, "Midnight Caller," Burbank, CA (1990-1991); Co-Producer, TV Series, "Midnight Caller," Burbank, CA (1989-1990); Executive Story Editor, TV Series, "Wiseguy," Hollywood, CA (1988-1989); Story Editor, The Slap Maxwell Story, North Hollywood, CA (1987-1988); Story Editor, Miami Vice, Universal City, CA (1987); Staff Writer, Miami Vice, Universal City, CA (1986-1987); Sports Columnist, Philadelphia Media Network, LLC (1984-1986); Author, Nonfiction Collection, "Writers' Fighters & Other Sweet Scientists" (1983); Sports Columnist, Chicago Sun-Times (1978-1984); Sports Columnist, Chicago Daily News (1977-1978); Sportswriter, The Washington Post (1975-1977); Reporter, The Baltimore Evening Sun (1970-1975); Copy Editor, The Salt Lake Tribune (1968); Editor, "The Great American Sports Page" **Career Related:** Professional-in-Residence, University of Utah (2004); Special Contributor, Sports Illustrated, Time Inc. (1998-2013) **Military Service:** U.S. Army (1968-1970) **Creative Works:** Writer, Esquire Magazine, Hearst Communications, Inc. (2016); Writer, Deadspin, Gizmodo Media Group (2016); Author, "A Better Goodbye" (2015); Editor, "Football" (2014); Author, "Sometimes They Even Shook Your Hand" (2011); Editor, "The John Lardner Reader" (2010); Co-Editor, "At the Fights" (2010); Co-Editor, "Fighter Still Remains" (2010); Author, "Twilight of the Long Ball Gods" (2005); Co-Executive Producer, "Tremors" (2002-2003); Writer, "The Outer Limits" (2000-2001); Producer, "The Outer Limits" (2000-2001); Consulting Producer, "Judge Advocate General" (1999-2000); Co-Executive Producer, "Lawless" (1996-1997); Associate Producer, "Ben Johnson: Third Cowboy on the Right" (1996); Co-Creator, "Xena: Warrior Princess" (1995); Co-Executive Producer, "Hercules" (1994-1996); Contributor, "The Best American Sports Writing" (1994); Creative Consultant, "The Untouchables" (1992-1993); Co-Executive Producer, "Reasonable Doubts" (1991-1992); Supervising Producer, "Midnight Caller" (1990-1991); Co-Producer, "Midnight Caller" (1989-1990); Consultant, "The Reader's Catalog" (1989); Executive Story Editor, "Wiseguy" (1988-1989); Story Editor, "The Slap Maxwell Story" (1987-1988); Story Editor, "Miami Vice" (1987); Staff Writer, "Miami Vice" (1986-1987); Commentator, NPR (1985-1986); Author, "Writers' Fighters and Other Sweet Scientists" (1983); Contributor, "Best Sports Stories" (1982-1986); Contributing Editor, "Panorama Magazine" (1980-1981); Contributor, "Best Sports Stories" (1975-1979); Syndicated Columnist, "UP Syndicate"; Author, Short Stories; Author, Short Stories, Thuglit; Author, Short Stories, Prague Revue; Contributor, Articles, The New York Times Company; Contributor, Articles to Playboy Enterprises; Contributor, Articles, Gentlemen's Quarterly; Contributor, Articles, Oxford American Magazine; Contributor, Articles, The National; Contributor, Articles, Los Angeles Times; Contributor, Reviews, Wall Street Journal **Awards:** PEN/ESPN Lifetime Achievement Award for Literary Sports Writing, PEN America (2016); Nat Fleischer Excellence in Boxing Journalism Award, Boxing Writers Association of America (1985); Best Sports Stories Award (1983-1984); Column Writing Award, Associated Press Sports Editors (1982); National Headliners Club Award (1980); Column Writing Award, Associated Press Sports Editors (1979) **Membership:** Writers Guild of America; The Phi Beta Kappa Society; Boxing Writers Association of America; Pacific Coast League Historical Society; The Baseball Reliquary **Marquis Who's Who Honors:** Albert Nelson Marquis Lifetime Achievement Award (2017) **Shipping Address:** 1709 Putney Road, Pasadena, CA, 91103

Jane Schuyler

Title: Fine Arts Educator **Industry:** Financial Services **Date of Birth:** 11/02/1943 **Place of Birth:** Flushing **State:** NY **Parents:** Frank James Schuyler; Helen (Oberhofer) Schuyler **Education:** PhD, Columbia University (1972); MA, Hunter College (1967); BA, Queens College (1965) **Career:** Professor Emerita of Fine Arts, York College (1996-Present); Professor, City University of New York (1993-1996); Associate Professor, City University of New York (1988-1992); Assistant Professor, York College, City University of New York, Jamaica, NY (1973-1987); Associate Professor, C.W. Post College, Long Island University, Greenvale, NY (1971-1973); Assistant Professor, Art History, Montclair State College, Upper Montclair, NJ (1970) **Career Related:** Director, Hampton Court Cooperative (1973-Present); Adjunct Associate Professor, Long Island University (1977-1978) **Civic:** President, United Community of Democrats, Jackson Heights, NY (1987-1989); International Fine Arts Committee, Women's Art Festival (1974-1976) **Creative Works:** Author, "Michelangelo's Serpent with Two Tails" (1995); Author, "Tiffany" (1992); Author, "Briggs Publishes Book on Tiffany Glass" (1992); Author, "The Female Holy Spirit (Shekhinah) in Michelangelo's Creation of Adam" (1987); Author, "The Malleus Maleficarum and Baldung's Witches' Sabbath" (1987); Author, "The Left Side of God: A Reflection of Cabala in Michelangelo's Genesis Scenes" (1986); Author, "Death Masks in Quattrocento Florence" (1986); Author, "Emperor John VIII Paleologus: Donatello's First Portrait Bust of a Living Person" (1986); Author, "La Fortuna di Paestum e la Memoria Moderna del Dorico" (1986); Author, "Dragons: East and West" (1986); Author, "The Cabalistic Doctrine of the Deity Reflected in Two Genesis Scenes of Michelangelo's Sistine Ceiling" (1985); Author; "Influences of Jewish Mysticism on Michelangelo's Sistine Ceiling" (1983); Contributor, Book Review, "James Beck's 'Italian Renaissance Painting'" (1982); Author, "The Occult and Art" (1978); Author, "Florentine Busts: Sculpted Portraiture in the Fifteenth Century" (1976); Contributor, Articles to Professional Journals **Awards:** Recipient, Research Award, Professional Staff Congress/CUNY (1990-1991); Summer Travel and Research Grantee, Columbia University (1969) **Membership:** President, United Community Democrats of Jackson Heights (1987-1989); President, Association of Neighborhood Democrats; Renaissance Society of America; College Art Association; National Trust Historical Preservation **Marquis Who's Who Honors:** Albert Nelson Marquis Lifetime Achievement Award (2017) **Why did you become involved in your profession or industry:** Dr. Schuyler became involved in her profession because her mother encouraged and motivated her through her work ethic. Her mother was the first in the family to graduate from college. Dr. Schuyler was the first in the family to earn a PhD degree. **What do you consider to be the highlight of your career:** The highlight of her career was to have a book published, as well as two articles in Wallace's "Michelangelo: Selected Studies in English." **Where will you be in five years:** In the next five years, Dr. Schuyler will be staying healthy and vigorous after surviving ovarian cancer. **Religion:** Roman Catholic **Shipping Address:** 3516 79th Street, Apt. 41, Jackson Heights, NY, 11372

Marshall Zane Schwartz

Title: Vice Chairman **Industry:** Medicine & Health Care **Company Name:** Drexel University College of Medicine **Date of Birth:** 09/01/1945 **Place of Birth:** Minneapolis **State:** MN **Parents:** Sidney Shay Schwartz; Peggy Belle (Lieberman) Schwartz **Marital Status:** Married **Spouse Name:** Michele Carroll Walker (10/16/1971) **Children:** Lisa; Jeffrey **Education:** Chief Resident in Pediatric Surgery, Boston Children's Hospital, Harvard Medical School (1977-1978); Senior Resident in Pediatric Surgery, Boston Children's Hospital, Harvard Medical School (1976-1977); Chief Resident in General Surgery, University of Minnesota (1975-1976); Research Fellow, University of Minnesota (1974-1975); Junior Resident in Pediatric Surgery, Boston Children's Hospital, Harvard Medical School (1973-1974); Resident in General Surgery, University of Minnesota (1971-1973); Intern, New York Hospital-Cornell Medical Center (1970-1971); MD, School of Medicine, University of Minnesota Medical School (1970); BS, College of Medical Science, University of Minnesota (1968) **Certifications:** Medical License, State of New Jersey (1998-2019); Medical License, Commonwealth of Pennsylvania (1996-2020); Medical License, State of California (1973-2017); Diplomate, American Board of Surgery, Inc.; Diplomate, American Board of Pediatric Surgery **Career:** Professor of Surgery and Pediatrics, School of Medicine, Drexel University (2004-Present); Surgeon-in-Chief, St. Christopher's Hospital for Children, (2005-Present); Chief, Division of Pediatric Surgery, St. Christopher's Hospital for Children (2005-Present); Senior Scholar, College of Population Health, Thomas Jefferson University (2005-Present); Vice Chairman, Department of Surgery, Drexel University College of Medicine (2003-Present); Professor, Department of Surgery and Urology, Wake Forest University School of Medicine (2017-Present); Member, Board Regents, American College of Surgeons (2009-Present); Vice Chairman, Board of Regents (2017-2018); Professor of Surgery, Temple University (2008-2016); Member, Surgery Residency Review Committee, Accreditation Council for Graduate Medical Education (2009-2015); Member, Board of Directors, Philadelphia Academy of Surgery (2005-2008); Professor of Surgery and Pediatrics, Thomas Jefferson University (1996-2004); Vice Chairman, Department of Surgery, Thomas Jefferson University (1996-2003); Vice Chairman, Department of Surgery, Dupont Hospital for Children (1996-2003); Associate Medical Director, Dupont Hospital for Children (1996-2001); Surgeon-in-Chief, Children's National Health System, Washington, DC (1992-1996); Chairman, Department of Surgery, Children's National Medical Center (1992-1996); Professor of Surgery and Pediatrics, The School of Medicine & Health Sciences, The George Washington University (1992-1996); Chairman, Faculty Executive Committee, School of Medicine, University of California, Davis (1991-1992); Professor of Surgery and Pediatrics, University of California, Davis (1986-1992); Chief of Pediatric Surgery, University of California, Davis (1983-1992) **Civic:** Member, Board of Directors, Gift of Life (2005-Present); Chairman, Health Policy Advisory Council, American College of Surgeons (2003-Present); Member, Board of Directors, American Pediatric Surgical Association Foundation(2002-2015); Member, Board of Directors, St. Christopher's Foundation for Children (2007-2014); Chairman, Medical Advisory Board, Gift of Life (2009-2011) **Creative Works:** Editorial Board Member, "Journal of the American College of Surgeons" (1999-Present); Editorial Board Member, "Journal of Pediatric Surgery" (1988-Present) **Awards:** Named, Alumnus of the Year, Department of Surgery, University of Minnesota (2017); Coe Medal for Distinctive Contributions to Pediatric Surgery, Pacific Association of Pediatric Surgeons (2014); Elected Honorary Fellow, Royal College of Surgeons of England (2013); President, American Pediatric Surgical Association (2011-2012); Research Award, American Society of Colon and Rectal Surgeons (2000); ASPEN-Rhodes Research Award (1999); Exemplary Performance Award, Helicopter Services Programmatic Subcommittee, University of California, Davis (1985); James W. McLaughlin Fund Award, University of Texas (1983) **Membership:** Member, Board of Regents, American College of Surgeons (2009-Present); Chairman, Health Policy and Advocacy Group (2016-2017); Vice Chairman, Board of Regents, American College of Surgeons (2017); President-Elect, President, American Pediatric Surgical Association (2011-2012); President, American Pediatric Surgical Association (2010-2011); Chairman, Program Committee, American Surgical Association (2007-2009); Chair, Advisory Council Chairs, American College of Surgeons (2005-2008); Chairman, Advisory Council for Pediatric Surgery, American College of Surgeons (2004-2008); Executive Committee, International Society of Surgery (2004-2007); Board of Governors, The American Pediatric Surgical Association (2001-2004); President, Pacific Association of Pediatric Surgeons (1997-1998) **Marquis Who's Who Honors:** Albert Nelson Marquis Lifetime Achievement Award (2017) **Religion:** Jewish **Business Address:** 160 E Erie Ave, 160 E Erie Ave, Philadelphia, PA, 19134 **Shipping Address:** 630 Black Rock Rd, Bryn Mawr, PA, 19010

William Schwartz

Title: Lawyer, Educator **Industry:** Law and Legal Services **Date of Birth:** 05/06/1933 **Place of Birth:** Providence **State:** RI **Year of Passing:** 2018-08-17 **Parents:** Morris Victor Schwartz; Martha (Glassman) Schwartz **Marital Status:** Married **Spouse Name:** Bernice Konigsberg (1/13/1957) **Children:** Alan Gershon; Robin Libby **Education:** LHD, Yeshiva University, With Honors (1998); LHD, Hebrew College, With Honors (1996); MA, Boston University (1960); Postgraduate Coursework, Harvard Law School (1955-1956); JD, Boston University, Magna Cum Laude (1955); AA, Boston University (1952) **Career:** University Professor, Yeshiva University (1991-Present); Of Counsel, Cadwalader, Wickersham & Taft LLP, New York, NY (1988-Present); Of Counsel, Cadwalader, Wickersham & Taft LLP, Washington, DC (1988-Present); Of Counsel, Cadwalader, Wickersham & Taft LLP, Charlotte, NC (1988-Present); Of Counsel, Cadwalader, Wickersham & Taft LLP, Houston, TX (1988-Present); Of Counsel, Cadwalader, Wickersham & Taft LLP, London, England (1988-Present); Of Counsel, Cadwalader, Wickersham & Taft LLP, Beijing, China (1988-Present); Of Counsel, Cadwalader, Wickersham & Taft LLP, Brussels, Belgium (1988-Present); Director, Massachusetts Probate Study (1976-Present); Vice President for Academy Affairs, Yeshiva University (1993-1998); Chief Academy Officer, Yeshiva University (1993-1998); Chairman, Special Committee on Police Procedures, City of Boston, MA (1991); Director, Center for Estate Planning, Boston University (1988-1991); Professor of Law, Boston University (1955-1991); Chairman, Special Committee on Police Procedures, City of Boston, MA (1989); Faculty Member, Frances Glessner Lee Institute (1988); Faculty Member, Harvard Medical School (1988); Faculty Member, National College of Probate Judges (1988); Dean, School of Law, Boston University (1980-1988); Of Counsel, Swartz & Swartz, P.C. (1973-1980); Faculty Member, Frances Glessner Lee Institute (1977-1979); Faculty Member, Harvard Medical School (1977-1979); Faculty Member, National College of Probate Judges (1977-1979); Roscoe Pound Professor of Law, Boston University (1970-1973) **Career Related:** Chairman, Board of Directors, UST Corp. (1993-2000); Member, Legal Advisory Board, New York Stock Exchange, Intercontinental Exchange, Inc.; Chairman, Governance and Nominating Committee, Viacom Inc.; Chairman, Compensation Committee, Viacom Inc. **Civic:** Honorary Chairman, Office of Public Information, United Nations (2014-Present); Honorary President, Fifth Avenue Synagogue, New York, NY (2001-President); Trustee, Hebrew College (1975-Present); Examiner of Titles, Commonwealth of Massachusetts (1964-Present); Chairman of the Board, Office of Public Information, United Nations (2010-2013); President, Fifth Avenue Synagogue, New York, NY (1997-2001); Chairman, City of Boston Committee Police Procedures (1991); Chairman, City of Boston Committee Police Procedures (1989); Special Counsel, Massachusetts Bay Transportation Authority (1979); Chairman, Legal Advisory Panel, National Commission Medical Practice (1972-1973) **Creative Works:** Property Editor, "Annual Survey of Massachusetts Law" (1960-Present); Author, "Revocable Inter-Vivos: Avoid Probate but Not Substantive Wills Rules" (2014); Author, "Strategies for Trusts and Estate in New York" (2014); Author, "Modifying Irrevocable Truths: Proceed but with Caution" (2013); Author, "The Art of Effectuating a Donor's Wishes" (2005); Author, "Amending Irrevocable Trusts" (2003); Author, "Does Time Heal All Wrongs?" (1999); Author, "Jewish Law and Contemporary Dilemmas and Problems" (1997); Author, "The Convention Method: The Unused Amending Superhighway" (1995); Author, "Estate Planning and Living Trusts" (1990); Author, "Future Interests and Estate Planning" (1986); Author, "Future Interests and Estate Planning" (1981); Author, "Massachusetts Pleading and Practice," Volumes 1-7 (1974-1980); Author, "Future Interests and Estate Planning" (1977); Author, "New Vistas in Litigation" (1973); Author, "Civil Trial Practice Manual" (1972); Author, "Comparative Negligence" (1970); Author, "A Products Liability Primer" (1970); Author, "Future Interests and Estate Planning" (1965); Editor, Law Review, Boston University (1954-1955) **Awards:** Judge Harold Tyler Award (2015); Distinguished Service Award, The Religious Zionists of America (1977); Homer Albers Award, Boston University (1955); John Ordronaux Prize (1955); William W. Treat Award; William O. Douglas Award **Membership:** Fellow, American College of Probate Counsel; ABA; The American Law Institute; Chairman, Task Force Tort Liability, Massachusetts Bar Association; New York State Bar Association; Association of the Bar of the City of New York; Honorary Member, National College of Probate Judges; Phi Beta Kappa **Bar Admissions:** New York State Bar Association (1989); State Bar of Massachusetts (1962); The District of Columbia Bar (1956) **Marquis Who's Who Honors:** Albert Nelson Marquis Lifetime Achievement Award (2017) **Shipping Address:** 860 5th Ave., Apt 4F, New York, NY, 10065

Anthony Walter Schweiger

Title: Managing Principal, CEO **Industry:** Business Management/Business Services **Company Name:** The Tomorrow Group, LLC **Date of Birth:** 11/25/1941 **Place of Birth:** Philadelphia **State:** PA **Parents:** Jerome Walter Schweiger; Hannah Schweiger **Marital Status:** Married **Spouse Name:** Katherine M. Kratt (1984); Sally Jane Grossman (8/4/1964, Divorced 1972) **Children:** David Michael; Suzanne Leigh; Jonathan Landau; Philip Miguel **Education:** MBA, Temple University (1968); BS in Economics, University of Pennsylvania (1964) **Certifications:** Master Certified Mortgage Banker (1988) **Career:** Secretary, Delaware Valley Industrial Resource Center (2015-Present); Director, United Financial Mortgage Corporation (2004-2006); Principal, E-brilliance LLC (2001-2010); Independent Director, Paragon Technologies Inc. (2001-2008); Acting Chief Operating Officer, WineAccess (1998-1999); Investor, Director, Input Technologies LLC (1998-1990); Acting Chief Executive Officer, Care Systems (1995-1996); Managing Director, Stafford Companies (1994-1995); Executive Vice President, First Advantage Mortgage Corporation (1993-1994); Director, Radian Group Inc. (1992-2012); Co-Founder, President, CEO, Executive Vice President, COO, Meridian Mortgage Corporation (1992); Co-Founder, President, CEO, Executive Vice President, COO, Meridian Mortgage Corporation (1987); Co-Founder, President, CEO, Executive Vice President, COO, Meridian Mortgage Corporation (1984); Director, Governance Chair, Secretary, Director, Delaware Valley Industrial Resource Center; Audit and Governance Chairman, Director, United Financial Mortgage Corporation; Director, Audit Chairman, Paragon Technologies, Inc; Managing Principal, CEO, Tomorrow Group LLC; Managing Director, RML Advisors **Career Related:** Board of Directors, Radian Group Inc. (1992-2012) **Civic:** Secretary, Board of Directors, Governance Chair, Delaware Valley Industrial Resource Center (2008-Present); Chairman, ACHIEVEability (2008-2012); Chairman, Philadelphia Committee to End Homelessness (2005-2007); General Chairman, Jaycee Football Classic (1969); Assistant Secretary, New Jersey Jaycees (1969); Jewish Federation of Greater Philadelphia **Creative Works:** Contributor, Articles, Mortgage Banking Industry Publications **Awards:** Ernst P. Schumacher Award, Mortgage Bankers of America **Membership:** Board of Governors, MBA America (1988-Present); President, White Manor Country Club (1991-1992); Board of Directors, New Jersey Mortgage Bankers Association (1970-1975); Free Masons **Marquis Who's Who Honors:** Albert Nelson Marquis Lifetime Achievement Award (2017) **To what do you attribute your success:** Mr. Schweiger attributes his success to his work ethic, and his hands-on approach to every aspect of his business. **Why did you become involved in your profession or industry:** Mr. Schweiger grew up in mortgage banking and real estate businesses. **What do you consider to be the highlight of your career:** The highlight of Mr. Schweiger's career has been serving as the governance chair of Radian Group for 20 years. **Where will you be in five years:** In five years, Mr. Schweiger will be attending the Oscars for his novel, which was made into a movie. **Hobbies:** Golf; Furniture refinishing; Gardening **Political Affiliations:** Republican **Religion:** Jewish **Shipping Address:** 3803 Baldwin Lane, Newtown Square, PA, 19073 **Website:** http://www.thetomorrowgroup.com

David Willson Scofield

Title: Lawyer **Industry:** Law and Legal Services **Company Name:** Peters Scofield A Professional Corporation **Date of Birth:** 10/17/1957 **Place of Birth:** Hartford **State:** CT **Parents:** Leslie Willson Scofield; Daphne Winifred (York) Scofield **Education:** JD, University of Utah (1983); AB in Biological Science, Cornell University (1979) **Career:** Founding Partner, Peters Scofield A Professional Corporation, Salt Lake City, UT (2004-Present); President, Parsons, Kinghorn, Peters, Salt Lake City, UT (1996-1997); Founding Partner, Parsons, Kinghorn, Peters, Salt Lake City, UT (1992-2004); Partner, Callister, Duncan & Nebeker, Salt Lake City, UT (1989-1992); Associate, Callister, Duncan & Nebeker, Salt Lake City, UT (1987-1989); Associate, Parsons & Crowther, Salt Lake City, UT (1983-1987) **Career Related:** Member, Advisory Committee on Professionalism, Utah Supreme Court (2003-Present); Member, Advisory Committee on Utah Rules of Civil Procedure (2002-2014) **Civic:** Member, Utah Supreme Court Advisory Committee, Utah Rules of Civil Procedure (2003-Present); Chairman, Cultivation Committee (1995-1996); Foundation Board, Westminster College (1994-1996) **Creative Works:** Author, "Trial Handbook for Utah Lawyers" (1994); Member, Utah Law Review (1981-1983); Contributor, Annual Supplement to Trial Handbook, Articles to Legal Journals **Awards:** Recipient, Outstanding Young Men of America (1986) **Membership:** ABA; Association of Trial Lawyers of America; Utah Trial Lawyers Association; Salt Lake County Foundation Bar Association; Outstanding Young Men of America; Zeta Psi **Bar Admissions:** United States District Court of Utah; Utah State Bar; United States Court of Appeals for the Tenth Circuit (1990); United States District Court of Hawaii (1997); United States District Courts for the Eastern and Western Districts of Arkansas (2013); United States District Courts for the District of Colorado (2010); Eastern District of Michigan (2010); Western District of Oklahoma (2010); Northern District of Oklahoma (2017); United States Court of Appeals for the Ninth Circuit (1995); Supreme Court of the United States (1996); United States Court of Federal Claims (1997) **Marquis Who's Who Honors:** Albert Nelson Marquis Lifetime Achievement Award (2017) **Hobbies:** American history; Writing; Sports; Scuba diving **Religion:** Congregationalist **Shipping Address:** 7933 Majestic Ridge Dr., Cottonwood Heights, UT, 84121

Gordon L. Scofield, PhD

Title: Mechanical Engineer (Retired) **Industry:** Engineering **Date of Birth:** 09/29/1925 **Place of Birth:** Huron **State:** SD **Parents:** Perry Lee Scofield; Zella (Reese) Scofield **Marital Status:** Married **Spouse Name:** Nancy Lou Cooney (12/27/1947) **Children:** Cathy Lynn; Terrence Lee **Education:** PhD in Mechanical Engineering, The University of Oklahoma (1968); MME, University of Missouri, Rolla, MO (Now Missouri University of Science and Technology) (1949); Bachelor's Degree in Mechanical Engineering, Purdue University (1946) **Career:** Dean of Engineering, Vice President, South Dakota School of Mines and Technology (1984-1986); President, South Dakota Mines Foundation (1982-1990); Distinguished Professor of Mechanical Engineering, South Dakota School of Mines and Technology (1981-1988); Assistant Vice President for Academy Affairs, South Dakota School of Mines and Technology (1981-1983); Head, Mechanical Engineering Department, Professor of Mechanical Engineering, Michigan Technological University (1969-1980); Professor, Associate Professor, Assistant Professor, University of Missouri (1947-1969); Graduate Assistant, University of Missouri (1947-1969); Instructor of Mechanical Engineering, South Dakota State University (1946-1947) **Career Related:** Member, Board of Directors, Accreditation Board for Engineering and Technology, Inc. (1994-2000); Consultant, Naval Air Weapons Station China Lake, U.S. Navy (1956-1971) **Military Service:** Naval Reserve, U.S. Navy (1943-1946) **Awards:** Excellence in Engineering Education Award, SAE International (1999); Alumni Achievement Award, University of Missouri, Rolla, MO (Now Missouri University of Science and Technology) (1975); Science Faculty Fellow, National Science Foundation (1966-1967) **Membership:** President, SAE International (1977); The American Society of Mechanical Engineers; American Society for Engineering Education; Sigma Xi, The Scientific Research Honor Society; The Tau Beta Pi Association, Inc.; Pi Tau Sigma, South Dakota State University; The Honor Society of Phi Kappa Phi **Business Address:** 3213 W Main St., Ste 314, Rapid City, SD, 57702

Gerald Wesley Scott

Title: Ambassador **Industry:** Military & Defense Services **Date of Birth:** 08/07/1940 **Place of Birth:** Oklahoma City **State:** OK **Education:** MA, Naval War College (2000); MA, Johns Hopkins University (1969); BS in Foreign Service, Georgetown University (1962) **Career:** Senior Advisor, United States Delegation to the United Nations General Assembly (2001-2015); Retired (2000); State Department Representative, Naval War College, Newport, RI (1998-2000); Ambassador, Banjul, Gambia (1996-1998); Deputy Chief, Mission, American Embassy, Kinshasa, Republic of the Congo (1993-1995); Political Counselor, American Embassy, Nairobi, Kenya (1992-1993); Political Counselor, American Embassy, Kinshasa, Zaire (1988-1992); Deputy Chief, Mission, American Embassy, Mbabane, Swaziland (1985-1988); Advisor, Political and Security Affairs, United States Mission to United Nations, New York, NY (1983-1985); Political Officer, American Embassy, Rome, Italy (1980-1983); Vice Consul, American Consulate General, Danang, Vietnam (1973-1975); Commissioned Foreign Service Officer (1969) **Military Service:** Lieutenant, U.S. Naval Reserve (1962-1967) **Awards:** William R. Rivkin Award, American Foreign Service Association (1992) **Membership:** American Foreign Service Association; Sovereign Military Order of Malta; Sons of the American Revolution; General Society Sons of the Revolution; The Lotos Club; The Army and Navy Club; Venerable Order of St. John of Jerusalem; The Commonwealth Club **Marquis Who's Who Honors:** Albert Nelson Marquis Lifetime Achievement Award (2017) **Religion:** Roman Catholic **Shipping Address:** 612 W Franklin Street, Richmond, VA, 23220

T. Gordon Scott, PhD

Title: Chemistry Professor, Mathematics Instructor, Writer **Industry:** Education/ Educational Services **Date of Birth:** 11/27/1941 **Place of Birth:** Laconia **State:** NH **Year of Passing:** 2018-09-04 **Parents:** William Stafford Scott; Jeanne Richardson Scott **Marital Status:** Widowed **Spouse Name:** Elizabeth Mary Winterberg (3/11/1995, Deceased) **Education:** MA, University of Cambridge, England (1970); PhD, University of Illinois (1969); BA Cantab, Gonville and Caius College, University of Cambridge, England (1965); AB, University of Pennsylvania (1963) **Certifications:** Professional Teaching Certificate, Commonwealth of Pennsylvania; Postgraduate Teaching License, Commonwealth of Virginia **Career:** Associate Professor of Chemistry, Winston-Salem State University (2004-2009); Adjunct Instructor of Pharmacology, National College (Now American National University), Danville, VA (2001-2003); Adjunct Professor of Natural Sciences, Danville Community College, Danville, VA (2000-2004); Instructor of Mathematics, Winona Independent School District, Texas (1998-2000); Employee, Chemical Education Consultant USA, Hawkins, TX (1998-2000); Associate Professor of Chemistry, Jarvis Christian College, Hawkins, TX (1992-1998); Associate Professor of Chemistry, Union College, Barbourville, KY (1989-1991); Associate Professor of Chemistry, Knoxville College, Tennessee (1987-1989); Associate Professor of Chemistry, Bryan College, Dayton, TN (1984-1986); Adjunct Professor of Organic Chemistry, Salem College (Now Salem University), WV (1982-1983); Associate Professor of Chemistry, Alderson Broaddus University, Philippi, WV (1981-1984); Supervisor in Secondary Studies, Westminster Academy, Carmichaels, PA (1975-1979); Consultant in Science and Mathematics, Uniontown, PA (1972-1975); Lecturer in Biochemistry, University of California, Santa Barbara (1971); Assistant Professor in Chemistry, Oberlin College, Ohio (1969-1970); Teaching Assistant, University of Illinois (1965-1967); Instructor of Mathematics, Chemistry and Astronomy, Pittsylvania County Schools, VA **Career Related:** Adjunct Science Instructor, Hargrave Military Academy, Chatham, VA (2003); Consultant, Transition State Associates, Danville, VA (2002-2004); Edgewood-Aberdeen Research, United States Army, Aberdeen Proving Ground, MD (1993); Visiting Professor, Louisiana College, Pineville, LA (1992); Undergraduate Research Mentor, National Science Foundation, New Orleans, LA (1992); Research Associate, EPA, Philadelphia, PA (1988); Research Associate, DuPont, Philadelphia, PA (1963) **Civic:** Ambassador, Creekside Terrace (2013-Present); Musician, Danville Recorder Consort, Danville Area Choral Arts Society **Military Service:** Researcher, Aberdeen-Edgewood Laboratory, Anti-Biological Warfare Unit, ARO (Now U.S. Army Edgewood Chemical Biological Center (ECBC)); Consultant, Demonstrated Potentially Viable Weapon to Detect and Protect Against Biological Attack, ARO (Now U.S. Army Edgewood Chemical Biological Center (ECBC)) **Creative Works:** Contributor, Articles, Journal of the American Chemical Society (2003); Contributor, Articles, Journal of Chemistry Crystallographic (1998); Contributor, Articles, Journal of the American Chemical Society (1972); Contributor, Articles, Journal of the American Chemical Society (1970); Author, "Spectroscopic Model Studies of NAD(H)" (1969); Co-author, "Synthetic Procedures in Nucleic Acid Chemistry" (1968); Contributor, Articles, Journal of the American Chemical Society (1967) **Awards:** Grantee, National Science Foundation (1996-1999); Grantee, Robert A. Welch Foundation (1996-1998); Grantee, Army Research Office (1993-1995); Thouron Awardee, Gonville & Caius College, Cambridge University (1963-1965) **Membership:** Director, American Scientific Affiliation (1998); Chairman, International Education Committee, Rotary International (1977-1981); American Chemical Society; Cambridge University Chemical Society (Now ChemSoc) **What do you consider to be the highlight of your career:** Dr. Scott is most proud of working at colleges that didn't have great resources. He was able to enrich the lives of students and prepare them for the next step, whether that was employment or graduate school. **Hobbies:** Baritone vocal solos; Exploring ideas; Renaissance music (Treble and tenor recorder); Astronomy **Shipping Address:** 3895 Old Vineyard Road, Apt. 128, Winston-Salem, NC, 27104

Jerome Chilwell Scowcroft

Title: Attorney at Law **Industry:** Law and Legal Services **Company Name:** Roosevelt Law Center **Date of Birth:** 05/17/1947 **Place of Birth:** Pocatello **State:** ID **Parents:** Harold Scowcroft; Alberta Mary (Chilwell) Scowcroft **Marital Status:** Married **Spouse Name:** Corinne Gail Cox (3/12/1983) **Children:** Jason Trevor Scowcroft; Brian Jonathan Scowcroft **Education:** LLM in Taxation, University of Washington (2001); JD, Duke Law, With Honors (1978); Master's Degree in Research Psychology, UC San Diego (1973); BA, Stanford University (1969) **Career:** Associate, Schwabe, Williamson & Wyatt PC (1985-Present); Editor, Lamorte Burns & Co. (1981-1985); Legal Advisor, Lamorte Burns & Co. (1981-1985); Associate, Haight, Gardner, Poor & Havens (Now Holland & Knight LLP) (1978-1981) **Career Related:** Adjunct Professor, University of Washington (1988-Present); Lecturer in Admiralty Law, University of Washington (1988-1989) **Military Service:** U.S. Army (1970-1972) **Creative Works:** Case Editor, Journal of Maritime Law and Commerce (1987-Present); Contributing Editor, "U.S. Maritime Arbitration," International Council for Commercial Arbitration (1983-Present); Board of Advisors, "Arbitration Award Digest," Maritime Advertisement Services (1981-Present); Contributor, Articles, Professional Services **Awards:** Honoree, AV Preeminent Attorney, Martindale-Hubbell (2014); Fellow, U.S. Department of Health & Human Services **Membership:** Vice Chairman, Carriage of Goods Committee, Maritime Law Association of the United States (1991-Present); ACCPNW; Urban Financial Services Coalition; ABA; World Trade Club; The International Propeller Club of the United States **Bar Admissions:** Washington State Bar Association (1986); New York State Bar Association (1980) **Marquis Who's Who Honors:** Albert Nelson Marquis Lifetime Achievement Award (2017); Distinguished Humanitarian (2017) **To what do you attribute your success:** Dr. Scowcroft attributes his success to his high-quality work, having a good mind, and relating well to people. **Why did you become involved in your profession or industry:** Dr. Scowcroft became involved with his profession because he was always intellectually-oriented, and gifted in both language and mathematical skills. He grew up in an intellectual environment in Ogden, UT, and decided to pursue a legal career for the community involvement aspect. **Where will you be in five years:** In five years, Mr. Scowcroft intends to pursue his photography hobby and possibly teach. **Hobbies:** Photography **Political Affiliations:** Republican **Religion:** Episcopalian **Shipping Address:** 11320 Roosevelt Way N.E., Roosevelt Law Center, Seattle, WA, 98125

James Lawrence Seale Jr., PhD

Title: Agricultural Studies Educator **Industry:** Agriculture **Company Name:** University of Florida **Date of Birth:** 04/12/1949 **Place of Birth:** Memphis **State:** TN **Parents:** James Lawrence Seale; Mary Helen (Keefe) Seale **Marital Status:** Married **Spouse Name:** Zoe Haynes Seale **Education:** PhD, Michigan State University (1985); Postgraduate Coursework, The University of Chicago (1978-1979); BA, The University of Mississippi (1972) **Career:** Professor of Agricultural Economics, University of Florida, Gainesville, FL (1995-Present); Associate Professor of Agricultural Economics, University of Florida, Gainesville, FL (1990-1995); Assistant Professor of Agricultural Economics, University of Florida, Gainesville, FL (1985-1990); Specialist, Michigan State University, Fayoum, Arab Republic of Egypt (1980-1983); Agricultural Advisor, Harvard Institute for International Development, Abyei, Sudan (1978); Agricultural Volunteer, Peace Corps, Tondo, Zaire (1973-1975) **Career Related:** Honorary Visiting Professor, The University of Leicester, England (1995); Visiting Professor, The University of Leicester, England (1994, 1992) **Civic:** Volunteer, Agricultural Business Services, Wenrock International, Russia (1998); Volunteer, Farmer to Farmer, Wenrock International (1994); Volunteer, Farmer to Farmer, UOCA, Namibia (1994) **Creative Works:** Editor, Journal of Agricultural and Applied Economics, Special Edition (2002-2003); Editor, Journal of Agricultural and Applied Economics (1998-2001); Co-Author, "Advances in Econometrics, a Research Annual: International Evidence on Consumption Patterns," Jai Press (1989); Contributor, Articles to Professional Journals **Awards:** Honoree, Research of the Year, University of Florida (2006-2007); Honorary Fellow, The University of Leicester (1995); Senior Research Fellow, McKethan-Matherly (1991-1994); Research Fellow, McKethan-Matherly (1986-1988); Research Fellow, Cairo University (1980-1983); Traveling Scholar, University of Michigan (1979); Scholar, National Institute of Mental Health, The University of Chicago (1978-1979) **Membership:** American Economic Association; Agricultural & Applied Economics Association; International Association of Agricultural Economists; International Agricultural Trade Research Consortium; Gamma Sigma Delta **Marquis Who's Who Honors:** Albert Nelson Marquis Lifetime Achievement Award (2017) **Why did you become involved in your profession or industry:** Dr. Seale entered his profession because he was inspired by his experience as an agricultural volunteer for the Peace Corps in Tondo, Zaire, between 1973 and 1975. **What do you consider to be the highlight of your career:** The highlight of Dr. Seale's career has been his work in international consumption and cross-country demand analysis. **Hobbies:** Scuba diving; Karate **Religion:** Episcopalian **Shipping Address:** PO Box 110240, UF, Department of Food and Resources, Gainesville, FL, 32611

Selvyn Seidel

Industry: Education/Educational Services **Date of Birth:** 05/14/1905 **Place of Birth:** Long Branch **State:** NJ **Parents:** Abraham; Anita (Stoller) Seidel **Marital Status:** Married **Spouse Name:** Deborah Lew (6/21/1970) **Children:** Emily **Education:** Diploma in Law, Oxford University (1968); JD, University of California, Berkeley (1967); BA, University of Chicago (1964) **Career:** Partner, Latham & Watkins, New York City, NY (1985-2006); Advisory Board Member, New York University Law Schools Center for International Arbitration; Linacre College Lecturer, Oxford University; Founder, Fulbrook Capital Management LLC; Co-founder, Burford Group Ltd; Co-founder, Burford Advisors LLC **Career Related:** Instructor, Practicing Law Institute (1980-1981, 1984); Adjunct Professor, School of Law, New York University (1974-1984) **Civic:** Board of Directors, Citizen Scholarship Fund of America (1995-2000) **Creative Works:** Contributor, Articles, Professional Journals **Membership:** Art Law Committee, New York City Bar Association (1997-2000); International Law committee, New York City Bar Association (1989-1992); Federal Courts Committee, New York City Bar Association (1982-1985); Board of Directors, Boalt Hall Alumni Association (1980-1982); American Bar Association; New York County Bar Association; New York City Bar Association **Bar Admissions:** D.C. Bar; D.C. Court of Appeals (1982); New York State Bar (1970)

Patricia Clark Seifert

Industry: Medicine & Health Care **Company Name:** Independent Cardiac Consultant **Date of Birth:** 05/08/1905 **Parents:** Thomas W. Clark; Kathleen E. (O'Malley) Clark **Marital Status:** Married **Spouse Name:** Gary F. Seifert, PhD **Children:** Kristina S. Leighty; Philip A. (Deceased) **Education:** MS in Nursing, Catholic University of America (1988); Associate Degree in Nursing, Northern Virginia Community College (1976); BA in History, Trinity College (1967) **Certifications:** RN, State of Virginia; RN, District of Columbia; Operating Room Nurse; First Assistant Nurse **Career:** Independent Perioperative Consultant (2017-Present); Education Coordinator, Inova Fairfax Hospital, Inova Heart and Vascular Institute, Falls Church, VA (2002-Present); Editor-in-Chief, AORN Journal (2008-2012); Innovations Liaison, Sandel Medical Industries, Chatsworth, CA (2002); Coordinator, Cardiovascular Services, Arlington Hospital, Virginia (2000-2002); Manager, Open Heart Surgery, Halifax Medical Center, Daytona Beach, FL (1997-1998); Operating Room Coordinator, Cardiac Surgery, Alexandria Hospital, Virginia (1995-1997); Operating Room Coordinator, Cardiac Surgery, Arlington Hospital, Virginia (1989-1997); Administrative Director, Washington Hospital Center (1988-1989); Head Nurse, Cardiac Surgery, Fairfax Hospital, Falls Church, VA (1976-1988) **Career Related:** Lead Coordinator, Nursing Organizations Alliance (2001-2003); Member, Advisory Board, Ethicon Endo-Surgery Nursing, Surgical Information Systems; Lecturer, Author, Consultant in Field **Creative Works:** Editor, E-Book, "Core Curriculum for the RN First Assistant" (2014); Contributor, Book Chapters, "Alexander's Care of the Patient in Surgery, 15th Edition" (2014); Contributor, Book Chapters, "Core Curriculum for the RN First Assistant, 6th Edition" (2014); Contributor, Book Chapters, "Anesthesia Nursing, 6th Edition" (2012); Contributor, Book Chapters, "Alexander's Care of the Patient in Surgery, 14th Edition" (2010); Co-author, Book, "Assisting in Surgery: Patient Centered Care" (2009); Contributor, Book Chapters, "Anesthesia Nursing, 5th Edition" (2008); Contributor, Book Chapters, "Cardiac Nursing: A Companion to Braunwald's Heart Disease" (2008); Co-author, Book, "Tea & Toast for the Perioperative Nursing Spirit" (2006); Contributor, Book Chapters, "Surgical Technology, 4th Edition" (2005); Contributor, Book Chapters, "Core Curriculum for the RN First Assistant, 4th Edition" (2005); Author, Book, "Cardiac Surgery" (2002); Contributor, Book Chapters, "The RN First Assistant: An Expanded Perioperative Role, 3rd Edition" (1999); Contributor, Book Chapters, Certified Nurse Operating Room Study Guide, Revised Edition" (1999); Contributor, Book Chapters, "Perioperative Care Planning, 2nd Edition" (1996); Author, Book, "Cardiac Surgery" (1994); Contributor, Book Chapters, "Cardiovascular Nursing, 7th Edition" (1991); Author, Book, "Clinical Assessment Tools for Use with Nursing Diagnosis" (1989); Contributor, Numerous Articles, Professional Journals **Awards:** Legacy of Service Award, Inova Health System (2014); Outstanding Achievement in Mentoring Award (2014); Jerry G. Peers Distinguished Service Award, AORN Inc. (2007); National Excellence Award, AORN Inc. (2004); Key to the City Award, Lake Charles, LA (1999); National President's Award, AORN Inc. (1992); Nurse of the Year Award, Virginia Nurses Association (1984) **Membership:** Advisory Board, Sigma Theta Tau (2014-Present); Council on Cardiovascular Surgery and Anesthesia, American Heart Association (2013-Present); Writing Group, American Heart Association (2013); Resident Nurse First Assistant, AORN Inc. (2004); Secretary, AORN Inc. Foundation (1999-2001); National President, AORN Inc. (1999-2000); National President-Elect, AORN Inc. (1998-1999); National Board Director, AORN Inc. (1994-1998); President, Northern Virginia Chapter, AORN Inc. (1994-1995); National Nominating Committee, AORN Inc. (1991-1993); President, Eta Alpha Chapter, Sigma Theta Tau (1990-1992); Board of Directors, District 8, Virginia Nurses Association (1987-1991); Fellow, American Academy of Nursing; Virginia Henderson Fellow, Sigma Theta Tau; American Association for the History of Nursing **Achievements:** Wrote the first textbook (Cardiac Surgery, Mosby, 1994) on the perioperative nursing care of the patient undergoing cardiac surgery; Developed the first written explication of the American Nurses Associations's Code of Ethics for perioperative nurses; chaired the first   AORN Ethics Committee that published the "Explications for Perioperative Nursing," 2001-2002. Sole RN member of the writing group for American Heart Association's Scientific Statement, Patient Safety in the Cardiac Operating   Room: Human Factors and Teamwork, 2013. **Hobbies:** Reading; Travel **Political Affiliations:** Independent **Shipping Address:** 6502 Overbrook Street, Falls Church, VA, 22043

Lisa K. Selin, PhD

Title: Physician **Industry:** Medicine & Health Care **Company Name:** University of Massachusetts Medical School **Date of Birth:** 04/08/1952 **Place of Birth:** Helsinki **Education:** PhD, University of Manitoba (1993); Postdoctoral Fellow, University of Massachusetts Medical School (1992-1995); Fellow in Infectious Diseases, University of Manitoba, Winnipeg, Canada (1984-1986); FRCP, Dalhousie University (1984); Resident in Internal Medicine, Dalhousie University (1980-1984); Medical Intern, Dalhousie University, Halifax, Canada (1979-1980); MD, Dalhousie University (1979); BSc, Dalhousie University (1974) **Career:** Professor, University of Massachusetts Medical School (2008-Present); Associate Professor, University of Massachusetts Medical School (2001-2008); Assistant Professor, University of Massachusetts Medical School (1996-2001); Instructor, University of Massachusetts Medical School (1995-1996) **Awards:** Research Grant, National Institute of Allergy and Infectious Disease, National Institutes of Health (1999-Present); Clinical Investigator Award, National Institutes of Health (1996-1999); Medical Council of Canada Student Fellowship, Medical Council of Canada (1986-1991); Izaak Walton Killam Scholarship, Izaak Walton Killam Foundation (1984-1986); Dalhousie Entrance Scholarship, Dalhousie University (1970) **Membership:** Canadian Infectious Disease Society; American Association of Immunologists **Marquis Who's Who Honors:** Albert Nelson Marquis Lifetime Achievement Award (2017); Distinguished Humanitarian (2017) **To what do you attribute your success:** Dr. Selin attributes her success to an extremely tenacious tenacity that can overcome anything; she keeps on going and ask a new question, remaining on the optimistic side. Even if experiment fails, Dr. Selin can see the positive side. **Why did you become involved in your profession or industry:** Dr. Selin wanted to be a doctor since she was about six years old. Around the age of five, she developed bacterial meningitis, and wanted to cure people like how she was cured. When she was ten, she read about Marie Curie, who won Nobel Prizes and discovered many things, like radiation. So, in addition to becoming a doctor, Dr. Selin wanted to become a scientist and earn a PhD. **Where will you be in five years:** In five years, Dr. Selin wishes to continue to educate, so long as she gets funding for studying how vaccines take and what sequence, and how many at a time. She would still hope to contribute to the research of chronic fatigue, as data on the immune system is quite irregular. **Hobbies:** Painting; Cross-country skiing; Swimming; Gardening; Travelling **Business Address:** 368 Plantation Street, AS9-2041, Worcester, MA, 01605 **Website:** http://profiles.umassmed.edu/profiles/display/130063

Paul Sellin, PhD

Title: Distinguished Professor Emeritus **Industry:** Education/Educational Services **Company Name:** University of California, Los Angeles **Date of Birth:** 11/14/1930 **Place of Birth:** Everett **State:** WA **Year of Passing:** 2017-10-23 **Parents:** Petrus Sellin; F. Amelia (Josephson) Sellin **Marital Status:** Married **Spouse Name:** Agatha Weststrate (9/21/1957) **Children:** Mark Eric; Christine Petra; Britt Amelia **Education:** PhD, The University of Chicago (1963); MA, The University of Chicago (1955); BA, Washington State University, Pullman, WA (1952) **Career:** Distinguished Professor Emeritus, University of California, Los Angeles (1993-Present); Distinguished Research Professor, University of California, Los Angeles (2015); Full Professor, University of California, Los Angeles (1966-1993); Assistant Professor, University of California, Los Angeles (1966-1993); Assistant Dean, Department of Arts & Sciences, Roosevelt University, Chicago, IL (1959-1966); Associate Professor, Roosevelt University, Chicago, IL (1959-1966); Lecturer, Roosevelt University, Chicago, IL (1959-1966) **Career Related:** Guest Research Scholar, Stockholms University (1993); Professor, English Literature, Stockholms University (1981-1988); Visiting Scholar, Vrije Universiteit Amsterdam (1980-1981); Co-Founder, Netherlandic Studies Programs, University of California, Los Angeles; Past Chairman, Netherlandic Studies Programs, University of California, Los Angeles; Co-Founder, International Overseas Programs, University of California, Los Angeles; Past Chairman, International Overseas Programs, University of California, Los Angeles **Civic:** Member, School Board, Bethel Lutheran School, Encino, CA (1995-Present); Member, Board of Directors, Scandinavian American Cultural and Historical Foundation, Thousand Oaks, CA (2003-2012); President, The American-Scandinavian Foundation, Thousand Oaks, CA (2003-2005); Member, School Board, Bethel Lutheran School, Encino, CA (1989-1991); Member, Infantry School, Fort Benning, GA (1952); Member, ROTC Washington State University (1948-1952); Member, Camp Atterbury, National Guard, Indiana **Military Service:** With Military Intelligence, U.S. Army Reserve, Chicago, IL (1954-1956); Platoon Leader, H Company, Second Battalion, 19th Infantry Regiment, 24th Division, U.S. Army (1953-1954); With 19th Infantry Regiment, 24th Division, U.S. Army (1952-1954); Second Lieutenant, U.S. Army (1952-1953) **Creative Works:** Treasurer, "Treason and the Tower: El Dorado and the Murder of Sir Walter Raleigh" (2011); Author, "So Doth, So Is Religion: John Donne and Diplomatic Contexts in the Reformed Netherlands, 1619-1620" (1988); Author, "John Donne and Calvinist Views of Grace, Amsterdam" (1983); Editor, "Daniel Heinsus On Plot in Tragedy" (1971); Translator, "Daniel Heinsus On Plot in Tragedy" (1971); Author, "Daniel Heinsius and Stuart England: With a Short-title Checklist of the Works of Daniel Heinsius" (1968); Treasurer, "Raad van Advies The Low Countries"; Consulting Editor, "The Netherlands"; Consulting Editor, "The Oxford Dictionary of the Renaissance"; Contributor, Articles, Professional Journals **Awards:** National Endowment of the Humanities Grantee (1989); Grantee, ACLS (1970-1989); Grantee, The American Philosophical Society (1970-1989); National Endowment of the Humanities Grantee (1982); Fullbright Travel Grantee (1980); National Endowment of the Humanities Grantee (1973); Named Fellow, Roosevelt University, Amsterdam (1963-1964); Named Hendrick Willem van Loon Fellow (1959-1960) **Membership:** UCLA Center Medieval and Renaissance Studies; Modern Language Association; Executive Board, American Association for Netherlands Studies; International Association for Neo-Latin Studies; American Association for Neo-Latin Studies; John Donne Society; Milton Society; ACLU; Southern Poverty Law Center; Alumni Association, University of Chicago; Alumni Association, Washington State University; Pi Alpha Theta; Gamma Xi; Alpha Tau Omega **Marquis Who's Who Honors:** Albert Nelson Marquis Lifetime Achievement Award (2017) **What do you consider to be the highlight of your career:** The highlight of Dr. Sellin's career has been his current project involving previously discounted translation of 450 AD work. **Hobbies:** Reading; Music; Literature **Political Affiliations:** Democrat **Religion:** Lutheran **Shipping Address:** 110 Wood Rd Apt A106, Los Gatos, CA, 95030

Paul M. Sengpiehl

Title: Lawyer, State Official **Industry:** Law and Legal Services **Date of Birth:** 10/10/1937 **Place of Birth:** Stuart **State:** NE **Parents:** Arthur Paul; Anne Marie (Andersen) Sengpiehl **Marital Status:** Married **Spouse Name:** June S. Cline (6/29/1963) **Education:** JD, Illinois Institute Technology Chicago-Kent College of Law (1970); MA in Public Administration, Michigan State University (1961); BA, Wheaton College (1959) **Certifications:** Minister Ordination (2009); License to Minister (2007) **Career:** Attorney (Present); Local Government Law Columnist, Chicago Daily Law Bulletin (1975-1984); Hearing Referee, Illinois Department of Labor (1983-1984); Assistant Attorney General, Court of Claims Division, Attorney General of Illinois (1976-1983); Special Assistant, Attorney General, Illinois Department of Labor (1973-1976); Legal Counsel, Illinois Department of Local Government Affairs(1972-1973); Management Officer, Illinois Department of Local Government Affairs (1971-1972); Supervisor, Illinois Municipal Retirement Fund (1966-1971); Administrative Assistant, Chicago Department of Urban Renewal (1962-1965) **Career Related:** Ordained Minister, Cook County Jail (Present); Chairman of the Board, American Baptist Cook County Jail Ministry (1996-Present); Political Science Instructor, Judson College (1963) **Civic:** Board Chairman, Cook County Jail Ministry (2006-Present); Cook County Correctional Chaplaincy Council (1996-Present); Treasurer, Cook County Correctional Chaplaincy Council (1996-2006); Representative, Alternate State Central Committeeman, 7th Congressional District (1996); Elected Delegate, Republican National Convention (1996); Elected Committeeman, Oak Park Township Republican Organization (1994-1998); Deputy Chairman, Cook County Jail Ministry (1993-1996); People's Choice Care Party Candidate, Village President, Oak Park Village (1993); Elected Alternate Delegate, Delegate Republican National Convention (1992); Republican Candidate, Cook County Recorder of Deeds (1984) **Creative Works:** Author, "The Centennial Graduation Class of Wheaton College"; Author, "The Class of 1959 Remembered" (2009); Two Musical Compositions Performed Publicly **Membership:** Cook County Chapter (1982-1987); President, Cook County Chapter (1997-Present); State Secretary, John Ericsson Republican League Illinois (1983-1985, 1995-Present); Honorable Past President of the State, John Ericsson Republican League of Illinois (2007); Small Business Committee, Oak Park-River Forest Chamber of Commerce (1991-2000); State Tax Section Council, Illinois State Bar Association (1979-1982, 1984-1985); Chairman, Chicago Bar Association (1981-1982); Vice Chairman, Chicago Bar Association (1980-1981); Secretary, Chicago Bar Association (1979-1980); Chairman, Legislative Subcommittee, Chicago Bar Association (1978-1979); Chairman, Editor, Newsletter, Illinois State Bar Association (1977-1978); Co-Editor, Local Government Newsletter, Illinois State Bar Association (1976-1977); Local Government Law Section Council, Illinois State Bar Association (1973-1979); Local Government Committee, Chicago Bar Association; State and Municipal Tax Committee, Chicago Bar Association; Vice Chairman, Local Government Law Section, Illinois State Bar Association **Bar Admissions:** Supreme Court of the United States (1982); Illinois (1971) **Religion:** Baptist **Shipping Address:** 727 N Ridgeland Ave., Oak Park, IL, 60302

David Michael Sever

Title: Professor Emeritus **Industry:** Education/Educational Services **Company Name:** Southeastern Louisiana University **Date of Birth:** 02/21/1948 **Place of Birth:** Canton **State:** OH **Parents:** Robert Garret Sever; Martha Jane (Grimm) Sever **Marital Status:** Married **Spouse Name:** Marlis Ann Lyon (8/30/1970) **Children:** Philip; Robert **Education:** PhD, Tulane University (1974); MS, Ohio University (1971); BS, Ohio University (1970) **Career:** Professor Emeritus, Southeastern Louisiana University (2015-Present); Scholar-in-Residence, Southeastern Louisiana University (2015-Present); Major Kenneth Dyson Endowed Chair, Southeastern Louisiana University (2012-2015); Professor, Southeastern Louisiana University (2004-2015); Department Head, Southeastern Louisiana University (2004-2011); Professor, St. Mary's College, Notre Dame, IN (1987-2004); Biology Department Chairman, St. Mary's College, Notre Dame, IN (1980-1989); Associate Professor, St. Mary's College, Notre Dame, IN (1977-1987); Assistant Professor, St. Mary's College, Notre Dame, IN (1974-1977) **Career Related:** External Review Committee Member, Smith College (1999); Dean's Advisory Council Member, College of Arts and Sciences, Ohio University (1998-2004); Panel Member, National Science Foundation (1998, 1988) **Creative Works:** Contributor, More than 170 Articles, More Than 30 Scientific Journals; Editor, Two Books; Associate Editor, Journal of Morphology and Journal of Herpetology; Editorial Board Member, Copeia **Awards:** Distinguished Herpetologist, Herpetologists' League (2013); Excellence in Research Award, Southeastern Louisiana University (2009-2010); Significant Achievement Award, Ohio University (1993); Grantee, National Science Foundation (1987-2012); Honoree, TriBeta (1980); Outstanding Alumnus Award, Ohio University; Fellow, Indiana Academy of Science; Research Grantee, Government & Private Agencies **Membership:** President, Herpetologists' League (2018-2019); Annual Meeting and Invitations Chairman, Indiana Academy of Science (1988-1990); American Society of Ichthyologists and Herpetologists; Society for Study Amphibians and Reptiles; Herpetologists' League; Chicago Herpetological Society; Sigma Xi; International Society of Vertebrate Morphology **Marquis Who's Who Honors:** Albert Nelson Marquis Lifetime Achievement Award (2017) **Why did you become involved in your profession or industry:** Dr. Sever became involved in his career because of his time as an Eagle Scout for the Boys Scouts of America. He took interest in being out in nature and camping. **What do you consider to be the highlight of your career:** A highlight of his career was when he was named distinguished Herpetologist of the year by the Herpetologists' League. **Hobbies:** Golf; Travel; Reading **Business Address:** 15695 Strader Rd., Hammond, LA, 70403

John Shacter

Title: Technology, Strategic Planning and Education Consultant **Industry:** Consulting **Company Name:** JS Associates Management **Date of Birth:** 09/26/1921 **Place of Birth:** Vienna **Country of Origin:** Austria **Parents:** Jacob Shacter; Regina (Bursten) Shacter **Marital Status:** Married **Spouse Name:** Kathleen Williams (3/6/1947) **Children:** Suzanne; Linda **Education:** BSChemE, University of Pennsylvania (1943) **Career:** Founder JS Associates Management, Technology, Strategic Planning and Education Consultant, Kingston, TN (1983-1985); President, JS Associates Management, Technology, Strategic Planning and Education Consultant, Kingston, TN (1983-1985); Senior Consultant, Union Carbide Corporation, Oak Ridge, TN (1976-1983); Assistant to President, Consultant Manitoba Systems, Union Carbide Corporation, Oak Ridge, TN (1972-1976); Founder, Multi-Company Combined Operations Planning, Atomic Energy Commission, Union Carbide Corporation, Oak Ridge, TN (1966-1972); Director, Multi-Company Combined Operations Planning, Atomic Energy Commission, Union Carbide Corporation, Oak Ridge, TN (1966-1972); Manager, Corporate Planning and Management Systems, Union Carbide Corporation, New York City, NY (1958-1966); Corporate Projects and New Ventures, Union Carbide Corporation, New York City, NY (1956-1958); International Process Analysis, Frankfurt, Germany (1955); Process Design, Analysis Manager, Union Carbide Corporation, Oak Ridge, TN (1946-1955); Operations Supervisor, Union Carbide Corporation, Oak Ridge, TN (1944-1946); Research Development Engineer, Manhattan Atomic Project, Union Carbide Corporation, New York City, NY (1943-1944) **Career Related:** Adjunct Professor, Graduate Engineering Design, Economics, The University of Tennessee, Knoxville; Member, Advisory Panel, Management and Technology, American Academy of Arts & Sciences; Consultant, International Institute for Applied Systems Analysis, Laxenburg, Austria **Civic:** Volunteer Teacher, Basic Math; Volunteer Teacher, Money Management; Volunteer Teacher, Other Key Subjects **Creative Works:** News Columnist, Television and Radio Discussions; Host, Television and Radio Discussions; Contributor, Numerous Articles, Professional Journals **Awards:** Named, State's Outstanding Engineer, Tennessee Society of Professional Engineers (1992); Named, Outstanding Boss of the Year, American Society of Administrative Professionals; Named, Outstanding Engineer, American Institute of Chemical Engineers **Membership:** Fellow, American Institute of Chemical Engineers; Past President, American Institute of Chemical Engineers; American Association for the Advancement of Science; Seminars Chairman, American Management Association; Lecturer, American Management Association; Tennessee Society of Professional Engineers; Past President, The Torch Club; Past President, Rotary International; Past President, Professional Society; Society of Professional Journalists; Tennessee Retired Teachers Association; Chair, Key Issues and Choices, Oak Ridge Institute for Continued Learning; Tau Beta Pi **Marquis Who's Who Honors:** Albert Nelson Marquis Lifetime Achievement Award (2017) **Hobbies:** Water sports; Dance; Music **Shipping Address:** 851 Lawnville Rd Apt 301, Kingston, TN, 37763

Leigh S. Shaffer

Title: Psychology Professor **Industry:** Education/Educational Services **Date of Birth:** 03/08/1947 **Place of Birth:** Wichita **State:** KS **Year of Passing:** 2018-03-05 **Parents:** Edward Wesley Shaffer; Ruth D. Shaffer **Marital Status:** Married **Spouse Name:** Barbara Anne Benskin (8/14/1971) **Children:** Victoria Anne **Education:** PhD, Pennsylvania State University (1974); MA, Wichita State University (1971); BA, Wichita State University (1969) **Career:** Professor Emeritus, West Chester University, West Chester, PA (2009); Assistant Professor, West Chester University, West Chester, PA (1980-2009); Assistant Professor of Psychology, Nebraska Wesleyan University, Lincoln, NE (1977-1980); Assistant Professor of Psychology, Pennsylvania State University, McKeesport, PA (1974-1977) **Career Related:** Co-Editor, NACADA Journal (2009-2016); Acting Associate Provost, West Chester University (2002) **Creative Works:** Co-Author, "Voices from the Pagan Census" (2003); Contributor, Articles, Professional Journals **Awards:** The Leigh S. Shaffer NACADA Award, National Academic Advisors Association (2017) **Membership:** National Academic Advisors Association **Hobbies:** Golf **Shipping Address:** 1501 Strathmore Drive, Columbia, MO, 65203

William W. Shane

Title: C.H. Adams Fellow **Industry:** Education/ Educational Services **Company Name:** Monterey Institute for Research in Astronomy **Date of Birth:** 06/03/1928 **Place of Birth:** Berkeley **State:** CA **Parents:** Charles Donald Shane; Mary Lea (Heger) Shane **Marital Status:** Married **Spouse Name:** Clasina van der Molen Shane (4/22/1964) **Children:** Johan Jacob; Charles Donald **Education:** ScD, Leiden University, Netherlands (1971); Postgraduate Work, University of California, Berkeley, CA (1953-1958); BA, University of California, Berkeley, CA (1951) **Career:** C.H. Adams Fellow, Monterey Institute for Research in Astronomy, CA (1994-Present); Guest Professor, Astronomy, Leiden University, Netherlands (1988-1993); Professor Astronomy, Director, Astronomical Institute, Catholic University of Nijmegen, Netherlands (1979-1988); Senior Scientist, Leiden University, Netherlands (1971-1979); Research Associate, Leiden University, Netherlands (1961-1971) **Military Service:** U.S. Navy (1951-1953) **Membership:** Fellow, American Association for the Advancement of Science; Astronomical Society of the Pacific; Nederlandse Astronomenclub (Astronomical Society in Netherlands); American Astronomical Society; Member, Divisions H and K, International Astronomical Union; Phi Beta Kappa **Marquis Who's Who Honors:** Albert Nelson Marquis Lifetime Achievement Award (2017) **Shipping Address:** 9095 Coker Rd, Prunedale, CA, 93907

Richard Allen Sheaffer

Title: Electrical Engineer (Retired) **Industry:** Engineering **Company Name:** San Diego Gas & Electric **Date of Birth:** 05/30/1950 **Place of Birth:** Bronxville **State:** NY **Education:** MBA, Pepperdine University (1996); MSEE, University of Southern California (1975); BSEE, Pennsylvania State University (1972) **Certifications:** Registered Professional Engineer, State of California; Registered Professional Engineer, State of Florida **Career:** Manager, Grid Contract Services, San Diego Gas & Electric (2012-2016); Principal Engineer, San Diego Gas & Electric (2007-2012); Representative, Steam Generator Replacement Project, San Onofre Nuclear Generating Station Units 2 and 3, San Diego Gas & Electric (2005-2007); Representative, Decommissioning at San Onofre Nuclear Generating Station Unit 1, San Diego Gas & Electric (2000-2007); Senior Transmission Planner, San Diego Gas & Electric (1991-2000); Consultant, San Diego Gas & Electric (1990-1991); Electrical Engineer, Southern California Edison, Rosemead, CA (1980-1990); Electrical Engineer, Harris Controls Division, Melbourne, FL (1979-1980); Electrical Engineer, Southern California Edison, Rosemead, CA (1973-1979) **Career Related:** Project Leader, Arizona-California 7550 MW Path Rating (1997); Project Leader, Nomogram Study, Pacific and Southwest Transfer Subcommittee, Western Systems Coordinating Council (1991); Project Leader, Nomogram Study, Pacific and Southwest Transfer Subcommittee, Western Systems Coordinating Council (1988) **Creative Works:** Author, "1984 West-of-the-River Operating Study" (1985); Author, "1982 Disturbance Study" (1983) **Membership:** IEEE; Power Engineering Society; Phi Eta Sigma **Marquis Who's Who Honors:** Albert Nelson Marquis Lifetime Achievement Award (2017) **To what do you attribute your success:** Mr. Sheaffer attributes some of his success to his 1982 Disturbance Study, which was published in 1983, as well as his 1984 West-of-the-River Operating Study, which was published in 1985, leading to enhanced economy of electric system operation while maintaining reliability. He also credits his nature of not following the pack and not excepting that the way things are done are the only way to do things, but instead looking for new approaches and discoveries. **Why did you become involved in your profession or industry:** Mr. Sheaffer become involved in electrical engineering when he received an electric set at the age of 8, which piqued his lifelong interest in the field. **Where will you be in five years:** In the next five years, Mr. Sheaffer hopes to be recognized in writing and art. **Hobbies:** Painting; Writing **Shipping Address:** 658 Corte Raquel, San Marcos, CA, 92069

C. Norman Shealy

Title: Doctor **Industry:** Health, Wellness and Fitness **Company Name:** Shealy Wellness **Education:** Doctor of Science, Ryodoraku Research Institute of North America, Inc. (1979); PhD, Saybrook Institute (1977); MD, Duke University (1956); BS in Medicine, Duke University **Certifications:** Certification, Biofeedback Certification Institute of America (1999); American Board of Somnology (1992); Certification, American Board of Sexology (1991); Certification, Biofeedback Certification Institute of America (1990); Certification, American Board of Pain Management (1989-2012); American Board of Somnology (1989); American Board of Medical Psychotherapists (1988); Certification, Biofeedback Certification Institute of America (1987); Certification, Biofeedback Certification Institute of America (1982); Certification, American Board of Neurological Surgery (1965); Fellow, American College of Surgeons; Fellow, American College of Preventive Medicine; License, American Medical Association; License, Missouri State Medical Society; License, Greene County Medical Society; License, The Harvey Cushing Society, American Association of Neurological Surgeons; License, International Association for the Study of Pain; License, American Holistic Medical Association; License, Association for Applied Psychophysiology & Biofeedback; License, Association for Humanistic Psychology; License, Association for Research and Enlightenment; License, Fellow and Diplomate, American Board of Medical Psychotherapists; License, Society of Integrative Medicine **Career:** Professor of Energy Medicine, Holos University Graduate Seminary (2000-2009); Founding President, Chief Executive Officer, Holos University Graduate Seminary (2000-2008); Chair, Department of Energy Medicine, Greenwich University (1995-2000); Affiliated Faculty in Pain Management, University of the Pacific (1991-1996); Adjunct Faculty, Department of Psychology, Drury College (1990-1997); Chairman, American Academy of Pain Management Certification Examination Committee (1989-1997); Clinical Professor, Professor of Clinical Research, Forest Institute of Professional Psychology (1986-1999); Adjunct Faculty, Department of Psychology, Drury College (1982-1986); Clinical Associate, Department of Psychology, University of Wisconsin-La Crosse (1971-1982); Associate Clinical Professor of Neurosurgery, University of Minnesota Medical School (1970-1975); Assistant Clinical Professor of Neurosurgery, University of Wisconsin Medical School (1967-1974); Chief, Neurosurgery Department, Gundersen Clinic and Lutheran Hospital (1966-1971); Assistant Professor of Neurosurgery, Western Reserve University School of Medicine (1966); Senior Instructor in Neurosurgery, Western Reserve University School of Medicine (1963-1966); Teaching Fellow in Surgery, Harvard University School of Medicine (1962-1963); Assistant in Surgery, Washington University in St. Louis, Missouri (1957-1958); Assistant in Medicine, Duke University School of Medicine (1956-1957) **Creative Works:** Author, 34 Books **Awards:** Recipient, Pearl Award, Bio-Medical Synergistics Education Institute (2000); Recipient, Elmer and Alyce Green Award, International Society for the Study of Subtle Energies and Energy Medicine (1998); Recipient, Stress Award, American Institute of Stress (1997) **Membership:** Founding President, American Holistic Medical Association (1978-1980); President, Holos Institutes of Health; President Emeritus, Holos University Graduate Seminary; Professor Emeritus of Energy Medicine, Holos University Graduate Seminary; Professor Emeritus of Energy Medicine, Greenwich University; Board Member, Holos Institutes of Health; Board Member, Biogenics, II, LLC; Board Member, International Science of Mind Church for Spiritual Healing; Board Member, American Board of Scientific Medical Intuition; Advisory Board Member, The Healers; Advisory Board Member, American Board of Medical Psychotherapists, Professional Advisory Council; Advisory Board Member, Scottsdale Institute for Health & Medicine; Advisory Board Member, The Lawrence LeShan Institute, Inc. **Marquis Who's Who Honors:** Albert Nelson Marquis Lifetime Achievement Award (2017) **To what do you attribute your success:** Dr. Shealy attributes his success to his intuition and interest in safe and effective ways of dealing with health. **Why did you become involved in your profession or industry:** Dr. Shealy became involved in his profession because he has wanted to be a physician since he was four years old and went to medical school at the age of 19. **What do you consider to be the highlight of your career:** The highlight of Dr. Shealy's career was the discovery of TENS (Transcutaneous Electrical Nerve Stimulation) and his current research exploring the potential of scale activation in stem cells. **Where will you be in five years:** In five years, Dr. Shealy plans on continuing to help people with chronic diseases. **Hobbies:** Health; Gardening; Research; Writing **Shipping Address:** 5607 S 222nd Rd., Fair Grove, MO, 65648 **Website:** https://www.normshealy.com

Theodore L. Shear, PhD

Title: Archaeologist (Retired) **Industry:** Sciences **Date of Birth:** 01/05/1938 **Place of Birth:** Athens **Country of Origin:** Greece **Parents:** Theodore Leslie Shear; Josephine (Platner) Shear **Marital Status:** Married **Spouse Name:** Ione Doris Mylonas (6/24/1959) **Children:** Julia Louise; Alexandra **Education:** PhD, Princeton University (1966); MA, Princeton University (1963); AB, Princeton University, Summa Cum Laude (1959) **Career:** Emeritus Professor, Princeton University (2009-Present); Professor of Archaeology, American School of Classical Studies (1988-1994); Professor of Classical Archaeology, Princeton University (1979-2009); Associate Chairman, Department of Art and Archaeology, Princeton University (1976-1978, 1982-1983); Chairman, Program in Classical Archaeology, Princeton University (1970-1985); Associate Professor, Princeton University (1970-1979); Assistant Professor of Art and Archaeology, Princeton University (1967-1970); Assistant Professor, Bryn Mawr College (1966-1967); Instructor of Greek and Latin, Bryn Mawr College (1964-1966) **Career Related:** Member, Managing Committee, American School of Classical Studies (1972-Present); President, Princeton Junior School (1994-2006); Member, Princeton Junior School (1983-2006); Field Director, Ancient Agora of Athens (1968-1994); Trustee, William Alexander Procter Foundation (1982-1989); Member, Ancient Agora of Athens (1955, 1967); Member, Archaeological Expeditions to Greece and Italy (1953-1954, 1958, 1962-1963, 1965-1966) **Creative Works:** Author, "Trophies of Victory: Public Building in Periklean Athens" (2016); Author, "Kallias of Sphettos and the Revolt of Athens in 286" (1978); Contributor, Articles to Professional Journals **Awards:** White Fellow, American School of Classical Studies (1959-1960) **Membership:** Archaeological Institute of America; American Philological Association (Now Society for Classical Studies); College Art Association; Archaeological Society at Athens; The Century Association; Nassau Country Club; Princeton Club; Hellenic Yacht Club (Now Yacht Club of Greece); The Phi Beta Kappa Society **Political Affiliations:** Republican **Religion:** Episcopalian **Shipping Address:** 87 Library Pl., Princeton, NJ, 08540

Robert Sheath

Title: Professor **Industry:** Education/Educational Services **Company Name:** California State University San Marcos **Date of Birth:** 12/26/1950 **Place of Birth:** Toronto **Country of Origin:** ON/Canada **Parents:** Harry Gordon; Shirley Irene (Rose) Sheath **Education:** PhD, University of Toronto (1977); BSc, University of Toronto (1973) **Career:** Professor, California State University San Marcos (2007-Present); Provost, California State University San Marcos (2001-2006); Dean, College of Biological Science, University of Guelph, Ontario (1995-2001); Head, Department of Biology, Memorial University, St. Johns, Canada (1991-1995); Professor, University of Rhode Island, Kingston (1987-1991); Chairman, Department of Botany, University of Rhode Island, Kingston (1986-1990); Associate Professor, University of Rhode Island, Kingston (1982-1986); Assistant Professor of Aquatic Biology, University of Rhode Island, Kingston (1978-1982); National Research Council of Canada Postdoctoral Fellow, University of British Columbia (1977-1978) **Career Related:** Chair, Major Facilities Access Life Subcommittee, Natural Sciences and Engineering Research Council (2001); Member, Canada Research Chairs College of Reviewers (2000-2001); Chair, Natural Sciences and Engineering Research Council (1996-1997); Selection Committee, Life Sciences, Natural Sciences and Engineering Research Council (1996); Member, Evolution and Ecology Grant Selection Committee, Natural Sciences and Engineering Research Council (1994-1997) **Creative Works:** Editor, with J.D. Wehr and J.P. Kociolek (2015); Editor, Journal of Phycology, Phycological Society of America (2006-2011); Editor, Classification and Ecology of Freshwater Algae of North America, with J.D. Wehr (2003); Editorial Board, Japanese Phycological Society (2000-2005); Editorial Board, Phycological Society of America (1996-2000); Editorial Board, International Phycological Society (1993-1995); Associate Editor, British Phycological Society (1990-2001); Editor, Biology of the Red Algae, with K.M. Cole (1990); Editor, Freshwater and Marine Plants of Rhode Island, with M.M. Harlin (1988); Associate Editor, Phycological Society of America (1984-1989); Editorial Board, Phycological Society of America (1983-1986); Contributor, 151 Articles, Professional Journals **Awards:** Awards, California Water Board (2007-2014); Grantee, National Science Foundation (2001-2005); T. Christensen Prize Panel (2000); Darbaker Prize, Botanical Society of America (1997); Grantee, National Science and Engineering Research Council (1991-2002); Grantee, National Science Foundation (1980-1991); Harold C. Bold Award, Phycological Society of America (1976); G.A. Cox Gold Medal, University of Toronto (1973) **Membership:** Publications Committee Chair, Phycological Society of America (2001-2014); Board of Trustees, Phycological Society of America (2001-2004); Overseas Vice President, British Phycological Society (1997-1999); Freshwater Flora Committee, British Phycological Society (1993-2002); President, Phycological Society of America (1991-1992); Arctic Institute of North America **Shipping Address:** 333 S. Twin Oaks Valley Road, CSUSM Dept of Biological Sci, San Marcos, CA, 92096

Ali Sheikh

Title: President, IT Program Director **Industry:** Information Technology and Services **Company Name:** Anikini Inc. **Education:** MBA in Marketing and Finance, IIM Ahmedabad (1992); BS in Engineering, Jawaharlal Nehru Technological University Hyderabad (1990) **Certifications:** Certification in Integrated Resources Management, APICS **Career:** President, Anikini Inc.; IT Program Director, Anikini Inc.; Chief Solution Architect, Anikini Inc.; Project Manager, Anikini Inc.; Team Lead, Anikini Inc.; Area Sales Manager, Anikini Inc.; Global Project Manager, Infoware Systems **Creative Works:** Author, "Closure of the Helpdesk-A Geek Tragedy" (2012) **To what do you attribute your success:** He attributes his success to his upbringing, the world-class education that he was fortunate to receive, his habit of always learning something new and his sense of discipline and fairness at the workplace. **Why did you become involved in your profession or industry:** He started his career in the early 1990's and could see IT beginning to transform practically all facets of business, not to mention many aspects of life. He switched fields in 1997 and never looked back. **What do you consider to be the highlight of your career:** The "one highlight" is something that happened not once, but six times so far in his career. He has taken ownership of an "at risk" business / IT initiative, turning it around and delivering on time and on budget, with no compromise on quality or on the team spirit. **Where will you be in five years:** In the next five years, Mr. Sheikh would like like to transition from his current avatar of "outsider consultant brought in to lead and deliver things" to more of a "resident leader who will own it and see it through." His ideal position would be in a manufacturing industry or in an executive leadership position, responsible for delivering business improvement and transformation by using IT as an "enabler." **Hobbies:** Writing **Shipping Address:** 2025 Central Park Drive, #1365, Okemos, MI, 48864-1365 **Website:** http://www.anikini.com

Estherina Shems

Title: Child Psychiatrist **Industry:** Medicine & Health Care **Date of Birth:** 04/15/1932 **Place of Birth:** Tel Aviv **Country of Origin:** Israel **Parents:** Aaron Shems; Rachel (Yehuda) Shems **Marital Status:** Married **Spouse Name:** Donald Lewis Schotland (1/11/1976, Deceased 2015) **Education:** Honorary DSc, Lynchburg College (2009); Fellow, Adult Psychiatry, University of Pennsylvania (1960-1963); Rotating Intern, Lankenau Medical Center, Main Line Health (1958-1959); MD, Woman's Medical College of Pennsylvania (1958); BS, Lynchburg College, Cum Laude (1954) **Career:** Consultant, Early Intervention Programs, Community Council Health Systems, Philadelphia, PA (1981-2002); Clinical Associate, Psychiatry, Perelman School of Medicine, University of Pennsylvania (1979-1981); Administrative Staff, Philadelphia Psychiatric Center, Irving Schwartz Institute for Children and Youth (1964-1981); Assistant Instructor, Department of Psychiatry, Irving Schwartz Institute for Children and Youth (1964-1966); Assistant Instructor, Department of Psychiatry, Perelman School of Medicine, University of Pennsylvania (1962-1963); Child Psychiatry Affiliate, Youth Study Center of Philadelphia (1961-1963) **Career Related:** Invited Lecturer, Institute of Pediatrics, Chinese Academy of Medical Sciences, Peking Union Medical College, Beijing, People's Republic of China; Numerous Consultant/Teaching Positions in Field **Civic:** Vice Chairman, The Medical College of Pennsylvania (2002-2013); Executive Board, Trust Fund, Alumnae/i Association, The Medical College of Pennsylvania (2001-2015); Member, Trust Fund, Alumnae/i Association, The Medical College of Pennsylvania (1982-2001) **Awards:** Bertha Van Hoosen Award, American Medical Women's Association (2002); Lifetime Achievement Award, Virginia Foundation for Independent Colleges (2002); Richard H. Thornton Award for Excellence, Lynchburg College (1995); Distinguished Alumni Award, Lynchburg College (1990); T. Gibson Hobbs Outstanding Alumni Award, Lynchburg College (1969); Honoree, Outstanding Young Women of America (1967); Honoree, Outstanding Young Women of Pennsylvania (1967) **Membership:** The Honor Society of Phi Kappa Phi (1996-Present); Various Committees and Task Forces, American Medical Women's Association (1970-Present); Distinguished Lifetime Member, American Psychiatric Association (2013); Vice President for North America, Executive Board, Medical Women's International Association (1998-2001); U.S. Delegate and Session Co-Chairman, XXII Congress, Medical Women's International Association (1995); Lifetime Member, Executive Committee, Board of Directors, American Medical Women's Association (1992-1998); National Coordinator for United States of America, Medical Women's International Association (1992-1998); Scientific Research Committee, Medical Women's International Association (1990-1998); U.S. Delegate and Session Co-chairman, XX International Congress, Medical Women's International Association (1987); Councilor of Organization, American Medical Women's Association (1986-1988); Lifetime Member, Executive Committee, Board of Directors, American Medical Women's Association (1986-1988); U.S. Delegate and Session Co-Chairman, XIX International Congress, Medical Women's International Association (1984); Pennsylvania Psychiatric Society; Psychiatric Physicians of Pennsylvania; Various Offices, Chi Beta Phi National Scientific Honorary; Fellow, The College of Physicians of Philadelphia; Fellow, American Orthopsychiatric Association **Marquis Who's Who Honors:** Albert Nelson Marquis Lifetime Achievement Award (2017) **Hobbies:** Travel; Photography; Music; Reading **Shipping Address:** 1310 Wyngate Rd, Wynnewood, PA, 19096

Deming Sherman

Title: Lawyer **Industry:** Law and Legal Services **Company Name:** Locke Lord LLP **Date of Birth:** 07/22/1943 **Place of Birth:** Providence **State:** RI **Parents:** Edwin Fisk Sherman; Martha Amy (Parkhurst) Sherman **Marital Status:** Married **Spouse Name:** Jane Catherine Bauer (12/20/1966) **Children:** Melissa Jane; Nicholas Deming **Education:** JD, The University of Chicago (1968); BA, Amherst College, Massachusetts (1965) **Career:** Counsel, Locke Lord LLP (2015-Present); Deputy General Counsel, Locke Lord LLP (2008-2013); General Counsel, Edwards Wildman Palmer LLP (2005-2008); Managing Partner, Edwards & Angell LLP, Providence, RI (1986-1994); Partner, Edwards Wildman Palmer LLP (1975-2014); Associate, Locke Lord LLP (1969-1975) **Career Related:** Adjunct Professor, Roger Williams University Law School (2013-2014); Chairman, Litigation Department, Locke Lord LLP (1996-2005, 1983-1986); Co-Creator, Firm Ethics Seminar, Locke Lord LLP (1990-2013); Chairman, Executive Committee, Locke Lord LLP (1985-1986); Member, Executive Committee, Locke Lord LLP (1984-1986, 1979-1981) **Creative Works:** Member, Editorial Board, Rhode Island Bar Journal (1970); Lecturer, Conferences; Lecturer, Seminars **Awards:** Community Preservation Award, Providence Preservation Society (2012); Recognition for Guantanamo Work, District of Columbia Pro Bono Committee, United States District Court (2011); Award for Professionalism, Round Bar Association (2010); Antoinette F. Downing Volunteer Service Award (2008); Ralph P. Semonoff Award for Professionalism (2007); Providence Preservation Society's 50th Anniversary Hall of Fame (2006); Ken and Rebecca Phillips Award for Contribution to the WBNA Neighborhood and the City, West Broadway Neighborhood Association (2006); John Hazen White, Sr. Leadership Award, Rhode Island Philharmonic Orchestra (2005); Special Recognition Award, Rhode Island Arts and Business Council (2003); Rhode Island Philharmonic President's Award (1996); Elmwood Foundation Recognition Award (1992); Named Best Lawyer in America in Environmental and Business Commercial Law; Named, Super Lawyer **Bar Admissions:** United States Court of Appeals for the Second Circuit (1991); Massachusetts (1985); United States District Court District of Massachusetts (1985); United States Court of Appeals for the Eighth Circuit (1980); United States Court of Appeals for the First Circuit (1975); Supreme Court of the United States (1974); United States District Court for the District of Rhode Island (1970); Rhode Island (1968) **Marquis Who's Who Honors:** Albert Nelson Marquis Lifetime Achievement Award (2017) **Why did you become involved in your profession or industry:** Mr. Sherman's grandfather was an attorney and he also had some other relatives that were attorneys. This sparked his interest in the study and practice of the law. He always wanted to make sure that people did not have their rights infringed upon. **Shipping Address:** One Financial Plaza, Suite 2800, Lecke Lord LLP, Providence, RI, 02903

William Shields

Title: Physician **Industry:** Education/Educational Services **Company Name:** University of California, Los Angeles **Date of Birth:** 10/29/1941 **Place of Birth:** Salt Lake City **State:** UT **Education:** Residency in Neurology, School of Medicine, University of Utah (1973-1976); Residency in Pediatrics, LAC + USC Medical Center (1972-1973); Internship in Pediatrics, LAC + USC Medical Center (1971-1972); MD, School of Medicine, University of Utah (1971) **Certifications:** Pediatrics, American Board of Pediatrics (1978); Neurology with Special Qualifications in Child Neurology, American Board of Psychiatry and Neurology (1977) **Career:** Vice President, Pediatrics Epilepsy Research Foundation (2009-Present); Emeritus Professor, School of Medicine, University of California, Los Angeles (2009-Present); President, Child Neurology Foundation (2012-2015); Rubin Brown Professor, School of Medicine, University of California, Los Angeles (1999-2005); Professor, School of Medicine, University of California, Los Angeles (1990-2009); Associate Professor, School of Medicine, University of California, Los Angeles (1983-1990); Assistant Professor, School of Medicine, University of California, Los Angeles (1976-1983); Fellow, University of Utah, Salt Lake City, UT (1973-1976); Resident, University of Southern California, Los Angeles, CA (1971-1973) **Career Related:** Fellow, American Academy of Pediatrics **Civic:** President, Board Member, Epilepsy Foundation, Los Angeles, CA (1981-1988); Professional Advisory Board, Epilepsy Foundation of America, Landover, MD **Awards:** Service Award, American Epilepsy Society (1996) **Membership:** President, Child Neurology Society (2012-2015); Counselor, Child Neurology Society (1994-1996); President, Los Angeles County Epilepsy Society (1986-1989); Chairman, Professional Advisory Board, Los Angeles County Epilepsy Society (1981-1986); American Epilepsy Society; Professors of Child Neurology; American Academy of Neurology; National Institute of Neurologic Disease and Stroke **Marquis Who's Who Honors:** Albert Nelson Marquis Lifetime Achievement Award (2017) **To what do you attribute your success:** Dr. Shields attributes his success to his mentors, Dr. Spencer Snow and Dr. Patrick Bray. **Why did you become involved in your profession or industry:** Dr. Shields always had interest in medicine. He liked chemistry, but didn't want to stay in a lab; he wanted to deal with people. He specialized in child neurology because of Dr. Patrick Bray and his fascination in this field. **Shipping Address:** 5711 Stonecrest Drive, Agoura Hills, CA, 91301 **Website:** https://www.uclahealth.org/william-shields

Sam Sang-Koo Shim

Title: Accountant **Industry:** Financial Services **Company Name:** Shim & Company **Date of Birth:** 10/01/1942 **Place of Birth:** Tokyo **Country of Origin:** Japan **Parents:** Sang Taek Shim; Kum Ryon (Bae) Shim **Marital Status:** Married **Spouse Name:** Jae Hee Lee (7/12/1972) **Children:** Tammy; David **Education:** MS, University of Wisconsin-Madison (1975); MBA, Northern Illinois University (1970); BS, Seoul National University (1967) **Certifications:** Certified Valuation Analyst; Chartered Global Management Accountant; Certified Public Accountant, State of Illinois; Certified Government Financial Manager, Association of Government Accountants **Career:** Certified Public Accountant, Shim & Co. (2002-Present); Chief, Bureau of General Accounting, Illinois Department of Human Services (1997-2002); Chief Financial Officer, Illinois Department of Public Health (1983-1997); Auditor, Illinois Department of Public Health (1980-1982); Finance Consultant, Central Accounting Association (1977-1979); Accountant, Stewart-Warner Corporation (1972-1973); Accountant, Vaughn Manufacturing Company (1970-1972); Founder, Director, Metro City Bank, Atlanta, GA **Career Related:** Board of Directors, Metro City Bank, Doraville, GA (1982) **Civic:** President, Korean Association of Greater St. Louis (1982) **Membership:** President, Korean-American Association of St. Louis (2008-2010); American Institute of CPAs; National Association of Certified Valuators and Analysts; Association of Government Accountants; Illinois CPA Society; Missouri Society of CPAs **Marquis Who's Who Honors:** Albert Nelson Marquis Lifetime Achievement Award (2017) **Business Address:** 1600 Lebanon Avenue, Suite 105, 1600 Lebanon Avenue, Suite 105, IL, Belleville, 62221 **Shipping Address:** 1600 Lebanon Avenue, Suite 105, Shim & Co. CPA, Belleville, IL, 62221

W. Richard Shindle

Title: Musicologist, Educator **Industry:** Education/Educational Services **Company Name:** Kent State University **Date of Birth:** 11/02/1930 **Place of Birth:** Van Orin **State:** IL **Parents:** Ira William Shindle; Elsie Virginia Showalter **Education:** PhD in Musicology, Indiana University (1970); MusM in Musicology, Indiana University (1963); MusB, Illinois Wesleyan University (1959) **Career:** Professor Emeritus, Kent State University (1991-Present); Professor in Musicology, Kent State University (1966-1991); Instructor, Harpur College, Binghamton University, State University of New York (1964-1965); Librarian, Harpur College, Binghamton University, State University of New York (1964-1965); Research Assistant, Indiana University (1962-1964); Teacher, Calvert High School (1959-1960) **Career Related:** Summer Research Fellowship, Kent State University (1983); Summer Research Fellowship, Kent State University (1980); Summer Research Fellowship, Kent State University (1974); Fellowship, Indiana University (1965-1966); Research Assistant to Willi Apel, Indiana University (1962-1964); Founder, W. Richard Shindle Musicology Fund, Indiana University **Military Service:** Second Class Petty Officer, U.S. Navy (1951-1955) **Creative Works:** Contributor, "New Grove Dictionary of Music and Musicians, Second Updated Edition" (2001); Contributor, "Encyclopedia of Keyboard Instruments, Volume 1" (1994); Contributor, "Jean de Macque: Sieben Madrigale zu 5 und 6 Stimmen" (1987); Contributor, "Frescobaldi Studies" (1987); Contributor, "New Grove Dictionary of Music and Musicians, First Edition" (1980); Contributor, "Girolamo Frescobaldi: Keyboard Compositions Preserved in Manuscripts" (1968); Contributor, "Ercole Pasquini: Collected Keyboard Works" (1966) **Membership:** American Musicological Society, Inc.; The Pennsylvania German Society **Marquis Who's Who Honors:** Albert Nelson Marquis Lifetime Achievement Award (2017); Distinguished Humanitarian (2017) **To what do you attribute your success:** When Dr. Shindle's edition of the keyboard music of Ercole Pasquini first appeared in print, it caught the attention by the Italian organist and musicologist, Luigi Ferdinando Tagliavini, and he began to introduce it to his students. One of his students, James Johnstone, recorded the music, and another student, Paul Kenyon, also an organist and musicologist, has been updating the first volume according to the latest standards, appearing on the 50th Anniversary of the publication of his more or less pioneering edition. **Why did you become involved in your profession or industry:** The celebration of the Bach bicentennial of his death in 1950 and the Mozart bicentennial of his birth in 1956 created Dr. Shindle's interest in musicology. During his first year of study at Illinois Wesleyan University, he was introduced to the music of the Middle Ages and Renaissance, and it became apparent that his true interest was in musicology. **What do you consider to be the highlight of your career:** A highlight of Dr. Shindle's career was when he found the missing part of a book containing the alto voice for the second choir of a series of polychoral motets. He had been searching for it over a period of seven years, as it contain a number of motets by Giovanni de Macque for two and three choirs. The reason he was not able to locate it earlier is that it had been originally been miscatalouged. **Where will you be in five years:** Considering Dr. Shindle's age and for reasons of health, he is forced to limit his travel time and slow down. He will make every effort to maintain his mental abilities. **Hobbies:** Genealogy **Shipping Address:** 138 Willis Street, Apt. A, Westminster, MD, 21157

Eric Shooter

Title: Biology Professor **Industry:** Education/ Educational Services **Company Name:** Stanford University **Date of Birth:** 04/18/1924 **Place of Birth:** Mansfield **Parents:** Fred Shooter; Pattie (Johnson) Shooter **Career:** Professor of Neurobiology Emeritus, Stanford University (2004-Present); Chairman of Neuroscience PhD Program, Stanford University (1972-1982); Professor of Neurobiology, Stanford University (1987-2004); Professor, Chairman of Neurobiology Department, Stanford University (1975-1987); Professor of Genetics and Biochemistry, Stanford University (1968-1975); Associate Professor of Genetics, Stanford University (1963-1968); Biochemistry Lecturer, University College, London, United Kingdom (1953-1963); Senior Scientist, Biochemistry, Brewing Industry Research Foundation (1950-1953) **Career Related:** Co-founder, Board of Directors, Regeneron Pharmaceutical, Inc., Tarrytown, NY (1988-2014); Member, Teaching Staff, International School of Neuroscience, Praglia, Italy (1987-1993); Senior Consultant, Markey Charitable Trust, Miami, FL (1985-1989); Associate, Neuroscience Research Program, New York City, NY (1979-1989) **Creative Works:** Associate Editor, Annual Review of Neurosciences (1984-2001); Contributor, Articles, Professional Journals **Awards:** Ralph W. Gerard Prize, Society for Neuroscience (1995) **Membership:** Fellow, American Association for the Advancement of Science; Fellow, American Academy of Arts and Sciences; Fellow, Royal Society; National Academy of Sciences; American Philosophical Society; International Brain Research Organization; International Society of Neurochemistry; American Society for Neurochemistry; American Association of Biological Chemists; Society for Neuroscience; National Academy Medicine; Alpha Omega Alpha **Hobbies:** Travel **Business Address:** 370 Golden Oak Dr, CA, Portola Valley, 94028 **Shipping Address:** 370 Golden Oak Drive, Portola Valley, CA, 94028

Marion Priscilla Short

Title: Neurogenetics Educator **Industry:** Education/Educational Services **Date of Birth:** 06/12/1951 **Place of Birth:** Milford **State:** DE **Parents:** Raymond Calistus; Barbara Anne (Ferguson) Short **Marital Status:** Married **Spouse Name:** Michael Peter Klein **Children:** Asher Calistus Klein **Education:** Fellow in Neurology, Massachusetts General Hospital, Boston, MA (1986-1990); Fellow in Medical Genetics, Mount Sinai Medical Center, New York City, NY (1984-1986); Neurology Resident, University of Pittsburgh Health Center (1981-1984); Medical Resident in Internal Medicine, St. Lukes-Roosevelt Hospital, New York City, NY (1979-1981); Intern in Internal Medicine, Hahnemann Medical College Hospital, Philadelphia, PA (1978-1979); MD, Medical College of Pennsylvania (1978); Diploma, University of Edinburgh, Scotland (1975); BA, Bryn Mawr College (1973) **Certifications:** Diplomate, American Board of Internal Medicine; Diplomate, American Board of Psychiatry and Neurology **Career:** Director, Office of Science, American Medical Association (1997-2002); Program Director of Genetics, Transplantation and Clinical Research, American Medical Association, Chicago, IL (1997-2002); Senior Fellow, McLean Center for Clinical Medical Ethics, The University of Chicago (2003-2004); Fellow, McLean Center for Clinical Medical Ethics, The University of Chicago (2002-2003); Clinical Associate of Pediatric Neurosurgery, The University of Chicago (2000-2008); Assistant Professor, Department of Neurology, Pediatrics and Pathology, The University of Chicago (1995-2000); Assistant Professor, Department of Neurology, Harvard Medical School, Boston, MA (1990-1995); Assistant Neurologist, Massachusetts General Hospital, Boston, MA (1990-1995) **Civic:** Volunteer, Book Store **Creative Works:** Author, "Tales From the Pen & Other Confined Spaces" (2017) **Awards:** Fellow, Institute of Medicine, Chicago, IL (1999); Clinical Investigator Developer Award, National Institutes of Health (1988-1993) **Membership:** American Medical Association; American Academy of Neurology; American Society for Human Genetics; American College of Medical Genetics; American Association of Neurological Surgeons **To what do you attribute your success:** Dr. Short attributes her success to parental and family support. **Why did you become involved in your profession or industry:** She became involved in her profession because of the lifetime exposure to physicians. **What do you consider to be the highlight of your career:** A highlight of her career is becoming the clinical co-director of the Neurogenetics Clinic in Boston, Massachusetts. **Hobbies:** Piano **Shipping Address:** 212 Locust St SE Apt 106, Vienna, VA, 22180 **Website:** http://www.drpriscillashort.com

S. Richard Shostak

Title: Lawyer **Industry:** Law and Legal Services **Company Name:** Stein Shostak Shostak Pollack & O'Hara, LLP **Date of Birth:** 07/16/1931 **Place of Birth:** Omaha **State:** NE **Parents:** Max Reubin Shostak; Reva Ruth (Gross) Shostak **Marital Status:** Married **Spouse Name:** Carol Ruth Blumenthal **Children:** Stuart Robert; Dennis Alan; Cynthia Robin **Education:** JD, University of California, Berkeley (1956); BA, University of California, Berkeley (1953); AB, University of California, Berkeley (1951) **Career:** Of Counsel, Stein Shostak Shostak Pollack & O'Hara, LLP (2013-Present); Partner, Stein Shostak Shostak Pollack & O'Hara, LLP, Shanghai, China (2005-2013); Vice President, Stein Shostak Shostak Pollack & O'Hara, LLP, San Diego, CA (1976-2005); Partner, Stein Shostak Shostak Pollack & O'Hara, LLP, Los Angeles, CA (1960-1976); Deputy District Attorney, Santa Rosa, CA (1958-1959); Sonoma County District Attorney, Santa Rosa, CA (1958-1959); Associate, Geary, Spridgen & Moskowitz, Santa Rosa, CA (1956-1958); Vice President, Stein Shostak Shostak Pollack and O'Hara LLP, Washington, DC; Partner, Stein Shostak Shostak Pollack and O'Hara LLP, Los Angeles, CA; Partner, Stein Shostak Shostak Pollack & O'Hara, LLP, San Diego, CA; Partner, Stein, Shostak, Shostak & O'Hara, Washington, DC **Career Related:** Lecturer, University of California, Los Angeles Extension (1975-1992); Hearing Examiner, Police Commission, Los Angeles Police Department (1964-1979) **Civic:** Member, Committee for Production Sharing, Washington, DC (1989-1992); Secretary, Committee for 807, Washington, DC (1980-1988); Chairman, World Trade Week, Los Angeles, CA (1976) **Creative Works:** Author, "Mastering the United States Customs Laws and Regulations" (2016); Author, "US Customs Laws and Regulations" (1978-1980); Contributor, Articles, Professional Journals **Membership:** President, Foreign Trade Association of Southern California (1976-1978); Chairman, Board of Directors, Foreign Trade Association of Southern California (1976-1978); ABA; Los Angeles Chamber of Commerce **Bar Admissions:** United States Court of International Trade (1981); The District of Columbia (1980); Supreme Court of the United States (1960); United States Court of Appeals for the Federal Circuit (1960); California (1956); United States District Court Southern District of California (1956); United States District Court Central District of California (1956); United States Court of Appeals for the Ninth Circuit **Marquis Who's Who Honors:** Albert Nelson Marquis Lifetime Achievement Award (2017); Distinguished Humanitarian (2017) **Hobbies:** Golf **Business Address:** 865 S. Figueroa Street, Suite 1388, 865 S. Figueroa Street, Suite 1388, CA, Los Angeles, 90071 **Shipping Address:** 865 S Figueroa St Ste 1388, Stein Shostak Shostak Pollack & O'Hara, LLP, Los Angeles, CA, 90071

Jean-Philippe Siblet

Title: Museum Director **Industry:** Museums & Institutions **Company Name:** National Museum of Natural History **Date of Birth:** 03/29/1957 **Place of Birth:** Paris **Country of Origin:** France **Parents:** Guy Siblet; Suzanne Siblet **Marital Status:** Married **Spouse Name:** Corinne Siblet (6/16/1984) **Education:** Degree in Bird Censusing Methods, University of Burgundy (2000); Degree in Public Law, University Paris II Pantheon-Assas (1980) **Career:** Director, Natural Heritage Service, National Museum of Natural History, Paris, France (2007-Present); Director of Expertise, National Museum of Natural History, Paris, France (2017); Head, Nature Protection Service, Regional Direction of Environment, Paris, France (1988-2007) **Civic:** General Secretary, French Society of Ornithological Studies, Paris, France (2009-2014); President, Association Naturaliste d'Ouessant, Lampaul, France (2009-2014); President, Forest Naturalists' Association, Fontainebleau, France (2008-2014) **Awards:** Honoree, National Merit Order Officer Medal, French Republic President (2016); Honoree, National Merit Order Chevalier Medal, French Republic President (1997); Vermeil Medal, French Agriculture Academy **Membership:** WPCA; International Union for the Conservation of Nature, Gland, Switzerland; National Council of Nature Protection, Paris, France **Hobbies:** Bird watching **Shipping Address:** 1 Bis Rue Des Sablonnieres, Saint-Mammes, France, 77670 **Website:** http://www.jean-philippesiblet.com

Ruth S. Sides

Title: Music Educator **Industry:** Education/Educational Services **Parents:** John Daniel; I. Ruth Schulmeyer **Spouse Name:** Anthony Fred Sides (5/25/1972, Deceased 9/7/1997) **Children:** Rebecca Ruth Desenti; Connie Susanne Moore **Education:** BA, Baldwin Wallace College (Now Baldwin Wallace University) (1968) **Certifications:** Certified Teacher, State of Ohio (1968) Certified Teacher, State of Florida (1973) **Career:** Chair, Department of Fine Arts and Foreign Languages, South Lake High School, FL (2002-2005); Director of Choral Music, South Lake High School, FL (1993-2005); Director, Choral Music, Groveland High School (Now South Lake High School), FL (1972-2016); Director, Band, Ridgemont Local Schools, Ridgeway, OH (1967-1971); Director, Choruses, Ridgemont Local Schools, Ridgeway, OH (1967-1971) **Career Related:** Garden Community Choir, Winter Garden, FL; Assistant Conductor, Kings Ridge Singers **Civic:** Certified Judge, Florida BBQ Association, FL (2002-Present) **Creative Works:** Owner, Craftor, MAESTRO MADE-N **Awards:** Nominee, Disney's American Teacher, Walt Disney World (2001); Award, Teacherific Judge's Choice, Disney (2000); Honoree, Groveland High School Year Dedication (Now South Lake High School) (1975-1976); Honoree, Outstanding Young Women of America (1973); Honoree, Teacher of the Year, Hardin County Schools (1969-1970) **Membership:** Florida Vocal Association; Florida Music Educators Association **Marquis Who's Who Honors:** Albert Nelson Marquis Lifetime Achievement Award (2017) **To what do you attribute your success:** She attributes her success to a motto she created. This phrase she used in her classroom has managed to be used by most of her colleagues. Her plan for success: you need to plan, prepare, practice and perform. And if that doesn't work, the last is guaranteed for success in life. If you are patient and polite, the rest of the world will never know how smart or dumb you are and you will be successful. **Why did you become involved in your profession or industry:** She became involved in her profession because she was inspired by her high school band director. She liked what he did; everybody came to the band room to hang out and you felt you were part of a special group. She wanted to pass that feeling on to the next generation. **What do you consider to be the highlight of your career:** One of the highlights of her career includes being part of a team that was chosen as a Walt Disney World "teacherific" team, where they were awarded $10,000 for contributions to their school and community. **Hobbies:** Crafts; Cooking; Sewing; Traveling **Shipping Address:** 11844 Lake Minneola Shores, Minneola, FL, 34715

Joel D. Siegal

Title: Lawyer **Industry:** Law and Legal Services **Company Name:** Hellring Lindeman Goldstein & Siegal LLP **Place of Birth:** Plainfield **State/Country of Origin:** NJ **Parents:** Samuel Siegal; Florence (Ravitz) Siegal **Children:** Samuel; Evan **Education:** MA in International Relations, Stockholm University (1963); JD, Yale Law School (1961); BA in Political Science, University of Pennsylvania (1958) **Career:** Partner, Hellring Lindeman Goldstein & Siegal LLP, Newark, NJ (1970-Present); Law Clerk to the Honorary Phillip Forman, United States Court of Appeals for the Third Circuit (1963-1964); Law Clerk to the Honorary Arthur S. Lane, United States District Court (1961-1962). **Career Related:** Participant, Panelist, "The Big Trial as a Media Event," Media Bench Bar Dialogues, Sponsored by Rutgers Law School per Grant from S.I. Newhouse Foundation (1998); New Jersey Commissioner, The National Conference of Commissioners on Uniform State Laws (1991-1998); Member, Drafting Committee, Uniform Interstate Family Support Act; United States District Court Lawyers Advisory Committee (1991-1992); Member, Working Group of the Subcommittee on Commercial Litigation, Supreme Court of New Jersey Committee on Civil Case Management and Procedure (1983-1984); Author, "Non-matrimonial Claims in Matrimonial Actions," The Matrimonial Strategist (1985) **Awards:** AV Preeminent Rating (Highest Possible Rating in both Legal Ability and Ethical Standards), Martindale-Hubbell Judicial Edition (2017); Albert Nelson Marquis Lifetime Achievement Award for Career Longevity and Unwavering Excellence, Marquis Who's Who Publications Board (2017) **Membership:** President, The Association of the Federal Bar of New Jersey (1990-1992); Bergen County Bar Association; Essex County Bar Association; New Jersey State Bar Association; The Harmonie Club; Lifetime Fellow, American Bar Foundation; ABA **Bar Admissions:** New Jersey State Bar (1962); New York State Bar (1965); United States District Court of District of New Jersey (1962); United States Court of Appeals for the Third Circuit (1963); Supreme Court of the United States (1969); United States District Court Southern District of New York (1975); United States District Court Eastern District of New York (1975) **Marquis Who's Who Honors:** Albert Nelson Marquis Lifetime Achievement Award (2017) **Shipping Address:** 1 Gateway Ctr., Fl 8, Hellring Lindeman Goldstein & Siegal LLP, Newark, NJ, 07102

Arthur C. Silverman

Title: Member, Building Construction Lawyer **Industry:** Architecture & Construction **Company Name:** Rosenberg & Estis, P.C. **Date of Birth:** 06/13/1938 **Place of Birth:** Lewiston **State:** ME **Parents:** Louis A. Silverman; Frances (Brownstone) Silverman **Marital Status:** Married **Spouse Name:** Donna Zolov (6/18/1961) **Children:** Leonard; Daniel **Education:** JD, Columbia Law School, Columbia University (1964); BS in Industrial Management, Massachusetts Institute of Technology (1960); BS in Electrical Engineering, Massachusetts Institute of Technology (1960) **Career:** Member and Head of, Building Construction Group, Rosenberg + Estis, P.C. (2018-Present); Partner, Duane Morris LLP (2008-2018); Partner, Thelen LLP (Formerly Thelen Reid & Priest) (1989-2008); Partner, Golenbock & Barell (1972-1989); Associate, Golenbock & Barell, New York, NY (1968-1972); Associate, Baer & Marks, New York, NY (1965-1968); Law Clerk, Chief Judge Lumbard, United States Court of Appeals for the Second Circuit (1964-1965); Engineering Assistant, Missile and Space Vehicles and Ordnance Divisions, General Electric, Pittsfield, MA and Philadelphia, PA (1958-1962) **Career Related:** Lawyer, Owner Advisors, Owner Representatives and Construction Managers, Lehrer McGovern, Inc. (Now Lehrer LLC), Lehrer McGovern Bovis, Inc. (Now Lendlease Corporation), Boris Lend Lease LMB, Inc., Schal Bovis Inc., McDevitt Street Bovis Inc., and Bovis Lend Lease Americas (1979-2001); Lawyer, Owners and Developers; Lawyer, National September 11 Memorial & Museum; Lawyer, Jetblue Terminal, John F. Kennedy International Airport, The Port Authority of New York and New Jersey; Lawyer, iTech Uplink Facilities, Home Box Office, Inc.; Lawyer, New Harlem Campus, Lois V. and Samuel J. Silberman School of Social Work at Hunter College; Lawyer, Barbara Walters Campus Center, Sarah Lawrence College; Lawyer, New Learning Center, Barnard College; Lawyer, Eataly Restaurants and Food Markets, Eataly Net USA LLC, Flat Iron District and World Trade Center, New York City, NY and Prudential Center, Boston, MA **Civic:** Member, Commission Appointed by New York City Mayor Michael Bloomberg to Find Ways to Reduce Construction Costs of New York City Public Schools (2001); Member, Executive Committee, National Jewish Center for Learning & Leadership (Now CLAL) (1984-1990); Board of Governors, Massachusetts Institute of Technology Chapter, Hillel International (1979-1984); Past Chair, Board of Trustees, The Ramaz School, New York, NY **Creative Works:** Author, "Getting the Most for Owners in Construction Contracting," The Voice, Construction Users Roundtable (2009) **Awards:** Named, Top Rated Lawyers in Construction (2014-2015); Named, Super Lawyers Business Edition (2014-2015); Named, Avenue Magazine's Legal Elite (2010-2014); Named, Corporate Counsel's Best Lawyers (2011-2013); Named, America's Leading Lawyers, Chambers & Partners (2008-2017); Listed, The Best Lawyers in America, Construction Law Section, U.S. News & World Report L.P./Best Lawyers (2007-2018); Listed, New York Super Lawyers (2006-2018); Named, Super Lawyers Corporate Counsel Edition (2006-2013); Named, Leading Construction Lawyer in New York, Chambers & Partners; AV Preeminent Peer-Review Rated Attorney, State of Maryland, Martindale-Hubbell; Best Presentation in Moot Court, Columbia Law School **Membership:** Committee on Construction Law, Association of the Bar of the City of New York (2011-Present); Forum on the Construction Industry, ABA; Section of Litigation, Committee on Construction, ABA; Committee on Design Construction, Section of Real Property, ABA; Business Law Section, ABA; Section on Real Estate, New York State Bar Association; Dispute Resolution Section, New York State Bar Association; Section on Torts, New York State Bar Association; Section on Insurance and Commerce, New York State Bar Association; NYSSPE; Professional Member, Construction Specifications Institute; Federal Bar Council; Associate Member, National Society of Professional Engineers; Planning, Growth and Sustainability Committee, Higher Education Committee, Healthcare Committee, New York Building Congress **Bar Admissions:** Supreme Court of the United States (1971); New York (1965); United States District Court Eastern District of New York; United States District Court Southern District of New York **Marquis Who's Who Honors:** Albert Nelson Marquis Lifetime Achievement Award (2017); Distinguished Humanitarian (2017) **Religion:** Jewish **Business Address:** 733 3rd Avenue, New York, NY, 10017

Franklin H. Sim

Title: Orthopedic Surgery Educator **Industry:** Education/Educational Services **Company Name:** Mayo Clinic **Date of Birth:** 09/02/1940 **Place of Birth:** New Glasgow **Country of Origin:** Canada **Children:** Leslie; Sheridan **Education:** MD, Dalhousie University Medical School (1964) **Certifications:** Certified Orthopedic Surgery, State of Minnesota (1972) **Career:** Professor of Orthopedic Surgery, Mayo Clinic, Rochester, MN (1983) **Career Related:** Chair, Division of Orthopedic Oncology, Mayo Clinic (2000-Present) **Civic:** Physician, United States National Hockey Team **Military Service:** Second Lieutenant, The Black Watch (Royal Highland Regiment) of Canada, Germany (1961) **Awards:** Diversity Award (2012); Distinguished Award, Mayo Clinic (2003); Outstanding Service Award, Canadian Orthopedic Association (2000) **Membership:** Honorary Fellow, Royal Australian College of Surgeons; SICOT; American Medical Association; Orthopedic Practice Society; Orthopedic Research Society; Musculoskeletal Tumor Society; Minnesota Orthopedic Society; Mid-American Orthopedic Association; International Society of Limb Salvage; International Society of Intraoperative Radiation Therapy; International Skeletal Society; International Orthopedic Association; Board of Directors, Canadian Orthopedic Foundation; American Orthopedic Association; American Orthopedic Society of Sports Medicine; American College of Sports Medicine; American Academy of Orthopedic Surgeons; 20th Century Orthopedic Society; Honorary Member, Ruth Jackson Orthopedic Society; Sigma Xi, The Scientific Research Honor Society **Marquis Who's Who Honors:** Albert Nelson Marquis Lifetime Achievement Award (2017) **Shipping Address:** 1303 Woodland Drive SW, Rochester, MN, 55902

Cynthia Simms Smith

Title: Chief Financial Officer **Industry:** Financial Services **Company Name:** ARSG Inc **Education:** Associate's Degree, National Institute for Paralegal Arts and Sciences (1999) **Career:** Chief Financial Officer, ARSG Inc. (2009-Present); Owner, Sync USA (2008-Present); Owner, Marketing Professions (Now ARSG, Inc.) (1993-2009); Western Regional Manager, Perfect Endings/Culinary Sales (1992-1993); Partner, Exsell Brokerage (1988-1992); Regional Sales Manager, Main on Foods, Corporation (1985-1988); Retail Representative, Various Departments, Crown BBK (1980-1985); Employee, Fazio Markets **Awards:** Awards for Outstanding Sales and Merchandising, Crown BBK **Shipping Address:** 3870 E Eagle Drive, ARSG, Inc, Anaheim, CA, 92807

Simon John Simonian

Title: Transformer Evolutionary Futures Collaborator, Surgeon, Scientist, Educator, Writer, Spiritual Leader for Justice & Peace, Quaker Justice **Industry:** Medicine & Health Care **Company Name:** Interfaith Communities United for Justice and Peace **Date of Birth:** 04/20/1932 **Place of Birth:** Antioch **Country of Origin:** Turkey **Parents:** John Simon Simonian; Marie (Tomboulian) Simonian **Marital Status:** Married **Spouse Name:** Arpi Ani Yeghiayan (7/11/1965) **Children:** Leonard Armen; Charles Haig; Andrew Hovig **Education:** DSc, National Academy of Sciences of the Republic of Armenia, with Honors (1998); Chief Resident in Surgery, Boston City Hospital (Now Boston Medical Center) (1970-1974); Resident, Boston City Hospital (Now Boston Medical Center) (1970-1974); MA in Physiological Sciences, University of Oxford (1969); DSc in Nutrition, Immunology and Genetics, Harvard University (1969); MSc in Nutrition, Immunology and Genetics, Harvard University (1967); BA in Physiological Sciences, St. Edmund Hall, University of Oxford (1964); Resident, City Hospital, The University of Edinburgh (1959-1960); Resident, Birmingham Accident and Burns Hospital, University of Birmingham (1959-1960); Resident, Western General Hospital, NHS Lothian, The University of Edinburgh (1958-1959); Intern in Surgery, Royal Infirmary of Edinburgh, NHS Lothian, The University of Edinburgh (1957-1958) **Certifications:** License to Practice Medicine, Commonwealth of Virginia (1990); License to Practice Medicine, State of Michigan (1988); License to Practice Medicine, Commonwealth of Pennsylvania (1978); Diplomate, American Board of Surgery, Inc. (1977); License to Practice Medicine, State of Illinois (1974); License to Practice Medicine, Commonwealth of Massachusetts (1970); Certified in Education, Council of Foreign Medical Graduates (1970) **Career:** Centennial Celebration Speaker, Interfaith Communities United for Justice and Peace (2012-Present); Board Member, Interfaith Communities United for Justice and Peace (2012-Present); Chairman, Mission Statement Committee, Interfaith Communities United for Justice and Peace (2012-Present); Member, World Future Society (2014); Clinical Professor of Surgery, Georgetown University (1995-2006); Guest Lecturer, Georgetown University (1994); Active Attending Faculty, Fairfax Hospital, Inova (1992-2006); Clinical Associate Professor of Surgery, Georgetown University (1992-1995); President and Chief Executive Officer, Vein Institute of Metropolitan Washington, Inc. (1990-2006); Associate Attending Staff, Fairfax Hospital, Inova (1990-1992) **Career Related:** Founding Member, Science Board, Center for Regenerative Biology and Medicine, Indiana University (2001-2015); Member, International Consensus Panel, The Prevention, Investigation and Treatment of Venous Thromboembolism and Thrombophilia, Windsor, England (2005); Kwang Dong Lecturer, Annual Congress, Phlebological Society of Korea (2003); Biomedical Lecturer (2003); Member, Faculty and Moderator, International Consensus Panel on Thrombophilia, Limassol, Cyprus (2003); Venus Lecturer European Chapter Congress, International Union of Angiology (2003); Honorary Member, German International Forum for Phlebology and Minisurgery of Varicose Veins (2000); Lecturer, Ninth Pan-American Congress of Phlebology and Lymphology, International Union of Phlebology, Cordoba, Argentina (2000); Medical Consultant to Alan Hovaness (1998-2000); Consultant for Venous Vascular Surgery, Podiatry Residence Program, Northern Virginia Medical College (Now Virginia Commonwealth University) (1994-2000); Venus Lecturer, European Chapter Congress, International Union of Angiology (1999); Member, International Consensus Panel on Venous Thromboembolism, Greece (1999) **Civic:** Philanthropist, University of Southern California (2012-Present); Participant, Non Violent Peace Vigils (2011-Present); Affiliate, Entry into Manhood of Armenian Youth at Age (2011-Present); Philanthropist, University of California, Los Angeles (2009-Present); Philanthropist, Armenian Academy of Sciences (2008-Present); Philanthropist, Harvard Medical School (2007-Present); Philanthropist, Weill Cornell Medicine (2007-Present); Philanthropist, New York-Presbyterian Hospital (2007-Present) **Membership:** Leadership Council, NAASR (2012-Present); Board of Advisers, Museum of Musical Compositions of Alan Hovhaness (2007-Present); President's Club, AGBU (1990-Present); Attendee, Annual Meeting, European Academy of Arts and Sciences (2014); Clerk, Chairman Nominating Committee, Peace & Social Action Committee (2011-2012); Nominating Committee, Peace & Social Action Committee (2011-2012); Co-chairman, Alumni Giving Council, School of Public Health, Harvard University (2007-2009); Board of Directors, NAASR (2004-2006); Co-founder, Leadership Council, School of Public Health, Harvard University (2003-2009); European Academy of Arts and Sciences (2004); Past Chairman, Phlebological Surgery Section, American College of Phlebology (2003-2004) **Marquis Who's Who Honors:** Albert Nelson Marquis Lifetime Achievement Award (2017) **Religion:** Society of Friends **Business Address:** 817 W 34th St., Los Angeles, CA, 90089 **Shipping Address:** 1101 El Medio Ave, Pacific Palisades, CA, 90272

John Nelson Simons

Title: Associate Professor of Plastic Surgery **Industry:** Education/Educational Services **Company Name:** Mayo Foundation for Medical Education and Research **Date of Birth:** 09/19/1932 **Place of Birth:** Lawrence **State:** KS **Parents:** Dolph Collins Simons; Marie Nelson Simons **Children:** John, Jr.; Andrea; James; Suzanne; Melissa **Education:** Resident of Plastic Surgery, University of Kansas (1963-1965); CM, University of Minnesota (1963); Resident of General Surgery, Mayo Clinic (1959-1963); Intern in Medicine, University of Kansas (1958-1959); MD, University of Pennsylvania (1958); BA, University of Kansas (1954) **Certifications:** Certification, The American Board of Plastic Surgery, Inc. (1967); Certification, American Board of Surgery, Inc. (1964) **Career:** Private Practice, Paradise Valley, AZ (1981-2003); Private Practice, Scottsdale, AZ (1974-1980); Associate Professor of Plastic Surgery, Mayo Foundation for Medical Education and Research (Now Mayo Clinic), Rochester, MN (1972-1973); Head of Plastic Surgery Section, Mayo Foundation for Medical Education and Research (Now Mayo Clinic), Rochester, MN (1967-1973); Assistant Professor of Plastic Surgery, Mayo Foundation for Medical Education and Research (Now Mayo Clinic), Rochester, MN (1965-1972); Consultant in Plastic Surgery, Mayo Foundation for Medical Education and Research (Now Mayo Clinic), Rochester, MN (1965-1966) **Career Related:** Founder, Chief Executive Officer, Simons Wellness Center (2000-Present); Founder, Chief Executive Officer, Health Campus International, Consultants in Health Care Delivery, East Gulf Lake, MN (1973-Present); Designer, Financier, Sole Practitioner, Southwest Plastic Surgeons (1974-2003); Speaker in Field **Creative Works:** Author in Field **Awards:** Outstanding Ambulatory Surgical Facility in America, American Society of Ambulatory Surgeons (1987); Outstanding Young Men in America (1967) **Membership:** Vice Chairman of the Board, Park Inn International Hotel Management Company (1987-1997); American Society of Plastic Surgeons; American Association of Plastic Surgeons; American Society for Aesthetic Plastic Surgery, Inc. (Now ASAPS); Plastic Surgery Research; Western Surgical Association (Now WSA); Society of Head and Neck Surgeons (Now American Head and Neck Society) **Marquis Who's Who Honors:** Albert Nelson Marquis Lifetime Achievement Award (2017) **To what do you attribute your success:** Dr. Simons attributes his success to his unlimited ability and desire to work. He started working while he was young and he enjoys challenges that come with it. He also believes in being honest, staying informed, and enjoying life. **Why did you become involved in your profession or industry:** Dr. Simons became a doctor because the head of his university, who was also a doctor and family friend, spoke to him about medical school. He wanted to be involved in a profession where he could see instant results from his work. **What do you consider to be the highlight of your career:** The highlight of Dr. Simons' career is being in the operating room and operating on patients. **Hobbies:** Reading; Sports **Political Affiliations:** Republican **Shipping Address:** 10999 Pine Beach Peninsula Road, Brainerd, MN, 56401

David A. Simpson

Title: Professor of Neurology, Associate Professor **Industry:** Education/Educational Services **Company Name:** Michigan State University, University of Michigan **Date of Birth:** 03/29/1955 **Place of Birth:** Highland Park **State:** MI **Parents:** Fred Raymond Simpson; Mary Theresa (Rossi) Simpson **Marital Status:** Married **Spouse Name:** Anne M. Pawlak (10/20/1984) **Children:** Francis Simpson **Education:** DO, Kirksville College of Osteopathic Medicine, A.T. Still University (1983); MS in Human Anatomy, Wayne State University (1979); BS in Biology, Wayne State University, With Distinction (1977) **Certifications:** Certified Examiner, American Board of Psychology & Neurology, Inc.; Certified Examiner, American Board of Electrodiagnostic Medicine **Career:** Staff Neurologist, Michigan Institute for Neurological Disorders (1991-Present); Professor of Neurology, Michigan State University (2008); Associate Clinical Professor, Michigan State University (2001-2009); Assistant Clinical Professor, Michigan State University (2001-2009); Associate Clinical Professor, University of Michigan (1992-2002); Assistant Clinical Professor, University of Michigan (1992-2002); Resident in Neurology, Botsford General Hospital (Now Beaumont Health) (1988-1991) **Career Related:** Physician, Wheel-Chair Hockey League (1999-Present); MDA/ALS Center, Michigan Institute for Neurological Disorders (1991-Present); Director, MDA Clinic, Michigan State University (2001-2009); Co-Director, Muscular Dystrophy Clinic of Southeastern Michigan (1991-2009); Director of Fellowship Training in Neuromuscular Disease, Michigan Institute for Neurological Disorders; Lecturer, Fieldwork **Civic:** Carmelite Sisters for the Aged and Infirm; Muscular Dystrophy Association, Inc.; Food for the Poor, Inc.; Heifer Foundation **Military Service:** Lieutenant Colonel, U.S. Army (1997); Commissioned Second Lieutenant, U.S. Army (1979); Special Forces, U.S. Army; Special Operations Delta Force, U.S. Army **Creative Works:** Patentee; Contributor, Articles, Professional Journals; Chief Editor, "Journal of American College of Neurologists and Psychiatrists" **Awards:** Army Paratroop Medal, U.S. Army; Army Combat Medal, U.S. Army; Army Reserve Medal, U.S. Army; Army Achievement Medal, U.S. Army; Humanitarian Service Medal, U.S. Army; Army Commendation Medal, U.S. Army; Meritorious Service Medal, U.S. Army; Army Distinguished Service Medal, U.S. Army; Iraq Campaign and Southeast Asia Service Medal, U.S. Army; Legion of Merit, U.S. Armed Forces **Membership:** American Osteopathic Association; Michigan Osteopathic Association; American College of Neuropsychiatrists; Psi Sigma Alpha; Sigma Sigma Alpha; American Association of Neuromuscular and Electrodiagnostic Medicine **Marquis Who's Who Honors:** Albert Nelson Marquis Lifetime Achievement Award (2017) **To what do you attribute your success:** Dr. Simpson attributes his success to his commitment, dedication, and hard work. **Why did you become involved in your profession or industry:** Dr. Simpson became involved in his profession because of his dedication to the care of patients, no matter the color of their skin, their ability to pay, or their ethnic background. **What do you consider to be the highlight of your career:** A highlight of Dr. Simpson's career was his military service because he went all over the world. Another highlight was working in the MDA/ALS clinics. **Where will you be in five years:** In five years, Dr. Simpson will be retired and working at Disney or working in Traverse City, Mich. **Hobbies:** Golf; Skiing; Boating **Religion:** Roman Catholic **Shipping Address:** 19550 Laurel Drive, Livonia, MI, 48152

Dick W. Simpson, PhD

Title: Professor **Industry:** Education/Educational Services **Company Name:** University of Illinois at Chicago **Date of Birth:** 11/08/1940 **Place of Birth:** Houston **State:** TX **Parents:** Warren Weldon Simpson; Ola Ela (Felts) Simpson **Marital Status:** Single **Spouse Name:** Sarajane Avidon (3/22/1987, Deceased 3/29/2006) **Children:** Kate Donley; August Donley **Education:** MDiv, McCormick Theological Seminary (1984); PhD, Indiana University (1968); MA, Indiana University (1964); BA, The University of Texas (1963) **Certifications:** Ordained Minister, United Church of Christ **Career:** Professor, The University of Illinois at Chicago (1996-Present); Department Head, The University of Illinois at Chicago (2006-2012); Associate Professor of Political Science, The University of Illinois at Chicago (1972-1996); Assistant Professor, The University of Illinois at Chicago (1968-1971); Instructor, The University of Illinois at Chicago (1967-1968); Foreign Area Fellow, Ford Foundation, Africa (1966-1967); Research Assistant, Indiana University, Bloomington, IN (1965) **Career Related:** Honoree, Great Cities Fellow (2005-2006); Honoree, Great Cities Fellow (1997-1998); Executive Director, Clergy and Laity Concerned, Chicago, IL (1987-1989); Executive Director, Institute on Church and Urban-Industrial Society, Chicago, IL (1984-1986) **Civic:** Transition Team Member, Board President, Todd Stroger, Cook County (2006-2007); Transition Team, Illinois Attorney General Lisa Madigan (2003); Congressional Candidate (1994); Congressional Candidate (1992); State's Attorney, O'Malley and County Clerk Orr (1990-1991); Minister, United Church of Christ (1985-2005); Transition Team, Mayor Byrne, City of Chicago (1983); Transition Team, Mayor Washington, City of Chicago (1979); Alderman, City Council, City of Chicago (1971-1979); Campaign Manager, McCarthy for President, Illinois (1967-1968) **Creative Works:** Author, "The Good Fight" (2018); Author, "Teaching Civic Engagement Across the Disciplines" (2017); Author, "Winning Elections in the 21st Century" (2016); Author, "Twenty-First Century Chicago," Second Edition (2015-2016); Author, "Corrupt Illinois" (2015); Author, "Teaching Civic Engagement" (2013); Author, "African Democracy and Development" (2012); Author, "Twenty-First Century Chicago" (2012); Author, "The City, Revisited" (2011); Author, "Struggle for Power in Cities and States" (2009); Producer, "Teaching Politics" (2006); Political Adviser, "Teaching Politics" (2006); Author, "Inside Urban Politics" (2004); Author, "Rogues, Rebels, and Rubber Stamps" (2001); Author, "Winning Elections," Fourth Edition (1996); Editor, "Chicago's Future," Fifth Edition (1993); Author, "Politics of Compassion" (1989); Editor, "Chicago's Future," Fourth Edition (1988); Editor, "Chicago's Future," Third Edition (1983); Author, "Winning Elections," Third Edition (1981); Editor, "Chicago's Future," Second Edition (1980); Editor, "Chicago's Future" (1976); Author, "Strategies for Change" (1976); Author, "Winning Elections," Second Edition (1974); Author, "Winning Elections" (1972); Producer, "By the People" (1970); Political Adviser, "By the People" (1970) **Awards:** Lifetime Achievement Award, Political Science Education Section, American Political Science Association (2017); Excellence in Teaching Award, The University of Illinois at Chicago (2004); Excellence in Teaching Award, The University of Illinois at Chicago (2002); Excellence in Teaching Award, American Political Science Association (2002); Excellence in Teaching Award, The University of Illinois at Chicago (1997); Honoree, Humanities Institute Fellow, The University of Illinois at Chicago (1985-1986); Research Grant, Joyce, Amoco, Woods, McArthur, Crossroads, Carnegie, Wieboldt Foundations (1972-2009); Excellence in Teaching Award, The University of Illinois at Chicago (1971); Award, Clarence Darrow Community Center, Clergy And Laity Concerned, Independent Voters of Illinois Independent Precinct Organization; Award, City Club of Chicago; Award Society of Midland Authors **Membership:** Teaching and Learning Committee, American Political Science Association (2008-2010); Midwest Political Science Association; Past President, Illinois Political Science Association; Vice President, City Club of Chicago; Society of Midland Authors **Shipping Address:** University of Illinois at Chicago, Department of Political Science, 1007 W Harrison Street, MC 276 1102 BSB, Chicago, IL, 60607

Sandra Kay Simpson

Title: Operations Research Specialist **Industry:** Government Administration/Government Relations/Government Services **Company Name:** United States Government **Date of Birth:** 02/26/1949 **Place of Birth:** Rutland **State:** VT **Parents:** Freeman Edward Campbell; Ruth Gail (Smith) Campbell **Education:** MSc in International Relations, Troy State University, Europe (1991); MPA, Troy State University, Europe (1988); BA, University of Vermont, Burlington, VT (1971) **Career:** Defense Logistics Agency, United States Government, Wiesbaden, Germany (2007-2015); Theater Level Logistics Manager, United States Government, Wiesbaden, United States (2005-2007); Defense Logistics Agency, United States Government, Wiesbaden, Germany (2003-2005); Theater Level Logistics Manager, United States Government, Wiesbaden, Germany (2002-2003); Deputy Director Internal Logistics, United States Government, Wiesbaden, Germany (1999-2002); Maintenance Management Coordinator, United States Government, Wiesbaden, Germany (1994-1999); Property Accounting Officer, United States Government, Wiesbaden, Germany (1986-1993); Property Accounting Officer, United States Government, Fort Hood, TX (1982-1986); Assistant Logistics Officer, United States Government, Kitzingen, Germany (1979-1982); Instructor & Trainer, United States Government, Fort McClellan, AL (1975-1979) **Career Related:** Consultant, United States Government, Kaiserslautern, Germany (1994-Present) **Military Service:** US Army (1973-1993) **Membership:** Secretary, Wiesbaden/Mainz Retiree Council (1994-Present); Charter Member, Women in Military Service for American Memorial Foundation (Now Women's Memorial); Retiree Council, United States Army Europe (Now Army in Europe Retiree Council; The Oxford Club **Marquis Who's Who Honors:** Distinguished Humanitarian (2017) **Hobbies:** Photography; Marathons **Business Address:** CMR 467, Box 1505, AE, APO, 09096

Robert Ewald Sinclair

Title: Physician (Retired) **Industry:** Medicine & Health Care **Date of Birth:** 01/19/1924 **Place of Birth:** Columbus **State:** OH **Year of Passing:** 2018-03-09 **Parents:** George Albert Sinclair; Bertha Florence (Ewald) Sinclair **Marital Status:** Married **Spouse Name:** Mary Almira Underwood (3/31/1945) **Children:** Marcia Ann; Bonnie Sue **Education:** Chief Psychiatric Resident, Adolescent Unit, Columbus State Hospital (1965-1966); Resident in Neurology and Psychiatry, Columbus State Hospital (1964-1966); Intern, Mount Carmel Hospital, Columbus, OH (1952-1953); MD, The Ohio State University (1952); BA, The Ohio State University (1948) **Certifications:** Licensed Physician, State of Ohio; Licensed Physician, State of Colorado; Licensed Physician, State of Alabama; Licensed Physician, State of Kansas **Career:** Retired, The University of Alabama (1988); Professor of Medicine, The University of Alabama (1980-1988); Director, Russell Student Health Center and Hospital (1970-1980); Team Physician, Kansas State University (1970-1980); Director, Lafene Student Health Center and University Hospital (1966-1970); Director, Student Health Service, University of Cincinnati (1966-1970); Team Physician, University of Cincinnati (1966-1970); Director, Student Health Service, Denison University (1957-1964); Professor of Health Education, Denison University (1957-1964); Team Physician, Denison University (1957-1964); Private Practice in Medicine, Granville, OH (1957-1964); Private Practice in Medicine, Columbus, OH (1953-1957) **Career Related:** Member, Licking County Board of Health (1958-1959); Physician, Westinghouse Electric Corp., Columbus, OH (1953-1957); Assistant Zone Chief, Civilian Defense, Columbus, OH (1954-1957) **Civic:** Drug Abuse and Education Committee (1968-1970); Board of Directors, Social Health Committee, Cincinnati and Hamilton County (1967-1970) **Military Service:** U.S. Naval Reserve (1943-1946) **Awards:** Hall of Fame, West High Alumni Association (2004); Jonoree, Men of Achievement, International Biographical Centre (1975); Featured Listee, Moore's Who is Who in Ohio (1961) **Membership:** President, Southern College Health Association (1986); President, Central College Health Association (1972-1973); President, Ohio College Health Association (1970-1971); Newsletter Editor, Ohio College Health Association (1968-1970); President, Nu Sigma Nu Ohio State Alumni Association (1953-1954); American Medical Association; Ohio Medical Society; Kansas Medical Society; Alabama Medical Society; Columbus Academy of Medicine; Licking County Medical Society; Riley County Medical Society; Tuscaloosa County Medical Society; National Athletic Trainers Association; St. Andrews Society; Southern Medicine Association; Faculty Adviser, Delta Tau Delta; Nu Sigma Nu; Kiwanis International; Rotary International **Marquis Who's Who Honors:** Albert Nelson Marquis Lifetime Achievement Award (2017) **Hobbies:** Playing jazz music; DJing **Shipping Address:** Marcia Grauerholz, 21265 West 181st street, Olathe, KS, 66062

Alan Daniel Singer

Title: Artist, Professor **Industry:** Education/Educational Services **Company Name:** Rochester Institute of Technology **Date of Birth:** 06/19/1950 **Place of Birth:** New York **State:** NY **Parents:** Arthur B. Singer; Edith (Goulfine) Singer **Marital Status:** Married **Spouse Name:** Anna K. Sears (9/1/1979) **Children:** Nathaniel **Education:** Postgraduate Work, Pratt Institute (1976-1977); MFA, Cornell University (1975); BFA, The Cooper Union for the Advancement of Science and Art (1972); Coursework, Yale University (1971) **Career:** Professor, Department of Fine Art, Rochester Institute of Technology (1987-Present); Artist (1974-Present); Painter (1974-Present); Freelance Writer (1974-Present); Educator (1974-Present); Designer (1974-Present); Illustrator (1974-Present); Curator (1974-Present); Adult Education Instructor, New York Botanical Garden (1985-1988); Instructor, Asa Wright Nature Centre (1978-1980) **Career Related:** Illustrator, Levaquin (Now Johnson & Johnson Services, Inc.) (2006); Visiting Lecturer, Syracuse University (2006); Visiting Artist, Syracuse University (2006); Designer, Program Franklin Mint Graphics, TDK U.S.A. Corporation (1987); Designer of Impressions Illustration, Brooklyn Botanic Garden (1987); Designer of Exhibits, Brooklyn Botanic Garden (1987); Designer of Designs and Mechanicals, Long Island University Brochures (1986); Designer of Designs and Mechanicals, North Carolina Zoological Society (1986); Stamp Designer, Stamp Illustrator, USPS (1980-1981) **Creative Works:** Exhibitor, Hunt Institute for Botanical Documentation (2009-Present); Author, Essays, Journals; Co-Author, "Arthur Singer: Wildlife Art of an American Master," RIT Press (2017); Solo Exhibitor, Spectrum Gallery (2014); Artist, Jean Geisel Gallery (2014); Artist, The Little Theatre (2013); Artist, The Ink Shop (2012); Artist, Roger Tory Peterson Institute of Natural History (2012); Exhibitor, Windsor Whip Works Art Gallery (2011); Solo Exhibitor, Och Hee Gallery (2010); Artist, The Erie Canal Oxford Gallery (2010); Exhibitor, Arts & Cultural Council for Greater Rochester (2008); Solo Exhibitor, Redhouse Gallery (2007); Author, "Alan Singer, Selections" (2007); Exhibitor, Everson Museum of Art (2006); Exhibitor, Arts & Cultural Council for Greater Rochester (2005); Solo Exhibitor, Dyer Arts Center, Rochester Institute of Technology (2004); Exhibitor, The Mill Art Center and Gallery (2003); Exhibitor, National Postal Museum, Smithsonian Institute (2003); Solo Exhibitor, Hobart William and Smith Colleges (2001); Solo Exhibitor, The Mill Art Center and Gallery (2001); Author, "Traveling the Erie Canal by Watercolor" (2001); Exhibitor, Norman Rockwell Museum (2000); Exhibitor, Sonnenberg (2000); Author, "Botanica" (2000); Solo Exhibitor, Century Club of Rochester (1999); Author, "Wildlife Art" (1999); Exhibitor, Everson Museum of Art (1999); Solo Exhibitor, Upstairs Gallery, Gallery Arabesque (1998); Exhibitor, Royal Botanic Gardens, Kew (1997); Exhibitor, Buffalo Museum of Science (1997); Exhibitor, Monroe Community College (1997); Solo Exhibitor, Germanow-Coffey Gallery (1997); Exhibitor, Coffey Germanow Gallery (1995); Solo Exhibitor, Angel Fire Gallery (1993); Exhibitor, Memorial Art Gallery (1993); Exhibitor, Angel Fire Gallery (1992); Solo Exhibitor, 55 Mercer St. Gallery (1992); Solo Exhibitor, Haenah-Kent Gallery (1991); Exhibitor, Memorial Art Gallery (1991); Solo Exhibitor, Bali Miller Gallery (1988); Exhibitor, Rochester Institute of Technology (1988); Solo Exhibitor, National Museum of Natural History, Smithsonian Institution (1987); Exhibitor, National Academy Museum (1986); Exhibitor, Community Gallery, Brooklyn Museum (1985); Solo Exhibitor, 55 Mercer St. Gallery (1985); Artist, Slice of Life; Exhibitor, Bausch & Lomb Headquarters, Rochester, Mercer Gallery Monroe Community College; Author, Essays, Museum Catalogs; Author, Essays, Newspapers **Awards:** Recipient, Grant, FEAD (2014); Recipient, Faculty Development Grant (1997); Grantee, Rochester Institute of Technology (1991); Recipient, Certificate of Merit, The Society of Illustrators (1985); Recipient, Best of Year Award, PCS Coins (1983); Recipient, Purchase Award, Nassau Community College (1976); Recipient, President's Award, The National Arts Club (1975) **Membership:** President, Print Club of Rochester **Marquis Who's Who Honors:** Albert Nelson Marquis Lifetime Achievement Award (2017) **To what do you attribute your success:** Mr. Singer attributes his success to being persistent, having help from his community and taking the creative life one day at a time, but remaining true to his vision. **Why did you become involved in your profession or industry:** Mr. Singer entered his profession because he has been a visual artist all his life. He also began writing and teaching as a part of his vision of how to make his way in this community. **What do you consider to be the highlight of your career:** The highlights of Mr. Singer's career were the exhibitions and designs he had worked on with his father for the United States postage stamp series of birds and flowers of the 50 states. **Where will you be in five years:** Mr. Singer will most likely retire from teaching in five years and devote his remaining years to working in his community. **Hobbies:** Gardening; Guitar; Hiking **Shipping Address:** 3021 Elmwood Ave, Rochester, NY, 14618

David John Singstock

Title: Senior Technical Director **Industry:** Information Technology and Services **Company Name:** General Dynamics Information Technology, Inc. **Date of Birth:** 07/19/1940 **Place of Birth:** Oshkosh **State:** WI **Parents:** Arnold William Singstock; Viola Rufine (Gerdener) Singstock **Children:** Susan; Brian; Elissa; Timothy **Education:** MS, George Washington University (1975); BS, George Washington University, With Distinction (1973); BS, Maine Maritime Academy, With Distinction (1964); Coursework, U.S. Merchant Marine Academy (1959-1962) **Certifications:** Licensed Professional lMarine Engineer; Certified Associate Contracts Manager **Career:** Senior Technical Director, Missile Defense Agency, Aegis Ballistic Missile Defense, General Dynamics Information Technology, Inc., Arlington, VA (2001-2011); Deputy Director, Applied Ordnance Technology, Inc., Arlington, VA (1999-2001); Manager, Theater Ballistic Missile Defense, Marconi Systems Technologies Inc., Arlington, VA (1999-2001); R&D Manager, Theater Ballistic Missile Defense, Tracor Systems Technologies, Inc., Arlington, VA (1998-1999); Manager, Ship Self Defense, Vitro Corporation, Arlington, VA (1996-1997); Manager, Ships Program, ROH Incorporated, Arlington, VA (1993-1995) **Career Related:** Senior Naval Technical Member, Secretary of Defense Chartered Delegation of Senior United States Officials, Saudi Arabia (1991); COMNAVSEA Technical Representative, Northeast Quarter of the United States Logistics Support Study (1980) **Civic:** Vice President, Northern Neck Christian Men's Group of Virginia (2014-Present); Active, Local Property Owners Civic Organizations, Virginia, Maine (1970-Present); Assistant Scoutmaster, Boy Scouts of America, Dumfries, VA (1985-1990); Coach, Youth Soccer, Maine, Virginia (1976-1984); Instructor, The American National Red Cross, Seattle, WA (1967) **Military Service:** Retired, U.S. Navy (1993); Senior Technical Adviser, Operations Desert Shield and Desert Storm, Royal Saudi Naval Forces (1990-1991); Technical Director, Deputy Assistant, Secretary, Navy for International Programs, U.S. Navy (1988-1993); Program Manager, USS STARK (FFG 31) Restoration, Naval Sea Systems Command, U.S. Navy (1986-1988); Commander, U.S. Navy (1984); Director, Fleet Modernization Program, Space/Naval Warfare Systems Command, U.S. Navy (1983-1986); Ship Maintenance Manager, Chief Naval Operations, U.S. Navy, Washington, DC (1980-1983); Production/Repair Officer, Supervisor, Shipbuilding, U.S. Navy, Bath, ME (1976-1979); Planning and Quality Assurance Officer, Supervisor, Shipbuilding, U.S. Navy, Portsmouth, VA (1973-1976); Automatic Data Processing Financial Manager, CINCLANTFLT, U.S. Navy, Norfolk, VA (1971-1973); Engineer Officer, USS Harold J. Ellison (DD 864), U.S. Navy, Norfolk, VA (1969-1971); Combat Duty, Vietnam, U.S. Navy, USS GALLUP (PG 85) (1967); Various Sea Assignments, Including USS PLAINVIEW (AGEH 1), USS MATTABESSETTE (AOG 52) (1964-1968); Commissioned Ensign, U.S. Navy (1964) **Creative Works:** Featured Guest, "BEHIND MY WINGS, Untold Stories of Vietnam Vets"; Featured Guest, "Coles Point and Tidwells, Virginia"; "Life and Times, Back Then and Now" **Awards:** Excellence Award, Aegis Ballistic Missile Defense (2015); Missile Defense Award, National Defense Industrial Association (2005); Decorated Navy Commendation Medal; Republic of Vietnam Gallantry Cross Medal; Navy Unit Commendation, Vietnam; Joint Meritorious Unit Commendation; Meritorious Service Medals; Joint Service Commendation Medal; Navy Marine Corps Combat Action Ribbon, Vietnam; Certificate for Appreciation and Gratitude, Commander, Saudi Arabian Armed Forces; Kuwait Liberation Medal; Republic of Vietnam Gallantry Cross Unit Citation; Certificate of Special Congressional Recognition in Commemoration of Courageous Military Service to the United States of America in the Vietnam War **Membership:** Deputy Committee Chairman, Speaker, American Society of Naval Engineers (1988); Alpha Sigma Lambda (1971); National Contract Management Association; Military Officers Association of America; The National Eagle Scout Association; 32nd Degree Masons; Scottish Rite of Freemasonry, S.J., U.S.A.; Shriner International; VFW; The American Legion; DAV; Vietnam Veterans of America **Marquis Who's Who Honors:** Albert Nelson Marquis Lifetime Achievement Award (2017) **To what do you attribute your success:** Mr. Singstock's definition of success is faith in yourself, your religion, and your country, personal motivation, and drive. **Why did you become involved in your profession or industry:** Mr. Singstock's father grew up on a farm, and then he was a factory worker. His mother grew up in a city, but couldn't go to college because of financial situations. His grandfather was educated in business, and his family always pushed him and his sister to get a good education. He did a master's, but never finished a PhD. Throughout his entire childhood, it was ingrained in him to do better. **Hobbies:** Sailing; Jogging; Camping; Golf; Music; Volunteering **Political Affiliations:** Republican **Religion:** Methodist **Business Address:** PO Box 25997, Alexandria, VA, 22313 **Shipping Address:** 625 Blackbeard Pond Road, Hague, VA, 22469

Rosemarie Skaine

Title: Writer **Industry:** Writing and Editing **Date of Birth:** 06/11/1936 **Year of Passing:** 2017-03-29 **Parents:** Warren V. Keller; Marie W. Kuehner Keller **Education:** MA, University of Northern Iowa (1977); BA, University South Dakota, Vermillion, SD (1958) **Career:** Adjunct Instructor, Composition, Hawkeye Community College, Waterloo, IA (1998); Adjunct Instructor, Sociology, Wartburg College, Waverly, IA (1979-1980); Administrative and Legislative Assistant, President Kennedy's Consumer Advisory Council Chairperson, Ithaca, NY (1963); English Teacher, Ovid Central School, New York (1958-1960) **Career Related:** Keynote Speaker, The First Convocation of First Ladies: Building Bridges, Sharing Experiences, and Bridging the Gaps for Global Partnerships (2013); Keynote Speaker, Terrorism and the Youths of Africa (2013); Keynote Speaker, Elimination & Prevention All Forms of Violence Against Women & Girls New York (2013); Featured Author, 4th Anniversary Hostage-taking Radio Free Europe, Moscow Dubrovka House of Culture (2006); Speaking Tour, Women of Afghanistan Under the Taliban, South Dakota Center for the Book's Three Day Program, Maintaining Democracy in an Unstable World, Aberdeen, Brookings, Mitchell and Sioux Falls, SD (2002); U.S. Delegate, XII International Congress on Family Law, Havana, Cuba (2002); Presenter, American Family, Guilin, Shijiazhuang, Xian, China, University of Northern Iowa, Cedar Falls, IA (1993); Consultant, Institutes on Sexual Harassment, Adult Education Board YWCA, Waterloo, IA (1992); Consultant, Sexual Harassment, KCET Public Television, Los Angeles, CA (1991-1994); Court Testimony, Sexual Harassment, District Court, Waterloo, IA (1989-1999); Keynote Speaker, Interactive Dialogue Allure of Suicide Bombers, UN Commission, Suicide Warfare & Violence Against Women **Civic:** With, Obama-Biden Presidential Compaign (2008); Precint Chairperson, Ohama Presidential Primary Campaign (2007-2008); Panel Member, Women in Afghanistan, Cable Television Here and There, Cedar Falls, IA (2001); National Steering Committee, Honorary Member, Gore 2000 Presidential Campaign (2000); National Steering Committee, Honorary Member, Clinton-Gore Presidential Campaign (1996); Campaign Manager, James Skaine for U.S. Congress, Cedar Falls, IA (1972-1974); Voters Service Chair, President, League of Women Voters of Waterloo-Cedar Falls, Cedar Falls, IA (1964-1969) **Creative Works:** Editor, "Abuse An Encyclopedia of Causes, Consequences, and Treatments" (2015); Author, "Suicide Warfare: Culture, the Military, and the Individual as a Weapon" (2013); Author, "Women in Combat" (2011); Author, "Women of Afganistan in the Post Taliban Era: How Lives Have Changed and Where They Stand Today" (2008); Author, "Women Political Leaders in Africa" (2008); Author, "Female Suicide Bombers" (2006); Author, "Female Genital Mutilation: Legal, Cultural and Medical Issues" (2005); Author, "The Cuban Family: Custom and Change in an Era of Hardship" (2004); Author, "Paternity and American Law" (2003); Author, "The Women of Afghanistan Under the Taliban" (2002); Author, "Women College Basketball Coaches" (2001); Co-author, "A Man of the Twentieth Century: Recollections of Warren V. Keller, A Nebraskan" (1999); Author, "Women at War: Gender Issues of Americans in Combat" (1999); Author, "Power and Gender: Issues in Sexual Dominance and Harassment" (1996); Author, "Sexual Harassment: Questions and Answers, 2nd Revised Edition (1990); Author, "Questions and Answers about Sexual Harassment" (1980); Author, "Lessons in Love and Life"; Contributor, Articles, Professional Journals; Contributor, Articles, Encyclopedias **Awards:** Gustavus Myers Center Award for the Study of Human Rights in North America for the Outstanding Work on Intolerance in North America (1997) **Membership:** Alpha Kappa Delta; Lifetime Member, Pi Kappa Delta **Shipping Address:** 2215 Clay Street, Cedar Falls, IA, 50613

Herbert A. Sklenar

Title: Manufacturing Executive **Industry:** Manufacturing **Company Name:** Vulcan Materials Company **Date of Birth:** 06/07/1931 **Place of Birth:** Omaha **State:** NE **Parents:** Michael Joseph Sklenar; Alice Madeline (Spicka) Sklenar **Marital Status:** Married **Spouse Name:** Eleanor Lydia Vincenz (9/15/1956) **Children:** Susan A.; Patricia I. **Education:** Honorary LLD, Birmingham-Southern College (1996); MBA, Harvard University (1954); BSBA, University of Nebraska Omaha, Summa Cum Laude (1952) **Certifications:** Certified Public Accountant, State of West Virginia **Career:** Chairman Emeritus, Board of Directors, Vulcan Materials Company (1997-Present); Chairman, Vulcan Materials Company (1992); Chief Executive Officer, Vulcan Materials Company (1992); President, Vulcan Materials Company (1986); Chief Executive Officer, Vulcan Materials Company (1986); President, Vulcan Materials Company (1983); Chief Operating Officer, Vulcan Materials Company (1983); Executive Vice President, Vulcan Materials Company (1979); Chief Administration Officer, Vulcan Materials Company (1979); Executive Vice President of Finance and Administration, Vulcan Materials Company (1974); Vice President of Finance, Vulcan Materials Company (1972); Executive Vice President of Finance and Administration, Cudahy Packing Company (1967-1972); Secretary, Cudahy Packing Company (1967-1972); Financial Control Manager, Boise Cascade (1966-1967); Vice President, Marmac Corporation (1963-1966); Director, Marmac Corporation (1963-1966); Vice President, Parkersburg-Aetna Corporation (1956-1963); Comptroller, Parkersburg-Aetna Corporation (1956-1963) **Creative Works:** Co-Author, "The Automatic Factory: A Critical Examination" (1955) **Awards:** Inductee, Birmingham Business Hall of Fame, City of Birmingham, Alabama (2013); Inductee, Alabama Academy of Honor, State of Alabama (1997); Brotherhood Award, National Conference of Christians and Jews (Now National Conference for Community and Justice) (1993); Alumni Achievement Award, University of Nebraska Omaha (1977); Elizah Watts Sells Award, American Institute of CPAs (1965); Certificate of Merit, WVSCPA **Membership:** President, Rotary Club of Birmingham; The Country Club of Birmingham; Phi Eta Sigma; The Honor Society of Phi Kappa Phi, Omicron Delta Kappa The National Leadership Honor Society; Delta Sigma Pi **Marquis Who's Who Honors:** Albert Nelson Marquis Lifetime Achievement Award (2017); Distinguished Humanitarian (2017) **Political Affiliations:** Republican **Religion:** Presbyterian **Shipping Address:** 2809 Shook Hill Cir., Mountain Brk, AL, 35223

Thomas Raymond Skulina

Title: Lawyer **Industry:** Law and Legal Services **Date of Birth:** 09/14/1933 **Place of Birth:** Cleveland **State:** OH **Parents:** John J. Skulina; Mary B. (Vesely) Skulina **Education:** LLM, Case Western Reserve University (1962); JD, Case Western Reserve University (1959); AB, John Carroll University (1955) **Certifications:** Interstate Commerce Commission (1965) **Career:** Private Practice, Cleveland, OH (1997-Present); Partner, Skulina & Hill, Cleveland, OH (1990-1997); Partner, Skulina & McKeon, Cleveland, OH (1986-1990); Partner, Skulina, Fillo, Walters & Negrelli (1981-1986); Partner, Riemer, Oberdank & Skulina, Cleveland, OH (1978-1981); Employee, Consolidated Rail Corporation (1976-1978); Partner, Skulina & Stringer, Cleveland, OH (1967-1972); Assistant General Attorney, Penn Central Transportation Company, Cleveland, OH (1965-1978); Trial Counsel, Penn Central Transportation Company, Cleveland, OH (1965-1976); Attorney, Penn Central Transportation Company, Cleveland, OH (1960-1965) **Career Related:** Arbitrator, Council of Better Business Bureaus (2000-Present); Mediator, National Association of Securities Dealers (1997-Present); Mediator, Commercial, American Arbitration Association (1997-Present); Arbitrator, National Association of Securities Dealers (1996-Present); Arbitrator, Intercontinental Exchange, Inc. (1995-Present); Practicing Labor Arbitrator, Federal Mediation and Conciliation Service (1990-Present); Referee, Civil Service Commission, Cleveland, OH (1986-Present); Mediator, Contract Panel, U.S. Equal Employment Opportunity Commission (1999-2000); Mediator, Volunteer Panel, U.S. Equal Employment Opportunity Commission (1997-1999); Arbitrator, Municipal Securities Rulemaking Board (1994-1998); President, Civil Service Commission, Cleveland, OH (1977-1986); Teacher, Commercial Law, Practicing Law Institute, New York, NY (1970) **Civic:** Fact-Finder, State Employees Relations Board, Ohio (1986-Present); Referee, Cleveland Charter Revision Commission (1986-Present); Hearing Officer, Human Resource Commission, Summit County, Ohio (2000-2003); Special Counsel, Cleveland Charter Revision Commission (1988); Special Counsel, Ohio Attorney General (1983-1993); Special Counsel, North Olmstead, OH (1971-1975); Income Tax and Federal Fund Coordinator, Warrensville Heights, OH (1970-1977) **Military Service:** U.S. Army (1959) **Creative Works:** Contributor, Articles, Legal Journals **Membership:** Arbitrator, Practicing Labor, American Arbitration Association (1987-Present); Alternate Dispute Resolution Committee, American Bar Association (1998-2000); ADR Committee, Cleveland Metropolitan Bar Association (1997-2000); Chairman, Cleveland Metropolitan Bar Association (1997-1998); Alternate Dispute Resolution Committee, Ohio State Bar Association (1996-2000); Trustee, Cleveland Metropolitan Bar Association (1993-1996); Ethics and Professional Responsibility Committee, Ohio State Bar Association (1990-1991); Negligence Law Committee, Ohio State Bar Association (1989-1996); Junior Chairman, American Bar Association (1989-1996); Railroad and Motor Carrier Committee, American Bar Association (1988-1996); Grievance Committee, Cleveland Metropolitan Bar Association (1987-1993); Board of Governors, Litigation Section, Ohio State Bar Association (1986-1998); Federal Bar Association; Association for Conflict Resolution; National Academy of Arbitrators; Emeritus, National Association of Railroad Trial Counsel; International Association of Law, Ethics and Science; Public Sector, Labor and Employment Relations Association **Bar Admissions:** U.S. Supreme Court (1964); State of Ohio (1959) **Marquis Who's Who Honors:** Albert Nelson Marquis Lifetime Achievement Award (2017) **Political Affiliations:** Democrat **Religion:** Roman Catholic **Business Address:** 24803 Detroit Road, Suite 8, Westlake, OH, 44145 **Shipping Address:** 28605 Westlake Village Drive, Westlake, OH, 44145

Donald Carl Slack, PhD

Title: Agricultural Engineer, Educator **Industry:** Engineering **Date of Birth:** 06/25/1942 **Place of Birth:** Cody **State:** WY **Parents:** Clarence Ralbon Slack; Clara May (Beightol) Slack **Marital Status:** Married **Spouse Name:** Marion Arline Kimball (12/19/1964) **Children:** Jonel Marie; Jennifer Michelle **Education:** Honorary ED, Khon Kaen University, Thailand (2010); PhD in Agricultural Engineering, University of Kentucky (1975); MS in Agricultural Engineering, University of Kentucky (1968); BS in Agricultural Engineering, University of Wyoming (1965) **Certifications:** Registered Professional Engineer, States of Kentucky and Arizona **Career:** Professor, Arid Lands Sustainable Bioenergy Institute, University of Arizona (2018-Present); Professor of Watershed Management, University of Arizona (2006-Present); Cecil H. Miller Endowed Chair, University of Arizona (2006-Present); Professor, University of Arizona (1984-Present); Head, Department of Agricultural and Biosystems Engineering, University of Arizona (2012-2014); Honorary Researcher, Khon Kaen University, Thailand (2010); Consultant, Gila Valley Irrigation District (2010); Co-Director, Arid Lands Sustainable Bioenergy Institute, University of Arizona (2008-2012); Head, Department Agricultural and Biosystems Engineering, University of Arizona (1991-2009); Assistant Professor of Agricultural Engineering, University of Minnesota (1975-1984); Associate Professor of Agricultural Engineering, University of Minnesota (1975-1984); Research Assistant, University of Kentucky (1973-1975); Agricultural Engineering Adviser, University of Kentucky (1970-1973); Research Specialist, University of Kentucky (1966-1970); Assistant Civil Engineer, City of Los Angeles, California (1965) **Career Related:** Middle-East and Mediterranean Desert Development Program (1997-Present); Advisory Team, Cearan Foundation for Meteorology and Hydrology (1995-Present); The World Bank Group (1992-Present); Portek International Pte, Ltd (1989-Present); Desert Agricultural Technology Systems, City of Tucson, Arizona (1985-Present); Consultant, Desert Whale Jojoba Company (2014); Consultant, State of Arizona (2012); Visiting Professor, Khon Kaen University, Thailand (2009); Fulbright Fellow, Khon Kaen University, Thailand (2009); Consultant, International Center for Agricultural Research in the Dry Areas (2005); Visiting Professor, Department of Irrigation, La Universidad Autónoma Chapingo, Mexico (2000); Consultant, F.J. Hansen Institute World Peace, San Diego State University, San Diego, CA (1997-2005); Agricultural Research Institute of Chile (1997); Visiting Professor, Department of Atmospheric Science, Universidade Federal de Campina Grande, Brazil (1997); Mexico Institute of Water Technology (1997); International Advisory Panel, Matrou Resources Management Project, The World Bank Group (1996-2000); Technology Adviser, Active Management Area, City of Tucson, Arizona (1996-2000); Malawi Environmental Monitoring Project (1996); Deputy Program Support Manager, Research Irrigation Support Project for Asia and the Near East (1987-1994); Department of Water Resources, State of Arizona (1985-1995); Water Management Synthesis II (1985); Winrock International (1984); Board of Directors, Watershed Management Group, Inc.; Member, Board of Directors, Sonoita Vineyards; Fellow, American Society of Civil Engineers **Creative Works:** Contributor, Articles to Professional Journals **Awards:** Recipient, Premio Nacional de Riego y Drenaje, El Colegio Mexicano de Ingeneros en Irrigación, La Universidad Autónoma Chapingo (2016); Recipient, Award of Excellence In Global Education (2014); Honoree, Named Administrator Of Year, College of Agricultural and Life Sciences, The University of Arizona (2012-2013); Recipient, Kishida International Award, American Society of Agricultural and Biological Engineers (2011); Honoree, Named Administrator of the Year, College of Agricultural and Life Sciences, The University of Arizona (2004-2005); Honoree, Arizona Section Engineer of the Year, American Society of Agricultural Engineers (1993); Recipient, Outstanding Journal Paper Award, American Society of Civil Engineers (1988) **Membership:** Engineer Accreditation Council, Accreditation Board for Engineering and Technology (2010-Present); Program Evaluator, Accreditation Board for Engineering and Technology, American Society for Engineering Education (2001-Present); American Society of Agricultural Engineers; American Society of Agricultural and Biological Engineers; Lifetime Member, United States Committee on Irrigation and Drainage; Sons of the American Revolution; Master Knight, Brotherhood of Knights of the Vine; Lifetime Member, Rocky Mountain Elk Foundation; Lifetime Member, Thai Society of Agriculture Engineering; Lifetime Member, Wyoming Wildlife Federation; Sigma Xi, The Scientific Research Honor Society; Tau Beta Pi; Alpha Epsilon; Gamma Sigma Delta; Board of Directors, International Dryland Development Commission; International Dryland Development Commission, Cairo, Egypt **Hobbies:** Hunting; Camping; Hiking; Building model railroads; Fishing **Political Affiliations:** Democrat **Religion:** Lutheran **Shipping Address:** 9230 E Visco Pl, Tucson, AZ, 85710

O. Temple Sloan Jr.

Title: Business Executive **Industry:** Business Management/Business Services **Company Name:** Trail Creek Investments, Inc., Highwoods Properties **Date of Birth:** 02/21/1939 **Place of Birth:** Sanford **State:** NC **Parents:** Orris Temple Sloan; Thelma (Hamilton) Sloan **Marital Status:** Married **Spouse Name:** Carolyn Myers (12/11/2010); Carol Carson (Deceased) **Children:** Kay Carson Henline; O. Temple, III; Mark H. **Education:** LLD, Northwood University, Honoris Causa, Midland, MI (2007); BBA, Duke University (1961) **Career:** Founder, Trail Creek Investments, Inc. (2009-Present); Chairman, Trail Creek Investments, Inc. (2009-Present); Chairman, Highwoods Properties, Inc., Raleigh, NC (1994-Present); Employee, Al Smith Buick Dodge and Mazda Company (1988-2004); Co-Founder, Highwoods Properties, Inc., Raleigh, NC (1978-1994); Employee, Southern Equipment Company (1970-2004); Founder, General Parts International, Inc., Raleigh, NC (1961-2013); Employee, Southern Finance Company (1959-1961); Chairman, Sheser Creek Co., LLC; Chairman, Investors Management Corporation

Career Related: Board of Directors, Golden Corral (2004-2014); Board of Directors, Lowe's Companies, Inc. (2004-2011); Lead Director, Executive Committee, Audit Committee, Board of Directors, Lowe's Companies, Inc. (2004-2011); Board of Directors, Bank of America Corporation, North Carolina (1996-2009); Trustee, Presbyterian Homes, Inc., Raleigh, NC (1985-1995); Board of Directors Carquest Auto Parts, Raleigh, NC (1974-2005); Lead Director, Lowe's Companies, Inc.; Lead Director, Executive Audit and Compensation Committees, Bank of America Corporation, Charlotte, NC **Civic:** National Advisory Board Officer, Boy Scouts of America (2014-Present); Chair, Annual Campaign, Southeast Raleigh YMCA (2011-Present); Occoneechee Council, Boy Scouts of America (1967-Present); Chairman, Santa Fe Trail Campaign, Philmont Scout Ranch, Boy Scouts of America (2015); Honorary Co-Chairman, Capital Campaign, YMCA of the Triangle (2014-2015); Chairman, We Build People Campaign, Young Men's Christian Association (2011-2012); National Executive Board, Boy Scouts of America (2004-2014); Executive Board, Capital Campaign Chairman, Occoneechee Council, Boy Scouts of America (2004-2007); Athletic Council, Duke University (2003-2006); Campaign Chairman, United Way of the Greater Triangle (2000); Board of Directors, World Games, Special Olympics, The Joseph P. Kennedy, Jr. Foundation (1998-1999); Chairman, Financial Committee, Centennial Authority (1995-2005); Trustee, Centennial Authority (1995-2005); Trustee, St. Andrews University (1990-1999); Trustee, William Peace University (1987-1997); Board of Visitors, William Peace University (1985-1987); Trustee, Boys & Girls Homes of North Carolina (1973-2002); Vice Chairman, Board of Trustees, William Peace University; Former Chairman, Board of Advisors, The Salvation Army USA; Vice President, Supply Group, Boy Scouts of America; Officers Committee, Boy Scouts of America; Honorary Co-Chairman, Capital Campaign, Meredith College; Honorary Chairman, Capital Campaign, YMCA of the Triangle; Past Treasurer, Past Vice President, Occoneechee Council, Boy Scouts of America; Elder, First Presbyterian Church, Raleigh, NC **Awards:** Inductee, Raleigh Hall of Fame (2016); Honoree, North Carolina Chambers (2014); Inductee, North Carolina Entrepreneur Hall of Fame (2014); A.E. Finley Distinguished Service Award, Greater Raleigh Chamber of Commerce (2012); Inductee, North Carolina Business Hall of Fame (2010); Silver Buffalo Award, Boy Scouts of America (2010); Silver Antelope Award, Boy Scouts of America (2009); Honoree, Entrepreneur of Year, Ernst & Young Global Limited (2008); Lifetime Achievement Award, Triangle Award, Motor & Equipment Manufacturers Association (2005); Honoree, Outstanding Business Leader, Northwood University (1999); Honoree, Distinguished Service Citation, The Automotive Hall of Fame (1997); Distinguished Eagle Scout Award, Boy Scouts of America (1992); Automotive Man of Year Award, Automotive Warehouse Distributors Association Inc. (1989); Scholarship Award, Automotive Warehouse Distributors Association Inc. (1977); Lifetime Achievement Award, Motor & Equipment Manufacturers Association; District Award of Merit, Boy Scouts of America; Eagle Scout Award, Boy Scouts of America; Silver Beaver Award, Boy Scouts of America **Membership:** Chairman, Automotive Warehouse Distributors Association Inc. (1976-1977); Director, Automotive Warehouse Distributors Association Inc. (1967-1980); Past President, The Fifty Group; The Abaco Club at Winding Bay; Desert Mountain Club; Carolina Country Club, Raleigh, NC **Marquis Who's Who Honors:** Albert Nelson Marquis Lifetime Achievement Award (2017) **Hobbies:** Fishing; Hunting; Ranching **Shipping Address:** 3026 Randolph Dr, Raleigh, NC, 27609

Allie Maitland Smith, PhD

Title: Engineering Educator (Retired) **Industry:** Engineering **Company Name:** The University of Mississippi **Date of Birth:** 06/09/1934 **Place of Birth:** Lumberton **State:** NC **Parents:** Allie McCoy Smith; Emma Hattie (Wright) Smith **Marital Status:** Married **Spouse Name:** Sarah Louise Whitlock (6/16/1957) **Children:** Sara Leianne; Hollis Duval; Meredith Lorren **Education:** PhD in Aerospace Engineering, North Carolina State University, Raleigh, NC (1966); MS in Aerospace Engineering, North Carolina State University, Raleigh, NC (1961); BME, North Carolina State University, with Honors (1956) **Career:** Emeritus Professor, The University of Mississippi (2008-Present); Emeritus Dean, The University of Mississippi (2000-Present); Professor of Mechanical Engineering, The University of Mississippi (1979-2008); Dean, School of Engineering, The University of Mississippi (1979-2000) Adjunct Professor, The University of Tennessee Space Institute, Tullahoma, TN (1967-1979); Research Supervisor, Sverdrup/ARO, Inc., Arnold Air Force Base, TN (1966-1979); Research Project Engineer, RTI International, Durham, NC (1962-1966); Member of Technical Staff, Bell Telephone Laboratories, Burlington, NC (1960-1962); Instructor then Assistant Professor Extension, NC State University (1958-1962); Development Engineer, Western Electric Company (1957-1960); Associate Engineer, Glenn L. Martin Company, Baltimore, MD (1956-1957) **Career Related:** Keynote Lecturer, Third International Conference on Hydroscience and Engineering, Berlin, Germany (1998); Chair, Plenary Session, Third International Conference on Hydroscience and Engineering, Berlin, Germany (1998); Chair, Plenary Session, Conference on Management of Landscapes Disturbed by Channel Incision (1997); Presiding Officer, Plenary Session, International Conference on Hydroscience and Engineering (1995); Session Chair, Conferences on Theoretical and Applied Mechanics, SECTAM (1994); Presiding Officer, Plenary Session, International Conference on Hydroscience and Engineering (1993); Operations Committee, Conferences on Theoretical and Applied Mechanics, SECTAM (1990-1999); Policy Committee, Conferences on Theoretical and Applied Mechanics, SECTAM (1990-1999); Board of Directors, Scholarship Board, Mississippi Mineral Resources Institute, The University of Mississippi; Executive Chairman, 14th Southeastern Conference on Theoretical and Applied Mechanics, SECTAM; Executive Committee, 13th-16th Conferences on Theoretical and Applied Mechanics, SECTAM; Organizing Committee, International Scientific Advisory Board; Conference on Management of Landscapes Disturbed by Channel Incision **Civic:** General Chairman, Engineering Deans Institute, American Society for Engineering Education (1991) **Creative Works:** Author, Articles and Reviews, Professional Journals; Editor, "Radiative Heat Transfer" (1997); Editor, "Solution Methods for Radiative Heat Transfer in Participating Media" (1996); Editor, "Radiative Heat Transfer: Theory and Applications" (1993); Editor, "Fundamentals of Radiation Heat Transfer" (1991); Editor, "Radiation Heat Transfer: Fundamentals and Applications" (1990); Editor, "Developments in Theoretical and Applied Mechanics," Vol. XIV (1988); Editor, "Fundamentals and Applications of Radiation Heat Transfer" (1987); Associate Editor, Journal of Thermophysics and Heat Transfer (1986-2007); Editor, "Thermophysics of Spacecraft and Outer Planet Entry Probes" (1977); Editor, "Radiative Transfer and Thermal Control" (1976); Associate Editor, Journal, American Institute of Aeronautics and Astronautics (AIAA) (1975-1977); Author, "Fundamentals of Silicon Integrated Device Technology, Volume I: Oxidation, Diffusion and Epitaxy" (1967) **Awards:** Scholar, Sigma Pi Fraternity International; Supernumerary Director, Alabama-Mississippi Section, American Institute of Aeronautics and Astronautics (AIAA) (1994-2000); Hermann Oberth Award, American Institute of Aeronautics and Astronautics (AIAA) (1984-1985); Space Shuttle Flag Challenger Plaque, American Institute of Aeronautics and Astronautics (AIAA) (1984); Thermophysics Award, American Institute of Aeronautics and Astronautics (AIAA) (1978) **Membership:** Chairman, Radiation Heat Transfer II Session, The American Society of Mechanical Engineers, St. Louis, MO (2002); Chairman, Radiative Heat Transfer I and II Sessions, The American Society of Mechanical Engineers, Pittsburgh, PA (2000); Host, Engineering Deans Institute, American Society for Engineering Education (1991); President, Northeast Mississippi Chapter, National Society of Professional Engineers (1990-1991); National Publication Committee, American Institute of Aeronautics and Astronautics (AIAA) (1979-1983); Chairman, Terrestrial Energy Systems Technical Committee, American Institute of Aeronautics and Astronautics (AIAA) (1979-1981); General Chairman, Aerospace Sciences Meeting, AIAA (1979); Aerospace Heat Transfer Committee, The American Society of Mechanical Engineers (1975-2007) **Marquis Who's Who Honors:** Albert Nelson Marquis Lifetime Achievement Award (2017); Distinguished Humanitarian (2017) **Shipping Address:** 4108 Fearrington Post, Pittsboro, NC, 27312

Diana Marie Smith

Title: Business Educator **Industry:** Education/ Educational Services **Date of Birth:** 10/25/1940 **Place of Birth:** Des Moines **State/Country of Origin:** IA **Parents:** Nathan Henry Kitchen; Helen (Hall) Kitchen **Marital Status:** Widowed **Spouse Name:** Robert Nelson Smith (1/26/1971, Deceased 12/7/2004) **Children:** Stephen **Education:** MA, Drake University, Des Moines, Iowa (1971); BA, Drake University, Des Moines, Iowa (1968) **Certifications:** Certified Teacher, State of Iowa **Career:** Instructor, Computers, St. Paul Church and Saks Incorporated, Des Moines, Iowa (2000-2006); Computer Operating, IRS, Des Moines, Iowa (1988); Lead Specialist II, Northwest Bank, Des Moines, Iowa (1978-2002); Secretary, Shive-Hattery Architecture & Engineers, Des Moines, Iowa (1976-1990); Typist, Central Life Assurance Co., Des Moines, Iowa (1976-1979); Instructor, Adult Education, Des Moines Independent Community School District (1969-2001); Teacher, Business, Computers, Des Moines Public Schools (1968-2000); Typist, Polk County Auditor, Des Moines, Iowa (1968); Stenographer, Polk County Welfare Department (Now Polk County DHS), Iowa Department of Human Services, Des Moines, Iowa (1960-1967) **Career Related:** Beauty Consultant, Mary Kay (1993-Present); Instructor, Authorized Training Associate Program for WordPerfect (1994); Independent Computer Consultant **Civic:** Sunday School Teacher, Burns United Methodist Church-Des Moines, Iowa (2006-Present); Chair, Memorial Committee, Burns United Methodist Church-Des Moines, Iowa (1988-Present); Sunday School Teacher, Burns United Methodist Church-Des Moines, Iowa (1992-1998); Secretary, Administrative Board, Burns United Methodist Church-Des Moines, Iowa (1983-2004); Sunday School Teacher, Burns United Methodist Church-Des Moines, Iowa (1961-1983) **Why did you become involved in your profession or industry:** Ms. Smith started teaching Sunday school at church, and her love for the professional grew. **Hobbies:** Reading; Computers **Political Affiliations:** Democrat **Shipping Address:** 3944 36th St., Des Moines, IA, 50310

Gary F. Smith

Title: Lawyer **Industry:** Law and Legal Services **Company Name:** Gary F. Smith, Attorney at Law **Date of Birth:** 02/15/1948 **Place of Birth:** New York **State:** NY **Parents:** Seba F. Smith; Cecelia Maryann (Ambrosio) Smith **Marital Status:** Widower **Spouse Name:** Eileen Marie Grosso (8/23/1969), Deceased (6/11/2013) **Children:** Evan Gary Smith **Education:** JD, Fordham University (1970-1973); BA, Iona College, Summa Cum Laude (1966-1970) **Career:** Sole Practitioner, Gary F. Smith, Attorney at Law Private Practice, Hauppauge, NY (1986-Present); Private Practice, Westbury, NY (1979-1986); Partner, Koozman & Hartman, New York, NY (1977-1979); Associate, Koozman & Hartman, New York, NY (1974-1977); Attorney, Metropolitan Life Insurance Co., New York, NY (1973-1974) **Awards:** Honoree, Cornelian Honor Society, Iona College, New Rochelle, NY (1970); Phi Beta Kappa Award, Long Island Phi Beta Kappa Alumni Association, Hempstead, NY (1966) **Membership:** ABA; New York State Bar Association; Suffolk County Bar Association; Phi Alpha Delta **Marquis Who's Who Honors:** Albert Nelson Marquis Lifetime Achievement Award (2017) **Why did you become involved in your profession or industry:** Mr. Smith became involved in his profession after coming from a humble blue collar background and having good debating skills. His family always commented how good he would be in law. He has wanted to go to law school since the fifth grade. **Where will you be in five years:** In five years, God willing, Mr. Smith will be doing what he is doing now. **Hobbies:** Golf; Fishing; Jogging; Bible research **Shipping Address:** 140 Fell Ct. Ste 303, Gary F. Smith Attorney at Law, Hauppauge, NY, 11788 **Website:** http://www.garyfsmithesq.com

George Bundy Smith Sr.

Title: Lawyer, State Appeals Court Judge **Industry:** Law and Legal Services **Date of Birth:** 04/07/1937 **Place of Birth:** New Orleans **State:** LA **Year of Passing:** 2017-08-28 **Parents:** Sidney R. Smith; Beatrice (Bundy) Smith **Marital Status:** Married **Spouse Name:** Alene L. Smith (1964) **Children:** George Smith, Jr.; Beth Beatrice **Education:** Honorary LLD, Albany Law School (2006); Honorary LLD, Fordham University School of Law (2004); Master's of Judicial Process, University of Virginia School of Law (2001); LLM of Judicial Process, University of Virginia (2001); PhD, New York University (1974); MA in Political Science, New York University (1968); LLB, Yale University (1962); BA, Yale University (1959); Honorary LLD, Brooklyn Law School; Honorary Doctorate, St. Thomas Aquinas College **Certifications:** Certification in Political Studies, Institut d'Etudes Politiques (1958) **Career:** Partner, George, Bundy, Smith and Associates PC (2012); Partner, Chadbourne & Parke LLP (2006-2011); Associate Judge, New York State Court of Appeals (1992-2006); Associate Justice, Appellate Division, First Department, Supreme Court of the State of New York (1987-1992); Judge, Supreme Court of the State of New York (1979-1986); Judge, Civil Court of the City of New York (1975-1979); Interim Judge, Civil Court of the City of New York (1975-1976); Administrator, Model Cities, City of New York (1974-1975); Law Clerk to Hon. Harold Stevens, Appellate Division, First Department, State of New York (1972-1974); Law Clerk to Hon. Edward Dudley (1967-1971); Law Clerk to Hon. Jawn Sandifer (1964-1967); Staff Attorney, Legal Defense and Educational Fund, NAACP (1962-1964) **Career Related:** Appointed Member, New York State Ethics Commission Unified Court System (1989-1990); Adjunct Professor, Criminal Procedure and Constitutional Law, Fordham University (1981-2012) **Civic:** Trustee, Horace Mann-Barnard School, Bronx, NY (1977-1999); Board of Directors, Harlem-Dowling Westside Center for Children and Family Services; Alumni Trustee, Phillips Academy, Andover, MA; Founding Member, Cardozo Law School National Center for Access to Justice, New York, NY; Trustee, Grace Congressional Church, Harlem, NY **Creative Works:** Co-Author, "You Decide: Applying the Bill of Rights to Real Cases"; Contributor, Articles, Professional Journals **Awards:** William Nelson Cromwell Award, New York County Lawyers Association (2005) **Membership:** Vice President, Association of the Bar of the City of New York (1988-1989); Chairman, Metropolitan Black Bar Association (1984-1988); President, Harlem Lawyers Association; Judicial Friends; American Bar Association; National Bar Association; New York State Bar Association; The Network of Bar Leaders; Founding Member, Metropolitan Black Bar Association; Chair, Board of Directors, Metropolitan Black Bar Association **Bar Admissions:** District of Columbia (1980); State of New York (1963); U.S. Supreme Court; Second Circuit, U.S. Court of Appeals; Fourth Circuit, U.S. Court of Appeals; U.S. District Court, Eastern District, State of New York; U.S. District Court, Southern District, State of New York; U.S. District Court, Western District, State of New York **Marquis Who's Who Honors:** Albert Nelson Marquis Lifetime Achievement Award (2017) **Shipping Address:** 549 W 123rd. Street, Apt. 13F, New York, NY, 10027

Ian C.P. Smith, PhD

Title: Biophysicist (Retired) **Industry:** Sciences **Company Name:** Innovative Biodiagnostics, Inc. **Date of Birth:** 09/23/1939 **Place of Birth:** Winnipeg **Country of Origin:** Canada **Parents:** Cormack Smith; Grace Mary Smith **Marital Status:** Married **Spouse Name:** Eva Gunilla Landvik (3/27/1965) **Children:** Brittmarie; Cormack; Duncan; Roderick **Education:** Honorary DSc, Polish Academy of Science, Krakow (2006); Honorary DSc, Brandon University (2001); Honorary Diploma, Technology, Red River College (1996); Honorary DSc, University of Winnipeg (1990); Honorary PhD, University of Stockholm (1986); PhD, Cambridge University, England (1965); MS, University of Manitoba (1962); BS, University of Manitoba (1961) **Career:** President, Innovative Biodiagnostics Incorporated (2013-2017); Director General, Institute Biodiagnostics, Winnipeg, Canada (1992-2013); Director General, National Research Council, Ottawa, Canada (1987-1991); Research Officer, Division of Biological Sciences, National Research Council, Ottawa, Canada (1967-1987); Member, Research Staff, Bell Telephone Laboratories, Murray Hill, NJ (1966-1967); Fellow, Stanford University (1965-66); With, Manitoba Technology Accelerator Medical Device Commercialization Center; Chief Executive Officer, Center for Imaging Technology Commercialization **Career Related:** Member, Advisory Board, Cancer Care Manitoba (2007-Present); St. Boniface Hospital Research Enterprise (2006-Present); President, Innovative Biodiagnostics Inc. (2013-2017); Chairman, Board of Directors CIMTEC (2011-2017); Member, Executive Board, Manitoba Health Research Council (2007-2012); Executive Committee Member, Economic Technology Innovation Council (2006-2008); Novadaq (2004-2006); Western Life Sciences Fund (2002-2008); Board of Directors, Manitoba Institute Cell Biology, Genome Prairie, Ontario Centres of Excellence, Cognosis Canada Inc., Biomed. Commercialization Can., Spectex Pty., Magnetic Resonance Vets., IMRIS Inc., DIASPEC Holdings, ENSIS Growth Fund Board of Governors, University of Manitoba, Canada (2000-2006); Keystone Ventures (1999-2002); Loeb Institute, Ottawa, Canada (1999-2001); Chairman, Manitoba Health Research Council (1998-2002); Allied Scientist, Health Sciences Center (1993); St. Boniface Hospital (1992); Ontario Cancer Foundation (1989-1991); Ottawa General Hospital (1989-1998); Ottawa Civic Hospital (1985-1998) **Civic:** Science Advisory Board, Thunder Bay Research Institute (2018-Present); President, Smart Winnipeg (2013-Present); Executive Committee, Province of Manitoba Premier's Economic Advisory Board (2004-Present); Premier's Economic Advisory Board (2001-Present); Advisory Board, Smart Winnipeg (2000-2003) **Creative Works:** Contributor, Book Chapters; Contributor, Articles, Professional Journals **Awards:** Officer of the Order of Canada (2009); Outstanding Achievement Award, Government of Canada (2008); Distinguished Alumni Award, University of Manitoba (2007); Paul Harris Award, Rotary Club (2006); Queen's Jubilee Medal (2012, 2003); Senior Scientist Award, Sigma Xi (1995); Organon Teknika Award, Canadian Society of Clinical Chemists (1987); Herzberg Award (1986); Barringer Award, Canadian Spectroscopy Society (1979); Manitoba Order of the Buffalo Hunt; Order of the Star of Romania **Membership:** Ontario Centres of Excellence; Biophysical Society of Canada; Canada Biochemical Society; Biophysical Society of North America; International Union for Pure and Applied Biophysics; Fellow, Royal Society of Canada; Past President, Alumni Association, University of Manitoba **Marquis Who's Who Honors:** Distinguished Humanitarian (2017) **Shipping Address:** 63 Shier Drive, MB, Winnipeg, Canada, R3R 2H2

Jack Carl Smith

Title: Foreign Trade Consultant **Industry:** Consulting **Company Name:** American Foreign Policy Council **Date of Birth:** 09/11/1928 **Place of Birth:** Cleveland **State:** OH **Parents:** John Carl Smith; Florence Agnes (O'Rourke) Smith **Marital Status:** Married **Spouse Name:** Nannette June Boyd (12/1/1962) **Children:** Colleen Wentworth Jones **Education:** Postgraduate Coursework, Baldwin Wallace University (1958); BA, Ohio University (1954); Coursework, Baldwin Wallace University (1948-1951) **Career:** Special Advisor, American Foreign Policy Council, Washington, DC (1990-Present); Publisher, Penton Publishing Co., Cleveland, OH (1964-1990); Principal, Publishing Representative Business, Cleveland, OH (1961-1964); Representative, Flying Tiger Line, Inc., Los Angeles, CA (1958-1961) **Career Related:** Director, National Distribution Terminals, Central Cleveland Corporation **Civic:** Trustee, Presidential Task Force; Trustee, Republican Senatorial Inner Circle Council of Logistics Management; Trustee, United States Business and Industry Council **Military Service:** Diplomate, Air Education and Training Command, U.S. Air Force Reserve (1958-1962); U.S. Air Force (1954-1958) **Membership:** American Management Association; Material Handling Institute; American Trucking Associations; National Council of Physical Distribution Management; Family Motor Coach Association; Recreation Vehicle Industry Association; North American Business Press; Magazine Publishers Association (Now Association of Magazine Media); Sigma Xi, The Scientific Research Honor Society; International Platform Association; Sigma Delta Chi (Now Society of Professional Journalists); Wings, New York, NY **Marquis Who's Who Honors:** Albert Nelson Marquis Lifetime Achievement Award (2017); Distinguished Humanitarian (2017) **Shipping Address:** 457 Devonshire Court, Bay Village, OH, 44140

R. Stephen Smith

Title: Professor of Surgery **Industry:** Education/Educational Services **Company Name:** University of Florida **Date of Birth:** 11/26/1955 **Place of Birth:** Russellville **State:** AR **Marital Status:** Married **Spouse Name:** Nellie Shinmon Smith **Children:** Ryan Michael; Nicole Rieko **Education:** Fellow in Trauma/Surgical Critical Care, St. Mary Medical Center (1986-1987); Resident in General Surgery, School of Medicine, University of Kansas (1981-1986); MD, University of Arkansas (1981); BS in Biology, Arkansas Tech University, With Highest Honors (1977) **Certifications:** Diplomate, American Board of Surgery, Inc. (2016); Licensed to Practice Medicine, State of Florida (2015); Licensed to Practice Medicine, State of South Carolina (2012); Diplomate, ASSET (2012); Licensed to Practice Medicine, Commonwealth of Pennsylvania (2010); Licensed to Practice Medicine, Commonwealth of Virginia (2008); Certificate of Special Qualifications in Critical Care (2008); Licensed to Practice Medicine, State of Oklahoma (2006); Diplomate, American Board of Surgery, Inc. (2005); Certified FCCS Instructor (2003); Certified Aviation Medical Examiner (2000); Certified in Pediatric Advanced Life Support (1999); Certificate of Special Qualifications in Critical Care (1998); Diplomate, American Board of Surgery, Inc. (1995); Registered Diagnostic Medical Sonographer (1994); Board Certified, Surgical Critical Care (1989); Certificate of Special Qualifications in Critical Care (1989); Diplomate, American Board of Surgery, Inc. (1987); Board Certified General Surgery (1987); Licensed to Practice Medicine, State of California (1986); Certified in Advanced Trauma Life Support (1986); Licensed to Practice Medicine, State of Kansas (1982); Certified in Advanced Cardiac Life Support (1981); Licensed to Practice Medicine, State of Arkansas (1981) **Career:** Professor, Clinical Surgery, University of Florida (2015-Present); Surgeon, Shands Hospital, University of Florida (2015-Present); Palmetto Richland Hospital, Palmetto Health (2012-Present); Professor, Clinical Surgery, University of South Carolina (2012-2015); Adjunct Professor, Surgery, Temple University School of Medicine (2011-2012); Surgeon, Allegheny General Hospital, Allegheny Health Network (2011-2012); Western Pennsylvania Hospital, Allegheny Health Network (2011-2012); Forbes Medical Center, Allegheny Health Network (2011-2012); Interim Chair, Department of Surgery, The Virginia Tech Carilion School of Medicine and Research Institute (2010); Professor, Surgery, The Virginia Tech Carilion School of Medicine and Research Institute (2009-2011); Clinical Professor, Surgery, The University of Virginia (2009-2011); Surgeon, Carilion Roanoke Medical Center, Carilion Clinic (2008-2011); Vice Chair, Director, Surgical Education, Carilion Clinic (2008-2011); Clinical Professor, Anesthesiology, The University of Kansas Medical Center (2004-2007); Professor, Surgery, The University of Kansas Medical Center (2000-2008); Clinical Associate Professor, Anesthesiology, The University of Kansas Medical Center (1995-2000); Surgeon, Regional Medical Center, Via Christi Health (1994-2008); Surgeon, Wesley Medical Center, C-HCA, Inc. (1994-2008); Associate Professor, Surgery, The University of Kansas Medical Center (1994-2000); Surgeon, VA Palo Alto Health Care System, U.S. Department of Veterans Affairs (1992-1994); Surgeon, Highland Department of Emergency Medicine (1991-1994); Clinical Assistant Professor, Surgery, University of California, Davis (1991-1994); Clinical Assistant Professor, Surgery, Uniform Services University (1991-1994); Surgeon, Santa Clara Valley Medical Center (1990-1994) **Career Related:** Fellow, American College of Surgeons (1992) **Military Service:** Captain, Medical Corps, U.S. Navy (1981-2006) **Awards:** Best Teacher Award, University of South Carolina (2014); St Luke's Award, Via Christi Medical Center (2003); J. Bradley Aust Award, Western Surgical Association (1998); Meritorious Service Medal, U.S. Navy (1994); Southwest Asia Service Ribbon, U.S. Navy (1991); Sea Service Ribbon, U.S. Navy (1991); National Defense Ribbon, U.S. Navy (1991); Kuwaiti Liberation Medal, U.S. Navy (1991); Overseas Service Ribbon, U.S. Navy (1989); Achievement Medal, U.S. Navy (1989); Humanitarian Service Ribbon, U.S. Navy (1989); Unit Citation Ribbon, U.S. Navy (1987) **Membership:** Past Chair, Ultrasound Users Group, American College of Surgeons (2011-Present); Committee on Trauma, American College of Surgeons (2009-Present); Multi-Center Trials Committee, Western Trauma Association (2005-Present); Board of Directors, Western Trauma Association (2014-2017); The Halsted Society (2014); Society of Surgical Chairs (2012-2015); Chair, Program Committee, Western Trauma Association (2009-2011); Program Committee, Western Trauma Association (2008-2012); Councilor, SWSC (2008-2009); Publications Committee, Western Trauma Association (2007-2011); President, Kansas Chapter, American College of Surgeons (2007-2008); Chairman, Ultrasound Users Group, American College of Surgeons (2006-2011) **Business Address:** 1600 SW Archer Road, Gainesville, FL, 32610 **Shipping Address:** 1913 Sprucewood Way, Port Orange, FL, 32128 **Website:** http://surgery.med.ufl.edu/category/acute-care-surgery/r-stephen-smith

Raoul N. Smith, PhD

Title: Professor Emeritus **Industry:** Education/Educational Services **Company Name:** Northeastern University **Date of Birth:** 05/15/1938 **Place of Birth:** West Warwick **State:** RI **Parents:** Luke Joseph Smith; Lucienne Smith **Marital Status:** Married **Spouse Name:** Mary Frances Hand (11/12/1966) **Children:** Stephen Edward; Timothy Luke **Education:** PhD, Brown University (1968); AM, Brown University (1964); AB, Brown University (1963) **Career:** Professor Emeritus, Northeastern University (2000-Present); Vice President, Chinaedu Corporation (2000-2002); Computer Science Professor, Northeastern University (1983-2000); Research Director, Northeastern University (1985-1986); Visiting Professor, Jilin University (1985); Graduate Schools Director, Northeastern University (1984-1985); Principal Member, Technical Staff, GTE Laboratories (1983); Senior Member, Technical Staff, GTE Laboratories (1981-1983); Associate Linguistics Professor, Slavic Languages & Literatures, Northwestern University (1973-1980); Assistant Professor, Northwestern University (1968-1973); Instructor, Northwestern University (1967-1968) **Career Related:** Chairman, Board of Directors, Cognitive Computers, Newton, MA (1985-1987); Principal, Raoul N. Smith and Associates; Consultant, Museum of Russian Icons; Head, Center for Icons Studies, Museum of Russian Icons **Civic:** Director, Acton Historical Society (2002-2004); Trustee, Acton Historical Society (1988-1990); Member, AIDS Action Committee (1985-1988); Incorporator, Higgins Armory Museum **Military Service:** With, U.S. Air Force (1957-1961) **Creative Works:** Editor, Journal of Icon Studies (2010-Present); Author, "Dictionary of Artificial Intelligence" (1989); Author, "The Language of Jonathan Fisher" (1985); Co-author, "Lexical-Semantic Relations" (1980); Author, "Probabilistic Performance Models of Language" (1973) **Awards:** Grantee, National Endowment for the Humanities (1975-1979); Grantee, The American Philosophical Society (1974); Grantee, American Council of Learned Societies (1974); Grantee, National Science Foundation (1971); Grantee, National Science Foundation (1966-1967); Air Force Intelligence (1957-1963); Research Fellow, Museum of Russian Icons **Membership:** Co-chair, Special Interest Group on Computer and Human Interaction, ACM, Inc (1981-1985); Union Club; Museum of Russian Icons **Marquis Who's Who Honors:** Albert Nelson Marquis Lifetime Achievement Award (2017) **To what do you attribute your success:** Dr. Smith attributes his success to intellectual curiosity. **Why did you become involved in your profession or industry:** Dr. Smith became involved in his profession because it interested him. He also credits his dissertation advisor, who was a great role model. **What do you consider to be the highlight of your career:** Dr. Smith is most proud of his publication, "The Language of Jonathan Fisher." **Hobbies:** Antiques **Shipping Address:** 206 Nagog Hill Rd., Acton, MA, 01720

Thomas J. Smith

Title: Educator, Researcher **Industry:** Education/ Educational Services **Marital Status:** Married **Spouse Name:** Mary Jill Clemens (8/25/1962) **Children:** Steven Thomas; Michael Karl **Education:** PhD in Physiology, University of Wisconsin-Madison (1977); MSc in Molecular Biology/Biochemistry, University of California, San Diego (1966); BA in Chemistry and Molecular Biology, University of Wisconsin-Madison (1962) **Certifications:** Board Certified Professional in Ergonomics (1995); Certified Human Factors Professional (1995) **Career:** Research Associate, School of Kinesiology, University of Minnesota, Minneapolis, MN (1996-Present); Supervisor, Human Factors Research Group, Twin Cities Research Center, U.S. Bureau of the Mines, Minneapolis, MN (1987-1996); Assistant Professor, School of Kinesiology, Simon Fraser University, Burnaby, BC, Canada (1980-1987) **Career Related:** Chair, Professional Standards, Education Standing Committee, International Ergonomics Association, Geneva, Switzerland (2006-Present); Editorial Board, Theoretical Issues in Ergonomics Science Journal (2000-Present) **Civic:** Dakota County Extension Committee, Minnesota (2006-2009) **Creative Works:** Monograph Editor, Human Factors & Ergonomics Society (2000-2006); Contributor, Articles, Professional Journals **Awards:** Grant, Minnesota Department of Transportation (2007); Grant, Minnesota Department of Transportation (2004); Grant, Minnesota Department of Transportation (2001); Grant, Minnesota Department of Transportation (1998) **Membership:** Human Factors & Ergonomics Society **Marquis Who's Who Honors:** Albert Nelson Marquis Lifetime Achievement Award (2017) **Why did you become involved in your profession or industry:** Mr. Smith was greatly inspired by his father, who established the first civilian human factors laboratory in the United States in 1947. He and his father co-authored papers together. **Hobbies:** Bicycling; Wilderness camping; Canoeing; Writing; Gardening **Shipping Address:** 625 Hampshire Drive, Mendota Heights, MN, 55120

Oles Smolansky

Title: Professor Emeritus **Industry:** Education/Educational Services **Company Name:** Lehigh University **Date of Birth:** 05/02/1930 **Place of Birth:** Ukraine **Country of Origin:** Ukraine **Parents:** Mykola S.; Irene (Pliuto) S. **Marital Status:** Married **Spouse Name:** Bettie Moretz (12/29/1966) **Children:** Holly; Alexandra; Nicholas **Education:** PhD, Columbia University (1959); MA, Columbia University (1955); BA, New York University (1953) **Career:** Emeritus, University Professor, Lehigh University, Bethlehem, PA (2005-Present); University Professor, Lehigh University, Bethlehem, PA (1985-2005); Professor, Lehigh University, Bethlehem, PA (1970-1985); Associate Professor, Lehigh University, Bethlehem, PA (1966-1970); Assistant Professor, Lehigh University, Bethlehem, PA (1963-1966); Instructor, University of California, Los Angeles (1960-1962) **Creative Works:** Author, "The Soviet Union and the Arab East Under Khrushchev" (1974); Author, "The USSR and Iraq: The Soviet Quest for Influence" (1991); Co-Editor, "Russia and America: From Rivalry to Reconciliation" (1993); Co-Editor, "Regional Power Rivalries in the New Eurasia: Russia, Turkey, and Iran" (1995); Co-Editor, "The Lost Equilibrium: International Relations in the Post-Soviet Era" (2001); Contributor, Articles, Professional Journals **Awards:** Marshall Shulman Award, American Association for Advancement of Slavic Studies (1992); Research Fellowship, Ford Foundation, New York City, NY (1980-1981); Senior Research Joint Fellowship, Research Institute on Communist Affairs and Middle East Institute, Columbia University, New York City, NY (1972-1973); Joint Fellowship, Rockefeller Foundation and Ford Foundation, New York City, NY (1962-1963) **Membership:** International Studies Association **Marquis Who's Who Honors:** Albert Nelson Marquis Lifetime Achievement Award (2017) **To what do you attribute your success:** Dr. Smolansky attributes his success to an interest in international politics, hard work and luck. **Why did you become involved in your profession or industry:** He became involved in his profession because of his background growing up in the Soviet Union and Nazi Germany, experiencing World War II, and life in postwar Germany. **What do you consider to be the highlight of your career:** A highlight of his career was researching, writing and publishing the book on the USSR and Iraq. **Where will you be in five years:** In five years, only God knows where he will be. **Hobbies:** Music; Sports **Political Affiliations:** Democrat **Religion:** Greek Orthodox **Shipping Address:** 1036 Resolution Drive, Bethlehem, PA, 18017

Skipi Lundquist Smoot, PhD

Title: Psychologist **Industry:** Social Work **Date of Birth:** 04/10/1934 **Place of Birth:** Aberdeen **State:** WA **Parents:** Warren Duncan Dobbins; Miriam Stephen (Bishop) Dobbins **Marital Status:** Married **Spouse Name:** Edward Lee Smoot (1973); Harold Richard Lundquist (6/2/1951, Divorced 3/1973) **Children:** Lake Donald (Deceased); Kurt Richard (Deceased); Mark David (Deceased); Ted Douglas **Education:** PhD, California School of Professional Psychology (Now Alliant International University) (1985); MA, Pepperdine University (1980); BA in Psychology, College of William and Mary (1978) **Certifications:** Licensed Clinical Psychologist, State of California; Licensed Marriage and Family Therapist, State of California **Career:** Private Practice, Cognitive Psyche Therapy for Adolescents and Adults (1995-Present); Clinical Director, Career Ambitions Unlimited (1991-1998); Clinical Director, Psychological Decisions (1991-1994); Psychologist, Psychological Center (1985-1991); Psychologist, Mental Health Association of Orange County (1984-1985); Psychotherapist, California State Police (1983-1984); Psychotherapist, California State Police (1982-1983); Psychotherapist, Orange County Child Guidance (1981-1982); Psychotherapist, College Hospitals (1979-1981); Owner, McDonald's (1965-1976); Operator, McDonald's (1965-1976); Owner, McDonald's (1965-1976); Operator, McDonald's Restaurants (1965-1976) **Career Related:** Psychological Consultant, Seminars and Workshops (1991-1998) **Creative Works:** Author, "Maturation: The Adult Paradigm, The Missing Link for Resolution of Anxiety" (2011) **Membership:** American Psychological Association; California Psychological Association **Hobbies:** Music; Travel; Research **Political Affiliations:** Democrat **Business Address:** 23072 Lake Center Drive, Suite 209, Lake Forest, CA, 92630 **Shipping Address:** 6 Chamonix, Laguna Niguel, CA, 92677

Linda Snow Yates-Williams

Title: Real Estate Broker **Industry:** Real Estate **Company Name:** Legacy Realty of the Lowcountry **Date of Birth:** 07/20/1938 **Place of Birth:** St. Louis **State:** MO **Parents:** Robert Anthony Jerrue Armstrong; June Alberta (Crowder) Armstrong **Marital Status:** Married **Spouse Name:** John Williams (2006); Alan Yates (1981, Divorced 2002, Deceased 2004); Charles Russell Snow (11/26/1958, Divorced 1979) **Children:** Sean Webster; Cathryn Louise; Christopher Armstrong; Heather Highstone **Education:** EdD, Auburn University (1998); MEd, Auburn University (1975); BBA, Auburn University (1973) **Certifications:** Certified Professional Secretary **Career:** Associate Broker, Legacy Realty of the Lowcountry (2013-Present); Broker-in-Charge, EXIT Hilton Head Realty (2008-2013); Broker-in-Charge, Exit Island Realty, Bluffton, SC (2006-2008); Real Estate Salesperson, Exit Realty Beaufort (2003-2005); Real Estate Salesperson, Apex Realty, Beaufort, SC (2002-2003); President, Power Communications Inc., Cashiers, NC (1994-1998); Owner, Power Communications Inc., Cashiers, NC (1994-1998); Board of Directors, Corporate Secretary, Hilltop Associates Inc (1992-1999); Legal Word Processing Assistant, Kilpatrick & Cody (Now Kilpatrick Townsend & Stockton LLP) (1990-1994); Legal Assistant, Rice & Keene, Atlanta, GA (1987-1990); Secretary, Rice & Keene (1987-1990); Operations Manager, Talent Tree Staffing (1985-1987); Owner, DataOne, Inc. (1984-1985); Recruiter, DataOne, Inc. (1984-1985); Employment Coordinator, Fulton Federal Savings Bank (1983-1984); Division Head Placement, Division Solutions Group, Atlanta, GA (1981-1983); Area Vice President, Enterprise Lenders, LLC; Loan Agent, Enterprise Lenders, LLC ; Marketing Director, Electronic Collection Division, American Financial Credit Services, Inc., Greenville, SC; Regional Coordinator, Southeast Region, World Connect Communications, Tulsa, OK; Regional Marketing Representative, World Connect Communications, Tulsa, OK **Career Related:** Adjunct Instructor, Mercer University (1981-1982); Adjunct Instructor, Perimeter College, Georgia State University (1980-1984); Executive Legal Secretary, Swift, Currie, McGhee & Hiers (1979-1980); President, Professional Secretaries Association (1975); Business Instructor, Southern Union State Community College (1974-1975); Radio Advertising, WAUD, Auburn, AL (1970-1975); Executive Legal Secretary, Samford, Torbert, Denson & Horsley (1969-1971); Radio Announcer, Meet The Public; Director, Academy Planning, Universidad De Monterrey; Chairman, Education Division, Universidad De Monterrey; Part-Time Faculty Member, Educational Administration, Universidad De Monterrey **Civic:** Vice President, Board Trustees, Family Promise of Beaufort County (2007-Present); Corporate Secretary, Steele Creek Marina & Campground (2006-Present); Vice President, Board Trustees, EXIT Realty Beaufort **Creative Works:** Columnist, Neon News Flash (1995) **Awards:** Honoree, Top Sales (2006); Honoree, Top Producer (2006); Honoree, Top Listing Agent (2005); Honoree, International Poet of Merit, International Society of Poets (1996); Inductee, International Poetry Hall of Fame, International Society of Poets (1996) **Membership:** Founding Laureate Member, International Society of Poets (2006); Charter Member, Paralegal Association Beaufort County (1993-1994); Secretary, Paralegal Association Beaufort County (1993-1994); NAWBO; National Association of Personnel Services; Distinguished Member, International Society of Poets; Cashiers Writers Group, NC Writers' Network; The 90/10 Club; Sunscribers; Phi Delta Kappa International; Alpha Xi Delta **Marquis Who's Who Honors:** Albert Nelson Marquis Lifetime Achievement Award (2017) **Hobbies:** Golf; Writing poetry; International travel **Political Affiliations:** Republican **Religion:** Presbyterian **Shipping Address:** 66 Concession Oak Dr., Bluffton, SC, 29910

Jean Maclean Snyder

Title: Lawyer **Industry:** Law and Legal Services **Company Name:** Law Office of Jean Maclean Snyder **Date of Birth:** 01/26/1942 **Place of Birth:** Chicago **State:** IL **Parents:** Norman Fitzroy Maclean; Jessie (Burns) Maclean **Marital Status:** Married **Spouse Name:** Joel Martin Snyder (9/4/1964) **Children:** Jacob Samuel; Noah Scot **Education:** JD, University of Chicago (1979); BA, University of Chicago (1963) **Career:** Teaching Team Member, Intensive Trial Practise Workshop, University of Chicago (2009-Present); Principal, Law Office of Jean Maclean Snyder (2004-Present); Of Counsel, University of Chicago Law School (2004-2005); Independent Advisor, Midwest Coalition Human Rights (2000-2010); Trial Counsel, The MacArthur Justice Center, University of Chicago Law School (1997-2004); Principal, Law Office of Jean Maclean Snyder, Chicago, IL (1993-1997); Partner, D'Ancona & Pflaum, Chicago, IL (1979-1992) **Civic:** Board of Directors, Citizens Alert (2005-2007) **Creative Works:** Editor-in-Chief, Litigation Magazine (1987-1988); Contributor, Articles, Professional Journals **Awards:** Excellence Award, U.S. District Court, Northern District, State of Illinois (2012) **Membership:** Co-Chair, Section Litigation Task Force on Gender, Racial, and Ethnic Bias (1998-2001); Standing Committee on Strategic Communications (1996-2001); American Civil Liberties Union of Illinois (1996-1999); Board of Directors, Lawyers for the Creative Arts (1995-1997); Co-Chair, First Amendment and Media Litigation Committee (1995-1996); Member Council, Litigation Section, American Bar Association (1989-1992) **Bar Admissions:** Seventh Circuit, U.S. Court of Appeals (1981); State of Illinois (1979); U.S. District Court, Northern District, State of Illinois (1979) **Shipping Address:** 4845 S Kenwood Avenue, Chicago, IL, 60615

Mark E. Sobel, PhD

Title: Executive Officer Emeritus **Industry:** Medicine & Health Care **Company Name:** American Society for Investigative Pathology **Date of Birth:** 04/14/1949 **Place of Birth:** New York **State:** NY **Parents:** Abraham David Sobel; Selma Etta (Spitzer) Sobel **Education:** Medical Intern, Pediatrics, Boston Children's Hospital, Harvard Medical School, Boston, MA (1975-1976); Clinical Fellow, Pediatrics, Boston Children's Hospital, Harvard Medical School, Boston, MA (1975-1976); PhD, Biomedical Sciences, The City University of New York (1975); MD, Icahn School of Medicine at Mount Sinai, New York, NY (1975); BA, Brandeis University (1970) **Certifications:** Diplomate, National Board of Medical Examiners **Career:** Executive Officer Emeritus (2018); Senior Executive Director, American Society for Investigative Pathology, Bethesda, MD (2001-2018); Chief, Molecular Pathology Section, National Cancer Institute, NIH, Bethesda, MD (1992-2001); Senior Investigator, National Cancer Institute, National Institutes of Health, Bethesda, MD (1983-1992); Research Associate, NIH, Bethesda, MD (1980-1983); Research Associate, National Institutes of Health,, Bethesda, MD (1976-1979) **Career Related:** Director, Concepts in Molecular Biology Course, American Society Investigative of Pathology, Bethesda, MD (1987-1999); Visiting Scientist, Max Planck Institute for Biochemistry, Martinsried bei Munchen, Germany (1979-1980) **Civic:** Captain, Commissioned Corps of the U.S. Public Health Service (1975-2001) **Creative Works:** Contributor, Articles, Professional Journals **Awards:** Commendation Medal, Commissioned Corps of the U.S. Public Health Service (1989); Various Awards **Membership:** National Advisory Committee, PMC, National Center for Biotechnology Information, U.S. National Library of Medicine (2007-2011); Advisory Board, Federation of American Societies for Experimental Biology (2006-2011); Advisory Board, Minority Access to Research Careers (2006-2011); Board of Directors, AAHRPP (2001-2008); President, American Society for Investigative Pathology (1999-2000); President, Association for Molecular Pathology (1999); Vice President, American Society for Investigative Pathology (1998-1999); President-Elect, Association for Molecular Pathology (1998); Vice President-Elect, American Society for Investigative Pathology (1997-1998); Of Council, American Society for Investigative Pathology (1995-1997); Secretary, Association for Molecular Pathology (1995-1997); American Society for Biochemistry and Molecular Biology; Phi Beta Kappa; Alpha Omega Alpha; Sigma Xi; Phi Beta Kappa **Hobbies:** Classical music; History **Religion:** Jewish **Shipping Address:** 1801 Rockville Pike, Ste 350, ASIP, Rockville, MD, 20852

Jaroslaw Sobieski

Title: Aerospace Engineer **Industry:** Engineering **Company Name:** NASA Langley Research Center **Date of Birth:** 03/11/1934 **Place of Birth:** Wilno **Country of Origin:** Poland **Parents:** Stanislaw Sobieszczanski; Sabina Sobieszczanski **Marital Status:** Widowed **Spouse Name:** Wanda Dlugosz (1958, Deceased 2008) **Children:** Margaret Ann; Ian Patrick **Education:** Doctor of Engineering, Warsaw University of Technology (1964); MS in Aerospace, Warsaw University of Technology (1957); BS in Aerospace., Warsaw University of Technology (1955) **Certifications:** Certified Chartered Engineer, Royal Aeronautical Society (1968) **Career:** Distinguished Research Associate, NASA Langley Research Center, Hampton, VA (2006-Present); Senior Research Scientist, NASA Langley Research Center, Hampton, VA (2001-2006); Manager, Computational AeroScience Team, NASA Langley Research Center, Hampton, VA (1996-2001); Multidisciplinary Research Coordinator, NASA Langley Research Center, Hampton, VA (1994-2001); Chief Scientist, NASA Langley Research Center, Hampton, VA (1993-1996); Head, Research Office, NASA Langley Research Center, Hampton, VA (1979-1993); Aerospace Engineer, NASA Langley Research Center, Hampton, VA (1971-1989); Associate Professor, St. Louis University (1966-1971); Research Associate, Norwegian University of Science and Technology, Trondheim, Norway (1964-1966); Assistant and Adjunct Professor, Warsaw University of Technology, Warsaw, Poland (1955-1964); Consultant, Polish Aircraft Industries, Warsaw, Poland (1957-1964) **Career Related:** Delft University of Technology, Netherlands (2010-Present); PhD Committee Member, Massachusetts Institute of Technology (2009-Present); Virginia Polytechnic Institute (2004-Present); Faculty Member, The George Washington University (1971-2003); Faculty Member, University of Virginia (1992-1999); President, Consultant Engineer, Technical Analysis Optimization, Inc., Hampton, VA (1982-1992); Presentation Lecturer, United States of America, United Kingdom, Australia, China, Japan, Brazil, Germany, Norway, Denmark, France, Portugal, Belgium, Israel and Holland **Civic:** President, Civic Association, Hampton, VA (1987-1988) **Military Service:** Lieutenant, Polish Airforce (1955) **Creative Works:** Co-author, "Multidisciplinary Design Optimization" (2015); Co-Editor, Structural Optimization Journal (1989-2005); Contributor, Articles, Professional Journals; Contributor, Chapters, Books; Lecturer in Field **Awards:** Exceptional Service Medal, National Aeronautics and Space Administration (2005); Wright Brothers Medal, SAE International (2005); Exceptional Engineering Achievement, National Aeronautics and Space Administration (1988); National Award for Multidisciplinary Design Optimization, AIAA (1986) **Membership:** Founding Chairman, Technical Committee, Multidisciplinary Design Optimization, AIAA; Fellow, AIAA; Executive Board, International Society Structural and Multidisciplinary Optimization (1992-2003); Co-founder, International Society Structural and Multidisciplinary Optimization; Soaring Society of America; The National Institute of Aerospace **To what do you attribute your success:** Dr. Sobieski attributes his success to persistence. **Why did you become involved in your profession or industry:** Dr. Sobieski was always an enthusiast for aviation. **What do you consider to be the highlight of your career:** The highlight of Dr. Sobieski's career was earning the National Aeronautics and Space Administration Medal for Exceptional Service. **Where will you be in five years:** In five years, he will be in Hampton, Virginia. **Hobbies:** Skiing; Sailing; Soaring; Boating **Political Affiliations:** Republican **Religion:** Catholic **Shipping Address:** 518 Elizabeth Lake Drive, Hampton, VA, 23669

Scott A. Sommer

Title: Owner, Complimentary and Alternative Medicine Practitioner **Industry:** Medicine & Health Care **Company Name:** NLC Health Center **Education:** MS in Traditional Oriental Medicine, College of Oriental Medicine, University of the Pacific, Magna Cum Laude (1998); BS in Nutritional Science, University of California, Davis (1994) **Certifications:** Master in Nutritional Response Testing (2006); Advanced Nutritional Response Testing, Dr. Freddie Ulan **Awards:** Rising Sun Award, Systemic Formulas (2009); Golden Sun Award, Systemic Formulas (2006); Rising Sun Award, Systemic Formulas (2005); Million Dollar Award, Ulan Associates; Platinum Award for Outstanding Service to the Community, Justin Toal of Standard Process **To what do you attribute your success:** Mr. Sommer attributes his success to his knowledge of nutrition and technology, a desire to create an impact in the lives of others, and an ability to research and develop new techniques. **Why did you become involved in your profession or industry:** Mr. Sommer became involved in his profession through the inspiration he received from his father, who was an organic farmer. **What do you consider to be the highlight of your career:** Every day is a highlight to Mr. Sommer because he witnesses people healing and getting better from long-term maladies using complimentary and alternative health care practices. Good health and optimal health is possible using a natural and wholesome approach. **Where will you be in five years:** In five years, Mr. Sommer hopes to complete his book and promote it by traveling across the country. He also wants to establish a school to educate other doctors about acupuncture and wellness techniques. It will be a one to two year program with an internship. He plans to invite all kinds of doctors including naturopaths, chiropractors, acupuncturists, medical doctors, and dentists and teach about a different view of the body by combining ancient wisdom and modern technology. **Hobbies:** Organic vegetable gardening; Cycling; Hiking; Photography; Community service; Spending time with family and friends; Reading; Attending seminars; Kayaking **Religion:** Christian **Shipping Address:** 8788 Greenback Lane, Suite 104, NLC Health Center, Orangevale, CA, 95662 **Website:** http://www.acupunctureadvantage.net

Janet Evelyn Sommerville

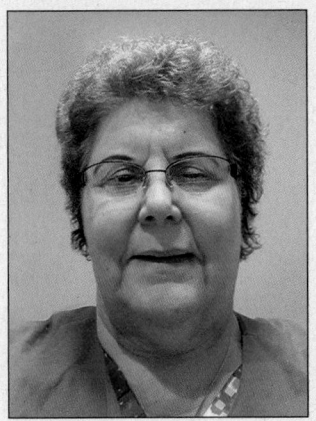

Title: Pediatrics Nurse **Industry:** Medicine & Health Care **Company Name:** Ascension Health **Date of Birth:** 09/16/1954 **Place of Birth:** Saginaw County **State:** MI **Parents:** William Henry Quaderer; Alice Mary (Louch) Quaderer **Marital Status:** Married **Spouse Name:** Ronald Sommerville (5/3/1985) **Education:** AD, Delta College (1980); Coursework, Mercy College **Certifications:** Registered Nurse, State of Michigan; Certified, Pediatrics Nurse; Certified, Pediatrics, American Academy of Family Physicians, Registered Nurse, State of Tennessee **Career:** Registered Nurse, Staff Nurse, Pre-Administration Testing Unit, Saint Thomas West Hospital, Saint Thomas Health, Ascension (2002-Present); Charge Nurse, Saint Joseph Mercy Health System, Trinity Health (1990-1992); Pontiac Staff, Saint Joseph Mercy Health System, Trinity Health (1985-1990); Staff, Charge Nurse, St. Mary's Medical Center (Now St. Mary's of Michigan, Ascension), Saginaw, MI (1981-1985); Assistant Nurse, Manager, Pre-Administration Testing Unit, Saint Thomas West Hospital, Saint Thomas Health, Ascension **Civic:** Member, St. Philips Church **Awards:** Various Awards **Membership:** Nurses' Health Study, Harvard Medical School (1980-Present); MI Nurses Association **Marquis Who's Who Honors:** Albert Nelson Marquis Lifetime Achievement Award (2017) **To what do you attribute your success:** Ms. Sommerville attributes her success to her own personal commitment to nursing, wanting to help and teach people to get well and get that back into their communities, and for them to spread the word of the healthcare they get at Saint Thomas. She also attributes her success to the compassion she feels about taking care of the patients, which includes all aspects. In pre-admission testing, they are the first line at Saint Thomas West to set that impression for them, that they are a very caring and high level hospital. They do provide excellent care for the patients, they have an excellent staff, and provide the patient with the overall great care they deserve. **Why did you become involved in your profession or industry:** She became involved in her profession because growing up, during her high school years, she did a lot of babysitting. She always wanted to be there to help, and being a babysitter, being a waitress, and then going to be a nursing assistant in 1974, helped her towards that direction. She feels she is compassionate, a good listener, and she stays on top of things. **What do you consider to be the highlight of your career:** A highlight of her career is the compassion from her peers. She was nominated for a star award when she first came into pre-admission testing. She was given an assignment to pilot to see if she could get more people to come in to do more pre-admission testing prior to their surgery. This was so people could be more prepared and not cancel surgeries due to blood work, as well as getting further details about their health. This resulted in better communication between the surgical scheduling and pre-admission testing. She was very excited and proud to be a part of that. **Where will you be in five years:** In 5 years, she will be continuing her nursing career. **Hobbies:** Reading; Walking; Movies; Volunteering at the library **Religion:** Catholic **Shipping Address:** 2722 Douglas Ln., Thompsons Station, TN, 37179

Jan Sonander

Title: Physician **Industry:** Medicine & Health Care **Education:** MD, University of California, Davis, CA; MS, University of California, Davis, CA; BS, University of California, Davis, CA **Certifications:** Board Certified Physician, The American Board of Family Medicine, Inc. **Awards:** Best Doctors in Sonoma County (2016); Best Doctor of Sonoma County (2012); Patient Satisfaction Excellence Award, St. Joseph Health System, Sonoma County, CA (2009); Readers' Choice Award, The Press Democrat **Membership:** Former Chief-of-Staff, Santa Rosa Memorial Hospital; Former President, Sonoma County Medical Association; California Medical Association; American Academy of Family Physicians **Marquis Who's Who Honors:** Albert Nelson Marquis Lifetime Achievement Award (2017); Distinguished Humanitarian (2017) **To what do you attribute your success:** Dr. Sonander attributes his success to his passion for helping patients. **Why did you become involved in your profession or industry:** Dr. Sonander became involved in his profession to help others and make a difference. **What do you consider to be the highlight of your career:** The highlight of Dr. Sonander's career was when he practiced obstetrics from 1987 until 2008. **Where will you be in five years:** In five years, Dr. Sonander intends to continue helping others and building his practice. **Hobbies:** Sailing; Skiing **Business Address:** 11 Doctors Park Drive, Santa Rosa, CA, 95405 **Shipping Address:** 1820 Sonoma Ave Ste. 11, Santa Rosa, CA, 95405

Leon Spicer, PhD

Title: Animal Scientist **Industry:** Education/ Educational Services **Company Name:** Oklahoma State University **Date of Birth:** 08/18/1955 **Place of Birth:** Portage **State:** WI **Parents:** Melville H. Spicer; Marcella Spicer **Marital Status:** Married **Spouse Name:** Maria T. Torres **Children:** Anna M.; Michael; Melissa V. **Education:** PhD, Michigan State University (1984); MS, University of Idaho (1979); BS, University of Minnesota (1977) **Career:** Professor, Oklahoma State University (1998-Present); Associate Professor, Oklahoma State University (1993-1998); Assistant Professor, Oklahoma State University (1988-1993); Instructor, Pennsylvania State University (1984-1988) **Career Related:** Visiting Professor, Stanford University (2005) **Creative Works:** Editorial Board, Journal of Animal Science (1993-1995); Contributor, Article, Professional Journals **Awards:** Regents Distinguished Research Award, Oklahoma State University (2013); Regents Teaching Award, Oklahoma State University, National Institutes of Health (2010); Grantee, U.S. Department of Agriculture (2005); Pfizer Animal Health Physiology Award, American Dairy Science Association (2004); Grantee, U.S. Department of Agriculture (1993) **Membership:** President, Sigma Xi, the Scientific Research Honor Society (1999-2000); American Dairy Science Association; Endocrine Society; American Society of Animal Scientists **Marquis Who's Who Honors:** Albert Nelson Marquis Lifetime Achievement Award (2017) **Hobbies:** Travel; Scuba diving; Running **Shipping Address:** 911 W Eskridge Avenue, Stillwater, OK, 74075

Bruce E. Spivey

Title: Ophthalmologist, Educator, Health Facility Manager **Industry:** Medicine & Health Care **Date of Birth:** 08/29/1934 **Place of Birth:** Cedar Rapids **State:** IA **Parents:** William Loranzy Spivey; Grace Loretta Spivey **Marital Status:** Married **Spouse Name:** Patti Amanda Birge (12/20/1987) **Children:** Lisa; Eric **Education:** Honorary DSc, Coe College (1978); MEd, University of Illinois (1969); MS, The University of Iowa (1964); MD, The University of Iowa (1959); BA, Coe College, Cum Laude (1956) **Certifications:** Diplomate, American Board of Ophthalmology **Career:** Chief Executive Officer, Columbia-Cornell Care, Network Physicians, New York City, NY (1998-2001); Chief Executive Officer, Columbia- Cornell Care, New York, NY (1997-2000); Chief Executive Officer, Northwestern Healthcare Network, Chicago, IL (1992-1997); President, Chief Executive Officer, California Healthcare Systems, Bay Area, CA (1986-1992); Executive Vice President, Chief Executive Officer, American Academy of Ophthalmology, San Francisco, CA (1977-1993); President, Director, California Pacific Medical Center, San Francisco, CA (1976-1991); Professor, Chairman, Department of Ophthalmology, California Pacific Medical Center, San Francisco, CA (1971-1987); Dean, School of Medical Sciences, University of the Pacific, San Francisco, CA (1971-1976) **Career Related:** Trustee, MedEx (Now United Healthcare Global), Baltimore, MD (1999-Present); Board of Directors, MedEx (Now United Healthcare Global), Baltimore, MD (1999-Present); Board Secretary, MedEx (Now United Healthcare Global), Baltimore, MD (1999-Present); Deputy Executive Vice President, Council of Medical Specialty Societies (2002-2008); Trustee, Board Secretary, PrimeSight, San Francisco, CA (1996-1999); National Board of Directors, Volunteer Hospitals of America, Northern California (1991-1996); Trustee, Ophthalmic Mutual Insurance Company, A Risk Retention Group (1988-2007); Board of Directors, Board Secretary, Ophthalmic Mutual Insurance Company, A Risk Retention Group (1988-2007); Special Medical Advisory Group, United States Department of Veteran Affairs (1987-1993); National Advisory Council, National Eye Institute, National Institutes of Health (1987-1992); Chairman, Board of Directors, Volunteer Hospitals of America, Northern California (1985-1987); President, American Board of Medical Specialties (1980-1982); Vice President, American Board of Medical Specialties (1978-1980); President, Council of Medical Specialty Societies (1975-2008); Board of Directors, Reliance Group Holdings Inc., New York City, NY; 42 Named Lectures in Field **Civic:** Life Trustee, Coe College (2013-Present); Founder, International Council of Ophthalmology Foundation (2001-Present); Helen Keller International (1999-Present); International Council of Ophthalmology (1985-Present); Board of Directors, United States-China Educational Exchange, Institute of International Education, Inc. (1979-Present); Founder, Pacific Vision Foundation (1977-Present); Chair, Pacific Vision Foundation (2001-2018); Chairman, MedBiquitous Consortium (2001-2007); Trustee, MedBiquitous Consortium (2000-2007); Trustee, Coe College (1985-2013); Foundation, American Academy of Ophthalmology (1981-2011) **Military Service:** Captain, U.S. Army (1964-1966); 85th Evacuation Hospital, U.S. Army, Vietnam (1965-1966) **Awards:** Laureate Award, Highest Award of the American Academy of Ophthalmology (2015); Marshall M. Parks, M.D. Silver Medal, American Association for Pediatric Ophthalmology and Strabismus, Children's Eye Foundation (2015); Kitty Carlisle Hart Award, New York Glaucoma Research Institute (2014); Fellow, All India Collegium of Ophthalmology, All India Ophthalmology Society, Hyderabad, India (2013); Bruce E. Spivey Fund for Risk Management Studies, Ophthalmic Mutual Insurance (2012); Honorary Award in Ophthalmology, Societa Oftalmologica Italiana (2012); Guest of Honor, American Academy of Ophthalmology (2011); Scroll of Appreciation, Foundation of the American Academy of Ophthalmology (2010); EnergEYES Award by the AAO Young Ophthalmologists, American Academy of Ophthalmology (2010); Jose Rizal International Gold Medal, Asia-Pacific Academy of Ophthalmology (2009); Regional Achievement Award, International Agency for the Prevention of Blindness (2008); Afro-Asian Congress of Ophthalmology/Congress of Moroccan Ophthalmological Society Recognition (2007); International Blindness Prevention Award, American Academy of Ophthalmology (2007); Bronze Star, U.S. Army (1966) **Membership:** Honorary Member, Association of University Professors of Ophthalmology (2013-Present); European Academy of Sciences & Arts (2011-Present); Chairman, Pacific Vision Foundation, San Francisco, CA (2003-Present); Most Venerable of the Hospital of St John of Jerusalem (1999-Present); Trustee, International Council of Ophthalmology (1985-Present); Academia Ophthalmologica Internationalis (1981-Present); Board of Directors, Pacific Vision Foundation, San Francisco, CA (1978-Present); American Ophthalmological Society (1976-Present); **Marquis Who's Who Honors:** Albert Nelson Marquis Lifetime Achievement Award (2017) **Shipping Address:** 945 Green St., Apt 10, San Francisco, CA, 94133

Robert Dale Springer

Title: President **Industry:** Military & Defense Services **Company Name:** bsone, Inc. **Date of Birth:** 01/17/1933 **Place of Birth:** Millheim **State:** PA **Parents:** Simon Peter Springer; Ruth Olive (McCool) Springer **Marital Status:** Married **Spouse Name:** Bonnie Joan Brubaker (8/30/1953) **Children:** Robert Dale, Jr.; Debra K. Springer Miller; Curtis A.; Michele L. Becker; Tania **Education:** Distinguished Graduate, Air Force Air Command and Staff College, Air War College, The Air University, Montgomery, AL (1972); MS in International Affairs, The George Washington University (1969); BA in Social Science, The George Washington University (1964) **Certifications:** Certified Command Pilot **Career:** President, bsone, Inc. (1999-2013); President, NovaLogic Systems (1999-2007); Retired (1988); Vice Commander-in-Chief, Military Airlift Command, United States Air Force, Scott Air Force Base, St. Clair County, IL (1987-1988); Inspector General, United States Air Force (1984-1987); Commander, 21st Air Force, United States Air Force, McGuire Air Force Base, Joint Base McGuire-Dix-Lakehurst, Burlington County, NJ (1984-1987); Commander, Air Force Manpower and Personnel Center, United States Air Force, Randolph Air Force Base, Texas (1982-1984); DCS-Personnel, Military Airlift Command, United States Air Force, Scott Air Force Base, St. Clair County, IL (1981-1982); Commander, 322nd Airlift Division, United States Air Force, Ramstein Air Base, Federal Republic of Germany (1980-1981); Commander, 435th Tactical Airlift Wing, United States Air Force, Rhein-Main Air Base, Federal Republic of Germany (1978-1980); Chief of Intelligence, Pleiku Air Base, South Vietnam (1965-1966); Commissioned Second Lieutenant, United States Air Force (1953) **Career Related:** Chairman, Advisory Board, First Bank (2012-Present); Member, Advisory Board, First Bank (1997-Present); Media Consultant (1989-Present); Lecturer (1989-2008); Member, Board of Directors, NovaLogic Systems (1999-2009); Director, Air Force Commissary Service, San Antonio, Texas (1982-1984); Director, Army-Air Force Exchange Service, Dallas, Texas (1982-1984); Chairman, Board of Directors, Air Force Welfare Board, San Antonio, Texas (1982-1984) **Civic:** Chairman, Air Force Memorial Advisory Committee, Air Force Association (2012-Present); Active Member, Air Force Memorial Advisory Committee, Air Force Association (2007-Present); Director, North Carolina Military Foundation (2006-2009); Trustee, Falcon Foundation (1996-2008); Vice Chairman, Air Force Memorial Foundation (1998-2007); President, Air Force Memorial Foundation (1996-1998); Founding Executive Director, Air Force Memorial Foundation (1992-1996); Trustee, Aerospace Education Foundation (1992-1994) **Military Service:** Lieutenant General, United States Air Force **Awards:** Presidential Citation, Air Force Association (1984); Decorated Defense Distinguished Service Medal; Air Force Distinguished Service Medal; Legion of Merit; Air Medal; Bronze Star; Distinguished Flying Cross **Membership:** Trustee, Arnold Air Society & Silver Wings (1993-2001); Senior Vice President, Airlift-Tanker Association (1989-1994); Executive Director, Arnold Air Society & Silver Wings (1990-1993); Air Force Association; Military Officers Association of America; Daedalians; 33rd Degree, Masons **Marquis Who's Who Honors:** Albert Nelson Marquis Lifetime Achievement Award (2017) **To what do you attribute your success:** Mr. Springer attributes his successes to education, his mentors, and his family. **Why did you become involved in your profession or industry:** Mr. Springer became involved in his profession in 1952 as an aviation cadet for the United States Air Force, and after three years as a B-29 navigator at Yokota Air Base in Japan, he went on to pilot training. **What do you consider to be the highlight of your career:** The highlight of Mr. Springer's career was his founding of the Air Force Memorial Foundation and the development of the United States Air Force National Memorial on October 14, 2006, commending the selfless dedication of the men and women who have served, or are serving, in the United States Air Force and its predecessor organizations. **Hobbies:** Golf; Reading **Religion:** Lutheran **Shipping Address:** PO Box 2003, Pinehurst, NC, 28370 **Website:** http://www.airforcemag.com/Wingman/Magazine%20Documents/2015/September%202015/w0915memorial.pdf

Wilma Marie Springer

Title: Elementary School Educator (Retired) **Industry:** Education/Educational Services **Date of Birth:** 01/13/1933 **Place of Birth:** Goshen **State:** IN **Marital Status:** Married **Spouse Name:** Walter Frederick Springer (05/25/1957) **Children:** Anita Daniel; Timothy; Mark **Education:** MS, Bradley University (1960); BA, Goshen College (1956) **Career:** Retired (2001); Teacher, Baxter Elementary School, Bellflower, CA (1996-2001); Teacher, Williams Elementary School, Lakewood, CA (1993-1996); Teacher, Woodruff Elementary School (1992-1993); Teacher, Jefferson Elementary School, Bellflower, CA (1989-1992); Teacher, Lindstrom Elementary School, Lakewood, CA (1970-1989); Teacher, Bellflower Unified School District (1968-2001); Teacher, Bellflower Unified School District, California (1960-1961); Teacher, Metamora Grade School, Illinois (1957-1959); Teacher, Topeka Elementary School, IN (1956-1957) **Career Related:** Administrative Coordinator for the Nation's Report Card, National Assessment of Educational Progress (2009, 2011, 2013, 2015) **Civic:** Educator Delegate, People to People Ambassadors Program, Russia (2004); Educator Delegate, People to People Ambassadors Program, South Africa (2003); Bellflower City Council (1988); Board of Directors, Women's Ministries of Crystal Cathedral, Garden Grove, CA (1978-1988); Petition Circulator, Various State Initiatives (1987-1988); State Senator and Assemblyman Campaigns (1986-1987); School Board Campaign (1984); Member, Bethany Baptist Church **Awards:** Ambassador of Zion Award, Friends of Zion Museum, Jerusalem, Israel (2015); Presidential Citation Award, Calagary, Alberta (2008); Grantee, Instructional Improvement Program, State of California (1986-1987); Recognition Award, Regional Educational Television Advisory Council (1986); Cathedral Star Award, Women's Ministries of Crystal Cathedral (1985); Distinguished Toastmaster, Distinguished District **Membership:** Founder's District Governor, Toastmasters International (2001-2002); President, Bellflower Education Association (1991-1995); National Education Association, Delegate, National Convention (1986-1987, 1990, 1992-1995); California Teachers Association, Delegate (1986, 1994); Vice President, Bellflower Education Association (1989-1991); Treasurer, Bellflower Education Association (1988-1989); Elementary Director, Bellflower Education Association (1986-1988); Delta Kappa Gamma **To what do you attribute your success:** Teachers and educators have inspired her to reach higher. **Why did you become involved in your profession or industry:** Her desire has always been to help others become the best they can be. **What do you consider to be the highlight of your career:** A highlight of her career was joining Toastmasters, because it gave her the confidence to achieve communication and leadership skills to use in any situation. **Where will you be in five years:** In five years, she will be continuing to assist others in achieving their full potential. **Hobbies:** Quilting; Painting **Religion:** Baptist **Shipping Address:** 3180 Marna Ave, Long Beach, CA, 90808

Grace Spruch

Title: Physics Professor (Retired) **Industry:** Education/Educational Services **Company Name:** Rutgers, the State University of New Jersey **Date of Birth:** 11/19/1926 **Place of Birth:** New York **State:** NY **Parents:** Isadore Marmor; Mollie (Pogel) Marmor **Marital Status:** Single **Spouse Name:** Larry Spruch (1950-2006) **Education:** PhD, New York University (1955); MS, University of Pennsylvania (1949); BA, Brooklyn College (1947) **Career:** Professor, Rutgers, the State University of New Jersey (1975-Present); Associate Professor, Rutgers, the State University of New Jersey (1969-1975); Research Scientist, New York University, New York, NY (1968-1969); Associate Research Scientist, New York University (1965-1967); Visiting Associate Professor, Rutgers, the State University of New Jersey (1964-1965); Associate Research Scientist, New York University (1955-1956, 1958-1963); Instructor, The Cooper Union, New York, NY (1957-1958) **Career Related:** Member, Interview Team, China US Physics Examination and Application Program (1985, 1986); Honorary Research Associate in Applied Science, Harvard University, Cambridge, Massachusetts (1977-1978); Honorary Associate, Nieman Foundation for Journalism, Harvard University (1977-1978); Science Secretary, International Conference Luminescence, New York City (1961) **Creative Works:** Referee, American Journal of Physics (1973-Present); Author, "Squirrels at my Window" (2000); Author, "Such Agreeable Friends" (1983); 21 Astounding Science Quizzes (1982); Co-Author, The Ubiquitous Atom (1974); Co-Editor: Luminescence of Organic and Inorganic Materials (1962); Translator, (M. Franon) Holography (1974); Co-Translator, (R. Jungk) "The Big Machine" (1968); Contributing Editor, International Science and Technology Magazine (1955-1960); Contributor, Articles, Professional Journals **Awards:** Recipient, Lifetime Achievement Award, Brooklyn College Alumni Association (2002); Humanities Grantee, Department of Higher Education, New Jersey (1989-1990); Grantee, Center for Technology Studies, New Jersey Institute for Technology (1986-1987); Grantee, Center for Energy and Environmental Studies, Princeton University (1981); Fellow, American Association of University Women, Oxford University (1963-1964); Scholar, New York State Regents, Brooklyn College (1943-1947) **Membership:** ACLU; American Physical Society; Chapter President, Phi Beta Kappa (1978-1982); Sigma Xi; Sigma Pi Sigma; Honorary Member, Pi Delta Epsilon **Marquis Who's Who Honors:** Albert Nelson Marquis Lifetime Achievement Award (2017) **Hobbies:** Tennis; Swimming; Hiking; Classical music; Ballet **Shipping Address:** 14 E. Eighth Street, Apartment 5B, New York, NY, 10003

Jean Mary St. Germain

Title: Medical Physicist **Industry:** Medicine & Health Care **Company Name:** Memorial Sloan Kettering **Year of Passing:** 2017-12-13 **Education:** MS, Rutgers University; BS, Marymount Manhattan College, New York City, NY **Certifications:** Certified, American Board of Health Physics; Licensed Medical Physicist, State of New York **Career:** Vice Chair for Clinical Academic Affairs, Memorial Sloan Kettering Cancer Center (2010-Present); Corporate Radiation Safety Officer (2010-Present); Attending Physicist, Memorial Sloan-Kettering Cancer Center (2006-Present); Acting Chair, Department of Medical Physics, Memorial Hospital (2007-2010); Associate Attending Physicist, Memorial Sloan-Kettering Cancer Center (1993-2006); Clinical Assistant Professor, Cornell University Medical College, New York City, NY (1979-1994); Instructor, Radiology, Cornell University Medical College, New York City, NY (1971-1978); Assistant Physicist, Cornell University Medical College, New York City, NY (1968-1971); Fellow, Department of Medical Physics, Memorial Hospital, New York City, NY; U.S. Public Health Service Fellow of Radiological Health, Rutgers, The State University of New Jersey **Career Related:** Vice Chair, Panel on Medical Health Physics, American Board of Medical Physics (2004-2008); Chair, Panel on Medical Health Physics, American Board of Medical Physics (1993-2000); Consultant in Field **Creative Works:** Author, "The Nurse and Radiotherapy" (1978); Contributor, Articles, Medical Journals **Awards:** Marvin M.D. Williams Award (2015); Distinguished Service Award, American Association of Physicists in Medicine (2005); Failla Memorial Lecture Award **Membership:** Failla Memorial Lecturer, Health Physics Society (1999); Treasurer, American Academy of Health Physics (1996-1999); Fellow, Health Physics Society; President, New York Chapter, Health Physics Society; President, Medical Health Physics Section, Health Physics Society; Fellow Secretary, American Association of Physicists in Medicine; Board of Directors, American Association of Physicists in Medicine; Regional Director, National Society of Arts and Letters; President, New York Chapter, National Society of Arts and Letters; National Music Chair, National Society of Arts and Letters; National Career Awards Chair, National Society of Arts and Letters; Past President, Radiological and Medical Physics Society New York; Governors Board, American Institute of Physics; Treasurer, Iota Sigma Pi; President, V Chapter, Iota Sigma Pi **Marquis Who's Who Honors:** Albert Nelson Marquis Lifetime Achievement Award (2017) **Business Address:** 1275 York Ave #84, New York, NY, 10065 **Shipping Address:** 1675 York Ave., Apt 29M, New York, NY, 10128

Kermit LeMoyne Staggers II, PhD

Title: History and Political Science Professor, State Legislator, Municipal Official **Industry:** Education/Educational Services **Company Name:** University of Sioux Falls **Date of Birth:** 11/02/1947 **Place of Birth:** Washington **State:** PA **Parents:** Kermit LeMoyne Staggers; Christine Ruby (Scherich) Staggers **Marital Status:** Married **Spouse Name:** June Ann Wenda (8/22/1970) **Children:** Ayn Kristen Staggers-Bird; Kyle Lee **Education:** PhD, Claremont Graduate University (1986); MA in History, University of Idaho (1975); BS, University of Idaho (1969) **Certifications:** Certification in Theological Studies, Sioux Falls Seminary (2009) **Career:** Emeritus Professor of History and Political Sciences, University of Sioux Falls (2016-Present); Sioux Falls City Council (2012-Present); Sioux Falls City Council (2002-2010); South Dakota Senate, Pierre, SD (1995-2002); Lecturer, History, University of Maryland, University College Europe, Heidelberg, Germany (1988-1989); Professor of History and Political Sciences, University of Sioux Falls (1982-2016); Adjunct Instructor, History, University of St. Francis, Joliet, IL (1982); Instructor, History, College Lake County, Grayslake, IL (1981-1982); Visiting Instructor, History, Trinity International University, Deerfield, IL (1980); Instructor, History, Northwestern College, Orange City, IA (1979-1980); Lecturer, History, Chapman University, Orange, CA (1979); Instructor, History, University of Idaho, Moscow, IA (1977); Instructor, History, Troy State University (1975-1976) **Career Related:** Lecturer, Diplomatic Academy, Ukrainian Foreign Ministry (2001); Lecturer, Mohyla Academy, National University of Kiev (2001); Malone Faculty Fellow (1993); Expert Analyst, Political and Social Issues, Local Radio and TV **Civic:** Board of Directors, Siouxland Heritage Museums, Sioux Falls, SD (2015-2016); Board of Directors, Siouxland Heritage Museums, Sioux Falls, SD (2006-2010); Chair, Senate Transportation Committee (1997-1999) **Military Service:** Captain, U.S. Air Force (1970-1976) **Creative Works:** Contributor, Articles, Professional Journals **Awards:** Guardian of Small Business Award, National Federation of Independent Business (1996) **Membership:** President, Great Plains Political Science Association (2000-2001); Federalist Society; Fulbright Association; Historical Society; Conference on Faith and History; Kiwanis; Phi Alpha Theta; Phi Kappa Phi; National Eagle Scout Association **Marquis Who's Who Honors:** Albert Nelson Marquis Lifetime Achievement Award (2017) **To what do you attribute your success:** Dr. Staggers attributes his success to persistence and the support of his wife, June. **Why did you become involved in your profession or industry:** Dr. Staggers entered his field because he enjoyed the subjects of history and politics. **What do you consider to be the highlight of your career:** The highlight of Dr. Staggers' career was leading the movement to abolish the South Dakota state inheritance tax and in the process, saving South Dakota residents millions of dollars. **Where will you be in five years:** In five years, Dr. Staggers will be on a Fulbright scholarship to Ukraine, working on a history manuscript. **Hobbies:** Book collecting; Travel **Political Affiliations:** Republican **Shipping Address:** 616 E Wiswall Place, Sioux Falls, SD, 57105

Harry Stainrook

Title: Photographer **Industry:** Media & Entertainment **Company Name:** Harry Stainrook, Ltd. **Date of Birth:** 01/11/1937 **Place of Birth:** Philadelphia **State:** PA **Parents:** Millward M. Stainrook; Janet Stainrook **Marital Status:** Married **Spouse Name:** Judith Anne (May 21, 1966) **Children:** Jennifer; Eric **Education:** BA, Rutgers, the State University of New Jersey (1970) **Career:** Principal, Owner, Harry Stainrook, Ltd., New York City (2006-Present); Retired, Manufacturers and Traders Trust Co. (1997); Executive Vice President Trust And Investments, Manufacturers and Traders Trust Co., Buffalo (1985-1997); Executive Vice President, Trust And Investments, First Pennsylvania Bank (1981-1985); Senior Vice President Commercial Group, First Pennsylvania Bank (1978-1981); Vice President International Department, First Pennsylvania Bank, Philadelphia (1975-1978); Vice President, Manager, London Office, First Pennsylvania Bank, Philadelphia (1973-1975); Assistant Vice President Branch Department, First Pennsylvania Bank, Philadelphia (1964-1973); Manager Bank Operations, First Pennsylvania Bank, Philadelphia (1956-1961) **Civic:** Former Chairman, Board of Directors, Greater Buffalo Opera Company; Former President, Buffalo Philharmonic Orchestra; Academy of Vocal Arts, Philadelphia **Military Service:** With, US Army (1961-1964) **Creative Works:** Performer, Haddonfield Yoga Center, (2011-2014); Excel Art and Framing Gallery, New York City (2008-2014); Featured Artist, Fine Art Gallery (2008-2014); Featured Artist, Third Street Gallery, Philadelphia (2011-2014); Featured Artist, Markeim Arts Center, Haddonfield, New Jersey (2011-2014); Featured Artist, Perkins Center Arts, Moorestown (2013-2014); Featured Artist, Philadelphia Sketch Club (2011); Featured Artist, Collectors Gallery, Albright Knox Art Museum (2007-2009); Featured Artist, Art Dialogue Gallery, Buffalo (2006, 2007-2008); Featured Artist, Stedman Gallery, Rutgers, the State University of New Jersey (2007-2008); Performer, Art Dialogue Gallery Amaryllis Buffalo (2006, 2008) **Membership:** Western New York Artists Group; World Future Society; Institute of Noetic Sciences; Saturn Club **Religion:** Lutheran **Shipping Address:** P.O. Box 230002, Harry Stainrook, Ltd., New York, NY, 10023

Jerome Merlin Stanley, PhD

Title: Professor of Music **Industry:** Education/Educational Services **Date of Birth:** 10/06/1941 **Place of Birth:** Mount Vernon **State:** IL **Parents:** Monty Merlin Stanley; Mildred C. Combs **Marital Status:** Married **Spouse Name:** Josette Gladys Thevenin (8/10/1974) **Children:** Nicholas Anthony **Education:** PhD, University of Cincinnati (1983); MusM, Miami University, Oxford, OH (1965); MusB, Washington University, St. Louis, MO (1963) **Certifications:** Professional Music Certificate, American Institute Musical Studies, Graz, Austria (1977) **Career:** Director, Oxford Arts Trio for Piano, Violin, and Cello (2010-Present); Professor Emeritus, Miami University, Oxford, OH (2004); Associate Professor, Miami University, Oxford, OH (1984-2004); Assistant Professor, Miami University, Oxford, OH (1973-1984); Instructor, Miami University, Oxford, OH (1965-1973); Graduate Assistant, Miami University, Oxford, OH (1963-1965); Piano Instructor, St. Louis, MO (1958-1963) **Career Related:** Affiliate, Miami University, Oxford, OH (1963-Present); MUDEC Scholar (1997); Resident Professor, Miami University Dolibois European Center (MUDEC) (1987-1989); Visiting Scholar, MUDEC, Grand Duchy, Luxembourg (1979); Concert Pianist, St. Louis, MO (1959-1963) **Civic:** Music Therapy Consultant, Child Life Division, Children's Hospital, Cincinnati, OH (1983-1986); Competition Adjudicator, Various Youth Orchestras, Indiana and Ohio (1971-1982) **Military Service:** U.S. Army (1966-1968) **Creative Works:** Author, "The Making of a Music Academy" (2016); Author, "William Holder and His Position in 17th Century Philosophy and Music Theory" (2002); Author, "Historic Parallels in the Arts" (1995) **Awards:** Development Grantee, Stanford University (1986); Development Grantee, Miami University, Oxford, OH (1986); Ella Lyman Cabot Trust Grantee, Cambridge, MA (1983-1984); Research Grantee, London, England (1979); Research Grantee, Brussels (1979); Research Grantee, Miami University, Oxford, OH (1979); Faculty Grantee, Study in Austria, Miami University, Oxford, OH (1977); St. Louis Symphony Young Artist Award (1962) **Membership:** Adviser, Phi Mu Alpha Sinfonia (1971-1979); Pi Kappa Lambda **Marquis Who's Who Honors:** Albert Nelson Marquis Lifetime Achievement Award (2017) **To what do you attribute your success:** Valuable help from mentors and a passion for the art of music led to Dr. Stanley's success. **Why did you become involved in your profession or industry:** Dr. Stanley began studying piano at five years of age. He continued throughout his life and when the decision came to decide on college, he chose to pursue music. Through the help of mentorship, he was able to receive scholarships. **What do you consider to be the highlight of your career:** The highlight of Dr. Stanley's career was teaching at the Miami University Dolibois European Center in the Grand Duchy of Luxembourg, where he gave lectures on music and visual arts and organized student study trips to major European cities. **Hobbies:** Gardening; Photography **Shipping Address:** 5735 Brown Road, Oxford, OH, 45056

Helen Camille Stanley

Title: Composer, Pianist, Musician **Industry:** Media & Entertainment **Place of Birth:** Tampa **State:** FL **Parents:** Edward Stanley; Lucy Gage (Crehore) Stanley **Marital Status:** Widowed **Children:** Helen Marjorie **Education:** BS, Muskingum University (1961); MusM, Florida State University (1954); MusB, College-Conservatory of Music, University of Cincinnati (1951) **Career:** Independent Composer (1963-Present); Independent Lecturer (1963-Present); Independent Pianist (1963-Present); Composer-in-Residence, Florida Contemporary Ensemble, Jacksonville, FL (1986); Pianist, Florida Contemporary Ensemble, Jacksonville, FL (1986); Composer, St. Paul's By-the-Sea, Jacksonville Beach, FL (1976); Conductor, St. Paul's By-the-Sea, Jacksonville Beach, FL (1976); Instructor, Music in Communications, Jones College, Jacksonville, FL (1965-1966); Instructor, Music and Fine Arts, Jacksonville University, Jacksonville, FL (1962-1967) **Career Related:** Consultant, Beaches Fine Arts Series, Neptune Beach, FL (1973-Present); Consultant, Microtonal Passages, Trombone Sonata (2012) **Civic:** Society of Mayflower Descendants in the State of Florida (1987-Present) **Creative Works:** Public Lecturer, Background of Recorded Music (2007-Present); Composer, "Locrian Lament" (2012); Composer, "Procession" (2011); Composer, Vocal, "Prospero Speaks" (2011); Composer, "Lydian Legend for Piano" (2010); Composer, "Aeolus for Piano" (2009); Composer, "Concerto Romantico" (2006); Composer, "Phrygiana for Piano" (2005); Composer, "Dorian Diversion in Functional Chromaticism" (2003); Orchestral Works on Compact Disc, "Fanfare for Orchestra," All American Celebration by Owensboro Symphony, Conducted by Nicholas Palmer (1999); Orchestral Works on Compact Disc, "Passacaglia, Concerto Romantico," St. Petersburg Philharmonic, Prague, Czech Republic (1997); Orchestral Works on Compact Disc, "Fanfare for Orchestra," Warsaw National Philharmonic Orchestra and Owensboro Symphony (1994); Composer, "Rhapsody for Electronic Tape and Orchestra" (1972); Composer, "Allegro, Passacaglia," Sonata for Trombone and Piano, Various Instrumental and Vocal Works; Composer, "Evocation I for Piano"; Composer, Website Theme Music, "The Living Music Foundation" **Awards:** Outstanding Achievements in Classical Music, Jacksonville, FL (1997); Jacksonville Community Foundation Award (1994); Art Ventures Fund Award (1992); Anthem Descant Award, St. Paul's By-the-Sea (1980); Composition Commission Award (1972); C. Hugo Grimm Ensemble Composition Award, Cincinnati, OH (1951); Pogner Music Composition Award, Cincinnati, OH (1950) **Membership:** ASCAP; American Keyboard Artists; Performing Arts Directory; Pi Kappa Lambda; American Composers Forum **To what do you attribute your success:** Ms. Stanley attributes her success to luck, determination, and perseverance. **Why did you become involved in your profession or industry:** Ms. Stanley became involved in her composition career at a very young age. She was lucky to have a piano in her childhood home. She was lucky to have a generous mother who obtained the best possible teachers when she wouldn't leave the piano alone. She was lucky to have a God-given gift of talent, according to Hans Barth, the international composer, pianist, inventor, and pedagogue, who believed in her gifts in music when she was only a teenager. He also told her that she must pursue a college degree and that he hoped that she would study orchestration with Dohnanyi, who had appeared on some of the New York series of concerts, as had Barth. She was lucky as a student at the Cincinnati Conservatory of Music to be there with a host of other students willing and bale to perform her music as she pursued a college degree. She was lucky to win a master's fellowship at Florida State University with Ernst von Dohnanyi, an international composer, pianist, and conductor, as her major professor. She had the determination to continue to study no matter what may intervene and to explore composing music in all available media such as symphony orchestra voices, micro-tones, or electronic. She had the opportunity to ask American international composer, Aaron Copland, what his advice would be to a young composer. Copland's answer was that a composer has to be somebody. All the above answers, involvement and success in being a composer all led to international travel, premieres, and recordings of many compositions. **What do you consider to be the highlight of your career:** Among all the amazing things in Ms. Stanley's career, a small, inspiring moment is very touching. She walked into the Warsaw National Symphony rehearsal only to realize that she was hearing a clarinet practicing a theme from a composition that she wrote. **Hobbies:** Art; Nature **Shipping Address:** 12047 Aladdin Road, Jacksonville, FL, 32223

Mary Louise Stanley Weinkauf

Title: Clergywoman (Retired), Educator **Industry:** Religious **Company Name:** Evangelical Lutheran Church in America **Date of Birth:** 09/22/1938 **Place of Birth:** Eau Claire **State:** WI **Parents:** Joseph Michael Stanley; Marie Barbara (Holzinger) Stanley **Marital Status:** Single **Spouse Name:** Alan D. Weinkauf (10/12/1962, Deceased 2000) **Children:** Stephen; Xanti **Education:** MDiv, Lutheran School of Theology at Chicago (LSTC), Chicago, IL (1993); PhD, University of Tennessee (1966); MA, University of Tennessee (1962); BA, University of Wisconsin-Eau Claire (1961) **Career:** Retired (1991); Part-Time Instructor, Columbia College (1989-1991); Professor, Head of English Department, Dakota Wesleyan University, Mitchell, SD (1969-1989); Assistant Professor of English, Adrian College (1966-1969); Graduate Assistant, University of Tennessee (1961-1966); Instructor **Career Related:** Director, Sayner Campus, Lay School for Mission (2006-2013); Pastor, Calvary Evangelical Lutheran Church; Pastor, Siloa Lutheran Church; Pastor, Ontonagon Faith; Pastor, White Pine, MI **Civic:** President, Pastime Club, Adult Day Care Center, North Central Wisconsin Thrivent Finance for Lutherans (2007-2010); Pastime Club, Adult Day Care Center, North Central Wisconsin Thrivent Finance for Lutherans (2006); Affiliate, Fortune Lake Lutheran Camp (2003-2004); Affiliate, Lakeland Area Food Pantry (2000-2009); Board Member, Lutheran Campus Ministry Committee for Wisconsin and Upper Michigan (1996-2002); Member, Board of Directors, Ontonagon Habitat for Humanity (1995-1997); Trustee, The Delta Kappa Gamma Educational Foundation (1986-1990); Supply Preacher, Northern Great Lakes Synod, Evangelical Lutheran Church in America **Creative Works:** Co-Author, "Murder Most Poetic: The Mystery Novels of Ngaio Marsh" (1996); Author, "Hard-boiled Heretic: The Lew Archer Novels of Ross Macdonald" (1994); Author, "Sermons in Science Fiction" (1994) **Membership:** Vice President, AAUW (2013-Present); Chapter President, The Alpha Eta Society (2008-2010); State President, DKGSI (1983-1985); President, South Dakota State Poetry Society (1982-1983); State Vice President, DKGSI (1979-1983); Division President, AAUW (1978-1980); Member, State Board, DKGSI (1972-1989); NCTE; SDCTE; Science Fiction Research Association; Popular Culture Association; The Milton Society of America; President, Local Chapter, DKGSI; Sigma Tau Delta; Pi Kappa Delta; The Honor Society of Phi Kappa Phi **Marquis Who's Who Honors:** Albert Nelson Marquis Lifetime Achievement Award (2017); Distinguished Humanitarian (2017) **To what do you attribute your success:** Dr. Stanley Weinkauf attributes her success to blessings, good health, and God's guidance. **Why did you become involved in your profession or industry:** She became involved in her profession because she loved school and church. **What do you consider to be the highlight of your career:** A highlight of her career was having students become pastors. **Where will you be in five years:** In five years, she will likely be at her current address. **Hobbies:** Music; Piano and organ for the choir; Gardening; Yard work; Reading **Political Affiliations:** Democrat **Religion:** Evangelical Lutheran Church in America **Shipping Address:** 8991 Highland Dr., Woodruff, WI, 54568

Michael D. Stanton-Hicks

Title: Anesthesiologist, Consultant **Industry:** Medicine & Health Care **Company Name:** Cleveland Clinic **Date of Birth:** 06/03/1931 **Place of Birth:** Adelaide **Country of Origin:** Australia **Parents:** Cedric Stanton-Hicks; Florence (Haggett) Perrin **Marital Status:** Married **Spouse Name:** Ursula Koch (8/27/1985); Kristina Litsmark (8/4/1969, Divorced 8/1984) **Children:** Erik Michael; Leif Neal **Education:** MD, University of Dusseldorf (1984); Resident, Royal Postgraduate Medical School, London and Lasarettet Köping (1966-1968); Bachelor of Medicine, Bachelor of Surgery, Adelaide University (1962); Intern, Queen Elizabeth Hospital, Adelaide, Australia (1961-1962) **Certifications:** Diplomate, American Board of Pain Medicine, Interventional Pain Practice (2002) **Career:** Consultant, Pain Management, Cleveland Clinic (2012-Present); Consultant, Anesthesiology and Intensive Care (2012-Present); With, Center for Functional Neurosurgery (2009-Present); Staff Physician, Shaker Pediatrics Pain Program (2008-Present); Professor, Lerner College of Medicine, Case Western Reserve University, Cleveland, OH (2004-Present); Vice Chairman, Pain Management and Research, Institute for Anesthesiology & Intensive Care (2006-2012); Vice Chairman, Pain Management and Research Division, Cleveland Clinic Foundation (1998-2006); Director, Pain Management Center, Cleveland Clinic Foundation (1988-1998); Professor, Johannes Gutenberg University, Mainz, Germany (1986-1997); Professor, Director, Pain Clinic and Research, Johannes Gutenberg University, Mainz, Germany (1986-1988); Acting Chairman, University of Colorado Health Sciences Center, Denver, CO (1985-1986); Vice Chairman, University of Colorado Health Sciences Center, Denver, CO (1983-1985); Professor, University of Colorado Health Sciences Center, Denver, CO (1983-1986); Professor, Chairman, University of Massachusetts Medical School, Worcester, MA (1975-1983); Assistant Professor, University of Washington Medical School, Seattle, WA (1972-1975); Tutor, Staff Anesthesiologist, Queen Elizabeth Hospital, Adelaide, Australia (1970-1972); Instructor, Anesthesiology, University of Washington Medical School, Seattle, WA (1969-1970) **Career Related:** Consultant, Peripheral Neurostimulation Technologies (2012); Science Advisor, Reflex Sympathetic Dystrophy Association (2006); Advisor, American Academy of Disability Evaluating Physicians (2000-2002); Medical Examiner, Industrial Commission of Ohio; Member, Ohio Pain Advisory Committee, Department of Health; Member, Liaison Committee, Medical Board, Ohio Pain Committee; Appointment to Governor's Task Force on Compassionate Care, Department of Health, Ohio; Board of Directors, World Institute of Pain; Consultant, Neurological Devices; Advisory Committee, Center for Devices & Radiological Health, Federal Drug Administration **Civic:** With, Pharmacy & Therapeutic Committee, Bureau of Workers Compensation, Ohio (2008) **Military Service:** Squadron Leader, Reserve Royal Australian Air Force (1962-1965) **Creative Works:** Editorial Board, Pain Physician (2002-Present); Executive Editor, Pain Practice Journal (2001-Present); Author, "Pain Management: A Cleveland Clinic Guide" (2009); Author, "CRPS: Current Diagnosis and Therapy" (2005); Section Editor, Complex Regional Pain Syndrome (2002); Author, "Reflex Sympathetic Dystrophy: A Reappraisal" (1996); Author, "Pain and Sympathetic Nervous System" (1990); Author, "Reflex Sympathetic Dystrophy" (1989); Author, "Illustrated Manual of Regional Anesthesia" (1988); Author, "Chronic Low Back Pain" (1982) **Awards:** Named, Best Doctors in America (2010-Present); Named, Best Pain Management Physician, Beckers Association Review, Best Doctors in America (2013); Lifetime Achievement Award, New York and New Jersey Society of Interventional Pain Physicians (2013); Lifetime Achievement Award, North American Neuromodulation Society (2010); Lifetime Achievement Award, American Society of Interventional Pain Physicians (2007); Distinguished Service Award, European Society of Regional Anesthesia (2003); Distinguished Award, Reflex Sympathetic Dystrophy Association (2002); Named, Scientist of the Year, American Herschel Society (1991-1992); Australian University Commission on Mature Age Scholar (1953-1960) **Membership:** Board of Directors, Stim Q Corp. (2014); President, American Neuromodulation Society (1994-1998); President, American Academy of Medical Infrared Imaging (1994-1995); Board of Directors, American Academy of Medical Infrared Imaging (1991-1995); President, American Society of Regional Anesthesia (1989-1990); Board of Directors, American Society of Regional Anesthesia (1979-1991); Fellow, Royal College of Surgeons; Fellow, Royal College of Anesthetists, Fellow, American Academy of Pain Medicine; Fellow, Interventional Pain Practice; International Association for the Study of Pain; World Institute of Pain; Irish College of Anesthetists; American Society of Regional Anesthesia **Marquis Who's Who Honors:** Distinguished Humanitarian (2017) **Political Affiliations:** Republican **Religion:** Anglican **Shipping Address:** 11405 Clearfield Lane, Chardon, OH, 44024

Michael Starr

Title: Lawyer **Industry:** Law and Legal Services **Company Name:** Holland & Knight LLP **Date of Birth:** 07/20/1948 **Place of Birth:** New York City **State:** NY **Parents:** Son of; Harry Starr; Gertrude (Spitz) Starr **Marital Status:** Married **Spouse Name:** Marsha Talan (9/5/1982) **Children:** 2 Children; Rachel Talan; Garret Matthew **Education:** JD, Yale University, New Haven, CT (1979) PhD in Philosophy, University of Michigan (1976) BA, Binghamton University, State University of New York, Summa Cum Laude (1970) **Career:** Member, Labor & Employment Law Department, Holland & Knight LLP (2009-Present); Member, Labor & Employment Law & Litigation Practice Group, Hogan & Hartson LLP (Now Hogan Lovells) (2002-2009); Chairman, Employment & Labor Relations Department, Squadron, Ellenoff, Plesent & Sheinfeld, LLP (Now Hogan Lovells) (1997-2002); Of Counsel, Parker Chapin Flattau & Kimpl, New York, NY (1988-1997); Attorney, Kaye, Scholer, Fierman, Hays & Handler (Arnold & Porter Kaye Scholer LLP), New York, NY (1980-1988); Law Clerk to Circuit Judge Abner J. Mikva, United States Court of Appeals for the District of Columbia (1979-1980); Clerk, Center for Law and Social Policy (1978) **Career Related:** Member, Alternative Dispute Resolution Advisory Council, United States District Court Eastern District Court of New York (2016-Present); Mediator, United States District Court Southern District of New York (2009-Present); Member, Pro Bono Panel, United States Court of Appeals for the Second Circuit (2005-Present); Pro-Bono Civil Appeal Panel, United States Court of Appeals for the Second Circuit (2002-Present); Mediator, United States District Court Eastern New York (1998-Present); Mediator, United States District Court Eastern District of New York (1992-Present); Early Neutral Evaluator, United States District Court Eastern District of New York (1992-1998); Member, Board of Arbitrators, National Association of Securities Dealers (1995-2003); Member, Board of Directors, Court Appointed Special Advocates, New York, NY (1982-2000) **Civic:** Member, Board of Trustees (2012-2016); Member, Board of Arbitrators, National Association of Securities Dealers (NASD) (1995-2003); Member, Board of Directors, National CASA Association (1983-2000); Member, Human Resources Committee, Partnership for New York City (1990-1998) **Creative Works:** Employment Law Columnist, "National Law Journal" (1998-Present); Member, Editorial Advisory Board, "Sexual Harassment and Sexual Discrimination," James Publishing (1994-Present); Author, "The Muddle of 'Motivating Factor' Volume 35, Using the Logic of Human Action to Inform Employment Discrimination Law," Hofstra Labor & Employment Law Journal (2018); Author, "Sex Stereotyping in Employment: Can the Center Hold?," The Labor Lawyer (2006); Columnist, Employment Law Section, "National Law Journal" (1996-2013); Member, Board of Editors, "The Corporate Counselor," Leader Publications (1996-2002); Author, "Who's the Boss? The Globalization of United States Employment Law," The Business Lawyer (1996); Member, Board of Editors, "Employment Law Strategist," Leader Publications (1994-2002); Co-Author, "Gender Bias in the Courts: The Father Child Perspective," Father & Child Legal Defense & Education Fund (1993); Author, "Accommodation and Accountability: A Strategy for Judicial Enforcement of Institutional Reform Decrees," Alabama Law Review (1981); Author, "The Mental Hospitalization of Children and the Limits of Parental Authority," The Yale Law Journal (1979); Editor, "The Yale Law Journal" (1978-1979) **Awards:** Featured Listee, Best Lawyers in America in Labor and Employment Law (2008-Present); Featured Listee, New York Super Lawyers (2006-Present); Wilson Fellow (1970) **Membership:** Fellow, American Bar Foundation (2011-Present); Fellow, The College of Labor and Employment Lawyers Inc. (2006-Present); Chambers USA, America's Leading Lawyers for Business (Now Chambers & Partners) (2005-Present); Second Circuit, Federal Bar Council (2003-Present); Association of the Bar of the City of New York (1980-Present); Section on Labor and Employment Law, ABA (1980-Present); Special Committee on the United States in a Global Economy, Association of the Bar of the City of New York (1995-2000); Committee on Labor and Employment Law, Association of the Bar of the City of New York (1989-1992); Committee on Civil Rights, Association of the Bar of the City of New York (1985-1988); Board of Directors, Council of New York Law Associates (1982-1986); Committee on Children and the Law, Association of the Bar of the City of New York (1984-1985) **Bar Admissions:** United States Court of Appeals for the Ninth Circuit (2015); United States Court of Appeals for the Second Circuit (2000); Supreme Court of the United States (1986); United States District Court Southern District of New York (1981); United States District Court Eastern District of New York (1981); New York (1980); United States Court of Appeals for the District of Columbia Circuit (1980) **Marquis Who's Who Honors:** Albert Nelson Marquis Lifetime Achievement Award (2017) **Business Address:** 31 W 52nd St., New York, NY, 10019 **Shipping Address:** 10 E. End Ave., Apt 7F, New York, NY, 10075 **Website:** https://www.linkedin.com/in/michaelstarresq

Howard Loucks Steele, PhD

Title: Economic Development Consultant, Author **Industry:** Consulting **Date of Birth:** 01/27/1929 **Place of Birth:** Pittsburgh **State:** PA **Parents:** Howard Bennington Steele; Ruby Alberta (Loucks) Steele **Marital Status:** Married **Spouse Name:** Elaine Haddock (8/23/1997); Jane R. Cornelius (7/30/1977, Divorced 1996); Sally E. Funk (6/6/1952, Divorced 1977) **Children:** John F.; David A.; Patricia A.; Jennifer L. **Education:** PhD, University of Kentucky (1962); MS, Pennsylvania State University (1952); BS, Washington and Lee University (1950) **Career:** Economic Development Consultant (1997-Present); Foreign Economic Development Service, Economic Research Service, Office of International Cooperation and Development, U.S. Department of Agriculture, Washington, DC (1971-1997); Foreign Economic Development Service, United States Department of Agriculture, Washington, DC (1971-1997); Associate Professor, Ohio State University, Columbus, OH (1964-1971); Associate Professor, Clemson University, South Carolina (1957-1964); Assistant Professor, Clemson University, South Carolina (1956-1957); Owner, H.L. Steele Bulk Milk Hauling, Greenville, PA (1955-1960); Sales Manager, Greenville Dairy Company (1952-1956) **Career Related:** Liaison Officer, Inter-American Institute for Cooperation on Agriculture, U.S. Department of Agriculture (1993-1997); Office of Deputy Administrator, USAID, Washington, DC (1990-1997); Office of the Director, Technical Assistance Division, USAID, Washington, DC (1988-1990); Project Manager, Bureau for Latin America and Caribbean, USAID, Washington, DC (1984-1988); Project Manager, USAID, Sri Lanka (1982-1984); Project Manager, USAID, Honduras (1980-1982); Project Manager, USAID, Bolivia (1977-1980); Project Manager, USAID, Guatemala (1976-1977); Instructor, University of Maryland, College Park, MD (1974-1976); Partner, Kingwood Acres Farm, Rockwood, PA (1966-1998); Visiting Professor, Universidade de Sao Paulo, Piracicaba, Brazil (1964-1966) **Creative Works:** Author, "More Food Soldier Encounters" (2010); Author, "Bushels and Bales: A Food Soldier in the Cold War" (2008); Author, "Food Soldier" (2002); Author, "Your Tax Dollars at Work (I'd Rather Have Gone Business Class!)" (1998); Author, "A 200 Year History of Some Descendants of the Pioneer James Steel of Castleblaney, Ireland, Mount Pleasant, PA" (1994); Author, "Comercializacao Agricola" (1971); Contributor, Articles, Professional Journals **Awards:** Certificate of Merit, U.S. Department of Agriculture (1992); Certificate of Merit, U.S. Department of Agriculture (1975); One of the Outstanding Young Men in the JCI, Inc. (1965); National Forensic Union Award **Membership:** Sons of the American Revolution; Masons; International Association of Agricultural Economists; Agricultural and Applied Economics Association; Shriners; Sigma Nu; Gamma Sigma Delta **Marquis Who's Who Honors:** Albert Nelson Marquis Lifetime Achievement Award (2017) **Shipping Address:** 5204 Holden Street, Fairfax, VA, 22032

Diane Evelyn Steen-Hinderlie

Title: Social Worker (Retired), Musician **Industry:** Social Work **Date of Birth:** 06/13/1947 **Place of Birth:** Duluth **State:** MN **Parents:** Julian Sem Steen; Evelyn Synnove (Helgaas) Steen **Marital Status:** Married **Spouse Name:** John Richard Olson (7/21/1989); John Peter Hinderlie (6/27/1971, Divorced 1987) **Children:** Peder Donald; Erik Steen **Education:** MusB, University of Minnesota and Other Institutions (1991); Postgraduate Coursework, Hamline University (1989-1991); BA in Social Psychology, Asian Studies, St. Olaf College, Cum Laude, Phi Beta Kappa (1969) **Certifications:** Licensed Social Worker, State of Minnesota; Nationally Certified Teacher of Music (NCTM), MTNA **Career:** Member, Workshop and Children's Ministry, Augsburg College Youth and Family Institute, Trinity Congregation (2009, 1998-2006); Founding Director, Fair Pay Institute, Minneapolis, MN (1995-2009); Small Group Leader, Mount Olive Lutheran Church, Children's Hospital, Minneapolis, MN (1993-1998); Faculty Teacher, Stenson Suzuki Studios and Home Studio, St. Louis Park, MN (1988-1992); Administrator, Family Child Care Facility, St. Louis Park, MN (1986-1990); Clergy Team Member, Youth Choir Director, First Lutheran Church, St. Louis Park, MN (1983-1986); Clergy Team Member, Jubilation Singers, Bethel Lutheran Church, Rochester, MN (1978-1983); Clergy Team Member, Exchange Program, Lutheran World Federation, Göppingen, Germany (1973-1977); Social Worker, Child Care Licensing, Hennepin County Welfare Department, Minneapolis, MN (1970-1973) **Career Related:** Founder, Organization and Curriculum, Early Childhood Organization for Education with Singing (1993-Present); Trainer, United for a Fair Economy, (1997-Present); Board, Teacher, Children's Garden Program, Concordia Language Villages (2005-2008); Member, Root Causes of Violence Action Team Initiative for Violence-Free Families, Fourth Judicial District, MN (1997-2007); Board of Directors, Midwest Council, National Peace Institute Foundation, Grinnell, Iowa (1991); First Music Teacher for Prince's Godson (1989-1992); Co-leader, German-American Youth Group Exchange (1979-1982); Co-founder, Family Day Care Certificate Program and Babygarten Classes (1970-1973); Presenter in Field **Civic:** Allies of St. Louis Park (2017-Present); Co-founder, Anti-torture Committee, Women Against Military Madness (2005-Present); Volunteer, People of Faith Peacemakers (1995-Present); Volunteer, FairVote Minnesota (1994-Present); Member, Muslim-Christian Relations Council, Minnesota Council of Churches (1994-Present); Founder, People for Reforming Early Start Time for Teens Organization, Minneapolis, MN (1993-Present); Member, Youth Host Committee, NAACP Convention, Minneapolis, MN (1995); Charter Member, U.S. Holocaust Memorial Museum (1993); Volunteer, Jewish Community Relations Council (1992-2003); Volunteer, Feminists in Faith/Reimagining; **Creative Works:** Performer, Nordic-American Psalmodikonforbundet (1997-Present); Study Area Co-organizer, Editorial Adviser, Suzuki Association of the Americas (1987-Present); Author, "A+=Baby Church School" (2002); Author, "School Start Time/Teen Sleep Deprivation" (1996-1997); Author, "Left-Right, Up-Down Balancing," 7th International Socio-economics Conference, Washington D.C. (1995); Author, "Carts vs. Horses II," Research Symposium, Suzuki Association, Chicago, IL (1992); Author, "Mother Tongue Singing/ Voice Method" (1988); Recording Artist, Member of the Ensemble, Record/Cassettes, Nowell Sing We (1986) **Awards:** Most Active Volunteer, FairVote Minnesota (2017); Cited Work in, State Affiliate of the Year Award, Minnesota Music Teachers Association (2011); Appreciation Certificate, Quilt, Mt. Olive Lutheran Church and Trinity Lutheran Congregation (2009, 1997); Book Feature, "A Tribute to Outstanding Minnesota Women," by Marilyn Chelstrom (2001); Listee, "Minnesota Profiles," Minnesota Historical Society (1994); Honoree, Honor Roll, Mendota Mdewakanton Dakota Tribal Community (1999); Asset Builder of the Month, Children First Initiative, St. Louis Park, MN (1997); Winner with "Carts vs. Horses II", 5th International Suzuki Association of Americas Conference Research Symposium Competition (1992); Service Pin, American Lutheran Church Women (1981); Appreciation Plaque, Christian Boy and Girl Scouts of Germany (1977) **Membership:** Charter Member, Norway House (2004-Present); Associate Member, Norwegian Memorial Church (1994-Present); Lodge Trustee, Sons of Norway (1991-Present); VoiceCare Network (1991-Present); Minnesota Music Teachers Association (1989-Present); National Lutheran Choir Academy (1987-Present); Charter Member, Center for Victims of Torture (1985-Present); Amnesty International (1983-Present); United Nations Association (1973-Present); National Association of Teachers of Singing (1987); Christ Lutheran Church on Capitol Hill; AE911Truth; Minnesota Metropolitan Branch, Women's International League for Peace and Freedom **Marquis Who's Who Honors:** Albert Nelson Marquis Lifetime Achievement Award (2017) **Political Affiliations:** Green Party **Religion:** Lutheran **Shipping Address:** 2829 Yosemite Ave., S, Fair Pay Institute, Minneapolis, MN, 55416

Dimitrios Stefanidis, PhD

Title: Vice Chair of Education, Chief of Minimally Invasive and Bariatric Surgery **Industry:** Education/Educational Services **Company Name:** Indiana University **Parents:** Maria Stefanidis; Konstantinos Stefanidis **Marital Status:** Married **Spouse Name:** Evie Anastasiadou **Children:** Maria Nefeli; Constantine **Education:** Leadership Scholar, McColl School of Business, Queens University (2012-2013); Bariatric Surgery Fellow, Carolinas Medical Center, Carolinas HealthCare System (2005-2006); Research Fellow, Tulane University (2004-2005); General Surgery Resident, University of Texas Health, San Antonio, TX (1999-2004); General Surgery Intern, School of Medicine, Aristotle University of Thessaloniki, Greece (1998-1999); PhD, Rheinishe Friedrich Wilhems Universitat, Bonn, Germany (1998) **Certifications:** Licensed to Practice Medicine, State of Indiana (2016-Present); Diplomate, ASMBS (2010-Present); Diplomate, American College of Surgeons (2008-Present); Licensed to Practice Medicine, State of North Carolina (2006-Present); Certified in Basic Life Support (1999-Present); Diplomate, Educational Commission for Foreign Medical Graduates (1997-Present); Diplomate, American Board of Surgery, Inc. (2005-Present); Certified in Robotic Surgery (2011); Certified, TEAMSTEPPS (2010); Certified in the Fundamentals of Laparoscopic Surgery (2010); Certified in Fundamentals of Energy Use (2017), Certified in Advanced Cardiac Life Support (2001-2009); Certified in Advanced Trauma Life Support (1999-2007) **Career:** Professor, Surgery, Department of Surgery, Indiana University (2017-Present); Vice Chair, Education, Department of Surgery, Indiana University (2016-Present); Chief, MIS/Bariatrics, Department of Surgery, Indiana University (2016-Present); Director, Skills Lab, Department of Surgery, Indiana University (2016-Present); Medical Director, Bariatric Program, IUH North Hospital, Indiana University (2016-Present); Attending Surgeon, IUH North Hospital, Indiana University (2016-Present); Visiting Associate Professor, Department of Surgery, Indiana University (2016-2017); Surgical Director, Simulation Center, Carolinas HealthCare System (2014-2016) **Career Related:** Patient Education and Simulation Committee, American College of Surgeons, Consortium of Accredited Education Institutes (2015-Present); Robotic surgery Task Force, Society of American Gastrointestinal and Endoscopic Surgeons (2015-Present); Safe Cholecystectomy Task Force, Society of American Gastrointestinal and Endoscopic Surgeons (2014-Present); Research Committee, American Society of Metabolic and Bariatric Surgery (2012-Present); Multi-institutional Education Research Group, Association for Surgical Education (2012-Present); Quality and Safety Committee, Society of American Gastrointestinal Endoscopic Surgeons (2010-Present); Fellow, American College of Surgeons (2005-Present); Fellow, American Society for Metabolic and Bariatric Surgery (2005-Present) **Civic:** Board Member, Society for American Gastrointestinal and Endoscopic Surgeons (2017-Present); Board of Directors, Institute for Surgical Excellence (2016-Present); Chair, Guidelines Committee, Society of American Gastrointestinal Endoscopic Surgeons (2016-Present); Chair, Program Committee, Association for Surgical Education (2016-Present); Chair, Society for Simulation in Healthcare Novice Grant Review (2015-Present); Co-Chair, Research and Development Committee, American College of Surgeons, Consortium of Accredited Education Institutes (2015-Present) **Creative Works:** Editorial Board Member, "Research in Surgical Education," American College of Surgeons (2017-Present); Guest editor, "American Journal of Surgery," (2016-Present); Reviewer, "Journal of Surgical Education" (2011-Present); Reviewer, "Annals of Surgery" (2009-Present); Reviewer, "Surgical Innovation" (2009-Present); Associate Editor, "Journal of the Society for Simulation in Healthcare" (2008-Present); Editorial Board Member, "American Journal of Surgery," Association for Surgical Education (2008-Present); Reviewer, "Surgery" (2008-Present); Reviewer, "Journal of the American College of Surgeons" (2008-Present); Reviewer, "Surgical Endoscopy" (2007-Present); Reviewer, "Journal of the Society for Simulation in Healthcare" (2006-Present); Reviewer, "The American Journal of Surgery" (2006-Present) **Awards:** Paper of Distinction Award, Association for Surgical Education (2016); Presidential Citation, Society for Simulation in Healthcare (2016); Bronze Touchstone Award, Carolinas HealthCare System (2016); Outstanding Service Award, Carolinas HealthCare System (2016) **Membership:** Consortium of Accredited Education Institutes, American College of Surgeons (2009-Present); Society for Simulation in Healthcare (2007-Present); Society of Robotic Surgery (2006-Present); Southeastern Surgical Congress (2005-Present); Society for American Gastrointestinal and Endoscopic Surgeons (2004-Present); Association for Surgical Education (2004-Present); Association of Academic Surgery (2004-Present); American Medical Association (2000-Present) **Business Address:** 545 Barnhill Drive, Room 125, Indianapolis, IN, 46202 **Shipping Address:** 13779 Pinto Drive, Carmel, IN, 46032 **Website:** https://medicine.iu.edu/faculty/26941/stefanidis-dimitrios

David Eric Stein

Title: Physicist, Defense Analyst, Futurist, Military Officer (Retired) **Industry:** Military & Defense Services **Education:** Diplomate, United States Air Force Air War College (1996); Diplomate, U.S. Naval War College (1995); Diplomate, United States Air Force Air Command and Staff College (1982); MS in Physics, University of Florida (1977); Postgraduate Coursework, University of Florida (1971-1972); BS, University of Florida, with High Honors (1971) **Career:** Operations Analyst 5, JT3, LLC (2008-2016); Operations Research Analyst, IT & Enterprise Solutions, Northrop Grumman Corporation (2003-2008); Operations Research Analyst, CACI International Inc (2000-2003); Operations Research Analyst, Army Digitization Office (1999-2000); Operations Research Analyst, Joint Chiefs of Staff (1998-1999); Operations Research Analyst, Office of the Assistant Secretary of the Air Force (1996-1997); Operations Research Analyst, Joint Chiefs of Staff (1996); Operations Research Analyst, Office of the Assistant Secretary of the Air Force (1995); Member, United States Air Force Scientific Advisory Board (1994-1995); Operations Research Analyst, Computer Systems Center Incorporated (1992-1994); Member, United States Air Force Systems Command, Joint Base Andrews, Prince George's County, Maryland (1992); Fellow Engineer, Westinghouse Electric Corporation (1990-1991); Electrical Engineer Specialist, LTV Aircraft Products Group (1987-1990); Radar Data and Imagery Analyst, 6585th Test Group, Holloman Air Force Base, Otero County, New Mexico (1983-1987); Field Engineer, Radar Systems Test and Evaluation, Rome Air Development Center and Lincoln Laboratory, Massachusetts Institute of Technology (1981-1983); Project Engineer, Advanced Surveillance Concepts, Rome Air Development Center (1979-1981); National Science Foundation Research Assistant, University of Florida, Gainesville, FL (1974-1976); Instructor, Department of Physics, University of Florida, Gainesville, FL (1971-1974) **Career Related:** Consultant, Advanced Research Workshop, NATO, Bad Windsheim, Germany (1994-Present); Short Course Instructor, Radar Technicians, The George Washington University (1991-1997); Advisory Associate Editor, Advanced Research Workshop, NATO, Bad Windsheim, Germany (1988); Adjunct College Faculty, The George Washington University (1982-1984) **Civic:** President, Center for Transcultural Foresight, Inc. (2010-2012); Advisory Board, Institute for the Future, AACC (2008-2010); Executive Board of Directors, Center for Frontier Sciences (2006-2009) **Military Service:** Lieutenant Colonel, U.S. Air Force Reserve (1994-1999); Major, U.S. Air Force Reserve (1989-1994); Captain, U.S. Air Force Reserve (1987); Captain, U.S. Air Force (1979-1987); First Lieutenant, U.S. Army (1977-1979) **Creative Works:** Editor-in-Chief, "FUTUREtakes" (2003-2011); Associate Science Editor, "Frontier Perspectives" (2000-2008); Editor-in-Chief, The ACES Journal (1987-1993); Contributor, Articles to Professional Journals **Awards:** Fellow, Alpha Foundation's Institute for Advanced Study (2002-2004); Distinguished Service Award, The Applied Computational Electromagnetics Society (1994); Named, J. Hillis Miller Memorial Scholar, University of Florida, Gainesville, FL **Membership:** Fellow, AIAS (2002-2004); American Physical Society; American Association of Physics Teachers; World Affairs Councils of America; World Future Society; The Army and Navy Club; Philosophical Society of Washington; Florida Blue Key; The Phi Beta Kappa Society; Sigma Pi Sigma, American Institute of Physics; Omicron Delta Kappa; Phi Kappa Phi; Fellow, Ford Foundation **Shipping Address:** PO Box 571433, Las Vegas, NV, 89157

John C. Stein

Title: Lawyer **Industry:** Law and Legal Services **Company Name:** Boccardo Law Firm **Date of Birth:** 05/08/1939 **Place of Birth:** Flint **State:** MI **Parents:** Joseph Aloyosius Stein; Gertrude (Carlin) Stein **Marital Status:** Married **Spouse Name:** Dorothea Ruel (11/20/1965) **Children:** John Jr.; Lisa; Peter; Thea **Education:** Certificate, Military Justice School (Now Naval Justice School), Newport, RI (1968); JD, University of California, Hastings, College of Law, San Francisco, CA (1966); BA, University of San Francisco (1963) **Career:** With, The Boccardo Law Firm, San Jose, CA (1971-Present); Owner, The Boccardo Law Firm, San Jose, CA (1981-1999); Deputy City Attorney, Office of the City Attorney, City of San Francisco (1969-1971) **Career Related:** Lecturer, University of Santa Clara Law School (1985-Present); Judge Pro Tempore, Santa Clara County Superior Court (1981-Present); Judge Pro Tempore, San Francisco County Superior Court (1978-Present); Lecturer, University of California, Hastings, College of Law, San Francisco, CA **Civic:** Board of Directors, Katherine Delmar Burke School for Girls, San Francisco, CA (1988-1992); Planning Organization, The Richmond, San Francisco, CA (1985-1988) **Military Service:** Captain, United States Marine Corps (1966-1969) **Awards:** Trial Lawyer of the Year, Consumer Attorneys of California, San Jose, CA **Membership:** Fellow, American College of Trial Lawyers; Association of Trial Lawyers of America (Now American Association for Justice); Consumer Attorneys of California; American Board of Trial Advocates **Bar Admissions:** United States District Court for the Fourth Circuit for the State of California (1969); The State Bar of California (1966) **Hobbies:** Golf; Skiing; Scuba Diving **Political Affiliations:** Democrat **Religion:** Roman Catholic **Shipping Address:** 111 W Saint John St., Ste. 400, Boccardo Law Firm, Inc., San Jose, CA, 95113

Paul David Stein

Title: Cardiologist **Industry:** Medicine & Health Care **Company Name:** Michigan State University **Date of Birth:** 04/13/1934 **Place of Birth:** Cincinnati **State:** OH **Parents:** Simon Stein; Sadie (Friedman) Stein **Marital Status:** Married **Spouse Name:** Janet Louise Tucker (8/14/1966) **Children:** Simon; Douglas; Rebecca **Education:** Graduate Coursework in Electrical Instrumentation, Massachusetts Institute of Technology (1965); Research Fellow, Harvard Medical School, Boston, MA (1964-1966); Fellow in Cardiology, Mount Sinai Hospital, New York, NY (1963-1964); Fellow in Cardiology, University of Cincinnati (1962-1963); Medical Resident, Jewish Hospital, Cincinnati, Ohio (1961-1962); Medical Resident, Gorgas Hospital, Panama Canal Zone (1960-1961); Intern, Jewish Hospital, Cincinnati, Ohio (1959-1960); MD, University of Cincinnati (1959); BS in Physics, University of Cincinnati, with Honors (1955) **Career:** Professor, Department of Osteopathic Medical Specialties, College of Osteopathic Medicine, Michigan State University (2012-Present); Director of Research, St. Mary Mercy Hospital, Livonia, MI (2010-2011); Visiting Professor, Department of Osteopathic Medical Specialties, College of Osteopathic Medicine, Michigan State University (2009-2011); Director of Research Education, St. Joseph Mercy Oakland Hospital, Pontiac, MI (2005-2009); Professor of Medicine, Full-Time Affiliate, Wayne State University, Detroit, MI (2003-2015); Director of Research, St. Joseph Mercy Oakland Hospital, Pontiac, MI (2000-2004); Medical Director of Cardiovascular Rehabilitation, Henry Ford Hospital, Detroit, MI (1994-2000); Professor of Medicine, Case Western Reserve University, Cleveland, Ohio (1994-2000); Adjunct Professor of Physics, Oakland University, Rochester, MI (1985-2001); Director of Cardiovascular Research, Henry Ford Hospital, Detroit, MI (1976-1994); Professor of Research Medicine, College of Medicine, University of Oklahoma, Oklahoma City, OK (1973-1976); Associate Professor of Medicine, University of Oklahoma, Oklahoma City, OK (1969-1973); Assistant Professor of Medicine, Creighton University, Omaha, NE (1967-1969); Assistant Director, Cardiac Catheterization Laboratory, Baylor University Medical Center, Dallas, Texas (1966-1967) **Career Related:** Master Fellow, President, American College of Chest Physicians (1992); Fellow, Council on Circulation, American Heart Association, Inc. (1972); Fellow, Council on Clinical Cardiology, American Heart Association, Inc. (1971); Fellow, American College of Physicians; Fellow, Royal Society of Health; Fellow, American College of Cardiology; Fellow, American Society of Mechanical Engineers **Military Service:** Captain, United States Air Force Reserve (Retired) **Creative Works:** Author, "Pulmonary Embolism, Third Edition" (2016); Author, "Pulmonary Embolism, Second Edition" (2007); Author, "Pulmonary Embolism" (1996); Author, "A Physical and Physiological Basis for the Interpretation of Cardiac Ausculation: Evaluations Based Primarily on Second Sound and Ejection Murmurs" (1981); Contributor, Articles, Professional Journals **Awards:** Walter F. Patenge Medal of Public Service Award, College of Osteopathic Medicine, Michigan State University (2017); Research Excellence Award, College of Osteopathic Medicine, Michigan State University (2013); Daniel Drake Award, College of Medicine, University of Cincinnati (2009); Plaque Recognition, St. Joseph Mercy Hospital (2007); Laureate Award, Michigan Chapter, American College of Physicians (2003); Lifetime Achievement Award, Michigan Chapter, American Heart Association, Inc. (2002); Medal of Recognition for Outstanding Contributions, American College of Chest Physicians (1998); Aristotle Gold Medal, Aristotle University of Thessaloniki (1993) **Membership:** President, Laennec Society (1984); Honorary Member, Neumomadrid Society **Marquis Who's Who Honors:** Albert Nelson Marquis Lifetime Achievement Award (2017); Distinguished Humanitarian (2017) **Shipping Address:** 1011 Hampshire Drive, Bloomfield Hills, MI, 48302

Arnold D. Steinberg

Title: Dentist **Industry:** Medicine & Health Care **Date of Birth:** 10/25/1930 **Place of Birth:** Warsaw **Country of Origin:** Poland **Parents:** Morris Aaron Steingberg; Leila Merium (Baum) Steinberg **Marital Status:** Married **Spouse Name:** June Bender (6/14/1953) **Children:** Steven; Barbara; Ruth; Mark **Education:** MS in Biochemistry, College of Medicine, University of Illinois (1964); DDS, Northwestern University (1954) **Career:** Director, Dental Information and Learning Technologies (1998-2006); Practice in General Dentistry (1956-1994); Associate Attending Dentist, Michael Reese Hospital (1958-1979) **Career Related:** Professor in Biochemistry and Periodontics, University of Illinois Hospital & Health Sciences System (1976-Present); Director, Lincoln Dental Caries Study (1963-1971) **Military Service:** Captain, U.S. Air Force (1956); Dentist, U.S. Air Force (1956); 1st Lieutenant, U.S. Air Force (1954) **Creative Works:** Contributor, Articles, Professional Journals **Awards:** Research Grant, University of Illinois (2005-2006); Research Grant, College of Dentistry (2001-Present); Curriculum Development Grant (1996-2000); Harold Berk Award For Excellence In The Field Of Oral Health Care To The Disabled (1997); Grant, Calcitek Corporation (1988-1992); Grant, Collagen Corporation (1981-1983); Grant, National Institutes Of Health (1970); Grant, Epilepsy Foundation (1967, 1970) **Membership:** Fellow, International College of Dentists; American College of Dentists; Academy of General Dentistry; Academy of Dentistry for the Handicapped **Marquis Who's Who Honors:** Albert Nelson Marquis Lifetime Achievement Award (2017) **Why did you become involved in your profession or industry:** He was inspired by one of his teachers from high school. **Hobbies:** Computers **Political Affiliations:** Republican **Religion:** Jewish **Shipping Address:** 3724 Arcadia St., Skokie, IL, 60076

John Madison Stembridge

Title: President **Industry:** Business Management/ Business Services **Company Name:** Stanbridge Furniture **Education:** Bachelor's Degree, Bob Jones University (1960) **Career:** President, Stembridge Furniture (1968-Present); President, Stembridge Real Estate Company Inc. (2011-2013); Associate, Americans for a Safe Israel (1985-2013); Vice President, Stembridge Real Estate Company Inc. (1968-2012) **Civic:** Candidate, Local District, United States Congress (1989); Mayor, North Miami, FL (1973-1975); Lobbyist for Israel-Global Relations **Creative Works:** Host, "John Stembrdige Inspirational Hour Weekly" (1975-1980); Founder, "Greater Miami Inspirational Concert Series" (1970-1980) **Awards:** Leadership Award, Jewish National Fund (2006); Business of the Year Award, Greater North Miami Chamber of Commerce (2003); Martin Luther King Brotherhood Award (1983); Shropshire Foundation Award, Civitan International **Membership:** Vice-Chairman, Bicentennial Committee, The United States Conference of Mayors (1975); Board Member, Holocaust Memorial Miami Beach; Board Member, Jewish National Fund; Governor, Tropical District, Civitan International; Board Member, Florida Furniture Dealers Association **Marquis Who's Who Honors:** Albert Nelson Marquis Lifetime Achievement Award (2017) **Shipping Address:** 545 NE 125th St., Stanbridge Furniture, North Miami, FL, 33161 **Website:** https://www.linkedin.com/in/john-stembridge-3129252a

Annabel K. Stephens

Title: Adjunct Professor **Industry:** Education/Educational Services **Company Name:** The University of Alabama **Date of Birth:** 04/17/1947 **Place of Birth:** New Albany **State:** MS **Parents:** Carl H. Stephens; Ruth Nell Kuykendall Stephens **Marital Status:** Married **Spouse Name:** Pat L. Dunbar **Education:** DLS, Columbia University, New York City, NY (1988); MLS, Vanderbilt University Peabody College, Nashville, TN (1970); BA, Mississippi University for Women, Columbus, MS (1968) **Career:** Adjunct, College of Communication & Information Sciences, The University of Alabama (2007-Present); Associate Professor, College of Communication & Information Sciences, The University of Alabama (1995-2007); Assistant Professor, College of Communication & Information Sciences, The University of Alabama (1985-1995); Part-time Instructor, College of Communication & Information Sciences, The University of Alabama (1984-1985); Director, Jennie Stephens Smith Public Library (1982-1983); Branch Head, Memphis Public Library (1972-1979); Librarian, Memphis Public Library (1970-1972); Librarian, Muscle Shoals Regional Library (1968-1969) **Civic:** Volunteer, Turning Point Domestic Violence and Sexual Assault Services (2012-Present); Volunteer, Hospice of West Alabama (2009-Present); Board of Directors, West Alabama AIDS Outreach, Tuscaloosa, AL (2003-Present); Volunteer, University Presbyterian Church Food Pantry (2002-Present) **Awards:** Beta Phi Mu Award for Distinguished Service in Library Education, American Library Association (2016); Inductee, Hall of Fame, College of Communication and Information Sciences, The University of Alabama (2015); Knox Hagood Award, College of Communications and Information Sciences, The University of Alabama (2007); Lifetime Achievement Award, Alabama Library Association (2006); Eminent Librarian Award, Alabama Library Association (2006); Ruth Blackburn Community Service Award, West Alabama AIDS Outreach (2004); Librarian of the Year Award, Alabama Chapter, Beta Phi Mu (2004); Humanitarian Award, Alabama Library Association (2002); Steven L. Mann Award, Mystic Krew of Druids **Membership:** Lifetime Member, American Library Association; Reference and User Service Association; Public Library Association; ALISE; Alabama Library Association **Marquis Who's Who Honors:** Albert Nelson Marquis Lifetime Achievement Award (2017); Distinguished Humanitarian (2017) **To what do you attribute your success:** Dr. Stephens attributed her success to encouragement and examples from her family and several professional mentors. **Why did you become involved in your profession or industry:** Public libraries provide great benefit to individuals and communities. As a professional librarian and as a professor, Dr. Stephens had the privilege of both helping people use public libraries and preparing future librarians to make incredible differences in the lives of individuals and communities. As a profession, librarians continue to offer worlds of information and knowledge that should be available to all. **What do you consider to be the highlight of your career:** The highlight of her career was receiving professional awards such as the national Phi Beta Mu Award for Distinguished Service in Library Education, the Alabama Library Association Lifetime Achievement Award, and induction into the College of Communication and Information Sciences Hall of Fame. **Hobbies:** Travel; Reading; Movies; Plays **Religion:** Presbyterian **Shipping Address:** 11851 Grandview Dr., Northport, AL, 35475

Keir B. Sterling

Title: Historian, Educator **Industry:** Education/Educational Services **Date of Birth:** 01/30/1934 **Place of Birth:** New York **State:** NY **Year of Passing:** 2017-01-03 **Marital Status:** Married **Spouse Name:** Anne Cox Diller **Children:** Duncan Diller; Warner Strong; Theodore Craig **Education:** PhD, Columbia University (1973); Professional Diploma, Columbia University (1965); MA, Columbia University (1963); BS, Columbia University (1961) **Career:** Open University Lecturer, Richmond, VA (2012-2016); Independent Historian, Author (2008-2016); Historian, United States Army Combined Arms Support Command, Fort Lee, VA (1998-2008); Ordnance Branch Historian, United States Army Ordnance Center and School, Fort Lee, VA (1994-1998); Ordnance Branch Historian, United States Army Ordnance Center and School, Aberdeen Proving Ground, Maryland (1983-1994); Adjunct Professor, Pace University, New York, NY, Pleasantville, NY (1977-1983); From Assistant Adjunct Professor to Associate Adjunct Professor, Pace University, New York, NY, Pleasantville, NY (1971-1977); Adjunct Instructor of History, Pace University, New York, NY, Pleasantville, NY (1966-1971); Research Grantee, England (1965-1966); Assistant to Dean, School of General Studies, Columbia University, New York, NY (1959-1965) **Career Related:** Chair Historian, Archivist Committee, International Federation of Mammalogy (2007); Grant Reviewer, Teaching American History Program, United States Department of Education (2003-2005); Chair, Adams-Pendleton Book Prize Committee, Society for History in the Federal Government (2002-2013); Instructor, Army Logistics Management College, Fort Lee, NJ (1995-2008); Judge, Annapolis National History Day Competition, University of Maryland (1993-2008); Community College (1987-1994); American Trust for the British Library (1986-1989); Steering Committee Section, Mammalogy, International Union of Biological Sciences (1985-2007); National Science Foundation (1983-2016); Visiting Professor, Mercy College, Westchester Community College, King's College, Nyack College and University of Wisconsin (1983); Visiting Professor, Mercy College, Westchester Community College, King's College, Nyack College and University of Wisconsin (1978-1989); Active Columbia University Seminar on History and Philosophy of Science (1976-1983); Co-Project Director, American Ornithologists Union Centennial History Project (1976-1989); Visiting Professor, Mercy College, Westchester Community College, King's College, Nyack College and University of Wisconsin (1975); Graduate School, State Colleges of New Jersey (1974-1975); Consultant, Arno Press, Inc. (1973-1978); Assistant Dean, Rockland Community College, State University of New York, Suffern (1971-1973) **Civic:** Board Member, League of Women Voters, Richmond, Virginia (2014-2016); Co-Vice President, College Hills Civic Association, Richmond, VA (2006-2007); President, Rhinebeck Historical Society, New York (1982-1983); Boy Scout Leader, Seattle, WA, Fort Devens, MA, New York, NY, Tarrytown, NY (1953-1977); Eagle Scout, Seattle, WA, Fort Devins, MA, New York, NY, Tarrytown, NY **Military Service:** US Army (1954-1956) **Creative Works:** General Editor, Contributor, "The International History of Mammalogy" (1987-Present); Contributing Author, "Centennial History of the American Ornithologist Union" (2016); Contributing Author, "Science in Uniform, Uniforms in Science" (2007); Contributing Author, "Military Communications: Ancient Times to the 21st Century" (2007); Contributing Author, "Dictionary of American History, Third Edition" (2003); Contributing Author, "Encyclopedia of World Environmental History" (2003); Contributing Author, "Ground Warfare: An International Encyclopedia" (2002); Senior Editor, Contributor with R. Harmond, G. Cevasco, and L. Hammond, "Biographical Dictionary of American and Canadian Naturalists and Environmentalists" (1997) **Awards:** Recipient, Editor's Quill Award, International Association of Torch Clubs (2003); Grantee, IREX (1982); Grantee, National Science Foundation (1981-1982); Grantee, Pace University (1980-1981); Grantee, American Society of Mammalogists (1978); Grantee, National Geographic Society (1977); Grantee, Theodore Roosevelt Memorial Fund, American Museum of Natural History (1967) **Membership:** Board Member, League of Women Voters, Richmond, VA (2013-2016); Council Member, Association for the Bibliography of History (1994-1998); Member, Archives Committee, American Ornithologists' Union (1976, 1977); Society for History in the Federal Government; History of Science Society; Co-Chairman, Centennial History Committee, American Ornithologists' Union; 75th Annual Committee, American Society of Mammalogists **Marquis Who's Who Honors:** Albert Nelson Marquis Lifetime Achievement Award (2017) **Political Affiliations:** Democrat **Religion:** Episcopalian **Shipping Address:** 7104 Wheeler Road, Richmond, VA, 23229

Walter W. Stern III

Title: Lawyer **Industry:** Law and Legal Services **Date of Birth:** 03/25/1946 **Place of Birth:** Cincinnati **State:** OH **Parents:** Walter W. Stern, Jr.; Harriet Louise Stern **Marital Status:** Single **Children:** Rachael Louise **Education:** JD, Marquette University, Milwaukee, WI (1974); BA in Social Science, Carthage College, Kenosha, WI, Cum laude (1969) **Certifications:** Certified Family Mediator, WIPCOD **Career:** Lawyer, Private Practice (2007-Present); Lawyer, Private Practice, Union Grove, WI (1991-2007); Administrative Appeals Officer, Kenosha County Department of Social Services, Kenosha, WI (1990-1994); Senior Partner, Caviali & Stern, Kenosha, WI (1985-1991); Senior Partner, Joling, Rizzo, Willems, Stern & Burroughs (1982-1985); Partner, Anderson & Stern, Kenosha, WI (1978-1982); Lawyer, Private Practice, Kenosha, WI (1974-1978) **Career Related:** Fellow, American Academy of Forensic Sciences (1981-Present); Lecturer in Criminal Law, Carthage College (1976-2005); Fellow, American Academy of Forensic Sciences **Civic:** The Epilepsy Foundation of Southern Wisconsin (2003-Present); Professional Member, Continental-Pinnacle (2017); Candidate for Circuit Judge (2005); Youth Leadership Council, Kenosha, WI (1995-1997); Hearing Examiner, General Relief (1990-1995); Volunteer Instructor, Domestic Violence Intervention Project, Kenosha, WI (1984-1995); Educator, Domestic Violence Project (1983-1994); Community Co-founder, Woman's and Children's Horizons (1982); Guardian Ad Litem in Field (1974-1980); Director of Switchboard Community Services (1972-1975) **Military Service:** Second Lieutenant, Illinois National Guard, Western Military Academy, Alton, IL (1964) **Creative Works:** Author, Draft, New Chapter 51 Standards for Mental Commitments (1974) **Awards:** Achievement Award for Professional Experience, Continental-Pinnacle (2017); Outstanding Achievement in the Law, Who's Who in American Law (2017); Industrial Leader Award, Who's Who in American Law (2017); Recognition, Easter Seals (2004-2005) **Membership:** Advisory Branch, NAMI **Bar Admissions:** Illinois (1999); Supreme Court of the United States (1983); United States Court of Appeals for the Seventh Circuit (1981); Wisconsin (1974); United States District Court for the Eastern District of Wisconsin (1974); United States District Court for the Western District of Wisconsin (1974) **Marquis Who's Who Honors:** Albert Nelson Marquis Lifetime Achievement Award (2017) **To what do you attribute your success:** Mr. Stern attributes his success to being a client-centered attorney who is not afraid of work or difficult cases. **Why did you become involved in your profession or industry:** After Mr. Stern served as a high school teacher in Chicago, Ill., he decided to go to law school. He completed law school at Marquette University. He became involved because he wanted to make a difference in terms of advocating people's rights, namely people who were average individuals, and whose rights have often been ignored. **What do you consider to be the highlight of your career:** The highlight of Mr. Stern's career occurred just recently, within the past year and a half, when he became engaged in wrongful deaths cases concerning excessive force used by police officers. He thinks he has been very successful in advocating the rights of the individuals who were harmed by excessive force. **Where will you be in five years:** Mr. Stern expects to be retired in approximately a year. He fully expects to be on the golf course and enjoying his retirement. **Hobbies:** Fishing; Hunting; Jogging; Reading; Creative writing; Fencing **Shipping Address:** 920 85th Street, Apt. 123, Kenosha, WI, 53143

Diana Lynn Carr Stevens

Title: Elementary School Educator (Retired) **Industry:** Education/Educational Services **Date of Birth:** 12/12/1950 **Place of Birth:** Waterloo **State:** IA **Parents:** Marcus Henry Carr; Clarissa Ann (Funk) Carr **Marital Status:** Married **Spouse Name:** Paul John Stevens **Children:** Drew Spencer **Education:** MA in Liberal Arts, Baker University, Baldwin, KS (1989); BS, Mid-America Nazarene College (Now MidAmerica Nazarene University) (1973) **Career:** Elementary Teacher, Olathe School District #233 (1975-2014) **Career Related:** Guest Teacher, Olathe Public Schools **Creative Works:** Artist, Delta Kappa Gamma Bulletin (2001); Artist, ARC Exhibit, National Art Education Association (1968); Exhibitor, Olathe Public Library; Exhibitor, Hidden Glen Art Festival; Exhibitor, Olathe Medical Center; Exhibitor, Buddy Roger's Playhouse; Exhibitor, College Church of the Nazarene; Exhibitor, Charcoal Portraits, MidAmerica Nazarene University; Exhibitor, Charcoal Portraits, Rolling Ridge Elementary School; Author, Poetry, DKG Bulletin; Artist, Newspapers; Artist, Charcoal Portraits, Patrons **Awards:** Honoree, Teacher Appreciation Night, Olathe North High School (2017); Nominee, Emporia State Master Teacher (2010-2011); Summer Reading Grantee, Olathe Public Schools (2008, 2011); Recipient, Outstanding Service Award (2009); Reading Grantee (2007); Recipient, Excellence in Education Award, Olathe Public Schools Foundation (2002); Recipient, Action Grant, Olathe School District (1996-1997); Recipient, Certificate of Recognition for Teaching 25 Years in Kansas, The University of Kansas **Membership:** Olathe Chapter, Daughters of the American Revolution (2015-Present); Board Member, OPS-REA (2018-2019); Second Vice President, Beta Omega (2006-2010); National Education Association; Kansas Education Association; Social Committee, Olathe Chapter, Olathe Education Association; College Church of the Nazarene; Professional Affairs Committee Member, Delta Kappa Gamma; National Honor Society; Membership Chairman, Beta Omega; Membership Committee Chairman, Local Chapters, Delta Kappa Gamma **Marquis Who's Who Honors:** Albert Nelson Marquis Lifetime Achievement Award (2018) **Hobbies:** Portrait art; Reading; Walking; Genealogy **Shipping Address:** 217 S. Montclaire Drive, Olathe, KS, 66061

Elwood C. Stevens Jr.

Title: Special Counsel **Industry:** Law and Legal Services **Company Name:** Domengeaux Wright Roy & Edwards, L.L.C. **Place of Birth:** Opelousas **State:** LA **Children:** Three Stepdaughters **Education:** JD, Paul M. Hebert Law Center, Louisiana State University (1979) **Career:** Special Counsel, Domengeaux, Wright, Roy & Edwards LLC (2009-Present); Lawyer, Hunter & Plattsmier (1981-Present); Lawyer, Sole Practice (2000-2009); Law Clerk to the Honorable John M. Shaw, U.S. District Court, Western District, State of Louisiana (1979-1981); Lawyer, Partner, Kleinpeter, Schwartzberg & Stevens **Career Related:** Charter Member, Fellow, Louisiana Bar Foundation **Military Service:** JAG Corps, U.S. Army (1970-1973) **Awards:** Best Lawyers in America, U.S. News and World Report (2018); A/V Preeminent Peer Rated for Highest Level of Professional Excellence (2017); Top Lawyers of Acadiana, Acadiana Profile Magazine (2017); Best Lawyers in America, U.S. News and World Report (2016); Honoree, Super Lawyers **Membership:** President, Board of Directors, Lafayette, St. Landry and St. Mary Parish Bar Association; Litigation Section, American Bar Association; Co-Chairman, Toxic Torts and Mass Litigation Subcommittee, American Bar Association; American Association for Justice; Bar Association of the Federal Fifth Circuit; Board of Governors, Louisiana Association for Justice; Council of Directors, Louisiana Association for Justice; President's Advisory Council, Louisiana Association for Justice; Executive Committee, Louisiana Association for Justice; The Bar Association of the Fifth Federal Circuit; Master, Acadiana Chapter, American Inns of Court; Past President, Board of Directors, Lafayette-Acadiana Chapter, Federal Bar Association **Bar Admissions:** State of Louisiana; Fifth Circuit, U.S. Court of Appeals; U.S. Supreme Court **To what do you attribute your success:** Mr. Stevens attributes his success to the incredible strength, courage, and moral compass he observed and absorbed from his mother. **Why did you become involved in your profession or industry:** After serving as a legal assistant to five military lawyers in the U.S. Army JAG Corps, Mr. Stevens knew he wanted to be an attorney. **What do you consider to be the highlight of your career:** The highlight of Mr. Stevens' career was working on the Hurricane Katrina trial against the U.S. Army Corps of Engineers. He is proud of his work in that two-month case. **Where will you be in five years:** Mr. Stevens sees himself continuing to represent victims of negligence and corporate misdeeds for the next ten years, and helping to mentor young attorneys. **Shipping Address:** 556 Jefferson Street, Suite 500, Domengeaux Wright Roy & Edwards LLC, Lafayette, LA, 70501 **Website:** http://www.wrightroy.com/attorney/elwood-c-stevens-jr

Rosemary Anne Stevens, PhD

Title: Medicine and Public Health Historian, Artist **Industry:** Media & Entertainment **Date of Birth:** 03/18/1935 **Place of Birth:** Bourne **Country of Origin:** England **Parents:** William Edward Wallace; Mary Agnes (Tricks) Wallace **Marital Status:** Married **Spouse Name:** Jack D. Barchas (8/9/1994); Robert B. Stevens (1961-1983, Divorced) **Children:** Carey; Richard **Education:** Honorary Degree, Rutgers, The State University of New Jersey (1995); Honorary Degree, Northeast Ohio Medical University (1995); Honorary Degree, Hahnemann University (1988); PhD, Yale University (1968); MPH, Yale University (1963); Diploma in Social Administration, Manchester University (1959); BA, University of Oxford (1957) **Career:** DeWitt Wallace Distinguished Scholar of Social Medicine and Public Policy, Department of Psychiatry, Weill Cornell Medical College (2005-Present); Professor Emeritus, University of Pennsylvania, Philadelphia, PA (2001-Present); Stanley I. Sheerr Endowed Term Professor, University of Pennsylvania, Philadelphia, PA (1997-2001); Dean, School of Arts and Sciences, University of Pennsylvania, Philadelphia, PA (1991-1996); Senior Fellow, Leonard Davis Institute of Health Economics, University of Pennsylvania (1980-2005); Professor of History and Sociology of Science, University of Pennsylvania (1979-2000); Academic Visitor, London School of Economics and Political Science (1973-1974); From Assistant Professor to Professor, Yale University (1968-1976); Visiting Lecturer, Johns Hopkins University (1967-1968); Guest Scholar, The Brookings Institution, Washington, DC (1967-1968); Academic Visitor, London School of Economics and Political Science (1962-1964); Fellow, American Academy of Medicine **Civic:** Board of Directors, Milbank Memorial Fund (1980-2017) **Creative Works:** Presentation, "A Time of Scandal: Charles R. Forbes, Warren G. Harding and the Making of the Veterans Bureau," Warren G. Harding Society, Cincinnati, OH (2017); Presentation, "A Time of Scandal: Charles R. Forbes, Warren G. Harding and the Making of the Veterans Bureau," United States Department of Veteran Affairs, Washington, DC (2017); Presentation, "A Time of Scandal: Charles R. Forbes, Warren G. Harding and the Making of the Veterans Bureau," C-Span (2016); Author, "A Time of Scandal: Charles R. Forbes, Warren G. Harding and the Making of the Veterans Bureau," Johns Hopkins University Press, Baltimore, MD (2016); Author, "The Public-Private Health Care State" (2007); Author, "Welfare Medicine in America, New Edition" (2003); Author, "Medical Practice in Modern England: The Impact of Specialization and State Medicine, New Edition" (2003); Author, "In Sickness and in Wealth: American Hospitals in the Twentieth Century, Revised Edition" (1999); Author, "American Medicine and the Public Interest, Revised Edition" (1998); Author, "In Sickness and in Wealth: American Hospitals in the Twentieth Century" (1989); Author, "Alien-Doctors: Foreign Medical Graduates in American Hospitals" (1978); Author, "Welfare Medicine in America" (1974); Author, "Foreign Trained Physicians and American Medicine" (1972); Author, "American Medicine and the Public Interest" (1971); Author, "Medical Practice in Modern England: The Impact of Specialization and State Medicine" (1966); Co-Editor, "History and Health Policy in the United States: Putting the Past Back In"; Contributor, Articles to Professional Journals; Contributor, Chapters to Books **Awards:** Recipient, Lifetime Achievement Award, American Association for the History of Medicine, Incorporated (2002); Recipient, Carlson Award for Extraordinary Contributions to the History of Medicine, Weill Cornell Medical College, Cornell University (2000); Recipient, Investigator Award in Health Policy Research, Robert Wood Johnson Foundation (1998-2003); Recipient, Nicholas E. Davies Award, Piedmont Healthcare (1997); Recipient, Welch Medal of Distinction in History of Medicine, American Association of History Medicine, Incorporated (1990); Recipient, Arthur Viseltear Award, History of Public Health, American Public Health Association (1990); Recipient, Baxter Foundation Prize of Distinction in Health Services Research (1990); Recipient, James A. Hamilton Book Award, American College of Healthcare Executives (1990); Fellow, John Simon Guggenheim Foundation (1984-1985); Recipient, Frohlich Medal, Royal Society of Medicine (1986); Recipient, Bellagio Study and Conference Scholarship (1984); Recipient, Rockefeller Humanities Fellowship (1982-1983) **Membership:** Chairman, History and Philosophy of Science, American Association for the Advancement of Science (2002-2003); National Academy of Medicine; American Sociological Association; American Association for History of Medicine, Incorporated; The College of Physicians of Philadelphia; Former Public Member, American Board of Pediatrics; Educational Commission for Foreign Medical Graduates; Josiah Macy Jr. Foundation; American Public Health Association; Association of University Programs in Health Administration; Various National Medical Organizations **Marquis Who's Who Honors:** Albert Nelson Marquis Lifetime Achievement Award (2017) **Hobbies:** Oil painting; Music **Shipping Address:** 171 W 71st St Apt 3C, New York, NY, 10023

Donald Steward

Title: Managing Director **Industry:** Business Management/Business Services **Company Name:** Problematics LLC **Place of Birth:** Buffalo **State:** NY **Education:** PhD in Computer Science, University of Wisconsin (1973); MS in Mathematics, Stanford University (1962); BS in Physics and Mathematics, Iowa State University of Science and Technology (1953) **Career:** Managing Director, Problematics LLC, Napa, CA (1996-Present); Professor Emeritus, Department of Computer Science, California State University, Sacramento, CA (1978-1996); Professor, Business Systems, Virginia Commonwealth University, Richmond, VA; Nuclear Engineer, General Electric; Programmer, Computer Systems, Burrough Research Laboratories; Developer, Econometric Modeling, Social Systems Research Institute, University of Wisconsin; Professor, Computer Science, California State University, Sacramento, CA; Contract Employee, Detect Violations of Arms Control Agreements, U.S. Arms Control and Disarmament Agency **Career Related:** Visiting Scholar, Massachusetts Institute of Technology **Civic:** Participant, Mississippi Summer Freedom Project (1964) **Creative Works:** Author, "Solving Today's Problems to Achieve a Better World," ResearchGate (2017); Author, "Software Engineering with Systems Analysis and Design", Brooks/Cole Publishing Company, Cengage Learning (1987); Author, "Systems Analysis and Management: Structure, Strategy and Design," Petrocelli Books (1981); Contributor, Many Papers; Developer, Computer Program, "Explainer" **Marquis Who's Who Honors:** Albert Nelson Marquis Lifetime Achievement Award (2017) **Why did you become involved in your profession or industry:** Dr. Steward's interest in his career was prompted by his father, who was very interested in science. **Shipping Address:** 1000 Banbury Ct., Napa, CA, 94558

S. Evelyn Stewart

Title: Psychiatrist **Industry:** Medicine & Health Care **Company Name:** Massachusetts General Hospital, Harvard University **Date of Birth:** 05/23/1969 **Place of Birth:** Sault Ste. Marie **Country of Origin:** ON/Canada **Parents:** Terry Stewart; Miriam Stewart **Education:** Research Fellowship, McLean Hospital (2003-2004); Early Investigator Postgraduate Fellowship, Canadian Institutes of Health Research (2002-2003); MD, Dalhousie University, Canada (1996); BA in Comparative Religion, Dalhousie University, Canada (1991); BS in Chemistry, Dalhousie University, Canada (1991) **Certifications:** Diplomate in Psychiatry, Royal College of Physicians and Surgeons, Canada (2002) **Career:** Director, Pediatrics, OCD Program, University of British Columbia (2010-Present); Assistant Professor, Massachusetts General Hospital, Harvard University, Boston, MA (2007-Present); Director, Brain Behavior and Development Theme, British Columbia Children's Research Institute (2016); Director of Research, Child Psychiatry, British Columbia Children's Hospital (2016); Associate Professor, University of British Columbia (2010); Instructor of Psychiatry, Massachusetts General Hospital, Harvard Medical School, Boston, MA (2005-2007); Research Fellow, Harvard University, Boston, MA (2002-2005) **Career Related:** Co-Director, International OCD Genetics Collaborative (2011-Present); Faculty, Psychiatric and Neurodevelopmental Genetics Unit (2007-Present); Pediatric Psychopharmacologist (2005-Present); OCD and Related Disorders Clinical Psychiatrist, Massachusetts General Hospital (2005-2010); Director, OCD PGY3 Residency Teaching Module (2005-2010); Director of Research, Obsessive Compulsive Disorder Institute, McLean Hospital, Belmont, MA (2005-2010); Scientific and Clinical Advisory Boards, Tourette Syndrome Association, International OCD Foundation **Membership:** Anxiety and Depression Association of America; Canadian Psychiatric Association; American Academy of Child and Adolescent Psychiatry; Canadian Academy of Child and Adolescent Psychiatry **Hobbies:** Running **Shipping Address:** 4350 Osler Street, BC, Vancouver, Canada, V6H 2X7

Mark H. Stoler

Title: Professor Emeritus **Industry:** Education/Educational Services **Company Name:** University of Virginia **Date of Birth:** 03/01/1954 **Parents:** Leonard Stoler; Evelyn (Yellen) Stoler **Marital Status:** Married **Spouse Name:** Paula Maria Piccini (6/12/1977) **Children:** Leah Elizabeth; Abby Rebecca **Education:** Chief Resident, University of Rochester Medical Center, Rochester, NY (1983-1984); Resident in Pathology, University of Rochester Medical Center, Rochester, NY (1981-1983); Intern in Pathology, University of Rochester Medical Center, Rochester, NY (1980-1981); Intern in Medicine, Rochester General Hospital (1980); MD, University of Rochester (1980); BA in Biology, University of Rochester, Magna Cum Laude (1976) **Certifications:** Diplomate, The American Board of Pathology; Diplomate, American Board of Cytopathology; Diplomate, National Board of Medical Examiners **Career:** Professor Emeritus of Pathology, Health Sciences Center, University of Virginia (2011); Professor Emeritus of Gynecology, Health Sciences Center, University of Virginia (2011); Professor of Pathology, Health Sciences Center, University of Virginia (1997-2011); Professor of Gynecology, Health Sciences Center, University of Virginia (1997-2011); Associate Professor of Pathology, University of Virginia Health System (1993-1997); Attending Pathologist, University of Virginia Health System (1993-1997); Attending Pathologist, Cleveland Clinic (1989-1993); Assistant Professor of Pathology, University of Rochester Medical Center, Rochester, NY (1985-1989); Assistant Professor of Laboratory Medicine, University of Rochester Medical Center, Rochester, NY (1985-1989); Assistant Professor of Oncology, University of Rochester Medical Center, Rochester, NY (1988-1989); Attending Pathologist, University of Rochester Medical Center, Rochester, NY (1985-1989); Fellow in Surgical Pathology, University of Rochester Medical Center, Rochester, NY (1984-1985); Fellow in Cytopathology, University of Rochester Medical Center, Rochester, NY (1984-1985); Instructor of Pathology, University of Rochester Medical Center, Rochester, NY (1983-1985); Instructor of Laboratory Medicine, University of Rochester Medical Center, Rochester, NY (1983-1985) **Awards:** Israel Davidsohn Award for Distinguished Service, American Society for Clinical Pathologists (2012); Distinguished Science Achievement Award, American Society for Colposcopy and Cervical Pathology (2011); George F. Stevenson Distinguished Service Award, American Society for Clinical Pathologists (2003); Young Investigator Award, Academy of Clinical Laboratory Physicians and Scientists (1983) **Membership:** Fellow, Molecular Pathology Committee, College of American Pathologists (1989-Present); Fellow, Cell Markers Committee, College of American Pathologists (1989-Present); Board of Directors, American Society for Clinical Pathology (2000-2012); President, American Society for Clinical Pathology (2009-2010); Fellow, College of American Pathologists; American Association for the Advancement of Science; American Medical Association; American Society for Investigative Pathology; American Society of Cytology; International Society of Gynecological Pathologists; Arthur Purdy Stout Society; The Phi Beta Kappa Society **Marquis Who's Who Honors:** Albert Nelson Marquis Lifetime Achievement Award (2017) **Why did you become involved in your profession or industry:** Dr. Stoler always knew he wanted to be in the field of medicine. **Hobbies:** Fishing; Baking **Shipping Address:** 6103 Indian Ridge Dr., Earlysville, VA, 22936

Michael Howard Stone

Title: Psychiatrist **Industry:** Social Work **Company Name:** Michael H. Stone, MD **Date of Birth:** 10/27/1933 **Place of Birth:** Syracuse **State:** NY **Parents:** Moses Howard Stone; Corinne (Gittleman) Stone **Marital Status:** Married **Spouse Name:** Beth Janine Eichstaedt; Clarice Joan Kestenbaum (Divorced 1979) **Children:** David; John **Education:** MD, Cornell University (1958); BA, Cornell University (1954) **Certifications:** Diplomate, American Board of Psychiatry and Neurology **Career:** Professor of Clinical Psychiatry, Columbia College of Physicians and Surgeons, New York, NY (1988-Present); Professor of Clinical Psychiatry, Cornell Medical College, New York, NY (1985-1988); Professor of Clinical Psychiatry, Mount Sinai School of Medicine, New York, NY (1984-1985); Clinical Director, Department of Psychiatry, University of Connecticut, Farmington, CT (1980-1984); Professor of Psychiatry, University of Connecticut, Farmington, CT (1980-1984); Associate Professor, Cornell Medical College, New York, NY (1977-1980); Assistant Professor of Psychiatry, Columbia College of Physicians and Surgeons, New York, NY (1973-1977); Residency in Psychiatry, Columbia College of Physicians and Surgeons, New York, NY (1963-1966); Consultant, Personal Disorder Institute, New York, NY; Medical Director of the Addiction Clinic, Orange Regional Medical Hospital, Middletown, NY; Director of Research, Middletown Psychiatric Center, New York **Career Related:** Visiting Professor of Psychiatry, Albert Einstein Medical Center, New York, NY (1987-Present); Lecturer in Field (1987-Present); Hematology Fellowship, National Institutes of Health (1961-1963); Professor of Clinical Psychiatry, Columbia College of Physicians and Surgeons; Board Member, Musica Sacra; Editorial Board Member, Journals of Personality Disorders and Psychodynamics in Psychiatry; Associate Editor, Journal of Violence and Gender; Fellow, American Psychiatric Association **Civic:** Patron, Metropolitan Opera and New York City Ballet **Creative Works:** Appearances, Current Forensic Topics, Radio and TV (2010-2011); Radio Show, "The Gradations of Evil Scale," San Francisco with Phil Hendrie (2009); Editor, "The Anatomy of Evil" (2009); Host, TV Show, "Most Evil" (2006-2007); Editor, "Personality Disorders: Treatable and Untreatable" (2006); Author, "The Fate of Borderline Patients" (1990); Editor, "Essential Papers on Borderline" (1985); Editor, "Treating Schizophrenic Patients" (1983); Editor, "Borderline Disorders" (1981); Author, "The Borderline Syndromes" (1980); Contributor, Over 250 Articles, Professional Journals **Awards:** Best Paper, American Academy of Psychoanalysis (2017); Lifetime Service Award, National Association of Forensic Counselors **Membership:** American Psychopathology Association; American College of Psychiatrists; Royal College of Psychiatrists in England; International Society of the Study of Personality Disorders; National Association of Forensic Counselors; Board Member, Musica Sacra; Reform Club of London; Edition Board of Personality and Mental Health, Faculty, Columbia Psychoanalytic Institute; College of Psychiatrists; Mexican Academy of Forensic Investigators; Phi Beta Kappa **Marquis Who's Who Honors:** Distinguished Humanitarian (2017) **To what do you attribute your success:** Dr. Stone attributes his success to a big capacity for work, little need for sleep, knowing many languages, traveling, lecturing on six continents, and getting familiar with many different cultures. **Why did you become involved in your profession or industry:** Dr. Stone always wanted to become a physician since he was ten years old. **What do you consider to be the highlight of your career:** The highlight of Dr. Stone's career was his TV series on the Discovery Channel called "Most Evil." **Where will you be in five years:** In five years, Dr. Stone will either be in New York City or underground in New York City. **Hobbies:** Piano; Collecting rare books; Languages **Political Affiliations:** Independent **Religion:** Jewish **Shipping Address:** 225 Central Park W, Apartment 114, New York, NY, 10024

William Edward Stone

Title: Academic Administrator, Consultant **Industry:** Education/Educational Services **Company Name:** eAdvancement Consortium **Date of Birth:** 08/13/1945 **Place of Birth:** Peoria **State:** IL **Parents:** Dean Proctor Stone; Katherine (Jamison) Stone **Marital Status:** Married **Spouse Name:** Deborah Ann Duncan **Children:** Jennifer; Allison; Molly **Education:** MBA, Stanford University (1969); AB, Stanford University (1967) **Career:** Principal, eAdvancement Consortium (2001-Present); Consultant in Educational Advancement, Stanford University (2001-Present); President Emeritus, Stanford Alumni Association, Stanford University (2001-Present); President, Stanford Sierra Programs LLC, South Lake Tahoe, CA (1998-2001); Director, Stanford Sierra Programs LLC, South Lake Tahoe, CA (1998-2001); President, Stanford Alumni Association Division, Stanford University (1998-2001); Director, Stanford Alumni Association Division, Stanford University (1998-2001); President, Stanford Alumni Association (1990-1998); CEO, Stanford Alumni Association (1990-1998); President, Alpine Chalet, Inc., Alpine Meadows, CA (1987-2001); Director, Alpine Chalet, Inc., Alpine Meadows, CA (1987-2001); Executive Director, Stanford Alumni Association (1977-1990); Assistant to President, Stanford University (1971-1977); Assistant Dean, Stanford University (1969-1971) **Career Related:** Secretary, University ProNet, Inc. (1996-2000); President, Council of Alumni Association Executives (1991-1992); Chairman, Board of Directors, University ProNet, Inc. (1990-1992); Vice President, Council of Alumni Association Executives (1990-1991); Director, Council of Alumni Association Executives (1989-1993); Trustee, Council for Advancement and Support of Education (1988-1991) **Civic:** Board Member, Stanford Emeriti Council (2010-Present); Board of Governors, Stanford Associates (2010-2014); President, Stanford Emeriti Council (2008-2010); President, Stanford Emeriti Council (2006-2008); Vice President, Stanford Emeriti Council (2003-2006); Director, Stanford Historical Society (2002-2010); Trustee, Watkins Discretionary Fund (1979-1982); Chairman, Board of Directors, Faculty Club Nominating Committee, Stanford University (1979-1981); Board of Directors, North County YMCA (1975-1976); Community Advisory Board, Stanford University; Women's Community Center, Stanford University **Creative Works:** Oral History for Stanford Historical Society **Awards:** Governors Award, Stanford Associates (2010); Award of Merit, Stanford Associates (2005); Steuben Apple Award (2002); Tribute Award Council for Advancement and Support of Education (1991); K.M. Cuthbertson Award, Stanford University (1987) **Membership:** Stanford Faculty Club **Marquis Who's Who Honors:** Albert Nelson Marquis Lifetime Achievement Award (2017) **To what do you attribute your success:** Mr. Stone attributes his success to practicing organizational management and leadership with a sense of humor. **Why did you become involved in your profession or industry:** Coming from a banking family in Illinois, Mr. Stone was sent to boarding school at a young age due to a lack of teachers in his town. He was placed at very good schools and made his way to Stanford University, where he remained for the rest of his life. **What do you consider to be the highlight of your career:** The highlight of Mr. Stone's career was bringing in talent and leadership over many years. He was also proud to have helped with the development and construction of the Alumni Center, which is an amazing venue for events. **Shipping Address:** 1061 Cathcart Way, Stanford, CA, 94305

Neil Ralph Stout, PhD

Title: History Educator (Retired) **Industry:** Education/Educational Services **Company Name:** The University of Vermont **Date of Birth:** 08/12/1932 **Place of Birth:** Marietta **State:** OH **Parents:** Ralph Plumly Stout; Carrie Baker Stout **Marital Status:** Widowed **Spouse Name:** Marilyn Blumenstiel (9/8/1956, Deceased 12/3/2017) **Children:** Hilary Ann; Peter Neil (Deceased 12/24/2015) **Education:** PhD, University of Wisconsin (1961); MS, University of Wisconsin (1958); BA, Harvard University (1954) **Career:** Professor Emeritus, Department of History, The University of Vermont, Burlington, VT (2000-Present); Professor, Department of History, The University of Vermont, Burlington, VT (1964-2000); Assistant Professor, Department of History, Texas A&M University, College Station, TX (1961-1964) **Career Related:** Editor, Vermont Historical Society, Montpelier, VT (1993-1994); President, New England Historical Association, Worcester, MA (1979-1980) **Civic:** Chair, Buildings and Grounds, The Cathedral Church of St. Paul, Burlington, VT (2006-Present); Archivist, The Cathedral Church of St. Paul, Burlington, VT (2005-Present); President, Friends of Fletcher Free Library, Burlington, VT (2009-2011); Senior Warden, The Cathedral Church of St. Paul, Burlington, VT (2008-2009); Junior Warden, The Cathedral Church of St. Paul, Burlington, VT (2007-2008); Vestry Member, The Cathedral Church of St. Paul, Burlington, VT (2006-2009); Trustee, Fletcher Free Library (2005-2007); Vice President, Friends of Fletcher Free Library, Burlington, VT (2001-2009); Historian, Green Mountain Hash House Harriers (1990-1994); Historian, Vermont State Historical Preservation Advisory Council, Montpelier, VT (1990-1994) **Military Service:** U.S. Army, France (1954-1956) **Creative Works:** Author, "The History Student's Vade Mecum," IMEHA (2012); Author, "The History Student's Vade Mecum," IMEHA (2008); Author, "The Perfect Crisis" (1976); Author, "Royal Navy in America, 1760-1775" (1973); Contributor, Articles, Professional Journals **Membership:** Preservation Burlington; Friends the Fletcher Free Library, Burlington, VT; Fleming Museum of Art, University of Vermont; Lake Champlain Maritime Museum; Green Mountain Club; Green Mountain Hash House Harriers; Green Mountain Athletic Association; Local Motion; Vermont Historical Society; Center for Research on Vermont; Organization of American Historians **Marquis Who's Who Honors:** Albert Nelson Marquis Lifetime Achievement Award (2017) **To what do you attribute your success:** Dr. Stout attributes his success to hard work and a love of learning. **Why did you become involved in your profession or industry:** He became involved in his profession because it is a whole lot easier than farming. **What do you consider to be the highlight of your career:** A highlight of his career is preparing students for the world. **Where will you be in five years:** In five years, he will be still active at 90. **Political Affiliations:** Liberal **Religion:** Episcopalian **Shipping Address:** 129 Robinson Pkwy, Burlington, VT, 05401

Wayne Ralph Strasbaugh

Title: Lawyer **Industry:** Law and Legal Services **Company Name:** Ballard Spahr LLP **Date of Birth:** 07/20/1948 **Place of Birth:** Lancaster **State:** PA **Parents:** Wayne Veily Strasbaugh; Jane Irene (Marzolf) Strasbaugh **Marital Status:** Married **Spouse Name:** Carol Lynne Taylor (6/8/1974) **Children:** Susan; Wayne T.; Elizabeth **Education:** JD, Harvard University, Cum Laude (1979); PhD in History, Harvard University (1976); AM in History, Harvard University (1971); AB, Bowdoin College, Summa Cum Laude (1970) **Career:** Senior Counsel, Ballard Spahr LLP, Philadelphia, PA (2018- Present), Chairman, Tax Group, Ballard Spahr LLP (2001-2015); Partner, Ballard Spahr LLP, Philadelphia, PA (1988-2018); Associate, Ballard Spahr LLP, Philadelphia, PA (1984-1988); Associate, Morgan Lewis & Bockius, Philadelphia, PA (1982-1984); Associate, Jones Day Reavis & Pogue, Cleveland, OH (1979-1982) **Civic:** Director, The Church Foundation (2011-Present); Board of Managers, Pennsylvania Society of Sons of the Revolution (2008-Present) **Membership:** Chairman, Committee, ABA (2007-2009); Regent, American College of Tax Counsel (2003-2009); Chairman, Philadelphia Bar Association (1999-2000); Vice-chairman, Philadelphia Bar Association (1997-1998); Secretary-treasurer, Philadelphia Bar Association (1996); Council Member, Philadelphia Bar Association (1995); Chairman, Committee, ABA (1992-1994); Chairman, Federal Tax Committee, Philadelphia Bar Association (1992); Tax Section, ABA; American College of Tax Counsel; Tax Section, Philadelphia Bar Association; Tax Section, New York State Bar Association **Bar Admissions:** United States District Court Eastern District of Pennsylvania (1983); Pennsylvania (1983); United States Court Appeals for the Federal Circuit (1982); United States Tax Court (1980); United States Court of Federal Claims (1980); State of Ohio (1979); United States District Court Northern District of Ohio (1979) **Marquis Who's Who Honors:** Lifetime Achievement 2016 **Religion:** Episcopalian **Business Address:** 1735 Market Street, 51st Floor, Philadelphia, PA, 19103 **Shipping Address:** 139 W Springfield Ave, Philadelphia, PA, 19118

Renate Strelau

Title: Historical Researcher, Artist **Industry:** Fine Art **Date of Birth:** 02/01/1951 **Place of Birth:** Berlin **Country of Origin:** Germany **Parents:** Wernerr Ernst Strelau; Gerda Gertrud (Bargel) Strelau **Education:** MFA, American University (1991); MA, American University (1985); BA, University of California, Berkeley (1974) **Certifications:** Certificate, Arabic Language Proficiency, Johns Hopkins University (1976) **Career:** Research Assistant, Iranian Embassy, Washington, DC (1975-1980) **Creative Works:** Shaolin Kung Fu Competitor/Performer, International Chinese Martial Arts Tournament, Santa Monica, CA (2017-2018); Shaolin Kung Fu Competitor/Performer, International Chinese Martial Arts Tournament, Pasadena, CA (2017); Exhibitor, Group Show, International Art Exhibit, India (2015); Exhibitor, One-Woman Show, Will Rogers State Beach, Pacific Palisades, Los Angeles, CA (2014); Exhibitor, One-Woman Show, Woodley Park, Lake Balboa, CA (2012); Exhibitor, One-Woman Show, Sylvan, North Hollywood, CA (2010); Exhibitor, One-Woman Show, 7538, Reseda, CA (2009-2010); Exhibitor, One-Woman Show, Sherman Way, San Fernando Valley, CA (2008); Exhibitor, One-Woman Show, Bank of America Corporation, Arlington, VA (2004-2005); Exhibitor, Group Show, Khoja Gallery, Arlington, VA (2002); Exhibitor, Group Show, Watkins Gallery, American University (1999); Exhibitor, One-Woman Show, Riggs Bank, Arlington, VA (1994-1995); Exhibitor, One-Woman Show, Cafe Espresso, Berkeley, CA (1973); Represented Artist, Permanent Collection, C. Law Watkins Memorial Collection, American University Museum, Washington, DC **Membership:** American Historical Association; Organization of American Historians; Lifetime Member, Society for Historians of American Foreign Relations **Marquis Who's Who Honors:** Albert Nelson Marquis Lifetime Achievement Award (2017) **Business Address:** PO Box 371444, Reseda, CA, 91377 **Shipping Address:** 7538 Nestle Ave., Reseda, CA, 91335

Harvey Alan Alan Strickon

Title: Attorney **Industry:** Law and Legal Services **Company Name:** Paul Hastings LLP **Date of Birth:** 11/09/1947 **Place of Birth:** Brooklyn **State:** NY **Parents:** Milton Strickon; Norma (Goodhartz) Strickon **Marital Status:** Married **Spouse Name:** Linda Carol (Meltzer) Strickon (7/2/1972) **Children:** Joshua Andrew; Meredith Cindy (Moses); Erica Stacey (Rosenberg) **Education:** JD, New York University School of Law (1971); BBA, Bernard M. Baruch School of Business and Public Administration (Now Zicklin School of Business, Baruch College), The City College of New York (1968) **Career:** From Partner to Counsel, Paul Hastings LLP, New York, NY (1991-Present); From Associate to Partner, Kaye, Scholer, Fierman, Hays & Handler (Now Arnold & Porter Kaye Scholer LLP), New York, NY (1980-1991); Associate, Moses & Singer, New York, NY (1973-1980); Law Clerk to Honorable George Rosling, U.S. District Court Judge, Eastern District of New York, Brooklyn, NY (1971-1973) **Career Related:** Chair, Complaint Mediation Panel, The Association of the Bar of the City of New York; Attorney Grievance Committees, Appellate Division, First Judicial Department, New York State Supreme Court; Mediation Panel, U.S. District Court for the Eastern District of New York; Mediation Register, U.S. Bankruptcy Court, Eastern District of New York; Mediation Register, U.S. Bankruptcy Court, Southern District of New York **Civic:** Nassau County Republican Committee, Great Neck, NY (1982-Present); Candidate, District Court Judge, Nassau County, Third District Court, North Hempstead, NY (2012); Vice Chairman, Board of Directors, Flushing Community Volunteer Ambulance Corps, Flushing, NY (1987-1992); Chairman, Board of Directors, Flushing Community Volunteer Ambulance Corps, Flushing, NY (1981-1986) **Creative Works:** Co-Author, "Enforcing Judgments and Collecting Debts in New York" (1996) **Awards:** Award for Alumni Achievement, Bernard M. Baruch College, The City University of New York (2018); Super Lawyer, Thomson Reuters (2011); Super Lawyer, Thomson Reuters (2007-2009) **Membership:** American Bar Association; Former Chair, Committee on Professional Discipline, The Association of the Bar of the City of New York; The Association of Commercial Finance Attorneys, Inc.; New York Law Institute **Bar Admissions:** U.S. Tax Court (2006); U.S. District Court, State of Connecticut (1996); U.S. District Court, State of Arizona (1991); U.S. District Court, Western District, State of New York (1981); U.S. District Court, Northern District, State of New York (1980); U.S. Supreme Court (1975); Second Circuit, U.S. Court of Appeals (1973); U.S. District Court, Southern District, State of New York (1973); U.S. District Court, Eastern District, State of New York (1973); State of New York (1972) **Marquis Who's Who Honors:** Albert Nelson Marquis Lifetime Achievement Award (2017) **Hobbies:** Travel; Food and wine; Collecting books, art, fountain pens, and timepieces **Political Affiliations:** Republican **Religion:** Jewish **Shipping Address:** 200 Park Avenue, Mezzanine, New York, NY, 10166 **Website:** http://www.paulhastings.com

John Fred Stroud Jr.

Title: Judge (Retired) **Industry:** Law and Legal Services **Company Name:** Arkansas Court of Appeals, Arkansas Supreme Court **Date of Birth:** 10/03/1931 **Place of Birth:** Hope **State:** AR **Parents:** John Fred Stroud; Clarine (Steel) Stroud **Marital Status:** Married **Spouse Name:** Marietta Kimball (6/1/1958) **Children:** John Fred, III (Deceased 2016); Ann Kimball White; Tracy Steel Waters **Education:** LLB, University of Arkansas (1960); BA, University of Arkansas (1959); Coursework, Hendrix College, Conway, AR (1949-1951) **Certifications:** Certified Mediator, Arkansas Bar Association **Career:** Mediator, Arbitrator and Neutral Evaluator, ADR, Inc. (2005-2016); Chief Judge, Arkansas Court of Appeals, Little Rock, AR (2001-2004); Judge, Arkansas Court of Appeals, Little Rock, AR (1996-2001); Partner, Smith, Stroud, McClerkin, Dunn & Nutter (1981-1995); Associate Justice, Arkansas Supreme Court, Little Rock, AR (1980); Partner, Smith, Stroud, McClerkin, Dunn & Nutter (1963-1979); Legislative Assistant, United States Senator John L. McClellan (1962-1963); City Attorney, City of Texarkana, AR (1961); Partner, Stroud & McClerkin (1959-1962) **Career Related:** Fellow, American Bar Foundation **Civic:** Advisory Board, Donald W. Reynolds Institute on Aging (2006-2015); Campaign, United Way of Greater Texarkana (1988); President, Caddo Area Council, Boy Scouts of America (1971-1973); Chairman, Texarkana Regional Airport Authority (1966-1967); Trustee, Arkansas Nature Conservancy; Board of Directors, Arkansas Community Foundation; Board Member, United Methodist Foundation of Arkansas; President, Red River Valley Association; Commissioner, Red River Compact Commission; Vice Chairman, Arkansas Water Code Study Commission; Former Chairman, Council on Ministries, Texarkana United Methodist Church **Military Service:** Lieutenant Colonel, U.S. Air Force (1951-1956); Jet Pilot, U.S. Air Force (1951-1956); Retired Reservist **Creative Works:** Comments Editor, Law Review, Arkansas Law School **Awards:** Golden Gavel Award (2015); Presidential Award of Excellence (2014-2015); Joint Presidential Award of Excellence, Arkansas Bar Association and Arkansas Bar Foundation (2007); Golden Gavel Award (2006); Charles L. Carpenter Memorial Award (1997-1998); Presidential Award of Excellence (1997-1998); C.E. Ransick Award of Excellence, Arkansas Bar Association (1990-1991); Award of Exceptional Accomplishment, Arkansas State Chamber of Commerce (1986); Outstanding Alumnus of University of Arkansas School of Law (1980); C.E. Palmer Award, Texarkana Chamber of Commerce (1979); Award of Exceptional Accomplishment, Arkansas State Chamber of Commerce (1972); One of Five Outstanding Young Men of Arkansas (1967); Outstanding Young Man of Texarkana (1966); Distinguished Graduate, Aviation Cadets (1953); Silver Beaver Awards, Boys Scouts of America; Eagle Scout Awards, Boys Scouts of America; Distinguished Eagle Scout Award **Membership:** Chairman, Arkansas Chapter, American Bar Foundation (2011-2013); Chairman, Trust Committee, Arkansas Bar Foundation (2003-2006); President, Texarkana Country Club (1990-1992); President, Arkansas Bar Association (1987-1988); Chairman, Arkansas Chapter, American College Trust and Estate Counsel (1986-1991); President, Texarkana Bar Association (1982-1983); Chairman, Executive Council, Arkansas Bar Association (1979-1980); Chairman, Arkansas Bar Foundation (1974-1975); President, Texarkana Chamber of Commerce (1969); President, Texarkana Rotary (1965-1966); ABA; Past Chairman, Four States Area Estate Planning Council; State Bar of Texas; Past President, Miller County Bar Association; Southwest Arkansas Bar Association; Northeast Texas Bar Association; Board of Directors, University of Arkansas Law Alumni Society; Association of Attorney-Mediators; President, Blue Key; Kappa Sigma Fraternity; Chairman, Former Chairman of the Board, Former Head Usher, Committee for Building for Construction of Family Life Center **Bar Admissions:** Supreme Court of Texas (1988); Supreme Court of the United States (1963); Arkansas Supreme Court (1959) **Hobbies:** Tennis; Golf; Hunting; Fishing **Religion:** Protestant **Shipping Address:** 405 Walnut Street, Texarkana, AR, 71854

Scott Wallace Stucky

Title: Chief Judge **Industry:** Law and Legal Services **Company Name:** United States Court of Appeals for the Armed Forces **Date of Birth:** 01/11/1948 **Place of Birth:** Hutchinson **State:** KS **Parents:** Joe Edward; Emma Clara (Graber) Stucky **Marital Status:** Married (8/18/1973) **Spouse Name:** Jean Elsie Seibert **Children:** Mary-Clare; Joseph **Education:** Honorary LLD, Collegium Augustinianum, Philadelphia, PA (2016); LLM, George Washington University, with High Honors (1983); MA, Trinity University, San Antonio (1980); JD, Harvard University (1973); BA, Wichita State University, Kansas, Summa Cum Laude (1970) **Career:** Adjunct Professor, George Washington University School of Law (2016-Present); Judge, United States Court of Appeals for the Armed Forces, Washington (2006-Present); General Counsel, United States Senate Armed Services Committee (2003-2006); Principal Minority Counsel, United States Senate Armed Services Committee (2001-2003); General Counsel, United States Senate Armed Services Committee (1996-2001); Legislative Counsel, U.S. Air Force, Washington (1983-1996); Chief, Docketing & Service Branch, Nuclear Regulatory Commission, Washington (1982-1983); Associate, Ginsburg, Feldman & Bress, Washington (1978-1982); Lecturer, Business Law, Maria Regina College, Syracuse, NY (1977) **Career Related:** Colonel, Appellate Military Judge, U.S. Air Force Court of Criminal Appeals (2001-2003); Air Reserve Personnel Center (1998-1999); Colonel, Appellate Military Judge, U.S. Air Force Court of Criminal Appeals (1997-1998); U.S. Air Force Judiciary (1995-1997); Senior Reservist, Air Force Legal Services Agency (1991-2001); Colonel, Appellate Military Judge, U.S. Air Force Court of Criminal Appeals (1991-1995); Congressional Fellow, Office of Senator John Warner (1986); Reserve Judge Advocate, U.S. Air Force Reserve, Washington (1982-2003) **Civic:** Board of Directors, Adoption Service Information Agency (2004-2007); Board of Directors, Adoption Service Information Agency (1998-2002) **Military Service:** Captain, United States Air Force (1973-1978) **Creative Works:** Contributor, Articles, Professional Journals **Awards:** Decorated Meritorious Service Medal with Two Oak Leaf Clusters; Legion of Merit **Membership:** Board of Directors, Appellate Judges Education Institution (2012-Present); Appellate Judges Conference Executive Committee, Appellate Judges Conference Executive Board, American Bar Association; Reserve Officers Association; Judges Advocates Association; The Army and Navy Club, Washington; Federal Bar Association; National Board of Directors, Phi Alpha Theta; Phi Delta Phi; Phi Kappa Phi; Sigma Phi Epsilon; National Board of Directors, Omricon Delta Kappa (2006-2010); National Commander-in-Chief, Military Order of the Loyal Legion of the United States (1993-1995); National Vice Commander, Military Order of the Loyal Legion of the United States (1989-1993); National Treasurer, Military Order of the Loyal Legion of the United States (1987-1989); Wichita State University Alumni Association (1986-1992); Chapter Vice Commander, Sons of Union Veterans Civil War (1986-1988); State Commander, Recorder, Military Order of the Loyal Legion of the United States (1984-1992); Chapter President, Wichita State University Alumni Association (1981-1986) **Bar Admissions:** U.S. Court of Appeals, DC Circuit (1979); District of Columbia Bar (1979); U.S. Supreme Court (1976); U.S. Court of Military Appeals (1974); U.S. Court of Appeals, 10th Circuit (1973); U.S. District Court, Kansas (1973); Kansas State Bar (1973) **Marquis Who's Who Honors:** Distinguished Humanitarian (2017) **Political Affiliations:** Republican **Religion:** Episcopalian **Shipping Address:** 11004 Homeplace Ln., Potomac, MD, 20854

Bernhard Stumpf

Title: Associate Professor **Industry:** Medicine & Health Care **Company Name:** University of Idaho **Date of Birth:** 09/21/1948 **Place of Birth:** Neustadt an der Weinstrasse **Country of Origin:** Germany **Parents:** Josef Stumpf; Katharina (Cervinka) Stumpf **Education:** Doctor Rerum Naturalium, Saarland University, Saarbrücken, Germany (1981); Diploma in Physics, Saarland University, Saarbrücken, Germany (1975) **Career:** Associate Professor, Physics Department, University of Idaho, Moscow, ID (1988-Present); Visiting Associate Professor, Physics Department, University of Windsor, Canada (1986-1988); Associate Research Scientist, Atomic Beams Laboratory, New York University (1985-1986); Instructor of Physics, New York University, New York, NY (1984-1986); Assistant Research Scientist, Atomic Beams Laboratory, New York University, New York, NY (1984-1985); Research Associate, Joint Institute for Laboratory Astrophysics, University of Colorado, Boulder (1981-1984); Research Assistant, Physics Department, Saarland University, Saarbrücken (1976-1981) **Career Related:** Secretary, National Association of Academies of Science (2004-2006); Chairman, Northwest Conference, American Physical Society, Moscow, ID (2004); Chairman, Conference on Atomic and Molecular Collisions Excited States, Moscow, ID (1990) **Creative Works:** Contributor, Articles to Professional Journals **Awards:** Dr. Eduard-Martin Prize for Excellence in Dissertation Research, Saarland University, Saarbrücken, Germany (1983); Postdoctoral Fellow, German Science Foundation, University of Colorado (1981-1983) **Membership:** Secretary, National Association of Academies of Science (2004-2006); Chairman, Northwest Conference, American Physical Society, Moscow, ID (2004); German Physical Society; American Association for the Advancement of Science; American Association of University Professors; Optical Society of America; American Chemical Society **Hobbies:** Cats; Fine dining **Religion:** Roman Catholic **Shipping Address:** 825 W C St., Moscow, ID, 83843

Patricia Ann Suggs

Title: Artist **Industry:** Fine Art **Date of Birth:** 03/17/1936 **Place of Birth:** Reedley **State:** CA **Parents:** Charles Kofoed; Dorothy Rema (Prouty) Kofoed **Marital Status:** Married **Spouse Name:** Robert Reed Suggs (7/28/1961) **Children:** Richard William **Education:** Coursework, Leighton Fine Art Academy, San Francisco, CA (1974-1981) **Career:** Pastel Landscape Painter; Floral Painter **Career Related:** Judge, Fine Arts Club, Santa Clara County (1997); Judge, Fine Arts Club, Santa Clara County (1991); Judge, Fine Arts Club, Alameda County Fair (1990-2003); Judge, Fine Arts Club, Sonoma County Fair (1990); Judge, Fine Arts Club, The Peninsula (1984-1998); Judge, Fine Arts Club, Northern California (1984-1998); Judge, Fine Arts Club, San Joaquim Valley (1984-1998); Judge, Fine Arts Club, California County Fairs (1984-1998); Teacher, Workshops, State of California; Teacher, Workshops, State of New Mexico **Creative Works:** Exhibitor, Group Shows, Hurrington Gallery (2014); Exhibitor, Group Shows, Binney & Smith Gallery, Slater Memorial Museum of Norwich Free Academy (2006); Exhibitor, Group Shows, Lone Star Pastel Society (2003); Exhibitor, Group Shows, The Butler Institute of American Art (2003); Exhibitor, One-woman Shows, New Museum Los Gatos (1998); Exhibitor, Group Shows, Fremont Art Association (1993); Exhibitor, Group Shows, Ashland Gallery (1990); Exhibitor, Group Shows, Runnings Gallery, Seattle, WA (1990); Exhibitor, Group Shows, Pastel Society of the West Coast (1989-1994); Exhibitor, One-woman Shows, Gadabout Gallery, Los Gatos, CA (1986); Exhibitor, One-woman Shows, Great Western Savings & Loan, Fremont, CA (1982); Exhibitor, One-woman Shows, Rosicrucian Egyptian Museums, Rosicrucian Order, San Jose, CA (1982); Exhibitor, Group Shows, Pastel Society of America (1980); Exhibitor, One-woman Shows, Group 21, Los Gatos, CA (1978); Exhibitor, Group Shows, Society of Western Artists (1976-1993) **Awards:** Los Angeles Great American Art Works Pastel Award, Degas Pastel Society (2006); Daler Rowney Award (2006); Gold Medallion, Society of Western Artists (2005); Canson Award, Pastel Society of Oregon (2003); Pastel Journal Award (2002); H.K. Holbein Award (2001); Faber Castill Award (2001); Best of Show Award, Fremont Art Association (1993); Grumbacher Award Medallion, NLAPW (1993); Best Pastel Plaque, Pastel Society of America (1993); First Place in Pastels, Society of Western Artists (1993); Award of Merit, Pastel Society of the West Coast (1991); Best Floral Award, Pastel Society of America (1980); Leann Simpson Heim Memorial Award; Master Circle Award, Society of Western Artists **Membership:** Chairman, Society of Western Artists (1998); Treasurer, IAPS (1994-2013); Director of Exhibitions, Allied Artists West (1991-1992); Board Member, Pastel Society of America (1986-2008); Board of Trustees, Society of Western Artists (1986-1996); Advisory Board, Pastel Society of the West Coast (1984-2013); Triton Museum of Art; IAPS; Society of Western Artists; NLAPW **Marquis Who's Who Honors:** Albert Nelson Marquis Lifetime Achievement Award (2017) **Shipping Address:** 4127 Beebe Cir., San Jose, CA, 95135

Theodore T. Suh

Industry: Education/Educational Services **Education:** MD, PhD, University of Cincinnati (1998); BA, Harvard University (1988) **Career:** Associate Clinical Professor, University of Michigan **Awards:** Top Medical Director, International Association of Top Professionals (2017) **Membership:** American Geriatric Society; Gerontological Society of America **Hobbies:** Hiking; Travel

James Gerald Sullivan

Title: Small Business Owner **Industry:** Business Management/Business Services **Date of Birth:** 09/13/1935 **Place of Birth:** Bad Axe **State:** MI **Parents:** John Thomas Sullivan; Frances Eugena (O'Henley) Sullivan **Marital Status:** Married **Spouse Name:** Florence Marie Tack (9/12/1959) **Children:** Kevin Michael (Deceased); Kathleen Marie **Education:** Coursework, Highland Park College (1959-1960); Coursework, University of Detroit - Mercy (1957-1958); Coursework, Central Michigan University **Career:** Owner, Jerry's Barber Shop, Kinde, Bad Axe, MI (1963-Present); Senior Member, MoneySports.Com Investor Relations (2014); Senior Member, GNLD International (2013-2015); Independent Ionways Associates (2013); Distributor, Alka Viva Distributor (2013); Water Specialist, Alka Viva Distributor (2013); Water Distributor, Ionized Antioxidant (2010); Director, ASEA (2010); Distributor, ASEA (2010); Regional Manager, Primerica Financial Services, Michigan (2010); Elected Member, Executive Committee, Veterans Club, National Rural Letter Carriers' Association (2009); Distributor, Water Specialist, Enagic USA Inc. (2009); Regional Manager, Primerica Financial Services, Bad Axe, MI (1985-2008); Rural Letter Carrier, United States Postal Service, Bad Axe, MI (1982-1998); Sales Representative, WLEW Radio Station, Bad Axe, MI (1981-1982); Sales Representative, Thumb Blanket, Bad Axe, MI (1980-1981); Treasurer, Colfax Township, Bad Axe, MI (1979-1990); Purchasing Agent, Walbro Corporation, Cass City, MI (1979-1980); Purchasing Agent, Thumb Electrical Cooperative, Ubly, MI (1966-1979) **Career Related:** Michigan Chapter, National Rural Letter Carriers' Association (2015); Professional Tee.Com Golf Partnership (2014); Elected President, Armed Forces Veterans Club (2011); Assistant National Secretary, Armed Forces Veterans Club (2011); Treasurer, Armed Forces Veterans Club (2011); Distributor, Ionized Antioxidant Water (2010); Enagic Distributor Water Specialist (2009); Elected Member, Executive Committee, Veterans Club, National Rural Letter Carriers' Association (2009); Notary Public, State of Michigan (1968); Loss Clerk, Toplis & Harding Wagner & Gliddon, Detroit, MI (1959-1961); Inventory Control Clerk, Carrick Products Co., Royal Oak, MI (1957-1959); Independent Distributor, Alkaline Antioxidant Ionized Multi-Clustered Water; National Secretary, Armed Forces Veterans Club, National Rural Letter Carriers' Association; Treasurer, Armed Forces Veterans Club, National Rural Letter Carriers' Association **Civic:** President, Huron County Township Association, Michigan (1988-1990); Leader, Boy Scouts of America, Bad Axe, MI (1975-1977); Eucharistic Minister, Lector, Ushers Club, Sacred Heart Church **Military Service:** U.S. Army (1954-1956) **Creative Works:** Honoree, National Profile Plus (2017) **Awards:** Featured, National Profile Plus Magazine (2017) **Membership:** President, Tip of the Thumb Dance Club (2005-Present); Re-elected National Secretary-Treasurer, National Armed Forces Veterans Club, National Rural Letter Carrier Association (2012); President, Bad Axe Lions Club, Lions Club International (2009-2010); President, Bad Axe Lions Club, Lions Club International (2006-2007); State Secretary, Michigan Division, National Rural Letter Carriers Association (1999-2015); President, Huron County Rural Letter Carriers Association (1988-2003); President, Bad Axe Lions Club, Lions Club International (1979-1980); President, Community Club (1976-1977); President, 4-H Club (1948-1950); The American Legion; Lion Tamer, Chaplain, Lions Club International; Council 1546, Knights of Columbus **Marquis Who's Who Honors:** Distinguished Humanitarian (2017) **Hobbies:** Gardening; Golfing; Swimming; Fishing **Political Affiliations:** Republican **Religion:** Roman Catholic **Shipping Address:** 122 W Richardson Rd, Bad Axe, MI, 48413

Stanley Eugene Summers

Title: Mechanical Engineer **Industry:** Engineering **Company Name:** Ketema A&E **Date of Birth:** 10/02/1925 **Place of Birth:** Sterling **State:** CO **Parents:** Matthew Marion Summers; Hazel J. (Snider) Summers **Marital Status:** Married **Spouse Name:** Jaclyn A. Marquart (10/15/1977); Dorothy E. Hanneman (Married 6/5/1944, Divorced 10/1977) **Children:** Daniel E.; Shirley A. Stephanie Ann; Jeffrey Eugene **Education:** University of California, Los Angeles **Career:** Mechanical Engineer, Senior Aerospace Ketema, El Cajon, CA (1990-2015); Mechanical Engineer, Ametek Calmec (1959-1990); Mechanical Engineer, Interstate Engineering, El Segundo, CA (1947-1959) **Awards:** Recipient, Snoopy Award, NASA (2004); Recipient, Spirit of Excellence Award (1992); Recipient, MacDonnell Douglas President's Award (1991); Recipient, NASA Achievement Award (1971); Recipient, Douglas Aircraft VIP Award (1968) **Membership:** American Society of Mechanical Engineers **Marquis Who's Who Honors:** Albert Nelson Marquis Lifetime Achievement Award (2017) **Hobbies:** Woodworking; RC models **Political Affiliations:** Republican **Religion:** Baptist **Shipping Address:** 2576 Katherine Ct., El Cajon, CA, 92020

Christine Johnson Suppes

Title: Writer, Online Publishing Executive **Industry:** Apparel & Fashion **Company Name:** Jewels by Christine, Fashionlines **Date of Birth:** 03/03/1953 **Place of Birth:** Los Angeles **State:** CA **Parents:** Robert Johnson; Jane Johnson **Marital Status:** Divorced **Spouse Name:** Patrick Suppes (1979, Divorced 2012) **Children:** Alexandra Christine; Michael Patrick **Career:** Chief Designer, Jewels by Christine (2002-Present); Publisher, Editor-in-Chief, www.Fashionlines.com, Stanford, CA (1999-2007); President, Gravure at Home, Stanford, CA (1997-2001); Editorial Assistant, San Francisco Examiner (1972-1973) **Career Related:** Freelance Fashion Writer (1999-Present); Advertising Consultant, Clarum Corporation, Palo Alto, CA (1997-Present); Advertising Consultant, Gravure Corporation, Dallas, TX (1997-2000) **Civic:** Supporter, Planned Parenthood (2016-Present); Supporter, Pacific Council on International Policy (2013-Present); Organizer, Teacher's Fund, Bing School, Stanford, CA (1995-Present); Supporter, St. Vincent de Paul Society; Supporter, American Red Cross, Palo Alto (2001); Peninsula Chapter, NARAL, Palo Alto (1997-2000); Supporter, Friends of The Costume Institute, The Metropolitan Museum of Art; Modern Art Council, San Francisco; Supporter, The Couture Council Museum, Fashion Institute of Technology **Creative Works:** Author, "Electric Fashion" (2015); Author, "Clinic" (1985); Author, "Amanda Prescott" (1984); Contributor, Reviews, San Francisco Chronicle **Membership:** Fine Art Museum of San Francisco; Couture Circle; Fashion Group International; Federation Francaise de la Couture; National Museum of Women in the Arts; SFMOMA Director's Circle; Friends of the Costume, Institute for the Metropolitan Museum of Art; Cantor Center for Visual Arts; Founding Grant Society, Stanford University **Marquis Who's Who Honors:** Albert Nelson Marquis Lifetime Achievement Award (2017) **Shipping Address:** 1335 Cowper Street, Palo Alto, CA, 94301

Diana Suttenfield

Title: Co-Founder **Industry:** Fine Art **Company Name:** Boarman Arts Center **Date of Birth:** 11/20/1944 **Place of Birth:** Washington **State:** DC **Education:** BFA, Maryland Institute College of Art, Baltimore, MD (1972) **Career:** Co-Founder, Boarman Arts Center, Martinsburg, WV (1982-1992); Co-Founder, German Street Gallery, Shepherdstown, WV (1973-1976) **Civic:** Donor, 26 Paintings, Local Hospice (2014); Founder, Friends of the Shepherdstown Riverfront (2002-2005); President, Friends of the Shepherdstown Riverfront (2002-2005) **Creative Works:** Exhibitor, U.S. Department of State (2008); Author, "Elegy for Barns" (2002); Exhibitor, Art in Embassies (1999-2008); Exhibitor, Baltimore Watercolor Society (1987); Exhibitor, Washington County Museum of Fine Arts (1984); Exhibitor, Aqueous Open (1983); Author, "The C and O Canal-An Illustrated History" (1981); Author, "Harpers Ferry-Pen and Ink Drawings" (1979); Author, "Martinsburg Sketchbook" (1978); Author, "Shepherdstown Sketchbook" (1976); Exhibitor, Johns Hopkins University; Exhibitor, Fall Exhibition, Pastel Society of America; Exhibitor, The National Arts Club; Exhibitor, Shades of Pastel, Maryland Pastel Society; Exhibitor, Mary Bell Galleries, Chicago, IL; Exhibitor, Callen McJunkin Gallery, Charleston, WV; Exhibitor, AIIA, Sheperdstown, WV **Awards:** Grantee, 40 Year Retrospective, Washington County Museum of Fine Arts, Hagerstown, MD (2015); Award, Maryland Pastel Society (1993); Award, Pastel Society of America (1993); Award, Maryland Pastel Society (1991); Award, Pastel Society of America (1991); Baltimore Water Color Society (1987); Woman of the Year in Art, West Virginia Women's Commission (1985); Artist of the Year, Women's Garden Council Club (1985) **Membership:** Lyme Art Association; Jefferson Arts Council; Ogunquit Arts Collaborative **Marquis Who's Who Honors:** Albert Nelson Marquis Lifetime Achievement Award (2017) **Why did you become involved in your profession or industry:** Ms. Suttenfield became involved in her profession because it is a way that she can communicate with people. Her landscapes resonate with people. **What do you consider to be the highlight of your career:** A highlight that stood out in Ms. Suttenfield's career is when her work was selected as part of the Arts in Embassies program. Her work traveled to different embassies around the world and represented the United States. She thought that it was terrific. **Hobbies:** Reading; Traveling; Walking **Business Address:** PO Box C, Shephardstown, WV, 25443

Paul J. Sutton

Title: Lawyer **Industry:** Law and Legal Services **Company Name:** Sutton Magidoff LLP **Date of Birth:** 06/16/1939 **Place of Birth:** New York **State:** NY **Parents:** Jack Schwartzberg; Frances (Drexler) Schwartzberg **Marital Status:** Married **Spouse Name:** Edith Diane Bers Sutton (9/18/1976) **Children:** Daniel Richard Bers; Lily Anna Bers **Education:** JD, Brooklyn Law School (1967); Coursework in Welding Metallurgy, University of California, Los Angeles (1963); Bachelor of Science in Biomedical Engineering, New York University (1962); Coursework, Industrial Management, Columbia University (1960) **Certifications:** Certified Welder, State of California **Career:** Founding Partner, Sutton Magidoff LLP, New York, NY (2009-Present); Chairman, Patent & Intellectual Property Practice, Greenberg Traurig, New York, NY (2000-2009); Chairman, Thelen Reid & Priest LLP, New York, NY (1995-2000); Senior Partner, Sutton, Basseches, Magidoff & Amaral, New York, NY (1982-1995); Partner, Sutton & Magidoff, New York, NY (1974-1982); Partner, Miskin & Sutton, New York, NY (1971-1974); Patent Counsel, Gulf and Western Industries, Inc., New York, NY (1969-1971); Patent Attorney, Darby & Darby, New York, NY (1967-1969); Patent Attorney, Nolte & Nolte, New York, NY (1965-1967); Design Engineer, Missiles & Space Systems Division, Douglas Aircraft Company, Los Angeles, CA (1962-1963) **Career Related:** Member, Editorial Panel, World Intellectual Property Review, London, England (2008-Present); Adjunct Professor, New York University Polytenchic School of Engineering (Now New York University Tandon School of Engineering) **Civic:** Chief Judge, American Intellectual Property Law Association, New York, NY (1981); Arbitrator, New York City Civil Court (1979-1986); Co-Founder, Hallen Center for Education, Mamaroneck, NY (1975) **Creative Works:** Author, "Commercial Law" (1971) **Membership:** Ethics and Professional Responsibilities Committee, ABA; Patent, Trademark and Copyright Section, ABA; Antitrust Law, New York State Bar Association; Patent and Trademarks Section, New York State Bar Association; The District of Columbia Bar; American Intellectual Property Law Association; New York Intellectual Property Law Association; American Judges Association; Trial Lawyers Association; East Hampton Licensing Executives Society Club; Yacht Licensing Executives Society Club; ABA; New York State Bar Association; The District of Columbia Bar **Hobbies:** Sailing; Photography; Computers **Shipping Address:** 300 Central Park W., Apt 16G, New York, NY, 10024

Richard Rockwell Swann

Title: Lawyer, Banker **Industry:** Law and Legal Services **Date of Birth:** 05/07/1940 **Place of Birth:** Orlando **State:** FL **Parents:** Pervie P. Swann; Maesther (Mears) Swann **Education:** JD, Duke University (1963); AB, Duke University (1961) **Career:** Member, Swann Hadley Stump Dietrich & Spears, P.A. (2011-Present); Member, Swann & Hadley (Now Swann Hadley Stump Dietrich & Spears, P.A.) (1990-2011); Member, Swann & Haddock, Orlando, FL (1963-1990) **Career Related:** Former Chairman, Board, American Pioneer, Inc., Orlando, FL; American Pioneer Savings Bank, Orlando, Fl; First Fidelity Savings & Loan, Orlando, FL; Director, Florida Next Foundation (2011-Present); Surrey Homes, LLC (Now Surrey Homes USA), Orlando, FL (2008-Present); Commercial Vehicle Insurance Company, SC (2004-Present); Property General, Inc., Orlando, FL (2003-Present); General Counsel, Director, Jefferson National Title Insurance Co. (1997-2003): American Heritage Homes USA, Inc. (1995-2000); Board of Visitors, Terry Sanford School Institute of Public Policy (Now Sanford School of Public Policy), Duke University (1989-1992); Director, Appointed by Governor Graham, Florida High Speed Rail Commission, Orlando, FL (1984-1988); Board of Governors, Overseas Investment Reins (1978-1982); Director, Overseas Private Investment Corporation, Washington, DC (1977-1982); Appointee of Governor Askew, Orange County Expressway Authority, Orlando, FL (1973-1975); Orange County Budget Commission, Orlando, FL (1971); Junior Achievement Board, Downtown Orlando Council (1969-1971); Member, Junior Achievement Board, Orlando, FL (1964-1968) **Membership:** ABA; The Florida Bar; Orange County Bar Association **Bar Admissions:** The Florida Bar (1963) **Political Affiliations:** Democrat

Jason W. Swindle Sr.

Title: Senior Partner **Industry:** Law and Legal Services **Company Name:** Swindle Law Group, P.C. **Parents:** Buck Swindle; Carol Swindle **Marital Status:** Married **Spouse Name:** Shea Burton (8/26/2001) **Children:** Jason Swindle Jr. (Jake); Reagan Burton **Education:** Honorary JD, Walter F. George School of Law (Now Mercer University School of Law), Mercer University, GA (2001); Third-Year Law Student Intern, District Attorney's Office - Coweta Judicial Circuit (2000); BBA in Marketing, Georgia Southern University (1997) **Career:** Partner, Criminal Defense Attorney, Swindle Law Group, P.C. (2012-Present); Partner, Criminal Defense Attorney, Drummond and Swindle P.C. (Now Swindle Law Group, P.C.) (2005-2012); Owner, Jason W. Swindle P.C. (Now Swindle Law Group, P.C.) (2003-2005); Associate, Word and Simmons P.C. (Now Johnson, Word & Simmons) (1998-2003) **Career Related:** Representative, Coweta Judicial Circuit on the Board of Governors for the State Bar of Georgia (2017-Present); Adjunct Professor, Criminology Department, University of West Georgia (2011-Present); Millennium Honor Roll, National Rifle Association (2000); Business Advisory Council, National Republican Congressional Committee; Hunting Advisory Committee, Georgia Outdoor News **Civic:** President, Chairman of the Board, West Georgia Autism Foundation (2017-Present); Fundraising Committee, Young Life (2015); Supporter, Autism Speaks, Inc. (2013); Speaker, Rotary International; Speaker, Kiwanis International; Speaker, Optimist International; Speaker, Academic Institutions; Speaker, Advocacy Groups **Creative Works:** Author, "The Truth About Confessions" (2013); Author, "High Court Strikes Down DUI Law" (2013); Syndicated Legal Columnist; Contributor, Articles to Times-Georgian, Douglas County Sentinel; Contributor, Articles to Professional Journals **Awards:** Super Lawyer in Criminal Defense, Super Lawyers (2017); Legal Elite Super Lawyer, Criminal Defense Legal Counsel, Rating Top 10 Lawyers in the State of Georgia (2016); Georgia's Top Rated Lawyers (2014); Named on the List of "Lawyers You Should Know"; Voted "Best Law Firm" in Carroll County, Reader's Choice Awards; Top 100 Lawyers, The National Trial Lawyers; Top 100 Criminal Defense Lawyers in Georgia, The National Trial Lawyers **Membership:** Board of Governors, The Bar Association of Carroll County (2015); The NCDD; Atlanta Bar Association; The Federalist Society; Georgia Association of Criminal Defense Lawyers; Lions Club International; Criminal Law Section, State Bar of Georgia; National Rifle Association; Carroll County Chamber of Commerce **Bar Admissions:** State Bar of Georgia (2003); Supreme Court of Georgia; United States Court of Appeals for the Eleventh Circuit; United States Court of Appeals for the Federal Circuit; United States District Court for the Middle District of Georgia; United States District Court for the Northern District of Georgia **Why did you become involved in your profession or industry:** Mr. Swindle became involved in his profession after seeing the movie, "To Kill a Mockingbird" when he was very young. He thought to himself, "Well, that's what I want to be when I grow up." Now, he loves what he does so much that he feels like he doesn't work. **What do you consider to be the highlight of your career:** One of the highlights of Mr. Swindle's career was during a trial involving aggravated assault with a motor vehicle. His client ran into a couple of businesses and tried to run over one of the business owners. Mr. Swindle was doubtful about their chances going in and during the case. Though a five year prison sentence was offered in the beginning, an offer of probation was given during the trial. When bringing this to his client, the client refused, and the end result was an acquittal on all charges. The trust Mr. Swindle's client had in his ability to represent him well really stood out and meant a lot to him. **Hobbies:** Hunting; Gardening; Watching FCC Football **Political Affiliations:** Conservative Liberal **Religion:** Protestant **Shipping Address:** 310 Tanner St., Swindle Law Group, P.C., Carrollton, GA, 30117

Assad Taha, PhD

Title: Acute Care Surgeon **Industry:** Medicine & Health Care **Company Name:** LAHEY CLINIC **Date of Birth:** 12/12/1955 **Place of Birth:** Nabatieh **Country of Origin:** Lebanon **Parents:** Muhyddin S. Taha; Hind (Jaber) Taha **Marital Status:** Married **Spouse Name:** Dima **Children:** Sarah; Maya; Rami **Education:** PhD in Physiology, University of Toledo (1992); Surgery Resident, Medical College of Ohio, Toledo, OH (1982-1985); Surgery Resident, Good Samaritan Hospital, Cincinnati, OH (1980-1982); MD, American University of Beirut (1980); BS in Biology, Chemistry, American University of Beirut (1976); LB in Mathematics, International College, Beirut, Lebanon (1973) **Certifications:** Certification in Surgical Critical Care, American Board of Surgery (1987-2027); Diplomate, American Board of Surgery (1986-2016); Certified Specialist in General Surgery, Royal College of Surgeons (1991) **Career:** Chief of Acute Care Surgery, Lahey Hospital and Medical Center, Boston, MA (2018-Present); Professor of Surgery, Morehouse School of Medicine, Grady Memorial Hospital, Atlanta, GA (2015-Present); General and Emergency Surgery, Bahaman Hospital (2009-2015); Associate Professor of Surgery and Physiology, Trauma and Critical Care, American University of Beirut (1993-2009); Associate Professor of Surgery, Medical College of Ohio (1991-1994); Assistant Professor of Surgery, Medical College of Ohio (1986-1991); Instructor in Surgery, Medical College of Ohio (1985-1986) **Career Related:** Associate Trauma Medical Director, Marcus Trauma Center, Grady Hospital, Atlanta, GA (2017-Present); Chief of Trauma and Critical Care, Morehouse School of Medicine, Grady Hospital, Atlanta, GA (2015-Present); Consultant, Trauma and Emergency Surgery, International Committee on Red Cross, Geneva, Switzerland (2009-2017) **Civic:** Trauma Outcome Performance Improvement Course (2016); Value Analysis Certification Course (2016); Just Culture, Training for Managers (2016); Workplace Accountability Champion Certification (2016); Overseas Security Advisory Council (2011); President, Parent Committee, American Community School (2008) **Creative Works:** Editorial Board, European Journal of Emergency Surgery and Intensive Care (1995-2005); Editorial Board, General Surgery and Laparoscopy and Intensive Care (1990-1995); Contributor, Articles, Professional Journals; Contributor, Chapters, Books; Deliverer, Lectures and Presentations **Awards:** American Medical Association Physician Recognition Award (2000, 1997, 1991); Grantee, American University of Beirut, University Research Board (1993-2000); Grantee, Ohio Lions (1987-1992); American Medical Association Physician Recognition Award (1987) **Membership:** Fellow of Royal College of Surgeons of Canada (1992); Fellow of American College or Surgeons (1988); Royal Society of Medicine; American University of Beirut Alumni Association; Disaster Medical Assistant Team; American Physiologic Society; European Association for Trauma and Emergency Surgery; Society for Critical Care Medicine; American Trauma Society **To what do you attribute your success:** Dr. Taha attributes his success to determination, open mindedness, adaptability, and hard work. **Why did you become involved in your profession or industry:** He aspires for excellence with a team spirit that benefits patients, students, and colleagues. He also seeks an overall mix as an outstanding clinician, dedicated researcher, energetic educator and effective administrator **What do you consider to be the highlight of your career:** Dr. Taha likes people and he communicates effectively with them. He does very well working with teams and is always building consensus while supporting team members at many levels **Where will you be in five years:** In five years, he will be practicing acute care surgery, together with teaching, research and administration. **Hobbies:** Spending time with his family; Chess; Soccer **Shipping Address:** 3104 Alexander Circle NE, Atlanta, GA, 30326

Ben Johnson Talbott Jr.

Title: Lawyer **Industry:** Law and Legal Services **Company Name:** Bardenwerper, Talbott & Roberts, PLLC **Date of Birth:** 05/02/1940 **Place of Birth:** Louisville **State:** KY **Parents:** Ben Johnson Talbott; Elizabeth (Farnsley) Talbott **Marital Status:** Married **Spouse Name:** Sandra Riehl (10/19/1963) **Children:** Elizabeth; Betty; John; Ben; Sandra **Education:** LLB, Harvard Law School, Harvard University (1964); AB, Xavier University, Magna Cum Laude (1961) **Career:** Senior Partner, Bardenwerper, Talbott & Roberts, PLLC, Louisville, KY (2004-Present); Partner, Talbott & Talbott, PLLC, Louisville, KY (2000-2004); Partner, Westfall, Talbott & Woods, Louisville, KY (1980-2000); Partner, Middleton, Reutlinger & Baird, Louisville, KY (1968-1980); Associate, Middleton, Reutlinger & Baird, Louisville, KY (1965-1968); Law Clerk, Chief Judge Henry Brooks, United States District Court of Kentucky, Louisville, KY (1964-1965) **Career Related:** Attorney, University of Louisville (1980-1995); Attorney, Louisville General Hospital (1974-1983); Attorney, Louisville and Jefferson County Board of Health (1974-1980); Attorney, Stitzel-Weller Distillery (1970-1972) **Civic:** Vice President, Board of Directors, Historic Homes Foundation, Inc. (2002-2006); Board of Directors, Historic Homes Foundation, Inc. (2000-2001); Board of Directors, Historic Homes Foundation, Inc. (1995-1997); Board of Directors, Defense Enterprise Fund (1994-2006); Chairman, Board of Regents, Whitehall (1993-2001); Board of Directors, The Kentucky Center for the Arts Foundation (1980-2006); Advisor, Attorney, Historic Homes Foundation, Inc. (1978-1998); Vice President, Historic Homes Foundation, Inc. (1978); Chairman, Louisville Theatrical Association (1977-1978); President, Louisville Orchestra (1976-1986); Chairman, Financial Committee, University of Louisville (1976); President, Louisville Theatrical Association (1975-1976); Board of Directors, Macauley Theatre (1975); Vice Chairman, University of Louisville (1975); Treasurer, Louisville Lung Association (1975); Board of Directors, Louisville Lung Association (1974-1975); President, Louisville 15, Station WKPC-TV (1974); Secretary, University of Louisville (1974); Board of Directors, Historic Homes Foundation, Inc. (1972-1978); Board of Directors, Louisville 15, Station WKPC-TV (1972-1974); Board of Directors, Louisville Theatrical Association (1971-2000); Advisor, Jefferson County Capital Construction Committee (1971); Board of Directors, TARC Advisory Committee (1971); Trustee, University of Louisville (1970-1979); Board of Regents, Locust Grove (1970-1975); Board of Directors, University of Louisville Medical School Fund Organization; Board of Directors, University of Louisville Foundation; Past Member, Pendennis Club; Past Member, University Club Louisville; Past Member, Defense Research and Trial Lawyers Association; Treasurer, University of Louisville; Secretary, Macauley Theatre; Board Member, Louisville Orchestra; Treasurer, Locust Grove; Advisory Board, Louisville 15, Station WKPC-TV **Awards:** Named, Outstanding Young Man of Louisville, Louisville Jaycees (1976); Listed, Bar Registry of Preeminent Lawyers; Recipient, AV Rating, Martindale-Hubbell **Membership:** Board of Directors, Kentucky Society of Mayflower Descendants (2009-Present); Treasurer, The Honor Society of Phi Kappa Phi, University of Louisville (1990-Present); Financial Committee Member, General Society of Mayflower Descendants (2009-2011); President, Harvard Law School Alumni Association of Kentucky (1989-2005); Board of Directors, Louisville Bar Association; Chairman, Kentucky Bar Association (1989); Secretary, Harvard Law School Alumni Association of Kentucky (1965); Sons of the American Revolution; ABA; Society of Colonial Wars in the State of Florida; Kentucky Society of Colonial Wars; Society of Mayflower Descendants in the State of Florida; Second Deputy Governor, Kentucky Society of Mayflower Descendants; Past, Acting Governor, Kentucky Society of Mayflower Descendants; Treasurer, Kentucky Society of Mayflower Descendants; Assistant Treasurer, General Society of Mayflower Descendants; General Practice Session of Continuing Legal Education, Kentucky Bar Association; Aldren Kindred of America; General Society of Colonial Wars; St. Andrews Club; The Filson Historical Society; The Country Club of Florida; Big Sand Lake Club; Board of Directors, Louisville Boat Club; Secretary, Louisville Boat Club; Louisville Country Club; Gulf Stream Bath and Tennis Club; Board of Directors, The Honor Society of Phi Kappa Phi, University of Louisville; Board and Officer, Alcohol Council of Louisville **Bar Admissions:** United States Court of Appeals for the Sixth Ciruit (1967); Kentucky (1965) **Hobbies:** Golf; Tennis; Skiing; Fishing **Shipping Address:** 1000 N Hurstbourne Pkwy., Ste 200, Bardenwerper, Talbott & Roberts, PLLC, Louisville, KY, 40223

Peter J. Tamburro Jr.

Title: Teacher **Industry:** Education/Educational Services **Date of Birth:** 01/20/1947 **Place of Birth:** Hoboken **State:** NJ **Parents:** Peter James Tamburro; Rose Catherine (Verta) Tamburro **Marital Status:** Single **Spouse Name:** Andrea Everitt Huber (1976-1998) **Children:** Peter James, III; Christopher Harding; Matthew Everitt **Education:** MAT in Social Studies, Trenton State College (1973); BA in Political Science, Dickinson College (1969) **Certifications:** Secondary School Teacher in Social Studies, New Jersey Department of Education **Career:** Teacher, The Frisch School (2005-2013); Teacher, Hanover Park Regional High School District (1976-2005); Teacher, Morris School District (1973-1976) **Career Related:** Board of Trustees, Morris County Historical Society (2016-Present); Teacher of New Jersey History (2013-2017); Table Tennis Coach, The Frisch School (2006-2012); Chess Coach (2005-2013); Adjunct Professor, William Paterson University (1999-2000); Curriculum Advisory Committee, Washington Township, Morris County (1996-1997); Assistant Basketball Coach, Hanover Park Regional High School (1994-2001); Historical Committee (1994-1997); Fellow, National Council of Basic Education (1993); Fellow, Woodrow Wilson National Fellowship Foundation (1991); Volleyball Coach (1990-1998); Assistant Basketball Coach, Caldwell University (1989-1993); Consultant for Developing Advanced Placement History Programs, Hanover Park Regional High School District (1989-1992); Reader, Advanced Placement Exams, Hanover Park Regional High School District (1989-1992); ETS Consultant, History Commission, Hanover Park Regional High School District (1989-1992); Fellow, Taft Institute Two Party Government, Fairleigh Dickinson University (1984); Cross Country Coach (1983-2003); Judge, Bicentennial Committee **Civic:** Republican County Committeeman, Town of Morristown (2002-2003); Team Captain, Republican National Convention (2000); Scoutmaster, Boy Scouts of America (1994-1997); Historical Commission, Washington Township, Morris County (1994-1996); Legislative Aide, Office of Assemblyman Robert Martin (1985-1989); Republican County Committeeman, Hanover, NJ (1984-1988) **Military Service:** U.S. Army (1969-1971) **Creative Works:** Internet Radio Host, "Openings for Amateurs"; Managing Editor, American Chess Magazine (2016-Present); Columnist, The British Chess Magazine Limited (2014-Present); Italian Translation of "Openings for Amateurs," "Teoria e Pratica delle Aperture Schacchistiche" (2016); Editor, Atlantic Chess News Annual (2014-2017); Author, "Openings for Amateurs" (2014); Feature Writer, Chess Life for Kids (2006-2017); Editor, "Teaching Chess Step by Step," Kasparov Chess Foundation (2006); Editor, Atlantic Chess News (2000-2002); Author, "Learn Chess from the Greats" (2000); Columnist, Chessmates, Newark Star Ledger, New Jersey On-Line LLC (1997-2015); Nationally Syndicated Columnist, U.S. Chess Federation (1994-2001); Author, "Gateway to Morris" (1993); Feature Writer, Chess Life Magazine (1973-2015); Editor, Atlantic Chess News (1973-1976) **Awards:** Chess Journalists of America (2009-2010); Winner, Metropolitan Yeshiva League Chess Team Champions (2007-2009); Chess Journalists of America (2006); Journalist of the Year, Chess Journalists of America (2006); Chess Journalists of America (2002-2003); Winner, Cross Country State Section Championships (2000-2002); Cross Country, Morris County Coach of the Year (2000); Chess Journalists of America (1995-1997); New Jersey's Outstanding Teacher of History, National Society Daughters of the American Revolution (1990); Grantee, Geraldine R. Dodge Foundation (1987); Winner, Cross Country State Section Championships (1987); Grantee, National Science Foundation (1978) **Membership:** Treasurer, New Jersey State Chess Federation (2014-2016); Chief Negotiator, Hanover Park Regional Educational Association (2003-2005); President, Chess Journalists of America (1997-2003); President, Hanover Park Regional Educational Association (1995-2001); National Chairman, Historical Committee, United States Chess Federation (1994-1999); Vice President, Hanover Park Regional Educational Association (1994-1995); Vice President, Chess Journalists of America (1990-1997); New Jersey Education Association; Morris County Historical Society **Marquis Who's Who Honors:** Albert Nelson Marquis Lifetime Achievement Award (2017) **Hobbies:** Rare books; Chess, New Jersey history **Political Affiliations:** Republican **Shipping Address:** 22 Budd Street, Morristown, NJ, 07960

Winston Tannis

Title: Founding Executive Chair, Lawyer, Mediator, Arbitrator, Consultant, Author, Editor, Entrepreneur, Publisher, Artist, Singer-Songwriter, Actor, Motion Picture Filmmaker **Industry:** Publishing **Company Name:** Beacon Publications Global **Date of Birth:** 07/19/1966 **Country of Origin:** ON/CA **Parents:** Sana T. Nesrallah Tannis; George N. Tannis **Marital Status:** Divorced **Spouse Name:** Alexandra Cork (Divorced 1997) **Education:** LLD, The Beacon Institute for Advanced Studies, Ottawa, Canada (2000); LLB/JD, Faculty of Law, Queen's University, Kingston, Ontario, Canada (1994); BA in Philosophy and Political Science, Western University, Cum Laude (1989) **Career:** Founding Publisher, The Neo-Republican (2015-Present); Founding Publisher, WG Magazine (2015-Present); Founding Publisher, New America Today & Tomorrow (2014-Present); Founder, EchoEternity Entertainment and Publishing (2014-Present); Founding Chair, President, Distinguished Professor, The Beacon Institute for Advanced Studies (2008-Present); Founding Chair, Creator, Counsel, Winston Tannis International, Ottawa, Canada (2003-Present); Founding Publisher, The Beacon Letters/Les Lettres du Balise (2002-Present); Founding Director, Tannis & Associates International, Toronto, Canada (1997-Present); Law Clerk to Chief Justice Barry L. Strayer, Federal Court of Canada, Court Martial Appeal Court of Canada and the Supreme Court of Canada (1995); Associate Counsel, Stikeman Elliot, Toronto, Canada (1994-1997); Counsel, Davies Ward, Toronto, Canada (1993); Corporate Development Director, Cast Community/Ontario Design, Toronto, Canada (1990-1991); Assistant Investment Advisor, HSBC Securities, Toronto, Canada (1989-1990); Marketing, Fashion Show and Conference Planning Director, The Inn at Manitou, Toronto, Canada (1987-1990); Student Police Officer, Residence Advisor, Tennis Professional, Western University, Ontario, Canada (1987-1989); Tennis Professional, The Inn at Manitou, McKellar, Toronto, Canada (1987-1988); Commentator, Writer, Glebe Report, Ottawa, Canada (1984-1985); Restaurant Executive and Worker, McDonald's Restaurants, Pepper's Ottawa, Canada (1983-1985); Club Supervisor, Tennis Professional, St. James Tennis Club, Ottawa, Canada (1983-1985); Child Program Supervisor, Planner, St. James Community Center, Ottawa, Canada (1983-1985); Kitchen, Cafeteria Assistant, Carleton University, Ottawa, Ontario, Canada (1970); Newspaper Distributor, Ottawa Journal, Ottawa Citizen, Globe & Mail (1970); Founding Managing Director, Creator, The WG Group **Career Related:** Founding Chair, Beacon Library Civilization (2012-Present); Counsel, Beacon Library Civilization (2012-Present); Founding Chair, The Winston George Foundation (2006-Present); Counsel, The Winston George Foundation (2006-Present); Founding Chair, Beacon Watch International (1989-Present); Counsel, Beacon Watch International (1989-Present); Founding President, Queen's Annual Business Law Symposium, Queen's University (1993-1998); Director, Queen's Annual Business Law Symposium, Queen's University (1993-1998); Editor-in-Chief, Queen's Annual Business Law Symposium, Queen's University (1993-1998) **Civic:** Chair, The Winston George Foundation, (2002-Present); Counsel, The Winston George Foundation, (2002-Present); Founding Chair, The Beacon Institute For Advanced Studies (2000); Secretary-Treasurer, Queen's Law (1994); Executive Member, UWO Entrepreneur & Philosophy Club (1985-1989); President, Graduating Class, Glebe Collegiate Institute (1984-1985) **Military Service:** Commander-and-Chief, New America **Creative Works:** Founding Publisher, The Neo-Republican (2015-Present); Founding Publisher, WG Magazine (2015-Present); Founder, EchoEternity Entertainment (2014-Present); Founding Publisher, New America Today & Tomorrow, Beacon Publisher (2014-Present); Founding Publisher, The Beacon Letters (2002-Present); Editor-in-Chief, Queen's Annual Business Law Symposium, Queen's University (1993-1998); Contributor, Articles to Professional Journals; Musician; Pianist; Lyricist; Vocalist; Producer, "Corporate Governance Reform with Stanley Hartt QC"; Author, "The Pillars of Justice & Law"; Author, "The Columns of America"; Author, "The Bridges To The Spirit" **Awards:** International Recognition Award, Wikipedia (2005-Present); Named, Queen's Law Scholar (1991-Present); Platinum Pen, Queen's Annual Business Law Symposium (1998); David Sabbath Tax Policy Award, Queen's Law, Queen's University (1994); National Silver Medal, Canadian Corporate Securities, Toronto, Canada (1994); Gold Medal, Western University, Ontario, Canada (1989); Winner, Athlete of the Year (1982); Named, Ontario Scholar (1980-1985); Winner, Athlete of the Year (1980); Listee, American Registry of Top Executives **Membership:** IMDB; The Law Society of Upper Canada; St. James Tennis Club; Yahoo.ca; The Beacon Society **Hobbies:** Tennis; Soccer; Running; Bicycling; Football; Hockey; Baseball; Weightlifting; Travel; Reading; Architecture; Volleyball; Basketball; Skiing; Skating **Shipping Address:** 200-481 Percy Street, Winston Tannis International, ON, Ottawa, Canada, KIS 4B1

Byron D. Tapley

Title: Professor of Aerospace Engineering **Industry:** Education/Educational Services **Company Name:** The University of Texas at Austin **Date of Birth:** 01/16/1933 **Place of Birth:** Charleston **State:** MS **Parents:** Ebbie Byron Tapley; Myrtle (Myers) Tapley **Marital Status:** Married **Spouse Name:** Sophia Philen (8/28/1959) **Children:** Mark Byron; Craig Philen **Education:** PhD in Engineering Mechanics, The University of Texas at Austin (1960); MS in Engineering Mechanics, The University of Texas at Austin (1958); BS in Mechanical Engineering, The University of Texas at Austin (1956) **Certifications:** Registered Professional Engineer, State of Texas **Career:** Clare Cockrell Williams Centennial Chair, Department of Aerospace Engineering and Engineering Mechanics, The University of Texas at Austin (1984-Present); Director, Center for Space Research, The University of Texas at Austin (1983-Present); Professor, Department of Aerospace Engineering and Engineering Mechanics, The University of Texas at Austin (1960-Present); Director, The Texas Space Grant Consortium, National Aeronautics and Space Administration (1990-2001); Woolrich Engineering Professor, The University of Texas at Austin (1974-1980); Chairman, Department of Aerospace Engineering and Engineering Mechanics, The University of Texas at Austin (1966-1977); Mechanical Engineering Instructor, The University of Texas at Austin (1958); Engineer, Structural Mechanics Research Laboratory, The University of Texas at Austin (1954-1958) **Career Related:** Member, Mission PI, GRACE Mission, National Aeronautics and Space Administration (1997-Present); Vice Chair, NAC Science Committee, National Aeronautics and Space Administration (2009-2013); Chair, NAC Earth Systems Subcommitee, National Aeronautics and Space Administration (2009-2013); Member, AGU Whitten Medal Selection Committee, National Aeronautics and Space Administration (2009-2010); Member, Advisory Council Committee, National Aeronautics and Space Administration (2006-2009); Chairman, Committee on Earth Studies, National Research Council, National Academy of Sciences (1988-1991); Member, Aerospace and Space Engineering Board, National Research Council, National Academy of Sciences (1984-1986); Chairman, Geodesy Committee, National Research Council, National Academy of Sciences (1981-1984); Chairman, Region IV, Engineering Council on Professional Development, National Aeronautics and Space Administration (1974-1976); Member, Panel I, Committee on Space Research, National Aeronautics and Space Administration (1974-1976); Member, Advisory Committee on Guidance Control and Navigation, National Aeronautics and Space Administration (1966-1967); Member, Space Science Board, National Research Council, National Academy of Sciences; Panel Member, National Research Council, National Academy of Sciences; Member, Technological Roadmap Investigation, National Aeronautics and Space Administration **Creative Works:** Associate Editor, Journal of Geophysical Research (1979-1981); Associate Editor, Journal of Guidance and Control (1978-1979); Editor, Celestial Mechanical Journal (1976-1979); Author, "Statistical Orbit Determination," Elsevier **Awards:** Exceptional Public Service Medal, National Aeronautics and Space Administration (2009); Charles A. Whitten Medal, American Geophysical Union (2001); Dirk Brouwer Award, American Astronautical Society (1995); Public Service Medal, National Aeronautics and Space Administration (1995); Mechanics and Control of Flight Award, American Institute of Aeronautics and Astronautics (1989); Exceptional Scientific Achievement Medal, National Aeronautics and Space Administration (1983); Fellow, American Association for the Advancement of Science; Fellow, American Institute of Aeronautics and Astronautics; Fellow, American Geophysical Union, NASA Exceptional Service Medal, 2018 **Membership:** President, Division of Dynamic Astronomy, American Astronautical Society (1988-1989); President, Geodesy Section, American Geophysical Union (1984-1986); Chairman, Astrodynamics Committee, American Institute of Aeronautics and Astronautics (1976-1978); International Astronomical Union; Society of Engineering Science Inc.; IEEE; American Academy of Mechanics; The American Society of Mechanical Engineers; National Academy of Engineering; The Tau Beta Pi Association, Inc.; The Honor Society of Phi Kappa Phi; Sigma Gamma Tau; Pi Tau Sigma; Sigma Xi, The Scientific Research Honor Society **Marquis Who's Who Honors:** Albert Nelson Marquis Lifetime Achievement Award (2017) **Hobbies:** Sailing; Cross country biking; Backpacking **Shipping Address:** 5603 Lands End St., Austin, TX, 78734 **Website:** http://www.ae.utexas.edu/faculty/faculty-directory/tapley

Herman H. Tarnow

Industry: Law and Legal Services **Education:** JD, Syracuse University College of Law **Bar Admissions:** New York; Connecticut; Florida; United States Supreme Court **Why did you become involved in your profession or industry?** Mr. Tarnow became involved in his profession because in the early stages of his career, he practiced criminal law, family law and EEOC work in federal court. By 1979, he realized that he was so intensely involved in each area that he was spreading himself thin. He decided to choose his favorite of the three fields, and he chose family. Mr. Tarnow enjoys having the ability to make people happy by finding reasonable solutions to their problems. Mr. Tarnow has recently written an article in "Strategies for Family Law in Florida," an Aspatore Law Book. The title of his article was "The View from My Side of the Desk: Sex and the City-One Episode Too Many." **Where will you be in 5 years?** In five years, Mr. Tarnow hopes to establish the practice so that it will continue as he moves into other interests.

Giulio Tarro, PhD

Title: Virologist **Industry:** Health, Wellness and Fitness **Company Name:** Foundation T. & L. de Beaumont Bonelli for Cancer Research **Date of Birth:** 07/09/1938 **Place of Birth:** Messina **Country of Origin:** Italy **Parents:** Emanuele Tarro; Emanuela (Iannello) Tarro **Children:** Giuseppe **Education:** Honorary Degree in Social Sciences, Bonakè University, Cote d'Ivoire (2010); Honorary MSc in Biomedical Technologies, ASAM University, Italy (2008); Honorary Degree in Bioethics, The Constantinian University, RI (1996); Honorary Degree in Immunology, St. Theodora Academy, NY (1991); Honorary Degree in Medicine, Pro-Deo State University, NY (1989); Postgraduate Coursework in Medical and Biological Sciences, Roman Academy (1979); PhD in Virology, Università degli Studi di Napoli Federico II (1971); Postgraduate Coursework in Nervous Diseases, Università degli Studi di Napoli Federico II (1968); MD, Università degli Studi di Napoli Federico II (1962) **Career:** Emeritus, D. Cotugno Hospital for Infectious Diseases (2006-Present); President, Ethic Committee, D. Cotugno Hospital for Infectious Diseases (1998-2007); Head of Department Diagnostic Laboratories, D. Cotugno Hospital for Infectious Diseases (2003-2006); Chief of Virology Division, D. Cotugno Hospital for Infectious Diseases (1973-2006); Professor, Microbiology, College of Medicine, Università degli Studi di Napoli Federico II (1972-2006); Professor, Immunology, College of Medicine, Università degli Studi di Napoli Federico II (1972-2006); Professor, Oncologic Virology, College of Medicine, Università degli Studi di Napoli Federico II (1971-1985); Research Fellow, Consiglio Nazionale delle Ricerche (1966-1974); Research Chief, Consiglio Nazionale delle Ricerche (1974); Assistant Professor, Research Pediatrics, College of Medicine, University of Cincinnati (1968-1969); Research Associate, Division of Virology and Cancer Research, Cincinnati Children's Hospital Medical Center (1965-1968) **Career Related:** President, Norman Academy (2009-Present); Adjunct Professor in Biology, College of Science and Technology, Temple University (2007-Present); Chairman, Committee on Biotechnologies and Virusphere, World Academy of Biomedical Technologies, UNESCO (2007-Present); Member, President De Beaumont Bonelli Foundation for Cancer Research (1978-Present); National Committee on Health (2015); Ethics Committee, Basilicata Oncologic Hospital (2005-2013); Member, Campania Technology and Ecology Center (2004-2012); President, Science Committee, Gonzaga University (2008-2009); Medical Director, Italian Pharmacotherapic Institute (2006-2007); Vice Chairman, General Secretary Science Advisory Board, Unihart Biotech Pharma Limited (2005-2007); European Group for Economic Interest, Research and Development (2003-2007); Head of Medicine Department, Università degli Studi di Napoli Federico II (2000-2005); Science Coordinator, Extracorporeal Hyperthermia in HCV Patients, First Circle Medical, Inc. (2000-2003) **Civic:** President, Studiorum Universitas Ruggero II (2013-Present); Honorary Rector, Studiorum Universitas Ruggero II (2003); Honorary Member, Universitas Sancti Cyrilli (2001); Member, International Computing Science Academy, United Nations (1997); Member, University Pro Deo (1994); Lieutenant Colonel, Marina Militare (1993-1995) **Creative Works:** Editor-in-Chief, Fratres (2004-Present); Editor-in-Chief, Journal of Vaccine Research and Development (2015); Author, "Cancer Should be Only a Zodiac Sign" (2014); Author, "Medicine is Life" (2013); Author, "Campania Land of Poisons" (2012); Author, "Health Without Borders, Fifth Edition" (2012); Editor-in-Chief, Cotugno News (2003-2009); Author, "Safety No Limits" (2008); Author, "Health Without Borders" (2004); Author, "Pocket File Research Collection, Sixth Edition" (2003); Author, "Bioethics and Culture of Prevention" (2001) **Awards:** Gold Coliseum Award (2015); Wojtila-Roncalli International Award (2013); Knight Grand Cross, Cernetic Imperial Order (2013); Rilancio Italia Award (2013); Gold Medal for 50 Years as a MD (2013); International Prize (2012); Gold Medal, The Royal House Of Maharaja Adinda Aranan (2012); Gold Medal, Norman Academy (2012); International Peace Award (2011); Global Education Sanremo Award (2011); National Award for Solidarity (2010); Grand Prix Solidarite (2010); Melvin Jones Fellowship, Lions Clubs International (2010); Lifetime Achievement Award, Sbarro Health Research Organization, Temple University (2009); Silver Medal, President Giorgio Napolitano (2008); Melvin Jones Fellowship, Lions Clubs International (2008); Grand Cross, International Academy of the State of Wyoming (2008) **Membership:** Honorary President, Italian Association for Viral Study and Research (2009-Present); Vice President, Italian Society for Immuno-Oncology (1975-Present); District Director of Rare Diseases (2014-2015); Vice President of Board, Lions Clubs International (2014-2015); Director of Rare Diseases, Lions Clubs International (2013-2015); International Director, Lions International Stamp Club, Lions Clubs International (2012-2014) **Marquis Who's Who Honors:** Albert Nelson Marquis Lifetime Achievement Award (2017) **Religion:** Roman Catholic **Shipping Address:** Via Posillipo 286, Naples, Italy, 80123

Cora Hodge Taylor

Title: Coordinator of Contract Programs **Industry:** Social Work **Company Name:** Edith Nourse Rogers Memorial Veterans Hospital **Date of Birth:** 11/25/1942 **Place of Birth:** Fayetteville **State:** NC **Marital Status:** Married **Spouse Name:** Charles L. Taylor, Jr. (6/26/1965) **Children:** Charles L. Taylor III; John M. **Education:** MSW, The University of North Carolina at Chapel Hill (1965); BS, North Carolina College (Now North Carolina Central University) (1963) **Career:** Coordinator, Contract Programs, Edith Nourse Rogers Memorial Veterans Hospital, U.S. Department of Veterans Affairs (1993-Present); Supervisory Social Worker of Geriatrics and Long Term Care, Edith Nourse Rogers Memorial Veterans Hospital, U.S. Department of Veterans Affairs, Bedford, MA (1991-2000); Field Instructor, Smith College School for Social Work (1986-1989); Field Instructor, School of Social Work, Boston University (1979-1987); Chief Social Worker, Regional Health Center, Wilmington, MA (1978-1979); Field Instructor, Regional Health Center, Wilmington, MA (1978-1979); Clinical Social Worker, Edith Nourse Rogers Memorial Veterans Hospital, U.S. Department of Veterans Affairs, Bedford, MA (1973-1991, 1965-1968); Instructor, Tufts University; Consultant to Primary Care Residents, Tufts University **Civic:** Deacon, First Congregational Church (1986-Present); Member, Board of Commissioners, Housing Authority of Atlantic Beach, South Carolina (2003-2004); Member, Town Meeting, Billerica, MA (1981-2000); Women Veterans' Coordinator, Social Work Leadership Training Program, Edith Nourse Rogers Memorial Veterans Hospital, U.S. Department of Veterans Affairs (1998); Precinct Clerk, Billerica, MA (1981-1982, 1989); Precinct Chairman, Billerica, MA (1984-1986); Volunteer, Food Pantry, U.S. Department of Veterans Affairs **Membership:** Director, LWC (1970-1973); Academy of Certified Social Workers, National Association of Social Workers; The African American Club in the Villages; Altar Angel, Hope Lutheran Church; On Our Own; Women of Hope **Marquis Who's Who Honors:** Albert Nelson Marquis Lifetime Achievement Award (2017) **What do you consider to be the highlight of your career:** Ms. Taylor considers the highlight of her career to be initiating the day hospital treatment program for veterans. Through the program , staff encouraged veterans to get involved with fundraising projects like car washes, and then used the money to benefit the veterans. She felt it empowered them. **Hobbies:** Line dancing; Playing card games **Shipping Address:** 2031 Ridge Spring Dr, The Villages, FL, 32162

Estelle Wormley Taylor

Title: Language Educator, Dean **Industry:** Education/Educational Services **Company Name:** Howard University **Date of Birth:** 01/12/1924 **Place of Birth:** Washington **State:** DC **Parents:** Luther Charles Wormley; Wilhelmina Wormley **Marital Status:** Married **Spouse Name:** Ivan Earle Taylor (12/26/1953) **Education:** PhD, The Catholic University of America (1969); MA, Howard University (1947); BS, Miner Teachers College, Magna Cum Laude (1945) **Career:** Professor Emeritus, Howard University (1991); Director, Expository Writing Program, Graduate School of Arts and Sciences, Howard University (1988-1991); Associate Dean, College of Liberal Arts, Howard University (1985-1986); Professor, Howard University (1976-1991); Chairman, Department of English, Howard University (1976-1985); Associate Provost, Federal City College, Washington, DC (1974-1975); Professor, Instructor, District of Columbia Teachers College (1963-1976); Teacher, Eastern Senior High School, Washington, DC (1955-1963); Teacher, Junior High School, Washington, DC (1952-1955); Instructor in English, Howard University (1947-1952) **Career Related:** Member, Advisory Board, Humanities Institute, Montgomery College (1997-Present); Secretary of Education, Higher Education Licensure Commission, Office of the State Superintendent of Education (1993-Present); Co-Chair, Steering Committee to Revise Characteristics of Excellence (1992-1993); Member, Middle States Commission on Higher Education (1988-1990); Member, Middle States Commission on Higher Education (1984-1987); Member, Central Executive Committee, Folger Institute for Renaissance and 18th Century Studies (1982-1991) **Civic:** Secretary, Vice Chairman, Higher Education Licensure Commission, Office of the State Superintendent of Education (1995-Present); Commissioner, Higher Education Licensure Commission, Office of the State Superintendent of Education (1993-Present); Member, Advisory Board, College of Arts and Services, Howard University (2002); Member, Selection Board, Foreign Agricultural Service, United States Department of Agriculture (2002); First Vice President, Order of the Daughters of the King Episcopalian Church Diocese, Washington, DC (1994-1998); Co-Chairman, Planning Committee, Centennial Celebration of the Andrew Rankin Chapel, Howard University (1994); Member, Humanities Council of Washington, DC (1990-1991); Vice Chairman, University of the District of Columbia (1983); Trustee, University of the District of Columbia (1979-1983) **Creative Works:** Contributing Editor, "A Howard Reader" (1997) **Awards:** Recipient, Alumni Award for Distinguished Postgraduate Achievement in Education and Literature (1997); Named, Distinguished Alumni, Howard University (1995); Recipient, Rockefeller/ Aspen Institute Fellowship (1978-1979); Recipient, Southern Fellowship (1968-1969) **Membership:** Recording Secretary, Capital City Chapter, The Links, Incorporated (1995-Present); Assembly Delegate, Modern Language Association of America (1994-Present); Recording Secretary, Capital City Chapter, The Links, Incorporated (1991-1993); Corresponding Secretary, Capital City Chapter, The Links, Incorporated (1989); Vice President, Capital City Chapter, The Links, Incorporated (1979-1981); National Association for Equal Opportunity in Higher Education; The College Language Association; Shakespeare Association of America; Public Member, American Foreign Service Association **Marquis Who's Who Honors:** Albert Nelson Marquis Lifetime Achievement Award (2017) **Why did you become involved in your profession or industry:** Dr. Taylor's great-aunt Emma Frances Grayson Merritt inspired her to become a teacher. She made a huge contribution to education. **What do you consider to be the highlight of your career:** The most rewarding part of Dr. Taylor's career is when her students stay in touch with her. **Political Affiliations:** Democrat **Shipping Address:** 3221 20th St NE, Washington, DC, 20018

Laurence Thomas

Title: Professor **Industry:** Education/Educational Services **Company Name:** Syracuse University **Education:** PhD, University of Pittsburgh (1976); Honorary LLD, New England College; MA, University of Pittsburgh; BA in Philosophy, University of Maryland **Career:** Professor, Philosophy and Political Science, Syracuse University (1989-Present) **Career Related:** Visiting Professor, University of South Africa (2002); Presenter, Kovler Lectures, Medical School of the University of Cape Town, South Africa (1997); Visiting Scholar, Religion Department, University of Michigan (1994); Andrew Mellon Faculty Fellow, Harvard University (1978-1979) **Creative Works:** Author, "The Family and the Political Self" (2005); Contributor, "Raisons Politiques: Etudes De Pensée Politique" (2003); Author, "Upside-Down Equality: A Response to Kantian Thought" (2003); Author, "Forgiving the Unforgivable" (2002); Author, "The Moral Self in the Face of Injustice" (2001); Author, "Autonomie" (2000); Author, "Trusting Under Pressure" (1999); Author, "Sexual Orientation and Human Rights" (1999); Author, "Vessels of Evil" (1993); Featured, Education Section, The New York Times (1992); Author, "Living Morally: A Psychology of Moral Character" (1989); Board of Consulting Editors, The Encyclopedia of Ethics; Author, Over 100 Articles **Awards:** Teacher of the Year, Syracuse University (1993); NEH Award (1981) **Membership:** American Society for Political and Legal Philosophy (1976-Present); American Philosophical Association (1971-Present); Fellow, National Humanities Center (1982-1983) **Shipping Address:** 502 Walnut Ave Apt 2, Syracuse, NY, 13210

Paul Thomas, PhD

Title: Science Educator **Industry:** Education/Educational Services **Date of Birth:** 12/01/1929 **Place of Birth:** Sligo **State:** PA **Parents:** Milton Ivan Thomas; Maude Hazel Thomas **Marital Status:** Married **Spouse Name:** Dorothy Marie McGinnett **Children:** Mona Lee Callahan **Education:** PhD in Ministry, Drew University (1980); PhD, University of Michigan (1964); MS, University of Michigan (1962); MA, University of Michigan (1959); BA, Allegheny College (1958) **Career:** Pastor, United Church of Christ (1995-2013); Professor of Biology, Edinboro University (1968-1990); Chairman, Biology Department, Edinboro University (1968-1990); Visiting Professor, Johns Hopkins University (1968); Research Fellow, California Institute of Technology (1967-1968); Assistant Professor, Point Loma Nazarene University (1964-1966); Instructor of Biology, Houghton College (1959-1962) **Career Related:** Visiting Scholar, Harvard University (1993) **Civic:** School Board Member, Union City, PA (1969-1975) **Creative Works:** Author, "W. Edwards Deming: Improving Quality in Colleges and Universities"; Author, "Easter Urges Us to Look at Death"; Author, "A Christian Looks at Death"; Author, "Pennsylvania Fish Commission"; Author, "Fishes of Erie County"; Author, "Fishes of Pymatuning"; Contributor, Articles, Professional Journals **Membership:** National Audubon Society; Sigma Xi, The Scientific Research Honor Society; The Honor Society of Phi Kappa Phi **Hobbies:** Hiking; World traveling **Political Affiliations:** Conservative **Shipping Address:** 87 W High Street, Union City, PA, 16438

Pauline Frances Thomassen

Title: Medical and Surgical Nurse (Retired) **Industry:** Health, Wellness and Fitness **Date of Birth:** 01/19/1939 **Place of Birth:** Cleveland **State:** OH **Parents:** Henry Clifford Nichols; Mabel Pauline (Hill) Nichols **Marital Status:** Married **Spouse Name:** Ruben Thomassen (10/10/1979) **Children:** Rhonda; Terry; Diana; Philipp; Jody; Barbara **Education:** BSN, Seattle Pacific University, Magna Cum Laude (1986); BA in Psychology, Southern Colorado State College (1975); AA in Nursing, Southern Colorado State College (1974) **Certifications:** RN, State of Washington **Career:** Clinical Spine Educator, Swedish Hospital Medical Center, Seattle, WA (1998-2002); Preceptor, Orientation of Registered Nurses and Student Registered Nurses, Swedish Hospital Medical Center, Seattle, WA (1975-2002); Staff Nurse, III Orthopedic Unit, Clinical Spine Educator, Swedish Hospital Medical Center, Seattle, WA (1975-2002) **Career Related:** Medical Mission, Mexico (2008-2009); Medical Mission, Mississippi Katrina Relief (2006-2007); Medical Mission, Official Camp Nurse, Camp Li-WA, Mexico (2006); Medical Mission, Official Camp Nurse, Camp Li-WA, Fairbanks, AK (2006); Medical Mission, Mexico (2006); Medical Mission, Philippines (2004); Lecturer, College of Nursing, Raleigh Fitkin Memorial Hospital, St. Petersburg, Russia (2003); Guest Speaker, American Academy of Orthopedic Surgeons, Dallas, TX (2002); Medical Mission, Official Camp Nurse, Camp Li-WA, Fairbanks, AK (2002); Guest Speaker, Degenerative Lumbar Spinal Techniques, Cadaver Workshop, University of Washington, Seattle, WA (2001); Medical Mission, Clinic for Street Children, Honolulu Police Department (2001); Medical Mission, Satipo, Peru (2000); Lecturer, Manzini, Swaziland, South Africa (1999); Planning Task Force, Faculty, National Nurses Conference, The Nurse and Spinal Surgery, Cleveland, OH **Creative Works:** Contributing Author, "Making Sense of Minimally Invasive Spine Surgery" (1998); Author, "Spinal Disease and Surgical Interventions" (1995) **Membership:** National Association of Orthopedic Nurses **Marquis Who's Who Honors:** Albert Nelson Marquis Lifetime Achievement Award (2017); Distinguished Humanitarian (2017) **To what do you attribute your success:** Ms. Thomassen has wanted to be a nurse since she was a child. A high school counselor told her she would never amount to anything. In 1974, she proved the counselor wrong and became a nurse. **What do you consider to be the highlight of your career:** A highlight of Ms. Thomassen's career was when she was sent to Alaska to take care of a man who had been in ice. It took a year for her to write about the experience for a bachelor's thesis. **Shipping Address:** 21301 13th Pl. W, Lynnwood, WA, 98036

James W. Thompson

Title: Partner **Industry:** Law and Legal Services **Company Name:** Thompson Painter Law P.C. **Date of Birth:** 10/22/1936 **Place of Birth:** Dallas **State:** TX **Parents:** John Charles Thompson; Frances (Van Slyke) Thompson **Marital Status:** Married **Spouse Name:** Linda Ball Dozier (5/2/1998); Marie Hertz (6/26/1965, Deceased 1995) **Children:** Elizabeth; Margaret; John **Education:** JD, University of Montana (1962); BS, University of Montana (1958) **Certifications:** Certified Public Accountant, State of Montana **Career:** Partner, Thompson Painter Law P.C., Billings, MT (2015-Present); Partner, Thompson Law Firm PLLC, Billings, MT (2007-2014); Partner, Guthals Hunnes Reuss Thompson PC, Billings, MT (2004-2007); Partner, Wright Tolliver Guthals Law Firm PC, Billings, MT (1999-2003); Partner, McNamer Thompson Law Firm PC (1993-1998); Partner, McNamer, Thompson, Werner & Stanley, Professional Corporation (1990-1993); Partner, McNamer & Thompson Law Firm PC (1986-1989); Partner, McNamer, Thompson & Cashmore (1973-1986); Partner, Felt, Speare & Thompson, Billings, MT (1966-1972); Attorney, City of Billings (1964-1966); Assistant Attorney, City of Billings (1963-1964); Associate, James R. Felt, Billings, MT (1964-1965); Associate, Cooke, Moulton, Bellingham & Longo, Billings, MT (1962-1964); Instructor, Business Administration, University of Montana, Missoula, MT (1960-1961); Instructor, Business Administration, Eastern Montana College, Billings, MT (1959-1960); Accountant, Arthur Young & Company, New York City, NY (1959) **Career Related:** Member, Advisory Council, School of Fine Arts, University of Montana (1997-2001); Board of Directors, Associated Employers of Montana, Inc. (1989-1998) **Civic:** President, Our Montana, Inc. (2000-Present); Board of Directors, Our Montana, Inc. (1997-Present); Board of Trustees, Billings Community Action Program (Now District 7 Human Resources Development Council) (1975-Present); Board of Directors, Rimrock Opera Company (1998-2013); Chairman, Board of Ethics, City of Billings (2001-2006); Treasurer, Rimrock Opera Company (1998-2002); Board of Directors, Foundation of Montana State University, Billings, MT (1992-1998); Board of Directors, Billings Area Business Incubator, Inc. (1991-1994); Board of Directors, Downtown Billings Association (1986-1990); Board of Directors, Montana Institute Arts Foundation (1986-1989); Board of Directors, United Way of Yellowstone County (1973-1981); Member, Diocesan Executive Council (1972-1975); Member, City Development Agency (1972-1973); Member, Billings Transit Commission (1971-1973); President, Billings Community Action Program (Now District 7 Human Resources Development Council) (1970-1975); President, Billings Symphony Society (1970-1971); Member, City-County Air Pollution Control Board (1969-1970); Member, Yellowstone County Legal Services Board (1969-1970); Vice President, Billings Community Action Program (Now District 7 Human Resources Development Council) (1968-1970); Board of Directors, Billings Studio Theater (1967-1973); Member, Billings Zoning Commission (1966-1969); Co-Organizer and Volunteer Attorney, Billings Community Action Program (Now District 7 Human Resources Development Council) (1965-1968) **Membership:** President, Yellowstone Area Bar Association (1985-1986); Board of Directors, Yellowstone Area Bar Association (1983-1987); President, Yellowstone Chapter, Elks, Kiwanis (1974-1975); President, Billings Alumni Association, Sigma Chi (1963-1965); ABA; American Academy of Estate Planning Attorneys; National Academy of Elder Law Attorneys **Bar Admissions:** Montana (1962) **Marquis Who's Who Honors:** Distinguished Humanitarian (2017) **Religion:** Episcopalian **Business Address:** 176 S 32nd St. W., Ste 4, Billings, MT, 59102 **Shipping Address:** 123 Lewis Ave., Billings, MT, 59101 **Website:** http://www.estatelawmontana.com

Jewel Thompson, PhD

Title: Music Educator **Industry:** Education/Educational Services **Company Name:** Hunter College, The City University of New York **Date of Birth:** 10/27/1935 **Place of Birth:** Kinsale **State:** VA **Parents:** Waverly Edward Taylor; Ella Joyce (Holman) Taylor **Spouse Name:** Leon Everette Thompson (6/10/1961, Deceased 6/1983) **Children:** Sonca Patrice; Miya Kateri **Education:** PhD, Eastman School of Music (1982); MA, Eastman School of Music (1960); BS, Virginia State University (1956) **Career:** Professor, Hunter College, The City University of New York (1997-Present); Associate Professor, Hunter College, The City University of New York (1990-1996); Assistant Professor, Hunter College, The City University of New York (1985-1990); Fellow, Ford Foundation (1974-1977); Adjunct Assistant Professor, Hunter College, The City University of New York (1972-1985); Assistant Professor, WVU Tech, Montgomery, WV (1968-1972); Assistant Professor, West Virginia State University (1967-1968); Assistant Professor, Virginia State University, Petersburg, VA (1960-1962); Fellow, Hattie M. Strong Foundation (1959-1960) **Career Related:** National Music Director (2004-2006); Eastern Area Music Director, The Links, Inc. (1995-2003); Minister of Music, Choirmaster, Abyssinian Baptist Church, New York, NY (1983-2007); Organist, Abyssinian Baptist Church, New York, NY (1978-1983) **Civic:** Delegate, International Women's Leadership Association (2015); Chair, Arts Program, The Links, Inc. (1989-1993); Scholarship Selection Committee, United Negro College Fund; Music Director, Area and National Levels; American Music Center, Inc. **Creative Works:** Contributor, "International Dictionary of Black Composers," Fitzroy Dearborn Publishers, Chicago, IL, London, England (1999); Author, "Samuel Coleridge-Taylor: The Development of His Compositional Style," The Scarecrow Press, Inc., Metuchen, NJ, London, England (1994); Composer, "Lord I Want to Be a Christian," SATB, Alto Solo, Morning Star Publishers, Fenton, MO; Composer, "I'm Free at Last," Mixed Choir, SSA Chorus, Tenor Solo, Morning Star Publishers, Fenton, MO; Composer, "Were You There," SATB, Soprano Solo, Piano, Morning Star Publishers, Fenton, MO; Composer, "Hush! Somebody's Calling My Name," SATB, Soprano Solo, Morning Star Publishers, Fenton, MO; Composer, "I Been in de Storm So Long," SATB, Soprano Solo, Piano, Morning Star Publishers, Fenton, MO; Composer, "Stand By Me," SATB, Soprano and Baritone Solo, Piano, GIA Publications, Inc., Chicago, IL; Composer, "Can I Ride," SATB, Baritone Solo, Men's and Women's Trios, GIA Publications, Inc., Chicago, IL **Awards:** Music of the African Diaspora Award (2013); Diamond of Faith Award, Abyssinian Baptist Church (2007); Outstanding Ministry Award, Council of Churches of New York City (2005); Hunter College Presidential Award for Excellence in Service (1998); Dame of Honour, Knights of Malta (1982); Grantee, Prince Hall Masons (1977-1978) **Membership:** Community Arts Advisory Counsel, New Jersey Symphony Orchestra (2013-Present); American Society of Composers; American Women Composers, Inc.; Music Theory Society of New York State; Advisory Counsel, International Women's Leadership Board **Marquis Who's Who Honors:** Albert Nelson Marquis Lifetime Achievement Award (2017) **Hobbies:** Travel; Art **Business Address:** 695 Park Avenue, New York, NY, 10065

David M. Thoms

Title: Lawyer **Industry:** Law and Legal Services **Company Name:** Warner Norcross + Judd LLP. **Place of Birth:** New York **State:** New York **Parents:** Elizabeth A. Thoms; Theodore C. Thoms **Marital Status:** Married **Spouse Name:** Susan S. Thoms, MD **Education:** LLM in Taxation, Wayne State University School of Law; JD, University of Detroit Mercy; Master of Urban Planning, Wayne State University; BA, Kalamazoo College **Civic:** Treasurer, Visiting Committee for European Sculpture and Decorative Arts, Detroit Institute of Arts; Tanahill Society; Hillwood Museum and Gardens International Committee; Board of Directors, Kalamazoo Institute of Arts; Board of Directors, French American Foundation; Past President, Alliance Francaise of Grosse Pointe, French Festival of Detroit; Financial and Estate Planning Council of Metropolitan Detroit; Past Chairman, The Salvation Army Southeast Michigan; Board of Directors, Detroit Symphony; Planned Giving Committee, Children's Hospital Foundation of Michigan; Planned Giving Committee, Wayne State University; Planned Giving Committee, Kalamazoo College; Planned Giving Committee, Henry Ford Health System; Advisor, Detroit Chamber Music Society; Past President, Federation of Alliances Francaises **Awards:** Belmondo Award, Government of France; Prix Charbonnier, Federation of Alliances Francaises–USA; William Booth Award, Salvation Army; Officier dans l'Ordre des Palms Academiques, Government of France; Order of Dali, Dali Museum; Order of Salvadore Award, Salvadore Dali Museum, Florida **Membership:** New York State Bar Association; City Bar Association of the City of New York; Michigan State Bar Association; Oakland County Bar Association; Kalamazoo County Bar Association; Metropolitan Detroit Bar Association; Financial and Estate Planning Council of New York; Financial and Estate Planning Council, Metropolitan Detroit; Financial and Estate Planning Council, Western Michigan **Bar Admissions:** New York; Michigan **To what do you attribute your success:** Mr. Thoms attributes his success to intellectual curiosity, hard work, devotion and subject matter. **Why did you become involved in your profession or industry:** He became involved in his profession because it was an extension of his education. **What do you consider to be the highlight of your career:** A highlight of his career was his interaction with people, and innovative problem solving. **Where will you be in five years:** In five years, he hopes to still be serving clients and the community. **Hobbies:** Music; Art history; Architectural history; Travel; Tennis **Religion:** Protestant Christian **Shipping Address:** 2000 Town Center, Suite 2700, Warner Norcross + Judd LLP, Southfield, MI, 48075

Thorsteinn Thorsteinsson

Title: Civil Engineer **Industry:** Engineering **Company Name:** University of Iceland **Date of Birth:** 09/05/1951 **Place of Birth:** Reykjavik **Country of Origin:** Iceland **Parents:** Thorsteinn Vilhelm Jonsson; Kristin Palsdottir **Education:** BS in Civil Engineering, University of Iceland (1974) **Certifications:** Registered Civil Engineer, Icelandic Ministry of Industry and Commerce (1974) **Career:** Researcher, University of Iceland (1991-Present); Adjunct Professor, University of Iceland (1985) **Career Related:** Member, National Arbitration Committee for Planning and Building Issues, Reykjavik (1996-Present); Consulting Engineer (1974-Present) **Civic:** Vice President, Icelandic Athletic Association (1993-2002) **Membership:** Area Technical Officer, International Association of Athletics Federations (1996-Present); Fellow, International Association of Athletics Federations; Associate, Icelandic Society Civil Engineers **Shipping Address:** Bergstadastraeti 45A, Reykjavik, Iceland, 101

Rosemary Thorstenson VanArsdel, PhD

Title: English Studies Educator **Industry:** Education/Educational Services **Date of Birth:** 09/01/1926 **Place of Birth:** Seattle **State:** WA **Parents:** Odin Thorstenson; Helen Catherine (McGregor) Thorstenson **Marital Status:** Widowed **Spouse Name:** Paul P. VanArsdel, Jr. (7/7/1950, Deceased 1/1994) **Children:** Mary M.; Andrew P. **Education:** PhD, Columbia University (1961); MA, University of Washington (1948); BA, University of Washington (1947) **Career:** Distinguished Professor Emeritus, University of Puget Sound, Tacoma, WA (1987-Present); Professor, English, University of Puget Sound, Tacoma, WA (1977-1987); Director, Semester Abroad, University of Puget Sound, Tacoma, WA (1977); Director, Writing Institute, University of Puget Sound, Tacoma, WA (1976-1986); Director, Legal English Program, School of Law, University of Puget Sound, Tacoma, WA (1973-1977); Associate Professor, University of Puget Sound, Tacoma, WA (1970-1977); Chair, Department of English, University of Puget Sound, Tacoma, WA (1970-1975); Assistant Professor, University of Puget Sound, Tacoma, WA (1967-1969); Acting Instructor, University of Washington, Seattle, WA (1961-1963); Graduate Teaching Assistant, Columbia University, New York, NY (1948-1950) **Career Related:** Visiting Professor, Gonzaga University (1977); Visiting Professor, Pacific Lutheran University (1977); Visiting Professor, Whitman College (1977); Visiting Professor, Willamette University (1977); Fellow, Royal Society of Literature **Creative Works:** Editorial Board Member, "Victorian Review" (1990-Present); Author, "Victorian Periodicals, Aids to Research: A Selected Bibliography on the Internet, Ninth Edition" (2009); Author, "Florence Fenwick Miller: Victorian Feminist, Journalist, Educator" (2001); Author, "Periodicals of Queen Victoria's Empire, An Exploration" (1996); Author, "Victorian Periodicals and Victorian Society" (1994); Author, "Victorian Periodicals: A Guide to Research, Volume II" (1989); Author, "George Eliot: A Centenary Tribute" (1982); Editorial Board, A Union List of Victorian Serials (1979-1985); Author, "Victorian Periodicals: A Guide to Research, Volume I" (1978); Editorial Board Member, "Wellesley Index to Victorian Periodicals, 1824-1900" (1968-1988); Contributor, Articles, Encyclopedias; Contributor, Articles, Professional Journals **Awards:** Van Arsdel Prize, Research Society of Victorian Periodicals (1990-Present); Distinguished Alumnae Award, Broadway High School, Seattle, WA (1991); Distinguished Professorship (1987); Doris Bronson Morrill Award, Kappa Kappa Gamma (1982); Achievement Awards, National Council of Teachers of English **Membership:** President, Research Society for Victorian Periodicals (1981-1983); Director, National Council of Teachers of English (1974-1977); Modern Language Association; Oxford Bibliographical Society **Marquis Who's Who Honors:** Albert Nelson Marquis Lifetime Achievement Award (2017) **Shipping Address:** 5051 50th Avenue NE, Apt. 10, Seattle, WA, 98105

William Grant Tifft, PhD

Title: Astronomy Professor, Scientist (Retired) **Industry:** Education/Educational Services **Company Name:** University of Arizona **Date of Birth:** 04/05/1932 **Place of Birth:** Derby **State:** CT **Parents:** William Charles Tifft; Marguerite Howe (Hubbell) Tifft **Marital Status:** Widowed **Spouse Name:** Janet Ann Lindner Homewood (6/2/1965, Deceased); Carol Ruth Nordquist (6/9/1957, Divorced 7/1964) **Children:** Jennifer Gail Tifft; William John Tifft; Amy Kathleen (Tifft) Lyons; Patricia Ann Homewood (Stepson); Susan Frances Homewood (Stepdaughter, Deceased); Hollis Richard (Homewood) Rose (Stepdaughter) **Education:** Postdoctoral Fellow, Australian National University, Canberra, Australia (1958-1960); Postdoctoral Fellow, National Science Foundation (1958-1960); PhD, Astronomy and Physics, California Institute of Technology (1958); Pre-Doctoral Fellow, National Science Foundation (1954-1958); AB, Astronomy, Harvard College, Magna Cum Laude (1954) **Career:** Professor Emeritus, The University of Arizona, Tucson, AZ (2002-Present); Principal Scientist, Scientific Association for the Study of Time in Physics and Cosmology (2000-Present); Professor, The University of Arizona, Tucson, AZ (1973-2002); Associate Professor, Director of Space Astronomy Laboratory, The University of Arizona, Tucson, AZ (1964-1973); Astronomer, Lowell Observatory, Flagstaff, AZ (1961-1964); Research Associate, Vanderbilt University, Nashville, TN (1960-1961); Affiliate, Steward Observatory, Tucson, AZ **Creative Works:** Author, "Redshift Key To Cosmology" (2014); Co-Editor, "Modern Mathematical Models of Time and Their Applications to Physics and Cosmology" (1997); Co-Editor, "International Conference on Modern Mathematical Models of Time and their Application to Physics and Cosmology" (1996); Co-Author, "Revised New General Catalog" (1973); Blogger, Williamtifft.wordpress.com; Contributor, More than 100 Articles to Professional Journals **Awards:** Finalist, First Scientist Astronauts Program (1965); Among Top 10 Winners, Westinghouse Talent Search (Now Regeneron Science Talent Search) (1950); Grantee, National Aeronautics and Space Administration; Grantee, National Science Foundation, Office of Naval Research, Research Corp. (Now Research Corporation For Science Advancement), NASA **Membership:** Founder, Heritage Fund for Arts and Science (2016); Fellow, American Astronomical Society; International Astronomical Union; Former Principal Scientist, Scientific Association for the Study of Time in Physics and Cosmology; Division: Galaxies and Cosmology, International Astronomical Union; Division VIII: Galaxies and the Universe, International Astronomical Union; Commission 28: Galaxies, International Astronomical Union; Commission 47: Cosmology, International Astronomical Union **Marquis Who's Who Honors:** Albert Nelson Marquis Lifetime Achievement Award (2017) **To what do you attribute your success:** Dr. Tifft attributes his success to his unwavering belief in the scientific method. **Why did you become involved in your profession or industry:** Dr. Tifft knew since he was in fourth grade that he wanted to be a scientist, and by the eighth grade, an astronomer. **What do you consider to be the highlight of your career:** The highlight of Dr. Tifft's career was the discovery of redshift quantization and the marriage to his beloved wife, Janet. **Shipping Address:** 6532 N Cibola, AZ, Tucson, 85718 **Website:** https://williamtifft.wordpress.com

Ralph F. Tilden

Title: Music Educator (Retired) **Industry:** Education/Educational Services **Date of Birth:** 02/10/1930 **Place of Birth:** High Point **State:** NC **Parents:** Thomas Alphonso Tilden; Ruth Eugenia (Fulton) Tilden **Education:** MusM, University of Cincinnati College-Conservatory of Music (1954); MusB, University of Cincinnati College-Conservatory of Music (1952) **Certifications:** Certified Teacher, State of Florida **Career:** Professor, Edison Community College (Now Florida SouthWestern State College), Fort Myers, FL (1966-1995); Music Teacher of Theology, St. James Cathedral School, Orlando, FL (1960-1965); Organ Professor, University of Cincinnati College-Conservatory of Music (1954-1960) **Career Related:** Organist, Choirmaster, St. Luke's Episcopal Church, Fort Myers, FL (1965-1995); Organist, Choirmaster, Cathedral Church of St. Luke, Orlando, FL (1960-1965); Organist, Choirmaster, The Calvary Church, Cincinnati, OH (1954-1960); Organ Recitalist, United States; Organ Recitalist, France; Organ Recitalist, England **Civic:** Volunteer, Activist, ACLU (1960-Present); Volunteer, Activist, National LGBTQ Task Force (1960-Present); AIDS Support Council, Mountain Television Network, Boone, NC (1999) **Creative Works:** Composer, "Assumpta Est Maria" (2000); Composer, "His Voice as the Sound" (1997); Composer, "Come, Holy Spirit, Come" (1987) **Membership:** Dean, American Guild of Organists; Association of Anglican Musicians; Organ Historical Society; Standing Commission on Liturgy and Music; Episcopal Diocese of Western North Carolina **Marquis Who's Who Honors:** Albert Nelson Marquis Lifetime Achievement Award (2017); Distinguished Humanitarian (2017) **Hobbies:** Antique collecting; Gardening **Political Affiliations:** Democrat **Religion:** Episcopalian **Shipping Address:** 1705 Pope Ct., Wilmington, NC, 28405

William Milton Timmons, PhD

Title: Producer, Freelance Writer, Publisher, Filmmaker, Cinema Arts Educator (Retired) **Industry:** Writing and Editing **Date of Birth:** 04/21/1933 **Place of Birth:** Houston **State:** TX **Parents:** Carter Charles Timmons; Gertrude Monte (Lee) Timmons **Marital Status:** Divorced **Spouse Name:** Pamela Cadorette (12/24/1975, Divorced) **Education:** PhD, University of Southern California (1975); MA, University of California, Los Angeles (1961); BS, University of Houston (1958) **Certifications:** Teaching Certificate, Los Angeles Unified School District (1960) **Career:** Chairman, Department of Cinema, Los Angeles Valley College, Van Nuys, CA (1970-1991); Professor, Speech and Drama, Sam Houston State University, Huntsville, TX (1963-1967); Operations Assistant, Columbia Broadcasting System, Hollywood, CA (1961-1962); Teaching Fellow, University of California, Los Angeles (1960-1961); Production Assistant, Station KUHT-TV, Houston, TX (1956-1957); Production Assistant, Station KUHT-TV, Houston, TX (1953-1954); Staff Announcer, Station KMCO, Conroe, TX (1951-1952); Child Actor, Houston Junior Theater (1945-1946) **Career Related:** Co-Founder, Center for Inquiry, Los Angeles, CA (1999); Producer, Station KPFK, Los Angeles, CA (1983-1995); Proofreader, Consultant, Focal Press Publishing Company, New York, NY (1983-1992); Co-Founder, Atheists United (1982); Publisher, Academic Associates, Los Angeles, CA (1976-2000); Associate Producer, Tom Sawyer and Huckleberry Finn, Pasadena Playhouse (1960); Producer, Children's Program, Station KPFK, Los Angeles, CA (1959-1960); Staff Announcer, Station KPFK, Los Angeles, CA (1959-1960); Producer, KUHT-TV (1953); Member, Independent Investigations Group, Center for Inquiry; Lecturer, Center for Inquiry, Los Angeles, CA; Saxophone Player, High School Band; Media Director, Independent Investigations Group, Center for Inquiry; Lecturer, Critical Thinking, Center for Inquiry **Civic:** President, High School Junior Class; President, High School Senior Class; President, Alpha Rho Chapter, Alpha Epsilon Rho, University of California, Los Angeles Chapter, The National Honorary Broadcasting Society **Military Service:** US Naval Reserve (1954-1956) **Creative Works:** Author, "The Scroll Seekers - Who Created the New Testament?" (2017); Author, "2084 - A Tale of Post America" (2008); Author, "Regarding an Angel's Flight" (2004); Author, "Everything About the Bible That You Never Had Time to Look Up" (2003); Producer, Educational Series, Cable Television (1993-2003); Author, "Orientation to Cinema" (1986); Producer, "Ghosts Never Die" (1981); Author, "Lucifer's Handbook - A Critique of Popular Religion" (1977); Producer, "Love Song" (1976); Producer, Director, Numerous Educational Films (1963-2003); Producer, Director, Weekly Radio Programs, Campus Comments (1963-1967); Producer, "The People, Yes" (1963); Associate Editor, Literary Yearbook, University of Houston (1957); Actor, Various Plays, University of Houston; Contributor, Articles to Magazines; Producer, Approximately 200 Television Programs **Awards:** Recipient, Golden Pen Award, Atheists United (2003); Recipient, Certificate of Appreciation, Center for Inquiry West (2000); Recipient, Certificate of Appreciation, Los Angeles Valley College (1993); Recipient, Award for Video Production, Atheists United (1993); Recipient, Teaching Fellowship, University of California, Los Angeles (1960); Nominee, Most Outstanding Student, University of Houston (1957); Recipient, Scholarship, Writer's Conference, Boulder, CO (1957); Named, Honorary Texas Ranger, State of Texas, Austin, TX (1946); Grantee, The James Hervey Johnson Charitable Educational Trust; Named, Personalities of America **Membership:** Associate Member, Society of Motion Picture and Television Engineers (1978-1992); Directory of American Film Scholars (1975); Mensa International Limited; Alumni Association, University of Southern California School of Cinematic Arts; Red Masque Players; Los Angeles Chapter, American Humanist Association; Alpha Epsilon Rho, University of California, Los Angeles Chapter; Delta Kappa Alpha; Ethical Culture Society of Los Angeles; Center for Inquiry; Atheists United; University Film & Video Association; Independent Film & Television Alliance; University Film Association; Informational Film Producers of America **Marquis Who's Who Honors:** Albert Nelson Marquis Lifetime Achievement Award (2017) **Hobbies:** Reading literary classics; Writing; Viewing latest movies; Participating in various civic organizations; Screening a large collection of films and educational programs for a local retirement homed educational programs for residents of a retirement home and educational television programs to the residents of his retirement home **Political Affiliations:** Democrat **Business Address:** 925 E Villa St., Apt 202A, Pasadena, CA, 91106 **Shipping Address:** 925 E Villa St Apt 202A, CA, Pasadena, 91106 **Website:** https://www.miltontimmons.com

Ilona L. Tobin

Title: Psychologist, Marriage and Family Therapist **Industry:** Medicine & Health Care **Company Name:** Dr. Ilona L. Tobin **Date of Birth:** 04/15/1943 **Place of Birth:** Trenton **State:** MI **Parents:** Frank John Kotyuk; Marjorie Cathalean (Lines) Kotyuk **Education:** EdD, Wayne State University, Detroit, MI (1978); MA, Michigan State University, East Lansing, MI (1975); MA, Eastern Michigan University, Ypsilanti, MI (1968); BA, Eastern Michigan University, Ypsilanti, MI (1965) **Certifications:** Licensed Psychologist, State of Michigan; Certified Sex Therapist; Certified Sex Educator and Counselor; Licensed Marriage and Family Therapist, State of Michigan; Diplomate, American Board of Sexology **Career:** Private Practice, Clinical Psychology, Birmingham, MI (1983-Present); Psychologist, Professional Psychotherapy and Counseling Center, Farmington Hills, MI (1980-1983); Director, Treatment, Alternative Lifestyles, Inc., Orchard Lake, MI (1979-1980); Psychotherapist, Identity Center, Inc., Mount Clemens, MI (1974-1979); Professor, Macomb Community College, Mount Clemens, MI (1974-1979); Teacher, Counselor, Willow Run Public Schools (Now Ypsilanti Community Schools), Ypsilanti, MI (1966-1972) **Career Related:** Datemate Coach (2005-Present); Teacher, Medical Education, St. Joseph's Hospital (Now Trinity Health), Pontiac, MI (1993-1998); Lecturer, Wayne State University, Detroit, MI (1977-1988); Recruitment Director, Upward Bound Program, Eastern Michigan University, Ypsilanti, MI (1969-1972) **Civic:** Member, Republican Presidential Round Table (2001); Advisory Board, Woodside Medical Center for Chemically Dependent Women (1984-1986); Vice President, Executive Board, Birmingham Community Women's Center (1984-1985); President, Executive Board, Birmingham Community Women's Center (1984-1985); Board of Directors, HAVEN of Oakland County (1984-1985); Board of Directors, Oakland Counselors Association (1984-1985); Co-chairman, Birmingham Families in Action (1982-1983); Board of Directors, Birmingham Community Women's Center **Creative Works:** Author, "Love's 4 Magnetic Forces Creating a Strong, Healthy Relationship," Publish Green (2017) **Awards:** Fellow, National Institute of Mental Health (1976-1978); Wayne State University Scholar (1976-1978) **Membership:** Mass Media Consultant, Michigan Psychological Association (1983-Present); Legislature Committee, Crisis Intervention Network, Michigan Psychological Association (1992-1994); American Psychological Association; ASCD; American Association of Sexuality Educators, Counselors & Therapists; Pi Lambda Theta; Phi Delta Kappa International **Marquis Who's Who Honors:** Albert Nelson Marquis Lifetime Achievement Award (2017) **To what do you attribute your success:** Dr. Tobin attributes her success to her loving and devoted mother of blessed memory, Marjorie C. Kotyuk. **Why did you become involved in your profession or industry:** She became involved in her profession because of her distinguished teachers and professors inspired her to learn and teach. **What do you consider to be the highlight of your career:** A highlight of her career was receiving her doctorate and graduate education while working full time. **Where will you be in five years:** In five years, she will be renovating old synagogues in Israel. **Hobbies:** Read; Listen to R&B and Jazz; College football and basketball mostly Michigan State **Political Affiliations:** Republican **Religion:** Jewish **Business Address:** 801 S. Adams Road, Suite 210, Birmingham, MI, 48009 **Shipping Address:** 1017 Pilgrim Ave., Birmingham, MI, 48009 **Website:** http://www.drilonatobin.com/?page_id=3

Frances Eileen Todd

Title: Pediatrics Nurse Practitioner, Health Care Transformation Advocate **Industry:** Medicine & Health Care **Company Name:** Los Angeles County Health Agency, SEIU 721 **Date of Birth:** 08/20/1950 **Place of Birth:** Hawthorne **State:** CA **Parents:** James Clark Nailen; Jean Eleanor (McGinty) Nailen **Marital Status:** Married **Spouse Name:** Steven Charles Todd (10/25/1975) **Children:** Amanda Kathryn **Education:** Doctorate in Public Administration, University of La Verne (2013); Master's Degree in Health Administration, University of La Verne, California (2000); Postgraduate Coursework, California State College, Long Beach, CA (1985); BSN, California State College, Long Beach, CA (1982); ASN, El Camino Junior College (1974); RN, State of California **Certifications:** Certified Public Health Nurse, State of California; Certified Pediatric Nurse Practitioner; Certified Nurse Practitioner; Certified Provider of Pediatrics and Advanced Life Support, American Heart Association; Certified Community College Teacher, State of California; Certification, Drug Enforcement Agency **Career:** Health Care Transformation Advocate, County Health Management, SEIU 721 (2015-Present); Pediatric Nurse Practitioner, Harbor-UCLA Medical Center, West Carson, CA (1985-2015); Pediatric Liaison Nurse, Harbor-UCLA Medical Center, West Carson, CA (1984-1990); Evening Shift Relief Charge Nurse, Harbor-UCLA Medical Center, West Carson, CA (1977-1985); Clinic Nurse II, Harbor-UCLA Medical Center, West Carson, CA (1977-1985); Clinic Nurse I, Harbor-UCLA Medical Center, West Carson, CA (1974-1977); Nursing Attendant, St. Earne's Nursing Home, Inglewood, CA (1973) **Career Related:** Steward, Service Employees International Union, Local Union 721 (1995-Present); Lecturer, Department of Pediatrics, UCLA School of Medicine (1980-Present); Co-chair, Interdisciplinary Practice Committee, Harbor-UCLA Medical Center, West Carson, CA (2013-2016); Neonatal Steering Committee, Harbor-UCLA Medical Center, West Carson, CA (1993-2015); Member, Interdisciplinary Practice Committee, Harbor-UCLA Medical Center, West Carson, CA (1986-2015); National Nurse Consultant, FluMist, MedImmune (2007); National Nurse Consultant, Synagis, MedImmune (2006); Member, Perinatal Steering Committee, Harbor-UCLA Medical Center, West Carson, CA (1991-2006); Lecturer, Faculty Department, Pediatrics, David Geffen School of Medicine, University of California, Los Angeles (1980-2015); Tutor, Compton College (1988); Clinical Instructor, Compton College (1987-1988); Lecturer in Field **Civic:** Member, Integration Advisory Board, Los Angeles Board of Supervisors (2015-Present); Ad Hoc Committee for RSV Prophylaxis in Los Angeles County (2003-2006); Member, Pre Hospital Care Sub Committee, EMS Commission, Los Angeles County (1987-1991); Past Co-Chairperson, Parent Support Group, Sherrie's Schools, Lomita, CA **Creative Works:** Author, "Insurance patterns of neonates admitted to a NICU (Doctoral Dissertation)," University of La Verne (2013); Co-author, "Preventing RSV infection for infants at risk: Current and emerging Strategies," The Clinical Adviser (2010); Co-producer, "Pavilion of Orchids Show," South Bay Pavilion Mall (1998-2000); Co-Author, "Judge's Handbook," Peruvian Paso Horse Registry of North America (1990); Content Reviewer, Pediatric Curriculum, Emergency Nurse's Association (1988); Author, "Reye's syndrome Triage," Journal of Emergency Nursing (1986); Author, "Stab Wound to the Heart," Journal of Emergency Nursing (1986); Author, "Pediatric Emergency: A Clinician's Reference," Journal of Emergency Nursing **Awards:** Recipient, Special Recognition, PDLN (1987); Honoree, Outstanding Pediatric Nurse, Harbor-UCLA Medical Center (1983); Honoree, Outstanding Pediatric Nurse, Harbor-UCLA Medical Center (1979) **Membership:** North American Peruvian Horse Association (2005-Present); American Society of Public Administration (2008-Present); American Opal Society (2001-Present); Local 721 (1974-Present); Executive Committee, California Premature Infant Coalition (2008-2011); Executive Committee, California Premature Infant Health Coalition (2008-2009); National Association of Pediatric Nurse Practitioners (1985-1988, 2007-2009); Show Chair, American Opal Society (2005); Peruvian Paso Horse Registry of North America (1978-2005); Judge's Accreditation Committee, Peruvian Paso Horse Registry of North America (1998-2000); Co-Chairman, Judge's Accreditation Committee, Peruvian Paso Horse Registry of North America (1988-1998); Emergency Nurses Association (1988-1991); Care of Pediatrics in Emergency Medicine Committee, Los Angeles Pediatric Society and the American Academy of Pediatrics (1986-1990); Vice President, PDLN (1988-1989); President, PDLN (1987); Los Angeles Pediatrics Society (1985-1986); SNAC, El Camino College (1972-1974); Service Employees International Union **Hobbies:** Peruvian paso horses; Orchids; Lapidary cutting and design with opals **Business Address:** PO Box 1953, Lomita, CA, 90717 **Shipping Address:** 1321 W M St., Wilmington, CA, 90744

Anthony J. Tomassoni

Title: Emergency Physician, Medical Toxicologist **Industry:** Medicine & Health Care **Company Name:** Yale University **State:** NJ **Education:** Fellow, University of Cincinnati Hospital (1995); Resident, University of Cincinnati Hospital (1993); MD, UMDNJ - New Jersey Medical School, The State University of New Jersey (1989); MS in Human Biochemistry, Fairleigh Dickinson University (1984); BA in Science Education, Fairleigh Dickinson University (1979) **Certifications:** Certified in Medical Toxicology, American Board of Emergency Medicine (1997); Certified in Emergency Medicine, American Board of Emergency Medicine (1994); Registered Master Maine Guide **Career:** Emergency Physician & Medical Toxicologist, Yale School of Medicine (2007-Present); Medical Director, Yale New Haven System Center for Emergency Preparedness and Disaster Response, Yale New Haven Health (2007-Present); Consultant, Medical Toxicology, Emergency and Disaster Medicine Education (1996-2012); Developer to Medical Director, Northern New England Poison Center, Maine Medical Center, Portland, ME (1995-2006); Emergency Physician/Medical Toxicologist, Northern New England Poison Center, Maine Medical Center, Portland, ME (1995-2006); Vice President, Quince Integrated Computer Systems, Inc., Whippany, NJ (1983-1989); Educator/Developer, Fair Lawn Board of Education (1979-1985) **Career Related:** Fellow, American Academy of Clinical Toxicology (2014); Fellow, American College of Emergency Physicians; Fellow, American College of Medical Toxicology; Medical Team Manager, FEMA Urban Search and Rescue Task Force MA-1, Beverly, MA **Civic:** FEMA Urban Search and Rescue; NDMS Disaster Medical Assistance Team; Emergency Medical Services; Public Health Preparedness **Creative Works:** Co-author, "Toxic Industrial Chemicals and Chemical Weapons: Exposure, Identification, and Management by Syndrome," Emergency Medicine Clinics of North America (2014); Co-author, "The Global Burden of Road Injury: Its Relevance to the Emergency Physician," Emergency Medicine International (2014); Co-author, "Mass Arsenic Poisoning and the Public Health Response in Maine," Disaster Medicine and Public Health Preparedness (2013); Co-author, "Resource Allocation: an Approach for Enhancing Hospital Resiliency," Journal of Business Continuity & Emergency Planning (2011); Contributor, Scientific Papers and Abstracts, Professional Journals; Contributor, Three Toxicology Texts, International EM Text, and Other Electronic References **Awards:** National Teaching Faculty Award, American College of Emergency Physicians (2010); Faculty Teaching Award in Emergency Medicine, Yale Emergency Medicine (2008) **Membership:** Advanced Hazmat Life Support Scientific Advisory Committee; American College of Emergency Physicians; American College of Medical Toxicology; Board of Trustees, American Academy of Clinical Toxicology; Wilderness Medical Society; Past Chair, American Association of Poison Control Centers Council of Medical Directors **Business Address:** 464 Congress Avenue, Suite 260, New Haven, CT, 06519 **Shipping Address:** 173 Hilldale Road, Bethany, CT, 06524

Patricia Short Tomlinson, PhD

Title: Distinguished Professor Emeritus, Nurse, Social Psychologist **Industry:** Education/Educational Services **Company Name:** University of Minnesota **Date of Birth:** 07/08/1933 **Place of Birth:** Valley City **State:** ND **Parents:** Florence Marie Short; Aubrey Niles Short **Marital Status:** Widowed **Children:** Cara Kirsten; Niles **Education:** Honorary PhD, University of Tampere, Finland (2005); PhD, Oregon State University (1984); MSN, University of Washington (1973); BSN, University of Minnesota (1957) **Certifications:** RN, Minnesota Board of Nursing, State of Minnesota (1985); RN, Oregon State Board of Nursing (1971); RN, California State Board of Nursing (Now California Board of Registered Nursing) (1957) **Career:** Professor Emeritus, University of Minnesota, Minneapolis, MN (2001-Present); Fulbright Visiting Professor, University of Tampere, Finland (2001); Visiting Professor, National Yang-Ming University, Taipei, Taiwan (1997); Visiting Professor, University of Bergen, Norway (1995-1996); Professor, University of Minnesota, Minneapolis, MN (1985-2001); Associate Professor, OHSU, Portland, OR (1973-1985) **Career Related:** Founding Director, Family Health Consultants, St. Paul, MN (2002-Present); Fellowship in Community Mental Health Administration, The University of North Carolina at Chapel Hill (1972-1973); Fellowship, National Institutes of Health (1972-1973) **Civic:** Board of Directors, National Council on Family Relations (1996-1999); Chair, Family Health Section, National Council on Family Relations (1996-1999) **Creative Works:** U.S. National Editor, Scandinavian Journal of Caring Sciences (2000-Present); Editorial Board Member, Scandinavian Journal of Caring Sciences (2000-Present); Contributor, Articles, Professional Journals **Awards:** Senior Fulbright Scholar (2006-Present); Nursing Alumni Award, University of Minnesota (2009); Fulbright Scholarship (2001); Award For Excellence in Clinical Research, American Association of Critical-Care Nurses (1995) **Membership:** Associate, Nordic College of Caring Science **Marquis Who's Who Honors:** Albert Nelson Marquis Lifetime Achievement Award (2017) **To what do you attribute your success:** Dr. Tomlinson attributes her success to curiosity, special concern, and commitment to learning, helping, and caring for children. **Why did you become involved in your profession or industry:** Ever since Dr. Tomlinson was a small child, she really wanted to be a nurse. She grew up in a family that inspired aspiration and always kept busy. Both her mother and father were teachers on the Indian reservation in South Dakota; her father died when she was very young. That inspired her to go into teaching. Her whole family are teachers. Her brother is a professor, her sister was a primary school teacher, and her son and daughter are professors; her granddaughter, who is 14-years-old, said that since her whole family are teachers, she will have to be a professor as well and is planning a career in bioscience. **What do you consider to be the highlight of your career:** The highlight of Dr. Tomlinson's career that stands out the most is the opportunity to teach and to learn alternative views of health delivery, community, linkages, and the role of nursing in Norway, Finland and Taiwan. **Hobbies:** Traveling; Sumi-e Painting; Writing **Political Affiliations:** Liberal **Religion:** Protestant **Shipping Address:** 16250 Pacific Highway, Unit 64, Lake Oswego, OR, 97034

Joseph B. Tompkins Jr.

Title: Lawyer **Industry:** Law and Legal Services **Company Name:** Sidley Austin LLP **Date of Birth:** 04/04/1950 **Place of Birth:** Roanoke **State:** VA **Parents:** Joseph Buford; Rebecca Louise (Johnston) T. **Children:** Edward Graves; Claiborne Forbes **Education:** Master in Public Policy, JD, Harvard University (1975); BA in Politics, Washington and Lee University, Summa Cum Laude (1971) **Certifications:** 4th Circuit, US Court of Appeals (1993); 7th Circuit, US Court of Appeals (1991); 6th Circuit, US Court of Appeals (1985); 3rd Circuit, US Court Appeals (1983); US District Court DC (1982); 11th Circuit, US Court Appeals (1982) **Career:** Partner, Sidley & Austin LLP, Washington, DC (1982-Present); Deputy Chief of Fraud, Section Criminal Division, United States Department of Justice, Washington, DC (1980-1982); Associate Director, Office of Policy and Management Analysis Criminal Division, United States Department of Justice, Washington, DC (1979-1980); Associate, Sidley & Austin LLP, Washington, DC (1975-1979) **Civic:** Virginia Board of Health Professions, Richmond, VA (1984-1992); Chairman, Virginia Board of Health (1986-1988, 1990-1991); Vice Chairman, Virginia Board of Health (1984-1986) **Creative Works:** Contributor, Articles, Professional Journals **Membership:** White Collar Crime Committee, Criminal Justice Section, ABA (1980-Present); Chairman, Task Force on Computer Crime, ABA (1982-1992); Virginia Bar Association; The District of Columbia Bar Association; The Phi Beta Kappa Society **Bar Admissions:** United States Court of Appeals for the Second Circuit (2010); United States Court of International Trade (1996); United States Court of Appeals for the Fourth Circuit (1993); United States Court of Appeals for the Seventh Circuit (1991); United States Court of Appeals for the Ninth Circuit (1985); United States Court of Appeals for the Federal Circuit (1985); United States Court of Appeals for the Sixth Circuit (1985); United States Court of Appeals for the Third Circuit (1983); United States Court of Appeals for the 11th Circuit (1982); United States Court of Appeals for the District of Columbia (1982); United States Court of Appeals for the Fifth Circuit (1977); Supreme Court of the United States (1977); District of Columbia (1976); Virginia (1975) **Shipping Address:** 1501 K Street N.W., Suite 600, Sidley Austin LLP, Washington, DC, 20005

Marian Tonjes

Title: Professor Emerita **Industry:** Education/Educational Services **Company Name:** Western Washington University **Date of Birth:** 02/16/1929 **Place of Birth:** Rockville Centre **State:** NY **Parents:** Millard Warren; Felicia E. (Tyler) Benton **Spouse Name:** Charles F. Tonjes (Divorced 1965, Deceased) **Children:** Jeffrey Charles; Kenneth Warren **Education:** EdD, University of Miami (1975); MA, University of New Mexico (1969); BA, University of New Mexico (1951) **Certifications:** Certification, University of New Mexico (1966) **Career:** Professor Emerita, Western Washington University (1994-Present); Professor Emerita, University of New Mexico (1995); Director of Summer Study at Oriel College, Oxford University, England (1976-1993); Professor of Education, Western Washington University, Bellingham, WA (1975-1994); Assistant Professor, United States International University, San Diego, CA (1972-1975); Associate Director, Visiting Instructor Florida Center Teacher Training Materials, University of Miami (1971-1972); Research Assistant, Reading, Southwestern Cooperative Educational Laboratory (1969-1971); Teacher of Secondary Development Reading, Rio Grande High School (1967-1969); Teacher of Remedial Reading, Zia Elementary School (1965-1967); Teacher of Music, Physical Education, Sunset Mesa Day School, Albuquerque, NM (1963-1964); Director of Recreation, Stuyvesant Town Housing Project, New York, NY (1951-1953) **Career Related:** Adjunct Professor, University of New Mexico (1995-Present); Keynote Speaker, American Reading Forum, Sanibel Island, FL (2008); Symposium Chair, World Congress, Manila (2004); Speaker, European Conference on Reading, Tallinn, Estonia (2003); International Travel Advisor, Vantage Deluxe Travel (2002-2005); Invited Guest, Russian Reading Association, Moscow (1992); Visiting Professor, University of Guam, Mangilao (1989-1990); Visiting Professor, Adult Education, Palomar Junior College, California (1974); Reading Supervisor, Manzanita Center (1968); Consultant in Field **Civic:** Tour Director, In the Footsteps of Dickens, England (2001); Trustee, White Mountain School (2000-2006); Read by Three Committee, Albuquerque Business and Education Compact (1999-2002); Honorary Trustee, Lomonosov School, Moscow, Russia **Creative Works:** Invited Keynote Banquet Speaker, American Reading Forum, Sanibel, FL (2008-Present); Co-Author, "Integrated Content Literacy, Fifth Edition" (2006); Author, "Integrated Content Literacy" (1999); Author, "Teaching Reading/Thinking Study Skills in Content Classroom, Third Edition, Secondary Reading, Writing and Learning" (1991) **Awards:** Named, Alumnae Volunteer of Year, White Mountain School (2006); Nominee, Professional Outstanding Alumna, McDaniel College (2005); Recipient, Outstanding Teacher Educator Award, International Reading Association (1981); Grantee, Training Teacher Trainers (1975); National Defense Education Act Fellow, Oklahoma State University (1969) **Membership:** Delta Delta Delta; Committee on International Development in North America, International Reading Association (1991-1996); Travel, Interchange and Study Tours Committee, International Reading Association (1984-1986); Chairman, Board of Directors, American Reading Forum (1983-1985); Workshop Director, Southwest Regional Conferences, International Reading Association (1982); Non-Print Media and Reading Committee, International Reading Association (1980-1983); Pendulum Society; American Reading Forum; International Reading Association; Past Chapter President, PEO; World Congress in Reading, Buenos Aires, Argentina; European Council of International Schools; European Conference in Reading; United Kingdom Reading Association; Circumnavigators; International Society of Roadway Travelers; Oxonian and Friend of Oriel College **Hobbies:** Miniatures; Reading; Bridge; Art; Travel; Cooking **Religion:** Presbyterian **Shipping Address:** 900 Solano Drive N.E., Albuquerque, NM, 87110

Saul Touster

Title: Law Educator **Industry:** Education/Educational Services **Date of Birth:** 10/12/1925 **Place of Birth:** Brooklyn **State/Country of Origin:** NY **Parents:** Ben Touster; Bertha (Landau) Touster **Marital Status:** Married **Spouse Name:** Irene Tayler (1/14/1978); Helen Davidson (11/23/1954, Divorced 1967) **Children:** Natasha Ann; Jonathan Bach **Education:** JD, Harvard University (1948); AB, Harvard University, Magna Cum Laude (1944) **Career:** Professor Emeritus, Brandeis University, Waltham, MA (1993); Professor, Brandeis University, Waltham, MA (1980-1993); Director, Legal Studies, Humanities, Professions Programs, Brandeis University, Waltham, MA (1980-1993); Professor, Law, City University of New York Graduate School (1974-1980); Professor, Law, John Jay College of Criminal Justice (1974-1980); Acting President, Richmond College, City University New York (1973-1974); Professor, City College of New York (1971-1973); Provost, City College of New York (1971-1973); Academy Vice President, City College of New York (1971-1973); Professor, Law and Social Sciences, State University of New York College at Old Westbury (1969-1971); Member, Adjunct Faculty, Medicine, Education, Psychology, University at Buffalo (1964-1969); Assistant to President, University at Buffalo (1966-1968); Professor, Law, University at Buffalo (1955-1969); Lawyer, New York City, NY (1949-1955) **Career Related:** Visiting Professor, Boston College Law School (1994); Visiting Professor, Summer Program, University of Brussels (1968); Legislative Consultant, New York State Law Review Commission (1956-1961) **Military Service:** Lieutenant Junior Grade, U.S. Naval Reserve (1944-1946); U.S. Navy (1943-1946) **Creative Works:** Author, "From My Life" (2017); Author, "Surrealism and the Art of Samuel Bak, in Between Worlds" (2002); Editor, Introduction, "Beyond Words: A Holocaust History in Sixteen Woodcuts" (2001); Author, Introduction, "Beyond Words: A Holocaust History in Sixteen Woodcuts" (2001); Editor, Introduction, "A Survivors' Haggadah" (1998); Author, Introduction, "A Survivors' Haggadah" (1998); Author, "Still Lives and Other Lives" (1966); Contributor, Articles, Legal Periodicals **Awards:** Fellow, National Endowment of the Humanities (1978); Legal History Fellow, American Bar Foundation (1977-1978); Philippine Liberation Medal (1944-1945) **Membership:** Board of Advisers, International Institute of Boston; Phi Beta Kappa **Bar Admissions:** New York (1949) **Marquis Who's Who Honors:** Albert Nelson Marquis Lifetime Achievement Award (2017) **Hobbies:** Writing poetry **Shipping Address:** 180 Beacon St, Boston, MA, 02116

Teryl Archer Townsend-Viner

Title: Artist, Educator **Industry:** Fine Art **Date of Birth:** 05/09/1938 **Place of Birth:** Coronado **State:** CA **Parents:** Robert Lee Townsend; Elizabeth (Archer) Townsend **Marital Status:** Widowed **Children:** Shawn Elizabeth Speers; Don Philip Speers, Jr. **Education:** Coursework with Glen Bradshaw (1980-1985); Coursework with Carl Molno (1971-1974); Coursework with Edgar Whitney (1971-1973); Coursework with Chen Chi (1971); Coursework with Millard Sheets (1971); Coursework with Edward Betts (1971); Coursework with Robert E. Wood (1971) **Career:** Freelance Teacher, Nantucket, MA (1974-1988); Freelance Teacher, Houston, TX (1974-1988); Freelance Teacher; Freelance Painter, Owner Teryl Townsend Gallery, Nantucket, MA **Civic:** Community Board, Wavery House, New Canaan, CT; Board of Trustees, Vero Beach Museum of Art; Deacon, St. Mark's Episcopal Church, New Canaan, CT **Creative Works:** Exhibitor, Solo Shows, Betty Barker Gallery (1998); Exhibitor, Solo Shows, South Wharf Gallery (1982-1983); Featured, "Watercolor Energies," Frank West (1982); Exhibitor, Solo Shows, The Little Gallery (1981); Exhibitor, Solo Shows, Stephen F. Austin State University (1979); Exhibitor, Solo Shows, The Kirby Gallery (1977); Exhibitor, Solo Shows, Robert Rice Gallery, Houston, TX (1976); Designer, Book Covers; Exhibitor, Group Shows, Washington, DC; Exhibitor, Group Shows, James Hunt Barker Gallery, Palm Beach, FL; Exhibitor, Group Shows, James Hunt Barker Gallery, Nantucket, MA; Exhibitor, Group Shows, Gregory Gallery, Darien, CT; Exhibitor, Group Shows, Hospice House, Vero Beach, FL; Exhibitor, Solo Shows, Art League of Houston; Exhibitor, Solo Shows, Potomac Gallery; Exhibitor, Solo Shows, Nantucket, MA **Awards:** Award Winner, New Canaan Society for the Arts (1998); Award Winner, New Canaan Society for the Arts (1996); First Place Award, Spectrum Exhibition, Southwestern Watercolor Society (1995); Award Winner, New Canaan Society for the Arts (1995); Merit Award, Nantucket Artists Association (1986); Award, Southwestern Watercolor Society (1984); Merit Award, Nantucket Artists Association (1983); Various Awards, Houston Watercolor Society (1982-1983); Merit Award, Nantucket Artists Association (1982); Merit Award, Art League Houston (1982); Merit Award, Nantucket Artists Association (1980); Award, Southwestern Watercolor Society (1978); Century Award, Rocky Mountain National Watermedia Society (1977); Merit Award, Southern Watercolor Society (1977); Merit Award, Art League Houston (1977); Third Place Award, National Small Painting Show (1976); Various Awards, Houston Watercolor Society (1975-1976); Merit Award, Art League Houston (1975); Award, Southwestern Watercolor Society (1974-1976); Century Award, Rocky Mountain National Watermedia Society (1974) **Membership:** Executive Committee, Nantucket Artists Association (1986-1987); Advisor, Professional Standards, Houston Watercolor Society (1976-1982); Advisor, Cultural Committee, Houston Chamber of Commerce (1975-1976); President, Houston Watercolor Society (1974-1975); American Watercolor Society; National Watercolor Society; Rocky Mountain National Watermedia Society; Southwestern Watercolor Society; Board of Directors, Nantucket Artists Association; Advisor, Nantucket Artists Association; Vice President, Houston Watercolor Society; Nantucket Chamber of Commerce; New Canaan Society for the Arts **Marquis Who's Who Honors:** Albert Nelson Marquis Lifetime Achievement Award (2017) **To what do you attribute your success:** Ms. Townsend-Viner attributes her success to hard work, and being committed to and loving the career she's chosen. **Why did you become involved in your profession or industry:** Ms. Townsend-Viner became involved in her profession because she was struck by lightning in her late 20s, and decided to follow the arts rather than physics. She does believe the two of them are closely related. **What do you consider to be the highlight of your career:** One of the highlights of Ms. Townsend-Viner's career was being struck by lightning. **Where will you be in five years:** In five years, Ms. Townsend-Viner plans on being right where she is. **Hobbies:** Theology; Philosophy; Entertaining **Religion:** Episcopalian **Business Address:** 1 Beachside Drive, Orchid, FL, 32963 **Shipping Address:** 913 Orchid Point Way, Vero Beach, FL, 32963

Philip Charles Trackman

Title: Biochemist **Industry:** Medicine & Health Care **Company Name:** Boston University Goldman School of Dental Medicine **Date of Birth:** 07/15/1953 **Place of Birth:** Montclair **State:** NJ **Parents:** John C. Trackman; Irene (Boveri) Trackman **Spouse Name:** Susan Kirkpatrick Troxler, October 24, 1979 (div. 2004) **Children:** Louisa; Eric **Education:** PhD, Brandeis University (1983); PhD in Biochemistry, Boston University (1980); BA in Chemistry, College Wooster, Ohio (1975) **Career:** Professor of Molecular and Cell Biology, Boston University Goldman School of Dental Medicine (2013-Present); Research Assistant Professor of Biochemistry, Boston University (1987-Present); Director of Oral Biology Research, Boston University Henry M. Goldman School Dental Medicine (2011-2013); Professor of Periodontology and Oral Biology, Boston University Goldman School of Dental Medicine (2004-2013); Associate Professor of Periodontology and Oral Biology, Boston University Goldman School of Dental Medicine (2000-2004); Assistant Professor, Periodontology and Oral Biology, Boston University Goldman School Dental Medicine (1992-2000); Team leader, Novo Laboratories, Inc. (1986-1987); Project Leader, Novo Laboratories, Inc. (1986-1987); Staff Researcher, Novo Laboratories, Inc., Wilton, CT (1983-1984) **Creative Works:** Contributor, Articles, Numerous Professional Journals; Contributor, Chapters, Books **Membership:** Associate Member, American Chemical Society; Sigma Xi; Boston Section, American Association of Dental Research; American Society of Bone and Mineral Research; American Society of Matrix Biology; International CCN Society; International Association of Dental Research; American Diabetes Association **Religion:** Protestant **Business Address:** Boston U Goldman Sch Dental Medicine 700 Albany St., #201, Boston, MA, 02118-2518 **Shipping Address:** 700 Albany Street, Boston, MA, 02118

Kim Trainor Davis

Title: Owner, President **Industry:** Corporate Communications & Public Relations **Company Name:** Nomiss Communication **Marital Status:** Married **Education:** BA in Journalism, Texas Tech University (1988) **Career:** Owner, Nomiss Communication; President, Nomiss Communication **Civic:** Past Marketing Chair, Local Branch, United Way Worldwide; Government Relations Committee, Local Chamber of Commerce; Past Member, National CASA Association; Board Member, Sondra's Song **Marquis Who's Who Honors:** Albert Nelson Marquis Lifetime Achievement Award (2017) **To what do you attribute your success:** Ms. Trainor Davis attributes her success to her honesty and ability to build good relationships. She surrounds herself personally and professionally with positive people who know more than she does. Her favorite quote is, "Live as if you were to die tomorrow. Learn as if you were to live forever." She hopes to learn something every day. **Why did you become involved in your profession or industry:** Ms. Trainor Davis became involved in her profession because she knew she wanted to go into journalism since she won an essay contest in the sixth grade. **What do you consider to be the highlight of your career:** The highlight of Ms. Trainor Davis' career was finally taking the leap of faith to begin her own business and not only seeing it survive but also thrive. Now, the business is celebrating 10 years as a nationally recognized media relations and crisis communications firm. **Where will you be in five years:** In the coming years, Ms. Trainor Davis plans on experiencing continued business growth and possibly expanding into the publishing field. **Hobbies:** Sports; Reading **Business Address:** 3305 81st St., Ste 3, Lubbock, TX, 79423 **Shipping Address:** 3910 100th St., Lubbock, TX, 79423 **Website:** http://www.nomisscom.com

Nang Tri Tran, PhD

Title: Electrical Engineer, Material Scientist **Industry:** Education/Educational Services **Company Name:** University of Minnesota, Ecosolar International **Place of Birth:** Binh Dinh **State:** Vietnam **Parents:** Cam Tran; Cuu Thi Nguyen **Spouse Name:** Thu-Huong Tran **Children:** Helen; Florence; Irene; Kenneth **Education:** PhD in Solid State Materials and Device Physics, Osaka Prefecture University, Japan (1979); MEE, Kyushu Institute of Technology (1975); BEE, Kyushu Institute of Technology (1973); Postdoctoral Research Coursework, Harvard University; Postdoctoral Research Coursework, University of California, Irvine **Career:** President, Ecosolar International (2008-Present); Adjunct Professor, University of Minnesota (2001-Present); Executive, Khanti Inc. (1996-Present); Consultant, American Thin Films (2007-2010); Senior Staff Scientist, Imation Corporation (1996-2007); Senior Research Scientist, 3M (1985-1996); Research Scientist/Senior Engineer, Arco Solar Industries (1980-1984); Engineer, Sharp Electronics Corporation (1979-1980); Research Associate, University of California, Irvine (1979-1980) **Career Related:** Fellow, Rotary International (1968-1979); Invited Speaker, Universities, Vietnam, and Japan; Lecturer, Seminars and Workshops; Technology Committees, Various International Conferences; Editor, Technical Journals; Reviewer, Technical Proposals **Creative Works:** Author, "My Journey: The Collected Poems of Binh an Tran" (2003); Author, Poem Collections, Unpublished **Membership:** Director, Phat An Temple (2000-2009); Senior Life Member, IEEE; JSAP; New York Academy of Sciences **Marquis Who's Who Honors:** Albert Nelson Marquis Lifetime Achievement Award (2017) **To what do you attribute your success:** Dr. Tran attributes his success to his love to help people and wanting to contribute something in his capacity to society. In addition, he enjoys what he's doing and chooses to see things in more positive ways. His motto for his R&D activities is "Don't think. Do!" He believes each individual, regardless of their socioeconomic conditions, has their own special skill that can be developed to the fullest through hard working, dedication, opportunities, and education. **Why did you become involved in your profession or industry:** Dr. Tran became involved in his profession because he was good at math and physics in high school. That had led him to choose science and engineering as his major in colleges. In his view, the engineering field is more objective and therefore one can draw a more accurate conclusion from the data. **What do you consider to be the highlight of your career:** One of the highlights of Dr. Tran's career that stands out the most is his contribution to the digital mammography. It can help screen and hopefully prevent breast cancers in millions of women worldwide. In addition, through the formation of Ecosolar International, he has been able to help enhance the living quality of thousands of people in low-income communities in Vietnam. **Business Address:** PO Box 28658, Saint Paul, MN, 55128 **Shipping Address:** 7970 Demontreville Trail N, Lake Elmo, MN, 55042 **Website:** http://www.ecosolarcity.org

Robert E. Tranquada

Title: Professor Emeritus **Industry:** Education/Educational Services **Company Name:** University of Southern California School of Medicine **Date of Birth:** 08/27/1930 **Place of Birth:** Los Angeles **State:** CA **Parents:** Ernest Alvro Tranquada; Katharine (Jacobus) Tranquada **Marital Status:** Married **Spouse Name:** Janet Martin (8/31/1951) **Children:** John Martin; Katherine Anne; James Robert **Education:** Honorary, LHD, Charles R. Drew University of Medicine and Science (2015); DSc, Charles R. Drew University of Medicine and Science (2015); Honorary DSc, Pomona College (2007); Honorary DSc, Worcester Polytechnic Institute (1985); Fellow in Diabetes, University of Southern California (1959-1960); Fellow in Diabetes and Metabolic Diseases, University of California, Los Angeles (1958-1959); Resident, Veterans Affairs Greater Los Angeles Healthcare System, United States Department of Veterans Affairs (1957-1958); Resident in Medicine, David Geffen School of Medicine, University of California, Los Angeles (1956-1957); Intern in Medicine, David Geffen School of Medicine, University of California, Los Angeles (1955-1956); MD, Stanford University (1955); BA, Pomona College (1951) **Certifications:** Diplomate, American Board of Internal Medicine **Career:** Professor Emeritus, University of Southern California (1997-Present); Norman Topping/National Medical Enterprises Professor of Medicine, University of Southern California (1992-1997); Norman Topping/National Medical Enterprises Professor of Public Policy, University of Southern California (1992-1997); Professor of Medicine, University of Southern California (1986-1992); Dean, School Medicine, University of Southern California (1986-1991); Chancellor, Dean, University of Massachusetts Medical School (1979-1986); Associate Dean School of Medicine, University of Southern California (1976-1979); Regional Director, Central Region, The Department Health Services, Los Angeles County (1974-1976); Associate Dean, School of Medicine, University of Southern California (1969-1976); Medical Director, Los Angeles County+University of Southern California Medical Center, The Department Health Services, Los Angeles County (1969-1974); Chairman, Department of Community Medicine, University of Southern California (1967-1970); Associate Professor, University of Southern California (1964-1968) **Career Related:** Chair, Task Force on Health Care Access, Los Angeles County (1992-1994) **Civic:** Member, Board of Directors, Martin Luther King, Jr. Community Hospital (2012-Present); Member, Board of Directors, Huntington Medical Research Institutes (2006-Present); Chairman Emeritus, Board of Overseers, Claremont University Consortium (2006-Present); Chairman Emeritus, Board of Trustees, Pomona College (2000-Present); Emeritus, School of Applied Life Sciences, Keck Graduate Institute (2000-Present); Vice Chairman, The Ralph M. Parsons Foundation (2008-2012); Board Trustee, AltaMed Health Services Corporation (2008-2011); Member, Board of Directors, Mt. San Antonio Gardens (2006-2015); Chairman, Good Hope Medical Foundation (2006-2014); Member, Board of Directors, Congressional Homes, Inc. (2006-2014); Chair, Association of Governing Boards of Universities and Colleges (2002-2003); Chairman, Local Initiative Health Authority, Los Angeles County (2001-2005); Member, Board of Directors, Ralph M. Parsons Foundation (2000-2017); Chairman, Board of Overseers, Claremont University Consortium (2000-2006); Council President, Association of Governing Boards (2000-2003); Vice-Chairman, Board of Trustees, School of Applied Life Sciences, Keck Graduate Institute (1997-2000); Member, Board of Directors, Good Hope Medical Foundation (1994-2016); Governing Board, Local Initiative Health Authority, Los Angeles County (1994-2007); Member, Board of Directors, Community Health Councils (1993-2012); Board Fellow, Claremont University Court (1991-2000); Chairman, Board of Trustees, Pomona College (1991-2000); Member, Board of Directors, Alliance for Children's Rights (1991-1995); Member, Independent Commission on the Los Angeles Police Department (1991-1992); Member, Board of Directors, Keck Hospital of University of Southern California (1988-1991); Member, Board of Trustees, Barlow Respiratory Hospital (1987-1989); Member, Board of Trustees, Orthopedic Hospital, Shriners Hospitals for Children (1986-1991); Member, Board of Trustees, Charles R. Drew University of Medicine and Science (1986-1995) **Awards:** Recipient, Fellowship, The Milbank Foundation (1967-1972); Inductee, Phi Beta Kappa, Pomona College; Named, Distinguished Military Graduate, Stanford University; Inductee, Alpha Omega Alpha; Recipient, Stanford Medical Alumni J.E. Wallace Sterling Distinguished Alumni Award, University of Southern California School of Medicine; Recipient, Elaine Stevely Hoffman Award, National Medical Fellowships, Inc. **Membership:** Fellow, American Association for the Advancement of Science; American Antiquarian Society; Institute of Medicine, The National Academy of Medicine; California Medical Association; Los Angeles Academy of Medicine; LACMA; American Medical Association **Marquis Who's Who Honors:** Albert Nelson Marquis Lifetime Achievement Award (2017) **Shipping Address:** 900 E Harrison Ave., Apt H4, Pomona, CA, 91767

Lawrence Alan Tritle

Title: History Professor **Industry:** Education/Educational Services **Company Name:** Loyola Marymount University **Date of Birth:** 10/13/1946 **Place of Birth:** Glendale **State:** CA **Parents:** Robert Charles Tritle Jr.; Dorothy (Brown) Tritle **Marital Status:** Married **Spouse Name:** Najwa Al-Qattan (8/15/2009); Margaret Burlington (1/31/1970, Deceased 8/24/2000) **Education:** PhD, University of Chicago (1978); MA, University of South Florida, Tampa, FL (1972); BA, University of California, Los Angeles (1968) **Career:** Author, Consultant (2016-Present); Professor, Loyola Marymount University, Los Angeles, CA (1978-2016); Daum Professor, Loyola Marymount University, Los Angeles, CA (2012); Marie Chilton Chair of Humanities, Loyola Marymount University, Los Angeles, CA (1988) **Career Related:** Visiting Professor, University of California, Los Angeles (1992); Visiting Professor, Loyola University Chicago (1990-1991); Visiting Professor, Loyola University Chicago (1981-1982) **Military Service:** Lieutenant, U.S. Army, Vietnam (1968-1971) **Creative Works:** Editor, "Oxford Handbook of Warfare in the Classical World" (2013); Author, "A New History of the Peloponnesian War" (2010); Editor, "Alexander the Great: A New History" (2009); Editor, "Alexander's Empire, From Formulation to Decay" (2007); Author, "The Peloponnesian War" (2004); Editor, "Crossroads of History Age of Alexander" (2003); Author, "From Melos to My Lai: War & Survival" (2000); Editor, "Text and Tradition: Studies in Greek History & Historiography" (1999); Editor, "Balkan Currents" (1998); Editor, "The Greek World in the Fourth Century " (1997); Author, "Phocion the Good" (1988) **Awards:** Fellow, National Endowment for The Humanities, University of Pennsylvania (1979) **Membership:** Chair, Committee of Ancient History, American Philological Association (1997-1999); Association of Ancient Historians; Society of Mayflower Descendants; American Legion; Society for Classical Studies **Marquis Who's Who Honors:** Albert Nelson Marquis Lifetime Achievement Award (2017) **Political Affiliations:** Democrat **Business Address:** 8235 Gulana Ave., Playa del Rey, CA, 90293

Alvin W. Trivelpiece, PhD

Title: Scientist (Retired) **Industry:** Sciences **Company Name:** Sandia National Laboratories **Date of Birth:** 03/15/1931 **Place of Birth:** Stockton **State:** CA **Parents:** Alvin Stevens Trivelpiece; Mae (Hughes) Trivelpiece **Marital Status:** Single **Spouse Name:** Shirley Ann Ross (3/23/1953, Deceased 4/26/2009) **Children:** Craig Evan; Steve Edward; Keith Eric **Education:** PhD in Electrical Engineering and Physics, California Institute of Technology, Pasadena, CA (1958); MEE, California Institute of Technology, Pasadena, CA (1955); BEE, California Polytechnic State University, San Luis Obispo, CA (1953) **Career:** Board of Trustees, Atomic Testing Museum (2017-Present); Consultant, Sandia National Laboratories, Albuquerque, NM (2000-2017); Consultant, Lawrence Livermore National Laboratory (2009-2014); President, Lockheed Martin Corporation (1996-2000); Director, Oak Ridge National Laboratory, Oak Ridge, TN (1989-2000); Vice President, Lockheed Martin Corporation (1995); Vice President, Martin Marietta (1989-1995); Executive Officer, American Association for the Advancement of Science, Washington, DC (1987-1988); Director, Office of Energy Research, U.S. Department of Energy, Washington, DC (1981-1987); Corporate Vice President, SAIC, La Jolla, CA (1978-1981); Vice President, Maxwell Technologies, San Diego, CA (1976-1978); Assistant Director, Atomic Energy Commission, Washington, DC (1973-1975); Professor, Physics, University of Maryland, (1966-1976); Associate Professor, University of California, Berkeley (1959-1966); Assistant Professor, University of California, Berkeley (1959-1966); Fulbright Scholar, Delft University of Technology, Delft, Netherlands (1958-1959) **Career Related:** Founding Board Member, American Council on Global Nuclear Competitiveness (2006-2012); Secretary, American Council on Global Nuclear Competitiveness (2006-2012); Treasurer, American Council on Global Nuclear Competitiveness (2006-2012); Chairman, Committee on Science and Technology in Kazakhstan, National Research Council, National Academy of Sciences (2006-2007); Workshop Chairman, National Academy of Sciences (2004); Workshop Chairman, Russian Academy of Sciences, Yekaterinburg, Russia (2004); Member, Committee on Technical Issues Related to Comprehensive Test Bane Treaty, National Academy of Sciences (2000-2002); Chairman, Committees, Small Innovative Firms, Nuclear Cities, Russia (2001); Chairman, Tennessee Technology Development Corporation (1998-2000); President, Tennessee Technology Development Corporation (1998-2000); Chairman, Tennessee Advisory Commission on Intergovernmental Relations (1996-1999); Member, Commission on Physical Sciences, Mathematics, and Applications, National Academy of Sciences (1993-1996); Member, Tennessee Advisory Commission on Intergovernmental Relations (1993-1996); Chairman, Advisory Committee, Federal Networking Council (1992-1996); Chairman, Coordinating Council for Education (1991-1993); Chairman, Mathematical Sciences Education Board, National Academy of Sciences (1990-1993); Head Delegate, Conference on Energy and Global Ecological Problems, National Academy of Sciences (1989); Head Delegate, Conference on Energy and Global Ecological Problems, Soviet Academy of Sciences (1989) **Creative Works:** Author, "Principles of Plasma Physics" (1973); Author, "Slow-Wave Propagation in Plasma Wave Guides" (1967); Contributor, Articles, Professional Journals **Awards:** Prize, Global Energy International (2009-2014); Tennessee Outstanding Service Commendation, Senate Joint Resolution #530 (2000); Distinguished Associate Award (2000); Outstanding Engineer Award, Region 3, IEEE (1995); Named Distinguished Alumnus, California Institute of Technology, Pasadena, CA (1987); Gold Medal for Distinguished Service, United States Secretary of Energy (1986); Named Distinguished Alumnus, California Polytechnic State University, San Luis Obispo, CA (1978) **Membership:** Fellow, John Simon Guggenheim Foundation (1966); Fellow, IEEE; Fellow, American Association for the Advancement of Science; Fellow, American Physical Society; NAE; American Association of University Professors; International Award Committee, Global Energy International; American Association of Physics Teachers; American Nuclear Society; National Press Club; Capital Hill Club; Tau Beta Pi; Sigma Xi **Marquis Who's Who Honors:** Albert Nelson Marquis Lifetime Achievement Award (2017) **Shipping Address:** 14 Wade Hampton Trl, Henderson, NV, 89052

Susanne Tropez-Sims

Title: Professor, Associate Dean of Clinical Affiliations, Clerkship Director **Industry:** Education/Educational Services **Company Name:** Meharry Medical College **Date of Birth:** 04/13/1949 **Place of Birth:** New Orleans **State:** LA **Parents:** Maxwell Sterling Tropez; Ethel (Ross) Tropez **Marital Status:** Married **Spouse Name:** Michael Milroy Sims (2/18/1995); James Carnell White (4/10/1971, Divorced 1992) **Children:** Lisa; Janifer; James Carnell **Education:** MPH, University of North Carolina at Chapel Hill (1982); MD, University of North Carolina at Chapel Hill (1975); BS, Bennett College (1971) **Certifications:** Diplomate, American Board of Pediatrics **Career:** Associate Dean of Clinical Affiliation, Meharry Medical College (2006-Present); Pediatric Clerkship Director, Meharry Medical College (2005-Present); Curriculum Committee Chair, Meharry Medical College (2003-Present); Joy McCann Professor, Meharry Medical College (2006-2010); Associate Dean of Academy Support, Meharry Medical College (2005-2006); Chair, Meharry Medical Service Foundation (2000-2002); Chair, Pediatrics Department, Meharry Medical College (1997-2005); Professor of Pediatrics, Meharry Medical College (1997-2005); Chief, Ambulatory Care Division, Louisiana State University (1989-1997); Associate Professor of Pediatrics, LSU Health New Orleans (1988-1997); Director, Pediatrics Emergency Room Division, Louisiana State University (1988-1989); Director, Pediatrics Day Clinic, University of North Carolina at Chapel Hill (1982-1988); Assistant Professor, University North Carolina at Chapel Hill (1982-1988); Acting Director, Pediatrics Day Clinic, WakeMed Health & Hospitals (1979-1982); Pediatrician, Carl R. Darnell Army Medical Center, U.S. Army (1976-1977); Resident of Pediatrics, UNC Health Care (1977-1979); Resident of Pediatrics, UNC Health Care (1975-1976) **Career Related:** Chair, Health Information Network Board, National Education Association 2011-Present); Dom Committee, National Medical Association (2011-Present); Chair, Pediatrics Section, National Medical Association (2011-2013); Chair, Health Network Board, National Education Association (2011-2012); Chair, Pediatrics Section, National Medical Association (2009-2012); Vice-Chair, Pediatrics Section, National Medical Association (2009-2011); Chair, Health Information Network Board, National Education Association (2000-2002); School Health Committee Chair, Local Chapter, American Academy of Pediatrics (1993-1996); National Committee of School Health (1992-1999); Clinical Director of Maternal and Child Health Units, Department of Health, The City of New Orleans (1992-1997); Chief of Community Pediatrics and Adolescent Medicine Division, Department of Health, The City of New Orleans (1992-1997); Faculty Development Fellowship, University of North Carolina at Chapel Hill School of Medicine (1985-1987); Pediatrician, Shelley Child Development Center (1981-1988); Child Medical Examiner Program (1979-1988); Fellowship in Preventive Medicine (1979-1982) **Civic:** Chair, LDM Committee, Clark Memorial United Methodist Church (2011-Present); Chair, Building Committee, Clark Memorial United Methodist Church (2005-2010); Chairman, Membership Care Committee, Clark Memorial United Methodist Church (2001-2006); Chair, Board of Trustees, Clark Memorial United Methodist Church (2001-2006); Chair, Administrative Board, Cornerstone United Methodist Church (1993-1996); Chair, Education Committee, United Methodist Church (1991-1992); Chairman, Pastor Parish Committee, Longview Baptist Church of Raleigh (1987-1988); Chairman, Pastor Parish Committee, Longview Baptist Church of Raleigh (1982-1984); Chairman, United Methodist Women, Walnut Terrace Child Development Center (1982-1983); United Methodist Women, Walnut Terrace Child Development Center (1981-1983) **Military Service:** Pediatrician, Carl R. Darnell Army Medical Center, U.S. Army (1976-1977) **Creative Works:** Contributor, Articles, Professional Journals **Awards:** Pre-Alumnae Clinical Faculty of Year Teaching Award (2011-2012); Listee, America's Top Pediatricians, Consumers Research Council of America (2009) **Membership:** Gold Humanism Honor Society, Arnold P. Gold Foundation (2013); School Health Committee, American Academy of Pediatrics; Child Abuse and Neglect Committee, North Carolina Pediatric Society; Adolescent Pregnancy Committee, North Carolina Pediatric Society; Louisiana Pediatric Society; Ambulatory Pediatric Association; Adolescent Pregnancy Coalition, United Way; National Alumnae Association, Bennett College **Marquis Who's Who Honors:** Distinguished Humanitarian (2017) **Political Affiliations:** Democrat **Shipping Address:** 509 Banshire Court, Brentwood, TN, 37027

Monroe Eugene Trout

Title: Health Administrator **Industry:** Medicine & Health Care **Company Name:** American Healthcare Systems (Now Premier) **Date of Birth:** 04/05/1931 **Place of Birth:** Harrisburg **State:** PA **Parents:** David Michael Trout; Florence Margaret (Kashner) Trout **Marital Status:** Married **Spouse Name:** Sandra Louise Lemke (6/11/1960) **Children:** Monroe Eugene; Timothy William (Deceased) **Education:** Honorary LLD, University of the Cumberlands (2003); Honorary LLD, Penn State Dickinson Law, The Pennsylvania State University (1996); Honorary LLD, Bloomfield College (1994); JD, Penn State Dickinson Law, The Pennsylvania State University (1969); LLB, Penn State Dickinson Law, The Pennsylvania State University (1964); Resident in Internal Medicine, Naval Medical Center Portsmouth (1959-1961); Intern, Great Lakes Naval Hospital (1957-1958); MD, University of Pennsylvania (1957); AB, University of Pennsylvania (1953) **Certifications:** Cerified in Medicine, Commonwealth of Pennsylvania; Certified in Medicine, State of New York **Career:** Chairman Emeritus, American Healthcare Systems, Inc. (1995-Present); Interim CEO, Cytran Inc. (1996); Chairman, American Healthcare Systems, Inc. (1987-1995); President, American Healthcare Systems, Inc. (1986-1995); Chief Executive Officer, American Healthcare Systems, Inc. (1986-1995); Board of Directors, American Healthcare Systems, Inc. (1986-1995); Senior Vice President, Sterling Drug, Inc. (1978-1986); Director of Medical Affairs, Sterling Drug, Inc. (1978-1986); Board of Directors, Sterling Drug, Inc. (1978-1986); Executive Committee Member, Sterling Drug, Inc. (1978-1986); Vice President, Sterling Drug, Inc. (1974-1978); Director of Medical Affairs, Sterling Drug, Inc. (1974-1978); Medical Director, Winthrop Laboratories (1970-1974); Vice President, Winthrop Laboratories (1968-1970); Medical Director, Sterling Drug, Inc. (1968-1970); Director of Drug Regulatory Affairs, Pfizer Inc. (1964-1968); Chief of Medical Department, Harrisburg State Hospital (1961-1964) **Career Related:** Chairman, Board of Directors, Cytyc, Inc. (Now Hologic, Inc.) (1998-2002); Chairman, Board of Directors, AEIX (1990-1995); Co-Chairman, Health Commission, County of San Diego (1992-1994); Special Lecturer in Legal Medicine, Penn State Dickinson Law, The Pennsylvania State University (1970-1993); Trustee, Penn State Dickinson Law, The Pennsylvania State University (1970-1993); Trustee, School of Health Administration, Arizona State University (1988-1991); Research Board Member, Sterling Drug, Inc. (1977-1986); Member, The Joint Commission (1976-1980); Secretary, Commission on Medical Malpractice, Department of Health, Education and Welfare (1971-1973); Endowed Director and Curator, National Churchill Museum, Fulton, MO; Endowed Chairs in Pharmacology and Surgery, UC San Diego; Endowed Vision Research Chair, University of Wisconsin; Founder of Professorship in Vision Research, University of Wisconsin; Chairman, Board of Directors, iNeedMD, Inc.; Adjunct Associate Professor, Arnold and Marie Schwartz College of Pharmacy, Long Island University **Civic:** Board of Directors, The International Churchill Society (2016-Present); Trustee, Baptist Health Foundation (1999-2007); Board of Directors, East Tennessee Historical Society (2003-2004); Board of Directors, Knoxville Opera, Tennessee (2001-2004); Board of Directors, Knoxville Symphony Orchestra, Tennessee (2001-2004); Trustee, The San Diego Museum of Art (1996-1998); President, Board of Trustees, University of California San Diego Foundation (1994-1997); Trustee, Thornton Pavilion, UC San Diego (1990-1997); International Dinner Chairman, B'nai B'rith International (1994); Co-Chairman, National Health Committee (1992); Board of Visitors, Penn Nursing Science (1988-1992); Trustee, St. Vincent DePaul Center for the Homeless (1987-1990); International Dinner Chairman, B'nai B'rith International (1989); Trustee, Morehouse School of Medicine (1980-1989); Vice-Chairman, Morehouse School of Medicine (1980-1989); George H.W. Bush Campaign Committee (1988); Chairman of the Board, American College of Legal Medicine (1983-1987); Trustee, Cleveland Clinic (1971-1987); Trustee, Albany Medical Center (1977-1986) **Military Service:** Regimental Surgeon, 3rd Marine Division, US Navy (1953-1961) **Creative Works:** Editorial Board Member, Medical Malpractice Prevention (1985-1990); Editorial Board Member, Forensic Science (1971-1990); Author, "Winter Galley" (2008); Editorial Board Member, Regulatory Toxicity and Pharmacology, Elsevier (1981-1987) **Awards:** Lifetime Leadership Award, University of the Cumberlands (2014); Eponym, Monroe E. Trout Day, Knox County Tennessee (March 13, 2007); Caring Servant Award (2005); Knoxville Philanthropist of the Year (2004); Visionary Award, Baptist Health Foundation (2002); 100 Most Influential Delts of Twentieth Century, Delta Tau Delta (2000); Gold Medal Award, American College of Legal Medicine (1999); Civis Universitatus Award, UC San Diego (1997); Salvation Army Tradition of Caring Award (1996); Alumni Achievement Award, Delta Tau Delta (1996) **Membership:** President, Medical Executives (1975-76); Bridge Bronze Life Master; President, American College of Legal Medicine **Political Affiliations:** Republican **Religion:** Lutheran **Shipping Address:** 7010 N. Palladium Court, Appleton, WI, 54913

Mary Theresa Troxell

Title: Geriatrics Services Professional (Retired) **Industry:** Medicine & Health Care **Company Name:** Fountains Retirement Communities **Date of Birth:** 08/29/1950 **Place of Birth:** Syracuse **State:** NY **Parents:** Henry Flynn; Mary (McDermott) Flynn **Children:** Melissa Lee **Education:** BSN, University of Pennsylvania (1971) **Certifications:** Certified Quality Improvement Specialist; Certified Gerontological Nurse Specialist; Certified Case Manager **Career:** Chief Operating Officer, Fountains Retirement Communities, Tucson, AZ (2000-Present); Chief Compliance Officer, Fountains Retirement Communities, Tucson, AZ (2000-Present); Vice President of Health Operations, Fountains Retirement Communities, Tucson, AZ (2000-Present); Retired (2016); Regional Director, Operations and Marketing for Southwest, Enlivant (2016); Regional Director, Western Operations, Senior Lifestyle (2010-2016); Chief Executive Officer, Unison Healthcare (1999-2000); Executive Vice President of Operations, Unison Healthcare (1998-1999); Senior Vice President, Clinical and Ancillary Operations, Unison Healthcare (1996-1998); Vice President, Clinical Operations, SunQuest Healthcare, Phoenix, AZ (1994-1996); Director, Professional Services, Unison Healthcare, Phoenix, AZ (1991-1994); Program Manager, Enforcement and Compliance Licensure and Certification, State of Arizona, Phoenix, AZ (1989-1991); Program Manager, Long Term Care Licensure and Certification, State of Arizona, Phoenix, AZ (1987-1989); Team Leader, Surveyor Health Care Licensure, State of Arizona, Phoenix, AZ (1985-1987); Director of Nursing, Desert Haven Care Center, Phoenix, AZ (1983-1984); Quality Assurance Nurse, Long Term Care, Maricopa County, Phoenix, AZ (1981-1983); Director of Nursing, Hillhaven, Phoenix, AZ (1979-1981); Supervisor, Neonatal Intensive Care Unit, St. Joseph's Hospital Health Center, Syracuse, NY (1976-1979) **Civic:** Developer, Legislation for Adult Care Homes, State of Arizona (1990); Developer, Health Care Licensure Laws, State of Arizona (1990) **Creative Works:** Author, "Clinical Operations Series" (1997); Author, "Director of Nursing Manual" (1996); Author, "Quality Improvement, Restorative Nursing: A Key to Quality" (1992); Author, "Licensure Procedures" (1990) **Membership:** National Quality Committee, American Health Care Association (1996-1997); LTC Nurses Council, American Health Care Association (1995); National Multi-Facility Committee, American Health Care Association (1993-1996); National Facility Standards Committee, American Health Care Association (1992-1996); Chair, Legislative Committee, Arizona Health Care Association (1992-1994); Chair, Development and Revision Nursing Facility Laws, Arizona Health Care Association (1992-1994); Vice President, Region XI, American Health Care; National Gerontological Nurses Association; Quality Improvement Nurses Association; Regional Vice President, Region XI Advisory Committee, American Health Care Association; Regional Vice President, Board of Directors, American Health Care Association **Marquis Who's Who Honors:** Albert Nelson Marquis Lifetime Achievement Award (2017) **Shipping Address:** 10224 E Sahuaro Dr, Scottsdale, AZ, 85260

Donald Lynn Trump

Title: Oncologist **Industry:** Medicine & Health Care **Company Name:** Inova Schar Cancer Institute **Date of Birth:** 07/31/1945 **Place of Birth:** Greencastle **State:** IN **Education:** Postgraduate Studies, Department of Medicine, Johns Hopkins University, Baltimore, MD (1970-1975); MD, Johns Hopkins University, Baltimore, MD (1970); BA in Human Biology, Johns Hopkins University, Baltimore, MD (1967) **Certifications:** Subspecialty Boards, Medical Oncology, American Board of Internal Medicine (1977); Diplomat, American Board of Internal Medicine (1973); License to Practice Medicine, State of Wisconsin; License to Practice Medicine, State of Maryland; License to Practice Medicine, State of North Carolina; License to Practice Medicine, Commonwealth of Pennsylvania; License to Practice Medicine, State of New York **Career:** Executive Director, Inova Schar Cancer Institute, Falls Church, VA (2015-Present); Chief Executive Officer, Inova Schar Cancer Institute, Falls Church, VA (2015-Present); President, Roswell Park Cancer Institute, Buffalo, NY (2007-2015); Chief Executive Officer, Roswell Park Cancer Institute, Buffalo, NY (2007-2014); Professor of Medicine, University at Buffalo, Buffalo, NY (2002-2014); Professor of Molecular Pharmacology and Oncology, Roswell Park Cancer Institute, Buffalo, NY (2002-2014); Senior Vice President of Clinical Research, Roswell Park Cancer Institute, Buffalo, NY (2002-2007); Chairman, Department of Medicine, Roswell Park Cancer Institute, Buffalo, NY (2002-2007); Chief, Division of Hematology/Oncology, School of Medicine, University of Pittsburgh, Pittsburgh, PA (1998-2002); Active Staff, UPMC-Shadyside, Pittsburgh, PA (1998-2002); Chief, Division of Medical Oncology, School of Medicine, University of Pittsburgh, Pittsburgh, PA (1996-1998); Deputy Director for Clinical Investigations, University of Pittsburgh Cancer Institute, Pittsburgh, PA (1992-2002); Professor, Department of Medicine and Urology, School of Medicine, University of Pittsburgh, Pittsburgh, PA (1992-2002); Professor, Department of Medicine, School of Medicine, Duke University, Durham, NC (1988-1992); Associate Professor, Department of Medicine, University of Wisconsin-Madison (1984-1988); Associate Professor, Department of Human Oncology, University of Wisconsin-Madison (1984-1988); Active Staff, University of Wisconsin Hospitals and Clinics, Madison, WI (1981-1988); Staff Oncologist, William S. Middleton Memorial Veterans Hospital, Madison, WI (1981-1988); Consultant, Madison General Hospital, Madison, WI (1981-1988); Consultant, St. Mary's Hospital, Madison, WI (1981-1988); Assistant Professor, Department of Medicine, University of Wisconsin-Madison (1981-1984); Assistant Professor, Department of Human Oncology, University of Wisconsin-Madison (1981-1984); Assistant Professor, The Sidney Kimmel Comprehensive Cancer Center, John Hopkins University, Baltimore, MD (1977-1981); Assistant Professor, Department of Medicine, School of Medicine, John Hopkins University, Baltimore MD (1977-1981); Active Staff, John Hopkins Hospital, Baltimore, MD (1977-1981); Clinical Assistant Professor, Sidney Kimmel Medical College, Thomas Jefferson University, Philadelphia, PA (1976-1977); Staff Oncologist, Naval Regional Medical Center, Philadelphia, PA (1975-1977); Instructor, Department of Medicine, School of Medicine, John Hopkins University, Baltimore, MD (1974-1975) **Civic:** External Advisory Board, Fox Chase Cancer Center (2009-Present); Medical Advisory Board, Johns Hopkins Kimmel Cancer Center (2009-Present); Clinical and Translational Research Committee, American Association for Cancer Research (2009-Present); Board of Directors, National Coalition for Cancer Research (2008-Present); Board of Directors, American Association of Cancer Institutes (2007-Present); Membership Committee, The Buffalo Club (2008-2014); Board of Directors, Buffalo Niagara Partnership (2008-2014); Board of Directors, Roswell Park Cancer Institute (2007-2014); Board of Directors, Health Research Incorporated, Menands, NY (2004-2014) **Awards:** Inductee, Johns Hopkins University Society of Scholars (2009); Honoree, Best Doctors in America (1994, 1999, 2002-2004, 2007-2008); Honoree, America's Top Doctors for Cancer (2005-2008); Honoree, Person of the Year in Science, Vectors Pittsburgh (2001); Scholar, Joseph Burchenal Lectureship, Memorial Sloan Kettering Cancer Center (2001); Fellow, American College of Physicians (1987) **Membership:** Science Policy and Government Affairs Committee, American Association for Cancer Research (2007-Present); American Urological Association for Education and Research Inc. (2000-Present); Society of Urologic Oncology (1999-Present); Society for Basic Urologic Research, Inc. (1998-2000); American Association for the Advancement of Science (1978-Present); American Society of Clinical Oncology (1978-Present); American Association for Cancer Research (1977-Present); American College of Healthcare Executives (2000-2002); American Federation for Clinical Research (1979-2000); American Association for Cancer Education (1987-1992); The New York Academy of Sciences (1976-1992) **Marquis Who's Who Honors:** Albert Nelson Marquis Lifetime Achievement Award (2017) **Shipping Address:** 11744 Stuart Mill Road, Oakton, VA, 22124

Lawrence Benson Trygstad

Industry: Law and Legal Services **Company Name:** Trygstad, Schwab & Trygstad **Date of Birth:** 04/22/1937 **Place of Birth:** Holton **State:** MI **Marital Status:** Married **Spouse Name:** Ann Trygstad (1963) **Children:** Kevin Rollenhagen; Michael Trigg; Shanon Trygstad; David Trygstad **Education:** JD, University of Southern California Gould School of Law (1967); BA, University of Michigan (1959) **Career:** Partner, Trygstad, Schwab and Trygstad (2004-Present); President, Trygstad Law Corporation (1980-2004); Partner, Trygstad and Odell (1971-1980); Legal Council, California Teachers Association, United Teachers (1968-1971) **Career Related:** Instructor, Teacher, Negotiation, University of California **Civic:** Board of Directors, George Washington Carver Foundation (1970-1985) **Membership:** American Bar Association; California Bar Association; Consumer Attorneys California; Los Angeles County Bar Association; National Organization of Lawyers for Education Associations; American Associate Justice; Consumer Attorneys, Los Angeles; Phi Alpha Delta **Bar Admissions:** California (1968); U.S. Supreme Court (1974) **Marquis Who's Who Honors:** Albert Nelson Marquis Lifetime Achievement Award (2017) **Why did you become involved in your profession or industry:** His father was a Justice of the Peace and also worked in the Sheriff's office and ran for Sheriff in the county where he grew up. His involvement is what made Mr. Trygstad think about becoming a lawyer. **Shipping Address:** 4209 Aleman Dr., Tarzana, CA, 91356

Tom Chunghu Tsai, PhD

Title: Chemical Engineer **Industry:** Engineering **Date of Birth:** 10/24/1948 **Place of Birth:** Kaohsiung **Country of Origin:** Taiwan **Parents:** Shu Tsai; Kwei (Kao) Tsai **Marital Status:** Married **Spouse Name:** Joyce Chionhwa Pai (12/17/1974) **Children:** Wayne; Jimmy Payne **Education:** DSChemE, Purdue University (1975); MSChemE, Purdue University (1973); BSChemE, National Taiwan University (1970) **Certifications:** Registered Professional Engineer, State of Texas **Career:** Lead Process Engineering Manager, The Dow Chemical Company (1995-2015); Reaction Engineering Technology Expert, The Dow Chemical Company (1995-2015); Process Engineering Associate, The Dow Chemical Company (1988-1995); Consultant Engineer, Founder, TDS Associates (1983-1988); Senior Engineer, Bechtel Corporation (1980-1983); Senior Process Engineer, CE-Lummus Company (Now ALSTOM) (1975-1980) **Career Related:** International Advisory Board, Encyclopedia of Chemical Processing and Design (1995-Present) **Civic:** Board of Directors, The High School for the Performing and Visual Arts (1993-1995); President, Chinese Community Center Chinese School PTO (1985-1986) **Military Service:** Second Lieutenant, Republic of China Army, Taiwan (1970-1971) **Creative Works:** Contributor, "Encyclopedia of Chemical Processing and Design" (2005-2006); Contributor, "Encyclopedia of Chemical Processing and Design" (1994-1996); Contributor, "Unit Operations Handbook" (1992); Contributor, "Encyclopedia of Chemical Processing and Design" (1990); Contributor, "Refining & Petrochemical Technology Yearbook" (1987); Contributor, "Pyrolysis: Theory and Industrial Practice" (1983); Contributor, "Ethylene-Keystone to the Petrochemical Industry" (1980); Contributor, "Kirk-Othmer Encyclopedia of Chemical Technology" (1980); Contributor, Articles, Professional Journals **Awards:** Environmental Care Award, The Dow Chemical Company; Process Technology Gold Award, The Dow Chemical Company; Technology Center Awards, The Dow Chemical Company **Membership:** President, Taiwanese Chorus of Greater Houston (2005-2006); President, Association of Chinese Organizations of Houston (2003); President, Association of Chinese American Professionals (2002-2003); President-Elect, Association of Chinese American Professionals (2001-2002); Vice President, Association of Chinese American Professionals (2000-2001); Division Chairman, Association of Chinese American Professionals (1988-1989); American Institute of Chemical Engineers **Marquis Who's Who Honors:** Albert Nelson Marquis Lifetime Achievement Award (2017) **Why did you become involved in your profession or industry:** Mr. Tsai was always fascinated with chemical engineering. It was like magic working with chemicals and transforming material wastes into something valuable. **What do you consider to be the highlight of your career:** One highlight of Mr. Tsai's career was becoming one of the first key people to develop a process to convert wastes into useful products. Not only did he destroy wastes, but he converted it into desirable material at the same time, which was like converting trash into treasure. **Shipping Address:** 1710 Ravenel Lane, Sugar Land, TX, 77479

Mikhail Tsypkin

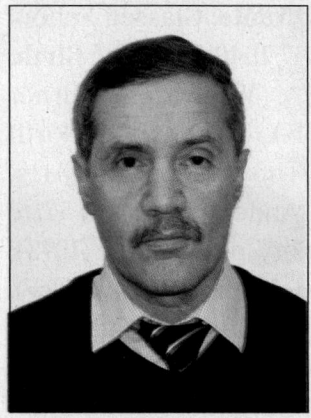

Title: Vibration Engineer **Industry:** Engineering **Company Name:** Vibration Specialty Corporation **Date of Birth:** 04/20/1953 **Place of Birth:** Kutaisi **State/Country of Origin:** PA **Marital Status:** Married **Education:** MS in Computer Science, Saint Petersburg State University, Saint Petersburg, Russia (1994); MEE, Saint Petersburg Electrotechnical University, Saint Petersburg, Russia (1976) **Career:** Field Service Engineer, Vibration Specialty Corporation, Philadelphia, PA (2001-Present); Vibration Analyst, Central Ship Electrical Engineering, Technology Research Institute, Saint Petersburg, Russia; Vibration Analyst, VibroAcoustical Systems and Technologies, Inc., Saint Petersburg, Russia **Creative Works:** Contributor, 12 Publications, Russian Magazines; Contributor, Nine Publications, Proceedings of Scientific Conferences; Contributor, One Publication, IEEE Magazine **Membership:** Category III, Vibration Institute; IEEE **To what do you attribute your success:** Mr. Tsypkin attributes his success to hard work, enjoying his profession, and learning as much as he can. **Hobbies:** Soccer; Theater; Opera; Stamp collecting; Art museums **Business Address:** 100 Geiger Road, Philadelphia, PA, 19115 **Shipping Address:** 9908 Bustleton Avenue, Apt. C10, Philadelphia, PA, 19115

Arthur Turner

Title: Artist, Educator **Industry:** Fine Art **Company Name:** Glassell School of Art, The Museum of Fine Arts **Date of Birth:** 11/17/1940 **Place of Birth:** Houston **State:** TX **Parents:** Lloyd T. Turner; Modest A. (Wainwright) Turner **Education:** MFA, Cranbrook Academy of Art (1966) BA, University of North Texas (1962) **Career:** Instructor, Glassell School Art, The Museum Fine Arts, Houston, Texas (1968-Present); Guest Instructor, Anderson Ranch Arts Center, Aspen, CO (1985); Guest Instructor, University of Houston (1973); Assistant Professor, Madison College (Now James Madison University), Harrisonburg, VA (1966-1968); Instructor, Birmingham Art Association, MI (1965-1966) **Creative Works:** Exhibitor, Group Show, Gestural and Geometric Abstraction, Mobile Museum of Fine Arts, Mobile, AL (2018); Exhibitor, Group Show, Moody Gallery, Houston, Texas (2016); Exhibitor, Group Show, United Nations in Vienna, UNIS (2003); Exhibitor, 41st Annual Exhibition, Texas Watercolor Society, San Antonio, Texas (1990); Exhibitor, Group Show, Perception Galleries, Houston, Texas (1989-1990, 1987); Exhibitor, Group Show, Texas Artists: A Group Exhibition, Moody Gallery, Houston, Texas (1989, 1987, 1985); Exhibitor, Group Show, Nave Museum, Victoria, Texas (1987); Exhibitor, Group Show, Aspen Institute (1986, 1984); Exhibitor, Group Show, Houston Festival, Two Houston Center (1986); Exhibitor, Group Show, Houston Printmakers, Goethe-Institut (1986); Exhibitor, Group Show, Texas Visions, Transco Tower (Now Williams Tower) (1986); Exhibitor, Group Show, Printmaking '86, Galveston Artists Guild, Texas (1986); Exhibitor, Group Show, Gateway Gallery Experience, Dallas Museum of Art (1984); Exhibitor, Group Show, Chicago Navy Pier Art Fair (1984); Exhibitor, Group Show, Stavanger Museum, Norway (1982); Exhibitor, Group Show, Jurgen Schweinbraden, Berlin, Germany (1980); Contributor, Numerous Workshops; Exhibitor, Group Show, McAllen International Museum, Texas; Exhibitor, Group Show, Morgan Gallery, Kansas City, KS; Creator, Video Tape, Color Perceptions, Cataloged by the Smithsonian Institution; Exhibitor, Permanent Collection, The Museum of Fine Arts, Houston, Texas; Exhibitor, Permanent Collection, First City National Bank, Bellaire, Texas; Exhibitor, Permanent Collection, Alcoa Corp., Detroit, MI; Exhibitor, Permanent Collection, Cranbrook Academy of Art, Bloomfield Hills, MI; Exhibitor, Permanent Collection, Del Mar College, Corpus Christi, Texas; Exhibitor, Permanent Collection, AT&T, New York City, NY; Exhibitor, Permanent Collection, East Tennessee State University, Johnson City, TN; Exhibitor, Permanent Collection, Dresser Industries Inc., Houston, Texas **Membership:** Texas Watercolor Society; Visual Arts Society of Texas (VAST) **What do you consider to be the highlight of your career:** Mr. Turner enjoyed teaching for three summers in Austria. The classroom was a 14th century castle. He was included in a group show in Vienna at the American Embassy. **Where will you be in five years:** In five years, Mr. Turner hopes to still be teaching and painting. **Shipping Address:** 2419 Julian St, Houston, TX, 77009

James Ukropina

Title: Lawyer **Industry:** Law and Legal Services **Company Name:** O'Melveny & Myers **Date of Birth:** 09/10/1937 **Place of Birth:** Fresno **State:** CA **Marital Status:** Married **Education:** JD, University of Southern California; MBA, Stanford University; BA, Stanford University **Membership:** Director, Lockheed Martin Corporation (1995-2012); Director, Internet Brands Inc. (2006-2011); Director, Central Natural Resources Inc. (1999-2009); Independent Director, IndyMac BanCorp. Inc. (2001-2006); Vice Chairman, Board of Trustees, Stanford University (1999-2000); Member, Board of Directors, TCW Group, Inc. (1999-2000); Chief Executive Officer, Chairman, Pacific Enterprises (1989-1991); Director, Lockheed Martin Corporation (1988-1995); Executive Vice President, General Counsel, Pacific Enterprise (1986-1989); Executive Vice President, General Counsel, Santa Fe International Corporation (1981-1985); Director, Pacific Mutual Holding Company; Director, W.M. Keck Foundation; Presiding Director, Lockheed Martin Corporation; Director, E&J Gallo Winery; Director, Pacific Life Mutual Holding Company; Director, Security Pacific Corporation; Director, Trust Company of the West; Director, Miller's Outpost; Director, California Chamber of Commerce; Director, California Business Roundtable; Trustee, Occidental College; Director, Executive Service Corps of the Southern Advisory Council, Stanford Graduate School of Business; Director, KCET; Director, California Economic Development Corporation **Bar Admissions:** The State Bar of California **Shipping Address:** 400 S. Hope Street, 19th Floor, O'Melveny & Myers LLP, Los Angeles, CA, 90071

James A. Unruh

Title: Bank Executive **Industry:** Financial Services **Company Name:** Alerion Capital Group LLC **Date of Birth:** 03/22/1941 **Place of Birth:** Goodrich **State:** ND **Marital Status:** Married **Spouse Name:** Candice Leigh Voight (4/28/1984) **Children:** Jeffrey; Julie **Education:** MBA, University of Denver (1964); BSBA, University of Jamestown (1963); Honorary LLD, Drexel University **Career:** Founding Principal, Alerion Capital Group LLC, Scottsdale, AZ (1998-Present); Chairman, Board of Directors, Chief Executive Officer, Unisys Corp., Detroit, MI (1991-1997); President, Chief Executive Officer, Unisys Corp., Detroit, MI (1990-1991); Executive Vice President, Unisys Corp., Detroit, MI (1986-1989); Executive Vice President of Finance, Unisys Corp., Detroit, MI (1986); Senior Vice President of Finance, Burroughs Corporation (Now Unisys Corp.), Detroit, MI (1984-1986); Vice President, Finance of Burroughs Corporation (Now Unisys Corp.), Detroit, MI (1982-1984); Vice President of Finance, Memorex Corporation, Santa Clara, CA (1980-1982); Vice President of Finance, Fairchild Camera & Instrument, California (1979-1980); Vice President of Treasury and Corporate Development, Fairchild Camera & Instrument, California (1976-1979); Director, Corporate Planning and Analysis, Fairchild Camera & Instrument, California (1974-1976) **Career Related:** Board of Directors, VTI Instruments Inc.; Board of Directors Worldlink, Inc.; Board of Directors, Steton Technology Group, Inc.; Board of Directors, BioVigilant Corporation; Board of Directors, LumenIQ Corporation; Board of Directors, CSG Systems International, Inc.; Board of Directors, Tenet Healthcare Corporation; Board of Directors, Qwest Communications International Inc.; Board of Directors, Prudential Financial Corporation **Civic:** Trustee, Chairman, Board of Directors, University of Jamestown **Creative Works:** Author, "Customers Mean Business: Six Steps to Building Relationships That Last" **Awards:** National Leadership Award of Excellence, State of North Dakota; Honoree, Chief Executive Officer of the Year, Enterprise Awards; Eleanor Roosevelt Humanitarian Award **Membership:** Association for Corporate Growth **Marquis Who's Who Honors:** Albert Nelson Marquis Lifetime Achievement Award (2017) **Hobbies:** Photography; Philanthropy; Golf **Political Affiliations:** Republican **Religion:** Protestant **Shipping Address:** 7702 E Doubletree Ranch Rd., Ste. 350, Alerion Capital Group LLC, Scottsdale, AZ, 85258

Leslie Raymond Usui

Title: Apparel Executive (Retired) **Industry:** Business Management/ Business Services **Company Name:** Satyuga Inc, Masktique LLC **Date of Birth:** 02/02/1946 **Place of Birth:** Wahiawa **State:** HI **Parents:** Raymond Isao Usui; Joyce Mitsuyo (Muramoto) Usui **Marital Status:** Married **Spouse Name:** Annie On Nor Hom (10/23/1980) **Children:** Atisha Feng Shui Keao Usui **Education:** Postgraduate Studies in Buddhist Psychology, Naropa Institute, Boulder, CO (1974); MEd in Education Foundations-Philosophy, University of Hawaii (1972); Professional Fifth Year Diploma in Elementary Education-Biology, University of Hawaii (1972); Bachelor of Arts in Zoology, University of Hawaii (1969); Coursework, Church College of Hawaii (1965) **Certifications:** Certified Minister, Universal Life Church (1974); Licensed to Perform Marriage Ceremonies, State of Hawaii (1974); Certified Teacher, State of Hawaii **Career:** Business Consultant (2012-2017); Creator, "ShopMy-Center" Virtual E-Commerce Project (2005-Present); President, Masktique LLC. (2003-Present); President, Director, Satyuga Inc. (1982-Present); Vice President of Communications, Director, Hawaii Pacific Channel (2001-2005); Vice President, Director, Green Organic Village Inc. (1997-1999); Building Design Consultant, Kaumana Iki Retirement Homes (1997-1998); Vice President, Director, Satyuga Inc. (1975-1981); New Age Magazine Distributor, Hawaii (1973-1974); Special Education Tutor, Department of Education, Hawaii (1971-1973); Flight Steward, United Airlines, Honolulu (1970) **Civic:** Co-Founder, High School Senior Prom Project (2001-Present); Founder, Organic Mosquito Control Project (1983-Present); National Tax Limitation Committee (1988-1989); Advisory Board, United States Senatorial Business Board, Washington, DC (1988); Director, Palpung Foundation (1984-2005); Co-Founder, Director, Maitreya Institute (1982-1985); Charter Member, Citizens Against Government Waste (1981); Co-Founder, Director, Church of Life (1979); Advisory Board, Kagyu Dharma National Board (1975-1992); Co-Founder, Director, President, Situ Rimay Chuling dba Kagyu Thegchen Ling Meditation Center (1974-2003); Member, National Federation of Independent Business; Member, Citizens For a Sound Economy **Creative Works:** Composer, CD, "Refugee" (1991); Composer, "Song to Chenrayzee" (1976); Composer, "Song to Karmapa" (1976); Author, "The Early History of Tibetan Buddhism in Hawaii" (1976); Creator, Yogarden Organic Sculpture **Awards:** Honorable Discharge, Hawaii Army National Guard (1972) **Membership:** Charter Member, Citizens Against Government Waste; Silversword Status, Nature Conservancy; Cousteau Society; Hawaiian Humane Society; National Geographic Society; PBS Hawaii **Marquis Who's Who Honors:** Albert Nelson Marquis Lifetime Achievement Award (2017) **Hobbies:** Music; Gardening; Poetry; Koi ponds; Aviary and related gardens; Numismatics **Political Affiliations:** Independent **Religion:** Buddhist **Business Address:** PO Box 161257, Honolulu, HI, 96816

Gene C. Valentine

Title: Chief Executive Officer **Industry:** Financial Services **Company Name:** Financial West Group, Inc. **Date of Birth:** 06/19/1950 **Place of Birth:** Washington **State:** DC **Parents:** John N. Valentine; Jane S. Valentine **Education:** BS in Psychology, Bethany College (1972); Coursework, University of Vienna, Austria (1971-1972) **Career:** Chairman, CEO, Pacific Asset Group Inc. (Now Financial West Group), Westlake Village, CA (1985-Present); Vice President of Marketing, Christopher Weil & Company Inc., Sherman Oaks, CA (1982-1985); Director of Land Acquisitions, Subsidiary of Windfarms Ltd, Chevron, San Francisco, CA (1980-1982); Owner, Horizon Realty, San Francisco, CA (1978-1982) **Career Related:** Board of Directors, Financial West Group; Board of Directors, Paradox Holdings; Founder, Chairman, Director, Second Byte Foundation; Founder, Chairman, Peace Point Farms Equestrian Center and Foundation, Bethany, WV **Military Service:** Lieutenant, U.S. Navy (1987); Honorable Discharged, U.S. Navy (1978); Commissioned Ensign, U.S. Navy (1972) **Membership:** Board of Directors, Los Angeles Chapter, International Association for Financial Planning (1982-1987); NASD (Now Financial Industry Regulatory Authority); Founder, Veterans Recovery Foundation **Marquis Who's Who Honors:** Albert Nelson Marquis Lifetime Achievement Award (2017) **Hobbies:** Horseback riding; Sailing; Tennis; Golf; Running **Political Affiliations:** Republican **Religion:** Episcopalian **Shipping Address:** 748 South Meadows Parkway Suite A9-333, Financial West Group, Reno, NV, 89521

Knox Van Dyke, PhD

Title: Pharmacologist **Industry:** Pharmaceuticals **Company Name:** West Virginia University Medical School **Date of Birth:** 06/23/1939 **Place of Birth:** Chicago **State:** IL **Parents:** Peter Fred Van Dyke; Marjory Eleanor Van Dyke **Education:** PhD in Biochemistry, St. Louis University Medical School, Missouri (1966); BA in Chemistry, Knox College, Galesburg, IL (1961) **Career:** Professor of Biochemistry, Pharmacology, West Virginia University Medical School, Morgantown, WV (1966) **Career Related:** Consultant, Drug Industry Cancer Biologics of America, Lexington, KY (1989-Present) **Civic:** Member, Kentucky Colonels (2002-2008) **Creative Works:** Author, Co-Author, Seven Separate Books on Luminesence Biotechnology **Membership:** New York Academy of Sciences; American Society for Pharmacology and Experimental Therapeutics **Marquis Who's Who Honors:** Albert Nelson Marquis Lifetime Achievement Award (2017) **Hobbies:** Travel; History; Baseball **Political Affiliations:** Independent **Shipping Address:** 106 Morgan Drive, Morgantown, WV, 26505

Frederick Van Fleteren

Title: Philosopher **Industry:** Education/Educational Services **Company Name:** LaSalle University **Date of Birth:** 07/14/1941 **Place of Birth:** St. Clair Shores **State:** MI **Parents:** Frederick Van Fleteren; Marion Elizabeth Van Fleteren **Education:** PhD in Ancient Philosophy, National University of Ireland (1971); MA, Villanova University (1968); BA, Villanova University **Certifications:** Ordained Priest, Augustinian Monks (1967-1978) **Career:** Professor, LaSalle University (1984-Present); Associate Editor, Augustinian Studies, Villanova University (1972-Present); Executive Director of Hospice, Our Lady Lourdes Hospital, Binghamton, NY (1979-1982); Assistant Administrator, Crozer-Chester Health System (1978); Associate Professor, Villanova University (1972-1978) **Creative Works:** Author, "Augustine and Philosophy," Augustinian Studies (2010); Author, "Spiritus et littera. Beiträge zur Augustinus-Forschung. Festschrift zum 80. Geburtstag von Cornelius Petrus Maier OSA. Res et Signa 6. Cassiciacum 39 Würzburg. Förster et alii. Augustinus bei Echter," Augustinian Studies (2010); Author, "Theologische Verwandtshaft. Augustinus von Hippo und Josef Rartzinger/Benedikt XVI by Joseph Lom C. Quy. Echter. Verlag," Augustinian Studies (2009); Author, "Augustinus: Spuren und Spiegelungen seines Denkens, Band I. Von Anfängen bis zur Reformation. Band 2. Von Descarres bis in die Gegenwart," Augustinian Studies (2009); Author, "Augustine and Anselm's Libertate Arbitrii," International Anselm Conference, Canterbury, England (2009); Co-translator, "Augustine, Husserl, and Heidegger on the Question of Time," Mellon Press (2008); Co-author, "Augustinus und das Corpus Spirituale," Theologie und Glaube (2007); Editor, "Martin Heidegger's Interpretation of Saint Augustine: Sein und Zeit und Ewigkeit," Mellon Press (2005); Author, "Per Speculum et in Aenigmate in Anselm and Augustine," Proceedings of Anselm Conference (2002); Author, "Peace and War in Augustine of Hippo," Conflict and Peace Conference, The International Association for the History of Religions (2005); Author, "Augustine and the Beginnings of Theology as a Science," Universität Tubingen (2004); Lecturer, "Augustine, Mysticism, and the Liberal Arts," School of Theology, University of Cambridge (2003); Reviewer, "Phillip Cary's Augustine's Discovery of the Inner Self," Augustinian Studies (2002); Lecturer, "Perspectives on American Philosophy," Universität Eichstätt (2002); Translator, "Collectanea Augustiniana" **Awards:** Visiting Fellowship, Fondazione di Bruno Kessler (2002, 2007, 2010) **Membership:** Clare Hall Cambridge **Marquis Who's Who Honors:** Albert Nelson Marquis Lifetime Achievement Award (2017) **Business Address:** 1900 W Olney Ave., Philadelphia, PA, 19141 **Shipping Address:** 212 W 1st Ave., Apt 19, Conshohocken, PA, 19428

Jaroslav Vanek

Title: Economist, Educator **Industry:** Education/Educational Services **Date of Birth:** 04/20/1930 **Place of Birth:** Prague **Country of Origin:** Czechoslovakia **Year of Passing:** 2018-05-09 **Parents:** Josef Vanek; Jaroslava (Tucek) Vanek **Marital Status:** Married **Spouse Name:** Wilda M. Marraffino (12/26/1959) **Children:** Joseph; Francis; Rosemarie; Steven; Teresa **Education:** PhD, Massachusetts Institute of Technology (1957); Degree in Statistics, La Chancellerie des Universités de Paris (1951) **Certifications:** License in Economics, Geneva, Switzerland (1954) **Career:** Professor Emeritus, Cornell University (1996-Present); Director of Program Participation, Cornell University (1969-1996); Director of Labor-Managed Systems, Cornell University (1969-1996); Carl Marks Professor, International Studies, Cornell University (1969-1996); Director, Program Comparative Economic Development, Cornell University (1968-1973); Professor, Economics, Cornell University (1966-1996); Member, Faculty, Cornell University (1964-1996); Adviser, Agency for International Development (1964); Instructor, Harvard University (1957-1963); Assistant Professor, Harvard University (1957-1963) **Career Related:** Founding President, S.T.E.V.E.N. Foundation (1985-Present); Member, National Advisory Board of Economics, National Science Foundation (1969-1970) **Creative Works:** Translator, "Sjednocená teorie spolecenských systému" (2013); Contributor, "Advances in the Economic Analysis of Participatory and Labor-Managed Firms, Volume 12" (2011); Contributor, "Advances in the Economic Analysis of Participatory and Labor-Managed Firms, Volume 11" (2011); Contributor, "Advances in the Economic Analysis of Participatory and Labor-Managed Firms, Volume 10" (2007); Contributor, "Advances in the Economic Analysis of Participatory and Labor-Managed Firms, Volume Seven" (2003); Author, "Unified Theory of Social Systems: A Radical Christian Analysis" (2000); Author, "Destructive International Trade: from Justice for Labour to Global Strategy" (1998); Author, "Toward Full Democracy, Political and Economic, In Russia" (1993); Author, "Crisis and Reform: East and West: Essays in Social Economy" (1989); Contributor, "Advances in the Economic Analysis of Participatory and Labor-Managed Firms, Volume Two" (1987); Author, "The Labor-Managed Economy" (1977); Author, "Self-Management: Economic Liberation of Man" (1975); Author, "The Participatory Economy" (1971); Author, "The General Theory of Labor-Managed Market Economies" (1970); Author, "Maximal Economic Growth" (1968); Author, "Estimating Foreign Resource Needs for Economic Development" (1966); Author, "General Equilibrium of International Discrimination" (1965); Author, "The Natural Resource Content of United States Foreign Trade, 1870-1955" (1963); Author, "International Trade: Theory and Economic Policy" (1962); Author, "The Balance of Payments, Level of Economic Activity and the Value of Currency" (1962); Translator, Manuscripts on Solar Technology; Inventor, Solar Steam Engines; Inventor, Solar Pumps; Inventor, Solar Refrigerators; Inventor, Solar Cookers **Marquis Who's Who Honors:** Albert Nelson Marquis Lifetime Achievement Award (2017) **Religion:** Roman Catholic **Shipping Address:** 414 Triphammer Rd., Ithaca, NY, 14850

Janet Frances Schafbuch Velicer-Geiger

Title: Elementary School Educator (Retired) **Industry:** Education/Educational Services **Date of Birth:** 08/27/1941 **Place of Birth:** Cedar Rapids **State:** IA **Parents:** Allan Jacob Schafbuch; Geraldine Frances (Stuart) Schafbuch **Marital Status:** Married **Spouse Name:** James Joseph Geiger (10/27/2007); Leland Frank Velicer (8/17/1963, Deceased 12/27/2000) **Children:** Mark Allan; Gregory Jon; Daniel James **Education:** MS in Food Science and Human Nutrition, Iowa State University (1966); BS in Home Economics Education, Iowa State University (1963) **Certifications:** Certified in Elementary Education, Michigan State University (1976) **Career:** Fourth Grade Teacher, Wardcliff Elementary School, Okemos, MI (1995-2001); Fourth/Fifth Grade Teacher, Gifted and Talented Alternative Program, Hiawatha Elementary School, Okemos, MI (1994-1995); Elementary School Teacher, Wardcliff Elementary School, Okemos, MI (1978-1994); Elementary School Teacher, Winans Elementary School, Waverly, MI (1976-1978); Substitute Teacher, Pennsylvania and Michigan (1967-1976); Home Economics Teacher, Cardinal O'Hara High School, Springfield, PA (1965-1966); Chemistry Teacher, Monsignor Bonner and Archbishop Prendergast Catholic High School, Drexel Hill, PA (1964-1965) **Career Related:** Michigan Education Exchange Opportunity Program, Germany (1999); Chairman, Wellness Committee, Okemos Public Schools (1993-1995); Executive Council, Okemos Education Association; Computer Coordinator; Great Books Coordinator; Member, District Committee on Mathematics, Computers, Substance Abuse and Cable Television; Evaluation Committee, Okemos Public Schools; Okemos Education Association Delegate, Instructional Council **Civic:** Leadership Council, National Institute for the Clinical Application of Behavioral Medicine (1998-2011); Chaperone, Spanish Club Exchange, Benton Community High School, Spain (2003); Chaperone, Spanish Club Exchange, Benton Community High School, Spain (2001); Chaperone, Spanish Club Exchange, Benton Community High School, Costa Rica (1999); Chaperone, Spanish Club Exchange, Benton Community High School, Mexico (1995); Faculty Representative, Bonding Election Steering Committee, Okemos Public Schools (1991); Faculty Representative, Taking Our Schools into Tomorrow Committee (1990-1991); Chaperone, German Club Exchange, Okemos Public Schools (1990); Chaperone, German Club Exchange, Okemos Public Schools (1987); Faculty Representative, Strategic Planning Steering Committee (1989-1990); Co-President, Okemos Music Patrons (1984-1986); Member, Board of Directors, Okemos Music Patrons (1981-1986); Faculty Representative, Community Use of Schools Advisory Committee (1984-1985); Faculty Representative, Building Utilization Advisory Committee (1983-1984); Faculty Representative, Citizens Advisory Committee (1982-1983); Swimming Instructor, American National Red Cross (1959-1961); Lifeguard, American National Red Cross (1957-1959) **Creative Works:** Author/Producer/Film Editor, "The Integrated Arts Program of the Okemos Elementary Schools," Okemos Public Schools (1983); Author/Producer/Film Editor, "Wardcliff School Documentary" (1982); Producer, Annual Classroom Plays and Musicals **Awards:** Classrooms of Tomorrow Teacher Award, Department of Education, State of Michigan (1990); General Foods Fund Fellowship (1963-1964) **Membership:** Program Committee, Lansing Woman's Club (2005-2006); Social Committee, Lansing Woman's Club (2003-2004); National Education Association; National Retired Teachers Association, AARP; Michigan Association of Retired School Personnel; Michigan Education Association; Executive Council, Okemos Education Association; Delegate, Instructional Council, Okemos Education Association; Fellow, Michigan Council of Teachers of Mathematics; Lifetime Fitness Athletic Club; Sparrow Michigan Athletic Club; Michigan State University Alumni Club; Iowa State University Alumni Club; Kappa Delta; Ulysseans **Hobbies:** Swimming; Reading; Hiking; Travel; Classical and Folk Music; Attending Cultural Events; Photography **Political Affiliations:** Democrat **Religion:** Unitarian Universalist **Shipping Address:** 9046 Cottonwood Street, Lenexa, KS, 66215

Paul M. Velt

Title: Radiologist **Industry:** Medicine & Health Care **Parents:** Irwin Velt; Beulah Velt **Marital Status:** Married **Spouse Name:** Lynn Pugan (2/4/1979) **Children:** Jennifer; Eric **Education:** MD, Vrije Universiteit Brussel (1979) **Certifications:** Certificate of Added Qualification, American Board of Radiology (1999); Certified Radiologist, American Board of Radiology (1985) **Career:** Chief, Radiology, Suncoast Imaging Partners, Spring Hill, FL (2002-Present); Associate Radiologist, The Ide Group, Rochester, NY (1999-2001); Associate Radiologist, Monroe Radiology, Rochester, NY (1997-1999); Associate Radiologist, Braff Associates, Clifton Springs, NY (1985-1997) **Membership:** American Medical Association; Society of Breast Imaging; Society of Interventional Radiology; American College of Radiology **Marquis Who's Who Honors:** Albert Nelson Marquis Lifetime Achievement Award (2017) **Shipping Address:** 19221 Inlet Cove Ct., Lutz, FL, 33558

Karl Geza Verebey, PhD

Title: Toxicologist, Pharmacologist, Educator **Industry:** Sciences **Company Name:** Ammon Analytical Laboratory, True Lox, North Shore Medical Labs **Date of Birth:** 03/12/1938 **Place of Birth:** Budapest **Country of Origin:** Hungary **Parents:** Karoly Verebey; Etelka (Szabo) Verebey **Marital Status:** Married **Spouse Name:** Debra Adler (11/22/1940) **Children:** Todd; Marc; Rita **Education:** Post-Doctoral Fellow in Neurology, Weill Cornell Medicine, Cornell University (1972-1973); PhD in Pharmacology, Biochemistry, Weill Cornell Medicine, Cornell University (1972); Pre-Doctoral Fellow, Department of Pharmacology, Weill Cornell Medicine, Cornell University (1968-1972); MA in Molecular Biology, City University of New York (1968); BA in Physiology, Hunter College (1965); AA in Humanities, Eotvos Jozsef Secondary School, Budapest, Hungary (1956) **Certifications:** Board Certified Clinical Laboratory Director, American Board of Bioanalysis; Diplomat, American Board of Forensic Toxicology; Licensed Clinical Laboratory Director, Department of Health, State of New York; Licensed Clinical Laboratory Director, Department of Health, State of New Jersey; Former Inspector, Department of Health and Human Services, National Laboratory Certification Program; Former Inspector, Department of Health and Human Services, College of American Pathologists; Licensed Director in Hematology, State of New York; Licensed Director in Clinical Chemistry, State of New York; Licensed Director in Blood pH and Gas, State of New York; Licensed Director in Endocrinology, State of New York; Licensed Director in Hematology, State of New York; Licensed Director in Blood Lead, State of New York; Licensed Director in Erythrocyte Protoporphirin, State of New York; Licensed Director in Forensic Toxicology, State of New York **Career:** With, North Shore Medical Labs (2013-2015); With, True Lox Labs (2013-2015); Director of Toxicology, Ammon Analytical Laboratory, Hillside, NJ (1999-2013); President, LeadTech, North Bergen, NJ (1992-2001); Director, LeadTech Corporation, North Bergen, NJ (1992-2001); Director of Toxicology, Institute for Basic Research, Staten Island, NY (1992-1995); Chief Toxicologist, Department of Health, City of New York, NY (1989-1992); Clinical Laboratory Director, Psychiatric Diagnostic Laboratories of America, South Plainfield, NJ (1982-1989); Senior Consultant in Forensic Toxicology, Pharmacology and Behavior, Biobehavioral Research Foundation Inc. (1981-1998); Director of Clinical Pharmacology, New York State Division, Substance Abuse Services Testing and Research Laboratory (1973-1988); Research Associate in Pharmacology, Weill Cornell Medicine, Cornell University (1972-1973) **Career Related:** Director of Clinical Laboratory, LeadTech, North Bergen, NJ (1992-2001); Director of Toxicology, Consolidated Clinical Laboratories, Institute For Basic Research, Staten Island, NY (1992-1995); Advisor, Subcommittee on Trace Metals, Analysis to National Committee on Clinical Laboratory Standards (1992); Chief Toxicologist, Department of Health, Bureau of Laboratories, City of New York, NY (1989-1992); Inspector, National Laboratory Certification Program, Department of Health and Human Services (1989); Assistant Director, Division of Substance Abuse Services, Testing and Research Laboratory, Brooklyn, NY (1984-1988); Director of Clinical Laboratory, Psychiatric Diagnostic, Laboratories of America, South Plainfield, NJ (1982-1989); Research Professor of Psychiatry, New York Medical College, Valhalla, NY (1981-1990); Associate Professor of Psychiatry, SUNY Downstate Medical Center (1978-2000); Director of Clinical Pharmacology, Division of Substance Abuse Services, Testing and Research Laboratory, Brooklyn, NY (1973-1988); Supervisor, Laboratory Technologist, St. Mary's Hospital, Brooklyn, NY (1968-1975) **Creative Works:** Co-Author, "Rapid, Sensitive Micro Blood Lead Analysis: A Mass Screening Technique for Lead Poisoning," Journal of Toxicology (1991); Editorial Board Member, Journal of Addictive Diseases (1981); Former Member, Editorial Board, Advances in Alcohol and Substance Abuse; Contributor, Articles to Professional Journals; Contributor, Lectures to Scientific Meetings; Contributor, Abstracts to Scientific Meetings; Co-Author, "A New Approach to Treating Arthritic Conditions on a Long-term Basis, Without Adverse Side Effects" **Awards:** Abraham Lincoln Award, American Hungarian Foundation (2013); Listed, National Faculty Directory, SUNY Downstate Medical Center (1996); Electee, Hall of Fame, Hunter College, City University of New York (1989); Grantee, "Analytical Method Development for 6-Beta Naltrexol in Urine," Narcotic and Drug Research Inc. (1985); Grantee, DuPont Pharmaceutical (1985); Grantee, "Clinical Pharmacology of Naltrexone," Narcotic and Drug Research Inc. (1979-1981) **Membership:** Honoree, "American Men and Women of Science" (1997-1998); Honoree, University Professor "National Faculty Directory (1986); Honoree, American Men and Women of Science" (1986) **Marquis Who's Who Honors:** Albert Nelson Marquis Lifetime Achievement Award (2017) **Political Affiliations:** Conservative **Religion:** Jewish **Business Address:** 600 Bloy St, 600 Bloy St., Hillside, NJ, 07205

William J. Vereen

Title: Chairman, Chief Executive Officer, President **Industry:** Business Management/Business Services **Company Name:** Riverside Properties Holding Corporation **Date of Birth:** 09/07/1940 **Place of Birth:** Moultrie **State:** GA **Parents:** William Coachman Vereen; Mary Elizabeth Vereen **Marital Status:** Widowed **Spouse Name:** Lula Evelyn King Vereen (Deceased 9/10/2016) **Children:** Elizabeth Vereen Zeanah; William Coachman Vereen **Education:** BS in Industrial Management, Georgia Institute of Technology (1963); High School Diploma, Culver Military Academy, Culver, IN (1959) **Certifications:** Captain, US Marine Corp **Career:** Treasurer, Riverside Manufacturing Company (1984-2014); Chief Executive Officer, Riverside Industries, Inc. (1984-2014); Chief Executive Officer, Riverside Manufacturing Company (1984-2012); President, Riverside Industries, Inc. (1977-2014); President, Riverside Manufacturing Company (1977-2012); Vice President, Director, Moultrie Cotton Mills (1969-1979); Employee, Riverside Manufacturing Company, Moultrie, GA (1967-2014); Executive Vice President, Riverside Industries, Inc., Moultrie, GA (1973-1977); Executive Vice President, Riverside Manufacturing Company (1970-1977) **Career Related:** Member, World Economic Forum, Davos, Switzerland (1999-2009); Member, Governors Development Council (1993-1995); Tyner Eminent Scholar Chair Holder, College of Human Sciences, Florida State University (1993-1994); President, Riverside Uniform Rentals, Inc., Moultrie, GA (1980-2012); Board of Directors, President, Riverside Manufacturing Co., Gesellschaft mit beschränkter Haftung, Germany (1979-2007); Chief Executive Officer, Riverside Manufacturing Co. Ltd., Ireland (1977-2007); Vice President, Riverside Uniform Rentals, Inc., Moultrie, GA (1971-1980); President, Right Image Corp.; President, G.A. Rivers Corp., Riverside Manufacturing Co. Ltd., United Kingdom; Chief Executive Officer, G.A. Rivers Corp., Riverside Manufacturing Co. Ltd., United Kingdom; Board of Directors, Textile Clothing Technology Corporation; Board of Directors, Georgia Power Co.; Board of Directors, Gerber Scientific, Inc.; Board of Directors, Blue Cross/Blue Shield, Georgia; Board of Directors, Cerulean Companies, Inc.; Board of Directors, Georgia Chamber of Commerce; Georgia Board of Trade and Tourism; Georgia Research Alliance; Georgia Corporation for Industrial Development; Member, Trilateral Commission for Apparel Labeling, NAFTA; Southern Regional Advisory Director Bank of America, Georgia (Formerly Nations Bank, N.A.); Adviser Textile and Apparel Tariffs and Quotas, United States Department of State Board **Civic:** Managing Trustee, Community Welfare Association (Vereen Family Foundation), Moultrie, GA (1970-Present); Member, Board of Directors, Moultrie-Colquitt County Development Authority (1973-1977); Member, Leadership Georgia (1972); Trustee, Pineland School, Moultrie, GA (1971-1975); Trustee, Colquitt County Cancer Society (1969-1973); Director, Moultrie-Colquitt County United Way (1968-1975); Director, Moultrie YMCA (1968-1975); Trustee, Georgia Council of Economic Education; Trustee, American Apparel Education Foundation; Advisory Board, Georgia Technical School of Textile and Fiber Engineering; Elder, First Presbyterian Church; Board of Directors, Moultrie Colquitt County Boys and Girls Clubs; Board of Directors, Moultrie Colquitt County Art Center **Military Service:** Captain, US Marine Corps Reserve (1963-1967) **Awards:** Winner, Lifetime Achievement Award, North American Association of Uniform Manufacturers & Distributers (2018); Inductee, Georgia Hall of Fame, Boys and Girls Club (2017); Decorated, Bronze Star with Combat V; Decorated, Purple Heart **Membership:** World Economic Forum (1999-2009); Chairman, International Apparel Federation, Berlin, Germany (1991-1992); Chairman, American Apparel Manufacturers Association (1990-1991); Board of Directors, National Association of Uniform Manufacturers and Distributors (1988-1991); Board of Directors, American Apparel Manufacturers Association (1980-2001); Trustee; Capital City Club, Atlanta, GA; Commerce Club, Atlanta, GA; Sunset Country Club; Georgia Chamber of Commerce; Elks; Kiwanis; Sigma Alpha Epsilon; Vice President, American Apparel Education Foundation **Marquis Who's Who Honors:** Albert Nelson Marquis Lifetime Achievement Award (2017) **Religion:** Presbyterian **Shipping Address:** PO Box 1663, Moultrie, GA, 31776

Donald Verene, PhD, LHD

Title: Philosopher **Industry:** Education/Educational Services **Company Name:** Emory University **Date of Birth:** 10/24/1937 **Place of Birth:** Galesburg **State:** IL **Parents:** Phillip Nelson Verene; Eleanor Louise (Grant) Verene **Marital Status:** Married **Spouse Name:** Molly Katherine Black (10/13/1960) **Children:** Christopher Phillip **Education:** LHD, Knox College (1990); PhD in Philosophy, Washington University in St. Louis (1964); MPhil, Washington University in St. Louis (1962); AB, Knox College, Cum Laude (1959) **Career:** Director, Institute for Vico Studies, Emory University (1996-Present); Charles Howard Candler Professor of Metaphysics and Moral Philosophy, Emory University (1990-Present); Research Fellow, Università degli Studi di Roma "La Sapienza" (1996); Faculty, Philosophy Department, Università degli Studi di Roma "La Sapienza" (1996); Visiting Professor, University of Toronto (1994); Seminar Director, Folger Shakespeare Library (1994); Visiting Fellow, Pembroke College, University of Oxford (1988); Professor Chair, Philosophy Department, Emory University (1982-1988); Professor, The Pennsylvania State University (1980-1982); Associate Professor, The Pennsylvania State University (1971-1980); Visiting Associate Professor, The Pennsylvania State University (1970); Associate Professor, Northern Illinois University (1969-1971); Assistant Professor, Northern Illinois University (1964-1969); Visiting Assistant Professor, Washington University in St. Louis (1964) **Career Related:** Fellow, Accademia Nazionale dei Lincei (2005-Present) **Civic:** President, The Metaphysical Society of America (2008-2009); President, Hegel Society of America (1992-1994) **Creative Works:** Author, "Metaphysics and the Modern World" (2016); Author, "James Joyce and the Philosophers at Finnegans Wake" (2016); Author, "Vicoa's New Science: A Philosophical Commentary" (2015); Author, "Moral Philosophy and the Modern World" (2013); Author, "The Origins of the Philosophy of Symbolic Forms: Kant, Hegel and Cassirer" (2011); Author, "Giambattista Vico: Keys to the "˜New Science: 'Translations, Commentaries, and Essays'" (2009); Author, "A Course of Life: An Autobiography" (2009); Author, "Speculative Philosophy" (2009); Author, "The History of Philosophy: A Reader's Guide: Including a List of 100 Great Philosophical Works from the Pre-Socratics to the Mid-Twentieth Century" (2008); Author, "Hegel's Absolute: An Introduction to Reading the "˜Phenomenology of Spirit'" (2007); Translator, "L'arte Dell'Educazione Umanistica" (2006); Translator, "La Filosofia e il Ritorno Conoscenza di Sea" (2003); Author, "Knowledge of Things Human and Divine: Vico's New Science and Finnegans Wake" (2003); Author, "The Art of Humane Education" (2002); Translator, "Filosofiiata i Zavrastaneto Kam 'Sebepoznanietoa'" (2001); Author, "Philosophy and the Return to Self-Knowledge" (1997); Author, "The Philosophy of Symbolic Forms, Volume Four: The Metaphysics of Symbolic Forms" (1996); Translator, "Novoto Iskustva na Autobiografija" (1996); Author, "The High Road of Humanity: The Seven Ethical Ages of Western Man" (1995); Author, "Vico nel Mondo Anglosassone" (1995); Co-Editor, "Giambattista Vico: Signs of the Metaphysical Imagination" (1994); Author, "The New Art of Autobiography: An Essay on the "Life of Giambattista Vico Written by Himself" (1991); Translator, "1985, Vico and Joyce" (1987); Translator, "Vicos Wissenschaft der Imagination" (1987); Translator, "Vico y el Pensamiento Contemporaneo" (1987); Author, "Hegel's Recollection: A Study of Images in the "˜Phenomenology of Spirit'" (1985); Author, "Vico's Science of Imagination" (1981); Translator, "Simbolo, Mito e Cultura" (1981); Author, "Symbol, Myth, and Culture: Essays and Lectures of Ernst Cassirer 1935-1945'" (1981); Author, "Hegel's Social and Political Thought: The Philosophy of Objective Spirit" (1980); Author, "Vico and Contemporary Thought" (1979); Author, "Giambattista Vico's Science of Humanity" (1976); Editor, "Sexual Love and Western Morality: A Philosophical Anthology" (1972); Editor, "Man and Culture: A Philosophical Anthology" (1970); Translator, "La Scienza della Fantasia"; Contributor, Articles to Professional Journals **Awards:** Paul Weiss Founders Medal for Lifetime Achievement in Philosophy, Metaphysical Society of America (2018); Galileo Prize (1998); Grantee, National Endowment of the Humanities (1993) **Marquis Who's Who Honors:** Albert Nelson Marquis Lifetime Achievement Award (2017) **Why did you become involved in your profession or industry:** Dr. Verene entered his profession because he was a philosophy major in college and began reading philosophy in high school on his own. **Shipping Address:** 1291 Oakdale Road NE, Atlanta, GA, 30307

Barry Stephen Verkauf

Title: Gynecologist, Reproductive Endocrinologist **Industry:** Medicine & Health Care **Company Name:** University of South Florida School of Medicine, Barry S. Verkauf, MD, MBA, LLC **Date of Birth:** 12/28/1940 **Place of Birth:** Tampa **State:** FL **Parents:** Oscar Verkauf; Rose (Freeman) Verkauf **Marital Status:** Married **Spouse Name:** Arline Laviage (08/20/1964) **Children:** Stefanie; Leslie **Education:** Resident in Obstetrics-Gynecology, Johns Hopkins University, Baltimore, MD (1966-1972); Fellow in Obstetrics-Gynecology, Johns Hopkins University, Baltimore, MD (1966-1972); Surgical Intern, Tulane University (1965-1966); MD, Tulane University (1965); MBA, University of South Florida (1997) **Certifications:** Certified, American Board of Obstetrics and Gynecology, Inc. (1974); Diplomate, Division of Reproductive Endocrinology and Infertility, American Board of Obstetrics and Gynecology, Inc. (1980); Certified Physician Executive, American Association for Physician Leadership (2005) **Career:** Affiliate Professor of Obstetrics and Gynecology, Morsani College of Medicine, University of South Florida (2018-Present); Professor of Obstetrics and Gynecology, Morsani College of Medicine, University of South Florida (2003-2018); Director of the Menopause Center, Morsani College of Medicine, University of South Florida (2003-2018); Private Practice, The Reproductive Medicine Group LLC, Tampa, FL (1981-2010); Founder, The Reproductive Medicine Group LLC, Tampa, FL (1981-2010); President, The Reproductive Medicine Group LLC, Tampa, FL (1981-2010); Partner, The Reproductive Medicine Group LLC, Tampa, FL (1981-2010); Associate Professor of Obstetrics and Gynecology, Morsani College of Medicine, University of South Florida, Tampa, FL (1979-2003); Director, Division of Reproductive Endocrinology and Infertility, Morsani College of Medicine, University of South Florida (1974-1985); Assistant Professor of Obstetrics and Gynecology, Morsani College of Medicine, University of South Florida, Tampa, FL (1974-1979) **Career Related:** Editorial Board, Hillsborough County Medical Association, Inc. (2017-Present); Board of Censors, Hillsborough County Medical Association, Inc. (2017-Present); Peer Review Organization, KEPRO (2012-Present); Delegate to AMA, Society for Reproductive Endocrinology and Infertility (2000-2016); Organon Inc. Fertility Insurance Task Force (2000-2003); Vice President, Board of Directors, St. Joseph's Women's Hospital (1981-1983); Consultant in Gynecology, Regional Hospital, MacDill Air Force Base, Tampa, FL (1977-1985); Consultant in Gynecology, VA Hospital, Tampa, FL (1974-1977) **Military Service:** Major, Medical Corps, US Army (1972-1974) **Creative Works:** Contributor, Chapters, Books; Contributors, 24 Scientific Articles, Medical Journals; Author, "Evolution of an Academic Department," Obstetrics and Gynecology at the University of Florida (2011); Author, "Practicing Medicine Profitability" (2000); Author, "Congenital Malformations of the Female Reproductive Tract" (1993) **Awards:** Distinguished Service Award, American Society of Reproductive Medicine (2017); Who's Who for Executives and Professionals (2015); Leading Physicians of the World (2012); Marquis Who's Who (2011); Cambridge Who's Who Registry Among Physicians and Professionals (2011); Best Doctors in America, Woodward/White, Inc. (2005); Distinguished Physician Certificate, Florida Medical Association (2000, 2006); Castle-Connolly Guide to Best Doctors in Florida (1996-2014); Who's Who in the South and Southeast (1996) **Membership:** Fellow, American Board of Obstetrics and Gynecology, Inc.; American Fertility Society; Society for Reproductive Endocrinology and Infertility; The Society of Reproductive Surgeons; South Atlantic Association of Obstetricians and Gynecologists; Florida Society of Reproductive Endocrinology and Infertility; Omicron Delta Kappa; Johns Hopkins Medical & Surgical Association, Johns Hopkins University; Hillsborough County Medical Association, Inc.; American Association for Physician Leadership; American College of Healthcare Executives **Marquis Who's Who Honors:** Albert Nelson Marquis Lifetime Achievement Award (2017) **To what do you attribute your success:** Dr. Verkauf attributes his success to focused hard work. **Why did you become involved in your profession or industry:** Dr. Verkauf entered the field of medicine because he enjoyed dealing with people, and wished to enter a profession where he did that. **What do you consider to be the highlight of your career:** The highlight of Dr. Verkauf's career was the completion of his training at Johns Hopkins. **Where will you be in five years:** In five years, he will transition to a consulting role. **Hobbies:** Golf; Reading **Political Affiliations:** Republican **Religion:** Jewish **Shipping Address:** 4922 W Bay Way Dr, Tampa, FL, 33629

Christopher Michael Vichiola

Title: Writer, Educator **Industry:** Government Administration/Government Relations/Government Services **Date of Birth:** 04/27/1959 **Place of Birth:** Bridgeport **State:** CT **Parents:** Michael Richard Vichiola; Delores (Distaci) Vichiola **Education:** Training Class on How to Get Democrats Elected into Federal, State, and Local Offices, Attorney General Eric Scheinderman (2018); Coursework, Training Conference, Amnesty International (2018); Coursework, Women's Leadership Training Forum with Jessica Knight Henry and Hillary Clinton (2018); BA, Western Connecticut State University (1983); AS, Western Connecticut State University (1981); Graduate, Colonel James "Bo" Gritz's Special Forces Green Beret On-Field Medical Surgical School; Coursework on Cyber Security, Congressman Jim Himes **Certifications:** Certified Nursing Assistant; Certified in Horticulture, Home Depot Product Authority, LLC; Certified Forklift Operator, Home Depot Product Authority, LLC; Certified Power Equipment Operator, Home Depot Product Authority, LLC **Career:** Member, Congressional Democratic Party (2010-Present); Member, Government Accountability Project, National Museum African American History & Culture, Smithsonian Institute (2010-Present); Sales Associate, Evelyn Ryan Macdonald's Restaurant (2009-Present); Coordinator, Extended Warranty Program, Home Depot (2007-Present); Customer Service Program Specialist, Home Depot Product Authority, LLC (2006-Present); Power Equipment Specialist, Home Depot (2006-Present); Teacher, Center for Action, Kamiah, ID (1997-Present); Martial Arts Teacher, American Bujinkan Dojo, Danbury, CT (1993-Present); Member, President Bill Clinton Commendation Christopher Vichiola (2012); Inventory Specialist, Walmart Inc. (2011); Advisor, President Barack Obama's Kitchen-Cabinet (2009-2017); Toys Sales Associate, Walmart Inc. (2007); Clerk, A&P Foodmart (1999-2003); Sales Representative, Home Depot (1998-2009); Safety Captain, Fertilizer, Toxic Fertilizer Program, Home Depot (1998-2009); Power Equipment Specialist, Home Depot (1998-2009) **Career Related:** Behavior Counselor, Children and Adults, Ability Beyond Disability Agency (2011-Present); Educator, Consultant, Primerica Financial Services, Danbury, CT (1997-Present); Educator, Christic Institute Law Firm, Washington, DC (1995-Present); Advisor, Barack Obama's Kitchen Cabinet (2013) **Civic:** Educator, Rev. Jesse L. Jackson's Rainbow Coalition (1992-Present); Founding Sponsor, Tuskegee Red Tail Squadron (2018); Security Marshal, March for Our Lives (2018); Security Marshal, People's Climate March (2018); Women's March Alliance Project (2018); Board of Directors, Kenny Graham's West Fourth Street Professional Basketball Summer League (2018); Security Marshal, Women's March (2018); Reelection Campaign Member, Mayor Bill de Blasio (2018); Training Captain, Leadership Circle, Democratic National Committee (2018); Po Murray Gun Reform Alliance Project (2018); Training Captain, Connecticut Democratic Party (2018); Position, Hillary Clinton's Youth Alliance Program for Voting Rights (2018); Position, NARAL Women's Protective Rights Agency with Executive Director Sarah Croucher (2018); Position, Hillary Clinton Onward Together to get Democratic Candidates Elected (2018) **Creative Works:** Author, "The Real Story of Christopher Vichiola and Colonel Gritz" (1997); Author, "The Real Story of Christopher Vichiola's and Colonel Gritz's Training" (1997); Author, "Above the Law - The Real Story's Files," (1995); Author, "Above the Law Part II," (1995); Producer, "Making a Killing: Guns, Greed and the National Rifle Association" **Awards:** Stand With Honor Roll Christopher Vichiola Award, National Law Enforcement Memorial Museum (2018); Award, Dr. Jordan Metzel Sports Good Health and Good Wellness Training Class Summit (2018); Award, Founding Sponsor for the Statue of Liberty Museum (2018); Certificate, Women's Training Forum (2018); Award for Sponsoring a Brave New Films Movie Ending Privatized Prisons (2018); Award for Sponsoring a New Films Movie on Immigration Reform (2018); Award for Work with the Syrian Refugee Crisis, Mark Heidel, Hais Agency (2018); Award for Outstanding Work Performance on Her Presidential Campaign, Presidential Candidate Hillary Clinton (2017); Award for Outstanding Contribution to the Holcombe Rucker Entertainers' Basketball Professional Classic, Greg Marius (2016); Award, Elizabeth Sawyer, Brave New Films (2016); Award for Work with Climate Reality Project, Al Gore (2016); Award for Co-Sponsoring President Obama's Iran Treaty (2015); Award for Investigative Work at Abu Garihb Prison and Guantanamo bay Prison, Senator Diane Feinstein (2015) **Membership:** Member, DCCC (2010-Present); National Museum of African American History and Culture, Smithsonian Institute; Amnesty International Organization; H.A.L.T. Attorneys Organization; Drug Policy Alliance Organization; National Democratic Committee; Southern Poverty Law Center; Martin Luther King Jr. Educational Foundation; United Nations Global Citizenship Program, UNESCO; Founding Member, Statue of Liberty Museum **Shipping Address:** 24 Topstone Drive, Danbury, CT, 06810

Jared Steven Videll

Title: Cardiologist **Industry:** Medicine & Health Care **Date of Birth:** 04/09/1947 **Place of Birth:** Philadelphia **State:** PA **Parents:** Harry Videll; Rose (Malken) Videll **Marital Status:** Married **Spouse Name:** Sherry Lynn Horowitz, Esq (1/15/2012); Cyta Trocki (12/27/1969, Deceased) **Children:** Haviv Elana; Mikhael Alon; Samara Pilar **Education:** Research Fellow, Nuclear Cardiology, Deborah Heart and Lung Center (1981-1982); Fellow of Cardiovascular Diseases, Einstein Healthcare Network (1979-1981); Resident, Chief Resident, Internal Medicine, Atlantic City Medical Center (Now AtlantiCare) (1976-1979); DO, Philadelphia College of Osteopathic Medicine (1976); EdB, University of Miami (1969) **Career:** Chairman of Clinical Medicine, Medical Director, Girard Medical Center (1997-2010); Director of House Staff, Intensive Care Unit-Cardiac Care Unit, North Philadelphia Health System (1994-1997); Director of House Staff, Intensive Care Unit-Cardiac Care Unit, Lower Bucks Hospital, Prime Healthcare (1992-1994); Co-Chairman of Intensive Care, Cardiac Stress Laboratory, Memorial Hospital (Now The Guthrie Clinic) (1987-1990); Director, Cardiac Stress Laboratory, Memorial Hospital (Now The Guthrie Clinic) (1987-1990); Cardiologist, Clinical Laboratory, Physician Care, Professional Corporation, Towanda, PA (1987-1990); Director of Clinical Laboratory, Physician Care, Professional Corporation, Towanda, PA (1987-1990); Assistant Director of Cardiology, Pritikin Longevity Center, Downington, PA (1984-1987); Director of Employee Health Services, Deborah Heart and Lung Center (1982-1984) **Career Related:** Medical Director, Local Chapter, American Cancer Society, Inc. (1989-1990); State Peer Reviewer, KEPRO (1989-1990) **Military Service:** Lieutenant Master Class, U.S. Army Reserve; Deputy Commander, Combat Support Hospital, Kuwait, U.S. Army Reserve **Membership:** Fellow, American Society of Angiology; Pennsylvania Osteopathic Medical Association; American Osteopathic Association; Alumni Association, Philadelphia College of Osteopathic Medicine; International Society of Endovascular Specialists; International Society of Internal Medicine; Society of General Internal Medicine; American College of Chest Physicians **Marquis Who's Who Honors:** Albert Nelson Marquis Lifetime Achievement Award (2017) **Hobbies:** Travel; Fishing **Shipping Address:** 111 Presidential Blvd., Ste 208, Bala Cynwyd, PA, 19004

James Walter Villaveces

Title: Allergist **Industry:** Medicine & Health Care **Date of Birth:** 11/04/1933 **Place of Birth:** San Luis Obispo **State:** CA **Parents:** Robert Villaveces (Deceased 1988); Solita (Combariza) Villaveces (Deceased) **Marital Status:** Partner **Spouse Name:** Rita (40-year Long-term Companion) **Education:** Intern, Sawtelle Veterans Affairs Hospital, Los Angeles, CA (1960-1961); Honorary MD, School of Medicine, University of California, San Francisco (1960); BA, University of California, Los Angeles (1955) **Certifications:** American Board of Allergy and Immunology (1974, 1993); Diplomate, American Board of Allergy and Immunology **Career:** Allergist, Ventura, CA (1984-Present); Co-Chief, Allergy Division, Ventura Medical Center, Ventura, CA (1969-1987); Speaker, Earth Day in Ventura County (1974); Teaching Fellow, Pediatrics Allergy, White Memorial Medical Center, Los Angeles, CA (1966-1967); Preceptorship, Adult Allergy, Los Angeles County and USC Medical Center, Los Angeles, CA (1964-1966); Member, Air Pollution Control Board Ventura County, CA; Partner, Earth Day Country Air Pollution Containment; Co-Director, Allergy Clinic Ventura County Hospital; Lecturer, Immunoglobulin Therapy, Wellpoint, CA; Lecturer, Radioallergosorbent Test, Wellpoint, CA **Career Related:** Researcher, Dartmouth University Hospital (Now Dartmouth-Hitchcock) (2008); Consultant, Sprixx (2001); Inventor, Sprixx (2001); Member, Western RAST Panel Forum, Pharmacy and Theraputics Committee, WellPoint Health Networks Inc. (1991-1996); Consultant, WellPoint Health Networks Inc. (1991-1996); Consultant, Allergy/Immunology, Blue Cross (1991-1996); Cities Street-Tree Guide, Blue Cross Southern California, Wellpoint, CA (1984-1985); Peer Reviewer, Blue Cross Southern California, Wellpoint, CA (1984-1985); Cities Street-Tree Guide, Blue Cross Southern California, Wellpoint, CA (1980); Peer Reviewer, Blue Cross Southern California, Wellpoint, CA (1980); Medical Invention Consultant, Inventor's International Co., Inc. (1970-1973); Co-founder, Botanical Weed Allergy Walks (1970); Consultant, Enviracaire HEPA Filter Co. (1970); Yearly Lecturer, Allergy-Immunology Pediatrics, Ventura County Hospital Residency Program (1968-1983); Co-director of Allergy Clinic, Ventura County Hospital (1968-1983); Screener of Medical Inventions Submissions, Inventor's International Inc. (1968); Student Body Vice President, Ventura Junior College (1952); Student Commissioner of Activities, Ventura High School Consultant, Clinic Ventura Hospital (1951); Member, Bee-Sting, Avoidance and Treatment Bulletin Public Group; Consultant in Field; Lecturer, Allergies and Medical Hospital Infections, University of California, Los Angeles; Lecturer, More than 100 Lectures in Ventura County on Allergies and the History of Infections in Hospitals; Peer Reviewer in Field; Speaker to California Newspaper Editors, Biltmore Hotel, Santa Barbara, CA **Civic:** Medical Member, Air Pollution Control Committee, American Lung Association of Ventura County (1971-1974); Judge, Ventura Science Fair (1970-1985); Board Director, American Lung Association of Ventura County (1969-1985); President, American Lung Association of Ventura County; Liaison, Ventura County Air Pollution Control Board; Liaison, Ventura Medical Society **Creative Works:** Singer, "Our Lady Coach," University of California, Los Angeles (1956); Dancer, "Our Lady Coach," University of California, Los Angeles (1956); Writer, Film Editor, Actor, Educational Film, "Alcohol: Drinking and Driving"; Writer, Film Editor, Actor, Educational Film, "Alcohol: Drinking and Driving, Spanish Translation"; Writer, Producer, Editor, Films; Stage Singer; Stage Actor; Featured Lecturer, Channel 2 Los Angeles TV, "History of Alcohol from Aztec to Present in Mexico"; Contributor, Publications on Pollen and Mold as it Relates to Allergies; Author, Presenter, Paper on Research and Treatment of Chronic Sinus Headaches, American College of Allergy, Asthma and Immunology **Awards:** America's Top Physicians, Consumers Research Council of America (2003-2005); Commendation, County Board of Supervisors, Ventura, CA (1974); Winning Dancer Trophy, Las Vegas Sahara Hotel Invitational Dinner (1974) **Membership:** Mensa International (1956-Present); President, Gold Coast Tri-County Allergy Society (1987); Fellow, American Academy of Allergy, Asthma & Immunology; Emeritus Member, American Academy of Allergy, Asthma & Immunology; California Society of Allergy, Asthma and Immunology; California Medical Association; Ventura County Medical Association; Founding Board Member, Ventura County Sports Hall of Fame **Hobbies:** Writing; Photography; Lecturing; Pistol target shooting; Fishing **Political Affiliations:** Republican **Religion:** Non-Denominational Christian **Shipping Address:** 241 Agnus Drive, Ventura, CA, 93003

Arlen Ellard Viste, PhD

Title: Professor Emeritus **Industry:** Education/Educational Services **Company Name:** Augustana University **Date of Birth:** 08/13/1936 **Place of Birth:** Austin **State:** MN **Parents:** Arthur E. Viste; Edith L. (Kehret) Viste **Marital Status:** Widowed **Spouse Name:** Elizabeth Ann Lindbeck (6/14/1959, Deceased 12/14/2010) **Children:** Solveig; David; Mark **Education:** PhD in Chemistry, The University of Chicago (1962); BA, St. Olaf College (1958) **Career:** Professor Emeritus, Augustana University (2002-Present); Stanley L. Olsen Chair of Moral Values (1999-2002); Professor, Augustana University (1973-2002); Associate Professor, Augustana University (1968-1973); Assistant Professor, Augustana University (1964-1968); Assistant Chemistry Professor, St. Olaf College (1962-1963) **Career Related:** Affiliate, Sabbatical Work, Quantum Chemistry, Elizabethtown College (1994); Sabbatical Researcher, Abo Akademi, Turku, Finland (1981-1982); Visiting Research Associate Professor, University of Waterloo (1973); Faculty Member, Research Participation Program, Argonne National Laboratory, Office of Science, U.S. Department of Energy (1970-1971); Researcher, Molecular Orbital Theory, Professor Harry B. Gray; Researcher, X-Ray Crystallography, Dr. Stanley Siegel; Researcher, Electron Paramagnetic Resonance, Dr. Juan McMillan; Researcher, Raman Spectroscopy, Professor Donald Irish; Researcher, Relativistic Quantum Chemistry, Professor Pekka Pyykko; Researcher, Professor John Ranck; Student Faculty Research, Augustana University; Participant, Molecvue (Molecular Computation and Visualization in Undergraduate Education) **Civic:** Visitor, Stephen Ministry, Our Savior's Lutheran Church, Sioux Falls, SD (1992-Present); Leader, Stephen Ministry, Our Savior's Lutheran Church, Sioux Falls, SD (1992-Present); Board Member, The Center for Western Studies, Augustana University; Volunteer, The Center for Western Studies, Augustana University **Creative Works:** Co-Editor, "Memoirs of John August Froemke, 1893-1988," Augustana College (1988); Contributor, Articles, Professional Journals **Awards:** Named Orin M. Lofthus Distinguished Professor, Augustana College (1989-1992); Named National Science Foundation Fellow, Columbia University (1963-1964) **Membership:** American Chemical Society; Royal Society of Chemistry; South Dakota Academy of Science; MACTLAC; The Phi Beta Kappa Society; Sigma Xi, The Scientific Research Honor Society **Marquis Who's Who Honors:** Albert Nelson Marquis Lifetime Achievement Award (2017) **Hobbies:** DNA genealogy **Political Affiliations:** Democrat **Religion:** ELCA Lutheran **Shipping Address:** 1500 W 30th St, Sioux Falls, SD, 57105

Suzanne Anne Vlamis

Suzanne Vlamis, left, presents her book "Africa Endangered" © 2017 to Dr. Jane Goodall in New York, April 10, 2017

Title: Owner, Director **Industry:** Other **Company Name:** Suzanne Vlamis Photography **Parents:** Steve Anthony Vlamis; Anne Lillian Vlamis **Education:** BA in English, Minor in Sociology, Long Island University, Brooklyn, NY (1966); Coursework, School of Visual Arts; Coursework, The New School **Certifications:** Intensive Film Summer Workshop, New York University (1989) **Career:** Owner, Director, Suzannevlamis.com (2017-Present); Special Projects Editor, Associated Press Photo Archives, Associated Press (1998-2009); News Features Supervising Photo Editor, Associated Press, New York City, NY (1985-1998); Staff Photographer, Associated Press, New York City, NY (1973-1985); Editorial Assistant to Victor Riesel, New York City, NY (1969); Freelance Photographer, New York City, NY (1967-1972); Copy Assistant to Features Editor, Brides Magazine, Condé Nast, New York City, NY (1967-1968) **Career Related:** Documenting Endangered Species, Indigenous Cultures and Landscapes in Africa, Antarctica, Australia and Alaska (2008-Present); Science and Health Researcher, Dr. Joy C. Zagoren, PhD, New York City, NY (1999-Present); Freelance Photographer, New York Daily News; Freelance Photographer, Fortune Magazine; Freelance Photographer, MD Magazine; Freelance Photographer, USIA; Freelance Photographer, Jersey City Journal; Published Photographer for Presidential Campaign and Inauguration of Richard Nixon, Associated Press; Published Photographer for Presidential Campaign and Inauguration of Gerald Ford, Associated Press; Published Photographer, Presidential Campaign and Inauguration of Jimmy Carter, Associated Press; Published Photographer, Presidential Campaign and Inauguration of Ronald Reagan, Associated Press; Covered, 1976 Summer Olympics, Montreal and Quebec, Canada; Covered, 1984 Summer Olympics, Los Angeles, CA; Published Photographer, Super Bowl; Published Photographer, United Nations; Published Photographer, Broadway; Sports Photographer; Published Photographer, Fashion, Art and Culture Scene; Published Photographer, Restoration of the Statue of Liberty; Published Photographer, Centennial Restoration of St. Patrick's Cathedral; Published Photographer, Building of Equitable Tower **Civic:** Board Member, Sarah Herzog Hospital, Jerusalem, Israel (2002-Present); Member, Community Emergency Response Team, Upper East Side, NY (2002-Present); Vice President, Sarah Herzog Hospital, Jerusalem, Israel (2002-2013); Vice President of Zoning Committee, 79th St. Neighborhood Association (2002-2003) **Creative Works:** Author, "Antarctica Endangered" (2018); Author, "Africa Endangered" (2017); Photographer, Exhibit, "Welfare Island - A Spirit of Place Past," The Roosevelt Island Historical Association (Now Roosevelt Island Historical Society) (2009); Photographer, "9/11 Commemorative Photo Exhibition," Gallery of Graphic Arts (2001); Photographer, "9/11 Commemorative Photo Exhibition," Morning Calm Gallery (2001); Photographer, "The Sports 100: The 100 Greatest Athletes of the 20th Century" (1999); Photographer, "The Olympics at 100: A Celebration in Pictures" (1995); Photographer, "Jazz Musicians" (1991); Photographer, "Restoring Lady Liberty" (1986); Photographer, "Moments in Time: 50 Years of Associated Press News Photos" (1985); Photographer, "One Day in Our World, Moments in Time: 60 Years of Associated Press News Photos" (1985); Photo Editor, "John Wayne: A Tribute" (1979); Photographer, "Welfare Island and Other Photographs," Long Island University (1972); Production Assistant, "Cable Doctor"; Production Assistant, "Speak Out"; Photographer, "American Photographers"; Photo Editor, "Bing Crosby"; Art Reviewer, The Jersey City Journal **Awards:** Associated Press Managing Editor Award for Top Feature Photography, Statue of Liberty Historic Restoration, Associated Press (1984); First Prize, Feature Story, "Centennial Restoration, St. Patrick's Cathedral," New York Press Photographers Association (1979); Photographers Sports Award, World Press (1975); National Press Photographers Association **Membership:** New York Press Photographers Association, Inc.; Associate, American Film Institute; Ocean Conservancy; Cousteau Society; World Wildlife Fund; National Audubon Society; George Eastman House, New York City Collector's Club; Sierra Club; The Jane Goodall Institute; African Wildlife Foundation; Catskill Animal Sanctuary; National Geographic Society **Marquis Who's Who Honors:** Albert Nelson Marquis Lifetime Achievement Award (2017); Distinguished Humanitarian (2017) **Why did you become involved in your profession or industry:** Ms. Vlamis became involved in her profession because of her parents. They both love the arts and always encouraged her interests. **Hobbies:** Collecting Fine Arts and Illustrated Books; Yoga; Dancing **Political Affiliations:** Independent **Religion:** Roman Catholic **Shipping Address:** 405 E 82nd St., Apt 3E, New York, NY, 10028 **Website:** https://www.suzannevlamis.com

Alvin Volkman, PhD

Title: Professor Emeritus, Physician (Retired), Research Scientist **Industry:** Education/Educational Services **Company Name:** East Carolina University **Date of Birth:** 06/10/1926 **Place of Birth:** Brooklyn **State:** NY **Year of Passing:** 2018-05-03 **Parents:** Henry Philip Volkman; Sarah Lucille Silverstein Volkman **Marital Status:** Divorced **Spouse Name:** Winifred Joan Grinnell (6/12/1947, Divorced 8/1967) **Children:** Karl Frederick; Nicholas James; Rebecca Jane Evans; Margaret Rose W.; Natalie Volkman; Debra **Education:** PhD, University of Oxford, England (1963); Resident to Senior Resident, Pathology Assistant, Peter Bent Brigham Hospital, Boston, MA (1956-1960); Research Fellow, Department of Anatomy, Case Western Reserve School of Medicine (1952-1954); Intern, Mount Sinai Hospital, Cleveland, OH (1951-1952); MD, University at Buffalo, The State University of New York (1951); BS, Union College (1947) **Certifications:** Board Certified Pathologist, State of North Carolina; Diplomate, National Board of Medical Examiners; Diplomate, Anatomic Pathology, American Board of Pathology **Career:** Professor Emeritus, Brody School of Medicine, East Carolina University, Greenville, NC (1995-Present); Associate Dean, Brody School of Medicine, East Carolina University, Greenville, NC (1997); Associate Dean of Research and Graduate Studies, Brody of School Medicine, East Carolina University, Greenville, NC (1989-1995); Acting Chairman, Department of Pathology, Brody School of Medicine, East Carolina University, Greenville, NC (1989-1990); Professor, Department of Pathology, Brody School of Medicine, East Carolina University, Greenville, NC (1977-1995); Assistant Member to Associate Member, Trudeau Institute, Saranac Lake, NY (1966-1977); Assistant Professor, Pathology, College of Physicians and Surgeons, Columbia University (1960-1966) **Career Related:** Chairman, Immunological Sciences Study Section, National Institutes of Health (1977-1979); Member, Immunological Sciences Study Section, National Institutes of Health (1975-1979) **Military Service:** Lieutenant, U.S. Naval Reserve (1954-1956) **Creative Works:** Contributor, Articles, Scientific Journals **Awards:** American Cancer Society Scholarship (1961-1963); Arthritis and Rheumatism Foundation Fellow (1952-1954) **Membership:** American Association for the Advancement of Science; American Society of Investigative Pathology; American Association of Immunologists; American Society of Hematology; Reticuloendothelial Society; American Society of Microbiologists; New York Academy of Sciences; Honorary Lifetime Member, Society of Leukocyte Biology **Marquis Who's Who Honors:** Albert Nelson Marquis Lifetime Achievement Award (2017) **Why did you become involved in your profession or industry:** Dr. Volkman had a cousin that was a physician whom he admired very much, and also a close friend that was a physician, so he decided to go into medicine. **Shipping Address:** 1324 Forest Acres Dr, Greenville, NC, 27834

Dolph William von Arx

Title: Food Products Executive **Industry:** Business Management/Business Services **Date of Birth:** 08/30/1934 **Place of Birth:** St. Louis **State:** MO **Parents:** Adolph William von Arx; Margaret Louise (Linderer) von Arx **Marital Status:** Married **Spouse Name:** Sharon Joy Landolt (12/21/1957) **Children:** Vanessa Von Arx Gilvarg; Eric S.; Valerie L. **Education:** LHD, Saint Augustine's University (1988); BSBA, Washington University in St. Louis (1961) **Career:** Chairman, Planters LifeSavers Company (Now KraftFoods) (1988-1991); Chief Executive Officer, Planters LifeSavers Company (Now KraftFoods) (1988-1991); President, RJ Reynolds (1987-1988); Chief Executive Officer, RJ Reynolds (1987-1988); Executive Vice President of the General Management Group, T.J. Lipton Inc. (Now Unilever United States) (1973-1987); Executive Vice President of Marketing, Gillette Personal Care Division (1969-1972); Vice President of Marketing, Purina (1964-1969); Account Executive, Compton Advertising (1961-1964) **Career Related:** Chairman, Morrison's (1996-1998); Board of Directors, Multi-Foods International LTD; Board of Directors, Hospital Partners of America, Inc.; Board of Directors, Northern Trust Corporation; Board of Directors, Cree, Inc.; Board of Directors, Ruby Tuesday Inc.; Board of Directors, BMC Fund, Inc.; Board of Directors, Aqua Scent, Inc.; Chairman, Juice Technologies; Chairman, Sanibel Captiva Trust Company **Civic:** Former Board Member, The Everglades Foundation (2011-2014); Former Chairman, SWFEDA (2004-2009); Former Member, Board of Directors, Artis–Naples (1994-2009); Former Chairman, Health Care Systems (1995-2005); Former Chairman, NCH Healthcare System (1994-1999); Former Chairman of the Board of Trustees, School of Business, Wake Forest University (1988-1996); Former Member, Board of Visitors, University of North Carolina at Chapel Hill (1988-1992); Former Member, Board of Directors, Forsyth Medical Center, Novant Health (1988-1992); Former President, Board of Trustees, North Carolina Dance Theater (Now Charlotte Ballet) (1989-1990); Executive Committee Member, Sanibel Captiva Trust Company; Former Chairman, Conservancy of Southwest Florida; Former Board Member, FGCU Foundation, Florida Gulf Coast University; Former Board of Directors, Florida Arts Council; Former Board of Directors, Reynolda House Museum of American Art **Membership:** Board of Directors, The Belle Haven Club (1983-1987); Naples Yacht Club; The University Club of New York; Linville Ridge Country Club; Port Royal Club **Marquis Who's Who Honors:** Albert Nelson Marquis Lifetime Achievement Award (2017) **Hobbies:** Tennis **Shipping Address:** 3663 Rum Row, Naples, FL, 34102

John M. Vranish

Title: Electrical Engineer Emeritus, Researcher **Industry:** Engineering **Company Name:** Goddard Space Flight Center **Date of Birth:** 05/20/1939 **Place of Birth:** Brainerd **State:** MN **Parents:** John Paul Vranish; Louise Ann (Jenkins) Vranish **Marital Status:** Married **Spouse Name:** Dorothy Jean Ward (6/27/1980) **Children:** John Christopher; Anthony Brian **Education:** MEE, George Washington University (1973); BEE, U.S. Military Academy (1962) **Career:** President, Vranish Innovative Technologies (2006-Present); Emeritus Member, Goddard Space Flight Center (2006-Present); Staff Engineer, Space Mechanisms and Space Robotics, Goddard Space Flight Center, Greenbelt, MD (1986-2006); Staff Engineer, Robotics Research, National Bureau Standards, Gaithersburg, MD (1982-1986); Staff Engineer, Robotics Research, Naval Surface Weapons Center, White Oak, Silver Spring, MD (1971-1982) **Career Related:** Consultant, U.S. Congress (1996); Consultant, U.S. Congress (1987); Consultant, U.S. Congress (1983); Technology Task Force, Office of Secretary Defense (1981-1982); Fact Finding Committee (1981); Speaker in Field **Military Service:** Captain, U.S. Army (1962-1970) **Creative Works:** Contributor, Articles, Professional Journals; Inventor, Final Development, Patent Applications in Preparation, "Virtual Feel" Smart Tools; Inventor, Final Development, Patent Applications in Preparation, Multi-Sense Capacitors (Proximity, Heat, Material Properties, Surface Properties); Inventor, Final Development, Patent Applications in Preparation, Rotary Piston Engines; Inventor, Final Development, Patent Applications in Preparation, Interference Traction Drives **Awards:** Award, Goddard Space Flight Center (2004-Present); Nominee for 2019 Induction, National Inventor's Hall of Fame, NASA/Goddard Space Flight Center (2018); 100 Award, R&D Magazine (2006); Inventor of the Year, Goddard Space Flight Center (2004-2005); Bose Award, Design News Magazine (1997); 100 Award, R&D Magazine (1997); Inventor of the Year, Goddard Space Flight Center (1992-1996); Grantee, Productivity Enhancement Program, Department of Defense (1979); Outstanding Service as a Mentor, NASA Robotics Academy Program; Exceptional Service Medal, NASA; Exceptional Achievement Technology Medal; Exceptional Engineering Achievement Medal **Membership:** Robotics International, Society of Manufacturing Engineers **Hobbies:** Sports; Physical fitness; Military history **Shipping Address:** 900 Truro Lane, Crofton, MD, 21114 **Website:** http://www.johnvranish.com

Eric Armin Wagner, PhD

Title: Sociologist (Retired); Professor Emeritus **Industry:** Education/ Educational Services **Company Name:** Ohio University **Date of Birth:** 05/31/1941 **Place of Birth:** Cleveland **State:** OH **Parents:** Armin Erich Wagner; Florence (Edwards) Wagner **Marital Status:** Divorced **Education:** PhD, University of Florida (1973); MA, University of Florida (1968); AB, Ohio State University (1964) **Career:** Professor Emeritus, Ohio University, Athens (1997); Chairman, Sociology and Anthropology, Ohio University, Athens (1994-1997); Chairman, Sociology and Anthropology, Ohio University, Athens (1986-1991); Professor, Ohio University, Athens (1983-1997); Vice Chairman, Faculty Senate, Ohio University, Athens (1982-1984); Associate Professor, Ohio University, Athens (1975-1983); Chairman, Sociology and Anthropology, Ohio University, Athens (1974-1978); Assistant Professor, Ohio University, Athens (1973-1975); Instructor, Sociology, Ohio University, Athens (1968-1973) **Civic:** President, Planned Parenthood of Southeast Ohio (Now Planned Parenthood Southeast, Inc.) (1992-1994); Director, Planned Parenthood of Southeast Ohio (Now Planned Parenthood Southeast, Inc.) (1990-1996); Elder, Deacon, Presbyterian Church USA **Creative Works:** Contributor, Articles, Professional Journals **Awards:** Founder's Citation, Ohio University Board of Trustees (2003) **Membership:** Secretary, U.S. Orienteering Federation (Now Orienteering USA) (1980-1982); Vice President, U.S. Orienteering Federation (Now Orienteering USA) (1979-1980); President, Midwest Association for Latin American Studies (1979-1980); Director, U.S. Orienteering Federation (Now Orienteering USA) (1976-1982); Secretary-treasurer, U.S. Orienteering Federation (Now Orienteering USA) (1976-1979); International Sociological Association; Delta Sigma Phi **Marquis Who's Who Honors:** Albert Nelson Marquis Lifetime Achievement Award (2017) **To what do you attribute your success:** The emphasis his family put on education in everything they did. **Why did you become involved in your profession or industry:** He was always interested in history and geography, and teaching was always something he was interested in; he is an academic at heart. **What do you consider to be the highlight of your career:** He is most proud of having won multiple teaching awards. **Religion:** Presbyterian **Shipping Address:** 8620 NW 13th St., Lot 76, Gainesville, FL, 32653 **Website:** https://www.ohio.edu/outlook/FoundersCitation1.cfm

Bruce Corlett Waldo

Title: Hospital Administrator **Industry:** Medicine & Health Care **Company Name:** Aurora Behavioral Health System **Date of Birth:** 09/15/1950 **Place of Birth:** Seattle **State:** WA **Education:** MPA, University of Washington (1974); BA in Sociology, University of Washington (1972) **Career:** Chief Executive Officer, Aurora Behavioral Health System (2010) **Creative Works:** Contributor, Articles, Professional Journals **Awards:** Lifetime Achievement Award, State of Arizona (2014) **Membership:** EGALA **Marquis Who's Who Honors:** Albert Nelson Marquis Lifetime Achievement Award (2017) **Hobbies:** Fishing **Business Address:** 395 County Road 2482, Mineola, TX, 75773

William D. Waldock

Title: Aerospace Transportation Executive **Industry:** Aviation **Company Name:** Embry-Riddle Aeronautical University **Date of Birth:** 08/04/1952 **Place of Birth:** Fort Worth **State:** TX **Parents:** Wallace Gordon Waldock; Annabelle (Wolfe) Waldock **Marital Status:** Married **Spouse Name:** Barbara A. Wisler (9/14/1974) **Children:** Andrew; Kathleen **Education:** Postgraduate Studies, Kennedy-Western University; Master of Aeronautical Science, Embry-Riddle Aeronautical University, with Honors (1982); Coursework, Miami-Dade College, Miami, FL (1977-1978); BA in History, University of Florida (1975) **Certifications:** Certified Forensic Examiner, Board of Engineering & Technology, American College of Forensic Examiners; Certified Safety Specialist, World Safety Organization; Certified Level 3 in Homeland Security, American Board for Certification in Homeland Security; Private Pilot **Career:** Director, Robertson Aviation Safety Center, Embry-Riddle Aeronautical University (1995-Present); Associate Director, Center of Aerospace Safety Education, Embry-Riddle Aeronautical University (1986-Present); Chief Investigator of Aircraft Accidents, Embry-Riddle Aeronautical University (1991-Present); Professor of Aeronautical Science, Embry-Riddle Aeronautical University (1982) **Career Related:** President and Chief Consultant, Systems Safety, Inc. (1990-Present); Consultant, American West Airlines (1996-1999); Presenter, Numerous Safety Conferences **Military Service:** Lieutenant Commander, US Coast Guard (1975-1996) **Creative Works:** Contributor, Various Articles, Professional Publications; Guest, Various Television Programs **Awards:** Who's Who in Safety (1991); General Spruance Award (1990) **Membership:** President, Arizona Chapter, International Society of Air Safety Investigators (1987-Present); SAFE Association; Aircraft Owners and Pilots Association; Aircraft Rescue and Firefighting Working Group; American Society of Safety Engineers; World Safety Organization **Marquis Who's Who Honors:** Albert Nelson Marquis Lifetime Achievement Award (2017) **Why did you become involved in your profession or industry:** He became involved in his profession when he was serving in the United States Coast Guard. He has always been interested in accident investigations, and after retiring from the reserves he became involved with boat investigations. **Shipping Address:** 2128 Ewin Drive, Prescott, AZ, 86305

George J. Walendowski

Title: Professor **Industry:** Education/Educational Services **Date of Birth:** 03/25/1947 **Place of Birth:** Han-Minden **Country of Origin:** Germany **Parents:** Stefan Walendowski; Eugenia (Lewandowska) Walendowski **Education:** Certificate in Finance Accounting, Villanova University (2007); Certificate in Organizational Leadership, Villanova University (2007); Certificate in Business Analysis, Villanova University (2007); Master Certificate, Villanova University (2006); Certificate in Leadership, Cornell University (2006); Certificate, Institute of Management Accountants, Inc. (2004); MBA, California State University, Los Angeles (1972); BS, California State University, Los Angeles (1970); AA, Los Angeles City College (1968) **Certifications:** Certificate in Tackling the Challenges of Big Data, Massachusetts Institute of Technology (2014); Fall of Roman Empire, University of Cambridge (2013); Certificate in Globalization, University of Oxford (2012); Chartered Economist in Athens and Fifth Century Intellectual Revolution, University Cambridge (2012); Certificate in Financial Planning & Control Managing People, Duke University (2011); Certified Project Manager, Stanford University (2010); Certificate in Economics, National Association for Business Economics (2010); Certified Chartered Accountant, International Financial Reporting (2010); Certificate in Strategic Decision and Risk Management (2010); Certificate in New Economic Powers, University of Oxford (2008); Certified Community College Instructor in Accounting and Management, State of California; Certificate in Business Strategy Achieving Competitive Advantage, Cornell University; Certificate in Measuring and Improving Business Performance, Cornell University **Career:** Business Analyst, Hughes Aircraft Company (1993-1995); Business Management Specialist, Hughes Aircraft Company (1986-1992); Program Controls Specialist, Hughes Aircraft Company (1984-1986); Financial Planning Specialist, Hughes Aircraft Company (1983-1984); Senior Financial Analyst, Hughes Aircraft Company (1979-1983); Accounting Analyst, Unocal Corporation (1978-1979); Data Control Supervisor, Unocal Corporation (1976-1978); Accountant, Unocal Corporation (1972-1976); Adjunct Associate Professor Emeritus, Hughes Aircraft Company **Career Related:** Reviewer, Conference Papers (2011-Present); Online Tutor in Mathematics and Finance (2011-Present); Adjunct Professor in Accounting and Business, Pasadena City College (2003-2007); Adjunct Associate Professor in Accounting, Los Angeles City College (1999-2012); Accounting Advisory Committee Member, Los Angeles City College (1999); Adjunct Professor in Accounting and Business, Pasadena City College (1996-2001); Accounting Advisory Committee Member, Los Angeles City College (1989); Accounting Advisory Committee Member, Los Angeles City College (1987); Accounting Advisory Committee Member, Los Angeles City College (1984); Adjunct Associate Professor in Accounting, Los Angeles City College (1980-1997); Adjunct Associate Professor in Business Mathematics, Los Angeles City College (1976-1980); Oxford Education Society; OUSSG **Civic:** Scholarship Committee Member, Teachers of Accounting at Two-Year Colleges (2007); Republican President's Task Force (1986) **Creative Works:** Editorial Board Member, Delta Pi Epsilon (2008-2009); Editorial Review Board Member, "Management in Practice," Society for the Advancement of Management (2007-2013); Proposal Reviewer, Delta Pi Epsilon (2005); Reviewer, "Academy of Management Learning and Educated Journal" (2003); Editorial Advisory Board Member, "Strategic Finance and Management Accounting Quarterly," Institute of Management Accountants, Inc. (2002-2013); Reviewer, "Business Policy and Strategy Division," Academy of Management (2002-2004); Editorial Review Board Member, "Advanced Management Journal," Society for the Advancement of Management (1999-2013) **Awards:** Book Reviewer Award, Chartered Management Institute (2011); Outstanding Reviewer Award, Business Policy and Strategy Division, Academy of Management (2004); Republican Congressional Order of Freedom Award, NRCC (1995); Republican Congressional Certificate of Appreciation, NRCC (1993); Vice-Presidential Certificate of Commendation, Republican National Hall of Honor (1992); Inductee, Honor Roll Life Member, Republican Presidential Task Force (1989); Inductee, Registered Life Member Commission, Republican Presidential Task Force (1986) **Membership:** Innovative Teaching Award Committee, Teaching and Curriculum Section, American Accounting Association (2004-2005); Program Review Committee, Midwest Finance Association (2002); Eastern Finance Association (2000); Selection Committee, International Conference, Society for the Advancement of Management (2000); Two-Year College Issues Committee, Teaching and Curriculum Section, American Accounting Association (1998-1999); Program Revision Committee, Management Education and Development Division, Academy of Management (1998-1999); Competitive Manuscript Committee, American Accounting Association (1997-1998) **Political Affiliations:** Republican **Religion:** Roman Catholic **Shipping Address:** 426 N Citrus Avenue, Los Angeles, CA, 90036

Betty Jane Walker

Title: Co-Founder, Teacher, Author **Industry:** Religious **Company Name:** Jonathan House Ministries **Place of Birth:** Lufkin **State:** TX **Parents:** John Copeland; Mary Alice Copeland **Marital Status:** Married **Spouse Name:** Bobby Glenn Walker (12/24/1952) **Children:** Kerry Dale Walker-Rogers; Robin Elizabeth Pemberton-Rochester; William Bradley Walker-Lufkin **Education:** High School Diploma **Certifications:** Certified in Healing and Deliverance; Certified Pastor, Lufkin, TX **Career:** Co-Founder, Jonathan House Ministries Inc. (2000-Present); Teacher, Jonathan House Ministries Inc. (2000-Present); Author, Jonathan House Ministries Inc. (2000-Present); Cashier; Bookkeeper **Civic:** Secretary-Treasurer, Ministry **Creative Works:** Author, "Family Life Today!!!"; Author, "Trust Me, Child"; Author, "God's Flower Garden"; Author, "To Keep Or Not To Keep"; Author, Books on Healing and Deliverance **To what do you attribute your success:** Ms. Walker attributes her success to listening to the voice of the Lord Jesus and following what he opens the door for her to do for him and his kingdom. **Why did you become involved in your profession or industry:** Ms. Walker and her husband were called to the ministry by the Lord following the supernatural healing of their grandson, Jonathan, who had suffered from seizures for more than four years, starting at the age of two. They gladly followed the open doors the Lord had for them. **What do you consider to be the highlight of your career:** One thing that has struck Ms. Walker the most throughout her career is the fact that so many of God's people are not able to live the lives the Lord intended for them because of sins they have committed, and things that their parents and grandparents have done in their lives. She has been astounded by the number of people who are divorced and have broken families, as well as the number of families that are negatively affected by the abuse of drugs and alcohol, which is then passed down to their children. She knows that is not God's plan for his people, and is committed to helping others. **Where will you be in five years:** In five years, Ms. Walker hopes that she and her husband will continue doing what the Lord has called them to do, and that they well have deliverance and healing centers in many cities and states. **Hobbies:** Gardening; Antiques; Cooking; Entertaining **Religion:** Christian **Shipping Address:** PO Box 5936, Jonathan House Ministries, Rochester, MN, 55903 **Website:** http://www.jonathanhouseministries.com

Deward E. Walker Jr., PhD

Title: Professor Emeritus of Anthropology and Ethnic Studies **Industry:** Education/Educational Services **Company Name:** University of Colorado Boulder **Date of Birth:** 08/03/1935 **Place of Birth:** Johnson City **State:** TN **Parents:** Deward Edgar Walker; Matilda Jane (Clark) Walker **Marital Status:** Married **Spouse Name:** Candace J. Arroyo **Children:** Alice; Deward Edgar III; Mary Jane; Sarah; Daniel; Joseph Benjamin **Education:** PhD in Anthropology, University of Oregon (1964); Postgraduate Studies, Washington State University (1962); Honorary BA in Anthropology, University of Oregon (1961); Coursework, University of the Americas (1958-1959); Coursework, Eastern Oregon College (1956-1958, 1953-1954) **Career:** Professor, University of Colorado Boulder (1969-Present); Associate Dean, Graduate School, University of Colorado Boulder (1973-1976); Research Associate, University of Colorado Boulder (1969-1973); Associate Professor, University of Idaho, Moscow, ID (1967-1969); Research Collaborator, Washington State University (1967-1969); Assistant Professor of Anthropology, Washington State University, Pullman, WA (1965-1967); Assistant Professor of Anthropology, The George Washington University (1964-1965); Professor Emeritus, Anthropology and Ethnic Studies, University of Colorado Boulder; Associate Chair, Department of Ethnic Studies, University of Colorado Boulder **Career Related:** Founder, Chief Executive Officer, Vice President, Walker Research Group, Ltd. (1970); Smithsonian Institute; Affiliate, Tribes of Nevada, Hopi, Lacota and Dakota; Invited Lecturer on American Indian Sacred Geography, Harvard University **Civic:** Member, Technology Steering Panel, Hanford Environmental Dose Reconstruction Project (1988-1995); Basalt Waste Isolation Project, Hanford, WA (1986-1988); Advisor of Native American Affairs, Walker Research Group; Founder, Walker Research Group, Chief Executive Officer, Walker Research Group **Military Service:** U.S. Army (1954-1962) **Creative Works:** Founder, Co-Editor, Northwest Anthropological Research Notes (1966-Present); Editor, "Plateau Volume: Handbook of North American Indians" (1971-1998); Author, More than 250 Publications **Awards:** Fellow, National Science Foundation (1961); Fellow, National Defense Education Act (1961) **Membership:** Fellow, American Anthropological Association (1973-1974); Executive Committee Member, Society of Applied Anthropology (1970-1979); Treasurer, Society of Applied Anthropology (1976-1979); Editor, Human Organization (1970-1976); Chairman, Society of Applied Anthropology (1960-2000); Expert Witness, Human Organization; Consultant, Society of Applied Anthropology; High Plains Applied Anthropologist; American Association for the Advancement of Science; American Academy of Political and Social Sciences; Northwest Anthropological Conference **Hobbies:** Geology; Mining; Ranching **Shipping Address:** PO Box 4147, Boulder, CO, 80306

Donald Burke Walker

Title: Music Educator (Retired), Archivist (Retired), Composer (Retired) **Industry:** Education/Educational Services **Date of Birth:** 12/18/1941 **Place of Birth:** Ventura **State:** CA **Parents:** Marion Russell Walker; Dorothy Burke Walker **Marital Status:** Married **Spouse Name:** Ellen Iris Amsterdam (8/20/1993); Harrie Alley (Divorced) **Children:** Nathaniel Burke; Anthony Cannon **Education:** MA in History, California State University, Sacramento (1992); MLS, University of California, Berkeley (1974); PhD in Music, University of California, Berkeley (1971); MA in Composition, University of California, Berkeley (1966) **Career:** Retired (2004); University Archivist, University of the Pacific, Stockton, CA (1991-2003); Organist, St. Paul's United Methodist Church, Stockton, CA (1980-2000); Visiting Assistant Professor, Oregon State University, Corvallis (1979); Visiting Assistant Professor, Sonoma State University, Rohnert Park, CA (1977-1978); Visiting Assistant Professor, University of South Florida, Tampa, FL (1975-1977); Visiting Assistant Professor, Sonoma State University, Rohnert Park, CA (1973-1974) **Career Related:** History Columnist, San Joaquin Farm Bureau Federation, Stockton, CA (1990-1998) **Civic:** Exhibitor, Historian Exhibition, Catalog and Exhibit, Italian Presence in San Joaquin Valley (1994); Editor, Quarterly Publication, San Joaquin County Historical Society, Lodi, CA (2000-2003); Archivist, San Joaquin County Historical Society (1989-2003) **Creative Works:** Composer, Seven Psalms (2003); Composer, Symphony #5 (2002); Musician, Numerous Compositions on VVM Label **Awards:** Grantee, Composer in Community, Oakland, CA (1997); Honoree, National Endowment for the Humanities (1977) **Membership:** American Music Center **Marquis Who's Who Honors:** Distinguished Humanitarian (2017) **Political Affiliations:** Democrat **Shipping Address:** 1733 Brighton Hill Ct., San Marcos, CA, 92078

Gail Flanagan Walker

Title: Interim Director Womens & Children **Industry:** Medicine & Health Care **Company Name:** Samaritan Medical Center, Watertown NY **Date of Birth:** 09/26/1946 **Place of Birth:** New York **State:** NY **Parents:** Matthew Garrett Flanagan; Edith Alexandria (Russell) Flanagan **Marital Status:** Married **Spouse Name:** Bruce Lee Walker (4/8/1972) **Children:** Erin Edria; Kendra Leigh **Education:** MS in Nursing Administration, The University of New Hampshire (1990); BS in Nursing, Adelphi University (1971) **Certifications:** Diplomate in Nursing, Mount Sinai Medical Center (Now Icahn School of Medicine at Mount Sinai) (1966); Registered Nurse, Mount Sinai Medical Center (Now Icahn School of Medicine at Mount Sinai), New York City, NY **Career:** Interim Director Women & Children, Samaritan Medical Center, Watertown, NY (Feb 2018-present); Per-Diem Clinical Project Manager, HealthAlliance Hospital, UMass Memorial Health Care, Leominster, MA (2016-218); Director of Maternal Child Health, Lawrence General Hospital, Lawrence, MA (2002-Present); Director of Women, Infants and Children, HealthAlliance Hospital, UMass Memorial Health Care, Leominster, MA (2014-2016); Interim Manager, Birthing Center, HealthAlliance Hospital, UMass Memorial Health Care, Leominster, MA (2013-2014); Interim Manager, Family Birth Center, Northwestern Medical Center, St. Albans, VT (2013); Interim Manager, Women & Newborn Care Unit, South County Hospital, South County Health, Wakefield, RI (2012-2013); Chair, Massachusetts Perinatal Team (2011-2012); Director, Maternal Child Health/Education/IV Services, Lawrence General Hospital, Lawrence, MA (2002-2011); Director of Maternal Child Health, Lowell General Hospital (1999-2002); Manager of Center for Women and Infants, Saint Vincent Hospital, Worcester, MA (1997-1999); Program Director, Women's and Children's Health, Optima Health, Manchester, NH (1995-1997); Director, Maternal-Child Health and Intravenous Therapy, Catholic Medical Center, Optima Health, Manchester, NH (1986-1995); Instructor of Staff Development, Holy Family Hospital (1984-1986); Instructor of Staff Development, ProHealth Waukesha Memorial Hospital, ProHealth Care (1982-1983); Nurse Recruiter, Family Hospital, Milwaukee, WI (1981-1982); Instructor of Staff Development, St. Mary's Health System (1978-1980); Instructor, Central Maine Medical Center (1972-1978); Head Nurse, Pediatrics Department, Mount Sinai Medical Center (Now Icahn School of Medicine at Mount Sinai) (1971-1972); Head Nurse, Neonatal Department, Mount Sinai Medical Center (Now Icahn School of Medicine at Mount Sinai) (1969-1971); Staff Nurse, Neonatal Department, Mount Sinai Medical Center (Now Icahn School of Medicine at Mount Sinai) (1966-1969) **Career Related:** Member, Mayor's Committee on Prenatal Care, Task Force on Prenatal Care, State of New Hampshire **Civic:** Member, Board of Incorporators, Optima Health (1994-1997); Member, Board of Directors, Home Health & Hospice Care (1990-1994); Visiting Nurse, Home Health & Hospice Care (1990-1994) **Awards:** Four-Time Recipient, Champions of Excellence Award (2015-2016); Certificate of Appreciation, Commissioner of Massachusetts Department of Public Health (2011); "I Make It Happen" Award, Catholic Medical Center (1990) **Membership:** Association of Women's Health, Obstetric and Neonatal Nurses; Board of Directors, New Hampshire Chapter, American SIDS Institute; Sigma Theta Tau International Honor Society of Nursing **Marquis Who's Who Honors:** Albert Nelson Marquis Lifetime Achievement Award (2017) **Hobbies:** Skating; Cross Stitch; Reading **Shipping Address:** 41 Gordon Dr, Londonderry, NH, 03053

Matthew Walker Wallace

Title: Entrepreneur **Industry:** Business Management/Business Services **Date of Birth:** 01/07/1924 **Place of Birth:** Salt Lake City **State:** UT **Parents:** John McChrystal Wallace; Glenn (Walker) Wallace **Marital Status:** Married **Spouse Name:** Susan Struggles (7/11/1981); Constance Cone (6/22/1954, Deceased 5/1980) **Children:** Matthew; Anne **Education:** Master's Degree in City Planning, Massachusetts Institute of Technology (1950); BA, Stanford University (1947) **Career:** Chairman, Wallace Associates (1969-1998); President, Arizona Ranch & Metals Company (1969-1984); President, Idaho TV Corporation, ABC, Inc. (1976-1978); President, Wallace-McConaughy Corporation (1955-1969); Vice President, National Planning and Research, Inc. (1953-1955); Principal Planner, Planning Board, City of Boston (1950-1953) **Career Related:** Member, Advisory Board, Arnold Machinery Company (1988-Present); Director, Roosevelt Hot Springs Corporation (1978-Present); Member, Community Board, Wells Fargo (2000); Director, First Interstate Bank, Salt Lake City (Now First Interstate BancSystem) (1956-1990); Member, Advisory Board, Mountain Bell Telephone Company (1975-1985) **Civic:** Chairman, Utah State Arts Council, Salt Lake City (1977); President, Downtown Planning Association, Salt Lake City (1970); Chairman, Honorary Board, Planned Parenthood Federation of America Inc.; Member, Humanities and Sciences Council, Stanford University; Board of Visitors, Law School, Stanford University; Member, Athletics Board, Stanford University; Alumni Association Executive Board, Stanford University; Member, Advisory Board, School of Law, University of Utah; Lifetime Director, Utah Symphony; Chairman, Arts Advisory Council, Westminster College; Chairman, Capital Campaign, Westminster College; Board of Directors, The Nature Conservancy **Military Service:** Junior-Grade Lieutenant, U.S. Navy (1944-1946) **Awards:** Recipient, Volunteer Heroes Award, The International Olympic Committee (2002); Recipient, Lifetime Achievement Award, NAIOP (1997); Recipient, Minuteman Award, Utah National Guard (1994); Recipient, Governor's Award In The Arts (1991); Honoree, University of Utah Chapter, The Honor Society of Phi Kappa Phi (1989); Recipient, Distinguished Service Award, Utah Symphony (1988); Recipient, Contribution Award, Downtown Planning Association (1977); Honoree, Paul Harris Fellow, Rotary International; Recipient, Athletic Awards for Tennis, Skiing, and Golf **Membership:** President, Flat Rock Club (1994-1998); Board of Directors, The Arts Alliance (1991); Chairman of the Board, Utah Institute of Fine Arts (1977); President, Cottonwood Country Club (1959-1963); American Institute of Certified Planners, APA; Director, Alta Club; Director, Salt Lake Country Club; The Springs Club; President, Downtown Planning Association **Marquis Who's Who Honors:** Albert Nelson Marquis Lifetime Achievement Award (2017) **Shipping Address:** 2230 E Parleys Ter, Salt Lake City, UT, 84109

Emily Mitchell Wallace, PhD

Title: Writer, Editor, Educator, Scholar **Industry:** Writing and Editing **Company Name:** Bryn Mawr College **Date of Birth:** 11/17/1933 **Parents:** George Lafayette Mitchell; Prewitt Carlisle (Evans) Mitchell **Marital Status:** Married **Spouse Name:** Gregory Merrill Harvey (6/14/1969); Robert Arthur Wallace (6/8/1954, Divorced 1954) **Education:** PhD, Bryn Mawr College (1965); MA, Bryn Mawr College (1959); BA, Southwest Missouri State University (Now Missouri State University) (1958) **Career:** Research Associate, Center of Visual Culture, Bryn Mawr College (2001-Present); Chair, English Department, Curtis Institute of Music, Philadelphia (1979-1983); Leader, Interdisciplinary Seminar, Yale University, New Haven (1979); Chair, English Department, Curtis Institute of Music, Philadelphia (1976-1978); Visiting Assistant Professor, Swarthmore College (1969-1970); Visiting Assistant Professor, Swarthmore College, Pennsylvania (1967-1968); Assistant Professor, University of Pennsylvania, Philadelphia (1962-1967); Instructor, University of Pennsylvania, Philadelphia (1962-1967); Teacher of Literature, Shipley School, Bryn Mawr College, Pennsylvania (1959-1960); History and Literature Tutor, Curtis Institute of Music, Philadelphia (1957-1958) **Career Related:** Member, Advisory Committee, Rosenbach Museum & Library (1980-Present); Member, Sponsoring Committee, Marianne Moore Fund for Poetry, Bryn Mawr College (1975-Present); Interdisciplinary Research Scholar in Poetry, The Cooper Union for the Advancement of Science and Art (1984-1985); Visual Arts Curriculum Consultant, The Cooper Union for the Advancement of Science and Art (1984-1985); Writer, Photographic Essays; Writer, Multimedia Lectures for Scholarly and Academic Audiences; Writer, PowerPoint Lecturer's Conferences; Writer, University Symposia; Writer, Museum Symposia **Civic:** Lifetime Member, Friends of the Bryn Mawr College Library, Bryn Mawr College (1996-Present); Shareholder, The Library Company of Philadelphia (1981-Present); Member, Board of Directors, The American Foundation, Bok Tower, Florida (1976-1986); Member, Yale Library Associates, Yale University Library **Creative Works:** Author, "'America' in Ezra Pound in Context" (2010); Author, "Why Not Spirits?-The Universe is Alive, in Ezra Pound and China" (2003); Guest Editor, "PAIDEUMA, Special James Laughlin Volume" (2002); Author, "Saffron Honey: A Love Song by William Carlos Williams, in The Idea and The Thing in Modernist American Poetry" (2001); Author, "Some Friends of Ezra Pound in the Yale Review" (1986); Author, "Athena's Owls: The Education of Marianne Moore and Hilda Doolittle, Bryn Mawr '09, in Poesis" (1985); Author, "Youthful Days and Costly Hours: The Education of Ol' Ez and Billy Williams at Penn," University of Pennsylvania Conference Papers (1983); Guest Editor, "W.C. Williams Review, Centennial Issue" (1983); Author, "A Bibliography of William Carlos Williams" (1969) **Membership:** Modern Language Association; Arts and Sciences Faculty Member, Harvard Humanities Center; Connecticut Academy of Arts and Sciences; Association of Literary Scholars and Critics; Emily Dickinson Society; H.D. Society; Ezra Pound Society; President, William Carlos Williams Society; Marianne Moore Society; Wallace Stevens Society; Henry James Society; Ernest Hemingway Society; Merion Cricket Club **Marquis Who's Who Honors:** Albert Nelson Marquis Lifetime Achievement Award (2017) **Hobbies:** Chess; Music; Traveling; Gardening; Tennis **Political Affiliations:** Democrat **Shipping Address:** 123 S Broad St., Fl 24, c/o Gregory M. Harvey, Philadelphia, PA, 19109

Reggie Walton

Industry: Law and Legal Services **Date of Birth:** 02/08/1949 **Place of Birth:** North Charleroi **State:** PA **Marital Status:** Married **Spouse Name:** Debra Walton **Children:** Danon **Education:** Honorary LLD, West Virginia State University (2008); JD, American University (1974); BA, West Virginia State University (1971) **Career:** Presiding Judge, U.S. Foreign Intelligence Surveillance Court (2013-Present); Judge, U.S. Foreign Intelligence Surveillance Court (2007-Present); Judge, U.S. District Court for the District of Columbia (2001-Present); Deputy Presiding Judge, Criminal Division, Superior Court, District of Columbia Courts (1991-2001); Associate Judge, Superior Court, District of Columbia Courts (1991-2001); Senior Adviser for Crime, The White House (1991); Associate Director, Office of National Drug Control Policy (1989-1991); Deputy Presiding Judge, Superior Court, District of Columbia Courts (1986-1989); Associate Judge, Superior Court, District of Columbia Courts (1981-1989); Executive Assistant United States Attorney, U.S. Department of Justice (1980-1981); Chief Career Criminal Unit, U.S. Department of Justice (1979-1980); Assistant United States Attorney, U.S. Department of Justice (1976-1980); Staff Attorney, Defender Association of Philadelphia (1974-1976) **Career Related:** Judicial Circuit Council, U.S. Court of Appeals District of Columbia Circuit (2004-Present); Faculty Member, The National Judicial College (1999-Present); Instructor, Harvard University, (1994-Present); Chairman, National Prison Rape Elimination Commission, National Institute of Corrections (2004-2009); Instructor, SEAK, Inc. (1997); Instructor, Criminal Practice Institute, Public Defender Service for the District of Columbia (1996-1997); Central and East European Law Initiative Reform Project, American Bar Association (1996); Instructor, SEAK, Inc. (1993); Instructor, U.S. Department of Justice (1993); Faculty Member, School of Law, George Washington University (1992-1994); Distinguished Guest Lecturer, Lincoln University (1991); Lecturer, Albany State University (1991); Instructor, Traffic Court Seminary, American Bar Association (1987); Instructor, Traffic Court Seminary, American Bar Association (1984); Instructor, Georgetown Law (1983-2000); Lecturer, District of Columbia Bar (1980); Lecturer, Offices of the United States Attorneys (1979-1981); Lecturer, Graterford Correctional Facility, Pennsylvania Department of Corrections (1974-1976); Instructor, National Institute for Trial Advocacy **Civic:** Co-Chairman, Public Safety Committee, District of Columbia Agenda Project, Federal City Council (1995-Present); Board of Directors, Robert A. Shuker Scholarship Fund (1993-Present); Hillcrest Children and Family Center (1994-1996); Board of Directors, National Center for Missing & Exploited Children (1990-1991); DC Care (1990); Honorary Member, Capitol Ballet (1989); Big Brothers Task Force on Interscholastic Programs, District of Columbia Public Schools (1987) **Creative Works:** Author, "Black Judges on Justice: Perspectives From The Bench"; Contributor, Articles, Professional Journals **Awards:** Honoree, All Sports Hall of Fame (2009); Community Service Award, National Organization Black Law Enforcement Executives (2008); Leadership in Education Award, American University (2007); Lifetime Achievement Award, Ringgold School District (2007); Honoree, Alumni Wall of Fame, West Virginia State University (2004); Honoree, The Rams Club Hall of Fame, Ringgold School District (2001); Angel Award, Mount Sinai Baptist Church (2000); North Star Award, American University Washington College of Law (2000); Distinguished Alumni Award, American University (1999); Friendship Award, Best Friends Foundation (1998); Honorable Robert A. Shuker Memorial Award, National Association of Assistant U.S. Attorneys (1997); William H. Hastie Award, Judicial Council, National Bar Association (1993); Secretary's Award, U.S. Department of Veterans Affairs (1990); James R. Waddy Meritorious Service Award, Alumni Association, West Virginia State College (1990); County Spotlight Award National Association Counties (1990); Dean's Award, American University Washington College of Law (1989); Distinguished Service Award, Young Lawyers Section, District of Columbia Bar (1989); H. Carl Moultrie Award, District of Columbia Branch, NAACP (1989) **Membership:** Delegate, National Conference of State Trial Judges, American Bar Association (1986); Lawyer Competency Committee, American Bar Association (1984-1987); Criminal Instructions Committee, District of Columbia Bar (1984-1986); Advocates Association, National Institute Trial Advocacy; American Inns of Court Foundation; The American Law Institute **Bar Admissions:** District of Columbia **Marquis Who's Who Honors:** Albert Nelson Marquis Lifetime Achievement Award (2017) **Hobbies:** Cooking; Traveling **Political Affiliations:** Republican **Business Address:** 5240 Reno Road NW, Washington, DC, 20015 **Shipping Address:** 333 Constitution Avenue NW, E. Barrett Prettman United States Courthouse, Washington, DC, 20001

Harold J. Wanebo

Title: Surgeon, Cancer Investigator, Educator **Industry:** Medicine & Health Care **Company Name:** Chemo Enhanced **Date of Birth:** 02/12/1935 **Place of Birth:** Denver **State/Country of Origin:** CO **Parents:** Clifford P. Wanebo; JoAnn (Curtin) Wanebo **Marital Status:** Married **Spouse Name:** Claire Anne Wanebo **Children:** John Eric; Michael David; Jacqueline Elise **Education:** Senior Surgical Fellow, Memorial Sloan-Kettering Cancer Center, New York (1971-1973); Surgical Resident, University of California, San Francisco Medical Center (1967-1969); Fellow in Tumor Immunology, Memorial Sloan-Kettering Cancer Center, New York (1965-1967); Surgical Resident, University of California, San Francisco Medical Center (1963-1965); Resident, Cornell Medical Division, Bellevue Hospital, New York (1962-1963); Intern, Cornell Medical Division, Bellevue Hospital, New York (1961-1962); MD, University of Colorado (1961); BS, Regis College (1957) **Career:** Professor of Surgery, Boston University Medical School (2006-2016); Professor of Surgery, Director of Surgical Oncology, Brown University, Providence, RI (1987-2007); Consultant, Clinical Immunology Service, Memorial Sloan-Kettering Cancer Center, New York (1977-1990); Professor of Surgery, Chief, Division of Surgical Oncology, University of Virginia, Charlottesville, VA (1977-1987); Associate Scientist, Memorial Sloan-Kettering Cancer Center, New York (1977-1983); Assistant Professor of Surgery, Weill Cornell Medicine, Cornell University (1975-1977); Assistant Attending Surgeon, Memorial Sloan-Kettering Cancer Center, New York (1974-1977); Associate, Memorial Sloan-Kettering Cancer Center, New York (1973-1977); Instructor of Surgery, Weill Cornell Medicine, Cornell University (1973-1975); Clinical Assistant, Attending Surgeon, Memorial Sloan-Kettering Cancer Center, New York (1973-1974); Founder, Chemo Enhanced, Providence, RI **Career Related:** Advanced Training Council, American Head and Neck Society (1997-2002); Consultant, Ad Hoc Study Section, Allergy and Infectious Diseases, National Institutes of Health; Endowed Chair, Harold Wanebo Professorship of Surgical Oncology, Rodger Williams Medical Center, Providence, RI; Associate Editor, Gastric Cancer, Japan; International Adviser, Journal of Surgical Association, Taiwan, China **Military Service:** Major, U.S. Army (1969-1971) **Creative Works:** Editor, "Regional Therapy of Malignancy," Surgical Clinics of North America (2008); Editor, "Surgical Management for Pelvic Malignancy" (2005); Editor, "Surgery for Gastrointestinal Cancer" (1996); Editor, "Colorectal Cancer" (1993); Contributor, Journal of Cancer Education (1988-1992); Editor, "Common Problems in Cancer Surgery" (1990); Editor, "Hepatic and Biliary Cancer" (1987); Editor, Surgical Clinics of North America; Editorial Board Member, Head and Neck, Annals of Surgical Oncology; Contributor, Presentation Papers, Books, Articles to Professional Journals; Author, Over 290 Peer Reviewed Articles, Clinical and Scientific Journals **Awards:** Special Award, University of Colorado Medical School (2007); Special Award, University of Colorado Medical School (2007); Junior Faculty Clinical Fellowship Award, American Cancer Society (1974-1977); Bronze Star Medal; Commendation Medal with Device; Grant Award, NCI, Society of Surgical Oncology, and American Cancer Society **Membership:** American College of Surgeons; American Association for Cancer Education; American Association for Cancer Research; American Association of Immunologists; American Cancer Society; American Surgical Association; American Society of Clinical Oncology; Association of American Physicians and Surgeons; Medical Society of the State of New York; Medical Society of Rhode Island; Medical Society of Virginia; Naffziger Surgical Society; New England Surgical Society; New York Academy of Sciences; New York Surgical Society; Society for Surgery of the Alimentary Tract; Society of Surgical Oncology; Society of University Surgeons; Southeastern Surgical Congress; Southern Surgical Association; American Head & Neck Society **Marquis Who's Who Honors:** Albert Nelson Marquis Lifetime Achievement Award (2017) **To what do you attribute your success:** Dr. Wanebo attributes his success to his wife, Claire Anne, who was a Bellevue Hospital nurse. She was very helpful and supportive of his medical efforts. They have three children. Their daughter, Jaqueline, is a pediatrician, and their son, John, is a neurosurgeon while their son, Michael, is a nuclear engineer. Both sons attended the U.S. Naval Academy in Annapolis, Md. and served for several years in the U.S. Navy. **Why did you become involved in your profession or industry:** Dr. Wanebo has always had an interest in medical science. **Hobbies:** Skiing; Fishing; Music; Classical music **Religion:** Catholic **Business Address:** 1165 N Main Street, Providence, RI, 02904 **Shipping Address:** 116 Poppasquash Road, Bristol, RI, 02809 **Website:** https://www.bumc.bu.edu/busm/profile/harold-wanebo

Patricia Ann Wanley

Title: Medical and Surgical Nurse **Industry:** Medicine & Health Care **Date of Birth:** 09/24/1948 **Place of Birth:** Cincinnati **State/Country of Origin:** OH **Parents:** Charles Henry Wanley; Georgina Helen (Masterson) Wanley **Education:** AS, University of Indianapolis (1969) **Certifications:** Registered Nurse, State of Arkansas; Registered Nurse; State of Indiana; Registered Nurse, State of Maryland **Career:** Research Nurse, National Institutes of Health (2005-Present); Acting Nurse Manager, Holy Cross Hospital, Silver Spring, MD; Private Physician, Chevy Chase, MD; Staff Nurse, Chevy Chase, MD; Staff Nurse in Home Health, Baptist Memorial Health Care Corporation, Hardy, AK; Staff Nurse, Indiana University Health **Civic:** Volunteer, American Diabetes Association; Volunteer, The Humane Society of the United States **Awards:** Honoree, Outstanding Volunteer, American Diabetes Association; Honoree, Business and Professional Women's Nursing Scholar; Honoree, Viva Campbell Nursing Scholar **Membership:** American Nurses Association, Inc.; Maryland Nurses Association **Marquis Who's Who Honors:** Albert Nelson Marquis Lifetime Achievement Award (2017) **Shipping Address:** 2601 Camelback Lane, Apartment 12, Silver Spring, MD, 20906

Alan Warne

Title: Continuing Education Educator, Consultant **Industry:** Education/Educational Services **Date of Birth:** 08/24/1945 **Place of Birth:** Pierre **State:** SD **Parents:** Maynard L. Warne; Ione P. Warne **Marital Status:** Married **Spouse Name:** Joan Caulfield (9/7/1996) **Children:** Alan M. Jr.; Andrea W. White; Amy N. **Education:** EdD in Continuing Education, Temple University (1978); MA in Educational Psychology, Eastern Kentucky University (1970); BA in Political Science, Arizona State University (1967) **Career:** Vice President, Operations, Silver Fox Associate, Kansas City, MO (2007-2011); Senior Program Manager, Medical Center, University of Kansas, Kansas City, MO (2002-2007); President, Chief Executive Officer, Entrepreneurial Education Foundation, Kansas City, MO (2000-2001); Chief Executive Officer, Vice President for Programs, People to People International, Kansas City, MO (1986-1999); Executive Director, National Council for International Visitors, Washington D.C. (1981-1985); Executive Director, Philadelphia Council for International Visitors (1977-1981); Director, International Student and Scholar Services, Temple University, Philadelphia, PA (1971-1977); Director, International Student Services, University of Kentucky, Lexington, KY (1968-1971); Foreign Student Advisor, Arizona State University, Tempe, AZ (1966-1968) **Career Related:** Peer Grant Reviewer, U.S. Department of Education (2005-Present); Member, Continuing Medical Center Statewide Advisory Board and Governing Committee, University of Kansas, Kansas City, KS (2002-Present); Member, Continuing Medical Education Advisory Committee (2002-Present); Managing Director, The Brain Inc., Kansas City, MO (2000-2011); Academic Program Consultant, Rockhurst University, Kansas City, MO (2000); Planning Consultant, Kauffman Center for Entrepreneurial Leadership, Kansas City, MO (2000) **Civic:** President, Vice President, Park University Board of Visitors, Parkville, MO (1995-2001); Board Member, Arts Committee, Mayor's UN Day Committee, Kansas City, MO (1990-1996); Site Planning Committee, Kansas City School District, Kansas City, MO (1990-1991); Scholarship Committees Representative, University of Missouri, Kansas City, MO (1986-2005); Founding Board Member, Consortium for International Citizen Exchange, Washington D.C. (1981-1985); Board Member, Vice Chair, National Council for International Visitors, Washington, DC (1978-1981); Founding Board Member, Caruthers' Arts Alliance, Kansas City, MO **Creative Works:** Contributor, Curriculum Guide, Expo 92, Kansas City-Seville; Contributor, National Professional Newsletter, Management/Program Planning Articles; Contributor, Admissions Guide, "International Student: A Model for the Education of Foreign Students" **Awards:** Delegate Leader, Baltic Nations, Ambassadors, Inc. (1999); Thematic Specialist, Citizen Initiatives, Six U.S. Cities, Institute of International Education (1981); Grantee, Educational Travel Grant, Ministry of Education of the People's Republic of China (1975) **Membership:** Membership Committee, Kansas City Club (1993-Present); Educational, Scholarship, Planning Committees, Rotary Club International (1999-2012); Regional Chair, Coordinator of National Job Registry, Executive Committee, Association of International Educators (1967-2000); Fellow, Rotary Club International; Society of Government Meeting Professionals **Marquis Who's Who Honors:** Distinguished Humanitarian (2017) **Hobbies:** Volunteerism; Travel; Cinema; Theater; Organizational Development **Shipping Address:** 9909 Jefferson St, Kansas City, MO, 64114

Richard Warren

Title: Partner **Industry:** Law and Legal Services **Company Name:** Bradley, Arant, Boult & Cummings LLP **Date of Birth:** 09/24/1951 **Place of Birth:** Nashville **State:** TN **Parents:** Richard Fenton Warren, Sr.; Kathryn Lorene (Wilson) Warren **Marital Status:** Married **Spouse Name:** Catherine Ashley Lawrence (6/3/1972) **Children:** John Richardson; Stephen Fenton **Education:** JD, Vanderbilt University (1976); BA, Birmingham Southern College (1973) **Career:** Partner, Bradley, Arant, Boult & Cummings LLP (2008-Present); Partner, Boult, Cummings, Conners & Berry, Nashville, TN (1976) **Career Related:** Fellow, Nashville Bar Foundation **Civic:** Active Volunteer, Professional, Civic and Community Affairs **Awards:** Honoree, Nashville Member of the Year (2014); Honoree, Best of the Bar in Real Estate, Nashville Business Journal (2012); Honoree, Outstanding Member, Nashville Chapter, NAIOP (2011); Honoree, Nashville's 101 Top Lawyers in Real Estate (2011); Honoree, Nashville Real Estate Lawyer of the Year, Chambers USA (2009); Honoree, Mid-South Super Lawyers in Real Estate Law (2007-2014); Honoree, The Best Lawyers in America in Real Estate Law (2005-2018) **Membership:** President, Governmental Relations Committee, Nashville Chapter, NAIOP (2008); Chair, Governmental Relations Committee, Nashville Chapter, NAIOP (2006-2007); Chair, Partnerships and Limited Liability Companies (2002-2006); Board of Directors, Nashville Chapter, NAIOP (1999-2014); Chair, Partnerships and other Investment Vehicles, ABA (1999-2001); Vice Chair, Partnerships and other Investment Vehicles, ABA (1993-1998); Chair, Real Property Section Committee on Syndication and Securities, ABA (1990-1993); Tennessee Bar Association; Former Chair, Real Estate Committee, Nashville Bar Association; National, Board of Directors, Nashville Chapter, NAIOP; Nashville District Counsel, Urban Land Institute; Capital Markets Committee, Urban Land Institute **Bar Admissions:** U.S. District Court, Middle District, State of Tennessee (1978); Sixth Circuit, U.S. Court of Appeals (1977); State of Tennessee (1976) **Hobbies:** Long-distance running; Baseball; Reading **Political Affiliations:** Democrat **Religion:** Presbyterian **Shipping Address:** 1600 Division Street, Suite 700, Bradley, Arant, Boult & Cummings LLP, Nashville, TN, 37203

John Rosser Washburn

Title: Entrepreneur **Industry:** Financial Services **Company Name:** Washburn & Associates **Date of Birth:** 07/24/1943 **Place of Birth:** Hopewell **State:** VA **Parents:** Winthrop Doane Washburn; Mary Virginia (Overstreet) Washburn **Marital Status:** Married **Spouse Name:** Rebecca Mary (Wells) Washburn (9/1991) **Children:** Amanda Ashley Washburn; Eric Joseph Harrison; Leo M. Cicone; Suzann Weldon **Education:** Coursework, Stanford University (1986-1987); Coursework, Williams College (1985); Coursework, University of Richmond Extension (1967-1969); Coursework, Louisburg Junior College (1963-1964) **Career:** President and CEO, Washburn & Associates; Senior VP, E Com Consultant, Inc. (1988-Present); VP Principal Agent, Washburn Insurance and Financial Services Group, Richmond, VA (1996-2005); Owner, Washburn Insurance and Financial Services Group, Richmond, VA (1996-2005); Investment Consultant, JA-GO Enterprises, Richmond, VA (1982-1998); Corporate Credit Management, Owens & Minor, Inc., Richmond, VA (1974-1988); Regional Credit and Sales Supervisor, Moores Building Supplies, Inc., Roanoke, VA (1969-1974); Loan Interviewer, Central Fidelity Bank, Richmond, VA (1967-1969); Assistant Manager, Liberty Loan Corporation, Richmond, VA (1965-1967) **Career Related:** Board of Directors, Mathews Yacht Club (2012-Present); Board Member, Pharmacy Advisory Board, Greenwoods State Bank (2007-Present); Retail Pharmacy Specialist, Washburn & Associates (2003-Present); President, Washburn & Associates (2003-Present); CEO, Washburn & Associates (2003-Present); Executive Senior Vice President, E-Com Consultant, Inc., Richmond, VA (1998-Present); Retail Pharmacy Consultant, Washburn Enterprises (1970-Present); Board of Directors, Pharmacy Advisory Board (2007-2013); Senior Vice President, American Wellness Alliance, Immune Health Management Group LLC (2005-2006); Charter Member, Nations Business Consultant Group, Tysons Corner, VA (1998-2003); Partner, Nations Business Consultant Group, Tysons Corner, VA (1998-2003); Director, Forbes Clinical Research Group, Richmond, VA (1995-2005); Vice President, Forbes Clinical Research Group, Richmond, VA (1995-2005); Agent, New York Life Insurance Co., Richmond, VA (1994-1998); Secretary-treasurer, Multi-Enterprises, Inc., Richmond, VA (1988-1998); Board of Directors, DaneVest Capital LLC (1972) **Civic:** American Museum of National History (1982-Present); U.S. Defense Committee (1981-Present); National Republican Congressional Committee (1980-Present); YMCA (1979-2006); Member, Credit Research Foundation **Military Service:** Vessel Examiner Officer, U.S. Coast Guard Auxiliary (2007-Present); Flotilla Commander, U.S. Coast Guard Auxiliary (2009-2011) **Awards:** National Quality Award, National Association of Life Underwriters (1996-1997); Appreciation Certificate for Outstanding Service, National Association of Credit Management (1980-1981) **Membership:** Director, National Association of Credit Management (1983-Present); National Association of Life Underwriters (1985-2005); President, Central Virginia Section, National Association of Credit Management (1979-1980); Chairman, Legislative Committee, National Association of Credit Management (1977-1979); International Platform Association; National Association of Credit Management; American Management Association; National Wildlife Federation; Virginia Association of Life Underwriters; American Pharmacists Association; Congressional Club; Hopewell Yacht Club; Mathews Yacht Club; Classic Yacht Club of America **Marquis Who's Who Honors:** Who's Who in America; Who's Who in Finance and Business; Who's Who in the World; 2017 Marquis Industry Leaders; Marquis Who's Who for Excellence in Pharmacy Consulting **To what do you attribute your success:** He attributes his success to the advice of his father, and his example of working hard. **Where will you be in five years:** In 5 years, he hopes to be retired. **Hobbies:** Boating; Sports **Religion:** Episcopalian **Business Address:** PO Box 477, Dutton, VA, 23050 **Shipping Address:** 244 Wading Creek Rd, Dutton, VA, 23050

Leonard M. Wasserman

Title: Consultant, Adjunct Professor **Industry:** Consulting **Company Name:** New York City Economic Development Corporation, Brooklyn Law School **Education:** JD, Brooklyn Law School (1973); BA, Columbia University **Career:** Consultant, New York City Economic Development Corporation; Adjunct Professor, Brooklyn Law School **Civic:** Active Volunteer, Local Homeless Shelter; Active Volunteer, Masbia Food Kitchen; Active Volunteer, Our Place; Active Volunteer, The Urban Land Institute; Active Volunteer, The New Israel Fund **Awards:** A/V Preeminent Rated Attorney, Martindale-Hubbell **Membership:** The Jewish Study Advisory Board, Jewish Theological Seminary; New York State Bar Association; American Bar Association **Marquis Who's Who Honors:** Albert Nelson Marquis Lifetime Achievement Award (2017) **To what do you attribute your success:** Mr. Wasserman cares about achieving public benefits through the socially sensitive and equitable realization regarding urban development projects. **Why did you become involved in your profession or industry:** Mr. Wasserman became involved in his profession because, after college, he found an opportunity as an intern with a New York City program in administration. While there, he engaged with young college graduates to help them enter the municipal world for work. He had thoughts of pursuing a degree in urban planning, but his supervisor suggested he become a lawyer. **What do you consider to be the highlight of your career:** A highlight of Mr. Wasserman's career was the achievement of the 42nd Street project, which completely changed the quality of life in Manhattan, was the highlight of his career. **Where will you be in five years:** In five years, Mr. Wasserman intends to continue to be recognized in the field, mentor others, and continue teaching. **Hobbies:** Teaching small groups of adults in Jewish text study **Religion:** Jewish **Shipping Address:** 110 William Street, Floor 4, NYC Economic Development Corp, New York, NY, 10038

Olle M. Wastberg

Title: Communication Consultant, Writer, Diplomat **Industry:** Consulting **Date of Birth:** 05/06/1945 **Place of Birth:** Stockholm **Country of Origin:** Sweden **Parents:** Erik Wastberg; Greta (Hirsch) Wastberg **Marital Status:** Married **Spouse Name:** Inger Claesson (2/21/1968) **Children:** David; Elias **Education:** BA, University of Stockholm (1972) **Career:** Governments Committee on Public Service (2017-Present); Board, Raoul Wallenberg Academy (2013-Present); Partner, Industricentralen Inc. (2010-Present); Chair, Isaak Hirsch Foundation (2006-Present); Chair of the Government's Committee on Democracy (2014-2016); Jury, The European Council Raoul Wallenberg Award (2012-2017); Government Coordinator, Raoul Wallenberg Centennial (2011-2012); Board President, Swedish Foundation for International Cooperation in Research and Higher Education (2010-2016); Board President, Thiel Art Gallery (2010-2011); General Director, Swedish Institute Board (2005-2010); Consul, General of Sweden to New York (1999-2004); Board President, Swedish Broadcasting Corporation (1996-1999); Board President, Nordic Investment Bank (1992-1994); Undersecretary of State for Financial Affairs, Ministry of Finance, Stockholm, Sweden (1991-1993); Board, Stockholm Stock Exchange (1988-1992); President, Swedish Newspaper Promotion Association (1983-1991); Board, Stockholm Stock Exchange (1979-1983); Parliament Member (1976-1982); President, Aktieframjandet (1976-1982); Research Fellow, Business and Society Research Center (1971-1976); Journalist, Political Department, Expressen (1968-1971); Teacher, Political Science, University of Stockholm (1967-1968) **Career Related:** President, Southwest Fund (2014-Present); Governor's Globalization Council Board, Sweden American Foundation (2009-Present); Partner, Ethico (2010-2012); Board of Directors, Swedish Institute of Alexandria (2007-2011); President, Bertil Ohlin Institute (1996-2000); Government Committees, South Africa Consumer Politics and Stock Market, Swedish Delegate Meeting, Ministry of Finance (1992); Group of Ten, IMF (1991-1993); Working Party 3, OECD (1991-1993) **Civic:** Board, Sweden American Foundation (2009-Present); Board Chair, Swedes Worldwide (2009-2013); Chair, Stockholm City Theatre (1996-1999); Board, Swedish Public Art Association (1988-1992); President, Executive Committee, Liberal Party (1982-1983); Chair, Friends of Hebrew University of Jerusalem (1979-1983); Board of Directors, Liberal Party (1972-2000); Vice President, Liberal Youth Sweden (1969-1971); Political Secretary, Liberal Youth Sweden (1966) **Military Service:** Head of Department, Swedish Psychological Defense **Creative Works:** Editor-in-Chief, Expressen (1994-1995); Author, Books on African Problems, Immigration Politics, and Economic Topics; Contributor, Articles, Professional Journals **Awards:** H.M. The King's Medal (2013); Karl Staaf Liberal Gold Medal (2013); Swedish Man of the Year, New York (2003); Gold Medal, Swedish Marketing Group (1982) **Membership:** President, Isaac Hirsch Foundation (2008-Present) **Marquis Who's Who Honors:** Albert Nelson Marquis Lifetime Achievement Award (2017); Distinguished Humanitarian (2017) **Political Affiliations:** Liberal **Shipping Address:** Bellmansgatan 6, Stockholm, Sweden, 118 20

Joan Marie Watkins

Title: Osteopathic Physician, Occupational Medicine Physician **Industry:** Medicine & Health Care **Date of Birth:** 01/01/1943 **Place of Birth:** Anderson **State:** IN **Parents:** Curtis David Watkins; Dorothy Ruth (Beckett) Watkins **Marital Status:** Divorced **Spouse Name:** Stanley G. Nodvik (12/25/1969, Divorced 4/1974) **Education:** MPH, University of Illinois (1989); Resident in Occupational and Preventive Medicine, University of Illinois (1988-1990); MA, Health Professions Education, University of Illinois at Chicago (1986); DO, Philadelphia College of Osteopathic Medicine (1972); Certificate of Graduate Physical Therapy, The Ohio State University (1966); BS, West Liberty University (1965) **Certifications:** Diplomate, American Board of Emergency Medicine (1983-1993); Diplomate, American College of Occupational and Environmental Medicine; Diplomate, American Board of Preventive Medicine; Diplomate, National Board of Osteopathic Medical Examiners **Career:** Consultant in Field (2006-Present); Corporate Medical Director of Occupational Health Service, University Community Hospital (Now Florida Hospital Tampa), Adventist Health System (1992-2006); Director, Emergency Center, Mercy Hospital & Medical Center (1984-1988); Emergency Osteopathic Physician, Mercy Hospital and Medical Center (1982-1990); Emergency Osteopathic Physician, St. Francis Hospital (1981-1982); Emergency Osteopathic Physician, Shore Medical Center (1979-1981); Emergency Osteopathic Physician, Cooper University Health Care (1974-1979); Resident in Physical Medicine and Rehabilitation, University of Pennsylvania (1973-1974); Member, Tampa Occupational Health Services; Affiliated Associate Professor of Environmental & Occupational Health, College of Public Health, University of South Florida **Creative Works:** Playwright, "Waiting for DO"; Contributor, "Hamilton and Hardy's Industrial Toxicology, Sixth Edition" **Membership:** President, Florida Association of Occupational and Environmental Medicine (1999-2001); Fellow, International Academy of Independent Medical Evaluators; Fellow, American College of Occupational and Environmental Medicine; Fellow, American College of Preventive Medicine **Marquis Who's Who Honors:** Albert Nelson Marquis Lifetime Achievement Award (2017) **To what do you attribute your success:** Dr. Watkins attributes her success to her hard work and grit, as well as her access to education. **Why did you become involved in your profession or industry:** Dr. Watkins wanted to become a physician since she was 8 years old. She has always loved science and people and never once regretted her decision to enter this field. **What do you consider to be the highlight of your career:** The highlight of Dr. Watkin's career was the privilege of treating wonderful people. In regards to her academic career, a highlight for her was having the opportunity to contribute a chapter to "Hamilton and Hardy's Industrial Toxicology, Sixth Edition." **Where will you be in five years:** Dr. Watkins is very happy in Florida. She hopes to be where she can contribute, hopefully near the water. **Hobbies:** Sailing; Needle crafts; Swimming **Shipping Address:** 4306 Harbor House Dr., Tampa, FL, 33615 **Website:** http://health.usf.edu/publichealth/eoh/ocmed/faculty

Brenda Bennett Watson

Title: Insurance Company Executive **Industry:** Insurance **Company Name:** TIP National, LLC **Date of Birth:** 08/26/1940 **Place of Birth:** Decatur **State:** GA **Parents:** Robert Joseph Bennett; Clarissa Mae (Weekes) Bennett **Marital Status:** Widowed **Spouse Name:** James Leigh Watson (9/9/1995, Deceased 4/3/2017); James H. Pair, Jr. (4/4/1969, Divorced 8/1992) **Children:** Richard S. Pair; Randall J. Pair; Ronald G. Pair (Deceased 12/23/2017) **Education:** Student, DeKalb College (1971); Student, New York College of Insurance **Certifications:** Licensed Property and Casualty Agent; Licensed Surplus Lines Agent, National **Career:** President, CEO, Managing Partner, TIP National, Inc. (2007-Present); Executive Vice President, Board of Directors, Chandler Insurance Managers Inc. (2003-2006); Executive Vice President, Director, LaGere-Walkingstick Insurance Agency, Chandler, OK (1988-2002); President, Walkingstick-LaGere-Pair Underwriting Managers, Inc., Chandler, OK (1986-1988); Executive Vice President, Partner, Pair Underwriting Managers Inc., Atlanta, GA (1982-1986); Senior Vice President, Alexander-Howden, Atlanta, GA (1968-1982); Underwriter, Tharpe & Associates, Atlanta, GA (1965-1968); Underwriter, W. K. Stringer Company, Atlanta, GA (1961-1965) **Career Related:** Executive Vice President, National American Insurance Company, Austin, TX (1999-2003); Executive Vice President, National American Insurance Company, Chandler, OK (1987-2006); Executive Vice President, Board of Directors, Chandler Insurance Ltd., Cayman Islands (1985-2004) **Civic:** Director, Past President, Gateway to Prevention and Recovery (1994-1998); Cancer Society, Lincoln County, Oklahoma **Awards:** TIP National, LLC (2017); Best Places to Work (2010-2011); Insurance Woman of the Year (1981); Woman of the Year, National Association of Insurance Women (1979-1980); Top U.S. Specialty Broker, Insurance Business America **Membership:** President, Atlanta Chapter, National Association of Insurance Women (1978-1979); Past President, Atlanta Insurance Women Association **To what do you attribute your success:** Ms. Watson attributes her success to her dedication, hard work, and mentors who were willing to let her advance. **Why did you become involved in your profession or industry:** Ms. Watson became involved in her profession because once she started, she found she had a passion for the specialty insurance market. **What do you consider to be the highlight of your career:** Ms. Watson considers the highlight of her career to be mentoring hundreds of other men and women in the insurance industry. **Where will you be in five years:** Ms. Watson wants to remain in the same position, but just grow her volume and add more programs. **Hobbies:** Reading; Snow skiing; Gardening; Traveling; Food and wine tasting in the United States and Europe **Political Affiliations:** Republican **Religion:** Episcopalian **Shipping Address:** 1900 NW Expressway, Suite 860, Tip National, LLC, Oklahoma City, OK, 73118 **Website:** http://www.tipnational.com

Raymond Coke Watson Jr., PhD

Title: Lead Consultant **Industry:** Engineering **Company Name:** RC Watson & Associates **Date of Birth:** 08/31/1926 **Place of Birth:** Anniston **State:** AL **Marital Status:** Married **Spouse Name:** Charlotte Bagley Watson **Children:** Lee; Coke; Anne; Joseph **Education:** Certificate, Radio Engineering, Auburn University (1942); BS, Jacksonville State College (1953); MS Engineering, University of Alabama (1955); MS, University of Florida (1959); PhD, California Coast University & University of Florida (1995); MBA, California Coast University (2003) **Certifications:** Communications Consultant, Federal Communications Commission (1949); Registered Professional Engineer, State of Alabama (1958) **Career:** Owner & Lead Consultant, RC Watson & Associates (1980-Present); President & Professor, Southeastern Institute of Technology (1976-2003); CEO, Vision Technologies Systems, Inc. (2000-2003); Chief Engineer, Chief Scientist, Teledyne Brown Engineering (1990-2001); Associate Professor, Director, Continuous Education, University of Alabama in Huntsville (1970-1976); VP Research, Brown Engineering Company (1960-1970; Founder & Head, Physics and Engineering Department, Jacksonville State College (1954-1960); Owner & Chief Engineer, Dixie Service Company (1948-1954) **Career Related:** Adjunct Associate Professor, University of Alabama Huntsville Graduate Center (1961-1970) **Civic:** Chairman, Engineering Advisory Board, Alabama A&M University **Military Service:** Active Duty, U.S. Navy, WWII (1944-1946) **Creative Works:** Author, Over 340 Publications, Including 4 History Books; Contributor, Articles, Professional Journals; Contributor, Reports, Professional Journals; Official Editor, Wikipedia **Awards:** Public Service Award for Lunar Exploration, National Aeronautics and Space Administration; Science Faculty Fellowship, National Science Foundation **Membership:** IEEE; AIAA; Optical Society of America; Operations Research Society of America; Institute Management Science (Now Informs); SPIE; Institute of Industrial and Systems Engineers **Marquis Who's Who Honors:** Albert Nelson Marquis Lifetime Achievement Award (2017) **Hobbies:** Writing **Political Affiliations:** Republican **Religion:** Protestant (Baptist) **Shipping Address:** P.O. Box 1485, RC Watson & Associates, Huntsville, AL, 35807

Rollin J. Watson, PhD

Title: Tenured Associate Professor **Industry:** Education/Educational Services **Company Name:** Somerset Community College **Date of Birth:** 07/25/1941 **Place of Birth:** Syracuse **State:** NY **Marital Status:** Married **Spouse Name:** Norma Osborne (5/20/1967) **Children:** David O.; Juliana Watson-Dick; Jennifer Mary **Education:** Fellow, University of Kentucky (1996); Honorary Doctor of Public Administration, Union College, Barbourville, KY (1992); PhD in American Studies, University of Maryland, College Park, MD (1975); Fellow, University of Maryland (1969) **Career:** Consultant, Administrator, Local Schools (2013-Present); Retired (2013); Tenured Associate Professor, Somerset Community College, Kentucky (1999-2013); President, Somerset Community College, Kentucky (1989-1999); Vice President to President, Hiwassee College, Madisonville, TN (1984-1989) **Career Related:** Board Member, Numerous Agencies and Associations **Civic:** Consultant, Safe Schools America (1995-Present); Library Board, University of Kentucky, Lexington, KY (1996-2007); Somerset-Pulaski County Developmental Foundation (1992-1999); Supporter, God's Kitchen **Military Service:** U.S. Army Reserve **Creative Works:** Author, "The School as a Safe Haven"; Author, "Spending a Lifetime: Careers of City Managers" **Awards:** Citation, University of Kentucky (1999); State Senate Citation, Commonwealth of Kentucky (1999) **Membership:** History and American Studies Associations **Marquis Who's Who Honors:** Albert Nelson Marquis Lifetime Achievement Award (2017) **Why did you become involved in your profession or industry:** Dr. Watson became involved in his profession because he took an interest in local government when he worked for a newspaper in high school. He became a club reporter. He became interested in writing and he enjoyed it. He got involved in a lot of historic things in Americana and American histories. **What do you consider to be the highlight of your career:** A highlight of Dr. Watson's career was his college presidencies. **Hobbies:** Swimming; Weightlifting; Bicycling; Reading **Shipping Address:** 359 Bolton Drive, Somerset, KY, 42503

Ross Leslie Watts

Title: Finance Educator **Industry:** Education/Educational Services **Company Name:** National Taiwan University **Date of Birth:** 11/10/1942 **Place of Birth:** Hamilton **Country of Origin:** Australia **Parents:** Leslie R. Watts; Elsie B. (Horadam) Watts **Marital Status:** Married **Spouse Name:** Nancy M. Lamb (7/17/2010); Helen Clare Firkin (1/15/1966, Divorced 2007) **Children:** Andrew David; James Michael **Education:** PhD, The University of Chicago (1971); MBA, The University of Chicago (1968); Honorary Bachelor's in Commerce, University of Newcastle (1966) **Career:** Distinguished Chaired Professor, Accounting Research Center, National Taiwan University (2013-Present); Director, Accounting Research Center, National Taiwan University (2013-Present); Erwin H. Schell Professor Emeritus of Management, Massachusetts Institute of Technology (2013-Present); Erwin H. Schell Professor of Management, Massachusetts Institute of Technology (2007-2013); Professor, Sloan School, Massachusetts Institute of Technology (2005-2007); William H. Meckling Professor, University of Rochester (1998-2005); Endowed Chair, Rochester Telephone Corporation. (1986-1998); Professor, Simon School of Management, University of Rochester (1984-1986); Associate Professor, Simon School of Management, University of Rochester (1978-1984); Assistant Professor, Simon School of Management, University of Rochester (1971-1978); Instructor, Graduate School of Business, The University of Chicago (1969-1970); Accountant, Forsythe & Co., Newcastle, Australia (1964-1966); Audit Clerk, Forsythe & Co., Newcastle, Australia (1960-1964) **Career Related:** Honorary Professor, City University of Hong Kong (1996-Present); Visiting Professor, Massachusetts Institute of Technology (2002); Distinguished Lecturer, Hong Kong University of Science and Technology (1994); Professor of Commerce, University of Newcastle (1974-1976) **Creative Works:** Member, Advisory Board, Bank of America Journal of Applied Corporate Finance (1994-Present); Consultant Editor, Journal of Contemporary Accounting and Economics (2005-Present); Director, Accounting Research Network (1997-Present); Editor, Accounting Research Network (1997-Present); Co-Editor, Journal of Accounting and Economics (1979-Present); Consulting Editor, Asia Pacific Journal of Accounting & Economics (1998-2005); Editor, Journal of Accounting Abstracts (1995-1997); Contributor, Continental Bank Journal of Applied Corporate Finance (1988-1994); Member, Advisory Board, Midland Corporate Finance Journal (1983-1988); Member, Editorial Board, Contemporary Accounting Research (1983-1985); Contributor, Australian Journal of Management (1976-1981); Contributor, Journal of Financial Economics (1974-1989); Associate Editor, Journal of Accounting Research (1972-1978); Contributor, Articles, Professional Journals **Awards:** Inductee, Australian Accounting Hall of Fame (2016); Award, University of Newcastle (2013); Inaugural Lifetime Achievement Award, American Accounting Association (2013); Seminal Research Award, American Accounting Association (2004); Outstanding Educator Award, American Accounting Association (2000); Excellence Award, University of Rochester (1996); Award, Alpha Kappa Psi Foundation (1985); Notable Contribution Award, American Institute Of Certified Public Accountants (1980); Notable Contribution Award, American Institute Of Certified Public Accountants (1979) **Membership:** American Finance Association; Institute of Chartered Accountants in Australia; Ford Foundation; American Accounting Association **Hobbies:** Rugby; Tennis; Golf; Bike riding **Business Address:** National Taiwan University, Taipei City, Taiwan, 10617 **Shipping Address:** 22 Park St., Arlington, MA, 02474

David R. Webb

Title: Chief Executive Officer **Industry:** Business Management/Business Services **Company Name:** Synbal **Date of Birth:** 11/10/1944 **Place of Birth:** Taft **State:** CA **Parents:** David R. Webb; Maude (Glynn) Webb **Marital Status:** Married **Spouse Name:** Lila Lee Schupach (6/18/1966) **Children:** Scott; Linly **Education:** PhD in Immunology, Rutgers, The State University of New Jersey (1971); MA, California State University, Fullerton (1968); BA, California State University, Fullerton (1966) **Career:** Chief Executive Officer, Synbal, Inc. (2017-Present); Adjunct Professor, Department of Integrative Structural and Computational Biology, The Scripps Research Institute (2011-Present); Chairman of the Board, Sorrento Therapeutics, Inc. (2013-2014); Adviser, Physical Sciences in Oncology, The Scripps Research Institute (2011-2014); Site Director, Celgene, San Diego, CA (2006-2011); Vice President of Research, Celgene, San Diego, CA (2003-2011); Vice President, Drug Discovery, Syrrx, Inc., (2001-2003); Corporate Vice President, Research, OSI Pharmaceuticals (1999-2003); Chief Scientific Officer, Vice President Research, Cadus Pharmaceuticals (1995-1999); Adjunct Professor of Microbiology, New York College of Medicine (1995-1999); Consulting Professor, Graduate Program in Cancer Biology, Stanford University School of Medicine (1988-1995); Distinguished Scientist, Director, Institute of Immunology and Biological Sciences, Syntex (1987-1995); Adjunct Associate Professor, Columbia University College of Physicians and Surgeons (1979-1987); Member, Roche Institute of Molecular Biology (1973-1987) **Career Related:** Member, President's Advisory Council, California State University San Marcos (2013-Present); Scientific Consultant (2011-Present); Member, Innovation Advisory Council of the Vice Chancellor for Research, University of California, San Diego (2011-Present); Member, Board of Directors, La Jolla Institute for Allergy & Immunology (2011-Present); Member, Board of Directors, BIOCOM (2006-Present); Member, Board of Directors, CONNECT (2006-Present); Member, Scientific Advisory Board, Axiom Biotechnologies (Now Axiom Life Sciences Group, LLC) (1998-2002); Member, Board of Directors, Axiom Biotechnologies (Now Axiom Life Sciences Group, LLC) (1997-2000); Chairman, Veterans Affairs Study Section, National Science Foundation (1990-1993); Member, Study Section, American Cancer Society, Inc. (1985-1987); Member, Study Section, National Science Foundation (1981-1983) **Civic:** Member, Council of the Mid-Winter Conference of Immunology (2007-Present); Member, Industry Advisory Council, Sanford Consortium for Regenerative Medicine (2007-Present); Honorary Co-Chair, Annual Gala, California Division, American Cancer Society, Inc. (2016); Honorary Chairman, Cancer Action Network, American Cancer Society, Inc. (2014-2015); Member, Scientific Advisory Board, Keystone Symposia on Molecular and Cellular Biology (2010-2012); Member, Honorary Co-Chair Partnership Council, Border Region, California Division, American Cancer Society, Inc. (2008-2009); Chairman, Merit Review Board for Oncology, United States Department of Veterans Affairs (1993-1994); Member, Merit Review Board for Oncology, United States Department of Veterans Affairs (1993); Member, Merit Review Board for Oncology, United States Department of Veterans Affairs (1991); Ad Hoc Member, Immunology Study Section, American Cancer Society, Inc. (1985-1986); Member, Ad Hoc Technical Review Group on Developmental Therapeutics, National Institutes of Health (1983); Member, Ad Hoc Technical Review Group on Developmental Therapeutics, National Institutes of Health (1983); Guest Member, Fellowship Advisory Committee, Damon Runyon (1982); Guest Member, Fellowship Advisory Committee, Damon Runyon (1982) **Creative Works:** Member, Editorial Advisory Board, "Biochemical Pharmacology" (2008-Present); Member, Editorial Advisory Board, "Progress in Immunology" (1994-Present); Editorial Board Member, "Journal of Immunology" (1992); Editorial Board Member, "Journal of Interferon and Cytokine Research" (1990-2000); Editorial Board Member, "Journal of Immunology" (1988); Editorial Board Member, "Lymphokine Research" (1987); Editorial Board Member, "Clinical Immunology and Immunopathology" (1987); Editorial Board Member, "Journal of Immunology" (1985); Editorial Board Member, "Lymphokine Research" (1984); Editorial Board Member, "Journal of Immunology" (1983); Editorial Board Member, "Clinical Immunology and Immunopathology" (1983) **Awards:** Named, Honorary Chairman, American Cancer Society Cancer Action Network (2006); Recipient, Rising Star Award, American Cancer Society, Inc. (2006); Recipient, Distinguished Alumni Award, California State University, Fullerton (1988) **Membership:** American Association for the Advancement of Science; American Society of Microbiology; Sigma Xi, The Scientific Research Honor Society; The American Association of Immunologists, Inc.; Clinical Immunology Society; Fellow, The New York Academy of Sciences; Collegium Internationale Allergolicum; American Society of Hematology; American Association for Cancer Research **Shipping Address:** 2747 Llama Ct, Carlesbad, CA, 92009

Carol Weber

Title: Associate Professor **Industry:** Education/ Educational Services **Date of Birth:** 05/05/1950 **Place of Birth:** New York City **State:** NY **Parents:** Eduardo Martinez; Jacqueline Sheehan Martinez **Children:** Julia Martinez Weber; Andres Martinez Weber **Education:** MD, Tufts University (1981); BA, Williams College (1972); Coursework, Mount Holyoke College (1968-1970) **Certifications:** Certified in Internal Medicine Geriatrics **Career:** Associate Professor, New York Medical College, Valhalla, NY (1986-Present); Attending Physician, St. Vincent's Hospital, New York, NY (1985-Present); Chief Resident, St. Vincent's Hospital, New York, NY (1984-1985); House Officer, St. Vincent's Hospital, New York, NY (1983-1984); House Officer, Mount Sinai Hospital, New York, NY (1981-1983) **Career Related:** Consultant in Field **Civic:** Board of Trustees, Corlears School, New York, NY (1987); Board of Directors, Khaniqahi Nimatullahi, New York **Creative Works:** Editorial Board Member, Postgraduate Medicine; Contributor, Articles to Professional Journals and Chapters to Books **Awards:** Grantee, United States Public Health Service, New York, NY (1995); Grantee, New York State Deptartment of Health, New York, NY (1993-1995); Grantee, McKinney Healthcare for Homeless, New York, NY (1993-1994) **Membership:** Fellow, American College of Physicians; Fellow, American College of Preventive Medicine; Alpha Omega Alpha **What do you consider to be the highlight of your career:** The highlight of Dr. Weber's career was bringing health care to homeless persons and hospital administration in West Africa. **Hobbies:** Nature walks; Swimming; Traveling **Shipping Address:** 493 Piedmont K, Delray Beach, FL, 33484-5080

Carleton Lloyd Weidemeyer

Title: Lawyer **Industry:** Law and Legal Services **Company Name:** Southern Municipal Corporation, Carleton L. Weidemeyer, P.A. Law Office **Date of Birth:** 06/12/1933 **Place of Birth:** Hebbville **State:** MD **Education:** JD, Stetson University, St. Petersburg, FL (1961); BA in Political Science, University of Maryland (1958) **Career:** President, Carleton L. Weidemeyer, P.A. Law Office (1982-Present); President, Southern Municipal Corporation (1997-2015); Assistant Public Defender, Sixth Judicial Circuit of Florida (1981-1983); Partner, Wightman, Weidemeyer, Jones, Turnbull and Cobb, Clearwater, FL (1968-1982); Assistant Public Defender, Sixth Judicial Circuit of Florida (1966-1969); Partner, Kalle and Weidemeyer, St. Petersburg, FL (1965-1968); Research Assistant, Second District Court of Appeal, Florida Courts (1961-1965) **Career Related:** Lecturer, Various Genealogical Societies (1995-1998); Guest Lecturer on Appellate Procedure, Stetson University Law School (1978-1980); International Law Committee, American Federation of Musicians (1977-1980); Director, First National Bank, Belleair Bluffs, FL (1977-1978); Director, Florida Bank of Commerce, Clearwater, FL (1975-1977); Director, Clearwater Yacht Club (1975-1977) **Civic:** Trustee, Jeanne Pisano Memorial Trust (2008-Present); Trustee, Francis G. Prasse Memorial Scholarship Trust (1984-Present); Trustee, Tampa Bay Research Institute (2001-2012); Board of Directors, Pinellas Center for the Visually Impaired (Now Lighthouse of Pinellas) (2000-2005); Board of Directors, Pinellas Center for Visually Impaired (1999-2000); Advisory Committee, Florida Sheriffs Youth Ranches (1997-2001); Co-Chairman, Squadron VX-4, VW-2 Navy Reunion Committee (1996-2009); Planned Giving Committee, The Arc Tampa Bay (1996-2001); Co-Chairman, Music Committee, Clearwater Jazz Holiday (1980-1981); Board of Advisers, Musicians Insurance Trust (1977-1980) **Military Service:** U.S. Navy (1951-1954) **Creative Works:** Contributor, Maryland Genealogical Society Journal (1990-Present); Publisher, Weidemeyer World Quarterly (2000-2007); Author, "History of Musicians' Association of Clearwater," Local 729, American Federation of Musicians (1999); Pinellas County Estate Planning Council, National Association of Estate Planners & Councils (1997-2005); Author, "Baltimore County's Second District: Inhabitants During the Emerging Thirties," Self-Published (1990); Author, "Area History of Baltimore County" (1990); Performer, Clearwater Jazz Holiday (1980-1983); St. Paul Church Orchestra (1979-1980); Editor, Ad Lib Magazine (1978-1981); Author, "Know Your Copyright Law" (1977); Leader, "Polka Dots," The Jazz Notes (1976-2007); Florida Historical Society (1973-1976); "The Ole Buds" Dixieland Band, Washington, DC (1955-1958); Performer, "This Is Your Navy Radio Show" (1951-1952); Author, "Johann Hermann Weidemeyer: His Descendants and Collateral Kindred," Legacy Publishing; Author, "Arbitration of Entertainment Claims" **Awards:** Shipmate of the Year, Fleet Reserve, Annapolis, MD (2014-2015); Life Membership Award, Sertoma International (2005); President's Award, Lighthouse of Pinellas (2005); Patron of Jazz Award, Suncoast Classic Jazz Society, Inc. (2003); Professional Service Award, Tampa Bay Research Institute (1999); President's Award, UPARC of Tampa Bay (1998); Shriner's Hospital Award (1992); Sertoma Centurian Award, Florida Sheriffs Association (1991) **Membership:** Presiding Justice, Largo Elks Club BPOE (2013-Present); Morton Plant Mease Health Care Foundation (2009-Present); Pinellas Community Foundation (1995-Present); Pinellas Genealogy Society, Inc. (1995-Present); Pinellas County Estate Planning Council, National Association of Estate Planners & Councils (1997-2005); Vice President, Clearwater Chapter, Sertoma (1989-1992); Board of Directors, Clearwater Breakfast, Sertoma (1984-2006); President Emeritus, Musicians Association of Clearwater (1981); President, Southern Conference of Musicians (1979-1980); American Federation of Musicians (1979-1980); President, Musicians Association of Clearwater (1976-1981); Secretary-Treasurer, Florida-Georgia Musicians Conference (1974-1976); National Rifle Association of America; Florida Historical Society; Maryland Historical Society; Clearwater Historical Society; Dunedin Historical Society; Catonsville Historical Society; Greater St. Petersburg Musicians Association; American Federation of Musicians; National Genealogical Society; Maryland Genealogical Society; Augustan Society, Inc.; Genealogical Society of Pennsylvania; Carroll County Genealogical Society, Inc. **Bar Admissions:** 11th Circuit, U.S. Court of Appeals (1982); District of Columbia Circuit, U.S. Court of Appeals (1976); District of Columbia (1971); Fifth Circuit, U.S. Court of Appeals (1967); U.S. Supreme Court (1966); Middle District of Florida, U.S. District Court (1963); State of Florida (1961); Senior Bar Section, American Bar Association; Federal Bar Association; Probate Division, Clearwater Bar Association **Marquis Who's Who Honors:** Albert Nelson Marquis Lifetime Achievement Award (2017) **Hobbies:** Genealogical and historical research; Music **Shipping Address:** 2261 Belleair Road, Clearwater, FL, 33764

Florence May Weinberg, PhD

Title: Modern Language and Literature Educator (Retired) **Industry:** Education/Educational Services **Date of Birth:** 12/03/1933 **Place of Birth:** Alamogordo **State:** NM **Parents:** Steven Horace Byham; Olive Gladys (Edgington) Byham **Marital Status:** Married **Spouse Name:** Kurt Weinberg (5/8/1955, Deceased 1996) **Education:** Resident, The Hambidge Center for the Creative Arts & Sciences (2009-2010, 2003-2007, 1999-2001); PhD, University of Rochester (1968) **Career:** Author, Novels (1999-Present); Professor of French, Trinity University, San Antonio, TX (1989-1999); Chairman, Department of Modern Languages and Literature, Trinity University, San Antonio, TX (1989-1995); Professor, Spanish, Trinity University, San Antonio, TX (1989-1999); Director, International Studies, St. John Fisher College, Rochester, NY (1983-1986); Professor, Modern Languages, St. John Fisher College, Rochester, NY (1975-1989); Chairman, Department of Modern Languages, St. John Fisher College, Rochester, NY (1972-1979); Associate Professor, Modern Languages, St. John Fisher College, Rochester, NY (1971-1975); Assistant Professor, Modern Languages, St. John Fisher College, Rochester, NY (1967-1971); Instructor, Modern Languages, St. John Fisher College, Rochester, NY (1967) **Creative Works:** Author, "Dolet" (2015); Author, "Anselm: a Metamorphosis" (2013); Author, "Unruhe im Paradies" (2012); Author, "Unrest in Eden" (2011); Author, "El Jesuita y el brujo" (2011); Author, "El Jesuita y la Tormenta" (2011); Author, "El Jesuita y la Caridad" (2011); Author, "Sonora Wind" (2009); Author, "Seven Cities of Mud" (2008); Author, "Sonora Moonlight" (2008); Author, "The Storks of La Caridad" (2005); Author, "Apache Lance, Franciscan Cross" (2005); Author, "Sonora Wind, Ill Wind" (2002); Author, "Longs désirs" (2002); Author, "I'll Come to Thee By Moonlight" (2002); Author, "Les Leçons du rire" (2000); Author, "Gargantua in a Convex Mirror" (1986); Author, "The Cave" (1986); Author, "The Wine and the Will" (1972) **Awards:** Pinnacle Book Achievement Award (2015, 2014, 2012); Finalist, Indie Next Generation Book Award (2012); Arts & Letters Award, Friends of the San Antonio Public Library (2012); Finalist, Indie Book Award (2012); New Mexico Book Award (2011); Finalist, Indie Next Generation Book Award (2010); Finalist, Eric Hoffer Award (2009); Alumna of the Year Award, Park University (2008); Finalist, New Mexico Book Award (2007-2008); Finalist, WILLA Literary Award (2006); Research Grant, Ludwig Vogelstein Foundation (1986); Grantee, National Endowment for the Humanities (1983); Senior Fellowship, National Endowment for the Humanities (1979-1980); Grantee-in-Aid, American Council of Learned Societies (1974-1975) **Membership:** Modern Language Association; PEN; Renaissance Society of America; Sixteenth Century Society & Conference; Women Writing the West; Toastmasters International **To what do you attribute your success:** Dr. Weinberg had wonderful parents and a fine education thanks to Park College (now Park University) and a series of excellent professors who guided he graduate work. **Why did you become involved in your profession or industry:** She became involved in her profession because she loved languages and fine literature from an early age and realized she could make a career teaching those subjects (especially French and Spanish language and literature) at the university level. **What do you consider to be the highlight of your career:** A highlight of her career was receiving the Best Teacher vote from students in 1988. **Where will you be in five years:** In five years, she will probably be behind her computer writing another novel. **Hobbies:** Swimming; Hiking; Weightlifting **Political Affiliations:** Democrat **Religion:** Catholic **Shipping Address:** 331 Royal Oaks Dr., San Antonio, TX, 78209 **Website:** http://florenceweinberg.com/

Marcia S. Weiner

Title: Judge **Industry:** Law and Legal Services **Company Name:** Bexar County **Date of Birth:** 04/12/1934 **Place of Birth:** Chicago **State:** IL **Parents:** A.C. Spitzer; Esther Spitzer **Marital Status:** Widow **Spouse Name:** Dr. Bernard K. Weiner (Deceased) **Children:** Audrey; Jodi; Karen **Education:** JD, St. Mary's University School of Law (1970); BA in History and English, St. Mary's University, Summa Cum Laude (1965) **Certifications:** Lifetime Teacher's Certificate (1965) **Career:** Justice of the Peace, Precinct 2, Bexar County, TX (2000-2009); Chief Counsel, U.S. Department of Housing and Urban Development San Antonio Area Office (1984-1997); Attorney-Adviser, HUD (1971-1984) **Civic:** First Secretary, Federal Bar Association, San Antonio, TX; Volunteer, Legal Awareness and Benefits Counseling Office, Texas Area Agency on Aging; Vice President, Alamo Unit No. 2, American Legion Auxiliary; Vice President, National Association of Retired Federal Employees; Board of Directors, AARP; Board of Directors, Summit Oaks Chapter, Harp and Shamrock Society of Texas; Bexar County Bail Bond Board; Committee for Judicial Conduct, State of Texas and the Judges Diversionary Committee; Speaker, Schools and Neighborhood Meetings **Awards:** Honoree, Woman Inspiring Change, Harvard Women's Law Association (2014); Honoree, International Black And White Ball (2010); Legion of Honor, Precinct 2, Bexar County (2008); Woman of the Year, American Business and Professional Women's Association of San Antonio (2006); Honoree, Business and Professional Women of Texas (2004); Honoree, Business and Professional Women of San Antonio (2003); Leigh Curry Award for Outstanding Chief Counsel (1994) **Membership:** Fellow, San Antonio Bar Foundation; Fellow, Texas Bar Foundation; AARP; National Association of Retired Federal Employees; Harp and Shamrock Society of Texas **Bar Admissions:** Texas **Marquis Who's Who Honors:** Albert Nelson Marquis Lifetime Achievement Award (2017); Who's Who Top Lawyers (2017) **To what do you attribute your success:** She attributes her success to her faith in God, and to the people in her life that encouraged her to be the best that she could be. **Why did you become involved in your profession or industry:** After her father passed away when she was 3 years old, her mother raised her and taught her to make the world a better place. Her first major was teaching, and then she moved into law. **What do you consider to be the highlight of your career:** The highlight of her career was being able to positively affect change in her community. She focused on getting children and their parents into counseling and meaningful community service. She also made it a point to empower mothers, and raise their self-esteem, and that of the juveniles who appeared in her court. **Hobbies:** Reading; Gardening; Traveling **Religion:** Jewish **Shipping Address:** 6603 Moss Oak Drive, San Antonio, TX, 78229

Jacob Weintz

Title: Investment Banker (Retired) **Industry:** Financial Services **Date of Birth:** 06/27/1926 **Place of Birth:** New York **State:** NY **Parents:** Jacob Frederick Weintz; Grace (Cortelyou) Weintz **Marital Status:** Married **Spouse Name:** Elisabeth Hamlin Brewer (12/26/1955, Deceased August 22, 2007) **Children:** Elizabeth Weintz Cerf; Polly Weintz Sanna; Eric Cortelyou; Kar **Education:** Honorary Doctor in Finance Management, Norwich University (2001); MBA, Harvard University (1951); BA, Stanford University (1948); Coursework, Norwich University (1943-1944) **Career:** Limited Partner, Goldman, Sachs Group L.P. (1984-1999); Partner, Goldman, Sachs & Co. (1965-1984); Associate, New Business Department, Goldman, Sachs & Co. (1954-1965); Associate, Buying Department, Goldman, Sachs & Co., New York, NY (1951-1954); Salesman, Vick Chemical Company, New York, NY (1948-1949) **Civic:** Leadership Council, Harvard School of Public Health, Pace University Financial and Audit and Investment Committee (1997-Present); Trustee, Sierra Club Foundation (1984-1990, 1992-1998); BENS-ED Commission on Fundamental Defense Management Issues (1991-1992); Board of Directors, The Forum World Affairs, Stamford, CT (1988-1994); President, Harvard University Business School Alumni Association (1988-1990); Trustee, Norwich University, Stanford University (1985-1995); Vice Chairman, Board of Directors, Guiding Eyes for the Blind (1984-1993); Trustee, Federation of Protestant Welfare Agencies, Pace University (1981-1997); President, Chairman, Board of Directors, Stonebridge Condominium Association, Snowmass Village, CT (1978-1985); Member, Executive Committee, Greenwich Republican Town Committee, Connecticut (1962-1969); Chairman, Board of Directors, New York Young Republicans Club (1957-1958); Trustee, Harbor Lights Foundation, New York, NY; Trustee, Martin B-26 Marauder Historical Society, National Lighthouse Museum, Staten Island, NY; Former Delegate, Council of Governing Boards, Albany, NY; The Task Force on Defense Spending; The Economy and the Nation's Security; Member, Stanford in Washington Council; Visiting Board Member, Freeman Spogli Institute for International Studies at Stanford **Military Service:** U.S. Army Air Forces (1944-1945) **Awards:** Stanford Gold Spike Award (1992); Recipient, La Medaille de la Ville de Paris (1990) **Membership:** Board Member, Martin B. Historical Society (2015-Present); President, Flying Scot Sailing Association; (1968-1969); Ambassadors Round Table, Stamford, CT; Bond Club of New York; Newcomen Society in North America; Down Town Association; Harvard Club of New York City; Riverside Yacht Club; Theta Chi **Political Affiliations:** Republican **Religion:** Episcopalian **Business Address:** 77 Water Street, 9th Floor, New York, NY, 10005 **Shipping Address:** 43 Jones Park Drive, Riverside, CT, 06878

Armand Berl Weiss

Title: Economist **Industry:** Financial Services **Date of Birth:** 04/02/1931 **Place of Birth:** Richmond **State:** VA **Parents:** Maurice Herbert Weiss; Henrietta (Shapiro) Weiss **Marital Status:** Single **Spouse Name:** Judith Bernstein (5/18/1957, Deceased) **Children:** Jo Ann Michele; Rhett Louis **Education:** DBA, George Washington University (1971); MBA, Wharton School of Finance, University of Pennsylvania (1954); BS in Economics, Wharton School of Finance, University of Pennsylvania (1953) **Certifications:** Certified Lifetime Association Executive **Career:** President, Weiss Publishing Company, Inc. (2013-Present); Adjunct Professor, American University (1989-1991); Chairman, Board of Directors, CFO, Rail Digital Corporation (1988-1991); Adjunct Professor, American University (1979-1981); Chairman of the Board, President, CEO, Associations International Inc. (1978-2017); Vice President, Treasurer, Technical Frontiers, Inc. (1978-1980); Project Director and Technical Assistant to the Vice President, System Planning Corporation (1977-1978); Senior Economist, National Commission on Supplies and Shortages (1976-1977); Co-Founder, U.S. Strategic Petroleum Reserve (1975); Director of System Integration, Federal Energy Administration, Washington, DC (1974-1976); Project Director, Logistics Management Institute, Washington, DC (1968-1974); Senior Economist, Center for Naval Analyses, Arlington, VA (1965-1968); Special Assistant to the Auditor General, U.S. Department of the Navy (1964-1965); Senior Vice President, Weiss Publishing Company, Inc., Richmond, VA (1960-2013) **Career Related:** Class Coordinator, Wharton School, University of Pennsylvania (2015-Present); Chairman, Dranesville Budget Task Force, Fairfax County, Virginia (2013-Present); President, Washington Management and Business Association (1993-Present); Treasurer, Fairfax County Democratic Committee (1992-Present); Resident Associate, Smithsonian Institute (1973-Present); Second Vice President, Budget & Taxation Committee (2013-2016); McLean Planning Committee, Virginia (2012-2016); Treasurer, Chair, Finance and Audit Committee, Fairfax County Water Authority (2012-2016); Dranesville District Democratic Committee, Virginia (2003-2017); Assisted Then-President Bill Clinton and Vice President Al Gore Transition at the White House (1993); Secretary, Board of Directors, Management Services International, Inc. (1989-1990); Vice President, Board of Directors, Leaders Digest Inc. (1987-1988); Associate Professor, George Mason University (1984); Vice President, Condo News International, Inc. (1981); President, National Council on Associations for Policy Sciences (1971-1977); Visiting Lecturer, George Washington University (1971); Chairman, Advisory Group, Defense Economic Advisory Council, Department of Defense (1970-1974); Chairman, U.S. Delegate, Session Chairman, NATO Conference on Operational Research in Industrial Systems, France (1970); NATO Symposium on Cost-Benefit Analysis, The Hague, Netherlands (1969); Treasurer, National Jewish Youth Conference (1948-1952); Fellow, American Association for the Advancement of Science **Civic:** Chairman, Archives and Library Committee (2009-Present); George Washington University Emeritus Society (2009-Present); University of Pennsylvania Emeritus Society (2003-Present); Advisory Board, University of Pennsylvania Mid-Atlantic Region (2003-Present); National Eagle Scout Association (1970-Present) **Military Service:** Officer, U.S. Navy (1954-1965) **Creative Works:** Editor, "The Democrat" (1997-2000); Publisher, "Special and Individual Needs Technology (SAINT) Newsletter (1987-1988); Publisher, "Journal of Parametrics" (1984-1988); Publisher, "IEEE Scanner" (1983-1989); Editor, "Condo World" (1981); Co-Editor, "Toward More Effective Public Programs: The Role of Analysis and Evaluation" (1975); Editor, "Operation Research and Management Science Today" (1974-1987); Co-Editor, "The Relevance of Economic Analysis to Decision Making in the Department of Defense" (1972); Associate Editor, "Operations Research" (1971-1975); Editor, "Operations Research and Systems Analysis Today" (1971-1973); Co-Editor, "Systems Analysis for Social Problems" (1970); Editor, "Feedback" (1969-1993); Editor, "Cost-Effectiveness Newsletter" (1966-1970) **Awards:** Founder's Award, Wharton School, Washington, DC (2008); Hero of Hope, Rutgers University Rally for a Cure (2004); Gold, Two Silver, Three Bronze Medals, Northern Virginia Senior Olympics (2001); Lifetime Service Award, Wharton School, Washington, DC (2000); Moving Spirit Award, Washington Operations Research and Management Science Council (1994); Joseph Wharton Award, Wharton School, Washington, DC (1991) **Membership:** New Ventures Committee, Greater Washington Society Association Executives (1995-1997); Delegate, National Association of the Academies of Science (1991-1993); Past President, Washington Academy of Science (1991-1992) **Marquis Who's Who Honors:** Albert Nelson Marquis Lifetime Achievement Award (2017) **Political Affiliations:** Democrat **Religion:** Jewish **Shipping Address:** 6516 Truman Lane, Falls Church, VA, 22043

Earle B. Weiss

Title: Senior Pulmonary Research Scientist **Industry:** Medicine & Health Care **Company Name:** Brigham and Women's Hospital **Date of Birth:** 11/23/1932 **Place of Birth:** Waltham **State:** MA **Parents:** Murray E. Weiss; Ruth R. (Pill) Weiss **Marital Status:** Married **Spouse Name:** Ruth Lithwick (12/1/1963) **Children:** Ilana; Joshua **Education:** Fellow, National Heart Institute, Boston City Hospital (1964-1966) Resident, Boston City Hospital (1962-1964); Intern, King's County Hospital, Brooklyn, NY (1961-1962); MD, Albert Einstein College of Medicine, New York City, NY (1961); MS in Biochemistry, Massachusetts Institute of Technology, Cambridge, MA (1957); BS in Biology-Chemistry, Northeastern University, With Honors, Boston, MA (1955) **Certifications:** Diplomate in Pulmonary Diseases, American Board of Internal Medicine (1970) **Career:** Medical Director, Foundation for Research in Bronchial Asthma and Related Diseases (1988-Present); Senior Consultant, Foundation for Research in Bronchial Asthma and Related Diseases (1988-Present); Senior Physician, St. Vincent Hospital, Worcester, MA (1990); Senior Pulmonary Research Scientist, Department of Anesthesia Research Laboratories, Brigham and Women's Hospital, Boston, MA (1989-2004); Professor, Medicine, University of Massachusetts Medical School (1977-1990); Director, Division of Respiratory Diseases, St. Vincent Hospital, Worcester, MA (1971-1989); Acting Medical Director, St. Vincent Hospital (1985-1987); Associate Medical Director, St. Vincent Hospital, Worcester, MA (1984-1985); Associate Chief of Medicine, Tufts Medical Service, Boston City Hospital (1969-1971); Associate Physician, Tufts Medical Service, Boston City Hospital (1967-1973); Director, Pulmonary Physiology Laboratory, Boston City Hospital (1964-1971); Founding Director, Respiratory Intensive Care Unit, Boston City Hospital (1964-1971); Senior Attending Physician, Pulmonary and Medical Service, Boston City Hospital (1964-1971); Senior Research Associate, Tufts Lung Station (1964-1971) **Career Related:** Appointed Honorary Member, Department of Astronomy, Wellesley College (2013-Present); Medical Director, Foundation for Research in Bronchial Asthma and Related Diseases, University of Guadalajara, Mexico (1980-Present); Lecturer in Medicine, Tufts University (1978-Present); Special Assistant to Director, Astronomy Department and Whitin Observatory, Wellesley College (2011); Visiting Professor, Faculty of Medicine, Department of Anesthesia, Harvard Medical School, Harvard University (1990-2002); Professor, Extraordinario Faculty Medicine, University of Guadalajara, Mexico (1982); Visiting Professor, University of Guadalajara, Mexico (1977); Professor of Extraordinario Faculty of Medicine, University of Guadalajara, Mexico (1977); Associate Professor of Life Sciences, Worcester Polytechnic Institute, MA (1976-1990); Consultant, Medical Devices Advisory Panel, Food and Drug Administration (1975-1977); Visiting Professor, University of Guadalajara, Mexico (1973); Tuberculosis Consultant, Commonwealth of Massachusetts (1972-1989); Director, Regional Inpatient Tuberculosis and Outpatient Tuberculosis Clinic, Worcester County (1972-1989); Associate Professor of Medicine, University of Massachusetts Medical School (1971-1977) **Military Service:** Captain, U.S. Air Force Reserve (1965-1970) **Creative Works:** Editorial Board Member, Journal of American College of Chest Physicians (1979-Present); Contributor, "On Earth as it is in Poetry" (2018); Author, "Footprints in the Sands of Time, Poems," Miles Press (2017); Exhibitor, "Impressionistic Photography" (2015); Exhibitor, Danforth Museum, Framingham, MA (2015); Exhibitor, "Impressionism in Photography," The Morse Institute Exhibition (2015); Contributor, "Faded Shadows, A Book of Poems" (2013); Contributor, "The Best Poems and Poets" (2005); Contributor, "The Colours of Life" (2003); Author, "Bronchial Asthma, Third Edition" (1993); Editor, Pulmonary Section, Practical Cardiology (1985-1987); Author, "Bronchial Asthma, Second Edition" (1985); Author, "Status Asthmaticus" (1978); Author, "Bronchial Asthma" (1976) **Awards:** Sarah F. Whiting Medal, Department of Astronomy, Wellesley College (2013); Named One Of America's Top Physicians, Staff Physicians, Brigham and Women's Hospital (2003); Chadwick Medal for Meritorious Contribution in Respiratory Diseases, Massachusetts Thoracic Society (1990); Named Extraordinary Professor, University of Guadalajara Faculty of Medicine (1977); Named Extraordinary Professor, University of Guadalajara Faculty of Medicine (1977) **Membership:** Co-founder, Clinical Assembly, American Thoracic Society (1971-Present); Representing Counselor, American Thoracic Society (1979-1982); President, Massachusetts Thoracic Society (1976-1978); Representative, ANSI Medical Technology Advisory Board, American Thoracic Society (1973-1975); Founder, Medical Devices Committee, American Thoracic Society (1972-1979); Chairman, Medical Devices Committee, American Thoracic Society (1972-1979); Medical Education Committee, American Thoracic Society (1972-1974); Associate Fellow, Royal College of Physicians (1971-1980) **Marquis Who's Who Honors:** Albert Nelson Marquis Lifetime Achievement Award (2017-2018) **Shipping Address:** 57 South St, Natick, MA, 01760

Roger Stanley Wells

Title: Software Engineer (Retired) **Industry:** Engineering **Company Name:** Boeing **Date of Birth:** 04/13/1949 **Place of Birth:** Seattle **State:** WA **Parents:** Stanley A. Wells; Margaret Wells **Education:** BS, Oregon State University (1977); Postgraduate Coursework, University of Texas at Austin (1973-1974); BA, Whitman College (1971) **Career:** Data and System Analyst, Boeing, St. Louis, MO (2015-2016); Leadership Institute, South Puget Sound (2012); Computer Process Specialist, Boeing, Seattle, WA (2005-2013); Software Builder, Volt Technical Resources (2004-2005); Technical Advisor, E-corps, Washington Service Corps (2002-2004); Senior Product Engineer, Wind River, Beaverton, OR (2000-2001); Manager Configuration, New Edge Network, Inc., Vancouver, WA (2000); Senior Project Engineer, Illuminet, Olympia, WA (1993-2000); Private Practice, Seattle, WA (1989-1992); Software Analyst, Lundy Financial Systems, San Dimas, CA (1986-1989); Software Engineer, Conrac Corporation, Duarte, CA (1985); Software Engineer, Conrac Corporation, Clackamas, OR (1984-1985); Computer Engineer, Saudi Aramco, Dhahran, Saudi Arabia (1983-1984); Software Evaluation Engineer, Tektronix, Inc., Beaverton, OR (1979-1983) **Career Related:** Advisor to Chair, Cascadia Con, North American Science Fiction Convention (2003-2005); Member, Executive of the Year 2000 Committee, Illuminet, Olympia, WA (1998-1999) **Civic:** Volunteer, Local Senior Center; Leader, Diversity Council, Boeing (2011); Diversity Council, Boeing (2010-2013); Volunteer Disaster Responder, Boeing (2006-2013); Volunteer, American Red Cross (2004-2006); Volunteer, PASCO (2003-2004); Volunteer, AmeriCorps, Yakima, WA (2002-2003); Board of Directors, Foundation for the Preservation of Science Fiction and Fantasy Memorabilia, Salem, OR (1996-2012); Co-Founder, Oregon Science Fiction Conventions, Inc. (1979-1981); Board of Directors, Oregon Science Fiction Conventions, Inc. (1979-1981); President, Oregon Science Fiction Conventions, Inc. (1979-1981); Board of Directors, Lydia Whitney Foundation, Collinsville, CT **Membership:** President, American Institute of Parliamentarians (1997-1998); District 32 Parliamentarian, Toastmasters International (1996-1999); Chapter Vice President, American Institute of Parliamentarians (1996-1997); Area Governor, Toastmasters International (1994-1995); Club President, Toastmasters International (1980); IEEE; American Philatelic Society; Disabled American Veterans; National Association of Parliamentarians; Fantasy Amateur Press Association; Northwest Science Fiction Society; Mensa; AMC, Inc.; Los Angeles Science Fantasy Society; Melbourne Science Fiction Club; Boeing Leadership Network Retirees; Past Member, Board of Governors, International Platform Association **Marquis Who's Who Honors:** Albert Nelson Marquis Lifetime Achievement Award (2017) **Hobbies:** Traveling; Public speaking; Science fiction; Stamp collecting (philately) **Shipping Address:** 3901 Cook St Apt 3, Yakima, WA, 98902

Francine Evans Weston, PhD

Title: Secondary School Educator (Retired) **Industry:** Education/Educational Services **Date of Birth:** 10/08/1946 **Place of Birth:** Mount Vernon **State:** NY **Parents:** John Joseph Pisaniello; Frances (Fantino) Pisaniello **Education:** PhD, New York University, New York City, NY (1991); MA, Lehman College, Bronx, NY (1973); BA, Hunter College, New York City, NY (1968) **Certifications:** Commissioner of Deeds, Westchester County, NY (2017); NYSED-Speech, Permanent (1973); NYSED-English 7-12, Permanent (1973); Water Safety Instructor, American Red Cross (Now The American National Red Cross) (1967-1976) **Career:** Program Director for the Public Safety Magnet Program (2003-2007); Program Developer for the Cadet Academy of Public Safety, Police, Fire and Emergency Medical Response (2001-2003); Advisor, L'Envoi Yearbook, Yonkers Public Schools (2003-2005); Co-advisor, L'Envoi Yearbook, Yonkers Public Schools (2001-2003); Mercy College Adjunct Professor, College Link English (2001); Sponsor, Class of 2000, Yonkers Public Schools (1997-2000); Nominating Chairperson, Reader's Digest Heroes in Education (Now Trusted Media Brands, Inc.) (1996); Chairperson, Nominating Committee, Blue Ribbon Schools (1995); Part-Time Instructor, Business English Teacher, Adult Basic Education Program, Yonkers Board of Education (1991-1992); Regents and RCT Testing Coordinator (1990-1994); Project Coordinator for Open Houses, Orientations, Dedications and Ceremonies (1988-1994); Scantron Coordinator (1988-2007); Staff Directory Coordinator (1988-1998); Part-Time Instruction, Communications Skills, National Teacher Exam Review, Yonkers Teacher Center (Now Richard Gazzola Teacher Center of Yonkers) (1987-1991); Chairperson, Middle States Steering Committee (1985-1988); Stage Lighting Designer (1980-1997); Sponsor, Class of 1981 (1979-1981); Roosevelt High School (1977-2007); Drama Director, John Burroughs Jr. High School, Yonkers, NY (1973-1976); Creative Drama Teacher, John Burroughs Jr. High School, Yonkers, NY (1972-1973); Yonkers Public Schools (1968-2007) **Career Related:** Freelance Stage Lighting Designer (1997-2011); Stage Lighting Designer, Yonkers Male Glee Club (Now The Male Glee Club of Yonkers) (1980-1989); Stage Lighting Designer, Master Electrician, Board Operator & Player, Iona Summer Theatre Festival (1979-1982); Master Electrician, New York University Summer Musical Theatre (1980-1981); Player & Stage Lighting Specialist, Greystone Actors' Studio (1980); Stage Lighting Designer & Player, New Rochelle Civic Theatre (1977-1979); American Academy of Dramatic Arts Summer/Evening Programs, New York City, NY (1975-1976); Water Safety Instructor, Yonkers Jewish Community Center (1971-1975); Aquatic Director, Pinsly Day Camp, Tarrytown, NY (1971-1974) **Civic:** Yonkers Police Department (Now City of Yonkers Police Department), Auxiliary Police Unit, City of Yonkers, NY (2016-Present); Inspector, Director of Administrative Services, Police Auxiliary, City of Yonkers, NY (2016-Present); Chairperson, Transition Committee, Police Auxiliary, City of Yonkers, NY (2016-Present); The First Precinct Community Council (2014-Present); Planning Board Member, National Night Out Against Crime Celebration, The First Precinct Community Council (2014-Present); Yonkers 10th Ward, Ninth District (2013-Present); Elected Corresponding Secretary, Grassy Sprain Civic Association (2009-Present) **Creative Works:** Editor, Command Post Dispatch Quarterly (1995-2013); Author, "A Descriptive Comparison of Computerized Stage Lighting Memory Systems With Non-Computerized Systems" (1991); Author, "A Hat for Louise" (1984); Author, "Old Memories: Beautiful and Otherwise" (1984); Literary Editor, "Beautifully Old" (1984); Community Theater Actress, "The Lottery" (1980); Community Theater Actress, "Trifles" (1980); Community Theater Actress, "A Touch of the Poet" (1979) **Awards:** Auxiliary Police Unit, City of Yonkers, NY, Outstanding Service Award (2017); Service Appreciation Award for 24 Years. City Council; President's Recognition Citation, Yonkers 10th Ward, 9th District (2017); Volunteer of the Year, 10th Ward, City of Yonkers, NY (2017); Certificate of Merit, New York State Assembly, 94th Assembly District (2017); Certificate of Merit, The New York State Senate, 40th Senate District (2017); Certificate of Appreciation, Westchester County Board of Legislators (2017); Westchester County Executive's Certificate of Achievement (2017); Certificates of Appreciation, First Precinct Community Council (2014-2017); Active Outstanding Volunteer Award, Therapy Dog Handler for Belgian Tervuren Dog, "Jaz", Therapy Dogs International (2014) **Membership:** NYSRPA (2017-Present); Benefactor Member, National Rifle Association of America (2015-Present); Yonkers Historical Society (2015-Present); North East Yonkers Republican Club (2013-Present); NRSC (2012-Present); The First Precinct Community Council (2009-Present); International Association of Women Police (2007-Present); American Belgian Tervuren Club (ABTC) (1995-Present); Port Chester Obedience Training Club (1995-Present) **Marquis Who's Who Honors:** Albert Nelson Marquis Lifetime Achievement Award (2017) **Political Affiliations:** Republican **Religion:** Roman Catholic **Shipping Address:** 88 Grassy Sprain Rd, Yonkers, NY, 10710

Thomas French Whayne, PhD

Title: Professor, Cardiologist, Educator, Writer **Industry:** Medicine & Health Care **Date of Birth:** 08/25/1937 **Place of Birth:** Fort Leavenworth **State:** KS **Parents:** Thomas French Whayne, Sr.; Mary Lutenia (Porter) Whayne **Marital Status:** Married **Spouse Name:** Eugenia McDonald Ingram (6/22/1963) **Children:** Thomas French III; James Givens; Katherine Ingram **Education:** PhD, University of California San Francisco; MD, University of Pennsylvania; BA, University of Pennsylvania **Certifications:** Certified in Cardiovascular Disease, American Board of Internal Medicine (1974); Diplomate, American Board of Internal Medicine (1972) **Career:** Professor, Cardiovascular Medicine, University of Kentucky (1998-Present); Clinical Professor, Medicine, University of Kentucky (1977-1998); Associate Professor, Medicine, The University of Oklahoma, Oklahoma City, OK (1972-1977); Assistant Professor, Medicine, The Ohio State University, Columbus, OH (1970-1972); Fellow, Cardiovascular Disease, University of Toronto, Ontario, Canada (1969-1970); Fellow, Cardiovascular Disease, Cardiovascular Institute, San Francisco, CA (1966-1969) **Career Related:** Staff Cardiologist, Lexington Clinic (1977-1998); Associate Member, Oklahoma Medical Research Foundation (1972-1977); Lecturer in Field; Presenter in Field; Presenter, Spanish Presentations, Spanish Speaking Countries **Civic:** Supporter, Rotary Club of Lexington; Supporter, Vesper Boat Club, Philadelphia, PA; Supporter, University of Pennsylvania Rowing; Supporter, Perelman School of Medicine, University of Pennsylvania; Supporter; Supporter, Department of Hispanic Studies, University of Kentucky; Supporter, Gill Heart & Vascular Institute, University of Kentucky **Military Service:** Medical Corps, U.S. Army Reserve (1963-1972) **Creative Works:** Contributor, Abstracts; Contributor, Chapters, Books; Contributor, Articles, Professional Journals; Contributor, Multiple Spanish Articles, Professional Journals **Awards:** Best Doctors in America (2009-Present); Research Achievement Award of the International College of Angiology, Vienna, Austria (2017); Man of the Year, Oklahoma Heart Association (1975-1976) **Membership:** Fellow, American College of Physicians; Fellow, International College of Angiology, Inc.; Fellow, The College of Physicians of Philadelphia; Fellow, American Heart Association, Inc.; Fellow, American College of Cardiology Foundation; Vesper Boat Club; Rotary International **Bar Admissions:** PhD, Biochemistry, University of California, San Francisco, CA (1970); Resident, The New York Hospital (1964-1966); Intern, The New York Hospital (1963-1964); MD, University of Pennsylvania (1963); AB, Chemistry, University of Pennsylvania (1959) **Marquis Who's Who Honors:** Albert Nelson Marquis Lifetime Achievement Award (2017) **To what do you attribute your success:** Dr. Whayne attributes his success to being able to combine true medical practice of medicine, academia and writing successfully. **Why did you become involved in your profession or industry:** Dr. Whayne became involved in his profession because he had a desire to make a difference. **What do you consider to be the highlight of your career:** The highlight of Dr. Whayne's career was making the first international presentation in the Spanish language. **Hobbies:** Spanish language; Golf; Scuba diving; Photography; Exercise; Rowing **Religion:** Presbyterian **Business Address:** 900 S Limestone, Lexington, KY, 40536 **Shipping Address:** 26 Ave of Champions, Nicholasville, KY, 40356

Lois Deimel Whealey

Title: Humanities Scholar (Retired) **Industry:** Education/Educational Services **Date of Birth:** 06/20/1932 **Place of Birth:** New York City **State:** NY **Parents:** Edgar Bertram Deimel; Lois Elizabeth (Hatch) Washburn **Marital Status:** Married **Spouse Name:** Robert Howard Whealey (7/2/1954) **Children:** Richard William; David John; Alice Ann **Education:** Master's Degree in Social Science, Ohio University (2007); MA in Political Science, Ohio University (1975); MEd, University of Michigan (1955); BA in History, Stanford University (1951) **Career:** Administrative Assistant, Humanities Conference, Ohio University, Athens, OH (1983); Administrative Assistant, Humanities Conference, Ohio University, Athens, OH (1974-1976); Teacher, Eighth Grade English & Social Studies, Slauson Junior High School (Now Slauson Middle School), Ann Arbor, MI (1958-1959); Teacher, Sixth Grade, Amerman School (Now Amerman Elementary School), Northville, MI (1957-1958); Teacher, Adult Basic Education, United States Air Force, Oxford, England (1956-1957); Teacher, Seventh Grade, Fort Knox Dependent Schools, Kentucky (1955-1956); Teacher, Fifth Grade, Swayne School (Now Owyhee Combined School), Owyhee, NV (1952-1953) **Career Related:** Volunteers, America (AmeriCorps VISTA) with Rural Action (1996-1998); Part-Time Instructor, Ohio University (1975); Part-Time Instructor, Athens, OH (1966-1968) **Civic:** Athens Community Television, Cable Channel 9 (Now Athens Community Television, Inc.) (2006-Present); Secretary, Ohio Women Inc. (1997-Present); Board of Directors, Ohio Women Inc. (1995-Present); Co-Chair, Unitarian Universalist Service Committee, National Volunteer Network (Now National Volunteer Caregiving Network) (2003-2005); Board President, Organize! Ohio (2001-2007); Board of Directors, Unitarian Universalist Service Committee (2001-2003); Board of Directors, Organize! Ohio (1999-2007); Ohio Outreach Liaison, National Town Meeting for a Sustainable America (1999); Vice President, Ohio Alliance for the Environment (1998); Board of Directors, Ohio Alliance for the Environment (1994-1998); Vice President, Tri-County Vocational School Board (Now Tri-County Career Center), Nelsonville, OH (1988-1989); Member, Advisory Committee, Ohio River Valley Water Sanitation Commission (Now ORSANCO) (1986-1995); Secretary, Ohio Environmental Council (1986-1990); President, Athens City School District Board of Education (1985); Board of Directors, Ohio Environmental Council (1984-1990); Member, Tri-County Vocational School Board (Now Tri-County Career Center), Nelsonville, OH (1984-1990); Member, Athens City School District Board of Education (1984-1990); Vice President, Athens City School District Board of Education (1984); Chair, New Day for Equal Rights Amendment, Athens, OH (1982); Vice President, Black Diamond Girl Scout Council (Now Girl Scouts of Black Diamond) (1980-1986); Member, Ohio Coordinator Committee, International Women's Year (1977); Treasurer, Athens County Regional Planning Commission (1976-1978); Board of Directors, Ohio-Meadville District Unitarian-Universalist Association (1975-1981); Member, Athens County Regional Planning Commission (1974-1978); Executive Committee, Democracy Over Corporations; Host, Women Today and Yesterday, ACTV **Creative Works:** Contributor, Articles, Professional Journals **Awards:** Social Justice Award for Contributions Over a Lifetime, United Campus Ministry (Now UCM), Ohio University (2016); Nora Price Award, SEOH Planned Parenthood (2009); Social Justice Award, United Campus Ministry (Now UCM), Ohio University (2008); Spirit Award, League of Women Voters of Athens County (2002); Award For Individual Contribution Over a Lifetime, Ohio Alliance Environment (2002); Outstanding Feminist, Athens Herstory Celebration (2002); Peacemaker, Appalachian Peace & Justice Network (1998); Community Service Award, Athens County Community Services Council (1998); Donna Chen Women's Equity Award, Ohio University (1994); How-To Award, Educational Press Association of America (1990); Woman of Achievement, Black Diamond Girl Scout Council (Now Girl Scouts of Black Diamond) (1987); Thanks Badge, Black Diamond Girl Scout Council (Now Girl Scouts of Black Diamond) (1986); Unsung Unitarian Universalist Award, Ohio-Meadville District Unitarian Universalist Association (1984) **Membership:** President, Ohio Board, American Association of University Women (1995-2004); President, Athens Branch, American Association of University Women (1993-2001); President, Athens Branch, American Association of University Women (1989-1990); President, League of Women Voters of Athens County (1975-1977); President, Athens Branch, American Association of University Women (1969-1970); Phi Kappa Phi (Now The Honor Society of Phi Kappa Phi); Pi Lambda Theta; League of Women Voters; Executive Committee, Democracy Over Corporations **Marquis Who's Who Honors:** Albert Nelson Marquis Lifetime Achievement Award (2017) **Political Affiliations:** Democrat **Religion:** Unitarian Universalist **Shipping Address:** 14 Oak St, Athens, OH, 45701

Thomas Beardsley Wheeler

Industry: Insurance **Date of Birth:** 08/02/1936 **Place of Birth:** Buffalo **State/Country of Origin:** NY **Parents:** William Henry Wheeler; Ruth (Matthews) Wheeler **Marital Status:** Married **Spouse Name:** Anne Tuck Robertson (11/25/1961) **Children:** Elizabeth Wheeler Soule; Wendy Wheeler MacDonald **Education:** BA, Yale University (1958) **Certifications:** Chartered Life Underwriter **Career:** Chairman, Massachusetts Mutual Life Insurance Co., Springfield, MA (1999-2000); Chairman, Chief Executive Officer, Massachusetts Mutual Life Insurance Co., Springfield, MA (1996-1999); President, Chief Executive Officer, Massachusetts Mutual Life Insurance Co., Springfield, MA (1988-1996); President, Massachusetts Mutual Life Insurance Co., Springfield, MA (1987-1988); Executive Vice President, Massachusetts Mutual Life Insurance Co., Springfield, MA (1983-1986); General Agent, Massachusetts Mutual Life Insurance Co., Boston, MA (1972-1983); Sales Representative, Assistant General Agent, Massachusetts Mutual Life Insurance Co., Boston, MA (1962); Sales Representative, IBM, White Plains, NY (1961-1962) **Career Related:** Chairman, Board of Directors, DLB Acquisition Corp. (1995-1999); Chairman, Board of Directors, Massachusetts Business Roundtable (1993-1996); Chairman, Board of Directors, Oppenheimer Acquisistion Corp. (1990-1999); Board of Directors, Textron, Inc.; President, Jobs for Massachusetts **Civic:** Chairman, Springfield College (1995-1998); Massachusetts State Chairman, United States Olympic Committee (1995-1996); Trustee, Basketball Hall of Fame, Springfield, MA (1991-2005); Trustee, American College, Bryn Mawr, PA (1987-1990); Trustee, Springfield Orchestra Association (1985-1999); Trustee, Springfield College (1985-1998); Trustee, Baystate Health Systems, Inc., Springfield, MA (1983-1992); Trustee, Woods Hole Oceanographic Institute; Board of Directors, Estate Works, Genworth Financial **Military Service:** Lieutenant, US Naval Reserve (1958-1960) **Creative Works:** Co-Author, "Managing Sales Professionals" (1984) **Membership:** President, Yale Club of Southwest Florida (2004-2005); Board of Directors, Health Insurance Association of America (1990-1993); President, Boston Chapter, American Society of Chartered Life Underwriters (1980-1981); President, Massachusetts Association of Life Underwriters (1976-1977); Secretary, Chapoquoit Yacht Club (1973-1975); President, Boston Underwriters Association (1972-1973); The Links, New York, NY; Naples Yacht Club; Woods Hole Golf Club, Massachusetts; Hole Wall Golf Club, Maples, FL; Port Royal Club of Florida; Colony Club, Springfield, MA; Yale Club of New York; Million Dollar Round Table; Springfield Life Underwriters Association; American Society of Chartered Life Underwriters; Pioneer Valley Chapter, American Society of Chartered Life Underwriters **Hobbies:** Golfing; Boating; Art; Antiques; Music **Political Affiliations:** Republican

Edward F. Whipps

Title: Principal **Industry:** Law and Legal Services **Company Name:** Edward F. Whipps & Associates **Date of Birth:** 12/17/1936 **Place of Birth:** Columbus **State:** OH **Parents:** Rusk Henry Whipps; Agnes Lucille (Green) Whipps **Marital Status:** Married **Spouse Name:** Martha J. Whipps **Children:** Edward Scott; Rusk Huot; Sylvia Louise; Rudyard Christian **Education:** JD, The Ohio State University (1961); BA, Ohio Wesleyan University (1958) **Career:** Principal, Edward F. Whipps and Associates, Columbus, OH (2000-Present); Partner, Whipps and Wistner, Columbus, OH (1995-1999); Principal, Edward F. Whipps and Associates, Columbus, OH (1993-1994); Partner, Thompson, Hine and Flory, Columbus, OH (1981-1993); Partner, McConnaughey, Stradley, Mone & Moul, Columbus, OH (1979-1981); Partner, George, Greek, King, McMahon & McConnaughey, Columbus, OH (1966-1979); Associate, George, Greek, King & McMahon, Columbus, OH (1961-1966) **Career Related:** Founder, Creative Living Inc. (1969-Present); Trustee, Creative Living Inc. (1969-Present); Trustee, Unverferth House Inc. (1989); Vice President, Unverferth House Inc. (1989); Trustee, Eagle Scholarship Trust **Civic:** President, Walden Ravines Association (1993-Present); President, Board of Psychology, State of Ohio (2001-2002); President, Walden Ravines Association (1993-1996); Board of Psychology, State of Ohio (1992-2002); Trustee, Walden Ravines Association (1992-1996); President, Board of Education, Upper Arlington Schools (1978-1979); Board of Directors, Ohio Wesleyan University Alumni Association (1975-1979); Board of Education, Upper Arlington Schools (1971-1980) **Creative Works:** Television Host, "The Ohio Wesleyan Experience" (1984-Present); Television Host, "Lawyers on Call" (1982-Present); Television Host, "USA Today" (1982-1986); Television Host, "Bridging Disability" (1981-1982); Television Host, "Upper Arlington Plain Talk" (1979-1982) **Awards:** Distinguished Alumnus, Delta Tau Delta Fraternity **Membership:** Vice President, Highlands Golf Club (2005-2015); Director, Highlands Golf Club (2001-2015); Trustee, Upper Arlington Area Chamber of Commerce (1978-1980); National Vice President, Delta Tau Delta (1976-1978); ABA; Columbus Bar Association; Association of Trial Lawyers of America; Ohio Academy of Trial Lawyers; Franklin County Trial Lawyers Association; Columbus Bar Foundation; Columbus Chamber of Commerce; Lawyers Club; Barrister Club; Columbus Athletic Club; National Football Foundation and Hall of Fame; Columbus Touchdown Club; Downtown Quarterback Club; Ohio State University Faculty Club; Ohio State University Golf Club **Bar Admissions:** United States Court of Appeals for the Sixth Circuit (1980); State of Mississippi Judiciary (1965); United States District Court for the Northern District of Ohio (1964); Supreme Court of the United States (1963); United States Court of Claims (1963); United States District Court for the Southern District of Ohio (1962); Supreme Court of Ohio (1961); Ohio **Marquis Who's Who Honors:** Albert Nelson Marquis Lifetime Achievement Award (2017) **Hobbies:** Golf; Scuba diving **Political Affiliations:** Republican **Religion:** Methodist **Shipping Address:** 51 Highland Court, Pataskala, OH, 43062

Thomas Russell Whitaker, PhD

Title: English Literature Educator, Professor Emeritus **Industry:** Education/ Educational Services **Company Name:** Yale University **Date of Birth:** 08/07/1925 **Place of Birth:** Marquette **State:** MI **Parents:** Joe Russell Whitaker; Sarah Genevieve (Houk) Whitaker **Marital Status:** Married **Spouse Name:** Lililan Ann Schoenberger Traub (6/2003); Joan Horwitt (1999, Divorced 2002); Dorothy Vera Barnes (Married 6/17/1950, Deceased 12/1995) **Children:** Thomas O'Hara; Sarah Mae; Mary Beth; Gwendolyn Anne **Education:** PhD, Yale University (1953); MA, Yale University (1950); BA, Oberlin College, Summa Cum Laude (1949) **Career:** Frederick W. Hilles Professor Emeritus of English (1995-Present); Frederick W. Hilles Professor of English, Yale University, New Haven, CT (1989-1995); Professor of Theater Studies, Yale University (1986-1995); Chairman, English Department, Yale University (1979-1985); Professor of English, Yale University (1975-1988); Professor of English, University of Iowa (1966-1975); Literature Teacher, Goddard College, Plainfield, VT (1964-1966); Professor, Oberlin College (1963-1964); Associate Professor, Oberlin College (1959-1963); Assistant Professor, Oberlin College (1955-1959); English Instructor, Oberlin College (1952-1955) **Civic:** US Army (1944-1946) **Creative Works:** Advisor, Yale National Initiative (2002-2012); Author, "Mirrors of Our Playing: Paradigms and Presences in Modern Drama" (1999); Writer and Advisor, Yale-New Haven Teachers Institute National Demonstration Project (1998-2002); Author, "Narrator Video Script: Excellence in Teaching: Agenda for Partnership" (1997); Chairman, Editorial Board, "On Common Ground"(1993-2009); Editor, "Teaching in New Haven: The Common Challenge" (1991); Author, "Swan and Shadow: Yeats's Dialogue with History Second Edition" (1989); Author, "William Carlos Williams, Revised Edition" (1989); Author, "Tom Stoppard, Augmented Edition" (1984); Author, "Tom Stoppard" (1983); Author, "Fields of Play in Modern Drama" (1977); Editor, Iowa Review (1974-1977); Editor, "Twentieth Century Interpretations of the Playboy of the Western World" (1969); Author, "William Carlos Williams" (1968); Author, "Swan and Shadow: Yeats's Dialogue with History" (1964) **Awards:** Recipient, Seton Elm and Ivy Award, City of New Haven and Yale University (2005); Fellow, NEH-Huntington (1981); Recipient, Harbison Award for Gifted Teaching, Danforth Foundation (1972); Fellow, American Council of Learned Societies (1969-1970) **Membership:** Modern Language Association **Marquis Who's Who Honors:** Albert Nelson Marquis Lifetime Achievement Award (2017); Distinguished Humanitarian (2017) **Why did you become involved in your profession or industry:** Dr. Whitaker grew up as the son of a teacher who was a professor at the University of Wisconsin and Peabody College; when Dr. Whitaker went to college, there were so many teachers that he admired. He has incorporated his love of history and literature into his career. **Shipping Address:** 20 Sconset Ln, Guilford, CT, 06437

George White

Title: Founder **Industry:** Media & Entertainment **Company Name:** Eugene O'Neill Theater Center **Date of Birth:** 08/16/1935 **Place of Birth:** New London **State/Country of Origin:** CT **Parents:** Nelson Cooke White; Aida (Rovetti) White **Marital Status:** Married **Spouse Name:** Elizabeth Conant Darling (7/5/1958) **Children:** George Conant; Caleb Ensign; Juliette Darling **Education:** Honorary ArtsD, Connecticut College (1994); Coursework, The Shakespeare Institute (1959); MFA, Yale University (1961); BA, Yale University (1957); Coursework, Universite Paris-Sorbonne (1956) **Career:** Founding Chairman, The Florence Academy of Art (2004); Executive Director, Johnny Mercer Foundation (1999-2006); Acting Director, Department of Art and Art History, Hunter College (1972-1973); Guest Lecturer, Wagner College (1970); Adviser, Director, Theatre One, Connecticut College for Women (1967-1970); Founder, President, Eugene O'Neill Memorial Theatre Foundation (1965-2000); Administrative Vice President, Score Productions, Paramount Pictures (1963-1965); Production Coordinator, Talent Associates (1961-1963); Assistant Manager, International Ballet Festival, Nervi, Italy (1955); Stage Manager, Imperial Japanese Azumakabuki Co. (1955); Regional Theater Consultant, National Educational TV Network **Career Related:** Nominating Committee, Antoinette Perry Awards (1998-2002); Administrative Committee, American Theater Wing (1997); Nominating Committee, Antoinette Perry Awards (1994-1996); Nominating Committee, Antoinette Perry Awards (1988); Director, "Anna Christie," Beijing Center for Dramatic Theater (1987); Guest Director, Chinese Theater Association, Beijing (1987); Guest Director, Hedgerow Theatre (1986); Director, Actors Theater of Minnesota (1986); Nominating Committee, Antoinette Perry Awards (1984-1986); Guest Director, Chinese Theater Association, Beijing (1984); Director, "Anna Christie," Beijing Center for Dramatic Theater (1984); Director, Actors Theater of Minnesota (1983, 1982); Director, Hartman Repertory Theatre (1980); Director, Actors Theater of Minnesota (1980, 1979); Member, Connecticut Commission on Arts (1978-1993); Professor, Theater Administration Program, Yale University (1978-1991); United States Delegate, International Theatre Institute, Congress, Moscow, Russia (1973); Guest Administrator, Australian National Playwrights Conference (1973); Board Member, American National Theatre and Academy (1967-1968); Member, Executive Committee, Theatre Library Association (1967) **Civic:** Member, Waterford Republican Town Meeting, Connecticut (2001-Present); Trustee, Mitchell College (1994-Present); Trustee, National Theatre Conference (1973-Present); Member, National Council on the Arts (1992-1997); Presidential Appointment, National Council of the National Education Association (1992); Member, Waterford Republican Town Meeting, Connecticut (1975-1977); Trustee, Connecticut Education Telecommunications Corp (1973-1983); Trustee, Connecticut Public TV (1973-1983); Board of Directors, Manhattan Theatre Club (1970-1980); Trustee, Goodspeed Opera House (1966-1968); Magazine Executive Committee, Yale Drama Alumni (1963-1973); Board Member, Boston Conservatory; Trustee, Arts International; Board of Directors, The Day Publishing Company; Board of Directors, RKO Pictures; Board of Directors, American Academy of Dramatic Arts; Trustee, Eastern Connecticut Symphony; Trustee, Dance Arts Council; Trustee, Connecticut Opera Association; Chairman, Mystic Seaport International Council; Board of Directors, Rehearsal Club; Board of Directors, Center for Inter-American Relations; Board of Directors, Theater of Latin America; Board of Directors, Metropolitan Opera Guild Performance; Member, Yale Alumni Board; Board of Overseers, Drama Department, Brandeis University; Advisory Board, American Musical Theatre Program; Advisory Board, Hartford Conservatory; Advisory Board, Arts & Business Council; Advisory Board, Brandeis Creative Arts Award Jury; **Military Service:** District Captain, United States Coast Guard Auxiliary (2011-Present); Division Commander, United States Coast Guard Auxiliary (2008-2010); Flotilla Commander, United States Coast Guard Auxiliary **Creative Works:** Actor, Television Series, "Citizen Soldier" (1959-1961); Appearance, Off-Broadway Production, "John Brown's Body" **Awards:** Russian American Friendship Award (2016); American Theatre Hall of Fame (2011); Special Citation, New England Theatre Conference (1998); Contribution to Connecticut Arts Award, Quinnipiac University (1989); Lifetime Contribution to Theatre Award, American Theater Award (1989); Chevalier des artes et des lettres and Officer, France (1983); Contributions to State Award, Connecticut Magazine (1981); Distinguished Service Award (1981); Cultural Exchange Grantee, People's Republic of China (1980); Distinguished Citizen's Award, Town of Waterford (1976); Public Service Award, New London County Bar Association (1975); Margo Jones Award (1968); Special Citation, New England Theatre Conference (1968) **Membership:** Fellow, Royal Society of Arts; College of Fellows of the American Theatre; Honorary Member, Chinese Theatre Association; Bohemian Club **Shipping Address:** 22 New Shore Rd., Waterford, CT, 06385

R. Stephen White

Title: Physics Professor **Industry:** Education/ Educational Services **Company Name:** University of California **Date of Birth:** 12/28/1920 **Place of Birth:** Ellsworth **State:** KS **Parents:** Byron F. White; Sebina (Leighty) White **Education:** Honorary DSc, Southwestern College (1971); PhD, University of California, Berkeley (1951); MS, University of Illinois (1943); AB, Southwestern College (1942) **Career:** Professor Emeritus of Physics Department, Research Physicist, University of California, Riverside (1992-Present); Chairman, Department of Physics, University of California, Riverside (1970-1973); Director, Institute of Geophysics and Planetary Physics, University of California, Riverside (1967-1992); Physics Professor, University of California, Riverside (1967-1992); Head, Department of Particles and Fields, Space Physics Laboratory Aerospace Corp., El Segundo, CA (1962-1967); Physicist, Lawrence Radiation Laboratory, Berkeley, Livermore, CA (1948-1961) **Career Related:** Lecturer, University of California, Berkeley (1953-1954, 1957-1959) **Military Service:** Officer, US Naval Reserve (1944-1946) **Creative Works:** Author, "Energy for the Public: The Case for Increased Nuclear Fission Energy" (2006); Author, "Why Science?" (1998); Author, "Space Physics" (1970); Contributor, Articles to Professional Journals **Awards:** Recipient, Department of Energy Award **Membership:** Executive Committee, American Physical Society (1972-1974); Fellow, American Association for the Advancement of Science; American Astronomical Society; American Geophysical Union **Shipping Address:** 715B Mas Amigos Street, Santa Barbara, CA, 93105

Robert White

Title: Board of Directors **Industry:** Financial Services **Company Name:** Alostar Bank of Commerce **Date of Birth:** 11/01/1946 **Place of Birth:** Chicago **State:** IL **Parents:** Melvin White; Margaret (Hoffman) White **Marital Status:** Married **Spouse Name:** Penelope K. Bloch (12/22/1985); Gail Janet Edenson (Married 6/29/1969, Divorced 12/1982) **Education:** JD, University of Michigan (1972); BS in Accountancy, University of Illinois (1968) **Career:** Board of Directors, Alostar Bank of Commerce (2011-Present); Board of Directors, EnerTech Environmental California, LLC (2011-Present); Board of Directors, Federal Power Commission PropCo, LLC (2009-Present); Board of Directors, Syncora Holdings Ltd. (2008-Present); Board of Directors, Coinmach Service Inc. (2009-2011); Executive Vice-President, Maguine Properties Inc. (2009-2010); Chief Executive Officer, O'Melvey Consultant LLC (2001-2003); Chair, Reorganization and Restructuring Department, O'Melveny & Myers, LA (1986-2001); Partner, O'Melveny & Myers, LA (1980-2007); Associate, O'Melveny & Myers, LA (1972-1979); Staff Auditor, Haskin & Sells, Chicago, IL (1968-1969) **Career Related:** Member, Los Angeles Productivity Commission (1993-1996); Lecturer, University of California, Los Angeles (1993); Lecturer, Practicing Law Institute, San Francisco and New York City (2001-Present); Lecturer, UCLA Bankruptcy Institute (1993); Lecturer, Southwestern Legal Foundation, Dallas, TX (1991); Lecturer, Practicing Law Institute, San Francisco and New York City (1989-1993); Lecturer, Professional Education Systems, Inc., Phoenix, AZ (1989); Lecturer, Professional Education Systems, Inc., Los Angeles, CA (1989); Lecturer, Professional Education Systems, Inc., Los Angeles, CA (1987); Lecturer, Professional Education Systems, Inc., Dallas, TX (1987); Visiting Lecturer, University of Michigan Law School, Ann Arbor (1986) **Civic:** Committee, National Bankruptcy Conference (2004-Present); Vice Chair, Partnership Committee, American Cancer Society (2003-Present); Member, Los Angeles Board of Directors, American Cancer Society (1995-Present); Active, American Cancer Society (1989-Present); Active, Constitutional Rights Foundation (1980-Present); Chapter Chair, American Cancer Society (2011) **Membership:** Board of Governors, Financial Lawyers Conference (1986-Present); Executive Committee, Los Angeles County Bar Association (1982-Present); Litigation Section, Commercial Law and Bankruptcy Committee, ABA (1972-Present); President, Financial Lawyers Conference (1990-1991); Board of Governors, Association of Business Trial Lawyers (1983-1985); Commercial Law and Bankruptcy Section, Chairman, Federal Courts Committee, Los Angeles County Bar Association (1981-1982); Fellow, American College of Bankruptcy; American Bankruptcy Institute **Bar Admissions:** New York (1985); United States Court of Appeals for the Sixth Circuit (1984); United States Court of Appeals for the Fifth Circuit (1983); United States Court of Appeals for the Ninth Circuit (1978); Supreme Court of the United States (1977); California (1972); United States District Court Central District of California (1972); United States District Court Eastern District of California (1972); United States District Court Southern District of California (1972) **Marquis Who's Who Honors:** Albert Nelson Marquis Lifetime Achievement Award (2017) **Shipping Address:** 2971 Club Drive, Los Angeles, CA, 90064

William Fredrick White

Title: Lawyer **Industry:** Law and Legal Services **Company Name:** Michael Best & Friedrich LLP **Date of Birth:** 09/30/1948 **Place of Birth:** Elmhurst **State:** IL **Parents:** William Daniel White; Carol Ruth (Laier) White **Marital Status:** Married **Spouse Name:** Kathie Jean Nichols (5/27/1979) **Children:** Nicholas Roland; Andrew William **Education:** JD, Antioch School of Law (Now University of the District of Columbia David A. Clarke School of Law) (1976); BA, University of Illinois (1970) **Career:** Lawyer, Law Office of William F. White, LLC (2017-Present); Partner, WhiteFish Partners (2016-Present); Member, Management Committee, Michael Best & Friedrich LLP, Madison, WI (2008-2010); Managing Partner, Michael Best & Friedrich LLP, Madison, WI (2002-2006); Chair, Land and Resources Legal Practice Area, Michael Best & Friedrich LLP, Madison, WI (1999-2002); Partner, Michael Best & Friedrich LLP, Madison, WI (1988-2015); Chairman, Associate Development Committee, Michael Best & Friedrich LLP (1988-1996); Associate, Michael Best & Friedrich LLP, Madison, WI (1982-1988); Director of Litigation, National Treasury Employees Union, Washington, DC (1981-1982); Associate General Counsel, National Treasury Employees Union, Washington, DC (1979-1981); Assistant Counsel, National Treasury Employees Union, Washington, DC (1977-1979); Interim Executive Director, Common Cause, Washington, DC (1977); Member, United States Department of Labor (1976) **Career Related:** Secretary, Medical Physics Foundation (1994-Present); Director, Medical Physics Foundation (1988-Present); Member, Board of Directors, Medical Physics Publication Company, American Association of Physicists in Medicine **Civic:** Director, First United Methodist Church Foundation, First United Methodist Church, Madison, WI (2011-Present); Member, Board of Governors, Madison Community Foundation (2009-Present); Board Member, Security and Dividend Section, The Capital Region Economic Development Corporation (2005-Present); Director, Madison Museum of Contemporary Art (2000-Present); Co-Chair, Friends of Hudson River Park (1999-Present); Chair, Board of Trustees, Madison Museum of Contemporary Art (1998-Present); Chairman, Airport Commission, County of Dane, WI (1994-Present); Chancellor Wisconsin Annual Conference, First United Methodist Church, Madison, WI (1992-Present); Member, Airport Commission, County of Dane, WI (1991-Present); Board of Directors, Veridian Foundation (2005-2007); Madison Program Chair, Public Affairs Council, County of Dane, WI (2000-2002); Member, Team Terrace Transportation Committee, County of Dane, WI (1996-1997); Secretary, Board of Directors, Downtown Madison, Inc. (1995-2001); Chairman, Legal Services Committee (1992-1996); General Council in Finance and Administration (1991-2000); Chairman, Madison Chapter, Arthritis Foundation (1991-1992); Board of Directors, Natural Heritage Land Trust (1988-1991); Board of Directors, Perinatal Foundation (Now Wisconsin Association for Perinatal Car) (1984-1996); Board of Directors, Madison Chapter, Arthritis Foundation (1984-1992); Board of Directors, Executive Committee, Mediation Program, Dane County Bar Association (1983-1990); Chairman, Public Health Commission, Madison & Dane Counties (1983-1989); Chair, Transportation Committee, Transferable Development Rights Task Force, County of Dane, WI; Director, The Capital Region Economic Development Corporation; Apartment Association of South Central Wisconsin; Vice President/President Olbrich Botanical Society; **Awards:** Wisconsin Super Lawyers, Land & Resources/Zoning (2005-Present); Best Lawyers in America (1995-Present); Lawyer of the Year, Land Use and Zoning Law/Litigation, Madison, WI (2015); Top Rated Lawyer, Land Use and Zoning, American Lawyer Media (2013); Top Rated Lawyer, Land Use and Zoning, Martindale-Hubbell (2013); Lawyer of the Year, Land Use and Zoning Law/Litigation, Madison, WI (2012); Pro Bono Lifetime Achievement Award, Dane County Bar Association (2011); Lawyer of the Year, Land Use and Zoning Law, Madison, WI (2011); WINGRA Recognition Award, Wisconsin National Guard (2006) **Membership:** Board of Directors, Medical Physics Foundation (1987-Present); Director, Transportation Development Association of Wisconsin (1999-2003); Executive Committee, Transportation Development Association of Wisconsin (1999-2003); Former Member, ABA; Former Member, The District of Columbia Bar; Dane County Bar Association; Secretary, Health Law Section, State Bar of Wisconsin **Bar Admissions:** United States District Court Western District of Wisconsin (1982); State of Wisconsin (1982); United States Court of Appeals for the Seventh Circuit (1982); United States Court of Appeals for the Tenth Circuit (1982); United States Court of Federal Claims (1978); United States District Court District of Columbia (1976); United States Court of Appeals for the District of Columbia Circuit (1976) **Marquis Who's Who Honors:** Albert Nelson Marquis Lifetime Achievement Award (2017) **Political Affiliations:** Democrat **Religion:** Methodist **Shipping Address:** 2708 Lakeland Ave., Madison, WI, 53704

Brooks M. Whitehurst

Title: President, Chemical Engineer **Industry:** Engineering **Company Name:** Whitehurst Associates, Inc. **Date of Birth:** 04/09/1930 **Parents:** David Brooks; Bessie Ann (Lowry) Whitehurst **Marital Status:** Married **Spouse Name:** Carolyn Sue Boyer (7/4/1951) **Children:** Garnett; Anita; Robert **Education:** Honorary PhD, International Biographical Centre (2018); Honorary LittD, International Biographical Center, Cambridge, England (2013); Honorary DSc, Roanoke College (2012); BS, Virginia Polytechnic Institute and State University (1951) **Certifications:** Registered Professional Engineer, State of North Carolina **Career:** President, Whitehurst Associates, Inc., New Bern, NC (1981-Present); Manager of Special Projects, Long Range Planning, Texasgulf, Inc., Aurora, NC (1980-1981); Manager of Engineering Services, Texasgulf, Inc., Aurora, NC (1967-1980); Project Engineer, Texaco Inc., Richmond, VA (1963-1966); Senior Process Development Engineer, Virginia-Carolina Chemical Corporation, Richmond, VA (1956-1963); Senior Process Assistant, American Enka Corp., Lowland, TN (1951-1956) **Career Related:** Presenter, Paper, Solar World Forum, Brighton, England (1981); Instructor, Consultant, Alternate Sources of Energy, Community College and University; Lecturer, Virginia Polytechnic Institute and State University; Lecturer, Roanoke College **Civic:** Active Member, Wood Enterprise Institute; Chairman, State Advisory Council on Career Education (1977-Present); Chairman, Governor's Task Force Volunteers in the Workplace (1981); Governor's Liaison for Education and Business (1978-1979); Co-Chairman, North Carolina State Superintendent Task Force on Secondary Education (1974-1975); North Carolina State Advisory Committee on Trade and Industrial Education (1971-1977) **Creative Works:** Contributor, Scientific Papers **Awards:** World Academy of Great Minds, International Biographical Centre (2018); Sir Isaac Newton Legacy of Honor Award for Recognition in Chemical Engineering, International Biographical Centre (2016); Engineering Hall Of Fame (2014); Named, Honorary Director General of the International Biographical Centre (2010); Recipient, Commendation, United States President (1981); Inductee, Engineering Hall of Fame in the Field of Chemical Engineering, International Biographical Centre; Gold Medal, International Biographical Center **Membership:** Board of Directors, American Institute of Chemists (1980-1984); President, North Carolina Institute of Chemists (1975-1977); American Institute of Chemical Engineers; National Society of Professional Engineers; North Carolina Society of Professional Engineers; Royal Society of Chemistry **Marquis Who's Who Honors:** Distinguished Humanitarian (2017) **Shipping Address:** 1983 Hoods Creek Dr, New Bern, NC, 28562

Carolyn Raye Whitener

Title: Artist, Commercial Artist, Interior Designer **Industry:** Fine Art **Company Name:** Colorvision Inc. **Date of Birth:** 02/02/1941 **Place of Birth:** Corpus Christi **State:** TX **Parents:** Rayburn N. Hamilton; Alice G. Hamilton **Children:** Mark Dwain; Rynn Rayna **Education:** Coursework, University of Science and Arts of Oklahoma (1981-1985); Coursework, Oklahoma State University (1970) **Career:** Owner, Clynn's Designs, Oklahoma City, OK (1969-Present); Motivational Speaker, Women's Groups and Universities (2011); Commercial Artist, Co-Owner, Colorvision, Inc., Oklahoma and Texas (1979-2007); Co-Owner, W&W Cattle Ranches, Oklahoma (1973-2007); Co-Owner, Honk N Hollers, Stillwater, OK (1962-1975) **Career Related:** Member, Advisory Council, Status of Oklahoma Woman (2001-Present); Commercial Design Consultant, One and Two Dimensional Rendering Drawings for Colorvision, Rynn's Lawncare & Landscaping, Oklahoma City (1997-Present); Consultant, Tele-Weight, Buena Vista, Co (1985-1992); Director, Staging and Backdrops, New York (1973-1974); Director, Staging and Backdrops, Stillwater, OK (1973-1974); Plaintive, Craig v. Boren Equal Rights Case (1972-1976) **Civic:** Advisory Member, Governor's Oklahoma Commission on the Status of Women (2000-Present); Active Member, Grady County Environmental Coalition (1991-1992) **Awards:** Recipient, Hall of Fame Award for a Chickasha, Oklahoma (2016); Recipient, Phi Alpha Delta Award (2012); Named, Oklahoma Woman Hall of Fame, Governor Brad Henry (2009); Named, Chickasha High School Students Hall Of Fame (2009); Named, Oklahoma's First Person, Oklahoma Commission on the Status of Women (2001); Named, Governor Commendation Award, Governor Frank Keating (2001); Recipient, State of Oklahoma Citation Award, Representative Richard Phillips and Senator Mike Fair (2001); Named, Woman of the Year, Oklahoma City Council, Beta Sigma Phi (1997-1998); Named, One Person Who Made a Difference, League of Women Voters (1997); President's Prestigious Award, Oklahoma State University (1996); Recipient, Outstanding Community Service Award, Ninnekah, OK (1992); Recipient, Outstanding Service Award, Beta Sigma Phi (1992); Recipient, Evening Lions Homecoming Window Design Awards, Beta Sigma Phi (1966-1968) **Membership:** Decorations Committee, All 1950s and 1960s Chickesha Oklahoma High School Alumni Class (1989-Present); Oklahoma Association of Family Community and Education; Grady County Extension Homemakers; Oklahoma City Newcomer's Club; Beta Sigma Phi; Career Homemakers Club, Sparta, NC; Senior River Loving Life; Rockport Art Center and Docent; Phi Alpha Delta; Rockport Women's Club; Motivation Speaking College Students and Organizations **Marquis Who's Who Honors:** Albert Nelson Marquis Lifetime Achievement Award (2017) **Political Affiliations:** Republican **Religion:** Methodist **Shipping Address:** 504 Spyglass St., Rockport, TX, 78382

Daniel Whitman

Title: Government Agency Administrator **Industry:** Government Administration/ Government Relations/Government Services **Date of Birth:** 08/09/1946 **Place of Birth:** Ann Arbor **State:** MI **Parents:** Sam Whitman; Pearl Sapirstein Whitman **Education:** PhD, Brown University, Providence, RI (1979); MA, Boston University (1974); BA, Oberlin College (1968) **Career:** Assistant Professor, Cross Cultural Communications, American University (2009-Present); Assistant Professor, Foreign Policy, American University, Washington (2008-2012); Deputy Director, Office of Public Diplomacy, African Bureau, US Department State (2007-2009); Oral Historian, Association for Diplomatic Studies and Training, Arlington, VA (2006-2007); Public Affairs Officer, US Embassy, Yaounde, Cameroon (2005-2006); Public Affairs Officer, US Embassy, Haiti (1999-2001); Program Development Officer, US Embassy, Pretoria, South Africa (1995-1999); Press Officer, US Embassy, Madrid (1989-1993); Press Officer, US Embassy, Copenhagen (1986-1989); Foreign Service Officer, US Department State, Washington (1985-2009); Program Director, Delphi Research Associates, Washington (1981-1983); Fulbright Professor, Marien Ngouabi University, Brazzaville, Republic of the Congo (1979-1981); French-English Interpreter, US Department State, Washington (1969-1984); French Teacher, Thayer Academy, Braintree, MA (1968-1972) **Career Related:** Press Officer, Bureau of Population, Refugees, and Migration, US Department of State (2016); Senior Advisor, US President's African Leaders Summit (2014); Public Affairs Officer, Temporary Duty, US Embassy, Malabo, Equatorial Guinea; Public Affairs Officer, Temporary Duty, US Embassy, Juba, Republic of South Sudan; Public Affairs Officer, Temporary Duty, US Embassy, Banjul, Gambia; Public Affairs Officer, Temporary Duty, US Consulate, Lagos; Public Affairs Officer, Temporary Duty, US Embassy, Accra, Ghana; Public Affairs Officer, Temporary Duty, US Embassy, Conakry, Guinea **Civic:** Faculty Sponsor, No Lost Generation, American University (2016); Board Member, Public Diplomacy Alumni Association (2016); President, Virtual Educa Foundation (2014-2016); Member, Public Diplomacy Council (2014-2016); Member, DACOR (Diplomats and Consular Officers Retired) (2012-2016); Founding Board Member, Asian Scholarship Fund, Washington (2008-2015) **Creative Works:** Author, Nonfiction, "Answer Coming Soon"; Author, Nonfiction, "Outsmarting Apartheid: An Oral History of South Africa's Cultural and Educational Exchange with the 1960-1999" (2014); Author, "Blaming No One" (2012); Author, "Crank: In Favor of the Outnumbered" (2006); Author, Nonfiction, "A Haiti Chronicle: The Undoing of a Latent Democracy" (2004); Author, "One Step Up: A Buyer's Guide to Stringed Instruments" (1995); Author, Travel Book, "Madrid Inside Out" (1992); Author, "Kaidara: A Translation with Commentary" (1988); 45 Articles on Demand for the New York Times, the Foreign Service Journal, State Magazine, the Foreign Service Journal, Ba Shiru, Parabola, Research in African Literatures, French Colonial Studies, and others **Membership:** American Foreign Service Association; Public Diplomacy Alumni Association; Programs Africa and Freedom Endowment; Advisor, US Center for Diplomacy **Marquis Who's Who Honors:** Albert Nelson Marquis Lifetime Achievement Award (2017) **Shipping Address:** 3630 39th St NW Apt F534, Washington, DC, 20016

Michele A. Whitham

Title: Owner **Industry:** Law and Legal Services **Company Name:** Whitham Law, LLC **Education:** JD, Cornell University (1988); MS in Human Development, Cornell University (1987); MA in Teaching in Education, Cornell University (1971); BA, Cornell University, Cum Laude (1970) **Awards:** Top Rated Lawyer in Boston, Martindale-Hubbell (2015); A/V Preeminent Rated Attorney, Martindale-Hubbell (2015); 15-Year Anniversary with A/V Preeminent Rating; Massachusetts and New England Super Lawyers **Membership:** Board of Directors, Lex Mundi; Society of Fellows, Boston Bar Foundation; Massachusetts Bar Association; Unified Court System of the State of New York; Trainer, Community Dispute Resolution Program; American Bar Association; The Phi Beta Kappa Society **Bar Admissions:** First Circuit, U.S. Court of Appeals; U.S. District Court, State of Massachusetts **Marquis Who's Who Honors:** Albert Nelson Marquis Lifetime Achievement Award (2017); Distinguished Humanitarian (2017) **Why did you become involved in your profession or industry:** Ms. Whitham became involved in her profession because she grew up in an academic family, and assumed she would become a professor and follow in the family business and footsteps. She was on the faculty and part of a multidisciplinary group at Cornell from 1976 to 1988. The more time she spent in academia, she began to realize that law would be a great companion and would enable her to take part in changing the world and making a difference. **Where will you be in five years:** In five years, Ms. Whitham would like to shift into a guru role to the legal community, and participate in groups and programs. **Shipping Address:** 11 King Avenue, Medford, MA, 02155

Ralph E. Whittington

Title: 1) Consultant 2) Curator (Retired) **Industry:** Museums & Institutions **Company Name:** 1) Museum of Sex 2) Library of Congress **Date of Birth:** 01/13/1945 **Place of Birth:** Washington **State:** DC **Parents:** Ralph John Whittington; Mildred May Whittington **Spouse Name:** Jennifer Kay Rutland (6/7/1969, Divorced) **Children:** Amanda Anne **Education:** Honorary PhD, Institute for Advanced Study of Human Sexuality (2012); Diploma, Surrattsville High School, Clinton, MD (1963) **Career:** Consultant, Institute for Advanced Study of Human Sexuality (2010-Present); Consultant, Museum of Sex, New York, NY (2001-Present); Consultant, Erotic Heritage Museum, Las Vegas, NV (2011-2012); Curator, Main Reading Room, Library of Congress, Washington, DC (1985-2000); Searcher, Library Materials Locator, Library of Congress, Washington, DC (1976-1985); Deck Attendant, Library of Congress, Washington, DC (1963-1976) **Creative Works:** Contributor, Dictionary of International Biography (2008-2009); Featured, Documentary, American Stag, Westlake Entertainment Group (2008); Featured, Documentary, Xperimental Euros, Other Cinema (2007) **Awards:** Named, Most Influential Professional, International Bank of Commerce (2015) **Why did you become involved in your profession or industry:** Mr. Whittington became involved in his profession while he worked at the Library of Congress. He realized how important the collections were and knew the library had nothing in genres like sexuality. Mr. Whittington started collecting things that were important in the 1970s and 1980s and it came together quite well. His collection was so extensive that he was contacted by the owner of the Museum of Sex, which at the time hadn't opened its doors yet. It took two years, and a 16-foot U-Haul truck to get his collection out of his home and into the museum. Mr. Whittington's collection totaled 938 boxes. **Hobbies:** Collecting vinyl records **Shipping Address:** 9204 Greenfield Ln, Clinton, MD, 20735

Wolfgang Lothar Wiese, PhD

Title: Physicist (Retired) **Industry:** Sciences **Company Name:** National Institute of Standards and Technology **Date of Birth:** 04/21/1931 **Place of Birth:** Tilsit **Country of Origin:** Germany **Parents:** Werner Max Wiese; Charlotte (Donath) Wiese **Marital Status:** Married **Spouse Name:** Gesa Ladehoff (10/12/1957) **Children:** Margrit Wiese; Cosima Wiese **Education:** Honorary PhD, Christian-Albrechts-Universität zu Kiel (1993); PhD, Christian-Albrechts-Universität zu Kiel (1957); BS, Christian-Universität zu Kiel (1954) **Career:** Research Associate, National Institute of Standards and Technology (2005-Present); Chief of Atomic Physics Division, National Bureau of Standards and Technology (1991-2004); Chief of Atomic and Plasma Radiation Division, National Bureau of Standards and Technology (1978-1991); Chief of Plasma Spectroscopy Section, National Bureau of Standards and Technology (1962-1977); Research Physicist, National Bureau of Standards and Technology (1960-1962); Research Associate, University of Maryland (1958-1959) **Career Related:** Lecturer, University of California (1963-1964) **Creative Works:** Co-Author, "Spectral Data for Highly Ionized Atoms: Ti, V, Cr, Mn, Fe, Co, Ni, Cu, Kr, and Mo," American Institute of Physics (2000); Co-Author, "Atomic Transition Probabilities of Carbon, Nitrogen, and Oxygen, A Critical Data Compilation," American Institute of Physics (1996); Co-Author, "Atomic Transition Probabilities: Scandium through Manganese," American Institute of Physics (1988); Co-Author, "Atomic Transition Probabilities: Iron Through Nickel," American Institute of Physics (1988); Co-Author, "Atomic Transition Probabilities, Volume II: Sodium Through Calcium," American Institute of Physics (1969); Co-Author, "Atomic Transition Probabilities, Volume 1: Hydrogen Through Neon - A Critical Data Compilations," United States Government Publishing Office (1966) **Awards:** Recipient, Distinguished Postdoctoral Award, University of Maryland (2003); Recipient, Distinguished Career in Science Award, Washington Academy of Sciences (1992); Recipient, Humboldt Award (1986); Recipient, Gold Medal Award (1971); Recipient, A.S. Fleming Award, United States Chamber of Commerce (1971); Recipient, Fellowship, John Simon Guggenheim Memorial Foundation (1966); Recipient, Silver Medal Award, United States Department of Commerce (1962); Recipient, Fellowship, American Physical Society; Recipient, Fellowship, The Optical Society; Recipient, Fellowship, Washington Academy of Sciences **Membership:** International Astronomical Union **Marquis Who's Who Honors:** Albert Nelson Marquis Lifetime Achievement Award (2017) **Religion:** Lutheran **Shipping Address:** 8229 Stone Trail Drive, Bethesda, MD, 20817

Jay Spencer Wiginton

Title: Independent Industrial Consultant **Industry:** Retail/Sales **Date of Birth:** 09/21/1941 **Place of Birth:** Lubbock **State:** TX **Year of Passing:** 2018-08-23 **Parents:** Clarence Elbert Wiginton; Faye (George) Wiginton **Marital Status:** Married **Spouse Name:** Laverne Shook (6/18/1993); Billye Kay Freitag (11/28/1968, Divorced 2/1993) **Children:** Lauren; Lindsay, Lee **Education:** MS, Texas Tech University (1968); BS, Texas Tech University (1963) **Career:** Equine Sales Specialist, Merial (1993-2009); General Manager, ProVets (1991-1993); Sales Manager, Western Region, Allflex USA Inc. (1987-1991); District Manager, Agri-Sales Associates, Inc. (ASA), San Antonio, Texas (1985-1987); Director, Field Development, V.A. Snell & Company Division, Great Plains Chemical Company, San Antonio, TX (1984-1985); Southwest Regional Manager, V.A. Snell & Company Division, Great Plains Chemical Company, San Antonio, TX (1983-1984); General Manager, V.A. Snell & Company Division, Great Plains Chemical Company, San Antonio, TX (1978-1983); National Account Manager, Custom Division (1976-1978); Regional Sales Manager, Zoecon Corporation, Central Life Sciences, Dallas, TX (1974-1976); Director, Marketing, Syntex Laboratories, West Texas Territory, Des Moines, IA (1973-1974); Far East Regional Manager, Syntex Laboratories, West Texas Territory, Des Moines, IA (1972-1973); Regional Sales Representative, Syntex Laboratories, West Texas Territory, Lubbock, TX (1970-1972); Sales Representative, Syntex Laboratories, West Texas Territory, Lubbock, TX (1968-1970); Independent Industrial Consultant **Military Service:** U.S. Army, Vietnam (1964-1966) **Membership:** Texas Grain and Feed Association; Texas Cattle Feeders Association; Association of Chemical Industry of Texas; Texas Chemical Council; Kappa Sigma Fraternity **Marquis Who's Who Honors:** Albert Nelson Marquis Lifetime Achievement Award (2017) **Religion:** Disciples of Christ **Shipping Address:** 335 Charon Pt, Spring Branch, TX, 78070

Subhashie Wijemanne

Title: Assistant Professor of Neurology **Industry:** Education/Educational Services **Company Name:** The University of Texas at San Antonio **Year of Passing:** 2017-10-04 **Children:** Two Daughters **Education:** Fellowship, Baylor College of Medicine (2014); Residency, Tufts University (2012); Intern, Lahey Hospital & Medical Center (2009); MD, Faculty of Medicine, University of Peradeniya (2000) **Certifications:** License to Practice Medicine, State of Texas (2012-Present); License to Practice Medicine, Commonwealth of Massachusetts (2008-2012); Certified, American Board of Neurological Surgery; Certified, American Board of Psychiatry and Neurology **Career:** Assistant Professor, Neurology, The University of Texas at San Antonio (2014-Present); Chief Resident, Tufts University School of Medicine, Boston, MA (2011-2012) **Creative Works:** Contributor, Articles, Professional Journals **Awards:** MRCP, Royal College of Physicians, London, England (2007); Dr. Barr-Kumar Kulasinghe Memorial Prize in Surgery (2000) **Membership:** American Academy of Neurology; International Parkinson and Movement Disorder Society; Texas Neurological Society **To what do you attribute your success:** Dr. Wijemanne attributed her success to her dedication, and being willing to put the time in. **Why did you become involved in your profession or industry:** Soon after she graduated from medicine school, she had a chance to practice neurology and got interested in movement disorders. Early in her training, she became interested in her specialization. Her father is a physician so medicine was something she always wanted to go into. **Hobbies:** Travel; Cooking; Music; Playing Piano; Tennis **Business Address:** 8300 Floyd Curl Dr., San Antonio, TX, 78229 **Shipping Address:** 17803 La Cantera Ter., Apt 12418, San Antonio, TX, 78256

David Eric Wilcox

Title: Electrical Engineer, Educator, Consultant, Federal Agency Executive, President, Chief Executive Officer **Industry:** Engineering **Company Name:** Global Skills Exchange Corporation **Date of Birth:** 09/04/1939 **Place of Birth:** Cortland **State:** NY **Parents:** James A. Wilcox; Lucille C. (Fiske) Wilcox **Marital Status:** Married **Spouse Name:** Phillipa Ann Wilcox (1/23/1977) **Children:** Terri L.; Cindy A.; Jana L. **Education:** Postgraduate Coursework, State University of New Jersey, Rutgers University (1980-1983); MEE, University of Bridgeport (1977); MS in Counseling and Human Resources, University of Bridgeport (1977); Postgraduate Business Coursework, Marist College (1976); Postgraduate Coursework, Electronic Engineering, Syracuse University (1965); BEE, University at Buffalo (1961) **Certifications:** Registered Professional Engineer, State of New York (1968) **Career:** President, Global Skills Exchange Corporation, Alexandria, VA (2003-Present); Chief Executive Officer, Global Skills Exchange Corporation, Alexandria, VA (2003-Present); Executive Deputy Director, National Skills Standards Board, Washington, DC (1998-2003); President, Wilcox Industries Corporation (1973-1998); Director of Sales, Mercom Corporation, Winooski, VT (1970-1973); Research Engineering Manager, Input/Output Devices Section, Air Force Research Laboratory, Rome, NY (1961-1970) **Career Related:** Board Member, Mercom Corporation (1970-1973); Board of Directors, Principal, Executive Effectiveness Inc., New York, NY; Instructor, Dale Carnegie & Associates, Inc. **Civic:** Examiner, New York State Excelsior Program (1995); Orange County Private Industry Council (1995); Treasurer, Board of Directors, Family Counseling Service, Inc. (1980-1984); Board Chairman, New York State Jaycees (1973-1974); President, New York State Jaycees (1972-1973); Vice President, Board of Directors, Special Olympics, New York (1972-1973); Director, JCI, Inc. (1970-1971); Various National Committees; Various Advisory Committees **Military Service:** Lieutenant, U.S. Air Force (1961-1965) **Creative Works:** Author, "Information System Sciences" (1965); Contributor, Articles, Professional Journals **Membership:** IEEE; Society for Information Display; NYSSPE; International Transactional Analysis Association; American Society for Quality; Platform - The International Platform Association; SHRM; ICE **Marquis Who's Who Honors:** Albert Nelson Marquis Lifetime Achievement Award (2017) **Religion:** Methodist **Shipping Address:** 1410 King Street, Suite 400, Global Skills Exchange Corporation, Alexandria, VA, 22314 **Website:** http://www.skillsdmo.com

Janet Wilder

Title: Performing Company Executive **Industry:** Media & Entertainment **Company Name:** Spokane/Coeur d'Alene Opera **Date of Birth:** 12/08/1944 **Place of Birth:** Pampa **State:** TX **Parents:** Robert; Jean **Marital Status:** Married **Spouse Name:** Ward Wilder **Children:** Suzanne; Robert **Education:** BS, University of Colorado (1966) **Certifications:** California Teaching Certification; Teacher Certification, Chicago National Association of Dance Masters; Cecchetti Teacher Certification, Cecchetti Council of America **Career:** Owner, Director, Academy of Dance, Spokane Valley, WA (1994-2007); Resident Choreographer, Occasional Corps Performances, Spokane/Coeur d'Alene Opera (1987-2006); Choreographer, Producer, Director, Coeur d'Alene Summer Theatre, Idaho (1991-1996); Co-Founder, Director, Theatre Ballet Spokane (1987-1994); Co-Owner, Co-Director, Ballet Arts Academy, Spokane (1987-1994); Director, Ballet Arts, San Antonio, TX (1983-1985); Dancer, Omaha Ballet (1979-1981); Instructor, Co-Director, Entenman School of Dance, Bellevue, NE (1978-1981); Artistic Director, Performing Company Executive, Ballet Spokane (2003-2009); Artistic Director, Dance Theatre Northwest, Spokane, WA (1994-2004); Artistic Director, San Antonio Dance Theatre (1983-1985); Artistic Director, Dakota Repertory Dance Company, Rapid City, SD (1975-1977); Instructor, Marguerite Phares School of Dance, Sacramento, CA (1985-1987); Instructor, Capitol City Ballet, Sacramento, CA (1985-1987); Instructor, Spokane Ballet, Washington (1981-1983); Instructor, Julie Ward School of Dance, Rapid City, SD (1972-1977); Fitness/Dance Instructor, American Wives' Club, Ghedi, Italy (1969-1971); Teacher, Santa Venetia Middle School, San Rafael, CA (1967-1968) **Career Related:** Dance Education Delegate to China, People to People, Bejing (1996); Ballet Advisory Board Member, MusicFest Northwest, Spokane, WA (2000-Present); Greater Spokane Music & Allied Arts Festival (1988-2000); Founder, Member, Inland Northwest Dance Association, Spokane, WA (1989-Present) **Civic:** Volunteer, Medical Lake Elementary School (2007-2008); Vice President, Inland Northwest Dance Association (2002-2004); Member, Entertainment Committee, Diamonds & Divas, Spokane, WA (2000-2005); Committee Member, First Night Spokane, WA (2003); Member, Officer, Parent Teacher Association, Rapid City, SD (1975-1977); Member, Rapid City Service League (1975-1977) **Creative Works:** Author, "Terms Every Dancer Should Know"; Writer, Producer, Director, "The Toy Shelf"; Choreographer, Over 150 Ballets, Operas and Musicals **Awards:** Director-in-Charge, Teen Group Community Service Honorable Mention, Chase Youth Commission (2001); Director-in-Charge, Teen Group Creativity Award (2000); Jim Chase Asset Builder (1997); Washington State Dance School Director, Bowl Games of America-CocaCola Olympic City (1996); Dance Excellence, International Festival for Young Dancers (1992-1995); Outstanding Young Women of America, Outstanding Young Women of America Program (1973); Outstanding Member, Ellsworth Officer's Wives' Club (1977); Ghedi Air Force Wives' Club (1971) **Marquis Who's Who Honors:** Albert Nelson Marquis Lifetime Achievement Award (2017) **Hobbies:** Writing; Scuba diving; Boating; Painting **Shipping Address:** 18614 W Buckboard Ave., Medical Lake, WA, 99022

Ann Meagher Williams

Title: Hospital Administrator (Retired) **Industry:** Health, Wellness and Fitness **Date of Birth:** 05/28/1929 **Place of Birth:** Hull **State:** MA **Parents:** James Francis Meagher Mullins; Dorothy Frances (Meagher) Mullins **Marital Status:** Widowed **Spouse Name:** Joseph Arthur Williams (5/15/1954) **Children:** James G. (Deceased); Mara A.; A. Scott (Deceased); Gordon M.; Mark J.; Antoinette M.; Andrea M.; **Education:** Honorary Degree, Cape Cod Community College (2009); MS, Boston College, Chestnut Hill, Newton, MA (1952); BS, Chestnut Hill College, Philadelphia, PA (1950) **Career:** Realtor, James E. Murphy, Inc., Osterville, MA (1995-2005); Director, Community Affairs, Cape Cod Hospital, Hyannis, MA (1977-1995); Realtor, James E. Murphy Inc., Hyannis, MA (1968-1977); Owner, Operator, Chatterlane, Osterville, MA (1961-1966); Assistant Manager, Roxbury Businessmen's Exchange, Boston, MA (1956-1966); Radioisotope Biologist, United States Air Force Cambridge Research Center, Bedford, MA (1952-1955) **Civic:** Member, Executive Committee, Cape Cod Chamber of Commerce Educational Foundation (1999-Present); Board of Directors, Cape Cod Chamber of Commerce Educational Foundation (1997-Present); Member, Executive Committee, Cape Cod Regional Technical High School (1983-Present); Member, School Committee, Cape Cod Regional Technical High School (1978-Present); Board of Directors, YMCA Cape Cod (2004-2013); Member, Cape and Islands United Way (1988-1989); Board of Directors, Center for Individual and Family Services, Mid Cape, MA (1982-1987); Board of Directors, American Cancer Society, Mid Cape, MA (1981-1996); Board of Directors, Community Council, Mid Cape, MA (1977-1988); Board of Directors, Cape Cod Mental Health Association (1977-1982); Chairman, Finance Committee, City of Barnstable, MA (1969-1977) **Awards:** Named, Cape Cod Mercy Otis Warren Woman of the Year (2016); Recipient, Mission Impact Champion Award, YMCA Cape Cod (2010); Named, Volunteer of the Year, YMCA Cape Cod (2008); Recipient, Lifetime Achievement Award, Massachusetts Association of School Committees (2000); Recipient, President's Recognition Award, Cape and Islands United Way (1989); Recipient, Certificate of Appreciation, American Cancer Society, Inc. (1988, 1983); Named, Business Woman of the Year, Business Professional Women's Club (1982) **Membership:** Vice Chairman, Rotary Leadership Institute (2007-2012); Board Director, Pure Water for the World (2006-2012); Zone 31 Literacy Coordinator, Rotary International (2005-2006); Zone 31 Membership Coordinator, Rotary International (2004-2006); Regional Vice Chairman, Rotary Leadership Institute (2003-2007); Governor, Rotary Club of Osterville (2002-2003); Governor, Rotary International (2002-2003); Board Director, Greater Hyannis Chamber of Commerce (2002-2003); Area Representative, Rotary Club of Osterville (1999-2000); Assistant Governor, District 7950, Rotary Club of Osterville (1998-1999); President, Rotary Club of Osterville (1996-1997); Board Director, Rotary Club of Osterville (1993-1998); Board Director, Greater Hyannis Chamber of Commerce (1993-1998); Tales of Cape Cod; National Association for Hospital Development; Southeast Massachusetts Hospital Marketing & Public Relations; New England Society for Healthcare Communications; American Society for Healthcare Strategy and Marketing Development; Chestnut Hill College Alumni Association **Marquis Who's Who Honors:** Albert Nelson Marquis Lifetime Achievement Award (2017); Distinguished Humanitarian (2017) **Hobbies:** Community theater; World travel **Religion:** Roman Catholic **Shipping Address:** 39 Blossom Ave., #6, Osterville, MA, 02655

Janet L. Williams

Title: Environmental Research Technician **Industry:** Environmental Services **Company Name:** DuPage County **Date of Birth:** 01/12/1953 **Place of Birth:** Aurora **State:** IL **Children:** Patty; Betsy **Education:** AAS in Architecture, College of DuPage; Associate Degree in Computer Science, College of DuPage; Associate Degree in Geographic Information Systems, College of DuPage; Coursework in Cooking, College of DuPage **Certifications:** Certification, Homeland Security Community Emergency Response Team; Certification in Legal Issues and Practical Considerations, Lorman Education Services; Certification in Law of Easements; Certification in Principals of Real Estate Acquisitions, International Right of Way Association; Certification in First Aid and CPR; Certified Water Safety Instructor, American National Red Cross; Certification in Geographic Information Systems, Elmhurst College **Career:** Environmental Research Technician, DuPage County **Civic:** Leader, Environmental Club, Churchill School (1993-Present); Assistant Troop Leader to Troop Leader, Girl Scouts of America; Youth Leader, RLDS Church; Sunday School Teacher, RLDS Church; Co-Coordinator, Annual Olympic Day, Churchill School **Creative Works:** Author, Numerous Books **Awards:** Those Who Excel Award, School District 41 (2006-2007); Most Beautiful Garden Award (2004); Volunteer of the Year, Glen Ellyn Jaycees and the Glen Ellyn Park District (1998); Grantee in Field **Membership:** National Association of Professional Women; International Right of Way Association; SSAMCO Veterans Group, Benedictine University **Why did you become involved in your profession or industry:** Ms. Williams became involved in her profession after attaining an assistant Girl Scout leader position, at which point she began working on the environmental side through the school district. She was soon employed by the County of DuPage Public Works Department. **What do you consider to be the highlight of your career:** The most gratifying aspect of Ms. Williams' career is having been able to pass along her knowledge and opportunities to the Girl Scouts, public school students, and students in the environmental club through the years. She is also proud to have earned an AAS in architecture at a time when architecture was very much a man's field. **Where will you be in five years:** In five years, Ms. Williams hopes to continue in her current position and improve her knowledge both at work and in the environmental field. **Hobbies:** Flower and vegetable gardening; Decorating wedding cakes; Making candies; Cooking; Conducting cooking classes; Sewing; Crafts; Organizing and putting on parties; Volunteering at the park **Shipping Address:** 421 N County Farm Road, DuPage County Public Works, Wheaton, IL, 60187

Jonathan H. Williams

Title: Senior Research Scientist (Retired) **Industry:** Sciences **Company Name:** University of Georgia **Date of Birth:** 09/23/1948 **Place of Birth:** Middelburg **Country of Origin:** South Africa **Parents:** David H. Williams; Gwenyth A. Williams **Marital Status:** Married **Spouse Name:** Sheila A. Nicol (9/23/1952); Lucinda **Children:** Katherine A. Waters; Elise R.; Alexander J.; Suzannah R. **Education:** DPhil, University of Zimbabwe (1978); MPhil, University of Zimbabwe (1975); BSc in Agriculture, University of London, with Honors (1970) **Career:** Retired (2015); Director, Peanut Collaborative Research Support Program (CRSP), USAID (1998-2016); Senior Research Scientist, University of Georgia, Griffin, GA (1996-2015); Principal Scientist, ICRISAT, Hyderabad, India (1980-1996); Research Officer, Government Research and Specialist Services, Harare, Zimbabwe (1969-1980) **Career Related:** Chairman, CRSP Council, Cultural Practice (2005-Present); Director, Peanut Collaborative Research Support Program, Griffin, GA (1998-Present); Adviser, Shandong Peanut Research Institute, Quindao, China (1997-2000); Consultant, FAO, Rome, Italy (1996-1997); Consultant, United Nations Development Programme, China (1996-1997); Consultant, Programme des Nations Unies, Niamey, Niger (1994); Graduate Student Advisor, Universität Bonn; Graduate Student Advisor, Makerere University; Graduate Student Advisor, University of Georgia **Civic:** Chairman, School Board, ISH, India (1983-1985) **Military Service:** Sergeant, South African National Defence Force (1967-1980) **Creative Works:** Contributor, Articles, Professional Journals **Awards:** Special Service Award, The Association for International Agriculture and Rural Development (2013); Special Award for Service to the Peanut Industry, Georgia Peanut Commission (2012); Nominee for World Food Prize, University of Georgia (2010); Research and Education Award, Georgia Peanut Commission (2004); Farmers Coop Award for Contributions in Zimbabwe Oilseeds Industry (1979) **Membership:** American Peanut Research and Education Society; Kiwanis International **Marquis Who's Who Honors:** Albert Nelson Marquis Lifetime Achievement Award (2017) **To what do you attribute your success:** Dr. Williams attributes his success to his ability to work with scientists from both developing and developed countries and applying basic principles to be effective in a wide range of scientific and engineering disciplines. **What do you consider to be the highlight of your career:** The highlight of Dr. Williams' career was being nominated for the World Food Prize. **Where will you be in five years:** Over the next five years, Dr. Williams wants to work on reducing global warming by increasing photosynthesis on a sufficient scale so that carbon dioxide concentration goes down by bringing nutrient rich waters from depths in the blue oceans and distributing it across the surface using the currents. He also wants to work on improving food quality in Africa. **Hobbies:** Building His Own Home; Woodworking; Gardening; Invention **Political Affiliations:** Independent **Religion:** Episcopal **Shipping Address:** 2238 White Oak Rd, Burnsville, NC, 28714

Mark Leon Williams

Title: Professor **Industry:** Education/Educational Services **Company Name:** Florida International University **Date of Birth:** 07/25/1953 **Place of Birth:** Portsmouth **State:** VA **Parents:** Marvin L. Williams; Kathleen J. (Clements) Williams **Education:** PhD in Political Science, The University of Iowa (1983); Master of Arts in Political Science, University of Nebraska-Lincoln (1979); Bachelor of General Studies, The University of Iowa (1976) **Career:** Professor, Florida International University (2011-Present); Acting/Interim Dean, Florida International University (2013-2016); Chair, Department of Health Policy and Management, Florida International University (2011-2013); Professor of Behavioral Science, University of Texas School of Public Health (2003-2010); Associate Professor of Behavioral Science, School of Public Health, The University of Texas Health Science Center at Houston (1999-2003); Vice President, Behavioral Research, NOVA Research Company, Bethesda, MD (1994-1999); Vice President, Research, Affiliated Systems Corporation, Houston, Texas (1987-1994); Assistant Professor, University of St. Thomas, Houston, Texas (1983-1987); Visiting Assistant Professor, Department of Political Science, University of Rhode Island (1982-1983) **Career Related:** Accreditation Committee, Florida Department of Health, Monroe County (2015); HIV Prevention Track Co-chair, 17th Texas HIV/STD Conference (2009-2010); The SMART Project, Karolinska Institute and City of Stockholm (2007-2013); Voluntary Professor of Epidemiology & Public Health, University of Miami (2003-2008); Women's Hormone Replacement Project, Baylor College of Medicine (2002); Adherence to Long-term Therapies, World Health Organization (2001-2004); Office on AIDS, American Psychological Association (1999-2007); Office of AIDS Research, Office of the Director, National Institutes of Health (1998-1999); Mentor to New Investigators at Traditionally African American Colleges and Universities, National Institute of Drug Abuse (1996-1998); Voluntary Associate Professor of Epidemiology & Public Health, University of Miami (1994-2003); Board of Directors, HIV Advisory Board, Houston Health Department (1992-1994); Member, Advisory Board, Good Neighbor Health Clinic, Houston, Texas (1992-1994) **Civic:** Vestry, St. Stephen's Church (2013-2015); Board of Trustees, Executive Board, Bering-Omega Community Services (2002-2008) **Creative Works:** Peer Reviewer, American Journal of Public Health, New York City, NY (1994-Present); Editorial Board, AIDS and Behavior (2006-2012); International Editorial Board, AIDS Care (2003-2010); Associate American Editor, AIDS Care (1999-2003); Peer Reviewer, Addiction; Peer Reviewer, AIDS and Behavior; Peer Reviewer, AIDS and Public Policy; Peer Reviewer, Annals of Epidemiology; Peer Reviewer, BMC Infectious Diseases; Peer Reviewer, Culture, Health, and Sexuality; Peer Reviewer, Drug and Alcohol Dependence Epidemiology and Infection; Peer Reviewer, Family and Community Health; Peer Reviewer, Field Methods; Peer Reviewer, GBLT Health; Peer Reviewer, Global Public Health; Peer Reviewer, Health Education Research; Peer Reviewer, Health Promotion Practice; Peer Reviewer, Health Psychology; Peer Reviewer, International Journal of Drug Policy; Peer Reviewer, Journal of Drug Abuse; Peer Reviewer, Journal of Homosexuality; Peer Reviewer, Journal of the National Medical Association; Peer Reviewer, Journal of Primary Prevention; Peer Reviewer, Journal of Rural Health; Peer Reviewer, Journal of Urban Health; Peer Reviewer, Sexually Transmitted Infections and AIDS; Peer Reviewer, Social Science and Medicine; Peer Reviewer, Sociology of Health and Illness; Contributor, Chapters, Books; Contributor, Articles, Professional Journals; Lecturer in the Field **Awards:** Featured Alumnus, Nebraska Magazine (2014); 100 Great Health Administration Professors and Leaders, MHA (2013); Top Scholars, Florida International University (2013); Grantee, National Institute on Drug Abuse (1995, 1992, 1986) **Membership:** American Public Health Association; Society for Prevention Research **Marquis Who's Who Honors:** Albert Nelson Marquis Lifetime Achievement Award (2017) **What do you consider to be the highlight of your career:** It was meaningful to Dr. Williams to work with under-served populations. He considers his shining achievement the work he's done in the field of global HIV prevention and stabilization. **Where will you be in five years:** In five years, he would like to move into administration again; he has a contribution to make on the university level. **Hobbies:** Reading; Movies; Gardening **Business Address:** 11200 SW 8th St., Ste 446, Miami, FL, 33199 **Shipping Address:** 14849 SW 30th St., Miami, FL, 33185

Una Joyce Williams

Title: Social Worker (Retired), Clinical Social Worker **Industry:** Social Work **Company Name:** Veteran's Administration Medical Center **Date of Birth:** 06/24/1934 **Place of Birth:** Youngstown **State:** OH **Parents:** Samuel Wilfred Ellis; Frances Josephine (Woods) Ellis **Marital Status:** Divorced **Spouse Name:** John Allan Williams (Deceased) **Children:** Wendy Louise; Christopher Ellis; Sharon Elizabeth **Education:** MSW, Adelphi University (1963); BA, The University of Alabama (1957) **Certifications:** Diplomate in Clinical Social Work, National Association of Social Workers (1987-Present); Diplomate in Professional Counseling, International Academy of Behavioral Medicine, Counseling and Psychotherapy, Inc.; Certified in Counseling; Certified in Psychotherapy **Career:** Psychiatric Social Worker of Acute Psychiatric Treatment Services, Northport Veterans Affairs Medical Center, United States Department of Veterans Affairs (2000-2008); Medical Social Worker of Dialysis Services, Northport Veterans Affairs Medical Center, United States Department of Veterans Affairs (1998-2008); Therapist, Madonna Heights Family Clinic, SCO Family Services (1994-1999); Information Referral Counselor, Mental Health Association of Nassau County (1985-2002); Medical and Psychiatric Social Worker, Northport Veterans Affairs Medical Center, United States Department of Veterans Affairs (1974-2008); Psychiatric Social Work Supervisor, New York State Department of Mental Hygiene (1969-1972); Psychiatric Social Work Supervisor, Suffolk Psychiatric Hospital (1969-1972); Director, Huntington Program Senior Citizens, Town of Huntington (1963-1967) **Career Related:** Consultant, Senior Citizen Programs, Board of Education, Port Jefferson School District, New York (1961-1963); Consultant, Programs for Aging, Lutheran Social Services of New York (1959); Group Worker, United Methodist Children's Village, Selma, AL (1958-1959) **Civic:** Counselor, Project Liberty, Nassau County, New York (2002-2003); Secretary, Board of Trustees, Unitarian Universalist Fellowship of Huntington (1984); Chairman, Human Relations Committee, Town of Huntington (1970) **Awards:** Recipient, Member of the Year, German Philatelic Society (1987) **Membership:** American Board of Examiners in Clinical Social Worker (1988-Present); President, Chapter 30, Germany Philatelic Society (1990); National Association of Social Workers; American Association Family Counselors and Mediators **Marquis Who's Who Honors:** Distinguished Humanitarian (2017) **Hobbies:** Painting; Stamp collecting/philately; Vocal music; Piano music; Genealogy; Gardening **Shipping Address:** 316 Lenox Rd., Huntington Station, NY, 11746

David Williams Russell

Title: Lawyer **Industry:** Law and Legal Services **Date of Birth:** 04/05/1945 **Place of Birth:** Lockport **State:** NY **Parents:** David Lawson Russell; Jean Graves (Williams) Russell **Marital Status:** Married **Spouse Name:** Frances Yung Chung Chen (5/23/1970) **Children:** Bayard Chen; Ming Rennick **Education:** JD, Northwestern University, Cum Laude (1976); MBA, Dartmouth College (1969); AB, Dartmouth College (1967) **Career:** Founder, Russell Law Firm, Carmel, IN (2018-Present); Partner, Harrison Moberly, Indianapolis, IN (2004-2017); Partner, Bose McKinney & Evans LLP, Indianapolis, IN (1999-2004); Partner, Johnson, Smith, Pence, Densborn, Wright & Heath, Indianapolis, IN (1987-1999); Partner, Klineman, Rose, Wolf & Wallack, Indianapolis, IN (1983-1987); Lawyer, Winston & Strawn LLP, Chicago, IL (1976-1983); Law Clerk, Montgomery McCracken Walker & Rhoads, Philadelphia, PA (1975); Chief Financial Officer, Tougaloo College, Mississippi (1971-1973); Assistant to President for Planning, Tougaloo College, Mississippi (1969-1971); Mathematics Teacher, Lyndon Institute, Lyndonville, VT (1967-1968); English Teacher, Talledega College, Alabama (1967) **Career Related:** Director, Dartmouth Lawyers Association (2014-Present); Director, Outdoor Youth Experience Academy (2011-Present); Director and Chairman, Indiana District Export Council (2005-Present); Director and Vice Chairman, African University Foundation (2005-Present); Director, Asian Services of Indiana (2004-Present); Director and Chairman, Carmel Sister Cities (1999-Present); Director, Vice President and General Counsel, International Lawrence Durrell Society (1993-Present); Director, Vice President, Indiana Sister Cities (1988-Present); Board of Advisors, Indiana Economic Development Corporation (2005-2016); International Advisory Board, Maurer School of Law, Indiana University (2003-2017); Honorary Fellow, Center for International Legal Studies (2002); International Advisory Board, Supply Chain & Global Management Academy, Kelley Graduate School of Business, Indiana University (2001-2017); Director, Friends of Taiwan Association, Inc. (2001-2012); Director, Indianapolis Peace Games, Inc. (2000-2005); Board of Neutral Arbitrators, Financial Industry Regulatory Authority (FINRA) (1999-2017); Director, Asian American Alliance (1999-2008); Director, Writer's Center of Indiana (1999-2008); President, Carmel Sister Cities (1997-1999); Leader, Indiana Products Trade Fair, Kawachi-Nagano, Japan (1996); Board of Advisors, Center for International Business Education and Research, Krannert Graduate School of Management, Purdue University (1995-2016); Director, Vice President and General Counsel, Global Crossroads Foundation (1995-2003); Adjunct Professor, International Business Law, Kelley School of Business, Indiana University (1993-1995); Director, Indiana Swiss Foundation (1991-2002); Director, Secretary, Indiana Soviet Trade Consortium Inc. (1991-1999); President, World Trade Club of Indiana (1991-1992); Indiana District Enrollment Director, Dartmouth College (1990-1999); Director, Vice President, The International Center of Indianapolis (1988-1992); President, Forum for International Professional Services (1988-1989); Director, World Trade Club of Indiana (1987-2008); United States Department of Justice Indiana Delegate to U.S. China Joint Session on Trade, Investment & Economic Law, Beijing, China (1987); Lecturer on Indiana Law, Indiana Governor's Trade Mission, Tokyo, Japan (1986); Director, Forum for International Professional Services (1985-2010); Volunteer, Lawyers for Creative Arts (1977-1983); National Selection Committee, Administrative Fellowship Program, Woodrow Wilson National Fellowship Foundation (1973-1976); Consultant, Alfred P. Sloan Foundation (1972-1973); Woodrow Wilson National Fellowship Foundation Administrative Fellowships (1969-1972) **Awards:** Appointed, Sagamore of the Wabash, Governor of Indiana (2002); International Business Person of the Year, World Trade Club of Indiana (2002); Indiana Super Lawyer, Indiana Monthly and Indiana Law and Politics Magazines; Eponym, David Williams Russell Day, Mayor of Indianapolis; Daniel Webster National Scholarship, Dartmouth College; Eagle Scout **Membership:** Dartmouth Lawyers Association (2014-Present); Treasurer, Indiana State Bar Association (2002-Present); Chairman, Indiana State Bar Association (2002-2004); Co-Chairman, Written Publications Committee, Indiana State Bar Association (1997-1999); Past-Chairman, International Law Sections, Indiana State and Indianapolis Bar Associations (1990-1992); Past President and Secretary, Dartmouth Club of Indiana; American Bar Association; Indianapolis Bar Association; Indiana Association of Chinese Americans, Inc.; Chinese Music Society; International Bar Association; Zeta Psi Fraternity, Inc.; University Club of Indianapolis. **Bar Admissions:** State of Indiana (1983); State of Illinois (1976) **Marquis Who's Who Honors:** Albert Nelson Marquis Lifetime Achievement Award (2017) **Religion:** Presbyterian **Business Address:** 539 Arbor Drive, Carmel, IN, 46032

Charles Vert Willie, PhD

Title: Social Sciences Educator **Industry:** Education/Educational Services **Company Name:** Harvard University **Date of Birth:** 10/08/1927 **Place of Birth:** Dallas **State:** TX **Parents:** Louis James Willie; Carrie (Sykes) Willie **Marital Status:** Married **Spouse Name:** Mary Susannah Conklin (3/31/1962) **Children:** Sarah Susannah; Martin Charles; James Theodore **Education:** Honorary DHL, Morgan State University (2013); Honorary DHL, Emerson College (2008); Honorary JCD, Seabury-Western Theological Seminary (2005); Honorary DD, Episcopal Divinity School (2004); Honorary DHL, Haverford College (2000); Honorary PhD in Engineering Technology, Wentworth Institute of Technology (1996); Honorary DHL, Franklin Pierce College, Rindge, NH (1996); Honorary DL, Framingham State College (1992); Honorary DHL, Syracuse University (1992); Honorary DHL, Johnson C. Smith University, Charlotte, NC (1991); Honorary DHL, Rhode Island College (1983); Honorary DHL, Morehouse College (1983); Honorary MA, Harvard University (1974); Honorary DD, General Seminary (1974); Honorary DHL, Berkley Divinity School, Yale University (1972); PhD, Syracuse University (1957); MA, Atlanta University (1949); BA, Morehouse College (1948) **Career:** Professor Emeritus, Graduate School of Education, Harvard University (1999-Present); Charles William Eliot Professor of Education, Graduate School of Education, Harvard University (1998-1999); Professor of Education and Urban Studies, Graduate School of Education, Harvard University (1974-1998); Vice President, Syracuse University (1972-1974); Professor, Syracuse University (1968-1974); Chairman, Department of Sociology, Syracuse University (1967-1971); Associate Professor, Syracuse University (1964-1967); Instructor, Assistant Professor of Sociology, Syracuse University (1952-1963) **Career Related:** Overseer Emeritus, Boston Science Museum (2002-Present); National Advisory Committee, The History-Makers (2002-2006); Chairman, Board of Directors, Judge Baker Children's Center, Boston, MA (2001-2003); Co-Operator, Emerson Hospital, Concord, MA (1998-2006); Hogg Foundation Mental Health (1998-2002); Morehouse Research Institute (1997-2002); Board of Overseers, Boston Science Museum (1997-2001); National Advancement Committee, Maxwell School, Syracuse University (1992-2000); Commissioner, Presidential Commission on Mental Health (1977-1978) **Creative Works:** Co-Author, "A New Look at Black Families," Sixth Edition (2010); Co-Author, "Grass Roots Social Action" (2008); Co-Author, "The Black College Mystique" (2006); Co-Author, "A New Look at Black Families," Fifth Edition (2003); Co-Author, "Student Diversity, Choice and School Improvement" (2002); Co-Author, "Black Power/White Power in Public Education" (1998); Co-Author, "Controlled Choice" (1996); Co-Author, "Mental Health, Racism and Sexism" (1995); Author, "Theories of Human Social Action" (1994); Co-Author, "African-Americans and the Doctoral Experience" (1991); Co-Author, "The Education of African-Americans" (1991); "The Caste and Class Controversy on Race and Poverty," Second Edition (1989); Author, "Social Goals and Educational Reforms" (1988); Author, "Effective Education" (1987) **Awards:** Charles V. Willie Award, Eastern Sociological Society (2014-Present); Lifetime Achievement Award, American Association of Blacks Higher Education (2009); U.S. Speaker and Specialist Grant Award, U.S. State Department, The Bahamas (2007); Outstanding Contribution Award, Eastern Sociological Society (2006); Merit Award, Eastern Sociological Society (2006); Career Distinguished Scholarship Award, American Sociological Association (2005); Outstanding Teacher Award, Harvard University (2005); William Foote Whyte Award, American Sociological Association (2004); DuBois-Johnson-Frazier Award, American Sociological Association (2004); Arents Alumni Award, Syracuse University (2000); Outstanding Book Award for Mental Health, Racism and Sexism, Myers Center for Study of Human Rights (1996); Distinguished Career Award, Association of Black Sociologists (1996); Father John LaFarge, S.J. Award, Fairfield University (1995); Spirit of Public Service Award (1994); Robin M. Williams Distinguished Lectureship Award, Eastern Sociological Society (1994); Benjamin E. Mays Service Award, Morehouse College (1994); Distinguished Career Contribution Award, Committee on Role and Status of Minorities in Education, American Educational Research Association (1990); Family Scholar Award, Society for Study of Social Problems (1986); Lee-Founders Award, Society for Study Social Problems (1983); 50th Anniversary Distinguished Alumnus Award, Maxwell School, Syracuse University (1974) **Membership:** District Sorokin Lecturer, Eastern Sociological Society District Sorokin (2006); Vice President, American Sociological Association (1996-1997); Council, American Sociological Association (1995-1998); Council, American Sociological Association (1980-1983); President, Eastern Sociological Society (1974-1975); American Association of Blacks Higher Education; Board of Directors, Science of Society Research Council (1969-1976); Executive Council, Alpha Phi Alpha (1968-1974) **Marquis Who's Who Honors:** Distinguished Humanitarian (2017) **Shipping Address:** 41 Hillcrest Road, Concord, MA, 01742

Frank Wilson

Title: Orthopedist **Industry:** Medicine & Health Care **Company Name:** University of North Carolina at Chapel Hill **Date of Birth:** 12/29/1929 **Place of Birth:** Rome **State:** GA **Parents:** Frank Crane Wilson; Cheyney Bryan Wilson **Marital Status:** Married **Spouse Name:** Ann Habersham Irvin (Wilson) **Children:** Jennifer King-Wilson; Anna Habersham-Wilson (Deceased); Robin Wilson-Johnston **Education:** Executive Program in Health Policy and Management, Harvard University School of Public Health, Boston, MA (1980); Senior Annie C. Kane Fellow in Orthopedic Surgery, New York Orthopaedic Hospital, Columbia-Presbyterian Medical Center, New York, NY (1963); Resident, The New York Orthopaedic Hospital, Columbia-Presbyterian Medical Center, New York, NY (1960-1962); Assistant Resident, The New York Orthopaedic Hospital, Columbia-Presbyterian Medical Center, New York, NY (1960-1962); Junior Annie C. Kane Fellow in Orthopaedics, New York Orthopaedic Hospital, Columbia-Presbyterian Medical Center, New York, NY (1960-1962); Assistant Resident in Surgery, Columbia-Presbyterian Medical Center, New York, NY (1958-1959); MD, Medical College of Georgia, Augusta, GA (1954); BA, Vanderbilt University, Nashville, TN (1950); Graduate, The Darlington School, Rome, GA, Magna Cum Laude (1946) **Certifications:** Diplomate, American Board of Orthopaedic Surgery, Inc. (1984); Diplomate, American Board of Orthopaedic Surgery, Inc. (1966) **Career:** Kenan Distinguished Professor of Surgery/Orthopaedics, University of North Carolina at Chapel Hill School of Medicine, Chapel Hill, NC (1992-2002); Acting Assistant Dean, Graduate Medical Education, University of North Carolina at Chapel Hill School of Medicine, Chapel Hill, NC (1990-1991); Instructor in Literature, Undergraduate Honors Program, Departments of Humanities and English, The University of North Carolina at Chapel Hill, Chapel Hill, NC (1980-1999); Director, Musculoskeletal Course, The University of North Carolina at Chapel Hill School of Medicine, Chapel Hill, NC (1971-2000); Professor of Surgery/Orthopaedics, University of North Carolina at Chapel Hill School of Medicine, Chapel Hill, NC (1971-1991); Associate Professor of Surgery/Orthopaedics, University of North Carolina at Chapel Hill School of Medicine, Chapel Hill, NC (1968-1971); Chief, Division of Orthopaedics, University of North Carolina at Chapel Hill School of Medicine, Chapel Hill, NC (1967-1996); Assistant Professor of Surgery/Orthopaedics, University of North Carolina at Chapel Hill School of Medicine, Chapel Hill, NC (1965-1968); Instructor in Surgery/Orthopaedics, University of North Carolina at Chapel Hill School of Medicine, Chapel Hill, NC (1964-1965); Instructor in Orthopaedics, College of Physicians and Surgeons, Columbia University, New York, NY (1963) **Military Service:** Active Duty, Lieutenant, US Navy (1956-1958) **Creative Works:** Author and Researcher, "Replacement of the Knee Joint," Journal of Bone and Joint Surgery (1972); Contributor, Editor, More than 200 Publications; Author, Co-Author, 11 Books; Speaker, More than 300 Presentations **Awards:** Listee, One of 100 Leading Health Professionals, International Biographical Centre, Cambridge, England (2013); Listee, One of 100 Leading Health Professionals, International Biographical Centre, Cambridge, England (2010); Recipient, E. Burke Evans Award for Academic and Clinical Excellence (2009); Inductee, Alpha Omega Alpha Honor Medical Society (2007); Recipient, AOA-Smith & Nephew Distinguished Clinician-Educator Award (2003); Recipient, Distinguished Southern Orthopaedist Award, Southern Orthopaedic Association (1999); Recipient, Distinguished Orthopaedist Award, North Carolina Orthopaedic Association (1997); Named, Club Championship in Tennis (1997); Recipient, Distinguished Alumnus Award, Medical College of Georgia, Augusta University (1996); Named, Distinguished Faculty Award, University of North Carolina at Chapel Hill School of Medicine (1994); Recipient, Thomas Jefferson Award, University of North Carolina at Chapel Hill (1992); Recipient, Kenan Distinguished Professorship, University of North Carolina at Chapel Hill (1992) **Membership:** Thomas Wolfe Society (1980-Present); American Orthopaedic Association (1971-Present); American Academy of Orthopaedic Surgeons (1968-Present); President, Thomas Wolfe Society (1998-1999); President, The American Board of Orthopaedic Surgery, Inc. (1988-1989); President, Centennial, American Orthopaedic Association (1986-1987); The American Board of Orthopaedic Surgery, Inc. (1983-1989); American Board of Medical Specialties (1982-1994); Chair, Council of Academic Societies, Association of American Medical Colleges (1982-1983); President, Association of Orthopedic Chairmen (1977-1978); President, North Carolina Orthopaedic Association (1975); Association of Orthopedic Chairmen (1973-1991); Director, Musculoskeletal Curriculum, University of North Carolina at Chapel Hill School of Medicine (1972-2000); Faculty Council, University of North Carolina at Chapel Hill (1970-1973); American College of Surgeons (1965-1982); American Medical Association (1964-2015) **Marquis Who's Who Honors:** Distinguished Humanitarian (2017) **Shipping Address:** 603 Laurel Hill Rd, Chapel Hill, NC, 27514

James Wilson IV

Title: Surgeon (Retired) **Industry:** Medicine & Health Care **Date of Birth:** 03/11/1946 **Place of Birth:** Atlanta **State:** GA **Parents:** James Miller Wilson III; Sara Sharp **Marital Status:** Married **Spouse Name:** Lisa Vanlandingham **Children:** James Miller Wilson V; Robert Paul; Michael Simpson; Sara Ann **Education:** Resident, University of California, San Francisco, CA (1975-1980); Resident, New York Hospital-Cornell Medical Center (1972-1973); Intern, New York Hospital (1971-1972); MD, Duke University (1971); Coursework, Emory University **Certifications:** Diplomate, American Board of Surgery, American Board of Thoracic Surgery **Career:** Director, Cardiac Surgery, Mercy Hospital (2001-Present); Attending Staff, Good Samaritan Hospital, Cincinnati, OH (1994-Present); Associate Professor of Clinical Surgery, University of Cincinnati College of Medicine (1985-Present); Attending Staff, Children's Hospital, Cincinnati, OH (1984-Present); Attending Staff, Veterans Affairs Medical Center, Cincinnati, OH (1983-Present); Attending Staff, Deaconess Hospital, Cincinnati, OH (1982-Present); Attending Staff, University Hospital, Cincinnati, OH (1982-Present); Attending Staff, Jewish Hospital, Cincinnati, OH (1980-Present); Attending Staff, Bethesda Hospital, Cincinnati, OH (1980-Present); Attending Staff, Christ Hospital, Cincinnati, OH (1980-Present); Chairman, Department of Cardiovascular Surgery, Deaconess Hospital (1985-2001) **Career Related:** Member, Open Heart Surgery Advisory Committee, Ohio (1995-Present); Technical Advisory Panel on Cardiac Surgery; Chairman, National Quality Forum **Military Service:** Lieutenant Commander, Submarine Service, U.S. Navy (1973-1975) **Creative Works:** Contributor, Articles, Professional Journals **Membership:** Fellow, American College of Surgeons; Fellow, American College of Cardiology; Fellow, Cardiovascular Council, American Heart Association; Fellow, American College of Chest Physicians; American Medical Association, U.S. Naval Submarine League; UDT/SEAL Association; United States Submarine Veterans, Inc.; American Association for Thoracic Surgery; Thoracic Surgery Foundation; Association for Academic Surgery; American Physiological Society; Society of Thoracic Surgeons; Ohio State Medical Association; Cincinnati Academy of Medicine; Howard C. Nafziger Society **Marquis Who's Who Honors:** Albert Nelson Marquis Lifetime Achievement Award (2017) **Hobbies:** Music; Diving; Hiking; Skiing; Horses **Shipping Address:** 1589 Long Laurel Ridge Drive, Lakemont, GA, 30552

James Ross Wilson

Title: Professor Emeritus **Industry:** Education/Educational Services **Company Name:** California State University, Fresno **Date of Birth:** 11/25/1939 **Place of Birth:** Petaluma **State:** CA **Parents:** Stanley Thomas Wilson; Billie (Ross) Wilson **Marital Status:** Single **Spouse Name:** Elizabeth Ann Buckleman (12/29/1964, Divorced 1982) **Children:** Greg; Tom **Education:** MA, California State University, Fresno (1976); BA, Fresno State College (Now California State University, Fresno) (1961) **Career:** Professor of Mass Communication and Journalism, California State University, Fresno (1983-2009); General Manager/Faculty Advisor, KFSR-FM, California State University, Fresno (1983-2009); Weekend News Anchor, KMPH-FM News Radio, Fresno (1994-1996); Jazz Disc Jockey, KVPR-FM, Valley Public Radio, Fresno (1984-1990); News Assignment Editor, ABC-30, KFSN-TV, Fresno (1982-1983); Vice President and General Manager, KMJ/KNAX-FM, Fresno (1978-1982), Program Director, KMJ/KNAX-FM, Fresno (1971-1978); News Director, KMJ Radio (1967-71); News Reporter, KMJ Radio (1966-1967); News Director, KTIM Radio, San Rafael, CA (1966); News Director, KTOB Radio, Petaluma, CA (1965-1966); News Director, KVON Radio, Napa, CA (1965); Radio-Television Instructor, Department of Defense Information School, Fort Slocum, NY (1962-1965); Part Time News Director, KCEY Radio, Turlock, CA (1962); Fifth Grade instructor, Julien School, Turlock, CA (1961-1962); Part Time Announcer and News Anchor, KMJ Radio, Fresno, CA (1960-1962); Part Time News Reporter, KYNO Radio, Fresno, CA (1959); Summer vacation fill-in for Reporters and Sports Editor, Turlock Daily Journal, Turlock, CA (1957, 1958, 1959) **Military Service:** Instructor, Army/Defense Information School, Armed Forces Radio and Television Service, Fort Slocum, NY (1962-1965); Enlistee, U.S. Army (1962) **Creative Works:** Lead Co-Author, "Mass Media/Mass Culture," Fifth Edition, McGraw-Hill (2000); Co-Author, "Mass Media/Mass Culture," Fourth Edition, McGraw-Hill (1997) **Awards:** Grantee, California State University, Fresno (1987); Broadcast Excellence Award, Billboard Magazine (1976); Best News Documentary Award, California Associated Press Television-Radio Association (1973-1974); Best Newscast Award, CAPTRA (1971) **Membership:** Board of Directors, Treasurer, Central California Broadcasters Association, (1980-1983); Broadcast Educators Association (BEA); Association for Education in Journalism and Mass Communication (AEJMC); Alpha Epsilon Rho, the National Broadcasting Society; Phi Kappa Phi Honor Society **Marquis Who's Who Honors:** Albert Nelson Marquis Lifetime Achievement Award (2017) **Shipping Address:** 3846 Chessa Ln, Clovis, CA, 93619

Peggy Irene Mayfield Wilson

Title: Chemist (Retired) **Industry:** Sciences **Company Name:** Mobil Oil Corp. **Date of Birth:** 03/24/1927 **State:** TX **Parents:** Isaac Mayfield Newton; Ella Lockwood Mayfield **Marital Status:** Widowed **Spouse Name:** Irving Ray Dunlap, Jr. (Deceased); William W. Wilson III (7/25/1975, Deceased) **Education:** PhD in Chemistry, University of Texas, Austin (1952); BS in Chemistry, University of Texas, Austin, With Honors (1948) **Career:** President, Stone Gap Industrial Corp., Duncanville (1991-2000); President, Greater Duncanville Industrial Corp., TX (1991-2000); 1st Woman Group Manager Department Research, Mobil Research Development Corp., Dallas, TX (1984-1989); Research Technologist - First Woman Senior Research Technologist, Mobil Research Development Corp., Dallas, TX (1953-1984); Special Instructor, University of Texas, Austin (1952-1953); First Woman Cirt Council Member, Cedar Hill, TX **Career Related:** Regent, East Texas State University (Now Texas A&M University-Commerce) (1981-1987) **Civic:** Member, Bond Oversight Committee, CHISD (2013-2014); Active, Citizens Advisory Committee (2011); Active, Strategic Plan Committee & Community Advisory Committee (2010-2011); Chairman, Cedar Hill Comprehensive Plan Board (1997-1999); First Woman Council Member, City of Cedar Hill (1996-1998); Chairman, Board of Directors, Cedar Hill Economic Development Corp. (1994-1996); Founder, Economic Development, City of Cedar Hill, TX (1991-1996); Active, State Republican Executive Committee, TX (1971-1980); Board of Directors, Treasurer, Cedar Hill Comprehensive Plan Board; Advisory Board, Cedar Valley Community College; Board of Directors, Treasurer, International Museum of Cultures **Creative Works:** Developer, U.S. Patents in Oil Field Chemistry **Awards:** Cedar Hill Distinguished Character Lifetime Award, Cedar Hill Chamber of Commerce (2012); Golden Cedar Lifetime Award (2001); Jean Harris Award, Rotary (1998); Outstanding Republican Woman, Texas Federation of Republican Women (1973) **Membership:** American Chemical Society; World Affairs Council; Cedar Summit Book Club **Hobbies:** Gardening **Political Affiliations:** Republican **Religion:** Methodist **Shipping Address:** 1819 W. Belt Line Road, Cedar Hill, TX, 75104

Richard R. Wilson

Title: Lawyer **Industry:** Law and Legal Services **Company Name:** HCMP **Date of Birth:** 04/14/1950 **Place of Birth:** Pasadena **State:** CA **Parents:** Robert James Wilson; Phyllis Jean (Blackman) Wilson **Marital Status:** Married **Spouse Name:** Catherine Goodhugh Stevens (10/11/1980) **Children:** Thomas Randolph; Charles Stevens **Education:** JD, University of Washington (1976); BA, Yale University, Cum Laude (1971) **Career:** Management Committee, HCMP, Seattle, WA (1991-2007); Partner, HCMP, Seattle, WA (1987-2015); Partner, Hillis, Cairncross, Clark & Martin, Seattle, WA (1984-1987); Partner, Hillis, Phillips, Cairncross, Clark & Martin, Seattle, WA (1981-1984); Associate, Hillis, Phillips, Cairncross, Clark & Martin, Seattle, WA (1976-1981) **Career Related:** Board of Directors, Plymouth Housing Group, Seattle, WA (2001-Present); Lecturer, Various Bar Associations (1980-Present); President, Plymouth Housing Group (1998-2000); Trustee, Plymouth Housing Group (1994-2001); Board of Directors, Quality Child Care Services, Inc., Seattle, WA **Civic:** President, Church Corporation, Plymouth Congregational Church (2004-2005); Vice Chairman, 30th Reunion, Yale University Alumni Fund, New Haven, CT (2000-2001); Moderator, President, Church Council, Plymouth Congregational Church, Seattle, WA (1998-2000); Vice Chairman, Leadership Gifts Committee, Yale 25th Reunion, Yale University Alumni Fund, New Haven, CT (1995-1996); Chairman, Capital Campaign, Plymouth Congregational Church (1995); Western Washington Executive Committee, Yale Capital Campaign, Yale University Alumni Fund, New Haven, CT (1992-1997); Class Council, Yale University Alumni Fund, New Haven, CT (1991-1996); Vice Chairman, Medina Planning Commission (1990-1992); Chairman, Class Agents, Yale University Alumni Fund, New Haven, CT (1985-1987); Trustee, Performer, Gilbert & Sullivan Society (1984-1991); Class Agent, Yale University Alumni Fund, New Haven, CT (1971-2001) **Creative Works:** Contributor, Articles, Professional Journals **Awards:** Seattle's Best Lawyer of the Year in Litigation, Land Use and Zoning, Best Lawyers in America (2014); Leading Individual for Real Estate, Chamber's USA (2008-2016); Super Lawyer, Washington Law & Politics (1998-2016); Listee, Best Lawyers in America (1995-2016) **Membership:** Trustee, Kingsley Trust Association (2003-2006); President, Kingsley Trust Association (1996-1998); Director, Environmental and Land Use Law Section, Washington State Bar Association (1985-1988); Yale Association of Western Washington; American Bar Association; King County Bar Association **Bar Admissions:** Ninth Circuit, U.S. Court of Appeals (1977); State of Washington (1976); U.S. District Court, Western District, State of Washington (1976) **Marquis Who's Who Honors:** Albert Nelson Marquis Lifetime Achievement Award (2017) **Hobbies:** Acting; Singing; Rare book collecting **Religion:** Congregationalist **Shipping Address:** 5604 Lakeview Drive, Apt. I, Kirkland, WA, 98033

Stephanie R. Wilson

Title: Clinical Professor **Industry:** Health, Wellness and Fitness **Company Name:** University of Calgary **Marital Status:** Married **Spouse Name:** Ken Wilson **Children:** Two Children **Education:** MD, University of Alberta, with Distinction (1970); Resident in Radiology, Toronto General Hospital, University of Toronto; Intern, Foothills Hospital, University of Calgary **Career:** Clinical Professor, Radiology and Medicine, University of Calgary (2007-Present); Chief, Ultrasound, Toronto General Hospital, University Health Network (1984-2007); Professor, Radiology, University of Toronto (1984-2007) **Career Related:** Physician, Department of Diagnostic Imaging, Foothills Medical Centre, Alberta Health Services (2007-Present); Physician, Department of Medicine, Division of Gastroenterology, Foothills Medical Centre, Alberta Health Services (2007-Present) **Civic:** Co-President, International Contrast Ultrasound Society (2017); President, Canadian Association of Radiologists (1993) **Creative Works:** Co-Editor, "Diagnostic Ultrasound," Elsevier (1992); Contributor, More Than 130 Peer-Reviewed Publications; Presenter, More Than 400 International Conferences **Awards:** Honoree, Canadian Association for the Study of the Liver, Calgary, Canada (2017); Lifetime Achievement Award, SRU (2012); Joseph Holmes Pioneer Award, American Institute of Ultrasound in Medicine (2012); Jean A. Vezina Award for Excellence and Innovation in Radiology, Société Française de Radiologie (2011); Wightman-Berris Academy Award for Individual Teaching Excellence (2005); Gold Medal, Canadian Association of Radiologists (2001); Colin R. Woolf Award for Excellence in Continuing Education Teaching, University of Toronto (1992); Best Teacher Awards, Body Imaging Section, Department of Medical Imaging, University of Toronto (1991-2006); Gold Medal, International Contrast Ultrasound Society **Membership:** Radiological Society of North America; Canadian Association of Radiologists; SRU; American Institute of Ultrasound in Medicine **To what do you attribute your success:** Dr. Wilson attributes her success to being blessed with self-confidence. **Why did you become involved in your profession or industry:** Dr. Wilson decided early on that she wanted to become a full professor at the University of Toronto. The pathway was hard but she never thought it was harder for her as a woman than it was for a man. Dr. Wilson came from a very good family; her parents and her sisters are very accomplished. However, she was also from a very ordinary area of Canada. She didn't have mentors; she went to school, then medical school, and wound up in radiology. She got onto a research and academic path that lead her to be a world leader in what she does. From the day she graduated, she always had a full-time clinical position, eventually adding research and teaching. **What do you consider to be the highlight of your career:** A highlight of Dr. Wilson's career was collaborating with Dr. Peter Burns on an investigation of the imaging and diagnosis of tumors of the liver. **Hobbies:** Golfing; Relaxing with family **Business Address:** 1403 29 St., NW, AB, Calgary, Canada, T2N 2T9 **Shipping Address:** 2710-720 13 Ave., SW, AB, Calgary, Canada, T2R 1M5 **Website:** http://calgarygirlsschool.com/governance/honourary-council/dr-stephanie-wilson/

Kenneth Grant Winans

Title: President, Chief Investment Officer **Industry:** Financial Services **Company Name:** Winans Investments **State:** CA **Parents:** Frank G. Winans; Jeanne E. Winans **Marital Status:** Married **Spouse Name:** Debbie Wreyford Winans **Education:** Research Intern, EF Hutton & Company (Now HUTN, Inc.); MA in Finance, University of San Francisco; BA in Business Economics, University of San Diego **Certifications:** Registered Investment Advisor (1988); Chartered Financial Analyst; Chartered Market Technician (CMT) **Career:** President of Investment Management & Research, Winans International (Now Winans Investments) (1992-Present); Chief Investment Officer, Winans International (Now Winans Investments) (1992-Present); Investment Manager, Winans International (Now Winans Investments) (1992-Present); Founder, Winans International (Now Winans Investments) (1992-Present); Adjunct Faculty Member, Graduate Business, Saint Mary's College of California (1996-2001); Investment Advisor, Merrill Lynch & Company Inc. (Now Bank of America) (1990-1992); Technical Research Director, Compass Investment Group, Chicago, IL; Quantitative Researcher, Sutro & Co. Inc. **Career Related:** Competitor, Alpine Masters National Championships, U.S. Ski Association (Now U.S. Ski & Snowboard Association) (1998-1999); Competitor, U.S. Investing Championship, EF Hutton & Company (Now HUTN, Inc.) (1986); Competitor, Decathlon, Junior Olympics Track & Field Championships, USA Track & Field, Inc., Western Region (1981) **Civic:** Co-founder, The W Foundation (2002-Present); Co-founder, The Space Station Museum, Novato, CA (2011); Board of Trustees, Museum of American Finance, New York (2009); Board of Trustees, USS Hornet Museum, Alameda, CA; Board of Trustees, Chabot Space & Science Center, Oakland, CA; Board of Trustees, The W Foundation, Novato, CA; Board, San Francisco Fleet Week Association; Board, University of San Francisco Alumni Association; Board, Institute of Ecolonomics, Ridgway, CO **Military Service:** U.S. Army ROTC/Reserves (1984-1986) **Creative Works:** Author, "Investment Atlas II: Using History as a Financial Tool" (2016); Author, "Preferred Stocks: The Art of Profitable Income Investing" (2010); Author, "Investment Atlas: Financial Maps to Investment Success" (2008); Author, "Preffereds: Wall Street's Best-Kept Income Secrets" (2007); Columnist, Forbes Magazine; Invited Guest, Television Shows, Nationwide; Invited Guest, Radio Shows, Nationwide **Awards:** Independent Publisher (IPPY) Award (2017); Beverly Hills International Book Awards in U.S. History (2016); National Best Book Awards in Investments (2011); Honoree, U.S. Navy for a 45-Minute Flight in a Blue Angel F/A-18 Hornet Supersonic Fighter Plane (2009); Next Generation Indie Book Awards in Finance (2009); National Best Book Awards in Business (2007); Named One of the University of San Francisco's Most Celebrated Graduates in its 161-Year History (2004) **Membership:** Sons of the American Revolution; The Society of Colonial Wars in the State of New York; Board of Trustees, Society of California Pioneers, San Francisco, CA; Board of Trustees, The Holland Society of New York; The Saint Nicholas Society of the City of New York; The Order of the Founders and Patriots of America; Founding President, Market Technician Association (Now CMT Association), San Francisco Chapter; Senior Member, Chartered Financial Analyst (CFA) Institute, San Francisco Chapter; Member, Several Committees, Chartered Financial Analyst (CFA) Institute, San Francisco Chapter; Member, California Brokers of San Diego **To what do you attribute your success:** He attributes his success to following his instincts. He believes the key to long-term investment success is to correctly interpret investment history and apply it to today's financial climate. **Why did you become involved in your profession or industry:** He became involved in his profession after winning a high school competition. At 16-½-years-old, he walked into a Dean Witter office near Big Bear Lake, to open an investment account. He had recently won his high school economic class mock investing contest and calculated that he would have earned more money investing in stocks than his summer job of cleaning construction sites for his father's construction company. **What do you consider to be the highlight of your career:** The highlight that stands out in his career is successfully navigating the bull and bear markets since 1992. **Where will you be in five years:** In five years, he plans to continue working. Winans Investments will grow 100% and the W Foundation's activities will include an expanded space museum and a permanent financial history exhibit in the Bay Area. **Hobbies:** Scuba Diving; Traveling; Skiing; Riding Motorcycles; Tennis **Shipping Address:** 504 Redwood Blvd., Ste 320, Winans Investments, Novato, CA, 94947 **Website:** http://winansinvestments.com/about-winans-investments-capital-management-research/the-team/

Calhoun Winton

Title: Professor Emeritus **Industry:** Education/Educational Services **Company Name:** University of Maryland **Date of Birth:** 01/21/1927 **Place of Birth:** Ft. Benning **State:** GA **Parents:** George Peterson Winton; Dorothy (Calhoun) Winton **Marital Status:** Married **Spouse Name:** Elizabeth Jefferys Myers (6/30/1948, Deceased 12/26/2014) **Children:** Jefferys Hobart; William Calhoun **Education:** PhD, Princeton University (1955); MA, Princeton University (1954); MA, Vanderbilt University (1950); BA, University of the South (1948); Coursework, Georgia Institute of Technology (1944-1946) **Career:** Professor Emeritus, University of Maryland (1997-Present); Director of Research, Center for Humanities, University of Maryland, College Park, MD (1988-1990); Professor, University of Maryland, College Park, MD (1975-1997); Department Chairman, University of South Carolina, Columbia, SC (1970-1973); Professor, Department of English, University of South Carolina, Columbia, SC (1967-1975); Assistant Professor, Associate Professor, Assistant Dean, Graduate School, University of Delaware (1960-1967); Assistant Professor, University of Virginia, Charlottesville, VA (1957-1960); Instructor, Dartmouth College, Hanover, NH (1954-1957) **Career Related:** Delegate, Joint National Committee on Languages, Washington, DC (1995-1999); Delegate, Washington, DC (1986-1990) **Civic:** Board of Directors, Maryland Federation of Teachers, Baltimore, MD (1986-1989); President, Faculty Guild, University of Maryland (1986-1989) **Military Service:** Captain, U.S. Navy (1944-1967) **Creative Works:** Co-author, "Agent of Change" (2007); Contributor, Oxford Dictionary of National Biography (2004); Co-author, "Colonial Book in the Atlantic World" (2000); Editor, "John Gay and the London Theatre" (1993); Editor, "Plays of Aaron Hill" (1981); Author, "Sir Richard Steele" (1970); Author, "Captain Steele" (1964) **Awards:** John Carter Brown Library Fellow, Providence, RI (2003); John Carter Brown Library Fellow, Providence, RI (1995); Fulbright Commission Lecture Grantee, Ankara, Turkey (1979-1980); Folger Shakespeare Library Fellow, Washington, DC (1970); Guggenheim Foundation Fellow (1965-1966); American Philosophical Society Grantee (1960) **Membership:** Founder, American Society for 18th Century Studies (1970-Present); President, Eastern Central Society for 18th Century Studies (1987); Executive Board, Association of Princeton Graduate Alumni (1986-1990); Executive Committee Member, South Atlantic Chapter, Modern Language Association (1977-1980); Princeton Club, New York City, NY; Princeton Club, Washington, DC; Cosmos Club, Washington, DC; American Antiquarian Society; Literary Society of Washington **Marquis Who's Who Honors:** Distinguished Humanitarian (2017) **Hobbies:** Swimming; Collecting books **Political Affiliations:** Democrat **Religion:** Episcopalian **Shipping Address:** PO Box 3128, 1033 Eva Rd., Sewanee, TN, 37375

Mary Ann Wise Wiggins

Title: Small Business Owner (Retired), Educator (Retired) **Industry:** Education/Educational Services **Company Name:** Red River Parish Alternative School **Date of Birth:** 12/25/1940 **Place of Birth:** Coushatta **State:** LA **Parents:** George Wilkinson Wise, Sr.; Maitland (Allums) Wise **Marital Status:** Widow **Spouse Name:** Billy J. Wiggins (10/3/1981, Deceased 2009); Gerald D. Paul (Divorced 1977) **Children:** John Barron; James Gordon; Brenda Michelle; Marshall Wade; Winona Gail; Joseph James; Brian Alan; William Joshua; George Justin **Education:** MA in Principalship and Supervision, Louisiana Tech University (2005); Postgraduate Work, Northwestern State University (1994); Postgraduate Work, University of North Texas (1968); Postgraduate Work, Weatherford College (1967); BA, Northwestern State University (1964) **Certifications:** Curriculum Certified, Teacher Grades 2-11, State of Louisiana; Licensed, Insurance Agent; Certified, Private Pilot; Licensed Real Estate Agent, Nationwide Motel Brokers in Arkansas; Licensed Agent, Hunter & Associates Real Estate, Louisiana **Career:** Partner, Auctions and Estate Sales of Antique Furniture, Big Easy Emporium (2015-Present); Tax Preparer (1992-Present); Teacher, Ware Youth Center, Red River Parish Alternative School, Coushatta, LA (1998-2016); Teacher, Red River Parish Alternative School (1996-1998); Teacher, Springville Middle School (1994-1996); Owner, Manager, Mary Ann's Furniture & Hardware (1977-1997); Ambassador of Good Will, Vietnam (1971); Bookkeeper, Wise Department Store, Coushatta, LA (1966-1967); Teacher, Mineral Wells Independent School District (1967-1970); Teacher, U.S. Army Schools, Nuremberg, Germany (1964-1966) **Career Related:** Teacher, Louisiana Tech University (2002-2003); Leader, Louisiana Tech University (2002-2003); Vice Chairman, Instruction and Professional Development Committee, Louisiana Association of Educators (LAE) (1999-2002); Vice President, Louisiana Juvenile Detention Teachers Association (1999-2001); Committee Member, Instruction and Professional Development Committee, Louisiana Association of Educators (LAE) (1998-2000) **Civic:** Chairman, Pastor Relations, Hall Summit United Methodist Church (2014-Present); Chairman, Grand Bayou Resort Board of Commissioners (2011-Present); Member, Board of Directors, Hall Summit United Methodist Church (2008-Present); Affiliate, Grand Marshall Christmas Parade (2014); Chairman, Red River Parish Christmas Festival (2010-2013); Chairman, Christmas Parade (2010-2013); Chairman, Coushatta-Red River Chamber of Commerce (2010-2012); Candidate, District 24, Louisiana House of Representatives (2007); Member, Board of Directors, Hall Summit United Methodist Church (1994-2006); Chairman, United Way of Northwest Louisiana, Coushatta, LA (1987-1988); Chairman, American Cancer Society, Conway, AR (1972); Member, Cub Scout Den Mother Norwela Council (1970-1972); Brownie Scout Leader, Germany (1966); Member-at-Large, Relay for Life; Creator, Plan of Emergency Preparedness for Hall Summit United Methodist Church; Chairman, Going Green on the Red River Festival; Treasurer, Board of Directors, Hall Summit United Methodist Church; President, Political Action Committee, Red River Parish Association of Educators (LAE) **Creative Works:** Columnist, "Wise Old Owl," Coushatta Citizen (2003-2005) **Awards:** German-American Hospitality Award, Organization of German-American Women, Nuremberg, Germany (1965); Small Awards in Horsemanship, Mineral Wells, TX; Small Educator Awards, Texas; Small Educator Awards, Louisiana **Membership:** Board Chairman, Grand Bayou Resort Commission (2011-Present); Charter, Board of Directors, Coushatta-Red River Chamber of Commerce (2007); Chairman, Legislative Committee, Louisiana Association of Educators (LAE) (2000-2004); President, Red River Association of Educators (1998-2001); Vice President, Red River Association of Educators (1994); National Education Association; Former President, Coushatta-Red River Chamber of Commerce; U.S. Chamber of Commerce; Pi Kappa Sigma; Sigma Kappa **Marquis Who's Who Honors:** Distinguished Humanitarian (2017) **Hobbies:** Gardening; Swimming; Horseback riding; Reading; Computers; Weekenders with family; Landscaping **Political Affiliations:** Democrat **Religion:** Methodist **Shipping Address:** 6098 Highway 71, Big Easy Emporium, Coushatta, LA, 71019

Gregory Just Wismar

Title: Newspaper Columnist, Writer, Pastor **Industry:** Writing and Editing **Date of Birth:** 01/09/1946 **Place of Birth:** Jersey City **State:** NJ **Parents:** Adolph Harold Wismar; Norma Adela (Just) Wismar **Marital Status:** Married **Spouse Name:** Priscilla Emily Ames (6/7/1969) **Children:** Eric Andrew; Sarah Emily; Elizabeth Victoria; Jessica Eve **Education:** Post-Doctoral Research Fellow, Yale Institute of Sacred Music, Worship of the Arts (1991); Doctor of Ministry, Hartford Seminary (1990); MEd, Southern Connecticut State University (1977); MDiv, Concordia Seminary, St. Louis, MO (1971); BA, Concordia Senior College, Fort Wayne, IN (1967); AA, Concordia College, Bronxville, NY (1965) **Certifications:** Ordained to Ministry, The Lutheran Church - Missouri Synod (1971) **Career:** Emeritus Pastor, Christ the King Lutheran Church, Newtown, CT (2011-Present); Pastor, Christ the King Lutheran Church, Newtown, CT (1987-2011); Pastor, Messiah Lutheran Church, Lynnfield, MA (1983-1987); Pastor, Redeemer Lutheran Church, Gorham, ME (1978-1983); Pastor, St. Paul's Lutheran Church, Naugatuck, CT (1972-1978); Assistant Pastor, Immanuel Lutheran Church, Danbury, CT (1971-1972); Feature Writer, Travel and Restaurants, Heritage Villager, Southbury, CT; Writer, Concordia Publishing House; Tour Host, GLOBUS Travel International; Supply Pastor, Congregations, Connecticut; Supply Pastor, Congregations, New York **Career Related:** Archives Committee, New England District (1989-Present); Chairman, Commission on Worship, St. Louis, MO (2006-2010); Commission on Worship, St. Louis, MO (2001-2010); Commission on Worship, St. Louis, MO (1990-1995); Nominations Committee, St. Louis, MO (1985-1986); Vice President, New England District, The Lutheran Church - Missouri Synod, Springfield, MA (1979-1983) **Civic:** Secretary, Board of Regents, Concordia College, Bronxville, NY (1998-2001); Congressional Advisory Board, Newtown Family Life Center (1988-1990); Chairman, Lynnfield Arts Commission (1985-1987); Guest Chaplain, Massachusetts House of Representatives (1985); Guest Chaplain, United States Senate, Washington, DC (1982); Fort Williams Committee, Cape Elizabeth, ME (1981-1983); Guest Chaplain, United States Senate, Washington, DC (1977); Fifth District Connecticut Congressional Advisory Board, Waterbury, CT (1975-1979) **Creative Works:** Essayist, "Handbook to Lutheran Service Book" (2018); Contributor, "Handbook to Lutheran Service Book" (2018); Author, "At Every Turn" (2013); Author, "God Is For Us" (2010); Foreword Author, "LSB Concordance" (2008); Foreword Author, "Lutheran Service Book - Hymn Selection Guide" (2006); Author, "For All the Saints" (2005); Author, "The Joy of the Lord is Your Strength" (2004); Author, "Saints and Angels All Around" (1995); Editor, "Prayer for Worship: Collects" (1993); Author, "A Parish Portrait" (1990) **Awards:** Singles Champion, Heritage Village Tennis Open (2012); Church World Service/CROP Award (2011); Grantee of Clergy Renewal Award, Lilly Endowment Inc. (2000); Photography Award, Kodak International (1988); Service Award, NED Youth Commission (1987) **Membership:** Connecticut Master Chorale (2007-Present); Vice President, New England Lutheran Historical Society (1999-2014); Delta Phi Alpha German Honorary Fraternity **Marquis Who's Who Honors:** Albert Nelson Marquis Lifetime Achievement Award (2017) **To what do you attribute your success:** Mr. Wismar attributes his success to the blessing of God, encouragement from many diverse people, and a continuing curiosity about the world and all that is interesting in it. **Why did you become involved in your profession or industry:** Mr. Wismar became involved in his profession because of Lutheran clergy on both of his parents' sides of the family, who were great role models. **What do you consider to be the highlight of your career:** The highlight of Mr. Wismar's career has been using the gift of words and music to enrich the worship and devotional lives of many people through the writing of hymns and prayers, particularly when a collegiate choir with orchestral accompaniment perform an anthem he created. **Where will you be in five years:** In five years, Mr. Wismar hopes to still be writing and editing articles and helping out congregations in situations of need, as well as hosting tours to different corners of the world. He also hopes to, with his wife, continue watching their 15 grandchildren grow and develop. **Hobbies:** Creative writing; Choral participation; Racket sports; Gardening **Religion:** Lutheran **Shipping Address:** 979 Heritage Village, Apt. B, Southbury, CT, 06488 **Website:** http://www.gregoryjustwismar.com

John Wittemyer

Title: Lawyer **Industry:** Law and Legal Services **Company Name:** Moses, Wittemyer, Harrison & Woodruff, PC **Date of Birth:** 12/19/1939 **Place of Birth:** Boulder **State:** CO **Parents:** Leonard Wittemyer; Beatrice Augusta (Dickhut) Wittemyer **Marital Status:** Married **Spouse Name:** Nancy Jean Vincent (6/6/1964) **Children:** Jon Vincent; Christopher Glen; Luke Leonard **Education:** LLB, University of Colorado (1965); BS in Business, University of Colorado (1962); BSCE, University of Colorado (1962) **Career:** Partner, Moses, Wittemyer, Harrison & Woodruff, PC, Boulder (1973-Present); General Counsel, Platte River Power Authority (1975-2002); Chairman, Board of Directors, Crowley County Land and Development Company Subsidiary, Aetna Casualty and Surety Company, Ordway, CO (1970-1975); Chief Executive Officer, Crowley County Land and Development Company Subsidiary, Aetna Casualty and Surety Company, Ordway, CO (1970-1975); Private Practice, Boulder (1967-1973); District Attorney, First Judicial District, Alaska (1966-1967); Law Clerk, U.S. Supreme Court, Alaska (1965) **Membership:** American Bar Association; Colorado Cattlemen's Association; Boulder Bar Association; Colorado Bar Association; Country Club **Bar Admissions:** Alaska State Bar (1965); Colorado State Bar (1965) **Political Affiliations:** Republican **Religion:** Methodist **Shipping Address:** P.O. Box 4575, Boulder, CO, 80306

Irna Lynn Wolf, PhD, ABPP

Title: Psychologist **Industry:** Social Work **Date of Birth:** 08/30/1949 **Country of Origin:** South Africa **Parents:** John Wolf; Tolsa Wolf **Marital Status:** Married **Spouse Name:** Raymond Shamos (2/22/1976) **Children:** Lorin; Richard; Ilan; Troy **Education:** Postdoctoral Studies in Clinical Neuropsychology, Barrow Neurological Institute, Dignity Health, Phoenix, AZ (1997); Diplomate, Doctoral Specialty Program in School Psychology, Arizona State University, Tempe, AZ (1993-1995); PhD in Cognitive Systems and Behavioral Neuroscience, Department of Psychology, Arizona State University, Tempe, AZ (1991); MA in Psychology, Center for Visual Science, Affiliate Center for Brain Research, University of Rochester, Rochester, NY (1983); MFA, Department of Fine Arts, University of the Witwatersrand, Johannesburg, South Africa (1976); BFA, Department of Fine Arts, University of the Witwatersrand, Johannesburg, South Africa (1970) **Certifications:** Licensed, Professional Practice of Psychology in Arizona, Arizona State Board of Psychologist Examiners; Specialty Board Certification in School Psychology, American Board of Professional Psychology; Nationally Certified School Psychologist, National Association of School Psychologists; Certified School Psychologist, Arizona Department of Education; Diplomate, American Board of Forensic Examiners; Fellow of the College, American College of Forensic Examiners **Career:** Private Practice, Phoenix, AZ (1997-Present); Independent Contracted School Psychologist, Arizona; Independent Consultant, Children's Neuropsychological Assessment and Educational Planning CNAEPP Program, Barrow Neurological Institute, Dignity Health, Phoenix, AZ; Independent Research; Research Teaching Assistant, Arizona State University, Tempe, AZ; Director, Arizona Psychological Diagnostics, Phoenix, AZ; Specialist in Cognitive Neuropsychology and School Psychology **Career Related:** Lecturer in Field, Human Information Processing; Consultant, Human Information Processing; Outstanding Service, American Board of School Psychology **Civic:** Leadership and Community Service, Phoenix, AZ; Leadership and Community Service, Scottsdale, AZ **Creative Works:** Author, "A Mathematical Predictive System for the Oblique Effect," Arizona State University, Tempe, AZ; Author, "Some Implications of the Usage of the Dot, with Reference to the Work of Seurat and Art of the Present Time," University of the Witwatersrand, Johannesburg, South Africa; Contributor, Abstracts and Articles, Professional Journals; Contributor, Poster Presentations; Contributor, Lectures; Contributor, Scientific Paper Presentations **Awards:** Distinguished Service Award, American Board of School Psychology; Certificate of Appreciation, Paradise Valley Police Department; The Honor Society of Phi Kappa Phi, Arizona State University, Tempe, AZ; Graduate Student Researcher Award, Graduate College Student Advisory Board, Arizona State University, Tempe, AZ **Membership:** American Board of Professional Psychology; Examiner, SP: Specialty Board, American Board of Professional Psychology; Work Sample Reviewer, SP; Director and AASP Liaison, SP; Director of Mentoring, Specialty Academy American Board of Professional Psychology; Treasurer, Specialty Academy American Board of Professional Psychology; American Psychological Association; American Psychological Society; National Association of School Psychologists; Western Psychological Association; Arizona Psychological Association; Arizona State University Chapter, The Honor Society of Phi Kappa Phi **Marquis Who's Who Honors:** Albert Nelson Marquis Lifetime Achievement Award (2017) **Hobbies:** Painting; Drawing; Hiking; Swimming **Political Affiliations:** Republican **Shipping Address:** 4516 E Onyx Avenue, Phoenix, AZ, 85028

James Bok Wong, PhD

Title: Economics and Operations Analyst (Retired) **Industry:** Financial Services **Company Name:** James B. Wong Associates, Inc. **Date of Birth:** 12/09/1922 **Place of Birth:** Canton **Country of Origin:** China **Parents:** Gen Ham Wong; Chen (Yee) Wong **Marital Status:** Married **Spouse Name:** Betty Yeow (5/25/2002); Wai Ping Lim (8/3/1946, Deceased) **Children:** John; Jane Doris; Julia Ann **Education:** PhD, University of Illinois (1954); MS, University of Illinois (1951); BS in Chemical Engineering, University of Maryland, Summa Cum Laude (1950); BS in Agriculture, University of Maryland, Summa Cum Laude (1949) **Career:** Retired (1990); President, James B. Wong Associates, Inc., Los Angeles, CA (1981-1990); Director of International Technologies, Chemical Plastics Group, Dart Industries, Inc., Los Angeles, CA (1978-1981); Director of Economics and Operations Analysis, Chemical Plastics Group, Dart Industries, Inc., Los Angeles, CA (1972-1978); Chief Economist, Chemical Plastics Group, Dart Industries, Inc., Los Angeles, CA (1967-1972); Manager of Long Range Planning and Economics, Chemical Plastics Group, Dart Industries, Inc., Los Angeles, CA (1967); Supervisor of Planning and Economics, Chemical Plastics Group, Dart Industries, Inc., Los Angeles, CA (1966-1967); Senior Planning Engineer, Chemical Plastics Group, Dart Industries, Inc., Los Angeles, CA (1961-1966); Principal Planning Engineer, Chemical Plastics Group, Dart Industries, Inc., Los Angeles, CA (1961-1966); Process Design Engineer, Shell Development Company, Emeryville, CA (1955-1961); Research Engineer, Shell Development Company, Emeryville, CA (1955-1961); Chemical Engineer, Standard Oil of Indiana, Whiting, IN (1953-1955); Research Assistant, University of Illinois (1950-1953) **Career Related:** Chairman, Board of Directors, United Pacific Bank (1988-Present); Technical Consultant, Various Corporations **Civic:** Foundation Member, Asian American Education Commission (1971-1981); Grand Marshall, Chinese American Citizens Alliance; President, Board of Directors, Chinese American Citizens Alliance **Military Service:** Flying Tigers, United States Air Force, China, Burma, India, World War II (1943-1946) **Creative Works:** Author, "Silk Tiger" (2008); Author, "Jade Eagle" (2000); Contributor, Articles to Professional Journals **Awards:** History Makers Leadership Award, Museum of Chinese in America (MOCA) (2014); Named, Executive Order, Commodores (1982); Los Angeles Outstanding Volunteer Service Award (1977) **Membership:** Vice Commander, Veterans of Foreign Wars (1959); American Chemical Society; American Institute of Chemical Engineers; Sigma Xi, The Scientific Research Honor Society; The Tau Beta Pi Association, Inc.; The Honor Society of Phi Kappa Phi; Pi Mu Epsilon; Phi Lambda Upsilon; Phi Eta Sigma **Marquis Who's Who Honors:** Albert Nelson Marquis Lifetime Achievement Award (2017) **Why did you become involved in your profession or industry:** Dr. Wong became involved in his profession because Dart Industries was heavily into chemicals and plastic and needed a chief economist for the company because the chemical plastics was a major operation and they already sold the Rexall chain. DuPont had an economist and Union Carbon had a chief economist, so they had him become the chief economist because he knew chemical and plastics and it would be easy for him. They sent Dr. Wong to Harvard Business School and UCLA, and when he had enough education of economics, he assumed the role of chief economist for the chemical and plastics group, which was the largest group at Dart Industries. **Shipping Address:** 3843 Carnavon Way, Los Angeles, CA, 90027

Robert C.C. Wood

Title: Lawyer, Real Estate Developer **Industry:** Law and Legal Services **Date of Birth:** 04/08/1956 **Place of Birth:** Chicago **State:** IL **Parents:** Roy Edward Wood; Mildred Lucille (Jones) Wood **Marital Status:** Single **Spouse Name:** Jennifer Jo Briggs (10/1984) **Children:** Jacqueline Jones; Reagan Keith **Education:** JD, Dedman School of Law, Southern Methodist University (1982); BBA in Real Estate, Southern Methodist University (1979); BA in History, Southern Methodist University (1979) **Career:** Real Estate Investor and Developer, Dallas, TX (1998-Present); Private Practice, Dallas, TX (1995-Present); Partner, Welch & Wood Attorneys and Y2K Consultant, Dallas, TX (1998-2000); Principal, Robert Wood Consultants, Dallas, TX (1981-1984); Researcher, Acquisitions Officer, Amstar Financial Services, Inc., Dallas, TX (1979-1980); Appraiser, McClellan-Massey, Dallas, TX (1977-1979); Founder, Partner, Law Offices of Robert C.C. Wood **Career Related:** Executive Vice President, General Counsel, Rushmore Investment Advisors, Plano, TX (2002-2006); Vice President, National Consulting Coordinator, Financial Advisors Council, Callan Associates Inc., San Francisco, CA (1994-1995); Chairman, Advisory Council on Development, MediSend International (1991); Senior Pension Consultant Principal, Eppler, Guerin & Turner (1988-1993); National Accountants Manager, Lomas & Nettleton Company, Dallas, TX (1987-1988); General Counsel, Diversified Benefit Services, Inc., Dallas, TX (1984-1986); Consultant, Plan Marketing Companies (1983-1984); Lawyer, Private Practice, Dallas, TX (1983-1984) **Civic:** Chairman, Corporate Development Board, American Cancer Society, Inc. (1989-1995); Medisend Advisory Committee (1988-1994); Crusade Committee, American Cancer Society, Inc. (1987-1988); Special Events Committee, American Cancer Society, Inc. (1986-1987); Board of Directors, Dallas Unit, American Cancer Society, Inc. (1982-1987) **Creative Works:** Author, "Y2K - The Year 2000 Issue: How Y2K Affects the Markets" (1998); Author, "After the Congress Vote: How the Managers See Things Now" (1993); Author, "Electionomics: How the Money Managers View the Election" (1992); Member, Southern Methodist University Law Review (1981-1982); Contributor, Articles, Professional Publications; Rated, A/V Preeminent, Martindale-Hubbell **Awards:** Selected, Super Lawyers Texas, Robert C.C. Wood General Litigation, Business Litigation (2013-2018); American Jurisprudence Award Property Law (1978) **Membership:** State Bar of Texas; Philadelphia Bar Association; Phi Gamma Delta **Bar Admissions:** State of Texas (1983) **Marquis Who's Who Honors:** Albert Nelson Marquis Lifetime Achievement Award (2017); Distinguished Humanitarian (2017) **To what do you attribute your success:** Mr. Wood attributes his success to grace, hard work, and a lot of helpful people who have been willing to share their time and wisdom with him over the years. **Why did you become involved in your profession or industry:** Since Mr. Wood was four years old, he wanted to be lawyer. Since childhood, he has viewed lawyers as helpful to society. **What do you consider to be the highlight of your career:** During his career, Mr. Wood had one case that stood out. He was helping a family who was going through a divorce, and the child was having issues. There was a custody battle and he was up against 19 sets of lawyers, but he was able to win the case. Now, the child is thriving. **Hobbies:** Golf; Skiing; Tennis; Bicycling **Shipping Address:** 6688 N Central Expressway, Suite 1000, Law Offices of Robert CC Wood, Dallas, TX, 75206 **Website:** http://www.robert-wood.net

Thomas Edwin Woodhouse

Title: Co-Trustee **Industry:** Law and Legal Services **Company Name:** RFCRG Trust, RFTA Trust **Date of Birth:** 04/30/1940 **Place of Birth:** Cedar Rapids **State:** IA **Parents:** Keith Wallace Woodhouse; Elinor Julia (Cherny) Woodhouse **Marital Status:** Married **Spouse Name:** Kiyoko Fujiie (5/29/1965) **Children:** Miya; Keith; Leighton **Education:** JD, Harvard University (1965); AB, Amherst College, Cum Laude (1962) **Career:** Co-Trustee, RFCRG Trust (2014-Present); Co-Trustee, Ronald Family Trust A (2009-Present); Trust Administrator, Gordon P. Getty Family Trust (1994-2008); Sole Practice, Berkeley, CA (1990-2001); Trust Administrator, Ronald Family Trust A (1989-2008); Lasky, Haas, Cohler & Munter, San Francisco, CA (1982-1990); Assistant General Counsel, Natomas Co., San Francisco, CA (1975-1981); Associate, Graham & James LLP, San Francisco, CA (1974-1975); Partner, Woodhouse Lee & Davis, Singapore (1972-1974); Counsel, Private Investment Co. for Asia S.A., Tokyo, Japan (1969-1972); Attorney, United States Agency for International Development, Washington, DC (1968-1969); Adviser, United States Agency for International Development, Washington, DC (1968-1969); Associate, Chadbourne, Parke, Whiteside & Wolff, New York, NY (1965-1968) **Career Related:** CEO, Vallejo Investments Inc. (1997-2009); Of Counsel, Wilson, Sonsini, Goodrich & Rosati, Palo Alto, CA (1992-1995); Berkeley Police Reserve (1986-2011); President, Literature Quarterly, Zyazzyva (1985-1987); Chairman, Police Review Committee of Berkeley, Berkeley, CA (1980-1984); Board of Directors, Friends Association of Services for the Elderly (1979-1984); Clerk, Financial Committee, American Friends Service Committee, California (1979-1983); Instructor, Law Faculty, University of Singapore (1972-1974); Fellow, American Bar Foundation **Civic:** Chairman, Council of Friends, The Bancroft Library, University of California, Berkeley (2018-Present); Trustee, Council of Friends, The Bancroft Library, University of California, Berkeley (2014-Present); Treasurer, The Book Club of California (2008-2010); Friends of the Library, Amherst College (2005-2014); Mark Twain Luncheon Club (2002-2011); Chairman, Council of Friends, The Bancroft Library, University of California, Berkeley (2002-2003); Trustee, Dominican School of Philosophy & Theology (1998-2003); Trustee, Council of Friends, The Bancroft Library, University of California, Berkeley (1997-2002); Friends of the Library, Amherst College (1990-1997); Trustee, Freedom from Hunger (1989-1999) **Military Service:** U.S. Army (1958) **Awards:** A/V Ranking, Martindale-Hubbell **Membership:** Life Member, American Bar Foundation; The State Bar of California; Association Internationale de Bibliophilie; Harvard Club of New York; The University Club of San Francisco; The Book Club of California; The Roxburghe Club; The Grolier Club of New York; Faculty Club, University of California, Berkeley; Berkeley Country Club; Pacific-Union Club **Bar Admissions:** State of California (1975); U.S. Supreme Court (1969); State of New York (1966) **Marquis Who's Who Honors:** Albert Nelson Marquis Lifetime Achievement Award (2017); Distinguished Humanitarian (2017) **Political Affiliations:** Republican **Religion:** Roman Catholic **Shipping Address:** 1800 San Antonio Avenue, Berkeley, CA, 94707

Thomas Smith Woods

Title: Chief Executive Officer, Management Consultant **Industry:** Consulting **Company Name:** Tom Woods, Inc. **Date of Birth:** 05/26/1928 **Place of Birth:** Boston **State:** MA **Parents:** Thomas Smith Woods; Lucy (Harding) Woods **Marital Status:** Widowed **Spouse Name:** Patricia (7/21/1956, Deceased) **Children:** Brooke; Lawrence; David **Education:** MBA, Graduate School of Business Administration, Harvard University (1952); AB, Harvard University (1950) **Certifications:** Certified Management Consultant **Career:** President, Tom Woods, Inc., Winnetka, IL (1985-Present) Vice President, Reddy, Traver & Woods, Inc., Winnetka, IL (1980-1985); Vice President, Midwest Region, Rath & Strong, Inc., Lexington, MA (1967-1980); Manager, Midwest Region, Rath & Strong, Inc., Lexington, MA (1967-1980); Production Manager, Goodyear Tire & Rubber Co., Akron, Ohio (1955-1967); Research Assistant, Harvard Business School, Boston, MA (1953-1954) **Career Related:** Faculty Member, Harvard Business School; Teacher, Quality Assurance Courses, University of Connecticut; Teacher, Quality Assurance Courses, University of Akron; Teacher, Quality Assurance Courses, Motorola University **Civic:** Alzheimer's Foundation; Veterans of Foreign Wars **Military Service:** Lieutenant, United States Air Force (1952-1955) **Membership:** American Society for Quality Control; Air Force Association **To what do you attribute your success:** He attributes his success to luck, and the good fortune to have mentors like Dorian Shanin, from whom he learned a highly specialized technique called variation research. **Why did you become involved in your profession or industry:** He became involved in his profession while in the United States Air Force. There, he was working on the quality and reliability of jet and reciprocating engines. **What do you consider to be the highlight of your career:** The highlight of his career was moving from manufacturing to management consulting while working with Samsung in Seoul, Korea. He took his children and his wife with him, and when he finished his week with Samsung, they flew over the Himalayas and spent time in Tibet. **Where will you be in five years:** In five years, Mr. Woods hopes to continue to give back to others. **Hobbies:** Photography; Travel **Political Affiliations:** Republican **Religion:** Episcopalian **Shipping Address:** 501 Tidepointe Way, Apt 5202, Hilton Head Island, SC, 29928

Marlene Erdley Woodson-Howard

Title: Former State Senator **Industry:** Education/Educational Services **Company Name:** Joy of Watercolor, Inc. **Date of Birth:** 03/08/1937 **Place of Birth:** Ford City **State:** PA **Parents:** James Erdley; Susie (Lettrich) Erdley **Marital Status:** Widowed **Spouse Name:** Francis M. Howard (Deceased) **Children:** George Woodson; Bert Woodson; Robert Woodson; Daniel Woodson; David Woodson **Education:** EdD, Nova University (1981); MA, University of South Florida (1968); BS, Indiana University of Pennsylvania (1958) **Career:** President, Joy of Watercolor, Inc. (2016-2018); President, Pegasus Enterprises Inc. (1986-2000); Senator, State of Florida (1986-1990); Executive Director, Manatee Community College Foundation (1982-1986); Director, Institute of Advancement, Manatee Community College (Now State College of Florida, Manatee-Sarasota) (1982-1986); Professor of Mathematics, Manatee Community College (1970-1982) **Civic:** Candidate, Governor of Florida (1990); Former President, New College Library Association; Former President, Manatee Symphony; Former President, Sarasota Kiwanis; Board of Directors, Manatee Red Cross; Board of Directors, Manatee Players, Inc.; Vice President, Trustee, Florida Kiwanis Foundation **Membership:** Bradenton Section, Kiwanis International; ArtCenter Manatee; Florida Watercolor Society; Anna Maria Artist Guild, Art Center Sarasota, Board Member, Just for Girls, Bradenton **Marquis Who's Who Honors:** Albert Nelson Marquis Lifetime Achievement Award (2017) **To what do you attribute your success:** She attributes her success to hard work, a loving family, and good friends. **Why did you become involved in your profession or industry:** Ms. Woodson-Howard was granted a scholarship at a nearby teachers college, which brought her into teaching. Fundraising at the Manatee Community College Foundation was her first entry into the world of business and the community encouraged her to pursue a political career. **What do you consider to be the highlight of your career:** She considers the highlights of her career to be her election as the first female president of Sarasota Kiwanis in 78 years, and being the first woman (and only woman) elected to the Florida Senate from her district. **Where will you be in five years:** In the past six years, Ms. Woodson-Howard has started a new life as an artist and she has fallen in love with it. After submitting her work to art shows and uploading them as images to tablets, prints for fabric pillows, silk scarves, and shirts, her son, and granddaughter are helping her start an decor and apparel business. **Hobbies:** Painting **Political Affiliations:** Republican **Religion:** Roman Catholic **Shipping Address:** 12 Tidy Island Blvd., Bradenton, FL, 34210 **Website:** http://joyofwatercolor.com

Lester Ray Woodward

Title: Lawyer **Industry:** Law and Legal Services **Company Name:** Davis Graham & Stubbs LLP **Date of Birth:** 05/24/1932 **Place of Birth:** Lincoln **State:** NE **Parents:** Wendell Smith Woodward; Mary Elizabeth (Theobald) Woodward **Marital Status:** Married **Spouse Name:** Marianne Martinson (12/27/1958) **Children:** Victoria L. Woodward Eisele; Richard T.; David M.; Andrew E. **Education:** Honorary LLD, Bethany College (1974); LLB, Harvard University (1957); BSBA, University of Nebraska (1953) **Career:** Senior Counsel, Davis Graham & Stubbs, Denver, CO (2004-Present); Partner, Davis Graham & Stubbs, Denver, CO (1962-2004); Associate, Davis Graham & Stubbs, Denver, CO (1960-1962, 1957-1959) **Career Related:** Member, Board of Directors, International Development Enterprises (2006-2012); Teaching Fellow, Harvard Law School, Harvard University (1959-1960) **Civic:** President, Board of Education, Denver Public Schools (2003-2005); Member, Board of Education, Denver Public Schools (1999-2005); Chairman, Bethany College, Lindsborg, KS (1989-1992); Chairman, Public Education & Business Coalition, Denver, CO (1988-1989); Member, Board of Directors, Bethany College, Lindsborg, KS (1987-1995); Member, Board of Directors, Public Education & Business Coalition, Denver, CO (1985-1992); Chairman, Colorado Department of Higher Education, Denver, CO (1979-1981); Member, Colorado Department of Higher Education, Denver, CO (1977-1986); Member, Board of Directors, Bethany College, Lindsborg, KS (1966-1974) **Membership:** ABA; Colorado Bar Association; The American Law Institute **Bar Admissions:** Colorado (1957) **Marquis Who's Who Honors:** Albert Nelson Marquis Lifetime Achievement Award (2017) **Hobbies:** Skiing; Watching Denver Broncos football **Political Affiliations:** Republican **Religion:** Lutheran **Business Address:** 1550 17th St., Ste. 500, Denver, CO, 80202 **Shipping Address:** 111 N Emerson St., Apt 864, Denver, CO, 80218 **Website:** http://www.lesterwoodward.com

Carol Clayman Woody, PhD

Title: Researcher, Cyber Security Technical Manager **Industry:** Research **Company Name:** Carnegie Mellon University **Date of Birth:** 05/20/1949 **Place of Birth:** Bristol **State:** VA **Parents:** George Neal Clayman; Ida Mae Clayman **Marital Status:** Married **Spouse Name:** Robert William Woody (8/19/1972) **Education:** PhD in Information Systems, Nova Southeastern University (2004); MBA, Wake Forest University, with Distinction (1979); BS in Mathematics, College of William and Mary (1971) **Career:** Technical Manager of Cyber Security Engineering, Software Engineering Institute, Carnegie Mellon University (2010-Present); Senior Member, Technology Staff, Software Engineering Institute, Carnegie Mellon University (2001-Present); Co-owner, Sign of the Sycamore, Antiques (1975-2014); Consultant, Imagework Technologies Corporation, White Plains, NY (1998-2001); Career Project Manager, Yale University, New Haven, CT (1984-1997); Finance Design Supervisor, Business Systems, Lycoming Division, AVCO Industries, Stratford, CT (1982-1983); Supervisor, Programming and Technical Services, J.E. Baker Company, York, PA (1979-1982); Programmer, Blue Bell, Inc., Greensboro, NC (1975-1979); Analyst, Technology Coordinator, Blue Bell, Inc., Greensboro, NC (1975-1979); Systems Engineer, Citizens Fidelity Bank and Trust Company, Louisville, KY (1972-1975); Programmer Trainee, General Services Administration (1971-1972) **Career Related:** Executive Partner, Mason Business School, College of William and Mary (2016-Present); Invited Speaker, Raymond A. Mason School of Business, College of William and Mary (2016-2018, 1994); Invited Speaker, CISO Executive Program CMU Heinz School (2016-2017); Invited Speaker, Annual Security Applications Conference (ACSAC) (2015, 2012); Invited Speaker, Military Operations Research Society (MORS) (2007-2013); IEEE Distinguished Visitor (2004-2007); Invited Speaker, Consortium for School Networking, K-12 Networking Conference (CoSN) (2003, 2004); Aion Expert, Systems National Conference (1990); Speaker, National Fuse Conference (1989); Member, Data Processing Standards Board (1977); CICS/VS Advisory Council (1975) **Civic:** Williamsburg Coral Guild (2016-Present); Pittsburgh Concert Coral (2002-2015) **Creative Works:** Co-author, "Engineering Emergence: A Modeling and Simulation Approach," CRC Press (2018); Co-author, "Cyber Security Engineering: A Foundation for Operational Security," Addison-Wesely Professional (2016); Co-author, "Software Assurance, Computing Handbook Set, Chapman & Hall/CRC," Taylor & Francis Group (2012); Author, "Applying Security Risk Management to Internet Connectivity: K-12 Schools and School Districts," Lambert Academic Publishing (2009); Author, Various Manuals; Contributor, Articles, Professional Journals; Contributor, Chapters to Handbooks **Awards:** Honoree, Best Conference Paper, IEEE International Systems Conference (2009); Outstanding Alumni Award, Nova Southeastern University (2007); Grantee, Stephen Bufton Memorial Educational Foundation (1978-1979); Fellowship, IBM (1978); Merit Award, American Business Woman's Association (1978) **Membership:** SEI Representative, Object Management Group Software Assurance Task Force (2009-Present); Association for Computing Machinery (1997-Present); Regional Chairman, Delta Omicron (2006-2016); AIAA (2009-2013); Elected Senior Member, The Association for Computing Machinery (2009); Elected Senior Member, IEEE (2009); Distinguished Speaker, IEEE (2005-2007); Section Editor, IEEE (2003-2006); Upsilon Pi Chapter, The International Honorary Society for Computer Science, Nova Southeastern University (2003); The Association for Image Information Management (1999-2002); Project Management Institute (1996-2003); Shoreline Network Founder, NAFE (1993-1998); The Association for System Management (1990-1995); Regional Chairman, Delta Omicron (1979-1982); Chapter Vice President, ABWA Management, LLC (1978-1979); Alumni President, Delta Omicron (1973-1975) **Marquis Who's Who Honors:** Albert Nelson Marquis Lifetime Achievement Award (2017) **Hobbies:** Reading; Travel; Writing **Political Affiliations:** Republican **Religion:** Presbyterian **Shipping Address:** 105 Jones Mill Ln., Williamsburg, VA, 23185

Kenneth Rau Woolling

Title: Cardiovascular Disease Internist **Industry:** Medicine & Health Care **Date of Birth:** 03/06/1918 **Place of Birth:** Indianapolis **State:** IN **Year of Passing:** 2017-04-16 **Parents:** Kenneth Kaarta Woolling; Marie May Rau Woolling **Marital Status:** Married **Spouse Name:** Catherine Margaret McColl (3/20/1948) **Children:** Kenneth Rau Woolling, Jr.; Mary Catherine Woolling **Education:** MS in Medicine, Mayo Clinic School of Medicine, University of Minnesota (1951); Fellow, First Assistant, Internal Medicine, Mayo Clinic, Mayo Foundation for Medical Education and Research (MFMER), Rochester, MN (1948-1952); Resident, Internal Medicine, Marion County General Hospital (Now Eskenazi Health) (1947); Internship, Indianapolis City Hospital (Now Eskenazi Health) (1943-1944); MD, Indiana University School of Medicine (1943); Postgraduate Coursework, Harvard University (1939-1940); BA, Butler University, Magna Cum Laude (1939) **Certifications:** Diplomate, National Board of Medical Examiners; Diplomate, American Board of Internal Medicine; Diplomate, American Board of Cardiovascular Disease **Career:** Member, Medical Staff, Teacher Staff, Postgraduate Medical Education, Methodist Hospital (Now Indiana University Health Methodist Hospital, IU Health), Indianapolis, IN (1952-Present); Private Practice, Internal Medicine and Cardiovascular Diseases, Indianapolis, IN (1952-Present); Member, Medical Staff, Teaching Staff, Postgraduate Medical Education, Marion County General Hospital (Now Eskenazi Health), Indianapolis, IN (1952-Present); Founder and Director, Vascular Laboratory, Methodist Hospital, (Now Indiana University Health Methodist Hospital, IU Health) (1970-1973); Founder and Director, Peripheral Vascular Diseases Clinic, Methodist Hospital (Now Indiana University Health Methodist Hospital, IU Health) (1967-1972); Founder and Director, Peripheral Vascular Diseases Clinic, Indianapolis City and Marion County General Hospital (Now Eskenazi Health), Indianapolis, IN (1952-1968) **Career Related:** Member, Medical Advisory Committee, Butler University (1956-Present); Member, Medical Staff, St. Vincent Hospital (1952-Present); Member, Medical Staff, St. Francis Hospital (1952-Present); Member, Medical Staff, Winona Memorial Hospital (1952-Present); Charter Member, Medical Staff, Community Hospital, Indianapolis, IN (1952-Present) **Military Service:** Captain, Medical Corps, U.S. Army (1944-1946) **Creative Works:** Contributor, Scientific Articles, Professional Journals (1950-Present); Author, "Recollections of a Mayo Clinic Fellowship at Mid-Twentieth Century, 1948-1952" (2010) **Awards:** 50-Year Award, American Medical Association (1993); 50-Year Award, Freemasons (1989); 50-Year Award, Phi Delta Theta Fraternity (1985) **Membership:** Governor, State of Indiana, American Society of Angiology (1979-1980); Fellow, American College of Physicians; Fellow, American College of Chest Physicians; Council on Cardiology, American Heart Association, Inc.; American Medical Association; Sons of the American Revolution; International Union of Angiology; American Society of Internal Medicine; American Diabetes Association; Indiana State Medical Association (ISMA); Indiana American Diabetes Association; American Federation for Medical Research; The New York Academy of Medicine; North Central Clinical Society; Mayo Cardiovascular Society, Mayo Clinic; Indiana Historical Society; Reserve Officers Association of the United States; Indianapolis Medical Society; The American Legion; Shriners International; Scottish Rite and Mystic Tie Lodge, Masons; Contemporary Club of Indianapolis; Indianapolis Athletic Club; The Columbia University Club; Highlands Country Club; Phi Delta Theta Fraternity; Phi Kappa Phi; Phi Chi Medical Fraternity **Marquis Who's Who Honors:** Albert Nelson Marquis Lifetime Achievement Award (2017) **Religion:** Presbyterian **Shipping Address:** PO Box 80192, Indianapolis, IN, 46280

Robert L. Worthington-Kirsch

Title: Director of Research, Medical Director **Industry:** Medicine & Health Care **Company Name:** Vein Clinics of America **Date of Birth:** 01/22/1960 **Place of Birth:** Worcester **State:** MA **Marital Status:** Married **Spouse Name:** Kimberly Worthington-Kirsch (1982) **Education:** Residency in Diagnostic Radiology, Mercy Catholic Medical Center, Mercy Health System (1990); MD, University of Massachusetts Medical School, Worcester, MA (1986); BS, Massachusetts Institute of Technology (1981); High School Diploma, Boston Latin School (1977) **Certifications:** Registered Physician in Vascular Interpretation, American Registry of Diagnostic Medical Sonographers (2006-Present); Registered Vascular Technologist, American Registry of Diagnostic Medical Sonographers (2005-Present); Certificate, American Board of Venous and Lymphatic Medicine (2012); Unrestricted Medical License, State of Florida (2011-2015); Unrestricted Medical License, State of North Carolina (2011-2012); Unrestricted Medical License, District of Columbia (2011); Unrestricted Medical License, State of New Jersey (2010); Unrestricted Medical License, State of Washington (2010-2017); Unrestricted Medical License, State of California (2010-2016); Unrestricted Medical License, State of Georgia (2010-2014); Unrestricted Medical License, State of Maryland (2007); Diplomate in Diagnostic Radiology with Added Qualifications in Vascular and Interventional Radiology, American Board of Radiology (1995); Diplomate in Diagnostic Radiology, American Board of Radiology (1990); Unrestricted Medical License, Commonwealth of Pennsylvania (1987); Certificate, National Board of Medical Examiners (1987) **Career:** Medical Director for Pennsylvania, Vein Clinics of America (2016-Present); Director of Research, Vein Clinics of America (2015-Present); Network Physician, Vein Clinics of America (2012-Present); Medical Director, Vascular Access Centers, Philadelphia, PA (2010-2012); Section Head, Interventional Radiology, Pottstown Memorial Medical Center, Pottstown, PA (2008-2010); Staff Radiologist, Montgomery Radiology Associates, Pottstown, PA (2007-2008); Independent Practice, Image Guided Surgery Associates, PC, Philadelphia, PA (2002-2007); Affiliate, Interventional Radiology Practice, Roxborough Memorial Hospital, Philadelphia, PA (1997-2002); Staff Radiologist, Delaware Valley Imaging, Ltd, Bala Cynwyd, PA (1995-2002) **Career Related:** Consultant, Syntactx (2015-Present); Consultant, Prairie Education & Research Cooperative (2013-Present); Elected Fellow, American College of Phlebology (2014); Consultant, Veniti (2012-2013); Consultant, Physician Advisory Board, BTG International Ltd. (2012); Consultant, ProVation Medical (2007-2008); Consultant, Conceptus (2006-2007); Elected Fellow, Cardiovascular and Interventional Radiological Society of Europe (2006); Consultant, BioCompatibles, BTG International Ltd. (2004-2011); Consultant, Vascular Solutions, Inc. (2004-2010); Consultant, Terumo Medical Corporation (2004-2010); Consultant, Implanon Radiology Advisory Board, Organon Pharmaceuticals USA, Inc. (2004-2010); Consultant, BioCure (2002-2005); Elected Fellow, Society of Cardiovascular & Interventional Radiology (Now Society of Interventional Radiology) (2001); Consultant, Biosphere Medical, Inc. (1999-2010); Consultant, Boston Scientific Corporation (1998-2004); Affiliate, GHS - City Avenue Hospital, Philadelphia, PA (1995-1997); Affiliate, Delaware Valley Imaging, Ltd, Bala Cynwyd, PA (1995); Associate Attending Staff, Mercy Radiology Associates, Darby, PA (1991-1994); Junior Staff, Wister Radiology, Philadelphia, PA (1990-1991); Chief Resident, Mercy Catholic Medical Center, Darby, PA (1989-1990); Nursing Assistant, American Nurse, Inc., Boston, MA (1981); Orderly, Beth Israel Hospital, Boston, MA (1980-1981); Switchboard Operator, Massachusetts Institute of Technology Telecommunications, Massachusetts Institute of Technology, Cambridge, MA (1979); Immunology Research Assistant, Massachusetts Institute of Technology, Cambridge, MA (1978-1980); Inspector, Electronics Production Quality Control, Analogic Corporation, Wakefield, MA (1978); Scientific Presenter; Invited Lecturer; Fellow, Society of Interventional Radiology **Civic:** Mohel, Congregation Beth Yeshua, Philadelphia, PA (1983-Present) **Creative Works:** Contributor, Articles, Professional Journals; Contributor, Chapters to Books **Awards:** Editor's Recognition Award for Distinction in Reviewing, CardioVascular and Interventional Radiology (2007); Distinguished Reviewer Award, Journal of Vascular & International Radiology (2002-2004); Distinguished Faculty Award, Society of Interventional Radiology **Membership:** Chairman, CME Committee, American College of Phlebology; American Roentgen Ray Society; American Scientific Affiliation; Cardiovascular and Interventional Radiological Society of Europe; Christian Medical & Dental Association; Pennsylvania Radiological Society; Philadelphia Angiography and Interventional Radiology Society **Religion:** Jewish **Shipping Address:** 676 E Swedesford Road, Suite 170, Vein Clinics of America, Wayne, PA, 19087

Midori Yamanouchi

Title: Social Sciences Educator (Retired) **Industry:** Education/Educational Services **Date of Birth:** 01/08/1928 **Place of Birth:** Osaka **Country of Origin:** Japan **Parents:** Shin'ichi Yamanouchi; Fumiko (Urai) Yamanouchi **Spouse Name:** Edward J. Rynn (10/10/1975, Deceased 7/29/1987) **Education:** MA in Library Science, University of Michigan (1959); PhD, Michigan State University (1972); MA, Michigan State University (1958); AB, Sophia University International Division (1956); Student, University of Tampa (1950-1951); Diploma, Tokyo Kasai University (1948) **Career:** Vice President, Academy of Affairs, Lackawanna College (2006-2008); Professor, University of Scranton, Pennsylvania (1975-2006); Visiting Professor, Frostburg State University (1974-1975); Associate Professor, Livingston College, Salisbury, NC (1972-1974); Assistant Professor, Sociology and Anthropology, Fisk University, Nashville, TN (1970-1972); Assistant Professor, Sociology and Anthropology, Marshall University, Huntington, WV (1967-1970); Assistant Director, R&D, Sperry & Hutchinson Company, New York City, NY (1963-1964); Librarian, Bibliographer, Michigan State University (1964-1967); Librarian, Bibliographer, Michigan State University (1959-1963); Chief Research Associate, International Division, Sophia University, Tokyo, Japan (1952-1956) **Civic:** Board Member, Northeastern Pennsylvania Philharmonic (2014-Present); Board Member, Everhart Museum (2003-Present); Board Member, Northeastern Pennsylvania Philharmonic (2006-2013); Trustee, Lackawanna College (2002-2006); Member, Advisory Board, Diversity Institute, College of Misericordia, Dallas, PA (1999-2009); Member, Advisory Board, Northeastern Intermediate Unit School Board, Scranton, PA (1998-2008); Trustee, Tokyo Kasei University (1997-2006); Member, President Council, Cedar Crest College (1996-2002); Trustee, Lackawanna College (1995-2001); Trustee, Lacawac Sanctuary, Lake Ariel, PA (1993-2009); Member, Salem Township Library Board **Creative Works:** Translator, "In The Faraway Mountains and Rivers" (2005); Editor, "Sociological Viewpoint" (2004-2005, 1989-1991); Translator, "Listen to the Voices from the Sea" (2000); Associate Editor, Comparative Civilizations Review (1996-2001) **Awards:** Woman of the Year, International Biographical Center (2014); David Gray Award, Keystone College (2014); Honorary Professor, Karaganda Economic University, Kazakhstan (2009); Presidential Medallion, Keystone College (2009); UN Day Rinaldi Memorial Award, United Nations Association of the United States of America (2007); Educational Service Award, Wilkes Barre Board of Education, PA (2002); Seeley Service Medal, Lackawanna College (2001); Distinguished Contribution Award, International Organization for Unification of Terminological Neologisms (2000); Distinguished Sociologist Award, Pennsylvania Sociological Society (1987) **Membership:** United Nations Delegate, International Organization for Unification of Terminological Neologisms (1995-Present); Journal Editor, International Society for Comparative Study of Civilizations (1996-2001); Journal Editor, Pennsylvania Sociological Society (1996-2001); Editor, Newsletters, International Society for Comparative Study of Civilizations (1990-1993); Editor, Newsletters, Pennsylvania Sociological Society (1990-1993); President, Pennsylvania Sociological Society (1990-1991); Pennsylvania Sociological Society (1986-1989); Executive Board Member, International Society for Comparative Study of Civilizations (1978-2005); Executive Board Member, Association for General and Liberal Studies (1975-1978) **Shipping Address:** 1122 Salem Park Lane, Lake Ariel, PA, 18436

Phyllis Yampolsky

Title: Artist, Seminal Figure in Participation Arts **Industry:** Fine Art **Company Name:** The 4th Chakra Company **Place of Birth:** Philadelphia **State:** PA **Parents:** Louis Jacob Yampolsky; Bassia Yampolsky Green **Marital Status:** Married **Spouse Name:** Peter Forakis (6/12/1959, Divorced 1964) **Children:** Gia; Jozeph Peter **Education:** Student, Hans Hofmann Atelier, New York, NY (1956-1958); Student, Ecole Beaux Arts, Fontainbleau, France (1956); Student, Institute Allende, San Miguel de Allende, Mexico (1954-1955); Student, Philadelphia Museum of Art (1950-1952) **Career:** Owner, The 4th Chakra Company (2016-Present); Founder, President, Friends of McCarren Park, Inc., New York, NY (1988-Present); Co-founder, Instructor, Vermont College of Fine Arts (1981); Instructor, Vermont Community College, Springfield, VT (1979-1981); Instructor, Vermont Academy, Saxton's River, VT (1979-1981); Founder, Officer, Northeast Windham Council for the Arts, Vermont (1978-1979); Creator, Director, Portrait of Ten Towns, New York State Council on the Arts (1967-1970); First Artist-in-Residence, New York, NY (1966-1967); Founder, Director, Hall of Issues, New York, NY (1960-1961: Art Instructor, 92d Street Y, New York, NY (1958-1960); Founder, Director, Teacher, Workshop Yampolsky, New York, NY (1956-1966) **Career Related:** Presenter, Habitat II, UN Conference, Istanbul, Turkey (1996); Consultant, Organizer, Program Director, Habitat II CBO Host Committee, New York, NY (1995-1996); Panelist, Performance Artist, Arcosanti, AZ (1980-1981); Panelist, Performance Artist, Arcosanti, AZ (1977-1978); Facilitator, National Education Association (1970-1975); Writer, Director of Art Curriculum, Bennett College (1970); Writer, Director of Art Curriculum, Marylerose Academy, Albany (1969); Ontario Arts Council (1968-1970); Special Events Director, Youth Pavilion, World's Fair, San Antonio (1968); Consultant, Model Cities, Columbus, OH (1968); Creator, Director, Producer, Hoving Happenings (1966-1967); Philadelphia Bicentennial Commission; Smithsonian Institute Bicentennial Traveling Festival Kit Consultant **Civic:** President, McCarren Park Conservancy, Brooklyn, NY (1998-2007) **Creative Works:** Solo Show, CAVE Gallery, Brooklyn, NY (2000); Permanent Collection, Appeal Peace Conference, The Hague, Netherlands (1999); Solo Show, Stephen Gang Gallery, New York, NY (1999); Permanent Collection, W.A.F.E. Festival/Conference on the Environment, Brooklyn, NY (1998); Permanent Collection, March Against Cancer, Washington, DC (1998); Permanent Collection, Clinton Presidential Campaign and Inaugural Festivities (1997); Permanent Collection, Vice President Al Gore's Reinvention Revolution Conference, Washington, DC (1996-1997); Solo Show, 479 Gallery, New York, NY (1996); Permanent Collection, UN 50th Celebration, New York, NY (1995); Permanent Collection, UN Women's Conference, Beijing, China (1995); Permanent Collection, Clinton Presidential Campaign and Inaugural Festivities (1993); Solo Show, Loft Lawyers, New York, NY (1987); Solo Show, City Bank Gallery, Brooklyn, NY (1986); Solo Show, A Place Apart, New York, NY (1984); Solo Show, Marlboro College, Vermont (1981); Solo Show, Windham College, Vermont (1978); Solo Show, Stryke Gallery, New York, NY (1978); Solo Show, O.K. Harris and Susan Caldwell Galleries, New York, NY (1978); Solo Show, Graham Gallery, New York, NY (1977); Solo Show, Kulicke Gallery, New York, NY (1975); Solo Show, Walker Gallery, New York, NY (1974); Permanent Collection, American Town Hall Wall Systems, Robert Kennedy Presidential Primary (1968); Solo Show, Judson Gallery, New York, NY (1962); Solo Show, Judson Gallery, New York, NY (1960); Solo Show, Philadelphia Art Alliance (1953); Group Shows, Park Place Gallery, New York, NY, Brata Gallery, Cornell University, Dallas Museum of Fine Arts, Museum of Erotic Art, San Francisco, CA Museum of Erotic Art, Stockholm, Sweden, Whitney Museum, Weisner Gallery, New York, NY, City Without Walls Gallery, Newark, NJ, Green Gallery, New York, NY, Leo Castelli Gallery, New York, NY, Allan Stone Gallery, New York, NY, Franklin Furnace, New York, NY, Dorsky Gallery, New York, NY, Brooklyn Terminal Show, New York, NY, Food Stamp Gallery, New York, NY, ABC No Rio, New York, NY, Blue Mountain Gallery, New York, NY, Boriqua College, New York, NY, Philadelphia Museum of Art, Holland-Goldowsky, Chicago, IL, Peter David, Minneapolis, MN, McNay Institute, San Antonio, TX, Stephen Gang Gallery, New York, NY, The Cave, Brooklyn, NY, Brooklyn Brewery; Permanent Collections, Main Street Millennium, Washington, DC, Dallas Museum of Fine Arts, Museum of Erotic Art, President Clinton Library; Contributor, Articles, Professional Journals; Work Shared in Washington, DC, Istanbul, Turkey, and Beijing, China; Featured, The New Yorker **Awards:** Citizen's Committee for New York City (1990-Present); Betsy Barlow Rogers Award, Friends of McCarren Park, Inc. (1995); Cue Magazine (1967); Ecole Beaux Arts Scholar; Hans Hofmann Atelier Scholar; Grantee, Friends of McCarren Park, Inc.; J.M. Kaplan Fund; Andy Warhol Foundation; New York Foundation; Vincent Astor Foundation **Shipping Address:** 169 Java Street, Brooklyn, NY, 11222

Feng-Jen Yang, PhD

Title: Associate Professor **Industry:** Education/Educational Services **Company Name:** Florida Polytechnic University **Education:** PhD, Computer Science, Illinois Institute of Technology, Chicago, IL (1998-2001); MS, Computer Science, Florida International University, Miami, FL (1996-1998); MS, Computer Science, California State University, Chico, CA (1994-1995); BE, Information Engineering, Feng Chia University, Taichung, Taiwan (1985-1989) **Certifications:** IPv6 Sage; Certified JavaScript Developer **Career:** Associate Professor, Department of Computer Sciences and Information Technology, Florida Polytechnic University, Lakeland, FL (2015-Present); Assistant Professor, Department of Mathematics and Information Sciences, University of North Texas at Dallas, Dallas, Texas (2010-2014); Program Coordinator, Department of Mathematics and Information Sciences, University of North Texas at Dallas, Dallas, Texas (2009-2014); Assistant Professor, Computer Science Department, Prairie View A&M University, Prairie View, Texas (2002-2009); Assistant Professor, Computer Science Department, Rowan University, Glassboro, NJ (2001-2002); Part-time Instructor, Computer Science Department, Illinois Institute of Technology, Chicago, IL (2000-2001); Engineer, Computer and Communication Research Laboratory, Industrial Technology Research Institute, Hsinchu, Taiwan (1995-1996) **Career Related:** Reviewer, The Journal of Supercomputing; Reviewer, Journal of Artificial Intelligence and Application; Reviewer, International Conference on Artificial Intelligence; Reviewer, International Conference on Foundations of Computer Science; Reviewer, International Conference on Artificial Intelligence and Application; Reviewer, International Conference on Internet Studies; Editorial Board, International Journal on Artificial Intelligence and Applications **Military Service:** Lieutenant, Research Assistant, Army Reserve Officer of Science and Technology, Chung Shan Institute of Science and Technology, Republic of Korea Army (1989-1993) **Creative Works:** Author, "The Preparation of an Intelligent Tutoring System for Relational Algebra," Proceedings of the First International Conference on Applied Cognitive Computing (ACC'17), Las Vegas, NV, (2017); Author, Book Chapter, "A General Purpose Probabilistic Inference Engine," International Association of Engineers Conferences (2017); Author, "The User Interface Design of an Intelligent Tutoring System for Relational Database Schema Normalization," International Journal of Technology and Engineering Studies (2016); Author, "Engaging a Real-Life Student with a Virtual Tutor," International Journal of Computer Science and Innovation (2016); Author, "Crafting a Lightweight Bayesian Inference Engine," Proceedings of the World Congress on Engineering 2016 (WCE 2016), London, United Kingdom (2016); Author, "The Logical Modeling of a Virtual Tutoring System for Relational Database Schema Normalization," International Journal of Advanced Computer Technology (2015); Author, "An Overview of Natural Language Generation Systems Evaluation," Proceedings of the World Congress on Engineering and Computer Science 2015, San Francisco, CA (2015); Co-author, "Declarative Cyber Physical Systems Modeling to Facilitate Autonomous Vehicles Design," Proceedings of the Fourth International Conference on Connected Vehicles and Expo, Shenzhen, China (2015); Author, "The Determination of When to Teach What in a Virtual Tutoring System for Relational Database Schema Normalization," International Journal of Advanced Computer Technology (2014); Co-author, "The Student Modeling in a Virtual Tutoring System for Relational Database Schema Normalization," Proceedings of the 2014 International Conference on Advanced Computer Science and Engineering, Guangzhou, China (2014); Author, "The Systems Planning and Analysis for a Relational Database Schema Normalization Tutoring System," Proceedings of the 2014 International Conference on Applied and Theoretical Information Systems Research, Taipei, Taiwan (2014); Author, "A More Humanized Way to Query a Database System," ACM Inroads (2013); Author, "The Dynamic Curriculum Planning for a Database Design Tutoring System," Proceedings of the World Congress on Engineering and Computer Science 2013, San Francisco, CA (2013); Author, "A Generalized Practice of Discourse Analysis and Modeling," The Journal of Advanced Research in Scientific Computing (2012); Author, "A Framework of Discourse Analysis and Modeling," Proceedings of the World Congress on Engineering and Computer Science 2012 (WCECS 2012), San Francisco, CA (2012) **Awards:** Internal Seed Grant, Principal Investigator, "An Intelligent Mobile App for the Tutoring of Relational Database Schema Normalization," Florida Polytechnic University (2016); Internal Seed Grant, Principal Investigator, "The Implementation of a Domain Independent Bayesian Inference Engine," Florida Polytechnic University (2015) **Membership:** ACM Special Interest Group on Computer Science Education; ACM Computer Science Teachers Association; International Association of Engineers **Business Address:** 4700 Research Way, Lakeland, FL, 33805 **Shipping Address:** 1531 Shorewood Dr., Auburndale, FL, 33823

Nancy Lien Yang

Title: President **Industry:** Fine Art **Company Name:** Pastel Association of Tawain **Date of Birth:** 03/12/1948 **Place of Birth:** Taipei **Country of Origin:** Taiwan **Parents:** Yuh-Lin Chen; Wang-Yuh Wu **Marital Status:** Married **Spouse Name:** Kei-Hsiung Yang (6/10/1971) **Children:** Lawrence H.; Andrew **Education:** Coursework, The Jason Chang Workshop (2007-Present); Coursework, Studied Pastel Painting with Rae Smith, Katonah Art Center (2006-Present); Coursework, Studied Pastel Painting with Wende Caporale, Katonah Art Center (2006-Present); Coursework in Pastel Painting, With Rae Smith, Northern Westchester Center for the Arts (2000-2006); Coursework in Pastel Painting, Eith Wende Caporale, Northern Westchester Center for the Arts (1997-2006); Coursework in Watercolor, With P.J. Steadman, Northern Westchester Center for the Art (1997-2001); Master's Degree in Statistics, University of California, Berkeley (1971); Bachelor's Degree in Mathematics, University of California, Berkeley (1970) **Certifications:** Certificate, Daniel E. Greene Workshop (2002); Certificate, Daniel E. Greene Workshop (2000) **Career:** President, Pastel Association of Taiwan, Taipei, Taiwan (2012-Present); Board Member, Pastel Association of Taiwan, Taipei, Taiwan (2010-2012); Director, Department of Computer Services, Purchase College, State University of New York (1983-1996); Analyst, Department Computer Services, Purchase College, State University of New York (1979-1983) **Career Related:** Full Member, American Artists Professional League (2016-Present); Elected Member, Allied Artists of America (2015-Present); Member, Salmagundi Club (2015-Present); Full Member, Audubon Artists (2013-Present); Member, Spanish Pastel Society, Oveido, Spain (2011-Present); Signature Member, Pastel Society of America (2009-Present); North America Pastel Artists Association (2008-Present) **Civic:** Organizer, Fifth International Pastel Artists Invitational Exhibition (2017); Organizer, Fourth International Pastel Artists Invitational Exhibition (2014) **Creative Works:** Catalog of the Fifth International Pastel Artists Invitational Exhibition (2017); Exhibition, Pastel Society of America, Annual Exhibition, New York City, NY (2017); Annual Exhibition, Allied Artists of America, New York City, NY (2017); Exhibition, International Pastel Artists Invitational Exhibition, Taipei, Taiwan (2017); On-Line Exhibition, International Association of Pastel Societies (2017); Exhibition, The 57 Chang-Chi Show, Tokyo, Japan (2017); Annual Journal for Pastel Association of Taiwan (2016-2017); Exhibition, Taiwan and Japan Joint Art Show, Tokyo, Japan (2016); Exhibition, International Biennial Pastel in Spain, Oviedo, Spain (2016); Exhibition, Pastel Society of America, Annual Exhibition, New York City, NY (2015); Annual Exhibition, Allied Artists of America, New York City, NY (2015); Featured, Annual Journal for Pastel Association of Taiwan (2015); Annual Exhibition, Allied Artists of America, New York City, NY (2014); Exhibition, International Pastel Artists Invitational Exhibition, Taipei, Taiwan (2014); Catalog of the Forth International Pastel Artists Invitational Exhibition (2014); Exhibition, Pastel Society of America, Annual Exhibition, NYC, NY (2013); Exhibition, International Biennial Pastel in Spain, Oviedo, Spain (2013); Co-Exhibition, King Boutique Art Gallery, Taipei, Taiwan (2013); Exhibition, American Artists Professional League, New York City, NY (2012-2017); Exhibition, Taiwan and Japan Joint Art Show, Taipei, Taiwan (2012-2014); Annual Exhibition, Allied Artists of America, New York City, NY (2012); Exhibition, International Pastel Artists Invitational Exhibition, Taipei, Taiwan (2012); Exhibition, International Biennial Pastel in Spain, Oviedo, Spain (2011); Annual Exhibition, Audubon Artists, New York City, NY (2010-2017); Semi-Annual Exhibition, Pastel Association of Taiwan, Taipei, Taiwan (2010-2014); Exhibition, Pastel Society of America, Annual Exhibition, New York City, NY (2010-2011); Annual Exhibition, Allied Artists of America, New York City, NY (2010); Exhibition, International Pastel Artists Invitational Exhibition, Taipei, Taiwan, New York City, NY (2010); Exhibition, North America Pastel Artists Association, Annual Exhibition, New York City, NY (2008-2014); Exhibition, Katonah Village Library, Katonah, NY (2006-2013); Exhibition, Eastern Multimedia Corp., YangMei, Taiwan (2006-2010) **Awards:** Allen J. Smith Memorial Award, American Artists Professional League (2015); Richard C. Pionk Memorial Award, Audubon Artists (2014); Artemiranda Award, The Second Biennial International Pastel Show in Spain, Oviedo, Spain (2013); Silver Award, Chiang Kai-Shek Memorial Hall National Pastel Competition, Taipei, Taiwan (2012); Artemiranda Award, First Biennial International Pastel Show in Spain, Oviedo, Spain (2011); Best in Show Award, Village Gallery of Katonah First Juried Competition and Art Exhibition, Katonah, NY (2003); Edward Booth Scholarship; Levi Strauss Scholarship **Membership:** American Artists Professional League (2016-Present); International Association of Pastel Societies (2014-Present); Audubon Artists (2013-Present); Signature Member, Pastel Society of America (2009-Present); North America Pastel Artists Association (2008-Present); Salmagundi Club **Shipping Address:** 122 Dungsen Road, #4F, Yangmei Taoyuan, Taiwan, 326 **Website:** http://www.nancyyangart.com/Nancy_Yang_Art-home-5a.html

Yin Yeh, PhD

Title: Professor Emeritus **Industry:** Education/Educational Services **Company Name:** University of California, Davis **Date of Birth:** 11/01/1938 **Place of Birth:** Chungking **Country of Origin:** China **Parents:** Prof. Chai Yeh; Ida C. Yeh **Marital Status:** Married **Spouse Name:** Elizabeth Tang **Children:** Debra Yeh, MD; Tamara Yeh, Esq. **Career:** Edward A. Dickson Honorary Professor Emeritus, University of California, Davis (2013-Present); Professor Emeritus, University of California, Davis (2011-2013); Chair, Department of Applied Sciences, University of California, Davis (2008-2011); Co-Principal Investigator, Center for Biophotonics Science and Technology, University of California, Davis (2002-2011); Executive Committee, Graduate Group in Biophysics, University of California, Davis (2000-2008); Professor, University of California, Davis (1973-2011); Staff Scientist, Lawrence Livermore National Laboratory (1968-1973); Postdoctorate Fellow, Lawrence Livermore National Laboratory (1966-1968); Postdoctorate Fellow, Columbia Radiation Laboratory, New York, NY (1965-1966) **Career Related:** Senior Fellow, Japanese Society for the Promotion of Science (2001); Fellow, American Association for the Advancement of Science (1991); Roche Fellow (1980) **Creative Works:** Author, "Biophotonics Science and Technology," World Scientific (2018); Contributor, Articles and Book Chapters, Professional Journals **Awards:** Senior Fulbright Scholar, Taiwan (2012-2013) **Membership:** Fulbright Alumni, Sigma Xi (1965); American Association for the Advancement of Science; Senior Member, Japanese Society of Promotion Science; American Physical Society; Biophysical Society **Hobbies:** Photography **Shipping Address:** 1520 Sycamore Lane, Davis, CA, 95616

Ronald F. Young

Title: Neurosurgeon **Industry:** Medicine & Health Care **Company Name:** Neuroscience Institute, Los Robles Hospital **Date of Birth:** 01/04/1939 **Place of Birth:** Buffalo **State:** NY **Parents:** Frederick Earl Young; Ruth Henrietta (Cowan) Young **Marital Status:** Single **Spouse Name:** Sheila Marie Young (6/23/1962, Divorced 1990) **Children:** Scott Ronald; Anne Louise; Karen Lynn **Education:** MD, State University of New York, Buffalo (1965); BA, State University of New York, Buffalo (1961) **Certifications:** Diplomate, American Board of Neurological Surgery **Career:** Medical Director, Movement Disorder Center (2010-Present); Medical Director, Providence St. Joseph's Medical Center, Burbank, CA (2009-Present); Medical Director, Rotating Gamma Center Southern California, Anaheim, CA (2008-Present); Medical Director, Gamma Knife Center, Neuroscience Institute, Los Robles Hospital, Thousand Oaks, CA (2006-Present); Director, Northwest Gamma Knife Center and Northwest Neuroscience Institute, Northwest Hospital, Seattle, WA (1993-2010); Clinical Professor, University of California, Irvine (1993-1998); Chief of Neurosurgery, University of California Medical Center, Irvine, CA (1986-1993); Professor of Neurosurgery, University of California, Irvine (1986-1993); Associate Professor, University of California, Los Angeles (1977-1985); Assistant Professor in Neurosurgery, State University of New York, Syracuse (1973-1977); Resident in Neurosurgery, State University of New York, Syracuse (1969-1973); Resident in Neurosurgery, VA Hospital, Long Beach, CA (1966-1967); Intern, University of Minnesota Hospital, Minneapolis, MN (1965-1966); Medical Director, Gamma Knife Center and DBS Program, Swedish Hospital, Seattle, WA **Career Related:** Elizabeth Crosby Memorial Lecturer, University of Michigan, Ann Arbor, MI (1990); Medical Staff, Swedish Hospital, Seattle, WA, Providence St. Joseph's Medical Center, Burbank, CA, Los Robles Hospital, Thousand Oaks, CA; Fellow, American College of Surgeons **Civic:** Captain, U.S. Air Force Medical Corps (1967-1969) **Creative Works:** Author, "Spinal Cord Injury" (1981); Contributor, Articles, Professional Journals; Presentations, Professional Societies and Courses **Awards:** The Lauds & Laurels Award, Professional Achievement, University of California, Irvine, Alumni Association (1992); Elizabeth Crosby Medal, University of Michigan, Ann Arbor, MI (1990); Congress Medal, German Neurosurgical Society (1982); Irving F. Heyman Award in Clinical Neurology, State University of New York (1965) **Membership:** Chairman, International Leksell Gamma Knife Society (1995); President, Western Neurosurgery Society (1993-1994); Secretary, American Academy of Pain Medicine (1991-1993); Vice President, Western Neurosurgery Society (1990-1991); American Association of Neurological Surgeons; Congress of Neurological Surgery; Society of Neurological Surgeons **Marquis Who's Who Honors:** Distinguished Humanitarian (2017) **Shipping Address:** 754 Avenida Majorca, Unit A, Laguna Woods, CA, 92637

David Ross Young

Title: Oceanographer **Industry:** Sciences **Date of Birth:** 11/19/1937 **Place of Birth:** San Diego **State:** CA **Parents:** David Robert Young; Vivian Young **Marital Status:** Married **Spouse Name:** Jean Barlow (8/10/1968) **Children:** Kirsten Sheridan; Michael David; Anthony Frederic **Education:** PhD in Chemical & Biological Oceanography, Scripps Institution of Oceanography, San Diego, CA (1970); BA in Physics, Pomona College, Claremont, CA (1960) **Career:** Guest Worker, United States Environmental Protection Agency, Newport, OR (2015-Present); Retired (2016); Lecturer, Department of Physical Sciences, Oregon Coast Community College, Newport, OR (2002-2012); Research Environmental Scientist, United States Environmental Protection Agency, Newport, OR (1986-2015); Adjunct Professor, Department of Oceanography, Oregon State University College of Oceanic & Atmospheric Sciences, Corvallis, OR (1986-2006); Associate Professor, Department of Oceanography, Stony Brook University (1984-1986); Oceanographer, Dames & Moore Environmental Consultants, LA (1980-1984); Oceanographer, Southern California Coastal Water Research Project, LA (1970-1980); Research Assistant, Scripps Institution of Oceanography (1961-1970); Teaching Assistant, Department of Physics, University of California, Los Angeles (1960-1961) **Civic:** Environmental Tour leader, Lake Baikal, Siberia, Russia (2004, 1998, 1996, 1994, 1993) **Creative Works:** Contributor, Articles, Scientific Journals **Awards:** Science Achievement Award, United States Environmental Protection Agency (2014-2015, 2011, 2009, 2007, 2004-2005, 1995, 1992, 1990) **Membership:** Pacific Estuarine Research Society; Coastal & Estuarine Research Federation; Wetlands Conservancy **Hobbies:** Kayaking; Environmental conservation **Shipping Address:** PO Box 799, South Beach, OR, 97366

Yi-Hao Yu, PhD

Title: Medical Director of Endocrinology **Industry:** Medicine & Health Care **Company Name:** Greenwich Hospital - Yale New Haven Health **Education:** Fellowship in Endocrinology, Diabetes and Metabolism, College of Physicians and Surgeons, Columbia University (1999-2002); MD, New York University School of Medicine (1996); PhD, Cell and Molecular Biology, New York University School of Medicine (1989); Residency, Columbia University Medical Center; Internship, Columbia University Medical Center; BS, Fudon University, Shanghai, China **Career:** Medical Director of Endocrinology, Greenwich Hospital, Yale-New Haven Health System (2011-Present); Clinical Associate Professor of Medicine, Drexel University College of Medicine (2011-2012); Core Teaching Faculty, Easton Hospital (2009-2011); Physician, Easton Endocrinology Associates (2008-2011); Medical Director, Bristo-Myers Squibb (2007-2008); Principal Investigator, Division of Preventative Medicine and Nutrition, Columbia University Medical Center (2004-2007); Director, Adult Specialized Nutrition Support Service (2003-2007); Assistant Professor of Medicine, Columbia University College of Physicians and Surgeons (2002-2007) **Membership:** American Association of Clinical Endocrinologists; Obesity Medicine Association **Why did you become involved in your profession or industry:** Dr. Yu has been in his profession for about 30 years now. Initially he was doing medical research, but in 2001 he started practicing medicine and having satisfaction doing patient care. They are interconnected. **Shipping Address:** 560 Riverside Dr., Apt. 4D, New York, NY, 10027 **Website:** https://www.linkedin.com/in/yi-hao-yu-a0442419

Peter Zasuly

Title: Executive Producer, Director **Industry:** Media & Entertainment **Company Name:** Random Pictures **Education:** Bachelor's Degree, Tisch School of The Arts - Television, New York University (1986) **Career:** Executive Producer, Triage Entertainment, LEG (2008-Present); Director, Triage Entertainment, LEG (2008-Present); Executive Producer, Random Pics (2006-Present); Owner, Random Pics (2006-Present); Supervising Producer, Painless Productions (2004-2009); Executive Producer, Pilgrim Studios, Inc. (2005); Director, Pilgrim Studios, Inc. (2005); Producer, DME Productions (2004-2005); Director, DME Productions (2004-2005); Writer, DME Productions (2004-2005); Show Producer, Painless Productions (2004); Writer, Painless Productions (2004); Producer, Original Productions (2003); Director, Original Productions (2003); Writer, Original Productions (2003); Producer, Associated Television International (2002); Writer, Associated Television International (2002); Co-executive Producer, Tri-Crown (2001); Director, Tri-Crown (2001); Writer, Tri-Crown (2001); Supervising Producer, Film Garden Entertainment (2000) **Creative Works:** Executive Producer, Showrunner, Director, "Dallas Cowboys Cheerleaders: Making The Team,"; Showrunner, Director, "Ghost Hunters Season 1," SYFY Channel; Creator, Showrunner, Director, "US SWAT," TLC; Showrunner, Writer, "The Repossessors," Discovery; Executive Producer, Showrunner, Fine Living Scripps Networks; Show Producer, Writer, Director, "Cat People," Animal Planet; Supervising Producer, AKC National Agility Championships; Producer, Camera, "COPS," Fox; Showrunner, Writer, Comedy Series "Caught On Tape," RTL; Producer, Camera, "LAPD: Life On The Beat"; Director, 52 Episodes, Multiple Camera Show, "Realty Views," Time Warner Cable, New York City, NY **Awards:** Three Cine Golden Eagle Awards; Platinum, Gold, Silver Awards, Houston Film Festival; Multiple Awards for a Short Film, "Blueberry Blintzes"; Best of Palm Springs; Won Best of Show and Best Documentary at NYU Video Festival; Alumni Spirit Award **Membership:** Directors Guild of America; Producers Guild of America **Shipping Address:** 2214 23rd St., Santa Monica, CA, 90405

G. Sam Zeller, PhD

Title: Physicist **Industry:** Sciences **Company Name:** Fermi National Accelerator Laboratory **Place of Birth:** Chicago **State:** IL **Parents:** Gerard Zeller; Patricia (Repay) Zeller **Education:** PhD in Physics, Northwestern University (2002); MS in Physics, Northwestern University (1996); BA in Physics, Northwestern University (1994) **Career:** Physicist, Fermi National Accelerator Laboratory (2010-Present); Physicist, LaSalle Nation Lab (2008-2010); Physicist, Columbia University (2003-2008) **Career Related:** Neutrino Physicist, Co-Spokesperson of the MicroBooNE Experiment; Deputy Head, Neutrino Division at Fermilab **Creative Works:** Author, "Precision Measurement of the Electroweak Mixing Angle in Neutrino-Nucleon Deep Inelastic Scattering" **Awards:** Early Career Award, Department of Energy Office of Science (2012); Tanaka Dissertation Award (2003); Best Thesis in the American Physical Society **Membership:** American Physical Society; Illinois Heart Rescue Group **To what do you attribute your success:** Dr. Zeller attributes her success to great mentors who have helped her and encouraged her to stick with her career. **Why did you become involved in your profession or industry:** Dr. Zeller took a tour of the Fermi National Accelerator Laboratory, which made her want to further study physics and take this as a career path. She was trying to get out of a class in school and had no idea that it would lead to her career. **Hobbies:** Driving cars **Shipping Address:** 918 West State Street, Geneva, IL, 60134

Hongbin Zhao

Title: Artist **Industry:** Fine Art **Company Name:** HZ International Fine Arts **Date of Birth:** 08/15/1952 **Place of Birth:** Shanghai **Country of Origin:** China **Parents:** Chi-Zhen Zhao; Xue-Min Chen **Marital Status:** Married **Spouse Name:** Mei-Jun Gu **Children:** Hui-Jie Zhao **Education:** Honorary Doctorate of Arts, The Yorker International University (2006); Graduate Diploma in Fine Arts, Shanghai Jiao Tong University (1984-1985) **Career:** Freelance Artist, Warrandyte South, Australia (1988-Present); Chief Editor, Modern New Products Pictorial, ShanghaiTech University (1985-1988); Art Editor, Designer, Science Life Magazine, Municipal Science and Technology Association, Shanghai, China (1979-1985) **Civic:** Vice President, Chinese Cultural Heritage Research Institute of National Painting and Calligraphy, Ministry of Culture, China (2014) **Creative Works:** Published Artist, "Messenger and Philosopher of Traditional Chinese Culture: Xi Jinping, Zhao Hongbin, Ouyang Zhongshi" (2017); Published Artist, "Chinese Painting and Calligraphy Grandmaster Xu Beihong & Zhao Hongbin" (2017); Published Artist, "Leading China Art Masters" (2017); Published Artist, "China's New Famous Art Masterpieces-Zhao Hongbin" (2016); Artist, Sino-US Diplomatic Relation 37th Anniversary Commemorative Stamps, Outstanding Chinese Art Master Zhao Hongbin, United States Post Office (2016); Artist, "Chinese Art Circle: The Three Masters" (2015); Artist, Chinese Famous Oil Painter Zhao Hongbin Special Collector Edition, Post Office of China (2015); Artist, "Chinese Art Circle-The Three Masters" (2014); Artist, Chinese Famous Oil Painter Zhao Hongbin Special Collector Edition, Post Office of China (2014); One-Man Show, Monet of the Orient: Hongbing Zhao Oil Paintings Exhibition, Tokyo Metropolitan Art Museum (2012); Published Artist, "The Three Great Masters: Liu Dawei, Zhao Wuji, Zhao Hongbin (2011); Published Artist, "Sixty Years Six Artists" (2010); Published Artist, "Three Masters of Oil Paintings" (2010); Published Artist, "Eight Contemporary Great Masters in Fine Art" (2010); Published Artist, "Masters of Chinese Oil Painting: Hou Yimin, Zhan Jianjun, Zhao Hongbin" (2009); Published Artwork, "The Overseas Oil Painter of China: Zhao Hongbin" (2008); Published Artist, "The Most Influential Masters in Contemporary Arts" (2008); Published Artist, "Famous Teacher in Modern Time" (2008); Published Artist, "Artist Style" (2008); Artist, "Spring, The Beach" (2005); Artist, The Sun (2004); Artist, " Zhao Hongbin, Monet of the Orient" (1999); Group Show, Shanghai World Trade Center (1997-1999); Published Artwork, "The Paintings of Zhao Hongbin" (1997); Group Show, "Dr. Sun Yet-Sen Memorial Hall," Taipei, China (1997); Group Show, Art Gallery of South Australia (1995); Group Show, Chinese War Memorial Museum (1995); Group Show, New Parliament House, Canberra, Australia (1995); Group Show, National Gallery of Victoria, Australia (1994); Group Show, Art Gallery of New South Wales (1994); Published Artwork, "50 Australian Artists" (1994); Published Artwork, "Dictionary of the Achievements of the World of Chinese Artists" (1994); Group Show, Australian National Maritime Museum (1993); Group Show, International Exhibition, London, England (1993); Group Show, Sydney Opera House (1992); Group Show, National Gallery of Victoria, Australia (1992); Published Artwork, "Portraits of Australia" (1992); Group Show, Victoria Art Center (1991); Group Show, Shanghai National Art Gallery (1977-1985) **Awards:** Gold Award, 36th Korea International Painting and Drawing Art Exhibition, Gyeongbokgung Palace (2016); China Great Wall Cultural Award (2015); Gold Award, 16th Japan-China International Art Exhibition, Tokyo Metropolitan Art Museum (2012); Top Influential Artists Award, 14th Beijing International Art Expo (2011); Best Display Award, 6th China International Cultural Industries Fair (2011); Appointed Top Supplying Artists for China National Gifts, China Asia-Pacific Economic Development Research Center, China (2009); American Medal of Honor, American Biographical Institute (2002); Order of International Ambassadors, American Biographical Institute (2001); Macquarie Award (2000); Mary MacKillop Art Award Finalist (1995); Golden Academy Award for Lifetime Achievement, American Biographical Institute (1995); Five Hundred Leader of Influence, American Biographical Institute (1995); 20th Century Award for Achievement, International Biographical Centre, United Kingdom (1994-1995); International Man of the Year, International Biographical Centre, United Kingdom (1994-1995); Man of the Year, American Biographical Institute (1994); Bronze Medal, China Famous Figures Works, Exhibition of Arts Circles (1994); Macquarie Award (1994); Archibald Prize Finalist, Art Gallery of New South Wales (1994); First Prize, Ernest Henry Memorial Art Show (1992-1994) **Membership:** Lifetime Fellow, International Biographical Centre, United Kingdom; Chinese Celebrity's Association; National Calligraphers' Association of China; Vice President, National Culture Painting and Calligraphy Institute of Chinese Academy of Cultural Heritage Protection, Ministry of Culture, China **Marquis Who's Who Honors:** Albert Nelson Marquis Lifetime Achievement Award (2017) **Shipping Address:** 125 Highland Ave., Basking Ridge, NJ, 09720

T.C. Price Zimmermann, PhD

Title: Historian, Educator **Industry:** Education/Educational Services **Date of Birth:** 08/22/1934 **Place of Birth:** Bryn Mawr **State:** PA **Parents:** R.Z. Zimmermann; Susan (Goodman) Zimmermann **Marital Status:** Married **Spouse Name:** Margaret Upham Ferris Zimmermann **Education:** PhD, Harvard University (1964); MA, University of Oxford (1964); AM, Harvard University (1960); BA, University of Oxford (1958); BA, Williams College (1956) **Career:** Charles A. Dana Professor Emeritus of History, Davidson College, Davidson, NC (1999-present); Charles A. Dana Professor of History, Davidson College, Davidson, NC (1986-1999); Vice President of Academic Affairs, Davidson College, Davidson, NC (1977-1986); Professor of History, Reed College, Portland, OR (1973-1977); Chairman, Department of History, Reed College, Portland, OR (1973-1975); Associate Professor, Reed College, Portland, OR (1967-1973); Assistant Professor, Reed College, Portland, OR (1964-1967) **Career Related:** Fellowship, American Council of Learned Societies, New York, NY (1975-1976); Oregon Committee, National Endowment for the Humanities (1971-1977); Villa "I Tatti" Fellowship, Harvard University (1970-1971); Region 14 Selection Committee, Woodrow Wilson National Fellowship Foundation, Princeton, NJ (1967-1970); Fulbright Fellowship, Italy (1962-1964); Danforth Fellowship (1956-1962) **Civic:** Advisory Council, Botanical Gardens, University of North Carolina, Charlotte, NC (2007-2008); Rome Prize Jury, Post-Classical Humanistic Studies, American Academy in Rome (1993); Board of Advisors, Lowell Observatory (1988-1993); Board of Directors, Charlotte Opera Association, North Carolina (1980-1982); President, American Alpine Club, New York, NY (1979-1982); Board of Directors, North Carolina Outward Bound School, Morganton, NC (1978-1981); Board of Directors, American Alpine Club, New York, NY (1975-1983) **Creative Works:** Author, "Paolo Giovio: A Historian and the Crisis of Sixteenth-Century Italy," Italian Translation (2012); Author, "Paolo Giovio: The Historian and the Crisis of Sixteenth-Century Italy" (1995); Co-Editor, "Collected Works of Paolo Giovio" (1985); Author, "April in Alaska," Mazama, Portland, OR (1972); Contributor, Articles, Professional Journals **Awards:** The Helen & Stewart F. Blake Philanthropy Award, Opera Carolina (2015); Presidential Book Award, American Association for Italian Studies (1997); Helen and Howard R. Marraro Book Prize, American History Association (1996) **Membership:** Board of Advisers, Opera Carolina Endowment (2008-2010); Renaissance Society of America; Society of Italian Historical Studies; American Association of Italian Studies; The Phi Beta Kappa Society **Marquis Who's Who Honors:** Albert Nelson Marquis Lifetime Achievement Award (2017); Distinguished Humanitarian (2017) **Why did you become involved in your profession or industry:** Dr. Zimmermann always wanted to be a professor. He originally wanted to teach chemistry, but then changed to history after being inspired by his history professors at Williams College. **What do you consider to be the highlight of your career:** A significant moment in Dr. Zimmermann's life was participating in the first ascent of Mount Skarland in Alaska. **Hobbies:** Gardening **Shipping Address:** 16101 McAuley Road, Huntersville, NC, 28078

Robert Eugene Zipf Jr.

Title: Medical Laboratory Director, Legal Medicine Consultant, Clinical & Forensic Pathologist **Industry:** Medicine & Health Care **Company Name:** R.E.Zipf Pathology Associates **Date of Birth:** 09/18/1940 **Place of Birth:** Dayton **State:** OH **Parents:** Robert Eugene Zipf; Meriam (Murr) Zipf **Marital Status:** Married **Spouse Name:** Nancy J. Gaskell (9/11/1965) **Children:** Karin Lorene; Marjorie Kristine **Education:** Pathology Resident, Duke University Medical Center (1967-1973); Intern, Miami Valley Hospital, Premier Health, Dayton, OH (1966-1967); MD, The Ohio State University (1966); BA, DePauw University (1962) **Certifications:** Diplomate, American Board of Pathology **Career:** Board of Trustees, Nash Community College (2016-Present); Regional Forensic Pathologist, Rocky Mount, NC (1978-Present); Director of Laboratories, Nash Health Care Systems (1978-2006); Regional Forensic Pathologist, North Carolina (1978-2006); President, R.E. Zipf, PA, Pathology Associates, Rocky Mount, NC (1978-2005); Deputy Coroner, Franklin County, OH (1974-1978); Forensic Pathologist, Franklin County, OH (1974-1978); Director, Radioisotope Pathology, Riverside Methodist Hospital, OhioHealth, Columbus, OH (1974-1978); Assistant Professor, Duke University Health System, Durham, NC (1973-1974); Director, Autopsy Pathology, Duke University Health System (1973-1974); Director, Forensic Pathology, Duke University Health System, Durham, NC (1967-1972) **Career Related:** Founder, Clintrac Pathology Computers (2012-Present); Advisory Board Member, North Carolina Forensic Science Advisory Board (2012-Present); Board of Directors, Rocky Mountain District of Kiwanis International (1980-Present); Clinical Assistant Professor, School of Medicine, East Carolina University (1979-Present); Director, Forensic Toxicology Laboratory, Nash Health Care Systems, Rocky Mount, NC (1990-2000); Vice President, Computerized Office Systems (1986-2000); Director, School of Medical Technology, Atlantic Christian College (Now Barton College) (1983-1989); Adjunct Professor, School of Medical Technology, Atlantic Christian College (Now Barton College) (1980-1989); Director, Clinical and Diagnostic Laboratories, Nash General Hospital, Rocky Mount, NC (1978-2006); Chief, Pathology, Nash General Hospital, Rocky Mount, NC (1978-2006); Founder, Clintrac Pathology Software; Consultant, SMS Medical Software; Consultant in Medical Forensics; Consultant in Laboratory Management; Fellow, College of American Pathologists; Fellow, American Academy of Forensic Sciences; Fellow, American Society for Clinical Pathology **Civic:** Board of Directors, Nash Community College (2015-Present); Forensic Advisory Board, North Carolina Department of Justice (2012-Present); Board of Trustees, North Carolina Wesleyan College (2005-Present); Nash Chamber of Commerce (2005-Present); Advisor, Zipf Charitable Trust and Fund (1999-Present); Active Member, Mayor's Committee on Drug and Substance Abuse (1987-Present); Mentor, Nash-Rocky Mount Public Schools (1980-Present); Trustee, Local Area, United Fund (1979-1984); Board Member, Nash Health Care Foundation; Eagle Scout Leader, Boy Scouts of America; Supporter, Boy Scouts of America; Advisory Board, North Carolina Forensic Science **Military Service:** Consultant to Surgeon General, US Air Force (1972-1974); Chief Anatomic Pathologist, US Air Force (1972); Major, US Air Force (1967-1974) **Creative Works:** Contributor, Articles to Professional Journals **Awards:** Eagle Scout, Boy Scouts of America **Membership:** President, Nash County Medical Society (1995); President, Laboratory Users Group, The New York Academy of Sciences (1992); President, Advisory Board, SMS (1990); Laboratory Advisors Board, SMS (1989-1991); Clinical Advisory Board, SMS (1988-1991); President, Laboratory Users Group, The New York Academy of Sciences (1988-1990); President, SMS Clinical Advisory Board; Nash County Medical Society; Association of Clinical Scientists; American College of Nuclear Medicine; North Carolina Medical Society **Marquis Who's Who Honors:** Albert Nelson Marquis Lifetime Achievement Award (2017) **Shipping Address:** 120 Newby Court, Rocky Mount, NC, 27804

Monib A. Zirvi, PhD

Title: Dermatologist **Industry:** Medicine & Health Care **Company Name:** Summit Medical Group **Marital Status:** Married **Spouse Name:** Shazia **Children:** Usman; Aleena; Saif; Armaan **Education:** Resident in Dermatology, University of Pennsylvania (2001-2004); Intern, Robert Wood Johnson University Hospital, New Brunswick, NJ (2001); MD, Cornell University Medical College (Now Weill Cornell Medicine) (2000); PhD, Cornell University Medical College (Now Weill Cornell Medicine) (2000); BS in Engineering, Princeton University, Summa Cum Laude (1993) **Certifications:** Strategic Leadership in Healthcare Certificate, New York University/Summit Medical Group (2004) **Career:** Dermatologist, Summit Medical Group (2004-Present); Adjunct Clinical Instructor, Weill Cornell Medicine, New York City, NY (2004-Present); Attending Dermatologist, Overlook Medical Center, Atlantic Health Group (2004-Present) **Career Related:** Chair, Alumni Schools Committee for Northern Middlesex County, Princeton University (2004-Present); Investigator, Research Projects on Diagnostics for DNA Cancer Detection **Civic:** AmFAR; Summit Medical Group Foundation; Volunteer, Charitable Organizations **Creative Works:** Co-author, "Acquired Perforating Calcific Collagenosis After Topical Calcium Chloride Exposure," Journal of Cutaneous Pathology (2010); Co-author, "A Rapidly Growing Tumor and Dome-Shaped Yellow Papules on the Face," Archives of Dermatology (2005); Co-author, "Journal of Absence of BRAF V599E Mutation in Spitz Nevi" (2005); Co-author, "Multiplex PCR/LDR for Detection of K-ras Mutations in Primary Colon Tumors," Oncogene (1999); Co-author, "Ligase Detection Reaction for Identification of Low Abundance Mutations," Clinical Biochemistry (1999); Co-author, "Ligase-based Detection of Mononucleotide Repeat Sequences," Nucleic Acids Research (1999); Co-author, "Improved Fidelity of Thermostable Ligases for Detection of Microsatellite Repeat Sequences Using Nucleoside Analogs," Nucleic Acids Research (1999); Co-patentee, "Detection of Nucleic Acid Sequence Differences Using the Ligase Detection Reaction with Addressable Arrays"; Co-patentee, "Accelerating Identification of Single Nucleotide Polymorphisms and Alignment of Clones in Genomic Sequencing"; Co-author, "Adverse Drug Reactions of Dermatological Therapies" **Awards:** Honoree, Top Doctor, New York Metro Area, Castle Connolly Medical Ltd. (2012, 2014); Honoree, Top Doctor, U.S. World Report (2012); Patient's Choice Award (2011); Honoree, New Jersey Monthly Top Doctors (2009); Beerman-Johnson Resident Research Award, Robert Wood Johnson University Hospital (2003); Medical Scientist Training Program Fellowship, National Institutes of Health (1993-2000); William F. Keck Fellowship (1998); Robert C. Byrd Scholarship (1990) **Membership:** The Phi Beta Kappa Society (1992); Tau Beta Pi (1991); Associate, American Academy of Dermatology **Hobbies:** Playing Basketball **Shipping Address:** 19 Major Rd., Monmouth Junction, NJ, 08852 **Website:** http://www.summitmedicalgroup.com/doctor/mzirvi

Barnett Zumoff

Title: Endocrinologist, Researcher **Industry:** Medicine & Health Care **Company Name:** Icahn School of Medicine at Mount Sinai **Date of Birth:** 06/01/1926 **Place of Birth:** Brooklyn **State:** NY **Parents:** Abraham Zumoff; Stella Zumoff **Marital Status:** Widowed **Spouse Name:** Selma Silver (11/11/1951, Deceased 2015) **Children:** Janine; Francine; Linda **Education:** Resident in Medicine, University Service, Kings County Hospital, The City of New York (1954-1955); Resident in Anatomic and Clinical Pathology, Brooklyn Veterans Affairs Hospital (Now Brooklyn Campus, Veterans Affairs New York Harbor Health Care System) (1954-1955); Straight Medical Intern, Massachusetts Memorial Hospital (1950-1951); Rotating Intern, Brooklyn Jewish Hospital (Now Interfaith Medical Center) (1949-1951); Resident in Internal Medicine, Brooklyn Jewish Hospital (Now Interfaith Medical Center) (1949-1951); MD, Long Island College of Medicine (Now SUNY Downstate Medical Center) (1949); Postgraduate Coursework, Albany Medical College (1945-1947); AB, Columbia University (1945); Resident in Internal Medicine, Boston University Medical Center; Resident, Memorial Sloan Kettering Cancer Center **Certifications:** New York State Medical License (1955-2019); Diplomate, American Board of Endocrinology and Metabolism; Diplomate, American Board of Internal Medicine **Career:** Attending Physician, Tisch Hospital, Langone Hospitals, New York University (2005-Present); Chief Emeritus, Division of Endocrinology and Metabolism, Department of Medicine, Beth Israel Medical Center, Icahn School of Medicine at Mount Sinai (2000-Present); Professor, Albert Einstein College of Medicine (1994-Present); Adjunct Attending Physician, Mount Sinai School of Medicine (Now Icahn School of Medicine at Mount Sinai) (1988-Present); Attending Physician, Department of Medicine, Montefiore Medical Center (1987-Present); Attending Physician, Icahn School of Medicine at Mount Sinai (1982-Present); Attending Physician, Division of Endocrinology and Metabolism, Department of Medicine, Beth Israel Medical Center, Icahn School of Medicine at Mount Sinai (1981-Present); Attending Physician, Department of Medicine, Hospital for Joint Diseases (Now NYU Langone Orthopedic Hospital), Langone Hospitals, New York University (1981-Present); Professor, Icahn School of Medicine at Mount Sinai (1982-1994); Attending Physician, Mount Sinai School of Medicine (Now Icahn School of Medicine at Mount Sinai) (1982-1988); Chief, Division of Endocrinology and Metabolism, Department of Medicine, Beth Israel Medical Center, Icahn School of Medicine at Mount Sinai (1981-2000); Professor, Albert Einstein College of Medicine (1978-1982); Attending Physician, Department of Medicine, Montefiore Medical Center (1977-1982); Associate Professor, Albert Einstein College of Medicine (1971-1978); Assistant Professor, Albert Einstein College of Medicine (1965-1971); Attending Physician, Department of Oncology, James Ewing Hospital (1963-1982); Associate Attending Physician, Division of Neoplastic Medicine, James Ewing Hospital (1961-1963) **Career Related:** Visiting Physician, The Rockefeller University Hospital (1978-1984); Director of Cancer Endocrinology, Clinical Research Center, Montefiore Medical Center (1976-1984); Director, Montefiore Medical Center (1976-1981); Senior Investigator, Institute on Steroid Research (1963-1981); Assistant Director, Montefiore Medical Center (1961-1976) **Civic:** Vice President, Executive Board, NYTF - Folksbiene (1997-Present); President, Forward Association (1995-Present); President, Congress for Jewish Culture (1989-Present); Director, Altran Foundation for Innovation (1987-Present); President, The Workmen's Circle/Arbeter Ring, Inc. (1992-1996); President, Forward Association (1991-1992); President, The Workmen's Circle/Arbeter Ring, Inc. (1984-1988) **Military Service:** Medical Corps, U.S. Air Force (1951-1982); Retired Brigadier General, U.S. Air Force Reserve **Creative Works:** Editorial Board Member, Breast Disease - An International Journal (1987-Present); Editorial Board Member, Anticancer Research (1981-Present); Editorial Board Member, Journal of Clinical Endocrinology and Metabolism (1971-1976) **Awards:** Decorated Air Force Commendation Medal; Meritorious Service Medal; Combat Readiness Medal; Legion of Merit; Expert Marksmanship Medal **Membership:** The American Association of Clinical Endocrinologists; American Association for the Advancement of Science; American Medical Association; New York Diabetes Association; The Society of Air Force Flight Surgeons; Society of Medical Consultants to the Armed Forces; AMSUS - The Society of Federal Health Professionals; American Federation for Medical Research; Professional Section, American Diabetes Association; Aerospace Medical Association; Endocrine Society; The American Society for Clinical Investigation; Council on Arteriosclerosis, American Heart Association, Inc.; Alpha Omega Alpha; Who's Who in World Jewry **Marquis Who's Who Honors:** Albert Nelson Marquis Lifetime Achievement Award (2017) **Religion:** Jewish **Business Address:** 317 E 17th St., New York, NY, 10003 **Shipping Address:** 3710 Bedford Ave., Brooklyn, NY, 11229 **Website:** http://www.mountsinai.org/profiles/barnett-zumoff

Dave A. Zweifel

Title: Editor **Industry:** Writing and Editing **Date of Birth:** 05/19/1940 **Place of Birth:** Monroe **State:** WI **Parents:** Cloyence John Zweifel; Uva Lorraine (Skinner) Zweifel **Marital Status:** Married **Spouse Name:** Sandra Louise Holz (9/7/1968) **Children:** Daniel Mark; Kristin Lynn **Education:** BJ, University of Wisconsin (1962) **Career:** Editor Emeritus, "The Capital Times," Madison, WI (2008-Present); Editor, "The Capital Times," Madison, WI (1983-2008); Managing Editor, "The Capital Times," Madison, WI (1978-1983); City Editor, "The Capital Times," Madison, WI (1971-1978); Reporter, "The Capital Times," Madison, WI (1962-1971) **Career Related:** Vice President, Simpson Street Free Press (2001-Present); Member, Board of Directors, Evjue Foundation; Member, William T. Evjue Charitable Trust; Affiliate, Madison Newspapers Inc.; Affiliate, Capital Times Company; Affiliate, Friends of Monona Terrace; Affiliate, Swiss Center of North America, YP LLC **Civic:** Vice President, The Kids Fund, Madison, WI (1983-Present); Member, Board of Directors, UCP of Greater Dane County, Madison, WI (1984-1991); Affiliate, Wisconsin Historical Society **Military Service:** Lieutenant, U.S. Army (1963-1965); Colonel, U.S. National Guard **Awards:** Inductee, Hall of Fame, Wisconsin Newspaper Association (2011); Inaugural Watchdog Achievement Award, Wisconsin Freedom of Information Council (2011); Named Distinguished Journalism Graduate, University of Wisconsin (2003); Special Achievement Award, Society Professional Journalists (1996); Special Achievement Award, Society of Professional Journalists (1992); Named Investigative Reporter of the Year, Madison Press Club (1972); Inductee, Media Hall of Fame, Milwaukee Press Club **Membership:** Pulitzer Prize Juror, American Society of Newspaper Editors (2000-2001); President, Wisconsin Freedom of Information Council (1986-2000); Wisconsin Associated Press (1987-1988); Trustee, Wisconsin National Guard Association, Inc. (1975-1981); Wisconsin Newspaper Association; Society of Professional Journalists; Committee for Freedom of Information, American Society of Newspaper Editors; Wisconsin Alumni Association; Benevolent and Protective Order of Elks **Why did you become involved in your profession or industry:** Mr. Zweifel became involved in his profession because his family previously owned the paper. He knew that he wanted to go into the newspaper business when he was six years old. **Hobbies:** Baseball memorabilia collecting; Reading **Shipping Address:** 1922 Dondee Road, Madison, WI, 53716

ACCLAIMED LISTEES

71st Edition

Nola Jean Aalberts

Title: Social Worker, Administrator **Industry:** Social Work **Date of Birth:** 02/19/1941 **Place of Birth:** Orange City **State:** IA/USA **Parents:** Gradus C. Aalberts; Auriel Mae Aalberts **Education:** MS in Management, University of South Florida (1977); BASW, Gustavus Adolphus College (1963) **Career:** Specialist, Community Partnership for Protecting Children (2013-Present); Coordinator, Northwest Iowa Community Empowerment and Child Welfare Decategorization, Orange City, IA (2001-Present); Coordinator, Healthy Families Northwest Iowa (2001); Coordinator, Mission Stewardship in Central America and Ecuador, Reformed Church in America, Orange City, IA (1999-2001); Supervisor, Native American Ministries in Central America and Ecuador, Reformed Church in America, Orange City, IA (1999-2001); Director of Accreditation and Education, Foundation for Hospice & Home Care, Washington, DC (1986-1987); Director, Homemaker-home Health Aide Division, National Association for Home Care & Hospice, Washington, DC (1985-1989); Director, Homemaker-home Health Aide Section, Iowa Department of Public Health, Des Moines, IA (1983-1985); Program Director, National Home Caring Council, New York, NY (1980-1983); Program Associate, National Home Caring Council, New York, NY (1978-1980); Program Director, Homemaker-home Health Aide Service, Family Services Center, Clearwater, FL (1974-1978); Director, Head Start, North Iowa Community Action Organization, Mason City, IA (1973-1974); Director, Mitchell County Homemaker-home Health Aide Service, Osage, IA (1969-1973); Teacher, American School of Guatemala, Guatemala City, Guatemala (1969-1973); Volunteer, Peace Corps, Guatemala (1963-1965) **Career Related:** Adjunct Professor of Spanish, Northwestern College, Orange City, IA (2001-2002); Past Teacher, Seminars on Supervision in Home Care, State of New Jersey **Civic:** Member, Iowa Early Childhood Development Stakeholders (2003-Present); State Advisory Committee, Healthy Families Iowa Program (HOPES) (2001-Present); Member, Mayor's Task Force on Child Care, Orange City Iowa (2002) **Creative Works:** Contributor, Articles, Magazines; Co-Author, "Home Care Curricula for Supervision and Home Care Aides" **Awards:** Distinguished Alumni Award, Gustavus Adolphus College (1986); Special Contributions Award, Mental Center of North Iowa; Excellence in Education Award, National Association for Home Care & Hospice **Membership:** Board of Directors, Winnebago, NE; Iowa Empowerment Coordinators **Marquis Who's Who Honors:** Albert Nelson Marquis Lifetime Achievement Award (2017) **Shipping Address:** 315 Colorado Ave SW, Orange City, IA, 51041

Charles I. Abramson, PhD

Title: Regents Professor of Psychology **Industry:** Education/Educational Services **Company Name:** Oklahoma State University **Date of Birth:** 06/28/1956 **Place of Birth:** Brooklyn **State:** NY/USA **Parents:** Irving Abramson; Alexandra (Romaine) Abramson **Education:** PhD in Physiological Psychology, Boston University (1986); MA in Experimental Psychology, Boston University (1983); AB in Psychology, Boston University (1978) **Career:** Coordinator of International Activities, Psychology Department, Oklahoma State University (2010-Present); Regents Professor of Psychology, Oklahoma State University, Stillwater, OK (2007-Present); Adjunct Professor of Entomology, Oklahoma State University (2005-Present); Adjunct Professor of Plant Pathology, Oklahoma State University (2005-Present); Professor, School of International Studies, Oklahoma State University (2004-Present); Professor of Psychology, Oklahoma State University (2002-Present); Professor, Environmental Institute, Oklahoma State University (2002-Present); Adjunct Professor of Zoology (Now Department of Integrative Biology), Oklahoma State University (2002-Present) **Career Related:** Teaching Fellow, Institute for Teaching and Learning Excellence, Oklahoma State University (2016-Present); Faculty, Interdisciplinary Toxicology Program, Oklahoma State University (2015-Present); Co-Director, PetSci LLC, Stillwater, OK (2004-Present); Consultant, American Psychological Association, Undergraduate Consulting Service (1995-Present) **Creative Works:** Consulting Editor, "Behavioral Sciences" (2010-Present); Consulting Editor, "Methodology and History of Psychology" (2009-Present); Consulting Editor, "Bulletin of Insectology" (2008-Present); Consulting Editor, "Pesticidas: Revista de Ecotoxicologia e Meio Ambiente" (2005-Present); Consulting Editor, "Nutrition & Metabolism" (2005-Present); Associate Editor, "Journal of Mind and Behavior" (1986-Present) **Awards:** Award for Outstanding Contributions to International Relations, Federal Institute of Paribia, Joao Pessoa, Brazil (2017); Honoree, Colombian Academy of Exact, Physical and Natural Sciences (2016); Lawrence L. Boger Endowed Professorship Award, School of International Studies, Oklahoma State University (2014) **Membership:** The Phi Beta Kappa Society; Psychonomic Society; Sigma Xi; Phi Beta Delta Honor Society; American Association for the Advancement of Science; American Psychological Association; New York Academy of Sciences; Psychonomic Society; Phi Beta Kappa; Sigma Xi **Marquis Who's Who Honors:** Albert Nelson Marquis Lifetime Achievement Award (2017) **Shipping Address:** 4914 Clayton Ln., Stillwater, OK, 74075

John Carter Adams Jr.

Title: Insurance Company Executive **Industry:** Insurance **Company Name:** Brown & Brown **Date of Birth:** 06/13/1936 **Place of Birth:** Williston **State:** FL **Parents:** John Carter Adams; Katharine Anna (Beall) Adams **Marital Status:** Married **Spouse Name:** Leila Nora Johnson (11/28/1958) **Children:** Julia Katharine Rand; Ruth Anne Pickett **Education:** Honorary LHD, Embry-Riddle Aeronautical University (2008); BBA, University of Florida (1958) **Career:** Leadership Council, Brown & Brown Insurance (1999-2006); Executive Vice President, Brown & Brown Insurance (1999-2006); Executive Vice President of Operations, Hilb Group (1994-1999); Executive Vice President, Hilb Group (1993-1994); Chief Operating Officer, Hilb Group (1993-1994); Executive Vice President of Sales and Marketing, Hilb Group (1991-1993) **Career Related:** Chairman, Compensation Committee, Pioneer Bank (2009-2010); Chairman, Compensation Committee, CTLC (2009-2010); Executive Committee, CTLC (2005-2010); Audit Committee, CTLC (2004-2010) **Civic:** Elected Trustee Emeritus, Embry-Riddle Aeronautical University (2010); Trustee Emeritus, Embry-Riddle Aeronautical University (2010) **Military Service:** U.S. Naval Reserve (1953-1961) **Awards:** Inductee, Embry-Riddle Athletic Hall of Fame (2015); J. Saxton Lloyd Outstanding Community Service Award, Civic League Of The Halifax Area (2003); Citizen of the Year, Central Florida Council, Boy Scouts of America (2001); Citizen of the Year, Boys And Girls Club of Volusia and Flagler Counties (2000) **Membership:** Board of Directors, The Council of Insurance Agents & Brokers (1989-Present); Co-Chairman, Nominating Committee, The Council of Insurance Agents & Brokers (1998-1999); Chairman, The Council of Insurance Agents & Brokers (1997-1998); Vice Chairman, The Council of Insurance Agents & Brokers (1996-1997) **Marquis Who's Who Honors:** Albert Nelson Marquis Lifetime Achievement Award (2017) **To what do you attribute your success:** Mr. Adams attributes his success to working hard, starting early, and staying late. **Why did you become involved in your profession or industry:** Mr. Adams' uncle owned an insurance agency in Florida, and because he majored in insurance at the University of Florida, it was a natural progression for him to work there. **What do you consider to be the highlight of your career:** A career highlight for Mr. Adams was becoming chairman of the Council of Insurance Agents & Brokers. **Hobbies:** Body surfing; Handball; Racquetball; Running **Political Affiliations:** Republican **Religion:** Episcopalian **Shipping Address:** 1616 S Peninsula Dr., Daytona Beach, FL, 32118 _

Elaine G. Adevai

Title: Executive Director **Industry:** Health, Wellness and Fitness **Company Name:** New Vista for Families, Inc. **Education:** MS in Clinical Psychology, Rutgers, The State University of New Jersey (1970); BS in Pre-Medical Studies, Douglass College (1967) **Certifications:** Licensed Psychologist **Awards:** Recipient, Distinction Award, Staten Island Chapter, World of Women (2009) **Membership:** New York State Coalition Against Domestic Violence; Human Resources Administration; New York State Office of Children and Family Services **Marquis Who's Who Honors:** Albert Nelson Marquis Lifetime Achievement Award (2017) **To what do you attribute your success:** Ms. Adevai attributes her success to her perseverance and communication skills. **Why did you become involved in your profession or industry:** Ms. Adevai became involved in her profession after gaining experience as a psychologist and desiring to help others in need. **What do you consider to be the highlight of your career:** The highlight of Ms. Adevai's career was starting her own independent shelter. **Where will you be in five years:** In five years, Ms. Adevai hopes to expand her private practice and the program to accommodate a few more families. **Hobbies:** Reading; Cooking; Walking **Shipping Address:** 177 Lindenwood Rd., Staten Island, NY, 10308

Kenyette Adrine-Robinson

Title: Teacher, Writer, Poet, Artist, Photographer, Community Activist, Percussionist **Industry:** Education/Educational Services **Date of Birth:** 05/14/1951 **Place of Birth:** Cleveland **State:** OH **Parents:** James Leroy Adrine; Beatrice (Jones) Johnson **Marital Status:** Divorced **Children:** Jua **Education:** MEd, Kent State University, Ohio (1985); Teacher Intern, Positive Education Program, Cleveland, OH (1984-1985); MEd, Kent State University, Ohio (1980); BA, Kent State University, Ohio (1976) **Career:** Teacher, Child Management Program, Cleveland, OH (1991); Teacher, Cuyahoga County Juvenile Detention Center, Board of Education, Cleveland Metropolitan School District (1987-1991); Teacher, Cleveland Metropolitan School District (1986-2009); Resident Photographer, Teacher, Ann Arbor Art Association (1986); Residential Team, Case Management Therapist, Murtis H. Taylor Multi Services Center, Cleveland, OH (1985-1986); Tutor, Glenville Presbyterian Church, Cleveland, OH (1985-1986); Instructor, Department of Pan-African Studies, Kent State University (1978-1993) **Career Related:** Artists in Education Program, Ohio Arts Council, Columbus, OH (1989-Present); President, Kenyette Productions, Cleveland, OH (1976-Present); Goodwill Ambassador, Aruba (2011); Trustee, Poets' & Writers' League of Greater Cleveland (1991-2006); Trustee, New Day Press Inc. (1991-1999); Consultant, Northeast Ohio Women's Pre-Release Center, Cleveland, OH (1991); Instructor, Cleveland State University, First College (1990); Poets' & Writers' League of Greater Cleveland (1989-2007); New Day Press Inc. (1989-1999); Karamu House Inc., Cleveland, OH (1988-1999) **Civic:** Trustee, Community Christian Church, Euclid, OH (2001-2005) **Military Service:** Writer, Editor, Public Information Office, U.S. Army, Mainz, Germany (1983-1984); Public Information Specialist, Morale Support Activities, U.S. Army, Wiesbaden, Germany (1981-1983); U.S. Army (1969-1971) **Creative Works:** Editor, "The Ghetto in Me" (1994); Editor, "Love is a Child" (1992); Editor, "Black Image Makers" (1988); Author, "Be My Shoo-Gar" (1987); Author, "Thru Kenyette Eyes" (1978); Author, Poems **Awards:** Certificate of Recognition, Aruba Tourism Authority (1997); Certificate of Recognition, Educational Service Center of Cuyahoga County (1988); Honorable Mention, Verse Writers' Guild of Ohio (1988); Fela Sowande Award, Institute for African American Affairs (1976) **Membership:** Progressive Family Reunions Member, African American Travel Conference (2010-Present) **Marquis Who's Who Honors:** Albert Nelson Marquis Lifetime Achievement Award (2017); Distinguished Humanitarian (2017) **Hobbies:** Travel; Music; Photography; Drums; Meditation; History **Shipping Address:** 20131 Champ Dr., Euclid, OH, 44117

Alexey V. Akimov

Title: Chemistry Professor **Industry:** Sciences **Company Name:** University at Buffalo **Education:** PhD in Chemistry, Rice University, Houston, TX (2011); MA in Chemistry, Rice University, Houston, TX (2009); MSc, Lomonosov Moscow State University (2007) **Career:** Assistant Professor, University at Buffalo (2015-Present); Postdoctoral Research Associate, University of Southern California, Los Angeles, CA (2014-2015); Postdoctoral Research Associate, Brookhaven National Laboratory (2012-2014); Postdoctoral Research Associate, University of Rochester, New York (2012-2014); Summer Intern, LANS, LLC, Los Alamos, NM (2010-2011) **Creative Works:** Guest Editor, "Special Issue on Condensed Matter on Theory of Solar Energy Materials," Journal of Physics (2012); Contributor, Articles, Professional Publications; Reviewer, Various Professional Journals **Awards:** Stephen C. Hofmann Fellowship, Rice University (2010); Silver Medal, XXXVI International Mendeleev Olympiad in Chemistry (2002); Numerous Medals, Regional and Russian Olympiads in Chemistry for High School Students **Membership:** American Chemical Society (2010-Present) **Shipping Address:** 716 Natural Sciences Complex, University at Buffalo, Buffalo, NY, 14260

Shirley Jeanne Allen

Title: Humanities Educator (Retired) **Industry:** Education/Educational Services **Date of Birth:** 12/19/1941 **Place of Birth:** Tyler **State:** TX/USA **Parents:** Ralph Carnell Allen; Theressa Gunzell Allen **Marital Status:** Divorced **Spouse Name:** George Taylor **Education:** EdD, University of Rochester, Rochester, NY (1992); MA, Howard University, Washington, DC (1972); BA, Gallaudet University, Washington, DC (1966) **Career:** Professor, Rochester Institute of Technology, New York (1973-2001); Instructor, Dorm Supervisor, Gallaudet University, Washington, DC (1968-1973); Editorial Clerk, Internal Revenue Service, Washington, DC (1967) **Civic:** Visiting Board, Jarvis Christian College, Hawkins, TX (2000-Present) **Awards:** Inductee, Pioneer Hall of Fame, Jarvis Christian College (1992) **Membership:** Council of American Instructors of the Deaf; National Black Deaf Advocates; National Association of the Deaf **Marquis Who's Who Honors:** Albert Nelson Marquis Lifetime Achievement Award (2017) **Why did you become involved in your profession or industry:** Dr. Allen became involved in her profession after being inspired by her father, stepmother, grandmother, aunts, and uncles, who were all educators. **What do you consider to be the highlight of your career:** The biggest highlight of Dr. Allen's career was going to conferences and meetings and seeing her students being successful. Another highlight for her was becoming the first black deaf female to earn a doctoral degree. **Hobbies:** Reading; Writing **Religion:** Baptist **Shipping Address:** 9117 Vicksburg Ave., Texas City, TX, 77591

John R. Allison

Title: Lawyer, Author, Coach **Industry:** Law and Legal Services **Company Name:** The Coach for Lawyers LLC **Date of Birth:** 02/09/1945 **Place of Birth:** San Antonio **State:** TX/USA **Parents:** Lyle Forehand (Stepfather); Beatrice (Kaliner) Forehand **Marital Status:** Married **Spouse Name:** Rebecca M. Picard **Children:** Katharine A. Allison **Education:** JD, University of Washington School of Law (1969); BS, Stanford University (1966) **Certifications:** Certified Emergency Medical Technician, State of California (2015) **Career:** Owner, Coach for Lawyers, LLC (2012-Present); Attorney, Larson King (2010-2013); Assistant General Counsel, 3M Co. (2000-2010); Senior Counsel, 3M Co. (1994-2000); Principal, Betts, Patterson & Mines (1986-1994); Partner, Garvey, Schubert & Barer (1973-1986); Associate, Garvey, Schubert & Barer (1969-1973) **Career Related:** Board of Directors, Southern Minnesota Regional Legal Services (2002-2010); Chair, ABA (1992-1993); Chair Elect, ABA (1991-1992); Vice Chairman, Toxic and Hazardous Substances and Environmental Law Committee, ABA (1986-1991); Bar Examiner, Washington State Bar Association (1985-1994); Judge Pro Tempore, King County Superior Court (1983-1994); Chairman, Judicial Evaluation Polling Committee, Seattle-King County Bar Association (1982-1983); Judge Pro Tempore, Seattle Municipal Court (1979-1987); Lecturer, University of Washington (1970-1973); Lecturer, Business Law, Seattle University (1970) **Civic:** Member, Planning Committee, Mendocino Coast District Hospital (2017-Present); Board Member, Treasurer, Mendocino Coast Hospital Foundation (2016-Present); Emergency Medical Technician, Firefighter, Westport Volunteer Fire Department, California (2015-Present); Member, Finance Committee, Mendocino Coast District Hospital (2014-2017) **Creative Works:** Author, "The Art of Practicing Law: A Practical Guide for Lawyers" (2017); Author, "Transforming the Practice of Law: Reclaiming the Soul of the Legal Profession" (2015); Author, "Choosing Your Lawyer: An Insiders Practical Guide to Making a Really Good Choice" (2013) **Awards:** Order of the Coif (1969) **Membership:** Board of Bar Examiners, Washington State Bar Association (1984-1994); The District of Columbia Bar **Bar Admissions:** The District of Columbia (1973); Supreme Court of the United States (1973); Washington (1969) **Hobbies:** Reading; Hiking; Enjoying the outdoors **Business Address:** 4040 Civic Center Dr., Suite 200, San Rafael, CA, 94903 **Shipping Address:** PO Box 1205, Fort Bragg, CA, 95437 **Website:** http://www.coachlawyers.com

Richard P. Ames

Title: Nephrologist, Educator **Industry:** Medicine & Health Care **Company Name:** Mt. Sinai West Hospital **Date of Birth:** 08/04/1932 **Place of Birth:** Northampton **State:** MA **Parents:** Harold Leslie Ames; Effie Melissa (Crowley) Ames **Marital Status:** Married **Spouse Name:** Janet Ann Shaw (10/7/1961) **Children:** Patricia Jean; Brian Shaw **Education:** Fellow, New York Heart Association, Presbyterian Hospital, New York, NY (1961-1963); MD, Columbia University (1958); BA, Williams College, Cum Laude (1954) **Certifications:** Diplomate, American Board of Internal Medicine; Diplomate, American Board of Nephrology; Diplomate, American Board of Medical Oncology; Diplomate, American Board of Hematology; Specialist in Clinical Hypertension, American Society of Hypertension **Career:** Nephrologist, St. Luke's Roosevelt Hospital (Mt. Sinai West Hospital), New York, NY (1970-Present); Chief of Nephrology, St. Clare's Hospital, New York, NY (1998-2000); Associate Director of Nephrology, St. Luke's Roosevelt Hospital, New York, NY (1990-1993); Director, Physical Diagnosis, St. Luke's Roosevelt Hospital, New York, NY (1981-1994); Chief, Hypertension Clinic, St. Luke's Roosevelt Hospital, New York, NY (1973-1994); Investigator, Whitehall Foundation, New York, NY (1967-1970); **Career Related:** Clinical Professor, Columbia University, New York, NY (1989-2013); Director of Hypertension, American Health Foundation, New York City, NY (1972-1982) **Civic:** Assistant Surgeon, United States Public Health Service (1963-1965) **Creative Works:** Contributing Author, "Messerli's Cardiovascular Drug Therapy" (1996); Contributing Author, "Laragh and Brenner's Hypertension" (1995); Contributing Author, "Clinical Cardiovascular Therapeutics" (1989); Co-Editor, "Medical Symposium Drugs" (1988); Contributing Author, "Frontiers in Hypertension Reserve" (1981); Contributing Author, "Topics in Hypertension" (1980) **Awards:** Named, Top Doctor, U.S. News & World Report L.P. (2011-Present); Honoree, Top Metro Physician, Consumers Research Council (1998-Present); Honoree, Castle Connolly (1997-Present); Named Super Doctor, The New York Times Company (2009-2013) **Membership:** Fellow, American College of Physicians; Council For High Blood Pressure Research, Kidney Council, American Heart Association, Inc.; Charter Member, American Society of Hypertension; American Society of Nephrology; Phi Beta Kappa; International Society Nephrology; Association of American Physicians and Surgeons **Marquis Who's Who Honors:** Distinguished Humanitarian (2017) **Why did you become involved in your profession or industry:** Dr. Ames' brother-in-law is in medicine. **Business Address:** 1000 10th Ave., New York, NY, 10019 **Shipping Address:** 110 Sherwood Rd., Ridgewood, NJ, 07450

Bill Maxwell Anderson

Title: Artist, Educator **Industry:** Fine Art **Date of Birth:** 07/31/1941 **Place of Birth:** Mankato **State:** MN/USA **Parents:** Robert Arthur Anderson; June Anderson **Marital Status:** Married **Spouse Name:** Ausma Edite Leipins Anderson (8/5/1962) **Children:** Kerri; Craig **Education:** Graduate Coursework, Minnesota State University, Mankato, MN (1974); Graduate Coursework, University of California, Irvine, CA (1969); Graduate Coursework, California State University, Long Beach, CA (1964-1968); BS, Minnesota State University, Mankato, MN (1963) **Career:** Owner, Bill Anderson Art Gallery (1994-Present); Art Teacher, Muralist, East Los Angeles College, California (2001-2002); Art Teacher, Orange County School of the Arts (1985-1996); Art Teacher, Los Alamitos Unified School District, California (1980-2001); Art Teacher, Anaheim Union High School District, California (1973-1980); Art Teacher, Appleton West High School, Appleton, WI (1969-1973); Art Teacher, Long Beach Unified School District, California (1963-1969) **Creative Works:** Author, "Sunset Beach: Through the Eyes of Artist Bill Anderson (2017); Author, "Huntington Beach: Through the Eyes of Artist Bill Anderson" (2016); Author, "Seal Beach: Through the Eyes of Artist Bill Anderson" (2016); Author, "Baseball: Great American Pastime Through the Eyes of Artist Bill Anderson" (2016); Author, "The Female Form: Through the Eyes of Artist Bill Anderson" (2016); Author, "The Fantastic Horse: Through the Eyes of Artist Bill Anderson" (2016); Author, "Greece: Through the Eyes of Artist Bill Anderson" (2014); Author, "The Heritage Series: U.S. Military Joint Forces Training Base" (2014); Exhibitor, One-Man Show, Chaffey Community Museum of Art, Rancho Cucamonga, CA, Joint Forces Training Base, Los Alamitos, CA (2007); Exhibitor, "Summer Solstice", Millard Sheets Art Center, Pomona, CA (2004-2005); Exhibitor, Ontario Museum (2004); Painter, Murals (2002); East Los Angeles College Exhibitor, Vincent Price Art Museum (2000); Exhibitor, Luckman Fine Arts Complex, California State University, Los Angeles, CA (1995); Exhibitor, Museo Nacional de la Acuarela (1994); Author, "The Work of Bill Anderson" (1984); Exhibitor, Group Exhibit, "Olympic International Artist Exchange," Huntington Beach Art Center, CA (1984) **Marquis Who's Who Honors:** Albert Nelson Marquis Lifetime Achievement Award (2017) **To what do you attribute your success:** Mr. Anderson attributes his success to his wife, Ausma Edite Liepins Anderson. **Business Address:** 16812 S Pacific Coast Highway, Sunset Beach, CA, 90742 **Shipping Address:** 17831 San Leandro Lane, Huntington Beach, CA, 92647 **Website:** http://www.billandersonartgallery.com

Helene C. Andreu

Title: Dance Instructor **Industry:** Education/Educational Services **Company Name:** Henry Street Settlement **Date of Birth:** 11/08/1930 **Place of Birth:** New York **State:** NY/USA **Parents:** Gaston Andreu; Clotilde Jaureguibéhére **Education:** MA in Dance Education, Columbia University (1971); BA, The City University of New York (1953); Coursework, School of American Ballet (1948-1954) **Career:** Dance Instructor, Henry Street Settlement, New York, NY (1989-1998); Dance Instructor, Choreographer, Board of Education, Adult Education, New York, NY (1975-1992); Part-time Adjunct Lecturer, Dance, The City University of New York, New York, NY (1973-2002); Singer, Dancer, Choreographer, Ephrata Star Playhouse (1964-1967); Dance Instructor, Substitute, Board of Education After School Centers, New York, NY (1963-1973); Dance Instructor, Private Dance Studios, Brooklyn, NY (1959-1992); Singer, Dancer, Choreographer, American Savoyards, New York, NY (1957-1968) **Career Related:** Speech/English Tutor, The City University of New York (1989-1998) **Civic:** Volunteer Teacher, History of Dance, Institute of Brooklyn Lifelong Learning, Brooklyn College (2007-2008); Volunteer, Brooklyn Public Library Literacy Program **Creative Works:** Author, Photographer, Choreographer, "Dance - An Illustrated History" (2015); Author, Photographer, Choreographer, "Dance, Movement, and Nutrition" (2006); Author, Photographer, Choreographer, "Jazz Dance Styles and Steps" (2003); Author, Photographer, Choreographer, "Aerobic Razzmatazz" (2000); Author, Choreographer, "Jazz Dance: An Adult Beginners Guide" (1983) **Membership:** Actors Equity Association **Hobbies:** Gardening; Singing; Photography **Shipping Address:** 983 E 29th St., Brooklyn, NY, 11210

John W. Arlidge

Title: Consultant on Energy Resources and Regulation **Industry:** Consulting **Date of Birth:** 02/04/1933 **Place of Birth:** Rochester **State:** NY/USA **Parents:** Harold Wesley Arlidge; Grace Edith (Kempshall) Arlidge **Marital Status:** Married **Spouse Name:** Sandra Marie Koswar (2/4/1955) **Children:** James William; Edward John **Education:** BS, California State University, Los Angeles (1962) **Certifications:** Registered Professional Engineer, State of California; Registered Professional Engineer, State of Nevada; Registered Professional Engineer, State of Utah **Career:** Consultant on Energy Resources and Regulation, Las Vegas, NV (1995-Present); Senior Vice President, Government Affairs, Nevada Power Company (Now NV Energy) (1989-1993); Vice President, Nevada Electric Investment Company (1982-1989); Director, Nevada Electric Investment Company (1982-1989); Vice President, Resource Planning and Power Dispatch, Nevada Power Company (Now NV Energy) (1982-1989); Assistant to Vice President, Nevada Power Company (Now NV Energy) (1974-1982); Power System Resource Planning Research and Development, City of Los Angeles (1962-1974); Communications System Engineering Design and Purchase, City of Los Angeles (1961-1962); Deputy Sheriff of Los Angeles County (1954-1962) **Career Related:** Advisor, Electric-Lignite Sector, Ministry Industry and Trade, Warsaw, Poland (1992-1995); Advisory Council, Las Vegas District (1980-1992); Energy Engineering Planning Committee (1978); Western Utility Group on Federal Land (1977); Endangered Species Subcommittee Rail Issues Group, Edison Electrical Institute (1977); Consultant on Air, Land and Water, Western Regional Council (1977); Nevada Solar Energy Development Advisory Group (1976-1986); Nevada Advisory Board, Bureau of Land Management (1975-1977); Nevada Engineer's Advisory Committee on Geothermal Development (1974-1976); Advanced Energy System Divisional Committee, Electric Power Research Institute (1973-1992); Energy Task Force WEST (1972-1984); Advisory Committee, Secretary of Energy on Coal Resource Development; Research Advisory Board, University of Nevada; Trustee, Corporate Development, SciTech Nevada **Civic:** National Coal Council, U.S. Department of Energy (1988-1993); Nevada Advisory Board, The Nature Conservancy **Creative Works:** Contributor, Articles on Energy Resources, Various Publications **Why did you become involved in your profession or industry:** Mr. Arlidge became involved in his profession after leaving high school early to become an apprentice in the electrical field. **Shipping Address:** 975 Lizzie Lane, Saint George, UT, 84790

Matthew C. Armand

Title: Director of Administration **Industry:** Utilities **Company Name:** Lake County, Ohio Utilities **Education:** BBA, John Carroll University, University Heights, OH, Cum Laude (2004) **Career:** Director of Administration, Lake County, Ohio Utilities (2016-Present); Public Service Coordinator, Lake County, Ohio Utilities (2013-2016); Assistant Billing/Operations Manager, Lake County, Ohio Utilities (2011-2013); Billing Specialist, Lake County, Ohio Utilities (2007-2011) **Career Related:** Core Member, Professional Development Group, Lake County, Ohio Utilities (2013-Present); Rules & Regulation Committee, Lake County, Ohio Utilities (2013-Present); Facilitator, Public Information Committee, Lake County, Ohio Utilities (2013-Present); Facilitator, Newsletter Committee, Lake County, Ohio Utilities (2013-Present); Water Review Committee, Lake County, Ohio Utilities (2013-Present); Customer Service Committee, Lake County, Ohio Utilities (2011-2015); Professional Development Group, Lake County, Ohio Utilities (2008-2011); Organizer & Facilitator, "Lunch & Learn" Series for LCDU Employees, Lake County, Ohio Utilities; Leader, Upgrade of Projectors, ULAB; Research Contributor, Telephone Analysis and Upgrade, Lake County, Ohio Utilities **Creative Works:** Co-Creator, "New Customer Informational Packets," Lake County, Ohio Utilities (2015); Developer, Tracker & Monitor, "Customer Service Surveys," Lake County, Ohio Utilities (2014); Author, Informational Handout, "All You Need to Know About Water Mains," Lake County, Ohio Utilities; Author, Informational Handout, "Leak Detection Tips," Lake County, Ohio Utilities; Author, Informational Handout, "Proper Disposal of Grease," Lake County, Ohio Utilities; Author, Informational Handout, "What NOT to Put Down the Toilet," Lake County, Ohio Utilities; Author, Informational Handout, "Winter Tips to Prevent Pipes from Freezing," Lake County, Ohio Utilities **Awards:** "Cyanotoxin Testing Equipment Grant," Ohio EPA (2014); Academic Achievement Award, Office of Multicultural Affairs (2003); Academic Achievement Award, Office of Multicultural Affairs (2002) **Membership:** Finance & Budget Chairperson, Board of Trustees, Laketran (2013); Vice President, Board of Trustees, Laketran (2012-2018); Finance & Budget Chairperson, Board of Trustees, Laketran (2011); Board of Trustees, Laketran (2009-2012); Beta Gamma Sigma, Inc. (2005); Phi Eta Sigma (2002); American Water Works Association; Former Board of Public Transportation System, Laketran **Business Address:** 105 Main St., Floor 2, Painesville, OH, 44077

Richard Anthony Arnell

Title: Radiologist **Industry:** Medicine & Health Care **Date of Birth:** 08/21/1938 **Place of Birth:** Chicago **State:** IL/USA **Parents:** Tony Frank Yaki; Mary Martha (Oberman) Yaki **Marital Status:** Widowed **Spouse Name:** Paula Ann Youngberg (6/28/1964, Deceased 9/11/2015) **Children:** Carla Ann Arnell; Paula Marie Arnell; Paul Anthony **Education:** MD, The University of Iowa (1964); BA, Grinnell College (1960) **Certifications:** Diplomate, The American Board of Radiology; Diplomate, ABNM **Career:** Founder, Radiology Associates, LLC (2000-2001); President, Radiology Associates, LLC (2000-2001); President, Advanced Imaging Center (1993-2001); President, Moline Management Associates, LTD (1990-2017); Chairman, Metro MRI (1990-2015); President, Advanced Imaging Center (1990-2001); Partner, Advanced Imaging Center (1968-1993) **Career Related:** Medical Staff, Illinois Hospital (1995-2003); Medical Staff, Mercer Health (1994-2003); Medical Staff, UnityPoint Health (1992-2003); Medical Director, Radiology Department, United Medical Center (1992-1999); Chairman, Radiology Department, United Medical Center (1992-1994); Staff, United Medical Center (1989-1992); Director of Continuing Member Education Progressive for Physicians, Moline Lutheran Hospital (1979-1983); Board of Directors, Moline Lutheran Hospital (1977-1983); Vice President, Quad City HMO Health Plan (1979); Executive Committee Member, Midstate Foundation for Medical Care (1976-1979); Trustee, Midstate Foundation for Medical Care (1975-1979); Staff, Moline Lutheran Hospital (1968-1988); Staff, Moline Public Hospital (1968-1988); Clinical Lecturer, The University of Iowa **Civic:** President, Moline Management Associates, LTD (2014-2017); Chairman of Managing Committee, METRO MRI (1990-2013); Associate Chairman, Professional Division, United Way of Illinois (1985); Chairman, Lutheran Medical Center Foundation, Lutheran Medical Center (1984-1988); Chairman, United Health Foundation (1989-1991); President/Founder, Lutheran Medical Center Foundation, Lutheran Medical Center (1981-1984); **Military Service:** Major, Medical Corps, U. S. Army Reserve (1964-1970) **Awards:** Doctor of Distinction Award, Rock Island County Medical Society Alliance (1998); **Membership:** President, Independent Physicians Association of Western Illinois (1986); Vice President, Independent Physicians Association of Western Illinois (1985); Director, Independent Physicians Association of Western Illinois (1984-1986) **Marquis Who's Who Honors:** Distinguished Humanitarian (2017) **Business Address:** 615 Valley View Dr., Ste 101, Moline, IL, 61265 **Shipping Address:** 3904 7th Ave., Rock Island, IL, 61201

Patricia E. Arterberry

Title: Elementary School Educator (Retired) **Industry:** Education/Educational Services **Date of Birth:** 04/11/1947 **Place of Birth:** Huntingburg **State:** IN **Parents:** Otis T. Barnett; Fanny Delores Wessel **Marital Status:** Married **Spouse Name:** Ronnie G. Arterberry (10/15/1994) **Children:** Eric Alan; Randall Gene; Tony Gene **Education:** MA, University of Evansville (1973); BS, University of Evansville (1970) **Career:** Primary Grade Teacher, Tell City-Troy Township Schools; Grade 3 Teacher, Tell City-Troy Township Schools **Civic:** Active Member, Boy Scouts of America; Active Member, United Methodist Church; Trustee, Tell City Chapter, United Methodist Church **Awards:** Cross & Flame Religious Award, National Education Association (2008); District Award of Merit, Boy Scouts of America; Council Silver Beaver Award, Boy Scouts of America **Membership:** National Education Association; Indiana State Teachers Association; Tell City-Troy Township Classroom Teachers' Association; Order of the Eastern Star; DKGSI **Marquis Who's Who Honors:** Albert Nelson Marquis Lifetime Achievement Award (2017) **Why did you become involved in your profession or industry:** Mrs. Arterberry became involved in her profession because she likes to work with children. **What do you consider to be the highlight of your career:** Ms. Arterberry's son Eric, who teaches in New York, earned the "Outstanding Math Teacher of The Year Award" in 2015. **Shipping Address:** 9575 Sweetwater Rd., Tell City, IN, 47586

Charlene Sutter Arvizu

Title: Elementary School Educator **Industry:** Education/Educational Services **Company Name:** Berryessa Union School District **Date of Birth:** 03/01/1947 **Place of Birth:** San Jose **State:** CA/USA **Parents:** Joseph Carl Sutter; Marjorie Loreen (Nylin) Sutter **Marital Status:** Married **Spouse Name:** Ambrose Emanuel Arvizu (4/7/1980) **Children:** Joseph Todd Nottingham; Matthew Sutter **Education:** BA in Art, San Jose State University (1964); Master's Degree in Young Child Learning Needs, San Jose State University **Certifications:** Certified in Special Education in Grades K-14, San Jose State University (1969); Certified in K-9 Education, San Jose State University (1969); Certified Specialist in Learning Handicapped, San Jose State University (1969) **Career:** Kindergarten Teacher, Ruskin Elementary School, Berryessa Union School District (1974-Present); Resource Center Director, Grades K-5, Berryessa Union School District (1971-1973); Special Education Teacher, Grades K-12, Berryessa Union School District (1969-1971) **Career Related:** Consultant, Bureau of Education & Research (1990-Present); Lecturer, Bureau of Education & Research (1990-Present); Instructor, San Jose County Office of Education (1985-1994); Instructor, Chapman University (1985-1988); Instructor, Ohlone College, Fremont, CA (1980-1989); National Lecturer in Field; Consultant in Field; Presenter in Field **Creative Works:** Author, "Together We Can Make a World of Difference" (2009); Author, "Strengthening Your Kindergarten Using Thematic, Integrate Literature Based Strategies" (2002); Author, "Current Best Strategies to Help All Your Kindergartens to be Successful" (2002); Author, "Whole Language Strategies in the Classroom" (2001); **Awards:** Outstanding Teacher of the Year Award, Santa Clara Valley (2006); Teacher of the Year Award, Berryessa Union School District (2005-2006); Outstanding Teacher of the Year Award, Berryessa Union School District (2005); Award, Bureau of Education And Research (1998); **Membership:** International Literacy Association; California Reading Association; International Book Association for Young Readers; Children's Book Council; California School-Age Consortium; Planetary Citizens; SCBWI; DKGSI **Marquis Who's Who Honors:** Albert Nelson Marquis Lifetime Achievement Award (2017); Distinguished Humanitarian (2017) **Why did you become involved in your profession or industry:** Ms. Arvizu became involved in her profession because she wanted to be a teacher since she was in high school. Her cousin was a teacher and loved what she did. Ms. Arvizu focused on forming creativity in kindergarten, and molding children for the future was what she loved. **Hobbies:** Horseback riding; Historical hula dance; Snorkeling **Shipping Address:** 3010 Daurine Ct., Gilroy, CA, 95020

Joyce Charlene Atwood

Title: School System Administrator **Industry:** Education/Educational Services **Company Name:** Ohio University **Date of Birth:** 04/29/1943 **Place of Birth:** Chillicothe **State:** OH/USA **Parents:** Pearl Workman; Blanche (Martindill) Workman **Education:** Postgraduate Coursework, Ashland University (1992-2013); Postgraduate Coursework, The Ohio State University (1976-1988); MEd, Ohio University (1969); EdB, Ohio University (1965) **Certifications:** Certified Teacher; Certified Supervisor; Certified Administrator **Career:** Director of Resource Development, Ohio University (2008-Present); Assistant Superintendent for Curriculum and Instruction, Ohio University (2008-Present); Assistant Superintendent for Curriculum and Instruction, Chillicothe City School District (1993-2008); Administrative Assistant, Chillicothe City School District (1989-1993); Assistant Principal, Middle School, Chillicothe City School District (1988-1989); Teaching Leader in Reading Recovery, Chillicothe City School District (1986-1988); Early Education Reading Teacher, Chillicothe City School District (1973-1986); Elementary School Teacher, Chillicothe City School District (1965-1973) **Career Related:** Member, Child Care Advisory Board, Portsmouth, OH (1993-1995); Consultant, Study Skills for Management in Industry, Pickaway-Ross Joint Vocational School District (1984-1988) **Civic:** Church Scholarship Team, Walnut Street United Methodist Church (2014-Present); President, Altrusa Branch, Altrusa International, Inc. (2013); Philanthropic Education Organization Member, Walnut Street United Methodist Church (2012-2013); President, South Central Ohio Region, Big Brothers Big Sisters of America (2012-2013); President, YMCA Board (2010-2011); President, The Delta Kappa Gamma Society International (2010); Philanthropic Education Organizer, The Delta Kappa Gamma Society International (2010); Altrusa International, Inc. (2005-2010); Faith Formation, Walnut Street United Methodist Church (2004-2010) **Awards:** Nominee, Citizen of Year, Junior Chamber International, Inc. (2015); Educator Emeritus Award (2012); Recipient, Red Cross Hero (2008); Altrusa Maime L. Boss Award (2008); North Central Accreditation Award (2002); George Washington University Partnership Award (2002); Ohio Creative Staff Development Award, ACSD (1997); **Marquis Who's Who Honors:** Albert Nelson Marquis Lifetime Achievement Award (2017) **To what do you attribute your success:** Ms. Atwood attributes her success to her motivation and passion to help every student be the best that they can become. **Hobbies:** Reading; Gardening **Religion:** Methodist **Shipping Address:** 10 Overlook Dr., Chillicothe, OH, 45601

Lorraine Avery

Title: Senior Vice President for Diversity and Inclusion, Consultant **Industry:** Financial Services **Company Name:** Associated Banc-Corp (Retired) **Education:** Coursework in Business Administration, University of Wisconsin **Certifications:** Total Quality Management Designation; Special Designation for Training Customer Program Used by the Ritz-Carlton and Other High-Quality Companies **Awards:** Certified Contact Center Program, J.D. Power (2016); Woman of Courage, Confidence and Character, Girl Scouts of the Northwestern Great Lakes (GSNWGL) (2013); Woman of the Year, National Association of Professional Women (2012); Woman of the Year, International Women's Leadership Association (2012); Best and Brightest Award, University of Wisconsin (2000) **To what do you attribute your success:** Ms. Avery attributes her success to her personal passion for the service industry and for helping customers. She is also grateful for the many mentors she has had, the networks and organizations of which she has been a part, and her community involvement. **Why did you become involved in your profession or industry:** Ms. Avery became involved in her profession through her passion for customer service. **Where will you be in five years:** In five years, Ms. Avery hopes to move into a higher executive role and pursue more consulting opportunities. **Hobbies:** Writing; Sewing; Fishing; Bowling; Reading; Gourmet cooking; Animals; Caring for her pets **Business Address:** 1305 Main Street, 1305 Main Street, WI, Stevens Point, 54481 **Shipping Address:** 3346 Sandy Acres Drive, Plover, WI, 54467 **Website:** http://www.associatedbank.com

Anne Louise Ayers

Title: Estate Administrator, Counselor **Industry:** Education/Educational Services **Date of Birth:** 10/22/1948 **Place of Birth:** Albuquerque **State:** NM **Parents:** F. Ernest Ayers; Gladys Marguerite (Miles) Ayers **Marital Status:** Single **Education:** MEd, Seattle Pacific University (1971); BA, The University of Kansas (1970); Coursework, Virginia Polytechnic Institute and State University; Coursework, College of William & Mary; Coursework, Hampton University; Coursework, American University; Coursework, University of Washington **Certifications:** Court Appointed Estate Administrator, States of Maryland, Washington, and California (2008) **Career:** Probate Administration, California, Washington, and Maryland (2010-Present); Staff Consultant in Student Development, Central Washington University, Ellensburg, WA (1996-2013); Education Services Specialist, National Aeronautics and Space Administration Headquarters, Washington, DC (1989-1996); Member, The International Platform Association (1979-2009); Education Specialist, National Mine Health and Safety Academy, Beckley, WV (1979-1989); Education Specialist, U. S. Army Transportation School, Fort Eustis, Virginia (1977-1979); Education Service Specialist, General Educational Development Center, Fort Monroe, VA (1975-1977); Instructor of Psychology, Hampton University, Virginia (1973-1975); Director, Aerospace Defense Command Resident Education Centers for North Dakota and Montana, Chapman University, Orange, CA (1972-1974); Staff Consultant in Student Development, Central Washington University, Ellensburg, WA (1971-1972) **Career Related:** President, Appalachian Love Arts, Martinsburg, WV (1981-2016); Substitute Counselor, Berkeley County Schools (1997-2013); Teacher, Berkeley County Schools (1997-2013) **Civic:** Elected Social Chairman, Church Youth Group of 100 (1965-1966); Elected Faith Chairman, Church Youth Group of 100 (1965-1966); Volunteer, Methodist Church; **Creative Works:** Photographer, International Library of Photography (1992-2010) **Marquis Who's Who Honors:** Albert Nelson Marquis Lifetime Achievement Award (2017); Distinguished Humanitarian (2017) **To what do you attribute your success:** Dr. Ayers attributes her success to the saying, "Anything worth doing at all, is worth doing well." **Hobbies:** Traveling; Coin collecting/numismatics; Clarinet; Oboe; Enjoying life; Collecting mine gems; Building rock gardens; Artistic activities; Outdoor work; Auto repair **Religion:** Protestant **Shipping Address:** 9309 Falls Bridge Ln., Potomic, MD, 20854

Malvina F. Baica

Title: Mathematics Professor **Industry:** Education/Educational Services **Company Name:** University of Wisconsin **Date of Birth:** 11/03/1942 **Place of Birth:** Oravita **Country of Origin:** Banat Romania **Parents:** Adam Bunghiu; Cornelia (Stefan) Bunghiu **Marital Status:** Single **Spouse Name:** Adrian Baica (1963-2014) **Education:** PhD in Mathematics, University of Houston (1980); MS in Mathematics, Illinois Institute of Technology (1974); MS in Mathematics and Mechanics, University of Timisoara, Romania (1965); BS in Mathematics and Physics, University of Timisoara, Romania (1964) **Career:** Full Professor of Mathematics, Researcher, University of Wisconsin-Whitewater (1992-2016); Associate Professor, University of Wisconsin-Whitewater (1989-1992); Assistant Professor, University of Wisconsin-Whitewater (1984-1989); Assistant Professor, Valparaiso University (1983-1984); Assistant Professor, Marshall University, Huntington, WV (1981-1983); Assistant Professor, Marquette University, Milwaukee, WI (1980-1981); Assistant Professor, Western Illinois University, Macomb, IL (1978-1980) **Creative Works:** Author, "Several Star Problems in Analytic Number Theory" (2005); Co-Author, "Several Star Problems in Analytic Number Theory" (2005); Author, "The Algorithmic Solution of the Original Euclidean Fermat's Last Theorem" (2001); Author, "The Euler System for the Algebraic Number Theory and Mathematical Models in Pollution" (2000); Contributor, More than 80 Articles to Professional Journals on Algebraic Number Theory, Number Theory and Engineering; Contributor, Papers in Celestial Mechanics; Inventor, Theory of Algorithms in Computer Science; Reviewer, "Computer and Industrial Engineering" **Awards:** Nominee, Excellence in Research Award, University of Wisconsin (1989-Present); Honorary Diploma, Romanian ASTRA Association (2003); Recipient, Excellence in Research Award, University of Wisconsin (1988) **Membership:** New York Academy of Sciences; Former Member, Pi Mu Epsilon **Shipping Address:** 122 N Esterly Ave., Whitewater, WI, 53190

Sandra Lee Bailey

Title: Secondary School Educator, Department Chairman **Industry:** Education/Educational Services **Company Name:** Edmonds School District **Date of Birth:** 01/27/1946 **Place of Birth:** Redding **State:** CA **Parents:** Robert Jordan; Florence Husby **Marital Status:** Married **Spouse Name:** Tom Bailey (6/22/1974) **Children:** Rebecca; Heather **Education:** MA in International Relations, University of Washington (1970); BA in Social Science, Major in English, Minor in Physical Science, San Diego State University (1967); Student, University of Uppsala (1965-1966) **Certifications:** Certification, Secondary Teacher, California; Certification, K-12 Teacher, Washington **Career:** Department Chairman for Social Studies and Special Education Departments, Edmonds School District (1970-2000, 2009-2018); Social Studies Department Chairman, Numerous School and District Committees, Shoreline School District (2000-2009); Special Education Teacher, Shasta Union High School District (1968-1969); Tutor, San Diego School Urban League (1967-1968); English Teacher, Skiffgarden Hospital Uppsala, Sweden (1965-1966) **Career Related:** District Representative to the Puget Sound Educational Consortium, Teacher Trainer and Workshop Leader, Edmonds School District (1970-2006); Adjunct Professor of Social Studies Methods, Seattle University (2004); Adjunct Professor of Learning Styles, Seattle Pacific University (1994) **Civic:** Council President, Council Vice President, Teacher and Hospitality Leader, First Lutheran Church, Shoreline, WA (1978-2018); Russian Sister Churches Committee Member, Lutheran Synod of Seattle, WA (2005); Volunteer, Olympic Ballet Theater (1984-2003); Organizer, Regional Dance Festival (2000-2003) **Creative Works:** Contributor, Banpo Village Prehistoric Dig, China: Tradition and Transformation, ERIC, U.S. Department of Education (1999); Contributor, Various Articles, Professional Publications; Author, Teacher Leadership Articles, Puget Sound Educational Consortium **Awards:** Recipient, Excellence in Teaching Award Shoreline School District, Shorewood High School (2001); Recipient, Angel Award for 20 Years of Service, Olympic Ballet (1999); Fulbright-Hays Scholarship to China, U.S. Government (1999); Recipient, Excellence in Teaching Awards, Edmonds School District (1985-1988, 1991, 1995-1998); Recipient, Civic Service Award, Edmonds City Council (1995) **Membership:** Associate, National Education Association; Associate, Edmonds Education Association; Former Member, ASCD; Alpha Lambda Delta National Honorary Society **Marquis Who's Who Honors:** Distinguished Humanitarian (2017) **Political Affiliations:** Democrat **Shipping Address:** 18355 Ridgefield Rd., NW, Shoreline, WA, 98177

Harrison M. Bains Jr.

Title: Corporate Financial Executive (Retired) **Industry:** Financial Services **Date of Birth:** 07/08/1943 **Place of Birth:** Pasadena **State:** CA **Parents:** Harrison MacKellar Bains; Celeste Adele (Callahan) Bains **Marital Status:** Married **Spouse Name:** Leslie E. Tawney (3/7/1970) **Children:** Harrison MacKellar III; Tawney Elizabeth **Education:** MBA, University of California, Berkeley (1966); BA, University of Redlands, California (1964) **Career:** Retired (2004); Vice President, Treasurer, Bristol-Myers Squibb Co. (2002-2004); Acting CFO, Bristol-Myers Squibb Co., New York, NY (2002); Vice President, Treasurer, Bristol-Myers Squibb Co., New York, NY (1988-2002); Senior Vice President, Chase Manhattan Bank, New York, NY (1987-1988); Vice President, Treasurer, RJR Nabisco, Inc., Winston-Salem, NC (1985-1987); Senior Vice President, Treasurer, Nabisco Brands, Inc., East Hanover, NJ (1981-1985); Vice President, Treasurer, Nabisco Inc., East Hanover, NJ (1976-1981); Assistant Treasurer, Richardson-Merrell Inc. (1972-1976); Assistant Vice President, Citibank N.A. (1968-1972) **Membership:** Director, Cara Therapeutic, Inc. (2013-Present); Trustee, Park Avenue Armory (2007-Present); Trustee, Civil War Trust (2005-Present); Trustee, Mercer Global Funds (2005-Present); Former Trustee, Bank of America Funds; Overlook Hospital Foundation; The University of Redlands; Financial Executives Institute **Shipping Address:** 435 E. 52nd St., Apt. 9B, New York, NY, 10022

William Baker

Title: Lawyer **Industry:** Law and Legal Services **Company Name:** Baker, Baker. P.A. **Date of Birth:** 09/05/1946 **Place of Birth:** Baltimore **State:** MD/USA **Parents:** George William Baker; Jane (Parr) Baker **Marital Status:** Married **Spouse Name:** Christine Corbett (10/23/1982) **Children:** William Corbett; Brendan Parr; Laura Elizabeth **Education:** JD, University of Maryland (1971); BA, Saint Francis University, Loretto, PA (1968) **Career:** Partner, Baker, Baker P.A., Baltimore, MD (1972-Present); Law Clerk, Office of the Attorney General of Maryland (1969-1971) **Career Related:** Civil Case Mediator, Circuit Court for Baltimore County; Adjunct Professor, University of Maryland Francis King Carey School of Law; Lecturer, The Maryland Institute for Continuing Professional Education of Lawyers; Lecturer, National Business Institute, Inc.; Lecturer, Lorman Education Services **Civic:** Accessions Committee, The Baltimore Museum Of Art (2017-Present); Trustee, Hughes Foundation (2013-Present); Civil Mediator, District Court for Baltimore County (2001-Present); Civil Mediator, Circuit Court for Baltimore County (1997-Present); Arbitrator, Maryland Health Claims Arbitration Board (1984-Present) **Creative Works:** Sponsor, "Off the Shelf: Modern and Contemporary Artists' Books," The Walters Art Museum (2017); Sponsor, "Faberge and the Russian Crafts Tradition: An Empire's Legacy," The Walters Art Museum (2017); Co-Sponsor, "A Feast for the Senses: Art and Experience in Medieval Europe," The Walters Art Museum (2016-2017); Co-Sponsor, "Rinehart's Studio: Rough Stone to Living Marble," The Walters Art Museum (2015); Contributor, "Black's Law Dictionary, Tenth Edition" (2014, 2009); Co-Author, "Construction Lien Law in Maryland," Lorman Education Services (2003) **Awards:** Featured Listee, Bar Register of Preeminent Lawyers, Martindale-Hubbell **Membership:** President, Maryland Chapter, Mensa International (2006-2014); Secretary, Maryland Chapter, Mensa International (2006-2014); Co-Chairperson, Scholarship Program, Education and Research Foundation, Maryland Chapter, Mensa International (2001-2006); Special Committee on the Cost of Civil Litigation Task Force, Maryland State Bar Association, Inc. (1999-2000) **Bar Admissions:** U. S. Court of Appeals for the Fourth Circuit (1982); Supreme Court of the U. S. (1980); U.S. Tax Court (1978); U.S. District Court District of Maryland (1972); Maryland (1971) **Religion:** Roman Catholic **Business Address:** 409 Washington Ave Ste 909, Baltimore, MD, 21204 **Shipping Address:** 409 Washington Ave Ste. 909, Baker and Baker, PA, Baltimore, MD, 21204

Anand Balasubramanian

Title: Physician **Industry:** Medicine & Health Care **Company Name:** Houston North West Primary Care **Education:** MD, Thanjavur Medical College (1992); MD, Thanjavur Medical College, Tamil-nadu, India (1992) **Career:** Senior Medical House Officer in Internal Medicine and Geriatrics, Peter-borough District Hospital, Peterborough, England **Hobbies:** Reading; Listening to music; Traveling; Spending time with his friends and family **Website:** http://www.hnwprimarycare.com **Why did you become involved in your profession or industry:** Dr. Balasubramanian became involved in his profession because he comes from a long line of physicians. **Where will you be in five years:** In five years, Dr. Balasubramanian intends to work within his community and develop relationships with the older population.

Patricia Creel Baltzley

Title: Mathematics Educator **Industry:** Education/Educational Services **Company Name:** Montana State University **Date of Birth:** 12/14/1952 **Place of Birth:** Fort Benning **State:** GA/USA **Parents:** Buckner Miller Creel; Mary Madeleine (O'Neill) Creel **Marital Status:** Married **Spouse Name:** Joseph Leroy Deveney (5/28/2006); Jeffrey Lynn Baltzley (7/23/1988, Deceased 12/1996); Kevin Gerard Robinson (11/15/1975, Divorced 12/21/1981) **Children:** Kevin G., Jr.; Timothy Eugene **Education:** MS in Mathematics, Shippensburg University (1986); BA in Mathematics, Notre Dame College (1975); **Certifications:** Certified Advanced Professional, State of Maryland; Certified in Administration; Certified in Supervision **Career:** Adjunct Professor, Montana State University (2013-Present); Board Chair, Gardiner Public Schools (2013-Present); Independent Consultant, Mathematics Education (2012-Present); Director, Pre-K-12 Mathematics, Baltimore County Public Schools (2004-2012); Mathematics Supervisor, Grades 6-12, Baltimore County Public Schools, (1998-2004); Mathematics Specialist, K-12, Baltimore County Public Schools (1995-1998); Mathematics Program Developer, Center for Social Organization of Schools, Johns Hopkins University (1991-1995); Mathematics Teacher, Board of Education, Carroll County Public Schools (1978-1991); Accountant Trainee, MBNA Limited (1975-1976) **Career Related:** Board Chair, Gardiner Public Schools (2013-Present); Adjunct Professor, University of Maryland, Baltimore County (2009-2010); Adjunct Professor, Morgan State University (2009); Adjunct Professor, Loyola University Maryland (2000-2010); Adjunct Professor, Western Maryland College (Now McDaniel College) (1997-2003); Adjunct Professor, Johns Hopkins University (1995-1997); Adjunct Professor, Notre Dame College (1992-2005); Consultant, Center for Social Organization, Johns Hopkins University; Independent Consultant in Field **Civic:** Volunteer, The National Shrine of Saint Elizabeth Ann Seton (1986-1995); President, The National Shrine of Saint Elizabeth Ann Seton (1982-1986) **Awards:** Maryland Mathematics Educator of the Year (1997); Presidential Award for Excellence in Teaching Mathematics, National Science Foundation (1989) **Membership:** Professional Learning Co-Director, NCSM (2015-Present); President, Maryland Council of Supervisors of Mathematics (2000-2005); President, Maryland Council of Teachers of Mathematics (1991-1993); ASCD; National Council of Teachers of Mathematics; Council of Presidential Awardees in Mathematics; Montana ASCD; Learning Forward; Montana Council of Teachers of Mathematics **Marquis Who's Who Honors:** Distinguished Humanitarian (2017) **Shipping Address:** PO Box 881, Gardiner, MT, 59030

Claire Barabash, PhD

Title: Lawyer, Special Education Services Professional, Psychologist **Industry:** Law and Legal Services **Date of Birth:** 10/22/1940 **Place of Birth:** New York **State:** NY/USA **Parents:** Maurice Isaac Barabash; Sarah (Libowsky) Barabash **Marital Status:** Widow **Spouse Name:** William W. Nelkin (Deceased) **Children:** Gamble Nelkin; Tor Nelkin **Education:** JD, Brooklyn Law School (1994); PhD in School Psychology, New York University (1979); MS in Clinical Psychology, The City University of New York (1962); BA in Psychology, Brooklyn College, Magna Cum Laude, with Honors (1960) **Certifications:** Diplomate, American College of Forensic Examiners Institute; Licensed Psychologist, States of Alabama and New York; Licensed School Psychologist, State of New York; School District Administrator, State of New York **Career:** Forensic Consultant (1999-Present); Psychologist/Attorney, Private Practice (1995-Present); Executive Director, Spring Valley School (2011-2013); Private Practice, NY (1996-1999); Assistant Superintendent for Clinical Services, The New York City Department of Education (1991-1992); Deputy Assistant Superintendent, The New York City Department of Education, Brooklyn-East/Staten Island Region, NY (1982-1995); Regional Coordinator, Office of School Based Support Teams, Region VI, The New York City Department of Education (1979-1982); Clinical Supervisor, Bureau of Child Guidance, Richmond Center, The New York City Department of Education (1978-1979); School Psychologist, Bureau of Child Guidance, Richmond Center, The New York City Department of Education (1965-1978); School Psychologist, Yonkers Public Schools, NY (1963-1965); Psychology Intern, Brooklyn College Education Clinic, The City University of New York (1962-1963) **Career Related:** Adjunct Associate Professor, Long Island University, NY (1988-1993); Adjunct Associate Professor, New York University (1979-1980); Psychologist, Goodhue Center, The Children's Aid Society (1978-1982) **Creative Works:** Author, Books; Presenter in Field **Awards:** Brian Tomlinson Memorial Award for Outstanding Achievement in Psychology, New York University (1991); Outstanding Special Educator of the Year, Orthodox Jewish Teachers (1990) **Membership:** Chair, Mentoring Committee, Administrative Women in Education (1989-1990); President, New York City Association School of Psychologists (1979-1980); American Psychological Association; ABA; Academy for Public Education **Bar Admissions:** Alabama State Bar Association (2000); New York State Bar Association (1995); New Jersey State Bar Association (1994) **Hobbies:** Traveling; Reading; Spending Time with Family **Shipping Address:** 101 Clark St Apt 26D, Brooklyn, NY, 11201

Carlos Barajas-Lopez, PhD

Title: Professor **Industry:** Education/Educational Services **Company Name:** Instituto Potosino de Investigacion Cientifica y Tecnologica **Country of Origin:** Mexico **Marital Status:** Married **Spouse Name:** Marcela Miranda **Children:** Juan Carlos; Gerardo; Alma Rosa **Education:** Fellowship, Vollum Institute, Oregon Health Sciences University, Portland, OR (1989-1990); PhD, Department of Physiology, Faculty of Medicine, National Autonomous University of Mexico (1989); Fellowship, Intestinal Disease Research Unit, McMaster University, Canada (1986-1989); Honorary MSc, Department of Physiology, Faculty of Medicine, National Autonomous University of Mexico (1986); MD, Faculty of Medicine, National Autonomous University of Mexico (1983) **Career:** Investigator, Professor, División de Biología Molecular, Instituto Potosino de Ciéncia y Tecnológia (2002-Present); Graduate Faculty Member, Faculty of Medicine, Graduate Programme in Biomedical Sciences, National Autonomous University of Mexico (1996-Present); Associate Professor, Department of Anatomy and Cell Biology, Queen's University, Kingston, ON, Canada (1997-2009); Associate Professor, Department of Biomedical Sciences, McMaster University, Canada (1997); Graduate Faculty Member, Neuroscience and Behavioural Sciences of the Graduate Programme in Medical Sciences, McMaster University, Canada (1993-1997); Assistant Professor, Department of Biomedical Sciences, McMaster University, Canada (1991-1997); Assistant Professor, Vollum Institute, Oregon Health Sciences University, Portland, OR (1990-1991); Associate Teacher, Researcher, Medical Pharmacology, Department of Pharmacology, Faculty of Medicine, Autonomous National University of Mexico (1985); Associate Teacher, Researcher of Human Physiology, Department of Physiology, Faculty of Medicine, Autonomous National University of Mexico (1982-1985); **Career Related:** Medical Research Council Fellowship, Canada (1990-1991); Medical Research Council Fellowship, Canada (1988-1990); **Creative Works:** Contributor, Articles to Professional Journals; Contributor, Chapters to Books; Author, Multiple Scientific Reports **Awards:** National Researcher Level 3 Scholarship, CONACYT (2007); Career Scientist Award, Ontario Ministry of Health, Canada (1997-2002); Career Scientist Award, Ontario Ministry of Health, Canada (1992-1997); **Membership:** The American Digestive Disease Society; Society for Neuroscience; American Neurogastroenterology and Motility Society; Sociedad de Biofísicos Latinoamericanos; Sociedad Mexicana de Ciencias Fisiológicas **Shipping Address:** Margaritas 183, Col La Florida 2X Seccion., San Luis Potosi, Mexico, 78420

Patricia Louise Barber

Title: Adult Nurse Practitioner **Industry:** Medicine & Health Care **Date of Birth:** 01/11/1953 **Place of Birth:** St. Paul **State:** MN **Parents:** James Beck; Margaret Mary (Neagle) Beck **Education:** BSN, University of Minnesota (1975) **Certifications:** Certified Nurse Practitioner, University of Illinois (1978); Certified Registered Nurse, State of Colorado; Certified Registered Nurse, State of Illinois; Certified Registered Nurse, State of Minnesota; Certified Nurse Practitioner, State of Colorado; Certified Nurse Practitioner, State of Illinois; Certified Nurse Practitioner, State of Minnesota **Career:** Director of Online Education, Community College of Denver (2006-2008); Acting Chair of Nursing, Board of Directors, Community College of Denver (2006); Associate Professor of Nursing, Community College of Denver (2004-2006); Nurse Practitioner, South Denver Cardiovascular Associates (2003-2008); Associate Professor of Nursing, Health Education Center, Community College of Denver (1999-2012); Nurse Practitioner of In-Patient Service, Presbyterian/St. Luke's Medical Center, C-HCA, Inc. (1996-1999); Nurse Practitioner in Nephrology, Presbyterian/St. Luke's Medical Center, C-HCA, Inc. (1995-1996); Nurse Practitioner of Cardiovascular In-Patient Service, Presbyterian/St. Luke's Medical Center, C-HCA, Inc. (1993-1995); Emergency Room Nurse Practitioner, Presbyterian/St. Luke's Medical Center, C-HCA, Inc. (1990-1993); Transplant Coordinator, The University of Illinois at Chicago (1978-1990); Staff Nurse, University of Minnesota (1974-1975) **Career Related:** Consultant in Field (1983-Present) **Civic:** Co-Chairman, S/A Patient Services Committee (1983-1990) **Creative Works:** Editor, "Resource Manual for Transplant Coordinators" (1982) **Awards:** Faculty Gold Award, Colorado Community College System (2005) **Membership:** Speaker's Bureau, American Diabetes Association (1982-Present); Board of Directors, National Kidney Foundation, Inc. (1983-1990); Honorary Member, NATCO (1983); Co-Chairman, NATCO (1979-1990) **Hobbies:** Fundraising; Volunteering; Pet therapy **Shipping Address:** 1283 Monroe Street, Denver, CO, 80206

Verlyn Lloyd Barker, PhD

Title: Educator, Minister (Retired) **Industry:** Religious **Date of Birth:** 07/25/1931 **Place of Birth:** Auburn **State:** NE/USA **Parents:** Jack Lloyd Barker; Olive Clara (Bollman) Barker **Education:** DD, Doane College (1977); PhD, Saint Louis University (1970); Postgraduate Studies, The University of Chicago (1960-1961); STM, Yale University (1960); BD, Yale University (1956); AB, Doane College (1952) **Career:** Retired, Board of Homeland Ministries, United Church of Christ, Cleveland, OH (1996); Secretary, Ministry for Higher Education, Board of Homeland Ministries, United Church of Christ, New York, NY (1961-1996); Pastor, University of Nebraska-Lincoln (1956-1959); History, Doane College (1954-1955); Chaplain, Doane College (1954-1955) **Civic:** President, United Ministries in Higher Education (Now Ekklesia), New York, NY (1971-1977) **Creative Works:** Editor, "Science, Technology and the Christian Faith" (1990); Contributing Author, "The New Faith-Science Debate" (1989); Contributing Author, "Religious Colleges in America: A Selected Bibliography" (1988); Author, "Health and Human Values: A Ministry of Theological Inquiry and Moral Discourse," United Ministries in Education (1987); Author, "Premises about Education" (1981); Author, "Creationism, the Church and The Public School," United Ministries in Education (1981); Editor, "The Church and the Public School" (1980); Contributing Author, "Campus Ministry" (1964); Editorial Advisory Committee, Journal of Current Social Issues, United Church of Christ, Division of Higher Education; Contributor, Articles, Various Publications **Awards:** Honoree, Who's Who in Science & Technology, John Templeton Foundation; Honoree, Who's Who in Theology & Science, John Templeton Foundation **Membership:** President, Doane College Alumni Association (1957-1958); ACLU; American Association for the Advancement of Science; National Association for Science Technology and Society; Society for Health and Human Values; The American Academy of Political and Social Science; Academy of Political Science; American Studies Association; AAHEA; The Yale Club of New York City; John Templeton Foundation **Bar Admissions:** Ordained Minister, United Church of Christ (1956) **Marquis Who's Who Honors:** Albert Nelson Marquis Lifetime Achievement Award (2017); Distinguished Humanitarian (2017) **Shipping Address:** 420 S Marion Pky Unit 1001, Denver, CO, 80209

Mary L. Barnett

Title: Teacher **Industry:** Education/Educational Services **Company Name:** Missoula Community School **Date of Birth:** 05/01/1941 **Place of Birth:** Exeter **State:** CA **Parents:** Raymond Edgar Noble; Nena Lavere (Huckaby) Hope **Marital Status:** Married **Spouse Name:** Gary Allen Barnett **Children:** Alice Marie; Virginia Lynn **Education:** Postgraduate Studies, University of Idaho (1984-Present); Postgraduate Studies, University of Montana (1979-1982); BA, University of Pacific (1963) **Certifications:** Certified Life Elementary Teacher, State of California **Career:** Director, Mary's Munchkins Preschool, Missoula (1999-Present); Teacher, Headstart of Missoula (1998-1999); Teacher, Windsong Preschool, Missoula, MT (1995-1998); Teacher, Bonneville Elementary, Pocatello (1994-1995); Teacher, Greenacres Elementary, Pocatello (1993-1994); Teacher, School District #25, Pocatello, ID (1983-1993); Teacher, Fort Shaw-Simms School District, Fort Shaw, MT (1976-1983); Teacher, School District #1, Missoula, MT (1969-1973); Teacher, Visalia Unified School District, California (1966-1969); Teacher, San Francisco Unified School Primary Grades, South San Francisco (1963-1966); Teacher, Colegio Americano de Torreon, Mexico (1962-63); Teacher, Missoula Community School **Career Related:** Advisory Council, Missoula Aging Services (2006-Present); Beauty Consultant Mary Kay **Civic:** Deacon, Dean, Treasurer, Presbyterian Church (1997-Present); Moderator, Kendall Presbyterian Women (1991-Present); People to People Education Ambassador, Cairo (2007) **Awards:** People to People Ambassador to Cairo (2007); Scholar, Five Valleys Reading Association, Missoula, MT (1982); Scholar, Great Falls Scottish Rite (1981); Scholar, Great Falls American Association of University Women (1980); Scholar, Montana Delta Kappa Gamma Education Society, Great Falls, MT (1976) **Membership:** PW Moderator, Montana Association for Early Childhood Education (2009-Present); Secretary, Friendship Force Delegate Moderator, Missoula AEYC (2008-Present); Vice President, American Association of University Women (2002-Present); Vice President of Membership, Missoula Chapter, American Association of University Women (2002-Present); Contact Advisor, Missoula After 5, Business Professional Women's Foundation, Pocatello (1999-Present); 2nd Vice President, Delta Kappa Gamma (1996-Present); Book Chair, American Association of University Women (1995-Present); Secretary, Business Professional Women's Foundation, Pocatello (1993-Present); Secretary, Laubach Literacy Tutors (1993-Present); Treasurer (2012-2016) **Political Affiliations:** Democrat **Religion:** Presbyterian **Shipping Address:** 103 E. Crestline Drive, Missoula, MT, 59803

Evelyn Carol Barrett

Title: Secondary Education Teacher (Retired) **Industry:** Education/Educational Services **State:** MS/USA **Education:** Coursework, Numerous Continuing Education Courses (1950-1982); MBA in Accounting, Louisiana State University (1950); BS, Mississippi Southern College (University of Southern Mississippi), with High Honors (1947); Diploma, Perkinston Junior College (Now Mississippi Coast College), with Honors, Perkinston, MS (1945) **Certifications:** Recipient, Police Academy Certificate **Career:** Head, Department of Business Education, Merrimack High School (1971-1981); Teacher, Business Education, Merrimack High School, New Hampshire (1958-1990); Teacher, Milford High School, New Hampshire (1957-1958); Instructor, Shorthand, Illinois Commercial College (1951-1952); Clerk-Stenographer, Department of Physics, University of Illinois at Urbana-Champaign (1951-1952); Instructor, Mississippi Southern College (1950); Instructor of Typing, College of Commerce, Louisiana State University (1947-1950); Assistant, Secretarial Practice Office and Division of Research; Member, Community Crimeline **Career Related:** Instructor, Auditing, Rivier University (1982); Graduate Assistant, Louisiana State University (1947-1950); Registered Representative, R. Danais Investment Co., Manchester, NH; Account Executive, John, Edward & Co., Lebanon, NH; Independent Beauty Consultant, Mary Kay Cosmetics, Merrimack, NH; **Civic:** Senior Troop Leader, Switwater Council, Girl Scouts of the United States of America (1970-1972); **Awards:** Recipient, Excellence in Education Award, Merrimack Teachers Association (1985); Recipient, Chapter Award of Appreciation, Alpha Delta Kappa (1980); **Membership:** Secretary, Manchester College Women's Club (2006-Present); Secretary, Reeds Ferry Women's Club (2003-2006); President, Our Lady of Mercy Ladies Guild (2000); Treasurer, Manchester User's Group of Apple Computers (2000); Librarian, Northern New England Chapter, Embroiderers' Guild of America (1999-2004); New Hampshire State Immediate Past President, Alpha Delta Kappa (1998-2000) **Marquis Who's Who Honors:** Albert Nelson Marquis Lifetime Achievement Award (2017); Distinguished Humanitarian (2017) **To what do you attribute your success:** Ms. Barrett attributes her success to her mother telling her "to do your best, that is all you can do," and to try to do different things so it wouldn't be the same routine. **What do you consider to be the highlight of your career:** A highlight for Ms. Barrett was earning her MBA at Louisiana State University in 1950, when not too many women were in her class. **Religion:** Roman Catholic **Shipping Address:** PO Box 987, Merrimack, NH, 03054

William Frederick Barthel Jr.

Marquis Who's Who
18 98
Biographee

Title: Engineer, Electronics Company Executive **Industry:** Engineering **Date of Birth:** 07/14/1940 **Place of Birth:** Washington **State:** DC/USA **Marital Status:** Married **Spouse Name:** Barbara Joan Adams (11/18/1961) **Children:** William Frederick III **Education:** BS, McNeese State University (1972) **Career:** Vice President, Operations, Gables Engineering, Coral Gables, FL (1993-2008); Director, Quality, Gables Engineering, Coral Gables, FL (1991-1993); Engineering Manager, Performance Assurance, Digital Equipment Corporation, Andover, MA (1987-1991); Engineering Manager, Process Reliability, Digital Equipment Corporation, Andover, MA (1981-1987); Senior Engineering Scientist, Process Control Development, Rockwell International, Cedar Rapids, IA (1980-1981); Manager, Quality Assurance, Rockwell International, Cedar Rapids, IA (1979); Engineer, Quality Control, Rockwell International, Cedar Rapids, IA (1974-1979); Shop Manager, Electronics Unlimited, Lake Charles, LA (1968) **Military Service:** U.S. Air Force (1958-1962) **Membership:** American Institute of Chemists; American Chemical Society **Marquis Who's Who Honors:** Albert Nelson Marquis Lifetime Achievement Award (2017) **To what do you attribute your success:** Mr. Barthel attributes his success to working in emerging fields. **Political Affiliations:** Republican **Shipping Address:** 745 SE 25th Ln, Homestead, FL, 33033

David Barton

Title: Religious Studies Educator, Writer, Historian, Public Speaker, Researcher **Industry:** Religious **Company Name:** WallBuilders **Date of Birth:** 01/28/1954 **Place of Birth:** Austin **State:** TX/USA **Parents:** Charles Grady Barton; Hilda Rose (Seely) Barton **Marital Status:** Married **Spouse Name:** Cheryl Edith Little (3/18/1978) **Children:** Damaris Ann; Timothy David; Stephen Daniel **Education:** PhD in Theology and American History, Life Christian University (2014); Honorary DLitt, Ecclesia College (2009); Honorary DLitt, Pensacola Christian College (1997); Bachelor of Religious Education, Oral Roberts University (1976) **Career:** Founder, President, Wallbuilders (1988-Present); Elder, Aledo Cornerstone Church, Aledo, TX (1987-Present); Vice-Chairman, Republican Party of Texas (1997-2006); Principal, Aledo Christian School, Aledo, TX (1981-1988); President, Owner, Maranatha Construction Company, Custom Homes, Aledo, TX (1978-1988); Director, Aledo Christian Center Bible School, Aledo, TX (1978-1982) **Career Related:** Guest Speaker, Universities; Guest Speaker, Churches; Guest Speaker, Military Bases; Guest Speaker, Educational Trainings; Guest Speaker, Business Conferences **Civic:** Advisory Board Member, Mighty Oaks Warriors Programs, Mighty Oaks Foundation (2015-Present); Advisory Board Member, Parental Rights (2014-Present); Advisory Board Member, Patriot Academy (2013-Present); Board of Reference, Christian Film and Television Commission (2013-Present) **Military Service:** Honorary Commission as an Admiral, U.S. Navy (2009) **Creative Works:** Signature Historian, "The Founders' Bible" (2012); Author, "The Jefferson Lies" (2012); Author, "Capitol Guidebook" (2009); Author, "The Bible, Voters & The 2008 Elections" (2008); Author, "Separation of Church and State" (2007); Author, "Freemasonry and the Founding Fathers" (2005); Author, "Restraining Judicial Activism" (2003); Author, "The Second Amendment" (2000) **Awards:** Issachara Award, Bott Radio Network (2017); Commendation, Resolution of Alabama State Senate (2016); Honoree, Person of the Year, Family PAC (2016); Military Certificate of Appreciation, First Stryker Brigade Combat Team "Arctic Wolves," Fort Wainwright (2015); Commendation, South Carolina State Senate (2014); Honoree, National Hero of the Faith, Vision America (2011); Board of Directors Award, National Religious Broadcasters (2009) **Marquis Who's Who Honors:** Albert Nelson Marquis Lifetime Achievement Award (2017) **Shipping Address:** PO Box 397, c/o Misty Huddleston, Aledo, TX, 76008 **Website:** https://wallbuilders.com/bios/#tab-34c5fc6bd5eda685312

Linda May Bartoshuk, PhD

Title: Psychologist, Educator, Researcher **Industry:** Education/Educational Services **Company Name:** University of Florida Health **Place of Birth:** Aberdeen **State:** SD/USA **Parents:** Hubert Buswell; Edna Buswell **Marital Status:** Married **Spouse Name:** Charles Sommerfield (5/25/1969) **Children:** Daniel; Elizabeth **Education:** Honorary DSc, Carleton College (2001); PhD in Psychology, Brown University, Providence, RI (1965); MS in Psychology, Brown University, Providence, RI (1963); BA in Psychology, Carleton College, Northfield, MN (1960) **Career:** Bushnell Professor, Department of Community Dentistry and Behavioral Sciences, College of Dentistry, University of Florida Health, Gainesville, FL (2005-Present); Presidential Endowed Professor of Community Dentistry and Behavioral Science, College of Dentistry, University of Florida Health, Gainesville, FL (2005-Present); Professor, Section of Otolaryngology, Department of Surgery, Yale University (1989-2005); Professor Department of Psychology, Yale University (1989-2005); Professor, Yale University (1985-1988); Associate Professor, Department of Epidemiology and Public Health, Yale University (1976-1985); Associate Professor, Department of Psychology, Yale University (1976-1985); Assistant Professor, Department of Epidemiology and Public Health, Yale University (1971-1976); Research Psychologist, Natick Army Laboratories (1966-1970) **Career Related:** Fellow, John B. Pierce Foundation Laboratory, Yale University (1985-1989); Chairman, Gordon Conference on Chemical Senses (1978); Associate, John B. Pierce Foundation Laboratory, Yale University (1974-1985); Assistant, John B. Pierce Foundation Laboratory, Yale University (1970-1973); Affiliate Assistant Professor, Clark University (1966-1969); Lecturer, Brown University (1966-1968); Member, Various Committees, National Research Council, National Institutes of Health **Creative Works:** Consultant Editor, "Perception and Psychophysics" (1972-1986); Editor, "Chemical Senses" (1982-1984); Consultant Editor, "Sensory Processes" (1976-1979); Contributor, Articles, Professional Journals **Awards:** Innovative Research Award (2004); Kreshover Award, The National Academy of Sciences (2003) **Membership:** Council Member, National Academy of Sciences (2008-Present); President, American Psychological Society (2010) **Marquis Who's Who Honors:** Albert Nelson Marquis Lifetime Achievement Award (2017) **Shipping Address:** 5200 SW 25th Blvd., Unit 1218, Gainesville, FL, 32608

Kit Smyth Basquin, PhD

Title: Writer, Art Historian (Retired) **Industry:** Writing and Editing **Date of Birth:** 07/03/1941 **Place of Birth:** New York **State:** NY/USA **Parents:** Joseph Percy Smyth; Virginia Sandford (Gibbs) Smyth (Deceased) **Marital Status:** Divorced **Spouse Name:** Maurice Hanson Basquin (2/4/1967, Divorced 2/1984), Deceased **Children:** Susan; Peter Lee; William **Education:** PhD in Interdisciplinary Studies, Union Institute and University, Cincinnati, OH (2009); MA in Art History, Indiana University (1970); BA in History, Goucher College, Baltimore, MD (1963) **Career:** Retired from Associate for Administration, Department of Drawings and Prints, The Metropolitan Museum of Art (2008-2014); Independent Curator, Art Gallery, College of Staten Island (2009-2010); Assistant for Administration, The Metropolitan Museum of Art (2000-2008); Research Associate, Writer Brooklyn Museum of Art (2000); Exhibition Manager, William Doyle New York Galleries, New York, NY (2000); Marketing, William Doyle Galleries, New York, NY (1999); Grant Writer, Curator, Ten Chimney's Foundation, Inc. (1999); Curator, Marvin Lowe Retrospective, Indiana University Art Museum (1998); Director of Outreach, Milwaukee, Wisconsin Humanities Council (1995-1998); Curator of Education and Guest Curator, Haggerty Museum, Marquette University, Milwaukee, WI (1988-1995); Director, Kit Basquin Gallery, Milwaukee, WI (1981-1983); Director, Washington Gallery, Indianapolis, IN (1977-1979); Director, Washington Gallery, Frankfort, IN (1972-1977); Assistant Director, Public Relations, Indianapolis Museum of Art (1971-1972) **Career Related:** Member, MasterVoices (2016-Present); Member, Collegiate Chorale (2013-2016); Advisory Board Member, Gordon Parks Gallery, Metropolitan State University, Minneapolis, MN (2012-2013); Guest Curator, Wording the Image, Sherman Gallery, School of Visual Arts, Boston University (2010-2011); Guest Curator, Gallery of College States Island, City University of New York (2009-2010) **Civic:** Special Events Committee, University Club of New York (2016-Present); Alumnae Board, Spence School, New York (2014-2018); Library & Art Committee, University Club of New York (2011-2016); Member, Alumnae Board, Spence School, New York (2005-2013) **Creative Works:** Author, "Gaza City," Narrative Magazine (2017); Author, "Collecting A Life," Art in Print (2017); Letter to the Editor, "New York Magazine," New York Media LLC (2017) **Membership:** The University Club of New York (1988-Present); MasterVoices (2013-Present); St. Barts Singers (1999-Present); Uptown Sound (2009-2013); James Joyce Society; University Club of Milwaukee **Religion:** Episcopalian **Shipping Address:** 110 E End Ave., Apt. 14G, New York, NY, 10028

Jack Bass

Title: Communications Educator **Industry:** Education/Educational Services **Date of Birth:** 06/24/1934 **Place of Birth:** Columbia **State:** SC/USA **Parents:** Nathan Bass; Esther (Cohen) Bass **Marital Status:** Married **Spouse Name:** Nathalie Dupree (4/10/1994); Carolyn E. McClung (3/3/1957, Divorced 6/1984) **Children:** Kenneth; David; Elizabeth **Education:** PhD, Emory University (1998); MA, University of South Carolina (1976); AB, University of South Carolina (1956) **Career:** Citadel Fellow, Charleston, SC (2008-2010); Professor of Humanities and Social Sciences, College of Charleston, SC (1999-2008); Professor of Journalism, The University of Mississippi, Oxford, MS (1987-1999); Research Fellow/Project Director, University of South Carolina, Columbia, SC (1979-1985); Writer-in-residence, South Carolina State College (Now South Carolina State University), Orangeburg, SC (1975-1978); Research Scholar, Duke University, Durham, NC (1973-1975); Bureau Chief, The Charlotte Observer, Columbia, SC (1966-1973); Governmental Affairs Reporter, Editor, Columbia Newspapers (1963-1966); Editor, Publisher, West Ashley Journal, Charleston, SC (1961-1963); Copy Editor, The News and Courier (Now Post and Courier), Charleston, SC (1960-1961) **Civic:** Director, Southern Education Foundation, Atlanta, GA (1980-1988); Democratic Candidate, U.S. House of Representatives, Columbia, SC (1978) **Military Service:** Retired Commander, U.S. Navy **Creative Works:** Co-author, "The Palmetto State" (2009); Co-author, "Strom: The Complicated Personal and Political Life of Strom Thurmond" (2005); Co-author, "Ol' Strom" (1998); Author, "Taming The Storm" (1993); Co-editor, "The American South Comes of Age" (1987); Co-editor, "The American South Comes of Age" (1987); Author, "Unlikely Heroes" (1980); Co-author, "The Transformation of Southern Politics" (1976); Author, "Porgy Comes Home" (1972); Co-author, "The Orangeburg Massacre" (1970) **Awards:** Lifetime Achievement Award, South Carolina African-American Historical Commission (2012); South Carolina Governor's Award, SC Humanities Council (2011); Robert Kennedy F. Book Award Grand Prize (1994); First Distinguished Alumnus Award, College of Journalism, University of South Carolina (1984); Named South Carolina Journalist of the Year, Society Professional Journalists (1970); Named South Carolina Journalist of the Year, Society Professional Journalists (1968); Nieman Fellow (1965-1966) **Membership:** Authors Guild; South Carolina Academy of Authors **Hobbies:** Walking **Shipping Address:** 100 Queen St, Charleston, SC, 29401

Mary Ann Beckwith

Title: Art Educator **Industry:** Fine Art **Date of Birth:** 05/17/1945 **Place of Birth:** Philadelphia **State:** PA/USA **Parents:** Raymond Leonard Liss; Leona Mary Liss **Children:** Susan Lynn Allen; Carl **Education:** BA, Marygrove College, Detroit, MI (1967) **Career:** Professor Emeritus, Department of Visual and Performing Arts, Michigan Technological University (2012-Present); Professor, Department of Visual and Performing Arts, Michigan Technological University (2001-2012); Associate Professor, Department of Visual and Performing Arts, Michigan Technological University (1997-2001); Assistant Professor, Department of Visual and Performing Arts, Michigan Technological University (1994-1997); Lecturer, Department of Visual and Performing Arts, Michigan Technological University (1980-1994) **Career Related:** Executive Director, International Society of Experimental Artists (2010-Present); Co-Chairperson, Keweenaw Art Affair, Dollar Bay, MI (2006); Speaker, Annual Meeting, Michigan Watercolor Society, Bloomfield, MI (2004); Presenter, Annual Meeting, Michigan Watercolor Society, Bloomfield, MI (2004); Speaker in Field; Juror, Various Art Exhibitions; Instructor, Various Art Workshops; Coordinator, Various Workshops, Michigan Technological University **Creative Works:** Exhibitor, American Watercolor Society (2017); Featured Artist, "Unique Insights, The Society of Layerists In Multi-Media," University of New Mexico Press (2016); Featured Artist, "A Walk into Abstracts, Volume II" (2011); Exhibitor, American Watercolor Society (2010-2011) **Awards:** Jack Richeson Award, Watercolor USA Springfield Museum of Art (2008); Silver Medal Award, Audubon Artists (2007); Mary Bryan Award, Allied Artists of America (2007); Fredric Albrecht Award, American Watercolor Society (2007); Traveling Show Award, Adirondack National Exhibition of American Watercolors (2005-2006); Winsor Newton Award, Watercolor Society of Alabama (2006) **Membership:** Society of Layerists in Multi-Media (1999-Present); National Watercolor Society (1999-Present); Georgia Watercolor Society (1993-Present); International Society of Experimental Artists (1992-Present); Alabama Watercolor Society (1992-Present); Associate, Allied Artists of America (1989-Present); Pittsburgh Watercolor Society (1986-Present); Louisiana Watercolor Society (1984-Present); Michigan Watercolor Society (1982-Present); Associate, American Watercolor Society (1980-Present); Copper Country Community Arts Council (1975-Present) **Marquis Who's Who Honors:** Albert Nelson Marquis Lifetime Achievement Award (2017) **Shipping Address:** 49107 N Royce Rd, Hancock, MI, 49930

Thomas J. Bellows

Title: Political Scientist, Educator **Industry:** Education/Educational Services **Company Name:** The University of Texas at San Antonio **Date of Birth:** 08/15/1935 **Place of Birth:** Chicago **State:** IL/USA **Parents:** Charles Everett Bellows; Dorothy (Morrison) Bellows **Marital Status:** Widowed **Children:** Scott Anthony; Justin Thomas; Trevor Cullen; Ethan Forrest; Roderick Alan; Adrienne Marie; Jeannine Louise; Marshall Thomas; Derek **Education:** PhD, Yale University (1968); MA, Yale University (1960); MA, University of Florida (1958); BA, Augustana College (1957); Coursework, UCLA (1956-1957); Coursework, American University (1956) **Career:** Professor of Political Science, University of Texas, San Antonio (1981-Present); Director, Division of Social Policy Sciences, University of Texas, San Antonio (1981-1988); Department Chair, University of Arkansas (1971-1978); Assistant Professor, Professor of Political Science, University of Arkansas, Fayetteville (1967-1981) **Career Related:** Visiting Professor, National Chengchi University, Taiwan (1979); Visiting Lecturer, Departments of History and Political Science, Nanyang University, Singapore (1965) **Creative Works:** Author, "The Singapore Polity" (2018); Editor, American Journal of Chinese Studies (1999-2017); Author, "Confucianism and Pluralism in a Meritocratic Society: The Singapore Case" (2014); Author, "No Change in Sight: Party Politics and Taiwan's Legislative Yuan During the Global Economic Crisis" (2010); Author, "State Craft of Modern Texas: Perspectives on Politics and History" (with Felix Almaraz) (2007); Author, "The Republic of China's Legislative Yuan: A Study of Institutional Evolution" (2003); Author, "Taiwan and Mainland China" (2000); Author, "Conflict and Compromise: An Introduction to Political Science" (1992); Author, "Bridging Tradition and Modernization: The Singapore Bureaucracy" (with H. Winter) (1989); Author, "People and Politics: An Introduction to Political Science" (1985); Author, "Taiwan's Foreign Policy in the 1970's" (with H. Winter) (1976); Author, "Political Science: Introductory Essays and Readings" (1971); Author, "The People's Action Party of Singapore: Emergence of a Dominant Party System" (with S. Erikson and H. Winter) (1970) **Membership:** President, American Association for Chinese Studies (1998-2000); Southwest Conference on Asian Studies, Association for Asian Studies (1995); Phi Beta Kappa; Phi Kappa Phi; Pi Sigma Alpha **Religion:** Methodist **Shipping Address:** 1 UTSA Circle, UTSA, Dept. of Political Science & Geography, San Antonio, TX, 78249

Dick N. Bentley

Title: Senior Planning Manager **Industry:** Architecture & Construction **Company Name:** Pioneer Valley Planning Commission **Date of Birth:** 03/17/1937 **Place of Birth:** Chicago **State:** IL/USA **Parents:** Richard Bentley; Phoebe Wrenn (Norcross) Bentley **Marital Status:** Married **Spouse Name:** Carolyn Stiglic (9/10/1977) **Children:** Nicholas Northrup; Julia Wrenn **Education:** MFA, Norwich University (1992); BA, Yale University (1959) **Career:** Senior Planning Manager, Pioneer Valley Planning Commission, West Springfield, MA (1987-1988); Planning Director, Boston Housing Authority (1986-1987); Chief Planner, Mayor's Office Housing, Boston, MA (1983-1986); Chief Project Manager, Massachusetts Department of Community Affairs, Boston, MA (1978-1983); Chief Project Manager, Advisory Services for Better Housing, New York, NY (1975-1978); Chief Project Manager, Rose Associates, New York, NY (1973-1975); Chief Project Manager, Kate Maremont Foundation (1965-1970); Campaign Assistant, Illinois Volunteers of Stevenson (1964) **Career Related:** Instructor, Creative Writing, University of Massachusetts (2008-Present); Adjunct Professor, Western New England University (2000-2008); Instructor, Creative Writing, University of Massachusetts (1992-2003); Instructor, Creative Writing, University of Massachusetts (1997-1999); Affiliate, International City Management Association, Washington, DC (1982-1990); Instructor, Housing Development Specialist Program, Washington, DC (1971) **Civic:** Delegate, Democratic State Convention, Massachusetts (2011); Delegate, Democratic State Convention, Massachusetts (2008); Delegate, Democratic State Convention, Massachusetts (2000); Board of Governors, Groton School, Groton, MA (1990-1995); Governor's Appointee Massachusetts Mortgage Review Board (1984-1987) **Military Service:** U.S. Army (1960-1962) **Creative Works:** Author, "All Rise" (2014); Author, "A General Theory of Desire" (2007); Author, "Post-Freudian Dreaming" (2002); Managing Editor, "Peregrine Magazine" (1991-1993) **Awards:** Honoree, Best Nonfiction and Fiction, Paris Writers' Workshop (2012); Nominee, Pushcart Prize, Paris Writers' Workshop (2006); International Fiction Award, Paris Writers' Workshop (1994) **Membership:** Delegate, The AYA Assembly (2000-2003); APA; NAHRO; Mayflower Descendants in the State of New York; Founding Member, Association of Personal Historians; Harvard Club of Boston; Yale Club, Connecticut; Amherst Yacht Club **Shipping Address:** 24 N Prospect Street, Amherst, MA, 01002

Bijan Berenji, PhD

Title: Adjunct Professor **Industry:** Education/Educational Services **Company Name:** California State University, Los Angeles **Marital Status:** Single **Education:** PhD in Applied Physics, Stanford University (2011); Degree in Physics, University of California, Los Angeles (2001); Postdoctoral Coursework, University of California, Los Angeles **Career:** Adjunct Professor of Physics and Astronomy, California State University, Los Angeles (2015-Present); Adjunct Professor of Astronomy, El Camino College (2014-Present); Research Consultant, fiziSim LLC (2013-Present); Affiliated Post-Doctorate Position, Fermi Large Area Telescope Collaboration (2013-2016) **Creative Works:** Author, "Constraints on Axions and Axion-Like Particles from Fermi LAT Observations of Neutron Stars," Physical Review D (2016); Co-Author, Various Peer-Reviewed Publications **Awards:** Recipient, Recognition Award, NASA/Fermi Large Area Telescope Collaboration (2011) **Membership:** Phi Beta Kappa; American Physical Society; Affiliated Member, Fermi Large Area Telescope Collaboration **To what do you attribute your success:** Dr. Berenji attributes his success to hard work. **Why did you become involved in your profession or industry:** Dr. Berenji has always been interested in mathematics, computers and science. When he was in high school, he knew he would go into the sciences. **Hobbies:** Playing violin **Shipping Address:** 2245 Hillsbury Rd, Westlake Village, CA, 91361

Stephen Berman

Title: Neurologist **Industry:** Medicine & Health Care **Company Name:** White River Junction Veterans Medical Center, University of Central Florida **Date of Birth:** 03/15/1948 **Place of Birth:** Oak Park **Education:** PhD in Biochemistry, University of Illinois; MBA, University of Tennessee (2008); Resident in Neurology, Baylor College of Medicine, Houston, TX (1977-1980); Intern, Greater Baltimore Medical Center (1976-1977); MD, University of Illinois (1974); BS, University of Illinois, Champaign-Urbana (1970) **Certifications:** Certified, Society for Neurorehabilitation; **Career:** Chief, Neurology, White River Junction Veterans Medical Center, White River Junction, VT (2000-Present); Professor, Medicine Neurology, Dartmouth Medical College, Hanover, NH (2000-Present); Professor, Neurology, Louisiana State University, Shreveport, LA (1996-2000); Assistant Professor, Harvard Medical School, Boston, MA (1992-1996); Instructor, Neurology, Harvard Medical School, Boston, MA (1990-1992); Assistant Professor, Neurology, The University of Texas MD Anderson Cancer Center (1989-1990); Assistant Professor, Neurology, The University of Chicago (1983-1989); Fellow, Genetics and Muscle Disease, Baylor College of Medicine, Houston, TX (1980-1983) **Civic:** Medical Advisory Committee, Multiple Sclerosis Society, Shreveport, LA (1997-2000) **Membership:** Quality Standards Subcommittee, American Academy of Neurology (1998); Therapeutics and Technical Assessment Subcommittee, American Academy of Neurology (1998); Vice President, Illinois Chapter, Alpha Omega Alpha (1973-1974); Society for Neurorehabilitation; Phi Beta Kappa **Religion:** Jewish **Shipping Address:** 11736 Eagle Ray Lane, Orlando, FL, 32827

Jerzy Bernholc, PhD

Title: Drexel Professor **Industry:** Education/Educational Services **Company Name:** North Carolina State University **Date of Birth:** 02/12/1952 **Place of Birth:** Szczecin **Country of Origin:** Poland **Parents:** David Bernholc; Irene Bernholc **Marital Status:** Married **Spouse Name:** Alissa Seligman Bernholc **Children:** Stuart; Judith **Education:** Postdoctoral Fellow, T.J. Watson Research Center, IBM (1978-1980); PhD, Lund University (1977); BS, Lund University (1973) **Career:** Drexel Professor of Physics, NC State University (2000-Present); Co-director, Institute for Computational Science and Engineering (2008-2013); Director, Center for High Performance Simulation (2004-2017); Professor, NC State University (1990-2000); Associate Professor, NC State University (1986-1990); Senior Physicist, Corporate Research Laboratories, Exxon Mobil Corporation (1980-1986) **Career Related:** Visiting Distinguished Scientist, Oak Ridge National Laboratory (2002-Present); Consultant, Dow Chemical Company (1999-2004) **Awards:** Honoree, Who's Who in the World (2002-Present); Honoree, Who's Who in America (2001-Present); Honoree, American Men and Women of Science (1982-Present); Honoree, Outstanding Referee, American Physical Society (2011); Jesse Beams Award for Outstanding Research, Southeastern Section, American Physical Society (2003); Finalist, Computerworld Smithsonian Science Award (1997); Nominee, Computerworld Smithsonian Technology Leadership Award for Breakthrough Computational Science (1993); Alumni Outstanding Research Award, NC State University (1992); Outstanding Innovation Award for Work on "Electronic Structure of Point Defects in Solids," Research Division, IBM (1979); The King Oscar the Second Award, Sweden (1978); Award, Lund Mathematical Society (1972) **Membership:** Fellow, American Association for the Advancement of Science (2011); Fellow, Materials Research Society (2011); Past Chair, Division of Computational Physics, American Physical Society (2004); Chair, Division of Computational Physics, American Physical Society (2003); Chair Elect, Division of Computational Physics, American Physical Society (2002); Vice Chair, Division of Computational Physics, American Physical Society (2001); Fellow, American Physical Society (1991) **Marquis Who's Who Honors:** Albert Nelson Marquis Lifetime Achievement Award (2017) **Business Address:** NC State University, Dept of Physics, NC, Raleigh, 27695-8202 **Shipping Address:** 2309 Byrd St, Raleigh, NC, 27608-1411 **Website:** http://chips.ncsu.edu/~bernholc

Melissa Rose Berta

Title: Mathematics Professor **Industry:** Education/Educational Services **Date of Birth:** 04/29/1966 **Place of Birth:** Van Nuys **State:** CA/USA **Parents:** Alexander Rocco Yguado; Patricia Ann Yguado **Marital Status:** Married **Spouse Name:** Brad Braden Berta (7/12/1986) **Children:** Joseph Brandon; Lisa Marie **Education:** EdD in Educational Leadership, Argosy University, California (2007); MS in Mathematics and Statistics, University of Nebraska (1996); BS in Mathematics, California State University (1993); Marec Fellow, California State University, Northridge, CA (1991-1993); AS in Mathematics and Science, College of the Canyons (1989) **Certifications:** The Academic Senate California Community Colleges Accreditation Institute Certification (2009); Kaleidoscope Leadership Institute Certificate (2009); University of San Diego Leadership Academy VI Student Success Certification (2008); California Student Learning Outcomes and Assessment Institute Certification (2007); Orange Coast College Faculty Academy Certification (2007); California Teaching Institute Certification (2007); Girl Scout Junior Leadership Certification (2002); Child Development Core Certification (1989) **Career:** Professor, Orange Coast College, Costa Mesa, CA (1998-Present); Academic Senate Vice President and Delegate, Basic Skill Initiative Chair, Student Success Center Director, Orange Coast College (2008-2011); Title III Grant Project Director, Orange Coast College (2008-2011); Teach 3 Director, Orange Coast College (2007-2008) **Career Related:** Larson Minority Graduate Fellow, University of Nebraska (1994-1995); Marec Fellow, California State University, Northridge, CA (1991-1993) **Civic:** Leader, Girl Scouts of the United States of America, Rancho Santa Margarita, CA (1997-2005); Vice President, Academic Senate **Military Service:** Military Police Corps, U.S. Army (1984-1987) **Creative Works:** Vice President of the Academic Senate, Foster Youth College **Awards:** Outstanding Coast Colleague, Orange Coast College (2011); Certification of Appreciation for Five Years of Service, California Coast Community College District (2011); Academic Senate Commendation Resolution, Orange Coast College (2008-2010); Certificate of Appreciation, Orange Coast College (2008); **Membership:** Phi Delta Kappa International (2008) **Marquis Who's Who Honors:** Albert Nelson Marquis Lifetime Achievement Award (2017) **Why did you become involved in your profession or industry:** While Dr. Berta was a teaching assistant at the University of Nebraska they provided a "free ride" to pay for her education. That was when she fell in love with teaching. **Shipping Address:** 5244 Huntington Crest Lane, Cumming, GA, 30040

Suzanne A. Beutler, PhD

Title: Middle School Educator **Industry:** Education/Educational Services **Date of Birth:** 10/23/1930 **Place of Birth:** Cincinnati **State:** OH **Parents:** Robert Armstrong; Marguerite (Pierson) Armstrong **Marital Status:** Married **Spouse Name:** Frederick J. Beutler (1/5/1969) **Children:** Richard; Mark Ireland **Education:** BFA, University of Michigan (2000); PhD, University of Michigan (1974); MA, University of Michigan (1966); BA, University of Wisconsin (1954) **Certifications:** Certified Teacher **Career:** Middle School Teacher, Ann Arbor Public Schools **Career Related:** Visiting Lecturer, University of Michigan; Adjunct Lecturer, Eastern Michigan University **Creative Works:** Author, Manuals for Language Art Projects; Contributor, Articles, Professional Journals **Awards:** Service Key Award, Phi Delta Kappa International (1992); Teacher Recognition Award (1986); Recipient, Various Grants **Membership:** Rotary Club of Ann Arbor; Phi Delta Kappa International **Marquis Who's Who Honors:** Albert Nelson Marquis Lifetime Achievement Award (2017) **Hobbies:** Oil painting; Playing the trumpet in two bands and an orchestra **Shipping Address:** 1717 Shadford Rd, Ann Arbor, MI, 48104 **Website:** http://www.suzannebeutler.com

Anatoly Bezkorovainy, PhD

Title: Associate Chairman, Director of Educational Programs **Industry:** Medicine & Health Care **Company Name:** Rush University Medical Center **Date of Birth:** 02/11/1935 **Place of Birth:** Riga **Country of Origin:** Latvia **Parents:** Ignatius Bezkorovainy; Olga (Solovey) Bezkorovainy **Marital Status:** Married **Spouse Name:** Marilyn Grib (6/14/1964) **Children:** Gregory; Alexander **Education:** JD, Illinois Institute of Technology (1977); PhD, University of Illinois (1960); BS, University of Chicago (1956) **Career:** Professor Emeritus, Rush University Medical Center (2004-Present); Associate Chairman, Director of Educational Programs, Biochemistry Department, Rush University Medical Center (1980-2000); Professor of Biochemistry, Rush University Medical Center (1973-2004); Associate Professor, Rush University Medical Center (1967-1973); Faculty, Rush University Medical Center (1962-2005); Assistant Professor, Rush University Medical Center (1962-1967); Chemist, U.S. Department of Agriculture, Ames, IA (1961-1962); Research Associate, Oak Ridge National Laboratory, Oak Ridge, TN (1960-1961) **Career Related:** Lecturer, Dr. William M. Scholl College of Podiatric Medicine, North Chicago, IL (2000-2008) **Creative Works:** Author, "Science and Medicine in Imperial Russia," Lulu Press (2018); Translator, "I Have Received Much More Than I Have Deserved" (2015); Author, "History of Imperial Russia," (2014); Author, "All Was Not Lost" (2008); Co-Author, "Concise Biochemistry" (1995); Co-Author, "Biochemistry and Physiology of Bifidobacteria" (1989); Author, "Biochemistry of Nonheme Iron" (1980); Co-Author, "Basic Biochemistry," (1980); Author, "Basic Protein Chemistry" (1970); Contributor, Articles, Professional Journals **Awards:** 50-Year Member Award, American Chemical Society; Numerous Grants, National Science Foundation, National Institutes of Health, American Heart Association, Industrial Institutions **Membership:** American Chemical Society; American Society of Biological Chemists; American Dairy Science Association; National Science Foundation; National Institutes of Health; American Heart Association **Bar Admissions:** State of Illinois (1977) **Marquis Who's Who Honors:** Albert Nelson Marquis Lifetime Achievement Award (2017); Distinguished Humanitarian (2017) **Religion:** Eastern Orthodox **Shipping Address:** 25449 S Truro Drive, Sun Lakes, AZ, 85248

Zdzislaw Tadeusz Bieniawski, PhD

Title: Engineering Educator, Engineering Designer, Professor Emeritus **Industry:** Engineering **Company Name:** Universidad Politecnica de Madrid, Bieniawski Design Enterprises, The Pennsylvania State University **Date of Birth:** 10/01/1936 **Place of Birth:** Krakow **Country of Origin:** Poland **Marital Status:** Married **Spouse Name:** Elizabeth Hyslop (1964) **Education:** Honorary Degree, AGH University of Science and Technology (2010); Honorary DEng, Universidad Politecnica de Madrid (2001); PhD in Rock Engineering, University of Pretoria, South Africa (1968); MME in Engineering Mechanics, University of the Witwatersrand, Johannesburg, South Africa (1963); BS in Mechanical Engineering, University of the Witwatersrand, Johannesburg, South Africa (1961); Coursework, Gdansk University of Technology (1954-1958) **Career:** Distinguished Geological Engineering Professor, Universidad Politecnica de Madrid (2001-Present); President, Bieniawski Design Enterprises, Prescott, AZ (1996-Present); Professor Emeritus, Pennsylvania State University (1996-Present); Science, Technology & Society Professor, Pennsylvania State University (1994-1996); Mineral Engineering Professor, Pennsylvania State University (1977-1996) **Career Related:** Visiting Professor, AGH University of Science and Technology (2010); Visiting Professor, Cambridge University (1997); Visiting Professor, Harvard University (1990); Visiting Professor, Stanford University (1985) **Creative Works:** Author, "The Matter of Alma Mater" (2012); Author, "Beasts in the Onion Leaves and Renaissance Dialogues" (2006); Author, "Alec's Journey" (1999); Author, "Gaudeamus Igitur: Poems" (1997); Editor, "Milestones in Rock Engineering" (1996); Author, "Design Methodology in Rock Engineering" (1992); Author, "A Tale of Three Continents" (1991); Author, "Engineering Rock Mass Classifications" (1989); Author, "Aiming High: A Collection of Essays" (1988); Author, "Strata Control in Mineral Engineering" (1987); Author, "Rock Mechanics Design in Mining and Tunneling" (1984) **Awards:** Honoree, Bieniawski Auditorium, Universidad Politecnica de Madrid (2003); Rock Mechanics Research Award (1984); Honoree, Mayor's Proclamation, Bieniawski Day, City of State College, PA (1983); Distinguished Toastmaster International Award (1974) **Marquis Who's Who Honors:** Albert Nelson Marquis Lifetime Achievement Award (2017) **Business Address:** 1035 Scott Drive, Apt. 458, Las Fuentes Resort, Prescott, AZ, 86301

Terri Bigler

Title: Doctor **Industry:** Medicine & Health Care **Company Name:** Dignity Health **Education:** MD, School of Medicine, University of Nevada (1992) **Certifications:** Licensed to Practice Medicine, State of California (1994) **Career:** Specialist in Internal Medicine, Mercy General Hospital, Dignity Health; Specialist in Internal Medicine, Mercy Hospital Of Folsom, Dignity Health; Specialist in Internal Medicine, Mercy San Juan Medical Center, Dignity Health; Coordinator, Medical Groups, Medical Foundation, Dignity Health **Civic:** Advisory Committee, Physician Assistance Program, University of the Pacific **Awards:** Recipient, Distinguished Doctor Recognition (2016); Honoree, Best Doctor, Roseville Tribune, Gold Country Media (2016); Honoree, Top Ten Internal Medicine Doctors in Roseville, CA, Vitals.com (2014); Honoree, Most Compassionate Doctor (2009, 2011, 2012); Featured Listee, American Registry, American Top Doctors (2005-2012) **Membership:** American Board of Internal Medicine; American College of Physicians; Sierra Sacramento Valley Medical Society **What do you consider to be the highlight of your career:** Doing outpatient internal medicine in the city of Roseville, CA from May 2000 to Aug 2016 was a highlight, and the town newspaper, The Tribune, voted Dr. Bigler Best Doctor 2016. **Business Address:** 6401 Coyle Ave., Ste. 412, Carmichael, CA, 95608 **Shipping Address:** 8245 W Hidden Lakes Dr, Granite Bay, CA, 95746

Stephanie J. Bird, PhD

Title: Science and Engineering Ethics Educator, Policy Consultant **Industry:** Education/Educational Services **Place of Birth:** Los Angeles **State:** CA/USA **Parents:** Joseph Lester Bird; Jean Belle (Lay) Kendall **Marital Status:** Married **Spouse Name:** Lawrence W. Shannon (1976) **Education:** PhD, Yale University, New Haven, CT (1975); MPhil, Yale University, New Haven, CT (1973); MS, Yale University, New Haven, CT (1972); BA, University of California, Los Angeles (1971) **Career:** Independent Consultant, Wrentham, MA (2003-Present); Special Assistant to Provost, Massachusetts Institute of Technology (1992-2003); Lecturer, Massachusetts Institute of Technology, Cambridge, MA (1982-1992); Staff Scientist, Neurosciences Research Program, Boston, MA (1979-1982); Visiting Scholar, Massachusetts Institute of Technology, Cambridge, MA; Research Affiliate, Massachusetts Institute of Technology, Cambridge, MA **Career Related:** Fellow, Association for Women in Science (1996); Fellow, American Association for the Advancement of Science (1991); Research Fellow, Mellon Foundation, Massachusetts Institute of Technology (1982-1983) **Creative Works:** Founding Co-Editor-in-Chief, "Science & Engineering Ethics," Springer/Nature, Dordrecht, Netherlands (1995-Present); Author, Numerous Articles and Chapters in Neuroscience, Neuroethics and Research Ethics **Awards:** Professional Development Award, National Science Foundation (1984-1986) **Membership:** Secretary, Societal Impacts of Science and Engineering Section, American Association for the Advancement of Science (1996-Present); Chair, Social Issues Committee, Society for Neuroscience (2002-2005); President, Association for Women In Science (1990-1992); International Neuroethics Society; Association for Practical and Professional Ethics; Sigma Xi; The Research Honor Society **Business Address:** PO Box 2007, Wrentham, MA, 02093

Annette Kay Bisanz

Title: Nurse (Retired) **Industry:** Medicine & Health Care **Company Name:** The University of Texas MD Anderson Cancer Center **Date of Birth:** 07/03/1942 **Place of Birth:** Kalamazoo **State:** MI/USA **Parents:** Frank John Bisanz; Arlowyne Biddle (Fisher) Bisanz **Marital Status:** Single **Education:** MPH, University of Michigan, Ann Arbor, MI (1972); BSN, Marquette University, Milwaukee, WI (1966); Diploma in Nursing, Borgess School of Nursing, Kalamazoo, MI (1964) **Career:** Clinical Nurse Specialist, The University of Texas MD Anderson Cancer Center (1983-2012); Clinical Practice Coordinator, The University of Texas MD Anderson Cancer Center (1999-2003); Case Manager, The University of Texas MD Anderson Cancer Center (1996-1999); Discharge Planning Nurse, The University of Texas MD Anderson Cancer Center (1983-1996); Director, Education and Training, St. Lawrence Hospital, Lansing, MI (1979-1981); Supervisor, Lansing Visiting Nurses Association, Michigan (1969-1979); Staff Nurse, Hospital Ship HOPE, Sri Lanka (1968-1969) **Career Related:** Facilitator of Bereavement Support Groups, Houston Hospice (2000-Present); Co-Founder, Volunteer Interfaith Care Givers, DBA Senior Rides and More (1994-Present); Scientific Advisory Board Member, Colon Cancer Alliance (1999-2009) **Creative Works:** Contributor, Chapters, Various Books; Contributor, Articles, Various Professional Journals **Awards:** Staff Educator of the Year (2006); Ethics Career Development Award, Oncology Nursing Foundation (1996); Ethel Fleming Arceneaux Brown Foundation Outstanding Oncology Nurse Award (1995); Honoree, Outstanding Contribution to Clinical Nursing Practice, Texas Nurses Association (1993) **Membership:** Oncology Nursing Society **Marquis Who's Who Honors:** Albert Nelson Marquis Lifetime Achievement Award (2017) **Hobbies:** Swimming; Reading; Music; Flower arranging **Religion:** Roman Catholic **Shipping Address:** 26 Grants Lake Circle, Sugar Land, TX, 77479

William Lawrence Bitner III

Title: Banker (Retired), Educator (Retired) **Industry:** Education/Educational Services **Date of Birth:** 12/25/1930 **Place of Birth:** Harrisburg **State:** PA **Parents:** William Lawrence Bitner Jr.; Anna (Horstick) Bitner **Marital Status:** Married **Spouse Name:** Wylla Mae Bowman (6/9/1956) **Children:** Lizabeth Anne; Lynne Ellen Bitner Ackner **Education:** PhD in Administration, New York University; MA, Rutgers, The State University of New Jersey; EdB, Pennsylvania State University, Bloomsburg, PA **Career:** President, Evergreen Bancorp, Inc. (1980-1993); Chief Executive Officer, Evergreen Bancorp, Inc. (1980-1993); President, First National Bank of Glens Falls (1977-1993); Chief Executive Officer, First National Bank of Glens Falls (1977-1993); Senior Vice President, First National Bank of Glens Falls (1976); Associate Commissioner of Education, Department of Education, State of New York (1972-1976); Superintendent of Schools, Glens Falls City School District, New York (1963-1972); Assistant Superintendent of Schools, Plainview-Old Bethpage Central School District, New York (1961-1963); Assistant Superintendent of Schools, Scotch Plains-Fanwood School District, New Jersey (1958-1961); Teacher, Scotch Plains-Fanwood High School, New Jersey (1956-1957) **Career Related:** President, Association for the Advancement of International Education, United States Department of State (1971-1973); Board of Directors, Sandy Hill Corporation, Hudson Falls, NY; North America Medical Instrument Corporation **Civic:** Lake Champlain Cancer Research Organization, Inc., Burlington, VT (1988-Present); Director, New York State Health Care Trustees (1998-2001); Board of Directors, Glens Falls Hospital (1988-2001); Chairman, Community Lending Corporation, New York (1991-1992); Chairman of the Board, Hyde Collections, Glens Falls, NY (1985-1988) **Awards:** Recipient, Distinguished Service Award, Glens Falls YMCA (1992); Recipient, Distinguished Service Award, Independent Bankers Association of New York State (1991); Recipient, Outstanding School Administrator Award, New York (1976); Recipient, Special Award, Human Resources School (1975); Recipient, Distinguished Service Award, Bloomsburg University, Pennsylvania (1972); Honoree, National PTA Life Membership, Adirondack Council PTA (1972); Honoree, Charles F. Kettering Foundation Fellowship, Carleton College (1966) **Membership:** Honorary Member, Glens Falls Country Club (2014-Present); Glens Falls Country Club (1964-2014) **Marquis Who's Who Honors:** Albert Nelson Marquis Lifetime Achievement Award (2017) **Hobbies:** Golf; Squash; Coin collecting **Political Affiliations:** Republican **Shipping Address:** 54 Wincrest Drive, Queensbury, NY, 12804

John Blackmore

Title: Historian **Industry:** Education/Educational Services **Date of Birth:** 09/13/1931 **Place of Birth:** Washington **State:** DC/USA **Parents:** Philip (Guillou) Blackmore; Emily Van Patten **Marital Status:** Married **Spouse Name:** Setsuko Tanaka **Education:** PhD, University of California, Los Angeles, with Distinction (1970); BA, University of New Mexico (1953) **Career:** Faculty, Tsukuba University, Japan (1991-1995); Visiting Scholar, Tokyo University (1986-1990); Faculty, Department of Theoretical Physics, University of Vienna (1982-1985); Visiting Scholar, Cambridge University, England (1977-1979); Faculty, Harvey Mudd College, Claremont, CA (1972-1977); Assistant Professor, University of California (1971-1972) **Military Service:** US Air Force (1953-1955) **Creative Works:** Author, "A Guide to the Past From Homer To Locke" (2013); Author, "Three Strikes and You're Out, Fred" (2013); Author, "Assumption Dialogues II" (2012); Author, "Great Realists From Galileo to Planck" (2012); Author, "Franks Philosophy" (2012); Editor, "Assumption Dialogues" (2011); Editor, "Ludwig Boltzmann, Volume II" (2010); Author, "Causal Dialogues or What is Influence?" (2011); Editor, "Ludwig Boltzmann Vol. 1" (2010); Editor, "Ernst Mach's Prague, 1867-1895" (2010); Author, "Semantic Dialogues or Ethics vs. Rhetoric" (2010); Editor, "Ernst Mach's Graz" (2010); Editor, "Ernst March's Influence Spreads" (2009); Editor, "Ernst March's Philosophy Pro & Con" (2009); Editor, "Choosing a Philosophy or Looking for Deeper Assumptions" (2008); Editor, "Ernst Mach's Science" (2006); Editor, "Ernst Mach's Vienna, 1895-1930" (2001); Author, "Foundation Theory-An Attempt to be Basic" (2000); Editor, "Ludwig Boltzmann Vol. I" (1995); Author, "Ludwig Boltzmann, Volume II" (1995); Author, "Ernst Mach- A Deeper Look" (1992); Editor, "Ernst Mach Als Aussenseiter" (1985); Editor, "Philosophy of Mind" (1982); Editor, "Ludwig Boltzmann Band 8" (1982); Author, "The Gibraltar Dialogues" (1980); Author, "Ernst Mach-His Life, Work and Influence" (1972); Author, "A Guide to the Past from Homer to Locke" **Membership:** History of Science Society **Hobbies:** Reading; Stamp collecting; Hiking **Shipping Address:** 4932 Sentinel Drive, Apartment 201, Bethesda, MD, 20816

Paul Bradford Blanch

Title: Equipment Specialist (Retired) **Industry:** Education/Educational Services **Company Name:** Shands Hospital, University of Florida **Date of Birth:** 03/25/1949 **Place of Birth:** Boston **State:** MA/USA **Parents:** E T Blanch, MD; Ethel Blanch **Marital Status:** Married **Spouse Name:** Laurel A. Blanch **Children:** David; Kimberly **Education:** AA, The University of Chicago (1976); BA, Colby College, Waterville, ME (1972) **Certifications:** Registered Respiratory Therapist (1977-2018); Diplomate, Florida Society for Respiratory Care (1990-2008); Diplomate, American Association for Respiratory Care (1977-2008) **Career:** Courtesy Assistant, Anesthesiology, Department of Anesthesiology College of Medicine, University of Florida (1995-Present); Respiratory Equipment Specialist, Shands Hospital, University of Florida (1980-Present); Supervisor, Blood Gas and Stat Chemistry Laboratory, Shands Hospital, University of Florida (1975-1980); Staff Therapist, Shands Hospital, University of Florida (1974-1975); Staff Therapist, Seton Hospital (1973-1974); Technologist, Carney Hospital (1972-1973) **Career Related:** Instructor, Respiratory Care, Santa Fe Community College (1974-1990) **Civic:** Coach, Babe Ruth Baseball Program, Alachua, FL (1993-1997) **Creative Works:** Developer, Designer, Productizing Engineer pNeuton-S and pNeuton-A Transport Ventilators (2003); Co-developer, Designer, Hamilton MAX Transport Ventilator; Designer, Developer, MACS CPAP System; Original Designer, pNeuton-Mini Infant Transport Ventilator; Co-owner, Patent Holder, Airon's Intellectual Property; Owner, Operator, Innovative Medical Pneumatics and Consulting Company; Owner, Operator, Innovative Medical Pneumatics and Consulting Company; Co-Developer, Concept Engineer, Philps Vent Assist Ventilation Monitor **Awards:** American Respiratory Care Foundation's Dr. Allen DeVilbliss Literary Award (1999); Best Paper Published (1998-1999); American Respiratory Care Foundation's Best Original Paper Literary Award (1997); Best Original Paper Published (1996-1997); American College of Chest Physicians Young Investigator Award (1994); American Respiratory Care Foundation's Dr. Allen DeVilbliss Literary Award (1994); Best Paper Published (1993-1994); American Respiratory Care Foundation Literary Award (1992); Best Paper, Open Forum (1992) **Marquis Who's Who Honors:** Albert Nelson Marquis Lifetime Achievement Award (2017) **Hobbies:** Fishing; Gardening; Building custom fishing rods; Fly and jig tying **Political Affiliations:** Independent **Religion:** Episcopalian **Shipping Address:** 136 Turkey Ridge Road, Byrdstown, TN, 38549

Jerry Blavat

Industry: Media & Entertainment **Date of Birth:** 07/03/1940 **Place of Birth:** Philadelphia **State:** PA/USA **Parents:** Louis Blavat; Lucille Capuano **Children:** Kathi, Geraldine, Stacy, Deserie **Education:** Graduate, High School **Career:** Program Director, Geator Gold Radio Network, Pennsylvania, Delaware, Maryland, New Jersey (1989-Present); Radio Station Disc Jockey, WOND-AM, Atlantic City (2013-Present); Radio Station Disc Jockey, WBCB-AM, Bucks County and Trenton (2012-Present); Radio Station Disc Jockey, WTKU **Career Related:** Owner, Night Club Memories, Margate, NJ (1972-Present); Member, Nominating Committee, Rock & Roll Hall of Fame, Philadelphia, PA (1988-Present) **Civic:** Board of Directors, Performer Hero Scholarship Fund, Philadelphia (1963-1970); Board of Directors, Police Athletic League, Philadelphia (1966-1970); Fundraiser, Numerous Schools, Churches, Foundations, and Public Television **Creative Works:** Actor, "Mancation" (2012); Actor, "Cookie" (1989); Actor, "Desperately Seeking Susan" (1985); Actor, "Baby, It's You" (1983); Television Guest, "The Monkees"; Television Guest, "Mod Squad"; Television Guest, "Joey Bishop Show" Television Guest, "Tonight Show"; Television Guest, "Mike Douglas Show"; Television Guest, "Pat Boone Show"; Television Guest, "Merv Griffin Show" **Awards:** Person of the Year, Broadcast Pioneers (2016) **Membership:** Advisory Board, National Music Foundation (1989-Present); SAG-AFTRA; American Guild of Variety Artists

Ernest Everett Blevins

Title: Genealogist, Researcher, Historian, Preservationist, Archaeologist **Industry:** Sciences **Company Name:** West Virginia Division of Culture and History **Date of Birth:** 11/16/1968 **Place of Birth:** Spartanburg **State:** SC **Parents:** Maurice Everett Blevins; Anne Soule Lapham Blevins **Marital Status:** Married **Spouse Name:** Lisa Ann Schlosser (12/30/1975) **Children:** Savannah Gayle; Avery Everett (Deceased); Ana Grace; Cameren Everett; Ryal Austin; Cavanagh William; Isabella Noel (Deceased); Jasper Alden **Education:** Postgraduate Coursework in Public History, University of West Georgia, Carrollton, GA (2009); Postgraduate Coursework in Public History, Georgia State University, Atlanta, GA (2004-2006); Postgraduate Coursework in Public History, University of West Georgia, Carrollton, GA (2003-2006); MFA in History Preservation, Savannah College of Art and Design, Savannah, GA (2001); BS in Anthropology, College of Charleston, Charleston, SC (1992); BA in Studio Art, College of Charleston, Charleston, SC (1992) **Certifications:** Certified in Public History, University of West Georgia (2009) **Career:** Structural Historian, West Virginia State Historic Preservation office (2013-Present); Owner, Blevins Historical Research, Villa Rica, GA (1997-Present); Cultural Research Analysis (2013); Adjunct Professor, United States History, Middle Tennessee State University, Murfreesboro, TN (2010-2011); Enumerator, United States Census Bureau (2010); Archaeologist, Edwards-Pitman Environmental, Smyrna, GA (2007-2008); Architectural Historian, Historian III, Fluor Corporation (2007); Professor of History, Georgia Highlands College, Rome, GA (2005-2006) **Military Service:** Second Lieutenant, South Carolina State Guard, Charleston, SC (1998-1999) **Creative Works:** Author, "Sears Exploring My America Application: The Overland Dixie Highway" (2010); Author, "Always Looking North: The Carroll County Confederate Monument," Dixie Film Festival, Athens, GA (2010) **Awards:** Distinguished Service Award, Yellow District County, Heard County, GA (2012); **Membership:** Monuments Officer, Sons of Union Veterans of the Civil War (2012-Present) **To what do you attribute your success:** Mr. Blevins attributes his success to a love of history. **Why did you become involved in your profession or industry:** Mr. Blevins became interested in his profession after taking a college course that required him to create a family tree. His mother's side of the chart ended up being 20 feet long, and for his father's side he had to perform a great deal of research and investigation. **Where will you be in five years:** In 5 years Mr. Blevins will still be working in preservation, and will continue to write for the Charleston Gazette Mail. **Shipping Address:** 648 Wayside Dr., Charleston, WV, 25303

Kenneth Blum, PhD

Title: Pharmaceutical Executive, Educator (Retired), Neuroscientist, Psychiatric Geneticist **Industry:** Pharmaceuticals **Date of Birth:** 08/08/1939 **Place of Birth:** Brooklyn **State:** NY/USA **Parents:** Harry Blum; Lena Blum **Marital Status:** Life Partner **Spouse Name:** Margaret Madigan; Arlene Carol Schlessel (06/08/1963, Deceased) **Children:** Jeffrey Haris; Seth Howard; Moses Madigan (Stepson) **Education:** PhD, New York Medical College, Valhalla, NY (1968); MSc, New Jersey Medical School, Rutgers, The State University of New Jersey (1964); BSc, Columbia University, New York, NY (1961) **Career:** Honorary Lifetime Professor, Psychology, Institute of Psychology, Eötvös Loránd University, Budapest, Hungary (2016-Present); Founding President, United Scientific Science Group (2014-Present); Chairman, IGENE (2013-Present); Chief Scientific Officer, IGENE (2013-Present); Chief Scientific Advisor, Dominion Diagnostics (2011-Present); Chief Scientific Officer, LifeGen, Inc., La Jolla, CA (2008-Present); Director, LifeGen, Inc., La Jolla, CA (2008-Present); Chairman, Geneus Health LLC. (2017); Chief Scientific Officer, Geneus Health LLC. (2017); Former Chief Scientific Officer, RDSS (2016); Chief Scientific Advisor, Nupathways Inc. (2017); Chief Neuroscience Advisor, The Shores Treatment and Recovery (2017); Adjunct Full Professor, Department of Psychiatry, Boonshoft School of Medicine, Wright State University, Dayton, OH (2017); Chief Scientific Officer, Victory Nutrition International, LLC (2016-2017); Adjunct Full Professor, Keck School of Medicine, University of Southern California (2016-2017); Adjunct Research Professor, College of Medicine, University of Florida, Gainesville, FL (2009); Vice Chairman, LifeGen, Inc., La Jolla, CA (2008-Present); Director, Salugen Inc., San Diego, CA (2005-2008); Vice Chairman, Salugen Inc., San Diego, CA (2005-2008); Chief Scientific Officer, Salugen Inc., San Diego, CA (2005-2008) **Creative Works:** Co-author, "Molecular Neurobiology of Addiction Recovery: The 12 Steps Program and Fellowship" (2014) **Awards:** Psychiatry Selection Award, "Handbook of Psychiatric Genetics" (1997); Julius Axelrod (Nobel Laurate) Distinguished Speaker Award (1986); Book of the Month, "Handbook of Abusable Drugs" (1985) **Hobbies:** Song writing; Jazz **Religion:** Jewish **Shipping Address:** 101 Colorado St Apt 1702, TX, Austin, 78701

Therese A. Boisvert

Title: Credentialing Compliance Coordinator **Industry:** Business Management/Business Services **Company Name:** Logistics Health Incorporated **Place of Birth:** La Crosse **State:** WI/USA **Parents:** Walter Boisvert (Deceased); Joanne Boisvert (Deceased) **Marital Status:** Single **Education:** MEd, Education Media with Emphasis in Library Science, University of Wisconsin-La Crosse (1985); BS, Pre-Law Studies and Political Science, Minor in Sociology, University of Wisconsin-La Crosse (1982); Aquinas High School, La Crosse, WI **Career:** Credentialing Compliance Coordinator, Logistics Health Incorporated (2017-Present); Administrative Assistant, Vicar General and Vicar for the Clergy, The Roman Catholic Diocese of La Crosse (2011-2017); Occupational Health Department Specialist, Gundersen Lutheran Medical Center (1989-2011); Assistant Medical Librarian, St. Francis Hospital (1986-1989) **Civic:** Liaison to the Diocese, LaCrosse Council of Catholic Women; Secretary, La Crosse Deanery, PCCW; Secretary, Cathedral Council of Catholic Women; Former Chairperson and Secretary, Aquinas Education Commission; Education Committee, The Cathedral of St. Joseph the Workman **Awards:** Professional Woman of the Year, National Association of Professional Women; Sterling Registry of Outstanding Professionals; Continental Who's Who Registry of National Business Leaders; Stanford Who's Who; Presidential Who's Who **Membership:** Policy Committee, Cathedral Parish Council of Catholic Women; National Association of Professional Women **Marquis Who's Who Honors:** Distinguished Humanitarian (2017) **To what do you attribute your success:** Ms. Boisvert attributes her success to the support she receives from her parents and older brother. **Why did you become involved in your profession or industry:** Ms. Boisvert became involved in her profession after working in the medical field for more than 26 years. **What do you consider to be the highlight of your career:** The highlight of Ms. Boisvert's career was going back in the medical field after working her new with The Roman Catholic Diocese of La Crosse, and being able to utilize all of her skills. **Where will you be in five years:** Ms. Boisvert will be continuing to build her career **Hobbies:** Needlepoint; Ice Skating; Reading **Religion:** Catholic **Shipping Address:** 419 Jackson Street, La Crosse, WI, 54601

Laurence Boorstein

Title: Project Manager, Engineer **Industry:** Environmental Services **Company Name:** Green Powered Technology LLC **Date of Birth:** 01/22/1951 **Place of Birth:** Neuilly-sur-Seine **Country of Origin:** France **Parents:** Edward Boorstein; Regula Boorstein **Education:** MBA, Finance, Columbia Business School, New York, NY (1988); CE, Civil Engineer, Columbia University, New York, NY (1978); MS, Civil Engineering, Columbia University, New York, NY (1974); BA, History, Columbia College, New York, NY (1972) **Certifications:** Certified Project Manager, AECOM (2016) **Career:** Project Manager, Engineer, Green Powered Technology (2017-Present); Project Manager, Principal Economist, AECOM, Arlington, VA (2005-2016); Project Manager, Principal Economist, AECOM, New York, NY (1994-2005); Senior Economist, Soros Associates (1988-1994); Senior Economist, Frederic R. Harris, Inc., Planning Research Corporation (1983-1986); Senior System Planner, Frederic R. Harris Inc., Planning Research Corporation (1979-1983); Principal System Engineer, Frederic R. Harris, Inc., Planning Research Corporation (1977-1979); Systems Analyst, Frederic R. Harris, Inc. Division, Planning Research Corporation, New York, NY (1974-1977) **Awards:** 40-Year Service Award, AECOM **Membership:** American Society of Civil Engineers; American Mensa **To what do you attribute your success:** Mr. Boorstein attributes his success to hard work and education. **Why did you become involved in your profession or industry:** Mr. Boorstein graduated as an engineer 44 yrs ago, and worked his way up the totem pole. **Hobbies:** Keeping up with current affairs and a variety of different social media and news **Business Address:** 901 D Street SW, Washington, DC, 20024-2113 **Shipping Address:** 11990 Market Street, Unit 616, Reston, VA, 20190-6017 **Website:** http://www.larryboorstein.com

Charles Edward Booth

Industry: Religious **Date of Birth:** 02/04/1947 **Place of Birth:** Baltimore **State:** MD **Parents:** William Whiting Booth; Hazel Delsenior (Willis) Sutton **Education:** PhD in Ministry, United Theological Seminary, Dayton, OH (1990); Honorary DD, Virginia Seminary (Now Virginia University of Lynchburg) (1980); MDiv, Eastern Baptist Seminary (Now Palmer Theological Seminary of Eastern University) (1973); BA, Howard University (1969) **Certifications:** Ordained Baptist Pastor, Baltimore, MD (1970) **Career:** Pastor, Mt. Olivet Baptist Church, Columbus, OH (1978-Present); Pastor, St. Paul's Baptist Church, West Chester, PA (1970-1977) **Career Related:** Professor, Preaching, United Theological Seminary, Dayton, OH (1988-Present); Guest Lecturer, Hampton Ministers' Conference (1999); Guest Lecturer, Hampton Ministers' Conference (1995); Instructor, MTSO, Delaware, OH (1984-1985); Guest Lecturer, Hampton Ministers' Conference (1984); Instructor, Trinity Lutheran Seminary, Columbus, OH (1982-1983); Guest Preacher, Baptist World Youth Conference; Speaker in Field **Civic:** Advisory Board Member, Banc Ohio Community Development Association, Columbus, OH (1988-Present); Board of Directors, Columbus Urban League (1988) **Creative Works:** Author, "Stronger in my Broken Places; Claiming a Life of Fullness in God" (2014); Author, "The Prophetic Voice: Words for Today" (2011); Author, "Bridging the Breach: Evangelical Thought and Liberation in the African-American Preaching Tradition," Urban Ministries (2000); Author, "The Worker" (1985); Co-author, "Outstanding Black Sermons, Volume Three" (1982); Advisory Board, "The African American Pulpit"; Contributor, "From One Brother to Another: Voices of African American Men"; Contributor, "The Irresistible Urge to Preach: A Collectible of African American 'Call' Stories"; Contributor, "Outstanding Black Sermons, Volume Four"; Contributor, "Wisdom of the Ages: The Mystique of the African American Preacher"; Contributor, "Preaching with Sacred Fire: An Anthology of African-American Sermons, 1750-Present" **Awards:** Martin Luther King, Jr. Humanitarian Award, The Columbus Education Association (2014); James E. Stamps Alumni Recognition Award (1999); Vertner Woodson Tandy Award, Alpha Lambda Rho Chapter, Alpha Phi Alpha (1999); Humanitarian Service Award, Alpha Kappa Alpha Sorority, Inc. (1981); Dedicated Service Award, West Chester University (1977); Middler Scholarship, Eastern Baptist Seminary (Now Palmer Theological Seminary of Eastern University) (1971); Honoree, Honor Roll of Preachers, Ebony Magazine **Marquis Who's Who Honors:** Albert Nelson Marquis Lifetime Achievement Award (2017) **Political Affiliations:** Democrat **Shipping Address:** 7877 Grandley Court, Reynoldsburg, OH, 43068

John Ellis Bowlt, PhD

Title: Professor Emeritus, Director **Industry:** Education/Educational Services **Company Name:** University of Southern California **Date of Birth:** 12/06/1943 **Place of Birth:** London **Country of Origin:** England **Marital Status:** Married **Spouse Name:** Nicoletta Misler (1981) **Education:** PhD in Russian Literature and Art, University of St. Andrews (1971); MA in Russian Literature, University of Birmingham (1966); Honorary BA in Russian, University of Birmingham (1965) **Career:** Professor Emeritus, Department of Slavic Languages, University of Southern California (1988-Present); Professor of Slavic Language, The University of Texas at Austin (1971-1988); Director, Institute of Modern Russian Culture, University of Southern California **Career Related:** Fellow, International Research and Exchange Board (1996); Senior Fellow, Wolfsonian Foundation Award (1995); Fellow, International Research and Exchange Board (1994); Fellow, International Research and Exchange Board (1991); Fellow, International Research and Exchange Board (1988); Fellow, International Research and Exchange Board (1986); Fellow, National Humanities Institute, Yale University (1977-1978); Fellow, British Council, Moscow University (1966-1968) **Creative Works:** Contributor, Articles, Professional Journals; Author, Co-Author, Various Books **Awards:** Golden Pen Award, U.S. Institute of Theater Technology (2017); Distinguished Contributions to Slavic, East European, and Eurasian Studies Award, Association for Slavic, East European, and Eurasian Studies (2016); Order of Friendship, Russian Federation (2010); The Albert & Elaine Borchard Foundation, France (1995); Award, American Council of Learned Societies, Rome, Italy (1986); Award, American Council of Learned Societies, Paris, France (1981); Award, Mitchell Wolfson, Senior Foundation, Miami, FL **Membership:** American Association for the Advancement of Slavic Studies (Now Association for Slavic, East European, and Eurasian Studies); Association of Teachers of Slavic and East European Languages; Association of Russian-American Scholars in USA **Marquis Who's Who Honors:** Albert Nelson Marquis Lifetime Achievement Award (2017) **Hobbies:** Rare books; Dogs **Business Address:** 3501 Trousdale Parkway, Suite 255, Department of Language and Literature, Los Angeles, CA, 90089

Edward Lee Boyd

Title: Physicist, Computer Scientist **Industry:** Information Technology and Services **Date of Birth:** 11/27/1932 **Education:** BA, Lehigh University, Bethlehem, PA **Career:** Senior Technical Staff Member, IBM; Manager, Beverly Laboratories; Builder, Weapons for Military **Military:** U.S. Navy **Awards:** Various Outstanding Achievement Awards; Honorary Award, Kyoto University **Marquis Who's Who Honors:** Albert Nelson Marquis Lifetime Achievement Award (2017) **Hobbies:** Genealogy; Photography **Why did you become involved in your profession or industry:** Mr. Boyd became interested in his profession while he was a teenager during World War II; his father worked on airplanes for the Air Force.

James Joseph Brady

Title: Labor Arbitrator **Industry:** Education/Educational Services **Company Name:** Jacksonville University **Date of Birth:** 03/02/1936 **Place of Birth:** Jersey City **State:** NJ/USA **Parents:** James Brady; Anna (Shine) Brady **Marital Status:** Married **Spouse Name:** Sheila Hartney (7/24/1965) **Children:** Matthew; Michael; James **Education:** PhD in Economics, University of Notre Dame (1969); MA in Economics, University of Notre Dame (1963); BA, University of Notre Dame (1959) **Career:** Professor of Economics, Jacksonville University (1995-2003); President, Jacksonville University (1989-1995); President-elect, Jacksonville University (1988-1989); Vice President of Academic Affairs, Jacksonville University (1984-1988); Dean, College of Business, Jacksonville University (1983-1984); Dean, College Arts and Sciences, Jacksonville University (1979-1983); Assistant Professor, Old Dominion University, Norfolk, VA (1969-1979); Associate Professor, Old Dominion University, Norfolk, VA (1969-1979); Professor Economics, Old Dominion University, Norfolk, VA (1969-1979); Assistant Professor Economics, Indiana University, South Bend (1965-1969); Professional Baseball Player, Detroit Tigers (1955-1960) **Career Related:** Permanent Arbitrator, University of Florida, University of Central Florida (1999-Present); Special Magistrate, Florida Public Employees Relations Commission, Tallahassee, FL (1985-Present); Member, Federal Mediation and Conciliation Service Labor Panel (1985-Present); Private Labor Consultant, Jacksonville, FL (1978-1988) **Military Service:** U.S. Army (1959-1961) **Creative Works:** Author, "Arbitration Principles: Layoffs" (1989); Co-author, "Transportation Noise Pollution" (1970); Articles; Speaking Engagements **Awards:** Grantee, National Aeronautics and Space Administration, Norfolk, VA (1970) **Membership:** Board of Directors, Jacksonville Chamber of Commerce (1989-Present); Commercial Arbitrator, American Arbitration Association (1987-1989); Labor Arbitrator, American Arbitration Association (1965); Industrial Relations Research Association; Society of Professionals in Dispute Resolution **Marquis Who's Who Honors:** Albert Nelson Marquis Lifetime Achievement Award (2017) **To what do you attribute your success:** Mr. Brady attributes his success to great parents, teachers and hard work. **Hobbies:** Fishing; Cooking; Tennis; Reading non-fiction **Shipping Address:** 9601 Southbrook Dr., Apt N107, Jacksonville, FL, 32256

B. Brent Breedin

Title: Historian **Industry:** Writing and Editing **Company Name:** White House Weekly **Date of Birth:** 11/03/1925 **Place of Birth:** Beaufort **State:** SC/USA **Parents:** Berryman Brent Breedin; Jane Cunningham Dixon **Marital Status:** Married **Spouse Name:** Catherine McCuen Muller (2006); Allain Crenshaw (1959, Divorced 1978) **Children:** David Singleton; Sarah Breedin-Chase; Amelia Breedin-Twarogowski **Education:** BA, Washington and Lee University (1947) **Career:** Private Practice, Brent Breedin and Associates, Columbia, SC (1988-Present); Historian, White House Weekly, Washington, DC (1998-2003); Resident Manager, Hunt Energy and Mineral Company, Australia (1996-1997); Director of Public Relations, Rice University, Houston, TX (1981-1987); Director of Public Relations, Georgetown University, Washington, DC (1977-1979); Editor, Council on Library and Information Resources, Washington, DC (1972-1975); Editor, American College Public Relations Association, Washington, DC (1966-1971); Editor, Clemson University (1964-1966); Information Specialist, DuPont Co. (1960-1963); Press Secretary, U.S. Senator Strom Thurmond (1958-1959); Resident Manager, Hunt International Oil Company, Pakistan (1955-1958); Publicist, Clemson University (1952-1955); Sports Editor, Columnist, Daily Mail, Anderson, SC (1949-1952); Reporter, Caller-Times, Corpus Christi, TX (1947-1948) **Career Related:** Adviser, Houston Zoo (1981-1987); Adviser, Washington D.C. Library (1972-1976) **Civic:** Field School, Washington, DC (1972); Founding Member, Capital Hill Montessori, Washington, DC (1964) **Military Service:** U.S. Navy (1944-1945) **Membership:** National Press Club; Sigma Delta Chi **Marquis Who's Who Honors:** Distinguished Humanitarian (2017) **Hobbies:** Sports history; Movie history **Religion:** Episcopalian **Shipping Address:** 1829 Senate Street, Apt. 18B, Columbia, SC, 29201

Jeremy Brenes

Title: Homeopath, Researcher, President, Treasurer, Consultant, Founder **Industry:** Health, Wellness and Fitness **Company Name:** Homeopathic Village, Inc. **Date of Birth:** 12/18/1973 **Place of Birth:** Oklahoma City **State:** OK **Parents:** Alvaro Brenes; June Brenes **Marital Status:** Married **Spouse Name:** Wenling Yu (10/16/2009) **Education:** PhD in Homeopathy, British Institute of Homeopathy, London (2003); BS in Mathematics, University of Oklahoma, Norman, OK (1996) **Career:** President, Treasurer, Consultant, Founder, Homeopathic Village, Inc., Houston, TX (2003-Present); Processing Geophysicist, Western Geophysical, Houston, TX (1997-2001) **Creative Works:** Homeopathic Village Electronical Newsletter (2003-Present); Author, homeopathicvillage.net (2016); Co-Author, "Plants Remedy Index" (2012); Author, "Dice Roll Probability Tables" (2007); Author, "Homeopathic Repertory of Heavy Elements" (2006) Author, www.homeopathicvillage.net (2002) **Awards:** Accredited, Better Business Bureau **Membership:** History Channel Club; The Folio Society **Marquis Who's Who Honors:** Distinguished Humanitarian (2017) **Hobbies:** Reading; Gardening; Computers; Arms and armor collecting; Artwork collecting; Vintage toy collecting **Shipping Address:** 20707 Fertile Valley Lane, Richmond, TX, 77407 **Website:** http://www.homeopathicvillage.net

Allen Eugene Brennecke

Title: Attorney at Law **Industry:** Law and Legal Services **Company Name:** Moore, McKibben, Goodman & Lorenz, LLP **Date of Birth:** 01/08/1937 **Place of Birth:** Marshalltown **State:** IA/USA **Parents:** Arthur Lynn Brennecke; Julia Alice (Allen) Brennecke **Marital Status:** Married **Spouse Name:** Billie Jean Johnstone (6/12/1958) **Children:** Scott; Stephen; Beth; Gregory; Kristen **Education:** JD, College of Law, University of IA (1961); BBA, University of IA (1959) **Career:** Of Counsel, Moore, McKibben, Goodman & Lorenz, LLP., Marshalltown, Iowa (2000); Partner, Harrison Brennecke Moore Smaha & McKibben LLP (Now Moore, McKibben, Goodman & Lorenz, LLP.), Marshalltown, Iowa (1966-2000); Associate, Mote, Wilson & Welp (Now Moore, McKibben, Goodman & Lorenz, LLP.), Marshalltown, IA (1962-1966); Law Clerk to U. S. District Judge, Des Moines, IA (1961-1962) **Civic:** First United Methodist Church, Marshalltown, IA (1987-1989); Board of Trustees, Iowa Law School Foundation (1973-1986); Finance Chairman, Republican Party, Fourth Congressional District, Iowa (1970-1973); Marshall County Republican Party, Iowa (1967-1970); Board of Directors, Marshalltown YMCA (1966-1971) **Creative Works:** Contributor, Articles, Professional Journals **Awards:** Award of Merit, Iowa State Bar Association (1987) **Membership:** President, The Iowa State Bar Association (1990-1991); Chairman, House of Delegates, ABA (1984-1986); Board of Directors, National Judicial College, ABA (1982-1988); Board of Governors, ABA (1982-1986); American College of Trust and Estate Counsel; American College of Tax Counsel; American Bar Foundation; Mason; Promise Keepers; Fellow, ABA **Bar Admissions:** State of Iowa (1961) **Marquis Who's Who Honors:** Albert Nelson Marquis Lifetime Achievement Award (2017) **To what do you attribute your success:** Mr. Brennecke attributes his success to being blessed with a wonderful wife, five children and their spouses, 19 grandchildren, three great-grandchild, good friends and gifts from the Lord. **Why did you become involved in your profession or industry:** Mr. Brennecke became involved in his profession upon earning a juris doctor, which was a great and respected degree to have for business. **What do you consider to be the highlight of your career:** The highlights of Mr. Brennecke's career have included being honored as president of The Iowa State Bar Association and being named chairman of the House of Delegates of the ABA. **Where will you be in five years:** In five years, Mr. Brennecke hopes to still be involved in law. **Hobbies:** Golf; Travel; Sports **Political Affiliations:** Republican **Religion:** Methodist **Shipping Address:** 2011 Elmcrest Drive, Marshalltown, IA, 50158

Arline Roth Brick

Title: Adjunct Instructor **Industry:** Education/Educational Services **Company Name:** Capital Community College **Parents:** Irving K. Roth; Elizabeth S. Roth **Marital Status:** Married **Spouse Name:** Lawrence Samuel Brick (11/3/1974) **Children:** Jason; Sheri; Adam **Education:** MEd, University of Hartford, West Hartford, CT (1972); BA, University of Hartford, West Hartford, CT (1969) **Certifications:** Certified Teacher, State of Connecticut **Career:** Adjunct Instructor, Human Biology, Capital Community College, Hartford, CT (2003-Present); Teacher, Biology and Psychology, Bulkeley High School, Hartford, CT (1969-2003); **Civic:** Chairman, West Hartford Board of Education (1993-1995); Member, West Hartford Board of Education (1991-1995); Chairman, West Hartford Board of Education (1986-1989); **Awards:** Named, Citizen of the Year, West Hartford Education Association (1989-1990) **Marquis Who's Who Honors:** Albert Nelson Marquis Lifetime Achievement Award (2017) **Why did you become involved in your profession or industry:** Ms. Brick became involved in her profession when she started as a day camp counselor in her late teens. During her last year in college she tutored at The Salvation Army, and volunteered in an elementary school in the afternoon PE programs. After college, Mrs. Brick worked as a research associate in the education department at the University of Hartford and helped develop the Vista Program, and Teacher Core between the Hartford Board of Education and the Hartford School System. **Shipping Address:** 25 Cassandra Blvd., Apt 101, West Hartford, CT, 06107

Billy Jean Britt Jr.

Title: Economic Education Specialist, Elementary School Educator (Retired) **Industry:** Education/Educational Services **Company Name:** Federal Reserve Bank of St. Louis **Date of Birth:** 10/19/1952 **Place of Birth:** Pine Bluff **State:** AR **Parents:** Billy Jean Britt; Charlene Faver Britt **Marital Status:** Single **Education:** MEd, University of Arkansas, Fayetteville, AR (1983); BA in Elementary Education, University of Arkansas at Monticello (1973) **Certifications:** Certified in Gifted and Talented Education, State of Arkansas (1986) **Career:** Economic Education Specialist, Little Rock Branch, Federal Reserve Bank of St. Louis (2004-Present); Teacher, Monticello Elementary School (1987-2004); Teacher, Woodlawn Elementary School, Rison, AR (1973-1987) **Career Related:** Master Economics Teacher, Arkansas Council on Economic Education, Little Rock, AR (1993-2004); **Civic:** Member, Pulaski County Juvenile Services Board, Little Rock, AR (2004-Present); Co-chairman, The Jump$tart Coalition for Personal Financial Literacy, Little Rock, AR (2004-2010); **Creative Works:** Author, "Economics of the Forest" (1997) **Awards:** Arkansas Mathematics Teacher Award (2004); Bessie B. Moore Economic Education Award (2004) **Membership:** 32nd Degree, Scottish Rite Mason (2016-Present); Mason York Rite (2016-Present); Board of Directors, GATE, Council for Economic Education (2004-Present) **Marquis Who's Who Honors:** Albert Nelson Marquis Lifetime Achievement Award (2017) **Political Affiliations:** Republican **Religion:** Methodist **Shipping Address:** 4810 Highway 63, Risen, AR, 71665

Linda H. Brooke

Title: Human Resources Specialist **Industry:** Human Resources **Date of Birth:** 08/09/1943 **Place of Birth:** Chattanooga **State:** TN/USA **Parents:** Howard Derwent; Leola Ruth (Taylor) Hundley **Marital Status:** Married **Spouse Name:** James Edmondson Brooke (2/21/1970) **Education:** BS, University of Tennessee (1965) **Career:** Vice President of Human Resources, National Audubon Society (1999-2007); Vice President of Human Resources, Sunkyong America (1995-1998); Vice President of Human Resources, Creditanstalt (1989-1994); Vice President, Human Resources Subsidiary Liaison, Chemical Bank (1987-1989); Vice President, Director of Affirmative Action, Chemical Bank (1978-1987); Equal Employment Opportunity Consultant (1973-1978); Employment Consultant, Metropolitan Life Insurance Company (1969-1973); Placement Director, M. David Lowe, Houston, TX (1968-1969); Administrative Assistant, Cameron Iron Works, Houston, TX (1966-1967); Buyer Trainee, Foley's, Houston, TX (1965-1966) **Civic:** Redeemer Presbyterian Church **Membership:** Daughters of the American Revolution **Shipping Address:** 44 Gramercy Park N., Apartment 14D, New York, NY, 10010

Leslie Joan Brookes

Title: Medical/Surgical Nurse **Industry:** Medicine & Health Care **Date of Birth:** 10/08/1941 **Place of Birth:** Summit **State:** NJ/USA **Parents:** Joseph Mahood; Mildred Evelyn Thompson **Spouse Name:** Robert Arthur Brookes (Deceased) **Children:** Timothy Scott; Todd Jonathan **Education:** Diploma in Nursing, Rapid City Regional Hospital School of Nursing, Rapid City, SD (1977); BS, Elmira College, Elmira, NY (1963) **Career:** Office Assistant, Kolbach & Associates Investigations, Inc. (2003-2005); Staff Nurse, Rapid City Regional Hospital (1977-2003); Organist, Second Congregational Church, New London, CT (1969-1971); Substitute Elementary Teacher, Waterford Public Schools, Waterford, CT (1968-1969); First Grade Teacher, Meriden School District, Meriden, CT (1963-1968) **Civic:** Flute Player, New Horizons Band (1997-Present); Board of Directors, Westside Preschool, Rapid City, SD (1976) **Hobbies:** Music; Reading; Walking; Crossword puzzles; Crafts **Shipping Address:** 4115 Sunset Dr, Rapid City, SD, 57702

Blanche Parisi Brownell

Title: Partner, Secondary School Educator **Industry:** Education/Educational Services **Company Name:** ERB Holdings Ltd. **Date of Birth:** 10/27/1934 **Place of Birth:** Waterbury **State:** CT **Parents:** Gustavo Mario Parisi; Philomena Marie (Santoro) Parisi **Marital Status:** Married **Spouse Name:** Edwin Rowland Brownell (12/26/1967) **Children:** Elizabeth R.; Elaine B. Dorrans; Evelyn B. Mika; Nancy Brownell Servat **Education:** BBA, University of Miami, Coral Gables, FL (1956) **Certifications:** Certified Teacher, University of Miami (1962) **Career:** Partner, ERB Holdings Ltd., Coral Gables, FL (1967-Present); Teacher, Business Education, Beautification Committee, City of Coral Gables, FL (1987-1997); Corporate Secretary, E.R. Brownell & Associate Inc., Miami, FL (1968-1992); Teacher, Business Education, Miami Jackson Senior High School (1962-1968); Classified, Display Ad Rep, Miami Herald Publishing Co. (1962); Secretary, Advertising Department, Burdines Department Store, Miami, FL (1961); Classified, Display Ad Rep, Miami Herald Publishing Co. (1953-1956); Secretary, Radio and Electronic Equipment Co., Miami, FL (1952) **Career Related:** Photographer (2009-2011) **Civic:** Founder, Ladies Auxiliary, Dade County Society Surveying and Mapping, Tallahassee, FL (1973); Founder, Ladies Auxiliary, Florida Society Surveying and Mapping, Tallahassee, FL (1973) **Awards:** Outstanding Service Award, American Congress of Surveying and Mapping, Washington, DC (1973); Sponsor of the Year, Future Business Leaders of America, Tallahassee, FL (1965-1966) **Membership:** Secretary, Steering Committee, UM Womens Guild (2005-2009); Corresponding Secretary, University of Miami Woman's Guild (2005-2007); Riviera Country Club; Country Club of Coral Gables; Coral Gables Garden Club; Coral Gables Woman's Club; Coral Cables Music Club; Gilded Lilies; Elkettes **Marquis Who's Who Honors:** Distinguished Humanitarian (2017) **What do you consider to be the highlight of your career:** The highlight of Ms. Brownell's career was her marriage and children. **Hobbies:** Crafts; Ballroom Dancing; Gardening; Travel; Computers; Sketching **Religion:** Roman Catholic **Shipping Address:** 1207 Sorolla Avenue, Coral Gables, FL, 33134

John G. Bruhn, PhD

Title: University Provost (Retired), Dean (Retired) **Industry:** Education/Educational Services **Date of Birth:** 04/27/1934 **Place of Birth:** Norfolk **State:** NE **Parents:** John Franz Bruhn; Margaret Constance (Treiber) Bruhn **Education:** PhD, Yale University (1961); MA, University of Nebraska (1958); BA, University of Nebraska (1956) **Certifications:** Certified Clinical Sociologist **Career:** Retired (1999); Provost, The Pennsylvania State University, Harrisburg, PA (1995-1999); Dean, The Pennsylvania State University, Harrisburg, PA (1995-1999); Vice President of Academic Affairs and Research, The University of Texas at El Paso (1991-1995); Chairman, Department of Preventive Medicine and Community Health, School of Allied Health Sciences, The University of Texas Medical Branch at Galveston (1990-1991); Special Assistant to President for Community Affairs, School of Allied Health Sciences, The University of Texas Medical Branch at Galveston (1981-1991); Dean, School of Allied Health Sciences, The University of Texas Medical Branch at Galveston (1981-1991); Acting Dean, School of Allied Health Sciences, The University of Texas Medical Branch at Galveston (1980-1981); Associate Dean for Community Affairs, The University of Texas Medical Branch at Galveston (1972-1981); Professor of Preventive Medicine and Community Health, The University of Texas Medical Branch at Galveston (1972-1981); Professor, Department of Human Ecology, University of Oklahoma Medical Center (1969-1972); Chairman, Department of Human Ecology, University of Oklahoma Medical Center (1969-1972); Member faculty, University of Oklahoma Medical Center (1962-1972); **Career Related:** Adjunct Professor of Sociology, Northern Arizona University (2000-2011); Professor of Management and Policy Sciences, School of Public Health, The University of Texas Health Science Center at Houston (1975-1995); Consultant in Field **Civic:** Member, United Way of the Greater Capitol Region, Harrisburg, PA (1998-1999); Board of Directors, Leadership Harrisburg (1997-1999); **Awards:** Frances Young Community Heroes Award, Scottsdale (2005); Pluralism Award, The Association of Schools of Allied Health Professions (1994); Fellowship, WHO (1991); John Fogarty International Fellowship (1989) **Marquis Who's Who Honors:** Albert Nelson Marquis Lifetime Achievement Award (2017) **Why did you become involved in your profession or industry:** Mr. Bruhn was influenced by role models. His adviser at the University of Nebraska was a very important role model in regards to arts and sciences. Also, his father and grandfather were in the retail shoe business in Nebraska gave him positive work ethic and organization skills. **Shipping Address:** 8864 E Surrey Ave, Scottsdale, AZ, 85260

Betty Freeze Bryce-Tubb

Title: Music Educator **Industry:** Education/Educational Services **Date of Birth:** 10/06/1932 **Place of Birth:** Oklahoma City **State:** OK **Parents:** Eugene Woodrow Freeze; Otha Merle Perkins **Marital Status:** Married **Spouse Name:** Curtis O'Connor Tubb (12/30/1969); Boyd Junior Bryce (1948-1965) **Children:** Donna Bryce Lacquement; DiAnn Bryce Neff; Tara Elizabeth Tubb Foster **Education:** BMus in Piano, Oklahoma City University (1966) **Certifications:** Certified Piano Teacher, State of Alabama **Career:** Private Music Teacher, Independent Piano Teacher, Mobile (1988-Present); Faculty Member, Wrights Girls School, Mobile (1986-1987); Private Music Teacher, Cross City, FL (1980-1985); Faculty, Mobile Christian School (1971-1973); Faculty, Tonsmeire's School of Music, Mobile, AL (1970-1971); Private Music Teacher, Oklahoma City (1960-1970) **Career Related:** Adjudicator, National Guild of Piano Teachers (1962-1991) **Membership:** Treasurer, Mobile Music Teachers Association (2001-2002); President, Mobile Music Teachers Association (1972-1974); Music Teachers National Association; Alabama Music Teachers Association; Adjudicator, Treasurer, Chair, Scholarship Committee, National Guild of Piano Teachers; Scholarship Chairman, Mobile Music Teachers Association; Sigma Alpha Iota **Hobbies:** Heritage **Political Affiliations:** Republican **Religion:** Church of Christ **Shipping Address:** 1200 Somerby Dr., Apt 1918, Mobile, AL, 36695

Edward A. Buchanan, PhD

Title: Educator **Industry:** Education/Educational Services **Date of Birth:** 08/28/1937 **Place of Birth:** Newark **State:** NJ/USA **Parents:** Osborne Buchanan; Edna Dorothy (Weber) Buchanan **Marital Status:** Married **Spouse Name:** Gladys J. Buchanan (8/28/1965) **Children:** Roger; Becky **Education:** PhD, Southern Baptist Theological Seminary (1970); MRE, New York Theological Seminary (1962); AB, Rutgers, the State University of New Jersey (1959) **Certifications:** Ordained Minister, Southern Baptist Church **Career:** Associate Dean, Ministry Studies, Southeastern Baptist Theological Seminary, Wake Forest, NC; Senior Professor, Education, Southeastern Baptist Theological Seminary, Wake Forest, NC; Professor, Education, Bethel Seminary, Bethel University, St. Paul, MN; Director, Continuing Education, Bethel Seminary, Bethel University, St. Paul, MN; Dean, Academy Affairs, Lancaster Bible College, Pennsylvania; Professor, Lancaster Bible College, Pennsylvania; Associate Professor, Psychology and Education, Grand Rapids Baptist College, Michigan; Teacher, Central School, Middlesex, NJ **Career Related:** Director, Grow in His Word, Inc. **Creative Works:** Author, "Christian Heritage II" (2006); Author, "The Bible Handbook II" (2005); Author, "The Bible Handbook" (2004); Author, "Christian Heritage" (2004); Author, "The Teaching Church," Harvest Publications (1988); Contributor, Articles, Professional Journals **Awards:** Excellence in Teaching Award, Southeastern Baptist Seminary (1994); Lilly Endowment Inc. ATS Grant, Seminary Retention Study, Association of Theological Schools (1987) **Membership:** American Psychological Association; ASCD; American Educational Research Association; National Society for the Study of Education **Marquis Who's Who Honors:** Albert Nelson Marquis Lifetime Achievement Award (2017) **Religion:** Southern Baptist **Shipping Address:** 1113 Silent Brook Road, Wake Forest, NC, 27587

Linda Buchin Sullivan

Title: Co-founder, President **Industry:** Biotechnology **Company Name:** Metrics Champion Consortium **Date of Birth:** 03/28/1959 **Place of Birth:** Boston **State:** MA **Parents:** Stanley I. Buchin; Jacqueline C. Buchin **Marital Status:** Married **Spouse Name:** Michael H. Sullivan **Children:** Andrew H.; Courtney L. **Education:** MBA, Amos Tuck School of Business, Dartmouth College, Hanover, NH (1989); BS in Biology and Environmental Science, Trinity College, Hartford, CT (1981) **Career:** President, Metrics Champion Consortium, Indianapolis, IN (2013-Present); Chief Operating Officer, Metrics Champion Consortium, Indianapolis, IN (2013-Present); Co-Founder, Metrics Champion Consortium, Indianapolis, IN (2006-Present); Vice President of Operations, Metrics Champion Consortium, Indianapolis, IN (2006-2013); Consultant, Knowledge Management Manager, Towers Perrin (1990-2002); Consultant, Mercer, Boston, MA (1989-1990); Research Associate, Health Effects Institute, Cambridge, MA (1984-1987); Conference Planner, Health Effects Institute, Cambridge, MA (1984-1987); Science Teacher, Buckingham, Brown & Nichols School, Cambridge, MA (1982-1984); Varsity Girls' Rowing Coach, Buckingham, Brown & Nichols School, Cambridge, MA (1982-1984); Varsity Girls' Rowing Coach, The Phillips Exeter Academy, Exeter, NH (1981-1982); Science Teaching Fellow, The Phillips Exeter Academy, Exeter, NH (1981-1982) **Career Related:** Author, "Chapter 30: How Quality Performance Metrics Enable Successful Change," Re-Engineering Clinical Trials: Best Practices for Streamlining the Development Process, Elsevier (2015); Presenter in Field **Awards:** Tuck Scholar, Dartmouth College (1989); Honoree, Order of the Arrow, Boy Scouts of America **Membership:** Athlete Representative, United States Lightweight Women's National Rowing Committee (1983-1984); Methods and Processes Domain Task Force, Clinical and Translational Science Awards Program, National Center for Advancing Translational Sciences, National Institutes of Health; DIA **Why did you become involved in your profession or industry:** In 2005, Ms. Sullivan was working in the field of drug development clinical trials at ExaroMed. During this time, it was her task the facilitate meetings for a client who had gathered 16 top pharma customers in order to get them to agree on a course that would include performance metrics which would be reported. At the end of the process, drug companies recognized the importance of these efforts and suggested the formation of an industry group so that other vendors would be able to take advantage of this type of collaboration. **Shipping Address:** 471 Morningbird Court, Carmel, IN, 46032 **Website:** http://metricschampion.org

Jo Buffalo

Title: Professor Emerita, Artist **Industry:** Education/Educational Services **Company Name:** Cazenovia College **Date of Birth:** 12/02/1948 **Place of Birth:** Cleveland **State:** OH/USA **Parents:** Richard Trevor Gross; Dolores Rice **Education:** MFA in Illustration, Syracuse University, Syracuse, NY (1985); BFA in Ceramics, Syracuse University, Syracuse, NY (1973) **Career:** Professor, Cazenovia College (2006-Present); Jurist, Ceramics, Annual State Scholastic Awards, Syracuse, NY (1995-Present); Professor Emerita, Cazenovia College (1986-Present); Owner, Operator, Jo Buffalo Studio (1972-Present); Co-Chair/Chair, Program Assessment Committee, Cazenovia College, New York (2003-2006); Chair, Search Committee for the Vice President for Academic Affairs, Cazenovia College, New York (2002-2003); Coordinator, Committee for the New Art and Design Building, Cazenovia College, New York (2001-2003); Steering Committee Middle States Self Study, Cazenovia College, New York (2001-2003); Long-Range Planning Committee, Cazenovia College, New York (2001-2002); Center Chair for the Center for Art and Design, Cazenovia College, New York (1999-2002); Elected Vice President of the Board, Cultural Resources Council, Syracuse, NY (1995-1996); Jurist, New York State Fair, Syracuse, NY (1995); Jurist for Grants, Empire State Craft Alliance, Syracuse, NY (1994); Jurist, "Art That Tells a Story," Civic Center, Syracuse, NY (1993); Jurist, Twelfth Annual Congressional Art Competition for High School Students, Rome, NY (1993); Panel of Experts, "Open Forum," Everson Museum of Art, Syracuse, NY (1992); Arts Area Coordinator, BS Program, Cazenovia College, New York (1989-1992) **Career Related:** Board of Directors, Cultural Resources Council, Syracuse, NY (1994-1996); Book Review, Studio Art, Westco Publishing (1994); Chairperson, Grant Redistribution Panel, New York State Council on the Arts, Syracuse, NY (1993); Celebrity Tour, Everson Museum of Art, Syracuse, NY (1992) **Civic:** Pet Therapy Volunteer, Psychiatric Ward, University Hospital, Syracuse, NY **Creative Works:** Illustrator, "Dispersal and Habitat Preferences of the Black tailed Prairie Dog", University of Colorado, Fort Collins, CO (1984); Illustrator, Bureau of Land Management Cultural Series #13," Archaeological Resources in South Western Colorado", Denver, CO (1980-1982); Various Collections **Awards:** Presidential Scholarship, Cazenovia College (1999); James Renwick Senior Fellowship, National Museum of American Art, Smithsonian Institution, Washington, DC (1997); Museum Purchase, Everson Museum of Art, Syracuse, NY (1985) **Membership:** MENSA **Marquis Who's Who Honors:** Albert Nelson Marquis Lifetime Achievement Award (2017) **Shipping Address:** 501 Scoville Ave, Syracuse, NY, 13203-1128

Robert L. Bumgarner

Title: Pathologist **Industry:** Media & Entertainment **Date of Birth:** 10/15/1944 **Place of Birth:** Long Beach **State:** CA **Education:** Resident Intern, Naval Medical Center Portsmouth, Virginia (1975-1979); MD, Michigan State University (1974); BS in Physics, Michigan State University (1967) **Certifications:** Diplomate, Anatomical Pathology and Clinical Pathology, The American Board of Pathology (1979) **Career:** Senior Manager, Leidos (2013-Present); Contractor, Leidos (2013-Present); Principal Medical Scientist, Defense Threat Reduction Agency, Science Applications International Corporation (2004-Present); Laboratory Medic, Chemical, Biological, Radiological, Nuclear, and Explosive Materials (2004-2013); Director, Leidos (2002-2007); Fleet Surgeon, Fleet Medical Intel Officer (2002); Fleet Surgeon, U.S. Pacific Fleet (1999-2001); Director, Armed Forces Radiobiology Research Institute, Uniformed Services University (1991-1995); Commanding Officer, Director for Undersea Medicine and Radiation Health, U.S. Navy, Washington, DC (1986-1991); Captain, U.S. Navy (1986); Force Medical Officer, Commander of Submarine Force, U.S. Pacific Fleet (1984-1986); Director, Navy Drug Screening Laboratory, Navy & Marine Corps Public Health Center (1983); Chief of Laboratory, Naval Submarine Medical Research Laboratory (1979-1983); Commissioned Ensign, U.S. Navy (1967); Nuclear Test Personnel, Chemical, Biological, Radiological, Nuclear, and Explosives; Senior Navy Pathologist, Naval Medical Center San Diego; Civil Air Patrol Laboratory Accreditation Inspector, Navy Medical Center San Diego; Principal, Armed Forces Institute of Pathology Board of Science, Navy Medical Center San Diego; Director of Ancillary Services, Breast Health Center, NCMSD; Head, Pacific Area of Responsibility, Department of Blood and Tissue Banks, Naval Medical Center San Diego **Career Related:** Submarine Line Officer, U. S. Navy (1971-Present) **Membership:** Fellow, College of American Pathologists (1996-1999); Lead Laboratory Accreditation Inspector, College of American Pathologists (1996-1999) **Business Address:** PO Box 4077, VA, Merrifield, 22116 **Shipping Address:** PO Box 4077, Merrifield, VA, 22116 **Website:** https://www.linkedin.com/in/robert-l-bumgarner-md-77843519

Richard Burgin

Title: Writer, Educator, Editor **Industry:** Education/Educational Services **Date of Birth:** 06/30/1947 **Place of Birth:** Brooklyn **State:** NY **Parents:** Richard Burgin; Ruth (Posselt) Burgin **Marital Status:** Divorced **Spouse Name:** Linda Kinnard Harris (9/7/1991) **Children:** Richard Daniel **Education:** MPhil in Modern American Literature, Columbia University, New York, NY (1980); MA, Columbia University, New York, NY with High Honors (1969); BA, Brandeis University, Waltham, MA with Honors (1968) **Career:** Professor of Communications and English, Saint Louis University (2003-2013); Associate Professor, Saint Louis University (1996-2003); Associate Professor, Drexel University, Philadelphia, PA (1984-1996); Editor, New York Arts Journal, New York, NY (1975-1980); Instructor of English, Tufts University, Medford, MA (1970-1974) **Career Related:** Visiting Lecturer, University of California, Santa Barbara (1981-1983) **Creative Works:** Editor, "Boulevard Magazine" (1985-Present); Author, "Hide Island"(2014); Author, "Shadow Traffics" (2011); Author, "Rivers Last Longer" (2010); Composer, "The Trouble with Love" (2008); Author, "The Ecco Anthology of Contemporary American" (2008); Author, "The Conference on Beautiful Moments" (2007); Author, "The Identity Club: New and Selected Stories" (2005); Composer, "Cold Ocean" (2005); Composer, "Don't Go There" (2005); Author, "Stories and Dream Boxes" (2002); Composer, "Doll of Dreams" (2002); Composer, "House of Sun" (2001); Author, "The Spirit Returns: Stories" (2000); Author, "Don't Think: Collection of Short Stories"; Composer, "In All of the World" (2000); Author, "Ghost Quartet" (1999); Editor, "Jorge Luis Borges: Conversations" (1998); Author, "Fear of Blue Skies" (1998); Author, "Private Fame" (1991); Author, "Man Without Memory" (1989); Author, "Conversations with Isaac Bashevis Singer" (1985); Author, "Conversations with Jorge Luis Borges" (1969); Contributor, Articles to Magazines **Awards:** Recipient, Pushcart Press Prize (1982, 1986, 1998, 2002, 2007) **Membership:** National Book Critics Circle; St. Louis Writers Guild **Hobbies:** Travel; Sports **Shipping Address:** 7507 Byron Pl., Fl 1, Saint Louis, MO, 63105

Dierdre A. Burgman

Title: Counsel **Industry:** Law and Legal Services **Company Name:** Sullivan & Worcester **Date of Birth:** 03/25/1948 **Place of Birth:** Logansport **State:** IN **Education:** LLM, Yale University (1985); JD, Valparaiso University (1979); BA, Valparaiso University (1970) **Career:** Counsel, Sullivan & Worcester (2004-2006); Counsel, Salans (2000-2004); Consultant, Salans (1999-2000); Of Counsel, Vandenberg & Felieu, New York, NY (1995-1999); General Counsel, Hudson River Park Conservancy (1992-1995); Deputy Inspector General, State of New York (1992-1995); Senior Vice President, General Counsel, New York State Urban Development Corporation (1992-1995); Associate, Cahill Gordon & Reindel (1985-1992); Associate, Dewey, Ballantine, Bushby, Palmer & Wood, New York, NY (1981-1984); Professor of Law, Valparaiso University (1980-1981); Law Clerk to Chief Judge, Indiana Court of Appeals, Indianapolis, IN (1979-1980) **Civic:** National Council Emeritus, School of Law, Valparaiso University (2006-2007); National Council, School of Law, Valparaiso University (2001-2006); Chairman, School of Law, Valparaiso University (1989-1992); Board of Visitors, School of Law, Valparaiso University (1986-1995) **Awards:** Indiana Bar Foundation Scholar (1978) **Membership:** Member of the Foundation, New York County Lawyers Association (2003-Present); Committee on Professional Standards of Attorney Conduct, New York State Bar Association (2002-Present); Finance and Personnel Committee, New York County Lawyers Association (2003); Board of Directors, New York County Lawyers Association (2002-2003); Council on Judicial Administration, Association of the Bar of the City of New York (1997-1999); House of Delegates, New York State Bar Association (1994-1998); Executive Committee, Board of Directors, New York County Lawyers Association (1992-1995); Board of Directors, New York County Lawyers Association (1991-1997); Committee on Professional and Judicial Ethics, Association of the Bar of the City of New York (1991-1995); Chairman, New York County Lawyers Association (1990-1993); Insurance Coverage Litigation Committee, American Bar Association (1990-1992); Committee on Professional Responsibility, Association of the Bar of the City of New York (1988-1991) **Bar Admissions:** U.S. District Court, Eastern District, State of New York (1992); District of Columbia (1988); U.S. Supreme Court (1985); District of Columbia and Second Circuits, U.S. Court of Appeals (1984); Seventh Circuit, U.S. Court of Appeals (1982); U.S. District Court, Southern District, State of New York (1982); State of New York (1982) **Marquis Who's Who Honors:** Albert Nelson Marquis Lifetime Achievement Award (2017) **Shipping Address:** 345 E 56th Street, Apt. 5C, New York, NY, 10022

J. Bryan Burton

Title: Music Educator **Industry:** Education/Educational Services **Company Name:** West Chester University **Date of Birth:** 11/10/1948 **Place of Birth:** Lubbock **State:** TX **Parents:** John Clark Burton; Geraldine (Wolf) Burton **Education:** MusD in Music Education, University of Southern Mississippi (1986); MA, Western State Colorado University (1973); MusB in Music Education, West Texas A&M University (1970) **Career:** Co-Director, Samuel Barber Institute for Music Educators (2008-Present); Chair, Music Education Department, West Chester University, Pennsylvania (2008-Present); Director, Post-Baccalaureate Teacher Certification Program, West Chester University, Pennsylvania (2001-Present); Coordinator, Graduate Studies, West Chester University, Pennsylvania (1997-Present); Professor of Music Education, West Chester University, Pennsylvania (1991-Present); Music Theatre Director, Assistant Professor of Music, Frostburg State University, Maryland (1986-1991); Director of Bands, Frostburg State University, Maryland (1986-1991); Graduate Assistant, University of Southern Mississippi, Hattiesburg, MS (1984-1986); Music Coordinator, Director, High School Band, Kirbyville Consolidated Independent School District, Texas (1982-1984); Band Director, Comfort Independent School District, Texas (1980-1982); Band Director, General Music, Bronte Independent School District, Texas (1979-1980); Band Director, Humanities, Jal Public Schools, New Mexico (1978-1979); Band Director for Humanities, Orient-Macksburg Community Schools (1976-1978) **Creative Works:** Editorial Board Member, Music Education Journal (2011-Present); Contributing Editor, Editorial Board Member, "New Grove Dictionary of American Music" (2006-Present); Editorial Board Member, "International Journal of Music Education" (2001-Present); Editorial Committee, ISME World Conference Proceedings (2012); Contributor, Native American Music Chapter, "Multicultural Perspectives in Music Education Third Edition" (2010); Contributor, "World Music and Traditional Transformations, Second Edition" (2010); Contributor, "Moving Within the Circle, Contemporary Native American Music and Dance, Second Edition," Native American Museum of Eastern North America (2008); Contributor, Music in Central Java (2007); Contributor, World Music and Traditional Transformations (2007); Author, "Moving Within the Circle: Contemporary Native American Music and Dance Second Edition" (2007); Contributor, Music in Brazil (2006); **Membership:** Eastern Representative, Society for Music Teacher Education (1998-2004) **Marquis Who's Who Honors:** Albert Nelson Marquis Lifetime Achievement Award (2017); Distinguished Humanitarian (2017) **Shipping Address:** 441 Webb Road, Chadds Ford, PA, 19317

Evan Calkins

Title: Physician **Industry:** Education/Educational Services **Company Name:** State University of New York at Buffalo **Date of Birth:** 07/15/1920 **Place of Birth:** Newton **State:** MA **Parents:** Grosvenor Calkins; Patty (Phillips) Calkins **Marital Status:** Married **Spouse Name:** Virginia Brady (9/9/1946) **Children:** Sarah Calkins Oxnard; Stephen; Lucy McCormick; Joan; Benjamin; Hugh; Ellen Rountree; Geoffrey; Timot **Education:** Assistant Resident, Medicine, Johns Hopkins University (1948-1950); Intern, Medicine, Johns Hopkins University (1946-1947); MD, Harvard University (1945); AB, Harvard University (1942); Diploma, Milton Academy (1939) **Certifications:** President, National Association of Geriatric Education Centers (1992-1993) **Career:** Professor Emeritus, State University of New York at Buffalo (1990-Present); Head, Division of Geriatrics/gerontology, State University of New York at Buffalo (1978-1990); Head, Gerontology Section, Buffalo VA Medical Center (1978-1990); Director, Medicine, E.J. Meyer Memorial Hospital (1968-1978); Chairman, Department of Medicine, State University of New York at Buffalo (1965-1977); Head, Department of Medicine, Buffalo General Hospital (1961-1968); Professor of Medicine, State University of New York at Buffalo (1961-1990); Medical Practice, Specializing in Rheumatology, Buffalo, NY (1961-2012); Assistant Professor of Medicine, Harvard University (1952-1961); Member, Arthritis Unit, Massachusetts General Hospital (1952-1961); Chief Resident Physician, Massachusetts General Hospital (1951-1952); Medical Practice, Specializing in Rheumatology, Boston, MA (1951-1961); National Research Council Fellow, Medical Sciences, Harvard University (1950-1951) **Career Related:** Private Practice, Rheumatology and Geriatrics (2001-2012); Partner, Promedicus Health Group (1998-2001) **Military Service:** Captain, Medical Corps, U.S. Army (1946-1948); Captain, Medical Corps, U.S. Army (1943-1945) **Awards:** Lifetime Achievement Award, Network in Aging of Western New York, Inc. (2010); Laureate Award, New York Upstate Chapter, American College of Physicians (1998); Freeman Award, Gerontological Society of America (1991); Milo D. Leavitt Award, American Geriatrics Society (1986); Presidential Citation for Community Service (1983) **Membership:** Master, American College of Physicians (1989); Chair, Clinical Medical Section, Gerontological Society of America (1989); Master, American College of Rheumatology (1986) **Bar Admissions:** President, National Association of Geriatric Education Centers (1992-1993) **Marquis Who's Who Honors:** Albert Nelson Marquis Lifetime Achievement Award (2017); Distinguished Humanitarian (2017) **Shipping Address:** 3799 Windover Dr, Hamburg, NY, 14075

Magda Campbell

Title: Psychiatrist, Child Psychiatrist **Industry:** Education/Educational Services **Company Name:** New York University **Date of Birth:** 01/22/1928 **Place of Birth:** Subotica **Country of Origin:** Yugoslavia **Parents:** Bela Pijukovi; Maroka (Lipzvencvic) Pijukovi **Marital Status:** Widowed **Spouse Name:** Francis P. Campbell, MD **Children:** Maria D.; John F. **Education:** MD, University of Belgrade, Yugoslavia (1953) **Certifications:** Diplomate in Psychiatry and Child Psychiatry, American Board of Psychiatry and Neurology, Inc. **Career:** Professor Emeritus, New York University (1995-Present); Retired (1995); Professor of Psychiatry, New York University (1963-1995); Director of Training Education, New York University (1990-1991); Director, Division of Child Adolescent Psychiatry, New York University (1987-1991); Teaching Assistant, New York University (1963) **Creative Works:** Co-author, "Clinical Evaluation of Psychotropic Drugs for Psychiatric Disorders" (1993); Co-author, "Child and Adolescent Psychopharmacology" (1985); Contributor, Over 225 Articles, Professional Journals; Contributor, Chapters, Books **Awards:** Grantee, National Institute of Mental Health (1973-1995); First Virginia Q. Anthony Outstanding Woman Leader Award, American Academy of Child and Adolescent Psychiatry (2013) **Membership:** Life Fellow Emeritus, American College of Neuropsychopharmacology; Life Fellow, American Academy of Child and Adolescent Psychiatry; American Psychiatric Association **Religion:** Roman Catholic **Shipping Address:** 333 E. 30th St., Apt. 7C, New York, NY, 10016

Luís Campos

Industry: Writing and Editing **Parents:** Manuel de Jesus Campos; Luz Navarro **Education:** Graduate, Benjamin Franklin High School, New York, NY (1952) **Career:** Puzzle creator, United Feature Syndicate, New York, NY (1984-Present); Member, Advisory and Inventory Staff, House of Fabrics, Inc., Sherman Oaks, CA (1963-1982) **Military Service:** With, US Army (1952-1954) **Creative Works:** Editor, VOL.NO. Poetry Magazine (1983) **Achievements:** Achievements include patents in field; has published over 12,000 puzzles **Hobbies:** Poetry; Drawing **Religion:** Roman Catholic

Robert Carlson

Title: Financial Planner **Industry:** Financial Services **Company Name:** Center for Retirement Security, Inc. **Education:** JD, University of Virginia (1982); MS in Accounting, University of Virginia (1982); BS in Financial Management, Clemson University, with High Honors (1979) **Certifications:** The District of Columbia Bar (1982); CPA, State of Maryland **Career:** President, Center for Retirement Security, Inc. (1992-Present); Editor, Bob Carlson's Retirement Watch, Eagle Products, LLC (1991-Present); Principal, R.C. Carlson Advisers (1988-1994); Editor, Tax Wise Money (1985-1997); Editor, Financial Independence (1983-1985); Editor, Tax Savings Report (1983-1985); Law Clerk, U.S. Department of Education (1982-1983); Law Clerk, U.S. Department of Justice (1982); Managing Member, Carlson Wealth Advisors, LLC, FMG Suite **Career Related:** Defined Contribution Plan Advisory Committee, Virginia Retirement Systems (2011-Present); Commissioner, The Fairfax County Redevelopment and Housing Authority, Fairfax County Government, VA (2008-Present); Chairman, Fairfax County, Virginia Retirement System (1995-Present); Trustee, Fairfax County, Virginia Retirement System (1992-Present); Trustee, Virginia Retirement System (2000-2005); Member, Virginia Fiscal Alternative Commission (1989-1991) **Civic:** Treasurer, Friends of Michael Frey (2011-Present); Treasurer, Northern Virginia Republican Business Forum (1990-Present); Defined Contribution Plan, Advisory Committee, Virginia Retirement System (2011); Chairman, Republican Committee, Sully District, Fairfax County Government, VA (2004-2010); Member, Butler for Congress (1992-1994); Member, Atoka Country Supper Committee (1989-1992); **Creative Works:** Co-author, "Personal Finance After 50 for Dummies" (2015); Co-author, "Personal Finance for Seniors for Dummies" (2010); Author, "Invest Like a Fox...Not Like a Hedgehog" (2007); Author, "New Rules of Retirement" (2005); Author, "New Rules of Estate Planning" (2003); Author, "Estate Planning Strategies, Second Edition" (1998); Author, "Tax Wise Money Strategies" (1995); Author, "Retirement Tax Guide, Revised Fourth Edition" (1994); Author, "How to Slash Your Mutual Fund Taxes, Second Revised Edition" (1991); Author, "How to Slash Your Mutual Fund Taxes" (1990); Author, "Retirement Tax Guide" (1989); Author, "How to Handle and Win a Federal Tax Appeal" (1988); Author, "199 Loopholes That Survived Tax Reform" (1987); Author, "Tax Savings Through Short-Term Trusts" (1985) **Awards:** Honoree, One of Outstanding Young Men of America, JCI (Junior Chamber International), Inc. (1983) **Membership:** Chairman, SDC (2004-2010); A.C.C. Ltd; The Honor Society of Phi Kappa Phi, Phi Gamma Sigma **Shipping Address:** PO Box 222070, Chantilly, VA, 20153

William Allan Caro

Marquis Who's Who
18 98
Biographee

Title: Physician, Professor **Industry:** Medicine & Health Care **Company Name:** Northwestern University **Date of Birth:** 08/16/1934 **Place of Birth:** Chicago **State:** IL **Parents:** Marcus Rayner Caro; Adeline Beatrice (Cohen) Caro **Marital Status:** Married **Spouse Name:** Joan Peters (10/18/1997, Deceased); Ruth Fruchtlander (6/15/1959, Deceased) **Children:** Mark Stephen; David Edward **Education:** Earl D. Osborne Fellow, Dermal Pathology, Armed Forces Institute of Pathology (1966-1967); Resident in Dermatology, Hospital of the University of Pennsylvania (1964-1966, 1961-1962); Resident in Internal Medicine, University of Illinois (1960-1961); Intern, Cook County Hospital, Chicago, IL (1959-1960); MD, University of Illinois (1959); **Certifications:** Diplomate, ABD (1986) **Career:** Retired (2015); Professor in Dermatology, Northwestern University (1981-2015); Dermatologist, Private Practice, Chicago, IL (1967-2015); Associate Professor of Dermatology, Northwestern University (1967-1981); Assistant Professor of Dermatology, Northwestern University (1967-1981) **Career Related:** Member, Medical Executive Committee, Northwestern Memorial HealthCare (1977-1979); Attending Physician, Northwestern Memorial HealthCare (1972-2015); Attending Physician, Wesley Memorial Hospital (1969-1972); **Civic:** Member, Medicine Advisory Board, University of Illinois College of Medicine (1988-Present); Member, Executive Committee, Northwestern Medicine (1988-1991); Board of Directors, Northwestern Memorial HealthCare (1988-1991); Member, Board of Directors, Northwestern Medicine (1987-2000) **Military Service:** Captain, Medical Corps, U.S. Army Reserve (1962-1964) **Creative Works:** Associate Editor, Year Book for Pathology and Clinical Pathology (1977-1980); Editorial Board Member, Cutis (1975-2014); Editor, Chicago Dermatological Society (1971-1973) **Awards:** Recipient, Gold Medal, Chicago Dermatological Society (2011); Clark W. Finnerud Award, Dermatology Foundation (2002); Founders Award, Chicago Dermatological Society (1992); Gold Award for Science Exhibit, American Academy of Dermatology (1970) **Membership:** Vice President, American Dermatological Association (2004-2005); Board of Directors, The American Society of Dermatopathology (1995-2000); Board of Directors, American Dermatological Association (1993-1998); President, Board of Directors, The American Society of Dermatopathology (1996-1997); **Marquis Who's Who Honors:** Albert Nelson Marquis Lifetime Achievement Award (2017) **What do you consider to be the highlight of your career:** The highlight of Dr. Caro's career is the relationships he developed with his patients over the years. **Shipping Address:** 2323 McDaniel Ave., Apt. 3123, Evanston, IL, 60201

Arthur Helmut Carrieri

Title: Researcher, Physicist **Industry:** Research **Date of Birth:** 06/15/1953 **Place of Birth:** Philadelphia **State:** PA **Parents:** Philip Carrieri; Margot Carrieri **Marital Status:** Single **Education:** MS, Pennsylvania State University (1978); BA, Temple University (1976) **Career:** Senior Research Physicist, Edgewood Chemical Biological Center, Research, Development, and Engineering Command, U.S. Army Aberdeen Proving Ground, Maryland (1983-2014) **Creative Works:** Contributor, Articles, Professional Journals **Awards:** Research and Development Achievement Awards, U.S. Army (2009); Research and Development Achievement Awards, U.S. Army (2001); Research and Development Achievement Awards, U.S. Army (1999); Research and Development Achievement Awards, U.S. Army (1994) **Marquis Who's Who Honors:** Albert Nelson Marquis Lifetime Achievement Award (2017) **Hobbies:** Scuba diving **Political Affiliations:** Democrat **Religion:** Roman Catholic **Shipping Address:** 667 Knollwood Court, Bluffton, SC, 29909

Stuart Edwin Cart

Industry: Consulting **Date of Birth:** 05/08/1944 **Place of Birth:** Bluffton **State:** IN/USA **Parents:** Cyril Joseph; Anna Irene Cart **Education:** BS in Electrical and Electronics, Indiana Institute of Technology, Fort Wayne (1969) **Career:** Technology Director, Stavatti Aerospace, Buffalo (2003-Present); Engineering Analyst, National Air Intelligence Center, Dayton, OH (1979-2001); Project Engineer, Naval Avionic Facility (1969-1979); Instructor, Purdue University, Indianapolis (1969-1979) **Career Related:** With, Clean Blast LLC; Consultant in Field **Creative Works:** Author, "Data Systems"; Author, "Practical Electronics" **Achievements:** Invention of no-operator training equipment; Design of Department of Defense configuration management for software configuration management; Design of electro-magnetic interference filters for pyrotechnic devices; Design of surface mount technology for space applications; Design of integrated circuits for cerebral implants **Hobbies:** Boating; Camping; Tennis; Dance **Political Affiliations:** Conservative

Thomas Allen Carter

Title: Engineering Executive (Retired) **Industry:** Engineering **Date of Birth:** 07/12/1935 **Place of Birth:** Cincinnati **State:** OH/USA **Parents:** Fernando Albert Carter; Mary Gladys (Gover) Carter **Marital Status:** Married **Spouse Name:** Janet Tucker (10/14/1956) **Children:** Barry Everett; Duane Allen; Sarita Anne **Education:** BBA, Jones College, Cum Laude (1982); AB, Jones College (1980) **Certifications:** Certified Construction Inspector **Career:** Estimator, Independent Mechanical Design Co., Inc. (1996-2005); Chief Engineer, D.A.M.S., Inc., Orlando, FL (1984-1991); Secretary, Blacando Development Corp., Orlando, FL (1980-1984); Private Practice, Orlando, FL (1978-1980); Contract Administrator, Red Lobster Restaurants, Orlando, FL (1976-1978) **Career Related:** Consultant in Field **Military Service:** Master Chief, U.S. Navy (1954-1976) **Membership:** Fleet Reserve Association; Armed Forces Top Enlisted Association; Rafman Club Orlando; American Legion; Disabled American Veterans; National Pinochle Association; Navy SeaBee Veterans of America **Marquis Who's Who Honors:** Albert Nelson Marquis Lifetime Achievement Award (2017) **Hobbies:** Bowling; Tennis; Travel **Political Affiliations:** Democrat **Religion:** Methodist **Shipping Address:** 4128 Arajo Ct, Belle Isle, FL, 32812-2805

Barry Cartmill

Title: President, Chief Executive Officer, Lead Information Architect and Consultant **Industry:** Information Technology and Services **Company Name:** BECIT, Inc. **Marital Status:** Married **Children:** Two Children **Education:** MBA in Management Information Systems, University of Minnesota (1984); MA in Psychology, Morehead State University (1979); BA in Psychology and Sociology, Morehead State University **Certifications:** Certified Solution Designer, WebSphere MQ, IBM; Certified System Administrator, WebSphere MQ, IBM; Certified Solution Developer, WebSphere Message Broker, IBM; Certified Solution Expert, MQSI, IBM; Certified Specialist, MQSI, IBM; Certified Technical Trainer, The Chauncey Group International; Professional Certificate in C-Programming on Unix, Dutchess Community College **Career:** President, Chief Executive Officer, Lead Architect, Consultant, BECIT, Inc. (2002-Present); Lead Integration Specialist/Architect, iSOA Group (2012-2016); Senior System Engineer, Architect, Mainline Information Services, Inc. (2010-2011); Senior Architect, Consultant, BMC Software, Inc. (2009-2010); Senior Architect, Consultant, MQSoftware (Now BMC Software, Inc.) (2002-2009); Principal Consultant, Instructor, MessageQuest (1998-2002); Advisory Programmer, IBM (1991-1998) **Awards:** Various Awards **Membership:** IEEE; Association for Computing Machinery **To what do you attribute your success:** Mr. Cartmill attributes his success to hard work, persistence, dedication, adaptability, his goal-oriented nature, and his interpersonal relations. His flexible application of business, technical, and social skills have also been important to his success. **Why did you become involved in your profession or industry:** Mr. Cartmill became involved in the information technology sector more than 30 years ago because of the opportunities it provided him to create applications and systems, which would improve business operations, as well as the quality of life for everyone. He has specialized in software for more than 20 years in messaging, application integration, and mediation for more than 15 years, and service-oriented architecture and enterprise service business for more than 12 years. **Where will you be in five years:** In five years, Mr. Cartmill plans to grow BECIT, Inc. by expanding into other related technical areas, including process management application services. **Hobbies:** Sports; Music; Spending time with his wife, two children, and four grandchildren **Shipping Address:** 12 Baker Court, Wappingers Falls, NY, 12590 **Website:** https://www.linkedin.com/in/barry-cartmill-5839431

James E. Cavanagh Jr.

Title: Medical Educator **Industry:** Education/Educational Services **Company Name:** Florida State University College of Medicine **Date of Birth:** 01/31/1930 **Place of Birth:** Plattsburgh **State:** NY **Parents:** James Ellsworth Cavanagh; Marjorie Carroll Cavanagh **Marital Status:** Widowed **Spouse Name:** Susan Caldwell Dodd (10/9/1976, Deceased 2013); Elizabeth Brady Cavanagh (8/25/1951, Divorced 1975) **Children:** Ralph Carroll Cavanagh; Robert Ellsworth Cavanagh; John Henry Cavanagh; Caitlin Cavanagh Wold; Mary Harwood Dodd (Stepchild); Anna Walker Dodd (Stepchild); Robert Howe Dodd, Jr. (Stepchild) **Education:** Chief Surgical Resident, Dartmouth Affiliated Hospitals, Geisel School of Medicine (1961); Surgical Resident, Dartmouth Affiliated Hospitals, Geisel School of Medicine, Dartmouth College (1959-1961); Surgical Resident, Boston City Hospital (1955-1957); Surgical Intern, Boston City Hospital (1954-1955); MD, Harvard Medical School, Harvard University (1954); Diploma, Geisel School of Medicine, Dartmouth College (1952); BA, Dartmouth College (1951) **Certifications:** Diplomate, American College of Surgeons (1967); Diplomate, American Board of Surgery, Inc. (1963) **Career:** Faculty, Department of Biomedical Sciences, College of Medicine, Florida State University (2001-Present); Clinical Associate Professor, Full Time Volunteer, Department of Anatomy, College of Medicine, Florida State University (2001-Present); General Surgical Practice, Tallahassee Memorial Hospital (1976-1997); General Surgical Practice, Portsmouth Hospital, C-HCA, Inc. (1962-1976); Chief Surgical Resident, Dartmouth Affiliated Hospitals, Geisel School of Medicine, Dartmouth College (1961); Member, Department of Surgery, Charleston Naval Hospital, U.S. Navy (1957-1959); Secretary, Geisel School of Medicine, Dartmouth College, Class of 1952 (1952) **Career Related:** Member, Admissions Committee, College of Medicine, Florida State University (2001-Present) **Civic:** Member, Water Resources Committee, Leon County, Tallahassee, FL (1999-2015) **Military Service:** Lieutenant, U.S. Navy (1959-1961) **Creative Works:** Contributor, Articles, Professional Surgical Journals **Awards:** Eagle Scout Award, National Council, Boy Scouts of America (1947) **Membership:** Senior Member, New England Surgical Society (1975-Present) **Hobbies:** Tennis; Bird Photography **Shipping Address:** 3950 Bellac Rd., Tallahassee, FL, 32303

Warren A. Cebulko

Title: Supervisor **Industry:** Medicine & Health Care **Company Name:** Advocate Health Care **Education:** MBA, DePaul University (1995); BS in Accounting, DePaul University (1974) **Career:** Supervisor, Coding Education and Compliance, Advocate Health Care **Civic:** Supporter, American Heart Association, Inc.; Blood Donor, American Heart Association, Inc.; Supporter, March of Dimes; Volunteer, Local Church **Membership:** American Health Information Management Association; Institute of Management Accountants **To what do you attribute your success:** Mr. Cebulko attributes his success to his education and driven nature. **Why did you become involved in your profession or industry:** Mr. Cebulko became involved in his profession due to his accounting and finance background. **Where will you be in five years:** In five years, Mr. Cebulko intends to venture into a management position within the health care sector. **Hobbies:** Traveling **Shipping Address:** 18429 Lange Street, Lansing, IL, 60438

Raul Adrian Cernea

Title: Engineer **Industry:** Engineering **Company Name:** SanDisk Corp. **Date of Birth:** 05/30/1949 **Place of Birth:** Ploiesti **Country of Origin:** Romania **Parents:** Neculai Cernea; Elena Cernea **Education:** Diploma in Physics Engineering, Polytechnic Institute, Bucharest, Romania (1972) **Career:** Senior Fellow, Western Digital Corp. (formerly SanDisk Corp.), Milpitas, CA (1990-Present); Design Engineer, SEEQ Tech., Milpitas, CA (1984-1990); Research Engineer, International Council for Computers in Education, Bucharest, Romania (1972-1984) **Creative Works:** Contributor, Scientific Papers, Professional Journals; Conference Presentations **Shipping Address:** 889 Agnew Rd, Santa Clara, CA, 95054

Imogene Klutts Chambers

Title: School System Administrator (Retired) **Industry:** Education/Educational Services **Date of Birth:** 08/06/1928 **Place of Birth:** Okfuskee County **State:** OK **Parents:** Odes Klutts; Lillie (Southard) Klutts **Marital Status:** Widowed **Spouse Name:** Richard Lee Chambers (5/27/1949, Deceased 11/17/1995) **Education:** EdD, Oklahoma State University (1980); MS, Oklahoma State University (1974); BA, East Central University (1948) **Certifications:** Certificate for Superintendent of Schools, Department of Education, The State of Oklahoma (1983-1988); Registered School Business Administrator, ASBO International (1976); Life Certified Teacher in High School Mathematics, Department of Education, The State of Oklahoma **Career:** Retired (1996); Financial Accounting Consultant, Oklahoma State Department of Education, The State of Oklahoma (1987-1992); Treasurer, Bartlesville Public Schools (1985-1994); Assistant Superintendent of Business Affairs, Bartlesville Public Schools (1980-1987); Employee, Bartlesville Public Schools (1950-1994); High School Mathematics Teacher, Marlow Public Schools (1948-1949) **Career Related:** Administrator, Oklahoma Schools Insurance Association (1993-1996); Director, Plaza National Bank of Bartlesville (Now BOK Financial) (1984-1994); Treasurer, Oklahoma Schools Insurance Association (1982-1996)
Civic: Member, First United Methodist Church, Bartlesville, OK (1950-Present) **Creative Works:** Author, "The Evolution of School Financial Accounting: The United States from 1910 to 1980 and Oklahoma from 1907 to 1980" (1980); Contributor, Articles, Publications; Presenter, Workshops to Implement a Uniform Cost Accounting System in Oklahoma Public Schools Based on the National Center for Education Statistics Publication Mandated by Oklahoma Department of Education **Awards:** Eagle Service Award, ASBO International (1993) **Membership:** ASBO International; Life Member, The Oklahoma Retired Educators Association; Life Member, Washington County Retired Educational Personnel Association; Life Member, Alumni Association, Oklahoma State University; Life Member, Alumni Association, East Central University **Marquis Who's Who Honors:** Albert Nelson Marquis Lifetime Achievement Award (2017) **What do you consider to be the highlight of your career:** The highlight of Ms. Chambers career was receiving the Eagle Service Award for outstanding service to school, community and profession from the Association of School Business Officials (ASBO) International in Boston, MA in 1993, with her husband by her side. **Political Affiliations:** Democrat **Religion:** Methodist **Shipping Address:** 911 SE Greystone Pl., Bartlesville, OK, 74006

Robert Leslie Chandler

Title: Healthcare Marketing, Communication Executive **Industry:** Medicine & Health Care **Company Name:** MaxAscent LLC **Date of Birth:** 03/03/1948 **Place of Birth:** Philadelphia **State:** PA **Parents:** Joel Leslie Chandler; Evelyn Laney (DeLaney) Chandler **Marital Status:** Married **Spouse Name:** Pamela Lin Gemmell (9/22/2002) **Children:** Jillian Delaney; Morgan Lindsey; Brooks Robert **Education:** MBA in Hospital Administration, Wagner College (1980); MS, Ohio University (1972); BS, Bowling Green State University (1971) **Career:** President, MaxAscent LLC. (2014-Present); Chief Executive Officer, MaxAscent LLC. (2014-Present); President Emeritus, Chandler Chicco Co (2014-Present); President, Chandler Chicco Co (1995-Present); President, inVentiv Health (2012-2014); Senior Vice President, Marketing and Communications, inVentiv Health (2011-2014); Executive Vice President, Burson-Marsteller, New York, NY (1982-1995); Vice President, Assistant Administrator Marketing, Public Affairs, Methodist Hospital, Brooklyn (1976-1982); Director, Community Relations, Henry Ford Wyandotte Hospital, Wyandotte, MI (1974-1976); Internal Communications Editor, Public Affairs Department, Owens Corning, Toledo, OH (1972-1974); Director, Public Relations, Athens Mental Health Center, Athens, OH (1972) **Career Related:** Special Consultant, American Society of Hospital Marketing and Public Relations (1989-1990); Special Consultant, American Hospital Association (1989-1990); Speaker, Numerous Communications Conferences **Civic:** Member, Board of Directors, New York Chapter, American Heart Association, Inc. (1990-1991); Member, Budget Committee, United Way Michigan (1975-1976); **Creative Works:** Contributor, Articles, Professional Journals **Awards:** Communique Lifetime Achievement Award (2014); Pharmavoice Top 100 Award In Healthcare (2014); Individual Lifetime Achievement SABRE Award (2010); Health Care Agency of the Decade Award (2010); EU Healthcare Consultancy of the Year Award, Holmes Report (2008-2009); Honoree, Best Agency to Work For, Holmes Report (2001-2008); Healthcare EU Consultancy of the Year Award, Puerto Rico Week (2008); Agency of the Year Award, Holmes Report (2002-2007); **Membership:** American Society of Healthcare Marketing and Planning; American College of Healthcare Executives; Healthcare Communications & Marketing Association; Healthcare Marketing & Communications Council; Kappa Tau Alpha; Public Relations Society of America; Sigma Delta Chi, Society of Professional Journalists **Hobbies:** Running **Business Address:** 170 Rumson Rd, MaxAscent LLC., Rumson, NJ, 07760

Kent Lowell Chaplin

Title: Chief Executive Officer, Founder **Industry:** Consulting **Company Name:** Avatar Global Consulting **Date of Birth:** 04/13/1953 **Place of Birth:** Los Angeles **State:** CA/USA **Marital Status:** Married **Spouse Name:** Deanna Chaplin **Children:** Gabrielle; Yasmine **Education:** MA, U.S. Naval War College, Georgetown University (1987); BA, University of California (1977) **Career:** Chief Executive Officer, Avatar Global Consulting (2010-Present); Founder, Avatar Global Consulting (2010-Present); Vice President Strategic Development, Harrington & Reed Global Resources (2009) **Career Related:** Consultant, Inner Quest (2000-2011) **Military Service:** Colonel, U.S. Air Force (1979-2009) **Awards:** Decorated Bronze Star, U.S. Air Force **Membership:** The Cyber Security Forum Initiative; Black Hat; Intelligence Community; Association for Intelligence Officers **Why did you become involved in your profession or industry:** Mr. Chaplin became involved in his profession due to his prior experience as an intelligence officer and college professor. He led global organizations during periods of crisis and rapid change, and provided critical economic, political, and military analysis to the highest levels of government. **Hobbies:** Politics **Shipping Address:** 8628 Copper Knoll Ave, Las Vegas, NV, 89129 **Website:** http://www.avatarglobalconsult.co.za

Richard Lee Chappell

Title: Biology Educator, Neuroscientist **Industry:** Education/Educational Services **Date of Birth:** 03/09/1938 **Place of Birth:** Buffalo **State:** NY/USA **Parents:** G. Howard Chappell; Gertrude Lyth (Myers) Chappell **Marital Status:** Widowed **Spouse Name:** Alice Carol Merckens (9/6/1968, Deceased) **Children:** Carol; Dreux **Education:** PhD in Biophysics, Johns Hopkins University, Baltimore, MD (1970); BSEE in Electrical Engineering/Physics, Princeton University (1962) **Career:** Research Professor, Department of Physiology and Biophysics, Jacobs School of Medicine and Biomedical Sciences, University at Buffalo (2016-Present); Professor Emeritus, Hunter College, CUNY (2012-Present); Senior Research Scientist, The Marine Biological Laboratory, Woods Hole, MA (2011-Present); Chair, Antarctic Program Task Force, National Council, Boy Scouts of America (2008-2012); Chairman, Council of Executive Officers, CUNY (2001-2008); Executive Officer, PhD Program in Biology, The Graduate Center, CUNY, New York, NY (1993-2008); Chairman, Department, Hunter College, CUNY, New York, NY (1987-1990); Professor, Hunter College, CUNY, New York City, NY (1980-2012); Associate Professor, Hunter College, CUNY, New York City, NY (1975-1979); Assistant Professor of Biology, Hunter College, CUNY, New York City, NY (1970-1974) **Career Related:** Chairman, Physiology and Neuroscience Subprogram, City University of New York, New York, NY (1986-1988); Consultant, Bell Laboratory, Murray Hill, NJ (1982-1983) **Civic:** Chairman, Science Development Program, Inc., New York, NY (1980-2007) **Military Service:** Lieutenant, U.S. Navy (1962-1966) **Creative Works:** Author, "Antarctic Scout" (1959); Contributor, Articles to Professional Journals **Awards:** Grantee, National Science Foundation (2006-Present); Grantee, National Eye Institute, National Institutes of Health (1971-2004); Antarctic Medal, U.S. Congress (1959); Chappell Peak, Antarctica Named in His Honor **Membership:** President, The American Polar Society (1997-2000); Vice President, The American Polar Society (1989-1997); Board of Directors, The Explorers Club (1972-1975); Fellow, The Explorers Club; The Association for Research in Vision and Ophthalmology; IEEE; The Marine Biological Laboratory Society; Sigma Xi, The Scientific Research Honor Society

Andrea Lea Charters

Title: Attorney **Industry:** Law and Legal Services **Place of Birth:** Cooperstown **State:** NY **Education:** JD, Harvard Law School, Harvard University, Cum Laude (1989); BA in History and Political Science, Yale University, Magna Cum Laude (1984); Coursework, Mohawk Valley Community College, State University of New York; Coursework, Washington University; Coursework, University of Missouri **Civic:** The Rotary Club of Rosslyn-Fort Myer; Volunteer, Operation Crossroads Africa, Lesotho, Africa **Awards:** Recipient, A/V Rating, Martindale-Hubbell **Membership:** Advisory Board Member, InsideCounsel, SuperConference (2013); The Yale Club of Washington, DC; Harvard Club of Washington, DC; Harvard Law School Association; Harvard Law School Women's Alliance; Association of Corporate Counsel **Marquis Who's Who Honors:** Albert Nelson Marquis Lifetime Achievement Award (2017) **To what do you attribute your success:** Ms. Charters attributes her success to her mother's encouragement; she always supported extra-curricular high school and college activities that pointed toward law. **Where will you be in five years:** In five years, Ms. Charters aims to expand her business. **Hobbies:** Hiking; Book clubs; Attending alumni functions; Theater; Traveling **Shipping Address:** 1600 N Oak St Apt 1130, Arlington, VA, 22209

James Leonard Checkel

Title: Researcher **Industry:** Research **Company Name:** Mayo Foundation for Medical Education and Research **Date of Birth:** 11/01/1959 **Place of Birth:** Rochester **State:** MN **Education:** AA, Rochester Vocational-Technical Institute, MN (1980) **Career:** Neurology Researcher, Mayo Clinic, Mayo Foundation for Medical Education and Research (2011-Present); Township Supervisor, Ashland Township, Dodge Center, MN (2009-Present); County Farm Bureau, Dodge County Farm Bureau, Dodge Center, MN (2002-Present); Farmer, Checkel Farm, Kasson, MN (2000-Present); Cell Technologist, Mayo Foundation for Medical Education and Research (1980) **Civic:** Chair, Dodge County Association (2013-Present); Member, Dodge County Association (2009-Present); Voting Member, Minnesota Farm Bureau (2010); Township Supervisor, Ashland Township, Dodge Center (2009-2010); President, Dodge County Farm Bureau, Dodge Center (2002-2010); Board Member, Great Northern Oliver Collectors; Member, Agricultural Advisory Committee, Great Northern Oliver Collectors **Awards:** Farmer of the Year, Dodge County Minnesota Conservation (2014); Outstanding Alumnus (2014) **Membership:** The Science Advisory Board (2008-Present); National Soybean Growers Association (2006-Present); National FFA Alumni (2004-Present); National Corn Growers Association (2002-Present); Hart-Parr Oliver Collectors of America (2002-Present); World Future Society (2007-2015); International Eosinophil Society (2002-2015); National Farm Toy Museum (2003-2007); Antique Barbed Wire Collectors of America (2001-2009); Board of Directors, Kasson Mantorville Lions; Fairview Family Counsel; Family Advisory Committee, Mayo Clinic, Kasson, MN; Great Northern Oliver Collectors, Minnesota Soybean Growers Association; Minnesota Livestock Coalition; Southeast Minnesota Agriculture Alliance; Minnesota BioAlliance; Minnesota Foundation for Responsible Animal Care; Agriculture Advisory Council, Southwest Minnesota State University; Agriculture Advisor, Oliver Kelly Farm, Elk River, MN; Dodge County Farm Bureau Board of Directors; Dodge County Corn and Soybean Growers; Dodge County Historical Society; Ashland Township Supervisor; Dodge County Association of Townships; Dodge County Planning Commission **Marquis Who's Who Honors:** Albert Nelson Marquis Lifetime Achievement Award (2017); Distinguished Humanitarian (2017) **Hobbies:** Farming; Reading **Shipping Address:** 64265 220th Ave, Kasson, MN, 55944

Robert Douglas Chelberg

Title: Military Officer **Industry:** Military & Defense Services **Date of Birth:** 09/01/1938 **Place of Birth:** Ironwood **State:** MI **Marital Status:** Married **Spouse Name:** Victoria **Children:** Robert; Kathryn **Education:** MBA, New Mexico State University (1973); BS, U.S. Military Academy at West Point (1961) **Career:** Consultant, TASC (2010-2016); Senior Fellow, Joint Forces Staff College (2001-2011); Consultant, Northrop Grumman (2006-2010); Senior Advisor of European Affairs, Economic Development Partnership (1999-2011); Program Manager, Defense Threat Reduction Agency, European Field Office (2003-2006); Senior Consultant, European Region, Cubic Applications, Inc. (1998-2003); Managing Director, European Region, Cubic Applications Inc. (1995-1998); Deputy Director, George C. Marshall European Center for Security Studies (1994-1995); Chief of Staff, U.S. European Command, Stuttgart, Germany (1991-1993); Special Advisor to Secretary-General, NATO (1990-1991); Special Assistant to Supreme Allied Commander Europe for Harmonization and Verification, Supreme Headquarters (1990); Chief Policy and Programs Branch, Policy Division, Supreme Headquarters Allied Powers Europe (1987-1990); Executive to Supreme Allied Commander Europe (1986-1987); Assistant Chief of Staff, Plans and Policy, Allied Forces Southern Europe (1986); Chief of Staff, Deputy Commanding General, Fort Jackson, South Carolina (1983-1986) **Civic:** Vice President of Membership, Transatlantic Council, Boy Scouts of America, Brussels, Belgium (2004-2008); District Commissioner, Transatlantic Council, Boy Scouts of America, Brussels, Belgium (1987-1990) **Military Service:** Lieutenant General, U.S. Army (1991-1993); Commissioned Second Lieutenant, U.S. Army (1961) **Awards:** Honoree, New Mexico State University Business School Hall of Fame (2001); Recipient, Army Exceptional Civilian Service Award (1995); Recipient, Distinguished Eagle Scout Award (1990); Outstanding Alumnus Service Award Lake Superior State University (1986); Recipient, Veteran of the Year Award VFW Post 3676 (1985); Defense Distinguished Service Medal; Army Distinguished Service Medal; Defense Superior Service Medal with Oak Leaf Cluster, Legion of Merit; Bronze Star with Four Oak Leaf Clusters; 10 Air Medals **Membership:** President, Wounded Veterans Relief Fund (2016-Present); President, Wounded Warriors South Florida (2015-2016); South Carolina State Vice President, Military Officers Association America (1999-2003); President, Federation of German-American Clubs (1994-1996) **Marquis Who's Who Honors:** Albert Nelson Marquis Lifetime Achievement Award (2017) **Hobbies:** Swimming; Traveling; Volunteer work **Shipping Address:** 100 Lakeshore Drive, Apt 1551, North Palm Beach, FL, 33408

Jon Arsen Chilingerian, PhD

Title: Professor, Director **Industry:** Education/Educational Services **Company Name:** Brandeis University **Place of Birth:** Boston **State:** MA **Marital Status:** Married **Spouse Name:** Dianne Irene Chilingerian **Children:** Two Children **Education:** PhD in Management, Massachusetts Institute of Technology (1987); MPA, Northeastern University (1975); BA in Political Science, Northeastern University (1973) **Career:** Director, Executive MBA Program for Physicians, Heller School, Brandeis University (2015-Present); Program Instructor, Director, AHRQ T-32 PhD Training Program in Health Services Research, Heller School, Brandeis University (2010-Present); Director, Executive Education, Heller School, Brandeis University (2007-Present); Chair, PhD and MBA Health Care Concentrations, Heller School, Brandeis University (2004-Present, 1995-1998); Visiting Scholar, Professor, Organizational Behavior and Healthcare Management, INSEAD, Fontainebleau, France (1997-Present); Adjunct Professor, Public Health and Community Medicine, Tufts School of Medicine (1995-Present); Brandeis Director, MD-MBA Program with Tufts Medical School (1995-Present); Professor, Heller School, Brandeis University (1989-Present) **Career Related:** Program Director, Maine Physician Executive Leadership Program (2012-Present); Program Director, The American College of Surgeons (2005-Present); Program Director, Tufts School of Medicine-Brandeis University Health Leadership Academy (2014-2015); Program Director, Massachusetts Medical Society (2013, 2009); Scientific Committee of the 11th International Conference on DEA, Samsun, Turkey (2013); Program Director, AATS (2012); Scientific Committee of the 10th International Conference on DEA, Natal, Brazil (2012); Steering Committee, 21st Century Health Care Curriculum, Harvard University (2011-2013) **Awards:** Dr. Royce Laycock Recognition of Excellence, American College of Surgeons (2016); Top 20 Professors of Health Care Management (2015-2016); Health Care Division for Excellent Paper Reviews, Academy of Management (2010, 2007); Myron D. Fotler Exceptional Service Award, Academy of Management (2010); Teaching Award MD-MBA Program, Tufts School of Medicine (2008) **Marquis Who's Who Honors:** Distinguished Humanitarian (2017) **Why did you become involved in your profession or industry:** Dr. Chilingerian became involved in his profession because he wanted to increase effectiveness through innovation. Over the years, he has worked in government, health and human services, and in the Office of Management and Budget in the city of Austin. He has thrived in roles where he was able to bring state-of-the-art management to government organizations. **Business Address:** 415 South Street, 415 South Street, Waltham, MA, 02453

Suzanne Christian

Title: Branch Manager **Industry:** Financial Services **Company Name:** LPL Financial **Parents:** Judge Peirson M.; Gertrude (Engel) Hall **Children:** Colleen Schmidt; Carolyn Christian; Claudia Christian; Cynthia Geary **Education:** MA, Redlands University (1979); BA, University of California, Los Angeles (1956) **Certifications:** Certified Financial Planner **Career:** Branch Manager, LPL Financial (2002-Present); Woman of Instructor, Island Empire Magazine (2012); Barron's Top Women's Advisors (2012); Branch Manager, Hornor, Townsend & Kent, Claremont (1996-2002); Senior Accountant Executive, Waddell & Reed (1986); Financial Planner, Waddell & Reed (1982-1996); Department Chair, Claremont Unified Schools (1981-1984); Instructor, Claremont Unified Schools (1972-1984); Instructor, L.A. City Schools (1958-1959) **Career Related:** Former Corporate Member, Pilgrim Place Foundation; Claremont Lecturer **Civic:** Board of Directors, Casa Colina Hospital (1994-2003); Treasurer, Fine Arts Scripps College (1993-1994); Former Member, Board of Directors, American Cancer Society (1988-1995); Professional Advisory Committee, YWCA-Inland Empire (1987); Claremont Chamber of Commerce; Claremont Rotary International; Former Member, Board of Directors, Galileo Society, Harvey Mudd College **Creative Works:** TV Cable Host, "Money Talks with Suzanne Christian" (1992-2008); Author, "Strands in Composition" (1979) **Awards:** Athena International Businesswoman of Year Award (1997) **Membership:** President, Estate Planning Council of Pomona Valley, Inc. (2001-2002); Board of Directors, Estate Planning Council Pomona Valley (2000-2007); Board of Directors, Harvey Mudd College Galileo Society (1997-1998); HTK Top Ten Leader (1996-2003); President, Board of Directors, Claremont Chamber of Commerce (1994-1995); President's Council, Circle of Champions (1994-1995); Silver Crest Award (1994-1995, 1985-1987); President, Curtain Raisers Club Garrison (1972-1975); President, Chairman's Club, Kappa Kappa Gamma (1970-1974); Foothill Philharmonic; Rotary International; Financial Planning Association; Patriots Club **Hobbies:** Tennis; Gardening; Archaeology **Shipping Address:** 419 Yale Avenue, Claremont, CA, 91711

Francesco Antonio Cipriani, PhD

Title: Academic Administrator (Retired) **Industry:** Education/Educational Services **Date of Birth:** 09/28/1933 **Place of Birth:** New York **State:** NY **Parents:** Domenico Cipriani; Maria (DiGiesi) Cipriani **Marital Status:** Married **Spouse Name:** Judith Pellathay (8/9/1959) **Children:** Maria; Frank; Michael; Dominique **Education:** PhD, New York University (1969); MEd, New York University (1961); AB in Political Science, Queens College (1955) **Career:** Retired (2000); College President, Farmingdale State College (1978-2000); Vice President, Administration, Farmingdale State College (1969-1978); Assistant to President, Farmingdale State College (1966-2969); Assistant Dean, Farmingdale State College (1964-1967); History Professor, Farmingdale State College (1964); Administrative Assistant to the Vice President, Business Affairs, New York University (1961-1964) **Civic:** Chairman, Long Island Regional Advisory Council on Higher Education; Chairman, Board of Directors, Regional Industrial Technical Education Council of Long Island, Inc.; Board Chairman, Long Island Regional Ashfill; Trustee, Long Island Power Authority; Member, Long Island Bi-County Planning Board (Now Long Island Regional Planning Council); **Military Service:** Captain, U.S. Air Force (1955-1957) Navigator and In-flight Instructor **Awards:** Inductee, Aviation Hall of Fame, Farmingdale State College (2017); Honoree, Knight, Government of Italy (1992) **Membership:** Middle States Commission on Higher Education; Consortium of Long Island Italian American Organizations, Inc.; Order of Merit of the Italian Republic **Marquis Who's Who Honors:** Albert Nelson Marquis Lifetime Achievement Award (2017); Distinguished Humanitarian (2017) **Why did you become involved in your profession or industry:** Dr. Cipriani was inspired to start his career when he joined the U.S. Air Force after college as a navigator, then a navigation instructor. He was hired as an industrial engineer at New York University and completed an MA and PhD. **What do you consider to be the highlight of your career:** Dr. Cipriani is most proud of transforming Farmingdale State College from a two-year agricultural/tech college into a bachelor's and master's degree-granting institution. He was involved in maintaining the environment and air quality of Long Island through his 20-year position as chair of the Suffolk Environmental Quality Council. He continued that involvement via the Long Island Bi-County Planning Board. **Political Affiliations:** Independent **Religion:** Roman Catholic **Shipping Address:** 23 Broadview Ave, Kings Park, NY, 11754

Sandra Helen Becker Clark

Title: Geologist **Industry:** Sciences **Company Name:** United States Geological Survey **Date of Birth:** 07/27/1938 **Place of Birth:** Kansas City **State:** MO **Parents:** LuVern Becker; Mildred Becker **Children:** Holly; Brett (Deceased); Ken (Deceased) **Education:** PhD, University of Idaho (1968); MS, University of Idaho (1964); BS, University of Idaho (1963); Coursework, Iowa State University (1956-1960) **Career:** Scientist Emeritus, United States Geological Survey, Reston, VA (2001-Present); Geologist, Eastern Mineral Resource Surveys Team, United States Geological Survey, Reston, VA (1996-2001); Deputy Chief for Mineral Resource Assessments, Office of Mineral Resources, United States Geological Survey, Reston, VA (1995-1996); Geologist, Commodity Specialist, Eastern Mineral Resources Branch, United States Geological Survey, Reston, VA (1980-1995); Equal Employment Opportunity Officer, United States Geological Survey, Reston, VA (1976-1980); Participant, Departments Manager of Development Program, United States Department of Interior, Washington, DC (1975-1976); Member, Alaska Gas Pipeline Task Force, United States Department of Interior, Washington, DC (1974-1975); Staff Geologist, Office of Mineral Resources, United States Geological Survey, Washington, DC (1972-1974); Geologist, Alaskan Mineral Resources Branch, United States Geological Survey, Menlo Park, CA (1967-1972); Geologist, Cominco America, Inc., Spokane, WA (1966-1967); Field Assistant, Bear Creek Mining Company, Spokane, WA (1965); Teaching Assistant, College of Mines, University of Idaho, Moscow, ID (1964-1966); Field Assistant, Idaho Bureau Mines and Geology, Moscow, ID (1963-1964) **Awards:** Recipient, Gold World Medal, New York Festivals Film and Video Competition (2003); Recipient, Silver Screen Award, International Film and Video Festival (2002); Recipient, Gold Screen Award, National Association of Government Communicators (2002); Recipient, Stewardship Award (1996); Summer Fellow, National Science Foundation (1996); Recipient, Meritorious Service Award, Department of Interior (1995); Graduate Fellow, National Science Foundation (1963-1964) **Membership:** Vice President, Geologic Division of Retires (2002-2009); Chairman, Commission of Fluorite and Barite, International Association of Genesis Ore Deposits (1996-2000); Delegate, American Association of Petroleum Geologists (1995-1996); Delegate, American Association of Petroleum Geologists (1992-1993) **Hobbies:** Scuba diving; Snorkeling; Photography; Camping; Figure skating; Cross-country skiing; Painting; Jewelry making **Shipping Address:** 11151 Timberhead Ct., Reston, VA, 20191

Carolyn Joan Cline, PhD

Title: Plastic and Reconstructive Surgeon **Industry:** Medicine & Health Care **Date of Birth:** 05/15/1941 **Place of Birth:** Boston **State:** MA/USA **Parents:** Paul S. Cline; Elizabeth (Flom) Cline **Education:** Resident, Plastic Surgery, St. Francis Hospital, San Francisco, CA (1979-1982); Fellow, Microvascular Surgery, Department of Surgery, University of California, San Francisco, CA (1978-1979); Resident, Surgery, Stanford University Medical Center (1976-1978); Intern, Internal Medicine, University of Wisconsin Hospital Center for Health Science, Madison, WI (1975-1976); MD, University of Miami (1975); Diploma, Washington School of Psychiatry (1972); PhD in Psychology, Washington University (1970); Intern, Clinical Psychology, St. Elizabeth's Hospital, Washington, DC (1966-1967); MA, University of Cincinnati (1966); BA, Wellesley College (1962) **Certifications:** Diplomate, American Board Plastic and Reconstructive Surgery **Career:** Freelance Writer, Professional and Popular Publications (1995-Present); Practice, Medicine Specializing in Plastic and Reconstructive Surgery, San Francisco, CA (1982-1995); Sole Practice, Clinical Psychology, Washington, DC (1970-1973); Chief Psychologist, Kingsbury Center for Children, Washington, DC (1969-1973); Research Fellow, National Institutes of Health, Washington, DC (1968-1969); Psychologist, Alexandria Community Mental Health Center, Alexandria, VA (1967-1968); Research Assistant, Physiology, Psychology Department, University of Cincinnati (1964-1965); Research Assistant, Physiology, Laser Laboratory, Children's Hospital Research Foundation, Cincinnati, OH (1964); Research Assistant, Harvard University Dental School, Boston, MA (1962-1964) **Creative Works:** Contributor, Chapters, Plastic Surgery Textbooks; Contributor, Articles, Professional Journals **Membership:** American Society of Plastic and Reconstructive Surgeons; Royal Society of Medicine; California Medicine Association; California Society of Plastic and Reconstructive Surgeons; San Francisco Medical Society **Hobbies:** Writing; Painting **Shipping Address:** 1340 Clay Street, Unit 603, San Francisco, CA, 94109

John Cogswell

Title: Financial Consultant, Telecommunications Industry Executive (Retired) **Industry:** Financial Services **Date of Birth:** 10/18/1933 **Place of Birth:** Southampton **State:** NY/USA **Parents:** John W. Cogswell; Lucy A. (McCurdy) Cogswell **Marital Status:** Married **Spouse Name:** Patricia A. Morrissey (6/18/1955) **Children:** Julie A.; Catherine J.; Jonathan P. **Education:** MS, Dartmouth College (1956); AB, Dartmouth College (1955) **Certifications:** Professional Engineer **Career:** Secretary-Treasury, New England Telephone Co., Boston, MA (1983-1990); Division Manager of Finance, New England Telephone Co., Boston, MA (1971-1983); Construction Program Engineer, New England Telephone Co., Boston, MA (1969-1971); Manager of Economics, American Telephone Co., New York, NY (1968-1969); Engineer, American Telephone Co., New York, NY (1965-1968); Staff Accountant, New England Telephone Co., Boston, MA (1963-1965); Planning Engineer, Pittsfield, Massachusetts, New England Telephone Co., Boston, MA (1961-1963); Engineer, New England Telephone Co., Boston, MA (1956-1961) **Career Related:** Treasurer, Board of Directors, Neighborhood Health Plan, Boston, MA (1986-1988, 1990-1998); President, Neighborhood Health Plan (1988-1990) **Civic:** Trustee, Needham Historical Society, Inc. (2014-Present); Trustee, Deaconess-Glover Hospital (1991-Present); Needham Town Meeting (2015-2018); Board of Directors, VNA Care Network Foundation (2008-2018); Treasurer, 128 Business Council (2008-2011); Treasurer, Living Care Villages of Massachusetts (2007-2010); Treasurer, North Hill Retirement Community (2007-2010); Chairman, Needham Board Selectmen (2006); Board of Directors, North Hill Retirement Community (2005-2010); Board of Directors, Living Care Villages of Massachusetts (2005-2010); Chairman, Board of Directors, Provider Service Network (2003-2005); Board of Directors, Beaconess-Waltham Hospital (2002); Board of Directors, HealthPoint (2001-2004); Board of Directors, Massachusetts Hospital Association (2000-2003); Chairman, Bridgewater Goddard Park Medical Associates (2000-2002); Chairman, Needham Board Selectman (2001) **Military Service:** Second Lieutenant, Captain, U.S. Army Reserves (1955-1963) **Awards:** Class of 1955 Award, Dartmouth College (2003); Volunteer of the Year, Combined Health Appeal of America (1992) **Membership:** Board of Directors, Financial Executive Institute (1988-1990); Board of Directors, Financial Management Association (1977-1979); President, Treasurer's Club of Greater Boston (1987-1988); President, Republican Club, New Providence, NJ (1966-1968) **Religion:** Episcopalian **Shipping Address:** 865 Central Avenue, Apartment O506, Needham, MA, 02492

Arthur M. Cohen

Title: Partner **Industry:** Law and Legal Services **Company Name:** Hawkins Delafield & Wood LLP **Place of Birth:** New York **State:** NY **Parents:** Samuel Cohen; Rose Cohen **Marital Status:** Married **Spouse Name:** Susan Horowitz (12/1/1991) **Children:** Samara; Adam **Education:** JD, Brooklyn Law School, Magna Cum Laude (1975); **Career:** Partner, Hawkins Delafield & Wood LLP (1983-Present); Associate, Hawkins Delafield & Wood LLP (1975-1983) **Career Related:** Speaker, Municipal Bonds, New York City Economic Development Corporation (2017); **Civic:** Oheb Shalom Congregation, South Orange, NJ **Creative Works:** Articles Editor, "Brooklyn Law Review" **Awards:** Lifetime Achievement Award, Council of Development Finance Agencies (2016); Super Lawyer in New York Metropolitan Area, Government Finance (2006-2017) **Membership:** National Association of Bond Lawyers; Council of Development Finance Agencies; New York State Economic Development Council; New York State Bar Association; **Bar Admissions:** State of New York **Marquis Who's Who Honors:** Albert Nelson Marquis Lifetime Achievement Award (2017); Distinguished Humanitarian Award (2017); Continental Who's Who Pinnacle Professional Member (2017) **To what do you attribute your success:** Mr. Cohen attributes his success to a strong work ethic, as well as his pride in his practice, clients, and legal firm. **Religion:** Jewish **Shipping Address:** 250 Greenwich Street, Floor 41, Hawkins Delafield & Wood LLP, New York, NY, 10007 **Website:** http://www.hawkins.com

Nancy Lee Collins

Title: Mathematician, Educator, Poet **Industry:** Education/Educational Services **Company Name:** St. James AME Church **Date of Birth:** 05/17/1925 **Place of Birth:** St. Louis **State:** MO **Parents:** Charles Alonzo Roberts; Leno Rosie (Squires) Roberts **Marital Status:** Single **Spouse Name:** Major Charles Brown Sr. (12/23/1946, Deceased 1984) **Children:** Major Charles Brown Jr.; Victor Ivy Brown **Education:** MA in Counseling, Washington University in St. Louis (1968); MEd, Saint Louis University (1955); BA, Harris-Stowe State University (1947) **Certifications:** Certified Elementary School Counselor, State of Missouri; **Career:** Supervisor, Computer Mathematics Laboratory, Meramec Community College (Now St. Louis Community College) (1989-1990); Secondary School Counselor, Saint Louis Public Schools (1967-1987); Adult Basic Education Teacher, Saint Louis Public Schools (1967-1972); Elementary School Teacher, Saint Louis Public Schools (1947-1987) **Civic:** Special Advocate Volunteer, Juvenile Court, St. Louis, MO (1989-1995); Member, Executive Board, Women's Missionary Society, Saint James AME Church; Peer Counselor, Older Adult Services Information Systems **Creative Works:** Artist, CD, "For God and Country" (2004); Author, "Potpourri and Remembrances" (2003); Contributor, Poetry, National Library of Poetry (1997); Co-Editor, "Profiles and Silhouettes: The Contribution of Black Women in Missouri" (1979); Author, Poem on the Heritage of Black Americans **Awards:** Honoree, Reflections of a Legacy, National Association of University Women (2017); 70-Year Member Award, Delta Sigma Theta Sorority, Inc. (2015); **Membership:** Membership Chairman, Missouri Conference, AMEC Women's Missionary Society (1995); Recruitment Chairman, Missouri Conference, AMEC Women's Missionary Society (1995); Local President, Missouri Conference, Lay Organization (1993-1995); **Marquis Who's Who Honors:** Albert Nelson Marquis Lifetime Achievement Award (2017) **Why did you become involved in your profession or industry:** Ms. Collins became involved in her profession because she was inspired by the field of education. Further, she enjoyed nurturing neighborhood children. **Political Affiliations:** Democrat **Religion:** African Methodist Episcopalian **Shipping Address:** 955 Jeanerette Dr, University City, MO, 63130

John Paris Colvis

Title: Mathematician, Research Scientist, Aerospace Engineer (Retired) **Industry:** Engineering **Date of Birth:** 06/30/1946 **Place of Birth:** St. Louis **State:** MO/USA **Parents:** Louis Jack Colvis; Jacqueline Betty (Beers) Colvis **Marital Status:** Married **Spouse Name:** Barbara Carol Davis (9/3/1976); Nancy Ellen Fritz (3/15/1969, Divorced 9/16/1974) **Children:** Michael Scott Colvis; Rebecca Jo (Colvis) Reiter; Bruce W. J. Zimmerly (Stepchild); Belinda Jo Zimmerly (Stepchild) **Education:** BS in Mathematics, Washington University in St. Louis, St. Louis, MO (1977); Coursework, University of Missouri, St. Louis (1966, 1972-1975); Coursework, University of Missouri, Rolla (1968-1969); Coursework, Palomar College, San Marcos, CA (1968); Coursework, Meramec Community College, St. Louis, MO (1964-1965) **Career:** Senior System Engineer II, Missile Defense Center, Raytheon Integrated Defense Systems, Woburn, MA (2009-2016); Staff Engineer, United Launch Alliance, Denver, CO (2007-2009); Senior Engineer, Lockheed Martin Astronautics Co. Space Launch Systems, Denver, CO (1995-2006); Senior Engineer, Martin Marietta Astronautics Group, Space Launch Systems Co., Denver, CO (1987-1995); Senior System Safety Engineer, Martin Marietta Astronautics Group, Strategic Systems, Co., Denver, CO (1981-1987); Associate System Safety Engineer, McDonnell Douglas Astronautics Co., St. Louis, MO (1978-1981) **Career Related:** Researcher in Field **Military Service:** Lance Corporal, U.S. Marine Corps, Vietnam (1966-1968) **Membership:** President, Colorado Home Educators' Association (1989); Post 4171, Veterans of Foreign Wars; Khe Sanh Veterans Inc.; Chapter 907, Vietnam Veterans of America **Hobbies:** Camping; Hiking; Swimming; Ballroom Dancing **Religion:** Evangelical **Shipping Address:** 45 Victoria Ln, Templeton, MA, 01468 **Website:** http://www.johnpariscolvis.com

Gary O. Concoff

Title: Partner **Industry:** Law and Legal Services **Company Name:** Rufus-Isaacs, Acland & Grantham LLP **Date of Birth:** 06/28/1936 **Place of Birth:** Los Angeles **State:** CA/USA **Marital Status:** Married **Spouse Name:** Jean F. Concoff (6/23/1963) **Children:** Cory N.; Andrew L. **Education:** LLB, Harvard Law School, Harvard University (1962); BBA in Business Administration and Accounting, University of California, Los Angeles (1958) **Career:** Attorney, TroyGould Attorneys (1996-Present); Partner, Mitchell Silberberg (Now Mitchell Silberberg & Knupp LLP) (1988-1995); Partner, Sidley Austin LLP (1981-1988); Partner, Kaplan, Livingston et al, Beverly Hills, CA (1965-1981); Associate, Kaplan, Livingston et al, Beverly Hills, CA (1965-1981); Associate, O'Melveny & Myers LLP (1962-1965); Partner, Rufus-Isaacs, Acland & Grantham LLP, Beverly Hills, CA **Career Related:** Adjunct Professor, Law Lecturer, University of California, Los Angeles (1980-1982); Founder, Entertainment Symposium, University of California, Los Angeles (1976-1978); Co-Chair, Entertainment Symposium, University of California, Los Angeles (1976-1978) **Military Service:** Second Lieutenant, U.S. Army (1958) **Creative Works:** Speaker, Moderator, Organizer, and Co-Chair, Several Programs, Cannes Film Festival (2009-2014); Contributor, Articles, Professional Journals **Awards:** Outstanding Practitioner of the Year, Anderson School of Management, University of California, Los Angeles **Membership:** Board of Directors, British Academy of Film and Television Arts (2001-2002); Chairman, Forum Committee, Motion Picture and Television Division, ABA (1987-1992); Los Angeles County Bar Association (1963); American Bar Association; Board of Trustees, Los Angeles Copyright Society; The State Bar of California **Bar Admissions:** State of California (1963) **Marquis Who's Who Honors:** Albert Nelson Marquis Lifetime Achievement Award (2017) **Why did you become involved in your profession or industry:** Mr. Concoff became involved in his profession because early on in his career, one of his supervisors commented that he was born to be a motion picture lawyer. **Shipping Address:** 640 Hightree Road, Santa Monica, CA, 90402

Lucinda D. Conger

Title: Librarian (Retired) **Industry:** Library Management/Library Services **Date of Birth:** 06/11/1941 **Place of Birth:** Fort Bragg **State:** NC **Parents:** Meredith Moore Dickinson; Ann Oliver Nee Mumford Dickinson **Marital Status:** Widowed **Spouse Name:** Bruce C. Conger (6/25/1966, Deceased) **Education:** Student, Wesley Theological Seminary (1990); MLS, Rutgers, The State University of New Jersey (1964); BA, Harvard College (1963) **Career:** Chief, Reader Services Branch, United States Department of State (1994-2000); Reference Librarian, United States Department of State, Washington, DC (1976-2000); Reference Librarian, Yale University, New Haven, CT (1973-1975); Serials Librarian, Albion College (1971-1973); Director of Reclassification, Albion College (1970-1971); Compact Storage Librarian, Princeton University (1966-1970); Reference Librarian, Library of Congress, Washington, DC (1966); Cataloger, Library of Congress, Washington, DC (1965); **Civic:** Volunteer, Washington National Cathedral (1976-Present); Volunteer, Smithsonian Museum of Natural History (2001-2012); Secretary, Washington DC Local Society (2001); **Creative Works:** Columnist, Database Magazine (1980-1990); Author, "Online Command Chart" (1981, 1977); Contributor, Articles, Various Professional Journals **Awards:** The Foot Soldier Award, The Archaeological Institute of America, Boston (2018); Roll of Honour Award, National Society of Colonial Dames (2010); Secretary Career Achievement Award (2000); Government Computer News Award (1992) **Membership:** Registrar, Maryland Society of the Colonial Dames of America (2014-Present); Secretary, Washington Society of the Archaeological Institute of America (2001-Present); Daughters of the American Revolution; Archaeological Institute of America; National Society of the Colonial Dames of America **Marquis Who's Who Honors:** Distinguished Humanitarian (2017) **Why did you become involved in your profession or industry:** Ms. Conger became involved in her profession after becoming friendly with a music librarian in college. She found that as a librarian, there was a large range of interests that one could develop. Ms. Conger was excited at the prospect of having the ability to work in different types of libraries with a degree in library science. **Political Affiliations:** Democrat **Religion:** Episcopalian **Shipping Address:** 4906 Jamestown Rd, Bethesda, MD, 20816

Billie Marie Connor-Dominguez

Title: Librarian (Retired) **Industry:** Library Management/Library Services **Date of Birth:** 10/04/1934 **Place of Birth:** Brighton **State:** MO **Parents:** Clifford Delmar Batten; Naomi Marie (Calhoun) Batten **Marital Status:** Married **Spouse Name:** Ramon Dominguez (9/10/1999); John Michael Connor (12/18/1968, Deceased 1978); Eugene Lee Struble (6/2/1962, Divorced 1968) **Education:** MLS, Rutgers, The State University of New Jersey (1959); Graduate Coursework, University of Guanajuato, Mexico (1956); BS, Southwest Missouri State University, Springfield, MO (1955) **Career:** Librarian (1996-2007); Manager, Business/Economics, Science/Technology/Patents, Water and Power Library, Los Angeles Public Library (1996-2007); Subject Department Manager, Science/Technology/Patents, Los Angeles Public Library (1979-1996); Subject Department Manager, Business/Economics, Los Angeles Public Library (1977-1979); Senior Librarian, Business/Economics, Los Angeles Public Library (1970-1977); Subject Specialist, SCAN, Los Angeles Public Library (1969-1970); Information Specialist, Business and Technology Service, Wichita Public Library (1962-1968); Extension Library, Southwest Regional Library, Bolivar, MO (1959-1962); Teacher, Auburn High School (1955-1958) **Civic:** Board of Directors, Community Career Development, Inc., Los Angeles, CA (2008-2010, 1995-2002) **Creative Works:** Editor, Communicator (1995-2007); Co-compiler, "Ottemiller's Index to Plays in Collections, Seventh Edition" (1988); Co-compiler, "Ottemiller's Index to Plays in Collections, Sixth Edition" (1976); Editor, Communicator (1971-1974); Co-compiler, "Ottemiller's Index to Plays in Collections, Fifth Edition" (1971) **Awards:** Support Staff Award, Library Mosaics and Council Library/Media Technicians (2002); Rose Vormelker Award, Southern California Chapter, Special Libraries Association (2002); Eponym, Billie Connor Award for Outstanding Contributions, Southern California Chapter, Special Libraries Association (1994) **Membership:** Board of Directors, Business Economic Science and Technology Friends (2012-Present); Board of Directors, Bruckman Rare Books Friends (2012-Present); Co-Chair, Acquisitions, Board of Directors, Culinary Historians of Southern California (2007-Present); President, Southern California Chapter, Special Libraries Association (1998-1999); Lifetime Member, Librarians Guild; Lifetime Member, American Federation of State **Marquis Who's Who Honors:** Albert Nelson Marquis Lifetime Achievement Award (2017) **To what do you attribute your success:** Mrs. Connor-Dominguez attributes her success to hard work. **Shipping Address:** 1707 Micheltorena Street, Apt. 312, Los Angeles, CA, 90026

Edward Gage Conture, PhD

Title: Speech Language Pathologist, Educator, Researcher **Industry:** Education/Educational Services **Company Name:** Vanderbilt University **Date of Birth:** 01/30/1945 **Place of Birth:** Winchester **State:** MA/USA **Parents:** Edward Joseph Conture; Helen Gage Conture **Marital Status:** Married **Spouse Name:** Patricia E. Kenyon **Children:** Brendan Gage; Tara Ki-Young Kim **Education:** PhD, University of Iowa (1972); MA, Northwestern University, Evanston, IL (1968); BS, Emerson College, Boston, MA (1967) **Certifications:** Licensed Speech-language Pathologist, North Carolina Board of Examiners for Speech-Language Pathologists and Audiologists (2013-Present); Board-certified Specialist, Fluency and Fluency Disorders, American Board of Fluency and Fluency Disorders (2001-Present); Licensed Speech-language Pathologist, Tennessee Department of Health (1997-Present); Certification, American Speech-Language-Hearing Association (1972-Present) **Career:** Professor Emeritus, Department of Hearing and Speech Sciences, Vanderbilt University, Nashville, TN (2013-Present); Professor of Hearing and Speech Sciences, Vanderbilt University, Nashville, TN (1997-2013); Director of Graduate Studies, Department of Hearing and Speech Sciences, Vanderbilt University, Nashville, TN (1997-2013); **Awards:** Distinguished Alumni Award, Department of Speech-Language Pathology and Audiology, University of Iowa (2007); Honors of the Association, American Speech, Language and Hearing Association (2007); **Marquis Who's Who Honors:** Albert Nelson Marquis Lifetime Achievement Award (2017); Distinguished Humanitarian (2017) **Why did you become involved in your profession or industry:** Dr. Conture became involved in his profession because he enjoys blending of humanistic elements with science. **What do you consider to be the highlight of your career:** Dr. Conture considers the highlights of his career to be his year abroad studying with Dr. Herman Kolk at Nijmegen University in The Netherlands, his consulting work in Bulgaria through the Fulbright Senior Specialist program, and receiving the Honors of the Association from the American Speech, Language and Hearing Association in 2017. **Where will you be in five years:** In five years, Dr. Conture intends to enjoy the company of his wife, Patricia E. Kenyon, his children, and his faithful dog, Willie. He also aims to continue appreciating things like herbs, cooking, professional and recreational reading and writing, travel, and long walks. **Shipping Address:** 53 Westall Avenue, Asheville, NC, 28804

Donald A. Cool, PhD

Title: Technical Executive **Industry:** Oil & Energy **Company Name:** Electric Power Research Institute **Marital Status:** Married **Education:** PhD in Radiation Biology, School of Medicine and Dentistry, University of Rochester (1983); MS in Radiation Biology, School of Medicine and Dentistry, University of Rochester (1981); BS in Biology, Houghton College (1978) **Career:** Technical Executive, Radiation Safety, Electric Power Research Institute (2015-Present); Senior Adviser, Radiation Safety and International Liaison, Office of Nuclear Material Safety and Safeguards, U.S. Nuclear Regulatory Commission, Washington, DC (2003-2015); Director, Division of Industrial and Medical Nuclear Safety, Office of Nuclear Material Safety and Safeguards, United States Nuclear Regulatory Commission, Washington, DC (1995-2003); Branch Chief, Radiation Protection and Health Effects Branch, Office of Nuclear Regulatory Research, U.S. Nuclear Regulatory Commission, Washington, DC (1989-1995); Health Physicist, Office of Nuclear Material Safety and Safeguards, U.S. Nuclear Regulatory Commission, Washington, DC (1982-1989) **Career Related:** Co-chair, National Council on Radiation Protection and Measurements, Council Committee 1 (2015-Present); International Commission on Radiological Protection (ICRP) Main Commission (2013-Present); Chairman, International Commission on Radiological Protection (ICRP) Committee 4, Practical Application of Recommendations (2013-Present); Council Member, National Council on Radiation Protection and Measurements (2013-Present); Program Chair, National Council on Radiation Protection and Measurements, 51st Annual Meeting (2015); Fellow, Health Physics Society (2014); International Commission on Radiological Protection (ICRP) Committee 4, Practical Application of Recommendations (2001-2013); United States Representative, Radiation Safety Standards Advisory Committee, International Atomic Energy Agency (IAEA) (1996-2002) **Creative Works:** Author, "The new mandate and work of ICRP Committee 4", Proceedings of the Fourth International Symposium on the System of Radiological Protection, Annals of the ICRP, (2018); Author, "Overview of ICRP Committee 4: application of the Commission's recommendations", Proceedings of the Third International Symposium on the System of Radiological Protection, Annals of the ICRP (2016); Co-author, "Review of the ICRP System of Protection: the Approach to Existing Exposure Situations," Annals of ICRP (2015) **Awards:** Meritorious Service Award, Nuclear Regulatory Commission (2012); Senior Level and Senior Executive Performance Awards, Nuclear Regulatory Commission **Membership:** Sigma Xi, The Scientific Research Honor Society; Radiation Research

Fred M. Cooper

Title: Physicist **Industry:** Sciences **Date of Birth:** 04/01/1944 **Place of Birth:** New York **State:** NY/USA **Parents:** Erwin E. Cooper; Lottie Silverman Cooper **Marital Status:** Married **Spouse Name:** Catherine L. Laforte (11/20/1986); Necia Grant (6/1972, Divorced 4/1982) **Children:** Lottie Grant Cooper; David Grant Cooper **Education:** PhD in Physics, Harvard University (1968); BS in Physics, City College of New York, Summa Cum Laude (1964) **Career:** External Professor, Santa Fe Institute (2010-Present); Visiting Scholar, Harvard University (2013-2014); Staff Member, T-4 Los Alamos National Labs (2010-2012); Program Director, Theoretical Physics, National Science Foundation (2002-2009); Group Leader, Los Alamos National Laboratories, New Mexico (1995-2000); Staff Member, Santa Fe Institute (1991-2006); Staff Member, Los Alamos National Laboratories, New Mexico (1975-1990); Assistant Professor, Belfer Graduate School of Science, Yeshiva University, New York, NY (1970-1975); Instructor, Cornell University, Ithaca, NY (1968-1970); **Career Related:** Panelist, High Energy Physics Advisory Panel and Sub-Panels (2003-Present); Organizer, Harold Morowitz Memorial Fest (2017); Chairman, Heineman Prize Selection Committee, American Physical Society (2010); Visiting Professor, Boston College (1998-1999); Organizer, Slansky Memorial Conference (1998); Organizer, Carruthers Fest (1996); Organizer, ECT Workshop on the Quark-Gluon Plasma, Trento, Italy (1994); Visiting Professor, University New Hampshire, Durham, NH (1993-1994); Co-Organizer, Santa Fe Summer Physics Workshop (1991-2000); Visiting Professor, Brown University, Providence, RI (1989-1990); **Civic:** President, Board of Directors, Kagyu Shenpen Kunchab Buddhist Center, Santa Fe, NM (1989-Present); County Committeeman, Bronx Democratic Party (1973-1975) **Creative Works:** Co-Author, "Supersymmetry and Quantum Mechanics," World Scientific (2001); Editor, Proceedings of the Santa Fe Workshop on Intermittency (1990); Editor, Recent Advances in Particle Physics, Annals of the New York Academy (1974); Author, More than 200 Published Papers in Various Physics Journals; Editor, Proceedings **Awards:** Principal Investigator, Laboratory Directed Research and Development Grant (1995-2000); United States-Israel Binational Science Foundation Grant (1993-1996); Co-Principal Investigator, High Energy Physics Department of Energy Grant (1990-2002); Investigator, Department of Energy Grant (1975-2002); **Membership:** Vice Chair, Chair, APS Heineman Prize Selection Committee (2009-2010); American Physical Society; Former Vice Chairman, Physics Section, New York Academy of Sciences; Founder, National Science Foundation Physics Theory Net, Large Hadron Collider Theory Initiative **Marquis Who's Who Honors:** Albert Nelson Marquis Lifetime Achievement Award (2017)

May M. Coryell

Title: Language Educator **Industry:** Education/Educational Services **Company Name:** Middlesex Community College **Date of Birth:** 06/22/1951 **Place of Birth:** Cleveland **State:** OH **Parents:** Franklin Mercer Coryell; Giuliana Coryell **Marital Status:** Life Partner **Spouse Name:** Margaret Batchelder (2/28/1987) **Education:** MA, School of International Training, Brattleboro, VT (1980); BA, Marietta College, Ohio (1973) **Career:** Professor, English as Second Language Coordinator, Middlesex Community College, Middletown, CT (1989-Present); English as Second Language Teacher, American Language Academy, Fay School, Southborough, MA (1984-1988); English as Second Language Teacher, American Language Academy, Lyndon Institute, VT (1980-1984); English Teacher, Palau High School, Koror, Palau (1978-1979); Teacher, Airai Elementary School, Koror, Palau (1975-1977); Trainee, English as Second Language Teacher, Peace Corps, Bukavu, Zaire (1974); Elementary School Teacher, St. Paul's School, Athens, OH (1973-1974) **Civic:** Volunteer, Peace Corps, Palau (1975-1978) **Awards:** Member of the Year, Congress of Connecticut Community College (2008); Merit Award, Connecticut Community College (2008); Returned Peace Corps Volunteer Award, Beyond War Organization (1987) **Membership:** NAFSA; Recording Secretary, Treasurer, The ConnTESOL Organization (1990-2005); TESOL International Association; Friends of Micronesia; Boston Area Returned Peace Corps Volunteers; American Coaster Enthusiasts; Coaster Zombies; Western New York Coaster Club; Alpha Gamma Delta **Marquis Who's Who Honors:** Albert Nelson Marquis Lifetime Achievement Award (2017) **Hobbies:** Reading; Travel; Musicals; Roller coaster riding **Shipping Address:** 1660 Limahana Circle, Apt. 107, Lahaina, HI, 96761

Mary-Patricia Tross Cottrell

Title: Bank Executive **Industry:** Financial Services **Date of Birth:** 04/24/1934 **Place of Birth:** Seattle **State:** WA/USA **Parents:** Alfred Carl Tross; Alice-Grace (O'Neal) Tross **Marital Status:** Married **Spouse Name:** Richard Smitt Cottrell (5/17/1969, Deceased 1995) **Education:** BBA, University of Washington (1955) **Career:** Senior Vice President, Corporate Services, Union Savings Bank (1997-2013); Vice President, Corporate Services, Lafayette American Bank (1995-1997); Vice President, Cash Management, Centerbank (1992-1995); Vice President, Cash Management, Connecticut Region, JPMorgan Chase & Co. (1991-1992); Senior Vice President, Cash Management Services, Citytrust (1990-1991); Vice President, Corporate Financial Services, Citytrust (1983-1990); Vice President, Union Trust Company (1978-1983); Head, Corporate Services, Union Trust Company (1978-1983); Vice President, Union Trust Company (1976-1978); Assistant Vice President, Union Trust Company (1969-1976); Assistant Treasurer, Union Trust Company (1967-1968); Data Processing Consultant, Stamford, CT (1965-1966); Customer Education Instructor, IBM (1958-1965); Systems Service Representative, IBM (1955-1958) **Civic:** Volunteer, PAWS (2017-Present); Tree Advisory Committee, City of Norwalk (2017-Present); Treasurer, Board of Directors, Lockwood-Mathews Mansion Museum (2015-Present); Board of Directors, Lockwood-Mathews Mansion Museum (2013-Present); Board of Directors, Family and Children's Agency (1982-Present); Trustee, Norwalk Seaport Association, Inc. (2012-2016); President, Board of Directors, Danbury Visiting Nurses of Western Connecticut Home Care (2006-2007); Board of Directors, Danbury Visiting Nurses of Western Connecticut Home Care (2003-2016); Chairman, Stamford Rehabilitation Center (2003-2004); Chairman, Gaylord Specialty Healthcare (2003-2004); Board of Directors, Danbury Cemetery Association (2002-2004) **Membership:** Board of Directors, New England Automated Clearing Housing Association (1995-1997); Director, President, Fairfield County Bankers Association (1984-1985); Chairman, Board of Directors, Electronic Funds Transfer Association (1983-1984) **Marquis Who's Who Honors:** Albert Nelson Marquis Lifetime Achievement Award (2017); Distinguished Humanitarian (2017) **Political Affiliations:** Republican **Religion:** Roman Catholic **Shipping Address:** 5 Seaside Place, Norwalk, CT, 06855

Patrick Campbell Coughlan

Title: Lawyer, Mediator **Industry:** Law and Legal Services **Company Name:** Conflict Solutions Inc. **Date of Birth:** 05/28/1940 **Place of Birth:** Orange **State:** NJ/USA **Parents:** Gerald Noel Coughlan; Carter (Van Schaick) Coughlan **Marital Status:** Married **Spouse Name:** Joyce Miskuf **Children:** Kimberly Campbell; Devon Gerald; Carter Turner **Education:** JD, Duke University (1965); BA, Duke University (1962) **Certifications:** Certified Mediator, Financial Industry Regulatory Authority (2009-Present) **Career:** President, Conflict Solutions, Naples, FL (1992-Present); President, Conflict Solutions, Portland, ME (1992-Present); Finance Chair, Community Foundation of Collier County (2016); President, Resolve Disputes, Inc. North America (1989-1992); Principal, Coughlan Associate (1987-1988); Chair, Board of Appeals, Raymond, ME (1985-1998); President, Kingsley Pines, Inc. (1984-2010); City Attorney, City of La Habra Heights, Westlake Village, CA (1981-1984); City Attorney, City of La Habra Heights, Rolling Hills, CA (1981-1984); City Attorney, City of La Habra Heights, Avalon, CA (1981-1984); City Attorney, City of La Habra Heights, California (1979-1984); City Attorney, City of Seal Beach, California (1978-1984); City Attorney, City of San Fernando, California (1977-1982); Partner, Richards, Watson & Gershon, Los Angeles, CA (1975-1984); City Attorney, City of Rancho Palos Verdes, California (1975-1982); Associate, Richards, Watson & Gershon, Los Angeles, CA (1974); Partner, Alley, Maass, Rogers & Lindsay, Palm Beach, FL (1972-1974); Judge, Municipal Court, Ocean Ridge, FL (1970-1972) **Career Related:** Speaker in Field, American Bar Association in Ethics Mediation (2011); Partner, Atlanean Partners LLC (1986-2010) **Civic:** Director, Admirals Watch at Windstar (2009-2011, 2004-2005); Mediator, Private Adjudication Center, Duke University (1998-2002); Director, Private Adjudication Center, Duke University (1994-2002) **Military Service:** Captain, US Air Force (1965-1968) **Creative Works:** Co-Author, "A Practical Guide to Superior Court Practice in Maine" (2013); Co-Author, "Mediation in Maine" (2013) **Awards:** Honoree, Named Best Lawyers In America (2008-Present); Honoree, Super Lawyer in New England (2007-Present); Honoree, Super Lawyer in Florida (2007-Present) **Membership:** CPR Commercial Litigation Panel (2007-Present); Board of Directors, International Academy of Mediators (1999-Present); Speaker, ABA (2011); International Institute of Conflict Prevention and Resolution (2010) **Bar Admissions:** Maine (1985); California (1974); Supreme Court of the United States (1968); Florida (1965) **Marquis Who's Who Honors:** Albert Nelson Marquis Lifetime Achievement Award (2017) **Shipping Address:** 75 Pearl Street, Suite 430, Conflict Solutions, Portland, ME, 04101

Donna Cretan

Title: Critical Care and Neonatal Nurse **Industry:** Medicine & Health Care **Company Name:** Mark Twain Medical Center **Date of Birth:** 05/18/1939 **Place of Birth:** Minneapolis **State:** MN **Parents:** Howard Robert Bjerke; Frances E. (Warner) Bjerke **Marital Status:** Married **Spouse Name:** Nestor Nicholas Cretan (1/24/1959) **Children:** Colette; John; Christopher; Bernadette **Education:** BSN, Sacred Heart University, Fairfield, CT (1986); ADN, Contra Costa College (1973) **Certifications:** Certificate, ILCA; Registered Nurse, State of Connecticut **Career:** Staff Nurse, Mark Twain Medical Center, Dignity Health, San Andreas, CA (2002-Present); Staff Nurse, Greenwich Hospital, Yale New Haven Health (1993-2002); Staff Nurse, Community Hospital, Santa Rosa, CA (1989-1993); Nurse Manager, St. Joseph Medical Center, Stamford, CT (1974-1989); Consultant, St. Joseph Medical Center, Stamford, CT (1974-1989) **Career Related:** Tutor, English as Second Language, Literacy Volunteers and Advocates (1997-Present) **Civic:** Volunteer Nurse, Americares Free Clinic, Norwalk, CT (1994-Present); Literacy Volunteer, English as Second Language Institute (1997-1998); Cultural Homestay International, Cohasset, MA (1991-1995); California Area, AFS-USA, Inc. (1991-1993); Secretary, Historical Society, Sebastopol, CA (1989-1992); AFS-USA, Inc. (1983-1984); Host Parent, New Canaan A Better Chance, New Canaan, CT (1982-1984); People Link, Petaluma, CA **Membership:** The American Nurses Association, Inc.; ILCA; Neonatal Network; The Association of Women's Health, Obstetrics and Neonatal Nurses **Marquis Who's Who Honors:** Albert Nelson Marquis Lifetime Achievement Award (2017); Distinguished Humanitarian (2017) **Hobbies:** Lactation promotion; Photography **Shipping Address:** 22865 Northrup Ct, Columbia, CA, 95310

Eugene "Gene" W. Cross

Title: Engineer **Industry:** Engineering **Company Name:** Lockheed Space Systems Company **Date of Birth:** 10/06/1946 **Education:** Professional Studies in Optics, University of California, Los Alamos (1982-1983); Professional Studies in Optics, University of Wisconsin-Madison (1979); Professional Studies in Optics, Short Courses, SPIE (1978-2010); Graduate Studies in Geophysics, Eastern New Mexico University (1975); BS in Geophysics, Eastern New Mexico University (1974); Coursework, Advanced Radar Prediction and Image Analysis, U.S. Air Force Institute of Technology (1973); Coursework, Photo-Interpretation and Image Analysis, Armed Forces Air Intelligence Training Center (1970); Coursework, Geology and Astronomy, New Mexico State University (1967-1970); AA in Humanities and Science, Cerritos College (1966) **Career:** Consultant, AMP Optics, LLC, San Diego, CA (2017-Present); Engineer Emeritus, Lockheed Martin, Sunnyvale, CA (2017-Present); Optics Engineer, Senior Staff, Lockheed Missiles and Space (1999-2008); Optics Engineer, Senior Staff, Advanced Technology Center, Lockheed Space Systems Company, Palo Alto and Sunnyvale, CA (1999-2007); Senior Optics Engineer, KLA-Tencor (1997-1998); Senior Optics Manufacturing Engineer, Perkin-Elmer Applied Optics Division, Corning OCA (Now Newport Precision Optics and II-VI) (1996-1997); Senior Optics Engineer, Consultant, Imagyn (1995-1996); Optics Engineer, Senior Staff, Circon-ACMI (Now Olympus-ACMI), Stamford, CT (1993-1994); Optics Engineer, Consultant, National Solar Observatory, Sunspot, NM (1986-1992); Senior Optics Engineer, Hughes Aircraft Company (1985-1991); Senior Optics Engineer, Grumman Space Systems, Irvine, CA (1984-1985); Optics Engineer, Staff Member, Los Alamos National Laboratory, Los Alamos, NM (1981-1984); Senior Member of the Technical Staff, Xerox Electro-Optical Systems (1980-1981) **Civic:** Public Outreach, Telescope SME, and Programs Chairman, Peninsula Astronomical Society (2002-Present); Optical Engineer, Manzanita Observatory, Tierra Astronomical Institute, San Diego, CA (1986-1991); Optical Engineer, Eastbay Astronomical Society (1986) **Membership:** Co-Chair, "Optical Alignment-2" Symposium, SPIE, Crystal City, VA (1984) **Marquis Who's Who Honors:** Albert Nelson Marquis Lifetime Achievement Award (2017) **Shipping Address:** 473 School Street, Fremont, CA, 94536 **Website:** https://www.linkedin.com/in/genecross

Nancy Ruth Crossley

Title: Federal Agency Administrator **Industry:** Government Administration/Government Relations/Government Services **Date of Birth:** 02/02/1944 **Place of Birth:** San Jose **State:** CA/USA **Parents:** Edward Crossley; Ruth Flesher Crossley **Education:** Diploma, San Francisco Business School (1964) **Career:** U.S. Geological Survey (1997); International Program Specialist, U.S. Geological Survey, Menlo Park, CA (1989-1997); International Program Specialist, U.S. Geological Survey, Reston, VA (1988-1989); Administrator, U.S. Geological Survey, Menlo Park, CA (1965-1988) **Career Related:** Secretary, National Chinese Officers' Language School, Taipei, Taiwan (1962-1963) **Civic:** Volunteer, Lee Memorial Health Systems, Cape Coral, FL (2001-2002); Entertainment Ticket Seller, The Jamaica Bay Club **Membership:** AARP **Marquis Who's Who Honors:** Albert Nelson Marquis Lifetime Achievement Award (2017) **Hobbies:** Travel; Swimming; Games; Puzzles; Volunteering **Shipping Address:** 36 Berkley Circle, #343, Fort Meyers, FL, 33907

Alfred T. Culliford III

Title: Professor of Surgery **Industry:** Medicine & Health Care **Company Name:** NYU School of Medicine **Marital Status:** Married **Spouse Name:** Susan **Education:** Fellow, Thoracic Surgery, NYU School of Medicine (1974-1976); Clinical Fellow, American Cancer Society, Inc. New York, NY (1973-1974); Resident, General Surgery, NYU School of Medicine (1970-1974); Intern, Surgery Hospital, University of Cincinnati (1969-1970); Doctorate, New York Medical College, Valhalla, NY (1969); Bachelor's Degree in Biology, St. Bonaventure University, with Honors, St. Bonaventure, NY (1965) **Certifications:** Certified Fellow, American College of Surgeons (2008); Certified Fellow, American College of Surgeons (1997); Certified in Thoracic Surgery, The American Board of Thoracic Surgery, Inc. (1977); Diplomate, National Board of Medical Examiners (1977); Certified in Surgery, American Board of Surgery (1975); Diplomate, National Board of Medical Examiners (1974); Diplomate, National Board of Medical Examiners (1970); Medical License, State of New York **Career:** Professor, Surgery, NYU School of Medicine (1998-Present); Associate Professor, Surgery, NYU School of Medicine (1981-1998); Assistant Professor, Surgery, NYU School of Medicine (1978-1981); Clinical Instructor, Surgery, NYU School of Medicine (1976-1978) **Career Related:** Attending Surgeon, NYU School of Medicine (1976-Present); Attending Surgeon, Bellevue Hospital, The City of New York (1976-Present); Attending Surgeon, VA NY Harbor Health Care System, Manhattan Campus (1976-Present) **Military Service:** Major, 74th Field Hospital, U.S. Army Reserve (1972-1978) **Creative Works:** Contributor, Articles, Professional Journals; Presenter, Numerous Organizations **Membership:** American Medical Association; The Medical Society of the State of New York; American College of Surgeons; Association of Academic Surgery; The Society of Thoracic Surgeons; New York Society for Thoracic Surgery; American Heart Association, Inc.; American Association for Thoracic Surgery; Alpha Omega Alpha Honor Medical Society **Hobbies:** Fishing; Hiking **Business Address:** 550 First Ave, New York, NY, 10016 **Shipping Address:** 9 Iroquois Trl, Harrison, NY, 10528

Aneta Joan Cupp

Title: Music Educator **Industry:** Education/Educational Services **Company Name:** Memorial Hall School **Date of Birth:** 12/30/1940 **Place of Birth:** Bonham **State:** TX/USA **Parents:** Emmett Morgan Northcutt; Hattie Faye (Taylor) Northcutt **Marital Status:** Married **Spouse Name:** Charles Daniel Cupp (3/8/1980) **Children:** Daniel Emmett (Deceased) **Education:** MEd, University of Houston (1983); MusB, University of North Texas (1963) **Certifications:** Lifetime Teaching Certificate **Career:** Substitute Teacher, Memorial Hall School (2000-Present); Substitute Teacher, Houston Independent School District (1996-2000); Secretary to Recreation Music Director, Houston Parks and Recreation Department (1968); Secretary to Recreation Music Director, Houston Parks and Recreation Department (1964-1966); Teacher, Elementary Itinerant Music, Houston Independent School District (1963-1996); Secretary, Health Workshop, University of North Texas (1963) **Career Related:** Leader, Elementary Classroom Teacher Music In-Service, Houston Independent School District (1974) **Creative Works:** Piano Lab System **Awards:** Certificate of Award, Burbank Elementary School (1993); Certificate of Appreciation, Burbank Elementary and Parent-Teacher Organization (1984); Inductee, Hall of Honor, Houston Independent School District (1982); Certificate of Appreciation, Houston Independent School District (1981); Teacher of the Year, Houston Independent School District (1976); Certificate of Recognition, Teacher of the Year Competition, Houston Independent School District (1975-1976); Certificate of Appreciation, AAU Bi-Centennial Project, Houston, TX (1975); Letters of Endorsement (1975); National Teacher of the Year (1975); Nominee, Teacher of the Year Award, Field Elementary School, Houston, TX (1975); Finalist, Teacher of the Year Competition, Field Elementary School, Houston, TX (1975); Featured in "Outstanding Elementary Teachers of America Book" (1974); Honoree, Outstanding Young Educator, Human Resources Committee, Houston Junior Chamber of Commerce (1970); Honoree, Jim Collins Scholar, Corsicana Senior High School (1959) **Membership:** Congress of Houston Teachers **To what do you attribute your success:** Ms. Cupp attributes her success to her determination, organizational skills, and faith in God. **Why did you become involved in your profession or industry:** Ms. Cupp comes from a musical family, and always had a love for music. **What do you consider to be the highlight of your career:** The highlight of Ms. Cupp's career was the piano lab she established with her own system of teaching. **Political Affiliations:** Conservative **Religion:** Non-Denominational **Shipping Address:** 1237 Althea Drive, Houston, TX, 77018

Jeffrey S. Cutter

Title: Secondary Education Educator, Music Educator **Industry:** Education/Educational Services **Date of Birth:** 07/20/1956 **Place of Birth:** Royal Oak **State:** MI/USA **Parents:** George E. Cutter; Joy G. (Dolby) Cutter **Education:** Master in Educational Leadership and Administration, Wayne State University (1994); MusB, Wayne State University, With Distinction (1978); MEd, Wayne State University **Certifications:** Certified Teacher, State of Michigan **Career:** Band Director, Paul K. Cousino High School (2006-2012); Curriculum Consultant, Warren Consolidated Schools (2000-2006); Performing Arts Facilitator, Warren Woods Adult & Community Education, Warren Woods Public Schools (1980-2006) **Career Related:** Executive Director, Southeast Michigan Arts Forum Weekend School of Music (2011); Program Director, Southeast Michigan Arts Forum Weekend School of Music (2001); Entertainment Director, Detroit Lions, Ltd. (1999-2003); Program Assistant, Detroit Lions, Ltd. (1975-1999); Program Coordinator, Entertainment & Special Events Department, Michigan State Fair, LLC (1975-1997) **Civic:** Chairman, Council of Commissions, City of Warren (2006); Chairman, Cultural Commission, City of Warren (1999); Vice-Chairman, Council of Commissions, City of Warren (1996-2006); President, Friends of Music, Wayne State University; Chairman, Warren-Centerline Thanksgiving Parade Committee Inc. **Awards:** State Chair Award, American School Band Directors Association (2016); State Chair Award, American School Band Directors Association (2014); Outstanding Volunteer, City of Warren (2010); Government Service Award, Warren Historical & Genealogical Society (2008) **Membership:** President Emeritus, American School Band Directors Association (2006-2010); National President, American School Band Directors Association (2005-2006); Treasurer, American School Band Directors Association Education Foundation, American School Band Directors Association; Warren Symphony Society/Motor City Symphony Orchestra; President, Warren Concert Band; Treasurer, Warren Concert Band; Michigan School Band and Orchestra Association **Shipping Address:** 32774 McConnell Street, Warren, MI, 48092

Nancy Daggett Jensen

Title: Private Piano Teacher **Industry:** Education/Educational Services **Date of Birth:** 09/10/1942 **Place of Birth:** Los Angeles **State:** CA **Parents:** Daniel Thomas Daggett; Louise Helen (Kuljian) Daggett **Marital Status:** Married **Spouse Name:** Sven Oxfeldt Jensen (11/19/1978) **Children:** Lori; Brian **Education:** MA, San Jose State University (1967); BA, San Jose State University (1964) **Certifications:** Certified Master Teacher, Music Teachers National Association **Career:** Private Piano Teacher, Los Altos, CA (1967) **Career Related:** Artistic Chair of Steinway Society **Awards:** Master Teacher Award, Music Teacher National Association (1991) **Membership:** Board of Directors, Steinway Society The Bay Area (2015-Present); Artistic Director, Steinway Society The Bay Area (2010-Present); Piano Panel Chair North, Certificate of Merit, MTAC (2007-2013); President, Los Altos Branch, MTAC (1993-1994); President, Los Altos Branch, MTAC (1985-1986); President, Los Altos Branch, MTAC (1982-1983); State Chair, Certificate of Merit, MTAC (1974-1979); President, Los Altos Branch, MTAC (1972-1974); CAPMT **Marquis Who's Who Honors:** Albert Nelson Marquis Lifetime Achievement Award (2017) **Why did you become involved in your profession or industry:** Ms. Daggett Jensen received a piano on her tenth birthday and knew right away that playing it was what she was meant to do. Since then, she has shared her passion for playing piano with others. **Shipping Address:** 1655 Clay Dr, Los Altos, CA, 94024 **Website:** https://www.linkedin.com/in/nancy-daggett-jensen-0ba06176

Ilene H.R. Danse

Title: Physician, Educator, Toxicologist, Designer, Sculptor **Industry:** Medicine & Health Care **Company Name:** University of California **Place of Birth:** New York **State:** NY **Parents:** Jack Homnick; Henrietta Homnick **Marital Status:** Married **Spouse Name:** James Atherton Danse **Children:** Arthur Raisfeld; Robin Raisfeld **Education:** Coursework, Brooklyn Museum Art School; Coursework, Art Students League; Coursework, Pratt Institute; MD, New York University (1964); BS, City University of New York (1960) **Certifications:** Diplomate, National Board of Medical Examiners; Diplomate, American Board of Internal Medicine; Diplomate, American Board of Toxicology **Career:** Associate Clinical Professor, Department of Epidemiological and Preventive Medicine, University of California, Davis (1991-Present); Independent Medical Examiner, Toxicology and Internal Medicine, Department of Industrial Relations, State of California (1985-Present); Associate Clinical Professor, Department of Medicine, Division of Occupational and Environmental Medicine, University of California, San Francisco (1986-2006); Principal, ENVIROMED Health Services, Inc., Novato, CA (1984-1999); Senior Advisor, Chevron Environmental Health Center, San Pablo, CA (1982-1984); Acting Chairperson of Clinical Pharmacology, Northport VA Hospital, Long Island, NY (1978-1983); Director of Clinical Pharmacology and Toxicology, School of Medicine, State University of New York, Stony Brook (1978-1983); Associate Professor of Pharmacology, State University of New York, Stony Brook (1977-1983); Associate Professor of Internal Medicine, State University of New York, Stony Brook (1975-1983) **Career Related:** Consultant in the Fields of Toxicology, Pharmacology, Environmental, Occupational and Internal Medicine (1984-2000); Board Member, Scientific Advisors, American Council on Science and Health; Scientific Review Panel, Hazardous Substances Database, National Library of Medicine **Creative Works:** Author, "Common Sense Toxics in the Workplace" (1991); **Membership:** Fellow, American College of Physicians; Fellow, American College of Clinical Pharmacology; American Association for the Advancement of Science; American Academy of Clinical Toxicology; Environmental Health and Safety Section, American Chemical Society; American College of Occupational Medicine; Occupational Medicine Section, American Industrial Hygiene Association; American College of Toxicology; American Society for Pharmacology and Experimental Therapeutics; Society of Toxicology; Western Occupational Medical Association **Business Address:** P.O. Box 578, Novato, CA, 94948

Deborah Ann Davenport

Title: Elementary School Educator **Industry:** Education/Educational Services **Company Name:** El Paso Independent School District **Date of Birth:** 08/12/1962 **Place of Birth:** Fort Still **State:** OK **Parents:** Andres Norte; Mary Helen Norte **Education:** MEd in Curriculum and Instruction, Grand Canyon University (2007); EdB, University of Texas at El Paso (1984) **Certifications:** Certified in Kindergarten Endorsement (1990) **Career:** Teacher, Aoy Elementary School (1994-2017); Teacher, Alamo School (1985-1994) **Awards:** Teacher of the Day, El Paso Times (1998) **Membership:** District VIII President, Alpha Delta Kappa (2018-Present); Secretary, Alpha Delta Kappa (2010-2012); Chapter President, Alpha Delta Kappa (2008-2010) **Marquis Who's Who Honors:** Albert Nelson Marquis Lifetime Achievement Award (2017); Distinguished Humanitarian (2017) **Why did you become involved in your profession or industry:** Eight other members of Ms. Davenport's family were in education. **Business Address:** PO Box 972031, El Paso, TX, 79997 **Shipping Address:** 8709 McFall Drive, El Paso, TX, 79925

Ernest Roy Davidson

Industry: Education/Educational Services **Date of Birth:** 10/12/1936 **Place of Birth:** Terre Haute **State:** IN **Parents:** Roy Emmette Davidson; Opal Ruth (Hugunin) Davidson **Marital Status:** Married **Spouse Name:** Reba Faye Minnich (1/27/1956) **Children:** Michael Collins; John Philip; Mark Ernest; Martha Ruth **Education:** Honorary PhD, Uppsala University (2000); Honorary DEng, Rose-Hulman Institute of Technology (1998); PhD, Indiana University (1961); BSc, Rose-Hulman Institute of Technology (1958) **Career:** Professor, University of Washington, Seattle (2002-Present); Chairman, Department of Chemistry, Indiana University, Bloomington (1999-2002); Distinguished Professor, Indiana University, Bloomington (1986-2002); Professor, Indiana University, Bloomington (1984-1986); Professor, University of Washington (1968-1984); Associate Professor, University of Washington (1965-1968); Assistant Professor of Chemistry, University of Washington (1962-1965); Postdoctoral Fellow, National Science Foundation, University of Wisconsin-Madison (1961-1962) **Career Related:** Adjunct Professor, University of North Carolina, Chapel Hill (2005-2009); Visiting Scholar, University of North Carolina (2002); Boys-Rahman Lecturer, Royal Society Chemistry (2002); Technion, Israel (1985); Visiting Professor, IMS, Japan (1984); Distinguished Visiting Professor, Ohio State University (1974-1975) **Creative Works:** Editor, Journal of Computational Physics (1975-1998); Editor, International Journal of Quantum Chemistry (1975-Present); Editor, Journal of Chemical Physics (1976-1978, 1998-Present); Editor, Chemical Physics Letters (1977-1984); Journal of the American Chemical Society (1978-1983); Editor, Journal of Physical Chemistry (1982-1990); Editor, Accounts of Chemical Research (1984-1992); Editor, Theoretica Chimica Acta (1985-1998); Editor, Chemical Reviews (1986-1998); Contributor, Numerous Articles on Density Matrices and Quantum Theory of Molecular Structure, Professional Journals **Awards:** National Medal of Science (2002); Schrodinger Medal (2001); Hirschfelder Prize in Theoretical Chemistry (1997-1998); Guggenheim Fellow (1974-1975); Laureate, l'Academie Internationale des Sciences Moleculaires Quantiques (1971); National Science Foundation Fellow, Indiana University (1961); Union Carbide Fellow, Rose-Hulman Institute of Technology (1958) **Membership:** Fellow, American Physical Society; Sigma Xi; National Academy of Sciences; American Chemical Society; American Academy of Arts and Sciences; Indiana Academy of Science; Phi Lambda Upsilon; Tau Beta Pi

Gretchen Davis Hammer

Title: Psychotherapist (Retired) **Industry:** Medicine & Health Care **Date of Birth:** 04/13/1934 **Place of Birth:** Lynn **State:** MA **Parents:** Laurence Frederic Davis; Helen Graves Davis **Marital Status:** Married **Spouse Name:** Kenneth Frederick Hammer (7/12/1958) **Children:** Karin Hammer-Williamson; Laurence; Karol; Peter; Richard **Education:** MEd, Lyndon State College (1985); BA, Lyndon State College (1974) **Certifications:** Certification, William Glasser Institute of Reality Therapy, State of California (1986); Certified in Experimental Education, Grades 1-12, State of Vermont (1974); Certified Psychotherapist, State of Vermont **Career:** Psychotherapist, Private Practice (1989-2005); School Psychologist, St. Johnsbury Academy (1992-1999); Director of Guidance, Concord School District (1991-1992); Director, Guidance, St. Johnsbury Public Schools (1982-1989); Director of Guidance, Concord School District (1979-1982) **Civic:** Honorary Board Member, Northeastern Vermont Regional Hospital (2012-Present); Board of Visitors, Lyndon State College (2001-Present); Member, William Glasser Institute-United States, California (1985-Present); Board Chair, Northeastern Vermont Regional Hospital (2004-2008); Board of Trustees, Northeastern Vermont Regional Hospital (2001-2012); Board Chair, Vermont Children's Aid Society (1975-1980); Founding Member, Youth Services, St. Johnsbury Community Justice Center (1975); Vermont Children's Aid Society (1972-2004); **Membership:** Board of Trustees, Northeastern Vermont Regional Hospital (2000-2011); American Counseling Association; Board Chair, Northeastern Vermont Regional Hospital; Honorary Board Chair, Northeastern Vermont Regional Hospital; Hospital Auxiliary; Caledonia County Republican Committee; Northeast Kingdom Restorative Justice Council **Marquis Who's Who Honors:** Albert Nelson Marquis Lifetime Achievement Award (2017) **To what do you attribute your success:** Ms. Hammer attributes her success to her supportive family, including her parents, husband, and children, as well as the excellent teachers and mentors she's had throughout her career. **Why did you become involved in your profession or industry:** Ms. Hammer became involved in her profession due to her love for children and her interest in helping them achieve a quality childhood. **What do you consider to be the highlight of your career:** Ms. Hammer considers the highlight of her career a reunion hosted for her by the Concord School District. All of the students she had counseled were part of the event. **Where will you be in five years:** In five years, Ms. Hammer intends to spend plenty of time with her grandchildren. **Shipping Address:** 210 Winter St., St. Johnsbury, VT, 05819

Peter Francis De Nicola

Title: Tax Executive **Industry:** Financial Services **Company Name:** Fujifilm Holdings America Corporation **Date of Birth:** 10/28/1954 **Place of Birth:** New York **State:** NY **Parents:** Louis Joseph De Nicola; Nancy Eleanor (Maddi) De Nicola **Marital Status:** Married **Spouse Name:** Charlotte Rebecca White (9/2/1998) **Education:** MBA, New York University (1978); BS, New York University (1976) **Certifications:** Certified Public Accountant, State of Connecticut; Certified Public Accountant, State of New York **Career:** Director of Taxes, FujiFilm Holdings America Corporation (2009-Present); Paul Harris Fellowship, Rotary International (2008); Group Tax Manager, FujiFilm Holdings America Corporation (2007-2009); Tax Manager, FujiFilm USA, Inc., Valhalla, NY (1999-2006); Associate Tax Manager, FujiFilm USA, Inc. (Now FujiFilm Holdings America Corporation) (1994-1998); Senior Tax Analyst, FujiFilm USA, Inc. (Now FujiFilm Holdings America Corporation) (1991-1993); Tax Manager, Siemens AG (1989-1991); Director of Taxes, AI International Corporation (1985-1988); Tax Manager, Emery Air Freight Corporation (1983-1985); Tax Manager, General Signal Corporation (1981-1983); Accountant, Main Hurdman (1978-1981); Founder, P.F. DeNicola, Inc. (1976-1984); **Career Related:** Iconographic Consultant, A.P. Giannini Exhibit, Rome, Italy (2004) **Creative Works:** Author, "Legal Liability of Tax Return Preparers" (1978); Contributor, "Palm Springs Weekend"; Contributor, Articles to Professional Journals; Contributor, Chapters to Books **Awards:** Rotarian of Year, Rotary International (2006); **Membership:** Treasurer, Financial Executives International (2017-Present); Director, Financial Executives International (2016-Present); Treasurer, District 7230, Rotary International (2015-Present); Director, Tax Executives Institute (2014-Present); President, Stamford Tax Association (2012-Present); Regional Vice President, Tax Executives Institute (2014-2015); Treasurer, Hudson Valley Chapter, Junior Achievement USA (2011-2012); Director, Hudson Valley Chapter, Junior Achievement USA (2009-2015); President, Tax Executives Institute, Westchester-Fairfield Chapter (2008-2009); Director, Mount Pleasant Rotary Foundation, Rotary International (2007-2016); **To what do you attribute your success:** Mr. De Nicola attributes his success to the work ethic instilled in him by his parents. **Why did you become involved in your profession or industry:** Mr. De Nicola became involved in his profession because he developed an interest in taxation as an undergraduate accounting student. **What do you consider to be the highlight of your career:** One of the highlights of Mr. De Nicola's career has been becoming head of tax for a global Fortune 500 company. **Business Address:** PO Box 4637, Stamford, CT, 06907

Thomas Deming

Title: Publishing Executive **Industry:** Publishing **Company Name:** Deming Fund **Date of Birth:** 05/04/1954 **Place of Birth:** Chicago **State:** IL/USA **Parents:** Anthony A. Dziurdzik; Josephine Andracki Dziurdzik **Marital Status:** Married **Spouse Name:** Mary Ann Jadowic (1976) **Children:** Mark Thomas; Emily Marie; William Joseph **Education:** MBA, DePaul University (1986); BS in Accounting, DePaul University (1976) **Certifications:** Certified Public Accountant, State of Illinois **Career:** Co-chief Executive Officer, Co-founder, Deming Fund (Now Money for Women/Barbara Deming Memorial Fund, Inc.) (2008-Present); Corporate Vice President, McDougal Littell Parent Co., Houghton Mifflin (Now Houghton Mifflin Harcourt) (1996-2007); Vice President of Financial Planning & Operations, McDougal Littell Publications, Inc., Evanston, IL (1996-2007); Vice President of Finance, Harper Collins Publishers (1995-1996); Vice President, Treasurer, Harper Collins Publishers (1992-1995); Vice President, Treasurer, Macmillan/McGraw-Hill School Publications Co. (Now McGraw-Hill Education), Lake Forest, IL (1991-1992); Treasurer, Macmillan/McGraw-Hill School Publishing Company (Now McGraw-Hill Education), Lake Forest, IL (1990-1991); Vice President of Finance and Administration, Scott, Foresman & Co., Glenview, IL (1990); Vice President of Finance, Scott, Foresman & Co., Glenview, IL (1988-1989); Vice President, Controller, Scott, Foresman & Co., Glenview, IL (1983-1988); Assistant Controller, Scott, Foresman & Co., Glenview, IL (1981-1983); Accountant, Arthur Andersen & Co., Chicago, IL (1975-1981) **Membership:** Financial Executives International; AICPA, Association of International Certified Professional Accountants; Illinois CPA Society; Ledger & Quill, DePaul University; Beta Alpha Psi; Delta Mu Delta; Beta Gamma Sigma **Hobbies:** Golf; Target shooting **Shipping Address:** 230 S Prairie Ave, Arlington Heights, IL, 60005

Suzanne Denk

Title: Owner, President, Co-Author **Industry:** Health, Wellness and Fitness **Company Name:** Psychological Wellness Center, Inc.

Florence L. Denmark-Wesner, PhD

Title: Distinguished Professor **Industry:** Education/Educational Services **Company Name:** The City University of New York **Date of Birth:** 01/28/1931 **Place of Birth:** Philadelphia **State:** PA/USA **Parents:** Morris Levin; Minnerva (Sharkis) Levin **Marital Status:** Married **Spouse Name:** Robert W. Wesner; Stanley J. Denmark (6/7/1953, Divorced 1973) **Children:** Valerie; Pamela (Deceased); Richard **Education:** DHL, Alleghany College (1998); Doctor of Psychology, Illinois School of Professional Psychology, Argosy University (1995); LHD, Cedar Crest College (1988); LHD, Massachusetts School of Professional Psychology (Now William James College) (1985); PhD, University of Pennsylvania (1958); AM, University of Pennsylvania (1954); AB, University of Pennsylvania (1952) **Career:** Adjunct Professor, The City University of New York (1990-Present); Robert Scott Pace Distinguished Professor of Psychology, Pace University (1988-Present); Chairman, Psychology Department, Pace University (1988-Present); Professor of Psychology, The City University of New York (1984-1990); Affiliate, Doctoral Faculty of Psychology, The City University of New York (1967-1987); Professor, The City University of New York (1964-1990); Instructor, The City University of New York (1964-1990); Lecturer in Psychology, The City University of New York (1959-1966) **Creative Works:** Co-Editor, "Engendering Psychology" (2000); Co-Editor, "Females and Autonomy: A Life-Span Perspective" (1999); Co-Editor, "Violence and the Prevention of Violence" (1995); Editor, "Psychology: The Leading Edge Into the Unknown" (1980); Co-Editor, "Women: Dependent or Independent Variable?" (1975) **Awards:** Distinguished Contributions to International Psychology Award, American Psychological Association (1999); Inter-American Award, Inter-American Society of Psychology, Inc. (1997); Distinguished Contributions to International Psychology Award, American Psychological Association (1996); Distinguished Career Award, The Association for Women in Psychology (1996); Margaret Floy Washburn Award, New York State Psychological Association (1996) **Membership:** Psychology Advisory Committee, The New York Academy of Sciences (1971-Present); President, Division 52, American Psychological Association (1999); Committee on Accreditation, American Psychological Association (1998); President, Academy Division, New York State Psychological Association (1990-1991); Board of Directors, Eastern Psychological Association (1988-1991); President, Division of Social Psychology, New York State Psychological Association (1989-1990); President, International Council of Psychologists (1989-1990) **Marquis Who's Who Honors:** Distinguished Humanitarian (2017) **Shipping Address:** 301 E 87th St., Apt 21A, New York, NY, 10128

Richard Arthur DeRemee

Title: Internist, Educator, Researcher (Retired) **Industry:** Medicine & Health Care **Date of Birth:** 07/04/1933 **Place of Birth:** Red Wing **State:** MN **Parents:** Arthur Eugene DeRemee; Anna Helen (Vinquist) DeRemee **Marital Status:** Married **Spouse Name:** E. Lucille Fogelstrom (3/17/1956) **Children:** Bo Arthur (1963); Brita Lyn (1961); Lisa Carol (1959) **Education:** Resident in Internal Medicine and Pulmonary Disease, Mayo Clinic, Mayo Foundation for Medical Education and Research, Rochester, MN (1962-1966); Intern, William Beaumont General Hospital, El Paso, TX (1959-1960); MD, University of Minnesota (1959); BS, University of Minnesota (1959); BA, Gustavus Adolphus College (1955) **Certifications:** Diplomate, American Board of Internal Medicine; Diplomate in Pulmonary Disease, American Board of Internal Medicine **Career:** Friedrich Wegener Memorial Lecturer, Lübeck, Germany (1992); Professor of Medicine, Mayo Medical School, Mayo Foundation for Medical Education and Research, Rochester, MN (1983-1996); Associate Professor of Medicine, Mayo Medical School, Mayo Foundation for Medical Education and Research, Rochester, MN (1977-1983) **Career Related:** Consultant in Internal Medicine and Pulmonary Disease, Mayo Clinic, Mayo Foundation for Medical Education and Research, Rochester, MN (1966-1996) **Civic:** President, South Woodley Civic Association, Virginia (1960-1962) **Military Service:** Captain, Medical Corps, U.S. Army (1959-1962) **Creative Works:** Author, "Once Upon a Jet Plane" (2017); Poet, "A String of Pearls" (2014); Author, "From Boys to Men: The Summer of 54" (2012); Author, "From a Solitary Room: Stories and Essays" (2008); Co-Author, "The Mick-Rick Debates: Controversies in Contemporary Christianity" (2007); Co-Author, "Mick-Rick Essays on the Sacred & Profane" (2007); Author, "Time and the Mystery of Consciousness" (2003); Contributor, More than 200 Scientific Papers **Awards:** Recipient, Distinguished Alumni Award, Mayo Clinic, Mayo Foundation for Medical Education and Research (2013); Recipient, Sesquicentennial Award, Gustavus Adolphus College (2012); Honoree, Named to Red Wing High School Wall of Honor (2000); Recipient, Alumni Citation, Gustavus Adolphus College (1982); Recipient, Judson Daland Travel Award, Mayo Foundation (1966); Recipient, Certificate of Achievement, US Army (1962) **Membership:** President, Mayo Chapter, Sigma Xi (1988-1989); President, Gustavus Adolphus Alumni Association (1979-1980) **Political Affiliations:** Independent **Religion:** Lutheran **Shipping Address:** 2209 5th Ave NE, Rochester, MN, 55906

Louise Fay Despres

Title: Secondary School Educator **Industry:** Education/Educational Services **Company Name:** New Canaan High School **Date of Birth:** 02/29/1944 **Place of Birth:** New Haven **State:** CT **Parents:** Frederick Taylor Fay; Ruth Jean (Lowery) Fay **Marital Status:** Married **Spouse Name:** Robert Leon Despres (2/16/1974) **Children:** Frederick Leon **Education:** MA in French, Middlebury College, Paris, France (1973); MA in Teaching French, Brown University (1968); BA in French, Connecticut College for Women (Now Connecticut College) (1966); Coursework in Organ, Studied with Nadia Boulanger, American School of Music (Now Fontainebleau Schools, Fontainebleau Associations), Fontainebleau, France (1965) **Certifications:** Certified Spanish Teacher, Secondary Level (7-12), State of Connecticut (1980-2012); Certified French Teacher, Secondary Level (7-12), State of Connecticut (1967-2012) **Career:** Accepted Teacher, New Advanced Placement French Audit (2011-2012); Substitute Teacher, Spanish, New Canaan High School (2011-2012); Teacher, Comparative Literature, New Canaan High School (2011-2012); Mentor to New Teacher, New Canaan High School (2009-2010); Independent Study Committee, New Canaan High School (2008-2011); Independent Study Advisor, New Canaan High School (2007-2011); **Civic:** Volunteer, Fellowship Committee, Hyde Park Union Church (2017-Present); Housing and Hunger Committee, Williamsburg Presbyterian Church (2015-Present); **Creative Works:** Contributor, Cultural Booklet, "French in Connecticut" (1970) **Awards:** Pegasus Pride Award, Connecticut Council of Language Teachers (2001); Advanced Placement Teacher Recognition Award, New England College Board (1994) **Membership:** President, Chapter BQ, P.E.O. Sisterhood, Williamsburg, VA (2016-2018) **Marquis Who's Who Honors:** Albert Nelson Marquis Lifetime Achievement Award (2017); Distinguished Humanitarian (2017) **To what do you attribute your success:** Mrs. Despres attributes her success to her late mentor, Rebecca Satterlee Robbins, who taught French at New Haven High School in Connecticut. **Why did you become involved in your profession or industry:** Mrs. Despres became involved in teaching because she had a love for it since early childhood. Her mother gave her French lessons before her school offered them, and she loved the language so much that it became her career. Both her father and aunt were teachers. **What do you consider to be the highlight of your career:** A highlight of Mrs. Despres' career was teaching Advanced Placement French, a college-level class, for more than 30 years. **Where will you be in five years:** In five years, Mrs. Despres hopes to be a senior-citizen volunteer in Williamsburg, Virginia. **Shipping Address:** 5844 S Stony Island Avenue, 7H, Chicago, IL, 60637

Terry Lee DeVassie

Title: Newspaper Executive (Retired) **Industry:** Business Management/Business Services **Company Name:** Preston-Strat Investments **Date of Birth:** 10/27/1939 **Place of Birth:** Columbus **State:** OH **Parents:** Robert William DeVassie; Laura Belle (VanOrsdel) DeVassie **Marital Status:** Married **Spouse Name:** Lola Faye Sandifer (6/21/1964) **Children:** Trevor Lane; Thad Lamont **Education:** BA in Industrial Design and Advertising, The Ohio State University (1964) **Career:** Partner, Preston-Strat Investments (1993-Present); Managing Partner, WW Circulation Consulting Group (2002-2005); President, Creative Inserts Co. (1992-2006); Chief Executive Officer, Creative Inserts Co. (1992-2006); Assistant Circulation Director, Columbus Dispatch (1981-2001); Circulation Manager, Columbus Dispatch (1979-1981); State Circulation Manager, Columbus Dispatch (1977-1979); Assistant to Circulation Director, Columbus Dispatch (1971-1977); Division Manager, Columbus Dispatch (1970-1971); Clerk, Columbus Dispatch (1957-1970); Station Manager, Columbus Dispatch (1957-1970) **Career Related:** Architect-Designer, Eagle Real Estate/Builders, Columbus, OH (1968-1970); Extrusion Designer, Plaskolite, Inc., Columbus, OH (1968-1969); Owner, TLD Design, Columbus, OH (1964-1969); Designer, TLD Design, Columbus, OH (1964-1969); Public Speaker; Newspaper Circulation Management; Hospital Information Services **Civic:** Director, Shriners Hospital for Children, Ohio Donor Relations Committee, Cincinnati, OH (2005-Present); Member, Board of Governors, Simon Kenton Council, Boy Scouts of America (1998-2002) **Creative Works:** Designer, Drive-up Newspaper Rack; Patentee, Graphic Inserts for Newspaper Racks **Awards:** President's Award, International Circulation Managers Association (1992); President's Award, Ohio News Media Association (1986); President's Award, Ohio News Media Association (1984); Founder President's Award, Ohio Circulation News Media Association (1982) **Membership:** Chairman of the Board, Ohio Masonic Home Foundation (2012-Present); Trustee, Benevolent Foundation, Ohio Masonic Home, Shriners (2007-Present); Board Chairman, Shriners (2007-Present); Emeritus Member, Board of Trustees, Shriners (2005-Present); Imperial Public Relations Committee, Shriners (1995-2012); Chairman, Endowment, Wills and Gifts, Shriners Hospital for Children, Shriners (1998-2000) **Marquis Who's Who Honors:** Distinguished Humanitarian (2017) **Hobbies:** Landscaping; Architecture; Golf **Political Affiliations:** Republican **Religion:** Methodist **Shipping Address:** 6330 Grassmere Dr, Westerville, OH, 43082

Philip A. Digati

Title: Lawyer **Industry:** Law and Legal Services **Company Name:** Philip A. Digati, P.A. **Date of Birth:** 05/19/1933 **Place of Birth:** Brooklyn **State:** NY **Parents:** Peter Digati; Rose Digati **Marital Status:** Widowed **Spouse Name:** Rosemarie (Deceased) **Children:** Elizabeth; Matthew **Education:** JD, Brooklyn Law School (1962); Undergraduate Coursework, U.S. Merchant Marine Academy; Undergraduate Coursework, St. John's University; Undergraduate Coursework, St. Francis Preparatory School **Career:** Lawyer, Philip A. Digati, P.A., Fort Lauderdale, FL; Staff/Trial Attorney, Royal Globe Insurance Company; Independent Real Estate Title Closer, Title Guaranty Company; Pioneer Title Insurance Company (Now Pioneer Title Agency); Security Title Guaranty Company, New York; Independent Trial Counsel for Insurance Companies in NY and FL **Career Related:** Speaker, Various Legal Seminars **Civic:** Vice President, Hollywood Hills Homeowners Association; Lay Director, Catholic Cursillo Movement in the Archdioceses of Miami; Eucharist Minister, Nativity Catholic Church, Hollywood, FL **Military Service:** With, U.S. Army (1954-1956); With, U.S. Army National Guard (1952-1954); With, U.S. Naval Reserve (1951-1952) **Membership:** New York State Bar Association; Bay Ridge Lawyers Association; Columbian Lawyers Association, Inc.; The Florida Bar; Broward County Bar Association; Broward County Trial Lawyers Association; Knights of Columbus; Boy Scouts of America; The Optimates Society; Third Order of Saint Francis; Legion of Mary; The American Legion **Bar Admissions:** The Florida Bar (1975); New York State Bar Association (1962) **To what do you attribute your success:** Mr. Digati attributes his success to his upbringing and educational opportunities. **Why did you become involved in your profession or industry:** Mr. Digati became involved in his profession because as a young man he worked at an insurance company where he was exposed to lawyers. This sparked his interest in law and his desire to seek justice and fairness for all. **What do you consider to be the highlight of your career:** The highlight of Mr. Digati's career was reaching a successful trial verdict in a very difficult case. **Where will you be in five years:** In five years, Mr. Digati intends to continue practicing law. **Religion:** Roman Catholic **Business Address:** 633 SE 3rd Ave Ste 4F, Philip A. Digati, P.A., Fort Lauderdale, FL, 33301

Michael A. DiTeresa

Title: Physician, Internist **Industry:** Medicine & Health Care **Company Name:** Tomball Adult Internal Medicine **Education:** MD in Internal Medicine, The University of Texas Southwestern Medical Center, Dallas, Texas (2000); Bachelor's Degree, Rice University, Magna Cum Laude (1996); Residency in Internal Medicine, Baylor Health Care System **Career:** Physician, Tomball Adult Internal Medicine **Awards:** On-Time Doctor Award (2014); Compassionate Doctor Award (2013); Compassionate Doctor Recognition (2009-2013); On-Time Doctor Award (2008); Patients' Choice Award (2008) **To what do you attribute your success:** Dr. DiTeresa attributes his success to his focus on his patients and remaining as humble as possible. **Why did you become involved in your profession or industry:** Dr. DiTeresa became involved in this profession because his seventh-grade biology teacher sparked his interest in medicine and health care. **Where will you be in five years:** In five years, Dr. DiTeresa intends to streamline his practice and treat younger patients. **Hobbies:** Reading; Working on antique cars; Traveling **Business Address:** 425 Holderrieth Blvd Ste 209, Tomball, TX, 77375 **Shipping Address:** 6103 Coral Ridge Rd, Houston, TX, 77069 **Website:** https://www.linkedin.com/in/michael-diteresa-7b6ab863

Michael Bernard Dompierre

Title: Assistant Vice President for Academic Affairs **Industry:** Education/Educational Services **Company Name:** St. Charles Community College **Date of Birth:** 05/07/1953 **Place of Birth:** Negaunee **State:** MI **Parents:** Bernard A. Dompierre; Ursula (nee Messner) Dompierre **Marital Status:** Widowed **Spouse Name:** Jo Anne C. Rocklage **Children:** Amanda Rocklage-Dompierre; David Rocklage-Dompierre **Education:** PhD, University of Michigan, Ann Arbor, MI (1981); MA, University of Michigan, Ann Arbor, MI (1978); BS, Northern Michigan University, Marquette, MI (1975) **Career:** Assistant Vice President, Academic Affairs, St. Charles Community College, Cottleville, MO (1989-Present); Assistant Professor, Economics, University of Missouri (1982-1989); Instructor, Economics, University of Missouri (1980-1982) **Career Related:** Ex-officio Member, Curriculum Committee; Administer, National and State Grant Funding for Career and Technical Programs **Membership:** Association for Career & Technical Education; Missouri Community College Association; Missouri Association for Career and Technical Education; MCCTA **Marquis Who's Who Honors:** Distinguished Humanitarian (2017) **Business Address:** St. Charles Community College, Cottleville, MO, 63376 **Shipping Address:** 119 Long And Winding Road, Saint Peters, MO, 63376

Dewey L. Douglas

Title: Assistant Professor **Industry:** Education/Educational Services **Company Name:** William Carey University **Parents:** Dewey Douglas; Evelyn Douglas **Marital Status:** Married **Spouse Name:** Jill Douglas **Children:** Jessica **Education:** MFA, The University of Southern Mississippi (2006); BFA, The University of Southern Mississippi (1975); AA, Copiah-Lincoln Community College, Wesson, MS (1972) **Career:** Assistant Professor, Department of Theatre and Communication, William Carey University, Hattiesburg, MS (2006-Present); Graduate Instructor, Department of Theatre and Dance, University of Southern Mississippi (2005-2006); Instructor, Northern Arizona University, Flagstaff, AZ (1998-2002); Technology Director, Northern Arizona University, Flagstaff, AZ (1998-2002); Technology Instructor, Northern Arizona University, Flagstaff, AZ (1998-2002); Properties Artisan, South Coast Repertory, Costa Mesa, CA (1994-1997) **Career Related:** Affiliate, Arizona TheatreWorks, Flagstaff, AZ (1997-1998); Founding Member, Dramaturge, Playwright-in-Residence, Babylonian Productions, Hollywood, CA (1995); Technical Director, Babylonian Productions, Hollywood, CA (1995); Scenic Carpenter, "Divas: Simply Singing," Hollywood, Los Angeles, CA (1994-1996); Staff Lighting Technician, Staff Scenic Carpenter, South Coast Repertory, Costa Mesa, CA (1991-1997); Freelance Technician (1991-1993); Affiliate, Spectrum DesignStudios, Fullerton, CA (1988-1989) **Creative Works:** Playwright, "A Cowboy Christmas Carol"; Playwright, "The Gospel"; Playwright, "Old African"; Playwright, "Ajax"; Playwright, "Whore of Babylon"; Playwright, "The Princes and the Dragon"; Designer, Various Productions; Technical Worker, Various Productions; Playwright, Various Productions; Director, Various Productions; Actor, Various Productions; Author, Short Stories; Author, Poems; Author, Saturday Afternoon Literary Journal **Awards:** Excellence in Directing Award, Kennedy Center American College Theatre Festival Region IV (2016); Excellence in Scenic Design Award, Kennedy Center American College Theatre Festival Region IV (2014); Excellence in Directing Award, Kennedy Center American College Theatre Festival Region IV (2011-2013); Named Scenic Design Teaching Artist of the Year, Kennedy Center American College Theatre Festival Region IV (2010); Excellence in Directing Award, Kennedy Center American College Theatre Festival Region IV (2009); Excellence in Technology Award, Kennedy Center American College Theatre Festival Region IV (2007-2008); Honoree, National Chancellor's List of Graduate Students (2004-2006) **Marquis Who's Who Honors:** Albert Nelson Marquis Lifetime Achievement Award (2017); Distinguished Humanitarian (2017) **Shipping Address:** 29 Sandy Ln, Hattiesburg, MS, 39402

Carol Dovan-van Schenkhof

Title: International Opera Singer, Voice Teacher **Industry:** Education/Educational Services **Company Name:** Carol Dovan-van Schenkhof Studios **Date of Birth:** 04/20/1942 **Place of Birth:** Reading **State:** PA/USA **Parents:** Harry Hammond Dougherty; Magdalen Mary Doviak **Marital Status:** Married **Spouse Name:** Mark Anton van Schenkhof (2/18/1995); John William Heierman (9/4/196, Divorced 7/6/1986) **Education:** Coursework in Vocal Pedagogy, Westminster Choir College, Rider University (2004); Coursework in Vocal Pedagogy, Oberlin College and Conservatory (2000-2002); Coursework in Vocal Pedagogy, Westminster Choir College, Rider University (1992, 1996); Coursework, Mannes School of Music, The New School (1980); Coursework, Hunter College (1971); MA in Ethno-Musicology, Hunter College (1970); Coursework, The Juilliard School (1964-1965, 1970); BA, Chatham University (1964) **Career:** Career Voice Teacher, Carol Dovan-van Schenkhof Studios, Port Washington, NY (1980-Present); Voice Instructor, Fordham University (2010); Voice Teacher, Stony Brook University (1998-1999); Professional Coordinator, Music Advisory Council, Port Washington Public Library (1985-1987); Opera Lecturer, C.W. Post Campus, Long Island University (1982-1983); Visiting Artist, Lecturer, Escola de Música do Conservatório Nacional, Lisbon, Portugal (1976); Visiting Artist, Lecturer, Nacional de Radiodifusão (Now Rádio e Televisão de Portugal) (1976); Visiting Artist, Lecturer, Ewha Women's University, Seoul, Korea (1975); Resource Professional, Lincoln Center for the Performing Arts (1972); Voice Teacher, School of Music, Chatham University (1964) **Creative Works:** Performer, Amicus Quartet (1987-1993); Performer, Festival Chamber Players (1985); Performer, With Composer Jeanne Singer, New York City Recitals (1983-1987) **Awards:** Scholar, Aspen Music Festival and School (1964); Recipient, First Place Award, Youth Auditions, Pittsburgh Concert Society (1963); Voice Scholarships, Music Festival and School Auditions, Chautauqua Institution (1962-1963); Recipient, First Place Award, Youth Auditions, Pittsburgh Concert Society (1962); Recipient, First Place Award, Competition, Pittsburgh Musicians Union (1962) **Membership:** Executive Board, Associated Music Teachers League (1994-Present); New York Singing Teachers' Association, Inc.; American Guild of Musical Artists; Adjudicator, National Association for Music Education; Adjudicator, Eastern Region Auditions, National Association of Teachers of Singing **Marquis Who's Who Honors:** Albert Nelson Marquis Lifetime Achievement Award (2017); Distinguished Humanitarian (2017) **Religion:** Episcopalian **Shipping Address:** 6 Hillview Ave, Port Washington, NY, 11050

Joseph Peter Drennan

Title: Attorney, Counsellor at Law **Industry:** Law and Legal Services **Date of Birth:** 04/15/1956 **Place of Birth:** Albany **State:** NY **Parents:** Richard Peter Drennan; Ann Marie (Conlon) Drennan **Marital Status:** Married **Spouse Name:** Adriana Sonia Miramontes (9/26/1987) **Children:** Patricia Solange; Monica Adriana; Michael Robert, Jr. **Education:** JD, Catholic University of America, Washington, DC (1981); BA in Political Science, University of Richmond (1978) **Career:** Private Practice, Washington, DC and Alexandria, VA (1981) **Career Related:** Adjunct Faculty Member, University of Baltimore (2007-2013); Adjunct Faculty Member, Germanna Community College, Fredericksburg, VA (1995-2000); Teacher, Criminal Justice Law Practice and Procedure, Health Care Law, Civil Rights Law, Constitutional Law, Copyright and Trademark Litigation, Bankruptcy Law, Defense of Claims Under the Alien Tort Claims Act; Litigation on Behalf of Victims of State Sponsored Terrorism **Membership:** Association of Trial Lawyers of America (Now American Association for Justice); National Association of Criminal Defense Attorneys; National Legal Aid & Defense Association; District of Columbia Bar; American Bankruptcy Institute; American Bar Association; Virginia Trial Lawyers Association; Trial Lawyers Association of Metropolitan Washington, DC; Alexandria Bar Association; Lifetime Member, Waterville Historical Society, New York; Oneida County Historical Society, New York; NAACP; Cleveland Club of Washington, DC; Bar Association of the District of Columbia **Bar Admissions:** U.S. Supreme Court (2016); U.S. District Court, Western District, State of West Virginia (2013); U.S. Bankruptcy Court, Eastern District, State of Virginia (1991); U.S. District Court, State of Maryland (1990); Fourth Circuit, U.S. Court of Appeals (1987); U.S. District Court, Eastern District, State of Virginia (1987); District of Columbia Circuit, U.S. Court of Appeals (1984); State of Virginia (1984); Federal Circuit, U.S. Court of Appeals (1983); U.S. District Court, District of Columbia (1983); District of Columbia (1981) **To what do you attribute your success:** Mr. Drennan attributes his success to his education and the support of his mentors. **Why did you become involved in your profession or industry:** Mr. Drennan became involved in his profession because he always wanted to be an attorney. In fact, when he was in second grade, a Sister of the Order of Saint Joseph called his mother and noted that he would most certainly grow up to be an exceptional lawyer. **Business Address:** 218 N Lee Street, Alexandria, VA, 22314

Amy Dryman

Industry: Medicine & Health Care **State:** NY/USA **Parents:** Sylvia Dryman; Irving Dryman **Education:** DSc, Johns Hopkins University School of Hygiene and Public Health, (Now Johns Hopkins Bloomberg School of Public Health), Baltimore, MD (1987); BA, Yale University, New Haven, CT (1981) **Career:** Manager, Pfizer, Inc., New York, NY (2001-2004); Assistant Director, Pfizer, Inc. (1999-2001); Project Leader, Pfizer, Inc. (1993-1999); Consultant, Pfizer, Inc. (1993); Research Scientist, Research Associate, Johns Hopkins Bloomberg School of Public Health, Baltimore, MD (1987-1988) **Civic:** Charities Relevant to Professional and Personal Concerns **Creative Works:** Contributor, Research Papers to Professional Journals **Membership:** American Statistical Association; Alpha Chapter, Delta Omega Honorary Society in Public Health; The New York Academy of Sciences; American Public Health Association; Drug Information Association **Marquis Who's Who Honors:** Albert Nelson Marquis Lifetime Achievement Award (2017) **Why did you become involved in your profession or industry:** Dr. Dryman became involved in her profession because she wanted to contribute to an improved understanding of risk factors for mental disorders. **Hobbies:** News; Watching Sports; Exercise **Shipping Address:** 21242 16th Ave, Bayside, NY, 11360 **Website:** http://www.amy-dryman.com

Arthur Dudley

Title: Lawyer **Industry:** Law and Legal Services **Company Name:** Butzel Long **Date of Birth:** 06/06/1951 **Place of Birth:** Detroit **State:** MI **Parents:** Arthur Dudley; Lethia Mae (Green) Dudley **Marital Status:** Married **Spouse Name:** Doreen Shepherd (6/24/1972) **Children:** A. Frederick; Alexander C. **Education:** JD, Yale University (1977); MA, Yale University (1977); BA, Harvard College, Cum Laude (1973) **Career:** Board President, Martin Luther King Jr. Education Center Academy, MI (1995-Present); Shareholder, Butzel Long, Professional Corporation, MI (1988-Present); Partner, Burnham, Connolly, Oesterle and Henry, MI (1987-1988); Shareholder, Donovan, Hammond, Ziegelman, Roach and Sotiroff, Professional Corporation, MI (1983-1987); Associate, Coudert Brothers LLP, NY (1977-1983); Guest Lecturer, Kingdom Business Institute, MI **Career Related:** Adjunct Professor, College Business Administration, University of Detroit Mercy (1990-1995); Securities Advisory Committee, Corporate and Securities Bureau, Michigan Department of Commerce **Civic:** Board Secretary, Michigan Minority Supplier Development Council (2013-Present); Board of Directors, Detroit Employment Solutions Corporation (2012-Present); Director, Michigan Minority Supplier Development Council (2012-Present); Board Chairman, Legal Aid and Defender Association (2011-Present); Director, Altimetrik Corporation (2000-Present); Professional Services Chairman, Michigan Minority Supplier Development Council (1994-2005); Board Secretary, Michigan Minority Supplier Development Council (2007-2010); Director, Legal Aid and Defender Association (2002-2009); Director, One Stop Capital Shop (2000-2003); Board Chairman, One Stop Capital Shop (2000-2003); Ann Arbor Director, Detroit Urban League (1995-2001); Vice Chairman, Detroit Urban League (1995-2001); **Creative Works:** Editor, "Yale Studies in Public World Order" **Awards:** Named One of Michigan Super Lawyers M & A (2006-2015); Named to Business Top Lawyers in Metro Detroit (2011-2012); Award, Chambers USA American, Leading Lawyers Business Corporation (2009-2012); Seven Gems Award, MMBDC Professional Service Section (2006); Named to Best Lawyers in America, Corporate Law (2005-2015); Hampton Award, Black United Fund (2005); National Merit Scholar **Membership:** ABA; Former Co-chairman, State Regulation Securities Committee, Business Law Section, State Bar of Michigan; **Bar Admissions:** Admitted to Practice, State Bar of Michigan (1983) **Marquis Who's Who Honors:** Albert Nelson Marquis Lifetime Achievement Award (2017) **Business Address:** 150 W Jefferson Ave., Ste 100, Detroit, MI, 48226 **Website:** https://www.butzel.com/attorneys-detail/arthur-dudley.html

Stanley Dudrick

Title: Surgeon **Industry:** Medicine & Health Care **Company Name:** St. Mary's Hospital **Date of Birth:** 04/09/1935 **Place of Birth:** Nanticoke **State:** PA **Parents:** Stanley Francis Dudrick; Stephania Mary (Jachimczak) Dudrick **Marital Status:** Married **Spouse Name:** Theresa M. Keen (6/14/1958) **Children:** Susan Marie; Paul Stanley; Carolyn Mary; Stanley Jonathan; Holly Anne; Anne Theresa **Education:** Honorary MA, Yale University (1999); MD, University of Pennsylvania (1961); BS, Franklin and Marshall College, Cum Laude (1957) **Certifications:** Certification, Board of Nutrition Specialists (2008); Diplomate, American Board of Surgery (1968) **Career:** Professor, Surgery, Commonwealth Medical College, Scranton, PA (2013-Present); Consulting Surgeon, Honorary Staff, Pennsylvania Hospital, Philadelphia, PA (2012-Present); Adjunct Clinical Professor, Temple University School Medical, Philadelphia, PA (2012-Present); Professor, Surgery Emeritus, Yale University School of Medicine, New Haven, CT (2012-Present); Honorary Staff, Yale New Haven Hospital, New Haven, CT (2011-Present); Medical Director, Physician Assistant, Misericordia University, Dallas, PA (2011-Present); Consulting Surgeon, Bridgeport Hospital, Yale University, New Haven Health Systems (2009-Present); Director Emeritus, St. Mary's Hospital, Waterbury, CT (2008-Present); Adjunct Clinical Professor, Surgery, Quinnipiac University, Hamden, CT (1996-Present); Consulting Surgeon, Yale New Haven Hospital, New Haven, CT (2005-2011) **Career Related:** Academy Practice Specializing in Surgery, Dallas, TX (2012-Present); Professor, Yale University, New Haven, CT (1999-Present); Adjunct Professor, Quinnipiac University (1996-Present); Academy Practice Specializing in Surgery, Waterbury, CT (1994-Present); Honorary Surgery Staff, Pennsylvania Hospital, Philadelphia, PA (1991-Present); Chairman, Department of Surgery, University of Pennsylvania (2004-2008); Academy Practice Specializing in Surgery, Bridgeport, CT (2002-2013); Director, Surgery Program, St. Mary's Hospital, Waterbury, CT; Director, Surgery Program, University of Pennsylvania (2002-2008); Associate Chairman, Department of Surgery, University of Pennsylvania (2002-2004) **Civic:** Trustee, Franklin and Marshall College (1985-Present); Board Member, Numerous Organizations **Creative Works:** Editorial Board Member, Numerous Publications; Editor, Numerous Publications **Awards:** Numerous Awards in Field **Membership:** Several Organizations **Business Address:** 56 Franklin Street, Waterbury, CT, 06706 **Shipping Address:** 40 Beecher Street, Naugatuck, CT, 06770

Fortune Anthony Dugan

Industry: Medicine & Health Care **Date of Birth:** 08/31/1944 **Place of Birth:** Dallas **State:** TX/USA **Parents:** Albert Francis Dugan; Ruth (Welsch) Dugan **Marital Status:** Married **Spouse Name:** Sandra Mary Duracher, (1968); **Children:** Fortune Anthony, Bridget Ann **Education:** Fellow in Cardiology, Duke University Medical Center, Durham, NC (1973-1975); Resident in Medicine, Louisiana State University Division, Charity Hospital of Louisiana, New Orleans, LA (1969-1971); Straight Medical Intern, Louisiana State University Division, Charity Hospital of Louisiana, New Orleans, LA (1968-1969); MD, Louisiana State University, New Orleans, LA (1968); BS, Louisiana State University, Cum Laude, New Orleans, LA (1966) **Certifications:** Diplomate in Internal Medicine and Cardiovascular Disease, American Board of Internal Medicine; Board Certified in Interventional Cardiology **Career:** Medical Director, Cardiac Catheterization Laboratory, East Jefferson General Hospital (1999-Present); Medical Director, Cardiac Catheterization Laboratory, Tulane University School of Medicine, New Orleans, LA (1998-Present); Medical Director, Cardiology, East Jefferson General Hospital, New Orleans, LA (1998-Present); Member, Staff, Department of Cardiology, East Jefferson General Hospital, Metairie, LA (1979-Present); Clinical Associate Professor, Department of Medicine, Tulane University School of Medicine, New Orleans, LA (1979-1985) **Career Related:** Visiting Staff, Charity Hospital, New Orleans, LA (1979-1985) **Military Service:** Major, U.S. Army (1971-1973) **Creative Works:** Contributor, Articles, Professional Journals **Awards:** Keith Collins Memorial Award (2016); Laureate Award, Louisiana Chapter Representative (2008); Named Top Cardiologist, New Orleans Magazine (1993-1994, 1998, 2001-2014); Outstanding Alumnus Award, University of New Orleans College of Science (1997); Named Best Doctors in America (1996-2019); Bel Award (1968); Hall of Fame, Louisiana Chapter, American College of Physicians; Decorated Army Commendation Medal **Membership:** Silver Torch Award, American Heart Association (1994); Governor, American College of Cardiology (1993-1996); President, American College of Cardiology (1993-1996); Vice President, Louisiana Chapter, American College of Cardiology (1991); President, New Orleans Academy of Internal Medicine (1989-1990); Fellow, American College of Cardiology; Society for Cardiovascular Angiography and Interventions; International Society of Cardiovascular Interventionists; Fellow, Council on Clinical Cardiology, American Heart Association; American Society of Internal Medicine **Hobbies:** Exercise **Religion:** Catholic **Shipping Address:** 3009 Palm Vista Dr, Kenner, LA, 70065-1560

Henry Edward Dugan Jr.

Title: Managing Partner **Industry:** Law and Legal Services **Company Name:** Dugan, Babij, Tolley & Kohler LLC **Place of Birth:** Baltimore **State:** MD **Parents:** Henry Dugan; Rita Dugan **Marital Status:** Married **Spouse Name:** Caroline A. Griffin **Children:** Camille E. Campanile; B. Teague Dugan **Education:** JD, University of Maryland (1973); BA, The Catholic University of America (1966) **Career:** Managing Partner, Founder, Dugan Babij Tolley Kohler LLC (1980-Present); High School Teacher, Baltimore, MD **Civic:** President, Maryland State Bar Association, Inc. (2011-2012); Board Member, Homewood House, The Johns Hopkins University **Awards:** Named to Super Lawyers (2007-2018); Named to Top 100 Maryland Super Lawyers (2012-2014); Named, Lawyer of the Year in Medical Malpractice Law for the Baltimore Area, Best Lawyers (2011); Leadership in Law Award, Daily Record (2011); Named, Trial Lawyer of the Year, Maryland Association for Justice, Inc. (2010); Named One of the 500 Leading Plaintiff's Lawyers in America, Law Dragon (2007); Named to America's Leading Lawyers; Honoree, "A/V" Rating by Martindale-Hubbell; Named One of the Top 100 Trial Lawyers in America, National Trial Lawyers Association; Finalist, Best Lawyers; Named, Top 100 Maryland Litigation Lawyers, American Society of Legal Advocates **Membership:** Former President, Maryland State Bar Association, Inc.; ABA; Baltimore County Bar Association; The Bar Association of Baltimore City; Prince George's County Bar Association; American Association for Justice; Maryland Association for Justice, Inc.; WVAJ; Trial Lawyers Association of Metropolitan Washington, DC; Life Fellow, American Bar Foundation; The Wranglers; Life Fellow, Maryland Bar Foundation; **Bar Admissions:** West Virginia (2003); The District of Columbia (2002); Maryland (1983) **Marquis Who's Who Honors:** Albert Nelson Marquis Lifetime Achievement Award (2017); Distinguished Humanitarian (2017) **To what do you attribute your success:** Mr. Dugan attributes his success to good fortune, good parents, good teachers, good partners, and a good family. **Why did you become involved in your profession or industry:** Mr. Dugan became involved in his profession to help others. **What do you consider to be the highlight of your career:** The highlight of Mr. Dugan's career was his ability to assist the families of babies who had suffered brain injuries via medical negligence. **Where will you be in five years:** In five years, Mr. Dugan aims to continue helping people. **Business Address:** 1966 Greenspring Drive, Ste 500, Timonium, MD, 21093 **Website:** http://www.medicalneg.com

Laurence Richard Dusold

Title: Supervisory Senior Scientist (Retired) **Industry:** Sciences **Company Name:** Food and Drug Administration **Date of Birth:** 11/15/1944 **Place of Birth:** Chicago **State:** IL **Parents:** Henry E. Dusold; Colette M. Dusold **Marital Status:** Widowed **Spouse Name:** Karen A. Marsh (8/29/1970) **Children:** Amy; Lauren; Patricia; Amanda **Education:** BS In Chemistry, Purdue University; MS in Chemistry, University of North Carolina Chapel Hill; Post Graduate Work Wayne State University, Detroit, Michigan **Career:** Private Consulting (2017-Present); Supervisor, Senior Computer Scientist, Food and Drug Administration (2011-2017); Senior Scientist, Computing Advisor, Food and Drug Administration (2008-2011); Information Technology Director, Science Computing, Food and Drug Administration, Washington, DC (2006-2008); Deputy, Information Technology Director, Science Computing, Food and Drug Administration, Washington, DC (2004-2006); Chief Telecommunications and Science Computer Support, Food and Drug Administration, Washington, DC (1986-2003); Senior Chemist, Computer Specialist, Division of Chemistry and Physics, Food and Drug Administration, Washington, DC (1981-1986); Chemist, Computer Specialist, Division of Chemistry and Physics, Food and Drug Administration, Washington, DC (1975-1981); Research Chemist, Residue Analysis and Methods Investigation Branch Bureau, Food and Drug Administration, Washington, DC (1971-1975) **Career Related:** Member, Federal Engineering Planning Group, Department of Health and Human Services (1990-1995); Faculty, Evening Division, University of Maryland (1973-2000) **Creative Works:** Editorial Board Member, Science Computing and Automation (1990-2003); Contributor, Articles to Professional Journals, Chapters to Books **Awards:** 50th Year Award, American Chemical Society; 50th Year Award, AAUP; Distinguished Career Service Award, FDA **Membership:** Vice Chairman, Potomac Chapter, Association Computing Machinery (1993-1996); Chairman, SIGAPL, D.C. Chapter, Association Computing Machinery (1978-1991); Co-Chairman, APL Users Group (1977-1987); New York Academy of Science; Alpha Chi Sigma; Phi Lambda Upsilon; Sigma Xi; American Association of University Professors; American Chemical Society; IEEE; IEEE Computer Society; Greater Washington Federal Agency **Marquis Who's Who Honors:** Albert Nelson Marquis Lifetime Achievement Award (2017) **Hobbies:** Traveling in Europe **Political Affiliations:** Democrat **Religion:** Roman Catholic **Shipping Address:** 307 Stonewall Rd, Catonsville, MD, 21228

Thomas Roy Dye

Title: Political Science Professor **Industry:** Education/Educational Services **Company Name:** Florida State University **Date of Birth:** 12/16/1935 **Place of Birth:** Pittsburgh **State:** PA **Parents:** James Clair Dye; Marguerite Ann (Dewan) Dye **Marital Status:** Married **Spouse Name:** Joan Grace Wohleber (6/29/1957) **Children:** Roy Thomas; Cheryl Price **Education:** PhD, University of Pennsylvania (1961); MA, The Pennsylvania State University (1959); BA, The Pennsylvania State University (1957) **Career:** Professor Emeritus, Political Science, Florida State University (1998-Present); McKenzie Professor, Government, Florida State University (1991-1998); Director, Policy Sciences, Florida State University (1978-1991); Professor, Department of Government, Florida State University (1968-1972); Chairman, Department of Government, Florida State University (1968-1972); Associate Professor, University of Georgia, Athens, GA (1963-1968); Head, Department of Political Science, University of Georgia, Athens, GA (1963-1968); Assistant Professor, Political Science, University of Wisconsin-Madison (1962-1963) **Career Related:** Visiting Professor, Political Studies, The University of Arizona (1976); Visiting Professor, Political Studies, Bar Ilan University, Ramat Gan, Israel (1972) **Military Service:** First Lieutenant, U.S. Air Force (1961-1962) **Creative Works:** Author, "Who's Running America? The Obama Reign" (2013); Author, "Who's Running America? The Bush Restoration" (2013); Author, "Politics in States and Communities (15th Edition)" (2013); Author, "Politics in America, 10th Edition" (2013); Author, "Understanding Public Policy, 14th Edition" (2012); Co-Author, "The Irony of Democracy: An Uncommon Introduction to American Politics, 15th Edition" (2011); Author, "Politics in Florida" (2007); Author, "Power and Society, 10th Edition" (2005); Author, "Who's Running America? The Bush Restoration" (2002); Author, "Top Down Policymaking" (2000); Author, "Politics in Florida" (1998); Author, "Politics in America" (1994); Author, "Who's Running America? The Clinton Years" (1994); Author, "American Federalism: Competition Among Governments" (1990); Author, "Who's Running America? The Bush Era" (1990); Author, "Power Elites and Organizations" (1987); Author, "Who's Running America? The Conservative Years" (1986); Author, "Who's Running America? The Reagan Years" (1983); Author, "American Politics in the Media Age" (1983); Author, "The Determinants of Public Policy" (1980); Author, "Who's Running America? The Carter Years" (1979); Author, "Who's Running America?" (1976); **Membership:** President, Southern Political Science Association (1976-1977); Vice President, Southern Political Science Association (1974-1975); **Shipping Address:** 550 Okeechobee Blvd, Apt 1710, West Palm Beach, FL, 33401

Lynne Earley

Title: School Librarian (Retired) **Industry:** Education/Educational Services **Company Name:** Abington Heights School District **Date of Birth:** 10/04/1955 **Place of Birth:** Scranton **State:** PA **Parents:** John George; Nancy Lou Archibald **Marital Status:** Married (12/28/1990) **Spouse Name:** John A. Earley **Children:** Bethany A.; Jennifer L. Hennessy; Karen E. Johnson **Education:** Master's Degree, Drexel University, Philadelphia (1981); BS, Millersville University, Pennsylvania (1977) **Career:** Retired (2016); School Librarian, Abington Heights School District, Clarks Summit, PA (1987-2016); Librarian, Scranton Public Library (1984-1987) **Career Related:** Council Member, Clarks Green (2007-Present); President, Abington Council Governments, Clarks Green, PA (2009-2011) **Membership:** Vice President, Clarks Green Borough Council (2014-Present) **Why did you become involved in your profession or industry:** Ms. Earley became involved in her profession because she has always loved books. She began working as a volunteer at the storefront library on Main Street in Abington. She put books away at the library for the teachers, and achieved an award for her work. **Shipping Address:** 115 N. Abington Road, Clarks Green, PA, 18411

Dorothy Elizabeth Ebert

Title: County Clerk (Retired) **Industry:** Government Administration/Government Relations/Government Services **Date of Birth:** 04/16/1941 **Place of Birth:** Beaver Dam **State:** WI **Parents:** Merlin Ebert; Gertrude Ebert **Marital Status:** Single **Education:** Diploma, High School, Beaver Dam, WI **Career:** County Clerk, Dodge County, Juneau, WI (1983-2003); Deputy County Clerk, Dodge County, Juneau, WI (1967-1982); Secretary, Household Financial Corporation, Beaver Dam, WI (1958-1967); Receptionist, Household Financial Corporation, Beaver Dam, WI (1958-1967) **Civic:** Past Board of Directors, Dodge County Chapter, American Cancer Society, Inc. **Membership:** President, Wisconsin County Clerks Association (1998-1999); Vice President, Wisconsin County Clerks Association (1997-1998); Secretary, Wisconsin County Clerks Association (1996-1997); Treasurer, Wisconsin County Clerks Association (1995-1996); Historian, Wisconsin County Clerks Association (1994-1995) **Marquis Who's Who Honors:** Albert Nelson Marquis Lifetime Achievement Award (2017) **Hobbies:** Bowling; Golf; Calligraphy; Singing; Bell choir; Travel **Political Affiliations:** Republican **Religion:** Lutheran **Shipping Address:** 213 Francis Ct, Beaver Dam, WI, 53916

Nathan E. Eden

Title: President **Industry:** Law and Legal Services **Company Name:** Nathan E. Eden P.A. **Date of Birth:** 03/24/1944 **Place of Birth:** Key West **State:** FL **Parents:** Delmar M. Eden; Lois (Archer) Eden **Marital Status:** Married **Spouse Name:** Deniece L. Eden (10/2001); Cindy Pike (1/4/1964, Divorced 3/1984) **Children:** Jennifer S. Eden **Education:** JD, College of Law, Stetson University, Magna Cum Laude (1969); BA, University of Florida (1966) **Career:** Partner, Eden & Nevius (2007-Present); Attorney, Law Offices of Nathan E. Eden (2002-Present); Private Practice, Key West, FL (2002-Present); Of Counsel, Lazzara and Paul, P.A., Tampa, FL (1982-Present); Special Master, 16th Judicial Circuit, State of Florida (2007); Partner, Browning, Eden, Sireci and Klitenick (1999-2002); Private Practice, Key West, FL (1984-1999); Partner, Feldman and Eden and Predecessors, Key West, FL (1970-1984); Associate, Nelson, Stinnett, Surfus, et al, Sarasota, FL (1969) **Career Related:** Board Attorney, Utility Board of Key West (1974-Present); **Awards:** Honoree, Leading American Attorney in Florida, American Research Corporation (1998-Present); Honoree, A.V. Preeminent, Martindale-Hubbell (1985-Present); Honoree, Distinguished Lawyer, The Expert Network (2017); Honoree, Top Rated Lawyers in Litigation, Martindale-Hubbell (2016); Ten Best Client Satisfaction Award, American Institute of Criminal Law Attorneys (2015-2018); Ten Best Client Satisfaction Award, American Institute of Personal Injury Attorneys (2015-2018); Honoree, Top Lawyers in Florida (2014-2018); Honoree, Registry of Executives, Professionals & Entrepreneurs, The American Registry, World Wide Who's Who (2014); Honoree, Top 100 Trial Lawyers, National Trial Lawyers (2013-2018); Honoree, A.V. Preeminent "" Judicial Edition, Martindale-Hubbell (2013-2018); Honoree, Top Rated Lawyers, The American Lawyer, South Florida Legal Leaders (2013-2016); Honoree, Top Rated Lawyer in Personal Injury Law (2013) **Bar Admissions:** U. S. Court of Appeals for the Eleventh Circuit (1982); U.S. Court Appeals of the Fifth Circuit (1969); U. S. District Court Southern District of Florida (1969); United States District Court Middle District of Florida (1969); Florida Board of Bar Examiners (1969) **Marquis Who's Who Honors:** Albert Nelson Marquis Lifetime Achievement Award (2017) **What do you consider to be the highlight of your career:** A highlight of Mr. Eden's career was working on a number of high-profile criminal cases, including Key West's "Big Pine 29" marijuana smuggling trial, the largest in U.S. history since 1984. Other representative cases include Key West's "Bubba Bust," Miami's "Operation Giraffe," and Miami's "Operation Tick Talk." **Political Affiliations:** Democrat **Business Address:** 302 Southard St., Ste 205, Key West, FL, 33040

Frank K. Edmondson Jr.

Title: Lawyer (Retired) **Industry:** Law and Legal Services **Date of Birth:** 08/27/1936 **Place of Birth:** Newport **State:** RI/USA **Parents:** Frank Kelley Edmondson, Sr.; Margaret Russell Edmondson **Marital Status:** Married **Spouse Name:** Elaine Sueko Kaneshir; Christiane Semirot (3/5/1959, Divorced 9/1969) **Children:** Mylene Anne; Yvonne Marie; Catherine May **Education:** JD, University of Puget Sound (1982); MBA, SIU (1978); BBA, Indiana University (1958) **Certifications:** Admitted to Practice, United States District Court Western District of Washington (1983) **Career:** Contracts Officer, Office of Administrator for the Courts, Washington Supreme Court, Washington Courts (1992-1999); Financial Service Officer, Office of the Administrator for the Courts, Washington Courts (1990-1992); Legal Representative, Washington Centennial Commission (1987-1990); Contracts Officer, Washington Courts (1989); Assistant Contracts Administrator, Washington's Lottery (1985-1987); Contracts Specialist, Washington's Lottery (1982-1985) **Career Related:** Scholarship Committee Member, Washington State Employees Credit Union (WSECU) (1995-2001) **Civic:** Mock Trial Program Committee, Youth and Government Program, YMCA of the USA (1994-1996); Board of Directors, Chambers Creek Foundation, Tacoma, WA (1981-1990); Pro Bono Panel Member, Puget Sound Legal Assistance Foundation (Now Columbia Legal Services) (1985-1990) **Military Service:** Retired, Pilot with over 1,000 Flight Missions, U.S. Air Force (1979); Advanced through Grades to Major, U.S. Air Force (1969-1979); Commissioned Second Lieutenant, U.S. Air Force (1959) **Membership:** National Council, Seattle University School of Law Alumni Society (1997-2003); Special District Counsel, Washington State Bar Association (1993-1995); Liaison to Washington State Bar Association, Government Lawyers Bar Association of Washington (1989-1993); President, Government Lawyers Bar Association of Washington (1987-1989); First Vice President, Government Lawyers Bar Association of Washington (1986-1987); Secretary, Government Lawyers Bar Association of Washington (1985-1986); College Club of Seattle; Beta Gamma Sigma, Inc. **Bar Admissions:** Washington State Bar Association (1982) **Marquis Who's Who Honors:** Albert Nelson Marquis Lifetime Achievement Award (2017) **Hobbies:** Travel; Reading; Woodworking **Shipping Address:** 2442 35th Ave W, Seattle, WA, 98199

Carl F. Eiberger II

Title: Principal **Industry:** Financial Services **Company Name:** Carl F. Eiberger & Associates **Date of Birth:** 01/17/1931 **Place of Birth:** Denver **State:** CO **Parents:** Carl Frederick Eiberger I; Madeleine Anastasia (Ries) Eiberger **Children:** Eileen; Carl Eiberger III; Mary; James **Education:** MBA, Denver University (1959); JD, University of Notre Dame, Magna Cum Laude (1954); BS in Chemistry, University of Notre Dame, Magna Cum Laude (1952) **Career:** Attorney-at-Law & Principal, Carl F. Eiberger & Associates, Denver, CO (1996-Present); Partner, Eiberger, Stacy, Smith & Martin, Denver, CO (1979-1996); Partner, Rovira, DeMuth & Eiberger, Denver, CO (1957-1979); Sole Practice (1954-1955) **Career Related:** Lawyer Designation, American Arbitration Association (1966); Assistant Bar Examiner, Colorado Bar Association (1963-1968); Co-founder, Labor Law Steering Committee and Section, Colorado Bar Association; Chairman, Economics of Law Practice Committee, Colorado Bar Association; Chairman, Economics of Law Practice Committee, Denver Bar Associations; Board of Governors, Colorado Bar Association; Lecturer, Labor Law and Continuing Legal Education in Other Subjects Across the United States; Arbitrator, American Arbitration Association **Civic:** General Counsel, Pro Bono, Denver Symphony Orchestra (1975-1984); **Military Service:** Korean Army War Veteran, United States Army; Judge Advocate General, U.S. Army, Fort Lewis, WA **Awards:** Certificate of Special Congressional Recognition for Outstanding and Invaluable Service to the Community, United States Congress (2017); Lifetime Achievement Award, Notre Dame Club of Denver (2016); Recognized 60 Years by Denver and Colorado Bar Associations (2014); Eisenhower Citizen Ambassador of the US Silent Hero of Notre Dame (2006); Michael McCafferty Distinguished Service and Lifetime Award, University of Notre Dame The Law School (2002); Named Man of the Year, Notre Dame Law Club of Denver, University of Notre Dame (1966); **Membership:** Executive Committee, Notre Dame Law Association (1998-Present); Board of Directors, Notre Dame Law Association (1965-Present); Nominated President, Denver Bar Association (1984); United States District Court for the District of Colorado; United States Court of Appeals for the Tenth Circuit; United States Court of Appeals for the Eleventh Circuit; Supreme Court of the United States; Admitted to Practice, Various Tax Courts; Federal District Courts; Admitted to Practice, 14 State Courts **Marquis Who's Who Honors:** Albert Nelson Marquis Lifetime Achievement Award (2017); Distinguished Humanitarian (2017)

Earl Otto Ellison

Title: Consultant, Computer Scientist **Industry:** Consulting **Company Name:** Securitas Services **Date of Birth:** 04/26/1938 **Place of Birth:** Elizabeth **State:** NJ/USA **Parents:** Thorleif Ellison; Reidun (Anderson) Ellison **Marital Status:** Married **Spouse Name:** Judith Roque Impoc (2/2/1997) **Children:** Reidun Impoc; Arnfinn Alejandro **Education:** Postgraduate Coursework, American University, Washington, DC (1964-1966); BS, American University, Washington, DC (1964) **Career:** Consultant, Securitas Critical Infrastructure Services (2013-Present); President, Teledesic Services, Inc., Washington, DC (1997-Present); Network Security Consultant, Northrop Grumman Corporation, McLean, VA (2002-2013); Computer Systems Contracting Officer, General Services Administration, Washington, DC (1977-1997); Contract Negotiator, Information Technology Service, General Services Administration, Washington, DC (1967-1977); Management Instructor, Federal Supply Service, General Services Administration, Washington, DC (1965-1967); Methods Analyst, Automation Industries, Consolidated American Services, Inc., Management Consultant Subsidiary, Washington, DC and Los Angeles, CA (1965); Tax Accountant, Trust Department, National Bank of Washington (1964-1965); Head, Supplies and Equipment at Pentagon, C & P Telephone Co. (Now Verizon), Arlington, VA (1956-1962) **Civic:** Judge, Ballroom Dancing, United States Ballroom Dancing Association (1986-1996); Judge, Eastern Seaboard (1986-1996); Swimming and Diving Coach, Pike Branch Swim and Tennis Club, Alexandria, VA (1966-2001) **Military Service:** U.S. Naval Reserve (1961-1962): Navy Patrol Bomber Squadrons VP661 and VP66, Cuban Missile Crisis, U.S Navy, NAS Leeward Point, Cuba (1961) **Creative Works:** Author, "Revenue Code of 1962: Effects on the Multi-National Firm" (1965) **Membership:** Trustee, Sons of Norway (2002-2014); Counselor, Sons of Norway (1996-1997); President, Sons of Norway, Washington Chapter (1994-1995); International Delegate to Convention, Washington Chapter President, Sons of Norway (1994); Executive Board, Beethoven Society of America (1993-2009); Vice President, Sons of Norway (1993); Counselor, Sons of Norway (1993); International Delegate to Convention, Sons of Norway (1988); Principal Building Fund, Sons of Norway (1985-2007); Investment Advisory, Sons of Norway (1979-2015); Beethoven Society of America; Norwegian Society **Marquis Who's Who Honors:** Albert Nelson Marquis Lifetime Achievement Award (2017) **Religion:** Presbyterian **Shipping Address:** 6324 Telegraph Rd, Alexandria, VA, 22310 **Website:** http://www.earlottoellison.com

Susan Embretson, PhD

Title: Professor **Industry:** Education/Educational Services **Company Name:** Georgia Institute of Technology **Education:** PhD, University of Minnesota (1973); BA, University of Minnesota, Summa Cum Laude (1967); Diplomate, Central High School (1962) **Career:** Professor of Psychology, School of Psychology, Georgia Institute of Technology (2004-Present); Professor of Psychology, The University of Kansas (1983-2004); Associate Professor of Psychology, The University of Kansas (1978-1983); Assistant Professor of Psychology, The University of Kansas (1974-1978); Research Associate, Measurement Service Center, University of Minnesota (1973-1974) **Creative Works:** Author, "Understanding Examinees' Responses to Items: Implications for Measurement," Educational Measurement: Issues and Practice (2016); Co-author, "Reliability of Diagnosing Broad and Narrow Skills with the Multicomponent Latent Trait Model: A Study of Middle School Mathematics," Quantitative Psychology Research (2015); Co-author, "Item Generation," The Wiley Handbook of Psychometric Testing (2015); Co-author, "Effects of Reducing the Cognitive Load of Mathematics Items on Student Performance," Numeracy (2015); Author, "The Multicomponent Latent Trait Model for Diagnosis: Applications to Heterogeneous Test Domains," Applied Psychological Measurement (2015); Co-author, "Using Cognitive Complexity to Measure Psychometric Properties of Mathematics Assessment Items," Multivariate Behavior Research (2014); Co-author, "Using Cognitive Complexity to Measure Psychometric Properties of Mathematics Assessment Items," Multivariate Behavior Research (2014); Co-author, "The Impact of Personality and Test Conditions on Mathematical Test Performance," Applied Measurement in Education (2013); Co-author, "A Multicomponent Latent Trait Model for Diagnosis," Psychometrika (2013); Co-author, "The Impact of Scaling and Measurement Methods on Individual Differences in Growth," Handbook of Developmental Research Methods (2012) **Awards:** Career Contribution Award, National Council on Measurement in Education (2013); Distinguished Lifetime Achievement Award, American Educational Research Association: Assessment and Cognition (2011); Distinguished Scientific Contribution Award, Division Five, American Psychological Association (2001) **Membership:** President, The Psychometric Society (1999); President, SMEP (1997-1998); Division of Measurement, Evaluation and Statistics, American Psychological Association (1991); President, Division Five, American Psychological Association (1990-1991); Charter Fellow, American Psychological Society (1990); Fellow, American Psychological Association (1984) **Business Address:** 654 Cherry Street NW, School of Psychology, Georgia Institute of Technology, Atlanta, GA, 30313 **Shipping Address:** 654 Cherry Street NW, School of Psychology, Georgia Institute of Technology, Atlanta, GA, 30313 **Website:** http://www.psychology.gatech.edu/people/faculty/339

Janos Endrenyi, PhD

Title: Engineer **Industry:** Engineering **Date of Birth:** 11/09/1927 **Place of Birth:** Budapest **Country of Origin:** Hungary **Year of Passing:** 10/2/2017 **Parents:** Sandor Endrenyi; Lilly (Szegvari) Endrenyi **Marital Status:** Married **Spouse Name:** Edith Bernat (12/5/1956) **Education:** PhD, University of Toronto, ON, Canada (1972); MS, University of Waterloo, ON, Canada (1965); Diploma in Engineering, Budapest University of Technology and Economics (1951) **Career:** Principal Scientist Emeritus, Ontario Hydro, Toronto, ON, Canada (1992-2007); Principal Research Engineer, Ontario Hydro, Toronto, ON, Canada (1990-1992); Head, Reliability and Statistics Section, Ontario Hydro, Toronto, ON, Canada (1979-1990); Research Engineer, Research Division, Ontario Hydro, Toronto, ON, Canada (1959-1979); Engineer, Ontario Hydro, Toronto, ON, Canada (1957-1959); Research Engineer, Research Institute for Electric Power, Budapest, Hungary (1952-1956); Teaching Assistant, Budapest University of Technology and Economics (1949-1952) **Career Related:** Adjunct Professor, University of Toronto (1983-2014); Adjunct Associate Professor, University of Toronto (1980-1983); Lecturer, University of Toronto (1972-1980); Speaker, Seminars, Worldwide **Creative Works:** Author, "Old Times, Evil Times, 2nd Edition" (2016); Author, "Old Times, Evil Times, 1st Edition" (2011); Author, "Reliability Modeling in Electric Power Systems," Russian and Chinese Editions (1978); Author, "Electric Shock Prevention (in Hungarian)" (1956); Contributor, Papers, Professional Journals **Awards:** Probability Method Applied in Power Systems Society Award (2004) **Membership:** President, Toronto Mozart Society (2001-2011); Fellow, IEEE; Board of Directors, Toronto Mozart Society **Marquis Who's Who Honors:** Albert Nelson Marquis Lifetime Achievement Award (2017) **Shipping Address:** 201-80 Front Street E, Apt. 201, Toronto, ON, Canada, M5E 1T4

Joseph Michael Englot

Title: Director of Infrastructure Security **Industry:** Engineering **Company Name:** HNTB **Date of Birth:** 05/05/1950 **Place of Birth:** New York **State:** NY **Parents:** Joseph Englot; Mary (Yanoschak) Englot **Marital Status:** Married **Spouse Name:** Jane Frances Mines (10/9/1982) **Children:** Brendan Joseph; Michael Edmund **Education:** MCE, Brooklyn Polytechnic Institute (Now New York University Tandon School of Engineering) (1972); BCE, Brooklyn Polytechnic Institute (Now New York University Tandon School of Engineering) (1972) **Certifications:** Registered Professional Engineer, State of New York **Career:** Associate Vice President, HNTB (2005-Present); National Director of Infrastructure Security, HNTB (2005-Present); Chief of Design, The Port Authority of New York and New Jersey (2003-2005), Chief Structural Engineer, The Port Authority of New York and New Jersey (1992-2002); Assistant Chief Structural Engineer, The Port Authority of New York and New Jersey (1989-1992); Principal Engineer, The Port Authority of New York and New Jersey (1988-1989); Senior Engineer, The Port Authority of New York and New Jersey (1984-1988); Engineer, The Port Authority of New York and New Jersey (1980-1984); Associate Engineer, The Port Authority of New York and New Jersey (1975-1980); Assistant Engineer, The Port Authority of New York and New Jersey (1972-1975) **Career Related:** Guest Lecturer, Engineering Universities; Guest Lecturer, Civil Engineering Seminars; Guest Lecturer, Construction Trade Associations **Creative Works:** Contributing Author, NIST Community Resilience Planning Guide for Transportation; Contributor, Articles, Professional Publications **Awards:** Honoree, Disaster Resiliency Fellowship, National Institute of Standards and Technology (2014-2017); Engineer of the Year Award, NYSSPE (2008); PEGASUS Award, National Society of Professional Engineers (2005); Roebling Award, Met Section American Society of Civil Engineers (2005) **Membership:** Blast and Impact Resistant Design Committee, American Institute of Steel Construction Standards (2004-2005); Committee on Steel Bridges, Transportation Research Board, National Academy of Sciences (2002-2008); Blue Ribbon Panel for Bridge and Tunnel Security, American Association of State Highway and Transportation Officials (2002-2003) **Business Address:** 350 5th Ave., Fl 57, New York, NY, 10118

Athema Louise Etzioni

Title: Veterinary Pathologist **Industry:** Medicine & Health Care **Company Name:** Purdue University **Date of Birth:** 11/04/1976 **Place of Birth:** New Orleans **State:** LA/USA **Parents:** Rodney Omar Gerard Casimire; Celestine Bernade Casimire **Marital Status:** Married **Spouse Name:** Baruch Nisan Etzioni (5/30/2003) **Children:** Akebalan Yao Etzioni; Nyela Aziza Etzioni; Zariya Omera Etzioni; Imaan Chasia Etzioni **Education:** MS in Veterinary Clinical Pathology, Purdue University, West Lafayette, IN (2005); DVM, Tuskegee University, Alabama (2001); BS in Biology, Pre-Medicine, Chemistry, Xavier University of Louisiana, New Orleans, LA (1997) **Career:** Veterinary Clinical Pathologist, Tuskegee University College of Veterinary Medicine (2015-Present); Associate Professor of Clinical Pathology, Tuskegee University College of Veterinary Medicine; Associate/Relief Veterinarian, South College Veterinary Clinic **Membership:** American Academy of Health Administrators; American Veterinary Medical Association; American Society of Veterinary Clinical Pathology; Omega Tau Sigma; Phi Zeta; Lifetime Member, Sigma Xi **Hobbies:** Dance; Capoiera; Needlecrafts; Reading **Shipping Address:** 908 S. Main Street, Tuskegee, AL, 36083

Raymond Peyton Ewing

Title: Figurative Sculptor **Industry:** Fine Art **Date of Birth:** 07/31/1925 **Place of Birth:** Hannibal **State:** MO **Parents:** Larama Angelo Ewing; Winona Fern (Adams) Ewing **Marital Status:** Married **Spouse Name:** Audrey Jane Schulze (5/7/1949) **Children:** Jane Ann (Deceased) **Education:** MA in Humanities, The University of Chicago (1950); BA, William Jewell College (1949); AA, Hannibal LaGrange University (1948) **Career:** Figurative Sculptor (1991-Present); Visiting Professor (1990-1991); Professor, Medill School of Journalism, Northwestern University, Evanston, IL (1989-1990); Associate Professor, Graduate Corporate Public Relations Program, Medill School of Journalism, Northwestern University, Evanston, IL (1986-1989); Founding Director, Graduate Corporate Public Relations Program, Medill School of Journalism, Northwestern University, Evanston, IL (1986-1989) **Career Related:** Book Columnist (1968-1970); Public Relations Director, Chicago Magazine (1966-1967); **Civic:** Member, House Commerce Committee, Private Sector Foresight Task Force (1982-1983); **Military Service:** U.S. Army (1943-1946) **Creative Works:** Editor, "Handbook of Communications in Corporate Restructuring and Takeovers" (1992); Author, "Managing the New Bottom Line" (1987); Author, "Mark Twain's Steamboat Years" (1981); **Awards:** Distinguished Professional Contributions Award, Issues Management Association (1994); Honorable Order Hannibal Award (1986); Golden Trumpet Award, Publicity Club of Chicago (1979); Silver Anvil Award for Business Special Events, Public Relations Society of America (1976); Golden Trumpet Award, Publicity Club of Chicago (1972) **Membership:** Chairman, National Public Affairs Section, Public Relations Society of America (1984); Chairman, Issues Management Association (1983-1984); Founder, Issues Management Association (1981-1983); President, Issues Management Association (1981-1983); President, Insurers Public Relations Council (1980-1981); Public Relations Society of America; National Sculpture Society; Mensa; World Future Society; Trends and Perspective Council, United States Chamber of Commerce **Marquis Who's Who Honors:** Albert Nelson Marquis Lifetime Achievement Award (2017) **Why did you become involved in your profession or industry:** Mr. Ewing became involved in his profession after he left the U.S. Army, during which he decided that he wanted to earn his living as a writer and understand why the United States government drafted him at the age of 18. After being in the field for eight years as a journalist, 17 years as a corporate communications director, eight years as an issues management director in the Strategic Planning Department, and six years as a professor with Northwestern University, Mr. Ewing started his career in figurative sculpting.

Tasheema L. Fair

Industry: Medicine & Health Care **Education:** MD, The University of Tennessee Health Science Center (2005) **Certifications:** Board Certified in Obstetrics and Gynecology **Awards:** Army Commendation Medal; Army Achievement Medal **Hobbies:** Shopping; Traveling; Reading; Running; Exercising

Daphne Janice Fairbairn

Title: Professor Emerita **Industry:** Education/Educational Services **Company Name:** University of California **Date of Birth:** 01/28/1949 **Place of Birth:** Ottawa **Country of origin:** ON/Canada **Parents:** Gordon Fairbairn; Mary Rioux **Marital Status:** Married **Spouse Name:** Derek Anthony Roff **Children:** Graham Fairbairn Roff; Robin Jane Roff **Education:** PhD in Zoology, Institute of Animal Resource Ecology, University of British Columbia, Vancouver, BC, Canada (1976); BS in Biology, Carleton University, Ottawa, ON, Canada, With Honors (1971) **Career:** Professor Emerita, Department of Biology, University of California, Riverside (2016-Present); Research Professor, Department of Biology, University of California, Riverside (2016-2017); Professor of Biology, University of California, Riverside (2001-2016); Chair, Department of Biology, Concordia University, Montreal, QC, Canada (1998-2001); Professor, Department of Biology, Concordia University, Montreal, QC, Canada (1994-2001) **Career Related:** Fellow, American Association for the Advancement of Science (2008-Present); President, Society for the Study of Evolution (2015) **Creative Works:** Contributor, Articles, Professional Journals **Awards:** Faculty of Arts and Science Nominee, Concordia University Research Award (1997); Concordia Council on Student Life Teaching Excellence Award (1994); Science and Engineering Scholarship (1971-1975) **Membership:** ESEB (1987-Present); Society for the Study of Evolution (1983-Present) **Marquis Who's Who Honors:** Albert Nelson Marquis Lifetime Achievement Award (2017) **To what do you attribute your success:** Mr. Fairbairn attributes her success to hard work combined with unquenchable curiosity and commitment to learning, and to generous support from scholarships, fellowships and research grants from the Canadian Natural Sciences and Engineering Research Council and the American National Science Foundation. She also attributes success to the support of her spouse and children, who always encouraged her success and often enthusiastically joined in her research adventures. **Why did you become involved in your profession or industry:** Ms. Fairbairn became a professor of biology because of a passion for learning about the natural world and particularly about ecology and evolution. **What do you consider to be the highlight of your career:** One highlight that stood out was the publication of her book, "Odd Couples: Extraordinary Differences between the Sexes in the Animal Kingdom," (Princeton University Press, 2013), which is the culmination of several decades of thought and research on sexual differences and animal diversity. **Shipping Address:** 4461 Picacho Drive, Riverside, CA, 92507 **Website:** http://www.biology.ucr.edu/people/faculty/Fairbairn.html

Kay Fangerow

Title: Nurse **Industry:** Medicine & Health Care **Company Name:** Westside Park School, Federally Qualified Health Center **Date of Birth:** 06/27/1952 **Parents:** Byron Frederick Mayfield; Wilma Jean (Bickford) Mayfield **Children:** David Andrew; Sarah Elizabeth **Education:** MS in Health Care Administration, University of LaVerne (1991); BS in Nursing, California State University, Long Beach, Magna Cum Laude (1975); Coursework, Oral Roberts University (1970-1971) **Career:** Coordinator, Montclair Clinic (2010-Present); Director, Westside Park School, Federally Qualified Health Center (2002-Present); Director, Westside Park School Based Health Center, Federally Qualified Health Center (2010); Program Manager, Child and Family Health Services, Deputy Director, San Bernardino County Department of Public Health, California (2007-2010); Nursing Coordinator, Early Intervention Program for Drug and Alcohol Exposed Infants, SART Project (2005-2010); Grant writer, County Health Department, San Bernardino, CA (2005-2010); Coordinator, School-Based and School-Linked Health Care Services, County Health Department, San Bernardino, CA (1994-2005); Staff Nurse of Pediatrics Services, Parkview Community Hospital, Riverside, CA (1982-2007); Supervising Public Health Nurse, County Health Department, San Bernardino, CA (1976-2006); Staff Nurse of Pediatrics Service, Riverside Community Hospital, California (1975-1976); Staff Nurse of Pediatrics Service, Long Beach Memorial Hospital (1974-1975) **Career Related:** Adjunct Professor of Community Health BSN & MSN programs, School of Nursing, California Baptist University (2011-Present); Consultant, American Home Health, Santa Ana, CA (1986-2000); Presenter in Field **Civic:** Board Member, Knotts Family Agency (2013-Present); Treasurer, Community Clinic Association, San Bernadins County, California (2011-2014); Member, Community Action Council, San Bernardino County Youth Justice Center (1999-2004); Instructor, Inland Counties Chapter, American Cancer Society, Riverside, CA (1977-2000) **Creative Works:** Co-Author, Abstracts, American Public Health Association **Awards:** Named, Public Health Nurse of the Year (2002); Recipient, Recognition for Child Abuse Prevention and Supervision **Membership:** Chair, San Bernardino County Child Death Review Team (2008-2010); Coding Compliance Chair, Technical Assistance Team, National Assembly School Based Health Center (2008-2009); Convention Presenter, Technical Assistance Team, National Assembly School Based Health Center (2005-2007); Chair, San Bernardino County Child Death Review Team (2005-2006) **Political Affiliations:** Democrat **Shipping Address:** 29041 Elder Creek Ln, Highland, CA, 92346

Sally R. Faron

Title: Performing Arts Association Administrator **Industry:** Consulting **Company Name:** La Musica **Date of Birth:** 10/27/1931 **Place of Birth:** Augusta **State:** ME/USA **Parents:** Allan Harvard; Edith Robinson Rogers **Marital Status:** Widowed **Spouse Name:** Louis Charles Faron (1974) **Education:** MA, Boston University (1957); AB, Wellesley College (1953) **Career:** President, La Musica, Sarasota, FL (2014-Present); Secretary, La Musica, Sarasota, FL (1989-2015); Executive Director, La Musica, Sarasota, FL (1989-2017); Administrative Assistant, Bach Aria Festival and Institute, Stony Brook, NY (1981-1986); Acting Head, Barnard School for Girls, New York, NY (1972-1973); Principal, Barnard School for Girls, New York, NY (1966-1974); Administrator, Barnard School for Girls New York, NY (1961-1974); Teacher, Barnard School for Girls New York, NY (1961-1974); Assistant to Headmaster, The MacDuffie School, Springfield, MA (1960-1961); Teacher, House in the Pines, Norton, MA (1953-1955, 1959-1960); Academic Dean House in the Pines, Norton, MA (1953-1955, 1959-1960); Teacher, Beverly High School, Beverly, MA (1955-1957) **Civic:** Board of Directors, Arts and Cultural Alliance of Sarasota County (2009-Present); Member, Cultural Executive Committee, Arts and Cultural Alliance of Sarasota County (1992-Present); Member, TDC Task Force, Arts and Cultural Alliance of Sarasota County (2009); Board of Directors, Key Chorale, Sarasota, FL (2004-2011); Member, Advisory Council, Bach Aria Festival and Institute, Stony Brook, NY (1980-1990); Founder, Suffolk Music Guild, Inc., Stony Brook, NY (1980-1986); President, Suffolk Music Guild, Inc., Stony Brook, NY (1980-1986); Chairman, Young Artists Competition, Suffolk County, Stony Brook, NY (1979-1986); President, Board of Directors, Suffolk Symphony Guild, Smithtown, NY (1975-1980) **Creative Works:** Editor, "Overtures & Artichokes" (1976); Contributor, "Encyclopedia Indians of the Americas" **Awards:** Founder's Medal, Barnard School for Girls (1973); Assistant to Grantee, National Institute of Mental Health, National Institutes of Health (1965-1967) **Membership:** Chamber Music America (1992-1999) **Marquis Who's Who Honors:** Albert Nelson Marquis Lifetime Achievement Award (2017) **Why did you become involved in your profession or industry:** Ms. Faron always enjoyed chamber music more than symphonies, and orchestras etc. **Shipping Address:** 5062 Sandy Cove Ave, Sarasota, FL, 34242 **Website:** http://www.lamusicafestival.com

Carmine J. Fasulo

Industry: Civil Service **Education:** AS in Accounting, Bryant & Stratton College, Buffalo, NY **Career:** Retired; Window Clerk, USPS **Civic:** Volunteer, St. Jude Childrens Research Hospital **Hobbies:** Reading Mysteries; Exercising

Steven Robert Federman

Title: Physicist, Researcher **Industry:** Research **Company Name:** The University of Toledo **Date of Birth:** 11/19/1949 **Place of Birth:** New York City **State:** NY **Parents:** Joseph M. Federman; Adele L. (Strome) Federman (Deceased) **Children:** Rebecca Paulette **Education:** PhD, New York University (1979); MS, New York University (1976); BS, Polytechnic Institute of Brooklyn (1971) **Career:** Professor, The University of Toledo (1998-Present); Associate Professor, The University of Toledo (1993-1998); Assistant Professor, Department of Physics and Astronomy, The University of Toledo (1988-1993); Technical Staff, Jet Propulsion Laboratory, Pasadena, CA (1985-1988); National Research Council Associate, Jet Propulsion Laboratory, Pasadena, CA (1983-1985); Lecturer, The University of Texas at Austin (1983); Postdoctoral Fellow, The University of Texas at Austin (1979-1982); Postdoctoral Fellow, New York University, New York, NY (1979); Senior Research Technician, Hospital for Special Surgery, Weill Cornell Medicine, New York, NY (1972-1975) **Creative Works:** Scientific Editor, "The Astrophysical Journal" (2008-2017); Technical Editor, Atomic and Molecular Spectroscopy, "Journal of the Optical Society of America B" (2004-2011); Contributor, Articles, Professional Journals **Awards:** Fellow, American Association for the Advancement of Science (2017); Fellow, American Physical Society (2002) **Membership:** Past Chair, Laboratory Astrophysics Division, American Astronomical Society (2015-2017); Chair, Laboratory Astrophysics Division, American Astronomical Society (2013-2015); Past President, Commission 14 (Atomic and Molecular Data), International Astronomical Union (2009-2012); President, Commission 14 (Atomic and Molecular Data), International Astronomical Union (2003-2009); Astronomical Society of the Pacific; American Physical Society; American Association for the Advancement of Science; Optical Society of America; Sigma Xi, The Scientific Research Honor Society **Marquis Who's Who Honors:** Albert Nelson Marquis Lifetime Achievement Award (2017) **To what do you attribute your success:** Mr. Federman attributes his success to a combination of hard work and his ability to solve interesting problems. **Why did you become involved in your profession or industry:** Mr. Federman became involved in his profession because of a very interesting research project he conducted in his quest for a PhD. **Where will you be in five years:** In five years, Mr Federman intends to be researching and traveling for pleasure and research. **Shipping Address:** 4029 W Bancroft St., Apt D, Ottawa Hills, OH, 43606

Earl W. Ferguson

Title: Cardiologist, Healthcare Executive **Industry:** Health, Wellness and Fitness **Company Name:** Sun Biomedical Tech Inc. **Date of Birth:** 08/29/1943 **Place of Birth:** Lebanon **State:** PA **Parents:** Warren Earl; Norma Laura (Wilson) F. **Marital Status:** Married **Spouse Name:** Sun Hye Paik (5/1/1998) **Children:** Steven Mark; Matthew Earl; Erin Lee **Education:** MD, PhD in Physiology, University of Texas, Galveston, TX (1970); BA in Chemistry, Baylor University (1965) **Career:** Chief Executive Officer, Sun Biomedical Technologies (2000-2016); Director, Aerospace Medicine and Occupational Health, NASA, Washington, DC (1993-1996); Colonel, U.S. Air Force (1984-1995); Commander, US Air Force Medical Center, Wiesbaden, Germany (1990-1993); Adjunct Professor of Physiology, Uniformed Services University of Health Sciences, Bethesda, MD (1984-1993); Deputy Command Surgeon, Military Airlift Command, Scott AFB (1988-1990); Commander, U.S. Air Force Hospital, Little Rock AFB, AR (1986-1988); Director of Hospital Services, U.S. Air Force Medical Center, Scott AFB, IL (1984-1986); Associate Professor of Physiology, Medicine and Military Medicine, Uniformed Services University of Health Sciences, Bethesda, MD (1980-1984); Chief of Cardiology, Director of Cardiology Training Program, Wilford Hall U.S. Air Force Medical Center, Lackland AFB, TX (1983-1984); Assistant Commandant, Uniformed Services University of Health Sciences, Bethesda, MD (1977-1982); Faculty Senate, Uniformed Services University of Health Sciences, Bethesda, MD (1979-1980); Assistant Professor of Biochemistry, Medicine and Military Medicine, Uniformed Services University of Health Sciences, Bethesda, MD (1976-1980); Staff Cardiologist, Director of Coronary Care, Wilford Hall U.S. Air Force Medical Center, Lackland AFB, TX (1975-1976); Research Associate of Cardiology, VA Hospital, Durham, NC (1974-1975); **Career Related:** Consultant, NASA (1997-Present); Corporate Board, Ridgecrest Regional Hospital (1997-Present); Director, Pertexa/Radekal (2013-Present); Clinical Professor, Health Policy & Management Health Science Center, Loma Linda University (2005-2018); Board of Directors, California Health Information Partnership and Services Organization (2010-2018) **Creative Works:** Author, "American Healthcare Reform: Fixing the Real Problems" (2014); Editorial Board, Telemedicine and eHealth Journal (1996-2003, 2007-2012) **Awards:** Ashbel Smith Distinguished Graduate (1993-Present); Grantee, Walter Reed Army Institute of Research (2002-2015) **Shipping Address:** 1500 McLean St., Suite 132, Ridgecrest, CA, 93555

Harry Finley

Title: Artist, Museum Director **Industry:** Museums & Institutions **Company Name:** Museum of Menstruation and Women's Health **Date of Birth:** 07/18/1942 **Place of Birth:** Long Branch **State:** NJ **Parents:** George Finley; Marjorie Finley **Education:** Postgraduate Coursework, University of Florida (1969-1971); Postgraduate Coursework, University of Florida (1966); BA, Johns Hopkins University (1964) **Career:** Museum Founder, Museum of Menstruation and Women's Health, New Carrollton, MD (1994-Present); Director, Museum of Menstruation and Women's Health, New Carrollton, MD (1994-Present); Artist (1971-Present); Graphic Designer, Department of the Army, Washington, DC and Germany (1971-2004); Founder, www.finleyart.com; Director, www.finleyart.com; Founder, www.mum.org; Director, www.mum.org **Military Service:** U.S. Army (1971-1974); U.S. Army (1964-1966) **Creative Works:** Artist, Portraits; Artist, Cartoons; Artist, Illustrations; Artist, Landscapes **Awards:** Thomas Jefferson Award, Department of Defense (1974); Keith L. Ware Award, Department of the Army (1974); Decorated Commendation Medal for Civilian Service, Department of the Army **Hobbies:** Astronomy; Cultural History; Classical Music; Languages; Emily Dickinson **Political Affiliations:** Independent **Shipping Address:** 5905 Mentana St, New Carrollton, MD, 20784

Sarah Maude Merritt Finley

Title: Retired **Industry:** Government Administration/Government Relations/Government Services **Company Name:** State of Georgia Clayton County DFCS **Date of Birth:** 11/19/1946 **Place of Birth:** Atlanta **State:** GA **Parents:** Genius Merritt; Willie Maude (Wright) Merritt **Marital Status:** Widowed **Spouse Name:** Craig Wayne Finley (8/10/1968) **Children:** Craig Wayne Jr.; Jarret Lee **Education:** Postgraduate Studies, Atlanta University (1968-1969); BA, Spelman College (1968) **Certifications:** Certified GPS/MAPP Leader (2001); Social Service Worker **Career:** Retired, State of Georgia (1972-2004); Social Services Worker, Department of Family and Children Services, Clayton County, Jonesboro, Georgia (2001-2004); Social Services Case Manager, Placement Resource Development Northwest Area Office (2000); Social Worker, Fulton County Department Family and Children Services (1972-2000); Counselor, Assistant to the Project Director, Right Way Home Project Northwest Area Office (1998-1999); Retired, Fulton County Department Family and Children Services (1998); Title VI Customer Service Coordinator, Central City/North Area Office, Fulton County Department Family and Children Services, Atlanta (1990-1998); Casework Supervisor, Fulton County Department Family and Children Services (1976-1998); Child Attendant, Fulton County Juvenile Court (1972); Job Placement Advisor, Marsh Draughton Business College (1971-1972) **Career Related:** Board of Directors, E.D. Cubed, Inc.; South Fulton County; Spelman's Team of Alumni Recruiters, Spelman College; Supervisor, "Count on Me" Video, Georgia Department of Human Resources (1987) **Civic:** Volunteer Coordinator, Family Support Program, Family Support Group of Atlanta Detachment of Second Army Maneuver Training Command; Volunteer, Family Support Council, 87th Maneuver Area Command (Now Fourth Brigade, 87th Division) (1991-1993); Delegate, Fort McPherson Army Family Symposium (1992); Delegate, Third Annual Worldwide US Army Reserve Family Support Conference, St. Louis (1992) **Creative Works:** Author, Memoir Life Plan, WestBow Press (2018) **Membership:** Fulton County Retired Employees Association; National Alumnae Association, Spelman College; Women's Auxiliary Georgia, VFW **Hobbies:** Poetry; Reading; Volunteer work; Stress management; Writing **Political Affiliations:** Democrat **Religion:** Methodist **Shipping Address:** 2678 Peyton Woods Trl SW, Atlanta, GA, 30311

Joseph A. Flaherty

Title: Chancellor Emeritus **Industry:** Medicine & Health Care **Company Name:** Adtelem Global Education **Date of Birth:** 06/01/1946 **Education:** Resident in Pediatrics, University of Illinois (1971-1975); MD, University of Illinois (1971); BS, University of Illinois (1968); Coursework in Sociology, University of London **Certifications:** Diplomate, American Board of Psychiatry; Diplomate, American Board of Geriatrics **Career:** President, Advocate Behavioral Partners (1997-Present); Professor of Psychiatry, The University of Illinois at Chicago (1976-Present); Dean, College of Medicine, The University of Illinois at Chicago (2004-2011); Head of Psychiatry, The University of Illinois at Chicago (1998-2004); Deputy Head of Psychiatry, The University of Illinois at Chicago (1991-1998); Chief Psychiatrist, Jesse Brown VA Medical Center, U.S. Department of Veterans Affairs (1976-1978) **Career Related:** Researcher in Field; Founder, Research Groups in Neurological Science **Civic:** Consultant, Trinity House, Chicago, IL (1975-1990) **Creative Works:** Contributor, Over 200 Papers, Professional Journals; Editor, Books; Co-author, Books; Contributor, Book Chapters **Awards:** Eponym, Chair for Child Psychiatry, The University of Illinois at Chicago; Featured Listee, America's Best Doctors, Castle Connolly Medical Ltd. **Membership:** Distinguished Fellow, America Psychiatric Association; Fellow, The American College of Psychiatrists; Board Member, University of Illinois Foundation; Committee Member, WHO; Committee Member, Health and Medicine Division, National Academy of Sciences; Committee Member, National Institutes of Health **Marquis Who's Who Honors:** Albert Nelson Marquis Lifetime Achievement Award (2017) **Why did you become involved in your profession or industry:** Mr. Flaherty always wanted to be in medicine. He wanted to be a family medicine doctor in a small town, but he went into academia. **What do you consider to be the highlight of your career:** Having an interaction with one of his first patients and being the dean of the largest U.S. medical school at the University of Illinois were highlights for Mr. Flaherty. **Shipping Address:** 400 Alton Rd., Apt. 1610, Miami Beach, FL, 33139

Keith George Fleer

Title: Lawyer, Film Company Executive **Industry:** Law and Legal Services **Company Name:** Fleer Law **Date of Birth:** 02/28/1943 **Parents:** Samuel Robert Fleer; Sophia M. (Scherer) Fleer **Education:** JD, American University (1967); BA in Government, American University (1964) **Career:** Partner, Loeb & Loeb LLP, Century City, CA (1998-Present); Partner, Sinclair Tenenbaum, Emanuel & Fleer, Beverly Hills, CA (1989-1998); Partner, Denton Hall Burgin and Warrens, Beverly Hills, CA (1987-1988); Vice President of Business Affairs, Warner Bros. Entertainment Inc., Beverly Hills, CA (1984-1988); Executive Vice President, Simon/Reeves/Landsburg Productions, Beverly Hills, CA (1982-1984); Senior Vice President of Business and Legal Affairs, Melvin Simon Productions, Inc., Beverly Hills, CA (1978-1981); Associate, Schiff, Hirsch & Schreiber Professional Corporation, Beverly Hills, CA (1977); Senior Counsel, Avco Embassy Pictures, Hollywood, CA (1976); Associate, Kaye, Scholer, Fierman, Hays & Handler, New York, NY (1972-1975); Associate, Gettinger, Gettinger & Manheimer, New York, NY (1968-1972); Assistant Director of Athletics, Fordham University (1967-1968) **Career Related:** Adjunct Professor, Law Center, University of Southern California (Now USC Gould School of Law) (1995); Guest Lecturer, University of West LA Law School (1979-1980); Legislative Counsel, New York State Assemblyman (1969-1970) **Civic:** Planning Committee, Entertainment Law, University of Southern California (2006-Present); Planning Committee, University of California, Los Angeles (1982-Present); Board of Trustees, American University (1992-1997); Dean's Advisory Council, American University **Creative Works:** Business Editor, American University Law Review (1966-1967) **Awards:** Stafford H. Cassell Award, American University Law School (1979); Alumni Award, American University (1967); Bruce Hughes Award, American University (1964) **Membership:** President, Los Angeles Copyright Society (1988-1989); Trustee, Los Angeles Copyright Society (1983-1990); Academy of Motion Picture Arts and Sciences; ABA; Beverly Hills Bar Association **Bar Admissions:** State of California (1976); The District of Columbia (1968); New York (1968) **Marquis Who's Who Honors:** Albert Nelson Marquis Lifetime Achievement Award (2017) **Shipping Address:** 11611 Montana Ave., Apt 203, Los Angeles, CA, 90049

Charles Gallagher Flinn

Title: Lawyer, Priest **Industry:** Law and Legal Services **Date of Birth:** 02/22/1938 **Place of Birth:** Fort Lauderdale **State:** FL/USA **Parents:** Robert Galloway; Gertrude (Gallagher) Flinn **Education:** PhD, Catholic University (Now The Catholic University of America) (2010); MA, Catholic University (Now The Catholic University of America) (2001); ThM, Westminster Theological Seminary (1994); BD, University of London (1980); LLB, University of Virginia (1962); AB, Princeton University (1959) **Certifications:** Ordained as Priest, Ministry Episcopal Church (1992); Ordained as Deacon, Ministry Episcopal Church (1991) **Career:** Vice-chancellor, Episcopal Diocese, Quincy, IL (1996-2010); Vicar, Trinity Episcopal Church, Monmouth, IL (1994-1996); Curate, Grace Episcopal Church, Brunswick, MD (1991-1993); Attorney, Arlington School Board (Now Arlington Public Schools) (1981-1993); County Attorney, County of Arlington, VA (1981-1993); Deputy County Attorney, County of Arlington, VA (1975-1981); Assistant County Attorney, County of Arlington, VA (1972-1975); Assistant Commonwealth's Attorney, County of Arlington, VA (1971-1972); Assistant Counsel, Office of General Counsel, U.S. Navy, Washington, DC (1963-1971); Associate, Charles B. Fulton, Esq., West Palm Beach, FL (1962-1963) **Career Related:** President, Nathanael Institute, Arlington, VA (2001-Present); Adjunct Faculty, Protestant Episcopal Theological Seminary, Alexandria, VA (1999-2000); Visiting Lecturer in Biblical Language, Reformed Theological Seminary, Orlando, FL (1997-2000); Visiting Lecturer in Biblical Language, Reformed Theological Seminary, Metropolitan D.C. (1997-2000) **Awards:** Harry L. Carrico Pro Bono Award, Legal Services, Northern Virginia (2005) **Membership:** Director-at-Large, Virginia Council School Board of Attorneys (1988-1993); Board of Directors, Virginia Local Government Attorneys Association (Now Local Government Attorneys of Virginia, Inc.) (1988-1992); American Oriental Society; Princeton Club of New York; Society Sons of American Revolution; Society Sons of American Colonists **Bar Admissions:** The District of Columbia Bar (1970); Supreme Court of the United States (1966); The Florida Bar (1962); Virginia State Bar (1962) **Marquis Who's Who Honors:** Albert Nelson Marquis Lifetime Achievement Award (2017); Distinguished Humanitarian (2017) **Shipping Address:** PO Box 100921, Arlington, VA, 22210

Gregory Charles Flood

Title: International Human Resources Management Consultant **Industry:** Consulting **Date of Birth:** 09/04/1946 **Place of Birth:** Yonkers **State:** NY **Parents:** Harold Austin Flood; Anne Marie (Wallace) Flood **Marital Status:** Married **Spouse Name:** Catherine Virginia Predham (12/9/1967) **Education:** BS, University at Albany (1973) **Career:** International Human Resources Management Consultant (2008-Present); Secretary, FAO Finance Committee (1998-2007); From Establishments Officer to Chief Recruitment and Staffing Branch, UN Food and Agriculture Organization, Rome, Italy (1980-2008); Personnel Administrator to Associate Program Budget Coordinator, New York State Education Department, Albany, NY (1977-1980); Personnel Technician, Rensselaer County Civil Service Commission (1974-1977) **Civic:** President, American International Club of Rome (2004-2006); President, American International Club of Rome (1996-1998); Treasurer, American International Club of Rome (1995-1996); Volunteer Firefighter, East Greenbush Fire Department (1974-1980); President, East Greenbush Republican Club, New York (1974) **Military Service:** Interior Communications Electrician, Petty Officer 2nd Class, U.S. Navy (1966-1970) **Membership:** Board Member, Carolina Friends of Foreign Services (2015-Present); Quartermaster, Post 7313, Veterans of Foreign Wars of the United States (2014-Present); President, West Triangle Chapter, United Nations Association of the USA (2013-2014); Vice President, West Triangle Chapter, United Nations Association of the USA (2011-2012); Founding Member, Association for Human Resources Management in International Organizations; Member, International Public Management Association; Member, American Society of Public Administration **Hobbies:** Reading; Computer programming; Badminton; Stage craft **Religion:** Roman Catholic **Business Address:** 1015 Fearrington Post, Pittsboro, NC, 27312

Gwendolyn Sue Foote

Title: Educator **Industry:** Education/Educational Services **Company Name:** Nautilus Middle School, Miami Dade County Public School District **Date of Birth:** 04/09/1953 **Place of Birth:** Oklahoma City **State:** OK/USA **Parents:** Maj. John T. Foote (ret); Dorothy Clow Foote **Marital Status:** Single **Children:** Shawn Robert Scarbrough **Education:** EdD, Instructional & Special Education Degree, Nova Southeastern University (2014); EdB in Elementary Education & Special Education, Oglala Lakota College, South Dakota (2005); Interdisciplinary Studies in Art, Psychology, and Intercultural Studies, University of Texas (1985); BS in Biomedical Science, College of Veterinary Medicine, Texas A&M University (1975) **Certifications:** Certified Teacher (2000); Registered Medical Technologist (1977) **Career:** Educator Coach for Future City Challenge, Green School Challenge (2011-Present); SECME & Science Fair Coordinator (2010-Present); Science Teacher, Nautilus Middle School, Miami Beach, FL (2006-Present); Science Department Chair, Teacher, Nautilus Middle School/International Baccalaureate World School, Science Competition Coach, STEAM School Liaison, Fairchild Challenge Lead Teacher (2014-2017) **Career Related:** Miami-Dade County Council, Vice President of Education (2018-Present); Teacher of Educators through Seminars and Workshops, Grant Writer (2003-Present) **Civic:** Rehabilitator, Federal Fish and Wildlife, State of Texas (1983-1987); Wildlife Rehabilitator, Lectures and Seminars, Conservation of Wildlife (1983-1987) **Creative Works:** United Nations Educational Human Civil Rights Program, Namibia, Africa (1995); Featured Artist, Exhibitions in Dallas, TX, Denver, CO, Las Vegas, NV, Rocky Mountain Region, CO, Australia, France, Ireland, England, and Universal Studios (1983-1995) **Awards:** Bronze Award, Fairchild Challenge (2015-2018); Finalist, Dream in Green Program, WE-LAB Award (2015-2018); STEM EXPO SECME Teacher of the Year Award (2013); Green School Challenge Educator and Future City Challenge Awards (2011-2018); Miami Beach PTSA Awards (2011-2017) **Membership:** Vice President, International Senior Citizens Association (1994-1997) **Marquis Who's Who Honors:** Albert Nelson Marquis Lifetime Achievement Award (2017); World Who's Who (2018) **Business Address:** Nautilus Middle School, Miami Beach, FL, 33140 **Shipping Address:** 16850-112 Collins Avenue, #226, Sunny Isles Beach, FL, 33160 **Website:** https://gwenfoote.weebly.com

Paul Sheldon Foote

Title: Professor of Accounting **Industry:** Education/Educational Services **Company Name:** California State University, Fullerton **Date of Birth:** 05/22/1946 **Place of Birth:** Lansing **State:** MI **Parents:** Harlon Sheldon Foote; Frances Norene Rotter **Marital Status:** Married **Spouse Name:** Badri Seddigheh Hosseinian (10/25/1968) **Children:** David R. Foote; Sheila P. Rossi **Education:** PhD, Michigan State University (1983); Advanced Professional Certificate in Accounting, New York University (1975); Postgraduate Coursework, New England School of Law (1971-1972); MBA, Harvard University (1971); BBA, University of Michigan (1967) **Career:** Professor, Department of Accounting, Mihaylo College of Business and Economics, California State University, Fullerton, CA (1989-Present); Visiting Professor, Claremont McKenna College, Claremont, CA (2014); Lecturer, University of California, Riverside, CA (2008-2009); Associate Dean, Chapman University, Orange, CA (2004-2005); Professor, Sultan Qaboos University, Muscat, Oman (1994-1996); Associate Professor, Pepperdine University, Malibu, CA (1987-1989); Assistant Professor, New York University (1983-1987); Assistant Professor, Oakland University, Rochester, MI (1982-1983); Associate Professor, Saginaw Valley State University, University Center, MI (1981-1982); Assistant Professor, University of Windsor, Canada (1979-1981); Instructor, University of Michigan, Flint, MI (1978-1979); Lecturer, Accounting, Michigan State University, East Lansing, MI (1977); Manager of Planning and Development, Singer Sewing Machine Company, Africa/Middle East (1974-1975); Pro Manager, Citibank, Beirut, Bombay, Mumbai, and New York, NY (1972-1974); Investment Analyst, Mutual of New York, New York, NY (1971); Market Analyst, U.S. Department of Commerce, American Embassy, Tehran, Iran (1970); **Military Service:** Lieutenant, U.S. Army, Vietnam (1968-1969) **Creative Works:** Editorial Board, Journal of Business Forecasting (1983-Present); Author, "Corporate Profitability: Determinants and Forecasts" (1983) **Awards:** Outstanding Faculty Recognition, California State University, Fullerton, CA (2000); Outstanding Faculty Finalist, School of Business Administration and Economics Executive Council, California State University, Fullerton, CA (1999); Doctoral Consortium Fellow, Haskins and Sells (1977); Loomis-Sayles Fellow, Harvard University (1969-1971); **Membership:** American Accounting Association; Life Member, United States Chess Federation **Marquis Who's Who Honors:** Albert Nelson Marquis Lifetime Achievement Award (2017) **Business Address:** 800 N State College Blvd., Fullerton, CA, 92831 **Website:** https://www.linkedin.com/in/paulsheldonfoote

James Foster

Title: Advertising and Public Relations Executive **Industry:** Advertising & Marketing **Date of Birth:** 05/14/1933 **Place of Birth:** Kansas City **State:** MO/USA **Parents:** Wendell Foster; Lillian M. (East) Foster **Education:** Postgraduate Work, Drake University (1957); BA, Drake University (1955) **Career:** President, Reputation Management Strategies, Durango, CO (1999-Present); Chairman Emeritus, Brouillard Communications (1999-2003); Chairman, Brouillard Communications (1997-1999); Chairman, Chief Executive Officer, Brouillard Communications (1994-1997); President, Chief Executive Officer, Brouillard Communications Division, New York, NY (1984-1994); Executive Vice President, General Manager, Brouillard Communications Division, New York, NY (1981-1984); Public Relations and Advertising Executive, J. Walter Thompson Co., New York, NY (1979-1999); Senior Vice President, General Manager, Brouillard Communications Division, New York, NY (1979-1981); Vice President of Public Affairs, Western Union Corp., Upper Saddle River, NJ (1973-1979); Vice President, J. Walter Thompson Co., New York, NY (1970-1973); Public Relations and Advertising Executive, J. Walter Thompson Co., New York, NY (1961-1973); Reporter, Editor, Des Moines Register (1951-1961) **Civic:** Board of Directors, Rocky Mountain PBS (2008-Present); Fort Lewis College Foundation (2004-Present); Chairman, Rocky Mountain PBS (2013-2016); Vice Chair, Rocky Mountain PBS (2011-2013); Board Treasurer, Rocky Mountain PBS (2010-2011); Chairman, Fort Lewis College Foundation (2008-2011); Board of Directors, Music in the Mountains, Inc., Durango, CO (1999-2009); Vice President, Fort Lewis College Foundation (2006-2008); Secretary, Fort Lewis College Foundation (2005-2006); President, Music in the Mountains, Inc., Durango, CO (2000-2003) **Membership:** Union League Club; Glacier Club **Marquis Who's Who Honors:** Albert Nelson Marquis Lifetime Achievement Award (2017) **Religion:** Presbyterian **Business Address:** 1472 E. Third Avenue, Durango, CO, 81301

Daniel M. Fowler

Title: Lawyer **Industry:** Law and Legal Services **Company Name:** Fowler Schimberg & Flanagan PC **Date of Birth:** 03/25/1950 **Place of Birth:** Chicago **State:** IL/USA **Marital Status:** Married **Spouse Name:** Julia M. Duffy **Children:** Douglas M, Peter M **Education:** JD, University of Denver (1975); BA, Monmouth College (1972) **Career:** President, Fowler, Schimberg, Flanagan & McLetchie P.C., Denver, CO **Membership:** ABA; Colorado Bar Association; Denver Bar Association; Defense Research Institute; Federation of Defense & Corporate Counsel; Colorado Defense Lawyers Association; Denver Athletic Club; Lakewood Country Club **Bar Admissions:** Wyoming (1994); Colorado (1975); U.S. District Court of Colorado (1975); U.S. Court of Appeals for the Tenth Circuit (1975) **Hobbies:** Motorcycle touring; Skiing; Boating; Travel; Golf **Business Address:** 1640 Grant Street, Suite 150, 1640 Grant Street, Suite 150, CO, Denver, 80203 **Shipping Address:** 1640 Grant Street, Suite 300, Fowler, Schimberg & Flanagan, P.C., Denver, CO, 80203

James M. Fragomeni, PhD

Title: Mechanical Engineer, Educator **Industry:** Engineering **Company Name:** Engineering and Science Consulting Services **Date of Birth:** 09/24/1962 **Place of Birth:** Columbus **State:** OH **Parents:** John Fragomeni; Kathleen Fragomeni **Marital Status:** Single **Education:** Summer Faculty Fellow, Materials & Manufacturing Directorate, Air Force Office of Scientific Research, Wright-Patterson Air Force Base (1998); Summer Faculty Fellow, Marshall Space Flight Center, NASA (1996-1997); PhD, Purdue University (1994); Graduate Research Assistant, Engineering Research Center, Purdue University (1986-1994); MS in Engineering, Purdue University (1988); BS in Metallurgical Engineering, University of Pittsburgh (1985); Summer Research Intern, Research Center, Allegheny Ludlum Steel Corporation (1984) **Certifications:** Greenbelt Certification, Six Sigma (2012); Certification, Construction Quality Management, U.S. Army Corps of Engineers (2009); Certification, Quality Technician, American Society for Quality (2005) **Career:** Assistant Professor, University of Detroit Mercy (2000-2004); Assistant Professor, Ohio University (1997-2000); Assistant Professor, The University of Alabama (1995-1997); Assistant Researcher, Department of Defense Analysis Center, Purdue University (1995) **Career Related:** Adviser, Guidepoint Global, LLC (2008-Present); Mechanical Engineering Consultant, Engineering and Science Consultant Service (2008-Present); Quality Systems Manager, Distel Tool and Machine Company (2008-2010); Metallurgical Engineering Consultant, Westmoreland Mechanical Testing & Research, Inc. (2007-2009); Adjunct Instructor, University of Detroit at Ford (2001-2005) **Civic:** Knights of Columbus (2006-Present); **Awards:** Honoree, Prestigious National Honor Society (2010-2012); Named to Top Two Hundred, American Biographical Institute (2010); Named to Outstanding Intellectuals of the 21st Century, American Biographical Institute (2009-2010) **Membership:** Ambassador, General Cultural Convention, American Biographical Institute (2006-Present); Lifetime Deputy Governor, American Biographical Institute (2005-Present) **Marquis Who's Who Honors:** Albert Nelson Marquis Lifetime Achievement Award (2018) **To what do you attribute your success:** Dr. Fragomeni attributes his success to hard work and staying focused and goal oriented to complete the tasks and projects that need to be completed. **Why did you become involved in your profession or industry:** Dr. Fragomeni became involved in his profession because he was interested in science, engineering, and technology and making contributions in these fields. **Political Affiliations:** Conservative **Business Address:** PO Box 1446, Royal Oak, MI, 48068 **Website:** www.jamesmfragomeni.com/

Francine Frankel, PhD

Title: Political Science Professor **Industry:** Education/Educational Services **Company Name:** University of Pennsylvania **Date of Birth:** 08/31/1935 **Place of Birth:** New York **State:** NY **Parents:** William Goldberg; Dora (Tuchschneider) Goldberg **Marital Status:** Married **Spouse Name:** Douglas Vernon Verney (11/28/1975) **Education:** PhD, University of Chicago (1965); MA, Johns Hopkins University (1958); BA, City College of New York (1956) **Career:** Founding Director, Center of Advanced Study of India, University of Pennsylvania (2006-2014); Madan Lal Sobti Professor, Study of Contemporary India, University of Pennsylvania, Philadelphia, PA (2004-2006); Director, Center of Advanced Study of India, University of Pennsylvania, Philadelphia, PA (1992-2006); Professor, University of Pennsylvania, Philadelphia, PA (1979-2014); Professor, South Asian Studies, University of Pennsylvania, Philadelphia, PA (1978-2014); Associate Professor, University of Pennsylvania, Philadelphia, PA (1970-1979); Assistant Professor, University of Pennsylvania, Philadelphia, PA (1965-1970) **Career Related:** Founding Member, University of Pennsylvania Institute for Advanced Study of India, New Delhi, PA (1995-2014); Delegate, South Asian Specialists to China (1986); Visiting Member, Institute of Advanced Study (1976); Resident Scholar, Bellagio Study and Conference Center (1975); Member-at-large, Commission of International Relations, National Academy of Sciences (1973-1979); **Creative Works:** Author, "India's Political Economy 1947-2004, Second Edition" (2005); Editor, Contributor, "The India-China Relationship: What the United States Needs to Know" (2004); Editor, Contributor, "Transforming India, Social and Political Dynamics of Democracy" (2000); Editor, Contributor, "Bridging the Non-Proliferation Gap: India and the United States" (1995); Author, "India's Political Economy, 1947-1977, The Gradual Revolution, Chinese Edition" (1990); Editor, Contributor, "Dominance and State Power in Modern India, Decline of a Social Order," Two Volumes (1989-1990); Author, "India's Political Economy, 1947-1977, The Gradual Revolution" (1978); Author, "India's Green Revolution" (1971); **Awards:** Scholar in Residence, Woodrow Wilson International Center for Scholars (2006-2007); Scholar in Residence, Woodrow Wilson International Center for Scholars (1997-1998); Social Science Research Council (1989-1991); Smithsonian Institution (1983-1986); Grantee, American Institute of Indian Studies (1979-1980) **Membership:** American Political Science Association; Association of Asian Studies; Council of Foreign Relations **Marquis Who's Who Honors:** Albert Nelson Marquis Lifetime Achievement Award (2017) **Shipping Address:** 104 Pine St, Philadelphia, PA, 19106

John Franks

Title: Anesthesiologist **Industry:** Medicine & Health Care **Company Name:** Vanderbilt University **Date of Birth:** 04/09/1929 **Place of Birth:** Pueblo **State:** CO **Marital Status:** Married **Spouse Name:** Mary Franks; Kathryne Jean Sammon (12/27/1951, Deceased 5/1999) **Children:** John Alec; William Thomas; Margaret Lila; Elizabeth Ellen **Career:** Professor Emeritus, Vanderbilt University (1999-Present); Director of Division of Organ Transplant Anesthesia, Vanderbilt University (1989-1998); Professor, Vanderbilt University (1987-1998); Director of Research Division, Vanderbilt University (1987-1998); Interim Chairman, Department of Anesthesiology, Vanderbilt University (1993-1994); Resident in Anesthesiology, Vanderbilt University Medical Center (1984-1986); Chief of Hematology Division, VA Eastern Colorado Health Care System, U.S. Department of Veterans Affairs (1983); Associate Chief of Staff, Research Division, VA Eastern Colorado Health Care System, U.S. Department of Veterans Affairs (1969-1982); Associate Director, University of Colorado Denver (1969-1981); Director, Clinical Research Center, University of Colorado Denver (1969-1981) **Awards:** Grantee, Vanderbilt University (1992-1996); Grantee, VA Eastern Colorado Health Care System, U.S. Department of Veterans Affairs (1969-1983); Grantee, University of Colorado (1963-1969, 1964-1982); **Membership:** Fellow, American Association for the Advancement of Science; American Society of Anesthesiologists; The American Physiological Society; Central Society for Clinical and Transnational Research; International Society on Thrombosis and Haemostasis, Inc.; Society of General Physiologists **Marquis Who's Who Honors:** Albert Nelson Marquis Lifetime Achievement Award (2017) **Shipping Address:** 216 Vaughns Gap Road, Nashville, TN 37205

George Wilson Freas II

Title: Computer Scientist, Consultant, Inventor **Industry:** Information Technology and Services **Company Name:** Freas Consulting, LLC **Date of Birth:** 10/27/1955 **Place of Birth:** Franklin **State:** KY **Parents:** George Wilson Freas; Audrey Carolyn Freas **Marital Status:** Divorced **Spouse Name:** Cynthia Anne Fleming (2/1984, Divorced 10/1990) **Children:** Alexander Morange **Education:** MS in Computer Science, University of Alabama in Huntsville (1994); BS in Computer Science, Western Kentucky University (1979) **Certifications:** IT Security Administrator, NASA (2007, 2017) **Career:** Lead Design Architect, Remote Advanced Payload Test Rig (RAPTR), Boeing International Space Station, Marshall Space Flight Center, Alabama (2009-Present); President/Owner, Freas Consulting, LLC (Formerly Synergistic Consultants) (1991-Present); Payload Ground Test Software Lead, Marshall Space Flight Center, Alabama (2003-2018); Ares 1 Instrument Unit Avionics Software, Marshall Space Flight Center (2008); Software Technical Liaison, Centrifuge Rack Interface Controller, Boeing International Space Station (1999-2002); Software Consultant, Bell South Telecommunications, Birmingham, AL (1995-1998); Graphics Software Engineer, Schematic Capture Software, Intergraph Corporation, Huntsville, Alabama (1990-1991); Software Engineer, FOG-M Embedded Trainer, Computer Sciences Corporation, Redstone Arsenal, Alabama (1986-1990); Lead Graphics Software Engineer, NECIP Train Traffic Control, Computer Sciences Corporation, Huntsville, Alabama (1981-1986); Scientific Software Engineer, Engineering Document Generator (EDGE), Computer Sciences Corporation, Marshall Space Flight Center, Alabama (1980-1981) **Creative Works:** Author, "Canny Canon-Abridged Version" (2016) **Awards:** Boeing Stars in Alabama Team Achievement Award for Remote Advanced Payload Test Rig, RAPTR (2018); Rotary National Stellar Award for Software Toolkit for Ethernet Lab Like Architecture (STELLA) Software Team (2013); NASA Spaceflight Awareness Award, NASA Marshall Space Flight Center (2010); Boeing Meritorious Invention Award, for Remote Advanced Payload Test Rig, RAPTR (2009) **Membership:** Committee Advisor, American Astronautical Society; International Space Station Utilization Technical Committee (2012-Present) **Marquis Who's Who Honors:** Albert Nelson Marquis Lifetime Achievement Award (2017); Marquis Who's Who Top Engineers (2018); Who's Who in the South and Southwest, Marquis Who's Who (1997-2001, 2010-2013); Who's Who in America, Marquis Who's Who (1998-2014); Who's Who in Science and Engineering, Marquis Who's Who (2000-2001, 2003-2004, 2008-2009, 2011-2012); Who's Who in the World, Marquis Who's Who (1998, 2000-2003, 2005-2007, 2009) **Political Affiliations:** Progressive Democrat **Religion:** Christian, Presbyterian **Business Address:** PO Box 2885, Huntsville, AL, 35804 **Shipping Address:** 1011 Humes Ave NE, Huntsville, AL, 35801

J.P. Ladyhawk Freeman

Title: Vicar, Underwater Exploration, Security and Transportation Executive, Fashion Model **Industry:** Other **Date of Birth:** 02/21/1951 **Place of Birth:** Berkeley **State:** CA/USA **Parents:** Gilbert Richard Freeman; P.M. (Ann) Raistrick **Marital Status:** Married **Spouse Name:** Beverly Herman (November 19, 2016) **Children:** Jennifer Patricia; Simon L.G.; Schneider F. **Education:** Graduate, Air War College, U.S. Air Force (1988); Master's Degree in Aviation Management, Embry-Riddle Aeronautical University (1986); Graduate, Computer Institute, Dept of Defense (1984); Graduate, USAF Command and Staff College (1986); Graduate US Marine Corps College (1986); BA in English, Davis & Elkins College (1973); Graduate, USAF Weapons Controller School (1973); Graduate Emergency Medical Technician, City College of Chicago; Graduate Paramedic, University of Trier (Germany); Coursework in Psychology, Davis & Elkins College; Coursework in Theology/Philosophy, Davis & Elkins College; Coursework in Music, Davis & Elkins College; Coursework in Aviation Science/Aeronautical Engineering, Embry-Riddle Aeronautical University **Certifications:** Certified Radar Air Traffic Controller (2003); Ordained Vicar, The Universal Church (2002) **Career:** Vicar (2002-Present); Retired (2005); Fashion Model (1996-2001); Director, FLEET International Explorations and Services Company (1995-1997); Systems Performance Specialist, Sport & Spine Rehab. (1994-1995); Director of Special Projects, Regional Hospital, U.S. Air Force Academy (1993-1994); Chief, Airport Management Division, U.S. Air Force (1991-1993); Deputy Base Commander, NATO (1989-1991); Support Chief of Staff, North American Aerospace Defense Command (1987-1989); Commander, Joint U.S. Forces Operation Raleigh (1986); Chief of Wing Radar Standardization/Evaluation, Royal Air Force (1980-1983); Member, 56th Special Operations Rescue for Southeast Asia, NKP Royal Thai Air Force Base (1974-1975); Reporter Associated Press (1971-1972) **Career Related:** Paralyzed Veterans of America Senior Legislature Advocate, U.S. Congress for College (2002-2005) **Awards:** Honoree, Named One of the Six Top Support Officers, U.S. Air Force (1986-1987); Honoree, Named Administration Officer of the Year, U.S. Air Force (1986) **Hobbies:** Writing; Skiing; Horseback riding; Painting; Music **Religion:** Anglican **Shipping Address:** 5913 Amber Station Ave, Las Vegas, NV, 89131

Sidney Frisch Jr.

Title: Lawyer, Real Estate Broker, Insurance Broker **Industry:** Law and Legal Services **Company Name:** Frisch & Frisch Chartered, Kroeschell, Inc. **Date of Birth:** 10/25/1940 **Place of Birth:** Evanston **State:** IL **Parents:** Sidney Frisch; Helen Frisch **Marital Status:** Married **Spouse Name:** Deborah A. King (8/27/1988) **Children:** Lauren; Michelle **Education:** JD, University of Illinois (1965); BS in Finance, University of Illinois (1962) **Certifications:** Licensed Insurance Broker, State of Illinois **Career:** President, Frisch Real Estate Group, Chicago, IL (1993-Present); President, Frisch & Frisch, Chartered, Inc., Chicago, IL (1977-Present); General Counsel, Kroeschell, Inc., Arlington Heights, IL (1966-Present); Vice President, Kroeschell, Inc., Arlington Heights, IL (1966-Present); General Counsel, Weber-Stephen Products (1966-2010); Vice President, Weber-Stephen Products (1966-2010); Vice President, Ontario Indemnity Group SPC, Grand Cayman, Cayman Islands; Consultant, Ontario Indemnity Group SPC, Grand Cayman, Cayman Islands **Career Related:** Member, Secretary Jim Edgar's Advisory Committee to Revise Illinois Business Corporation Act (1984); Lecturer, Seminars in Corporation and Mechanics in Law **Civic:** Vice President, University of Chicago Cancer Research Foundation, The University of Chicago Medicine Comprehensive Cancer Center (1984); Associate Board Member, University of Chicago Cancer Research Foundation, University of Chicago Medicine Comprehensive Cancer Center (1982) **Military Service:** Lieutenant, US Naval Reserve (1962-1969) **Creative Works:** Member, Editorial Committee, Illinois Business Corporation Act Annotated (1983); Author, "Attorney's Guide to Negotiation" (1979); Author, "Illinois Mechanic's Liens" (1972); Assistant Editor, "Illinois Law Forum," Illinois College of Law, University of Illinois at Urbana-Champaign (1964-1965) **Awards:** Certificate of Appreciation, The Chicago Bar Association (1983); Honoree, Order of the Coif, Illinois College of Law, University of Illinois at Urbana-Champaign, University of Illinois Board of Trustees (1965) **Membership:** Illinois Bar Association (1966-Present); ABA (1966-Present); Chairman, Corporate Law Committee, The Chicago Bar Association (1983-1984) **Bar Admissions:** Supreme Court of the U.S. (1986); Colorado Bar (1977); United States District Court for the Middle District of Georgia (1974); United States Court of Appeals for the Seventh Circuit (1968); Illinois (1966); United States District Court for Northern District of Illinois (1966) **Marquis Who's Who Honors:** Albert Nelson Marquis Lifetime Achievement Award (2017) **Business Address:** 14 N Peoria St., Ste 2E, Chicago, IL, 60607

Mary Patricia Garrahan-Masters

Title: Social Worker (Retired), Writer **Industry:** Social Work **Date of Birth:** 06/06/1951 **Place of Birth:** Philadelphia **State:** PA/USA **Parents:** Francis Edward Garrahan; Mary Patricia McElduff Garrahan **Education:** Master of Social Sciences, Law and Social Policy, Bryn Mawr College, Bryn Mawr, PA (1983); BA in Sociology, Villanova University, with Honors (1973); Coursework, Georgetown University (1971-1972); Facultad Filosofia y Letras, Madrid, Spain **Career:** Medical Social Worker, Philadelphia VA Medical Center, U.S. Department of Veterans Affairs, Philadelphia, PA (1988-1990); Medical Social Worker, VA Medical Center Lebanon, U.S. Department of Veterans Affairs, Lebanon, PA (1985-1988); Teacher, Delaware County Community College, Media, PA (1984); Social Service Director, Dowden Nursing Home, Newtown Square, PA (1980-1984); Director, Admissions, St Francis County House, Darby, PA (1981); Geriatrics Case Worker, Schuylkill County Office of Senior Services, Pottsville, PA (1974-1979) **Career Related:** Part-Time Social Worker, Delta-T Group, Bryn Mawr, PA (1992-1997); Part-Time Staff Coordinator, Garrahan Equipment Inc., Havertown, PA (1973-1992) **Civic:** Associate Member, National Committee, Washington, DC (1993-1999); Representative, National Committee, Washington, DC (1993-1999); Eucharistic Minister, St. Richard's Roman Catholic Church, Barnesville, PA (1974-1979) **Creative Works:** Contributor, Poetry, Lynx Magazine, Villanova University **Membership:** International Hypnosis Hall of Fame Guild Inc.; NARFE; Associate, Society of Friends of Touro Synagogue; Alpha Zeta Delta; Alpha Xi Delta; Disabled American Veterans; Animal Cat Rescue; American Diabetes Association **Marquis Who's Who Honors:** Albert Nelson Marquis Lifetime Achievement Award (2017) **To what do you attribute your success:** Ms. Garrahan-Masters attributes her success to being raised by her mother and grandmothers, as well as being integrated into what is old and what is new. **Why did you become involved in your profession or industry:** Ms. Garrahan-Masters became involved in her profession because she was interested in social work. Her father believed in social justice and coming up with solutions to problems that worked. **Hobbies:** Astronomy; Cats; Dutch County, Pennsylvania; Greek America **Shipping Address:** 501 Harriet Ln, Havertown, PA, 19083 **Website:** http://prabook.com/web/person-view.html?profileId=498214

Mary Jane Gavin

Title: Medical/Surgical Nurse (Retired) **Industry:** Medicine & Health Care **Date of Birth:** 09/01/1941 **Place of Birth:** Prairie Du Chen **State:** WI/USA **Parents:** Frank Grant Wolf; Mary Elizabeth Wolf **Marital Status:** Married **Spouse Name:** Alfred William Gavin (11/9/1963) **Children:** Catherine Heidi Elizabeth; Carol Alfred Eric; Scott **Education:** Postgraduate Work, Deepmuscle Training Ltd (1980); BS, University of Wisconsin-Madison (1964); RN, University of Wisconsin-Madison (1964); Coursework, North Central College (1959-1961); Postgraduate Work in Deep Muscle Therapy **Career:** Retired (2006); Home Response Nurse, Milwaukee VA Medical Center, U.S. Department of Veterans Affairs; Staff Nurse, University of Wisconsin Hospitals and Clinics Authority **Civic:** Unit Chair, American Legion Auxiliary Badger Girls State (1991-2005); Member, Auxiliary Task Force for the Handicapped, Eastside Wisconsin Evangelical Lutheran Church and School (1993); Active Member, Wisconsin Chapter, The American Legion **Awards:** Scholarship, University of Wisconsin-Madison **Membership:** Unit 501, American Legion Auxiliary (2012-2015); President, Unit 429, American Legion Auxiliary (1990-2005); American Library Association; Disabled American Veterans Auxiliary **Marquis Who's Who Honors:** Albert Nelson Marquis Lifetime Achievement Award (2017); Distinguished Humanitarian (2017) **Shipping Address:** 702 Fairmont Ave, Madison, WI, 53714

Evelyn Geer Clement, PhD

Title: Librarian, Educator (Retired) **Industry:** Education/Educational Services **Date of Birth:** 09/01/1926 **Place of Birth:** Springfield **State:** MA/USA **Parents:** Elihu Geer; Helen (Schenck) Geer **Marital Status:** Divorced **Spouse Name:** J.R. Clement (9/9/1946, Divorced 1972) **Children:** James Randall Clement; Timothy Bruce Clement; Susan Lynn Henson; Marc Weldon Clement; Audrey Hart Ethriedge **Education:** PhD, Indiana University, Bloomington, IN (1975); MLS, University of Oklahoma (1966); BA, The University of Tulsa, With Honors (1965) **Career:** Retired (1995); Member, Standing University Library Committee, Memphis State University (1986-1987); Director, Center for Instructional Service and Research, Memphis State University (1985-1995); Chairman, Women's Task Force, Memphis State University (1984-1985); Member, Faculty Tenure and Promotion Appeals Committee, Memphis State University (1980-1982); Chairman, Academy Senate, Memphis State University (1979-1980); Member, Standing University Library Committee, Memphis State University (1975-1980); Professor, Chairman of Library Science, Memphis State University (1972-1985); Special Instructor, University of Oklahoma, Norman, OK (1966-1970); Learning Resources Librarian, Oral Roberts University, Tulsa, OK (1966-1968); Librarian, Tulsa City-County Library (1960-1966) **Career Related:** Regional Trustee, Geer Family Association (2001-2007); Director, Media Consortium, Tennessee Regents (1993-1995) **Civic:** Board of Administration, Harvard Park Village Neighborhood Association (2005-2010) **Creative Works:** Editor, "No Other Generation" (1975); Editor, "Bibliographic Control of Nonprint Media" (1972); Contributor, Articles, Professional Journals **Awards:** Doctoral Fellow, United States Office of Education, Title II-B, Indiana University (1968-1971) **Membership:** American Library Association; Afghanistan Perceivers of Oklahoma; Pi Gamma Mu; Beta Phi Mu; Phi Alpha Theta **Marquis Who's Who Honors:** Albert Nelson Marquis Lifetime Achievement Award (2017) **What do you consider to be the highlight of your career:** When she got a bachelor's degree **Hobbies:** Reading; Crossword puzzles **Political Affiliations:** Republican **Religion:** Presbyterian **Shipping Address:** 6014 S Marion Place, Tulsa, OK, 74135

Ronald Walter Genini

Title: History Educator **Industry:** Education/Educational Services **Company Name:** Central Unified School District **Date of Birth:** 12/05/1946 **Place of Birth:** Oakland **State:** CA **Parents:** William Angelo Genini; Irma Lea (Gays) Genini **Marital Status:** Married **Spouse Name:** Roberta Mae Tucker (12/20/1969) **Children:** Thomas; Justin; Nicholas **Education:** MA, University of San Francisco (1969); BA, University of San Francisco (1968) **Certifications:** Secondary Education Teacher, State of California; Administrative Services Credential **Career:** Teacher, Central Unified School District, Fresno, CA (1970-2004) **Career Related:** Guest Contributor, Time Line Films (2006); Guest Appearance, History Channel Program "UFO Hotspots" (2003); United States History Exam Development Team, Golden State University, San Diego, CA (1989-1993); Judge, State History Day, Sacramento, CA (1986-1994); Securer, Placement of State-Registered Landmarks **Civic:** Active Member, Good Company Players, Fresno, CA (2000-2001); St. Anthony's School Board, Fresno, CA (1980-1984); Fresno City and County Historical Society (1975-1978); Board of Directors, Fresno Area 6 Neighborhood Council (1973-1974) **Creative Works:** Author, "California: On the Edge of American History," CreateSpace (2017); Editorial Assistant, "Fight of the Eagle" (2013); Editorial Assistant, "The Invincible Quest" (2007); Featured, Documentary, "The Woman with the Hungry Eyes", Director Hugh M. Neely, Time Line Films (2006); Cited Authority, Theda Bara Entry, Encyclopedia Britannica Online; American Women in History (1999); Author, "Theda Bara" (1996); Author, "Darn Right It's Butch" (1994); Author, "Romualdo Pacheco" (1985); Contributor, Articles to Professional Journals; Cited Authority, Romualdo Pacheco Entry, Biographical Directory, U.S. Congress **Awards:** Teacher Cares Award, California State Assembly and Fresno City Council (1996); Honoree, One Of the Outstanding Young Educators in America, Fresno Jaycees (1978) **Membership:** Mount Vernon Ladies Association; California Retired Teachers Association; Smithsonian Institute; Carmel Bach Festival; San Joaquin Parkway and Conservation Trust **Marquis Who's Who Honors:** Albert Nelson Marquis Lifetime Achievement Award (2017) **Why did you become involved in your profession or industry:** It was the only thing available for Mr. Genini in late 60s as a history major. **Hobbies:** Writing history; Motion picture script writing; Commercial acting **Political Affiliations:** Independent **Religion:** Roman Catholic **Shipping Address:** 1486 W Menlo Avenue, Fresno, CA, 93711

Dona Alden Coe Gibbons

Title: Senior System Analyst **Industry:** Technology **Company Name:** Troy University **Date of Birth:** 03/09/1975 **Place of Birth:** Springfield **State:** MA **Parents:** Arthur Coe Gibbons; Virginia Elaine Fife Gibbons **Education:** MS in Applied Computer Science, Columbus State University, Georgia (2007); BS in Software Engineering, Auburn University (2000); BS in Computer Engineering, Auburn University (2000); BEE, Auburn University (2000) **Certifications:** Certified CompTIA Network Professional (2003) **Career:** Educational Technology Senior System Analyst, SQL Programmer, Troy University eCampus, Troy Online (2010-Present); Education Technology Coordinator, Engineer, Troy University eCampus (2006-2010); Systems Integration and Software Development Manager, Engineer, Troy State University Southeast Regions (2004-2006); Network Specialist, Institutional support eArmyU, Troy State University, Southeast Regions (2002-2004); Government Contractor, U.S. Army, Ft. Benning, Columbus, GA (1999-2002); Thinkpad Product Specialist, Server Gas Analyst, IBM Personal Systems Group, Research Triangle Park, NC (1996-1998) **Awards:** Staff Spirit Award, eTroy (2013); Outstanding Achievement Award, IBM (1998) **Membership:** IEEE; Association for Supervision and Curriculum Development, Columbus State University Alumni; Mathematics Association of America; Association of Computing Machinery; **Marquis Who's Who Honors:** Albert Nelson Marquis Lifetime Achievement Award (2017) **Shipping Address:** PO Box 341, Ariton, AL, 36311

John R. Gibson

Title: Software Engineer **Industry:** Engineering **Company Name:** Rockwell Collins (Retired) **Date of Birth:** 12/24/1948 **Place of Birth:** Murfreesboro **State:** TN **Parents:** Donald Cotis Gibson; Sara Elizabeth Garner **Marital Status:** Divorced **Spouse Name:** Corinne de Marie Pallatto (9/2/1978, Divorced 7/1989) **Career:** Software Engineer, Rockwell Collins, Warner Robins, GA (2007-2013); Software Tester, Boeing Service Company, Colorado Springs, CO (2005); Embedded Programming, AOA Inc., Westlake Village, CA (2002-2004); Software Engineer, EDO Technical Services Operations, Edwards Air Force Base (1997-2001); Software Tester, EER Systems, Inc., Ridgecrest, CA (1996-1997); Computer Engineer, U.S. Air Force, Edwards Air Force Base, California (1993-1995); Science Computer Programmer, Boeing Computer Support Services, Ridgecrest, CA (1990-1991); Computer Programmer, Analyst, Computer Sciences Corporation, Ridgecrest, CA (1984-1990); Computer Programmer, Analyst, Computer Sciences Corporation, Colorado Springs, CO **Civic:** Treasurer, Antelope Valley Libertarian Party (2000-2002); Candidate for California State Senate, Antelope Valley Libertarian Party (2000) **Military Service:** Resigned, U.S. Air Force (1983); Captain, U.S. Air Force (1977); Commissioned 2nd Lieutenant, U.S. Air Force (1973) **Creative Works:** Contributor, Articles, News-letters; Contributor, Articles **Membership:** President, California Checker Association (1999-2005) **Political Affiliations:** Libertarian **Shipping Address:** 1023 Ridge Avenue, Tuscumbia, AL, 35674

Joanne Marie Gigliotti

Title: Artist, Arts Administrator **Industry:** Fine Art **Company Name:** Batik-Designs **Date of Birth:** 06/12/1945 **Place of Birth:** Pittsburgh **State:** PA **Parents:** Joseph F. Gigliotti; Anna Maria (Costantini) Gigliotti **Children:** Jennifer L. Valli; Robert J. Valli **Education:** MEd in Art, The Pennsylvania State University (1978); BFA in Painting, Design and Sculpture, Carnegie-Mellon University (1967) **Certifications:** Certificate in Design, Carnegie-Mellon University (1967) **Career:** Artist, Administrator, Batik-Designs.com (2011-Present); Artist, Administrator, BatikTile.com (1995-Present); Advisor, Women's Council, Smithsonian (1995); Senior Program Coordinator, Visual Arts Specialist, Smithsonian (1994-1995); Chair, Women's Council, Smithsonian (1992-1994); Secretary, Women's Council, Smithsonian (1989-1992); Member, Women's Council, Smithsonian (1988-1995); Director, Studio Arts Department, Smithsonian (1987-1995); Project Director, Discover Graphics, Smithsonian (1987-1995); Consultant, Administrator, The Fine Arts Connection, Inc., State College, PA (1983-1987); Art and Framing Consultant, Eli's Art Gallery, State College, PA (1981-1982); Founder, Director, Commercial Operation, Washington, DC (1980-1982); Director, HUB Arts and Craft Centre, University Park, PA (1978-1980); Self-Employed Exhibiting Artist, 60 One-Woman Shows, Accompanying Presentations (1967-1978) **Career Related:** Coordinator, Second American Batik Design Competition (2013-2014); Art Services, Presentation Work (2007-2009); Creative Computer Coach (2006-2008) **Civic:** Women's Issues Project, Womens Informational Needs (2002-2003) **Creative Works:** Featured Presenter, Remarkable Indonesia Fair, Consulate of the Republic of Indonesia, Chicago Hilton, Illinois (2016); Featured Presenter, World Bank/International Monetary Fund Summer Meeting, Atrium, IMF, Washington, DC (2016); Featured Presenter, Batik Demonstration, Representing Indonesia, 10 ASEAN Countries, USABC 30th Galla Event, Four Seasons Hotel, Washington, DC (2014); Featured Presenter, "Show and Tell," The National Textile Museum, Symposium, Celebration of World Batik Day (2012) **Awards:** Named, First Place Winner, First American Batik Design Competition (2011-2012) **Membership:** The George Washington University Museum and The Textile Museum; National Cryptologic Museum; American Alliance of Museums; Women in Museums Network; Phi Kappa Phi **Marquis Who's Who Honors:** Albert Nelson Marquis Lifetime Achievement Award (2017) **Political Affiliations:** Democrat **Shipping Address:** 69 Bralan Court, Gaithersburg, MD, 20877 **Website:** http://www.batik-designs.com

O.L. Gilbert

Title: Attorney **Industry:** Law and Legal Services **Company Name:** Gilbert & Albiston **Spouse:** Laura Bloom Gilbert **Children:** Four Children; Eight Grandchildren **Education:** JD, College of William and Mary (1975); BSBA, Old Dominion University (1972) **Bar Admissions:** Virginia State Bar **Career:** Trial Lawyer (1975-Present); Substitute Judge, Commonwealth of Virginia (2015-2017) **Military:** U.S. Naval Reserve (1967-1974) **Awards:** Lawyer of the Year, Personal Injury Litigation, Best Lawyers (2011, 2013, 2017); Best Lawyers in America **Memberships:** ABA; Expertise: Victims law for personal injury (car accidents, malpractice, etc.) **Hobbies:** Golf **To what do you attribute your success:** Mr. Gilbert attributes his success to hard work, preparation, and a lot of personal experience with people. He became a lawyer because he wanted to help people.

Melva Theresa Giles

Title: Nursing Professor, Researcher, Clinical Specialist, Assistant Chairperson **Industry:** Medicine & Health Care **Company Name:** Pierce College **Place of Birth:** Baltimore **State:** MD **Marital Status:** Single **Spouse Name:** Mr. Hargett Jr. (Deceased); Mr. Owens Jr. (Deceased); Mr. Giles (Deceased) **Children:** Meya Elizabeth Hargett **Education:** EdD, Pepperdine University (1993); MSN, California State University, Dominguez Hills, CA (1988); BSN, California State University, Los Angeles, CA (1981); Associate Degree in Nursing, Catonsville Community College, MD (1970); RN, California **Career:** Professor of Nursing, Pierce College (1989-Present); Professor, Graduate School of Nursing Science, University of Phoenix (2002-2007); Clinical Nurse Specialist, County of Los Angeles (1987-1989); Educator, County of Los Angeles (1987-1989); Guest Lecturer, Research Education Institute, University of California, Los Angeles, CA (1987-1988); Director of Professional Development, Department of Nursing, Pierce College; Director of Research, Department of Nursing, Pierce College; Associate Chairperson, Department of Nursing, Pierce College **Career Related:** Nursing Researcher (2011-Present); Statewide Graduate School Nursing (1990-1998); Lecturer, California State University, Dominguez Hills, CA **Civic:** Educational Ambassador to the People's Republic of China; U.S.-Sino Nursing Forum **Creative Works:** Author, "Decision Making Styles and Effective Problem Solving"; Author, "Development and Evaluation of an Information Index for Community College Based on Senate Bill 533"; Author, "Re-engineering the Traditional Nursing Curriculum"; Author, "Perspectives on Alzheimer's Disease: Clinical, Academic, Research and Management"; Contributor, Articles, Chi Eta Phi's Glowing Lamp Journal **Awards:** Nominated, Ethel Witkin's Research Award; Recipient, Distinguished Scholarship Award; Recipient, Certificates of Appreciation, Chi Eta Sorority, Inc., Delta Chapter **Membership:** Fellow, Nightingale Society; California Nurses Association; Council of Black Nurses; Future Society; Association of Pan African Doctoral Scholars, Inc.; Phi Delta Kappa; Sigma Theta Tau; Chi Eta Phi, Delta Chapter; Gamma Tau (at Large); Nursing Research Group, Beijing, China; Editorial Board, Journal of Chi Eta Phi Sorority, Inc.; Healthy People, Healthy Communities Through Nursing Contributions, Sigma Theta Tau **Marquis Who's Who Honors:** Albert Nelson Marquis Lifetime Achievement Award (2017) **Hobbies:** Playing the piano; Playing the violin; Reading; Traveling **Shipping Address:** 3057 Tourmaline Ln, Palmdale, CA, 93550

Stephen Gill

Title: Physicist (Retired) **Industry:** Sciences **Date of Birth:** 11/13/1938 **Place of Birth:** Baltimore **State:** MD **Parents:** Robert Lee Gill; Charlotte (Olmsted) Gill **Marital Status:** Married **Spouse Name:** Margaret Ann Gaskins (12/21/1961) **Children:** Elizabeth Olmsted; Richard Paschall **Education:** PhD, Harvard University (1964); MA, Harvard University (1961); BS, Massachusetts Institute of Technology (1960) **Career:** Chief Scientist, Votan Corporation (1981-1999); Chairman, Board, Votan Corporation (1981-1985); Founder, President, Votan Corporation (1979-1991); Chief Scientist, Artec Associates, Inc. (1977-1991); Founder, President, Artec Associates, Inc. (1972-1977); Manager, Shock Dynamics Department, Physics International Company (1970-1972); Head, High Energy Gasdynamics, Physics International Company (1968-1970); Head, High Energy Gasdynamics, Stanford Research Institute (1965-1968); Research Physicist, Stanford Research Institute (1964-1965); **Career Related:** Founder, Director, Chief Financial Officer, Stephen & Margaret Gill Family Foundation (1999-Present); Founder, Chief Scientist, Magnetic Pulse Inc. (1985-1999) **Civic:** San Francisco Symphony Association; San Francisco Museum of Art **Membership:** IEEE; Lifetime Member, American Physical Society; Lifetime Member, American Mathematics Society; Massachusetts Institute of Technology Alumni Association; **Political Affiliations:** Republican **Religion:** Episcopalian **Shipping Address:** 32 Flood Cir, Atherton, CA, 94027

Dennis M. Gingold

Title: Chairman of the board **Industry:** Law and Legal Services **Company Name:** The Reserve Trust Company **Date of Birth:** 06/23/1949 **Place of Birth:** Plainfield **State:** NJ **Marital Status:** Married **Spouse Name:** Anne Carol Pearson (1970) **Children:** Stacy Michele; Samantha Anne **Education:** LLD, Rollins College, with Honors (2007); Postgraduate Studies, State University of New York, Buffalo (1975-1976); LLM in International Law, New York University (1975); Postgraduate Studies, Princeton University (1974-1975); Postgraduate Studies, New York University (1974-1975); JD, Seton Hall University (1974); BA, Rollins College (1971) **Career:** Principal, PennAveOne LLC (2013-Present); Partner, Gingold Guilder (Now Gingold Law Firm PLLC) (2012-Present); Lead Counsel, Cobell Plaintiffs in Cobell vs. Salazar (1996-2012); Lead Banking Partner, Squire, Sanders & Dempsey, Washington, DC (1985-1988); Partner, Dickstein, Shapiro & Morin, Washington, DC (1990-1993); Partner, Foley, Hoag & Eliot (Now Foley Hoag LLP), Washington, DC (1988-1990); Partner, Kirkland & Ellis LLP, Denver, CO and Washington, DC (1982-85); Partner, Gorsuch, Kirgis, Campbell, Walker & Grover, Denver, CO (1980-1982); Regional Counsel, 12th National Bank Region, Office of the Comptroller of the Currency, U.S. Department of the Treasury, Denver, CO (1979-80); Attorney-Advisor, Office of the Comptroller of the Currency, U.S. Department of the Treasury, Washington, DC (1976-1979) **Creative Works:** Senior Member, Seton Hall University Law Review (1972-1973) **Awards:** National Litigator of the Month, The American Lawyer (2009); Commencement Speaker, Rollins College (2007); Most Influential Individuals in Banking, American Banker Newsletter (1995); Top 20 Banking Lawyer, The National Law Journal (1983); Reginald Heber Smith Fellow (1975-1976) **Bar Admissions:** Admitted to Practice, U.S. Court of Appeals for the Eleventh Circuit (1997); Admitted to Practice, U.S. Court of Appeals for the Ninth Circuit (1991); Admitted to Practice, U.S. District Court for the District of Columbia (1989); Admitted to Practice, Supreme Court of the United States (1985); Admitted to Practice, U.S. Court of Appeals for the Tenth Circuit (1984); Admitted to Practice, U.S. District Court for the District of Colorado (1981); Admitted to Practice, U.S. District Court for the District of New Jersey (1974); New Jersey State Bar Association (1974) **Business Address:** 1717 Pennsylvania Avenue, 9th Floor, Washington, DC, 20006

Raymond Girvigian

Title: Architect (Retired) **Industry:** Architecture & Construction **Date of Birth:** 11/27/1926 **Place of Birth:** Detroit **State:** MI **Parents:** Manoug Girvigian; Margaret Girvigian **Marital Status:** Widowed **Spouse Name:** Beverly Rae Bennett (9/23/1967, Deceased 2005) **Children:** Dr. Michael Raymond Girvigian **Education:** MA in Architecture, University of California, Berkeley (1951); BA in Architecture, University of California, Berkeley, with Highest Honors in Architecture (1950); AA, University of California, Los Angeles (1947) **Certifications:** California State Board Architectural License #C-1812 (1957) **Career:** Owner/Principal, Raymond Girvigan FAIA, South Pasadena, CA (1968-2017); Owner/Principal, Raymond Girvigan AIA, Los Angeles, CA (1957-1968); With, Hutchason Architects, Los Angeles, CA (1952-1957) **Career Related:** Chairman Emeritus, California State Capitol Commission (1998); Chairman Emeritus, California Historical Buildings Code (1993); Co-Founder, Chairman, California State Capitol Commission (1985-1998); Co-Founder, Chairman, Governing Board, California Historical Buildings Code (1976-1991); Co-Founder, Chairman, South Pasadena Cultural Heritage Commission (1971-1977); **Civic:** Member, St. James' Episcopal Church, South Pasadena, CA **Military Service:** U.S. Army (1944-1946) **Creative Works:** Restoration Architect, Castle Green Apartments, Pasadena, CA (1994-1997); Restoration Architect, Bradbury Building, Los Angeles Retrofit/Rehab (1984-1987); Co-Editor, Producer, Historical Monographs of Memorial Coliseum (1984); Restoration Architect, Robinson Gardens Landmarks, Beverly Hills, CA (1983-1992); Restoration Architect, Pasadena Central Library (1982-2015); Co-Editor, Producer, Historical Monographs of Pan Pacific Auditorium (1980); Restoration Architect, California State Capitol (1975-1982); Co-Editor, Producer, Historical Monographs of California's State Capitol (1975); Restoration Architect, Workman/Temple Homestead (La Puente Rancho), City of Industry, California (1974-1981); Restoration Architect, Mount Pleasant House Museum, Heritage Square, Los Angeles, CA (1972-1995); **Awards:** Recipient, Joseph P. Thomas Founders Award, American Institute of Architects (2011); Recipient, Heritage Preservation Award, City of South Pasadena, California (2010-2011); Recipient, Lifetime Achievement Award, California Preservation Foundation (2007); **Membership:** State Preservation Coordinator, American Institute of Architects (1970-1989) **Marquis Who's Who Honors:** Lifetime Achievement Award (2018); Who's Who in "America" (1986-2018); Who's Who in the World" (1996-2018) **Political Affiliations:** Democrat **Religion:** Episcopalian **Business Address:** PO Box 220, South Pasadena, CA, 91031

Norman Goldstein

Title: Clinical Professor of Dermatology **Industry:** Education/Educational Services **Company Name:** Icahn School of Medicine **Place of Birth:** Brooklyn **State:** NY/USA **Marital Status:** Married **Education:** MD, SUNY Downstate Medical Center (1959); Degree, Columbia College (1955); Resident of Dermatology, Skin and Cancer Hospital, Bellevue Hospital, New York University **Career:** Senior Faculty Member, Mount Sinai Hospital and School of Medicine; Clinical Professor of Dermatology, Mount Sinai Medical Center, Icahn School of Medicine at Mount Sinai; Chief of Dermatology, U.S. Army; Chief of Dermatology, Director of Research and Education Foundation Laboratory, Honolulu Medical Group **Creative Works:** Author, "The Skin You Live In" (1978); Contributor, Numerous Books on Tattoo Art; Contributor, More than 200 Published Medical Articles, Book Chapters and Editorial Columns **Awards:** Commendation for 50 Years of Practice, American Medical Association (2009); Laureate Award, American College of Physicians (2005); Original Research and Prevention of Skin Cancers Award, American Academy of Dermatology (1972); Fellow, American College of Physicians; Named, Leading Physician of the World, International Association of Dermatologists **Marquis Who's Who Honors:** Albert Nelson Marquis Lifetime Achievement Award (2017) **Business Address:** 5 E 98th St., Fl 5, New York, NY, 10029 **Shipping Address:** 1510 Lexington Ave., Apt 4B, New York, NY, 10029

Miguel Gonzalez-Gerth, PhD

Title: Literature Educator, Language Educator **Industry:** Education/Educational Services **Company Name:** The University of Texas at Austin **Date of Birth:** 08/15/1926 **Place of Birth:** Mexico City **Country of Origin:** Mexico **Year of Passing:** 7/18/2017 **Parents:** Gen. Miguel Gonzalez-Cadena; Claire E. Gerth **Marital Status:** Married **Spouse Name:** Tita Valencia (10/9/1994); Betty Brumbalow (Deceased) **Education:** PhD, Princeton University (1970); MA, Princeton University (1960); MA, The University of Texas at Austin (1955); BA, The University of Texas at Austin (1950) **Career:** Professor Emeritus, The University of Texas at Austin (2001-2017); Professor in Spanish, The University of Texas at Austin (1995-2001); Professor in Comparative Literature, The University of Texas at Austin (1995-2001); Professor in Spanish, The University of Texas at Austin (1987-1995); Associate Professor in Spanish, The University of Texas at Austin (1973-1987); Assistant Professor in Spanish, The University of Texas at Austin (1965-1972); Instructor in Romance Languages, Bryn Mawr College (1960-1965); Master of Spanish, The Lawrenceville School (1956-1958); Master of French, The Lawrenceville School (1956-1958) **Career Related:** Consultant, Ransom Center, The University of Texas at Austin (1972-2017); Consultant, Educational Testing Service (1960-1975); Consultant, The College Board (1960-1970) **Civic:** Board of Directors, Humanities Texas (2007-2017) **Military Service:** Captain, U.S. Navy **Creative Works:** Author, "Looking For The Horse Latitudes" (2007); Author, "Nueve Musas Eroticas" (2005); Author, "The Brandywine in Winter" (2004); Author, "La Lengua Fracturads," Ediciones Calle de Cerezas, Mexico (2003); Author, "En Busca de las Calmas Ecuatoriales" (1996); Author, "T.E. Lawrence, Richard Aldington, and the Death of Heroes" (1994); Author, "The Musicians and Other Poems" (1991); Author, "Labyrinth of Imagery: Ramon Gomez de la Serna's Novelas de la Nebulosa" (1986); Editor, "Texas Quarterly" (1972-1978) **Awards:** Pro Bene Meritis Award, College of Liberal Arts, The University of Texas at Austin (2006) **Marquis Who's Who Honors:** Albert Nelson Marquis Lifetime Achievement Award (2017) **Hobbies:** Collecting antiques, art, and books; Nature watching **Shipping Address:** 303 E 42nd Street, c/o Tita Valencia, Austin, TX, 78751

Martin Eli Gordon

Title: Physician, Educator **Industry:** Education/Educational Services **Company Name:** Yale School of Medicine **Date of Birth:** 08/15/1921 **Place of Birth:** Kiev **Country of Origin:** Russia **Parents:** Isadore Gordon; Belle Gordon **Marital Status:** Widowed **Spouse Name:** Evelyn E. Gordon (3/17/1946, Deceased) **Children:** Jeffrey I. Gordon; Judy I. Dienstag **Education:** Junior to Chief Medical Resident, VA Hospital, CT (1949-1951); Intern, University of Chicago Clinics (1946-1947); MD, Yale University (1946); BS, Kent State University (1943) **Certifications:** Diplomate, American Board of Internal Medicine; Diplomate, National Medical Boards **Career:** Author, Creator, Production of Medical Educational Exhibits, Devices and Films, Medical Films, LLC, CT (1956-Present); Clinical Instructor to Clinical Professor, Medicine, Yale School of Medicine, CT (1951-Present); Consultant, Practice in Gastroenterology, CT (1955-1991); Private Consultant, Gastroenterologist, Various Hospitals, CT (1955-1991); Consultant, Gastroenterologist, Department of University Health, Yale University, CT; Acting Chief to Chief, Gastroenterology Section, VA Hospital, CT **Career Related:** Honorary Trustee, Yale Medical Library (1989-Present); Chairman, Trustee, Cushing/Whitney Medical Library Associates (1989-Present); Associate Fellow, Pierson College, Yale University (1979-Present) **Civic:** Attending Physician, Free Clinic, University City, MO (2007-Present); Chair, Lifetime Board of Trustees, Cushing/Whitney Library Associates, Yale University (1994-Present) **Military Service:** Senior Assistant Surgeon, U.S. Public Health Service (1947-1949); **Creative Works:** Author, Producer, Director, Various Medical Educational Films, (1971-Present); Creator, Education Films **Awards:** Health and Medical Media Annual Awards (2005-Present); AMWA Award (2006); Dean's Peter Parker Medal for Outstanding Contributions to Medicine and the Well Being of the Yale University School of Medicine (2004) **Membership:** Archives Committee, American College of Gastroenterology (1991-1993); Delegate to National, Yale Alumni Association (1989-1994) **Marquis Who's Who Honors:** Albert Nelson Marquis Lifetime Achievement Award (2017) **To what do you attribute your success:** Dr. Gordon attributes his success to knowing many patients, each a learning event and good fortune. **Why did you become involved in your profession or industry:** Dr. Gordon became involved because of human needs. **What do you consider to be the highlight of your career:** One of the highlights in Dr. Gordon's career was winning awards with Medical Films, LLC. **Business Address:** 1 McKnight Pl Apt 437, Saint Louis, MO, 63124

David F. Gossom

Industry: Law and Legal Services **Place of Birth:** Wichita Falls **State:** KS/USA **Education:** JD, School of Law, Texas Tech University (1981) **Civic:** Volunteer, Paws for Greatness; Volunteer, Campfire Girls of Wichita Falls **Awards:** AV Preeminent Attorney (2013) **Membership:** Council of School Attorneys, Texas Association of School Boards, Inc.; Council of School Attorneys, National School Boards Association **Hobbies:** Training retrievers

Edward Earl Gotts

Title: Clinical Psychologist, Researcher **Industry:** Research **Company Name:** MultiTED Associates **Date of Birth:** 05/25/1933 **Place of Birth:** Los Angeles **State:** CA **Parents:** Earl Gotts; Norma Stone Gotts **Marital Status:** Widowed **Spouse Name:** Shirley Jean Lund (9/10/1955, Deceased 2/13/2014) **Children:** Gregory; Gary; Kimberly **Education:** Postdoctoral Fellow, University of Colorado Medical Center (1971-1972); PhD, The University of Texas at Austin (1966); United States Public Health Service Research Fellow, University of Texas (1965-1967); MA, Whitworth University, Spokane, WA (1962); Intern in College Teaching, Washington State University, Pullman, WA (1960-1961); BA, Whitworth University, Spokane, WA (1960) **Career:** Adjunct Faculty Member, Massachusetts School of Professional Psychology (Now William James College) (2004-2012); Pre-Doctoral Internship Director, APPIC (1993-2002); Psychologist, Evansville Psychiatric Children's Center, Indiana (1992-1993); Clinical Director, Evansville Psychiatric Children's Center, Indiana (1992-1993); Psychologist, King's Daughters' Hospital Rehabilitation Center (1994-2003); Chief Psychologist, Madison State Hospital, Indiana (1986-2003); Psychologist, Hospital Corporation of America's Huntington Hospital (1984-1986); Psychologist, John Marshall Medical Service (1984-1986); Director, School-Family Relations Study (1984-1985); Chief Psychologist, Huntington State Hospital (1983-1986); Clinical Professor of Medical Psychology, Marshall Medical School, West Virginia (1983-1986); Principal Consultant, "The Family Room," Community Action Program Evansville (CAPE), Evansville, IN (1982-1984); Client Service Director, Shawnee Hills CMHC, Charleston, WV (1982-1983); School-Family Relations Research Program (1981-1983); Consultant, Journal of School Psychology (1980-1991); Commission Invited Panelist, "Improving Basic Education Skills of Appalachian Children," Appalachian Regional (1979); Long-term Follow-up, Project Hope (1977-1981); Director, Television for Effective Parenting, USOE (1975-1976); Director, Division of Childhood and Parenting, Appalachia Educational Laboratory, Charleston, WV (1974-1983); Psychology Director, Developmental Training Center, Indiana University Bloomington (1972-1974) **Civic:** Certified Lay Speaker, North United Methodist Church, Madison, IN (1999-2015) **Military Service:** Captain, U.S. Air Force (1953-1957) **Creative Works:** Author, "Multicultural Tasks of Emotional Development Test" (2017); Author, "The Clinical Interpretation of the MMPI-2" (2005) **Political Affiliations:** Independent **Religion:** Christian **Shipping Address:** 217 Wildwood Dr, Madison, IN, 47250

Ronald Gougher

Title: Language Educator **Industry:** Education/Educational Services **Company Name:** West Chester University **Date of Birth:** 07/27/1939 **Place of Birth:** Allentown **State:** PA **Parents:** Samuel Franklin Gougher; Beatrice Dorothy (Shanaberger) Gougher **Children:** Robert **Education:** Advanced Certificate, Goethe Institute, Munich, Germany (1969); Postgraduate Coursework, University of Pennsylvania (1964-1975); Postgraduate Coursework, Harvard University (1964); MA, Lehigh University (1964); Postgraduate Coursework, Stanford University (1963); Postgraduate Coursework, Albright College (1962); BA, Muhlenberg College (1961) **Career:** Campus Director, Experiment in International Living, West Chester University (1972-1992); Chairman, Department of Foreign Languages, West Chester University (1977-1996); Director, International Education, West Chester University (1974-1983); Coordinator, German Studies, West Chester University (1972-2005); Associate Professor, German, West Chester University (1969-2005); Instructor, German, Lehigh University (1965-1969); Teacher, German, Moravian Seminary for Girls (1965-1969) **Career Related:** Director, American-European Studies Program, West Chester University and Soros Foundation, Kazakhstan (1998-Present); Director, American-European Studies Program, West Chester University and Soros Foundation, Albania, Bosnia, Kyrgystan, Mongolia (1997-Present); Consultant, Franklin Mint (1992-Present); President, World Learning Inc. (1992-Present); Delegate to Israel (2014); Delegate to Cuba (2012); Delegate to Egypt (2012); Delegate to China (2010); Delegate to Vietnam, Cambodia (2007); Director, American-European Studies Program, West Chester University and Soros Foundation, China, Haiti, Zimbabwe, Argentina, Immaculata University (2005); Director, American-European Studies Program, West Chester University and Soros Foundation, Georgia (2003); Director, American-European Studies Program, West Chester University and Soros Foundation, Kosovo (2001-2002); Director, American-European Studies Program, West Chester University and Soros Foundation, Azerbaijan (1999) **Civic:** Citizen Ambassador Program, Israel (2014); Citizen Ambassador Program, Cuba (2012); Citizen Ambassador Program, Egypt (2012); Citizen Ambassador Program, China (2010); Citizen Ambassador Program, Vietnam, Cambodia (2007) **Awards:** Soros Foundation (1990-Present); Grantee at Immaculata University (2005); **Membership:** American Association of Teachers of German; ACTFL; Northeast Conference on the Teaching of Foreign Languages; International Platform Association; Smithsonian Institution; Ruffed Grouse Society **Political Affiliations:** Republican **Religion:** Lutheran **Shipping Address:** 3309 Windsor Lane, Thorndale, PA, 19372

Arnold Harold Graf

Title: Financial Planner, Owner (Retired) **Industry:** Financial Services **Company Name:** Nebsco Financial Services, Inc. **Date of Birth:** 10/30/1930 **Place of Birth:** Buffalo **State:** NY **Parents:** John Edward Graf; Rose Ruth (Tyman) Graf **Marital Status:** Single **Spouse Name:** Rita Mary DiFlorio (8/3/1981, Deceased); Joan Nensel (9/1/1956, Divorced 1980) **Children:** Jenny; David; Laurie; Paul; Ellen; Amy **Education:** MA in International Relations, The U.S. Army War College (1975); Postgraduate Studies, Command and General Staff College (1966); BS in Economics, University of Pennsylvania (1968); Coursework, Rutgers, The State University of New Jersey (1955-1958) **Career:** Finance Associate, Allstate LSA Securities (Now Allstate Insurance Companies) (2002-2006); Chief Executive Officer, Nebsco Financial Service LTD (1981-2004); President, Nebsco Financial Service LTD (1981-2004); Career General Agent, Aetna Inc. (1975-1980); Senior Superintendent Agencies, Insurance Company of North America (Now Chubb) (1972-1975); Regional Manager, Southland Life Insurance Company (1970-1972); Field Marketing Director, National Liberty Corporation (1968-1970); District and Regional Manager, Franklin Life Insurance Company (1960-1968); Special Agent, Provident Mutual Life Insurance Company of Philadelphia (1959-1960); Personnel Director, Container Corporation of America (1957-1959); Shift Supervisor, Campbell Soup Company (Now CSC BRANDS, L.P.) (1956-1957) **Career Related:** National Insurance and Financial Service (2007-Present) **Civic:** Major Donor, Rotary International (1958-Present); Major Donor, Marple Newtown School District (2002-2005, 1995-2000); **Military Service:** Colonel, U.S. Army (1975); Commissioned 2nd Lieutenant, U.S. Army (1952); Served in Vietnam, U.S. Army; Served in Korea, U.S. Army **Awards:** Citation for Meritorious Service, Rotary International (2005); Recipient, Humanitarian Award, Four Chaplains Memorial Foundation (1996); Fellow, The Gundaker Foundation, Inc., Rotary District 7450 (1990) **Membership:** Life Manager, Penn National Insurance (2007-2009); Chair, District 7450, Rotary International (2000-2006); Director, NAIFA-PA (2000-2004); Foundation Trustee, Serra International (1998-2000); Governor, District 28, Serra International (1996-1998); Governor, Rhode Island District, Rotary International (1990-1991); President, Newton Square Club, Rotary International (1987-1988); President, Delaware County Association of Life Underwriters; 32nd Degree Masons **Political Affiliations:** Republican **Religion:** Roman Catholic; Episcopalian; Anglican **Shipping Address:** 1047 Bidwell Circle, Charleston, SC, 29414

Alma Eleanor Graham

Title: Editor, Writer, Educational Consultant **Industry:** Writing and Editing **Date of Birth:** 11/13/1936 **Place of Birth:** Raleigh **State:** NC **Parents:** David Robert Graham; Irene G. (Knott) Graham **Education:** MA in Contemporary Literature, Columbia University (1970); BA in English, University of North Carolina at Chapel Hill, With Honors (1958) **Career:** Consultant (2001-Present); Freelance Author (1987-1990); Corporate Consultant (1987-1990); Editorial Manager, McGraw-Hill Education (1976-1987); Executive Editor, McGraw-Hill Education (1976-1987) **Career Related:** Consultant in Bias-Free Language (1978-1980); Images Consultant, U.S. Information Agency (1978-1980); Featured Speaker, Berlin Conference, The Aspen Institute (1977); Woodrow Wilson Fellowship (1958-1959) **Civic:** Trustee, The Cathedral Church of Saint John the Divine (1994-1999); President, Laymen's Club **Creative Works:** Editor, "New World Outlook," General Board of Global Ministries (1991-2001); Author, "Basic Map Skills" (1991); Author, "McGraw-Hill Educational Software" (1988); Author, "Our Nation, Our World," Third Edition (1988); Author, "North Carolina: The Land and Its People" (1988); Author, "Our Nation, Our World," Second Edition (1986); Co-Author, Bridging Worlds Through General Semantics (1984); Author, "Our Nation, Our World" (1983); Co-Author, "Success With Words" (1983); Co-Author, "Guidelines for Equal Treatment of the Sexes" (1972); Executive Editor, "American Heritage Dictionary," Houghton Mifflin Harcourt (1970-1975) **Awards:** Honoree, 50 Extraordinary Women of Achievement, National Conference of Christians and Jews (Now National Conference for Community and Justice) (1978); Honoree, Trail Blazer in Environmental Law, National Law Journal, ALM Media Properties, LLC; Honoree, American Leading Lawyer for Business, Chambers & Partners; Honoree, Best Lawyers in America; Honoree, A/V Preeminent, Martindale-Hubbell; Honoree, SuperLawyers; Nominee, Environmental Leadership Counsel, Environmental Law Institute; Honoree, Leading Lawyer for Environment, Legal 500 **Membership:** National Organization for Women; The Associated Church Press; National Council for the Social Studies; Organization for Equal Education of the Sexes; **Marquis Who's Who Honors:** Albert Nelson Marquis Lifetime Achievement Award (2017) **Shipping Address:** PO Box 117, East Arlington, VT, 05252 **Website:** http://www.goodwinlaw.com/professionals/k/kirsch-laurence

Nessa Grainger

Title: Artist **Industry:** Fine Art **Date of Birth:** 09/15/1934 **Place of Birth:** Atlantic City **State:** NJ **Parents:** Barnet Posner; Pauline (Gittelman) Posner **Marital Status:** Married **Spouse Name:** Murray Grainger **Children:** Richard Greenbaum; Margie Friedman **Education:** Postgraduate Studies, Pennsylvania Academy of Arts (1962-1964); Postgraduate Studies, Tyler School of Art, Temple University, PA (1959-1960); BFA, Philadelphia Museum School (1955) **Career Related:** Workshop Presenter in Field; Teacher, The Banana Factory; Resident Artist, Pennsylvania; Painting Teacher, Pennsylvania; Somerset Art Association, New Jersey; Artist in Residence, Lafayette College, Easton, PA (2008) **Creative Works:** One-Woman Show, Wired Gallery, Bethlehem, PA (2007); One-Woman Show, The Baum School of Art, Allentown, Pennsylvania (2007); One-Woman Show, Gallery on Main, PA (2007); One-Woman Show, Connections Gallery (2006); Exhibition, Freyberger Gallery, Pennsylvania State University (2002); One-Woman Show, Louisa Melrose Gallery, NJ (2001); One-Woman Show, Pen and Brush, Inc., New York, NY (2000); Exhibition Pen and Brush Club, New York, NY (2000); One-Woman Show, Somerset Art Association, New Jersey (1998); One-Woman Show, Van Eck Global Gallery, New York, NY (1998); Exhibition, California Watercolor Society (1998); Exhibition, San Diego Watercolor Society (1997); One-Woman Show, Warner-Lambert Corporate Headquarters, Morris Plains, NJ (1996); Exhibition, American Watercolor Society Annual Exhibition (1995, 2006, 2008); One-Woman Show, Ocean County Artists Guild (1994); One-Woman Show, Elliott Museum, Stuart, FL (1993); One-Woman Show, The Interchurch Center, New York, NY (1992); One-Woman Show, Douglas College, New Jersey (1990); Exhibition, National Academy of Design, (1981, 1992, 1996); Exhibition, Watercolor Society of Alabama; Adirondacks National Exhibition, Old Forge, NY (1998); Exhibition, Pennsylvania Watercolor Society at Bucknell University, Lewisburg, PA (1998); Exhibition, National Watercolor Society of Oklahoma (1998, 1999); Exhibition, Kilpatrick Galleries, Oklahoma City (1998-1999) **Awards:** Mark Freeman Award, National Society of Painters, Sculptors (2009-Present); Nicholas Reale Award (1993-Present); Watercolor Award, New Jersey (2009); Liquitex Award, National Society of Painters in Casein & Acrylic (2007) **Membership:** Rocky Mountain Watercolor Society (1997-Present) **Shipping Address:** 706 S.W. 18th Street, Boynton Beach, FL, 33426

Patrick Alexander Grant

Title: Non Profit Association Chair, President/Chief Executive Officer **Industry:** Nonprofit & Philanthropy **Company Name:** Western Stock Show Association **Date of Birth:** 11/14/1945 **Place of Birth:** Denver **State:** CO **Parents:** Edwin Hendrie Grant (Deceased); Mary Belle (McIntyre) Grant (Deceased) **Marital Status:** Married **Spouse Name:** Carla Clyde Yancey (8/16/1975) **Children:** Mary Cameron; Swede Tamazin; Alexis Hendrie Guinan **Education:** JD, Drake University (1976); MBA, Denver University (1973); Navy Supply Corps School (1968); BA, Colgate University, with Honors (1967); Officer Candidate School, U.S. Navy Reserve **Career:** Chairman, Board of Directors, Western Stock Show Association (2016-Present); Vice Chair, Capital Campaign Committee, Western Stock Show Association (2016-Present); President, National Western Stock Show (1990-2010); Chief Executive Officer, National Western Stock Show (1990-2010); Chairman, Audit Committee, Colorado General Assembly (1989-1990); Chairman, Judiciary Committee, Colorado General Assembly (1988-1992); Chairman, Legal Services Committee, Colorado General Assembly (1988-1989); Vice-Chairman, Financial Committee, Colorado General Assembly (1987-1988); State Representative, Colorado General Assembly (1985-1992) **Career Related:** Local U.S. Bank Advisory Board (2003-2004); Board of Directors, Colorado Sports Hall of Fame (1992-1998); Colorado Council of Elected Officials for Soviet Jewry (1985-1992); Colorado Special Task Force, Tort Liability and Insurance (1985) **Civic:** Executive Board, Denver Council, Boy Scouts of America (1997-Present); Roundup Riders of the Rockies (1989-Present); Board of Directors, Four-Mile House (2012-2014); Board of Directors, Urban Farm, Colorado State University System (2007-2010); Water Future Panel, University of Denver (2007); Board Member, National Cattlemen's Beef Association (2006-2014); Board of Directors, Mountain States Employers Council, Inc. (2006-2011) **Military Service:** Officer, U.S. Navy Reserve (1967-1971); Lieutenant, Junior Grade, Republic of South Viet Nam **Awards:** Evans Award, University of Denver (2011); New York Medal of Honor, Ellis Island (2007); The Denver & Colorado Travel Industry Hall of Fame, VISIT DENVER (2005); **Membership:** Vice Chairman, Western Stock Show Association; Chairman, Long Range Planning Group, Western Stock Show Association; Board of Directors, Chairman, Association of Rodeo Committees; **Bar Admissions:** Colorado Bar Association (1977) **Marquis Who's Who Honors:** Albert Nelson Marquis Lifetime Achievement Award (2017) **Political Affiliations:** Republican **Religion:** Episcopalian **Shipping Address:** 106 S University Blvd Unit 4, Denver, CO, 80209

Constance Udean Greaser

Title: Communications Executive, Researcher **Industry:** Corporate Communications & Public Relations **Date of Birth:** 01/18/1938 **Place of Birth:** San Diego **State:** CA **Parents:** Lloyd Edward Greaser; Udean Greaser **Education:** Executive MBA, University of California, Los Angeles (1981); MA, University of Southern California (1968); Postgraduate Coursework, School of Foreign Service, Georgetown University (1967); Postgraduate Coursework, Graduate School for Foreign Service, University of Copenhagen (1963); BA, San Diego State College (1959) **Career:** Manager, Communications Service, American Honda Motor Co., Inc., Torrance, CA (1990-2002); Head of Publications, RAND Corporation, Santa Monica, CA (1974-1990); Vice President, SAGE Publications, Beverly Hills, CA (1970-1974); Editorial Director, SAGE Publications, Beverly Hills, CA (1970-1974); Manager, Computerized Typesetting Department, Continental Graphics, Los Angeles, CA (1967-1970); Supervisor, Engineering Support Services Division, Arcata Data Management, Hawthorne, CA (1964-1967); Supervisor, Mercury Publication Ltd, Fullerton, CA (1962-1964) **Civic:** Board of Directors, JWC Domestic Violence Prevention Program (2007-2010); Global Cooperation for Better World (1988); National Information Standards Organization (1987-1993); National Committee, Million Minutes of Peace Appeal (1986) **Creative Works:** Co-author, "Quick Writer-Word Processing Center Operations Manual" (1984); Co-author, "Quick Writer: Build Your Own Word Processing Users Guide" (1983); Editor, "Urban Research News" (1971-1974); Managing Editor, "Comparative Political Studies" (1971-1974); **Awards:** Berber Award for Outstanding Woman in Graphic Arts, Graphic Arts Technical Foundation (1989); **Membership:** Executive Co-Chair, The Women's Company (2016-2017); Chair, Los Angeles Valley Chapter, Southern California Women for Understanding (2004-2006); President, Women in Business (1977-1978); National Board of Directors, Society for Scholarly Publishing; Society for Technical Communication; **Marquis Who's Who Honors:** Albert Nelson Marquis Lifetime Achievement Award (2017) **Why did you become involved in your profession or industry:** Ms. Greaser fell in love with books when she was about four years old, and never deviated from her plan to be deeply involved with books and writing for the rest of her life. **What do you consider to be the highlight of your career:** The highlight of Ms. Greaser career was travelling independently around the world with two friends for six months from 1961 to 1962. **Shipping Address:** 78299 Kensington Avenue, Palm Desert, CA, 92211

Nancy L. Green

Title: Media Marketing Strategist **Industry:** Advertising & Marketing **Company Name:** Nancy Green & Associates **Date of Birth:** 01/19/1942 **Place of Birth:** Lexington **State:** KY **Parents:** William S. Loughridge; Nancy O. (Green) Loughridge **Education:** EdD, Nova Southeastern University (2003); MA in Journalism, Ball State University (1971); Postgraduate Studies, University of Minnesota (1968); Postgraduate Studies, University of Kentucky (1968); BA in Journalism, University of Kentucky (1964) **Career:** Chief Executive Officer, Nancy Green & Associates, Richmond (2017-Present), Assistant Director of Marketing and Enrollment Management, External Relations Ivy Tech. Community College (2010-2017); Chief Executive Officer, Nancy Green & Associates, St. Louis (2009-2010); Executive Director, External Relations, Ivy Tech Community College, Richmond (2010-2014); Chief Executive Officer, AVP, Marketing and Communications, West Virginia School of Osteopathic Medicine (2009-2010); President, STL Distribution Service (2008-2009); Vice President of Circulation, LEE Enterprises, St. Louis (2008-2009); Publisher, The Courier (2004-2008); Vice President of Circulation, LEE Enterprises, Davenport (2002-2008); Director of Circulation/Distribution, Sales & Marketing, Lee Enterprises (2000-2002); Vice President of Communications, Georgia GLOBE, University Systems (1999-2000); Vice President of Advancement, Clayton College & State University, Morrow, GA (1996-1999); Executive Director of Advancement, Clayton State College, Morrow, GA (1994-1996); Assistant to President, Newspaper Division, Gannett Co., Inc., Washington (1992-1994); President, Publishing, News-Leader, Springfield, MO (1989-1992); President, Publishing, Palladium-Item, Richmond, IN (1985-1989); General Manager, Student Publications, University of Texas, Austin (1982-1985); Adviser, Student Publications, University of Kentucky, Lexington (1971-1982); Teacher of Journalism, Publications Director, Elmhurst High School, Fort Wayne, IN (1970-1971); Assistant Publications and Public Information Specialist, West Virginia Department of Education, Charleston (1969-1970) **Civic:** Board of Directors, Student Press Law Center (1975-2005); Atlanta Chapter, AIWF (1995-2000) **Awards:** Honoree, Distinguished Alumni, School of Journalism and Media, University of Kentucky (2017); Dr. Martin Luther King Award, Richmond, Indiana (2017) **Membership:** Vice Chairman, Institute of Rural Journalism & Community Issues (2007-Present) **Marquis Who's Who Honors:** Distinguished Humanitarian (2017) **Shipping Address:** 320 S 48th St., Richmond, IN, 47374

Jane Green Schaller

Title: Pediatrician **Industry:** Medicine & Health Care **Company Name:** Tufts University **Date of Birth:** 06/26/1934 **Place of Birth:** Cleveland **State:** OH **Parents:** George Green; May Alice (Wing) Green **Children:** Robert Thomas; George Charles; Margaret May **Education:** Fellow of Immunology, Children's Hospital, University of Washington (1963-1965); Resident in Pediatrics, Children's Hospital, University of Washington, Seattle, WA (1960-1963); MD, Harvard University, Cum Laude (1960); AB, Hiram College, Ohio (1956) **Certifications:** Diplomate, American Board of Pediatrics; Diplomate, American Board of Medical Examiners **Career:** Retired (2010); Distinguished Professor, School of Medicine, Tufts University (1995-2010); Karp Professor of Pediatrics, School of Medicine, Tufts University (1983-2010); Chairman, Department of Pediatrics, School of Medicine, Tufts University School of Medicine (1983-1998); Pediatrician-in-Chief, New England Medical Center (1983-1998); Professor of Pediatrics, University of Washington Medical School (1975-1983); Head, Division of Rheumatic Diseases, Children's Hospital, Seattle, WA (1968-1983); Faculty, School of Medicine, University of Washington (1965-1983) **Career Related:** Adjunct Professor of Diplomacy, The Fletcher School of Law and Diplomacy, Tufts University (1998-2000) **Civic:** Member, Advisory Committee, Middle East Division (1998-Present); Chairman, Advisory Committee, Children's Rights Division, Human Rights Watch (1995-Present); Advisory Council, Women's Commission for Refugee Women and Children (1994-Present); Trustee, Boston Chamber Music Society (1985-Present) **Creative Works:** Contributor, Articles, Professional Journals **Membership:** Executive Director, American College of Rheumatology, International Pediatrics Association (2004-Present); Executive Committee, Physicians for Human Rights (1986-Present); Board Membership, The Partnership for Maternal, Newborn and Child Health (2007-2010); Board Membership, Global Alliance for Vaccines and Immunization (2006-2010); President, American College of Rheumatology, International Pediatrics Association (2001-2004); President-Elect, American College of Rheumatology, International Pediatrics Association (1998-2001) **Marquis Who's Who Honors:** Albert Nelson Marquis Lifetime Achievement Award (2017) **Shipping Address:** 737 Olive Way Apt 2505, Seattle, WA, 98101

Virginia Greenleaf Koch

Title: Painter **Industry:** Fine Art **Date of Birth:** 08/28/1925 **Place of Birth:** Chicago **State:** IL **Parents:** William Henry Greenleaf; Henrietta Irene (Moser) Greenleaf **Marital Status:** Single **Spouse Name:** Henry Koch (8/20/1962, Deceased); William Greenough (1951, Deceased); Aley Allan (1945, Divorced) **Children:** Diedra G.; William G. **Education:** Coursework with Gene Davis (1968-1970); Postgraduate Coursework, American University (1956-1957); Coursework with Robert Brackman (1946); Coursework, Yale University (1943-1945); **Civic:** Member, National Symphony of Washington, DC Committee (1970-Present); Member, Georgetown Citizens' Association, Washington, DC (1971-1975); Board of Directors, Arts Council of Nantucket **Creative Works:** Exhibitor, Group Shows, Diane Birdsall Gallery, Old Lyme, CT (2008-2014); Exhibitor, Group Shows, Pet Connections, Old Lyme, CT (2005-2006); Exhibitor, Group Shows, Cooley Gallery (2004-2006); Exhibitor, Solo Exhibit, Christy Lawrence Gallery, Old Lyme, CT (2003); Exhibitor, Group Show, Cooley Gallery (2003); Exhibitor, Group Show, Rittenhouse Fine Arts Gallery, Philadelphia, PA (2002); Exhibitor, Group Shows, Old Lyme (1991-2002); Exhibitor, Group Show, Alva Gallery, New London, CT (2001); Exhibitor, Solo Exhibit, Gallery at Essex Meadows (2001); Exhibitor, Solo Exhibit, Nantucket, MA (1995-1998); Exhibitor, Group Show, Corcoran Gallery (1992-1993, 1975); Exhibitor, Solo Exhibits, Nantucket, MA (1991-1993, 1982-1989, 1977); Exhibitor, Group Show, Maritime Museum (1990-1991); Exhibitor, Group Show, Phillips Collection, Washington, DC (1989); Exhibitor, Solo Exhibits, Main Street Gallery, Boston, MA (1987-1989, 1983, 1976-1981); Exhibitor, Solo Exhibit, Gallery 124, New York, NY (1983); Exhibitor, Group Show, Parsons Drefyss Gallery, New York, NY (1976-1977); Exhibitor, Solo Exhibits, Studio Gallery, Washington, DC (1976, 1974, 1972, 1970); Exhibitor, Group Show, University of Maryland (1975); Exhibitor, Solo Exhibit, In Town Gallery, Cleveland, OH (1973); Exhibitor, Solo Exhibit, Art League of Northern Virginia (1973); **Membership:** Studio Gallery, Foundry Group of Women Painters; Artists' Equity; Art League of Virginia; Art Foundation of Nantucket History; Old Lyme Historic Foundation **Marquis Who's Who Honors:** Albert Nelson Marquis Lifetime Achievement Award (2017) **What do you consider to be the highlight of your career:** Ms. Greenleaf Koch is most proud of working in Gene Davis' studio in Washington, DC Davis was a remarkable teacher and mentor for Greenleaf Koch.

Lyubomira Gribble

Title: Language Educator (Retired) **Industry:** Education/Educational Services **Company Name:** Ohio State University **Parents:** Deyan I. Parpulov; Rayna N. Parpulova **Spouse Name:** Charles Edward Gribble (Married 9/20/1982, Deceased 2016) **Children:** Elizabeth R. **Education:** PhD, Ohio State University, Columbus, OH (1990); PhD, Bulgarian Academy of Science, Sofia, Bulgaria (1975) **Career:** Retired (2016); Assistant Curator, Hilandar Research Library, Ohio State University (2007-2014); Examiner Responsible, International Baccalaureate Organization, Geneva (2003-2007); Assistant Professor, Ohio State University (1992-1999); Senior Research Associate, Bulgarian Academy of Science (1974-1983) **Awards:** IREX Russian Language Teachers Summer Fellowship, International Research & Exchanges Board (1990); Jacob Javits Fellowship (1987-1989); Grant, United States Office of Education and Ohio State University (1987-1988); National Graduate Training Fellowship (1986-1987); Fulbright Fellowship, United States Office of Education (1979); Grant, Bulgarian Academy of Science (1979, 1974) **Membership:** Modern Language Association; Early Slavic Studies Association; Bulgarian Studies Association; Association of Women Slavic Studies; American Association for Teachers of Slavic & East European Languages; Phi Kappa Phi; Dobro Slovo **Shipping Address:** 3494 Manchester Drive, Powell, OH, 43065

Campbell Arthur Griffin Jr.

Title: Retired Lawyer **Industry:** Law and Legal Services **Date of Birth:** 07/17/1929 **Place of Birth:** Joplin **State:** MO **Parents:** Campbell Arthur Griffin; Clara M. (Smith) Griffin **Marital Status:** Married **Spouse Name:** Margaret Ann Adams (10/19/1958) **Children:** Campbell A., III; Laura Ann Davis **Education:** JD, University of Texas (1957); MA in Accounting, University of Missouri (1952); BA, University of Missouri (1951); AA, Joplin Junior College (1949) **Career:** Partner, Vinson & Elkins, LLP, Houston, TX (1968-1992); Management Committee, Vinson & Elkins, LLP, Houston, TX (1981-1990); Partner in Charge, Vinson & Elkins, LLP, Dallas, TX (1986-1989); Associate, Vinson & Elkins, LLP, Houston, TX (1957-1967) **Career Related:** Adjunct Professor, Administrative Science, Jesse H. Jones Graduate School of Business, Rice University (1992-1994) **Civic:** Board of Directors, Cornell Companies, Inc. (1996-2000); President, Windcliff Property Owners Association, Estes Park, CO (1995-1996); Councilman, City of Hunters Creek Village, Texas (1993-1995); Board of Directors, Houston Pops Orchestra (1982-1987); Member, Official Board, Bethany Christian Church, Houston, TX (1962-1969); Active, St. Martin's Epsicopal Church, Houston, TX **Military Service:** Staff Sergeant, U.S. Army Audit Agency, San Antonio, TX (1952-1954) **Membership:** Director, Villa D'Este Condominium Owners Association (2004-2008); Director, Houston Racquet Club (1992-1994); Director, Texas Business Law Foundation (1988-2000); Chairman, Texas Business Law Foundation (1988-1989); Business Law Section Chairman, State Bar of Texas (1974-1975); **Bar Admissions:** Texas State Bar (1957) **Marquis Who's Who Honors:** Albert Nelson Marquis Lifetime Achievement Award (2017) **Why did you become involved in your profession or industry:** Mr. Griffin always wanted to be either a lawyer, doctor, or accountant so he could own his own business. Law school became the alternative. He started out wanting to be a tax lawyer, but in visiting with the law firm, they had already filled the vacancy in the tax department and asked if he wanted to do corporate work. He spent half a day with the then-corporate-partner of the firm, and when they told him how much they would pay him he asked when they wanted him to show up. Becoming a corporate lawyer was a wonderful decision for him. **What do you consider to be the highlight of your career:** A highlight of Mr. Griffin's career was when he took 14 Lawyers with him from the Houston home office to the Dallas office he opened. The office now has 150 lawyers. **Shipping Address:** 1000 Uptown Park Boulevard, Apt. 201, Houston, TX, 77056

James Robb Grover, PhD

Title: Chemist, Editor **Industry:** Sciences **Company Name:** Brookhaven National Laboratory **Date of Birth:** 09/16/1928 **Place of Birth:** Klamath Falls **State:** OR **Parents:** James Richard Grover; Marjorie Alida (van Groos) Grover **Marital Status:** Widowed **Spouse Name:** Barbara Jean Ton (4/14/1957) **Children:** Jonathan Robb; Patricia Jean **Education:** PhD, University of California, Berkeley (1958); BS, University of Washington, Seattle, Summa Cum Laude, Valedictorian (1952) **Career:** Research Collaborator, Brookhaven National Laboratory, Upton, NY (1993-Present); Senior Chemist, Brookhaven National Laboratory, Upton, NY (1978-1993); Chemist with Tenure, Brookhaven National Laboratory, Upton, NY (1967-1977); Chemist, Brookhaven National Laboratory, Upton, NY (1963-1967); Associate Chemist, Brookhaven National Laboratory, Upton, NY (1959-1963); Research Associate, Brookhaven National Laboratory, Upton, NY (1957-1959) **Career Related:** Visiting Professor, Institute for Molecular Science, Okazaki, Japan (1986-1987); Visiting Scientist, Max Planck Institute for Dynamics and Self-Organization, Göttingen, Germany (1975-1976); Associate Editor, Annual Review of Nuclear Science, Annual Reviews Inc., Palo Alto, CA (1967-1977); Consultant, Lawrence Livermore National Laboratory (1962) **Military Service:** U.S. Navy (1946-1948) **Creative Works:** Author, Portland's Gold (2018); Contributor, Articles, Professional Journals **Membership:** Chairman, Nuclear Chemistry and Technology, American Chemical Society (1989); American Chemical Society; American Physical Society; Triple Nine Society; Sigma Xi; Phi Beta Kappa; Phi Lambda Upsilon; Zeta Mu Tau; Pi Mu Epsilon **Political Affiliations:** Independent **Religion:** Presbyterian **Shipping Address:** 1536 Pinecrest Ter, Ashland, OR, 97520

Angelo Guastaferro

Title: Science Administrator **Industry:** Education/Educational Services **Date of Birth:** 06/04/1932 **Place of Birth:** Hoboken **State:** NJ **Parents:** Carlo Guastaferro; Rafaela Nancy (Gioffi) Guastaferro **Marital Status:** Married **Spouse Name:** Eleanor Lago (9/12/1954) **Children:** Carl; Mark; John Brian **Education:** Diplomate, Advanced Management Program, Harvard University (1984); MBA, Florida State University (1963); BS in Mechanical Engineering, New Jersey Institute of Technology (1954) **Career:** Executive Partner, Florida Institute of Technology (1998-Present); Lecturer, Florida Institute of Technology (1998-Present); Executive Consultant, Williamsburg, VA (1998-Present); AG Consultant, Williamsburg, VA (1998-Present); President, View Corporation, Newport News, VA (1996-1998); Chief Executive Officer, View Corporation, Newport News, VA (1996-1998); Chairman of the Board, View Corporation, Newport News, VA (1996); Executive Director, Lockheed Missiles & Space Company (Now Lockheed Martin Corporation) (1994-1996); Vice President, Lockheed Missiles & Space Company (Now Lockheed Martin Corporation) (1985-1996); Program Director, Lockheed Missiles & Space Company (Now Lockheed Martin Corporation) (1985-1996); Deputy Director, Ames Research Center, National Aeronautics and Space Administration (1981-1985); Employee, National Aeronautics and Space Administration (1963-1985); Director of Planetary Programs, National Aeronautics and Space Administration (1979-1981); Deputy Manager, Viking Project, National Aeronautics and Space Administration (1974-1976) **Career Related:** Chairman, Board of Directors, View Corporation (1995-2002); Member, Board of Trustees, International Space University (1993-1996); Member, Science Advisory Committee, New Jersey Institute of Technology **Civic:** Chair, Board of Directors, Hampton Roads Technology Council **Military Service:** U.S. Air Force (1955-1958) **Awards:** Honoree, Distinguished Alumnus New Jersey Institute of Technology (1997); Honoree, Eminent Engineer, The Tau Beta Pi Association, Inc. (1989); Honoree, Presidential Meritorious Rank (1982); Space Systems Medal, AIAA (1982); Exceptional Service Medal (1981); Langley Special Achievement Award National Aeronautics and Space Administration (1974, 1977-1978); **Membership:** President, Mars First Landing Society (1978-1979); Fellow, AIAA; Fellow, American Astronautical Society; Board of Directors, International Astronautical Federation; **Marquis Who's Who Honors:** Albert Nelson Marquis Lifetime Achievement Award (2017) **Shipping Address:** 149 Roger Smith, Williamsburg, VA, 23185

Paul Joseph Guglielmino

Title: Educator **Industry:** Education **Date of Birth:** 05/19/1942 **Place of Birth:** Brooklyn **State:** NY **Parents:** Carl Guglielmino; Rose (Loreto) Guglielmino **Marital Status:** Married Spouse Name: Lucy Margaret Madsen (7/31/1965) **Children:** Joseph Allen; Margaret Rose Guglielmino-Perez **Education:** EdD, University of Georgia (1978); MA, Grady School of Journalism, University of Georgia (1970); BA in English, The Citadel - The Military College of South Carolina (1964) **Career:** Associate Professor, Florida Atlantic University (1994-2009); Assistant Professor, Florida Atlantic University (1986-1994); Executive Director, Florida Atlantic University (1986-1994); Adjunct Professor Management, Florida Atlantic University (1981-1986); Director, Center for Management, Florida Atlantic University (1978-1981) **Career Related:** Doctoral Dissertation Juror, Universite de Paris (2012); **Military Service:** First Lieutenant, Adjutant General Corp, Transfer Point, U.S. Army, Fort Devens, MA (1964-1966); Captain, Infantry, 3220th Headquarters Company, U.S. Army **Creative Works:** Contributing Author, The Journal of Education Finance (2010); Review Board, International Journal of Self-Directed Learning (2007-2012); Review Board, Human Resource Development Quarterly, University of Minnesota (2006); Review Board, Human Resource Management Journal, University of Michigan (2006); Contributing Author, SAM Advanced Management Journal (2006); Presenter, International Congress for School Effectiveness and Improvement (2006); Contributing Author, Expanding Your Readiness for Self-Directed Learning: A Workbook for the Learning Preference Assessment (2005); Presenter, ASTD National Conference (2003); Contributing Author, The American Management Association Handbook of E-Learning: Effective Design, Implementation and Technology Solutions (2003); Contributing Author, Preparing Learners for E-learning (2003); Contributing Author, Getting the Most from E-learning (2003); Contributing Author, Current Developments in E-learning and Self-Directed Learning (2003) **Awards:** Tradition of Excellence Award, Florida Atlantic University (2004); Malcolm Knowles Memorial Award in Self-Directed Learning (2002); International Travel Grantee, Universite de Paris & FAU Foundation, Inc. (1999); Honoree, University Distinguished Teacher of the Year, Florida Atlantic University (1998) **Membership:** Board Member, International Self-Directed Learning Symposium (1992-Present); Beta Gamma Sigma, Inc. (1994); The Honor Society of Phi Kappa Phi (1991); Scientific Council, Centre d'Etudes de Populations de Pauvrete et de Politiques Socio-Economiques, Grand Duche de Luxembourg (1990); **Marquis Who's Who Honors:** Albert Nelson Marquis Lifetime Achievement Award (2017)

Frank Guliuzza

Industry: Education/Educational Services **Date of Birth:** 02/02/1957 **Place of Birth:** Marion **State:** OH **Parents:** Frank Guliuzza; Mary Guliuzza **Education:** PhD, University of Notre Dame, South Bend, IN (1990) **Career:** Dean of Academic Affairs, Patrick Henry College, Purcellville, VA (2008); Chair, Department of Political Science & Philosophy, Weber State University, Ogden, UT (1990-2008) **Career Related:** American College Moot Court Association, (2009-2016); President, American Mock Trial Association (2015); Chair, Pre-Law Advisors' National Council, Durham, NC (2007-2008); President, Western Association Pre-Law Advisors (2001-2007); Chair, Weber County Republican Party, Ogden, UT (1997-1999) **Civic:** Vice Chairman, Utah Republican Party, Salt Lake City, UT (2001-2003) **Creative Works:** Co-Author (with Tim Garrison), "Before The Paper Chase" (2012); Author, "Over The Wall" (2011) **Awards:** Utah Professor of the Year, Council for Advancement & Support Education, Carnegie Foundation for the Advancement of Teaching (2003) **Political Affiliations:** Conservative **Religion:** Baptist

Gershon Hait

Title: Professor Emeritus, Pediatric Cardiologist **Industry:** Medicine & Health Care **Company Name:** Albert Einstein College of Medicine **Date of Birth:** 05/10/1927 **Parents:** Nahum Hait; Leah Hait **Marital Status:** Married **Spouse Name:** Doris J. Coburn (3/20/1957) **Children:** Jonathan; Yael **Education:** Fellow in Pediatric Cardiology, Albert Einstein College of Medicine (1962-1964); Resident, John H. Stroger Jr. Hospital of Cook County, Cook County Health and Hospitals System (1961-1962); Fellow in Pediatric Cardiology, John H. Stroger Jr. Hospital of Cook County, Cook County Health and Hospitals System (1959-1960); Fellow in Pediatric Cardiology, John H. Stroger Jr. Hospital of Cook County, Cook County Health and Hospitals System (1954-1956); Intern, Michael Reese Hospital (1952-1953); MD, University of Lausanne, Switzerland (1952) **Career:** Professor Emeritus, Albert Einstein College of Medicine (2005-Present); Professor in Pediatrics, Albert Einstein College of Medicine (1979-2005); Director of Pediatric Cardiology, Albert Einstein College of Medicine (1966-1985); Instructor, Pediatrics, Albert Einstein College of Medicine (1962-1964) **Career Related:** Staff Member, Bronx Municipal Hospital Center; Montefiore Cardiac Consultant, Department of Health, Bronx, NY; Montefiore Cardiac Consultant, Department of Health, Staten Island, NY; Montefiore Cardiac Consultant, Department of Health, Rockland County, NY **Military Service:** Served to Lieutenant, Medical Corps, Israeli Defense Forces (1956-1959) **Creative Works:** Contributor, Articles, Professional Journals **Awards:** Grantee, NIH; Grantee, American Heart Association, Inc. **Membership:** American Physiology Society; APS-SPR; American Academy of Pediatrics; American Federation for Medical Research; American Heart Association, Inc.; American College of Cardiology Foundation; Sleep Research Society; American Academy of Sleep Medicine **Why did you become involved in your profession or industry:** Dr. Hait became involved in his profession after he finished his medical studies in Switzerland, at which point there weren't too many medical schools left in Europe after the war. He then had the opportunity to work in cardiology in Chicago and enjoyed it. **Religion:** Jewish **Business Address:** 1300 Morris Park Ave, Bronx, NY, 10461 **Shipping Address:** 14 Withington Rd., Scarsdale, NY, 10583

Edward C. Halbach Jr.

Title: Law Educator **Industry:** Education/Educational Services **Company Name:** UC Berkeley School of Law **Date of Birth:** 11/08/1931 **Place of Birth:** Clinton **State:** IA **Parents:** Edward Christian Halbach, Sr.; Lewella (Sullivan) Halbach **Marital Status:** Married **Spouse Name:** Janet Elizabeth Bridges (07/25/1953) **Children:** Kristin Lynn; Edward Christian III; Kathleen Ann; Thomas Elliot; Elaine Diane **Education:** LLD, University of Redlands (1973); LLM, Harvard University (1959); JD, University of Iowa (1958); BA, University of Iowa (1953) **Career:** Professor Emeritus, UC Berkeley School of Law (1996-Present); Professor, UC Berkeley School of Law (1963-1996); Dean, UC Berkeley School of Law (1966-1975); Associate Professor, UC Berkeley School of Law (1959-1962) **Military Service:** First Lieutenant, U.S. Air Force (1953-1956) **Creative Works:** Reporter, Volume 4, Restatement of Law of Trusts (2012); Reporter, Volume 3, Restatement of Law of Trusts (2007); Reporter, Volumes 1 and 2, Restatement of Law of Trusts (2003); Author, "Principles and Techniques of Estate Planning" (1995); Reporter, Third Restatement, Prudent Investor Rule (1992); Author, "Summary of the Law of Trusts" (1990, 1998, 2004, 2007); Author, "Fundamentals of Estate Planning" (1983, 1986, 1987, 1989, 1991, 1993, 1995); Co-author, "Materials on Future Interests" (1977); Co-author, "Death, Taxes and Family Property" (1977); Author, "Use of Trusts in Estate Planning" (1975, 1981, 1984, 1986, 1991); Reporter, Uniform Probate Code (1969); Co-author, "Problems and Materials on Decedents Estates and Trusts" (1965, 1973, 1981, 1987, 1993, 2000, 2006); Co-author, "California Will Drafting" (1965, 1977, 1992) **Awards:** TREAT Award for Excellence, National College of Probate Judges; Tweed Merit Award for Continuing Legal Education, American Law Institute; A.J. Casner Reporter's Chair, American Law Institute; Elected to Estate Planning Hall of Fame, NAEPC; RV Wellman Award, The National Conference of Commissioners on Uniform State Laws; Lifetime Achievement Award, Boalt Hall Alumni Association, UC Berkeley School of Law **Membership:** Chairman, Committee, Individual Rights and Responsibilities Section, ABA; Chairman, Committee, Real Property, Trust and Estate Law, ABA; Director, Probate and Trust Division, ABA; Section Chairman, ABA; Iowa State Bar Association; Advisor, Restatement of the Law Second, American Law Institute; ABA; NAEPC; American College of Trust and Estate Counsel American College of Tax Counsel; Vice President, International Academy of Estate and Trust Law; President, International Academy of Estate and Trust Law; **Marquis Who's Who Honors:** Albert Nelson Marquis Lifetime Achievement Award (2017) **Shipping Address:** 679 San Luis Road, Berkeley, CA, 94707

John H. Hammer II

Title: Hospital Administrator (Retired) **Industry:** Medicine & Health Care **Date of Birth:** 12/27/1943 **Place of Birth:** Bartlesville **State:** OK **Parents:** John Henry Hammer; Lucy (Macias) Hammer **Children:** John Henry; Erica; Megan **Education:** MBA, University of Illinois (1984); Coursework, University of Maryland, University College Europe (1968-1969); BBA, St. Joseph's College (1966) **Career:** Construction Projects Coordinator, University of Illinois (2010-2013); Assistant Director of Operations & Maintenance, University of Illinois (1997-2007); Vice President, United Samaritans Medical Center, Presence Health (1988-1995); Vice President, Lakeview Medical Associates (1984-1988); Director of Personnel, Lakeview Medical Associates (1980-1984); President, Employees Credit Union (1974-1980); Assistant Director of Human Resources, St. Catherine Hospital, Community Healthcare System (1974-1980); Project Manager, Economic & Manpower Corporation (1971-1973) **Career Related:** Member, Education Commission, St. Mary's School (2009-2010); Member, Advisory Board, McKinley Health Center, University of Illinois (2002-2007); Chairman, Junior Achievement of Danville (1993-1995); Vice Chairman, Junior Achievement of Danville (1991-1992); Board of Directors, Junior Achievement of Danville (1990-1995); Chairman, Program Committee, De La Garza Career Center (1974-1980); Board of Directors, East Central Illinois Health Systems Agency, Alterna-Care Home Health System; Board of Directors, East Central Illinois Health Planning Organization; Board of Directors, Vermilion Area Community Health Center, Aunt Martha's **Military Service:** Lieutenant Colonel, U.S. Air Force Reserve (1974-1993); Captain, U.S. Air Force (1967-1971) **Awards:** Honoree, Communications Squadron Commander of the Year, U.S. Air Force Reserve (1990,1987-1988,); Honoree, Outstanding Company Grade Officer of the Year, Grissom Air Force Base, Reserve Officers Association (1977) **Membership:** Post 210, The American Legion (2015-Present); Performance Partnership Program Implementation Team, University of Illinois (1998-1999); Task Force on Human Resources, Illinois Health and Hospital Association (1997-1998); President, Danville South Chapter, Rotary International (1991-1992); Board of Directors, Rotary International (1990-1992); Illinois Private Industry Council (1987-1988); President, Indiana Society Hospital Personnel Administration (1979-1980); Chairman, Membership Committee, Indiana Society Hospital Personnel Administration (1976-1977); Reserve Officers Association of the United States; American College of Healthcare Executives **Religion:** Roman Catholic **Shipping Address:** 218 W. Ellsworth Street, Westville, IL, 61883

Leroy Hampton

Title: Chemicals Executive (Retired) **Industry:** Sciences **Date of Birth:** 04/20/1927 **Place of Birth:** Ingalls **State:** AR **Parents:** Ed Levi Hampton; Kitty Annie (Larry) Hampton **Marital Status:** Married **Spouse Name:** Anne Neris Herndon (7/11/1954) **Children:** Mary Louise; Gloria Stanley Lamar; Cedric Leroy; Candice LaNeris **Education:** MS, Denver University (1960); BS, University of Colorado (1950) **Certifications:** Registered Pharmacist, States of Colorado and Michigan **Career:** President, Chairman, Dow Chemical Employees Credit Union (1992); Vice President, Dow Chemical Employees Credit Union (1991); President, Dow Chemical Employees Credit Union (1985); Research Associate, The Dow Chemical Company (1981-1986); President, Dow Chemical Employees Credit Union (1979); Manager, Issue Analysis, The Dow Chemical Company (1976-1980); Director, Dow Chemical Employees Credit Union (1975-1995); Manager, Minority Employee Relations, Northeast Region (1970-1975); Recruiting Manager, Northeast Region (1968-1970); Recruiting Supervisor, The Dow Chemical Company, Midland, MI (1967-1968); Development Leader, The Dow Chemical Company (1963-1967); Development Chemist, The Dow Chemical Company (1961-1963); Professional Scientist, Chemist in Charge, The Dow Chemical Company (1958-1961); Scientist, Chemist, The Dow Chemical Company, Golden, CO (1953-1958); Registered Pharmacist, Rocky Mountain Drug Company, Denver, CO (1950-1953) **Career Related:** Owner, Operator, Hardware Store, Denver, CO (1965-1967); Member, Community Advisory Panel, The Dow Chemical Company, Michigan Operations **Civic:** Member, Midland, Dow Community Advisory Panel (2001-2005); Deacon, Memorial Presbyterian Church, Midland, MI (1995-1997); Director, Affirmative Action, Saginaw Valley State University, University Center, MI (1987-1990); Treasurer, Midland Association for Retarded Citizens (1986-1987); Deacon, Memorial Presbyterian Church, Midland, MI (1985-1987); Vice President, Midland Association for Retarded Citizens (1985-1986); Board of Directors, Midland Association for Retarded Citizens (1982-1988); Vice President, Midland Board of Education (1981-1982); Secretary, Midland Board of Education (1979-1980); Member, Midland Board of Education (1978-1982); Board of Directors, The American National Red Cross, Midland, MI (1974-1976) **Membership:** President, Midland Club, Kiwanis (1976-1977); American Chemical Society; American Pharmaceutical Association; Michigan Pharmacists Association; League of Women Voters of the Midland Area; Alpha Phi Alpha **Marquis Who's Who Honors:** Albert Nelson Marquis Lifetime Achievement Award (2017) **Religion:** Presbyterian **Shipping Address:** 2206 Burlington Dr, Midland, MI, 48642

Patricia Hancock

Title: Artist **Industry:** Fine Art **Date of Birth:** 04/01/1956 **Place of Birth:** Columbia **State:** SC/USA **Parents:** William Edwards Hancock; Joan Marie Moore Hancock **Education:** Postgraduate Work, Virginia Commonwealth University (1980-1981); BFA, University of Georgia (1979); Student, Queens College (1973-1975) **Career:** Artist (1981-Present); Art Teacher, Thornwell School, Clinton, SC (1979-1980) **Civic:** NADA Charitable Trust; Congaree National Forest; Co-Operative Ministry; Richland Library Foundation; Samaritan's Purse **Membership:** Daughters of the American Revolution; National Society of Children's Book Writers and Illustrators **Marquis Who's Who Honors:** Albert Nelson Marquis Lifetime Achievement Award (2017) **Hobbies:** Sewing; Walking; Dancing; Fashion; Bible Study **Religion:** Presbyterian **Shipping Address:** 806 Poinsettia St, Columbia, SC, 29205

Margie Lee Handley

Title: Real Estate Developer, Business Executive **Industry:** Real Estate **Date of Birth:** 09/29/1939 **Place of Birth:** Bakersfield **State:** CA/USA **Parents:** Robert E. Harrah; Jayne A. (Knoblock) Harrah **Marital Status:** Widow **Spouse Name:** Leon C. Handley Sr. (10/28/1975, Deceased) **Children:** Steven Daniel Lovell (Deceased); David Robert Lovell; Ronald Eugene Lovell **Certifications:** General Engineering "A" Contractors License **Career:** President, Frank R. Howard Foundation (1993-Present); President, Harrah Industries, Inc., Willits, CA (1981-Present); President, Hot Rocks, Inc., Willits, CA (1983-1989); Vice President, Microphor, Inc., Willits, CA (1974-1981); Owner, Operator, Lovell's Tack 'n Togs, Yreka, CA (1970-1973); Owner, Operator, Shasta Pallet Co., Montague, CA (1969-1970) **Career Related:** General Partner, Madrone Professional Group, Willits, CA (1982-Present); Member, Selective Service Systems, Local Board State of California (2002-2011); Appointed Member, State of California Economic Strategy Panel (1995-2000); Co-partner, Running Wild Ostrich Farm (1994-2012); Coordinator, State of California Timber Transition (1994-1995); Active, State of California Employment Training Panel (1993-1995); Board of Directors, N-Tech; Board of Directors, National Bank of the Redwoods; Board of Directors, NBR Mortgage Co.; Board of Directors, Willits Electronics Assembly, Inc.; Board of Directors, Redwood Empire Bancorp; Member, California Transportation Commission **Civic:** Member, Mental Health Advisory Board, Mendocino County, CA (2015-Present); Member, California Rural Development Council (1998-Present); Member, California Small Business Roundtable (1996-Present); Member, California State Republican Central Committee (1985-Present); Northern California Network, Adventist Health (2014-2016); Director, Frank R. Memorial Hospital (2014-2016); Advisory Board, North Valley Bank (2010-2014); President, Mendocino County Employer's Council (2007-2011); Chairman, Mendocino County Schwarzenegger for Governor (2006) **Awards:** Volunteer Award, A Heart For Willits (2000, 2013); Notable American Women (2011); Woman of Distinction, Soroptimist International (1991); Agricultural Fair Woman of the Year, Mendocino 12th District (1987) **Membership:** Director, Seabiscuit Heritage Foundation (2015-Present); President, Rotary (2004-2005); Director, Rotary (2001-2006); Northern Coast Builders Exchange; Honorary, Willits Chamber of Commerce; Rotary **Marquis Who's Who Honors:** Distinguished Humanitarian (2017) **Shipping Address:** 235 Haehl Creek Ct, Willits, CA, 95490

John-Cyril Patrick Hanisko, PhD

Title: Electronics Engineer, Physicist **Industry:** Sciences **Date of Birth:** 03/17/1937 **Place of Birth:** Detroit **State:** MI/USA **Parents:** John Joseph Hanisko; Pauline Victoria (Vrabel) Hanisko **Education:** PhD in Physics, Wayne State University (1988); MA, Wayne State University (1972); MSEE, University of Detroit Mercy (1965); BEE, University of Detroit Mercy (1963) **Career:** Consultant, SCAT Systems, Southfield, MI (2003-Present); Technology Specialist, Eaton, Southfield, MI (1994-2003); Staff Engineer, TRW (Now ZF Friedrichshafen AG), Farmington Hills, MI (1980-1994); Project Engineer, Bendix Corporation, Troy, MI (1976-1980); Consultant, Southfield, MI (1975-1976); Research Engineer, Udylite Corporation, Warren, MI (1973-1975); Staff Engineer, Kent-Moore Corporation, Warren, MI (1971-1973); Senior Engineer, Eastman Kodak Company, Rochester, NY (1967-1968); Research Engineer, Boeing, Seattle, WA (1965-1967); Engineer, Burroughs, Inc., Detroit, MI (1962-1965) **Civic:** Member, National Tax Limitation Committee, Washington D.C.; Member, National Right to Life Committee, Washington D.C.; Member, The Catholic League; Supporter, Blinded American Veterans Foundation; Member, Legacy Society, Christendom College; Member, Legacy Society, Thomas Aquinas College; Pro-bono Tutor, Students; Volunteer Table Waiter, Capuchin Soup Kitchen **Creative Works:** Contributor, Articles, Professional Journals **Awards:** Sudan Relief Award (2017); Commanders Club Award, DAV (2016-2017); Excellence In Engineering Award, Transportation Electronics Division, TRW (Now ZF Friedrichshafen AG) (1987-1989); Honoree, Named Design of the Year, EDN Magazine, AspenCore (1977) **Membership:** Senior Member, IEEE; Fellowship of Catholic Scholars; Institute for Theological Encounter with Science and Technology **Marquis Who's Who Honors:** Albert Nelson Marquis Lifetime Achievement Award (2017) **Why did you become involved in your profession or industry:** Dr. Hanisko became involved in his profession because many of the understandings of life are taken from the sciences. It seemed to fit with his personality, as well as his intellectual and personal curiosities. **Hobbies:** Reading; Writing; Fitness; Socializing **Political Affiliations:** Conservative Independent **Religion:** Roman Catholic **Shipping Address:** 21888 Murray Crescent Dr, Southfield, MI, 48076

Edwin Leland Harper, PhD

Title: Corporate Financial Executive **Industry:** Financial Services **Date of Birth:** 11/13/1941 **Place of Birth:** Belleville **State:** IL **Parents:** Horace Edwin Harper; Evelyn Ruth (Wright) Harper **Marital Status:** Married **Spouse Name:** Lucy Davis (8/21/1965) **Children:** Elizabeth Allen; Peter Edwin **Education:** PhD, University of Virginia (1968); BA, Principia College, With Honors (1963) **Career:** Senior Vice President of Government Relations, Association of American Railroads (2000-2010); Chief Operating Officer, Assurant Inc. (1998-2000); Chief Executive Officer, Assurant Inc. (1998-2000); Executive Vice President and Chief Financial Officer, American Security Group Fortis, Association of American Railroads (1997-2000); Chairman, Commodore Applied Technologies, Association of American Railroads (1997); Chief Executive Officer, Commodore Applied Technologies, Association of American Railroads (1997); President, Association of American Railroads (1992-1997); Chief Executive Officer, Association of American Railroads (1992-1997); Acting Co-Chief Executive Officer, Campbell Soup Company, Camden, NJ (1991-1992); Senior Vice President, Campbell Soup Company, Camden, NJ (1986-1992); Chief Financial Officer, Campbell Soup Company, Camden, NJ (1986-1992); Director, Overhead Door Corp. (Now Dallas Corp.) (1983-1986); Executive Vice President, Overhead Door Corp. (Now Dallas Corp.) (1983-1986); Chairman, Federal Property Review Board (1982-1983); Chairman, President's Council on Integrity and Efficiency in Government (1982-1983); Assistant to President Ronald Reagan (1981-1983) **Career Related:** Board of Directors, Allied Capital (2005-2010); Chairman, White House Fellows Selection Committee (1990-1991) **Creative Works:** Contributor, Articles, Professional Journals **Awards:** Special Commendation, Association of Federal Investigators (1983); Executive Government Award, Opportunities Industrialization Corporation of America (1982); Person of the Year Award, Washington Chapter, The Institute of Internal Auditors (1982); Louis Brownlow Award (1969); Grantee, Ford Foundation (1965) **Membership:** National Academy of Public Administration; Financial Executives Institute; Economic Policy Public Affairs Committee, U.S. Chamber of Commerce; Metropolitan Club of Washington; Raven Society; Omicron Delta Kappa **Marquis Who's Who Honors:** Albert Nelson Marquis Lifetime Achievement Award (2017) **Political Affiliations:** Republican **Shipping Address:** 4210 S Douglas Road, Miami, FL, 33133

Duncan Hartley, PhD

Title: Fine Art Photographer/Owner, Fundraising Executive **Industry:** Fine Art **Company Name:** Duncan Hartley Fine Art Photography **Date of Birth:** 09/27/1941 **Parents:** Harold Shephard Hartley; Catherine Carmichael (Hursley) Hartley **Marital Status:** Married **Spouse Name:** Adrienne Ashley (8/19/1971) **Education:** PhD in English Literature, Wayne State University, Detroit, MI (1971); MA in English History, Wayne State University, Detroit, MI (1966); BA in English History, University of Michigan (1964) **Career:** Owner, Duncan Hartley Fine Art Photography (2008-Present); Associate Dean, Development and Alumni Affairs, Case Western Reserve University School of Medicine, Cleveland, OH (1996-2003); Director of Individual Giving, Memorial Sloan Kettering Cancer Center, New York, NY (1984-1996); Executive Director of the President's Council, Memorial Sloan Kettering Cancer Center, New York, NY (1984-1996); Director, Capital Gifts, Greater New York Council, Boy Scouts of America, New York, NY (1980-1984); Director, Planned Giving, Carroll College (Now Carroll University), Waukesha, WI (1978-1980); Administrator, Educational Resources, Chapter Liaison, Young President's Organization (YPO), New York City, NY (1973-1978); **Civic:** Member, Communications Committee, Princeton United Methodist Church (2016-Present); Senior Philanthropic Adviser, St. Jude Children's Research Hospital (2003-2008); Donor, Harvard Medical School, Harvard University **Creative Works:** Contributor, "The Art of the CEO" (2013); Author, "The Sociology of the Arts" (1975); Author, "Shakespeare's Living Cities"; Exhibitor, Executive Arriving at PanAm Building with Joseph Albers Mural in Background; Exhibitor, Bicentennial Crowd in New York Awaiting the Arrival of the Tall Ships, World Trade Center in Background, National September 11 Memorial & Museum; Exhibitor, Over 150 Archival Photographs, Private Collections, 10 Major National Museums and Special Collections **Membership:** Princeton Photography Club (2014-Present); KelbyOne (2006-Present); Tim Grey (2006-Present); The Metropolitan Museum of Art; New-York Historical Society; Princeton University Art Museum; The Princeton Club of New York **Why did you become involved in your profession or industry:** Dr. Hartley grew up in a family dedicated to the arts. His mother attended art school, and later opened an art gallery. His father was a poet, a Thoreau scholar and wood sculptor. He began a career in professional photography while in the eighth grade when he was offered a job working in a darkroom. He held that job until he graduated college and stuck to it with the profession. **Religion:** Presbyterian **Shipping Address:** 40 Edgemere Dr, Kendall Park, NJ, 08824 **Website:** http://duncanhartley.com

Irene Janofsky Hartzell, PhD

Title: Author, Educational Consultant, Psychologist, Mediator **Industry:** Education/Educational Services **Company Name:** Kids Like Learning **Parents:** Leonard S. Janofsky; Annelies Janofsky **Children:** Mark Hartzell **Education:** PhD in Counseling Psychology, University of Oregon, Eugene, OR (1970); MA in Counseling Psychology, University of California, Berkeley, CA (1965); BA in Psychology, University of California, Berkeley (1963); Vor-Diplom in Psychology, LMU, Munich, Germany (1961) **Certifications:** Certified Mediator, Center for Dialog and Resolution, Tacoma, WA (2010); Advanced Paralegal Certificate, Edmonds Community College, WA (2010) **Career:** Founder, Kids Like Learning, LLC (2015-Present); Small Claims Court Mediator, Riverside County, CA (2008-2009); Small Claims Court Mediator, Pierce County, WA (2009-2014); Clinical Psychologist, Kaiser Permanente, Woodland Hills, CA (1979-1994); Clinical Instructor, Pediatrics, College of Medicine, University of California, Irvine (1975-1978); Director, Parent Education, Children's Hospital, Orange, CA (1975-1978); Staff Psychologist, VA Medical Center, Long Beach, CA (1973-1974); School Psychologist, Lake Washington School District, Kirkland, WA (1971-1972); Staff Psychologist, VA Medical Center, Seattle, WA (1970-1971) **Civic:** Member, King County Human Resources Commission (2006) **Creative Works:** Publisher and Author, "A Wizard's Guide to Study Skills" (2018); Author, "The Study Skills Advantage" (1986); Contributor, Articles to Professional Journals **Awards:** Fellowship, United States Vocational Rehabilitation Administration, University of Oregon (1966-1967) **Membership:** Life Member, American Psychological Association (APA); Member, National Association of School Psychologists (NASP) **Marquis Who's Who Honors:** Albert Nelson Marquis Lifetime Achievement Award (2017) **Business Address:** 1425 Broadway Box 467, Seattle, WA, 98122 **Shipping Address:** 37 Via Santo Tomas, Rancho Mirage, CA, 92270 **Website:** http://www.KidsLike Learning.com

Nancy Melissa Harvey

Title: Artist, Poet, Media Consultant **Industry:** Fine Art **Date of Birth:** 03/31/1934 **Place of Birth:** Atlanta **State:** GA/USA **Parents:** Alfred Alonzo Ettinger; Helen Rosella (Puntney) Ettinger **Marital Status:** Married **Spouse Name:** Dale Gene Harvey (8/23/1957) **Children:** Howard Russell; Andrew Dale; Renee Jeannine (Deceased 1988) **Education:** Master's Degree in Human Services, Great Falls College Montana State University, Montana (1987); BA, University of Montana (1957) **Certifications:** Certified Teacher, State of Montana **Career:** Librarian, Art Teacher, Cut Bank High School (1979-1994); Media Specialist, Librarian, Flathead High School, Kalispell, MT (1971-1979) **Career Related:** Media Specialist, Grades K-12 **Civic:** Volunteer, Bigfork Art & Cultural Center **Creative Works:** Contributor, Back Porch Magazine (2011-2012); Author, "Bluffs" (2000); Contributor, Poetry, Arts in Montana; Contributor, Poetry, Montana Arts Magazine; Contributor, Poetry, Poetry Today Quarterly; Contributor, Poetry, Today's Poets Anthology; Contributor, Newspapers **Awards:** Grantee, Montana Committee for the Humanities (1987); Grantee, Montana Committee for the Humanities (1985); Mary Brennan Clapp Poetry Award, Montana Arts Foundation (1973); Silver Anniversary Who's Who of American Women **Membership:** Treasurer, Tangled Roots Chapter, Montana State Genealogical Society (1990-Present); Chapter President, Delta Kappa Gamma (1994-1996); Lifetime Member, AAUW; Phi Kappa Phi; Montana Retired Educators Association; Great Books Foundation Classes; Montana Library Association; Montana Association for Gifted and Talented Education **Marquis Who's Who Honors:** Albert Nelson Marquis Lifetime Achievement Award (2017); Distinguished Humanitarian (2017) **Why did you become involved in your profession or industry:** Ms. Harvey was published at the age of 14, and that inspired her to keep writing. **Hobbies:** Music; Painting; Creative writing; Photography **Political Affiliations:** Democrat **Religion:** Presbyterian **Shipping Address:** 33424 Orchard Hills Drive, Bigfork, MT, 59911

Mary Newgeon Hawkes

Title: Educator, Minister (Retired) **Industry:** Education/Educational Services **Date of Birth:** 06/27/1934 **Place of Birth:** Thessaloniki **Country of Origin:** Greece **Parents:** William Emory Hawkes; Jessie Newgeon Hawkes **Marital Status:** Single **Education:** EdD in Religious Education, Columbia University Teachers College and Union Theological Seminary, New York, NY (1983); MA in Religious Education, Hartford Seminary (1958); AB in Music Organ, Doane College (Now Doane University) (1956) **Certifications:** Ordained to Ministry, United Church of Christ (1980) **Career:** Acting Coordinator of Educational Ministries, Centre Congregational Church, Brattleboro, VT (2006-2008); Education Partner, UCCNY (1999-2002); Pastor, First Congregational Church, Deer River, NY (1998-2002); United Community Church, Carthage, NY (1998-2002); Interim Site Manager, Ingraham House Retreat Center, Bristol, CT (1997-1998); Interim Minister, United Churches of Christ, NY, CT (1994-1998); Pastor, United Church of Christ, North Bennington, VT (1988-1994); Interim Minister, United Churches of Christ, NY, CT and VT (1986-1988); Secretary of Educational Programs, United Church Board for Homeland Ministries (1981-1985) **Career Related:** Resource Person, UCCNY Women (1999-2002); Vice President, Village Ecumenical Ministry (Now Carthage VEM), Carthage, NY (1999-2002); President, Village Ecumenical Ministry (Now Carthage VEM), Carthage, NY (1999-2002) **Civic:** President, Adam Hawkes Family Association (2009-Present); Editor, Newsletter, Adam Hawkes Family Association, Saugus, MA (2002-Present); Member, Spiritual Life Communications (2002-Present); Guest Preacher (2002-Present); Organist (2002-Present) **Creative Works:** Editor, Intergenerational Resources CESA (1981-1985); Editor, Sing to God (1981-1984); Co-author, Festivals of Christmas (1981-1983); Editor, Festivals of Christmas (1981-1983); Co-author, "Go and Tell" (1978); Editorial Board, Songs of Mary Nations (1971) **Awards:** Honoree, Brattleboro Branch, Women of Distinction, AAUW (2013); Doane Builder Award, Doane College (Now Doane University) (1981) **Membership:** Brattleboro Branch, Women of Distinction, American Association of University Women (Now AAUW) (2013); President, American Association of University Women (Now AAUW) (2010-2014); Secretary, American Association of University Women (Now AAUW) (2006-2010); **Marquis Who's Who Honors:** Albert Nelson Marquis Lifetime Achievement Award (2017); Distinguished Humanitarian (2017) **Hobbies:** Music; Traveling; Reading **Political Affiliations:** Democrat **Religion:** United Church of Christ **Business Address:** 52 Missionary Rd.,+ Ste 214, Cromwell,CT, 06416

Roland B. Hawkins

Title: Radiation Oncologist **Industry:** Medicine & Health Care **Company Name:** Ochsner Health System **Date of Birth:** 02/10/1940 **Place of Birth:** St. Louis **State:** MO **Marital Status:** Married **Spouse Name:** Nancy **Children:** Two Children **Education:** Resident, Radiation Oncology, Mallinckrodt Institute of Radiology, Washington University Medical Center, St. Louis, MO (1984-1987); First Year Resident, Radiation Oncology, Washington University Medical Center, St. Louis, MO (1980-1981); MD, Washington University in St. Louis (1980); Postdoctoral Research Fellow, James Franck Institute, The University of Chicago (1969-1971); PhD in Molecular Biology, Washington University in St. Louis (1967); BS in Physics, Washington University in St. Louis School of Engineering & Applied Science (1962) **Certifications:** Certified in Radiation Oncology, American Board of Radiology (1987); Licensed Physician, State of Louisiana; Licensed Physician, State of Missouri **Career:** Radiation Oncologist, Ochsner Medical Center, Ochsner Health System, New Orleans, LA (1989-Present); Clinical Assistant Professor, School of Medicine, Tulane University (1989-1999); Radiation Oncologist, Watson Clinic, Lakeland Regional Health, Lakeland, FL (1988-1989); Radiation Oncologist, Department of Radiation Medicine, Florida Hospital Orlando (1987-1988); Primary Care Physician, Ambulatory Care Department, Division of Health and Hospitals, City of St. Louis, MO (1981-1984); Research Associate, School of Medicine, Washington University in St. Louis (1976-1977); Assistant Professor, Biochemistry, School of Medicine, Saint Louis University (1971-1976); **Career Related:** Research in Radiation Biology **Military Service:** Major, U.S. Army Reserve (1979-1987); Reserve, U.S. Army (1970-1979); Active Duty, U.S. Army (1967-1969); Major, U.S. Army Medical Corps Captain, Medical Service Corps, U.S. Army **Creative Works:** Contributor, Chapters, Medical Books; Contributor, Articles, Professional Journals **Membership:** American Society of Therapeutic Radiology and Oncology **Marquis Who's Who Honors:** Albert Nelson Marquis Lifetime Achievement Award (2017) **To what do you attribute your success:** Dr. Hawkins attributes his success to training in science and medicine. **Why did you become involved in your profession or industry:** Dr. Hawkins became involved in his profession because his science experience led him to medicine. **Hobbies:** Reading; Golf; Swimming **Political Affiliations:** Democrat **Business Address:** 1514 Jefferson Highway, New Orleans, LA, 70121 **Shipping Address:** 150 Broadway St., Apt 808, New Orleans, LA, 70118

Maxine Shoemaker Heath, PhD

Title: Instructor (Retired), Assistant Professor (Retired) **Industry:** Education/Educational Services **Company Name:** University of Illinois **Place of Birth:** Los Angeles **State:** CA **Parents:** George Estell Shoemaker; Muriel May Scott Shoemaker **Marital Status:** Single **Spouse Name:** James Edward Heath (4/2/1955, Deceased 2017) **Children:** Cynthia Heath-Smith; Pamela Diewald; Jessica Breitbarth **Education:** Postdoctoral Fellowship in Radiation Biology (1978-1981); PhD in Entomology, University of Florida (1978); MS in Entomology, University of Florida (1976); MLS, University of California, Los Angeles (1961); BA in English Literature, University of California, Los Angeles **Certifications:** Certified Entomologist **Civic:** Troop Leader, Girl Scouts of America; Regent, Llano Uplift Chapter, National Society of Daughters of the American Revolution; President, Chapter IG, Texas P.E.O. Sisterhood; Chaplain Clara Barton; Detached Tent #3, Daughters of Union Veterans of the Civil War; Chairman, Red Barn Craft Group; Volunteer, Programs on United States Historical People and Events, Civic Groups, Genealogical Societies, Texas **Creative Works:** Author, "The Cicadas of North America North of Mexico, Second Edition" (2017); Co-author, "The Cicadas of Argentina with New Records, a New Genus and 15 New Species," with Allen F. Sanborn (2014); Co-author, "The Cicadas of North America North of Mexico," with Allen F. Sanborn (2012); Author, Co-author, More Than 40 Published Scientific Papers **Membership:** The Honor Society of Phi Kappa Phi; Society of Southwestern Entomologists; National Society of Daughters of the American Revolution; Sigma Xi; Entomological Society of America; National Society United States Daughters of 1812; Daughters of Union Veterans of the Civil War; Sons of the American Revolution Auxiliary; P.E.O. Sisterhood; Red Barn Craft Group **To what do you attribute your success:** Dr. Heath attributes her success to the support she received from her husband and family. **Why did you become involved in your profession or industry:** Dr. Heath became involved in her profession through her husband, James Edward Heath. **What do you consider to be the highlight of your career:** The highlight of Dr. Heath's career was publishing "The Cicadas of North America North of Mexico." **Where will you be in five years:** Five years from now, Dr. Heath intends to be living in Texas and still contributing to both her community and science. **Hobbies:** Contributing to several genealogical and veteran organizations; Lecturing on United States history; Scientific and historical research **Shipping Address:** 104 Hummingbird Cir, Buchanan Dam, TX, 78609

James Heck, PhD

Title: Academic Administrator **Industry:** Education/Educational Services **Date of Birth:** 08/26/1930 **Place of Birth:** Columbus **State:** OH **Parents:** Arch O. Heck; Frances (Agnew) Heck **Marital Status:** Married **Spouse Name:** Jo Ann Gatton (11/18/1950) **Children:** Janice M.; Judith L.; J. Jeffrey **Education:** PhD, The Ohio State University (1967); MA, The Ohio State University (1961); EdB, The Ohio State University (1953) **Career:** Executive Director of WUSF Advancement, WUSF Public Media (2002-2003); Professor, WUSF Public Media (2002-2003); General Manager, WUSF Public Media (1990-2002); Professor, WUSF Public Media (1990-2002); General Manager, Station WSFP-TV/FM (Now WGCU Public Media) (1990-1996); Dean, School of Extended Studies & Learning Technologies, University of South Florida (1986-1990); General Manager, Public Broadcasting Station WUSF-TV/FM, University of South Florida (1986-1990); General Manager, Public Broadcasting Station WSFP-TV/FM, University of South Florida (1986-1990); Special Assistant to Provost, University of South Florida (1986-1990); Director of Office Technology, University of South Florida (1986-1990); Director, Office of Technology, University of South Florida (1984-1986) **Career Related:** Member of Board Administrative Representatives, WUSF Public Media (1999-2002); Member, Center for Digital and Computational Video, University of South Florida (1999-2002); Co-chair, International Workshop on Digital and Computational Video, University of South Florida (1999, 2000); Chairman, Southeast Region Conference, Association for Experiential Education (1988); Chairman, Planning Committee for the Academic Fellows Working Reunion, The American Council for Education (1972, 1979, 1985); Chairman, Council Fellows, The American Council on Education (1981-1982); Executive Committee Member, Council Fellows, The American Council on Education (1980-1983); Vice Chairman, Council Fellows, The American Council on Education (1980-1981) **Military Service:** U.S. Air Force (1953-1955) **Creative Works:** Co-author, "Educational Administration: Selected Readings, Second Edition" (1971); Co-author, "Analysis of Educational Change in Ohio Public Schools" (1968); Co-author, "Educational Administration: Selected Readings" (1965); Co-author, "Selected Readings" (1962); Co-author, "Counseling" **Awards:** Robert F. Summer Lifetime Award (2013); Best Comprehensive Grassroots Program Award, APTS (1999); **Marquis Who's Who Honors:** Albert Nelson Marquis Lifetime Achievement Award (2017) **Religion:** Presbyterian **Shipping Address:** 12912 Terrace Springs Dr, Tampa, FL, 33637

Mary Jo Heeb

Title: Professor Emeritus **Industry:** Education/Educational Services **Company Name:** The Scripps Research Institute **Date of Birth:** 09/20/1942 **Place of Birth:** Louisville **State:** KY/USA **Parents:** John J. Holzknecht; Mary Rose Bohn Holzknecht **Marital Status:** Married **Spouse Name:** James M. Thomas (2005); Michael Heeb (1962, Divorced 1987) **Children:** Angela Heeb Platenberg; Randall Heeb; Derek Heeb; Cynthia Heeb Clark **Education:** PhD in Biochemistry, Georgetown University (1983); MS in Microbiology, University of Florida (1968); BS in Chemistry, University of Florida (1966) **Career:** Professor Emeritus (2014-Present); Associate Professor (1999-2014); Assistant Member, Science Association (1993-1999); Science Association (1988-1992); Postdoctoral Fellow, The Scripps Research Institute, La Jolla, CA (1983-1988); Research Group Leader, Hazelton Labs, Vienna, VA (1975-1978, 1981-1982); Instructor of Chemistry, University of North Carolina, Wilmington, NC (1973-1975); Math Teacher, Wilmington, NC (1971-1972); Research Assistant, University of Miami (1969-1971); Technician, University of Florida (1963-1965) **Career Related:** Consultant, U.S. Department of the Interior, Wrightsville Beach, NC (1972-1973) **Civic:** Active in the Catholic Worker and Other Organizations that Serve the Poor and Homeless **Creative Works:** Contributor, 77 Publications in Scientific Journals; Presenter, Over 70 Presentations at Scientific Conferences **Awards:** Co-chair, Four International Society on Thrombosid and Haemostasis, Inc. Sessions (2004-2007); Invited Speaker, Six Times, International Society on Thrombosis and Haemostasis (1989-1993); Highest Score, American Heart Association, Inc. Fellowship Applications (1987); Wilhelm Turk Prize, Austrian Society of Hematology (Now Austrian Society of Hematology and Oncology) (1986) **Membership:** American Society of Hematology; International Society on Thrombosis and Haemostasis **Marquis Who's Who Honors:** Albert Nelson Marquis Lifetime Achievement Award (2017) **Hobbies:** Hiking; Camping; Travel **Political Affiliations:** Democrat **Religion:** Catholic **Shipping Address:** 2432 Front St, San Diego, CA, 92101

Petra Jean Hegstad DeKrey

Title: Elementary School Educator (Retired), Reading Teacher **Industry:** Education/Educational Services **Date of Birth:** 05/27/1944 **Place of Birth:** Oakland **State:** CA **Parents:** Lorentz Reginald Hegstad; Hazel Dorothy (Danielson) Hegstad **Marital Status:** Widowed **Spouse Name:** Donald DeKrey (7/13/2002, Deceased); Curtis Wayne Martel (4/30/1966, Divorced 1989) **Children:** Christopher W. Martel; Peter L. Martel; Loren R. Martel **Education:** MEd in Elementary Education, Bemidji State University (1989); EdB in Elementary Education, Concordia College (1966); BS in German, Concordia College (1966) **Certifications:** Certified in German; State of Minnesota; Certified in Elementary Education, State of Minnesota; Certified Reading Consultant, State of Minnesota; Certified Remedial and Developmental Reading Teacher in K-12, State of Minnesota **Career:** Retired (2005); Eighth Grade Reading Teacher, Horizon Middle School (2004-2005); Chapter I Reading Teacher, Moorhead Junior High School, Moorhead Area Public Schools (1993-2004); Student Newspaper Adviser, Moorhead Junior High School, Moorhead Area Public Schools (1993-2001); Teacher, English Reading, Rochester Public Schools (1992-1993); Chapter I Reading Teacher, Bug-O-Nay-Ge-Shig (1986-1992); **Career Related:** Member, License Committee, District 152 (2000-2002); Practice Test Writer; Teacher, Minnesota Reading Standards Tests Prep Classes; Teacher, Reading Strategies and Techniques to Junior High School Students in to Help Ensure Success in Passing the Mixed Reading Standards Test **Civic:** Election Judge (2015-Present); Volunteer, Sanford Medical Center (2006-Present); Member, Auxiliary, North Country Regional Hospital, Sanford Health (2006-Present); Secretary, Sons of Norway, Lodge i-500 (2016-2017); **Membership:** Honor Council, Northland Reading Council (1986); President, Northland Reading Council (1985-1986); **Marquis Who's Who Honors:** Albert Nelson Marquis Lifetime Achievement Award (2017); Distinguished Humanitarian (2017) **To what do you attribute your success:** Ms. DeKrey attributes her success to her parents who encouraged her at all times, had a successful marriage and strong family values. Her mom had a background in education and her dad had a business background. Her mom was very supportive of all the teachers her children had. **Why did you become involved in your profession or industry:** Ms. DeKrey became involved in her profession because of her mom and because she had very good teachers herself. **What do you consider to be the highlight of your career:** A highlight of Ms. DeKrey's career was making the decision to go back and work a masters degree and attaining it. **Shipping Address:** 1902 Lakeview Dr, Bemidji, MN, 56601

Debora A. Henderson

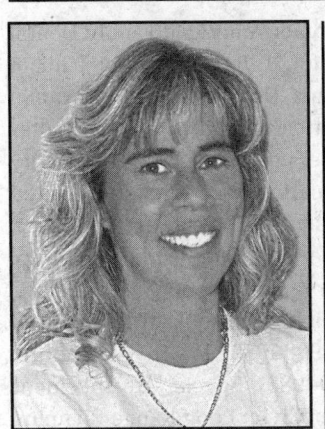

Title: Previous Owner **Industry:** Business Management/Business Services **Company Name:** 7-Eleven **Place of Birth:** Petersburg **State:** VA/USA **Children:** Amber **Education:** Associate Degree in Computer Technology, Electronic Computer Programming Institute **Career:** Manager, 7-Eleven, Inc. **Awards:** Highest Core Earnings Award (2004); Award for Operational Excellence (2003); Best Operating Earnings Award (2001-2002) **To what do you attribute your success:** Ms. Henderson attributes her success to her determination, personal drive, work ethic, confidence, motivation and hard work, as well as the support she receives from her family, colleagues and friends. **What do you consider to be the highlight of your career:** The most gratifying aspect of Ms. Henderson career is managing a 7-Eleven successfully. **Where will you be in five years:** In five years, Ms. Henderson hopes to see her team succeed together, and would like to purchase more investment properties. **Hobbies:** Diving; Sailing; Snorkeling; Traveling; Visiting Islands; Visiting the Great Barrier Reef; Caring for Her Two Dogs, Jackson and Bug **Business Address:** 2910 Patterson Avenue, Richmond, VA, 23221 **Shipping Address:** 1416 Leicester Rd, Richmond, VA, 23225

Paula Louise Henderson Setters

Title: Physics Teacher (Retired) **Industry:** Education/Educational Services **Date of Birth:** 07/18/1949 **Place of Birth:** Kay Jay **State:** KY/USA **Parents:** Louis Henderson; Lora (Bruce) Henderson **Marital Status:** Married **Spouse Name:** Charles Mullikin Setters **Children:** Philip Bennett; Lora Elizabeth; Jonas R. Lamb; Charles J. Lamb; Christopher Kelly; Sarah Haavistola **Education:** Postgraduate Coursework, Western Kentucky University (1992); MA in Science Education, The University of Alabama (1974); BS in Physics, Western Kentucky University (1970) **Certifications:** Certified Teacher, State of Kentucky (1970) **Career:** Adjunct Instructor, Campbellsville University (2003-2005); Physics Instructor, Campbellsville University (2002-2003); Adjunct Instructor, Campbellsville University (1998-2002); Teacher, LaRue County High School, Hodgenville, KY (1976-1999); Teacher, Homewood High School, AL (1971-1975); Teacher, Warren Central High School, Bowling Green, KY (1970-1971) **Career Related:** Site-Based Council, LaRue County High School (1996-1999); Professional Development Presenter, American Equity Investment Life Holding Company, Charleston, WV (1995-1998); Kentucky Instructional Technology Leaders, Frankfort, KY (1994-1998); Strategic Planning Committee, LaRue County Board of Education (1992-1999); Research Assistant, Department of Energy, TRAC, Los Alamos National Laboratory (1991) **Civic:** Chair, LaRue County Relay for Life (2000-2001); Chair, Special Programs, United Methodist Women, Hodgenville, KY (1990); President, Special Programs, United Methodist Women, Hodgenville, KY (1980-1982); President, Hodgenville Elementary (1980-1981) **Membership:** Kentucky Retired Teachers Association; Elizabethtown Hardin LaRue Retired Teachers Association **Marquis Who's Who Honors:** Albert Nelson Marquis Lifetime Achievement Award (2017) **Why did you become involved in your profession or industry:** Ms. Henderson Setters became involved in her profession because she always enjoyed helping people learn, and has always had a knack for mentoring. When she was younger, would always play teacher with her friends. As for physics, she was always interested in learning how things worked, so it was very natural for her to gravitate towards it. **What do you consider to be the highlight of your career:** Ms. Henderson Setters feels most proud when her students tell her what an impact she's had on them. **Political Affiliations:** Republican **Religion:** Methodist **Shipping Address:** 2877 Tanner Rd, Hodgenville, KY, 42748

William Grant Hennigar

Title: Dentist **Industry:** Medicine & Health Care **Company Name:** American Family Dental Group **Date of Birth:** 12/25/1947 **Place of Birth:** Buffalo **State:** NY/USA **Parents:** William Grant Hennigar; Donnette (Glaeser) Hennigar **Marital Status:** Divorced **Spouse Name:** Jennie Carcaud (Divorced) **Children:** William Grant III; Charlotte Carcaud; Travis Welshofer (Deceased); Brittany Lines **Education:** JD, Cleveland State University (1992); DMD, University of Pennsylvania (1973); AB, Colgate University (1970) **Certifications:** Certification, United States Dental Institute (1985); Certificate, University of Rochester (1975) **Career:** President, Grand Island, Cheektowaga, NY (1988-Present); Partner, American Family Dental Group, Professional Corporation, Cheektowaga, NY (1982-1997); Harvard University Health Inc., Cambridge, MA (1974) **Career Related:** Committee Member, Nichols School Athletic Hall of Fame (2014, 2010); Alumni Board, Nichols School, Buffalo, NY (1988-1989); Board of Directors, West River Homeowners Association, Grand Island, NY (1985-1988); Special Advancement Committee, Eastman Institute Oral Health University Rochester **Civic:** Long Range Planning Committee, Grand Island, NY (1998) **Military Service:** Captain, US Coast Guard (1989-Present) **Awards:** Inductee, Athletic Hall of Fame, Nichols School (2005) **Membership:** Fellow, Academy of General Dentistry; American Dental Association; ABA; New York State Bar Association; International Association of Orthodontics; American Academy Dental Group Practice; International Association of Dentists; Erie County Bar Association; New York State Dental Society; Erie County Dental Society; Eighth District Dental Society; American Dental Association; Buffalo Launch Club; Phi Kappa Psi; Psi Omega; United States Power Squadron **Marquis Who's Who Honors:** Distinguished Humanitarian (2017) **Hobbies:** Volleyball; Boating; Softball; Genealogy; Running **Political Affiliations:** Libertarian **Religion:** Episcopalian **Business Address:** 2025 Whitehaven Road, Grand Island, NY, 14072 **Shipping Address:** PO Box 574, American Family Dental Group, Grand Island, NY, 14072

Ernest Charles Hickson

Title: Finance Executive **Industry:** Financial Services **Date of Birth:** 07/14/1931 **Place of Birth:** Los Angeles **State:** CA **Parents:** Russell Arthur Hickson; Marilyn Louise (Mambert) Hickson **Marital Status:** Married **Spouse Name:** Janice Beleal (9/5/1959) **Children:** Arthur; Jennifer; Barton **Education:** Postgraduate Coursework, UCLA Anderson School of Management (1961-1963); BS, University of Southern California (1961) **Certifications:** Licensed Real Estate Broker, State of California (1956) **Career:** Principal Chairman, TMN Capital Incorporated (2009-Present); Senior Partner, TMH Resources and Affiliates, Laguna Niguel, CA (1982-Present); President, First Hawaiian Development, Honolulu, Hawaii (1976-1982); Chief Executive Officer, First Hawaiian Development, Honolulu, Hawaii (1976-1982); Executive Vice President, Sonnenblick Goldman (Now Sonnenblick Development LLC), Los Angeles, CA (1973-1976); President, USF Investors, NYSE (1971-1973); Chief Executive Officer, USF Investors, NYSE (1971-1973); Director, United States Financial, Inc., NYSE, San Diego, CA (1970-1973); President, Shelter Corporation LLC (1968-1972); Chief Executive Officer, Shelter Corporation LLC (1968-1972); Vice President, City Bank, Honolulu, Hawaii (1967-1970); Senior Loan Officer, City Bank, Honolulu, Hawaii (1967-1970); Vice President, County National Bank (Now Wells Fargo), Orange, CA (1964-1967); Assistant Vice President, Union Bank, Los Angeles, CA (1960-1964); Credit Supervisor, Atlantic Richfield Company (ARCO), Los Angeles, CA (1955-1960) **Career Related:** Expert Witness in Finances **Military Service:** Staff Sergeant, U.S. Air Force (1951-1954) **Creative Works:** Editor, "Financial Marketing" (1978-1983); Author, "The Developers" (1978) **Awards:** Executive Award, Graduate School of Credit and Financial Management, Stanford University (1964); Associates Award, The National Institute of Credit, University of California, Los Angeles (1959) **Membership:** USC Associates, University of Southern California; President's Circle, University of Southern California; Urban Land Institute; The Pacific Club, Honolulu, Hli; Outrigger Canoe Club, Honolulu, HI; Phi Gamma Delta **Marquis Who's Who Honors:** Albert Nelson Marquis Lifetime Achievement Award (2017) **Hobbies:** Tennis; Walking; Writing; Swimming **Shipping Address:** 960 Hayne Rd, Hillsborough, CA, 94010 **Website:** http://tmhcompanies.com

Peter B. Hilton, PhD

Title: Associate Professor **Industry:** Education/Educational Services **Company Name:** Saint Xavier University **Education:** PhD in Curriculum Design, The University of Illinois at Chicago (2004); MA in Teaching, Concentration in Reading, National Louis University (1986); MA in Individualized American Studies, University of Oregon (1977); BA in Epistemology, San Jose State University (1970) **Certifications:** Certified Online Instructor (2015) **Career:** Associate Professor, Saint Xavier University (2004-Present); Teacher, Graduate Courses, Saint Xavier University (1992-Present); Teacher, Staff Development Courses, Saint Xavier University (1992-Present); Teacher, Education Foundation Courses, Saint Xavier University (1992-Present) **Career Related:** Middle School Teacher, Lincoln, IL (1986-1991); Presenter, National Middle School Association Convention; Presenter, International Reading Association National Convention; Presenter, Association for the Advancement of Curriculum National Conference; Presenter, American Educational Research Association National Conference; Presenter, Journal of Curriculum Theorizing: Curriculum and Pedagogy National Conference; **Military Service:** US Army, Vietnam **Creative Works:** Contributor, "Subject Matter as Experience," Guide to Curriculum in Education, Sage Publishing, Thousand Oaks, CA (2015); Contributor, "Sage's Encyclopedia of Curriculum," Sage Publishing, Thousand Oaks, CA (2009); Contributor, "A Pathway Toward Curriculum, Pedagogies of the Imagination: Mythopoetic Curriculum in Educational Practice," London, United Kingdom (2008); Author, "Fictionalized Autobiography as Curriculum: Relationships in the Making of a Teacher Educator," The University of Illinois at Chicago (2004) **Awards:** Recipient, Saint Xavier Award, Saint Xavier University (2013) **Membership:** American Educational Research Association; International Literacy Association **To what do you attribute your success:** Dr. Hilton attributes his success to his ability to build relationships with his students. **Why did you become involved in your profession or industry:** During his tour in Vietnam, Dr. Hilton saved children from a burning bus and ever since then he knew he had to help children. He became involved in his position through his experience as a reading instructor. **What do you consider to be the highlight of your career:** The highlight of Dr. Hilton's career was studying with William H. Schubert at the University of Illinois in Chicago. He is also proud of getting the award from Saint Xavier - a service award that goes to one faculty member every year. Being elected as senate president two years ago. **Business Address:** 3700 W 103rd St., Chicago, IL, 60655

Richard Hirtzel, PhD

Title: Political Science Professor **Industry:** Education/Educational Services **Date of Birth:** 02/01/1929 **Place of Birth:** Chicago **State:** IL/USA **Parents:** Frederich E. Hirtzel; Sarah F. Swank **Marital Status:** Married **Spouse Name:** Connie Kay Olsen (10/16/1964) **Children:** Thomas; Lori; Tammie; Carrie **Education:** PhD in Political Science, University of Utah, Salt Lake City, UT (1967); MS, Brigham Young University, Provo, UT (1962); BS, Brigham Young University, Provo, UT (1956) **Career:** Professor Emeritus of Political Science, Western Illinois University (1968-1991); Associate Professor, Winona State College (1966-1968) **Career Related:** Member, Consultant, The United States Army War College (1969-1982) **Civic:** Member, The Church of Jesus Christ of Latter-day Saints (1952-2014); Member, Church Employment Resources Center, American Fork, UT (1991-1995); **Military Service:** Civilian Personal Officer, Hill Air Force Base, Utah (1961-1965); Korean Communication Zone, U.S. Army, Republic of Korea (1952-1953); Colonel, U.S. Army Reserve **Creative Works:** Author, "Career Opportunities in International Relations" (1983); Author, "Career Opportunities in Political Science" (1982); Author, "Military & Economic Aid To Indonesia: A Case Story,"(1967); Author, "Adam Lambert of Lancaster County and Dauphin County, Pennsylvania and August County, Virginia"; Author, "Anastasia Mueller (Miller) of Fuetzen, Waldshut, Baden, Germany and Athens, St. Clair County, Illinois"; Author, "Ancestors from Fuetzen : Waldshut, Baden, Germany"; Author, "Ancestors from Ofterdingenm, Schwarzwald Kreis, Wuerttemberg, Germany"; Author, "Ancestors from Waldshut, Baden, Germany : Muller, Gleichauf, Bomma, Staub, Bausch Families"; Author, "The Ancestors of George William Hirtzel"; Author, "The Ancestors of Richard D. Hirtzel"; Author, "The Ancestors of Sarah Ferne Swank (Hirtzel) of Effingham County, Illinois and North Hollywood, California"; Author, "Benedict Miller of Effingham County, Illinois"; Author, "David Lambert of Lancaster County and Dauphin County, Pennsylvania and Augusta County, Virginia and Gallia County, Ohio"; Author, "Denny and Southard/Suddarth, Immigrants to Early America"; Author, "Denny Families in Early Northumberland County and Lancaster County, Virginia" **Awards:** Decorated U.S. Army Meritorious Medal With Oak Leaf Cluster; Army Commendation Medal; National Defense Service Medal; United Nations Service Medal; Bronze Service Stars; Korean Service Medal, Republic of Korea; Academy Award, Illinois Governor **Membership:** Military Officers Association of America; Reserve Officer Association of the United States; Pi Sigma Alpha **Shipping Address:** 2120 N. 900 W., Pleasant Grove, UT, 84062

Christina G. Hoagland

Title: Occupational Therapist (Retired), Industrial Drafter **Industry:** Health, Wellness and Fitness **Date of Birth:** 07/18/1954 **Place of Birth:** Long Beach **State:** CA **Parents:** Joseph Richard Hoagland; Dorothy Marian (Bell) Hoagland **Marital Status:** Married **Spouse Name:** Theresa J. Feuerborn **Education:** AS in Industrial Drafting Technology, Mount San Antonio College (1985); BS in Occupational Therapy, Loma Linda University (1975) **Certifications:** Certified Brain Injury Specialist (2008); Registered Occupational Therapist **Career:** Retired (2013); Staff Occupational Therapist Coordinator, Grand Junction Community Hospital (2000-2013); Floating Staff Occupational Therapist, Grand Junction Community Hospital (2000-2013); Occupational Therapist, Independent Living Skills Training Supervisor, Interim Home Health Care (1998-2008); Floating Staff Occupational Therapist, St. Mary's Rehabilitation Center, Grand Junction, CO (1995-1997); Floating Staff Occupational Therapist, Hilltop Rehabilitation Hospital, Grand Junction, CO (1992-1995); Occupational Therapist, Linda R. Brown, Visalia, CA (1992); Staff Occupational Therapist, Corona Community Hospital (1990-1992); Re-entry Occupational Therapist, Rancho Los Amigos, Downey, CA (1989-1990); Industrial Drafter, Amerex Corporation, Riverside, CA (1985-1988); Staff Occupational Therapist, Glendale Adventist Medical Center (1978-1979); Staff Occupational Therapist, Hinsdale Sanitarium and Hospital (1977-1978); Occupational Therapist, Yuka Mission Hospital, Zambia, Africa (1976-1977) **Career Related:** Board Member, Brain Injury Trust Fund (2006-2010) **Civic:** Member and Community Presenter, Grand Valley Brain Injury & Epilepsy Support Group; Assistant, Creative Writing and Poetry Workshops **Creative Works:** Drawings and Paintings Hung in Members' Shows, Grand Junction Art Center, Veteran's Art Center **Membership:** Charter Board Member, Colorado Traumatic Brain Injury Trust Fund (2005-2010); American Occupational Therapy Association; Occupational Therapy Association of Colorado; National Museum of Women in the Arts; Western Colorado Center for the Arts **Why did you become involved in your profession or industry:** Ms. Hoagland graduated as occupational therapist and then moved forward to brain injury where she was told not to go back to occupational therapy and was retrained to be a drafter. **Hobbies:** Yoga; Poetry; Bicycling; Gardening; Daily dog walking; Memoirs; Pencil drawing; Acrylic and watercolor painting; Printmaking; Pottery; Sculpture; Graphic art **Political Affiliations:** Progressive Democrat **Religion:** Seventh-day Adventist **Shipping Address:** 578 N 26th St, Grand Junction, CO, 81501

Matthew Ryan Holland

Title: Chief Executive Officer **Industry:** Medicine & Health Care **Company Name:** Synergistic Creations **State:** CA **Marital Status:** Married **Education:** Doctoral Coursework in Psychology, Capella University (2013-Present); Journeyman Classification in Communication and Navigation Systems, Community College of the Air Force (2004); Diplomate in Psychology, Pasadena City College (1994) **Career:** Chief Executive Officer, Synergistic Creations (2014-Present); Co-Founder, Synergistic Creations (2014-Present); Regional Director, Willamette Valley, Mid-Valley Behavioral Care Network (2010-2016); Care Coordinator, Linn County Mental Health, EASA (2010-2015); Consultant in Field (2008-2012); Program Manager, Trillium Family Services (2007-2010); Administrator, Trillium Family Services (2007-2010); Treatment Team Leader (2007); Therapeutic Guide, Catherine Freer Wilderness Therapy Programs (2006-2009) **Career Related:** Volunteer Consultant, Youth Era (2016-Present); Contributing Blogger, The Huffington Post, LinkedIn Pulse (2015-2018) **Civic:** Addictions and Mental Health Planning and Advisory Council, Oregon (2013-Present); Past Chairman, Addictions and Mental Health Planning and Advisory Council, Oregon (2013-Present); Behavioral Health Prevention and Promotion Sub-Committee, Addictions and Mental Health Planning and Advisory Council, Oregon (2013-Present); Behavioral Health Collaborative, Standards of Care and Competencies Workgroup, Oregon (2017); Panel Member, Substance Abuse and Mental Health Services Administration (2017); Certified Community Behavioral Health Clinics Advisory Group, Oregon (2016) **Military Service:** Senior Airman, 353rd Special Operations Group, U.S. Air Force (2000-2004); 353 SOMXS Wizards AFSOC MC 130 Maintenance Magic **Creative Works:** Contributor, Articles, Professional Journals Including the Huffington Post **Membership:** Oregon Entrepreneurs Network Technology Association of Oregon **Marquis Who's Who Honors:** Marquis Who's Who for Excellence in Behavioral Health and Mental Health Care **Why did you become involved in your profession or industry:** Mr. Holland became involved in his profession because having worked in a broken system for many years, navigating the loop holes to provide care for clients, he knew that there must be a better way to provide more consistent care, not just on a monthly basis, but on a daily basis, to help people be more connected with themselves and their providers. **Hobbies:** Arts; Music; Books; Outdoors; Family **Shipping Address:** 1356 Pressler Court S, Salem, OR, 97306 **Website:** https://www.myknktd.com

Vernon Daughty Holleman

Title: Internist, Educator **Industry:** Medicine & Health Care **Company Name:** Baylor Scott & White Health, Texas A&M College of Medicine **Date of Birth:** 10/01/1931 **Place of Birth:** Brownwood **State:** TX/USA **Parents:** Vernon Edgar Holleman; Olene Nollie (Reece) Holleman **Marital Status:** Married **Spouse Name:** Shirley Eyvonne Roberts (4/26/1961) **Children:** Richard; Joel; Douglas **Education:** Residency, Internal Medicine, Scott and White Clinic and Hospital, Texas (1959-1962); Intern, Scott and White Clinic and Hospital, Texas (1958-1959); MD, Baylor University (1958); BA in Chemistry and Biology, Howard Payne College (1953) **Certifications:** Diplomate, American Academy of Pain Management **Career:** Associate Clinical Professor, Texas A&M College of Medicine (2016-Present); Medical Staff Member, Scott and White Hospital (1962-Present); Associate Professor of Internal Medicine, Texas A&M College Medicine (1982-2016); Director, Division of General Internal Medicine, Santa Fe Center, Texas (1985-2003); Medical Director, Santa Fe Employees Hospital Association (1985-2005); Director, Division of General Internal Medicine, Santa Fe Center (1985-2005); President, Medical Staff, Santa Fe Memorial Hospital (1979-1983); Assistant Chief Physician, Santa Fe Employees Hospital Association (1962-1985); Medical Staff Member, Santa Fe Memorial Hospital (1962-1983) **Career Related:** Medical Director, Consolidated Associations of Railroad Employees (1997-Present); Adjunct Faculty, Ohio College of Podiatric Medicine (1982-1986); Clinician, Ohio College of Podiatric Medicine (1982-1986) **Civic:** Board of Directors, Santa Fe Memorial Foundation; Honorary Chairman, Physicians Advisory Board, Texas National Representative Congressional Committee **Awards:** Distinguished Alumnus, Howard Payne University (2016); Board of Trustees Service Award, Scott and White Healthcare (2012); 50 Year Staff Service Award, Scott and White Clinic (2012); Press Ganey Focus Award, Scott & White (2007); Honorary Award, Santa Fe Memorial Foundation (2004) **Marquis Who's Who Honors:** Albert Nelson Marquis Lifetime Achievement Award (2017); Distinguished Humanitarian (2017) **Why did you become involved in your profession or industry:** Dr. Holleman's hero was David Livingstone, and he knew that becoming a doctor was always his calling. After completing his internship, he was planning on going into general practice. However, his instructors talked him into going into internal medicine. **Religion:** Baptist **Business Address:** 1605 S 31st St., Temple, TX, 76508

Jack E. Holmes, PhD

Title: Emeritus Political Science Professor **Industry:** Education/Educational Services **Date of Birth:** 05/16/1941 **Place of Birth:** Wichita **State:** KS **Parents:** Herbert Paul Holmes; Marguerite Elizabeth (Duerr) Holmes **Marital Status:** Married **Spouse Name:** Linda Sue Pacheco (12/28/1996) **Children:** Valerie; Jacqueline; Cynthia; Elizabeth **Education:** PhD in International Studies, University of Denver (1972); MA, University of Denver (1967); BA, Knox College (1963) **Career:** Professor, Hope College, Holland, MI (1987-Present); Chairman, Department of Political Science, Hope College, Holland, MI (1999-2004); Chairman, Department of Political Science, Hope College, Holland, MI (1988-1995); Associate Professor, Hope College, Holland, MI (1976-1987); Assistant Professor, Hope College, Holland, MI (1975-1976); District Assistant, Congressman Don Brotzman, Denver, CO (1973-1975); **Civic:** Campaign Co-Chairman, Ottawa County Republicans, Holland, MI (2007-Present); Member and Policy Sub-Committee Vice-Chair of Michigan Republican State Committee (2014-Present); Michigan Presidential Elector (2016); Ottawa County Bush for President (2004); Chairman, Congressional District, Republican Party (2003-2007); Ottawa County Bush for President (2000); Delegate, Republican National Convention (2000); Chairman, Ottawa County Republicans, Holland, MI (1997-2002); Campaign Chairman, Ottawa County Republicans, Holland, MI (1982-1996); **Military Service:** Captain, U.S. Army (1967-1969); Assigned to Politico-Military Section of Army General Staff **Creative Works:** Author,, "240 Years of Foreign Policy Moods in a Democracy Which Grew Into a Superpower: What It Means for IR Theory" in Oxford Encyclopedia of Empirical International Relations Theory (2018); Author, "Ambivalent America: Toward a Steadier and Safer Response to World Trends" (2011); Co-Author, "American Government Essentials and Perspectives" (1998); Co-Author, "American Government Essentials and Perspectives" (1994); Co-Author, "American Government Essentials and Perspectives" (1991); Author, "The Mood/Interest Theory of American Foreign Policy" (1985) **Awards:** Hall of Fame, Michigan Model United Nations **Membership:** International Studies Association; American Political Science Association; Holy Cross Wilderness Defense Fund **Marquis Who's Who Honors:** Albert Nelson Marquis Lifetime Achievement Award (2017) **Why did you become involved in your profession or industry:** Dr. Holmes always had an interest in working with young people and passing his knowledge onto them. He wanted to get them interested in politics and national affairs. **Political Affiliations:** Republican **Religion:** Presbyterian **Shipping Address:** 4128 Byron Rd, Hudsonville, MI, 49426

Eleanor B. Howe

Title: Librarian (Retired), Educator (Retired) **Industry:** Library Management/Library Services **Date of Birth:** 10/13/1941 **Place of Birth:** Baltimore **State:** MD **Parents:** Eugene Winkelmann Bruns; Esther I. Benson Bruns Haugh **Children:** Sarah E. Michalak; David J. Michalak **Education:** Master of Education, Millersville University of Pennsylvania, Millersville, PA (1994); Master of Science in Library Science, Clarion University of Pennsylvania, Clarion, PA (1993); BA, Vassar College, Poughkeepsie, NY (1963) **Certifications:** Elementary Education Teacher, Commonwealth of Pennsylvania (1994); Social Studies Teacher, Commonwealth of Pennsylvania (1987); School Librarian, K-12, Commonwealth of Pennsylvania (1992); Social Studies Teacher, 7-12, State of New York (1963) **Career:** Co-Chair, Library Science Department K-12, Pine-Richland School District, Gibsonia, PA (2003-2007); Librarian, Pine-Richland High School, Gibsonia, PA (2001-2007); Librarian, Washington Park School, Washington, PA (1999-2001); Librarian, Shady Side Academy Senior School, Pittsburgh, PA (1993-1999); Adjunct Instructor, Department of Library Science, Clarion University of Pennsylvania (1996-1997) **Career Related:** Member, Media Selection and Review Committee, Pennsylvania School Librarians Association (1995-2012); Staff Member, Learning and Media, Journal of the Pennsylvania School Librarians Association (2001-2011); Member, Double-blind Review Panels, International Association of School Librarianship (2002-2007); Chair, Research Special Interest Group, International Association of School Librarianship (2001-2007); USA Director, International Association of School Librarianship (2001-2007) **Civic:** Volunteer, Alumnae and Alumni of Vassar College (AAVC), Poughkeepsie, NY (2000-Present); Volunteer Meditation Leader, Kearns Spirituality Center, Pittsburgh, PA (2008-2016); Study Leader, Osher Lifelong Learning Institute, Carnegie Mellon University, Pittsburgh, PA (2012-2014) **Creative Works:** Author, Professional Articles, Publications and Manuals (1994-2012); **Awards:** Who's Who Industry Leaders, Marquis Who's Who (2017); Intergenerational Honor Choir, American Choral Directors Association of Pennsylvania (2011-2012) **Membership:** Pennsylvania School Librarians Association (PSLA); International Association of School Librarianship (IASL); American Library Association (ALA) **What do you consider to be the highlight of your career:** One of Ms. Howe's greatest highlights was having the assistant superintendent write her a letter saying that her library department K-12 direct report of 2004 was the best direction support ever submitted. **Shipping Address:** 4499 Birchwood Lane, Allison Park, PA, 15101

Harold Aaron Huckins

Title: Chemical Engineer **Industry:** Engineering **Company Name:** Princeton Advanced Technology, Inc. **Date of Birth:** 11/28/1924 **Place of Birth:** Cambridge **State:** MA **Parents:** Harold Aaron Huckins; Julia E. (Nugent) Huckins **Marital Status:** Widowed **Spouse Name:** Elizabeth L. Kearns (11/15/1952, Deceased 8/2017) **Children:** Richard W.; Robert M.; Christopher N.; Patricia A.; Leslie K. **Education:** Graduate Coursework in Chemical Engineering, University of Pittsburgh (1952); Graduate Coursework in Business Administration, Boston University (1949); Associate Degree in Mechanical Engineering, Lowell Institute (1946); BSChemE, Northeastern University, Boston, MA (1945) **Career:** Founder, President, International Consultant, Firm for Chemical Processing, Materials, Environmental, Multiclient Reports, Technical Legal Cases Expert Witness, Princeton Advanced Technology, Inc. (1985-2017); Initiative Chairman, World's First Advanced Materials Conference with 29 Technology Societies (1984); Chairman, World's First Electrical Car Conference with Princeton University (1978); Vice President, Technology Assessment, Halcon Science Design, New York, NY (1974-1985); Technical Director, Vice President of Technical Operations, Oxirane Chemical Company, Princeton, NJ (1969-1974); Manager, Pilot Plants, Project Manager, Director, Vice President, Project Evaluation-process Design, Scientific Design Company, Inc., New York, NY (1953-1969); Senior Process Engineer, Project Manager, Chemical Division, Koppers Company, Pittsburgh, PA (1949-1953); **Career Related:** Fellow, American Institute of Chemical Engineers (1977-Present); Chairman, Entrepreneurial Forum (1994-1999); New Technology Committee, American Institute of Chemical Engineers (1985-1993); Director Association, Consultant Chemists and Chemical Engineers, New York, NY (1985-1993); Director, Management Division, American Institute of Chemical Engineers (1980-1982); Director, Member to Chair, Joint Engineering Council, John Fritz Engineering Entrepreneur Medal Award Committee (1979-1989); National Speaker Bureau, American Institute of Chemical Engineers (1977-1994); Director, Chairman, Materials Engineering Sciences Division, American Institute of Chemical Engineers (1977-1990); Director, Materials Technical Institute, St. Louis, MO (1976-1985) **Awards:** Chemical Engineering Practice Award (1994); Highest Industrial Award, American Institute of Chemical Engineers **Membership:** American Institute of Chemical Engineers (1947-Present); American Chemical Society; National Association of Corrosion Engineers; Mensa International; **Political Affiliations:** Republican **Shipping Address:** 1423 Eagle Pointe Way, Chesapeake, VA, 23322

Donna L. Hudson, PhD

Title: Computer Science Educator **Industry:** Education/Educational Services **Company Name:** University of California, San Francisco **Date of Birth:** 07/16/1946 **Place of Birth:** Fresno **State:** CA **Parents:** David Harder; Elvera Marie (Hegquist) Harder **Marital Status:** Married **Spouse Name:** Samuel E. Hudson **Education:** PhD in Computer Science, University of California, Los Angeles (1981); MS in Mathematics, California State University, Fresno (1972); BS in Mathematics, California State University, Fresno (1968) **Career:** Professor, University of California, San Francisco (1992-Present); Associate Professor, University of California, San Francisco (1988-1992); Assistant Professor, University of California, San Francisco (1982-1988); Assistant Professor, University of California, Davis (1981-1982); Lecturer, California State University, Fresno (1975-1981) **Career Related:** Director, Medical Information Resources, Fresno Medical Education Program, University of California, San Francisco (1982-Present); Fellow, American Association for Medical Systems and Informatics; Fellow, Institute of Medical and Biological Engineering, University of Leeds; Fellow, IEEE; Fellow, AIMBE; Lifetime Fellow, IEEE **Creative Works:** Associate Editor, "International Journal of Computers and Their Applications"; Contributor, Articles, Professional Journals **Awards:** Distinguished Service Award, IEEE (2013); Faculty Research Award, The Honor Society of Phi Kappa Phi; Honoree, Alumnus of the Year, College of Science and Mathematics, California State University, Fresno **Membership:** Board of Directors, International Society for Computers and Their Applications; Senior, IEEE; Beta Gamma Sigma; The Honor Society of Phi Kappa Phi; Past Chair, Life Sciences Community, IEEE **Marquis Who's Who Honors:** Albert Nelson Marquis Lifetime Achievement Award (2017) **Hobbies:** Traveling **Political Affiliations:** Democrat **Business Address:** 155 North Fresno Street, Fresno, CA, 93704 **Shipping Address:** 363 W Vartikian Avenue, Fresno, CA, 93701

Eliza Hudson-Zonn

Title: Director of Nursing **Industry:** Medicine & Health Care **Company Name:** Arc/Morris **Date of Birth:** 12/12/1956 **Place of Birth:** Monrovia **Country of Origin:** Liberia **Parents:** Hartzell Gleh Killen; Joan Eliza (Roberts) Killen **Spouse Name:** Mawuli Sonny Zonn (Married 7/31/1988); Henry Clay Hudson (7/1979, Divorced 4/1985) **Children:** Kimberly Clayde **Education:** BSN, University of Southern Mississippi (1984); BA in Psychology, University of Southern Mississippi (1984) **Certifications:** RN, States of New Jersey, Texas and Virginia **Career:** Director of Nursing, Medical Day Care Center, New Community Extended Care, Newark, NJ (2003-Present); Supervising Nurse, Interim Healthcare, Inc., Morristown, NJ (1990-Present); Private Duty Nurse, Maxim Healthcare, Inc., South Orange, NJ (1990-Present); Director of Nursing, American Red Cross of Morris - Home and Hospital Skilled Home Care (2015-2016); Director of Nursing, Better Care Nursing Health Services, Bloomfield, NJ (2007-2008); Supervisor, St. Mary's Life Center, Pope John Paul II Pavilion, Orange, NJ (2007); Staff Nurse, United Children's Hospital, Newark, NJ (1989-1992); Staff Nurse, Montclair General Hospital, New Jersey (1989-1991); Critical Care Nurse, National Staffing Association Inc., East Orange, NJ (1988-2004); Private Nurse, Beth Israel Medical Center, Newark, NJ (1988-1992); Critical Care Nurse, Midpoint Professional Agency, East Orange, NJ (1988) **Career Related:** Charge Nurse, Community Psychiatric Center, Houston, TX (1993) **Civic:** Human Rights Advocate, Movement for Justice in Africa (1975-Present); Member, Leadership Counsel, Southern Poverty Law Center (2003); Coordinator, Health Services Director, Liberian Community Association, New Jersey (2001); Women's Refugees Health Advocate, Union Sierra Leone for Liberia (1990-1995); Counselor, St. Elmo Baptist Church (1982); Membership Recruiter, Student Unification Party, Monrovia, Liberia (1975-1976); Rural Health Volunteer, Red Cross Liberia, Monrovia, Liberia (1973-1974) **Awards:** Recipient, Southern Baptist Convention Scholarship (1978-1984); National Baptist Convention Scholar (1972-1984); Recipient, Public Service Award, East Mississippi Baptist Women Convention (1972) **Membership:** National Association for the Advancement of Colored People; National Association of Professional Women; National Staffing Association for Skilled Home Care Nursing; Founding Member, Suehn Academy Alumni Association **Political Affiliations:** Democrat **Shipping Address:** 64 Hillyer St, Orange, NJ, 07050

Cynthia Cox Huntting

Title: Artist **Industry:** Fine Art **Date of Birth:** 09/02/1936 **Place of Birth:** San Francisco **State:** CA **Parents:** E. Morris Cox; Margaret (Storke) Cox **Marital Status:** Divorced **Spouse Name:** Edward Tyler Huntting, Jr. (3/8/1969, Divorced 1974) **Education:** Diploma, San Francisco Art Institute (1959); BA, Smith College (1958) **Career:** Artist, Private Practice, San Francisco, CA (1968-Present); Artist, World Affairs Council of Northern California (1964-1967); Artist, Staff, Pace Program, Stanford University (1962-1964); Artist, Emporium White House (1958-1961) **Career Related:** Modern Art Council Board, San Francisco Museum of Modern Art (1970-1978) **Civic:** Junior League of San Francisco **Creative Works:** Artist, Oil and Acrylic Paintings; Artist, Commercial Art **Membership:** Emeritus Member, Town and Country; Emeritus Member, California Tennis Club **Why did you become involved in your profession or industry:** Ms. Huntting became involved in her profession because she wanted to make a living doing creative work that she enjoyed. **Hobbies:** Tennis; Fly-fishing **Political Affiliations:** Republican **Religion:** Episcopalian **Shipping Address:** 2562 Treasure Dr., Apt S4002, Santa Barbara, CA, 93105

Margo Hutz Allman

Title: Sculptor, Painter **Industry:** Fine Art **Date of Birth:** 02/23/1933 **Place of Birth:** New York **State:** NY **Parents:** Werner H. Hutz; Avis (Newcomb) Hutz **Marital Status:** Married **Spouse Name:** William B. Allman (2/19/1954) **Children:** Avis Louise; David Drue **Education:** Coursework, University of Delaware (1970); Coursework, Hans Hofmann School of Fine Arts(1953); Coursework, Moore College of Art & Design (1955) **Career Related:** Artist-in-Residence, Canakkale Seramik, Kale Group, Turkey (1995) **Civic:** Member, Board of Directors, Robert Small Dance Company, New York, NY (1979-1980) **Creative Works:** Exhibitor, Group Shows, "Layering Constructs," Delaware Art Museum and The Delaware Contemporary (2015); Exhibitor, Group Shows, "Dream Streets," Delaware Art Museum (2015); Exhibitor, Group Shows, Syne Exhibit, West Chester University (2014); Exhibitor, Group Shows, "Affinities Women Artists," Regional Center for Women in the Arts (2014); Solo Exhibitor, The Delaplaine Visual Arts Education Center (2013); Solo Exhibitor, Blue Streak Gallery (2012); Exhibitor, Group Shows, The Art Trust, West Chester, PA (2011-2012); Exhibitor, Group Shows, Villanova University, Pennsylvania (2011); Exhibitor, Group Shows, Serpentine Gallery, West Chester, PA (2011); Exhibitor, Group Shows, Delaware Art Museum, Wilmington, DE (2010); Exhibitor, Group Shows, Gallery 919, SYNE Group, Wilmington, DE (2010); Exhibitor, Group Shows, Widener University, Chester, PA (2009); Exhibitor, Group Shows, Coral Springs Museum of Art, Florida (2009); Exhibitor, Group Shows, The Delaplaine Visual Arts Education Center, Frederick, MD (2009); Solo Exhibitor, Main Line Unitarian Church, Devon, PA (2009); Exhibitor, Group Shows, "Staying the Course Two Women Retrospective," Towson University, Maryland (2008); Solo Exhibitor, "Retrospective," West Chester University (2008); Exhibitor, Group Shows, "Parallel Visions," Vonderau Museum, Germany (2007); Exhibitor, Group Shows, Art Scene (2006); Solo Exhibitor, Garrubbo Bazan Gallery, West Chester, PA (2005); Exhibitor, Group Shows, Garrubbo Bazan Gallery (2005); Exhibitor, Group Shows, Moore College of Art & Design (2005); Exhibitor, Group Shows, The Delaware Contemporary, Wilmington, DE (2005); Exhibitor, Group Shows, The Art Trust, West Chester, PA (2005); Exhibitor, Group Shows, The Regional Center for Women in the Arts (2003); Exhibitor, Group Shows, Chester County Art Association, West Chester, PA (2003) **Awards:** Distinguished Alumnae Award, Moore College of Art & Design (1998); Landscape Prize, Wilmington Trust Bank (1969) **Membership:** Philadelphia Museum of Art; **Marquis Who's Who Honors:** Albert Nelson Marquis Lifetime Achievement Award (2017) **Shipping Address:** 307 Whitestone Road, Avondale, PA, 19311

Winifred Prince Hyson

Title: Composer, Music Educator **Industry:** Media & Entertainment **Date of Birth:** 02/21/1925 **Place of Birth:** Schenectady **State:** NY **Parents:** David Chandler Prince; Winifred Notman Prince **Marital Status:** Married **Spouse Name:** Charles David Hyson (9/7/1946) **Children:** David Prince; Pamela Chandler; Christopher Perry **Education:** Postgraduate Coursework in Music, American University (1967); Postgraduate Coursework in Physics, Harvard University (1946); BA in Physics, Radcliffe College, Magna Cum Laude (1945) **Career:** Originator and Director, Music Theory Program, Maryland State Music Teachers Association (1979-1982); Research Assistant, Gordon McKay Engineering Laboratory, Harvard University (1946-1947); Private Teacher, Piano, Music Theory, Composition **Creative Works:** Composer, "Salute to President Lincoln" (2010); Composer, "Another Way to Be" (2008); Composer, "Spanish Dance Fantasy" (2002); Composer, "Somewhere in the Wild" (2002); Composer, "Ladies First"; Composer, "Forgotten Wars"; Composer, "View From Sandburg"; Composer, "Breathing Naturally"; Composer, "Somewhere in the Wild" **Awards:** Grant, Arts Council Montgomery County, Maryland (1999); Grant, Meet The Composer, Inc. (1987); Grant, Meet The Composer, Inc. (1982) **Membership:** National League of American Pen Women; American Society of Composers; National Council of Teachers of Mathematics; Maryland State Music Teachers Association; ACME; Honorary Member, Friday Morning Music Club; Mu Phi Epsilon; Phi Beta Kappa **Marquis Who's Who Honors:** Albert Nelson Marquis Lifetime Achievement Award (2017) **Shipping Address:** 9707 Old Georgetown Road, Apt. 1112, Bethesda, MD, 20814

Vasanth Iyer, PhD

Title: Instructor **Industry:** Education/Educational Services **Company Name:** Mansfield University of Pennsylvania **Date of Birth:** 05/29/1964 **Place of Birth:** Madurai **Country of Origin:** India **Parents:** Srinivas Subramanian; Rajameenkshi Subramanian **Marital Status:** Married **Spouse Name:** Indira Iyer **Children:** Puja; Pranav **Education:** PhD in Computer Science, Florida International University, Miami, FL (2013); PhD, ABD in Computer Science, International Institute of Information Technology, Hyderabad, India (2012); MS in Computer and Information Science, University of New Haven (1989); BEE in Electronic and Communication Engineering, Osmania University (1985) **Certifications:** CISCO Network Programming, UNH (2003); Microsoft Windows Programming, University of California, Berkeley (1992-1994) **Career:** Faculty, Mansfield University; Assistant Professor, University of Central Missouri; Visiting Assistant Professor, Department of Computer Science, Oklahoma State University; Postdoctoral Research Scientist, TIGER Institute, Tennessee State University; Collaborator, IIIT-H, Institute of Infocomm Research, Canon Information Systems; Real-Time Kernel, Iconics Inc., Foxborough, MA; Smart Phones Department, Catalytic Software, Seattle and Hyderabad, WA; Browser and Security Department, NetManage, Cupertino, CA; Snap-In Server Administrator, MacAfee, Santa Clara, CA; Browser Plug-ins Department, Silicon Energy, Alameda, CA **Career Related:** Technical Program Committee Member, International Conference on Computer Intelligent Systems and Networking (2018); Associate Editor, Academic Journal of Information Security (2017); Track Chair, Technical Program Committee Member, IEEE (2017); Technical Program Committee Member, World Symposium on Computer Applications & Research (2017) **Civic:** Air Force Summer Faculty Fellowship Program (2018); Participant, Air Force Summer Faculty Fellowship Program (2017) **Creative Works:** Contributor, Mortal Combat Game Keyboard Interface, DirectX Team, Microsoft (2005); Contributor, Jim Hensen Muppetier Display, Disney World (1991) **Awards:** Microsoft Azure for "Research Cloud Computing Services for Computing Fixed Matrix Similarity Score Instead of Real-time Dynamic Range Measured from Data Stream Using Big-Table Approach" Project (2015-Present); Student Travel Grantee, ICDM, IEEE International Conference on Data Mining (2011) **Membership:** The Order of the Computing Professionals (2013); Professional Member, ACM; IEEE **Business Address:** 31 S Academy Street, Mansfield, PA, 16933 **Shipping Address:** 37 Spring Pond Road, Painted Post, NY, 14870

Stanley Jacobson

Title: Professor Emeritus, Biologist **Industry:** Education/Educational Services **Company Name:** Tufts University **Date of Birth:** 08/24/1937 **Place of Birth:** Chicago **State:** IL **Marital Status:** Married **Spouse Name:** Avis G. Jacobson (1960) **Children:** Arthur S. Jacobson **Education:** PhD in Anatomy, Northwestern University (1963); MS in Anatomy, Northwestern University (1961); BS in Zoology, University of Illinois (1959) **Career:** Professor, Department of Anatomy, Tufts University (1975-Present); Associate Professor, Department of Anatomy, Tufts University (1971-1975); Assistant Professor, Department of Anatomy, Tufts University (1967-1971); Research Associate, Northwestern University (1965-1967); Research Biologist, Veterans Affairs Research Hospital of Chicago (1965-1967); Emeritus Research Biologist, Division of Neuroscience, National Institutes of Health (1963-1965); U.S. Public Health Service Research Fellow, Northwestern University (1959-1963) **Career Related:** Fulbright Scholar, Department of Anatomy, School of Medicine, Makerere University, Uganda (2011-2012); Visiting Scholar, Department of Neuroscience, University of California, San Diego (2003); Visiting Professor, Department of Neuropharmacology, The Scripps Research Institute (1994-1995); Weizmann Institute of Science, Rehovot, Israel (1981-1982); Cytologist, Neurosurgical Service, Massachusetts General Hospital (1975-1981); Visiting Associate Professor, Department of Neurosciences, Medische Faculteit, Erasmus University Rotterdam, The Netherlands (1973-1974); Assistant Professorial Lecturer, The George Washington University (1964-1965) **Civic:** Reviewer, Applications for Fulbright Awards in Sub-Sahara Africa, Council for International Exchange of Scholars (2013-2015) **Creative Works:** Author, "Neuroanatomy for the Neuroscientist, Third Edition" (2017); Contributing Author, "Integrated Neuroscience and Neurology" (2014); Contributing Author, "Introduction to the Neurosciences"; Contributing Author, "Integrated Neuroscience and Neurology, Second Edition"; Contributor, Articles, Professional Journals **Awards:** Letter of Commendation for Undergraduate Teaching, Tufts University (2013-2015, 2008-2011, 2006, 2004, 1997-2002, 1995, 1993); Fulbright Scholar, Makerere University, Uganda (2011-2012); Letter of Commendation for Excellence in Teaching, Tufts University (1991, 1986-1987, 1980-1982, 1978, 1975-1976); Fulbright Fellow, United States Department of State; Fellow, Royal Society of Arts **Membership:** American Association for the Advancement of Science; American Association of University Professors; Association of Medical Education in Europe; American Association of Anatomists; Society of Neuroscience **Business Address:** 136 Harrison Ave, Boston, MA, 02111 **Website:** http://www.stanleyjacobsonphd.com

David M. Jaffe

Industry: Fine Art **Children:** Two Daughters **Education:** AS in Science, State University of New York (1981) **Career:** Graphic Designer, Top Advertising Agencies, New York; Art Director, Top Advertising Agencies, New York; Fine Artist **Career Related:** Lecturer, Military Tactics, Israeli Army (1983-1986); Chairman, Israel Bonds, Development Corporation for Israel, Freeport, NY (1983) **Civic:** Cantor, Del Prado Minyan Condominium, Aventura, FL (2012-Present); Watercolor Teacher, Del Prado Minyan Condominium, Aventura, FL; Donor, Foundation for Advancement in Cancer Therapy; Jewish Community Services of South Florida **Military Service:** U.S. Army (1943-1946) **Creative Works:** Designer, Cover of Wonder Bread Package; Artist, Framed Watercolor Portrait of President H.W. Bush; Artist, Watercolor Portrait of Albert Einstein; Exhibitor, Various Artwork **Awards:** Bronze Medal, U.S. Army; Three Battle Stars, U.S. Army; Certificate of Recognition, Secretary of Defense, U.S. Government **Marquis Who's Who Honors:** Albert Nelson Marquis Lifetime Achievement Award (2017) **Why did you become involved in your profession or industry:** Mr. Jaffe became involved in his profession because of World War II. **What do you consider to be the highlight of your career:** A highlight of Mr. Jaffe's career was serving his country. **Shipping Address:** 3375 N Country Club Drive, Apt. 1108, Aventura, FL, 33180

Ravinder Kumar Jain, PhD

Title: Dean, Professor Emeritus **Industry:** Education/Educational Services **Company Name:** University of the Pacific **Country of Origin:** India **Marital Status:** Married **Spouse Name:** Terumi T. Takahashi **Education:** Elected Fellow, Churchill College, Cambridge University, England (1985-1986); MPA in Management and Public Policy, Harvard University (1980); PhD in Civil Engineering, Texas Tech University (1971); MS in Civil Engineering, California State University, Sacramento (1968); BS in Civil Engineering, California State University, Sacramento (1961); **Certifications:** Certified Professional Engineer, State of California; Board Certified Environmental Engineer **Career:** Dean, Professor Emeritus, University of the Pacific, School of Engineering and Computer Science (2013-Present); Dean, Professor, School of Engineering and Computer Science, University of the Pacific (2000-2013); Associate Dean of Research and International Engineering, College of Engineering, University of Cincinnati (1992-2000); Founding Director, United States Army Environmental Policy Institute, Champaign, IL (1990-1992); Chief, Environmental Division, United States Army Civil Engineer, Champaign, IL (1971-1989); Research Assistant, Texas Tech University, Lubbock, TX (1969-1971); Senior Engineer, Development and Resources Corporation, Sacramento, CA (1968-1969); Associate Engineer, California Department of Water Resources, Sacramento, CA (1964-1968) **Career Related:** Elected Member, European Academy of Sciences and Arts (2016); Advisory Board Member, National Academy of Sciences, Washington, DC (1993-1994); Consultant, Environmental Engineering Industrial Organizations, Federal and State Agencies **Creative Works:** Co-Author, "Management of Research and Development, Second Edition" (1997); Editor, "Environmental Technologies and Trends" (1996); Co-Author, "Environmental Assessment" (1993); Co-Author, "Management of Research and Development" (1989) **Awards:** Recipient, Founder's Gold Medal, National Society of Professional Engineers (1989); Honoree, Named Federal and Army Engineer of the Year, U.S. Army and National Society of Professional Engineers (1989); Decorated for Meritorious Civilian Service, United States Military (1988) **Membership:** Fellow, American Society of Civil Engineers; American Academy of Environmental Engineers; American Society of Engineering Education; Fellow, American Association for the Advancement of Science; Association of Environmental Engineering Professors; Elected Member, American Academy of Environmental Engineers **What do you consider to be the highlight of your career:** The highlight of Dr. Jain's career was being named "Federal and Army Engineer of Year" by the United States Army and the National Society of Professional Engineers in 1989.

John Edward Jamieson Jr.

Title: Chaplain **Industry:** Religious **Company Name:** Holy Redeemer Hospice **Date of Birth:** 03/05/1945 **Place of Birth:** Philadelphia **State:** PA **Parents:** John Edward Jamieson; Frances (Hayes) Jamieson **Marital Status:** Married **Spouse Name:** Marilyn T. Haws (6/8/1968) **Children:** Douglas Stuart; Heather Lynn; Mark Stuart **Education:** PhD, Christian Bible College, Rocky Mount, NC (1990); MDiv, Reformed Episcopal Seminary, Philadelphia, PA (1970); BA, University of Pennsylvania (1967) **Certifications:** Ordained to Ministry, Baptist Church (1978); Ordained to Ministry, Reformed Episcopal Church (1970); Board Certified Expert, The American Academy Experts in Traumatic Stress **Career:** Chaplin, Holy Redeemer Hospice; Director of Patient Support, Atlanticare (2003-2010); Director of Pastoral Care, Atlanticare (1988-2003); Pastor, Grace Bible Chapel (1988-1995); Paramedic, Mobile Intensive Care Unit, West Jersey Health System, Camden, NJ (1983-1988); Operations Coordinator, Emergency Medical Services Division, Aid Ambulance Service (1982-1983); Pastor, Hammonton Baptist Church (1978-1981) **Career Related:** Vice President, Board of Trustees, Central Ocean City Union Chapel (1998-Present); Co-Chairman, Institutional Medical Ethics Committee, Atlantic City Medical Center, Atlanticare (1996-Present); Minister, Pastoral Care, Cornerstone Church (2000-2002); Vice Chairman, Institutional Medical Ethics Committee, Atlantic City Medical Center, Atlanticare (1988-1996) **Civic:** Emergency Medical Services Task Force, State of New Jersey (2009-Present); Chaplain, Ocean City Volunteer Fire Department (1993-Present); Executive Vice President, Reformed Bible Institute of Delaware Valley (2000-2001); Member, Board of Directors, Atlantic County Unit, American Cancer Society, Inc. (1988-1990); Program Coordinator, Cansurmount Support Program, Answers4Families (1988-1990) **Creative Works:** Editor, "Biblical Bioethics" (1990) **Membership:** Fellow, The American Academy Experts in Traumatic Stress; Board Certified Expert, The American Academy Experts in Traumatic Stress; American Association of Christian Counselors; Southern Jersey Ethics Alliance; International Critical Incident Stress Foundation, Inc.; Master Chaplain, Federation of Fire Chaplains; National Center for Crisis Management **Marquis Who's Who Honors:** Albert Nelson Marquis Lifetime Achievement Award (2017) **Political Affiliations:** Republican **Shipping Address:** 1111 Lakeside Dr, Egg Harbor Township, NJ, 08234

Ronald R. Janke

Title: Lawyer **Industry:** Law and Legal Services **Company Name:** Law Offices of Ronald Janke **Date of Birth:** 03/02/1947 **Place of Birth:** Milwaukee **State:** WI **Parents:** Robert Erwin Janke; Elaine Patricia (Wilken) Janke **Marital Status:** Married **Spouse Name:** Mary Ann Burg Janke (7/3/1971) **Children:** Jennifer; William; Emily **Education:** JD, Duke University (1974); BA, Wittenberg University, Cum Laude (1969) **Career:** Owner, Law Offices of Ronald Janke (2011-Present); Partner, Jones Day (1984-2010); Associate, Jones Day, Cleveland, OH (1974-1983) **Career Related:** Advisory Committee, U.S. Environmental Protection Agency; Advisory Committee, Ohio Environmental Protection Agency; Fellow, American College of Environmental Lawyers **Civic:** Chairman, Ohio Water Resources Council Advisory Group **Military Service:** U.S. Army, Vietnam (1970-1971) **Membership:** Chairman, Environmental Control Committee, American Bar Association (1980-1983); Ohio State Bar Association (1974); Greater Cleveland Bar Association; Past Chairman, Business Law Section, American Bar Association **Bar Admissions:** State of Ohio (1974) **Marquis Who's Who Honors:** Albert Nelson Marquis Lifetime Achievement Award (2017) **To what do you attribute your success:** Mr. Janke attributes his success to his ability to learn and follow developments in the field. **Political Affiliations:** Republican **Religion:** Christian **Shipping Address:** 105 Easton Lane, Moreland Hills, OH, 44022

Charles Dean Jeffries, PhD

Title: Microbiology Educator, Research Scientist, Dean **Industry:** Education/Educational Services **Date of Birth:** 04/09/1929 **Place of Birth:** Rome **Country of Origin:** Italy **Parents:** Andrew Jones Jeffries; Rachel Lucinda (Ringer) Jeffries **Marital Status:** Married **Spouse Name:** Virginia Mae Alford (9/6/1953) **Education:** PhD, University of Tennessee (1958); Postgraduate Coursework, Purdue University (1955-1956) MS, University of Tennessee (1955); BS, University of North Georgia (1950) **Career:** Adjunct Instructor, College of Health Professions, Davenport University (2005); Guest Lecturer (2000-2003); Dean, Ross University School of Medicine, Roseau, West Indies (1998-2000); Dean, Basic Sciences, Ross University School of Medicine, Roseau, West Indies (1997-1998); Professor, Ross University School of Medicine, Roseau, West Indies (1996-2000); Chair, Department of Microbiology and Immunology, Ross University School of Medicine, Roseau, West Indies (1996-2000); Professor Emeritus, Wayne State University, Detroit, MI (1996); Voluntary Professor, Department of Biological Sciences, Wayne State University, Detroit, MI (1990-1996); Assistant Dean for Curriculum Affairs, School of Medicine, Wayne State University, Detroit, MI (1975-1980); Director, Graduate Programs, School of Medicine, Wayne State University, Detroit, MI (1975-1980); Professor, Wayne State University, Detroit, MI (1970-1996); **Career Related:** Consultant, VA Medical Center, Allen Park, MI (1989-1992); Guest Researcher, Center for Disease Control and Prevention, U.S. Department of Health and Human Services, Atlanta, GA (1980-1981); Vice President, Board of Basic Sciences, State of Michigan (1970-1972); **Civic:** President, Saline Area Senior Council, MI (2009-2013); President, Academy Senate, Wayne State University (1989-1992); EPA Advisory Panel, American Institute of Biological Sciences (1979-1980); Scientific Advisory Board, Michigan Cancer Foundation (1970-1979) **Military Service:** U.S. Army (1951-1953) **Awards:** Grantee, National Science Foundation (1959-1969); Grantee, National Institutes of Health (1958-1970) **Membership:** Chairman, Medical Mycology Division, American Society for Microbiology (1977-1978); **Marquis Who's Who Honors:** Albert Nelson Marquis Lifetime Achievement Award (2017) **Why did you become involved in your profession or industry:** After graduating high school, he got a summer job with a warehouse group at a hospital. Dr. Jeffries became interested in becoming a pharmacist, and got experience working with microbiological samples and laboratory experience. Because he went to college with ROTC training, he was commissioned at an infantry and then decided to change his commission into the medical service corps. **Shipping Address:** 590 Berkshire Dr, Saline, MI, 48176

Sandra Jemison, PhD

Title: Educational Association Administrator, Educator **Industry:** Education/Educational Services **Company Name:** Thumbs Up Service Agency **Parents:** James Johnson; Virginia Johnson **Marital Status:** Married **Spouse Name:** Walter Jemison (3/16/1974) **Children:** Stephen; Lance **Education:** PhD, University of Alabama (2002); EdS, University of Alabama (1988); MA, University of Alabama (1975) **Certifications:** Certified Teacher, Instructional Leadership, State of Alabama; Certified School Psychologist, State of Alabama **Career:** Director, Thumbs Up Service Agency, Tuscaloosa, AL (2005-Present); Federal Programs Administrator, Tuscaloosa City Schools (2000-2004); Elementary Director, Tuscaloosa City Schools (1996-2000); Chapter I Supervisor, Tuscaloosa City Schools (1992-1996); School Psychologist, Tuscaloosa City Schools (1988-1992); School Psychometrist, Tuscaloosa City Schools (1979-1988); Special Education Teacher, Tuscaloosa City Schools, Alabama (1974-1979); Special Education Teacher, Hale County Board of Education, Greensboro, AL (1973-1974) **Career Related:** Assistant Professor, Education and Psychology, Stillman College (2005-Present); Mayor's Pre-Kindergarten Committee, Stillman College (2005-Present); Consultant, Rural Districts, Alabama **Civic:** Board Member, Skyland SDA School, Tuscaloosa, AL (2004-Present); Board Member, Tombigbee Girl Scout Council, Inc., Tuscaloosa, AL (2004-Present); Personal Ministries Leader, Tuscaloosa Skyland Church (2004) **Creative Works:** Contributor, Articles, Professional Journals **Awards:** Breakthrough Literacy Award, NABSE (2000); Grantee, Patricia Roberts Harris Fellowship, University of Alabama (1994-1995) **Membership:** National Education Association; Alabama ASCD; National Association of School Psychologists; Phi Delta Kappa **Marquis Who's Who Honors:** Albert Nelson Marquis Lifetime Achievement Award (2017) **Hobbies:** Reading; Cooking **Shipping Address:** 9908 Fieldstone Lane, Tuscaloosa, AL, 35405

Shirley Shimmick Jennett

Title: Home Care Management Executive, Nurse **Industry:** Medicine & Health Care **Date of Birth:** 05/01/1937 **Place of Birth:** Jennings **State:** KS **Parents:** William Shimmick; Mabel C. (Mowry) Shimmick **Marital Status:** Married **Spouse Name:** Albert J. Kukral (4/16/1977, Divorced 1990); Nelson K. Jennett (8/20/1960, Divorced 1972) **Children:** Jon W.; Cheryl L. **Education:** Diplomate, Research Hospital School Nursing, Kansas City, MO (1958) **Certifications:** Certified Geriatrics Care Manager (2009-Present); Registered Nurse, State of Missouri; Registered Nurse, State of Colorado; Registered Nurse, State of Texas; Registered Nurse, State of Illinois **Career:** President, Care Management & Resources, Inc. (1996-Present); Professional Geriatric Care Manager, Care Management & Resources, Inc. (1996-Present); Executive Director, Hospice of Metro Denver (Now The Denver Hospice) (1988-1994); Director, Patient and Family Services, Hospice of Metro Denver (Now The Denver Hospice) (1988); Volunteer, Hospice of Metro Denver (Now The Denver Hospice) (1984-1988); Primary Care Nurse, Hospice of Metro Denver (Now The Denver Hospice) (1984-1988); Admissions Coordinator, Hospice of Metro Denver (Now The Denver Hospice) (1984-1988); Team Manager, Hospice of Metro Denver (Now The Denver Hospice) (1984-1988); Owner, Medical Placement Services, Lakewood, CO (1980-1984); Manager, Medical Placement Services, Lakewood, CO (1980-1984); Staff Nurse, Lutheran Hospital, SCL Health (1969-1979); Head Nurse, Lutheran Hospital, SCL Health (1969-1979); Nurse Recruiter, Lutheran Hospital, SCL Health (1969-1979); Staff Nurse, St. Anthony Hospital, Centura Health (1968-1969); Staff Nurse, NacNeal Hospital (1964-1965); Staff Nurse, Rush Oak Park Hospital (1963-1964); Head Nurse, Hotel Dieu Hospital (1962-1963); Head Nurse, Penrose-St. Francis Health Services (1960-1962); Head Nurse, Research Hospital School Nursing, Kansas City, MO (1958-1960); Staff Nurse, Research Hospital School Nursing, Kansas City, MO (1958-1960) **Membership:** Council of Former Board Members, National Hospice and Palliative Care Organization (1995-Present); Board of Directors, National Hospice and Palliative Care Organization (1992-1995); NAFE; NAWBO; Aging Life Care Association; Denver Business Women's Network; Home Care Resources; President, Board of Directors, Colorado Hospice Organization; Representative, Rocky Mountain Region, National Hospice Board of Directors **Marquis Who's Who Honors:** Albert Nelson Marquis Lifetime Achievement Award (2017) **Religion:** Church of Religious Science **Shipping Address:** 3360 S Holly Pl, Denver, CO, 80222 **Website:** https://denverhcr.com

William H. Jeynes

Title: Education Educator **Industry:** Education/Educational Services **Company Name:** Witherspoon Institute **Date of Birth:** 03/27/1957 **Place of Birth:** New York **State:** NY **Parents:** Paul Hettich; Enid Phillips Jeynes **Marital Status:** Married **Spouse Name:** Hyelee Jung Jeynes (6/17/1986) **Children:** Isaiah; Elisha; Luke **Education:** PhD, The University of Chicago (1997); MEd, Harvard University (1993); PhD, Freedom University (1992); Doctor of Ministry, Freedom University (1986); BA, University of Wisconsin (1979) **Career:** Senior Fellow, Witherspoon Institute (2010-Present); Professor, California State University, Long Beach (2001-Present); Assistant Professor, Hillsdale College, Michigan (1999-2001); Lecturer, National Louis University, Evanston, IL (1999); Lecturer, Roosevelt University, Schaumburg, IL (1999) **Career Related:** Adviser, Family Research Project, Harvard University, Cambridge, MA (2005-Present); Speaker, Family Research Project, Harvard University, Cambridge, MA (2005-Present); Advisor, Speech Writer, Various United States Politicians, including United States Presidential Candidates (2004-Present); Architect, South Korean Economic Stimulus Package to Arise from Asian Economic Crisis (1998); Writer, President George W. Bush; Writer, President Barack Obama; Speaker, Peking University; Advisor or Consultant for United States Government, Europe, and the South Korean, Russian and Chinese Governments **Civic:** President, God's Love Ministries, Huntington Beach, CA (1978-Present) **Creative Works:** Advisor, Speech Writer, Various United States Politicians, including United States Presidential Candidates (2004-Present); Author, "Wiley Handbook of Christianity and Education" (2018); Author, "What Would Christ Do?" (2016); Author, "Ministering Spirituality to Families" (2015); Author, "School Choice: A Balanced Approach" (2014); Author, "International Handbook of Protestant Education" (2012); Author, "Getting Closer to God" (2012); Author, "Parental Involvement and Academic Success" (2011); Author, "Family Factors and Children's Educational Success" (2010); Author, "A Call for Character Education and Prayer in the Schools" (2010); Author, "American Educational History: School, Society and the Common Good" (2007) **Awards:** Recipient, Distinguished Achievement Award, American Educational Research Association (2015); Recipient, California Distinguished Scholar, California State Senate (2012); Recipient, California Distinguished Scholar, California State Assembly (2012) **Membership:** Chair, Religion and Education Special Interest Group, American Educational Research Association (2004-2017) **Marquis Who's Who Honors:** Albert Nelson Marquis Lifetime Achievement Award (2017) **Shipping Address:** 6572 Red Coach Dr, Huntington Beach, CA, 92647

Kay L. Johannes

Title: Docent, Co-chair of the Friends of Art Counsel **Industry:** Museums & Institutions **Company Name:** John Michael Kohler Arts Center **Date of Birth:** 07/03/1952 **Place of Birth:** Milwaukee **State:** WI **Parents:** James Ben Johannes; Evelyn (Horne) Johannes **Marital Status:** Married **Spouse Name:** Alexander David Bub (01/05/1982) **Children:** David A. **Education:** BS in Instructional Technology, Rochester Institute of Technology (1977); AAS in Visual Communications, Milwaukee Area Technical College (1972) **Career:** Retired; Senior Salestrack Specialist, The Northwestern Mutual Life Insurance Company, Milwaukee, WI (1987-2012); Audio Visual Producer, Photography Unlimited, Milwaukee, WI (1982-1987); Owner, Johannes, Milwaukee, WI (1980-1982); Producer, Johannes, Milwaukee, WI (1980-1982); Designer, Multimedia, AV Centrum, Stockholm, Sweden (1979-1980); Visual Designer, Pohlman Studios, Milwaukee, WI (1977-1979); Animator, Pohlman Studios, Milwaukee, WI (1977-1979); Audio Visual Technician, Nicolet High School, Glendale, WI (1972-1975) **Career Related:** Owner, Wisconsin Off Road Adventures, LLC (2005-Present); Chair, Visual Communications Advisory Board, Milwaukee Area Technical College (1990-2005) **Civic:** Member, Board of Appeals, Town of Sherman, WI (2014-Present); Co-chairman, Friends of the Arts Council, John Michael Kohler Arts Center, Sheboygan, WI (2013-Present); Volunteer Docent, John Michael Kohler Arts Center, Sheboygan, WI (2013-Present); Volunteer, Big Brothers Big Sisters of Ozaukee, WI (1978-1991) **Awards:** TEST **Membership:** American Mensa, Ltd. (1977-Present); Royal Matron, Order of Amaranth, Inc.; Worthy High Priestess, The Order of the White Shrine of Jerusalem **Why did you become involved in your profession or industry:** Ms. Johannes entered this field when she got a job in insurances for the visual arts. **Hobbies:** Motorcycles; Computer Web Design **Religion:** Methodist **Shipping Address:** W4802 Knuth Rd, Random Lake, WI, 53075

Dolores Yuille Johns

Title: Director, Federal Programs (Retired) **Industry:** Education/Educational Services **Company Name:** Roanoke City Public Schools, VA **Date of Birth:** 09/27/1934 **Place of Birth:** Altavista **State:** VA **Parents:** William Everett Yuille; Helen Ruth (Dabney) Yuille **Marital Status:** Married **Spouse Name:** William Lawrence Johns Junior (4/19/1957) **Children:** Deborah; Linda; Lawrence; Anthony **Education:** EdD, Virginia Polytechnic Institute and State University (1981); MS in Marketing Education, Virginia Commonwealth University (1970); BS in Business Education, Virginia State University (1955) **Certifications:** Licensed Professional Counselor, Commonwealth of Virginia; Certified Teacher, Commonwealth of Virginia **Career:** Director, Federal Programs, Roanoke City Public Schools (1985-2000); Supervisor, Guidance Counselor, Roanoke City Public Schools (1982-1984); Associate Professor, Virginia Western Community College, Roanoke, VA (1980-1982); Teacher-Educator, Virginia Polytechnic Institute and State University, Blacksburg, VA (1975-1979); Director, Special Services, Virginia Western Community College, Roanoke, VA (1970-1975); Teacher, Marketing Education, Roanoke City Public Schools, VA (1965-1969) **Career Related:** Consultant, Presenter, International Literacy Association (1993); Consultant, Presenter, U.S. Department Education (1992); Consultant, Virginia Department of Federal Programs, Richmond, VA (1990-1991); Consultant, Presenter, International Literacy Association (IRA) (1990); Consultant, Presenter, U.S. Department Education (1989); Consultant, Presenter, International Literacy Association (1988); Consultant, Virginia Department of Federal Programs, Richmond, VA (1988); Consultant, Presenter, Virginia State Board of Education (1987-1988) **Civic:** Board of Directors, YWCA, Roanoke, VA (1989); Member, Health Services Board, Catawba Hospital (1988-1991); Director, Educational Services, High Street Baptist Church, Roanoke, VA (1985-1999); **Awards:** Living Legends First in Service Award, Alpha Kappa Alpha Sorority, Inc. (2008); Virginia Blue Ridge Behavioral Health Care Award (2004); Roanoke City Mother of Year in Education (1996); Virginia Board of Education Leadership Achievement Award (1992, 1989, 1987); United States Department Educational Leadership Achievement Award (1992, 1989, 1987) **Membership:** NAACP Life Member (2013), President, Omnia Bona (1975-1977); NAFEPA; International Literacy Association; Virginia State Reading Association; Virginia Association of Federal Educators **Marquis Who's Who Honors:** Albert Nelson Marquis Lifetime Achievement Award (2017) **What do you consider to be the highlight of your career:** The highlight of Ms. Johns' career was becoming the first black faculty member at Virginia Western Community College. **Religion:** Baptist

Edmond C. Johnson

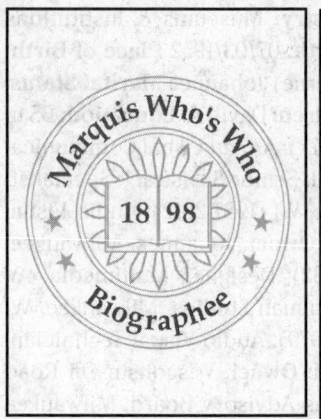

Title: Social Sciences Educator (Retired) **Industry:** Education/Educational Services **Company Name:** Social & Behavioral Sciences and Education **Date of Birth:** 01/06/1947 **Place of Birth:** Ft. Worth **State:** TX **Parents:** Kimber Daniel; Helen Louise Johnson **Spouse Name:** Naomi Charlotte Blom **Education:** MA in Sociology, University of Texas at Arlington (1997); BS in Sociology, Union College, Lincoln, NE **Career:** Chair, Department of Humanities, Social & Behavioral Sciences and Education (2013-Present); Social Science Instructor, Barton Community College, Great Bend, KS (1999-Present); Advisor, Barton Community College (2001-2017); Sociology Instructor, Tarrant County Junior College, Fort Worth, Texas (1998-1999); Sociology Instructor, Weatherford College, Texas (1997-1999) **Civic:** Walk a Mile in Her Shoes: International Men's March to Stop Rape, Sexual Assault & Gender Violence **Awards:** Distinguished Instructor Award, Barton Community College (2017); Award of Excellence, National Institute for Staff and Organizational Development, University of Texas (2006) **Membership:** American Sociological Association **Business Address:** P.O. Box 1393, Great Bend, KS, 67530 **Shipping Address:** P.O. Box 1393, Great Bend, KS, 67530

Mary Powell Johnson

Title: Freelance Arts Writer **Industry:** Writing and Editing **Date of Birth:** 09/23/1927 **Place of Birth:** Baltimore **State:** MD **Parents:** Frederick Manke; Marie Rosina (Walter) Manke **Marital Status:** Married **Spouse Name:** Maurice P. Johnson (7/1/1955); Alvin H. Walker (6/21/1947, Divorced 1955) **Children:** Carol Joy **Education:** Diploma, Johns Hopkins University, Baltimore, MD (1963) **Career:** Arts Reviewer, Anne Arundel County, The Baltimore Sun (1997-Present); Arts Writer, Patch Media, Severna Park, Annapolis, MD (2011-2012); Reviewer, Concerts and Theater, Severna Park Voice, Severna Park, MD (1998-2009); Reporter, Severna Park Voice, Severna Park, MD (1998-2009); Associate Director, Centennial Planning and Programs, Johns Hopkins University, Baltimore, MD (1973-1977) **Career Related:** Inactive Member, Journalism & Women Symposium (2002-Present); Member, American Theatre Critics Association (2000-Present) **Civic:** Member, National Museum of Women in the Arts (1998-Present); Board Director, Performing Arts Association of Linthicum (Now Maryland Concert Series), Linthicum, MD (1995-Present) **Membership:** American Association of University Women; Journalism & Women Symposium; American Theater Critics Association; Annapolis Opera; Ballet Theater of Maryland, Inc.; Live Arts Maryland; Annapolis Summer Garden Theater; Compass Rose Theater; Metropolitan Opera Guild **Marquis Who's Who Honors:** Albert Nelson Marquis Lifetime Achievement Award (2017) **To what do you attribute your success:** Ms. Johnson attributes some of her success to Joel Markowitz for the past decade, the founder of DCMetroTheaterArts. Shes respects all of the work that he has done. Joel Markowitz invited Mrs. Johnson to be Senior Writer from the beginning of DCMetroTheaterArts and she enjoyed working with him. **Why did you become involved in your profession or industry:** Ms. Johnson started arts coverage in the Serverna Park Voice. **Political Affiliations:** Democrat **Religion:** Lutheran **Shipping Address:** 267 Bowline Rd, Severna Park, MD, 21146 **Website:** http://dcmetrotheaterarts.com

Maryanna Morse Johnson

Title: Owner **Industry:** Other **Company Name:** MJM Associates **Date of Birth:** 12/21/1936 **Place of Birth:** Oxford **State:** MS **Parents:** Hugh McDonald Morse; Anna Sullivan (Virden) Morse **Marital Status:** Divorced **Children:** Julianna; Hunter; Cynthia; Capp **Education:** BSN, Texas Woman's University, Cum Laude (1986); Student, Mississippi University for Women (1957) **Certifications:** Registered Nurse, Texas **Career:** Owner, MJM Associates, Dallas, TX (2014-Present); Owner, MM Johnson Network India, Boulder, CO (1998-2016); Owner, MJM Associates, Boulder, CO (1990-2014) **Career Related:** Health Promotion Consultant (1986-Present) **Awards:** Lane Zunker Excellence Award (1999) **Membership:** Sigma Theta Tau **Marquis Who's Who Honors:** Albert Nelson Marquis Lifetime Achievement Award (2017) **Hobbies:** Golfing; Hiking; Jogging; Cross-country skiing **Political Affiliations:** Republican **Religion:** Anglican **Shipping Address:** 3342 Dorado Beach Drive, Dallas, TX, 75234

Richard Darrell Johnson

Title: Management Consultant **Industry:** Consulting **Company Name:** Ventures 33, LLC **Date of Birth:** 08/01/1935 **Place of Birth:** Columbus **State:** OH **Parents:** Darrell Dean Johnson; Gretchen Price (Motz) Johnson **Marital Status:** Married **Spouse Name:** Ann Elizabeth Sektnan (4/9/1960) **Children:** Julie Ann; Jennifer Lynn; Douglas Richard **Education:** MBA, Ohio State University (1962); BA in Industrial Engineering, Ohio State University (1958) **Certifications:** CPA, State of Illinois; CPA, State of Ohio; Certificate in Computer Processing, Institute for the Certification of Computing Professionals; Registered Professional Engineer, State of Ohio **Career:** Dean's Advisory Council, Fisher College of Business, The Ohio State University (2006-Present); Manager, Ventures 33, LLC (2004-2015); Ventures 33, LLC (2004-2015); Chairman, VIA International Limited, Chicago, IL (1998-1999); President, VIA International Limited, Chicago, IL (1992-1999); Retired Partner, Accenture, Chicago, IL (1991); Managing Partner, Change Management, Andersen Consulting, Chicago, IL (1986-1991); Managing Partner, Education Consulting, Arthur Andersen & Company, Chicago, IL (1979-1986); Managing Partner, Professional Education, Arthur Andersen & Company, Chicago, IL (1977-1979); Chairman, Advisory Council, Arthur Andersen & Company (1976-1978); Country Managing Partner, Iran, Afghanistan and Pakistan, Arthur Andersen & Company, Tehran, Iran (1975-1977) **Civic:** Long Range Planning Committee, Ravinia Festival (1996-Present); Trustee, Ravinia Festival, Highland Park, IL (2006-2013); Vice Chairman, Board of Directors, The Ohio State University Alumni Association (2001-2004); Board of Directors, The Ohio State University Alumni Association (1999-2004); Chairman, Development Committee, Ravinia Festival, Highland Park, IL (1999-2002); Vice Chairman, Ravinia Festival, Highland Park, IL (1999-2002); Ruth Weimer Mount Leadership Initiatives Fund (1997-2001); Trustee, Ravinia Festival, Highland Park, IL (1997-2004) **Military Service:** First Lieutenant, U.S. Air Force (1958-1961) **Awards:** Distinguished Service Award, Ohio State University (2006); Significant Sig Award, Sigma Chi Fraternity (2002); Distinguished Alumni Award, Fisher College of Business, Ohio State University (2002) **Membership:** Emeritus Member, President's Club, Ohio State University (2000-Present); Chairman, President's Club, Ohio State University (1996-1998); Vice Chairman, President's Club, Ohio State University (1995-1996) **Marquis Who's Who Honors:** Albert Nelson Marquis Lifetime Achievement Award (2017); Distinguished Humanitarian (2017) **Hobbies:** Skiing; Boating; Travel; Golf; Classical music **Shipping Address:** 351 Sussex Lane, Lake Forest, IL, 60045

Robert Alan Johnson

Title: Of Counsel **Industry:** Law and Legal Services **Company Name:** Buchanan Ingersoll & Rooney PC **Date of Birth:** 06/18/1944 **Place of Birth:** Harrisburg **State:** PA **Parents:** Harry Andrew Johnson; Minna Melissa (Ebert) Johnson **Marital Status:** Married **Spouse Name:** Selina Braham Pedersen Johnson (8/25/1979) **Children:** Isabella P.; Robert A., Jr. **Education:** JD, Harvard University (1969); BA, Washington & Jefferson College (1966) **Career:** Of Counsel, Buchanan Ingersoll & Rooney PC (2016-Present); Shareholder, Buchanan Ingersoll & Rooney PC (1977-2015); Associate, Buchanan Ingersoll & Rooney PC, Pittsburgh (1969-1976) **Civic:** Member, Board of Directors, Chatham Baroque (2004-Present); Member, Board of Directors, River City Brass Band Charitable Endowment, Pittsburgh, PA (2000-Present); Member, Board of Directors, CTC Foundation (1999-Present); Member, Board of Directors, Friends of the Music Library (Carnegie Library of Pittsburgh) (1995-Present); Member, Board of Directors, Renaissance & Baroque (1994-Present); Member, Board of Directors, Early Music America (2002-2014); Member, Board of Directors, Presbyterian Association of Chautauqua, New York (2005-2011); Member, Board of Directors, River City Brass Band (1986-1995); Member, Board of Directors, Pittsburgh Opera (1985-1994); President, Bach Choir of Pittsburgh (1979-1981) **Creative Works:** Contributor, Legal Articles, Professional Journals; Presenter, Papers, Legal Seminars **Awards:** Honoree, Best Lawyers in America (1989-Present) **Membership:** Chairman, Allegheny Tax Society (1982-1983); Fellow, American College of Tax Counsel; Fellow, American College of Employee Benefits Counsel, Inc.; Fellow, American Bar Foundation; American Bar Association; Allegheny County Bar Association; Pittsburgh Tax Club, Duquesne Club **Bar Admissions:** Pennsylvania (1969) **Marquis Who's Who Honors:** Albert Nelson Marquis Lifetime Achievement Award (2017) **Hobbies:** Collecting classical music recordings **Political Affiliations:** Republican **Religion:** Presbyterian **Business Address:** Buchanan Ingersoll & Rooney PC, Pittsburgh, PA, 15219 **Shipping Address:** 100 Denniston St., Apt 302, Pittsburgh, PA, 15206 **Website:** http://www.bipc.com/robert-johnson

Robert E. Johnson, PhD

Title: Provost, Dean of Faculty **Industry:** Religious **Company Name:** Central Baptist Theological Seminary **Marital Status:** Married **Spouse Name:** Rebecca **Children:** Rebekah; Robert; Eryn; Nick **Education:** PhD in Church History, Southwestern Baptist Theological Seminary (1984); MDiv, Southwestern Baptist Theological Seminary (1977); Bachelor's Degree in Religious Studies, University of Richmond **Career:** Provost, Dean of Faculty, Midwestern Baptist Theological Seminary (1998-Present); Associate Professor of Church History, Midwestern Baptist Theological Seminary (1992-1998); Professor of Church History, Faculdade de Educação Teológica de São Paulo (1979-1992) **Civic:** Board Member, Lyric Opera of Kansas City; Council of Opera Member, The Metropolitan Opera **Creative Works:** Author, "A Global Introduction to Baptist Churches" **Membership:** The Phi Beta Kappa Society; American Historical Association; American Society of Church History; American Academy of Religion; The Ecclesiastical History Society **Marquis Who's Who Honors:** Albert Nelson Marquis Lifetime Achievement Award (2017) **To what do you attribute your success:** Dr. Johnson attributes his success to his hard work, creativity and networking skills. **Why did you become involved in your profession or industry:** Dr. Johnson became involved in his profession because of his educational background, and his interest in theological education and church activities. **Where will you be in five years:** In five years, Dr. Johnson intends to help his institution become well-positioned in its mission as a higher educational institute in theological studies, and to publish philosophies and directions that contribute to the field. **Hobbies:** Attending the opera **Shipping Address:** 6601 Monticello Rd, Shawnee, KS, 66226-3513 **Website:** http://www.cbts.edu

Steven Jonas

Title: Preventive Medicine Physician, Author **Industry:** Medicine & Health Care **Company Name:** Stony Brook University **Date of Birth:** 11/22/1936 **Place of Birth:** New York **State:** NY **Parents:** Harold Jacob Jonas; Florence Jane (Kyzor) Jonas **Marital Status:** Married **Spouse Name:** Chezn Jonas; Linda Sue Friedman (11/23/1971, Divorced); Josephine Gear (6/19/1964, Divorced) **Children:** Jacob Henry; Lillian Sara; Mark Scott Newman **Education:** MS, New York University (1997); MPH, Yale University (1967); MD, Harvard University (1962); BA, Columbia College, Cum Laude (1958) **Career:** Professor Emeritus, School of Medicine, Stony Brook University (2014-Present); Professor, Graduate Program of Public Health, School of Medicine, Stony Brook University (2004-Present); Professor, Department of Preventive Medicine, School of Medicine, Stony Brook University (1983-2014); Associate Professor, Department of Community and Preventive Medicine, School of Medicine, Stony Brook University (1974-1983); Attending Physician, Nassau University Medical Center, East Meadow, NY (1973-1986) **Career Related:** Adjunct Professor of Legal Education, Touro College Jacob D. Fuchsberg Law Center, Huntington, NY (1998-2006); Adjunct Associate Professor of Medical Education, Texas College of Osteopathic Medicine, University of North Texas, Fort Worth, TX (1980-1985) **Civic:** Senior Advisor, U.S. Preventive Services Task Force (1984-1989) **Creative Works:** Contributor, Gorunbikerun (2017-Present); Monthly Contributor, USA Triathlon Blog (2013-Present); Senior Editor, Politics, Greanvillepost.com (2005-Present); Columnist, Quarterly, American Medical Athletic Association (1999-Present); Editorial Board, Quarterly, American Medical Athletic Association (1988-Present) **Awards:** Outstanding Service Recognition Award, United University Professions (2011); Top Ten Most Influential Public Health Professor Award, Health Hawk (2010); Distinguished Alumni Award, School of Public Health, Yale University (2010); Duncan Clark Lifetime Achievement Award, Association for Prevention Teaching and Research (2006) **Membership:** Medical Education Committee, New York Academy of Medicine (1983-1992); Committee Chairman, American College of Preventive Medicine (1979-1982); President, Association for Prevention Teaching and Research (1977-1978) **Hobbies:** Bicycling; Pacewalking; Running; Weightlifting; Triathlon/duathlon competition; Skiing **Political Affiliations:** Democrat **Religion:** Jewish **Shipping Address:** PO Box 843, East Setauket, NY, 11733

Ben Block Burton Jones II

Title: Accountant, Law Clerk **Industry:** Law and Legal Services **Company Name:** MS Office of Attorney General/MS Department of Transportation **Date of Birth:** 11/02/1962 **Place of Birth:** Jackson **State:** MS **Parents:** Ben Block Burton Jones; Suda Mae Leech Drowns **Education:** Vocational Masters of Communication Technology, National Radio Institute, McGraw-Hill Continuing Education Center (2002); BS in Accounting, Belhaven College, Jackson, MS (1997); Post-graduate Studies, Thomas Cooley School of Law, Lansing, MI (1992); Post-graduate Studies in Spanish Literature, Mississippi College, Clinton, MS (1992) **Certifications:** Certification, eDiscovery, Arkfeld Professional Education (2014); Commercial Radio Telegraph Operator (2003); Commercial Radio Operator (2002); Ship Radar Endorsement (2002); Emergency Program Manager, FEMA-EMI (2003); Advanced Emergency Program Manager, FEMA-EMI (2007); State EMA Director of Endorsement (2007) **Career:** Special Assistant to Chief Counsel, Law Clerk, Mississippi Attorney General, Mississippi Department of Transportation (2007-Present); President-Owner, Accoutre Systems Inc. (2001-Present); Law Clerk, Forman Perry Watkins Krutz & Tardy (2004-2007); Private Practice in Accounting, SBS Business Service Inc., Jackson, MS (2001-2004) **Career Related:** Member, Intermodal and Public Transit Law and Emerging Technology Law Committees, Legal Resources Group, Transportation Research Board, National Research Council/National Academies (2011-Present) **Civic:** Member, DHS-SHARES HF Interoperability Working Group (2015-Present); Member, Advisory Committee, Mississippi VOAD (2006-2008); Member, NCS RM-HF Network **Creative Works:** Author, "Affordable Care Act: Practitioner's View of Individual Mandate, Spanish Edition" (2017); Author, "White Paper: The Disconnectedness of IoT" (2016); Author, "Affordable Care Act: Practitioner's View of Individual Mandate" (2015-2016); Co-Author, "Protecting the Federal Interest" (2011) **Awards:** Longevity Award, State Guard Association of the United States (2010, 2015); National Commander-in-Chief Recognition, Sons of Union Veterans (2014); Certificate of Commendation, National Communications Systems Shared Resources (2003); Volunteer of the Year, Mississippi VITA, Internal Revenue Service (2002) **Membership:** President, Ceremonial Divan, Shriners (2017); IEEE; Taxation Section, ABA; Associate Member, Association of Certified Fraud Examiners; NALA; Past Master, Canton Lodge #28 F&AM; Secretary, Past Master, Circle Lodge #638; F&AM Masonic Lodge; Crown of Charlemagne; The Society of The Lees of Virginia **Shipping Address:** 246 Highland Place Drive, Jackson, MS, 39211 **Website:** https://www.linkedin.com/in/ben-block-jones-ii-81392a80

Cynthia M. Jones, PhD

Title: Professor, Eminent Scholar **Industry:** Education/Educational Services **Company Name:** Old Dominion University **Education:** Postdoctoral Associate, Department of Natural Resources, Cornell University (1984-1985); PhD in Oceanography, University Of Rhode Island (1984); Graduate Research Associate, University of Rhode Island (1980-1982); Graduate Research Assistant, University of Rhode Island (1977-1978); MS in Oceanography, Graduate School of Oceanography, University of Rhode Island (1973); BA in Zoology, Boston University (1968) **Career:** Professor, Department of Ocean, Earth, and Atmospheric Sciences, Old Dominion University (2003-Present); Eminent Scholar, Old Dominion University (2003-Present); A.D. and Annye L. Morgan Endowed Chairperson of Science, Old Dominion University (2009-2014); Professor, Department of Biological Sciences, Old Dominion University (1998-2003); Associate Professor, Department of Biological Sciences, Old Dominion University (1993-1998); Assistant Research Professor, Department of Biological Sciences, Old Dominion University (1988-1993) **Civic:** Member, Scientific and Statistics Committee, Mid-Atlantic Fishery Management Council **Awards:** Faculty Excellence Award, College of Sciences, Old Dominion University (2011); Named Outstanding Professor, State Council of Higher Education for Virginia (2005); Named Virginia Professor of the Year, Carnegie Foundation (2004); Honoree, Most Significant Paper, American Fisheries Society (2004); Nominee, Outstanding Faculty, State Council of Higher Education for Virginia (2004); Outstanding Achievement Award, Friends of the Library, Old Dominion University (2004); Named Outstanding Virginia Scientist (2003); Finalist, Outstanding Faculty, State Council of Higher Education for Virginia (2003); **Membership:** Fellow, American Association for the Advancement of Science; Early Life History Section, American Fisheries Society; Marine Fisheries Section, American Fisheries Society; Education Section, American Fisheries Society; Computer Section, American Fisheries Society; The Association for the Sciences of Limnology and Oceanography; Education Section, Ecological Society of America; Statistical Ecology Section, Ecological Society of America; Theoretical Ecology Section, Ecological Society of America; The Phi Beta Kappa Society; Phi Sigma; Sigma Xi **What do you consider to be the highlight of your career:** There were several highlights, including Dr. Jones being named Virginia Scientist of the Year, being given the State Council for Higher Education Award, and being named Virginia Professor of the Year for the Carnegie Foundation for the Advancement of Teaching. **Business Address:** 800 W 46th St., Norfolk, VA, 23508

John W. Jones

Title: Entrepreneur **Industry:** Business Management/Business Services **Company Name:** J. Jones Enterprises **Date of Birth:** 11/15/1942 **Place of Birth:** Wenatchee **State:** WA **Parents:** Richard F. Jones; Hazel F. (Hendrix) Jones **Spouse Name:** Deborah G. Matthews (4/24/1993); Melissa L. Meyer (6/22/1968, Divorced 1982) **Children:** John E.; Jennifer L. **Education:** BBA in Business/Economics, Western Washington University, Bellingham (1966) **Career:** Owner/Director of Operations, J. Jones Enterprises (1994-Present); Private Investor, Bellevue (Now J. Jones Enterprises) (1987-1994); Owner/Manager, Jones Building, Seattle, WA (1978-1986); Owner/Manager, Northwest Inboards, Bellevue, WA (1974-1978); Manager, Jones Building, (1969-1978); Trainee, Jones Building, Seattle, WA (1967-1969) **Career Related:** Chairman, BOMA Health & Wellness Trust (1986); Trustee, BOMA Health & Welfare Trust (1982-1986); Chairman, Seattle Fire Code Advisory Board (1984-1986); Member, Seattle Fire Code Advisory Board (1979-1986) **Military Service:** U.S. Marine Corps Reserve (1966-1972) **Membership:** Former Trustee, Seattle Building Owners Managers Association (1979-1986); Former Member, Building Owners Managers International; American Association of Individual Investors; Benevolent & Protective Order of Elk; BoatUS; Financial Committee, Seattle Yacht Club (1987-Present); Life Member, National Rifle Association; Specialty Equipment Marketing Association **Why did you become involved in your profession or industry:** Mr. Jones has a long history in business. He was initially involved with his father's real estate investment in Seattle as a manager of the property's parking garage. Later, he became part owner of the building, and years down the line, he bought out the other owners to become solely responsible for the property. Additionally, in the mid-'70s, Mr. Jones took a turn selling high-performance boats, which were made primarily in California. **What do you consider to be the highlight of your career:** Mr. Jones considers his work with the Seattle Fire Code Advisory Board, on which he served as chairman, to be one of the highlights of his career. He also spent time assisting the building owners and management association's health and welfare initiatives, during which he assisted with unions for maintenance workers. This experience was particularly rewarding.

Stephen Jones

Title: Lawyer **Industry:** Law and Legal Services **Company Name:** Jones, Otjen, Davis & Boyd **Date of Birth:** 07/01/1940 **Place of Birth:** Lafayette **State:** LA **Parents:** Leslie William Jones; Gladys A. (Williams) Jones **Marital Status:** Married **Spouse Name:** Sherrel Alice Stephens (12/27/1973); Virginia Hadden (Deceased) **Children:** John Chapman (Deceased); Stephen Mark; Leslie **Education:** LLB, University of Oklahoma (1966); **Career:** Judge, Oklahoma Court of Appeals (1982); Advisory Committee on Court Rules, Oklahoma Court of Criminal Appeals (1980); Civil Jury Instruction Committee, Oklahoma Supreme Court (1979-1981); Special United States Attorney, Northern District of Oklahoma (1979); Special Prosecutor, Special Assistant District Attorney, State of Oklahoma (1977); Staff Counsel Censure Task Force, House of Representatives, Impeachment Inquiry (1974); Member, United States Delegate to North Atlantic Assembly, NATO (1968); Special Assistant to United States Senator Charles H. Percy and United States Representative Donald Rumsfeld (1968); Legal Counsel to the Governor of Oklahoma (1967); Administrative Assistant to Congressman Paul Findley (1966-1969); Personal Assistant to Richard M. Nixon, New York, NY (1964); Secretary, Republican Minority Conference, Texas House of Representatives (1963); Managing Partner, Jones, Otjen & Davis, Enid, OK **Career Related:** Senior Council, Oklahoma Commissioner Insurance (2011-Present); Advisory Council, Center for American History, University of Texas, Austin, TX (2007-Present); Instructor, Phillips University (1982-1990); Adjunct Professor, University of Oklahoma (1973-1976); Board of Directors, Council on the National Interest Foundation **Civic:** Senior Counselor, Oklahoma Communications Insurance (2011-Present); Republican State Financial Committee Member (2010); Advisory Board Member, Center for American History, University of Texas at Austin (2007-2010); Member, Republican State Financial Committee (2006-2010); Appointed Chief of Defense Counsel, United States District Court, Oklahoma City, United States Versus Tim McVeigh, Oklahoma City Bombing Case (1995-1997); Special Counsel to the Governor of Oklahoma (1995); U.S. Senate (1990); Republican Nominee, Oklahoma Attorney General (1974) **Creative Works:** Author, "Vernon's Oklahoma Forms Second Criminal Practice & Procedure Volumes I, II" (1999); Author, "Others Unknown: The Oklahoma City Bombing Case and Conspiracy" (1998); Co-Author, "France and China, The First Ten Years, 1964-1974" (1991); Author, "Oklahoma and Politics in State and Nation, 1907-1962" (1974) **Membership:** Garfield County Bar Association; Beacon Club **Bar Admissions:** Oklahoma

William R. Jones

Title: Database Administrator, IT Specialist, Data Management Specialist **Industry:** Information Technology and Services **Company Name:** Oracle **Date of Birth:** 09/27/1952 **Place of Birth:** Morgantown **State:** KY **Parents:** James Edward Jones; Mahalia Jane (Kuykendall) Bratton **Marital Status:** Married **Spouse Name:** Marina del Pilar Lagario (11/20/1981) **Education:** MS in Information Science, Capella University (2002); Coursework, University of Tennessee (1987-1990); BS, Excelsior College (1984); AA, Excelsior College (1982) **Certifications:** Diplomate, CompTIA Network+ (2009); Diplomate, CompTIA Security+ (2009); Certified Computer Professional, Oracle Professional 10g (2007) **Career:** IT Specialist, Defense Finance Accounting Services, Oracle (2012-Present); Database Administrator, Oracle (2012-Present); Database Engineer, Advanced Micro Devices, Inc. (2006-Present); IT Specialist, U.S. Department of Veteran Affairs (2010-2012); Programmer, Texas Department of Public Safety (2005-2006); Database Administrator, Volt (2001-2002); Database Administrator, Alistia Inc., Austin, TX (2000-2001); Database Administrator, Acxiom (1998-2000); Open Systems Product Support Representative, BMC Software, Inc., Austin, TX (1995-1998); Database Administrator, Tennessee Valley Authority (1992-1995); Programmer-analyst, Tennessee Valley Authority (1990-1992); Engineering Associate, Tennessee Valley Authority, Chattanooga, TN (1986-1990) **Career Related:** Teaching Assistant on Compuserve, ZD Net University (1996) **Civic:** Team Leader, Web Page Regional Judging Team, Information Superhighway Competition on Blacks in Government and The Alliance of Black Technical Organizations **Military Service:** Leading Petty Officer, U.S. Ship Cimarron, U.S. Navy, Pearl Harbor, HI (1984-1985); Calibration Technician, Naval Oceanographic Facility, U.S. Navy, Ford Island, HI (1981-1984); Supervisor, Radar Work Center, U.S. Ship Midway, U.S. Navy, Yokosuka, Japan (1980-1981) **Awards:** Educational & Research Foundation Essay Scholarship, Mensa International (1988); Grosswirth-Salny Essay Scholarship; Web Page Design Award, Magellan **Membership:** HyperText Markup Language Writer's Guild; Association for Computing Machinery; Black Data Processing Associates; Data Warehousing Institute; Veterans of Foreign Wars; Intertel; Tennessee State Numismatic Society; American MENSA; The American Legion **Why did you become involved in your profession or industry:** Mr. Jones started in hardware work and as his career progressed he got involved in operating systems **Political Affiliations:** Republican **Shipping Address:** 5823 Beatle Dr., Apt H, Indianapolis, IN, 46216

Manfred Kaminsky

Title: Physicist **Industry:** Sciences **Company Name:** Surface Treatment Science International **Date of Birth:** 06/04/1929 **Place of Birth:** Koenigsberg **Country of Origin:** Germany **Parents:** Stephan Kaminsky; Kaethe (Gieger) Kaminsky **Marital Status:** Married **Spouse Name:** Elisabeth Moellering (5/1/1957) **Children:** Cornelia K.B.; Mark-Peter **Education:** PhD in Physics, Philipps University of Marburg, Magna Cum Laude, Germany (1957); German Research Society Fellow, Research Assistant, Physical Institute, Philipps University of Marburg (1953-1957); First Diploma, Physics, University of Rostock, Germany (1951); German Research Society Fellow, Graduate Assistant, Physics, University of Rostock (1950-1952) **Career:** Sole Proprietor, Surface Treatment Science International, Hinsdale, IL (1986-Present); Director, Tribology Program, Argonne National Laboratory (1984-1986); Director, Surface Science Center-CTR Program, Argonne National Laboratory (1974-1980); Senior Physicist, Argonne National Laboratory (1970-1986); Associate, Argonne National Laboratory (1962-1970); Assistant Physicist, Argonne National Laboratory (1959-1962); Research Associate, Argonne National Laboratory (1958-1959); Senior Assistant, Physical Institute, Philipps University of Marburg (1957-1958); Lecturer, Medical Technology, University of Rostock (1952) **Career Related:** National Research Council Committee on Tribology, Office of Technology Assessment, U.S. Congress (1986-1988); Consultant, Office of Technology Assessment, U.S. Congress (1986); Symposium Chairman, International Conference on Metallurgical Coatings (1985-1993); E.W. Mueller Lecturer, University of Wisconsin, Milwaukee, WI (1978); Guest Professor, Institute for Energy, Institut National de la Recherche Scientifique (1976-1982); Fellow, American Physical Society **Creative Works:** Co-Editor, "Dictionary of Terms for Vacuum Science and Technology" (1980); Co-Editor, "Surface Effects in Controlled Fusion Devices" (1976); Editor, "Radiation Effects on Solid Surfaces" (1976); Co-Editor, "Surface Effects on Controlled Fusion" (1974) **Awards:** Fellow, Japanese Society for the Promotion of Science (1982); Named, Outstanding New Citizen of the Year, Citizenship Council of Chicago (1968) **Membership:** Honorary Member, AVS (1986); Chairman, Fusion Division, International Union for Vacuum Science, Technique and Applications (1984-1986); Senior, Trustee, AVS (1982-1984); Chairman, Fusion Technology Division, AVS (1980-1981); Co-Founder, Great Lakes Chapter, Director, AVS (1968-1970); Chairman, Midwest Section, AVS (1967-1968); American Chemical Society; Scientific Research Society of America; American Society for Research; American Association for the Advancement of Science **Marquis Who's Who Honors:** Albert Nelson Marquis Lifetime Achievement Award (2017) **Shipping Address:** 300 Galen Drive, Apt. 506, Key Biscayne, FL, 33149

Robert B. Kaplan

Title: Emeritus Professor of Applied Linguistics, Emeritus **Industry:** Education/Educational Services **Company Name:** University of Southern California **Date of Birth:** 09/20/1929 **Place of Birth:** New York **State:** NY **Parents:** Emanuel B. Kaplan; Natalie Kaplan **Marital Status:** Widowed **Spouse Name:** Audrey A. Lien (4/21/1951) **Children:** Robin Ann Kaplan Gibson; Lisa Kaplan Morris; Robert Allen **Education:** PhD, University of Southern California (1962); MA, University of Southern California (1957); BA, Willamette University (1952); Student, Syracuse University (1948-1949); Student, Champlain College (1947-1948) **Career:** Professor Emeritus, University of Southern California, Los Angeles, CA (1995-Present); Professor, Applied Linguistics, University of Southern California, Los Angeles, CA (1976-1995); Director, American Language Institute, University of Southern California, Los Angeles, CA (1986-1991); Associate Dean, Continuing Education, University of Southern California, Los Angeles, CA (1973-1976); Associate Professor, Director, English Communication Program for Foreign Students, University of Southern California, Los Angeles, CA (1972-1976); Instructor, Coordinator, Assistant Professor, English Communication Program for Foreign Students, University of Southern California, Los Angeles, CA (1965-1972) **Career Related:** Syndicate, Visiting Senior Professor, Graduate School, Applied Language Studies, Meikai University, Urayasu City, Chiba, Japan (1998-2000); President, Faculty Senate, University of Southern California (1989-1990); President-Elect, Faculty Senate, University of Southern California (1988-1989); Consultant, Field Service Program, National Association for Foreign Student Affairs, (1964-1984); Advisory Board, International Comparability Study of Standardized Language Exams, University of Cambridge Local Exams **Civic:** International Education Research Foundation (1986-1994); Board of Directors, International Bilingual School, Los Angeles, CA (1986-1991) **Military Service:** Infantry, U.S. Army, Korea **Awards:** Recipient, University of Southern California Faculty Lifetime Achievement Award (2005); Award for Distinguished Scholarship and Service, American Association for Applied Linguistics (1998); Fulbright Senior Scholar, New Zealand (1992); Fulbright Senior Scholar, Hong Kong (1986); Fulbright Senior Scholar, Australia (1978) **Membership:** Vice President, President, American Association for Applied Linguistics (1992-1994); First Vice President, President, Teachers of English to Speakers Other Languages (1989-1991) **Marquis Who's Who Honors:** Albert Nelson Marquis Lifetime Achievement Award (2017) **Business Address:** P.O. Box 577, Port Angeles, WA, 98362

Frank Albert Kapral, PhD

Title: Science Educator **Industry:** Education/Educational Services **Company Name:** The Ohio State University **Date of Birth:** 04/12/1928 **Place of Birth:** Philadelphia **State:** PA **Parents:** John Kapral; Erna Louise (Melching) Kapral **Marital Status:** Married **Spouse Name:** Esther McKenzie (5/10/2003); Marina Garay (11/22/1951) **Children:** Gloria; Robert **Education:** PhD, University of Pennsylvania (1956); BS, University of the Sciences in Philadelphia (1952) **Career:** Professor Emeritus, Department of Molecular Virology, Immunology and Medical Genetics, The Ohio State University (1995-Present); Professor, Department of Medical Virology, Immunology And Medical Genetics, The Ohio State University (1969-1995); Associate Professor, Department of Medical Microbiology, The Ohio State University (1966-1969); Chief of Microbiology, Philadelphia General Hospital (1965-1966); Chief of Microbiology Research, Philadelphia General Hospital (1964-1966); Assistant Chief of Microbiology Research, Philadelphia Veteran Affairs Medical Center (Now Corporal Michael J. Crescenz Veteran Affairs Medical Center) (1962-1966); Associate Microbiologist, Philadelphia General Hospital (1962-1964); Associate In Microbiology, University of Pennsylvania, Philadelphia, PA (1958-1966); University of Pennsylvania (1952-1966) **Career Related:** Consultant, Procter & Gamble (1981-1987); Consultant, Center for Disease Control and Prevention, United States Department of Health and Human Services, Atlanta, GA (1980) **Civic:** Active Member, Central Ohio Diabetes Association (1992-1993) **Military Service:** U.S. Army (1946-1947) **Creative Works:** Contributor, Articles, Professional Journals **Awards:** Grantee, Central Ohio Diabetes Association (1992-1993); Research Grantee, National Institutes of Health (1959-1995); Fellow, American Academy of Microbiology, American Society for Microbiology; Fellow, Infectious Diseases Society of America **Membership:** American Association for the Advancement of Science; American Society for Microbiology; American Association for Immunologists; Sigma Xi **Marquis Who's Who Honors:** Albert Nelson Marquis Lifetime Achievement Award (2017) **Political Affiliations:** Democrat **Religion:** Roman Catholic **Shipping Address:** 873 Clubview Blvd S, Columbus, OH, 43235

Jeanne Elinor Karison, PhD

Title: Educator **Industry:** Education/Educational Services **Company Name:** Roanoke-Chowan Community College **Date of Birth:** 09/05/1949 **Place of Birth:** Washington **State:** DC **Parents:** Henry Karison; Barbara Karison **Marital Status:** Single **Children:** Elaine Lesgold Martha Thomas **Education:** Postdoctoral Work in Early Childhood Education, Auburn University at Montgomery (1993-1995); Postdoctoral Work in Early Childhood Education, Alabama State University (1993-1995); PhD in Curriculum and Instruction, Auburn University, Auburn, AL (1993); MEd in Elementary Education, University of Virginia (1972); Postgraduate Work, University of Virginia (1971-1980); EdB in Elementary Education and English, Old Dominion University (1971) **Certifications:** Certified in Early Childhood Education; Certified in Elementary Education **Career:** Faculty, English Developmental Program, Roanoke-Chowan Community College, Ahoskie, NC (2009-Present); Coordinator, Lateral Entry Program, Roanoke-Chowan Community College, Ahoskie, NC (2007-Present); Adviser, College Transfer and Nursing Programs, Roanoke-Chowan Community College, Ahoskie, NC (2007-Present); Coordinator and Faculty, Developmental Reading and English Program, Roanoke-Chowan Community College, Ahoskie, NC (2007-2009); **Civic:** Volunteer, Murfreesboro Historical Society Gift Shop (2005-Present); Coordinator and Parade Marshall, Neptune Festival (2001-Present); Monitor, Sandman Triathlon (2001-Present); Volunteer, Chowan University, Watermelon Festival (2006); Volunteer, Murfreesboro Candlelight Tour (2005) **Creative Works:** Story Editor, "A Dance in Paradise," Lee Chavis (2010); Editor, "Enz - Introduction to Education, 1E, Textbook Review," Kendall/Hunt Publishers (2005); Author, "Facilitating Research in Education: A Guidebook to the Basics of Participating in the Process," Department of Graphics Communications, Chowan College (2004-2005) **Awards:** Service Award for Years of Dedicated Service, Roanoke-Chowan Community College (2017); Inductee, International Women's Leadership Association (2012); Honoree, Outstanding Graduate, Auburn University (1993) **To what do you attribute your success:** Dr. Karison attributes her success to Mr. Alf Mapp and Mr. Andrew C. Muse. **Why did you become involved in your profession or industry:** Dr. Karison became involved in her profession because she loves learning and teaching. **What do you consider to be the highlight of your career:** A highlight of Dr. Karison's career was figuring out the importance of maintaining a positive outlook on life and sharing that with others. **Religion:** Methodist **Business Address:** 109 Community College Road, 109 Community College Road, Ahoskie, NC, 27910

Barbara Stein Katz

Title: Special Education Teacher **Industry:** Education/Educational Services **Date of Birth:** 07/22/1933 **Place of Birth:** Springfield **State:** MA **Parents:** Harry Stein; Pearl (Black) Stein **Marital Status:** Married **Spouse Name:** Charles M. Katz (7/14/1957) **Children:** Helen L.; Robert A. **Education:** MA in Educational Psychology in Learning Disabilities, American International College, Springfield, MA (1979); BS, American International College, Springfield, MA (1956) **Certifications:** Certified in Elementary Education, Moderate Special Needs, State of Massachusetts **Career:** Special Education Teacher, Public Schools, Chicopee, MA (1978-1998); Gillingham Remedial Teacher, Public Schools, Longmeadow, MA (1975-1978); Elementary Teacher, Springfield Public Schools (1956-1960) **Career Related:** Proprietor, Lynn Katz Photography **Civic:** Reader, Lower Pioneer Valley Collaborative (1998-2002); President, Kodimoh Synagogue Women's Group, Springfield, MA (1972-1974); Troop Leader, Girl Scouts of the USA, Longmeadow, MA (1967-1970) **Awards:** Horace Mann Grantee (1988) **Membership:** National Education Association; National Trust for Historic Preservation; The Trustees of Reservations; Massachusetts Teachers Association; Lifetime Member, JGS Lifecare, Inc.; Lifetime Member, World Mizrachi; Lifetime Member, Hadassah, The Women's Zionist Organization of America, Inc. **Marquis Who's Who Honors:** Albert Nelson Marquis Lifetime Achievement Award (2017) **Shipping Address:** 407 Bliss Rd, Longmeadow, MA, 01106

Charleen Verena Kavleski

Title: Conceptual Artist, Sculptor **Industry:** Fine Art **Date of Birth:** 11/19/1942 **Place of Birth:** Ellenville **State:** NY **Education:** Graduate Coursework in Fine Arts, State University of New York, New Paltz (1965-1972); BS, State University of New York, New Paltz (1964); Coursework, Herron School of Art and Design, Indiana University (1964); AAS, Orange County Community College, SUNY (1964); AA, Orange County Community College, SUNY (1963) **Career:** Antiques and Art Dealer, Brockmann's Antique Center, Milford, NY (1983-2009); Art Advisor, Editor, Literary and Art Magazine, Robert J. Kaiser Middle School, Monticello Central School District, NY (1989-1999); Art Teacher, Monticello Central School District, New York (1968-1999) **Career Related:** Board Member, Amos Eno Gallery(2014-Present); Albatross Antiques and Art Dealer, South Fallsburg, NY (2009-Present); Board Member, Amos Eno Gallery (2014-2016) **Creative Works:** Exhibit, Catskill Art Society, Livingston Manor, NY (2018); Member Exhibition, Amos Eno Gallery, NY (2018); Exhibit, 128th Annual Member Exhibit, Sylvia Wald and Po Kim Art Gallery, National Association of Woman Arts, Inc., New York, NY (2017); Exhibit, "The Summer Member Show," Catskill Art Society, Livingston Manor, NY (2017); Solo Exhibition, Amos Eno Gallery, New York, NY (2016); Annual Exhibitions, National Association of Women Artists, Inc. (1992-2016); Solo Exhibition, Amos Eno Gallery, New York, NY (2014); Exhibition, Shops at the Loom (2014); Solo Exhibition, Amos Eno Gallery, New York, NY (2012); Exhibition, Albany Center Gallery (2008-2012); Exhibition, Catskill Artists Gallery, Liberty, NY (2007-2011); Solo Exhibition, Amos Eno Gallery, New York, NY (2010, 2007); Exhibit, 139th Annual National Association of Women Artists, Inc. (2010); Exhibition, Plotkin Gallery, Dobbs Ferry, NY (2006); Solo Exhibition, Amos Eno Gallery, New York, NY (2005); Touring Exhibition, Millennium Collection, National Association of Women Artists, Inc., NY (1992-2005); Solo Exhibition, Amos Eno Gallery, New York, NY (2003); Exhibition, Beck Gallery, Hurleyville, NY (2003) **Awards:** National Association of Women Artists Award (2016); Elizabeth Horman Member Award for Digital Art, 125th National Association of Women Artists Exhibition (2014); Catalog, National Association of Women Artists, Inc. (2013-2014); Featured, Catskill Artists Gallery, Liberty, NY (2011) **Membership:** National Association of Women Artists, Inc.; New York State Art Teachers Association; New York Retired Teachers Association (Now NYSRTA); Catskill Art Society; National Museum of Women in the Arts; Albany Center Gallery; The Museum of Modern Art; Whitney Museum of American Art; Guggenheim Museum (Now The Solomon R. Guggenheim Foundation); Samuel Dorsky Museum of Art; Amos Eno Gallery **Marquis Who's Who Honors:** Albert Nelson Marquis Lifetime Achievement Award (2017) **Shipping Address:** PO Box 454, South Fallsburg, NY, 12779

Ann Terese Kelly

Title: Elementary and Secondary School Educator (Retired) **Industry:** Education/Educational Services **Company Name:** Bishop DuBourg High School **Date of Birth:** 01/29/1954 **Place of Birth:** St. Louis **State:** MO **Parents:** Robert Victor Kelly (Deceased); Mary Magdalen (Debrecht) Kelly **Marital Status:** Single **Education:** Coursework, The College at Brockport (1994, 1997, 2000, 2009); Coursework, Webster University (1990, 1999); Coursework, University of Missouri, St. Louis (1978-1979, 1986-1988, 1995); EdB in Elementary Education, University of Missouri, St. Louis (1977) **Certifications:** K-8 Certified **Career:** Teacher, Bishop DuBourg High School, St. Louis, MO (2005-Present); Teacher, Grade Five, Our Lady of Sorrows, St. Louis, MO (1988-2005); Teacher Grade Seven, Our Lady of Sorrows, St. Louis, MO (1986-1988); Teacher, Grades 6-8, St. Raphael the Archangel, St. Louis, Missouri (1979-1986); Teacher Fourth Grade, Assumption School, O'Fallon, Missouri (1977-1979); Teacher, Fourth Grade, St. Paul School, MO (1974-1975) **Career Related:** DataStreme Local Implementation Team Leader for the American Meteorological Society, Maury Project for Oceanographic Studies, American Meteorological Society/National Oceanic and Atmospheric Administration (2000-Present); Workshop Presenter, Maury Project for Oceanographic Studies, American Meteorological Society/National Oceanic and Atmospheric Administration (1994-Present); Teacher-trainer, Science Olympiad, St. Louis, Missouri (1987-Present); Presenter, Weather Workshops (1991-Present); Trainer, Archdiocese of St. Louis (1994-2002); Trainer, Grade Five Developmental Approaches in Science and Health (1993) **Awards:** Recipient, Woodie Flower Finalist Award (2015); Recipient, Eastern Missouri Volunteer Of Year Award, FLL (2012); Recipient, Heart Of DB Award, Bishop DuBourg High School (2009); Recipient, Shining Star Award, St. Louis Science Center (2002) **Membership:** NSTA; Science Teachers of Missouri; American Meteorological Society **Marquis Who's Who Honors:** Albert Nelson Marquis Lifetime Achievement Award (2017) **Why did you become involved in your profession or industry:** It was a passion that Ms. Kelly had to help form the future of our country and our world and if she can help students grow and benefit, be good students, take care of the earth and themselves, that's what she wanted to do. **Hobbies:** Singing; Dance; Photography **Religion:** Roman Catholic **Business Address:** 5850 Eichelberger, St. Louis, MO, 63109 **Shipping Address:** 303 Church St, O'Fallon, MO, 63366

Ronald G. Kelsey

Title: Military Officer, Environmental Engineer (Retired) **Industry:** Military & Defense Services **Date of Birth:** 07/22/1944 **Place of Birth:** Omar, Town of Orleans **State:** NY **Parents:** Lynwood Jerome Kelsey; Dorothy Mable (Simpkins) Kelsey **Marital Status:** Widowed **Spouse Name:** Linda York (3/24/1987, Deceased 12/12/2006) **Children:** Grant A.Kelsey **Education:** MA in Business Management, Central Michigan University (1981); MS in Engineering, Virginia Polytechnic Institute and State University (1974); BS in Civil Engineering, Norwich University (1965) **Career:** Retired (2004); Senior Environmental Engineer, Federal Aviation Administration Partnership, Northrop Grumman Corporation, Leesburg, VA (1999-2004); Senior Environmental Planner, URS Corp, Hunt Valley, MD (1999); Director, Government Environmental Services, Envirohealth Marketing, Equinox International, Frederick, MD (1995-1996); Director, Government Environmental Services, AWK Group of Companies, Turtle Creek, PA (1995); Senior Environmental Engineer, Meta, Inc., Gaithersburg, MD (1992-1995) **Career Related:** Presenter, Intellectual and Developmental Disabilities, Non-profit Organizations and Frederick Community College Transition Fair **Civic:** Volunteer Support, The Arc of Frederick County, MD; Volunteer Support, Alan P. Linton Emergency Shelter; Supporter, Daily Life Activities for His Son; Presenter, Regarding His Son with Developmental Disabilities; Participant, Parent Support Group Luncheons **Military Service:** Retired, U.S. Army Corps of Engineers (1992); Advanced through grades to Colonel, U.S. Army Corps of Engineers (1988); Commissioned Second Lieutenant, U.S. Army Corps of Engineers (1965) **Awards:** Decorated Legion of Merit with Two Oak Leaf Clusters; Bronze Star Medal; Meritorious Service Medal with One Oak Leaf Cluster; Army Commendation Medal with one Oak Leaf Cluster; National Defense Service Medal with Bronze Service Star; Vietnam Service Medal (Five Campaigns); Army Service Ribbon; Three Overseas Service Ribbons; Multinational Force and Observers Medal (Sinai of Egypt); Republic of Vietnam Campaign Medal; Republic of Vietnam Gallantry Cross Unit Citation; Parachute Badge; Army Staff Identification Badge **Membership:** President, Society of American Military Engineers (1991-1992); American Society of Civil Engineers; Water Environment Federation; Master Mason w/Hiram Lodge 819; Lifetime Member, VFW; American Legion; Army Engineer Association; Association of the United States Army; Army Historical Foundation **Hobbies:** Jogging; Reading; Travel; Environmental issues **Political Affiliations:** Republican **Religion:** Lutheran **Shipping Address:** 525 Sage Hen Ct, Frederick, MD, 21703

J. Robert Kemmerly

Title: Obstetrician **Industry:** Medicine & Health Care **Date of Birth:** 08/15/1936 **Place of Birth:** Baton Rouge **State:** LA **Parents:** Carl Edward Kemmerly; Edith May (Wright) Kemmerly **Education:** MD, Louisiana State University (1960); Summer Student, Perkins School of Theology, Southern Methodist University (1957-1959); BS, Louisiana State University (1956) **Certifications:** Diplomate, American Board of OB-GYN **Career:** Practice in Medicine, Obstetrics-Gynecology, Minden, LA (1966-2010); Resident, Southern Baptist Hospital, New Orleans, LA (1963-1966); Intern, Southern Baptist Hospital, New Orleans, LA (1960-1961); Founding President, The Women's Clinic A Medical Corporation **Career Related:** Medical Director, Minden Medical Center (2002-2004); President, Medical Staff, Minden Medical Center (1988-1989); President, Medical Staff, Minden Medical Center (1976-1977); Clinical Assistant Professor, Louisiana State University Medical Center, Shreveport, LA (1972-1982); President, Medical Staff, Minden Medical Center (1972); Board of Directors, Peoples Bank & Trust Co., Minden, LA; Fellow, American College of OB-GYN **Civic:** Chairman of the Administrative Board, Pastor of the Committee, Delegate to State and National Conferences, U.S. Air Force (1962-1963); First United Methodist Church, Minden, LA **Creative Works:** Contributor, Articles, Epidural Anesthesia Provided in Labor by Obstetricians **Awards:** Award for Best Fellow Presentation Paper, "Elective Induction of Labor Compared to Spontaneous Labor: Outcome Analysis," American College of Obstetricians and Gynecologists (1997) **Membership:** President, Webster Parish Medical Society (1986-1996); American Medical Association; Louisiana State Medical Association; Southern Medical Association; Member Emeritus, Medical Societies of Louisiana **Marquis Who's Who Honors:** Albert Nelson Marquis Lifetime Achievement Award (2017) **Hobbies:** Painting houses and assistant ramps **Shipping Address:** 215 Fernwood Lane, Minden, LA, 71055

Dorothy Irene Kendall

Title: Secondary School Educator **Industry:** Education/Educational Services **Place of Birth:** Karnes City **State:** TX **Parents:** Alger Hugh Kendall, Sr. (Deceased); Adelia Irene (Rasor) Kendall (Deceased) **Marital Status:** Single **Education:** MEd, University of Houston, Victoria, TX (1980); BBA, The University of Texas at Austin (1967) **Certifications:** Certified Teacher, State of Texas (1969) **Career:** Retired (2006); Teacher, Victoria High School (1967-2006) **Career Related:** Owner, Kendall's Boutique, Victoria, TX (1974-1977); Owner, The Open Door Boutique, Karnes City, TX (1970-1974); Coach, Victoria High School (1968-1973) **Civic:** Sponsor, Victoria High School Christian Club, Victoria, TX (1993-2006); Sponsor, Student Council, Victoria High School (1989-1992); Teacher, Sunday School, Northside Baptist Church, Victoria, TX (1968-1977); Sponsor, Baptist Young Women's Association, Victoria, TX (1968-1975); Donor, St. Jude Children's Research Hospital; Donor, Feed the Children **Awards:** Outstanding Teacher, National Honor Roll of Outstanding American Teachers (2006); Recipient, Leadership Certificate, DuPont (1992) **Membership:** Lifetime Member, National Education Association; Lifetime Member, Texas State Teachers Association; Lifetime Member, Texas Exes **Marquis Who's Who Honors:** Albert Nelson Marquis Lifetime Achievement Award (2017); Marquis Who's Who Lifetime Achievers; Who's Who in America; Who's Who in the World; Who's Who of American Women **To what do you attribute your success:** Dr. Kendall attributes her success to her faith in God and the encouragement and love she received from her parents and brother. **Why did you become involved in your profession or industry:** Dr. Kendall became involved in her profession after a great deal of prayer led her to the decision to teach. She felt that this was what the Lord wanted her to do. **What do you consider to be the highlight of your career:** A highlight of Dr. Kendall's career was the realization that each student was like a treasure box waiting to be opened. The realization that each one had a special talent, gift or purpose just waiting to be discovered. **Where will you be in five years:** In five years, Dr. Kendall cannot foresee the future so she has to say she doesn't know. **Hobbies:** Photography; Traveling; Horseback riding; Tennis; Basketball **Political Affiliations:** Republican **Religion:** Baptist **Shipping Address:** 931 E Calvert Ave, Karnes City, TX, 78118

Christian Randolph Kerns

Title: Chemist **Industry:** Sciences **Date of Birth:** 04/08/1953 **Place of Birth:** Fredericksburg **State:** VA **Parents:** Terrill D. Kerns; Mary Barbe Kerns **Education:** BS in Chemistry, West Virginia University (1978) **Career:** Chemist, Adecco, Leominster, MA (2002-2008); Engineer, Spectro Analytical Instruments GmbH, Fitchburg, MA (2000-2001); Chemist, Aerotek Sciences, Fort Lauderdale, FL (1999-2000); Chemist, Harbor Branch Oceanographic Institution, Florida Atlantic University, Fort Pierce, FL (1997); Chemist, Florida Department of Agriculture and Consumer Services, Tallahassee, FL (1986-1996) **Civic:** President, United Methodist Men, Wesley United Methodist Church, Worcester, MA (2010-2012); Membership and Evangelism Committee, Wesley United Methodist Church, Worcester, MA (2002-2008); Chairman, Mission Committee, St. Paul's United Methodist Church, Tallahassee, FL (1994-1996) **Awards:** Layman of the Year, Wesley United Methodist Church, Worcester, MA (2018); Science Excellence award, American Biographical Institute (2011); Honoree, Man of the Year, American Biographical Institute (2011); Honoree, First Team All State Colorado Men's Basketball Team (1971) **Membership:** American Chemical Society; Past President, Lions Club International; Honorary Member, Phi Theta Kappa Honor Society **Marquis Who's Who Honors:** Albert Nelson Marquis Lifetime Achievement Award (2017) **Hobbies:** Stained glass art **Religion:** Methodist **Shipping Address:** 176 Maple Avenue, Unit 1-24, Rutland, MA, 01543

Rosemary Joan Kijowski

Title: Volunteer **Industry:** Religious **Company Name:** St. Mary of Mount Virgin Church **Date of Birth:** 02/13/1948 **Place of Birth:** Perth Amboy **State:** NJ **Parents:** John Raymond Kijowski; Rosaria Rosica Kijowski **Children:** Robert John Kijowski; Edward Raymond Kijowski **Education:** MA, The College of New Jersey, Ewing, NJ (1976); BA, The College of New Jersey, Ewing, NJ (1970) **Certifications:** Certified Fitness Nutritionist, State of California (2004); Certified Music Teacher, K-12, State of New Jersey (1970) **Career:** Owner, The Body Shoppe for Women (2003-2012); General Manager of Fitness Center, The Body Shoppe for Women (2003-2012); Talent Show Adviser, Woodrow Wilson Middle School (1998-2005); Vocal and Music Director, Board of Education, Edison Local School District (1970-2005); Peer Leadership Adviser, Woodrow Wilson Middle School (2000-2001) **Career Related:** Assistant Coach, Odyssey of the Mind, Edison, NJ (1984-1990) **Civic:** Eucharistic Minister, St. Mary of Mount Virgin Church, Parish of the Visitation; Eucharistic Minister, Saint Peter's Healthcare System; Volunteer, Castle of Dreams Animal Rescue **Awards:** Honoree, Teacher of the Year, Edison Township Education Association (1998, 2004-2005) **Membership:** The New Jersey Association of Women Business Owners; Associate, Edison Township Education Association; Associate, New Jersey Education Association; Associate, National Association for Music Education; Associate, New Jersey Retired Educators Association; Associate, New Jersey Music Educators Association **Marquis Who's Who Honors:** Albert Nelson Marquis Lifetime Achievement Award (2017); Distinguished Humanitarian (2017) **Why did you become involved in your profession or industry:** When Ms. Kijowski was in fifth grade, she won three years of accordion lessons along with a brand new accordion. This started her formal music studies. She was intense on learning, continually being promoted year after year to more challenging heights. **Shipping Address:** 52 Riverview Avenue, Edison, NJ, 08817

John Henry Killmaster III

Title: Art Professor Emeritus **Industry:** Education/Educational Services **Company Name:** Boise State University **Date of Birth:** 12/02/1934 **Place of Birth:** Allegan **State:** MI **Parents:** John H. Killmaster; Ora Mae (Backus) Killmaster **Marital Status:** Married **Spouse Name:** Rosemary Olson (1996) **Children:** John Henry, IV; Karen; Dana **Education:** MFA, Cranbrook Academy of Art, Bloomfield Hills, MI (1969); BA, Hope College, Holland, MI, Cum Laude (1968) **Career:** Professor of Art Emeritus, Boise State University (1997-Present); Professor of Art, Boise State University (1970-1997); Assistant Professor of Art, Ferris State College, Big Rapids, MI (1969-1970); Assistant Professor of Art, Ferris State College, Big Rapids, MI (1966-1967); Designer, LaDriere Inc. (Now LaDriere Digital Arts Studio), Detroit, MI (1953-1963); Designer, Ambrose & Associates (1953-1963); Artist, Ambrose & Associates (1953-1957) **Creative Works:** Contributor, Art, "Killmaster: Art & Soul," Christopher R. Schnoor (2017); Exhibitor, "Close to Home: Our Own Spectacular Parks," St. George Art Museum (2015); Exhibitor, Annual Exhibitions, Western States Arts Federation (2013-2014); Exhibitor, "Alchemy 2 International Enamel Exhibition" (2013); Exhibitor, "Era Messages," Museum of Contemporary Craft" (2011); Exhibitor, "Sustain-Expand Idaho Triennial," Boise Art Museum (2010); Exhibitor, "Surfacing," The Oakland Art Gallery (2009); Exhibitor, "The Killmaster Collection - A 60 Year Perspective," The Herrett Center for Arts and Science (2007); Exhibitor, "Drawing Power," The National Automotive History Collection (2006); Exhibitor, The Whatcom Museum, Bellingham, WA (2005); Exhibitor, "International Juried Enamel Exhibition," The Evergreen State College, Olympia, WA (2003); Exhibitor, "International Enamel Exhibition," Richmond Art Center (2002); Exhibitor, Random Modern Gallery, Tacoma, WA (2000); Exhibitor, "American Enamels," Random Modern Gallery (2000); Exhibitor, "Fifth International Juried Enamel Exhibit," Velvet da Vinci Gallery, San Francisco, CA (2000); Exhibitor, Canadian Clay, Glass & Enamel Gallery (Now Canadian Clay and Glass Gallery), Waterloo, ON, Canada (1999); Exhibitor, "Second Annual International Juried Enamel Exhibit," In Sight Gallery (1997); Exhibitor, "Contemporary American, Canadian & European Enamels," School of Art Collection and Galleries, Kent State University (1994); Exhibitor, Veste Coburg, Coburg, Germany (1994); Exhibitor, Yaroslavl Art Museum (1994) **Awards:** Lifetime Achievement Award, The Enamelist Society, Inc. (2001); Sudden Opportunity Grant, Commission on the Arts, State of Idaho (1991); Fourth Annual Jack A. Schaefle Award for Excellence in the Arts, Commission on the Arts, City of Boise, Idaho (1990) **Membership:** Northwest Designer Craftsmen; The Enamelist Society, Inc. **Marquis Who's Who Honors:** Albert Nelson Marquis Lifetime Achievement Award (2017) **Shipping Address:** 2373 S Annett Street, Boise, ID, 83705

Jeannie J. Kinzie, MD

Title: Radiation Oncologist (Retired) & Nuclear Medicine Physician (Retired) **Industry:** Medicine & Health Care **Date of Birth:** 03/14/1940 **Place of Birth:** Great Falls **State:** MT **Parents:** James Wayne Jones; Lillian Alice (Young) Jones **Marital Status:** Single **Spouse Name:** Joseph Lee Kinzie (3/26/1965, Divorced 9/1982) **Children:** Daniel Joseph **Education:** Fellowship in Nuclear Medicine, University of Colorado (1996-1998); MBA, University of Phoenix (1997); Resident in Therapeutic Radiology, Washington University in St. Louis (1968-1971); Intern in Surgery, The University of North Carolina at Chapel Hill (1965-1966); MD, Washington University in St. Louis (1965); BS, Montana State University (1961); Coursework, Oregon State University (1960) **Certifications:** Diplomate, The American Board of Radiology (1972), Diplomate, American Board of Nuclear Medicine (1998) **Career:** Retired (2008); Staff Radiologist, VA Eastern Colorado Health Care System, U.S. Department of Veteran Affairs (2003-2008); Assistant Clinical Professor of Nuclear Medicine, University of Colorado (1998-2005); Radiology Professor (Radiation Oncology), University of Colorado (1985-1995); Director of Radiation Oncology, University of Colorado Hospital, UCHealth (1985-1991); Associate Professor of Radiation Oncology, Wayne State University (1980-1985); Associate Professor of Radiology, The University of Chicago (1978-1980); Assistant Professor of Radiology, The University of Chicago (1975-1978) **Career Related:** Chairman, Faculty Promotion Committee, University of Colorado School of Medicine (1988-1989); Consultant, Center for Devices and Radiological Health, U.S. Food and Drug Administration (1986-1991); Consultant, VA Eastern Colorado Health Care System, U.S. Department of Veteran Affairs (1985-1998); Consultant, Denver Health (1985-1995); Consultant, Rose Medical Center, C-HCA, Inc. (1986-1995); Scientific Advisory Board, Cancer League of Colorado (1985-1988); Examiner, The American Board of Radiology (1985-1988) **Civic:** Member, Faith Bible Chapel **Creative Works:** Associate Editor, International Journal Radiation of Oncology, Biology and Physics, Elsevier, Inc. (1985-1995); **Awards:** Grantee, National Institutes of Health (1973-1975); Fellow, American College of Radiology (1984) **Membership:** Delegate, House of Delegates, Colorado Medical Society (1993-1995, 1998-2000); Alternate Delegate, House of Delegates, Colorado Medical Society (1989-1992, 1996-1998); President, Rocky Mountain Oncology Society (1991-1993); Board of Directors, Rocky Mountain Oncology Society (1989-1993); Board of Directors, Denver Unit, American Cancer Society, Inc. (1986-1987); **Marquis Who's Who Honors:** Albert Nelson Marquis Lifetime Achievement Award (2017) **Political Affiliations:** Republican **Religion:** Christian, Protestant

Raymond Klebba

Title: Property Manager **Industry:** Consulting **Company Name:** Arkay Consulting Services **Date of Birth:** 04/16/1934 **Place of Birth:** Chicago **State:** IL **Parents:** Raymond Aloysius; Marie Cecelia (Tobin) Klebba **Marital Status:** Married **Spouse Name:** Margaret Mistak **Children:** Anne; Daniel; Mary; Theresa **Education:** Student, Loyola University, Chicago, IL (1954-1956) **Certifications:** Certified Property Manager, Institute of Real Estate Management (1970) **Career:** President, Arkay Consulting Services (2012-Present); Real Estate Broker, Tempo Real Estate, Inc., Chicago, IL (1998-2011); Business Manager, St. Matthias Parish, Chicago, IL (1995-1998); Branch Manager, Bank of Highwood, Deerfield, IL (1990-1994); Vice President, Director, Mid-American National Bank, Chicago, IL (1983-1990); Real Estate Manager, Broker, Strobeck, Reiss School Management Co., Chicago, IL (1970-1983); Vice President, General Manager, Strobeck, Reiss School Management Co., Chicago, IL (1968-1970); President, Midland Warehouses, Chicago, IL (1961-1968); Correspondent, Representative, Western Railroad Association and Western Military Bureau, Chicago, IL (1956-1961) **Civic:** Board of Advisors, Senior Center **Creative Works:** Silverliners Singing Duo With Ms. Peggy Mistak **Awards:** Chicagoland Individual Casting Champion (1999-Present) **Membership:** Vice President, Chicago Angling & Casting Club **Hobbies:** Painting; Fishing; Bicycling; Casting; Singing **Shipping Address:** 2150 Bouterse Street, Apt. 106, Park Ridge, IL, 60068

Donald Kline

Title: Professional Food Technologist **Industry:** Sciences **Date of Birth:** 07/06/1948 **Place of Birth:** Chicago **State:** IL **Parents:** Ralph Waldo Kline; Theresa (Donato) Kline **Marital Status:** Single **Spouse Name:** Christine Janet Kennedy (8/23/1972, Deceased 2/24/2010) **Children:** Bethany Amber; Torah-Ann Shiloh; Nathaniel Darwin Kennedy; Abraham Newton Kennedy; Seth-Andrew Brigham Kennedy **Education:** BS, Northern Illinois University, DeKalb, IL (1974); BS, Roosevelt University (1974); AS, Kishwaukee College, Malta, IL (1971); AA, South Suburban College, South Holland, IL (1969) **Certifications:** Certified Natural Health Professional, The National Association of Certified Natural Health Professionals (2003); Certified Nutritional Consultant; The American Association of Nutritional Consultants (1998); Certification for Thermal Process Control of Low-Acid Canned Foods, University of Wisconsin (1974) **Career:** With, Kline Consulting Services, LLC, New Oxford, PA (2017-Present); Research Fellow, UTZ Quality Foods, LLC, Hanover, PA (2016-2017); Director of Technical Services, Research & Development, UTZ Quality Foods, LLC, Hanover, PA (2002-2016); Director of Quality Assurance, UTZ Quality Foods, LLC, Hanover, PA (1995-2002); Director of Quality Assurance, Hanover Foods Corp., Hanover, PA (1994-1995); Senior Research Associate, Nabisco Biscuit Co., East Hanover, NJ (1992-1994); Quality Assurance Research and Development Manager, Snyder's of Hanover, Hanover, PA (1982-1992); President, Abinadi Enterprises International Corp., Nappanee, IN (1980-1982) **Career Related:** Innovative Snack Food Product Development **Civic:** Secretary, New Oxford Municipal Authority (2017-Present); First Assistant, Gettysburg Ward, High Priest Group (2017-Present); Trustee, Masonic Hebron Lodge No. 465 (2016-Present); Ordained, Office of High Priest, The Church of Jesus Christ of Latter-day Saints (2014-Present) **Membership:** Grand Commandery of Knights Templar of Pennsylvania (2013-Present); 32nd Degree Scottish Rite Mason, Hebron Lodge No 465 (2009-Present); National Association of Certified Natural Health Professionals (2003-Present) **Hobbies:** Collecting rare coins and postal stamps; Fossils **Political Affiliations:** Republican **Religion:** The Church of Jesus Christ of Latter-day Saints **Shipping Address:** 10 Kevin Dr, Kline Consulting Services, Snack Food R&D and Holistic Healthcare, New Oxford, PA, 17350

Wiley Eugene Knott

Title: Electronics Engineer (Retired) **Industry:** Engineering **Date of Birth:** 03/18/1938 **Place of Birth:** Muncie **State:** IN **Parents:** Joseph Wiley Knott; Mildred Viola (Haxton) Knott **Children:** Brian Evan **Education:** Postgraduate Coursework, Georgia College (1987); Postgraduate Coursework, Union College (1970-1973); BSEE, Tri-State University (1963) **Career:** Part-time Business Consultant (1972-2003); Principal Engineer, Boeing, Everett, WA (1993-1995); Lead Engineer, Boeing, Everett, WA (1992-1993); Facilities, Plant Operations and Maintenance Engineer, Boeing, Everett, WA (1991-1992); Base Manager, Military Division, Boeing, Castle Air Force Base (1990-1991); Senior Specialist Engineer, Military Division, Boeing, Wichita, KS (1989-1990); Customer Support Manager, Military Division, Boeing, Wichita, KS (1985-1989); Logistics Manager, Military Division, Boeing, Wichita, KS (1984-1985); Senior Specialist Engineer, Military Division, Boeing, Wichita, KS (1981-1984); Specialist Engineer, Military Division, Boeing, Wichita, KS (1979-1981); Senior Publications Engineer, General Electric, Pittsfield, MA (1977-1979); Group Leader, General Electric, Pittsfield, MA (1967-1979); Technical Publications Engineer, GE, Pittsfield, MA (1965-1977); Associate Aircraft Engineer, Lockheed Corporation (Now Lockheed Martin Corporation), Marietta, GA (1963-1965) **Career Related:** Member, Museum of Aviation (1987-1995); American Security Council (1975-1990); National Republican Congressional Committee (1979-1987); Republican National Committee (1979-1987); Joint Presidential/Congressional Steering Committee (1982-1986); State Adviser, U.S. Congressional Advisory Board (1981-1986); Republican Presidential Task Force (1981-1986); National Republican Senatorial Committee (1979-1986); Republican Political Action Committee (1979-1986); Adviser, Junior Achievement (1978-1979); Active, Junior Achievement (1978-1979) **Military Service:** U.S. Army (1956-1959) **Membership:** Life Member, National Rifle Association; Founding Sponsor, National Army Museum; Life Member, National Defense Industrial Association; Life Member, Association of the U.S. Army; Life Member, Air Force Association; Golf Clubmakers Association; American Family Association; Heidelberg American High School Alumni Association; Overseas Brats; Military Brats; Amateur Radio Relay League; The Heritage Foundation; Gun Owners of America; Illinois Railway Museum; U.S. Golf Association; Life Member, PGA Tour Partners; Perry Country Club; Life Member, MLB Insiders Club **Marquis Who's Who Honors:** Albert Nelson Marquis Lifetime Achievement Award (2017) **Political Affiliations:** Conservative **Religion:** Presbyterian **Shipping Address:** 109 Holbeck Ct, Warner Robins, GA, 31088

Robert Allan Kolb

Title: Professor Emeritus **Industry:** Education/Educational Services **Company Name:** Concordia College **Date of Birth:** 06/17/1941 **Place of Birth:** Fort Dodge **State:** IA **Parents:** Ralph Orrin Kolb; Eva Ann (Holm) Kolb **Marital Status:** Married **Spouse Name:** Pauline Joanne Ansorge Kolb (8/14/1965) **Education:** LLD, Concordia University Irvine (2008); LLD, Concordia University (2005); LLD, Valparaiso University (2000); PhD, University of Wisconsin-Madison (1973); Master of Sacred Theology, Concordia Seminary (1968); MDiv, Concordia Seminary (1967); BA, Concordia College, Fort Wayne (1963) **Career:** Emeritus Professor; Professor, Concordia Seminary (1993-2009); Acting President, Concordia University, St. Paul (1990-1991); Professor, Concordia University, St. Paul (1986-1993); Chairman, Division of Religion, Concordia University, St. Paul (1982-1987); Associate Professor, Concordia University, St. Paul (1981-1986); Faculty Member, Concordia University (1977-1993); Executive Director, Center for Reformation Research, Concordia Seminary (1972-1977) **Career Related:** Chairman, The Lutheran Church Missouri Synod (1990-1992); Member, Theology & Church Relations, The Lutheran Church Missouri Synod (1984-1992) **Civic:** Member, Contribution Committee, International Congress for Luther Research (1993-Present); Board Member, Lexington-Hamline Community Council (1980-1990); Ordained to Ministry, Lutheran Church (1972) **Creative Works:** Author, "Luther's Wittenberg World" (2018); Author, "Martin Luther and the Enduring Word of God" (2016); Co-editor, "The Oxford Handbook of Martin Luther's Theology" (2014); Author, "Luther and the Stories of God" (2012); Co-author, "The Lutheran Confessions" (2012); Author, "Martin Luther, Confessor of the Faith" (2009); Co-author, "The Genius of Luther's Theology" (2008); Editor, "Lutheran Ecclesiastical Culture, 1550-1675" (2008); Author, "Bound Choice, Election and Wittenberg Theological Method" (2005); Co-editor, "The Book of Concord" (2000); Author, "Martin Luther as Prophet, Teacher and Hero" (1999); Co-editor, "The Sixteenth Century Journal" (1994-1997); Associate Editor, "The Sixteenth Century Journal" (1973-1993) **Awards:** Hermann Sasse Preis, Selbständige Evangelisch-Lutherische Kirche (2013) **Membership:** Membership Committee, American Society of Church History (1984-1989); President, Sixteenth Century Society & Conference (1980-1981); Council Member, American Society of Church History (1978-1981); Society for Reformation Research **Marquis Who's Who Honors:** Albert Nelson Marquis Lifetime Achievement Award (2017); Distinguished Humanitarian (2017) **Religion:** Lutheran **Shipping Address:** 801 Seminary Pl, Saint Louis, MO, 63105

David Benjamin Kopel

Title: Lawyer **Industry:** Law and Legal Services **Company Name:** Independence Institute **Place of Birth:** Denver **State:** CO/USA **Parents:** Gerald Henry Kopel; Dolores B. Kopel **Marital Status:** Married **Spouse Name:** Deirdre Frances Dolan (1987) **Education:** JD, University of Michigan (1985); BA in History, Brown University (1982) **Career:** Research Director, Independence Institute, Golden, CO (1992-Present); Assistant Attorney General, Colorado State Attorney General, Denver, CO (1988-1992); Assistant District Attorney, Manhattan District Attorney, New York, NY (1986-1988); Associate, Sullivan & Cromwell, New York, NY (1985-1986) **Career Related:** Adjunct Professor, Sturm College of Law, Denver University (2009-Present); Adjunct Professor, School of Law, New York University (1998-1999) **Membership:** Vice-Chair, Colorado State Advisory Commission on Civil Rights, Colorado (2016-Present) **Bar Admissions:** Sixth Circuit, U.S. Court of Appeals (2010); Ninth Circuit, U.S. Court of Appeals (2010); 11th Circuit, U.S. Court of Appeals (2010); Third Circuit, U.S. Court of Appeals (2009); Seventh Circuit, U.S. Court of Appeals (2009); Eighth Circuit, U.S. Court of Appeals (2003); Fourth Circuit, U.S. Court of Appeals (2003); Fifth Circuit, U.S. Court of Appeals (1999); District of Columbia Circuit, U.S. Court of Appeals (1997); Tenth Circuit, U.S. Court of Appeals (1988); U.S. District Court, State of Colorado (1988); Second Circuit, U.S. Court of Appeals (1988); U.S. District Court, Eastern and Southern Districts, State of New York (1986); State of New York (1986); State of Colorado (1986) **Marquis Who's Who Honors:** Albert Nelson Marquis Lifetime Achievement Award (2017) **Why did you become involved in your profession or industry:** Mr. Kopel was inspired to pursue law because both of his parents were lawyers. **What do you consider to be the highlight of your career:** A highlight of Mr. Kopel's career was when he was a part of the oral argument team in the Supreme Court of the United States case District of Columbia vs. Heller. **Hobbies:** Skiing; Golf; Amateur radio **Political Affiliations:** Democrat **Religion:** Catholic **Shipping Address:** 727 E 16th Avenue, Independence Institute, Denver, CO, 80203 **Website:** http://www.davekopel.org

Joseph William Kovach

Title: Doctor **Industry:** Medicine & Health Care **Company Name:** Joseph W. Kovach and Associates, Ltd. **Date of Birth:** 10/04/1946 **Place of Birth:** Hammond **State:** IN **Parents:** William Charles Kovach; Florence (Miotka) Kovach **Education:** School Psychologist Intern, School District 164, Park Forest, IL (1986); PsyD in Clinical Psychology, The Chicago School of Professional Psychology (1986); Pre-Doctoral Intern, Chicago-Read Mental Health Center (1983-1984); Illinois Institute of Technology (1981); MA in Psychology, Roosevelt University (1974); **Certifications:** Diplomate, American College of Forensic Examiners Institute; Licensed School Psychologist, State of Illinois; Licensed School Psychologist, State of Indiana; Licensed School Psychologist, State of Missouri; Certified Marriage and Family Therapist, State of Indiana **Career:** President, Joseph W. Kovach and Associates, Ltd. (1985-Present); Professor, Calumet College of St. Joseph (1984-Present); Chairman, Department of Psychology, Calumet College of St. Joseph (1984-Present); Former Chairman, Department of General Education, Calumet College of St. Joseph (2006-2015); Former Chairman, Department of Natural and Social Sciences, Calumet College of St. Joseph (1993-2014); Director, Buzan Centre of Chicago (1992-2008); Director, Educational Research Exchange (1988-2001) **Career Related:** Oxford Round Table: Women's Rights, Oxford, England (2004); Psychologist, Nonmilitary Support Services for Military and Families, United States Army (2001); Presenter, International Conference of the Role of Social Science in the Development of Education, Business and Government Entering the 21st Century, Kaunas Lithuania (1998); Adjunct Faculty, Thornton Community College (Now South Suburban College) (1997-1998); Member, 24th International Congress on Arts and Communications, Keble College, Oxford University, Oxford, England (1997); Assistant Program Director, Chicago-Read Mental Health Center (1987-1989); Supervisor, Loyola University Health System, Neurology (1980-1983); Adjunct Faculty, Purdue University Calumet (Now Purdue University Northwest) (1976-1989); Research Associate, Neurology, Stritch School of Medicine, Loyola University (1976-1978) **Creative Works:** Columnist, Business in Review/The Times; Columnist, Executive Excellence and Personal Excellence; Columnist, Northwest Indiana Business Journal; Columnist, Talking to the Boss **Awards:** Distinguished Alumni, The Chicago School of Professional Psychology (2016) **Membership:** American Psychological Association; International Conference of Police Chaplains **Marquis Who's Who Honors:** Albert Nelson Marquis Lifetime Achievement Award (2017); Distinguished Humanitarian (2017) **Shipping Address:** 1426 Oak Park Dr, Munster, IN, 46321

Pauline Kra

Title: Professor of French **Industry:** Education/Educational Services **Company Name:** Yeshiva University **Date of Birth:** 07/30/1934 **Place of Birth:** Lodz **Country of Origin:** Poland **Parents:** Edward Skornicki; Nathalie Skornicki **Spouse Name:** Leo Dietrich Kra (3/10/1955) **Children:** David Theodore; Andrew Jason **Education:** MA, Queens College (1990); PhD, Columbia University (1968); MA, Columbia University (1963); BA, Barnard College (1955); Student, Radcliffe College (1951-1953) **Career:** Professor Emerita, Yeshiva University, New York, NY (1999-Present); Senior Programmer, Section of Genetic Medicine, Department of Medicine, University of Chicago (2007-2013); Senior Programmer Analyst, Department of Biomedical Informatics, Columbia University, New York, NY (1998-2007); Professor, Yeshiva University, New York, NY (1982-1999); Associate Professor, Yeshiva University, New York, NY (1974-1982); Assistant Professor of French, Yeshiva University, New York, NY (1968-1974); Lecturer, Queens College (1964-1965) **Creative Works:** Author, "The Manuscript of Claude Dupin's Commentary on Montesquieu's 'Esprit des lois'" (2016); Author, "The Role of China in Montesquieu's 'Esprit des lois'" (2016); Editor, "Voltaire, De la paix perpetuelle," "Les Å'uvres Completes de Voltaire," The Voltaire Foundation, University of Oxford (2016); Author, "Lyttelton, George," "The Encyclopedia of British Literature 1660, 1789," DayBlackwell Publishing (2015); Editor, "Voltaire, Lettre d'un ecclesiastique sur le pretendu retablissement des jesuites dans Paris," "Les Å'uvres Completes de Voltaire," the Voltaire Foundation, University of Oxford, (2013); Editor, "Voltaire, L'Epitre aux Romains," "Les Å'uvres Completes de Voltaire," the Voltaire Foundation, University of Oxford (2011); Author, "La Defense des Lettres persanes," Cahiers Montesquieu, No. 9, University of Bordeaux (2005); Author, "La Religion dans les Penses de Montesquieu," Revue Montesquieu No. 7. Universite Stendhal-Grenoble (2005); Contributor, "Automating terminological networks to link heterogeneous biomedical databases." Medinfo, American Medical Informatics Association (2004-2011); Contributor, Annotation of Montesquieu, "Lettres Persanes," "Oeuvres Completes, Vol. I," the Voltaire Foundation, University of Oxford (2004); Author, "The Concept of National Character in 18th Century France," Cromohs (2002); Author, "Rousseau et la politique du caractere national," Politique et Nation (2001) **Membership:** Modern Language Association of America; American Society for Eighteenth-Century Studies; La Societe Francaise d'etude du Dix-Huitieme Siecle; La Societe Montesquieu; Association for Computers and the Humanities; Association for Literary and Linguistic Computing **Marquis Who's Who Honors:** Albert Nelson Marquis Lifetime Achievement Award (2017) **Shipping Address:** 10914 Ascan Avenue, Apt. 4H, Forest Hills, NY, 11375 **Website:** http://www.paulinekra.info

Andrew Thomas Kreig

Title: Trade Association Executive **Industry:** Law and Legal Services **Company Name:** Justice Integrity Project **Date of Birth:** 02/28/1949 **Place of Birth:** Chicago **State:** IL **Parents:** Albert Arthur Kreig; Margaret Theresa (Baltzell) Kreig **Education:** JD, University of Chicago (1990); MSL, Yale University (1983); AB, Cornell University (1970) **Career:** Executive Director, Justice Integrity Project (2010-Present); President, Chief Executive Officer, Wireless Communications Association International, Inc., Washington (1996-2008); Associate, Latham & Watkins (1991-1993); Law Clerk to U.S. District Judge Mark L. Wolf, Boston, MA (1990-1991); Freelance Author (1985-1989); Freelance Journalist (1985-1989); Freelance Lecturer (1985-1989); Media Director, Connecticut House Speaker, Hartford, CT (1984); Writer-Editor, Hartford Courant (1970-1984) **Civic:** Board Member, Illinois State Society (2017-Present); Co-Chair, Fixed Wireless Committee Coalition (2000-2013); Senior Fellow, Schuster Institute, Brandeis University (2009-2012) **Creative Works:** Author, "Presidential Puppetry" (2013); Author, "Spiked: How Chain Management, Second Edition" (1988); Author, "Spiked: How Chain Management" (1987) **Awards:** Ford Foundation Fellow, Yale Law School (1982-1983) **Membership:** American Bar Association; American Society of Newspaper Editors; American Society of Journalists and Authors; National Press Club; Overseas Press Club **Bar Admissions:** The District of Columbia Bar (1991); Massachusetts Bar Association (1991); Illinois State Bar Association (1991) **Marquis Who's Who Honors:** Albert Nelson Marquis Lifetime Achievement Award (2017); Continuous listings since mid-1990s in "Who's Who In America" and "Who's Who In the World" **Why did you become involved in your profession or industry:** Mr. Kreig became involved in his profession after starting out as a research fellow at the university and a writer. He started writing during the Watergate era, and he developed a passion for seeing what made Washington work. He felt that the stories presented in the news did not always reflect the totality of the situation, so he performed research development with the Justice Integrity Project, a non-partisan investigative reporting agency that was founded with other senior reporters. He remains active and on the board and is still editing stories and conferences. **Business Address:** 701 Pennsylvania Ave NW Apt PH8, 701 Pennsylvania Ave NW Apt PH8, Washington, DC, 20004

Layne Edwin Kruse

Title: Attorney **Industry:** Law and Legal Services **Company Name:** Norton Rose Fulbright US LLP **Date of Birth:** 08/15/1951 **Place of Birth:** Emporia **State:** KS **Education:** JD, Yale Law School (1977); MSc, London School of Economics (1974); BA in Economics, Texas A&M University, Summa Cum Laude (1973) **Certifications:** Certified in Civil Trial Law, Texas Board of Legal Specialization **Career:** Partner, Norton Rose Fulbright US LLP, Texas (2013-Present); Member, Fulbright & Jaworski L.L.P., Texas (1978-2013); Law Clerk to Honorable John R. Brown, United States Court Appeals for the Fifth Circuit (1977-1978) **Career Related:** Panelist, GCR Live 3rd Annual Antitrust Litigation USA, New York (2017); Competition Law v. Tax Breaks & Local Incentives, ABA 65th Antitrust Law Spring Meeting, Washington, DC (2017); Moderator, "Telemedicine: Are Old Definitions Restricting Competition?" ABA 64th Antitrust Law Spring Meeting, Washington, DC (2016); Moderator, "Defending Civil Antitrust Suits in the Aftermath of Criminal Prosecutions," ABA Antitrust Spring Meeting, Washington, DC (2014); Speaker, Antitrust Update for Petroleum Marketing, ABA Petroleum Marketing Attorneys Association, Washington, DC (2014); Speaker, Antitrust, Securities Fraud and Other Business Torts in Texas, State Judges Conference (2014); Moderator, Class Actions After Comcast, ABA Antitrust Spring Meeting, Washington, DC (2013) **Creative Works:** Co-author, "Business and Commercial Litigation in Federal Courts, Fourth Edition" (2017); Co-author, "A Practitioner's Guide to Class Actions" (2017); Contributor, Model Jury Instructions in Civil Antitrust Cases (2016); Co-author, "US: Energy," The Antitrust Review of the Americas (2015) **Awards:** Named Lawyer of the Year, Best Lawyers (2011, 2016, 2017); Named Client Service All-Star, The BTI Consulting Group (2016); Named to Top 100 Houston Super Lawyers, Texas Super Lawyers (2014-2016); Named Texas Super Lawyer, Thomson Reuters (2003-2016) **Membership:** Chairman, Exemptions & Immunities Committee, Antitrust Section, ABA; Ethics and Professionalism Committee, ABA; Litigation Section, ABA; Fellow, ABA; Fellow, Texas Bar Foundation; Fellow, Houston Bar Foundation; Board of Directors, The World Affairs Council of Greater Houston **Bar Admissions:** Admitted to Practice, State Bar of Texas (1978); Admitted to Practice, ABA; Admitted to Practice, Houston Bar Association; Admitted to Practice, The District of Columbia Bar **Marquis Who's Who Honors:** Albert Nelson Marquis Lifetime Achievement Award (2017) **Business Address:** 1301 Mckinney St., Ste 5100, Houston, TX, 77010

Vendulka Kubalkova, PhD

Title: Professor **Industry:** Education/Educational Services **Company Name:** University of Miami **Education:** Visiting Fellow, Department of International Relations, Australian National University (1980-1981); Visiting Fellow, Balliol College, Oxford, United Kingdom (1980-1981); PhD, Lancaster University, England (1979); Postdoctoral Research Fellow, Department of International Relations, Research School of Pacific Studies, Australian National University, Canberra, Australia (1977-1981); Postdoctoral Research Fellow, Department of Political Studies, University of Otago, Dunedin, New Zealand (1974-1976); JUDr, Law School, Charles University (1969); Degree in Music, State Conservatoire, Prague, Czech Republic (1966) **Career:** Visiting Professor, Prague School of Economics (2016-Present); Professor, Department of International Studies, University of Miami (1989-Present); Organist, Episcopal Church Center (1991-1997); Visiting Professor, Graduate School of International Relations, University of Miami (1988-1989); Senior Research Fellow, Center for Russian and East European Studies, Stanford University (1988-1989); Associate Professor, Reader in Political Science, University of Queensland (1987-1988); Research Associate, University of California, Berkeley (1987-1988) **Career Related:** Formerly Assistant Provost, University-Wide International Studies; Director, Mater's Program in International Administration, Association of Professional Schools of International Affairs; Chair, Interim Chair, Department of International Studies, University of Miami **Creative Works:** Co-Author, "Marxism-Leninism and Theory of International Relations, Reissued" (2016); Co-Editor, "International Relations in a Constructed World" (1998); Co-Author, "Marxism and International Relations," Oxford University Press (1989) **Awards:** Invited Member, Alpha Epsilon Lambda, National Graduate Society (1996-Present); Recipient, Australian Senior Fulbright Fellowship; Recipient, Olin Fellowship, Faculty of International Studies, Prague School of Economics (2018) **Membership:** Board of Dante Fascell Fellow, United States Department of State, Washington, DC (1994-Present); Judge, Board of the National Education Security Program, United States Department of Defense, Washington, DC (1994-Present); Committee for International Relations of the Vice-President, Charles University, Prague, Czech Republic (1990-Present) **Bar Admissions:** Czechoslovak Republic (1991) **Marquis Who's Who Honors:** Albert Nelson Marquis Lifetime Achievement Award (2017) **Shipping Address:** 8050 SW 78th St, Miami, FL, 33143

Walter Anthony Kukull, PhD

Title: Professor of Epidemiology; Director National Alzheimer's Coordinating Center **Industry:** Medicine & Health Care **Company Name:** University of Washington **State:** USA **Parents:** Anthony Kukull; Winnifred Kukull **Marital Status:** Married **Spouse Name:** Diane **Children:** Megan; Anthony; Benjamin **Education:** PhD in Epidemiology, University of Washington (1983); MS, Western Washington University (1974); BA, University of Washington (1971) **Career:** Professor of Epidemiology, Department of Epidemiology, University of Washington, Seattle, WA (1998-Present); Founding Director, National Alzheimer's Coordinating Center, University of Washington (1999-Present); Principal Investigator, Numerous National Institutes of Health Grants, Co-Principal Investigator, Alzheimer's Disease Patient Registry/ACT (1986-2000); Co-investigator, Alzheimer's Disease Research Center, University of Washington (1986-2000) **Career Related:** Member, Executive Committee, Alzheimer's Disease Genetics Consortium, University of Pennsylvania (2009-Present); Member, Executive Committee, National Cell Repository for Alzheimer's Disease, Indiana University (2009-Present); Member, External Advisory Board, Alzheimer's Disease Centers, Various Universities; Peer Reviewer, Numerous Study Sections, National Institutes of Health **Military Service:** U.S. Navy (1966-1969) **Creative Works:** Senior Associate Editor, "Alzheimer's and Dementia"; Editorial Board Member, "Alzheimer's Disease and Associate Disorders"; Reviewer, Numerous Journals; Contributor, Articles, Scientific Journals; Contributor, Abstracts, Scientific Journals; Contributor, Book Chapters; Invited Presenter, National and International Meetings **Awards:** Fellow, American Association for the Advancement of Science; Fellow, American College of Epidemiology; Fellow, American Academy of Neurology **Membership:** Society of Epidemiology Research; American Public Health Association; ASA; AAN; AAAS; American College of Epidemiology; Royal Society of Medicine **Marquis Who's Who Honors:** Albert Nelson Marquis Lifetime Achievement Award (2017) **Why did you become involved in your profession or industry:** Dr. Kukull really enjoyed and did well in research. **What do you consider to be the highlight of your career:** Dr. Kukull is most proud of his 18 years of involvement with the National Alzheimer's Coordination Center. He currently serves as the center's director. **Hobbies:** Music; Travel; Family **Shipping Address:** 17327 2nd Ave NW, Seattle, WA, 98177 **Website:** http://www.alz.washington.edu

Corinne Kyle

Title: Management Consultant **Industry:** Consulting **Date of Birth:** 01/04/1930 **Place of Birth:** New York **State:** NY **Parents:** Nathan Silverman; Janno (Harra) Silverman **Marital Status:** Divorced **Spouse Name:** Alec Kyle (8/29/1959, Divorced 2/1969) **Children:** Joshua; Perry (Deceased); Julia **Education:** MA, Harvard University (1953); BA, Bennington College (1950) **Career:** Survey Research Consultant (1999-2001); Associate, Krog & Partners, Inc. (1997-1999); Director of Research, George H. Gallup International Institute (1991-1997); Vice President, Response Analysis Corporation (1986-1991); Manager of Social Research, The Gallup Organization, Princeton, NJ (1982-1986); Vice President, Director of Research, Total Research Corporation, Princeton, NJ (1981-1982); Senior Associate, Periodical Studies Service, Inc. (1978-1981); Consultant, Program Planning and Control, Government Studies and Systems, Philadelphia, PA (1972-1978); Senior Associate, Government Studies and Systems, Philadelphia, PA (1970-1972); Founding Partner, The Philadelphia Group (1967-1970); Senior Research Associate, Marketing Science Institute, Inc., Philadelphia, PA (1964-1967); Research Analyst, McKinsey & Company, New York, NY (1963-1964); Co-Founder, The Financial Index Company, New York, NY (1960-1963); Chief Editor, The Financial Index Company, New York, NY (1960-1963); Associate Editor, The Inter-University Case Program, New York, NY (1956-1960) **Career Related:** Visiting Professor, Fairleigh Dickinson University (1993); Visiting Professor, Fairleigh Dickinson University (1990-1991); Lecturer on Research Methods, Temple University (1981-1982); West Orange Advocates **Civic:** Livingston Vision 20/20 Committee (2013-Present); Livingston Citizens Budget Advisory Committee (2013-2015); Institutional Review Board, Montclair State University (2011-2014); Essex County Democratic Committee, Inc. (2010-2012); Vice President, West Orange Board of Education (2007-2008); President, West Orange Board of Education (2004-2005); West Orange Board of Education (2002-2008); Chair, Princeton Regional Planning Board (1997-1999); Chair, OnePrinceton (1996-1997); Chair, Borough Task Force on Consolidation, Princeton, NJ (1995) **Creative Works:** Contributor, Articles, Professional Journals **Membership:** Citizens Budget Advisory Committee (2013-2015); West Orange Advocates **Marquis Who's Who Honors:** Albert Nelson Marquis Lifetime Achievement Award (2017); Distinguished Humanitarian (2017) **Shipping Address:** 104 E Cedar Street, Livingston, NJ, 07039

Lawrence Anthony LaJohn, PhD

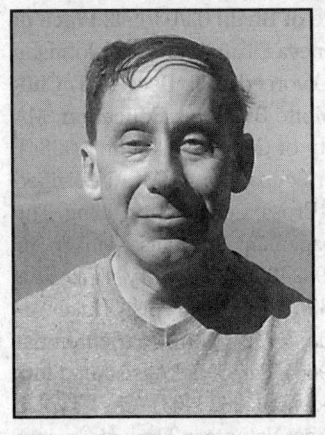

Title: Research Scientist **Industry:** Sciences **Company Name:** University of Pittsburgh **Date of Birth:** 04/23/1949 **Place of Birth:** Jamestown **State:** NY/USA **Parents:** Anthony Raymond LaJohn; Anne Theresa LaJohn **Education:** Postdoctoral Fellow, Department of Applied Mathematics, University of Western Ontario, London, ON, Canada (1990-1993); PhD in Theoretical Chemistry, Minor in Mathematics, Clarkson University (1990); MS in Theoretical Chemistry, Minor in Mathematics, Clarkson University (1988); Graduate Work, Queens University, Canada (1982-1984); Graduate Work, Southern Illinois University (1978-1982); Graduate Work, University of Notre Dame (1977-1978); MS in Biochemistry, George Washington University (1976); BA in Chemistry, Ohio Northern University (1971) **Career:** Research Scientist, Department of Physics and Astronomy, University of Pittsburgh, Pennsylvania (1993-Present); Research Assistant, Miles Laboratories, Elkhart, IN (1976-1977); Chemist, National Institutes of Health, Bethesda, MD (1972-1976) **Career Related:** Adjunct Physics Instructor, University of Pittsburgh; Adjunct Physics Instructor, Carnegie Mellon University; Adjunct Physics Instructor, Duquesne University; Adjunct Physics Instructor, CCAC **Creative Works:** Contributor, Articles, Physical Review A, Physical Review Letters, Journal of Physics A, Journal of Physics B, Journal of Chemical Physics, Chemical Physics Letters, and Journal of Theoretical Chemistry; Presenter, Results of Research, Conferences, DAMOP, ICPEAK, and ICAP **Membership:** American Chemical Society; American Mathematical Society; American Physical Society; Sigma Xi; Planetary Society **Why did you become involved in your profession or industry:** Dr. LaJohn became involved in his profession because he fell in love with what he was doing while working at his first research job at National Institutes of Health. **Where will you be in five years:** In five years, Dr. LaJohn would still like to be active in research and to continue teaching. **Hobbies:** Weightlifting; Bowling; BBQ ribs **Business Address:** 4227 5th Avenue, Pittsburgh, PA, 15213

Arline Joan LaMear

Title: Librarian, Writer, Mayor **Industry:** Library Management/Library Services **Company Name:** Columbia River Maritime Museum **Date of Birth:** 06/19/1939 **Place of Birth:** Yuma **State:** AZ/USA **Parents:** Arnold Jesse Bauska; Agnes Jean Bauska **Marital Status:** Married **Spouse Name:** Clifford Galen LaMear (7/24/1999); Charles Gordon Luton (Divorced) **Children:** Todd Luton; Scott Luton **Education:** MEd, James Madison University (1980); BA, Occidental College, Los Angeles, CA (1960) **Career:** Mayor, Astoria, OR (2015); Research Librarian, Columbia River Maritime Museum, Astoria, OR (1997-2016); School Librarian, Kings Park Elementary School, Springfield, VA (1976-1997); School Secretary, Kings Park Elementary School, Springfield, VA (1972-1976); Teacher, Wattana Academy, Bangkok, Thailand (1969-1970); Teacher, Public Schools, Fayetteville, NC (1962-1963); Teacher, Lighthouse Elementary School, Pacific Grove, CA (1960-1962) **Civic:** Astoria City Council (2008-Present); Astoria Planning Commission (2003-2008); Court Appointment Special Advocate (2001-2013); President, Virginia Educational Media Association (1995-1996); Virginia Delegate, White House Conference for Libraries and Information Services, Washington, DC (1991) **Creative Works:** Author, "Lewis & Clark: The Astoria Cats" (2002) **Membership:** President, Northern Coast Women's Political Caucus (2007-2008); Scholarship, American Association of University Women (2006); President, American Association of University Women (2005-2007); Secretary, Friends of Columbia River Maritime Museum (2003); Clatsop County Commission on Children and Families; Astoria Rotary **Marquis Who's Who Honors:** Distinguished Humanitarian (2017) **Hobbies:** Volkswalking; Travel **Political Affiliations:** Democrat **Religion:** Unitarian Universalist **Business Address:** 1792 Marine Drive, Astoria, OR, 97103 **Shipping Address:** 288 Franklin Avenue, Astoria, OR, 97103

Janet Allison LaMotte

Title: Management Consultant (Retired) **Industry:** Consulting **Date of Birth:** 03/03/1942 **Place of Birth:** Norfolk **State:** VA **Parents:** Dr. Charles Nelson Johnson Jr.; Geneva Elizabeth (Baird) Johnson **Marital Status:** Single **Spouse Name:** Larry LaMotte (8/30/1964, Divorced 1979, Deceased) **Children:** Lori Louise LaMotte Velasquez (Deceased); Lisa Renee LaMotte Buchholz **Education:** MA in Human Relations, University of Oklahoma (1986); BA, University of Central Oklahoma (1984); AA, Rose State College (1982) **Certifications:** Certified Open Water Scuba Diver, YMCA; Certified Advanced Swimming and Life Saving, The American National Red Cross; Certified in Sailing, The American National Red Cross **Career:** Worldwide Inventory Management Specialist, Tinker Air Force Base (1987-1998); Supply Specialist, Tinker Air Force Base (1982-1987); Secretary, Tinker Air Force Base (1981-1982); Accounting Clerk, Tinker Air Force Base (1980-1981); Clerk-Typist, Tinker Air Force Base (1979); Clerk-Typist, Defense Logistics Agency, Alexandria, VA (1978-1979); Procurement Clerk, Federal Aviation Administration, Oklahoma City, OK (1965-1966); Personnel Assistant, State Board of Control, Austin, TX (1964-1965); Secretary, IRS, Richmond, VA (1962-1963); Clerk-Typist, IRS, Dallas, TX (1962); Clerk-Typist, U.S. Army, Dallas, TX (1961) **Civic:** Volunteer, Findagrave.com (2011-2017); Volunteer, CONTACT Crisis Helpline (1986-1989); Safety Chairman, National PTA, Kensler Elementary School, Wichita, KS (1974-1975) **Awards:** Exceptional Service Award, Gerrity Chapter, Air Force Association (1998); Member of the Year Award, Oklahoma Air Force Association (1996); Exceptional Service Award, Air Force Association (1996); Medal of Merit Award, Air Force Association (1995); First Place, New Recruitment, Tinker Management Association (1994); Best Area Bulletin Award, K-3 Newsletter, Oklahoma State Toastmasters (1992-1993); Outstanding Service Award, Area K-3 Governor, Oklahoma State Toastmasters (1991-1992); Outstanding Education Vice President Award, Area K-3 Toastmasters (1988); Scholarships, Tinker Management Association (1981-1985) **Why did you become involved in your profession or industry:** Ms. LaMotte became involved in her career after being inspired by United States President John F. Kennedy, who spoke to graduating high school seniors in the DC area, encouraging them to pursue careers in government service. **What do you consider to be the highlight of your career:** One of the highlights of Ms. LaMotte's career was being a passenger on a training flight in a KC-135 tanker with the Kentucky Air National Guard while refueling F-16 Falcon Fighters over Kansas. **Religion:** United Methodist **Shipping Address:** 9525 Ridgeview Dr, Oklahoma City, OK, 73120

Elizabeth Jane Landerholm

Title: Education Educator **Industry:** Education/Educational Services **Company Name:** Northeastern Illinois University **Place of Birth:** Oak Park **State:** IL **Parents:** Daniel R. LaBar; Dorothy E. LaBar **Marital Status:** Married **Spouse Name:** Wayne A. Landerholm (6/6/1964) **Children:** Arthur Scott **Education:** EdD in Curriculum and Instruction, Northern Illinois University (1980); MS in Teaching, University of Chicago (1966); BA in Sociology, DePauw University (1963) **Certifications:** Certification, Luminous Energy Medicine, Four Winds Society (2014); Certified in Early Childhood Education, State of Illinois; Certified in Elementary Education, State of Illinois **Career:** Energy Healing Practitioner, Sacred Star Path (2014-Present); Educational Consultant, Children's Center of Cicero-Berwyn (2012-Present); Professor Emerita, Northeastern Illinois University (2012-Present); Founder, Sacred Star Path, Energy Healing (2014); Outreach Consultant, Northeastern Illinois University (2012-2014); Student Teaching Supervisor in the Republic of Korea, Northeastern Illinois University (2009-2012); Professor, Northeastern Illinois University (1993-2012); Associate Professor, Northeastern Illinois University (1986-1992); Project Director, Children's Development Center (1984-1986); Assistant Professor, Roosevelt University (1980-1983); Student Teaching Supervisor, National College of Education, National Louis University (1970-1979); Teacher, Chicago Board of Education (1966-1969) **Career Related:** Evaluator, Fulbright Hayes Study Abroad Group (2008-2009); Principal Investigator, Early Reading First Grant, U.S. Department of Education (2004-2008); Project Coordinator, Early Childhood Cohort, Illinois Professional Learning Partnerships (1999-2004); Project Director, McCosh Even Start (1994-2003); Therapist, The Theraplay Institute (1980-1984) **Civic:** Educational Consultant, Children's Center of Cicero-Berwyn (2012-Present); Outreach Consultant, Innovation Grant, Northeastern Illinois University (2012-2014) **Awards:** Fulbright Grant, Jamaica (2006-2009); Early Reading First Grant, Department of Education, Washington, DC (2004-2008); Illinois Professionals Learning Partnerships Grant (1999-2004); McCosh Even Start Grant, Illinois State Board of Education (1994-2003) **Marquis Who's Who Honors:** Albert Nelson Marquis Lifetime Achievement Award (2017) **Why did you become involved in your profession or industry:** Dr. Landerholm became inspired when she studied abroad for one year in Japan. **What do you consider to be the highlight of your career:** Seeing a student she mentored receive their PhD. **Hobbies:** Art **Shipping Address:** 1129 Robinhood Lane, LaGrange Park, IL, 60526

Diana J. Landes

Title: President **Industry:** Insurance **Company Name:** D&L Landes Company **Place of Birth:** Queens **State:** NY **Education:** MBA, Columbia University (1977); BA in Economics, University at Buffalo (1975) **Certifications:** Licensed Property and Casualty Insurance Broker, State of New York; Licensed Life and Health Insurance Broker, State of New York **Career:** Product Director, Johnson & Johnson Services, Inc. **Civic:** Volunteer, Local Police Department; Volunteer, University at Buffalo Foundation, Inc.; Volunteer, Affiliates, University at Buffalo Foundation, Inc. **Membership:** Columbia Business School Alumni Club of New York; Alumni Association, University at Buffalo; Alumni Association, Columbia University; Greater New York Chamber of Commerce **Marquis Who's Who Honors:** Albert Nelson Marquis Lifetime Achievement Award (2017) **To what do you attribute your success:** Ms. Landes attributes her success to her perseverance and business development skills. **Why did you become involved in your profession or industry:** Ms. Landes became involved in her profession because it was her father's business. **What do you consider to be the highlight of your career:** The highlight of Ms. Landes' career was working with church medical insurance committees. **Hobbies:** Listening to Music; Watching Movies; Reading **Business Address:** PO Box 20344, NY, New York, 10021 **Shipping Address:** 233 E 69th St Apt 10E, New York, NY, 10021

Diana Lennox Latta

Title: Interior Designer **Industry:** Other **Company Name:** Retired **Date of Birth:** 08/05/1936 **Place of Birth:** Lahaina **State:** HI **Parents:** Duncan Stewart; Jean Marjorie (Anderson) Lennox Sr. **Spouse Name:** Arthur McKee Latta (Married, 1/26/1957, Deceased 12/3/83) **Children:** Mary-Stewart; Marion McKee Latta de Vogel **Education:** Student, University of Washington, Seattle (1954-1956); Graduate, The Bishop's School, La Jolla, CA (1954) **Career:** Vice President, Secretary, Director, JADSL Corporation, Anacortes, WA (1999-Present); Senior Staff Designer, Chancellor's Inc., Bellingham, WA (1992-1993); Designer's Assistant, Frank J. Lincoln Interiors, Inc., Vero Beach, Locust Valley, New York (1987-1990); Owner, Designer, The Designery, Vero Beach (1983-1987); Design and Administrative Assistant to President, Design Studio Architectural & Interior Design Concepts, Inc., Vero Beach (1975-1982); Assistant to Senior Designer, Rablen-West Interiors, Vero Beach (1972-1975); Director, Vero Beach Branch of Wellington Hall Ltd., Thomasville, NC (1970-1972) **Civic:** Member, Key Leaders Board, Communities That Care Project, Edmonds School District, Washington (2001-2008); Council Member, Snohomish County Federated Health and Safety Network, Everett, WA (1999-2003); Advisory Committee, Safe and Drug Free Schools, Edmonds School District, Washington (1996-2002); Advisor to Steering Committee, The Malt Shoppe After School Program, Mill Creek, WA (1995-1997); Chairman, Mill Creek for Youth Committee, WA (1994); Founding Member, Indian River Land Trust, Vero Beach, FL, Vice-President and Treasurer (1989-1990) **Creative Works:** Leading Actress, "Oklahoma" (1966); Leading Actress, "The Laughmaker," Vero Beach Theatre Guild Productions (1964); Model, Holly Fashion Show, Vero Beach (1962-1969) **Awards:** Tennis Champion, Riomar Bay Yacht Club, Vero Beach (1966); Tennis Champion, Riomar Bay Yacht Club (1964) **Membership:** Asheville Area Alumnae Association, Kappa Kappa Gamma (2008-Present); McKee Botanical Garden, Vero Beach, FL, (2001-Present); Founding Member, N. Sound Alumnae Association, Kappa Kappa Gamma, Edmonds, WA (2002-Present); Advisory Board, University of Washington, Seattle Chapter, Kappa Kappa Gamma (1997-2000); Founding Member, Indian River Alumnae Club, Kappa Kappa Gamma, Vero Beach, FL (1968-1990); International Platform Association; Riomar Bay Yacht Club, Vero Beach, FL (1964-1990) **Hobbies:** Piano-playing/vocalizing; Books; Gardening; **Political Affiliations:** Republican **Religion:** Episcopalian **Shipping Address:** 509 Cokesbury Lane, Asheville, NC, 28803

Steven Lattimore, PhD

Title: Classicist (Retired) **Industry:** Education/Educational Services **Company Name:** University of California **Date of Birth:** 05/25/1938 **Place of Birth:** Bryn Mawr **State:** PA **Parents:** Richmond Lattimore; Alice Bockstahler Lattimore **Marital Status:** Single **Spouse Name:** Deborah Lee Nourse (7/14/1976, Divorced 7/1994) **Children:** Judith; Nicholas; Isabel **Education:** PhD, Princeton University (1968); MA, Princeton University (1964); BA, Dartmouth College (1960) **Career:** Professor Emeritus, University of California (2005-Present); Professor, University of California (1998-2006); Associate Professor, University of California, Los Angeles (1974-1998); Assistant Professor, University of California, Los Angeles (1967-1974); Assistant Professor, Intercollegiate Center for Classical Studies, Rome, Italy (1966-1967); Instructor, Haverford College, Haverford, PA (1965-1966); Instructor, Dartmouth College, Hanover, NH (1964) **Career Related:** Fellow, John Simon Guggenheim Memorial Foundation (1975-1976) **Civic:** Active Volunteer, Board Member, League of Women Voters, Ventura County, CA; Program Director, Organizing Public Forums, League of Women Voters, Ventura County, CA **Creative Works:** Translator, "Thucydides, Peloponnesian War" (1998); Author, "Isthmia Marble Sculpture" (1996); Author, "Marine Thiasos in Greek Sculpture" (1976); Author, "Isthmia Marble Sculpture" (1967-1980) **Awards:** Fellow, John Simon Guggenheim Memorial Foundation (1975-1976) **Membership:** Elected Member, German Archaeological Institute **Marquis Who's Who Honors:** Albert Nelson Marquis Lifetime Achievement Award (2017) **To what do you attribute your success:** The key to Dr. Lattimore's success was he was interdisciplinary in all different aspects. He had many specialties. **Why did you become involved in your profession or industry:** Dr. Lattimore's father inspired him, He was very close to him. When he became a scholar himself he respected his father even more and had more in common with him. When his father received as fellowship when he was 13-14, he took the whole family to Greece. **Where will you be in five years:** Dr. Lattimore will be continuing to enjoy retirement, and enjoy doing his good works and seeing his grandchild, family and good friends. **Hobbies:** Travel; Hiking **Political Affiliations:** Democrat **Religion:** Universalist Unitarian **Shipping Address:** 1146 Say Rd, Santa Paula, CA, 93060 **Website:** http://www.stevenlattimore.com

James Donald Lauter

Title: Stockbroker (Retired) **Industry:** Financial Services **Date of Birth:** 09/03/1931 **Place of Birth:** Los Angeles **State:** CA **Parents:** Richard Leo Lauter; Helen M. (Stern) Lauter **Marital Status:** Married **Spouse Name:** Neima Zwieli (2/24/1973) **Children:** Walter James (Deceased); Gary **Education:** BS, University of California, Los Angeles (1956) **Career:** Senior Vice President in Investments, Dean Witter Reynolds, Inc. (1961-1996); Branch Manager, Account Executive, Dean Witter Reynolds, Inc. (1961-1996); Account Executive Trainee, Dean Witter Reynolds, Inc. (1961); Market Research Manager, Germain's Inc. (1961) **Military Service:** US Army (1954-1956) **Awards:** Recipient, Sammy Award, Los Angeles Sales Executives Club (1961) **Membership:** President, Pasadena Bond Club (1995-1996); AARP; University of California, Los Angeles Alumni; Chancellor's Society; University of California, Los Angeles Fund; Bruin Athletic Club; Bruin Varsity Club; El Caballero Country Club **Marquis Who's Who Honors:** Albert Nelson Marquis Lifetime Achievement Award (2017) **Why did you become involved in your profession or industry:** Mr. Lauter started investing when he was 16. He had heard that Dean Witter wanted to hire brokers with sales backgrounds, and he the necessary experience with sales. It was how he won the Sammy Award when he was with Germain's Inc. for 5 years. He then went directly to Dean Witter because of the company's reputation for integrity, and worked there for 35 years. **What do you consider to be the highlight of your career:** Mr. Lauter's career highlights while at Dean Witter were when he attended training class in 1966; when he was ranked 3rd in volume in the country, and when he was promoted to vice president of the company. Outside of work, his three grandchildren make him very proud. **Hobbies:** Golf; Reading; Family time **Shipping Address:** 3717 Marfield Ave, Tarzana, CA, 91356

David J. Leciston

Title: Computer Engineer, Computer Scientist **Industry:** Sciences **Company Name:** U.S. Army **Date of Birth:** 12/25/1958 **Place of Birth:** Passaic **State:** NJ **Parents:** Alex Leciston; Rose (Kozmoski) Leciston **Marital Status:** Married **Spouse Name:** Deborah Ann Owens (12/30/1999); Wendie Sue Orr (2/3/1987, Divorced 10/1998); Diane Carol Hirth (6/19/1981, Divorced 4/1985) **Children:** Jennifer Ann; David Jonathan; Mary Rose **Education:** BS in Computer Science, Seton Hall University (1982) **Career:** Program Executive Officer, Intelligence and Electronic Ware and Sensors, Project Manager Distributed Common Ground System, U.S. Army, Computer Engineer, Aberdeen Proving Ground, MD (2010-Present); Project Manager, Distributed Common Ground Systems, U.S. Army (2005-2010); Computer Engineer, Communications-Electronics Command, Software Engineering Center, U.S. Army, Fort Monmouth, NJ (2001-2005); Computer Scientist, Communications-Electronics Command, Research and Development Engineering Center, Software Engineering Directorate, Fort Monmouth, NJ (1989-2001); Computer Scientist, Communications-Electronics Command, Research and Development Engineering Center, Software Engineering Directorate, Fort Huachuca, AZ (1987-1989) **Military Service:** First Lieutenant, U.S. Army (1983-1987) **Awards:** Secretary of the Army Award for Outstanding Achievement in Materiel Acquisition (1997, 1991) **Membership:** Initiative on Software Engineering as a Profession (1994-Present); Life and Senior Member, Association for Computing Machinery; Life Member, Armed Forces Communications-Electronics Association; Senior Member, IEEE **To what do you attribute your success:** Mr. Leciston attributes his success to parents that supported his interests. **Why did you become involved in your profession or industry:** Mr. Leciston became involved in his profession because of his interest in mathematics, science, and history. **What do you consider to be the highlight of your career:** Mr. Leciston is most proud of continuing to field improvements to system concepts he started over 30 years ago. **Hobbies:** Tabletop role-playing games; Tabletop historical wargames; Computers **Religion:** Catholic **Shipping Address:** 105 Deerfield Rd Apt F, Elkton, MD, 21921

Deokwoo Lee, PhD

Title: Professor **Industry:** Education/Educational Services **Company Name:** Youngsan University **Place of Birth:** Daegu **Country of Origin:** Republic of Korea **Marital Status:** Married **Education:** PhD in Electrical Engineering, North Carolina State University (2012); BEE in Electrical Engineering and Computer Science, Kyungpook National University, Republic of Korea (2007) **Career:** Assistant Professor, Youngsan University (2016-Present); Senior Researcher, Samsung Electronics (2013-2016); Postdoctoral Research Associate, Washington University in St. Louis (2013) **Military Service:** Sergeant, Republic of Korea Army (2002-2004) **Awards:** Galaxy S5 Contribution Award, Division of Mobile Communications, Samsung Electronics (2014) **Membership:** IEEE; The Korean Society of Automotive Engineers; Korea Multimedia Society; The Institute of Electronics, Information, and Communication Engineers; The Korean Institute of Communications and Information Sciences **To what do you attribute your success:** Dr. Lee always tries to understand any problem in an easy and simple way. That is how he can be involved in every task or project in an optimistic mood. **Why did you become involved in your profession or industry:** Dr. Lee has always wanted to model the world in a mathematical way. Other interests of his include geometric perspectives, image processing, and signal processing. His research involves trying to efficiently process and represent high-dimensional data. **Hobbies:** Reading history and culture; Running; Badminton **Religion:** Roman Catholic **Business Address:** 142, Bansong-dong, 142, Bansong-dong, INTL, Haeundae-gu, Busan, Korea South, 48015 **Shipping Address:** 204-4702, POSCO The Sharp Centum Park Apts, Jaesong-Dong, Haeundae-Gu, Busan, South, Korea 48050

Frances Lee

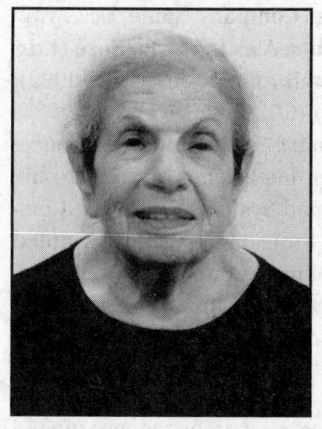

Title: Editor **Industry:** Writing and Editing **Date of Birth:** 01/06/1936 **Place of Birth:** New York City **State:** NY **Parents:** Murray Lee; Rose (Rothman) Lee **Education:** MA, New York University (1962); BA, Queens College, CUNY (1957) **Career:** Freelance Editor, Consultant (1988-Present); Editor, American Druggist Blue Book (1982-1988); Editor, New Price Report (1982-1984); Special Projects Coordinator, Motor Manuals, Hearst Book Division (Now Hearst Communications Inc.) (1981-1982); Editor, American Druggist Blue Book, Hearst Books/Business Publications Group (Now Hearst Communications Inc.) (1980-1981); Directory Editor, Photographic Division, United Business Publications, New York, NY (1971-1980); With, Industrial Water Engineering Magazine, New York, NY (1969-1971); With, American Electric Power Service Corp., AEP Operating Ideas, New York, NY (1966-1969); With, Gordon & Breach Science Publishers, Inc., New York, NY (1964-1966); **Civic:** Information Project Manager (2001-Present); Volunteer, New York City Opera (1988-Present); Chairman, Committee on New York City Cultural Concerns (1997-1998); Board of Directors, Co-chairman, Committee on New York City Cultural Concerns (1979-1997); Committee on City Management (1977-1992); Committee on New York City Charter, Revision Citizens Union (1975); Supervisor, Bronx Division, New York State Civil Defense (1953-1959) **Awards:** Meritorious Service Award (1986); Certificate of Honor, New York University Alumni Association (1985) **Membership:** Director Emerita, New York University Alumni Association (2007-Present); Secretary, East End Temple Sisterhood (2008-2014); Treasurer, Villa-Lobos Music Society (1992-1995); Secretary, New York Business Press Editors (1990-1991); Secretary, Villa-Lobos Music Society (1989-1991); Board of Directors, New York Business Press Editors (1988-1990); Board of Governors, New York University Club (1987-1989); Representative to Board of Directors, Federation, New York University Alumni Club (1984-1986); President, New York University Alumni Club (1982-1984); Vice President, New York University Alumni Club (1980-1982); Recording Secretary, New York University Alumni Club (1978-1980); Director, New York University Alumni Club (1976-1978); Chairman, Research Committee, Women's Equity Action League; New York Business Press Editors **Political Affiliations:** Republican **Religion:** Jewish **Shipping Address:** 170 2nd Avenue, Apartment 3E, New York, NY, 10003

Nelda S. Lee

Title: Art Appraiser **Industry:** Fine Art **Date of Birth:** 07/03/1941 **Place of Birth:** Gorman **State:** TX **Parents:** Olan C. Lee; Onis Lee **Children:** Jeanna Lea Pool **Education:** Coursework, University of Southern California (2000); Postgraduate Coursework, San Miguel de Allende Art Institute, Mexico (1965); Postgraduate Coursework, Texas Tech University (1964); BA in Fine Arts, University of North Texas (1963); AS, Tarleton State University (1961); Coursework, Texas Woman's University (1959-1960) **Certifications:** Certified Personal Property Appraiser, American Society of Appraisers (1972) **Career:** Self-Employed, Art Galleries Business (1967-Present); Head, Art Department, Ector High School, Odessa, TX (1963-1968) **Career Related:** Board of Directors, North American Art Exchange (1979-1980); Ector County Committee **Civic:** Board of Directors, Odessa Art Museum (1979-Present); Chairperson, Acquisition Committee, Odessa Art Museum (1979-Present); Odessa Appointee, Texas Commission for the Arts (1993-1995); Board of Directors, Ector County Cultural Center, Texas Business Hall of Fame (1980-1985) **Creative Works:** Exhibitor, Group Shows, El Paso, TX; Exhibitor, Group Shows, New Orleans, LA; Artist, Exhibitions in Mexico; Artist, Exhibitions in the United States; Contributor, Articles, Professional Journals **Awards:** State Area Award, YMCA of Odessa (2001): Honoree, Presenter for President Carter's Inauguration, Texas State Society (1977); Lifetime Membership for Outstanding Community Service, Odessa Chamber of Commerce (1969); Presenter, Special Award, YMCA of Odessa (1968); Designer-Craftsman Award, El Paso Museum of Fine Arts (1964); Honoree, Dean's List, Tarleton State University (1960-1961); Student Grant, Franklin Lindsay Foundation (1959-1962) **Membership:** Appraisers Association of America (1978-Present); Appraisers of Fine Arts Society (1978-Present); Century Club, Tarleton State University (1981); Senior Member, American Society of Appraisers (1980); President, National Texas Association of Art Dealers (1978-1988); Associate Member, American Society of Appraisers (1970-1972) **Marquis Who's Who Honors:** Albert Nelson Marquis Lifetime Achievement Award (2017) **Why did you become involved in your profession or industry:** Ms. Lee became involved in her profession after art dealers came to her to get her art appraised. **Shipping Address:** PO Box 14438, Odessa, TX, 79768

Raya Lee

Title: Librarian, Storyteller **Industry:** Library Management/Library Services **Company Name:** Medaille College **Date of Birth:** 03/14/1950 **Place of Birth:** Brooklyn **State:** NY **Parents:** George Schwartz; Ruth Schwartz **Children:** Franz Michael Then **Education:** Master of Music Librarianship, School of Information & Library Science, State University of New York, Buffalo (1977); Applied Bachelor of Music in Piano, State University of New York, Fredonia (1972) **Certifications:** Certified Suzuki Piano Teacher, Chautauqua Institute (1979); Certified Music Librarian, State Education Department, Albany, NY (1977) **Career:** Reference Librarian/Instructor, Medaille College (2009-Present); Librarian, Buffalo & Erie County Public Library (1974-Present); Music Librarian Chelsea Music Festival, NY (2016); Lecturer, New York Council Humanities (2007-2016); Music Librarian, Buffalo Philharmonic Orchestra, NY (1976-1979) **Career Related:** Buffalo Philharmonic Orchestra; Buffalo Philharmonic Chorus; Ars Nova Chamber Orchestra; Lake Placid Sinfonietta; Ithaca Community Orchestra; Binghamton Community Orchestra; Picadilly Symphony Orchestra; Theatre Figuren; Lecturer, Cornell University; Lecturer, Haydn Haus Vienna; Lecturer, Skidmore College; Lecturer, SUNY Albany; Lecturer, Italian Conference University of California, Los Angeles; Lecturer, Popular Music Conference, Rome Italy; Lecturer, Buffalo History Museum; Lecturer, Buffalo Naval Museum; Alto, Sing Mit Chorus, Haydn's Creation, St. Stephen's Cathedral, Vienna; Alto, Verdi's Requiem, Carnegie Hall, NY **Civic:** Archive Assistant, Kleinhans Music Hall (2015); Archive Assistant, Buffalo Philharmonic Chorus (2012); Education Committee Member, Buffalo Philharmonic Orchestra (1997-2017) **Creative Works:** Co-author with Edward Yadzinski, "Buffalo Philharmonic Orchestra: The BPO Celebrates the First 75 Years" (2010); Author, "Pan American Exposition: A Birds-Eye View of Sights and Sounds" (2001); Co-author with Edward Yadzinski (Article), "Kleinhans Music Hall and the BPO, A Story Told in Stereo" **Awards:** City of Buffalo Common Council, in Recognition of Public Library Service to the Community for 32 Years **Membership:** Society of Children's Book Authors & Illustrators; New York Chapter, Music Library Association; Librarians Union, Buffalo & Erie County Public Library **Hobbies:** Piano; Gardening **Shipping Address:** 87 Highland Drive, Williamsville, NY, 14221

Jeffrey Legum

Title: Holding Company Executive **Industry:** Business Management/Business Services **Date of Birth:** 12/16/1941 **Place of Birth:** Baltimore **State:** MD **Parents:** Leslie Legum; Naomi (Hendler) Legum **Marital Status:** Married **Spouse Name:** Harriet Cohn (11/10/1968) **Children:** Laurie Hope; Michael Neil **Education:** Diplomate, Chevrolet School of Merchandising and Management (1966); BS in Economics, The Wharton School, University of Pennsylvania (1963) **Career:** President, Professional Corporation Parts Company (1995-Present); Chief Executive Officer, Park Circle Company, DBA Park Circle Investments (1982-Present); President, Park Circle Company, DBA Park Circle Investments (1977-Present); Vice President, Director, Professional Corporation Parts Company (1967-Present); Employee, Park Circle Company, DBA Park Circle Investments, Baltimore, MD (1963-Present); Partner, Circle Limited Partnership, Glen Burnie, MD (1991-1999); President, Director, Legum Chevrolet-Nissan (1977-1989); President, Chief Executive Officer, Westminster Motor Company (1973-1997); President, One-Forty Corporation, Westminster, MD (1972-1997); Executive Vice President, Park Circle Company, DBA Park Circle Investments (1966-1977); Partner, Parkway Industrial Center, Dorsey, MD (1965-1991) **Career Related:** Chairman, Washington Zone (1982-1983); District Chairman, Chevrolet Dealers Council (1975-1977); Director, Executive Committee, United Consolidated Industries (1970-1973) **Civic:** Emeritus Trustee, John Hopkins Medicine (2013-Present); Fine Arts Accessions Committee, The Baltimore Museum of Art (2011-Present); Honorary Trustee, The Baltimore Museum of Art (2011-Present); Governor Member, Baltimore Symphony Orchestra (2010-Present); Executive Committee, The Baltimore Museum of Art (2006-Present); Investment Committee, Baltimore Hebrew Congregation (2002-Present); Trustee, Member, Financial Committee, Johns Hopkins Medical Institutes (1997-Present); Investment Committee, The Baltimore Museum of Art (1992-Present); Board of Governors, John's Hopkins Hospital - Wilmer Eye Institute (1991-Present) **Awards:** Honoree, Baltimore Hebrew Congregation Night of the Stars (2018); Eponym, Jeffrey Legum Day, Baltimore County Executive (2016); Recipient, Gold, Young Presidents' Organization (2016); Honoree, Minute of Gratitude, The Park School Board of Trustees (1994); Recipient, Philanthropy Leadership Award, Associated Endowment Fund (1993); Recipient, Cadillac Master Dealer Award (1991) **Membership:** Gold Member, Young Presidents Organization (1989-Present) **Business Address:** 1829 Reisterstown Rd, Baltimore, MD, 21208

Stephen Leuchtman, Esq.

Title: Lawyer **Industry:** Law and Legal Services **Company Name:** Bauchan Law Offices, P.C. **Date of Birth:** 10/14/1945 **Place of Birth:** Detroit **State:** MI **Parents:** Alexis C. Leuchtman; Frances J. (Boucher) Leuchtman **Marital Status:** Married **Spouse Name:** Jacque Ward (11/29/1991) **Children:** Stephen; John II; Lucinda **Education:** JD, University of Michigan (1970); BA, University of Michigan (1967) **Career:** Counsel, Bauchan Law Offices, P.C. (2001-Present); Attorney, Stephen N. Leuchtman, P.C., Detroit, MI (2001-Present); Counsel, Trowbridge Law Firm PC (2009-2015); Counsel, Ravid & Associates, P.C. (2005-2009); Founding Partner, Trowbridge Law Firm PC, Detroit, MI (1997-2001); Partner, Sommers, Schwartz, Silver & Schwartz, Southfield, MI (1980-1997); Associate, Tyler & Canham, Detroit, MI (1975-1980); Associate, Eggenberger, Eggenberger, McKinney & Weber, Detroit, MI (1970-1975) **Creative Works:** Contributor, Articles, Professional Journals **Membership:** ABA; Association of Trial Lawyers of America; American Board of Trial Advocates; Million Dollar Advocates Forum, LLC; State Bar of Michigan **Bar Admissions:** California (1993); United States Court of Appeals for the Sixth Circuit (1982); Michigan (1970); United States District Court for the Eastern District of Michigan (1970) **Hobbies:** Writing; Travel **Political Affiliations:** Democrat **Business Address:** 32100 Telegraph Rd Ste 200, Bingham Farms, MI, 48025 **Website:** http://www.leuchlaw.com

Winston Zai-Yang Li

Title: Language Educator **Industry:** Education/Educational Services **Date of Birth:** 10/22/1941 **Place of Birth:** Chengdu, Sichuan **Country of Origin:** China **Parents:** Yang-Han Li; Lian-Jing Wu Li **Marital Status:** Married **Spouse Name:** Dong-Yn Cathy Chiu **Children:** Timothy Cohen Leigh (Tianhai); Tianxu Li; Chiu-Fun Jennifer Chen **Education:** Diplomate, Oral Proficiency Interview Assessment Workshop for Chinese, Bemidji State University (2009); Coursework in Chinese Language Pedagogy, East Asian Languages and Cultural Studies, University of California, Santa Barbara (2006); Coursework, Summer Study Abroad Program, Beijing Language and Culture University, Beijing, China (2002); Diplomate in Accelerated Language Programs, Dartmouth College (1994); BA in Motion Picture and Video, Brooks Institute of Photography (1988); Diplomate in Performing Arts, Shanghai Film Academy (1962); **Career:** Director of International Development, Brooks Institute (2015-Present); President's Council, Brooks Institute (2015-Present); Special Envoy, Montanan Tech (2014-2015); International & Alumni Outreach, Brooks Institute (2013); Language Instructor, Cate School (1994-2013); Instructor in School Life Photography, Cate School (1994-1995); General Manager, Tony Rose Camera and Video (1993); General Coordinator, Brooks Institute (1991-1993); Assistant Professor, Brooks Institute (1990) **Career Related:** Adviser, North American Journal of Chinese Learning (2003-Present); Educational Adviser, National Young Leaders Conference (2005-2013) **Civic:** Volunteer, Chinese-American Community Board Meetings **Creative Works:** Leading Actor, "Returning Country Home" (1983); Actor, "Tiny Tot" (1983); Actor "Fire for a Send-off" (1982); Actor, "Happiness Sower" (1981); Actor, "Flying to Pacific Ocean" (1981); Actor, Films **Awards:** Honorary Shanghai Film Performing Artist Award (2016); Honorary Montana Citizen Award (2009); Educators in Digital Starlight Award (2003); Fulbright-Hays Scholarship, U.S. Department of Education (2002); Scholarship, Brooks Institute (1985-1989); Scholarship, UC Santa Barbara (1984-1985); Flying Apsaras Award, Ministry of Culture, People's Republic of China (1982) **Membership:** Board of Directors, Calligraphy Education Group, The Chinese Language Teachers Association (2001-Present); Association for Asian Studies (2001-Present); Executive Committee, Santa Barbara Chinese American Association (2001-Present); Executive Committee, East Asian Calligraphy Education Association (2001-Present); Chinese Language Association of Secondary-Elementary Schools (1994-Present) **Marquis Who's Who Honors:** Albert Nelson Marquis Lifetime Achievement Award (2017) **Shipping Address:** 5332 Parejo Dr, Santa Barbara, CA, 93111

Bruce Jared Lish

Title: Dentist **Industry:** Medicine & Health Care **Date of Birth:** 06/27/1969 **Parents:** Jerome Lish; Marion Lish **Marital Status:** Married **Spouse Name:** Cindy Michelle Rosenblum-Lish (8/15/1993) **Children:** Matthew; Jessica **Education:** DDS, New York University College of Dentistry (1994); BA in Biology, College of Arts & Science, New York University (1991) **Certifications:** Dental and Oral Surgery, Brookdale University Hospital Medical Center (1996) **Career:** Director, Division of Dentistry, Mount Sinai St. Luke's, Roosevelt Hospital (Now Mount Sinai West), New York, NY (2000-Present); Surgical Course Instructor, American and Canadian Technical Support 3M/IMTEC Implants (2000-Present); Private Practice, General & Implant Dentistry, Brooklyn, NY (1995-Present); Clinical Assistant Professor, Department of Pediatric Dentistry, New York University College of Dentistry (2008-2014); Clinical Assistant Professor, College of Dental Medicine, Columbia University (2000-2014); Residency Director, General Practice Program, Brookdale University Hospital Center, Brooklyn, NY (1998-2000); Clinical Assistant Professor, New York University College of Dentistry, New York, NY (1996-1998) **Civic:** Board of Directors, Areyvut (2010-Present); Founder, Dr. Molar Magic Foundation (2005-Present); Board of Directors, Dr. Molar Magic Foundation (2005-Present); Performer, Community Service Provider, Clown Doctor Program (1994-Present); **Creative Works:** Creator, Educational Dental Program, Dr. Molar Magic Show (1993-Present); Author, Chapter Five, "Mini Dental Implants Principles and Practice" (2012); Author, "Back For Seconds, Circus Bicuspid" (2012); Author, "Almost on Broadway, Circus Bicuspid" (2011); Creator, "Boss Clown, Circus Bicuspid," Family Entertainment (2010); Publisher, Magic Builder's Monthly (2000-2003); Author, "Sunday In The Park With Clowns, Circus Bicuspid" **Membership:** International Brotherhood of Magicians (2016-Present); American Academy of Pediatric Dentistry (2003-Present); Academy of General Dentistry (1996-Present); American Dental Association (1995-Present); Second District Dental Society (1995-Present); Society of American Magicians (1989-Present); Secretary-Treasurer, American Society of Dentistry for Children (2000-2001); New Dentist Committee, Second District Dental Society (1998-1999); Chapter President, Society of American Magicians (1998); American Society of Dentistry for Children (1995-2003); American Academy of Implant Dentistry **Marquis Who's Who Honors:** Albert Nelson Marquis Lifetime Achievement Award (2017) **Religion:** Jewish **Business Address:** 7224 Ave. T, Brooklyn, NY, 11234 **Shipping Address:** 7347 183rd St, Fresh Meadows, NY, 11366

Sylvia Elizabeth Little-Sweat

Title: Literature and Language Professor **Industry:** Education/Educational Services **Company Name:** Wingate University **Date of Birth:** 08/16/1941 **Place of Birth:** Monroe **State:** NC **Parents:** Joseph Dwight Pierce; Mary Juel Sheets **Marital Status:** Widowed **Spouse Name:** Samuel T. Sweet, Jr. **Children:** Wesley Lee Little; Ashley Elizabeth Bledsoe **Education:** ArtsD, Middle Tennessee State University, Murfreesboro, TN (1983); MA in English, University of North Carolina, Chapel Hill (1965); BA in English, University of North Carolina, Chapel Hill (1963); AA, Wingate College, North Carolina (1961) **Career:** Writer-in-Residence at Wingate University (2017-Present); Professor of English, Wingate University (1963-2018) **Career Related:** Symposium Presentations; Poetry Readings; Speeches **Creative Works:** Author, "The Goose River Anthology Coffee Table Book" (2012-2015); Author, "Montage: Memory and Metaphor, Poems" (2012); Author, "Crossing Boundaries: Words and Images" (2012); Co-Composer, "The Way Home" (2010); Author, "The Chalk Dust Chronicle: A Centennial Celebration, 1896-1996" (1996); Author, "Portrait on Pablo Aruda (Nobel Peace Prize)" **Awards:** Alumni Excellence in Service Award (2012); The Charles and Hazel Corts Award for Excellence in Teaching, Wingate University (2003); History Award, "The Chalk Dust Chronicle: A Centennial Celebration," Wingate University (1996); Spivey Instructorship (1995); Presidential Meritorious Service Award (1992); Phi Eta Sigma Teacher of the Year (1986); Delta Kappa Gamma (1986); Outstanding Young Women of America (1966); Phi Beta Kappa (1963); Outstanding Teachers in America (Multiple Years) **Membership:** DKGSI (1986-Present) **Hobbies:** Travel; Music; Cooking; **Political Affiliations:** Democrat **Religion:** Baptist **Shipping Address:** PO Box 342, Wingate, NC, 28174

Frederic H. Livingston

Title: Associate Principal **Industry:** Engineering **Company Name:** R. G. Vanderweil Engineers **Date of Birth:** 02/17/1948 **Place of Birth:** Bryn Mawr **State:** PA **Parents:** William Henry Livingston; Joan Holleyman Livingston **Marital Status:** Married **Spouse Name:** Christine Ann Dalrymple (9/15/1979) **Children:** Jason Matthew; Corey Bradford **Education:** BSME, Pennsylvania State University (1970) **Certifications:** Registered Professional Engineer, LEED Associated Press BD+C (2011); Registered Professional Engineer, LEED Accredited Professional (2009); Registered Professional Engineer, State of Nevada (2005); Registered Professional Engineer, State of Massachusetts (1981); Registered Professional Engineer, State of Pennsylvania (1978) **Career:** Associate Principal, Project Manager, R. G. Vanderweil Engineers, Boston, MA (1984-Present); HVAC Engineer, Charles T. Main, Boston, MA (1981-1984); HVAC Engineer, Kling Lindquist, Philadelphia, PA (1972-1981) **Awards:** Citation for Excellence in Federal Building Design for an EPA Building Project, General Services Administration (2002) **Membership:** American Society of Heating, Refrigeration and Air Conditioning Engineers (ASHRAE); American Society of Plumbing Engineers (ASPE) **Marquis Who's Who Honors:** Albert Nelson Marquis Lifetime Achievement Award (2017); Distinguished Humanitarian (2017) **To what do you attribute your success:** Mr. Livingston attributes his success to working well with people and listening. **Religion:** Episcopalian **Business Address:** 274 Summer St Bsmt, 274, Boston, MA, 02210

Mary LaVerne Loman, PhD

Title: Mathematics Professor (Retired) **Industry:** Education/Educational Services **Company Name:** University of Central Oklahoma **Date of Birth:** 06/10/1928 **Place of Birth:** Stratford **State:** OK **Marital Status:** Widowed **Spouse Name:** Coy E. Loman (12/23/1944, Deceased 1996) **Children:** Sandra Leigh; Loman Easton **Education:** PhD, University of Oklahoma (1961); MA, University of Oklahoma (1957); BS, University of Oklahoma (1956) **Career:** Professor Emeritus, University of Central Oklahoma (1993-Present); Professor, University of Central Oklahoma (1966-1993); Associate Professor, University of Central Oklahoma (1962-1966); Assistant Professor of Mathematics, University of Central Oklahoma (1961-1962); Graduate Assistant, Instructor, University of Oklahoma (1956-1961) **Awards:** Fellow, National Science Foundation (1965-1967) **Membership:** Vice President, Oklahoma Council of Teachers of Mathematics (1972-1976); Mathematical Association of America; National Council of Teachers of Mathematics; Higher Education Alumni Council of Oklahoma; Veterans of Foreign War Auxiliary National Organization; Delta Kappa Gamma **Shipping Address:** 300 Hadwiger Ave, Apt 226, Edmond, OK, 73034

Eugene F. Loveland

Title: Gas Industry Executive **Industry:** Oil & Energy **Company Name:** Transworld Oil USA, Inc. **Date of Birth:** 09/11/1920 **Place of Birth:** Anderson **State:** IN **Parents:** Irving Eugene Loveland; Clare (Macfarlane) Loveland **Spouse Name:** Joan King (8/4/1944) **Children:** Jeffrey; David C.; Peter F.; Mark; Laurie E. **Education:** BA, Wesleyan University, Middletown, CT **Career:** President, Transworld Oil USA, Inc., Houston, TX (1981-Present); Chairman, Chief Executive Officer, T.W. Oil Inc. (1983-1989); Vice President of Oil Products, Shell Oil Co., Houston, TX (1972-1980); Vice President, Central Marketing Region, Shell Oil Co. (1968-1971); Shell Oil Co. (1946-1980) **Career Related:** Board of Directors, Transworld Oil Ltd., Bermuda **Civic:** Chairman, Greater Houston Ice Skating Council (1989-Present); Director, Cultural Arts Council of Houston (1989-1993); Executive Committee, Houston International Festival (1992); Chairman, Development Commission, Fay School (1992); Board of Directors, Lyric Theatre, Houston, TX; American Dance Companies Chairman, Houston Ballet Foundation; Combined Arts Corporation Campaign, Houston, TX; **Military Service:** U.S. Naval Reserve (1943-1945) **Awards:** National Order of Merit, Country of Malta (2003); Distinguished Alumnus Award, Wesleyan University (1993); Decorated Distinguished Flying Cross; Two Air Medals **Membership:** Military and Hospitaller Order of St. Lazarus of Jerusalem **Shipping Address:** 4718 Hallmark Drive, Apt. 1002, Houston, TX, 77056

Herbert Augustus Lubs

Title: Professor Emeritus, Administrator, Genetics Educator **Industry:** Education/Educational Services **Company Name:** University of Miami **Date of Birth:** 01/07/1929 **Marital Status:** Married **Spouse Name:** Betty Lou Lubs (1999) **Education:** Chief Resident, Yale-New Haven Hospital, Connecticut (1959-1960); Resident in Medicine, Yale-New Haven Hospital (1957-1959); Intern, Yale-New Haven Hospital (1954-1955); MD, Yale University (1954); BA, Washington and Lee University (1950) **Career:** Professor Emeritus, University of Miami School of Medicine (2004-Present); Professor, Genetics, University of Troms, Norway (1992-1999); Professor, Department of Pediatrics, University of Miami School of Medicine, Florida (1979-2004); Director, Genetics Division, Mailman Center for Child Development, University of Miami School of Medicine, Florida (1979-2004); Associate Professor, Department Biophysics and Genetics, University of Colorado Medical Center, Denver, CO (1973-1979); Associate Professor, Department of Pediatrics, University of Colorado Medical Center, Denver, CO (1968-1979); Director, Yale Private Diagnostic Clinic, New Haven, CT (1964-1966); Assistant Professor of Medicine, Chief, Medicine Genetics Section, Yale School of Medicine, New Haven, CT (1963-1967); Clinical Investigator, VA Hospital, West Haven, CT (1960-1963); Instructor, Medicine, Yale School of Medicine, New Haven, CT (1959-1963); Special Trainee in Research and Genetics, National Institutes of Health, Department of Human Genetics, University of Michigan, Department of Biology, Yale University (1957-1963); Clinical Associate, Endocrinology Branch, National Cancer Institute, U.S. Public Health Service, Bethesda, MD (1955-1957) **Career Related:** Human Subjects Executive Review Committee, University of Miami School of Medicine (1984-Present); Co-Founder, Research Endowment, The Science Society and the Arts Conference (2017) **Civic:** NICHD Collaborative Study on Chorionic Villus Sampling and Amniocentesis (1984-Present); Site Visit Committees and Ad Hoc Review Committees, National Institutes of Health (1979-Present) **Awards:** Joseph P. Kennedy, Jr. International Award for Research in Mental Retardation (1986); Career Development Award, U.S. Public Health Service (1963-1973); **Membership:** Board of Directors, Genetic Services Committee, American Society of Human Genetics (1985-Present) **Marquis Who's Who Honors:** Albert Nelson Marquis Lifetime Achievement Award (2017); Distinguished Humanitarian (2017) **Hobbies:** Photography; Reading **Shipping Address:** 1055 W Joppa Rd., Unit 322, Towson, MD, 21204

Priscilla Mark Luce

Title: Non-Profit Consultant, Arts Management, Public Relations Executive **Industry:** Business Management/Business Services **Place of Birth:** New York **State:** NY **Parents:** S. Carl Mark; Patricia (Greenfield) Mark **Marital Status:** Divorced **Spouse Name:** Robert Warren Luce (7/19/1969, Divorced 2007) **Children:** James Warren Luce; David Mark Luce **Education:** BA, University of Pennsylvania **Career:** Executive Managing Director, Philadelphia Theatre Company (2013-2017); Consultant, Non-Profit Organizations (2003-2013); Vice President of Corporate Communications, TRW Inc. (2001-2003); Vice President of Marketing and Organization Communications, TRW Inc. (1994-2001); Vice President of TRW Information System and Services Communications, TRW Inc. (1992-1994); Director of Public Affairs and Advertising, TRW Inc., Cleveland, OH (1990-1992); Manager, External Communications, TRW Inc., Cleveland, OH (1988-1990); Manager, Community Relations, TRW Inc., Cleveland, OH (1985-1988); Manager, Civic Programs, TRW Inc., Cleveland, OH (1982-1985); Vice President, Barnes & Roche Inc., Philadelphia, PA (1971-1982); Assistant Director of Public Information, Mount Holyoke College, South Hadley, MA (1969-1971); President, The Albert M. Greenfield Foundation **Civic:** Member, Board of Visitors, Division of General, Thoracic and Fetal Surgery, Children's Hospital of Philadelphia (2017-Present); Board Member, Greater Philadelphia Cultural Alliance (2017-Present); President, The Albert M. Greenfield Foundation, Philadelphia, PA (1998-Present); Chairman, Development Committee, Cleveland State University Foundation (1998-2004); Trustee, The Albert M. Greenfield Foundation, Philadelphia, PA (1989-Present); Trustee, Cleveland State University Foundation (1996-2008); President, Philadelphia Theatre Company (2010-2014); Chairman, Ad Hoc Strategic Planning Committee, Philadelphia Theatre Company (2008); Trustee, Philadelphia Theatre Company (2007-2014); Chairman, Cleveland State University Foundation (2004-2008); Vice Chairman, Cleveland State University Foundation (1999-2004); Trustee, Western Reserve Historical Society (1999-2002) **Creative Works:** Executive Producer, Documentary Film, "Mr. Philadelphia: The Story of Albert M. Greenfield" **Awards:** Woman of Professional Excellence Award, YWCA Greater Cleveland (1990) **Marquis Who's Who Honors:** Albert Nelson Marquis Lifetime Achievement Award (2017) **Shipping Address:** 1034 Ingram Ct, Ambler, PA, 19002

Rita Doris Luck Rogers

Title: Family Nurse Practitioner (Retired) **Industry:** Medicine & Health Care **Date of Birth:** 02/06/1948 **Place of Birth:** Lincoln County **State:** KS **Parents:** Ernest F. Luck; Rea N. (Nelson) Luck **Marital Status:** Married **Spouse Name:** Eugene W. Rogers (3/15/1969) **Children:** R. Michelle; Sara J. (Deceased); Brandon G. **Education:** MSN, Fort Hays State University (1996); BSN, Fort Hays State University, Cum Laude (1992); Diploma, Wesley School of Nursing (Now Wesley College) (1969) **Career:** Contract Interim Director, Nursing, Ray E. Dillon Living Center, Hutchinson Regional Healthcare System (2014); Family Nurse Practitioner, Larned State Hospital, Kansas Department for Aging and Disability Services (2008-2014); Health Services Director, Asbury Park, Inc., Newton, KS (2005-2008); Interim Director Nursing, Presbyterian Manors (2004); Clinical Education Specialist, Presbyterian Manors, Wichita, KS (2003-2005); Interim Nurse Practitioner, StatCare Minor Emergency Clinic (2000); Nurse Consultant, Presbyterian Manors (1999-2003); Interim Director Nursing, Presbyterian Manors, Kansas City, MO (1999); Interim Director Nursing, Presbyterian Manors, Sterling, KS (1998-1999); Family Nurse Practitioner, Dr. Judith Butler, Superior, NE (1997-1998); Head Nurse, Jewell County Hospital, Mankato, KS (1977-1997); Evening Supervisor, Jewell County Hospital, Mankato, KS (1977-1997); Office Nurse, Dr. A.T. Llana, Superior, NE (1975-1976); Director, Jewell County Health Department (1973-1974); Public Health Nurse III, Jewell County Health Department (1973-1974); Charge Nurse, Mitchell County Hospital, FastHealth Corporation, Beloit, KS (1971-1972); **Career Related:** Member, Ethics Committee & Infection Control Committee, Larned State Hospital, Kansas Department for Aging and Disability Services (2008-2014); Medical Staff, Larned State Hospital, Kansas Department for Aging and Disability Services (2008-2014); Certified Leader, Aquatics Program, Arthritis Foundation (2004-2006); Independent Contractor, Nation's CareLink, LLC (2003-2012); Member, Nursing Standards Committee and Products Specifications Committee, Presbyterian Manors, (1998-2005) **Civic:** County and Club Leader, 4-H Youth Development, Mitchell County (2000-2010) **Awards:** Scholar, Kansas Nurses Foundation, Wesley Alumni (1995); Scholar, Dane G. Hansen Foundation (1994); Scholar, Fort Hays State University (1994); Scholar, Midwest Organ Bank (Now Midwest Transplant Network) (1994); Scholar, Kansas Health Foundation (1993) **Marquis Who's Who Honors:** Albert Nelson Marquis Lifetime Achievement Award (2017) **Shipping Address:** 309 N Columbus St, Jewell, KS, 66949

Priscilla Ann Mabie Stewart

Title: Art Historian **Industry:** Education/Educational Services **Company Name:** State College of Florida **Date of Birth:** 09/21/1926 **Place of Birth:** Iowa City **State:** IA **Parents:** Edward Charles Mabie; Grace Frances (Chase) Mabie **Marital Status:** Married **Spouse Name:** Thomas Wilson Stewart (8/28/1949, Deceased 4/1996) **Education:** EdS, Florida Atlantic University (1983); MA, University of South Florida (1971); BA, University of Iowa (1948) **Career:** Professor, Art History, Founder of Photography, Department of Fine and Performing Arts, Intercultural Humanities, State College of Florida (2009-Present); Professor, Art History, Department of Fine and Performing Arts, Intercultural Humanities, Founder Professor of Photography, Manatee Community College, Bradenton, FL (1959-Present); Coordinator, Elementary Art, Manatee County, Florida (1953-1959) **Career Related:** Organizer, Director, Pelican Perch Wild Bird Hospital, Bradenton, FL (1953-1985); Participant, Women's Archives University, Iowa Libraries **Civic:** Charter Member, Advisory Board to Dean of Liberal Arts, University of Iowa (1999-2009) **Membership:** President, Phi Beta Kappa Association (1984-1986); Phi Beta Kappa; Alpha Xi Delta; Phi Kappa Phi; President's Club, University of Iowa; Florida Association CCS, Sarasota-Manatee **Marquis Who's Who Honors:** Albert Nelson Marquis Lifetime Achievement Award (2017) **Religion:** Episcopalian **Shipping Address:** 2705 Riverview Blvd, Bradenton, FL, 34205

Robert James Macek

Title: Physicist **Industry:** Sciences **Company Name:** TechSource, Inc. **Date of Birth:** 07/14/1936 **Place of Birth:** Rapid City **State:** SD **Parents:** Joseph Bernard Macek; Esther Mary Macek **Education:** PhD, California Institute of Technology, Pasadena, CA (1964); BS, South Dakota State University, Brookings, SD (1958) **Career:** Senior Scientist, TechSource, Inc., Santa Fe, NM (2003-Present); Guest Scientist, Los Alamos National Laboratory (2003-Present); Dahrt Red Team, TechSource, Inc. (2004-2007); Project Leader, Los Alamos National Laboratory (1995-2003); Facility Operations Manager, Los Alamos National Laboratory (1993-1995); Program Manager, Los Alamos National Laboratory, New Mexico (1987-1993); Associate Division Leader, Los Alamos National Laboratory (1985-1986); Group Leader, Los Alamos National Laboratory (1976-1985); Alternate Group Leader, Los Alamos National Laboratory (1972-1975); Technical Staff Member, Los Alamos National Laboratory (1969-2003); Postdoctorate Research Associate, University of Pennsylvania, Philadelphia, PA (1966-1969); Graduate Research Assistant, California Institute of Technology, Pasadena, CA (1959-1964); Chemist, Shell Development Corporation, Emeryville, CA (1958); Chemistry Lab Assistant, South Dakota State University (1955-1958) **Career Related:** Accelerator, Advisory Board, Oak Ridge National Laboratory, Tennessee (2007-Present); Scientific Advisory Board, HiEnergy Technologies, Irvine, CA (2002-2006); Review Panel Member, European Organization of Nuclear Research, Geneva, Switzerland (2002); Expert Consultant, Atomic Energy Control Board of Canada, Ottawa, ON, Canada (2000-2001); Panel Member, Accelerator on Physics and Technology, U.S. Department of Energy, Washington, DC (1995-1996); Program Review Panel, High Energy Physics Program, Brookhaven, NY (1994); American Chemical Society (1956-1964) **Civic:** Rotary **Creative Works:** Contributor, Scientific Papers, Professional Journals **Awards:** Awards, Los Alamos National Laboratory **Membership:** IEEE; American Physical Society **Marquis Who's Who Honors:** Distinguished Humanitarian (2017) **Shipping Address:** 163 Laguna Street, Los Alamos, NM, 87544

Michael Daniel Madden

Title: Finance Company Executive **Industry:** Financial Services **Company Name:** BlackEagle Partners LLC **Date of Birth:** 02/16/1949 **Place of Birth:** Buffalo **State:** NY **Parents:** Daniel Francis Madden; Miriam (Catron) Madden **Marital Status:** Single **Children:** Daniel; Kristina; Megan; Michael **Education:** MBA, University of Pennsylvania, with Distinction (1973); BA in Economics, Le Moyne College, Magna Cum Laude (1971) **Career:** Managing Partner, Co-Founder, BlackEagle Partners LLC, New York, NY (2005-Present); Chairman, Chief Executive Officer, Hanover Capital LLC, New York, NY (1996-Present); Senior Partner, Questor Management Co., New York, NY (1999-2005); Partner, Beacon Group Holdings, New York, NY (1997-1999); Vice Chairman, Chief Origination Officer, Board of Directors, Paine Webber Inc., New York, NY (1995-1996); Executive Managing Director, Kidder, Peabody & Co., New York, NY (1993-1994); Co-Head of Worldwide Investment Banking, Lehman Brothers, New York, NY (1989-1993); Global Head of Investment Banking, Kidder, Peabody & Co. (1985-1988); Managing Director, Kidder, Peabody & Co. (1980-1985); Vice President, Kidder, Peabody & Co. (1977-1980); Associate, Kidder, Peabody & Co., New York, NY (1973-1977) **Career Related:** Board of Directors, Geologistics Corp.; Board of Directors, US LBM Holdings Corporation; Board of Directors, Rockford Products; Board of Directors, InStar Corp.; Board of Directors, Pinn Oak Mining; Board of Directors, Chef Solutions Inc.; Board of Directors, Transonic Systems Inc.; Lead Director, Stratus Corporation **Civic:** Canisius Preparatory School, Buffalo, NY (1992-Present); Chair, Board of Trustees, LeMoyne College, Syracuse, NY (1999-2003); Board of Directors, Catholic TV Center, New York, NY (1981-1985) **Awards:** Eponym, Madden School of Business, LeMoyne College (2012); Distinguished Alumnus, LeMoyne College (1998) **Membership:** American Petroleum Institute; MBA Association; University Club; The Creek; Longboat Key Club; Economic Club of New York **Hobbies:** Boxing; Hunting; Tennis; Coin collecting; Numismatics; Fishing **Political Affiliations:** Republican **Religion:** Roman Catholic **Business Address:** 5821 Gulf of Mexico Drive, Longboat Key, FL, 34228

Walt Magnussen, PhD

Title: Director **Industry:** Education/Educational Services **Company Name:** Texas A&M University **Education:** PhD, Texas A&M University (2003); MBA, University of Minnesota, Duluth (1989); BBA, University of Minnesota, Duluth (1989) **Career:** Director, The Academy, Texas A&M University (2003-Present); Director of Telecommunications, Texas A&M University **Military Service:** U.S. Air Force **Creative Works:** Contributor, Articles, IEEE; Contributor, Articles, Mission Critical Magazine **Awards:** Distinguished Faculty Award, Texas A&M University (2002) **To what do you attribute your success:** Dr. Magnussen attributes his success to his hallmark, which is understanding that collaboration is the way to get things done. **Why did you become involved in your profession or industry:** Dr. Magnussen became involved in his profession because he feels that this profession choose him. **Shipping Address:** 1501 Texas Ave S, The Academy, Texas A&M University, College Station, TX, 77840 **Website:** http://www.hopescreekranch.com/foals.html

Maureen Murphy Maloney, PhD

Title: Social Sciences Educator **Industry:** Education/Educational Services **Date of Birth:** 11/16/1941 **Place of Birth:** New York **State:** NY **Parents:** Cyril Bernard Murphy; Monique Jacques Murphy **Marital Status:** Married **Spouse Name:** Paul K. Maloney (12/5/1964) **Children:** Jennifer; Paula; Edward **Education:** PhD in Educational Leadership, University of Bridgeport, Summa Cum Laude (2003); MS in Applied Psychology, Fairfield University (1986); BS in Psychology, Sacred Heart University (1982); Diploma, School of Nursing, Holy Name Medical Center (1962) **Certifications:** Registered Nurse, State of New Jersey **Career:** Chairman, Department of Behavioral and Social Sciences, Housatonic Community College (2006-2007); Professor, Housatonic Community College (1993-2007); Head Nurse of Neurosurgery, NewYork Presbyterian/Columbia University Medical Center, NewYork-Presbyterian Hospital (1962-1965) **Career Related:** Adjunct Professor, Norwalk Community College (1987-1993) **Civic:** Volunteer Teacher, English as Second Language, Christ Church Episcopal, Alexandria, VA **Creative Works:** Author, "Faculty Participation in the Decision-Making Process: Impact Upon Job Satisfaction at CT Community Colleges" (2003) **Awards:** Award for Teaching Excellence And Distinguished Service, Housatonic Community College (2004) **Membership:** American Physical Society; ASCD; American Psychological Association; Condominium Christmas (Holiday) Fund; National Honor Society; The Phi Beta Kappa Society **Marquis Who's Who Honors:** Distinguished Humanitarian (2017) **To what do you attribute your success:** To Dr. Maloney, happiness is success. It's a feeling you done what you wanted to do. **Why did you become involved in your profession or industry:** Dr. Maloney became involved in her profession because she has always loved education, and was always a straight A student. She was in every honors society on the way up, which encouraged her. She was helped by being encouraged. Her parents couldn't send her to college because they didn't have the money. So she did it herself, and her husband was able to help her after they got married. **What do you consider to be the highlight of your career:** A highlight of Dr. Maloney's career was getting a doctorate. It was a tough time. Also receiving her Award For Teaching Excellence And Distinguished Service, Housatonic Community College in 2004. **Hobbies:** Reading; Skiing; Tennis; Classical music; Opera **Religion:** Roman Catholic **Shipping Address:** 1250 S Washington Street, Unit 417, Alexandria, VA, 22314

Rod David Margo

Title: Lawyer **Industry:** Law and Legal Services **Company Name:** Condon & Forsyth **Date of Birth:** 02/14/1950 **Place of Birth:** Johannesburg **Country of Origin:** South Africa **Parents:** Cecil Stanley Margo; Marguerite Giselle (Polne) Margo **Education:** DCL, McGill University, Montreal, QC, Canada (1979); LLB, University of Witwatersrand, Johannesburg, South Africa, Cum Laude (1973); Bachelor in Communications, University of Witwatersrand, Johannesburg, South Africa (1970) **Certifications:** Solicitor, New South Wales, Australia (2004) **Career:** Associate to Partner, Condon & Forsyth, Los Angeles, CA (1980) **Career Related:** Lecturer of Aviation Law, University of California, Los Angeles (1981-1998); Adjunct Professor of Law, Institute of Air and Space Law, Montreal, QC, Canada; Fellow, Royal Aeronautical Society **Creative Works:** Co-Author, "Shawcross & Beaumont on Air Law, Fourth Review Edition" (2009); Co-Author, "Montreal Convention, First Edition" (2007); Author, "Aviation Insurance, Third Edition" (2000) **Membership:** Los Angeles County Bar Association **Bar Admissions:** U.S. Supreme Court (2005); Solicitor, New South Wales, Australia (2004); District of Columbia (1996); State of California (1981); State of Georgia (1979) **Marquis Who's Who Honors:** Albert Nelson Marquis Lifetime Achievement Award (2017); Distinguished Humanitarian (2017) **Shipping Address:** 3036 Cavendish Drive, Los Angeles, CA, 90064

Kent S. Marshall, PhD

Title: Professor of Chemistry **Industry:** Education/Educational Services **Company Name:** Quinnipiac University **Date of Birth:** 02/04/1944 **Place of Birth:** Chillicothe **State:** MO **Parents:** John Ellen Marshall; Mildred Stuart Marshall **Marital Status:** Married **Spouse Name:** Lucretia Affie Marshall (8/16/1974) **Children:** Marie Grace Nierenberg; Tina Marie **Education:** PhD in Organic Chemistry, University of Oregon, Eugene, OR (1971) **Career:** Chemical Safety and Hygiene Officer, Quinnipiac University, Hamden, CT (1999-Present); Professor of Chemistry, Quinnipiac University, Hamden, CT (1973-Present); Postdoctoral Research Associate, University California, San Francisco (1971-1973) **Civic:** Officer, Grange-Local, Regional, Cheshire, CT (1999-2010) **Creative Works:** Contributor, Articles to Professional Journals **Membership:** American Chemical Society; Sigma Xi **Hobbies:** Ballroom dancing; Off-roading in his Jeep **Business Address:** 275 Mount Carmel Avenue, Tator Hall, Room 321, Hamden, CT, 06518 **Shipping Address:** 275 Mount Carmel Ave, Quinnipiac University, Chemistry Department, Hamden, CT, 06518

Dean F. Martin

Title: Distinguished Professor Emeritus **Industry:** Education/Educational Services **Company Name:** University of South Florida **Date of Birth:** 04/16/1933 **Place of Birth:** Woodburn **State:** IA **Parents:** Heman Martin; Frances R. Martin **Marital Status:** Married **Spouse Name:** Barbara Bursa Martin **Children:** Diane; Bruce; John; Brian; Eric **Education:** Postdoctoral Fellow, University College London (1958-1959); PhD, The Pennsylvania State University (1958); Honorary BA, Grinnell College (1955) **Career:** Distinguished University Professor Emeritus, University of South Florida (2006-Present); Director, Institute for Environmental Studies, University of South Florida (1989-Present); Associate Chairman for Development, University of South Florida (2000-2006); Distinguished University Professor, University of South Florida (1992-2006); Associate Chairman for Graduate Studies, University of South Florida (1988-2000) **Career Related:** Director, Class Fund, Grinnell College (1981-Present); Danforth/Sesquicentennial Lecturer, Grinnell College (1996); Member, Board of Directors, Research Foundation, University of South Florida (1995); Associate Member, Moffitt Cancer Center (1994-1995); Member, Alumni Association Board of Directors, Grinnell College (1989-1995); Member, Library Development Board, University of South Florida (1986-1990); **Civic:** Delegate, Governor's Conference on Library and Information Services, FL (1990); Lake Okeechobee Technical Advisory Committee II, Governor Martinez (1988-1990) **Creative Works:** Editorial Advisory Board, Technology and Innovation (2010-Present); Editorial Board, Journal of Environmental Science and Health (1970-Present); Editor Emeritus, Florida Scientist (2010-Present); Deputy Editor, Co-editor, Editor, Associate Editor, Journals and Books; Author, Books **Awards:** Featured Listee, American Men and Women of Science (1963-Present); University of South Florida Chemistry Lifetime Achievement Award (2017); Class of '56 Award, University of South Florida Alumni Association (2010); Honorary Membership Award, The Aquatic Plant Management Society, Inc. (2007); **Membership:** Fellow, The National Academy of Inventors, Inc. (2015); Charter Member, Academy of Inventors, University of South Florida (2009); Web Master, Tampa Bay Section, American Chemical Society (2004-2010); Chairman, Tampa Bay Section, American Chemical Society (2001); Chairman, Awards Committee, American Chemical Society (1988-1991); President, The Aquatic Plant Management Society, Inc. (1986-1987) **Political Affiliations:** Democrat **Religion:** Catholic **Business Address:** 4202 E Fowler Ave CHE 205, Tampa, FL, 33620 **Shipping Address:** 3402 Valencia Rd, Tampa, FL, 33618

George Whitney Martin

Industry: Writing and Editing **Date of Birth:** 01/25/1926 **Place of Birth:** New York **State:** NY/USA **Parents:** George Whitney; Agnes Wharton (Hutchinson) M. **Education:** LL.B., University of Virginia (1953); Student, Trinity College, Cambridge University, England (1950); BA, Harvard University (1948) **Career:** Writer (1959-2015); With, Emmet, Marvin & Martin, New York, NY (1955-1959) **Creative Works:** Author, "Opera at the Bandstand, Then and Now" (2014); Author, "The Battle of the Frogs and Mice, An Homeric Fable, Third Edition" (2013); Author, "Verdi in America Oberto Through Rigoletto" (2011); Author, "The Opera Companion, A Guide for the Casual Operagoer" Sixth Edition (2008); Author, "CCB: The Life and Century of Charles C. Burlingham, New York's First Citizen, 1858-1959" (2005); Author, "Verdi, His Music, Life and Times, Fourth Edition" (2001); Author, "Twentieth Century Opera, A Guide" (1999); Author, "Causes and Conflicts, The Centennial History of the Association of the Bar of the City of New York, 1870-1970, Second Edition" (1997); Author, "Aspects of Verdi, Second Edition" (1993); Author, "Verdi at the Golden Gate, San Francisco in the Golden Years" (1993); Author, "Aspects of Verdi" (1988); Author, "The Damrosch Dynasty, America's First Family of Music" (1983); Author, "Madam Secretary: Frances Perkins" (1976); Author, "Causes and Conflicts, The Centennial History of the Association of the Bar of the City of New York, 1870-1970" (1970); Author, "The Red Shirt and The Cross of Savoy, The Story of Italy's Risorgimento, 1748-1871" (1969); Author, "Verdi, His Music, Life and Times" (1963); Author, "The Battle of the Frogs and Mice, An Homeric Fable" (1962); Author, "The Opera Companion, A Guide for the Casual Operagoer" (1961); Contributor, Articles, Professional Journals and Magazines **Bar Admissions:** New York (1955)

Christopher P. Mastro

Title: Secondary School Educator **Industry:** Education/Educational Services **Company Name:** SUNY **Date of Birth:** 10/17/1946 **Place of Birth:** Schenectady **State:** NY **Parents:** George Mastro; Evelyn Mastro **Marital Status:** Married **Spouse Name:** Linda Mary Condon (06/27/1981) **Education:** Masters of Arts in Teaching in English, Saint Michael's College, Winooski, VT (1969); BA in English, Saint Michael's College, Winooski, VT (1968) **Career:** Education Supervisor, University at Albany (2002-Present); Education Supervisor, The College of Saint Rose, Albany, NY (2001-2002); English Teacher, Clayton A. Bouton High School, Voorheesville, NY (1971-1998); English Teacher, Mohonasen High School, Rotterdam, NY (1969-1971) **Career Related:** Volunteer, High School English Teacher, Hope House Inc., Colonie, NY (2002-Present); High School Basketball Coach (1971-1986); Speaker in Field **Awards:** Volunteer Teaching Award, Albany County Executive (2008); Outstanding Teacher Award, Golub (1990) **Membership:** New York State United Teachers **Marquis Who's Who Honors:** Albert Nelson Marquis Lifetime Achievement Award (2017) **Shipping Address:** 79 Van Wie Terrace, Albany, NY, 12203

George Atterbury Mathewson

Title: Lawyer **Industry:** Law and Legal Services **Date of Birth:** 03/31/1935 **Place of Birth:** Paterson **State:** NJ **Parents:** Joseph B. Mathewson; Christina A. (Atterbury) Mathewson **Marital Status:** Married **Spouse Name:** Ann Elizabeth Mathewson (7/31/1975) **Children:** James Lemuel **Education:** LLM, University of Michigan (1961); LLB, Cornell University, Ithaca, NY (1960); AB, Amherst College, Massachusetts, Cum Laude (1957) **Career:** Of Counsel, Banac and Mathewson, Manlius, NY (2002-2004); Private Practice, Syracuse, NY (1973-2002); Regional Attorney, New York State Department of Environmental Conservation, Liverpool, NY (1972-1973); Private Practice, Syracuse, NY (1966-1972); Attorney, Office of Special Legal Assistants; Trial Attorney, Federal Trade Commission, Washington, DC (1963-1965) **Career Related:** Adjunct Instructor in Business Law, Onondaga Community College, Syracuse, NY (1979-1984) **Civic:** Director, Milly's Pantry, Inc. (2009); Director, Finger Lakes Chamber Music Festival, Inc. (2007-2008); Vice President, Board of Directors, Yates County Arts Council, Inc. (2005); Vice President, Steuben County Historical Society (2005); Secretary, Board of Directors, Yates County Arts Council, Inc. (2004); Board of Directors, Yates County Arts Council, Inc. (2003-2006); Trustee, Steuben County Historical Society (2002-2005); Vice President, Manilus Chamber of Commerce (1997); Director, Manilus Chamber of Commerce (1995); President, Board of Directors, South Side Businessmen (1993); Vice President, Board of Directors, South Side Businessmen (1992); Board of Directors, South Side Businessmen (1988-1991); Elder, Onondaga Hill Presbyterian Church (1982-1985); Elder, Onondaga Hill Presbyterian Church (1979); Board of Directors, South Side Businessmen (1971-1972) **Creative Works:** Author, "A Boy Named Martin" (2014); Author, "Hidden Agenda" (2013); Author, "1984 Arrives in America" (2005) **Awards:** Patentee for Safety Device for Disabled Airplanes **Membership:** President, Onondaga Club (1989-1991); President, Vice President, Onondaga Club (1989); Board of Directors, Onondaga Club (1988-1989); New York State Bar Association; State and County Bar Association Committees; 50-Year Member, Onondaga County Bar Association; Kiwanis Club **Hobbies:** Lawn care; Bird watching; Walking; Reading; Writing **Political Affiliations:** Republican **Business Address:** PO Box 192, Lake George, NY, 12845 **Website:** http://www.georgeamathewson.com

John R. Mathiason

Title: Political Science Professor, Consultant **Industry:** Education/Educational Services **Company Name:** State University of New York **Date of Birth:** 08/05/1942 **Place of Birth:** Willmar **State:** MN **Marital Status:** Married **Spouse Name:** Jan Elizabeth Clausen (8/5/2004); Maria Cristina Sara-Serrano (11/15/1966, Deceased 2004) **Children:** John Michael; Pablo Andres **Education:** PhD, Massachusetts Institute of Technology, Cambridge, MA (1968); BA, St. Olaf College, Summa Cum Laude (1963) **Career:** Lecturer, College of Environmental Science and Forestry, State University of New York (2012-Present); Adjunct Professor, Institute of Public Affairs, College of Human Ecology, Cornell University (2012-Present); Professor of International Relations, Syracuse University (1999-2012); Adjunct Professor of Public Administration, New York University (1994-2001); Deputy Director, Division of Advancement of Women, UN Secretariat, New York (1987-1997); Senior Program Officer, UN Secretariat, New York (1980-1987); Social Affairs Officer, UN Secretariat, New York (1976-1980); Assistant Resident, Representative, UN Development Program, Islamabad, Pakistan (1974-1976); Associate Social Affairs Officer, UN Secretariat, New York (1971-1974); Assistant Professor of Communications, University of Washington (1968-1971); Expert, Social Aspects Agrarian Reform, Technical Cooperation Bureau, Caracas, Venezuela (1966-1967) **Career Related:** Editor-in-Chief, Journal of International Organizations Studies (2010-Present); Managing Director, Associates International Management Services (1997-Present) **Civic:** Board Chair, Comprehensive Planning Committee, Shandaken, NY (2001-2003) **Creative Works:** Author, "Internet Governance: The New Frontier of Global Institutions" (2008); Author, "Invisible Governance: International Secretariats in Global Politics" (2007); Author, "Eliminating Weapons of Mass Destruction: Prospects of Effective International Verification" (2004) **Awards:** Distinguished Adjunct Professor Award, Graduate School of Public Administration, New York University (1983) **Membership:** Association of Former International Civil Servants **Marquis Who's Who Honors:** Distinguished Humanitarian (2017) **Hobbies:** Hiking **Political Affiliations:** Democrat **Religion:** Lutheran **Shipping Address:** 538 Fayette Blvd, Syracuse, NY, 13224

Ann R. Matthews

Title: Speech-Language Pathologist (Retired) **Industry:** Education/Educational Services **Company Name:** Plano Independent School District **Education:** Master's in Speech and Language Pathology, American Speech-Language-Hearing Association **Hobbies:** Yoga; Baking; Writing; Spending Time with Her Family **Why did you become involved in your profession?** Ms. Matthews chose her career because she is passionate about working with children and families in need. She prepared for her profession by earning an undergraduate and master's degree. She also developed her personal gifts in order to more effectively help others. She places emphasis on the fact that people with disabilities are not defined by their disabilities. There is no such thing as an autistic child, only children with autism. In order to help the family and the child, this difference has to be understood.

George August Maul, PhD

Title: Professor of Oceanography **Industry:** Education/Educational Services **Company Name:** Florida Institute of Technology **Date of Birth:** 07/17/1938 **Place of Birth:** Brooklyn **State:** NY **Parents:** George Maul; Sophie Maul **Marital Status:** Married **Spouse Name:** Carole K. Maul **Children:** Anne K.; Patricia C. **Education:** PhD, University of Miami (1974); BS, SUNY Maritime College, With Honors (1960) **Certifications:** Licensed U.S. Merchant Marine Officer (1960-1992) **Career:** Professor of Oceanography, Florida Institute of Technology (1994-Present); Head, Department of Marine and Environmental Systems, Florida Institute of Technology (1994-2014); Adjunct Professor of Meteorology and Physical Oceanography, University of Miami (1977-1996); Research Oceanographer, NOAA (1969-1994); Commissioned Officer, U.S. Coast and Geodetic Survey (1960-1969) **Career Related:** Chairman, Group of Experts on Ocean Physics, IOCRAIBE, UNESCO (1992-1996); Intergovernmental Panel on Climate Change (1991-1995); IOC Group of Experts on the Global Sea Level Observing System (1989-2000); Vice President, Caribbean Subcommittee, Intergovernmental Oceanographic Commission, UNESCO (1989-1995); Chairman, Tsunami Steering Group of Experts, IOCARIBE, UNESCO (1987-2003); Chairman, Environment Programme Task Team on Climate Change, United Nations (1987-1996) **Military Service:** Lieutenant Commander, U.S. Coast and Geodetic Survey (1966-1969); Ensign, U.S. Coast and Geodetic Survey (1960-1961) **Creative Works:** Author, "The Oceanographer's Companion" (2017); Editor, "Small Islands: Marine Science and Sustainable Development" (1996); Editor, "Climatic Change in the Intra-Americas Sea" (1993); Author, "Introduction to Satellite Oceanography" (1985); **Awards:** Medalist, Florida Academy of Sciences (2016); Faculty Senate Excellence Award for Service, Florida Institute of Technology (2015); Faculty Senate Excellence Award for Teaching, Florida Institute of Technology (1998); Three Distinguished Authorship Awards, NOAA; Five Outstanding Performance Awards, NOAA; U.S. President's Council Volunteer Service Award; Silver Beaver Award, Boy Scouts of America; St. George Episcopal Award; **Membership:** Treasurer, SECOORA; Past President, SECOORA; American Geophysical Union; Marine Technology Society; American Meteorological Society; Florida Academy of Sciences; Sigma Xi; Sigma Xi; Phi Kappa Phi; Omicron Delta Kappa; Alpha Phi Omega **Marquis Who's Who Honors:** Albert Nelson Marquis Lifetime Achievement Award (2017) **Religion:** Episcopalian **Shipping Address:** 5959 S Highway A1A, Melbourne Beach, FL, 32951 **Website:** http://web2.fit.edu/faculty/profiles/profile.php?tracks=gmaul

Carol K. Mavromatis Crouse

Title: Elementary School Educator **Industry:** Education/Educational Services **Company Name:** Upper Darby School District **Parents:** George Mavromatis; Helen Mavromatis **Marital Status:** Widowed **Spouse Name:** David Crouse (Deceased 4/1998) **Education:** MEd in Curriculum and Instruction, Temple University (1981); EdB, Temple University (1972) **Career:** Science Curriculum Commission, Upper Darby School District (1974-2010); Elementary Teacher, Grades 1-5, Upper Darby School District, PA (1974-2010) **Career Related:** Highland Park Elementary School Learn and Serve Community Service Center (2004); Supervisor, Kids Care Club (2000-2002); Teacher, Advisory Board, Philadelphia Zoo (1995-2002); NASA Lunar Rock and Meteorite Education Program (1993-2010); Writing and Evaluation Team, REEP Environmental Education Program, Schuykill Valley Nature Center (1993-1994); Excellence Education Team, Hillcrest Elementary School, Pennsylvania (1987) **Civic:** Volunteer, Collenbrook Colonial Farm (2016-Present); **Awards:** Howard W. McComb Award, Phi Delta Kappa, Temple University (1981) **Membership:** Supervisor, UD Recording Department Extended Day Care (2004-2015); Co-Director, Upper Darby Recreation Tennis Tournament (1987-1996); National Science Teachers Association; Association for Supervision and Curriculum Development; Phi Delta Kappa International **Marquis Who's Who Honors:** Albert Nelson Marquis Lifetime Achievement Award (2017) **Shipping Address:** 202 N Drexel Avenue, Havertown, PA, 19083

Lea Stevens McChesney

Title: Anthropologist, Educator, Curator **Industry:** Museums & Institutions **Company Name:** Maxwell Museum of Anthropology **Date of Birth:** 12/31/1954 **Place of Birth:** Albany **State:** NY **Parents:** William J. McChesney; Susan Baldwin McChesney **Marital Status:** Married **Spouse Name:** Christopher John Burnett **Children:** Anne Miriam McChesney Burnett **Education:** PhD, New York University, New York, NY (2003); MPhil, New York University, New York, NY (1991); MA, Wesleyan University, Middletown, CT (1978); BA, Bard College, Annandale-on-Hudson, New York (1976) **Career:** Director, Alfonso Ortiz Center for Intercultural Studies, The University of New Mexico, Albuquerque, NM (2017-Present); Research Assistant Professor, Department of Anthropology, The University of New Mexico, Albuquerque, NM (2017-Present); Curator of Ethnology, Maxwell Museum, University New Mexico, Albuquerque, NM (2014-Present); Visiting Assistant Professor, Department of Sociology and Anthropology, The University of Toledo, Toledo, OH (2013-2014); Affiliated Faculty, Department Women's and Gender Studies, The University of Toledo, Toledo, OH (2012-2014); Research Assistant Professor, Department Sociology and Anthropology, The University of Toledo, Toledo, OH (2010-2013); **Career Related:** Editor, Peer-Reviewed Journal of the American Anthropological Association, "Museum Anthropology" (2016-Present); Research Associate, Peabody Museum, Harvard University, Cambridge, MA (2005-Present); Member, Association on American Indian Affairs Repatriation Working Group (2018); Principal Investigator, National Endowment for the Humanities Grant (2017) **Civic:** Board Member, Westport Citizens Action Coalition, Kansas City, MO (2001) **Creative Works:** Curatorial Contributor, "All the World is Here: Harvard's Peabody Museum and the Invention of American Anthropology," Peabody Museum (2017); Contributing Curator, "Sewing Seeds in the Garden, The Mulvaney Collection of African Art," University of New Mexico Art Museum (2015) **Awards:** Green Fund Grantee, Office of Sustainability, University of New Mexico (2015); **Membership:** Fellow, Society for Applied Anthropology; Council for Museum Anthropology; American Anthropological Association; Native American Art Studies Association; American Alliance of Museums **Marquis Who's Who Honors:** Albert Nelson Marquis Lifetime Achievement Award (2017); Distinguished Humanitarian (2017) **Business Address:** Maxwell Museum of Anthropology 500 University Blvd NE, Maxwell Museum of Anthropology, Albuquerque, NM 87131 **Shipping Address:** 431 Ash Street NE, Albuquerque, NM, 87106 **Website:** https://maxwellmuseum.unm.edu/about/people/lea-mcchesney

Raenell McDonough

Title: Musician, Organ Instructor, Humanities Teacher (Retired) **Industry:** Education/Educational Services **Company Name:** Texas A&M University **Date of Birth:** 08/19/1946 **Place of Birth:** Amarillo **State:** TX **Parents:** Ray Sam Roberts; Doris Winnie (Williams) Roberts **Spouse Name:** Jerome F. McDonough (12/21/1978, Deceased) **Children:** Brian Christopher **Education:** MEd, West Texas A&M University, Canyon, TX (1971); BA in Music Education, West Texas A&M University, Canyon, TX (1968) **Certifications:** Certified in Elementary Education; Certified in Music Education **Career:** Part-time Organ Instructor, West Texas A&M University (2017-Present); Humanities Teacher, West Texas A&M University (1972-Present); Retired (2016); Coach, Amarillo College (2000-2016); Accompanist, Amarillo College (2000-2016); Instructor, Music Theory and Organ, Amarillo College (2000-2016); Pianist, Amarillo Opera (1989-2016); Music Educator, West Texas A&M University, Canyon, TX (1972-1989); Piano Accompanist, West Texas A&M University, Canyon, TX (1973-1989); Performer, West Texas A&M University, Canyon, TX (1973-1989); Music Educator, Amarillo Independent School District (1968-1973) **Career Related:** Member, Textbook Committee, Amarillo Independent School District (1970) **Civic:** Member, Secretary Executive Board, Trustee, Amarillo Opera (2006-Present); Trustee, Amarillo Opera (2006-Present); Member, Friends of Aeolian Skinner, Amarillo, TX (2004-Present); Member, Amarillo Little Theatre Guild (1980-Present); Member, Friends of Fine Arts Association, West Texas A&M University, Canyon, TX (1980-Present); Organist, St. Paul Methodist Church, Amarillo, TX (1968-Present); Music Coordinator, St. Paul Methodist Church, Amarillo, TX (1968-Present); Member, Amarillo United Citizens Forum (2006); Member, Station KACV-TV PBS Organization, Amarillo, TX; Member, Amarillo Youth Choirs; Member, WTAMU Foundation, West Texas A&M University, Canyon, TX **Awards:** Bill and Louise Dee Volunteer Award, Amarillo Opera (1997-1998); Named in Outstanding Young Women of America (1980) **Membership:** Dean, Amarillo Chapter, American Guild of Organists (2015-Present); Secretary, Executive Board, Amarillo Art Force (2006-Present); Sub-Dean, American Guild of Organists (1990-1995); Amarillo Symphony Guild; Texas Community College Association **Hobbies:** Travel; Crafts; Reading; Theater **Shipping Address:** 6106 Dartmouth St, Amarillo, TX, 79109

Larry George McDougle, PhD

Title: Academic Administrator **Industry:** Education/Educational Services **Date of Birth:** 02/22/1941 **Place of Birth:** McComb **State:** OH **Parents:** Serge Glen McDougle; Emma Rowena (Rader) McDougle **Marital Status:** Married **Spouse Name:** Ruth Elnor Leader (8/18/1962) **Children:** Janet Lynne; Bradley Kent; Craig Andrew **Education:** Honorary Associate Degree in Education Administration, Owens Community College, Toledo, OH (2011); Doctorate in Educational Leadership, University of Findlay, with Honors, Findlay, OH (1998); PhD in Higher Education Administration, University of Toledo, Toledo, OH (1971); MA in Physics, Kent State University, Kent, OH (1965); BS in Mathematics, University of Findlay, Findlay, OH (1963); BS in Physics, University of Findlay, Findlay, OH (1963); BS in English, University of Findlay, Findlay, OH (1963) **Career:** President, Owens Community College, Toledo, OH (2010-2011); Chief Executive Officer, Owens Community College, Toledo, OH (2010-2011); Adjunct Professor, University of Toledo, Toledo, OH (2004-2009); President Emeritus, Northwest State Community College (2003); President, Northwest State Community College, Archbold, OH (1991-2003); Academy Dean, University of Toledo, Toledo, OH (1984-1991); Division Director, Southern Illinois University, Carbondale, IL (1979-1984); Division Director, Indiana University, Kokomo, IL (1976-1979); Provost, South Carolina Technology Systems, Columbia, SC (1972-1975); Department Chairman, Jacksonville Community College, Jacksonville, FL (1971-1972); Physics Instructor, University of Findlay, Findlay, OH (1966-1971); With, Quality Control, Eastman Kodak, Rochester, NY (1965-1966) **Career Related:** Trustee, Mercy College of Ohio, Toledo, OH (1992-2004); Member, Board of Directors, Northwest Ohio Regional Economic Development Association (1993-2003) **Civic:** Pastor, First Church of Christ, Napoleon, OH (2007-Present); Member, Board of Trustees, Great Lakes Christian College, Lansing, MI (2003-2007) **Creative Works:** Columnist, "Crescent-News Newspaper," Defiance, OH (2001-2003) **Awards:** Lifetime Career Achievement Award, University of Toledo, Toledo, OH (2014); Distinguished Alumnus Award, University of Findlay, Findlay, OH (2009) **Marquis Who's Who Honors:** Albert Nelson Marquis Lifetime Achievement Award (2017) **What do you consider to be the highlight of your career:** The highlight of Dr. McDougle's career is being able to witness the success of his students. **Hobbies:** Coin collecting/numismatics; Rare books; **Shipping Address:** 600 Rohm Dr, Napoleon, OH, 43535

Betsy Mickey McDowell, PhD

Title: Professor, Chair **Industry:** Education/Educational Services **Company Name:** Newberry College **Date of Birth:** 10/29/1950 **Place of Birth:** Winston-Salem **State:** SC **Parents:** James S. Mickey; Betty W. Mickey **Marital Status:** Married **Spouse Name:** Fred H. McDowell (August 31, 1996) **Children:** Thomas Scott Barnes **Education:** PhD in Nursing Science, University of South Carolina (1997); MSN, The University of North Carolina at Chapel Hill (1975); BSN, University of South Carolina (1971) **Certifications:** Certified Nursing Educator, National League for Nursing (2015); Licensed Registered Nurse, State of South Carolina (2014); Certified Critical-Care Registered Nurse in Pediatrics, American Association of Critical-Care Nurses (2010) **Career:** Chair, Department of Nursing, Professor of Nursing, Newberry College (2007-Present); Staff Nurse, Neonatal ICU, Self Regional Healthcare, Greenwood, SC (2002-2009); Nursing Faculty, Lander University (1971-2007); Staff Nurse, Pediatric ICU/Pediatric Intermediate ICU, Children's Hospital, Palmetto Health (1988-2002); Staff Nurse, Self Memorial Hospital (1971-1989); Staff Nurse, North Carolina Memorial Hospital, UNC Health Care (1973-1975); Head Nurse of Pediatrics, Self Memorial Hospital (1973) **Career Related:** Consultant, Newberry College (2006-2007) **Civic:** Weekly Children's Support Group Facilitator to Domestic Violence Shelter, MEG's House (1998-2007); Mentor, Maternal Child Leadership Academy, Indianapolis, IN (2006-2007) **Creative Works:** Editor, SPN News (2012-Present); Editorial Board Member, Chair, South Carolina Nurses Journal, Columbia (1987-2004); Contributor, Articles, Professional Journals **Awards:** Fellow, Academy of Nursing Education (2015); Recipient, Palmetto Gold Award, South Carolina Nurses Foundation (2006); Recipient, Nursing Excellence Award, South Carolina League for Nursing (2005); Recipient, Excellence in Teaching Award (2005); Recipient, President's Award, South Carolina Nurses Association (2003-2004); Recipient, Excellence in Maternal Child Health Nursing Practice Award (2002) **Membership:** Work Group Member, American Association of Critical-Care Nurses (2005-2006); Trustee, Neuman Systems Model International; Secretary, Neuman Systems Model International; the American Nurses Association, Inc.; Zeta Mu Chapter, Sigma Theta Tau International; Alpha Xi, Sigma Theta Tau International **Marquis Who's Who Honors:** Albert Nelson Marquis Lifetime Achievement Award (2017) **Business Address:** 2100 College Street, SCM 125, Newberry, SC, 29108 **Shipping Address:** 131 Annie Drive, Ninety Six, SC, 29666 **Website:** https://www.newberry.edu/faculty/details/mcdowell-betsy

Charles Robert McGhee

Title: Biology Professor **Industry:** Education/Educational Services **Company Name:** Middle Tennessee State University **Date of Birth:** 07/17/1934 **Place of Birth:** Chattanooga **State:** TN **Parents:** Buford Charles McGhee; Beatrice Parker **Marital Status:** Married **Spouse Name:** Anna Louise Cummings (6/13/1964) **Children:** John Robert; Jennifer Ann; Charles Brian **Education:** PhD, Virginia Polytechnic Institute and State University, Blacksburg, VA (1970); MA, Middle Tennessee State University, Murfreesboro, TN (1964); BS, Middle Tennessee State University, Murfreesboro, TN (1962) **Career:** Entomology Consultant, International Zoology (1969); Professor, Department of Biology, Middle Tennessee State University **Civic:** Member, Alaskan Air Command; Member, Ground Aerial Photography **Military Service:** 11th Air Force, U.S. Air Force (1954-1958) **Creative Works:** Contributor, Scientific Papers, Professional Journals **Awards:** The Long Rifle Award, Boy Scouts of America **Membership:** Fellow, Tennessee Academy of Science; American Arachnological Society; Charter Member, Association Southeastern Biologists; Phi Sigma Society; Sigma Xi, The Scientific Research Honor Society **Marquis Who's Who Honors:** Albert Nelson Marquis Lifetime Achievement Award (2017) **Hobbies:** Fishing; Photography; Writing; Genealogy; Poetry **Political Affiliations:** Independent **Shipping Address:** 4192 Betty Ford Road, Murfreesboro, TN, 37130

Langdon McIlroy Cooper

Title: Lawyer **Industry:** Law and Legal Services **Company Name:** Mullen Holland & Cooper P. A. **Date of Birth:** 04/27/1941 **Place of Birth:** Chicago **State:** IL **Parents:** George Langdon Cooper; Lois McIlroy Cooper **Marital Status:** Divorced **Spouse Name:** Mary H. Cooper (6/1964, Divorced) **Children:** Marya Ladd; Abigail Harrill **Education:** JD, University of North Carolina, Chapel Hill, NC (1969); BA, Duke University (1964) **Certifications:** Board Certification in Business and Consumer Bankruptcy, American Board of Certification; Board Certification in Bankruptcy Law, North Carolina State Bar Board of Legal Specialization **Career:** Managing Director, Mullen Holland & Cooper P. A., Gastonia, NC (1969-Present); Chairman, Mullen Holland & Cooper P. A., Gastonia, NC (1969-Present); Treasurer, Mullen Holland & Cooper P. A., Gastonia, NC (1969-Present) **Career Related:** Lecturer in Field **Civic:** Initial Director, Jobquest Program, Gastonia, NC **Creative Works:** Contributor, Articles to Professional Journals **Awards:** Named, North Carolina Legal Elite, North Carolina Business Journal (2013-Present); Named, Best Lawyers in America, U.S. News & World Report (2011-Present); Named, North Carolina Super Lawyers (2006-Present); Named, Top 100 Lawyers, North Carolina Charlotte Magazine, North Carolina Law & Politics (2009-2010); Named, North Carolina Legal Elite, North Carolina Business Journal (2005-2010); Rated A/V Preeminent Attorney, Martindale-Hubbell **Membership:** Panel of Trustees, United States Bankruptcy Court for the Western District of North Carolina (1975-Present); Board Governors, North Carolina Bar Association (1985-1988); ABA; North Carolina State Bar; Bankruptcy Lawyer Lecturer, National Association Bankruptcy Trustees; American Bankruptcy Institute; Bankruptcy Law Lecturer, North Carolina Bar Association; Gaston County Bar Association; Council of Certified Bankruptcy Specialists **Bar Admissions:** Washington (1992); United States District Court for the Western, Middle and Eastern Districts of North Carolina (1980); North Carolina; Supreme Court of the United States; United State Court of Appeals for the Fourth Circuit; United State Court of Appeals for the Third Circuit **Marquis Who's Who Honors:** Albert Nelson Marquis Lifetime Achievement Award (2017) **Business Address:** 301 S York St PO Box 488, Gastonia, NC, 28052

Diane Elaine McVey

Title: Accountant **Industry:** Financial Services **Company Name:** FirstEnergy Service Company **Date of Birth:** 04/20/1953 **Place of Birth:** Wilmington **State:** DE **Parents:** C. Granville McVey; Margaret M. (Lindell) McVey **Marital Status:** Single **Education:** MBA in Management, Fairleigh Dickinson University (1985); BS in Accounting, Goldey-Beacom College (1980); AA in Accounting, Goldey-Beacom College (1973) **Career:** Staff Accountant, GPU Service, Inc. (Now FirstEnergy Corporation), Reading, PA (2000-Present); Senior Accountant, FirstEnergy Corporation (2004-2013); Staff Accountant, FirstEnergy Corporation (2001-2004); Staff Accountant, GPU Service, Morristown, NJ (1995-2000); Staff Accountant, GPU Nuclear Corporation (1993-1995); Staff Analyst, GPU Nuclear Corporation, Parsippany, NJ (1980-1993); Assistant Accountant, NVF Corporation, Kennett Square, PA (1978-1980); Cost Accountant, FMC Corporation, Kennett Square, PA (1973-1975); Accountant, Audio Visual Arts, Wilmington, DE (1973) **Career Related:** Owner, Demac Consulting, Reading, PA (2000-2010); Owner, Demac Consulting, Dover, NJ (1988-2000) **Civic:** Commissioner, Board Adjustment, Dover, NJ (1994-2000); Elder, First Presbyterian Church, Rockaway, NJ (1986-2000); Session Member, First Presbyterian Church, Rockaway, NJ (1986-1991) **Military Service:** U.S. Army (1975-1978) **Awards:** U.S. Army Commendation Medal; Good Conduct Medal; Expert Shot Medal **Marquis Who's Who Honors:** Albert Nelson Marquis Lifetime Achievement Award (2017) **Why did you become involved in your profession or industry:** Ms. McVey was inspired to become involved in her profession during her senior year of high school. **Hobbies:** Playing computer games; Reading mystery books; Needle crafts **Political Affiliations:** Independent **Religion:** Presbyterian **Shipping Address:** 1525 Old Coach Road, Newark, DE, 19711

Steven E. Meier, PhD

Title: Associate Professor **Industry:** Education/Educational Services **Company Name:** University of Idaho **Education:** PhD, Washington State University, Pullman, WA (1991) **Certifications:** Certified Prevention Specialist, IC&RC (2009); Certified GAIN Local Trainer, Chestnut (2009); Certified Trainer, TIPS, Health Communications, Inc. (2009) **Career:** Director, Addictions Training Program, University of Idaho, Moscow, ID (2000-Present); Associate Professor, University of Idaho, Moscow, ID (1987-Present); Chairman, Institutional Review Board, University of Idaho, Moscow, ID (2005-2007) **Career Related:** TIPS Trainer, Meier Training & Consulting (2009-Present); Community Development Specialist, Meier Training & Consulting (2007-Present); Addictions Consultant, Meier Training & Consulting (1985-Present) **Civic:** Worthy Warden, Knights of Columbus, Moscow, ID (2009); Scoutmaster, Boy Scouts of America, Moscow, ID (2006-2009); Community Coalition Development Specialist **Military Service:** Sergeant, U.S. Navy (1972-1976) **Awards:** Named Drug Awareness Chairman of the Year, Benevolent and Protective Order of Elks (2014); Named Arrowman, Order of the Arrow, Boy Scouts of America (2009); District Award, Boy Scouts of America (2009); Named Elk of the Year, Benevolent and Protective Order of Elks (2006-2007); Grantee, Idaho Department of Health and Welfare (2002-2008); Addictions Training Grantee, Idaho Department of Health and Welfare (2000-2009) **Membership:** District Deputy, Benevolent and Protective Order of Elks (2009-Present); Executive Board Member, National Ski Patrol (2009); Drug Awareness Chairman, Benevolent and Protective Order of Elks (2005-2009); American Psychological Society **Marquis Who's Who Honors:** Albert Nelson Marquis Lifetime Achievement Award (2017) **What do you consider to be the highlight of your career:** Mr. Meier is most proud of the students he has advised and mentored, who have gone on to become doctors. **Hobbies:** Fly fishing; Skiing **Business Address:** 1031 N Academic Way, Coeur d' Alene, ID, 83814 **Shipping Address:** 1219 E Lakeside Ave, Coeur d' Alene, ID, 83814

Patricia Mell

Title: Lawyer, Employee Benefits Consultant **Industry:** Law and Legal Services **Company Name:** P. Mell Advisors **Date of Birth:** 12/15/1953 **Place of Birth:** Cleveland **State:** OH **Parents:** Julian Cooper; Thelma (Webb) M. Cooper **Marital Status:** Married **Spouse Name:** Dr. Steven Ragland **Education:** JD, Case Western Reserve University (1978); AB, Wellesley College, with Honors (1975) **Certifications:** Certified in Insurance, States of Illinois, Michigan, Pennsylvania, Wisconsin, Ohio, Maryland, Texas, California **Career:** Principal, P. Mell Advisors, IL (2007-Present); Dean, John Marshall Law School, Chicago, IL (2003-2007); Associate Dean for Academic Affairs, Michigan State University College of Law, East Lansing, MI (2000-2002); Professor of Law, Michigan State University College of Law, East Lansing, MI (1996-2003); Associate Professor of Law, Michigan State University College of Law, East Lansing, MI (1992-2003); Assistant Professor of Law, Widener University (Formerly Delaware Law School), Wilmington, NC (1986-1988); Visiting Assistant Professor, The University of Toledo College of Law (1985-1986); Visiting Assistant Professor, Capital University Law School, Columbus, OH (1984-1985); Secretary of State Corporations Counsel, State of Ohio, Columbus, OH (1982-1984); Assistant Attorney General, State of Ohio, Columbus, OH (1978-1982); Adjunct Professor, University of Phoenix **Career Related:** Mediator of Night Prosecutor's Program, Columbus, OH (1984-1985) **Civic:** National Black MBA (1986-Present); Orlando Park Chamber of Commerce (2015); Governing Board, Case Western Reserve University School of Law, Cleveland, OH (1985-1988); Century Club Ohio Democrats (1985-1986); Scholarship Screening Committee, Black American Law Student Association, University of Toledo College of Law (1985-1986); Chairman, Law Student Committee, Young Black Democrats, Columbus, OH (1982-1984) **Awards:** Recipient, Legacy of Opportunity Recognition, Glenn T. Johnson Chapter of the Black Law Students Association (2006); Recipient, C.F. Stardford Award (2005); Named, One of Chicago's 100 Most Influential Women, Crain's Chicago Business (2004); Honoree, Chicago Midwest, National Council of Negro Women (2003) **Membership:** Commercial Arbitrator, American Arbitration Association (1986-Present); National Black MBAs (1986-1991); ABA; National Bar Association; National Conference of Black Lawyers **Bar Admissions:** Michigan (1991-Present); Pennsylvania (1988); United States District Court for the Southern and North Districts of Ohio (1979); Ohio (1979) **Marquis Who's Who Honors:** Distinguished Humanitarian (2017) **Religion:** African Methodist Episcopal **Shipping Address:** 103 Windmill Road, Orland Park, IL, 60467 **Website:** http://www.pmelladvisors.com

Sári Menna

Title: Artist, Educator **Industry:** Fine Art **Date of Birth:** 09/29/1932 **Place of Birth:** San Francisco **State:** CA **Marital Status:** Married **Spouse Name:** Ferdinand Carlo Menna (3/10/1949) **Children:** Mark Menna; Diane Menna **Education:** Postgraduate Work, New York University (1987-1993); MFA, Hunter College (1974); BFA, Hunter College, Cum Laude (1968) **Career:** Art Teacher, New York City Department of Education (1971-1995); Substitute Teacher, Massapequa Public Schools (1968-1969) **Career Related:** Teacher, Cultural Workshop (1968); Volunteer Art Teacher, President's Economic Opportunity Center (1967-1968) **Civic:** Member, Queens Council on the Arts (2001-2005); Member, New York City Chapter, Women's Caucus Art (1982-1991); President, Creative Women's Collective (1982-1985) **Creative Works:** Online Exhibition, "Virtual Foresight," Women's Studio Center (1995-Present); Internet Installation, "The World's Women On Line" (1995-Present); Contributor, Women in the Arts Newsletter (2014); Online Exhibition, "Virtual Perspective," Melissa Wolf Fine Arts (2012); Exhibitor, James Brown House (2008); Exhibitor, ArtExpo New York, Redwood Media Group (2008); Exhibitor, Licartopen.org (2008); Exhibitor, "Women in the Arts," Venezuelan Center (2007); Exhibitor, Group Shows, Pier Show, Emerald Expositions, LLC (2006); Exhibitor, Medeung Gallery (2005); Exhibitor, Taller Boricua Gallery, JdBPAC (2005); Online Exhibition, "Virtual Fantasy," Melissa Wolf Fine Arts (2005); Exhibitor, Williamsburg Art & Historical Center (2004); Exhibitor, Broome Street Gallery, Parasol Projects (2004); Exhibitor, Women in the Arts Part II, Canajoharie, NY (2000); Exhibitor, Broome Street Gallery, Parasol Projects (2000); Exhibitor, Flat Iron Gallery (1999); Exhibitor, "Brooklyn Waterfront Artist's Collective 4th Annual Pier Show" (1998); Exhibitor, "Painterly Forms" (1997); Exhibitor, "Small Statement Show" (1997); Exhibitor, "Diversity" (1997); Exhibitor, "Openings" (1996); Exhibitor, Fine Arts Museum of Long Island (1996); Exhibitor, "ADA: Women and Information Technology" (1995-1996); Featured, "In Three Dimensions; Women Sculptors of the 90's" by Charlotte Streiffer Rubinstein, Snug Harbor Cultural Center & Botanical Garden, Newhouse Center for Contemporary Art, New York, NY (1995-1996); Video Installation, Computing Commons Gallery, Arizona State University, Tempe, AZ (1995-1996); Installation, "United Nations Fourth World Conference on Women," Beijing, China (1995-1996); Exhibitor, "Points of View" (1995); Exhibitor, "A Woman's Place" (1995); Exhibitor, "Visions of Reality" (1995); Exhibitor, "Hallelujah" (1994); Exhibitor, "Family Values" (1994); Exhibitor, "Garden of Delights" (1994); Exhibitor, "Small Works" (1993); Exhibitor, "Paintings and Paperworks," The City University of New York (1992); Exhibitor, "Women's Art" (1992); Exhibitor, "Salute to Women," National Museum of Women in the Arts, Washington, DC (1991); "An American Album," National Museum of Women in the Arts, Washington, DC (1991); "Themes: Music, Dance, Theater," Cork Gallery, Lincoln Center, New York, NY (1990); "Women's Visions: Themes from Nature," Nabisco Brands Gallery, New York, NY (1989) **Membership:** Women in the Arts Foundation (1980-Present); Executive Coordinator, Women in the Arts Foundation (1986); Creative Women's Collective; Women's Studio Center, New York Artists Equity Association, Inc. **Shipping Address:** 16625 Powells Cove Blvd Apt 12L, Beechhurst, NY, 11357

P. Evelyn Merk

Title: Librarian **Industry:** Library Management/Library Services **Date of Birth:** 12/08/1943 **Place of Birth:** Macon **State:** GA **Parents:** Charlie B. Merk; Gladys (Perry) Merk **Education:** MLS, Emory University (1987); MEd, University of Georgia (1973); BA, Mercer University (1966) **Career:** Library Consultant and Trainer, Houston County Public Library, Warner Robins, GA (2002-2006); Assistant Director, Houston County Public Library, Warner Robins, GA (1996-2002); Librarian, Houston County Public Library, Warner Robins, GA (1977-1996); Reference Librarian, Houston County Public Library, Warner Robins, GA (1976-1977); Technical Services Librarian, Houston County Public Library, Warner Robins, GA (1975-1976); School Media Specialist, Mary Persons School, Forsyth, GA (1973-1975); Teacher, Brantley County High School, Nahunta, GA (1970-1972); Teacher, Westside School, McDonough, GA (1968-1970); Teacher, East Laurens High School, Dublin, GA (1966-1968) **Civic:** Board of Directors, Warner Robins Community Concert Association (1991); Chairman, Warner Robins Day Care Center Inc. (1984-1985); Board of Directors, Warner Robins Day Care Center Inc. **Awards:** Bob Richardson Award, Georgia Library Association (2016); Honorary Member Award, Southeastern Library Association (2016) **Membership:** American Library Association, American Association of University Women, Business and Professional Women; Southeastern Library Association; Georgia Library Association **Marquis Who's Who Honors:** Albert Nelson Marquis Lifetime Achievement Award (2017) **Hobbies:** Reading; Travel **Shipping Address:** 293 Peachtree Circle, Warner Robins, GA, 31088

Yvonne F. Messner, PhD

Title: Physical Education Educator **Industry:** Education/Educational Services **Education:** PhD in Physical Education in Recreation and Health, Indiana University, With Honors **Career:** Assistant Professor in Physical Education, Azusa Pacific University (1996-2003); Assistant Professor in Physical Education, Winthrop University, Rock Hill, SC (1988-1996); Associate Professor in Physical Education, Director of Fitness, Ball State University, Muncie, IN (1986-1987); Associate Professor in Physical Education, Chair of Health and Physical Education Department, Women's Athletic Director, Grace College, Winona Lake, IN (1977-1985); Women's Athletic Director, Grace College, Winona Lake, IN (1963-1976); Director of Intramural Sports Program, Grace College, Winona Lake, IN (1963-1976); Assistant Professor in Physical Education, Grace College, Winona Lake, IN (1963-1976); Director of Women's Intramural and Extramural Sports, Grace College, Winona Lake, IN (1957-1963); Instructor in Health and Physical Education, Grace College, Winona Lake, IN (1957-1963); Physical Education Teacher, Coach, Warsaw Junior and Senior High School (1956-1957); Teacher, West Ward Elementary School, Warsaw, IN (1955-1956) **Creative Works:** Author, "Swimming Everyone," Second Edition (1992); Author, "Swimming Everyone" (1989); Author, "Camp Devotions" (1974); Author, "Campfire Cooking" (1973); **Membership:** South Carolina Park and Recreation Association; South Carolina Alliance of Health, Physical Education, Recreation, and Dance; American Alliance of Health, Physical Education, Recreation, and Dance **Marquis Who's Who Honors:** Albert Nelson Marquis Lifetime Achievement Award (2017) **Shipping Address:** 315 Canyonside Way, Apartment 299, Oceanside, CA, 92058

James Robert Metzler

Title: Musician, Adjunct Professor of Music (Retired) **Industry:** Education/Educational Services **Company Name:** Grand Valley State University **Date of Birth:** 06/20/1947 **Place of Birth:** Worcester **State:** MA **Year of Passing:** 06/28/2017 **Parents:** Robert Adolph Metzler; Olga Slonin **Marital Status:** Married **Spouse Name:** Diane Pearl Fought (8/27/1988) **Children:** Yurii Wynn Fought; Jeffrey David Metzler **Education:** Doctoral Studies in Organ and Musicology, University of Michigan, Ann Arbor, MI (1987); Diploma in Choir Training, American Guild of Organists (1977); Honorary Diploma, National College Music & Arts; Diploma, Cambridge Society of Musicians; MusM, Hartt College Music, University of Hartford (1975); MusB, Westminster Choir College (1969) **Career:** Adjunct Professor of Music, Grand Valley State University (2011-2016); Organist, Director of Music, Park Congregational Church, Grand Rapids, MI (2006-2013); Organist and Director of Music, Trinity Episcopal Cathedral, Little Rock, AR (1996-2006); Adjunct Professor in Organ, University of Toledo (1984-1989); Organist and Choirmaster, Trinity Episcopal Church, Toledo, Ohio (1972-1996); Organist and Choirmaster, First Presbyterian Church, Hartford, CT (1971-1972); **Career Related:** Performance Recital, Church of the Madeleine, Paris, France (2017) **Awards:** First Prize in Guild Exams, S. Lewis Elmer, American Guild of Organists (1977) **Membership:** Royal School of Church Music; American Guild of Organists; Organ Historical Society **Religion:** Catholic **Shipping Address:** 8734 Galloway Ct, Sylvania, OH, 43560

Marsha L. Meyers

Title: Licensed Social Worker **Industry:** Social Work **Date of Birth:** 12/03/1948 **Place of Birth:** Springfield **State:** OH **Parents:** Dennis Wathan; Juanita E. (Ratliff) Easterling **Marital Status:** Married **Spouse Name:** Wade Trent Meyers (10/5/1974) **Children:** Lindsay Dionne; Whitney Jane **Education:** BA in Sociology, Olivet Nazarene University, Bourbonnais, IL (1972) **Certifications:** Licensed Social Worker; Licensed Ohio-Counselor; Licensed Social Worker and Marriage & Family Therapist **Career:** Former Social Work Coordinator, Mercy Health Systems and Home Health Care, Urbana, OH **Career Related:** Former Board of Directors, Champaign County Chapter, American Cancer Society; Member, Advisory Board, Mercy Memorial Hospital, Home Health Care Hospice; Practicum Site Supervisor **Awards:** Social Worker of the Year, Cedarville University Chapter, Phi Alpha Theta (2000); Social Worker of the Year for Excellence in Small Departments, Ohio Society of Hospital Social Workers (1995) **Membership:** Society of Hospital Social Work Directors; Former Vice President, National American Association of Christians in Social Work **Shipping Address:** 223 College St, Urbana, OH, 43078

Wayne M. Meyers

Title: Microbiologist (Retired), Physician (Retired) **Industry:** Sciences **Date of Birth:** 08/28/1924 **Place of Birth:** Huntingdon **State:** PA **Parents:** John William Meyers; Carrie Venca (Weaver) Meyers **Marital Status:** Married **Spouse Name:** Esther Louise Kleinschmidt (8/26/1953) **Children:** Amy; George; Daniel; Sara **Education:** Honorary DSc, Juniata College, Huntingdon, PA (1986); Intern, Conemaugh Valley Memorial Hospital, Johnstown, PA (1959-1960); MD, Baylor College of Medicine (1959); PhD in Medical Microbiology, University of Wisconsin (1955); MS in Medical Microbiology, University of Wisconsin (1953); Diploma, Moody Bible Institute (1950); BS in Chemistry, Juniata College (1947) **Career:** Visiting Scientist, Armed Forces Institute of Pathology, Washington, DC (2005-2011); Assistant to Registrar, Leprosy Registry, Armed Forces Institute of Pathology, Washington, DC (2005-2011); Visiting Scientist, American Red Cross (2005-2011); Chief, Mycobacteriology Division, Armed Forces Institute of Pathology, Washington, DC (1989-2005); Research Affiliate, Tulane University (1981-2005); Registrar, Leprosy Registry, Armed Forces Institute of Pathology, Washington, DC (1975-2005); Consultant, Leonard Wood Memorial (1990-2004); Science Director, Leonard Wood Memorial (1987-1990) **Career Related:** Member, Board of Directors, Leonard Wood Memorial; Member, Board of Directors, Gorgas Memorial Institute of Tropical and Preventive Medicine **Civic:** Corporate Board of Directors, Damien-Dutton Society Leprosy Aid, Inc. (1996-Present); Member, Board of References, American Leprosy Missions (1988-Present); Member, Buruli Ulcer Task Force, World Health Organization (1998-2004); Program Consultant to Board of Directors, American Leprosy Missions (1988-2003); Advisory Board, Damien-Dutton Society Leprosy Aid, Inc. (1983-1996) **Military Service:** U.S. Army (1944-1946) **Creative Works:** Board of Directors, Journal of Leprosy (1978-1993); Contributor, Book Chapters; Contributor, Articles, Professional Journals **Awards:** Life Achievement Award, Alumni Association, Baylor College of Medicine (2009); Research Grantee, World Health Organization (1978-1987); Fellow, Allergy Foundation of America (1957-1958) **Membership:** President, Binford-Dammin Society of Infectious Disease Pathologists (1995-1996); President, International Leprosy Association (1988-1993); Secretary-Treasurer, Binford-Dammin Society of Infectious Disease Pathologists (1988-1991); Councillor, International Leprosy Association (1978-1988); **Political Affiliations:** Independent **Religion:** Protestant **Business Address:** 6825 16th St NW #54, Washington, DC, 20306 **Shipping Address:** 12202 Brittany Pl, Laurel, MD, 20708

Emanuel John Mickel, PhD

Title: Retired Language Educator **Industry:** Education/Educational Services **Company Name:** Indiana University **Date of Birth:** 10/11/1937 **Place of Birth:** Lemont **State:** IL **Parents:** Emanuel John Mickel; Mildred (Newton) Mickel **Marital Status:** Married **Spouse Name:** Kathleen Russell (05/31/1959) **Children:** Jennifer; Chiara; Heather **Education:** PhD, University of North Carolina (1965); MA, University of North Carolina (1961); BA, Louisiana State University (1959) **Career:** Professor Emeritus, Indiana University, Bloomington, IN (2015-Present); Retired (2015); Professor, Indiana University, Bloomington, IN (1973-2015); Chairman, Department of French and Italian, Indiana University (2009-2015); Chairman, Department of French and Italian, Indiana University, Bloomington, IN (1984-1995); Director, Medieval Studies Institute, Indiana University, Bloomington, IN (1976-1991); Associate Professor, Indiana University, Bloomington, IN (1968-1973); Associate Professor, University of Nebraska, Lincoln (1967-1968); Assistant Professor, University of Nebraska, Lincoln (1965-1967) **Career Related:** Consultant, National Endowment for the Humanities; Evaluator, ALVS Fellowship; Visiting Scholar, Pembroke College; Advisory Board Member, Mediaevalia (2007); Visiting Scholar, University of Cambridge (2006); Advisory Board Member, Nineteenth Century French Studies (1995-Present); French Advisor, Societe Rencesvals (1995-1998) **Military Service:** Captain, U.S. Army (1963-1965) **Creative Works:** Author, "Les Enfances Godefroi and Le Retour de Cornumarant" (1999); Author, "Jules Vernes" Complete Twenty Thousand Leagues Under the Sea (1992); Author, "Ganelon, Treason, and the '¯Chanson de Roland'" (1989); Author, "Eugene Fromentin" (1982); Co-editor, "Old French Crusade Cycle," 10 Volume, University of Alabama (1977-2003); Author, "Marie de France" (1974) **Awards:** Promoted to Officier, L'Ordre des Palmes Academiques (2011); Chevalier, L'Ordre des Palmes Academiques (1997); Lilly Open Fellow, Lilly Endowment Inc., Indianaoplis, IN (1981-1982); Grantee, National Endowment for the Humanities, Washington, DC (1978-1984) **Hobbies:** Music; Theater; Sports; Travel; Ancient Literature **Shipping Address:** 3749 E Cameron Ave, Bloomington, IN, 47401

Carol Susan Miller

Title: Elementary School Educator, Counselor **Industry:** Education/Educational Services **Date of Birth:** 01/10/1939 **Place of Birth:** Brooklyn **State:** NY **Parents:** Maurice Shapiro; Bess (Strauss) Shapiro **Marital Status:** Divorced **Spouse Name:** Stephen Herschel Miller (Divorced) **Children:** Mark Alan; David Charles **Education:** MA in Counseling Psychology, Lewis & Clark (1988); Coursework in Education, Queens College, CUNY (1959-1961); BS in Elementary Education, The Ohio State University (1959) **Certifications:** Certification in Basic Counselor Personnel Services, State of Oregon (1988); Certified Teacher, Grades K-6, California Department of Education (1966); Certified Teacher, Grades K-3, New York State Education Department (1959) **Career:** Advisory Board Member, St. Germaine Auxiliary for Child Abuse Prevention (Now Promises2Kids) (1998-Present); Breast Cancer Support Group Facilitator, Scripps Health (2000-2002); Advisory Board Member, Scripps Polster Breast Cancer Center, Scripps Health (1999-2001); Cancer Support Group Facilitator, American Cancer Society, Inc. (1992-1999); Advisory Board Member, American Cancer Society, Inc. (1994-1996); Substitute Elementary School Teacher, San Diego School Districts (1990-1991); Substitute Elementary School Teacher, San Diego School Districts (1967-1968); Elementary School Teacher, Horace Mann School, Beverly Hills School District (1966-1967); Teacher, Grades K-Three, Roosevelt Elementary School, Santa Monica Malibu Unified School District (1961-1966); Kindergarten Teacher, Hampton Street School, Mineola Public Schools (1959-1961) **Civic:** Volunteer, Moores Cancer Center, University of California, San Diego (2005-Present); Volunteer, Barnes Tennis Center, Point Loma, CA (2005-Present); Volunteer, Reach to Recovery, American Cancer Society, Inc. (1980-Present); Volunteer, Polinsky Children's Center, San Diego County (1991-2005); Coordinator, Reach to Recovery, American Cancer Society, Inc. (1991-1993); Scripps Polster Breast Care Center, Scripps Health, San Diego, CA (1982-1984); Leader, Boy Scouts of America (1977-1983); Citizen Advisory Committee, Lake Oswego, OR (1982) **Awards:** Volunteer of the Year, Health & Human Services Agency, County of San Diego (2002); Terese Lasser Award, American Cancer Society, Inc. (1993) **Membership:** League of Women Voters; Psi Chi, The International Honor Society in Psychology **Marquis Who's Who Honors:** Distinguished Humanitarian (2017) **Hobbies:** Tennis; Dance; Reading; Traveling; Writing **Political Affiliations:** Democrat **Religion:** Jewish **Shipping Address:** 6555 Caminito Northland, La Jolla, CA, 92037

Elizabeth Miller

Title: Mathematician **Industry:** Education/Educational Services **Company Name:** Rapides Parish Schools **Date of Birth:** 09/11/1939 **Place of Birth:** Alexandria **State:** LA **Education:** MS, Northwestern State University, Natchitoches, LA (1964); BS, Louisiana College (1962) **Certifications:** Certified Teacher, Louisiana **Career:** Substitute Teacher, Rapides Parish Schools, Alexandria, VA (1989-Present); Teacher, Forest Hill Academy (2000); Substitute Teacher, Holy Savior Menard Central High School, Alexandra Country Day School (1993-1998); Instructor, Communications College, Alexandria, VA (1987-1988); Substitute Teacher, Various Alexandria Schools (1982-1987); Human Service Worker II, Rapides Parish Office of Human Development, Alexandria, VA (1969-1982); Teacher, Rapides Parish Schools, Alexandria, LA (1967-1969); Instructor, Jefferson State Junior College, Birmingham, AL (1966-1967); Instructor, Itawamba Junior College, Fulton, MS (1965-1966); Teacher, Rapides Parish Schools, Alexandria, LA (1964-1965) **Membership:** Parliamentarian, Alexandria-Pineville Branch, American Association of University Women (2004); Secretary, Alexandria-Pineville Branch, American Association of University Women (2002-2004); American History Month Chair, Daughters of the American Revolution (1991-1994); **Marquis Who's Who Honors:** Albert Nelson Marquis Lifetime Achievement Award (2017) **Shipping Address:** 5821 Starling Circle, Alexandria, LA, 71301

Waenard Livingston Miller Jr.

Title: Cardiologist **Industry:** Medicine & Health Care **Date of Birth:** 03/01/1947 **Place of Birth:** Greenville **State:** SC **Parents:** Waenard Livingston Miller; Margaret Evelyn (Burns) Miller **Marital Status:** Married **Spouse Name:** Sheila McLawhorn Miller (12/20/1969) **Children:** Waenard Livingston, III; Bernyrd Carlysle **Education:** MS in Medical Management, The University of Texas (2000); Fellow in Cardiology, The University of Texas Southwestern Medical Center (1981-1983); Resident in Internal Medicine, The University of Texas Southwestern Medical Center (1979-1981); Intern in Internal Medicine, The University of Texas Southwestern Medical Center (1978-1979); MD, Medical University of South Carolina (1978); MS in Biology, Wright State University (1974); MS in Nuclear Physics, University of Tennessee (1970); BS in Physics, Clemson University (1969) **Certifications:** Diplomate, American Board of Internal Medicine; Subspecialty of Cardiovascular Disease **Career:** Laboratory Director, Cardiac Catheterization Lab, HCA Medical Center, Plano, TX (1994); Co-founder, Texas Heart Group (Now Legacy Heart Center) (1985); Private Cardiology Practice, Plano, TX (1983-2017) **Career Related:** Fellow, American College of Cardiology; Fellow, American Heart Association **Civic:** Trustee, Baylor Healthcare Systems (2004) **Military Service:** First Lieutenant, U.S. Air Force (1971-1974) **Awards:** Top Doctors In Texas, "Texas Monthly Magazine" (2004-2016) **Membership:** Councilor, Texas Division, American College of Cardiology (2004-2005) **Marquis Who's Who Honors:** Albert Nelson Marquis Lifetime Achievement Award (2017); Distinguished Humanitarian (2017) **Hobbies:** Traveling; Digital photography **Shipping Address:** 5118 Oak Knoll Lane, Frisco, TX, 75034 **Website:** http://newsstand.clemson.edu/mediarelations/miller-gift-establishes-endowed-chair-in-medical-physics

Marilyn D. Mintz

Title: Artist, Writer, Inventor, Business Person, Licensor **Industry:** Business Management/Business Services **Company Name:** The Sweetheart Arts Company, Inc. **Date of Birth:** 03/18/2017 **Place of Birth:** Philadelphia **State:** PA **Parents:** Milton A. Mintz; Mildred L. Mintz **Education:** MA in Film and TV, University of California, Los Angeles (1975); BFA in Theater, California Institute of the Arts (1972); Undergraduate Coursework, University of California, Santa Barbara (1968-1970) **Career:** Founder, President & Chief Executive Officer, The Sweetheart Arts Company, Inc., Los Gatos, CA (1990-Present); Founder, President & Chief Executive Officer, M.D.M. Company, Studio City, CA (1981) **Creative Works:** Author, Artist, Inventor, Designer, Composer, Performer, Actor, Director, Creator, "Marilyn D. Mintz, Series (1989-Present); Author, Designer & Creator, "The Martial Arts Films, Second Edition" (1983); Creator, Scriptwriter, "The Cartoonist" (1980); Scriptwriter, Creator, "Cartoon Pictures" (1979); Author, Designer, Creator, "The Martial Arts Films" (1978); Playwright, "A Man," Adaptation of Shakespeare's "Julius Caesar" (1972); Actor, California Shakespeare Festival (1970); Columnist, Images (1967-1968) **Where will you be in five years:** As Ms. Mintz looks to the future, she intends to continue contributing to the field of art while taking on new projects and opportunities as they arise. **Business Address:** P.O. Box 1411, Los Gatos, CA, 95031 **Shipping Address:** 15466 Los Gatos Blvd., Suite 109, P.M.B. 213, Los Gatos, CA, 95032

Thomas Anthony Mirante

Title: Secondary School Educator **Industry:** Education/Educational Services **Date of Birth:** 10/11/1931 **Place of Birth:** Utica **State:** NY **Education:** Studies with Earl George, David Diamond; Postgraduate Coursework, Colgate University (1964); MS in Music, Ithaca College (1955); BS in Music, State University of New York, Potsdam (1954) **Certifications:** Certified Music Teacher; Guidance Counselor, State of New York **Career:** Director of Music, Teacher, Oneida City Schools (1960-1992); Teacher of Music, Port Leyden Center School (1957-1960); Choral Director, First Infantry Division, Post Chapel U.S. Army, Fort Riley, KS (1956-1957); Pianist, Fifth Infantry Division Band, US Army, Fort Ord, CA (1955-1956) **Civic:** Trustee, Canastota Library Board (1986) **Awards:** Rockefeller Grantee American Music Center (1975); Grantee, New York State Council of Arts (1975) **Membership:** BMI; Madison County Music Teachers Association **Marquis Who's Who Honors:** Albert Nelson Marquis Lifetime Achievement Award (2017) **Hobbies:** Walking **Religion:** Roman Catholic **Shipping Address:** 208 N Main St, Canastota, NY, 13032

Len Mizrah, PhD

Marquis Who's Who
18 | 98
Biographee

Title: President, Chief Executive Officer **Industry:** Business Management/Business Services **Company Name:** Authernative, Inc. **Date of Birth:** 05/11/1948 **Place of Birth:** Kiev **Country of Origin:** Ukraine **Parents:** Benjamin Mizrah; Maria (Gutin) Mizrah **Marital Status:** Married **Spouse Name:** Zoya Gelvan (1/6/1989) **Education:** PhD, Institute of Physics, Kiev, Ukraine (1985); MS, Institute of Electron Technology, MIET, Moscow, Russia (1972) **Career:** Engineer Manager, MIPS Technologies, Inc. (Now Imagination Technologies Limited) (1998-Present); Department Manager, Hitachi Systems Micro Clinic, Pvt. Ltd. (1995-1998); Engineer Manager, Sun Microsystems, Inc. (Now Oracle) (1993-1995); Laboratory Manager, Fujitsu (1989-1993); Research Staff, The Institute of Physics, Kiev, Ukraine (1972-1989); Managing Partner, B Cubed Ventures LLC; President, Authernative, Inc. **Career Related:** Lecturer, Cogswell College (1993-1996) **Creative Works:** Patentee, 33 Patents in Field; Contributor, Articles, Professional Journals **Membership:** Senior Member, Institute of Electrical and Electronics Engineers (2016); American Physical Society; IEEE **Marquis Who's Who Honors:** Albert Nelson Marquis Lifetime Achievement Award (2017) **Shipping Address:** 9711 Amethyst Lane, Brentwood, TN, 37027

Susan Lynn Mogus

Title: Lead Technologist **Industry:** Technology **Company Name:** Trinitas Regional Medical Center **Education:** BS in Medical Technology, Slippery Rock University of Pennsylvania (1984) **Certifications:** Certified Medical Technologist **Membership:** Hockey Kicks Cancer; American Society for Clinical Pathology **Marquis Who's Who Honors:** Albert Nelson Marquis Lifetime Achievement Award (2017) **To what do you attribute your success:** Ms. Mogus attributes her success to her caring nature, dedication, and life experience. **Why did you become involved in your profession or industry:** Ms. Mogus became involved in her profession due to her genuine interest in the field of medicine. **Where will you be in five years:** In five years, Ms. Mogus hopes to continue to grow in the fields of health care and research. **Hobbies:** Reading; Hockey enthusiast **Shipping Address:** 660 Summer Street, Elizabeth, NJ, 07202 **Website:** http://www.susanmogus.com

Mitchell William Moncrieff

Title: Meteorologist **Industry:** Sciences **Company Name:** National Center for Atmospheric Research **Date of Birth:** 04/07/1944 **Place of Birth:** Shetland **Country of Origin:** Scotland **Parents:** Mitchell James; Eliza Agnes Moncrieff **Marital Status:** Married **Spouse Name:** Patricia Margaret Nicolson **Children:** Kerri Elizabeth **Education:** PhD in Atmospheric Physics, Imperial College, London (1970); BS in Mathematics, Aberdeen University, Scotland (1967) **Career:** Senior Scientist, Climate & Global Dynamics Laboratory, National Center for Atmospheric Research (2015-Present); Senior Scientist, Climate and Global Dynamics Division, Earth System Laboratory, National Center for Atmospheric Research (2010-2015); Senior Scientist, National Center for Atmospheric Research, Boulder, CO (1988-2010); Head, Cloud Systems Group, Mesoscale & Microscale Meteorology Division, National Center for Atmospheric Research (1994-2007); Reader, Imperial College (1987-1988); Lecturer, Department of Physics, Imperial College (1975-1986); Lecturer, Department of Meteorology, Imperial College (1972-1975); Post Doctoral Fellow, Imperial College (1970-1972); Senior Ambassador, Mesoscale and Microscale Meteorology Division, National Center for Atmospheric Research **Career Related:** Science Advisor, Center for Prototype Climate Modeling, New York, NY (2011-Present); Distinguished Lecturer, Indian Meteorological Society, Pune (2016); Editorial Advisory Board Member, Mathematics of Climate and Weather Forecasting, De Gruyter Open (2014); Science Advisor, Science Advisor, Associate Investigator, Australian Research Council Centre of Excellence for Climate Systems Science (2012); Head, Mesoscale Interactions Section Convective Storms Division (1986-1994); Visiting Scientist, National Center for Atmospheric Research, Boulder, CO (1986) **Civic:** Business Ambassador, Highlands and Islands Enterprise, Scotland (1996-Present) **Creative Works:** Contributor, Chapters, Various Books; Contributor, Over 150 Articles, Professional Journals **Awards:** Certificate of Excellence, National Center for Atmospheric Research (1999); Buchan Prize, Royal Meteorological Society (1982); Various Academic Awards, Aberdeen University (1966, 1964) **Membership:** Fellow, Royal Meteorological Society; American Meteorological Society **Shipping Address:** 1447 Kennedy Ct, Boulder, CO, 80303

Jay Parry Monge

Title: Lawyer **Industry:** Law and Legal Services **Company Name:** Monge Law Firm, PLLC **Date of Birth:** 03/15/1943 **Place of Birth:** New York City **State:** NY **Parents:** Joseph Paul Monge; Dorothy Emma (Oschmann) Monge **Marital Status:** Married **Spouse Name:** Elizabeth Ann Tracy (1994); Julia T. Burdick (1966, Divorced 1994) **Children:** Justin Parry; Lindsay Newton **Education:** LLB, University of Virginia (1969); AB, Harvard University (1966) **Career:** Partner, Mayer, Brown, LLP, Charlotte, NC (2000-2018); Managing Partner, Mayer, Brown, LLP, New York, NY (1981-1994); Partner, Mayer, Brown, LLP, New York, NY (1980-1999); Partner, Mayer, Brown, LLP, Chicago, IL (1976-1979); Associate, Mayer, Brown, Rowe & Maw, LLP, Chicago, IL (1969-1975) **Civic:** Trustee, Wagner College (1996-2002) **Creative Works:** Contributor, Legal Commentaries, Illinois Institute for Continuing Legal Education (2002, 1996, 1993, 1987, 1984, 1981, 1978, 1974) **Membership:** American Bar Association; Association of the Bar of the City of New York; Chicago Club; Charlotte City Club; Quail Hollow Club **Bar Admissions:** North Carolina (2003); New York (1981); Illinois (1969) **Marquis Who's Who Honors:** Albert Nelson Marquis Lifetime Achievement Award (2017) **Why did you become involved in your profession or industry:** Mr. Monge was inspired to enter law because his father was a lawyer. Also, law is a way for him to solve problems, and assist his clients in achieving their goals. **Business Address:** 333 W Trade St Unit 250, Charlotte, NC, 28202

John Ron Moore

Title: Manufacturing Executive **Industry:** Manufacturing **Date of Birth:** 07/12/1935 **Place of Birth:** Pueblo **State:** CO **Parents:** John E. Moore; Anna (Yesberger) Moore **Marital Status:** Married **Spouse Name:** Judith Russelyn Bauman (9/5/1959) **Children:** Leland; Roni; Timothy; Elaine **Education:** Graduate Coursework, Advanced Management Program, Graduate School of Business, Harvard University (1981); BS, University of Colorado (1959) **Career:** President, Chief Executive Officer, Midas International Corporation, Chicago, IL (1982-1998); President, Auto Group, Midas International Corporation, Chicago, IL (1976-1982); Vice President, General Manager, Midas, Toronto, ON, Canada (1972-1975); Distribution Manager, Midas International Corporation, Chicago, IL (1965-1971); Management Trainee, Montgomery Ward & Co., Denver, CO (1960-1965) **Civic:** Director, Chicago Crime Commission Trustee, University of Colorado Foundation **Membership:** Harvard Business School Alumni Association; University of Colorado Alumni Association; Chicago Council on Global Affairs; Economic Club of Chicago; Commercial Club of Chicago **Political Affiliations:** Republican **Shipping Address:** 930 Barclay Circle, Lake Forest, IL, 60045

Lloyd "Pete" A. Morley, PhD

Title: Electrical Engineering Educator **Industry:** Education/Educational Services **Company Name:** University of Alabama **Date of Birth:** 10/28/1940 **Place of Birth:** Provo **State:** UT **Parents:** John Morley, Jr.; Dorothea (Nielsen) Morley **Marital Status:** Married **Spouse Name:** Jo Ann Bryant (2/22/1975) **Children:** Paul Loring **Education:** PhD in Mining Engineering, University of Utah, Salt Lake City, UT (1971); BS in Mining Engineering, University of Utah, Salt Lake City, UT (1968) **Career:** Professor Emeritus, University of Alabama (2007-Present); Department Head, University of Alabama, Tuscaloosa, AL (2000-2004); Interim Department Head, University of Alabama, Tuscaloosa, AL (1999-2000); Associate Department Head, Electrical and Computer Engineering, University of Alabama, Tuscaloosa, AL (1997-1999); Professor, Electrical Engineering, University of Alabama, Tuscaloosa, AL (1996-2006); Endowed Chair, Mining Engineering, University of Alabama, Tuscaloosa, AL (1993-1999); Professor, Head, Department of Mineral Engineering, University of Alabama, Tuscaloosa, AL (1985-1993); Professor, Pennsylvania State University, University Park, PA (1980-1985); Associate Professor, Pennsylvania State University, University Park, PA (1975-1980); Assistant Professor, Mining Engineering, Pennsylvania State University, University Park, PA (1971-1975); Teaching Assistant, Research Associate, University of Utah, Salt Lake City, UT (1968-1971) **Career Related:** Consultant, Drummond Company, Inc., Birmingham, AL (1991-1998); Consultant, Pittsburg and Midway Coal Mining Company, Englewood, CO (1990-1998); Consultant, Jim Walter Resources, Inc., Brookwood, AL (1987-1998) **Civic:** Volunteer, IEEE **Military Service:** Staff Sergeant, U.S. National Guard (1958-1966) **Creative Works:** Author, "Mine Power Systems" (1990); Contributor, Articles, Professional Journals **Awards:** Technical Activities Hall of Honor, IEEE (2015); Richard M. Emerson Award, IEEE (2005); Hackney Outstanding Teaching Award, University of Alabama (2004); Third Millennium Medal, IEEE (2000); Hackney Faculty Leadership Award, University of Alabama (2000); Distinguished Service Award, IEEE Industry Applications Society (1995) **Membership:** Life Fellow, IEEE (1988-Present); Corporate Integrity Officer, IEEE (2006-2011); Vice President, Publications, IEEE (1999); Board of Directors, IEEE (1997-1999); Vice President, Technical Activities, IEEE (1997-1998) **Marquis Who's Who Honors:** Albert Nelson Marquis Lifetime Achievement Award (2017) **Hobbies:** Vintage vacuum-tube and high-end audio systems; Classic sports cars; Growing roses; **Shipping Address:** 2540 Saratoga Lane, Tuscaloosa, AL, 35406 **Website:** https://www.linkedin.com/in/lloyd-a-pete-morley-55ab5012

Drew A. Morris

Title: Attorney **Industry:** Law and Legal Services **Company Name:** Nachmias Morris & Alt, P.C. **Marital Status:** Married **Spouse Name:** Nicole S. Morris **Children:** Avery G.; Blake K. **Education:** MBA, Drexel University; LLM in Taxation, New York University School of Law; JD, The Pennsylvania State University, Cum Laude; BA, Brandeis University **Career:** Attorney, Shareholder, Nachmias, Morris & Alt, P.C. (2009-Present); Adjunct Law Professor, Charles Widger School of Law, Villanova University (2007-Present); Adjunct Law Professor, Temple University (2007-2010) **Membership:** American Bar Association; Pennsylvania Bar Association; Tax Group, Philadelphia Bar Association; Tax Council, Philadelphia Bar Association **To what do you attribute your success:** Mr. Morris attributes his success to just doing a very good job, so people will come to the practice through word of mouth. **Why did you become involved in your profession or industry:** Mr. Morris became involved in his profession because at the end of his first year of law school, instead of going back, he backpacked across Europe and ended up studying with Justice Anthony Scalia of the Supreme Court of the United States for about a month in Vienna. He came back and got a phone call from one of the deans, who asked him to play golf. He agreed and while they were golfing, the dean told him he was in the top 10% of his class. The dean encouraged him to send out resumes right away, as did friends of his, so he got a summer job at Schnader Harrison and when he finished school he got a job with them right away. **Business Address:** 20 Ash Street, Suite 200, 20 Ash Street, Suite 200, Conshohocken, PA, 19428 **Website:** http://www.nmapc.net/index.php/attorneys/morris

William Morris

Title: Founding Partner **Industry:** Law and Legal Services **Company Name:** The Morris Law Group **Education:** JD, York University **Certifications:** Certified Specialist in Civil Litigation **Career:** Founding Partner, The Morris Law Group; Founder, Accident Benefits Consultants, The Morris Law Group **Awards:** Emilius Irving Award, Hamilton Law Association (2006) **Membership:** President, Hamilton Law Association; President, Hamilton Medical-Legal Society; President, Hamilton Jewish Federation; President, B'nai Brith Canada **To what do you attribute your success:** Mr. Morris attributes his success to his empathy toward his clients. **Why did you become involved in your profession or industry:** Mr. Morris became involved in his profession because of his desire to help the less fortunate. He was inspired by his late mother. **Shipping Address:** 125 Main St E, Hamilton, ON, Canada, L8N 3Z3 **Website:** http://www.morrislawyers.com

Robert Parker Morse

Title: Investment Company Executive **Industry:** Business Management/Business Services **Company Name:** Morse Asset Management, Inc. **Date of Birth:** 05/08/1945 **Place of Birth:** Nyack **State:** NY **Parents:** Robert Willard Parker Morse; Julia (Larson) Morse **Marital Status:** Married **Spouse Name:** Sarah Morgan Cumings (9/23/1978) **Children:** Robert Bradley St. Clair; Parker Morgan; Sarah Spencer **Education:** Coursework in Advanced Currency Theory, Adelphi University Suffolk Centers (1970-1971); BS in Economics, The Wharton School, University of Pennsylvania (1967) **Career:** Director, Morse, Williams & Co. Inc. (1984-Present); Chief Executive Officer, Morse Asset Management, Inc. (2017); Partner, Evercore Wealth Management, LLC (2010-2013); Senior Portfolio Manager, Evercore Wealth Management, LLC (2010-2013); Chairman, Chief Executive Officer, Morse, Williams & Co. Inc., New York, NY (1981-2010); Senior Vice President, Partner, Campbell & Company, LP., New York, NY (1975-1980); Vice President, W.H. Morton Division, American Express Company, New York, NY (1970-1974); Former Chairman, Chief Executive Officer, Capital Guardian LLC, New York, NY **Career Related:** Board of Directors, Dialog Communications, eLottery, Inc. (2005-2006); Board of Directors, 860 United Nations Plaza, Inc., Stowe, VT (2001-2013) **Civic:** Chairman, Board, Chief Executive Officer, Capital Guardian Core Balanced Fund (2013-Present); Member, Sterling George Preservation Trust, Stowe, VT (2007-Present); Trustee, Chairman, Finance, The English-Speaking Union (1998-Present); Board of Associates, The Whitehead Institute, Massachusetts Institute of Technology (1996-Present); Chairman, CGS Management AG (2014-2016) **Military Service:** Lieutenant, US Naval Reserve (1967-1978) **Awards:** Wharton Club Award; National Mayflower Award; Certificate, Secretary of Defense **Membership:** American Defense Preparedness Association; The Pilgrims of the United States; The River Club; The Bond Club of New York, Inc.; United States Naval Institute; Union Club of the City of New York; New York Yacht Club; The Links Club **Marquis Who's Who Honors:** Albert Nelson Marquis Lifetime Achievement Award (2017) **Why did you become involved in your profession or industry:** Mr. Morse started his professional journey with a summer job back in 1959, after which he decided to attend The Wharton School, of the University of Pennsylvania. He was hired right after he got out of the service. His career choice was influenced by his father, who ran the Dime Savings Bank in New York. **Religion:** Episcopalian **Shipping Address:** 805 3rd Ave., Ste 1120, Morse Asset Management, Inc., New York, NY, 10022

Stephen Scott Morse, PhD

Title: Virologist, Epidemiologist, Immunologist, Educator **Industry:** Medicine & Health Care **Company Name:** Mailman School of Public Health, Columbia University **Date of Birth:** 11/22/1951 **Place of Birth:** New York **State:** NY **Parents:** Murray H. Morse; Phyllis Morse **Marital Status:** Married **Spouse Name:** Marilyn Gewirtz (2/1991) **Education:** PhD, University of Wisconsin-Madison (1977); MS, University of Wisconsin-Madison (1974); BS, The City College of New York (1971) **Career:** Professor, Mailman School of Public Health, Columbia University (2008-Present); Adjunct Faculty Member, The Rockefeller University, New York, NY (1996-Present); Director, USAID Predict Project (2009-2014); Director, Center for Public Health Preparedness, Mailman School of Public Health, Columbia University (2000-2005); Assistant Professor to Professor of Epidemiology, Mailman School of Public Health, Columbia University (1996-2008); Program Manager, Defense Advanced Research Projects Agency (1996-2000); Assistant Professor, The Rockefeller University, New York, NY (1988-1996); Research Associate, The Rockefeller University, New York, NY (1985-1988); Assistant Professor of Microbiology, Rutgers, The State University of New Jersey, New Brunswick, NJ (1981-1985); Instructor of Microbiology, School of Medicine, Virginia Commonwealth University, Richmond, VA (1980-1981) **Career Related:** National Science Advisory Board for Biosecurity (2014-Present); Standing Committee on Health Threats Resilience and Workforce Resilience, Institute of Medicine and National Academy of Sciences (2013-Present); Standing Committee, Department of Defense's Biodefense Programs, NAS-NRC (2012-Present); Committee on Biodefense Analysis and Countermeasures (2005-2008); Founding Chair, ProMED (Program for Monitoring Emerging Diseases (1993-1999) **Creative Works:** Associate Editor, Disaster Medicine and Public Health Preparedness (2016-Present); Editorial Board, Emerging Health Threats Journal (2013-Present); Editorial Board, Viral Immunology (2003-Present); Editorial Board, Biosecurity and Bioterrorism (2003-Present); Editorial Board, EcoHealth (2003-2010); Editorial Board, Emerging Infectious Diseases (2003-2006); Author, "Evolutionary Biology of Viruses" (1994); Author, "Emerging Viruses" (1993) **Awards:** Book "Emerging Viruses" Named Top 100 Science Books of the Century **Membership:** Chair, Microbiology Section, The New York Academy of Sciences (1996-1998); Vice Chair, Microbiology Section, The New York Academy of Sciences (1994-1996); **Marquis Who's Who Honors:** Albert Nelson Marquis Lifetime Achievement Award (2017) **Shipping Address:** 275 Central Park W Apt 11F, New York, NY, 10024

Linda Hays Mosely

Title: Surgeon **Industry:** Medicine & Health Care **Company Name:** Linda H. Mosely, MD, PC **Date of Birth:** 02/20/1941 **Place of Birth:** New Orleans **State:** LA **Parents:** Charles Hodge Mosely; Florence (Morley) Mosely Williams **Children:** One Son **Education:** Microsurgery Fellowship, Dr. Ralph Manktelow, Toronto General Hospital, Toronto, Canada (1979-1980); Plastic Surgery Residency, Yale Medical Center, New Haven, CT (1975-1977); Research Fellowship, Yale Medical Center, New Haven, CT (1975); Hand Surgery Fellowship, Dr. Harold Kleinert, Louisville, KY (1972); Clinical Surgery Fellowship, University of Louisville Medical Center, Louisville, KY (1972); General Surgery Residency, Mt. Sinai Hospital, New York, NY (1969-1970); Rotating Internship, Charity Hospital, New Orleans, LA (1968-1969); Medical Residency, CHNO - Tulane Service, New Orleans, LA (1968-1969); MD, Louisiana State University (1967) **Career:** Active Staff, Reston Hospital Center (2005-Present); Active Staff, Inova Alexandria (1980-Present); Active Staff, Inova Fairfax (1980-Present); Consultant in Plastic Surgery, John Fitzgerald Kennedy Hospital, Monrovia, Liberia (1979); Aesthetic Surgery, Clinical Planas, Barcelona, Spain (1978-1979); Part-Time Tutor Specialists, Middlemore Hospital Auckland, Otahuhu, NZ (1977-1978) **Career Related:** Presenter, Hypothenar Hammer Syndrome, Yale Alumni/Resident Meeting (2013); Fellow Emeritus, American College of Surgeons **Civic:** Plastic Surgeon Volunteer Work, Azogues, Ecuador (1988) **Creative Works:** Author, "Cumulative Trauma Disorders and Compression Neuropathies of the Upper Extremities," Occupational Hand & Upper Extremity Injuries & Diseases, Philadelphia, PA (1991); Co-Author, "Difficult Reconstruction of an Extensive Injury in the Lower Extremity With a Large Cross-Leg Microvascular Composite-Tissue Flap Containing Fibula," Plastic and Reconstructive Surgery Journal (1989) **Awards:** Listed, Top 101 Industry Experts, WorldWide Registry (2015); Executives, Professionals and Entreprenuers, World-Wide Registry (2014-2015); Top Doctor, Northern Virginia Magazine (2012-2015) **Membership:** Board of Directors, Medical Society of Northern Virginia (2006-Present); American Society for Surgery of the Hand (1988-Present); Medical Executive Committee, Inova Alexandria Hospital (2013-2014); President, Medical Society of Northern Virginia Women Physicians Group (2010-2013) **Marquis Who's Who Honors:** Albert Nelson Marquis Lifetime Achievement Award (2017) **Business Address:** 1860 Town Center Dr Ste 310, Reston, VA, 20190 **Website:** http://www.lindamoselyhandsurgery.com

William Wallace Mountcastle Jr.

Title: Philosophy and Religion Educator **Industry:** Religious **Company Name:** University of West Florida **Date of Birth:** 07/10/1925 **Place of Birth:** Hanover **State:** NH **Parents:** William Wallace Mountcastle; Grace Elizabeth (Zottarelli) Mountcastle **Marital Status:** Married **Spouse Name:** Barbara Kaye Teelin (10/19/1979); Ila M. Warner (Divorced) **Children:** Christine; Susan; Gregory; Eric; Cathleena; Dasha (Stepdaughter) **Education:** PhD, Boston University (1958); STB, Boston University (1954); BA, Whittier College (1951); Coursework, Embry-Riddle School of Aviation (Now Embry-Riddle University) (1940-1941); Coursework, Cleveland School of Art (1936-1938) **Certifications:** Ordained to Ministry, United Methodist Church (1954) **Career:** Professor, Philosophy and Religion, University of West Florida, Pensacola, FL (1969-Present); Emeritus M.L. Tipton Professor, University of West of Florida, Pensacola, FL (2003); M.L. Tipton Professor, Philosophy and Religion, University of West Florida, Pensacola, FL (1980-2003); Associate Professor, Philosophy and Religion, University of West Florida, Pensacola, FL (1969-1973); Professor, Philosophy, Florida Southern College, Lakeland, FL (1967-1969); Professor, Department of Philosophy, Nebraska Wesleyan University, Lincoln, NE (1963-1967); Head, Department of Philosophy, Nebraska Wesleyan University, Lincoln, NE (1960-1967); Associate Professor, Nebraska Wesleyan University, Lincoln, NE (1960-1963); Assistant Professor, Philosophy and Religion, High Point College, High Point, NC (1958-1960); Nebraska ANN Conference, United Methodist Church (1954-1995) **Civic:** Great Plains Conference, United Methodist Church (2015); Unitarian Universalist Church of Pensacola; United Methodist Church, Pensacola Beach, FL **Military Service:** Army Air Corps Pilot, Far East Air Command, 16th Communications Squadrant, Japan, U.S. Army Air Corps (1942-1948); Charter Member, World War II Memorial **Creative Works:** Author, "The Secret Ministry of Jesus" (2007); Author, "Science Fantasy Voices and Visions of Cosmic Religion" (1996); Author, "Religion in Planetary Perspective" (1979); Contributor, Articles, Professional Journals **Awards:** Several Outstanding Teaching Awards, University of West Florida **Membership:** National Education Association; United Faculty of Florida; American Academy of Religion; The American Philosophical Association; Phi Kappa Phi; Veterans for Peace; Pensacola United Universalist Church **Marquis Who's Who Honors:** Albert Nelson Marquis Lifetime Achievement Award (2017) **Political Affiliations:** Democrat **Shipping Address:** 2526 Bayou Boulevard, Pensacola, FL, 32503

Eileen Anne Mullen

Title: Personnel Director **Industry:** Business Management/Business Services **Company Name:** ASTM **Date of Birth:** 02/14/1943 **Place of Birth:** Philadelphia **State:** PA **Parents:** Joseph Gregory Mullen; Helen Rita (Kane) Mullen **Spouse Name:** William John Raschiatore (Deceased) **Education:** MA in English, Villanova University (1978); BS in English, St. Joseph's University (1967) **Certifications:** Certified Teacher, Commonwealth of Pennsylvania **Career:** Personnel Director, ASTM (2011-Present); Director, Human Resources, ASTM, Philadelphia, PA (1996-2011); Manager, Staff Training and Development, ASTM, Philadelphia, PA (1974-1996); Teacher, West Catholic Girls High School (1967-1974); Teacher, St. Anastasia School, Newtown Square, PA (1960-1967) **Career Related:** Instructor, Speech and Communications, Widener University, Chester, PA **Creative Works:** Contributing Author, Articles on Communications, Training Programs; Contributor, Articles, Professional Journals **Awards:** Outstanding Leadership as President Award, ATD (1981) **Membership:** President, Philadelphia/Delaware Valley Chapter, ATD (1980-1981); ASTD **Political Affiliations:** Democrat **Religion:** Roman Catholic **Business Address:** 100 Barr Harbor Drive, W. Conshohocken, PA, 19428 **Shipping Address:** 1401 Whispering Brooke Dr, Newtown Square, PA, 19073

James Mullen

Title: Lawyer **Industry:** Law and Legal Services **Company Name:** Morrison & Foerster, LLP **Parents:** James Joseph; Maria Isabel Mullen **Marital Status:** Married **Children:** Isabella Zenovia; Olivia Rasha; Samantha Maria **Education:** JD, Hastings College of Law, University of California, San Francisco (1997); PhD, Graduate School of Biomedical Sciences, The University of Texas (1994); BA, University of California, San Diego (1988) **Career:** Of Counsel, Morrison & Foerster, LLP, San Diego (2006-Present); Partner, Morrison & Foerster, LLP, San Diego (2009); Associate, Morrison & Foerster, LLP, San Diego (2003-2006); Associate, Knobbe, Martens, Olson and Bear, LLP, San Diego (1997-2003) **Civic:** Board of Trustees, Hastings Foundation (2016) **Bar Admissions:** United State Patent and Trademark Office (1999); California (1998) **Why did you become involved in your profession or industry:** Dr. Mullen was always interested in helping others. **Hobbies:** Brewing beer; Photography **Business Address:** 12531 High Bluff Dr Ste 100, San Diego, CA, 92130 **Shipping Address:** 12531 High Bluff Dr Ste 100, Morrison Foerster LLP, San Diego, CA, 92130

Margaret J. Murphey

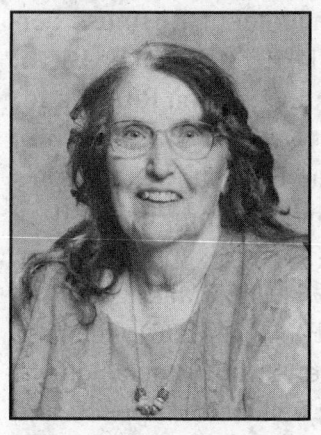

Title: Marriage and Family Therapist **Industry:** Social Work **Company Name:** Angel Rose Counselling **Parents:** Glen Roosevelt Wurster; Lucile Mildred Lopez **Marital Status:** Widowed **Spouse Name:** Russell Warren Murphey (6/20/1959, Deceased 2013) **Children:** Lucinda Huff; Rochelle Scott; Janice Sorenson **Education:** Therapy Intern, Counseling Center, California State University, Chico, CA (1989-1990); MA in Psychology, California State University, Chico, CA (1989); BA in Social Science, California State University, Chico, CA (1986); Postgraduate Coursework, La Salle University **Certifications:** International Christian Counselling License (2007) **Career:** School Counselor, Dishchii'bikoh Community School (1998-2006); Mental Health Counselor, Cibecue Indian Health Center, Cibecue, AZ (1990-1998); Therapist, Mental Health Clinic, Butte County, Chico, CA (1989-1990); Therapist, Family Service Association, Chico, CA (1987-1990); Welfare Worker, Shasta County Health and Human Services, Redding, CA (1979-1985); Secretary, Shasta County Personnel, Redding, CA (1978-1979); Claims Determiner, Employment Development Department, Redding, CA (1976-1978); Teacher, Desert Sands Unified School District, Indio, CA (1969-1972); Secretary, Folsom State Prison, Folsom, CA (1963-1966) **Career Related:** Kinisba Child Abuse Committee (1994-1998) **Civic:** Founder, Private Non-Profit Counseling Practice (2006-Present); Volunteer, Pacheco Elementary School, Redding, CA (1972-1976); Sunday School Teacher, Director, Vacation Bible School, Nazarene Church, Sacramento, CA (1958-1985); Teacher, Director, Vacation Bible School, Nazarene Church, Indio, CA (1958-1985); Teacher, Director, Vacation Bible School, Nazarene Church, Redding, CA (1958-1985) **Awards:** Indian Health Service Directors Award for Excellence (1997); School Bell Award, Pacheco Elementary School **Membership:** American Counseling Association; American Association of Christian Counselors; American Academy of Grief Counseling; Arizona School Counselors Association **Marquis Who's Who Honors:** Albert Nelson Marquis Lifetime Achievement Award (2017) **Hobbies:** Study of American Indian history; Sewing; Crafts; Travel; Bluegrass music **Shipping Address:** PO Box 647, Baker City, OR, 97814

Darryl Boyd Neill

Title: Professor **Industry:** Education/Educational Services **Company Name:** Emory University **Date of Birth:** 01/30/1946 **Place of Birth:** Durham **State:** NC **Parents:** Robert Neill; Lois Neill **Marital Status:** Married **Spouse Name:** Suzanne Snyder (10/13/1968) **Children:** Stephanie Letellier; Alexis; Stewart **Education:** PhD in Biopsychology, The University of Chicago (1971); BS in Biology, Eckerd College, St. Petersburg, FL (1967) **Career:** Goodrich C. White Professor of Psychology and Behavioral Neuroscience, Emory University (2011-Present); Faculty Member, Neuroscience and Behavioral Biology, Emory University (1997-Present); Professor of Psychology, Emory University (1986-Present); Faculty Member, Graduate Program in Neuroscience, Emory University (1985-Present); Faculty Member, Center for Behavioral Neuroscience, Emory University (1999-2008); Faculty Member, Graduate Program in Molecular and Systems Pharmacology (1999-2001); Chairman, Department of Psychology, Emory University (1997-2003); Director, Psychobiology Program, Department of Psychology, Emory University (1996-1997); Faculty Member, Graduate Program in Molecular Therapeutics and Toxicology, Emory University (1995-1999); Faculty Member, Graduate Program in Pharmacological and Physiological Sciences, Emory University (1989-1995); Collaborative Scientist, Yerkes Regional Primate Research Center (1981-1991); Associate Professor of Psychology, Emory University (1975-1986); Assistant Professor of Psychology, Emory University (1972-1975); Instructor in Psychology, Emory University (1971-1972) **Civic:** President, Board of Directors, Nicholas House, Atlanta, GA (1990-1994); Volunteer, Nicholas House, Atlanta, GA (1987-2002) **Awards:** Crystal Apple Teaching Award, Emory College Student Government (2014); TCP Champion Award, Transforming Community Project, Emory University (2010); Elected Fellow, Association for Psychological Science (2010); Invited Speaker, Emory University Convocation (2002); Faculty Appreciation Award, Interfraternity/Intersorority Council, Emory College (1999); Fox Award, Office of Disability Services, Emory University (1999); Excellence in Teaching Award, Emory Student Government Association (1996); Emory Williams Distinguished Teaching Award, Emory University (1995); Graduate Fellowships, National Science Foundation (1967-1971); **Membership:** Fellow, Association for Psychological Science; Society for Neuroscience **Marquis Who's Who Honors:** Distinguished Humanitarian (2017) **Political Affiliations:** Democrat **Religion:** Episcopalian **Business Address:** 36 Eagle Row, Atlanta, GA, 30322 **Shipping Address:** 1208 Blueberry Trl, Decatur, GA, 30033 **Website:** https://www.researchgate.net/profile/Darryl_Neill/publications

David Harold Neustadt

Title: Physician (Retired) **Industry:** Medicine & Health Care **Date of Birth:** 12/02/1925 **Place of Birth:** Evansville **State:** IN/USA **Parents:** Mose Neustadt; Leah (Epstein) Neustadt **Marital Status:** Married **Spouse Name:** Carolyn Jacobson (6/15/1952) **Children:** Susan Miriam; Jeffrey Bruce; Robert Alan **Education:** Resident, Gastroenterology, Lenox Hill Hospital, Northwell Health (1953-1954); Resident in Internal Medicine, Lenox Hill Hospital, Northwell Health (1951-1952); Intern, Morrisania City Hospital (Now Morrisania Diagnostic and Treatment Center), Gotham Health FQHC, Inc. (1950-1951); MD, University of Louisville (1950); Coursework, DePaul University (1946-1947); Coursework, DePaul University (1943-1944) **Career:** Retired (2013); Clinical Professor, Medicine, School of Medicine, University of Louisville (1974-2013); Consultant, Rheumatology, VA (1970-2013); Associate Professor, Clinical Medicine, School of Medicine, University of Louisville (1967-1975); President, Medical Staff, Jewish Hospital, KentuckyOne Health (1967-1969); Chief, Medicine, Jewish Hospital, KentuckyOne Health (1965-1967); Assistant Professor, Medicine, School of Medicine, University of Louisville (1963-1967); Head, Rheumatic Diseases Section, School of Medicine, University of Louisville (1960-1976); Chief, Arthritis Clinic, Louisville General Hospital (1960-1976); Medical Practitioner, Rheumatic Diseases, Louisville, KY (1954-2013); National Institutes of Health Trainee, Rheumatic Diseases, Lenox Hill Hospital, Northwell Health (1952-1953) **Career Related:** Adviser, Network for Continuing Medical Education (1983-Present) **Civic:** President, Kentucky Chapter, Arthritis Foundation; Chairman, Medical Science Committee, Kentucky Chapter, Arthritis Foundation **Military Service:** U.S. Army (1944-1946) **Creative Works:** Contributing Editor, Spondylitis Association of America (1989-Present); Editorial Board Member, Arthritis Care and Research Newsletter, Spondylitis Association of America (1989-Present); Co-editor, "Arthritis Abstracts" (1970-1975); Co-editor, "References Indexes" (1970-1975); Co-author, "Aspiration and Injection Therapy in Arthritis and Musculoskeletal Disorders" (1972); Author, "The Chemistry and Therapy of Collagen Diseases" (1963) **Awards:** Distinguished Rheumatologist Award, American College of Rheumatology (1997); Eponym, Dr. David H. Neustadt Library **Membership:** Advisory Board Member, Spondylitis Association of America (1986-Present); National Trustee, American Physicians Fellowship (1984-Present) **Marquis Who's Who Honors:** Albert Nelson Marquis Lifetime Achievement Award (2017); Distinguished Humanitarian (2017) **Religion:** Jewish **Shipping Address:** 211 W Oak St Apt 820, Louisville, KY, 40203

William A. Newton Jr.

Title: Pediatrician **Industry:** Education/Educational Services **Company Name:** Ohio State University **Date of Birth:** 05/19/1923 **Place of Birth:** Traverse City **State:** MI **Parents:** William Allen Newton; Florence Emma (Brown) Newton **Marital Status:** Married **Spouse Name:** Helen Patricia Goodrich **Children:** Katherine Germaine; Elizabeth Gale; William Allen; Nancy Anne **Education:** MD, University of Michigan (1946); BSc, Alma College, Cum Laude (1943) **Certifications:** Diplomate, American Board of Pathology; Diplomate, American Board of Pediatrics **Career:** Professor Emeritus, College of Medicine, Ohio State University (1989-Present); Professor, College of Medicine, Ohio State University (1965-Present); Faculty, College of Medicine, Ohio State University (1952-Present); Research Pathologist, Nationwide Children's Hospital, Columbus, OH (1989-1993); Chief of Pediatric Pathology, College of Medicine, Ohio State University (1952-1989); Director of Laboratories, Nationwide Children's Hospital, Columbus, OH (1952-1988); Chief, Division of Pediatric Hematology, College of Medicine, Ohio State University (1952-1982); Resident in Pediatrics, Children's Hospital of Philadelphia (1950); Resident in Pediatric Pathology, Oncology and Hematology, Children's Hospital of Michigan, Detroit, MI (1948-1950); Intern, Wayne County General Hospital, Detroit, MI (1947) **Career Related:** Chairman, Pathology Committee, Children's Cancer Study Group (1965-1991); Chairman, Pathology Committee, Intergroup Rhabdomyosarcoma Study Group; Chairman, Pathology Committee, Late Effects Study Group **Civic:** President, Cure of Childhood Cancer in China (2000-Present); Chairman, Executive Committee, Cancer Control Consortium of Ohio (1982-1986); Trustee, Executive Committee, Ohio Division, American Cancer Society (1972-1986); Advisory Committee on Childhood Cancer, American Cancer Society; Scientific Advisory Committee, Armed Forces Institute of Pathology **Military Service:** Captain, Medical Corps, U.S. Army (1950-1952); Brigadier General, Army Reserve **Creative Works:** Author, "By The Grace of God, My Story of Faith, Family and Medicine" **Membership:** President, Pediatric Pathology Club (1968-1969); President, Midwest Society for Pediatric Research (1964-1965); Council Member, Midwest Society for Pediatric Research (1960-1963); Society for Pediatric Research; American Pediatric Society; American Society of Clinical Oncology; International Society of Pediatric Oncology; Sigma Xi, The Scientific Research Honor Society; Phi Sigma Pi; American Association for Cancer Research; Committee on Cancer, Ohio State Medical Association **Political Affiliations:** Republican **Religion:** Baptist **Shipping Address:** 4823 Hazelton Etna Road SW, Pataskala, OH, 43062

John Nonna

Title: Lawyer **Industry:** Law and Legal Services **Company Name:** Squire Patton Boggs **Date of Birth:** 07/08/1948 **Place of Birth:** New York **State:** NY **Parents:** Angelo Nonna; Josphine (Visconti) Nonna **Marital Status:** Married **Spouse Name:** Jean Wanda Cleary (6/9/1973) **Children:** Elizabeth Nonna; Caroline Nonna; Marianne Nonna; Timothy Nonna **Education:** JD, New York University (1975); BA, Princeton University (1970) **Career:** Managing Partner, Squire Patton Boggs (2014-Present); Co-Managing Partner, Squire Patton Boggs (2012-2014); Partner, Dewey & LeBoeuf LLP (2008-2012); Partner, LeBoeuf, Lamb, Greene, and MacRae (1999-2007); Partner, Werner & Kennedy (1984-1999); Associate, Thelen Reid & Priest LLP (1977-1984); Law Assistant to the Honorable D.L. Gabrielli, Court of Appeals, State of New York (1975-1977) **Civic:** Board Member, Westchester County Legislators (2008-2011); Mayor, Village of Pleasantville (1995-2003); Deputy Mayor, Village of Pleasantville (1990-1995); Trustee, Village of Pleasantville (1990-1995); Acting Justice, Village of Pleasantville (1983-1989); Co-Chair, The Lawyers' Committee for Civil Rights Under Law; Board of Directors, The Lawyers' Committee for Civil Rights Under Law; Board of Trustees, Westchester Community College; Board of Governors, New York Athletic Club **Military Service:** U.S. Naval Reserve (1970-1975) **Creative Works:** Contributor, Articles, Professional Journals **Awards:** Congressional Medal of Achievement; Paul Harris Fellowship, Rotary International; Fellowship, American College of Trial Lawyers; Lifetime Fellowship, American Bar Foundation **Membership:** Co-Editor-in-Chief of Insurance Law Practice, New York State Bar Association (2016, 2000); Chair, Commercial and Federal Litigation Section, New York State Bar Association (1998-1999); Committee Chair, Torts and Insurance Practice Section, ABA (1992-1993, 1986-1987); United States Olympic Team (1980, 1972); Association of the Bar of the City of New York **Bar Admissions:** United States Court of Appeals for the District of Columbia Circuit (2007); Supreme Court of the United States (1998); United States Court of Appeals for the Fifth Circuit (1997); United States Court of Appeals for the Seventh Circuit (1988); United States Court of Appeals for the Ninth Circuit (1980); United States District Court for the Southern District of New York (1978); United States Court of Appeals for the Second Circuit (1978); New York (1976) **Marquis Who's Who Honors:** Albert Nelson Marquis Lifetime Achievement Award (2017) **Hobbies:** Fencing; Running; Piano **Shipping Address:** 21 Ashland Ave, Pleasantville, NY, 10570

Jo Anne W. Norris

Title: Curriculum Leader, School Counselor **Industry:** Education/Educational Services **Company Name:** Columbia Borough School District **Date of Birth:** 01/31/1953 **Place of Birth:** Roaring Spring **State:** PA **Parents:** C. Roscoe Wareham; Wilma Irene (Allen) Wareham **Marital Status:** Single **Spouse Name:** Raymond H. Norris (6/16/1973, Deceased) **Children:** Charles Norris (Deceased); Joanna Norris **Education:** EdD, Pupil Service Leadership, Widener University (2008); MEd in School Counseling, University of Delaware, Newark, DE (1992); BSEd in Communicative Disorders, West Chester University (1981) **Certifications:** Principal, K-12, PA (2010); Supervisor, Pupil Personnel Services, PA (2010); Licensed Professional Counselor, Commonwealth of Pennsylvania (2002); Licensed School Counselor (1996); Licensed National Counselor (1995); Certified School Counselor, State of Maryland (1993); Certified School Counselor, Commonwealth of Pennsylvania (1992) **Career:** Curriculum Leader, Special Education K-12, Columbia Borough School District, PA (2009-Present); School Counselor, Columbia Borough School District, PA (2006-Present); Intervention Specialist, Lancaster School District, PA (2002-2006); Child Development Counselor, Cecil County Public School, Elkton, MD (1993-2002); Staff Assistant, Dean's Office, University of Delaware, Newark, DE (1988-1993); Office Manager, Holy Family Church, Newark, DE (1985-1988); Executive Secretary, Keystone Auto Club, Philadelphia, PA (1973-1978) **Awards:** Honoree, Outstanding Member of the Year, University of Delaware Chapter, Kappa Delta Pi, International Honor Society in Education (1993) **Membership:** National Education Association; Association for Supervision and Curriculum Development; American School Counselors Association; Pennsylvania School Counselors Association; Pennsylvania State Education Association; Columbia Education Association; Kappa Delta Pi, International Honor Society in Education **Why did you become involved in your profession or industry:** Dr. Norris became involved in her profession after being listed with Continental Who's Who. **Hobbies:** Traveling; Computers; Desktop Publishing **Religion:** Roman Catholic **Shipping Address:** 1121 State Rd, Lincoln University, PA, 19352 **Website:** jawnorris7@gmail.com

Jacob Eugene Nyenhuis, PhD

Title: Interim Director **Industry:** Education/Educational Services **Company Name:** Hope College **Date of Birth:** 03/25/1935 **Place of Birth:** Mille Lacs County **State:** MN **Parents:** Egbert Peter Nyenhuis; Rosa (Walburg) Nyenhuis **Marital Status:** Married **Spouse Name:** Leona M. Nyenhuis (6/6/1956) **Children:** Karen J. Louwsma; Kathy J. Kurtze; Lorna J. Cook; Sarah Van Duyn N. **Education:** Honorary LittD, Hope College (2001); PhD in Classics, Stanford University (1963); AM in Classics, Stanford University (1961); AB in Greek, Calvin College (1956) **Career:** Interim Director, A.C. Van Raalte Institute, Hope College (2017-Present); Professor Emeritus, Hope College (2001-Present); Provost Emeritus, Hope College (2001-Present); Director, A.C. Van Raalte Institute, Hope College (2002-2015); Senior Research Fellow, A.C. Van Raalte Institute, Hope College (2001-2002); Provost, Hope College (1984-2001); Dean for Arts and Humanities, Hope College (1978-1984); Dean for Humanities, Hope College (1975-1978); Professor of Classics, Hope College (1975-2001); Professor, Wayne State University (1972-1975); Associate Professor, Wayne University (1967-1972); Chairman, Greek and Latin Department, Wayne State University (1965-1975); Director, Liberal Arts Honors Program, Wayne State University (1964-1975); Assistant Professor, Wayne State University (1962-1967) **Career Related:** Reviewer, Michigan Humanities Council (2006); Consultant, Kalamazoo College (2003-2004); Consultant, Albion College (2002-2003); Reviewer, Michigan Humanities Council (1999-2001); Reviewer, United States Department of Education (1993); Panelist, National Endowment for the Humanities (1991); Visiting Scholar, Green Templeton College (1989) **Civic:** Vice President, Board of Trustees, Calvin Theological Seminary (2003-2007); Executive Committee, Calvin Theological Seminary (2002-2007) **Creative Works:** Editor, Co-author/Author, Books; **Awards:** West Michigan Dutch-American Leadership Service Award (2017); Meritorious Service Award, Alumni Association, Hope College (2001) **Membership:** Emeritus, Managing Committee, The American School of Classical Studies at Athens (2002-Present); Board of Directors, Michigan Humanities Council (1996-1999); Councilor-at-Large, The Council on Undergraduate Research (1993-1999) **Marquis Who's Who Honors:** Albert Nelson Marquis Lifetime Achievement Award (2017); Distinguished Humanitarian (2017) **Hobbies:** Photography; Carpentry **Political Affiliations:** Democrat **Business Address:** PO Box 9000, Holland, MI, 49422 **Shipping Address:** 1274 St Andrews Dr, Holland, MI, 49423

Paul O'Connor

Title: Lawyer **Industry:** Law and Legal Services **Date of Birth:** 11/24/1936 **Place of Birth:** Paterson **State:** NJ **Parents:** Paul Daniel; Anne Marie Christopher **Children:** Steven Paul; Sheryl Lynn; Laura Ann **Education:** LLB, University of Virginia (1965); BS in Engineering, US Naval Academy (1959) **Career:** Trustee, Valley Trusts, Oakland, CA (1986-Present); General Council, Berg Holdings, Sausalito, CA (2007); Chief Executive Officer, Citation Builders (1986-1995); Senior Vice President, General Counsel, Singer Co., Stamford, CT (1980-1986); Partner, Winthrop, Stimson, Putnam & Roberts (1972-1980); Associate Firm, Winthrop, Stimson, Putnam & Roberts (1965-1972) **Military Service:** First Lieutenant, US Air Force (1959-1962) **Bar Admissions:** New York (1965); California (1959) **Shipping Address:** 323 Piper St, Healdsburg, CA, 95448

Michael A. O'Hara

Title: Attorney, Counselor-at-Law **Industry:** Law and Legal Services **Company Name:** Michael A. O'Hara, PLLC Attorney at Law **Education:** JD, Salmon P. Chase College of Law, Northern Kentucky University (1993); BS in History and Psychology, Thomas More College (1989) **Certifications:** Admitted to Practice, United States Court of Federal Claims (2002); Diplomate, Mediator Training Program, Mediation Center of Kentucky (2000); Licensed to Practice Law, Federal Court (1994) **Career:** Michael A. O'Hara PLLC Attorney at Law (2000-Present); Attorney, O'Connor, Acciani & Levy CO, LPA (1996-1999); President, The 5:20 Club, LLC (2005-Present) **Civic:** National Ski Patrol/Orphan Ski Outing, Redwood School and Orphanage (2004) **Awards:** Honoree, Recognized as the Nations One Percent, National Association of Distinguished Counsel (2015-2017); Recipient, Nationally Top Ten Ranked Attorney Award, National Academy of Family Law Attorneys (2016); Recipient, Top Ten Client Satisfaction Award, American Institute of Family Law Attorneys (2015) **Membership:** Northern Kentucky Bar Association; Cincinnati Bar Association; National Association of Criminal Defense Lawyers; Kentucky Justice Association **Bar Admissions:** Ohio State Bar Association (1997); Kentucky Bar Association (1994) **Marquis Who's Who Honors:** Albert Nelson Marquis Lifetime Achievement Award (2017); Distinguished Humanitarian (2017) **To what do you attribute your success:** Mr. O'Hara attributes his success to the ability to identify with those who have concerns and help organize their thoughts and write their prayers and get them on the path to achieve their dreams uninformative basis. The more of a relationship he has with his clients and the more they can share with him will be more trans formative. **Why did you become involved in your profession or industry:** The high school Mr. O'Hara went to prepared people for college, but for professions there were only three true professions he saw opportunity to make a lasting impact on someone: clergy, doctors or lawyers. He found law to be the path to go. **Where will you be in five years:** Mr. O'Hara plans on writing a book about establishing, using and rebuilding trust. **Hobbies:** Alpine skiing; Boating; Golf **Shipping Address:** 7000 Houston Rd Ste 27, Michael A. O'Hara PLLC, Florence, KY, 41042 **Website:** http://www.michaeloharaattorney.com/5.html

LeAnn Michelle Oliver

Title: Senior Advisor **Industry:** Government Administration/Government Relations/Government Services **Company Name:** U.S. Department of Energy **Parents:** George L. Oliver; Laura Maxine (Jennings) Oliver **Marital Status:** Married **Spouse Name:** Daniel Thomas **Education:** MPA, University at Albany (1980); BS, Willamette University (1977) **Certifications:** Certificate, National Commercial Lending School, American Bankers Association, Norman, OK (1982) **Career:** Senior Advisor, Office of the Chief Financial Officer, U.S. Department of Energy (2015-Present); Associate Chief Information Officer, IT Policy & Governance, U.S. Department of Energy (2014-2015); Senior Advisor, Clean Energy and Rural Development, U.S. Department of Energy (2012-2014); Program Director, Weatherization and State Energy Programs (2010-2012); Deputy Administrator, Cooperative Programs, Rural Development, United State Department of Agriculture (2006-2010); Acting Deputy, Associate Deputy Administrator, Entrepreneurial Development (2005-2006); Deputy Associate Administrator, Capital Access, U.S. Small Business Administration (2000-2005); Director, Division of Program Development, U.S. Small Business Administration (1995-2000); Acting Director, Office of Rural Affairs and Economic Development, U.S. Small Business Administration (1995); Acting Director, One Stop Office, Capital Shop Project (1994); Deputy Director, Office of Rural Affairs and Economic Development (1992-1994); Deputy Director, Program Development, Office of Economic Development (1989-1992); Financial Analyst, Policy and Program Development, U.S. Small Business Administration (1983-1989); Presidential Management Intern, U.S. Small Business Administration (1980-1983); Management Trainee, U.S. General Accounting Office, Albany, NY (1979-1980) **Career Related:** Treasurer, Lafayette Federal Credit Union (2004-2007); Assistant Treasurer, Lafayette Federal Credit Union (2000-2004); Member, Board of Directors, Lafayette Federal Credit Union (1986-2007) **Civic:** Women's Energy Network; Women's Council on Energy and the Environment; Women in Housing and Finance **Marquis Who's Who Honors:** Albert Nelson Marquis Lifetime Achievement Award (2017) **Hobbies:** Travel; Reading **Religion:** Roman Catholic **Shipping Address:** 3717 N Nelson St, Arlington, VA, 22207

Ann Louise Reuther Onton

Title: Senior Scientist **Industry:** Sciences **Company Name:** NanoViricides, Inc. **Date of Birth:** 09/29/1943 **Place of Birth:** Bridgeport **State:** CT **Marital Status:** Divorced **Spouse Name:** Aare Onton (1965, Divorced) **Children:** Alan David; Daryl John; Julie Ann **Education:** BS in Chemistry, Purdue University (1965) **Career:** Senior Scientist, NanoViricides, Inc. (2006-Present); Laboratory Manager, TheraCour Pharma, Inc. (2005-2006); Laboratory Assistant, University of San Diego (2003-2005); Manager, Research Development and Production, AllExcel Inc (2000-2003); Research Associate, Genaissance Pharmaceuticals Inc (1999-2000); Research Associate, Applied Biotech Concepts, Inc. (1995-1998); Chemist, Prototek, Enzyme Systems Products (1992-1993); Researcher, Cancer Prevention Study II, American Cancer Society, Inc. (1980-1990); Abstractor, Chemical Abstracts Service, American Chemical Society (1970-1972); Research Assistant, Geigy Chemical Corporation (1967-1970); Laboratory Chemist, Great Lakes Chemical Corporation (1965-1967) **Awards:** Grantee, National Institutes of Health (1996-1997) **Membership:** NAFE; AAUW; American Chemical Society; Association for Women in Science; National Association of Professional Women; American Composers Forum; U.S. Masters Swimming **Marquis Who's Who Honors:** Albert Nelson Marquis Lifetime Achievement Award (2017) **Business Address:** 50 Old Dairy Lane, Shelton, CT, 06484

James Thomas O'Reilly

Title: Lawyer, Educator, Writer **Industry:** Law and Legal Services **Company Name:** University of Cincinnati **Date of Birth:** 11/15/1947 **Place of Birth:** New York **State:** NY **Parents:** Matthew Richard O'Reilly; Regina (Casey) O'Reilly **Children:** Jean; Ann **Education:** JD, University of Virginia (1974); BA, Boston College, Cum Laude (1969) **Career:** Visiting Professor of Law, University of Cincinnati, Cincinnati, OH (1998-Present); Associate General Counsel, Procter & Gamble, Cincinnati, OH (1993-1998); Corporate Counsel, Procter & Gamble, Cincinnati, OH (1985-1993); Adjunct Professor in Administrative Law, University of Cincinnati, Cincinnati, OH (1980-1997); Senior Counsel for Food, Drug and Product Safety, Procter & Gamble, Cincinnati, OH (1979-1985); Counsel, Procter & Gamble, Cincinnati, OH (1976-1979); Attorney, Procter & Gamble, Cincinnati, OH (1974-1976) **Career Related:** Consultant, Congressional Office of Compliance (1995-1996) **Military Service:** U.S. Army (1970-1972) **Creative Works:** Author, "Medical Malpractice" (2014); Author, "Clergy Sexual Abuse" (2014); Author, "Executive's Guide to Food Safety Law" (2011); Author, "A Practitioner's Guide to Hospital Liability" (2011); Author, "Careers in Administrative Law" (2010); Author, "Punishing Corporate Crime" (2009); Author, "Brownreds Cleanup" (2008); Author, "Consumer Product Safety" (2008); Author, "Gangs and Law Enforcement" (2007); Author, "Ohio Personal Injury Practice" (2006); Author, "Ohio Tort Reform" (2005); Author, "Homeland Security Deskbook" (2004); Author, "Food Crisis Management Manual" (2002); Author, "Police Racial Profiling" (2002); Author, "Accident Prevention Manual" (2000); Author, "Product Warnings, Defects & Hazards" (1999); Author, "Indoor Environmental Health" (1997); Author, "Environmental and Workplace Safety for University and Hospital Managers" (1996); Author, "Elder Safety" (1995); Author, "Clean Air Permits Manual" (1994); Author, "United States Environmental Liabilities" (1994); Author, "American Bar Association Product Liability Resource Manual" (1993); Author, "RCRA and Superfund Practice Guide" (1993); Author, "Solid Waste Management" (1991); Author, "Ohio Products Liability Handbook" (1991); Author, "Toxic Torts Guide" (1991); Author, "Toxic Torts Strategy Deskbook" (1989) **Membership:** Chairman, AD Law Section, American Bar Association; Federal Bar Association; Chairman, Program Committee, Food and Drug Law Institute **Bar Admissions:** Sixth Circuit, U.S. Court of Appeals (1980); U.S. Supreme Court (1979); State of Virginia (1974) **Marquis Who's Who Honors:** Albert Nelson Marquis Lifetime Achievement Award (2017); Distinguished Humanitarian (2017) **Political Affiliations:** Democrat **Religion:** Roman Catholic **Shipping Address:** 24 Jewett Drive, Cincinnati, OH, 45215

Fran Marilyn Orenstein

Title: Chief Executive Officer **Industry:** Writing and Editing Company Name: Sunwriter, LLC **Date of Birth:** 10/31/1939 **Place of Birth:** Brooklyn **State:** NY **Parents:** Nathan Gitterman; Gertrude Celia Chall-Gitterman **Marital Status:** Divorced **Spouse Name:** Walter Orenstein (12/21/1958, Divorced 1977) **Children:** James Michael; Susannah Beth; Peter David **Education:** EdD, Nova Southeastern University (1993); MEd, The College of New Jersey (1976); BA, Brooklyn College (1960) **Certifications:** Certified Public Manager, State of New Jersey; Licensed Guidance Counselor, States of California and New Jersey; Certified Teacher, States of New Jersey and New York; Certified REIKI Master **Career:** Author, Poet, Editor, Founder, Sunwriter, LLC (2002-Present); Director of Editorial Service, Triad Publishing Company (2007-2010); Special Events/Disability Officer, AmeriCorps, State of New Jersey Department of Education (1998-2002); Program Development Specialist, State of New Jersey Department of Community Affairs (1988-1998); Senior Rehabilitation Counselor, New Jersey Division of Vocational Rehabilitation Services (1980-1988); Teacher, Content Specialist, East Windsor Regional Schools (1979-1980); Editor, Writer, University Communications (1975-1979); Teacher, Hilltop Academy (1973-1974) **Career Related:** Presenter, Educational Visions Group (1990-1998); Founder, New Jersey Coalition on Women and Disabilities **Civic:** Tutor, Assistant Teacher, Bluffton, SC (2006-2007); Board of Directors, Susan B. Komen Race for the Cure (1995-1999); Board of Directors, Newsletter Editor, Women's Agenda/New Jersey Law (1993-1996) **Creative Works:** Author, "First Footprints and Winding Ways" (2015); Author, "The Shadow Boy Mysteries" Series (2017); Author, "Danse Macabre" (2015); Author, "The Spice Trader's Daughter" (2014); Author, "Amber and the Magic Whipped-Cream Dress" (2014); Author, "The Calling of the Flute, Second Edition" (2014); Author, "Fat Girls from Outer Space, Third Edition" (2014); Author, "One Amber Too Many" (2013); Author, "Murder in Duplicate" (2013); "Murder in Disguise" (2018); Author, "Death in D Minor" (2013); Author, "Gaias Gift" (2012); Author, "Short Stories in Gallery of Voices" (2012); Author, "The Book of Mysteries" (2012); Author, "Reflections" (2012); Author, "The Calling of the Flute, First Edition" (2011); Author, "Fat Girls from Outer Space, Second Edition" (2011); Author, "The Mystery Under Third Base" (2010); Author, "The Spice Merchant's Daughter" (2010); Author, "The Gargoyles of Blackthorne" (2010); Author, "The Mystery of the Green Goblin" (2010) **Membership:** Sisters in Crime Desert Sleuths Chapter; Arizona State Poetry Society; National League of American Pen Women, Inc.; Florida State Poets Association, Inc.; American Mensa, Ltd.; Proctor, American Mensa, Ltd., SC, GA, FL

Rosalie Muller Wright Pakenham

Title: Magazine and Newspaper Editor **Industry:** Writing and Editing **Date of Birth:** 06/20/1942 **Place of Birth:** Newark **State:** NJ **Parents:** Charles Muller; Angela (Fortunato) Muller **Marital Status:** Married **Spouse Name:** Edward Michael Pakenham **Children:** James Anthony Meador Wright; Geoffrey Shepard Wright **Education:** BA in English, Temple University (1965) **Career:** Vice President and Editor-in-chief, Sunset Magazine, Sunset Publishing Corporation, CA (1996-2001); Assistant Managing Editor, Features, San Francisco Chronicle, Hearst Corporation (1987-1996); Features and Sunday Editor, San Francisco Chronicle, Hearst Corporation (1981-1987); Executive Editor, New West Magazine, New West Publications, CA (1977-1981); Editor, Scene Section, The San Francisco Examiner (1975-1977); Consulting Editor, Francis Ford Coppola's City of San Francisco Magazine (1975); Founding Editor, Billie Jean King's Womensports Magazine, CA (1973-1975); Managing Editor, Philadelphia Magazine, Metro Corp. (1969-1973); Associate Editor, Philadelphia Magazine, Metro Corp. (1962-1964); Managing Editor, Suburban Life Magazine, NJ (1960-1962) **Career Related:** Co-owner, Professionalediting.net (2009-Present); Editorial Consultant (2002-Present); Judge, National Magazine Awards (1998, 1999, 2005); International Association of Culinary Professionals (2002-2008); Council for the Advancement and Support of Education (1984); Chairman, Magazine Judges at Conference (1980); Participant, Publishing Proceedings Course, Stanford University (1977-1979); Teacher, Magazine Writing, University of California, Berkeley (1975-1976) **Civic:** Comprehensive Plan, Washington Township, York County, PA **Creative Works:** Contributor, Numerous Magazine Articles, Critiques, Reviews, Compton's Encyclopedia; Contributing Writer **Awards:** Named to Hall of Fame, American Association of Sunday and Feature Editors (1999) **Membership:** National Magazine Awards Judge, American Society of Magazine Editors (1998, 1999, 2005); Secretary, Women's Forum West (1994); Board of Directors, Women's Forum West (1993-2002); Publishers Task Force on Minorities in Newspaper Business, American Newspaper Publishers Association (1988-1989); Chronicle Minority Recruiter, American Newspaper Publishers Association (1987-1994); President, American Association of Sunday and Feature Editors (1987); First Vice President, American Association of Sunday and Feature Editors (1986) **Shipping Address:** 221 Pine Woods Rd, Wellsville, PA, 17365-9544

Gerald L. Paley

Title: Lawyer (Retired) **Industry:** Law and Legal Services **Date of Birth:** 09/11/1939 **Place of Birth:** Albany **State:** NY **Parents:** Arthur Paley; Mary (Peckner) Paley **Marital Status:** Married **Spouse Name:** Andrea Paley (10/25/15) Joyce R. (8/25/1961, Divorced 1985) **Children:** Jonathan; Eric; Suzanne **Education:** JD, Cornell University, with Distinction (1964); BA, Union College (1961) **Career:** Partner, Phillips, Lytle, Hitchcock, Blaine & Huber (Now Phillips-Lytle LLP), Rochester, NY (1987-1997); Partner, Nixon, Hargrave, Devans & Doyle (Now Nixon Peabody LLP), Rochester, NY (1964-1970); Associate Solicitor, United States Department of Labor, Washington, DC (1970-1972); Associate, Nixon, Hargrave, Devans & Doyle (Now Nixon Peabody LLP), Rochester, NY (1972-1987) **Creative Works:** Co-author, "How to Comply with Federal Employee Laws," London Publishing Company (1991); Co-author "Understanding Employee Regulations" (1984); Author, "Employers Handbook of Federal Labor Relations Law," London Publishing Company (1979) **Membership:** ABA; National Panel of Arbitrators of the American Arbitration Association; U.S. Federal Mediation and Conciliation Service **Bar Admissions:** New York (1964) **Marquis Who's Who Honors:** Albert Nelson Marquis Lifetime Achievement Award (2017) **Why did you become involved in your profession or industry:** Mr. Paley said, "It was the way it worked out." He had no interest in becoming a labor lawyer until he graduated from law school and entered a practice and he fell into it. It wasn't planned. **What do you consider to be the highlight of your career:** The one highlight of Mr. Paley's career that stood out the most was spending two years with the Federal Department of Labor in Washington. **Hobbies:** Piano; Tennis; Horseback riding **Political Affiliations:** Republican **Religion:** Jewish **Shipping Address:** 225 Allens Creek Rd, Rochester, NY, 14618

Dino Paravano

Title: Artist **Industry:** Fine Art **Date of Birth:** 11/09/1935 **Place of Birth:** Rome **Country of Origin:** Italy **Parents:** Domenico Paravano; Gemma Paravano **Marital Status:** Married **Spouse Name:** Maria Grazia Malinverni (January 25, 1964) **Children:** Daniela Maria; Paolo Carlo; Domenico **Career:** Studio Owner, Tuscon (1992-Present); Studio Owner, Sandton (1976-1993); Owner, Kempel's Gallery (1973-1975); Studio Owner, Johannesburg (1956-1975); Co-Owner, The Sandton Gallery (1970-1973) **Creative Works:** Group Exhibitor, Big Rock, Artist's Magazine, F+W Media, Inc. (2005); Exhibitor, "North of San Francisco, " Leigh Yawkey Woodson Art Museum (1993); Exhibitor, "Cheetah with Cubs" (1990); Exhibitor, "Pride's Proud Family," The Witte Museum; Group Exhibitor, Night Games **Awards:** Recipient, Hiram Blauvelt Art Museum Purchase Award (2007); First Place Landscape Category Award, Artist's Magazine Competition, F+W Media, Inc. (2005); Recipient, Second Place Award on Wild Cat Art, Night Games (2001); Recipient, Elliot Lipskin Award for Representational Painting, The Society of Animal Artists (1996); Recipient, Master of Wildlife Artist Award for Birds in Art, Leigh Yawkey Woodson Art Museum (1993); Recipient, Award of Excellence, The Society of Animal Artists (1990); Recipient, Various Interclub Skeet Shooting Trophies; Recipient, Various Interclub Trap Shooting Trophies; Recipient, Various Interclub Trap Shooting Trophies; Recipient, Various National Trap Shooting Trophies **Membership:** Pastel Society of America; The Society of Animal Artists **Religion:** Roman Catholic **Shipping Address:** 6758 W. Redcliff Way, Tucson, AZ, 85743

Arva Moore Parks

Title: Historian, Author **Industry:** Writing and Editing **Company Name:** Arva Parks & Company **Date of Birth:** 01/19/1939 **Place of Birth:** Miami **State:** FL **Parents:** Jack Moore; Anne (Parker) Moore **Marital Status:** Widowed **Spouse Name:** Robert Howard McCabe (6/1992, Deceased 1/2015); Robert Lyle Parks (8/1959, Divorced 1986) **Children:** Jacqueline Carey; Robert Downing; Gregory Moore **Education:** Honorary LLD, Barry University (1996); MA in History, University of Miami, Coral Gables, FL (1971); BA, University of Florida (1960); Coursework, Florida State University (1956-1958) **Career:** President, Arva Parks & Co., Miami, FL (1986-Present); Freelance Research Historian, Miami, FL (1970-Present); Acting Director, Chief Curator, Coral Gables Museum (2011-2012); Adjunct Professor, University of Miami, Coral Gables, FL (1986-1987); Consultant (1966-1970); Teacher, Everglades School for Girls (Now Ransom Everglades School), Miami, FL (1965-1966); Graduate Assistant, University of Miami, Coral Gables (1964-1965); Teacher, Miami Edison Senior High School (1963-1964); Teacher, Rollingcrest Junior High School, West Hyattsville, MD (1960-1963) **Career Related:** President, Centennial Press (1991-Present) **Civic:** Board Member, Dade Heritage Trust (2016-Present); Board Member, Historic St. Augustine, University of Florida (2013-Present); Trustee, University of Miami (1994-Present); Orange Bowl Committee (1989-Present) **Creative Works:** Author, "George Merrick: Son of the South Wind; Visionary Creator of Coral Gables" (2015); Author, "Miami - A Sense of Place" (2014); Co-Author, "Legendary Locals" (2013); Author, "Harry Truman and the Little White House in Key West" (2012); Co-Author, "Coconut Grove" (2010); Author, "Miami the Magic City," Revised Edition (2008); Author, "George Merrick's Coral Gables" (2006); Author, "The Forgotten Frontier" Revised Edition (2004); Co-Author, "Miami Then & Now" (2002) **Awards:** Women Who Make a Difference Award, Junior League of Miami (2018); Marcia Kanner Service Award, History Miami (2018); Alumni Hall of Fame, Miami Dade County Public Schools (2017); Florida Book Award, Nonfiction (2015); Distinguished Florida Author Award, Florida House (2014); Finer Womanhood Community Fellowship Award, Zeta Phi Beta Sorority, Inc. (2011); Honoree, Historian of the Year, Miami Woman's Club (2009); Rosiland R. Luduig Chairman Award, The American National Red Cross (2009); Historic President Carl Weinhard Lifetime Achievement Award (2009) **Marquis Who's Who Honors:** Albert Nelson Marquis Lifetime Achievement Award (2017) **Political Affiliations:** Democrat **Religion:** Methodist **Shipping Address:** 1240 SW 17th Terrace, Miami, FL, 33145

Douglas M. Patterson, PhD

Title: Finance Educator **Industry:** Education/Educational Services **Company Name:** Virginia Polytechnic Institute and State University **Date of Birth:** 01/16/1945 **Place of Birth:** Tallahassee **State:** FL **Parents:** Thomas Patterson; Ruth (MacLennan) Patterson **Marital Status:** Married **Spouse Name:** Sara Louise Lucas **Children:** Cara Beth; John Douglas **Education:** PhD, Graduate School of Business, University of Wisconsin-Madison, Madison, WI (1978); MBA, University of Wisconsin-Madison, Madison, WI (1972); BEE, University of Wisconsin-Madison, Madison, WI (1968) **Career:** Professor, Virginia Polytechnic Institute and State University (1999-Present); Associate Professor, Virginia Polytechnic Institute and State University (1986-1999); Assistant Professor, Virginia Polytechnic Institute and State University (1980-1985); Faculty Research Fellowship, Rackham Graduate School, University of Michigan (1979); Assistant Professor, University of Michigan (1978-1980); Lecturer, University of Michigan (1976-1977); Teaching Assistant, University of Wisconsin (1972-1973) **Career Related:** Faculty Senate, Virginia Polytechnic Institute and State University (2014-Present); Director, Program on Free Markets, Virginia Tech, Pamplin College of Business (2007-Present) **Creative Works:** Author, "An ARFIMA Model for Volatility Does Not Imply Long Memory," Nonlinear Time Series and Finance, Guadalajara University Press, Guadalajara, Mexico (2013); Co-Author, "A Test of the GARCH (1,1) Specification for Daily Stock Prices," Macroeconomic Dynamics (2010); Co-Author, "The Incidence of Informational Cascades and the Behavior of Trade Interarrival Times During the Stock Market Bubble," Macroeconomic Dynamics (2010); Co-Author, "Apparent Long Memory In Time Series as an Artifact of a Time-Varying Mean: Considering Alternatives to the Fractionally Integrated Model," Macroeconomic Dynamics (2010); Co-Author, "A New Bispectral Test for Nonlinear Dependence," Econometric Reviews (2009); Co-Author, "Detecting Epochs of Transient Dependence in White Noise," Money, Measurement and Computation, Palgrave Macmillian, New York, NY (2006) **Awards:** Recipient, Summer Research Grant, Department of Finance, Virginia Polytechnic Institute and State University (2009); Recipient, Summer Research Grant, Department of Finance, Virginia Polytechnic Institute and State University (2003) **Membership:** Director, Program on Exploring the Foundations of Capitalism and Freedom (2007-2017); Chairman, Pamplin College of Business Computer Committee (2000-2001) **Religion:** Methodist **Business Address:** 880 West Campus Drive, Blacksburg, VA, 24061 **Shipping Address:** 702 Crestwood Dr, Blacksburg, VA, 24060 **Website:** https://finance.pamplin.vt.edu

Ellen Tsatiri Pavlakos

Title: Sculptor **Industry:** Fine Art **Date of Birth:** 05/25/1936 **Place of Birth:** Athens **Country of Origin:** Greece **Parents:** Andrew Tsatiri; Katherine (Fliskanopoulou) Tsatiri **Marital Status:** Married **Spouse Name:** Andrew George Pavlakos (11/2/1952) **Children:** James; John Andrew **Education:** Coursework, National Academy of Design, New York, NY (1980-1981); Coursework, Norton School of Art, West Palm Beach, FL (1975-1979) **Creative Works:** Group Show, Gray Robinson Exhibit (2010-Present); Solo Show, 5th Avenue Art Gallery, Melbourne, FL (2014); Group Show, Scaling the Charts, Foosaner Art Museum (2014); Group Show, National Juried Exhibition Cornell Museum Art, Delray Beach, FL (2014); Group Show, Cultural Center, Stuart, FL (2014); Group Show, Court House Cultural Center (2014); Group Show, National Sculpture Competition, Marietta Cobb Museum of Art, Atlanta, GA (2012-2014); Group Show, Marietta Cabb Museum of Art, Atlanta, GA (2012-2013); Group Show, Museum of Art, Marietta, GA (2012); Group Show, Terrace Gallery, Orlando City Hall, Florida (2010); Group Show, Seminol State College, Sanford, FL (2010); Group Show, Tampa Group Show, International Airport (2009); Group Show, Thomas Center Galleries (2008); Group Show, The Deland Museum of Art, Florida (2007); Group Show, Melbourne International Airport, Florida (2007); Group Show, Albany Museum, Georgia (2006); Group Show, Turner Center for the Arts, Valdosta, GA (2006); Group Show, Gadsen Arts Center, Lake Wales, FL (2004); Group Show, Atlantic Center for the Arts (2004); Group Show, Seminol Committee College, Sanford, FL (2004); Group Show, Lake Wales Art Center, Florida (2004); Group Show, Welcoming Christ, Holy Name of Jesus Church, Florida (2004); Group Show, Oceola Art Center, Kissimmee, FL (2002); Group Show, Visual Arts Center of Northwest Florida, Panama City, FL (2002); Group Show, Brevard Museum of Arts and Science, Melbourne, FL (2002); Group Show, University of Florida Arts Center, Gainesville, FL (2001); Group Show, DeLand Museum of Art (2001); Group Show, Louisiana State University, Shreveport, LA (2000); Group Show, Mount Dora Art Center (2000); Group Show, 621 Gallery, Tallahassee, FL (1999); Group Show, Lee County Alliance of the Arts, Fort Myers, FL (1999); Group Show, Stephen Girard Relief, Girard College, Philadelphia, PA (1999) **Membership:** National Academic Artists Association; Medallic Sculpture Association; International Art Medal Federation; Chamber of Visual Arts, Greece **Marquis Who's Who Honors:** Albert Nelson Marquis Lifetime Achievement Award (2017) **Religion:** Greek Orthodox **Shipping Address:** 3609 Poseidon Way, Indialantic, FL, 32903

Charles Pereyra-Suarez

Title: Lawyer **Industry:** Law and Legal Services **Date of Birth:** 09/07/1947 **Place of Birth:** Paysandu **Country of Origin:** Uruguay **Parents:** Hector Pereyra-Suarez; Esther (Enriquez-Sarano) Pereyra-Suarez **Marital Status:** Married **Spouse Name:** Susan H. Cross (12/30/1983) **Children:** Peter; Katie **Education:** JD, Boalt Hall School of Law, University of California, Berkeley, CA (1975); Postgraduate Work, University of California, Los Angeles, CA (1970-1971); BA in History, Pacific Union College, Magna Cum Laude (1970) **Career:** Private Practice, Los Angeles, CA (1998-Present); Litigation Partner, Davis Wright Tremaine, Los Angeles, CA (1995-1998); Litigation Partner, McKenna & Cuneo, Los Angeles, CA (1986-1995); Private Practice, Los Angeles, CA (1984-1986); Senior Litigation Associate, Gibson, Dunn & Crutcher, Los Angeles, CA (1982-1984); Assistant United States Attorney, Criminal Division, U.S. Department of Justice, Los Angeles, CA (1979-1982); Trial Attorney, Appellate Attorney, Civil Rights Division, U.S. Department Justice, Washington D.C. (1976-1979); Staff Attorney, Western Center on Law and Poverty, Inc., Los Angeles, CA (1976); Federal Prosecutor, Los Angeles, CA; Judge Pro Tem, Superior Court of California, County of Los Angeles **Career Related:** Chair, Three Arbitrator Panels **Bar Admissions:** The District of Columbia (1980); State of California (1975) **Marquis Who's Who Honors:** Albert Nelson Marquis Lifetime Achievement Award (2017) **Political Affiliations:** Democrat **Business Address:** 800 Wilshire Blvd Ste 1200, Los Angeles, CA, 90017

Ruth G. Perez

Title: Associate Professor **Industry:** Education/Educational Services **Company Name:** Texas Tech University Health Sciences Center El Paso **Education:** Honorary PhD in Neurobiology, School of Medicine, University of Pittsburgh (1993); Honorary MS in Neuropsychobiochemistry, The University of Texas at El Paso (1987); BS in Biology, The University of Texas at El Paso (1972); Postdoctoral Training, Department of Neurology, Harvard Medical School, Center For Neurologic Diseases, Brigham and Women's Hospital **Career:** Associate Professor of Biomedical Sciences, Center of Emphasis in Neurosciences, Texas Tech University Health Sciences Center El Paso (2011-Present); Assistant Professor, University of Pittsburgh (2005-2011); Research Assistant Professor, School of Medicine, University of Pittsburgh (1999-2005); Postdoctoral Research Fellow, Brigham and Women's Hospital, Harvard Medical School (1993-1996); Postdoctoral Research Fellow, Associate Professor of Neurology, University of Pittsburgh's School of Medicine **Civic:** Invited Presenter, World CNS Summit: Targeting Neurodegeneration/Accelerating Therapeutics (2017); Keynote Speaker, Congreso de Bioingenieria, Tec de Monterrey, Chihuahua, MX (2014); Visiting Scholar, Fudan University School of Medicine, Shanghai, China (2011) **Creative Works:** Editorial Board, "Journal of Biological Chemistry" (2011-2016); Reviewer, National Institutes of Health, Several Foundations and Scientific Journals Including the Journal of Biological Chemistry, Journal of Neurochemistry and the Journal of Neuroscience **Awards:** Coldwell Foundation Award, Assessing Heart and Brain Effects of FTY720s (2017-2018); Grantee, Lizanell and Colbert Coldwell Foundation (2017); Grantee, Molecular Regulators of Dopamine Synthesis (2006); Grantee, Synuclein, Parkinson's Disease and Strategies for Neuroprotection (2001); New Faculty Award, Nathan Shock Center for Excellence, Allegheny University of the Health Sciences (1997-1998); Carl Storm Travel Fellowship **Membership:** American Chemical Society (2014-Present); International Society for Neurochemistry (2013-Present); Charter Member, Rio Grande Chapter, Society for Neuroscience (2012-Present); American Society for Biochemistry and Molecular Biology (2010-Present); American Association for the Advancement of Science (1998-Present); Society for Neuroscience (1997-Present); Joint Steering Committee for Public Policy, Society for Neuroscience (2002-2011); **Business Address:** 5001 El Paso Drive, MSB1 Ste 4002, El Paso, TX, 79905 **Shipping Address:** 6005 Alcalde St, El Paso, TX, 79912

Yeritza Perez-Perez, PhD

Title: Research Assistant **Industry:** Research **Company Name:** University of Illinois **Date of Birth:** 04/21/1988 **Place of Birth:** Arecibo **Country of Origin:** Puerto Rico **Parents:** Gerardo Perez-Lopez; Marilsa Perez-Mendez **Marital Status:** Single **Education:** PhD in Civil and Environmental Engineering, University of Illinois (2013-Present); MCE, University of Puerto Rico at Mayaguez (2013); BCE, University of Puerto Rico at Mayaguez (2011) **Career:** Research Assistant, University of Illinois (2013-Present); Teaching Assistant, University of Illinois (2015-2017); Research Assistant, University of Puerto Rico at Mayaguez (2012-2013) **Creative Works:** Co-author, "Automatic 3D Modeling of Structural and Mechanical Components from Point Clouds", Construction Research Congress (2018); Co-author, "Semantic-rich 3D CAD Models for Built Environments from Point Clouds: An End-to-End Procedure," Workshop on Computing for Civil Engineering (2017); Co-author, "3D Solid Geometric Modeling of the Built Environment via Semantically Segmented Point Clouds," Third International Conference on Civil and Building Engineering Informatics & Conference on Computer Applications in Civil and Hydraulic Engineering (2017); Co-author, "Semantic and Geometric Labeling for Enhanced 3D Point Cloud Segmentation," Construction Research Congress (2016) **Awards:** Nominee, Best Paper at ICCBEI & CCACHE, University of Illinois (2017); Best 2013 MSCE Research Award, First Abertis Chair Contest in Puerto Rico (2014); Inductee, Civil Engineering Honors Program, University of Puerto Rico at Mayaguez (2011); The Boeing Company Scholarship, University of Puerto Rico at Mayaguez (2010); Inductee, Honors Program, University of Puerto Rico at Mayaguez (2009-2010); Science, Mathematics & Research for Transformation Scholarship, University of Puerto Rico at Mayaguez (2008-2010); The Boeing Company Scholarship, University of Puerto Rico at Mayaguez (2008); Inductee, Honors Program, University of Puerto Rico at Arecibo (2008); Robert C. Byrd Honors Scholarship, University of Puerto Rico at Mayaguez (2007-2010); USA Funds Access to Education Scholarship, University of Puerto Rico at Mayaguez (2007-2010); Inductee, Student Advance Honor Program, University of Puerto Rico at Arecibo (2006-2008) **Membership:** Golden Key International Honour Society (2009-2013); American Concrete Institute (2008-2009); General Contractor Association (2008-2009); American Society of Civil Engineers (2008-2009); Integrated Science Multi Use Laboratory (2007-2008); Student Honor Program, University of Puerto Rico at Mayaguez (2006-2013) **Religion:** Catholic **Business Address:** 205 N Mathews Avenue, Office 3143, Urbana, IL, 61801

Barry S. Perlman

Title: Electrical Engineer (Retired), Researcher, Director **Industry:** Engineering **Date of Birth:** 12/05/1939 **Place of Birth:** Brooklyn **State:** NY **Parents:** Harold Wallace Perlman; Jane (Cohen) Perlman **Marital Status:** Married **Spouse Name:** Carolyn Amelia Francis **Children:** David Matthew **Education:** PhD in Electrophysics, New York University Polytechnic School of Engineering (1973); MSEE, New York University Polytechnic School of Engineering (1964); BEE, City College of New York (1961) **Career:** Research & Development Engineering Center Staff, Aberdeen, MD (2011-2012); Associate Director of Technology, Principal Scientist, Intel and Info Directorate (1999-2002); Chief of Applied Communications, Communications-Electronics Command, Fort Monmouth, New Jersey (1998-1999); Research & Development Engineering Center Staff, Communications-Electronics Command, Fort Monmouth, New Jersey (1997-1998); Chief, Radio Frequency and Electronics Division, Sensor and Electron Devices Directorate, Army Research Laboratory, Fort Monmouth, New Jersey, Adelphi, MD (1996-1997); Director of Electronics Division, Physical Sciences Directorate, Army Research Laboratory, Fort Monmouth, New Jersey (1995-1996); Chief of Microwave Photonic Devices Branch, Electronics and Power Source Directorate, Army Research Laboratory, Fort Monmouth, New Jersey (1988-1995); Head of Design Automation Research, RCA Laboratories, Princeton, NJ (1986-1988); Manager of Microwave Research Laboratory, RCA Laboratories, Princeton, NJ (1981-1986); Member of Technical Staff, RCA Laboratories, Princeton, NJ (1968-1981); Member of Technical Staff, Communications Laboratory, RCA Corp., New York, NY (1961-1968) **Career Related:** Advisor, High Frequency Electronics Group, RF Alliance (2010-Present); Member, RF Alliance OSD (2010-Present); DOD STEM Working Group, Science Technology Engineering & Technology Education (2009-Present) **Civic:** Instructor, American Heart Association, New Jersey (1978-1982); Chief, Rescue squad, East Windsor, New Jersey (1978-1982) **Creative Works:** Editorial Board Member, Wiley Journal, MW.MMW CAD (1992-Present); Editor, "Advances in Microwaves" (1974); Contributor, Articles to Professional Journals **Membership:** Technical Program Chair, COMCAS (2007-Present); Chairman, MTT Adcommunications (2002-Present); IMS Technology Program Committee, Circulations and Systems, Ultrasonics, Ferroelectrics and Frequency Control, Microwave Theory and Technology Society of IEE (1980-Present) **Hobbies:** Woodworking; Photography; Pistol/rifle target competition; Gardening; Gourmet cooking **Shipping Address:** 13864 E. Coyote Way, Fountain Hills, AZ, 85268

Carl J. Pernicone

Title: Partner, Attorney **Industry:** Law and Legal Services **Company Name:** Wilson Elser **Marital Status:** Married **Education:** JD, School of Law, Fordham University (1983); BA, Iona College, Summa Cum Laude (1980) **Civic:** Local Community Charitable Organizations **Awards:** Best Lawyers (2016-2017); Honoree, Top Attorneys in the New York Metro Area (2015-2017); Honoree, New York Super Lawyers (2009-2017); Honoree, New York Super Lawyers (2006) **Membership:** Environmental Law Committee, New York State Bar Association; Ad Hoc Litigation Committee, New York City Bar Association; New York County Lawyers' Association; Council on Litigation Management; Defense Research Institute; Litigation Committee, American Bar Association **To what do you attribute your success:** Mr. Pernicone attributes his success to his passion for his work, being very detail oriented, and staying current with emerging issues that can impact society. **Why did you become involved in your profession or industry:** Mr. Pernicone became involved in his profession because he comes from a family of lawyers, so it was a natural choice for him to follow. Also, he has always had an interest in political science, which has made for a natural flow as well. **What do you consider to be the highlight of your career:** The highlight of Mr. Pernicone's career was going before the second circuit with two wins. **Where will you be in five years:** In the coming years, Mr. Pernicone would like to have continued growth and success for the firm, with a special focus on emerging areas, such as energy, climate change, and hydraulic fracturing. **Hobbies:** Skiing; Golfing; Hiking **Business Address:** 150 E 42nd Street BSMT 1, New York, NY, 10017 **Shipping Address:** 1133 Westchester Ave, Wilson Elser, White Plains, NY, 10604 **Website:** http://www.wilsonelser.com

Edward B. Perrin, PhD

Title: Biomedical Researcher, Public Health Educator **Industry:** Education/Educational Services **Company Name:** University of Washington **Date of Birth:** 09/19/1931 **Place of Birth:** Greensboro **State:** VT **Parents:** J. Newton Perrin; Dorothy E. (Willey) Perrin **Marital Status:** Married **Spouse Name:** Carol Anne Hendricks (8/18/1956) **Children:** Jenifer; Scott **Education:** PhD, Stanford University (1961); MA in Mathematical Statistics, Columbia University (1956); Coursework in Statistics, University of Edinburgh, Scotland (1953-1954); BA, Middlebury College (1953) **Career:** Professor Emeritus, University of Washington (1999-Present); Senior Scientist, Veterans Affairs Puget Sound Health Care System, United States Department of Veterans Affairs (1994-2001); Overseas Fellow, Churchill College, University of Cambridge (1991-1992); Honorary Professor, West China Medical Center (Now Sichuan Medical University) (1988-1998); Chairman, Health Services Department, University of Washington (1983-1994); Professor, Health Services Department, Biostatistics Department, University of Washington (1975-1998); Adjunct Professor, Biostatistics Department, University of Washington (1975-1998); Professor, Biostatistics Department, University of Washington (1970-1972); Chairman, Biostatistics Department, University of Washington (1970-1972); Professor, University of Washington (1969-1970); Associate Professor, University of Washington (1965-1969); Assistant Professor, Department of Preventive Medicine, University of Washington (1962-1965); **Career Related:** Report Review Committee, National Research Council, National Academy of Sciences (2005-2012); Committee on National Statistics, National Academy of Sciences (1994-2000); Chairman, Science Advisory Committee, Medical Outcomes Trust (1994-1999); National Research Council Member, National Advisory Council, Agency for Health Care Policy and Research Department, United States Department of Health and Human Service (1994-1997) **Civic:** Health Services and Outcomes Research Methodology (1999-2004); Technology Board, Milbank Memorial Fund (1974-1976) **Creative Works:** Editorial Board Member, "Public Health Nursing" (1992-1998); Editorial Board Member, "Journal of Family Practice" (1978-1990) **Awards:** Recognition Award, Statistics Section, American Public Health Association (1989) **Membership:** Board of Directors, Puqet Sound Association (2015-Present); President, University of Washington Retirement Association, University of Washington (2011-2012) **Marquis Who's Who Honors:** Albert Nelson Marquis Lifetime Achievement Award (2017) **Shipping Address:** 116 Fairview Avenue N, Unit 728, Seattle, WA, 98109

Donald Leslie Petramale

Title: Insurance Company Executive (Retired) **Industry:** Insurance **Company Name:** D & D Ventures Inc. **Date of Birth:** 05/01/1935 **Place of Birth:** Chicago **State:** IL **Parents:** Domenico Petramale; Serafina (Martino) Petramale **Marital Status:** Married **Spouse Name:** Diana Mae Silvestri (8/3/1980) **Children:** Deborah; Dominick; Dean; Donna; Michele; Debbie; Terri; Danny **Education:** Coursework, Harper College (1990); LUTC Graduate, Elmhurst College (1968) **Certifications:** Licensed Real Estate Broker (1968-1996) **Career:** Owner, D & D Ventures Inc., Roselle, IL (1967-1996); Chief Executive Officer, D & D Ventures Inc., Roselle, IL (1967-1996); President, D & D Ventures Inc., Roselle, IL (1967-1996); Owner, D & D Office Machines Inc., Roselle, IL (1967-1996); Chief Executive Officer, D & D Office Machines Inc., Roselle, IL (1967-1996); President, D & D Office Machines Inc., Roselle, IL (1967-1996); Secretary, National Office Machine Dealers Association (Now Business Technology Association), Chicago, IL (1988) **Career Related:** Director, American Heritage S & C Association, Bloomingdale, IL (1975-1977) **Civic:** Committee Member, Holy Family Catholic Church, Inverness, IL (1990); Democratic Township Chairman, Bloomingdale Township, IL (1971); Chairman, Addison Lake Manor Park Association, Addison, IL (1961) **Awards:** First Place for Best Dressed Performer, USA World Showcase, Las Vegas Hilton, Las Vegas, NV (2008); Leading Insurance Agent Awards, American National Insurance Company, Chicago, IL (1953-1967); Gold Winner of Music, Chicago School of Music (1951); 25 Baseball Trophies **Membership:** Business Technology Association, Chicago, IL (1988) **Marquis Who's Who Honors:** Albert Nelson Marquis Lifetime Achievement Award (2017) **To what do you attribute your success:** Mr. Petramale attributes his success to various seminars and his family's curriculum. He lives by the following motto: "We build a ladder by which we climb." **Why did you become involved in your profession or industry:** Mr. Petramale became involved in his profession because he believes in the skills that one possesses to pursue one's dream. **What do you consider to be the highlight of your career:** A highlight of Mr. Petramale's career was singing in Italy, where his parents were born. **Where will you be in five years:** In five years, Mr. Petramale will be enjoying his life with his wife, family and friends, as well as reliving memories. **Hobbies:** Music; Baseball; Football; Traveling; Spending time with his grandchildren **Religion:** Roman Catholic **Shipping Address:** 4629 Sweetmeadow Cir, Sarasota, FL, 34238

Renee Danette Petrola

Title: Teacher, Author (Retired) **Industry:** Education/Educational Services **Company Name:** Mt. Sinai School District **Parents:** Phyllis Petrola **Education:** Master's Degree in Liberal Studies, Stony Brook University (1974); BA in Elementary Education and Teaching, Bethany College (1970) **Career:** Retired (2013); Sixth Grade Teacher, Writing, Mount Sinai School District, Mount Sinai, NY (1970-2013); Author, Self-Employed **Career Related:** Conflict Mediator; Counselor; Instructor, Swimming Lessons **Civic:** Volunteer, Beach Cleanups; Volunteer, Relay for Life, American Cancer Society, Inc.; Volunteer, Ride For Life Inc; Volunteer, ASPCA; Volunteer, Greenpeace **Creative Works:** Author, "The Healing Tree, Volume Three" Book Stand Publishing (2015); Author, "Woman on the Edge of Time" (2014); Author, "Primitive Dancer," Book Stand Publishing (2014) **Awards:** Professional of the Year in Education (2010); Certificate of Recognition, Elite American Educators **Membership:** Mt. Sinai Teachers Association, American Federation of Teachers; National Education Association **Marquis Who's Who Honors:** Albert Nelson Marquis Lifetime Achievement Award (2017); Distinguished Humanitarian (2017) **To what do you attribute your success:** Ms. Petrola attributes her success to her passion, as well as her listening and observational skills. **Why did you become involved in your profession or industry:** Ms. Petrola became involved in her profession because of the inspiration she received from her mother, Phyllis Petrola, who was also an elementary teacher, and her experience as a babysitter. **What do you consider to be the highlight of your career:** The highlight of Ms. Petrola's career was being recognized for her participation in the Walt Whitman Poetry Contest. Her students placed first two years in a row for anthology. Ms. Petrola also accompanied her principal to the Washington, DC to receive a Blue Ribbon Award, which is given to schools cited for exemplary high performance by the U.S. Department of Education. The teachers at her school had a brick installed at The Walt Whitman Walkway. **Where will you be in five years:** In five years, Ms. Petrola would like to continue to write and publish more books. **Hobbies:** Designing jewelry; Writing; Swimming; Kayaking; Spending time at the beach; Riding her bike; Running; Rescuing and adopting Irish Setters **Shipping Address:** 232 Parkside Ave, Miller Place, NY, 11764 **Website:** http://www.reneedanette.net/about.html

Ghery St. John Pettit

Title: President **Industry:** Consulting **Company Name:** Pettit EMC Consulting LLC **Date of Birth:** 04/06/1952 **Place of Birth:** Woodland **State:** CA **Parents:** Ghery DeWitt Pettit; Frances Marie (Seitz) Pettit **Marital Status:** Married **Spouse Name:** Marilyn Jo Van Hoose (7/28/1973) **Children:** Ghery Christopher; Heather Kathleen **Education:** BS in Electrical Engineering, Washington State University (1975) **Certifications:** Certified Engineer-in-training, State of Colorado; Certified Engineer-in-training, State of Washington; Certified Electromagnetic Compatibility Engineer, INARTE **Career:** President, Pettit EMC Consulting LLC (2015-Present); Electromagnetic Compatibility Engineer, Intel Corporation, DuPont, WA (1996-2015); Electromagnetic Compatibility Engineer, Intel Corporation, Hillsboro, OR (1995-1996); Electromagnetic Compatibility Lead Engineer, Tandem Computers Inc. (1991-1995); Manager of Electromagnetic Capability, Tandem Computers Inc. (1990-1991); Staff Engineer, Tandem Computers Inc. (1983-1990) **Career Related:** Member, CISPR Subcommittee I, MT7 (2017-Present); Member, CISPR Subcommittee I, MT8 (2017-Present); CISPR Representative to Advisory Committee on Electromagnetic Compatibility, IEC (2017-Present); Chair, International Special Committee on Radio Interference (CISPR) Subcommittee I, IEC (2016-Present); Member, United States Technical Advisory Group, CISPR Subcommittee I (2001-Present); Convener, CISPR Subcommittee I, WG3, IEC (2007-2012) **Civic:** Scoutmaster, Boy Scouts of America (1990-1993) **Awards:** Laurence G. Cumming Award, EMCS (2007); Third Millennium Award, IEEE (2000) **Membership:** Immediate Past President, IEEE EMCS (2014-2015); President, IEEE EMCS (2012-2013); President-Elect, IEEE EMCS (2011); Vice President of Conference Services, IEEE EMCS (2009-2010); Board of Directors, IEEE EMCS (2006-2011); Vice President of Communication Services, IEEE EMCS (2003-2008); Board Assessment Member, National Research Council, National Academy of Sciences (1999-2005); Board of Directors, IEEE EMCS (1999-2004); Chairman, Seattle Chapter, IEEE EMCS (1997-2000); Chairman, Santa Clara Valley Section, IEEE (1994-1995); Vice-Chairman, Santa Clara Valley Section, IEEE (1993-1994); Treasurer, Santa Clara Valley Section, IEEE (1992-1993); Aircraft Owners and Pilots Association; American Radio Relay League; Benefactor Member, National Rifle Association of America **Marquis Who's Who Honors:** Albert Nelson Marquis Lifetime Achievement Award (2017) **Hobbies:** Flying; Amateur Radio; Sailing **Political Affiliations:** Republican **Religion:** Presbyterian **Business Address:** 3131 Leeward Ct NW, Olympia, WA, 98502 **Website:** www.pettitemcconsulting.com

Gail Susan Phillips

Title: Teacher **Industry:** Education/Educational Services **Company Name:** Bowdish Middle School **Date of Birth:** 04/17/1962 **Place of Birth:** Spokane **State:** WA **Parents:** Vern Phillips; Jane Phillips **Education:** MA in Music Education, Eastern Washington University (1992); Bachelor of Music Education, Eastern Washington University (1985); Bachelor of Music Performance, Eastern Washington University (1985); AA, Spokane Falls Community College (1982) **Career:** Band Director, Orchestra, Music Exploratory, Central Valley School District (2017-Present); Band/Orchestra Director, Chase Middle School, Spokane Public Schools (2012-2017); Orchestra Director, Bowdish Middle School, Central Valley School District (2011-2012); Band Director, Medical Lake School District (2008-2011); Member, Strategic Planning Committee, West Valley School District (2007-2008); Substitute Teacher, Coeur d'Alene School District (2007-2008); Band Director, Kalles Junior High, Puyallup, WA (1997-2007); Band Director, Totem Middle School, Federal Way, WA (1994-1997); Elementary Band Director, Mead School District 354 (1993-1994); Band Director, Rainier Junior High, Auburn, WA (1992-1993); Brass and Marching Band Instructor, Imperials Summer Band Program (1992-1993); Elementary Band Director, Medical Lake School District (1991-1992); Director, Bands, Cascade Junior High, Auburn, WA (1988-1991) **Creative Works:** Flugelhorn with Spokane British Brass Band (2008-Present); Trumpeter, Coeur D'Alene Symphony Orchestra (2008-2012); West Valley Kiwanis String Ensemble (Violin) (2007-2010); Trumpeter, Tacoma Concert Band (1997-2007) **Awards:** Washington Music Educators Association Hall of Fame (2018); Innovating Washington State Distinguished (2013-2017); Outstanding Music Teacher (2015); Second Place, Washington State Autumn Leaf Festival (2015); First Place, Coeur D'Alene/Silverwood Jazz Festival (2014-2016); First Place, Junior Lilac Parade (2014-2016) **Membership:** Secretary, Board of Directors, British Brass Band (2010-2017); West Valley School District Strategic Planning Committee (2007-2008) **Marquis Who's Who Honors:** Albert Nelson Marquis Lifetime Achievement Award (2017); Distinguished Humanitarian (2017) **Why did you become involved in your profession or industry:** Ms. Phillips became involved in her profession because she loves kids. **Where will you be in five years:** In five years, Ms. Phillips will be continuing her work get students and teachers more involved in music. **Shipping Address:** PO Box 141165, Spokane Valley, WA, 99214

Deirdre K. Pierson

Industry: Law and Legal Services **Date of Birth:** 01/01/1900 **Education:** JD, Brooklyn Law School; MA, Columbia University, New York; BA, Boston University **Certifications:** New York **Career:** Attorney, Partner, Emmet, Marvin & Martin LLP, New York City (2001)

Anita Ellescas Plummer

Title: Artist **Industry:** Fine Art **Date of Birth:** 06/05/1944 **Place of Birth:** San Pedro **State:** CA **Parents:** Henry Declison Ellescas; Helen Robles Ellescas **Marital Status:** Married **Spouse Name:** Walter Allen Plummer III (7/25/1964) **Children:** Sean Allen; Kira Elise; Eric Drew **Education:** MA, California State University, Fullerton, CA (1994); BA, California State University, Fullerton, CA (1984) **Career:** Book Illustrator, Scholastic, New York, NY (1995-1996); Design Instructor, California State University, Fullerton, CA (1994-1996); Illustration Instructor, Learning Tree University, Irvine, CA (1994-1995); Illustrator, Textiles, Funny Bunny Cache, Santa Ana, CA (1982-1994); Conceptual Illustrator, Mattel Toys, El Segundo, CA (1988-1992); Illustrator Designer, Playskool, North Vale, NJ (1988-1992); Illustrator, DC Cook Pub. Co., Elgin, IL (1969-1980) **Career Related:** Designer/Illustrator, National Christmas Seal Association **Creative Works:** Author in Field **Membership:** California Art Club; Laguna Plein Air Painters Association; National Association Women Artists **Hobbies:** Antiques; Aerobics; Walking **Shipping Address:** 1872 Holly Tree Ln, Santa Ana, CA, 92705

Cindy Deborah Postell

Title: English Teacher **Industry:** Education/Educational Services **Company Name:** Jasper County School District **Date of Birth:** 08/14/1954 **Place of Birth:** Savannah **State:** GA **Parents:** George Robert Postell; Sallie Walker Postell **Education:** MEd, Georgia Southern University (1980); BJ, University of Georgia (1976); Graduate, Jenkins High School, Jenkins Independent Schools, With Honors (1972) **Career:** English Teacher, Jasper County School District (1985-Present); Substitute Teacher, Chatham County Board of Education (1991) **Career Related:** Local Board Member (2012-Present); School Crossing Guard (2012-Present); Campus Security (2012-Present) **Civic:** Choir Member, St. John the Baptist Cathedral (1982-Present) **Creative Works:** Singer, Savannah Philharmonic **Awards:** Certificate of Recognition for Papal Visit to United States, World Families (2015); Substitute Classified Worker Award, Chatham County, GA (2010-2012); Grand Prize, Monastery of the Holy Cross (2008); Certificate of Appreciation, Basilica of the National Shrine of the Immaculate Conception (2006-2010); Certificate of Appreciation, The Carter Center (2006); Certificate of Appreciation, Pope John Paul II Cultural Center, The Knights of Columbus (2005) **Membership:** Electa Chapter, Order of the Eastern Star **Marquis Who's Who Honors:** Albert Nelson Marquis Lifetime Achievement Award (2017) **Hobbies:** Knitting; Crocheting **Religion:** Catholic **Shipping Address:** 128 W 51st Street, Savannah, GA, 31405

William C. Powell

Title: Consumer Products Company Executive **Industry:** Business Management/Business Services **Company Name:** Home Entertainment and Decor Systems **Date of Birth:** 11/05/1948 **Place of Birth:** Burlington **State:** NC **Parents:** Thomas Edward Powell, Jr.; Annabelle (Council) Powell **Marital Status:** Married **Spouse Name:** Jacqueline Garrison (7/3/1976) **Children:** William C., Jr.; Ashley C. **Education:** MBA, Wake Forest University (1974); Postgraduate Coursework, Elon University (1972); BS, Virginia Military Institute (1971); Coursework, University of South Carolina (1968-1969) **Certifications:** Licensed Pilot; Certified Real Estate Broker **Career:** President, Home Entertainment and Decor Systems (1984-Present); Owner, Home Entertainment and Decor Systems (1978-Present); Owner, Ashwil Acres Farm (1981-2005); President, Bobbitt Laboratories, Burlington, NC (1977-1982); Vice President, Bobbitt Laboratories, Burlington, NC (1974-1977); North Carolina Administrative Associate, Carolina Biological Supply Company, Burlington, NC (1971-1991) **Career Related:** Chairman, Goat Island Maritime, Inc. (2011-Present); Member, Forest Realm, Inc. (2001-Present); Member, Poignard Compact, Inc. (2001-Present); Member, Powell Realm Inc. (2001-Present); Member, Board of Directors, Ran for North Carolina Senate (2000, 2002); Member, Goat Island Maritime, Inc. (2001-2011); Member, Merrymount Boat Slip Association, Inc. (1996-2005); Member, StratoNet, Inc. (1996-2001); Member, Merrymount Property Owners Association (1996-2000); Chairman of Board, Netpath Inc. (1995-1996); Member, Warren Land Company (1994-2005); Partner, Port Associates II (1992-2002); Vice President of Finance, Environmental Responsible Business, Inc. (1992-1997); Manager, Macon Farm (1992-1995); Member, Underground Storage Tank Specialists Inc. (1991-2000); Chairman of Board, Ensci Corporation Inc. (1991-1995); Partner, Port Associates (1987-2002); Member, Babcock School Alumni Council, Wake Forest University (1981-1985); President, Granite Diagnostics, Inc. (1981-1984); Owner, Powell Real Estate (1979-2001); Member, Board of Directors, Excalibur Lock Company, Inc.; Member, Board of Directors, Waubun Laboratories Inc. **Military Service:** Captain, U.S. Army Reserve (1971-1979) **Awards:** Third Place, Big Rock Blue Marlin Tournament (1998); Governor's Cup for Billfishing, State of North Carolina (1991); Bill Fish Certificates, State of North Carolina (1990); Sower's Award, Duke University (1985); Bill Fish Certificate, State of South Carolina (1983) **Marquis Who's Who Honors:** Albert Nelson Marquis Lifetime Achievement Award (2017) **Shipping Address:** 1109 W Front St, Burlington, NC, 27215

Martin Ford Puris

Title: Chairman, Chief Executive Officer **Industry:** Business Management/Business Services **Company Name:** Puris & Partners **Date of Birth:** 02/22/1939 **Place of Birth:** Chicago **State:** IL **Parents:** Martin Puris; Virginia Lee Puris **Marital Status:** Married **Spouse Name:** Mary M. Herrmann **Children:** Kimberly Mayo; Jason Patterson; Mary Elizabeth **Education:** Coursework, DePauw University **Career:** President, Chief Executive Officer, Ammirati & Puris, Inc., New York, NY (1974-1994); Vice President, Carl Ally, Inc., New York, NY (1966-1974); With, Young & Rubicam, Inc., New York, NY (1964-1966); With, Campbell-Ewald Co., Detroit, MI (1962-1964); Chairman, Chief Executive Officer, Puris & Partners; Chairman, Chief Executive Officer, Chief Creative Officer, Ammirati, Puris, Lintas, New York, NY; Chairman, Chief Executive Officer, Chief Creative Officer, Ammirati, Puris, Lintas, New York, NY **Career Related:** Vice Chairman, Sheltering Arms; Director, IPG Group (1995-1999); Board of Directors, American Society for the Prevention of Cruelty to Animals; Treasurer, Hampton Classic; Managing Director, New Things Investment Group; Media Advisor, President George H.W. Bush **Creative Works:** Author, "Comeback: How Seven Straight-Shooting Chief Executive Officers Turned Around Troubled Companies" (1999) **Awards:** Inductee, Creative Hall of Fame, The One Club (2013); Recipient, Awards, Cannes Film Festival **Membership:** Devon Yacht Club; Union Club; American Yacht Club; Nantucket Yacht Club; New York Yacht Club **Marquis Who's Who Honors:** Distinguished Humanitarian (2017) **Why did you become involved in your profession or industry:** Mr. Puris knew that he wanted to be a writer and advertising was a hot area when he got into it. **Where will you be in five years:** Continuing to grow the company. **Hobbies:** Sailing; Horseback riding **Political Affiliations:** Republican **Religion:** Roman Catholic **Shipping Address:** PO Box 839, Sagaponack, NY, 11962

Anne Marie Puto

Title: Reading Specialist **Industry:** Education/Educational Services **Date of Birth:** 07/20/1956 **Place of Birth:** Windber **State:** PA **Parents:** John Michael Puto; Ann Theresa (Biel) Puto **Marital Status:** Single **Education:** EdM in Educational Psychology, Indiana University of Pennsylvania (1989); EdM in Language Communications, University of Pittsburgh (1981); BS Elementary Education, University of Pittsburgh, Johnstown (1978) **Certifications:** Elementary Guidance Certification **Career:** Reading Specialist, Children's Aid Home, Somerset, PA (1999-Present); Reading Specialist, Appalachia Intermediate Unit 08, Altoona, PA (1979-Present); Reading Specialist, Upward Bound Program, St. Francis University, Loretto, PA (1994-2000); Reading Specialist, Appalachian Youth Service, Ebensburg, PA (1991-2004); Reading Specialist, Conemaugh Valley School District, Johnstown, PA (1978-1979) **Awards:** Service Award, Appalachian Youth Service (2017); Youth Advocacy Award, Appalachian Youth Service (1998, 1992) **Membership:** Board of Directors, Cambria County Literacy Council, Johnstown, PA (2016-Present); Board of Directors, Appalachian Youth Service, Ebensburg, PA (2012-Present) **Marquis Who's Who Honors:** Albert Nelson Marquis Lifetime Achievement Award (2017) **Hobbies:** Reading; Travel; Cross-country skiing; Needlecrafts; Theater **Shipping Address:** 1093 Tener St, Johnstown, PA, 15904

Arnold J. Quakkelaar

Title: Ministry Executive **Industry:** Religious **Company Name:** Genesis in Milwaukee Inc. **Date of Birth:** 07/09/1937 **Place of Birth:** Muskegon **State:** MI/USA **Marital Status:** Married **Spouse Name:** Norma Quakkelaar **Children:** Daniel; David; Douglas; Dale; Dean; Luanne (Deceased) **Education:** BS, Calvin College (1960) **Certifications:** Registered Professional Engineer, State of Wisconsin; Certified Service Executive, National Association of Service Managers **Career:** Director, Johnson Controls Inc. (1992-1995); International Vice President, Global Technical Services, Rockwell International (1980-1991); Director, Johnson Controls Inc. (1955-1980) **Career Related:** Chairman, Board of Directors, Operation Mercy and Elmbrook Church (1975-2011); Senior Elder, Elmbrook Church (1975-2011); Chair, Council, Building Expansion, Elmbrook Church (1975-2011); Board's Chief Delegate, American Technical Committee, International Standards Organization (1972-1977) **Civic:** CEO, Genesis, Milwaukee Inc. (2012-Present); Founder, Genesis, Milwaukee Inc. (2012-Present); CEO, Basics, Milwaukee Inc. (1995-Present); Founder, Basics, Milwaukee Inc. (1995-Present); Pinnacle Forum; Community Activism for Peace; Pastors United, Milwaulkee, WI; Advisor, Faith Ministries **Military Service:** U.S. Army Reserve **Creative Works:** Author, "Doing God's Work in Milwaukee" **Awards:** Milwaukee's Greatest Bridge-builder **Membership:** Leadership Foundations; Past President, Rotary International **Marquis Who's Who Honors:** Marquis Who's Who Lifetime Achievement Award (2017) **Hobbies:** Golf; Music; Writing **Political Affiliations:** Conservative **Religion:** Evangelical Christian, Follower of Jesus Christ **Business Address:** 2224 West Kilbourn Avenue, WI, Milwaukee, 53233 **Shipping Address:** 1724 Erin Lane, Waukesha, WI, 53188 **Website:** http://www.GENESlinMke.org

Jill M. Rabin

Title: Obstetrician, Gynecologist, Urogynecologist, Educator **Industry:** Medicine & Health Care **Date of Birth:** 05/20/1953 **Place of Birth:** Bronx **State:** NY **Parents:** Gilbert Rabin; Zita Rabin **Marital Status:** Married **Education:** Fellow, Long Island Jewish Medical Center, Northwell Health (1989-1992); Fellow, Memorial Sloan Kettering Cancer Center (1984); Resident, Albert Einstein College of Medicine (1981-1985); MD, SUNY Downstate Medical Center (1981); BA in Speech Pathology and Audiology/Premedical Studies, Hofstra University (1975) **Certifications:** Diplomate, American Board of Obstetrics and Gynecology (1987-Present); License to Practice Medicine, State of New York (1983) **Career:** Co-chief, Division of Ambulatory Care, Women's Health Programs, PCAP Services, Northwell Health; Associate Professor to Professor, Obstetrics and Gynecology, Donald and Barbara Zucker School of Medicine at Hofstra/Northwell; Co-director, Advanced Clinical Experience in Obstetrics and Gynecology, Donald and Barbara Zucker School of Medicine at Hofstra/Northwell; Director, Curriculum Development in Obstetrics and Gynecology, Donald and Barbara Zucker School of Medicine at Hofstra/Northwell **Career Related:** Hofstra University Gala Committee; Committee Chair, Library and Informatics Committee, Northwell Health; Consultant, The Dr. Oz Show, Harpo, Inc.; Presenter in Field **Civic:** Faculty Mentor, Hofstra Medical Students for Choice; Chair, UJA Committee of Physicians and Dentists, Northwell Health; Board Member, Office of Professional Medical Conduct, New York State Department of Health **Creative Works:** Reviewer, Professional Journals; Contributing Editor; Editorial Board; Guest Editor; Author, Books; Narrateur; Contributor, Chapters, Books; Contributor, Articles, Medical Journals; Contributor, Medically-Based Videos; Regular Contributor, Public Media **Awards:** Katz Women's Institute Research Award, Northwell Health; Grantee, New York State Department of Health; Research Grants **Membership:** Society of Women in Urology; Executive Board, Susan G. Komen Greater NYC; National League of American Pen Women (NLAPW) **To what do you attribute your success:** Dr. Rabin attributes her success to stellar mentorship, family encouragement, patients from whom she can learn as well as to care for and to commitment to ongoing learning and study. **Why did you become involved in your profession or industry:** Dr. Rabin became involved in her profession from the love of teaching and caring for her patients and students. **What do you consider to be the highlight of your career:** The day Dr. Rabin learned to listen to patients with her heart as well as her mind. **Business Address:** 270-05 76th Avenue, New Hyde Park, NY, 11040

Diane M. Radford, MD, FACS, FRCSEd

Title: Surgeon, Oncologist, Medical Director **Industry:** Health, Wellness and Fitness **Company Name:** Cleveland Clinic Foundation **Date of Birth:** 11/14/1957 **Place of Birth:** Irvine **Country of Origin:** Scotland **Parents:** Sidney Radford; Mary Margery (Parr) Radford **Marital Status:** Married **Spouse Name:** P. Evans **Education:** MD, Glasgow University (1991); Bachelor of Medicine, Bachelor of Surgery, Glasgow University (1981); BSc, Glasgow University, with Honors (1978) **Certifications:** Board Certified in General Surgery, American College of Surgeons **Career:** Medical Director, Breast Program, Cleveland Clinic, Hillcrest Hospital (2017-Present); Associate Professor of Surgery, Lerner College of Medicine of Case Western Reserve University (2017 - Present); Cleveland Clinic (2016-Present); Mercy Clinic (2008-2015); St. Louis Cancer and Breast Institute (1999-2008); Parkcrest Surgical Associates, St. Louis, MO (1996-2001); Assistant Professor of Surgery, Washington University, St. Louis, MO (1992-1996); Instructor in Surgery, Washington University, St. Louis, MO (1991-1992); Resident in Surgery, St. Louis University Hospital (1987-1991); Fellow in Surgical Oncology, Roswell Park Memorial Institute, Buffalo, NY (1985-1987); Registrar, Crosshouse Hospital, Kilmarnock, Scotland (1984-1985); Senior House Officer, Royal Infirmary, Edinburgh, Scotland (1983-1984); Senior House Officer, We. Infirmary, Glasgow (1982-1983); Junior House Officer, Monklands District General Hospital, Airdrie, Scotland (1982); Junior House Officer, Gartravel General Hospital, Glasgow, Scotland (1981-1982) **Creative Works:** Author, "Bless Your Little Cotton Socks"; **Awards:** First Prize, Resident's Competition, Missouri Chapter, American College of Surgeons Post-Training (1996-Present); Cleveland Clinic Caregiver Appreciation Award: Innovation (2017); Press Ganey Patient Satisfaction Award (2016); Woman of Distinction in the Sciences, Girl Scouts of Eastern Missouri (2012-2016); Patients' Choice Award (2012); Vitals Compassionate Doctor Award (2015); List of Castle Connolly Top Doctors in Surgery (2012-2014); STAR (Survivorship Training and Rehab) Certified Clinician (2014); Graduate, Leadership Certification Program, Joint program of Mercy and St. Louis University (2014); List of Best Doctors in America (2006); Fran Lefrak-Brown Illuminator Award, AMC Breast Cancer Research Center (Jointly with partners St. Louis Cancer & Breast Institute) (2010); Cleveland Clinic Caregiver Appreciation Award: Engagement Champion Caregiver Experience Survey **Hobbies:** Golf **Business Address:** 9500 Euclid Ave, Cleveland, OH, 44195 **Shipping Address:** 361 W. Edinburgh Drive, Highland Heights, OH, 44143 **Website:** http://www.dianeradfordmd.com

Manjula Raguthu

Title: Physician, Director **Industry:** Medicine & Health Care **Company Name:** Medwin Family Medicine & Rehabilitation **Education:** Postgraduate Diploma in Obstetrics and Gynecology (1993); MBBS, Guntur Medical College (1990) **Certifications:** Re-certified in Family Practice (2008); Board Certified in Family Practice (2001); Board Certified in Anti-aging and Integrative Medicine; Certification in Advanced Trauma Life Support; Certified Medical Coder; Certification in Medical Office Management Certification; Certified Compliance Officer **Civic:** Various Nonprofit Organizations; Provides Healthcare for Immigrant Children **Awards:** Best Family Physicians in America, Consumer's Research Council of America (2009); Best Family Physician, Consumer's Research Council of America (2008); Best Family Physicians in America, Consumer's Research Council of America (2006); Best Family Physician, Consumer's Research Council of America (2006); Best Family Physicians in America, Consumer's Research Council of America (2004); Exemplary Leadership Award (2001); 32nd Rank in Family Practice Boards in America; Distinction in Microbiology; Distinction in Ophthalmology; Overall Percentile of 97.3 in Medical School; Topper in Physiology, Surgery, and Obstetrics and Gynecology **Membership:** American Academy of Family Physicians; American Medical Association; American Association of Physicians of Indian Origin; Texas Academy of Family Physicians; American Anti-Aging Academy **Marquis Who's Who Honors:** Albert Nelson Marquis Lifetime Achievement Award (2017) **To what do you attribute your success:** Dr. Raguthu attributes her success to her hard work and dedication. **Why did you become involved in your profession or industry:** Dr. Raguthu became involved in her profession because of her desire to care for people. **What do you consider to be the highlight of your career:** The highlight of Dr. Raguthu's career is caring for her patients. **Where will you be in five years:** In the years to come, Dr. Raguthu intends to continue to build her practice. **Hobbies:** Badminton; Photography; Handicrafts **Business Address:** 315 Jose Marti Boulevard, Suite D, Brownsville, TX, 78526 **Website:** http://www.medwinfamily.com

Joy Rainey King

Title: Poet, Executive Secretary **Industry:** Fine Art **Date of Birth:** 08/05/1939 **Place of Birth:** Memphis **State:** TN **Parents:** Roy Henry Rainey; Margaret (Irvin) Rainey **Marital Status:** Widowed **Spouse Name:** Guy Robert King (12/24/1956) **Children:** William Lonnie; Cheryl King Ramsey **Education:** Honorary DLitt, World Academy of Arts and Culture, Paris, France; Diploma, Whitehaven High School, Memphis, TN (1957) **Career:** First National Bank of Southaven, MS (1973-1979); Medical Secretary, James Ballard, MD, Tupelo, MS (1969-1973); **Career Related:** Staff Writer, Majestic Records; Staff Writer, Countrywine Publishing Company **Creative Works:** Invited Poetry Reader, Speak Up Fest, Nairobi, Kenya (2012); Author, "From the Gazebo, Wonder of Words" (2003); Author, "America's New Hero"; Author, Poetry, Published in China, Cyprus, Croatia, Italy, India, Japan, Canada, Belgium, Finland and England; Author, Book, Mongolia; Author, Three Books, India; Author, Numerous Poems, 25 Poetry Books, Numerous Books; Songwriter, Songs of Love Foundation; Author, Poems, Local Newspapers and Numerous Anthologies; Interviewee, "Successful Women Speak Out"; Contributor, Poetry, "American Poetry in Mongolia"; Featured Biography, Pictures and Poems, The UB Post, Mongolia **Awards:** Official of Dignity Award, United Nations (2014); Circle of Light Award (2014); Nominee, Nobel Prize in Literature (2010); Nominee, Nobel Prize in Literature (2008); Nominee, Nobel Prize in Literature (2004); International Book of Gold Prize (2003); International Peace Prize, United Cultural Convention (2002); President's Recognition of Literary Excellence, National Authors Registry (1999-2000); Author of the Year, Edizoni University (Now University of Trento), Trento, Italy (1999); International Woman of the Year, International Biographical Centre, Cambridge, England (1998); Editor's Choice Award (1993-1994); Poet of the Month Award; Four-Time Winner, International Book of Gold Prizes, Four Collections of Poetry; International Best Poets Award, International Translation and Research Center, China; Lifetime Achievement Award, International Poets Academy, India **Membership:** Secretary, Southern Illinois Writers Guild, Illinois Humanities (1996-1998); International Society of Poets; Poets Guild; International Poetry Hall of Fame; Top Recorders Songwriters Association; Famous Poets Society; Metverse Muse, India; World Congress of Poets (Now United Poets Laureate International World Congress of Poets); World Poets Society, Greece; Vice President, World Congress of Arts, Sciences and Communications, Cambridge, England **Marquis Who's Who Honors:** Albert Nelson Marquis Lifetime Achievement Award (2017) **Religion:** Baptist **Shipping Address:** 3029 Willow Branch Ln, Herrin, IL 62948

Betty Rantze-Byrd

Title: Actor, Writer, Photographer **Industry:** Writing and Editing **Date of Birth:** 07/08/1949 **Place of Birth:** Oklahoma City **State:** OK **Parents:** Rolande Brown; Mary Louise Haner **Marital Status:** Married **Spouse Name:** Bill Byrd (9/16/1995) **Children:** Elizabeth Chase Rantze **Education:** Paralegal Degree, Capital University Law School, Columbus, OH (1975); Graduate Coursework, The OH State University, Columbus, OH (1974-1975); BA in Creative Writing and Theater, Minor in French, University of Arizona, Tucson, AZ (1974); Diploma, Ohio State University (1974) **Career:** Actor, Numerous Commercials, Films and Television Shows (1978-1993); Paralegal, Public Defender, Lewisburg, PA (1976-1977); Managing Editor, Ohio State University Dental Newsletter (1974-1975); Editor, The Spectator Newspapers, Columbus, OH (1974-1975) **Civic:** Volunteer, San Diego Family Recovery Center; Volunteer, Special Olympics, San Diego, CA; Volunteer, Meals-on-Wheels, San Diego, CA; Volunteer, Salvation Army **Creative Works:** Wildlife Photographer, Photographs in Private Collections Throughout the Country and Gallery Showings in California and New Mexico (2010-2017); Author, "Utopia, Texas" (2008); Author, "Trinity's Daughter" (2004) **Awards:** Second Place Ribbon, San Diego County Fair Exhibition of Photography (2016); Two Honorable Mention Ribbons, San Diego County Fair Exhibition of Photography (2013); EVVY Award (2009); Best Fiction Writer's Award, Santa Barbara Writers Conference (2004); Special Recognition, Commitment to Preserving San Diego County Fair as an Exhibition Photographic Competitor, California State Senate **Membership:** American Federation of Television and Radio Artists; Screen Actors Guild; National Charity League; Rancho Santa Fe Literary Society; Lifetime Member, National Geographic; Your Shot Photo Community, National Geographic; San Diego Zoo Global Community; Various Wildlife Foundations **Hobbies:** Photography; Golf; Travel; Walking; Scrapbooks **Shipping Address:** PO Box 2593, Rancho Santa Fe, CA, 92067

Ronald L. Rardin, PhD

Title: Engineering Educator **Industry:** Education/Educational Services **Company Name:** University of Arkansas **Date of Birth:** 05/03/1943 **Place of Birth:** Kansas City **State:** MO **Parents:** Eugene Murray Rardin; Virginia Shepherd Rardin **Marital Status:** Married **Spouse Name:** Blanca Q. Quiroga (9/3/1969) **Children:** Robert R. **Education:** PhD in Industrial and Systems Engineering, Georgia Institute of Technology (1974); MPA, University of Kansas, Lawrence, KS (1967); BA in Mathematics and Political Science, University of Kansas, Lawrence, KS (1965) **Career:** Distinguished Professor Emeritus, University of Arkansas, Fayetteville, AR (2013-Present); Distinguished Professor of Industrial Engineering, University of Arkansas, Fayetteville, AR (2007-2013); John and Mary Lib White Systems Integration Chair in Industrial Engineering, University of Arkansas, Fayetteville, AR **Career Related:** Program Director, National Science Foundation, Arlington, VA (2000-2003); Fellow, Institute for Operations Research and the Management; Fellow, Institute of Operations Research and Management Sciences **Creative Works:** Author, "Discrete Optimization, Optimization in Operations Research" **Awards:** Book of the Year, Institute of Industrial Engineers (1999); The David F. Baker Distinguished Research Award; Career Research Award **Membership:** Institute of Industrial Engineers; Mathematical Programming Society **Marquis Who's Who Honors:** Albert Nelson Marquis Lifetime Achievement Award (2017) **Shipping Address:** 8404 Warren Parkway, Apt. 122, Frisco, TX, 75034

John David Raymer

Title: Teacher, Founding Member **Industry:** Education/Educational Services **Company Name:** Holy Cross College Westville Education Initiative, Prison Studies Project **Date of Birth:** 07/09/1948 **Place of Birth:** Elkhart **State:** IN **Children:** Carolyn Mary McEachran; Janet Theresa Smith; Thomas Joseph **Education:** PhD, Ohio University, Athens, OH (1975); MA, National University of Ireland, Dublin, Ireland (1971); BA, Wittenberg University, Springfield, OH (1970); Postdoctoral, Purdue University, West Lafayette, IN **Certifications:** Certification in Midwest Technical Institute, Teaching Academy (2001); University Tours, France (1974) **Career:** Teacher, University of Notre Dame and Holy Cross College Westville Education Initiative, Prison Studies Project (2013-Present); Founding Member, Participant, University of Notre Dame and Holy Cross College Westville Education Initiative, Prison Studies Project (2012-Present); Lecturer, Purdue University, North Central Campus, Westville, IN (2008-Present); English Professor, Holy Cross College, Notre Dame, IN (1990-Present); Adjunct Lecturer, Saint Mary's College, Notre Dame, IN (2007-2008); Adjunct Assistant Professor, Indiana University, South Bend, IN (1989-1994) **Career Related:** Chairman, Department of English, Holy Cross College, Notre Dame, IN (2008-Present); Chairman, Promotions and Retention Committee (2005-Present); Co-Founder, Homework Tutoring Program (1995-Present) **Civic:** Senior Warden, St. Michael and All Angels Episcopal Church (2004-Present); Lecturer, St. James, Episcopal Cathedral, South Bend, IN (1996-Present) **Creative Works:** Contributing Editor, Louisville Reader (2007-Present); Contributing Editor, Associated Press Reading Focales, Kansas City, MO (2015); Contributing Editor, "The Hole in Me Since the Day You Died" by David Labrum (2005); Contributing Editor, Associated Press English Language Exam, Daytona Beach, FL **Awards:** Nominee, Michiana 55 Plus Volunteer Award (2012); Certificate of Appreciation Award (2012); Outstanding Board Member, Dismas House (2010); Outstanding Mentor, University of Notre Dame, Bound Students (2005); George Hixson Award, Kiwanis International (2004) **Membership:** Defenders of World Wildlife; Royal Society for the Prevention of Cruelty to Animals; National Audubon Society; Phi Kappa Phi National Scholastic Honor Society; Delta Epsilon Sigma National Catholic Scholastic Honor Society **Marquis Who's Who Honors:** Albert Nelson Marquis Lifetime Achievement Award (2017) **Hobbies:** Traveling; Swimming; Canoeing; Hiking; Reading; Painting **Political Affiliations:** Democrat **Religion:** Episcopalian **Shipping Address:** 1613 E Madison Street, South Bend, IN, 46617

Karen Reid

Title: Associate Professor of Psychology **Industry:** Education/Educational Services **Company Name:** New Mexico State University **Date of Birth:** 02/13/1953 **Place of Birth:** Augsburg **Country of Origin:** Germany **Parents:** Larry Edward Mills; Elizabeth Eunice Smith Mills **Education:** PhD, University of Nevada, Las Vegas, NV (2009); Education Specialist, Troy State University, Montgomery, AL (1980); MEd, University of Missouri, Columbia, MO (1977); BA, Stephens College, Columbia, MO (1974) **Career:** Associate Professor, Psychology, New Mexico State University (2012-Present); Assistant Professor, Psychology, New Mexico State University Alamogordo (2009-2012); Graduate Assistant, Part-time Instructor, University of Nevada, Las Vegas, NV (2003-2009) **Career Related:** Courseware Development Manager, Lead Instructional Developer, SDS International, Las Vegas, NV (1998-2003); Senior Test Administrator, Human Resources Research Organization, Lawton, OK (1997-1998); Registered Representative, Agent, USPA&IRA, Wichita Falls, TX (1995-1997) **Civic:** Assistant Division Head, Career and Technology Education (2016-Present); Board of Directors, Alamogordo Earth Day (2011-Present); Member, Career and Technology Education Career Expo, Alamogordo, NM (2009-Present); Member, Community Spelling Bee Team, Alamogordo, NM (2010-2013); Organizer, Member, Community Spelling Bee Team, Alamogordo, NM (2010); Vice President, Finance, Greater Las Vegas Chapter, ATD (2001-2003) **Military Service:** Education and Training Officer, U.S. Air Force (1978-1995) **Creative Works:** Contributor, Articles, Professional Journals **Awards:** Excellence Award, National Institute of Staff and Organization Development, Austin, TX (2012); Recognition Award, Graduate and Professional Student Association (2008-2009); Graduate Research Training Great Assistantship Grant, Graduate College, University of Nevada, Las Vegas, NV (2006); Decorated Meritorious Service Medal, Fifth Oak Leaf Cluster, U.S. Air Force **Membership:** American Psychological Association; American Evaluation Association; American Educational Research Association; Air Force Association **Shipping Address:** 1417 Rockwood, Alamogordo, NM, 88310

Ruth Reininghaus

Title: Artist (Retired) **Industry:** Fine Art **Date of Birth:** 10/04/1922 **Place of Birth:** New York **State:** NY **Parents:** Emil William Reininghaus; Pauline Rosa (Lazarisk) Reininghaus **Marital Status:** Married **Spouse Name:** Allen Joseph Smith (5/28/1960); George H. Morales (2/20/1944) **Children:** George James; Robert Charles **Education:** Coursework, The Art Students League (1964-1968); Coursework, The Frank Reilly School of Art (1963); Coursework, National Academy School of Design (1960-1961); Coursework, Hunter College (1940); Coursework in Oil Painting with Rudy Colao; Coursework in Oil Painting with Robert Maione; Coursework in Oil Painting with Morton Roberts and Frank Reilly; Coursework in Oil Painting with Robert Beverly Hale and Robert Philips **Career Related:** Art Instructor, Banker's Trust Company (1979-1999); Art Instructor, Kittredge Club for Women (1971-1998); Art Instructor, Banker's Trust Company (1971-1977) **Civic:** Active Member, Coast Guard Art Program; Active Member, Navy Art Cooperative and Liaison, U.S. Navy **Creative Works:** Exhibitor, Group Shows, Pastel Society of America (1988-Present); Exhibitor, Group Shows, John Lane Gallery (1992-1997); Exhibitor, Group Shows, Pen + Brush (1985-1995); Exhibitor, Group Shows, Regianni Gallery (1994); Exhibitor, Group Shows, Petrucci Gallery (1988-1994); Exhibitor, Group Shows, Mufalli Gallery (1983-1990); Exhibitor, Group Shows, Berkshire Art Museum (1970-1979); Exhibitor, Group Shows, Hammer Galleries (1974); Exhibitor, Group Shows, Far Gallery (1974) **Awards:** Magnifico Collage Award, American Artist Professional League (2016); Honoree, Named Woman of the Year, American Biographical Institute (2007); Helen G. Oehler Memorial Award (2006-2007); Mortimer Freehof Award, Salmagundi Club (2005-2007); Art Spirit Foundation Silver Medal for Excellence in Pastel, Salmagundi Club (2006); Second Prize for Pastel, Salmagundi Club (2006) **Membership:** Curator, Salmagundi Club (2003-2004); Curator, Salmagundi Club (1989-1997); Board of Directors, Catharine Lorillard Wolfe Art Club (1987-1997); Board of Directors, Pastel Society of America (1988-1990); Board of Directors, Washington Square Outdoor Art Exhibit (1983-1990); President, Salmagundi Club (1983-1987); Fellow, The American Artists Professional League; Knickerbocker Artists; Oil Pastel Association; Associate, Allied Artists of America, Inc.; The National Arts Club; Alpha Delta Pi **Marquis Who's Who Honors:** Albert Nelson Marquis Lifetime Achievement Award (2017) **Religion:** Lutheran **Shipping Address:** 222 E 93rd St Apt 26A, New York, NY, 10128

Nancy Reynolds

Title: Writer **Industry:** Writing and Editing **Company Name:** The George Balanchine Foundation **Date of Birth:** 07/15/1928 **Place of Birth:** San Antonio **State:** TX/USA **Parents:** Donald Worthington; Edith (Remick) R. **Marital Status:** Married **Spouse Name:** Brian Rushton (6/25/1983, Deceased 2005) **Children:** Ehren Reynolds **Education:** Postgraduate, Sarah Lawrence College, Bronxville, NY (1974-1977); Postgraduate, The University of Chicago (1974-1976); Postgraduate, Goethe Institut, Prien am Chiemsee, Germany (1972); BA, Art History, Columbia University, NY (1965); Coursework, Sorbonne, Paris (1962); Coursework, Martha Graham Center of Contemporary Dance, Inc., NY (1959); Coursework, Julliard School of Music, NY (1957); Coursework, School of American Ballet, NY (1953-1961); Coursework, School of American Ballet, NY (1951) **Career:** Concept Direction, George Balanchine Foundation Video Archives (1994-Present); Director of Research, The George Balanchine Foundation, NY (1994-Present); Associate Editor, International Encyclopedia of Dance (1998); Director of Research, Public TV Special, Balanchine, NY (1983-1984); Director, Research Book, "Choreography by George Balanchine: A Catalogue of Works" (1979-1982); Editor, Praeger Publications, NY (1965-1971); Dancer, New York City Ballet (1956-1961) **Career Related:** Co-publisher, Twentieth-Century Dance in Slides (1978-1993) **Creative Works:** Editorial Director, Balachine Catalogue (2008); Editor, "Remembering Lincoln" (2007); Author, "No Fixed Points: Dance in the Twentieth Century (2003); Author, "Dance Classics: Recommended for Teenagers, New York Public Library" (1991); Contributor, "Ballet: Bias and Belief," "Three Pamphlets Collected" and Other Dance Writings of Lincoln Kirstein (1983); Author, "In Performance" (1980); Author, "The Dance Catalogue: A Complete Guide to Today's World of Dance" (1979); Contributor, "School of Classical Dance," Vera Kostrovitskaya and A. Pisarev (1978); Author, "Repertory in Review: Forty Years of the New York City Ballet" (1977); Author, "Dance as a Theatre Art: Source Readings in Dance History from 1581 to the Present" (1974) **Awards:** Calliope, Special Award for Dance Writing, Dance Critics Association (2012); New York Dance and Performance Award, "Bessie" (2012) **Membership:** President, Dance Critics Association (1986-1987); Society of Dance History Scholars; Society for Dance Research; American Society for Theatre Research (ASTR); European Association of Dance Historians; International Federation for Theatre Research (IFTR) in Affiliation with Societe International des Bibliotheques et Musees des Arts du Spectacle (SIBMAS); **Shipping Address:** 9 Prospect Park W., Apartment 4C, Brooklyn, NY, 11215

Jo Ann Scholze Reynolds-Hufner

Title: Educational Administrator, Principal **Industry:** Education/Educational Services **Date of Birth:** 08/15/1941 **Place of Birth:** Sarasota **State:** FL **Parents:** Joseph Wendling Scholze; Frances (Amsden) Scholze **Marital Status:** Widowed **Spouse Name:** Frederick G. Hufner (1/16/1989, Deceased); James Hooks Reynolds (12/27/1959, Divorced 5/1985) **Children:** James Burton; Jamie Jo (Deceased) **Education:** EdD, Nova University (1987); MEd, Florida Atlantic University (1973); BS, Florida Atlantic University (1968); AA, Palm Beach Junior College (1967) **Certifications:** General Education, Physical Education, Education Administration; Health Masters of K-12, Education Administration **Career:** Principal, Adult Education Center (1994-1998); Personnel Specialist, Palm Beach County Public Schools (1993-1994); Principal, Wellington Landings Community Middle School, FL (1987-1993); Principal, Palm Beach, Public School (1983-1987); Assistant Principal, Forest Hill High School, West Palm Beach, FL (1979-1983); Dean, Congress Middle School, Boynton Beach, FL (1976-1979); Dean, Conniston Junior High School, West Palm Beach, FL (1973-1976); Teacher, J.I. Leonard High School, Lake Worth, FL (1968-1973) **Creative Works:** Author, Articles; Developer, Writing Curriculum; Poet **Awards:** Golden Poet Award (1987-1988) **Membership:** Palm Beach Chamber of Commerce; American Association of School Administrators; Florida Association of Secondary School Principals; National Association of Secondary School Principals **Marquis Who's Who Honors:** Albert Nelson Marquis Lifetime Achievement Award (2017) **Why did you become involved in your profession or industry:** When Ms. Reynolds-Hufner was younger, she had a teacher that inspired her to become involved in education. **Hobbies:** Reading **Political Affiliations:** Democrat **Religion:** Christian **Shipping Address:** 1017 Island Manor Drive, Greenacres, FL, 33413

Philip Rich

Title: Publishing Executive **Industry:** Publishing **Date of Birth:** 02/01/1940 **Place of Birth:** Nashua **State:** NH **Parents:** John Parker Rich; Olive Frances (Hussey) Rich **Marital Status:** Single **Spouse Name:** Leslie Ann Burke (6/14/1974, Divorced 1982) **Education:** Postgraduate Coursework, Princeton University (1962); MA, New York University (1962); AB, Harvard University, Magna Cum Laude (1961) **Career:** Editorial Consultant, Pittsfield, MA (2003-Present); Retired (2016); Editorial Director, Production Director, Berkshire House Publications, Lee, MA (1999-2003); Managing Editor, Production Editor, Berkshire House Publications, Lee, MA (1996-1999); Managing Editor, Berkshire House Publications, Lee, MA (1993-1996); Consultant Editor, Berkshire House Publications, Lee, MA (1992-1993); Vice President, Executive Editor, Book Creations Inc., Canaan, NY (1991-1992); Editor-in-Chief, Book Creations Inc., Canaan, NY (1980-1991); Editor, Book Creations Inc., Canaan, NY (1977-1980); Assistant Managing Editor, UpCountry Magazine, Berkshire Eagle, Pittsfield, MA (1976-1977); Editor, Houghton Mifflin Harcourt, Boston, MA (1964-1973) **Career Related:** Consultant **Shipping Address:** 10 Hazelwood Terrace, Pittsfield, MA, 01201

Roy Clark Richards

Title: Insurance Company Executive **Industry:** Insurance **Date of Birth:** 12/14/1942 **Place of Birth:** Philadelphia **State:** PA **Parents:** Riley Harry Richards; Eloise (Smith) Richards **Marital Status:** Married **Spouse Name:** Gloria Kay Wallis (2/13/1971) **Children:** Kristen Leigh; Geoffrey Stephen **Education:** MBA, University of Chicago (1967); BA, Carleton College, Magna Cum Laude (1965) **Certifications:** Chartered Property and Casualty Underwriter **Career:** Founder & Principal, Middle Age Renewal Training, Des Moines, IA (2010-Present); Executive Vice President, MJ Kelly of Iowa, Des Moines, IA (1993-2010); President, RDS Group, Des Moines, IA (1991-1993); Management Consultant, Self-Employed, Des Moines, IA (1988-1991); Vice President, Atlantic Management Services, San Antonio, TX (1987-1988); Senior Vice President, Chief Financial Officer, Western Employers Insurance Company, Santa Ana, CA (1984-1985); Director of Insurance Strategy, Continental Group, Inc., Stamford, CT (1980-1984); Assistant Corp. Controller, Booz Allen Hamilton Inc., New York, NY (1979-1980); Region Controller, Commercial Union Insurance Co., Camp Hill, PA (1975-1979); Senior Financial Analyst, Rockwell International, Pittsburgh, PA (1973-1975); Financial Analyst, Ford Motor Company, Dearborn, MI (1970-1973) **Military Service:** Officer, U.S. Navy (1967-1969) **Creative Works:** Host, Internet Podcast, "Middle Age Can Be Your Best Age" (2012-Present); Author, "WAKE UP CAPTAIN AND CREW: Restart Your Engines!" (2007); Author, "A Mid-Life Challenge WAKE UP!" (2006) **Awards:** Scholarship Recognition, Society of Property and Casualty Underwriters (1977) **Membership:** Phi Beta Kappa (1965); Society of Property and Casualty Underwriters **Marquis Who's Who Honors:** Albert Nelson Marquis Lifetime Achievement Award (2017) **To what do you attribute your success:** Mr. Richards attributes his success to realizing that you have to define what you are really good at and what you really want to do. He believes that people should not pursue careers that they are not enjoying, and that they should consider if they are really happy and balanced in their relationships, if they are joyful, if they are taking control of their lives, and if they are making sure that events don't take control of them. **Where will you be in five years:** Mr. Richards hopes to bring some other people in from different age groups to continue his work. **Hobbies:** Jogging; Hiking; Bike riding; Dramatics; College athletics; **Political Affiliations:** Republican **Religion:** Presbyterian **Shipping Address:** 1740 Cedarwood Circle, Clive, IA, 50325 **Website:** http://middleagerenewal.com

Bonnie Ring

Title: Psychologist/Minister **Industry:** Medicine & Health Care **Date of Birth:** 04/22/1940 **Place of Birth:** New York **State:** NY **Marital Status:** Single **Education:** EdD, Boston University (1972); EdM, Boston University (1964); BA, New York University (1962); Attended, Vassar College (1957-1959) **Certifications:** Spiritual Direction Institute, Mercy Center Burlingame (1988); Licensed Psychologist, State of California (1974); National Register of Health Service Providers (1974) **Career:** Spiritual Director and Retreat Leader (1990-Present); Psychologist, Private Practice (1976-Present); Adjunct Faculty in Pastoral Theology, Church Divinity School of the Pacific (1990-1994); Consultant, Western Region, AT&T (1982-1986); Host, Daily Psychological Call-In Talk Show, 560 KFSO, San Francisco, CA (1980-1981); Member, Training Staff, Executive Effectiveness Seminar, AMA (1978-1982); President, Bonnie Ring, EdD, A Psychological Corporation, San Francisco, CA (1977-1986); Associate Dean, California School of Podiatric Medicine, Samuel Merritt University, San Francisco, CA (1975-1977); Lecturer, University of California, Irvine (1973-1975); Lecturer, University of California, Santa Cruz (1971-1973); Associate Director of Clinical Services, University of California, Irvine (1973-1975); Counseling Psychologist, University of California, Santa Cruz (1969-1973); Training Associate, Coordinator Intern Program, University of California, State Wise Extensions (1967-1968); Research Assistant, UCLA (1966-1967); Training Specialist, Economic & Youth Opportunities Program (1966); Fellow, Center for Applied Behavioral Sciences, Boston University (1963-1965); Teaching Fellow, Questrom School of Business, Boston University **Civic:** Director, Elder Ministry, St. John's Episcopal Church, Oakland, CA (2004-2005); Ordained Episcopal Priest (1992) **Creative Works:** Author, "Women Who Knew Jesus" (2015, 2018) **Awards:** Honorary Life Member, Pi Lambda Theta **Membership:** Spiritual Directors International; National Register Health Service Psychologists; California Psychological Association; Pi Lambda Theta **Political Affiliations:** Democrat **Religion:** Progressive Christian **Shipping Address:** 2011 Carlos Street, Moss Beach, CA, 94038 **Website:** drbonniering.com

Carlos Rios-Velazquez

Title: Research Scientist **Industry:** Research **Company Name:** University of Puerto Rico at Mayaguez **Date of Birth:** 03/22/1966 **Place of Birth:** Playa de Ponce **Country of Origin:** Puerto Rico **Parents:** Angel Luis Rios-Vergara; Monserrate Velazquez-Cintron **Education:** Postgraduate Coursework, National Institutes of Health (2001); PhD in Bacteriology, University of Wisconsin-Madison (2000); MS in Biology, University of Puerto Rico, Mayaguez (1993); BS in Industrial Microbiology, University of Puerto Rico, Mayaguez (1989) **Certifications:** Licensed Secondary School Science Teacher, Department of Education, Puerto Rico (1989) **Career:** Associate Faculty, Biology Department, University of Puerto Rico, Mayaguez (2001-Present); Research Faculty, Upward Bound Science and Mathematics Program, Interamerican University of Puerto Rico at Ponce (2000-Present); Faculty, Pontifical Catholic University of Puerto Rico at Ponce (1994-1995); Faculty, Interamerican University of Puerto Rico at Arecibo (1993); Qualified Assessor, Interamerican University of Puerto Rico, San German (1992-1995); Research Professor, Upward Bound Science and Mathematics Program, Interamerican University of Puerto Rico, San German (1992-1995) **Career Related:** Co-director, Center for Hemispherical Cooperative in Research and Education in Engineering and Applied Science **Awards:** Microbe Minority Travel Award, American Society for Microbiology (2017); SACNAS Distinguished Scientist Award, The National Diversity in STEM Conference (2015); Faces of Bioscience, INDUNIV & PR BioAlliance (2015); Induction Ceremony Acts Dedication, Biology Honor Society (2015); President, Scientific Review Committee, SESO (2015) **Membership:** Adviser, Astrobiology and Exobiology Association (2015-Present); Founder, Society for the Advancement of Chicanos/Latinos and Native American in Science (2007-Present); Association of Future Teachers (1992-Present); American Society for Microbiology (1985-Present) **To what do you attribute your success:** Mr. Rios-Velazquez attributes his success to dedication and loving what he does. **Why did you become involved in your profession or industry:** Mr. Rios-Velazquez has a passion for finding microbes in order to solve problems. **Hobbies:** Poetry; Playing the Organ; Chess; Gardening **Religion:** Roman Catholic **Business Address:** 667 Calle Amapola, Mayaguez, PR, 00680

C. Frederick Risinger

Title: Social Studies Educator **Industry:** Education/Educational Services **Date of Birth:** 07/15/1939 **Place of Birth:** Paducah **State:** KY **Parents:** Charles Morris Risinger; Mary Neal (Barfield) Risinger **Marital Status:** Married **Spouse Name:** Margaret M. Marker (7/4/1994) **Children:** Donna Lyne (Deceased); Alyson; Laura; John **Education:** MA in History, Northern Illinois University (1968); EdB, Southern Illinois University (1961) **Career:** Director of Professional Development, School Services and Summer Sessions, Indiana University (1997-2004); Associate Director, Teacher Education, Indiana University (1995-2004); Director, National Clearinghouse for U.S.-Japan Studies, Indiana University (1990-2004); Associate Director, Social Studies Development Center, Indiana University (1986-1990); Coordinator, School of Social Studies, Indiana University (1973-1986); Teacher, Lake Park Community High School, Roselle, IL (1962-1973); Administrator, Lake Park Community High School, Roselle, IL (1962-1973); Coach, Lake Park Community High School, Roselle, IL (1962-1973); Broadcaster, WMOK Radio, Metropolis, IL (1955-1961) **Career Related:** Advisory Board Member, Learning Magazine, Boston, MA (1988-1999) **Civic:** President, National Social Studies Supervisors Association, Washington, DC (1985-1986); Executive Director, Indiana Council for the Social Studies, National Council for the Social Studies (1975-1987) **Creative Works:** Co-Author, "American History" (2010); Co-Author, "Scott Foresman Social Studies: K-6 Series" (2008); Co-Author, "Creating America" (2000); Co-Author, "Surfing Social Studies: The Internet Book" (1999); Co-Author, "America's Past and Promise" (1997); Co-Author, "America! America!" (1974); Editor, News and Notes on the Social Sciences (1973-1986) **Awards:** Irving Morrissett Award for Outstanding Contribution to Social Science Education (2011); Lifetime Achievement Award, Social Science Education Consortium (2011); Grantee, Teaching American History (2009-2010); Honoree, Teacher of the Year, DuPage County Education Association (Now DuPage Regional Office of Education) (1973); Numerous Public and Private Educational Grants **Membership:** President, Social Science Education Consortium (2006-2008); President, National Council for the Social Studies (1990-1991); ASCD; NCHE; Indiana Association of Historians; Phi Delta Kappa International **Marquis Who's Who Honors:** Albert Nelson Marquis Lifetime Achievement Award (2017) **Political Affiliations:** Democrat **Shipping Address:** 7039 E State Road 45, Bloomington, IN, 47408

John Robert Roberts

Title: Cardiothoracic Surgeon, Consultant **Industry:** Medicine & Health Care **Company Name:** Lynn Cancer Institute **Date of Birth:** 04/05/1959 **Place of Birth:** Athens **State:** TN **Parents:** Doyle Ford Roberts; Frankie Howard Roberts **Marital Status:** Single **Children:** Amanda; Timothy; John Anthony; Thomas **Education:** MBA, Auburn University (2003); Fellow in Thoracic Surgery, Brigham and Women's Hospital, Boston, MA (1993-1995); Fellow in Surgical Oncology, Johns Hopkins Hospital, Baltimore, MD (1992-1993); Resident Surgeon, Johns Hopkins Hospital, Baltimore, MD (1986-1992); MD, Yale University, with Honors (1985); AB, Duke University, Summa Cum Laude (1981) **Certifications:** Licensed Medical Practice, State of Tennessee; Licensed in State of Florida: Board Certified, Thoracic Surgery, American Board of Thoracic Surgery; Board Certified, General Surgery, American Board of Surgery **Career:** Thoracic Surgeon, Boca Raton Regional Hospital and Lynn Cancer Institute, Boca Raton, FL (2018-Present); Tri Star Medical Group, Nashville, TN (2011-2018); Southeastern Research Associates (2008); Thoracic Surgeon, Surgical Clinic, Nashville, TN (2003-2011); Chief, General Thoracic Surgery, Vanderbilt University, Nashville, TN (1997-2003); Assistant Professor, University of Pennsylvania, Philadelphia, PA (1995-1997) **Career Related:** Ingram Professor of Cancer Research, Vanderbilt University (1997-2009); Lecturer in Field; Richard Wilson Visiting Professor of Surgical Oncology, Harvard Medical School; Fellow, American College of Surgeons **Military Service:** Captain, U.S. Army Reserve (1995-2003) **Creative Works:** Reviewer, CHEST; Reviewer, Annals of Thoracic Surgery; Reviewer, Journal Thoracic and Cardiovascular Surgery; **Awards:** Resident Research Award, Johns Hopkins Hospital (1986); Grants in Field; Alfred Soffler Award, American College Chest Physicians **Membership:** Committee on Applicants, American College of Surgeons (2006-Present); Scholarship for Health Policy, American College of Surgeons (2003-Present); Master, American College of Chest Physicians; Workforce on Health Policy, Reform and Advocacy, Southern Thoracic Surgical Association; Society of Thoracic Surgeons; American Society of Clinical Oncology; Southern Association for Oncology; Society of Cell and Tissue Kinetics; Alpha Omega Alpha; Phi Kappa Phi **Marquis Who's Who Honors:** Albert Nelson Marquis Lifetime Achievement Award (2017) **Hobbies:** Taekwondo; Piano **Religion:** Baptist **Business Address:** 701 NW 13th Street, Boca Raton, FL, 33486 **Shipping Address:** 1216 SW Mulberry Way, Boca Raton, FL, 33486 **Website:** http://www.bocacare.com

A. Haeworth Robertson

Title: Actuary **Industry:** Insurance **Date of Birth:** 05/10/1930 **Place of Birth:** Oklahoma City **State:** OK **Parents:** Albert Haeworth Robertson; Bonnie Tennessee (Duckett) Robertson **Marital Status:** Divorced **Spouse Name:** Mary Adeline Kissee (2/3/1952, Divorced 7/1979) **Children:** Valerie Lynn; Alan Haeworth; Mary Kathryn **Career:** Private Practice, International Consultant, Actuary, Washington, DC, Kuwait, Turkey, Guyana, Zimbabwe, China, The Philippines (1988-Present); Managing Director, William M. Mercer, Inc. (Now Mercer LLC), Washington, DC (1978-1988); Chief Actuary, U.S. Social Security Administration, Baltimore, MD (1975-1978); Senior Actuary, International Labor Organization, Geneva (1973-1975); Private Practice International Consultant Actuary, Barbados and Ghana (1969-1972; President, First American Security Life Insurance Co. of Missouri, St. Louis, MO (1964-1968); Vice President, Actuary, W. Alfred Hayes & Co., St. Louis, MO (1960-1963); Actuary, Bowles, Andrews & Towne, Dallas, TX (1958-1960); Actuary, Wyatt Co., Washington, DC and Dallas, TX (1955-1958) **Career Related:** President, Founder, Retirement Policy Institute Inc. (1986-Present); Member, Education Benefits Board of Actuaries (1985-1995); Chairman, Retirement Board Actuaries, Department of Defense (1984-1995) **Civic:** Served to First Lieutenant, U.S. Air Force (1953-1955) **Creative Works:** Author, "The Siren of Sans Souci, (Revised and Expanded Edition)" (2015); Author, "The Siren of Sans Souci" (2014); Author, "The Silver Pendant" (2009); Author, "The Big Lie: What Every Baby Boomer Should Know About Social Security and Medicare" (1997); Author, "Social Security: What Every Taxpayer Should Know" (1992); Author, "The Coming Revolution in Social Security" (1981) **Awards:** Wynn Kent Communications Award, The Actuarial Foundation, Chicago, IL (2007); Robert J. Myers Publishing Service Award, American Academy of Actuaries (2004); Distinguished Alumni Award, Central High School, Oklahoma City, OK (1997); Arthur J. Altmeyer Award, Department of Health, Washington, DC (1978); Commissioner's Citation, U.S. Social Security Administration, Washington, DC (1976) **Membership:** Vice President, Society of Actuaries (1985-1987); Board of Governors, Society of Actuaries (1979-1981); Fellow, Society of Actuaries; Conference of Consulting Actuaries; American Academy of Actuaries; International Actuarial Association; International Association of Consulting Actuaries; Associate Member, U.K. Institute Actuaries (Now Institute and Faculty of Actuaries); Cosmos Club, The Travelers' Century Club; **Political Affiliations:** Republican **Religion:** Methodist **Shipping Address:** 2320 41st Street, Apartment 37, The Commons, Wilmington, NC, 28403

Joyce McPeake Robinson, PhD

Title: Independent Educational Consultant **Industry:** Education/Educational Services **Company Name:** Robinson Educational Consulting **Date of Birth:** 07/28/1941 **Place of Birth:** Newark **State:** NJ **Parents:** Salvatore Guinta; Wilhelmina (Cervetto) Guinta **Marital Status:** Married **Spouse Name:** Enders Anthony Robinson (8/8/1992); John David McPeake (6/15/1963, Divorced 1974) **Children:** John Paul; David Samuel **Education:** PhD, Boston University (1979); MA in English, Boston University (1965); BA in English, Tufts University (1962) **Career:** Private Independent Educational Consultant (2005-Present); Head of School Emeritus, Dwight School, New York, NY (2004-Present); Online Educator, Virtual Learning Academy (2011-2014); Director of Literacy and Technology Programs, Seacoast School of Technology, Exeter, NH (2008-2011); Director of Reading Programs, Massachusetts Public Schools (2004-2008); Head of School, Dwight School, New York, NY (1994-2004); Chairman of English, Dwight School, New York, NY (1994-1996); Chairman of English, Masters School, Dobbs Ferry, NY (1995-1996); Assistant Principal, Islamic Saudi Academy, Alexandria, VA (1991-1993); Director of Learning Resources in English, Fountain Valley School, Colorado Springs, CO (1989-1991); Chair of English, Broadwater Academy, Exmore, VA (1988-1989); Learning Specialist, Broadwater Academy, Exmore, VA (1988-1989); Chairman of English, Director of Reading Programs, Saint Andrew's School, Boca Raton, FL (1980-1988); Principal, Scituate Public Schools (1974-1980); Reading Specialist, Scituate Public Schools (1974-1980); Director, Christ Lutheran School, Scituate, MA (1971-1974); Reporter, Patriot Ledger, Quincy, MA (1967-1969); Reading and Learning Specialist, Manter Hall School, Cambridge, MA (1964-1967); Reading Specialist, Hingham Public Schools, MA (1963-1964) **Career Related:** Teacher, St. Thomas University, Miami, FL (1987-1988); School Evaluator, Florida Council of Independent Schools (1985-1988); Professor, Nova Southeastern University, Fort Lauderdale, FL (1984-1988) **Creative Works:** Author, "The Joy of Knowing How to Learn, Language Skills, Series 1: Spelling" (2017) **Membership:** Executive Board, Association for the Advancement of Educational Research (2009-Present); Board Member, Treasure Time (2004-Present); Founding Member, International Women's Review Board, National Council of Teachers of English (2008); President, Association for the Advancement of Educational Research (2006-2009) **Shipping Address:** 8 Dorothy E Lucey Dr, Newburyport, MA, 01950

Ross Utley Robinson

Title: Industrial Relations Specialist **Industry:** Business Management/Business Services **Company Name:** Cardinal Associates **Date of Birth:** 07/30/1928 **Place of Birth:** Minneapolis **State:** MN **Parents:** Howard Hadley Robinson; Doris (Utley) Robinson **Marital Status:** Widower **Spouse Name:** Barbara Aitken Brown (10/3/1953, Deceased) **Children:** Brian; Emily; Judith; Ross Stuart; Rachel; John **Education:** MS, Massachusetts Institute of Technology (1953); MA, Wesleyan University (1951); BA, Colgate University (1949) **Career:** Adviser, Established Program to Stimulate Competitive Research, National Aeronautics and Space Administration, Oklahoma (2002-Present); Technical Director, Norman Economic Development Coalition, Oklahoma (2003-2016); President, Cardinal Associates, Santa Fe, NM (1984-2002); President, Chief Executive Officer, Mesa Diagnostics, Los Alamos, NM (1984-1985); Vice President, Research and Development, ICL Scientific, Fountain Valley, CA (1981-1984); Vice President, ICL Scientific, California (1973-1983); Manager, Diagnostics Division, Abbott Laboratories, California (1973-1983); Manager, Hycel, TX (1981); Associate Director, Research and Development, Boehringer Mannheim, Tustin, CA (1979-1981); Director, Advanced Systems, Abbott Laboratories, North Chicago, IL (1953-1973) **Career Related:** Lecturer, University of New Mexico, Albuquerque, NM (1986-Present); Lecturer, University of California, Irvine, CA (1984) **Civic:** President, Board of Directors, Los Alamos Economic Development Corporation; Organizer, Biomedical Organization, New Mexico; City Economic Review Committee, New Mexico; Strategist, Regional Economic Planning, New Mexico; Deacon, Elder, Four Presbyterian Churches; Chair, Worship Committee, Presbyterian Church; Chair, Budget Committee, Presbyterian Church; Chair, Christian Education Committee, Presbyterian Church **Creative Works:** Contributor, Articles, Professional Journals **Awards:** Martin Award (2001) **Membership:** Task Force, Los Angeles Chamber of Commerce (1978); National Secretary, Association for the Advancement of Medical Instrumentation (1973-1975); Club President, Sigma Xi (1964-1965); American Chemical Society; American Association for the Advancement of Science; Presbyterian Association for Science, Technology and Christian Faith; Charter Member, Industrial Lobbying Organization, Medical Device Manufacturers Association; New Mexico Academy of Science; Oklahoma Academy for State Goals **Marquis Who's Who Honors:** Albert Nelson Marquis Lifetime Achievement Award (2017) **Religion:** Presbyterian **Shipping Address:** 2601 Wood Hollow St, Norman, OK, 73071 **Website:** http://www.ross-robinson.net

Sidney Rodnunsky

Title: Lawyer, Educator **Industry:** Law and Legal Services **Date of Birth:** 02/03/1946 **Place of Birth:** Edmonton **Country of Origin:** AB/Canada **Parents:** B. Rodnunsky; I. Rodnunsky **Marital Status:** Married **Spouse Name:** Teresita Asuncion **Children:** Naomi; Shawna; Rachel; Tevie; Claire; Donna; Sidney Junior **Education:** MBA, Fitchburg State University (2010); Graduate Diploma, University of Calgary (1990); BS, University of the State of New York (1988); JD, University of Alberta (1973); MEd, University of Calgary (1969); BEd, University of Alberta (1966) **Certifications:** Certified PMgr; Justice of the Peace (Retired) **Career:** Educator, Legal Counsel, Administrator, Canada; Former Governor, Grande Prairie Regional College; Regional Counsel, Her Majesty the Queen in Right of the Dominion of Canada **Career Related:** Past President, Aspenview, Alta Teachers Association, Grande Prairie Bar Association, District Bar Association; National Executive, Alberta Coordinator for Gifted Children; Ombudsman, SIG Coordinator, Mensa Canada **Civic:** Member, Helping Professions **Military Service:** Officer, Royal Canadian Air Force **Creative Works:** Author, Breathalyzer Casebook; Editor, "The Children Speak" **Awards:** Decorated, Knight Grand Cross Sovereign and Royal Order of Piast; Decorated, Knight Grand Cross Order of St. John the Baptist; Decorated, Knight Hospitaller Order of St. John of Jerusalem, Prince of Kiev, Prince of Trabzon, Prince and Duke of Rodari, Duke of Chernigov, Count of Riga, Count of St. John of Alexandria; Named, Honorable Order of Kentucky Colonels; Named, Admiral State of Texas; Recipient, Presidential Legion of Merit **Membership:** Law Society of Alberta; Law Society of Saskatchewan; Canada Bar Association; Canadian Institute of Management; Phi Delta Kappa **Bar Admissions:** Alberta; Saskatchewan **Marquis Who's Who Honors:** Distinguished Humanitarian (2017) **Hobbies:** Reading; Old-time radio; History; Old cars **Shipping Address:** 34 Clark Drive, BC, Port Alice, Canada, V0N 2N0

Kristen Ann Ross

Title: School System Administrator **Industry:** Education/Educational Services **Company Name:** Gombert Elementary School **Parents:** Alexander William Kalnes; Anna Marie Kalnes **Marital Status:** Widowed **Spouse Name:** Jesse Davis Ross (6/27/1992, Deceased); James Allen Ruebush (Divorced) **Children:** Julie Ann Lehman; Jennifer Louise Baltimore **Education:** EdD, Loyola University, Chicago, IL (1997); MEd, Northern Illinois University, DeKalb, IL (1988); EdB, Western Illinois University, Macomb, IL (1977) **Certifications:** Certified Reading Specialist, Northern Illinois University (1988); Elementary Education; Secondary English; Superintendent's Endorsement **Career:** Director of Education, Lost Boys Rebuilding Southern Sudan (2011-Present); Secretary of the Board, Lost Boys Rebuilding Southern Sudan (2011-Present); Reading Specialist, Anne Arundel County Public Schools, Brock Bridge Elementary School, Laurel, MD (2015-2017); Board of Directors, American Professionals Promoting Lithuanian Education (2012-2015); Instructor/Facilitator, American Professionals Promoting Lithuanian Education (2011-2014); Educational Consultant, Curriculum Development and Instructional Coaching, Youth Connection Charter Schools, Chicago, IL (2011-2013) **Career Related:** Presenter, CIES Conference, Washington, DC (2015); UNESCO's Mobile Learning Week, Paris, France (2014); Panel Discussion for FHI 360/USAID on Literacy Instruction in Countries in Conflict (2014); Education Alliance Conference (2014) **Civic:** Lions Club International (2014-Present); Secretary, Bowie Lions (2014-Present); Co-Planner, Bowie Green Expo (2014-Present); Governmental Relations Chair, Illinois Reading Council (1983) **Creative Works:** Grant Writer, Federal and International Grants **Awards:** Library of Congress Commendation for Effective Implementation of Best Practices in Literacy and Reading, Literacy at the Well Program (2014); E2T2 Grant, Federal Government (2006); Literacy Grantee, Federal Government (2006) **Membership:** Delegate, United States-Russian Education Conference, ASCD (1995); International Literacy Association; International Reading Association **Marquis Who's Who Honors:** Albert Nelson Marquis Lifetime Achievement Award (2017) **Hobbies:** Hiking; Book clubs; Knitting; Volunteer work with church and the Lions Club **Political Affiliations:** Progressive **Religion:** Christian **Shipping Address:** 12500 Kingsfield Lane, Bowie, MD, 20715

Janet K. Rossman

Title: Director **Industry:** Other **Company Name:** IDesign Intl, LLC **Parents:** Elmer Chris Rossman; Elizabeth Jean Schell **Marital Status:** Married **Children:** Alexander John Moazed; Christina Jean Moazed **Education:** BA in Human Environmental Design, Michigan State University (1976) **Career:** Director, IDesign Intl LLC, (2012-Present); Design Consultant, New York, NY (2000-Present); Designer, Culpen & Woods Architects, CT (1995-1997); Director of Design, SPGA Group, Inc., New York, NY (1984-1988); Project Designer, Bonsignore Brignati & Mazzotta Architects, New York, NY (1982-1984); Project Designer, Swanke Hayden Connell & Partners, New York, NY (1979-1981); Designer, Tilton & Lewis Associates, Chicago, IL (1977-1979); Dimitrios Economides Architects, MI (1974-1976); Instructor, Design Education Center, MI (1976) **Career Related:** American Society of Interior Designers; Institute of Business Designers; National Association of Female Executives; International Furnishings and Design Association **Civic:** St. George's Society of New York; English Speaking Union; Greenwich Historical Society; Putnam Hill Chapter Board; Independence Day Association Chair; Greenwich Country Day School Board **Awards:** Morna S. Kline Design Award; Kappa Omicron Nu National Honor Society **Membership:** General Society of Mayflower Descendants; National Society Daughters of the American Revolution; The National Society of The Colonial Dames of America; National Society Colonial Dames XVII Century **Marquis Who's Who Honors:** Albert Nelson Marquis Lifetime Achievement Award (2017) **Hobbies:** Genealogy; Travel **Political Affiliations:** Libertarian **Shipping Address:** 10 Sparrow Ln, Greenwich, CT, 06830

Carmen Sybile Sabau

Title: Chemist **Industry:** Sciences **Date of Birth:** 04/24/1933 **Place of Birth:** Cluj-Napoca **Country of Origin:** Romania **Parents:** George Grigorescu; Antoinette Marie (Chiriac) Grigorescu **Marital Status:** Married **Spouse Name:** Mircea Nicolae Sabau (7/11/1956) **Children:** Isabelle Carmen **Education:** PhD in Radiochemistry, Fridericiana University (Now Karlsruhe Institute of Technology) (1972); MS in Inorganic and Analytical Chemistry, C.I. Parhon University (Now University of Bucharest) (1955) **Career:** Chemist, Argonne National Laboratory, U.S. Department of Energy (1976-1998); Visitor Scientist, Karlsruhe Institute of Technology (1975-1976); Principal Chemist, Joint Institute for Nuclear Research (1974-1975); Chemist, Institutul de Fizica Atomica (1956-1974) **Career Related:** Fellow, Alexander von Humboldt-Stiftung/Foundation (1970-1972); Fellow, IAEA (1967-1968) **Creative Works:** Author, "Ion-exchange Theory and Applications in Analytical Chemistry" (1967); Contributor, Articles, Professional Journals **Membership:** American-Romanian Academy of Arts and Sciences; American Friends of the Alexander von Humboldt Foundation; Alpha: Friends of Antiquity; Rocky Mountain Region, Modern Language Association of America **Marquis Who's Who Honors:** Albert Nelson Marquis Lifetime Achievement Award (2017) **Shipping Address:** 689 Banbury Way, Bolingbrook, IL, 60440

Donald Robert Sadoway, PhD

Title: Materials Science Educator **Industry:** Education/Educational Services **Company Name:** Massachusetts Institute of Technology **Date of Birth:** 03/07/1950 **Place of Birth:** Toronto **Country of Origin:** Canada **Parents:** Donald Anthony Sadoway; Irene Mary (Romanko) Sadoway **Marital Status:** Married **Spouse Name:** Rebecca Rosenberg (12/19/2004, Divorced 7/2016); Anne Marie Mayes (1/4/1997, Divorced 6/2003); Sandra Lynn Mary Babij (9/8/1973, Divorced 9/1996) **Children:** Steven; Laryssa; Andrew **Education:** PhD in Chemical Metallurgy, University of Toronto (1977); Master of Applied Science in Chemical Metallurgy, University of Toronto (1973); Bachelor of Applied Science in Engineering Science, University of Toronto (1972) **Certifications:** Certified, Chemical Metallurgy **Career:** John F. Elliott Professor of Materials Chemistry, Massachusetts Institute of Technology (1999-Present); Professor of Materials Chemistry, Massachusetts Institute of Technology, Cambridge, MA (1992-Present); MacVicar Faculty Fellow, Massachusetts Institute of Technology (1995-2005); Associate Professor, Massachusetts Institute of Technology, Cambridge, MA (1982-1992); Assistant Professor of Materials Engineering, Massachusetts Institute of Technology, Cambridge, MA (1978-1982) **Creative Works:** Associate Editor, Journal of Materials Research (1995-2005); Contributor, Over 160 Articles on Electrochemistry and Physical Chemistry, Professional Journals; Patentee in Field **Awards:** John F. Elliott Lectureship Award, Association for Iron & Steel Technology (2017); Honorary Doctorate, University of Toronto (2013); Time 100 Most Influential People, Time Magazine (2012); 100 Most Influential People in the World, TIME Magazine (2012); Honorary Doctorate, Norwegian University of Science and Technology, Trondheim, Norway (2012); Bose Award (1997); Faculty Fellow in Industrial Ecology, AT&T (1993-1995); Graduate Student Council Teaching Award, Massachusetts Institute of Technology (1993); Graduate Student Council Teaching Award, Massachusetts Institute of Technology (1988); Professor T.B. King Memorial Award, Department of Materials Science and Engineering, Massachusetts Institute of Technology (1986); Graduate Student Council Teaching Award, Massachusetts Institute of Technology (1984); NATO Postdoctoral Fellow, National Research Council of Canada (1977) **Membership:** American Association for the Advancement of Science; Minerals, Metals and Materials Society; Electrochemical Society; International Society of Electrochemistry; Materials Research Society; Elected Member, Norwegian Academy of Technological Sciences **Business Address:** 77 Massachusetts Ave, Cambridge, MA, 02139

Cynthia Chen Sadowski

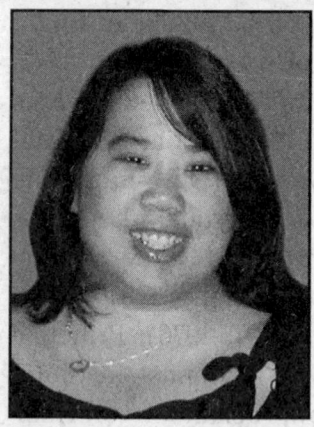

Title: Associate Principal Counsel **Industry:** Law and Legal Services **Company Name:** The Walt Disney Company **Date of Birth:** 03/30/1968 **Place of Birth:** Panorama City **State:** CA **Parents:** Joseph Tao Chen; Marjorie Wong Mishkin **Marital Status:** Married **Spouse Name:** Jeremy Richard Sadowski **Education:** JD, Loyola Law School, Los Angeles, CA (1992); BA, Pomona College, Claremont, CA (1989) **Career:** Associate Principal Counsel, Walt Disney Studios Motion Pictures (2000-Present); Legal Services, Walt Disney Studios Special Events Team, Walt Disney Studios Publicity Team, El Capitan Theatre, Hollywood, CA, Disney Studio Store, Hollywood, CA **Career Related:** Walt Disney Company Women Lawyers Network (2016-Present); Pro Bono Lawyer, Walt Disney Company Legal Pro Bono Adoption Program (2011-Present); California State Bar Foundation Representative, Disney Lawyers of Color (2017) **Membership:** Disney Lawyers of Color (2017-Present); Walt Disney Company Women Lawyers Network (2016-Present) **Bar Admissions:** State of California (1992) **Marquis Who's Who Honors:** Albert Nelson Marquis Lifetime Achievement Award (2017) **To what do you attribute your success:** Ms. Sadowski attributes her success to hard work, maintaining an optimistic outlook and focusing on solutions, not problems. **Why did you become involved in your profession or industry:** Ms. Sadowski wanted to be an entertainment lawyer since she was eight years old. **What do you consider to be the highlight of your career:** Ms. Sadowski acted as a lead attorney for the Walt Disney Studios in drafting, negotiating and closing a multi-million dollar deal that enabled the first wave of installation of digital cinema equipment in theaters throughout the United States. She has also been a part of many Disney movie premieres, from the premiere of "Pirates of the Caribbean: The Curse of the Black Pearl" at Disneyland Park to the premieres of "Star Wars: The Force Awakens" and Marvel's "The Avengers" in Hollywood. **Business Address:** 500 S Buena Vista Street, Burbank, CA, 91521

Joseph Robert Sahid

Title: Lawyer **Industry:** Law and Legal Services **Company Name:** Law Offices of Joseph R. Sahid **Date of Birth:** 02/14/1944 **Place of Birth:** Paterson **State:** NJ **Marital Status:** Married **Spouse Name:** Serra Yavuz **Children:** Annunziata; Joseph; Olivia **Education:** LLB, School of Law, University of Virginia (1968); BS, Rutgers, The State University of New Jersey (1965) **Career:** Private Practice, Law Offices of Joseph R. Sahid, New York, NY (1996-Present); Resident Partner, Barrack, Rodos & Bacine, New York, NY (1995-1996); Consultant, Cravath, Swaine & Moore, New York, NY (1994-1997); Partner, Cravath, Swaine & Moore (1977-1993); Associate, Cravath, Swaine & Moore (1972-1977); Consultant, President's Commission on Campus Unrest, Washington, DC (1970); Staff Member, U.S. National Commission on the Causes and Prevention of Violence, Washington, DC (1968-1969) **Military Service:** Lieutenant, U.S. Coast Guard Reserve **Membership:** Committee on Procedures for Judicial Discipline, New York State Bar Association (2015-Present); Cooperative and Condo Mediation Project, Association of the Bar of the City of New York (2006-Present); Legal Referral Service Panel, Association of the Bar of the City of New York (2004-Present); Council on Children, Association of the Bar of the City of New York (2003-Present); Committee on Professional Discipline, New York State Bar Association (2002-2012); Professional Responsibility, Association of the Bar of City of New York (2009-2012) Committee on Procedures for Judicial Discipline, Association of the Bar of the City of New York (2006-2009); Professional Responsibility, Association of the Bar of City of New York (2003-2006); Committee on Professional Discipline, Association of the Bar of the City of New York (2001-2003) **Bar Admissions:** State of New York; U.S. Federal Courts **Marquis Who's Who Honors:** Distinguished Humanitarian (2017) **Business Address:** 1065 Park Avenue, New York, NY, 10128

Judith-Ann Saks

Title: Artist **Industry:** Fine Art **Date of Birth:** 12/20/1943 **Place of Birth:** Anniston **State:** AL **Parents:** Julien David Saks; Lucy-Jane Saks **Marital Status:** Married **Spouse Name:** Haskell Rosenthal (12/22/1974) **Education:** Postgraduate Coursework, University of Houston (1967); BFA, Tulane University (1966); Coursework, Rice University (1962); Coursework, The Museum of Fine Arts, Houston (1962); Coursework, Texas Academy of Art (1957-1958) **Career Related:** Artist, American Revolution Bicentennial Project, Port of Houston Authority (1975-1976); Curator, Student Art Collection, University of Houston (1968-1972) **Creative Works:** Commissioned Artist, "'Celebrating America' Coloring Book" (2014); Commissioned Artist, St. Lukes Hospital Art Project CDA (2011); Commissioned Artist, "Martha 'Lady' Washington Pin" (2008); Group Show, Margolis Gallery, Congregation Beth Israel, Houston, TX (2005-2006); Group Show, Park Crest Gallery, Austin, Texas (1981); Group Show, Galerie Barbizon, Houston, TX (1980); Group Show, Meinhard Galleries, Houston, TX (1977); Group Show, Traveling Art Exhibit, Mississippi Art Association (1970-1971); One-Woman Show, Alley Gallery, Houston, TX (1969); Group Shows, Birmingham Museum of Art (1967) **Awards:** Albert Nelson Marquis Lifetime Achievement Award (2017); National First Place Award, Family Tree of Thomas Luther Choiniere (2017); Van Rensselaer Award (2016); Third Place Group Award, Fiber Arts, "Evening Cloak," National Society Daughters of the American Revolution (NSDAR), Texas (2016); National Third Place Award, Acrylic Painting, American Heritage, "China Painting" (2016); National Women in the Arts Recognition Award (2015); TXDAR Women in the Arts Award (2013); National Second Place Award, Acrylic Painting, "Lilly in White," National Society Daughters of the American Revolution (NSDAR) (2013); National Third Place Award, Acrylic Painting, "Liberty," National Society Daughters of the American Revolution (NSDAR) (2012); CDA Outstanding Service Award (2012); St. Luke's Hospital Art Project CDA (2011); National First Place Award, American Heritage Remembered - Houston, Cultural Events and Traditions (2010); First Place, Cultural Events and Traditions, South Central Division (2010) **Membership:** President, The National Society of the Colonial Dames of America (2018-Present) **Marquis Who's Who Honors:** Albert Nelson Marquis Lifetime Achievement Award (2017) **Why did you become involved in your profession or industry:** Ms. Saks became involved in her profession because she wanted to be an artist since she was a child. **Hobbies:** History; Genealogy **Shipping Address:** 2215 Briar Branch Dr, Houston, TX, 77042

Dilano K. Saldin

Title: Distinguished Professor **Industry:** Education/Educational Services **Company Name:** University of Wisconsin-Milwaukee **Date of Birth:** 08/26/1949 **Place of Birth:** Colombo **Country of Origin:** Sri Lanka **Parents:** Hamlin Mesrur Saldin; Muzeena Saldin **Education:** Research Fellow, Imperial College London (1981-1988); Junior Research Fellow, Wolfson College, Oxford, England (1976-1981); PhD in Materials, University of Oxford (1975); BA, University of Oxford (1971) **Career:** Distinguished Professor, University of Wisconsin-Milwaukee (1988-Present); Chairman, Department of Physics, University of Wisconsin-Milwaukee (2002-2008); Chairman, Department of Physics, University of Wisconsin-Milwaukee (2000-2001) **Creative Works:** Co-author, "Algorithm for Reconstruction of 3D Images of Nanorice Particles from Diffraction Patterns of Two Particles in Interdependent Randomly Orientations with an X-Ray Laser," Applied Sciences (2017); Author, "Ghost Imaging with X-rays," Physics (2016); Co-author, "Simulations on Time-Resolved Structure Determination of Uncrystallized Biomolecules in the Presence of Shot Noise," Structural Dynamics (2015); Co-author, "Use of Triple Correlations for the Sign Determinations of Expansion Coefficients of Symmetric Approximations to the Diraction Volumes of Regular Viruses," Structural Dynamics (2015); Co-author, "Enzyme Transient State Kinetics in Crystal and Solution from the Perspective of a Time-Resolved Crystallographer," Structural Dynamics (2014); Co-author, "Deducing Fast Electron Density Changes in Randomly Orientated Uncrystallized Biomolecules in a Pump-Probe Experiment," Philosophical Transactions of the Royal Society B (2014); Co-author, "Fiber Diffraction without Fibers," Physical Review Letters (2013); Co-author, "Three-Dimensional Single-Particle Imaging Using Angular Correlations from X-ray Laser Data," Acta Crystallogrphica A (2013); Co-author, "Extraction of Fast Changes in the Structure of a Disordered Ensemble of Photoexcited Biomolecules," Advances in Condensed Matter Physics, Hindawi Publishing Corporation (2013); Contributor, Over 150 Articles, Professional Journals **Awards:** Grantee, U.S. Department of Energy (2001-Present); Grantee, National Science Foundation (1994-Present); Grantee, Petroleum Research Fund (1990-1994); **Membership:** American Crystallographic Association; Fellow, American Physical Society; BioXFEL, Financed by the National Science Foundation **Marquis Who's Who Honors:** Albert Nelson Marquis Lifetime Achievement Award (2017) **To what do you attribute your success:** Dr. Saldin attributes his success to hard work. **Shipping Address:** 3135 N Maryland Ave, UWM Dept Of Physics, Milwaukee, WI, 53211 **Website:** https://uwm.edu/physics/people/saldin-dilano

Mona Lisa Saloy

Title: Author, Folklorist, Literature and Writing Professor **Industry:** Writing and Editing **Date of Birth:** 07/01/1950 **Place of Birth:** New Orleans **State:** LA **Parents:** Louis Saloy; Olga Fitch **Education:** PhD, Louisiana State University, Baton Rouge, LA (2005); MFA, Louisiana State University, Baton Rouge, LA (1988); MA, San Francisco State University, California (1982) **Career:** Conrad N. Hilton Endowed Professor, Coordinator of English, Dillard University (2014-Present); Visiting Associate Professor, University of Washington, Seattle, WA (2005-2007); Professor, Dillard University; Visiting Associate Professor, City College of San Francisco; Visiting Associate Professor, Laney College, Oakland, CA **Career Related:** Presenter, Atlanta Conference (2015); Guest Speaker, Smithsonian Black Creole Culture (2015); Speaker, Presenter, Purdue African American Cultural Center, New Orleans, LA (2008); Guest Writer, Lakeside School, Seattle (2008); Speaker, Guest Writer, Santa Barbara City College (2006); Speaker, Presenter, Annual Conference, American Folklore Society, Milwaukee, WI (2006); Speaker, Guest Writer, Savannah State University, Georgia (2003); Association of Writers & Writing Programs, Baltimore, MD (2003); Speaker, Jack Kerouac Conference on Beat Literature, University of Massachusetts Lowell (2003); Speaker, Presenter, Tom Dent Literary Festival, New Orleans, LA (2003); Moderator, Society for the Study of Southern Literature, Lafayette, LA (2002); Speaker, New Orleans Jazz & Heritage Festival (2001-2003) **Creative Works:** Author, "Second Line Home, New Orleans Poems" (2014); Author, "Red Beans & Ricely Yours: Poems" (2005) **Awards:** Nominee, Best Female Faculty, HBCU Digest (2014); Recipient, National Endowment for the Humanities, UNCF/Mellon Fellows (2012); Recipient, Andrew Mellon Faculty Fellowship (2012); Inductee, Phi Eta Sigma National Honor Society (2011-2012); Recipient, Cultural Economy Grant, Oakland, Research Mini Grant, Dillard University (2009); Recipient, Commissioned Poem Medal, National Constitution Center (2006); Recipient, Truman State University Award (2005); Recipient, Research Travel Grant, United Negro College Fund, Andrew W. Mellon Foundation (2004); Recipient, Creative Writing Award, Louisiana Board of Regents, Dillard University (2003); Recipient, Artie, Arts Excellence Award, Delta Sigma Theta Sorority (1996); Recipient, Dissertation Fellowship, National Endowment of the Humanities (1994-1995); **Membership:** Founding President, Seventh Ward Neighborhood Association (2012) **Marquis Who's Who Honors:** Distinguished Humanitarian (2017) **Hobbies:** Swimming; Gardening; Interior decorating; Languages **Political Affiliations:** Democrat **Religion:** Roman Catholic **Business Address:** P.O. Box 8411, New Orleans, LA, 70182

Robert B. Sanders, PhD

Title: Emeritus Professor **Industry:** Education/Educational Services **Company Name:** University of Kansas **Parents:** Robert Sanders; Lois (Jones) Sanders **Marital Status:** Married **Spouse Name:** Gladys Nealous **Children:** Sylvia Lynne; William Nealous **Education:** Postdoctoral Coursework in Biological Chemistry, University of Wisconsin, Madison, WI (1964-1966); PhD in Biological Chemistry, University of Michigan, Ann Arbor, MI (1964); MS in Biological Chemistry, University of Michigan, Ann Arbor, MI (1961); BS in Chemistry, Paine College, Augusta, GA, Summa Cum Laude (1959) **Career:** Professor Emeritus, University of Kansas, Lawrence, KS (2004-Present); Associate Vice Chancellor, University of Kansas, Lawrence, KS (1989-1996); Associate Dean, Graduate School, University of Kansas, Lawrence, KS (1987-1996); Professor of Biochemistry, University of Kansas, Lawrence, KS (1986-2004); Program Director, National Science Foundation, Washington, DC (1978-1979); Visiting Associate Professor, University of Texas Medical School, Houston, TX (1974-1975) **Career Related:** Consultant, Department of Education, Washington, DC (2002-2015); Educational Testing Service, New Jersey (2001-2004); Reviewer, Biology Texts, McGraw Hill (2000-2004); Vice President, National Physical Science Consortium (1994-1996); Consultant, Department of Education, Washington, DC (1983-1997); Consultant, National Science Foundation, Washington, DC (1983-1992); National Institutes of Health, Washington, DC (1977-1986); National Institutes of Health Postdoctoral Fellow (1974-1975); National Research Council, Washington, DC (1973-1993); Interx Research Corporation, Lawrence, KS (1972-1980); Battelle Memorial Institute Fellow (1970-1971); American Cancer Society Fellow (1964-1966) **Civic:** Board of Directors, American Lung Association, Plains Gulf Region, AL (2010-2012); Chairman, Board of Directors, American Lung Association of Central States (2008-2009); Chairman, Board of Directors, American Lung Association of Central States (2008-2009) **Military Service:** U.S. Army Reserve (1955-1962) **Creative Works:** Author, "Contributions of African American Scientists to the Fields of Science, Medicine, and Inventions," Second Edition (2015); Author, "Contributions of African American Scientists to the Fields of Science, Medicine, and Inventions" (2010) **Awards:** Bernard Gregory Award, American Lung Association (2014) **Membership:** American Association of University Professors; American Society of Biochemistry and Molecular Biology **Marquis Who's Who Honors:** Albert Nelson Marquis Lifetime Achievement Award (2017); Distinguished Humanitarian (2017) **Religion:** Methodist **Shipping Address:** 277 Lake Point Drive, Sanford, NC, 27332

Gerald Howard Sandler

Title: Computer Science Educator, Company Executive **Industry:** Technology **Date of Birth:** 09/17/1934 **Place of Birth:** New York **State:** NY **Parents:** Irving Sandler; Sally Sandler **Marital Status:** Married **Spouse Name:** Ann Sandler (Deceased) **Children:** Eric; Steven **Education:** MS, The City College of New York (1957); BS, The City College of New York (1956); Diplomate, Program for Senior Executives, Massachusetts Institute of Technology **Career:** Adjunct Professor of Computer Science, Farmingdale Campus, Polytechnic Institute of New York (1995-Present); President, GHS Enterprises (1995-Present); President, Grumman Data Systems & Services (Now Northrop Grumman Corporation) (1983-1995); Deputy Department Head, Grumman Aerospace (Now Northrop Grumman Corporation) (1981-1983); Grumman Aerospace Corporation (1963-1981); Systems Engineer, RCA (Now Technicolor) **Career Related:** Program Manager, Apollo/Lunar Module Program, Grumman Aerospace **Civic:** Chairman, Long Island Blood Services (1992-1993); Visiting Committee, Polytechnic University **Creative Works:** Author, "System Reliability Engineering, " Prentice Hall (1963) **Awards:** Recipient, Hirsch Award, Long Island Section, IEEE (1989) **Membership:** Director, Armed Forces Communications and Electronics Association International; Air Force Association; IEEE; Council of Information Management Executives; National Space Club & Foundation; Navy League of the United States; The New York Academy of Sciences **Marquis Who's Who Honors:** Albert Nelson Marquis Lifetime Achievement Award (2017) **To what do you attribute your success:** Mr. Sandler attributes his success to hard work, and his education. **Why did you become involved in your profession or industry:** Mr. Sandler became involved in his profession because he joined the U.S. Army after earning a master's. After his military service, he worked on military projects. **Hobbies:** Science; Cosmology; Microbiology; Life on other planets **Shipping Address:** 46 Bonnie Dr, Westbury, NY, 11590

James Kenneth Sanford

Title: Public Relations Executive **Industry:** Corporate Communications & Public Relations **Date of Birth:** 01/23/1932 **Place of Birth:** Clyde **Parents:** James Edward S. Peebles; Bernice (Crawford) Sanford **Education:** MA, University of North Carolina (1958); AB, University of North Carolina (1954); AA, Mars Hill College, North Carolina (1952) **Career:** Public Relations Consultant, Charlotte, NC (1994-Present); Director of Public Information and Publications, University of North Carolina, Charlotte (1964-1994); Editorial Writer, Winston-Salem Journal (1963-1964); News Editor, Winston-Salem Journal (1961-1963); Assistant State Editor, Winston-Salem Journal (1959-1961); Reporter, Copy Editor, Winston-Salem Journal (1957-1959); Public Relations Officer, Asheville United Appeal (1954) **Career Related:** Consultant, Commission on Future of Mars Hill College (1990-1991) **Civic:** Deacon Emeritus, Local Church (2010); Board of Trustees, Mars Hill College (2005); General Board Baptist, State Convention North Carolina (2000-2003); Member, Council on Christian Higher Education (2000-2003); President-Elect International House (2001-2002); President, Mars Hill College National Alumni Board (2001); Chairman, Board of Deacons, Local Church (1994-1995); Attractions Committee, Charlotte Convention and Visitors Bureau (1994); Advisory Committee, Station WTVI Public TV, Charlotte, (1986-1994) **Creative Works:** Author, "Charlotte and UNC Charlotte: Growing Up Together" (1996); Author, "Building Future From the Past: The History of Gaston College 1964-99" (1999); Author, The Mystique of Mars Hill: Stories of the College's 150 Years of Struggles, Survival and Triumph (2007); Co-Author, "Fifty Favored Years" (1972); Contributing Author, "The North Carolina Century: Tar Heels Who Made a Difference" (1900-2000) (2002); Contributor, Numerous Articles, Various Magazines and Newspapers **Awards:** Infinity Award, Charlotte Public Relations Society (1986); Lewis Gaston Award, College News Association Carolinas (1982) **Membership:** Chairman, Southeast District, Public Relations Society of America (1991); College News Association Carolinas; President, Charlotte Public Relations Society (1974); District Chairman, Council for Advancement and Support Education (1975-1976); Phi Kappa Phi; River Hills Lions Club; Editorial Board, Lake Wylie Pilot **Religion:** Baptist **Shipping Address:** 74 Fairway Ridge Lane, Wylie, SC, 29710

Danilo John Santini, PhD

Title: Energy Economist, Urban Systems Engineer **Industry:** Sciences **Company Name:** Argonne National Laboratory **Date of Birth:** 03/10/1945 **Place of Birth:** Louisville **State:** IL/USA **Parents:** Danilo Gene Santini; Mary Margaret (Dink) Brown **Marital Status:** Married **Spouse Name:** Tomma Jean Trent (12/28/1969-01/15/2015) **Children:** Laura Trent; Danilo Thomas **Education:** PhD in Urban Systems/Public Policy Analysis, Northwestern University (1976); MS in Business and Economics, Illinois Institute of Technology (1972); BArch, Massachusetts Institute of Technology (1968) **Career:** Senior Economist, Argonne National Laboratory, IL (2003-Present); Section Manager, Argonne National Laboratory, IL (1993-2008); Scientist, Argonne National Laboratory, IL (1980-1992); Assistant Scientist, Argonne National Laboratory, IL (1974-1979); High School Teacher for Mathematics and Science, George Washington High School, Charleston, WV (1968-1970) **Career Related:** Emeritus Member, Alternative Fuels Committee, Transportation Research Board (TRB), National Academy of Sciences, Washington, DC (2007-Present); Member, Alternative Fuels Committee, Transportation Research Board (TRB), National Academy of Sciences, Washington, DC (1989-Present); US Expert, Implementing Agreement on Hybrid and Electric Vehicles, International Energy Agency (2001-2014); Plug-In Hybrid Electric Vehicles, International Energy Agency, OECD/IEA (2011-2013); Member, Committee on Land Use, Vehicle Miles Travel & Energy, National Academy of Sciences (2007-2009); Member, Research Advisory Committee, American Transportation Research Institute (ATRI) (2003-2006); Operating Agent Study Manager, Information Exchange, International Energy Agency, OECD/IEA (2002-2005); Chairman, Alternative Fuels Committee, Transportation Research Board (TRB), Washington, DC (1996-2002); Architectural Draftsman, Teng & Associates, Chicago, IL (1971-1972); Architectural Draftsman, Bowman & Associates, Vecellio and Kreps, Charleston, WV (1963-1970) **Civic:** Trustee, Member Building Committee, Friendship United Methodist Church, Bolingbrook, IL (1991-1996) **Awards:** Barry D. McNutt Award, Society Automotive Engineers (Now SAE International) (2010); Best Paper Award, Alternative Fuels Committee, Transportation Research Board (TRB) (2010); Fellow, Northwestern University (1972-1974); Fellow, Illinois Institute of Technology (1970) **Membership:** Chapter President, International Association for Energy Economists (1985-1986); Society Automotive Engineers (Now SAE International); Transportation Research Board (TRB); **Shipping Address:** 6420 Double Eagle Drive, Unit 908, Woodridge, IL, 60517

Sonia Sarreals

Title: Data Processing Executive, Consultant **Industry:** Information Technology and Services **Date of Birth:** 09/17/1938 **Place of Birth:** New York **State:** NY **Parents:** Espriela Sarreals; Sadie Beatrice (Scales) Sarreals **Marital Status:** Single **Spouse Name:** Waldro Lynch (9/18/1981, Divorced 1983) **Education:** BA in Languages, City College of New York, Summa Cum Laude (1960) **Certifications:** Certification in French, Sorbonne and Paris, France (1961) **Career:** Technology Consultant, TEKsystems Inc., Reston, VA (1996-2008); Lead Technical Analyst, Automated Concepts, Inc., Arlington, VA (1992-1996); Senior Analyst, AT&T (1989-1992); Staff Data Processing Consultant, Cincinnati Bell Information Systems (1978-1989); Senior Programmer, McGraw-Hill Education, Hightstown, NJ (1973-1978); Project Leader, Touche Ross (Now Deloitte), New York, NY (1970-1973); Consultant, Babbage Systems Inc., New York, NY (1969-1970); Systems Engineer, IBM, New York, NY (1963-1969) **Career Related:** Dickman Institute Fellow, Columbia University (1960-1961) **Civic:** Elder, Lutheran Church of St. Andrew, Silver Spring, MD (1992-1996) **Awards:** Downer Scholar, City University of New York (1960) **Membership:** The Phi Beta Kappa Society **Marquis Who's Who Honors:** Albert Nelson Marquis Lifetime Achievement Award (2017) **Hobbies:** Needlecrafts; **Political Affiliations:** Lutheran **Religion:** Democrat **Shipping Address:** 13705 Beret Place, Silver Spring, MD, 20906

Robert Lee Schmitt

Title: Computer Scientist/Systems Engineer (Retired) **Industry:** Engineering **Date of Birth:** 10/01/1948 **Place of Birth:** Astoria **State:** NY **Parents:** Edward Schmitt; Margaret Louise (Gleason) Schmitt **Marital Status:** Married **Spouse Name:** Elsy Evagelene Burnett (06/1999) **Children:** Eric Jason Marin (Stepson); Alexis Michelle (Marin) Izumi (Stepdaughter) **Education:** Postgraduate Coursework in Systems Engineering, Stevens Institute of Technology (2005-2009): Doctoral Candidate in Developmental Psychology, University of Maryland (1994-1996); Graduate Diploma in Strategic Science, United States Naval War College (1991); Postgraduate Coursework in General Administration, University of Maryland (1979-1980); MS in Computer Science, Stony Brook University (1975); BS in Computer Science, Stony Brook University (1974); Coursework, Hofstra University (1972-1973); AAS in Data Processing, Farmingdale State College, State University of New York (1972) **Career:** Lead System Engineer, Department of Defense, Fort George G. Meade, Maryland (2003-2011); Acting Deputy Chief, Systems Engineering Office, Department of Defense, Fort George G. Meade, Maryland (2003); Acting Chief, Engineering Division, Department of Defense, Fort George G. Meade, Maryland (2002-2003); Systems Engineer, Department of Defense, Fort George G. Meade, Maryland (2001-2002); Systems Architect Implementation Engineer, Department of Defense, Fort George G. Meade, Maryland (2000-2001); Manager Year 2000 Compliance, Department of Defense, Fort George G. Meade, Maryland (1999); Systems Engineer, Department of Defense, Fort George G. Meade, Maryland (1997-1999); Standards, Training and Verification Engineer, Department of Defense, Fort George G. Meade, Maryland (1996-1997); Senior Computer Scientist, Department of Defense, Fort George G. Meade, Maryland (1995-1996); Deputy Director for Technology Fellow, Department of Defense, Fort George G. Meade, Maryland (1994-1995); Manager of System Acquisition, Department of Defense, Fort George G. Meade, Maryland (1989-1994); Computer Scientist, Department of Defense, Fort George G. Meade, Maryland (1986-1989); Senior Computer System Analyst, Department of Defense, Fort George G. Meade, Maryland (1985-1986) **Military Service:** U.S. Naval Reserve (1970-1979); U.S. Navy (1968-1970); US Naval Reserve (1967-1968) **Membership:** The Great Courses Research Advisory Panel, The Teaching Company LLC (2017-Present) **Shipping Address:** 3002 Viburnum Pl., Olney, MD, 20832

Berthold J. Schmutzhart

Title: Sculptor, Educator **Industry:** Education/Educational Services **Company Name:** Corcoran School of the Arts and Design, The George Washington University **Date of Birth:** 08/17/1928 **Place of Birth:** Salzburg **Country of Origin:** Austria **Parents:** Berthold Josef Schmutzhart; Anna (Valaschek) Schmutzhart **Education:** Coursework, University of Applied Arts, Vienna, Austria (1956) **Certifications:** Certified Federal Teacher, Austria **Career:** Professor Emeritus, Corcoran School of the Arts and Design, Washington, DC (1994-Present); Lecturer, Smithsonian Institution, Washington, DC (1968-1984); Professor, Corcoran School Art of the Arts and Design, Washington, DC (1963-1994); Chairman, Sculpture Department, Corcoran School Art of the Arts and Design, Washington, DC (1963-1994); Teacher, Longfellow School, Bethesda, MD (1960-1963); Sculptor, Washington, DC (1959-1960); Professor, Werkschulheim Felbertal, Ebenau, Austria (1951-1958) **Civic:** Member, Board of Directors, The Franz and Virginia Bader Fund (2006-2010); Chairman, The Franz and Virginia Bader Fund (2001-2006); Trustee, Arts for the Aging, Inc. (1990-1998); Member, Board of Directors, Franz Bader Gallery, Washington, DC (1981-1986); Chairman of the Board, Market Five Gallery, Washington, DC (1978-1982) **Creative Works:** Exhibitor, Group Shows, National Gallery of Modern Art, New Delhi, India (1990); Exhibitor, One-Man Shows, Franz Bader Gallery (1988); Exhibitor, One-Man Shows, Franz Bader Gallery (1986); Exhibitor, One-Man Shows, Franz Bader Gallery (1983); Exhibitor, One-Man Shows, Franz Bader Gallery (1981); Exhibitor, Group Shows, Hirshhorn Museum and Sculpture Garden, Washington, DC (1981); Author, "The Handmade Furniture Book" (1981); Exhibitor, One-Man Shows, Franz Bader Gallery (1978); Exhibitor, One-Man Shows, Fredericksburg Art Gallery, Virginia (1967-1973); Exhibitor, Group Shows, Birmingham Museum of Art, Birmingham, AL (1967); Designer, Fountain, Gallery of Modern Art, Fredericksburg, TX (1967); Exhibitor, Group Shows, Arkansas Art Center, Little Rock, AR (1966); Exhibitor, Group Shows, High Museum of Art, Atlanta, GA (1965); Exhibitor, Group Shows, National Collection of Fine Arts, Smithsonian Institution, Washington, DC (1961-1970) **Awards:** Silver Medal, National Audubon Society, Washington, DC (1971); First Prize for Sculpture, Louisville, KY (1968) **Membership:** President, DC Chapter, Artists Equity Association (1973-1975); President, American Austrian Society (1968-1970); Guild for Religious Architects; American Association of University Professors; Executive Committee, American Austrian Society; Soaring Society of America **Marquis Who's Who Honors:** Distinguished Humanitarian (2017) **Shipping Address:** 32 Layline Ln, Fredericksburg, VA, 22406

Deena Jo Schneider

Title: Lawyer **Industry:** Law and Legal Services **Company Name:** Schnader Harrison Segal & Lewis LLP **Education:** JD, Harvard University (1974); BA, Yale University, Magna Cum Laude (1971); Student, University of Michigan **Career:** Partner, Schnader, Harrison, Segal & Lewis, Philadelphia, PA; Member, Schnader, Harrison, Segal & Lewis, Philadelphia, PA **Civic:** Council Member, The Yale Club of Philadelphia; Co-director, Yale Alumni Schools Committee, Philadelphia, PA **Creative Works:** Contributor **Awards:** Honoree, Pennsylvania Super Lawyer (2004-2006) **Membership:** Antitrust Litigation Section, ABA; The Historical Society of the United States Court of Appeals for the Third Circuit, The Bar Association of the Third Federal Circuit; Appellate Courts Committee, Philadelphia Bar Association; Pennsylvania Bar Association **Bar Admissions:** Pennsylvania (1974); Supreme Court of the United States; United States Court of Appeals for the Third Circuit; United States Court of Appeals for the Eighth Circuit; United States District Court Eastern District of Pennsylvania **Marquis Who's Who Honors:** Albert Nelson Marquis Lifetime Achievement Award (2017) **Why did you become involved in your profession or industry:** Dr. Schneider became involved with her profession when she became interested in mathematics and took a few courses in constitutional law. She particularly enjoyed the analytical thinking behind those studies. **Hobbies:** Reading; Hiking; **Business Address:** 1600 Market Street, Ste 3600, Philadelphia, PA, 19103

Heiko Schoder

Title: Attending Physician **Industry:** Medicine & Health Care **Company Name:** Memorial Sloan Kettering Cancer Center **Date of Birth:** 10/03/1961 **Place of Birth:** Berlin **Country of Origin:** Germany **Education:** MBA, Yale University (2016); MD, Humboldt-Universität zu Berlin (1988) **Certifications:** Board Certified, Clinical Densitometry (2008-Present); Certification Board in Nuclear Cardiology (2001-Present); Board Certified, American Board of Nuclear Medicine (2000-Present); Board Certified, Nuclear Medicine, Germany (1999-Present); Board Certified, Diagnostic Radiology, Germany (1994-Present) **Career:** Deputy Chief, Molecular Imaging and Therapy Service, Department of Radiology, Memorial Hospital for Cancer and Allied Diseases (2013-Present); Professor, Radiology, Weill Cornell Medicine, New York, NY (2012-Present); Attending Physician, Department of Radiology/ Nuclear Medicine, Memorial Hospital for Cancer and Allied Diseases (2012-Present); Member, Memorial Hospital, Memorial Sloan Kettering Cancer Center, New York, NY (2012-Present); Associate Professor, Radiology, Weill Cornell Medicine, New York, NY (2007-2012); Associate Member, Memorial Hospital, Memorial Sloan Kettering Cancer Center, New York, NY (2006-2011); Associate Attending Physician, Department of Radiology/ Nuclear Medicine, Memorial Hospital for Cancer and Allied Diseases (2006-2011); Assistant Professor, Radiology, Weill Cornell Medicine, New York, NY (2001-2007); Assistant Member, Memorial Sloan Kettering Cancer Center, New York, NY (2001-2006); Assistant Attending Physician, Department of Radiology/ Nuclear Medicine, Memorial Hospital for Cancer and Allied Diseases (2001-2006); Clinical Instructor, Nuclear Medicine, UCLA Ahmanson Biological Imaging Center, University of California, Los Angeles, CA (2000); Clinical Instructor, Diagnostic Radiology, Krankenhaus Am Urban Berlin, Germany (1994) **Career Related:** Member, IND Committee, Memorial Sloan Kettering Cancer Center (2014-Present); Deputy Chief, Molecular Imaging and Therapy Service (2013-Present); Member, Leadership Group, Department of Radiology (2012-Present) **Creative Works:** Associate Editor, Journal of Nuclear Medicine (2016-Present); Member Editorial Board, Journal of Nuclear Medicine (2005-Present) **Awards:** Memorial Sloan Kettering Cancer Center, Department of Radiology, Faculty Award for Clinical Excellence (2016); Who is Who in America, Science and Engineering (2012-2017) **Membership:** Society of Nuclear Medicine and Molecular Imaging (2006-Present); Radiological Society of North America (2001-Present) **Business Address:** 1275 York Ave, Box 77, RM Schwartz 212, New York, NY, 10065

Brenda B. Schoonover

Title: Ambassador (Retired) **Industry:** Government Administration/Government Relations/ Government Services **Education:** Postgraduate Coursework, Howard University; BA, Morgan State University, Baltimore, MD **Career:** Chargé D'affaires, Ad Interim Minister, Counselor, American Embassy, Brussels, Belgium (2001-2004); Ambassador-in-Residence, Chapel Hill, NC (2000-2001); United States Ambassador to Togo, American Embassy, Lome, Togo (1998-2000); Member, Senior Seminar, United States Department of State, Washington, DC (1996-1997); Administrative Officer and Department Director, Office of Joint Administrative Services, American Embassy, Brussels, Belgium (1992-1996); Chief of Personnel, Bureau of European and Canadian Affairs, United States Department of State, Washington, DC (1988-1991); Bureau of Near East and South Asia, United States Department of State, Washington, DC (1978-1988); Foreign Service, United States Department of State, Tunis, Tunisia; Foreign Service, United States Department of State, Manila, Philippines; Foreign Service, United States Department of State, Colombo, Sri Lanka; Affirmative Action Officer, Government of Arlington County, Virginia; Director, School Partnership Program, Peace Corps, Washington, DC; Associate Director, Peace Corps, Tanzania; Administrator, Office Talent Search, Peace Corps, Washington, DC **Career Related:** President, American Diplomacy Online Magazine **Civic:** Volunteer, Peace Corps, Philippines (1961); Ex Officio, Advisory Board, Global Education, The University of North Carolina at Chapel Hill **Awards:** Career Achievement Award, Secretary of State (2004); Presidential Meritorious Award, United States (2003); Order of the Mono Award, The Togolese Government (2000); Capstone Fellow, National Defense University, Washington, DC (1997) **Membership:** Chairman, Advisory Committee, IntraHealth International, Inc. **Marquis Who's Who Honors:** Albert Nelson Marquis Lifetime Achievement Award (2017) **Shipping Address:** 108 Ironwoods Dr, Chapel Hill, NC, 27516

Sally Maria Schott

Title: Music Publisher, Arts Education Consultant, Music Festival Coordinator **Industry:** Media & Entertainment **Company Name:** Alliance Music Publications **Date of Birth:** 02/07/1943 **Place of Birth:** San Antonio **State:** TX **Parents:** Valentine Felix Schott, Jr.; Doris Faye Schott **Education:** MusM in Education, North Texas State University (1966); MusB, Oklahoma College of Women, Magna Cum Laude (1964) **Career:** Manager, Festival Department, American Classic Tours and Music Festivals (2017-Present); Founding Partner, Alliance Music Publications, Houston, TX (1994-Present); Choral Director, South Houston High School (1974-2004) **Career Related:** Supervisor, Student Teachers, Sam Houston State University (2008-Present); President, Schott Bradshaw Publications, LLC (2006-Present); President, Quaid/Schott Media Productions, LLC (2005-Present); Supervisor, University of Houston (2004-Present); Educational Consultant, Bay Area Chorus, Houston, TX (2004-2012); Minority Partner, AMC Music, Houston, Texas (1975-2006); Adjudicator, Choral Music Competitions; Educational Consultant, Multiple School Districts; Festival Department Manager, American Classic Music Festivals **Civic:** Advisory Board Member, Houston Boychoir (2013-Present); Educational Advisory Board, Houston Chamber Choir (2004-Present); Advisory Board, Bay Area Chorus (2004-Present) **Creative Works:** Collaborator, Six Music Sight Reading Books (2005-2017); Coordinator, Writing Team, "Sing!" (1988); Editor, "Howard Swan: Conscience of a Profession" (1987); Editor, "Something to Sing About" (1981); Producer, "Salamunovich: Chant and Beyond"; Producer, "Noble: Perpetual Inspiration"; Producer, "Snow"; Choral Conductor, "Charlene Archibeque: How to Make a Good Choir Sound Great!" **Awards:** Texas Choirmaster Award, Texas Choral Directors Association (2017); South Houston High School Faculty Hall of Honor (2013); School Bell Award, Houston Symphony School (2013); Distinctive Service Award, Bay Area Chorus (2008); Bay Area Chorus Excellence Award, Texas Choral Directors Association (2008); Named, Hall of Fame, University of Science and Arts of Oklahoma (1996); Teachers Make a Difference Award, KTRK-TV (1988); Leadership Award for Service to Music in Houston, Sigma Alpha Iota (1987); High School Teacher of the Year, Pasadena Independent School District, CA (1986) **Membership:** Newsletter Editor, American Choral Directors Association (2002-2004); President, American Choral Directors Association (2000-2002); Repertoire and Standards, American Choral Directors Association (1994-1998) **Political Affiliations:** Republican **Religion:** Methodist **Shipping Address:** 62 W Thymewood Pl, The Woodlands, TX, 77382

Ellen M. Scrivner, PhD

Title: Police Reform Consultant **Industry:** Consulting **Company Name:** Ellen Scrivner Consultant **Date of Birth:** 08/17/1939 **Place of Birth:** St. Louis **State:** MO **Parents:** John P. O'Shea; Dorothy Mary O'Shea-Hanley **Marital Status:** Married **Spouse Name:** Peter C. Scrivner (8/25/1962) **Children:** Anne Collins (Scrivner) Kuban; Thomas C. **Education:** PhD in Psychology, The Catholic University of America (1986); MS, St. Louis University (1963); BS, St. Louis University (1961) **Certifications:** Certification, American Board of Professional Psychology (2013); Licensed Psychologist, Board of Examiners, Maryland **Career:** Police Reform Consultant (2014-Present); Executive Fellow, Police Foundation, Washington (2012-Present); National Director, High Intensity Drug Traffic Program, Office of National Drug Control Policy, Executive Office of the President (2011-2012); Presidential Appointee, National Institute of Justice, United States Department of Justice Administration (2009-2012); Director, John Jay College of Criminal Justice Leadership Academy (2007-2009); Deputy Superintendent, Bureau of Administrative Services, Chicago Police Department (2004-2007); President, Public Safety Innovations, Washington, DC (2003-2004); Senior Advisor, FBI Office of Law Enforcement Coordination (2002-2004); Deputy Director, COPS Office, United States Department of Justice, Washington, DC (2000-2002); Police Psychologist, Prince Georges County, Maryland; Police Psychologist, Fairfax County, Virginia; Visiting Fellow, National Institute of Justice, United States Department of Justice **Career Related:** Invitee,Testimony for the Presidential Task Force on 21st Century Policing-Supervisory Leadership and Management Training **Civic:** Advisory Board, Local Initiatives Support Corporation, New York, NY (2003-2005) **Creative Works:** Author, "Online Diagnostic Center Guide for Law Enforcement" (2015); Author, "Community Policing in the New Economy" (2015); Author, "Police Psychology Into The 21st Century" (1995); Author, "Law Enforcement Families: Issues and Answers" (1994) **Awards:** Recipient, Women of Courage and Vision Award (2001); Recipient, Lifetime Achievement Award, United States Department of Justice (2000); Distinguished Service Award, American Psychological Association (1990); Recipient, OW Wilson Award, Academy of Criminal Justice Sciences **Membership:** Division President, American Psychological Association (1991-1992) **Marquis Who's Who Honors:** Albert Nelson Marquis Lifetime Achievement Award (2017) **Shipping Address:** 2959 W Gulf Dr Unit 102, Sanibel, FL, 33957

Thomas Lloyd Seifert

Title: Lawyer **Industry:** Law and Legal Services **Company Name:** Sterling Grace Capital Management LLC **Date of Birth:** 06/06/1940 **Place of Birth:** Boston **State:** MA **Parents:** Ralph Frederick Seifert; Hazel Bell (Harrington) Seifert **Marital Status:** Married **Spouse Name:** Ann Cecelia Berg (6/19/1965) **Education:** JD, Indiana University, Cum Laude (1965); BS, Indiana University, Cum Laude (1962) **Career:** General Counsel, Sterling Grace Capital Management LLC, New York, NY (1991-Present); Chief Legal Officer, Sterling Grace Capital Management LLC, New York, NY (1991-Present); Paul, Weiss, Rifkind, Wharton & Garrison, New York, NY (1987-1991); Finley, Kumble, Wagner, Heine, Underberg, Manley, Myerson & Casey, New York City, New York (1983-1987); Senior Vice President of Law, Petrie Stores Corporation, New York, NY (1982-1983); Chief Financial Officer, Petrie Stores Corporation, New York, NY (1982-1983); Vice President, Hanson Industries, Inc., New York, NY (1978-1982); General Counsel, Hanson Industries, Inc., New York, NY (1978-1982); Secretary, Hanson Industries, Inc., New York, NY (1978-1982); Secretary, The Marmon Group, Inc., Chicago, IL (1975-1978); General Counsel, The Marmon Group, Inc., Chicago, IL (1975-1978); Associate General Counsel, Canteen Corporation, Chicago, IL (1973-1975); Assistant Secretary, Canteen Corporation, Chicago, IL (1973-1975); Attorney, Amoco Corporation, Chicago, IL (1970-1973); Attorney, Essex Group, Inc. (Now Superior Essex Inc.), Fort Wayne, IN (1967-1970); Associate, Law Firm of Keck, Mahin & Cate, Chicago, IL (1965-1967) **Creative Works:** Notes Editor, "Indiana Law Journal" (1964-1965) **Awards:** Honoree, Indiana Track and Cross Country Hall of Fame (1993); Beta Gamma Sigma; The Order of the Coif **Membership:** ABA; New York State Bar Association; Association of the Bar of the City of New York; The Order of the Coif; Beta Gamma Sigma **Bar Admissions:** New York (1979); Illinois (1965); Indiana (1965) **Business Address:** 300 Park Avenue, New York, NY, 10022 **Shipping Address:** 15 W 53rd St Apt 31E, New York, NY, 10019

Michael Senra

Title: Assistant Professor **Industry:** Education/Educational Services **Company Name:** Lafayette College **Education:** PhD in Chemical Engineering, University of Michigan (2009); BS in Chemical Engineering, Cornell University (2003) **Career:** Assistant Professor, Department of Chemical and Biomolecular Engineering, Lafayette College (2013-Present); Visiting Assistant Professor, Department of Chemical and Biomolecular Engineering, Lafayette College (2011-2013) **Career Related:** Engineering Graduate School Mentor, University of Michigan (2008-2009); Graduate Student Research Assistant, University of Michigan (2004-2009); Intern, ConocoPhillips (2008); Graduate Research Instructor, University of Michigan (2005-2008) **Civic:** Volunteer, United Way **Membership:** American Chemical Society; American Institute of Chemical Engineers; American Chemical Educators **To what do you attribute your success:** Dr. Senra attributes his success to dedication and hard work. **Why did you become involved in your profession or industry:** From a very young age and through his graduate studies, a number of classmates, colleagues and friends envisioned Dr. Senra being in education. For him, the appeal of being an educator is the ability to help and mentor others while having a lot of freedom in developing your craft. The engineering part came only after taking high school chemistry. His high school chemistry teacher, Mr. Goodfellow, suggested that his abilities in chemistry and mathematics would be a good fit for chemical engineering. He was right. He also correctly predicted that Dr. Senra would receive a PhD. **What do you consider to be the highlight of your career:** Dr. Senra believes students most admire his desire to give constructive feedback in a very prompt manner, his availability to answer questions about courses, chemical engineering and their futures as well as his willingness to challenge them. Professionally, he tries to show dedication to his university, his profession and to his students, engaging them for advice and ideas about how to improve, not only on the student experience, but also the experience for faculty members and colleagues. **Hobbies:** Cooking; Traveling; Watching sports events; Watching performing arts events; Watching his students perform, whether in arts or athletics **Shipping Address:** 424 McCartney St Apt 1, Easton, PA, 18042 **Website:** https://che.lafayette.edu/

Douglas John Shackley

Title: President, CEO **Industry:** Utilities **Company Name:** Pacific Auxiliary Fire Alarm Company **Date of Birth:** 09/21/1938 **Place of Birth:** Oakland **State:** CA **Education:** Student, San Jose State University (1957) **Career:** President, CEO, Pacific Auxiliary Fire Alarm Company (1973-Present); Office Manager to General Manager, Pacific Auxiliary Fire Alarm Company (1967-1973) **Membership:** Board of Directors, Unilateral Apprenticeship and Training Committee, Western Burglar & Fire Alarm Association (2003-Present); Board Member, Automatic Fire Alarm Association (2004-2011); Two-Time President, Board Member, California Automatic Fire Alarm Association (1983-2009); Various Roles, California Automatic Fire Alarm Association (1982-2014) **Shipping Address:** 95 Boutwell Street, San Francisco, CA, 94124-1903 **Website:** http://www.pafa.com

Shirley Shedd

Title: Archivist **Industry:** Education/Educational Services **Company Name:** Evangel University **Date of Birth:** 12/03/1940 **Place of Birth:** Waukegan **State:** IL **Parents:** Edward Sigfried Hanson; Viola Amelia Hanson **Marital Status:** Married **Spouse Name:** Arthur Glenroy Shedd (7/27/1963) **Children:** Bradley Dean; Christy Lynn Wiebe; Timothy Allen **Education:** Coursework, University of Central Missouri (1987); Coursework, The University of Southern Mississippi (1984); MA in English, Missouri State University (1976); BS in English Education, Evangel University (1962) **Career:** Part-time Archivist, Evangel University (2007-Present); Professor Emeritus in Communication, Evangel University (2006-Present); Associate Professor in Communication, Evangel University (1981-2006); Assistant Professor in English, Central Bible College (Now Evangel University) (1976-1981); Journalism Teacher, Springfield Central High School (1963-1969); Media Adviser, Springfield Central High School (1963-1969) **Career Related:** Member, Springfield Area Archivists Committee (2007-Present); Independent Member, Missouri College Media Association (1990-2006); Member, Broadcast Education Association (1987-2006); National Vice President, Society for Collegiate Journalists (1981-2006); Associate Chair, Private Church-Related Colleges Committee, College Media Advisers (1981-2006); Member, Society of Professional Journalists **Civic:** National President, Evangel Auxiliary, Evangel University (1966-Present); Vice President, Local Chapter, Evangel Auxiliary, Evangel University (1966-Present); Chaplain, Local Chapter, Evangel Auxiliary, Evangel University (1966-Present); Historian, Evangel Auxiliary, Evangel University (1966-Present); Board Member, AGCU (2011) **Awards:** Tree of Honor Award, Evangel University (2015); Wall of Fame Award, Communication Department Alumnae, Evangel University (2014); Honoree, Advisers Hall of Fame, Missouri College Media Association (MCMA) (2006); Honoree, Sheridan C. Barker Adviser of Year, Society for Collegiate Journalists (2000); E.M. & Estella Clark Teaching Award (1998) **Membership:** Vice President, Alpha Gamma Chapter, DKGSI (1966-Present); Vice President, Alpha Gamma Chapter Delta State, DKSGI (1974-1976); President, DKGSI **Marquis Who's Who Honors:** Albert Nelson Marquis Lifetime Achievement Award (2017) **Hobbies:** Reading; Travel; Photography; Genealogy **Shipping Address:** 2540 W Swan St, Springfield, MO, 65807

Betty Jo Lester Sheehy

Title: Real Estate Company Executive, Investment Advisor **Industry:** Real Estate **Date of Birth:** 10/01/1936 **Place of Birth:** Baileysville **State:** WV **Parents:** Virgil Lester; Virginia Graham Lester **Spouse Name:** John D. Sheehy (9/21/1963, Divorced 1976) **Children:** John; Peter; Barbara **Education:** Coursework, New York Institute of Finance (1960); Coursework, Marshall University (1956) **Certifications:** Licentiate in Real Estate, Southampton College (Now Southampton Campus, Long Island University) (2002) **Career:** Owner, Betty Jo Sheehy Real Estate, Southampton, NY (2002-2014); Broker, Betty Jo Sheehy Real Estate, Southampton, NY (2002-2014); Vice President of Investments, Newbridge Securities, West Palm Beach, FL (2006-2007); Financial Adviser, Morgan Stanley, Southampton, NY (1991-2002); Associate Vice President, Morgan Stanley, Southampton, NY (1991-2002); Finance Consultant, Merrill Lynch, Bank of America Corporation, Short Hills, NJ (1984-1990) **Civic:** Benefactor, Parish Art Museum, Southampton, NY (1999-2010); Chapter President, New Jersey Symphony Women League, Short Hills, NJ (1977-1981); Volunteer, Red Cross of the Oranges, The American National Red Cross (1970) **Awards:** Honoree, Named Business Woman of the Year, National Congressional Committee (2006); Leadership Development Award, Merrill Lynch, Bank of America Corporation (1984-1990) **Hobbies:** Golf; Music; Reading; Running **Shipping Address:** 4230 50th Ave S Apt 3, Seattle, WA, 98118

Donald Sloane Shepard, PhD

Title: Political Science Professor **Industry:** Education/Educational Services **Company Name:** Brandeis University **Date of Birth:** 09/15/1947 **Place of Birth:** New York **State:** NY **Parents:** Bertram David Shepard; Marjorie (Haspel) Markley **Marital Status:** Married **Spouse Name:** Emily A. Maitin (8/17/1980) **Children:** Melissa R. Maitin-Shepard; Jeremy B. Maitin-Shepard **Education:** PhD, Harvard University (1976); MPP in Public Policy, Harvard University (1973); BA, Harvard University, with Highest Honors, Magna Cum Laude (1969) **Career:** Professor, Brandeis University, Waltham, MA (1991-Present); Associate Professor, Harvard University, Cambridge, MA (1980-1991); Director, Economic Research, Veteran's Affairs (Now United States Department of Veterans Affairs), West Roxbury, MA (1979-1985); Lecturer, Harvard University, Cambridge, MA (1977-1980); Senior Economist, Massachusetts Department of Public Health, Commonwealth of Massachusetts, Boston, MA (1970-1971) **Career Related:** Director, Cost and Value Work Group, Schneider Institutes of Health Policy, Brandeis University (2000-Present); Affiliated Faculty, Brown University, Providence, RI (1995-Present); Chair, Initiative on Under-Reporting under International Dengue Vaccine to Vaccination Committee (2012); Behavioral and Social Sciences for the Prevention of HIV/AIDS (2006-2012); National Institute of Drug Abuse (2004-2006) **Civic:** Partnership for Dengue Control (2010-Present); Member, Board of Directors, Mountain Sun Condominium-Quarters (2009-2014) **Creative Works:** Author, "Lifestyle Modification to Control Heart Disease: Evidence and Policy" (2010-2011); Guest Editor, Dengue Bulletin, World Health Organization (Now WHO) (2010-2011); Guest Editor, Administration and Policy in Mental Health (2005); Author, "Analysis of Hospital Costs: A Manual for Managers" (2000) **Awards:** Recipient, Award, World Bank (2014-Present); Recipient, Award, Bill & Melinda Gates Foundation (2011-Present); Named, Principal Investigator, National Institute on Drug Abuse and National Institute on Alcohol Abuse and Alcoholism (1993-Present); Recipient, Professional Award (2016); Fellow, American Society of Topical Medicine and Hygiene **Membership:** International Health Economics Association; American Society of Tropical Medicine and Hygiene; Phi Beta Kappa (Now The Phi Beta Kappa Society) **Marquis Who's Who Honors:** Albert Nelson Marquis Lifetime Achievement Award (2017) **Hobbies:** Cross-country Skiing; Swimming **Business Address:** 415 South St Rm 275, Waltham, MA, 02453

Judith R. Shepp

Title: Elementary School Educator (Retired) **Industry:** Education/Educational Services **Date of Birth:** 03/11/1942 **Place of Birth:** Dayton **State:** OH **Parents:** Rollin Labarr Rosser; Eloise (Comstock) Rosser **Marital Status:** Widowed **Spouse Name:** John W. Shepp (7/12/1969, Deceased 2008) **Children:** David; Edward; Cynthia **Education:** BS, Eastern Kentucky University (1964) **Career:** Special Educated Teacher, Lovell Elementary School (2003-2006); Primary Team Leader, Lovell Elementary School (2001-2009); Teacher, Orange County Public School (1992-2009); Teacher, Lake County, FL (1988-1989); Teacher, Brevard County, FL (1964-1969) **Career Related:** Faculty Representative, Orange County Classroom Teachers Association (1994-1997, 2001-2009); Board Member, Orange County Reading Association (1999-2007); Primary Team Leader, Maxey Elementary School, Winter Garden, FL, (1994-1995, 1997-1998); Member, Advisory Council, Maxey Elementary School (1996-1998) **Civic:** Vice President, GFWC Mount Dora Woman's Club, Inc. (1984-Present); Mentor, Take Stock in Children, Lake County Educational Foundation (2015-2018); President, Women's Communication of Fine Arts (2012-2014); Woman's Commission of Fine Arts (1986-1990); President, Magnolia Garden Circle (1984-1986); President, West Pasco Junior Woman's Club, New Port Richey, FL (1973-1975) **Awards:** Gold Key Award (2012); Disney Teacheriffic Award (1996); Named Clubwoman of the Year (1992) **Membership:** Florida Committee, General Federation of Women's Club Mount Dora (2012-Present); Treasurer, General Federation of Women's Club Mount Dora (2013-Present); President, General Federation of Women's Club Mount Dora (1990-1992, 2010-2012, 2018-2020); Mediator, General Federation of Women's Club Mount Dora (2015); Florida District Public Issues Chairman, General Federation of Women's Club Mount Dora (2012-2014); Newsletter Editor, Key Notes (1996-2012) **Marquis Who's Who Honors:** Albert Nelson Marquis Lifetime Achievement Award (2017) **To what do you attribute your success:** Ms. Shepp attributes her success to her mother, who encouraged her to enter teaching. **Why did you become involved in your profession or industry:** Ms. Shepp's mother influenced her to become a teacher. **Hobbies:** Reading; Golf **Shipping Address:** 30627 Round Lake Rd, Mount Dora, FL, 32757

Elizabeth M. Short, MD

Title: Emerita Professor of Medicine **Industry:** Education/Educational Services **Company Name:** Georgetown U SOM **Date of Birth:** 06/02/1942 **Place of Birth:** Boston **State:** MA/USA **Parents:** James Edward Meehan; Arlene (Mitchell) Meehan **Marital Status:** Married **Spouse Name:** Michael Allen Friedman (12/21/1975) **Children:** Lia Gabrielle; Hannah Ariel; Eleanor Elana **Education:** Postdoctoral Fellow, Renal Metabolism, UCSF School of Medicine (1972-1973); Postdoctoral Fellow in Human Genetics, Yale School of Medicine (1970-1972); MD, Yale School of Medicine, Cum Laude (1968); BA in Philosophy, Mount Holyoke College, Magna Cum Laude (1963) **Certifications:** Diplomate, American Board of Internal Medicine; Diplomate, American Board of Medical Genetics and Genomics **Career:** Professor Emerita, Clinical Medicine, School of Medicine, Georgetown University (2004-Present): Health Policy Consultant, U.S. Department of Health & Human Services (1996-2001); Associate Chief Medical Director, Academic Affairs, U.S. Department of Veterans Affairs (1992-1996); Deputy Associate Chief Medical Director, Academic Affairs, U.S. Department of Veterans Affairs (1988-1992) **Career Related:** Member, Committee on Scientific Education & Training, Office of Science & Technology Policy, White House (1996); Member, White House Task Force on Health Care Reform (1993); Member, National Child Health Advisory Council, National Institutes of Health (1990-1997); Member, ACGME (1988-1997); Member, House of Delegates, American Medical Association (1988-1996); Visiting Professor, Human Biology, Stanford University (1983-1986) **Civic:** Adviser, Capital Campaign, Autry Museum of the American West (2016-Present); Chair, Program Assessment Committee, Hillsides (2015-Present); Executive Committee, Hillsides (2011-Present); Western Council, Autry Museum of the American West (2008-Present); Class of 1963 Leadership Gift Committee, Mount Holyoke College (2008-Present); Cornerstone Chair, Class of 1963, Mount Holyoke College (2008-Present); Program Assessment Committee, Hillsides (2006-Present); Board of Directors, Hillsides (2003-Present); Reunion Co-chair, Class of 1968, Yale School of Medicine (2008, 2013, 2018); Chair, Strategic Planning Committee for Merger with University of Southern California, Pacific Asia Museum (2013-2014) **Awards:** Distinguished Alumni Award, Yale School of Medicine (2013) **Membership:** The American Society of Human Genetics (1972-Present); American Association for the Advancement of Science (1970-Present) **Marquis Who's Who Honors:** Albert Nelson Marquis Lifetime Achievement Award (2017) **Hobbies:** Textile Art; Weaving; Sailing **Shipping Address:** 3535 Ranch Top Rd, Pasadena, CA, 91107

Susan Richards Shreve

Title: Writer, Educator **Industry:** Education/Educational Services **Company Name:** George Mason University **Date of Birth:** 05/02/1939 **Place of Birth:** Toledo **State:** OH **Parents:** Robert Kenneth Richards; Helen (Greene) Richards **Children:** Porter; Elizabeth; Caleb; Kate **Education:** MA, University of Virginia (1969); BA, University of Pennsylvania (1961) **Career:** Professor, English Literature, George Mason University, Fairfax, VA (1976-Present) **Career Related:** Visiting Professor, Columbia University, New York, NY (1982-2000); Visiting Professor, Princeton University (1991-1993) **Creative Works:** Author, "More News Tomorrow" (2017); Author, "The Search For Baby Ruby" (2015); Editor, "The Search for Baby Ruby" (2015); Author, "The Lovely Shoes" (2011); Author, "You Are The Love Of My Life" (2012); Author, "A Memoir: Warm Springs: Traces of a Childhood" (2007); Author, "A Student of Living Things" (2006); Author, "Kiss Me Tomorrow" (2006); Author, "Under the Watson's Porch" (2004); Editor, "Dream Me Home Safely" (2003); Author, "Trout & Me" (2003); Author, "Blister" (2002); Author, "Plum & Jaggers" (2000); Author, "Goodbye, Amanda The Good" (2000); Author "Ghost Cats" (1999); Co-Editor, "Tales Out of School: Narratives on Education" (1999); Co-Editor, "How We Want to Live: Narratives on Progress" (1998); Author, "Glimmer" (1997); Author, "Joshua Bates in Trouble Again" (1997); Author, "Jonah, The Whale" (1997); Co-Editor, "Outside the Law: Narratives on Justice" (1997); Author, "Warts" (1996); Co-Editor, "How We Want to Live: Narratives on Progress" (1996); Author, "A Goalie" (1996); Author, "The Visiting Physician" (1995); Author, "Skin Deep: Women & Race" (1995); Author, "The Formerly Great Alexander Family" (1995); Author "Zoe and Columbo" (1995); Author, "Lucy Forever & the Stolen Baby" (1994); Author, "Amy Dunn Quits School" (1993); Author, "The Train Home" (1993); Author, "Daughters of the New World" (1992); Author, "Wait for Me" (1992); Author, "Joshua T. Bates In Charge" (1992); Author, "The Gift of the Girl Who Couldn't Hear" (1991); Author, "A Country of Strangers" (1989); Author, "Queen of Hearts" (1986); Author, "Lucy Forever and Miss Rosetree, Shrinks" (1985); Author, "How I Saved the World on Purpose" (1985); Author, "Dreaming of Heroes" (1984); Author, "The Flunking of Joshua T. Bates" (1984) **Awards:** National Endowment Arts Fiction Award (1982); John Simon Guggenheim Award in Fiction (1980); Jenny Moore Award, George Washington University (1978); Poets and Writers Award for Service to Writers **Membership:** Chairman, PEN/Faulkner Foundation; President, PEN/Faulkner Foundation; Phi Beta Kappa **Business Address:** 3506 35th Street NW, Washington, DC, 20016

Adam Louis Shrier

Title: Energy Expert, University Professor, Management Consultant **Industry:** Consulting **Company Name:** Global Development Opportunities, LLC **Date of Birth:** 03/26/1938 **Place of Birth:** Warsaw **Country of Origin:** Poland **Parents:** Henry Leon Shrier; Mathilda (Czamanska) Shrier **Marital Status:** Married **Spouse Name:** Diane Kesler (6/10/1961) **Children:** Jonathan; Lydia; Catherine; David **Education:** JD, Fordham University (1976); Postdoctoral Visitor, University Cambridge, England (1965-1966); Doctor of Engineering and Applied Science Yale University (1965); MS, Massachusetts Institute of Technology (1960); BS, Columbia University (1959); Completed Executive Education Programs at Harvard Business School, Wharton School of Business, Brookings Institution (1973-1982) **Career:** Adjunct Professor, International and Public Affairs, Columbia University (2005-Present); Adjunct Faculty, School of Public Policy, University of Maryland (2014-Present); President, Global Development Opportunities, Washington (1997-Present); Visiting Professor, Beijing Foreign Studies University, China (2012-2014); Course Leader, Continuing Legal Education, Terrapinn, Ltd. (2014); Course Leader, Continuing Legal Education, CWC Energy, Ltd. (2006-2012); Visiting Professor, International Business, Xiamen University, China (2003-2009); Adjunct Professor, International Business, American University (2000-2009); Managing Director, Specialty Tech. Associates, Washington (1988-1997); Manager of Policy and Planning, Exxon International Co., New York, NY (1986-1988); Coordinator of Corporate Business Dealings with Sensitive (Communist) Countries, Division Manager, Supply and Transportation, Exxon International Co., New York, NY (1983-1986); Corporate Planning Consultant, Secretary of New Business Investments, Exxon Corporation, New York City (1981-1982); President Solar Thermal System Division, Exxon Enterprises Inc. (1977-1981); General Manager Solar Energy Projects, Exxon Enterprises Inc. (1975-1977); Portfolio Manager, New Energy Systems, Exxon Enterprises Inc. New York, NY (1974-1975); Coordinator of Pollution Abatement Activities, Tanker Department, Exxon International Company, New York, NY (1972-1974); Head, Environmental Sciences Laboratory, Corporate Research, Esso Research & Engineering Company (1969-1972) **Business Address:** 4000 Cathedral Ave NW Ofc 318B, Washington, DC, 20016

Emmanuel Skordalakes, PhD

Title: Associate Professor **Industry:** Education/Educational Services **Company Name:** The Wistar Institute of Anatomy and Biology, University of Pennsylvania **Education:** Postdoctoral Coursework, University of California, Berkeley (2001-2006); PhD, University of London (2000); Trainee in Synthetic Chemistry, Peptide Synthesis Division, TRI (1993-1994); MSc in Chemical Research, University of London, London, UK (1992); BSc, Anglia Ruskin University, Cambridge, UK, With Honors (1991) **Career:** Adjunct Associate Professor, Department of Biochemistry and Molecular Biology, University of Pennsylvania (2013-Present); Associate Professor, Gene Expression and Regulation Program, The Wistar Institute of Anatomy and Biology (2012-Present); Adjunct Associate Professor, Department of Chemistry, University of Pennsylvania (2012-Present); Adjunct Assistant Professor, Department of Chemistry, University of Pennsylvania (2008-2011); Adjunct Assistant Professor, Department of Biochemistry and Molecular Biology, University of Pennsylvania (2007-2012); Assistant Professor, Gene Expression and Regulation Program, The Wistar Institute of Anatomy and Biology (2007-2011) **Career Related:** Lecturer in Field; Presenter, Conferences; Patentee in Field **Creative Works:** Contributor, 39 Articles, Professional Journals; Patents in Field; Ad Hoc Manuscript Reviewer, Science; Ad Hoc Manuscript Reviewer, EMBO; Ad Hoc Manuscript Reviewer, Cancer Research; Ad Hoc Manuscript Reviewer, Biomed Research International; Ad Hoc Manuscript Reviewer, NSMB; Ad Hoc Manuscript Reviewer, PNAS; Ad Hoc Manuscript Reviewer, Gen&Dev; Ad Hoc Manuscript Reviewer, JMB; Ad Hoc Manuscript Reviewer, MCB; Ad Hoc Manuscript Reviewer, Cellular and Molecular Life Sciences; Ad Hoc Manuscript Reviewer, Acta; Ad Hoc Manuscript Reviewer, Crystallography; Ad Hoc Manuscript Reviewer, BBA-Protein and Proteomics; Ad Hoc Manuscript Reviewer, Journal of the American Aging Association; Ad Hoc Manuscript Reviewer, Biochemistry; Ad Hoc Manuscript Reviewer, Human Genetics; Ad Hoc Manuscript Reviewer, Cell Research **Awards:** Nominee, Howard Hughes Medical Institute Award (2014); Pilot Project in Drug Discovery Award, The Wistar Institute of Anatomy and Biology (2014); Etter Award, American Crystallographic Association, Inc. (2012); Emerald Foundation Award (2009); Award, V Foundation for Cancer Research (2008) **Membership:** American Cancer Society, Inc.; American Chemical Society; American Crystallographic Association, Inc. **Marquis Who's Who Honors:** Albert Nelson Marquis Lifetime Achievement Award (2017) **Business Address:** 3601 Spruce St., Office 318, Philadelphia, PA, 19104

Charles Jim Slater

Title: Construction Company Executive **Industry:** Architecture & Construction **Company Name:** Snow Constructors, Inc. **Date of Birth:** 02/16/1949 **Place of Birth:** Munich **Country of Origin:** Germany **Parents:** Robert Marsh Slater; Mary Elizabeth (James) Slater **Marital Status:** Married **Spouse Name:** Kristie J. Alexander (5/11/1992); Pamela S. Senning (9/17/1974, Divorced 4/1992) **Children:** Mary Katherine; Robert Charles **Education:** BA in Political Science, University of Tennessee (1974) **Certifications:** Certified Safety and Health Manager; Certified for Professional Safety Management **Career:** Owner, Paradigm-5 (2014-Present); Contractor, Advisor, Duke Energy Absolute Consulting (2014-Present); Regional Safety Manager, Shaw Group, Inc. (2006-Present); Senior HSE manager, Fluor Corp. (2003-2006); Senior Safety Manager, Fluor Corp. (1996-2003); Safety and Risk Management Director, Harbert-Yeargin Inc. (1992-1996); Resident Engineer, Yeargin Inc. (1991); Resident Engineer, Yeargin Inc. (1991); Risk Management Manager, Yeargin Inc. (1990); Risk Management Manager, Yeargin Inc. (1985-1988); Safety and Medical Manager, Daniel International Co. (1983-1984); Safety Manager, Daniel International Co. (1981-1983) **Career Related:** National Safety Council, Washington, DC (1993-Present); Board of Advisors, Associate Builders and Contractors **Civic:** Kingsport Area Safety Council (1989); President, Tennessee Volunteers Firefighters Association, Sullivan County (1987-1989) **Membership:** Chapter President, American Institute of Constructors (1993-1994); Instructor, Construction Industry Cooperative Alliance (1992); American Society of Safety Engineers; National Safety Management Society; Charter, Safety Directors League; Construction Specifications Institute **Hobbies:** Golf; Chess; Reading; Cinematography **Shipping Address:** 2134 Cross Trail Ridge, Lockhill, SC, 29732

Robert Albian Smallwood Jr.

Title: Secondary Education Educator (Retired) **Industry:** Education/Educational Services **Date of Birth:** 10/03/1946 **Place of Birth:** Philadelphia **State:** PA **Parents:** Robert Albian Smallwood; Mildred May (Miller) Smallwood **Marital Status:** Married **Spouse Name:** Geraldine Ann Boozan (5/27/1972) **Children:** Amy Lynn; Daniel James **Education:** EdS in Educational Administration and Supervision, Rutgers University (Now Rutgers, The State University of New Jersey), New Brunswick, NJ (1983); MA in School Administration and Supervision, Rider College (Now Rider University), Lawrenceville, NJ (1976); BS in Commerce, Business Administration, Rider College (Now Rider University), Lawrenceville, NJ (1969) **Career:** Whole School Reform Site Facilitator, Dunn Junior High School (Now Dunn Middle School), Trenton Public Schools (1999-2005); Social Studies Teacher, Dunn Junior High School (Now Dunn Middle School) Trenton Public Schools (1997-1999); School Disciplinarian, Trenton Board of Education (Now Trenton Public Schools) (1994-1997); Teacher, Gifted and Talented Social Studies, Dunn Junior High School (Now Dunn Middle School) Trenton Public Schools (1989-1993); Acting Assistant Principal, Carroll Robbins Elementary School, Trenton Public Schools (1987-1988); Acting Assistant Principal, Junior High Schools #1, Trenton Public Schools (1987-1988); Acting Assistant Principal, Junior High Schools #5, Trenton Public Schools (1987-1988); Chairman, Social Studies Department, Junior High School #2, Trenton Public Schools (1984-1985); Teacher, US History, Junior High School #2, Trenton Public Schools (1983-1987); Acting Assistant Principal, Junior High School #2, Trenton Public Schools (1980-1983); School Disciplinarian, Trenton Board of Education (Now Trenton Public Schools) (1976-1984) **Career Related:** Middle School Principal (1998-2005); Districts Affirmative Action Advisory Council; National Teacher Corps Project; Trenton Area Financial Advisor **Civic:** Executive Committee (1996-1999); Trustee, New Jersey Council for Alcohol/Drug Education (1983-1999); President (1998-1999); Vice President (1996-1998); Acting Executive Director (1994-1995) **Military Service:** U.S. Army (1969-1972) **Awards:** Decorated Bronze Star; Army Commendation Medal with Oak Leaf Cluster; Joint Service Commendation Medal; Good Conduct Medal; National Defense Service Medal; Vietnam Service Medal; Vietnam Campaign Medal with Two Campaign Stars; Order of First Families of Maryland **Hobbies:** Genealogy; History **Political Affiliations:** Republican **Religion:** Baptist **Shipping Address:** 2 Leese Ave, Hamilton, NJ, 08609

Edith M. Smart

Title: Volunteer **Industry:** Education/Educational Services **Company Name:** Middleburg Elementary School **Date of Birth:** 09/10/1929 **Parents:** Edwin Katte Merrill; Helen Phelps (Stokes) Merrill **Marital Status:** Married **Spouse Name:** S. Bruce Smart, Jr. (9/10/1949) **Children:** Edith Minturn Smart-Moore; William Candler; Charlotte Merrill Smart-Rogan; Priscilla Smart-Schwarzenbach **Education:** Coursework, Barnard College (1949-1950); Coursework, Smith College (1947-1949) **Career:** Study Buddies Tutoring Program, Southport, CT Elementary School (2010-Present); Teacher, Middleburg Community Charter School (2009-2012); Trustee, Virginia Chapter, The Nature Conservancy (1992-2008); Trustee, Fairfield University (1987-1993); Trustee, Connecticut Chapter, The Nature Conservancy (1981-1991); Chairman, Westport, CT Nature Center of Environmental Activities (1981-1985); President, Near & Far Aid Association Inc. (1977-1979); Vice President, Near & Far Aid Association Inc. (1975-1977); Chairman, Southport-Westport Antiques Show (1974-1976); Treasurer, Near & Far Aid Association Inc. (1970-1975); Guide, Mill River Wetlands Committee (1967-1985); Instructor, Mill River Wetlands Committee (1967-1985); Leader, Northern Cook County Council, Girl Scouts of the United States of America (1962-1964); Elementary School Teacher, Gibson Island, MD (1959-1960); President, Nature Center of Environmental Activities, Westport, CT **Career Related:** Director, The Land Trust of Virginia (2002-2014); Director, Piedmont Child Care Center (1991-1997); Guide, National Aquarium (1985-1990) **Civic:** Vestryman, St. Timothy's Episcopal Church (1974-1976); Board Member, The Land Trust of Virginia **Membership:** The Fairfax Hunt Club; Upperville Garden Club **Marquis Who's Who Honors:** Albert Nelson Marquis Lifetime Achievement Award (2017) **Political Affiliations:** Independent **Religion:** Episcopalian **Shipping Address:** 20561 Trappe Road, Upperville, VA, 20184

Mieko Kotake Smith, PhD

Title: Educator **Industry:** Education/Educational Services **Date of Birth:** 09/19/1941 **Place of Birth:** Osaka **Country of Origin:** Japan **Parents:** Kohei Kotake; Toshiko Kotake **Marital Status:** Married **Spouse Name:** James Allen Smith **Children:** Six Children **Education:** PhD, Case Western Reserve University (1980); EdS, Kent State University (1972); MA, Kent State University (1972); BA, Tsuda College, Tokyo, Japan (1964) **Certifications:** Licensed Clinical Social Worker, State of Ohio **Career:** Professor, Cleveland State University (2000-Present); Professor, University of Akron (2014); Associate Professor, Cleveland State University (1993-2000); Assistant Professor, Cleveland State University (1990-1993); Consultant, Summit County Children Services Board, Akron, OH (1988-1990); Independent Consultant, Beachwood, OH (1987-1990); Director, Research and Training, Hill House Mental Health Rehabilitation and Research, Inc. (1982-1987); Director of Aftercare, Murtis Taylor Human Services System (1981-1982); Research Associate, Case Western Reserve University (1978-1981); Student Activities Coordinator, International Student Advisor, Cleveland State University (1972-1978) **Career Related:** Chief Evaluator, Consultant, Asian Services, Akron, OH; Director, Program Evaluation/Research, Ohio Program Evaluator's Group **Civic:** First Vice Chair, Board of Governors, Program Planning and Policy Committee Chair, Cuyahoga County Community Mental Health Board (Now Alcohol, Drug Addiction & Mental Health Services Board) Cleveland, OH (1998); Trustee, The Phoenix Society, Inc., Cleveland, OH (1996-1998) **Creative Works:** Co-Author, "Mental Health Practice with Children and Youth: A Strengths and Well-Being Model (Social Work Practice in Action)" (1998); Contributor, Chapters to Books; Contributor, Articles, Professional Journals **Awards:** Lifetime Achievement Award, National Association of Social Workers, Region 2, Ohio (2013); Grantee, U.S. Department of Health and Human Services, Cleveland, OH (1999-2001); Grantee, U.S. Department of Education (1999); Grantee, Ohio Department of Mental Health and Addiction Services (1999); Research Recognition Award, Ohio Program Evaluators' Group (1992); Grantee, Ohio Department of Mental Health and Addiction Services (1990); Grantee, Ohio Department of Mental Health and Addiction Services (1985) **Membership:** American Association of University Professors; National Association of Social Workers; American Evaluation Association **Marquis Who's Who Honors:** Albert Nelson Marquis Lifetime Achievement Award (2017) **Hobbies:** Reading **Political Affiliations:** Democrat **Religion:** Presbyterian **Shipping Address:** 30097 Yellow Feather Drive, Canyon Lake, CA, 92587

Paul Aikin Smith, PhD

Title: Physics Educator **Industry:** Education/Educational Services **Date of Birth:** 01/12/1934 **Place of Birth:** Bucaramanga **Country of Origin:** Colombia **Parents:** Pryor Timmons; Letha (Brubaker) Smith **Marital Status:** Married **Spouse Name:** Margaret Sue McCluggage (8/27/1958) **Children:** Valerie Anne; Amy Cheryl Smith-Dorff **Education:** PhD in Physics, Tufts University (1964); AM in Physics, Washington University, St. Louis, MO (1959); AB in Physics and Philosophy, Park College (1956) **Career:** Professor of Physics, Coe College, Cedar Rapids, IA (1981-Present); Associate Professor, Coe College, Cedar Rapids, IA (1970-1981); Assistant Professor of Physics, Coe College, Cedar Rapids, IA (1964-1970) **Career Related:** Delegate, Russian and Chinese Physics Departments (1983); National Council, The American Association of Physics Teachers (1974-1985) **Civic:** Advocacy Committee, PATCH Project, Cedar Rapids, IA (1993-Present); Clerk of Session, Central Park Presbyterian Church, Cedar Rapids, IA (1989-Present); Delegate to East Iowa Presbytery (1989-Present); Parliamentarian, Democratic Center Committee, Linn County (1974-Present); Commissioner to General Assembly, Presbyterian Church USA (1992); Secretary, Constitution Revisions Committee (1980); Secretary, Constitution Revisions Committee (1978); Secretary, Rules and Nominations Committee, Numerous Democratic Conventions (1974-1990); Secretary, Iowa Democratic Party (1974-1978); Secretary, Constitution Revisions Committee (1974) **Creative Works:** Creator, Computer-Based Publication Medium **Marquis Who's Who Honors:** Albert Nelson Marquis Lifetime Achievement Award (2017) **Why did you become involved in your profession or industry:** Dr. Smith majored in philosophy and physics. He ended up in the den of the person who made the first atomic bombs and was asked to teach an astronomy lab. After Mr. Smith earned a PhD, he was invited to a conference by the chairman of the physics department, who was interested in getting women into physics. **Hobbies:** Computer programming **Shipping Address:** 508 W Trilby Road, Apt. 201, Fort Collins, CO, 80525

Paul Lowell Smith

Title: Realtor, Senior Pastor **Industry:** Real Estate **Company Name:** Smitty Realty, Romar Beach Baptist Church **Date of Birth:** 07/05/1940 **Place of Birth:** Fairfield **State:** AL **Marital Status:** Married **Spouse Name:** Janet E. Lindsay (1/23/1964) **Children:** Janine Smith Shelby; Paul L., Jr.; Scott Lyndsay; Andrew Hamilton **Education:** ThD, New Orleans Baptist Seminary (1972); ThM, New Orleans Baptist Seminary (1965); BA, Samford University (1962) **Career:** President, MTS Investment Corporation (1995-Present); Senior Pastor, Romar Beach Baptist Church, Orange Beach, AL (1995-Present); President, Foley Plantation, Inc. (1994-Present); President, Smitty Realty, Inc., Saraland, AL (1975-Present); President, Lighthouse Gospel Productions (2011); President, MTS Investment Corporation, Saraland, AL (1989); President, Paul Lowell Smith Evangelistic Ministries (1974-1991); Pastor, First Baptist Church, Citronelle, AL (1972-1974); Pastor, Ethel Baptist Church, Mississippi (1970-1972); Pastor, Ruth Baptist Church, Mississippi (1968-1970); Pastor, Fulton Baptist Church, Alabama (1962-1966) **Career Related:** Land Development Consultant, Merchants National Bank, Mobile, AL (1985-1986) **Civic:** President, Citronelle Youth Football League (1982); Master of Ceremonies, Citronelle Oil Bowl Pageant (1982); Auctioneer, Various Charities, Mobile, AL (1980-1994); Foreign Mission Board, Southern Baptist Convention; Evangelist for Crusades in Ecuador, Antigua and Guyana **Creative Works:** Author, "Greek Mystery Religions" (1971); Contributor, Articles, Real Estate Investments and Development **Awards:** Pastor of the Year, Samford University (2005) **Hobbies:** Hunting; Fishing **Shipping Address:** PO Box 1492, Orange Beach, AL, 36561

Stuart Lewis Smith

Title: Community Volunteer **Industry:** Nonprofit & Philanthropy **Date of Birth:** 03/28/1936 **Place of Birth:** Richmond **State:** VA **Parents:** John Minor Botts Lewis Junior; Elise Davis Deyerle **Marital Status:** Married **Spouse Name:** Isaac Noyes Smith IV (4/30/1960) **Children:** Isaac Noyes V; Minor Botts; Lyle Davis; Lisa Lewis **Education:** BA in Sociology, Hollins College (1958) **Career:** Sales Associate, Clothes Consultant, The Worth Collection, Charleston, WV (1992-2002); West Virginia Sales Associate, Stanmar Homes, Sudbury, MA (1974-1981); Kindergarten Teacher, First Presbyterian Church School, Charleston, West Virginia (1960-1961); Home Service Caseworker, The American Red Cross, Richmond, VA (1958-1960) **Civic:** Volunteer, Various Community and State Organizations (2003-Present); Parks Commissioner, Chair, Long Range Planning Committee, Kanawha County Park Systems (1986-Present); Auxiliary, Charleston Area Medical Center (1986-2016); Fundraiser, Spirit of the Valley (2000-2011); Board Member, Spring Hill Cemetery; Committee Member, High Hopes Committee, YWCA (2004-2010); Steering Committee Member, Kanawha County Cares for Youth (2004-2007); Vice President, Coouskin Park Foundation; Volunteer, Habitat for Humanity (1990-2005); Member, Legislative Advisory Committee, Community Council, Children's Services, Charleston, WV (1985-1992); Residential Chair, Trustee, United Way (1977-1992) **Awards:** Master Gardner Emeritus, Garden Club of America (2018); Directors Award; 30 Year Board Leadership Award (2016); 30 Year Service Award, Ronald McDonald House (2015); Award, Garden Club of America (2012); 25 Years of Board Service Award (2012); Service Award, Ronald McDonald House, Charleston Area Medical Center Auxiliary (2011); 20 Years of Board Service Award, Ronald McDonald House (2002); Award, West Virginia State Garden Club (1985); Outstanding Community Leadership Award (2000) **Membership:** Ronald McDonald House and Charleston Area Medical Center Auxiliary; Park Foundation, Vice Chairman (2008-Present); Vice President, Friends Coonskin Park Foundation (2003-Present); Standing Leadership and Community Service Member (2012); Friends of Spring Hill Cemetery, Board Member (2010); Vice President (2005-2009); Garden Club of America, Diaectrons, National Vice-Chair, Scholarship Committee (1990); Robert E. Lee Memorial Association, West Virginia Director, Secretary to the Board (1975); National Society of Colonial Dames of America **Marquis Who's Who Honors:** Albert Nelson Marquis Lifetime Achievement Award (2017) **Hobbies:** Tennis; Traveling, Gardening, Fishing, Reading **Shipping Address:** 153 Abney Circle, Charleston, WV, 25314

Kristyn M. Snyer McKenna

Title: Attorney **Industry:** Law and Legal Services **Company Name:** Law Office of Kristyn Snyer McKenna **Education:** JD, Suffolk University Law School (1993); BA, College of the Holy Cross (1990) **Career:** Principal, Law Office of Kristyn Snyer McKenna **Civic:** Board Member, Merrimack Valley Catholic Charities; Board Member, Saint Camillus Catholic Church; Board Member, Boys and Girls Club of Greater Lowell **Awards:** Judge Blitzman Award (2008) **Membership:** Juvenile Justice Center, American Bar Association; American Academy of Criminal Defense Attorneys; Greater Lowell Bar Association; Massachusetts Juvenile Bar Association; National Association of Counsel For Children **To what do you attribute your success:** Ms. Snyer McKenna attributes her success to her hard work. **Why did you become involved in your profession or industry:** Ms. Snyer McKenna became involved in her profession because she always wanted to help and represent children. **What do you consider to be the highlight of your career:** The highlight of Ms. Snyer McKenna's career is having the ability to help her clients over the past 20 years. **Hobbies:** Singing; Biking **Business Address:** 9 Billerica Road, Law Office of Kristyn Snyer McKenna, Chelmsford, MA, 01824

Carl Lionel Soares

Title: Quality Assurance Professional, Metrologist **Industry:** Other **Company Name:** SE Regional Network **Date of Birth:** 09/14/1944 **Place of Birth:** New Bedford **State:** MA **Parents:** Lionel Francis Soares; Sarah Vincent (Flor) Soares **Marital Status:** Married **Spouse Name:** Maria T. Ortiz (7/9/2005); Jean Rosalee Bettencourt (11/11/1965, Divorced 10/1974) **Children:** Kevin Carl; Keith Christopher; Kenneth Craig **Education:** Coursework in Industrial Technology, Fitchburg State University (1980-Present) **Career:** Director of Facilities Services, Southeast Regional Network, Inc. (2006-Present); President, The Maids (1995-2006); Treasurer, The Maids (1995-2006); Manager, The Maids (1995-2006); Metrologist, Department Quality Director, Raytheon Company (1979-1996); Quality Control Superintendent, Raytheon Company (1982-1985); Computer-Controlled Test Equipment Technician, Raytheon Company (1966-1979); Quality Assurance Specialist, Cornell Dubilier (1965-1966) **Civic:** Vice President, First Night New Bedford (2003); Treasurer, First Night New Bedford (2003); Board of Directors, First Night New Bedford (1996-2005); Board of Directors, Zoological Society, Buttonwood Park Zoo (Now Buttonwood Park Zoological Society); Events Chairman Secretary, Zoological Society, Buttonwood Park Zoo (Now Buttonwood Park Zoological Society); Former Clerk, Southeastern Network Agencies; Former Chairman, Board of Directors, New Bedford Council on Substance Abuse; President, SEMCOA (Now Southeast Massachusetts Council on Addiction) **Military Service:** U.S. Navy (1962-1965) **Membership:** Rotary International; The American Legion **Marquis Who's Who Honors:** Albert Nelson Marquis Lifetime Achievement Award (2017); Distinguished Humanitarian (2017) **Hobbies:** Gardening; Bicycling; Records and CDs; Computers; Music; Playing bass guitar **Religion:** Roman Catholic **Shipping Address:** 205 Maple St, New Bedford, MA, 02740

Mary Sorrows Hughes

Title: Artist **Industry:** Fine Art **Date of Birth:** 10/28/1945 **Place of Birth:** Washington **State:** DC **Parents:** Dr. Howard Earl Sorrows; Martha Jane (Summerville) Sorrows **Marital Status:** Married **Spouse Name:** Frank Broox Hughes, MD (5/22/1967) **Children:** Broox Bradley **Education:** EdB, Centenary College of Louisiana (1978); BA in Art, Centenary College of Louisiana (1967); Coursework, American University, Bossier Parish Community College, Louisiana Tech University **Certifications:** Certification to Teach **Career:** Art Studio Owner, Freelance Artist, Shreveport, LA (1979-Present); Draftsman, Department of Civil Engineering, Texaco, Chevron U.S.A. Inc., New Orleans, LA (1967-1970) **Civic:** Board of Directors, Shreveport Art Guild, Friends of the Meadows Museum (2000-2003); Worker, Habitat for Humanity, Shreveport, LA (1994); Trustee, St. Luke's Methodist Church, Shreveport, LA (1993-1995); Worker, Habitat for Humanity, Shreveport, LA (1992); Artport Airport Exhibit and Fundraiser for AIDS, Shreveport, LA (1991-2015); President, Child Care Services, Inc. of Northwest Louisiana, Shreveport, LA (1991) **Creative Works:** Featured Artist, Country Roads Magazine (2010); Contributing Illustrator, "The New Creative Artist by Nita Leland" (2006); Featured Artist, Watercolor Magazine (2003); Featured Art Donor, Philadelphia House Auction and Fundraiser for AIDS (2003); Contributing Illustrator, "Splash 7: The Qualities of Light" (2002); Contributing Illustrator, "Floral Inspirations" (1998); Contributing Illustrator, "Best of Watercolor: Painting Color" (1997); Contributing Illustrator, "The Best of Watercolor" (1995) **Awards:** Special Award, Hoover Watercolor Society (2010); St. Cuthberts Mill Merchandise Award, Southwestern Watercolor Society (2009); Sidney Hoover Memorial Award, Hoover Watercolor Society (2009); Transparent Watercolor Award, Hoover Watercolor Society (2006); Jurors Choice Award, Hoover Watercolor Society (2006); President Award, International Show, Louisiana Watercolor Society (2005) **Membership:** President, Louisiana Artist Roster (1998); President, Louisiana Artists (1998); Signature Member, Watercolor West (1996); President, Louisiana Artist Roster (1994); President, Louisiana Artists (1994); Signature Member, Southwestern Watercolor Society (1991); President, Hoover Watercolor Society (1986); Medical Auxiliary Wives Club, St. Luke's United Methodist Church, Shreveport, LA (1976-2018) **Marquis Who's Who Honors:** Albert Nelson Marquis Lifetime Achievement Award (2017) **Hobbies:** Exercise; Gardening; Travel; Flute; Photography; Ancestry; Choir **Political Affiliations:** Democrat **Religion:** Methodist **Shipping Address:** 530 Atkins Avenue, Shreveport, LA, 71104

Dennis K. Spillane

Title: Lawyer **Industry:** Law and Legal Services **Company Name:** Office of Professional Discipline, New York State Education Department **Date of Birth:** 09/15/1953 **Place of Birth:** New York City **State:** NY **Parents:** Denis Joseph Spillane; Mary Kate (Sullivan) Spillane **Education:** Post-Masters Certificate in Business, Pace University (1992); MS in Taxation, Pace University (1986); JD, New York Law School (1978); BA, Manhattan College, Magna Cum Laude (1974) **Career:** Supervising Attorney, Office of Professional Discipline, New York State Education Department (1987-Present); Senior Adjunct Professor, Pace University Graduate Business School (1987-Present); Principal Attorney, New York State Tax Department, New York, NY (1985-1987); Assistant District Attorney, Borough of the Bronx, New York, NY (1978-1985) **Career Related:** Professor, Law and Taxation, Pace University (1987-Present) **Creative Works:** Author, "PCAOB and SEC Referrals to the Office of Professional Discipline: What New York CPAs Need to Know," The CPA Journal (2015); Author, "Representing a Licensed Professional in Administrative Disciplinary Proceedings," ABA Government, Law and Policy Journal (2005); Author, "PCAOB Enforcement: What to Expect," The CPA Journal (2004); Author, "New York State's Professional Disciplinary Process," Tax and Regulatory Bulletin (1994); Author, "Representing the Licensed Professional: A Primer," New York Law Journal (1990); Author, "New York's Right to Counsel-The Pendulum Swings," New York Law Journal (1983); Author, "Frisking the Fourth Amendment," Human Rights Law Journal (1982); Author, "Child Snatching," Human Rights Law Review (1978); Contributor, Articles to Professional Journals **Membership:** Connecticut Bar Association; New York State Bar Association; BADC **Bar Admissions:** Connecticut (1989); The District of Columbia Bar (1988); U.S. Court of Appeals for the Second Circuit (1988); Supreme Court of the United States (1988); United States Tax Court (1986); New York (1979); U.S. District Court Eastern District of New York (1979); U.S. District Court Southern District of New York (1979); U.S. Court of Federal Claims; United States Court of International Trade **Political Affiliations:** Conservative **Religion:** Roman Catholic **Shipping Address:** 11 Crusher Road, Bedford, NY, 10506

William M. Stall, PhD

Title: Weed Scientist, Educator **Industry:** Education/Educational Services **Date of Birth:** 04/14/1944 **Marital Status:** Married **Spouse Name:** Donna Duncan Stall (1983) **Education:** PhD in Vegetable Crops, University of Florida (1973); MS in Vegetable Crops, University of Florida (1969); BS in Botany and Plant Pathology, The Ohio State University (1967) **Career:** Professor Emeritus, University of Florida (2009-Present); Professor, University of Florida, Gainesville (1985-2009); Extension Specialist and Weed Management (1980-1988); Associate Professor, University of Florida, Gainesville (1980-1985); Extension Agent, Dade County Cooperative Extension Service (1974-1980) **Career Related:** Extension Specialist and Weed Management (1980-2009) **Creative Works:** Author, Book Chapters; Contributor, Articles, Professional Journals **Awards:** Outstanding Research Award, Florida Fruit and Vegetable Association (2001); Outstanding Weed Scientist Award, Florida Weed Science Society (2000); Extension Education Aides Award, American Society for Horticultural Science (1994, 2000); Outstanding Extension Award, Weed Science Society of America (1995) **Membership:** President, Florida Weed Science Society (1994-1995); Minor Use Committee, Weed Science Society of America (1991-1994); Director-at-Large, Florida State Horticultural Society (1985-1989); Director, Florida Weed Science Society (1985-1989); Chairman, IPM Working Group, American Society for Horticultural Science (1986); Vice President, Vegetable Section, Florida State Horticultural Society (1983); Florida Fruit and Vegetable Association **Marquis Who's Who Honors:** Albert Nelson Marquis Lifetime Achievement Award (2017) **Shipping Address:** 10101 SW 35th Place, Gainesville, FL, 32608

Russell Starkey

Title: Energy Executive (Retired) **Industry:** Oil & Energy **Date of Birth:** 07/20/1942 **Place of Birth:** Lumberport **State:** WV/USA **Parents:** Russell Bruce Starkey; Dorotha Mable (Field) Starkey **Marital Status:** Married **Spouse Name:** Joan McClellan (5/27/1966) **Children:** Christine; Pamela; Joanne **Education:** Graduate Student, North Carolina State University (1974-1975); Graduate Student, University of New Haven (1972-1973); Postgraduate Studies, U.S. Navy Schools (1964-1966); BS in Physics, Miami University, Oxford, OH (1964) **Career:** Retired Consultant (2010-Present); Vice President, General Manager, USEC Government Services (2009-2010); Vice President, American Centrifuge Project (2008-2009); Vice President of Operations, U.S. Enrichment Corporation, Paducah, KY (2005-2008); Plant General Manager, U.S. Enrichment Corporation, Paducah, KY (2001-2005); Training Manager, U.S. Enrichment Corporation, Paducah, KY (1998-2001); Consultant, U.S. Enrichment Corporation, Paducah, KY (1997-1998); From Director of the Industrial Electrotechnology Laboratory to Vice President and General Technology Manager, Advanced Energy Corporation (1993-1997); Executive Vice President, Energy Management Division, Hesco, Inc. (1993); Vice President, Nuclear Service Department, Brunswick Nuclear Project Department (1992-1993); Vice President, Brunswick Nuclear Project Department (1989-1992); Manager, Brunswick Nuclear Project Department (1988-1989); Manager, Nuclear Safety and Environmental Services Department, Carolina Power & Light Company, Raleigh, NC (1985-1988); Manager, Environmental Services, Carolina Power & Light Company, Raleigh, NC (1984-1985); Plant Manager, H. B. Robinson Steam Electric Plant, Hartsville, SC (1977-1983); Supervisor, Quality Assurance, Superintendent, Technology and Administration, Brunswick Steam Electric Plant, Southport, NC (1975-1977); From Senior Engineer, Nuclear Generation Section to Principal Engineer, Carolina Power & Light Company, Raleigh, NC (1973-1975) **Career Related:** Alumni Advisory Board, College of Arts and Science, Miami University, Ohio; Advisory Board, Lambda Chi Alpha Fraternity; Secretary, Treasurer, NROTC **Military Service:** Officer, Submarine Force, U.S. Navy (1964-1973) **Awards:** Alben Barkley Distinguished Citizen Award, McCracken County (2005); Named Honorary Kentucky Colonel **Membership:** American Nuclear Society; Kiwanis Club, Oxford, OH **Marquis Who's Who Honors:** Albert Nelson Marquis Lifetime Achievement Award (2017) **Hobbies:** Stamp collecting; Coin collecting **Political Affiliations:** Republican **Religion:** Lutheran **Business Address:** P.O. Box 189, Oxford, OH, 45056

Allan J. Sternstein

Title: Director of IP and Entrepreneurship Clinic, Professor of Intellectual Property **Industry:** Education/Educational Services **Company Name:** University of Arizona **Date of Birth:** 06/07/1948 **Place of Birth:** Chicago **State:** IL **Parents:** Milton Sternstein; Celia (Kaganove) Sternstein **Marital Status:** Married **Spouse Name:** Marilyn F. (Davis) Green **Children:** Jeffery A.; Amy R. Eisenstein; Julia S. Yob; Tracy Green Franklin; Jordan Green; Blake Green **Education:** JD, School of Law, Loyola University, Chicago, IL (1977); MS, University of Michigan (1972); BS, University of Illinois (1970) **Career:** Director, Intellectual Property and Entrepreneurship Clinic, James E. Rogers College of Law, University of Arizona (2015-Present); Professor of Intellectual Property, James E. Rogers College of Law, University of Arizona (2015-Present); Head of IP Litigation, Lathrop & Gage LLP (2014-2017); Chair IP Division, Lathrop & Gage LLP (2013-2017); Partner, Lathrop & Gage LLP (2013-2017); Director IP and IP Litigation Department, Dykema Gossett PLLC (2007-2013); Head of Intellectual Property Group, Dykema Gossett PLLC (2005-2007); Partner, Dykema Gossett PLLC (2005-2013); Managing Partner, Brinks Hofer Gilson Lione, Chicago, IL (1996-1999); Partner, Brinks Hofer Gilson Lione, Chicago, IL (1987-2005); Division Patent Counsel, Abbott Laboratories, Chicago, IL (1984-1987); Partner, Neuman, Williams, Anderson & Olson (1976-1984); Associate, Neuman, Williams, Anderson & Olson (1976-1979); Patent Agent, Sunbeam Corp., Oak Brook, IL (1974-1976) **Career Related:** Lecturer, University of Victoria, Victoria, BC, Canada (2004); Lecturer, Oxford University, Oxford, England (2003); Lecturer, University of Victoria, Victoria, BC, Canada (2002) **Creative Works:** Co-author, Designing an Effective Intellectual Property Compliance Program; Contributor, Articles, Professional Journals **Membership:** Committee Chairman, Intellectual Property Law Association of Chicago (1982); American Bar Association; Intellectual Property Owners Association; AIPLA **Bar Admissions:** U.S. District Court, Central District, State of Illinois (2013); U.S. District Court, Eastern District, State of Texas (2007); Fifth Circuit, U.S. Court of Appeals (2003); U.S. District Court, Eastern District, State of Wisconsin (2003); Federal Circuit, U.S. Court of Appeals (1982); Seventh Circuit, U.S. Court of Appeals (1979); U.S. District Court, Western District, State of Michigan (1990); U.S. District Court, Eastern District, State of Michigan (1986); U.S. District Court, Northern District, State of Ohio (1977); U.S. District Court, Northern District, State of Illinois (1977) **Marquis Who's Who Honors:** Albert Nelson Marquis Lifetime Achievement Award (2018) **Religion:** Jewish **Business Address:** 1145 N Mountain Avenue, Tucson, AZ, 85719

David Pentland Stewart

Title: Professor from Practice **Industry:** Education/Educational Services **Company Name:** Georgetown University Law Center **Date of Birth:** 12/24/1943 **Place of Birth:** Milwaukee **State:** WI **Parents:** James Pentland Stewart; Frederica (Stockwell) Stewart **Marital Status:** Married **Spouse Name:** Jennifer Kilmer (6/21/1986) **Children:** Daniel; Mary Elizabeth; Jason; Jonathan **Education:** LLM, New York University (1975); JD, Yale University (1972); MA, Yale University (1971); AB, Princeton University (1966) **Career:** Professor from Practice, Georgetown University Law Center (2014-Present); Visiting Professor of Law, Georgetown University Law Center (2008-2014); Assistant Legal Adviser (Senior Executive Service), U.S. Department of State, Washington, DC (1982-2008); Attorney Adviser and Special Assistant, Office of Legal Adviser, U.S. Department of State, Washington, DC (1976-1982); Associate, Donovan, Leisure, Newton & Irvine, New York, NY (1971-1976) **Career Related:** Co-Reporter, Restatement (Fourth), Foreign Relations Law of the United States (2014-2018); Elected Member, Inter-American Juridical Committee (2008-2016); American Law Institute (2004); Adjunct Professor, Johns Hopkins School of Advanced International Studies (2001-2012); Visiting Lecturer, National Law Center, George Washington University (1993-1999) **Creative Works:** Author, "International Criminal Law in a Nutshell," Second Edition (2018); Author, "The Foreign Sovereign Immunization Act: A Guide for Judges," Second Edition (2018); Co-Author, "International Human Rights in a Nutshell," Fifth Edition (2017); Co-Author, "International and Transnational Criminal Law," Second Edition (2014); Co-Editor, Digest of United States Practice in International Law," Multiple Volumes (1989-2005) **Awards:** Theberge Award for Private International Law, American Bar Association (2008); Charles Fahy Award for Distinguished Adjunct Faculty Teaching, Georgetown University (2003-2004); Vicennial Medal for Distinguished Service, Georgetown University (2003); Superior and Distinguished Honor Awards, Secretary's Career Achievement Award, U.S. Department of State **Membership:** President, American Branch of the International Law Association (2014-Present); President-Elect, American Branch of the International Law Association (2010-2014) **Bar Admissions:** District of Columbia (1976); Second Circuit, U.S. Court of Appeals (1973); U.S. District Court, Eastern District, State of New York (1973); U.S. District Court, Southern District, State of New York (1973) **Marquis Who's Who Honors:** Albert Nelson Marquis Lifetime Achievement Award (2017); Distinguished Humanitarian (2017) **Business Address:** 600 New Jersey Avenue NW, Hotung 6018, Washington, DC, 20001-2005 **Website:** https://www.law.georgetown.edu/faculty/stewart-david-p.cfm

David Witherington Stewart

Title: Novelist **Industry:** Publishing **Company Name:** Coreopsis Publications, LLC **Date of Birth:** 02/09/1939 **Place of Birth:** Marion **State:** IN **Parents:** Edgar Allen Stewart Jr.; Faye Maxine (Cummings) Stewart **Marital Status:** Married **Spouse Name:** Annette Louise Witherington (12/17/1962, Deceased 8/1999); Ruth Ada Valk (8/26/1961, Divorced) **Children:** Edna **Education:** BS in Physics, University of Florida, Gainesville, FL (1959) **Career:** Owner, General Manager, Coreopsis Publications (2004-Present); Owner, President, L&D Consulting, Titusville, FL (1996-2009); Program Developer, Manager, Florida Operations Space System Division, Rockwell International, Kennedy Space Center, Florida (1992-1996); Project Manager Advisor Program and Business Development, Rockwell International, Kennedy Space Center, FL (1991-1992); Manager, Advisory Program, Rockwell International, Kennedy Space Center, Florida (1989-1991); Project Manager, Advisory Programs, Rockwell International, Kennedy Space Center, FL (1985-1989); Project Manager of Design, Rockwell International, Kennedy Space Center, Florida (1984-1985); Project Manager of Software, Rockwell International, Kennedy Space Center, Florid (1982-1984); Supervisor, Orbiter Software, Rockwell International, Kennedy Space Center, Florida (1979-1981); Prime System Integrative Engineer Shuttle, Rockwell International, Kennedy Space Center, Florida (1978-1979); Lead Engineer of Avionics, Rockwell International, Kennedy Space Center, Florida (1975-1978); Lead Engineer Apollo, Rockwell International, Kennedy Space Center, Florida (1967-1974); Lead Engineer Sprint, Martin-Orlando, Orlando, FL (1966-1967); Lead Engineer Gemini-Titan, Martin Canaveral, Cape Canaveral, FL (1963-1966); Senior Engineer Atlas, General Dynamics/Convair, Cape Canaveral, FL (1959-1963) **Civic:** Volunteer, Treasurer, Brevard Humanity Center, Inc (2000-2006); President, Brevard Adult Literacy Volumes, Inc. (2000-2004); Chairman, Marine Resources Council of East Florida (2000-2002); Secretary, Space Coast Grant Profiles Network (1997-1999); Chairman, Marine Resources Council of East Florida (1996-1997); President-elect, Space Coast Development Commission (1995-1996); **Creative Works:** Author, "Seeking Success: A Memoir" (2016); Author, "Serious Consequences" (2013); Author, "Within the Wind: Seeking Spiritual Deliverance" (2010); Author, "Psychic Redemption" (2009) **Membership:** Institute of Certified Professional Managers; Accredited Professional Consultant, American Consultant League **Marquis Who's Who Honors:** Distinguished Humanitarian (2017) **Political Affiliations:** Republican **Religion:** Unitarian Universalist **Shipping Address:** PO Box 5869, Titusville, FL, 32783 **Website:** http://davidwstewart.com

Annsley Chapman Strong

Title: Interior Designer **Industry:** Architecture & Construction **Company Name:** Strong Studio Designs **Date of Birth:** 07/18/1947 **Place of Birth:** Paterson **State:** NJ **Parents:** Donald John Chapman; Margaret Lovell Brawley Chapman **Marital Status:** Married **Spouse Name:** George Gordon Strong, Jr. (11/30/1974) **Children:** George Gordon, III; Courtney Chapman Strong-Thomas; Meredith Annsley Strong-White; Alexis Palmer **Education:** BA, Wheaton College, Norton, MA (1969) **Certifications:** Interior Designers Guild, Beverly Hills, CA (1975); New York School of Design (1969) **Career:** Principal, Strong Studio Designs, La Canada, CA (1984) **Career Related:** Hathaway-Sycamores Child & Family Services Board, Pasadena, CA (2013-Present); Bishop Stevens Foundation Board, Episcopal Diocese of Los Angeles, Pasadena, CA (2007-Present); USC Verdugo Hills Hospital Foundation Board, Glendale, CA (2013-2016); "The Reader's Retreat," Pasadena Showcase House of Design (2013); Governing Board Chair, USC Verdugo Hills Hospital, Glendale, CA (2010-2012); Board Chair, Hathaway-Sycamores Child & Family Services, Pasadena, CA (2007-2009); Board Chair, USC Verdugo Hills Hospital Foundation, Glendale, CA (2006-2008); Wheaton College President's Commission, Norton, MA (2001-2005); Board Chair, Verdugo Hills Hospital Foundation, Glendale, CA (1998-2000); Co-founder, La Canada Sports Coalition, La Canada, CA (1996); Commissioner, AYSO Region 13, Pasadena, CA (1995-1997); Treasurer, AYSO Region 13, Pasadena, CA (1993-1995); Verdugo Hills Hospital Foundation Board, Glendale, CA (1987-2010); President, Verdugo Hills Hospital Women's Council, Glendale, CA (1984-1986); President, La Canada Junior Women's Club, La Canada, CA (1983-1984); Investment Management, Wells Fargo Bank, Beverly Hills, Los Angeles, CA (1975-1977); Wells Fargo Fund Advisory Corporation, San Francisco, CA (1971-1973); Fidelity Investment Management Services, Boston, MA (1969-1971) **Awards:** Celebrating Children Award, Hathaway-Sycamores (2014); Humanitarian Award, USC Verdugo Hills Hospital (2012); Bill Carroll Lifetimes Achievement Award, AYSO (2000); Women of the Year Award (1990); 20th Century Award, Pasadena YMCA **Hobbies:** Painting; Piano; Bridge; Golf **Political Affiliations:** Republican **Business Address:** 5455 Castle Knoll Road, La Canada Flintridge, CA, 91011

James Francis Suess

Title: Clinical Psychologist (Retired) **Industry:** Media & Entertainment **Company Name:** State University of New York **Date of Birth:** 08/08/1950 **Place of Birth:** Evanston **State:** IL **Parents:** James Francis Seuss; Rae Love (Miller) Seuss **Marital Status:** Married **Spouse Name:** Linda Grace Powell (7/3/1976) **Children:** Misty Lynne **Education:** PhD, The University of Southern Mississippi (1982); MS, The University of Southern Mississippi (1978); BS, The University of Southern Mississippi (1974) **Certifications:** Licensed Psychologist, State of New York; Licensed Psychologist, State of Alabama; Diplomate, American Board of Professional Psychology; Diplomate, American Board of Medical Psychotherapists; Diplomate, The Professional Academy of Custody Experts **Career:** Professor Emeritus, SUNY (2005-Present); Professor, Department of Psychology, South Alabama Medical Clinic (2001-2005); Associate Director, Jacobs School of Medicine and Biomedical Sciences, SUNY (1987-2005); Associate Director, ECMC, Buffalo, NY (1987-2005); Supervising Clinical Psychologist, Jacobs School of Medicine and Biomedical Sciences, SUNY (1984-1987); Supervising Clinical Psychologist, ECMC (1984-1987) **Career Related:** Adjunct Professor, Department of Psychology, University of South Alabama (2000-Present); Chief Executive Officer, Stillwood Clinical Group, Inc. (1998-Present); Clinical Director, Physicians' Psychiatric Clinic, Inc., Mobile, AL (1997-Present); Faculty Counsel, Jacobs School of Medicine and Biomedical Sciences, SUNY (1988-Present); Member, Speaker's Bureau, National Alliance on Mental Illness in Buffalo & Erie County (1986-Present); Consultant, Eerie County Department of Social Services (1985-Present); Visiting Professor, School of Medicine, Universidad Autonoma de Guadalajara (1985-Present) **Military Service:** With, United States Army Reserve, Special Operations, Weapons/Psychological Operations/Reconnaissance (2009-Present) **Creative Works:** Author, "Enduring My Journey Through Life: The Borderline Personality Disorders" (2005); Author, "Personality Disorder and Self Psychology" (1991); Author, "Annotated Bibliography of Sex Roles" (1972); **Awards:** Fellow, American Orthopsychiatry Association (Now Global Alliance for Behavioral Health and Social Justice); Fellow, Society for Personality Assessment **Membership:** Lifetime Member, The American Legion (2009-Present); Small Business Advisory Council, National Congressional Committee (2005-Present); **Marquis Who's Who Honors:** Albert Nelson Marquis Lifetime Achievement Award (2017) **Shipping Address:** 507 Evergreen Rd, Mobile, AL, 36608

John Dominic Sullivan

Title: Theater Producer **Industry:** Media & Entertainment **Date of Birth:** 10/06/1963 **Place of Birth:** La Crosse **State:** WI/USA **Marital Status:** Single **Education:** BFA in Theatre **Career:** Freelance Arts Consultant, La Crosse, WI (1993-Present); Managing Director, Fairbanks Shakespeare Theatre, Alaska (1997); Stage Manager, La Crosse Community Theatre, WI (1997); Play Producer, Great River Steamboat Company, La Crosse, WI (1996-1997); Assistant Director, Duluth Playhouse, MN (1985) **Creative Works:** Murder on the Mississippi's The Cabaret Killer **Awards:** Pacey Beers Scholarship Award, Theatre Department, University of Wisconsin - Superior (1985) **Political Affiliations:** Democrat **Religion:** Roman Catholic **Shipping Address:** W3691 County Road YY, La Crosse, WI, 54601

Rory E. Suomi, PhD

Title: Physical Education Educator **Industry:** Education/Educational Services **Date of Birth:** 05/07/1956 **Place of Birth:** Norwich **State:** WI **Marital Status:** Married **Spouse Name:** Joanne Suomi **Children:** Samara **Education:** PhD, Indiana University (1992) **Career:** Director, Special Needs Aquatic Program, University of Wisconsin-Stevens Point (1993-Present); Professor of Physical Education, University of Wisconsin-Stevens Point (1992); Professor of Health Sciences, University of Wisconsin-Stevens Point **Civic:** Women's Golf Coach, Special Olympics, Joseph P. Kennedy, Jr. Foundation for the Benefit of Persons with Intellectual Disabilities (2014-Present) **Creative Works:** Contributor, Article, "Joann Goes to China," PALAESTRA; Invited Speaker, Aquatic Therapy Program, Guangzhou, People's Republic of China **Awards:** Ethel & Ward Cable Family Faculty Hero Award, University of Wisconsin-Stevens Point (2017); Diversity Award, University of Wisconsin-Stevens Point (2015); Outstanding Researcher Award, Arthritis Foundation (2000); Robert W. Doucette Research Award, Arthritis Foundation (1999); Aquatic International Power Award, Hanley Wood Media, Inc. **Membership:** Alliance for Positive Health; ACSM; Lifetime Member, Wisconsin Health & Physical Education **Marquis Who's Who Honors:** Albert Nelson Marquis Lifetime Achievement Award (2017) **Hobbies:** Golf **Shipping Address:** 2300 4th Avenue, Stevens Point, WI, 54481

Phyllis Supino

Title: Medical Researcher **Industry:** Research **Company Name:** SUNY Downstate Medical Center **Date of Birth:** 12/30/1942 **Place of Birth:** New York **State:** NY **Marital Status:** Married **Spouse Name:** Rene Patrick Supino (6/7/1980) **Children:** Lisa Michelle; Christopher Davies **Education:** EdD in Science Education, Rutgers, the State University of New Jersey, New Brunswick, NJ (1976); BS in Biological Sciences, City College of New York (1964) **Career:** Professor, Medicine and Public Health, Director, Clinical Epidemiology and Clinical Research, Division of Cardiovascular Medicine, State University of New York Downstate College of Medicine, Brooklyn, NY (2008-Present); Adjunct Professor at Cornell Weill Medical College (2008-Present); Professor, Medicine and Public Health, State University of New York Downstate College of Medicine, Brooklyn, NY (2008-Present); Director, Clinical Epidemiology and Clinical Research, Division of Cardiovascular Medicine, State University of New York Downstate College of Medicine, Brooklyn, NY (2008-Present) **Career Related:** Director, Course, Principles of Research Methodology (2008-Present); Fellow, New York Academy of Medicine **Civic:** Volunteer, Morocco VI, U.S. Peace Corps, Washington, DC; Science Advisory Board, 15th-17th World Congress of Heart Diseases **Creative Works:** Publisher, "Principles of Research Methodology; Guide for Clinical Investigators," Springer Verlag (2012) **Awards:** Best Mentor of the Year Award, Mount Sinai School of Medicine (1998); Howard Gilman Award, Howard Gilman Foundation (1995); Phi Delta Kappa Award, Rutgers University (1976) **Membership:** American Society of Nuclear Cardiology and International Affiliates (2001) **Marquis Who's Who Honors:** Albert Nelson Marquis Lifetime Achievement Award (2017) **Shipping Address:** 46 Goodwin Terrace, Westwood, NJ, 07675

Kerry Peter Sutton

Industry: Graphic Design **Date of Birth:** 09/22/1944 **Place of Birth:** Matamata **State:** Waikato/New Zealand **Parents:** Alfred Sutton; Beatrice Frances Sutton **Education:** Student, Art Center College Design, LA (1966-1968); Diploma in Industrial Design, Wellington Polytechnic - Massey University, New Zealand (1964) **Career:** Designer, Auckland, New Zealand (1990) **Creative Works:** Designer, Inventor, I-ching Lucky Chime; Designer, Inventor, I-ching Incense Burner **Membership:** Royal Overseas League **Hobbies:** Travel

Benjamin Kinsell Swartz Jr., PhD

Title: Archaeologist, Educator **Industry:** Education/Educational Services **Company Name:** Ball State University **Date of Birth:** 06/23/1931 **Place of Birth:** Los Angeles **State:** CA **Parents:** Benjamin Kinsell Swartz; Maxine Marietta (Pearce) Swartz **Marital Status:** Married **Spouse Name:** Cyrilla Casillas (10/23/1966) **Children:** Benjamin Kinsell, III; Frank Casillas **Education:** PhD, University of Arizona, Tucson, AZ (1964); MA, University of California, Los Angeles (1958); BA, University of California, Los Angeles (1954); AA, Los Angeles City College, Summa Cum Laude (1952) **Career:** Professor Emeritus, Ball State University, Muncie, IN (2001-Present); Professor, Ball State University, Muncie, IN (1972-2001); Associate Professor, Ball State University, Muncie, IN (1968-1972); Assistant Professor of Anthropology, Ball State University, Muncie, IN (1964-1968); Research Associate, Klamath County Museum, Oregon (1961-1962); Curator, Klamath County Museum, Oregon (1959-1961) **Career Related:** Summer Visiting Professor, University of Nevada, Las Vegas (2009); Exchange Professor, University of Yaounde, Cameroon (1984-1985); Visiting Senior Lecturer, University of Ghana (1970-1971); Field Researcher, North America and West Africa; Executive Board, American Committee to Advance the Study of Petroglyphs and Pictographs; President, American Committee to Advance the Study of Petroglyphs and Pictographs; Representative, International Federation of Rock Art Organizations, American Committee to Advance the Study of Petroglyphs and Pictographs; Overseas Education Board of Rock Art Research; Advisory Board, American Committee for Preservation of Archaeological Collections; Fellow, American Association for the Advancement of Science **Civic:** Klamath County Chairman, Oregon Statehood Centennial (1959) **Military Service:** U.S. Navy (1954-1956) **Creative Works:** Author, "Rock Art and Posterity" (1991); Author, "Proceedings of the First International South African Rock Art Association Conference" (1991); Author, "Indiana's Prehistoric Past" (1981); Author, "West African Culture Dynamics" (1980); Contributor, Reviews, Articles, Professional Journals; Author, Books, Monographs in Field **Membership:** Indiana Academy of Science; Associate, Current Anthropology; Society of American Archaeology; International Committee of Rock Art; Sigma Xi; National Council, Lambda Alpha **Marquis Who's Who Honors:** Albert Nelson Marquis Lifetime Achievement Award (2017) **T Hobbies:** Walking; Travel **Shipping Address:** 805 W Charles Street, Muncie, IN, 47305

Theresa Rose Tack

Title: Women's Health Nurse **Industry:** Medicine & Health Care **Date of Birth:** 11/10/1940 **Place of Birth:** Luneburg **State:** VT **Parents:** Gustave L. Fournier; Blanche Rose Fournier **Marital Status:** Divorced **Children:** Lynelle Scullard; Karyn Terry; LeAnn Gomez **Education:** Diploma, Central Maine General Hospital (1961) **Certifications:** Certified, ACLS, American Heart Association; Certified, Neonatal Resuscitation, American Heart Association; Licensed Eucharistic Minister **Career:** Staff Nurse, Wasatch County Hospital, Heber City, UT (1985-1997); Staff Nurse, St. John's Hospital, Red Wing, MN (1979-1985); Staff Nurse, Cardiovascular Unit, Methodist Hospital, Houston, TX (1962-1965); Staff Nurse, Neurosurgery Unit, Hillcrest Medical Center, Tulsa, OK (1961-1962) **Civic:** Pastoral Care Team, Local Church; Habitat for Humanity; Meals of Hope; St. Monica's Episcopal Church; Miracles in Action; Empty Bowls **Creative Works:** Columnist, Nurses Notes in Wasatch Wave, Heber City, Utah (1990-1997) **Membership:** Association of Contemplative Sisters; Order of St. Luke **Marquis Who's Who Honors:** Distinguished Humanitarian (2017) **Hobbies:** Reading; Knitting; Crocheting; Tatting; Arts and Crafts **Religion:** Episcopalian **Shipping Address:** 5015 Cedar Springs Drive, Apt. 103, Naples, FL, 34110

Natalie J. Tackett

Title: State Agency Administrator **Industry:** Government Administration/Government Relations/Government Services **Company Name:** Missouri General Assembly **Place of Birth:** Wausau **State:** WI **Parents:** Roland Elsworth Kannenberg; Natalie (Zanon) Kannenberg **Marital Status:** Single **Spouse Name:** William Marshall Tackett (7/1975, Deceased) **Children:** Roland; Scott; Renee; William **Education:** PhD Candidate, University of Missouri MA in English, Northwest Missouri State University (1968); BA in English, Northwest Missouri State University, With Highest Honors (1966) **Career:** Director, Oversight Division, Missouri General Assembly, Missouri Legislature (1984-Present); Research Analyst, Missouri House of Representatives, Missouri Legislature (1981-1984); Research Director, Missouri Department of Revenue (1978-1981); Instructor of English, Northwest Missouri State University (1970-1978); Instructor of English, Tarkio College (1968-1970); Budget Analyst, Missouri House of Representatives; Research Director, Missouri Department of Revenue **Civic:** Member, Gratz & Mary Gunn Brown Foundation (2009-2010); President, Cole County Historical Society and Museum (1996-1998, 2004-2006); Councilman, Northwest Missouri Subarea Council, Area II Health Systems Agency (1976-1977); Governor's Advisory Council for Comprehensive Health Planning, State of Missouri (1976); Member, Community Leaders and Noteworthy Americans (1975-1976); President, Board of Directors, Nodaway County Health Center (1974-1976); Chairman, Citizen's Committee for a County Health Center, Nodaway County, Missouri (1972-1974); Member, Board of Directors, Nodaway County Health Center **Awards:** Recipient, Alex & Kathrine Hope Award (2003, 2009); Honoree, Show Me Missouri: Women Selected Biographies (1989); Honoree, Outstanding Contribution in the Area of Legislation, Missouri Division, AAUW (1987); Recipient, Woman of Distinction Award, AAUW (1984); Recipient, Outstanding Woman Award, Maryville Chapter, Soroptimist International of the Americas (1975); Recipient, Joy Of Achievement Award (1975) **Membership:** Legislative Committee, AAUW (1985-1987); President, Missouri Division, AAUW (1983-1985); Legislative Program Evaluation Society, National Conference of State Legislatures **Marquis Who's Who Honors:** Albert Nelson Marquis Lifetime Achievement Award (2017) **Shipping Address:** 2308 Jason Ct, Jefferson City, MO, 65109

Martha H. Talbot

Title: Secretary-Treasurer **Industry:** Business Management/Business Services **Company Name:** Lee Talbot Associates International **Date of Birth:** 08/03/1932 **Place of Birth:** San Francisco **State:** CA **Parents:** Francis Bourn Hayne; Anna (Walcott) Hayne **Marital Status:** Married **Spouse Name:** Dr. Lee M. Talbot **Children:** Lawrence Hayne Talbot; Russell Merriam Talbot **Education:** BA, Vassar College (1954) **Career:** Secretary-Treasurer, Lee Talbot Associates International, McLean (1991-Present); Secretary-Treasurer, Talbot Racing Associates, McLean, VA (1983-Present); Owner, Director, Talbot Hayne Vineyard, St. Helena, CA (1988-2013); Member, Treasurer, Fairfax County Park Authority, Fairfax, VA (1973-1977); Research Associate, Smithsonian Institution, Washington, DC (1966-1975); Assistant Coordinator, International Biological Programme, London (1966); Assistant Director, Southeast Asia Project, International Union for Conservation of Nature/ Natural Resources (1964-1965); Co-Director, East African Ecological Research Project, Kenya and Tanzania (1959-1963); Co-Founder, Assistant Director, Student Conservation Program, U.S. National Parks (1955-1959) **Career Related:** Honorary Director, Student Conservation Association (1987-Present); Defenders Wildlife National Council (2011-Present); Vice President, Rachel Carson Council (1998-Present); Treasurer, Rachel Carson Council (1994-1998); Rachel Carson Council (1975-1994); Board Director, Student Conservation Association (1966-1978, 1983-1987); Audubon Naturalist Society (1975-1978) **Civic:** Member, Advisory Council State of the Parks Program, National Parks Conservation Association (2010-Present); **Creative Works:** Co-Author or Editor, Six Books and Monographs; Contributor, 25 Articles, Various Professional Journals **Awards:** Lowell Thomas Award, The Explorers Club (2013); Flag Award, The Explorers Club (2007-2011); Honorary Award, The Explorers Club (2009); Co-Recipient, World Communications on Protected Areas East Asia Award (2005); Resolution of Honor (1999); Conservation Service Award, U.S. Department of the Interior (1986); Board Tribute to Co-Founder, Student Conservation Association (1984); Distinguished Alumna Award, Katharine Branson School (1981); Service Honor Award, Defenders of Wildlife (1974-1977); Outstanding Public Award The Wildlife Society (1963); Cinema Golden Eagle Award for Documentary Film (1968); Grantee, New York Zoological Society (1961) **Membership:** Treasurer, Washington Group (1990-1996); Treasurer (1984-1989); Board Director, Member Society Woman Geographers (1972-1975); Napa Valley Grape Growers Association; Rachels Network **Shipping Address:** 6656 Chilton Court, McLean, VA, 22101

Gerilyn Tandberg

Title: Associate Professor **Industry:** Education/Educational Services **Company Name:** Louisiana State University **Date of Birth:** 08/23/1942 **Place of Birth:** Rugby **State:** ND **Parents:** Otto Tandberg; Edna Tandberg **Marital Status:** Widowed **Spouse Name:** Maurice Berger (8/2/1980) **Education:** Postgraduate Work, The Courtauld Institute of Art; Postgraduate Work, Women's and Gender Studies Program, Louisiana State University (1995); PhD in Theater Arts, University of Minnesota (1973); MA, University of Minnesota (1969); BS in English, Minot State University (1963); BS in French, Minot State University (1963); BS in Education, Minot State University (1963); Postgraduate Work, California State University Long Beach; Postgraduate Work, The University of Texas at Austin; Postgraduate Work, Central Saint Martins, University of the Arts London **Career:** Costume Designer, Theatre Department, Louisiana State University (1973-2009); Historian, Department of Theatre, Louisiana State University (1973-2009); Assistant Professor, Minot State University (1966-1973) **Career Related:** Dress Journal Reviewer, Costume Society of America (1991-2003); Costume Consultant, Films (1975-2000); Board Director, Region 6 Conference, Costume Society of America (1996); Co-Chair, Region 6 Conference, Costume Society of America (1996); Costume Designer, The University of Tulsa (1986-1987); Member, Theatre Advisory Board, Louisiana State Arts Council, Louisiana Department of Culture Recreation and Tourism (1981-1982); Costume Designer, Central State University (1981-1982); State Chair, American College Theatre Festival, The John F. Kennedy Center for the Performing Arts (1976-1980); Critic (1975-1979); Lecturer, Field; Vice President, Theaters **Civic:** Public Relations Officer, Flotilla 4-10, U.S. Coast Guard Auxiliary (1980-2006); Public Relations Officer, Regional Division IV, U.S. Coast Guard Auxiliary (1980-2006) **Military Service:** Coast Guard Auxiliary **Creative Works:** Author, General Learning Press; **Awards:** Grantee, The Student Technology Fee (2000-2002); Grantee, Manship Foundation (1996); Recipient, Gold Medallion, The John F. Kennedy Center for the Performing Arts (1984); Recipient, Outstanding Service Citation, Southwest Theatre Association **Membership:** Board Member, Costume Society of America (1988-1991); Vice President, Costume Society of America (1988-1991) **Marquis Who's Who Honors:** Albert Nelson Marquis Lifetime Achievement Award (2017) **Hobbies:** Reading; Vintage clothing; Jewelry; Scrimshaw; Buttons **Political Affiliations:** Democrat **Religion:** Unitarian Universalist **Shipping Address:** 5954 Parkbriar Ct, Baton Rouge, LA, 70816

Theodore Calvin Taub

Title: Attorney (Retired) **Industry:** Law and Legal Services **Company Name:** Shumaker, Loop & Kendrick, LLP **Date of Birth:** 01/01/1935 **Place of Birth:** Springfield **State:** MA **Parents:** Samuel Taub; Sara Lee (Daum) Taub **Marital Status:** Married **Spouse Name:** Roberta Mae Ginsburg (8/23/1959) **Children:** Tracy; Andrew; Adam **Education:** JD, University of Florida (1960); AB, Duke University (1956) **Certifications:** Board Certified Real Estate Lawyer, The Florida Bar **Career:** Attorney, Shumaker, Loop & Kendrick, LLP, Tampa, FL **Career Related:** City Attorney, City of Temple Terrace, Florida (1974-2007); Assistant City Attorney, City of Tampa, Florida (1963-1967); City Attorney, City of Oldsmar, Florida; Panelist in Field **Civic:** Environmental Efficiency Study Commission, State of Florida (1986-1988); Local Government Management Efficiency Committee (1979); Chairman, Tampa-Hillsborough County Expressway Authority, Florida (1974-1984); Hillsborough County Charter Commission, Florida (1966-1969); Founder, Tampa Bay Performing Arts Center (Now David A. Straz, Jr. Center for the Performing Arts); Member, Numerous Other Civic Activities including Appointments by Governors H. Burn, R. Askew and R. Graham **Creative Works:** Author, Lecturer, More than 150 Articles to Professional Journals **Awards:** Listee, Super Lawyers in Florida; Listee, Bar Register of Pre-Eminent Lawyers; Listee, Best Lawyers in America **Membership:** Chairman, Committee on Housing and Urban Environmental (1989-1991); Chairman, Real Property Litigation Committee (1981-1986); President, Tau Epsilon Phi, Duke University, Durham, NC (1956); Fellow, American Bar Foundation; Board of Governors, American College of Real Estate Lawyers; President, Florida Jaycees (Now JCI Florida); Legal Counsel, United States Jaycees; Tau Epsilon Phi **Bar Admissions:** Florida (1960); United States District Court for the Middle District of Florida; Supreme Court of the United States **Marquis Who's Who Honors:** Albert Nelson Marquis Lifetime Achievement Award (2017) **To what do you attribute your success:** Mr. Taub attributes his success to hard work. **Why did you become involved in your profession or industry:** Mr. Taub became involved in his profession out of a desire to serve. **Hobbies:** Reading **Political Affiliations:** Democrat **Religion:** Jewish **Shipping Address:** 4937 Lyford Cay Rd, Tampa, FL, 33629

Dorothea F. Ten Eyck

Title: Real Estate Agent **Industry:** Real Estate **Date of Birth:** 12/02/1923 **Place of Birth:** Pulaski County **State:** VA/USA **Parents:** Orel Cronk Fariss; Esther Mildred (Rexrode) Fariss **Marital Status:** Married **Spouse Name:** Robert L. Ten Eyck (12/29/1994); John S. Kreeger (8/27/1965, Deceased); George Ten Eyck (1/4/1947, Deceased) **Children:** Wendy Ten Eyck-Hites; George Lancaster, III; Kirk Farris; Thomas Emmerson (Deceased); Catheryn Kreeger-Shrive **Education:** Coursework, Indiana University **Career:** Real Estate Agent, Mars Manufacturing Company (1975-1985); Secretary, Mars Manufacturing Company (1975-1985); Partner, Santee Builders (1960-1963); Market Researcher, Proctor & Gamble (1944-1947) **Civic:** President, Women's Committee, Cincinnati Art Museum; Advisory Committee, Cincinnati Art Museum; Docent Emeritus, Cincinnati Art Museum; Indian Hill Church **Marquis Who's Who Honors:** Albert Nelson Marquis Lifetime Achievement Award (2017) **Hobbies:** Golf; Gardening; Travel; Volunteering; Painting; Knitting **Political Affiliations:** Independent **Religion:** Presbyterian **Shipping Address:** 3435 Golden Avenue, Apt. 304, Cincinnati, OH, 45226

Frances Terry

Title: Psychiatric Nurse Practitioner **Industry:** Medicine & Health Care **Date of Birth:** 01/07/1930 **Parents:** Walter Louis Jefferson; Ruth Williams Jefferson **Education:** MSN, University of Washington, Seattle, WA (1981); BSN, Seattle University (1951) **Certifications:** Licensed Advanced Registered Nurse Practitioner, American Nurses Credentialing Center **Career:** Public Health Nurse, Seattle King County Health Department, Seattle, WA; School Nurse, Seattle Public Schools; Director, Health Services, Northwest Center Developmentally Challenged, Seattle, WA; Nursing Instructor, Seattle University; Nurse Case Manager, Mental Health, University of Washington; Nursing Instructor, Shoreline Community College, Seattle, WA; Psychiatric Mental Health Practitioner, University of Washington-Harborview Medical Center, Seattle, WA; Prescribing and Consulting Nurse, Community House Mental Health Agency, Seattle, WA; Staff Nurse, Providence Hospital, Seattle, WA; Health Enhancement-program Nurse, Central Area Senior Center, Seattle, WA **Career Related:** Diabetes Support Group Volunteer Facilitator, Joslin Diabetes Center, Seattle, WA **Civic:** Auditor, Church Council, Immaculate Conception Church, Seattle, WA; Member, Seattle Central College Foundation **Awards:** Honoree, Black Heritage Society of Washington State (2008); Honoree, Washington State Nurses Society Centennial Celebration (2008); Honoree, Knights of Peter Claver Ladies (2008); Community Service Award, Seattle University (2004); Named to the Hall of Fame, Washington State Nurses Association (2000); Named Outstanding Nurse, University Washington-Harborview Medical Center (1993) **Membership:** Certified Retired Nurse Ambassador Circle; American Nurses Credentialing Center; Mary Mahoney Professional Nurses Association; Life Member, American Nurses' Association; Life Member, Alpha Kappa Alpha Sorority **Shipping Address:** 1422 33rd Avenue S, Seattle, WA, 98144

Priscilla D. Thomas, PhD

Title: County Commissioner (Retired) **Industry:** Government Administration/Government Relations/Government Services **Company Name:** Chatham County **Date of Birth:** 10/26/1934 **Place of Birth:** Savannah **State:** GA **Parents:** Marte Edwards Baker; Henry Robinson **Marital Status:** Married **Spouse Name:** Nathaniel Thomas **Children:** Deborah Thomas Cooper **Education:** PhD in Philosophy and Education, University of St. Louis; MS in Elementary Education, Bradley University, Peoria, IL; BS, Savannah State College **Certifications:** Certified Commissioner; Certified Independent Meeting and Event Planner; Certified Travel Consultant; Extended Vision Certification, Atlanta University; Administrative Certification, University of Georgia **Civic:** Fairlawn Baptist Church; Economic Opportunity Authority; Young Men's Christian Association; Ralph Mark Gilbert Civil Rights Museum; Savannah Development and Renewal Authority; National Association of the Blind **Military Service:** U.S. Air Force **Awards:** Award, South Chapter, Boys and Girls Clubs of America (2018); Humanitarian Award, Worldwide Who's Who (2014); Professional of the Year in Public Service, Worldwide Who's Who (2014); Top Female Executive, Who's Who Publishers (2014); Outstanding Community Service Award, National Council of Negro Women, Inc. (2014); Eponym, "The Dr. Priscilla Thomas Library," The Chatham Area Transit Authority Library (2014); Very Important Person Member, Excellence in Nonprofit Management, Worldwide Who's Who (2013); Plaque for Many Years of Service, The Chatham Area Transit Authority Library (2012); National County Government Month Award, The National Association of Counties (2012); Eponym, Preschool Classroom, "The Dr. Priscilla D. Thomas Room," YMCA (2012); Eponym, Former Wheathill Road, "Priscilla D. Thomas Way," The City of Garden City (2010); Resolution Recipient, Honor for the Many Contributions Made to the City and State, The National Resolutions Committee of the Moles (2009); Mark of Excellence Award in the Field of Nonprofit, National Forum for Black Public Administrators (2009); Humanitarian Service Award, George Funeral Service Practitioners Association (2009); First Recipient, Lifetime Achievement Award, Ross King and the Board of Directors, The Association of County Commissioners of Georgia **Membership:** Founder, Executive Director, Summer Bonanza Partnership, Inc.; Founder, Executive Director, Chatham County Youth Commission; Association of County Commissioners of Georgia; National Association of County Commissioners; Former President, Iota Phi Lambda Sorority **Hobbies:** Reading; Traveling **Shipping Address:** 1727 Chester St, Savannah, GA, 31415

Sarah Elaine Thomas

Title: Music Educator **Industry:** Education/Educational Services **Company Name:** Retired **Date of Birth:** 08/08/1947 **Place of Birth:** Little Rock **State:** AR **Parents:** William Collins; Madie Murle (Stout) Collins **Marital Status:** Married **Spouse Name:** Gary Wayne Thomas (8/8/1970, Deceased 1991) **Education:** MEd, Dallas Baptist University (1997); MusB in Education, University of North Texas (1970) **Career:** Director of Fine Arts, Dallas Independent School District (2007-2017); Supervisor, Elementary Fine Arts, Lincoln Instructional Center (2005-2007); Music Teacher, Pleasant Grove Elementary School (2001-2005); Music Teacher, Kleberg Elementary School, Dallas, TX (1994-2001); Music Teacher, Lenore Kirk Hall Elementary School, Dallas, TX (1982-1994); Music Teacher, Winnetka Elementary School, Dallas, TX (1970-1982) **Career Related:** Presenter, Dallas Independent School District (1997-2005); Staff Development, Dallas Independent School District (1977-1997); Workshop Presenter, Texas Arts Council, Austin (1990-1994) **Civic:** Board of Directors, Chairman, Dallas All-City Elementary Choir (1991-2007); Director, Dallas All-City Elementary Choir (1999-2004); Board of Directors, Dallas PTA (1980-1982) **Awards:** Bayard H. Friedman Hero Award (2014); Service Above Self Award, Rotary International (2003); Named Class Act Teacher, Station KDFW-TV, Dallas (1992) **Membership:** Former Vice President, Dallas Music Teachers Association (1992); Lifetime Member, PTA; American Federation of Teachers; Delta Kappa Gamma; Music Educators National Conference; Rotary International **Hobbies:** Cooking; Sewing; Gardening; Travel **Shipping Address:** 2407 Norwich Ct, Arlington, TX, 76015

Yvonne Maree Thomas-John

Title: Artist **Industry:** Fine Art **Company Name:** Yvonne Maree Designs **Date of Birth:** 09/08/1944 **Place of Birth:** Leeton **Country of Origin:** Australia **Year of Passing:** 11/14/2017 **Parents:** Percy Edward; Gladys May (Markham) Thomas; **Spouse Name:** Michael Peter John, (8/20/1966); **Children:** Michael Christian, Stephen Edwin Dennis **Education:** AA, Interior Design Guild (1976); Coursework, University of California, Santa Barbara (1975) **Certifications:** Certificate, United Design Guild (1975) **Career:** Owner, Manager, Yvonne Maree Designs, Shelton, WA (1979-Present); Owner, Manager, Yvonne Maree Designs, Olympia, WA (1979-Present); Owner, Manager, Yvonne Maree Designs, Ventura, CA (1979-Present); Cosmetologist, Artist, Bernard's Hair Stylists, Ventura, CA (1974-1973); Designer, Percy Thomas Real Estate, Leeton, Australia (1960-1966) **Career Related:** Owner, Manager Y.M. Boutique, Griffith, Australia (1965-1966) **Creative Works:** Group Exhibit, World Bank, Washington (1996-1997); Group Exhibit, Gallery Brindabella, Oakville, ON, Canada (1996); Group Exhibit, Art Communications International, Philadelphia, PA (1996); Group Exhibit, United Nations Fourth World Conference on Women, Beijing, China (1995); Exhibit, Hargus Unique Gallery, Pomona, CA (1994); Group Exhibit, Hargus Unique Gallery, Pomona, CA (1994); Group Exhibit, Museum of Modern Art, Bordeaux, France (1993); Group Exhibit, Abney Galleries, New York, NY (1993); Group Exhibit, Northeastern Trade Center & Exposition Center, Massachusetts (1993); Group Exhibit, Museum of Modern Art, Miami, FL (1993); Group Exhibit, National Headquarters of American Society of Interior Designers, Washington (1992); Group Exhibit, Michael Stone Collection (1992); Group Exhibit, Funding Center, Alexandria, VA (1992); Group Exhibit, Maska International Gallery, Seattle, WA (1991); Group Exhibit, Washington Women in Art, Olympia, WA (1990); Group Exhibit, Timberland Library (1990); Group Exhibit, Ventura County Courthouse (1970); Solo Exhibit, Royal Museum of Sydney, Australia (1954); Represented in Permanent Collections, Royal Museum of Sydney, O'Toole Collection, Melbourne, Australia, National Museum Women in Arts, Washington, Patterson Collection, Michigan, Witherow Collection, Washington, Samaniego Collection, California, Ronald Reagan Collection, California; Artist, Ventura County General Hospital; **Awards:** Recipient, First Round Winner for Painting, Hathaway Competition (1970); Recipient, Ribbons, County Fairs, Australia (1950); **Membership:** American Platform Association **Hobbies:** Swimming; Tennis; Walking; Music; Reading **Political Affiliations:** Republican **Religion:** Roman Catholic **Business Address:** PO Box 1036, Shelton, WA, 98584

Norman W. Thoms

Title: Cardiovascular and Thoracic Surgeon (Retired) **Industry:** Medicine & Health Care **Date of Birth:** 11/05/1934 **Country of Origin:** Bahrain **Parents:** S. WM Wells; Ethel Scudder (Beth) Thoms **Marital Status:** Married **Spouse Name:** Anna J. Holmes (6/22/1962) **Children:** Sharon; Alice; Galena **Education:** Resident in Thoracic Surgery, Detroit General Hospital (1968-1970); Resident in General Surgery, Detroit General Hospital (1966-1968, 1960-1962); Intern, Blodgett Memorial Hospital, Grand Rapids, MI (1959-1960); University of Michigan (1959); BA, Oberlin College (1955) **Certifications:** Diplomate, American Board of Surgery; Diplomate, American Board of Thoracic Surgery **Career:** Retired (2006); Active Staff, Lawrence Memorial Hospital (2003-2006); Private Practice, Topeka, KS (1975-2003); Associate Professor, Wayne State University School of Medicine, Detroit, MI (1974-1975); Assistant Professor, Wayne State University School of Medicine, Detroit, MI (1970-1974); Surgery Instructor, Wayne State University School of Medicine, Detroit, MI (1968-1970) **Civic:** Medical Missionary, Muscat, Oman (1964-1965) **Military Service:** Officer, Medical Corps, U.S. Army (1962-1964) **Awards:** Hall Of Fame, Oberlin College Athletics (2011); Heart Of St. Francis Award (2010); Bal Jeffrey Award Stormont-Vail Foundation (1995); Regents' Award For Best Science Exhibit, American College of Chest Physicians (1972) **Membership:** Fellow, American Medical Association; Fellow, American College of Surgeons; Kansas Medical Society; Shawnee County Medical Society; Society of Thoracic Surgeons; Wayne State Surgical Society **Political Affiliations:** Republican **Religion:** Evangelical Christian **Shipping Address:** 5420 SE 37th Street, Tecumseh, KS, 66542

Clyde Thornsberry, PhD

Title: Microbiologist **Industry:** Sciences **Date of Birth:** 06/20/1930 **Place of Birth:** Pippa Passes **Parents:** Columbus B. Thornsberry; Ollie Mae (Sparkman) Thornsberry **Spouse Name:** Glenda L. Martin (5/13/1952) **Children:** Teresa; David; Robert **Education:** PhD, University of Kentucky, Lexington, KY (1966); BS, University of Kentucky, Lexington, KY (1958) **Career:** Director, Focus Biolnova, Inc., Franklin, TN (1993-Present); Director, Institute for Microbiological Research, Franklin, TN (1989-1993); Chief Antimicrobial Investigations Branch, Centers for Disease Control, Atlanta, GA (1966-1989); Director, Eurofins Medinet, Inc., Franklin, TN **Career Related:** Advisory Board, Several Pharmaceutical Companies (1980-Present); Chairman, Vice Chairman, Interscience Conference on Anti-Agents, Washington, DC (1989-1994); Lecturer in Field **Creative Works:** Contributor, Articles, Professional Journals **Awards:** BD Award for Research in Clinical Microbiology, American Society of Microbiology (2003) **Membership:** Fellow, Infectious Disease Society of America; American Society of Microbiology; American Academy of Microbiology; New York Academy of Sciences; World Health Organization Committees on Antibiotics; National Committee on Clinical Laboratory Standards **Marquis Who's Who Honors:** Distinguished Humanitarian (2017) **Hobbies:** Guitar; Music **Political Affiliations:** Democrat **Shipping Address:** 5228 Forsyth Road, Apt. 202, Macon, GA, 31210

Stelian-Doru Ticsa

Industry: Information Technology and Services **Education:** MD in Orthopedics and Plastic Surgery, Iuliu Hațieganu University of Medicine and Pharmacy, Cluj-Napoca, Romania **Career:** President, Chief Executive Officer, TIMMES, Inc., St. Petersburg, FL (1997-Present) **Membership:** AMA **To what do you attribute your success:** Dr. Ticsa attributes his success to his continuity and commitment to honor the oath that he took when he became a doctor. **Why did you become involved in your profession or industry:** Dr. Tisca became involved in his profession because there are 17 physicians in his family. He always excelled in mathematics and his father encouraged him to pursue a career in that field, but he chose medicine instead.

Natasha Marie Tiffany

Title: Physician, Researcher **Industry:** Medicine & Health Care **Company Name:** Oregon Oncology Specialists **Date of Birth:** 05/16/1970 **Place of Birth:** Portland **State:** OR **Parents:** Carson William Taylor; Gudrun Renate Taylor **Marital Status:** Married **Spouse Name:** Geoffrey Paul Tiffany (5/23/1993) **Children:** Emma Elizabeth; Matthew William **Education:** Chief Fellow, Hematology and Medical Oncology, Oregon Health and Science University (OHSU) (2003-2004); Fellowship in Hematology and Medical Oncology, Oregon Health and Science University (OHSU) (2001-2004); Internship and Residency in Internal Medicine, Harvard Medical School, Massachusetts General Hospital (The General Hospital Corporation) (1998-2001); MD, Oregon Health and Science University (OHSU), Cum Laude (1998); MusB in Piano Performance, Oberlin College and Conservatory (1992); BA in Neuroscience, Oberlin College and Conservatory (1992) **Certifications:** Board Re-certified, Medical Oncology (2015); Board Re-certified, Hematology (2014); Board Re-certified, Internal Medicine (2011); Board Certified, Medical Oncology (2005); Board Certified, Hematology (2003); Board Certified, Internal Medicine (2001) **Career:** Physician, Hematology Oncology of Salem (Now Oregon Oncology Specialists), Salem, OR (2004-Present) **Career Related:** Board of Directors, Willamette Clinical Research (Now Willamette Valley Cancer Institute) (2005-Present); Affiliate Assistant Professor, Department of Medicine, Division of Hematology and Medical Oncology, Oregon Health and Science University (OHSU) School of Medicine (2004-Present); Chair, Thoracic Oncology Committee, Salem Cancer Institute, Salem Health (2014-2016); Medical Oncology Director, Salem Cancer Institute, Salem Health (2013-2015); Vice Chair, Breast Cancer Committee, Salem Cancer Institute, Salem Health (2010-2015); Breast Cancer Committee, Salem Cancer Institute, Salem Health (2008-2015); Secretary-Treasurer, Willamette Clinical Research (Now Willamette Valley Cancer Institute) (2007); Line Committee, Salem Hospital Cancer Service (Now Salem Health Cancer Institute) (2004); Curriculum Committee, Internal Medicine Residency Program, Massachusetts General Hospital, The General Hospital Corporation (1999-2000) **Civic:** Secretary, Abiqua Academy (2015-Present); Board of Trustees, Abiqua Academy (2013-Present) **Creative Works:** Presenter, "Side Effect of Endocrine Therapy and the Breast Cancer Index," Cancer Symposium for Primary Care, Salem Hospital, Salem Health (2017); Presenter, "New Trends and Treatments in Breast Cancer: Cancer Symposium for Primary Care," Salem Hospital, Salem Health (2016); Presenter, Hot Topics in Breast Cancer, Salem Conference Center (2013)

Lynn P. Tishman, PhD

Title: Psychologist, Psychoanalyst **Industry:** Social Work **Date of Birth:** 04/03/1951 **Place of Birth:** Yonkers **State:** NY **Parents:** Neal Petrucci; Olga Petrucci **Marital Status:** Married **Spouse Name:** Peter V. Tishman (5/31/1992) **Children:** Steven; Linda; Anita **Education:** PhD in Clinical Psychology, Columbia University (2007); MSW, Silberman School of Social Work, Hunter College (1995); BA in Psychology, Hunter College, Summa Cum Laude (1993); AAS in Accounting, Westchester Community College (1971) **Certifications:** Licensed Psychologist, State of New York (2009); Certified Adult and Child Psychoanalyst, Institute of the Postgraduate Psychoanalytic Society, New York, NY (2002); Licensed Clinical Social Worker, New York (1995); Certified Psychoanalyst, Psychotherapist and Researcher; Certified Biofeedback Therapist, BCIA (1985); Licensed Massage Therapist, New York (1980) **Career:** Psychotherapist, Karen Horney Clinic, Fifth Avenue Center, Postgraduate Center, Payne Whitney Psychiatric Clinic, Columbia University, Columbia Presbyterian Hospital; Child Development Specialist and Researcher, Pacella Parent Child Center; New York Psychoanalytic Society & Institute **Career Related:** Lynn P. Tishman Scholarship Fund, Teachers College, Columbia University (2008-Present) **Membership:** American Psychological Association; Association for Applied Psychophysiology and Biofeedback; Postgraduate Psychoanalytic Society & Institute **Marquis Who's Who Honors:** Distinguished Humanitarian (2017) **Hobbies:** Running; Weightlifting; Bicycling; Yoga **Shipping Address:** 840 Park Avenue, Apt. 11A, New York, NY, 10075

Masayoshi Tomizuka, PhD

Title: Cheryl and John Neerhout, Jr. Distinguished Professor **Industry:** Education/Educational Services **Company Name:** University of California, Berkeley **Date of Birth:** 03/31/1946 **Place of Birth:** Tokyo **Country of Origin:** Japan **Parents:** Makoto Tomizuka; Shizuko (Nagatome) Tomizuka **Marital Status:** Married **Spouse Name:** Miwako Tomizawa (9/5/1971) **Children:** Lica; Yumi **Education:** PhD, Massachusetts Institute of Technology (1974); MS, Keio University (1970) **Career:** Cheryl and John Neerhout, Jr. Distinguished Professor, University of California, Berkeley (1998-Present); Professor, University of California, Berkeley (1986-Present); Roscoe and Elizabeth Hughes Professor, University of California, Berkeley (1996-1997); Associate Professor, University of California, Berkeley (1980-1986); Assistant Professor, University of California, Berkeley (1974-1980); Research Associate, Keio University (1974) **Creative Works:** Editor-in-Chief, "IEEE/ASME Transition on Mechatronics," Institute of Electrical and Electronics Engineers (1997-1999); Associate Editor, International Federation of Automatic Control (1993-2000); Technology Editor, "Journal of Dynamic Systems Measurement and Control," American Society of Mechanical Engineers (1988-1993); Associate Editor, "Control System Magazine," Institute of Electrical and Electronics Engineers (1986-1988); Contributor, Articles, Professional Journals; Author, "Research on Mechanical Control Systems" **Awards:** Grantee, State of California (2004-Present); Grantee, National Science Foundation (1993-Present); Honoree, Life Fellow, Institute of Electrical and Electronics Engineers (2017); Honoree, Life Fellow, American Society of Mechanical Engineers (2016); Lifetime Achievement Award, Technical Committee on Mechatronic Systems, International Federation of Automatic Control (2013); Grantee, State of California (1988-1993); Grantee, National Science Foundation (1986-1989); Grantee, State of California (1984-1986); Grantee, National Science Foundation (1981-1983); Grantee, National Science Foundation (1976-1978) **Membership:** Science Committee, Society of Mechanical Engineers (1993-2000); Chairman, Dynamic System and Control Division, American Society of Mechanical Engineers (1986-1987); Fellow, American Society of Mechanical Engineers; Fellow, IEEE; Fellow, International Federation of Automatic Control **Marquis Who's Who Honors:** Albert Nelson Marquis Lifetime Achievement Award (2017) **Hobbies:** Playing music **Business Address:** 5100B Etcheverry Hall, Berkeley, CA, 94720

Kelly A. Tomo

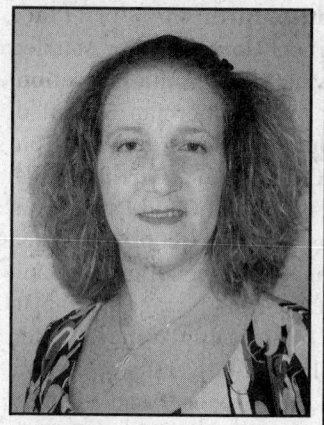

Industry: Pharmaceuticals **Place of Birth:** Sharon **Education:** Resident, Pharmaceutical Practice, Inova Health System (2004); PharmD, Ohio Northern University (2003) **Career:** Pharmacist, Inova Health System (2004-Present) **Membership:** American Society of Health-System Pharmacists; Cru; World Vision, Inc. **Hobbies:** Cross-stitching; Reading; Watching sports; Caring for her dog, Abby, and cat, Tiger

Lawrence C. Tondel

Title: Lawyer (Retired) **Industry:** Law and Legal Services **Company Name:** Sidley Austin, LLP **Date of Birth:** 04/09/1946 **Place of Birth:** New York **State:** NY **Parents:** Lyman Mark Tondel; Jean (Basch) Tondel **Marital Status:** Married **Spouse Name:** Sharyn A. Smith (8/3/1974) **Children:** Michael Lawrence (Deceased); Kathryn Chapman **Education:** JD, University of Michigan School of Law (1971); AB, Wesleyan University (1968); Coursework, Lawrenceville School (1964) **Career:** Senior Counsel, Sidley Austin LLP, New York, NY (2011-Present); Partner, Sidley Austin LLP, New York, NY (2001-2010); Senior Partner, Brown & Wood LLP, New York, NY (1997-2001); Partner, Brown & Wood LLP, New York, NY (1980-1997); Associate, Brown & Wood LLP, New York, NY (1971-1979) **Career Related:** Chairman, Annual International Forum Offshore Funds (1993-2000); International Business Conferences **Civic:** Member, Executive Committee, Parents Committee, Washington University, St. Louis, MO (2000-2002); Trustee, Elisabeth Morrow School, Englewood, NJ (1988-1993) **Membership:** American Bar Association; American Bar Foundation; American Law Institute **Bar Admissions:** New York (1972) **Marquis Who's Who Honors:** Albert Nelson Marquis Lifetime Achievement Award (2017) **Political Affiliations:** Republican **Religion:** Roman Catholic **Shipping Address:** 14 Gilmore Ave, Cresskill, NJ, 07626

Craig Aaron Tovey, PhD

Title: Engineering Educator **Industry:** Education/Educational Services **Company Name:** Georgia Institute of Technology **Date of Birth:** 10/01/1955 **Place of Birth:** Washington **State:** DC **Parents:** Henry Tovey; Bella Tovey **Marital Status:** Married **Spouse Name:** Gail Ann Foorman (6/11/2000); Duif Calvin (Divorced) **Children:** William Noah; Kendl SoonMee; David MinHyeok; Leo Oscar **Education:** PhD, Stanford University, California (1981); AB, Harvard College, Cambridge, MA, Magna Cum Laude (1977) **Career:** Professor, Georgia Institute of Technology, Atlanta, GA (1993-Present); Associate Professor, Georgia Institute of Technology, Atlanta, GA (1986-1992); Assistant Professor, Georgia Institute of Technology, Atlanta, GA (1981-1985) **Career Related:** Co-Director, Center for Biologically Inspired Design, Atlanta, GA (2006-2009); Research Fellow, Georgia Institute of Technology (1995-1999); Senior Research Associate, National Research Council, Monterey, CA (1990-1991); Consultant, AT&T Bell Laboratories, Weyerhaeuser Paper Co., Freddie Mac, Georgia (1984-1992) **Creative Works:** Editor, "Modeling in Industrial Engineering" **Awards:** Grantee, Biologically Inspired Design Education Grant (2009-Present); Golden Goose Award (2016); Sig-Econ Test of Time Award (2016); Auction-Based Coordination Grant, U.S. Army Research (2008-2009); Fundamentals & Applications Grant, National Science Foundation (2006-2009); Online Planning Methods Grant (2001-2005); Jacob Wolfowitz Prize, AJMMS (1989); Presidential Young Investigator Award, National Science Foundation (1985); Research Initiation Grant (1983-1985) **Membership:** INFORMS; Society of Neuroscience **Marquis Who's Who Honors:** Albert Nelson Marquis Lifetime Achievement Award (2017) **Why did you become involved in your profession or industry:** Dr. Tovey became involved in his profession because he always wanted to explain the unexplained through teaching and research. **What do you consider to be the highlight of your career:** The highlight of Dr. Tovey's career was winning the Golden Goose award in 2016. He won it because of two different pieces of research that came 15 years apart, fitting together beautifully in an unexpected way. **Hobbies:** Reading; Singing; Music **Religion:** Jewish **Shipping Address:** 4699 Kings Down Road, Atlanta, GA, 30338

Joseph E. Trader

Title: Orthopedic Surgeon **Industry:** Medicine & Health Care **Date of Birth:** 11/02/1946 **Place of Birth:** Milwaukee **State:** WI **Parents:** Edgar Joseph; Dorothy Elizabeth (Senzig) T. **Marital Status:** Married **Spouse Name:** Rhonda Sue Schultz; Janet Louise Burzycki (9/23/1972, Divorced 11/1987) **Children:** James; Jonathan; Ann Elizabeth **Education:** MD, Medical College of Wisconsin (1973); Marquette University (1964-1967) **Certifications:** Diplomate, American Board of Orthopedic Surgery **Career:** Orthopedic Surgeon, President, Orthopedic Association, Manitowoc, WI (1979-2011); Physician, Emergency Room, Columbia, St. Joseph's Hospitals, Milwaukee, WI (1972-1976) **Career Related:** Ethics Committee, Holy Family Memorial Medical Center (1995-2011); Chair, Institutional Review Committee (1995-2009); Executive Committee, Holy Family Memorial Medical Center (1985-1996); Chief of Staff, Holy Family Memorial Medical Center (1994-1996) **Civic:** President, Board of Directors, Holy Innocents Men's Choir; County Delegate, State Medical Society; Board of Directors, Trustee, Charitable Science and Education Foundation; Chairman, Cobia Committee; Vice President, Board Directors, Wisconsin Maritime Museum; Men's Choir, St. Francis Assisi; Cantor, Funeral Choir, St. Francis Assisi Parish; Board of Directors, President, Manitowoc Symphony Orchestra **Creative Works:** Contributor, Articles, Various Professional Journals **Awards:** Walter Zeit Fellow, Medical College of Wisconsin; Harris Fellow, Rotary International **Membership:** American College of Surgeons, American Academy of Orthopedic Surgeons; American Medical Association; Wisconsin State Medical Society; Wisconsin Orthopedic Society; Midwest Orthopedic Society; American College of Sports Medicine; Crown and Anchor; Wisconsin Maritime Museum; Manitowoc Yacht Club; Manitowoc Noon Rotary; Rotary International; Phi Delta Epsilon; Psi Chi **Hobbies:** Singing; Tennis; Skiing; Sailing; Golf **Religion:** Roman Catholic **Shipping Address:** 1021 Memorial Drive, Manitowoc, WI, 54220

John James Trautner

Title: Real Estate Executive (Retired) **Industry:** Real Estate **Date of Birth:** 12/04/1935 **Place of Birth:** Simpson **State:** MN **Parents:** John Sylvester Trautner; Oridena Francis (Baker) Trautner **Marital Status:** Single **Spouse Name:** Carol Lee Rowberry (7/1974, Divorced 5/1981); Donna L. Jones (5/1960, Divorced 12/1969) **Children:** Theresa; Carrie; John **Education:** MBA, University of Alaska (1998); BBA, University of Alaska (1970); BA, Community and Technical College, University of Alaska Anchorage (1968) **Certifications:** Licensed Commercial Pilot; Licensed Master, 100 Gross Ton, United States Coast Guard **Career:** Chief Executive Officer, Alyeska Management Services, Inc. (1985-2016); President, Gateway, Inc. (1976-1985); General Manager, Gateway, Inc. (1976-1985); Vice President, C. Bruce Ficke Investments (1974-1976); General Manager, C. Bruce Ficke Investments (1974-1976); Executive Director, City of Lost River (1973-1974); Management Consultant, State of Alaska (1972-1973); Director of Administration & Public Relations, Alyeska Resort (1970-1971); Administrator, Public Affairs, RCA Service Company (1965-1970) **Career Related:** Chairman, Multiple District 49 Council of Governors, Alaska District 49A Lions (1999-2000); Member, Multiple District 49 Council of Governors, Alaska District 49A Lions (1996-1997); Marriage Commissioner, Third Judicial District (1973-1993); Patents in Field **Civic:** Chairman, Girdwood Board of Supervisors, Municipality of Anchorage, Alaska (1992-1995); Chairman, Girdwood Community Council, The Federation of Community Councils (1976-1978); Fire Chief, Girdwood Volunteer Fire and Rescue, Inc. (1972-1975); Junior Inter-Fraternity Council (1957-1958) **Military Service:** Sergeant, U.S. Army (1953-1964) **Awards:** Recipient, Melvin Jones Fellowship, City of Chicago (1993-1994) **Membership:** North America Nature Photography Association; American Legion; Lions Clubs International; Disabled American Veterans; Alaska Airmen Association; San Francisco Tennis Club **Marquis Who's Who Honors:** Albert Nelson Marquis Lifetime Achievement Award (2017) **Hobbies:** Photography; Music; Art; Humanitarianism; Flying **Political Affiliations:** Republican **Religion:** Roman Catholic **Business Address:** P.O. Box 909, Girdwood, AK, 99587

Dennis D. Truax

Title: James T. White Endowed Chair, Head and Professor **Industry:** Education/Educational Services **Company Name:** Mississippi State University **Date of Birth:** 07/25/1953 **Place of Birth:** Hagerstown **State:** MD **Parents:** Bernard James Truax; Dorothy Hilda Truax **Marital Status:** Married **Spouse Name:** Jeanie Ann Knable (8/20/1977) **Children:** Courtney Lea Truax; Kelly Lyn Truax **Education:** PhD in Civil Engineering, Mississippi State University (1986); MS in Civil Engineering, Mississippi State University (1978); BS in Civil Engineering, Virginia Polytechnic Institute and State University (1976) **Certifications:** Certification, AED Operation, MEDIC First Aid International, Safety Office, Mississippi State University (2011) **Career:** Director, Mississippi Transportation Research Center, Mississippi State University (2014-Present); Bagley College Engineering Fellow, Mississippi State University, Starkville, MS (2006-Present); James T. White Chair, Civil and Environmental Engineering, Bagley College of Engineering, Mississippi State University, Starkville, MS (2006-Present); Head, Department of Civil Engineering, Mississippi State University, Starkville, MS (2006-Present); Professor, Civil Engineering, Mississippi State University, Starkville, MS (1996-Present); Co-Director, Mississippi Transportation Research Center, Mississippi State University, Starkville, MS (2006-2014); Associate Professor, Mississippi State University, Starkville, MS (1991-1996); Assistant Professor, Civil and Environmental Engineering, Mississippi State University, Starkville, MS (1986-1991); Instructor, Mississippi State University, Starkville, MS (1980-1986) **Creative Works:** Editorial Board Member, Professional Issues Journal, American Society of Civil Engineers (1999-Present) **Awards:** Honoree, Professional New Faces of Civil Engineering Mentor, American Society of Civil Engineers (2014-2016) **Membership:** Board Secretary, Treasurer, American Water Works Association (1998-Present); Scholarship Committee, American Society of Civil Engineers (1998-Present); Alabama-Mississippi Chapter, Scholarship Board of Directors, American Water Works Association (1994-Present); Advisor, Mississippi State Student Chapter, American Society of Civil Engineers (1981-Present); National Society of Professional Engineers (2016) **Marquis Who's Who Honors:** Albert Nelson Marquis Lifetime Achievement Award (2017); Distinguished Humanitarian (2017) **Political Affiliations:** Democrat **Religion:** Methodist **Business Address:** 501 Hardy Road, 235 Walker Engineering Bldg, Mississippi State, MS, 39762-9546 **Website:** http://www.cee.msstate.edu/people/faculty/dennis-truax

Emily Herrick Trueblood

Title: Artist, Librarian **Industry:** Fine Art **Date of Birth:** 08/13/1942 **Place of Birth:** Alexandria **State:** VA **Parents:** Lorman Chancellor Trueblood; Helen Julia (Smith) Trueblood **Marital Status:** Married **Spouse Name:** Ernest Theodore Patrikis (3/18/1972) **Education:** MS, Columbia University, New York, NY (1969); BA, University of Wisconsin, Madison, WI (1965); Student, University of Madrid (1962-1963); Student, Beloit College, Beloit, WI (1960-1962) **Career:** Chief Librarian, Federal Reserve Bank of New York, New York, NY (1985-1995); Librarian, Federal Reserve Bank of New York, New York, NY (1969-1995) **Creative Works:** Group Show Exhibition, Hofstra University Museum, Hempstead, NY (2016); Group Show Exhibition, Y Taipei Cultural Center in New York, New York, NY (2016); Group Show Exhibition, Old Print Shop, New York, NY (2012-2016); One- and Two-Person Shows, Old Print Gallery, Washington, DC (2011); One- and Two-Person Shows, Old Print Shop, New York, NY (2009); Group Show Exhibition, Ingbar Gallery, New York, NY (2009); Group Show Exhibition, Old Print Shop, New York, NY (2009); Group Show Exhibition, Old Print Shop, New York, NY (2007); Group Show Exhibition, International Miniature Art Biennial, QC, Canada (2007); Group Show Exhibition, Ingbar Gallery, New York, NY (2007); Group Show Exhibition, New-York Historical Society, New York, NY (2004-2005); Group Show Exhibition, New York Transit Museum (2003); Group Show Exhibition, New-York Historical Society, New York, NY (2001); Group Show Exhibition, Ingbar Gallery, New York, NY (2000-2001); Group Show Exhibition, Xylon 13, Winterthur, Switzerland (1997-2001); Group Show Exhibition, Bienal Internacional de Grabado, Spain (1997); Permanent Collections, The British Museum; Permanent Collections, New York Public Library; Permanent Collection, Cleveland Museum of Art **Awards:** Society of American Graphic Artists Award for Commitment and Contribution to the World of Fine Art Printmaking (2015); Silver Medal of Honor for Graphics, Audubon Artists (2001) **Membership:** Jury of Awards, Salmagundi Club (2004-2010); Vice President, Society of American Graphic Artists (2003-2006); Catharine Lorillard Wolfe Art Club, Inc.; The National Arts Club; Audubon Artists **Marquis Who's Who Honors:** Albert Nelson Marquis Lifetime Achievement Award (2017) **Hobbies:** Swimming; Hiking **Shipping Address:** 20 E 9th Street, Apt. 18C, New York, NY, 10003 **Website:** http://www.emilytrueblood.com

Rosalie Marie Uht, PhD

Title: Associate Professor **Industry:** Education/Educational Services **Company Name:** UNT Health Science Center **Date of Birth:** 08/03/1953 **Place of Birth:** New York **State:** NY/USA **Parents:** Charles Frederick Uht; Carol Kinzel Uhbt; Joan McKenzie Uht (Stepmother) **Marital Status:** Married **Spouse Name:** Walter J. Dowling (6/8/2013) **Education:** PhD, Stony Brook University (1990); BSN, School of Nursing, Columbia University (1980); BA in Music History, University of Southern California (1976); MD, Stony Brook University **Certifications:** Certified in Anatomic Pathology and Neuropathology, The American Board of Pathology **Career:** Associate Professor, Center for Alzheimer's & Neurodegenerative Diseases, The University of Oklahoma (2010-Present); Associate Neuropathology Professor, Department of Pathology, The University of Texas Southwestern Medical Center (2010-Present); Associate Professor, UNT Health Science Center (2008-Present); Assistant Research Biochemist, Department of Biochemistry and Molecular Genetics, University of Virginia (2000-2008); Assistant Professor, Department of Pathology, University of Virginia (2000-2007); Assistant Research Biochemist, Diabetes and Metabolism, University of California, San Francisco (1997-2000); Adjunct Instructor, Department of Medicine, Diabetes and Metabolism, University of California, San Francisco (1995-1997); Clinical Neuropathology Professor, Department of Pathology and Laboratory Medicine, University of California, San Francisco (1994-2000) **Career Related:** The New York Academy of Sciences (1981-1985) **Civic:** Active Community Member, Town of Westmore, VT (2009-2013); Active Member, Healthy Aging Council (2009-2013) **Creative Works:** Contributor, Molecular Endocrinology, Oxford University Press (2013); Contributor, BMC Genomics; Editor, Endocrinology **Awards:** President's Award for Excellence in Research, UNT Health Science Center (2012); Lieber Investigator Award, Brain Research Foundation (2003) **Membership:** American Association for the Advancement of Science; Endocrine Society; American Association of Neuropathologists; Sigma Xi, The Scientific Research Honor Society; Sigma Theta Tau International; Society for Neuroscience **Marquis Who's Who Honors:** Albert Nelson Marquis Lifetime Achievement Award (2017) **To what do you attribute your success:** Dr. Uht attributes her success to her own persistence. **Hobbies:** Music **Business Address:** 3400 Camp Bowie Boulevard, CBH 469, Fort Worth, TX, 76107

Gwen Justine Ulin

Title: Vice President of Engineering **Industry:** Engineering **Company Name:** TGI, Inc. **Date of Birth:** 11/08/1955 **Place of Birth:** Canal Zone **Country of Origin:** Panama **Parents:** Webster Beattie Ulin; Ann (Fletcher) Rainier **Marital Status:** Widowed **Spouse Name:** Lida Ohan (05/30/1992) **Children:** Nicole Ann Ulin **Education:** University of Delaware (1973-1978) **Career:** Vice President of Engineering, TGI Inc., Granada Hills, CA (2015-Present); Vice President of Engineering, IDEA, Inc., Seattle, WA (1996-Present); Senior Software Engineer, Source Photonics Inc., IDEA, Inc. (2001-2013); Senior System Designer, Litigation Sciences, Culver City, CA (1989-1996); Director of Engineering, Flight Safety Inc., Irving Independent School District, Irving, Texas (1987-1989); Director of Engineering, Flight Safety Inc., Independent School District, Malvern, PA (1986-1987); Systems Designer, DBS Films, Inc., Malvern, PA (1984-1986); Systems Design Consultant, Command Computer Services, New York, NY (1983-1984); Systems Design Consultant, Alpha Ro Inc., Wilmington, DE (1982-1983) **Creative Works:** Software Designer, Interactive Training on Aircraft System (1983) **Marquis Who's Who Honors:** Albert Nelson Marquis Lifetime Achievement Award (2017) **Hobbies:** Electronics; Stamp and Coin Collecting; Reading; Cooking; Hiking; Music **Shipping Address:** PO Box 33112, Granada Hills, CA, 91394

James M. Urnes Sr.

Title: Aerospace Engineer (Retired) **Industry:** Engineering **Company Name:** The Boeing Company **Date of Birth:** 09/13/1936 **Place of Birth:** Minneapolis **State:** MN **Parents:** Ambjourn M. Urnes; Cora J. Edming **Marital Status:** Married **Spouse Name:** Lois C. Urnes (8/22/1959) **Children:** Mark; Eric; James, Jr.; Paul; Joel **Education:** MS, Aerospace Engineering, University of Minnesota (1961); BS, University of Minnesota (1959); Coursework, St. Olaf College (1954-1956) **Career:** Manager of Engineering, The Boeing Company (1997-Present); Program Manager, Intelligent Flight Control System, Boeing Phantom Works (1996-Present); Branch Chief, McDonnell Douglas Company (1981-1997); Senior Engineer, McDonnell Douglas Co. (1968-1981); Engineer, McDonnell Aircraft Company, St. Louis, MO (1964-1968) **Career Related:** Engineer, Space Shuttle, F-4 Fighter Aircraft, FA-18 Fighter Aircraft **Military Service:** First Lieutenant, Headquarters, U.S. Air Forces in Europe, U.S. Air Force, Wiesbaden, Germany (1963-1964); First Lieutenant, 43rd Bomb Wing, U.S. Air Force, Fort Worth, TX (1961-1963); Maintenance Officer, Special Weapons Officer, U.S. Air Force **Creative Works:** Designer, Variable Camber Continuous Trailing Edge Flap to Reduce Drag on Commercial Aircraft (2010-2014); Inventor, Neural Network Fault Diagnostics, Patent (1999); Designer, Flight Test on NASA Research F-15 (1998); Designer, Propulsion Controlled Aircraft Flight Test for F-15 and MD-11 (1994); Designer, Damage Adaptive Control Flight Test (1991); Designer, Flight Control F/A-18 Flight Control System (1980); Designer, Flight Control F-4 Automatic Carrier Landing (1976) **Awards:** Recipient, Numerous Research Project Awards, The Boeing Company **Membership:** PTA President, Carrollton Oaks School; Board of Directors, Washington University and University of Missouri Joint Engineering Program; American Institute of Aeronautics and Astronautics; SAE International; Sigma Gamma Tau, Honorary Engineering Society at the University of Minnesota **Marquis Who's Who Honors:** Albert Nelson Marquis Lifetime Achievement Award (2017) **What do you consider to be the highlight of your career:** When a DC 10 aircraft crashed in Iowa due to losing power in the engine, Mr. Urnes was inspired to design a propulsion control system to compensate for unforeseen circumstances in powered flight. **Hobbies:** Gardening; Building model airplanes **Shipping Address:** 3561 Bostons Farm Dr, Bridgeton, MO, 63044

Charles Daniel Vail

Title: Veterinarian, Consultant **Industry:** Veterinary Care **Company Name:** Littleton Equine Medical Center **Date of Birth:** 06/11/1936 **Place of Birth:** Denver **State:** CO **Parents:** Allan Padan Vail; Katherine Marie (Phillips) Vail **Marital Status:** Married **Spouse Name:** Jean Williams Ebsen (6/15/1963) **Children:** Ellen Marie; David Elston **Education:** DVM, Colorado State University (1960); BS, Colorado Agricultural and Mechanical College (1958) **Career:** Equine Practitioner, Littleton Large Animal Clinic (1960-Present); Littleton Equine Medical Center (2007-2016); Track Veterinarian, Centennial Race Track, Littleton, CO (1962-1963); Assistant Veterinarian, Colorado Racing Commission, Littleton, CO (1958-1960) **Career Related:** Commissioner, Colorado Racing Commission (2007-Present) **Civic:** Examiner, Clinical Practitionary (2007-Present); Araphoe Chamber of Commerce Foundation (2004-Present); Selection Committee Member, Outstanding Biology Teacher Award, Colorado (1988-Present); President, Western Veterinarian Conference (2003); Development Council Member, Colorado State University (2002-2006); President-elect, Western Veterinarian Conference (2002); Vice President, Western Veterinarian Conference (2001); Friends Littleton Public Library/Museum (2000-2004); Western Veterinarian Conference (1997-2000); President, Animal Assistance Foundation, Denver, CO (1996-1997); Vice President, Animal Assistance Foundation, Denver, CO (1995-1996) **Creative Works:** Editor-in-Chief, "Equine Practice" (1986-2000); Contributor, Articles to Professional Journals **Awards:** Recipient, Meritorious Service Award, Western Veterinary Conference (2008); Recipient, Alumni Award, Colorado State University College Veterinary Medicine (1991); Recipient, Veterinarian of the Year Award, Colorado Veterinary Medical Association (1987) **Membership:** Clinical Proficiency Examination Faculty, American Veterinary Medical Association (2005-Present); President, Colorado State University Alumni Association (2001-2002); President, Arapahoe Town and Gown Society (2000); Vice President, Arapahoe Town and Gown Society (1999); President, Littleton Rotary Foundation (1992-1993); District Lifetime Member, President, American Association of Equine Practitioners (1985); Publications Committee, American Veterinary Medical Association (1981-1987); President, Colorado Veterinary Medical Association (1980); President, Denver Area Veterinary Medical Society (1975); Sigma Alpha Epsilon; Omicron Delta Kappa; Nottingham Club **Marquis Who's Who Honors:** Albert Nelson Marquis Lifetime Achievement Award (2017) **Hobbies:** Trout fishing; Reading **Shipping Address:** 5921 S Cherrywood Cir, Centennial, CO, 80121

Harry Edwin Vanden

Title: University Educator, Scholar **Industry:** Education/Educational Services **Company Name:** University of South Florida **Date of Birth:** 09/29/1943 **Place of Birth:** Wilmington **State:** DE **Parents:** Harry Edwin Vanden, Sr.; Rena Baker (Van Zandt) Vanden **Marital Status:** Single **Spouse Name:** Vera Esther Ballin (1967-1995) **Children:** David Jeffrey; Jonathan Harry **Education:** PhD, The New School (1976); Graduate Certificate, Latin American Studies, Syracuse University (1969); MA, Syracuse University (1969); BA, Albright College (1966); Diploma, Complutense University of Madrid (1965) **Career:** Professor Emerita, University South Florida, Tampa, FL (2017-Present); Visiting Professor, State University of Sao Paulo, Brazil (2007); Director of Institute for the Study of Latin America and the Caribbean, University South Florida, Tampa, FL (1993-1997); Assistant Professor to Professor, University South Florida, Tampa, FL (1975-2017); Expert, Instituto Nacional Administración Pública, Lima, Peru (1974-1975); Fulbright Scholar, U.S. Government, Lima, Peru (1973-1974); Adjunct Assistant Professor, Richmond College, City University of New York, New York, NY (1971) **Civic:** Member, Treasurer, National Religious-based N.G.O., Working Group, Peace in Latin America (2012-Present); Vice President, Board of Directors, WMNF, Tampa, FL (1990-1996); Board of Directors, Hispanic Services Council, Tampa, FL (1996-2003); International Election Observer, Venezuela Elections, The Carter Center (1998) **Creative Works:** Co-Editor, "The New Global Politics: Global Social Movements in the Twenty-First Century" (2017); Co-Author, "Politics of Latin America: The Power Game" (2002, 2006, 2008, 2012, 2015, 2018); Co-Editor, "Rethinking Latin American Social Movements" (2014); Co-Editor, "U.S. National Security Concerns in Latin America and the Caribbean: the Concept of Ungoverned Spaces and Sovereignty" (2014); Co-Editor, "Social Movements and Leftists Governments in Latin America" (2012); Co-Translator, Co-Editor, "José Carlos Mariátegui: An Anthology of His Writings" (2011); Author, "Latin America: An Introduction" (2011); Author, "A Bibliography of Latin American Marxism" (1991); Author, "National Marxism in Latin America" (1986) **Awards:** Choice Outstanding Academic Book Award (2009); Fulbright Research and Teaching Grant, São Paulo, Brazil (2007); National Endowment of the Humanities Grantee (1980); Fulbright Scholar, Peru (1975-1976) **Membership:** President, Society for Iberian and Latin America Thought (1983-1985); President, Southeastern Council on Latin America Studies (1988-1989) **Hobbies:** Judo; Swimming; Sailing **Political Affiliations:** Democrat **Business Address:** 4202 E. Fowler Avenue, Tampa, FL, 33620 **Shipping Address:** 15421 East Lake Burrell Drive, Lutz, FL, 33549

James Vasek

Title: Industrial Engineer **Industry:** Engineering **Company Name:** NXP Semiconductors **Year of Passing:** 10/4/2017 **Education:** MS in Physics, University of Wisconsin-Madison (1994); MS in Materials Science, University of Wisconsin-Madison (1994); BA in Physics, Rice University, Houston, TX (1991) **Career:** Capital and Capacity Manager, NXP Semiconductors (2008-Present); Research and Development Engineer, NXP Semiconductors (2002-2008); Process Engineering Manager, NXP Semiconductors (1998-2002); Process Engineer, NXP Semiconductors, Austin, TX (1994-1998) **Career Related:** Consultant, Brion Technologies, Santa Clara, CA (2003-2006) **Creative Works:** Contributor, Professional Publications **Awards:** Heaps Prize, Rice University (1991) **Hobbies:** Astronomy; Running; Reading **Shipping Address:** 2102 Cypress Point E, Austin, TX, 78746

John A. Vassallo

Title: Lawyer **Industry:** Law and Legal Services **Company Name:** Franklin, Weinrib, Rudell & Vassallo, P.C. **Date of Birth:** 08/19/1937 **Place of Birth:** New York **State:** NY **Parents:** John Vassallo; Gilda (Di Desidero) Vassallo **Marital Status:** Married **Spouse Name:** Lynne Vassallo **Children:** John C.; Elena L.; Edward F. **Education:** JD, Columbia University School of Law (1962); AB, Columbia College (1959) **Career:** Partner, Franklin, Weinrib, Rudell & Vassallo, P.C., New York, NY (1978-Present); Partner, Kurtz & Vassallo, New York, NY (1970-1978); Partner, Barovick & Konecky, New York, NY (1968-1970); Associate, Saxe, Bacon & O'Shea, New York, NY (1962-1968) **Creative Works:** Contributing Author, "Inside the Minds: Leading Divorce Lawyers" (2005) **Awards:** Top Professional of the Year in Law, International Association of Top Professionals (2017); Academia Europea Per Le Relazioni Economiche E Culturali Award for Bringing honor to the Italian-American Community (2003); Honoree, The Best Lawyers in America; A/V Rated Attorney, Martindale-Hubbell; Honoree, New York Metro Edition, Super Lawyer **Membership:** Diplomate, American College of Family Trial Lawyers; Board of Admissions, Board of Governors, American Academy of Matrimonial Lawyers **Bar Admissions:** Second Circuit, U.S. Court of Appeals (1965); U.S. District Court, Southern and Eastern Districts, State of New York (1964); New York State Board of Law Examiners (1962) **Marquis Who's Who Honors:** Albert Nelson Marquis Lifetime Achievement Award (2017); Who's Who in the East; Who's Who in America; Who's Who in the World **Hobbies:** Travel; Reading; His dog **Business Address:** 488 Madison Avenue, New York, NY, 10022 **Shipping Address:** 2 Hampton Road, Great Neck, NY, 11020

Ruth Vidrine Petry

Title: Principal (Retired) **Industry:** Education/Educational Services **Date of Birth:** 01/20/1947 **Place of Birth:** Eunice **State:** LA **Parents:** Adea Vidrine; Ruth Alice (Fox) Vidrine **Marital Status:** Married **Spouse Name:** Carson Clinton Petry (6/19/1976) **Education:** MEd, McNeese State University (1984); BA, Louisiana College (1971) **Certifications:** Certified Teacher and Principal, State of Louisiana **Career:** Adjunct Instructor, Louisiana State University Eunice (2004-Present); Principal, Rayne High School (2001-2004); Assistant Principal, Rayne High School, LA (1996-2001); Executive Director, Associated Professional Educators of Louisiana, Baton Rouge, LA (1995-1996); Instructional Assistant, Crowley Middle School (1994-1995); Teacher, Crowley Middle School (1991-1994); Master Teacher Assessor, Louisiana State Department of Education, Lafayette, LA (1990-1991); Teacher, Language Arts, Crowley Junior High School (1981-1990); Teacher, Jefferson Parish, Gretna, LA (1973-1981); Teacher, St. Tammany Parish, Mandeville, LA (1972-1973); Teacher, Jefferson Davis Parish, Jennings, LA (1970-1972) **Career Related:** Adjunct Professor of Education, Louisiana State University Eunice (2002-Present); Principal's Evaluation State Committee (1993); Member, State Selection Committee for Louisiana Teacher of the Year (1992-1993); Member, Teacher Evaluation Revision Panels, I, III, IV (1992-1993); Chairman, Spelling Bee, Crowley Junior High School (1992-1993); Member of Faculty In-service Team (1986-1989) **Civic:** Member, Louisiana Goals (2000); Member, School Financial Commission (1999-2000); Steering Committee on School Governance and Accountability (1994-1995); Member, Louisiana Governor-elect's Education Transition Team (1991-1992); Co-sponsor, National Junior Honor Society (1984-1990) **Awards:** Teacher of the Year, Crowley Junior High School (1985-1986) **Membership:** State Leadership Scholar (1993); State President, Association of Professional Educators of Louisiana (1992-1994); State President-elect, Association of Professional Educators of Louisiana (1991-1992); District VII State Executive Board, Association of Professional Educators of Louisiana (1990-1991); President, Acadia Chapter, Association of Professional Educators of Louisiana (1988-1992); Chapter President, DKGSI (1988-1990); Association of Professional Educators of Louisiana; Lafayette Association for Retarded Citizens; Louisiana Retired Teachers' Association **Marquis Who's Who Honors:** Albert Nelson Marquis Lifetime Achievement Award (2017) **Hobbies:** Music; Reading; Sewing **Political Affiliations:** Republican **Religion:** Baptist **Shipping Address:** 206 Bruce St, Lafayette, LA, 70503

Richard Carl Vie

Title: Chairman Emeritus **Industry:** Insurance **Company Name:** Kemper Corporation **Date of Birth:** 09/26/1937 **Place of Birth:** St. Louis **State:** MO **Marital Status:** Married **Spouse Name:** Joan Wilschetz Vie (1950) **Children:** Laura; Mark; Amy; Paul; Sarah; Todd **Education:** Coursework, University of Missouri; Coursework, Saint Louis University **Career:** Chairman/Chief Executive Officer Emeritus, Unitrin, Inc. (Now Kemper Corporation) (2005-Present); Chairman, Unitrin, Inc. (Now Kemper Corporation) (2006-2009); Chairman, Unitrin, Inc. (Now Kemper Corporation) (1999-2006); President, Unitrin, Inc. (Now Kemper Corporation) (1999-2006); Chief Executive Officer, Unitrin, Inc. (Now Kemper Corporation) (1999-2006); President, Unitrin, Inc. (Now Kemper Corporation) (1992-1999); Chief Executive Officer, Unitrin, Inc. (Now Kemper Corporation) (1992-1999); Senior Vice President, Unitrin, Inc. (Now Kemper Corporation) (1990-1992); Board of Directors, Unitrin, Inc. (Now Kemper Corporation) (1990-1992); Chief Executive Officer, United Insurance Company (1983-1990); President, United Insurance Company (1983-1990); Chairman, United Insurance Company (1983-1990); Board of Directors, United Insurance Company (1983-1990); President, Commonwealth Annuity and Life Insurance Company (1979-1982); Affiliate, Reliable Life Insurance Company (1962-1979) **Career Related:** Chairman, Life Insurance Conference (1994); Trustee, Life Underwriters Training Council, NAIFA **Civic:** Director, National Museum of the American Sailor Foundation (2017); Co-Chairman, Chicago Navy Memorial at Navy Pier, Chicago Navy Memorial Foundation Inc. (2012); Chairman, U.S. Navy Memorial, Washington, DC (2010-2017); Chairman, Military Outreach USA (2010); Affiliate, U.S. Navy Memorial, Washington, DC (2009-2015); Board of Directors, Valparaiso University (1995); Board of Directors, Concordia University Foundation, Concordia University (1985-1994); Board of Directors, Concordia University, Wisconsin; Board of Directors, Concordia University, Irvine; Several Military Support Boards, United Service Organizations (USO); Chicago Navy Memorial at Navy Pier Foundation, Chicago, IL **Military Service:** Lieutenant, U.S. Navy (1958-1962); Navy Pilot **Membership:** Chairman, The Executives Club of Chicago (2010); Racquet Club Ladue; Chicago Navy Memorial Foundation Inc. **Marquis Who's Who Honors:** Albert Nelson Marquis Lifetime Achievement Award (2017); Distinguished Humanitarian (2017) **Hobbies:** Charity work; Christian education; Charity work towards deployed military families **Shipping Address:** 511 Oakwood Avenue, Apt. 3C, Lake Forest, IL, 60045

John Stanley Vishneski

Title: Lawyer **Industry:** Law and Legal Services **Date of Birth:** 08/27/1963 **Place of Birth:** Virginia Beach **State:** VA **Parents:** John Stanley Vishneski; Antoinette Ann (Caracciolo) Vishneski **Marital Status:** Married **Spouse Name:** Jane Estelle Beard (5/28/1988) **Children:** John Joseph II; Peter Anthony; Robert Thomas; Elisabeth Katharine **Education:** JD, The University of Virginia (1988); BA, The University of Virginia (1985) **Certifications:** Admitted to Practice, U.S. District Court, District of Maryland (1992); Admitted to Practice, U.S. District Court for the District of Columbia (1992); Admitted to Practice, U.S. Court of Appeals for the Seventh Circuit (1991) **Career:** Partner, Reed Smith LLP **Civic:** Elder, Fair Oaks Presbyterian Church, Oak Park, IL (1989-Present) **Creative Works:** Contributor, Various Articles, Professional Journals **Awards:** Recipient, Unparalleled Champion of Lawyer-Made Music in Chicago 30 Years of Thanks, Chicago Bar Association (2016); Honoree, AV Preeminent Attorney; Honoree, Top-Ranked Attorney in Illinois, Chambers USA; Honoree, Second Highest Ranked Attorney Nationally, Chambers USA; Honoree, Legal 500; Honoree, Super Lawyer **Membership:** Orchestra Member, Chicago Bar Association (1988-Present); President, Jefferson Society (1985); Raven Society; The Phi Beta Kappa Society; Omicron Delta Kappa; Fellow, American College of Coverage and Extracontractual Counsel; Federal Trial Bar; Co-Chair, Asbestos Subcommittee, ABA; Co-Chair, Program Committee, ABA; Section of Litigation, Insurance Coverage Litigation, ABA; Insurance Information Counsel Illinois Policyholders Counsel Group; Board Member, Children's Memorial Hospital Foundation; Founder and Band Leader, Barristers Big Band; Founder, Annual Barristers Big Band Benefit Ball; Fair Use Quintet; American College of Coverage and Extra Contractual Counsel **Bar Admissions:** The District of Columbia Bar (1989); Illinois State Bar Association (1988); State Bar Association of North Dakota (1988) **Marquis Who's Who Honors:** Albert Nelson Marquis Lifetime Achievement Award (2017) **Hobbies:** Clarinet; Wine collecting; Racquetball **Shipping Address:** 162 N Lombard Avenue, Oak Park, IL, 60302

Peter von Braun, PhD

Title: Finance Company Executive **Industry:** Financial Services **Company Name:** Leyton Associates LLC **Date of Birth:** 06/24/1940 **Place of Birth:** Greenwich **State:** CT **Parents:** Carl Conrad von Braun; Martha Irwin (Moore) von Braun **Marital Status:** Married **Spouse Name:** Denene Jensen (9/26/1987); Elizabeth Esser (7/1/1967-12/1980) **Children:** Christina Stewart; Alexander Stewart **Education:** PhD, University of Cologne, Summa Cum Laude (1966); BA, Yale University, With High Honors (1964) **Career:** Managing Partner, Leyton Associates LLC, Greenwich, CT (1980-Present); Chairman, Ruspetro (1989-1999); Chief Executive Officer, Ruspetro (1989-1999); Chairman, American Microtrace, Virginia Beach, VA (1987-1995); Chief Executive Officer, American Microtrace, Virginia Beach, VA (1987-1995); Executive Director, Sight Programme, Embassy of The Sultanate of Oman, London, England (1977-1984); Chief International Program Developer, Order of St John (1977-1980); Partner, McKinsey & Company, New York, NY (1972-1977); Principal, McKinsey & Company (1972-1977); Associate, McKinsey & Company (1966-1972) **Career Related:** Chairman, Leix LLC, Riverside, CT (2000-Present); Managing Director, LabelADD, LLC, Greenwich, CT (1987-1999); Advisor, Republic of Turkey Ministry of National Defence; Lecturer, Harvard Business School, Harvard University **Civic:** Chairman, Anglican Service Training & Relief Organization (Now Episcopal Relief & Development) (1986-Present); Chairman, Battle Harbour Historic Trust (1972-Present); Vestryman, Trinity Church Wall Street (1977-1984); Board of Directors, Presiding Bishop's Fund for World Relief, New York, NY (1977-1981); Executive Board Member, Greenwich Council, Boy Scouts of America; Board of Education Member, Greenwich, CT; Episcopal Church Representative, Church World Service **Military Service:** U.S. Army (1958-1964); U.S. Navy (1956-1958) **Creative Works:** Author, "How to Save an Eye" (1981); Author, "How to Save a Life" (1977); Film Producer, "How to Save a Life" (1977); Author, "Die Verteidigung Indiens" (1968) **Awards:** Fulbright Scholar (1964-1966); Honoree, Decorated Knight of Grace and Knight of Justice, Order of St. John; Companion with Star, Order of Merit of the Republic of Cyprus; Honoree, Other Foreign and U.S. Decorations **Membership:** Cavalry, Guards Polo Club, London, England; New York Yacht Club; The Yale Club of New York City; Indian Harbor Yacht Club, Greenwich, CT; Battle Harbour Yacht Club, Newfoundland, NL, Canada; Commodore, The Stewart Society **Hobbies:** Sailing; Military history **Political Affiliations:** Republican **Religion:** Episcopalian **Shipping Address:** 34 A Homestead Lane, Greenwich, CT, 06831

Elizabeth J. Vosbeck

Title: Geneticist **Industry:** Medicine & Health Care **Date of Birth:** 05/24/1925 **Place of Birth:** Mankato **State:** MN **Parents:** Frederick William Just; Frances Beneta (Johnson) Just **Marital Status:** Married **Spouse Name:** William Frederick Vosbeck (8/2/1947) **Children:** Lee; William Frederick III; Lynn; Jon Scot; James Stephen **Education:** PhD in Human Genetics, The George Washington University (1975); MS in Anatomy, The George Washington University (1965); BBA, University of Minnesota (1947) **Career:** Laboratory Director of Cell Chromosome Analysis, Reproduction Genetics Center (1976-1987); Embryology Laboratory Instructor, The George Washington University (1965-1975); Lecturer, The George Washington University (1965-1975); Human Genetics Researcher, The George Washington University (1965-1975); Marketing Research Director, Minneapolis Regional Chamber (1947-1948) **Civic:** DAR Preservation, Jones Point Lighthouse, Alexandria, VA **Awards:** Grantee, National Institutes Of Health (1968-1970) **Membership:** National Society Daughters of the American Revolution; Sigma Xi, The Scientific Research Honor Society; Beta Gamma Sigma, Inc. **Hobbies:** Golf; Bridge; Genealogy; Astrology; Ice skating **Religion:** Protestant-Presbyterian **Shipping Address:** 9110 Belvoir Woods Parkway, Apartment 218, Fort Belvoir, VA, 22060

Mary Emma Wagner

Title: Science Educator **Industry:** Education/Educational Services **Company Name:** University of Pennsylvania **Date of Birth:** 06/20/1927 **Place of Birth:** Wilmington **State:** DE **Parents:** John Mercer Mertz; Emma Welch (Davis) Mertz **Marital Status:** Married **Spouse Name:** Daniel Hobson Wagner (9/10/1949) **Children:** David Hobson; Christopher Daniel; Thomas John; Elizabeth Ann **Education:** PhD, Bryn Mawr College (1972); MS, Bryn Mawr College (1966); BA, Mount Holyoke College (1948) **Career:** Lecturer Emeritus, University of Pennsylvania, Philadelphia, PA (1993-Present); Lecturer in Geology, University of Pennsylvania, Philadelphia, PA (1972-1993) **Creative Works:** Contributor, Articles, American Journal of Science; Contributor, Articles, Bulletin, Geological Society of America; Contributor, Articles, Geological Society of America, Centennial Volume; Contributor, Articles, Journal of Geology **Awards:** Grantee, Pew Foundation, University of Pennsylvania (1990); Grantee, University of Pennsylvania (1984-1987); Grantee, National Science Foundation, Bryn Mawr College (1977-1979) **Membership:** Board of Directors, Northeast Section, Geological Society of America (1984-1986); President, Philadelphia Geological Society (1984-1986); American Geophysical Union **Marquis Who's Who Honors:** Albert Nelson Marquis Lifetime Achievement Award (2017) **Shipping Address:** 51 Kendal Dr, Kennett Square, PA, 19348

Christine M. Waisanen

Title: Lawyer, Writer **Industry:** Law and Legal Services **Company Name:** Hill, Katzenstein & Waisanen **Date of Birth:** 05/27/1949 **Place of Birth:** Hancock **State:** MI **Parents:** Frederick B. Waisanen; Helen M. (Hill) Waisanen **Marital Status:** Married **Children:** Jeffrey Hunt; Erick Hill **Education:** JD, University of Denver (1975); BA, University of Michigan, with Honors (1971) **Career:** Founder, Hill, Katzenstein & Waisanen (1988-Present); Chief Writer, Hill, Katzenstein & Waisanen (1988-Present); Director, Cultural Affairs, City of Wilmington, DE (1987); Government Relations Specialist, ICI Americas, Inc., Wilmington, DE (1979-1987); Labor Relations Attorney, U.S. Chamber of Commerce, Washington, DC (1976-1979) **Civic:** Chairman, Delaware State Coastal Zone Industrial Control Board (1993-Present) **Membership:** President, University of Michigan Club of Delaware (1999-Present); Board of Directors, Women's Republican Club of Wilmington (1988-1993); Vice President, Junior League of Wilmington (1985-1986); Federal Bar Association **Bar Admissions:** The District of Columbia Bar (1978); Colorado State Bar (1975) **Marquis Who's Who Honors:** Distinguished Humanitarian (2017) **Why did you become involved in your profession or industry:** Ms. Waisanen was planning to pursue a PhD in psychology but was told that she wouldn't get a scholarship because she was a white woman. Her great-grandfather was a judge, and her cousins worked in law, so she followed in their footsteps. **What do you consider to be the highlight of your career:** Ms. Waisanen considers working on legislation to be the highlight of her career. She was involved with safety and health, as well as environmental issues, and women's employment opportunities. Additionally, she has achieved rewards through teamwork and her community-minded nature. **Religion:** Presbyterian **Shipping Address:** 1609 Mount Salem Ln, Wilmington, DE, 19806

Michael Waldman

Title: Economist, Educator **Industry:** Education/Educational Services **Company Name:** Cornell University **Date of Birth:** 05/12/1955 **Place of Birth:** Paterson **State:** NJ **Parents:** Henry Waldman; Nettie Waldman **Marital Status:** Married **Spouse Name:** Lisa Berki (7/18/1999); Karen Voris (7/9/1982, Divorced 1/1992) **Children:** David Henry; Emma Nicole **Education:** Postdoctoral Fellow, Department of Economics, University of California, Los Angeles (1982-1983); PhD in Economics, University of Pennsylvania (1982); BS in Economics, Massachusetts Institute of Technology (1977) **Career:** Charles H. Dyson Professor, Management, Professor, Economics, Johnson School Management, Cornell University, Ithaca, NY (1997-Present); Professor, Economics, College of Arts & Sciences, Cornell University ILR School (2011-2015); Director, Institute for the Advancement of Economics, Cornell University (2008-2012); Professor, Economics, Cornell University, Ithaca, NY (1991-1997); Professor, Economics, University of California, Los Angeles (1991-1993); Associate Professor, Economics, University of California, Los Angeles (1989-1991); Associate Professor, Economics, University of California, Los Angeles (1983-1989) **Career Related:** Visiting Professor, Economics, Graduate School of Business, University of Chicago (1999) **Creative Works:** Editor, Journal of Labor Economics (2009-Present); Co-Editor, Journal of Economic Perspectives (2000-2006); Associate Editor, The Quarterly Journal of Economics (2000-2014); Contributor, Chapters, Books; Referee, Reviewer, Several Peer-reviewed Journals **Awards:** Cornell-Tsinghua Dual Degree MBA Program Class of 2017 Gravitas Teaching Award (2017); AMBA Class of 2017 Core Faculty Teaching Award (2017); Co-Winner, RERCI Best Paper Award for Best Paper Published in the Review of Economic Research on Copyright Issues (2016); Robert F. Lanzillotti Prize for the Best Paper in Antitrust Economics, International Industrial Organization Conference (2008); Faculty Research Award, Johnson Graduate School of Management, Cornell University (2003); Warren C. Scoville Distinguished Teaching Award, Department of Economics, University of California, Los Angeles (1984-1986) **Membership:** Program Committee, Industrial Organization Society (2013); The Society of Labor Economists (2013); Program Committee, Industrial Organization Society (2009); American Economic Association (2004); Board Member, The Society for the Study of ASD and Social-Communication; SERCI; Royal Economic Society; The Econometric Society **Marquis Who's Who Honors:** Albert Nelson Marquis Lifetime Achievement Award (2017) **Hobbies:** Racquetball **Business Address:** 323 Sage Hall, Ithaca, NY, 14853

Neola Waller

Title: Secondary School Educator (Retired) **Industry:** Education/Educational Services **Date of Birth:** 02/14/1929 **Place of Birth:** Canadian County **State:** OK/USA **Parents:** Lewis Ray; Alma Marie (Liebscher) Shultz **Marital Status:** Married **Spouse Name:** William Waller, Junior (05/28/1949) **Children:** Mary Ann McKenney; Jeffrey Scott Waller **Education:** Master in Teaching of Science, College of William and Mary (1972); BA, Oklahoma State University (1949) **Career:** Secondary Mathematics Teacher, Virginia Beach City Public Schools, VA (1963-1993) **Civic:** Member, Virginia Women's Leadership Project; Chairman of the Administrative Board, Certified Lay Speaker, Lay Leader, Historian, Baylake United Methodist Church; Member, Virginia Beach Arts and Humanities Commission; Chair, Commission on the Status and Role of Women, Virginia Conference of the United Methodist Church; Delegate, Joint Conference of U.S. and Russia on Education; Member, United Methodist Mission Team to Cambodia **Creative Works:** Author, "The History of Baylake United Methodist Church" (2006-2016); Author, "The History of AAUW of Virginia" (1970-2010); Editor, Portion from 1955-2016, "The History of Baylake United Methodist Church" **Awards:** Secondary Mathematics Teacher of the Year for Virginia, Virginia Council of Teachers of Mathematics (1985) **Membership:** Board Member-at-Large, Educational Foundation, AAUW; Resolutions Chair, AAUW; Major Gifts Committee, Breaking Through Barriers, AAUW; Co-chair, Charting the Course Campaign, AAUW; President, AAUW of Virginia; Membership Vice President, AAUW of Virginia; Treasurer, AAUW of Virginia; Historian, AAUW of Virginia; President, AAUW of Virginia Beach (VA) Branch; Treasurer, AAUW of Virginia Beach (VA) Branch; Bylaws Chair, AAUW of Virginia Beach (VA) Branch; DKGSI; National Teachers of Mathematics (Now National Council of Teachers of Mathematics) **Marquis Who's Who Honors:** Albert Nelson Marquis Lifetime Achievement Award (2017) **Why did you become involved in your profession or industry:** Ms. Waller became involved in her profession because of her love of mathematics, and teaching allowed her to share this with thousands of students over her 30-year career. **What do you consider to be the highlight of your career:** Ms. Waller most memorable event occurred during her final year of teaching when students were recognized for making perfect scores on the College Board Mathematics Examination. Of all those students in southeast Virginia, in both public and private schools, half of them were her students. **Hobbies:** Travel; Reading; Music; Bridge **Shipping Address:** 3100 Shore Drive, Apartment PH 52, Virginia Beach, VA, 23451

Walter Denis Wallis, PhD

Title: Professor Emeritus **Industry:** Education/Educational Services **Company Name:** Southern Illinois University **Date of Birth:** 06/26/1941 **Place of Birth:** Sydney **Country of Origin:** Australia **Parents:** Walter Edwin Wallis; Olive May (Roche) Wallis **Marital Status:** Married **Spouse Name:** Elizabeth Ann Kaiser (11/15/2003) **Children:** Ralph (Deceased); Luke; Peter Kaiser (Stepson) **Education:** PhD, The University of Sydney (1968); BSc, The University of Sydney (1963) **Career:** Professor Emeritus, Southern Illinois University, Carbondale, IL (2008-Present); Professor, Southern Illinois University, Carbondale, IL (1985-2008); Associate Professor, The University of Newcastle, Australia (1975-1985); Senior Lecturer, The University of Newcastle, Australia (1970-1985); Lecturer of Mathematics, La Trobe University, Melbourne, Australia (1967-1970) **Creative Works:** Author, "One-Factorizations" (1997); Editor, "Computational and Constructive Design Theory" (1996); Author, "Combinatorial Designs" (1988); Co-Author, "Combinatorics-A First Course" (1985); Co-Author, "Combinatorial Theory: An Introduction" (1977); Co-Author, "Hadamard Matrices" (1972); Editor, "Journal of Combinatorial Mathematics and Combinatorial Computing"; Author, 20 Books; Co-Author, "Combinatorics-Room Squares"; Co-Author, "Sum-free Sets" **Membership:** Australian Mathematical Society; American Mathematical Society; Mathematical Association of America; Combinatorial Mathematical Society of Australasia; Founder, Australasian Conference on Combinatorial Mathematics and Combinatorial Computing; Founding Fellow, Institute of Combinatorics and Its Applications **Marquis Who's Who Honors:** Albert Nelson Marquis Lifetime Achievement Award (2017) **Why did you become involved in your profession or industry:** Dr. Wallis decided to enter his profession after he graduated, and met a couple of research mathematicians at conferences. He had an interest in mathematics from as far back as he could remember. **Hobbies:** Contract Bridge (ACBL Bronze Life Master) **Political Affiliations:** Green Party **Religion:** Atheist **Shipping Address:** 3117 Fawn Hill Dr, Evansville, IN, 47711

Marie Leclerc Walsh

Title: Nurse (Retired) **Industry:** Medicine & Health Care **Date of Birth:** 09/11/1928 **Place of Birth:** Providence **State:** RI **Parents:** Walter Normand Leclerc; Anna Mary (Ryan) Leclerc **Marital Status:** Married **Spouse Name:** John Breffni Walsh (6/18/1955) **Children:** George Breffni; John Leclerc; Darina Louise **Education:** MA, Columbia University (1955); BS, Columbia University (1954); Graduate, Waterbury Hospital School of Nursing (1951) **Career:** Disaster Services Nurse, Seattle-King County Chapter, The American National Red Cross (1990-1996); Disaster Services Nurse, Wichita, Kansas Chapter, The American National Red Cross (1985-1990); Adjunct Faculty, University of Virginia School of Continuing and Professional Studies (1981); Member, Disaster Steering Committee, Northern Virginia Community College (1976); Course Coordinator, Occupational Health Nursing, University Virginia School Continuing Education (1975-1977); Chairman, Disaster Nursing, Fairfax County Chapter, The American National Red Cross (1975); Clinical Nursing Instructor, St. Luke's Hospital, New York, NY (1957-1958); School Nurse Teacher, Agnes Russell School, Teachers College, Columbia University (1955-1956); Private Duty Nurse, St. Luke's Hospital, New York, NY (1953-1957); Team Leader, Hartford Hospital (1951-1953) **Career Related:** Research Librarian, Olive Garvey Center for Improvement Human Functioning, Inc. (1985); Research and Statistical Analyst, University of Virginia School of Continuing and Professional Studies (1975) **Civic:** President, McLean Newcomers and Neighbors (1999-2000); Vice President, McLean Newcomers and Neighbors (1997-1999); Election Officer, Election Board, Wichita, KS (1987-1988); Supervisor, Election Board, Wichita, KS (1987-1988); President, International Staff Wives, NATO, Brussels, Belgium (1978-1980); Vice President, International Staff Wives, NATO, Brussels, Belgium (1978-1980); County Committeewoman, Bergen County, NJ (1965-1966); Secretary, Democratic Party, Cresskill, NJ (1964-1966) **Membership:** American Association for the Advancement of Science; The New York Academy of Sciences; Sigma Theta Tau International; Pi Lambda Theta **Marquis Who's Who Honors:** Albert Nelson Marquis Lifetime Achievement Award (2017) **Hobbies:** Travel; Gardening **Shipping Address:** 8800 Prestwould Pl, McLean, VA, 22102

Ross Leslie Watts

Title: Finance Educator **Industry:** Education/Educational Services **Company Name:** National Taiwan University **Date of Birth:** 11/10/1942 **Place of Birth:** Hamilton **Country of Origin:** Australia **Parents:** Leslie R. Watts; Elsie B. (Horadam) Watts **Marital Status:** Married **Spouse Name:** Nancy M. Lamb (7/17/2010); Helen Clare Firkin (1/15/1966, Divorced 2007) **Children:** Andrew David; James Michael **Education:** PhD, The University of Chicago (1971); MBA, The University of Chicago (1968); Honorary Bachelor's in Commerce, University of Newcastle (1966) **Career:** Distinguished Chaired Professor, Accounting Research Center, National Taiwan University (2013-Present); Director, Accounting Research Center, National Taiwan University (2013-Present); Erwin H. Schell Professor Emeritus of Management, Massachusetts Institute of Technology (2013-Present); Erwin H. Schell Professor of Management, Massachusetts Institute of Technology (2007-2013); Professor, Sloan School, Massachusetts Institute of Technology (2005-2007); William H. Meckling Professor, University of Rochester (1998-2005); Endowed Chair, Rochester Telephone Corporation (1986-1998); Professor, Simon School of Management, University of Rochester (1984-1986); Associate Professor, Simon School of Management, University of Rochester (1978-1984); Assistant Professor, Simon School of Management, University of Rochester (1971-1978); Instructor, Graduate School of Business, The University of Chicago (1969-1970) **Career Related:** Honorary Professor, City University of Hong Kong (1996-Present); Visiting Professor, Massachusetts Institute of Technology (2002); Distinguished Lecturer, Hong Kong University of Science and Technology (1994); Professor of Commerce, University of Newcastle (1974-1976) **Creative Works:** Member, Advisory Board, Bank of America Journal of Applied Corporate Finance (1994-Present); Consultant Editor, Journal of Contemporary Accounting and Economics (2005-Present); Director, Accounting Research Network (1997-Present); Editor, Accounting Research Network (1997-Present); Co-Editor, Journal of Accounting and Economics (1979-Present) **Awards:** Inductee, Australian Accounting Hall of Fame (2016); Award, University of Newcastle (2013); Inaugural Lifetime Achievement Award, American Accounting Association (2013); Seminal Research Award, American Accounting Association (2004); Outstanding Educator Award, American Accounting Association (2000) **Membership:** American Finance Association; Institute of Chartered Accountants in Australia; Ford Foundation; American Accounting Association **Business Address:** National Taiwan University, Taipei City, Taiwan, 10617 **Shipping Address:** 22 Park St, Arlington, MA, 02474

Carol Ann Wehrheim

Title: Writer, Editor **Industry:** Writing and Editing **Date of Birth:** 12/18/1940 **Place of Birth:** Red Bud **State:** IL **Parents:** Elbert (Pete) Wehrheim; Fern Wehrheim **Marital Status:** Single **Spouse Name:** Charles Daniel Kuehner, Sr. (12/21/1981, 2003); Harrison Henry Bender (12/28/1969, Divorced 1976) **Education:** MA in Religious Education, McCormick Theological Seminary, Chicago, IL (1964); BA in Liberal Arts and Sciences, Southern Illinois University, Carbondale, IL (1962); Coursework in Education and Religion, University of Maine, Orono, ME, Towson State University, MD, McCormick Theological Seminary, Princeton Theological Seminary **Certifications:** Ordained Deacon and Ruling Elder, Nassau Presbyterian Church, Princeton, NJ **Career:** Writer, Editor, Princeton, NJ (1982-Present); Assistant Director, Doctor of Ministry Program, McCormick Theological Seminary (1979-1982); Secretary for Early Childhood Education, United Church Board for Homeland Ministries (1976-1979); Director, Woods Child Development Center (1974-1976); Director of Christian Education, St. John's United Church of Christ (1972-1974); Director of Christian Education, Hammond Street Congregational Church (1971-1972); Teacher, Union 90, Alton, ME (1970-1971) **Career Related:** Associate Readability Editor, Common English Bible Editorial Team (2011) **Creative Works:** Co-Editor, "Growing in God's Love" (2018); Author, "The Baptism of Your Child, Second Edition" (2018); General Editor, "Feasting on the Word Curriculum" (2010-2017); Author, "The Baptism of Your Child" (2006); Editor, "Seasons of the Spirit" (2000-2006); Author, "Growing Together" (2004); Author, "Getting It Together" (2002); Author, "The Great Parade" (1992); Author, "The Journey Ahead" (1990); Author, "The Storytelling Series" **Awards:** Honoree, Educator of the Year, The Association of Presbyterian Church Educators (2001); Recipient, Outstanding Young Woman of America, American Association of University Women (1968); Honoree, Distinguished Alumni, McCormick Theological Seminary **Membership:** American Association of University Women; Association of Presbyterian Church Educators **Marquis Who's Who Honors:** Albert Nelson Marquis Lifetime Achievement Award (2017); Distinguished Humanitarian (2017) **To what do you attribute your success:** Ms. Wehrheim attributes her success to her family. She somehow had the opportunity to do anything she wanted to do without criticism in her house. **What do you consider to be the highlight of your career:** The highlight of Ms. Wehrheim's career was publishing 18 board books of bible stories for toddlers, which were reviewed in the Philadelphia Enquirer. **Shipping Address:** 8 Ballantine Ln, Skillman, NJ, 08558

Cynthia Ellen Wein Lett

Title: Executive Director **Industry:** Business Management/Business Services **Company Name:** International Society of Protocol & Etiquette Professionals **Date of Birth:** 12/24/1957 **Place of Birth:** Takoma Park **State:** MD/USA **Parents:** Arthur Benjamin Wein; Mary Louise (Barker) Wein **Marital Status:** Married **Spouse Name:** Gerald Lee Lett (6/1/1991) **Children:** Cameron Barker Wein Lett **Education:** Masters, Antioch School of Law, Washington, DC (1983); BS, Purdue University, West Lafayette, IN (1979) **Career:** Executive Director, International Society of Protocol & Etiquette Professionals (2002-Present); Director, The Lett Group (1983-Present); President, Creative Planning International, Washington, DC (1983-Present); Director of Sales, The Ritz-Carlton Hotel Company, L.L.C., Washington, DC (1982-1983); Director of Sales, Sheraton Potomac Hotel, Rockville, MD (1981-1982); Sales Manager, The Sea Pines Resort, Hilton Head Island, SC (1980-1981); Marketing Researcher, Sheraton, Washington, DC (1979-1980) **Career Related:** President, The Lett Group (1996-Present); Etiquette Consultant, American Healthcare Institute (1989-Present); Corporate Affairs Manager, Chief Protocol, MCI Telecommunications Corp. (1992-1995); Director of Meetings, American Healthcare Institute (1991-1992); Director, Great Inns America, Annapolis, MD (1987-1989); Member, Great Inns America, Annapolis, MD (1987-1989) **Creative Works:** Editor, "Apropos!" (1996-Present); Author, "Modern Civility" (2015); Author, "That's So Annoying: An Etiquette Expert on the Worlds Must Irritating Habits and What You Can Do About Them" (2009); Editor, Travel Inn Style Newsletter (1990-1991); Author, "Getaway Innstyle, America's Fifty Best Inns" (1990) **Membership:** Executive Director, International Society of Protocol & Etiquette Professionals (2002-Present); Board of Governors, Foundation for International Meetings (1985-1986); American Society for Training and Development; Professional Convention Management Association; National Speakers Association; Washington Convention Visitors Association; Purdue Club; University Club; Platform Society **Marquis Who's Who Honors:** Albert Nelson Marquis Lifetime Achievement Award (2017) **Hobbies:** Gardening; Music; Photography; Travel **Business Address:** 13116 Hutchinson Way, Ste 100, Silver Spring, MD, 20906

Jasper A. Welch Jr.

Title: Security Company Executive, Consultant **Industry:** Consulting **Date of Birth:** 01/05/1931 **Place of Birth:** Baton Rouge **State:** LA **Parents:** Jasper Arthur; Oramay Ballinger Young Welch **Marital Status:** Single **Spouse Name:** Frances Carroll Wright (3/28/1953), Divorced (11/1984) **Children:** Jasper Arthur III; Carroll Welch Pawlikowski; Brent Ballinger **Education:** LHD, Honorable, Louisiana State University (2013); DSc, Honorable, Louisiana State University (2013); PhD in Physics, University of California, Berkeley (1958); MA in Physics, University of California, Berkeley (1954); BS in Physics, Louisiana State University (1952) **Career:** Assistant, Department Chief of Staff, U.S. Air Force (1981-1983); Defense Policy Coordinator, National Security Council (1979-1981); Assistant Chief of Staff for Analysis, U.S. Air Force (1975-1979); Chief Strategic Concepts, U.S. Air Force (1974-1975); Major General, U.S. Air Force (1975); Chief Strategic Analysis, Office of the Secretary of Defense (1971-1974); Chief Analyst, U.S. Air Force (1969-1971); Commissioned Officer Second Lieutenant, U.S. Air Force (1952) **Career Related:** Technology Consultant, Jasper Welch Associates (2012-Present); Technology Consultant, Jasper Welch Associates (1984-2011); Member, National Security Panel, University of California (2000-2007); Chairman, Military Advisory Panel to the Director of the CIA (1986-1998); Member, Advisory Council, National Aeronautics and Space Administration (1985-1989) **Civic:** Member, Foundation Board, Santa Fe Chamber Music Festival (1998-2004); Member, St. Andrews Episcopal Church (1969-1974); Youth Director, St. Matthews Episcopal Church (1965-1969) **Creative Works:** Author, "Atomic Theory of Gas Dynamic" (1965); Contributor, Articles, Science Journals; Contributor, Physical Review; Contributor, Strategic Review **Awards:** Recipient, Decorated Distinguished Service Medal with Oak Leaf Cluster; Recipient, Legion of Merit with Two Oak Leaf Clusters **Membership:** Member, National Academy of Engineers (1995-2005); American Geophysical Union; American Physical Society; Council on Foreign Relations **Hobbies:** Music; Theater; Gardening; Hiking; Racing sailboats **Shipping Address:** 2121 Kirby Dr Unit 4, Houston, TX, 77019

Eva Ella Mary Wells-Burton

Title: Insurance Salesperson, Primary School Educator **Industry:** Insurance **Date of Birth:** 09/12/1925 **Place of Birth:** Gillette **State:** WY **Parents:** Evart Rae Potts; Hazel Jemima Tharp Potts **Marital Status:** Widowed **Spouse Name:** Howard Dale Burton (6/7/1990, Deceased 12/28/2010); Edwin Harry Wells (1/25/1945, Deceased 1/21/1970) **Children:** Virginia; John; Harry; Valerie; Edella; Donna **Education:** Coursework, University of Wyoming (1942-1945) **Career:** Insurance Salesperson, Royal Neighbors of America, Rock Island, IL (1984-1991); Substitute Teacher, District I and at Sheridan County, Sheridan, WY (1964-1970); Teacher, District of Shasta County, Redding, CA (1949-1950); Teacher, District of Crook County (1946-1947); Teacher, District II of Campbell County, Weston, WY (1945-1946) **Career Related:** Insurance Counselor, Royal Neighbors of America, Sheridan and Glendo, WY (1989-1991) **Civic:** Church Choir **Creative Works:** Author, "Mystery in History: Legends of Currant Creek Ranch with Butch Cassidy and William H. Gottsche" (2004); Author, "Wyoming Legacy Little Powder School" (2000) **Awards:** Selling Goal in Fraternal Life Insurance, Three-Day Trip, Paradise Island, Bahamas **Membership:** President, American Legion Auxiliary (2001-2004); Royal Neighbors of America **Marquis Who's Who Honors:** Albert Nelson Marquis Lifetime Achievement Award (2017) **Hobbies:** Singing; Reading; Tutoring; Horseback riding **Political Affiliations:** Republican **Religion:** Methodist **Shipping Address:** 437 W Brundage Street, Sheridan, WY, 82801

Timothy Ray Wertime

Title: Music Educator **Industry:** Education/Educational Services **Company Name:** Wertime's Keyboard Studio **Date of Birth:** 04/10/1954 **Place of Birth:** Chambersburg **State:** PA **Parents:** Rudolf Milton Wertime; Phyllis Jane Wertime **Education:** Master's Degree in Sacred Music, Wittenberg University, Springfield, OH (1985); BA, Wittenberg University, Springfield, Ohio (1976) **Certifications:** Certified Water Safety Instructor, American National Red Cross (1975-1990); Certified Elementary Music Teacher, OH Department of Education; Certified Elementary School Teacher, Ohio Department of Education **Career:** Organist, St. John's Evangelical Lutheran Church, Mercersburg, PA (1995-Present); Teacher, Wertime's Keyboard Studio, Greencastle, PA (1992-Present); Choirmaster, St. John's Evangelical Lutheran Church, Mercersburg, PA (1995-2005); Music Teacher, Urbana City Schools, Urbana, OH (1986-1990); Organist, Northminster Presbyterian Church, Springfield, OH (1977-1992); Substitute Teacher, Clark County Schools, Springfield, Ohio (1977-1986); Substitute Teacher, Springfield City Schools, Springfield, OH (1977-1986); Director of Youth Choir, Covenant Presbyterian Church, Springfield, OH (1975-1976) **Career Related:** Director, Civic Boy Choir (1980-1992); Aquatics Director, Summer Camp (1976-1980) **Civic:** Ordained Presbyterian Deacon (1990-Present); Singer, Mercersburg Area Community Chorus (1990); Boy Scout Leader (1976-1980) **Creative Works:** Author, "English Liturgical Music of the Sixteenth Century (1984); Composer, "Magnificat-Song of Mary" (1984); Sportswriter, Photographer, "The Record Herald" (1973-1974); Author, "Forces and Factors Contributing to the Success of English Cathedral and College Choirs" **Awards:** Fellowship of Christian Athletes, Wittenberg University (1975-1976); 30-Year Honorary Teacher, Phi Delta Kappa International **Membership:** American Guild of Organists; Royal School of Church Music, England; Phi Delta Kappa International; Pennsylvania Music Educators Association; National Association for Music Education **Hobbies:** Walking; Hiking; Listening to Music; Playing Piano; Camping; Recitals; Concerts; Organist Every Sunday for Saint Johns Evangelical Lutheran Church, Mercersburg, PA **Political Affiliations:** Republican **Religion:** Presbyterian **Shipping Address:** 207 Leitersburg St, Greencastle, PA, 17225

Albert A. Wetherell, PhD

Title: Secondary School Educator (Retired) **Industry:** Education/Educational Services **Place of Birth:** Queens **State:** NY **Year of Passing:** 3/15/2018 **Parents:** Albert M. Wetherell; Hedwig D. Wetherell **Education:** PhD, St. John's University (1979); MA, Fordham University, The Jesuit University of New York (1967); BA, St. John's University (1965) **Career:** Retired (2004); Teacher, The New York City Department of Education (1967-2004); Member, Pastoral Council, St. Kevin RC Church; Sacristan, St. Kevin RC Church; Usher, St. Kevin RC Church **Career Related:** Member, John Paul II Cultural Center (Now Saint John Paul II National Shrine, Knights of Columbus) **Awards:** Achievement Award, American Federation of Teachers, AFL-CIO (2005); Bunzel Award, United Federation of Teachers (1992); Named Knight of the Grand Cross, Order of the Holy Sepulchre **Membership:** New York State Archives Partnership Trust; Polish Institute of Arts and Sciences of America; American Historical Association; Queens Historical Society; John Paul II Cultural Center (Now Saint John Paul II National Shrine); Józef Piłsudski Institute of America; Eastern Lieutenancy, Equestrian Order of the Holy Sepulchre of Jerusalem; Phi Alpha Theta; Phi Delta Kappa International **Marquis Who's Who Honors:** Distinguished Humanitarian (2017) **Hobbies:** Historical Research **Shipping Address:** 19312 47th Ave, Flushing, NY, 11358

Helen Lou White

Title: School Nurse Practitioner (Retired) **Industry:** Medicine & Health Care **Company Name:** Clemson University **Date of Birth:** 08/24/1936 **Place of Birth:** Caldwell **State:** KS **Parents:** Orville George Fauchier; Mildred Estelle (Garrison) Fauchier **Marital Status:** Married **Spouse Name:** Wayne Lee White (9/1/1957) **Children:** Michelle Lee; Dana Lynn; Jacki Lou **Education:** Diploma, St. Francis School of Nursing, Wichita, KS (1957) **Certifications:** Certified School Nurse, Pittsburg State University, Kansas (1983); National Certified School Nurse, Registered Nurse, State of Kansas **Career:** School Nurse, Director of Health Services, Unified School District # 353, Wellington, KS (1974-1994); Staff Nurse, Wellington Hospital and Clinic (1971-1974); Staff Nurse, St. Lukes Hospital, Wellington, KS (1961-1963); Staff Nurse, St. Francis Hospital, Wichita, KS (1957-1960) **Career Related:** Human Sexuality and AIDS Education Trainer for Elementary School Teachers (1989); Human Sexuality Teacher Trainer, Kansas Department of Education (1988); Advisory Council on Health and Physical Education, Kansas (1984-1990); Member, Planning Committee for Implementing School Nurse Certification Programs, Wichita State University (1984-1990) **Civic:** Director, Community Theater; Church Executive, United Methodist Women **Awards:** Kansas School Nurse of the Year, Kansas School Nurse Organization (1991) **Membership:** Legislative Co-chair, Kansas School Nurse Organization (2000-2005); Kansas Director, Board of Directors, National Association of School Nurses (1985-1989); Board of Directors, National Association of School Nurses (1985-1989); President, Kansas School Nurse Organization (1983-1985); President-elect, Kansas School Nurse Organization (1981-1983); American Nurses Association; Kappa Kappa Iota **Marquis Who's Who Honors:** Albert Nelson Marquis Lifetime Achievement Award (2017) **Why did you become involved in your profession or industry:** Ms. White became a nurse because of her admiration for the profession. **Hobbies:** Acting; Directing theater productions; Playing the piano; Singing; Travel **Political Affiliations:** Democrat **Religion:** Methodist **Shipping Address:** 438 E 20th St N, Wellington, KS, 67152

Polly Sears White

Title: Religious Organization Administrator (Retired) **Industry:** Religious **Date of Birth:** 01/29/1931 **Place of Birth:** Philadelphia **State:** PA **Parents:** W. Heyward Myers; Emily P. (Welsh) Myers **Marital Status:** Married **Spouse Name:** Peter White, MD (6/13/1953) **Children:** Katharine; Peter Jr. MD; Jennifer; Jeffrey **Education:** AB, Smith College (1953) **Career:** Program Director, Metro Toledo Churches United (1987-2001); Parish Secretary, St. Mary's Episcopal Church, Wayne, PA (1977-1985); Administrative Aide, Institute of Local and State Government, University of Pennsylvania, Philadelphia, PA (1953-1955) **Civic:** Member, Fort Meigs Cabinet (2005-Present); Perrysburg Area Historic Museum, Inc. (2002-Present); Secretary, Perrysburg Area Historic Museum, Inc. (2002-Present); Volunteer, Therapy Dogs International (2006-2014); Secretary, Board of Directors, Perrysburg Area Historic Museum (2001-2010); Volunteer Tour Guide, Downtown Toledo (1995-2002); Vice Chair, Operating Committee, First Call for Help of United Way, Toledo, OH (1993-2001); **Career Related:** Development, Spafford House Museum, Perrysburg Area Historic Museum, Inc. (2001); President, Perrysburg League of Women Voters (1995-1997); President, Perrysburg League of Women Voters (1995-1997); Member, Perrysburg Landmarks Commission (1992-1997) **Civic:** Member, Vestry, Altar Guild, Flower Guild, St. Timothy's Episcopalian Church (1993-1996); Board of Directors, Historic Perrysburg (1990-1996); Trustee, Historical Perrysburg (1990); Perrysburg League of Women Voters, Ohio (1986-1988); Member, Board of Directors, Wood County Planned Parenthood Council, Bowling Green, OH (1985-1986); President, Presbyterian Hospital Medical Auxiliary, Philadelphia, PA (1983-1985); Secretary-treasurer, Friends of Radnor Township Memorial Library, Wayne, PA (1978-1980 **Membership:** Co-President, Perrysburg Chapter, League of Women Voters (1999-2001) **Marquis Who's Who Honors:** Albert Nelson Marquis Lifetime Achievement Award (2017); Distinguished Humanitarian (2017) **What do you consider to be the highlight of your career:** Arranging church tours during the summer months, free of charge, well attended. They ran for 20 years. **Hobbies:** Tennis; Knitting; Bird watching; Gardening **Political Affiliations:** Democrat **Religion:** Protestant Episcopal **Shipping Address:** 525 E 6th St, Perrysburg, OH, 43551

Ralph Paul White

Title: Automotive Executive, Consultant **Industry:** Automotive **Date of Birth:** 08/01/1926 **Place of Birth:** Watertown **State:** MA **Parents:** Irving William White; Margaret Sarah (McGowan) White **Marital Status:** Widowed **Spouse Name:** Shirley Irene Christie (11/22/1947, Deceased) **Children:** Karin Ann; Eric John **Education:** Postgraduate Coursework, Yale University (1958-1959); BS in Industrial Engineering, Columbia University (1951) **Career:** Chairman, Troy Mills Inc. (1987-1989); Chief Executive Officer, Troy Mills Inc. (1983-1989); President, Troy Mills Inc. (1983-1986); Group Vice President, Parent Company, Ex-Cell-O, Troy, MI (1980-1983); President, Davidson Rubber Co., Dover, NH (1969-1980); Vice President, Davidson Rubber Co., Dover, NH (1966-1969); Partner, Management Consultant, Bavier, Bulger & Goodyear, New Haven, CT (1961-1966); Manager Data Processing, B.F. Goodrich Co., Shelton, CT (1956-1961); Instructor, Engineering Mechanics, University of Connecticut, Torrington, CT (1956-1957) **Career Related:** Board of Directors, D.G. O'Brien Co., Seabrook, NH; Board of Directors, Exeter Trust Co., Hampton, NH; Board of Directors, J.D. Cahill Co., Hampton, NH; Board of Directors, J.A. Wright Co., Keene, NH **Civic:** New Hampshire Business Finance Authority (1992-2004); Executive Board, Whittemore School of Business, University of New Hampshire, Durham, NH (1984-2002); Pease Development Authority, State of New Hampshire (1990-1993); Member, New Hampshire Industrial Development Authority (1985-1988); Member, New Hampshire Industrial Development Authority (1972-1980); Active in Fundraising and Advocacy, Alzheimer's Association **Military Service:** Infantry Officer, Second Lieutenant, World War II (1945) **Awards:** Inductee, Tau Beta Pi - The Engineering Honor Society **Membership:** Vice Chairman, New Hampshire Business and Industry Association (1984-1986); Board of Directors, New Hampshire Business and Industry Association (1970-1980); President, New Hampshire Business and Industry Association (1972-1973); American Institute of Industrial Engineers; Society of Automotive Engineers; Abenaqui Country Club; Rye Beach Club; Alzheimer's Association **Hobbies:** Skiing; Golf **Political Affiliations:** Republican **Religion:** Roman Catholic **Shipping Address:** 20 Chestnut St Apt N19, Exeter, NH, 03833

Jane K. Whitehead

Title: Archaeologist **Industry:** Sciences **Company Name:** Valdosta State University **Date of Birth:** 12/15/1944 **Parents:** George Goethals Whitehead; Norma Noreen Wiersig **Career:** Director, Archaeological Excavation Roman Baths, Carsulae, Italy (2004-Present); Professor, Valdosta State University, Georgia (2001-Present); Founding Editor, Etruscan News, New York, NY (2002-Present); Founding Editor, Etruscan Studies (1994-2000); Director, Archaeological Excavation Etruscan Settlement, La Piana, Italy (1982-2002) **Membership:** Founding Editor, Newsletter, U.S. Section, Istituto di Studi Etruschi ed Italici (2002); Fellow, National Explorers Club (1994); Fellow, Explorers Club; Phi Kappa Phi Honor Society **Hobbies:** Singing; Travel **Shipping Address:** 245 Pleasant Street, Laconia, NH, 03246

David Wayne Wicklund

Title: Lawyer **Industry:** Law and Legal Services **Company Name:** Shumaker, Loop & Kendrick **Date of Birth:** 08/07/1949 **Place of Birth:** St. Paul **State:** MN **Parents:** Wayne Glenwood Wicklund; Elna Katherine (Buresh) Wicklund **Marital Status:** Married **Spouse Name:** Susan Marie Bubenko (11/17/1973) **Children:** David, Jr.; Kurt; Edward **Education:** JD, The University of Toledo, Cum Laude (1974); BA, Williams College, Cum Laude (1971) **Career:** Partner, Shumaker, Loop & Kendrick (1981-Present); Associate, Shumaker, Loop & Kendrick (1974-1980) **Career Related:** Adjunct Instructor of Law, The University of Toledo (1988) **Creative Works:** Editor-in-Chief, Law Review, The University of Toledo (1974) **Awards:** Honoree, Best Lawyers in America (2009-2017); AV-Rated, Martindale Hubbell **Membership:** President, College of Law Alumni Association, The University of Toledo (1999-2000); Board of Governors, Antitrust Section, Ohio State Bar Association (1994-2001); Antitrust Section, ABA; Business Tort and Unfair Competition Committee, ABA; Civil Practice and Procedure Committee, ABA; Toledo Bar Association; Dean's Advisory Board, College of Law, The University of Toledo **Bar Admissions:** Ohio (1974) **Marquis Who's Who Honors:** Albert Nelson Marquis Lifetime Achievement Award (2017) **Why did you become involved in your profession or industry:** Mr. Wicklund grew up thinking of studying business or law, and law seemed more attractive as a profession. **Business Address:** 1000 Jackson St, Toledo, OH, 43604

Gary L. Widman

Title: President Emeritus **Industry:** Business Management/Business Services **Company Name:** Presidio Historical Association **Date of Birth:** 06/01/1936 **Place of Birth:** Fremont **State:** NE **Parents:** Benjamin H. Widman; Alice C. (Negley) Widman **Marital Status:** Single **Spouse Name:** Mary Margaret Donnelly (3/5/1972, Divorced 1988) **Children:** Andrew Scott; Natalie Claire Einhorn **Education:** LLM, University of Michigan (1966); JD, Hastings College of Law, University of California (1962); BS, University of Nebraska (1957) **Career:** President Emeritus, Presidio Historical Association (2016-Present); President, Presidio Historical Association (2007-2016); Senior Mediator, Concur Inc., Berkeley, CA (2001-2004); Professor of Law, School of Law, Santa Clara University (1998-1999); Chief Counsel, State Department of Parks and Recreation, Sacramento, CA (1995-1996); Attorney, Bronson, Bronson & McKinnon, San Francisco, CA (1988-1995); Director, Staff Attorneys, Ninth Circuit, U.S. Court of Appeals, San Francisco, CA (1985-1987); Of Counsel, Fulbright & Jaworski L.L.P. (1981-1985); Associate Solicitor, Department of the Interior, Washington, DC (1980-1981); Lecturer, University of California, Davis (1978); Lecturer, Boalt Hall (1977-1979); General Counsel, Council Environmental Quality, Executive Office of the President, Washington, DC (1974-1976); Professor, Hastings College of Law, University of California, San Francisco (1969-1980); Director of Resources and Environmental Law Program, Hastings College of Law, University of California, San Francisco (1969-1980); Associate Professor of Law, University of Denver (1966-1969) **Career Related:** Appointee, Governor P. Wilson, Bay-Delta Oversight Council (1993-1995); Trustee, Rocky Mountain Mineral Law Foundation (1977-1980); Trustee, Rocky Mountain Mineral Law Foundation (1969-1974) **Military Service:** U.S. Army (1957-1959) **Creative Works:** Author, "Legal Study of Oil Shale on Public Lands" (1969-2007); Project Director, "Legal Study of Oil Shale on Public Lands" (1969-2007) **Awards:** Recipient, Golden Bear Award, California Heritage Council (2014) **Membership:** President, Presidio Historical Association (2006-Present); Board Chairman, California Heritage Council (2006-2008); President, California Heritage Council (2004-2006); Vice President, Presidio Historical Association (2004-2006); Council Lawyers and Scientists, ABA (1984-1990); President, Trout Unlimited (1986-1990); Special Committee, Energy Law, ABA (1977-1982); Council, Section of Natural Resources, ABA (1975-1977); The State Bar of California **Bar Admissions:** Washington, DC (1982); California (1962) **Political Affiliations:** Independent **Shipping Address:** 28 Marinero Cir Apt 31, Tiburon, CA, 94920

Richard H. Wildnauer, PhD, MBA

Title: Life Science Executive, Independent Board Director **Industry:** Research **Company Name:** RHW Associates LLC **Date of Birth:** 02/14/1940 **Place of Birth:** New Kensington **State:** PA **Marital Status:** Married **Spouse Name:** Sharon Ann Novick (1/22/1966) **Children:** Tara Lynne **Education:** MBA in Management, Rider University (1974); PhD in BioChemistry, West Virginia University (1966); BS in Chemistry, Saint Vincent College (1962) **Certifications:** Masters Professional Director Certification **Career:** Founder, RHW Associates LLC (2007-Present); Non-executive Board Chairman, EuroMed Inc. (2009-2016), President, NeoStrata Company, Inc. (1995-2007); Chief Executive Officer, NeoStrata Company, Inc. (1995-2007); President, Baker Cummins Dermatologicals (1992-1995); Vice President of Technology and Business Development, Johnson & Johnson Company, (1988-1992); Vice President of Research and Development, Janssen Pharmaceutica, LLC (1982-1988); Director of New Product Development, Janssen Pharmaceutica, LLC (1979-1982); Senior Project Coordinator for New Products, Pharmaceutical Division, McNeil Laboratories (1977-1979); Associate Manager of Technology Planning, Exploratory Research Division, Johnson & Johnson Services, Inc. (1975-1977); Senior Research Associate in Skin Biology, Exploratory Research Division, Johnson & Johnson Services, Inc. (1967-1975); Trainee in National Institutes of Health, West Virginia University (1963-1966) **Career Related:** Board Director, Dynamis Skin Science Inc., Jenkintown, PA (2011-Present); Board Director, EuroMed Inc., Orangeburg, NY (2010-2016); NIH Postdoctoral Fellow, University of Kansas (1965-1967) **Civic:** Member, Board of Directors, United Way Central Jersey (2009-Present); Chief Volunteer Officer, United Way Central Jersey (1991-1993); Trustee, Board of Directors, United Way Central Jersey (1988-1995) **Creative Works:** Contributor, Scientific Articles to Professional Journals and Book Chapters in Dermatology, Skin Biology, Biochemistry and Polymer Sciences; Patents **Membership:** Counselor, SCORE (2011-Present); National Association of Corporate Directors; American College of Corporate Directors (ACCD); Society of Cosmetic Chemists; Society for Investigative Dermatology; American Academy of Dermatology **Marquis Who's Who Honors:** Albert Nelson Marquis Lifetime Achievement Award (2017); Distinguished Humanitarian (2017) **Hobbies:** Gardening; Walking; Travel **Religion:** Roman Catholic **Business Address:** 6 Pilgrim Run, East Brunswick, NJ, 08816

Louis Charles Willard, PhD

Title: Licensed Tax Preparer, Librarian **Industry:** Financial Services **Date of Birth:** 09/28/1937 **Place of Birth:** Tallahassee **State:** FL **Parents:** Bert Willard; Rose (De Milly) Willard **Marital Status:** Married **Spouse Name:** Nancy Booth (6/22/1963) **Children:** Michel Jonathan **Education:** PhD, Yale University (1970); MA, Yale University (1967); BD, Yale University (1965); BA, University of Florida (1959) **Career:** Stated Clerk, Presbytery of Tampa Bay (2013-2014); Director Accreditation and Institutional Evaluation, Association of Theological Schools in the U.S. and Canada (1999-2008); Librarian, Harvard Divinity School (1986-1999); Faculty, Harvard Divinity School (1986-1999); Librarian, Princeton Theological Seminary (1969-1986); Acting Librarian, Princeton Theological Seminary (1968-1969); Teaching Assistant, Yale Divinity School (1966-1968); Teacher, Tripoli Boys' School (1959-1962) **Career Related:** Licensed Tax Preparer (1992-Present); Programs and Committees Related to Preservation, American Theological Library Association (1970-Present); ATS Commission on Accrediting (1996-1999); Online Reference Resources, American Theological Library Association (1994-1999); Continuing Education, American Theological Library Association (1990-1992); Director, The Princeton Institute for Theological Librarianship (1979-1984); Chair, Microform Standards Committee, American National Standards Institute (1976-1992); Chair, Microform Standards Committee, National Information Standards Organization (1976-1992); Programs and Committees Related to Microforms, American Theological Library Association (1975-1990); Executive Secretary, Preservation Microform Program, American Theological Library Association (1970-1985); Accreditation Teams, ATS and Regional Associations (1969-1999) **Membership:** Ordained, Presbyterian Church (1965-2006); American Library Association; American Theological Library Association; Society of Biblical Literature; American Academy of Religion; Phi Beta Kappa; Chi Phi; Society for Values in Higher Education **Marquis Who's Who Honors:** Albert Nelson Marquis Lifetime Achievement Award (2017) **To what do you attribute your success:** The proudest moment of Dr. Willard's career was having his dissertation published. **Why did you become involved in your profession or industry:** Dr. Willard became involved in his profession not through inspiration, but through a series of organic events that transpired after he was not accepted into the military. **Shipping Address:** 1010 American Eagle Boulevard, Apt. 621, Sun City Center, FL, 33573

George Jacob Willauer, PhD

Title: American Literature Educator **Industry:** Education/Educational Services **Date of Birth:** 10/30/1935 **Place of Birth:** Philadelphia **State:** PA **Parents:** George Jacob Willauer, M.D.; Mary Catherine (Eshleman) Willauer **Marital Status:** Married **Spouse Name:** Cynthia Cameron Thun Willauer (6/11/1966) **Children:** George Jacob III; Elizabeth Christian **Education:** PhD, University of Pennsylvania (1965); MA, University of Pennsylvania (1959); BA, Wesleyan University (1957) **Career:** Chair, Department of English, Connecticut College, New London, CT (2000-2002); Dean of Academic Programs, Connecticut College, New London, CT (1997-2000); Charles J. MacCurdy Professor of American Studies, Connecticut College, New London, CT (1993-2002); Chair, Department of English, Connecticut College, New London, CT (1991-1994); College Marshal, Connecticut College, New London, CT (1989-2002); Professor, Connecticut College, New London, CT (1978-2002); Associate Professor, Connecticut College, New London, CT (1972-1978); Chair, Department of English, Connecticut College, New London, CT (1972-1977); Assistant Professor, Connecticut College, New London, CT (1966-1972); Instructor, Connecticut College, New London, CT (1962-1966); Assistant Instructor, University of Pennsylvania, Philadelphia, PA (1958-1962) **Career Related:** Mellon Foundation Visiting Faculty Fellow, Yale University (1998-1999); Visiting Faculty Fellow, Yale University (1993-1994); Visiting Professor of Literature, University of Dar es Salaam, Tanzania (1996); Instructor, Williams College and the Mystic Seaport Maritime Studies Program (1986-1988); Visiting Lecturer, Westminster College, Oxford, England (1982); English Speaking Union Fellow, Ireland (1972); English Speaking Union Fellow, England (1969) **Civic:** Honorary Trustee, Musical Masterworks (2013-Present); Trustee, Florence Griswold Museum (1978-Present); President, Lyme Public Library, Inc. (Now Lyme Public Library Foundation) (2003-2016); President, Community Foundation of Southeastern Connecticut (2000-2002); Trustee, Musical Masterworks (1998-2013); Lyme Public Library, Inc. (Now Lyme Public Library Foundation) (1997-2016); Trustee, Lyman Allyn Art Museum (1996-2004); Trustee, Lyme Land Conservation Trust (1996-2002); Trustee, Community Foundation of Southeastern Connecticut (1996-2002); Trustee, Lyme Public Library, Inc. (Now Lyme Public Library Foundation) (1995-1997); **Creative Works:** Editor, "A Lyme Miscellany: 1776-1976" (1977); Co-editor, "Original Discontent: Commentaries on the Creation of Connecticut's Constitution of 1818"; **Membership:** The Century Association, New York, NY; Acorn Club, New London, CT **Shipping Address:** 55-1 Beaver Brook Rd, Lyme, CT, 06371

Charles Wilson

Industry: Military & Defense Services **Date of Birth:** 09/06/1941 **Place of Birth:** Chicago **State:** IL **Parents:** Charles Wilson; Lorraine F. Wilson **Marital Status:** Married **Spouse Name:** Mona Dickerson (July 2, 1988) **Children:** Audrey; Angela; Andrew; Aaron **Education:** Military Diploma, Industrial College of Armed Forces **Career:** Financial Planner, Davis and Davis Planning (2016-Present); Sales Manager, Mass Mutual (1991-1997); Executive Director, Executive Leadership Program, Department of Defense, Washington, DC (1976-1988) **Career Related:** Military Liaison, Republic of China (1977-1980); Adjunct Professor, Park University, St. Louis (1977-1980); Municipal Consultant, City of Dayton, OH (1980); President, Advanced Ethonomics **Civic:** School Vice Chairman, Alexandria City Public School, Virginia (2003-Present); School Vice Chairman, Alexandria School Board; Advisory Board, Concerned Citizens Network, Alexandria, VA; Board of Directors, Advisory Board, Parent Leadership Training Institute **Military Service:** Lieutenant Colonel, U.S. Air Force (1986) **Membership:** Fellow, D.C. Life Under Writers Training Council; Chairman, Washington DC Area School Board; American Society of Training and Development; Human Rights Commission, International Personnel Management Association; Omega Psi Phi; Toastmasters; Queen St. Business **Achievements:** Achievements include invention of microwave oven carousel **Hobbies:** Flying **Political Affiliations:** Democrat **Religion:** Methodist

Mary Wilson

Title: Musician **Industry:** Other **Company Name:** University of West Virginia **Date of Birth:** 11/02/1939 **Place of Birth:** Minneapolis **State:** MN **Marital Status:** Married **Spouse Name:** Cecil B. Wilson **Education:** MusB, Northwestern University, Evanston, IL (1961) **Career:** Founder, Leader, Seneca String Quartet, Morgantown, West Virginia (1986-Present); Director Suzuki Program, Violin Teacher, West Virginia University (1977-Present); Private Teacher, Violin and Piano, Cleveland (1964-1977); Orchestra Band Director, Private Teacher, Deerfield Public Schools (1961-1964); Orchestra Band Director, Private Teacher, Lutheran Schools (1961-1964) **Civic:** Church Volunteer, Teaching and Music, Morgantown (1960-Present); Church Volunteer, Teaching and Music, Chicago, IL **Awards:** Studio Teacher of the Year, American String Teachers Association (2008, 2018); Outstanding Studio Teacher, West Virginia String Teachers Association (2011-2012); Distinguished Leader of the Year, WVMTA (2008); Outstanding Leadership Award, West Virginia University Community Music Program (2008); Outstanding Teacher Award (2005); State Outstanding Teacher of the Year, West Virginia Music Teachers Association (1996) **Membership:** District Chairman of Strings, West Virginia Music Teachers Association (1977-Present); State Officer Public (1989-Present); West Virginia String Teachers Association; American String Teachers Association; West Virginia Music Teachers Association **Shipping Address:** 237 Poplar Drive, Morgantown, WV, 26505

Roberta S. Wilson

Title: Learning Enhancement Coordinator **Industry:** Education/Educational Services **Company Name:** Southwest Tennessee Community College **Education:** MS in Management, Concentration in Nursing, Southern Nazarene University (1995) **Certifications:** Wound Care Certification **Career:** Learning Enhancement Coordinator, Southwest Tennessee Community College; Nurse, Wound, and Burn Care **Awards:** Nurse of the Year, Le Bonheur Children's Medical Center (2003); Methodist Star (2003); Best Beef Clubber, 4-H Beef Club; Number One in Showmanship for Beef Cattle, 4-H Beef Club **Membership:** Order of the Eastern Star; American Burn Association **Marquis Who's Who Honors:** Albert Nelson Marquis Lifetime Achievement Award (2017) **To what do you attribute your success:** Ms. Wilson attributes her success to never saying no, constantly reading, and being determined to obtain and use information. **Why did you become involved in your profession or industry:** Ms. Wilson became involved in her profession after she decided against a career as a veterinarian. **Where will you be in five years:** In five years, Ms. Wilson hopes to publish more of her work. **Hobbies:** Gardening; Sewing; Needlework **Shipping Address:** 7991 Bandye Lane, Bartlett, TN, 38133

Robert Marshall Wilson, PhD

Title: Distinguished Research Professor **Industry:** Education/Educational Services **Company Name:** Bowling Green State University **Date of Birth:** 10/18/1939 **Place of Birth:** Reading **State:** PA **Parents:** Robert Fitzpatrick Wilson; Eugenia (Kyle) Wilson **Marital Status:** Married **Spouse Name:** Antonia Gigliello (6/17/1967) **Children:** Daniel Lee; Laura Jean **Education:** Summer Faculty Fellow, University of Cincinnati (1972); Postdoctoral Fellow, Harvard University (1965-1967); PhD in Organic Chemistry, Massachusetts Institute of Technology (1965); BS in Chemical Engineering, The Pennsylvania State University (1961) **Career:** Distinguished Research Professor, Department of Chemistry, Center for Photochemical Sciences (Now Center for Pure and Applied Photosciences), Bowling Green State University (2005-Present); Fellow, Graduate School, University of Cincinnati (1988-Present); Interim Director, Center for Photochemical Sciences, Bowling Green State University (2013-2015); Professor Emeritus, Department of Chemistry, University of Cincinnati (2005); Head, Department of Chemistry, University of Cincinnati (1998-2004); Acting Head, Department of Chemistry, University of Cincinnati (1997-1998); Distinguished Research Professor, University of Cincinnati (1995-2005) **Career Related:** Advisory Board, Biomedical Research Center, Department of Chemistry, University of Cincinnati (1986-Present); Lecturer, "Pyridinium Salts as Photoinduced Electron Traps," Fourth International Conference on Physical and Theoretical Chemistry, Dublin, Ireland (2017); Lecturer, "Pyridinium Salts of Dihydrodioxins as Photoinduced Electron Traps in DNA Cleaving **Creative Works:** Co-Author, "Oxidation of Adenosine and Inosine: The Chemistry of 8-Oxo-7,8-dihydropurines, Purine Iminoquinones and Purine Quinones as Observed by Ultrafast Spectroscopy," American Chemical Society (2013); Co-Author, "Nitrenium Ions and Related Species in Photoaffinity Labeling," Nitrenes and Nitrenium Ions, Wiley Interscience (2013) **Awards:** Private Funding, Bowling Green Effort Foundation (2007-Present); Grant, Hoke S. and Stella Greene Chair in Biocatalysis (2006); Hans H. Jaffe Award for Distinguished Scholarship, Department of Chemistry, University of Cincinnati (2005) **Membership:** Co-organizer, Luminating Molecules Symposium, Central Region, American Chemical Society (2007); Organizer, Meetings, Ohio Photochemistry Society (2005); Organizer, Oesper Symposium (2004); Organizer, Meetings, Ohio Photochemistry Society (2002) **Hobbies:** Biology **Shipping Address:** 1420 Sheffield Dr, Bowling Green, OH, 43402 **Website:** https://www.bgsu.edu/arts-and-sciences/chemistry/faculty/r-marshall-wilson.html

Thomas Leon Wilson

Title: Physicist, Researcher **Industry:** Sciences **Date of Birth:** 05/21/1942 **Place of Birth:** Alpine **State:** TX **Parents:** Homer Marvin Wilson; Ogarita Maude (Bailey) Wilson **Marital Status:** Married **Spouse Name:** Joyce Ann Krevosky (5/7/1978) **Children:** Kenneth Edward Byron; Bailey Elizabeth Victoria **Education:** PhD, Rice University (1976); MA, Rice University (1974); BS, Rice University (1965); BA, Rice University (1964) **Career:** High-Energy Theoretical Physicist, National Aeronautics and Space Administration, Houston, TX (1969-2013); Employee, National Aeronautics and Space Administration, Houston, TX (1965-2011); Astronaut Instructor, National Aeronautics and Space Administration, Houston, TX (1965-1974) **Creative Works:** Author, Three Books; Contributor, Articles to Professional Journals **Awards:** Fellow, National Aeronautics and Space Administration (1969-1976); Hugo Gernsback Award, IEEE (1964) **Membership:** American Association for the Advancement of Science; American Nuclear Society; American Association of Physicists in Medicine; New York Academy of Sciences; American Physical Society **Marquis Who's Who Honors:** Albert Nelson Marquis Lifetime Achievement Award (2017) **Shipping Address:** 206 Woodcombe Dr, Houston, TX, 77062

Thomas Matthew Wilson III

Title: Of Counsel **Industry:** Law and Legal Services **Company Name:** Tydings & Rosenberg **Date of Birth:** 02/22/1936 **Place of Birth:** Ware **State:** MA **Parents:** Thomas Matthew Wilson, Jr.; Ann Veronica (Shea) Wilson **Marital Status:** Married **Spouse Name:** Deborah Ord Lockhart (2/10/1962) **Children:** Deborah Veronica; Leslie Lockhart; Thomas Matthew, IV **Education:** JD, University of Maryland (1971); BA, Brown University (1958) **Career:** Of Counsel, Tydings & Rosenberg (2012-Present); Partner, Tydings & Rosenberg (1979-2012); Assistant Attorney General, State of Maryland (1974-1979); Chief of Antritrust Division, State of Maryland (1974-1979); Sales Manager, Mideastern Box Manufacturing Company (1966-1974) **Career Related:** Fellow, American Bar Foundation **Creative Works:** Co-Author, "Intentional Grounding of an Implied Antitrust Exemption" (2011); Author, "An Unintended Consequence of Leegin" (2007); Author, "The Spectre of Double Recovery in Antitrust Federalism" (1989); Author, "Defending an Antitrust Action Brought by a State Attorney General" (1987); Editorial Advisory Board, "Bureau of National Affairs Antitrust and Trade Regulation Report" (1979-2016); Co-Author, "Reciprocity and the Private Plaintiff" (1972) **Awards:** Honoree, Best Lawyers in Baltimore Anti-Trust Law & Government Relations, Best Lawyers (2017); Honoree, A/V Preeminent Rated Super Lawyers, Martindale-Hubbell; Featured Listee, 23rd Edition, The Best Lawyers in America **Membership:** Antitrust Law and Monopolies Committee, Section on Business Law, International Bar Association (1983-Present); Section on Antitrust Law, American Bar Association (1974-Present); Coordinator, Committee on Legal Education, American Bar Foundation (1993-1994); Antitrust Section Council, American Bar Association (1990-1993); Chairman, State Antitrust Enforcement Committee, American Bar Association (1986-1989); Antitrust Subcommittee, Maryland State Bar Association (1975-1978); Section on Business Law, International Bar Association; Churchwarden's Chess Club; Annapolis Yacht Club; Metropolitan Club of the City of Washington **Bar Admissions:** U.S. Supreme Court (1977); Fourth Circuit, U.S. Court of Appeals (1976); State of Maryland (1972) **To what do you attribute your success:** Mr. Wilson attributes his success to his desire for helping others. **Political Affiliations:** Republican **Business Address:** 100 E Pratt Street, Floor 26, Baltimore, MD, 21202 **Shipping Address:** 19007 Brick Store Road, Hampstead, MD, 21074 **Website:** http://www.thomasmwilson.com

Walter Clinton Wilson, PhD

Title: Oil and Gas Industry Executive (Retired) **Industry:** Oil & Energy **Date of Birth:** 09/21/1942 **Place of Birth:** Brownwood **State:** TX **Year of Passing:** 9/12/2017 **Parents:** Henry Eliga Wilson; Lottie Mae (Palmore) Wilson **Marital Status:** Married **Spouse Name:** Debra M. Thompson (8/26/1965) **Children:** Walter Scott; Aimée Renee **Education:** Honorary PhD in Humanities, Howard Payne University (2009); Honorary HHD, Howard Payne University (2009); BS, Howard Payne University, Cum Laude (1965) **Certifications:** Certified Professional Accountant **Career:** Senior Vice President, EOG Resources, Inc., Houston, TX (1988-2000); Chief Financial Officer, EOG Resources, Inc., Houston, TX (1988-2000); Vice President, EOG Resources, Inc., Houston, TX (1987-1988); Controller, EOG Resources, Inc., Houston, TX (1987-1988); Financial Consultant, Superior Oil Company, Inc., Houston, TX (1985-1987); Assistant Controller, Superior Oil Co., Houston, TX (1982-1985); Financial Management, Exxon Mobil Corporation, USA, Kingsville, Corpus Christi, Houston, TX (1965-1981) **Career Related:** Member, Advisory Board, H. S. Grace & Co., Houston, TX (2001-Present) **Civic:** Trustee, Howard Payne University (2010-Present); Board of Directors, Lyric Performing Arts Company, Brownwood, Texas (2004-Present); Chairman, Lyric Performing Arts Company, Brownwood, TX (2004-2006); Chairman, Howard Payne University (2002-2004); Trustee, Howard Payne University, Brownwood, TX (1999-2008) **Military Service:** Lieutenant, U.S. Naval Reserve, Vietnam War (1966-1969) **Marquis Who's Who Honors:** Albert Nelson Marquis Lifetime Achievement Award (2017) **Political Affiliations:** Republican **Shipping Address:** 10112 Valley Forge Dr., Houston, TX, 77042

Richard Neill Winfield

Title: Lawyer **Industry:** Law and Legal Services **Date of Birth:** 01/20/1933 **Place of Birth:** Chicago **State:** IL/USA **Parents:** Richard Paul Winfield; Mary B. (Monaghan) Winfield **Marital Status:** Married **Spouse Name:** Deborah Mary Trainer (6/13/1959) **Children:** Richard Neill Junior; Pamela; Nicole **Education:** LLB, Georgetown University (1961); AB, Villanova University (1955) **Career:** Of Counsel, Clifford Chance US LLP (2002-Present); Partner, Clifford Chance US LLP (Formerly Known as Rogers & Wells), New York, NY (1969-2002); Associate, Royall, Koegel, Rogers & Wells, New York, NY (1967-1969); Assistant Counsel to Governor Nelson A. Rockefeller, Governor's Office, Albany, NY (1965-1967); Associate, Donovan, Leisure, Newton & Irvine, New York, NY (1961-1965); Presentations, Speaking Engagements, Lectures **Career Related:** Professor, Fordham Law School (2002-Present); Professor, Columbia Law School (2002-Present); Co-chairman, Board of Directors, Fund for Peace (2000-2004); Chairman, Board of Consultors, Villanova University School of Law, Pennsylvania (1980-2004); Chairman, Libel Litigation Conferences, Practising Law Institute, New York, NY (1979-2000); Faculty Communications Law Conferences (1977-2001) **Civic:** Chairman, World Press Freedom Committee (2006-2011); Treasurer & Co-founder, International Seniors Lawyers Project (2000-Present); Chairman, Board of Trustees, Convent Sacred Heart School, New York, NY (1987-1990); Member, Board of Visitors, School Languages and Linguistics, Georgetown University, Washington, DC (1987-1993) **Military Service:** Lieutenant, U.S. Navy (1955-1959) **Creative Works:** Author, "Exporting the Matrix: The Campaign to Reform Media Laws Abroad (2012); Co-author, "Breathing Life into Freedom of Information Laws: The Challenges of Implementation in the Democratizing World" (2013); Editor, Libel Litigation, PLI (1979, 1981, 1984, 1986, 1988, 1990, 1992, 1994, 1996, 1998, 2000) **Awards:** International Seniors Lawyers Project, Global Pro Bono Visionary Award (2015); First Amendment Award, Deadline Club (2002); **Membership:** Chairman, Media Law Reform Working Group, American Bar Association (ABA) (1996-Present); Central Europe and Eurasian Law Initiative; Co-founder, Board of Directors, Treasurer, International Senior Lawyers Project; Century Association; Association of the Bar of the City of New York; New York State Bar Association **Bar Admissions:** U.S. District Court for the Southern District of New York (1963); New York State Bar Association (1962); Virginia State Bar (1961) **Marquis Who's Who Honors:** Albert Nelson Marquis Lifetime Achievement Award (2017) **Political Affiliations:** Republican **Religion:** Roman Catholic **Shipping Address:** 40 5th Ave Apt 7E, New York, NY, 10011

Marianne Winter Miller Cohn

Title: Civic Activist **Industry:** Other **Date of Birth:** 01/15/1928 **Place of Birth:** Denver **State:** CO **Parents:** Henry Abraham Winter II; Esther (Sheflan) Winter **Marital Status:** Widowed **Spouse Name:** Dr. Isidore Cohn Jr. (Deceased 10/14/2015); Benjamin K. Miller (12/29/1948, Deceased 12/1972) **Children:** Judy Ellen (Deceased 2009); Philip Henry (Deceased 1996) **Education:** Coursework, Colorado University (1946-1947) **Civic:** Regional Vice Chairman, National Jewish Center (1999-Present); Chairman, Odyssey Ball of New Orleans Museum Art (1992-Present); National Board, National Jewish Health (1976-Present); Vice Chair, Arts Council of New Orleans (2007); Board of Directors, Church Artworks (2004); Vice President, Grants, Arts Council of New Orleans (2001); Board of Directors, Louisiana ArtWorks of Arts Council of New Orleans (2000-2006); Chairman, Board of Directors, Arts Council of New Orleans (1999); President, Arts Council of New Orleans (1997-1998); Vice President, Grants, Arts Council of New Orleans (1995-1996); Board of Directors, Louisiana State Museum (1994-2001); Treasurer, National Conference of Christians and Jews (1993-1994); National Board of Directors, National Conference of Christians and Jews (1993); Member, Governing Board, Louisiana State Museum (1992-2005); Secretary, National Conference of Christians and Jews (1991-1992); Board of Directors, Louisiana Council of Music and Performing Arts (1991-1992); Vice President of Development, Arts Council of New Orleans (1991-1992); President, Louisiana Museum Foundation (1989-1990); Member, Arts Council of New Orleans (1988-2009); Board of Directors, Jewish Endowment Foundation, New Orleans, LA (1987-1988); Executive Board, National Conference of Christians and Jews, New Orleans, LA (1987-1996); Chairman, Spouse Program Arrangements, American College of Surgeons National (1985); Member, Executive Board, Greater New Orleans Tourist and Convention Commission (1985); Chairman, Sun King Exhibit, Louis XIV, Louisiana State Museum (1984); Board of Directors, New Orleans Symphony Auxiliary (1980) **Awards:** Role Model Award, Young Leadership Council, New Orleans, LA (1998-Present); Chairman's Award, Arts Council of New Orleans (2012); Tzedakah Award, Jewish Endowment Foundation (2009); Robert S. Daniels MD Alumni Service Award, Louisiana State University School of Medicine (2006); Chairman's Award, National Jewish Center (1999); Humanitarian Award, National Jewish Center for Immunology and Respiratory Medicine (1995) **Political Affiliations:** Republican **Shipping Address:** 510 Iona St, Metairie, LA, 70005

Dorothy R. Wiswall, PhD

Title: Language Educator **Industry:** Education/Educational Services **Date of Birth:** 08/06/1947 **Place of Birth:** Alpirsbach **Country of Origin:** Germany **Marital Status:** Married **Spouse Name:** Thomas S. Wiswall (6/5/1976) **Children:** James; Karen **Education:** PhD, University of Michigan (1979); AM, University of Michigan (1972); AB, Cornell University (1971) **Career:** Adjunct Professor, Buffalo State College (2001-2015); Adjunct Professor, Canisius College, Buffalo, NY (1991-2003); Adjunct Professor, Niagara University (1981-1991); Teaching Fellow, University of Michigan, Ann Arbor, MI (1971-1975); Instructor, School for International Training, Brattleboro, VT (1971) **Career Related:** Tutor, Literacy New York Buffalo and Niagara, Inc. (2015-Present); Docent, Buffalo Museum of Science (2004-2015); Tutor, Literacy Volunteer, Buffalo, NY (2004-2010); Vice President, American Association of Teachers, German, Buffalo, NY (1998-2002); Workshop Presenter, BOCES, Buffalo, NY (1998-1999) **Civic:** Treasurer, Grand Island Community Chorus (2006-Present); Deacon, St. Timothy Lutheran Church, Grand Island, NY (2000-Present); Council Member, St. Timothy Lutheran Church, Grand Island, NY (1999-2005); President, Board of Directors, STLCC Child Care Center, Grand Island, NY (1995-1999) **Creative Works:** Author, "In the Seasons of My Mind" (2007); Author, "A Comparison of Selected Poetic and Scientific Works of Albrecht von Haller" (1981) **Awards:** State University of New York Chancellor's Award (2014-2015); Zontian of the Year, Zonta International Club, Buffalo, NY (2013); Second Prize, Faculty Division, Martin Luther King Poetry Contest, Canisius College (2003); Travel Grantee, University of Bern, Switzerland (1977) **Membership:** President, Zonta International Club, Buffalo (2008-2010); Secretary, Zonta International Club, Buffalo (2006-2008); Board of Directors, Zonta International Club, Buffalo (2004-2006); Vice President, American Association of Teachers of German (1998-2002); Phi Sigma Iota **Marquis Who's Who Honors:** Distinguished Humanitarian (2017) **Hobbies:** Swimming; Sewing; Violin; Poetry **Religion:** Lutheran **Shipping Address:** 1421 W River Road, NY, Grand Island, 14072 **Website:** http://www.dorothywiswall.com

Derish Michael Wolff

Title: Economist **Industry:** Financial Services **Company Name:** DM Wolff Everglades Associates **Date of Birth:** 05/14/1935 **Place of Birth:** Boston **State:** MA/USA **Parents:** Nathan Wolff; Ruth Mae (Derish) Wolff **Marital Status:** Married **Spouse Name:** Maureen Robinson **Children:** Jeffrey Scott; Hayley Beth **Education:** MBA, Harvard University, Cambridge, MA (1959); BA, University of Pennsylvania, Philadelphia (1957) **Career:** Chairman, Louis Berger, Inc., East Orange, NJ (2002-2010); President, Louis Berger, Inc. (1982-2002); Chief Executive Officer, Louis Berger, Inc. (1982-2002); Executive Vice President, Louis Berger, Inc. (1976-1982); Vice President, Louis Berger, Inc. (1968-1975); Chief Economist, Louis Berger, Inc. (1965-1967); Development Economist, Louis Berger, Inc., East Orange, NJ (1961-1965); Financial Analyst, Sigmund Werner, Inc., Belleville, NJ (1959-1961) **Career Related:** Visiting Lecturer, Massachusetts Institute of Technology (2001-2009); Director, Berger Group Holdings; Director, CHELBI; Director, Ammann & Whitney; Director, ABAM; Director, EA Engineering, Science & Technology; Director, Berger Devine Yaeger; Director, RBA Group; Guest Lecturer, U.N. Foreign Service Institute; **Civic:** Trustee, New Jersey Institute of Technology (2008-2011); Board of Overseers, New Jersey Institute of Technology (2006-2011); Member, Industry Advisory Panel, U.S. State Department (2001-2005); Member, Industry Advisory Panel, U.S. State Department (2001-2005); Member, Advisory Board, Huntsman Program, University of Pennsylvania (1997-2011); Member, Advisory Committee, New Jersey Institute of Technology (1995-2011); Advisory Committee, U.S. Trade and Development Program, U.S. State Department (1989-1992); Industrial Sector Advisory Committee, Department of Commerce (1988-1992); U.S. Presidential Trade Delegate to Japan, Department of State (1986); Class Chairman, PennGiving, University of Pennsylvania (1975-1982) **Creative Works:** Member, Editorial Board, Construction Business Review (1991-1995); Member, Editorial Board, Modern Engineering Tech (1978-1980); **Awards:** President's Medal for Lifetime Achievement, New Jersey Institute of Technology (2003) **Membership:** Vice Chairman, Building Futures Council (1998-2006); Steering Group/GATT Negotiations, Center for Strategic and International Studies (1989); Chairman, International Engineering and Construction Industries Council (1988-1990); Vice Chair, International Engineering Committee, American Consultant Engineers Council (1986-1993) **Marquis Who's Who Honors:** Albert Nelson Marquis Lifetime Achievement Award (2017) **Hobbies:** Skiing; Reading **Religion:** Jewish **Shipping Address:** 1881 Washington Ave Apt 16B, Miami Beach, FL, 33139

Vivien Perrine Woofter

Title: Interior Designer **Industry:** Other **Date of Birth:** 09/10/1930 **Place of Birth:** Weston **State:** WV **Parents:** Orie Ray Perrine; Hazel Lucille (Bostic) Perrine **Marital Status:** Married **Spouse Name:** Perry Wilson Woofter (10/5/1952) **Children:** James Perry; Lori Evan Hugh **Education:** Honorary LHD, West Virginia University (1998); BS in Home Economics, West Virginia University (1952) **Career:** Historic Conservation Advisor, Cultural Heritage Office, Overseas Buildings Operations, U.S. Department of State (2004-Present); Director of Interiors and Furnishings Division, Bureau of Overseas Buildings Operations, U.S. Department of State (1988-2004); Senior Interior Designer, U.S. Department of State (1981-1988); Head Interior Design, U.S. Department Health and Human Services (1977-1981); Head Interior Design, The White House (1976-1977); Interior Designer, General Services Administration, Washington, DC (1968-1976) **Career Related:** President, Visiting Committee, College of Creative Arts, West Virginia University (2001-Present); Board of Directors, WVU Foundation (1999-2010); Alumni Board, West Virginia University, Morgantown, VA (1994-2004); Volunteer Member, Designer Renovation, President's House Committee, West Virginia University (1996-2003) **Civic:** Restoration Work, The Metropolitan Theatre, Morgantown, VA (2003); Restoration, President's Home, West Virginia University, Morgantown, WV (1992); Restoration, Governor's Mansion, Charleston, WV (1980) **Creative Works:** Interior Designer, Riyadh Embassy, Saudi Arabia; Interior Designer, Ambassador's Residence, Paris, France; Interior Designer, Ambassador's Residence, Buenos Aires, Argentina; Interior Designer, Building Headquarters, U.S. Department of Health and Human Services; Federal Design Council of Excellence, Building Headquarters, U.S. Department of Health and Human Services (1979); Author, Developmental Furniture Standards- Physical Handicap, Congressional Record (1977) **Membership:** International Interior Design Association **Business Address:** U.S. Department of State, Washington, DC, 20522 **Shipping Address:** 900 N. Taylor Street, Unit 1010, Arlington, VA, 22203

Edward Slavko Yambrusic

Title: Lawyer **Industry:** Law and Legal Services **Date of Birth:** 03/09/1933 **Place of Birth:** Conway **State:** MA **Parents:** Michael Misko Yambrusic; Slavica Sylvia Yambrusic **Marital Status:** Married **Spouse Name:** Natalie Visniak (1990) **Education:** PhD in Public International Law, Catholic University of America (1984); JD, University of Baltimore (1966); Postgraduate Work, Law Center, Georgetown University (1961); Bachelor's Degree, Duquesne University (1957) **Certifications:** Diploma, International Law and International Relations, Center for Study and Research (1970); International Law, The Hague Academy, Netherlands (1969) **Career:** Attorney Adviser, Office of the Register of Copyrights (1969-1998); Private Practice, International and Immigration Law (1969); Copyright Examiner, U.S. Copyright Office, Library of Congress, Washington, DC (1960-1969) **Career Related:** President, AMCRO International (1995); Society of Federal Linguists (1980); Legal Counsel, National Ethnic Studies Assembly (1976); President, National Confederation of American Ethnic Groups, Washington, DC **Civic:** National Chairman, Croatian-American Bicentennial Committee; National Chairman, National Pilgrimage of Croatian-Americans to National Shrine of Immaculate Conception, Washington, DC; Vice President, Croatian Academy of America **Military Service:** Served to Captain, U.S. Army (1957-1959) **Creative Works:** Author, "Trade Based Approaches to the Protection of Intellectual Property" **Awards:** Certificate, 40 Years of Distinguished Service to the People of the United States of America, Librarian of Congress (1957-1998) **Membership:** American Bar Association; Maryland Bar Association; International Law Association; International Fiscal Association; American Society of International Law; Croatian Catholic Union of America; Croatian Fraternity Union of America **Bar Admissions:** U.S. Court of International Trade (1988); U.S. Supreme Court (1972); U.S. Court Customs and Patent Appeals (1972); State of Maryland (1969) **Shipping Address:** 4720 Massachusetts Avenue NW, Washington, DC, 20016

James F. York

Title: Professor of Electrical Engineering, Program Manager of Electrical Engineering Technology **Industry:** Education/Educational Services **Company Name:** Washington State Community College **Date of Birth:** 09/30/1938 **Place of Birth:** Huntington **State:** NY **Parents:** Randolph M. York; Helen F. York **Marital Status:** Married **Spouse Name:** Evelyn Yvonne Anderson (4/6/1962) **Children:** David Michael; Robert Alan **Education:** MS in Chemical Engineering, Ohio University, Athens, OH (1968); BS in Chemical Engineering, Purdue University, West Lafayette, IN (1961) **Career:** Professor, Electrical Engineering, Washington State Community College, Marietta, OH (2007-Present); Instructor, The Washington County Career Center, Washington County, OH (1999-Present); Principal Engineer, General Electric Plastics, Washington, WV (1987-1999); Research Manager, Borg-Warner Chemicals, Morgantown, WV (1974-1987); Administrative Manager, Borg-Warner Chemicals, Washington, WV (1964-1974); Senior Engineer, Borg-Warner Chemicals, Washington, WV (1961-1964) **Awards:** Award for Innovative Fire-Retardant Additive Product, IR-100 (1981) **Membership:** American Chemical Society **Marquis Who's Who Honors:** Albert Nelson Marquis Lifetime Achievement Award (2017) **Shipping Address:** 50 Cherry Hills Dr, Belpre, OH, 45714

Richard Yurko

Title: Lawyer **Industry:** Law and Legal Services **Company Name:** Yurko, Salvesen & Remz, PC **Date of Birth:** 10/30/1953 **Place of Birth:** Ottawa **Country of Origin:** Canada **Parents:** Michael Yurko; Catherine (Ewanishan) Yurko **Children:** Nathan; Daniel **Education:** JD, Harvard University, Cum Laude (1979); AB, Dartmouth College, Summa Cum Laude (1975) **Career:** Shareholder, President, Yurko, Salvesen & Remz, PC, Boston, MA (1995-Present); Chairman, Litigation Department, Hutchins, Wheeler & Dittmar, Boston, MA (1992-1994); Shareholder, Hutchins, Wheeler & Dittmar, Boston, MA (1992-1994); Hiring Partner, Widett, Slater & Goldman, Professional Corporation, Boston, MA (1992); Chairman, Litigation Department, Widett, Slater & Goldman, Professional Corporation, Boston, MA (1989-1991); Shareholder, Widett, Slater & Goldman, Professional Corporation, Boston, MA (1987-1992); Associate, Widett, Slater & Goldman, Professional Corporation, Boston, MA (1985-1987); Associate, Bingham, Dana & Gould, Boston, MA (1980-1985); Law Clerk, Judge James L. King, United States District Court for the Southern District of Florida, Miami, FL (1979-1980) **Career Related:** Teacher, Legal Research and Writing, Boston University School of Law **Creative Works:** Contributor, Articles, Legal Journals **Membership:** Treasurer, GLAD (2016-Present); Vice President, GLAD (2014-2015); Treasurer, GLAD (2012-2013); Board Member, GLAD (2009); Ad Hoc Committee, Creation Business Court, Boston Bar Association (1999-2000); Head Mentoring Committee, Boston Bar Association (1998-2004); ABA; Massachusetts Bar Association; Former Chairman, Antitrust Committee, Boston Bar Association; Former President, Frank J. Murray Inn Court; Phi Beta Kappa **Bar Admissions:** U.S. District Court District of Massachusetts (1980); U.S. Court of Appeals for the First Circuit (1980); Massachusetts (1979) **Business Address:** One Washington Mall, 11th Floor, Boston, MA, 02108

Neal Zierler, PhD

Title: Mathematician **Industry:** Sciences **Date of Birth:** 09/17/1926 **Place of Birth:** Baltimore **State:** MD **Marital Status:** Married **Spouse Name:** Jacqueline Stephan (1992); Betty Matsumoto (Divorced 1970) **Children:** Robert Eugene; Joan Mariye; Ann Michie **Education:** PhD, Harvard University (1959); AM, Harvard University (1949); Graduate, Japanese Language School, U.S. Navy (1946); AB, Johns Hopkins University (1945) **Career:** Technical Staff, Center for Communications Research, Institute of Defense Analysis, Princeton, NJ (1965-1996); Head, Sub-Department of Process Analysis, MITRE Corporation, Bedford, MA (1962-1965); Senior Scientist, ARCON Corporation (1961-1962); Supervisor, Information Processing Group, Jet Propulsion Laboratory, California Institute of Technology, Pasadena, CA (1960-1961); Technical Staff, Lincoln Laboratory, Massachusetts Institute of Technology, Lexington, MA (1954-1960); Technical Staff, Instrumentation Laboratory, Massachusetts Institute of Technology, Cambridge, MA (1952-1954); Mathematician, Physicist, Ballistic Research Laboratories, Aberdeen, MD (1951) **Career Related:** Fellow, IEEE **Military Service:** Lieutenant, U.S. Navy (1944-1946) **Creative Works:** Patentee, Error-Detecting and Error-Correcting Devices; Contributor, Articles, Professional Journals **Membership:** American Mathematical Society; Mathematical Association of America; American Physics Society **Hobbies:** Tennis; Skiing; Photography **Shipping Address:** 70 Golf Course Road, South Burlington, VT, 05403

George Zimmerman, PhD

Title: Physicist **Industry:** Sciences **Company Name:** George O. Zimmerman PhD **Date of Birth:** 10/20/1935 **Place of Birth:** Katowice **Country of Origin:** Poland **Parents:** Charles Zimmerman; Carolin Olga (Fisher) Zimmerman **Marital Status:** Married **Spouse Name:** Isa Kaftal (10/4/1964) **Education:** PhD, Yale University (1963); Wilson Fellow, Yale University (1959-1960); D.N. Clark Fellow, Yale University (1959-1961); MS, Yale University (1959); BS, Yale University (1958) **Career:** Professor Emeritus, Boston University (2001-Present); Director, Honors Program in Science & Engineering High School Students, Boston University (1964-1985); Chairman, Faculty Council, Boston University (1985-1986); Chairman, Department of Physics, Boston University (1973-1983); Associate Chairman, Department of Physics, Boston University (1971-1972); Professor, Boston University (1974-2001); Associate Professor, Boston University (1968-1974); Assistant Professor of Physics, Boston University (1963-1968); Research Associate, Yale University (1962-1963) **Career Related:** Co-chair, International Symposium on Jahn-Teller Effect (1999-2000); President, Super Solder Corp. (1997-1999); Visiting Scholar, Imperial College, London, United Kingdom (1997); President, Board of Directors, Kenmore Tower Corp. (1996-2002); President, Zerres Corp. (1992-1997); Visiting Scholar, Harvard University (1988); Visiting Scholar, Kamerling Onnes Laboratorium, Leiden, The Netherlands (1988); Visiting Scientist, Brookhaven National Laboratory (1980); Associate Physicist, University of California, San Diego (1973); Visiting Scientist, National Magnet Laboratory, Cambridge, MA (1964-1970); Staff, National Magnet Laboratory, Cambridge, MA (1964); Lecturer in Field **Civic:** Chairman, Boston University Planning Committee (1999, 2001); Board of Directors, The Symphony by the Sea **Creative Works:** Contributor, Articles on Low Temperature Physics, Phase Transitions, the Jahn-Teller Effect, Superconductivity, and History of Physics, Professional Journals; Patentee in Field **Awards:** Membership Advisory Committee, American Physical Society (2013-2015); Advisory Committee, American Institute of Physics (2011-2014) **Membership:** Advisory Committee, American Institute of Physics (2012-Present); Member at Large, Forum of the History of Physics, American Physical Society (2007-2010); Fellow, American Physical Society; American Institute of Physics; American Physical Society; American Association for the Advancement of Science; New York Academy of Sciences; Materials Research Society; American Chemical Society; Phi Beta Kappa; Sigma Xi **Hobbies:** Classical music; Photography **Business Address:** 566 Commonwealth Ave, Boston, MA, 02215

Natalia Louise Zunino, PhD

Title: Psychologist **Industry:** Medicine & Health Care **Date of Birth:** 11/23/1937 **Place of Birth:** New York **State:** NY **Parents:** Frank Anthony Zunino; Elizabeth (Delafield) Zunino **Marital Status:** Divorced **Spouse Name:** Philip Puschel (6/29/1974, Divorced 1978) **Education:** PhD, New York University (1982); MA, New York University (1975); MA, Columbia University (1962); BA, Mount Holyoke College, Massachusetts (1959) **Certifications:** Licensed Psychologist, State of New York; Licensed Psychologist, State of Connecticut **Career:** Supervisor, Center for Study of Anorexia and Bulimia (1995-Present); Supervisor, Metropolitan Institute for Training in Psychoanalytic Psychotherapy, New York, NY (1985-Present); Private Practice (1984-Present); Supervisor, Staff Psychotherapist, Eating Disorder Resource Center, New York, NY (1986-2004); Participant, Eastern Group, Psychotherapy Training Program (1997-1998); Member, Faculty, Center for Study of Anorexia and Bulimia, New York, NY (1987-1996); Participant, Intensive-External Program, Family Institute of Westchester, Harrison, NY (1990-1994); Psychotherapist, Family and Couple Treatment, Institute of Contemporary Psychotherapy, New York, NY (1988-1990); Staff Psychotherapist, Washington Square Institute, New York, NY (1984-1987); Staff Psychotherapist, Metropolitan Center for Mental Health, New York, NY (1983-1985); Researcher, Time-Life Books, New York, NY (1962-1967) **Career Related:** Executive Committee, Center for Study of Anorexia and Bulimia (2006-2014); Member, Intake Committee (1997-2014); Adjunct Assistant Professor, College of Staten Island, New York (1984-1986) **Creative Works:** Editor, "Sociology: The Study of Human Relationships" (1972); Editor, "Psychology: Its Principles and Applications" (1969); Senior Editor, Harcourt Brace Jovanovich, New York, NY (1967-1980); Contributor, Articles, Professional Journals **Membership:** American Psychological Association; National Eating Disorders Association **Marquis Who's Who Honors:** Albert Nelson Marquis Lifetime Achievement Award (2017) **Why did you become involved in your profession or industry:** Dr. Zunino became involved in her industry out of a desire to have a positive impact on other people's lives. **Hobbies:** Horseback riding; Gardening **Shipping Address:** 115 4th Ave Apt 7G, New York, NY, 10003

HONORED
LISTEES

71st Edition

ABDUL RAHMAN, MAI, T: Educational Researcher **I:** Education/Educational Services **CN:** Consultant **SC:** Palestine **PT:** Muhammad Abdul-Rahman; Salwa Sa'ed Eldeen Abdul-Rahman **MS:** Married **SPN:** Hassan Abdul-Ali **CH:** Muhammad Abdul-Ali; Omar Abdul-Ali; Iman Abdul-Ali; Salam Abdul-Ali **ED:** Doctoral, Howard University (2014); MA, Trinity University; BA, Drake University **CT:** Teaching Institute Certificate in College Teaching, Johns Hopkins University (2017); Certificate in Faculty Teaching, Howard University Graduate School (2014); Certificate in International Studies, Howard University Graduate School (2014) **C:** Educational Researcher; Writer; Teacher; Human Rights Evaluator; Affiliate, Transformational Leadership, Ethnic and Cultural Diversity, Human Rights, Teaching and Learning, Educational Policy, and Civil Rights, Historically Black Colleges **CIV:** Invited Speaker, Cultural Leadership: Transformational Journey (2017); Invited Speaker, Northeastern University Human Rights Institute (2016); Invited Speaker, U.S. Human Rights Cities Gathering (2016); Invited Speaker, United Methodist Church Human Rights Task Force (2014); Guest Lecturer, Howard University (2014); Invited Speaker, University of Maryland (2013); Invited Speaker, Jewish-Islamic Dialogue Society of Washington D.C. (2013); Invited Speaker, Howard Community College (2011-2013); Invited Speaker, Operation Understanding D.C. (2012-2016); Participant, Panel Discussion, Washington, D.C. Jewish Community Center (Now Edlavitch Jewish Community Center of Washington, D.C.) (2010); Invited Speaker, Center for South Asian and Middle Eastern Studies, University of Illinois (2009); Committee Member, D.C. Hunger Solutions (2005); Committee Member, Peace Commission of the Episcopal Diocese of Washington, D.C. (2001-2005); Invited Speaker, Sacred Circles Conference, Washington National Cathedral (2005); Invited Speaker, University of Pittsburgh (2004) **CW:** Author, "U.S. Homeless Student Population" (2017); Author, "Teaching Outside the Box: Beyond the Deficit Driven School Reforms" (2017); Author, "Arab American Women and the U.S. Gender Discourse" (2016); Author, "District of Columbia Black Homeless Youth: Limits and Possibilities" (2016); Co-author, "Ethnic and Cultural Diversity at HBCUs and Its Impact on Students, Faculty and Staff" (2015); Author, "Factors That Influence the Education of District of Columbia Black Homeless Youth: Racial Inequality, Poverty and Consecutive Educational Reform" (2015); Author, "Homeless Student Population: Homeless Youth Education, Review of Research, Classifications, Typologies, and the U.S. Federal Legislative Response" (2015); Co-author, "2015 DC Human Rights City Report: State of Human Rights in the District of Columbia as a Human Rights City" (2015); Co-author, "State of Human Rights in the District of Columbia" (2012); Co-author, "Diversity at Historically Black Colleges & Universities" (2012); Contributor, "Starting Off Right 2006: A School System in Transition" (2006); Author & Co-producer, "Arab Women Speak Out" (1998); Co-author, "Quality Management Savings at Al Hussein Hospital, Salt, Jordan" (1997); Author, "QM Practices & institutionalization of Q.A." (1997); Co-author, "Quality Assurance Guides: Health reform in Jordan" (1996); Co-editor, "Journal of Behavioral and Social Science" **AW:** Honoree, Human Rights Commissioner, The Council of the District of Columbia (2014) **MEM:** President, American-Palestinian Women's Association **H:** Reading; Biking; Swimming; Hiking **RE:** Islam **BA:** 5652 46th Place, Hyattsville, DC, 20781 **URL:** https://americanpalestinianwomen.wordpress.com/2016/12/12/standing-with-ourjewish-

ABDULRAUF, SALEEM I., T: Neurosurgeon-in-Chief **I:** Medicine & Health Care **CN:** Saint Louis University Hospital **ED:** Skull Base Neurosurgical Fellow, University of Arkansas for Medical Sciences (1998-1999); Vascular Neurosurgical Fellow, Yale School of Medicine (1997-1998); Neurosurgical Chief Resident, Henry Ford Hospital, Detroit, MI (1996-1997); Neurosurgical Resident, Henry Ford Hospital, Detroit, MI (1992-1996); Surgical Intern, Henry Ford Hospital, Detroit, MI (1991-1992); MD, School of Medicine, Saint Louis University (1991); BA in Biology, Washington University in St. Louis (1986) **CT:** License to Practice Medicine, State of Illinois (2001); License to Practice Medicine, State of Missouri (2000); Diplomat, American Board of Neurological Surgery; Certification, National Board of Medical Examiners **C:** Neurosurgeon-in-Chief, Saint Louis University Hospital (2008-Present); Director, Saint Louis University Center for Cerebrovascular and Skull Base Surgery, Saint Louis University Hospital (2008-Present); Chairman, Department of Neurosurgery, Saint Louis University School of Medicine (2011); Tenured Professor, Neurosurgery, School of Medicine, Saint Louis University (2009); Associate Professor, Neurosurgery, School of Medicine, Saint Louis University (2005-2009); Assistant Professor, Neurosurgery, School of Medicine, Saint Louis University(2000-2005); Program Director, Cerebrovascular and Skull Base Surgery Fellowship, Saint Louis University Hospital (2004); Director, Cerebrovascular and Skull Base Surgery Program, Saint Louis University Hospital (2000); Consultant Neurological Surgeon, Cardinal Glennon Children's Hospital, SSM Health (2000); Attending Staff, Neurological Surgery, Saint Louis University Hospital, SSM Health (2000); Assistant Professor, Neurological Surgery, University of Arkansas for Medical Sciences (1998-2000); Attending Staff, Neurological Surgery, Arkansas Children's Hospital (1998-2000); Consultant, Neurological Surgery, John L. McClellan Memorial Veterans Hospital (1998-2000); Attending Staff, Neurological Surgery, University of Arkansas for Medical Sciences (1998-2000); Instructor, Neurological Surgery, Yale School of Medicine (1997-1998); Assistant Director, Neuroscience Intensive Care Unit, Yale New Haven Hospital, Yale New Haven Health (1997-1998); Attending Staff, Neurological Surgery, Yale New Haven Hospital, Yale New Haven Health (1997-1998); Consultant, Neurological Surgery, Veterans Hospital West Haven Campus (1997-1998) **AW:** Award for Reference Text Book for Bypass Procedures in Neurosurgery (2016); Named to Best Doctor's in America (2003-2011); Named to One of the City's Top Neurological Surgeons, St. Louis Magazine (2005-2010); Featured Listee, "In Their Hands" (2002); Outstanding Resident Award, Board of Governors of Henry Ford Hospital (1997); Best Resident Paper Presentation, Michigan Association of Neurological Surgeons Annual Meeting (1994); Research Grants **MEM:** President, Walter E. Dandy Neurosurgical Society; Past Secretary General, World Federation of Neurosurgical Societies; Chairman, Neurosurgical Anatomy Committee, World Federation of Neurosurgical Societies; Past Vice President, Congress of Neurological Surgeons; Past Inaugural Chairman, International Division, Congress of Neurological Surgeons; Fellow, American College of Surgeons; American Medical Association; American Association of Neurological Surgeons; American College of Surgeons; American Heart Association, Inc.; Joint Section on Cerebrovascular Surgery, American Association of Neurological Surgeons and Congress of Neurological Surgeons; Joint Section on Tumors, American Association of Neurological Surgeons and Congress of Neurological Surgeons; Joint Section on Neurotrauma and Critical Care, American Association of Neurological Surgeons and Congress of Neurological Surgeons; North American Skull Base Society; The Society of University Neurosurgeons **BA:** 3635 Vista Ave, 5 FDT, Saint Louis University, St. Louis, MO, 63110 **ADD:** 50 Brighton Way Apt 3N, Saint Louis, MO, 63105 **URL:** http://neurosurgery.slu.edu/index.php?page=dr-abdulrauf—cv

ABT, HELMUT ARTHUR, T: Astronomer **I:** Sciences **CN:** Kitt Peak National Observatory **DOB:** 05/26/1925 **PB:** Helmstedt **SC:** Germany **PT:** Karl M. Abt; Margaret S. (Simon) Abt **CH:** Daniel D. **ED:** PhD in Astronomy, California Institute of Technology (1952); MS in Physics, Northwestern University (1948); BS in Mathematics, Northwestern University (1946) **C:** Associate Professor, Peking University (2005-Present); Astronomer Emeritus, Kitt Peak National Observatory, National Optical Astronomy Observatory, Tuscon, AZ (2000-Present); Professor Emeritus, Kitt Peak National Observatory, Tucson, AZ (1971-2000); Astronomer, Kitt Peak National Observatory, National Optical Astronomy Observatory, Tuscon, AZ (1959-1999); Assistant Professor, Research Assistant, Yerkes Observatory, The University of Chicago, Williams Bay, WI (1956-1959); Junior Research Astronomer, Lick Observatory, University of California, Mount Hamilton, CA (1952-1953) **CR:** Associate Professor, Peking University (1995); Associate Professor, Beijing Normal University (1990-2000); Lecturer, China (1985-2012); President, Astronomical Society of the Pacific (1967-1969); Council Member, American Astronomical Society (1965-1968); Fieldwork, Kitt Peak National Observatory, National Optical Astronomy Observatory (1955-1956); Chair, Committee on Aims, National Aeronautics and Space Administration; Founder, Van Biesbroek Award, American Astronomical Society; Founder, Y.C. Cheng Award for Outstanding Research by a Chinese Astronomer; Fellow, American Association for the Advancement of Science **CIV:** Astronomy Teacher, The Learning Curve, Tuscon, AZ (2009); Astronomy Teacher, The Learning Curve, Tuscon, AZ (2007); Secretary, Board of Directors, Arizona Friends of Chamber Music, Tuscon, AZ **CW:** Managing Editor, "Astrophysics Journal" (1971-1999); Author, Five Books; Contributor, 320 Articles to Professional Journals **AW:** Van Viesbroack Prixe (1997); Eponym, Asteroid 9423 **MEM:** American Astronomical Society; Astronomical Society of the Pacific; The American Institute of Physics **MH:** Albert Nelson Marquis Lifetime Achievement Award (2017) **H:** Reading; Chinese art; Travel; Music **ADD:** 5701 E Glenn Street, Apt. 132, Tucson, AZ, 85712

ABZUG, ROBERT HENRY, T: Audre and Bernard Rapoport Regents Chair of Jewish Studies, Professor of History and American Studies **I:** Education/Educational Services **CN:** University of Texas **DOB:** 05/02/1945 **PB:** New York **SC:** NY/USA **PT:** F. Seymour William Abzug; M. Frances (Wolff) Abzug **MS:** Married **SPN:** Penne Lee Restad (11/16/1980) **CH:** Benjamin Cameron; Johanna Wolff **ED:** PhD, University of California, Berkeley (1977); BA, Harvard University, Magna Cum Laude (1967) **C:** Audre and Bernard Rapoport Regents Chair in Jewish Studies, University of Texas (2011-Present); Professor, History and American Studies, University of Texas (1990-Present); Founding Director, Schusterman Center for Jewish Studies (2007-2017); Oliver H. Radkey Regents Professor, University of Texas (2002-2011); Director, Liberal Arts Plan, Honors Programs, University of Texas at Austin (1996-2002); Director/Chair, Department of American Studies, University of Texas at Austin (1990-1996); Director, Religious Studies Program, University of Texas at Austin (1989-1990); Associate Professor, History, University of Texas at Austin (1984-1990); Assistant Professor, History, University of Texas at Austin (1978-1984); Lecturer, University of California, Los Angeles (1977-1978); Instructor, University of California, Berkeley (1976); Co-Director, Gale Collaborative for the Study of Jewish Life in the Americas **CR:** Education Committee, Holocaust Museum Houston (2008-Present); Rollo May Scholarship Committee, Saybrook Institute, San Francisco, CA (2003-Present); Silver Spurs Teaching Fellowship (2015); Advisory Board, Israel Studies Institute (2012-2017); Board Member, Texas Jewish Historical Society (2009-2012); Board of Trustees, Beecher House Society (2004-2008); Chair, University of Texas, Carnegie Foundation Initiative on the Doctorate (2003-2006); Friends of the Dallas Public Library Award Prize Committee, Texas Institute of Letters (2002); Founding Board Member, Res Publica (2000-2009); Board of Directors, Austin Phi Beta Kappa Alumni Association (2000-2007); Board of Directors, Human Rights Documentation Exchange (2000-2002); Fellowship, John Simon Guggenheim Memorial Foundation (2000-2001); President, University of Texas Chapter of Phi Beta Kappa (1999-2001); Vice-President, New Texas Music Works (1998-2000); Board of Directors, New Texas Music Works (1998-2000); Texas Board of Advisers, Institute for the Humanities at Salado, Texas (1997-2002); President, American Studies Association of Texas (1995-1996); Eric Voegelin Visiting Professor, University of Munich (1990-1991); Centennial Teaching Fellowship, Friar Society (1988-1989); Special Recognition, Friar Society Centennial Teaching Fellowship (1987); Fellowship for Independent Study, National Endowment for the Humanities (1983-1984); Lewis Fellowship, Mabelle McLeod (1975-1976); Career Fellowship, Ford Foundation Graduate (1967-1972); Fellowship, Danforth Graduate (1967-1972); Fellowship, Woodrow Wilson Graduate (1967-1968); Knox Traveling Fellowship, Harvard University (1967-1968) **CW:** Editorial Board, Southern Jewish History (2012-Present); Series Editor, "Jean-Claude Grumberg, Three Plays" (2014); Interviewed on Screen, "Salinger" (2013); Author and Editor, Critical, Annotated, and Abridged Edition "The Varieties of Religious Experience" (2012); Editorial Board, Rhetoric and Public Affairs (2006-2012); Historical Consultant, Advisor, "Loving Henri" (2006); Author, "The Transatlantic Dialogue in Religion and Psychology: Paul Tillich, Erich Fromm, Rollo May and the Reformulation of Personal Meaning, 1934-1960, Political Cultures and the Culture of Politics: A Transatlantic Perspective (2005); Author, "Abolition and Religion," History Now: American History Online (2005); Author, "Befreiung," Gesamtgeschichte der Nationalsozialistischen Konzentrationslager (2005); Author, "A Modest Proposal," Insights: The Faculty Journal of the Austin Presbyterian Seminary (2004); Author, "America Views the Holocaust, 1933-1945: A Brief Documentary History" (1999); Author, "Theodore Dwight Weld," American National Biography (1999); Author, "The Deconversion of Rollo May," Review of Existential Psychology and Psychiatry (1999); Author, "Rollo May, Paul Tillich and Existential Psychotherapy in America," Existential Analysis (1996); Author, "Love and Will: Rollo May and the Seventies' Crisis of Intimacy," The Lost Decade: America in the Seventies (1996); Author, "Rollo May as 'Friend to Man'," Journal of Humanistic Psychology (1996); Chief Consultant, Script Writing and Editing, "Nightmare's End: The Liberation of the Camps" (1995); Author, "American Studies at the University

of Texas," Craft: The Newsletter of the CTI for History, Archaeology, and Art History (1995); Author, "The Liberation of the Concentration and Death Camps: Understanding and Using History," Dimensions: A Journal of Holocaust Studies (1995); Author, "The Liberation of the Concentration Camps," Liberation 1945, Exhibition Catalogue, U.S. Holocaust Memorial Museum, Washington, DC (1995); Author, "America and the Holocaust," Discovery (1995); Author, "The Holocaust and More Recent Cases of Genocide," Chronicle of Higher Education (1994); Author, "Paul Tillich," A Companion to American Thought (1994); Author, "Benjamin Rush," A Companion to American Thought (1994); Author, "Cosmos Crumbling: American Reform and the Religious Imagination" (1994); Author, "Introduction," G.I.s Remember (1993); Author, "Theodore Dwight Weld," Dictionary of Afro-American Slavery (1991); Author, "Exhibiting the Indescribable: Issues of Holocaust Photography," United States Holocaust Memorial Museum Newsletter (1990); Author, "The Need for an Archive of Humanistic Psychology," Journal of Humanistic Psychology (1990); Author, "Facing Survivors in Fiction and Film," Simon Wiesenthal Center Annual V (1988); Author, "Inside the Vicious Heart: Americans and the Liberation of Nazi Concentration Camps," Oxford University Press (1987); Author, "Invisible Victims: European Jews in the American Consciousness, 1940-1946," Dimensions: A Journal of Holocaust Studies (1986); Co-editor, "New Perspectives on Race and Slavery in America: Essays in Honor of Kenneth M. Stampp" (1986); Author, "Exploring Beginnings," The Biographer's Gift: Life Histories and Humanism (1983); Author, "Passionate Liberator: Theodore Dwight Weld and the Dilemma of Reform," Oxford University Press (1980); Author, "The Black Family During Reconstruction," Key Issues in the Afro-American Experience II (1971); Author, "The Copperheads: Historical Approaches to Civil War Dissent in the Midwest," Indiana Magazine of History (1970); Author, "The Influence of Garrisonian Abolitionists' Fears of Slave Violence on the Antislavery Argument, 1829-1840," Journal of Negro History (1970); Author, "The Spiritual Odyssey of Rollo May" **AW:** Outstanding Advising Certificate of Merit, National Academic Advising Association (2015); Faculty Appreciation Award, Texas Blazers (2004); Eyes of Texas Award (1996); Research Grant, Frederick Binkard Artz Summer, Oberlin College (1993); Summer Stipend National Endowment for the Humanities (1987); Small Travel Grant, University Research Institute (1987); Summer Grant, University Research Institute Matching (1987); Professor of the Year, Liberal Arts Council (1987); Grant-in-Aid, American Council of Learned Societies (1984); Fred Crawford Memorial Research Associate, Emory University (1983); Advanced Research Associate, U.S. Army Military History Institute (1983); Teaching Award, Liberal Arts Council, University of Texas (1983); Preferred Professor, Mortar Board Society, University of Texas (1982-1983); Special Recognition, Jean Holloway Award for Excellence in Teaching (1982); Summer Grant, University Research Institute, University of Texas (1981) **MEM:** Educator Associate, American Psychoanalytic Association; American Historical Association; Association for Jewish Studies; Association for Canadian Jewish Studies; Authors Guild; Organization of American Historians; Phi Beta Kappa Alumni Association; Society of Americanists; Society for U.S. Intellectual History; Texas Photographic Society; Beta Alpha Phi International Honor Society; Phi Beta Kappa **PA:** Democrat **RE:** Jewish **BA:** 128 Inner Campus Drive, Stop B7000, University of Texas, Department of

History, Austin, TX, 78712 **ADD:** 3504 Cactus Wren Way, Austin, TX, 78746 **URL:** http://www. robertabzug.com

ACEVEDO GIROD, MARTA TERESA, T: Partner **I:** Law and Legal Services **CN:** Girod Consulting **MS:** Married **SPN:** Bob Girod **ED:** Master's Degree, The Johns Hopkins University Applied Physics Laboratory LLC (1993); Bachelor's Degree, Loyola University Chicago **C:** Partner, Girod Consulting (2007-Present); Partner, A&N Consulting, LLC (1992-2007); Pulse Engineering, Westinghouse Electric Corporation (1989-1992) **CIV:** Work in Therapeutic Recreation, Riding Center **AW:** Honoree, Therapy Dog Training Course, National Capitol Therapy Dogs, Inc. (2008) **MEM:** AFCEA International **H:** Horse back riding; Swimming; Yoga; Building 3D legos; Doing Spanish classes with father **RE:** Catholic **ADD:** 3200 Roscommon Dr, Glenelg, MD, 21737

ACKERMAN ENGELMAN, ROSALYN, T: Artist **I:** Fine Art **CN:** EnglemanArt **PB:** Liberty **SC:** NY/USA **PT:** Nathan Ackerman; Lillie (Schultz) Ackerman **MS:** Married **SPN:** Irwin Engelman (11/24/1956) **CH:** Madeleine Florence; Marianne Leslie **ED:** MS, Art History and Museum Curatorship, University of Rochester, Rochester, NY (1978); BA in Fine Arts, The City College of New York (1958); Coursework, Art Students League of New York, New York, NY **CT:** Certified Teacher, City of New York, State of New York **C:** Vice President, Marketing, Praxis Media (1984-Present); Development Officer, Connecticut Public Broadcasting, Inc. (1982-1983); President, Westport-Weston Arts Council (Now Westport Arts Council) (1980-1981); Member, Metropolitan Arts Resources Committee, Rochester, NY (1977-1978); Researcher, Memorial Art Gallery, Rochester, NY (1975-1978); Co-chair, Arts, Westport Bicentennial Committee (1975-1976); Lecturer, Memorial Art Gallery (1972-1974); Fundraiser, Memorial Art Gallery (1972-1974); Docent, Memorial Art Gallery (1972-1974); Art Teacher, New Jersey (1964-1966); Art Teacher, New York, NY (1958) **CR:** President, National Corporate Theatre Fund (Now Theatre Forward) (1984); Treasurer, National Corporate Theatre Fund (Now Theatre Forward) (1982); Chairperson, Board of Directors, National Corporate Theatre Fund (Now Theatre Forward) (1981-1988); Board of Directors, Long Wharf Theatre, New Haven, CT (1980-1983) **CIV:** Chair, Board of Directors, Westport Arts Council (1982-Present); Board of Directors, Museum of Art Science and Industry (Now Discovery Museum and Planetarium) (1990); Performer, Long Wharf Theatre (1980-1984) **CW:** Artist, Permanent Collections, "Evil - A Matter of Intent," Hebrew Union College - Jewish Institute of Religion (2015-Present); Artist, Permanent Collections, Corporate Headquarters, AllianceBernstein L.P. (2015); Artist, Permanent Collections, "Cutting Edge Masters of Contemporary Art," International Exhibit, Grand Auditorium al Duomo, Florence, Italy (2014); Artist, Commissions, "To Inspire Lives" (2014); Artist, Commissions, "The Sexuality Spectrum," Hebrew Union College - Jewish Institute of Religion (2012-2013); Artist, Permanent Collections, "The Sexuality Spectrum," Hebrew Union College - Jewish Institute of Religion (2012-2013); Artist, Permanent Collections, "Plato Wall," Nina Torres Fine Art (2012); Artist, Commissions, Art Basel, Nina Torres Fine Art (2012); Artist, Commissions, "Manu Honda," Nina Torres Fine Art (2012); Artist, Commissions, Hudson Valley Center for Contemporary Art (2012); Artist, Commissions, International Wood Products, LLC (2012); Artist, One Woman Show, Art Museum of South Texas, Corpus Christi, TX (2008, 2011); Artist, One Woman Show, Memorial Art Gallery, Rochester,

NY (2011); Artist, Commissions, Florence Biennale (2011); Artist, Commissions, Hartnett Art Gallery, University of Rochester (2011); Artist, Permanent Collections, "Revelations: Women's Art from the Permanent Collection," Art Museum of South Texas (2011); Artist, One Woman Show, Museum in New York, Hebrew Union College - Jewish Institute of Religion, New York, NY (2008, 2010); Artist, One Woman Show, DeLorenzo Gallery, New York, NY (2008-2010); Artist, One Woman Show, Broadway Gallery, New York, NY (2010); Artist, One Woman Show, La Societe des Artistes Independants, Grand Palais, Paris, France (2010); Artist, One Woman Show, Agora Gallery, Miami, FL (2010); Artist, One Woman Show, Salon des Refuses (2010); Artist, Commissions, Memorial Art Gallery (2010); Artist, One Woman Show, Biennale Citta di Firenze (2007, 2009); Artist, One Woman Show, National Arts Club (2009); Artist, One Woman Show, Wally Findlay Galleries International, Inc., Palm Beach, FL (2009); Artist, One Woman Show, Florence Biennale (2009); Artist, One Woman Show, Grand Gallery, National Arts Club (2008); Artist, One Woman Show, Gallery 440, Brooklyn, NY (2008); Artist, One Woman Show, Etra Fine Art Gallery, Miami, FL (2005-2007); Artist, One Woman Show, Kaller Fine Arts (2007); Artist, One Woman Show, Master's Mystery Show, Miami, FL (2004-2006); Artist, One Woman Show, Caelum Gallery, New York, NY (2004-2006); Artist, One Woman Show, Art Basel, Etra Fine Art Gallery, Miami, FL (2006); Artist, One Woman Show, QCC Art Gallery CUNY, Bayside, NY (2005); Artist, One Woman Show, Phthalo Gallery, Bay Harbor Islands, FL (2005); Artist, One Woman Show, Barbara Gillman Gallery, Miami, FL (2004-2005); Artist, Exhibitions, Galleries, Norwalk Symphony Orchestra (2004); Artist, Exhibitions, Galleries, Master's Mystery Show, Florida International University (2004); Artist, One Woman Show, Art Miami LLC (2004); Artist, One Woman Show, Thomas Walsh Art Gallery, Fairfield University (2003); Artist, One Woman Show, Earthplace, Westport, CT (2003); Artist, One Woman Show, All Commemorative Show, National Arts Club (2002); Artist, One Woman Show, Florence Biennale (2002); Artist, One Woman Show, Florence Biennale (2002); Artist, One Woman Show, The Sidney Mishkin Gallery, Baruch College (2001); Artist, One Woman Show, Nico Gallery, Seattle, WA (2001); Artist, Commissions, Frontispieces of Substantive and Procedural Aspects International Criminal Law, The Hague, the Netherlands (2000); Artist, Exhibitions, Galleries, Art Galleries, Adelphi University (1999); Artist, Exhibitions, Galleries, National Arts Club, New York, NY (1999); Artist, One Woman Show, National Arts Club (1999); Artist, Exhibitions, Galleries, Nigerian Embassy (1998); Artist, Exhibitions, Galleries, Baruch College, New York, NY (1998); Artist, Exhibitions, Galleries, Kravetz Gallery, Temple Israel, New York, NY (1997); Artist, Exhibitions, Galleries, T'ZART, New York, NY (1994); Artist, Exhibitions, Galleries, Gronsky Gallery; Artist, Commissions, Queensborough Community College, Bayside, NY; Artist, Commissions, The New School, New York, NY; Artist, Commissions, Red Tie Media Inc.; Artist, Permanent Collections, Memorial Art Gallery AW: Sandro Botticelli Prize (2015); Honoree, International Marco Polo Art Ambassador, Venice, Italy (2015); ATIM Choice Award, Florence, ArtTour International Publications Inc. (2014); Master's Award, Cutting Edge Exhibition (2014); Lorenzo di Medici Gold Medal, Florence Biennale (2009); Honoree, Best in Show, National Arts Club (2009); Visual Arts Award, Florence Biennale (2007); Painting Award, The National Arts Club (2007); Gold Medal, Grumbacher Award, Thalo LLC (1998); Recipient, Citation, Town of Westport,

NY (1981); Commission, War Tribunal Court, The Hague, Netherlands **MEM:** University of Rochester Alumni Association; The National Arts Club **MH:** Albert Nelson Marquis Lifetime Achievement Award (2017) **H:** History; Opera; Art **BA:** 936 5th Avenue, New York, NY, 10021 **URL:** http://www.engelmanart.com

ADEGBEGE, AMBROSE ADEBAYO, T: Assistant Professor of Electrical and Computer Engineering **I:** Education/Educational Services **CN:** The College of New Jersey **ED:** Post Doctoral Research, Masdar Institute (2012); PhD, The University of Manchester, England (2011); Master's Degree, The University of Manchester, England (2006); Bachelor's Degree, Nigeria (2004) **C:** Assistant Professor, The College of New Jersey (2014-Present); Visiting Assistant Professor, The College of New Jersey (2013-2014) **MEM:** American Society for Engineering Education (2012-Present); IEEE Control Systems Society (2003-Present); IEEE CAS (2003-Present); Power and Energy Society, IEEE (2003-Present); The International Society of Automation (2003-Present); IEEE **H:** Tennis; Travel **BA:** 2000 Pennington Road, Armstrong Bldng Room 153, The College of New Jersey, Ewing, NJ, 08628

AHMAD, JAMEEL, T: Civil Engineer **I:** Engineering **CN:** Cooper Union for the Advancement of Science and Art **DOB:** 05/22/1941 **PB:** Lahore **SC:** Pakistan **PT:** Naseer Bakhsh; Iftikhar (Dean) Bakhsh **MS:** Married **SPN:** Rosalba Quiroz (3/31/1983) **CH:** Monica; Sidney **ED:** PhD, University of Pennsylvania (1967); MS, University of Hawaii (1964); BS, University of the Punjab (1962) **C:** Director, Institute for Urban Security, Cooper Union for the Advancement of Science and Art (2005-Present); Director, Center for Urban Infrastructure, Cooper Union for the Advancement of Science and Art (2005-Present); Senior Adviser, Verdant Power, Inc. (2003-Present); Chairman of Civil Engineering, Cooper Union for the Advancement of Science and Art (1980-Present); Professor of Civil Engineering, Cooper Union for the Advancement of Science and Art (1979-Present); Director of Research, C.V. Starr Research Foundation, Cooper Union for the Advancement of Science and Art (1983-2007); Associate Professor, Cooper Union for the Advancement of Science and Art (1971-1980); Assistant Professor, Cooper Union for the Advancement of Science and Art (1968-1971); Assistant Professor, Widener University (1967-1968); Research Fellow, University of Pennsylvania (1965-1967); East-West Center Fellow, University of Hawaii (1962-1965) **CR:** New York Fellow, Research Institute for the Study of Man (2002); Senior Adviser, Verdant Power, Inc.; Board of Advisers, Verdant Power, Inc. **CIV:** Vice President, Forest Hills Vilmanor Community Association, Inc. (1992); West Side Community Organization (1976) **AW:** Presidential Citation for 25 Years of Service, C.V. Starr Research Foundation, Cooper Union for the Advancement of Science and Art (2007); Abdus Salam Medal for Distinguished Research in Engineering Sciences, Pakistan League of America (1993); Outstanding Service Award, American Society of Civil Engineers (1985); Rossi Prize for Research (1971) **MEM:** American Society of Civil Engineers; American Society of Mechanical Engineers; American Society for Engineering Education; American Institute of Steel Construction; Structural Engineering Institute, American Society of Civil Engineers; Board of Directors, Pakistan League of America; Chi Epsilon, Inc.; The Honor Society of Phi Kappa Phi **MH:** Albert Nelson Marquis Lifetime Achievement Award (2017) **ADD:** 11031 63rd Drive, Forest Hills, NY, 11375

AHMED, S. BASHEER, T: Research Company Executive, Educator **I:** Consulting **CN:** Pearce Consultant Services **DOB:** 01/01/1934 **PB:** Kurnool, Andhra **SC:** India **PT:** S.M. Hussain; K.A. (Bee) Hussain **MS:** Married **SPN:** Alice Cordelia Pearce (1968) **CH:** Ivy Amina **ED:** PhD, Texas A&M University (1966); MS, Texas A&M University (1963); MA, Osmania University, Hyderabad, India (1957); BA, Osmania College, Kurnool (1955) **C:** President, Pearce Consulting (2000-Present); Professor Emeritus, Pace University (1993-2003); President, Princeton Economic Research, Inc. (1980-1999); Professor of Management Sciences, Lubin Graduate School Business, Pace University (1982-1992); Director, Doctoral Program, Pace University (1982-1992); Visiting Fellow, Princeton University, New Jersey (1977-1978); Professor, Western Kentucky University (1970-1980); Assistant Professor, Ohio University, Athens (1968-1970); Assistant Professor, Tennessee Technical University, Cookeville (1966-1968) **CR:** Consultant, Honeywell International Inc. (1985); Consultant, Institute for Energy Analysis, Oak Ridge, Tennessee (1975); Consultant, Oak Ridge National Laboratory (1969-1977) **CIV:** Member, Board of Directors, The Kennedy Center (1997-2000) **CW:** Author, "Technology, International Stability, and Growth" (1984); Editor, "Technology, International Stability, and Growth" (1984); Author, "Nuclear Fuel and Energy Policy" (1979); Author, "Quantitative Methods for Business" (1974) **AW:** Millennium Medal (2000); Centennial Medal, IEEE (1983); Achievement Award, Oak Ridge National Laboratory (1977) **MEM:** President, Systems, Man, and Cybernetics Society, IEEE (1980-1982); Fellow, American Association for the Advancement of Science **MH:** Albert Nelson Marquis Lifetime Achievement Award (2017) **H:** Travel; Health and fitness **PA:** Republican **ADD:** 817 Albemarle St., Bowling Green, KY, 42103 **URL:** https://relationshipscience.com/person/s-basheer-ahmed-5202946

AHMED, IQBAL, T: Psychiatrist **I:** Medicine & Health Care **DOB:** 08/23/1951 **PB:** Tumkur **SC:** India **PT:** Rahimuddin Ahmed; Arifa (Banu) Rahimuddin **MS:** Married **SPN:** Lisa Rose Ahmed (10/9/1983) **CH:** Yasmin Smith; Jihan Ahmed **ED:** Fellowship in Consultation, School of Medicine, Boston University (1979-1981); Resident in Psychiatry, University of Nebraska Medical Center (1976-1979); Bachelor of Medicine, Bachelor of Surgery, St.John's National Academy of Health Sciences and Bangalore University (1975); Intern, St. Martha's Hospital, Bangalore, India (1974-1975) **CT:** Diplomate in General Psychiatry, American Board of Psychiatry and Neurology, Inc.; Diplomate in Geriatric Psychiatry, American Board of Psychiatry and Neurology, Inc.; Diplomate in Psychosomatic Medicine, American Board of Psychiatry and Neurology, Inc. **C:** Faculty, Tripler Army Medical Center, Uniformed Services University (2010-Present); Attending Psychiatrist on the Consultation/Liaison and Geriatric Psychiatry Consultation Service, The Queen's Medical Center, Honolulu, Hawaii (1993-2010); Psychiatric Consultant on Geriatric, Neuropsychiatry and Psychopharmacology Issues, Hawaii State Hospital, Kaneohe, Hawaii (1992-2010); Associate Director of Consultation Liaison Psychiatry, New England Medical Center (Now Tufts Medical Center) (1989-1992); Director of Geriatric Psychiatry, Boston Medical Center (1988-1992); Director, Geriatric Neuropsychiatry Unit, Boston Medical Center (1985-1987); Staff Psychiatrist in Geriatric Psychiatry, Boston Medical Center (1983-1985); Staff Psychiatrist in Consultation Liaison Psychiatry, Boston Medical Center (1981-1987) **CR:** Member, Residency

Review Committee, ACGME (2013-Present); Editorial Board Member, Psychiatry Resident-In-Training Examination (PRITE) (2013-Present); Clinical Professor of Psychiatry, University of Hawai'i (2011-Present); Vice-Chair, Scientific Program Committee, American Psychiatric Association (2017-2019); Clinical Professor of Geriatric Medicine, University of Hawai'i (2010); Clinical Professor of Psychiatry, University of Hawai'i (2010); Consultant in Geriatric Psychiatry (2003-2010); Director of Psychopharmacology, Adult Mental Health Division, State of Hawaii (2003-2010); Consultant, Tripler Army Medical Center, Uniformed Services University (1997-2010); Professor, Department of Psychiatry, John A. Burns School of Medicine University of Hawai'i at Manoa (1997-2010); Vice Chairman of Education, Department of Psychiatry, The Queen's Medical Center (1999-2004); Program Director, General and Geriatric Psychiatry Residency Programs, University of Hawai'i (1998-2004); Vice Chairman, Department of Psychiatry, University of Hawai'i (1999-2001); Chief of Geriatric Psychiatry, Hawaii State Hospital (1994-1997); Associate Professor, Department of Psychiatry, John A. Burns School of Medicine University of Hawai'i at Manoa (1992-1997); President of Medical Staff, Hawaii State Hospital (1994-1995); Chief of Special Services, Hawaii State Hospital (1991-1994); Assistant Professor of Psychiatry, Tufts University School of Medicine (1987-1992); Director, Medical Student Education in Psychiatry, Boston Medical Center (1981-1987); Boston University School of Medicine (1981-1987) CW: Member, Editorial Board, The American College of Psychiatrists (2013-Present); Oral Examiner, ACGME (2013-Present); Author, "Spectrum of Psychotic Disorders - Neurobiology, Etiology and Pathogenesis" (2007); Co-editor, "Spectrum of Psychotic Disorders - Neurobiology, Etiology and Pathogenesis" (2007); Managing Editor, "eMedicine," Psychiatry Section; Screening Editor, American Journal of Geriatric Psychiatry; Contributor, Articles, Professional Journals; Contributor, Book Chapters AW: Distinguished Life Fellow, American Psychiatric Association (2013); Educator of the Year Award, American Association for Geriatric Psychiatry (2012); Outstanding Service Award, IAPA (2010); Diversity Award, American Association for Geriatric Psychiatry (2010); Fellow, Royal College of Psychiatrists, United Kingdom (2005); Irma Bland Award, American Psychological Association (2005); Finalist, Parker Palmer Courage to Teach Award, ACGME (2004); Honorary Faculty, Alpha Omega Alpha Honor Medical Society MEM: Board of Directors, American Association for Geriatric Psychiatry (2009-2012); Elected Honorary Faculty, Alpha Omega Alpha Honor Medical Society (2007); Registered Fellow, Royal College of Psychiatrists; American Psychiatric Association; Science Program Committee, American Psychiatric Association; Legislative Representative, State of Hawaii, American Psychiatric Association; Academy of Psychosomatic Medicine; The American College of Psychiatrists; Co-founder, International College of Geriatric Psychoneuropharmacology; American Neuropsychiatric Association MH: Albert Nelson Marquis Lifetime Achievement Award (2017); Distinguished Humanitarian (2017) H: Playing the Piano; Public Education Relative to Mental Health ADD: 2861 Kalawao St, Honolulu, HI, 96822

AHMED, MOHAMMED BASHEER, T: Psychiatrist, Educator **I:** Medicine & Health Care **DOB:** 06/07/1935 **PB:** Hyderabad **SC:** India **PT:** M. Quameruddin; Aziz Fatima Tahira **MS:** Married **SPN:** Shakila Khatoon (12/7/1967) **CH:** Sameer; Araj **ED:** MD, Dow Medical College (1960); BSc, Osmania University (1954) **CT:** Diplomate, American Board of Psychiatry, Geriatric Psychiatry (1991); Fellow, Royal College of Psychiatrist, London (1980); Fellow, Royal College of Physicians, Canada (1977); Diplomate, American Board of Psychiatry and Neurology (1975); Diplomate in Psychiatry, Royal College of Physicians, Edinburgh and London (1964); Certified in Administrative Psychiatry, Pain Management and Addiction Medicine **C:** Chairman, MCC for Human Services (1995-Present); Private Practice, Fort Worth, TX (1984-Present); Medical Director, New Horizon PHP Program, Fort Worth, TX (1997-2000); Director, Psychiatric Unit, Medical Plaza Hospital, Fort Worth, TX (1992-1997); Chief of Staff, Care Unit Hospital, Fort Worth, TX (1989-1994); Director, Department of Psychiatry, St. Joseph Hospital, Fort Worth, TX (1985-1989); Director, Psychiatric Department, John Peter Smith Hospital, Fort Worth, TX (1978-1982); Chief of Psychiatry, VA Hospital, Dayton, OH (1976-1978); Director, Sound View, Throngs Neck Community Mental Health Center, Bronx, NY (1971-1976); Director, Psychiatric Department, St. Louis County General Hospital, Clayton, MO (1969-1971) **CR:** Clinical Professor, Department of Psychiatry, University of Texas Health Science Center, Fort Worth, TX (1982-1998); Professor, Department of Psychiatry, University of Texas Southwestern Medical School, Dallas, TX (1978-1988); Professor, Department of Psychiatry, Wright State University Medical School, Dayton, OH (1976-1978); Assistant Professor of Psychiatry, Albert Einstein College of Medicine, New York City, NY (1971-1976) **CW:** Contributing Author, Administration of Mental Health (1980); Contributing Author, Group Counseling and Psychotherapy (1976); Author, Articles, Various Professional Journals; Editor, Various Books; Author, "My Story as a Muslim Emigrant in America: Psychiatry, Social Activism and Services" **AW:** Community Service Recognition Award, Islamic Society of North America (2009); Tarrant County Medical Society Humanitarian Award (2008); Hyderabad Culture Society Humanitarian Award (2008); Pakistan Community Service Recognition Award for Medical Service (2006); Daughters of Abraham Community Service Award (2005); Tarrant County Asian-American Chambers of Commerce Recognition Award for Outstanding Contributions in Medicine (2002); Radio Jhankar Award for Community Services (1995) **MH:** Albert Nelson Marquis Lifetime Achievement Award (2017); Who's Who in American Education, (2003-2009); Who's Who in the World (2000-2006); Who's Who in Medicine and Healthcare (2000-2006); Who's Who in America (1996-2010); Who's Who in Science & Engineering (1996-2006); Who's Who in the South and Southwest (1996-2005); Who's Who Among Human Services Professionals (1992-1999); Whos Who in the East (1977-1978) **H:** Travel; Photography **RE:** Islam **ADD:** 10 Home Place Ct, Arlington, TX, 76016

AHMED, MUTAHAR, T: Urologist, Oncologist, Clinical Assistant Professor **I:** Medicine & Health Care **CN:** Hackensack University Medical Center **ED:** Intern, New Jersey Medical School (Now Rutgers, The State University of New Jersey) (1997-1999); Resident, New Jersey Medical School (Now Rutgers, The State University of New Jersey) (1997-1999); MD, State University of New York Upstate Medical University, Syracuse, NY (1997); BA in Biochemistry, New York University (1993) **CT:** Certified Urologist, American Board of Urology; Diplomate, American Board of Urology; Fellow, American College of Surgeons **C:** Attending Clinician of Urology, Saint Barnabas Medical Center, West Orange, NJ (2008-Present); Affiliate Staff, Department of Urology, The Valley Hospital, Ridgewood, NJ (2005-Present); Clinical Assistant Professor, Rutgers New Jersey Medical School, Newark, NJ (2004-Present); Attending Clinician, The Stone Center of New Jersey, Newark, NJ (2003-Present); New Jersey Center for Prostate Cancer and Urology (2003-Present); Attending Clinician, Department of Urology, Hackensack University Medical Center, Hackensack, NJ (2003-Present); Attending Clinician, Department of Surgery, Holy Name Hospital, Teaneck, NJ (2003-Present); Urologist, New Jersey Center for Prostate Cancer and Urology; Director, Center for Bladder Cancer, Hackensack University Medical Center, Hackensack, NJ **CR:** Presenter in Field; Lecturer in Field **CIV:** Distressed Children & Infants International **CW:** Author, "Robot-Assisted Laparoscopic Management of Inflatable Penile Prosthesis Reservoir Migration Into Bladder With Utilization Of Cryopreserved Amniotic Membrane And Umbilical Tissue," American Urological Association Meeting (2017); Author, "Robot Assisted Laparoscopic Radical Cystectomy and Intracorporeal Neobladder Utilizing a Vaginal-Sparing and Staple Free Approach," American Urological Association Meeting (2017); Author, "The Use of Novel Curved-Tip Suction Device in Laparoscopic And Robotic Urologic Surgery," American Urological Association Meeting (2017); Author, "Vaginal Sparing Robotic Assisted Laparoscopic Anterior Pelvic Exenteration and Neo-Bladder Construction," 34th World Congress of Endourology (2016); Author, "Robot Assisted Laparoscopic Radical Cystectomy with Intracorporeal Ilael Conduit Urinary Diversion in a Male Who Underwent Prior Robotic Prostatectomy for Prostate Cancer," 34th World Congress of Endourology (2016); Author, "Salvage Robot-Assisted Radical Prostatectomy After Radiation and Inflatable Penile Prosthesis Implantation," 34th World Congress of Endourology (2016); Author, "Robot-Assisted Laparoscopic Inflatable Penile Prosthesis Removal and Re-insertion," 34th World Congress of Endourology (2016); Author, "Creation of a Robot-Assisted Boari Flap for Total Ureteral Replacement," 34th World Congress of Endourology (2016); Author, "Off-Clamp Right Robotic Partial Nephrectomy Using Intuitive Endo Wrist One Vessel Sealer," World Congress Urological Meeting (2013); Author, "Combined Robot Assisted Laparoscopic Cystectomy-Nephroureterectomy: An Initial Series," American Urological Association (2010); Author, "Extraperitoneal Laparoscopic Robotic Prostatectomy," American Urological Association Annual Meeting (2007); Author, "Four-Arm daVinciTM Surgical System for Extraperitoneal Laparoscopic Robotic Prostatectomies," American Urological Association Annual Meeting (2006); Author, "True Extraperitoneal Laparoscopic Robotic Prostatectomy (EP-LRP): A Large Series Experience at One Institute," American Urological Association Annual Meeting (2004); Author, "Tissue-Link DS 3.0TM Dissecting Sealer Device Assisted Partial Nephrectomy For Renal Masses A New Surgical Technique," American Urological Association Annual Meeting (2004); Author, "Decrease in Blood Loss in Patients Who Underwent Tissuelink Dissecting Sealer 3.0," American Urological Association Annual Meeting (2003); Author, "Extraperitoneal Robotic Prostatectomy: Comparison of Technique and Results at One Institution," American Urological Association Annual Meeting (2003); Contributor, Articles to Professional Journals **AW:** New York Metro Area Top Doctors (2014); Top Doctors, New York Media LLC (2014); Named, Top Cancer Doctor, New Jersey Insider Magazine (2013-2017); Named, Bergen County Top Doctor (2013-2017); Regional Top Urologist, Castle Connolly Medical Ltd (2013-2017); Honored, New Jersey Monthly's Top Doctors (2010-2017); Named, Outstanding American

Laparoscopic Fellow (2003); Recipient, Pfizer Scholars in Urology Award, American Urological Association (2003); Recipient, Gerald P. Murphy Scholars for Distinction in the Study of Prostate Cancer, Praecis Pharmaceuticals (2003); Recipient, Society of Laparoscopic Surgeons Resident Achievement Award **MEM:** Fellow, American College of Surgery; Society of Larapoendoscopic Surgeons; American Endourological Society; American Urological Association **BA:** 255 W Spring Valley Ave Ste 101, New Jersey Center for Prostate Cancer and Urology, Maywood, NJ, 07607 **ADD:** 255 W Spring Valley Ave Ste 101, NJ Ctr for Prostate Cancer and Urology, Maywood, NJ, 07607

ALARCON, RENATO DANIEL, T: Emeritus Professor of Psychiatry **I:** Education/Educational Services **CN:** Mayo Clinic College of Medicine **DOB:** 04/11/1942 **PB:** Arequipa **SC:** Peru **PT:** Jose R. Alarcon-Linares; Rosa Guzman de Alarcon **MS:** Married **SPN:** Graciela S. Alarcon (6/8/1967) **CH:** Patricia; Sylvia; Daniel **ED:** MPH, Johns Hopkins University (1972); MD, Cayetano Heredia University, Lima, Peru (1966) **CT:** Diplomate, American Board of Psychiatry and Neurology, Inc. **C:** Professor, Department of Psychiatry, School of Medicine, Emory University, Atlanta, GA (1993-Present); Vice Chairman, Department of Psychiatry, School of Medicine, Emory University, Atlanta, GA (1993-Present); Chief of Psychiatry Service, VA Medical Center, U.S. Department of Veterans Affairs, Atlanta, GA (1993-Present); Chief of Affective Disorders Program, School of Medicine, The University of Alabama at Birmingham (1991-1993); Chief of Adult Services, University of Alabama Hospital, The University of Alabama at Birmingham (1981-1992); Professor of Psychiatry, School of Medicine, The University of Alabama at Birmingham (1981-1983); Associate Professor of Psychiatry, Cayetano Heredia University, Lima, Peru (1976-1980); Assistant Professor of Psychiatry, Cayetano Heredia University, Lima, Peru (1972-1976); Resident in Psychiatry, School of Medicine, Johns Hopkins University (1968-1972); Fellow in Psychosomatic Medicine, School of Medicine, Johns Hopkins (1967-1968) **CR:** Examiner, American Board of Psychiatry and Neurology, Inc. (1989-Present); Consultant, Pan American Health Organization, Washington, DC (1974-1987) **CIV:** Affiliate, Amnesty International (1986); Active Member, Physicians for Social Responsibility (1982) **CW:** Co-Editor, "Enciclopedia Iberoam, Psiquiatria, Buenos Aires" (1990-1994); Associate Editor, "Acta Psiquiatrica Y Psicologica De America Latina" (1989-1994); Author, "Identidad de la Psiquiatria Latinoamericana" (1990); Author, "Psiquiatria" (1986); Author, "Psicoterapia" (1979); Book Review Editor, "Depression and Anxiety"; Editor, "Cull Div. and Mental Health"; Contributor, Articles, Professional Journals **AW:** Weng Tseng Award, WACP (2015); Named Exemplary Psychiatrist, NAMI (1992); Scholar, The Rockefeller Foundation (1988) **MEM:** President, American Society of Hispanic Psychiatry (1994-1996); Fellow, American Psychological Association; The American College of Psychiatrists; Group Advisory Psychiatrist, American Psychopathological Association **MH:** Albert Nelson Marquis Lifetime Achievement Award (2017) **H:** Reading history, fiction, and poetry; Listening to romantic and classic music; Collecting owls; Writing; Soccer; Biking **RE:** Roman Catholic **ADD:** 1 Lakeside Dr Apt 1602, Oakland, CA, 94612 **URL:** http://www.mayo.edu/research/faculty/alarcon-renato-d-m-d/bio-00028169

ALAV, FARAMARZ, T: Internist **I:** Medicine & Health Care **CN:** Alav Medical Corporation **DOB:** 01/26/1958 **PB:** Akstafa **SC:** Azerbaijan

PT: Ahmed Alav; Ashraf Abulmulla **MS:** Married **SPN:** Kristina Jailova (11/7/2000) **CH:** Leila; Emin; Emil **ED:** MD, Azerbaycan Tibb Universiteti (1980) **C:** Internist, Alav Medical Corporation (2007-Present); Physician in Internal Medicine, United Family Care (Now Pinnacle Medical Group), Fontana, CA (2001-2007); Telemetry Technician, St. Joseph Health|St. Joseph Hospital (1995-1998); Internist, Bonab Central Hospital, Bonab, Iran (1993-1994); Resident in Internal Medicine, Sinai-Grace Hospital, Wayne State University, Internal Medicine Residency (1988-2001); Cardiologist, Diagnostic Center, Baku, Azerbaijan (1988-1993); Fellow, Institute for Advanced Medical Studies, Baku, Azerbaijan (1986-1988); Emergency Unit Physician, Central Hospital Emergency Unit, Baku, Azerbaijan (1981-1986); Intern, Research Institute for Cardiology, Baku, Azerbaijan (1980-1981) **CW:** Contributor, Articles, Professional Journals **AW:** Award for Outstanding Performance and Service to the Community, State Board (1995) **MEM:** Society of General Internal Medicine; American College of Physicians **MH:** Albert Nelson Marquis Lifetime Achievement Award (2017) **ADD:** 570 Wooden Bridge Lane, Redlands, CA, 92373

ALDRICH, GEORGE HOOVER, T: State Legislator, Lawyer **I:** Law and Legal Services **DOB:** 02/25/1932 **PB:** St. Louis **SC:** MO/USA **PT:** Emmett Porter Aldrich; Hettie Barbara (Hoover) Aldrich **MS:** Married **SPN:** Rosemary Margaret Balmforth Aldrich (June 6, 1959) **CH:** Edward; Stephen; Robert **ED:** Honorary LLD, DePaul University (2006); LLM, Harvard Law School, Harvard University (1958); LLB, Harvard Law School, Harvard University (1957); BA, DePaul University (1954) **C:** Commissioner, Eritrea-Ethiopia Claims Commission, The Hague Justice Portal (2001-2009); Judge, IUSCT (1981-Present); Ambassador, U.S. Department of State (1977-1981); Deputy Special Representative to President, U.S. Department of State (1977-1981); Deputy Legal Adviser, U.S. Department of State (1969-1977); Assistant Legal Adviser, U.S. Department of State (1965-1969); Legal Adviser, U.S. Mission to NATO (1963-1965); Attorney, U.S. Department of Defense (1960-1963); Attorney, Secretary of the Navy (1959-1960) **CR:** Professor, Universiteit Leiden (1990-1997); Member, International Law Commission, United Nations (1981); U.S. Ambassador for Laws of War Negotiations (1974-1977) **CIV:** President, Executive Committee, American School of The Hague (1987-1988) **CW:** Member, Board of Editors, "American Journal of International Law," The American Society of International Law (1987-Present); Author, "The Jurisprudence of the Iran-United States Claims Tribunal" (1996); Author, "Negotiator: The Protocols to the 1973 Vietnam Peace Agreement"; Contributor, Articles, Professional Journals **AW:** Honoree, Distinguished Senior Executive, President Jimmy Carter (1980) **MEM:** Council on Foreign Relations; American Society of International Law; International Institute of Humanitarian Law **BAR:** Indiana State Bar Association (1958) **MH:** Albert Nelson Marquis Lifetime Achievement Award (2017) **H:** Spending time with his family; Spending time in St. Croix; Tennis; Sailing **ADD:** 24389 Oakwood Park Rd, St Michaels, MD, 21663

ALES, JOHN F. ESQ., T: Attorney **I:** Law and Legal Services **CN:** Law Offices of John Ales **PB:** New Orleans **SC:** LA/USA **PT:** Peter J. Ales; Lena Romano Ales **CH:** Elisabeth Ales Nolan; Laura Ales Guillen; John Forrest Ales **ED:** LLM in Taxation, Georgetown University (1980); JD, Louisiana State University (1973); BSBA, Louisiana State University (1970) **C:** Attorney at Law, Private Practice (1973-Present); Special Counsel, Florida Joint Underwriting

Association (1992-1995); Secretary, Department of Natural Resources, State of Louisiana (1992-1994); General Counsel, Department of Water, Jefferson Parish (1976-1979); Chief of Staff, Jefferson Parish President's Office (1973-1976); Special Counsel, Reinsurance Association of America; Special Counsel, Association of Bermuda Reinsures (Now ABIR); Special Counsel, Swiss Re; Special Counsel, American International Group, Inc.; Special Legal Counsel to the Chairman, Board of Commissioners, Miami Dade County **CIV:** Member, Advisory Council, United States Secretary of the Interior; Member, School Board, Catholic Diocese of East Baton Rouge; Louisiana Democratic National Committee; Member, Louisiana Democratic Central Committee; Member, Various Catholic Parishes' School Boards and Parish Councils; Member, Union Governing Board, Louisiana State University; President, Student Government Association, Louisiana State University; Student Member, Dean of Men's Disciplinary Committee, Louisiana State University; Student Member, Athletic Council, Louisiana State University **BAR:** Louisiana State Bar Association (1973); United States District Court Eastern District of Louisiana; United States District Court Western District of Louisiana; United States District Court Middle District of Louisiana; United States District Court Northern District of New York; United States Bankruptcy Court Middle District of Louisiana; United States Bankruptcy Court Eastern District of Louisiana; United States Bankruptcy Court Western District of Louisiana; United States Bankruptcy Court Southern District of Texas; United States Court of Appeals for the Fifth Circuit; United States Court of Appeals for the 11th Circuit; United States Tax Court **BA:** PO Box 14695, Law Offices of John Ales, Baton Rouge, LA, 70898 **ADD:** PO Box 14695, Law Offices of John Ales, Baton Rouge, LA, 70810

ALEXANDER, ANNE A., T: Retired **I:** Education/Educational Services **DOB:** 08/22/1927 **PB:** Bartlesville **SC:** OK/USA **PT:** Francis Willard Alexander; Cloe Gray Alexander **MS:** Single **CH:** Josiah A. Turner; Kathleen Jane Turner; Christopher R. Turner **ED:** MA, The University of Kansas (1980); Degree in Visual Art Education, The University of Kansas (1975) **CT:** Certified Teacher, State of Kansas; Certified Teacher, State of Missouri **C:** Sales Consultant, Transworld Systems Inc., Mission, KS (1991-2015); Art Teacher, North Kansas City Schools (1975-1988); Artist, Hallmark Cards, Kansas City, MO (1963-1964) **CR:** Private Artist, Kansas City, MO; Art Teacher, Kansas City, MO **CIV:** Member, Gladstone Planning Commission (2000-Present); Active Member, Sosland Series, Kansas City Public Library (1998-Present); Board Member, WomenSpeak Steering Committee, Kansas City, MO (1994-Present); Board Member, Forward, Kansas City, MO (1994-Present); Volunteer, Greater Kansas City Community (1968-Present); Participant, Consensus City Planning, Kansas City, MO (1994); Commissioner, Mayor's Key to the City Commission, Kansas City, MO (1993-1995); Chair, Tri-County Domestic Violence Board, Platte, Clay and Ray Counties (1990-1994); Participant, Women's Leadership Institute, Avila University, Kansas City, MO (1984); Commissioner, Human Relations Commission, Kansas City, MO (1982-1990); Commissioner, Metropolitan Commission on Status of Women, Kansas City, MO (1980-1982); Board Member, SafeHaven, Clay, Platte and Ray Counties (1978-1994); Board Member, Share, Kansas City, MO (1978-1979) **CW:** Restoration Artist, Historic Statues, Old St. Mary's Church, Kansas City, MO (1992-Present); Solo Exhibitor, Parkville Art Gallery (1986); Exhibitor, Missouri Artists Invitational, Riverfront, Jefferson City, MO

(1985); Exhibitor, Art in the Woods, Corporate Woods, Overland Park, KS (1982); Exhibitor, River Bend Art Show, Atchison, KS (1980); Exhibitor, Group Shows, Cottonstone Gallery, Jefferson City, MO (1979); Billboard Painting, 72nd and Oak, Gladstone, MO (1978); Represented Artist, Private Collections Throughout the United States **AW:** Rookie of the Year, Sales Professionals International (1997); Award, Missouri Artists Invitational, Riverfront, Jefferson City, MO (1985); Purchase Award, Art in the Woods, Corporate Woods, Overland Park, KS (1982); First Place Award, River Bend Art Show, Atchison, KS (1980) **MEM:** Board Member, Sales Professionals International (1996-1998) **H:** Reading; Gardening; Advocating for women's issues; Dining with friends **PA:** Independent **RE:** Episcopalian **ADD:** 3121 NE 59th Ter Apt 3, Gladstone, MO, 64119

ALEXANDER, ICIE MAE, T: Communications Executive **I:** Corporate Communications & Public Relations **DOB:** 04/10/1933 **PB:** Knoxville **SC:** TN/USA **PT:** Jasper J. Casey; Gracie L. (Taylor) Casey **MS:** Widowed **SPN:** William C. Alexander (7/14/1954, Deceased 1982) **CH:** Iva G. (Deceased); Billie Jean **ED:** Supervisor Diploma, Ohio State Extension (1972) **C:** President, International Training in Communications, Columbus, OH (2002-2003); Secretary, Labor Union, Columbus Development Center (1983-1986); Loan Officer, Columbus State School Federal Credit Union (1982-1989); Supervisor, Printing Department, Columbus Development Center (1970-1989); Instructor, Printing, Columbus State Institute, Ohio (1967-1970); Chairman, Ohio Federation of Women's Clubs **CR:** Treasurer, Corban Communications Research Council, Columbus, OH (2001-2003) **CIV:** Secretary, Finance Secretary, Youth Connections Inc. (2004-2006); Volunteer Receptionist, Corban Commons Senior Community (2004-2006); Mentor, Granville T. Woods School, Columbus, OH (2003-2004); Mentor, Cassady Elementary School, Columbus, OH (2000-2002) **CW:** Performer, "Black to the Truth" (2000) **AW:** Member of the Year, East Mount Olivet Baptist Church (2016); Dedicated Service Award, Mount Calvery Baptist District Association (2002) **MEM:** General Secretary, Mount Calvery Baptist District Association (2001); Chairman, Fundraising, East Columbus Democratic Club (1995-2003); East Mount Olivet Baptist Church; Mount Calvery Baptist District Association; East Columbus Civic Association; Franklin County Democratic Women's Club; Columbus Inner City Lions; President, Chairman Program, Columbus Inner City Lions; Co-chairman, Audit Committee, Columbus Inner City Lions; East Columbus Democratic Club; Community Service Club **H:** Sewing; Reading; Crossword puzzles **PA:** Democrat **RE:** Baptist **ADD:** 1100 E Broad Street, Apt. 306, Columbus, OH, 43205

ALEXIADES, MACRENE RENEE MD, PHD, T: Dermatologist Scientist Entrepreneur **I:** Medicine & Health Care **CN:** Dr. Macrene **DOB:** 09/02/1967 **PB:** New York **SC:** NY/USA **PT:** Gregory Alexiades; Sophia Alexiades **MS:** Married **CH:** Sophia Stella Armenakas; Anthony Emmanuel Armenakas **ED:** Resident in Dermatology, New York University School of Medicine, New York, NY (1998-2000); Intern in Medicine, Lenox Hill Hospital, New York, NY (1997-1998); PhD, Harvard University (1997); MD, Harvard Medical School, Harvard University (1997); BA, Harvard University (1989) **CT:** Board Certified in Dermatology (2009); Credentialed in Medicine and Surgery, European Union (2004); Licensed in Medicine and Surgery, Greece (2004); Licensed in Medicine and Surgery, State of Connecticut (2004); Diplomate, ABD (2002); Licensed in Medicine and Surgery, State

of New York (1998) **C:** Founder, Dr. Macrene (2009-Present); Owner, Dr. Macrene (2009-Present); Founder, Owner, NY Derm LLC (2005-Present); Attending Physician, Yale New Haven and West Haven Hospitals (2006-Present); Assistant Clinical Professor, Yale School of Medicine (2003-Present); President, Macrene Alexiades, MD, PhD, PC (2003-Present); Director of Dermatology and Laser Surgery, Macrene Alexiades, MD, PhD, PC (2003-Present); Attending Physician, Lenox Hill Hospital, New York, NY (2001-Present); Attending Physician, Yale/New Haven Hospital (2003); Director of Research and Laser Dermatology, Laser & Skin Surgery Center of New York (2001-2003); Chief Resident in Dermatology, New York University School of Medicine, New York, NY (2000-2001); Fulbright Scholar, University of Crete, Heraklion, Greece (1989-1990); Doctorate Researcher, Harvard University, Boston, MA (1991-1997); Teaching Assistant, Harvard University, Cambridge, MA (1990-1997); Tutor Supervisor, Harvard University, Cambridge, MA (1985-1989); Researcher, Harvard University, Cambridge, MA (1984-1989); Adjunct Clinical Professor, Syggros Hospital, University of Athens; Associate Clinical Professor, Yale School of Medicine **CR:** Scientific Advisor, Antiochian Orthodox Christian Archdiocese of North America (2006-Present); Admissions Interviewer Committee, Harvard Medical School (2002-Present); Consultant Dermatologist, L'oréal Paris (2005-2008); MD/PhD Program Steering Committee (1993-1994); Advanced Biomedical Sciences Committeee (1993-1995); Minority Recruitment Committee (1992-1995); MD/PhD Program Retreat Committee (1992-1994); Tutor Supervisor, Bureau of Study Counsel, Harvard University (1985-1989); Advisory Board, Allergan, Merz and Galderma **CIV:** Board of Directors, Archdiocesan Cathedral of the Holy Trinity (2009-Present); Board of Directors, Cutera (2008-Present); Board of Directors, Primaeva Medical (2008-Present); Chair, Afternoon School Board of Directors, Promenade Condominiums (2008-Present); Science and Research Advisor (2006-Present); Chairperson, The Chapin School (2004-Present); Board of Trustees, The Chapin School (2004-Present); Member, Parents Association (2004-2005); Art Committee, The Chapin School (2004-2005); Solicitation Coordinator, Fundraising Committee, The William Woodward, Jr. Nursery School (2001-2002); Volunteer, St. Francis House (1990-1994); Yoga Instructor, Vanderbilt Hall Athletic Facility, Boston, MA (1990-1992); Counselor, Peer Counseling, Harvard Medical School (1990-1992); Counselor, Rape Crisis Response, Cambridge, MA (1988-1989); Chair, Afternoon School Board of Directors, Cathedral School **CW:** Author, Numerous Publications; Contributor, Chapters to Books; Author, Textbook **AW:** Recipient, Beauty Quest Award, QVC (2014); Recipient, People's Choice Award, New York Post (2009); Honoree, Top Five Treatments, American Society for Laser Medicine and Surgery, Inc. (2008); Honoree, Top Ten Research Presentation, American Society for Laser Medicine and Surgery, Inc. (2007); Recipient, First Place Award, Journal of Drugs in Dermatology (2004); Recipient, Husik Prize (2001); Grantee, National Eye Institute, National Institutes of Health (1995); Recipient, Paul Dudley White Scholarship, Harvard University (1991); Recipient, Scholarship, Fulbright Foundation (1989-1990) **MEM:** Faculty, American Academy of Dermatology (2008-Present); Faculty, American Society for Laser Medicine and Surgery, Inc. (2001-Present); Director, American Society for Laser Medicine and Surgery, Inc. (2001-Present); Chairman, Research Committee, American Society for Dermatologic Surgery (2004-2006); Councilman,

Education and Research Committee, American Society for Dermatologic Surgery (2002-2006); Fellow, American Society for Laser Medicine and Surgery, Inc.; Fellow, American Academy of Dermatology; Fellow, Hellenic Medical Society of New York; Cosmetic Executive Women; Women's Dermatologic Society; Dermatology Foundation; Founder, Hellenic Society, Harvard University; Massachusetts Medical Society; Harvard Club of Greece; Editor, American Society for Dermatologic Surgery **MH:** Albert Nelson Marquis Lifetime Achievement Award (2017); Who's Who in America, Who's Who in the World, Who's Who Among American Women, Who's Who Among American Professionals **H:** Portraiture; Sculpture; Drawing; Painting; Skiing; Tennis; Yoga; Farming; Horticulture **RE:** Greek Orthodox Christian **ADD:** 530 E 76th St Apt 21H, New York, NY, 10021 **URL:** http://www.nyderm.org

AL-HAMDI, MOHANED, T: Assistant Professor **I:** Education/Educational Services **CN:** Kansas State University **ED:** PhD, Department of Economics, Kansas State University, Manhattan, KS (2005) **C:** Assistant Professor, Kansas State University (2008-Present) **CIV:** President of Board of Directors, Prairie Glen Place; Advisory Council, North Elementary School **CW:** Contributor, 24 Published Articles; Author, Two Translated Books **AW:** Teaching Award, Kansas State University (2016) **MEM:** American Economists Association; American Political Science Association; Interaction of Political Science Association **BA:** 327 Waters Hall, Kansas State University, Manhattan, KS, 66506 **URL:** https://www.researchgate.net/profile/Mohaned_Al-Hamdi

ALLAN, DAVID W., T: President **I:** Sciences **CN:** Allan's TIME **DOB:** 09/25/1936 **PB:** Mapleton **SC:** UT/USA **PT:** Sylvester Allan; Florence Allan **MS:** Married **SPN:** Edna Love (Ramsay) Allan (2/20/1959) **CH:** Shelli Allan-Owen; Karie Allan-Clingo; Sterling; Jeannette Allan-Colbert; Celeste Allan-Lambson; McKaylee; Nathan **ED:** Master's Degree, University of Colorado (1965); BS in Physics, Brigham Young University, Provo, UT (1960) **C:** Retired; President, Allan's Time Interval Metrology Enterprise; Senior Scientist, National Institute of Standards and Technology; Consultant, HP Development Company, L.P.; Consultant, Bliley **CR:** Fellow, The Institution of Navigation, Inc. (1999); Guest Speaker, Consultant to Director of the National Physical Laboratory, Israel (1987); Guest Scientist, Speaker, NIST, People's Republic of China (1982); Consultant, United Nations Development Program, New Delhi, India (1981); Visiting Professor, Istituto Elettrotecnico Nazionale Galileo Ferraris, Turin, Italy (1969); United States Expert, Consultative Committee for the Definition of the Second, Treaty of the Meter **CIV:** Volunteer Mission, Church, Republic of Cote d'Ivoire, West Africa (1997-1999); Stake President, Boulder Stake (1977-1987); Bishop, Boulder Second Ward (1966-1972); Volunteer Mission, Church, Eastern States (1956-1958) **CW:** Author, "It's About Time - Science Harmonized with Religion, Second Edition" (2016); Author, "It's About Time - Science Harmonized with Religion" (2014); Presenter, ION-GPS Conference, Salt Lake City, Utah (2001); Presenter, "Coordinate Time in the Vicinity of the Earth," International Astronomical Union Symposium on Relativity and Celestial Mechanics, Saint Petersburg, Russia (1985); Associate Editor, Frequency and Time, IEEE (1985); Presenter, "Practical Implications of Relativity for a Global Coordinate Time Scale," International Union of Radio Science, Helsinki, Finland (1978); Author, "Statistics of Atomic Frequency Standards," Proceedings of the IEEE (1966); Contributor, Articles, Professional

Journals; Contributor, Chapters, Books; Author, Over 100 Technical Papers **AW:** Joseph F. Keithley Award, IEEE (2018); Award for Seminal Work to the UFFC Community Regarding Time Determination, Time Prediction, Time Dissemination and Timekeeping Through Contributions to Atomic Frequency Standards, Space-Based Navigation, Time and Frequency Stability Analysis, Time-Scale Algorithms, and Timekeeping Devices, IEEE (2016); Time Lord Award, Edinburgh, Scotland (2011); Nominee in Physics, Gold Medal, Department of Commerce, NIST (1992); I. I. Rabi Award for Contributions to the Measurement and Characterization of Precise Time and Frequency Sources, IEEE (1984); Invention Award, U.S. Air Force (1978); International Research IR-100 Award (1972); Silver Medal, Department of Commerce, NIST (1968) **MEM:** Original Chair, Timing Sub-Committee, Civil GPS Service Interface Committee for Interfacing GPS, U.S. Department of Defense (1988); International Astronomical Union; Chair, Special Millisecond Pulsar Timing Subcommittee, Sigma Xi, The Scientific Research Honor Society; Radio Division, ITU; ITU Radiocommunication Sector; International Union of Radio Science; Senior and Honorary Lifetime Member, IEEE **H:** Jogging; Cross-country skiing; Mountain biking; Walking with his wife; Gardening **RE:** Latter-Day Saints **ADD:** PO Box 66, 650 W Big Springs Road, Fountain Green, UT, 84632 **URL:** https://en.wikipedia.org/wiki/David_W._Allan

ALMARAZ, DAVID, T: Trial Lawyer **I:** Law and Legal Services **CN:** Law Office of David Almaraz **ED:** JD, St. Mary's School of Law, San Antonio, TX (1977); MA in Elementary Education, The University of Texas at Austin (1972); BA in Political Science, The University of Texas at Austin (1970) **C:** Solo Practitioner, Law Office of David Almaraz, Laredo, Webb County, TX (1985-Present); Assistant United States Attorney, Sole Prosecutor of 5 Different Counties, Laredo Division, Southern District of Texas (1980-1985); Assistant District Attorney, Sole Prosecutor in the County, Starr County, TX (1978-1980) **CIV:** Appointed Judicial Selection Committee, United States Magistrate (1988-Present); President, Laredo Chapter, ACLU; Past Director, Texas Young Lawyers Association **AW:** Named, Texas Super Lawyer (2009-2012); Named, Top 100 Trial Lawyers, National Trial Lawyers **BAR:** Supreme Court of the United States; United States Court of Appeals for the Fifth Circuit; United States District Court Southern District of Texas; United States District Court Northern District of Texas; United States District Court Western District of Texas **BA:** 1802 Houston St, Law Office of David Almaraz, Laredo, TX, 78040 **URL:** https://www.davidalmarazlaw.com/untitled-c1n8o

ALTSCHULER, BRUCE ROBERT, T: Dentist, Chief Executive Officer **I:** Medicine & Health Care **CN:** Cobalt Research, LLC **DOB:** 02/17/1947 **PB:** Brooklyn **SC:** NY/USA **PT:** Frank Philip Altschuler; Sarah Gertrude (Cloder) Altschuler **MS:** Married **SPN:** Ruth Phyllis Gass (10/27/1974) **CH:** Joan Ellen; Wendy Karen; Cheryl Miriam **ED:** Residency in Advanced Clinical Dentistry, Elgin Air Force Base, Florida (1985-1986); DDS, Temple University, Philadelphia, PA (1971); BA, Brooklyn College (1967) **CT:** Licensed Dentist, States of New York, Maine, Connecticut, Pennsylvania, and Maryland **C:** Chief Executive Officer, Cobalt Research, LLC (2004-Present); Director of Research Development, Cobalt Research, LLC (1997-2003); Chief, Imaging Robotics Laboratory, Walter Reed Army Institute of Research Dental Research Detachment (Now U.S. Army Institute of Surgical Research), Fort Meade, MD (1995-1997); Air Force Research Liaison, Chief of Laser

Imaging, United States Army Institute of Dental Research (Now U.S. Army Institute of Surgical Research), Fort Meade, MD (1986-1994); Deputy of Optical Processing, Systems Avionics Division, Wright-Patterson Air Force Base, Ohio (1985); Chief, Avionics Advanced Systems Research Group, Information Processing Branch, Wright-Patterson Air Force Base, Ohio (1982-1984); Chief of Dental Computer and Laser Technology, United States Air Force School of Aerospace Medicine, Brooks Air Force Base, Texas (1980-1982); Chief of Dental Laser Holography, United States Air Force Dental Investigation Service (Now United States Dental Evaluation & Consultation Service), Brooks Air Force Base, Texas (1976-1980); Chief of Dental Consultation, Dental Sciences Branch, Brooks Air Force Base, Texas (1975-1976); Project Scientist of Dental Holography, Dental Sciences Branch, Brooks Air Force Base, Texas (1971-1974) **CR:** Chairman, SPIE Robotics and Machine Perception Technology Group (2006); Reviewer, National Institutes of Health Computer Aided Dentistry, Washington, DC (1987); Dental X-Ray Subcommittee 26, American National Standards Institute, Washington, DC (1980-1985); Department of Dental Diagnostic Service, University of Texas Health Science Center, San Antonio, TX (1980-1982); Clinical Assistant Professor, Department of Diagnosis and Roentgenology, University of Texas Health Science Center, San Antonio, TX (1976-1980) **CIV:** Volunteer, Howard County Radio Amateur Civil Emergency Service (2013-2018); Columbia Residential Architectural Committee (2013-2018); Delegate, Howard County Dental Association (2015-2017); Board of Advisers, Maryland Responds Medical Reserve Corps (2015-2017); Instructor, Advanced Disaster Life Support (2014); Campaign Coordinator, Avionics Laboratory Combined Federal Campaign, Dayton, OH (1984); Board of Directors, American Cancer Society, Bexar County, Texas (1980-1982); Public Education Committee (1980-1982); Special Award Judge, Alamo Regional Science Fair, San Antonio, TX (1980-1982) **MIL:** Colonel, U.S. Air Force (1986); Commissioned Captain, U.S. Air Force (1971) **CW:** Editor, "3-D Machine Perception" **AW:** 27th Annual Burka Award, Avionics Laboratory, Wright-Patterson Air Force Base (1983); U.S. Air Force Research and Development Award in Electro-Optic Systems, Secretary of Air Force Level **MEM:** Resident Architectural Committee (2015-Present); Society of Photo-Optical Instrumentation Engineers (2006); American Dental Association; International Association for Dental Research; Air Force Association; AFCEA International; Amateur Radio Relay League; National Defense Industrial Association; Amateur Radio Emergency Services; Maryland State Dental Association; Maryland Medical Reserve Corps.; Texas Dental Association; American Mensa, Ltd.; Advisory Board, Medical Reserve Corps.; Chairman, Robotics and Machine Perception Technology Group **H:** Photography; Computers **PA:** Republican **RE:** Jewish **ADD:** PO Box 458, Simpsonville, MD, 21150

ALTSHULER, KENNETH, T: Psychiatrist **I:** Medicine & Health Care **CN:** Dallas Psychoanalytic Institute **PB:** Paterson **SC:** NJ/USA **PT:** Jacob Altshuler; Altie (Freedman) Altshuler **MS:** Married **SPN:** Ruth Collins Sharp (12/4/1987); Gloria Seigel (1952-1981) **CH:** Steven; Lori; Dara **ED:** Honorary DSc, Gallaudet College (1972); Resident, New York State Psychiatric Institute (1955-1958); Intern, Kings County Hospital, Brooklyn, (1952-1953); MD, University of Buffalo (1952); BA, Cornell University (1948) **C:** Training Analyst, Dallas Psychoanalytic Institute (1986-Present); Stanton Sharp Professor of Psychiatry, University of Texas-Southwestern Medical School (2000-Present); Training Analyst,

New Orleans Psychoanalytic Institute (1979-1986); Stanton Sharp Professor, Chairman of Psychiatry, University of Texas-Southwestern Medical School (1977-2000); Project Director, Trauma and Sleep Physiology (1975-1977); Project Director, Essential Aspects of Deafness (1972-1976); Training Analyst, Columbia University Psychoanalytic Clinic for Training and Research (1969-1977); Professor, Columbia University, (1975-1977); Associate Clinical Professor, Columbia University (1971-1975); Assistant Clinical Professor, Columbia University (1967-1971); Research Associate, Columbia University (1963-1967); Instructor, Columbia University (1959-1963); Assistant in Psychiatry, Columbia University (1958-1959) **CR:** Chief, Deafness Unit, Rockland State Hospital (1966-1977); Consultant, National Institutes of Health; Director, American Board of Psychiatry and Neurology (1990-1997); President, American Board of Psychiatry and Neurology (1996); National Board of Medical Examiners (1986-1989); Chairman, Part II Psychiatry Committee (1988-1989); AACDP (1977-2000); President, AACDP (1990-1991) **CIV:** Co-Author, "Managing Sleep Complaints" (1982); Co-Editor, Family and Mental Health Problems in a Deaf Population (1963); Co-Editor, "Comprehensive Mental Health Service for the Deaf" (1966); Co-Editor, "Psychiatry and the Deaf" (1968); Co-Editor, "Expanded Mental Health Care for the Deaf" (1970); Co-Editor, "Depression: Mechanisms, Diagnosis and Treatment" (1986); Contributor, Articles, Professional Journals **CW:** Co-Author, "Managing Sleep Complaints" (1982); Co-Editor, Family and Mental Health Problems in a Deaf Population (1963); Co-Editor, "Comprehensive Mental Health Service for the Deaf" (1966); Co-Editor, "Psychiatry and the Deaf" (1968); Co-Editor, "Expanded Mental Health Care for the Deaf" (1970); Co-Editor, "Depression: Mechanisms, Diagnosis and Treatment" (1986); Contributor, Articles, Professional Journals **AW:** Wilson Award in Genetics and Preventive Medicine (1961); Distinguished Community Service Award, Dallas County Mental Health Association (1986); Prism Award (1992); Distinguished Alumnus Award, State University of New York, Buffalo (1993); Namesake, First Trailblazer Award, Dallas County Mental Health and Retardation Center (1996); Texas Star Award for Outstanding Community Service, Texas Mental Health Association (1997); Outstanding Psychiatrist, Texas Society of Psychiatric Physicians (1996); Outstanding Alumnus of the 1960s Decade, Columbia University (1996); Medical Leadership Award, Turtle Creek Manor (2003); Certificate of Achievement, Board of Hospital Psychiatry; Certificate of Significant Achievement, Deafness Program, New York State (1976); Certificate of Significant Achievement, Mental Health Connections Program (1995) **MEM:** President, Southern Association of Research Psychiatry (1993-1994) ; Founder, Vice President, Association Director, Medical Student Education in Psychiatry (1976-1977); Fellow, American Psychiatric Association; American College of Psychiatrists; American College of Psychoanalysts; American Medical Association; American Psychoanalytic Association; Association for Psychoanalytic Medicine; Texas Medical Society; Dallas County Medical Society; American Psychopathology Association **ADD:** 5227 Meaders Lane, Dallas, TX, 75229

AMBROSE, CHARLES T., T: Professor **I:** Education/Educational Services **CN:** University of Kentucky **ED:** MD, The Johns Hopkins University School of Medicine (1955) **C:** Professor, Pathogenic Microbiology, Department of Microbiology, Immunology and Molecular Genetics, University of Kentucky **CW:** Contributor, Article in Field, Annale d'Immunologie (1975); Author, "The Essential Role of Corticosteroid … in Hormones & the Immune

Response," J. & A. Churchill (1970); Contributor, Articles in Field, JEM (1969, 1966, 1964); Contributor, Articles, Professional Journals AW: Scholarship, LHD, Honoris Causa, Transylvania University (2009) ADD: 341 Arcadia Park, Lexington, KY, 40503

AMENT, MICHAEL S., T: Investor I: Financial Services PB: Elmira SC: NY/USA ED: MBA in Finance and International Business, New York University; BSBA, Georgetown University CT: Certified Count in Travels to Germany C: President, Ament International (2012-Present); Founder, Revision Skincare (1997-2015); Chief Executive Officer, Revision Skincare (1997-2015); Financial Specialist, Ernest + Whinney CIV: Executive Positions, Republican National Committee AW: Recipient, Commendation for Extraordinary Diplomatic Service, American Foreign Service Association MEM: Founder, Wine Tasting Society, Georgetown University H: Extensive international travel; Fitness; Culinary and wine indulgence RE: Protestant ADD: 11851 NW 6th St, Plantation, FL, 33325 URL: https://www.facebook.com/michael.ament2

ANDERSON, GORDON, T: President I: Publishing CN: Paragon House Publishers DOB: 11/16/1947 PB: St. Croix Falls SC: WI/USA PT: Erwin Louis Anderson; Eunice Arlene (Johnson) Anderson MS: Married SPN: Mary Jane Evenson (7/1/1982) CH: Tamara; Jayna; Greta; Evan ED: PhD in Philosophy Religion, Claremont Graduate School (1986); MA in Religion, Claremont Graduate School (1985); MDiv in Ethics, Union Theological Seminary, New York, NY (1980); BME, University of Minnesota (1975) C: Adjunct Professor, California Institute of Integral Studies, San Francisco, CA (2011-Present); Secretary General, Professors World Peace Academy, St. Paul, MN (1993-Present); Secretary General, Board of Directors, International Cultural Foundation, Washington, D.C. (1986-2009); Secretary General, Board of Directors, Professors World Peace Academy, New York, NY (1984-1993); Owner, Manager, Aerograph Aerial Photography, Claremont, CA (1981-1984); Engineer, Board of Directors, Gull Engineering Inc., Minneapolis, MN (1974-1980) CR: Board of Directors, Unification Theological Seminary (1988-96); Lecturer, Unification Theological Seminary, Barrytown, NY (1987-1996); Lecturer, 40 Countries including Europe, Africa, Asia and South America CIV: Board Member, Minnesota Legislative Evaluation Assembly (1999-Present); President, Paragon House Publishers (1996-Present); Trustee, University of Bridgeport, CT (1994-Present); Board of Directors, Paragon House Publishers (1993-Present); Chairman, Minnesota Legislative Evaluation Assembly (2007-2011); Citizens for a Better New Jersey (1986-1992) MIL: US Army, Vietnam (1969-1972) CW: Author, "Life, Liberty and the Pursuit of Happiness" (2009); Author, "The Philosophy of the United States" (2004); Publisher, International Journal on World Peace (2000); Associate Editor, "Family in Global Transition" (1997); Associate Editor, "Worldwide State of the Family" (1995); Editor, International Journal on World Peace (1994-2000); Associate Editor, "Morality and Religion in Liberal Democratic Societies" (1992); Associate Editor, International Journal on World Peace (1985-1994); Contributor, Articles to Professional Journals; Contributor, Chapters to Books MEM: World Future Society; American Academy of Religion; American Political Science Association; Peace and Justice Studies Association; Consortium on Peace Research MH: Albert Nelson Marquis Lifetime Achievement Award (2017) ADD: 3600 Labore Road, Suite 1, Paragon House, Saint Paul, MN, 55110 URL: http://www.pwpa.org

ANDREWS, ANTHONY HUNTER, T: Veterinary Educator, Writer, Consultant I: Education/Educational Services DOB: 08/16/1942 PB: Swindon SC: England PT: Harold Edward Andrews; Alice Winifred (Hunter) Andrews MS: Single SPN: Joan Margaret Isle (1/1/1966, Divorced 10/1972); Celia Josephine Tucker (10/21/1972, Divorced 2/1977) CH: Michael John; Mark Edward Alexander ED: PhD, University of London (1980); Bachelor's Degree in Veterinary Medicine, University of London (1966) CT: Registered Forensic Practitioner, Council of Registration Forensic Practitioners (2005); Diplomate, European College of Small Ruminant Health Management, Diplomate European College of Bovine Health Management (2004) C: Independent Veterinary Consultant (1997-Present); Recognized Specialist in Cattle Health and Production (1991-2017), European Veterinary Specialist in Bovine Health Management (2005-2017), Meat and Livestock Commission, Milton Keynes, England (1992); Senior Veterinary Officer, Meat and Livestock Commission, Milton Keynes, England (1973-1979); Senior Lecturer of Farm Animal Medicine, Royal Veterinary College, University of London (1979-1997); Royal Smithfield Club Fellow, Royal Veterinary College, University of London (1970-1973); Veterinary Surgeon, Isle of Wight, England (1968); Veterinary Surgeon, Cranleigh, Surrey, England (1967-1970); Veterinary Surgeon, Falmouth, Cornwall, England (1966-1967) CR: Director, Embryo Veterinary School (2005-2012); Chief Executive, European School of Veterinary Postgraduate Studies (2004-2013); Advisory Committee, Antibiotics, British Pharmaceutical Commission(2005-2009); Director, Responsible Use of Medicines in Agricultural Alliance (2003-2009); Veterinary Adviser, Tubney Charitable Trust (2001-2007); Member, Royal College of Veterinary Surgeons (1998-2007); Member, Food Standards Agency (2000-2005); Veterinary Consultant, Safeway Superstores Limited (2001-2004); Veterinary Consultant, Food and Agricultural Organization, World Bank, Kosovo (2001); Beef Assurance Advisory Panel, Minister Agriculture, Fisheries and Food (1999-2000); Social Economic Committee, European Economic Community, Brussels, Belgium (1989-1990); Veterinary Expert, Select Committee on European Community, House of Lords, London, UK (1989); Vice President, British Cattle Veterinary Association (1979-1982); President, British Cattle Veterinary Association (1980-1981); Secretary, British Cattle Veterinary Association (1976-1979); Examiner, Royal College of Veterinary Surgeons; Examiner, University of Edinburgh; Examiner, University of Dublin; Examiner, University of Cambridge; Examiner, University of London; European Veterinary Specialist, Bovine Health Management; Independent Consultant CW: Assistant Editor,"Black's Veterinary Dictionary, 22nd Edition" (2015); Assistant Editor, "Black's Veterinary Dictionary, 21st Edition" (2005); Livestock Editor, UK Veterinarian (1995-2005); Author, "Bovine Medicine Second Edition" (2004); Editor, "Bovine Medicine Second Edition" (2004); Editorial Board Member, British Veterinary Journal (1988-2002); Assistant Editor, "Black's Veterinary Dictionary, 20th Edition" (2001); Editor, "The Expectant Cow" (2000); Author, "The Health of Dairy Cattle," Blackwell Science (2000); Editor, "The Health of Dairy Cattle," Blackwell Science (2000); Author, "The Henston Veterinary Vade Mecum" (1984-2000); Assistant Editor, "Black's Veterinary Dictionary, 19th Edition" (1998); Executive Board Member, British Veterinary Journal (1995-1998); Author, "Bovine Medicine" (1992); Editor, "Bovine Medicine" (1992); Author, "Poisoning in Veterinary Practice" (1992); Author, "Outline of Clinical Diagnosis in Cattle" (1990); Author, "Growing Cattle Management and Disease Notes Management" (1985-1986); Author, "Calf Management and Disease Notes" (1983); Contributor, Articles, Professional Journals AW: First National Office of Animal Health Award for Contribution to Animal Health (2010); Recipient, Centenary Prize, Central Veterinary Society (1987); Recipient, William Hunting Award, British Veterinarian Association (1971); Recipient, Bewicke Award, Royal Veterinary College (1969) MEM: Former President, Goat Veterinarian Society (2014-Present); Second Opinion, Editorial Board, British Veterinary Association (1966-Present); Judge, Ceva Farm Animal Welfare Awards, British Veterinary Association (2014-2017); Chairman, Goat Veterinarian Society (1997-2014); Editorial Working Party for Cattle Practice, British Veterinary Association (2011-2013); Committee Member, Veterinary History Society (2007-2012); Director, Embryo Veterinarian School, British Veterinary Association (2005-2012); Council, British Veterinary Association (1976-1987, 1990-2011); Board Member, European College of Bovine Health Management (2008-2011); Fellow, Goat Veterinarian Society (2010); Chairman, Accreditation Committee, European College of Bovine Health Management (2005-2007); Senior Vice Chairman, Veterinarian Association for Arbitration and Jurisprudence (2004-2006); Council Member, European College of Bovine Health Management (1995-2006); Chairman, Veterinarian Association for Arbitration and Jurisprudence (2002-2004); Vice Chairman, European College of Bovine Health Management (2002-2004); Chairman, British Cattle Veterinarian Association (1998-2000); Senior, Hertfordshire and Bedfordshire Veterinarian Society (1997-1999); Vice Chair, British Cattle Veterinarian Association (1996-1997); Vice Chairman, Goat Veterinarian Society (1996-1997); President, Hertfordshire and Bedfordshire Veterinarian Society (1995-1997); Board Member, British Cattle Veterinarian Association (1995-1996); Council Member, Goat Veterinarian Society (1995-1996); Vice Chairman, Veterinarian Association for Arbitration and Jurisprudence (1996); Vice President, Hertfordshire and Bedfordshire Veterinarian Society (1993-1995); Council Member, Veterinarian Association for Arbitration and Jurisprudence (1994); Chairman, Science, Education and Marketing Committee, British Veterinary Association (1984-1987); Chairman, Large Animals Committee, British Veterinary Association (1983-1984); Senior Vice President, British Cattle Veterinarian Association (1981-1982); President, British Cattle Veterinarian Association (1980-1981); Vice President, British Cattle Veterinarian Association (1979-1980); Secretary, British Cattle Veterinarian Association (1976-1979); Fellow, Veterinary History Society; Royal College of Veterinary Surgeons, British Institute of Agricultural Consultants; Farmers Club; Royal Society of Medicine; European College of Bovine Health Management; Goat Veterinarian Society; Veterinarian Association for Arbitration and Jurisprudence; British Cattle Veterinarian Association; Hertfordshire and Bedfordshire Veterinarian Society; British Veterinary Association MH: Albert Nelson Marquis Lifetime Achievement Award (2017) H: Travel; Gardening; Reading; Writing, Walking RE: Church of England ADD: 25 Mardley Hill, Welwyn, United Kingdom, AL6 0TT

ANGRIST, BURTON MORRIS, T: Professor of Psychiatry (Retired) I: Education/Educational Services CN: New York University School of Medicine DOB: 07/15/1936 PB: New York SC: NY/USA PT: Alfred Angrist; Sylvia M. (Kasdan)

Angrist (Deceased) **MS:** Married **SPN:** Anna Marie Katan (4/2/1976) **CH:** Laurel S. Angrist (1980) **ED:** MD, Albert Einstein College of Medicine (1962); AB, Colby College (1958) **CT:** Diplomate, American Board of Psychiatry and Neurology, Inc. (1973) **C:** Professor, Department of Psychiatry, New York University School of Medicine (1980-2003); Staff Psychiatrist, New York Harbor Health Care System, United States Department of Veterans Affairs (1980-1998); Staff Psychiatrist, Bellevue Hospital, The City of New York (1967); Postdoctoral Fellowship, Psychopharmacology, NYU/Bellevue Hospital (1966-1968); Lifetime Fellow, American College of Neuropsychopharmacology; Fellow, Collegium Internationale Neuropsychopharmacologium **MIL:** U.S. Army Reserve (1964-1969) **CW:** Contributor, Articles, Professional Journals; Contributor, Chapters, Books **AW:** Grantee, National Institute of Mental Health, National Institutes of Health **MEM:** American College of Neuropsychopharmacology; Collegium Internationale Neuropsychopharmacollogium; American Alpine Club; Vulgarian Mountain Club **MH:** Albert Nelson Marquis Lifetime Achievement Award (2017) **H:** Outdoor sports; Hiking; Skiing; Canoeing; Rock climbing; Scuba diving **ADD:** 39 Nutmeg Rd, High Falls, NY, 12440

ANSARY, CYRUS A., T: President **I:** Financial Services **CN:** Investment Services International Company LLC **DOB:** 11/20/1933 **PB:** Shiraz **SC:** Iran **PT:** A. Russell Ansary; Jamali (Mostmand) Ansary **MS:** Married **SPN:** Janet C. Hodges (8/1/1970) **CH:** Douglas C.; Pary Ann; Jeffrey C.; Bradley C. **ED:** JD, Columbia University (1958); BS, American University (1955) **CT:** Certified in French Civilization, University of Paris (1966) **C:** Chairman Emeritus, Washington Mutual Investors Fund (2009-Present); Chairman, MACO Bancorp, Washington, D.C. (1988-1995); Chairman, American Funds Tax-Exempt Series I (1986-2008); Chairman, Fort Knox National Company (1985-2014); Chairman, J.P. Morgan Value Opportunities Fund (1985-2008); Chairman of the Board, Washington Mutual Investors Fund (1983-2008); Director, Metalurgica Campo Limpo Limitada, Sao Paulo, Brazil (1976-1980); Member, Supervisory Board, Deutsche Babcock & Wilcox AG, Oberhausen, Germany (1976-1980); Member, Supervisory Board, Fried. Krupp GmbH, Essen, Federal Republic of Germany (1975-1979); Vice Chairman of the Board, IK Investment A.G., Zurich, Switzerland (1974-1979); President, Investment Services International Company LLC, Washington, D.C. (1973-Present); Chairman of the Board, Campbell Music Company, Washington, D.C. (1968-1972); Chairman of the Board, Financial Dynamics Corporation, Washington, D.C. (1967-1972); Lecturer, School Business Administration, American University (1967-1971); Chairman and President, Woodland National Bank, Alexandria, Virginia (1963-1965); Chairman of the Board, John L. Lindstrom and Associates, Inc., Washington, D.C. (1962-1986); Chairman of the Board, Industry Reports, Inc., Washington, D.C. (1960-1972); Senior Partner, Ansary, Kirkpatrick and Rosse (1959-1972) **CIV:** Member, Penn Medicine Cardiovascular Institute Leadership Council (2009-Present); Member, Woodrow Wilson Council, Washington, DC (2000-2012); Chairman emeritus, American University Board of Trustees (1989-Present); President, Ansary Foundation, Washington, DC (1983-Present); Trustee, Washington Opera Society (1982-1989); Chairman of the Board of Trustees, American University (1981-1989); Trustee, Wolf Trap Foundation, Vienna, Virginia (1977-1982); Trustee, Fried Krupp Foundation, Essen, Germany (1977-1979); Director, International Law Institute (1976-1988); Trustee, American University (1968-1980) **MIL:** U.S. Marine

Corps Reserve (1959-1964) **MEM:** CFA Institute; The National Economists Club, Inc.; Washington Association of Money Managers; The National Press Club; The Economic Club of Washington, D.C.; The Economic Club of New York; Life Guard Society, Mount Vernon; Congressional Country Club; Chevy Chase Country Club; The Metropolitan Club of the City of Washington; Rotary International **BAR:** Virginia (1961); The District of Columbia (1960); Maryland (1959); Supreme Court of the United States (1966) **BA:** 3 Bethesda Metro Ctr Ste 700, Investment Services International Co LLC, Bethesda, MD, 20814

ANSLEY, SHEPARD, T: Lawyer **I:** Law and Legal Services **DOB:** 07/31/1939 **PT:** William Bonneau; Florence Jackson (Bryan) Ansley **MS:** Married (5/9/1970) **SPN:** Boyce Lineberger **CH:** Anna Ansley Davis; Florence Bryan **ED:** LLB, University of Virginia (1964); BA, University of Georgia (1961) **CT:** Georgia (1967) **C:** With, Carter, Terry and Co., Inc., Atlanta (2004-2012); With, Attkisson Carter & Co., Atlanta (2001-2004); With, Attkisson Carter & Akers Inc., Atlanta (1997-2000); Of Counsel, Carter & Ansley and Predecessor Firm Carter, Ansley, Smith & McLendon, Atlanta (1984-1991); Partner, Carter & Ansley (formerly Carter, Ansley, Smith & McLendon), Atlanta (1973-1984); Associate, Carter & Ansley (Formerly Carter, Ansley, Smith & McLendon), Atlanta (1967-1973) **CR:** Board of Directors, Secretary, CRM of America LLC, Queen Creek, AZ (2007-2014); Board of Directors, Secretary, CRM Co., LLC, Los Angeles County, CA; Board of Directors, Prime Bancshares, Inc.; Executive Vice President, Woodridge Realty, Inc.; Financial Consultant, Carter, Terry and Co., Inc.; President, Sodamaster Co. **CIV:** Board, Study Hall at Emmaus House, Inc. (1992-Present); Trustee, Atlanta Music Festival Association, Inc. (1975-Present); Board of Governors, Georgia Public Policy Foundation, Inc. (1999-2001); President, Study Hall at Emmaus House, Inc. (1988-1992); Visiting Board, Lineberger Cancer Research Center, University of North Carolina, Chapel Hill (1987-1992); Treasurer, Executive Committee, Board of Directors, Alliance Theatre Co., Atlanta (1974-1985); Vestry Member, St. Luke's Episcopalian Church, Atlanta (1971-1974); Board of Directors, Margaret Mitchell House, Inc.; Vice President, Board of Directors, Atlanta Preservation Center, Inc. **MIL:** Captain, US Army (1965-1967) **MEM:** American Bar Association; Georgia Bar Association; Atlanta Bar Association; Piedmont Driving Club **MH:** Distinguished Humanitarian (2017) **ADD:** 2505 Rivers Road N.W., Atlanta, GA, 30305

APPLE, DAINA DRAVNIEKS, T: Planning Commissioner **I:** Government Administration/Government Relations/Government Services **CN:** City of Benicia, California **DOB:** 07/06/1944 **PB:** Kuldiga **SC:** Latvia **MS:** Married **SPN:** Martin A. Apple (9/2/1986) **CH:** Almira Moronne; Deborah Apple; Nathan Apple; Pamela Apple; Rebeccah Apple **ED:** MA, University of California, Berkeley (1980); BSc, University of California, Berkeley (1977) **C:** Planning Commissioner, City of Benicia, CA (2016-Present); Director, Knowledge Management and Communications, United States Forest Service (2013-2015); Staff Assistant to the Deputy Chief for Research & Development, United States Forest Service, Washington, D.C. (2005-2014); Staff Assistant to Deputy Chief, Programs and Legislation, United States Forest Service, Washington, D.C. (2004-2005); Administrator, Workplace Relations, Pacific Southwest Region, United States Forest Service, Vallejo, CA (2002-2003); Policy Analyst, United States Forest Service (1998-2002); Strategic Planner, National Forest System RPA Staff, United States Forest Service (1995-1998); Assistant

Regulatory Officer, United States Forest Service, Washington, D.C. (1990-1995); Program Analysis Officer, Engineering, United States Forest Service, San Francisco, CA (1988-1990); Manager, Regional Land Use Appeals, United States Forest Service, San Francisco, CA (1986-1988); Economist, Pacific Southwest Research, United States Forest Service, Berkeley, CA (1976-1985) **AW:** Distinguished Service Award, Phi Beta Kappa Northern California Association, Inc.; Senior Executive Fellow, Harvard Kennedy School **MEM:** Chair, National Capital Society, Society of American Foresters (2000); Board of Directors, The American Latvian Association (1995-1997); National Secretary, Phi Beta Kappa Associations (1985-1988); President, Northern California, Phi Beta Kappa Associations (1982-1984); Fellow, Society of American Foresters; Fellow, The Phi Beta Kappa Society; Ecological Society of America; American Association for the Advancement of Science; American Institute of Biological Sciences; Washington Academy of Sciences; The New York Academy of Sciences; Sigma Xi; Fellow, Phi Beta Kappa Associates **MH:** Albert Nelson Marquis Lifetime Achievement Award (2017) **H:** Politics; Ballroom Dancing; Tennis; Films **ADD:** PO Box 905, Benicia, CA, 94510

ARABIAN, ARMAND, T: Associate Justice **I:** Law and Legal Services **CN:** Supreme Court of California **DOB:** 12/12/1934 **PB:** New York **SC:** NY/ USA **YOP:** 2018-05-15 **PT:** John Arabian; Aghavnie (Yalian) Arabian **MS:** Married **SPN:** Nancy Arabian (8/26/1962) **CH:** Allison Ann; Robert Armand **ED:** Honorary LLD, American College of Law (2001); Honorary LLD, Thomas Jefferson School of Law (1997); Honorary LLD (1997); Honorary, University of West Los Angeles (1994); Honorary LLD, Pepperdine University (1990); Honorary LLD, Southwestern School of Law (1990); LLM, University of Southern California (1970); JD, Boston University (1961); BSBA, Boston University (1956) **CT:** Admitted to Practice, United States Supreme Court (1966) **C:** Associate Justice, Supreme Court of California (1990-1996); Associate Justice, California Court of Appeals (1983-1990); Judge, Superior Court of Los Angeles (1973-1983); Judge, Municipal Court of Los Angeles (1972-1973); Private Practice Attorney, Van Nuys, California (1963-1972); Deputy District Attorney, LA County (1962-1963) **CR:** Adjunct Professor, School of Law, Pepperdine University (1996-1998) **MIL:** First Lieutenant, US Army (1956-1958) **CW:** Contributor, Various Articles to Professional Journals **AW:** Spirit Award, Americanism Educational League (2009); Fernando Award (2006); Women of LA Highlight Award (2005); Namesake, Reception Area, Chatsworth Superior Courthouse (2005); Ellis Island Medal Honor Award (2004); St. Gregory the Illuminator Medal, Karekin II Catholicos Yerevan (2004); Albert Einstein Gold Medal of Honor, Russian Academy of Natural Sciences (2003); Mekhitar Gosh Medal, Robert Kocharian (2001); St. James the Apostle Medal, Beatitude Torkom Manoogian (2001); Justice, Armand Arabian Resource and Communications Centers (1999); Mesrob Mashdots Medal, Aram I Catholicos (1999); Mekhitar Medal, Brotherhood in Venice (1999); Gold Medal of Honor of Peter the Great, Russian Academy of Science (1999); Outstanding Jurist of the Year, Malibu Bar Association (1996); Lifetime Achievement Award, San Fernando Valley Bar Association (1993); Pappas Distinguished Scholar, Boston University School of Law (1987); Recipient Stanley Lintz Memorial Award, San Fernando Valley Bar Association (1986); Leaders of Character Award, LA County Boy Scouts of America; Fernando Award, Foundation Inc. of the San Fernando Valley **BAR:** The State Bar of California (1962) **MH:** Albert Nelson

Marquis Lifetime Achievement Award (2017) **PA:** Republican **ADD:** 18875 Pasadero Drive, Tarzana, CA, 91356

ARCHERD, ROBERT, T: Academic Administrator **I:** Education/Educational Services **DOB:** 04/13/1940 **PB:** Rancho Palos Verdes **SC:** CA/USA **ED:** MS, Magna Cum Laude, Pepperdine University, LA (1976); BA, California State University, LA (1964) **CT:** K-9 Teaching Credential, University of California, Los Angeles (1970) **C:** Adjunct Assistant Professor, University of Southern California (2005-2006); Local District Elementary Mathematics Specialist, LA Unified School District (2002-2003); District K-12 Mathematics Coordinator, LA Unified School District (2001-2002); Central District Elementary Mathematics Specialist, LA Unified School District (2000-2001) **CR:** Chair, Mathematics Coordinator, LA Schools (1975-1980); Co-Creator, Elementary Bilingual Program (1970) **AW:** Outstanding Achievement Award, LA Unified School District Board of Education (2005); LAUSD District Teacher of Year, Center for the Advancement of Public Education, California Polytechnic School of Education (1992); Outstanding Contribution Award, LA City Teachers Mathematics Association **MEM:** President, LA City Teachers Mathematics Association (2003-2005); American Mensa **MH:** Albert Nelson Marquis Lifetime Achievement Award (2017) **H:** Art; Music; Guitar; Piano; Exercise **ADD:** 1837 Caddington Dr Unit 45, Rancho Palos Verdes, CA, 90275

ARDS, SHEILA, T: Professor (Retired) **I:** Education/Educational Services **CN:** University of Minnesota **MS:** Married **CH:** Two Daughters **ED:** PhD in Public Policy, Dissertation in Child Abuse and Neglect, Carnegie Mellon University (1982-1990) **C:** Retired, Faculty Member, University of Minnesota; Vice President, Community Development, South Carolina; Teacher, Policy, Humphrey Institute **CIV:** Former Member, NAACP; Former Member, Child Welfare Groups **CW:** Contributor, Articles, Professional Journals **MEM:** Alpha Kappa Alpha; Former Member, Jack and Jill of America; The Ladies of Saint Peters Savior Catholic Church; American Political Science Association; Former President, American Political Science Association; Former President, National Economics Association; Former Vice President, Association of Public Policy and Management **H:** Travel **ADD:** 9 Island View Ln, North Oaks, MN, 55127

ARLING, BRYAN JEREMY, T: Clinical Professor of Medicine **I:** Education/Educational Services **CN:** Georgetown University, The George Washington University **DOB:** 12/10/1944 **PB:** Minneapolis **SC:** MN/USA **PT:** Leonard Swenson Arling; Marion (Schroeder) Arling **MS:** Divorced **CH:** Elissa; Jeremy; Timothy **ED:** Resident in Internal Medicine, Stanford Affiliated Hospital, Stanford, CA (1970-1971); Intern, Stanford Affiliated Hospital, Stanford, CA (1969-1970); MD, Harvard University (1969); BA, University of Minnesota, Summa Cum Laude (1965) **CT:** Diplomate, American Board of Internal Medicine; Fellow, American College of Physicians **C:** Clinical Professor of Medicine, Georgetown University, Washington, D.C. (1997-Present); Clinical Professor of Medicine, The George Washington University, Washington, D.C. (1988-Present); Private Practice, Washington, D.C. (1977-Present); Assistant Professor of Medicine, The George Washington University Hospital, Washington, D.C. (1974-1977); Instructor, The George Washington University Hospital, Washington, D.C. (1973-1974); Chief Resident of Medicine, The George Washington University Hospital, Washington, D.C. (1973-1974); Administrator, Health Science Mental Health Administration, United States Department of Health and Human Services, North Bethesda, MD (1971-1973); Special Assistant, Health Science Mental Health Administration, United States Department of Health and Human Services, North Bethesda, MD (1971-1973) **CIV:** Reviewer, Pri-Med, American College of Physicians Jeopardy Examiners (2011); White House Fellows Regional Judge (2011); Vice President, Maret School (1994-1998); Trustee, Maret School (1991-1998); Member, Committee on Certifying and Recertifying Examiners (1992-1993); Question Relevance Reviewer, American Board of Internal Medicine (1991-1992); Member, Developmental Committee, Maret School (1985-1998); Member, Administrative Board, Chevy Chase United Methodist Church **MIL:** US Public Health Service (1971-1973) **AW:** Recipient, Highest Citation for Best Internist (2011); Named, One of Best Doctors in America, Woodward & White (2007); Honoree, Washington Consumers Checkbook (2007); Named, One of Best Doctors in America, Naifen & Smith (2001-2007); Named, Top Internists (2005); Named, Best Doctors in Town, Washington Magazine (2005); Named, Best Primary Care Physicians in America, Town & Country Magazine (2000); Named, Top Internists (1999); Named, Best Doctors in Town, Washington Magazine (1999); Named, Best Doctors in America, Southeast Region (1996); Named, Best Doctors in Town, Washington Magazine (1995); Named, Top Internists (1993); Named, Best Doctors in Town, Washington Magazine" (1993); Named, One of the Best Pediatricians and Internists (1987); Named, Best Doctors in Town, Washington Magazine (1986-1987) **MEM:** Advisory Council on Medical Educated, Harvard Medical School (2003-Present); Vice President, National Academy of Sciences, Washington, D.C. (2001-Present); Executive Committee, Academy of Medicine (1995-Present); Chairman, Medical School Alumni Meetings, Harvard Club of Washington, D.C. (2007); Fellow, American College of Physicians; American Medical Association; Medical Society of the District of Columbia; Smithsonian Associates; Friends of the Kennedy Center Volunteers; National Trust for Historic Preservation; Smithsonian's National Zoo & Conservation Biology Institute; Common Cause; American Civil Liberties Union; Physicians for Social Responsibility; Columbia Country Club; Bahamas Air-Sea Rescue Association **MH:** Albert Nelson Marquis Lifetime Achievement Award (2017) **H:** Scuba diving; Bridge; Smithsonian events **PA:** Moderate **RE:** Methodist **ADD:** 3803 Taylor St, Bethesda, MD, 20815

ARMSTRONG, WILLIAM TUCKER III, T: Lawyer **I:** Law and Legal Services **CN:** Langley & Banack, Inc. **DOB:** 11/13/1947 **PB:** Houston **SC:** TX/USA **PT:** William Tucker Junior; Jess A. Tucker (nee Nettles) **MS:** Married **SPN:** Nancy Bayliss Armstrong (2/18/1978) **CH:** Will; Anne; Daniel **ED:** JD, The University of Texas at Austin, with Honors (1972); BA, American University (1969) **CT:** United States Court of Appeals for the District of Columbia Circuit (1983); United States Court of Appeals for the Eleventh Circuit (1982); United States District & Bankruptcy Courts of Southern District of Texas (1978); United States Court of Appeals for the Fifth Circuit (1972) **C:** Shareholder, Langley & Banack, Inc., San Antonio, TX (1996-Present); Shareholder, Foster, Lewis, Langley, Gardner & Banack, San Antonio, TX (1976-1996); Associate, Foster, Lewis, Langley, Gardner & Banack, San Antonio, TX (1973-1976); Staff Counsel for Inmates, Texas Department of Criminal Justice, Huntsville, TX (1972-1973) **CIV:** President, Texas Council of School Attorneys (2003-2004); Director, South Texas Leukemia Society (1989-1992) **CW:** Contributor, Articles, Professional Publications **MEM:** Chairman, Texas Council of School Attorneys (2003-2004); Vice Chairman, Texas Council of School Attorneys (2002-2003); Director, Texas Council of School Attorneys (1999-2001); Director, Oak Hills Country Club (1998-2001); President, Texas Longhorn Club (1996-1997); President, San Antonio Longhorn Club (1993-1994); President, San Antonio Chapter, Ex-Students' Association of The University of Texas (1993-1994); Council of School Law, State Bar of Texas; Officer, Council of School Law, State Bar of Texas **BAR:** State of Texas (1972) **H:** Golfing **RE:** Methodist **ADD:** 213 Haskin Drive, San Antonio, TX, 78209

ARNT, GEORGIA LEE, T: Psychiatric Social Worker **I:** Medicine & Health Care **DOB:** 11/05/1940 **PB:** Poughkeepsie **SC:** NY/USA **PT:** George Christopher; Virginia Kelley Christopher **MS:** Married **SPN:** John Harold Arnt (12/6/1959) **CH:** Laura Lee; Cheryl Lee; Christopher Douglas **ED:** MSW, Rutgers, The State University of New Jersey (1978); BA in Social Work, Fairleigh Dickinson University, Cum Laude (1973) **CT:** Certified Social Worker, State of New York; Certified School Social Worker, State of New Jersey; Certified Psychoanalytic Psychotherapist, Institute of Mental Health Education; Certified Family Therapist, Ackerman Institute for the Family; Licensed Marriage and Family Therapist, State of New Jersey; Licensed Clinical Social Worker, State of New Jersey **C:** Psychoanalytic Psychotherapist, New Jersey Center for Psychotherapy, Englewood (1981-1985); Guidance Counselor, Wyckoff School District (1980-1982); Social Worker, Wyckoff School District (1980-1982); Social Worker, Fair Lawn School District (1978-1980); Social Worker, Division of Youth and Family Services, State of New Jersey, Hackensack (1974-1975) **CR:** Psychotherapist in Marriage and Family Counseling Services, Private Practice (1983-2002); Instructor, Midland Park Waldwick Adult School (1982-1986); Instructor, Fair Lawn Adult School (1983); Instructor, Paramus Community School (1983); Psychotherapist, Women's Counseling and Psychotherapy Service (1982) **CW:** Exhibitor, Hawthorne Public Library (2008); Exhibitor, Ridgewood Public Library (2006); Columnist, "Suburban News" (1983-1984) **MEM:** Mystery Writers of America; National Section, Sisters in Crime; Tri-state Section, Sisters in Crime; Central Jersey Section, Sisters in Crime; RWA **H:** Piano; Painting; Writing; Gardening; Skiing **RE:** Unitarian Universalist **ADD:** 411 Alpine Terrace, Ridgewood, NJ, 07450

ARUNDELL LEAKEY, JULIAN EDWIN, T: Toxicologist, Researcher **I:** Sciences **DOB:** 06/12/1951 **PB:** Settle **SC:** England **PT:** Robert Dove Leakey; Barbara Mary Leakey **MS:** Married **SPN:** Tatiana Ivanova Sergeeva (9/28/1999) **CH:** Laura Clair; Sharon Aileen **ED:** PhD, University of Dundee (1976); BSc, University of Dundee (1973) **CT:** Diplomate in Toxicology, American Board of Toxicology (1995) **C:** Research Fellow, University of Dundee (1978-1985); Research Fellow, National Institute of Environmental Health Sciences, Research Triangle Park, North Carolina (1977-1978) **CR:** Research Scientist, National Center for Toxicological Research, Jefferson, AK (1985-Present) **MEM:** Society of Toxicology **ADD:** 4817 Lafayette Avenue, Little Rock, AR, 72205

ASHWORTH, BRENT FERRIN, T: Owner **I:** Law and Legal Services **CN:** B. Ashworth's **DOB:** 01/08/1949 **PB:** Albany **SC:** CA/USA **PT:** Dell Shepherd Ashworth; Bette Jean (Brailsford) Ashworth **MS:** Married **SPN:** Charlene Mills (12/16/1970) **CH:** Amy; John; Matthew; Samuel (Deceased); Adam; David; Emily; Luke; Benjamin **ED:** JD, S.J. Quinney College of Law, The University of Utah (1975); BA, Brigham Young University

(1972) **C:** Of General Counsel, ZIJA International, Lehi, Utah (2012-Present); Owner, B. Ashworth's (2006-Present); Partner, Ashworth and Sandberg, Provo, Utah (2005-2012); Private Practice (2004-2005); Vice President, Neways, Springville, Utah (2003-2004); Of General Counsel, Neways, Springville, Utah (2003-2004); Vice President of Legal Affairs, Nature's Sunshine Products Inc, Provo, Utah (1977-2003); Secretary, Nature's Sunshine Products Inc, Provo, Utah (1977-2003); Of General Counsel, Nature's Sunshine Products Inc, Provo, Utah (1977-2003); Associate Attorney, Frandsen & Keller, Price, Utah (1976-1977); Assistant County Attorney, Carbon County, Price, Utah (1975-1976) **CR:** Board Member, Fort Douglas Military Museum (2009-Present); Affiliate, National Exhibits, Glen Beck Association (2016); Affiliate, National Exhibits, Glen Beck Association (2013-2014); With, Latter Day Saints Church Service, Missionary Church History Library (2007-2012) **CIV:** Active Member, Provo Landmarks Commission (1997-Present); Chairman, Provo Library Board (2003-2004); Chairman, Provo Landmarks Commission (2002-2005); Board Member, American Heritage School, American Fork, Utah (2002-2005); Member, Board of Directors, Provo Education Foundation (2001-2003); Member, Executive Board, Utah National Park Council, Boy Scouts of America (2000-2010); Founder, George E. Freestone Boy Scout Museum, Provo, Utah (2000-2008); Chairman, George E. Freestone Boy Scout Museum, Provo, Utah (2000-2008); Active Member, Provo Library Board (2000-2006); Member, Board of Directors, Celebration Health Foundation (1999-2007); Member, Board of Directors, Springville Museum of Art (1998-2001); Of General Counsel, Brigham Young Academy Foundation (1995-2001); Chairman, Provo LCOC Arts Subcommittee (1998-1999); Co-chairman, Sesquicentennial Committee, Provo Landmarks Commission (1998-1999); Member, Board of Directors, Utah County Chapter, The American National Red Cross (1988-1994); President, Deseret Village Association, Spani Fork, Utah (1988-1990); Chairman, Utah County Cancer Crusade Committee (1981-1983); Mayor Pro Tempore, Payson City, Utah (1982); City Councilman, Planning Commission, Payson City, Utah (1980-1982); Member, Board of Directors, Carbon County Nursing Home, Price, Utah (1976-1977); Of General Counsel, Carbon County Nursing Home, Price, Utah (1976-1977) **AW:** Outstanding Eagle Scout Award, Boy Scouts of America (2011); Silver Beaver Award, Boy Scouts of America (2006) **MEM:** Immediate Past Governor, Kiwanis International (2011-2012); Governor, Kiwanis International (2009-2010); Governor Elect, Kiwanis International (2008-2009); Lieutenant Governor, Utah-Idaho District, Kiwanis International (2001-2002); President, Kiwanis International (1997-1998); President, Emily Dickinson Society Utah (1995-1997); Vice President, Kiwanis International (1995-1996); Chancellor, Sons of the American Revolution (1992-1994); State Society President, Sons of the American Revolution (1991-1992); First Vice President, State Chapters, Sons of the American Revolution (1990-1991); Secretary, Intermountain Chapter, American Corporate Counsel Association (1990-1991); President, Utah County Chapter, Sons of the American Revolution (1989-1990); Secretary, Southeastern Utah Bar Association (1977); American Association of Justice; ABA; Utah State Bar; The National Society of the Sons of Utah Pioneers; Phi Eta Sigma; Phi Kappa Phi **BAR:** Admitted to Practice, Utah State Bar (1977) **MH:** Albert Nelson Marquis Lifetime Achievement Award (2017) **ADD:** 1377 Cambridge Ct, Provo, UT, 84604 **URL:** https://www.linkedin.com/in/brent-ashworth-1787b813/

ASKINS, ARTHUR J., **T:** Accountant **I:** Financial Services **DOB:** 12/02/1944 **PT:** William J. Askins; Rita M. (O'Brien) Askins **MS:** Married **SPN:** Nancy E. Paulsen (4/28/1979) **ED:** MA, Rider University (1971); BS, La Salle University (1967) **CT:** Certified, Chartered Institute of Management Accountants (2012); Specialization in Hospitality, Accounting and Management, AHLA; CPA, Commonwealth of Pennsylvania; CPA, State of New Jersey; Certified Fraud Examiner; Certified Hotel Administrator; Certified Gaming Commissioner, NIGA **C:** Accountant, Private Practice (1967-Present); Teacher, Cardinal Dougherty High School (1967-1970); Manager, Indian Gaming **CW:** Contributor, Articles, Professional Journals **AW:** Outstanding Volunteer Service Award, Big Brothers Big Sisters of America (1987); Management Award, Resorts Casino Hotel (1986); First Managers Award, Resorts Casino-Hotel (1986); Brotherhood Award, National Conference of Christians and Jews (Now National Conference for Community and Justice) (1983); Distinguished Service Award, Community Accountants (1982); Superstar Award, Resorts Casino Hotel (1982); Community Affairs Award, Institute of Management Accountants, Inc. (1978); Certificate of Commendation, Abington Township, PA (1967) **MEM:** Gaming Advisory Committee, The Institute of Internal Auditors (2008-Present); National Speaker, The Institute of Internal Auditors (2011-2012); Board of Directors, The Institute of Internal Auditors (1984-1989); National Board of Directors, Institute of Management Accountants, Inc. (1983-1985); Audit Committee, The Institute of Internal Auditors (1979-1983); President, South Jersey Shore Chapter, Institute of Management Accountants, Inc. (1979-1981); New Jersey Society of Certified Public Accountants; PICPA; Greater Atlantic City Chamber; Forensic CPA Society; Association of Certified Fraud Examiners, Inc.; American Institute of CPAs **PA:** Republican **RE:** Roman Catholic **BA:** P.O. Box 428, Youngstown, NY, 14174

ASKINS, NANCY ELLEN PAULSEN, **T:** Executive Director **I:** Health, Wellness and Fitness **CN:** Center of Renewal Retreat & Conference Center at Stella Niagara **DOB:** 11/02/1948 **PB:** St. Paul **SC:** MN/USA **PT:** Charles A. Paulsen; Stasia (Sawicki) Paulsen **MS:** Married **SPN:** Arthur J. Askins (4/28/1979) **ED:** PhD in Training and Performance Improvement, Capella University (2012); Postgraduate Coursework, Walden University (1988-1992); Postgraduate coursework, National Institute of Financial Education (1982-1985); Postgraduate Coursework, Temple University (1976); Postgraduate coursework, University at Buffalo (1974-1976); MEd, University of Cincinnati (1972); BS in Education, University of Cincinnati (1971); BS in Home Economic, University of Cincinnati (1970) **CT:** John Maxwell Certified Speaker-Trainer-Coach (2016-Present); Certified Coaching Practitioner, Certified Coaches Foundation (2015-Present); Certified Manager of Quality and Organizational Excellence, American Society for Quality (2000-Present); John Maxwell Certified Coach (2015); John Maxwell Certified Trainer (2015); Certified, Advanced Applied Urban Ministry, Niagara University (2012); Certified, Applied Urban Ministry, Niagara University (2009); Certified Gaming Supervisor, American Hotel & Lodging Educational Institute; Certified, Strategic Planning Facilitator **C:** Founder & Executive Consultant, Askins Learning Institute (2013-Present); Executive Director, Center of Renewal Retreat & Conference Center, Stella Niagara, NY (2005-Present); Adjunct Professor, Webster University, Memphis, TN (2003); Director of Quality, Hollywood Casino & Hotel Tunica, Robinsonville, MS (1998-2001); Coordinator, Training Services, Gulf Coast Business Services, Gulfport, MS (1996-1998); Vice President of Training and Associate Development, Grand Casino (Now Harrah's Gulf Coast), Caesars License Company, LLC, Biloxi, MS (1994-1996); Part-Time Instructor, Wellness Program, Holy Cross Hospital, Fort Lauderdale, FL (1991-1994); Director, Community and Volunteer Services, Holy Cross Hospital, Fort Lauderdale, FL (1991-1994); Director of Education Services, Holy Cross Hospital, Fort Lauderdale, FL (1990-1991); Director of Educational Development, Shore Memorial Hospital (Now Shore Medical Center), Somers Point, NJ (1986-1989); Instructor of Wellness, Shore Memorial Hospital (Now Shore Medical Center), Somers Point, NJ (1984-1988); Training Manager, Shore Memorial Hospital (Now Shore Medical Center), Somers Point, NJ (1984-1985); Training Director & Assistant Vice President, Collective Federal Savings & Loan Association, Egg Harbor City, NJ (1982-1984); Training Services Coordinator, Collective Federal Savings & Loan Association, Egg Harbor City, NJ (1981-1982); Executive Corporate Consultant, Askins Learning Institute, Youngstown, NY (2012-present); Owner & Executive Corporate Consultant, Askins Training & Consulting (1981-2012); Member, Women's Task Force, The Phoenix Companies, Inc. (1980-1981); Registered Representative, Securities Agent, Phoenix Equity Planning Corporation, Philadelphia, PA (1980-1981); Career Life Insurance Agent, Financial Planning Consultant, Phoenix Mutual Life Insurance Co., Philadelphia, PA (1978-1981); Student Affairs Administrator, Temple University, Philadelphia, PA (1976-1978); Adjunct Faculty Member in Education, SUNY Geneseo (1974-1976); Student Affairs Administrator, SUNY Geneseo (1974-1976); Teacher, Drug Awareness Coordinator, Adams Elementary School, Harlandale School District, San Antonio, Texas (1973-1974); Adjunct Faculty in Education, Texas Lutheran College (1972-1973); Student Affairs Administrator, Texas Lutheran College (1972-1973); Graduate Resident Advisor / Student Affairs, University of Cincinnati (1970-1972); Assistant Aquatic Supervisor, Cincinnati Recreation Commission (1969-1972) **CR:** National Seminar Leader, Educational Institute (2002-2005); Judge, Mississippi Quality Award (2002); Member, Board of Examiners, Malcolm Baldrige National Quality Award (2001-2003); Member, Board of Examiners, President's Quality Award (2000); Member, Board of Examiners, Tennessee Quality Award (2000); Member, Board of Examiners, Mississippi Quality Award (1999-2000); Adjunct Professor of Business and Social Sciences, Atlantic Cape Community College, Mays Landing, NJ (1986-1989); National Conference Speaker, American Society for Training and Development (Now ATD) (1984-1986); Instructor, Institute for Financial Education (Now National Institute of Financial Education) (1982-1985); Facilitator, Assertiveness Training Group; Facilitator, Interpersonal Communications Group; Facilitator, Organizational and Leadership Development, Seminars and Consultant; Workshop Presenter in Field; Speaker in Field; Writer in Field **CIV:** Lifetime Member, Girl Scouts of the United States of America (1956-Present); Lector, St. Bernard Catholic Church, Youngstown, NJ (2005-2012); Lector, Christ the King Catholic Church, Southaven, MS (1998-2003); Parish Council, St. Luke's Catholic Church, Coconut Creek, FL (1993-1994); Chairman, Women's Club, St. Luke's Catholic Church, Coconut Creek, FL (1992-1994); Member, Library Advisory Board, City of Margate, FL (1991-1994); Cantor, St. Joseph Roman Catholic Church, Somers Point, NJ (1979-1989); Parish Council, St. Joseph Roman Catholic Church, Somers Point, NJ (1984-1988) **CW:** "Askins Core

VALUES Paradigm & Implementation Model" (2012); "Core Values Implementation by Mid-Level Managers of a Faith-Based Healthcare System" (Award-Winning Doctoral Dissertation, 2012); Features Editor, Competitive Advantage Quality Division, American Society for Quality (2000-2003); Newsletter Editor, Robinsonville Rotary Club (1998-1999); Newsletter Editor, "National Business Women's Week," Biloxi Lighthouse Business & Professional Women **AW:** Award of Excellence for Outstanding Research, International Society for Performance Improvement (2013); SBMEF Scholarship, ABWA Management, LLC. (2010); Top Five Business Women Award, ABWA Management, LLC. (2010); Leadership Niagara Class of 2004. (2004); Women of Achievement, Business Professional Women of Clarksdale, MS (1999); Named Woman of the Year, Business Professional Women of Clarksdale, MS (1999); Gold Director Award, Carlson Learning Co., Inscape Publishing, Minnesota (1998); Rising Star Award, Carlson Learning Co., Inscape Publishing, MN (1997); Named Biloxi Career Woman of the Year, Biloxi Lighthouse Business & Professional Women (1995); Brotherhood-Sisterhood Achievers Award, National Conference of Christians and Jews (Now National Conference for Community and Justice) (1985); President's Award, Greater Mainland Chamber of Commerce (1983) **MEM:** Session Retreat Facilitator, ABWA Management, LLC. (2007-Present); Vice President, Human Capital, Virtual Chapter, Capella University (2013); Board of Directors, Niagara River Region Chamber of Commerce (2010-2012); Program & Professional Development Chairperson, ABWA Management, LLC., Western New York Charter, Falls Chapter (2009-2011); Youngest Careerist Chairperson, Business and Professional Women Buffalo/Amherst (2009); Individual Development Program Co-chairperson, Business and Professional Women Buffalo/Amherst (2004-2005); National Leadership Chair, BPW/USA (2004-2005); President, Greater Camden Association Life Underwriters (2003-2004); State President, Business and Professional Women of Mississippi (2003-2004); National Leadership Chair, Business and Professional Women /USA (2002-2003); State President-Elect, Business and Professional Women (2002-2003); Chairman, Matching Grants Committee, Rotary International (2001-2002); Regional Keynote Address, National Conference Session, Competitive Advantage Quality Division, American Society for Quality (2000-2003); President, Robinsonville Rotary Club (2000-2001); Instructor, AHLA (1999-2001); Chairperson, Long Range Planning Committee, Rotary International (1999-2001); Charter President, Business and Professional Women, Robinsonville, MS (1999-2000); President-Elect, Robinsonville Rotary Club (1999-2000); Group Study Exchange Committee, Rotary International (1999-2000); Youth Study Exchange Committee, Rotary International (1999-2000); State Legislative Chairman, Business and Professional Women of Mississippi (1999-2000); Northern Mississippi Chapter Charter President, AHLA (1999); Section, Robinsonville Rotary Club (1999); Legislative Committee Chairman, Business and Professional Women of Clarksdale (1998-2000); Chairperson, Biloxi Lighthouse Business & Professional Women (1997); State Second Vice President, Business and Professional Women of Mississippi (1996-1997); Education Committee, Greater Fort Lauderdale Chamber of Commerce (1993-1994); President, ATD Greater Broward/Ft. Lauderdale Chapter (1993); Diplomat, Greater Fort Lauderdale Chamber of Commerce (1992-1993); President-Elect, ATD (1992); Director, ATD (1991-1992) **H:** Reading; Swimming and resistance training; Music; Research on core values, mission

integration and organizational development **PA:** Democrat **RE:** Roman Catholic **BA:** Askins Learning Institute, 444 Lockport Street, Youngstown, NY, 14174 **ADD:** PO Box 428, 444 Lockport Street, Youngstown, NY, 14174

ASNIEN, PHYLLIS, T: Humanities Educator **I:** Education/Educational Services **CN:** Lakeland Community College **DOB:** 06/23/1937 **PB:** Cleveland **SC:** OH/USA **PT:** Morris Asnien; Rebecca Berman Asnien **MS:** Single **SPN:** Michael Jay Tabor (1973-1983) **CH:** Xanthe Rebecca Tabor **ED:** MA in American and English Literature, John Carroll University (1967); BS in Vocal Music Education, Ohio State University (1959) **C:** Adult Continuing Education Educator, Case Western University (2006-Present); Professor Emerita, Lakeland Community College, Kirtland, OH (2004-Present); Professor of the Humanities, Lakeland Community College, Kirtland, OH (1969-Present); Adjunct Faculty for Remedial Speech, Cuyahoga Community College, Cleveland, OH (1984); Teacher of English Literature, Composition and Dramatics, Westlake Senior High School (1964-1968) **CR:** Textbook Revisionist, HarperCollins Publishers, New York, NY (1990-1997) **CIV:** Board of Directors, Carl Jung Society, Cleveland, OH (1993-1995); Cleveland Art Museum **CW:** Author, "Humanities Considered" (1966); Dramatist, "A Sudden Conviction" (1966); Dramatist, "To the Sound of the Heartbeat" (1965) **AW:** Career Teacher Award, Ohio State University (1999) **MEM:** Charter Member; National Museum of Women in Arts; Delta Omicron **MH:** Albert Nelson Marquis Lifetime Achievement Award (2017) **H:** Singing; Swimming; Ikebana; Yoga **ADD:** 2243 S Overlook Road, Cleveland Heights, OH, 44106

ASSENSOH, AKWASI B., T: Historian, Educator **I:** Education/Educational Services **DOB:** 04/01/1946 **PB:** Dunkwa-on-Offin **SC:** Ghana **PT:** Opanin Kwabena Assensoh; Abena Amoatemaah **MS:** Married **SPN:** Yvette Marie Alex (5/7/1994); Irenita Benbow (1980, Divorced 1993) **CH:** Gloria; Philip; Sam; Kwadwo; Livingston Alex; Rose-Abena; Akwasi Bretuo Jr. **ED:** PhD in History, New York University (1984); MA in History, New York University (1982); BA in History and Political Science, Dillard University (1981); Advanced Diploma in Mass Communications and Journalism, School of Journalism and Television, Frilsham, England (1967); Diploma in Journalism, School Journalism and Television, Frilsham, England (1967) **C:** Professor Emeritus, University of Oregon (2012-Present); Mentor, University of Oregon (2012-Present); Professor Emeritus, Indiana University (2011-Present); Professor, African American and African Diaspora Studies, Indiana University (2002-Present); Director, Graduate Studies and Admissions, Indiana University (2004-2007); Research Professor, University of Maryland Eastern Shore (2004-2005); Member, Promotion Committee, Indiana University (2002-2005); Professor, Indiana University (1999-2011); Associate Professor, History, Indiana University (1995-2000); Visiting Scholar, Emory University (1989-1990); Director of Research, King Papers Project, Stanford University (1989-1990); Visiting Assistant Professor of History, Stanford University (1988-1989); Associate Professor of History, Southern University, Texas A&M University **CR:** Invited Lecturer in Field **CIV:** Acting Pastor, Second Baptist Church (1999-2001); Associate Minister, Second Baptist Church (1998-1999); Member, Board of Trustees, African Methodist Episcopal Church (1996-1997); Secretary-Treasurer, The Reverend Livingston Alex Partnership Foundation **CW:** Book Review Editor, Africa Today (2008-Present); Co-Review Editor, African and Asian Street Journal

(2006-Present); Contributing Editor, West Africa Magazine, London, England (2003-Present); Editorial Board Member, International Abraham Lincoln Journal (2000-Present); Editorial Board Member, Journal of Third World Studies (1988-Present); Author, "African Military History and Politics: Coups and Ideological Incursions; 1900-Present" (2001); Author, "African Political Leadership: A Comparative Study of Jomo Kenyatta, Julius K. Nyerere, and Kwame Nkrumah" (1998); Author, "Kwame Nkrumah of Africa: His Formative Years and the Shaping of his Nationalism and Pan-Africanism 1935-1948" (1990); Associate Editor, African Commentary Journal, Amherst, MA (1990); Associate Editor, King Papers Project, Stanford University (1989-1990); Editorial Board Member, "Africa and the World" (1987-1988); Author, "Reverend Dr. Martin Luther King, Jr., and America's Quest for Racial Integration" (1986); Author, "Campus Life" (1986); Author, "Essays on Contemporary International Topics" (1986); Author, "Africa in Retrospect" (1985); Author, "An Overview of Political Risk Reporting in Africa: The Liberian Example" (1985); Author, "Polygamy in the Ashanti Tribe of Ghana: A Histo-Political Overview" (1984); Managing Editor, International Observer Magazine, New Orleans, LA (1980-1981); Author, "Black Woman, An African Story" (1980); Participant, Television Programs (1978-1999); Participant, Radio Programs (1978-1999); Author, "Kwame Nkrumah: Six Years in Exile, 1966-1972" (1978); Sub-Editor, The Pioneer, Monrovia, Liberia (1970-1972); Sub-Editor, The Pioneer, Kumasi, Ghana (1969-1970); Contributor, Chapters to Books; Contributor, Articles to Professional Journals; Contributor, Reviews to Professional Journals; Contributor, Magazines; Contributor, Newspapers; Editor-in-Chief, Daily Listener, Saturday Chronicle; Editor-in-Chief, Daily Listener, Sunday Digest **AW:** Recipient, Fellowship, National Endowment for the Humanities (2011, 2000); Recipient, Research Conference Grant for Advancing Education Research, Spencer Foundation (2000); Recipient, Fulbright-Hays Faculty Fellowship, Johns Hopkins University (1986) **MEM:** President, United States Chapter, Association of Third-World Studies (2003-2004); PEN America; Royal African Society; International Federation of Journalists; American-Scandinavian Foundation; African Studies Association; National Geographic Society; The Southern Historical Association; American Historical Association; Associate, Smithsonian Institution; Alumni Association, New York University; National Alumni Association, Dillard University; Press Club of New Orleans; The Rosicrucian Order; Masons; Alpha Phi Alpha **MH:** Albert Nelson Marquis Lifetime Achievement Award (2017) **RE:** Baptist **ADD:** 1995 Potter Street, Eugene, OR, 97405

ATALLAH, DAVID, T: Associate Professor **I:** Education/Educational Services **DOB:** 08/22/1967 **PB:** Beirut **MS:** Married **SPN:** Rania Kalouche **CH:** Caroline; Sarah; Lisa Maria Conception **ED:** Master of Science in Clinical Research, University of Liverpool, United Kingdom (2017); Fellowship in Gynecologic Oncology and Breast Cancer, Surgery Institut Gustave Roussy, Villejuif, France (1999-2003); Fellowship in Gynecologic and Oncologic Surgery and Breast Cancer Surgery, Salpetriere University Hospital, Paris, France (1998-1999); Fellowship in Gynecologic Surgery, Breast Cancer Surgery, Deaconness Hospital, Paris, France (1997-1998); Residency in Obstetrics and Gynecology, Hotel Dieu de France University Hospital, Beirut, Lebanon (1994-1997); Coursework in Preliminary Surgery, General Surgery and Urology, Hotel Dieu de France University Hospital, Beirut, Lebanon (1993-1994); Coursework, Medical School, Saint

Joseph University, Beirut, Lebanon (1986-1993) **CT:** Certification in Visceral Surgery (2003); Doctor in Medicine (2003); Certification in Surgical Oncology (2002); European Diploma in Clinical Cancer Research (2002); Diploma in Vaginal Surgery, University of Lille, France (2002); Fellowship Diploma of the European Society of Surgical Oncology (2001); Diploma in Breast Cancer and Reconstructive Surgery, Paris, France (2000); Diploma in Urodynamics, Paris, France (1999); Diploma in Colposcopy and Cervico-Vaginal Pathology, Paris, France (1999); Gynecologic Surgery Fellowship Diploma, College of Medicine of Paris (1999); Obstetrics and Gynecology Diploma, License to Practice in Lebanon (1998); Urogynecology and Pelvic Floor Dysfunction Diploma, Paris, France (1998); Educational Commission for Foreign Medical Graduates Certification, United States of America (1993); Licence to Practice Medicine in Lebanon (1993) **C:** Head of obstetrics and gynecology department at Hotel-Dieu de France University Hospital (2018-Present); Representative, Saint Joseph University, Board of the Lebanese Medical Journal (2015-Present); Anatomy Instructor, Salpetriere University School of Nursing (1998-1999); Anatomy Instructor, Lebanese University School of Physiotherapy (1993-1997); Associate Professor of Obstetrics and Gynecology, Saint Joseph University, School of Medicine; Vice President of the Lebanese Gynecologic Oncologic Group **CR:** Presenter in Field **CW:** Reviewer, Annals of Surgical Oncology (2007-Present); Reviewer, International Journal of Gynecology and Obstetrics, Official Journal of FIGO (2007-Present); Editorial Board Member, Lebanese Medical Journal (2015); Contributor, Articles to Professional Journals; Contributing Author, Books **AW:** Research Grant Award, Research Board, Saint Joseph University (2014); Scholarship, Research Grant, Lingue Nationale Contre Le Cancer (2001-2002); Scholarship, European Society of Surgical Oncology (2000-2001); Fellow, European Society of Surgical Oncology (2000); Fellow, Medical College of Paris in Gynecologic Surgery (1999); Scholarship in Gynecologic Surgery, Medical College of Paris (1998-1999); Scholarship in Gynecologic Surgery, Raoul Follereau Institute (1997-1998); Best Thesis Award (1993); Dean's Honor List (1986-1993) **MEM:** French Society of Breast Cancer Pathology and Surgery; European Society of Gynecological Oncology; American Society of Clinical Oncology; International Gynecologic Cancer Society; Society of Gynecologic Oncology; International Continence Society; Lebanese Medical Society and Order of Physicians; Founding Member, Lebanese Society of Obstetrics and Gynecology; Founding Member, Lebanese Gynecologic Oncologic Group; Founding Member, Middle Eastern Mediterranean Association of Gynecologic Oncology; Executive Council Member, Pan-Arabian Research Society of Gynecological Oncology; Pan Arab Continence Society **ADD:** Obererle 58, c/o Malak Moubarak, Gelsenkirchen, Germany, 45897

AUNG, KENDRICK, T: Mechanical Engineer **I:** Engineering **CN:** Lamar University **DOB:** 06/05/1961 **PB:** Yangon **SC:** Myanmar **ED:** PhD, University of Michigan (1996); Master's Degree in Engineering, Asian Institute of Technology (1991); Bachelor's Degree in Engineering, Yildiz Technical University (1983) **C:** Associate Professor, Lamar University (2005-2011); Assistant Professor, Lamar University (2001-2004); Research Assistant Professor, University of Southern California (1999-2001); Research Fellow, Georgia Institute of Technology (1996-1998); Research Assistant, University of Michigan (1993-1996); Instructor,

Yildiz Technical University (1984-1988) **CIV:** Lamar University Representative, Texas Grant Consortium **AW:** Distinguished Faculty Fellowship for Teaching, Lamar University **MEM:** American Society for Engineering Education; American Society of Mechanical Engineers; Senior, AIAA; Combustion Institute **MH:** Albert Nelson Marquis Lifetime Achievement Award (2017) **ADD:** 3417 Ocean Ridge Circle, Seabrook, TX, 77586

AUSTIN, JOHN DAVID, T: Chess Coach, Financial Executive **I:** Recreational Facilities and Services **CN:** Kid Chess **DOB:** 01/16/1936 **PB:** Memphis **SC:** TN/USA **PT:** Thomas L. Austin; Vela M. (Davis) Austin **MS:** Married **SPN:** Marilyn C. Brewster (11/2/1985); Dorothy Clemans (12/31/1959, Divorced) **CH:** Laura Jan; David John; Christopher Brewster **ED:** BBA, Georgia State University (1961) **C:** Director, Kid Chess, Marietta, GA (2007-Present); COO, Atlanta Cutlery Corp, Conyers, GA (1993-1996); Vice President, Atlanta Cutlery Corp, Conyers, GA (1991-1996); CFO, Atlanta Cutlery Corp, Conyers, GA (1991-1996); Self-Employed, Marietta, GA (1990-1991); Executive Vice President, Citizens Federal Savings & Loan, Salisbury, NC (1988-1990); CEO, Citizens Federal Savings & Loan, Salisbury, NC (1988-1990); Board of Directors, Citizens Federal Savings & Loan, Salisbury, NC (1988-1990); President, Virginia Federal Savings and Loan, Richmond, VA (1986-1988); Board of Directors, Virginia Federal Savings and Loan, Richmond, VA (1986-1988); Executive Vice President, Virginia Federal Savings and Loan, Richmond, VA (1985); Senior Vice President, Virginia Federal Savings and Loan, Richmond, VA (1984); Acting President, Southeast National Bank, Malvern, PA (1978-1980); CEO, Southeast National Bank, Malvern, PA (1978-1980); Executive Vice President, Southeast National Bank, Malvern, PA (1975-1983); Senior Vice President, Southeast National Bank, Malvern, PA (1974-1975); Senior Vice President, 1st National Bank, Mobile, AL (1973-1974); Director, Corporate Planning, 1st National Bank, Mobile, AL (1973-1974); Vice President, North Carolina National Bank Corp., Charlotte, NC (1969-1973); General Auditor, North Carolina National Bank Corp., Charlotte, NC (1969-1973); Audit Manager, North Carolina National Bank Corp., Greensboro, NC (1968); Senior Tax Accountant, Price Waterhouse & Co., Miami, FL (1964-1967); Accountant, Price Waterhouse & Co., Atlanta, GA (1961-1964) **CR:** Lecturer in Field; Presenter in Field; Workshops in Field **CIV:** Board of Directors, St. John's Hospital; Board of Directors, Delaware County Community College Foundation; Board of Directors, Delaware County Economic Development Committee; Board of Directors, The Chester Group; Board of Directors, Chester County Mental Health Board; President, United Arts Council of Rowan; Chess Teacher, After School Programs **MIL:** U.S. Army (1957-1959) **MH:** Albert Nelson Marquis Lifetime Achievement Award (2017) **H:** Tournament chess; Studying languages; Baroque music and art **ADD:** 1303 Spring Gate Circle, Woodstock, GA, 30189

AUVILLE, FRANCES C., T: Educator **I:** Education/Educational Services **CN:** Mercer County Schools **SC:** USA **ED:** Postgraduate Coursework, Marshall University (1994-Present); Postgraduate Coursework, West Virginia University (1994-1998); MA in English, Marshall University (1970); BA in English, Concord College (Now Concord University), Athens, WV (1965) **C:** Assistant Principal, Mercer County Schools, Princeton, WV (1992-2001); Supervisor, Mercer County Schools, Princeton, WV (1989-1992); Teacher, Mercer County Schools, Princeton, WV (1983-1989); Instructor, Bluefield State College, Bluefield, WV (1969-1974); Teacher, Mercer County Schools,

Princeton, WV (1967-1969); Teacher, St. John School, Memphis, TN (1966-1967); Insurance Auditor, Treadwell & Harry Brokers, Memphis, TN (1964-1966); Payroll Clerk, Concord College (Now Concord University) (1959-1964) **CR:** Participant, Seminars, National Endowment of the Humanities, Washington, DC (1992); Participant, Seminars, National Endowment of the Humanities, Washington, DC (1988) **CIV:** Volunteer, Craft Memorial Library, Bluefield, WV (2001-Present); Volunteer, Hospital, Bluefield, WV (1974-1986); Representative Poll Worker, Bluefield, WV **CW:** Contributor, American Poetry Anthology (1991); Contributor, American Poetry Anthology (1988); Advisory Board, Children's Album Magazine, Concord, CA (1987-1990); Contributor, "Treasures of the Precious Moment" (1985); Contributor, "Art of Poetry" (1985); Contributor, American Poetry Anthology (1985); Contributor, American Poetry; Contributor, World of Poetry **AW:** Outstanding Poets, Treasures of the Precious Moment (1994); Golden Poet Award, World of Poetry (1991); Golden Poet Award, World of Poetry (1988); Language Arts Teacher of the Year, West Virginia English Language Arts Council (1986) **MEM:** National Council on Teachers of English; West Virginia English Language Arts Council; Consultant, West Virginia Writing Project; Phi Delta Kappa **H:** Spending time with grandchildren; Tennis **PA:** Republican **RE:** Presbyterian **ADD:** 510 Mountain View Avenue, Bluefield, WV, 24701

AVRUTIN, VITALIY, T: Research Assistant Professor **I:** Education/Educational Services **CN:** Virginia Commonwealth University **DOB:** 01/02/1964 **PB:** Shevchenko (Now Aktau) **SC:** Mangyshlak Peninsula/Kazakhstan **PT:** Semen Avrutin; Sofia Zhurakhovskaya Avrutin **MS:** Married **SPN:** Natalia Izyumskaya (4/14/2001) **CH:** Ksenia Avrutina; Maxim Alexander Aurutin **ED:** PhD in Physics and Mathematics, Russian Academy of Sciences (1999); MS, MISiS, National University of Science and Technology (1986) **C:** Research Assistant Professor, Department of Electrical and Computer Engineering, Virginia Commonwealth University, Richmond, VA (2010-Present); Research Associate, Virginia Commonwealth University, Richmond, VA (2004-2010); Visiting Research Scientist, Ulm University, Ulm, Germany (2001-2004); Research Scientist, IMT RAS, Chernogolovka, Russia (1999-2001); Junior Scientist, IMT RAS, Chernogolovka, Russia (1996-1999); Engineer, IMT RAS, Chernogolovka, Russia (1989-1996); Postgraduate Researcher, IMT RAS, Chernogolovka, Russia (1986-1989) **CW:** Contributor, Articles, Professional Journals in Field **AW:** Grantee, National Science Foundation; Grantee, Air Force Office of Scientific Research; Industry-Funded Grantee **MEM:** Materials Research Society; American Physical Society **ADD:** 1720 Fox Creek Cir, Hemrico, VA, 23238

AXILROD, STEPHEN H., T: Global Economic Consultant, Economist **I:** Consulting **DOB:** 06/21/1926 **PB:** New York City **SC:** NY/USA **PT:** Jacob James Axilrod; Pearl (Feltenstein) Axilrod **MS:** Married **SPN:** Katherine Podolsky Axilrod (7/1/1950) **CH:** Peter; Emily Axilrod Hildner; Richard **ED:** Postgraduate Coursework, The University of Chicago (1951-1952); MA, The University of Chicago (1950); AB, Harvard University, Magna Cum Laude (1948); Coursework, Southern Methodist University (1943-1944) **C:** Consultant, Global Economics and Markets, Private Practice (1994-Present); Consultant, International Organizations and Central Banks on Policy Operations (1994-Present); Vice Chairman, Nikko Securities International (Now SMBC Nikko Securities Inc.), New York City, NY (1986-1994);

Staff Director, Federal Open Market Committee, Washington D.C. (1981-1986); Secretary, Federal Open Market , Washington D.C. (1981-1986); Economist, Federal Open Market Committee, Washington D.C. (1978-1981); Staff Director, Monetary and Financial Policy, Federal Reserve Board, Washington D.C. (1976-1986); Economist, Domestic Finance, Federal Open Market Committee, Washington D.C. (1974-1978); Advisor to Board of Governors, Federal Reserve Board, Washington D.C. (1973-1976); Associate Director, Division of Research and Statistics, Federal Reserve Board, Washington D.C. (1970-1973) **CR:** Member, Board, Financial Services Volunteer Corps. (2005-2017); Member, Advisory Council, Central Bank of Oman (1993-1999); Member, Investment Committee, Japan Society (1987-2003); Advisor, Brookings Panel on Economic Activity, Washington D.C. (1986-1989); Chairman, Audit Committee, Financial Services Volunteer Corps (200-2017). **MIL:** U.S. Navy Seabees (1944-1946) **CW:** Author, "The Federal Reserve: What Everyone Needs to Know," Oxford University Press (2013); Author, "Inside the Fed: Monetary Policy & Its Management, Martin Through Greenspan to Bernanke, Revised Edition" (2011); Author, "Inside the Fed: Monetary Policy & Its Management, Martin Through Greenspan to Bernanke" (2009); Contributor, Articles, Books; Contributor, Articles, Newspapers; Contributor, Articles, Magazines; Contributor, Articles, Professional Journals **AW:** Phi Beta Kappa, Harvard College (1948) **MEM:** The Phi Beta Kappa Society **H:** Tennis; Writing poetry and prose; Reading; Hiking; Squash **PA:** Democratic **BA:** 30 Bokum Road, Essex, CT, 10028 **ADD:** 30 Bokum Road, Apt 256, Essex, CT, 06426

BABBEL, DAVID F., **T:** Professor Emeritus **I:** Education/Educational Services **CN:** The Wharton School, University of Pennsylvania **DOB:** 04/12/1949 **PT:** Frederick W. Babbel; June Babbel **MS:** Married **SPN:** Mary Jane Babbel **CH:** Tara Nicole Babbel Haglund; Elise Kiera Babbel Hahl; Karisa Rose Babbel McAllister; Tyson Frederick Babbel **ED:** Postdoctoral Fellow, Risk and Insurance, The Wharton School, University of Pennsylvania; Postdoctoral Studies, Financial Theory, The Haas School of Business, University of California at Berkeley; PhD in Finance, University of Florida; PhD Certificate of Latin American Studies, MBA in Finance and International Finance, University of Florida; BA in Economics and Philosophy, Brigham Young University, George Mason University **C:** Emeritus Professor, The Wharton School, University of Pennsylvania (2011-Present); Senior Advisor, Director of Insurance Economics Practice, Finance Group, Charles River Associates, Boston, MA, New York, NY (2006-2016); Visiting Distinguished Professor of Finance, Villanova University (2006); Full Professor of Insurance and Risk Management and Full Professor of Finance, The Wharton School, University of Pennsylvania (1998-2010); Senior Financial Economist, The World Bank (1995); Senior Advisor, Fixed Income Division, Financial Strategies, Capital Markets, Mortgage Securities, Goldman Sachs Asset Management Divisions, Insurance Services Group (1988-1992); Vice President, Goldman, Sachs, and Company, Pension and Insurance Department, New York, NY (1987); Associate Professor of Finance and Associate Professor of Insurance, The Wharton School, University of Pennsylvania (1985-1997); Assistant Professor of Finance and Insurance, Assistant Professor of International Finance, The Haas School, University of California at Berkeley (1978-1984); Financial Economist, Brazilian Capital Market Institute, Financial Research Division, Rio de Janeiro, Brazil (1976-1977); Pension Specialist, Financial

Sector, Development Department, Washington, DC; Founder, Insurance Services Group **CW:** Contributor, More than 130 Books and Scholarly Articles on Investment and Insurance Topics **AW:** Australian Innovation Award for Retirement Strategies (2017), Annual Prize for the Best Paper Published in the North American Actuarial Journal (2002); Graham and Dodd Award of Excellence, Association for Investment Management and Research (1997); Society of Actuaries Research Grant (1992-1996); Award for Best Feature Article, American Risk and Insurance Association (1989); Award for Best Feature Article, American Risk and Insurance Association (1989); Prochnov Foundation for Banking Studies Research Grant (1988); Harry J. Loman Foundation Research Fellowship (1986); Regents of California Junior Faculty Fellowship (1983-1984); Award for Best Communication, American Risk and Insurance Association (1983); Fulbright Fellow, United States Office of Education (1977); Fulbright-Hays Fellowship, United States State Department (1976); Various Academic Scholarships, Fellowships and Research Grants **MEM:** Risk Subteam Member, Society of Actuaries (2016); Advisory Panel, Critical Review of the United States Actuarial Profession (2005-2006); Valuation Tools Working Group, American Academy of Actuaries Valuation Task Force (1997-2002); Beta Gamma Sigma; American Finance Association; American Risk and Insurance Association; Past Member, American Economics Association; Past Member, Academy of International Business; Omicron Delta Epsilon **MH:** Albert Nelson Marquis Lifetime Achievement Award (2017) **H:** Baseball **RE:** Church of Jesus Christ of Latter-day Saints **ADD:** 215 Wakefield Rd, Bryn Mawr, PA, 19010

BABBITT, MARTHA E., **T:** Retired Teacher **I:** Education/Educational Services **DOB:** 11/04/1944 **PB:** Valley Falls **SC:** NY/USA **PT:** Nelson Benjamin; Pearl Leone Betts **MS:** Married **SPN:** Donald W. Babbitt, (July 8, 1995 - Deceased October 2017) **CH:** Mary Ellen Crowley; William Christopher; Kenneth Scott; Katharine Doreen Hubbard **ED:** MS in Education, Western Connecticut State University, Danbury, CT (1973); BS, New York State University College, Cortland, (1966) **C:** Retired (2007); Teacher, Amateur Radio Relay League, Education and Technology Progressive, Newtown, CT (2003-2007); Teacher, Newtown Middle School, Connecticut (1969-2007); Teacher, Scotia-Glenville Central Schools, Scotia, NY (1966-1969) **CR:** Master, Rensselaer County Pomona (2013-Present); Lecturer (2011-Present); Secretary, Hoosick Grange (2012-Present); Treasurer, Pomona Lecturers Association, New York State Grange (2011-Present); Gate Keeper Hoosick Grange (2009-2012); Teacher, Amateur Radio Relay League, Education and Technology Program, Hoosick Valley Central School (2008) **CIV:** Member of the Choir, Salem Covenant Church, Washington, CT (2001-2008); Secretary, Candlewood Amateur Radio Association; Secretary, Northville Amateur Radio Association; Building Upkeep, Salem Covenant Church **MEM:** Secretary, Northville Amateur Radio Associates (2006-2007); Candlewood Amateur Radio Association (2005-2007); Overseer, Bridgewater Grange #153 (2001-2007) **MH:** Albert Nelson Marquis Lifetime Achievement Award (2017) **H:** Painting (Specifically Houses) **ADD:** 65 Geary Rd, Valley Falls, NY, 12185

BABI, MELVIN J., **T:** Founding Partner **I:** Law and Legal Services **CN:** Babi Legal Group, PLLC **ED:** JD, University of Detroit Mercy School of Law (2006); BA in Business Administration and Corporate Finance, Wayne State University, Cum

Laude (2002); Coursework, European Union Law and International Business Law, Study Aboard Program, University of Baltimore **CT:** Licensed Real Estate Agent, State of Michigan **C:** Managing Partner, Babi Legal Group, PLLC; Chief Legal Officer, Knight Capital Partners **AW:** Named, Super Lawyers (2014-2016); Named, Crain's Detroit Top Attorneys (2014); Named, The Nationals Top 100 Lawyers Advocate; Golden Key Scholar, Wayne State University **MEM:** ABA; Chaldean American Bar Association; Consumer Bankruptcy Association; Chaldean Chamber of Commerce **BAR:** United States District Court for the Eastern District of Michigan (2008); Michigan (2007); Federal Courts **H:** Spending time with family; Golf; Going to the gym **BA:** 22710 Haggerty Rd Ste 151, Babi Legal Group PLLC, Farmington Hills, MI, 48335 **ADD:** 38940 Holsworth Ct, Farmington Hills, MI, 48331-1605

BACA, SARAH J.D, **T:** Controller **I:** Financial Services **CN:** Capitol Ford Lincoln **SC:** NM/USA **ED:** MBA, New Mexico Highlands University (2015); BA in Business Administration and Management, New Mexico Highlands University (2011); BA in Science in Exercise Science, Santa Fe Community College (2008); AS in Business Administration and Management, Santa Fe Community College (2008) **CT:** Certified Professional in Financial Services, Association of Finance and Insurance Professionals (2017) **C:** Controller, Capital Ford Lincoln (2014-Present); Director of Human Resources, Beaver Toyota Scion (2005-2014) **BA:** 4490 Cerrillos Rd, Capitol Ford Lincoln, Santa Fe, NM, 87507

BACON, GEORGE EDGAR, **T:** Pediatric Endocrinologist (Retired) **I:** Medicine & Health Care **DOB:** 04/13/1932 **PB:** New York City **SC:** NY/USA **PT:** Edgar Bacon; Margaret Priscilla (Anderson) Bacon **MS:** Married **SPN:** Grace Elizabeth Graham (6/30/1956) **CH:** Nancy; George; John **ED:** MS in Pharmacology, University of Michigan (1967); Resident in Pediatrics, Columbia-Presbyterian Medical Center (Now New York-Presbyterian Hospital) (1961-1963); Intern in Pediatrics, Duke University Health System (1957-1958); MD, Duke University (1957); BA, Wesleyan University (1953) **CT:** Diplomate, Subspecialty, Board of Pediatric Endocrinology, The American Board of Pediatrics **C:** Professor Emeritus, University of Michigan, Ann Arbor, MI (1986-Present); Pediatric Endocrinologist, Detroit Medical Center (Now DMC Main), Southfield, MI (1996-2001); Pediatric Endocrinologist, University Hospital, Michigan Medicine, University of Michigan, Ann Arbor, MI (1995-2007); Medical Director, Department of Pediatrics, Butterworth Hospital, Spectrum Health, Grand Rapids, MI (1991-1995); Professor of Pediatrics, Michigan State University, East Lansing, MI (1990-1995); Director of Medical Education and Research, Butterworth Hospital, Spectrum Health, Grand Rapids, MI (1990-1991); Chairman of Medical Practice Income Plan, Texas Tech University, Lubbock, Texas (1989); Chief of Staff Pediatrics, Lubbock General Hospital (Now UMC Health System) (1986-1990); Professor of Pediatrics, Chairman of Department, Texas Tech University, Lubbock, Texas (1986-1990); Associate Chairman, Department of Pediatrics, Michigan Medicine, University of Michigan, Ann Arbor, MI (1983-1986); Director of House Officer Programs, Department of Pediatrics, Michigan Medicine, University of Michigan, Ann Arbor, MI (1981-1986); Vice Chairman, Director's Advisory Council, University Hospital, Michigan Medicine, University of Michigan, Ann Arbor, MI (1981-1982); Member, Senate Assembly, Michigan Medicine, University of Michigan, Ann Arbor, MI (1978-1980); Chief of Pediatric Endocrinology Service, Department of Pediatrics, Michigan Medicine, University of Michigan, Ann Arbor, MI (1970-1983); Instructor, University of Michigan, Ann Arbor, MI (1963-1986) **CR:** Associate Vice Chairman of Medical Staff, C.S. Mott Children's Hospital, Michigan Medicine, University of Michigan (1978-1979); Executive Committee for Clinical Affairs, C.S. Mott Children's Hospital, Michigan Medicine, University of Michigan (1977-1979); Executive Committee for Clinical Affairs, C.S. Mott Children's Hospital, Michigan Medicine, University of Michigan (1975-1976); Professional Service Coordinator, C.S. Mott Children's Hospital, Michigan Medicine, University of Michigan (1973-1983); Chairman, Executive Committee, Von Voigtlander Women's Hospital, Michigan Medicine, University of Michigan (1973-1982) **MIL:** Captain, U.S. Army (1958-1961) **CW:** Author, "A Practical Approach to Pediatric Endocrinology, Third Edition" (1990); Author, "A Practical Approach to Pediatric Endocrinology" (1975); Contributor, Articles to Professional Journals **AW:** Pediatrician of the Year, Michigan Chapter, American Academy of Pediatrics (2002); Certificate of Achievement for Outstanding Service, United States Army (1961); Eponym, George E. Bacon Lecture in Pediatric Endocrinology, Department of Pediatrics, University of Michigan **MEM:** Alternate-at-Large, American Academy of Pediatrics (1995-2001); Council, Texas Chapter, American Academy of Pediatrics (1986-1989); Treasurer, Michigan Chapter, American Academy of Pediatrics (1983-1986); Fellow, American Academy of Pediatrics; American Pediatric Society, Society for Pediatric Research (Now APS-SPR); Pediatric Endocrine Society **MH:** Albert Nelson Marquis Lifetime Achievement Award (2017) **ADD:** 3911 Waldenwood Dr, Ann Arbor, MI, 48105

BAILEY, DIANE B., T: Director **I:** Law and Legal Services **CN:** Credit Suisse **ED:** LLB, Kings College, University of London (1997); MPA, Harvard J.F. Kennedy School of Government (1987); BA in Biology/Phycology, Lewis & Clark College (1981) **C:** Functional Head/Subject Matter Expert, CS Wroclaw Compliance Reviews CH & Global Coordination, Credit Suisse Ltd. (2016-Present); Head of Solution Partners, Legal and Compliance, Credit Suisse AG, Zürich, Switzerland (2011-2016); Senior Associate, Banking/Corporate Law Group, Ogier, Guernsey, Channel Islands (2008-2011); Associate, Investment Funds, Corporate Law Group, Carey Olsen, Guernsey, Channel Islands (2004-2008); Lawyer, Union Bank of Switzerland, London, United Kingdom (2004); Associate, Capital Markets, Derivatives Group, Allen & Overy, London, United Kingdom (2001-2004); Trainee Solicitor, Richards Butler International Law Firm, London, United Kingdom (1999-2001); Summer Intern, Richards Butler/SJ Berwin & Co, London, United Kingdom (1996); Consultant, Prudential Assurance Company (1991-1994); Investment Banker, Prudential Bache Securities, New York, NY (1987-1990); Summer Associate, Merrill Lynch, New York, NY (1987) **AW:** Honor Society, Girls State; Lions Club Scholarship; DAR Good Citizenship Award **MEM:** Executive Board, Harvard Club of Switzerland (2017-Present); Harvard Club of Switzerland (2015-Present); Appointed to GILA Committee (2008-2011); Guernsey International Legal Association (2006-2011); Harvard Club of London (1998-2004); Chairman, London Goodenough Trust Running Club (1998-2000); President, Law Student Society (1996-1997); Treasurer, Law Student Society (1995-1996); Harvard Club of New York (1987-1990); Junior Kennedy Student Government (1985-1986) **BAR:** Roll of Solicitors, England and Wales (2001) **H:** Running; Sailing; Films; Writing; Organizing events **ADD:** Bergstrasse 21a, Küsnacht, Switzerland, 8700

BAIRD, CHARLES, T: Lawyer (Retired) **I:** Law and Legal Services **DOB:** 04/18/1935 **PB:** DeLand **SC:** FL/USA **PT:** James Turner Baird; Ethelyn Isabelle (Williams) Baird **MS:** Married **SPN:** Byung-Ran Cho; Barbara Ann Fabian (6/6/1959, Divorced 1979) **CH:** C. Bruce Junior; Robert Arthur; Bryan James **ED:** JD, American University (1971); MBA, California State University (1966); Postgraduate Work, University of California, Los Angeles, CA (1962-1964); Bachelor's of Science in Mechanical Engineering, University of Miami (1958) **C:** Special Assistant, Policy of Compliance, United States Information Agency, Voice of America, Washington D.C. (1983-1984); Professor, Defense Systems Management College, Defense Acquisitions University, Fort Belvoir, VA (1982); Consultant Engineer, Bird Engineering Research Assistants, Vienna, VA (1969-1971); Aerospace Engineer, Naval Air Systems Command, Washington D.C. (1967-1969); Research Engineer, Naval Ordnance Laboratory, Corona, CA (1961-1967) **CR:** Consultant, Logistics Management Institute, McLean, VA (2002-2009); Consultant, TelcoExchange.com (1998-2001); Adjunct Professor, Florida Institute of Technology (1988); Consultant, Logistics Management Institute, McLean, VA (1986-1998); Consultant, IBM, Bethesda, MD (1984); Consultant, Booz, Allen & Hamilton, Inc., Bethesda, MD (1975-1982) **CIV:** Trustee, Galilee United Methodist Church, Arlington, VA (1983-1987); Board of Governors, School of Engineering, University of Miami (1957) **MIL:** Officer, U.S. Navy (1958-1961) **CW:** Contributor, Articles to Professional Journals; Inventor, Computer-Based Communications Systems for the Gravely Handicapped **MEM:** National Rifle Association; Virginia Trial Lawyers Association; Internet Society; Federal Communications Bar Association; Sigma Alpha Epsilon **BAR:** Supreme Court of the United States (1975); United States Court of Appeals for the Fourth Circuit (1974); United States District Court for the District of Columbia (1973); United States District Court Eastern District of Virginia (1971); Virginia (1971) **MH:** Albert Nelson Marquis Lifetime Achievement Award (2017) **ADD:** 5396 Gainsborough Dr, Fairfax, VA, 22032

BAKER, DANIEL R., T: Computer Company Executive **I:** Information Technology and Services **DOB:** 03/19/1932 **PB:** Copenhagen **SC:** Denmark **PT:** Arthur Baker; Molly (Needman) Baker **MS:** Married **SPN:** June Ellin Nebenzahl (10/2/1960) **CH:** David Charles; Jill Alison **ED:** Diploma, Realtors Institute, The University of Virginia (1972); Postgraduate Coursework, American University (1968-1969); Postgraduate Coursework, Fairleigh Dickinson University (1961-1964); BA, Brooklyn College (1957); Coursework, Tufts University (1949-1951) **C:** President, Data Associates, Fairfax Station, VA (1970-Present); Senior System Analyst, North American Rockwell Corporation, Roslyn, VA (1968-1970); Systems Analyst, ARES Corporation, McLean, VA (1966-1968); Systems Analyst, Wolf Research and Development Corporation, Bladensburg, MD (1965-1966); Senior Mathematician, Melpar, Inc., Falls Church, VA (1964-1965); Programmer Analyst, ITT, Paramus, NJ (1961-1964); Computer Programmer, Advanced Data Systems, Paramus, NJ (1959-1961); Mathematics Teacher, New York City Public Schools (1958-1959); Former President, Data Associates, Phoenix, AZ **CR:** Real Estate Broker **CIV:** Volunteer, Annual Fund Campaign, Tufts University (1976-Present); Group Leader, Dale Carnegie Sales Courses **MIL:** Korean War, U.S. Army (1954-1955) **AW:** Lifetime Award, Virginia REALTORS (1994-2005, 1992); Eagle Scout, Boy Scouts of America (1945); 5-year Million Dollar Sales Club Award, National Association Realtors

MEM: Director, Virginia REALTORS (1983-1997, 1977-1980); Vice President, Washington Tufts Club (1975); Northern Virginia Association of Realtors Pioneer Club; Charles Tufts Society; Packard Society, Tufts University **MH:** Albert Nelson Marquis Lifetime Achievement Award (2017) **H:** Art; Music; Antique automobile collector **ADD:** 15850 N 63rd Pl, Scottsdale, AZ, 85254

BAKER, HILDA HELLUMS, T: Founder, Chairman of the Board **I:** Recreational Facilities and Services **CN:** Cross Roads Camp and Conference Center, Inc. **DOB:** 01/04/1950 **PB:** Houston **SC:** TX/USA **PT:** J. Verrell Hellums; Sandra Shartle Hellums **MS:** Married **SPN:** Pat Baker **CH:** Jennifer McFarland Stover; Jeremy Carroll Derr; Nina Delores Derr **C:** Founder, CrossRoads Camp and Retreat Center (1996-Present); Chairman of the Board, CrossRoads Camp and Retreat Center (1996-Present) **CIV:** Volunteer, Christian Organizations **CW:** Author, "Stand at the Cross Roads" (2013) **MEM:** Co-Founder, Area 3:16 Church; Brazos Valley Emmaus Community **H:** Spending time with family and friends; Gardening; Horses **RE:** Christian **ADD:** 590 Cross Road, Caldwell, TX, 77836 **URL:** https://www.linkedin.com/in/hilda-hellums-baker-998a3838

BAKER, IAN ARCHBALD, T: Anthropologist, Author, Explorer, Educator, Photographer **I:** Education/Educational Services **CN:** University of Glasgow, Scotland **DOB:** 12/10/1957 **PB:** New York **SC:** NY/USA **PT:** John Milnes Baker; Virginia Lea Busser Baker **MS:** Single **ED:** PhD Candidate, Centre for the Social History of Health and Healthcare, University of Strathclyde, Glasgow, Scotland (2018); MPhil in Medical Anthropology, University College London (2010); Dean's Fellow, Graduate School of Religion, Columbia University (1990-1991); MA in English Literature, Lincoln College, University of Oxford (1985); BA in Art History, Middlebury College, Cum Laude (1980); Diploma, Phillips Academy, Andover, Massachusetts (1973-1975); Degree, Ringerike Realskole, Hønefoss, Norway (1971-1973) **C:** Author (1993-Present); Photographer (1993-Present); Research Associate, 'The Art and Science of Tantric Buddhism' Exhibition, Victoria and Albert Museum, London (2018); Curator, 'Tibet''s Secret Temple' Exhibition, Wellcome Collection, London (2015-2016); Managing Director, Rare Journeys Travel Seminars (2005-2014); Lecturer, California Literary & Prologue Society''s Distinguished Authors Series (2008); Instructor, Department of Buddhist Studies, Naropa University, Boulder, Colorado (2006-2007); Tibet Travel Expert, National Geographic Expeditions, National Geographic Partners, LLC, Washington DC (2006); Director, Kamalaya Wellness Sanctuary, Koh Samui, Thailand (2000-2005); Partner, Lotus Energy Solar Energy Solutions, Kathmandu, Nepal (1993-2000); Consultant in Tibetan and Himalayan Art, Togendo Collection, Kyoto, Japan (1990-1992); Study Tour Leader, Academic Travel Abroad in Nepal, Tibet, and Bhutan, Smithsonian Institution, Washington DC (1990); Academic Director, School for International Training in Kathmandu, Nepal (1984-1990); Academic Director, School for International Training in Ahmedabad, India (1983-1984) **CR:** Writer and Photographer, National Geographic Magazine (1999-2008) ; Founder, Red Panda Expeditions, Ltd. (1993-2005); Academic Adviser, University of Wisconsin (1985-1993); Nepal Research Associate, Foundation for Shamanic Studies (1985-1990) **CW:** Author, "Dragon's Milk: Alchemy and Altered States in Colonial-Era Burma (forthcoming 2020); Author, "Tibetan Yoga: Principles and Practices," Thames & Hudson (forthcoming 2019); Author, "Buddhas of the

Celestial Gallery," Palace Press (2012); Author, "The Heart of the World: A Journey to the Last Secret Place," Penguin Press (2004); Author, "The Dalai Lama's Secret Temple: Tantric Wall Paintings from Tibet," Thames & Hudson (2000); Author, "Celestial Gallery," Callaway Editions (2000); Author, "The Tibetan Art of Healing," Thames & Hudson (1997); Co-author, "Tibet: Reflections from the Wheel of Life," Abbeville Press (1993); Author, "Secret River: Journeys in the Himalayan Hidden Land of Pemakö"; Author, "The Secret Key to the Heart of Yoga: Pema Lingpa's Revelation of Spontaneous Enlightenment"; Author, "Drinking the Milk of Dragons: Travels Among the Alchemist Wizards of Burma"; Author, "The Secret Key to the Heart of Yoga: Pema Lingpa's Revelation of Spontaneous Enlightenment"; Contributor, Book Chapters; Contributor, Articles, Professional Journals; Featured Guest, Film and Television Programs; Featured Guest, Radio Interviews; Speaker and Lecturer **AW:** Recipient, Albert Nelson Lifetime Achievement Award, Marquis Who's Who (2018); Research Award, Wellcome Trust (2016); Presidential Award, Explorers Club (2016); Research Grant, Expeditions Council, National Geographic Society (2006-2007); Research Grant, Expeditions Council, National Geographic Society (2006); Honoree, Explorer for the Millennium Award, National Geographic Society (2000); Research Grant, Exploration Council, National Geographic Society (1998); Dean's Fellowship, Department of Religion, Columbia University (1990); Rolex Award for Enterprise: Himalayan Sacred Geography as Indigenous Conservation Paradigm (1990); Honoree, Presidential Scholar, Bread Loaf School of English, Lincoln College, University of Oxford (1985); Robert Gallagher Award for Distinguished Scholarship, Bread Loaf School of English, Middlebury, Vermont (1984); Research Grant, Explorers Club (1980) **MEM:** Fellow, Explorers Club; Fellow, The Saint Nicholas Society and Colonial Lords Manors; Fellow, Royal Society for Asian Affairs; Fellow, Royal Geographical Society **MH:** Albert Nelson Lifetime Achievement Award, Marquis Who's Who (2018) **ADD:** Cawdor Castle, North Lodge, Nairnshire, United Kingdom, IV12 5RB

BAKER, ROBERT B., **T:** Philosopher Educator **I:** Education/Educational Services **DOB:** 12/05/1937 **PB:** New York **SC:** NY/USA **PT:** Hal Murray Baker; Freda (Ginsburg) Baker **MS:** Married **SPN:** Arlene Shiela Bernstein Baker (11/28/1958) **CH:** Nathanial Edward; Meredith Harrison **ED:** Fellow, Department of Preventive and Community Medicine, Albany Medical College (1977-1978); Diplomate, Council of Philosophical Studies Institute on Medicine and Morals, Haverford College (1974); PhD, University of Minnesota (1967); Honorary BA in History, The City University of New York (1959) **C:** William D. Williams Professor, Union College (2006-Present); Director, Ethics Across the Curriculum, Union College (2005-Present); Professor of Philosophy, Union College (1989-Present); Chair, Subcouncil on Academic Integrity, Union College (2016-2015); Director, Health and Human Values Proseminar, Union College (1979-2003); Chair, Philosophy Department, Union College (2001-2002); Director, Center for Bioethics, Union College (2000-2002); Chair, Faculty Appeals Committee, Union College (1998-2001); Chair, Philosophy Department, Union College (1991-1996); Chair, Human Subjects Research Committee, Union College (1982-1995); Humanities Curriculum Project, Union College (1984-1988); Associate Professor, Union College (1980-1988); Coordinator, National Health Systems Term Abroad, Union College (1976-1990); Assistant Professor, Union College (1973-1980); Assistant Professor, Wayne State University (1969-1973);

President, Iowa Philosophical Society (1968-1969); Assistant Professor, University of Iowa (1967-1969); Instructor, University of Iowa (1965-1967); Instructor, University of Minnesota (1964-1965) **CR:** Professor of Bioethics, Clarkson University (2016-Present); Professor of Bioethics, Icahn School of Medicine at Mount Sinai (2016-Present); Fellow, The Hastings Center (2014-Present); Co-Chair, History of Medical Ethics Affinity Group, American Society of Bioethics and Humanities (2012-Present); Co-Directors, Masters of Bioethics Program, Albany Medical College (2000-Present); Scholar-in-Residence, American Society of Bioethics and Humanities (1998-Present); Founding Director, Bioethics Program, Icahn School Medicine at Mt. Sinai (2013-2015); Chair, Presidential Faculty Leadership Award, Union College (2014); Chair, Joint ASBH-ASBD Taskforce on Accreditation, American Society of Bioethics and Humanities (2010-2013); Consultant, CECA Taskforce on Ethics Codes, American Society of Bioethics and Humanities (2010-2013); Director Bioethics Program UGC, Icahn School Medicine at Mt. Sinai (2007-2013); Visiting Fellow, Center for Bioethics, University of Pennsylvania (1996-2012); Founding Chair, History of Medical Ethics Affinity Group, American Society of Bioethics and Humanities (1998-2011); Baccalaureate Keynote Speaker, Union College (2007); Advisory Committee on Ethics Standards, American Society of Bioethics and Humanities (2005-2007); Chair, Alden March Bioethics Institute, Albany Medical Center (2005-2006); Associate, Center for Medical Ethics, Albany Medical College (1997-2005); Academy Coordinator, Study of National Health Care Systems, Union College (1979-2004); Archives & History Committee, American Society of Bioethics and Humanities (1998-2003); Collegiate Board Professor, University of Mumbai (2002); Scholar-in-Residence, New York University (1998); Scholar-in-residence, New York University (1995); Visiting Scholar, Kennedy Institute of Ethics (1994-1995); Visiting Scholar, Wellcome Institute for the History of Medicine, Wellcome Trust (1994); Visiting Scholar, Wellcome Institute for the History of Medicine, Wellcome Trust (1987-1988); Director, Computers in Humanities Undergraduate Curriculum, Union College (1984-1988); Visiting Scholar, Kennedy Institute of Ethics (1982); Visiting Associate Professor, NYU Medical Center (Now NYU Langone Hospitals) (1981); Governor's Taskforce on Victimless Crime, Michigan (1972-1973); Project Director, Educator in Research Ethics, Albany Medical College **CW:** Editorial Board Member, "Bioethics" (2007-Present); Co-Editor, "The Cambridge World History of Medical Ethics," Cambridge University Press (2009); Co-Editor, With F. Elliston, "Philosophy and Sex," Prometheus Books (2009); Co-Editor, "Ethics and Epidemics," Elsevier (2006); Editor, "History Medical Ethics" (2005-2006); Editorial Board Member, "American Journal of Bioethics" (2000-2006); Co-Editor, "The American Medical Ethics Revolution: How the AMA's Code of Ethics Has Transformed Physicians' Relationships to Patients, Professionals and Society," Johns Hopkins University Press (1999); Co-Editor, With K. Wininger and F. Elliston, "Philosophy and Sex, Third Edition," Prometheus Books (1998); Co-Editor, "Legislating Medical Ethics: A Study of New York State's Do Not Resuscitate Laws," Kluwer Academic Publishers (1995); Co-Editor, "The Codification of Medical Morality: Historical and Philosophical Studies of the Formalization Of Medical Morality in the Eighteenth and Nineteenth Centuries Volume II, Anglo-American Medical Ethics and Medical Jurisprudence in the Nineteenth Century," Kluwer Academic Publishers (1995); Co-Editor, "The Codification of Medical

Morality: Historical and Philosophical Studies of the Formalization of Medical Morality in the Eighteenth and Nineteenth Centuries: Volume I, Medical Ethics and Etiquette in the Eighteenth Century," Kluwer Academic Publishers (1993); Co-Editor, "Rationing America's Health Care: The Oregon Plan and Beyond," Brookings Institution (1990); Co-Editor, "Philosophy and Sex, Second Edition, Prometheus Books (1984); Co-Editor, With F. Elliston, "Philosophy and Sex," Prometheus Books (1984); Co-Editor, With F. Elliston, "Philosophy and Sex," Prometheus Books (1975); Contributor, Chapters to Books; Contributor, Articles to Professional Journals **AW:** Certificate, Appreciation for Leadership, American Society of Bioethics and Humanities (2015-2016); Recipient, Presidential Faculty Leadership Award, Union College (2014); Grantee, John Conley Foundation (2008); Grantee, Fogarty Center, National Institutes of Health (2004-2008); Grantee, Nathan Litauer Foundation (2007); Co-Recipient, Collaborative Research Grant, National Endowment for the Humanities (1999-2002); Co-Recipient, Presidential Grant, Greenwall Foundation (2001); Honoree, Outstanding Academic Title Published in Field in 2000 (2001); Grantee, NEH-Earhart Foundation-Greenwall Foundation-Litauer-Milbank Memorial Funds (2000); Recipient, Wood Institute Fellowship, College of Physicians of Philadelphia (1996-1997); Grantee, American Philosophical Society (1994-1995); Values in Science and Technology Interdisciplinary Fellowship, New York University (1981-1982); Recipient, Mellon Fellowship, Union College (1976-1977); Recipient, Selected Fields Fellowship, National Endowment for the Humanities (1974-1975); Recipient, Summer Study Grant, Council of Philosophical Studies (1974); Recipient, Junior Research Fellowship, National Endowment for the Humanities (1969) **MEM:** Chair, History of Medical Ethics Group, American Society of Bioethics and Humanities (1998-Present); Committee on Medicine and Philosophy, American Philosophical Association (2006-2008); Visiting Scholar-in-Residence, Institute of Ethics, American Medical Association (2005); American Psychological Association; American Association of Historians of Medicine **MH:** Albert Nelson Marquis Lifetime Achievement Award (2017) **H:** Reading; Travel; Walking **ADD:** 1126 Waverly Pl, Schenectady, NY, 12308

BAKKENSEN, JOHN RESER, **T:** Lawyer **I:** Law and Legal Services **DOB:** 10/04/1943 **PB:** Pendleton **SC:** OR/USA **PT:** Manley John Bakkensen; Helen (Reser) Bakkensen **MS:** Married **SPN:** Ann Marie Dahlen (September 30, 1978) **CH:** Michael; Dana; Laura **ED:** JD, Stanford University (1968); AB, Harvard University, Magna Cum Laude (1965) **CT:** Admitted to Practice, State of Oregon (1969); Admitted to Practice, California (1969); Admitted to Practice, U.S. District Court, District of Oregon (1969) **C:** Partner, Miller Nash Graham & Dunn LLP (1968-1999); Lawyer, Private Practice; Arbitrator, Private Practice; Mediator, Private Practice; Special Master, Private Practice; Trustee, Private Practice **CR:** Lawyer Delegate to Ninth Circuit Judicial Conference (1980-1982) **CIV:** Past Board of Directors, The ARC of Multnomah County; Adviser, Portland Youth Shelter House **CW:** Co-Author, "Arbitration and Mediation, Supplement" (2000, 2008); Co-Author, "Advising Oregon Businesses" (1979) **MEM:** Counsel to Board of Directors, Associated General Contractors, Oregon-Columbia Chapter (1992); Legal Committee, Associated General Contractors, Oregon-Columbia Chapter (1991); Forum on Construction Industry, ABA; American Arbitration Association; Oregon State Bar; Arbitrator, Arbitration Service of Portland, Inc.; Multnomah Athletic Club **MH:** Albert Nelson

Marquis Lifetime Achievement Award (2017) **H:** Astronomy **ADD:** 1141 S.W. Mitchell Lane, Portland, OR, 97239-2822

BALDASSANO, CORINNE LESLIE, T: Senior Vice President of Programming and Marketing **I:** Advertising & Marketing **CN:** Take on the Day LLC **PB:** New York **SC:** NY/USA **ED:** MBA in Finance, New York University (1986); MA in Theatre, Hunter College (1975); BA, Queens College, Cum Laude (1970) **C:** Senior Vice President of Programming and Marketing, Take on the Day, LLC (2005-Present); Owner, Translucent Media (2001-2005); Vice President, Content LMiV (2000); Vice President of Broadcast Programming, Soundsbig.com (1999-2000); General Manager, Radio Division, Associated Press (1997-1999); Senior Vice President of Programming, Southwest Networks, Inc. (1995-1997); Vice President of Programming, Southwest Networks, Inc. (1994-1995); Vice President of Programming, Unistar Radio Networks (1994); Vice President of Programming, ABC Radio (1990-1994); Various Programming Positions, Local Radio Stations (1970-1989); Various Programming Positions, National Radio Stations (1970-1989) **CIV:** Vice Chair, Los Angeles Regional Alumni, Leonard N. Stern School of Business (2004-Present) **AW:** Honoree, One of 20 Most Influential Women in Radio, Radio Ink Magazine, Streamline Publishing, Inc. (1999, 2009-2010) **MEM:** Vice President, New York University Business Forum (1990-1991); Treasurer, New York University Business Forum (1990-1991); Board of Directors, New York University Business Forum (1988-1991) **MH:** Albert Nelson Marquis Lifetime Achievement Award (2017) **H:** American history; Travel; Theater; Dance; Music; Films **BA:** 149 S Barrington Ave Ste 728, Take on the Day LLC, Los Angeles, CA, 90049

BALL, JAMES DALE, T: Associate Professor Emeritus **I:** Education/Educational Services **CN:** Wake Forest Baptist Medical Center **PB:** Yale **SC:** MI/USA **PT:** B. Dale Ball; Francis M. Ball **MS:** Married **SPN:** Carole J. Ball **CH:** Victoria Hook; Christopher **ED:** MD, Feinberg School of Medicine, Northwestern University (1969); BA, Michigan State University (1965) **CT:** Diplomate, American Board of Radiology; Diplomate, American Board of Nuclear Medicine **C:** Associate Professor Emeritus, Wake Forest Baptist Medical Center (2015-Present) **MIL:** Major, U.S. Air Force **AW:** Quinn Award for Teaching Excellence (2007) **MEM:** Society of Nuclear Medicine; College of Nuclear Medicine; American Medical Association **H:** Dog obedience; Photography **PA:** Republican **RE:** Christian **ADD:** PO Box 26333, Winston Salem, NC, 27114

BALLARD, MARION, T: Software Development Company Executive **I:** Information Technology and Services **DOB:** 12/19/1939 **PB:** Montclair **SC:** NJ/USA **PT:** Alfred G. Scattergood; Helen F. (Galey) Scattergood **MS:** Married **SPN:** Frederic L. Ballard Jr. (12/20/1974) **CH:** William; Robert; Anne A. Ballard (Stepchild) **ED:** MBA, American University (1990); MA, University of Pennsylvania (1963); BA, Smith College (1961) **C:** Zone Chairman, Garden Club Of America (2016-Present); Former President, DataPlus, Inc, Washington, DC; Vice President, FINPAC Corporation, Narberth, PA; Mathematician, UNIVAC, Blue Bell, PA; Lecturer, Temple University, Philadelphia, PA **CR:** Quaker Motto Calendar (1999-Present); Former Executive Committee Member, Friends Committee on National Legislation; Board of Directors, Nurturing Minds; Democratic Precinct Chair **CIV:** Former Secretary of the Board, Sidwell Friends School; Former Board Chair, Washington Area Women's Foundation; Board Member, Sandy

Spring Friends School; Board of Directors, Planned Parenthood of Metropolitan Washington; Board of Directors, Levine School of Music; Board Member, Nurturing Minds **MEM:** Phi Beta Kappa; Sigma Xi **MH:** Albert Nelson Marquis Lifetime Achievement Award (2017) **ADD:** 4413 Chalfont Pl, Bethesda, MD, 20816

BANERJEE, ASHIS, T: Assistant Professor **I:** Education/Educational Services **CN:** University of Washington **ED:** PhD in Mechanical Engineering, University of Maryland (2009); MS in Mechanical Engineering, University of Maryland (2006); Bachelor's Degree in Technology, Manufacturing Science and Engineering, Indian Institute of Technology Kharagpur (2004) **C:** Assistant Professor, University of Washington (2015-Present); Research Scientist, Complex Systems Engineering Laboratory, Global Research Division, General Electric (2012-2015); Research Scientist, Computer Science and Artificial Intelligence Laboratory, Massachusetts Institute of Technology (2012); Postdoctoral Associate, Computer Science and Artificial Intelligence Laboratory, Massachusetts Institute of Technology (2009-2011); Graduate Research Assistant, University of Maryland (2004-2009); Trainee, Cadbury India Limited (2003) **CIV:** Program Committee, "Robotics: Science and Systems Conference" (2017) **CW:** Associate Editor, Conference Editorial Board, "International Conference on Automation Science and Engineering," IEEE (2017); Contributor, 47 Articles, Professional Journals **AW:** Recipient, Above & Beyond Silver Award, Global Research Division, General Electric (2013); Recipient, Most Cited Paper Award, Computer-Aided Design Journal (2012); Recipient, Best Session Presentation Award, American Control Conference (2011); Recipient, Best Dissertation Award, Department of Mechanical Engineering, University of Maryland (2009); Recipient, George Harhalakis Outstanding Graduate Student Award, Institute for Systems Research, University of Maryland (2009) **MEM:** IEEE; The American Society of Mechanical Engineers **H:** Hiking; Different foods; Reading novels **ADD:** 2126 N 137th St, Seattle, WA, 98133 **URL:** https://www.linkedin.com/in/ashisbanerjee/

BANKS, RICHARD CHARLES, T: Ornithologist (Retired) **I:** Sciences **DOB:** 04/19/1931 **PB:** Steubenville **SC:** OH/USA **PT:** Clinton Seeger Banks; Elizabeth Mae (Harter) Banks **MS:** Widowed **SPN:** Gladys Sparks (7/14/1967, Deceased 8/2009) **CH:** Randall C.; David R. **ED:** PhD, University of California, Berkeley, CA (1961); MA, University of California, Berkeley, CA (1957); BS, The Ohio State University (1953) **C:** Zoologist, United States Geological Survey, Washington D.C. (1997-2002); Zoologist, National Biological Service, Washington D.C. (1993-1997); Zoologist, United States Fish and Wildlife Service, Washington, D.C. (1966-1993); Curator, Birds and Mammals, San Diego Natural History Museum, San Diego, CA (1961-1966) **CR:** Research Associate, Smithsonian Institution, Washington, D.C. (2003-2015); Adjunct Professor, George Mason University, Fairfax, VA (1985); Research Associate, Smithsonian Institution, Washington, D.C. (1966-1990) **CIV:** First Lieutenant, U.S. Army, Korea (1953-1955) **MIL:** First Lieutenant, U.S. Army, Korea (1953-1955) **CW:** Standing Committee on Ornithological Nomenclature, International Ornithological Congress (2005-2015); Editor, Biological Society of Washington (2004-2006); Creator, Editor, Ornithological Newsletter (1976-1992) **AW:** Klamm Service Award, Wilson Ornithological Society (2008); Marion Jenkinson Service Award, American Ornithological Union (1998) **MEM:** Member, Washington Biologists' Field Club (1968-Present); American Association for

Zoological Nomenclature (2001-2003); President, American Ornithological Society (1994-1996); President-elect, American Ornithological Society (1992-1994); President, Wilson Ornithological Society (1991-1993); President, Washington Biologists' Field Club (1990-1993); First and Second Vice President, Wilson Ornithological Society (1987-1991); Vice President, American Ornithological Society (1987-1988); President, Biological Society of Washington (1979-1980); Secretary, American Ornithological Society (1968-1972); Fellow, American Ornithological Union; Honorary Member, Cooper Ornithological Society **MH:** Albert Nelson Marquis Lifetime Achievement Award (2017) **H:** Reading; Sports **ADD:** 3201 Circle Hill Rd, Alexandria, VA, 22305

BARBE, BETTY CATHERINE, T: Marketing Professional **I:** Advertising & Marketing **CN:** Primerica Financial Services **DOB:** 12/24/1930 **PB:** Chicago **SC:** IL/USA **PT:** Norbert Weishaar; Helen Weishaar **MS:** Widow **SPN:** Edward William (8/8/1953), Deceased **CH:** Leonard Walter; Roger Andrew **ED:** Coursework, University of Toledo (1970-1985) Diploma, National Institute of Practical Nursing Inc. (1950) **CT:** Life Licensed, Series Six Securities License, Certification, Fixed Annuity; Certification, Notary **C:** District Representative, Life License, Primerica Financial Service (2009-Present); Marketing Executive, Melaleuca, Inc., The Wellness Company (2003-2008); Tax Administrator, City of Perrysburg (1983-1998); Assistant City Clerk, Payroll, City of Perrysburg (1977-1983); Executive Secretary, Crow Aviation Group Inc (1973-1977); Secretary, Estimator, Grinnell Fire Protection (1972-1973); Vice President Secretary, Cost Accounting, Craftmaster Paint by Number (1970-1972); Hostess, Welcome Wagon International, Maumee, OH (1965-1970); Switchboard Operator, Accountant, Gorr Printing, Allstate Insurance, Muntz TV (1947-1953); Kresege Five and Dime (1946); Sears (1947) **CIV:** Reading Coach, Evening St. School (2001); Reading Coach, Park Elementary School (2001); Reading Coach, Bluffsview Elementary School (2001); Volunteer, Worthington Republican Women's Club (1999); Active Member, Big Sisters of Toledo (1979); Tutor, Ohio Reads; Volunteer, Partners for Citizenship and Character; Volunteer, Jamie Farr Ladies Professional Golf Association Golf Classic; Volunteer, New Albany Ladies Professional Golf Association Golf Classic; Active Member, YWCA; Member, Advisory Council, Ohio Bicentennial Commission; Secretary, Ohio Women's Policy and Research Commission; Vice Chair, Ohio Women's Policy and Research Commission; Association of Two Toledos, Spain; Vice Chair, Reader Sight Center, Toledo; Secretary, Reader Sight Center, Toledo; Volunteer, Passavant Hospital **AW:** Paul Harris Fellow, Dublin-Worthington Rotary (1999-2000) Honoree, Maumee Valley Council, Girl Scouts of the USA (1990) Woman of the Year, Business and Professional Women, Black Swamp Region II; Partnership for Citizenship & Character; Dedicated Tile, Chlois G. Ingram Spirit of Women Park, Ohio State University Wexner Medical Center **MEM:** President, Maumee Business and Professional Women (1995-1997); President, Maumee Valley Toastmasters (1989-1990); Presenter, Key to the Sea Business and Professional Women's Organization (1982-1984); President, Key to the Sea Business and Professional Women's Organization (1982-1984); Secretary, Toledo Opera Society Association; Vice President, Toledo Opera Society Association; Christ Child Society; Secretary, Maumee Chamber of Commerce; Treasurer, Samagama Club, Zonta II; Maumee Valley Historical Society; Secretary, Dublin-Worthington Chapter, Rotary International; Perrysburg Rotary; International Institute, National Notary Association; National Federation of Business and Professional Women **MH:** Albert Nelson Marquis Lifetime Achievement Award (2017) **H:** Football; Reading; Sewing; Crafts; Travel; Basketball **PA:** Republican **RE:** Roman Catholic **ADD:** 806 Drummond Ct, Columbus, OH, 43214

BARBER, JAMES WILLIAM, T: Theology Studies Educator, Director **I:** Education/Educational Services **CN:** Oral Roberts School of Theology **DOB:** 03/10/1952 **PB:** Charlotte **SC:** NC/USA **PT:** James William Barber; Mella Barber **MS:** Married **SPN:** Geraldine Brickhouse (12/21/1973, Divorced); Adeline P. D'Cruz **CH:** Christa Joy; Jamael Oronde; Johnathan William; Atiim Kiambu **ED:** DMin, Oral Roberts University, Tulsa, OK (1997) **CT:** Ordained Clergy and Missionary Teacher, World Ministry Fellowship (2008) **C:** Assistant Professor, Practical Theology, Oral Roberts School of Theology (2001-Present); Director, Field Education, Oral Roberts School of Theology, Tulsa, OK (2001) **CR:** Missionary Teacher, Barber Ministries Inc, Broken Arrrow, OK (2005-Present) **CW:** Director, "Discipleship in Local Church" **AW:** Outstanding Service Award, Oral Roberts University (2010); Outstanding Service Award, Oral Roberts University (2006) **MEM:** Fellow, Association of Theological Field Educators **MH:** Albert Nelson Marquis Lifetime Achievement Award (2017) **ADD:** 4405 S Hickory Ave, Broken Arrow, OK, 74011 **URL:** jbarber@oru.edu

BARDEN, GEORGE V., I: Government Administration/Government Relations/Government Services **DOB:** 01/20/1948 **PB:** Penn Yan **SC:** NY/USA **PT:** Gerald Barden; Helen Lou Barden **CH:** Peter; Thomas **ED:** Associate Degree, Agricultural & Technical College, Canton, NY (1968) **CT:** Certified Professional Soil Erosion and Sediment Control Specialist **C:** Watershed inspector Canandaigua Lake,, Ontario County Soil & Water Conservation District, Canandaigua, NY (1991-Present); Delegate, National Ground Water Resources, Russia (2001); Owner, Operator, Barden Tech. Services, Penn Yan (1984-1990); Designer, Design Draftsman, Sear Brown Associates, Rochester (1979-1983); Designer, Design Draftsman, MRB Group, Rochester, NY (1969-1978); General Construction Laborer, Penn Yan Builders (1967-1968); General Farm Laborer, Ej-Lo Farms, Penn Yan (1963-1966) **CR:** Representative, Watershed Task Force, Canandaigua Lake Watershed Commission **CIV:** President, Finger Lakes Concert Band (1984-2012) **AW:** Recognition Award, Canandaigua Lake Watershed Task Force (1998); Merit Award, New York State Conservation District Employees Association (1996); Special Project Award, New York State Conservation District Employees Association (1994); Map Competition Award, New York State Association of Professional Land Surveyors (1980); Service Award, Canandaigua Lake Watershed Council **MEM:** Delegation of Water Profiles and Citizen Ambassador, National Ground Water Association; Finger Lakes Water Works Association; New York State Building Officials Association; American Water Works Association; Finger Lakes Building Officials Association; American Design Drafting Association; American Institute of Design and Drafting **H:** Music; Woodworking; Furniture refinishing; Vegetable gardening

BARKER, BARBARA ANN, T: Ophthalmologist **I:** Medicine & Health Care **CN:** Private Practice **DOB:** 11/10/1943 **PB:** Paterson **SC:** NJ/USA **PT:** Earle Louis Barker; Dorothy Louise (Williamson) Barker **MS:** Married **SPN:** Joel Ira Papernik (7/28/1972) **CH:** Deborah; Ilana **ED:** Fellow, Cornea, Refractive Surgery, Mount Sinai School of Medicine/Beth Israel Medical Center (1981-1982); Fellow in Glaucoma, Mount Sinai School of

Medicine/Beth Israel Medical Center (1980-1981); Resident, Mount Sinai School of Medicine/Beth Israel Medical Center (1980); Intern, Beth Israel Medical Center (1977); MD, Mount Sinai School of Medicine (1976); MA, Rutgers University (1974); MS, Yale University (1967); BA, Connecticut College, Magna Cum Laude (1965) **CT:** Diplomate, American Board of Ophthalmology **C:** Private Practice, Ophthalmology, New York, NY (1983-2016) **CR:** Independent Contractor, New York Hotel and Motel Trades Council (2016-Present); Staff Member, Beth Israel Hospital (1982-Present); Staff Member, St. Luke's Hospital (1982-Present); Staff Member, Roosevelt Hospital (1982-Present); Staff Member, New York Eye and Ear Hospital (1982-Present); Assistant Clinical Professor, Mount Sinai School of Medicine, New York, NY (1982-Present); Research Assistant, Sloan Kettering Institute, New York, NY (1969-1972); Teacher, Riverdale Country Schools, New York, NY (1967-1968); Research Technician, The Rockefeller University, New York, NY (1965-1966); Fellow, American College of Surgeons; Fellow, New York Academy of Medicine **AW:** Best Paper Award, Beth Israel Medical Center (1989); Research Grant, Beth Israel (1983); Grantee, National Science Foundation (1966); Honor Award, American Academy of Ophthalmology (1955) **MEM:** American Medical Association; New York County Medical Association; Women's Medical Society of New York City; American Medical Women's Association; Phi Beta Kappa **MH:** Albert Nelson Marquis Lifetime Achievement Award (2017) **H:** Swimming; Reading; Theaters; Museums **ADD:** 11 E 86th Street, Apt. 18B, New York, NY, 10028

BARKER, ROBERT OSBORNE, T: Mediator, Educator (Retired) **I:** Law and Legal Services **CN:** County Court Mediation Services **DOB:** 06/13/1932 **PB:** Cleveland **SC:** OH/USA **PT:** Cecil Baker (Deceased 1994); Barbara Barker (Deceased 1991) **MS:** Partnership **SPN:** Pauline Barker **CH:** Debra; Dawn; Colleen; Stephen; Michael **ED:** Postgraduate Coursework in Public Relations, University of Florida (1996); Postgraduate Coursework in Quality Management, University of Wisconsin (1989); LLB, LaSalle University (1969); BA in Communications, Arts and Science, Michigan State University (1954); Coursework, Henry Ford Community College (1950) **CT:** Certification in Dispute Resolution, Seventh Circuit District, State of Florida (1995-Present); Certification in Mediation, Florida Supreme Court, Seventh Circuit District **C:** Mediator, County Court Mediation Services (1995-Present); Member, United Service Organizations (2013); Legislative Chair, Association of Florida Healthcare Auxiliaries and Volunteers (2007-2008); Professor Emeritus, Daytona State College (1994-2006); President, CEO, Barker Consultant Inc. (1987-1996); Resort Manager, Outrigger Beach Club, Ormond Beach, FL (1994-1995); Resort Manager, Oceanside 99 Condo, Ormond Beach, FL (1992-1993); National Merchandise and Marketing Manager, "Costa" del Mar Sunglasses, Ormond Beach, FL (1990-1991); Manager, Vice President Seminars and Materials Department, American Supplier Institute (Division of FoMoCo) (1987-1990); Manager, Vice President, National Association Manufacturers, Washington, D.C., Boston, MA, Detroit, MI (1972-1987); Manager, Goodyear Tire and Rubber Company, Detroit, MI (1971-1972); Dealer, Training Regional Manager, Sun Oil Company, Michigan (1959-1971); Advertising Manager, Bastian Blessing Company, Chicago, IL (1958-1959); Manager, Kaiser Aluminum Company, Chicago, IL (1956-1958); Public Relations Department, Ford Motor Company, Dearborn, MI (1953); Industry Executive and Lobbyist, National Association Manufacturers,

Washington, DC, Boston, MA, Detroit, MI **CR:** Board of Directors, Circuit County Mediation Services (2018-Present); Falcon Student Athlete Mentor, Daytona State College (2003-Present); Public Relations Chair, Media Chair, Florida Hospital Memorial Medical Center (1998-2014); Annual Giving Committee, Florida Hospital Foundation, Elected Board Member Foundation (2009-2012); Board Member, Florida Hospital Memorial Medical Center (2009-2012); Board of Directors, Florida Hospital Memorial Medical Center (2009-2012); Elected Auxiliary President, Adventist Hospital System, Florida Hospital Memorial Medical Center (2008-2010); Advisor, Junior Achievement, Daytona Beach, FL (2007-2008); Adjunct Professor, Public Relations, Advertising, Retailing, Sales Fundamentals, Global and International Marketing, Quality Service Management (1994-2006); Board of Directors, Dolphin Beach Club Condo (1991-1999); Owner, Dolphin Beach Club Condo (1981-2001); High School Football Players Recruiter, Michigan State University (1956-1991); Federal Lobbyist, National Association of Manufacturers (1972-1987); FACC Member, Florida Association; Public Relations Chair, Oceanside Hospital Reflections and Imaging Center (2011-Present) **CIV:** Board of Directors, Navy League Public Relations, Public Information Officer, Judge Advocate General (2011-Present); Member, Personnel Board, City of Daytona Beach (2006-Present); Vice President, Senior Advisor, Chapter Board, FPRA (1999-Present); Team Selection Scout, Florida Citrus Sports, New Year's Bowl, ABC Football Game and Camping World Bowl, Orlando, FL (1995-Present); Chairman, Group of Fans and Spartans, Michigan State University Football and Basketball (1990-Present); Ambassador, Daytona Beach Convention Visitors Bureau (2017-2018); Member, Choir and the Living Christmas Tree, White Chapel Church (2013-2018); Member, Focus Group, Florida Healthcare Plans Inc. (2013); Heritage Member, Ormond Memorial Art Museum (2004-2012); Advisory Team, United States Census Bureau, Enumerator and Finger Printing (2010); Survivor, Quintuple Bypass Open Heart Surgery (2010); Member, City of Daytona Beach Community Relations Council (2006-2009); Member, Worship Committee and Visioning Committee, St. James Episcopalian Church, Ormond Beach, FL (2005-2008); Board of Directors, Daytona and Ormond Beach Representative Club (2006-2007); Board of Directors, American Cancer Society (1991-2005); Ambassador, Daytona International Airport (1996-2002); Member, Elder Voice Focus Group, Genesis Elder Care (2001); Heritage Member, Ormond Memorial Art Museum (1991-2001); Member, Advisory Council Board, Council of Aging (1991-2000); Member, Executive Board of Directors, Volusia County Representative (1991-2000); Jazzmatazz Executive Committee Member, Ho-Ho Parade Executive Committee Member, Habitat for Humanity (1995-1999); Commissioner, Ormond Beach Quality of Life, Beautification and Planning Boards (1990-1999); Board of Directors, Daytona and Ormond Beach Representative Club (1991-1999); Community Associate Institute (1993-1997); Volusia Presidential Forum (1991-1999); Assistant Publicity Director, Board of Directors, Ormond Senior Games (1994-1996); Board of Directors, Building Association Managers (1991-1995); Volusia County Personnel Board (1991-1993); Dearborn City Beautiful Commissioner Emeritus (1970-1990); Lay Minister, Episcopal Church (1959-1989); Vestry, Episcopal Church (1981-1989); Resident Police Officer, Dearborn, MI (1968-1988); Board of Directors, Dearborn Civic Theatre (1980-1984); Township Trustee, Findlay, OH (1962); Minuteman, Greenfield Village; Guys and Dolls, Defiance, OH;

PTA President, Dearborn High School and Lindbergh Elementary School **MIL:** U.S. Naval Reserve (1949-1958); Air Force ROTC (1951-1954) **AW:** Outstanding Leadership Award, FHMMC Auxiliary (2009-2010); Advocate Award, American Heart Association (2008); Outstanding Award for Faculty Business, Daytona State College (2006); Outstanding Adjunct Faculty Award, Daytona State College (2005-2006); Award for Assistance to Student Athletes, Special Needs Awareness Program and Service Club, Athletic Department (2000-2001); Volunteer of the Year Award, American Cancer Society (1998); Gold, Silver and Bronze Medals, Ormond Senior Olympic Games (1992-1996); Olympian (1952); Honoree, President Donald Trump; Defense Award for Service During the Korean Conflict **MEM:** Chair, Michigan State Varsity Club (2013-Present); Board of Directors, Volusia/Flagler, American Heart Association (2002-Present); Board of Directors, Public Affairs, Public Relations Director, Daytona Beach Area Council, Navy League of the United States (2011-Present); Board of Directors, Historian, Florida Public Relations Society of America (2011-Present); Public Relations and Public Information Officer, GFHE-UF (2011-Present); Board of Directors Member, Gators for Higher Education (2008-Present); Michigan State University, Spartan (2000-Present); FPRA (1995-Present); Public Relations Society of America (1978-Present); Senior Advisor, Florida Public Relations Society of America (1978-Present); Member, Volusia Public Relations Chapter, Chicago Chapter (1959-Present); Chicago Chapter, Florida Public Relations Society of America (1959-Present); Historian, Florida Public Relations Society of America (2011-2012); Advocate, Gator Club (2008); Outreach Vice President, Volusia/Flagler County Gator Club (2007-2017); Volusia Flagler Member, Michigan State Varsity Club (2002-2012); Premier Health Seniors; Florida Hospital Memorial Systems; Michigan State University Spartan Fund; National Football Foundation; President, Senior Friends of Volusia/Flagler Counties (2000-2004); Vice President of Education, Volusia/ Flagler County Gator Club (1999-2002); Vice President, Florida Public Relations Society of America (1996-1998); President, Ormond Shrine Club (1994-1995); Ambassador, Chairman, Public Relations, Beautification, JazzMatazz, Social Committee, Ormond Beach Chamber of Commerce (1990-2002); President, Southfield Area Rotary (1987-1988); Director of Public Relations, Shriners, Detroit, MI (1984-1989); Delegate, National Republican Convention (1980); Dayton Beach Area Chair, Spartan Club Activities (1957); Lifetime Member, American Legion; Elks; Moose; Masons; Delta Tau Delta; Assistant State Coordinator, Driver Safety Instructor, Volunteer, AARP; Shriners, Provost Unit, Fez on Wheels and Veterans Unit; Florida Police Benevolent Association; Exchange Club; Director, Gator Club; Association Executives; Advertising Federation; Lifetime Member, Military Officers Association America; Lifetime Member, Michigan State University Football Players Association; Florida Sheriffs Association; Lifetime Member, Michigan State University Alumni Association; University of Florida Alumni Association Advocate; Past President, 5 Michigan State University Alumni Clubs; Alumni, Chicago Bears; Lifetime Member, Michigan State Varsity Club; President Trump's Advisory Council; Choir of Christmas Tree; Choir of White Chapel Church of God; YMCA; AMD Cancer Institute **H:** Swimming **PA:** Conservative Republican **RE:** Episcopalian **ADD:** 229 S. Ridgewood Ave Apt 613, Daytona Beach, FL, 32114-4334

BARLETTA, JOSEPH FRANCIS, T: Newspaper Executive, Lawyer **I:** Publishing **DOB:** 10/01/1936 **PB:** Punxsutawney **SC:** PA/USA **ED:** JD, Duquesne University (1963); AB, Marietta College (1959) **C:** U.S. Senior Associate, Independent Council (1997); Of Counsel, Firm Seyfarth Shows, San Francisco, CA (1996-1997); President, Murdoch Magazines (1994-1995); President, Chief Executive Officer, TV Guide (1993-1996); Senior Vice President, Chief Operating Officer-U.S., Thomson Newspapers, Inc., Des Plaines, IL (1992-1993); Executive Vice President, Chief Operating Officer, Director, Freedom Newspapers, Inc. (1987-1992); President, San Francisco Newspaper Agency (Chronicle and Examiner) (1982-1986); Partner, Seyfarth, Shaw, Fairweather & Geraldson (1981); Executive Vice President, General Manager, New York Daily News, Inc. (1977-1981); Vice President Director of Employee Relations, Vice President Director of Operations, Chicago Tribune (1970-1976); Labor Relations Manager, Dow Jones & Co. (1966-1970); Partner, Barletta and Barletta, Ellwood City, PA (1963-1966) **CIV:** Trustee Emeritus, University of San Francisco; Life Associate Trustee, Marietta College; Former Vice Chairman, Orange County Business Committee for Arts; Former Board of Directors, Orange County Performing Arts Center; Former Member, Chief Executive Roundtable, University of California, Irvine; Former Board of Governors, San Francisco Symphony; Napa Valley Symphony; Former Commissioner, California Public Utilities Commission, San Francisco; Former Member, Mayor's Fiscal Advisory Committee, San Francisco, CA; Formal Member, Cardinal's Committee of Laity, New York, NY **MEM:** The Lotos Club; New York Friars Club; San Francisco Family Club **BAR:** State of New York (1981); State of Illinois (1975); State of Pennsylvania (1963) **ADD:** 530 Westgate Drive, Napa, CA, 94558

BARNES, ROBERT VINCENT, T: Art Educator (Retired) **I:** Education/Educational Services **DOB:** 05/27/1948 **PB:** Flint **SC:** MI/USA **PT:** Albert J. Barnes; Mary Elizabeth (Morey) Barnes **MS:** Widowed **SPN:** Sandra E. Mathews-Barnes (12/20/1986), Deceased (2/3/2015) **CH:** Kathryn R. **ED:** Postgraduate Coursework, Cranbrook Academy of Art (1995); MA, Marygrove College (1997); Postgraduate Coursework, Central Michigan University (1976-1980); Postgraduate Coursework, University of Michigan (1973-1975); BA, Adrian College (1970); Postgraduate Coursework, Education Department, J. Paul Getty Museum; Postgraduate Coursework, Cincinnati Art Museum; Postgraduate Coursework, Marygrove College **CT:** Certified Art Teacher, Grades K-12, State of Michigan **C:** Private Art Teacher (2002-Present); Teacher, Genealogy, Adult Education Program, Mott Community College, Flushing, Fenton and Grand Blanc, MI (1976-1984); Instructor, Flint Institute of Arts (1975-1976); Teacher, Art, Flushing Community Schools, Michigan (1971-2002) **CR:** Kids Hope Mentor, Students, Fenton United Methodist Church (2000-Present) **CIV:** Member, Education Commission Fenton United Methodist Church (2000-2015); Member, Museum Board, City of Fenton (2009-2010); Committee Member, The Sesquicentennial of Genesee County, Flint, MI (1986); Co-Chairman, Fenton Civic Committee for New Museum (1985-1986); President, Museum Board, City of Fenton (1984-1986); Chairman, Fenton's 150th Anniversary Planning Committee (1984); Board Director, Past President, Flushing Area Historical Society; Past President, Fenton Historical Society; Past President, Flint Genealogical Society; Former Member, Flushing Jaycees; Former Member, Fenton Lions Club **CW:** Author, "Flushing Area Families" (1984); Author, "Flushing Area Families"

(1981); Editor, Flint Genealogical Quarterly (1981) **AW:** Orren Hart Award, Flushing Area Historical Society (1983); First Prize, Flushing Art Fair, Flushing Junior Women's League (1978) **H:** Pottery; Painting; Genealogy **RE:** Methodist **ADD:** 501 S East St, Fenton, MI, 48430 **URL:** http://whoswhoindustryleaders.com/2016/10/robert-vincent-barnes/

BARNES, HARRIS H. III, T: President **I:** Law and Legal Services **CN:** Barnes Law Firm, P.A. **DOB:** 09/17/1946 **PB:** Clarksdale **SC:** MS/USA **PT:** Harris Hastings Barnes; Jamye (Haskins) Barnes **MS:** Married **SPN:** Sandra S. Barnes (6/21/1969) **CH:** Patrick S.; Elizabeth Blair; Bryan Parrish **ED:** LLM, University of Florida (1980); JD, The University of Mississippi (1972); BA, Mississippi State University (1968) **C:** President, Barnes Law Firm, P.A. (2007-Present); Managing Partner, Barnes, Broom, Dallas & McLeod, PLLC, Jackson, MS (1996-2012) **CR:** Instructor, Continuing Education for CPAs **CIV:** Chairman, Advisory Board, Salvation Army, Gulfport, MS (1984-1985, 1987, 1992); Vice Chairman, Advisory Board, Salvation Army, Gulfport, MS (1991) **CW:** Author, "Financial Survival After Tax Reform" (1986); Author, "Financial Survival in the 80's" (1985) **AW:** Honorary Membership, National Association of Distinguished Counsel (2016); Named, Outstanding Young Man of America, The US Jaycee Foundation (1979); Fellow, Mississippi Bar Foundation **MEM:** President, Law Alumni Association, Mississippi State University (1990-Present); Chairman, Professionalism Committee, Mississippi State Bar Association (2003); President, Hinds County Bar Association (Now Capital Area Bar Association) (1999); Chairman, Taxation Section, Mississippi State Bar Association (1987-1988); Trustee, Mississippi Tax Institute; Past Chairman, Mississippi Tax Institute; Secretary-treasurer, Hinds County Bar Association (Now Capital Area Bar Association); Vice Chairman, Kiwanis International; Sergeant at Arms, Board of Directors, The Downtown Rotary Club, Rotary International **BAR:** Arkansas (2014); Tennessee (2013) **MH:** Albert Nelson Marquis Lifetime Achievement Award (2017) **H:** Reading; Weightlifting; Running; Tennis; Golf **PA:** Republican **RE:** Presbyterian **BA:** 5 River Bend Pl Ste A, Barnes Law Firm, Flowood, MS, 39232 **URL:** http://barnes-lawfirm.com/harris-trip-h.-barnes%2c-iii.html

BARNETT, WILLIAM ARNOLD, T: Oswald Distinguished Professor of Macroeconomics **I:** Education/Educational Services **CN:** University of Kansas **DOB:** 10/30/1941 **PB:** Boston **SC:** MA/USA **PT:** Marcus Jack Barnett; Elizabeth Leah (Forman) Barnett **MS:** Married **SPN:** Melinda Gentry (9/1/1991) **ED:** PhD, Carnegie Mellon University (1974); MS, Carnegie Mellon University (1972); MBA, University of California, Berkeley (1965); BS, Massachusetts Institute of Technology (1963) **C:** Director, Institute for Nonlinear Dynamical Inference, Moscow, Russia (2017-Present); Honorary Professor, Henan University, China (2015-Present); Director, Center for Financial Stability, New York, NY (2011-Present); Oswald Distinguished Professor of Macroeconomics, University of Kansas (2002-Present); Professor of Economics, Washington University in St. Louis (1990-2002); Stuart Centennial Professor of Economics, The University of Texas at Austin (1981-1990); Research Econometrician, Board of Governors of the Federal Reserve System, Washington, D.C. (1973-1981); System Development Engineer, Apollo Project, Rocketdyne Division, North American Aviation, Canoga Park, CA (1963-1967) **CR:** Fellow, World Innovation Foundation (2005-Present); Research Fellow, Johns Hopkins University Institute for Applied Economics, Global Health, and the Study of Business Enterprise (2014-Present); Visiting Professor, Duke University, Durham, NC (1987-1988); Organizer, Annual Symposia in Economic Theory and Econometrics, The University of Texas at Austin (1981-1990); Janey Briscoe Fellow, Institute for Constructive Capitalism, The University of Texas at Austin (1981-1990); Visiting Professor, Economics, Aix Marseille Université, Aix-en-Provence, France (1979) **CIV:** Member, Advisory Panel of Experts, Federal Reserve Bank of St. Louis (2004-2013); Consultant, European Central Bank, Frankfurt, Gemany (2004); Contract Selection Panel Member, National Institutes of Health, Washington, D.C. (1983) **CW:** Editor, Founder, Cambridge University Press Journal, Macroeconomic Dynamics (1997-Present); Editor, Cambridge University Press Monograph Series (1985-Present); Editor, Emerald Press Monograph Series, International Symposia in Economic Theory and Econometrics (1983-Present); Editor, Journal of Econometrics Special Issues (1985); Associate Editor, Journal of Business & Economic Statistics (1982-1997); Editor, Journal of Econometrics Special Issues (1979-1980); Contributor, More than 200 Articles, Professional Journals; Author, Editor, 41 Books **AW:** Honoree, Conference in Honor of William A. Barnett, Bank of England, London, England (2017); Recipient, John C. Wright Outstanding Graduate Mentor Award, University of Kansas (2017); Recipient, Balfour S. Jeffrey Research Award in the Humanities and Social Sciences (Higuchi Award), University of Kansas (2013); American Publishers Award for Professional and Scholarly Excellence (PROSE Award), Best Book Published in the Field of Economics (2012); Research Grantee, Hogg Foundation, Houston, TX (1983); Research Grantee, National Science Foundation, Washington, D.C. (1977-1989); Fellow, R.K. Mellon Foundation (1971-1973); Recipient, 45 Awards and Honors **MEM:** Program Chair, American Statistical Association (1992-Present); Fellow, American Statistical Association (1989-Present); Charter Fellow, Journal of Econometrics (1989-Present); Founder, President, Society for Economic Measurement (2013-2017); Senior Fellow, Institute for Constructive Capitalism, University of Texas at Austin; Fellow, Society for Economic Measurement; The Econometric Society; American Economic Association **MH:** Albert Nelson Marquis Lifetime Achievement Award (2017) **BA:** 1460 Jayhawk Blvd, Snow Hall, Rm 356, University of Kansas, Dept. of Economics, Lawrence, KS, 66045 **ADD:** 1904 Inverness Dr, Lawrence, KS, 66047 **URL:** https://econ.tepper.cmu.edu/barnett/welcome.html

BARR, JOHN B., T: Consultant, Chemist **I:** Sciences **DOB:** 11/08/1932 **PB:** Niagara Falls **SC:** NY/USA **PT:** Lorne Haworth Barr; Myra (Baldwin) Barr **MS:** Married **SPN:** Patricia Jane Kromer (9/18/1954) **CH:** Mark Kromer; John Robert; Kathryn Jean; Karen Patricia **ED:** PhD, Pennsylvania State University (1961); MS, University of Michigan (1956); BA, University at Buffalo (1954) **C:** Consultant, Carbon Fiber Industry (2002-Present); Consultant, Research Opportunities, Inc., Torrance, CA (1996-2001); Associate Research Scientist, Amoco Performance Products Inc., Alpharetta, GA (1991-1995); Senior Research Scientist, Amoco Performance Products Inc., Alpharetta, GA (1990-1991); Senior Research Scientist, Amoco Performance Products Inc., Parma, OH (1986-1990); Senior Research Scientist, Union Carbide Corporation, Parma, OH (1982-1986); Research Scientist, Union Carbide Corporation, Parma, OH (1971-1982); Senior Research Chemist, Union Carbide Corporation, Parma, OH (1962-1971); Research Chemist, Corning Inc. (1961-1962) **CR:** Shell Oil Company Fellow (1959) **CW:** Contributor, Articles, Professional Journals

AW: Award, American Chemical Society (2003) **MEM:** North American Thermal Analysis Society; American Carbon Society; American Chemical Society; Pi Lambda Upsilon; Sigma Xi **ADD:** 3445 Summit Trail, Cumming, GA, 30041

BARRACANO, HENRY RALPH, T: Oil Industry Executive **I:** Oil & Energy **DOB:** 04/08/1926 **PB:** Brooklyn **SC:** NY/USA **PT:** Ralph Henry Barracano; Josephine (Chianese) Barracano **MS:** Widowed **SPN:** Dorothy Sue Bartlow (Deceased May 10, 2010) **CH:** Ralph Robert (Deceased July 20, 2011); Susan Jo Barracano Ratterree; Linda Joyce Barracano Swartz **ED:** BSEE, The Pennsylvania State University (1948) **CT:** Registered Professional Engineer, Oklahoma **C:** Independent Consultant (1992-2007); Senior Project Manager, Hudson Engineering and Project Management Corporation (1990-1991); Independent Consultant (1983-1989); Staff Engineer to Assistant to Senior Vice President, Engineering and Construction, Saudi Arabian Oil Co. (1956-1983); Electrical Engineer, W.R. Holway & Associates, Tulsa, OK (1951-1956); Distribution Engineer, Public Service Company of Oklahoma, Tulsa, OK (1948-1951) **CIV:** Board of Directors, The Pinemont Apartments (2002-2003); Precinct Chair, Democratic Party, Harris County, TX (1984-1998); Precinct Judge, Harris County, TX (1984-1990) **MIL:** 1st Lieutenant, Signal Corps, U.S. Army (1943-1959) **AW:** Pennsylvania State Pioneer (1998); Alumni Fellow Award (1997); Outstanding Engineering Alumnus, The Pennsylvania State University (1993) **MEM:** Lifetime Senior Member, IEEE; Officer, IEEE; Resident Member, Petroleum Club of Houston; Northgate Country Club **MH:** Albert Nelson Marquis Lifetime Achievement Award (2017) **ADD:** 8215 Cypresswood Dr Apt 5402, Spring, TX, 77379

BARREDO, RITA M., T: Auditor (Retired) **I:** Financial Services **CN:** Defense Contract Audit Agency **DOB:** 06/24/1953 **PB:** Torrington **SC:** CT/USA **PT:** Avelino Barredo; Josephine (DiNoia) Barredo **ED:** MA in Public History, Central Connecticut State University (2010); MBA, University of Hartford (1990); MS in Accounting, University of Hartford (1984); BS in Accounting, Post University (1981); BA in History, University of Connecticut (1975) **CT:** Certified Public Accountant, State of Connecticut; Certified Information Systems Auditor; Diplomate, American College of Forensic Examiners Institute; Diplomate, American Board of Forensic Accountants; Certified Information Technology Professional; Certification in Homeland Security; Certified Government Auditing Professional; Certified Management Accountant; Certified Internal Auditor **C:** Auditor, Defense Contract Audit Agency, Lowell, MA (1985-2016); Timekeeper, Timex Group USA, Inc., Waterbury, CT (1976-1985) **CIV:** Member, Torrington Chapter, UNICO National (2006-Present) **MEM:** Corporator, Torrington Historical Society (2014-Present); Association of Professional Genealogists (2013-Present); Utah Genealogical Association (2006-Present); Continuing Professional Education Committee, CTCPA (1997-Present); Secretary, Waterbury Chapter, Institute of Management Accountants, Inc. (1994-Present); Social and Recreation Committee, CTCPA (1996-1997); Continuing Professional Education Committee, CTCPA (1989-1995); Association of International Certified Professional Accountants; American College of Forensic Examiners Institute; AWSCPA; The Institute of Internal Auditors; ISACA; New England Historic Genealogical Society; Connecticut Historical Society **H:** Genealogy; History; Reading **ADD:** 130 Dawes Ave, Torrington, CT, 06790

BARTO, SUSAN CAROL, T: Writer **I:** Writing and Editing **DOB:** 06/21/1941 **PB:** Brooklyn **SC:** NY/USA **PT:** William O. Forcellon; Eda (Birra) Forcellon **MS:** Single **SPN:** Harry W. Barto (3/11/1960, Deceased 8/20/2001) **CH:** William M. Barto (Deceased, 8/26/2000) **ED:** Coursework, Union College (1979-1982); Certification, Katherine Gibbs School (1960) **C:** Paralegal, Dempsey Dempsey & Sheenan (1980-1984); Legislative Aide to State Senator James Vreeland, Morris County, NJ (1977-1979); Executive Secretary, Union County Republican Committee, Westfield, NJ (1971-1979); Secretary, Presbyterian Synod of New Jersey, Synod of the Northeast, East Orange, NJ (1961-1962); Secretary to the Dean of Students, Montclair State University (1960) **CIV:** Lector, Our Lady of Lourdes (2015-2016); Teacher, CCD to First Grade, Our Lady of Lourdes (2012-2015); Head of Volunteers, Hunterdon Art Museum (2001-2010); Active Member, Library Board, Borough of New Providence (1979-1986); County Committee Woman, Union County Republican Committee, Westfield, NJ (1970-1982) **CW:** Author, "Palm Sunday" (2006); Author, Ten Short Stories **AW:** Plaque of Appreciation, Library Board, Borough of New Providence (1986) **MEM:** President, Friends of the Hunterdon Art Museum (1996-1999) **MH:** Albert Nelson Marquis Lifetime Achievement Award (2017) **H:** Reading **RE:** Presbyterian **ADD:** 1 Fisher Ct, Lebanon, NJ, 08833

BASAERI, HAMID, T: Research Assistant **I:** Education/Educational Services **CN:** University of Utah **ED:** Pursuing PhD in Mechanical Engineering, The University of Utah (Expected Completion 2019); MS in Mechanical Engineering, University of Tehran, Iran (2011-2014) **C:** Research Assistant, Utah Nanofab (2016-Present); Research Assistant, The University of Utah (2015-Present); Director of Research and Scientific Department, University of Tehran, Center of Advanced Systems and Technologies, Iran (2013-2015); Project Engineer, Research Assistant, University of Tehran, Center of Advanced Systems and Technologies, Iran (2011-2015) **ADD:** 325 University Vlg, Salt Lake City, UT, 84108 **URL:** https://www.researchgate.net/profile/Hamid_Basaeri

BATES, CHARLES WALTER, T: Attorney, Youth Development Volunteer, Writer, Philanthropist **I:** Law and Legal Services **DOB:** 06/28/1953 **PB:** Detroit **SC:** MI/USA **PT:** E. Frederick Bates; Virginia Marion (Nunneley) Bates **MS:** Single **ED:** MA, Michigan State University (2014); JD, William Mitchell College of Law (Now Mitchell-Hamline Law School (1984); Postgraduate Coursework, DePaul University (1979-1980); Master's Degree in Labor and Industrial Relations, Michigan State University (1977); BA in Social Sciences, Michigan State University, Cum Laude (1975) **CT:** Certified Senior Professional in Human Resources **C:** Educational Employment Coordinator, Cocoon House, Everett, WA (2015-2016); Public Records Officer, Washington State Administrative Office of Courts (2008-2014); Risk Management Coordinator, Washington State Administrative Office of Courts (2008-2014); Director of Human Resources, Washington State Ferries, Washington State Department of Transportation (2005-2007); Director of Administration, TransAlta USA, Inc., Centralia, WA (2002-2004); Corporate Secretary, TransAlta USA, Inc., Centralia, WA (2002-2004); Director of Human Resources Centralia Operations, TransAlta Corp., Washington (2000-2002); Director of Human Resources, PACCAR Automotive, Inc. (1997-2000); Director of Field Human Resources, PACCAR Automotive, Inc. Renton, WA (1997); Senior Internal Auditor, PACCAR, Inc, Bellevue, WA (1995-1997); Director of Human Resources and Counsel, Royal Seafoods, Inc., Seattle, WA (1994-1995); Director of

Human Resources, Royal Seafoods, Inc., Seattle, WA (1992-1994); Director of Employee Relations Counsel, Royal Seafoods, Inc., Seattle, WA (1992-1994); Director of Human Resources, Royal Seafoods, Inc., Seattle, WA (1991-1992); Manager of Human Resources, Western United States and Canada, Godfather's Pizza, Inc., Bellevue, WA (1985-1991); Manager of Human Resources, Western Division, Godfather's Pizza, Inc., Costa Mesa, CA (1984-1985); Personnel Manager, Consumer Foods Marketing Divisions and Saluto Pizza, General Mills, Inc., Minneapolis, MI (1982-1984); Personnel Manager, Consumer Foods Marketing, General Mills, Inc., Minneapolis, MI (1981-1982); Plant Assistant Personnel Manager, General Mills, Inc., Chicago, IL (1980-1981); Plant Personnel Assistant II, General Mills, Inc., Chicago, IL (1978-1980); Job Analyst, General Mills, Inc., Minneapolis, MI (1977-1978) **CR:** Instructor of Staffing, Professional Development Center, University of Washington, Tacoma, WA (2008), 2005; Board of Directors, Olympia Symphony Orchestra (2001-2002); Board of Directors, TransAlta USA Inc. (2000-2001); Board of Directors, TransAlta Investments LLC (2000-2001); Instructor of Employee Labor Relations, Lake Washington Technical College, Kirkland, WA (1992-1994) **CIV:** Truancy Board, Bremerton School District Community (2018-Present); The 400 Condominium Association Board of Directors (2018-Present); Secretary, The 400 Condominium Association Board of Directors (2018-Present); Assistant Scoutmaster, Boy Scouts of America (1971-Present); Commissioner, Scott Lake Drainage District (2008-2010); Member, Group Health Cooperative, Olympia Medical Center Council (2008-2009); Commissioner, Scott Lake Drainage District (2002-2005); Chairman, Bellevue Civil Service Commission (2000); Vice Chairman, Bellevue Civil Service Commission (1999); Bellevue Civil Service Commission (1997-2000); Sammamish Community Council, Bellevue (1990-1993); Member, East Bellevue Transportation Study Advisory Committee (1989-1992); Eagle Scout, Boy Scouts of America (1969) **CW:** Contributor, Articles to Professional Journals **AW:** Recipient, STAR Award, Cocoon House (2015); Recipient, Outstanding Eagle Scout Award, National Eagle Scout Association (2014); Recipient, Council Award of Merit, Silver Beaver (2010); Finalist, Washington Attorney Award of Excellence, Butch Blum/Washington Law and Politics Magazine (2003); Recipient, District Award of Merit, Boy Scouts of America (1991); Recipient, Vigil Honor, Designation Order of the Arrow, Boy Scouts of America (1990); Recipient, Vantage Recruiting Award, Recruitment Today Magazine (1989); Recipient, Scouter's Training Award, Boy Scouts of America (1979) **MEM:** Washington State Bar Association; Kitsap County Bar Association; Federal Bar Association for the Western District of Washington; National Eagle Scout Association **BAR:** United States Court of Appeals for the Ninth Circuit (2002); United States District Court for the Western District of Washington (1992); Washington (1990) **MH:** Albert Nelson Marquis Lifetime Achievement Award (2017) **H:** Camping; Hiking; Movies; Reading **ADD:** 400 Washington Avenue, #400, Bremerton, WA, 98337

BAUM, HERBERT MERRILL, T: Consumer Products Company Executive **I:** Manufacturing **DOB:** 12/06/1936 **PB:** Chicago **SC:** IL/USA **PT:** Jack William Baum; Ruth Frances (Ginsburg) Baum **MS:** Married **SPN:** Karen Rochelle Oberman (12/22/1983); Diane Jean Kale (11/1/1975, Divorced 9/1977) **ED:** BSBA, Drake University (1958) **C:** Chairman, Chief Executive Officer, Dial Corporation, Scottsdale, AZ (2000-2005); President, Chief Operating Officer, Hasbro,

Providence, RI (1999-2000); Chairman, Chief Executive Officer, Quaker State Corporation, Irving, TX (1993-1998); President, Campbell North and South America, Camden, NJ (1992-1993); Executive Vice President, Campbell USA, Camden, NJ (1989-1993); President, Campbell North America, Camden, NJ (1990-1992); President, Campbell USA, Camden, NJ (1985-1990); Senior Vice President, Campbell USA, Camden, NJ (1986-1989); Executive Vice President, United States Division, Campbell Soup Company, Camden, NJ (1984-1985); Vice President, Marketing, General Manager, Soup Division, Campbell Soup Company, Camden, NJ (1978-1984); Associate Director, Director, New Products, Campbell Soup Company, Camden, NJ (1978); Vice President, Account Director, Needham, Harper & Steers, Chicago IL (1969-1978); Account Executive, Doyle, Dane & Bernbach, Chicago, IL (1966-1969); Account Executive, Stern, Walters & Simmons, Chicago, IL (1962-1966); Board of Directors, Ocean Spray Cranberries, Inc. **CR:** Board of Trustees, Jupiter Medical Center Foundation, FL (2014-Present); Chairman, Jupiter Tequesta Humane Society, Jupiter, FL **MIL:** U.S. Army (1958-1959) **AW:** Ellis Island Medal of Honor (2017) **MH:** Albert Nelson Marquis Lifetime Achievement Award (2017) **PA:** Republican **ADD:** 5223 Center Street, Jupiter, FL, 33458

BEALS, L. ALAN, I: Business Management/ Business Services **DOB:** 01/10/1933 **PB:** Glens Falls **SC:** NY/USA **PT:** Edgar Vernon Beals; Ruth (Ackley) Beals **MS:** Married **SPN:** Sandra Gale Campbell (2/26/1982) **CH:** Vernon Alan; Catherine Ann; Kimberly Ruth; Jacob David Adair (Stepchild); Vicki Lynn Adair (Stepchild); Steven Montgomery Campbell (Stepchild); Gary Britt Campbell (Stepchild) **ED:** MPA, Syracuse University (1955); BA, Colgate University (1954) **C:** President and Chief Executive Officer, Savannah Area Chamber of Commerce (1990-1998); Executive Director, National League of Cities (1975-1990); Deputy Director, National League of Cities (1972-1975); Director of Federal Affairs, National League of Cities (1971); Director of Congressional Relations, National League of Cities (1970); Director of Publications, National League of Cities (1957-1959); Director of Town Affiliations, National League of Cities (1957-1959); Administrative Assistant, The City of Norfolk (1956); Intern, Richmond, Virginia (1955-1956) **CR:** United Way of Coastal Empire, Inc. (1995-1998); Executive Committee, Savannah Olympic Support Council (1991-1996); Member, Georgia Partnership for Excellence in Education (1990-1999); Chairman, Public Technology, Inc. (1986-1990, 1983-1985, 1978-1980); Executive Committee, International Union Local Authorities, The World Bank Group (1985-1990); Board of Directors, Center for Renewal Resources (1980-1983); Chairman, Council for International Urban Liaison (1980-1982); Lecturer, University of California, Los Angeles (1977-1981); Chairman, Academy for Contemporary Problems (1977-1978); Chairman, National Training and Development Service (1976-1977); Board of Directors, Public Technology, Inc. (1975-1990); Board of Directors, Academy for State and Local Government (1975-1990); Board of Directors National Training and Development Service (1975-1982); Board of Directors, National Association of Regional Councils (1975-1979); Founding Trustee, The Community Foundation for the National Capital Region (1971-1975); Chairman, Chicago Region, Federal Council (1968-1969); Regional Director, Great Lakes (1967-1970); Secretary, Public Officials Advisory Council, Office of Economic Opportunity (1966-1967); Director of Economic Operations Programs, Metropolitan

Fund (1965-1966); Lecturer in Government and Politics, University of Maryland (1959-1965); Executive Secretary, Maryland Municipal League (1959-1965) **CIV:** Brown Pelican Consulting, LLC (2011-Present); Management Consultant (1999-Present); ME&A (2012-2013); Local Government Consultant, Democracy International (2009-2010); President, Coastal Georgia Botanical Gardens (2006-2014); Association Development Adviser, DAI (2003-2006); Senior Policy Adviser of Local Government Reform, Project Macedonia (2002-2007); President, Convention and Visitors Bureau, Savannah (1990-1999) **CW:** Editor-in-Chief, "Nation's Cities Weekly," National League of Cities (1975-1990); Contributing Editor, "Nation's Cities Weekly," National League of Cities (1970-1975); Editor, "Maryland Municipal News," Maryland Municipal League (1959-1965) **AW:** Environmental Volunteer of the Year, United Way of the Coastal Empire (2014) **MEM:** Trustee, National Academy of Public Administration (1978-1981); The City Club of Washington; The Chatham Club **H:** Master gardener **RE:** Methodist **ADD:** 117 McIntosh Dr, Savannah, GA, 31406

BEAN-WATERS, FRANCENA, T: Community Liaison (Freelance) **I:** Education/Educational Services **CN:** GBS-NCNW, Inc. **DOB:** 10/31/1939 **PB:** Dowell **SC:** MD/USA **PT:** Leroy M. Bean, Sr.; Nina (Franklin) Bean **MS:** Divorced **CH:** Arthur B. Waters III; Merrell-Ayana Waters **ED:** MS in Educational Administration and Supervision, Morgan State University; BFA in Fashion Design, Maryland Institute College of Art **CT:** Certificate, Dorothy I. Height Leadership Development Institute, The National Council of Negro Women, Inc.; Certificate, National Foundation for Teaching Entrepreneurship; Certification in Fundraising and Development, Goucher College; Certification in Public Relations **C:** Educator; Organizational Leader; Community Organizer; Project Manager; Event Planner **CR:** CTE Department Chair; Adjunct Professor; Fashion Designer; Founder, GBS-NCNW, Inc., Spirit of a Woman Conference: Mind, Body, & Pocketbook! **CIV:** Board of Directors, Fieffe Foundation for Haiti; Various Positions, Greater Baltimore Section, The National Council of Negro Women, Inc.; Former Chair, Joshua Johnson Council, Baltimore Museum of Art; Former Committee Member, Kunta Kinte Foundation **CW:** Author, Book, "Couture Sewing" **AW:** Recipient, 100 Outstanding Black Women in Baltimore City Award, Ministerial Alliance; Recipient, Jewel of Baltimore Unsung Hero Award; Recipient, Citation for Community Service, Maryland General Assembly and Maryland House of Delegates; Recipient, Citation for Public Service, Mayor Kurt Schmoke; Recipient, Presidential Citation, Baltimore City Council for Community Service; Recognition, Maryland State Governor Martin O'Malley; Recognition, Baltimore City Mayor Stephanie Rawlings-Blake **MEM:** Lifetime Member, The National Council of Negro Women, Inc.; Honorary Lifetime Member, Greater Baltimore Section, GBS-NCNW, Inc.; National Association of Fashion and Accessory Designers **H:** Literature; Music; Traveling; Fashion and decor magazines; Films; Theatre (plays and dances); Museums; Events like convocations, artsy socials, teas, and dinners; Antiquing **PA:** Democrat **RE:** African Methodist Episcopal **ADD:** 3939 Roland Ave Apt 711, Baltimore, MD, 21211-2053

BEATON, ALBERT E., T: Professor Emeritus **I:** Education/Educational Services **CN:** Boston College **DOB:** 08/09/1931 **PB:** Boston **SC:** MA/USA **PT:** Albert E.; Annie MacEachen Beaton **MS:** Married **SPN:** Joan G. Flaherty Beaton **CH:** Albert E., III; Douglas L. **ED:** EdD, Harvard University,

Cambridge, MA (1964); EdM, Harvard University, Cambridge, MA (1956); BS, State Teachers College, Boston, MA (1955) **C:** Professor Emeritus, Boston College (2005-Present); Augustus Long Professor of Education, Boston College (2002-2005); Director, Center for the Study of Testing Evaluation, and Educational Policy, Boston College (1993-1998); Professor of Education, Boston College, Massachusetts (1990-2002); Director of Research, Educational Testing Service, Princeton, NJ (1981-1991); Director, Division of Measurement, Statistics and Data Analysis, Research, Educational Testing Service, Princeton, NJ (1970-1981); Advisor of Statistics and Data Analysis, Educational Testing Service, Princeton, NJ (1964-1970); IBM Research Fellow, Harvard University (1962-1964); Professor of Education, Boston College, Massachusetts (1960-1961); Director, Statistical Laboratory, Harvard University (1957-1962); Managing Director, Littauer Statistical Laboratory, Harvard University (1957-1959) **CR:** Visiting Lecturer, Stanford University, California (1988) Visiting Lecturer, Trinity College of the University of Dublin (1980); Visiting Lecturer, Dublin University (1980); Visiting Research Scientist, Educational Research Centre, Dublin, Ireland (1979-1980); Visiting Lecturer, Nuffic, The Hague, Netherlands (1970); Lecturer, Harvard University (1967); Visiting Lecturer, Princeton University (1966-1978) **CIV:** Consultant, Election Coverage, NBC (1966-1978) **CW:** Co-Author, "Advancing Human Assessment: Methodological, Psychological and Policy Contributions of ETS," Springer Open (2017); Co-Author, "Large-Scale Group-Score Assessment in Advancing Human Assessment," Springer (2017); Co-Author, "The NAEP Primer," (2011); Co-Author, "NAEP Trends: Main NAEP vs. Long-Term Trends," National Validity Study Panel (2010); Co-Author, "Secondary Analysis of the TIMSS Data" (2002); Co-Author, "The Impact of TIMSS on the Teaching and Learning of Mathematics and Science" (2000); Co-Author, "The Benefits and Limitations of International Educational Achievement Studies" (1999); Co-Author, "An Overview of the Third International Mathematics and Science Study" (1999); Co-Author, "Mathematics Achievement in the Middle School Years: IEA's Third International Mathematics and Science Study" (1996); Co-Author, "Science Achievement in the Middle School Years: IEA's Third International Mathematics and Science Study (1996); Contributor, Articles to Professional Journals **AW:** Recipient, Award for Technical Contribution to Educational Measurement, National Council on Measurement in Education (1988); Recipient, Senior Scientist Award, Educational Testing Service (1987); Recipient, Wilcoxon Award, Technometrics (1974) **MEM:** Honorary Member, International Association for the Evaluation of Educational Achievement (1998); Chairman, Technical Advisory Committee, International Energy Agency; American Statistical Association; Psychometric Society; American Educational Research Association **ADD:** 308 Main Street, Norfolk, MA, 02056

BEAUCHAMP, JOHN L., T: Senior Vice President of Wealth Management, Senior Consultant **I:** Business Management/Business Services **CN:** Merrill Lynch **MS:** Married **SPN:** Donna **CH:** Harrison; Annie **ED:** Bachelor's, The University of Alabama (1969) **CT:** Financial Advisor Certification, Series 65 (1993); Financial Advisor Certification, Series 63 (1980); Financial Advisor Certification, PC (1977); Financial Advisor Certification, Series 1 (1974); Licensed Investment Advisor; Registered Broker, Financial Industry Regulatory Authority, Inc. **C:** Senior Vice President, Bank of America Merrill Lynch (1978-Present) **AW:** Listee, Barron's Top 1,000 Financial Advisors,

Barron's Magazine (2012) **MEM:** Merrill Lynch Circle of Excellence; Former President, Alabama Securities Dealers Association; Charter Member, Investment Management Consultants Association; President's Cabinet, The University of Alabama **BA:** 569 Brookwood Vlg Fl 5, Merrill Lynch, Birmingham, AL, 35209 **URL:** https://fa.ml.com/alabama/birmingham/bwwa-team

BEAUPRE, ELAINE MARCIA KENOW, I: Government Administration/Government Relations/Government Services **DOB:** 06/04/1905 **PT:** Sylvester John D.; Marcella Marie (Karp) D. **MS:** Married **SPN:** James Francis Beaupre; Richard Thomas Kenow, January 25, 1964 (deceased); **CH:** Cheryl Marie; William Richard **C:** Consultant, Mary Kay Cosmetics (1997-Present); Part-time Pre-school Teacher Aide, Peace Lutheran School, Faribault, MN (1997-2001); Executive Director, Faribault Tourism Bureau (1986-1997); Executive Director, Faribault Area Chamber of Commerce (1986-1997); Executive Assistant, Faribault Area Chamber of Commerce (1985-1986); Manager, Public Relations, Faribault Area Chamber of Commerce (1984-1985); Assistant Manager, Nelson's Super Valu Deli, Minnesota (1979-1984); Sales Person, Karp's Shoe Store, Faribault, MN (1968-1979); Bookkeeper, Office Manager, Town & Country Inc., Faribault, MN (1964-1966); Medical Assistant, Doctors Ersfeld, McGroarty, Shelander, St. Paul, MN (1960-1964); Medical Secretary, Dr. Paul Bauer, Faribault, MN (1956-1960); Sales Person, Fabric Store, Faribault, MN **CR:** Member, Planning Committee, Minnesota C. of C. Executives Board Member, Vice President, Old Log Landing Association Crosslake, Minnesota (2004); Member, Advisory Board, Southeast Minnesota Private Industry Council (1991-1997); Member, Advisory Board, Small Business Development Center, Faribault, MN (1986-1997); Member, Advisory Board, Sales & Marketing Tech. Institute, Faribault, MN (1986-1997); Consultant, Faribault Festivals Inc. (1984-1997) **CIV:** Member, Advisory Board, Disaster Committee, Rice County Child Care, (1998-Present); Member, Project SIGHT, TRAM Committee, Multiple Sclerosis Rideathon Bike (1999-2000); Member, Redistricting Committee, Faribault Area-Cannon Valley Group, Girl Scouts of the United States of America (1998-1999); Member, Stop Teen Access to Tobacco Committee, Rice County Hospital (1997-2000); Citizens Liaison, Council for Corrections Facility, Faribault Member, Advisory Board, Downtown Development Committee (1994-1997); Board of Directors, River Bend Institute Art, Faribault, MN (1988); Board of Directors, Faribault Regional Center Community Support Employment Advisory Board (1987); Member, Advisory Committee, Historic Society for Alexander Faribault on History Register, Retired Director, Chamber and Tourism Bureau Faribault Area Chamber of Commerce **MEM:** Treasurer, Southeast Minnesota Executive Chamber Association (1995, 1996); President, Southeast Minnesota Executive Chamber Association (1994); Public Relations Secretary, Mid-America Chamber Executives **H:** Sewing; Crafts; Hiking; Canoeing; Horseback riding; Essential oil for organic home and personal uses **PA:** Democrat **RE:** Roman Catholic **ADD:** 2805 Hanson Ave, Faribault, MN, 55021-2937

BECK, EVA CAROL, T: Musician **I:** Media & Entertainment **DOB:** 10/09/1938 **PB:** San Antonio **SC:** TX/USA **PT:** Carl Addison Beck, Jr.; Seldon (Sandlin) Beck **MS:** Divorced **SPN:** Jay Kenneth Friedman (1962, Divorced 1974) **CH:** Erika Ann; David Jay **ED:** MusM, Indiana University (1964); Postgraduate Coursework, Yale University (1960-1961); MusB, University of Houston, Magna Cum Laude (1960) **C:** Assistant Principal, Symphony II (Now Chicago Philharmonic) (1989-2008); Acting

Assistant Principal Viola, Lyric Opera, Chicago, IL (1982-1983); Acting Assistant Principal Viola, Grant Park Symphony, Chicago, IL (1981-1982); Viola Section, Lyric Opera, Chicago, IL (1971-2015); Viola Section, Grant Park Symphony, Chicago, IL (1970-2009); Viola Section, Lyric Opera, Chicago, IL (1964-1966); Principal Viola, Florida Symphony, Orlando, FL (1961) **CR:** Examining Board, Chicago Federation of Musicians (1986-1988); Negotiator, Members Committee, Lyric Opera Orchestra (1986-1988); Delegate, International Conference of Symphony and Opera Musicians (1984-2009); Grant Park Symphony **MEM:** Mortarboard; Phi Kappa Phi **MH:** Albert Nelson Marquis Lifetime Achievement Award (2017) **H:** Cooking; Exercise; Playing in quartets with her friends **PA:** Democrat **ADD:** 161 W Harrison Street, Unit 1102, Chicago, IL, 60605

BEERY, ARTHUR, T: Artist **I:** Fine Art **DOB:** 03/04/1930 **PB:** Marion **SC:** OH/USA **PT:** Oscar O. Beery; Fern Rachel (Dutton) Beery **MS:** Single **SPN:** Norma Beery (8/27/1985), Deceased; Dolores J. Miller (6/1/1963), Deceased (1984) **CH:** Linda Beery Hindman; Laura Johnson **C:** Artist **CIV:** Contributor, Donations, Marion County Ohio Historical Society **MIL:** United States Navy (1950-1954) **CW:** Artist, Ohio Permanent Collection (2016); Artist, Ohio State Fair Exhibition (2015); Exhibitor, Butler National Exhibition (2014); Exhibitor, Barlow Art Center, Marion, OH (2014); Solo Exhibitor, Barlow Art Center, Marion, OH (2013); Solo Exhibitor, Butler National Midyear Show, Youngstown, OH (2011); Exhibitor, National Midyear Exhibition, The Butler Institute of American Art (2011); Exhibitor, Ohio State Fair (2009); Solo Exhibitor, The Jefferson Avenue Center, Ohio (2008); Exhibitor, All Ohio Exhibition (2007); Exhibitor, Ohio Art League, Richard M. Ross Art Museum, Ohio Wesleyan University, Delaware, OH (2006); Solo Exhibitor, Mansfield Art Center, Ohio (2006); Solo Exhibitor, Ohio Art League Show, Riffe Gallery, Ohio Arts Council (2005); Solo Exhibitor, Rhodes State Office Tower (2005); Solo Exhibitor, E.J. Thomas Performing Arts Hall, The University of Akron, Akron, OH (1979); Exhibitor, Galerie Cernuschi, Paris, France (1972); Exhibitor, The 23rd Grand Prix, Deauville, France (1972); Exhibitor, Rome, Italy (1972); Painter, Murals, United States Navy Minecraft Base, Charleston, SC (1954); Solo Exhibitor, New York, NY; Exhibitor, All Ohio Exhibition, Zanesville, OH; Creator, Ultramodern Techniques, Topological Space Forms; Creator, Ultramodern Techniques, Hyper Pointillism; Painter, Murals, "Elegance in American Cities"; Painter, 36 Paintings of 36 United States Cities; Exhibitor, The Butler Institute of American Art, Youngstown, OH; Exhibitor, Herbert F. Johnson Museum of Art, Cornell University, NY; Exhibitor, Sweet Briar College Gallery, VA; Exhibitor, Springfield Art Museum, MO; Exhibitor, Marion County Ohio Historical Society; Artist, Columbus Museum of Art **AW:** Professional Award, Ohio State Fair (2011); Third Award, Ohio State University (2009); Best of Show, New/AM Open National Show (2004); Oscar D'Italia Award, Accademia Italiana, Calvatone, Italy (1985); Watercolor USA Award (1971); Third Prize, All Ohio Exhibition, Zanesville, OH; Two Purchase Awards, The Butler Institute of American Art, Youngstown, OH **MH:** Albert Nelson Marquis Lifetime Achievement Award (2017) **H:** Travel **ADD:** 402 Fies Avenue, Marion, OH, 43302

BEETHAM STARK, NELLIE MAY, T: Author, Painter, Forest Ecologist **I:** Writing and Editing **DOB:** 11/20/1933 **PB:** Norwich **SC:** CT/USA **PT:** Theodore Benjamin Beetham; Dorothy Josephine (Pendleton) Beetham **MS:** Single **SPN:** Oscar Elder

Stark (10/1962, Deceased) **ED:** PhD; MA **C:** Professor of Forest Ecology, School of Forestry, University of Montana, Missoula, MT (1972-1992); Botanist, Ecologist, Desert Research Institute, Reno, NV (1966-1972); Botanist, Experimental Station, U.S. Forest Service, Old Strawberry, CA (1958-1966); Private Consultant, Philomath, OR **CR:** President, Camas Analytical Laboratory, Inc., Missoula, MT (1987-1992) **CW:** Author, "The Adventures of Leftenant Rundel" (2010); Author, "Midshipman Rundel" (2009); Author, "Humble Launching (2009); Author, "Mediterranean Madness" (2009); Author, "Thirteen Days of Christmas" (2005); Author, "So You Want to Build a Little Log Cabin in the Woods" (2002); Author, "Memories of Wren, Oregon" (1998); Author, "Will Your Family Survive the 21st Century" (1997); Author, "The Adventures of Leftenant Rundel" (1990); Author; Painter; Contributor, Articles, Numerous Professional Journals **AW:** Connecticut Award, Connecticut College (1986); Distinguished Daughter, Norwich, CT (1985) **MEM:** Task Force, Society of American Foresters (1987-1988); Chair, Ethics Committee, Ecological Society of America (1976); Chair, Ethics Committee, Ecological Society of America (1974) **MH:** Distinguished Humanitarian (2016) **H:** Metal detecting **RE:** Christian **ADD:** 36053 Blakesley Creek Road, Philomath, OR, 97370 **URL:** http://www.nbeethamstark.com

BEETON, ALFRED MERLE, T: Lab Administrator **I:** Sciences **CN:** Department of Commerce **DOB:** 08/15/1927 **PB:** Denver **SC:** CO/USA **PT:** Charles Frederick Beeton; Edna F. (Smith) Beeton **MS:** Married **SPN:** Ruth Elizabeth Holland (6/4/1966); Mary Eileen Wilcox (7/20/1945) **CH:** Maureen Ann; Heather Ann; Celeste Nadine; Jonathan Eugene; Daniel **ED:** Honorary DSc, University of Wisconsin, Milwaukee, WI (1996); PhD, University of Michigan (1958); MS, University of Michigan (1954); BS, University of Michigan (1952) **C:** Emeritus, Department of Commerce, Ann Arbor, MI (2002-Present); Senior Scientific Advisor, Department of Commerce, Washington, D.C. (1998-2002); Acting Chief Scientist, National Oceanic & Atmospheric Administration, Department of Commerce, Washington, D.C. (1996-1997); Director, Great Lakes Environmental Research Laboratory, National Oceanic and Atmospheric Administration, Department of Commerce, Ann Arbor, MI (1986-1996); Professor, Engineering and Natural Resources, University of Michigan, Ann Arbor, MI (1976-1986); Associate Dean, University of Wisconsin-Milwaukee Graduate School (1973-1976); Associate Director, Center for Great Lakes Studies, University of Wisconsin-Milwaukee (1969-1973); Professor, Zoology, University of Wisconsin-Milwaukee (1966-1976); Assistant Director, Center for Great Lakes Studies, University of Wisconsin-Milwaukee (1966-1969); Chief, Environmental Research, United States Bureau of Commercial Fisheries (1960-1965); Fishery Biologist, United States Bureau of Commercial Fisheries, Ann Arbor, MI (1957-1965); Director, Michigan Sea Grant; Director, Great Lakes and Marine Waters Center **CR:** Board of Directors, University of Michigan (2006-Present); President, Ecology Center, University of Michigan (2010-2013); Ocean Research Advisory Panel, National Oceanographic Partnership Program (2000-2002); Adjunct Professor, School of Public Health, University of Michigan (1999-2009); Chairman, Scientific Advisory Board, National Oceanographic and Atmospheric Administration (1998-2002); Council of Great Lakes Research Managers (1995-1997); Michigan Toxic Substance Control Commission (1987-1989); United States Chairman, Scientific Advisory Board International Joint Commission (1986-1991); Adjunct Visiting Professor, Oregon State University (1982); Adviser, WHO/Pan American Health Organization, Venezuela (1978); Environmental Studies Board, National Research Council, International Environmental Program Committee (1977-1982); Environmental Program Committee (1976-1982); Consultant, EPA (1973-1983); Adviser on Projects in Ghana, Laos and Yugoslavia, Smithsonian Institution (1972-1982); Metropolitan Sanitary District of Chicago (1968-1976); Lecturer, Civil Engineering, University of Michigan (1961-1965); Lecturer, Biology, Wayne State University (1957-1961); Instructor of Biology (1956-1957); Water Quality Criteria Committee, National Academy of Sciences Research Advisory Council, Wisconsin Department of Natural Resources **MIL:** Civil Engineer, U.S. Army (1967-1973) **CW:** Contributor, Chapters, Books; Contributor, Articles, Encyclopedia Britannica **MEM:** Executive Committee, Michigan Sierra Club (2006-2012); Board of Directors, Great Lakes Observing Systems (2006-2009); Board of Directors, Detroit Audubon Society (2002-2004); National Representative for the United States, International Association for Theoretical and Applied Limnology (1976-1995); Treasurer, American Society for Limnology and Oceanography (1962-1981); Michigan Academy of Science, Arts and Letters; International Association for Great Lakes Research **ADD:** 2761 Oakcleft Street, Ann Arbor, MI, 48103 **URL:** https://quod.lib.umich.edu/b/bhlead/umich-bhl-0399?view=text

BEHM, MARK EDWARD, T: Academic Administrator **I:** Education/Educational Services **DOB:** 04/21/1945 **PB:** Baltimore **SC:** MD/USA **PT:** Carl Behm; Margaret Anderson Behm **MS:** Married **SPN:** Linda Ann Walker (10/9/1976) **CH:** Scott Anderson; Craig Redgwick **ED:** MBA, Loyola University Maryland, Baltimore, MD (1980); BS, Economics, University of Maryland (1967) **C:** Consultant to the President, University of Maryland Eastern Shore (2017-Present); Partner, Towson Bypass LLC (2010-Present); Assistant to President, Towson University (2013-2015); Interim Vice President, Administration and Finance, Chief Financial Officer, Towson University (2011-2013); Interim Vice President, Administration, AACC (2005-2008); Vice President, Administrative Affairs, University of Maryland, Baltimore County (1986-2005); Director, Planning and Budget, University of Maryland, Baltimore County (1980-1986); Budget Officer, University of Maryland, Baltimore County (1976-1980); Assistant Comptroller, University of Maryland, Baltimore County (1973-1975); Product Area Administrator, Singer Company, Link Simulation Systems Division, Silver Spring, MD (1969-1973); Co-Owner, Applied Light Technology Company, Silver Spring, MD (1968-1969) **CR:** Delegate of Directors, National Association of College and University Business Officers; Delegate of Directors, Eastern Association of College and University Business Officers; Delegate of Directors, AURP **CIV:** Board Member, Talbot Mentors, Inc. (2015-Present); Board Member, Treasurer, Maryland University of Integrative Health (2015-Present) **MH:** Albert Nelson Marquis Lifetime Achievement Award (2017) **ADD:** 27942 Oaklands Cir, Easton, MD, 21601 **URL:** https://www.linkedin.com/in/mark-behm-8aaa476/

BELLEW, CAROLE K., T: Owner **I:** Business Management/Business Services **CN:** Bookkeeping Plus More **PB:** New York **SC:** NY/USA **PT:** Joakim Bellew; Mildred Bellew **MS:** Divorced **CH:** Judd; Luke **ED:** Coursework, Bentley University (1982-1986); AA, Business, Lasell College (1965) **C:** Realtor, Keller Williams (2005-Present); Owner, Bookkeeping Plus More (1986-Present) **MEM:** Treasurer, East Cambridge Planning Team; Open Space Trust Fund; Better Business Bureau; Board Member, Kendall Square Association; Green Ribbon Open Space Committee **H:** Knitting; Walking; Golfing **BA:** 257 Charles St, Bookkeeping Plus More, Cambridge, MA, 02141

BELLOVIN, SABRA M., T: Doctor **I:** Medicine & Health Care **CN:** Town Center Physicians, Southeastern Virginia Health System **ED:** MD, Eastern Virginia Medical School **CT:** Board Certified in Family Medicine; Licensed to Practice, Commonwealth of Virginia **C:** Doctor, Town Center Physicians, Southeastern Virginia Health Systems (1997-Present) **CR:** Consultant, Any Lab Test Now; Consultant, Your Home Advantage **AW:** Top 10 Doctors by State in Family Practice (2014); Compassionate Doctor (2009-2013) **MEM:** Medical Society of Virginia; American Academy of Family Physicians; International Lyme and Associated Diseases Society **H:** Listening to music; Yard sales; Running **BA:** 10980 Buckley Hall Road, Building 5, Mathews, VA, 23109 **ADD:** 512 Country Club Ct, Chesapeake, VA, 23322 **URL:** http://secure.intmednova.com/portal/default.aspx

BELT, DAVID LEVIN, T: Lawyer **I:** Law and Legal Services **CN:** Jacobs, Grudberg, Belt Dow & Katz Professional Corporation **DOB:** 01/13/1944 **PB:** Wheeling **SC:** WV/USA **PT:** David Homer Belt; Mae Jean (Duffy) Belt **MS:** Married **SPN:** Caroline Annmarie (7/22/1967) **CH:** David Clifford; Amy Elizabeth **ED:** LLB, Yale University (1970); BA, Yale University, Magna Cum Laude (1965) **C:** Lawyer, Hurwitz, Sagarin, Slossderg & Knuff LLC, Milford, CT (2001-Present); Partner, Jacobs, Grudberg, Belt Dow & Katz Professional Corporation, New Haven, CT (1974-Present); Partner, Jacob, Grudberg, Belt and Katz Firm, New Haven, CT (2011); Associate, Jacobs, Grudberg, Belt & Dow Professional Corporation, New Haven, CT (1970-1974) **CR:** Adjunct Professor, School of Law, Quinnipiac University (2004-Present); Fellow, The Connecticut Bar Foundation (2016) **MIL:** U.S. Army, Vietnam (1966-1967); First Lieutenant, U.S. Army Reserve (1965-1967) **CW:** Senior Topical Editor, Antitrust/Trade Regulation, Connecticut Bar Journal (2012-Present); Co-Author, "Connecticut Unfair Trade Practices, Business Torts and Antitrust" (2015-2016); Author, "Should the FTC's Current Criteria for Determining Unfair Acts or Practices Be Applied to Little FTC Acts?" (2010); Author, "Unresolved Issues Under the Unfair Trade Practices Act" (2008); Contributor, Articles, Professional Journals **AW:** Local Litigation Star, Benchmark Litigation (2009-2016); Connecticut Super Lawyer (2006-2016); Best Lawyers of America (2003-2016); America's Leading Lawyers for Business, Chambers U.S.A. (2003-2016); America Leading Lawyers for Business, Chambers USA (2003); Bronze Star Medal for Meritorious Achievement **MEM:** Connecticut Bar Association; The Phi Beta Kappa Society; Omicron Delta Epsilon **BAR:** U.S. District Court, State of Rhode Island (1981); U.S. District Court, Southern District, State of New York (1975); U.S. District Court, Eastern District, State of New York (1975); U.S. Supreme Court (1975); Second Circuit, U.S. Court of Appeals (1971); U.S. District Court, State of Connecticut (1970); State of Connecticut (1970) **MH:** Albert Nelson Marquis Lifetime Achievement Award (2017) **BA:** 147 Broad Street, Milford, CT, 06460 **ADD:** 168 Westwood Road, New Haven, CT, 06515 **URL:** http://www.hssklaw.com/Attorneys/David-L-Belt.shtml

BELTRAN, ELIO F., T: Artist, Author **I:** Retail/Sales **DOB:** 12/03/1929 **PB:** Havana **SC:** Cuba **PT:** Miguel Beltran Gonzales; Maria Antonia Marrero Albelo **MS:** Married **SPN:** Aurora A.

McIntosh-Beltrain (9/24/1994) **CH:** Maggie Beltran Sori; Maritza Beltran Pappas; Paul McIntosh (Stepson); Michael McIntosh (Stepson); Steven McIntosh (Stepson) **ED:** Honorary Diploma in Electromechanics, Fernando Aguado-Rico College of the Arts and Technological Education, Havana, Cuba (1948) **CT:** Certificate in Effective Executive Communication, Center for Professional Development, Temple University School of Business Administration (1981); Advanced Courses Certificate in Technological Knowledge of the Science of the Art of Illumination, Illuminating Engineering Society, New York City, NY (1968); Certification in Special Education for Advanced English Languish Proficiency, Cuyahoga College, Cleveland, OH (1965); English Language Post-Graduate Certificate, Ministry of Education, Havana, Cuba (1953); Teaching License, Ministry of Education, Havana, Cuba **C:** International Sales Regional Manager, Philips Lighting Holding B.V. (1984-1999); Sales Manager, Norelco (1979-1984); Assistant Chief Engineer to Regional Management, Royal-Dutch Shell Oil Company, Havana, Cuba (1949-1960) **CW:** Exhibition, "What Flows from Spain," Gallery of St. Augustine Art Association (2013); Author, "Back to Cuba: The Return of the Butterflies" (2003), Special Edition (2011); Exhibition, "Nostalgia: A Tribute to Cuban Master Daniel Serra Badué," Cintas Foundation Collection (1998); Artist, "Farewell," Bergen Museum (1995); Artist, "Festivity of St. John at the Hill of the Hermitage" (1993); Artist, "Destiny Unknown," Bergen Museum Collection (1989-1990); Exhibition, Jersey City Museum Collection, New Jersey; Artist, "The Night of the Exiles", Florida International University (1988); Artist, "Transitions", Exhibition, Museum of Modern Art of the Americas, Washington, D.C. Collection (1982); Artist, "The Balseros Series Collection," Various Museums in Connecticut, and Florida International University; Exhibition, Museum of Contemporary Art Chicago; Exhibition, Newark Museum; Exhibitor, Minnesota Museum of American Art; Artist, Various Pieces, Private Collections, Mexico, United States, United Kingdom and Spain; Author, Poems and Essays; Contributor, Poetry and Graphic Design, Popol Vuh, New Jersey City University **AW:** Special Nomination Award, The Visual Artist of the Year, Biographical Center of Cambridge University (2004); Silver Medal Award, French Academy of Arts, Sciences and Letters (2002-2003); Honorary Prize for Exceptional Artistic Achievement in Oil Painting, Bergen County of New Jersey (1997); Outstanding Latino of the Year in Art, The New Jersey Channel Network (1995); National Artist of the Year Painting Award, The New Jersey Channel Network (1994); Top Sales Award, Export Division, Philips Lighting Holding B.V. (1991-1992); Priority Fellowship Winner, New Jersey State Council on the Arts (1983-1984); Painting Award, Institute of International Education, Inc., Cintas Foundation, New York (1983-1984); Priority Award, New Jersey State Council on the Arts (1982-1983) **MEM:** Celia Viñas Cultural Association, Almeria, Spain (2001-2010); "La Musa Traviesa" Tertulia Literaria, Jersey City State College (1980-1990); St. Augustine Art Association, Florida; Pan American Circle of Culture, New York; Invited Participant, Flagler County Art Association **MH:** Albert Nelson Marquis Lifetime Achievement Award (2017) **ADD:** 1213 Sunningdale Ln, Ormond Beach, FL, 32174 **URL:** http://www.artofeliobeltran.com

BEMENT, ARDEN L. JR., T: David A. Ross Distinguished Professor Emeritus of Nuclear Engineering, Chief Global Affairs Officer Emeritus, Inaugural Director Emeritus **I:** Education/Educational Services **CN:** Purdue University **DOB:** 05/22/1932 **PB:** Pittsburgh **SC:** PA/USA **PT:** Arden Lee Bement; Edith Ardelia (Bigelow) Bement **MS:** Married **SPN:** Louise Capistrain (6/24/2001); Mary Ann Baroch (8/24/1952), (Deceased) **CH:** Kristine; Kenneth; Vincent; Cynthia; Mark; David; Paul; Mary Loretta; Kimberly Smiley (Stepchild); Robert Smiley (Stepchild); Suzanne Smiley (Stepchild) **ED:** PhD Honoris Causa, Michigan Technological University (2012); PhD Honoris Causa, University of Macau (2012); PhD Honoris Causa, University of Idaho (2010); PhD Honoris Causa, Korea Advanced Institute of Science and Technology (2010); PhD Honoris Causa, Colorado School of Mines (2004); PhD Honoris Causa, Case Western Reserve University (2000); PhD Honoris Causa, Cleveland State University (1989); PhD in Metallurgical Engineering, University of Michigan (1963); MS in Metallurgical Engineering, University of Idaho (1959); Degree in Metallurgical Engineering, Colorado School of Mines (1954) **C:** Director, Global Policy Research Institute, Purdue University, West Lafayette, ID (2010-2012); Director, National Science Foundation, Arlington, VA (2004-2010); Acting Director, National Science Foundation, Arlington, VA (2004); Director, National Institute of Standards and Technology, United States Department of Commerce, Gaithersburg, MD (2001-2004); Head, School of Nuclear Engineering, Purdue University, West Lafayette, ID (1998-2001); David A. Ross Distinguished Professor of Nuclear Engineering, Purdue University, West Lafayette, ID (1998-2001); Basil S. Turner Distinguished Professor of Materials Engineering and Electrical and Computer Engineering, Purdue University, West Lafayette, ID (1992-1998); Vice President of Science and Technology, TRW, Lyndhurst, OH (1990-1992); Vice President of Technological Resources, TRW, Lyndhurst, OH (1980-1989); Deputy, Research and Advanced Technology, U.S. Department of Defense, Washington, DC (1979-1980); Deputy Under Secretary, Research and Advanced Technology, Office of Materials Science, Defense Advanced Research Projects Agency, U.S. Department of Defense, Washington, DC (1979-1980); Director of Research and Advanced Technology, Office of Materials Science, Defense Advanced Research Projects Agency, U.S. Department of Defense, Washington, DC (1976-1979); Professor of Nuclear Engineering and Materials Science and Engineering, Massachusetts Institute of Technology (1970-1976); Senior Research Manager, Pacific Northwest National Laboratory, Battelle Memorial Institute, Richland, WA (1965-1970); Manager, Fuels and Materials Department, Pacific Northwest Laboratories, Battelle Memorial Institute (1968-1970); Manager, Metallurgy Research Department, Pacific Northwest Laboratories, Battelle Memorial Institute (1965-1968); Senior Research Fellow, General Electric Hanford Laboratories, Richland, WA (1954-1965) **CR:** Member, Statutory Board of Visitors, National Intelligence University, Bethesda, MD (2012-Present); Trustee, Skolkovo Institute for Science and Technology, Skolkovo, Russia (2012-Present); Director, Radian Research, Inc., Lafayette, IN (2011-Present); Member, Science Advisory Council, Skolkovo Foundation, Moscow, Russia (2010-2016); President, Indiana Academy of Science, Indianapolis, IN (2014-2015); Member, Board of Governors, Fermi National Accelerator Laboratory, Batavia, IL (1995-2001); Director, Lord Corporation, Carey, NC (1987-2001); Chair, Commission for Engineering and Technical Systems, National Research Council, Washington, DC (1986-1999); Member, Nuclear Operating Committee, Board of Directors, Commonwealth Edison Company, Chicago, IL (1994-1998); Director, Midwest Superconductivity Consortium, Purdue University, West Lafayette, IN (1992-1998); Member, Technology and Commercialization Advisory Committee, National Aeronautics and Space Administration, Washington, DC (1992-1997); Director, Keithley Instruments, Inc., Solon. OH (1984-1997); Member, National Science Board, National Science Foundation, Arlington, VA (1989-1995); Chair, Advisory Committee for Exploratory Research, Electric Power Research Institute, Inc., Palo Alto, CA (1987-1992); Chair, National Materials Advisory Board, National Research Council, Washington, DC (1984-1986); Chair, Statutory Visiting Committee, National Institute of Standards and Technology, Gaithersburg, MD (1980-1986); Technical Assistance Expert for Mexico and Taiwan, UN International Atomic Energy Agency, Vienna, Austria (1974-1976) **CIV:** Trustee, Lafayette Symphony Orchestra Company, Lafayette, IN (1993-1998); Trustee, Great Lakes Science Museum, Cleveland, OH (1990-1992); Trustee, Society for the Prevention of Violence, Cleveland, OH (1988-1992); Vice President, Board of Directors, Cleveland Opera Company, Cleveland, OH (1980-1991); Councilman, Richland City Council, Richland WA (1968-1970); Mayor Pro-tempore, Richland City Council, Richland WA (1968-1970); Chairman, Boards of Health, Mental Health and Mental Retardation, Benton and Franklin Counties, WA (1968-1970); Founder, Allied Arts Council for the Mid-Columbia Region, Richland, WA (1968-1970); President, Allied Arts Council for the Mid-Columbia Region, Richland, WA (1968-1970) **MIL:** Retired Lieutenant Colonel, Corps of Engineers, U.S. Army Reserve (1992); National Security Management Course, Industrial College of the Armed Forces, Washington, DC (1975); Research and Development Program Officer, Research Office, U.S. Army, Durham, NC (1967-1978); Command and General Staff College, U.S. Army, Ft. Leavenworth, KS; Brigade Shore Party Commander, 498th Engineer Amphibious Brigade, U.S. Army, Ft. Lawton, WA (1960-1967); Shore Party Commander's Course, Navy Pacific Amphibious Command, Coronado, CA; Engineering Officer's Career Course, U.S. Army, Ft. Belvoir, VA (1958); Engineering Construction Brigade, U.S. Army, Ft. Lewis, WA (1956); Company Commander, Active Duty, U.S. Army; Basic Officer's Course, Ft. Belvoir, VA (1956); Commissioned Second Lieutenant Corps of Engineers, U.S. Army, Colorado School of Mines (1954) **CW:** Member, Statutory Board of Visitors, National Intelligence University, Bethesda, MD (2012-Present); Trustee, Skolkovo Institute for Science and Technology, Skolkovo, Russia (2012-Present); Director, Radian Research, Inc., Lafayette, IN (2011-Present); Member, Science Advisory Council, Skolkovo Foundation, Moscow, Russia (2010-2016); President, Indiana Academy of Science, Indianapolis, IN (2014-2015); Member, Board of Governors, Fermi National Accelerator Laboratory, Batavia, IL (1995-2001); Director, Lord Corporation, Carey, NC (1987-2001); Chair, Commission for Engineering and Technical Systems, National Research Council, Washington, DC (1986-1999); Member, Nuclear Operating Committee, Board of Directors, Commonwealth Edison Company, Chicago, IL (1994-1998); Director, Midwest Superconductivity Consortium, Purdue University, West Lafayette, IN (1992-1998); Member, Technology and Commercialization Advisory Committee, National Aeronautics and Space Administration, Washington, DC (1992-1997); Director, Keithley Instruments, Inc., Solon. OH (1984-1997); Member, National Science Board, National Science Foundation, Arlington, VA (1989-1995); Chair, Advisory Committee for Exploratory Research, Electric Power Research Institute, Inc., Palo Alto, CA (1987-1992); Chair, National Materials Advisory Board, National Research Council,

Washington, DC (1984-1986); Chair, Statutory Visiting Committee, National Institute of Standards and Technology, Gaithersburg, MD (1980-1986); Technical Assistance Expert for Mexico and Taiwan, UN International Atomic Energy Agency, Vienna, Austria (1974-1976) **AW:** Distinguished Scholar Award, Indiana Academy of Science (2013); Inductee, Pan American Academy of Engineers (2012); Membership, Council of the Sagamores of the Wabash, Mitch Daniels, Governor of the State of Indiana (2012); William C. Redman Award, Department of Commerce (2012); Inductee, Indiana Academy of Science (2011); Order of the Legion of Honor, President Nicolas Sarkozy, France (2011); Navigator Award, Potomac Institute for Policy Analysis (2010); Imperial Order of the Rising Sun, Gold and Silver Star, Emperor of Japan (2009); National Engineering Award, American Association of Engineering Societies (2009); Recipient, Public Service Award, American Chemical Society (2006); Distinguished Career in Science Award, Washington Academy of Science (2006); Honorary Professor, Chinese Academy of Science Graduate School, President of the Chinese Academy of Science Graduate School (2005) **MEM:** Federation of Material Societies (1994-Present); Fellow and Distinguished Life Member, ASM International (1978-Present); Fellow, American Nuclear Society (1973-Present); Cosmos Club of Washington (1984-Present); Sigma Xi (1959-Present); American Chemical Society (2002-2015); American Physical Society (2010-2014); American Mathematical Society (1992-2012); American Society of Engineering Education (1992-2010); Fellow, American Association for the Advancement of Science (2006); ASM International (1954-1978); American Institute of Chemists; American Nuclear Society (1954-1973); Tau Beta Pi; American Ceramic Society; Society of Mechanical Engineers; American Association of Engineering Societies **H:** Stamp collecting; Art; Classical music; Opera; Classical novels; Cosmology; Natural history **PA:** Republican **RE:** Roman Catholic **ADD:** 3873 Heron Ct, Stow, OH, 44224

BENADE, LEONARD EDWARD, T: Managing Partner **I:** Law and Legal Services **CN:** Benade & Huggins LLP **PT:** Leo Edward Benade; Marietta Taylor Benade **MS:** Married **SPN:** Lynne Huggins **CH:** Tina Marie Blocher, Jennifer Lynn Pupa, Nicole Kathleen Benade **ED:** JD, California School of Law, With Honors (2014); PhD in Biochemistry, The George Washington University (1971); BA in Biology, University of Virginia, With Honors (1966) **CT:** Veterans Affairs Accredited Agent; Mediator, Family Financial Services, District Court; Advanced Family Practitioner, ACR; Mediator, Estates and Guardianship; Clerk of Court; Mediator, Superior Court; Mediator, Workers' Comp, North Carolina Bar Association **C:** Managing Partner, Benade & Huggins LLP, Hickory, NC (2007-Present); Arbitrator, Self-Employed, Hickory, NC (1997-2006); District Court Mediator, Self-Employed, Hickory, NC (1997-2006); Affiliate, L. E. Benade Consulting, Germantown, MD (1994-1997); Chief, Developmental Virology and Genetics Group, The American Red Cross, Rockville, MD (1988-1994); Head, Department of Virology, ATCC, Rockville, MD (1982-1988); Research Scientist, National Cancer Institute, Bethesda, MD (1981-1982); Senior Staff Scientist, Meloy Laboratories, Inc., Springfield, VA (1979-1981); Postdoctoral Fellow, Frederick Cancer Research Center, Frederick, MD (1977-1979); Senior Biomedical Analyst, JRB Associates, McLean, VA (1974-1976); Staff Scientist, Central Intelligence Agency, Washington, DC (1971-1973) **CR:** Lecturer in Biology, Northern Virginia Community College (1974-1977); Expert Witness, Congressional Hearings on Health Impact of OSHA Standards **CIV:** Affiliate, Mediator District Court-Community Mediation Center, The Conflict Resolution Center, Hickory, NC **CW:** Contributor, Articles, Professional Journals; Contributor, Abstracts, Professional Journals; Reviewer Professional Journals; Study Sections, National Institutes of Health **AW:** Named Advanced Practitioner, Academy of Family Mediators (2015); CALI Award, Constitutional Law. California School of Law **MEM:** Doctoral Thesis Advisor, University of Maryland (1984-1988); Chairman, Study Sections, NIAID, NIH (1987); Study Sections, NIAID, NIH (1987); Consultant, AnMed/BioSafe, Inc. (1985-1986); Study Sections, NIAID, NIH (1983); Honor Committee, University of Virginia (1963-1964); Student Council, University of Virginia (1962-1963); ABA; Workers' Comp Section, North Carolina Bar Association; ACR; Notary Public, Catawba County, NC; Republican Party, Catawba County, NC **MH:** Albert Nelson Marquis Lifetime Achievement Award (2017) **BA:** 2425 N Center St, Box 127, Benade & Huggins LLP, Hickory, NC, 28601 **ADD:** 64 28th Avenue Dr NW, Hickory, NC, 28601 **URL:** http://www.bhadr.com

BENDITT, THEODORE MATTHEW, T: Professor (Retired), Professor Emeritus **I:** Education/Educational Services **CN:** The University of Alabama at Birmingham **DOB:** 10/23/1940 **PB:** Philadelphia **SC:** PA/USA **MS:** Married **SPN:** Anne Rosamond Shaw (2/3/1968) **CH:** David Shaw Benditt **ED:** PhD, University of Pittsburgh (1971); MA, University of Pennsylvania (1967); JD, University of Pennsylvania (1965); AB, University of Pennsylvania (1962) **C:** Professor, The University of Alabama at Birmingham (1983-Present); Dean, School of Arts and Humanities, The University of Alabama at Birmingham (1984-1998); Associate Professor, The University of Alabama at Birmingham (1978-1983); Visiting Associate Professor, University of Pittsburgh (1979); Assistant Professor, University of Southern California, Los Angeles (1975-1978); Assistant Professor, Duke University, Durham, NC (1972-1975); Instructor, Duke University, Durham, NC (1970-1972) **CR:** Chair, Department of Philosophy, The University of Alabama at Birmingham (2011-2012); Interim Chair, Department of English, The University of Alabama at Birmingham (2006-2007); Chair, Department of Philosophy, The University of Alabama at Birmingham (1980-1983); Advisor, Law and Philosophy Minor, The University of Alabama at Birmingham; Chair, Search Committee, English Department Chairmanship, The University of Alabama at Birmingham; Faculty Coordinator, Mellon and National Endowment for the Humanities Fellowships, The University of Alabama at Birmingham; Chair, Honors Program Design Committee, The University of Alabama at Birmingham; Secretary, Faculty, The University of Alabama at Birmingham; Chair, Faculty, The University of Alabama at Birmingham; Member, Honors Council, The University of Alabama at Birmingham; Member, The University of Alabama at Birmingham Arts Advisory Board, The University of Alabama at Birmingham; Chair, University Works of Art Committee, The University of Alabama at Birmingham; Member, Town and Gown Advisory Board, The University of Alabama at Birmingham; Chair, Assessment Task Force, The University of Alabama at Birmingham; Member, Fringe Benefits Committee, The University of Alabama at Birmingham; Member, Campus Planning Committee, The University of Alabama at Birmingham; Member, Early Retirement Policy Committee, The University of Alabama at Birmingham; Member, Institutional Review Board, The University of Alabama at Birmingham; Coordinator, Benevolent Fund Drives, The University of Alabama at Birmingham; Chair, Faculty Promotion and Tenure Committee, School of Arts and Humanities, The University of Alabama at Birmingham; Chair, Faculty Affairs Committee, School of Arts and Humanities, The University of Alabama at Birmingham **CW:** Speaker, "Living in Jane Austen's World," Homewood Public Library (2015); Author, "Private Land Ownership and Its Limitations" (2015); Speaker, "Jane Austen and Crime," Annual General Meeting, The Jane Austen Society of North America, Louisville, KY (2015); Author, "Why Respect Matters" (2008); Author, "Acting in Concert or Going It Alone: Game Theory and the Law" (2004); Author, "The Virtue of Pride: Jane Austen as Moralist" (2003); Author, "Mental Illness and Commitment" (2002); Editor, Newsletter on Law and Philosophy, American Philosophical Association (2000-2005); Author, "Modest Judicial Restraint" (1999); Author, "Rights: Civil and Economic" (1999); Eco-Editor, "Philosophy Then and Now," Basil Blackwell (1998); Author, "The Research Demands of Teaching in Modern Higher Education" (1990); Author, "The Rule of Precedent" (1987); Author, "The Demands of Justice" (1985); Author, "A Functional Theory of Law" (1985); Author, "Surrogate Gestation: Law and Morality" (1983); Author, "Liability for Failing to Rescue" (1982); Author, "Law as Rule and Principle: Problems of Legal Philosophy," Stanford University Press (1982); Author, "Rights," Rowman and Littlefield (1978); Author, "Law and the Balancing of Interests" (1975); Author, "Legal Theory and Rules of Law" (1974); Author, "Happiness" (1974); Author, "The Public Interest" (1973); Reviewer, Professional Journals and Publishing Companies; Author, 17 Additional Publications; Editorial Board, Pacific Philosophical Quarterly **AW:** Recipient, Younger Humanist Fellowship, National Endowment of the Humanities (1974-1975) **MEM:** Regional Coordinator, Alabama Region, The Jane Austen Society of North America; Committee on the Defense of Professional Rights of Philosophers, American Philosophical Association; Committee on Philosophy and Law, American Philosophical Association; Program Committee, American Philosophical Association; Co-Leader, Case Study Sessions, Council of Colleges of Arts & Sciences; Grantmaking Panelist, Division of Research Programs, National Endowment for the Humanities; Grantmaking Panelist, Division of Education Programs, National Endowment for the Humanities; President, Alabama Philosophical Society; External Reviewer, Programs in Philosophy, University of Tennessee, Virginia Commonwealth University, The University of North Carolina at Greensboro, Baruch College, The City University of New York; Board of Trustees, Alabama Symphonic Association; Board of Trustees, Birmingham Summerfest; Board of Directors, Alabama Humanities Foundation; Board of Directors, Birmingham Festival of Arts; Board of Trustees, Opera Birmingham; Second Vice President, Opera Birmingham; Board of Directors, Southern Stories Foundation; Steering Committee, Institute for Religious Studies; Member, The Japan America Society of Alabama; Poet Laureate Committee, Birmingham Regional Arts Commission **BAR:** Pennsylvania (1966) **BA:** 900 13th St, 416 Humanities Bldg, Birmingham, AL, 35228 **ADD:** 73 Fairway Dr, Birmingham, AL, 35213

BENGLIS, LYNDA, T: Sculptor, Visual Artist **I:** Fine Art **DOB:** 10/25/1941 **PB:** Lake Charles **SC:** LA/USA **MS:** Widowed **SPN:** Anand Sarabhai (Life Partner, Deceased 2013); Gordon Hart (Divorced) **ED:** Honorary PhD, Kansas City Art Institute (2000); Student, Painting, Brooklyn Museum Art School (1965); BFA in Ceramics and Painting, H. Sophie Newcomb Memorial College, Tulane University,

New Orleans, LA (1964); Student, Yale Norfolk Summer School, Norfolk, CT (1963); Student, McNeese State University, Lake Charles, LA **C:** Assistant, Paula Cooper Gallery, New York, NY; Assistant to Klaus Kertess, Bykert Gallery, New York, NY; Teacher, Third Grade, Jefferson Parish, Louisiana **CR:** Visiting Artist, School of Visual Arts (1985-1987); Visiting Artist, University of Arizona (1982); Guggenheim Fellowship (1975); Visiting Artist, Princeton University (1975); Visiting Artist, University of Rochester (1970-1972) **CW:** Featured, Advertisement, Artforum (1974); Artist, Over 75 Solo Exhibitions, Nationally and Internationally (1969-1995); Collaborator, Print Research Institute of North Texas, University of North Texas **AW:** Co-Recipient, Lifetime Achievement in Contemporary Sculpture Award, International Sculpture Center (2017); Grantee, National Endowment for the Arts (1990); Grantee, National Council of Art Administration (1989); Grantee, Minos Beach Art Symposium, Delphi Art Symposium, and Olympiad of Art Sculpture Park, Republic of Korea (1988); Grantee, National Endowment for the Arts (1979); Artpark Grant, Australian Art Council Award (1976); Max Beckman Scholarship (1965); Yale-Norfolk Summer School Scholarship (1963) **MEM:** American Academy of Arts and Letters (2012) **URL:** https://en.wikipedia.org/wiki/Lynda_Benglis

BENNETT, WILLIAM P., T: Lawyer, Minister **I:** Law and Legal Services **DOB:** 08/28/1938 **PB:** Inglewood **SC:** CA/USA **PT:** George William Bennett; Lenora (Perry) Bennett **MS:** Married **SPN:** Hilda Rodriguez (12/29/2000); Linda L. Schneider (8/19/1961, Deceased 6/9/2000) **CH:** Greg; Mark; Carin **ED:** PhD in Ministry, Reformed Theological Seminary (1995); JD, University of Southern California (1964); MA in Specialized Ministry, Grace College & Theological Seminary (1964); BA, California State University, Long Beach (1961) **CT:** Licensed Real Estate Broker (1965); Certified Real Estate Investment Specialist; Certified Real Estate Management Specialist; Certified Family Law Specialist; Certified Lifetime Teaching Credential Specialized Subject; Ordained to Ministry, Reformed Church of America **C:** Owner, Pacific Coast Properties (1988-Present); Broker, Pacific Coast Properties (1988-Present); Associate Professor in Business and Real Estate Law, California State University, Long Beach (2010); Executive Director, Grandparents Rights Center (1998-2001); Senior Real Estate Attorney, Wise, Wiezorek, Timmons & Wise (1991-1994); Owner, Century 21 Pacific Coast Realty (1979-1988); Broker, Century 21 Pacific Coast Realty (1979-1988); Senior Partner, William P. Bennett Law Corporation (1978-2001); Associate Professor in Business and Real Estate Law, California State University, Long Beach (1965-1986); Partner, Powars, Tretheway & Bennett Law Corporation (1965-1978); Minister, Reformed Church in America; Certified Mediator, Religious Nonprofit Organizations; Certified Mediator, Religious Nonprofit Organizations; Consultant, Churches; Consultant, Religious Nonprofit Organizations **CR:** Department of Religious Studies, California State University Long Beach (2010); General Counsel, Crystal Cathedral Ministries (1995-2003); General Counsel, Campus Crusade for Christ (1991-1993); Arbitrator, American Arbitration Association Panel (1965-1995); Alumni President, California State University, Long Beach; Advisory Board, California State University, Long Beach; Superior Court Arbitrator, Los Angeles County; Pro Tempore Judge, Los Angeles County; Christian Conciliation Service, Los Angeles and Orange Counties; Business Advisory Board, Long Beach City College; Special Counsel, Churches Uniting in Global Mission, Calvary Chapel; Adjunct Professor

of Law, Trinity Law School; Lecturer, California State University Long Beach **CIV:** Administrator, Reformed Church in America, California (1999-2000); Executive Management Team, Arrowhead Springs Conference Center (1991-1994); Board of Directors, Long Beach Area March of Dimes (1973-1990); Legal Adviser, Long Beach Area March of Dimes (1973-1990); Executive Director, Legal Ministry, Campus Crusade for Christ; Director, Property Management, Campus Crusade; Director, Grandparents Rights Center; Executive Pastor, Shepherd's Grove Church **MIL:** Captain, U.S. Marine Corps (1975); Major, California State Reserve; Chaplain, California State Reserve **AW:** Honoree, Alumnus of the Year, Liberal Arts Department, California State University, Long Beach (2010); Business Person of the Year Award, Long Beach Area Chamber of Commerce (1987); Kiwanian of Year, Kiwanis International **MEM:** President, Seal Beach Chamber of Commerce (1989-1990); President, Southern California Investment Society (1988); President, Seal Beach Chamber of Commerce (1985-1986); Board of Directors, Long Beach Area Chamber of Commerce (1985-1986); President, Century 21 Orange County Brokers Council (1984); Board of Governors, Long Beach Bar Association (1970-1976); Pastoral Adviser, Alzheimer's Association; Interfaith Committee, Alzheimer's Association; California Chapter, Christian Legal Society; Director, Legal Ministries International; President, Kiwanis International; Lieutenant Governor, Kiwanis International **BAR:** U.S. Supreme Court (1993); State of California (1965); Ninth Circuit, U.S. Court of Appeals (1965) **H:** Academics; Speaking; Religion; Hiking; Travel **PA:** Republican **RE:** Christian **BA:** PO Box 2817, Orange, CA, 92859

BERACHA, MORIS, T: Business Development Chairman **I:** Business Management/Business Services **CN:** Celistics Holdings **CH:** Adriana; Alan; Alexandria; Andre **ED:** Master's Degree, Metropolitan University in Caracas Venezuela (1983) **C:** Miriq/Connect (2016-Present); Hispanopost Media Group (2015-Present); SKY Devices USA (2015-Present); Chairman, Business Development, Celistics Holdings (2008-Present); Movilway S.A (2008-Present); Sure destiny S.A (2008-Present); Bestinvest Casa de Bolsa, CA (1997-Present); Inversiones Planina Ca (1987-Present); Inmobiliaria Yacambu, C.A. (1987-Present); CORPORACION ACA NEW (1987-Present); Brown Montgomery Ltd. (2003-2009); Banco Caracas (1998-2001); Corporaci n Leibe CA (1994-2002); Westfalia Investment, Inc. (1990-2003); Cartonera del Caribe CA (1987-2012); Naragansa de Venezuela CA (1987-2012); ACCO Brands Manufacturing (1987-2012); Management Portfolio Financing Advisor, Beracha Group; Management Portfolio Financing Advisor, Financial Institutions; Management Portfolio Financing Advisor, Industrial Corporations; Management Portfolio Financing Advisor, Private Investors **CIV:** Supporter, Sponsor, Many Initiatives in Music and Education **MEM:** Cámara Venezolano Americana de Comercio e Industria; Asociación Venezolana de Ejecutivos; Instituto Venezolano Ejecutivos de Finanzas; Latin America Advisory Board **BA:** Plaza Colon 2 , Planta 15, Torre, Celistics Holdings, Madrid, Spain, 20846 **ADD:** Eden Rock, Cap Cana, Juanillo, Punta Cana, Provincia la Altagracia, Dominican Republic, 23000

BERESNEV, LEONID ALEKSEEVICH, T: Research Physicist **I:** Research **CN:** U.S. Army Research Laboratory **DOB:** 07/19/1947 **PB:** Bogovarovo **SC:** Russia **PT:** Aleksei Fyodorovich Beresnev; Klavdia Arsen'evna Beresneva **MS:** Married **SPN:** Galina Viktorovna Patrusheva (6/28/1980) **CH:** Pavel; Aleksei **ED:** PhD in Solid State Physics, Institute Solid State Physics, Chernogolovka,

Russia (1979); MS in Physics, Moscow Institute of Physics and Technology (1971); BS in Physics, Moscow Institute of Physics and Technology (1968) **CT:** Certified Radiophysics and Electronics **C:** Research Physicist, U.S. Army Research Laboratory (2004-Present); Fellow, American Society for Engineering Education (2000-2004); Contractor, U.S. Naval Research Laboratory (1999-2003); Leading Researcher, A.V. Shubnikov Institute of Crystallography, Russian Academy of Sciences, Moscow, Russia (1988-2003); Senior Researcher, A.V. Shubnikov Institute of Crystallography, Russian Academy of Sciences, Moscow, Russia (1982-1988); Junior Researcher, Organic Intermediates and Dyes Institute, Moscow, Russia (1971-1982) **CR:** Contractor, Technical Research Institute, Sterling VA and Wills Eye Hospital, Philadelphia, PA (2001-2002); Consultant, Beam Engineering for Advanced Measurements Co. (BEAM), Orlando, FL (2000-2002); Fellow, European Research Office (1999); Visiting Researcher, Technical University, Darmstadt, Germany (1993-1998); Visiting Professor, Technical University, Darmstadt, Germany (1992); Visiting Researcher, Technical University, Darmstadt, Germany (1991-1992) **CW:** International Exhibitions, CeBit (1996-1997); Contributor, 145 Articles, Professional Journals **AW:** Achievement Award for Technical Excellence, Department of the Army Research & Development (2013); Grantee, Deutsche Telekom AG, Germany (1993-1998); Grantee, Volkswagen-Stiftung Foundation, Germany (1992-1993); Grantee, W.E. Heraeus-Stiftung Foundation, Germany (1991) **MEM:** SPIE; OSA; Material Research Society; International Liquid Crystal Society; Directed Energy Professional Society **MH:** Albert Nelson Marquis Lifetime Achievement Award (2017) **BA:** 2800 Powder Mill Road, US Army Research Lab, Adelphi, MD, 20783 **ADD:** 10730 Faulkner Ridge Circle, Columbia, MD, 21044

BERGAN, EDMUND P. JR., T: Indendent Consultant **I:** Consulting **DOB:** 05/06/1950 **PB:** New York **SC:** NY/USA **PT:** Edmund Paul Bergan; Alice (Gordon) P. Bergan **MS:** Divorced **CH:** Annabel (Deceased); Caroline **ED:** JD, Fordham University (1975); BA, Holy Cross College, Cum Laude (1971) **C:** Retired, Active Practice (2015); General Counsel, Westford Asset Management LLC, Montreux, Switzerland (2007-2012); Chief Compliance Officer, Westford Asset Management LLC, Montreux, Switzerland (2007-2012); Chief Executive Officer, France Growth Fund Inc., New York, NY (2004); Vice Chairman, France Growth Fund Inc., New York, NY (2004); Senior Vice President, The Reserve, New York, NY (2006-2007); General Counsel, The Reserve, New York, NY (2006-2007); Secretary, The Reserve, New York, NY (2006-2007); Board Directors, The Reserve, New York, NY (2006-2007); Senior Regulatory Counsel, Proskauer Rose LLP, New York, NY (2005-2006); General Counsel, Alliance Fund Services (Now AllianceBernstein Global Investor Services, Inc.), New York, NY (1988-2003); Senior Vice President, Alliance Fund Services (Now AllianceBernstein Global Investor Services, Inc.), New York, NY (1994-2003); General Counsel, Alliance Fund Distributors (Now Alliance Bernstein Investment Research and Management, Inc.), New York, NY (1988-2003); Senior Vice President, Alliance Fund Distributors (Now Alliance Bernstein Investment Research and Management, Inc.), New York, NY (1994-2003); Assistant General Counsel, Alliance Capital Management L.P., New York, NY (1981-1988); Vice President, Alliance Capital Management L.P., New York, NY (1981-1988); Associate General Counsel, Security Industry Association, New York, NY (1977-1981); Vice President, Security Industry Association, New York, NY (1977-1981);

Staff Attorney, U.S. Securities and Exchange Commission, Washington, D.C. (1975-1977) **MEM:** River Run Country Club (2013-Present); Investment Advisers and Companies Committee, ABA (1999-2013); Federal Securities Committee, ABA (1982-2013); Investment Management Committee, Association of the Bar of the City of New York (1999-2009); Closed-End Fund Committee, The Investment Company Institute (1989-2003); Chairman, Closed-End Fund Committee, Investment Company Institute (1992-97); Securities and Exchange Commission Rules Committee, The Investment Company Institute (1986-2003); Various Subcommittees, The Investment Company Institute (1982-2003) **BAR:** New York (2013) **MH:** Albert Nelson Marquis Lifetime Achievement Award (2017) **H:** History **PA:** Independent **RE:** Roman Catholic **ADD:** PO Box 415, Davidson, NC, 28036

BERGER, LEV ISAAC, T: President **I:** Technology **CN:** California Institute of Electronics and Materials Science **DOB:** 06/23/1929 **PB:** Rostov **SC:** USSR **PT:** Isaac Mark and Sara (Poltevsker) Berger **MS:** Married **SPN:** Ninelle Rossine (7/2/1956) **CH:** Yuri **ED:** PhD in Technical Sciences, National University of Science and Technology, Moscow, Russia (1968); PhD in Physics, State University, Minsk, Russia (1959); MS in Physics, State University, Moscow, Russia (1955) **C:** President, California Institute of Electronics and Materials Sciences, Hemet, CA (1981-Present); Lecturer, Physics, University of San Diego (1989-1998); Lecturer Physics, San Diego State University (1981-1989); Senior Scientist, New England Research Center, Sudbury, MA (1979-1981); Professor, Polytechnic Institute, Moscow, Russia (1962-1977); Docent Physics, University of Metallurgy, Moscow, Russia (1960-1962); Physics Lecturer, University of Nonferrous Metals, Moscow, Russia (1956-1960) **CR:** Introscopy Research Institute, Moscow, Russia (1971-1977); Director, Division Institute of Special Purity Substances, Moscow, Russia (1962-1971) **CIV:** Advisory Board Member, CRC Handbook of Chemistry and Physics (2000-Present) **CW:** Author, "Semiconductor Materials" (1997); Author, "Ternary Diamond-like Semiconductors" (1969); Contributor, Articles to Professional Journals **AW:** Grantee, San Diego State University (1983) **MEM:** American Association for the Advancement of Science; Electronics and Thermal Measurements Committee, American Society for Testing and Materials; Executive Board, Society for Advancement of Material and Process Engineering; American Physical Society; American Association for Crystal Growth; Materials Research Society; National Association of Scholars **ADD:** 2115 Flame Tree Way, Hemet, CA, 92545

BERK, PAUL D., T: Internist, Research Scientist, Educator **I:** Education/Educational Services **CN:** Columbia University **DOB:** 04/03/1938 **PB:** Brooklyn **SC:** NY/USA **PT:** Charles Berk; Helen (Goell) Berk **MS:** Married **SPN:** Nicole Polak (1991); Aviva Ancona (7/4/1965, Divorced 8/1990) **CH:** Claire; Philip; Edward; David **ED:** Fellow, Hematology, Columbia-Presbyterian Medical Center, New York City, NY (1969-1970); Resident, Columbia-Presbyterian Medical Center, New York City, NY (1965-1966); Intern, Columbia-Presbyterian Medical Center, New York City, NY (1964-1965); MD, Columbia University, New York City, New York (1964); Honorary BA in Chemistry, Swarthmore College, Swarthmore, PA (1959) **CT:** Diplomate, American Board of Hematology (1972); Diplomate, American Board of Internal Medicine (1971); Qualifying Certificate, American Board of Internal Medicine (1970); Diplomate, National Board of Medical Examiners (1965); Certification, University of St.

Andrews, Scotland (1960) **C:** Professor, Department of Medicine, Columbia University College of Physicians and Surgeons, New York City, NY (2004-Present); Henry and Lillian Stratton Professor of Molecular Medicine, Mount Sinai School of Medicine, New York City, NY (1989-2004); Chief, Division of Liver Disease, Mount Sinai School of Medicine, New York City, NY (1989-2001); Acting Chief, Mount Sinai School of Medicine, New York City, NY (1989-1990); Professor of Biochemistry, Mount Sinai School of Medicine, New York City, NY (1987-1999); Albert and Vera List Professor of Medicine, Mount Sinai School of Medicine, New York City, NY (1980-1989); Professor of Medicine, Mount Sinai School of Medicine, New York City, NY (1977-2004); Chief, Division of Hematology, Mount Sinai School of Medicine, New York City, NY (1977-1989); Clinical Associate Professor, Georgetown University, Washington, D.C. (1975-1977); Chief, Section on Diseases of the Liver, National Institute Arthritis, Metabolism and Digestive Diseases, National Institutes of Health, Bethesda, MD (1973-1977); Clinical Assistant Professor of Medicine, Georgetown University, Washington, D.C. (1971-1975); Senior Investigator, National Cancer Institute, Bethesda, MD (1970-1973); Clinical Associate, Metabolism Branch, National Cancer Institute, Bethesda, MD (1966-1969) **CR:** Professor, Biochemistry and Molecular Biology, Mount Sinai School Medicine (1999-2004); Member, Advisory Council, National Institute of Diabetes and Digestive and Kidney Diseases (1990-1994); Adjunct Professor, Rockefeller University (1987-1989); Consultant in Liver Disease, National Institutes of Health (1977-1980) **CIV:** Senior Surgeon, United States Public Health Service (1975-1977, 1966-1969) **MIL:** Commissioned Officer, U.S. Public Health Service (1975-1977, 1966-1969) **CW:** Editor-in-Chief, Seminars in Liver Disease (1996-Present); Contributing Editor, "Polcythemia Vera" (1994); Contributing Editor, "Hepatic Transport and Bile Secretion" (1993); Contributing Editor, "Hans Popper: A Tribute" (1992); Editor-in-Chief, "Hepatology" (1991-1996); Contributing Editor, "Myelofibrosis and the Biology of Connective Tissue" (1984); Editor-in-Chief, Seminars in Liver Disease (1981-1990); Contributing Editor, "Frontiers in Liver Disease" (1981); Member, Editorial Board, "Liver" (1980-1993); Member, Editorial Board, "Artificial Organs" (1979-1992); Contributing Editor, "Chemistry and Physiology of the Bile Pigments" (1977); Contributor, Articles, Professional Journals **AW:** George Jamieson Humanitarian Award, American Liver Foundation (2004); Distinguished Service Award, American Association for the Study of Liver Disease (2003); Special Award, Columbia University College of Physicians and Surgeon (1992); Merck Award, Columbia University College of Physicians and Surgeon (1964); Mosby Book Award, Columbia University College of Physicians and Surgeons (1963); Fulbright Scholar, Department of Applied Mathematics, University of St. Andrews, Scotland (1959-1960); Ivy Medal, Swarthmore College (1959); Honorable Mention, Westinghouse Scientific Talent Search (1955); Columbia University College of Physician and Surgeons; George Jamieson Humanitarian Award **MEM:** Chairman, Board of Directors, American Liver Foundation (2000-2004); Councilor, Society for Experimental Biological Medicine (1993-1996); President, American Association Study of Liver Disease (1989); Councilor, International Association Study of Liver (1988-1991); Vice President, American Association Study of Liver Disease (1988); Councilor, American Association Study of Liver Disease (1985-1993); President, New York Society Study of Blood (1982-1983); Vice Chairman, National Polycythemia Vera Study Group (1978-1995); Sigma Xi; Phi Beta Kappa; Alpha Omega Alpha; American Physiology Society;

American Society for Clinical Investigation; Association of American Physicians; Fellow, American College of Physicians; Fellow, American College of Gastroenterology; American Society for Hematology; American Clinical and Climatological Association; Fellow, The Obesity Society; Research Society on Alcohol; The Harvey Society **MH:** Albert Nelson Marquis Lifetime Achievement Award (2017) **ADD:** 2500 Johnson Ave Apt 6N, Bronx, NY, 10463

BERNARD, ALEXANDER, T: Protective Services Official **I:** Other **DOB:** 04/23/1952 **PB:** Los Angeles **SC:** CA/USA **PT:** Louis Bernard; Hannah (Bergman) Bernard **MS:** Married **SPN:** Diana LoRee Winstead (12/17/1976) **CH:** Michael Alexander; Andrew Alexander **ED:** BS, California State University, Los Angeles, Summa Cum Laude (1989); AA, Los Angeles Valley College (1976) **C:** General Manager, Kern Law Enforcement Association (2003-2012); Sergeant, Police Services Division, Los Angeles World Airports (1995-2003); Police Officer, Los Angeles World Airports (1979-1995); Parking Meter Collector, Office of the City Clerk, City of Los Angeles (1973-1979) **CR:** Chairman, Commission on Peace Officer Standards and Training, State of California (2002, 2007-Present); Advisory Committee Member, Commission on Peace Officer Standards & Training, State of California (1999-2004); Vice Chairman, Commission on Peace Officer Standards and Training, State of California (2001) **CIV:** Active Member, Boy Scouts of America **CW:** Contributor, Articles, Professional Journals **MEM:** Lodge President, Fraternal Order of Police (2010-Present); State Trustee, Fraternal Order of Police (2010-Present); President, RPOAC (2006-Present); Board of Directors, RPOAC (2005-Present); State Board Director, PORAC (2006-2008); Vice President, Los Angeles Airport Police Supervisors Association (2003); State Board of Directors, PORAC (1984-1985, 1987-2003); President, Los Angeles Airport Police Supervisors Association (1999-2003); Secretary, PORAC (1999-2003); Vice President, Los Angeles Airport Police Supervisors Association (1997-1998); Executive Committee, PORAC (1994-2003); President, Los Angeles Airport Peace Officers Association (1994-1995); Ethnic Relations Committee, PORAC (1993-1994); Board of Directors, Los Angeles Airport Peace Officers Association (1992-1994); Chapter President, PORAC (1982-1987); Los Angeles Airport Peace Officers Association (1981-1989); NRA; Board of Directors, Los Angeles Airport Police Supervisors Association; California Peace Officers Association; Labor and Employment Relations Association; Lifetime Member, Law Enforcement Alliance of America; International Police Association; Lifetime Member, California Rifle and Pistol Association; Lifetime Member, Golden Key International Honor Society; Lifetime Member, The Honor Society of Phi Kappa Phi; Advisory Committee, Peace Officers Standards and Training **MH:** Albert Nelson Marquis Lifetime Achievement Award (2017) **H:** Travel; Collecting records **PA:** Republican **ADD:** 528 E Jenner St, Lancaster, CA, 93535

BERRYMAN, JAMES GARLAND, T: Physics/Geophysics Researcher, Applied Mathematics Researcher **I:** Sciences **CN:** Lawrence Berkeley National Laboratory **DOB:** 06/26/1947 **PB:** Hutchinson **SC:** KS/USA **PT:** Garland Hardesty Berryman; Alice Lucile (Pratt) Berryman **MS:** Married **SPN:** Marcia Ann Griffin (8/4/1973) **CH:** Rachel Lynne; Martin Andrew **ED:** Postdoctoral Appointment, University of Wisconsin, Madison (1975-1976); PhD in Condensed Matter Physics, University of Wisconsin-Madison (1975); MS in Physics, University of Wisconsin-Madison (1970); BA in Mathematics, The University of Kansas,

Lawrence, KS (1969); BS in Physics, The University of Kansas, Lawrence, KS (1969) **C:** Geological Senior Scientist, Lawrence Berkeley National Laboratory, Berkeley, CA (2006-Present); Physicist, Lawrence Livermore National Laboratory, Livermore, CA (1981-2006); Technical Staff, ATT Bell Telephone Laboratories, Whippany, NJ (1978-1981); National Science Foundation Fellow, Courant Institute, New York University (1977-1978); Research Geophysicist, Continental Oil Co., Ponca City, OK (1976-1977) **CR:** Fellow, Institute of Physics (2004) **CW:** Editorial Board, "International Journal of Engineering Science" (2007); Advisory Board, "International Journal for Numerical and Analytical Methods in Geomechanics" (2005); Editorial Board, Inverse Problems (2003-2006); Associate Editor, "Transactions on Geoscience and Remote Sensing," IEEE (1984); Associate Editor, "Journal of Mathematical Physics" (1979-1981); Contributor, Over 150 Articles, Professional Journals; Author, Numerous Conference Proceeding Paper; Author, Numerous Company Internal Reports **AW:** Outstanding Referee, American Physical Society (2008); Outstanding Referee, Society of Exploration Geophysicists (2007); Maurice A. Biot Medal for Contributions in Poromechanics, American Society of Civil Engineers (2005) **MEM:** Society of Exploration Geophysicists; American Geophysical Union; Acoustical Society of America; American Physical Society **MH:** Albert Nelson Marquis Lifetime Achievement Award (2017) **ADD:** 119 Siena Place, Danville, CA, 94506

BERSIN, RUTH HARGRAVE, T: Executive Director **I:** Religious **CN:** Refugee Immigration Ministry **DOB:** 09/16/1939 **PB:** LaPorte **SC:** IN/USA **PT:** Jacob Harold Hargrave; Rowena Adeline (Hullett) Hargrave **MS:** Widowed **SPN:** Richard Lewis Bersin (Deceased) **CH:** Jacob David Antonio; Rebekah Bersin-Funes **ED:** PhD, Graduate Theological Foundation (2008); PhD of Ministries, Graduate Theological Foundation (1994); MDiv, Yale Divinity School (1982); MA in Religion, Colgate Rochester Crozer Divinity School (1965); EdB, Indiana University (1962) **CT:** Fellow, American Association of Pastoral Counselors (2016); Ordained Priest (1984); Certificate, Association of Trauma Stress Specialists; Certified Fundraising Executive, National Society of Fund Raising Executives (Now Association of Fundraising Professionals) **C:** Priest Associate, Trinity Topsfield (1999-Present); Executive Director, Refugee Immigration Ministry (1998-Present); Pastoral Psychotherapist, New England Pastoral Institute (2004-2016); Pastoral Psychotherapist, Greater Lowell Pastoral Counseling Center (1997-2004); Director, The Trauma Center, Brookline, MA (1996-1999); Associate Priest, Grace Episcopal Church, Lawrence, MA (1996-1999); Priest, St. Monica and St. James, Capitol Hill, Washington, DC (1995-1996); Assistant Priest, Church of the Good Shepherd, Burke, VA (1994); Assistant Director, InterFaith Conference of Metropolitan Washington (1992-1993); Executive Director, TELL Japan (1989-1992); Director, Special Projects, Episcopal Social Services, Bridgeport, CT (1987-1989); Priest, St Luke's Church, Bridgeport, CT (1985-1989); Priest, St. Peter's Episcopal Church, Cheshire, CT (1983-1985); Refugees Services Coordinator, Episcopal Social Services, Bridgeport, CT (1982-1987); Director, Educational Development Center, Commodore, Japan (1972-1975) **CR:** New England Pastoral Institute (2004-2015); National Director, Interfaith Spiritual Care Givers (2002-2004); Episcopal Diocese of Massachusetts (1996-2004); Chaplain, Washington National Cathedral (1995-1996); Chairman, Task Force on Violence Against Women, Episcopal Diocese of Washington (1995-

1996); Episcopal Diocese of Washington (1995); Episcopal Congregation, United States Naval Base, Yokosuka, Japan (1989-1992); Ecumenical Commission Diocese of Connecticut (1984-1989) **CIV:** Board of Directors, Peace at Home (2003-2004); Wider Mission Commission Diocese of Massachusetts (2001-2004); Leader, NOVA Trauma Team, Oklahoma City, OK (1995); Refugee Welfare Committee, Church World Service (1986); Refugee Advisory Council, Connecticut (1984-1989); Board of Directors, Women's Crisis Center, Norwalk, CT (1980-1983); National Coalition Against Sexual Assault; Massachusetts Immigrant and Refugee Advocacy Coalition; Boston Theological Institute Working Group on Restorative Justice; Women's Crisis Committee Diocese of Massachusetts; Task Force on Domestic Violence, Lowell, MA; Strategy and Action Committee, Massachusetts Council of Churches; Democratic Town Committee, Boxford, MA **CW:** Author, "Let's Bergin" (1974); Author, "English Through Folk Songs," (1974); Author, "Theological Literacy in the Twenty First Century"; Author, "Healing Traumatic Memories: A Spiritual Journey"; Author, "Outside the Gates," BTI **AW:** Humanitarian Award, School of Theology, Boston University (2007) **MEM:** Board of Directors, Association of Refugee Service Providers (2010-Present); American Association of Pastoral Counselors; Certificate, Association of Trauma Stress Specialists; International Society for Traumatic Stress Studies; National Society of Fund Raising Executives (Now Association of Fundraising Professionals); The Assembly of Episcopal Chaplains; Chair, National Committee, Certification Standards **MH:** Albert Nelson Marquis Lifetime Achievement Award (2017) **H:** Music; Swimming; Reading; Gourmet cooking **PA:** Democrat **RE:** Episcopalian **BA:** 6 Pleasant Street, Suite 612, Refugee Immigration Ministry, Malden, MA, 02148 **ADD:** 4 Holmes Road, Boxford, MA, 01921 **URL:** http://www.r-i-m.net

BESHEER, NORMAN O., T: Chief Executive Officer, Chairman **I:** Business Management/Business Services **CN:** Gunter Pest Management **DOB:** 12/21/1928 **PB:** Independence **SC:** MO/USA **PT:** Grace Malinda (White) Besheer; Royal Pleasant Besheer **MS:** Married **SPN:** Patricia Ann Gunter (6/25/1949) **CH:** Kimbrough A. Besheer; Christie E. Besheer Biggs; Jay G. Besheer; Zachary N. Besheer **ED:** JD, University of Missouri-Kansas City (1955); BA in History and Government, University of Missouri-Kansas City (1953) **C:** Chairman of the Board, Gunter Pest Management (1998-Present); Chief Executive Officer, President, Treasurer, Gunter Exterminating Company (Now Gunter Pest Management) (1979-1998); Vice President, General Counsel, Gunter Exterminating Company (Now Gunter Pest Management) (1971-1979); Counsel, The Gas Service Company (Now Heritage Propane); Assistant Secretary, The Gas Service Company (Now Heritage Propane); Corporate Secretary, North Penn Gas Company, Port Allegany, PA; Counsel, North Penn Gas Company, Port Allegany, PA; Counsel, Kansas City Life Insurance Company; Associate, Swanson Midgley LLC; Associate, Langworthy, Matz & Linde; Investigator, Kansas City Public Service Company (Now Kansas City Area Transportation Authority) **CIV:** Chancel Choir, Broadway United Methodist Church (Now Keystone United Methodist Church); Chairman of Trustees, Broadway United Methodist Church (Now Keystone United Methodist Church); Chairman, Stewardship & Finance Committee, Broadway United Methodist Church (Now Keystone United Methodist Church); Lay Member to United Methodist Church Annual Conference, Broadway United Methodist Church (Now Keystone United Methodist Church); Member,

Various Committees, Broadway United Methodist Church (Now Keystone United Methodist Church) **MIL:** Commissioned Major, U.S. Marine Corps (1968-1982); U.S. Marine Corps (1946-1948); Honorary Plank Owner, U.S.S. Missouri (SSN-780) Nuclear Attack Submarine; Honorary Plank Owner, U.S.S. Harry S. Truman (CVN-75) Aircraft Carrier **CW:** Contributor, Missouri Bar Journal (1960); Contributor, Kansas City Law Review (1954) **AW:** World War II Victory Medal; China Service Medal; Japanese Occupation Medal; Asiatic-Pacific Campaign Medal; Organized Marine Corp Reserve Medal; Honoree, DeMolay Legion of Honor, DeMolay International; Man of the Year Award, Missouri Pest Management Association; Man of the Year Award, Kansas Pest Control Association **MEM:** Kansas City Metropolitan Bar Association; Lawyers Association of Kansas City; Past Dean, DeMolay International; Mother Preceptory, DeMolay International; Past President, Greater Kansas City Council, Navy League of the United States; National Director, Central Midwest Area, Navy League of the United States; President, Central Midwest Area, Navy League of the United States; Past President, WABA; Board Member, WABA; Past President, Friends of Sacred Structures; Board Member, Friends of Sacred Structures; Past President, U.S.S. Atlanta Reunion Association; Past President, Missouri Pest Management Association; Board member Missouri Pest Management Association; Past President, Kansas Pest Control Association; Honorary Life Member, Kansas Pest Control Association; Past President, Pest Management Association of Greater Kansas City; Past National Vice President, National Pest Management Association; Regional Vice President, National Pest Management Association Pestworld; Director, National Pest Management Association Pestworld; Blue Lodge, Masons, Port Allegany, PA; York Rite Freemasonry; Ararat Shrine Temple; Board of Directors, Secretary, Vice President, President, The Native Sons and Daughters of Greater Kansas City; Alexander Majors Chapter, Sons of the American Revolution; Lifetime Member, United States Marine Corps Reserve Officers Association; Marine Corps Mustang Association; Advisory Committee, Country Club Right of Way; Steering Committee, Kansas City Light Rail Implementation; Board of Directors, Better Business Bureau of Greater Kansas City; Vice President, Alumni Association, University of Missouri-Kansas City; Board Member, Alumni Association, University of Missouri-Kansas City; Vice President, Law Alumni Association, University of Missouri-Kansas City; Board Member, Law Alumni Association, University of Missouri-Kansas City; Founding Member, Law Foundation, School of Law, University of Missouri-Kansas City; Lifetime Member, Boy Scouts of America; Honorary Warrior, Mic-O-Say Tribe, Boy Scouts of America; The International Legal Honor Society of Phi Delta; Tau Kappa Epsilon; Pi Chi Omega; Honorary Admiral, Missouri Navy; Honorary Colonel, Commonwealth of Kentucky **BAR:** Pennsylvania (1965); Missouri (1955) **H:** Travel; Participating in historic organizations; Reading historic novels; Reading biographies of American presidents; Watching old movies; Studying foreign languages **PA:** Republican **RE:** Methodist **BA:** 220 W 72nd Street, Gunter Pest Management, Inc, Kansas City, MO, 64114

BEST, FRANKLIN JR., T: VP General Counsel, Insurance Operations and Corporate Secretary **I:** Law and Legal Services **CN:** Penn Mutual Life Insurance Company **DOB:** 12/14/1945 **PB:** Lock Haven **SC:** PA/USA **PT:** Franklin L.; Hazel M. (Yearick) **MS:** Married **SPN:** Kimberly R. (5/1/1982) **ED:** Postgraduate Coursework,

Columbia University (1994); JD, University of Pennsylvania (1970); BA, Yale University (1967) **C:** Vice President, General Counsel, Insurance Operations, Corporate Secretary, Penn Mutual Life Insurance Co. (2011-Present); Counsel, Secretary, Penn Insurance and Annuity Co., Philadelphia, PA (1996-Present); Managing Corporate Counsel, Penn Mutual Life Insurance Co., Philadelphia, PA (1999-2011); Counsel, Assistant Secretary, Penn Insurance and Annuity Co., Philadelphia, PA (1983-1996); Assistant General Counsel, Penn Mutual Life Insurance Co., Philadelphia, PA (1978-1999); Assistant Counsel, Penn Mutual Life Insurance Co., Philadelphia, PA (1974-1977); Associate, MacCoy, Evans & Lewis, Philadelphia, PA (1970-1974) **CR:** Lecturer, Pennsylvania Bar Institute (1976-1984) **CIV:** West Pikeland Township Open Spaces Committee (1987-1999); Board of Directors, Center City South Neighborhood Association (1979-1980); President, Center City South Neighborhood Association (1978-1979); Member, Committee of Seventy (1978-1984); Secretary, Washington Square Association (1977-1987) **CW:** Co-author, "Life and Health Insurance Law" (2008); Author, "Pennsylvania Insurance Law" (1991); Contributor, Articles, Professional Journals **MEM:** Executive Committee, International Claim Association (1995-Present); Treasurer, International Claim Association (2005-2010); President, International Claim Association (2002-2003); Secretary, International Claim Association (1995-2000); Executive Committee, International Claim Association (1979-1981, 1985-1988); American Bar Association; Philadelphia Bar Association; International Claim Association; Chair, The Defense Research Institute; Yale Club of Philadelphia **BAR:** Pennsylvania Bar (1970) **MH:** Albert Nelson Marquis Lifetime Achievement Award (2017) **ADD:** 1179 Dunsinane Hl, Chester Springs, PA, 19425

BETTS, BARBARA LANG, T: Lawyer, Real Estate Agent, Rancher **I:** Law and Legal Services **CN:** The Hayes Law Firm **DOB:** 04/28/1926 **PB:** Anaheim **SC:** CA/USA **PT:** W. Harold Lang; Helen (Thompson) Lang **MS:** Married **SPN:** Bert A. Betts (7/11/1962); Roby F. Hayes (7/22/1948, Deceased) **CH:** John Chauncey, IV; Frederick Prescott; Roby Francis, II **ED:** LLB, Balboa University (Now Alliant International University) (1951); BA, Stanford University, Magna Cum Laude (1948) **C:** Of Counsel, The Hayes Law Firm (2004-Present); Private Practice, Sacramento, CA (1962-Present); Private Practice, San Diego, CA (1960-Present); Private Practice, Oceanside, CA (1952-1968) **CR:** Secretary, International Production Associates, Inc. (1968-Present); Member, Steering & Development Committee, Metro Air Park (1989-2004); Margaret M. McCabe, M.D., Inc. (1977-1978); Vice President, Isle & Oceans Marinas, Inc. (1970-1980); Vice President, W.H. Lang Corp. (1964-1969); City Attorney, Carlsbad, CA (1959-1963); Partner, Roby F. Hayes & Barbara Lang Hayes (1952-1960) **CIV:** Co-chairman, California Democratic State Central Committee (1960-1962); Co-chairman, 28th Congressional District Alternate Delegate, DNC (1960); Vice Chairman, City of Carlsbad Planning Commission (1959); Member, City of San Diego Planning Commission (1959); Member, California Democratic State Central Committee (1958-1966); Vice President, Oceanside Diamond Jubilee Committee (1958); President, Oceanside-Carlsbad Junior Chambrettes (1955-1956); Candidate, California State Assembly, 77th Assembly District (1954); Chairman, Traveler's Aid International (1952-1953); Co-sponsor, All American B-24 Liberator, The Collings Foundation **CW:** Co-author, "A Citizen Answers" **AW:** Named To Fullerton Union High School Wall Of Fame (1986); Block

S Award, Stanford University; Certificate of Appreciation, California Supreme Court and The State Bar of California **MEM:** Regent, Oceanside Chapter, National Society Daughters of the American Revolution (1960-1961); Local President, AAUW (1959-1960); Legislative Committee, AAUW (1958-1959); Assistant State Legislative Chairman, AAUW (1958-1959); President, Soroptimist International, Oceanside-Carlsbad (1958-1959); President, President's Council, Mexico (1958-1959); Chairman, South District Legislation, Business Professional Women's Foundation (1958-1959); Vice President, Oceanside Chamber of Commerce (1958); Director, Oceanside Chamber of Commerce (1957-1959); Secretary, Oceanside Chamber of Commerce (1957); Secretary of Public Affairs, San Diego and Imperial Counties (1954); Director, Oceanside Chamber of Commerce (1953-1954); President, President's Council, San Diego and Imperial Counties; ABA; American Judicature Society; National Rifle Association of America; International Municipal Lawyers Association; The State Bar of California; San Diego County Bar Association; Second Air Division, Eighth Air Force, Heritage League; National Trust for Historic Preservation; Secretary-Treasurer, North San Diego County Association Chamber of Commerce; San Diego Regional Chamber of Commerce; San Diego History Society; Fullerton Junior Assistance League; Life Member, California Scholarship Federation; Loyola Guild of Jesuit High School; Barrister, Stanford; Barrister, Sacramento; Associate, The Distinguished Flying Cross Society; Stanford Mothers; The Phi Beta Kappa Society; The Heritage Foundation **MH:** Albert Nelson Marquis Lifetime Achievement Award (2017) **ADD:** 1830 Avenida Del Mundo Unit 1609, Coronado, CA, 92118

BETTS, DOROTHY ANNE, I: Education/Educational Services **DOB:** 11/03/1946 **PB:** Washington **SC:** DC/USA **PT:** Thomas Joseph Salb; Elizabeth Anne (McGee) Salb **MS:** Married **SPN:** Jerold Le-Roy Betts (6/14/1975) **CH:** Ellen Marie; Matthew Connor (Grandson) **ED:** MA in Education, The University of New Mexico (1976); BS in Elementary Education, The University of New Mexico (1968) **CT:** Certified Teacher, States of New Mexico, Colorado **C:** Preschool Paraprofessional Cortez, CO (2006-2009); Teacher, Albuquerque Public Schools (1999-2004); Educational Assistant, Albuquerque Public Schools (1993-1999); Teacher, Albuquerque Public Schools (1980-1984); Teacher, Albuquerque Public Schools (1969-1979); Teacher, Gustine Unified School District, California (1968-1969); Co-Owner, Stork News New Mexico **CIV:** Coordinator, Pennies for Patients, Zuni Elementary School, Leukemia & Lymphoma Society (2001); Volunteer, Our Lady of Victory Church, Dolores, CO; Volunteer, Saint Margaret Mary Church, Cortez, CO; Volunteer, Dolores Schools, Dolores, CO **MEM:** Vice President, DKGSI (2000-2002); President, DKGSI (1984-1986); Vice President, DKGSI (1982-1984) **H:** Travel; Spending time and doing things with family, friends, and pets; Crafts; Playing board games **RE:** Roman Catholic **BA:** PO Box 1646, Dolores, CO, 81323

BEUTLER, LARRY E., T: Distinguished Professor Emeritus **I:** Education/Educational Services **CN:** Palo Alto University **DOB:** 02/14/1941 **PB:** Logan **SC:** UT/USA **PT:** Edward Beutler; Beulah (Andrus) Beutler **MS:** Married **SPN:** Jamie Lynn Beutler (2004) **CH:** Jana; Kelly; Ian David; Gail **ED:** PhD, University of Nebraska, Lincoln (1970); MS, Utah State University (1966); BS, Utah State University (1965) **CT:** License to Practice Psychology, State of California (1991-2009); Diplomate, American Board of Medical Psychotherapists (1984-2000); License to Practice Psychology, State of Arizo-

na (1979-1991); License to Practice Psychology, State of Texas (1971-1990); Licensed Practicing Psychologist, State of North Carolina (1971-1979); Certified North Carolina School Psychologist (1971-1973); Diplomate, American Board of Professional Psychology **C:** Retired (2016); Distinguished Professor Emeritus, Palo Alto University (2013); Consulting Professor Emeritus, Psychiatry and Behavioral Sciences, Stanford University School of Medicine, (2002-2013); Distinguished Professor, Clinical Psychology, William McInnes Chair, Palo Alto University (2002-2013); Professor Emeritus, University of California, Santa Barbara (2002); Professor, University of California, Santa Barbara (1990-2002); Professor, The University of Arizona, Tucson, AZ (1979-1990); Associate Professor, Baylor College of Medicine, Houston, TX (1973-1979); Assistant Professor, Stephen F. Austin State University, Nacogdoches, TX (1971-1973); Assistant Professor, Medical Psychology, Duke University, Asheville, NC (1970-1971) **CR:** Associate Editor, Advances in Psychotherapy: Evidence Based Practices (2005-Present); Scientific Advisory Board, John Wiley and Sons, Inc. (2000-2011); Editor, Journal of Clinical Psychology (1991-2005); Editor, Journal of Consulting and Clinical Psychology (1991-1996); Associate Editor, Journal of Consulting and Clinical Psychology (1985-1991) **CIV:** Member, Center for Violence Through Relationships; Volunteer, Community Health Centers **AW:** Distinguished Service Award, Division 52, American Psychological Association (2016); Distinguished Contributions Award (2015); Award for Contributions to Minority Education, Division 53, American Psychological Association (2015); Eponym, Larry E. Beutler Award for Excellence in Clinical Psychology, Palo Alto University/Pacific Graduate School of Psychology (2008); Honors Award, Minho University, Braga, Portugal (2008); Distinguished Scientific Contributions Award, American Psychological Association, Society for Clinical Psychology (2007); Certificate of Appreciation to the Palo Alto Medical Reserve Corps, Palo Alto City Council (2006); Career Achievement Award, Society of Clinical Psychology (2004); Jerome Fisher Memorial Award, University of California, San Francisco, CA (2003); American Psychological Association Presidential Citation (2002); Distinguished Research in Psychology, University of California, Santa Barbara (2002); Distinguished Research Award, California Psychological Association (2001); Distinguished Research Award, Society for Psychotherapy Research (2000); Gold Medal Award and Rosalee G. Weiss Award and Memorial Lecture, American Psychological Foundation (1999); Certificate of Meritorious Service, Division of Clinical Psychology, American Psychological Association (1998); Visiting Scholar Award, Gaspar de Portola' Catalan Studies Program (1992); Award for Distinguished Contributions to the Profession of Psychology, Arizona Psychological Association (1990); Research Award, Association for Specialists in Group Work (1987-1988); Award for Academic Contribution to Psychology, Arizona Psychological Association (1987); Meritorious Service Award, Arizona State Psychological Association (1985-1986); Recognition of Merit, Journal of Consulting and Clinical Psychology (1984); Contributor, Articles, Professional Journals; Reviewer, Books; Contributor, Chapters, Books **MEM:** Founding Member, Animals and Society (2005-Present); Fellow, Academy of Clinical Psychology (1994-Present); Fellow, American Psychological Society (1992-Present); President, Division 12, American Psychological Association (2002); Fellow, President-Elect, Division 12, American Psychological Association (2001); President, Division 29, American Psychological Association (1997); Fellow, President-Elect, Division 29, American Psychological Association (1996);

Past President, Society for Psychotherapy Research (1988-1989); President, Arizona Group Psychotherapy Society (1987-1988); President, Society for Psychotherapy Research (1986-1988); President-Elect, Arizona Group Psychotherapy Society (1986-1987); American Group Psychotherapy Association (1985-1992); Executive Board, Association of Medical School Professors of Psychology (1985-1987); President-Elect, Society for Psychotherapy Research (1985-1986); American Association for the Advancement of Science (1981-2000); Southern Arizona Psychological Association (1979-1990); Arizona State Psychological Association (1979-1990); President, Division 12, Section 2, American Psychological Association (1979); Fellow, International Academy of Eclectic Psychotherapists; Society for the Exploration of Psychotherapy Integration **MH:** Albert Nelson Marquis Lifetime Achievement Award (2017) **H:** Horseback riding; Equine therapy **PA:** Democrat **ADD:** 2620 Piedra Verde Ct, Placerville, CA, 95667 **URL:** https://en.wikipedia.org/wiki/Larry_E._Beutler

BHADURI, MOINAK, T: PhD Candidate in Mathematical Sciences, Graduate Student Researcher **I:** Sciences **CN:** University of Nevada, Las Vegas **ED:** BSc in Statistics, St. Xavier's College, Kolkata, India (2010); Pursuing PhD in Statistics, University of Nevada, Las Vegas **CT:** Mentorship Certification, Graduate College, University of Nevada, Las Vegas (2017); Rebel Research and Mentorship Certification, Graduate College, University of Nevada, Las Vegas (2017) **CR:** PhD Candidate in Mathematical Sciences, University of Nevada, Las Vegas (2012-Present); Instructor, University of Nevada, Las Vegas (2012-Present); Postgraduate Position, Specialization in Mathematical Statistics and Probability, Indian Statistical Institute, Kolkata, India (2011-2012) **CW:** Contributor, Articles to Academic Journals; Presentations, Scientific Conferences and Workshops **AW:** Wolzinger Family Research Scholarship, The Wolzinger Family, College of Sciences, University of Nevada, Las Vegas (2016) **MEM:** Student Member, American Statistical Association; Statistical Society in London; Institute of Mathematical Statistics; Bernouli Society for Mathematical Statistics and Probability **H:** Writing; Reading; Hiking; Freelance writing **ADD:** 1450 E Harmon Ave Apt 216B, Las Vegas, NV, 89119

BHATTACHARYA, RABI, T: Professor of Mathematics **I:** Education/Educational Services **CN:** University of Arizona **DOB:** 01/11/1937 **PT:** Hrishikesh Bhattacharya; Sailabala Bhattacharya **MS:** Married **SPN:** Bithika Banerjee (11/11/1967) **CH:** Urmi; Deepta **ED:** PhD in Statistics, University of Chicago (1967); MS in Statistics, University of Calcutta, India **C:** Professor of Mathematics, University of Arizona (2002-Present); Professor of Mathematics, Indiana University, Bloomington, IN (1982-2002); Associate Professor of Mathematics, University of Arizona (1972-1982); Assistant Professor of Statistics, University of California, Berkeley (1967-1972) **CR:** Guggenheim Fellowship, John Simon Guggenheim Memorial Foundation (2000); Fellow, Institute of Mathematical Statistics **CW:** Contributor, "Contemporary Mathematicians," Berkhauser (2016); Co-Author, "A Course in Mathematical Statistics and Large Sample Theory (2016); Co-Author, "Nonparametric Inference on Manifolds" (2012); Associate Editor, "Sankhya" (2008-2011); Co-Author, "Random Dynamical Systems" (2007); Co-Author, "A Basic Course in Probability Theory" (2007); Associate Editor, "The Annals of Applied Probability" (2006-2009); Associate Editor, "Statistica Sinica" (2002-2008); Associate Editor, "The Annals of Probability" (2000-2002); Co-Author, "Stochastic Processes with Applications" (1990); Co-Author,

"Asymptotic Statistics" (1990); Associate Editor, "Econometric Theory" (1985-1999); Associate Editor, "The Journal of Multivariate Analysis" (1985-1992); Associate Editor, "The Journal of Statistical Planning and Inference" (1984-1988); Associate Editor, "The Annals of Probability" (1976-1981); Co-Author, "Normal Approximation and Asymptotic Expansions" (1976); Contributor, Research Articles, Professional Journals **AW:** Alexander von Humboldt Forschungs Prize (1993-1994) **MEM:** American Mathematical Society; Institute of Mathematical Statistics **MH:** Albert Nelson Marquis Lifetime Achievement Award (2017) **ADD:** 4901 N Fort Verde Trail, Tucson, AZ, 85750

BIRD, WENDELL R., T: Senior Partner **I:** Law and Legal Services **CN:** Bird, Loechl, Brittain & McCants **PT:** Raleigh Milton Bird; R. Jean Bird **MS:** Married **SPN:** Julie Worthington **ED:** DPhil, University of Oxford (2012); JD, Yale Law School (1978); BA, Vanderbilt University, Summa Cum Laude (1975) **C:** Senior Partner, Bird, Loechl, Brittain & McCants, Atlanta, GA (1986-Present); Law Clerk to Judge, United States Court of Appeals, Fifth Circuit, Birmingham, AL (1979-1980); Law Clerk to Judge, United States Court of Appeals, Fourth Circuit, Durham, NC (1978-1979) **CR:** Lecturer, Washington Non-Profit Tax Conference (1982-Present); Adjunct Professor, Emory University School of Law, Atlanta, GA (1985-1990) **CW:** Author, "Press and Speech Under Assault," Oxford University Press (2016); Co-Author, "Federal and State Taxation of Exempt Organizations" (1994); Co-Author, "CCH Federal Tax Service" (1988-2000); Editorial Board, "The Yale Law Journal" (1977-1978); Contributor, Articles, Professional Journals **AW:** Visiting Scholar, Emory University School of Law (2012-Present); Egger Prize, Yale Law School (1978) **MEM:** Life Member, American Law Institute; American Bar Foundation; Co-Chairman, Subcommittee on Charitable Contributions, ABA (2002-Present); Litigation, ABA; Taxation Section, ABA; Committee on Exempt Organizations, ABA; Past Chairman, Subcommittee on Religious Organizations, ABA; Past Chairman, Subcommittee on State and Local Taxes, ABA **BA:** 1150 Monarch Plaza, 3414 Peachtree Road, Bird, Loechl, Brittain & McCants, Atlanta, GA, 30326 **ADD:** 3414 Peachtree Rd NE Ste 1150, Bird, Loechl, Brittain & McCants, Atlanta, GA, 30326

BJORKMAN, SYLVIA JOHNSON, T: School Psychologist, (Currently Part- Time, Retired) **I:** Medicine & Health Care **CN:** Pitt County Schools, Greenville NC **SC:** North Carolina **PT:** William A and Alice W Johnson, Fairmont, NC **MS:** Married **SPN:** Dr. David R Bjorkman **CH:** William Eric and John David **ED:** MS, CAS School Psychology East Carolina University 1984; Administration (1993); MA Education UNC Chapel Hill (1979); BA Psychology UNC-Greensboro, Magna Cum Laude (1976) **CT:** Licensed Psychological Associate, Health Care Services Provider, School Psychologist II, Curriculum Instructional Specialist **C:** Part-Time School Psychologist, Pitt County Schools (2015-Present); School Psychologist, Pitt County Schools (1984-2014); Student Services Coordinator, Section 504, Teacher Assistance/Intervention Teams and NC SIP Math Improvement Grant, Pitt County Schools (2008-2014) **CR:** Part Time Private practice, East Carolina Behavioral Specialists (2004-2005); Contracted Consultant, Infohandler Corporation, Durham, NC (2015-2018) **CIV:** Friends of Photography, Greenville Museum of Art (2014-Present); Political Committee Member, Cypress Group, Sierra Club (2017-2018); Secretary, Greenville Museum of Art (2018); Executive Committee Member, Cypress Group, Sierra Club (2014-2016); Eucharistic Minister,

St. Paul's Episcopal Church, Greenville, NC **CW:** Presenter, National Conferences on School-Based Wraparound (1996-2014); Local Staff Development Facilitator, School Crisis Intervention (1996-2014); Author, "Environmental Ratings and Children's Social Behavior: Implications for the Assessment of Day Care Quality," American Journal of Orthopsychiatry (1986); Author, "Influence of Day Care on Social Behavior in Kindergarten," American Journal of Orthopsychiatry; Presenter, AHEC, NCDPI Conferences **AW:** Delta Kappa Honorary Sorority in Education (2014-Present); NC School Psychologist Innovative Practice Award, North Carolina School Psychology Association (NCSPA) (2010) **MEM:** North Carolina School Psychologist Association, Sierra Club, Delta Kappa Honorary Sorority **MH:** Albert Nelson Marquis Lifetime Achievement Award (2017) **H:** Music; Playing guitar in a Celtic/folk musical group in Greenville, NC; Photography; Genealogy research; Travel **ADD:** 3314 Cadenza Street, Greenville, NC, 27858

BLACKBURN, LARRY H., T: Instructor of Construction Science, Builder (Retired) **I:** Architecture & Construction **DOB:** 11/13/1948 **PB:** Houston **SC:** TX/USA **PT:** Ephraim S.; Hollie B. Blackburn **MS:** Married **SPN:** Judith L. McCubbin (1977) **CH:** Wendy L.; Ashley G.; Courtney L.; Kelly L. **ED:** PhD in Strategic Management, California Coast University, Santa Ana, CA (2007); MBA, California Coast University, Santa Ana, CA (2004); BBA in Accounting, University of Houston, Texas (1973) **C:** Professional Builder, E.E. Reed Construction, L.P., Houston, Texas (2003-Present); Professional Builder, Linbeck Group, LLC, Houston, Texas (1994-2002); Professional Builder, LeBlanc, Houston, Texas (1989-1993); Professional Builder, E.G. Lowry, Houston, Texas (1974-1988); Classified, FBI, Houston, Texas (1970-1973) **CR:** Principal, Owner, Blackburn Investment Properties, Houston, Texas (1980-2000) **CIV:** Pastoral Advisor, St. Edwards Catholic Church, Houston, Texas (2004-2006); Parish Council, St. Ambrose Catholic Church, Houston, Texas (2000-2004); School Board Member, St. Pius X Catholic High School, Houston, Texas (2000-2003); Chairman Committee, St. Pius X Catholic High School, Houston, Texas (2000-2003); Coach, YMCA, Houston, Texas (1984-1994); Cub Master, Boy Scouts of America, Houston, Texas (1984-1988); Construction Advisor, Career and Recovery Resource, Inc., Houston, Texas **MIL:** Sergeant, Fleet Marine Forces Pacific, United States Marine Corps (1968-1974) **CW:** Author, "Empowered High-Performance Teams in Construction" (2008) **AW:** ABC Merit Award, Regions Financial Center, Greenway Plaza, Houston, Texas (2016); ABC National Eagle Award, Texas Instruments Research Development Engineering Facility, Sugar Land, Texas (2014); ABC National Eagle Award, Veteran's War Memorial, Fort Bend County, Texas (2013); Excellence in Construction Award, Granite Office Towers, Sugar Land, Texas (2008); Excellence in Construction Award, St. Lukes Community Medical Center (Now CHI St. Luke's Health - The Woodlands Hospital), CHI St. Luke's Health, The Woodlands, Texas (2002); Outstanding Carpenter Apprentice Award, U.S. Department of Labor (1967); Excellence in Construction Award, NFL Texans Marketing Center, Houston, Texas; National Defense, Meritorious Service, Honorable Service, Cold War and Viet Nam Era, Marine Rifleman Sharpshooter, United States Marine Corps **MEM:** The Delta Epsilon Tau Honor Society; Sons of the American Revolution; Associate, California Coast University Alumni Association; Associate, University of Houston Alumni Association; The American Legion; Military Order of the Crusades; The Sons of the Republic of Texas; Founders of

North America; Magna Charta Barons; Order of the Crown of Charlemagne in the USA; Plantagenet Society **MH:** Who's Who in America **H:** Golf **PA:** Independent **RE:** Roman Catholic **ADD:** 12823 Mimosa Spring Drive, Tomball, TX, 77377

BLACKLIDGE, RAYMOND M., T: Senior Vice President, Secretary **I:** Insurance **CN:** Modern USA Insurance Company **DOB:** 05/17/1960 **PB:** Fort Belvoir **SC:** VA/USA **PT:** Martin H. Blacklidge; Carol Ann (Fiarito) Blacklidge **MS:** Married **SPN:** Lisa Blacklidge **CH:** Robert Mark; Jonathon Michael; Sara Kathryn **ED:** JD, John Marshall Law School (1985); BA, Southern Illinois University (1982) **CT:** Admitted to Practice, United States Supreme Court (2009); Admitted to Practice, Middle District of Florida, United States District Court (2003); Admitted to Practice, State Florida Court (2002); Admitted to Practice, State of Florida (1996); Admitted to Practice, Northern District of Illinois, United States District Court (1986); Admitted to Practice, State of Illinois (1986) **C:** Part Owner, Senior Vice President and Secretary, Modern USA Insurance Company (2007-Present); Senior Vice President, Secretary, American Traditions Insurance Company (2006-Present); Sole Practice, Tampa, FL (2002-Present); Sole Practice, West Chicago, IL (1986-Present); General Partner, Blacklidge Insurance Holdings, LLP; Sole Practice, West Chicago (1992-2002); Partner, Corporate Secretary, Grief, Bus & Blacklidge, Professional Corporation, Illinois (1987-1992) **CR:** Title Insurance Agent, Attorney's Title Insurance Fund (1994-Present); Treasurer, USF Delta Chi Housing Corporation (2002–Present); Registered Lobbyist, State of Florida (1994-Present); Regional Manager and Counsel, Alliance of American Insurers (1992-1996); Of Counsel, Edward J. Boltz, Christopher C. Benfante and David E. Caddigan (1993-1994); Board of Directors, Senior Vice President, General Counsel and Secretary, The Jerger Company, Inc.; Mobile Homeowners Insurance Agencies, Inc.; Jerger & Sons, Inc.; Board of Directors, General Counsel, Secretary Mobile USA Insurance Company, Inc., Mobile United Property & Casualty Insurance Company, Inc.; Board of Directors, Senior Vice President, General Counsel, Secretary and Treasurer, MHIA Premium Finance Company; Director, Senior Vice President, Secretary and Treasurer, Mobile Adjustment Company, Inc.; Arbitrator, 18th Judicial Circuit **CIV:** Scoutmaster, Troop 148, Boy Scouts of America (1999-Present); Board of Directors, West Chicago R.R. Days, Inc. (1988-1994); Alderman, City of West Chicago (1989-1994); Representative, Winfield Township Precinct, DuPage County (1991-1994); President, USF Delta Chi Housing Corporation; School Board Member; President, Board of Directors, West Chicago Clean and Proud, Inc. **CW:** Editor-in-Chief, Marshall Opinion (1985) **MEM:** Trustee, Knights of Columbus (1985-Present); Board of Directors, Member Florida Insurance Council (1996-Present); Licensed Member, Florida Health, Life and Variable Annuity Agent (2001-Present); Brief Grader, National Appellate Advocacy Competition (2009-2010); President, Lodge 37, Woodmen of the World (2001-2002); Florida Authorized House Counsel (1996-2000); Government Affairs Committee, Alliance of American Insurers; Alliance of Southern Regional Advisory Committees; Gavel Society; Vice President, Columbian Club; Business Law Section, Florida Bar Association; St. Petersburg Bar Association; Founder, American Traditions Insurance Company; Founder, Modern USA Insurance Company; Homeowner's Division, Florida Property & Casualty Association; Florida Based Property Insurers CEO Group Inc. **BAR:** Illinois Trial Bar (1991) **MH:** Albert Nelson Marquis Lifetime Achievement Award (2017) **H:** Traveling;

Boating; Bicycling; Walking **PA:** Republican **RE:** Roman Catholic **ADD:** 602 Flamingo Drive, Madeira Beach, FL, 33708

BLEAM, LAURA JANE, T: Pediatric Nurse **I:** Medicine & Health Care **CN:** Montgomery County Community College **DOB:** 03/27/1940 **PB:** New Britain **SC:** PA/USA **PT:** Andrew Y. Jr. Michie; Edna (Tagert) Michie **MS:** Single **SPN:** Brian L. Bleam (4/8/1978, Deceased 10/1996) **CH:** Jennifer Lynn Bleam **ED:** Postgraduate Studies, Villanova University (1991); MSN, Gwynedd-Mercy University (1985); MA, Villanova University (1971); BSN, Alderson Broaddus University, Philippi, WV (1963) **CT:** Registered Nurse, Elementary Counselor, Commonwealth of Pennsylvania **C:** Professor Emeritus, Montgomery County Community College, Blue Bell, PA (2003-Present); Associate Professor, Pediatrics Nursing, Montgomery County Community College (1972-2004); Nursing Instructor, Gwynedd-Mercy University (1967-1969); Instructor, Grand View Hospital School of Nursing (Now Grand View University), Sellersville, PA (1963-1967) **CIV:** Board of Deacons, New Britain Baptist Church (1992-Present); Church Clerk, New Britain Baptist Church (2000-2005); Chairman, Deacon's 250th Anniversary, New Britain Baptist Church (1997-2004); Chairman, New Britain Baptist Church (1995-1996); Vice Chairman, New Britain Baptist Church (1993-1995); Former Board of Directors, Bucks County, American Lung Association; Admission Counselor, Pennsylvania Masonic Villages; Member, Church Relations Committee, New Britain Baptist Church **CW:** Contributor, Articles, Newspapers **MEM:** Worthy Matron, Doylestown Chapter, Order Of The Eastern Star (1975-1976, 2005-2006); Chairman, Order Of The Eastern Star (1991-1993); Board of Directors, Order Of The Eastern Star (1987-1993); National Society Daughters of the American Revolution; International Girl Scout, Girl Scouts of the United States of America; National League for Nursing; Pennsylvania League for Nursing; Lifetime Member, Alderson Broaddus Nursing Alumni Association; Gwynned-Mercy College of Nursing Honor Society; Sigma Theta Tau **MH:** Albert Nelson Marquis Lifetime Achievement Award (2017) **ADD:** 555 N Broad St Apt 109A, Doylestown, PA, 18901

BOCK, PHILIP E., T: Retired **I:** Sciences **DOB:** 03/03/1939 **PB:** Ba, Fiji **PT:** Henry H. Bock Beryl E. Bock (nee Christie) **MS:** Married **SPN:** Margaret Bock (18/8/1962) **CH:** Michael Philip David Ross Fiona Margaret **ED:** BSc, University Melbourne (1959) **C:** Senior Lecturer in Geology, Royal Melbourne Institute Technology, Australia (1966-1997) **CIV:** Honorary Associate, Marine Invertebrates Museum Victoria (1979-Present); Educator, University Third Age, Nunawading, Australia (1995) **AW:** Order of Australia Medal (OAM) 2018); Ellis Medal of International Bryozoology Association (IBA) (2016) **ADD:** 32 Swayfield Road, Mount Waverley, VIC, Australia, 3149

BOCZKO, IAN , I: Law and Legal Services **MEM:** Phi Beta Kappa

BODNAR, PETER O., T: Managing Partner **I:** Law and Legal Services **CN:** BodnarMilone LLP **DOB:** 03/19/1945 **PB:** Queens **SC:** NY/USA **PT:** John Bodnar; Edith (Schultz) Bodnar **MS:** Married **SPN:** Robin Weiser **CH:** Jessica Weiser McCarthy; Jill Kurlanzik; Lauren Raivetz **ED:** JD, Fordham University (1970); BA in Government, New York University (1966) **C:** Principal, BodnarMilone LLP, White Plains, NY (1999-Present); Principal, Law Offices of Peter O. Bodnar, White Plains, NY

(1998-1999); Partner, Bender & Bodnar, White Plains, NY (1980-1998); Partner, Bodnar & Greene, Professional Corporation, White Plains, NY (1977-1980); Private Practice, White Plains, NY (1973-1977); Confidential Law Secretary, Hon. Evans V. Brewster, Family Court and County Court, Westchester County, New York (1970-1973) **CR:** Managing Member, Organica USA II LLC (2004-2007); Supervisory Board, Vertis Environmental Finance, KFT, Budapest, Hungary (2002-2009); Organica RT, Budapest, Hungary (2001-2007); Chief Executive Officer, Organica USA, Inc. (1998-2007); President, Chief Executive Officer, P.A.J. America Ltd./The Olo Corp. (1990-1997); Lecturer, Family Law Section, New York State Bar Association; Lecturer, Family Law Section, Westchester County Bar Association; Lecturer, Pace Women's Justice Center, Elisabeth Haub School of Law at Pace University; Lecturer, Appellate Division, Second Department, Law Guardian Program; Fellow, American Academy of Matrimonial Lawyers; Fellow, International Academy of Family Lawyers **CIV:** Trustee, Ossining, NY (1975-1977) **AW:** Best Lawyers in America (1995-Present); Honoree, Best Family Lawyer (2013); Super Lawyers **MEM:** Chair, Long Range Planning, Family Law Section, New York State Bar Association (2008-Present); Executive Committee, Family Law Section, New York State Bar Association (2000-Present); American Bar Foundation; Executive Committee, Family Law Section, Westchester County Bar Association (1992-Present); Vice President, New York State Chapter, American Academy of Matrimonial Lawyers (2012-2013); Board of Managers, American Academy of Matrimonial Lawyers (2009-2012); Parliamentarian, American Academy of Matrimonial Lawyers (2007-2008); Chair, Executive Committee, Family Law Section, Westchester County Bar Association (2000-2002); Family Law Section, ABA; Westchester County Bar Association; International Academy of Family Lawyers; American Academy of Matrimonial Lawyers; International Academy of Collaborative Professionals; Association of Collaborative Lawyers of Rockland-Westchester; Board of Governors, New York State Chapter, American Academy of Matrimonial Lawyers **BAR:** State of New York; U.S. District Court, Southern District, State of New York; U.S. Supreme Court **MH:** Albert Nelson Marquis Lifetime Achievement Award (2017) **BA:** 140 Grand Street,Suite 401, BodnarMilone LLP, White Plains, NY, 10601 **URL:** http://www.bodnarmilone.com

BOLAND, WINNIFRED JOAN, T: Librarian (Retired) **I:** Library Management/Library Services **DOB:** 09/05/1931 **PB:** Watrous **SC:** Saskatchewan/ Canada **PT:** Charles Frederick Fisher; Mary Jane Little **MS:** Widowed **SPN:** William Guy Boland (2/16/1968, Deceased 4/23/2015) **CH:** Thomas Richard; James Patrick **ED:** MLS, University of Washington (1965); BLS, McGill University (1955); BA, University of Saskatchewan (1952) **C:** Volunteer Reference Librarian, Washington State Library (1990-2000); Instructor, Library School, University of Washington (1969-1970); Head Reference Librarian, Undergraduate Library, University of Washington (1968-1970); Reference Librarian, Undergraduate Library, University of Washington (1966-1968); Reference Librarian, The Seattle Public Library (1962-1965); Reference Librarian, University of Saskatchewan (1957-1961); Reference Librarian, Provincial Library (1955-1957) **CR:** Member, Citizen's Advisory Committee, Washington State Library (2002-2005) **CIV:** Officer, Precinct Committee, Thurston County Democrats (1998-2002); Lobbyist, Washington Coalition Against Censorship, State of Washington (1965-1985) **CW:** Contributor, Articles on Censorship

Issues **AW:** Recipient, Scholarship, Government of Saskatchewan (1954); Recipient, John L. McKinnon Trophy, Saskatchewan Technical Collegiate (1949) **MEM:** Washington Library Association (1984-Present); Contact Person, Thurston County Chapter, American Civil Liberties Union (1995-2002); Friends of Clinton Presidential Foundation; Friends of Washington State Library; Southern Poverty Law Center; People for the American Way; National Coalition Against Censorship; Beta Phi Mu, Library Honor Society **MH:** Albert Nelson Marquis Lifetime Achievement Award (2017) **H:** Reading; Public speaking **PA:** Democrat **RE:** Protestant **ADD:** 5035 Donnelly Dr SE, Olympia, WA, 98501

BOLLENDORF, ROBERT F., I: Education/Educational Services **DOB:** 09/11/1946 **PB:** Kenosha **SC:** WI/USA **PT:** Lucile Bollendorf; Fred Bollendorf **MS:** Married **SPN:** Linda **CH:** Becky; Bryan **ED:** EdD, Northern Illinois University; MS, Southern Illinois University; BA, St. Joseph's College **CT:** Clinical Psychologist; Addictions Counselor **C:** Human Services Department, College of DuPage **CIV:** Chairman, Bike/Pedestrian Committee, Lisle High School Boosters; Volunteer, Pads Homeless Shelter; Volunteer, Sharing Connections Furniture Bank **CW:** Sober Spring; Flight of the Loon; Autumn Snow; Witch of Winter; Summer Heat; The Challenger; A Rose by any Other Name **AW:** Illinois Community College Teacher of the Year, College of DuPage **MEM:** Certification Board, Illinois Alcohol and Other Drugs of Abuse **H:** Swimming; Bicycling; Writing; Skiing **RE:** Catholic **ADD:** 2498 Sun Valley Rd, Lisle, IL, 60532

BOOMERSHINE, DONALD EUGENE, T: Municipal Official (Retired) **I:** Business Management/Business Services **DOB:** 10/05/1931 **PB:** Brookville **SC:** OH/US **PT:** Harold Everett; Elsie (Rhoads) Boomershine **MS:** Married **SPN:** Patti Watsom (5/29/1985); Marilyn Sullivan (8/29/1953, Deceased) **CH:** Jeffrey; Alan; Andrew Raine (Stepson) **ED:** Postgraduate Coursework, University of Oklahoma National Senior Commercial Lending School (1974); Bank Management, Stonier Graduate School of Banking, Rutgers, The State University of New Jersey (1972); Northwestern University, Financial Public Relations Graduate School (1965); BS, Bowling Green State University, OH (1953) **C:** President, Better Business Bureau Central of Alabama, Birmingham, AL (1982-2007); Chief Executive Officer, Better Business Bureau Central of Alabama, Birmingham, AL (1982-2007); Vice President, Sales Manager Division, Metropolitan Development Board (1980-1982); Vice President of Community Development, Metropolitan Development Board (1980-1982); Vice President, Birmingham Trust National Bank (1978-1980); Vice President, National Division, Birmingham Trust National Bank (1965-1978); Business Development Representative, Exchange Security Bank, Birmingham, AL (1961-1965); Assistant Cashier, Exchange Security Bank, Birmingham, AL (1961-1965); Senior Sales Representative, IBM, Dayton, OH (1957-1961); Junior Executive, Program Frigidaire Division, General Motors Corporation, Dayton, OH (1955-1957) **CR:** Business Advisory Council, Sorrell College of Business, Troy University (1991-Present); Interim Executive Director, Alabama Public TV (2012); Chairman, Atlanta-Birmingham Branch, Federal Reserve Board (1991-1997); Chairman, Business Tomorrow Conference, University of South Alabama (1976); Educational Chairman Associate, Industries Alabama (1975-1977); Auburn University (1975) **CIV:** Vice President, National Veteran's Day, United States Naval Academy (1988-2011); Blue and Gold Board, United States Naval Academy (1972-2011);

Designated Information Officer, United States Naval Academy (1982-2004); Founder, Board of Directors, Alabama Jump Start Coalition (2002); Board of Directors, Downtown YMCA, Metropolitan YMCA (1992-1997); Alumnus, Leadership Birmingham (1991); General Chairman, Corporation Director, United States World Youth Games (1973); Board of Directors, Alabama Association of Independent Colleges and Universities (1967); Volunteer, Alabama Association of Independent Colleges and Universities (1967); Founder, Birmingham Touchdown Club (1966); Founder, Downtown Action Committee **MIL:** Retired Colonel, U.S. Marine Corps Reserve (1984); Second Lieutenant, U.S. Marine Corps (1953) **AW:** ARC: Completed 50 years as a Leader and Volunteer (2017); Golden Falcon Award (2015); Community Alliance Church Youth Leadership Award (2011); Yacht Leadership Development Program Award (2011); Significant Sig Award, National Sigma Chi (2011); Lifetime Achievement Award, Federal Reserve Bank of Atlanta (2009); Hall Of Fame, Birmingham Better Business Bureau, Inc. (2006); Alabama Senior Citizen Hall of Fame (2005); Alumni Community Service Award, Bowling Green State University (2001); Commandant's Director Award (1999); Outstanding Broadcasters Cooperation Award, Alabama Broadcasters Association (1998); Commandant Award, United States Naval Academy (1994); Alumni Hall of Fame, Brookville High School (1991); Eponym, Donald E. Boomershine Day (1985); Eponym, Reserve Day, Birmingham, AL (1983) **MEM:** Lifetime Member, Founding Member, United States Marine Corps League (2013-Present); Appointed Interim Executive Director, Alabama Public Television (2012); National Sigma Chi (2011); Founding Member, Board of Directors, Summit Club (2004); Marine Corps Reserve Officers Association (1974-1976); Diplomats of Birmingham (1973); Kiwanis International (1971); Founder, Alabama Native Sons and Daughters (1971-1972); Bank Marketing Association (1971); Alabama Industrial Development Council; Southern Industrial Council; Life Member, Birmingham Chamber of Commerce; Vestavia Club; The Club **MH:** Albert Nelson Marquis Lifetime Achievement Award (2017) **H:** Life long handball player **ADD:** 183 Highland Park Dr, Birmingham, AL, 35242

BORENE, SCOTT M., T: Founder, Managing Attorney **I:** Law and Legal Services **CN:** Borene Law Firm, P.A. **MS:** Married **SPN:** Penny Ann Van Kampen **CH:** Andrew Borene **ED:** JD, William Mitchell College of Law (Now Mitchell Hamline School of Law) (1978); Bachelor's Degree, Harvard University (1970) **CT:** Admitted to Practice, Immigration Courts, U.S. Department of Justice **C:** Founder, Borene Law Firm, P.A. (1987-Present); Managing Attorney, Borene Law Firm, P.A. (1987-Present) **CIV:** Chair, Council of the Global Employment Institute, International Bar Association (2013-Present); Chair, North Dakota Petroleum Council (2013-Present); Director, Board of Governors, American Immigration Lawyers Association (1997-2003); National Chair, Liaison Committee, INS Nebraska Service Center (2000-2002); National Chair, INS Headquarters Adjudications Liaison Committee, American Immigration Lawyer's Association (1999); Vice Chair, Immigration and Nationality Law Committee, International Law Section, ABA (1995-1998); Co-chair, Immigration Law Committee, International Bar Association; Past Chair, Immigration Section, MSBA **AW:** Honoree, AV-Rated Attorney, Martindale-Hubbell (1994-Present); Honoree, Lawyer of the Year in Immigration Law, Best Lawyers in America (2016, 2018); President's Commendation Award "For Setting a New Standard

in INS Headquarters Liaison (2000, 2003); Super Lawyer for Immigration Law **MEM:** International Section Council, MSBA; American Immigration Lawyers Association; NAFSA; International Bar Association; Associate Individual Member, NACUA; Charter Member, American Immigration Law Foundation; Harvard Club of Minnesota **H:** Playing tennis on a competitive level; Travel; Foreign policy; Public policy **BA:** 80 S 8th St Ste 3950, Borene Law Firm, P.A., Minneapolis, MN, 55402

BOSE, SANDIP , I: Oil & Energy **C:** Principal Research Scientist, Schlumberger Limited, Cambridge, MA (1997-Present) **CW:** Presenter in Field **MEM:** IEEE; Society of Exploration Geophysicists; SPWLA

BOSKIN, JOSEPH, T: History Professor, Director of Urban Studies **I:** Education/Educational Services **CN:** Boston University **DOB:** 08/10/1929 **PB:** Brooklyn **SC:** NY/USA **CH:** Julie; Lori; Deborah **ED:** PhD in History, University of Minnesota, Minneapolis, MN (1959); MA in History, New York University (1952); BA in History, State University of New York, Oswego, NY (1951) **C:** Emeritus Professor of American Social History & African-American Studies, Boston University (1970-Present); Associate Professor, University of Southern California, Los Angeles, CA (1960-1969); Adjunct Professor, State University of Iowa (1959-1960) **MIL:** U.S. Army (1952-1954) **AW:** Outstanding Teacher, University of Southern California (1968); Outstanding Teacher, University of Southern California (1964); Russall Sage Research Grant; Research Grant, National Institute of Mental Health; Emmy Award for "The Negro In American Culture" **MEM:** American Association of University Professors (1960-Present); Advisory Board, International Humor Society (1970) **MH:** Albert Nelson Marquis Lifetime Achievement Award (2017); Distinguished Humanitarian (2017) **ADD:** 4 Sparks Pl, Cambridge, MA, 02138

BOSWELL, JAMES AURTHUR JR., I: Education/Educational Services **DOB:** 03/21/1953 **PB:** Pittsburgh **SC:** PA/USA **PT:** James A. Boswell; Pauline R. Boswell **MS:** Married **SPN:** Olivia Boswell **ED:** MA in English, Slippery Rock University, Pennsylvania (1980); BA, Slippery Rock University, Pennsylvania, Summa Cum Laude (1975) **C:** Professor, Harrisburg Area Community College (1994-Present); Instructor, Sprint/United Technology Institute for High School Students (1993-1997); Adjunct Instructor in Junior Level American Literature, College of St. Francis at Holy Spirit Hospital (1990); Associate Professor, Harrisburg Area Community College (1988-1994); Assistant Professor, Harrisburg Area Community College (1984-1988); Instructor, Harrisburg Area Community College (1981-1984); Adjunct Instructor, Community College of Allegheny County (1981); Graduate Assistant, Slippery Rock University (1979-1980) **CIV:** Volunteer Instructor for Reading and Writing, Melrose Project; Instructor in Report Writing to High School Engineering Students; United Way; Deacon Church Brethren **CW:** Editor, "The World According to Siggy" (1988); Contributor, Articles, Professional Journals; Editor, Articles, Professional Journals; Contributor, Poetry, Professional Journals **AW:** Honoree, Exemplary Teaching in Developmental Education, Pennsylvania Association of Developmental Educators (2002); Honorary Membership, Phi Theta Kappa Honor Society (2000); Certificate of Appreciation, Learning Center (1993); Award of Gratitude from Black Student Union Members (1989); Award of Gratitude from Black Student Union Members (1986); Certificate of Recognition of Service to Faculty Council (1984); High Academic Achievement Award, Slippery Rock University (1975) **MEM:** Modern Language Association; Pennsylvania Association of Developmental Educators; NCTE; The Mid-Atlantic Writing Centers Association; Assembly for Teaching English Grammar **MH:** Albert Nelson Marquis Lifetime Achievement Award (2017) **ADD:** 676 S 82nd Street, Harrisburg, PA, 17111

BOUTWELL, ANNE , I: Fine Art **PB:** Dakha **SC:** India **PT:** Raymond Stulting; Dolores Lilly Yaukey **ED:** MFA, Temple University (1996); Student, University Washington, Seattle (1991-1992); BA in Philosophy, Grinnell College (1984) **C:** Professor of Art, Appalachian State University, Boone, NC (1996-Present); Head Jewelery Designer, Faces of Time, Madison, CT (1987-1990) **CW:** Featured Artist, Ashes to Ashes (2007); Featured Artist, Funerary Urns (2006); Exhibited Artist **AW:** 64-Year Pin, Kappa Kappa Gamma **MEM:** Life Member, Society of North Am. Goldsmiths **ACH:** Achievements include development of adapting digital design and creation process for the studio jeweler **H:** Spending time with her three sons, eight grandchildren and four great-grandsons; Preparing for the arrival of her great-granddaughter **PA:** Independent **RE:** Quaker

BOVERIE, PATRICIA, T: Professor, Director **I:** Education/Educational Services **CN:** The University of New Mexico **MS:** Married **CH:** Three Children **ED:** PhD, The University of Texas at Austin (1990); Postdoctoral Coursework, The University of British Columbia; Postdoctoral Coursework, Harvard University; Master's Degree in Clinical Psychology, The University of Texas at El Paso; Bachelor's Degree in Business, The University of Texas at El Paso **C:** Professor of Organized Information and Learning Sciences Program, The University of New Mexico (1990-Present); Director of Organized Information and Learning Sciences Program, The University of New Mexico (1990-Present); Professor, Department of Psychology, Central Washington University; Director of Master's Program in Organized Development, Central Washington University **CW:** Co-Author, "My Passion and Work, and Happiness," Sigma Press (2008); Co-Author, "Transforming Work: The Five Keys to Developing and Sustaining Trust, Commitment and Passion in the Workplace," Perseus, Hachette Book Group (2001); Contributor, Articles to Professional Journals **AW:** Recipient, Global HRD Leadership Award, World HRD Congress (2009) **MEM:** Former Member, International Positive Psychology Association **H:** Taking and teaching ballet classes **BA:** 1 OILS, MSC05 3020, The University Of New Mexico, Albuquerque, NM, 87131 **ADD:** 9716 Admiral Emerson NE, Albuquerque, NM, 87111 **URL:** https://oils.unm.edu/people/directory/patricia-boverie

BOWEN, WAYNE DARRELL, T: Upjohn Professor of Pharmacology **I:** Education/Educational Services **CN:** Brown University **DOB:** 11/11/1952 **PB:** Petersburg **SC:** VA/USA **PT:** Herbert Edward Bowen, Jr.; June Eleanor Bowen **MS:** Married **SPN:** Barbara E. Bowen **ED:** Ad Eundem Honorary Degree, Brown University (1990); PhD in Biochemistry, Cornell University (1981); BS in Chemistry, Morgan State University, Summa Cum Laude (1974); Summer Intern Undergraduate Mentor, National Institutes of Health **C:** Upjohn Professor of Pharmacology, Brown University (2008-Present); Chair, Department of Molecular Pharmacology, Physiology & Biotechnology, Division of Biology and Medicine, Brown University (2007-Present); Professor of Biology, Department of Molecular Pharmacology, Physiology & Biotechnology, Division of Biology and Medicine, Brown University

(2004-Present); Adjunct Professor of Molecular Biology, Cell Biology, and Biochemistry, Division of Biology and Medicine, Brown University (1991-2004); Adjunct Professor of Neuroscience, Division of Biology and Medicine, Brown University (1991-2004); Chief, Unit on Receptor Biochemistry and Pharmacology, Drug Design and Synthesis Section, National Institute of Diabetes and Digestive and Kidney Diseases, National Institutes of Health (1991-2004); Associate Professor of Biology, Biochemistry Section, Division of Biology and Medicine, Brown University (1989-1991); Assistant Professor of Biology, Biochemistry Section, Division of Biology and Medicine, Brown University (1983-1989); Tutor, Cornell University (1977-1978); Teaching Assistant, Cornell University (1975-1976); Medicinal Chemist, Smith, Kline, and French Laboratories (1974) **CR:** Graduate Program Thesis Committee, Brown University (2005-Present); Undergraduate Research Supervisor, Brown University (2004-Present); Human Biology Concentration Advisor, Brown University (2004-Present); Co-Director, Molecular Pharmacology and Physiology Graduate Program, Division of Biology and Medicine, Brown University (2005-2009); Postdoctoral Fellowship Advisor, Brown University (2004-2014); Minority Supplement Advisory Committee, National Institute of Diabetes and Digestive and Kidney Diseases, National Institutes of Health (1996-2004); Member, Neuropharmacology and Neurochemistry Review Committee, National Institute of Mental Health, National Institutes of Health (1992); Member, Cellular Neurobiology and Psychopharmacology Study Section, National Institute of Mental Health, National Institutes of Health (1989-1991) **CIV:** Lecturer, Seminars, Classical High School (2016); Lecturer, Seminars, Morgan State University (2015); Lecturer, Seminars, University of Hawaii at Hilo (2014); Lecturer, Seminars, United States National Library of Medicine, National Institutes of Health (2014); Lecturer, Seminars, The University of North Carolina at Chapel Hill (2014); Lecturer, Seminars, Classical High School (2013); Lecturer, Seminars, National Institute on Drug Abuse, National Institutes of Health (2012); Lecturer, Seminars, Meharry Medical College (2011); Lecturer, Seminars, Harvard University (2010); Lecturer, Seminars, Wayne State University (2010); Lecturer, Seminars, COSI (2010); Lecturer, Seminars, National Center for Minority Health and Health Disparities, National Institutes of Health (2010); Lecturer, Seminars, University of Rhode Island (2010); Lecturer, Seminars, The F. Ivy Carroll Symposium: 50 Years of Research, RTI International (2010); Lecturer, Seminars, Brown University (2009-2010); Speaker, Sigma Receptors: Viable Therapeutic Targets for Medication Development, American Association of Pharmaceutical Scientists (2008); Lecturer, Seminars, Indiana University (2007); Lecturer, Seminars, Morehouse College (2007); Speaker, Annual Meeting, American Association for Cancer Research (2006-2017); Speaker, Annual National Training Conference, Blacks in Government (2005-2006); Lecturer, Seminars, National Alliance on Mental Illness (2005); Lecturer, Seminars, University of South Florida (2005); Speaker, International Meeting on Neurobiology of the Skin (2004); Speaker, Annual Scientific Meeting, College on Problems of Drug Dependence (2004); Speaker, Gordon Research Conference on Glycolipid and Sphingolipid Biology (2002); Lecturer, Seminars, National Institute on Aging, National Institutes of Health (2002); Lecturer, Seminars, Virginia Commonwealth University (2002); Lecturer, Seminars, Morgan State University (2001-2002); Lecturer, Seminars, National Cancer Institute, National Institutes of Health (2002); Lecturer, Seminars, Hampton University (2001) Lecturer, Seminars, Brown University (2000-

2002) **CW:** Contributing Author, Articles, Molecular Pharmaceuticals (2017); Contributing Author, Articles, Clinical Case Reports and Reviews (2016); Contributing Author, Articles, Journal of Pharmacology and Experimental Therapeutics (2015-2016); Contributing Author, Articles, Natural Product Communications (2013); Contributing Author, Articles, Nano Letters (2012); Interviewee, "Science Makers," The History Makers (2012); Contributing Author, Articles, Journal of Pharmacology and Experimental Therapeutics (2009); Contributing Author, Articles on Cellular Signaling (2009); Contributing Author, Articles, Journal of Pharmacology and Experimental Therapeutics (2009); Contributing Author, Articles, Journal of Biological Chemistry (2008); Contributing Author, Articles, Neuropsychopharmacology (2007); Editor, "Sigma Receptors: Chemistry, Cell Biology and Clinical Implications" (2007); Contributing Author, Articles, Pharmacology Biochemistry and Behavior (2004); Contributing Author, Articles, European Journal of Pharmacology (2004); Contributing Author, Articles, Psychopharmacology (2004); Contributing Author, Articles, Journal of Medicinal Chemistry (2003); Contributing Author, Articles, Bioorganic & Medicinal Chemistry Letters (2002-2003); Contributing Author, Articles, European Journal of Pharmacology (2001-2002); Contributing Author, Articles, Journal of Medicinal Chemistry (2001) **AW:** Honoree, 700 Most Cited Scientists, Institute for Scientific Information (2006-Present); Ralph J. Cazort Lectureship, Meharry Medical College (2011); Grantee, Predoctoral Training Program in Transdisciplinary Pharmacological Sciences, National Institute of General Medical Sciences (2010-2015); Grantee, RI-STAC (2010-2011); Grantee, National Institute on Drug Abuse, National Institutes of Health (2008-2011); Recipient, Salomon Award, Office of Vice President for Research, Brown University (2007); Recipient, Jack and Linda Gill Lectureship, The Gill Foundation of Texas, Indiana University (2007); Recipient, Award of Recognition for Research in Receptor Biochemistry and Pharmacology, Morgan State University (2002); Recipient, Special Recognition Award, National Institutes of Health (2000); Recipient, Certificate of Recognition, Speakers Bureau, National Institutes of Health (2000); Grantee, National Cancer Institute, National Institutes of Health (1997-2000); Recipient, Certificate of Appreciation, Howard Hughes Medical Institute, Montgomery County Public Schools, National Institutes of Health (1996-1997); Recipient, Award of Appreciation, Morgan State University (1996); Honoree, Sterling's Who's Who (1996); Honoree, Distinguished Panel Member, Black Scientists and the Biomedical Research Enterprise, National Institutes of Health (1996); Intramural Research Program Grantee, National Institute of Diabetes and Digestive and Kidney Diseases, National Institutes of Health (1991-2004); Recipient, Recognition Award, Daniel Hale Williams Medical Society and Office of Minority Medical Affairs, Division of Biology and Medicine, Brown University (1991); Honoree, Men of Achievement (1989); Grantee, National Institute of Neurological Disorders and Stroke, National Institutes of Health (1988-1991) **MEM:** Core Facilities Advisory Committee, Brown University (2017-Present); Brown University Steering Committee, New England Association of Schools and Colleges (2016-Present); Council of Consultants, Gerson Lehrman Group (2006-Present); Scientific Advisory Board, Affichem Pharmaceuticals (2006-Present); External Advisory Committee, MBRS/SCORE Program, Florida Agricultural and Mechanical University (2005-Present); External Advisory Committee, Research Centers in Minority Institutions Grants, Morgan State University (2001-Present); Tenure Review Committee for

Chairman, Department of Pathology and Laboratory Medicine, Brown University (2017); Search Committee, Department of Pathology and Laboratory Medicine, Brown University (2016-2017); Associate Dean of Minority Affairs Search Committee, Alpert Medical School, Brown University (2016); President's Deficit Reduction Committee, Brown University (2014-2015); Professional Development Committee, Society for Neuroscience (2012-2016); Provost's Search Committee for Dean of Medicine and Biology, Brown University (2012-2013); Minorities in Cancer Research Council, American Association for Cancer Research (2011-2016); Chair, Nuclear Magnetic Resonance Spectroscopist Search Committee, Structural Biology Facility, Department of Molecular Pharmacology, Physiology and Biotechnology, Brown University (2011-2012) **MH:** Albert Nelson Marquis Lifetime Achievement Award (2017) **H:** Music; Photography; Sailing; Chinese martial arts; Drumming **ADD:** 8 Spring House Ln, Cumberland, RI, 02864

BOWLES, BARBARA LANDERS, T: Investment Executive (Retired) **I:** Financial Services **DOB:** 09/17/1947 **PB:** Nashville **SC:** TN/USA **PT:** Corris Landers (Deceased); Rebecca Landers Jennings (Deceased) **MS:** Married **SPN:** Earl Stanley Bowles (11/27/1971) **CH:** Terrence Earl **ED:** MBA in Finance, University of Chicago (1971); BA in Mathematics, Fisk University (1968) **CT:** Chartered Financial Analyst **C:** President, Landers Bowles Family Foundation (2008-Present); Chairman of the Board, Fisk University (2013-2018); Vice Chairman, Profit Investments (2006-2007); Chairman, The Kenwood Group Inc. (2000-2006); President, The Kenwood Group Inc.(1989-2006); Chief Executive Officer, The Kenwood Group Inc. (1989-2006); Founder, The Kenwood Group Inc. (1989-2006); Vice President, Investor Relations, Kraft, Inc. (Now The Kraft Heinz Company) (1984-1989); Assistant Vice President, Beatrice Companies, Inc. (1981-1984); Bank Official, Vice President, First National Bank of Chicago (1968-1981) **CR:** Board of Directors, WEC Energy Group (1998-Present); Board of Directors, Hospira, Inc. (2008-2015) **CIV:** Board of Directors, Ann & Robert H. Lurie Children's Hospital of Chicago; Board of Directors, Chicago Urban League; Council Member, Graduate School of Business, University of Chicago; Director, Museum of Science and Industry, Chicago **MEM:** Trustee, Fisk University (1998-Present); Lifetime Member, National Association for the Advancement of Colored People **MH:** Albert Nelson Marquis Lifetime Achievement Award (2017) **H:** Tennis; Bridge **RE:** United Church of Christ **ADD:** 5015 S Ellis Ave, Chicago, IL, 60615

BRADY, MARY ROLFRES, T: Music Educator **I:** Education/Educational Services **DOB:** 11/26/1933 **PB:** St. Louis **SC:** MO/USA **PT:** William Henry Rolfes; Helen Dorothy (Slavick) Rolfes **MS:** Married **SPN:** Donald Sheridan Brady (8/29/1953) **CH:** Joseph William; Mark David; Douglas Sheridan; John Rolfes; Todd Christopher **ED:** Coursework, University of Southern California (1972-1973); Coursework, University of California, Los Amgeles (1967); Coursework, Stanford University (1951-1954) **C:** Private Piano Teacher, Los Angeles, CA (1955-Present); Television Performer; Radio Performer **CR:** Legislation Coordinator, Board of Directors, Philharmonic Affiliates, Los Angeles, CA (1978-1980); President of the Board, President, Junior Philharmonic Committee, Los Angeles, CA (1975-1976) **CIV:** Los Angeles Trustee, St. Francis Medical Center (1984-1988); Trustee, St. Vincent Medical Center (1984-1988); Board of Directors, Hollygrove-Los Angeles Orphans Home, Inc. **MEM:** President,

Los Angeles Chapter, Stanford Women's Club of Southern California (1977-Present); American College of Musicians Club; Springs Country Club **MH:** Albert Nelson Marquis Lifetime Achievement Award (2017) **ADD:** 72 Colgate Dr, Rancho Mirage, CA, 92270

BRANCA, JOHN, T: Lawyer **I:** Law and Legal Services **CN:** Ziffren Brittenham LLP **DOB:** 12/11/1950 **PB:** Bronxville **SC:** NY/USA **PT:** John Ralph Branca; Barbara (Werle) Branca **ED:** JD, University of California, Los Angeles (1975); AB in Political Science, Occidental College, Cum Laude (1972) **C:** Partner, Ziffren, Brittenham, LLP, Los Angeles, CA (1981-Present); Chairman, MusiCares Foundation (2007-2009); Associate, Hardee, Barovick, Konecky & Braun, Beverly Hills, CA (1977-1981); Associate, Kindel & Anderson, Los Angeles, CA (1975-1977) **CR:** Consultant, Various Music Industry Organizations, Los Angeles, CA (1981-Present); Consultant, New York State Assembly, Mount Vernon, NY (1978-1982); Chair Emeritus, MusiCares Foundation; Member, Board of Trustees, Grammy Museum Foundation; Board of Trustees, Occidental College; Board of Trustees, UCLA Law Entertainment & Media Law & Policy Program Advisory Council; Board of Trustees, UCLA Pauley Pavilion Renovation Campaign Committee; Chairman, Musi Cares Capital Campaign **CIV:** Consultant, Board of Trustees, Occidental College Musician's Assistance Program (1995); Consultant, Board of Trustees, UCLA Law School Committee; Consultant, Board of Trustees, UCLA Athletic Department **CW:** Editor-in-Chief, UCLA-Alaska Law Review (1974-1975); Contributor, Articles, Professional Journals **AW:** Named, One of The 100 Power Lawyers in Entertainment, The Hollywood Reporter (2010); UCLA Alumnus of Year Award (2010); Occidental College Alumnus of Year Award (2010); Outstanding Alumnus of Year Award, L.A. City College (2010); Named, Entertainment Lawyer of Year, American Lawyer Magazine (1981); Bancroft-Whitney Award **MEM:** Patent Trademark and Copyright Law Section, ABA; Phi Alpha Delta; Sigma Tau Sigma **BAR:** State of California (1975) **MH:** Albert Nelson Marquis Lifetime Achievement Award (2017) **H:** Art; Antiques; Music; Real estate **BA:** 1801 Century Park W Fl 7, Ziffren Brittenham LLP, Los Angeles, CA, 90067 **URL:** michellen@ziffrenbrittenham.com

BRANDON, RAYMOND WILSON, T: CEO **I:** Financial Services **CN:** Brandon Financial Planning, Inc. **DOB:** 03/11/1959 **PB:** Memphis **SC:** TN/USA **PT:** Elvis Denby Brandon, Jr.; Helen (Deupree) Brandon **MS:** Married **SPN:** Dana Stallings Brandon (9/21/1996) **CH:** Emma Ann; Ben Wilson **ED:** MBA, University of Texas (1983); BA, Vanderbilt University (1981) **CT:** Phi Beta Kappa, Magna Cum Laude **C:** CEO, Brandon Investments, Inc., Memphis, TN (1983-Present); President, Chairman, Investment Committee, Brandon Financial Planning, Inc., Memphis, TN (1983) **CR:** Vice President, Brandon Underwriting Specialists, Inc., Memphis, TN; Paul Harris Fellow, Rotary **MEM:** Sergeant-at-Arm, Rotary (2014); Vice President, Rotary (2007); President, Memphis Chapter, Financial Planning Association (1988-1989); Board of Directors, Memphis Institute of Certified Financial Planners; Chartered Financial Analyst Institute; Racquet Club of Memphis; Phi Beta Kappa; Treasurer, Board of Directors, Rotary **H:** Swimming; Running; Travel; Magic; Public speaking **RE:** Presbyterian **BA:** 5101 Wheelis Road, Suite 112, Brandon Financial Planning, Memphis, TN, 38117

BRANNON, JEAN, T: Education Educator **I:** Education/Educational Services **CN:** Brannon Properties LLC **DOB:** 06/22/2017 **PT:** Ervin Lewis Estes; Helen (Martin) Estes **CH:** Michael George; Sandra-Jean **ED:** Master's Degree, Fairfield University (1972-1973) **C:** Professor, Alamo County College District (1980-2004); Instructor, University of North Carolina at Greensboro (1974-1978) **CR:** Consultant in Field **CW:** Patentee, Sa-Mitch Hospital Gown **MEM:** American Association of University Professors; National Association of Realtors; French International Culinary Society; Texas Junior College Teachers Association; National League for Nursing; Sigma Theta Tau **H:** Dance; Music; Travel **ADD:** 9233 Gloxinia Dr, San Antonio, TX, 78266 **URL:** https://www.brannonproperties.com

BRANSON, HARLEY KENNETH, T: Finance Company Executive **I:** Financial Services **CN:** Flying Palms LLC **DOB:** 06/10/1942 **PB:** Ukiah **SC:** CA/USA **PT:** Harley; Clara Branson **CH:** Erik Jordan **ED:** JD, Santa Clara University (1968); BS in Accounting and Finance, San Jose State University (1965) **C:** President, Flying Palms LLC, San Diego, CA (1995-Present); Chief Executive Officer, Flying Palms LLC, San Diego, CA (1995-Present); Executive Vice President, Bumble Bee Seafoods, San Diego, CA (1985-1989); General Counsel, Bumble Bee Seafoods, San Diego, CA (1985-1989); Corporate Secretary, Bumble Bee Seafoods, San Diego, CA (1985-1989); Group General Counsel, Castle & Cooke, Inc., San Diego, CA (1983-1985); Division Counsel, Ralston Purina Company (Now Nestle Purina Petcare Company), San Diego, CA (1978-1983); Private Practice, San Diego, CA (1969-1978); Judge, United States Court of Appeals for the Ninth Circuit San Diego, CA (1968-1969); Law Clerk, United States Court of Appeals for the Ninth Circuit, San Diego, CA (1968-1969) **BAR:** California (1969-1998) **MH:** Albert Nelson Marquis Lifetime Achievement Award (2017) **ADD:** 6724 Landon Ln, Bethesda, MD, 20817

BRASWELL, JACKIE BOYD, T: State Agency Administrator **I:** Real Estate **CN:** Rayner Real Estate **DOB:** 02/15/1938 **PB:** Leon County **SC:** FL/USA **PT:** Chalmer Parks Boyd; Kathryn Iris (Johnson) Boyd **MS:** Married **SPN:** Fletcher Braswell (11/28/1957) **CH:** Flecia Lori; Carmen Ethelee **ED:** Master's Degree in Educational Administration (1976); BS, Florida State University (1964) **CT:** Licensed Real Estate Sales Associate, State of Florida (2005); Certified Educator, Valdosta State University (1968); Certified in Rayner Real Estate, Tallahassee, FL; Licensed Administrator, State of Florida **C:** Real Estate Associate, Rayner Real Estate (2005-Present); Director of Educational Affairs and Policy, Florida Lottery (1999-2005); Business-Vocational Teacher, Department of Career Education, Lincoln High School (1975-1999); Chairman, Department of Career Education, Lincoln High School (1975-1999); Teacher of Business Education, James S. Rickards High School, Tallahassee, FL (1970-1975); Teacher of Business Education, Berrien High School, Berrien County Board of Education, Nashville, GA (1966-1969); Single Manager, U.S. Air Force, Moody Air Force Base (1958-1961) **CR:** Co-Owner, Rundown Farms, Tallahassee, FL (1969-Present); Financial Manager, Rundown Farms, Tallahassee, FL (1969-Present); Governor's Mentoring Initiative Lottery Mentoring Program (1999-2005); President, Eight Out Investment Group (1993-2003) **CIV:** Annual Fundraiser Committee, PACE Center for Girls, Inc (2005-2008); Fundraising Committee, Boys & Girls Clubs of the Big Bend (2005-2006); Fundraising Committee for Annual Dinner, Boys & Girls Clubs of the

Big Bend (2005-2006); Sponsorship Chairman, Capital Cultural Center, Chukker Challenge (1997-1998); Fundraising Chairman, District School Superintendents Campaign (1996); Invited Delegate to China, Citizens Ambassador Program, People International (1995); Chairman, Representatives to Florida Commission on Education Reform and Accountability, Speaker of the Florida House of Representatives (1991-1993); Appointed Member, Representatives to Florida Commission on Education Reform and Accountability, Speaker of the Florida House of Representatives (1991-1993); Vice Chairman, Florida Department of Education, Gov. Bob Martinez (1990-1991); Appointee, Florida Department of Education, Gov. Bob Martinez (1987-1990) **CW:** Editor, In Touch (1979-1980); Contributor, Articles, Professional Journals **AW:** Selectee, Harvard Institute for Higher Education (1991); Merit Award, National FFA Organization (1974) **MEM:** Gold-Sustaining Member, Political Action Committee, Florida Realtors (2008-2015); Treasurer, Capital Gains Club (2000); Governmental Relations, LCTA (1991); Parliamentarian, LCTA (1988-1989); President, Leon Vocational Association (1988-1989); President-Elect, Leon Vocational Association (1987-1988); Secretary-Treasurer, LCTA (1987-1988); Charter Member, National Museum of Women in the Arts; National Business Education Association; Florida Vocational Association (Now FACTE); Florida Business Education Association; Public Relations Chairman, LCTA; Dance Arts Guild; Leon County Farm Bureau; Quill and Scroll; Honor Society of Phi Kappa Phi **MH:** Albert Nelson Marquis Lifetime Achievement Award (2017) **PA:** Republican **BA:** 7006 N Meridian Road, Rayner Real Estate, Tallahassee, FL; 32312

BRAUER, STEPHEN FRANKLIN, T: Diplomat, Manufacturing Company Executive **I:** Engineering **CN:** Hunter Engineering Co. **DOB:** 09/03/1945 **PT:** Arthur John Brauer Jr.; Jane (Franklin) Brauer **MS:** Married **SPN:** Camilla Thompson Brauer (6/12/1971) **CH:** Blackford Fitzhugh; Rebecca Randolph; Stephen Franklin Jr. **ED:** Honorary LLD, Washington University (1997); BA, Westminster College (1967); Coursework, Washington and Lee University (1963-1964) **C:** Chairman, Hunter Engineering Co., St. Louis, MO (2001-Present); U.S. Ambassador to Belgium (2001-2003); President, Hunter Engineering Co., St. Louis, MO (1981-2001); Executive Vice President, Hunter Engineering Co., St. Louis, MO (1978-1981); Sales and Marketing Official, Hunter Engineering Co., St. Louis, MO (1971-1978) **CR:** Partner, St. Louis Cardinals (1996-Present); Director, Ameren Corp. (2006-2013); Private Client Board, Bank of America (1996-2003); Board of Directors, Boatmen's Trust Co., St. Louis, MO (1986-1996) **CIV:** Trustee, Washington University in St. Louis (1991-Present); Trustee, Missouri Botanical Garden (1988-Present); Chairman, Board of Trustees, Washington University in St. Louis (2009-2014); Member, National Board, Smithsonian Institute, Washington, D.C. (1993-1999); Member, Missouri 21st Judicial District Commission (1992-1996); Civilian Aide, Secretary of the Army (1991-1995); Honorary Consul, Belgian Government (1987-2001) **MIL:** 1st Lieutenant, U.S. Army (1968-1970) **AW:** Henry Shaw Medal, Missouri Botanical Gardens (2003); Spirit of Enterprise Award, Missouri Republican Party (1999); Dean's Award, Washington University School of Engineering (1998); Technology Award, St. Louis Regional Commerce Growth Association (1993); Recognition of Outstanding Business Leadership Award, U.S. House of Representatives (1993) **MEM:** St. Louis Consular Corps.; St. Louis Civic Progress; St. Louis Country Club; Everglades Club, Palm Beach, CA **MH:** Albert Nelson Marquis Lifetime Achievement Award (2017) **PA:** Republican **RE:** Episcopalian **BA:** 11250 Hunter Dr, Hunter Engineering Co., c/o Bernie Kurtz, Bridgeton, MO, 63044

BRAULT, LORAIN, T: Healthcare Executive **I:** Medicine & Health Care **DOB:** 01/03/1944 **PB:** Chicago **SC:** IL/USA **PT:** Theodore Frank Hahn; Victoria Jean (Pribyl) Hahn **MS:** Married **SPN:** Donald R. Brault (4/29/1971) **CH:** Kevin David Brault **ED:** MSN, California State University, Long Beach (1977); BSN, California State University, Long Beach (1973); AA in Nursing, Long Beach City College (1963) **CT:** Registered Nurse, State of California; Certified Nurse Practitioner (1976) **C:** Consultant, Student Health Education (2008-Present); Professor Emeritus, Fullerton College, Fullerton, CA (2006-Present); Director, Student Health Service, Fullerton College (1999-2006); Vice President, Hospital Council of Southern California, Los Angeles, CA (1992-1999); President, Hospital Home Health Agency of California and Related Companies, Torrance, CA (1985-1992); Chief Executive Officer, Hospital Home Health Agency of California and Related Companies, Torrance, CA (1985-1992); Vice President, Hospital Home Care Corporation, Santa Ana, CA (1983-1985); Regional Director, Nursing and Support Services, American Medical International Inc., Beverly Hills, CA (1979-1983); Director, Master of Nursing Program, California State University, Long Beach (1977-1979); Director, Nursing, Canyon General Hospital, Anaheim, CA (1973-1976) **CR:** Lecturer, Board of Governors, Long Beach City College Foundation, Long Beach, CA (2007-Present); State Chairman, United States Department of Health & Human Services (2002-2003); Local Chairman, United States Department of Health & Human Services (2002-2003); Lecturer, California State University, Fullerton, CA (1999-2006); Lecturer, California State University, Los Angeles (1996-1999); Advisor, Nursing Institute (1990-1991); Guest Lecturer, Department of Public Health, University of California, Los Angeles (1986-1987); Consultant, AMI, Inc., Saudi Arabia (1983); Invited Lecturer, China Nurses Association (1983); Chairman, California Association for Health Services at Home; State President, Health Service Administration of California Community Colleges; Director, City of Long Beach Public Health Department; Chairman, Board of Directors, City of Long Beach Public Health Department; Professional Conference Speaker; Professional Conference Writer; Grant Director **CIV:** Member, Board of Governors, Long Beach City College Foundation, Long Beach, CA (2006-Present); President-elect, Board of Governors, Long Beach City College Foundation, Long Beach, CA (2017-2018); President, Long Beach Cares, Long Beach, CA (2009-2010); Member, Board of Directors, Long Beach Cares, Long Beach, CA (2008-2017); State President, Health Service Administration of California Community Colleges (2004-2005); Member, Health Service Administration of California Community Colleges (1999-2006); Faculty Member, California State University, Fullerton (1999-2005); Adviser, Home Health Masters Program, California State University, Los Angeles (1998); Member, Board of Directors, Department of Health and Human Services, Long Beach, CA (1996-2006); Chairman, Editorial Advisory Board, California Nursing (1995-1996); Faculty Member, California State University, Los Angeles (1993-1996); Chairman, Department of Heath and Human Services, Long Beach, CA (1991-1992); Consultant, NSI, Inc., Beverly Hills, CA (1991-1992); Consultant, NSI, Inc., Gardena, CA (1991-1992); Consultant, Maxim Home Care, Beverly Hills, CA (1991-1992); Member, City of Long Beach Empowerment Zone: EZ Working Group (1991); Chairman, California Association of Health Services at Home, Sacramento, CA (1990-1992); Board of Governors, SCAN Health Plan (1989-1990); Associate Clinical Professor, Nursing, University of Southern California (1988-1993); Commissioner, Secretary's Commission on Nursing, Department of Health Services, Washington, D.C. (1988); Clinical Consultant, King Faisal Hospital, Saudi Arabia (1984) **CW:** Author, "Community College Health Services: Who are We?" (2005); Author, "Smoking Prevention and Cessation in a Community College" (2004); Author, "Book Reviews" (2000); Author, "Health Care Industry Must Prepare for Year 2000 Problem" (1998); Author, "Office of Statewide Planning Releases Statistics for Hospital Community Benefits" (1997); Author, "New Strain of Staph Bacteria Could Prove Deadly" (1997); Author, "Building a Good Working Relationship with Physicians" (1992); Author, "Home Health Care: The Changing Picture" (1991); Author, "Home Health Care is the Place to Be" (1991); Author, "Case Management: Ambiguous at Best" (1991); Author, "No Place Like Home" (1990); Chairman, Editorial Advisory Committee, Registered Nurse Times, Nurseweek (1988-2000); Author, "Quality Assurance in a Home Care IV Therapy Program" (1988); Author, "Evaluating the Quality Assurance Program" (1988), Author, "Capitated Service Agreements with HMO's: High Risk-Low Yield-High Demand" (1988); Author, "Data Processing: A Guide to System Selection" (1987); Author, "1980s Reorientation to Home Health Care" (1987); Author, "Determining if Home Health is Right for Your Hospital" (1984); Author, "Planning and Development of a Masters Degree Program in Critical Care" (1979); Presenter in Field; Contributor, Articles, Professional Journals; Contributor, Chapters, Books; Editorial Advisory Boards, Nursing Journals **AW:** Distinguished Alumni, College of Health and Human Services, California State University, Long Beach (2013); Inductee, Hall of Fame, Long Beach City College, Long Beach, CA (2012); Making Democracy Work Award, League of Women Voters, Long Beach, CA (2008); Inductee, Hall of Fame, Downey Union High School, Downey, CA (2007); Distinguished Alumni, Long Beach City College, Long Beach, CA (2004); Grantee, Public, County, Private and State (1998-2006); Women Who Make a Difference, Soroptimist International, Long Beach, CA; Leadership Award, Health Service Administration of California Community Colleges, California; Lillian O'Brien Award for Outstanding Dedication and Commitment to Home Care, California Association for Health Services at Home, Sacramento, CA; Grantee, Health And Human Services Advanced Nurse Training **MEM:** President-elect, Board of Governors, Long Beach City College Foundation, Long Beach, CA (2018-2020); State President, Healthcare Service Administration for California Community Colleges (2004-2005); Section President, Healthcare Service Administration for California Community Colleges (2003-2004); Chairman, Board of Directors, California Association for Health Services at Home (1990-1993); Vice President, Women in Health Administration (1990); Secretary, Women in Health Administration (1989); Board of Directors, California Association for Health Services at Home (1988-1993); National Association for Home Care & Hospice; American Organization of Nurse Executives; American College of Health Care Executives; Southern California Public Health Association; California Association of Nurse Leaders; Nurse Executives Council; Soroptimist International of Long Beach; Sigma Theta Tau; Phi Kappa Phi **BAR:** Certified Nurse Practitioner (1976); Registered Nurse, State of California **MH:**

Albert Nelson Marquis Lifetime Achievement Award (2017) **H:** Traveling around the world; Photography **PA:** Democrat **RE:** Christian **ADD:** 1032 E Andrews Dr, Long Beach, CA, 90807

BRAXTON, KERRY E. ESQ., T: Assistant General Counsel **I:** Law and Legal Services **CN:** Lincoln Property Company **SC:** Texas/United States **ED:** MBA, Executive Program In-House Counsel, Boston University; JD, Texas Southern University Thurgood Marshall School of Law; BA, University of Texas Arlington **C:** Assistant General Counsel, Lincoln Property Company; Senior Counsel, FedEx Office; Of Counsel, Squire Patton Boggs **CR:** Dallas County Community College District Paralegal Program, Adjunct Professor **MIL:** United States Naval Academy, Annapolis, MD, Congressional Nomination **CW:** Author, Real Estate and Insurance Legal Publications Speaker, National and International Legal Conferences **AW:** Texas Top-Rated Lawyer, Martindale Hubbell; AV Preeminent Attorney, Martindale Hubbell; Top 1% of American Professionals, The American Registry of Business & Professional Excellence **MEM:** State Bar of Texas - Texas Bar College, Corporate Counsel Section, Real Estate Section, Texas Minority Counsel Program Inaugural Steering Committee; Dallas Bar Association - Corporate Counsel Section, Real Property Law Section, Minority Attorney Business Development Initiative Inaugural Co-Chair, Media Relations Committee Co-Chair; Texas General Counsel Forum Board of Directors; Association of Corporate Counsel Chief Legal Officer Global Network; NAA/NMHC Joint Legislative Committee; RIMS The Risk Management Society Government Affairs Committee **BAR:** State Bar of Texas, United States District Court, Northern District of Texas, Dallas **MH:** Who's Who in America for Achievements in Law, Marquis Who's Who in America **BA:** 2000 McKinney Ave Ste 1000, Lincoln Property Company, Dallas, TX, 75201 **URL:** http://www.kerrybraxton.com

BRENNAN, STEPHAN Y., T: Managing Shareholder **I:** Law and Legal Services **CN:** Iliff, Meredith, Wildberger & Brennan, P.C. **PB:** Fresno **SC:** CA/USA **PT:** William E. Brennan and Laura F. Young **MS:** Married **SPN:** Lisa M. Brennan **CH:** Sarah E. Brennan and Catherine C. Brennan **ED:** JD, University of Maryland School of Law, with Honors (1992); BA, University of San Diego, with Honors (1986) **C:** Managing Shareholder at Iliff, Meredith, Wildberger & Brennan, P. C. (2010-Present); Managing Shareholder, Iliff & Meredith, P.C. (2007-2009); Shareholder, Iliff & Meredith, P.C. (2003-2007); Associate, Iliff & Meredith, P.C. (1995-2003); Associate, Semmes, Bowen & Semmes (1994-1995); Staff Attorney, Semmes, Bowen & Semmes (1992-1993) **CIV:** Junior Warden St. Margaret's Episcopal Church, Annapolis, MD (2016-Present); President, Arc of the Central Chesapeake Region (2014-Present); Member, Board of Directors, Arc of the Central Chesapeake Region (2004-Present); Vestry Member, St. Margaret's Episcopal Church, Annapolis, MD (2008-2011); Treasurer, Two Past Terms, Arc of the Central Chesapeake Region; Past Mentor, Maryland Professionalism Center, Inc.; Vice-President, Arc of the Central Chesapeake Region; Continuing Legal Education Presentations **CW:** Author, "Cybersecurity, Hacking and Wire Fraud," Continuing Legal Education Lecture/Program, Minnesota Lawyers Mutual Insurance Company/Maryland Defense Counsel, Inc. (2018); Author, "Avoid Civil Claims and Disciplinary Complaints Caused by Problems with the Three Cs: Competence, Communication and Conflicts," Continuing Legal Education Lecture/Program, Minnesota Lawyers Mutual Insurance Company/Howard County Bar Association (2018); Author,

"Fee Sharing Agreements: The Interaction of Contracts Between Lawyers and the Rules of Professional Conduct," Trial Reporter (2016); Author, "Ethical Duties Arising from Medical Liens, and Their Effect in Personal Injury Cases," Trial Reporter (2015); Author, "Practitioners' Guidelines for Attorney Advertising," Trial Reporter (2014); Author, "The Law Practice Lifecycle: Insurance," Trial Reporter (2013); Author, "Managing Your Statute of Limitations (and What to Do When You Screw Up)," Trial Reporter (2012); Co-author, "Rule of Expert Witnesses in Legal Malpractice Cases," Maryland Bar Journal (2007); Author, "Fee Disputes: Things to Think About," Anne Arundel County Bar Association Barrister (2007); Co-author, "Settlement Recommendations: High Risk Behavior for Maryland Attorneys," MSBA Annual Meeting (2002); Co-author, "Ex Parte Communication with Former Employees of an Adverse Party, or a Potential Adverse Party: Maryland Lawyers Proceed at Their Own Risk," Trial Reporter (1998) **AW:** Super Lawyers, Maryland (2014-Present); Best Lawyers in America (2018); Outstanding Chapter Volunteer of the Year, The Arc Maryland (2018); Top 100 (2017); Philanthropy Award, The Arc Central Chesapeake Region (2015); Outstanding Chapter Volunteer of the Year, The Arc Maryland (2011); AV Preeminent Rating, Martindale-Hubbell; America's Top 100 Civil Defense Litigators, Maryland; American Bar Foundation Fellow **MEM:** Board of Trustees, James C. Cawood, Jr. American Inn of Court (2008-Present); James C. Cawood, Jr. American Inn of Court (2003-Present); Anne Arundel County Bar Association (2003-Present); Mentor, Maryland Professionalism Center, Inc. of the Court of Appeals of Maryland (2013-2014); President, James C. Cawood, Jr. American Inn of Court (2012-2013); Mentor, Professionalism Commission of the Court of Appeals of Maryland (2011-2012); President-Elect, James C. Cawood, Jr. American Inn of Court (2011-2012); Treasurer, James C. Cawood, Jr. American Inn of Court (2010-2011); Bar Association of Baltimore City (1992-2003); Maryland Pattern Jury Instruction Committee, Civil, Maryland State Bar Association; Appellate Practice Committee, Maryland State Bar Association; Litigation Section, Maryland State Bar Association; Lawyers Professional Liability Consortium, ABA; Center for Professional Responsibility, ABA; District of Columbia Bar Association; Fellow, Maryland Bar Foundation; Fellow, Litigation Counsel of America **BAR:** The District of Columbia Court of Appeals (1995); United States District Court District of Maryland (1995); Court of Appeals of Maryland (1992); United States Court of Appeals for the Fourth Circuit; United States District Court for the District of Columbia; United States Court of Appeals for the District of Columbia Circuit **H:** Traveling; Reading; Forestry; Boating; Fishing **RE:** Episcopalian **BA:** 8055 Ritchie Hwy Ste 201, Iliff, Meredith, Wildberger & Brennan, P.C., Pasadena, MD, 21122

BRENNECKE, ALLEN EUGENE, I: Other **DOB:** 01/08/1937 **PB:** Marshalltown **SC:** IA/USA **PT:** Arthur Lynn Brennecke; Julia Alice (Allen) Brennecke **SPN:** Billie Jean Johnstone (June 12, 1958) **CH:** Scott; Stephen; Beth; Gregory; Kristen **ED:** JD, University Iowa (1961); BBA, University Iowa (1959) **C:** Of Counsel, Moore, McKibben, Goodman & Lorenz, LLP, Marshalltown (2000-Present); Partner, Harrison, Brennecke, Moore, Smaha & McKibben, Marshalltown (1966-2000); Associate, Mote, Wilson & Welp, Marshalltown, IA (1962-1966); Law clerk, U.S. District Judge, Des Moines (1961-1962) **CIV:** United Methodist Church, Marshalltown (1978-1981, 1987-1989); Board of Trustees, Iowa Law

School Foundation (1973-1986); Finance Chairman, Republican Party, Fourth Congressional District, IA (1970-1973); Board of Directors, Marshalltown YMCA (1966-1971); Marshall County Republican Party, IA (1967-1970) **CW:** Contributor, Articles, Professional Journals **MEM:** Board of Directors, National Judicial College (1982-1988); Chairman, House of Delegates, American Bar Association (1984-1986); Board of Governors, American Bar Association (1982-1986); American College of Trusts and Estates Counsel; American College Tax Counsel, American Bar Foundation; President, Iowa Bar Association (1990-1991); Masons; Promise Keepers **BAR:** Iowa (1961) **H:** Golf; Travel; Sports **PA:** Republican **RE:** Methodist

BRENNER, M. HARVEY, T: Professor **I:** Education/Educational Services **CN:** UNT Health Science Center; Johns Hopkins University **PB:** New York City **SC:** NY/USA **ED:** Fellow, Institute for Patient Safety, UNT Health Science Center (2016-Present); PhD in Medical Sociology, Yale University (1966); MA in Sociology, Yale University (1964); BA in Economics and History, The City University of New York, with Honors (1962) **C:** Professor, Department of Behavioral and Community Health, UNT Health Science Center (2008-Present); Professor Emeritus, Johns Hopkins University (2004-Present); Professor, Department of Social and Behavioral Sciences, UNT Health Science Center (2008-2010); Chair, Professor, Department of Social and Behavioral Sciences, UNT Health Science Center (2005-2008); Professor, Chair, Epidemiology, Institute for Health Sciences, Technical University of Berlin (1996-2005); Professor, Health Policy and Management, Johns Hopkins University (1979-2004); Associate Professor, Epidemiology and Public Health, and Sociology, Yale School of Medicine (1972); Assistant Professor, Epidemiology and Public Health, and Sociology, Yale School of Medicine (1966-1971); Associate in Research, Epidemiology and Public Health, and Sociology, Yale School of Medicine (1965-1966); Research Staff, Wakoff Research Center, Staten Island Mental Health Society (1963-1964) **CR:** Visiting Professor, Medical University of Hannover, Institute of Epidemiology, Social Medicine and Health Research (1994-1997, 2014-Present); Visiting Professor, Technical University of Berlin (2005-2014); Visiting Professor, Yale University (2001-2003); Visiting Professor, Harvard University (1977); Consultant, Several Parliaments, Countries in Europe; Consultant, World Health Organization, Geneva, Switzerland and Copenhagen, Denmark; Expert Testimony, Joint Economic Committee, United States Congress; Expert Testimony, Committee on Science, Space, and Technology; Expert Testimony, House Judiciary Committee; Expert Testimony, United States Department of Labor; Expert Testimony, Centers for Disease Control and Prevention; Expert Testimony, U.S. Senate Committee on Environment and Public Works **CIV:** Member, American Public Health Association **CW:** Author, "Estimating the Effects of Economic Change on National Health and Social Well-being" (1984); Author, "Mental Illness and the Economy" (1973); Reviewer, Professional Journals; Contributor, Numerous Articles, Professional Journals; Presenter, Professional/Scientific Meetings **AW:** Fellow, Institute for Patient Safety, UNT Health Science Center (2016-Present); UNTHSC Research Award, UNT Health Science Center (2005); Major Career Award for Excellence, American Public Health Association (1997); Career Award for Scientific Excellence (1996) **MEM:** American Association for the Advancement of Science; Phi Beta Kappa; American Public Health Association; American Sociological Association **BA:** 3500 Camp Bowie Blvd, University of North

Texas Health Science Center, Fort Worth, TX, 76107 **ADD:** 3500 Camp Bowie Blvd, UNT Health Science Center, Fort Worth, TX, 76107 **URL:** https://www.unthsc.edu/school-of-public-health/dr-m-harvey-

BRICEL, TANIA ELIZABETH, T: Owner, President, Chief Executive Officer, Chief Designer **I:** Business Management/Business Services **CN:** Colour Creations-Progressive Marketing Ltd. **DOB:** 08/31/1957 **PB:** Vancouver **SC:** British Columbia/Canada **PT:** Marko Leon Bricel; Liselotte Elizabeth Ringer-Bricel **MS:** Divorced **ED:** Bachelor's of Commerce, Marketing and International Business, Concordia University (1980) **CT:** Certified, Canadian Ski Instructors Alliance **C:** Owner, Colour Creations-Progressive Marketing Ltd. (1998-Present); President, Colour Creations-Progressive Marketing Ltd. (1998-Present); Chief Executive Officer, Colour Creations-Progressive Marketing Ltd. (1998-Present); Chief Designer, Colour Creations-Progressive Marketing Ltd. (1998-Present); Product Manager, Skin Care Division, Avon Canadian Head Office (1985-1987); Assistant Marketing Manager, Cosmetic and Hair Care Divisions Head Office, Revlon (1980-1985) **CR:** Consultant, Interior Design **CIV:** ADL **MEM:** Canadian Ski Instructors Alliance **H:** Professional skiing; Windsurfing; Sailing; Golf; Tennis **RE:** Roman Catholic **BA:** 2170 Dunwin Dr. Unit 2, Mississauga, ON, Canada, L5L 5M8 **ADD:** Stone Grove, 2417 Old Carriage Rd. Bungalow 8, Mississauga, ON, Canada, L5C 1Y6 **URL:** http://www.stanfordwhoswho.com/Tania.Bricel.7135926.html#biography

BRIDGES, LINDELL C., I: Environmental Services **ED:** Master's Degree in Geology, University of Arkansas, Fayetteville, AR (1982); Bachelor of Science in Geology, University of Arkansas, Fayetteville, AR (1980) **CT:** Certified Professional Geologist, American Association of Petroleum Geologists **AW:** Peppard-Souders Scholarship (1980) **H:** Reading about history, science and religion; Skiing; Canoeing; Hiking

BRILLIANT, RICHARD, T: Art Historian, Educator (Ret) **I:** Education/Educational Services **CN:** Columbia University **DOB:** 11/20/1929 **PB:** Boston **SC:** MA/USA **PT:** Frank Brilliant; Pauline (Apt) Brilliant **MS:** Married **SPN:** Eleanor Luria (6/24/1951) **CH:** Stephanie; Livia; Franca; Myron **ED:** PhD, Yale University (1960); MA, Yale University (1957); LLB, Harvard University (1954); BA, Yale University, Magna Cum Laude (1951) **C:** Retired (Present); Professor Emeritus, Art History and Archeology, Columbia University, New York, NY (2004-Present); Anna S. Garbedian Professor in the Humanities, Columbia University, New York, NY (1990-2004); Professor of Art History and Archaeology, Columbia University, New York, NY (1970-2004); Visiting Professor, Princeton University (1986); Visiting Mellon Professor of Fine Arts, University of Pittsburgh (1971); Assistant Professor to Professor, Chairman, Department of Art History, University of Pennsylvania, Philadelphia, PA (1962-1970) **CR:** Consultant, New-York Historical Society (2004-2005); Director, Italian Academy for Advanced Studies in America, Columbia University (1996-2000); Visiting Professor, Scuola Normale Superiore, Pisa, Italy (1988); Consultant, WNET-TV, New York, NY (1984-1989); Chairman, Governing Board, The Society of Fellows in the Humanities, Columbia University (1981-1984); Visiting Professor, Scuola Normale Superiore, Pisa, Italy (1980); Visiting Professor, Scuola Normale Superiore, Pisa, Italy (1974) **CW:** Author, "Death: From Dust to Destiny," Reaktion Press, London, England (2017); Co-Editor, With Dale Kinney, "Use and Reuse, Spolia and Appropriation in Art" (2011); Guest Curator,

New York Historical Society (2006); Guest Curator, Minneapolis Institute of the Arts (2003-2004); Author, "My Laocoon" (2000); Author, "Un Americano a Roma" (2000); Guest Curator, Jewish Museum, New York, NY (1997); Exhibitor, Jewish Museum, New York, NY (1997); Author, "Facing the New World" (1997); Author, "Commentaries on Roman Art" (1994); Author, "Portraiture" (1991); Editor, Art Bulletin (1990-1994); Co-Curator, Exhibition Center for African Art, New York, NY (1990); Co-Author, "The Fayum Portraits" (1988); Author, "Visual Narratives" (1984); Author, "Pompeii: A.D. 79" (1979); Author, "Roman Art" (1974); Author, "The Arts of the Ancient Greeks" (1973); Author, "Arch of Septimius Severus in the Roman Forum" (1967); Author, "Gesture and Rank in Roman Art" (1963); Author, More than 100 Articles and Reviews **AW:** Distinguished Scholar Award, College Art Association (2005); Honoree, Senior Fellow, National Endowment for the Humanities (1972-1973); Fellowship, John Simon Guggenheim Memorial Foundation (1967-1968); Fellowship, American Academy in Rome (1960-1962); Fulbright Grantee, Rome, Italy (1957-1959) **MEM:** Managing Committee, American School of Classical Studies (1974-2007); American Academy of Arts & Sciences; Connecticut Academy of Arts and Sciences, Yale University; American School of Classical Studies; College Art Association; Corresponding Member, German Archaeological Institute, Berlin, Germany; The Phi Beta Kappa Society **BAR:** Massachusetts (1954) **MH:** Albert Nelson Marquis Lifetime Achievement Award (2017) **H:** Reading; Traveling; Wine **PA:** Democrat **ADD:** 400 E 56th St Apt 12N, New York, NY, 10022

BRITT, JOSEPH JOHN, T: Religious Studies Educator **I:** Education/Educational Services **CN:** Vatican Embassy **DOB:** 07/13/1948 **PB:** Baltimore **SC:** MD/USA **PT:** Joseph John Britt; Lottie Elizabeth (Zielinski) Britt **ED:** MA, Northeastern University, Boston, MA (1972); AB in History, Boston College (1970) **C:** Chief Archivist, Vatican Embassy, Washington, DC (2010-Present); Xaverian Brothers, Baltimore, MD (1970-Present); Director, Educational Programs, Curator, Pope John Paul II Cultural Center, Washington, DC (2004-2010); Historical Researcher, Xaverian Brothers, Baltimore, MD (2003-2004); Teacher, Paltarokas School, Panevezys, Lithuania (1997-2002); Teacher, St. Joseph Regional High School, Montvale, NJ (1993-1997); Teacher, Malden Catholic High School, Massachusetts (1983-1993); Teacher, St. Joseph Regional High School, Montvale, NJ (1981-1983); Teacher, Malden Catholic High School, Massachusetts (1976-1981); Teacher, Notre Dame High School, Utica, NY (1973-1976); Teacher, Malden Catholic High School, Massachusetts (1970-1973) **CIV:** Board of Directors, Minutemen Boston Council, Boy Scouts of America, Boston, MA (1985-1993) **CW:** Author, "Xaverian Brothers in East Africa" (2004) **AW:** Silver Beaver Award, Boy Scouts of America (1987) **MH:** Distinguished Humanitarian (2017) **H:** Photography; Camping; Science fiction; History **RE:** Roman Catholic **ADD:** 7513 Jackson Avenue, Takoma Park, MD, 20912

BRITTON, RUTH ANN, T: Educator **I:** Education/Educational Services **CN:** Cochise College **DOB:** 04/04/1943 **PB:** Fort Smith **SC:** AR/USA **PT:** Ralph M. Wright; Margaret E. (Reising) Wright **MS:** Married **SPN:** Joseph D. Britton (9/25/1965, Deceased 5/2017) **CH:** Beth; Meg; Jo **ED:** MS, Kansas State University (1978) BA in Elementary Education, Concordia Teachers College (Now Concordia University Chicago), River Forest, IL (1965) **CT:** Certified in Reading K-12 Education; Certified in Elementary Education; Certified in Developmental Reading; Certified Nationally in Developmental

Education **C:** Faculty Emeritus, Cochise College (2012-Present); Instructor, Cochise College, Arizona (1993-2006); Department Head, Cochise College, Arizona (1993-2005); Director, Junior High School Reading Laboratory, Hillsborough County Public Schools, Tampa, FL (1986-1992); Chapter I Reading Teacher, Montgomery County Public Schools, Christianburg, VA (1982-1986); Teacher, Second and Fifth Grade, Manhattan City Schools, Kansas (1977-1978, 1969); Teacher, Fifth Grade, School District of Pickens County (1966-1968) **CIV:** Secretary, Board of Directors, Legacy Foundation of South East Arizona (2012-Present); Philanthropy Committee Chair, Legacy Foundation of South East Arizona (2010-Present); Governance Chair, Cochise County Education Foundation (2010-2017); Sierra Vista Regional Health Center Foundation, Secretary (2009-2012) **CW:** Co-Author, "Reading Handbook for Parents"; Co-Author, "Making Connections" **AW:** Inductee, Hall of Fame, Cochise College (2017); Named, Outstanding Instructor, Cochise College (1999-2000); Excellence in Education, National Institute for Staff and Organizational Development (1997-1998); Teacher of the Year, Texas Commission on Jail Standards (1989-1990); Recipient, Helping Hands Award for Volunteer Service, Seventh Corps., US Army (1980) **MEM:** Chair, Governor's Commission for Service Learning and Volunteerism (2002-2015); Former Member, International Reading Association; Literacy Volunteers; College Reading and Learning Association; Numerous Church Committees **MH:** Albert Nelson Marquis Lifetime Achievement Award (2017) **H:** Cooking, Gardening, Personal reading; Counted cross stitch; Music **PA:** Republican **RE:** Lutheran **BA:** PO Box 3921, Sierra Vista, AZ, 85636 **ADD:** 3115 E San Xavier Rd, Sierra Vista, AZ, 85635

BRODSKY, BEVERLY ANNE, T: Writer, Consultant, Spiritual Counselor **I:** Writing and Editing **DOB:** 06/23/1950 **PB:** Philadelphia **SC:** PA/USA **PT:** Louis Singer; Florence Elaine Singer **MS:** Married **SPN:** Bruce Brodsky (8/17/1980) **CH:** Lauren Fay **ED:** Diploma, Pilot Program, Hawaii Institute of Unified Physics with the Resonance Academy (2015); BA in Psychology, Vassar College, Cum Laude, Poughkeepsie, NY (1977) **CT:** Ordained to Ministry, Los Angeles Community Church of Religious Science (2003) **C:** President, San Diego International Association for Near Death Studies, San Diego, CA (2002-Present); Freelance Book Editor & Writer, El Cajon, CA (2003-2009); Founder, Proprietor, All One Light (2004-2007); Co-Founder, Wisdom, Wealth, Wellness, Vista, CA (2004-2006); Business Analyst, Naval Air Technical Data and Engineering Service Center (NATEC), San Diego, CA (1998-2002); Inventory, Systems, & Computer Analyst, ASO/NAVICP, Philadelphia, PA (1978-1998); Spiritual Life Coach **CR:** President, Delaware Valley Near Death Studies, Ardmore, PA (1996-1998); Speaker, Internet Programs, Workshops and Seminars **CIV:** Founding Board Member, American Center for the Integration of Spiritual Transformative Experiences (2009-Present); Director, Los Angeles Community Church of Religious Science (2006-Present); Community Group Leader, Institute of Noetic Sciences (Now IONS), Petaluma, CA (2003-2006) **CW:** Contributor, Book, "The Art of Purposeful Being, Second Edition" Philip Winkelmans (2017); Featured, "The Art of Purposeful Being," Philip Winkleman, Hay House (2017); Featured, "Pathways to Peace," Christine Spencer (2012); Featured, Documentary, "Luminous World Views" (2011); Featured, Documentary, "New Light on Near Death: Come Home to Perfection" (2009); Featured, Documentary, "Home and Back" (2009); Assistant Producer, Bonus Feature, "Reflections:

Beyond and Back," "Life Before Her Eyes" (2008); Featured, "God Wants to Talk to You," Philip Winklemans (2007); Featured, Jerusalem Post (2006); Featured, "Lessons from the Light," Dr. Kenneth Ring (2006); Featured, "They Saw Beyond Death," Arvin Gibson (2006); Featured, "The New Children and Near-Death Experiences," P.M.H. Atwater (2003); First Person Interviewed on NDE Program, Israeli Public Radio (2003); Featured, "Nothing Better than Death," Kevin Williams (2002); Featured, "Children of the New Millennium," P.M.H. Atwater (1999); Contributor, Book, "The Art of Purposeful Being" by Philip Winkelmans (1999); Featured, BBC Documentary, "The Human Body: An Intimate Universe, New Light on Near Death" (1998); Featured, McCall's Magazine (1993); First New Death Experience Program, New Tang Dynasty Chinese Satellite Television (Now New Tang Dynasty Television) **AW:** Scholarship, Vassar College (1975-1976) **MEM:** Donor, Board of Directors, International Foundation for Survival Research (2004-Present); Leader, International Association for Near Death Studies, San Diego Chapter (2001-Present); Leader, Media Consultant, International Association for Near Death Studies (1992-Present); Board of Directors, Seattle International Association for Near Death Studies (2002-2007); Newsletter Editor, Seattle International Association for Near Death Studies (2002-2007); Associate, Phi Beta Kappa (Now The Phi Beta Kappa Society) (2001); Secretary, Phi Beta Kappa (Now The Phi Beta Kappa Society) (2001); Afterlife Research and Education Institute, Inc. **MH:** Albert Nelson Marquis Lifetime Achievement Award (2017) **ADD:** 12031 Via Felicia, El Cajon, CA, 92019 **URL:** http://bevbrodsky.com

BROG, DAVID, T: Air Force Officer, Consultant **I:** Consulting **CN:** IRD, Inc. **DOB:** 08/11/1933 **PB:** Manchester **SC:** CT/USA **PT:** Israel Brog; Pesha (Blonstein) Brog **MS:** Married **SPN:** Verda Anna Raney (11/9/1959) **CH:** Kai Ling; Tov Binyamin **ED:** MS, University of Southern California (1967); BA, University of Pittsburgh (1955) **C:** President, IRD, Inc., Silver Spring, MD (1982-Present); Domestic and International Consultant, IRD, Inc., Silver Spring, MD (1982-Present) **CIV:** Executive Director, Air Warrior Courage Foundation **MIL:** Deputy Chief of Staff, Operations, Command Control and Communications Countermeasures, U.S. Air Force (1981-1982); Director, Readiness and Electronic Combat, Headquarters, U.S. Air Force (1981); Advanced Through Grades to Colonel, U.S. Air Force (1978); Commissioned Second Lieutenant, U.S. Air Force (1956) **CW:** Contributor, Articles, Professional Journals **AW:** Decorated Distinguished Flying Cross; Legion of Merit; Air Medal With 12 Oak Leaf Clusters; Distinguished Graduate, U.S. Air Force Air War College **MEM:** President, Red River Valley Fighter Pilots Association; Association of Old Crows; Air Force Association **RE:** Jewish **ADD:** PO Box 877, Silver Spring, MD, 20918

BROGDEN, STEPHEN, T: Library Director (Retired) **I:** Library Management/Library Services **CN:** CSU Channel Islands **DOB:** 09/26/1948 **PB:** Des Moines **SC:** IA/USA **PT:** Paul M. Brogden; Marjorie (Kueck) Brogden **MS:** Single **SPN:** Melinda L. Raine (1983-2014) **CH:** Nathan **ED:** MA, University of Iowa (1972); BA, University of Iowa (1970) **CT:** Wine Education and Management Certificate (UCLA, 2016) **C:** Library Faculty Member, California State University Channel Islands (2015-Present); Adjunct Faculty Member, University of North Texas (2010-2018); Board Member, Folk Alliance Region-West (FAR-West)(2008-2017); Director, City of Thousand Oaks Library (1999-2014); Deputy Director, City of Thousand Oaks Library (1990-1999); Head of

Fine Arts, Des Moines Public Library (1980-1990); Road Manager, Bill and Bonnie Hearne (1976-1979); Visiting Lecturer, The University of Arizona (1975-1976); Director Harwood Foundation, The University of New Mexico, Taos (1972-1975); Caretaker, Eya Fechin Branham Ranch, Taos, NM (1970-1972) **CR:** Board Member, Ventura County Library Foundation (2017-Present); Board Member, Pacific Pioneer Broadcasters (2005-2008, 2009-2015); Chair, Metropolitan Cooperative Library System (2001) **CIV:** Board of Directors, Thousand Oaks Library Foundation (1999-2014); Board Member, Pacific Pioneer Broadcasters (2005-2007, 2009-2011); Vice President, Hospice of the Conejo (2004-2005) **MEM:** President, Films for Iowa Libraries (1983-1986); President, Metro Des Moines Library Association (1980); American Library Association; California Library Association **MH:** Albert Nelson Marquis Lifetime Achievement Award (2017) **ADD:** 5736 Skyview Way, Unit H, Agoura Hills, CA, 91301

BROOKS, SHARON DIANE, T: Of Senior Counsel **I:** Law and Legal Services **CN:** Bristol-Myers Squibb **PT:** Bernard Edward Brooks; Alice Lillian Brooks **ED:** JD, Georgetown University Law Center, Georgetown University (2000); MPH, Yale University (1986); BA, University of Illinois (1984) **C:** Of Senior Counsel, Research & Development Law, Bristol-Myers Squibb Company (2015-Present); Of Senior Counsel, Development & Regulatory Law Group, Amgen Inc., Thousand Oaks, CA (2007-2015); Attorney, Alston & Bird LLP, Washington, D.C. (2004-2007); Attorney, OFW Law, Washington, D.C. (2000-2004); Law Clerk, American Cancer Society, Washington, D.C. (2000); Senior Data Analyst, University Research Co., LLC, Bethesda, MD (1992-1994); Epidemiologist, CSR, Incorporated, Washington, D.C. (1988-1992); Database Manager, Cardiac Arrhythmia Center, MedStar Washington Hospital Center, MedStar Health, Washington, D.C. (1986-1988); Database Analyst, Cardiac Arrhythmia Center, MedStar Washington Hospital Center, MedStar Health, Washington, D.C. (1986-1988); Policy Analyst, Project HOPE, The Center for Health Affairs, Bethesda, MD **CIV:** Member, Institutional Review Board, Project HOPE, The Center for Health Affairs, Bethesda, MD (1996-2003) **CW:** Contributor, Reports to Public Health Publications **BAR:** Washington (2001); Maryland (2000) **MH:** Albert Nelson Marquis Lifetime Achievement Award (2017) **ADD:** 416 Burd St, Pennington, NJ, 08534 **URL:** https://www.martindale.com/thousand-oaks/california/sharon-d-brooks-2137324-a

BROWN, BILL, T: Bank Executive **I:** Financial Services **CN:** 1) Net Power, LLC, 2) 8 Rivers Capital, LLC **DOB:** 06/09/1955 **PB:** Waynesville **SC:** NC/USA **PT:** Glenn William Brown; Evelyn Myralyn (Davis) Brown **MS:** Married **SPN:** Amy Margaret Moss (4/14/1984) **CH:** Elizabeth Quinn; Lauren Alexandra **ED:** JD, Duke University School of Law (1980); BS in Political Science, Massachusetts Institute of Technology (1977); BS in Biology, Massachusetts Institute of Technology (1977) **C:** CEO, NET Power, LLC (2010-Present); Co-founder, 8 Rivers, Durham, NC (2008-Present); CEO, 8 Rivers, Durham, NC (2008-Present); Energy Innovation Fellow, Duke University (2013-2014); Chairman, Palmer Labs, LLC (2008-2014); Professor of Law, Duke University School of Law (2008-2013); Global Co-head Listed Derivatives, Morgan Stanley, New York, NY (2007-2008); Head of US FX Sales, Morgan Stanley, New York, NY (1997-2007); Head of US EM and Non-$ Debt Sales, Morgan Stanley, New York, NY (2003-2005); Principal, Morgan Stanley, New York, NY (1997); Global Head of FX and Fixed Income Sales, American International Group, Inc.,

Greenwich, CT (1996-1997); Executive Director, Goldman Sachs, London, England (1994-1996); Vice President, Goldman Sachs, New York, NY (1990-1994); Partner, Sidley Austin LLP, New York, NY (1988-1989); Corporate Law Associate, Sidley Austin LLP, New York, NY (1984-1987); Corporate Law Associate, Donovan, Leisure, Newton & Irvine, New York, NY (1980-1984) **CR:** Board Member, Council for Economic Development (2016-Present); Senior Lecturing Fellow, Duke University School of Law (2013-2014); Professor of Practice, Duke University School of Law (2009-2014); Visiting Professor of Practice, Duke University School of Law (2008-2010) **CIV:** Board of Visitors, Duke University School of Law (2014-Present); Board of Directors, East Durham Children's Initiative (2013-2016); Visiting Professor, Duke University School of Law (2008-2009); Corporate Advisory Board, School of American Ballet (2003-2007); Alumni Association Board, Duke University School of Law (2001-2003); Session Member, First Presbyterian Church of Greenwich (2000-2003) **CW:** Editorial Board, Duke Law Journal, Duke University School of Law (1978-1980) **MEM:** American Bar Association; The New York Society of Security Analysts, Inc.; AFSA; President, Karl Taylor Compton Lecture Series Committee, Massachusetts Institute of Technology; President, Massachusetts Gamma Chapter, Phi Delta Theta; Massachusetts Institute of Technology; Political Science Department Washington Fellowship **BAR:** New York State Bar (1980) **MH:** Albert Nelson Marquis Lifetime Achievement Award (2017) **RE:** Presbyterian **BA:** 406 Blackwell St Ste 410, Net Power Llc, Durham, NC, 27701

BROWN, CAROL ANN, T: Librarian (Retired) **I:** Library Management/Library Services **DOB:** 03/07/1948 **PB:** Denver **SC:** CO/USA **PT:** Truman Veach Yowell; Mary Margaret Yowell **MS:** Married **SPN:** Robert Ray Brown (9/15/1974) **CH:** Nancy Ann **ED:** MLS, Emporia State University, Kansas (1998); BA, Western State Colorado University, Gunnison, CO (1971); AA, Western Wyoming Community College, Rock Springs, WY (1969) **C:** Library Director, Hay Library, Western Wyoming Community College (2006-2011); Associate Librarian, Interim Library Director, Hay Library, Western Wyoming Community College (2005-2006); Library Technician to Associate Librarian, Western Wyoming Community College (1972-2005) **CR:** Judge, Women Writing the West (2015); Judge, Women Writing the West (2011-2013); President, Para-Professional Association, Western Wyoming Community College (2003-2004) **CIV:** President, Business and Professional Women, Rock Springs, WY (2001-2003) **AW:** Grantee, Wyoming State Library, Cheyenne, WY (2005); Recipient, Performance Incentive Award, Western Wyoming Community College (2004-2005); Grantee, Wyoming State Library, Cheyenne, WY (2003) **MEM:** Section Chair, Wyoming Library Association (2003-2004); Executive Council, Wyoming Library Association (2003-2004); American Library Association; Mountain Plains Library Association **MH:** Albert Nelson Marquis Lifetime Achievement Award (2017) **H:** Reading; ATV riding; Horseback riding; Snowmobiling **ADD:** 2713 Briarwood Ln, Rock Springs, WY, 82901

BROWN, DALE, T: Federal Agency Administrator **I:** Government Administration/Government Relations/Government Services **DOB:** 05/27/1954 **PB:** New York **SC:** NY/USA **PT:** Bertram S. Brown; Beatrice Joy (Gilman) Brown **ED:** BA, Antioch College (1976) **C:** Disability Policy Consultant, Veterans Staffing Network, (2013-2014); Senior Policy Expert, EconSys Corporation (2009-2010); Senior Manager, LD Online (2006-2009); Member, Youth Team, Department of Labor (2002-2005); Policy Advisor, Office of Disability Employment Policy,

Department of Labor (2001-2005); Manager, National Conference of Youth with Disabilities (2000); Program Manager, Job Accommodation Network (1997-1999); Program Manager, Labor Committee, President's Committee on Employment of People with Disabilities (1996-1998); With, Interagency Technology Assistance Coordinating Team, President's Committee on Employment of People with Disabilities (1992-1994); Agency Representative, President's Committee on Employment of People with Disabilities (1991-1993); Program Manager, Work Environment and Technology Committee, President's Committee on Employment of People with Disabilities (1988-1994); Member, New Products Development Team, President's Committee on Employment of People with Disabilities (1987-1990); Youth Development Committee, President's Committee on Employment of People with Disabilities (1986-1988); Program Manager, Labor Committee, President's Committee on Employment of People with Disabilities (1985); Program Manager, Committee on Library and Information Services, President's Committee on Employment of People with Disabilities (1984-1986); Program Manager, Handicapped Concerns Committee, President's Committee on Employment of People with Disabilities (1982-1985); Writer, President's Committee on Employment of People with Disabilities (1979-1982); Research Assistant, American Occupational Therapy Association (1978-1979) **CR:** Consultant in Field; Member, Task Force on Learning Disabilities, Rehabilitation Services Administration (1981-1983); General Assembly Speaker, National Convention, General Federation of Women's Clubs (1981) **CIV:** Board of Directors, Lourie Mitchell Employment Center (2008-Present); Advisory Committee, Learning Disability Online Website (2005-Present); Advisory Board, International Center for Disability Resources on the Internet (2003-Present); Judge, Ten Outstanding Young Americans, United States Junior Chamber of Commerce, Jaycees (2003); Board of Directors, Council on Quality and Leadership (2001-2005); Committee on Youth with Disabilities, Presidential Task Force on Employment of Adults with Disabilities (1999-2002); Representative, Committee on Federal Government as Model Employer; Delegate, National Writer's Union (1999); Representative, Interagency Committee, Handicapped Employees (1998-1999); Professional Advisory Board, National Attention Deficit Disorder Association (1996-1999); Special Assistant for People with Disabilities, Federally Employed Women (1991-1992); Member, Blue Ribbon Panel, National Telecommunications Access for People with Disabilities (1989-1994); Chair, Conference on Information Technology for Users With Disabilities (1989); Member, Congressional Task Force, Rights and Empowerment of Americans with Disabilities (1988-1990); Board of Directors, American Coalition for Citizens with Disabilities (1985-1986); Board of Directors, Closer Look National Information Center (1980-1983); President, Association of Learning Disabled Adults (1979-1980) **CW:** Author, Civil Service Career Coach Column, NARFE Magazine (2009-2012); Author, "The Federal Government A Place to Work and a Place to Serve" (2007); Author, "Steps to Independence for People with Learning Disabilities" (2005); Guest Editor, "Learning Disability and Career Development" (2002); Guest Editor, "Career Planning and Adult Development Journal" (2002); Co-Author, "Job-Hunting Tips for the So-Called Handicapped" (2001); Author, "Learning A Living Guide to Planning Your Career and Finding a Job for People with Learning Disabilities, Attention Deficit Disorder and Dyslexia" (2000); Member, Editorial Board, "In the Mainstream" (1994-1998); Author, "Learning Disabilities and Employment" (1997); Guest Editor, "Learning Disabilities Research and Practice"

(1990-1996); Author, "Working Effectively with People Who Have Learning Disabilities and Attention Deficit Hyperactivity Disorder" (1995); Author, "I Know I Can Climb the Mountain" (1995); Co-Editor, "Learning Disabilities Quarterly Americans with Disabilities Act and Learning Disabilities" (1992); Author, "Pathways to Employment for People with Learning Disabilities" (1991); Director, "Part of the Team: People with Disabilities in the Workforce" (1990); Member, Editorial Board, "Learning Disabilities Focus" (1988-1990); Author, "They Could Have Saved Their Homes" (1982); Member, Editorial Board, "Perceptions" (1981-1983); Author, "What Color is Your Parachute"; Contributor, Various Columns in Newspapers **AW:** Recipient, Honor Award, Department of Labor (2004); Recipient, Voices Campaign Award (2004); Honoree, Ten Outstanding Young Americans, U.S. Junior Chamber of Commerce (1994); Recipient, Arthur S. Fleming Award (1992); Recipient, Gold Screen Award, National Association Governor Communicators (1991); Recipient, Special Achievement Award, President's Committee on Employment of People with Disabilities (1991); Recipient, Individual Achievement Award, National Council on Communications Disorders (1991); Recipient, Personal Achievement Award, Women's Program, Department of Labor (1989); Recipient, Margaret Byrd Rawson Award (1989); Recipient, Blue Pencil Award, National Association of Government Communicators (1986); Grantee, Foundation for Children with Learning Disabilities (1982) **MEM:** Representative, Interagency Committee on Handicapped Employees (1989-1991); Board of Directors, Learning Disabilities Association of America (1986-1991); Founder, President, National Network of Learning Disabled Adults (1980-1981); Member, American Library Association; National Association Government Communicators **PA:** Democrat **ADD:** 4570 Macarthur Boulevard N.W., Apartment 104, Washington, DC, 20007 **URL:** DoB:27-05-1954

BROWN, DOUGLAS COLTON, I: Law and Legal Services **DOB:** 09/02/1948 **PB:** New York **SC:** NY/USA **PT:** Robin Colton Brown; Catherine (Snyder) Brown **ED:** JD, California Western University (1973); BA, Ohio Wesleyan University (1970) **C:** Private Practice in Law (1977-Present); Judge Advocate General, Marine Corps (1973-1977) **CIV:** Captain, US Marine Corps (1973-1977) **MEM:** National Association of Criminal Defense Attorneys; California Attorneys for Criminal Justice; San Diego Criminal Defense Lawyers Club **BAR:** United States District Court for the Central District of California (1987); United States Court of Appeals for the Ninth Circuit (1980); California (1979); United States District Court for the Southern District of California (1979); Supreme Court of the United States (1978); Washington (1973) **H:** Travel

BROWN, JUDITH GWYN, T: Author, Illustrator, Painter **I:** Fine Art **DOB:** 10/15/1933 **PB:** New York **SC:** NY/USA **PT:** Philip S. Brown; Freida C. (Robinson) Brown **ED:** Postgraduate Work, Parsons School of Design, The New School (1956-1957); BA, New York University (1956); Coursework, Cooper Union for the Advancement of Science and Art (1951-1952) **C:** Illustrator, New York, NY (1958-Present); Instructor, New York, NY (1958-Present) **CIV:** Volunteer, Animal Welfare Groups, New York and Massachusetts **CW:** Illustrator, "Cry of Victory"; Illustrator, "Mandy"; Illustrator, "The Best Christmas Pageant Ever"; Illustrator, "King of the Dollhouse"; Illustrator, "The Happy Voyage"; Illustrator, "Alphabet Dreams"; Illustrator, "The Mask of the Dancing Princess"; Featured in Permanent Collections, Boston Public Library, Metropolitan Museum of Art, Huntington Library, Universities **MH:** Albert Nelson Marquis

Lifetime Achievement Award (2017) **H:** Reading 19th century books **ADD:** 522 E 85th Street, Apt. 5W, New York, NY, 10028

BROWNWOOD, DAVID, T: Senior Counsel **I:** Law and Legal Services **CN:** Cravath, Swaine & Moore LLP **DOB:** 05/24/1935 **PB:** Los Angeles **SC:** CA/USA **PT:** Robert Scott Osgood; Ruth Elizabeth (Bellamy) Brownwood **MS:** Married **SPN:** Susan Sloane Jannick; Sigrid Carlson (1956-1972) **CH:** Jeffrey Owen; Kirsten; Scott David; Daniel Stuart **ED:** LLB, Harvard University, Magna Cum Laude (1964); AB, Stanford University, with Distinction (1956) **C:** Senior Counsel, Cravath, Swaine & Moore, LLC, New York, NY (2003-Present); Partner-in-Charge, London Office (1995-2001); Managing Partner for Legal Staff, Cravath, Swaine & Moore, LLC, New York, NY (1983-1986); Recruiting Partner, Cravath, Swaine & Moore, LLC, New York, NY (1978-1982); Partner, Cravath, Swaine & Moore, LLC, New York, NY (1973-2003); Associate, Cravath, Swaine & Moore, LLC, New York, NY (1968-1972); Lecturer of Law, Kenya Institute of Administration, Lower Kabete (1967-1968); Lecturer of Law, University of Khartoum, Sudan (1966-1967); Associate, McCutchen, Doyle, Brown & Enersen, San Francisco, CA (1964-1966); Law Clerk, Ropes & Gray, Boston, MA (1963) **CR:** President (1988-1993); Chairman, Executive Committee (1983-1988); Treasurer, New York Law Institute (1978-1983) **CIV:** Secretary, Greenwich Historical Society (2009-Present); Trustee, Greenwich Historical Society (2008-Present); Vice Chair, Greenwich Historical Society (2016); Secretary, Greenwich Historical Society (2011-2016); Board of Directors, Greenwich Historical Society (2010-2011); President, Board of Trustees, Greenwich Library (2008-2010); Trustee, Greenwich Library (2003-2010); Treasurer, Royal Oak Foundation (2004-2009); Board of Directors, Royal Oak Foundation (2003-2009); Board of Directors, Collegiate Chorale, New York City (2005-2008); President, Benjamin Franklin House Foundation (2002-2007); Co-Chairman, 50th Reunion Gift, Stanford University (2005-2006); Committee on University Resources, Harvard University (1991-2006); Co-Chairman, 40th Reunion Gift, Stanford University (2003-2005); Board of Advisers, Stanford University Trust, U.K. (1995-2002); Member, Harvard Law School Visiting Committee, Harvard University (1995-2001); Member, National Board, Outward Bound USA (1993-1996); President, Board of Governors, Stanford Associates (1994-1995); Board of Governors, Stanford Associates (1993-1995); Vice Chairman, New York Major Gifts Committee, Stanford University (1993-1995); Co-Chair, Eastern Council, Stanford University (1993); Executive Committee, New York Council, Stanford University (1992-1995); New York Regional Committee Campaign, Harvard Law School, Harvard University (1991-1995); Co-Chairman, Board of Directors, Literacy Assistance Center, New York City (1987-1994); Board of Directors, Literacy Assistance Center, New York City (1983-1994); National Chair, Law School Fund, Harvard University (1991-1993); President, Board of Trustees, Greenwich Country Day School (1988-1992); Keystone Regional Vice Chair, Centennial Campaign, Stanford University (1986-1992); Trustee, Greenwich Country Day School (1985-1992); Co-Chairman, Harvard University Law School 25th Reunion Gift (1988-1989); Vice President, Greenwich Country Day School (1986-1988) **MIL:** Captain, U.S. Air Force Reserve, Massachusetts Air National Guard (1961-1966); Fighter Pilot, Air Defense Command, 1st Lieutenant, U.S. Air Force (1956-1961) **CW:** Member, Editorial Board, Harvard University Law Review (1963-1964) **AW:** Centennial Medallion, Stanford University; Stanford Associates Award **MEM:** Board of Governors, The Field Club of

Greenwich (2011-2014); Chairman, Business and Membership Committee, Alumni Association, Stanford University (2008-2011); Board of Directors, Alumni Association, Stanford University (2004-2011); Chairman, Finance Committee, Alumni Association, Stanford University (2006-2008); Fellow, American Bar Foundation; Fellow, New York State Bar Foundation; ABA; New York State Bar Association; Association of the Bar of the City of New York; Siasconset Casino Association; Harvard Club of New York City; Great Harbor Club; Sankaty Head Golf Club; The Pilgrims Society; Round Hill Club **BAR:** State of New York (1969); State of California (1965) **MH:** Albert Nelson Marquis Lifetime Achievement Award (2017) **BA:** 825 8th Avenue, 46th Floor, Cravath, Swaine & Moore LLP, New York, NY, 10019 **ADD:** 296 Old Church Road, Greenwich, CT, 06830

BRUMBAUGH, HARLEY A., T: Founder, Director **I:** Education/Educational Services **DOB:** 10/23/1934 **PB:** Renton **SC:** WA/USA **PT:** Aaron Emery Brumbaugh; Alice Jane Brumbaugh **ED:** Master's Degree in Music Education, Central Washington University (1962); BEd, Central Washington University (1957) **C:** Professor of Music, Bellevue Community College (1972-1992); Director of Choral Music, Renton School District, WA (1963-1972); Director of Instrumental Music, Port Angeles School District (1962-1963); Supervisor of Music, Ketchikan School District, Ketchikan, Alaska (1959-1962) **CR:** Founder, Voices of the Valley Chorale (2010); Director, Voices of the Valley Chorale (2010); Vice President, East Side Musician's Association (1995-1997); Lead Trumpet/Vocalist, Kings of Swing jazz Band, White Nights Festival, St. Petersburg, Russia (1992); Co-founder, Washington Association of Community Bands, Bellevue (1986); Conductor, Tacoma All-City Honor Choir (1982-1986); Conductor, Celebration Singers, Nandi, Fiji (1985); Conductor, Celebration Singers Australian Youth Music Festival, Melbourne, Australia (1983); Conductor, Tahiti Typhoon Benefit Radio Broadcast, Papeete, French Polynesia (1983); Guest Appearance, Saturday with Saldonia; Guest Appearance, The Don Lane Show; Guest Appearance, The Daryl Somers Show (1982-1983); Conductor, University of Mexico Concert Series, Mexico City (1981); Festival Conductor, Olympic Penninsula Massed Choir, Chimacum, Washington (1979); National Chairman for Community and Two-year Colleges, Music Educator's National Conference, Chicago, Illinois (1977-1978); Conductor, All Southeastern Alaska Massed Choir, Ketchikan/Skagway (1974-1978); Conductor, All-Bellevue Massed Choir (1975); Member, Puget Sound Choral Director's Association, Seattle, Washington (1973-1975); Chairman, Northwest Music Educator's Conference, Portland (1972-1973); Clinician, Northwest Music Educator's Conference, Portland (1972-1973); Vice President, Washington Jazz Educator's Association, Yakima (1970-1972); Clinician, Washington Music Educator's Conference, Yakima (1970); Trumpeter, Seattle Opera Orchestra (1966-1967); Singer, Seattle Opera Chorus (1964-1965); Leader, Harley's Horns-A-Plenty!; Lead Trumpet, Jackie Souders Orchestra; Lead Trumpet, Max Pillar, Norm Hougy; Lead Trumpet, Archie Kyle; Lead Trumpet, Hank Ohstus; Lead Trumpet, Ted Carper; Lead Trumpet, Red Shepherd; Lead Trumpet, Ben Blakeman; Lead Trumpet, Reg Hudman; Lead Trumpet, Terry King; Lead Trumpet, The Many Sounds of Nine Orchestra; Trumpet Player, Marion Hutton; Trumpet Player, Eartha Kitt; Trumpet Player, Morey Amsterdam; Trumpet Player, Kay Starr; Trumpet Player, Frankie Laine; Trumpet Player, Vick Schoen; Trumpeter, Mel Torme; Trumpeter, Nelson Riddle; Trumpeter, Lawrence Welk; Trumpeter, Tex Beneke; Trumpeter, Tennessee Ernie

Ford; Trumpeter, Seattle Symphony; Trumpeter, Seahawks Band; Trumpeter, Sonic Six; Trumpeter, Seattle World's Fair Band **CIV:** Conductor, Voices of the Valley Choral (2010); Conductor, Renton City Concert Band (1985-2003); Founding Member, Entertainment Board, Renton River Days Annual Festival (1985-2001); Co-founder/producer, Snoqualmie Valley Arts Live (1992-1996); Co-founder, Washington Association of Community Bands, Bellevue (1986); Founding Member, Bellevue Jazz Festival (1974); Director, The Valley Community Players, Renton, Washington (1965); Founder, The Valley Community Players, Renton, Washington (1965); Founder, Celebration Singers **MIL:** Principal Trumpet Player, 52nd Army Band, Ford Ord, CA **CW:** Recorder, Albums (2016); Arranger, "Molly Malone" (1970-1974); Composer, "Drums of God"; Composer, "No Greater Love"; Composer, "Tattered Sandals"; Composer, "Four Riverside Reflections"; Author, "Riverside Reflections"; Composer, "Snoqualmie Falls Mill Town Images"; Director, "Sounds of Freedom!" **AW:** Special Award for Being an Outstanding Foreign Musical Group, University of Mexico (1980-1981) **MEM:** Board Member, Snoqualmie Valley Historical Society (2003); International Trumpet Guild; Poets West; Washington State Historical Society; Renton Historical Society **MH:** Who's Who in America; Who's Who in American Education **H:** History; Reading; Walking **RE:** Christian **ADD:** 524 Orchard Avenue NE, North Bend, WA, 98045

BRUN, FRANCISCO, T: Intensive Care Unit Medical Director **I:** Medicine & Health Care **CN:** Vituity Healthcare **SPN:** Brenda (07/05/2003) **ED:** MD, Boonshoft School of Medicine, Wright State University (1998); BS, Wright State University (1991); Fellow, Critical Care Medicine, University of Pittsburgh Medical Center; Resident, Internal Medicine, Akron General Medical Center **CT:** Certified in Critical Care Medicine, American Board of Internal Medicine; License to Practice Medicine, Commonwealth of Pennsylvania; License to Practice Medicine, State of Florida; License to Practice Medicine, State of Arizona; License to Practice Medicine, State of California **C:** Intensive Care Unit Medical Director, Good Samaritan Hospital, Vituity, CEP America, LLC (2017-Present); Intensive Attending, Regional Medical Center of San Jose (2011-2017); Chairman, Bioethics Committee, Regional Medical Center of San Jose (2011-2017); Vice Chair, Internal Medicine Department, Regional Medical Center of San Jose (2011-2017); Fellow, American Medical Association **CR:** Assistant Professor, Medicine, Thomas Jefferson University (2005-2008) **MEM:** Society of Critical Care Medicine; American College of Chest Physicians; American Society of Addiction Medicine; NCS **ADD:** 18 Chapel Cove Dr, San Rafael, CA, 94901 **URL:** https://health.usnews.com/doctors/francisco-brun-473581

BRUNSON, BURLIE A., T: Aerospace Transportation Executive **I:** Engineering **CN:** Lockheed Martin Corporation **DOB:** 04/28/1945 **PB:** Bakersfield **SC:** CA/USA **PT:** Burlie B. Brunson; Mary Helen (Self) Brunson **MS:** Married **SPN:** Lois L. Corbett (4/25/1968) **CH:** Marci L.; Meredith L. **ED:** MBA, The George Washington University School of Business (1995); PhD, Oregon State University (1983); MS, Oregon State University (1972); Fulbright Scholar, Geology, Central University, Ecuador (1968); BS, U.S. Naval Academy, with Honors (1967) **CT:** Certified, Lean-Six Sigma Operations Improvement; Certified Competitive Intelligence Professional; AACSB Certified Professional Faculty **C:** Founder, President, Chief Operating Officer Emeritus, DCG, LLC (2012-Current); Senior Vice President, Chief Strategy Officer, Logistics Specialties Inc., Layton, UT (2011-2012); Vice Pres-

ident, Programs, Plans and Analysis, Lockheed Martin Corporation, Bethesda, MD (1999-2011); Vice President, Washington Operations, Lockheed Martin Corporation (1995-1999); Director, Maritime Systems, Lockheed Corporation, Calabasas, CA (1992-1994); Vice President, ASW, Lockheed Sanders Inc., Nashua, NH (1991-1992); Executive Vice President, Chief Operations Officer, Planning Systems Inc., McLean, VA (1989-1991); Senior Vice President, Technical Director, Planning Systems Inc. (1988-1989); Vice President, Planning Systems Inc. (1986-1988); Principal Scientist, Planning Systems Inc. (1981-1986); Research Physicist, Naval Ocean Research and Development Activity, Bay St. Louis, MS (1978-1981); Research Oceanographer, Naval Ocean Systems Center, San Diego, CA (1972-1978); Research Assistant, Oregon State University, Corvallis, OR (1970-1972) **CR:** Board of Advisors, Intufo, LLC; Guest Lecturer, Reformed Theological Seminary; Adjunct Faculty, The George Washington University School of Business **CIV:** Council of Advisors, Office of Executive Programs, Robert H. Smith School of Business, University of Maryland ; Member, Board of Advisors, The George Washington University School of Business; Board of Directors, Greater Washington Chapter, U.S. Naval Academy Alumni Association; Board of Advisors, College of Earth, Ocean, & Atmospheric Sciences, Oregon State University **MIL:** U.S. Navy (Retired); Commissioned Officer, U.S. Navy, Pensacola, FL (1968-1970) **CW:** Contributor, Articles, Professional Journals **AW:** Distinguished Alumni Achievement Award, The George Washington University School of Business (1997); Man of the Year, Fullerton College (1966) **MEM:** Beta Gamma Sigma (1995); Sigma Xi (1978); Phi Kappa Phi (1972); Navy League of the United States; National Defense Industrial Association; U.S. Naval Academy Alumni Association **PA:** Republican **RE:** Presbyterian **ADD:** 711 Potomac Knolls Drive, McLean, VA, 22102

BRUSCH, JOHN LYNCH, T: Medical Director **I:** Health, Wellness and Fitness **CN:** Cambridge Health Alliance **DOB:** 11/03/1943 **PB:** Boston **SC:** MA/USA **PT:** Charles Brusch; Margaret Agnes (Lynch) Brusch **MS:** Married **SPN:** Married Patricia Gahan (5/12/1973) **CH:** Amy Claire; Meaghan; Patrick **ED:** Resident in Infectious Disease, New England Medical Center, Boston, MA (1971-1974); Resident in Medicine, New England Medical Center, Boston, MA (1970-1971); Intern, New England Medical Center, Boston, MA (1969-1970); MD, Tufts University School of Medicine (1969); BS in Chemistry and Biology, Tufts University (1965) **CT:** Diplomate, American Board of Geriatrics; Diplomate, American Board of Infectious Disease; Diplomate, American Board of Internal Medicine **C:** Senior Consultant, Youville Hospital (2007-; 2012); Attending Physician, Division of Infectious Diseases, Cambridge Health Alliance, Cambridge, MA (1976-Present); Medical Director, Somerville Hospital (2001-2015); Chief of Medicine, Somerville Hospital (1999-2009); Clinical Associate, Massachusetts General Hospital, Boston, MA (1996-2009); Director, Community Medicine, Youville Hospital (1995-2007); Chief of Medicine, Youville Hospital, Cambridge, MA (1991-2007); Assistant Chief of Medicine, Brighton Public Health Service Hospital, Boston, MA (1974-1976) **CR:** Staff, Cambridge Health Alliance, Community Health Advisory Council (2012-Present); Member, Cambridge Bio Safety Committee (2011-Present); Board of Directors, North Cambridge Coop Bank (2001-Present); Assistant Professor of Medicine, Harvard Medical School (2001-Present); Associate Chief of Medicine, Cambridge Health Alliance (1999-Present); Chief Editor, Medscape Medical Director, Primary Care Unit, Cambridge Hospital

(2015); Infectious Disease Section, Medscape Medical Director, Primary Care Unit, Cambridge Hospital (2015); Director, Hospital Board, Cambridge Health Alliance (2003-2012); Senior Consultant, Spaulding Hospital (2011) **CIV:** Board of Directors, Council on Aging, Belmont, MA (2000-2009) **MIL:** Uniform Branch USPHS (1974-1976) **CW:** Chief Editor, Infectious Disease (2014); Managing Editor, Emedicine Medscape (2001-2014); Editor, "Endocarditis Essentials" (2011); Co-author, "Infective Endocarditis: Management in the Era of Intravascular Devices" (2007); Editor, "Infective Endocarditis: Management in the Era of Intravascular Devices" (2007); Co-author, "Infective Endocarditis" (1996); Contributor, Articles, Professional Journals **AW:** Nancy Kahn Award (2010) **MEM:** Fellow, American College of Physicians; Knight Commander, Equestrian Order of the Holy Sepulchre; Infectious Disease Society of America; American Society of Microbiology **MH:** Albert Nelson Marquis Lifetime Achievement Award (2017) **RE:** Roman Catholic **BA:** 1493 Cambridge St, Cambridge, MA, 02139 **ADD:** 52 Radcliffe Rd, Belmont, MA, 02478

BRYSON, EARLENE, T: Director of Administrative Services **I:** Business Management/Business Services **CN:** Reseda Church of Christ **ED:** Associate Degree, Sawyer Business College **CT:** Administrative Management Certification **C:** Director of Administrative Services, Reseda Church of Christ (2017-Present); Keynote and Motivational Speaker (1985-Present); Vice President, Phoenix House (1999-2015) **CIV:** Ambassador for Christian Education; Crusade for Women's Empowerment; Advocate for Ministries to Youth **CW:** Author, "He Keeps On Blessing Me" **AW:** Recipient, Woman of Faith Award, Los Angeles Bible College (2017); Recipient, Outstanding Leadership, The International Women's Leadership Association (2015) **MEM:** National Association of Professional Women; The Leadership Council; San Fernando Valley Chapter, NAACP; Advisory Board, United Christian Women of the Churches of Christ **MH:** Distinguished Humanitarian (2017) **RE:** Christian **ADD:** 27642 Ennismore Ave, Canyon Country, CA, 91351 **URL:** https://www.linkedin.com/in/earlene-bryson-30a38519

BUCHANAN-BOARDMAN, CHARLES EDWARD SEAN, T: President **I:** Financial Services **CN:** Assiduus Falcon Networking, LLC **DOB:** 02/14/1981 **PB:** Las Vegas **SC:** NV/USA **PT:** Patricia Danielle Boardman, MS, MBA; Sgt. Larry W. Tarin, USAF Vietnam **MS:** Single **ED:** MS in International Real Estate, Chapman Graduate School of Business, Florida International University (2015); MBA in Finance and Accounting, Regis University (2012); BS in Accounting, Liberty University (2012); BS in Accounting, Liberty University **CT:** REFM Certification in Excel for Real Estate Level One; Undergraduate Certification in Real Estate Management; Certified Microsoft Office Specialist in Excel 2007; Undergraduate Certification in Advanced Accounting; Customer Service Certification **C:** President, Assiduus Falcon Networking, LLC (2018-Present); Analyst in Corporate Accounting, Park Hotels & Resorts (2017-Present); Senior Accountant, Navistar, Inc. (2016-2017); Staff Accountant, Leidos (2015-2016); Fixed Assets Accountant III, Leidos (2012-2015); Associate Auditor, SAIC (2011-2012); Accounting Specialist, Lawler-Wood, LLC (2011); Staff Accountant, Able Body Labor (2007-2010); Full-Charge Bookkeeper, Terra West Management Service (2007); Accounts Payable Specialist, Avw Telav Inc. (2006-2007) **CR:** Founded Assiduus Falcon Networking, LLC in 2018 in the City of Manassas Park, VA **MEM:** Sons of the American Revolution; Sons of the American Colonists;

St. George's Society of New York; American Institute of Professional Bookkeepers; Institute of Management Accountants **H:** Genealogy - He is a descendant of the Candler family of Coca-Cola and a great great grandnephew of Marcus Daly, Montana's Copper King **RE:** Christian **ADD:** 170 Market St Apt 430, Manassas Park, VA, 20111 **URL:** http://www.washingtondcwealth.com/

BUCKLEY, CHRISTOPHER HENRY JR., T: Environmental Lawyer **I:** Law and Legal Services **DOB:** 07/16/1940 **PB:** New Haven **SC:** CT/USA **PT:** Christopher H. Buckley; Margaret Elaine (McKeon) Buckley **MS:** Married **SPN:** Marguerite Mae Buckley (9/2/1972) **CH:** Marisa Marguerite; Mark Raymond **ED:** LLB, Harvard University (1967); BA, University of Notre Dame, South Bend, IN (1962) **C:** Partner, Gibson, Dunn & Crutcher LLP, Washington, DC (1990-2008); Partner, Beveridge & Diamond PC, Washington, DC (1976-1990); Associate, Covington & Burling LLP, Washington, DC (1967-1975) **CR:** Founder and Chair, Environment & Natural Resources Practice Group, Gibson, Dunn & Crutcher LLP; Executive Committee, Gibson, Dunn & Crutcher LLP, Washington, DC; Lecturer, Environmental Litigation, Environmental Regulatory Programs **CIV:** President, Barker Foundation (1988-1989); Chairman, Board of Directors, Atlantic Salmon Federation; Executive Committee, Everglades Foundation; Board Member, Bonefish & Tarpon Trust; Executive Committee, Board Member, Environmental Law Institute; Founder, Chair, Environment & Natural Resources Practice Group, Gibson, Dunn & Crutcher, Washington, DC **MIL:** First Lieutenant, U.S. Army (1962-1964) **CW:** Contributor, Numerous Articles, Professional Journals; Contributor, Chapters Related to Trial Law, Books; Lecturer, Environmental Law, Natural Resources Law and Trial Advocacy **AW:** The Lee Wulff Conservation Award, Atlantic Salmon Federation (2015); One of the Best Environmental Lawyers, America's Leading Lawyers for Business, Chambers USA; Best Lawyers in America; Guide to the World's Leading Environmental Lawyers; Who's Who Legal: USA - Environment; Environment Expert Guide; Washingtonian's Best Environmental Lawyers List; Super Lawyers, Washington, DC **MEM:** American Bar Association; Federal Bar Association **BAR:** 11th Circuit, U.S. Court of Appeals (2005); Sixth Circuit, U.S. Court of Appeals (2004); Tenth Circuit, U.S. Court of Appeals (2004); Ninth Circuit, U.S. Court of Appeals (2000); Federal Circuit, U.S. Court of Appeals (2000); U.S. District Court, State of Colorado (1999); U.S. Claims Court (Now Court of Federal Claims) (1991); U.S. District Court, State of Maryland (1990); Fourth Circuit, U.S. Court of Appeals (1983); U.S. Supreme Court (1979); U.S. District Court, District of Columbia (1968); District of Columbia Circuit, U.S. Court of Appeals (1968); Pro Hac Vice in Numerous Other Federal and State Courts **MH:** Albert Nelson Marquis Lifetime Achievement Award (2017) **H:** Fly fishing **ADD:** 122 Anglers Way, Islamorada, FL, 33036

BUCKLEY, JOHN JOSEPH JR., I: Business Management/Business Services **DOB:** 10/05/1944 **PB:** Evanston **SC:** IL/USA **PT:** John Joseph; Mary Ruth (Smith) B. **MS:** Married **SPN:** Sarah Amelia Puceloski (May 16, 1970) **CH:** Ruth Mary; Patricia Kimberly; John Joseph III **ED:** MBA, George Washington University (1969); AB, Kenyon College (1966) **C:** President, Jack Buckley & Associates, College Station, Texas (2001-Present); President, Chief Executive Officer, St. Joseph Health Systems, Bryan, Texas (2005-2009); Chief Executive Officer, St. Joseph Regional Health Center, Bryan, Texas (2004-2008); Interim Chief Executive Officer, St. Joseph Regional Health Center, Bryan, Texas

(2003-2004); Interim Chief Operating Officer, St. Joseph Campus of Via Christi Medical Center, Wichita, Kansas (2003); Interim President, Chief Executive Officer, St. Mary's Hospital of East St. Louis, Illinois (2002); President, Southern Illinois Healthcare Enterprises, Carbondale, Illinois (1992-2001); Senior Vice President, Mercy Health System, Cincinnati (1988-1991); President, St. Joseph's Hospital and Medical Center, Phoenix (1984-1988); Chief operating officer, Harrington Cancer Center, Amarillo (1982-1984); President, St. Anthony's Development Corporation, Amarillo (1982-1984); President, St. Anthony's Hospital, Amarillo, Texas (1979-1984); Vice President, St. Joseph's Hospital and Medical Center, Phoenix (1976-1979); Associate Administrator, St. Joseph's Hospital and Medical Center, Phoenix (1974-1976); Assistant Administrator, St. Joseph's Hospital and Medical Center, Phoenix (1971-1974); Assistant Administrator, Maricopa County General Hospital, Phoenix (1969-1971); Assistant, Center Health Organization Transformation; Fellowship, Faculty Department and School **CR:** Member, External Advisory Board, College of Business, Southern Illinois University (2000-Present); External Advisory Board Member (2004-Present); Executive-in-Residence, Health Policy and Management, TAMU Health Science Center, School of Rural Public Health, HPM Department MHA Program (2009-Present); Chairman, TAMU Health Science Center, School of Rural Public Health (2004-2011); President Southern Illinois Hospital Services, Health Services Southern Illinois, Regional Health Plan (1992-2001); Faculty and Candidates Master of Hospital Administration, Health Policy Management Department, School of Rural Public Health; Advisor to Deans Department, Chairs and Faculty Graduate and Undergraduate Levels, Southern Illinois University **CIV:** Alumni Council, Kenyon College (1998-2003); Active Member, Staten Island Edge (1995-2003); President, Kenyon College (2001-2002); Trustee, Kenyon College, Gambier, OH (1991-1995); President, Mercy Services Corporation (1984-1988); Board of Directors, Greater Phoenix Affordable Health Care Foundation (1984-1988); Active Amarillo Alliance of Community Service Executives; Amarillo Area Academy Health Center Corporation; Amarillo Area Hospital Home Care; Amarillo Foundation for Health and Science; Panhandle Chapter, Texas Society to Prevent Blindness; Amarillo Junior League; Children's Oncology Services of Texas Panhandle; Amarillo Diocesan Coordinator of Health Affairs; Administrative Committee, Amarillo **MEM:** Fellow, American College of Healthcare Executives; Trustee, The Prenatal Clinic (2000-Present); Chair, Leadership Council, St. Mary's Catholic Church (2009-Present); Management and Leadership Board of Trustees, The George Washington University Alumni Association for Health Services (1988-2013); Secretary Treasurer, Texas Association Voluntary Hospital (2008-2009); HOSPAC (2006-2009); Trustee, Illinois Hospital Association (1995-2001); President, Alumni Association, Delta Phi (1988-2000); Trustee, Catholic Health Association U.S. (1985-1991); Trustee, Texas Hospital Association (1983-1984); Arizona Hospital Association; Arizona Kidney Foundation **PA:** Republican **RE:** Roman Catholic

BUKOVAC, MARTIN JOHN, T: Horticulturist, Educator/Researcher **I:** Education/Educational Services **CN:** Michigan State University **DOB:** 11/12/1929 **PB:** Johnston City **SC:** IL/USA **PT:** John Bukovac; Sadie (Fak) Bukovac **MS:** Married **SPN:** Judith Ann Kelley (9/5/1956) **CH:** Janice Louise **ED:** Doctorate Honoris Causa in Agriculture, Universität Bonn, Germany (1995); PhD, Michigan

State University (1957); MS, Michigan State University (1954); BS, Michigan State University, with Honors (1951) **C:** National Science Foundation Senior Postdoctoral Fellow, University of Oxford, University of Bristol, England (1965-1966); Professor, Michigan State University, East Lansing, MI (1963); Associate Professor, Michigan State University, East Lansing, MI (1961-1963); Assistant Professor in Horticulture, Michigan State University, East Lansing, MI (1957-1961) **CR:** Collaborator, Agricultural Research Service, U.S. Department of Agriculture (1982-2003); President, Martin J. Bukovac Inc. (1996-2001); Member, International Advisory Board, Division of Life Sciences, Center for Nuclear Studies, Atomic Energy Commission, Grenoble, France (1993-2000); Science Exchange Lecturer, NAIST (2000); Donald L. Reichard Memorial Lecturer, The Ohio State University (1999); Kermit Olson Memorial Lecturer, University of Minnesota (1997); Monselise Memorial Lecturer, The Hebrew University of Jerusalem (1994); Agricultural Research Service B.Y. Morrison Memorial Lecturer (1994); Visiting Professor, The Ohio State University (1990); Member, Agricultural Research Advisory Committee, Eli Lilly and Company, Indianapolis, Indiana (1971-1988); Commencement Speaker, Michigan State University (1986); Guest Researcher, Institute Obstbau und Gemusebau, Universität Bonn, Germany (1986); Batjer Memorial Lecturer, Washington State Horticultural Society (1985); Consultant, Department of Agriculture, China (1984); Distinguished Lecturer, Department of Science and Technology, China (1984); Guest Researcher, Horticultural Research Institute, Budapest, Hungary (1983); Visiting Professor, University of Zagreb, Yugoslavia (1983); Visiting Professor, University of Guelph, Ontario, Canada (1982); Visiting Professor, The Ohio State University (1982); John A. Hannah Distinguished Lecturer, Michigan State Horticultural Society (1980); Guest Lecturer, Serbian Science Council, Fruit Research Institute, Cacak, Yugoslavia (1979); Visiting Professor, Japan Society for the Promotion Science, Osaka Prefecture University (1977); Distinguished Visiting Professor, New Mexico State University (1976); Guest Lecturer, Polish Academy of Sciences (1974); Visiting Scholar, Virginia Polytechnic Institute and State University, Blacksburg (1973); National Academy of Sciences Exchange Lecturer, Council of Academies, Yugoslavia (1971); Adviser, IAEA, Vienna (1961); Visiting Lecturer, Japan Atomic Energy Research Institute (1958) **CIV:** Board of Directors, Michigan State University Press (1983-1992); President, Okemos Music Patrons, Michigan (1973-1974) **MIL:** First Lieutenant, U.S. Army (1951-1953) **CW:** Author, "The Cuticular Membrane: a dynamic interface between plant and environment," Periodicum Biologorum (2005); Member, Editorial Advisory Board, Center for Agriculture and Bioscience International (1989-2003); "Co-author, "Studies on water transport through the sweet cherry fruit surface," Planta (2000); Member, Executive Advisory Board, "Encyclopedia of Agricultural Sciences" (1991-1996); Co-author, "Rheological properties of enzymatically isolated tomato fruit cuticle," Plant Physiology (1995); Co-author, "Spray Droplet: Plant surface interaction and deposit formation as related to surfactants and spray volume," New Zealand Forest Research Institute (1995); Co-author, "Interaction between 2-(1-naphthyl) acetic acid and micelles of nonionic surfactants in aqueous solution," Journal of Agricultural Food Chemistry (1992); Co-author, "Peroxidase and IAA oxidase activities and peroxidase isoenzymes from the pericarp of seeded and seedless 'Redhaven' peach fruit," Journal of Plant Growth Regulation (1992); Co-

author, "Evidence by gel filtration for solubilization of NAA by nonionic surfactant micelles," HortScience (1990); Co-author, "A system for photographically studying droplet impaction on leaf surfaces," American Society of Agricultural and Biological Engineers (1986); Co-author, "Cherry fruit development: Indoleacetic acid oxidase isoenzymes in the seed," Physiologia of Plantarium (1983); Co-author, "Phthalimide-inhibition of the ethylene effect on sex expression in monoecious cucumber plants," American Society of Horticultural Science (1983); Co-author, "Composition of tomato fruit cuticle as related to fruit growth and development," The Plant Cuticle, Academic Press (1982); Co-author, "Peach leaf surfaces: Changes during expansion with special reference to spray application," American Society of Horticultural Science (1979); Co-author, "Ontogenetic variations in the composition of peach leaf wax," Phytochemistry (1979); Author, "Herbicide entry into plants," Herbicides Physiology, Academic Press (1976); Co-author, "Carbon Input," Carbon, Productivity, Waverly Press (1975); Co-author, "Cherry fruit abscission: A role for ethylene in mechanically induced abscission of immature fruits," American Society of Horticultural Science (1975); Co-author, "Characterization of the components of plant cuticles in relation to the penetration of 2,4-D," Annual Applied Biology (1971); Co-author, "Preferential polar pathways in the cuticle and their relationship to ectodesmata" (1970); Co-author, "Some physical kinetic considerations in penetration of naphthaleneacetic acid through isolated pear leaf cuticle," Physiologia of Plantarum (1969); Co-author, "Histochemical changes in the developing abscission layer of fruits of Prunus cerasus" (1969); Co-author, "A histochemical study of abscission layer formation in the bean," American Journal of Botany (1969); Co-author, "Ion uptake by cells enzymically isolated from green tobacco leaves," Plant Physiology (1965); Author, "Modification of the vegetative development of Phaseolus vulgaris with N, N–dimethylaminomaleamic acid," American Journal of Botany (1964); Co-author, "Mechanisms of ion uptake by leaves of higher plants as revealed by radioisotropes," Second Annual Oak Ridge Radioisotope Conference (1964); Co-author, "Induction of parthenocarpic growth of apple fruits with gibberellins A3 and A4," Botany Gazette (1963); Co-author, "Gibberellin Effects on Photoperiod-controlled growth of Weigela," Nature (1959); Co-author, "Comparative biological effectiveness of the Gibberellins," Nature (1958); Co-author, "Absorption and Mobility of Foliar Applied Nutrients," Plant Physiology (1957); Member, International Editorial Board, "Horticultural Science"; Contributor, 373 Articles, Professional Journals **AW:** Spiridon Brusina Medal, Croatian Society for Natural Sciences (2004); Recipient, Gold Veitch Memorial Medal, Royal Horticultural Society (2003); Inductee, Hall of Fame, American Society of Agricultural and Biological Engineers (2001); Alexander von Humboldt Research Prize (1995); Outstanding Paper Award, American Society of Agricultural and Biological Engineers (1995); Eponym, Bukovac Distinguished Lecturer Michigan State Horticultural Society (1995); Outstanding Researcher Award, American Society of Agricultural and Biological Engineers (1988); Dennis R. Hoagland Award, American Society of Plant Biologists (1988); Hatch Memorial Medallion Award, U.S. Department of Agriculture (1987); Industry Man of Year Award, National Cherry Festival (1987); Distinguished Faculty Award, Michigan Association of Governing Boards (1986); Carroll R. Miller Award, American Society of

Agricultural and Biological Engineers (1980); Joseph Harvey Gourley Award, American Society of Agricultural and Biological Engineers (1969, 1976); Marion Meadows Award, American Society of Agricultural and Biological Engineers (1975); Citation of Appreciation, American Society of Agricultural and Biological Engineers (1975); M.A. Blake Award for Distinguished Graduate Teaching, American Society of Agricultural and Biological Engineers (1975); Distinguished Service Award, Michigan Horticultural Society (1974); Distinguished Faculty Award, Michigan State University (1971); Citation for Meritorious Research, American Horticultural Society (1970); Research Award, Kedzie Chapter, Sigma Xi **MEM:** President, Sigma Xi (1978-1979); President, American Society of Agricultural and Biological Engineers (1974-1975); Fellow, American Association for the Advancement of Science; Fellow, American Society for Horticultural Science; Honorary Member for Life, American Society of Agricultural and Biological Engineers; National Academy of Sciences; American Chemical Society; American Society of Plant Biologists; National Research Council; International Union of Biological Sciences; The Botanical Society of America; Societas Physiologiae Plantarum Scandinavica; The Japanese Society of Plant Physiologists; International Society for Horticultural Science; Society for Experimental Biology; Honorary Member, Croatian Society of Plant Physiologists; Faculty Club, Michigan State University; The Honor Society of Phi Kappa Phi; Gamma Sigma Delta **MH:** Albert Nelson Marquis Lifetime Achievement Award (2017) **BA:** 1066 Bogue St Rm A288, MSU, Dept of Horticulture, Plant and Soil Sciences Building, East Lansing, MI, 48824

BULLOCK, PETER BRADLEY, T: Former Company Chairman and Chief Executive Officer **I:** Business Management/Business Services **DOB:** 06/09/1934 **PB:** Tipton **SC:** England **PT:** William Horace Bradley; Catherine (Garner) Bullock **MS:** Married **SPN:** Joyce Rea (11/1/1958) **CH:** Claire Elizabeth; Bradley Locke; Penelope Jane Bradley-Hembrow **ED:** BSc, University of London **CT:** Chartered Engineer, United Kingdom; Charted Marketer, United Kingdom **C:** Chairman, Scala Collections Ltd. (1997-2006); Chairman, James Dickie PLC (1995-1998); Chairman, London & Geneva Securities Ltd. (1990-2001); President, Director, AMV, France (1986-1990); Chairman, Neill Tools Ltd. (Now Spear & Jackson UK) (1983-1990); Group Chief Executive, Spear & Jackson UK (1983-1990); Group Chief Executive, James Neill Holdings PLC (1983-1989); Joint Managing Director, Electrolux, United Kingdom (1976-1983); Employee, Thomas Potterton Ltd. (1966-1967); Employee, Fibreglass Ltd. (1965-1969); Employee, National Coal Board (1959-1965); Director, Electrolux, United Kingdom; President, Managing Director, Flymo Ltd. (Now Husqvarna AB) **CR:** Board of Directors, 600 Group PLC (1998-2004); Board of Directors, Syltone PLC (1990-1999); Wetherby Consultants Ltd (1990-1996); The Paterson Photax Group Ltd (1992-1994) **MIL:** British Army (1956-1958) **AW:** Queens Award for Technology (1983); Queens Award for Export (1982) **MEM:** Energy Institute; Chartered Institute of Marketing; Leander Club; Phyllis Court Club **H:** France and all things French **RE:** Church of England **ADD:** 5 Old Brewery Lane, Henley-on-Thames, United Kingdom, RG9 2DE

BUMBLEBURG, JOSEPH, T: Attorney Senior Member **I:** Law and Legal Services **CN:** Ball Eggleston PC **PB:** Lafayette **SC:** IN/USA **PT:** Theodore Joseph Bumbleburg; Elizabeth Mary (Delaney) Bumbleburg **MS:** Married **SPN:** Married Constance J. Peterson, December 26, 1966; **CH:**

Theodore William; Amy Ann **ED:** Honorary AS in Community Service, Ivy Technology Community College, Lafayette, IN (2013); AB, University of Notre Dame (1958); JD, Maurer School of Law Indiana University (1961) **C:** Senior Member, Ball Eggleston, PC (1964-Present); Governor, American Red Cross (1976-1981) **CR:** Trial Lawyer **CIV:** Secretary, Tippecanoe County Sheriff's Merit Board (1968-Present); Chairman, Ivy Tech Community College (2000-2002); Vice-Chairman, Ivy Tech Community College (1998-2000); State Trustee, Ivy Tech Community College (1992-2007); Member, Community Advisor, Council, School of Nursing, Purdue University (1979-1985); National Board of Governors, American Red Cross (1975-1981); Member, National Board of Governors, American Red Cross (1975-1981); Member, Pastoral Council, St. Mary's Cathedral (1974-1978); President, City of Lafayette Police Civil Service Commission (1972-1975) Advisor to Registrants, Selective Service System (1972-1975); Board of Directors, United Way, Lafayette, IN (1972-1975); Commissioner, City of Lafayette Police Civil Service Commission (1971-1975); Vice President, City of Lafayette Police Civil Service Commission (1971-1972); Member, Lafayette Board of Zoning Appeals (1970-1971); Member, Pastoral Council, St. Mary's Cathedral (1968-1970); Advisor to Registrants, Selective Service System (1967-1969); Former President/Chairman of the Greater Lafayette Chamber of Commerce, The United Way of Greater Lafayette and Capital Fund Foundation; Former State Trustee, Ivy Tech Community College of Indiana; Judge Advocate, Department of Indiana American Legion **MIL:** Captain, Judge Advocate, US Army, Fort Gordon, GA (1961-1964); Retired Lieutenant Colonel, US Army Reserve **AW:** Named, Official Founder of Ivy Technical Community College (2015); Eponym, Campus Street, Ivy Tech Community College, Lafayette Region Leadership in Law Distinguished Barrister, The Indiana Lawyer (2014); Listee, Super Lawyers (2013); Recipient, Chancellor's Award, Lafayette Region, Greater Lafayette Commerce, Ivy Tech Community College (2013); Listee, Best Lawyers in America (2011-2012); Recipient, Grand Marquis Award for Community Service (2010); Recipient, Medal of Honor, Daughters of the American Revolution (2009); Recipient, Harriman Award for Distinguished Volunteer Service, American Red Cross (2004); Academy of Law Alumni Fellow, Mauerer School of Law (2002); Academy Alumni Fellow, Mauer Indiana University School of Law (2002); Distinguished Service Award, Department of Indiana, American Legion (2001); Recipient, Harriman Award for Distinguished Volunteer Service, American Red Cross (1992); Named, Post II Legionnaire of Year, American Legion (1982-1983); Recipient, President of the United States Citation for Community Achievement (1979); Recipient, Certificate of Appreciation, Chief of Naval Education (1978); Recipient, Gold Award, United Way (1978); Recipient, Certificate of Appreciation, American Red Cross (1972); Decorated, Army Commendation Medal, Meritorious Service Medal; Inductee, Jefferson High School Alumni Hall of Fame; Recipient, Chancellor's Award for Distinguished Service; Listee, Best Lawyers in America for Mediation; Recipient, Good Scout Award, Sagamore Council Boys Scouts of America **MEM:** Indiana Judge Advocate (1999-Present); Named, Disting Barrister, Indiana Lawyers Leadership in Law Series (2014); Chairman, Greater Lafayette Chamber of Commerce (1988-1989); Board of Directors, Greater Lafayette Chamber of Commernce (1986-1991); National Security Council, American Legion (1970-1983); Academy of Alumni Fellows of the Indiana University School of Law (Bloomington), Tippecanoe County, Indiana;

ABA; Associate Member, Indiana Trial Lawyers; Reserve Officers Association; Fellow, Master, Indiana Bar Foundation; Indiana Bar Association; Knights of Columbus; Honorary Member, Phi Theta Kappa **BAR:** United States Court of Appeals for the Federal Circuit (1985); Supreme Court of the United States (1970); United States Court of Appeals for the Seventh Circuit (1970); United States District Court for the Northern District of Indiana (1964); United States Court of Military Appeals (1962); Indiana (1961) **H:** Traveling; Antique sales; Woodworking **PA:** Democrat **RE:** Roman Catholic **ADD:** 726 Owen St, Lafayette, IN, 47905 **URL:** http://www.ball-law.com/service/joseph-bumbleburg

BUMPAS, STUART M., T: Lawyer **I:** Law and Legal Services **CN:** Locke Lord **DOB:** 10/07/1944 **PB:** Little Rock **SC:** AR/USA **PT:** Hubert Wayne Bumpas; Martha Conway (Maryman) Gaylord **MS:** Married **SPN:** Diane Ellen DeWare (10/1/1977) **ED:** LLM, The George Washington University (1973); JD, The University of Texas (1969); BA, Brown University (1966) **C:** Partner, Looke Lord LLP (2008-Present); Partner, Locke, Liddell & Sapp, Dallas, TX (1999-2007); Partner, Locke, Purnell, Rain, Harrell, Dallas, TX (1974-1998); Assistant, Commissioner, IRS, Washington D.C. (1973-1974); Attorney Adviser, Office of the Chief Counsel, Washington D.C. (1969-1972) **CR:** Adjunct Professor, Employee Benefits, Southern Methodist University, Dallas, TX (1975); Lecturer, Washington Non-Profit Legal & Tax Conference; Lecturer, American Law Institute; Lecturer, Annual, Non-Profit Organizations Institute **CIV:** Board of Directors, Callier Center for Communication Disorders, Dallas, TX (1984-Present); National Counsel, American Heart Association, Inc., Dallas, TX (1979-Present); Board of Directors, Dallas Grand Opera Association (1984); Vice President, Dallas Grand Opera Association (1984); Executive Committee, Meadows School of Arts, Southern Methodist University, Dallas, TX; Board of Directors, Friends of Alzheimer's Disease Center, The University of Texas Southwestern Medical Center; Board of Directors, Goodwill Industries of Dallas, Inc.; Member, Mayor's Commission on International Development; Member, Task Force on Arts and Culture, Dallas, TX; Trustee, The Lamplighter School; General Counsel, The Hockaday School; General Counsel, Dallas Museum of Art; Trustee, Dallas Museum of Art; Member, Executive Committee, Dallas Museum of Art; Trustee, Southwestern Medical Foundation; Member, The Chancellor's Council, The University of Texas System; Member, Advisory Committee, Meadows Museum **CW:** Contributor, Articles, Professional Journals **MEM:** Member, Exempt Organizations Committee, ABA; Former Chairman, Legal Aspects of Arts Committee, State Bar of Texas; Dallas Bar Association; Business Advisory Committee; American Council On Germany; Council, Foreign Relations, The Dallas Petroleum Club; Council, Foreign Relations, Brook Hollow Golf Club; Council, Foreign Relations, The Idlewild Club; The Society of the Cincinnati; Coral Beach & Tennis Club **BAR:** The District of Columbia (1972); Texas (1969) **RE:** Episcopalian **BA:** 2200 Ross Ave Ste 2800, Locke Lord LLP, Dallas, TX, 75201

BURKE, ANNE M., I: Other **DOB:** 02/03/1944 **PB:** Chicago **SC:** IL/USA **ED:** JD, IIT/Chicago-Kent College of Law (1983); BA in Education, DePaul University (1976) **CT:** Trial Bar, Federal District Court (1987); Seventh Circuit, United States Court of Appeals (1985); Federal Court Northern District of Illinois (1983) **C:** Associate justice, Illinois Supreme Court, Chicago (2006-Present); Judge, First District, Illinois Appellate Court,

Chicago (1995-1996, 1996-2006); Special Counsel to Governor, Child Welfare Services, State of Illinois (1994-1995); Judge, Illinois Court Claims (1987-1994); Private Practice (1983-1994); Physical Education Teacher, Chicago Park District **CIV:** Founder, Chicago Special Olympics **AW:** Grantee, Kennedy Foundation **H:** Dance; Antiques

BURNETT, ARTHUR LOUIS SR., T: Judge **I:** Law and Legal Services **CN:** Federal Judicial Center **DOB:** 03/15/1935 **PB:** Spotsylvania County **SC:** VA/USA **PT:** Robert Louis Burnett; Lena Victoria (Bumbry) Burnett **MS:** Married **SPN:** Ann Lloyd (May 14, 1960) **CH:** Darnellena; Arthur Louis II; Darryl; Darlisa; Dionne **ED:** Graduate, Federal Executive Institute (Now Center for Leadership Development), U.S. Office of Personnel Management (1978); LLB, New York University (1958); BA, Howard University, Summa Cum Laude (1957) **CT:** Admitted to Practice, Supreme Court of the United States (1964); Admitted to Practice, United States District Court District of Maryland (1963) **C:** Vice President of Administration, NAADPC (2004-Present); National Executive Director, NAADPC (2004-Present); Faculty, The National Judicial College (1974-Present); Faculty, The National Judicial College (1970-Present); Senior Judge, Superior Court, District of Columbia Courts (1998-2013); Judge, Superior Court, District of Columbia Courts (1987-1998); United States Magistrate, United States District Court for the District of Columbia (1980-1987); Associate General Counsel, U.S. Office of Personnel Management (1979-1980); Assistant General Counsel, Legal Advisory Division, United States Civil Service Commission (1975-1978); United States Magistrate, United States District Court for the District of Columbia (1969-1975); Legal Adviser, Metropolitan Police Department, District of Columbia (1968-1969); General Counsel, Metropolitan Police Department, District of Columbia (1968-1969); Assistant, United States Attorney's Office for the District of Columbia (1965-1968); Attorney to Acting Deputy Chief General, Crimes Section, The United States Department of Justice (1960-1965); Special Assistant, United States Attorney's Office, District of Maryland (1961-1963); Special Assistant, United States Attorney's Office, Southern District of Illinois (1961-1963); Attorney General's Honor Program Attorney, Fraud Section Criminal Division, The United States Department of Justice (1958) **CR:** Adjunct Professor, School of Law, Howard University (1998-2011); Adjunct Professor, The Catholic University of America Columbus School of Law (1997-2008); Judge-in-Residence, Children's Defense Fund (1998-2004); President, Federal Magistrate Judges Association (1983-1984); Program Participant, Judicial Conference, US Court of Federal Claims Bar Association (1979); Chairman, National Conference Specialized Court Judges, ABA (1975); Chairman-Elect, National Conference Specialized Court Judges, ABA (1974-1975); Acting Chairman, National Conference Specialized Court Judges, ABA (1974-1975); Program Chairman, Annual Meeting, Federal Magistrate Judges Association (1974); Program Participant, Circuit Judicial Conference, United States Court of Appeals District of Columbia Circuit (1974); Program Chairman, Annual Meeting, National Conference Specialized Court Judges, ABA (1973) **CIV:** Secretary, National Association for Children of Alcoholics (2010-Present); Member, Board of Directors, National Association for Children of Alcoholics (2000-Present); Member, Board of Directors, NCADD (2010-2014); Member, Board of Directors, Fellowship of Christian Athletes (2000-2003) **CW:** Editor, "Directory of Minority Judges of U.S." (1997-2009); Co-Chairman, Editorial Board,

"Criminal Justice Magazine," ABA (1997-2000); Member, "Law Review," New York University (1957-1958) **AW:** Recipient, Sarah Harper Humanitarian Award, National Bar Association (2014); Recipient, Wiley A. Branton Civil Rights Award, National Bar Association (2014); Honoree, Named To Hall Of Fame (2014); Recipient, Lifetime Achievement Award, The John Carroll Society (2010); Recipient, The President's Award, The National Black Prosecutors Association (2010); Recipient, President's Award, National Bar Association (1996, 2005, 2006, 2009); Recipient, International Community Corrections Association Judicial Award, National Bar Association (2006); Recipient, Spirit Of Excellence Award (2005); Recipient, Raymond Pace Alexander Award, National Bar Association (2004); Recipient, E. Francis Stradford Award, National Bar Association (2004); Recipient, Earl Kintner Award, Federal Bar Association (2002); Recipient, State Justice Initiatives Award, ABA (2002); Recipient, Judicial Award Of Excellence, Trial Lawyers Association of Metropolitan Washington, DC (1999); Recipient, Award Of Excellence, National Conference of State Trial Judges, ABA (1999); Recipient, Ollie Mae Cooper Award, The District of Columbia Bar (1997); Recipient, The President's Award, National Bar Association (1996); Recipient, President's Award, Federal Bar Association (1994); Recipient, Judge Edward R. Finch Law Day USA Speech Award, ABA (1991); Recipient, Franklin N. Flaschner Judicial Award, ABA (1985); Recipient, Outstanding Distinguished Service Award, Federal Bar Association (1983); Recipient, Meritorious Service Award, U.S. Office Of Personnel Management (1980); Recipient, Distinguished Service Award, United States Civil Service Commission (1978); Recipient, Distinguished Service Award, Federal Bar Association (1978); Recipient, Sustained Superior Performance Award, United States Attorney General Robert F. Kennedy (1963); Recipient, Founders Day Award, New York University (1958) **MEM:** Chair, Advisory Committee on Substance Abuse, ABA (2010-Present); Advisory Committee on Substance Abuse, ABA (2005-2012); Task Force on Improving Opportunities for Minorities (Now Standing Committee on Minorities in Judiciary), ABA (1988-2009); Standing Committee on Unmet Legal Needs of Children, ABA (2003-2006); Chairman, Audit Committee, Federal Bar Association (1999-2006); Chairman, Judicial Council, The District of Columbia Bar (2000-2001); Standing Committee on Substance Abuse, ABA (1995-1999); President, Prettyman-Leventhal Inn of Court, American Judicature Society (1994-1995); Secretary, Administrative Law and Regulatory Practice Section (1993-1995); Employment Discrimination Committee, ABA (1992-1995); Chairman, Administration of Justice Section, Federal Bar Association (1983-1984, 1995-1997); Chair, Civil Right and Chairman, Committee on Criminal Rules and Evidence, ABA (1993-1997); Prettyman-Leventhal Inn of Court, American Judicature Society (1991-1994); Conference of United States, ABA (1990-1994); Liaison Representative of Administrative Law and Regulatory Practice Section to Administrative Assistant Secretary, ABA (1991-1993); Chairman, Professional Ethics Committee, Federal Bar Association (1991-1993); Recipient, Judge Edward R. Finch Law Day USA Speech Award, ABA (1991); Council of Administrative Law and Regulatory Practice Section, ABA (1987-1990); Section Coordinator, Federal Bar Association (1987-1988); Chairman, Federal Litigation Section, Federal Bar Association (1984-1985); President, District of Columbia Chapter, Federal Bar Association (1984-1985); Deputy Chairman, Administration of Justice Section, Federal Bar Association (1983-1984);

Chairman, Standing Committee on U.S. Magistrate, Federal Bar Association; Chairman, Professional Ethics Committee, Judicial Council, National Bar Association; Assistant Secretary, National Bar Association; The Phi Beta Kappa Society; Omega Psi Phi Fraternity Inc.; Fellow American Bar Foundation **BAR:** The District of Columbia Bar (1958) **MH:** Albert Nelson Marquis Lifetime Achievement Award (2017) **H:** Farming; Writing **ADD:** 6229 32nd Pl NW, Washington, DC, 20015

BURNS, MARVIN G., T: Lawyer **I:** Law and Legal Services **CN:** Marvin G. Burns, a Law Corporation **DOB:** 07/03/1930 **PB:** Los Angeles **SC:** CA/US **PT:** Milton Burns; Belle (Cytron) Burns **MS:** Widowed **SPN:** Barbara Irene Fisher (Deceased) **CH:** Scott Douglas; Jody Lynn; Bradley Frederick **ED:** LLB, Harvard University (1954); BA in Political Science and Economics, University of Arizona (1951) **C:** Principal, Marvin G. Burns, a Law Corporation (1991-Present); Lawyer, De Castro et al (1985-1991); Lawyer, Burns & Resnick (1982-1985); Lawyer, Fulop, Rolston, Burns and McKittrick (1955-1982) **MIL:** U.S. Army (1955-1956) **MEM:** Beverly Hills Tennis **BAR:** State of California (1955) **MH:** Albert Nelson Marquis Lifetime Achievement Award (2017) **BA:** 10537 Clearwood Court, Los Angeles, CA, 90077 **ADD:** 10537 Clearwood Court, Los Angeles, CA, 90077-2019 **URL:** https://www.linkedin.com/in/marvin-burns-16aa3712

BURSON, THOMAS DANIEL, I: Machinery **DOB:** 01/07/1936 **PB:** Hartselle **SC:** AL/USA **PT:** Daniel Webster Burson; Ardia Burson **MS:** Married **SPN:** Mary Frances Wilson (6/7/1958) **CH:** Kelly Frances; Robyn Elizabeth; Thomas Scott **ED:** MBA, University of Southern California (1969); BME, Auburn University, Alabama, With High Honors (1958) **C:** Vice President, General Manager, Space Transportation Division, McDonnell Douglas Astronautics Co., Huntington Beach, CA (1989-1996); Vice President, Deputy General Manager, McDonnell Douglas Astronautics Co., Huntington Beach, CA (1987-1988); Vice President, Fiscal Management, McDonnell Douglas Astronautics Co., Huntington Beach, CA (1984-1987); Vice President of Operations, McDonnell Douglas Astronautics Co., Huntington Beach, CA (1983-1984); Vice President, General Manager, McDonnell Douglas Corp., Monrovia, CA (1979-1983); Vice President of Fiscal Management, McDonnell Douglas Corp., Monrovia, CA (1976-1979); Director, Contracts and Pricing, Actron Division, McDonnell Douglas Corp., Monrovia, CA (1971-1976); Vice President, Hycon Co., Monrovia, CA (1969-1971); Director of Marketing, Hycon Co., Monrovia, CA (1967-1971); Assistant to President, Hycon Co., Monrovia, CA (1966-1967); Manager, Customer Contracts, Hycon Co., Monrovia, CA (1963-1966); Assistant Manager, Contract Administration, Hycon Co., Monrovia, CA (1961-1963) **CR:** Chairman, Commercial Space Transportation Advisory Committee, Secretary Transportation (1996) **MIL:** U.S. Navy Reserves (1961-1967); Commissioned Officer, U.S. Navy (1958-1960) **AW:** George M. Law Spencer Transportation Award, American Institute of Aeronautics and Astronautics (1996) **MEM:** American Institute of Aeronautics and Astronautics; American Society of Mechanical Engineers; National Contract Management Association; Phi Kappa Phi; Tau Beta Pi; Pi Tau Sigma; Beta Gamma Sigma; Kappa Alpha **ADD:** 19731 Seashore Circle, Huntington Beach, CA, 92648-3037

BURSTEIN, STEPHEN D., T: Neurosurgeon **I:** Medicine & Health Care **CN:** Neurological Surgery P.C. **DOB:** 04/10/1934 **PB:** Brooklyn **SC:** NY/USA **MS:** Married **SPN:** Ronnie Sue **CH:** Alissa **ED:** MS

in Neurosurgery, University of Minnesota; Resident in Neurosurgery, Mayo Foundation for Medical Education and Research; Intern, The Johns Hopkins Hospital; MD, SUNY Downstate Medical Center; BA, University of Michigan **CT:** Diplomate, American Board of Neurological Surgery **C:** Senior Partner, Neurological Surgery P.C.; Former Chief of Neurosurgery, South Nassau Communities Hospital; Former Chief of Neurosurgery, Franklin General Hospital **MIL:** Lieutenant, Third Division, US Navy Reserve, Okinawa, Japan **AW:** Fellow, American College of Surgeons **MEM:** Past President, Brooklyn Chapter, Alpha Omega Alpha Honor Medical Society; Past President, New York State Neurosurgical Society; Former Executive Director, New York State Neurosurgical Society **MH:** Albert Nelson Marquis Lifetime Achievement Award (2017) **ADD:** 43 Chestnut Hill, Roslyn, NY, 11576

BURTI, CHRISTOPHER L. SR., T: Vice President, Senior Legal Counsel **I:** Insurance **CN:** Statewide Title, Inc. **PB:** Muroc **SC:** CA/USA **PT:** Louis Burti Landa; Johanna Renate (Schmidt) Landa **MS:** Married **SPN:** Linda Carol Pipkin (9/15/1973) **CH:** Christopher Louis, Jr.; Erika Pipkin **ED:** JD, School of Law, University of North Carolina (1979); BS in Management, East Carolina University (1975) **C:** Vice President, Statewide Title, Incorporated, Greenville, NC (1994-Present); Legal Counsel, Statewide Title, Incorporated, Greenville, NC (1994-Present); Partner, Lewis & Burti, Farmville, NC (1982-1994); Associate, Lewis, Lewis & Lewis, Farmville, NC (1979-1982) **CR:** Attorney, Falkland, NC (1989-Present); Attorney, Farmville, NC (1982-1984) **CIV:** President, North Carolina Land Title Association (2002-Present); Board of Directors, Farmville Child Development Center (2000-Present); Board of Directors, Farmville Community Arts Council (2002); Board of Directors, Farmville Community Arts Council (2000); Board of Directors, Farmville Charitable Services (1987-1989); Board of Directors, Farmville Child Development Center (1983-1984); Board of Directors, Farmville Community Arts Council (1983-1984); Cubmaster, Farmville Troop 25, Boy Scouts of America **MIL:** Volunteer, U.S. Army (1970-1972) **CW:** Contributor, "Statewide Title, Inc. Newsletter and Legal Memorandum," Real Property Law Section, Campbell Law Observer **MEM:** Chairman, Cable Communications Committee (1991); Board of Directors, North Carolina Municipal Attorneys Association (1988-1989); Board of Directors, Farmville Chamber of Commerce (1982-1983); Farmville Country Club; Past Master, Masons; Past District Deputy Grand Master; Phi Sigma Pi; Beta Gamma Sigma; The Honor Society of Phi Kappa Phi; Chair, Senior Lawyers Division, North Carolina Bar Association; Board of Governors, North Carolina Bar Association; Transitioning Lawyers Commission, North Carolina Bar Association; Pitt County Bar Association **BAR:** U.S. District Court, Eastern District, State of North Carolina (1983); State of North Carolina (1979) **H:** Sailing; Skiing; Woodworking; Photography **PA:** Democrat **RE:** Episcopalian **BA:** 3364 N Contentnea Street, Statewide Title, Inc., Farmville, NC, 27828

BUSER, STEPHEN, T: Emeritus Professor of Finance **I:** Education/Educational Services **CN:** The Ohio State University **ED:** PhD in Economics, Boston College (1972); AB in Economics, Princeton University (1969) **C:** Professor Emeritus, The Ohio State University (2002-Present); Visiting Professor of Finance, The University of Chicago (2015-2016); Historian, American Finance Association (2004-2013); Member, Board of Directors, State Teachers Retirement System of Ohio (2005-2007); Visiting Professor of Finance, Massachusetts Institute of Technology (2004); Visiting Professor of Finance, Massachusetts Institute of Technology (1997);

Associate Dean, Fisher College of Business, The Ohio State University (1995-2002); Chair, Department of Finance, The Ohio State University (1992-2003); Coordinator, Student Investment Program, The Ohio State University (1988-2002); Professor of Finance, The Ohio State University (1986-2002); Visiting Associate Professor of Finance, The University of Chicago, Booth School of Business (1983-1984); Associate Professor of Finance, The Ohio State University (1979-1986); Assistant Professor of Finance, The Ohio State University (1975-1979); Financial Economist, Federal Deposit Insurance Corporation (1974-1975); Assistant Professor of Economics, Southern Illinois University (1972-1975) **CW:** Former Co-editor, The Journal of Finance (1988-1995); Associate Editor, Journal of Housing Research; Associate Editor, Housing Policy Debate; Former Associate Editor, American Real Estate and Urban Economics Association Journal; Manuscript Referee, Journal of Financial Economics; Manuscript Referee, Journal of Financial and Quantitative Analysis; Manuscript Referee, The Journal of Business; Manuscript Referee, Journal of Money, Credit and Banking; Manuscript Referee, Housing Finance Review; Manuscript Referee, Financial Management; Manuscript Referee, Financial Review; Manuscript Referee, Journal of Financial Research; Manuscript Referee, Management Science; Manuscript Referee, Journal of Economics and Business; Manuscript Referee, Journal of Macroeconomics; Author, Articles, The Journal of Business; Author, Articles, Journal of Risk and Insurance; Author, Articles, Journal of Financial Economics **AW:** Participant, Presidential Transition Team, Obama-Biden Administration (2008) **MEM:** American Finance Association **MH:** Albert Nelson Marquis Lifetime Achievement Award (2017) **ADD:** 2748 Andover Rd, Columbus, OH, 43221 **URL:** https://news.osu.edu/faculty-experts/a%E2%80%93m/buser-stephen.html

BUSSEL, JAMES B., T: Pediatrician **I:** Medicine & Health Care **CN:** Weill Cornell Medicine **PT:** John David Bussel; Lili Renata Bussel **MS:** Married **SPN:** Charlotte Anne Cunningham-Rundles (11/13/1982) **CH:** Amy Christine Cunningham-Bussel **ED:** Fellow in Pediatrics Hematology/Oncology, Memorial Sloan-Kettering Cancer Center, New York-Presbyterian Hospital (1979-1981); Resident, Cincinnati Children's Hospital (1976-1978); Intern in Pediatrics Hematological Oncology, Cincinnati Children's Hospital (1975-1976); MD, Columbia University (1975); BS, Yale University, Cum Laude (1971) **CT:** Diplomate in Pediatrics Hematology Oncology, American Academy of Pediatrics (1981); Diplomate in Pediatrics, American Academy of Pediatrics (1979) **C:** Professor of Pediatrics, New York-Presbyterian Hospital, Weill Cornell Medicine (1999-Present); Attending Pediatrician, New York-Presbyterian Hospital, Weill Cornell Medicine (1999-Present) **CR:** Lecturer in Field **CW:** Contributor, Articles to Professional Journals **AW:** Recipient, King Faisal International Prize of Medicine (2012); Named, One of Top Doctors in New York (2007); Recipient, Alpha Award for Contributions in Immunohematology, American Blood Resources Association (1998); Listee, Top Doctors, Castle Connolly Medical Ltd. **MEM:** American Society of Hematology; American Society of Pediatric Hematology/Oncology **MH:** Albert Nelson Marquis Lifetime Achievement Award (2017) **ADD:** 115 E 67th Street, Apt. 9B, New York, NY, 10065

BUTHIAU, DIDIER NICOLAS, T: Physician **I:** Medicine & Health Care **CN:** American Hospital of Paris **DOB:** 01/19/1953 **PB:** Dreux **SC:** France **PT:** Albert Louis Buthiau; Douceline Michele

Colaneri **MS:** Single **SPN:** Sylvie Helene Beedham (6/30/1984, Divorced 12/2004) **CH:** Norman; Candice **ED:** Intern, Hospital of Paris (1980-1984); MD, Faculty of Medicine, Paris, France (1979) **C:** Teaching Director, Education Offices, Paris, France (1992-Present); Consultant, Clinic & Hospitals, Paris, France (1988-Present); Clinical Chief, Hospital of Paris (1984-1988); Associate Professor, Faculty of Medicine, Paris, France **CR:** Associate Member, American Hospital of Paris (2007); Consultant in Field **CIV:** Expert, Health Department, France (1998-Present) **CW:** Author, "Meet the Professor, ASCO" (2008); Author, "Meet the Professor, ASCO" (2005); Author, "Virtual Endoscopy" (2002); Author, "CT and MRI in Oncology" (1995); Author, "Clinical CT and MRI" (1991); Inventor in Field **AW:** National Academy of Medicine Prize, Paris, France (1994) **MEM:** American Association for the Advancement of Science; The New York Academy of Sciences **MH:** Albert Nelson Marquis Lifetime Achievement Award (2017) **H:** Music; Diving; Painting **ADD:** 3 Rue Casimir Pinel, Neuilly-Sur-Seine, France, 92200

BYRNE, GRANVILLE BLAND III, T: Attorney **I:** Law and Legal Services **CN:** Byrne, Davis & Hicks, P. C. **DOB:** 01/26/1952 **PB:** San Antonio **SC:** TX/USA **PT:** Granville Bland; Mary (Dowling) Bland **MS:** Married **SPN:** Monique Renée Wise (1999) **CH:** Peyton Smith; Fulton Buckner; Monique Renée-Christienne **ED:** MA, Candler School of Theology, Emory University (2018); JD, Harvard University (1978); AB in English and Mathematics, The University North Carolina at Chapel Hill (1974) **C:** Principal, Byrne, Davis & Hicks, P.C., Atlanta, GA (2003-Present); Principal, Byrne, Moore & Davis, P.C., Atlanta, GA (1999-2002); Principal, Byrne, Eldridge, Moore & Davis, Professional Corporation, Atlanta, GA (1994-1999); Partner, Swift, Currie, McGhee & Hiers, Atlanta, GA (1984-1994); Associate, Swift, Currie, McGhee & Hiers, Atlanta, GA (1978-1983) **CIV:** Elder, Session First Presbyterian Church of Atlanta (1999-2002); Elder, Session First Presbyterian Church of Atlanta (1993-1996) **MEM:** ABA; Atlanta Bar Association; The Phi Beta Kappa Society; Phi Eta Sigma; Delta Phi Alpha; Order of the Grail; Order of the Old Well, The University of North Carolina at Chapel Hill **BAR:** United States Court of Appeals for the Eleventh Circuit (1981); United States District Court for the Northern District of Georgia (1978); United States Court of Appeals for the Fifth Circuit (1978); State of Georgia (1978) **MH:** Albert Nelson Marquis Lifetime Achievement Award (2017) **PA:** Democrat **RE:** Presbyterian **BA:** 3565 Piedmont Rd NE, Bldg Four, Ste 380, Byrne, Davis & Hicks, PC, Atlanta, GA, 30305 **URL:** https://www.martindale.com/atlanta/georgia/g-bland-byrne-iii-855980-a

CAINE, CLIFFORD J., T: Educational Administrator, Consultant **I:** Education/Educational Services **DOB:** 05/28/1933 **PB:** Watertown **SC:** SD/USA **PT:** Louis Vernon Caine; Elizabeth Matilda (Holland) Caine **ED:** Postgraduate Coursework, Harvard University (1976); PhD, University of Minnesota (1975); JD, University of Minnesota (1958); BA, Macalester College (1955) **C:** Education Consultant, Breck School, Golden Valley, MN (1994-2012); Director, Student Affairs, Breck School, Golden Valley, MN (1986-1994); Director, Student Service, Breck School, Golden Valley, MN (1985-1986); Assistant Headmaster, St. Paul Academy and Summit School, St. Paul, MN (1970-1985); Director, Administrative Policies Study, Macalester College (1969-1970); Lecturer, University of Minnesota (1966-1968); Director, Men's Residence Halls, Macalester College (1959-1963); Director, Student Union, Macalester College (1959-1963); Coordinator, Neighborhood Seminar

Program **CIV:** Ruling Elder, United Presbyterian Church (1962-Present); Clerk Session, The House of Hope Presbyterian Church (1983-1984); Member, Board of Directors, Family Service, St. Paul, MN (1973-1979); Member, Board of Directors, Hallie Q Brown Community Center, Inc. (1972-1973) **CW:** Author, "Hollyhocks" (2013); Author, "The College Entrance Predictor" (1988); Author, "How To Get Into College" (1985); Contributor, Articles, Professional Journals **AW:** Named to Hall of Fame, Minnesota State High School; Named to Hall of Fame, United States Professional Tennis Association; Named to Hall of Fame, Macalester College Athletics **MEM:** President, Minnesota Association of Secretaries to School and College Admissions Officers (1978-1979); Macalester College Alumni Association; Past President, Girls Tennis Association of Minnesota; United States Professional Tennis Association; Minnesota State Bar Association; National Association for College Admission Counseling; American Studies Association; The University Club of St. Paul; President, College Counseling, Minnesota State University **BAR:** Minnesota State Bar Association (1958) **MH:** Albert Nelson Marquis Lifetime Achievement Award (2017) **ADD:** 456 Summit Ave Apt 303, Saint Paul, MN, 55102

CALDWELL, BILLY R., T: Geologist **I:** Sciences **DOB:** 04/20/1932 **PB:** Newellton **SC:** LA/USA **PT:** Leslie Richardson Caldwell; Helen Merle (Clark) Caldwell **MS:** Widowed **SPN:** Carolyn Marie Heath (Deceased) **CH:** Caryn; Jeana; Craig **ED:** PhD, University of Cambridge (2004); MA, Texas Christian University (1970); BA, Texas Christian University (1954) **CT:** Certified Petroleum Geologist No. 2476, American Association of Petroleum Geologists; Certified Professional Geologist No. 7464, American Institute of Professional Geologists; Licensed Professional Geoscientist No. 3112, State of Texas **C:** Adjunct Geology Professor, Tarrant County College, Fort Worth, TX (1971-Present); Independent Geological Consultant, Fort Worth, TX (1971-Present); Manager, Outdoor Living Inc. (1963-1971); Science Teacher, Lake Worth Independent School District (1960-1963); Geologist, Geological Engineering Services, Inc., Fort Worth, TX (1954-1960) **CR:** Petroleum and Environmental Geology Consultant, Fort Worth, TX (1971-Present) **CIV:** Board of Directors, Greater Fort Worth Builders Association (1973); Past Chairman, Environmental Management Committee, Fort Worth, TX; Director, Fort Worth Jaycees **CW:** Author, "The History of the Fort Worth Basin," The Professional Geologist (2012); Author, "Geology in The Bible," Exposure Publishing (2005); Author, "Barnett Shale Production Potentials" (2000); Author, "Geological Investigations in Environmental Studies," The Professional Geologist (1991) **AW:** Buster Kirkpatrick Award for the Director of the Year, Fort Worth Jaycees (1966-1967) **MEM:** American Institute of Professional Geologists; American Association of Petroleum Geologists; Geological Society of America, Inc.; FWGS; Texas Association for Environmental Education **MH:** Albert Nelson Marquis Lifetime Achievement Award (2017) **H:** Travel; Cruise ship lectures **PA:** Republican **RE:** Baptist **ADD:** 305 Bodart Lane, Fort Worth, TX, 76108-3804

CALDWELL, MARK DONALD, T: Educational Sales Executive **I:** Retail/Sales **CN:** Mackin Educational Resources **DOB:** 10/23/1954 **PB:** New York **SC:** NY/USA **PT:** Roy Arthur Caldwell; Beverly Jean (Kline) Caldwell **ED:** BA, State University of New York (1976); AAS, Morrisville College (1974) **CT:** Library Fellowship, Dominican University, Illinois **C:** President, Woodstock Square

Inc. (1987-Present); Executive Vice President, Magazine and Paperback Marketing Institute, Des Plaines, IL (1986-Present); Vice President, Midwest Region, Time Inc., Southern California, Chicago (1984-1986); Circulation Sales Manager, Time Inc., Southern California (1981-1984); Sales Representative, Time Inc., Houston and New York City (1978-1981); Wine Merchant, Wine Merchants Ltd., Syracuse, NY (1977-1978) **CR:** Board of Directors, Morningstar Publication Inc., Santa Barbara, CA **MEM:** National Association of Convenience Stores; Food Marketing Institute; Mid-American Periodical Distributors; Morrisville College Alumni Corp.; Museum of Contemporary Art; Chicago Art Institute; Oak Brook Polo Club **MH:** Albert Nelson Marquis Lifetime Achievement Award (2017) **ADD:** 122 Willow St, South Hampton, NY, 11968 **URL:** https://www.linkedin.com/in/mark-caldwell-75116aa2/

CALLAHAN, DANIEL JOHN, T: President **I:** Research **CN:** The Hastings Center **DOB:** 07/19/1930 **SC:** WA/USA **PT:** Vincent Francis Callahan; Anita (Hawkins) Callahan **MS:** Married **SPN:** Sidney Cornelia de Shazo (6/5/1954) **CH:** Mark Sidney; Stephen Daniel; John Vincent; Peter Thorn; Sarah Elisabeth; David Lee **ED:** Honorary DHL, Charles University, Prague, Czech Republic (2008); Honorary DHL, State University of New York (2006); Honorary DHL, Oregon State University (1997); Honorary DHL, Williams College (1992); Honorary DHL, University of Colorado (1990); Honorary DSc, University of Medicine and Dentistry of New Jersey (1981); PhD, Harvard University (1965); MA, Georgetown University (1957); BA, Yale University (1952) **C:** Co-Director, Yale-Hastings Program in Ethics and Health Policy (2009); Senior Research Scholar, The Hastings Center (1997-2009); Resident Scholar, Aspen Institute for Humanistic Studies (1975); Co-Founder, President, The Hastings Center (1969-1996); Staff Associate, Population Council (1969-1970); Executive Editor, The Commonwealth, New York, NY (1961-1968) **CR:** Senior Research Scholar, Yale University (2004-Present); Senior Lecturer, Harvard Medical School (1998-Present); Honorary Professor, Charles University Medical School, Prague, Czech Republic (1997-Present); Senior Fellow, Harvard Center for Population and Development Studies (1996); Consultant, Medical Ethics, Judicial Council, American College of Physicians (1979-1986); Special Consultant, National Endowment of the Humanities (1979); Committee Member, American Medical Association (1972-1982); Commission on Population Growth and the American Future (1970-1971); Visiting Professor, University of Pennsylvania (1970); Visiting Professor of Theology, Marymount College (1966); Visiting Assistant Professor of Religious Studies, Brown University (1965); Visiting Assistant Professor of Religion, Temple University (1964) **CIV:** Advisory Committee on Scientific Integrity, United States Department of Health and Human Services (1991-1993); Trustee, University of Pennsylvania Medical Center (1987-1991); National Advisory Board, Health Promotion Program, Henry J. Kaiser Family Foundation (1987-1991); National Advisory Board, New York Panel and HIV Screening (1987); Public Member, American Board of Medical Specialties, New York Science and Education Policy Association (1985-1991); New York Task Force on Life and Law (1985-1987); Public Member, American Board of Medical Specialties (1982-1987); Selection Committee, Rockefeller Foundation Program in Humanities (1980); Elector, National Medal for Literature (1979-1983); New York Council for Humanities (1975-1979); Selection Committee, Ford-Rockefeller Program in Population Policy (1975-1978); New York State Health Advisory Council (1975-1976); National Book Award Committee (1975); Advisory Committee to Director, Center for Disease Control, United States Department of Health and Human Service **CW:** Editorial Advisory Board, Technology in Society (1981-Present); Advisory Board, Science, Technology and Human Values (1979-Present); Author, "Taming the Beloved Beast" (2009); Editor, "Medicine and the Market" (2006); Author, "Medicine and the Market Equity v. Choice" (2006); Author, "What Price Better Health: Hazards of the Research Imperative" (2003); Editor, "The Role of Complementary and Alternative Medicine" (2002); Editor, "Promoting Healthy Behavior" (2000); Author, "False Hopes: Why America's Quest for Perfect Health is a Recipe for Failure" (1998); Editor, "A World Growing Old" (1995); Editor, "What Price Mental Health?" (1995); Author, "The Troubled Dream of Life: Living with Morality" (1993); Author, "What Kind of Life: The Limits of Medical Progress" (1990); Author, "Setting Limits: Medical Goals in an Aging Society" (1987); Advisory Board, American Journal of Bioethics (1985-1996); Editor, "Applying the Humanities" (1985); Editor, "Representation and Responsibility" (1985); Editor, "Abortion: Understanding Differences" (1984); Editor, "Ethics, the Social Sciences and Policy Analysis" (1983); Advisory Board, Criminal Justice Ethics (1982); Author, "The Teaching of Ethics in the Military" (1982); Advisory Board, Environmental Ethics (1982); Advisory Board, Encyclopedia of Life Sciences (1982); Advisory Board, Business and Professional Ethics (1981); Editor, "The Roots of Ethics" (1981); Editor, "Ethics in Hard Times" (1981); Editor, "Ethics Teaching in Higher Education" (1980); Editor, "Ethical Issues in Population Aid" (1980); Editor, "Knowing and Valuing" (1979); Editor, "Morals, Science and Sociality" (1978); Editor, "Knowledge, Value and Belief" (1977); Editor, "Science, Ethics and Medicine" (1976); Co-Editor, "Ethical Issues in Human Genetics" (1973); Author, "The Tyranny of Survival" (1973); Author, "Ethics and Population Limitation" (1971); Editor, "The American Population Debate" (1971); Author, "Abortion: Law, Choice and Morality" (1970); Editor, "The Catholic Case for Contraception" (1969); Author, "The New Church" (1966); Editor, "Secular City Debate" (1966); Author, "Honesty in the Church" (1965); Editor, "Federal Aid and Catholic Schools" (1964); Author, "The Mind of the Catholic Layman" (1963); Co-Editor, "Christianity Divided: Protestant and Roman Catholic Theological Issues" (1961) **AW:** Bioethics Leadership Award, Johns Hopkins University (2006); Centennial Medal, Harvard Graduate School of Arts and Sciences (2006); Morrison Prize, Massachusetts Institute of Technology (2002); Career Achievement Award, Society for Bioethics and Medical Humanities (2001); Washington Irving Book Award (1999); ARCHON Award, Sigma Theta Tau International Honor Society of Nursing (1999); Joseph Leiter Award, National Library of Medicine (1999); Scientific Freedom and Responsibility Award, American Association for the Advancement of Science (1996); President Cabinet Award, University of Texas (1995); James H. Hamilton Book Award, American College of Healthcare Executives (1990); Business Enterprise Trust Fellow (1989-1995); Henry Knowles Beecher Award, The Hastings Center (1989); Book of Year Award, American Journal of Nursing (1987); Daryl J. Mase Distinguished Leadership Award (1987); Tekolste Scholar, Independent Hospital Association (1986); One of 200 Outstanding Young Men Leaders, Time Magazine (1974); Thomas More Medal (1970) **MEM:** Senior Scholar, Harvard Graduate Society (1994-2008); Council, Harvard Graduate Society (1989-1992); Board of Directors, Society for Study Social Biology (1987-1995); Institute of Medicine, National Academy of Sciences; American Association for Advancement Humanities; Fellow, American Association for the Advancement of Science **MH:** Albert Nelson Marquis Lifetime Achievement Award (2017) **H:** Writing **ADD:** 42 Whitman Street, Hastings-on-Hudson, NY, 10706

CALLAWAY BRABANT, SARAH, T: Sociologist, Educator **I:** Education/Educational Services **CN:** University of Louisiana at Lafayette **DOB:** 11/18/1932 **PB:** LaGrange **SC:** GA/USA **PT:** Enoch Callaway; Jennie Louisa Crowell Callaway **MS:** Married **SPN:** Wilmee MacNair (1973); Wilmer Everett Mac Nair (1953, Divorced 1968) **CH:** Jennie Crowell; Enoch Callaway; Anne Delebart **ED:** PhD, University of Georgia (1973); MA, Memphis State University (Now University of Memphis) (1968); BS, Memphis State University (Now University of Memphis) (1967); Coursework, Auburn University (1952-1953); Coursework, Newcomb College (1950-1952) **CT:** Thanatology Certification; Certified Family Life Educator; Certified Sociological Practitioner **C:** Professor Emeritus of Sociology, University of Louisiana at Lafayette (2001-Present); Professor, University of Southwestern Louisiana (Now University of Louisiana at Lafayette), Lafayette, LA (1983-2001); Associate Professor, University of Southwestern Louisiana (Now University of Louisiana at Lafayette), Lafayette, LA (1977-1983); Visiting Assistant Professor of Anthropology, Louisiana State University (1974); Assistant Professor of Sociology, University of Southwestern Louisiana (Now University of Louisiana at Lafayette), Lafayette, LA (1973-1977); Visiting Assistant Professor of Anthropology, Louisiana State University (1973); Instructor of Sociology, Memphis State University (Now University of Memphis) (1968-1970) **CIV:** Co-founder, The Grief Center of Southwest Louisiana (Now Healing House) (1997-2008); Volunteer, The Grief Center of Southwest Louisiana (Now Healing House) (1997-2008); Vestry, Episcopal Church (1996-1998); Vestry, Episcopalian Church (1984-1987); President of the Board, Acadiana Task Force on AIDS, Faith House, Lafayette, LA (1982-1983); Volunteer, Steering Committee, UMC Rape Crisis Center (1980-1989); Co-founder, Lafayette Commission on the Needs of Women (1977-1979); First President, Lafayette Commission on the Needs of Women (1977-1979); Vice Chair, Digging for Treasure Ministries; Secretary, Digging for Treasure Ministries; Treasurer, Digging for Treasure Ministries; Board of Directors, Acadiana Chapter, Compassionate Friends; Consultant, Acadiana Chapter, Compassionate Friends; **CW:** Author, Â"Mending the Torn Fabric: For Those Who Grieve and Those Who Want to Help Them; Â" Contributor, Over 70 Chapters and Articles, Professional Publications **AW:** Sarah Brabant Trail Blazer Award, University of Louisiana at Lafayette (2016); Kathleen Blanco Award in Excellence and Leadership (2015); Alice Dunbar Nelson Award, Students for the Advancement of Women, University of Louisiana at Lafayette (2013); Making a Lifetime of Difference Award, League of Women Voters (2011); Oliver-Sigur Humanitarian Service Award, Louisiana Council on Human Relations (2011); Jefferson Award for Outstanding Community Service (2006); Citizen of the Year, Woodmen of the World Life Insurance Society (2006); President's Daily Point of Light Award (2001); Sertoma Service to Mankind Award (2000); Angel Award, Blue Cross and Blue Shield of Louisiana (2000); Distinguished Book Award, Mid-south Sociological Society (1998); Distinguished Service to Families Award, Louisiana Council on Family Relations (1996); Recognition Award, American Sociological Practice Association (1995); Woman of Achievement Award, Zonta International (1989); Dr. Charles Blair Mental Health Award, Mental Health Association (1989); Blue Key Alumni Faculty Excellence Award (1986); Outstanding Alumna for Community Service Award, Phi Mu (1986); Volunteer Activist Award, Acadiana, LA (1985); Distinguished Professor Award, University Southwestern Louisiana Foundation (Now University of Louisiana Lafayette Foundation) (1980); Martin Luther King Humanitarian Service Award, Lafayette Council on Human Relations (1978); Research Award, American Personnel and Guidance Association (1977) **MEM:** Vice President, Mid-South Sociological Society (1976-1977); American Sociological Association; American Association of University Professors; Association for Death Education and Counseling; Association for Applied and Clinical Sociology **MH:** Albert Nelson Marquis Lifetime Achievement Award (2017) **PA:** Democrat **RE:** Catholic **ADD:** 149 Memory Ln, Lafayette, LA, 70506

CAMPBELL, JOAN VIRGINIA LOWEKE, T: Language Educator **I:** Education/Educational Services **CN:** Blacksburg High School **DOB:** 11/08/1942 **PB:** Detroit **SC:** MI/USA **PT:** George Paul Loweke; Lolamae (Weians) Loweke **MS:** Married **SPN:** James Bachelder Campbell (7/26/1975) **CH:** James Bachelder Loweke Campbell **ED:** Coursework, Virginia Polytechnic Institute and State University (2011-Present); Coursework in Chinese Language and Culture, Virginia Polytechnic Institute and State University (2011-Present); BA in Spanish, Virginia Polytechnic Institute and State University (1990); Coursework, Millersville University (1990); Coursework, Millersville University, PA (1983-1984); Coursework, Estudio Sampere, Madrid, Spain, Virginia Polytechnic Institute and State University (1982); Coursework, Virginia Polytechnic Institute and State University (1980-1990); BA in English, Virginia Polytechnic Institute and State University (1977); Coursework, Virginia Polytechnic Institute and State University (1976-1977); Coursework, Stuttgart University, Germany (1970-1971); Coursework, Salzburg University, American Institute for Foreign Study, Austria (1968); BA in German, French and Education, Hope College (1965); Coursework, University of Cologne, University of Washington, Germany (1964) **CT:** Course Completion Certificates in Psychology, Gifted Education, Computer Study, University of Virginia (1990-1999); Certified Secondary Teacher, Commonwealth of Virginia (1977); Certified Secondary Teacher, State of Kansas (1972); Certified Secondary Teacher, State of Michigan (1965) **C:** Teacher of French I-IV, Blacksburg High School, Virginia (1977-2000); Teacher of Spanish I and II, Blacksburg High School, Virginia (1986-2000); Teacher of German I-IV, Highland Park High School, Topeka, KS (1975-1976); Teacher of French I and II, Teacher of Senior English, Yearbook Teacher, Oskaloosa High School, Oskaloosa, KS (1974-1975); Teacher of German I and II, Central Junior High School, Lawrence, KS (1972-1974); Assistant Instructor, German I and II, University of Kansas, Lawrence, KS (1971-1972, 1969-1970); Teacher of French I and II, Teacher of German I and II, Grand Haven Junior High School, Grand Haven MI (1965-1969) **CR:** Chaperone, Educational Adventures, Quebec City, Montreal, Canada (1990-2000); Audio Visual Committee, Montgomery County Foreign Language Collaborative Group, Blacksburg, VA (1984-1987); Chaperone, Paris, France, American Institute for Foreign Study (1982); Chaperone, Madrid, Spain, American Institute for Foreign Study (1982); Chaperone, Vichy, France, American Institute for Foreign Study (1979-1980); Teacher of French, YMCA

Evening Courses, Teacher of Spanish, YMCA Evening Courses, Blacksburg, VA (1976-1980); Chaperone, Salzburg, Austria, American Institute for Foreign Study (1968-1970); Area Administrator, Summer and Winter Programs Abroad for Western Michigan (1968-1969), American Institute for Foreign Study (1968-1969); Convention Presenter in Field, Montgomery County Public Schools **CIV:** Member, International Host Family Organization, Virginia Polytechnic Institute and State University, Blacksburg, VA (1977-2000) **CW:** Author, "The Gothic Cathedral" (1995) **AW:** Recognized, Virginia Governor's School Outstanding Educator (1990); Rockefeller Fellow, Rockefeller Association and National Endowment for the Humanities (1986); Fulbright Fellow, Goethe-Institut (1976); University of Kansas Scholarship, Barcelona, Spain (1976); Fulbright Exchange Fellow to University of Stuttgart, Germany, University of Kansas (1970-1971); National Defense Education Act Fellow to Montana State University, Bozeman, Montana (1966) **MEM:** Virginia Education Association (1977-2000); State and Region IV U.S. Recognition Effort, Dedication and High Scores on National French Exams (1981-2000); District Administrator, Le Grand Concours-Nat. French Exams, National Association of Teachers of French (1980-2000); Montgomery County Education Association (1977-2000); Conference Attendant, National Foreign Language (1993); Northeast Conference Presenter, National Foreign Language (1993); Northeast Conference Member, National Foreign Language (1993); Conference Presenter, National Foreign Language (1986-1990); The American Association of Teachers of Spanish and Portuguese (1986-1990); Conference Attendant, National Foreign Language (1986); Co-Chair, Virginia Chapter, National German Exams, American Association of Teachers of German (1984-1987); State Nominating Committee, American Association of Teachers of German (1984-1987); Secretary, Virginia Executive Committee, American Association of Teachers of German (1977-1986); Chair, State Nominating Committee, American Association of Teachers of German (1984-1985); Representative, Blacksburg High School, Montgomery County Education Association, National Association of Teachers of French (1980-1982); Founder, La Society Honoraire de Français for Outstanding Students in French, Blacksburg Chapter, National Association of Teachers of French (1977); National Association of Professional Women; State Committee, American Association of Teachers of French; Lifetime Member, American Association of Teachers of German; American Association of Teachers of French; American Conference on the Teaching of Foreign Languages **H:** Studying Chinese; Gardening; Hiking; Traveling; Classical music; Art history **PA:** Republican **RE:** Presbyterian **ADD:** 3003 Mclean Court, Blacksburg, VA, 24060

CANNON, KIM, T: Lawyer **I:** Law and Legal Services **CN:** Davis & Cannon LLP **DOB:** 10/15/1948 **PB:** Salt Lake City **SC:** UT/USA **PT:** Morris Nibley Cannon; Bette Jeanne (Decker) Sage **MS:** Married **SPN:** Susan Margaret Clinch (9/6/1986); Jane B. Howard (6/10/1972, Divorced 9/1985) **CH:** Sage; Meredith **ED:** JD, University of Colorado (1974); BA, Dartmouth College (1970) **CT:** U.S. District Court, State of Wyoming (1974); Tenth Circuit, U.S. Court of Appeals (1974) **C:** Partner, Davis & Cannon, LLP, Sheridan, WY (1994-Present); Partner, Burgess, Davis, Carmichael & Cannon, Sheridan, WY (1990-1994); Partner, Burgess & Davis, Sheridan, WY (1974-1990) **CR:** Fellow, The International Academy of Trial Lawyers **CIV:** Chairman, Rhodes Scholarship Selection Committee, Wyoming (1998-2005); Chair, Commission on Judicial Conduct and Ethics (2001-2003); Commission on Judicial

Conduct and Ethics (1997-2001); Chairman, Wyoming Environmental Quality Council (1992-1996); Wyoming Outdoor Council, Lander, WY (1987-1991); Wyoming Theater, Inc., Sheridan, WY (1986-1991); President, Sheridan County Fulmer Public Libraries (1980-1985) **MEM:** Board of Directors, The International Academy of Trial Lawyers (2012-Present); Vice President, Dartmouth Lawyers Association (1998-2010); President, Sheridan Bar Association (1982); Board of Directors, Wyoming Trial Lawyers Association **BAR:** State of Wyoming (1974) **H:** Polo; Training horses; Fly fishing; Skiing **BA:** 40 S Main Street, Davis & Cannon, LLP, Sheridan, WY, 82801 **ADD:** 40 S Main Street, Davis & Cannon, Sheridan, WY, 82801

CANTILLI, EDMUND JOSEPH, T: Professor Emeritus **I:** Education/Educational Services **CN:** NYU Tandon School of Engineering **DOB:** 02/12/1927 **PB:** Yonkers **SC:** NY/USA **PT:** Ettore Cantilli; Maria (deRubeis) Cantilli **MS:** Married **SPN:** Nella Franco (5/15/1948) **CH:** Robert; John; Teresa; Duane Brooks **ED:** PhD in Transportation Planning and Engineering, NYU Tandon School of Engineering (1972); Postgraduate Coursework, Urban Planning and Public Safety, New York University (1968-1971); Certificate of Graduation, Yale University Bureau of Highway Traffic (1957); BS, Columbia University (1955); AB, Columbia University (1954) **CT:** Registered Professional Engineer, State of New York; Registered Professional Engineer, State of New Jersey; Registered Professional Engineer, State of California; Registered Professional Planner, State of New Jersey; Certified Safety Professional, Board of Certified Safety Professionals; Certified Planner, AICP, APA; Certified Forensic Engineer, BCFE **C:** Professor Emeritus, NYU Tandon School of Engineering (1990-Present); Expert Witness for Accident Cases (1995-2012); President, EJC Safety Associates, Inc. (1989-1995); Executive Director, International Institute for Safety in Transportation, Inc. (1977-1995); Professor, Transportation and Safety Engineering, NYU Tandon School of Engineering (1969-1990); President, Urbitran Associates (1973-1981); Supervising Engineer, Safety Research and Studies, The Port Authority of New York and New Jersey (1955-1969) **CR:** Teacher, Italian (1969-Present); Teacher, Algebra (1969-Present); Teacher, Traffic Engineering (1969-Present); Teacher, Urban Planning (1969-Present); Teacher, Transportation Planning (1969-Present); Teacher, Urban and Transportation Geography (1969-Present); Teacher, Land Use Planning (1969-Present); Teacher, Aesthetics (1969-Present); Teacher, Environment (1969-Present); Teacher, Industrial (1969-Present); Teacher, Traffic and Transportation Safety Engineering (1969-Present); Teacher, Human Factors Engineering (1969-Present); Teacher, Ethics for Engineers (1969-Present); Teacher, Consultant Transportation and Traffic Safety Engineering (1969-Present); Teacher, Community Planning (1969-Present); Teacher, Traffic Engineering (1969-Present); Teacher, Transportation Planning (1969-Present); Teacher, Accident Reconstruction (1969-Present); Teacher, Environmental Impacts (1969-Present); Consultant (1969-Present); Forensic Engineer (1969-Present); Accident Reconstructionist (1969-Present); Expert Witness, Transportation Accident Litigation (1969-Present); Visiting Professor, Transportation Safety Engineering, Instituto Superior Tenico, Universidade de Lisboa, Lisbon, Portugal (1987-1997); Advisor to Doctorate Students, Politecnico di Milano, Milan, Italy (1980-1998); Advisor to Doctorate Students, NYU Tandon School of Engineering (1969-1994) **MIL:** U.S. Army (1950-1951, 1945-1949) **CW:** Translator, "The Difficult Word" (1988); Translator, "The New Word" (1988); Translator, "The Ancient Word" (1988); Author, "Transportation System Safety" (1979); Editor, "There Is No Death That Is Not Ennobled by So Great A Cause" (1976); Calligrapher, "There Is No Death That Is Not Ennobled by So Great A Cause" (1976); Author, "Programming Environmental Improvements in Public Transportation" (1974); Author, "Transportation and the Disadvantaged: The Poor, the Young, the Elderly, the Handicapped" (1974); Co-Editor, "Traffic Engineering Theory and Control" (1973); Editor, "Transportation and Aging" (1971); Editor, "Pedestrian Planning and Design" (1971); Contributor, Articles, Professional Journals; Contributor, Articles, Trade Journals Novels **MEM:** Fellow, American Society of Civil Engineers; Fellow, Institute of Transportation Engineers; Fellow, National Academy of Forensic Engineers; National Society of Professional Engineers; Charter Member, APA; Certified Member, AICP, APA; The American Society of Safety Engineers; The New York Academy of Sciences; NAPARS; International Association for Accidents and Traffic Medicine; Human Factors and Ergonomics Society; International System Safety Society; Sigma Xi, The Scientific Research Honor Society; Mensa International Limited **MH:** Albert Nelson Marquis Lifetime Achievement Award (2017) **ADD:** 134 Euston Rd S, West Hempstead, NY, 11552 **URL:** http://cedb.asce.org/CEDBsearch/record.jsp?dockey=0034065

CANTILO, PATRICK HERRERA, T: Partner **I:** Law and Legal Services **CN:** Cantilo & Bennett, L.L.P. **DOB:** 03/19/1954 **PB:** Santiago **SC:** Chile **PT:** Luis Cantilo (Deceased); Yvonne Cantilo (Deceased) **MS:** Married **SPN:** Judy Elliott (8/5/2013) **CH:** Michael; Daniel; Nicholas **ED:** JD, The University of Texas at Austin (1980); BA, The University of Texas at Austin, with Honors (1977) **C:** Partner, Cantilo & Bennett L.L.P., Austin, TX (1999-Present); Partner, Cantilo Maisel & Hubbard L.L.P., Dallas, TX (1993-1999); Partner, Rubinstein & Perry, Austin, TX (1987-1993); Counsel, Freytag, Perry, LaForce, Rubinstein & Teofan, Austin, TX (1986-1987); Partner, Davis, Cantilo, Welch & Ewbank, Austin, TX (1985-1986); Associate, Davis & Davis Professional Corporation, Austin, TX (1983-1985); Counsel to Receiver, Texas Department of Insurance (1980-1983) **CIV:** Officer, Board of Directors, KUT; Officer, Board of Directors, The Austin Theatre Alliance; Officer, Board of Directors, Texas Appleseed **CW:** Contributor, "The Perfect Receiver," International Association of Insurance Receivers (2010-2018); Contributor, Articles, Professional Journals **AW:** Honoree, Best Lawyers in America, Super Lawyers (2009-Present) AV Rated Martindale Hubbell **MEM:** Receiver's Handbook Committee, National Association of Insurance Commissioners (1991); Continuation of Benefits Working Group, Contracts and Services, National Association of HMO Regulators (1989); Joint Committee, National Association of HMO Regulators (1986); Advisory Committee, National Association of HMO Regulators (1986); Liquidators Task Force Advisory Committee, National Association of Insurance Commissioners (1986); Chairman, Finance Subcommittee, National Association of Insurance Commissioners (1986); Advisory Committee for HMO, National Association of Insurance Commissioners (1986); ABA; Travis County Bar Association (Now Austin Bar Association); Austin Young Lawyers Association, Austin Bar Association; Society of Insurance Receiver's Charter Principal; Past President, International Association of Insurance Receivers; Past Board Member, Board of Directors, International Association of Insurance Receivers; NAMCP **BAR:** United States Court of Federal Claims (2017); Supreme Court of the United States (1994); United States Court of Appeals for the Fourth Circuit (1994); United States Court of Appeals for the Fifth Circuit (1989); United States

District Court Eastern District of Texas (1989); United States District Court Southern District of Texas (1989); United States District Court Northern District of Texas (1988); United States District Court Western District of Texas (1983); State of Texas (1980) **MH:** Albert Nelson Marquis Lifetime Achievement Award (2017) **PA:** Democrat **RE:** Roman Catholic **BA:** 11401 Century Oaks Ter Ste 300, Cantilo & Bennett, L.L.P., Austin, TX, 78758 **URL:** http://www.cb-firm.com/

CAPRARO, FRANZ, T: Accountant **I:** Financial Services **CN:** GLSC & Co., PLLC **DOB:** 11/19/1941 **PB:** Thuringia **SC:** Germany **PT:** Ernst Capraro; Lia (Loeschmann) Baeuscher **MS:** Married **SPN:** Daniela DiPauli (12/26/1964) **CH:** Monica L. **ED:** BBA, University of Miami, Cum Laude (1964) **CT:** Certified Public Accountant, State of Florida **C:** Partner, GLSC & Co., PLLC, Miami, FL (1996-Present); Private Accounting Practice, Davie, FL (1995-1996); Vice President, The Hampton Roads, Inc., Miami Beach, FL (1984-1995); Vice President, The Foundlings, Inc., Miami Beach, FL (1984-1995); Vice President, Washington Storage Co., Miami, FL (1984-1995); Vice President, The Novecento Corp., Miami, FL (1984-1995); Executive Vice President, The Wolfson Initiative Corp., Miami, FL (1984-1995); Partner, Deloitte Haskins & Sells, Miami, FL (1966-1984) **CR:** Treasurer, The Journal of Decorative and Propaganda Arts, Miami, FL (1986-1998); Attendee, National Security Forum, U.S. Air War College, Montgomery, AL (1993) **CIV:** Treasurer, Mitchell Wolfson Family Foundation, Miami, FL (1985-Present); Member, Executive Committee, University of Miami Citizens Board, Coral Gables, FL (1987-2011); Trustee, Greater Miami Opera Finance Committee (1991-1996); Board of Directors, Louis Wolfson II Media History Center, Miami, FL (1987-1995); First Lieutenant, U.S. Army Finance Corps, France (1965-1966) **MIL:** First Lieutenant, Finance Corps, U.S. Army (1964-1966) **AW:** Certificate of Appreciation, City of Miami Beach (1987); Honorary Conch, City of Key West (1987) **MEM:** Treasurer, Schlaraffia Costa Aurea (1986-1987); American Institute of Certified Public Accountants; Florida Institute of CPAs; Life Member, U.S. Air War College Alumni Association **H:** Reading; Travel **RE:** Roman Catholic **BA:** 6303 Blue Lagoon Drive, Suite 200, GLSC & Co., PLLC, Miami, FL, 33126 **ADD:** 2821 SW 116th Avenue, Davie, FL, 33330

CARALEY, DEMETRIOS JAMES, T: Political Science Professor, Writer, Publisher **I:** Education/Educational Services **DOB:** 06/22/1932 **PB:** New York City **SC:** NY/USA **PT:** Christopher Caraley; Stella (Psaras) Caraley **ED:** MPhil, Columbia University (1962); PhD, Columbia University (1962); BA, Columbia University, Summa Cum Laude (1954) **C:** President, Academy of Political Science (1992-Present); Janet H. Robb Professor of Social Sciences, Barnard College and Columbia University (1980-Present); Editor, Political Science Quarterly (1973-Present); Professor of Political Science, Barnard College and Columbia University (1968-Present); Member, Faculty, Barnard College and Columbia University, New York City, NY (1959-Present); Chairman, Barnard Department of Political Science, Columbia University (1965-1995); Director, Graduate Program in Public Policy and Administration, Columbia University (1978-1985) **CR:** Visiting Scholar, Russell Sage Foundation (1995-1996) **CIV:** Chairman, North Tarrytown Planning Board (1977-1979); Deputy Mayor and Acting Mayor, City of North Tarrytown (1972-1973); Member, North Tarrytown Board of Trustees (1971-1973); Member, North Tarrytown Zoning Board Appeals (1970-1971) **MIL:** With United States Navy Reserve (1954-1956) **CW:** Author, "American

Hegemony: Preventive War, Iraq, and Imposing Democracy" (2004); Author, "September 11, Terrorist Attacks and U.S. Foreign Policy" (2002); Author, "The New American Interventionism" (1999); Co-author, "American Leadership, Ethnic Conflict, and the New World Politics" (1997); Author, "Critical Issues for Clinton's Domestic Agenda" (1994); Author, "Volatilities in the New World Politics" (1993); Author, "The President's War Powers" (1984); Co-author, "National Security and Nuclear Strategy" (1983); Author, "Doing More with Less" (1982); Co-author, "Urban Policymaking" (1979); Co-author, "The Making of American Foreign and Domestic Policy" (1978); Co-author, "American Politics and Public Policy" (1978); Author, "City Governments and Urban Problems" (1977); Author, "American Political Institutions in the 1970's" (1976); Co-author, "Governing the City" (1969); Author, "Politics of Military Unification" (1966); Author, "New York City's Deputy Mayor & City Administrator" (1966); Author,, "Party Politics and National Elections" (1966) **MEM:** President, Board of Directors, Academy Political Science (1992-Present); APSA; The University Club of New York; The Phi Beta Kappa Society **PA:** Democrat

CARANGELO, ROBERT F., T: Partner **I:** Law and Legal Services **CN:** Weil, Gotshal & Manges LLP **ED:** JD, New York Law School, Cum Laude (1991); BA, Fairfield University, Fairfield, CT (1988) **C:** Partner, Litigation Department, Weil, Gotshal & Manges LLP, New York, NY; Member, Securities Litigation Practice, Weil, Gotshal & Manges LLP, New York, NY **CR:** Member, Nominating Committee, Weil, Gotshal & Manges LLP, New York, NY; Chairman, Board of Health, Town of Greenwich; Member, Board of Trustees, Brunswick School **CW:** Managing Editor, "New York Law School Law Review," New York Law School **AW:** Honoree, Super Lawyers (2013-2017); Leading Securities Lawyer, New York Super Lawyers **MEM:** Executive Board, Moot Court, New York Law School **BAR:** Connecticut (1992); New York (1992); Supreme Court of the United States; United States Court of Appeals for the Second Circuit; United States District Court Eastern District of New York; United States District Court Northern District of New York; United States District Court Southern District of New York **MH:** Albert Nelson Marquis Lifetime Achievement Award (2017) **BA:** 767 5th Ave Fl CONC1, Weil, Gotshal & Manges LLP, New York, NY, 10153 **ADD:** 80 Circle Dr, Greenwich, CT, 06830

CARASSO, ALFRED SAMUEL, T: Mathematician **I:** Sciences **CN:** National Institute of Standards and Technology **PT:** Samuel Carasso; Renee (Ades) Carasso **MS:** Married **SPN:** Beatrice Kozak (6/12/1964) **CH:** Adam Leonard; Rachel Lisa **ED:** PhD in Mathematics, University of Wisconsin (1968); BSc in Physics, The University of Adelaide (1960) **C:** Mathematician, National Institute of Standards and Technology, Gaithersburg, Maryland (1982-Present); Professor, The University of New Mexico, Albuquerque (1976-1981); Associate Professor, The University of New Mexico, Albuquerque (1972-1976); Assistant Professor of Mathematics, The University of New Mexico, Albuquerque (1969-1972); Assistant Professor of Mathematics, Michigan State University, East Lansing (1968-1969); Research Assistant, Graduate School, University of Wisconsin-Madison (1962-1968); Meteorologist, Bureau of Meteorology, Adelaide, Australia (1960-1962) **CR:** Consultant, Center for Computing Sciences, Institute for Defense Analyses (1996-2003); Visiting Staff Member, Los Alamos National Laboratory, New Mexico (1972-1982) **CW:** Contributor, Articles,

Professional Journals **MEM:** Society for Industrial and Applied Mathematics; American Mathematical Society; Cosmos Club **MH:** Albert Nelson Marquis Lifetime Achievement Award (2017) **RE:** Jewish **ADD:** 18 War Admiral Ct, North Potomac, MD, 20878 **URL:** www.alfredcarasso.com

CARMANY, GEORGE WALTER III, T: Finance Company Executive, Consultant **I:** Financial Services **CN:** GW Carmany and Co Inc. **DOB:** 03/21/1940 **PB:** New York **SC:** NY/USA **PT:** George Walter Carmany Jr.; Merle (Harrold) Carmany **MS:** Married **SPN:** Judith Jermain Lawrence (4/27/1968) **CH:** George W.W.; Elizabeth C. Perreten **ED:** BA, Amherst College (1962) **C:** Adviser, Health Care Policy, Harvard Medical School (2014-Present); Senior Adviser, Essex Woodlands Health Ventures (2010-Present); President, G.W. Carmany & Co., Inc., Boston, MA (1994-Present); Senior Executive Vice President, The Boston Company (1990-1993); Senior Executive Vice President, American Express Bank, Ltd., New York, NY (1981-1990); Senior Vice President, American Express Company, New York, NY (1975-1981); Vice President, Bankers Trust Company, New York, NY (1966-1971) **CR:** Director, Remedy Partners, Darien, CT (2013-Present); Director, Breath America Inc., Nashville, TN (2012-Present); Senior Adviser, Brown Brothers Harriman, Boston, MA (2008-Present); Director, Macquarie Infrastructure Corporation, New York, NY (2004-Present); Senior Adviser, EnGeneIC Pty. Ltd., Sydney, Australia (2003-Present); Director, SunLife Finance, Inc., Toronto, Canada (2004-2010); Vice Chairman, Computerized Medical Systems, St. Louis, MO (2001-2008); Chairman, Helicon Therapeutics, Farmingdale, NY (1999-2005) **CIV:** Member, Advisory Committee, Education, Harvard Medical School (2012-Present); Vice President, Alumni Council, Amherst College (2007-Present); Member, President's Circle, The National Academies, Washington, DC (2002-2008); Chairman, Board of Associates, The Whitehead Institute, Cambridge, MA (2001-2003); Vice Chairman, Lifespan, Inc., Providence, RI (1997-2002); Chairman, The New England Medical Center Hospitals, Boston, MA (1996-1997); Trustee, Bentley University, Waltham, MA (1990-2012); Executive Member, Bentley University, Waltham, MA (1990-2012) **MIL:** Lieutenant, U.S. Naval Reserve (1962-1966) **AW:** Distinguished Service Award, National Maritime Historical Society (2014); New York Yacht Club Medal (2012); Eminent Service Medal, Amherst College (2012); Distinguished Service Award, Amherst College (2001) **MEM:** Trustee, New York Yacht Club (1996-2013); Commodore, Shinnecock Yacht Club (1983-1987); Long Island Wyandanch Club; Racquet and Tennis Club; Royal Sydney Yacht Squadron; Somerset Club; Fort Worth Boat Club **MH:** Albert Nelson Marquis Lifetime Achievement Award (2017) **H:** Ocean racing; Game fishing; Hunting **BA:** 50 Congress St Ste 936, GW Carmany and Co Inc., Boston, MA, 02109 **ADD:** 46 Chestnut Street, Boston, MA, 02108

CARMI, SHLOMO, T: Engineering Educator **I:** Education/Educational Services **CN:** University of Maryland, Baltimore County **DOB:** 07/18/1937 **PB:** Cernauti **SC:** Romania **PT:** Shmuel Carmi; Haia (Marcovici) Carmi **MS:** Married **SPN:** Rachel Aharoni (12/23/1963) **CH:** Sharon; Ronen-Itzhak; Lemore **ED:** PhD, University of Minnesota (1968); MS, University of Minnesota (1966); BS, University of the Witwatersrand, Cum Laude (1962); Coursework, Technion, Israel Institute of Technology (1958-1960) **C:** Professor Emeritus, Mechanical Engineering, College of Engineering and Information Technology, University of Maryland, Baltimore County (2012-Present); Dean Emeritus, College of Engineering and Information Technology, University of Maryland, Baltimore County (2012-Present); Professor of

Mechanical Engineering, University of Maryland, Baltimore County (1996-2012); Chair, Department of Mechanical Engineering, University of Maryland, Baltimore County (2006-2010); Dean, College of Engineering and Information Technology, University of Maryland, Baltimore County (1996-2006); Professor and Head, Department of Mechanical Engineering and Mechanics, Drexel University, Philadelphia, Pennsylvania (1986-1996); Head, Department of Mechanical Engineering and Mechanics, Drexel University, Philadelphia, PA (1986-1996); Professor, Mechanical Engineering, Wayne State University (1978-1986); Associate Professor, Mechanical Engineering, Wayne State University (1973-1978); Assistant Professor, Mechanical Engineering, Wayne State University (1972-1973); Assistant Professor, Mechanical Engineering, Wayne State University (1968-1970); Research Assistant, University of Minnesota (1963-1968); Research Fellow, University of Minnesota (1963-1968); Research Engineer, West Rand Gold Mining Company, Krugersdorp, South Africa (1962-1963) **CR:** Chair, National Mechanical Engineering Department Heads Committee (1996-1997); Congressional Fellow, Science & Technology Adviser to U.S. Senator Carl Levin (1985-1986); Research Specialist, Detroit Edison Company (1983); Sabbatical I. Taylor Chair (1977-1978); Research Specialist, Ford Motor Company (1973-1974, 1976-1977); Senior Lecturer, Technion, Israel Institute of Technology (1970-1972); Speaker in Field **MIL:** Israeli Defense Forces (1956-1958) **CW:** Associate Editor, "Journal of Fluids Engineering" (1981-1984); Editor, Three Books in Field; Contributor, Many Articles, Professional Journals; Contributor, Reviews, Professional Journals **AW:** Lifetime Achievement Award, District of Columbia Council of Engineering and Architectural Societies (2008); Faculty Research Award, Wayne State University (1970); South African Technion Society Scholarship, Technion, Israel Institute of Technology (1960-1962); Prize, Transvaal Chamber of Mines (1961); Research Grant, U.S. Department of Energy; Research Grant, Office of Research, U.S. Army; Research Grant, National Science Foundation; Research Grant, National Institute for Standards and Technology; Research Grant, National Institutes of Health; Research Grant, Advanced Research Project Agency; Research Grant, Office of Science Research, U.S. Air Force **MEM:** Board of Governors, The American Society of Mechanical Engineers (2008-2011); Senior Vice President of Education, The American Society of Mechanical Engineers (2003-2006); Vice President of Engineering Education, The American Society of Mechanical Engineers (2000-2003); Dean's Council, American Society for Engineering Education (1996-2006); Evaluator, Mechanical Engineering Programs, ABET (1988-1996); Fellow, The American Society of Mechanical Engineers; American Physical Society; Golden Key Honor Society; Sigma Xi; The Tau Beta Pi Association, Inc.; Pi Tau Sigma; The Honor Society of Phi Kappa Phi **MH:** Albert Nelson Marquis Lifetime Achievement Award (2017) **ADD:** 2 Aston Ct, Owings Mills, MD, 21117

CAROL, JOY HAUPT, T: Author, Educator, Retreat Leader **I:** Writing and Editing **DOB:** 04/28/1938 **PB:** Lincoln **SC:** NE/USA **PT:** Wilson J. Haupt; Alma J. (Weilage) Haupt **ED:** MA in Spirituality, General Theological Seminary (1998); Honorary LHD, Nebraska Wesleyan University (1994); Postgraduate Coursework, New York University (1974-1975); MA in Counseling Psychology, University of Maryland (1968); Postgraduate Coursework, Scarritt University (1960-1961); BA in Education, Nebraska Wesleyan University (1959) **CT:** Spiritual director, chaplain, Red Cross volunteer **C:** Author; Speaker; Retreat and Workshop Leader; Preacher (1998-Present), Director of Development, International Women's

Tribune Center, New York City, NY (1996-1997); Director, International Programs, Christian Children's Fund, Richmond, VA (1993-1995); Director, Asia/Pacific Region, Save the Children, Westport, CT (1984-1993); Program Development Officer, Cultural Information Services, New York City, NY (1983-1984); Program Officer, Ford Foundation, New York City, NY (1980-1982); Staff Member, United Nations Development Program, Suva, Fiji (1979-1980); Associate Executive Director, YWCA Brooklyn (1978); Founder, Director, Union Center for Women, Brooklyn, NY (1973-1976); Psychological Counselor, Public and Private Schools (1969-1973); Teacher, Director, Project Head Start, Various Public Schools (1964-1968); Project Director, Methodist Church Education Systems, Karachi, Pakistan (1961-1963); Teacher, Director, Project Head Start, Various Public Schools (1959-1960) **CR:** Trauma Response Assistance for Children (2002-2003); Consultant, United Nations/World Council Churches, New York and Asia (1984); Consultant, United Nations/World Council Churches, New York and Asia (1976-1977); Women's Organizations, Oslo, Norway (1974) **CIV:** Board of Directors, Nebraska Wesleyan University (1992-Present); Board of Directors, Vietnamese Memorial Association, Central Europe Institute (1990-Present); Volunteer, Central Park Conservancy (2002-2005); Volunteer Chaplain, American Red Cross (2001-2005); Spiritual Director (1997-2005); Volunteer, Chaplain, Bellevue Hospital (1997-1998); Hospice Volunteer (1994-1998); Volunteer, Support Groups for Brain Tumor Patients, Local Hospitals, Richmond, VA (1992-1994); National Convener, United States Forum on Vietnam, Cambodia, Laos, New York (1990-1995); Co-Founder, Self-Help Community Center, CHIPS, Brooklyn, NY (1972-1975); Co-Founder, Volunteer, Project Reach Youth, New York City, NY (1965-1968); National Advisory Council, United Methodist Church **CW:** Author, "Seasons of Joy" (2015); Author, "The Fabric of Friendship" (2006); Author, "Journeys of Courage" (2004); Author, "Towers of Hope" (2002); Author, "Finding Courage" (2002); Author, "Already I Feel the Change" (1989); Author, "Official Report on End of International Women's Decade," United Nations Development Program (1985); Author, "But We're Not Afraid to Speak Anymore" (1976); Author, "You Don't Have to be Rich to Own a Brownstone" (1971); Contributor, Numerous Articles to Magazines **AW:** Outstanding Woman, Brooklyn, NY (1970); Outstanding Women of America (1966); Outstanding Educator in the United States, United States Jaycees, Colorado (1966) **MEM:** American Association of University Women; National Organization of Women; Women's International League for Peace and Freedom; Society for International Development **H:** Writing; Reading; Hiking; Music; Gardening; Singing **BA:** 3460 Caroline Blvd, # 206D, Penney Farms, FL, 32079 **ADD:** PO Box 62, Penny Farms, FL, 32079 **URL:** http://www.joycarol.com

CARPENTER, PAMELA PRISCO, T: Bank Executive **I:** Education/Educational Services **CN:** State Street Corporation **DOB:** 07/12/1958 **PB:** Norwood **SC:** MA/USA **PT:** Francis Joseph Prisco; Helene Louise (Swartz) Prisco **CH:** Charles; Craig; Cameron **ED:** Postgraduate Work, Boston State College (1980-1981); Graduate Certificate, Universidad de Salamanca (1980); BA, Harvard University, Summa Cum Laude (1980); Phi Beta Kappa **CT:** Certified Spanish Teacher, Commonwealth of Massachusetts; Licensed Real Estate Associate, State of Massachusetts **C:** Vice President of International Trade, Royal Bank of Scotland (2009-Present); Vice President, Investor Services Division, State Street Corporation

(2009-2015); Vice President of International Trade Banking, Sovereign Bank (Now Santander Bank, N. A.) (2003-2009); Vice President of Global Finance Institutions, Fleet National Bank (1980-2003); Spanish Teacher, Grades K-Two, IES Language School, IES Languages (1991-1992); Substitute Teacher in Bilingual Education, The English High School (1979-1980); Private Spanish Tutor; Private French Tutor **CIV:** Secretary Parent-Teacher Association, C.J. Prescott Elementary School, Norwood Public Schools (1995-1997); President, Parent Advisory Board, Mulberry Childcare and Pre-school Center (Now Mulberry Learning Centre) (1991-1994); Mentor, Hyde Park High School Partnership, BankBoston (1990) **AW:** Recipient, Excellence Award, Royal Bank of Scotland (2009-2016); Recipient, Scholarship, Radcliffe Club of Boston (1976) **MEM:** The Phi Beta Kappa Society **MH:** Albert Nelson Marquis Lifetime Achievement Award (2017) **RE:** Catholic **ADD:** 549 Neponset St, Norwood, MA, 02062

CARR, EDWARD, T: Lawyer **I:** Law and Legal Services **CN:** Vinson & Elkins LLP **DOB:** 07/31/1962 **PB:** Borger **SC:** TX/USA **ED:** JD, UCLA School of Law (1987); AB, Stanford University, with Honors and Distinction (1984) **C:** Partner, Vinson & Elkins, Houston (1997-Present); Associate, Vinson & Elkins, Houston (1988-1997) **CR:** Speaker in Field; Lecturer in Field **CW:** Contributing Author, "Business and Commercial Litigation in Federal Courts" (2016); Contributing Author, "Business and Commercial Litigation in Federal Courts" (2011); Contributing Author,"Business and Commercial Litigation in Federal Courts" (2005); Contributing Author, "Texas Legal Ethics," American Legal Ethics Library, Cornell University (1998); Contributing Author, Business and Commercial Litigation in Federal Courts (1998); Member, Editorial Board, "UCLA Law Review" (1986-1987); Member, "UCLA Law Review" (1985-1987); Contributor, Articles, Professional Journals **MEM:** Standing Committee on Texas Disciplinary Rules of Professional Conduct, State Bar of Texas (2007-2013); Chair, District 4B Grievance Committee, State Bar of Texas (2003-2004); Lifetime Fellow, Texas Bar Foundation; Fellow, Texas Bar College; Lifetime Member, American Judicature Society; Federal Bar Association; Houston Bar Association; Antitrust Law and Litigation Section, ABA **BAR:** Admitted to Practice, United States District & Bankruptcy Courts of the Southern District of Texas (1989); Admitted to Practice, United States Court of Appeals for the Fifth Circuit (1989); Admitted to Practice, United States Court of Appeals for the Federal Circuit (1989); The District of Columbia Bar (1989); State Bar of Texas (1988) **ADD:** PO Box 52398, Houston, TX, 77052

CARRERE, CHARLES SCOTT, T: Judge **I:** Law and Legal Services **DOB:** 09/26/1937 **PB:** Dublin **SC:** GA/USA **CH:** Daniel Austin **ED:** LLB, Stetson University (1961); BA, University of Georgia, Athens, GA (1959) **C:** Visiting Professor of Law, Cumberland School of Law, Samford University (1998-1999); Visiting Law Professor, College of Law, Stetson University (1997-1998); Judge, Pinellas County, FL (1980-1996); Partner, Harrison, Greene, Mann, Rowe & Stanton (1970-1980); Chief Trial Attorney, U.S. District Court, Middle District, State of Florida (1968-1969); Assistant U.S. Attorney, U.S. District Court, Middle District, State of Florida (1968-1969); Chief Trial Attorney, U.S. District Court, Middle District, State of Florida (1965-1966); Assistant U.S. Attorney, U.S. District Court, Middle District, State of Florida (1963-1966); Law Clerk to U.S. District Judge, Orlando, FL (1962-1963) **AW:** Alumnus of Year Award, Stetson Student Bar Association (1998); Judicial Appreciation Award,

St. Petersburg Bar Association (1996) **MEM:** State Bar of Georgia; The Florida Bar; Phi Beta Kappa **BAR:** State of Florida (1961); State of Georgia (1960) **RE:** Presbyterian **ADD:** PO Box 7177, Seminole, FL, 33775

CARROL, EDWARD NICHOLAS, T: Psychologist **I:** Social Work **DOB:** 06/22/1943 **PB:** Newark **SC:** NJ/USA **PT:** Wilfred Carrol; Ruth (Gluck) Carrol **MS:** Married **SPN:** Virginia Paisley Herbruck (10/6/1996); Anne Marie McDonald (5/27/1973, Divorced 5/1989) **CH:** Abbe Galen **ED:** PhD, University of Delaware (1979); MA, University of Delaware (1975); MA, New York University (1970); BA, Columbia University (1965); Dissertation Research, Jefferson Medical College, Thomas Jefferson University, Philadelphia, PA **CT:** Diplomate, American Academy of Pain Management **C:** Director, Pain Psychology Section, Pain Management Center, VA Medical Center, Cleveland, OH (2003-2009); Clinical Director, Pain Management Center, Huron Road Hospital, East Cleveland, OH (1986-1988); Founder, Director, Pain Clinic, VA Medical Center, Cleveland, OH (1979-2003) **MEM:** International Association for the Study of Pain; Midwest Pain Society **H:** Dogs; Classical, country, and jazz organ music **PA:** Republican **RE:** Jewish **ADD:** 10880 Cedar Road, Munson, OH, 44026-3630

CARSON, KENNETH WAYNE, T: Science Educator **I:** Education/Educational Services **CN:** Round Rock Opportunity Center **DOB:** 10/14/1957 **PB:** Dallas **SC:** TX/USA **PT:** Gerald W. Carson; Jane G. Carson **MS:** Married **SPN:** Connie Stried (2010); Natalie C. Anderson (10/19/1981, Deceased 5/26/2004) **CH:** Sarah E.; Hannah L.; Stephanie L. (Stepchild); Samantha A. (Stepchild) **ED:** MEd in Educational Leadership, Texas State University (2010); Coursework in Educational Administration, University of North Texas, Denton, TX (1980-1981); EdB in Secondary Education, University of North Texas, Denton, TX (1980); Coursework, Culver-Stockton College, Canton, MO (1976-1978) **C:** Middle School Science Teacher, Round Rock Opportunity Center, Round Rock, TX (2005-Present); Middle School Science Teacher, Quincy Junior High School, Quincy, IL (1993-2005); Affiliate, Insurance Sales and Service, Trust GDC, Hannibal, MO (1991-1993); Head Coach, Softball, Assistant Football Coach, Culver-Stockton College, Canton, MO (1989-1991); Assistant Football Coach, Quincy University (1987-1989); Coach, Hannibal High School, Hannibal, MO (1984-1987); Biology Teacher, Hannibal High School, Hannibal, MO (1984-1987); Coach, Richardson West Junior High School, Richardson, TX (1980-1984); English Teacher, Richardson West Junior High School, Richardson, TX (1980-1984); Biology Teacher, Richardson West Junior High School, Richardson, TX (1980-1984) **CR:** Head, Science Department, Round Rock Opportunity Center, Round Rock, TX (2015-Present); Team Leader, Round Rock Opportunity Center, Round Rock, TX (2011-Present); Pilot Program, Next Generation Digital Classroom, Round Rock Opportunity Center, Round Rock, TX (2014-2017); Emerging Science Leader Cohort, Round Rock Opportunity Center, Round Rock, TX (2010-2013); Site-Based Committee, Round Rock Opportunity Center, Round Rock, TX (2009-2011); Middle School Science Collaborative, Round Rock Opportunity Center, Round Rock, TX (2009-2010); Superintendent's Retreat, Round Rock Opportunity Center, Round Rock, TX (2007); District Advisory Committee, Round Rock Opportunity Center, Round Rock, TX (2006-2008); Collaborative Teacher, Round Rock Opportunity Center, Round Rock, TX (2005-2008); Lead Teacher,

Quincy Junior High School, Quincy, IL; Technology Team, Quincy Junior High School, Quincy, IL **CIV:** Elder, First Christian Church, Hannibal, MO (1999-2005); Treasurer, Hannibal Arts Council (1998-2002); Treasurer, Hannibal Community Theatre (1996-2000); Deacon, First Christian Church, Hannibal, MO (1986-1999); Sponsor, Sim City Team Competition, Quincy Junior High School, Quincy, IL; Coach, YMCA Little League; Affiliate, HAC Celebrity Waiters Benefit; Sponsor, Wilderness Experience in Canada; Choir; Sunday School Teacher, First Christian Church, Hannibal, MO; Chairman, Ministerial Search Committee, First Christian Church, Hannibal, MO; Vice-President of the Board, First Christian Church, Hannibal, MO **CW:** Contributor, Tejas Trax; Blogger **AW:** Texas Regional Collaborative for Excellence in Science Teaching (2011-2014); Grantee, DATE, Round Rock Opportunity Center (2009-2011); Grantee, Partners in Education, Round Rock Opportunity Center, Round Rock, TX (2009); Teacher of the Year, Round Rock Opportunity Center, Round Rock, TX (2006); Grantee, Northern Illinois Outdoor Education, Quincy Junior High School, Quincy, IL **MEM:** BMW Car Club of America; NSTA; International Society for Technology in Education (ISTE); The Science Teacher Association of Texas (STAT); Quincy Community Theatre; Shelbina Clowns and Criers Theatre; Hannibal Community Theatre; Mark Twain Men's Chorale; Cosmopolitan Singers; Jaycees **MH:** Albert Nelson Marquis Lifetime Achievement Award (2017) **H:** Restoring old BMW cars **RE:** Christian **ADD:** 750 Sunny Slope Road, Liberty Hill, TX, 78642

CARTER, GLENN THOMAS "TOM", T: Lawyer, Clergyman **I:** Law and Legal Services **CN:** Seventh-Day Adventist Church **DOB:** 07/20/1934 **PB:** Beaumont **SC:** TX/USA **PT:** Glenmore Rust Carter; Sarah Elizabeth (Woods) Carter **MS:** Married **SPN:** Janette Lucile Mullikin (8/1/1954) **CH:** Penny Lucile Soucy; Sylvia Lee DeVries **ED:** JD, Emory University (1967); BA, Union College (1956) **CT:** Ordained to Ministry, Seventh-Day Adventist Church (1960) **C:** Georgia-Cumberland Conference Executive and Association Boards, Calhoun, GA (2017-Present); Director Planned Giving and Trust Services, Southern Union of Seventh-Day Adventists, Decatur, GA (2009-2014); Special Legal Counsel, Georgia Cumberland Conference of Seventh-Day Adventists (2000-2009); Director, Trust Services General Conference of Seventh-Day Adventists, Silver Spring, MD (1985-2000); Director of Trust Services, Pacific Union Conference Seventh-Day Adventists, Westlake Village, CA (1982-1985); Director, Public Affairs, Southwestern Union Conference of Seventh-Day Adventists, Burleson, TX (1980-1982); Associate Director, Trust Services, Southwestern Union Conference of Seventh-Day Adventists, Burleson, TX (1980-1982); Associate Director, Trust Services, General Conference of Seventh-Day Adventists, Washington, DC (1976-1980); Director, Trust Services, Texaco and Texas Conference of Seventh-Day Adventists, Amarillo and Fort Worth, TX (1969-1976); Special Legal Adviser, Georgia-Cumberland Conference of Seventh-Day Adventists, Decatur, GA (1968-1969); Pastor, Texas, Wyoming, and Georgia (1956-1965); **CR:** Paul Harris Fellow, Rotary **CW:** Author, "The 19th Century Odyssey of John and Judith: From the Battlefields of the Civil War to Spiritual Battles on the Texas Frontier" (2007); Author, "Developing Ethical Standards In Charitable Fundraising, Trust & Estates" (1994); Author, "Liberty Magazine on the Supreme Court and Same-Sex Marriage"; Author, "Treason vs Treason" **AW:** Trust Services Honorary Director, General Conference of Seventh-Day Adventists (2014); American Jurisprudence Prize, Litigation Lawyers Co-Op (1967) **BAR:**

State of California (1984); U.S. District Court, Northern District, State of Texas (1981); District of Columbia (1976); State of Maryland (1976); U.S. Supreme Court (1976); State of Texas (1969); State of Georgia (1968) **H:** Jogging; Reading; Travel **RE:** Seventh-Day Adventist **ADD:** 4200 Herendeen Carter Drive, Douglasville, GA, 30135

CARTER, LYNDA , T: Actress **I:** Fine Art **DOB:** 06/06/1905 **PB:** Phoenix **SC:** AZ/USA **MS:** Married **SPN:** Robert Altman (1/29/1984); Ron Samuels (5/28/1977, Divorced 1982) **CH:** 2 Children **ED:** Student, University of Arizona **CR:** Beauty and Fashion Director, Maybelline Cosmetics; Professional Motivational Speaker **CIV:** Honorary Crusade Chairman, American Cancer Society (1985-1986); Honorary Chairperson, Exceptional Children's Foundation (1987-1988) **CW:** Actor, "Super Troopers 2" (2018); Actor, "Supergirl" (2016); Actor, "Skin Wars" (2014); Actor, "Two and a Half Men" (2013); Actor, "Tattered Angel" (2007); Actor, "Smallville" (2007); Actor, "Slayer" (2006); Actor, "Tempbot" (2006); Actor, "Sky High" (2005); Actor, "The Dukes of Hazzard" (2005); Actor, "Law and Order SVU" (2005); Actor, "The Creature of the Sunny Side Up Trailer Park" (2004); Actor, "Terror Peak" (2003); Actor, "Hope and Faith" (2003); Actor, "Super Troopers" (2001); Actor, "Someone to Love Me: A Moment of Truth Movie" (1998); Actor, "A Prayer in the Dark" (1997); Actor, "When Friendship Kills" (1996); Actor, "She Woke Up Pregnant" (1996); Actor, "Family Blessings" (1996); Actor, "Lightning in a Bottle" (1993); Actor, "Daddy" (1991); Actor, "Posing: Inspired by Three Real Stories" (1991); Actor, "Mike Hammer: Murder Takes All" (1989); Actor, "Stillwatch" (1987); Actor, "Partners in Crime" (1984); Actor, "Rita Hayworth: The Love Goddess" (1983); Actor, "Hotline" (1982); Actor, "Born to Be Sold" (1981); Actor, "The Last Song" (1980); Actor, "Wonder Woman" (1976-1979); Actor, "A Matter of Wife...and Death" (1976); Actor, "The New Original Wonder Woman" (1975); Actor, "Bobbie Jo and the Outlaw" (1976) **AW:** Golden Eagle Award (1986); Recipient, Hispanic Woman of the Year Award (1983); Named Miss World, Represented United States (1972) **ADD:** 9200 Harrington Drive, Potomac, MD, 20854

CASON, ROGER L., T: Chemical Company Executive, Educator, Consultant **I:** Business Management/Business Services **DOB:** 08/13/1930 **PB:** Madison **SC:** WI/USA **PT:** Hulsey Cason; Eloise (Boeker) Cason **MS:** Married **SPN:** June Ely Macnabb (6/12/1952) **CH:** David Allan; Diane Louise; Nancy Lynn **ED:** MA in Liberal Studies, University of Delaware (1998); MBA, University of Delaware (1977); MS in Mechanical Engineering, University of Rochester (1952); BS in Mechanical Engineering, University of Rochester, with High Distinction (1951) **CT:** Registered Professional Engineer, State of Delaware (Inactive) **C:** Consultant, For-Profit Organizations (1993-2009); Consultant, Non-Profit Organizations (1993-2009); Principal Consultant, DuPont, Wilmington, DE (1983-1992); Business Analysis Manager, DuPont, Wilmington, DE (1975-1983); Staff Business Analyst, DuPont, Wilmington, DE (1971-1975); Senior Mechanical Engineer, DuPont, Houston, TX (1963-1970); Production Supervisor, DuPont, Houston, TX (1963-1970); Mechanical Supervisor, DuPont, Houston, TX (1963-1970); Engineer, DuPont, Charleston, WV (1955-1962); Supervisor, DuPont, Charleston, WV (1955-1962) **CIV:** Treasurer, Delaware Chamber Music Festival (2000-2004) **MIL:** Civil Engineer Corps, U.S. Navy (1952-1955) **CW:** Contributor, Articles, Professional Journals **MEM:** Regional President, National Model Railroad Association, Inc. (2008-2010); Regional Secretary, National Model Railroad Association, Inc. (2006-2008); National Development Manager, National Model Railroad Association, Inc. (2006-2008); National Trustee, National Model Railroad Association, Inc. (2004-2005); Regional Director, National Model Railroad Association, Inc. (2000-2004); Commander, Wilmington Sail and Power Squadron (1995-1996); Commander, Wilmington Sail and Power Squadron (1988-1989); Senior Navigator, Wilmington Sail and Power Squadron; Master Model Railroader, National Model Railroad Association, Inc.; Tau Beta Pi; Phi Beta Kappa; Associate, Sigma Xi; Beta Gamma Sigma; IEEE **MH:** Albert Nelson Marquis Lifetime Achievement Award (2017); Distinguished Humanitarian (2017) **H:** Bridge; Traveling; Photography; Model building **PA:** Republican **RE:** Episcopalian **ADD:** 410 Bayberry Lane, West Grove, PA, 19390

CASS, DARRELL L., T: Director of Fetal Surgery **I:** Health, Wellness and Fitness **CN:** Cleveland Clinic **DOB:** 06/16/1964 **PB:** North Hollywood **SC:** CA/USA **MS:** Single **CH:** Harrison, Hannah **ED:** MD, University of California, Los Angeles (1991); AB, Stanford University, California (1986) **CT:** Certification in Pediatric Surgery, American Board of Surgery (2002); Certification in General Surgery, American Board of Surgery (2000) **C:** Director of Fetal Surgery, Cleveland Clinic (2017); Associate Professor, Michael E. DeBakey Department of Surgery, Baylor College of Medicine, Houston, TX (2001) **CR:** Co-Founder, Texas Children's Fetal Center (2001); Co-Director, Texas Center of Fetal Surgery, Houston, TX (2001-2017); Speaker in Field **MIL:** Colonel, US Army Reserves **CW:** Contributor, Over Seven Chapters, Books; Contributor, Over 125 Articles, Peer-Reviewed Journals **AW:** Alpha Omega Alpha, University of California, Los Angeles School of Medicine (1991); Fellow, American College of Surgeons; Fellow, American Academy of Pediatrics; Grantee, American Heart Association; Grantee, Juvenile Diabetes Association; Listed, Best of the Best, Houston Chronicle Newspaper **MEM:** International Fetal Medicine and Surgery Society; Society of University Surgeons; Association for Academic Surgery **H:** Exercise; Running; Snow skiing; Wine collecting **BA:** 9500 Euclid Ave, A120, Cleveland, OH, 44195 **ADD:** 24150 Woodside Ln, Beachwood, OH, 44122 **URL:** https://www.researchgate.net/profile/Darrell_Cass

CEPURITIS, TALIVALDIS, T: Partner **I:** Law and Legal Services **CN:** Olson & Cepuritis Ltd. **ED:** JD, New York University (1965); MSE in Chemical Engineering, University of Michigan; BSE in Chemical Engineering, University of Michigan **C:** Partner, Olson and Cepuritis Ltd. **CW:** Author, "Guide to Patents and Patent Activities"; Author, "Commentary on the Keeping and Preservation of Records of Invention and Specimens" **AW:** Named, Illinois Super Lawyer (2008-2013); Named, Top Lawyers in Illinois, Leading Lawyers, Law Bulletin Media (2005-2012); Named, Illinois Super Lawyer (2005-2006) **BAR:** New York; Michigan; Illinois; Washington, D.C.; Supreme Court of the United States; United States Court of Appeals for the Federal Circuit; United States Court of Appeals for the District of Columbia Circuit; United States Court of Appeals for the Third Circuit; United States Court of Appeals for the Sixth Circuit; United States Court of Appeals for the Seventh Circuit; United States District Court for the Northern District of Illinois; United States Patent and Trademark Office **BA:** 20 North Wacker Drive, 36th Floor, Olson & Cepuritis Ltd., Chicago, IL, 60606 **ADD:** 20 N Wacker Dr Fl 36, Olson & Cepuritis Ltd., Chicago, IL, 60606

CHADSEY, HAROLD A., T: Engineer **I:** Engineering **MS:** Married **SPN:** Carol Ellen **ED:** PhD, Kennedy-Western University (2001); MS, American University (1995); BS, Centenary College (1982) **CT:** Certified, Project Management, George Washington University (2012) **C:** Physicist, U.S. Department of the Navy (2004-2016); Atomic Frequency Standards (1995-2004); GPS Timing, Precise Time & Time Interval (1993-2004); Timing and Clock Adviser, U.S. Coast Guard, Alexandria, VA (1989-2004); Astronomer, U.S. Naval Observatory, Washington, D.C. (1989-2004); Astronomer, U.S. Naval Observatory, Miami, FL (1985-1989) **CIV:** Chairman, Fairfax County Public Schools Science Fair Grand Prize Judges (2004-2017); Mentor, High School Students, Department of the Navy, U.S. Naval Observatory (2002); Judge, High School Science Fairs, Fairfax County Public Schools (1998-2017); Judge, High School Science Fairs, Washington, D.C. Public Schools (1991-2002) **CW:** Author, "An Automated Quality Control System for Cesium Frequency Standards" (2001) **AW:** Meritorious Civilian Federal Service Award (2016); Safety Representative, Naval District of Washington (2002) **MEM:** Project Management Institute (2012); President, Northern Virginia Radio Control (1997); El Karubah Shriners **MH:** Albert Nelson Marquis Lifetime Achievement Award (2017) **H:** Building and flying remote control airplanes; Private pilot **ADD:** 11931 Appling Valley Rd, Fairfax, VA, 22030

CHAKRABORTY, PRATYUSH, T: Postdoctoral Scholar **I:** Education/Educational Services **CN:** University of California, Berkeley **PB:** Kolkata **SC:** India **MS:** Married **SPN:** Vijaya Goswami **ED:** PhD in Electrical and Computer Engineering, University of Florida, Gainesville, FL (2016); MEE in Electrical and Computer Engineering, University of Florida, Gainesville, FL (2013); MEE in Electrical Engineering, Indian Institute of Technology, Mumbai, India (2011); BEE in Electrical Engineering, Jadavpur University, Kolkata, West Bengal, India (2006) **C:** Postdoctoral Scholar, Department of Mechanical Engineering, University of California, Berkeley (2012-Present); Teaching Assistant, University of Florida, Gainesville, FL (2012); Teaching Assistant, IIT Bombay (2009-2011); Senior Marketing Executive, Industrial Solutions and Services, Siemens Corporation, Kolkata, India (2009); Marketing Executive, Industrial Solutions and Services, Siemens Corporation, Kolkata, India (2007-2008); Graduate Trainee Engineer, Industrial Solutions and Services, Siemens Corporation, Kolkata, India (2006-2007) **CR:** Fellowship, University of Florida, Gainesville, FL (2011-2015) **CIV:** Poster Competition Judge, Graduate Student Research Day, University of Florida, Gainesville, FL (2015); Poster Competition Judge, Graduate Student Research Day, University of Florida, Gainesville, FL (2014); Poster Competition Judge, Graduate Student Research Day, University of Florida, Gainesville, FL (2013) **CW:** Contributor, Book Chapters; Contributor, Articles, Professional Journals; Contributor, Peer-Reviewed Publications; Contributor, Poster Presentations; Contributor, Talks **AW:** All India Rank-98, Graduate Aptitude Test in Engineering (2009); Certificate of Appreciation for Excellent Performance and Noteworthy Contribution to Siemens' Objective (2009); Outstanding Excellence Award, "Project monitoring-An Excel way," Siemens Corporation (2007) **MEM:** Reviewer, IEEE Conference on Decision and Control; Reviewer, American Control Conference; Reviewer, IEEE Transactions on Smart Grid; Reviewer, IEEE Transactions on Power Systems **ADD:** 2000 Walnut Avenue, Apt. G204, Fremont, CA, 94538 **URL:** http://www.pratyushchakraborty.com

CHALK, BARBARA A., **T:** Clinical Coordinator (Retired) **I:** Medicine & Health Care **CN:** Sentara Norfolk General Hospital **DOB:** 05/01/1936 **PB:** Watertown **SC:** NY/USA **PT:** Herbert Graham Chalk; Julia Rosemead (Donaldson) Chalk **MS:** Single **ED:** Diploma in Nursing, House of Good Samaritan Hospital, Watertown, NY (1957) **C:** Clinical Coordinator, Neurosurgery Operating Room, Sentara Norfolk General Hospital, Virginia (1975-2000); Head Nurse, Neurosurgery Operating Room, University of Virginia Hospital, Charlottesville, VA (1959-1975); Staff Nurse, Operating Room, House of Good Samaritan Hospital (1957-1959) **CR:** Vice President, AURN (1984-1985); President-elect, American Association of Neuroscience Nurses (1981-1982); Publicity Chairman, Southeastern Chapter of Virginia, American Association of Neuroscience Nurses (1981); Clinical Core Curriculum Communications, Surgical Core Curriculum Communications, American Association of Neuroscience Nurses (1980-1984); President, Southeastern Chapter of Virginia, American Association of Neuroscience Nurses (1979-1980); Publicity Chairman, Southeastern Chapter of Virginia, American Association of Neuroscience Nurses (1978); National Treasurer, Board of Directors, American Association of Neuroscience Nurses (1975-1979); Chairman, Admission Commission, American Association of Neuroscience Nurses (1973-1975) **CIV:** Board of Directors, Parkinson Disease Association, Virginia Beach, VA (2003-Present); Volunteer, Sentara Norfolk General Heart Hospital (2000-Present); Volunteer, Parkinson Support Group (2000-Present); Pledging Money Towards Nursing Scholarship **CW:** Co-editor, "Core Curriculum for Operating Room Nurses-Neurosurgery"; Contributor, Articles to Professional Journals **AW:** Certificate of Merit, Parkinson Disease Association, Virginia (2001); Dr. Walter Atkinson Award **H:** Needlepoint; Ceramics **RE:** Episcopalian **BA:** Sentara Norfolk General Hospital, 600 Gresham Drive, Norfolk, VA, 23507 **ADD:** 944 Adelphi Road, Virginia Beach, VA, 23464

CHAMBERLAIN, DAVID ALLEN, **T:** Artist, Musician, Poet, Consultant, Educator, Designer **I:** Fine Art **DOB:** 08/11/1949 **PB:** Canton **SC:** OH/USA **PT:** Clifford Ivan Chamberlain; Nancy (Allen) Chamberlain **MS:** Life Partner **SPN:** Janet **CH:** Lura; Ezra **ED:** MLA, Landscape Architecture and Design, University of Colorado (2002); MFA in Sculpture, Printmaking, and Photography, University of Pennsylvania (1977); Postgraduate Coursework, Teaching Studio, The Art Institute of Colorado (1972); Diploma, Centre Audio-Visuel Langues Modernes, Vichy, France (1972); BA in Architecture and Design, Princeton University (1971) **CT:** Certificate, The Art Institute of Colorado (1973) **C:** Adjunct Associate Professor, Design and Creativity, Golisano Institute of Sustainability, Rochester Institute of Technology, Rochester, NY (2013-2014); Visiting Professor of Design, College of Art, Architecture and Humanities, Clemson University, Clemson, SC (2004-2005); Adjunct Professor, Introduction to the Arts, Sculpture, Drawing and Poetry, Art & Music Department, Rivier College, Nashua, NH (1991-1994); Visiting Professor of Creativity, Fine Arts Department, University of South Carolina, Columbia, SC (1990-1991); Presidential Fellow, Fine Arts Department, University of South Carolina, Columbia, SC (1990-1991) **CR:** Visiting Artist, Missouri Valley College, Marshall, MO (2017); Visiting Artist, Rochester Institute of Technology, Rochester, NY (2013-2014); Fellow, Executive Seminar, The Aspen Institute, Aspen, CO (2000); Guest Speaker, "Man in the Arena," Haverford School, Haverford, PA (2000); Visiting Artist, Haverford School, Bryn Mawr, PA (1999); Visiting Artist, Bradford College (1998); Visiting Artist, Clemson University, Clemson, SC (1997-1998); Visiting Artist, African Institute of Art, FUNDA Soweto, South Africa (1997); Guest Speaker, "Architecture and Composition," Department of Architecture, Clemson University (1997); Visiting Artist, Princeton University, Princeton, NJ (1996); Visiting Artist, Williams College (1995); Visiting Artist, Rhode Island School of Design, Providence, RI (1995); Visiting Artist, Purnell School, Pottersville, NJ (1995); Visiting Artist, Bradford College (1994); Guest Speaker, "Reflections on Creativity," American Institute of Architects Convention, Highlands, NC (1994); Visiting Artist, College of Charleston (1994); Visiting Artist, University of South Carolina (1994); Visiting Artist, University of Pennsylvania (1993); Guest Speaker, "Neurons, Notes, and Sketches," Conference on Art and Mathematics, Albany, NY (1993); Guest Speaker, "On the Creative Process," Empire State Plaza Art Collection, Albany, NY (1993); Visiting Artist, State University of New York, Albany (1992-1993); Guest Speaker, "Music Into Sculpture," Conference on Art and Mathematics, Albany, NY (1992); Guest Speaker, "Creativity and Fulfillment," Conference on Health and Spirituality, Boston, MA (1991); Panelist, Conference on World Affairs, University of Colorado, Boulder, CO (1990-1998); Visiting Artist, University of South Carolina (1990); Visiting Artist, Pine Manor College (1989); Visiting Artist, Bentley College (1988); Visiting Artist, Simon's Rock/Bard College (1988); Visiting Artist, Pine Manor College (1987); Speaker, Various Events **MIL:** Vietnam (1965) **CW:** Group Show, The Drawing Room Art Gallery, Cos Cob, CT (2011-Present); Group Show, Artisan's Loft Gallery, Putneyville, NY (2011-Present); Group Show, Art3Gallery, Manchester, NH (2010-Present); Group Show, Rochester Contemporary, Rochester, NY (2010-Present); Group Show, Edgewater Gallery, Middlebury, VT, Greenwich, CT (2009-Present); Group Show, Renjeau Gallery, Natick/Wellesley, MA (2008-Present); Group Show, Art Services International, Westport, CT (2007-Present); Group Show, Fast One Frame and Gallery, Wethersfield, CT (2006-Present); Group Show, McGrath and Braun, Denver, CO (2000-Present); Group Show, Alpers Fine Arts, Andover, MA (1998-Present); Group Show, Spheris Gallery, Walpole, NH (1997-Present); Group Show, Llynn Strong Gallery, Greenville, SC (1997-Present); Group Show, JRS Gallery, Providence, RI (1993-Present); Group Show, Renjeau Gallery, Concord, MA (1989-Present); Vocalist, Arranger, "Cahoots" (1974-Present); Vocalist, Arranger, "The Class of 1971 Quartet" (1968-Present); Solo Show, Morris Gallery, Missouri Valley College, Marshall, MO (2017); Solo Show, Geisel Gallery, Bausch and Lomb Center, Rochester, NY (2013); Group Show, "New Acquisitions," DeCordova Museum of Art (1999-2000); Publisher, "Media Jukebox," deCordova Sculpture Park and Museum, Lincoln, MA (1999); Solo Show, Muse a Muse Gallery, Tokyo, Japan (1997-1999); Solo Show, Consulate of Japan, San Francisco, CA (1997-1998); Group Show, "Summer Duets," Brooks Center for the Arts, Clemson University (1997-1998); Group Show, "New Acquisitions," DeCordova Museum of Art (1997); Group Show, Madison Avenue Gallery, Memphis, TN (1996-1999); Solo Show, "Retrospective: Solos, Duets and Concertos," Muskegon Art Museum, Michigan (1996); Solo Show, "Duetts," Delaware Museum of Art, Wilmington, DE (1995); Group Show, Art Thomas Gallery, Charleston, SC (1994-1998); Group Show, "New Acquisitions," DeCordova Museum of Art (1994-1995); Group Show, "New Directions: Contemporary Art from the Currier," Currier Museum (1994); Group Show, Aspen Grove Fine Arts, Aspen, CO (1993-1998); Group Show, Miller Gallery, Cincinnati, OH (1992-1998); Creator, "David Chamberlain" Artistry in Motion" (1992); Author, "A View from the Edge" (1991); Solo Show, MacLaren/Markowitz Gallery, Boulder, CO (1991); Group Show, MacLaren/Markowitz Gallery, Boulder/Broomfield, CO (1990-2000); Consultant, "Sculpture Walk Project," Facility of Planning, University of South Carolina, Columbia, SC (1990-1991); Author, "Melodic Form: The Sculpture of David Chamberlain" (1990); Solo Show, "Retrospective," McKissick Museum of Art, Columbia, SC (1990); Group Show, Clark Gallery, Lincoln, MA (1989-2010); Group Show, Joanne Lyon Galleries, Aspen, CO (1989-1991); Solo Show, "Retrospective," The Art Complex Museum, Duxbury, MA (1988); Solo Show, Pucker Gallery, Boston, MA (1988); Solo Show, Arlene McDaniel Galleries, Simsbury, CT (1988); Group Show, National Invitational Sculpture Show, Biennial, Hartford, CT (1987-1993); Solo Show, Gibson Gallery, State University of New York, Potsdam (1987); Group Show, Main Street Gallery, Nantucket, MA (1986-1995); Group Show, Richard Green Gallery, Guilford, CT (1986-1991); Group Show, Gallery on the Green, Lexington, MA (1986-1989); Group Show, Contemporary Sculpture at Chesterwood, Stockbridge, MA (1986-1988); Solo Show, Arlene McDaniel Galleries, Simsbury, CT (1986); Group Show, CAFA Exhibition, New Britain Museum of Art, New Britain, CT (1986); Author, "Best Poems of 1995: Distinguished Poets of America," National Library of Poetry; Participant, Various Solo Shows; Representative, Various Art Galleries; Participant, Various Commissions; Participant, Various Art Collections; Contributor, Various Art Institutions; Contributor, Various Musical Works; Contributor, Articles, Journals **AW:** Grantee, Clemson Advancement Foundation, Clemson University (2004); Grantee, University of Colorado, Denver, CO (2001); Grantee, The Aspen Institute (2000); Emergency Grantee, Krasner-Pollack Foundation (1999); Grantee, Indochina Arts Project, Ford Foundation (1994); Grantee, K.B.K. Foundation (1994); Top Gun Award, Plum Island Ultra-light Flying Club (1992-1993); Individual Artist Grantee, South Carolina Arts Commission (1991); Grantee, K.B.K. Foundation (1991); Editor's Choice Award for "A View from the Edge" (1991); Grantee, High Meadow Foundation (1990); Red Ribbon Award for "Search for Perfection," American Film Festival (1982); Grantee, Ford Venture Fund, University of Pennsylvania (1975-1977); Faculty Grantee, Purnell School (1972-1973); University Records, Track and Field, Princeton University, Princeton, NJ (1967-1969); Grant, Kodak, Rochester, NY; Grant, FujiFilm and Media, Columbia, SC; Grant, Papeteries Canson and Montgolfier, Annonay, France; Grant, Royal Talens BV Oil Paints, Apeldoorn, Netherlands; Grant, Takach Press Corporation, Albuquerque, NM; Grant, South African Airlines; Grant, American Airlines; Grant, Korean Airlines; Grant, Trans World Airlines **MEM:** President, The Princeton Club of Rochester (2014-Present); National Committee, Princeton Prize in Race Relations, The Princeton Club of Rochester (2010-Present) **MH:** Albert Nelson Marquis Lifetime Achievement Award (2017) **H:** Singing in jazz quartets; Fishing; Building and flying ultralight planes; Golf **ADD:** 7731 Lake Rd, Sodus Point, NY, 14555 **URL:** https://www.webwire.com/ViewPressRel.asp?aId=179460

CHAMBERLAIN, STUART HAY JR., **T:** Radio News Writer (Retired) **I:** Writing and Editing **CN:** ABC Radio **DOB:** 08/21/1943 **PB:** New York **SC:** NY/USA **PT:** Stuart Hay Chamberlain; Mary Elinor (Wilson) Chamberlain **MS:** Single **ED:** BA in Journalism, The Pennsylvania State University, University Park, PA (1965); William Benton Fellow in Broadcast Journalism, The University of Chicago, 1983-1984.

C: Writer, ABC Radio, New York, NY (1977-2010); Editor, ABC Radio, New York, NY (1977-2010); Writer, NBCUniversal Media, LLC, New York, NY (1976-1977); Producer, Station WPSX-TV, University Park, PA (1968-1976); Director, WPSX-TV, University Park, PA (1968-1976); News/Program Director, WCPA, Clearfield, PA (1966-1968); Announcer, WMAJ, State College, PA (1961-1966) **CR:** Adjunct Instructor, Brooklyn College (1987-1998) **AW:** Best News Analysis Feature or Commentary Award, Writers Guild of America (2010); Best News Analysis Feature or Commentary Award, Writers Guild of America (2007); Best Radio News Spot Script Award, Writers Guild of America (2002-2004); Best Radio News Spot Script Award, Writers Guild of America (1998); Best Radio News Spot Script Award, Writers Guild of America (1995); Best Radio News Spot Script Award, Writers Guild of America (1993); Best Radio News Spot Script Award, Writers Guild of America (1989); Best Radio News Spot Script Award, Writers Guild of America (1986); Grantee, William Benton Fellowship, The University of Chicago (1983-1984) **MEM:** Writers Guild of America; The Amateur Comedy Club, New York; The Lambs, New York; BPOE #1600, State College, PA **H:** Theater; Running **PA:** Republican **RE:** Episcopalian **ADD:** 50 Atlantic Ave, West Sayville, NY, 11796

CHAN, JONATHAN S., I: Medicine & Health Care **ED:** Doctorate, University of Alberta (2004) **AW:** Named One of Top 40 Under 40, Rising Young Business Star, Avenue Magazine (2015)

CHANG, CHIA-HWA "LYDIA" CHU, T: Artist **I:** Fine Art **PB:** Shanghai **SC:** China **SPN:** M.H. Chang **CH:** Victor; Mona **ED:** Bachelor's Degree in Economics, Utopia University **C:** Lecturer in Chinese Calligraphy, Hunter College; Lecturer in Painting, Continuing Education Program, Columbia University; Tutor in Chinese Calligraphy, Columbia University; Instructor in Chinese Language, United Nations International School; Instructor, Chinese Classical Literature, United Nations **CR:** Invited Lecturer, Asia Society; Invited Lecturer, Metropolitan Museum of Art; Invited Lecturer, Massachusetts Institute of Technology; Invited Lecturer, United Nations; Invited Lecturer, Long Island University; Invited Lecturer, Riverside Church **CW:** Featured Artist, Greeting Card, "Golden Fish," UNICEF International Art Committee, United States National Committee; Artist, "New Year's Offering," "Gold Fish," "Spring," UNICEF International Art Committee; Artist, "Hermitage in Autumn"; Exhibiting Artist, Annual Art Exhibitions of the United Nations; Exhibiting Artist, United States People for the United Nations Gallery; Exhibiting Artist, Community Art Gallery; Exhibiting Artist, Aspen Institute for Humanist Studies; Exhibiting Artist, Fairfield University; Exhibiting Artist, School of Chinese Brushwork; Exhibiting Artist, Wustum Museum of Fine Arts; Exhibiting Artist, Riverside Church Arts Gallery; Exhibiting Artist, RAA Art Gallery; Exhibiting Artist, Hunter Arts Gallery; Exhibiting Artist, Ziegfeld Gallery; Exhibiting Artist, Massachusetts Institute of Technology; Exhibiting Artist, Columbia University; Featured Artist, Cover of United Nations Secretariat News **ADD:** 549 W 123rd Street, Apt. 19F, New York, NY, 10027 **CHANG, MONA MEI-HSUAN, T:** Research Data Coordinator (Retired) **I:** Technology **CN:** Memorial Sloan-Kettering Cancer Center **PB:** New York City **SC:** NY/USA **PT:** Meng-Hsiu Chang; Lydia Chia-Hwa (Chu) Chang **ED:** MPhil in Medical Informatics, Columbia University (1999); MA in Medical Informatics, Columbia University (1997); BA in Computer Science and Biochemistry, Columbia University (1985) **C:** Research Data Coordinator, Memorial Sloan-Kettering Cancer Center, New York City, NY (2002-2006);

Trainee in Medical Informatics, National Library of Medicine, Columbia University, New York City, NY (1999-2001); Computer Programmer Analyst, New York Hospital, Cornell University Medical Center, New York City, NY (1992-1996); Data Manager, New York Hospital, Cornell University Medical Center, New York City, NY (1990-1992) **MEM:** Chairman, Computer Committee for Data Managers, Cancer and Leukemia Group B (1990-1992); Iota Sigma Pi **MH:** Albert Nelson Marquis Lifetime Achievement Award (2017) **H:** Chinese butterfly harp; Chinese watercolor painting **BA:** 549 W 123Rd St Apt 19F, New York, NY, 10027

CHANG, JONGWHA, T: Assistant Professor **I:** Education/Educational Services **CN:** The University of Texas **ED:** Doctoral Degree, College of Pharmacy, The University of Michigan (2009-2012) **BA:** 500 W University Blvd, El Paso, TX, 79902 **ADD:** 7472 Meadow Sage Dr, El Paso, TX, 79911

CHAPPELL, BARBARA KELLY, T: Child Welfare Consultant **I:** Consulting **DOB:** 10/17/1940 **PT:** Arthur Lee Kelly; Katherine (Martin) Kelly **CH:** Kelly Katherine **ED:** MSW, University of South Carolina (1974); BA in English, University of South Carolina (1962); BA in Education, University of South Carolina (1962) **C:** Accreditation Coordinator, South Carolina Department of Mental Health (1997-2004); Social Worker IV, South Carolina Department of Mental Health (1997-2004); Executive Director, New Pathways (1992-1997); Administrator, Department of Juvenile Services, State of Maryland (1989-1992); Child Welfare Consultant, Children's Foster Care Review Board, S.C. Department of Administration (1985-1989); Director, Children's Foster Care Review Board, S.C. Department of Administration (1975-1985); Officer of Child Advocacy, Children's Foster Care Review Board, S.C. Department of Administration (1975-1985); Child Welfare Consultant, Edna McConnell Clark Foundation (1974-1975); Supervisor, Juvenile Placement and Aftercare, South Carolina Department of Juvenile Justice (1970-1972); Caseworker, South Carolina Department of Social Services (1969-1970); Teacher of English, Alamo Heights High School (1965-1967); Teacher of English, Hawai'i State Department of Education (1962-1965) **CR:** Lecturer in Field **CIV:** Coordinator, Child's Rights to Parents, Columbia (1970-1975) **CW:** Contributor, Articles, Professional Journals **MH:** Albert Nelson Marquis Lifetime Achievement Award (2017) **RE:** Episcopalian **ADD:** 2215 Westchase Rd, Fort Collins, CO, 80528

CHASE, KENNETH HUNTINGTON, T: Associate **I:** Law and Legal Services **CN:** Davis, Polk & Wardwell LLP **DOB:** 07/17/1944 **PB:** New York City **SC:** NY/USA **PT:** Hollis H. Chase; Beverly Huntington (Seaman) Chase **MS:** Single **SPN:** Mary Bain (3/2/1990, Divorced 2010); Jeanne-Nicole Ledoux (2/14/1971, Divorced 1984) **ED:** LLB, University of Pennsylvania (1969); AB, University of Pennsylvania (1966) **C:** Associate, Davis, Polk & Wardwell LLP, New York City, NY (1980-2004); Secretary, Counsel, The Reserve Fund, Inc., New York City, NY (1977-1980); Assistant Secretary, Assistant Counsel, American General Capital Management, Inc., New York City, NY (1972-1977); Assistant Secretary, American General Funds, New York City, NY (1971-1977); Assistant Secretary, American Investors Fund, Inc., Greenwich, CT (1969-1970) **CR:** Association of the Bar of the City of New York (1971-Present); Art Committee (1973-1975) **CIV:** Benevolence Committee, West End Collegiate Church (2003-Present); West End Collegiate Church (2000-Present); Chair, Henry Hudson 400 Committee (2009-2010); Elder, West End Collegiate Church (2003-2007); Deacon,

West End Collegiate Church (2001-2003); Deacon, English Neighborhood Reformed Church, Ridgefield, NJ (1978-1980); Cemetery Treasurer, English Neighborhood Reformed Church, Ridgefield, NJ (1978-1980); Secretary, Conductor's Club (1975-1978); Vice President, Bar Harbor Festival (1970-1980); Trustee, Bar Harbor Festival (1970-1980) **MEM:** Trustee, New Amsterdam History Center, New York City, NY (2006-Present); Secretary, New Amsterdam History Center, New York City, NY (2004-Present); Board of Managers, Sons of the Revolution in the State of New York (1982-Present); Chair, Book Awards Committee, Sons of the Revolution in the State of New York (1979-Present); Sons of the Revolution in the State of New York (1970-Present); Secretary, Sons of the Revolution in the State of New York (2017); President, University of Pennsylvania Club of New York (1976-1978); Color Guard, Sons of the Revolution in the State of New York (1973-1982); The Saint Nicholas Society; The Society of the Cincinnati; Society of Colonial Wars; Phi Kappa Psi Fraternity; Ancient and Honorable Artillery Company of Massachusetts **BAR:** New York (1970) **MH:** Albert Nelson Marquis Lifetime Achievement Award (2017) **H:** American history **PA:** Democrat **RE:** Reformed Church in America **ADD:** 60 Riverside Dr Apt 9F, New York, NY, 10024

CHASE, NICHOLAS J., T: Attorney **I:** Law and Legal Services **CN:** Egerton, McAfee, Armistead & Davis, P.C. **ED:** JD, University of Tennessee College of Law, Cum Laude (2004); BA, University of Tennessee, Summa Cum Laude **C:** Attorney, Egerton, McAfee, Armistead, & Davis, P.C. (2005-Present); Law Clerk, Egerton, McAfee, Armistead, & Davis, P.C. (2003-2005) **CR:** Adjunct Professor, Mergers and Acquisitions, University of Tennessee College of Law (2010-Present) **CIV:** Former Chair, Helen Ross McNabb Center **CW:** Co-Author, "Recovery of Damages for Lost Profits: The Historical Development" (2016) **AW:** M&A Advisor of the Year Award for Transaction of the Year in the Information Technology Sector (2011); Transaction of the Year in the Professional Services Award, Business-to-Business Sector (2011); Mid-South Rising Star, Super Lawyers; AV Rating, Matindale-Hubbell **MEM:** Hamilton Burnett Inns of Court; Knoxville Estate Planning Council; ABA; Tennessee Bar Association; Knoxville Bar Association **BAR:** Tennessee; United States District Court Eastern District of Tennessee **BA:** 900 S Gay St Fl 14, Egerton, McAfee, Armistead & Davis, P.C., Knoxville, TN, 37902 **URL:** http://emlaw.com/attorneys/chase.php

CHATTERJEE, DEBABRATA, T: Surgeon (Retired) **I:** Medicine & Health Care **DOB:** 12/01/1937 **PB:** Chandernagore **SC:** India **PT:** Debendranath Chatterjee; Nandarani (nee Mukherjee) Chatterjee **MS:** Widow **SPN:** Jana Roy (11/15/2004, Deceased 8/7/2015); Adele Patricia Powell (9/17/1971, Deceased 3/30/1999) **CH:** Crispin Dara; Justin Sanjay **ED:** Honorary Doctorate, International Institute for Advanced Studies (2016); Coursework, Law, University of London (2002-2006); CM, University of Liverpool, England (1973); University Research Fellow, University of Liverpool, England (1965-1967); MB, University of Calcutta, India (1960); BS, University of Calcutta, India (1960); LRCP, MRCS, DRCOG, Royal College of Surgeons, England **C:** Retired (2002); Medical Practitioner, South Uist, Scotland (1982-2002); Consultant, General Surgeon, Daliburgh, Sacred Heart Hospital, South Uist, Scotland (1982-2002); Consultant, General Surgery, Spire Harpenden Hospital, Harpenden, England (1978-2002); Consultant, Surgeon, North West Thames Regional Health Authority, Royal London Hospital,

Plymouth General Hospital, Edinburgh, Scotland (1977-1981); Lecturer, Consultant, General Surgeon, University Hospital of the West Indies, Jamaica (1974-1977); Assistant General Surgeon, Northern Ireland (1971-1974); Senior Surgical Registrar, Tutor, Assistant General, Surgery, UCC, Ireland (1970-1971); Surgical Registrar, London, Liverpool, Leeds, England (1965-1970); House Surgeon, Medicine, Surgery, Gynaecology, Orthodontics, Urology, Nil Ratan Sircar Medical College & Hospital, Calcutta, Kent, England (1960-1964) **CR:** Teacher, Researcher, Service Administrator, London, Leeds, Liverpool, Cork, Jamaica, Edinburgh, Scotland (1965-Present); Examiner, The University of the West Indies (1974-1977); University Undergraduate and Postgraduate Teacher (1965-1981); Emeritus Professor, Surgery, Government of West Bengal, Calcutta; Distinguished Professor, The Bibliotheque: World Wide Society; Researcher in Field **CW:** Author, "Essays on Philosophy and Literature" (2016); Author, "Philosophical Basis of Mahayana Buddhism" (2010); Author, "Perpetual Peace of Kant" (2003); Author, Eight Books of Verse, Bharavi, Calcutta, India; Contributor, Articles, Professional Journals **AW:** Outstanding Scholar Award, International Institute for Advanced Studies (2002-Present); Glory of India Award, India International Friendship Society (2005); Distinguished Professor Award, The Bibliotheque: World Wide Society (2003); Best Teacher, The University of the West Indies (1976); Research and Publications Grantee, The University of the West Indies, Mona, Jamaica (1974-1976); Grantee, Medical Education and Research Council, Belfast, Ireland (1972-1973); Grantee, Medical Research Council of Ireland (1971); Grantee, Medical Research Committee, University of Liverpool (1966-1967) **MEM:** Charles Darwin Associate, The New York Academy of Sciences (1999); Fellow, The Royal College of Surgeons of Edinburgh; Fellow, Royal Society of Medicine; Senior Fellow, The International College of Surgeons; Fellow, Association of Surgeons of Great Britain and Ireland; American Association for the Advancement of Science; British Science Association; Founding Member, British Association of Surgical Oncology; Member, Society of American Gastrointestinal and Endoscopic Surgeons; Founding Member, British Society of Minimal Invasive Surgeons; British Medical Association; Hospital Consultants and Specialists Association; European Association for Endoscopic Surgery; Lifetime Member, Rationalist Press Association **MH:** Albert Nelson Marquis Lifetime Achievement Award (2017) **H:** History of Philosophy; Playing Indian Classical Musical Instruments **ADD:** 26 Aldwickbury Crescent, Harpenden, United Kingdom, AL5 5RR

CHATTERTON, ROBERT TREAT JR., T: Professor **I:** Education/Educational Services **CN:** Northwestern University **DOB:** 08/09/1935 **PB:** Catskill **SC:** NY/USA **PT:** Robert Treat Chatterton; Irene (Spoor) Chatterton **MS:** Married **SPN:** Carol J.; Astrida J. Vanags (6/4/1966, Divorced 1977); Patricia A. Holland (6/26/1956, Divorced 1965) **CH:** Ruth Ellen; William Matthew; James Daniel; Derek Scott **ED:** Postdoctoral Fellow, Medical School, Harvard University (1963-1965); PhD, Cornell University (1963); MS, University of Connecticut (1959); BS, Cornell University (1958) **C:** Professor, Feinberg School of Medicine, Northwestern University, Evanston, IL (1979-Present); Associate Professor, University of Illinois College of Medicine (1972-1979); Assistant Professor, University of Illinois College of Medicine (1970-1972); Research Associate, Oncology Division, Institute of Steroid Research, Montefiore Medical Center, Bronx, NY (1965-1970) **CR:** Member, National Scientific

Advisory Board, Susan Love MD Cancer Research Foundation (2003-Present); Reviewer, Integrative and Clinical Endocrinology and Reproduction Study Section, National Institutes of Health (2010); Grants Program, Swiss National Science Foundation (2009); Breast Cancer Research Program, U.S. Army Medical Research and Material Command, Department of Defense (2009); Scientific Review Committee, Health Services and Policy Research, Northwestern University (2009); Postdoctoral Fellowship Program, Komen Foundation Breast Cancer (2008); Breast Cancer Research Program, U.S. Army Medical Research and Material Command, Department of Defense (2008); President-elect, Sigma Xi, The Scientific Research Society (2007-2009); Prostate Cancer Research Program, U.S. Army Medical Research and Material Command, Department of Defense (2006-2012); Loan Reimbursement Program, National Institutes of Health (2006-2009); Breast Cancer Research Program, U.S. Army Medical Research and Material Command, Department of Defense (2006); NCI, RPHB-B Study Section, National Institutes of Health (2004-2005); Uniformed Services University of the Health Sciences, Exploratory Cancer Program, Department of Defense (2003); Prostate Cancer Research Program, U.S. Army Medical Research and Material Command, Department of Defense (2002-2004); Breast Cancer Research Program, U.S. Army Medical Research and Material Command, Department of Defense (2002-2004); Director, Immunoassay Facility, Robert H. Lurie Comprehensive Cancer Center, Northwestern University (2000-2002); Chairperson, Radiation Safety Committee, Northwestern University (2000-2002); Director, Shared Clinical Laboratories, Northwestern Medical Faculty Foundation Inc., Northwestern University (1999-2014); Director, Clinical Laboratories, Obstetrics-Gynecology Department, Northwestern University (1996-1999); March of Dimes (1995); Research Council, Northwestern University Medical School (1993-1995); Reviewer, National Institutes of Health (1992-1994); Chairman, Research Committee, Chicago Association of Reproductive Endocrinologists (1991-1993); Ad Hoc Review, National Science Foundation (1990-1992); Chairperson, Committee on Intellectual Property, Northwestern University (1987-1995); Chairperson, Intellectual Properties Committee, Northwestern University (1987-1995); President, Chicago Association of Reproductive Endocrinologists (1987-1988); President-elect, Chicago Association of Reproductive Endocrinologists (1986-1987); Secretary, Chicago Association of Reproductive Endocrinologists (1985-1986); Chairperson, Prentice Hospital Research Committee, Northwestern University (1982-1992); Chairperson, Institutional Review Board, Northwestern University (1982-1983); Animal Care and Use Committee, Northwestern University (1980-1985); Chairperson, Animal Care and Use Committee, Northwestern University (1980-1983); Scientific Advisory Committee, Program for Applied Research on Fertility Regulation, Agency for International Development (1976-1982); Reviewer, Scientific Journals **CIV:** Deacon, Presbyterian Church (1977-Present); Mamaroneck-Larchmont Jaycees (1966-1969); External Vice President, Mamaroneck-Larchmont Jaycees **CW:** Author, Co-author, 214 Peer-reviewed Scientific Articles; Author, Co-author, 38 Review Articles; Presenter, 212 Scientific Papers, National Scientific Meetings **AW:** Grantee, National Institutes of Health (1995-2010); Grantee, National Science Foundation (1995-1998); Grantee, United States Army Research Laboratory (1987-1994); Grantee, National Science Foundation (1975); Grantee, National Institutes

of Health (1972-1990); Grantee, United States Agency for International Development (1971-1986) **MEM:** President, Chicago Association of Reproductive Endocrinologists (1987-1988); American Association for the Advancement of Science; American Association of Clinical Research; American Association for Cancer Research; Society for the Study of Reproduction; Society for Gynecologic Investigation; Endocrine Society; American Chemical Society; The New York Academy of Sciences; The Honor Society of Phi Kappa Phi; Sigma Xi **MH:** Albert Nelson Marquis Lifetime Achievement Award (2017) **H:** Art; Oil painting **RE:** Presbyterian **BA:** 710 N Fairbanks Court, Chicago, IL, 60611 **ADD:** 6001 N Knox Ave, Chicago, IL, 60646 **URL:** https://www.scholars.northwestern.edu/en/persons/robert-treat-chatterton-jr

CHAUDHARI, SHISHIR, T: Chief Executive Officer **I:** Business Management/Business Services **CN:** iBusiness Solution LLC **PT:** Brij Bhushan Kishore; Sumitra Chaudhari **MS:** Married **SPN:** Geetika Chaudhari **CH:** Samriddh; Ameya Vikram **ED:** MBA in Marketing, Institute of Business Management, Chhatrapati Shahu Ji Maharaj University, Kanpur (1993); Diploma in Computer Management, DATAPRO (1993); BS, Chhatrapati Shahu Ji Maharaj University, Kanpur (1990) **C:** Chief Executive Officer, xPert Solutions, Inc. (2015-Present); President, NMS IT Services Inc. (2014-Present); Chief Executive Officer, iBusiness Solution LLC (2006-Present); Director, Consulting Practice, WOW Global Corporation LLC & Group Companies (2003-2006); Account Manager, Infotech Consulting (Now Mindteck) (2000-2003); Business Analyst, Fortune 500 Systems Inc., Harrisburg, PA (2000); Manager, CEAT Financial Services Ltd. (1997-2000); Branch Manager, Prudential Capital Markets Ltd., India (1996-1997); Market Analyst, Sterling Securities Ltd. (Now Ruia Group), Delhi, India (1993-1995); Management Trainee, JK White Cement Works, India (1993) **CIV:** Volunteer, Cumberland Valley Midget Football Association **AW:** Honoree, Pride of India, Mana TV (2016); Great Achiever of India, Front for National Progress (1999) **H:** Youth football; Cricket **ADD:** 5000 Lenker Street, Suite 200, iBusiness Solution LLC, Mechanicsburg, PA, 17050 **URL:** http://www.ibusinesssolution.com

CHAUDHRY, HUMAYUN JAVAID, T: President, Chief Executive Officer **I:** Medicine & Health Care **CN:** Federation of State Medical Boards **DOB:** 11/17/1965 **PB:** Karachi **SC:** Pakistan **PT:** Hukam Chaudhry; Riffat Sultana (Bhatti) Chaudhry **MS:** Married **SPN:** Nazli Tabasum Iqbal (6/7/1992) **CH:** Shaun Hatim; Haris Iqbal **ED:** SM, Harvard School of Public Health (2001); Resident, Internal Medicine, Winthrop University Hospital, Mineola, NY (1992-1995); Intern, St. Barnabas Hospital, Bronx, NY (1991-1992); DO, New York College of Osteopathic Medicine (1991); MS, New York University (1989); BA, New York University (1986) **CT:** Diplomate, American Osteopathic Board of Internal Medicine (2006-2016); Diplomate, American Board of Internal Medicine (1996-2006); Licensed Physician and Surgeon, State of New York; Diplomate, National Board, Osteopathic Medical Examiners **C:** President, Chief Executive Officer, Federal State Medical Boards (2009-Present); Commissioner, Suffolk County Department Health Services, New York (2007-2009); Assistant Dean, Health Policy, New York College of Osteopathic Medicine, Old Westbury, NY (2005-2007); Clinical Associate, Professor of Medicine, New York College of Osteopathic Medicine, Old Westbury, NY (2003-2013); Assistant Dean for Pre-Clinical Education, New York College of Osteopathic Medicine, Old

Westbury, NY (2003-2005); Medical Director, New York College Osteopathic Medicine, Old Westbury, NY (2003-2005); Staff Member, Winthrop University Hospital, New York (2001-2007); Attending Physician, Academy Health Care Center, New York College Osteopathic Medicine (2001-2007); Chairman, Department of Medicine, New York College of Osteopathic Medicine, Old Westbury, NY (2001-2007); Assistant Professor of Medicine, New York College of Osteopathic Medicine, Old Westbury, NY (1997-2003); Attending Physician, Director, Medical Education, Long Beach Medical Center, New York (1996-2001); Attending Physician, Family Care Center, Long Beach, NY (1996-1999); Attending Physician, Island Park New York Medical Care (1996-1998); Chief Medical Resident, Winthrop University Hospital, Mineola, NY (1995-1996) **CR:** Reporter, News Editor, TV Anchorman, Third World Broadcasting Network, New York City, NY (1986-1995) **CIV:** Board Member, Multifaith Forum of Long Island (2000-2007) **MIL:** Major, U.S. Air Force Reserve (2002-2013); Captain, U.S. Air Force Reserve (1999-2002) **CW:** Medical Licensing and Discipline in America (2012); Author, "Fundamentals of Clinical Medicine" (2004); Member, Editorial Board, New Physician (1991-1999); Contributor, Article to Professional Journals **AW:** Fellow, Royal College of Physicians of Edinburgh (2017); Laureate Award, American College of Physicians (2005); Regents College Scholar, State of New York, Albany, NY (1982); Recipient, Essay Competition Award, New York City Fire Department (1979) **MEM:** President, American College of Osteopathic Internists (2008-2009); President, Association of Osteopathic Directors and Medical Educators (2007-2009); Secretary-Treasurer, American College of Osteopathic Internists (2006-2007); Fellow Master, Nassau West District President, American College of Physicians (2000-2007); Board of Directors, American College of Osteopathic Internists (1999-2006); Treasurer, Association of Osteopathic Directors and Medical Educators (2003-2004); Board of Directors, Association of Osteopathic Directors and Medical Educators (2001-2003); Board of Directors, New York College of Osteopathic Medicine Alumni Association (2000-2002); President, Nassau Society of Internal Medicine (1999-2000); President, New York College of Osteopathic Medicine Alumni Association (1998-2000); Board of Directors, New York State Society of Internal Medicine (1996-2000); Vice President, Nassau Society of Internal Medicine (1998-1999); Board of Directors, Nassau Society of Internal Medicine (1996-1998); Secretary, Board of Directors, New York College of Osteopathic Medicine Alumni Association (1995-1998); President, Resident Physicians Section, New York State Society of Internal Medicine (1995-1996); Amnesty International; American College of Osteopathic Internists; American Medical Association; Association of Military Surgeons; Southern Poverty Law Center; New York State Osteopathic Medical Society; Harvard Alumni Association; Harvard Club, New York; The University Club of Washington DC **H:** Reading; Cinema; Travel **RE:** Muslim **BA:** 400 Fuller Wiser Rd Ste 300, Federation State Medical Boards, Euless, TX, 76039

CHAVEZ, TERESA, T: Bank Operations Officer (Retired) **I:** Financial Services **DOB:** 01/10/1935 **PB:** Los Angeles **SC:** CA/USA **PT:** Flavio F. Chavez; Marie S. Chavez **ED:** BA in Liberal Studies, California State University, Los Angeles (1982); AA, East Los Angeles College (1975) **C:** Operations Officer, MUFG Union Bank, N.A. (1979-1994); Trainer Courses, MUFG Union Bank, N.A. (1960-1994); Various Banking Positions, MUFG Union Bank, N.A. (1960-1994) **MEM:** Historian, Glassell

Park Improvement Association; Former President, Associated Alumnae and Alumni of the Sacred Heart; Northeast Los Angeles Democratic Club; Secretary, Toastmasters International **MH:** Albert Nelson Marquis Lifetime Achievement Award (2017) **ADD:** 3921 Filion St, Los Angeles, CA, 90065

CHAVIS, GLENN, T: Historian **I:** Pharmaceuticals **DOB:** 12/03/1940 **PB:** High Point **SC:** NC/USA **PT:** Roy Lloyd Chavis; Ruth Elmira Chavis **MS:** Married **SPN:** Gladys Faye McBee (10/10/1958) **CH:** Rory Keith; Trey Emilliano **ED:** BA in English, Johnson C. Smith University, Charlotte, NC (1963) **C:** District System Specialist, Abbott Laboratories (1995-2000); Account Executive, Abbott Laboratories (1991-1995); Vision Specialist, Abbott Laboratories (1988-1990); National Recruiting Consultant, Abbott Laboratories (1974-1988); Minority Recruiter and Professional Pharmaceutical Representative, Abbott Laboratories (1973-1974); Professional Pharmaceutical Representative, Abbott Laboratories (1971-1973); Professional Hospital Representative, Abbott Laboratories, North Chicago, IL (1969-1970) **CR:** Diversity Task Force, Abbott Diagnostics, Abbott Laboratories (1998-2000); Antibiotic Consultant Panel, Abbott Diagnostics, Abbott Laboratories (1971-1973); Cardiovascular Consultant Panel, Abbott Diagnostics, Abbott Laboratories (1970-1972) **CIV:** Member, High Point Sesquicentennial Commission (2007); Trustee, United Way Greater High Point (2003-2007); Member, Chairman, City High Point Citizens Advisory Committee (2002-2006); Trustee, High Point Museum (2003-2005); Member, Southside Revitalization Steering Committee, High Point (2004); Member, High Point 311 Bypass Gateway Committee (2003); Member, Kivett Dr. Gateway Committee, High Point, NC (2003); Member, High Point Racial Healing (2002); Researcher, Column Writer, News-Record, Greensboro, NC (2002); Member, Undo Racism Task Force, High Point (2001); Trustee, High Point Regional Hospital (1986-1994) **CW:** Researcher, African American Exhibit, High Point Museum & Historical Park (2006); Contributing Researcher and Writer "African American Heritage Guide" (2005) **AW:** Walsh Award (2006); Chairman's Award, High Point Visitor's Bureau (2005) **MH:** Albert Nelson Marquis Lifetime Achievement Award (2017) **PA:** Conservative **RE:** Methodist **ADD:** 137 Orville Dr, High Point, NC, 27260

CHEN, GONGYIN, T: Lead Research Scientist **I:** Sciences **CN:** Varex Imaging Corporation **MS:** Married **SPN:** Ming Wei **CH:** Jiming; Andy **ED:** PhD in Nuclear Engineering, Massachusetts Institute of Technology (2001); MS in Nuclear Engineering, Massachusetts Institute of Technology (1999); BE in Engineering Physics, Tsinghua University (1991) **C:** Lead Research Scientist, Security & Inspection Products, Varex Imaging Corporation (2007-Present); Principal Engineer, Security & Detection Systems, L3 Technologies, Inc. (2002-2006); Teaching Assistant, Massachusetts Institute of Technology (1997-2001); Research Assistant, Massachusetts Institute of Technology (1997-2001); Lecturer, Engineering Physics, Tsinghua University (1991-1997); Assistant Professor, Engineering Physics, Tsinghua University (1991-1997) **H:** Sailing; Hiking **BA:** 6811 Spencer St, Varex Imaging Corporation, Las Vegas, NV, 89119 **URL:** http://www.vareximaging.com/

CHERNOW, BART, T: Retired **I:** Medicine & Health Care **DOB:** 06/26/1947 **PB:** New York **SC:** NY/USA **ED:** MD, State University of New York (1976); BA, Queens College (1968) **C:** Vice Provost of Technological Advancement, University of Miami (2007-2010); Vice President of Special Programs

and Resource Strategy, Miller School of Medicine, University of Miami (2007-2010); Professor of Medicine, University of Miami, Miami, FL; Chief Technology Officer, GMP Companies, Inc., Fort Lauderdale, FL (2004-2006); President, Chief Executive Officer, GMP Companies, Inc., Fort Lauderdale, Florida (1999-2004); Vice Dean for Research and Technology, School of Medicine, Johns Hopkins University School of Medicine (1997-1999); Program Director, John Hopkins University/Sinai Hospital Program in Internal Medicine (1990-1997); Physician-in-Chief, Sinai Hospital (1990-1997); Professor of Medicine, Anesthesia and Critical Care, Johns Hopkins University School of Medicine, Baltimore, MD (1990-1999); Associate Director, Surgical ICU, Massachusetts General Hospital (1986-1990); Associate Professor of Anesthesia, Harvard Medical School, Boston (1986-1990); Head of Academy Affairs, Bethesda Naval Hospital (1985-1986); Director, Research Department, Critical Care Medicine, Bethesda Naval Hospital (1981-1985); Endocrine Fellow, National Naval Medical Center (1979-1981); Internal Medicine Resident, National Naval Medical Center (1977-1979); Internal Medicine Intern, National Naval Medical Center, Bethesda, MD (1976-1977) **CR:** Adjunct Professor of Medicine, Johns Hopkins University School of Medicine (1999-2009) **CIV:** Commander, Medical Corps, U.S. Naval Reserve (1969-1986) **CW:** Editor-in-Chief, "Critical Care Medicine" (1990-1997); Editor, "Pharmacologic Approach to the Critically Ill Patient" (1983, 1988, 1994) **AW:** Recipient, Alumni Achievement Award, SUNY Downstate College of Medicine (2016); Recipient, Presidential Citation, Society of Critical Care Medicine (1997); Recipient, Achievement Award, American College of Nutrition (1995) **MEM:** Master Fellow, Chair and Founder, CHEST Foundation (1996-2002); Regent, American College of Chest Physicians (1990-1998); President, American College of Chest Physicians (1996-1997); Fellow, American College of Physicians; American College of Critical Care Medicine; Society of Critical Care Medicine **MH:** Albert Nelson Marquis Lifetime Achievement Award (2017) **ADD:** 4240 Galt Ocean Dr, Apt 2404, Fort Lauderdale, FL, 33308

CHIACCHIERINI, RICHARD PHILIP, T: Health Service Executive **I:** Consulting **CN:** R. P. Consulting, LLC **DOB:** 03/21/1943 **PB:** Elmira **SC:** NY/USA **PT:** Frank Andrew Chiacchierini; Grace Rose (Spallone) Chiacchierini **MS:** Married **SPN:** Kathleen O. (O'Grady) Chiacchierini (8/14/1965) **CH:** Paul Thomas; Lisa Marie **ED:** PhD in Statistics, Virginia Polytechnic Institute and State University (1973); MS in Experimental Statistics, North Carolina State University (1967); BS in Mathematics, St. Bonaventure University (1965); Diploma, Watkins Glen Central School District, New York (1961) **C:** President, R. P. Consulting, LLC, Gaithersburg, MD (2016-Present); President, R.P. Chiacchierini & Associates, LLC, Rockville, MD (2002-2016); Senior Vice President for Statistical Services, C. L. McIntosh and Associates, Inc., Rockville, MD (1999-2002); Vice President for Statistical Services, C. L. McIntosh and Associates, Inc., Rockville, MD (1994-1999); Director, Division of Biometric Sciences, Office of Surveillance and Biometrics, Center for Devices and Radiological Health, Food and Drug Administration, Rockville, MD (1993-1994); Chief Scientist Officer, U.S. Public Health Service Commissioned Corps (1987-1991); Director, Division of Biometric Sciences, Office of Science and Technology, Center for Devices and Radiological Health, Food and Drug Administration, Rockville, MD (1985-1993); Chief, Statistics Branch, Division of Life Sciences, Office of Science and Technology, Center for Devices and Radiological Health, Food and Drug Administration (1984-1985); Chief, Ionizing Radiation and Statistics Branch, Division of Risk Assessment, Center for Devices and Radiological Health, Food and Drug Administration, Rockville, MD (1982-1984); Chief, Statistics Section, Epidemiologic Studies Branch, Division of Biological Effects, Bureau of Radiological Health, Food and Drug Administration, Rockville, MD (1979-1982); Senior Statistician, Epidemiologic Studies Branch, Division of Biological Effects, Bureau of Radiological Health, Food and Drug Administration, Rockville, MD (1973-1979); Chief, Statistics Section, Office of Radiation Programs, Environmental Protection Agency, Washington, D.C. (1972-1973); Outside-the-Service Trainee, Virginia Polytechnic Institute and State University, Blacksburg, VA (1970-1972); Junior Statistician, Radiation Bioeffects Program, National Center for Radiological Health, Rockville, MD (1967-1970) **CR:** Chairman, Board of Directors, Commissioned Officers Association of the USPHS Inc. (1991-Present); Chairman, Device Clinical Trials Workshop, Food and Drug Administration (1993); Chairman, Tenth Conference on Radiation and Health, American Statistical Association (1992); Chairman, Force Management Work Group, U.S. Public Health Service Commissioned Corps (1990-1994); Co-Chairman, Ninth Conference on Radiation and Health, American Statistical Association (1990); Chairman, Epidemiology Training Steering Committee, U.S. Public Health Service (1989-1992); Chairman, Centennial Science Symposium, U.S. Public Health Service Commissioned Corps (1989); Board of Directors, Commissioned Officers Association of the USPHS Inc. (1988-1994); Scientist Professional Advisory Committee, U.S. Public Health Service (1987-1991); Commissioner's Task Force on Recruitment and Retention of Biostatisticians, Food and Drug Administration (1987); Surgeon General's Committee on Career Development, U.S. Public Health Service (1987); Adjunct Faculty of Statistics, Virginia Polytechnic Institute and State University (1981-1990); Epidemiology Training Steering Committee, U.S. Public Health Service (1979-1994); Chairman, Board of Directors, Bennington Community Association (1978); Interagency Epidemiology Working Group, U.S. Public Health Service (1976-1980); Invited Speaker, Various Presentations **MIL:** Commissioned Officer, U.S. Public Health Service (1967-1994) **CW:** Contributor, Articles, Academic Emergency Medicine (2017); Contributor, Articles, Lasers in Surgery and Medicine (2014); Associate Editor, Cephalagia (2013-2018); Contributor, Articles, Spine (2012); Contributor, Articles, American Heart Journal (2011); Contributor, Articles, Journal of Cardiac Failure (2011); Contributor, Articles, The New England Journal of Medicine (2010); Contributor, Articles, Journal of Clinical Sleep Medicine (2010); Contributor, Articles, Transfusion (2005); Contributor, Articles, Urology (1999); Contributor, Articles, Medical Devices and Diagnostics Industry (1996); Editorial Board, Clinical Trials Advisor (1995-1999); Editorial Board, Statistics in Medicine (1991-1996); Contributor, Articles, Quality Control (1991); Radiation Research (1990); Contributor, Articles, Proceedings of the ASA Conference on Radiation and Health (1989); Contributor, Articles, Proceedings of the Biopharmaceutical Section of the American Statistical Association (1987); Contributor, Articles, Proceedings of the Social Statistics Section of the American Statistical Association (1986); Contributor, Articles, Journal of Occupational Medicine (1985); Contributor, Articles, Proceedings of the Biopharmaceutical Section of the American Statistical Association (1985); Contributor, Articles, Proceedings of the Seventh International Congress of Radiation Research (1983); Radiation Research (1982); Contributor, Articles, Symposium on Biological Effects, Imaging

Techniques, and Dosimetry of Ionizing Radiations (1981); Contributor, Articles, Detection of Cancer: Part II (1980); Contributor, Articles, Application of the Dose Limitation System for Radiation Protection (1979); Contributor, Articles, Reduced Dose Mammography (1979); Radiation Research (1979); Contributing Author, "Breast Carcinoma: The Radiologists Expanded Role" (1977); Contributor, Articles, Journal of the American Statistical Association (1977); Contributing Author, Radiation Biology of the Fetal and Juvenile Mammal (1969) **AW:** Meritorious Service Medal, U.S. Public Health Service (1994); Outstanding Unit Citation, U.S. Public Health Service (1994); Unit Commendation, U.S. Public Health Service (1992); Exemplary Service Medal, Office of the Surgeon General (1990); Outstanding Service Award, Center for Devices and Radiological Health (1990); Unit Commendation, U.S. Public Health Service (1987-1990); Outstanding Service Medal, U.S. Public Health Service (1987); Citation, U.S. Public Health Service (1987); Citation, U.S. Public Health Service (1985); Service Commendation Medal, U.S. Public Health Service (1977); Group Commendation, Food and Drug Administration (1977); Honoree, Superior Scholastic Achievement, The Honor Society of Phi Kappa Phi, Virginia Polytechnic Institute and State University (1972); National Science Foundation Fellow, NC State University (1965-1967); Medal for Highest Grade Point Average in Mathematics, St. Bonaventure University (1965) **MEM:** Chairman, FDA Device Clinical Trials Workshop (1993); Chairman, American Statistical Association Tenth Conference on Radiation and Health (1992); Chairman, Commissioned Officers Association (1991); Chairman, PHS Commissioned Corps Force Management Work Group (1990-1994); Co-Chairman, American Statistical Association Ninth Conference on Radiation and Health (1990); Chairman, Public Health Service Epidemiology Training Steering Committee (1989-1992); Chairman, Commissioned Corps Centennial Science Symposium (1989); Board of Directors, Commissioned Officers Association (1988-1994); Public Health Service Scientist Professional Advisory Committee (1987-1991); Commissioner's Task Force on Recruitment and Retention of Bio-statisticians (1987); Surgeon General's Committee on Career Development (1987); Public Health Service Epidemiology Training Steering Committee (1979-1994); Interagency Epidemiology Working Group (1976-1980); American Statistical Association; The Honor Society of Phi Kappa Phi; Commissioned Officers Association of the USPHS Inc.; Military Officers Association of America **MH:** Albert Nelson Marquis Lifetime Achievement Award (2017) **H:** Golf; Boating; Travel **RE:** Roman Catholic **ADD:** 17003 Horn Point Drive, Gaithersburg, MD, 20878 **URL:** http://www.rpcaconsulting.com

CHOI, JIN OUK, T: Assistant Professor **I:** Education/Educational Services **CN:** University of Nevada, Las Vegas **ED:** PhD, The University of Texas at Austin, Texas (2014); MS, The University of Texas at Austin (2011); BS, Korea University, Seoul, Korea (2010) **C:** Assistant Professor, University of Nevada, Las Vegas, NV (2016-Present); Postdoctoral Fellow, City University of Hong Kong, Hong Kong (2015-2016); Postdoctoral Research Associate, Iowa State University, Ames, IA (2014-2015); Postdoctoral Fellow, The University of Texas at Austin (2014); Graduate Research Assistant/Teaching Assistant, The University of Texas at Austin (2011-2014) **AW:** Recipient, ExCEEd Fellowship, American Society of Civil Engineers (2018); Named, Outstanding Reviewer, Journal of Management in Engineering, American Society of Civil Engineers (2017); Named, Outstanding Reviewer, Journal of Construction Engineering and Management, American Society of Civil

Engineers (2017); Named, Outstanding Reviewer, Journal of Management in Engineering, American Society of Civil Engineers (2016); Named, Outstanding Reviewer, Journal of Construction Engineering and Management, American Society of Civil Engineers (2016); Recipient, International Scholarship, AACE International (2015); Recipient, International Scholarship, American Association of Cost Engineers International (2013); Recipient, Centre for Excellence in Project Management Scholarship, Richard & Shirley Tucker Endowed Excellence Fund in Construction Engineering and Project Management (2011); Recipient, National Science and Engineering Scholarship, Korea Student Aid Foundation (2004-2010) **MEM:** Academic Advisor, Construction Industry Institute Modularization Comunity for Business Advancement (2012-Present); American Society of Civil Engineers; Korean-American Construction Engineering and Project Management Association **BA:** 4505 S Maryland Pkwy, University Of Nevada, TBE-B 370, Las Vegas, NV, 89154

CHOI, SUNGHWAN, I: Medicine & Health Care **PB:** 1964 **ED:** Doctorate Degree, Kyungpook National University (2007); Master's Degree, Kyunghee University (1994); Bachelor's Degree, Kyunghee University (1989) **C:** Psychiatrist **CR:** Author; Columnist **MIL:** Captain, US Army (1997) **CW:** Author, "Cross-Cultural Study Between East and West"; Author, "Psychology of Contradiction" **AW:** Recipient, Award for Crime Prevention and Social Contribution, Ministry of Justice, Republic of Korea (2008) **MEM:** Korean Neuro-Psychiatric Association

CHOUDHURY, RAJIN, T: Cardiac Electrophysiologist, Cardiologist **I:** Medicine & Health Care **CN:** Heart Rhythm Service **ED:** Postgraduate Degree in Cardiac Electrophysiology and Pacing, Heart Rhythm Management Centre, Cardiovascular Department, Universitair Ziekenhuis, Vrije Universiteit Brussel (2016-2017); EHRA Clinical Fellowship in Invasive Cardiac Electrophysiology, Department of Cardiac Electrophysiology, AZ Sint-Jan Hospital Brugge-Oostende AV, Belgium (2014-2015); Resident Medical Officer, ILS Hospitals (2010-2011); Fellow in Cardiology, IMSP Institutul de Cardiologie (2007-2009); Resident in Internal Medicine, Universitatea de Stat de Medicina si Farmacie Nicolae Testemitanu (2004-2007); Intern, Universitatea de Medicina si Farmacie Grigore T. Popa (2002-2003); Bachelor's in Medicine and Surgery, Universitatea de Medicina si Farmacie Grigore T.Popa (1996-2002); Cardiac Electrophysiology and Pacing Fellow, Queen Elizabeth II Halifax Infirmary, Heart Rhythm Service, Division of Cardiology, Department of Medicine, Dalhousie University, Halifax, Canada **CR:** Hosted, Eastern India Interventional Cardiology Conclave, Calcutta, India (2011); Speaker in Field **CW:** Contributor, Articles, Professional Journals **AW:** Fellowship Grant for Postgraduate Training in Cardiac Electrophysiology and Pacing, Brussels University, Medtronic Europe (2016); Award of Recognition for Outstanding Service to Patients and Cardiology, Al Qassimi Hospital, Ministry of Health, United Arab Emirates (2015); Asia Pacific Heart Rhythm Society Fellowship Award Grant, European Heart Rhythm Association (2014); Certificate, European Heart Rhythm Association Induction & Award Ceremony, Asia Pacific Hear Rhythm Society (2014) **MEM:** European Heart Rhythm Association Young Electrophysiologists Community (2015); Asia Pacific Heart Rhythm Society (2015); Emirates Medical Association, Emirates Cardiac Society (2012-2015); European Heart Rhythm Association (2011-2015); Elected

Fellow, Gulf Heart Association (2014); Physician, Heart Rhythm Society (2013); Moldavian Society of Cardiologists (2009-2015); Middle East Critical Care Assembly (2011); Lifetime Member, Indian Medical Association (2011); Associate Lifetime Member, Indian Society of Critical Care Medicine (2011); European Society of Cardiology **H:** Travel **ADD:** 808-5885 Cunard Street, Halifax, NS, Canada, B3K 1E3

CHOUKAS-BRADLEY, JAMES R., T: Lawyer **I:** Law and Legal Services **CN:** McCarter & English, LLP **DOB:** 09/11/1950 **PB:** Hartford **SC:** CT/USA **PT:** William Lee Bradley; Paula Ann (Elliott) Bradley **MS:** Married **SPN:** Melanie Rose Choukas (6/21/1975) **CH:** Sophia Crane; Jesse Elliott **ED:** JD, Georgetown University, Cum Laude (1980); BA, University of Vermont, Cum Laude (1974) **C:** Partner, McCarter & English, LLP (2014-Present); Director, Miller, Balis & O'Neil PC, Washington, D.C. (2014-Present); Executive Committee and Management Principal, Miller, Balis & O'Neil PC, Washington, D.C. (1993-1997); Member, Vice President, Miller, Balis & O'Neil PC, Washington, D.C. (1985-2014); Associate, Miller, Balis & O'Neil PC, Washington, D.C. (1980-1984); Research Associate, Schlossberg-Cassidy & Associates, Washington, D.C. (1978-1980); Contributing Reporter, The Lewiston Sun (1976); Assistant to City Manager, Berlin, New Hampshire (1975-1977); Editor, Publisher, Creative Director, Ad Lib, Gorham, NH (1974-1975); Reporter, The Berlin Reporter (1973-1974); Editor, The Berlin Reporter (1973-1974); Reporter, The Groveton News (1973-1974); Editor, The Groveton News (1973-1974); Reporter, The Northland News (1973-1974); Editor, The Northland News (1973-1974) **CR:** President, Sugarloaf Citizens' Association, Dickerson, MD (2012-2014); Legal Advisor, First Vice President, Sugarloaf Citizens' Association, Dickerson, MD (1987-2000); Pioneer in Joint Action and Public Financing; Speaker in Field; Of Counsel, Colorado Springs Utilities; Of Counsel, Louisiana Municipal Gas Authority; Of Counsel, Clarke-Mobile Counties Gas District; Of Counsel, Black Belt Energy Gas District; Of Counsel, Public Authority of Colorado Energy; Of Counsel, Central Plains Energy Project; Of Counsel, Municipal Gas Authority of Mississippi; Of Counsel, Tennessee Customer Group; Of Counsel, Alabama Municipal Distributors Group; Of Counsel, Southeast Alabama Gas District; Counsel, Public Gas Partners; Of Counsel, Municipal Gas Authority of Georgia; Of General Counsel, Lower Alabama Gas District; Of General Counsel, Tennessee Energy Acquisition Corporation **CIV:** Chairman, Sugarloaf Mountain Records Inc. (2008-Present); President, Sugarloaf Mountain Records Inc. (2008-Present); Director, Piedmont Environmental Foundation (2004-Present); President, Sugarloaf Citizens Association (2014-2016); Youth Soccer Coach, Montgomery Soccer Inc. (2005-2006); Youth Soccer and Flag Football Coach, Seneca Sports Association (1999-2005); President, Montgomery Dukes (1987-1992); President, D.C. Dukes Athletic Club, Washington, DC (1978-1981); Committee Chairman, Berlin Bicentennial Commission, Berlin, NH (1975-1976); Board Member, Friend of Ten Mile Creek and Sugarloaf Citizens Association **CW:** Band Founder and Songwriter, Rhododendron Road (2005-Present); Performer, "Rising Tide" (2010); Co-author, "Report on Dynamics of Natural Gas Markets and Projected Gas Prices for 2005 and Beyond" (2005); Author, "The Early Days" (1975); Vocalist; Musician; Songwriter **AW:** Inductee, The Phi Beta Kappa Society (1974); Regents Scholar, State of New York (1968) **MEM:** Friends of Rock Creek; Montgomery Countryside Alliance; Americana

Music Association; MS Natural Gas Association; Alabama Natural Gas Association; Tennessee Gas Association; National Association of Bond Lawyers; Washington Area Music Association; Energy Bar Association; Audubon Naturalist Society; The University Club of Washington DC; American Farmland Trust; Randolph Mountain Club; Phi Beta Kappa **BAR:** United States Court of Appeals for the Sixth Circuit (1993); United States Court of Appeals for the Fourth Circuit (1990); United States Court of Appeals for the Tenth Circuit (1985); United States Court of Appeals for the Eleventh Circuit (1984); United States Court of Appeals for the District of Columbia Circuit (1981); The District of Columbia Bar (1980) **MH:** Albert Nelson Marquis Lifetime Achievement Award (2017) **H:** Hiking; Music recording; United States history; Guitar; Piano **PA:** Independent **RE:** Christian **BA:** 1015 15th St NW 12th Fl, McCarter & English LLP, Washington, DC, 20005

CHOWDHURY, MOHAMMED ANDALEEB, T: Cardiology **I:** Medicine & Health Care **CN:** Vanderbilt University Medical Center **SC:** Bangladesh **ED:** Advanced Heart Failure and Transplantation Fellow, Vanderbilt University Medical Center, Nashville, TN (2017-2018); MD, University of Toledo Medical Center (2017); Cardiovascular Medicine Fellow, University of Toledo Medical Center, Toledo, OH (2015-2017); Internal Medicine Resident, University of Toledo Medical Center, Toledo, OH (2012-2015); Internal Medicine/Cardiology Resident, Al Qassimi Hospital, Sharjah, United Arab Emirates (2010-2012); Cardiology Resident, Gulf Medical College Hospital and Research Center, Ajman, United Arab Emirates (2008-2009); Cardiology Resident, National Heart Institute, Cairo, Egypt (2007-2008); MS, Gulf Medical University (2007); MBBS, Gulf Medical University (2005) **CT:** Specialist in Clinical Hypertension, American Society of Hypertension (2016); Certified, American Board of Internal Medicine (2015); Testamur Status in Examination of Special Competence in Adult Echocardiography, National Board of Echocardiography (2014) **C:** Externship, Consultative Gastroenterology, Emory Hospital, Atlanta, GA (2011); Cardiology Senior House Officer, James Cook University Hospital, Middlesbrough, United Kingdom (2009-2010); Research Associate to Professor, Alaa Ismail Professor of Surgery, Ain Shams University, Cairo, Egypt (2007-2008); Dean, National Hepatology and Tropical Medicine Research Institute (2007-2008); Medical Officer, Ain Shams Medical University Hospital, Cairo, Egypt (2006-2007) **CW:** Contributor, ResearchGate; Contributor, Articles, Professional Journals **AW:** Winner, Thomas Walsh Research Symposium (2017); Winner, Thomas Walsh Research Symposium (2016); Top 25 investigators, American Society of Echocardiography (2016) **MEM:** Royal College of Physicians of the United Kingdom (2011); American Society of Hypertension; American College of Cardiology; American Society of Echocardiography; Heart Failure Society of America **BA:** 1211 Medical Center Dr, Nashville, TN, 37232 **ADD:** Apt 1106, 905 20th Avenue South, Nashville, TN, 37203

CHRISTENSEN, DORIS ANN, T: Antique Dealer, Researcher, Writer **I:** Research **CN:** All That & Everything **DOB:** 12/31/1938 **PB:** Safford **SC:** AZ/USA **PT:** Joseph Solomon Welson; Bernice Beatrice (Blasius) Van Order **MS:** Widowed **SPN:** Donald Edward Christensen (4/22/1967, Deceased) **ED:** Coursework, Eastern Arizona College (1961-1966) **C:** Antique Dealer, All That & Everything, Graham, WA (1995-Present); Office Manager, Heller Co.

Realtors, Federal Way, WA (1990-1994); Secretary to President, United Homes Corp., Federal Way, WA (1969-1989); Secretary to Dean of Admissions, Eastern Arizona College, Thatcher, AZ (1963-1967) **CW:** Author, "Lets Laugh" (2008); Author, "Road to Rhyme in the United States" (2006); Newsletter Editor, Violin Bottle Collector's Association, United States (1995-1998); Author, "Violin Bottles, Banjos, Guitars and Other Novelty Glass" (1995); Author, "Violin Bottles"; Author, "Car Faces" **AW:** Outstanding Citizenship Award, American Legion, Safford, AZ (1957); Good Citizen's Certificate, Daughters of the American Revolution (Now National Society of the American Revolution) (1957) **MEM:** Violin Bottle Collectors Association, United States (1995-2018) **MH:** Albert Nelson Marquis Lifetime Achievement Award (2017) **H:** Collecting violin-shaped bottles; Writing; Helping with antique and collectible shows part-time **ADD:** 9908 196th Street E, Graham, WA, 98338

CHU, HORN D., T: Chemical Engineer **I:** Sciences **DOB:** 09/09/1933 **SC:** China **PT:** Johnson S.T. Chu; Daisy (Hsia) Chu **MS:** Married **SPN:** Pik Yu Cheung (6/23/1962) **ED:** PhD, The University of Alabama (1965); MS, University of Pennsylvania (1963); MS, Waseda University, Tokyo, Japan (1961); BS, Waseda University, Tokyo, Japan (1959) **C:** President, Berkorp Inc., Haddonfield, NJ (1981-Present); Senior Process Engineer, MacAndrews & Forbes Incorporated, Camden, NJ (1979-1981); Assistant Professor, Adjunct Professor, Rutgers, The State University of New Jersey, New Brunswick, NJ (1971-1979); Project Engineer, Selas Corporation, Dresher, PA (1965-1971) **CW:** Contributor, Articles, Professional Journals **MEM:** Fellow, American Institute of Chemists; Fellow, American Institute of Chemical Engineers; Fellow, American Chemical Society; Fellow, Institute of Food Technologists; Fellow, American Association for the Advancement of Science; Fellow, Sigma Xi **MH:** Albert Nelson Marquis Lifetime Achievement Award (2017) **BA:** 6 S Haddon Ave Ste 2, Berkorp Inc., Haddonfield, NJ, 08033 **ADD:** 61 Festival Dr., Voorhees, NJ, 08043

CHUNG, JOHN DAVID PHD, T: Principal Scientist **I:** Sciences **CN:** KindredBio **ED:** Postdoctoral Researcher, Cell Culture Bioengineering, Massachusetts Institute of Technology (1994-1996); PhD, Massachusetts Institute of Technology (1994); BS, University of California, Santa Barbara (1986) **C:** Consultant, Chung Bioengineering Consulting (2005-Present); Principal Scientist, KindredBio (2018) Adjunct Professor, Department of Chemistry, Mendocino College (2014-2017); Adjunct Instructor of Mathematics & Chemistry, Woodland College (2015-2016); Bioprocess Engineer, Dendreon (2003); Scientist, Abgenix/Boehringer Ingelheim (2001-2003); Scientist, Celera/Arris Pharmaceutical (1997-2000); Summer Intern, Amgen (1986) **ADD:** PO Box 1, Millbrae, CA, 94030

CHVATAL, PATRICIA J., T: Chvatal Law Office **I:** Law and Legal Services **CN:** Owner **DOB:** 07/06/1950 **PB:** Walla Walla **SC:** WA/USA **PT:** Joseph J. Chvatal; Mary R. (Doherty) Chvatal **MS:** Single **CH:** Two Daughters **ED:** JD, Gonzaga University, Cum Laude (1976); BA, Carroll College, Magna Cum Laude (1972) **C:** Owner, Chvatal Law Firm (1990-Present); Partner, Carroll, Chvatal and Heye, Richland, Washington (1981-Present); Partner, Carroll and Chvatal, Richland, Washington (1979-1981); Junior Partner, Bennett, Carroll and Chvatal, Richland, Washington (1978-1979); Associate, Bennett and Carroll, Richland, Washington (1976-1978); Lecturer, Seminars on Law, State of Washington **CIV:** Board of Directors, United

Way (1979-1980); Board of Directors, Northwest Women's Law Center, Seattle, Washington; Member, City Council Planning Commission, City of Richland, WA; First Woman President, Benton Franklin Bar Association; Board of Directors, The Arc; Board of Directors, Tri-Cities Prep; Board of Trustees, Carroll College, Helena, Montana **CW:** Contributor, Articles, Professional Journals **AW:** Albert J Yankapal Award for Community Service, Washington State Bar Association **MEM:** President, Washington Women's Political Caucus (1981); President, Richland Chapter, Business Professional Women's Foundation (1977-1979); League of Women Voters; AAUW; Washington Women United; Catholic Daughters of the Americas; Past President, Tri-City Women Lawyers; Washington Women Lawyers; Altrusa International **BAR:** Washington State Bar Association (1976) **MH:** Albert Nelson Marquis Lifetime Achievement Award (2017) **PA:** Democrat **RE:** Roman Catholic **BA:** 1111 Jadwin Ave, Chvatal Law, Richland, WA, 99352 **URL:** http://www.chvatallaw.com/About-Us/Patricia-J-Chvatal.shtml

CIULLO, ROSEMARY C., T: Psychologist **I:** Medicine & Health Care **DOB:** 03/16/1951 **PB:** Chicago **SC:** IL/USA **PT:** Lenard Ciullo (Deceased, 1998); Anna Auriemma Ciullo (Deceased, 1991) **ED:** Doctorate in Psychology, The School of Professional Psychology at Forest Institute, with High Distinction (1986); MA, Governors State University, University Park, Illinois (1977); BA, The University of Illinois at Chicago (1974) **CT:** Diplomate in Child and Adolescent Psychology, International College of Professional Psychology (2005) **C:** Psychologist, Private Practice, IL (1995-2000); Henry Horner Children's Center (1987-1993); Private Practice, (1998-2000); Ada McKinley Foster Care (1974-1977); St. Ann's Hospital (1969-1980); **CIV:** Cursillo Group; Former Volunteer, Women's Choice Services **CW:** Co-contributor, Article, "Small Group Interaction and Behavior in Latency-Age Children," Sage Publications, Inc. (1988) **MEM:** American Psychological Association; Prescribing Psychologists Register; American Association of Suicidology; Association for Psychological Science; American Orthopsychiatry Society; Illinois Psychological Association **MH:** Albert Nelson Marquis Lifetime Achievement Award (2017) **H:** Reading; Workshops in Continuing Education; Volunteering; Writing **ADD:** 604 S Fairfield Ave, Lombard, IL, 60148

CLAGETT, VIRGINIA, T: County Official **I:** Government Administration/Government Relations/Government Services **DOB:** 07/18/1943 **PB:** Washington **SC:** DC/USA **PT:** William; Virginia **ED:** BA in History, Smith College (1965); Coursework, University of Geneva **C:** Member District 30, Maryland House of Delegates (1994-2011); Councilwoman, Anne Arundel County Council, Annapolis, MD (1974-1994); Chairman, Anne Arundel County Council, Annapolis (1984-1991); Assistant Reporter, Triangle Pub. & Radio Station, Philadelphia (1966-1968) **CIV:** Vice chairman Baltimore Regional Planning Council (1984-Present); Trustee, Hammond-Harwood House (1978-Present); Trustee, Chesapeake EPA (1976-Present); Member, Alcohol and Drug Abuse Advisory Committee (1985-Present); Member, Anne Arundel County Agricultural Advisory Committee (1978-Present); Board of Directors, Historic Annapolis, Inc. **MEM:** American Business Women's Association; Legislative Committee, Maryland Association of Counties **H:** Tennis; Gardening; Horseback riding **PA:** Democrat **RE:** Episcopalian **ADD:** P.O. Box 1, West River, MD, 20778

CLARK, ALICIA GARCIA, T: Political Party Official **I:** Government Administration/Government Relations/Government Services **PB:** Vera Cruz **SC:** Mexico **PT:** Rafael Garcia Aully; Maria Luisa (Cobos) Garcia **MS:** Married **SPN:** Edward E. Clark (10/20/1970) **CH:** Edward E., Jr. **ED:** MSChemE, Universidad Nacional Autonoma de Mexico (1951) **C:** Sales Promotion and Advertising Manager, Celanese Mexicana, Celanese Corporation, Mexico City, Mexico (1965-1970); Sales Promotion Manager, Celanese Mexicana, Celanese Corporation, Mexico City, Mexico (1960-1965); Laboratory Manager, Celanese Mexicana, Celanese Corporation, Mexico City, Mexico (1953-1960); Chemist, Celanese Mexicana, Celanese Corporation, Mexico City, Mexico (1951-1953); Technical Assistant, Celanese Mexicana, Celanese Corporation, Mexico City, Mexico; Co-Founder, Liz Claiborne **CR:** Chairman, Celebrity Series (1989-1991); President, San Marino Guild of Huntington Hospitals, California (1981-1982); Mexico Olympic Committee (1968) **CIV:** Board of Advisers, Pasadena Symphony Orchestra and POPS (2006-Present); Managing Director, Los Angeles Opera (1995-Present); President, Hispanics for Los Angeles Opera, Los Angeles Opera (2013); Founder, Co-chair, Hispanics for Los Angeles Opera, Los Angeles Opera (2008-2013); Life Trustee, Los Angeles Opera (2006); Redcat Theater Council (2002-2006); Club 100 (1996-1999); Board of Directors, Guild Opera Company (1994-1996); Founder, Co-chair, Hispanics for Los Angeles Opera, Los Angeles Opera (1991-1999); Coordinator, Libertarian State Parties (1991-1998); President, Board of Directors, Opera League of Los Angeles (1990-1996); President, San Marino Woman's Club (1989-1990); Chair, Libertarian Party (1981-1983); President, San Marino Guild Huntington Memorial Hospital (1981-1982) **AW:** Medal, Pro Conscious World Association, A.C. Mexico (2011); Philanthropic Leadership Award, Los Angeles Music and Art (2011); Zachary Society Honor Award (2001); Placido Domingo Award (2000); Star of the Arts Award, Mexican Cultural Institute (1998); Heroes Los Angeles Award, Hispanic Traditions and Heritage Council (1995); Award, Fashion Group (1970); Placido Domingo Award **MEM:** Treasurer, Fashion Group (1969-1970) **MH:** Albert Nelson Marquis Lifetime Achievement Award (2017) **H:** Reading; Traveling **PA:** Libertarian **RE:** Catholic **ADD:** 437 S Orange Grove Boulevard, Apt. 5, Pasadena, CA, 91105 **URL:** http://people.com/archive/ed-clark-is-the-libertarian-partys-headstrong-candidate-for-the-white-hous

CLARKE-PEARSON, DANIEL L. MD, T: Chair **I:** Education/Educational Services **CN:** University of North Carolina at Chapel Hill **DOB:** 09/10/1948 **PB:** Indio **SC:** CA/USA **PT:** Donald; Francis **MS:** Married **SPN:** Kathleen **CH:** Don; Emily; Mary; Michael **ED:** Fellow, Gynecologic Oncology, Duke University Medical Center, Durham, NC (1979-1981); Intern, Resident, Obstetrics & Gynecology, Duke University Medical Center, Durham, NC (1975-1979); MD, Case Western Reserve University (1975); BA, Harvard University (1970) **CT:** Diplomate, Obstetrics & Gynecology, American Board of Obstetrics and Gynecology; Diplomate, Gynecological Oncology, American Board of Obstetrics and Gynecology; Diplomate, National Board of Medical Examiners **C:** Robert A. Ross Distinguished Professor, Chair, Department of Obstetrics and Gynecology, University of North Carolina at Chapel Hill (2005-Present); Professor, Gynecologic Oncology, Duke University Medical Center, Durham, NC (1987-2005) **CR:** Fellow, American College of Surgeons; Fellow, American Congress of Obstetricians and Gynecologists **CW:** Contributor, Over 250 Scientific Papers, Peer-Reviewed Journals; Contributor, More Than 50 Chapters, Textbooks; Author, Three Textbooks **AW:** Ranked Second in the United States, U.S. News & World Report, Department of Obstetrics and Gynecology, School of Medicine, University of North Carolina at Chapel Hill (2017); Ranked 11th in the United States, U.S. News & World Report, Department of Obstetrics and Gynecology, School of Medicine, University of North Carolina at Chapel Hill (2016); Ranked First in North Carolina, U.S. News & World Report, Department of Obstetrics and Gynecology, School of Medicine, University of North Carolina at Chapel Hill (2016); Ranked First in the Southeast, U.S. News & World Report, Department of Obstetrics and Gynecology, School of Medicine, University of North Carolina at Chapel Hill (2016) **MEM:** President, Society of Gynecologic Oncology (2010); Society of Pelvic Surgeons **MH:** Albert Nelson Marquis Lifetime Achievement Award (2017) **BA:** CB 7570, University of North Carolina, Chapel Hill, NC, 27599 **ADD:** 3009 Old Clinic Building, CB 7570, School of Medicine, Chapel Hill, NC, 27599

CLEMENGER, MARIE ELENA ELENA, I: Financial Services **ED:** Master's Degree in Accounting and Credit; BS in Accounting and Working in Finance **CT:** Registered Tax Professional, Internal Revenue Service **MEM:** National Society of Tax Professionals

CLEMENTE, FRANK M. JR., T: Chief Geotechnology Engineer **I:** Engineering **CN:** AECOM **DOB:** 11/03/1941 **PB:** New York **SC:** NY/USA **PT:** Frank F. Clemente; Catherine Clemente **ED:** PhD, Tulane University, New Orleans, LA (1984); MCE, New York University, New York, NY (1967); BE, Cooper Union, New York, NY (1966) **CT:** Certification in Civil Engineering, State of Louisiana (1984); Certification in Structural Engineering, State of Hawaii (1974); Certification in Civil Engineering, State of Louisiana (1973); Certification in Professional Engineering, State of New York (1971) **C:** Chief Geotechnology Engineer, AECOM, New York, NY (2002-Present); Chief Geotechnology Engineer, TAMS Consultants, Inc., New York, NY (1988-2002); Professional Associate, Parsons Brinckerhoff, Honolulu, HI (1967-1984) **CR:** Geotechnology Project Manager, Soils and Foundations Committee, Mayoral Commission to Revise New York City Building Code (2002-2007); Soils and Foundations Committee, Mayoral Commission to Revise New York City Building Code (2002-2007); Academic Fellow, Tulane University, New Orleans, LA (1982-1983); Lecturer on Soil-Structure Interaction in Ocean Engineering, University of Hawaii, Honolulu, HI (1982); Adjunct Instructor, Theoretical Soil Mechanics, Cooper Union, New York, NY (1967); Foundation Engineer, Terminal Four, New Staten Island Ferry Terminal, New York, NY; Foundation Engineer, Halawa and Keehi Interchanges; Design Principal, Halawa and Keehi Interchanges **CW:** Contributor, Articles, Professional Journals **AW:** Silver Award, Earth Tech (2007); President's Gold Award, Earth Tech (2007); Outstanding Technology Chairman, American Society of Civil Engineers (1974-1975) **MEM:** President, Hawaii Chapter, American Society of Civil Engineers (1980); American Society of Engineering Education; Charter Member, Deep Foundations Institute; Earthquake Engineering Research Institute **MH:** Albert Nelson Marquis Lifetime Achievement Award (2017) **ADD:** 185 Park Row, Apt. 5G, New York, NY, 10038

CLIFF, KARISSA, T: Director **I:** Business Management/Business Services **CN:** Fruit of the Loom, Inc. **ED:** EdD, Trevecca Nazarene University **C:** Director, Fruit of the Loom, Inc. **CW:** Author, Poem, "Yes, They're My Children"

COCHRAN, MELODIE T., T: Chayil Maison **I:** Business Management/Business Services **CN:** Chief Executive Officer **DOB:** 01/06/1962 **ED:** BSEE, University of California, Los Angeles (1985) **CT:** Diplomate, Global Entrepreneurs Institute, La Red Business Network (2013); Certified Enterprise Coach, Nehemiah Project International Ministries (2013); Diplomate, Biblical Entrepreneurship Business Program, Nehemiah Project International Ministries (2012); Certified Six Sigma Green Belt (2004); Diplomate, Dream Interpretation School (1992); Diplomate, Living Water Bible College Certificate Program (1990) **C:** Owner, Chayil Maison Hair Salon (2017-Present); Information Technologist, Navigation Systems Division, Northrop Grumman Corporation; Webmaster, Northrop Grumman Corporation **CIV:** Volunteer, His Life Ministries **CW:** Producer, "Spooknight"; Developer "WEBSAR"; Developer, "Process Champion," Northrop Grumman Corporation **AW:** Teacher of the Year Award, Nehemiah Project International Ministries (2015); Teacher of the Year, Le Nouvel Horizon (2015) **MEM:** Alpha Kappa Alpha Sorority, Inc.; National Society of Black Engineers **H:** Worshiping God; Playing basketball; Water skiing; Snow skiing; Interpreting dreams **RE:** Christian **BA:** 512 W. 7th Street, Los Angeles, CA, 90014 **ADD:** 5200 Premiere Hills Cir Apt 245, Woodland Hills, CA, 91364 **URL:** https://www.chayilmaison.com

COE, JUDITH LYNN, T: Automobile Manufacturing Company Administrator (Retired) **I:** Manufacturing **DOB:** 10/04/1945 **PB:** Washington **SC:** DC/USA **PT:** Raymond G.; Lynn (Pulliam) Coe **ED:** BA in Mathematics, Converse College (1967) **CT:** Executive Secretary Certification, Washington School for Secretaries (1968) **C:** Retired (1995); Zone Manager's Secretary, Pontiac Division, GM Corp., Washington, DC (1987-1995); Secretary to Assistant Zone Managers, Pontiac Division GM Corp., Atlanta, GA (1983-1987); Secretary to Regional Manager, Electro-Motive Division GM Corp., Atlanta, GA (1972-1983); Secretary to Vice President and Secretary, Nonprescription Drug Manufacturers Association, Washington, DC (1968-1972) **MEM:** Salvation Army Women's Auxiliary in Washington; Peace Center Peacekeepers; Greenville Art Museum Association; Greenville Women Giving; Commerce Club; Poinsett Club; Upstate Republican Woman; Greenville County Republican Women's Club **H:** Attending Lectures; Attending author's talks; Museums; Musicals **PA:** Republican **ADD:** 707 Quail Run, Greenville, SC, 29605

COHEN, STEVEN ARTHUR, T: 1) Writer 2) Flight Attendant **I:** Aviation **CN:** 1) Steven Arthur Cohen Communications 2) United Airlines **DOB:** 09/09/1951 **PB:** Wichita **SC:** KS/USA **PT:** William Cohen; Celia (Friedman) Cohen **MS:** Single **ED:** Graduate, Leadership Fairfax (2009); BS in Journalism, University of Kansas (1973) **C:** Writer, Steven Arthur Cohen Communications, Amsterdam, Netherlands (1982-Present); Editor, Salt River Project Public Utility, Phoenix, AZ (1979-1981); Communications Consultant, Phoenix, AZ (1977-1979); Reporter, Hollywood Sun-Tattler (Now Hollywood Sun) (1975-1977); Reporter, The Wichita Eagle (1973-1975) **CR:** Leadership, Fairfax Inc. (2009); Scriptwriter, Fiesta Bowl Parade, Phoenix, AZ (1978-1980) **CIV:** Board of Directors, Langley Residential Support Services, McLean, VA (2009-2012); Commercial Anglo Dutch Society (1996-2002); Green Cross International (1993); Newsletter Columnist, American Chamber of Commerce in the Netherlands (1989-2001); Educational Publicity Station Director, KAET-TV, Phoenix, AZ (1980); National Member Chairman (1980); Ad2 Phoenix, Phoenix, AZ (1978-1981);

1st Annual American Heart Association, Inc., Golf Classic, Scottsdale, AZ (1978) **CW:** Author, Exhibition Catalog, "Anne Frank in the World: 1929-1945" (1985) **MEM:** Phoenix Chapter President, KU Alumni Association (1980); Commercial Anglo Dutch Society; Lifetime Member, KU Alumni Association **MH:** Albert Nelson Marquis Lifetime Achievement Award (2017) **H:** Swimming; Traveling; Education **RE:** Jewish **ADD:** 12937 Centre Park Cir Apt 307, Herndon, VA, 20171

COHN, ANDREW, T: Lawyer **I:** Law and Legal Services **CN:** Hale and Dorr **DOB:** 01/17/1945 **PB:** New York **SC:** NY/USA **PT:** Maurice John Cohn; Margaret Ethel (Gordon) Cohn **MS:** Married **SPN:** Marcia Bliss Leavitt (7/10/1977) **CH:** Marisa Leavitt; David Herman **ED:** JD, Yale University (1975); PhD, Harvard University (1972); AM, Harvard University (1970); BA, University of Pennsylvania (1966) **C:** Senior Partner, Wilmer Hale, Boston, MA (1980-2016); Associate, Hill & Barlow, Boston, MA (1976-1980); Law Clerk to Presiding Justice, First Circuit, U.S. Court of Appeals, Providence, RI and Boston, MA (1975-1976) **CR:** President, CEO, Longwood Medical Energy Collaboration, Inc. (2016-Present); Chairman, Energy Group, Hale and Dorr (1992-Present); Chairman, Real Estate Department, Hale and Dorr (1991-1997); Chairman, Executive Committee, Hale and Dorr (1990-1991); Consultant for Juvenile Justice Standards Project, American Bar Association and Institute for Judicial Administration, New York, NY (1973-1974); Law And Social Science Fellow, Russell Sage Foundation (1972-1974); Research Fellow, Massachusetts Institute of Technology and Harvard University Joint Center for Urban Studies, Cambridge, MA (1969-1971); Research Fellow, University College, Nairobi, Kenya (1968); Harvard Medical Center; Beth Israel Medical Deaconess Center; Boston Children's Hospital; Brigham & Woman's Hospital; Dana-Farber Cancer Institute; Joslin Diabetes Center; Rockefeller Fellow, University of Florida Journal of Law & Public Policy **CIV:** Advisor, Newton Community Schools Foundation, Massachusetts (1987-1988); Advisory Committee, Senior Partners for Justice; Treasurer, Volunteer Lawyers Project **CW:** Note and Project Editor, Yale Law Journal, New Haven, CT (1974-1975); Contributor, Articles, Professional Journals; "Reducing the Civil Justice Gap by Enhancing the Delivery of Pro-Bono Legal Assistants to Indigent Pro-Se Litigants" **MEM:** Chairman, Real Estate Section, Boston Bar Association (1995-1997); Treasurer, Yale Law School Association, Massachusetts (1985-1987); Environmental Controls Committee, Business Law Section, American Bar Association; American College of Real Estate Lawyers **BAR:** First Circuit, U.S. Court of Appeals (1976); U.S. District Court, State of Massachusetts (1976); State of Massachusetts (1975) **MH:** Albert Nelson Marquis Lifetime Achievement Award (2017) **PA:** Democrat **RE:** Jewish **ADD:** 29 Jameson Road, Newton, MA, 02458

COLAIANNI, JOSEPH VINCENT, T: Judge **I:** Law and Legal Services **CN:** Squire Patton Boggs **DOB:** 03/19/1933 **PB:** Detroit **SC:** MI/USA **PT:** Pasquale Colaianni; Marie D. (Mastrantonio) Colaianni **MS:** Widowed **SPN:** Rita Milena Roll (10/13/1962, Deceased) **CH:** Marie Elena; Joseph Vincent; Michael Philip; Vincent Gerard **ED:** JD, George Washington University, With Honors (1961); Postgraduate Work, Wayne State University (1956-1958); BEE, University of Detroit Mercy (1956) **C:** Chair of Intellectual Property, Patton Squire Boggs (1998-Present); Managing Partner, Pennie & Edmonds (1984-1998); Judge, U.S. Court of Federal Claims (1977-1984); Trial Judge, U.S. Court of Federal Claims (1973-1977); Commissioner, U.S. Court of Federal Claims (1970-1973); Trial

Attorney, Civil Division, U.S. Department of Justice (1965-1970); Associate of the Firm, Fay and Fay (1965) **CR:** Adjunct Professor, American University (1997-Present); Senior Adviser, Advisory Council, U.S. Court of Federal Claims (1984-Present); Advisory Committee on Patents and Trademarks, U.S. Department of Commerce (1987-1989); Adjunct Professor, American University (1984-1987); Scientific Liaison Committee, Science Court (1976-1984); Professor, Graduate School, Patent Resources Institute; Advisory Committee, U.S. Patent and Trademark Office **CIV:** Board of Directors, Lido Civic Club (2000-Present); Advisory Board, Holy Rosary, Washington, DC (1984-Present); President's Cabinet, University of Detroit Mercy (1982-Present); Commission on Future, College of Engineering (1995-1996); Co-President, Parents Association, University of Maryland (1991-1997); Board of Directors, Lido Civic Club (1982-1990); Trustee, Western University of Health Sciences (1982-1985); President, Board of Directors, Lido Civic Club (1981); President, Parent-Teacher Association Tilden Middle School, MCPS (1979-1981); District Heights Recreation Council, Maryland (1969-1970); Board of Directors, Henson Valley Montessori School **CW:** Advisory Board "Patent, Trademark and Copyright Journal" (1984-1991); Law Review, George Washington University (1960-1961) **AW:** Honoree, Alumnus of Year, College of Engineering, University of Detroit Mercy (2008) **MEM:** American Bar Association; Federal Bar Association; Patent & Trademark Office Society; Insignis; The International Legal Honor Society of Phi Delta Phi; Eta Kappa Nu, IEEE; Omicron Delta Kappa; Phi Delta Kappa International **BAR:** District of Columbia (1964); State of Ohio (1963); State of Michigan (1962) **MH:** Albert Nelson Marquis Lifetime Achievement Award (2017) **ADD:** 6309 Windermere Circle, North Bethesda, MD, 20852

COLE, STAN A., T: 1. Director 2. Executive Vice President **I:** Other **CN:** 1. CGH Global Emergency Management Strategies 2. CGH Global **MS:** Married **ED:** Degree in Occupational Safety/Fire Science, Columbia Southern University (2011); Associate's, American InterContinental University (2008) **C:** Corporate Fire Chief, CGH Global Emergency Management Strategies LLC (2011-Present); Fire Safety Chief, Afghanistan Theater, Task Force Power (2011-2012); Operational Readiness Inspector, Task Force Safe (2008-2010); Fire Chief, AAAA (2004-2008) **AW:** VIP Registry of Executives, Professionals and Entrepreneurs, Worldwide Who's Who (2013-2014) **MEM:** International Association of Fire Chiefs; International Society of Fire Service Instructors; Firefighter Nation; National Fire Protection **ADD:** 606 Lakeshore Ct, Monroe, GA, 30655 **URL:** https://www.linkedin.com/in/stan-a-cole-484a0140/

COLKET, MEREDITH B. III, T: Senior Fellow **I:** Research **CN:** United Technologies Research Center **PT:** Meredith Colket, Jr.; Julia Colket **MS:** Married **SPN:** Kathleen Colket **CH:** Alexander; Laura; Caroline **ED:** PhD in Aerospace and Mechanical Sciences, Princeton University (1976); MA in Aerospace and Mechanical Sciences, Princeton University (1974); BS in Engineering Physics, Cornell University (1970) **C:** Professor, Combustion Fundamentals, Department of Engineering and Science, Rensselaer at Hartford, Rensselaer Polytechnic Institute (2003); Postdoctoral Research Associate, Mechanical Engineering Department, Purdue University (1975-1976); Research Assistant, Department of Aerospace and Mechanical Sciences, Princeton University (1974); Affiliate, Project Approving Alternative Fuels for Jet Aircraft, National

Aeronautics and Space Administration; Affiliate, Contract Supporting Micro-Gravity Projects, National Aeronautics and Space Administration **CR:** Fellow, Combustion Institute; Associate Fellow, AIAA **MIL:** Army Captain, Signal Corps **CW:** Associate Editor, "Combustion Science and Technology" (2008-Present); Invited Presenter, "Evolution of Reaction Kinetics: From Small Molecules to Real Fuels," Seventh Annual Fuel and Combustion Research Meeting, Multi-Agency Coordinating Council for Combustion Research, Boulder, CO (2014); Invited Presenter, "Challenges and Uncertainties in Use of Surrogate Fuels for Emulating Combustor Performance," 52nd AIAA Aerospace Sciences Meeting, National Harbor, MD (2014); Invited Presenter, "Use of Alternate Fuels for Aviation: Concerns of GT Industry," Sixth Annual Fuel and Combustion Research Meeting, Multi-Agency Coordinating Council for Combustion Research, Washington, DC (2013); Invited Presenter, "Fuel Research at UTRC," Fifth Annual Fuel Research Meeting, Multi-Agency Coordinating Council for Combustion Research Sandia National Laboratories, Livermore, CA (2012); Invited Presenter, "Use of Kinetic Models to Predict Fuel Impact on Engine Performance," Fourth Annual Fuel Research Meeting, Multi-Agency Coordinating Council for Combustion Research Argonne National Laboratories, Chicago, IL (2011); Invited Presenter, "Chemical Kinetic Concerns for Non-Petroleum Derived Jet Fuel," Joint Propulsion Conference, Nashville, TN (2010); Invited Presenter, "Combustion Rules and Tools for Alternative Fuels," Third Annual Fuel Research Meeting, Multi-Agency Coordinating Council for Combustion Research, Princeton, NJ (2010); Reviewer, Student Papers, Northeast Regional Conference, AIAA (2005); Editor, Publications Committee, "Proceedings of the Combustion Institute" (2002-2005); Contributor, Articles, Professional Journals; Patentee in Field **AW:** Weapon Systems and Platforms Project-of-the-Year Award, Strategic Environmental Research and Development Program (SERDP) (2011); Leadership Award, United Technologies Corporation — Pratt & Whitney Division (2002); Honoree, Best Paper, AIAA (2000); Leadership Award, United Technologies Corporation — Pratt & Whitney Division (1998); Outstanding Achievement Award, United Technologies Research Center (1997); Outstanding Achievement Award, United Technologies Research Center (1992); Special Award, United Technologies Research Center (1990); Special Award, United Technologies Research Center (1989); Numerous Contract Awards (1985-2018) **MEM:** Advisory Committee, Development and Evaluation of Gas Fuel Interchangeability Criteria/Methodologies, California Energy Commission, State of California (2012-Present); Scientific Committee, International Sooting Flame Workshop (2012-Present); Review Panel, Combustion Program, National Science Foundation (2017); Board of Governors, American Society for Gravitational and Space Research (2016-2018); Review Panel, Physical Sciences Informatics System, National Aeronautics and Space Administration (2016); Chairman, Review Panel, Physical Sciences Informatics System, National Aeronautics and Space Administration (2015); Review Panel, Engineering Laboratory, National Institute of Standards and Technology, U.S. Department of Commerce (2014); Chairman, Science Concept Review Panel, BRE Program, National Aeronautics and Space Administration (2013); Review Panel, ACME Program in CIR, National Aeronautics and Space Administration (2012); Advisory Committee, Kinetics Study of Alternative (HRJ & FT) Jet Fuels, Air Force, Research Laboratory, U.S. Air Force (2011-2012);

Stakeholder Committee, Improved Two-Phase Model for JP-8 and Alternative Fuels, AFRL SBIR, U.S. Air Force (2011-2012); International Advisory Committee, Combustion Energy Frontier Research Center, Princeton University (2010-2014); Committee on CyberInfrastructure on Combustion Science, U.S. Nuclear Regulatory Commission (2009-2011); Review Panel, ACME Program in CIR, National Aeronautics and Space Administration (2010); Expert Review Panel, Combustion Technologies to Achieve California (2007); Board of Directors, Combustion Institute (2006-2018); Advisory Committee, Implication of Natural Gas Interchangeability, California Energy Commission, State of California (2006-2010); Chairman, Surrogate Fuels Working Group for Jet Fuel (2006-2009); Review Panel, Combustion and Plasma Systems, National Science Foundation (2005); Review Panel, Capstone Turbine Corporation (2004); Science Concept Review (SCR) Panel, Flame Design Experiment, National Aeronautics and Space Administration (2002); Committee on Task Group on Research on the International Space Station, U.S. Nuclear Regulatory Commission (1999-2002); Chairman, Eastern States Section, Combustion Institute (1994-2002); Vice Chairman, Eastern States Section, Combustion Institute (1994-2002); Arrangements Chairman, Eastern States Section, Combustion Institute (1994-2002); Advisory Committee, Poster Session Coordinator, 21st International Symposium on Combustion (1987); American Chemical Society; Combustion Institute; American Society of Gravitational and Space Research; American Association for the Advancement of Science **H:** Tennis; Bridge; Hiking; Biking **ADD:** 36 Gatewood, Avon, CT, 06001 **URL:** https://www.researchgate.net/profile/Meredith_Colket

COLLARS, SHIRLEY, T: Small Business Owner **I:** Research **CN:** Emerson Research Services **DOB:** 07/26/1937 **PB:** Bluff City **SC:** TN/USA **PT:** Clifford Miller Coffey; Velma Christine (Houser) Coffey **MS:** Single **SPN:** Roy Emerson Collars (1956-2003) **CH:** Roy Allen; Brett Wayne **C:** Field Representative, US Department of Commerce (2005-Present); Owner, Operator, Emerson Research Services, Hattiesburg (1989-Present); Freelance Interviewer, Hattiesburg, MI (1983-1989); Field Interviewer, U.S. Department Commerce, Dallas (1979-1983); Office Assistant, Bookkeeper, J. Morgan Construction, Inc., Biloxi, MI (1967-1970); Bookkeeper, First National Bank of Baltimore, Baltimore City, MD (1955-1956) **MEM:** American Marketing Association; National Genealogical Society; National Humane Society; Marketing Research Association **H:** Genealogy; History; Needlecrafts **ADD:** P.O. Box 4635, Biloxi, MS, 39535

COLLINS, DELWOOD CHARLIE, T: Biomedical Researcher, University Administrator (Retired) **I:** Medicine & Health Care **DOB:** 10/07/1937 **PB:** Cairo **SC:** IL/USA **MS:** Married **SPN:** Patricia Ann Burg (5/18/1981) **CH:** Robert; Susan; Christina **ED:** National Institutes of Health Postdoctoral Fellow in Biochemistry, Worcester Foundation for Experimental Biology, Shrewsbury, MA (1965-1967); PhD in Physiology, University of Georgia (1966); MS in Zoology, University of Georgia (1963); BS in Biology, Emory University (1959) **C:** Associate Vice President for Research and Graduate Studies, University of Kentucky (2002-2007); Senior Research Career Scientist, VA Medical Center, Lexington, KY (1999-2007); Adjunct Professor of Physiology, University of Kentucky College of Medicine (1994-2007); Professor of Gynecology and Obstetrics, University of Kentucky College of Medicine, Lexington, KY (1991-2007); Professor of Biochemistry, University of Kentucky College of

Medicine (1991-2007); Chair, Construction Review Committee, NCRR (2002-2005); Vice Chancellor for Research and Graduate Studies, University of Kentucky Medical Center (1991-2002); Associate Research Career Scientist, VA Medical Center, Lexington, KY (1991-1999); Acting Vice President for Research and Graduate Studies, University of Kentucky (1994-1995); Collaborating Scientist, Yerkes Regional Primate Research Center, Emory University School of Medicine (1970-1995); Associate Research Career Scientist, VA Medical Center, Atlanta, GA (1983-1991); Adjunct Professor of Pathology, Emory University School of Medicine (1982-1991); Adjunct Professor of Gynecology and Obstetrics, Emory University School of Medicine (1982-1991); Associate Professor of Biochemistry, Emory University School of Medicine (1981-1991); Professor of Medicine, Emory University School of Medicine (1976-1991); Adjunct Professor of Biology, Emory University (1972-1991); Associate Chief of Staff for Research and Development, VA Medical Center, Decatur, GA (1987-1988); Director, Hormone Research Laboratory, Division of Endocrinology, Department of Medicine, Emory University School of Medicine (1976-1985); Professor of Medicine, Emory University School of Medicine (1976-1981); Associate Professor of Medicine, Emory University School of Medicine (1972-1976); Assistant Professor of Medicine, Emory University School of Medicine (1969-1972); Medical Research Associate, Medical Research Council of Canada, Department of Biochemistry, University of Ottawa, Ontario (1968-1969); Research Scientist, Endocrinology Section, Department of National Health and Welfare (1967-1968); Fellow, Steroid Biochemistry Training Program, Worcester Foundation for Experimental Biology, Shrewsbury, MA (1965-1967) **CW:** Reviewer, Steroids; Reviewer, Endocrinology; Reviewer, Journal of Clinical Endocrinology and Metabolism; Reviewer, American Journal of Physiology; Reviewer, Biology of Reproduction; Reviewer, Fertility and Sterility; Reviewer, Journal of Andrology; Reviewer, Endocrine Journal; Reviewer, Proceedings of Experimental Biology and Medicine; Reviewer, Cancer Research; Reviewer, Teriogenology; Reviewer, Journal of the National Cancer Institute; Reviewer, Prostate **MEM:** Endocrine Society; American Physiological Society; American Chemical Society; American Society of Andrology; International Society for the Study of Reproduction; International Society for the Study of Steroid Hormones; American Association for Cancer Research; American Association for the Advancement of Science; Sigma Xi; American Society of Reproductive Medicine; Society for Experimental Biology and Medicine **MH:** Albert Nelson Marquis Lifetime Achievement Award (2017) **ADD:** 1937 Long Pond Walk, Lexington, KY, 40502

COLLINS, DENNIS GLENN, T: Mathematics Professor (Retired) **I:** Education/Educational Services **DOB:** 06/26/1944 **PB:** Gary **SC:** IN/USA **PT:** Glenn Collins; Irene Martha (Richman) Collins **MS:** Married **SPN:** Barbara Jean Hamilton (07/14/1979) **CH:** Glenn H. **ED:** PhD, Illinois Institute of Technology (1975); MS, Illinois Institute of Technology (1970); BA, Valparaiso University (1966) **C:** Chairman, Personnel Committee, University of Puerto Rico, Mayaguez (1994-1995); Assistant Professor to Professor of Mathematics, University of Puerto Rico, Mayaguez (1982-2009); Assistant Professor, Valparaiso University, Valparaiso, IN (1979-1982); Instructor, University of New Orleans (1976-1979); Temporary Instructor, Michigan State University, East Lansing, MI (1975-1976) **CR:** Presenter, Lectures in Field; Blog, Quantum History Institute (2013);

Detection of Some Malignant 2-D Tumors, Purdue Northwest - North Central, Purdue University (2010); Continuous Symmetry of Wedge and Other Shapes, University of Notre Dame, IN (2010); Toward a Mathematical Origin of Species, 7th Biennial Emergy Research Conference (2010); Moral Codes III, Department of Mathematical Sciences, University of Puerto Rico, Mayaguez (2009); Architecture Case Study in Transformative Factorization, Annual ISSS Meeting, Madison, WI (2008); Visiting Scholar, University of Puerto Rico, Mayaguez (2003-2004); Visiting Scholar, Michigan State University (1988-1989, 1996-1997); Judge, Computer Science, International Science and Engineering Fair, San Juan, Puerto Rico (1987) **CW:** Lecturer, "Toward Thermodynamics and Emergy of Picture and Other Puzzle Solving", Tri-State MAA, Valparaiso University (2018); Author, Three Papers on the Topic of Emergy Synthesis 9, Center for Environmental Policy, Gainesville, FL; Author, "Toward Max and Min Symmetry of Order 24 Groups," Butler University, Indianapolis, IN; Meetings, Mathematical Association of America; Number Blocks Talk, Trine University, Angola, IN (2014); Energy-Simplicity Talk, Gainesville, FL (2014); Talk, "Approximating Continuous Symmetry of Some Systems & Solids," Akron, OH (2012); Founding Fathers Postcards (2012); Talk, "Measuring Symmetry of a Finite Group," University of Indianapolis (2011); Author, "Conflict in History Measuring Symmetry, Thermodynamic Modeling and Other Work" (2011); Author, "Some Continuous Empower -Z Models Political Spectrum Models," University of Florida, Gainesville, FL (2010); Composer, "Meditation" (2010); Author, Examples of Measuring Continuous Symmetry (2008); Composer, "Amadis Lullaby" (2007); Composer, "New Orleans Serenade" (2006); Composer, Short Columbus Cantata and Short Spaceship Cantata, Short Cosmic Cantata, "One Size Fits All," (2001); Creater, Postcards of 120 Mathematicians and Physicists (1983-2001) **AW:** Fellow, National Science Foundation (1966-1967) **MEM:** American Mathematical Society; Mathematical Association of America; American Chemical Society; The New York Academy of Sciences; Society for Industrial and Applied Mathematics; St. Louis Chapter, American Mathematical Society (2013); Informatics and Cybernetics, American Mathematical Society (1990); Dialog Committee to Rector, American Mathematical Society (1997-2003); Fourth Energy Conference, American Mathematical Society (2006); Talk on Symmetry, American Mathematical Society (2007); Conflict in History, American Mathematical Society (1971); SPIE; President, Sigma Xi, The Scientific Research Honor Society (2003-2004) **MH:** Lifetime Achievement **RE:** Lutheran **ADD:** 7108 Grand Blvd, Hobart, IN, 46342

COLLINS, MELANIE JEAN, T: Reading Interventionist **I:** Education/Educational Services **CN:** Metro Nashville Public Schools **DOB:** 12/05/1954 **PB:** Madison **SC:** Tennessee **PT:** William Daniel Hunt, Jr.; Betty Jean Hunt **MS:** Married **SPN:** Paul Vernon Collins, Jr. (12/17/1983) **ED:** MEd, Covenant College (1997); BS, University of Tennessee (1979) **CT:** Certified Legal Secretary **C:** Reading Specialist, Metro Nashville Public Schools (2004-Present); Teacher, First Grade, Metro Nashville Public Schools (2002-2004); Teacher, First Grade, Lighthouse Christian School, Nashville, TN (2000-2002); Teacher, Fifth Grade, Woodbine Christian Academy, Nashville, TN (1999-2000); Principal, Lord's Chapel Christian Academy, Nashville, TN (1996-1999); Teacher, Kindergarten, Mount Juliet Christian Academy, Juliet, TN (1992-1995); Legal Secretary, Office of Joe Binkley Junior, Nashville, TN (1986-1991); Paralegal, Office of Joe Binkley Junior, Nashville, TN (1986-1991) **CIV:** Secretary, Murfreesboro Soroptomist Club, Tennessee (1990-1991); President, Davidson County Legal Secretaries, Nashville, TN (1988-1989); President, Tennessee Association Legal Secretaries, Nashville, TN (1987-1989) **CW:** Contributor, Poetry, Literacy Publications **AW:** Named Legal Secretary of the Year, Davidson County Legal Secretaries (1990) **MEM:** President, Middle Tennessee Reading Association (2007-2008); Secretary, The Cedars Club of Nashville (2005-2006); Board of Directors, Metropolitan Nashville Education Association (2005-2006); National Education Association; International Reading Association **H:** Reading; Travel **ADD:** 798 Walnut Ridge Dr, La Vergne, TN, 37086

COLLINS, NANCY W., T: Senior Vice-President **I:** Financial Services **CN:** Landbank Investment **DOB:** 12/20/1933 **PB:** Charlotte, North Carolina **PT:** Ward William Whisnant; Marjorie Adele (Blackburn) Whisnant **MS:** Single (divorced) **SPN:** Richard F. Chapman (5/29/1982), Divorced (1992); James Quincy Collins Jr. (4/25/1959), Divorced (1974) **CH:** James Quincy Collins, III; Charles Lowell Collins; William Robey Collins **ED:** MS in Personnel Administration, The University of North Carolina at Chapel Hill (1967); Postgraduate Fellowship, Cornell University, Ithaca, NY (1955-1956); AB in Journalism, The University of North Carolina at Chapel Hill (1955); Coursework, Queens University of Charlotte (1951-1953) **C:** Senior Vice President, Landbank Investments (2015-Present); Assistant to Chairman, Landbank Investments (2010-2015); Executive Director, The Marconi Society (2006-2009); Assistant to Chairman, Novo Holdings A/S, Menlo Park, CA (2000-2006); Assistant to President, Palo Alto Medical Foundation (1981-2000); Assistant Director, Hoover Institution, Stanford University (1979-1981); Corporate Development Officer, Graduate School of Business, Stanford, CA (1978-1979); Assistant Director, Tour, Tokyo, Hong Kong, Singapore, Bangkok (1972, 1965); Director, Administration, Sloan Executive Program, Stanford University (1968-1978); Program Director, Girl Scouts of the United States of America, Hampton, VA (1959-1960); Freelance Journalist, London, England, Paris, France and Frankfurt, Germany (1956-1959); Junior Executive Placement Director, Scofield Placement Agency, San Francisco, CA (1956); Personnel Assistant, R.H. Macy & Co., New York, NY (1955) **CR:** Board of Directors, American Healthway Systems, Inc., Palo Alto, CA; Secretary, Treasurer, Chapman Research Fund, Carmel Valley, CA; Trustee, Pacific Graduate School of Psychology, Palo Alto, CA; Board of Directors, Women's Programs, Coro Foundation, San Francisco, CA **CIV:** Committee Member, Homeless Program, Menlo Park Presbyterian Church; Board of Directors, National Center for Equine Facilitated Therapy; Fundraising Consultant, Stanford University Equestrian Center, Stanford, CA; Member, Personnel Board, City of Menlo Park, CA; Member, Charter Review Committee, San Mateo County, CA; Member, Executive Council, Stanford Area Council, Boy Scouts of America; Singles Leadership Team, Menlo Park Presbyterian Church, Menlo Park, CA; Member Board of Directors, National Center Equine Facilitated Therapy **CW:** Editor, "Have a Great Day: Today and Every Day of Your Life," Bay Sports Publishing (2004); Author, "Love at Second Sight," New Horizon Press (2004); Editor, "In Good Taste," Wimmer Brothers (1991); Author, "Women Leading: Making Tough Choices on the Fast Track," Viking, Penguin (1988); Author, "Professional Women and Their Mentors," Prentice-Hall (1983); Author, "A Socio-Psychological Evaluation of Twelve Industrial Engineers as Related to Creative an Managerial Effectiveness," The University of North Carolina Press (1966); Author, Short Stories; Author, Poems; Contributor, Articles, Magazines; Contributor, Articles, Newspapers **AW:** Grantee, Richardson Foundation (1967); Fellowship, Cornell Graduate School (1955-1956) **MEM:** Menlo Circus Club; General Society of Mayflower Descendants; National Society Daughters of the American Revolution; Peninsula Women's Network; Commonwealth Club; Overseas Press Club of America; Kappa Delta **MH:** Albert Nelson Marquis Lifetime Achievement Award (2017) **H:** Horseback riding and dressage; Tennis; Ballroom dancing **RE:** Protestant **ADD:** 1850 Oak Ave, Menlo Park, CA, 94025-5842

CONKLIN, DONALD RANSFORD, T: Pharmaceutical Executive (Retired) **I:** Pharmaceuticals **CN:** Schering-Plough Corporation **DOB:** 09/10/1936 **PB:** Bound Brook **SC:** NJ/USA **PT:** Walter Ransford Conklin; Dorothy Ann (Haase) Conklin **MS:** Married **SPN:** Elizabeth Heckman (2009); Louise Sealey (7/13/1960, Deceased 2005) **CH:** Elizabeth; Edward **ED:** Honorary PhD, Kean University (2006); Diplomate, Graduate Program for Management Development, Harvard University (1970); MBA, Rutgers, The State University of New Jersey (1961); BA, Williams College (1958) **C:** President of Health Care Products, Schering-Plough Corporation, Kenilworth, NJ (1994-1996); President of Pharmaceutical Operations, Schering-Plough Corporation, Kenilworth, NJ (1985-1994); Senior Vice President, International Headquarters, Schering-Plough Corporation, Kenilworth, NJ (1984-1996); Executive Vice President of Pharmaceutical Operations, Schering-Plough Corporation, Kenilworth, NJ (1984-1985); Group Vice President of Pharmaceutical Operations, Schering-Plough Corporation, Kenilworth, NJ (1983); Regional Director, President, Latin America Division, Schering-Plough Corporation, Miami, FL (1980-1983); Vice President of International Marketing, Schering-Plough Corporation, Kenilworth, NJ (1977-1979); Director of Marketing, Europe Division, Schering-Plough Corporation, Lucerne, Switzerland (1975-1976); Director of Marketing, Schering Corp. U.S.A. (Now Schering-Plough Corporation), Kenilworth, NJ (1970-1974) **CIV:** Vice Chair, Kean University Foundation Board (2001-2008) **MEM:** Ocean Reef Club, Key Largo, FL; Canoe Brook Country Club, Summit, NJ; Former Board Member, Ventiv Health, Vertex Pharmaceuticals **MH:** Albert Nelson Marquis Lifetime Achievement Award (2017) **H:** Tennis; Fishing **PA:** Independent **ADD:** 66 Youngs Rd, Basking Ridge, NJ, 07920

CONKLIN, GEORGE HENRY, T: Professor Emeritus, Sociologist, Educator **I:** Education/Educational Services **DOB:** 04/09/1941 **PB:** Dumont **SC:** NJ/USA **PT:** Richard Brown Conklin; Heloise Sealey Conklin **MS:** Married **SPN:** Verna Gibble (8/21/1965) **CH:** Heather; Wendy; Dawn **ED:** PhD, University of Pennsylvania (1971); AB, Colgate University (1963) **C:** President of the International Association of Torch Clubs, 2017-2020; Professor Emeritus of Sociology, North Carolina Central University, Durham, NC (1978-Present); President, Durham/Chapel Hill Chapter, International Association of Torch Clubs (2008-2010; 2015-2016); Professor Emeritus, North Carolina Central University (2008); Vice President, International Association of Torch Clubs (2007-2008); President, Durham-Chapel Hill Torch Club (2003-2004); Chair, Faculty Senate, North Carolina Central University (1999-2000); Associate Professor, Sweet Briar College (1974-1978); Assistant Professor, Syracuse University (1969-1974) **CR:** Trustee, Torch Foundation (2017-2018); Vice Chairman, Faculty Assembly, University of North Carolina (2002-2003) **CIV:** Planning Commissioner, Durham City-

County Planning Department (2000-2005); Airport Commissioner, Raleigh-Durham Airport Authority (1990-1999); Chair, Board of Adjustment, Durham City-County Planning Department (1984-1990) **CW:** Editor, "Sociation Today"(2003-2018); Contributor, Articles to Professional Journals, Chapters to Books and Educational Software **AW:** Sociology Award, "Sociation Today" (1998); Grantee, Computer-Based Instructional Materials; Grantee, National Science Foundation, Lilly Endowment (1982-1993); College Teaching Improvement Grantee, Fund for Improvement of Post-Secondary Education (FIPSE) (1982-1986); Research Grantee, American Institute of Indian Studies (1968); Fulbright Grantee, United States Educational Foundation in India (1963-1964) **MEM:** President, North Carolina Sociological Association (1998-1999); International Sociological Association; Southern Sociological Association; Webmaster, Editor, "Sociation Today" (2003-2018) **H:** Collecting antique phonographs **PA:** Liberal **RE:** Presbyterian **ADD:** 2905 Scuppernong Ln, Durham, NC, 27703

COOK, GRANT, T: Senior Counsel, Commercial Trial Lawyer **I:** Law and Legal Services **CN:** The Faubus Firm **PB:** Ft. Worth **SC:** TX/USA **PT:** Buster Cook; Lorene Cook **MS:** Divorced **CH:** Kelly; Kyle (Deceased) **ED:** LLB, Baylor Law School, Baylor University (1961); Undergraduate Coursework, Tulane University (1958) **CT:** Diploma, A.A. White Mediation Institute (Now A.A. White Dispute Resolution Center), University of Houston Law Center (2003) **C:** Senior Counsel, The Faubus Firm (2014-Present) **CR:** Texas Film Commission, Appointed by Governor Mark White (1986); Texas Judicial Council, Appointed by Governor Dolph Briscoe (1978-1982) **CW:** Contributor, Articles, Professional Journals **AW:** Fellowship, American College of Trial Lawyers (1983-Present); America's Most Honored Professional (2017); Best Lawyers in Texas, The Wall Street Journal (2017); Texas Super Lawyers, Texas Monthly (2006-2016); Houston's Top Lawyers, H Texas, Bayou City Publishing, LLC (2006); Houston's Top Lawyers, H Texas, Bayou City Publishing, LLC (2004); Texas Super Lawyers, Texas Monthly (2003-2004) **MEM:** Associate Member, American Board of Trial Advocates (2010-Present); Founding Member, School Law Section, State Bar of Texas (1970); Chairman, School Law Section, State Bar of Texas (1970); Houston Bar Association; The Bar Association of the Fifth Federal Circuit; New York State Bar Association **BAR:** New York (2007); Supreme Court of the United States (1970); United States Court of Appeals for the Eleventh Circuit (1963); United States Court of Appeals for the Fifth Circuit (1963); United States District Court for the Eastern District of Texas (1963); United States District Court for the Northern District of Texas (1963); United States District Court for the Southern District of Texas (1963); United States District Court for the Western District of Texas (1963); Texas (1961) **H:** Golf; Hunting quail **RE:** Methodist **BA:** 1001 Texas Ave Ste 1100, The Faubus Firm, Houston, TX, 77002 **URL:** http://www.faubusfirm.com/grant_cook.html

COOK, JAY D. MD, FAAM, T: Neurology Consultant **I:** Medicine & Health Care **CN:** Banner Health **PB:** Denver **SC:** CO/USA **MS:** Married **CH:** Two Children; Five Stepchildren **ED:** Coursework in Immunology, National Institutes of Health (1974-1976); Laboratory Training in Immunology, National Cancer Institute, National Institutes of Health (1974-1976); Fellow in Pediatric Neurology, Duke University Health System (1972-1973); Resident in Neurology, Duke University Health System (1971-1972); Resident in Pediatrics, Duke University Health System (1970-1971); Intern

in Pediatrics, Duke University Health System (1969-1970); MD, Duke University (1968); BS, Purdue University (1965) **CT:** Diplomate in Child Neurology, The American Board of Psychiatry and Neurology, Inc. (1977); Diplomate, The American Board of Pediatrics (1975); Licensed to Practice Medicine, State of Maryland (1974); Licensed to Practice Medicine, State of North Carolina (1971); Licensed to Practice Medicine, State of Texas **C:** Consultant Neurologist, Banner Health (2006-Present); Retired (2005) Interim Director of Child Neurology, The University of Texas Southwestern Medical Center (2002-2005); Clinical Professor of Neurology, The University of Texas Southwestern Medical Center (2001-2005); Assistant Medical Director, Institute of Metabolic Disease, Baylor University Medical Center at Dallas, Baylor Scott & White Health (1999-2001); Associate Professor, The University of Texas Medical Branch at Galveston (1993-1999); Director of Pediatric Neurology, The University of Texas Medical Branch at Galveston (1993-1999); Medical Staff, Children's Health (1993); Medical Director of Pediatrics, Dallas Rehabilitation Institute (Now Baylor Institute for Rehabilitation), Baylor Scott & White Health (1993); Professor of Pediatrics, College of Medicine, King Saud University (1992); Consultant Child Neurologist, King Faisal Specialist Hospital & Research Center (1991-1992); Consultant of Child Neurology, Texas Scottish Rite Hospital for Children (1990); Associate Professor of Clinical Neurology, The University of Texas Southwestern Medical Center (1983-1990); Director of Child Neurology, Texas Scottish Rite Hospital for Children (1978-1990); Chief of Neuromuscular Disease, Department of Neurology, Veterans Administration Hospital and University of Texas Health Science Center (Now The University of Texas Southwestern Medical Center) (1976-1983); Assistant Professor, Veterans Administration Hospital and University of Texas Health Science Center (Now The University of Texas Southwestern Medical Center) (1976-1983); Assistant Professor, Department of Pediatrics, Children's Health (1976-1979); Medical Investigator, Medical Neurology Branch, National Institute of Neurological and Communicative Disorders, National Institutes of Health (1975-1976); Clinical Associate, Medical Neurology Branch, National Institute of Neurological and Communicative Disorders, National Institutes of Health (1973-1976) **CR:** Consultant in Field **CIV:** Pharmacy Therapeutics Committee (2007-Present); Member, Advisory Board, International Foundation for Alternating Hemiplegia of Childhood (1997-2000); Committee to Review Research-related Financial Disclosures (1998-1999); Curriculum Committee, The University of Texas Medical Branch at Galveston (1997-1999); Quality Standards Subcommittee, The University of Texas Medical Branch at Galveston (1996-1999); Pharmacy and Therapeutics Committee (1995-1997); American Neurological Review Committee (1998); Chair, Carol Krusen Symposium (1978-1990); Dallas Intertribal Medical Committee **CW:** Physician Reviewer, National Medical Reviews (2000-2001); Contributor, Articles, Medical Journals **AW:** Honoree, Top Neurologist, IAHCP (2017); Honoree, Top Docs, U.S. News Report (2012); Honoree, Selected for Patient's Choice (2011-2012); Honoree, Selected for Top Docs, Phoenix, Arizona (2011-2012); Honoree, Selected as Physician of the Month, Cardon Children's Medical Center, Banner Health (2010); Honoree, Voted One of the "Top Docs," Phoenix, Arizona (2009); Honoree, Voted one of the Best Child Neurologists in Dallas (2004); Honoree, Voted One of the Best Doctors of America (1999, 2002-2003); Honoree, Outstanding Teacher, St. Vincent's Clinic (1997-1998); Featured Listee, The

Best Doctors in America - Central Region (1996-1997); Honoree, One of the Twenty Outstanding Individuals of Dallas, D-Magazine (1989); Honoree, One of Ten Outstanding Individuals in the Dallas Medical Community, Dallas Chamber of Commerce (1989); Recipient, Medical School Award (1969); Recipient, Scholarship, Duke University (1968-1969); Recipient, Hamilton Watch Award (1965); Recipient, President's Scholastic Award (1962-1964); Recipient, Various Research Grants **MEM:** American Medical Association (1992, 1999); Neurological Rehabilitation Society (1992); Professors of Child Neurology (1987); American Academy of Neurology (1979); Child Neurology Society (1977); Omicron Delta Kappa; Phi Eta Sigma **MH:** Albert Nelson Marquis Lifetime Achievement Award (2017) **ADD:** 2605 Cherry Sage Dr, Flower Mound, TX, 75022

COOK, QUENTIN, T: Church Administrator **I:** Religious **CN:** The Church of Jesus Christ of Latter-Day Saints **DOB:** 09/08/1940 **PT:** J. Vernon Cook; Bernice (Kimball) Cook **MS:** Married (11/30/1962) **SPN:** Mary Gaddie **CH:** Kathryn Cook Knight; Quentin Laurance; Joseph Vernon III **ED:** Honorary Doctor of Laws, Utah State University (2012); JD, Stanford University (1966); BS, Utah State University (1963) **C:** General Authority, The Church of Jesus Christ of Latter-Day Saints (1996-Present); Church Leader, The Church of Jesus Christ of Latter-Day Saints, Council of the Twelve, Salt Lake City, UT (2007); Vice Chairman, Sutter Health/ California Healthcare Systems, San Francisco, CA (1996); President, CEO, California Healthcare Systems, San Francisco, CA (1994-1995); Interim President, CEO, California Healthcare Systems, San Francisco, CA (1993-1994); Partner, Carr, McClellan, Ingersoll, Thompson & Horn, Burlingame, CA (1969-1993); Associate, Carr, McClellan, Ingersoll, Thompson & Horn, Burlingame, CA (1966-1969) **CIV:** Member, Board of Visitors, Brigham Young University Law School, Provo, UT (1994-1996); Lay Leadership Service, Local Latter Day Saints Church (1967-1996); Member, Advisory Board, Utah State University, Logan, UT (1985-1995); City Attorney, Pro Bono, Town of Hillsborough, California (1982-1993) **BAR:** California (1966) **BA:** 47 E. South Temple, Latter Day Saints Church, Salt Lake City, UT, 84150

COOK WIGGINS, CYNTHIA , I: Other **ED:** BA, North Texas State University (1969) **C:** Decorator **CW:** Painter **AW:** Inducted, Daughters of the American Revolution (Now National Society Daughters of the American Revolution (NSDAR)) (2016) **MEM:** Plein Air Artists Group

COOKE, SARA MULLIN, T: Daycare Administrator **I:** Education/Educational Services **DOB:** 12/29/1935 **PB:** Philadelphia **SC:** PA/USA **PT:** Charles Henry Graff; Elizabeth (Mullin) Brandt Graff **MS:** Divorced **SPN:** Peter Fischer Cooke (Married, 7/29/1963, Divorced, 7/1984) **CH:** Anna Cooke Woodward; Peter Fischer Junior; Elizabeth Cooke Haskins; Laina Cooke Driscoll; Sara Reynolds Lowe **ED:** BE in Child Education, Westchester State Teachers College (1956); AA, Bennett College (1955); BA, Madeira School (1953) **C:** Secretary Class, McLean, Virginia (2000-2018); Coordinator, Elderhostel Program, Landmarks Society (1992-1993); Coordinator, Master of Educational Ceremonies, Philadelphia Society for Preservation Landmarks (1991-1993); Fundraiser, Children's Hospital, Philadelphia (1989-1992); President, Women's Committee, Children's Hospital, Philadelphia (1987-2008); With, F.C.I. Marketing Co-ordinators Inc., New York City, New Canaan, CT (1980-1986); Teacher, Tarleton School, Devon, PA (1963-1964); Teacher, Chestnut Hill

Academy, Pennsylvania (1962-1963); Teacher, Sara Bircher's Kindergarten, Germantown, PA (1958-1962); Assistant to Teacher, 1st Grade, The Woodlyn School (1956-1958) **CR:** Member, Children's Hospital Christmas Boutique Benefit (2000-2017); Private Daycare and Doctor's Assistant (1994-2010); Private Day Caretaker, Special Care, Inc. (1988-2012) **CIV:** Volunteer, Trump Headquarters; Volunteer, McCain Headquarters; Founding Member, Supporter, Barnes Foundation (2015); Art Museum of Philadelphia (2012); Member, Episcopal Community Service (2007); Volunteer, Pediatrics Oncology Section, Children's Hospital of Philadelphia (2007); Teacher, Chestnut Hill Sunday School (2005-2013); Kindergarten Teacher, Sunday School (2004-2013); President, Volunteer, Political Fest in Laura Bush Library (2000); Volunteer, Republican National Convention (2000); Volunteer with Parents of Very Sick Children, Connelly Family Resource Center, Children's Hospital of Philadelphia (1999-2015); Co-Chairman, Benefit, St. Martin in the Fields, London (1997); Gimbel Award Committee (1994); Alternate Delegate, Republican National Convention (1992); Commonwealth Board, Medical College of Pennsylvania (1984-1999); Women's Board (1977-2015); Auxiliary Board, Children's Hospital of Philadelphia (1970-1976) **AW:** Volunteer of the Year, Children's Hospital (2010); Award, Blue Bell Republican Headquarters, McCain-Palin Campaign (2008); Nominee, Pennsylvania Society (2004); Silver Cup Award, Children's Hospital, Philadelphia (2002); Volunteer Service Award, Alumnae Association, Madeira School (1997-2018) **MEM:** Garden Committee, National Society of Colonial Dames (1988-Present); Health Representative, Pennsylvania Association of Hospital Auxiliaries; Lifetime Member, Pennsylvania Society; National Society of Colonial Dames of Pennsylvania; Pennsylvania Society Republicans; Philadelphia Cricket Club; Corbett for Governor, Blue Bell Headquarters; Corbett Toomey Campaign, Conshohocken Headquarters; Corbett Wolf Campaign for Governor; Romney Obama Campaign (2012); Chairman, Children's Hospital Botique Luncheon (2010-2015); Co-Chairman, Daisy Day Children's Hospital (2001); Class Secretary, Alumnae Association, Madeira School (1998-2018) **H:** Golf; Tennis; Antiques; Dog owner of Oliver; Animals **PA:** Republican **RE:** Episcopalian **ADD:** 20 Haws Lane G26, Flourtown, PA, 19031

COOPER, ALAN S., T: Of Counsel **I:** Law and Legal Services **CN:** Westerman Hattori Daniels & Adrian LLP **DOB:** 06/13/1942 **PB:** Louisville **SC:** Kentucky, USA **PT:** Rudey Cooper; Rosalie (Schwartz) Cooper **MS:** Married **SPN:** Linda Morguelan Klein (4/18/1999); Maxine Jacobs (8/13/1966, Deceased) **CH:** Lauren K.; Jennifer D. **ED:** JD, Vanderbilt University (1968); BA, Vanderbilt University (1964) **C:** Of Counsel, Wiley Rein LLP (2011-2015); Partner, Howrey LLP (2005-2011); Partner, Shaw Pittman Potts & Trowbridge, Washington, D.C., New York City, NY, Los Angeles, CA, London, England (1997-2005); Member, Board of Directors, Shareholder, Banner & Witcoff, Ltd., Washington, D.C., Chicago, IL, Boston, MA (1995-1997); Partner, Schyler, Banner, Birch, McKie & Beckett, Washington, D.C. (1974-1994); Associate, Schyler, Birch, Swindler, McKie & Beckett, Washington, D.C. (1972-1974); Associate, Browne, Schuyler & Beveridge and Browne, Beveridge & DeGrandi, Washington, D.C. (1968-1972); Law Clerk, United States District Court for the Middle District of Tennessee (1967-1968) **CR:** Adjunct Professor, Georgetown University Law Center (1985-2003); Adviser on Trademark Law to the United States Development to Diplomatic Conference on Revision of Paris Convention for

Protection of Industrial Property, Nairobi, Kenya (1981) **CW:** Author, Chapter on Ethics, "Strategic Practice Before the Trademark Trial and Appeal Board," ABA **MEM:** Faculty Member, National Institutes on Trademark Litigation, ABA (1978-1979); International Trademark Association; The District of Columbia Bar; Bar Association of the District of Columbia; Tennessee Bar Association; Bethesda Country Club **BAR:** Supreme Court of the United States (1980); United States Supreme Court of Appeals for the Federal Circuit (1975); The District of Columbia (1969); United States District Court District of Columbia (1969); Tennessee (1968) **MH:** Albert Nelson Marquis Lifetime Achievement Award (2017) **RE:** Jewish **BA:** 1250 Connecticut Ave NW Ste 850, Westerman Hattori Daniels & Adrian LLP, Washington, DC, 20036

COOPER, BYRON STANLEY, T: Internist **I:** Medicine & Health Care **CN:** Byron S. Cooper, MD PLLC **DOB:** 05/21/1947 **PB:** Washington **SC:** DC/USA **PT:** Joseph David Cooper; Ruth (Zeidner) Cooper **MS:** Married **SPN:** Jane Ann Kanter (February 5, 1978) **CH:** Joseph; Allison **ED:** MD, Washington University, St. Louis (1973); BA, Johns Hopkins University (1969) **CT:** Certification in Pulmonary Disease (1982); Certified in Internal Medicine, ABIM (1978) **C:** Clinical Professor, George Washington University (1981) **MEM:** Alternate Delegate, American Medical Association (2000-2004); President, Medical Society of DC (1998-1999); President, American College of Chest Physicians, DC Thoracic Society (1994); Fellow American College of Physicians **H:** Photography; Running; Computers **BA:** 2440 M Street N.W., Suite 810, Washington, DC, 20036 **ADD:** 1120 19th ST NW #200, Washington, DC, 20036

COOPER, THOMAS DAVID, T: Metallurgical Engineer, Consultant **I:** Mining & Metals **DOB:** 04/07/1932 **PB:** Dayton **SC:** OH/USA **PT:** Arnold Leroy Cooper; Edna Catherine (Guthrie) Cooper **MS:** Widowed **SPN:** Katherine Ann Ambrose (12/26/1953, Deceased) **CH:** Theresa Deborah; Michael Bruce; Stephen Jeffrey **ED:** MS in Metallurgical Engineering, Ohio State University (1964); BS in Metallurgical Engineering, University of Cincinnati (1955) **CT:** Registered Professional Engineer, Ohio; Certified Acquisition Professional, Air Force Level III **C:** Senior Program Manager, Universal Technology Corporation, Dayton, OH (1995-2014); Division Chief, Systems Support, United States Air Force Materials Laboratory, Wright-Patterson Air Force Base, Ohio (1991-1995); Branch Chief, Materials Integrity, United States Air Force Materials Laboratory, Wright-Patterson Air Force Base, Ohio (1976-1991); Section Chief, Branch Chief, Various Branches, United States Air Force Materials Laboratory, Wright-Patterson Air Force Base, Ohio (1961-1976); Project Engineer, Senior Project Engineer, United States Air Force Materials Laboratory, Wright-Patterson Air Force Base, Ohio (1956-1961); Junior Engineer, Westinghouse Electric Corporation, Pittsburgh, PA (1955-1956); United States Delegate, NATO Air Corps 82; Advisory Board Member, National Materials Advisory Board; Advisory Board Member, Engine Structural Integrity Program; Advisory Board Member, Army Stationing and Installation Plan **CR:** Presenter, Mehl Honor Lecturer, American Society for Nondestructive Testing (1991); Presenter in Field; Associate Fellow, American Institute of Aeronautics and Astronautics; Fellow, Advanced Technology Awareness Council **MIL:** Captain, U.S. Air Force Reserve (1956-1958) **CW:** Co-Editor, "Prevention of Structural Failure: The Role of Quantitative Nondestructive Evaluation"(1975); Co-Editor, "Oxide Dispersion Strengthening" (1966); Contributor, Chapters

to Books, Articles to Professional Journals **AW:** United States Air Force, Meritorious Civilian Service Award (1992); Arch T. Colwell Cooperative Engineering Medal, Society of Automotive Engineers (1992); Franklin Kolk Air Transport Award, Society of Automotive Engineers (1991); Dayton Area Outstanding Engineers and Scientists Award (1990); Distinguished Alumnus Award, University of Cincinnati, College of Engineering (1972); Certificate of Merit, Air Force Systems Service Award, Air Force Systems Command **MEM:** Honorary Member, Aerospace Materials Division, Society of Automotive Engineers (1995); Lifetime Member, Past Chairman, Advanced Technology Awareness Council, First Chairman of Materials Testing and Quality Control Division, American Society for Metals International; American Society of Nondestructive Testing; Chairman, Engineering Processes Subdivision, Society of Manufacturing Engineers; Chairman, Structural Materials Committee, American Institute of Metallurgical Engineers; Air Force Association; Honorary Member, Performance Review Board Member, Chairman, Aerospace Materials Division, Society of Automotive Engineers; Dayton Engineers Club; Tau Beta Pi; Air Force Dayton Chapter, Sigma Xi **ADD:** 542 Rader Drive, Vandalia, OH, 45377

COOPER MCCALL, MAXINE, T: Publisher, Minister, Educator, Writer **I:** Publishing **CN:** Western Piedmont Community College **PT:** Lloyd Edison Cooper; Minnie Belle (Rector) Cooper **MS:** Married **SPN:** Donald Jackson McCall (10/15/1960) **ED:** MA in English, Appalachian State University (1965); BS in English, Appalachian State University, Magna Cum Laude (1960) **C:** Owner, C&M Resources, Drexel, NC (1997-Present); Adjunct Faculty English Department, Western Piedmont Community College, Morganton, NC (1990-Present); Coordinator, Grades K-12, Burke Schools Coordinator for Language Arts, Foreign Language, Gifted Programs (1972-1990); Teacher, Administrator, Burke County Public Schools, Morganton, NC (1960-1990); English Teacher, Gifted Programs, Valdese and Drexel High School (1960-1971); English Teacher, Appalachian State University, Boone, NC (1959-1960) **CR:** Board of Directors, Warner Press (2010-Present); Christian Education Consultant, Conference Leader, Church of God Ministries, Anderson, IN (1982-Present); Board of Directors, Warner Press (2008); Consultant, Church Growth and Planting Board of Church Extension, Anderson, IN (1990-2001); Educational Consultant, Grades K-12, Burke County Public Schools, Morganton, NC (1960-1990) **CIV:** Member, Founding Board of Directors, North Carolina Delta Kappa Gamma Educational Foundation (2014-Present); Board of Directors, Warner Press (2010-Present); Co-Founder, Facilitator, Christians Broadcasting Hope, National Bible Conference, Western North Carolina (1981-Present); Guest Speaker, Various Church and Civic Organizations in Burke County, North Carolina (1971-Present); Co-Chair, North Carolina Delta Kappa Gamma Educational Foundation Committee (2011-2014); Member, Co-China Educational Foundation Committee (2010-2014); Member, North Carolina Delta Kappa Gamma Committee (2009-2011); Board of Directors, The History Museum of Burke County, Morganton, NC (2003-2009); Founding Board of Directors, History Museum of Burke County, Morganton, NC (2003-2009); Board of Directors, Warner Press (2007-2008); Board of Trustees, Anderson University, Indiana (1988-2003); Task Force Implementation Team, Area Administrator Association, Church of God (1997-1998); Governance and Policy Task Force and Implementation Team, Area Administrator Association Church of God

(1988-1993); Chairperson, Area Administrator Association, Church of God (1988); Secretary, Area Administrator Association, Church of God, Anderson, IN (1984-1987); State Representative, Consultant, Long-Range Planning, Church of God (1984) **CW:** Author, Graphic Designer, "They Won't Hang A Woman," Heritage Edition (2008); Editor, Graphic Designer, "Silver Wings and a Gold Star" (2003); Co-Author, Graphic Designer, "Posthumorously Berk" (2000); Author, "Etched in Granite" (1999); Author, Graphic Designer, "Guidebook to the Trail of Faith" (1998); Editor, "A Handful of Stars" (1996); Author, "What Mean These Stones?" (1993); Author, "They Won't Hang a Woman" (1972) **AW:** Willie Parker Peace History Book Award, North Carolina Society of Historians (2008); Barringer Award, North Carolina Society of Historians (2008); President's Award (2005); Willie Parker Peace History Book Award (2005); Willie Parker Peace History Book Award, North Carolina Society of Historians (2003); Willie Parker Peace History Book Award, North Carolina Society of Historians (1993) **MEM:** Board of Directors, North Carolina Society Historians (2007-Present); President, Delta Kappa Gamma (2008-2012); Secretary, Delta Kappa Gamma (2004-2008) **H:** Travel; Theater; Films; Antiques; History **RE:** Church Of God **ADD:** PO Box 487, Drexel, NC, 28619

COPELAND, ROBERT G., **T:** Lawyer **I:** Law and Legal Services **DOB:** 03/15/1941 **PB:** San Diego **SC:** CA/USA **PT:** Glenn Howard Copeland; Luella Louise (Schmid) Copeland **MS:** Married **SPN:** Lynne Newman (10/10/1993); Harriet S. Smith (6/27/1964-1977) **CH:** Katherine Louise; Matthew Robert; Zachary Newman **ED:** JD, University of Southern California Law School (1966); AB in Political Science, Occidental College (1963) **CT:** Certified in Advance Mediation, National Conflict Resolution Center **C:** Partner, Sheppard Mullin Richter & Hampton LLP (2008-Present); Partner, Duane Morris LLP (2004-2008); Partner, Luce, Forward Hamilton & Scripps, LLP (1995-2004); Partner, Gray, Cary, Ware & Freidenrich, San Diego, CA (1966-1995) **CIV:** Founder, The Thomas C. Ackerman Foundation (1995-Present); Co-Chair, Advisory Board, Scripps Green Hospital (2009-2012); President, The Thomas C. Ackerman Foundation (1995-2012); Board Member, San Diego Yacht Club Sailing Foundation; Board Member, Any Body Can Youth Foundation; Board Member, Sailing Events Association of San Diego **CW:** Contributor, California State Bar Business Law Section Corporation Guide; Contributor, ABA Business Law Section Manual on Acquisition Review, Model Stock Purchase and Model Asset Purchase Agreements; Contributor, Chapters, Books; Contributor, Articles, Professional Journals; Frequent Speaker in Field **AW:** Named, Super Lawyer for San Diego (2007-Present); Named, Best Lawyers in San Diego, San Diego Magazine (2001-Present); Named, The Best Lawyers in America (1987-Present); Named, San Diego 500-The Book of Influential Business Leaders (2016); AV Preeminent Rating, Martindale Hubbell **MEM:** Mergers & Acquisitions Committee, Business Law Section, ABA (1987-2012); The State Bar of California; San Diego County Bar Association; Firm Representative, Chairmen's Roundtable **BAR:** United States District Court Southern District of California (1967); State of California (1966) **MH:** Albert Nelson Marquis Lifetime Achievement Award (2017) **H:** Shooting; Fly fishing; Hiking; Racquetball **ADD:** 13 Lake Helix Dr, La Mesa, CA, 91941 **URL:** https://www.sheppardmullin.com/rcopeland

CORINTHIOS, MICHAEL JEAN GEORGES, **T:** Electrical Engineer **I:** Engineering **CN:** Polytechnique Montreal **DOB:** 01/19/1941 **PB:** Cairo **SC:** Egypt **PT:** Jean George Corinthios; Gisele Michel (Cabbabe) Corinthios **MS:** Married **SPN:** Maria Scigalski (11/18/1967) **CH:** Angela; Gisele; John **ED:** PhD, University of Toronto (1971); Master of Applied Science, University of Toronto (1968); BSc, Ain Shams University, Cairo, Egypt (1962); Coursework, Leonardo Da Vinci Art Institute, Cairo, Egypt (1952-1956) **C:** Professor, Polytechnique Montreal (1977-Present); Assistant Professor, Polytechnique Montreal, Montreal, Quebec, Canada (1971-1974); Engineer, Litton Systems Canada (Now Northrop Grumman Corporation), Toronto, Canada (1968-1969); Engineer, Bell Canada, Toronto, Ontario, Canada (1965-1966); Engineer, Radio Transmission, Abu Zaabal, Cairo, Egypt (1962-1965) **CR:** President, Corinthian Games Ltd., Montreal, Canada (1980-Present); International Conference on Electrical, Electronic, and Computer Engineering, Ain Shams University, Cairo, Egypt (2004); Invited Professor, National Technical University of Athens, Greece (1998-1999); Academy Visitor, Imperial College of Science, Technology and Medicine, London, England (1992-1993); Chairman, Second International Spectral Workshop, Montreal, Canada (1986); Visiting Scientist, University of Nice Sophia Antipolis, France (1979-1980); Speaker, Sixth International Conference on Artificial Intelligence, American University, Cairo, Egypt **CW:** Author, "Hypercubes, Kronecker Products and Sorting in Digital Signal Processing" (2016); Author, "Signals, Systems, Transforms and Digital Signal Processing with MATLAB" (2009); Inventor, Ministers Chess, "New Laplace Z and Fourier Related Transforms," Proceedings of the Royal Society A, Mathematical, Physical & Engineering Sciences, Volume 463 (2007); Author, "Louis Bruens" (1995); Author, "Paintings Reproduced in Guide Vallee" (1993); Author, "Analyse des Signaux Ecole Polytechnique" (1982); Author, "How to Patent Your Invention" (1971); Author, More than 60 Scientific Papers; Contributor, Chapters to Books; Contributor, Numerous Papers to Scientific and Professional Journals **AW:** Nominated, Achievement Medal, Institute of Electrical Engineers (Now The Institution of Engineering and Technology) (2005); Recipient, First Prize, Art Competition, Montreal Chapter, The New York Academy of Sciences (1979); Mary H. Beatty Fellow, University of Toronto (1969) **MEM:** Lifetime Fellow, IEEE; ITT, Inc.; Institute of Electrical Engineers (Now The Institution of Engineering and Technology) **ADD:** 4488 Rue Sherbrooke Ouest, Westmount, QC, Canada, H3Z 1E6

CORMIER, JASON L., **T:** Neurosurgeon **I:** Medicine & Health Care **CN:** Acadiana Neurosurgery **C:** Neurosurgeon, Acadiana Neurosurgery, PatientPop Inc. **CR:** Owner, Interval Training Center, Orangetheory Fitness **CIV:** Affiliate, Numerous Homeless Societies **MEM:** Congress of Neurological Surgeons; American Association of Neurological Surgeons; Louisiana State Medical Society; Lafayette Parish Medical Society; American College of Surgeons; Pituitary Network Association; North American Neuromodulation Society; International Council of Motorsport Sciences; International Convention for the Safety of Life at Sea; Subcortical Surgery Group **BA:** 1103 Kaliste Saloom Rd Ste 204, Acadiana Neurosurgery, PatientPop Inc., Lafayette, LA, 70508 **URL:** http://www.motorsportssafetygroup.com

CORPUZ, LAURA BALATBAT, **T:** Interlibrary Loan Coordinator, Writer **I:** Writing and Editing **CN:** Bradley University Library **DOB:** 08/14/1943 **PB:** Hagonoy **SC:** Philippines **PT:** Igmedio Libao Balatbat; Sofia Garcia Balatbat **MS:** Married **SPN:** Ricarte Santos Corpuz (10/25/1969) **CH:** Alona Corpuz Dawson; Allan Balatbat Corpuz; Alyse Corpuz Ringenberg **ED:** LAS, Illinois Central College, East Peoria, IL (1983); BS in Elementary Education, National Teachers College, Manila, Philippines (1966) **CT:** Certified K-9 Teacher, State of Illinois (1974) **C:** Interlibrary Loan Coordinator, Bradley University Library, Peoria, IL (1978-Present); Interlibrary Loan Assistant, Illinois Valley Library Systems, Peoria, IL (1990-1992); Music Teacher YWCA Peoria, IL (1969-1978); Teacher, Philippine Public School, Philippines (1966-1969) **CR:** Charter Member, National Women History Museum (2014-Present); Member, National Association of Professional Women (2011-Present); Asian Pacific Islander Speaker, Federal Correctional Institution, Pekin, IL (2016); International Speaker, Bensenville Home Society Adoption Agency, Bensenville, IL (1995-2015); Coordinator, Cultural Booth and Fashion Show coordinator, IGNITE PEORIA Annual Event, Filipino-American Society of Central Illinois; Past President, Advisor, Peoria Area Friends of International Students, Bradley University; Treasurer, Membership Co-Chairperson, WCBU FM 89.9 **CIV:** Board Member, Filipino-American Society of Central Illinois (2012-Present); Volunteer Reader & Editor, WCBU 89.9, Peoria Public Radio (1990-Present); Coordinator, Glencoe McGraw Hill (1992-1993); St. Vincent de Paul Parish Peoria, IL; Alzheimer's Disease Research; American Bible Society; American Diabetes Association; American Heart Association; American Indian Relief Council; American Legion National Headquarters; AMVETS National Science Foundation; Boys Town; Braille Books for Blind Children; Capuchin Franciscans; Carl Farley's Catholic Relief Services; Christian Appalachian Project; Companions of St. Anthony, Covenant House, Cross Catholic Outreach; Disabled Veterans National Foundation; Easter Seals; Feeding North America's Hungry Children; Franciscan Apostolic Sisters; Franciscan Friars; Help Hospitalized Veterans, George Bush Presidential Center; Help the Vets; March of Dimes; Memorial Sloan Kettering Cancer Center; Maryknoll Fathers and Brothers; Miraculous Medal; National Association of Blind Veterans, National Federation of the Blind; National Shrine of St. Jude; Nationwide Children's Hospital; Northern Plains Reservation; Paralyzed Veterans of America; Priests for Life; Province of St. Mary; Sacred Heart Southern Mission; Salisian Mission; Shriner's Hospital for Children; SmileTrain; St. Joseph's Indian School; St. Labre Indian School; Society of the Divine Savior; Society of the Little Flowers; United Service Organization; Veterans of Foreign Wars; Wounded Warrior Project **CW:** Co-Author, "Filipino Pagbasa at Pagsulat sa Piling Larangan Sining," C&E Publishing Inc. (2017); Author, "Remembering Rizal Voices from the Diaspora" (2011) **AW:** Recipient, Outstanding President Award, Filipino-American Society of Central Illinois (2011) **MEM:** Treasurer, Peoria Area Friends of International Students (2013-Present); Board Member, Filipino-American Society of Central Illinois (2012-Present); Board Member, Peoria Area Friends of International Students (1989-Present); President, Filipino-American Society of Central Illinois (2008-2011) **MH:** Distinguished Humanitarian (2017) **H:** Writing poetry; Crocheting; Knitting; Flower arranging; Gardening **RE:** Roman Catholic **BA:** 1501 W. Bradley Avenue, Bradley University Library, Peoria, IL, 61625 **ADD:** 609 Countryside Dr, Germantown Hills, IL, 61548

CORROTHERS, HELEN GLADYS, T: Criminal Justice Consultant **I:** Law and Legal Services **DOB:** 03/19/1937 **PB:** Montrose **SC:** AR/USA **PT:** Thomas Curl; Christene (Farley) Curl **SPN:** Edward Corrothers (12/17/1968, Divorced 1983) **CH:** Michael Edward **ED:** Postgraduate Coursework, California Coast University (1981-Present); Graduate, Institute Criminal Justice, Executive Center for Continuing Education, University of Chicago (1973); Graduate, Officer Leadership School, Women's Army Corps School (1965); BS in Business Administration Management, Roosevelt University (1965); AA in Liberal Arts, Arkansas Baptist College, Magna Cum Laude (1955) **C:** Criminal Justice Consultant (1996-Present); Fellow, United States Department of Justice, Washington D.C. (1992-1995); Commissioner, United States Sentencing Commission, Washington D.C. (1985-1991); Commissioner, United States Parole Commission, Burlingame, CA (1983-1985); Superintendent, Women's Unit, Arkansas Department of Correction, Pine Bluff, AR (1971-1983); Social Interviewer, Arkansas Department of Correction, Grady, AR (1970-1971); Director, Housing, Giessen Depot, Germany (1967-1969) **CR:** Instructor, Women and Crime, University of Maryland, College Park, MD (1994); Board of Directors, Volunteers of America (1985-1994); Member, United States Attorney General's Correctional Policy Study Team (1987); Board of Directors, Volunteers in Courts (1979-1983); Member, American/Canadian Study Team, Mexico Penal System, American Correctional Association, Islas Marias, Mexico (1981); Member, Board of Visitation, Jefferson-Lincoln Circuit Court, 6th Division, Juvenile, Pine Bluff, AR (1978-1981); Instructor, Corrections, University of Arkansas Pine Bluff (1976-1979); Member, Crimes and Law Enforcement, Arkansas Commission (1975-1978) **CIV:** Board of Directors, Baptist Mission Foundation of Maryland/Delaware, Columbia, MD (1993-1998); Member, National Advisory Board, Department of Criminal Justice, Xavier University, Cincinnati, OH (1993-1997); Board of Directors, Committee Against Spouse Abuse (1982-1983); Member, Arkansas Commission on Status of Women (1976-1978); Former Board Member, Volunteers of America; Sunday School Teacher **MIL:** Captain, U.S. Army (1969); Chief Military Personnel, U.S. Army, Fort Meyer, VA (1965-1967); U.S. Army (1956) **AW:** Excellence Award, American Chaplains Association (2009); Appreciation Certificate, Office for Victims of Crime (1994); E.R. Cass Correctional Achievement Award, American Correctional Association (1993); Testimonial for Service to the Federal Judiciary Administrative Office of Courts (1991); Outstanding Victim Advocacy Award, National Center for Victims of Crime (1991); William H. Hastie Award, The National Association of Blacks in Criminal Justice (1986); Correctional Service Award, Volunteers of America (1984); Outstanding Woman of Achievement Award, Station KATV-TV, Little Rock, AR (1981); Woman of Achievement Award, Arkansas Press Women (1980); Human Relations Award, Arkansas Education Association (1980) **MEM:** Member, Ethics Committee, American Correctional Association (2003-Present); Member, Past President Council, American Correctional Association (1998-Present); Member, Delaware Assembly, American Correctional Association (1993-Present); Chairman, Retirees Committee, American Correctional Association (2005-2007); Member, President's Field Advisory Task Force, American Correctional Association (2005-2007); Chairman, Correctional Awards Committee, American Correctional Association (2001-2005); Chairman, Research Council, American Correctional Association (1997-2000);

President, American Correctional Association (1990-1992); Treasurer, American Correctional Association (1980-1986); Vice President, American Correctional Association (1986-1988); Local Parliamentarian, Delta Sigma Theta (1983); Local Secretary, Delta Sigma Theta (1976-1979); NAFE; National Organization of Hispanics in Criminal Justice; American Society of Criminology; National Council on Crime and Delinquency; Arkansas Association of Chiefs of Police; North American Association of Wardens & Superintendents; Honorary Member, Arkansas Sheriffs' Association **MH:** Distinguished Humanitarian (2017) **H:** Reading; Music **RE:** Baptist **ADD:** 3104 Beaver Wood Ln, Silver Springs, MD, 20906

COTA, HAROLD MAURICE, T: Professor Emeritus **I:** Education/Educational Services **CN:** California Polytechnic State University **MS:** Single **SPN:** Judy (1959, Deceased 2017) **CH:** Michael; Becky; Cindy **ED:** PhD in Chemical Engineering, The University of Oklahoma, Norman, OK (1966); MS in Chemical Engineering, Northwestern University, Evanston, IL (1961); BS in Chemical Engineering, University of California, Berkeley (1959) **CT:** Diplomate, American Academy of Environmental Engineers and Scientists; Registered Engineer, State of California **C:** Professor Emeritus, California Polytechnic State University, San Luis Obispo, CA (2005-Present); Educator Engineering, California Polytechnic State University, San Luis Obispo, CA (1966-2005); Research Engineer, Lockheed Martin Corporation, Sunnyvale, CA (1960-1962); Teaching Assistant, The University of Oklahoma, Norman, OK (1962-1966) **CR:** Assistant Project Engineer, FMC Corporation (1959); Affiliate, San Diego Gas & Electric (1955-1958) **CIV:** Chairman, Research Screening Committee, California Air Resources Board (1996-Present); Sponsor Representative, Troop 303, Boy Scouts of America (1990-2000); Member, Scientific Review Committee, BACT, South Coast Air Quality Management District (1994-1996); Member, Research Screening Committee, California Air Resources Board (1985-1995); Member, Board of Directors, Environmental Research Foundation (1978-1992); Member, Regional Water Quality Control Board, State of California (1970-1984); Chairman, Regional Water Quality Control Board, State of California (1976-1977); Scout Master, Troop 7, Boy Scouts of America; Board Member, California Research Committee **AW:** Charles W. Gruber Association Leadership Award, Air & Waste Management Association (2007); Lyman A. Ripperton Award, Air Pollution Control Association; Distinguished Educator Professor Achievement **MEM:** Fellow, Air & Waste Management Association; American Institute of Chemical Engineers; American Academy of Environmental Engineers and Scientists; Institute of Noise Control Engineering; Board for Professional Engineers, Land Surveyors, and Geologists, State of California **MH:** Albert Nelson Marquis Lifetime Achievement Award (2017) **RE:** Methodist **ADD:** 1210 Woodside Dr, San Luis Obispo, CA, 93401

COX, BARBARA, T: Physical Therapist **I:** Health, Wellness and Fitness **CN:** Self-Employed **ED:** BS in Physical Therapy, University of Texas at Austin (1960); Diploma, Calhoun High School (1957) **C:** Physical Therapist, Independent Contract P.T. (1961-2013) **ADD:** 3328 Tuckaleechee Pike, Maryville, TN, 37803 **URL:** https://www.linkedin.com/in/barbara-cox-3b094260

COX, MARGARET PHD, T: Educator **I:** Education/Educational Services **CN:** King's College London **DOB:** 07/17/1939 **PB:** London **SC:** England **PT:**

Edgar Horace Samuel; Winifred Olive (Foyle) Samuel **MS:** Single **SPN:** Jack Cox, (2/23/1963, Deceased 5/1986) **CH:** Simon Francis; Nicholas William; Katherine Margaret Jacqueline **ED:** PhD in Atomic Physics, University of London (1966); BSc in Experimental Physics, University of London (1961) **CT:** Certified Chartered Physicist (1996) **C:** Professorial Fellow, The University of Melbourne (2004-Present); Professor Emerita, Information Technology in Education, Department of Education and Professional Studies, Dental Institute, King's College London (2004-Present); Professor, Information Technology in Education, King's College London (1998-2004); Lecturer to Senior Lecturer, King's College London (1982-1998); Research Fellow to Senior Research Fellow, Surrey University, Guildford, England (1972-1981); Research Officer, UCL (1964-1965) **CR:** Member, Independent Advisory Unit for Computer Based Learning, Hatfield, England (1995-Present); Chair-Person, Board of Trustees, Independent Advisory Unit for Computer Based Learning, Hatfield, England (2003-2010); Vice President, Chairman, Advisory Unit Trust, England (1999-2010) **CIV:** Active, Liberal Democratic Party, Guildford, England (1975-Present); President, National Conference University Professors (2014-2018) **CW:** Editorial Board Member, "Generic Robotics" (2011-Present); Educational Consultant, "Generic Robotics" (2011-Present); Editorial Board Member, "International Journal for Science Education" (1997-Present); Editorial Board Member, "Journal for Computer Assisted Learning" (1985-Present); Contributor, Chapters, Books; Contributor, Over 200 Articles, Professional Journals; Contributor, Official Reports; Contributor, Educational Software Packs **AW:** Honoree, Professorial Fellow, The University of Melbourne (2003-Present); Honoree, Appointed Visiting Professor, University of Portsmouth (2017); Recipient, Lifetime Achievement Award, NAACE (2017); Recipient, Lifelong Fellowship, Mirandanet (2013); Recipient, BETT Award (2012); Recipient, Research Project of the Year Award, King's College London (2012); Recipient, Lifelong Fellowship in Information Technology, Teacher Education Association (2012); Selectee, Celebrating Social Science Project, Economic and Social Research Council (2011); Recipient, Medical Futures Awards (2011); Recipient, Fellowship, King's College London (2011); Honoree, Runner Up, STELi Excellence in Education Award (2010); Recipient, Lifelong Fellowship, NAACE (2006); Honoree, Officer of the Order of the British Empire (2001); Recipient, Percy Abbot Prize (1961) **MEM:** International Association for Dental Research (2014-Present); President, National Conference of University Professors (2013-Present); Institution Member, Association for Dental Education in Europe (2005-Present); Fellow, Institute of Physics (2003-Present); American Educational Research Association (1990-Present); British Education Research Association (1985-Present); Institute of Physics (1963-Present); British Computer Society's Expert Panel on ICT Education (1985-2013); British Computer Society's Strategy Committee (2004-2008); Founding Member, National Energy Education Forum (1993-1998); Founding Member, London Mental Models Group (1986-1997); Lifetime Member, Society for Information Technology and Teacher Education; Committee on International Physics Education; Lifetime Member, RSPCA; Guildford Opera Company; Godalming Operatic Society **H:** Singing opera; Dance; Piano; Swimming; Skiing; Philately **PA:** Liberal Democrat **RE:** Anglican Church of England **ADD:** 17 Clandon Rd, The Old Vicarage, Guildford, United Kingdom, GU1 2DR

CRAFT, EDMUND COLEMAN JR., **T:** Automotive Parts Manufacturing Executive (Retired) **I:** Automotive **DOB:** 12/23/1939 **PB:** Plainfield **SC:** NJ/USA **PT:** Edmund Coleman Craft; Ruth Irene (Morrell) Craft **MS:** Married **SPN:** Gail Christensen **CH:** Edmund Coleman III; Elisabeth Gordon; William Todd **ED:** Coursework, Graduate Executive Program, University of Minnesota (1984); Postgraduate Coursework, Syracuse University (1963-1964); BS, Lycoming College (1963) **C:** Retired (2001); Senior Advisor, Global Aftermarket (2000-2001); Vice President, Donaldson Company, Inc., Minneapolis, MN (1983-2000); Director, Hydraulics Division, BorgWarner Inc., Wooster, OH (1979-1983); Vice President, Hydraulics Division, BorgWarner Inc., Wooster, OH (1975-1979); Employee, BorgWarner Inc., Letchworth, Hertfordshire, England (1970-1975); Administrative Assistant to Chairman, BorgWarner Inc., Chicago, IL (1969-1970); Employee, BorgWarner Inc., Detroit, MI **CIV:** Executive Committee, Junior Achievement of the Upper Midwest (1994-2000); Board of Directors, Junior Achievement of the Upper Midwest (1993-2000); Division Chairman, United Way of Wayne and Holmes Counties, Wooster, OH (1974) **MEM:** Vice President, Beaufort Rowing Club (2012-2014); Board Member, Beaufort Rowing Club (2012); Board of Directors, Filter Manufacturers Council (1991-2000); Chairman, Filter Manufacturers Council (1989-1991); Vice Chairman, Filter Manufacturers Council (1985-1989); Dataw Island Yacht Club **MH:** Albert Nelson Marquis Lifetime Achievement Award (2017) **H:** Golfing **PA:** Republican **RE:** Presbyterian **ADD:** 1025 Curisha Point N, Saint Helena Island, SC, 29920

CRAGG, GORDON MITCHELL, **T:** Special Volunteer **I:** Medicine & Health Care **CN:** National Cancer Institute **DOB:** 09/04/1936 **PB:** Cape Town **SC:** South Africa **PT:** Ernest Lynn Cragg; Doris Jessie (Mitchell) Cragg **MS:** Married **SPN:** Jacqueline Claire Tuers (12/30/1966) **ED:** DPhil, Oxford University, England (1963); BSc, Rhodes University, with Honors, Grahamstown, South Africa (1956) **C:** Chief, Natural Products Branch, National Cancer Institute, Frederick, MD (1989-2004); Chemist, National Cancer Institute, Bethesda, MD (1988-1989); Expert, Natural Products Branch, National Cancer Institute, Bethesda, MD (1984-1987); Assistant to Director, Cancer Research Institute (Now Center for Convergence of Physical Science and Cancer Biology), Arizona State University (1980-1984); Senior Research Chemist, Cancer Research Institute, (Now Center for Convergence of Physical Science and Cancer Biology), Arizona State University (1979-1980); Senior Lecturer, University of Cape Town (1973-1979); Senior Lecturer, University of South Africa, Pretoria, South Africa (1966-1972); Scientific Research Officer, National Chemical Research Laboratory, Council for Scientific and Industrial Research, Pretoria, South Africa (1965) **CW:** Co-Author, "Biosynthetic Products for Cancer Chemotherapy" (1985); Author, "Organoboranes in Organic Synthesis" (1973); Contributor, Various Articles to Professional Journals **AW:** Four Merit Awards, National Institutes of Health [1991, 2004 (2), 2010]; Honorary Member, American Society of Pharmacognosy (2003); William L. Brown Award for Plant Genetic Resources, Missouri Botanical Garden (2006); Medalha Reitor Martins Filho, Federal University of Ceara, Fortaleza, Brazil (2006); Fellow, American Society of Pharmacognosy (2008); Old Rhodian Award, Rhodes University, South Africa (2008); Doctor of Science Honoris Causa, Rhodes University (2010); Norman R. Farnsworth Excellence in Botanical Research Award, American Botanical Council

(2013) **MEM:** President, The American Society of Pharmacognosy (1998-1999); American Chemical Society; The American Society of Pharmacognosy; International Union of Pure and Applied Chemistry; American Association for the Advancement of Science; Phytochemical Society of North America; South African Chemical Institute; Society for Economic Botany **RE:** United Methodist Church **ADD:** 552 Russell Ave, Gaithersburg, MD, 20877

CRAKES, GARY, **T:** Professor Emeritus **I:** Education/Educational Services **CN:** Southern Connecticut State University **DOB:** 07/02/1953 **PB:** Southington **SC:** CT/USA **PT:** Harry Fremont; Frances Katherine (Koth) Crakes **MS:** Married **SPN:** Deborah Jean MacArthur (August 14, 1976) **CH:** Andrew David; Jeffrey Alan; Timothy Scott **ED:** PhD in Economics, University of Connecticut (1984); MA in Economics, University of Connecticut (1976); BA in Economics, Central Connecticut State University (1975) **C:** Professor Emeritus, Southern Connecticut State University (2011-Present); Professor, Southern Connecticut State University, New Haven (1989-2011); Chairman, Department of Economics and Finance, Southern Connecticut State University, New Haven (1991-1996); Associate Professor, Southern Connecticut State University, New Haven (1985-1989); Visiting Professor, Health Center, School of Dental Medicine, University of Connecticut, Farmington (1988); Assistant Professor, Southern Connecticut State University, New Haven (1980-1985); Instructor, University of Connecticut, Hartford (1979-1980); Research Assistant, Health Center, University of Connecticut, Farmington (1976-1979) **CR:** President, Maher, Crakes & Associates, Cheshire, CT (1987-Present); Economic Expert Witness **CIV:** Member, State of Connecticut Senior Economist Examination Committee, Hartford (1987) **CW:** Contributor, Articles, Professional Journals **AW:** Honored for Pro Bono Work on Behalf of World Trade Center Victim Families, Association of Trial Lawyers of America (2004); Schools of Business Outstanding Teacher Award (1998); University Teacher of the Year Award (1987); Richard D. Irwin Fellow, Irwin Publication Co., Homewood, IL (1983-1984); Fellow, University of Connecticut (1983) **MEM:** American Association of University Professors; American Economic Association; Eastern Economic Association; National Association of Forensic Economics; Omicron Delta Epsilon **H:** Golf; Fishing **PA:** Democrat **ADD:** 860 Ward Lane, Cheshire, CT, 06410

CRAWLEY, CHERYL, **T:** Educational Leadership Consultant, Superintendent (Retired) **I:** Education/Educational Services **CN:** Educational Leadership **SC:** USA **PT:** Donald Schultze; Margaret Schultze **MS:** Married **SPN:** Edward Marckx (3/23/1996) **CH:** Damara Crawley Chambers **ED:** PhD, University of California, Berkeley (2008); MA, California State University, East Bay, Hayward, CA (1976); BS, Montana State University, Bozeman (1965) **CT:** Certified Superintendent, States of Montana and Oregon; Standard Administrator and Principal, States of Montana and Oregon; Teacher and Community College Instructor, States of California and Montana; Independent Contractor License, State of Montana **C:** Educational Leadership Consultant, Personal Coaching for New Superintendents and Principals (2013-Present); Superintendent of Schools, Great Falls Public Schools (2007-2013); Superintendent of Schools, Ross Valley, Marin County, California (2004-2007); Superintendent of Schools, The Dalles, Oregon (1997-2004); Superintendent of Public Schools, Joseph, OR (1994-1997); Director of Student Services, Salem - Keizer School District, Salem, OR (1986-1994); Assistant Superintendent,

Hardin, Crow Agency, Fort Smith Public Schools (1983-1986); Teaching Assistant, Departments of Anthropology and Linguistics, University of California, Berkeley (1982); Director of Bilingual Education and Federal Programs, Hardin, Crow Agency, Fort Smith Schools, Montana (1978-1982); Research Consultant, Social Science Research Group, Xerox Corporation (1977); Teaching Assistant, Departments of Anthropology and Linguistics, University of California, Berkeley (1976-1978); Work-Study, Department of Anthropology, California State University, East Bay, Hayward, CA (1974-1976); Caseworker, Alameda County Welfare Department, Oakland, CA (1973-1974); Manager, Customer Service and Special Order, US Navy Exchange, Taiwan, Taipei, Taiwan (1970-1973); Accountant, Non-appropropriated Fund, Headquarters, US Army Europe, Heidelberg, Germany (1966-1969); Clerk-Typist for Commander in Chief, Headquarters, US Army Europe, Heidelberg, Germany (1966) **CR:** Member of the Board, Montana Quality Schools Coalition (2008-2013); Academic Affairs Committee, University of Great Falls, Great Falls, MT (2008-2013); California Governor's High Achieving School Districts Summit (2006); Board Member, Marin County Special Education Local Area Plan (2006); Chairman, Confederation of Oregon School Administrators Resolutions Committee (2002-2004); Chairman, Oregon Association of School Executives Legislative Issues Committee (2000-2001); Member (1998-2003); Leadership America, Class of 1997 (1997); Co-President, Mid-Willamette Valley Region, Oregon Association of Central Office Administrators, Confederation of Oregon School Administrators (1992-1994); President, Mid-Willamette Valley Region, Oregon Association of Central Office Administrators, Confederation of Oregon School Administrators (1990-1992); Oregon Governor's Task Force for Long Range Plan for Developmental Disabilities Services in Oregon (1987-1988); Keynote Speaker, Montana Association for Bilingual Education (1987); Conference Chair, Montana Association for Bilingual Education (1981)' Montana Association for Bilingual Education (1979-1985); Member, Indian Bilingual Advisory Council, Plains Region (1979-1981); Colloquium Participant, Confronting the Myths About Bilingual Education, Office of Bilingual Education and Minority Languages Affairs, United States Department of Education, Washington, D.C.; Various Leadership Institutes **CIV:** Member, Rotary International (1994-Present); President, Rotary Club of Great Falls, Montana (2014-2015); Western States Affiliate Board, American Heart Association (2009-2013); Board of Health, Cascade County and City of Great Falls, Montana (2007-2013); Board Member, Economic Development Authority, Great Falls, MT (2007-2013); Senior Examiner, Baldridge National Quality Award, Department of Commerce, Washington, D.C. (2006); Delegate, Oregon Economic Summit (2003-2004); Oregon Business Council (2002-2003); Examiner, Baldridge National Quality Award, Department of Commerce, Washington, D.C. (2001-2005); Rotary Area Representative, Columbia Gorge Region, Rotary District 5100 (2001-2004); President, Rotary Club of The Dalles, Oregon (1998-1999); The Dalles Area Chamber of Commerce, Government Affairs Committee, The Dalles, Oregon (1997-2004); Leadership America, Washington, D.C. (1997); Member, Rotary Club of The Dalles, Oregon (1994-2004); Treasurer, Board of Directors, Wallowa Valley Mental Health Clinic, Wallowa County, Oregon (1994-1997); Board of Directors, Garten Foundation, Salem, OR (1993-1994); Oregon Symphony Association in Salem (1989-1992); Volunteer, March of Dimes, Oregon (1989-1990); Member, Public Health

Board, Marion County, Oregon (1987-1994); President, Cat Club of the Yellowstone, Billings, MT (1985-1986); President, Friends of the Clarence E. Smith Museum of Anthropology, California State University, Hayward (1975-1976); Board of Directors, Numerous Nonprofit Organizations; Member, Board of Directors, Garten Foundation, Salem, OR **CW:** Editor, Contributor, "Thoughts 'n Things"," Bilingual Materials Development Center (1981-1986); Editor, Contributor, "Montana Bilingual Education Newsletter," Bilingual Materials Development Center (1981-1983); Contributor, National Clearinghouse for Bilingual Education (1981); Co-Author, "A Behavioral View of Office Work," Xerox Corporation (1978); Editor, Linguistic Anthropology, Kroeber Anthropological Society Papers, University of California, Berkeley (1976-1978); Contributor, "Confronting the Myths About Bilingual Education: Improving Public Information Strategies, Colloquium IV in A Bilingual Meeting of the Minds: Working Papers from the OBEMLA Leadership Colloquium," Rosslyn, VA; Various Lectures, Workshops, Presentations and Keynote Speeches, Organizations, Conferences and Other Engagements **AW:** Honoree, Native American Honor Ceremony, Great Falls Public Schools (2013); Recipient, Health Equity Award, American Heart Association (2012); Named, Regional Superintendent of the Year, School Administrators of Montana (2009); Recipient, Salute to Success Award, Oregon School Boards Association (2003); Recipient, Oregon Governor's Sustainability Award (2003); Recipient, Oregon Office of Energy's High Performing School Award (2002); Named, Woman of Distinction, The Dalles Chronicle (2001); Recipient, Award, Leadership America (1996); Recipient, Award, Horace Mann Society (1994); Recipient, Robert H. Lowie Graduate Fellowship, University of California, Berkeley (1977); Recipient, Montana Federation of Women's Clubs Four-Year Scholastic Scholarship, Montana State University, Bozeman, MT (1961) **MEM:** American Anthropological Association; American Association of School Administrators; Council on Anthropology and Education; Montana Historical Society; Montana Wilderness Association; Rotary International; School Administrators of Montana; Sierra Club; Society for Linguistic Anthropology; University of California, Berkeley Alumni Association **H:** Photography; Travel **BA:** 612 Linden Drive, Great Falls, MT, 59404

CRISPO, RICHARD, I: Fine Art **DOB:** 01/13/1945 **PB:** Brooklyn **SC:** NY/USA **PT:** Frank C. Crispo; Irene M. (Lamont) Crispo **ED:** ThD, Collegii Romani, Rome, Italy (1977); PhD, Collegii Romani, Rome, Italy (1976); MFA, Trinity Hall Cambridge (1975) **C:** Coordinator, Arts in Corrections Art Project, Soledad State Prison (1976-1983); Counselor, Interim, Inc., Monterey, CA (1976); Instructor, Ethnic Studies, Monterey Peninsula College (1976); Founder, Museum on Wheels (1973-1974); Founder, World Folk Art Collection, Monterey, CA (1972); Instructor, Art, Monterey Peninsula College (1968-1969); Instructor, Public School Art, Monterey Peninsula Unified School District, California (1967-1972); Instructor, Art History, Hartnell College; Visiting Instructor, Interdisciplinary Studies Department, Porter College; Visiting Lecturer, University of California, Santa Cruz, CA; American Cultural Specialist to Latin America for United States **CR:** Priest, North America Old Roman Catholic Church; Contributing Artist, Half-Mile-Long Mural, Soledad State Prison; Artist, 53 Murals; Solo Exhibitor, 78 Shows **CW:** Contributor, Articles, Art Journals; Exhibitor, Internationally; Exhibitor, Library of Congress; Exhibitor, Bibliotheque Nationale de France, Paris; Exhibitor, The National Museum of

Western Art Tokyo, Japan; Exhibitor, Museo de Arte Moderno, Mexico City, Mexico; Exhibitor, The Print Center, Philadelphia, PA; Exhibitor, Oakland Museum of California; Exhibitor, Crocker Art Museum, Sacramento, CA; Exhibitor, Monterey Museum of Art; Exhibitor, Harrison Memorial Library, Carmel, CA; Exhibitor, Museo di Belle Arti Lugano, Switzerland; Exhibitor, Smithsonian Institution **AW:** United Nations Educational Award (1971-1973); 1st Prize, California State Fair (1964); Grantee, California Arts Council; Recipient, 36 Awards **MEM:** Pacific Grove Art Center; Carmel Art Association; Foundation for the Community of Artists; Artists Equity **ADD:** PO Box 1952, Carmel, CA, 93921 **URL:** http://dickcrispoartist.com/

CRIVARO, ALAN J., T: Attorney at Law **I:** Law and Legal Services **CN:** Law Offices of Alan J. Crivaro **PB:** Iowa City **SC:** IA/USA **MS:** Married **ED:** JD, Creighton University, Ahmanson Law Center (1980), BA, University of Southern California (1977) **C:** Senior Deputy Public Defender, Orange County, CA (1984-2011), Private Practice, Newport Beach, CA (2011-Present) **CR:** Chair, Member, OCBA Administration of Justice Committee (1992-1999, 2007-Present); Presenter, Criminal Law, OCBA Bridging the Gap (2015-2018); Founding Member, Criminal Law Section, Orange County Bar Association (2015-2016); Workshop Judge, Orange County Bar Association College of Trial Advocacy, Criminal & Civil (1992-2017) **CIV:** Pro Bono Work; Past Director, Orange County Bar Association; Past President, Director, Orange County Bar Foundation; Past President, Director, Constitutional Rights Foundation of Orange County; Past President, Master Bencher, William P. Gray Legion Lex Inn of Court **CW:** Co-author, "When To Ask, When To Tell: Navigating California's Recent Ban-the-Box Legislation," Orange County Lawyer Magazine (2018); Co-author, "The Honorable Mary Kreber Varipapa, Part of the Solution at OC Community Court," 60 Orange County Lawyer 28 (2018); Co-Author, 3 Chapters, "California Criminal Law: Procedure and Practice," CEB Publications **AW:** AV Rating, Martindall-Hubbell (1993-Present); Harmon G. Scoville Award, Orange County Bar Association (2016); Volunteer of the Year Award, Constitutional Rights Foundation of Orange County (2014); Certificate of Appreciation, Constitution Day, California Assembly (2014); Mock Trial Coach of the Year, CRF-OC (2005); Orange County Bar Foundation Distinguished Society of Fellows Award **MEM:** ABA (2000-Present); California Public Defender's Association (1992-Present); Orange County Bar Association (1985-Present) **BAR:** California (1984) **BA:** 3857 Birch St Ste 603, Law Offices of Alan J. Crivaro, Newport Beach, CA, 92660 **URL:** https://www.avvo.com/attorneys/92660-ca-alan-crivaro-290296.html#!

CROFT, VICKI FAYE, T: Librarian Emeritus **I:** Library Management/Library Services **CN:** Washington State University **DOB:** 01/13/1948 **PB:** St. Louis **SC:** MO/USA **PT:** Floyd Merle Keating; Vivian W. Keating Sorensen **MS:** Married **SPN:** Willard A. Swanson (2006) **ED:** MSLS, University of Illinois, Champaign-Urbana (1971); BS, Dana College, Blair, NE (1970) **CT:** Certified Distinguished Member, Academy of Health Information Professionals **C:** Professor Emerita, Washington State University (2014-Present); Head, Animal Health Library, Washington State University, Pullman, WA (1976-2014); Science Library, University of Nebraska, Lincoln, NE (1971-1976) **CR:** Fellow, Medical Library Association (2017-Present); Planning Committee, Medical Library Association (1977-Present); Medical Library Association (1977-Present); National Planning Committee, Medical Library Association

(2012-2013); Veterinary Information Resources Committee (2011-2014); Communications and Public Relations Committee (2011-2014); One Health Program Committee Task Force (2010-2013); Chair, Medical Library Association, Pacific Northwest Chapter (2004); Fourth-Seventh International Conferences, Animal Health Information Professionals (2003-2013); Executive Board Member, Medical Library Association, Pacific Northwest Chapter (2003-2005); Sister Library Committee, International Cooperation Section, Medical Library Association (1999-2003); Executive Board Member, Pacific Northwest Chapter Treasury, Medical Library Association (1993-1996); Pacific Northwest Chapter, Medical Library Association (1993-1996); Chairman, Contributed Papers, First International Conference on Animal Health Information Professionals, Reading, England (1992); Veterinary Medical Libraries Section, Medical Library Association (1986-1987) **CIV:** Volunteer Medical Librarian, St. Joseph's Regional Medical Center, Idaho (2015-Present) **CW:** Editor, Pets Section, Magazines for Libraries (1989); Editor, Pets Section, Magazines for Libraries (1986); Editor, Pets Section, Magazines for Libraries (1982); Contributor, Articles, Professional Journals **AW:** Erich Meyerhoff Prize, Medical Library Association (2018); Animal Health Information Specialists Founders Award, International Conference, Medical Library Association (2013); Daniel T. Richards Award, Collection Development Section, Medical Library Association (2010) **MEM:** Lifetime Member, Pacific Northwest Chapter, Medical Library Association; American Veterinary Medical History Society; Inland Northwest Health Science Libraries; Distinguished Member, Academy of Health Information Professionals; Medical Library Association; Veterinary Medical Libraries Section, Medical Library Association; Pacific Northwest Chapter, Medical Library Association; International Cooperation Section, Medical Library Association **H:** Exercise; Travel **RE:** Lutheran **ADD:** 2800 27th Street, Clarkston, WA, 99403

CROPPER, ANDRE D., T: EO/IR Engineering Fellow & Chief Engineer **I:** Engineering **CN:** Raytheon Company, Space and Airborne Systems **DOB:** 08/04/1961 **PB:** Port-of-Spain **SC:** Trinidad and Tobago **PT:** Anthony Cropper; Vilma V. (Skinner) Cropper **MS:** Married **SPN:** Natalie Rogers (1995) **CH:** Iala Kitanyea Cropper (12/2/2004) **ED:** PhD, Virginia Polytechnic Institute and State University (1995); MSEE, Howard University (1987); BSEE, Howard University (1984) **CT:** Optical Systems Engineering Certification (2012); Stage Gate Process Certification (2007); Miller Heiman Conceptual & Strategic Selling Certification (2007); Diplomate, Infrared Technology Program, SPIE (2005); Frontline Leadership Certification (2003); Diplomate, Project Management Certificate Program (2000); Certified in in Value Based Product Development; Certified in Failure Mode & Effect Analysis **C:** Electro-Optical Infrared Engineering Fellow, Raytheon Company (2013-Present); Hyperspectral Imaging Technical Subject Matter Expert (2013-Present); Technical Subject Matter Expert, Spectral (2008-Present); Chief Scientist of Integrated Regulatory Review Service, DRS Defense Solutions (2011-2013); Director of Advanced Technologies, DRS Defense Solutions (2011-2013); Chief Scientist, Director of the Office of Disruptive Technologies, ITT Inc. (2009-2011); Senior Staff Scientist, CTO Office and Director of Disruptive Technologies, Space Systems Division, ITT Inc. (2007-2009); Technology Development Manager for New Business, Strategic Planning and Business Development Office, Defense Space

Systems Division, ITT Inc. (2006-2007); Technology Development Manager, Remote Sensing Systems, Electronic and Sensor Products Group, Industries Space Systems Division, ITT Inc. (2004-2005); Technology Development Manager, Remote Sensing Systems, Electronic and Sensor Products Group, Commercial & Government Systems, Business Unit, Eastman Kodak Company (2003-2004); Adjunct Professor, Department of Electrical & Computer Engineering, Clarkson University (2000-2005); Research Associate, Image Extraction Group, Commercial & Government Systems, Business Unit, Eastman Kodak Company (2000-2003); Engineering Manager, Image Extraction Group, Commercial & Government Systems, Business Unit, Eastman Kodak Company (2000-2003); OLED Application Project Manager, Research & Development Division, Eastman Kodak Company (1999-2000); Senior Research Scientist, Active Materials and Device Directorate, Corning Incorporated (1998-1999); Corning Inc. Researcher, Clarkson University (1997-1999); Project Leader, AC-Plasma Displays Global Measurements, Fontainebleau Research Center, Corning Incorporated, France (1997-1998) **CR:** Battlespace, Survivability & Discrimination Committee, Military Sensing Symposia (2015-Present); Co-Chair, BSD, Targets, Backgrounds and Discrimination Session, Military Sensing Symposia (2015-Present); Employee Resource Group, Raytheon American Indian Network, Raytheon Company (2013-Present); Independent Panel Reviewer, Nonproliferation Research and Development, United States Department of Energy (2008-Present); Member, Faculty of Engineering Curriculum Committee, Norfolk State University (1995-1996); Director, Engineering Enrichment Program, Morgan State University (1992); Chairperson, Engineering Technology Program, Norfolk State University (1990-1992); Director, Engineering Enrichment Program, Morgan State University (1990); Consultant, Advance Controls and Equipment Services, Freeport, Bahamas (1990); Team Member, Advisory Committee, School of Technology, Norfolk State University (1988-1992) **CIV:** Invitee, Indigenous Peoples Section, International Association for Impact Assessment (2017); Invited Speaker, RAIN ERG Brown Bag Lunch and Learn, Raytheon Company (2016); Graduation Keynote Address, Native American Future Stewards Program, Rochester Institute of Technology, Rochester (2016); Invited Speaker, Native American Students Body, Cornell University (2016); Speaker, Keynote Address, Fifteenth Annual New England Science Symposium (2016); Invited Motivational Speaker, Flying Fish Swim Club, Trinidad & Tobago (2015); Invited Speaker, Region Six Conference, American Indian Science and Engineering Society, Ithaca, NY (2015); Invited Speaker, Leadership Summit, American Indian Science and Engineering Society, Santa Ana Pueblo, NM (2014); Invited Speaker, Region Six Conference, American Indian Science and Engineering Society, Ithaca, NY (2013); Invited Speaker, Career Day, Thornell Road Elementary School, Rochester, NY (2013); Invited Speaker, Hyperspectral Research, University of Puerto Rico at Mayaguez (2008); Kalinago Carib Representative, Trinidad and Tobago Indigenous People Conference (2008); Invited Speaker on VBLD, VOC & Green Belt Certification Process, ITT India (2007); Keynote Address, Caribbean Youth Science Forum, NIHERST, Trinidad & Tobago (2006); Invited Speaker, Region Six Conference, American Indian Science and Engineering Society, Ithaca, NY (2005); Kalinago Carib Representative, Trinidad and Tobago Indigenous People Conference (2005); Trinidad & Tobago Caribbean Representative, United Confederation of Taino People (2004-2011);

Member, Corporate Advisory Board, American Indian Science and Engineering Society (1996-2016) **CW:** Author, "Target Detection and Identification Performance of Hyperspectral Imagers⬚," Military Sensing Symposia, Gaithersburg, MD (2018); Author, "Comparison of Techniques to Model and Measure Spatial Resolution in Hyperspectral Imaging Sensors," Military Sensing Symposia, Gaithersburg, MD (2018); Author, "ACES HY Wide Field-of-Regard, High Resolution Imager Upgrade⬚," Military Sensing Symposia, Gaithersburg, MD (2018); Author, "Component and System-Level Advances in Airborne Full-Spectrum Hyperspectral Imaging," Military Sensing Symposia, Gaithersburg, MD (2018); Author, "Atmospheric Effects on Long Stand-Off HSI Applications," Military Sensing Symposium Conference, NATO (2017); Author, "Hyperspectral Imaging in Tropical Environments," OSA Hyperspectral Imaging & Sounding of the Environment, Leipzig, Germany (2016); Author, "Atmospheric Effects on Long stand-off HSI applications," National Conference, American Indian Science and Engineering Society (2016); Author, "System-Level Performance Modeling for Next Generation Dual-Band HSI Sensors," Military Sensing Symposia (2016); Author, "Impact of Focal Plane Persistence on Performance of the ACES HY Hyperspectral Imaging Sensor," Military Sensing Symposia (2016); Author, "Atmospheric Turbulence in Long Stand-Off HSI Performance Modelling," Military Sensing Symposia (2016); Author, "Quantitative Analysis of Errors from Keystone and Smile in Hyperspectral Imagers," Military Sensing Symposia (2016); Author, "ACES HY Airborne Maritime Collection of Hyperspectral Data," National Military Sensing Symposia (2016); Author, "Atmospheric Effects on Long stand-off HSI Applications," SPIE (2016) **AW:** Recipient, Inventor Award for Multi Sensor Payload Performance Metric, Raytheon Company (2016); Inductee, Hall of Fame as a Pioneer in the Field of Science and Engineering, Fatima College, Trinidad & Tobago (2015); Recipient, Inventor Award for Deterministic Method and Model for HSI Systems A2AD Metric of Detection and Hyperspectral Imaging/Lidar Imaging Multimode Sensor, Raytheon Company (2015); Named, Professional of the Year, American Indian Science and Engineering Society (2014); Recipient, STAR Award, Raytheon Company (2014); Recipient, Inventor Award for Full Spectral Compact Single Focal Plane Hyperspectral Imaging System, Raytheon Company (2014); Recipient, Inventors - Who Makes Things Work in Rochester Award, Rochester Museum and Science Center (2006); Recipient, Caribbean ICONS in Science Technology & Innovation Award, NIHERST (2006); Recipient, National ICONS in Science & Technology Award NIHERST (2005); Recipient, IPT Leadership Development Program Award, C&GS Business Unit, Eastman Kodak Company (2002); Recipient, Visiting Alumni Lecture Series Award, Howard University (2000); Honoree, Excellent Leadership as Campus Manager of Howard University, Awareness Quality Improvement Team, Corning Incorporated (1999); Recipient, Howard University Recruiting Award, Awareness Quality Improvement Team, Corning Incorporated (1998); Recipient, Broadening Diversity Efforts Award, Society of Black Professionals, Corning Incorporated (1997) **MEM:** SPIE (1999-Present); Fellow, American Indian Science and Engineering Society (1992-Present); IEEE (1983-Present); Session Chair, Defense and Security Symposium, The International Symposium on Optical Science and Technology, Long-Range Imaging Conference, SPIE (2016); Secretary, Executive Committee, Rochester Section, IEEE (2013); Vice President, Technology

Management Council, Rochester Chapter, IEEE (2013); President, Board of Directors, American Indian Science and Engineering Society (2012-2014); President, Technology Management Council, Rochester Chapter, IEEE (2009-2010); Publishing Board, American Indian Science and Engineering Society (2008-2014); Treasurer-secretary, Board of Directors, American Indian Science and Engineering Society (2008-2011); Vice-President, Engineering Management Society, Rochester Chapter, IEEE (2007-2008); Education and Fundraising Chair, American Indian Science and Engineering Society (2006-2008) **MH:** Albert Nelson Marquis Lifetime Achievement Award (2017) **H:** Swimming; Teaching adults and children how to swim; Science; Art; Scuba diving; Outdoor activities; Dancing; Reading **PA:** Independent **RE:** Roman Catholic **ADD:** 6 Ridgeview Ct, Pittsford, NY, 14534

CROW, RITA JANE, T: Secondary School Educator **I:** Education/Educational Services **CN:** Cyril Independent School District **PT:** Wilson Douglas Ryland; Margaret Elizabeth Ryland **MS:** Married **ED:** MS in Behavioral Science, Cameron University, Lawton, OK (1993); BA in Business, Sul Ross State **CT:** Certified, Texas State Education Agency (2003); Certified, Provisional Teaching, Oklahoma Education Association (1981) **C:** Teacher, Calhoun County Independent School District, Port Lavaca, TX (2017); Teacher, Calhoun County Independent School District, Port Lavaca, TX (2006-2016); Teacher, Kingsville Independent School District, Texas (2002-2006); Teacher, Cyril Independent School District, Oklahoma (1991-2002); Department Chair, Cyril Independent School District, Oklahoma (1991-2002); Teacher, Bridgecreek Independent School District, Newcastle, OK (1989-1991); Teacher, Apache Independent School District, Oklahoma (1981-1988); Teacher, Uvalde Independent School District, Texas (1971-1980) **CR:** Presenter, Caddo County Teachers Association, Fort Cobb, OK (2001-2002) **CIV:** Quilt Guild (2016); Adviser, National Honor Society (1990-2002) **AW:** Teacher of the Year, Texas Education Association (2006); Teacher of the Year, Oklahoma Education Association (1995); Teacher of the Year, Oklahoma Education Association (1985) **MEM:** President, Association of Texas Professional Educators (2010-2013); Secretary, Association of Texas Professional Educators (2006-2008); Masonic Lodge (1995-2002); Association of Texas Professional Educators; Delta Kappa Gamma **MH:** Albert Nelson Marquis Lifetime Achievement Award (2017) **H:** Scuba diving; Painting; Playing piano; Walking; Spending time with family **PA:** Independent **ADD:** 107 Belle Ln, Port Lavaca, TX, 77979

CRUM, ALBERT B., T: Psychiatrist **I:** Medicine & Health Care **DOB:** 11/17/1931 **PB:** Omaha **SC:** NE/USA **PT:** J. Rufus Crum; Alberta (McCreary) Crum **MS:** Married **SPN:** Rosa Maria Hennessy Y. Sinclair **CH:** Rosa Maria Crum O'Brien; Elsie Crum McCabe; Alberta Crum Fousek **ED:** MS, New York University (1987); Honorary DSc, University of Redlands, California (1974); Residency in Psychiatry and Stress Management, Columbia University Psychiatric Institute, New York-Presbyterian Hospital (1961-1963); Research Resident, Creedmoor Institute for Psychobiological Studies, Queens Village, New York (1958-1959); Medical Intern, Columbia University Division, Bellevue Hospital Center, The City of New York (1957-1958); MD, Harvard Medical School (1957); BS, University of Redlands, California (1953) **CT:** Diplomate, American Board of Forensic Examiners; Diplomate, American Board of Forensic Medicine; Fellow, Royal College of Physicians & Surgeons in Psychiatry; New York State Medical License C: Stress Management and Forensic Expert, Private Practice, Brooklyn Heights, NY (1963-2003); Captain, U.S. Air Force, Chief of Neuropsychiatric Service, Continental Air Command Headquarters, (1959-1961); Expert in Glutathione Science CR: Chairman, Selection Committee, Albert Schweitzer Humanitarian Award, (1986-Present); President, The ProImmune Company, LLC (1997-Present); Clinical Professor, Departments of Behavioral Sciences and Management Sciences, New York University (1987-2002); Co-Chair, United States Coordinating Committee for Nomination of His Holiness the Dalai Lama XIV of Tibet for the Nobel Peace Prize (1986-1989) CIV: Board of Directors, Burdick International Ancestry Library (1985-Present); Chairman, Advisory Board, New York University College of Dentistry (1988-1996); Board of Directors, Albert Schweitzer Fellowship (1982-2002); Member, Brooklyn Heights Association (1970-1996); Permanent Class Agent, Class of 1957, Harvard Medical School, Harvard University; President, Stress Watchers, Inc. MIL: Captain, U.S. Air Force (1959-1961) CW: Author, "The 10-Step Method of Stress Relief: Decoding the Meaning and Significance of Stress," CRC Press (2000); Lecture, "Aequanimitas Revisited," Omega Chapter, Omicron Kappa Upsilon, New York University (1986); Contributor, Articles, Professional Journals; Contributor, Abstracts, Professional Journals; Author, "Glutathione Synthesis: Unraveling the Pleiotropic Paradox and its Vital Immune Roles," John Wiley & Sons Publishers; Author, Copyrighted Manuscript, "Unique Features and Key Advantages of Immune Formulation 200® (also known as Vitamin GSH-S)" AW: Inductee, Distinguished Hall of Fame, Omaha Central High School (2005); Citizen of the Year Award for Achievements In Medicine and Human Understanding, Brooklyn, NY (1989); Honoree, Distinguished Lecturer, Omega Chapter, Omicron Kappa Upsilon, New York University College of Dentistry (1986); Bicentennial Award, National Jogging Association (1976); Gold Medal with a Sacred Embedded Relic of Pope Saint John XXII (1974); Distinguished Service Award, "Young Man of the Year," Brooklyn Junior Chamber of Commerce (1966); Harvard Medical School Student Research Fellowship; Merited Honor Grades for Research, Harvard Medical School MEM: Fellow, Royal College Physicians and Surgeons in Psychiatry; National Board of Medical Examiners; Medical Council of Canada; Harvard Club of New York; Lifetime Member, Sigma Xi; Mensa; Eagle Scout, Boy Scouts of America; Ranger Scout, Boy Scouts of America MH: Albert Nelson Marquis Lifetime Achievement Award (2017) H: Jogging; Studying world religions; History ADD: 64 E Market St, Rhinebeck, NY, 12572 URL: http://proimmuneco.com/albert/index.html

CRUZ, JOSE BEJAR JR., T: Professor Emeritus I: Education/Educational Services CN: Ohio State University DOB: 09/17/1932 PB: Bacolod City SC: Philippines PT: Jose P. Cruz; Felicidad (Bejar) Cruz MS: Married SPN: Stella E. Rubia, Esq. CH: Fe E. Cruz-Langdon; Ricardo A.; Rene L. (Deceased); Sylvia C. Cruz-Loebach; Loretta C. Cruz-Spray ED: PhD in Electrical Engineering, University of Illinois (1959); MEE, Massachusetts Institute of Technology, Cambridge, MA (1956); BEE, University of the Philippines, Summa Cum Laude (1953) CT: Licensed Professional Engineer, State of Illinois; Licensed Professional Engineer, State of Ohio; Professional Electrical Engineer, Philippines C: Professor Emeritus, Ohio State University, Columbus, OH (2010-Present); Distinguished Professor of Engineering, Ohio State University, Columbus, OH (2004-2010); Howard D. Winbigler

Chair in Engineering, Ohio State University (1997-2004); Professor of Electrical Engineering, Ohio State University, Columbus, OH (1992-2004); Dean, College of Engineering, Ohio State University (1992-1997); Professor, Department of Electrical and Computer Engineering, University of California, Irvine (1986-1992); Chairman, Department of Engineering, University of California, Irvine (1986-1990); Visiting Professor, Massachusetts Institute of Technology (1973); Associate Member, Center for Advanced Study, University of Illinois (1967-1968); Professor of Electrical Engineering, University of Illinois (1965-1986); Research Professor, Coordinated Science Laboratory (1965-1986); Associate Professor, University of Illinois (1961-1965); Assistant Professor, University of Illinois (1959-1961); Instructor, University of Illinois (1956-1959); Research Assistant, Massachusetts Institute of Technology, Cambridge, MA (1954-1956); Instructor of Electrical Engineering, University of the Philippines, Quezon City, Philippines (1953-1954) CR: Project Advisory Group on Engineering and Science Education Project, Department of Science and Technology, Republic of the Philippines (1993-1998); National Council of Engineering Examiners (1984-1986); Professional Engineering Examinations Committee, State of Illinois (1984-1986); General Chairman, Conference on Decision and Control (1975); Visiting Professor, Harvard University (1973); President, Dynamic Systems; Theory Committee, American Automatic Control Council (1967); Visiting Associate Professor, University of California, Berkeley (1964-1965); Fellow, American Association for the Advancement of Science CIV: Board of Trustees, Mapua Institute of Technology (Now Mapua University) (2016-Present); Board of Directors, Ohio Chapter, The Intelligent Transportation Society of America (1994-1998); Vice-Chairman, Ohio Chapter, The Intelligent Transportation Society of America (1994-1998); Board of Trustees, National Regulatory Research Institute (1993-1997); Board of Trustees, Orton Family Foundation (1993-1997); Board of Directors, EWI (1993-1997); Chairman, Board of Directors, TRC Inc. (1992-1997) CW: Associate Editor, "Journal of Optimization Theory and Applications" (1980-Present); Co-author, "Signals in Linear Circuits, Translated Into Spanish" (1978); Co-author, "Feedback Systems, Translated Into Polish" (1977); Associate Editor, "Journal of the Franklin Institute" (1976-1982); Co-author, "Feedback Systems, Translated Into Chinese" (1976); Co-author, "Signals in Linear Circuits" (1974); Author, "System Sensitivity Analysis" (1973); Co-author, "Feedback Systems" (1972); Editor, "Transitions on Automatic Control," Control Systems Society, IEEE (1971-1973); Co-author, "Engineering of Dynamic Systems" (1969); Co-author, "Introductory Signals and Circuits" (1967); Associate Editor, "Transitions on Circuit Theory," IEEE (1962-1964); Series Editor, "Advances in Large Scale Systems Theory and Applications"; Contributor, Articles on Network Theory; Contributor, Articles on Automatic Control Systems; Contributor, Articles on System Theory; Contributor, Articles on Sensitivity Theory of Dynamical Systems; Contributor, Articles on Large Scale Systems; Contributor, Articles on Dynamic Games; Contributor, Articles on Dynamic Scheduling in Manufacturing Systems; Contributor, Science Technology Journals AW: Lifetime Achievement Award, University of the Philippines (2010); James H. Mulligan Education Medal, IEEE (2009); Education Society Lifetime Achievement Award, IEEE (2009); Founders Lecture Award, Philippine-American Academy of Science and Engineering (2001); Diamond Award (1999); Richard E. Bellman Control Heritage

Award, American Automatic Control Council (1994); Honoree, Most Outstanding Overseas Alumnus, College of Engineering, Alumni Association, University of the Philippines (1990); Richard M. Emberson Award, Control Systems Society, IEEE (1989); Most Outstanding Alumnus Award, Alumni Association of America, University of the Philippines (1989); Halliburton Engineering Education Leadership Award (1981); Curtis W. McGraw Research Award, American Society for Engineering Education (1972); Purple Tower Award, Beta Epsilon, University of the Philippines (1969); Honoree, Named Outstanding 100 Alumni Over 100 Years, College of Engineering, University of the Philippines; Academician, National Academy of Science and Technology, Philippines 2012; Member US National Academy of Engineering, 1980. MEM: Chairman, Life Member Committee, IEEE (2014-2015); Membership Committee, National Academy of Engineering (2003-2007); Chair Emeritus, American Association for the Advancement of Science (2005-2006); Council, American Association for the Advancement of Science (2005-2006); Chairman, American Association for the Advancement of Science (2004-2005); Chairman-elect, American Association for the Advancement of Science (2003-2004); Chairman, Peer Committee, for Electronics Engineering, National Academy of Engineering (2003-2004); Vice-Chairman, Peer Committee, for Electronics Engineering, National Academy of Engineering (2002-2003); Peer Committee for Electronics Engineering, National Academy of Engineering (2000-2004); Committee on Diversity in Engineering Workforce, National Academy of Engineering (1999-2001); Vice-chairman, International Federation of Automatic Control (1999); Secretary, American Association for the Advancement of Science (1998-2003); Chairman, Board of Directors, Philippine-American Academy of Science and Engineering (1998-2000); Chairman, International Federation of Automatic Control (1996); Academic Advisory Board, National Academy of Engineering (1994-1997); Vice-chairman, International Federation of Automatic Control (1993); Section Committee for Section on Engineering, American Association for the Advancement of Science (1991-1994); Policy Committee, International Federation of Automatic Control (1987-1993); Membership Committee, National Academy of Engineering (1987-1990); Peer Committee on National Agenda for Career-long Education for Engineers, National Academy of Engineering (1986-1988); Vice-chairman, Technology Board, International Federation of Automatic Control (1984-1987); Chairman, Control Systems Society, IEEE (1984-1985); Vice President of Publication Activities, Control Systems Society, IEEE (1984-1985); Executive Committee, Control Systems Society, IEEE (1982-1985); Chairman, Technology Activities Board, Control Systems Society, IEEE (1982-1983); Vice President of Technological Activities, Control Systems Society, IEEE (1982-1983); Committee for Electronics Engineering, National Academy of Engineering (1982); President,, Philippine-American Academy of Science and Engineering (1982); Chairman, Theory Committee, International Federation of Automatic Control (1981-1984); Vice-chairman, Publications Board, Control Systems Society, IEEE (1981); Chairman, Panel of Technological Editors, Control Systems Society, IEEE (1981); Chairman, TAB Periodicals Committee, Control Systems Society, IEEE (1981); Chairman, PUB. Society Publications Committee, Control Systems Society, IEEE (1981); Director, Control Systems Society, IEEE (1980-1985); Co-founder, Philippine-American Academy of Science and Engineering (1980); Technology Activities Board, Control Systems

Society, IEEE (1979-1983); President, Control Systems Society, IEEE (1979); Administrative Committee, Control Systems Society, IEEE (1978-1980); Education Medical Committee, Control Systems Society, IEEE (1977-1979); Vice President of Finance and Administrative Activities, Control Systems Society, IEEE (1976-1977); Chairman, Awards Committee, Control Systems Society, IEEE (1973-1975); Educational Activities Board, Control Systems Society, IEEE (1973-1975); Administrative Committee, Control Systems Society, IEEE (1966-1975); Chairman, Linear System Committee, Group on Automatic Control, IEEE (1966-1968); Awards Policy Committee, American Society for Engineering Education; Terman Awards Committee, American Society for Engineering Education; Congress International Program Committee, International Federation of Automatic Control; Philippine Engineers and Scientists Organization; Correspondent, The National Academy of Future Scientists and Technologists; Philippine Engineers and Scientists Organization; Sigma Xi; The Honor Society of Phi Kappa Phi; Eta Kappa Nu, IEEE **MH:** Albert Nelson Marquis Lifetime Achievement Award (2017) **H:** Violin; Swimming **ADD:** 1437 Fountaine Drive, Columbus, OH, 43221 **URL:** http://www.ece.osu.edu/~cruz

CULVER, MICHAEL PATRICK, T: Music Educator, Composer **I:** Media & Entertainment **DOB:** 10/24/1948 **PB:** Memphis **SC:** TN/USA **PT:** Charles Lawrence Culver; Ruth Enid (Boone) Culver **MS:** Married **SPN:** Linda Marie Szymanski (12/17/1966) **CH:** Erik-Jon; Ezra Charles; Soren Bernard **ED:** MFA in Music Composition, Bard College (1993); BA in Music Composition, Empire State College (1989); AA in Music, Ulster County Community College (1975) **C:** Tutor, Evaluator, Empire State College, New Paltz, NY (1992-1996); Private Practice, Bloomington, NY (1975-1996) **CW:** Composer, "String Quartet 3 Metaleptic" (2017); Composer, "Four Variations for Piano" (2008); Composer, "Lontano Series," Tape Recorder, Piano (2007); Composer, "Itinerary," Tape Recorder, Piano (2005); Composer, "Non Liquet," String Quartet (2004); Composer, "Occasional Chairs," Ten Trio Sonatas (2002); Composer, "Pronaos: Structural Trio for Seven Instruments" (1998); Composer, "Stevedores," Violin, Bass Clarinet, Piano (1996); Composer, "Her Sleeping Form Shifting," Oboe, Viola, Piano (1994); Composer, Medium of Exchange, Flute, Cello, Piano (1992); Composer, Four Georgics, String Quartet (1991); Composer, Two Etudes, Electronic Sound Sources (1990); Performances: Circumstance for 2 Pianos; John Cage Memorial Concert, Nudelman, Culver (1981-1992); Composer, Ontic Emanations, Music for Piano (1980-1987); Composer, Dadaloop, Magnetic Tape (1979) **MH:** Albert Nelson Marquis Lifetime Achievement Award (2017) **ADD:** 166 Apple Hill Road, Hurley, NY, 12443

CULVER, VICKY, T: Art Gallery Coordinator, Artist **I:** Fine Art **CN:** Guild of Creative Art **DOB:** 08/31/1948 **PB:** Liverpool **SC:** United Kingdom **ED:** BSc in Graphic Design, Photography and Communications, Manchester Metropolitan University (1969) **C:** Coordinator of Gallery Exhibits, Guild of Creative Art, Shrewsbury, NJ (2000-Present); Volunteer, Guild of Creative Art (1987-2018); Freelance Graphic Designer, Ottawa, Ontario, Canada (1984-1987); Employee, Banfield Advertising, Ottawa, Ontario, Canada (1981-1984); Employee, Department of Industry, Trade and Commerce, Ottawa, Ontario, Canada (1974-1979); Employee, Longman Educational Publishers, Harlow, England (1974-1979) **CW:** Exhibitor, All Things Local, Redbank, NJ (2018); Brookdale CC CVA Gallery Exhibit for Guild Members (2018); Brookdale CC Art Alliance Gallery Exhibit (2018); Solo Exhibitor, Terner House Gallery (2009); Solo Exhibitor, Dolphin Watch Gallery, Corolla, NC (2009); Exhibitor, Group Show, Art Alliance of Monmouth County, Red Bank, NJ (2009); Solo Exhibitor, Brookdale Community College Western Monmouth Campus, Freehold, NJ (2008); Solo Exhibitor, Oceanic Free Library, Rumson, NJ (2008); Solo Exhibitor, McKay Imaging Gallery, Red Bank, NJ (2007); Solo Exhibitor, Guild of Creative Art, Shrewsbury, NJ (2007); Solo Exhibitor, Small World Coffee, Princeton, NJ (2006); Solo Exhibitor, Georgian Court University (2006); Solo Exhibitor, Monmouth Beach Cultural Center (2005); Solo Exhibitor, West Long Branch Public Library (2005); Solo Exhibitor, Powys Gallery (2004); Solo Exhibitor, Metuchen Library (2003); Solo Exhibitor, Black Box, Asbury Park, NJ (2001); Solo Exhibitor, Guild of Creative Art, Shrewsbury, NJ (1998); Solo Exhibitor, Little Silver Borough Hall, NJ (1998); Solo Exhibitor, Poricy Park Nature Center, Middletown, NJ (1998); Solo Exhibitor, Art and Attic Gallery, Red Bank, NJ (1997); Solo Exhibitor, PNC Bank, Howell, NJ (1997); Exhibitor, Group Show, Guild of Creative Art, Shrewsbury, NJ; Exhibitor, Group Shows; Contributor, Articles, Professional Journals **AW:** Award, Art Exhibit, Mixed Media, Arts Society of Monmouth Country (2018); Honorable Mention, Edgy Show, Guild of Creative Art (2017); Alice Tendler Award for Innovation, Eyesights Open Juried Photography Exhibit, Guild of Creative Art (2017); Second Place in Mixed Media, Art Society of Monmouth County (2017) **MEM:** Audubon Artists; Guild of Creative Art; Art Alliance of Monmouth County; Freehold Art Society; Belmar Arts Council; Freehold Art Gallery; Art Society of Monmouth County; Noyes Museum of Art, Stockton University; Monmouth Arts; Wainright House Museum **MH:** Albert Nelson Marquis Lifetime Achievement Award (2017) **H:** Traveling; Cooking; Audio books **ADD:** 39 Forrest Hill Dr, Howell, NJ, 07731 **URL:** https://www.linkedin.com/in/vicky-culver-93177427

CUNNINGHAM, FRANCIS, I: Fine Art **DOB:** 01/18/1931 **PB:** New York **SC:** NY/USA **PT:** Francis De Lancey Cunningham; Marcia (Davis) Cunningham **MS:** Married **SPN:** Katharine Spalding (9/18/1954) **CH:** Marcia; Katharine **ED:** Postgraduate Studies, The Art Students League (1955-1959); AB, Harvard College (1953) **C:** Founder, Co-Director, New York Academy of Art (1983-1985); Founder, Co-Director, The New Brooklyn School Life Drawing, Painting & Sculpture (1980-1983); Teacher, The Art Students League New York (1980-1983); Teacher, Brooklyn Museum Art School (1962-1980); Artist in Residence, The Sense of Place, Manhattan, KS (1974); Teacher, City College of New York (1962-1965) **MIL:** Captain, U.S. Marine Corps Forces Reserve (1953-1957) **CW:** Solo Exhibition, St. Francis College, Brooklyn, NY (2009); Solo Exhibition, Laurel Tracey Gallery (2000, 2002-2004, 2006, 2008-2009); Group Exhibit, Federation Modern Painters, New York, NY, Art Students League of New York, Galerie Susanne Ho/Jriis, Copenhagen, Denmark (2002); Group Exhibit, National Academy Design, The Tel Aviv Museum of Art (1999); Solo Exhibition, Pro Persona Gallery, Stockholm, Sweden (1998); Solo Exhibition, First St. Gallery, New York, NY (1995); Solo Exhibition, Gallerihuset, Copenhagen, Denmark (1995); Solo Exhibition, Marsh Gallery University Richmond, VA (1989); Solo Exhibition, Danish Consulate, New York, NY (1987); Solo Exhibition, New Brooklyn School Life Drawing, Painting and Sculpture, New York, NY (1982); Group Exhibit, Forum Gallery, New York, NY (1979); Solo Exhibition, Hirschl & Adler Galleries, New York, NY (1967, 1970, 1975); Solo Exhibition, Welles Gallery, Lenox, Massachusetts (1971); Solo Exhibition, Michelson Gallery, Washington, DC (1971); Solo Exhibition, Distelheim Galleries, Chicago, IL (1970); Solo Exhibition, The Berkshire Museum, Pittsfield, MA (1969); Solo Exhibition, Harry Salpeter Gallery, New York, NY (1966); Solo Exhibition, Waverly Gallery, New York, NY (1964); Group Exhibit, Pennsylvania Academy; Group Exhibit, Botler Institute; Group Exhibit, Numerous Others **AW:** Recipient, Benjamin West Clinedinst Memorial Medal for Exceptional Artistic Merit, Artists' Fellowship Inc. (2004); Recipient, Bogliasco Foundation Fellowship (1997); Recipient, Joseph Raskin Award, Audubon Artists (1985); Recipient, Certificate of Merit, Audubon Artists (1980); Recipient, Minnie Stern Award, Audubon Artists (1977); Recipient, Salmagundi Award, Audubon Artists (1973); Grantee, Louis Comfort Tiffany Foundation (1973); Recipient, Purchase Award, Berkshire Museum (1968); Recipient, Peebles Award (1965) **MEM:** Member, Board of Directors, Audubon Artists (1988); Century Association; National Academician; National Academy of Design **MH:** Albert Nelson Marquis Lifetime Achievement Award (2017) **ADD:** 789 W End Ave Apt 11D, New York, NY, 10025

CUNNINGHAM, GARY ALLEN, T: Lawyer (Retired) **I:** Law and Legal Services **CN:** Bishop Cunningham & Andrews **DOB:** 07/04/1940 **PB:** Seattle **SC:** WA/USA **PT:** Chester Martin Cunningham; Elsie Annette (Peterson) Cunningham **MS:** Married **SPN:** Marilyn Phyllis Thunman (6/13/1964) **ED:** JD, University of Washington (1965); Bachelor of Engineering, Yale University (1962) **C:** Retired (2017); Partner, Bishop Cunningham & Andrews, Bremerton, WA (1967-2017); Deputy Prosecutor, Office of the King County Prosecuting Attorney, King County, WA (1965-1967) **CIV:** Board of Directors, Great Peninsula Conservancy (2000-2016); Board of Directors, Hood Canal Environmental Council, Seabeck, WA (1970-Present); President, Board of Directors, Great Peninsula Conservancy (2000-2002); President, Board of Directors, Kitsap Land Trust, Bremerton, WA (1993-2000); Board of Directors, Kitsap Land Trust, Bremerton, WA (1989-2000); President, Kitsap County Estate Planning Council (1985); Secretary, Board of Directors, Olympic Peninsula Kidney Center, Bremerton, WA (1980-2007); President, Board of Directors, Hood Canal Environmental Council, Seabeck, WA (1978, 1974) **AW:** Professionalism Award, Kitsap County Bar Association (2012) **MEM:** President, Kitsap County Bar Association (1975-1976); Kitsap Golf & Country Club; Bremerton Rotary Club, Rotary International **BAR:** Supreme Court of the United States (1993); United States Court of Appeals for the Ninth Circuit (1967); Washington (1965); United States District Court for the Western District of Washington (1965) **MH:** Albert Nelson Marquis Lifetime Achievement Award (2017) **H:** Golf; Hiking; Cross-country skiing; Foreign travel **ADD:** 8411 Sunset Ln NW, Seabeck, WA, 98380

CURCIO, JOSEPH R., T: President, Shareholder **I:** Law and Legal Services **CN:** Curcio Law Office **ED:** JD, John Marshall Law School (1956); Student in History, DePaul University **C:** President, Curcio Law Offices, Chicago, IL (1956-Present) **AW:** Leonard M. Ring Lifetime Achievement Award, Illinois Trial Lawyers Association (2009); Super Lawyers, Illinois; Leading Lawyer, Leading Lawyers Network **MEM:** American Board of Trial Advocates (1992-Present); American Association for Justice; Chicago Bar Association; Illinois Trial Lawyers Association; Life Member, Million Dollar Advocates Forum **BA:** 161 N Clark Street, Curcio Law Office, Chicago, IL, 60601 **URL:** https://www.curcio-law.com

CURTIS, JAMES L., **T:** Psychiatrist **I:** Medicine & Health Care **CN:** Columbia University **DOB:** 04/27/1922 **PB:** Jeffersonville **SC:** GA/USA **PT:** Will Curtis; Francis (Hall) Curtis **MS:** Married **SPN:** Vivian Alzine Rawls (12/11/1948) **CH:** Lawrence; Paul **ED:** Honorary Doctorate of Science, University of Michigan (2014); Honorary Doctorate of Science, Albion College (1992); Intern, Wayne County General Hospital, Eloise, MI (1947); MD, University of Michigan Medical School (1946); BA, Albion College (1944) **CT:** Diplomate, American Academy of Addiction Psychiatry (1994); Certificate in Psychoanalysis, Columbia University (1954); Diplomate, American Board of Psychiatry and Neurology, Inc. (1952) **C:** Clinical Professor Emeritus, The College of Physicians and Surgeons, Columbia University (2000-Present); Director, Department of Psychiatry, Harlem Hospital Center, New York City, NY (1982-2000); Clinical Professor, Psychiatry, The College of Physicians and Surgeons, Columbia University, New York, NY (1982-2000); Clinical Professor, Psychiatry, New York Medical College, New York, NY (1980-1982); Associate Dean, Associate Professor, Psychiatry, Weill Cornell Medical College, New York, NY (1968-1980); Instructor to Clinical Assistant Professor, SUNY Downstate Medical Center, Brooklyn, NY (1954-1968); Resident, Psychiatry, SUNY Downstate Medical Center, Brooklyn, NY (1949-1950); Resident, Psychiatry, Wayne County General Hospital, Eloise, MI (1948) **MIL:** Captain, U.S. Air Force (1952-1954) **CW:** Author, "Memoirs of a Black Psychiatrist: A Life of Advocacy for Social Change" (2017); Author, "Affirmative Action in Medicine" (2003); Author, "Blacks, Medical Schools and Society" (1971); Contributor, Articles, Professional Journals **MEM:** Fellow, American Psychiatric Association; Fellow, The American Orthopsychiatric Association; Fellow, American Psychoanalytic Association; Fellow, American Psychoanalytic Association **MH:** Albert Nelson Marquis Lifetime Achievement Award (2017) **PA:** Democrat **RE:** Congregationalist **ADD:** 1207 Barnes St, Albion, MI, 49224

CUSTODIO, CHRISTIAN M., **T:** Physiatrist **I:** Medicine & Health Care **CN:** Memorial Sloan Kettering Cancer Center **ED:** MS in Engineering, Cornell University (1992); MD, University of Medicine and Dentistry of New Jersey (Now Rutgers New Jersey Medical School), Rutgers, The State University of New Jersey; Resident, Mayo Foundation for Medical Education and Research (MFMER); Fellowship, Mayo Foundation for Medical Education and Research (MFMER) **CT:** Board Certified, American Academy of Physical Medicine and Rehabilitation; Board Certified, Electrodiagnostic Medicine **C:** Program Director, Cancer Rehabilitation Fellowship Program, Memorial Sloan Kettering Cancer Center **BA:** 515 Madison Avenue, Front 5, Memorial Sloan Kettering Cancer Center, New York, NY, 10022 **ADD:** 400 E 70th Street, Apt. 1205, New York, NY, 10021

CZUMA, STANISLAW J., **T:** Historian (Retired) **I:** Education/Educational Services **DOB:** 10/26/1935 **PB:** Warsaw **SC:** Poland **PT:** Wladyslaw Czuma; Wanda Ligon Czuma **MS:** Married **SPN:** Ingrid Zollinger **CH:** Lesley **ED:** PhD in Oriental Art, University of Michigan, Ann Arbor, MI (1968); Graduate Studies in Southeast Asia and India, Faculté des Lettres, Sorbonne, Paris, France (1960-1961); Graduate Studies in Indology, Calcutta University (Now University of Calcutta), Kolkata, West Bengal, India (1958-1959); Graduate Studies, Banares Hindu University, Varanasi, Uttar Pradesh, India (1958-1959); Postgraduate Training Camp,

Inventory and Preservation of Art Monuments in the Western Part of Poland, Breslau and its Vicinity (1957); MA in Western Art, Jagiellon University (Now Jagiellonian University in Krakow), Krakow, Poland (1957); BA in Western Art, Jagiellon University (Now Jagiellonian University in Krakow), Krakow, Poland (1953) **C:** Retired (2005); Maxeen J. Stone Visiting Professor of Asian Art, Case Western Reserve University, Cleveland, Ohio (1990-2000); Adjunct Professor, History of Oriental Art, Case Western Reserve University, Cleveland, Ohio (1973-1990); George P. Bickford Curator of Indian and Southeast Asian Art, The Cleveland Museum Art, Cleveland, OH (1972-2005); Curator of Oriental Art, Brooklyn Museum, Brooklyn, NY (1970-1972); Postdoctoral Curatorial Training Program, Cleveland Art Museum, Cleveland, OH (1968-1969); Research Assistant, Oriental Art Archives Project, History of Art Department, University of Michigan (1962-1964) **CW:** Co-author, "Treasures from The Cleveland Museum of Art," London/New York, Scala Publishers (2012); Author, "A Classic Jain Bronze," The Cleveland Museum of Art Members Magazine (2002); Exhibition, "Treasury of the World Jewelled Arts of India in the Age of the Mughals: the Al-Sabah Collection, Kuwait National Museum," The Cleveland Museum of Art (2002); Supplementary Exhibition, Mughal Paintings and Jewels, The Cleveland Museum of Art's Asian Galleries (2002); Author, "Stalking the Western Tibetan Style," The Cleveland Museum of Art Members Magazine (2001); Author, "Two Vessels from Ancient India," The Cleveland Museum of Art Members Magazine (2001); Exhibition, "Object in Focus: Toward a Definition of an Early "Western Tibetan" Style," The Cleveland Museum of Art (2001); Author, "The Cleveland Museum's Krishna Govardhana and the Early "Phnom Da Style" of Cambodian Sculpture," Ars Orientalis, Festschrift in Honor of Walter Spink (2000); Exhibition, "Object in Focus: Kneeling Male Figure," The Cleveland Museum of Art (2000); Author, Catalog, "Masterworks of Asian Art, The Cleveland Museum of Art," The Cleveland Museum of Art (1998); Author, "East Meets West," The Cleveland Museum of Art Members Magazine (1998); Exhibition, "Dance of the Gods: Indian Art Inspired by Music," The Cleveland Museum of Art (1996); Author, "Some Tibetan and Tibet Related Acquisitions of The Cleveland Museum of Art," Oriental Art Volume XXXVIII, No. 4 (1992-1993); Author, "The Kailasanatha Temple at Ellora," Makaranda, Essays in Honor of Dr. James C. Harle (1990); Author, "Ivory Sculpture," Art and Architecture of Ancient Kashmir, Marg Publication, Bombay, India (1989); Author, "A Unique Addition to the School of Kashmiri Ivories," The Bulletin of The Cleveland Museum of Art, Volume LXXV, No. 8 (1988); Author, Exhibition Catalog, "Kushan Sculpture: Images from Early India," The Cleveland Museum of Art (1985); Exhibition, "Kushan Sculpture: Images from Early India," The Cleveland Museum of Art, Asia Society, New York, Seattle Art Museum (1985-1986); Author, "Mon-Dvaravati Buddha," The Bulletin of The Cleveland Museum of Art, Volume LXVII, No. 7 (1980); Author, "The Case of the Buried Fragments," The Bulletin of The Cleveland Museum of Art, Volume LXVI, No. 7 (1979); Author, "Mathura Sculpture in the Cleveland Museum Collection," The Bulletin of The Cleveland Museum of Art, Volume LXIV, No. 3 (1977); Author, Exhibition Catalog, "Indian Art from the George P. Bickford Collection," The Cleveland Museum of Art (1975); Exhibition, "Indian Art from the George P. Bickford Collection," The Cleveland Museum of Art, University of Texas, University of Florida, Phoenix Art Museum, University of California, University of Michigan (1975-1977); Author, "A Masterpiece of Early Cambodian Sculpture,"

The Bulletin of The Cleveland Museum of Art, Volume LXI, No. 4 (1974); Author, "A Gupta Style Bronze Buddha," The Bulletin of The Cleveland Museum of Art, Volume LVII, No. 2 (1970); Co-author, Exhibition Catalog, "Ancient Cambodian Sculpture," Asia Society, New York: Asia Society (1969); Co-Exhibition, "Ancient Cambodian Sculpture," Asia Society, New York (1969); Author, "The Brahmanical Rashtrakuta Monuments of Ellora" (1968); Author, "Momograph of the Painter Friedrich Pautsch" (1957) **MEM:** Association for Asian Studies; Asia Society **MH:** Albert Nelson Marquis Lifetime Achievement Award (2017) **H:** Travel; Reading; World history; Politics **ADD:** 2448 Woodmere Dr, Cleveland, OH, 44106

D'AGOSTINO, RALPH BENEDICT JR., **T:** Professor **I:** Education/Educational Services **CN:** Wake Forest University School of Medicine **ED:** Postdoctoral Coursework, The Jackson Laboratory (2003); PhD in Statistics, Harvard University (1994); MA in Statistics, Harvard University (1989); BA in Mathematics, Bowdoin College (1988) **C:** Professor, Wake Forest Institute for Regenerative Medicine, Wake Forest School of Medicine (2010-Present); Professor, Clinical and Translational Science Institute, Wake Forest School of Medicine (2010-Present); Professor with Tenure, Department of Biostatistical Sciences, Wake Forest School of Medicine (2004-Present); Director, Biostatistics Core, Comprehensive Cancer Center, Wake Forest School of Medicine (2004-Present); Consultant, Senior Director, Biostatistics, Target Health Inc. (1997-Present); Associate Professor, Department of Public Health Sciences, Wake Forest School of Medicine (1999-2004); Consultant, Harvard Medical School (1994-2003); Assistant Professor, Department of Public Health Sciences, Wake Forest School of Medicine (1994-1999); Research Assistant, New England Biomedical Research Foundation (1992-1994); Research Assistant, Harvard Medical School (1991-1994); Research Assistant, Statistical Consultant, Massachusetts General Hospital (1990-1994); Statistical Consultant, Staff Statistician, Eunice Kennedy Shriver Center (1989-1994); Research Assistant, Department of Physics, Harvard University (1989-1991); Research Assistant, Department of Environmental Sciences and Physiology, Harvard University (1989); Research Assistant, The Framingham Heart Study, Thompson Medical Food and Drug Administration, Hoechst Roussel Pharmaceuticals (1988-1994); Research Assistant, Department of Biostatistics, Harvard University (1988) **CR:** Faculty Member, ASCO/AACR Methods in Clinical Cancer Research Course, Vail, CO (2015-Present); Elected Member, Graduate Faculty Council, Wake Forest Graduate School (2014-Present); Chair, Safety and Toxicity Review Committee, Comprehensive Cancer Center, Wake Forest School of Medicine (2010-Present); Chair, Clinical Research Oversight Committee, Comprehensive Cancer Center, Wake Forest School of Medicine (2004-Present); Interval Advisory Board, Comprehensive Cancer Center, Wake Forest School of Medicine (2004-Present); Research Awards Day Committee, Wake Forest School of Medicine (2017); Co-Director, Biomedical Informatics Graduate Program, Wake Forest School of Medicine (2015-2016); Graduate School Tuition & Compensation Committee, Wake Forest School of Medicine (2015-2016); CTSA Review Task Group, Wake Forest School of Medicine (2011-2012); Development of Novel Clinical and Translational Methodologies Program, Translational Science Institute, Wake Forest School of Medicine (2007-2010); Protocol Review Committee, Comprehensive Cancer Center, Wake Forest School of Medicine (2004-

2012); Departmental Promotions Committee, Division of Public Health Sciences, Wake Forest School of Medicine (2004-2010); Recruitment, Retention, Promotion, and Tenure Committee, Wake Forest School of Medicine (2004-2007); Assistant Dean Search Committee, Wake Forest School of Medicine (2004); Dean's Advisory Committee, Wake Forest School of Medicine (2003-2004); Chair, Biostatistics Consulting Committee, Department of Public Health Sciences, Wake Forest School of Medicine (2002-2003); Social/Morale Committee, Department of Public Health Sciences, Wake Forest School of Medicine (2000-2009); Biostatistician Search Committee, Department of Public Health Sciences, Wake Forest School of Medicine (2000-2003); Biostatistics Faculty Search Committee, Department of Public Health Sciences, Wake Forest School of Medicine (1999); Graduate Medical Education/Continuing Medical Education Sub-Committee of LCME Self Study, Wake Forest School of Medicine (1999-2001); Adjunct Assistant Professor, Department of Biostatistics, The University of North Carolina at Chapel Hill (1998-2004); Continuing Medical Education (CME) Committee, Wake Forest School of Medicine (1998-2001); Chair, Departmental Education Committee, Department of Public Health Sciences, Wake Forest School of Medicine (1997-1999); Curriculum for 2002 Phase III Committee on Student Evaluation, Wake Forest School of Medicine (1997-1998); Biostatistics Faculty Search Committee, Department of Public Health Sciences, Wake Forest School of Medicine (1997-1998); Departmental Workshop Committee, Department of Public Health Sciences, Wake Forest School of Medicine (1997); Departmental World Wide Web Committee, Department of Public Health Sciences, Wake Forest School of Medicine (1996); Departmental Education Committee, Department of Public Health Sciences, Wake Forest School of Medicine (1995-1996); Co-chair, Biostatistician Search Committee, Department of Public Health Sciences, Wake Forest School of Medicine (1995) CW: Associate Editor, Statistics in Medicine (2017-Present); Chief Statistical Editor, Biochimica et Biophysica Acta Clinical (2014-2017); Fellow, American Statistical Association (2013); Statistical Associate Editor, Arthroscopy, The Journal of Arthroscopy & Related Surgery (2008-2017); Associate Editor, Journal of Cardiac Failure (2002-2005); Editorial Board, Current Controlled Trials in Cardiovascular Medicine (2000-2005); Associate Editor, American Journal of Epidemiology (1998-2003); Reviewer, Biometrics; Reviewer, American Journal of the Medical Sciences; Reviewer, Annals of Epidemiology; Reviewer, Archives of General Psychiatry; Reviewer, Archives of Internal Medicine; Reviewer, Arthroscopy; Reviewer, Communications in Statistics; Reviewer, Diabetes; Reviewer, Diabetes Care; Reviewer, European Journal of Clinical Investigation; Reviewer, Health Services and Outcomes Research Journal; Reviewer, Journal of the American Geriatrics Society; Reviewer, Journal of the American Medical Association; Reviewer, Journal of the American Statistical Association; Reviewer, Journal of Educational and Behavioral Statistics; Reviewer, The American Statistician; Reviewer, Stroke; Invited Lecturer in Field; Contributor, Chapters, Books; Contributor, Over 300 Articles, Professional Journals; Contributor, Over 100 Abstracts AW: Established Investigator in Clinical Sciences Award, Wake Forest School of Medicine (2016); Outstanding Senior Faculty Research Award, Division of Public Health Sciences, Wake Forest University School of Medicine (2009); Travel Grant Award, American Diabetes Association (1997); Presidential Poster Presentation, American Diabetes Association (1997); Young Investigators Travel Award, Teratology Society (1994); Research Grants MEM: American Statistics Association (1990-Present); Secretary, Treasurer, Biometrics Section, American Statistical Association (2003-2005); Program Chair, Health Policy Statistics Section, American Statistical Association (2000); Representative, Council of Sections, Section on Statistics in Epidemiology, American Statistical Association (1999-2001); Program Chair, Section on Statistics in Epidemiology, American Statistical Association (1998); European Association for the Study of Diabetes (1996-2001); American Heart Association (1996-2000); American Diabetes Association (1995-2012); The Biometric Society (1994-2012) ADD: 620 Staffordshire Road, Winston-Salem, NC, 27104

DAHMES, ROBERT A., T: Psychiatrist **I:** Medicine & Health Care **CN:** Robert A. Dahmes, MD **ED:** Fellow, Louisiana State University; Resident in Psychiatry, Louisiana State University; Intern, LSU Health New Orleans; MD, LSU Health New Orleans (1975) **CT:** Certified in Psychiatry, American Board of Psychiatry and Neurology, Inc.; Licensed to Practice Medicine, State of Louisiana **CW:** Contributor, Textbook of Child Psychological Disorders; Contributor, Medical Brochures **AW:** Honoree, Best Doctors in Louisiana (2017) **MH:** Albert Nelson Marquis Lifetime Achievement Award (2017) **H:** Playing in a rock and roll band **ADD:** 2401 Cumberland Ct, New Orleans, LA, 70131

DALEY, SANDRA, I: Fine Art **DOB:** 02/28/1940 **PB:** Fargo **SC:** ND/USA **PT:** Cecil Raymond Daley; Margaret (Anderson) Daley **ED:** MFA with High Distinction, California College Arts and Crafts, Oakland, (1965); AB, Cum Laude, Oberlin College, Ohio (1961) **CW:** Co-editor, Contemporary Photographer Magazine (1960); Featured Artist, with Andy Warhol and Roy Lichtenstein; Featured Artist, with Nicholas Quennell; Producer and Director, Experiments in Art and Technology; Producer and Director, London Mysteries (1964); Producer and Director, Robert Having His Nipple Pierced (1970); Producer and Director, Patti Having Her Knee Tattooed (1971); Producer and Director, Live Mixed Media Performance with Alan Lanier and Patti Smith, Cine Probe, The Museum of Modern Art, New York, NY (1971); Director, Cine Portraits of Leonard Cohen, Edie Sedgwick, Gregory Corso, Incredible String Band, Lucy Colella, Arthur C. Clark, Harry Smith, et. al., The Hotel Chelsea (1965-1975) **H:** Writing, drawing

DALIMONTE, JO-ANN, T: Pediatric Nurse Practitioner, Registered Nurse, School Nurse Practitioner **I:** Medicine & Health Care **CN:** Somerville School System, Boston University Student Health Services **DOB:** 06/04/1941 **PB:** Boston **SC:** MA/USA **PT:** John Frisoni; Jennie (Gangarossa) Frisoni **MS:** Married **SPN:** Anthony Dalimonte (10/19/1963) **CH:** John Anthony; Denise Marie; Mark Andrew; Susan Ellen **ED:** RN, St. Elizabeth's Hospital, School of Nursing, Boston, MA (1962) **CT:** Certified Pediatric Nurse Practitioner, Health Science Center, University of Colorado (1986); Certified School Nurse Practitioner, Health Science Center, University of Colorado (1985) **C:** School Nurse Practitioner, Somerville Public Schools, Somerville, MA (2000-2010); Nurse Practitioner, Department of Youth Services, Health Care of Southeast Massachusetts, Abington, MA (1993-1994); Nurse Practitioner, Eunice Kennedy Shriver Center, University of Massachusetts Medical School, Waltham, MA (1987-1992); Nurse Practitioner, Perkins School for the Blind, Watertown, MA (1985-1986); Camp Nurse, Camp Rotary YMCA, Boxford, MA (1983); Nurse, Student Health Services, Boston University (1979-1985); Counselor, Weight Loss Medical Center, Reading, MA (1979); Private Duty Nurse, Central Registry, Boston, MA (1966-1981); Staff Nurse, Malden Hospital (1962-1963); College Health Nurse Practitioner, Boston University **CR:** Visiting Resource, Westboro State Hospital (1992-1994); Court Advocate in Child Custody Cases (1992); Health Educator, St. Patrick's School, Stoneham, MA (1985-1986) **CIV:** Boston Archdiocesan Council of Catholic Nurses (1997-Present); Colonial Chorus, Reading Community Singers, Reading, MA (1995-Present); Liturgical Minister, St. Patrick's Church, Stoneham, MA (1993-Present); Performer, Church Show, Saint Pius X Church, South Yarmouth, MA (2015); Boston Archdiocesan Council of Catholic Nurses (1997-2004); Visiting Resource for a Child in Foster Care, Department of Social Services (1997); Liturgical Minister, St Patrick's Church, Stoneham, MA (1993-2004); Volunteer, Food Pantry, Malden, MA (1993); Volunteer, Visiting Resource, Westboro State Hospital (1992-1994); Volunteer, Court Advocate, Child Custody Cases (1992); Volunteer Health Educator, St. Patrick School, Stoneham, MA (1985-1986); Active Member, Stoneham Red Cross (1975-1988); Parent Teacher Association, Stoneham Public Schools (1970-1986); Attendee, St. Timothy Roman Catholic Church, The Villages, FL; Pianist, The Villages Regional Hospital, The Villages, FL; Pianist, Moffitt Cancer Center, The Villages Regional Hospital, The Villages, FL **CW:** Performer, Singer, Mandolin Player, Folk Group, The Villages, FL; Contributor, Articles, Professional Journals **MEM:** Vice President, Stoneham Garden Club (1992-1994); North Shore Nurse Practitioner Association (1990-2000); Massachusetts School Nurse Organization; Massachusetts Coalition of Nurse Practitioners; Mother Cabrini Nurses Guild **MH:** Albert Nelson Marquis Lifetime Achievement Award (2017) **H:** Music; Singing; Community theater; Mandolin; Swimming; Piano **PA:** Independent **RE:** Roman Catholic **ADD:** 806 Gaffney Street, The Villages, FL, 32162

DANAHER, MALLORY, T: Writer, Chief Financial Officer **I:** Business Management/Business Services **CN:** Sheets.com **PB:** St. Paul **SC:** MN/USA **PT:** James Albert; Helen Rose (Feely) Millett **MS:** Married **SPN:** Thomas C. Danaher (1985) **CH:** Kristen Vigard **ED:** BA, University of Minnesota **C:** Chief Financial Officer, Sheets.com; Chief Financial Officer, Mallory Inc.; Chief Financial Officer, Happy Camper Inc.; Chief Financial Officer, PerfectLinens.com **CIV:** Director, David Horowitz Freedom Center, serves on Governance Committee of DHFC; Board of Regents of Center For Security Policy **CW:** Actress, Originated Role of Mrs. Greer, "Annie"; Actress, Originated Role of Ginger, "The Best Little Whorehouse in Texas"; Actress, "Dodsworth"; Actress, "House of Blue Leaves," The Berkshire Theatre Festival; Actress, "Kennedy's Children," Directed by Olympia Dukakis, Amherst College; Actress, "Edward Albee's 'Everything in the Garden' and 'Full Moon and High Tide,'" Directed by Shelley Winters, The Actors Studio; Actress, "Tornado", with Margaret Colin, Lincoln Center Library Theater; Actress, "Stella", Goethe, Nat Horn Theatre; Actor, "The Human Voice", Deutsches Haus, New York University; Actress, "Loose Connections", Judith Anderson Theatre; Actress, "Love of Life"; Actress, "Another World"; Actress, "Hunter"; Actress, "Thirtysomething"; Actress, "Superior Court"; Actress, "Divorce Court"; Actress, "The Judge"; Actress, "Eischied: Only the Pretty Girls Die"; Actress, "Tootsie"; Actress, "Hell Hath No Fury"; Actress, "Alone in the Dark"; Actress, "Tied to a Chair"; Manager, The Stilettos; Ten Sexiest Women over 40,

"Oprah Winfrey Show"; Five One-Woman Photo Exhibitions; Author, "Fatherless Child"; Executive Producer, "Three Lives"; Co-Producer and Lead Actress, "Deleting Spam"; Co-Producer, "Epic Proportions,"; Producer, "Handicapped People in their Formal Attire," The Actors Studio; Producer, The Fantasticks; Columnist, Frontpage Mag; Columnist, Truth Revolt; Columnist, American Thinker; OpEd Writer, New York Post; Performer, Arcadia Film's "Gender Agenda," EWTN **AW:** Recipient, Producer of Best Feature Film, IndieFest Film Festival; Recipient, Best Leading Actress, IndieFest Film Festival **MEM:** Lector, St. Michael's Church, NYC (2014-2018); Head Lector, Church of Our Savior (2004-2013); Chairman of Auditions, The Actors Studio (2002-2006); Lector, St Victor's Church, L.A. **MH:** Albert Nelson Marquis Lifetime Achievement Award (2017) **RE:** Roman Catholic **ADD:** 484 W. 43rd Street, Apartment 42S, New York, NY, 10036

D'ANGELO, DEBBI, T: Director of Research Evaluation and Assessment **I:** Education/ Educational Services **CN:** Berkeley Unified School District **ED:** MA in Educational Leadership and Administration, General, University of San Francisco (2002); BA in Sociology, University of California, Santa Cruz **C:** Director of Evaluation, Assessment and Research, Berkeley Unified School District (2010-Present); Director of Educational Technology, Monterrey Peninsula Unified School District (2006-2011); Director of Accountability, Monterrey Peninsula Unified School District (2006-2011); Director of Student Information, Monterrey Peninsula Unified School District (2006-2011); Headmaster, Horizons Academy, Maui, HI (2005-2006); Chief Executive Officer, Horizons Academy, Maui, HI (2005-2006); Director of Curriculum, Campbell Union School District (2002-2005); Director of Instruction, Campbell Union School District (2002-2005); Director of Accountability, Campbell Union School District (2002-2005); Principal, Campbell Union School District (1998-2002); Vice Principal, Campbell Union School District (1995-1998); Lead Teacher, Mountain View School District (1985-1995); Affiliate, San Joaquin County Office of Education (1984-1985) **MEM:** Association of California School Administrators; Association for Supervision and Curriculum Development; CUE; California Association for Bilingual Education; National Council of Teacher of Mathematics **ADD:** 649 Sheffield Dr, Alameda, CA, 94502

DANIELS, CAROLINE, T: Information Technology Executive (Retired) **I:** Information Technology and Services **CN:** Aircraft Technical Publishing (Retired) **DOB:** 12/11/1948 **PB:** San Francisco **SC:** CA/USA **PT:** William L. Daniels; Gladys Daniels **CH:** Martin Wernick; Katherine Wernick **ED:** Postgraduate Coursework, Babson College (1994); Postgraduate Coursework, Harvard University (1983-1985); BA in Psychology, University of Colorado (1970); Coursework, University of Dijon, France (1965) **C:** Chief Executive Officer, Chairman, Board of Directors, Aircraft Technology Publishing (1984-2015); President, Aircraft Technology Publishing, Brisbane, CA (1984-1986); Executive Vice President, Aircraft Technology Publishing, Brisbane, CA (1982-1984); Vice President, Aircraft Technology Publishing, San Francisco, CA (1980-1982); Operations Manager, Aircraft Technology Publishing, San Francisco, CA (1975-1980); Library Supervisor, Aircraft Technology Publishing, San Francisco, CA (1973-1975); Co-Founder, Aircraft Technical Publishers (1973); Export Agent, Air Oceanic Shippers, San Francisco, CA (1972-1973) **CR:** Co-Chair, Northern California Chapter, Women Corporate Directors

CIV: Co-Chair, Women Corporate Directors, Past Board of Directors Member, Junior Achievement of Bay Area, San Francisco Opera Guild **AW:** Recipient, Pathfinder Award, Forever Influential, San Francisco Business Times **MEM:** Board of Directors, Executive Committee, Chairman Safety & Training Committee, Chairman, General Aviation Manufacturing Association; Board of Directors, Financial Committee, Academy of Art University, San Francisco, CA; President, Advisory Board, Embry Riddle Aeronautical University; Trustee, Embry Riddle Aeronautical University **MH:** Albert Nelson Marquis Lifetime Achievement Award (2017) **H:** Golf; Cooking; Gardening **RE:** Christian **ADD:** 1000 Green Street, Apartment 704, San Franciso, CA, 94133

DANKO, GEORGE, T: Engineering Educator **I:** Education/Educational Services **CN:** University of Nevada **DOB:** 04/03/1944 **PB:** Budapest **SC:** Hungary **PT:** Gyorgy Danko; Ilona (Mihaly) Danko **MS:** Married **SPN:** Emoke Danko **CH:** Reka **ED:** DSc, Hungarian Academy of Sciences, Budapest, Hungary (2010); PhD, Hungarian Academy of Sciences, Budapest, Hungary (1985); PhD, Budapest University of Technology and Economics (1976); MS in Applied Mathematics, Eotovs University of Sciences, Budapest, Hungary (1975); BSME, Budapest University of Technology and Economics (1968) **CT:** Certified Ski Instructor, Professional Ski Instructors of America **C:** Professor, Mining Engineering, University of Nevada, Reno, NV (1995-Present); Associate Professor, University of Nevada, Reno, NV (1990-1995); Research Associate, University of Nevada, Reno, NV (1986-1990); Associate Professor, Budapest University of Technology and Economics (1979-1986); Fellow, Hungarian Academy of Sciences, Budapest, Hungary (1975-1979); Assistant Professor, Budapest University of Technology and Economics (1968-1975) **CR:** Portrait Artist, Life Portrait and Graphic Art, Reno, NV (2017-Present); Consultant, Sierra Science, Reno, NV (1990-Present); Chairman, High-Level Radioactive Waste Management Conference (1991-1992); Portrait Artist, Life Portrait and Graphic Art, Reno, NV (1987-1992) **CIV:** Committee Representative, Truckee River Steering Committee, Reno, NV (1993-1994) **CW:** Author, "Model Elements and Network Solutions of Heat, Mass and Momentum Transport Processes" (2016); Author, "Warming-up and Cooling of Electrical Machinery" (1982); Co-Author, "Methods for the Calculation of Pipeline Transients" (1976); Contributor, Articles to Professional Journals; Author, Computational Energy Dynamics (CED) Software and the MULTIFLUX Code **AW:** Grantee, NIOSH (2009-Present); Grantee, United States Department of Energy (1991-Present); Grantee, Clarkson Company (1992-1998); Grantee, United States Bureau Mines (1986-1997) **MEM:** IFAC (1995-Present); American Society of Mechanical Engineers, ISES (1993-1994); Society of Mining Engineers; American Nuclear Society **H:** Skiing; Camping; White-water kayaking and rafting; Photography **ADD:** 4861 Idlewild Dr, Reno, NV, 89519

DAS, KAL, T: Head of Global Bank and Institutional Finance & Restructuring Practice Group **I:** Law and Legal Services **CN:** Seward & Kissel LLP **DOB:** 06/23/1956 **PB:** Kolkata **SC:** India **PT:** Amulyaratan Das; Chaitaly (Mitra) Das **MS:** Married **SPN:** Pia Mukherjee Das, MD (2/18/1986) **CH:** Sabrina; Rahul **ED:** LLM, New York University (1989); Diploma, Associate's Diploma Chartered Institute of Arbitrators (1980); Barrister-at-Law, The Honourable Society of Lincoln's Inn (1979) **C:** Partner, Seward & Kissel LLP (1993-Present);

Head of Global Bank and Institutional Finance & Restructuring Practice Group, Seward & Kissel LLP (1993-Present); Associate, Seward & Kissel LLP (1990-1993); Associate, Milbank, Tweed, Hadley & McCloy, LLP (1988-1990); Associate, White & Case LLP (1983-1988); Associate, Malcolm A. Hoffmann (1981-1982); Barrister-at-law, Fountain Court Temple (1980-1981) **CIV:** President, Friends of International Students House Inc. (2015); Lifetime Vice President, International Students House (1987); Member, Board of Trustees, Skidmore College, Saratoga Springs, NY; Member, Board of Directors and Vice President, New York University Law School Alumni Association **CW:** Editor, "Company Law" (1980) **AW:** Honoree, Banking & Finance Law Firm of the Year in New York, Global Law Experts (2016-2017); Honoree, New York Super Lawyers (2006-2010, 2012-2017); Legal Award for Project Finance Law Firm of the Year, Large Tier, Corporate International Magazine (2013-2014); Deal Maker of the Year Award, Finance Monthly (2014); Award for Project Finance Law Firm of the Year, Large Tier, International Global Law Experts (2013); Honoree, Best Structured Finance Law Firm of the Year, InterContinental Finance Magazine (2013); Honoree, Legal 500; Fellow, The American College of Investment Counsel; Lifetime Achievement Award **MEM:** Board of Trustees, The American College of Investment Counsel (2004-2007); Annual Meeting Co-Chairman, The American College of Investment Counsel (1998); Board of Trustees, Skidmore College; American Bankers Association; Panel Member, American Arbitration Association; The Honourable Society of Lincoln's Inn; The Wine Society; IBWS; Metropolitan Club, NYC; Metropolitan Club, Washington, D.C.; Carlton Club, London; Board of Directors and Vice President, New York University Law School Alumni Association; Panel Member, The American Securitization Forum; Strategic Research Institute; Practicing Law Institute; ABA; New York City Bar Association **BAR:** Barrister and Solicitor, Australia (1984); New York (1983); Advocate, Supreme Court, India and Delhi High Court (1981); The Bar Council, England (1979); Admitted to Practice, Wales (1979) **MH:** Albert Nelson Marquis Lifetime Achievement Award (2017) **H:** Traveling **BA:** 1 Battery Park Plz Fl 21, Seward & Kissel LLP, New York, NY, 10004 **ADD:** 107 W 89th St PH A and B, New York, NY, 10024

DAUB, HAL, T: Senior Counsel **I:** Law and Legal Services **CN:** Husch Blackwell LLP **PB:** Fayetteville **SC:** NC/USA **PT:** Harold J. Daub; Eleanor M. Daub (Deceased) **MS:** Married **SPN:** Mary Wurdeman Daub **CH:** Natalie Wilhelm; John Daub; Tammy Hoysgaard **ED:** JD, College of Law, University of Nebraska-Lincoln (1966); BSBAdm, Washington University in St. Louis (1963) **C:** Former Mayor of Omaha, NE (1997-2001); Partner, Blackwell Sanders, LLP (1992-1997); Former Partner, Deloitte (1989-1992); Former Member, United States Congress, Ways and Means Committee (1981-1989) **CR:** Chairman, Presidentially Appointed, Social Security Advisory Board; Senate, Social Security Advisory Board; Elected Regent, University of Nebraska-Lincoln; Mentor, Rotary Club of Omaha; Mentor, Optimist International **CIV:** Affiliate, Capitol Campaign, Madonna School; Affiliate, Various Charitable Events **AW:** Hope is Help Award, Autism Action Partnership (2017); Named Distinguished Eagle Scout, Boy Scouts of America, Mid-America Council; Silver Beaver Awards in Scouting, Boy Scouts of America, Mid-America Council; Citizen of the Year, Boy Scouts of America, Mid-America Council; Inductee, Omaha Chamber of Commerce Business Hall of Fame; Humanitarian Award, Grand Lodge AF & AM of Nebraska; Toastmasters International; Named

33rd Degree Mason **MEM:** Chairman, "Be a Hero" Luncheon, Salvation Army; Chairman, Tree of Lights, Salvation Army; Board Member, Boy Scouts of America, Mid-America Council; Board Member, Salvation Army; Board Member, Autism Actions Partnership; Board Member, Wounded Warrior Family Support and Fatherhood Family Initiative; VFW Post 2503; Post 112, The American Legion; "40 & 8," The American Legion; Reserve Officers Association of the United States **PA:** Republican **BA:** 13330 California St Ste 200, Husch Blackwell, LLP, Omaha, NE, 68154 **URL:** https://en.wikipedia.org/wiki/Hal_Daub

DAUCHY, ESTELLE P., T: Associate Director of International Research **I:** Nonprofit & Philanthropy **CN:** Campaign for Tobacco Free Kids **ED:** PhD in Economics, University of Michigan (2007); Diploma of Profound Studies in International Economics, University Paris I Pantheon-Sorbonne (2000); BS in Applied Economics, University Paris-Dauphine (1999) **C:** Associate Director of International Research, Campaign for Tobacco-Free Kids (2016-Present); Assistant Professor of Economics, The New Economic School, Moscow, Russia (2012-2016); Assistant Professor of Economics, Peking University HSBC Business School, Shenzhen, China (2010-2012); Online Professor, Principia College (2010-2011); Senior Economist, Ernst and Young/QUEST Group (2007-2010); Research Assistant, School of Law, University of Michigan (2005); Research Assistant, Ross School of Business, University of Michigan (2004-2006); Teaching Assistant, University of Michigan (2003-2007) **CR:** Research Assistant to Joel Slemrod and Michelle Hanlon, Office of Tax Policy Research, University of Michigan (2004, 2006) **CW:** Reviewer, FinanzArchiv/Public Finance Analysis (2015-Present); Reviewer, International Review of Economics and Finance (2014-Present); Reviewer, Journal of Public Economics (2013-Present); Reviewer, International Tax and Public Finance (2010-Present); Co-author, "Cross-Country Evidence on the Preliminary Effects of Patent Box Regimes on Patent Activity and Ownership" (2015); Reviewer, National Research University Higher School of Economics Centre for Advanced Studies, Program for Individual Research Grants (2013); Reviewer, Applied Stochastic Models in Business and Industry (2008); Co-author, "International Tax Policy, Acquisition of Innovative Assets, and Innovative Activity"; Co-author, "Taxation and Inequality: Active versus Passive Channels"; Co-author, "The Tax-Adjusted Q Model of Corporate Investment After Accounting for Intangible Assets: Theory and Evidence from Temporary Investment Tax Incentives"; Co-author, "Investor Valuations of Japan's Adoption of a Territorial Tax Regime: Quantifying the Direct and Competitive Effects of International Tax Reform"; Author, "The Efficiency Cost of Asset Taxation in the U.S. After Accounting for Intangibles"; Co-author, "Asymmetric Institutions Equalizing Symmetry in Gravity: Taxation and Trade in the OECD"; Co-author, "International R&D Sourcing and Knowledge Spillover: Evidence from OECD Patent Owners"; Co-author, "Federal Income Tax Revenue Volatility Since 1966"; Co-Author, "The Impact of Tax Rebates on Firm Value: Evidence from High Tech Certificates Announcements in China"; Author, "Private School Competition and Public School Performance in Arizona" **AW:** Research Grant, International Tax Policy Forum (2016) **MEM:** Association of Public Economic Theory (2012-Present); International Institute of Public Finance (2010-Present); Midwest Economics Association (2007-Present); National Tax Association (2005-Present); American Economic Association (2009-Present); The

National Economists Club (2009-Present); Tax Economist Forum (2007-Present); Committee on the Status of Women in the Economics Profession (2004-2007); European Network for Tobacco Control **H:** Running; Swimming; Reading; Traveling **BA:** 1400 I St NW Ste 1200, Campaign for Tobacco Free Kids, Washington, DC, 20005 **URL:** https://www.nes.ru/dataupload/files/CV/2016/Resume-Estelle-Dauchy-December-2015.pdf

DAUGHADAY, DOUGLAS ROBERT, T: Senior Project Engineer **I:** Engineering **CN:** The Aerospace Corporation **PB:** Highland Park **SC:** NJ/USA **PT:** Robert Owings Daughaday; Mary Daughaday **MS:** Married **SPN:** Ilene D. Eichel, (2/14/1987) **CH:** Brian Douglas **ED:** MSEE, University of Southern California (1979); BSEE, WVU Tech, Cum Laude (1976) **C:** Senior Project Engineer (2014-Present); Project Engineer, The Aerospace Corp. (2004-Present); Engineering Specialist, The Aerospace Corp., El Segundo, CA (1996-2004); Project Engineer, The Aerospace Corp., El Segundo, CA (1993-1996); Manager, The Aerospace Corp., El Segundo, CA (1987-1993); Member, Technology Staff, The Aerospace Corp., El Segundo, CA (1984-1987); Laboratory Engineer, Garrett Airesearch, Torrance, CA (1980-1984); Senior Engineer, Litton G&CS, Woodland Hills, CA (1979-1980); Member, Technology Staff, Hughes Aircraft Co., Culver City, CA (1977-1979) **MEM:** IEEE; ACM; President, Assembly #22, The Society of American Magicians; Instructor, National Association of Underwater Instructors; Life Member, University of South Carolina Alumni Association; Life Member, Eta Kappa Nu **H:** Photography; Computers **PA:** Republican **ADD:** 2385 Roscomare Road, Apartment F1, Los Angeles, CA, 90077

DAVE, BHAVANA J., T: Professor, Associate Director **I:** Medicine & Health Care **CN:** University of Nebraska Medical Center **MS:** Married **ED:** ABMG Clinical Fellowship, Clinical Cytogenetics, Munroe Meyer Institute for Genetics and Rehabilitation, University of Nebraska Medical Center, Omaha, NE (1995-1998); Postdoctoral Fellowship, Cancer Cytogenetics, The University of Texas MD Anderson Cancer Center (1991-1994); PhD, Cancer Research, The Maharaja Sayajirao University of Baroda (1990); MS in Microbiology, Gujarat University, Ahmedabad, India (1978); BS in Microbiology, Chemistry, Gujarat University, Ahmedabad, India (1976) **CT:** Diplomate, American Board of Medical Genetics and Genomics (2012, 2002); Certified Clinical Specialist in Cytogenetics, National Certification Agency (1992) **C:** Program Director, Clinical Cytogenetics and Clinical Molecular Genetics Training Program, American Board of Medical Genetics and Genomics (2015-Present); Professor, Departments of Pediatrics, Pathology/Microbiology, MMI, and Genetics, Cell Biology and Anatomy, University of Nebraska Medical Center, Omaha, NE (2010-Present); Associate Director, Human Genetics Laboratories, Munroe Meyer Institute (MMI), Biology and Anatomy, University of Nebraska Medical Center, Omaha, NE (2001-Present); Associate Member, Fred and Pamela Buffett Cancer Center, University of Nebraska Medical Center, Omaha NE (1998-Present); Associate Professor, Departments of Pediatrics and Pathology/Microbiology, Munroe Meyer Institute, University of Nebraska Medical Center, Omaha, NE (2004-2010); Assistant Professor, Departments of Pediatrics and Pathology/Microbiology, Munroe Meyer Institute, University of Nebraska Medical Center, Omaha, NE (1998-2004); Clinical Fellow, Research Associate, Munroe Meyer Institute for Genetics and Rehabilitation, University of Nebraska Medical Center, Omaha NE (1995-

1998); Research Associate, Department of Cell Biology, M.D. Anderson Cancer Center, Houston TX (1994-1995); Junior Scientific Officer, Gujarat Cancer and Research Institute, Ahmedabad, India (1988-1991); Research Assistant, Cell Biology Division, Gujarat Cancer and Research Institute, Ahmedabad, India (1982-1987) **CR:** Member, Promotion and Tenure Committee, Munroe-Meyer Institute, University of Nebraska Medical Center, Omaha, NE (2015-Present); Member, Research and Development Committee, Human Genetics Lab (2002-Present); Member, Departmental Quality Management Committee, Human Genetics Lab (1999-Present); Member, Distinction through Quality Committee, Munroe-Meyer Institute, University of Nebraska Medical Center, Omaha, NE (1999-Present) **CIV:** Member, Board of Trustees, Hindu Temple, Omaha, NE (2009-Present); Volunteer, The American National Red Cross (2002-Present); Volunteer, American Cancer Society, Inc. (2002-Present); Volunteer, Hindu Temple, Omaha, NE (2000-Present); Volunteer, Nebraska Chapter, Leukemia and Lymphoma Society (1998-Present); Grant Review Committee, Michael Smith Foundation for Health Research, British Columbia, Canada (2012-2015); Grant Proposal Review, Michael Smith Foundation for Health Research, British Columbia, Canada (2002) **CW:** Editorial Board, Cogent Medicine (2015-Present); Editorial Board Member, Advances in Medicine- Genetics (2013-Present); Associate Editor, BioMedCentral Medical Genetics (2009-Present); Reviewer, American Journal of Hematology; Reviewer, American Journal of Medical Genetics; Reviewer, Atlas of Genetics and Cytogenetics in Oncology and Haematology URL; Reviewer, Blood; Reviewer, Breast Disease; Reviewer, British Journal of Hematology; Reviewer, Cancer Genetics; Reviewer, Cancer Genetics and Cytogenetics; Reviewer, Clinical Cancer Research; Reviewer, GENE; Reviewer, Genes Chromosomes and Cancer; Reviewer, Hematological Oncology; Reviewer, International Research Journal of Medicine and Medical Sciences; Reviewers, Journal of Clinical Pathology; Reviewer, Journal of National Cancer Institute; Reviewer, Journal of Neurological Sciences; Reviewer, Journal of Pediatric Genetics; Reviewer, Journal of Pediatric Infectious Diseases; Reviewer, Lab Medicine; Reviewer, Leukemia Research; Reviewer, Modern Pathology; Reviewer, Neoplasia; Reviewer, Pediatric Blood and Cancer; Reviewer, PLoS ONE; Reviewer, Sensors; Contributor, Over 100 Articles, Professional Journals; Contributor, Chapters, Books; Author, Over 200 Abstracts; Presenter in Field **AW:** Shri R. J. Kinariwala Cancer Research Lifetime Achievement Award, The Gujarat Cancer Society and Gujarat Cancer & Research Institute (2016); Award for Meritorious Abstract, U.S. National Committee for International Union Against Cancer (1994, 1998); Lymphoma Research Foundation of America Fellowship Award (1997); Young Investigator Travel Award, American Association for Cancer Research (1994); Bhaikaka Inter-University Award for Best Research Paper Publication (1987); Sitaram Joglekar Award for Best Presentation, The Indian Association for Cancer Research (1986); Recipient, Research Grants **MEM:** Cancer Genomics Consortium and the Cytogenomics Array Group (2011-Present); American Society of Human Genetics (2001-Present); American Association for Cancer Research (1991-Present); Fellow, American College of Medical Genetics (2002-Present); Fellow, Leukemia and Lymphoma Society of America (1998); American Society of Preventive Oncology (1995); Lifetime Member, Indian Association for Cancer Research; Lifetime Member, Indian Society of Oncology; Society of

Pediatric Oncology; Lifetime Member, The Indian Society of Cell Biology **MH:** Albert Nelson Marquis Lifetime Achievement Award (2017) **ADD:** 13407 Tregaron Cir, Bellevue, NE, 68123 **URL:** https://www.unmc.edu/chmr/members/Dave.html

DAVID, IVO, I: Fine Art **DOB:** 11/22/1934 **PB:** St. Leucio Sannio, Italy, November 22, 1934 **SC:** St. Leucio Sannio, Italy, November 22, 1934 **PT:** Arduino David; Clarice-Olga (Lepore) David **MS:** Widower **SPN:** Nancy Pugliese (September 26, 1962) (Deceased November 1997) **ED:** Graduate, International Academy Micenei, Reggio, Italy (1976); Graduate, Academy of Fine Arts Paestum Academy, Italy (1975); MFA, Academy Fine Arts, Naples, Italy (1958); Graduate, Lyceum of Science, Italy **CT:** Licensed Real Estate Broker, State of New Jersey **C:** Art Advertising Consultant, Union Center Realty Corp. (1975-Present); President, Broker, Developer, Union Center Realty Corp. (1972-Present); Architectural Designer, Raritan Center, Edison, NJ (1970-1975); Chief Architect, Design Federal Warehouses, Newark (1966-1974); Planning Designer, Candeub/Fleissig Associate, Newark (1963-1966) **MIL:** With, Italian Air Force **CW:** Featured Artist, Backus Museum Fort Pierce, FL (2007-2010); Featured Artist, Vero Beach Art Club, Vero Beach Museum, FL (2007-2010); Numerous One-Man Shows in US and Europe including City Hall Paris (1999), Musee d'Unet, France (2001), Ramapo University, New Jersey (2002), Chateau Briand Grandroom, New York (2003, 2005, 2007, 2009), Biennale International dell'Arte Contemporanee, Florence, Italy (2004), Merk & Co., Inc.; Author, "Manifesto of Fusionism" (1956); Author, "Memories of an Artist" (1981); Founder, New Art Style of Fusionism (1956) **MEM:** Greater Union County Association Realtors; Backus Museum (Fort Pierce); Vero Beach Art Museum; Vero Beach Art Club **H:** Tennis **ADD:** 3662 2nd Pl, SW Vero Beach, FL, 32968-3172

DAVIES, CATHERINE EVANS, T: Professor of Linguistics **I:** Education/Educational Services **CN:** The University of Alabama **DOB:** 01/31/1946 **PB:** New York **SC:** NY/USA **PT:** Daniel R. Davies; Winifred Evans Davies **ED:** PhD in Linguistics, University of California, Berkeley (1986); MA in Foreign Language Education, Stanford University (1968); BA in German and French, Pomona College (1967) **CT:** State of California Secondary Teaching Credential (1968) **C:** Professor of Linguistics in the Department of English, The University of Alabama (1989-Present); Visiting Assistant Professor, Linguistics Program and Academic Coordinator of the English Language Institute, University of Florida, University of Florida (1986-1989); Teacher of German and French, South San Francisco Unified School District (1968-1974); Affiliated Faculty Member, Summersell Center for the Study of the South in the Department of History; Affiliated Faculty Member in the German Applied Linguistics Program, Department of Modern Languages and Classics **CR:** Executive Secretary, Southeastern Conference on Linguistics (SECOL) (2016-Present); Coordinator, Interdisciplinary Undergraduate Linguistics Minor, College of Arts and Sciences, The University of Alabama (2015-Present); Member, Linguistics in Higher Education Committee, Linguistic Society of America (2014-2016); Chair of the English Department of the University of Alabama (2009-2014); Editorial Advisory Board for the TESOL Quarterly (2009-2012); Director of Graduate Studies (2006-2009); Chair of University Research Advisory Committee for Arts and Humanities (2006-2008); Director of the M.A.-TESOL Program (1990-2004); Member, Advisory Board, Digital Humanities Initiative, University Libraries, The University of Alabama; Faculty Senate (2001-2004); Editorial Board Member, Southern Journal of Linguistics; Reviewer for various scholarly journals: TESOL Quarterly, Journal of Applied Linguistics, Humor, Journal of Pragmatics, System, Pragmatics and Language Learning; Research Grantee, National Science Foundation Collaborative Research Grant #0317553 (with Michael Picone) (2003-2004); Research Grantee, Symposium on Language Variety in the South, Historical and Contemporary Perspectives; Research Grantee, National Endowment for the Humanities #RZ-50220 (with Michael Picone) (2004-2008); Grantee, Alabama Humanities Foundation (2002) **CIV:** League of Women Voters of Greater Tuscaloosa, Tuscaloosa County Democratic Party Executive Committee, Alabama Humanities Foundation Speakers Bureau **CW:** "Culture, Gender, Ethnicity, Identity in Discourse: Exploring Crosscultural Communicative Competence in American University Contexts." To appear in Language Learning, Discourse and Cognition: Studies in the tradition of Andrea Tyler, (eds. Vyv Evans and Lucy Pickering). Amsterdam and New York: John Benjamins (Human Cognitive Processing Series) (2018); "Southern American English in Alabama," To appear in Speaking of Alabama: The History, Diversity, Function, and Change of Language, Thomas Nunnally, (ed.), The University of Alabama Press (2018); "On the Relationship between Interaction and Language Learning: A Usage-based Perspective Grounded in Interactional Sociolinguistics." In Usage-Inspired L2 Instruction: Researched Pedagogy (co-eds. Andrea Tyler, Lourdes Ortega, Mariko Uno, & Lauren Park), pp. 75-91. Amsterdam and New York: John Benjamins Publishing (2018); "Performing Southernness in Country Music," with Caroline Myrick, In Language Variety in the New South: Change and Variation (LAVIS IV), (eds. Jeffrey Reaser, Eric Wilbanks, Karissa Wojcik, and Walt Wolfram), pp. 78-96. Raleigh: The University of North Carolina Press (2018); "Sociolinguistic Approaches to Humor." The Routledge Handbook of Language and Humor, pp. 472-488, Salvatore Attardo, ed. New York, NY: Routledge (2017); "Performing Southernness in Country Music across Five Generations." International Country Music Journal. pp. 37-58 (2017); "Twitter as political discourse: The case of Sarah Palin," Discourse, Politics, and Women as Global Leaders (eds., Diana Boxer and John Wilson), pp. 93-120. Amsterdam: John Benjamins (2015); "Humor in intercultural interaction as both content and process in the classroom" HUMOR: International Journal of Humor Research. 28(3): 375-395 (2015); "Introduction" with Michael D. Picone, In New Perspectives on Language Variety in the South: Historical and Contemporary Approaches, Michael D. Picone and Catherine Evans Davies (eds.). pp. 1-15. Tuscaloosa: The University of Alabama Press (2015); "Southern storytelling: Historical and contemporary perspectives," In New Perspectives on Language Variety in the South: Historical and Contemporary Approaches, Michael D. Picone and Catherine Evans Davies (eds.). pp. 399-421. Tuscaloosa: The University of Alabama Press (2015); "Reaching across the partisan divide: The linguistic construction of an oppositional country music voice", International Country Music Journal. pp. 114-145 (2014); "Cross-cultural Humor." The Encyclopedia of Humor (Salvatore Attardo, ed.) Thousand Oaks, CA: Sage Publications (2014); "Dialect Humor." Encyclopedia of Humor Studies. (Salvatore Attardo, ed.) Thousand Oaks, CA: Sage Publications (2014); "An interview with Robin Tolmach Lakoff," Journal of English Linguistics, (Vol. 38, 369-376) (2011); "Training your taste buds: The language of success in diabetes 'self-efficacy,'" with Linda Knol and Lori Turner. In Language, Body, and Health, McPherron, P. & Ramanathan, V. (eds). pps. 171-190. Munich: De Gruyter Mouton (2011); "We had a wonderful time: Individual sibling voices in the joint construction of a family ethos through narrative performance." Narrative Inquiry, 20(1) 20-36 (2010); "Joking as boundary negotiation among 'good old boys': 'White trash' as a social category at the bottom of the southern working class in Alabama," HUMOR: An International Journal of Interdisciplinary Studies, 23(2) 179-200 (2010); "Southern American English in Alabama," Tributaries, Journal of the Alabama Folklife Association, in a special issue on Alabama's Linguistic Tributaries, 10, pp. 71-90 (2008); "We digress: Kathryn Tucker Windham and southern storytelling style," Storytelling, Self, Society: An Interdisciplinary Journal of Storytelling Studies, 4(3), pp. 167-184 (2008); "Southern politeness," entry for the New Encyclopedia of Southern Culture, volume 5 "Language," Michael Montgomery and Ellen Johnson (eds.), pp. 174-177. Chapel Hill, NC: University of North Carolina Press (2007); "Language and identity in discourse in the American South: Sociolinguistic repertoire as expressive resource in the presentation of self," In Selves and Identities in Narrative and Discourse, Bamberg, M., De Fina, A., & Schiffrin, D. (eds.). pp. 71-88. Amsterdam: Benjamins (2007); "Gendered sense of humor as expressed through aesthetic typifications," Journal of Pragmatics, 38, pp. 96-113 (2006); "English and ethnicity: Introduction," In English and Ethnicity, Janina Brutt-Griffler and Catherine Evans Davies (eds.), pp. 1-15. Symposium volume from University of Alabama Department of English, Palgrave Press (Signs of Race Series) (2006); "Learning the discourse of friendship," In Language in Use: Cognitive and Discourse Perspectives on Language and Language Learning, pp. 85-99, Andrea E. Tyler, Mari Takada, Yiyoung Kim, and Diana Marinova (eds.). Washington, DC: Georgetown University Press (Georgetown University Round Table on Languages and Linguistics) (2005); "Discourse strategies in the context of crosscultural institutional talk: Uncovering interlanguage pragmatics in the university classroom," co-authored with Andrea Tyler. In Interlanguage Pragmatics: Exploring Institutional Talk, pp. 133-156, Kathleen Bardovi-Harlig and Beverly Hartford, (eds.). Mahwah, NJ: Lawrence Erlbaum Associates (in the Second Language Acquisition Research Series) (2005); "Developing awareness of crosscultural pragmatics: The case of American/German sociable interaction," Multilingua: Journal of Cross-Cultural and Interlanguage Communication, 23.3, pp. 207-231 (2004) **AW:** Keynote address at the Southeast Regional TESOL Conference (SETESOL), Birmingham, AL (2017); "Expanding Our Perspectives on Humor and Pedagogy." Plenary lecture at 5th Annual Humor Conference, Dallas, TX (2015) **MEM:** Graduate Faculty, The University of Alabama; International Pragmatics Association; Linguistic Society of America; Southeastern Conference on Linguistics (SECOL); American Dialect Society; American Anthropological Association; Society for Linguistic Anthropology; The International Society for Humor Studies (ISHS) **H:** Choral singing with Prentice Concert Chorale, Tuscaloosa, AL **BA:** Box 870244, Department of English, The University of Alabama, Tuscaloosa, AL, 35487-0244 **ADD:** 930 Wallace Wade Ave, Tuscaloosa, AL, 35401 **URL:** https://english.ua.edu/user/57

DAVIS, JEREMY MATTHEW, T: Supervising Chemist **I:** Sciences **CN:** Orange County Water District **DOB:** 08/05/1953 **PB:** Bakersfield **SC:** CA/

USA **PT:** Joseph Hyman Davis; Mary Davis **MS:** Married **SPN:** Bernadette Sobkiewicz (8/28/1976, Divorced) **CH:** Andrew Jeremy; Christopher Peter **ED:** Masters of Public Administration, California State University Long Beach (1983); BS in Biological Sciences, University of California, Irvine (1974) **CT:** Certificate in Facilities Management, University of California, Irvine (2006) **C:** Supervising Chemist, Orange County Water District (1984-Present); Chemist, Orange County Water District (1977-1984) **CIV:** Member, St. James Anglican Church **CW:** Contestant, "Jeopardy!" (2001); Contributor, Papers in Field **AW:** Recipient, Distinguished Toastmaster Award, Toastmasters International (2010); Honoree, Named Laboratory Person Of Year, California Water Environment Association (1984) **MEM:** President, Watermeisters Club, Toastmasters International (1996, 1999, 2003, 2008); Governor, Division C, Toastmasters International (2001-2002); Governor, Founder's District Area C-5, Toastmasters International (1999-2001); Mensa International; Intertel; Triple Nine Society **MH:** Albert Nelson Marquis Lifetime Achievement Award (2017) **RE:** Anglican **ADD:** 550 Paularino Ave Apt H202, Costa Mesa, CA, 92626

DAVIS, JACK C., T: Lawyer **I:** Law and Legal Services **CN:** Loomis Law Firm **ED:** JD, Harvard University (1964); Diplomate in History, University of Wisconsin-Madison **C:** Senior Partner, Loomis Law Firm **CIV:** President, Lansing Regional Chamber of Commerce **AW:** Promise Community Champion Award, Lansing Promise (2017); Outstanding Philanthropy Award, Lansing Economic Foundation, Lansing Regional Chamber of Commerce; Community Service Pioneer Award, Lansing, Michigan; Outstanding Attorney Award; Service Dedication Award, State of Michigan; Distinguished Citizen Award, Boy Scouts of America; Distinguished Volunteer Attorney Award, SBM; Boy and Man Award, Boys & Girls Clubs of America **MEM:** Chair, Regional Art Museum **H:** Travel **BA:** 124 W Allegan St Ste 700, Loomis Law Firm, Lansing, MI, 48933

DAVIS, JOHN WARREN, T: Consultant, Real Estate Broker **I:** Consulting **DOB:** 02/14/1946 **PB:** York **SC:** PA/USA **PT:** Frank Asbury Davis, Jr.; Lillian Margaret (Billings) Davis **ED:** Postgraduate Coursework, Walden University (1992-Present); Graduate in Overseas Procurement, Kellogg Brown & Root Procurement Academy, Houston, TX (2005); MS in Acquisition and Contract Management, West Coast University, Los Angeles, CA (1987); AA in Real Estate, San Diego City College (1976); BA in Political Science, Drake University, Des Moines, IA (1968) **CT:** Certified Professional Contract Manager, NCMA **C:** Contractor, Consultant, GM15 (2005-2006); Subcontract Administrator, Kellogg, Brown & Root, Houston, TX (2005-2006); Senior Vice President, Azan Corporation Group, San Diego, CA (2001-2003); Defense Contract Manager, Defense Contract Management Command (1998-2000); Procurement Analyst, General Service, 102-12 COMNAVAIRPAC (1988-1998); Contract Specialist, General Service, 1102-12 Navy Space Systems Activity (1986-1988); Contract Specialist, Warranted Ordering Officer, General Service, 1102-11 Naval Weapons Station (1984-1986); Contract Intern, Contract Administrator, Office of Naval Research, Stanford University (1980-1984); Clerk GS, 3 Naval Ocean Systems Center (1979-1980); Real Estate Sales Staff (1972-1979) **CR:** Chairperson for Electronic Data Interchange Society of Logistics Engineers (1995); Delegate, San Diego State University to the National Academy Conference for Contract Management Educators (1993); Delegate, San Diego State University to the National Academy Conference

for Contract Management Educators (1992); Professional Consultant, Computer Applications, Inc. (1992); Delegate, San Diego State University to the National Academy Conference for Contract Management Educators (1991); Chairman, Curriculum Review Committee for Acquisition; Technology Program Committee; Golden Hill Planning Committee, City of San Diego; Adjunct Professor, San Diego State University; Fellow, National Contract Management Association **CIV:** Founding Sponsor, U.S. Army Museum; Patron, San Diego Opera; Golden Hill Planning Committee, City of San Diego **MIL:** U.S. Army, Vietnam War (1968-1972) **CW:** Author, "Palm Springs Salad" (2000); Author, "Paperless Contracting: The EDI Revolution" (1995); Contributor, Articles to Professional Publications and Magazines **AW:** Mariners Award, Holland American Lines (2016); Army Commendation Medal; Hall Of Honor, VFW (2011); Seven Continents Award, ITN Magazine (2010); Decorated War Medal, Sons of the American Revolution; Travel Forte Award **MEM:** Lifetime Member, Certified Professional Contract Manager, National Contract Management Association; Lifetime Member, National Chapter, California and San Diego Chapters, Sons of the American Revolution; Lifetime Member, VFW; San Diego Writers and Editors Guild; Lifetime Member, Past President, Author's Guild; Great Books Discussion Group, San Diego, CA; Black Tie Club International; Lifetime Member, National Society of Sons of American Colonists; Lifetime Member, National Society Sons of Colonial New England; Lifetime Member, Order of Founders of North America **MH:** Albert Nelson Marquis Lifetime Achievement Award (2017) **H:** Swimming; Traveling **RE:** Episcopalian **ADD:** 1128 26th Street, San Diego, CA, 92102

DAVIS-HARRIS, JEANNETTE GARDRINE, T: Microbiologist, Historian, Educator **I:** Sciences **PB:** Glastonbury **SC:** CT/USA **YOP:** 2017-09-06 **PT:** James Robert Davis; Jeannette Gardrine (Nelson) Davis **CH:** Paul Anthony; Catherine Gardrine **ED:** EdD, University of Massachusetts (1974); MEd, University of Massachusetts (1972); Degree, Westfield State College (1971); Degree, Boston University (1962); BS, University of Massachusetts, Amherst (1953) **C:** Educational Specialist, Massachusetts Department of Education, Quincy, MA (1991-1992); Educational Specialist, Massachusetts Department of Education, Chicopee, MA (1987-1991); Instructor, Black Studies, Elder Hostel, Western New England College, Springfield, MA (1985); Visiting Lecturer, African History, Our Lady Elms College, Chicopee, MA (1984); Visiting Lecturer, Elms College, Chicopee, MA (1984); Adjunct Lecturer, Afro-American Studies, University of Massachusetts (1982-1984); Visiting Lecturer, American International College (1981); Corporator, Easthampton Savings Bank (1980-1990); National Board Consultant, Parting Ways Museum of Afro-American Ethnohistory Inc., Plymouth, MA (1980); Educational Specialist, Massachusetts Department of Education, West Springfield, MA (1978-1987); Adjunct Instructor, Springfield Technical Community College (1977); Adjunct Associate Professor, Springfield College (1976); Adjunct Instructor, Holyoke Community College (1975); Adjunct Instructor, Holyoke Community College (1973); Educational Administrator, American Forum for International Study, Cleveland, OH (1972-1973); Photographer, American Forum for International Study, Cleveland, OH (1972-1973); Visiting Lecturer, American International College (1971-1973); Teacher, Black Studies Program, Springfield Public Schools (1969-1978); Chairman, Social Studies Department, Black Studies Program, Springfield

Public Schools (1969-1978); Community Organizer, Northern Educational Services Inc., Springfield, MA (1967-1969); Cultural and Educational Programmer, Northern Educational Services Inc., Springfield, MA (1967-1969); Teaching Assistant, Anthropology, University of Massachusetts (1967-1968); Graduate Research Assistant, Microbiology, University of Massachusetts, Amherst, MA (1965-1966); Bacteriologist-in-charge, Lahey Clinic, Boston, MA (1958-1965); Virologist, Massachusetts Department of Public Health, Boston, MA (1956-1958); Research Instructor, Massachusetts Department A, Amherst, MA (1955-1956); Chemist, Massachusetts Department A, Amherst, MA (1955-1956); Medical Missionary, Order of the Holy Cross, Bolahun, Liberia (1953-1955); Bacteriologist, Order of the Holy Cross, Bolahun, Liberia (1953-1955); Chairman, Social Studies Department, Black Studies Program, Classical High School; Consultant, African & Afro-American Studies, Elder Hostel, Western New England College; Teacher, Black Studies Program, Classical High School **CR:** Corporator, Easthampton Public Library (1985-1986); Chairman, Easthampton Town Charter Commission (1985-1986); Massachusetts Governor's Special Commission, Commemoration of the 350th Anniversary of the African Arrival in Massachusetts (1984-1988); Mayor's Committee, 350th Celebration, Springfield, MA (1983-1986); Board of Directors, World Affairs Council, Connecticut Valley (1983-1984); Executive Committee Member, Station WGBY-TV (1980-1983); Board of Tribunes, Station WGBY-TV (1979-1983); Trustee, Springfield Library & Museum Association (1979-1983); Intern, Massachusetts State Senate (1976) **CIV:** Chair, Easthampton Board of Selectmen (1995); Vice Chair, Easthampton Board of Selectmen (1994); Chair, Easthampton Board of Selectmen (1989-1990); Vice-chair, Easthampton Board of Selectmen (1988); Elected Member, Easthampton Board of Selectmen (1987-1996); Town Meeting Member, Easthampton Board of Selectmen (1987-1996) **CW:** Author, "The Missionary" (2017); Author, "The Struggle for Freedom, The History of African Americans in Western Massachusetts" (2013); Author, "Holyoke Transcript Telegram" (1986-1987); Author, "A History of the World" (1985); Documentary Exhibit, The African-Afro-American Connection (1982-1990); Co-author, "Unfinished Journey" (1980); Author, "Springfield's Ethnic Heritage: The Black Community" (1976) **AW:** Brethren Community Service Award (1985); Grantee, Massachusetts Foundation Humanities & Public Policy (1982); Award, Museum Research Archaeology **MEM:** Executive Board, Massachusetts Association of Supervision & Curriculum Development (1981-1985); President, Western Massachusetts Branch, Association for the Study Afro-American Life & History (1980-1981); National Association of Supervision & Curriculum Development **MH:** Albert Nelson Marquis Lifetime Achievement Award (2017) **ADD:** 15 Reservation Road, Easthampton, MA, 01027

DAWSON ODELL PINCHING, DEBORAH A., T: Special Education Educator **I:** Education/Educational Services **DOB:** 06/28/1954 **PB:** Travis Air Force Base **SC:** CA/USA **PT:** John R. Dawson; Ruth A. (Patchell) Dawson **MS:** Married **ED:** EdM, New Mexico State University (1991); BA in Education, Elementary Education and Special Education, New Mexico State University (1976) **CT:** Certified in Elementary and Special Education Teaching, State of New Mexico **C:** Assistive Technologist, Carlsbad Municipal Schools (1991-Present); Owner, Assistant Technologist, Debs Technologies (1999-2011); Special Education Teacher, Carlsbad Municipal Schools (1979-

2004); Assistant Technology Evaluator, Carlsbad Municipal Schools (1979-2004) **CR:** President, Carlsbad Blind/Low Vision Support Group, Carlsbad, NM (2010-Present) **CIV:** Foster Parent Trainer, New Mexico Human Service Department, Carlsbad, NM (1988-1991); Foster Parent (1984-1991) **CW:** Presenter, Social Work Disabilities Conferences, Las Cruces, NM **MEM:** National Education Association; Board Member, Choices; Pilot Club International **MH:** Albert Nelson Marquis Lifetime Achievement Award (2017); Distinguished Humanitarian (2017) **H:** Crocheting; Computer programming; Cooking **RE:** Nazarene **BA:** PO Box 3190, Carlsbad, NM, 88221

DAY, EDWARD FRANCIS JR., T: Lawyer **I:** Law and Legal Services **DOB:** 11/04/1946 **PB:** Portland **SC:** ME/USA **PT:** Edward Francis Day; Anne (Rague) Day **MS:** Married **SPN:** Claire Anne Nicholson (6/27/1970) **CH:** Kelley Ann; John Edward **ED:** LLM in Taxation, New York University School of Law (1976); JD, The University of Maine School of Law, Cum Laude (1973); BA, Saint Anselm College (1968) **C:** Counsel, McElroy, Deutsch, Mulvaney & Carpenter, LLP, Morristown, NJ (2004-2013); Counsel, Carpenter, Bennett & Morrissey, Newark, NJ (1999-2004); Senior Partner, Carpenter, Bennett & Morrissey, Newark, NJ (1994-1998); Partner, Carpenter, Bennett & Morrissey, Newark, NJ (1979-1993); Associate, Carpenter, Bennett & Morrissey, Newark, NJ (1974-1978); Associate, Hannoch, Weisman, Stern & Besser, Newark, NJ (1973-1974) **CR:** Vice Chairman, Main Steel, Tinton Falls, NJ (2007-2011); Executive Vice President, Main Steel, Tinton Falls, NJ (1999-2007); General Counsel, Main Steel, Tinton Falls, NJ (1999-2007); Instructor, Employee Benefits and Commercial Law, The American College of Financial Services, Valley Forge, PA (1981-1982) **CIV:** National Ski Patrol, Denver, CO (1985-Present); Scoutmaster, Monmouth Council, Boy Scouts of America, Ocean Township, NJ (1987-1990); Vice-Chairman, Allenhurst Planning Board, Borough of Allenhurst, New Jersey (1985-1987); Vice-Chairman, Board of Adjustment, Borough of Allenhurst, New Jersey (1983-1985) **MIL:** Military Police Corps, US Army (1968-1970) **CW:** Editor, "Maine Law Review" (1972-1973) **AW:** Named, One of the Outstanding Young Men of America (1979); Recipient, Ford Foundation Scholarship (1966-1968) **MEM:** Secretary, Deal Golf & Country Club (1991-1992); Board of Directors, Deal Golf & Country Club (1985-1992); Vice President, Jersey Coast Club of Red Bank (1976-1977); ABA; Appalachian Mountain Club; Estate Planning Council of Northern New Jersey, National Association of Estate Planners & Councils; Essex County Bar Association; National Association of the 10th Mountain Division, Inc., Aspen, CO; Sawgrass County Club, Ponte Vedra Beach, FL; The Carnoustie Golf Club, Scotland; TPC Sawgrass, Ponte Vedra Beach, FL; Jumping Brook Country Club, Neptune, NJ; The American Legion; Forsgate Country Club **BAR:** New York (1981); United States Tax Court (1974); New Jersey (1973) **MH:** Albert Nelson Marquis Lifetime Achievement Award (2017) **H:** Golf; Piano **RE:** Roman Catholic **BA:** 2 Hance Ave, Tinton Falls, NJ, 7724 **ADD:** 225 Spier Ave, Allenhurst, NJ, 07711 **URL:** https://www.lawyercentral.com/edward-f-day-jr-interactive-profile–20-406721.html

DAY, JOHN , I: Law and Legal Services **ED:** JD, The University of New Mexico (1995)

DE BRIER, DONALD PAUL, T: Executive Vice President, Corporate Secretary (Retired) **I:** Oil & Energy **CN:** Occidental Petroleum Corporation **DOB:** 03/20/1940 **PB:** Atlantic City **SC:** NJ/USA **PT:** Daniel deBrier; Ethel deBrier **MS:** Married

SPN: Nancy Lee McElroy (8/1/1964) **CH:** Lesley Anne; Rachel Wynne; Danielle Verne **ED:** JD, University of Pennsylvania, with Honors (1967); BA in History, Princeton University (1962) **C:** Executive Vice President/General Counsel, Occidental Petroleum Corporation (2012-2016); Senior Vice President/General Counsel/Corporate Secretary, Occidental Petroleum Corporation (1993-2012); General Counsel, BP Exploration Operating Company Limited, London, England (1989-1993); Associate General Counsel, Standard Oil Co. Inc., Cleveland, OH (1987-1989); Vice President of Law, Kennecott Corp., Salt Lake City, UT (1983-1989); Vice President/General Counsel, Gulf Resources & Chemical Corporation, Houston, TX (1976-1982); Associate, Patterson Belknap Webb & Tyler LLP, New York, NY (1970-1976); Associate, Sullivan & Cromwell LLP, New York, NY (1967-1970) **CIV:** Oregon Shakespeare Festival (2016-Present); Member, Board of Trustees, NPR (2010-Present); Member, Board of Trustees, KCRW (2010-Present); Member, Board of Directors, Los Angeles Philharmonic Association (1995-Present) **MIL:** Lieutenant, U.S. Naval Reserve (1962-1974) **MEM:** Chairman, Advisory Board of Governors, Riviera Golf and Tennis Club (2002-2004); California Club **BAR:** Ohio (1987); Utah (1983); Texas (1977); New York (1967) **MH:** Albert Nelson Marquis Lifetime Achievement Award (2017) **H:** Golfing; Tennis **ADD:** 699 Amalfi Dr, Pacific Palisades, CA, 90272 **URL:** https://www.bloomberg.com/research/stocks/people/person.asp?personId=293312&privcapId=293286

DEADWYLER, SAMUEL, T: Professor **I:** Education/Educational Services **CN:** Wake Forest University **CH:** Three Children **ED:** PhD in Psychology, Stony Brook University (1973); Undergraduate Coursework, San Diego, CA **C:** Professor, Department of Physiology & Pharmacology, Wake Forest University (1978-Present); Affiliate, UCI (1973-1978) **CR:** Vice Chairman, Department of Physiology & Pharmacology, Wake Forest University (1999-2008); Former Co-Director, NIDA Center on the Neurobiological Basis of Drug Abuse, Department of Physiology & Pharmacology, Wake Forest University; Affiliate, Several NIH Grant Review and Policy-Making Panels; President, Major Societal Organizations in the Neuroscience Area; Board Member, Major Societal Organizations in the Neuroscience Area **AW:** Service Award (2017); WFSM Senior Investigator Basic Science Award, School of Medicine, Wake Forest University (2003); Senior Scientist Career Award, NIH **H:** Bike riding out in the country **BA:** Wake Forest Baptist Medical Center, Medical Center Boulevard, Winston-Salem, NC, 27157 **ADD:** 853 Montrachet Court, Lewisville, NC, 27023 **URL:** http://www.wakehealth.edu/Faculty/Deadwyler-Samuel-A.htm

DEAN, DAVID, T: Partner **I:** Law and Legal Services **CN:** Sullivan Papain Block McGrath & Cannavo P.C. **PB:** Chicago **SC:** IL/USA **PT:** John Dean; Carmelita Dean **MS:** Married **SPN:** Ellen Dean (10/15/1976) **CH:** Jeffery; Christopher; Lisa; Lauren **ED:** JD, Georgetown University Law Center (1961); Bachelor's Degree, School of Foreign Service, Georgetown University (1958) **C:** Partner, SPBMC - Sullivan Papain Block McGrath & Cannavo P.C. (1997-Present); Owner, SPBMC - Sullivan Papain Block McGrath & Cannavo P.C. (1997-Present) **CR:** Lecturer, Various Law Schools; Lecturer, Various Bar Associations; Various Federal Courts **CW:** Contributor, Articles, Professional Journals **AW:** Honoree, Lawyer of the Year, Best Lawyers (2018); Honoree, New York's Top Lawyers, Super Lawyers; Featured Listee, Best Lawyers in America; A/V-Rated Attorney, Martindale-Hubbell; Honoree, One of America's Great Trial Lawyers **BAR:** State

of New York (1962) **H:** Going to the theater **BA:** 120 Broadway, Floor 18, Sullivan Papain Block McGrath & Cannavo PC, New York, NY, 10271 **URL:** https://www.triallaw1.com/attorney/david-j-dean

DEBENEDETTI, PABLO GASTÓN, T: Dean for Research, Class of 1950 Professor in Engineering and Applied Science, Professor of Chemical and Biological Engineering **I:** Education/Educational Services **CN:** Princeton University **DOB:** 03/30/1953 **PB:** Buenos Aires **SC:** Argentina **PT:** Sergio Isaias Debenedetti; Francine Fanny (Lehmann) Debenedetti **MS:** Married **ED:** PhD in Chemical Engineering, Massachusetts Institute of Technology (1985); MS in Chemical Engineering, Massachusetts Institute of Technology (1981); BS in Chemical Engineering, Buenos Aires University (1978) **C:** Dean for Research, Princeton University (2013-Present); Class of 1950 Professor in Engineering and Applied Science, Princeton University (1998-Present); Professor, Chemical Engineering, Princeton University (1994-Present); Vice Dean, School of Engineering and Applied Science, Princeton University (2008-2013); Director of Graduate Studies, Department of Chemical Engineering, Princeton University (1990-1991, 1992-1994, 2006-2008); Department Chair, Chemical Engineering, Princeton University (1996-2004); Associate Professor, Chemical Engineering, Princeton University (1990-1994); Assistant Professor, Chemical Engineering, Princeton University (1985-1990); Research Engineer, O de Nora Impianti Elettrochimici, Milan, Italy (1978-1980) **CR:** Mason Lecturer, Department of Chemical Engineering, Stanford University (2015); Bird, Stewart and Lightfoot Lecturer, Department of Chemical and Biological Engineering, University of Wisconsin (2014); McCabe Lecturer, Department of Chemical and Biomolecular Engineering, NC State University (2014); Smith Lecturer, School of Chemical Engineering, Cornell University (2013); Fredrickson Lecturer, University of Minnesota (2012); Lowrie Lecturer, The Ohio State University (2012); Ruckenstein Lecturer, University at Buffalo (2011); Kelly Lecturer, Purdue University (2008); Smith Distinguished Lecturer, University of California, Davis (2007); Abbott Lecturer, Rensselaer Polytechnic Institute (2007); Rilley Lecturer, University of Notre Dame (2007); Patten Distinguished Lecturer, University of Colorado, Boulder, CO (2006); Katz Lecturer, Chemical Engineering, University of Michigan (2005); Collaboratus Distinguished Lecturer, Rutgers, The State University of New Jersey (2003); Berkeley Lecturer, Chemical Engineering, University of California, Berkeley (2003); Cary Lecturer, Georgia Institute of Technology (1998); Wohl Memorial Lecturer, University of Delaware (1997); Katz Memorial Lecturer, The City University of New York (1997); Vaughan Lecturer, California Institute of Technology (1992) **CW:** Member, Editorial Board, "Proceedings of the National Academy of Sciences" (2013-Present); Co-Author, Over 300 Scientific Articles, Professional Journals (1985-Present); Member, Editorial Board, "Chemical Engineering Education" (2000-2009); Member, Editorial Board, "Journal of Chemical Physics" (2006-2008); Member, Editorial Board, "Industrial and Engineering Chemical Research" (2001-2004); Member, Editorial Board, "Journal of Supercritical Fluids (1998-2004); Author, "Matastable Liquids, Concepts and Principles" (1996) **AW:** Guggenheim Medal, Institution of Chemical Engineers (2017); Benjamin Garver Lamme Award, American Society for Engineering Education (2014); Elected Fellow, American Institute of Chemical Engineers (2013); Elected Fellow, American Physical Society (2012); Institute Lecturer, American Institute of Chemical Engineers (2013); Elected Member, National

Academy of Sciences (2012); Elected Fellow, American Association For the Advancement of Science (2011); Distinguished Teacher Award, Princeton University School of Engineering and Applied Science (2008); President's Award for Distinguished Teaching, Princeton University (2008); Elected Fellow, American Academy Arts and Sciences (2008); Hildebrand Award, American Chemical Society (2008); Walker Award, American Institute of Chemical Engineers (2008); Excellence In Teaching Award, Princeton University Engineering Council (2004-2007); Prausnitz Award in Applied Chemical Thermodynamics (2001); Elected Member, National Academy of Engineering (2000); Professional Progress Award, American Institute of Chemical Engineers (1997); Guggenheim Fellow (1991); Camille and Henry Dreyfus Teacher Scholar (1989); National Science Foundation Presidential Young Investigator (1987); European Economic Community Fellow (1978) **MEM:** Fellow, American Association for the Advancement of Science; Fellow, American Institute of Chemical Engineers; Fellow, American Physical Society; American Chemical Society **BA:** 91 Prospect Ave, Princeton University, Office of the Dean for Research, Princeton, NJ, 08540 **URL:** http://research.princeton.edu/dean/bio/

DEBS, RICHARD, T: Investment Executive **I:** Financial Services **CN:** Morgan Stanley **DOB:** 10/07/1930 **PB:** Providence **SC:** RI/USA **MS:** Married **SPN:** Barbara Knowles Debs (7/19/1958) **ED:** Graduate, Advanced Management Program, Harvard Business School, Harvard University (1973); PhD, Princeton University (1963); LLB, Harvard Law School, Harvard University (1958); MA, Princeton University (1956); Postgraduate Studies, The American University in Cairo (1952-1953); BA, Colgate University, Summa Cum Laude (1952) **C:** Advisory Director, Morgan Stanley (1987-Present); Chairman, Morgan Stanley Saudi Arabia (2011-Present); Founding President, Morgan Stanley International (1976-1987); Managing Director, Morgan Stanley (1976-1987); Chief Operating Officer, Federal Reserve Bank of New York (1973-1976); First Vice President, Federal Reserve Bank of New York (1973-1976); Senior Vice President, Federal Reserve Bank of New York (1973); Vice President, Open Market Operations, Federal Reserve Bank of New York (1972); Vice President, Loans and Credits, Federal Reserve Bank of New York (1969-1972); Vice President, Government Bonds and Securities, Federal Reserve Bank of New York (1969-1972); Secretary of Bank, Federal Reserve Bank of New York (1965-1969); Assistant Counsel, Federal Reserve Bank of New York (1964-1969); Legal Department, Federal Reserve Bank of New York (1960-1964) **CR:** Chairman, R.A. Debs & Co.; Advisor, the Nissho-Iwai Corporation; Advisor, Dai-Ichi Mutual Life Insurance Company; Chairman, The Malaysia Fund; Advisor, Bank Julius Baer; Chairman, Mizuho Securities USA; Director, Mizuho Bank, Ltd. (Formerly Mizuho Corporate Bank); Director, Gulf International Bank; Co-chair, Advisory Council, Middle East Institute, Columbia University; Advisor, The Industrial Bank of Japan, Ltd.; Advisor, U.S. Delegation, Annual Meetings, International Monetary Fund; Advisor, U.S. Delegation, Annual Meetings, International Bank for Reconstruction and Development, The World Bank; Director, Aubrey G. Lanston & Co.; Director, IBJ Whitehall Bank & Trust Company; Principal Contact, OPEC Countries, Federal Reserve Bank of New York; Advisory Council, United Gulf Group Company Limited **CIV:** Chairman, American University of Beirut (1994-Present); Vice Chairman, American University of Beirut (1981-1994); Trustee, Barenboim-Said Foundation; Trustee, The Federation of Protestant Welfare Agencies;

Trustee, Institute of International Education, Inc.; Trustee Emeritus, Carnegie Endowment for International Peace; Pro-bono Financial Advisor, President Sadat, Egypt; Field Staff Trustee, American University of Beirut; Chairman, Carnegie Hall; Co-Chair, Middle East Program, Carnegie Endowment for International Peace; President Debs Foundation **CW:** Author, "Islamic Law and Civil Code" (2010); Founder, Islamic Law Library Collection, Harvard University; Contributing Author, Articles, Professional Journals **AW:** Research Fellow on Islamic Law, Harvard University & Princeton University (1958-1959); Scholar, Fulbright Association; Fellow, Ford Foundation; Recipient, Cedars of Lebanon Medal, Government of Lebanon; Recipient, King Abdul Aziz Medal, Government of Saudi Arabia; Recipient, Lifetime Achievement Award, National Academy of Design; Recipient, Award, Third Street Music School Settlement; Recipient, Award, The Federation of Protestant Welfare Agencies; Recipient, Award, ABANA; Recipient, Award, Harvard Law School, Harvard University **MEM:** Global Public Policy Group, Reuters-Carnegie; International Advisory Board, Morgan Stanley; International Policy Committee, U.S. Chamber of Commerce; Chairman, Subcommittee on International Economic Development, U.S. Chamber of Commerce; Visiting Committee, Middle East Center, Harvard University; Alternate Member, Federal Open Market Committee, Federal Reserve Bank of New York; Advisory Council, American Institute of Banking; Savings Bond Committee, State of New York; Take Stock in America Committee, Carnegie Commission; Steering Committee on International Banking, Federal Reserve Bank of New York; FOMC Committee on Foreign Currency, Federal Reserve Bank of New York; Chairman, Treasury Committee on Fiscal Agency Operations, Federal Reserve Bank of New York; Board of Directors, American Council on Germany; Middle Eastern Law Committee, ABA; Council on Foreign Relations; Chairman, American Chamber of Commerce in Egypt; Board of Governors, Foreign Policy Association; Greater New York Chamber of Commerce; Japan Society; The Economic Club of New York; Asia Society; The Century Association; Larchmont Yacht Club; The River Club; The Phi Beta Kappa Society; Visiting Committee, Center for International Affairs; Group of Thirty; Group of Eight; Chairman, International Council, The Bretton Woods Committee; Vice Chairman, U.S.-Saudi Arabian Business Council; the Carnegie Commission on the Role of the Multinational Development Banks; Advisory Committee, Private Sector Development, The World Bank; Visiting Committee, Near Eastern Program, Princeton University; Chairman, International Committee, New York Stock Exchange; Advisory Committee, Federal Reserve Bank of New York; The Volcker Commission, National Commission on the Public Service; Business Advisory Council, Russian-American Bankers Forum; Business Advisory Council, European Bank for Reconstruction and Development; U.S./Middle East Project; Chairman, International Advisory Council, American University of Beirut; Executive Committee, Carnegie Hall; Advisory Committee, International Monetary Fund; Visiting Committee, Columbia University; Task Force on Pay Reform, U.S. Office of Personnel Management; EUSBC; U.S. Overseas Cooperative Development Council **BAR:** New York State Bar Association (1960); ABA; Association of the Bar of the City of New York **MH:** Albert Nelson Marquis Lifetime Achievement Award (2017) **ADD:** 1 Beekman Pl Apt 7A, New York, NY, 10022

DECKER, JOSEPHINE, T: Health Facility Administrator **I:** Medicine & Health Care **CN:**

Sparks Medical Foundation **DOB:** 05/24/1933 **PB:** Barling **SC:** AR/USA **PT:** Ralph Snider; Ada A. (Claborn) Snider **MS:** Married **SPN:** William Arlen Decker (February 4, 1952) **CH:** Peter A. **ED:** MS in Business Administration, Kennedy Western University (1987); BS in Health Management, Kennedy Western University (1986) **C:** Business Administrator, Holt Krock Clinic (Now Sparks Medical Foundation), Fort Smith, AR (1970-Present); With, Holt Krock Clinic (Now Sparks Medical Foundation), Fort Smith, AR (1952-Present); Retired (2004); Regional Director, Holt Krock Clinic (Now Sparks Medical Foundation), Fort Smith, AR (1999-2004); With, Southwestern Bell Telephone Company, Fort Smith, AR (1951-1952) **CIV:** Board of Directors, Sparks Credit Union; Board of Directors, Bost Foundation; Board of Directors, Crisis Center for Women; Board of Directors, Sparks Women's Center; Board of Directors, Leadership Fort Smith; Member, Advisory Council, Northside High School, Fort Smith, AR; Member, Advisory Council, Southside High School, Fort Smith, AR; Member, Advisory Council, Fort Smith Girls Shelter; Member, Advisory Council, Fort Smith Credit Bureau **MEM:** Credit Women International; Society of Certified Consumer Credit Executives **MH:** Albert Nelson Marquis Lifetime Achievement Award (2017) **ADD:** 504 E Sequoyah St, Muldrow, OK, 74948

DEHAY, JERRY MARVIN, T: Co-Owner **I:** Education/Educational Services **CN:** Recollections Antiques and Collectible **DOB:** 11/21/1939 **PB:** Brownwood **SC:** TX/USA **PT:** Marvin Edward DeHay; Willie Marie (Daniell) DeHay **MS:** Married **SPN:** Marilyn Ann Lethco (7/28/1973); Dana Lea Laxson (5/29/1960, Divorced 6/30/1973) **CH:** Colin; Beva; Sue; David (Deceased); Deanna **ED:** PhD, University of North Texas (1978); MBA, Texas A&M University (1966); BBA, Texas A&M University (1962) **C:** Dean's Council, College of Business Administration, Tarleton State University (2011-Present); Co-Owner, Recollections Antiques and Collectibles, Brownwood, TX (1996-Present); Chief Executive Officer, JMD Consultant, Brownwood, TX (1994-Present); Professor, Business Administration, Howard Payne University (2001-2004); Director, Small Business Development Center, Tarleton State University, Stephenville, TX (1987-1989); Dean, College of Business Administration, Tarleton State University, Stephenville, TX (1983-1994); Director, Small Business Institute, Tarleton State University, Stephenville, TX (1983-1987); Director, Small Business Institute, East Texas State University (Now Texas A&M University-Commerce) (1979-1983); Professor, East Texas State University (Now Texas A&M University-Commerce) (1979-1983); Associate Professor, Business, Hardin Simmons University, Abilene, TX (1978-1979); Assistant Professor, Marketing, East Texas State University (Now Texas A&M University-Commerce) (1977-1978); Instructor, Mathematics, Brownwood State School (1976-1977); Coordinator, Food Marketing, Northeast Campus, Tarrant County College, Hurst, TX (1973-1975); Director, Continuing Education, Howard Payne University (1971-1973); Assistant Professor, Business, Howard Payne University, Brownwood, TX (1969-1973); Instructor, Marketing, Texas A&M University, College Station, TX (1966-1969); Sales Manager, Procter & Gamble, Corpus Christi, TX (1962-1965) **CR:** Advisory Board, Small Business Development Center **CIV:** President, Executive Board, West Central Texas Council of Governments (2015-Present); Brownwood Retail Advisory Committee (2010-Present); Brownwood Tourism Board (2009-Present); Board of Trustees Doulas MacArthur Academy of

Freedom (2007-Present); Brownwood City Council (2007-Present); Board of Directors, Brownwood Heritage Association (2006); President, Brown County Historical Society (1999); Vice-Chairman, Brownwood Building Standards Commission (1997-2007); Trustee, Mullin Independent School District (1979); Secretary, Board of Trustees, Brownwood Independent School District (1972); Chairman, Regional Advisory Board, Small Business Administration, Dallas, TX; Board of Directors, Brown County Historical Society; Board Member, Guy D. Newman Honors Academy, Howard Pain University **CW:** Author, Presenter, PBS Business File (1985); Co-Author, "Supervision" (1984); Contributor, Poems, Anthologies **AW:** Top Faculty Advisor Award, Pi Sigma Epsilon (1983); Outstanding American of the Bi-Centennial Era (1976); Outstanding Educator of America (1973-1975) **MEM:** President, West Central Texas Council of Governments (2015-Present); Vice President, West Central Texas Council of Governments (2012-Present); Secretary, Treasurer, West Central Texas Council of Governments (2011-Present); Board of Directors, National Button Society (2009-2012); President, Texas State Button Society (2007-2008); National President, Pi Sigma Epsilon (1987); Administrative Vice President, Pi Sigma Epsilon (1985-1986); Educator, Vice President, Pi Sigma Epsilon (1984-1985); Educator Member, Sales & Marketing Executives of Fort Worth; Mu Kappa Tau; Delta Sigma Pi; British Button Society **MH:** Albert Nelson Marquis Lifetime Achievement Award (2017) **H:** Writing; Singing **RE:** Baptist **ADD:** 801 Quail Run, Brownwood, TX, 76801

DEITERS, JOAN ADELE PHD, T: Spiritual Director **I:** Religious **CN:** Sisters of Charity **DOB:** 04/28/1934 **PB:** Cincinnati **SC:** OH/USA **PT:** Alfred Harry Deiters; Rose Catherine (Rusche) Deiters **ED:** Master in Christian Spirituality, Creighton University (1985); PhD, University of Cincinnati (1967); BA, College Mount St. Joseph (1963) **CT:** Certified Psychoanalyst, Westchester Institute for Training in Psychoanalysis and Psychotherapy (2000); Sisters of Charity, Roman Catholic Church (1952); Licensed Psychoanalyst, New York State **C:** Matthew Vassar Junior Chair, Vassar College, Poughkeepsie, New York (1978-1996); Professor of Chemistry, College Mount St. Joseph (1969-1978) **CW:** Contributor, Various Articles to Professional Journals; Contributor, Publications, American Chemical Society **MEM:** Sigma Xi; National Association for Advancement of Psychoanalysis, American Chemical Society **BA:** 5900 Delhi Road, Mt. St. Joseph, OH, 45051

DEL GIUDICE, MICHAEL, T: Chief Planning Officer, Director **I:** Education/Educational Services **CN:** University of Colorado, Denver **PB:** Providence **SC:** RI/USA **MS:** Married **SPN:** Jorge Navarro **ED:** MLA, School of Environmental Design, University of Georgia, With Honors (1992); BFA, San Francisco Art Institute, With Honors (1978); AA, Franconia College (1974) **C:** Chief Planning Officer, University of Colorado, Denver Anschutz Medical Campus (2012-Present); Director, University of Colorado, Denver Anschutz Medical Campus (2012-Present); Associate Principal, US Director of Campus Planning, AECOM (2011); Senior Associate, US Director of Campus Planning, AECOM (2009-2010); Senior Associate, US East Director of Campus Planning, EDAW (2006-2009); Senior Associate, Institution/Community Planning & Design, Wallace Roberts & Todd, LLC (2004-2006); Associate, Institution/Community Planning & Design, Wallace Roberts & Todd, LLC (1999-2004); Instructor, Graduate/Undergraduate Studios, School of Architecture, Florida International University, Miami, FL (1998-

2004); Urban Planning & Design, Wallace Roberts & Todd, LLC (1994-1999); Urban Designer, Maryland National Capital Parks and Planning (1993); Instructor, Undergraduate Studio Courses, School of Environmental Design, University of Georgia, Athens, GA (1990-1992); Founding Partner, Custom Charter Yachts, LLC, Westport, CT (1982-1988); Private Practice, Institutional Planning **MEM:** Association of American Medical Colleges (2012); American Planning Association (2007); Society of College and University Planners (2003) **H:** Reading; Painting; Gardening **BA:** 1945 Wheeling Street, Suite F540, University Of Colorado, Denver, Aurora, CO, 80045 **ADD:** 10771 East 28th Place, Denver, CO, 80045 **URL:** http://www.ucdenver.edu/about/departments/InstitutionalPlanning/Pages/AboutUs.aspx

DEL RISCO, GILDA, T: Professor, Executive Director for the School of Curriculum **I:** Education/Educational Services **CN:** Kean University **DOB:** 02/14/1949 **PB:** Bayamo **SC:** Cuba **PT:** Carlos Manuel Cespedes; Anicia (Labaut) Cespedes **MS:** Married **SPN:** Jose Miguel Del Risco (10/4/1969) **CH:** Joseph Michael; George; Charles **ED:** PhD, Seton Hall University (2001); MA, Kean University, New Jersey (1995); BA, Kean University, New Jersey (1991) **C:** Professor, Executive Director, The School of Curriculum and Teaching, Kean University, Union, NJ (2017-Present); Assistant Professor, Kean University, Union, NJ (2001-2008); Adjunct Professor, Kean University (1995-2001); Chair, Kean University (2007-2010); Teacher Trainer, Elizabeth Board of Education (1997-2001); Teacher, Elizabeth Board of Education, New Jersey (1991-1997) **CR:** Key Note Speaker, NJTESOL/NJBE (2016); Coordinator, Professor, Educational Units Exhibit (1997-1999) **AW:** Teacher of the Year, RMHC/HACER (2012) **MEM:** English as Second Language; Teachers of English to Speakers Other Languages **H:** Reading; Education; Travel **BA:** 505 N Broad St, Elizabeth, NJ, 07208 **ADD:** 244 North Avenue, Hillside, NJ, 07205

DELAPLAINE, GEORGE BIRELY JR., T: Business Administrator (Retired) **I:** Business Management/Business Services **DOB:** 12/09/1926 **PB:** Frederick **SC:** MD/USA **PT:** George B. Delaplaine; Ruth (Carty) Delaplaine **MS:** Married **SPN:** Elizabeth Barker (8/12/1955) **CH:** George III; James; Edward; John **ED:** BBA, Johns Hopkins University (1948) **C:** Vice President, Frederick Brick Works, Inc. (1989-2015); From Reporter to Publisher, The Frederick News-Post (1949) **CR:** Chairman of the Board, GS Communications **CIV:** Secretary, The National Museum of Civil War Medicine (2016); Former Board Member, Blue Cross, Blue Shield of Maryland; The Delaplaine Foundation, Inc.; Delaplaine Visual Arts Center; The Delaplaine Arts Center at Mount St. Mary's University **AW:** Silver Beaver Scout Award (2002); Maryland Entrepreneur of the Year Award, Ernst & Young Global Limited (1999); Distinguished Eagle Scout Award, Boy Scouts of America (1997); Honoree, Honorary American Farmer, National FFA Organization (1987) **MEM:** Kiwanis International; Fraternal Order of Eagles; The US Jaycee Foundation; The Grand Lodge of Maryland **MH:** Albert Nelson Marquis Lifetime Achievement Award (2017); Distinguished Humanitarian (2017) **PA:** Republican **RE:** Episcopalian **BA:** PO Box 3829, Great Southern Enterprises, Frederick, MD, 21705 **ADD:** 11732 Old Annapolis Rd, Frederick, MD, 21701

DELEON, JEAN M., I: Education/Educational Services **CN:** University of Texas Southwestern Medical Center **DOB:** 05/02/1966 **PB:** Washington **SC:** DC/USA **PT:** Antonio de Leon; Lillian de

Leon **MS:** Married **SPN:** Linda Ryan **CH:** Taylor Ryan **ED:** Physical Medicine and Rehabilitation Residency Program, University of Texas Health Science Center at San Antonio (1993-1996); MD, College of Medicine, University of Oklahoma (1992); BA in Asian Studies, Rice University (1988) **CT:** Board Certified in Physical Medicine and Rehabilitation **C:** Professor, University of Texas Southwestern Medical Center at Dallas, Dallas, TX (2012-Present); Medical Director, Outpatient Wound and Hyperbaric Clinic, University of Texas Southwestern Medical Center, Dallas, TX (2014-2016); Medical Director, Wound Care, Baylor Specialty Hospital, Baylor Health Care System, Dallas, TX (1996-2012) **BA:** 5323 Harry Hines Boulevard, MC 9055, University of Texas Southwestern Medical Center, Dallas, TX, 75390 **ADD:** 2708 Dublin Park Drive, Parker, TX, 75094 **URL:** https://www.linkedin.com/in/jean-deleon-59007063

DEMETRIADI, PETER MICHAEL, T: Director **I:** Business Management/Business Services **CN:** Anglo Danish Oil Company Limited **DOB:** 01/04/1953 **PB:** Glasgow **SC:** Scotland **PT:** Colonel Michael Anthony Demetriadi (Deceased); Nancy Anna (Rodocanachi) Demetriadi (Deceased) **MS:** Married **SPN:** France Marie Ann Nicole Bodson (9/6/1980) **CH:** Jennifer; Guy; James **ED:** BA in Scandinavian Studies, UCL with Honours (1975) **CT:** Certificate in Petrochemical Feedstocks, Oxford College of Petroleum Studies (1984); Certificate in Finnish Language and Culture, Lappeenranta Summer University, Finland (1974); License in The Science of Nutrition, The Open University **C:** Managing Director, Anglo Danish Oil Company Limited (1997-Present); Trading Consultant, Tricon International, Ltd., Houston, TX (2007-2014); Managing Director, Midland Petrochemical Ltd. (1997-2007); General Manager, Sunkyong Chemical Trading, Inc. (1992-1997); Manager, Aromatics Trading, Mitsui & Co. Benelux S. A./N. V., Brussels, Belgium (1989-1992); Manager, Energy Futures, Cargill Investor Services, Ltd., London, England (1987-1989); Manager, Petrochemicals Trading, Cargill, Geneva, Switzerland (1987); Manager, Naphtha Trading, Cargill, Geneva, Switzerland (1986); Petrochemicals Trader, Tradax S.A., Cargill Group, Geneva, Switzerland (1979-1986); Grain Trader, Tradax, London, England (1975-1979) **CR:** Smallholder, Stud Farmer (2000-Present); Consultant in Commodity Training **CIV:** Esquire, Order of St. John **MIL:** Marksman (.303) Proficiency Badge, Combined Cadet Force **MEM:** MCC; The Army and Navy Club; Henley Royal Regatta; Energy Institute; The Warmblood Breeders Studbook UK **MH:** Albert Nelson Marquis Lifetime Achievement Award (2017) **H:** Music; Riding horses **RE:** Church of England **ADD:** Moat House Farm, Earsham Street, Wingfield, Diss, United Kingdom, IP21 5RH **URL:** https://www.linkedin.com/in/peter-demetriadi-ba967aa5/

DENNIS, PATRICIA LYON, T: Elementary Education Educator **I:** Education/Educational Services **DOB:** 06/13/1933 **PB:** Rockford **SC:** TN/USA **PT:** Howard Stanton Lyon; Dora Hester (Maynard) Lyon **MS:** Widowed **SPN:** Norman Bryan Dennis Jr. (1/12/1957, Deceased 1/1985) **CH:** Sarah Dennis Banks; Rebecca Dennis Hampton **ED:** Postgraduate Coursework, University of Missouri (1996); Postgraduate Coursework, University of Missouri, Kansas City, MO (1994); Postgraduate Coursework, University of Kansas (1982-1992); MA, University of Missouri (1977); Postgraduate Coursework, Auburn University (1972-1973); BS, George Peabody College (1955) **CT:** Certified Teacher; Certified Library Media Specialist, Kan; Elementary Classroom Teacher,

States of North Carolina, Michigan, Missouri and Alabama **C:** Instructor, Continuing Education, Johnson County Community College, Children's Class, Overland Park, KS (1999-2010); Library Media Specialist, Washington Elementary School, Olathe, KS (1977-1999); Second and Third Grade Teacher, Fairview Elementary School, Olathe, KS (1974-1977); First and Fourth Grade Teacher, Trinity Christian Day School, Montgomery, AL (1970-1972); Second Grade Teacher, Edgewood Academy, Wetumpka, AL (1969-1970); Second Grade Teacher, Librarian, Goose Air Force Base Dependent School, Labrador, Canada (1965-1967); Kindergarten Teacher, Gladden Elementary School, Richards-Gebaur Air Force Base, Missouri (1964-1965); Special Reading Teacher, First Grade Teacher, McDonald Elementary School, K.I. Sawyer Air Force Base, Michigan (1961-1963); Kindergarten Teacher, Clark Air Force Base, Philippines (1957-1958); Third Grade Teacher, Ray Street Elementary School, High Point, NC (1955-1956); Instructor, Continuing Education, Kansas State Extension, Children's Class, Olathe, KS **CIV:** Library Committee (2004-Present); Adult Choir (2004-Present); Pastoral Care and Counseling Committee, Village Presbyterian Church (2004-Present); Congregation, Village Presbyterian Church, Prairie Village, KS (2004-Present); Congregation, Leawood Baptist Church, Leawood, KS (1974-2004); Primary Subcommittee, Chairperson, Kansas State Reading Circle (1998-1999); Commissioner, Book Review Committee, Kansas State Reading Circle Commission, Topeka, KS (1997-1999); Commissioner, Book Review Committee, Kansas State Reading Circle Commission, Topeka, KS (1994-1996); Church Librarian (1990-1993); Chaperone, Traveling Companion, Miss America-Kansas Scholarship Pageant, Pratt, KS (1989-1998); Board of Directors Scholarship Pageant, Kansas City, MO (1988-1996); Sunday School Department Director (1987-1988); Commissioner, Book Review Committee, Kansas State Reading Circle Commission, Topeka, KS (1985-1991); Children's Choir Director, Leawood Baptist Church (1979-1984); Youth Choir Director, Rock Spring Church, Wetumpka, AL (1969-1970); President, Preschool Board, Gunter Air Force Base (1968-1969); Children's Choir Director, K.I. Sawyer Air Force Base, MI (1960-1962); Pianist and Organist, K.I. Sawyer Air Force Base, MI (1960-1962) **MIL:** Military Spouse, United States Air Force (1957-1971) **AW:** Nominee, Kansas Master Teacher Award (1985-1988); Algernon Sydney Sullivan Award, George Peabody College **MEM:** PEO (2005-Present); Alumnae Chapter, Sigma Alpha Iota (1975-Present); Vice President, Community Scholarship Board (2004-Present); Harp Trio Program (2011); Sweet Adelines Barbershop Chorus, Kansas City (2008-2010); Olathe Seniors Serving Schools Choral Group (2002-2007); Vice President, Alpha Delta Kappa (2004-2006); President, Community Scholarship Board (2002-2004); Vice President, Olathe Culture Group (2002-2004); Community Scholarship Board (2002-2003); President, Alpha Delta Kappa (2002-2003); Secretary, Alpha Delta Kappa (1999-2002); Presenter, Kansas Association of School Librarians (1990-1997); Treasurer, Sigma Alpha Iota (1954); Modern Language Association; National Education Association; Kansas City Lyric Opera Guild; Kansas City Lyric Opera Guild; Kansas Reading Association **H:** Harp; Piano; Voice; Dance; Physical fitness **PA:** Republican **RE:** Baptist **ADD:** 10525 S Chesney Ln, Olathe, KS, 66061

DENNIS, EVERETTE, **T:** University Administrator, Foundation Executive, Educator, Author **I:** Education/Educational Services **CN:** Northwestern University-Quatar **DOB:** 08/15/1942 **PB:** Seattle **SC:** WA/USA **PT:** Everette Eugene; Kathryn Marie (Platt) D. **MS:** Married **SPN:** Emily Thompson Smith (1988) **ED:** Postdoctoral Work, Harvard University (1978-1979); PhD, University of Minnesota (1974); MA, Syracuse University (1966); BS, University of Oregon (1964) **C:** Dean, Chief Executive Officer, Northwestern University, Qatar (2011-Present); Chief Operating Officer, International Longevity Center (1999-2011); Felix E. Larkin Distinguished Professor, Graduate School of Business, Fordham University (1997-2011); Founding President, American Academy in Berlin (1996-2000); Senior Vice President (1994-1997); Vice President (1989-1994); Founding Executive Director, Gannett Freedom Forum Media Studies Center, Columbia University, New York City, NY (1984-1996); Professor, Dean, School of Journalism, University of Oregon, Eugene, OR (1981-1984); Director, Graduate Program, School of Journalism and Mass Communication, University of Minnesota, Minneapolis, MN (1978-1981); Assistant Professor, Associate Professor, Professor, University of Minnesota, Minneapolis, MN (1972-1981); Assistant Professor, Kansas State University (1968-1972); Information Officer, Department of Mental Health, State of Illinois, Chicago, IL (1966-1968) **CR:** Board, World Innovation Summit for Health (2015-Present); Former Trustee, International Museum of Photography; International Institute of Communications; Center for International Journalists; Councilor, American Antiquarian Society; Chair, Advisory Board, Fred Rogers Center; Member, Board of Governors, Academic Doha, Qatar; American Chamber of Commerce; Doha Member Advisory Committee, Transfer and Interpretation Centers; Qatar Foundation **CW:** Author, Editor, "Understanding Media in the Digital Age" (2011); Author, Editor, "Other Voices: The New Journalism in America Newsed" (2011); Author, Editor, "Finding the Best Business School" (2006); Author, Editor, "Understanding Mass Communication," 7th Edition (2002); Author, Editor, "Media and Democracy" (1998); Author, Editor, "Publishing Books" (1997); Author, Editor, "Media and Public Life" (1997); Author, Editor, "American Communication Research" (1996); Author, Editor, "Media and Children" (1996); Author, Editor, "Media-Black and White" (1996); Author, Editor, "Media and Congress" (1997); Editor-in-Chief, "Media Studies Journal" (1987-1996); Author, Editor, "Radio-The Forgotten Medium" (1995); Author, Editor, "The Culture of Crime" (1995); Author, Editor, "Demystifying Media Technology" (1993); Author, Editor, "Higher Education in the Information Age" (1993); Author, Editor, "America's Schools and the Mass Media" (1993); Author, Editor, "Beyond the Cold War" (1991); Author, Editor, "Of Media and People" (1992); Author, Editor, "Media and the Environment" (1991); Author, Editor, "Media Debates" (1991) 3rd Edition (2006); Author, Editor, "Reshaping the Media" (1989); Author, Editor, "Media Freedom and Accountability" (1989); Author, Editor, "The Cost of Libel" (1989); Author, Editor, "Basic Issues in Mass Communication" (1984); Author, Editor, "New Strategies for Public Affairs Reporting" (1983); Author, Editor, "Reporting Processes and Practices" (1981); Author, Editor, "Justice Hugo Black and the First Amendment" (1978); Author, Editor, "Enduring Issues in Mass Communication" (1978); Author, Editor, "The Media Society" (1978); Author, Editor, "Other Voices: The New Journalism in America" (1973); Author, Editor, "The Magic Writing Machine" (1971) **AW:** John Henry Newman Fellow, Fordham University (2002-2003); Distinguished Service Award, University of Oregon (2002); Global Media Research Award, Center for Global Media (2002); Eleanor Blum Award for Research (2004); Inducted Oregon Journalism Hall Of Achievement (2001); Fellow, Center For Journalism and Democracy, University of Southern California; H. Kreighbaum Under 40 Award (1982); University of Oregon Webfoot Award (1985); John F. Kennedy School Government Research Fellow (1981); East-West Communication Institute, HI (1976); Liberal Arts Fellow in Law, Harvard University (1978-1979); Visiting Nieman Fellow (1980); Summer Fellow, Stanford University (1969) **MEM:** President, Association Education in Journalism and Massachusetts Communications (1983-1984); International Communications Association; Council on Foreign Relations; Century Association (New York); Harvard Club (New York) **ADD:** 76 Quaker Hill Dr, Croton on Hudson, NY, 10520

DEPIERRO, MICHAEL JOSEPH, **I:** Telecommunications **DOB:** 12/09/1938 **PB:** New Rochelle **SC:** NY/USA **PT:** Richard dePierro; Josephine (DeBella) dePierro **MS:** Married **SPN:** Dolores M. Lopardi (9/17/1960) **CH:** Richard; Jeanette; Therese; Ten Grandchildren **ED:** BSEE, Fairleigh Dickinson University (1970); AAS in Engineering Technology, RCA Institutes (1965) **C:** Retired (2014); Manager, State of New Jersey, Trenton (1994-2014); Systems Manager, Bell Atlantic Corporation, Newark, NJ (1983-1994); Staff Manager, New Jersey Bell Telephone Company, Newark, NJ (1970-1983); Senior Technology Aide, Bell Telephone Laboratories, Whippany, NJ (1965-1970); Engineering Technician, Adler Electronics, New Rochelle, NY (1962-1965) **CR:** Councilman, Parsippany, NJ (1981-Present); President, Municipal Alliance Committee, Parsippany, NJ (1983-1997); Director, Morris County School Boards Association (1977-1981) **CIV:** Chairman, Republican Club, Parsippany, NJ (1978-Present); Committeeman, Parsippany Republican Committee (1975-Present); League President, Morris County League Municipalities (1985-1997); Council President, Parsippany Township (1982-1997); Member, School Board, Parsippany Board of Education (1975-1981); Past Committee Chairman, Troop 215, Boy Scouts of America **MIL:** Veteran, U.S. Air Force (1956-1962) **CW:** TV Show Producer, "Parsippany Spotlight" (1996-1998); Emcee "Parsippany Spotlight" (1996-1998) **AW:** Honoree, Rescue and Recovery Squad, Parsippany Township (1998); Recognition Plaque, Parsippany Area Chamber of Commerce (1997); Plaque, New Jersey Chapter, U.S. Olympic Committee (1992); Recognition Plaques, Parsippany Board of Education (1981); Plaques and Proclamations from NJ Governor, President of New Jersey Bell, Bell Atlantic, State Senators, Congressmen, Assemblymen, County Freeholders, Rotary, Unico, and Sons of Italy **MEM:** Committee, Association of Government Accountants (1998-Present); Life Member, Scholarship Committee, Post 249, The American Legion (1995-Present); Committee, Post 1084, VFW (1995-Present); President, Parsippany Chapter, Rotary International (1974-Present); Director, Parsippany Area Chamber of Commerce (1988-1997); Chairman, New Jersey Chapter, U.S. Olympic Committee (1980-1992); Fellow, Parsippany Chapter, Rotary International; Chair, Scholarship Fund, Order Sons and Daughters of Italy in America; IEEE **MH:** Albert Nelson Marquis Lifetime Achievement Award (2017); Who's Who in Science and Engineering; Who's Who in Technology **H:** Golf; Internet surfing; Science fiction movies and books **PA:** Republican **RE:** Roman Catholic **ADD:** 5 Fernwood Place, Parsippany, NJ, 07054

DER KALOUSTIAN, VAZKEN MOVSES, **T:** Professor Emeritus **I:** Education/Educational Services **CN:** McGill University **DOB:** 10/27/1937 **PB:** Musa Dagh **SC:** Turkey **PT:** Movses Der Kaloustian; Anahid (Khatchadourian) Der Kaloustian **MS:**

Married **SPN:** Lena Sethian (6/21/1970) **CH:** Sarine; Daria **ED:** Fellow, Department of Pediatrics, Genetics Unit, The Johns Hopkins Hospital (1982); Fellow, Department of Cell Biology and Genetics, Medical Faculty, Erasmus University, Rotterdam, The Netherlands (1974); MSc, The Johns Hopkins University (1968); Fellow in Human Genetics, Department of Pediatrics, The Johns Hopkins University (1966-1968); Resident in Pediatrics, Boston Children's Hospital , Harvard University (1964-1966); Assistant Resident in Pediatrics, American University of Beirut (1963-1964); MD, American University of Beirut, Lebanon (1963); Rotating Intern, American University of Beirut (1962-1963); BSc, American University of Beirut, Lebanon (1959); Diploma, International College, Beirut, Lebanon (1956); Diploma, Hamazkayin Armenian College, Beirut, Lebanon (1955) **CT:** Diplomate, Canadian College of Medical Geneticists (1989); Diplomate, American Board of Medical Genetics and Genomics (1987); Diplomate, The American Board of Pediatrics (1967); Diplomate, Educational Commission for Foreign Medical Graduates (1962); Licensed to Practice Medicine, Lebanon; Licensed to Practice Medicine, Commonwealth of Massachusetts; Licensed to Practice Medicine, State of Maryland; Licensed to Practice Medicine, Quebec, Canada **C:** Professor Emeritus, of Pediatrics and Human Genetics, McGill University (2009-Present); Director, Medical Genetics Training Program, McGill University (2004-2007); Visiting Professor of Pediatrics, American University of Beirut (2000-2005, 1996-1998); Clinical Director, Division of Medical Genetics, Montreal Children's Hospital (1994-2003); Professor of Pediatrics and Genetics, McGill University (1988-2009); Head, Division of Medical Genetics, Montreal Children's Hospital, McGill University (1987-1994); Visiting Professor of Pediatrics, McGill University (1986-1988); Director, National Unit of Human Genetics, American University of Beirut (1981-1986); Founder, National Unit of Human Genetics, American University of Beirut (1981-1986); Professor of Pediatrics, American University of Beirut (1981-1986); Associate Professor of Pediatrics, American University of Beirut (1978-1981); Visiting Associate Professor of Pediatrics, Division of Medical and Biochemical Genetics, Montreal Children's Hospital, McGill University, Montreal, Canada (1976-1977); Associate Professor of Pediatrics, American University of Beirut (1975-1976); Assistant Professor of Pediatrics, American University of Beirut (1970-1975); Instructor of Pediatrics, American University of Beirut (1968-1970); Teaching Fellow in Pediatrics, Harvard University (1965-1966) **CIV:** Armenian Medical International Committee (1994-2000); President, Central Executive, Hamazkayin Armenian Educational and Cultural Association (1990-1998, 1986-1988); Central Council of the Armenian Catholicosate of Cilicia (1983-1990); Advisory Board, Karagueuzian Foundation for Child Welfare in Lebanon (1970-1986) **CW:** Editorial Board Member, Armenian Medical Reviews (2006-Present); Guest Editor, American Journal of Medical Genetics (2004); Author, Book, "Congenital Anomalies of the Ear, Nose, and Throat," Oxford University Press (1997); Editorial Board Member, Dysmorphology and Clinical Genetics (1992-1994); Editorial Board Member, The Birth Defects Encyclopedia (1990); Editorial Board Member, The American Journal of Medical Genetic (1989-1999); Author, "The Kidney in Genetic Disease (Genetics in Medicine & Surgery)," Churchill Livingstone (1986); Editorial Board Member, The American Journal of Medical Genetics (1981-1989); Editorial Board Member, The Lebanese Science Bulletin (1985-1986); Author, "Genetic Diseases of the Skin," Springer-Verlag (1979); Author, "Genetic Diseases of the Skin", Springer -Verlag (1979); Reviewer, Various Medical Journals; Contributor, 161 Articles in Medical and Scientific Professional Journals; Contributor, 15 Chapters to Medical Books; Author, Three Medical Books **AW:** Medal of the Armenian Catholicosate of Cilicia, Level of Prince (2010); Gold Medal Award, Alumni Association, American University of Beirut (2007); Fellowship Award, National Institutes of Health (1966-1968); Hamazkayin Medal, Armenian Educational and Cultural Association; Dean's Honor List, American University of Beirut **MEM:** International Scientific Advisory Committee, The Cyprus Institute of Neurology & Genetics (2008-Present); International Board of Medical Advisers, Yerevan State Medical University (2007); Teratology Society (1998-2001); AMGQ (1998-2009); Advisory Board, Canadian Angelman Syndrome Society (1996-2005); Medical Advisory Board, Canadian Organization for Rare Disorders (1996); American College of Medical Genetics and Genomics (1993-1995); Canadian College of Medical Geneticists (1989-2009); The American Society of Human Genetics, Incorporated (1987-2009); European Paediatric Research Society (1981-1986); LebPedSoc (1968-1986); Lebanese Medical Society (1963-1986); Alpha Omega Alpha Honor Medical Society; Johns Hopkins University Chapter, The Johns Hopkins University; Lebanese Association for the Advancement of Science **MH:** Albert Nelson Marquis Lifetime Achievement Award (2017) **ADD:** 456 Melbourne Avenue, Mount Royal, QC, Canada, H3P 1H2

DER-HOUSSIKIAN, HAIG, T: Linguist, Educator (Retired) **I:** Education/Educational Services **DOB:** 08/16/1938 **PB:** Heliopolis **SC:** Egypt **PT:** Vagharsh Der-Houssikian; Adrine (Karalian) Der-Houssikian **MS:** Married **SPN:** Gaylynne Hall (8/27/1961) **ED:** PhD in Linguistics, University of Texas at Austin (1969); MA in Political Science and Public Administration, American University of Beirut, Lebanon (1962); BA in Political Science and Public Administration, American University of Beirut, Lebanon (1961); Coursework, American University in Cairo, Egypt (1957-1959) **C:** Professor Emeritus, University of Florida, Gainesville (2003-Present); Professor, University of Florida, Gainesville (1977-2003); Chairman, Department of African and Asian Languages and Literature, University of Florida, Gainesville (1982-1991); Director, Linguistics Programs, University of Florida, Gainesville (1984-1985); Director, Center for African Studies, University of Florida, Gainesville (1973-1979); Associate Professor, University of Florida, Gainesville (1972-1977); Director, Linguistics Programs, University of Florida, Gainesville (1971-1972); Assistant Professor of African Languages and Linguistics, University of Florida, Gainesville (1967-1972); Research Associate, Fulbright-Hays Doctoral Dissertation Grant, University of Dar-es-Salaam, Tanzania (1966-1967) **CR:** Reviewer, African Book Publication Review (1996-Present); Panelist, U.S. Department of Education, Washington D.C. (1975-2015); Graduate Council, University of Florida (1988-1991); Visiting Professor of African Linguistics, University of Zimbabwe, Harare (1989); Consultant, U.S. Information Agency Academic Specialist Grant, Brazzaville, Congo (February 1988); Short Term Senior Fulbright Lecturer, Universite Marien Ngouabi, Brazzaville, Congo (February-March, 1981); Specialist Grant Consultant to the Universite De Ouagadougou, U.S. Information Agency, Burkina Faso (1981); Senior Fulbright Lecturer, Universite Du Benin, Lome, Togo (1979-1980); Senior Fulbright Lecturer, Universidade De Luanda, Angola (1972-1973); Invited Participant in One-week "Scholar Diplomat" Conference in Reference to East Africa, U.S. State Department (1970); Grant Proposal Evaluator, Social Sciences and Humanities Research Council of Canada; U.S. Information Agency Academic Specialist Grant, Universite Marien Ngouabi **CW:** Author, "TEM, Grammar Handbook" (1980); Author, "TEM, Communication and Culture" (1980); Author, "TEM, Special Skills" (Tem, also known as Cotocoli, is a north central language in Togo belonging to the Gur/Voltaic family of languages) (1980); Co-Editor, "Language and Linguistics Problems in Africa" (1977); Compiler, "A Bibliography Of African Linguistics" (1972); Contributor, Chapters, Linguistics Books **AW:** Grantee, ACTION (1980-1981) **MEM:** African Linguistics Bibliographer, Modern Language Association (1967-1974); Linguistics Society of America; African Studies Association; Southeastern Conference on Linguistics; Phi Kappa Phi **MH:** Albert Nelson Marquis Lifetime Achievement Award (2017) **H:** Reading; Hiking; Travel **RE:** Armenian Apostolic **ADD:** 218 NW 30th St, Gainesville, FL, 32607

DEVINE, MICHAEL BUXTON, T: Attorney, Barrister, Arbitrator, Law Professor **I:** Law and Legal Services **CN:** Northumbria University Law School **DOB:** 10/25/1953 **PB:** Des Moines **SC:** IA/USA **PT:** Cleatie Hiram Devine Jr.; Katherine Ann (Buxton) Devine **MS:** Single **ED:** LLM in International Business Legal Studies, University of Exeter, England (1988); Diploma in Advanced International Legal Studies, University of the Pacific, Salzburg, Austria (1986); JD, Drake University, Des Moines, Iowa (1980); MPA, Drake University, Des Moines, Iowa (1980); BA Cum Laude, St. Olaf College, Northfield, Minnesota (1976); Associated Colleges of the Midwest (ACM) Student Research Fellow, The Newberry Library, Chicago, Illinois (1976); St. Olaf Term Abroad at St. Peter's College, University of Oxford, England (1975) **CT:** Fellow in International Commercial Arbitration, Chartered Institute of Arbitrators (FCIArb), London, England **C:** Senior Lecturer and Program Leader, LLMs in Commercial Law, International Commercial Law, and International Trade Law (2010-Present); Arbitrator, Chartered Institute of Arbitrators (2008-Present); Barrister: Magdalen Chambers, Exeter, England, Door Tenant (2001-Present); Professor, University of Wisconsin-La Crosse, College of Business Administration, La Crosse, Wisconsin, Assistant Professor of Business Law (Domestic and International) (2005-2010); Lecturer and Course Leader, The Robert Gordon University, Aberdeen Business School, Department of Law, Aberdeen, Scotland; LLM in International Commercial Law (2001-2004); Part-Time Lecturer, University of Kent at Canterbury, Kent Law School, Canterbury, England (2000, 2001); Chambers of Donald Gordon, London, England, Tenant (1999-2001); Chambers of Maire-Claire Sparrow, London, England (1996-1999); Pupil Barrister, Lafili, VanCrumbrugghe & Partners, Association d'Avocats, Brussels, Belgium (1995); Pupil Barrister, Office of the General Counsel and Secretary, Philips Electronics UK Ltd., London, England (1994); Pupil Barrister, Chambers of Alan Tyrrell, QC, London, England (1993-1994); Associate, Pavelic & Levites PC, New York, NY (1989-1992); Associate, Christianson, Hohnbaum & George, Des Moines, Iowa (1989); Judicial Law Clerk, Judicial Branch of the State of Iowa, Burlington, Iowa (1987-1988); Associate, Bump & Haesemeyer PC, Des Moines, Iowa (1980-1985); Law Professor, Northumbria University Law School, Newcastle upon Tyne, England **CR:** Member, Congress of Fellows, Center for International Legal Studies, Salzburg, Austria (2008-Present); Member, College of Arbitrators,

Center for International Legal Studies, Salzburg, Austria (2008-Present); Fellow, Chartered Institute of Arbitrators, London, England (2008-Present); Member, Society of Legal Scholars in Great Britain and Ireland (2002-Present); Volunteer Judge/Arbitrator, Willem C. Vis International Commercial Law Arbitration Moot, Vienna, Austria (2008-Present); Volunteer Judge/Arbitrator, Foreign Direct Investment (FDI) International Arbitration Moot, Various Venues (2008-Present); International Law Intern, Herbert Oppenheimer, Nathan & Vandyk, Solicitors, City of London, England (1986) **CIV:** Donor, Des Moines YMCA Camp Camperships (2013-Present); Donor, St. Olaf College, Drake University Law School, University of Exeter Law School; State of Iowa Friendship Force Mission to China (1984); City of Des Moines, Iowa Friendship Force Exchange with West Berlin, West Germany (1982) **CW:** Deputy Editor, International Law News, American Bar Association (2016-Present); Assistant Editor, Journal of International Trade Law & Policy (2005-2009); Various Law Review Publications **AW:** Student Led Teaching Awards, Northumbria University Law School (2015, 2017); Finalist, Law Teacher of the Year for the Northeast of England, Northern Law Awards (2016); Pi Alpha Alpha Public Affairs and Administration Honor Society, Drake University Chapter (1978); Phi Alpha Theta History Honor Society, St. Olaf College Chapter (1976); St. Olaf College Scholarships (1973-1976); St. Olaf College Grant (1972-1973) **MEM:** Council on International Affairs, New York City Bar Association (1990-1992); Treasurer, Iowa Chapter, Federal Bar Association (1984-1985); Executive Committee, Federal Bar Association (1984-1985); Chairman, State of Iowa, Federal Bar Association/US Small Business Administration Export Assistance Program (Pro Bono) (1983-1985) **BAR:** Ireland (King's Inn of Court, Dublin, 2004), Northern Ireland (Inn of Court of Northern Ireland, Belfast, 2000), England & Wales (Gray's Inn of Court, London, 1995); US Court of Appeals, Federal Circuit (1990); US Court of International Trade (1990); US District Court, Southern District of New York (1990); Colorado (1988); New York (1987); Wisconsin (1987); District of Columbia (1986); Minnesota (1986); Nebraska (1985); US Supreme Court (1985); Iowa (1980); International Section on Dispute Resolution, American Section on International Law, New York State Section on International Law, Iowa State Section on International Law and New York City Bar Associations; General Council of the Bar of England and Wales; Bar European Group **MH:** Albert Nelson Marquis Lifetime Achievement Award (2017) **PA:** Democrat **RE:** Presbyterian **ADD:** 55 Renforth Close, Gateshead, United Kingdom, NE8 3JF

DEWEESE, ELDONNA ROSE, T: Librarian **I:** Library Management/Library Services **DOB:** 11/07/1940 **SC:** MO/USA **PT:** Osborne Kuhn DeWeese; Helena Elizabeth DeWeese **ED:** MA, Missouri State University (1984); MLS, Emporia State University (1969); EdB, Missouri State University (1962) **CT:** Certified English Teacher, State of Missouri; Certified Speech Teacher, State of Missouri **C:** Collection Development Librarian, Southwest Baptist University, Bolivar, MO (2002-2003); Interim Dean, University Librarian, Southwest Baptist University, Bolivar, MO (2000-2002); Collection Development Librarian, Southwest Baptist University, Bolivar, MO (1991-2000); Computer Software Distributor, Micro-Magic Systems Inc, Bolivar, MO (1985-1988); Graduate Assistant, Missouri State University, Springfield, MO (1982-1985); Reference Librarian, Missouri State University, Springfield, MO (1982-1985); Administrative Librarian, Southwest Baptist

University, Bolivar, MO (1972-1982); Reference Librarian, Southwest Baptist University, Bolivar, MO (1969-1972); English Teacher, Pierce City High School, Pierce City, MO (1962-1968); Speech Teacher, Pierce City High School, Pierce City, MO (1962-1968); Librarian, Pierce City High School, Pierce City, MO (1962-1968) **CW:** Editor, Southern Baptist Periodical Index (1987-Present); Production Manager, Southern Baptist Periodical Index (1987-Present); Author, Poetry, "Grist" **AW:** The Betty Hurtt Meritorious Service Award for Admirable and Exceptional Contributions to the Baptist Library and Archive Profession, ALABI (2013) **MEM:** American Library Association; The American Society for Indexing; Missouri State Poetry Society; Missouri Library Association; ALABI **MH:** Albert Nelson Marquis Lifetime Achievement Award (2017) **H:** Reading; Church choir; Poetry writing **RE:** Baptist **BA:** 1600 University Avenue, Southwest Baptist University, Bolivar, MO, 65613 **ADD:** 504 N Benton Avenue, Apt. 3, Bolivar, MO, 65613

DEWITT, EULA, T: Enrolled Agent, Accountant (Retired) **I:** Financial Services **CN:** IRS **DOB:** 02/05/1948 **PB:** Conway **SC:** SC/USA **PT:** Joseph DeWitt; Ethel Maude (Parmley) DeWitt **CH:** Andre Carter; David Carter; John Ramos, III (Stepchild) **ED:** PhD, Lighthouse Christian College (2011); DDiv Lighthouse Christian College, Magna Cum Laude (2000); ThM, Lighthouse Christian College (1998); BS in Accounting and Economics, The City University of New York (1981) **CT:** Certified Enrolled Agent, IRS (2007); Certificate, Bethlehem Bible College (1990) **C:** Staff, Public Speakers Bureau, IRS, New York, NY (1985-Present); Field Agent, IRS, New York, NY (1981-Present); Instructor for Revenue Agents, IRS, New York, NY (1986-2005); Junior Accountant, Kenneth Laventhol, CPA Firm, New York, NY (1981) **CR:** Notary Public, Division of Licensing Services, State of New York **CIV:** Associate Minister, Bethel Baptist Church (2000-Present); Missionary Evangelist, Wartburg Lutheran Home for Seniors (1999-Present); Member, Prison Ministry Team to Rikers Island, Bethlehem Missionary Church (1996-Present); First Corinthian Baptist Church (1993-Present); Leader, Altar Workers Ministry (1991-Present); Tutor, York College, The City University of New York (1991-Present); Sunday School Teacher, Bethlehem Missionary Church (1977-Present); Missionary, Jamaica (2000); Missionary, West Indies (2000); Missionary, Kano State, Nigeria (1997); Missionary, Jos State, Nigeria (1997); Missionary, Benue State, Nigeria (1997); Various Baptist Churches (1996); Missionary, Guyana (1995); Missionary, England (1993); Missionary, Belize (1991); Guest Speaker, Sixth Annual Convention, Hunter College (1991); Exploring Division of Greater New York (1991); Catholic Charities Archdiocese of New York (1991) **CW:** Author, Newsletters; Contributor, Articles, Professional Journals **MEM:** Board of Directors, Institute of Management Accountants, Inc. (1982-Present); President, Institute of Management Accountants, Inc. (2007); President, Toastmaster's 21 Club (2004-2005); President, Institute of Management Accountants, Inc. (1997); Able Toastmaster, ATM, Toastmaster's 21 Club (1996); Vice President, Professional Education, Institute of Management Accountants, Inc. (1994-1995); Vice President, Toastmaster's 21 Club; Board Governor, Stuart Cameron McCloud Society; Director, Member Services, York College Alumni Association **MH:** Albert Nelson Marquis Lifetime Achievement Award (2017) **H:** Photography; Reading **ADD:** 16518 144th Ter, Jamaica, NY, 11434

DEY, RADHESHYAM CHANDRA, T: Supervisory Cytologist **I:** Medicine & Health Care **CN:** Howard

University Hospital **DOB:** 01/30/1950 **PB:** Kolkata **SC:** India **PT:** Bhairab Dey; Satyabala Dey **MS:** Married **SPN:** Indrani Roy Chowdhury (7/5/1981) **CH:** Smita; Anita; Ishan **ED:** Postgraduate Studies, Albert Einstein School Medicine, New York, NY (1997); Postgraduate Studies, Laval University, Quebec City, Canada (1995); Certified In Life Science, University of Calcutta (1974); MSc, University of Calcutta (1972); BSc, Bangabasi College, Calcutta, India (1970) **CT:** Certified Quality Assurance, Inspector's Inspection Laboratory, College of American Pathologists (2005, 2008); Certified in Basic American Sign Language Course, Gallaudet University (1989); Certified in Leadership Management, Educational Development, Quality Improvement and Equal Opportunity, Walter Reed Army Medical Center (1989); Brooke Army Medical Center (now San Antonio Military Medical Center), San Antonio, TX (1983); Registered Cytotechnologist, American Society of Clinical Pathologists, International Academy Cytology, States of California, Maryland **C:** Cytopathology Inspector, Howard University Medical Center, Washington D.C. (2014-Present); Health Science Specialist, Supervisory Cytologist, Baltimore Veterans Affairs Medical Center (2008-Present); Team Member, USCAP, Baltimore, MD (2014); Laboratory Inspector, College of American Pathologists (2012); Chief Cytotechnologist, United Medical Laboratory, McLean, VA (2007-2008); Supervisory Cytologist, Walter Reed Army Medical Center (now Walter Reed National Military Medical Center), Washington D.C. (1988-2005); Cytotechnologist, National Health Laboratory, Vienna, VA (1988); Cytology Specialist, Medical Center, Supreme Headquarters, , Allied Powers Europe, Mons, Belgium (1985-1987); Cytology Specialist, U.S. Army Hospital, Fort Campbell, KY (1983-1985); Biological Science Assistant, Walter Reed Army Institute for Research, Washington D.C. (1980-1983); Associate, Anthropology Survey of India, Indian Museum, Calcutta, India (1977-1978); Research Fellow, University of Calcutta (1975-1977) **CR:** Member Dubrovnik-Cavtat, Geneva, Switzerland (2014); Member Dubrovnik-Cavtat, Pondicherry, India (2013); Member Dubrovnik-Cavtat, Paris, France (2013); Member Dubrovnik-Cavtat, Croatia (2012); USCAP, Vancouver, Canada (2012); American Society of Cytopathology, Las Vegas (2012); American Society of Cytopathology, Baltimore (2011); European Congress of Cytology, Istanbul, Turkey (2011); European Congress of Cytology, Edinburgh, Scotland (2010); European Congress of Cytology, Lisbon, Portugal (2009); European Congress of Cytology, Athens, Greece (2004); Presenter in Field, Indian Statistical Institute, Calcutta, India (1999) **CW:** Contributor, Professional Journals, Pathology Conferences **AW:** Bronze Award, U.S. Government Federal Executive Board, Baltimore, MD (2013); Services Award, Department of Veterans Affairs, Baltimore, MD (2011); Leadership Symposia Award, Baltimore, MD (2010); Commander's Award, Walter Reed Medical Center, U.S. Army (1997); Excellence in Teaching Award, National Capital Region Consortium Pathology Residency, (1997); Decree Of Merit for Outstanding Contribution to Medicine and Health Care (1995); Anthropological Survey of India Fellowship, University of Calcutta (1976); Decorated, Commendation Medal, U.S. Army; Decorated, Achievement Medal, U.S. Army; Decorated, Good Conduct Medals, U.S. Army **MEM:** Fellow, International Academy of Cytology; American Association for the Advancement of Science; Life Member, DAV; Indian Academy of Cytologists; Indian Anthropology Society; American Society of Clinical Pathologists; American Society of Cytopathology; American Anthropology Association; Life Member, American

Legion **MH:** Albert Nelson Marquis Lifetime Achievement Award (2017) **H:** Soccer; Swimming; Running; Travel; Theater **ADD:** 4404 Camley Way, Burtonsville, MD, 20866

DIAMOND, RICHARD S., T: Managing Partner **I:** Law and Legal Services **CN:** Diamond & Diamond P.A. **PB:** Newark **SC:** NJ/USA **PT:** Robert Diamond; Arlene Diamond **MS:** Married **SPN:** Denise Diamond **CH:** Jonathan; Tyler **ED:** JD, Seton Hall University (1985); BA in Economics, Rutgers, The State University of New Jersey (1982); BBA, Rutgers, The State University of New Jersey (1982) **CT:** Certified Matrimonial Trial Lawyer, Supreme Court, New Jersey Courts; Certified Divorce Mediator, New Jersey Courts; Court Appointed Economic Mediator, New Jersey Courts; Court Appointed Divorce Early Settlement Panelist, Somerset County; Court Appointed Divorce Early Settlement Panelist, Union County; Court Appointed Divorce Early Settlement Panelist, Essex County; Court Appointed Divorce Early Settlement Panelist, Hunterdon County **C:** Managing Partner, Law Firm of Diamond & Diamond P.A., Millburn, NJ (1992-Present); Law Secretary, Hon. Burton Ironson, JSC (1985-1986); Partner, Diamond Hodes & Diamond, Springfield, NJ; Associate, Law Firm of Robert Diamond, Springfield, NJ **CR:** Speaker, Broadcasts; Guest Lecturer, Broadcasts **CW:** Contributor, Articles, Professional Journals **MEM:** Lecturer, New Jersey State Bar Association; Speaker, New Jersey State Bar Association; Early Settlement Panelist, Somerset County, New Jersey State Bar Association; Essex County Bar Association; Union County Bar Association **BAR:** U.S. District Court, State of New Jersey (1991); State of Florida (1991); State of New Jersey (1985) **MH:** Albert Nelson Marquis Lifetime Achievement Award (2017) **ADD:** 225 Millburn Avenue, Suite 208, Millburn, NJ, 07041 **URL:** http://www.DiamondandDiamond.com

DICK, ROBERT B., T: Contractor **I:** Sciences **CN:** National Institute for Occupational Safety and Health, Centers For Disease Control and Prevention **DOB:** 08/20/1942 **PB:** Grand Rapids **SC:** MI/USA **PT:** David J. Dick; Alyce C. (Usher) Dick **MS:** Single **SPN:** Margaret M. Mackey (11/29/1969, Deceased 6/13/2002) **CH:** Michael; Anthony; Kevin **ED:** PhD, Oklahoma State University (1972); MA, University of South Dakota (1966); BA, Michigan State University, Cum Laude (1964) **C:** Director of Research Science, National Institute for Occupational Health and Safety, Centers For Disease Control and Prevention, Cincinnati, OH (1990-Present); Research Psychologist, National Institute for Occupational Health and Safety, Centers For Disease Control and Prevention, Cincinnati, OH (1982-1989); Branch Chief, Alcohol, Drug Abuse and Mental Health Division, Region IV, Centers for Disease Control and Prevention, Atlanta, GA (1978-1982); Health Services Representative, Division of Health Services, Region IV, Centers for Disease Control and Prevention, Atlanta, GA (1974-1978); Mental Health Consultant, National Institute of Mental Health, Region IV, Centers for Disease Control and Prevention, Atlanta, GA (1972-1974); Member, Narcotic Addict Rehabilitation Branch, National Institute of Mental Health, Los Angeles, CA (1967-1969) **CIV:** Secretary, IHM Athletic Boosters (1987-1993) **MIL:** Captain, Communication Corps, U.S. Public Health Service **CW:** Member, Editorial Advisory Board, NeuroToxicology and Teratology, Elmsford, NY (1989-Present); Contributor, Articles, Professional Journals **AW:** Commendation Medals, U.S. Public Health Service **MEM:** American Psychological Association; International Neurotoxicology Association; AMSUS; Behavioral Toxicology Society; Commissioned Officer, Commissioned Officers Association of the USPHS Inc.; Sigma Xi **MH:** Albert Nelson Marquis Lifetime Achievement Award (2017) **H:** Sports; History; Model railroading **ADD:** 6930 Gammwell Dr, Cincinnati, OH, 45230

DICKERSON, JOHN ROBERT, T: Engineer **I:** Engineering **DOB:** 10/08/1930 **PB:** Detroit **SC:** MI/USA **PT:** James Eldridge; Edith Barrie Dickerson **MS:** Married **SPN:** Barbara Marie Gannon (2/7/1969); Jacqueline Bowman (6/14/1952, Divorced 9/1967) **CH:** Robert Floyd; Diane Lynn; Edward Michael Gannon **C:** Off-Site Manager of Vehicle Build Operations, Production, Show and Impact Test and Development Section, Chrysler Corporation (Now FCA US LLC) (1978-1989); Manager, Vehicle Build Operations, Chrysler Corporation (Now FCA US LLC) (1984-1988); Product Development Engineer, Chrysler Corporation (Now FCA US LLC) (1978-1984); Supervisor, Fleet Engineering, American Motors Corporation (1972-1978); Owner, Chief Financial Officer, J. Robert Dickerson & Associates (1969-1972); Senior Stylist Designer, Chrysler Corporation (Now FCA US LLC) (1964-1969); Engineer, Chrysler Corporation (Now FCA US LLC) (1964-1969); Senior Stylist Designer, Chrysler Corporation (Now FCA US LLC) (1961-1964); Senior Stylist Designer, Chrysler Corporation (Now FCA US LLC) (1957-1961) **CR:** Assistant Executor, Multimillion Dollar Estate, Malibu, California (2005-2008); Director, Woodfield Reforestation Project (2006-2007); Chairman, Advisory Committee, Technical Communications (2001-2002); Member, Signatory Party to United Nations, American Motors Corporation (1974-1978); Engineering Representative, Automotive Vehicle Bid Consortium, U.S. General Services Administration (1974-1978); Design Consultant, J. Robert Dickerson & Associates (1969-1973); Consultant, Wayne State University (1971-1972); Stylist Design Consultant, Creative Industries, Detroit, Michigan (1970-1971) **CIV:** Member, Republican Senatorial Committee (2002-Present); Member, Republican Presidential Task Force (2000-Present); Charter Member, Republican National Committee (2000-Present); Contributor, 100th Anniversary of the Automobile, Detroit Historical Museum, Detroit Historical Society (2000); Organizer, 100th Anniversary of the Automobile, Detroit Historical Museum, Detroit Historical Society (2000); Sponsor, Starr Commonwealth; Founding Sponsor, National Museum of the United States Army **MIL:** U.S. Air Force (1950-1952) **CW:** Author, "One Goal is Not Enough" (2001); Author, "How to Build a 50 Foot Yacht" (1972) **AW:** Recipient, Design Award, U.S. General Services Administration (1980); Recipient, Recognition Award, Probate Court, Judicial Council of California **MEM:** United States Olympic Committee; asbe Foundation; National Rifle Association of America; Senior Men's Club of Grosse Pointe **H:** Flying; Boating; Golf; Travel; Gardening; Painting; Target shooting **PA:** Republican **ADD:** 7501 E Thompson Peak Pkwy Unit 313, Scottsdale, AZ, 85255

DIEHL, STEPHEN ANTHONY, T: Human Resources Consultant **I:** Human Resources **DOB:** 03/15/1942 **PB:** Brooklyn **SC:** NY/USA **PT:** Anthony Stephen Diehl; Paula (Kula) Diehl **MS:** Married **SPN:** Barbara Lynn Marschman (8/3/1968) **ED:** Postgraduate Coursework in Business, New York University (1967-1973); BS, Long Island University (1963) **C:** Senior Vice President, Human Resources Director, Greenpoint Savings Bank, New York City, NY (1977-1995); Vice President, Marketing Director, Greenpoint Savings Bank, Brooklyn, NY (1969-1977) **CR:** Town Council Member, Morrisville, NC (2009-2013); Human Resources Consultant (1997-Present); Director, Human Resources,

New York City Marathon, New York Road Runners (1996-2001); Officer, Director, New York Chapter, SHRM (1995-2001) **MEM:** President, Savings Banks Officers Forum (1986-1987); Chairman, Human Resources Officers Forum (1980-1981); Chairman, New York City Marketing Forum (1975-1976); Chairman, Savings Banks Marketing Forum, New York State (1973-1974) **MH:** Albert Nelson Marquis Lifetime Achievement Award (2017) **H:** Photography; Video; Stereo **PA:** Democrat **RE:** Roman Catholic **ADD:** 112 Bruington Ct, Morrisville, NC, 27560

DIETHELM, ARNOLD, T: Professor of Surgery Emeritus **I:** Education/Educational Services **CN:** The University of Alabama at Birmingham School of Medicine **DOB:** 01/13/1932 **PB:** Baltimore **SC:** MD/USA **PT:** Oskar Arnold Diethelm; Grace (Gillespie) Diethelm **MS:** Married **SPN:** Nancy Lee Lane (6/21/1951) **CH:** Nancy Elizabeth; Linda Lane; Eugene Arnold (Deceased); Ellen Jeanette; Richard Gillespie **ED:** Honorary DSc, The University of Alabama (1993) Research Fellow, Harvard University Medical School (1966-1967) Research Fellow, Peter Bent Brigham Hospital, Boston, MA (1965-1966); From Intern to Resident in Surgery, New York Presbyterian Hospital-New York Weill Cornell Center (1958-1965) MD, Cornell University (1958) AB, Washington State University (1953) **CT:** Board Certified in General Surgery, American Board of Surgery **C:** Professor Emeritus, Department of Surgery, The University of Alabama at Birmingham School of Medicine (2000-Present) Member, Faculty, The University of Alabama at Birmingham Hospital (1967-Present) Chairman, Department of Surgery, The University of Alabama at Birmingham Hospital (1982-2000); Professor, Surgery, The University of Alabama at Birmingham Hospital (1973-2000) Vice Chairman, Department, The University of Alabama at Birmingham Hospital (1973-1982); Assistant of Surgery, Peter Bent Brigham Hospital, Boston, MA (1965-1966); Instructor, Cornell University Medical School (1964-1965) **CR:** Member, Residency Review Committee for Surgery, Accreditation Council for Graduate Medical Education (1994-Present); Chairman, Accreditation Council for Graduate Medical Education (1997-1999) **CW:** Contributor, More Than 200 Articles to Medical Journals; Author, "Order from Chaos"; Speaker in Field **MEM:** President, American Society of Transplant Surgeons (1991-1992) President, Southern Surgical Association (1989); Director, American Board of Surgery (1987-1993) American Association for the Advancement of Science; American College of Surgeons; American Medical Association; American Society of Nephrology; American Surgical Association; Association for Academic Surgery; The Transplantation Society **MH:** Albert Nelson Marquis Lifetime Achievement Award (2017) **ADD:** 3248 Sterling Rd, Birmingham, AL, 35213 **URL:** https://www.doximity.com/pub/arnold-diethelm-md

DILL, ELLEN RENÉE, T: Educator, Minister, Writer **I:** Education/Educational Services **DOB:** 01/02/1949 **PB:** Detroit **SC:** MI/USA **PT:** Clarence Lorenzo Dill; Melvin Elizabeth (Knowles) Dill **MS:** Divorced **CH:** Christopher Edward Brown; Crystal Elizabeth Brown **ED:** DMin, Chicago Theological Seminary (1999); ABD in Sociology and Ethics, Northwestern University, Evanston, IL (1988); MDiv, Garrett Evangelical Seminary, Evanston, IL (1979); BA in Sociology and Education, Nazareth College of Michigan, Nazareth, MI (1972) **CT:** Ordained Minister (2003); Licensed Missionary, Methodist Church (2003); Ordained Minister (1985); Ministry, United Methodist Church (1974); Certified in Education, State of Nevada; Certified in Education, State of Georgia; Certified in Education,

State of Michigan **C:** Ministerial Staff, Union Chapel Methodist Church (2012-Present); Web Master, Riverside School (2006-Present); Council Chairperson, Union Chapel Methodist Church (2012-Present); RTI Coordinator, Riverside School (2006-Present); Ministerial Staff, STAMEZ (2011-2012); Chairperson, STAMEZ (2011-2012); Teacher, Grades K-5, CCSD (2007-2011); Educator, Riverside School (2006-2011); Educator, Cornerstone Academy (2006-2007); Educator, Heritage Academy (2005-2006); Webmaster, Tracy McGregor Elementary School (2000-2005); Teacher, Tracy McGregor Elementary School, Detroit, MI (1999-2005); Pastor, Immanuel United Methodist Church (1999); Pastor, United Campus Ministry, Winona State University (1995-1999); Pastor, Woodlawn United Methodist Church, Chicago, IL (1990-1993); Assistant Spiritual Director, Walk to Emeritus (1988-1992); Pastor, Community United Methodist Church, Markham, IL (1988-1990); Pastor, Clair-Christian United Methodist Church, Chicago, IL (1984-1988); Associate Pastor, First United Methodist Church Temple, Chicago, IL (1982-1984); Pastor, St. Luke United Methodist Church, Chicago, IL (1980-1982); Teacher, Eastside Vicariate School, Detroit, MI (1972-1977); Teaching Assistant, Head Start St. Agnes Church, Detroit, MI (1966-1968) **CR:** Member, Minnesota Conference of Council Ministries (1995-Present); Chairperson, Administration Council, Union Chapel Church (2013-2014); Minister, International Missionary Church (2003); Adjunct Professor, Winona State University, Minnesota (1998-2008); Winona Cultural Diversity Task Force (1997-1999); Board Member, Project Fine (1997-1999); Chairperson, Commission on Religion and Race, Minnesota Conference (1997-1999); Medical Ethics Committee, Community Memorial Hospital, Winona, MN (1995-1999); Winona Area Ministerium (1995-1999); Invocation Speaker, United Theological Seminary, Twin Cities (1995); State of Minnesota Cultural Dynamics Project (1994-1997); Minnesota Conference Clergy Mentor (1994-1996); Member, Minneapolis Council of Churches (1994-1996); Adjunct Faculty, United Theological Seminary, Twin Cities (1994-1996); Chairperson, Minnesota Conference Committee on Religion & Race (1995); Clinical Pastoral Education examiner, St. Paul, MN (1995); Invocation, Annual Meeting, National Association for the Advancement of Colored People, Minneapolis, MN (1995); Invocation, Chicago City Council Meetings (1993); Invocation, Chicago City Council Meetings (1991); Spiritual Director, Men's Walk to Emmaus (1991); Commission on the Status & Role Women, Northern Illinois Conference (1991-1993); United Methodist Foundation, University of Chicago (1990-1993); Chicago Clergy Ethics Study Group (1990-1993); Member, Southern District Board of Ministry (1988-1993); Church Building & Location (1988-1993); Invocation, Chicago City Council Meetings (1990); Assistant Spiritual Director, Walk Emmaus (1988-1992); Marcy-Newberry Foundation (1988); Southern District Council Ministries (1984-1988); Southern District Strategy Committee (1984-1988); Member, Detroit Conference of Elders Orders (1985); Coordinator, North Central Ethnic-minority Clergywomen's Conference, Chicago, IL (1983); Conducted Seminar, Women in Ministry, Garrett Evangelical Seminary (1981); Teaching Fellow in Church and Society, Garrett Evangelical Theological Seminary (1980); Protestant Chaplain, Wayne County Youth Home, Detroit, MI (1975-1977); Founder, St. Agnes Gazette Newspaper (1964-1966); Editor, St. Agnes Gazette Newspaper (1964-1966); Former Chairman, Southern District Board of Education; Member, Monitoring Committee, Northern Illinois Conference; Configuration Committee,

Western District Laboratory School; Planning Committee, Western District Laboratory School; Member, National Education Association; Building Committee Member, Covenant United Methodist Church **CIV:** Charter Member, Atlanta Meetup Optimist Club (2014-Present); Member, Minnesota Cultural Dynamics Project (1994-1997); Carroll M. Felton Junior Housing Foundation (1992-1993); Assistant Dean, Pembroke Institute (1992); Board of Directors, Marcy-Newberry Association (1986-1988); Child Serve Community Council, Chicago, IL (1984-1988); Board Member, Austin Christian Law Center (1983-1993); Participant, Worship Service, Free Soviet Jewry (1983); Board of Directors, Garrett-Evangelical Seminary (1978); Founder, St. Agnes Girls Club (1965-1967); Area Chair, Mayor's Committee to Keep Detroit Beautiful (1965-1966); Invocation, City of Chicago City Council; Holy Name Cathedral, Chicago, IL **CW:** Editorial Adviser, "The Christian Ministry Journal" (1987-Present); Webmaster, Tracy McGregor Elementary School (2000-2005); Co-Author, Abstract, American Academy of Rheumatology (1990); Co-author, "Teachers Guide: Two Hundred Years of American Methodism" (1981); Contributor, Articles, Professional Journals, Websites, Blogs; Editorial Adviser, Writer, "The Christian Ministry" **AW:** Recognition for Teaching, Governor Jennifer Granholm (2003); State of Minnesota Cultural Dynamics Education Project (1997); Black Methodist for Church Renewal Leadership Award (1988); Hartman Fellow (1981); Dempster Graduate Fellow (1980); Hartman Scholar (1979); Citation for Excellence in Journalism, Michigan Press Association (1978); Citation, Mayor's Committee to Keep Detroit Beautiful (1966); Pastor's Award, Woodlawn United Methodist Church; Pastor's Award, Clair-Christian United Methodist Church, Winona, MN; Pastor's Award, Immanuel United Methodist Church **MEM:** National Education Association; Georgia Association of Educators; Optimist International; AARP **MH:** Albert Nelson Marquis Lifetime Achievement Award (2017) **H:** Reading; Sewing; Teaching; Writing; Studying; Computer technology; Travelling; Volunteering **PA:** Democrat **RE:** Methodist **ADD:** 37 Little Silver Ct SE, Smyrna, GA, 30080-8020

DINES, PHILIPP L., T: Medical Director, Division of Geropsychiatry and Geropsychiatry Fellowship, Associate Professor of Psychiatry, Case Western Reserve University **I:** Medicine & Health Care **CN:** University Hospitals Cleveland Medical Center **DOB:** 01/06/1950 **PB:** Cleveland **SC:** OH/USA **PT:** Lazaros Christos Dines; Penelope Dines **MS:** Married **SPN:** Niki Dines **CH:** Anastasia Maria Dines **ED:** Fellow in Research Biological Psychiatry, University Hospitals, Cleveland, Ohio (1988); Resident, University Hospitals, Cleveland, Ohio (1985); Intern, School of Medicine, Case Western Reserve University (1984); MD, School of Medicine, Case Western Reserve University (1984); PhD in Electrical Engineering and Applied Physics, Case Western Reserve University (1977); MSEE and Applied Physics, Case Western Reserve University (1975); BSEE, Cleveland State University (1972) **CT:** Certified in Geriatric Psychiatry, American Board of Psychiatry and Neurology, Inc.; Certified in General Psychiatry, American Board of Psychiatry and Neurology, Inc.; Lapsed Certification in Forensic Addictions Psychiatry, American Board of Psychiatry and Neurology, Inc. **C:** Training Medical Director, Geropsychiatry Fellowship Program, University Hospitals Cleveland Medical Center, Cleveland, Ohio (2008-Present); Medical Director, Neurogeropsychiatry Inpatient Program, University Hospitals Cleveland Medical Center, Cleveland, Ohio (2008-Present); Medical Director, Inpatient Neurogeropsychiatric Service,

University Hospitals Cleveland Medical Center (2007-Present); Medical Director, Geriatric Psychiatry Fellowship Program, University Hospitals Cleveland Medical Center (1988-Present); Medical Director of Geropsychiatry at University Hospitals of Cleveland (2018); Associate Professor of Psychiatry, School of Medicine, Case Western Reserve University (2016); Psychiatry Division Chief, Ahuja Medical Center, University Hospitals (2014-2016); Research Project Electrical Engineer for Defense Contractor Developing Detection Systems and Signal Theory for United States Navy, Gould Incorporated (1977-1980) **CR:** Independent Forensic Neuropsychiatric Practice including Medical Consult to Cuyahoga County Probate Court, Summit County Probate Court and State Medical Board of Ohio; Full Time Administrative, Clinical and Research Faculty, Division of Geropsychiatry, University Hospitals Cleveland Medical Center; Member, Pharmacy Committee for Psychiatry, University Hospitals Cleveland Medical Center; Member, Quality Committee for Psychiatry, University Hospitals Cleveland Medical Center; Medical Director, University Hospitals Geropsychiatry Fellowship; Member, Clinical Competency, Education Committees and Core Psychiatric Faculty, Psychiatric Residency Program, University Hospitals Cleveland Medical Center **CIV:** Member, Medical Advisory Board, NAMI; Former Member, Alzheimer's Medical Advisory Board; Former Board Member, Historic Greek Orthodox Annunciation Church, Cleveland; Donor to Nature Conservatory, Conservation Advocacy, Cleveland Natural History, Art, Historic and Science Museums **CW:** Author, Several Chapters on Adult and Geriatric Sleep Hygiene, Distinguishing Panic Disorder from Seizures, Life Expectancy and Geriatric Depression; Contributor, Book Chapters; Contributor, Articles, Professional Journals in Psychiatry and Neurology; Numerous Psychiatric Forensic Reports and Opinions for Client Courts and Attorneys for Over 20 Years; Published Confidential and Secret Engineering Work in Signal Detection Theory for the United States Navy When Working as an Electrical Project Engineer **AW:** Honoree, Lifetime Distinguished Fellow, American Psychiatric Association (2018); Award for 25 Years of Excellence in Service, University Hospitals Case Medical Center (2013); Honoree, Accepted Future Leaders in Psychiatry Program, Emory University (2008); Honoree, Distinguished Fellow, American Psychiatric Association (1998) **MEM:** Lifetime Distinguished Fellow, American Psychiatric Association (2018); Vice President, Medical Staff and Medical Director, Windsor Laurelwood (Now Windsor Laurelwood Center for Behavioral Medicine) (2005); President, Cleveland Psychiatric Society (2000); President-elect, Cleveland Psychiatric Society (1999); American Association for Geriatric Psychiatry; American Association for Forensic Psychiatry **MH:** Albert Nelson Marquis Lifetime Achievement **H:** History; Music; Travel; Science **PA:** Independent **RE:** Greek Orthodox **BA:** 10524 Euclid Ave Ste 7107, W.O. Walker Center, Cleveland, OH, 44106-5080 **ADD:** 3678 Cinnamon Way, Westlake, OH, 44145-5700 **URL:** https://www.uhhospitals.org/find-a-doctor/dines-philipp-1680

DINES, DAVID MICHAEL, I: Medicine & Health Care **DOB:** 02/04/1948 **PB:** New York **SC:** NY/USA **PT:** Aaron Dines; Yvette Harriet Dines **ED:** MD, New Jersey College Medicine (1974); BA in Biology, Lehigh University, Bethlehem, PA (1970) **CT:** Diplomate, American Board of Surgery **C:** Adjunct Professor, Cornell University Medical College, New York, NY (1983-Present); Clinical Professor of Orthopedic Surgery, Albert Einstein College of Medicine, New York, NY (1998-2010);

Chairman, Department of Orthopedic Surgery, Albert Einstein College of Medicine, New York, NY (1996-2007); Fellow, American Academy of Orthopedic Surgery, Chicago (1981); Fellow, Hospital of Special Surgery, New York, NY (1980); Resident in Orthopedic Surgery, Hospital Special Surgery, New York, NY (1976-1979); Resident in Orthopedic Surgery, New York Hospital Cornell, New York, NY (1974-1976); Clinical Professor of Orthopedic Surgery, Weill Cornell Medical College, New York; Senior Orthopedic Attending, Hospital for Special Surgery, New York, NY **CR:** Director of Medical Services, Association of Tennis Professionals (2004-Present); Medical Advisor, Florida (1994-Present); Team Physician, US Tennis Association (1999-Present); Presenter in Field, Trustee Board, Journal of Shoulder and Elbow Surgery (2005-Present); Team Physician, US Davis Cup Tennis Team (2000-2004); Team Physician, New York Mets (1991-1997) **CIV:** Fundraiser, Hospital Special Surgery, New York, NY (1979-Present) **CW:** Contributor, More than 100 Articles, Professional Journals **AW:** Named one of Best Orthopedic Surgeons (2005-Present); Best Doctors in America (1999-Present); Best Doctors in New York, New York Magazine (1996-Present); Recipient, Lifetime Achievement Award, American Academy of Orthopedics (2010); John Chanley Memorial Award, University of Liverpool, England (1996) **MEM:** Fellow, American Academy of Orthopedic Surgeons (2005-Present); Medical Director, Association of Tennis Professionals (2005-Present); Membership Committee, American Orthopedic Association (1998-Present); President, American Shoulder and Elbow Society (2005); Associate Director, Association Team Professional Medical Society (1991); Academy Orthopedic Society of America **H:** Tennis; Golf; Politics

DIVITA, JAMES J., **T:** Writer, Researcher, Social Studies Educator (Retired) **I:** Education/Educational Services **CN:** Marian University **DOB:** 01/20/1938 **PB:** Chicago **SC:** IL/USA **PT:** Charles V. Divita; Theresa Rohde Divita **MS:** Married **SPN:** Mary Frances Beckmeyer (8/22/1964) **CH:** Lawrence; Mary Theresa; Michael; Anne **ED:** PhD, University of Chicago (1972); AM, University of Chicago (1960); BA, DePaul University, Chicago, IL (1959) **C:** Professor Emeritus, History, Marian University (2003-Present); Professor of History, Marian University (1976-2003); Chairman, Department of History and Political Science, Marian University (1983-2002); Associate Professor of History, Marian University, Indianapolis, IN (1970-1976); Chairman, Department of History and Political Science, Marian University (1974-1975); Assistant Professor of History, Marian University (1964-1970); Instructor of History, Marian University, Indianapolis, IN (1961-1964) **CR:** Chairman, American Catholic Historical Association Regional Meeting, Indianapolis, IN (1998); President, Indiana Religious History Association, Indianapolis, IN (1987-1997) **CW:** Author, "Origins of German Catholicism and Protestantism in Indianapolis" (2016-17); Author, "One Parish Family (St. Gabriel)" (2013); Author, "Sister as Schoolmarm: Studies in Indiana German-Americana" (2012); Author, "Sirviendo al Immigrante" (2009); Author, "Serving the Immigrant" (2008); Author, "Indianapolis Italians," Arcadia Publishers (2006); Author, "Return to Splendor" (2003); Author, "Splendor of the South Side" (2000); Author, "L'Italia on the White River" (1995); Author, "Workers' Church" (1994); Author, "Rejoice and Remember" (1992); Author, "Ethnic Settlement Patterns in Indianapolis" (1989); Author, "History of St. Christopher Speedway" (1987); Author, "Indianapolis Cathedral" (1986); Author, "The Italians of Indianapolis" (1984); Author,

"Slaves to No One" (1981); Contributor, Chapters, Books; Contributor, Articles, Professional Journals; Contributor, Articles, Encyclopedias (American Midwest, The Italian American Experience, Indianapolis) **AW:** President's Award, Italian Heritage Society of Indiana (2011); Fadely History Award, Marion County Indianapolis Historical Society (2006); "Dr. James J. Divita Day, 28 July 2003", Mayor of Indianapolis; Franciscan Values Award (2003); IRHA Excellence Award (2001); Teaching Excellence Award, Marian University (1998); IRHA Excellence Award (1995); Grantee, National Endowment of the Humanities (1984); Grantee, National Endowment of the Humanities (1981); Grantee, National Endowment of the Humanities (1977) **MEM:** Board Member, Indiana German Heritage Society (2014-Present); President, Italian Heritage Society of Indiana (2004-2006); Vice President, Italian Heritage Society of Indiana (1998-2004); Assistant Secretary, Indianapolis Literary Club (1989-1992); Library Committee Chairman, Indiana Historical Society (1983-1994); Life Member, American Historical Association; Life Member, Italian Heritage Society of Indiana; Member, American Catholic Historical Association, American Italian Historical Association, Historical Landmarks Foundation of Indiana **MH:** Albert Nelson Marquis Lifetime Achievement Award (2017) **RE:** Roman Catholic **ADD:** 3208 Acacia Dr, Indianapolis, IN, 46214

DIXON, MARTHA LEE PH.D., **T:** Anatomist, Physiologist, Educator **I:** Education/Educational Services **CN:** Diablo Valley College **DOB:** 01/27/1944 **PB:** San Diego **SC:** CA/USA **PT:** Dick Dixon; Clara Lowe **MS:** Single **ED:** Post-doctoral Fellow, York University, Toronto; PhD in Biophysics, University of California (1983); Graduate Work in Physiology (1970); Standard Secondary Teaching Credential in Biology, San Francisco State University (1970); BA in Physiology, University of California, Berkeley (1966) **C:** Professor, Diablo Valley College, Pleasant Hill, CA (1993-Present); Instructor, Peralta Community College, Oakland, CA (1989-1994); Director, Tissue Network, Bay Area Tumor Institute, Oakland, CA (1989-1993); Staff Scientist, Lawrence Berkeley National Laboratory, Berkeley, CA (1987-1989); Postdoctoral Fellow, Scientist, Instructor, York University, Toronto, Canada (1983-1987); Teacher, Lowell High School, San Francisco, CA (1970-1972) **CW:** Reviewer, Textbook Publishers (1994-Present) **AW:** NSF Individual Postdoctoral Fellowship (1980); NIH Biophysics Training Grant, NIH Training Grants (1970-1980); Unified School Workshop Grants, California State Scholarship (1961-1965), Charles Shewking, George Kondall Scholarship, Kiwanis Scholarship, Sears Roebuck Foundation Scholarship for Leadership **MEM:** Human Anatomy and Physiology Society; AFT; American Civil Liberties Union; Greenpeace **MH:** Albert Nelson Marquis Lifetime Achievement Award **H:** Swimming; Travel **PA:** Democrat (Liberal) **BA:** 321 Golf Club Road, Pleasant Hill, CA, 94523 **ADD:** 4154 Piedmont Ave Apt 2, Oakland, CA, 94611

DIXSON, DIANE ELIZABETH, **T:** Librarian **I:** Library Management/Library Services **DOB:** 09/26/1943 **PB:** Washington **SC:** DC/USA **ED:** Graduate, Financial Management School (2002); BA in English, George Mason University (1978); BA in German, George Mason University (1978) **C:** Docent, Library of Congress **CIV:** Member, Board of Directors, LC Full (2001-2008); Chair, Supervisory Committee, Library of Congress FCU (1982-1990) **AW:** Recipient, First Place in Photography, Employees' Art Show (2016); Recipient, Credit Anion Achievement Award (2015) **MEM:** National Association of Tax Professionals **MH:** Albert

Nelson Marquis Lifetime Achievement Award (2017) **H:** Travel; Classical music; Beach; Tennis **RE:** Roman Catholic **ADD:** 2914 Strathmeade St, Falls Church, VA, 22042

DOBBS, JOHN MCGREGOR, **T:** Physicist **I:** Sciences **CN:** Ryalside Institute **DOB:** 06/30/1936 **PB:** Hankow **ED:** PhD, University of Pennsylvania; MS, University of Pennsylvania; BSME, University of Pennsylvania **C:** Private Practice Consultant, Physicist, Engineer (2008-Present); Founder, President, Ryalside Institute, Cambridge, MA (2008-Present); Corporate Fellow, Analogic Corporation (2008-2011); Vice President, Chief Scientist, Analogic Corporation, Peabody, MA (1992-2008); Director, Bioinstrumentation Developmental Milligen Division, Millipore, Burlington and Milford, MA (1989-1992); Founder, Chairman, Chief Technical Officer, Autogen Instruments, Beverly, MA (1988-1989); Private Practice Consultant, Product Development, Boston Area (1986-1988); President, Chief Executive Officer, Ion Beam Technology, Beverly, MA (1984-1986); Vice President, Chief Scientist, Analogic Corporation, Wakefield, MA (1981-1984); Vice President, Technical Director, General Ionex, Newburyport, MA (1980-1981); Principal Engineer, Division Manager, Analogic Corporation, Wakefield, MA (1975-1980); Private Practice Consultant Engineer, St. Louis, MO and Boston, MA (1973-1975); Assistant Professor, Washington University in St. Louis (1966-1973) **AW:** 31 Patents in Medical Imaging; Instrumentation and Climate Change **MEM:** Fellow, IEEE; Life Member, IEEE; International Biochar Initiative; The International Society for Ecological Economics; The American Association of Physicists in Medicine; American Physical Society **MH:** Albert Nelson Marquis Lifetime Achievement Award (2017) **ADD:** 145 Mount Auburn St, Cambridge, MA, 02138 **URL:** http://www.ryalside.org

DOBBS-WARD, WANDA LOUISE, **T:** Principal **I:** Education/Educational Services **CN:** Thornell Road Elementary School **DOB:** 02/16/1927 **PB:** Hebron **SC:** IL/USA **PT:** Willie S. Dobbs; Ada S. (Burnett) Dobbs **MS:** Widowed **SPN:** William David Ward, Sr. (6/4/1950), Deceased (12/24/2009) **CH:** Susan Jean Ward-Stare; William David, Jr.; Steven Carl **ED:** CAS, State University of New York, Brockport, NY (1982); MS, State University of New York, Geneseo, NY (1972); BS, MacMurray College (1969) **C:** New York State Higher Education Committee (1987-Present); Supervisor, Student Teachers, Nazareth College, Rochester, NY (1990-1992); Chairman, New York State Teacher Center Conference (1989-1991); Coordinator, Developer, Greater Rochester Staff Development Council (1984-1990); Founder, Director, Pittsford Teacher Center (1984-1990); Principal, Thornell Road Elementary School (1983-1984); Director, Pittsford Continuing Education (1981-1990); Liaison, Overseas School-to-School Programs, Pittsford, NY (1979-1983); Liaison, Overseas School-to-School Programs, Zagreb, Croatia (1979-1983); Liaison, Overseas School-to-School Programs, Belgrade, Serbia (1979-1983); Director, Pittsford Teacher Center (1978-1983); Teacher, Kindergarten Classes, Barker Road Elementary School, Pittsford, NY (1968-1978); Producer, Director, Council Teacher Center Department (1974); Director, Founder, President, K Board, Danville, IL (1965-1966); Teacher, First and Third Grade, Public Schools, Creve Coeur, IL (1950-1952); Teacher, First through Forth Grade, Eighth Grade Music, Two-room School, Literberry, IL (1946-1947); Co-Chairman, State Teacher Center Conference; Consultant Staff Development Programs, New York; Conductor, Local, State and National Workshops on Early

Childhood Readiness, Starting Teacher Charter Approach to Staff Development; Consultant, Mentor/Intern Program, West Irondequoit School District; Regional Consultant, Instructor Magazine **CR:** Organizer, Developer 10 Kindergarten Classes, Danville, IL (1965) **CIV:** Active Member, Rochester Philharmonic Organization **AW:** Professional Education Award, New York State Delta Kappa Gamma Society (2018); Woman of Distinction, Delta Kappa Gamma Society International (2007); Wanda Ward Lifetime Achievement Award (2005); State Woman of the Year, Women's Club, Pittsford, NY (2000); New York State Achievement Award (1990); Service Award, Phi Delta Kappa (1988); Distinguished Alumnae, MacMurray College (1984); Distinguished Service Award, Parent Teacher Student Association (1982); Lifetime Membership Award, Parent Teacher Student Association (1969); Lifetime Membership Award, Parent Teacher Student Association (1965); Woman of the Year, Commercial News (1965); Lifetime Membership Award, Parent Teacher Student Association (1963); Lifetime Achievement Award, Danville, Illinois School District; Lifetime Achievement Award, Women's Club, Pittsford, NY **MEM:** International Nominations Committee, Delta Kappa Gamma Society International (2004-2008); President, Charter Member, Pittsford New York Women's Club (2001-2002); International Northeastern Regional Director, Delta Kappa Gamma Society International (1990-1992); International Chair Member, Communications Committee, Delta Kappa Gamma Society International (1988-1990); President, New York State, Delta Kappa Gamma Society International (1987-1989); President, Alpha Xi Chapter, Delta Kappa Gamma Society International (1980-1982); President, Pittsford Teachers Association (1976-1977); Women's Club; Danville School District; President, Local Executive Board, Association of Supervision and Curriculum Development; National Association of Education for Young Children; New York State Teachers Association; Parent Teacher Student Association; Phi Beta Mu; Delta Kappa Gamma Society International **H:** Art (Oil, Watercolor and Crayon) **PA:** Republican **RE:** Methodist **ADD:** 81 Linden Avenue, Apt. 507, Rochester, NY, 14610

DODGE, WILLIAM R., **T:** Founder, Chief Financial Officer, Emergency Physician **I:** Medicine & Health Care **CN:** Access Mind Institute **ED:** MD, F. Edward Herbert School of Medicine, Uniformed Services University of Health Sciences (1997); Master's Degree in Medical Management, University of Southern California; Cardiovascular Emergencies Fellowship, Stanford University; Emergency Medicine Residency, NMCSD **CT:** Board Certified Emergency Medicine Physician **C:** Founder, Access Mind Institute (2016-Present); Chief Financial Officer, Access Mind Institute (2016-Present); Emergency Physician, Access Mind Institute (2016-Present); Emergency Physician, Private Practice **CR:** Staff Member, Clinical Faculty, Mission Hospital, UCLA **MIL:** Emergency Medicine Physician, Operation Enduring Freedom **AW:** Honoree, Physician of Excellence, Orange County Medical Association (2017) **MEM:** Fellow, American Academy of Emergency Medicine; Fellow, American College of Emergency Physicians **MH:** Albert Nelson Marquis Lifetime Achievement Award (2017) **ADD:** 25941 Rapid Falls Road, Laguna Hills, CA, 92653 **URL:** https://accessmindinstitute.com/about-us

DODSON, DARYL THEODORE, **I:** Media & Entertainment **DOB:** 10/09/1934 **PB:** Warrensburg **SC:** MO/USA **PT:** Theodore Dodson; Ada Marie (Ayres) Dodson **ED:** BS, Central Missouri State

University (1956) **CR:** Manager, Phantom of the Opera (1992-2003); Manager, Les Miserables (1988-1992); Manager, New York and U.S. Tour, Paris Opera Ballet (1988); Manager, Porgy and Bess (1986-1987); Manager, La Cage Aux Folles (1987); Manager, New York Engagement, The Golden Land (1985); Manager, The Wiz (1983-1984); General Manager, John Curry Skating Company (1984); Manager, U.S. Tours, Amadeus (1982-1983); Manager, U.S. and Canada Tour, Sweeney Todd (1982); Manager, American Tour, Royal Ballet England (1981); President Pine Cone Enterprises, Ltd. (1977-1981); Proprietor Pine Cone Inn, Haverhill, New Hampshire (1978-1981); Manager, Opera House, John F. Kennedy Center, Washington (1981); Manager, American Tour, National Ballet Cuba (1979); Member, Advisory Panel, Vermont Council on Arts (1978); Manager, American Tour, First Cultural Exchange, People's Republic of China and U.S. (1978); Member Governor S.C.'s Council of the Arts (1974) **MIL:** With, U.S. Army (1957-1959) **CW:** General Manager, American Ballet Theatre (1968-1977); Production Manager, American Ballet Theatre (1963); Stage Manager, American Ballet Theatre (1961); Production Stage Manager, American Ballet Theatre (1961); Regisseur, Chicago Opera Ballet (1960); Assistant Stage Manager, American Ballet Theatre, New York, NY (1960); Assistant Director The Mikado, New York City Opera (1959) **AW:** National Touring Broadway Achievement Award (2003) **MEM:** Member Theta Chi; Theta Alpha Phi **RE:** Episcopalian

DOLGIN, STEPHEN M., **T:** Secondary School Educator **I:** Education/Educational Services **DOB:** 12/22/1949 **PB:** San Francisco **SC:** CA/USA **PT:** David Aubrey Dolgin; Ruth (Ogurak) Dolgin **ED:** Postgraduate Work, San Francisco State University (1989); MBA in Health Services Management, Golden Gate University (1982); MSW, University of Minnesota (1976); BA, University of Minnesota (1972) **C:** Substitute Teacher, Oakland Military Institute, San Francisco Unified School District, California (2017-Present); Math Teacher, Oakland Military Institute (2016-2017); Teacher, San Francisco Unified School District (1991-2015); Veterans Service Officer, Dakota County, Minnesota (1987); Social Insurance Claims Examiner, Social Security Administration, Richmond, CA (1982-1984); Social Caseworker, Contra Costa County Social Services Department, Richmond, CA (1979-1981); Social Worker, U.S. Army (1976-1979) **CR:** Internship for Teachers, Global Climate Change, Lawrence Livermore National Laboratory (1991) **CIV:** Toastmasters International (2015-Present); Admissions Partner Program Volunteer, U.S. Coast Guard Academy (2005-Present); Toastmasters International (1982-1992); Tutor, Learning Center, Coast Guard Island, Alameda, CA **MIL:** Lieutenant Colonel, U.S. Army Reserve (1979-2001); Lieutenant Colonel, U.S. Army Reserve (1973-1976) **AW:** Squadron Officer of the Year Award, Civil Air Patrol (1980); Decorated Army Expert Field Medical Badge; U.S. Naval Sea Cadet Corps; Army Commendation Medal, U.S. Army; Meritorious Service Medal; Distinguished Service Ribbon, U.S. Naval Sea Cadets; California Cadet Corps (Special Projects Officer); Competent Toastmaster Award **MEM:** Chapter Vice President, ROTC Affairs, Association of the U.S. Army (2016-Present); Vice President of the Army, Department of the Golden West, Reserve Officers Association (2014-Present); Assistant Sub-Region Director, Naval Sea Cadets (2006-Present); Assistant Senior Regional Director, Naval Sea Cadets (2002-2005); Lieutenant Colonel, Cadet Program Officer, Civil Air Patrol; Association of the United States Army; American Philatelic Society; Coast Guard Auxiliary; Navy League of the United States; Air Force Association; American

Legion, The Forty and Eight; Military Officers Association (MOAA) **H:** Running; Military history, honoring our troops and veterans; Computers; Collecting stamps and vinyl records from the 50s-70s **ADD:** 1400 Carpentier Street, Apt. 306, San Leandro, CA, 94577

DONAHE, PEGGY YVONNE, **T:** Educator, Librarian, English Elementary Teacher **I:** Education/Educational Services **DOB:** 05/05/1940 **PB:** Bismarck **SC:** ND/USA **PT:** Fred Rattei Porter; Austie Mahre Porter **MS:** Single **SPN:** Robert Charles Donahe (6/17/1967, Deceased 3/7/2013) **CH:** Noel Charles **ED:** MA, Northern State University (1970); BA in Elementary Education, University of North Dakota (1964); BS, Trinity Bible College **CT:** Certified in Bilingual Reading Endorsement, Library Media, State of Utah; Certified, Reading and Gifted Education Endorsement, State of North Dakota **C:** Academic Department Head, Bureau of Indian Affairs School, Shiprock Agency, United States Department of the Interior (2003-2005); Librarian, Aneth Community School, Aneth, UT (1994-2006); Gifted Teacher, Aneth Community School, Aneth, UT (1994-2006); English Teacher, Title I, Standing Rock Community School, Fort Yates, ND (1989-1994); Gifted Educator, Title I, Standing Rock Community School, Fort Yates, ND (1989-1994); Language Arts Teacher, Grades Four Through Eight, Richland 44 School District, Abercrombie, ND (1969-1989); Fourth Grade Teacher, Britton-Hecla School District, Britton, SD (1967-1969); Fifth Grade Teacher, Ashley Public School (1964-1967) **CR:** Chief School Reform Leader, School Reform Communications (2000-2005); Curriculum Leader, Aneth Communications School, Aneth, UT (1997-2005); President of the Board, Tao Dine Library Association, Shiprock, NM (1995-2006); Member, Wahpeton Zoning Communications (1987-1990); President, Investment Club (1985-1989); Reading Presenter, State, Regional & National Conference (1980-1998); President, North Dakota Reading Association, Wahpeton, ND (1979-1989); President, League of Women Voters (1970-1989); Affiliate, Community Projects, League of Women Voters (1970-1989) **CIV:** Troop Leader, Girl Scouts of the United States of America (2000-2003); Scout Master, Boy Scouts of America (1998-2004); Election Reporter, American Broadcasting Company (1981-1989) **CW:** Artist, Paintings and Chalk; Contributor, Columns to Newspapers; Contributor, Articles to Professional Journals **AW:** Named, Professional of the Year (2012); Named, Employee of the Year, Aneth Community School, Aneth, UT (2003); Named, Employee of the Year, Aneth Community School, Aneth, UT (2000); Educator Award, Education Program, National Aeronautics and Space Administration (1998-2006); Named, Employee of the Year, Aneth Community School, Aneth, UT (1996); Citation, Delta Kappa Gamma **MEM:** President, DKGSI (2008-Present); Charter Member, National Museum Women in Arts (1986-Present); Chairman, Aneth Child Study Team, International Literacy Association (2001-2005); State President, International Literacy Association (1984-1986); American Association of University Women; Chairman, National Defense Education Act; Resolution Committee Member, National Defense Education Act; Resolution Committee Member, National Education Association; State Vice President, Delta Kappa Gamma; Lifetime Member, Remington Who's Who **MH:** Albert Nelson Marquis Lifetime Achievement Award (2017) **H:** Reading; Knitting; Bridge; Puzzles; Crafts; Painting; Computers **ADD:** 1137 Westmore Ave, Wahpeton, ND, 58075

DOREIAN, PATRICK, **T:** Social Network Analyst, Educator **I:** Education/Educational Services **CN:** University of Ljubljana **DOB:** 10/01/1942

PB: Cambridge **SC:** England **PT:** Harold Doreian (Stepfather); Tove Jensen **MS:** Married **SPN:** Esther Sales (5/24/1981) **CH:** Leeza; Brian Sales; Fracka Future **ED:** MA in Sociology, University of Essex, Colchester, England (1966); BSc in Mathematics, University of Leicester, England (1964) **C:** Research Faculty, Faculty of Social Sciences, University of Ljubljana (2009-Present); Professor Emeritus, University of Pittsburgh (2006-Present); Professor, University of Pittsburgh (1981-2006); Associate Professor, University of Pittsburgh (1972-1981); Visiting Associate Professor, University of Pittsburgh (1971-1972); Lecturer, University of Essex (1967-1971) **CR:** Chair, Department of Sociology, University of Pittsburgh (1999-2006); Centennial Professor, London School of Economics (2002); Chair, Mathematics and Sociology Section, American Sociological Association (2001-2002); Keynote Speaker, International Social Networks Conference, London, England (1995); Visiting Professor, University of California, Irvine (1980); Gast Professor, Institute for Advanced Studies (1974) **CIV:** Member, National Resources Defense Council **CW:** Editor, Social Networks (2006-Present); Co-Author, Understanding Large Temporal Networks and Spatial Networks: Exploration, Pattern Searching, Visualization and Network Evolution (2014); Editor, Journal of Mathematical Sociology (1982-2005); Author, Editor, Books and Monographs; Contributor, Articles to Professional Journals, Chapters to Books; Author, "Advances in Network Clustering and Blockmodeling," John Wiley & Sons, Inc. **AW:** Recipient, Harrison White Outstanding Book Award (2007); Honoree, University of Cambridge Chapter, American Sociological Association (2005); Honoree, Blockmodeling Award, Cambridge University Press (2005); Recipient, Honorary Senator Award, University of Ljubljana (2004); Recipient, Simmel Award, International Network for Social Network Analysis (1995) **MEM:** Board of Directors, International Network for Social Network Analysts (1996-2006); Editorial Board Member, International Network for Social Network Analysts **MH:** Albert Nelson Marquis Lifetime Achievement Award (2017) **H:** Movies; Travel; Wine; Soccer **PA:** Progressive **ADD:** 122 Yorkshire Dr, Pittsburgh, PA, 15208

DORNETTE, W. STUART, T: Lawyer, Educator **I:** Law and Legal Services **CN:** Taft, Stettinius & Hollister **DOB:** 03/02/1951 **PB:** Washington **SC:** DC/USA **PT:** William Henry Lueders Dornette; Frances Hester Dornette **MS:** Married **SPN:** Martha Louise Mehl (11/19/1983) **CH:** Marjorie Frances; Anna Christine; David Paul **ED:** JD, University of Virginia (1975); AB, Williams College (1972) **C:** Partner, Taft Stettinius & Hollister, Cincinnati, OH (1983-Present); Associate, Taft Stettinius & Hollister, Cincinnati, OH (1975-1983) **CR:** Adjunct Professor, University of Cincinnati (1988-1991); Instructor of Law, University of Cincinnati (1980-1987); Trial Work in Commercial Matters; Representative, Various Sports Entities **CIV:** Chair, Zoological Society of Cincinnati (2016-Present); Board of Directors, Zoological Society of Cincinnati (2006-Present); Hamilton County Republican Executive Committee (1982-Present); Board of Visitors, University of Cincinnati Law School (2002-2006); Board of Trustees, Cincinnati Parks Foundation (1995-2004); Ohio Board of Bar Examiners (1991-1993); Board of Directors, Zoological Society of Cincinnati (1983-1994) **CW:** Co-Author, "Federal Judiciary Almanac" (1984-1987) **AW:** Municipal Litigator of the Year, Best Lawyers, Cincinnati, OH (2017) **MEM:** City Gospel Mission; Federal Bar Association; Ohio State Bar Association; Cincinnati Bar Association; American Physical Society **BAR:** U.S. Supreme Court (1980);

Sixth Circuit, U.S. Court of Appeals (1977); District of Columbia (1976); State of Virginia (1975); State of Ohio (1975); U.S. District Court, Southern District, State of Ohio (1975) **MH:** Albert Nelson Marquis Lifetime Achievement Award (2017) **RE:** Methodist **BA:** 425 Walnut Street, Suite 1800, Cincinnati, OH, 45202 **ADD:** 329 Bishopsbridge Drive, Cincinnati, OH, 45255

DOUGLAS, DONNA, T: Realtor **I:** Real Estate **CN:** Elevate Real Estate with Donna Douglas at United Country, Staples Property Group **DOB:** 05/18/1953 **PB:** Baton Rouge **SC:** LA/USA **PT:** Joffre Jones; Melba Jones **MS:** Married **SPN:** Benny Joe Douglas **ED:** Coursework, School of Auctioneering (1983); Coursework, Sam Houston State University (1971) **CT:** Accredited Buyer's Representative **C:** Realtor, Lake Palestine Branch, Lake Palestine Real Estate - Frankston Texas Real Estate (2008-Present); Texas Licensed Auctioneer, Douglas Auction Service (1983-1999); Executive Secretary, Drilco, Smith International (1975-1982) **CR:** Owner, Douglas Plant Farm (1996-Present) **CIV:** Board Member, Economic Development Committee, Coffee City **AW:** Broker Agent Award, Certificate of Excellence (2016); DFW Five-Star Professional Real Estate Award (2013-2018); Honoree, VIP Woman of the Year for Outstanding Excellence and Dedication to Her Profession and the Achievement of Women, NAPW (2013-2014) **MEM:** National Association of Realtors; Texas Association of Realtors; Greater Tyler Association of Realtors, NAVICA; Palestine Area Association of Realtors, NAVICA; Henderson County Association of Realtors, MetroTex, Dallas Association of Realtors; National Rifle Association; Sarcoidosis Research Foundation; Lighthouse Baptist Chapel **H:** Collecting antiques; Journaling; Water sports; Kayaking **PA:** Republican **RE:** Christian **BA:** 7500 State Highway 155, United Country Lake Palestine, Frankston, TX, 75763 **URL:** http://www.realtordonnadouglas.com

DOVE, DONALD AUGUSTINE, T: Urban Planner, Educator **I:** Health, Wellness and Fitness **CN:** White House Conference on Aging **DOB:** 08/07/1930 **PB:** Waco **SC:** TX/USA **PT:** Sebert Constantine Dove; Amy Delmena (Stern) Dove **MS:** Married **SPN:** Cecelia Mae White (2/9/1957) **CH:** Angela; Donald; Monica Gilstrap; Celine; Cathlyn Cwiek; Dianna Diress; Jennifer; Austin **ED:** MA in Public Administration, University of Southern California (1966); BA, California State University (1951) **C:** Panelist, White House Conference on Aging, Washington, DC (1970-Present); Adviser, White House Conference on Aging, Washington, DC (1970-Present); Panelist, International Conference on Energy Use Management (1981); Adviser, International Conference on Energy Use Management (1981); Chief, L.A. Region Transportation Study, State of California (1975-1984); Chief of Environmental Planning, California Department of Transportation (1972-1975); Environmental Coordinator, California Department of Public Works, Sacramento, CA (1971-1975); Director, Transportation Employment Project, State of California (1966-1971); Supervisor, Demographic Research, California Department of Public Works (1960-1966); Planning & Development Consultant, D. Dove Associates, Los Angeles, CA (1959-1960) **CR:** Guest Lecturer, Universities (1969-1993) **CIV:** Chairman, Lynwood City Planning Commission, California (1982-2004); President, Neighborhood Esteem/Enrichment Techniques Institute (1992-1993); Member, Delegate, Archdiocesan Pastoral Council (1979-1986); President, Area Pastoral Council (1982-1983); Member, Delegate, Compton Community Development Board, California (1967-1971) **MIL:** U.S. Army (1952-1954) **CW:** Author,

"Preserving Urban Environment" (1976); Author, "Small Area Population Forecasts" (1966) **MEM:** President, California Association Management (1987-1988); Secretary, Optimists Club (1978-1979); Co-founder, Association of Environmental Professionals (1973); Transportation Chairman, American Institute of Planners (1972-1973); Los Angeles County Democratic Central Committee; American Institute of Certified Planners; America Planning Association **MH:** Albert Nelson Marquis Lifetime Achievement Award (2017) **PA:** Democrat **RE:** Roman Catholic **ADD:** 11356 Ernestine Ave, Lynwood, CA, 90262

DRAKE, ELISABETH, T: Associate Director (Retired) **I:** Engineering **CN:** Massachusetts Institute of Technology **DOB:** 12/20/1936 **PB:** New York **SC:** NY/USA **PT:** John Martin Mertz; Ruth (Johnson) Mertz **MS:** Single **SPN:** Alvin William Drake (7/31/1957, Divorced 1984, Deceased) **CH:** Alan Lee (Deceased) **ED:** ScD in Chemical Engineering, Massachusetts Institute of Technology (1966); BS in Chemical Engineering, Massachusetts Institute of Technology (1958) **CT:** Registered Professional Engineer, Commonwealth of Massachusetts **C:** Emeritus Staff Member of Energy Laboratory, Massachusetts Institute of Technology (2007-Present); Consultant of Energy Laboratory, Massachusetts Institute of Technology (2000-2007); Director of Energy Laboratory, Massachusetts Institute of Technology (1994-1995); Consultant, Arthur D. Little Inc., Cambridge, MA (1990-1994); Associate Director of New Technology, Energy Laboratory, Massachusetts Institute of Technology (1989-2002); Vice President of Risk Management of Hazardous Industries, Arthur D. Little Inc., Cambridge, MA (1976-1988); Manager of Risk Analysis, Arthur D. Little Inc., Cambridge, MA (1977-1982); Chair of Chemical Engineering Department, Northeastern University, Boston, MA (1972-1976); Visiting Professor, Massachusetts Institute of Technology, Cambridge, MA (1973-1974); Lecturer, University of California, Berkeley (1971); Senior Staff, Arthur D. Little Inc., Cambridge, MA (1966-1976); Vice President of Risk Management of Hazardous Industries, Arthur D. Little Inc., Cambridge, MA (1958-1972); Staff Engineer, Arthur D. Little Inc., Cambridge, MA (1958-1964) **CR:** Monitor Report Review Committee, National Research Council, National Academy of Sciences (2008-Present); Vice Chair, Committee on Chemical Demolition, National Research Council, National Academy of Sciences (2004-2007); Member of National Research Council, National Academy of Sciences (2002-2004); Vice Chair, Committee on Review and Evaluation on Army Chemical Stockpile Disposal Program, National Research Council, National Academy of Sciences (1993-1998); Member of Managing Board, American Institute of Chemical Engineers (1988-1990); Corporate Manager, Massachusetts Institute of Technology (1981-1986); Member, Technology Pipeline Safety Standards Committee, United States Department of Transportation (1980-1985); Report Review Work, National Academy of Engineering **CIV:** Member, The Green Team **CW:** Co-Author, "Sustainable Energy: Choosing Among Options, Second Edition" (2010); Co-Author, "Sustainable Energy: Choosing Among Options," MIT Press (2005); Contributor, Articles to Professional Journals; Co-Author, "AIChE/Center for Chemical Process Safety Guidelines for the Safe Automation of Chemical Processes" **AW:** Recipient, Westinghouse Award for Safe Automation Based in the CCPS Book (2002); Recipient, TJ Hamilton Award for Government Service, American Institute of Chemical Engineers (1990) **MEM:** Board of Directors, American Institute of Chemical

Engineers (1987-1990); Fellow, American Institute of Chemical Engineers; American Association for the Advancement of Science; Membership Committee, National Academy of Engineering; American Chemical Society; Sigma Xi; Advisory Committees, United States Environmental Protection Agency; Advisory Committees, Department of Energy; Advisory Committee, United States Coast Guard; Advisory Committee, United States Department of Defense; Committee overseeing the United States Chemical Weapons Stockpile Disposal Program, National Academy of Engineering **H:** Environmental activism; Gardening; Working with others; Music; Reading **ADD:** 80B Seminary Ave Apt 154, Auburndale, MA, 02466 **URL:** https://www.engineergirl.org/Engineers/Directory/2935.aspx

DRAUGHON, SCOTT, **T:** Lawyer, Social Worker, Educator **I:** Law and Legal Services **CN:** Franklyn Youth Academy **DOB:** 07/17/1952 **PB:** Muskogee **SC:** OK/USA **ED:** Graduate Coursework in Master Gardener Training (1998-Present); MSW, University of Oklahoma, Norman, OK (1992); Postgraduate Coursework, Oxford University, Oxford, England (1978); JD, University of Tulsa, Oklahoma (1977); BA, Oklahoma State University (1974); AA, Tulsa Junior College (1972) **CT:** Certified Special Education Teacher; Certified School Counselor, All Grade Levels; Licensed Social Worker with Clinical Specialty Certification; Certified Teacher, Social Studies **C:** Private Practice Social Worker (1994-Present); Private Practice Financial Planning, Tulsa, OL (1984-Present); Sole Law Practice, Tulsa, OK (1979-Present); School Counselor, Franklyn Youth Academy, Tulsa Public School (2007-2013); Social Worker, Hospice of Green Country, Inc. (2000-2004); Clinical Social Worker, Cushing Regional Hospital, Oklahoma (1996-1999); Legal Counsel, Tulsa City-County Health Department (1996-1997); Aftercare Department Coordinator, Tulsa Boys' Home (1992-1994); In-House Council, Steeple Nickel House (1986-1987); Stockbroker (1983-1993); Contracts Analyst, Rockwell International (1982-1983) **CIV:** Member, Keeping Tulsa Beautiful Task Force (2003-Present); 20th Anniversary Committee Leadership, Tulsa, Inc. (1992-Present); Member, Tri-County Council on Aging (2003-2004); Graduate, Oklahoma Aging Advocacy Leadership Academy (2000); Volunteer Docent, Tula, OK (1999-2000); Vice Chairman, Oklahoma Human Rights Commission (1999); Member, Oklahoma Human Rights Commission (1997-2000); Member, Executive Board, Tulsa Association, Volunteer Administrators (1994-1995); Tulsa County Regional Planning Coordinator, Board Services to Children and Youth (1992-1995); Member, Executive Committee Corporation, Volunteer Council of Greater Tulsa (1990); Member, Indian Affairs Commission, City of Tulsa (1989-1991); Eastern Oklahoma Chapter, March of Dimes (1989-1990); Registered Lobbyist, Oklahoma Credit Union League Affiliate (1988-1990); International Council of Tulsa (1987-1991); Chairman, Public Relations Committee, Executive Committee, Tulsa Human Rights Commission (1987-1988); Board of Directors, Arts and Humanities Council, Tulsa, OK (1982-1983); Volunteer, Greyhound Rescue **AW:** Regional Finalist, White House Fellowships (1990); S. Halden Pendleton Award; National Association of Accountants Award; Commendation Award for Service on the Oklahoma Human Rights Commission, Oklahoma Governor Frank Keating **MEM:** Will Rogers Rotary Club (1982-1993); Oklahoma Bar Association; Phi Delta Phi; Lifetime Member, Master Mason, Millenium Lodge; Lifetime Member, 32nd degree Mason, Scottish Rite; Lifetime Member, Akdar Shrine; Cushing Rotary Clubs; Cherokee Nation of Oklahoma;

Wolf Clan; Mayoral Appointee, Indian Affairs Commission of the City of Tulsa, Human Rights Commission; Mayflower Descendants; Sons of the American Revolution; Sons of Union Veterans **MH:** Albert Nelson Marquis Lifetime Achievement Award (2017) **H:** Travel; Photography; Reading; Gardening; Cooking **RE:** Methodist **ADD:** 10125 S 94th East Pl, Tulsa, OK, 74133

DRESBACH, DAVID PHILIP, **T:** Financial Consultant, Educator **I:** Financial Services **DOB:** 02/23/1947 **PB:** Columbus **SC:** OH/USA **PT:** Donald Philip Dresbach; Marilyn Jo (Armstrong) Dresbach **MS:** Married **SPN:** Mary Louise Mathes (11/29/1980); Vicki Elaine Smith (2/25/1966, Divorced 1980) **CH:** Chad; Andrew **ED:** MA, Ohio University (1972) **C:** President, Dresbach & Associates, Inc., St. Paul, MN (1995-Present); Senior Managing Consultant, Public Finanical Management (2003-2005); Manager, Evensen Dodge Investment Advisers (Now Evensen Dodge International, Inc) (2001-2003); Senior Vice President, Evensen Dodge Investment Advisers (Now Evensen Dodge International, Inc) (2000-2003); Coordinator, Vice President, Higher Education Group, Springsted Incorporated, St. Paul, MN (1993-1995); Vice President, Evensen Dodge, Inc. (Now Evensen Dodge International, Inc), Minneapolis, MN (1985-1993); Manager, Evensen Dodge, Inc. (Now Evensen Dodge International, Inc), Minneapolis, MN (1983-1984); Administrator, State of Minnesota, St. Paul, MN (1979-1982); Administrator, State of Ohio, Columbus, OH (1977-1979); Regional Manager, State of Ohio, Columbus, OH (1973-1977); Administrator, Ohio University (1969-1973) **CR:** Lecturer, University of Minnesota, Minneapolis, MN (1980-1984); Adjunct Professor, University of Minnesota, Minneapolis, MN (1980-1984); Lecturer, Metropolitan State University, Minneapolis, MN (1980); Adjunct Professor, Metropolitan State University, Minneapolis, MN (1980); Lecturer, Columbus Technical College (1976-1979); Adjunct Professor, Columbus Technical College (1976-1979); Lecturer, Franklin University, Columbus, OH (1975); Adjunct Professor, Franklin University, Columbus, OH (1975); Lecturer, Ohio University (1969-1974); Adjunct Professor, Ohio University (1969-1974) **CIV:** Member, Solid Waste Management Advisory Board, Dakota County, MN (1992-2004); Chairman, Solid Waste Management Advisory Board, Dakota County, MN (2000-2003); Soccer Coach, Grove City Kids Association (1977-1979); Chairman, Grove City Kids Association (1977-1979) **CW:** Author, Poetry Anthologies (1993); Author, Poetry Anthologies (1990-1991); Author, Poetry Anthologies (1970); Contributor, Articles, Professional Journals **AW:** Named, Boss of the Year, ABWA Management, LLC, St. Paul, MN (1980) **MEM:** Chairman, FPA – Minnesota (2001); President, FPA – Minnesota (2000); Board of Directors, Minnesota Society, Institute of Certified Financial Planners; American Association of Individual Investors; Financial Planning Association; Minneapolis Institute of Art; Academy of American Poets **MH:** Albert Nelson Marquis Lifetime Achievement Award (2017) **H:** Reading; Painting; Traveling; Golf; Writing **ADD:** 710 Mager Ct, Saint Paul, MN, 55118

DREW, SHARON LEE, **T:** Sociologist (Retired) **I:** Sciences **DOB:** 08/11/1946 **PB:** Los Angeles **SC:** CA/USA **PT:** Hal Bernard Drew; Helen Elizabeth (Hammond) Drew **CH:** Keith; Charmagne **ED:** Graduate Coursework, California State University, Dominguez Hills (1988-1992); BA, California State University, Long Beach (1983) **C:** Case Worker, Department of Public Social Services, Los Angeles County (1978-2011); Clerical Support, Compton Unified School District, CA (1967-1978) **CIV:**

Lay Minister, St. Luke's Episcopal Church, Long Beach, CA (1998-2004); Lay Reader, St. Luke's Episcopal Church, Long Beach, CA (1998-2004); Volunteer, AIDS Project, Long Beach, CA (2003); Volunteer, Older Adult Center, California State University, Dominguez Hills (1994); Member, Los Angeles Caregiver's Network (1993-1994); Project Coordinator, Parent Education Leadership Development Project, California Tomorrow (1990); Employee Volunteer, Dominguez High School, Compton, CA (1972-1973); Den Mother, Boy Scouts of America, Compton, CA (1971-1972) **AW:** Certificate, Parent Education Leadership Development Project, California Tomorrow (1990) **MEM:** Treasurer, Xi Chapter, Alpha Kappa Delta (1992-1995); International Society for Exploring Teaching and Learning (1992-1994); Chairperson, Dominguez Hills Gerontology Association (1990-1991); Southern California Chapter, American Statistical Association (1990-1991) **H:** Yiddish culture and language; Genealogy; Gardening **ADD:** 927 N Chester Ave, Compton, CA, 90221

DREWS, STEVEN JEFFREY, **T:** 1) Clinical Microbiologist 2) Associate Professor **I:** Sciences **CN:** 1) ProvLab Alberta 2) University of Alberta **DOB:** 10/03/1969 **ED:** Fellowship in Clinical Microbiology, University of Toronto (2006); PhD in Specialty Experimental Medicine, University of British Columbia (2003); Msc in Specialty Pathology and Laboratory Medicine, University of British Columbia (1998); BSc in Cell and Developmental Biology, University of British Columbia (1994); BA in Political Science, University of British Columbia (1992) **CT:** Board Certified Clinical Microbiologist, Canada; Board Certified Clinical Microbiologist, United States of America **C:** Associate Professor, Department of Microbiology, Immunology, and Infectious Diseases, University of Calgary, Calgary, Alberta, Canada (2013-2014); Clinical Microbiologist, Virologist, ProvLab Alberta (2009-2017); Assistant Professor, Department of Microbiology, Immunology, and Infectious Diseases, University of Calgary, Calgary, Alberta, Canada (2009-2013); Assistant Professor, Department of Laboratory Medicine and Pathobiology, University of Toronto, Toronto, Ontario, Canada (2007-2009); Assistant Professor, Samuel Lunenfeld Research Institute, Mount Sinai Hospital, Toronto, Ontario, Canada (2007-2009); Clinical Microbiologist, Head of Molecular Diagnostics, Ontario Public Health Laboratories (2006-2009); Present Rank Associate Professor, Laboratory of Medicine and Pathology, Faculty of Medicine, University of Alberta **CW:** Author, 150 Academic Publications Including Peer Reviewed Articles, Abstracts, Book Chapters **MEM:** American Association for the Advancement of Sciences (2015-Present); Canada Council, Association of Medical Microbiology and Infectious Diseases (2012-Present); Diplomate, American Board of Medical Microbiology (2007-Present); Fellow, Canadian College of Microbiologists (2007-Present); CIHR College of Reviewers (2017) **H:** Working Out; Sports; Watching Football **ADD:** 3628 114 St NW, Edmonton, AB, Canada, T6J 1L9

DRUM, BRUCE ALAN, **T:** Physicist **I:** Sciences **CN:** U.S. Food and Drug Administration **DOB:** 05/18/1947 **PB:** Wauseon **SC:** OH/USA **PT:** Virgil Drum; Clela Drum **MS:** Married **SPN:** Pamela Joy Neff (6/16/1973) **CH:** River (Rachel); Kevin; Erin **ED:** PhD, Biophysics, The Ohio State University, Columbus, OH (1973); BSc, Physics, The Ohio State University, Columbus, OH (1969) **C:** Physicist, U.S. Food and Drug Administration, Center for Devices and Radiological Health, Office of Device Evaluation (1994-Present); Assistant Professor, Wilmer Eye Institute, Johns Hopkins University, Baltimore,

MD (1984-1991); Research Faculty, Department of Ophthalmology, George Washington University, Washington, DC (1975-1984); Postdoctoral Fellow, Wilmer Eye Institute, Johns Hopkins University, Baltimore, MD (1973-1974) **CR:** Independent Vision Consultant, Columbia, MD (1985-Present); Co-Founder, Close Consulting Corporation, Vision Research Associates, Inc., Baltimore, MD (1985-1994); Member, Close Consulting Corporation, Vision Research Associates, Inc., Baltimore, MD (1985-1994) **CIV:** The Planetary Society; Member, Union of Concerned Scientists; Central Maryland Chorale, Laurel, MD; Federation of American Scientists; Greater Washington Educational Telecommunications Association (WETA); Chesapeake Bay Foundation; National Parks Foundation; The Clinton Foundation **CW:** Contributor, Articles, Professional Journals; Contributor, Book Chapters; Speaker, Presentations, Scientific Conferences; Editor, Published Conference Proceedings **AW:** Group Recognition Award, CDRH, U.S. Food and Drug Administration (2017); Group Recognition Award, CDRH, U.S. Food and Drug Administration (2014); Outstanding Service Award, U.S. Food and Drug Administration (2011); Group Recognition Award, CDRH, U.S. Food and Drug Administration (2011); Group Recognition Award (2004); Special Recognition Awards, Center for Devices and Radiological Health, U.S. Food and Drug Administration (2004); Special Recognition Awards, Center for Devices and Radiological Health, U.S. Food and Drug Administration (2003); Clear Science Communications Award, U.S. Food and Drug Administration (2003); Outstanding Service Award, U.S. Food and Drug Administration (2001); Group Recognition Award (2001); Group Recognition Award (1998); Special Recognition Awards, Center for Devices and Radiological Health, U.S. Food and Drug Administration (1998); Special Recognition Awards, Center for Devices and Radiological Health, U.S. Food and Drug Administration (1996); Group Recognition Award (1996); Group Recognition Award (1995); Grantee, National Eye Institute, NIH (1988-1991); Grantee, National Eye Institute, NIH (1985-1989); Grantee, National Eye Institute, NIH (1981-1984); Grantee, National Eye Institute, NIH (1975-1982); Postdoctoral Fellow, The Johns Hopkins Wilmer Eye Institute, The Johns Hopkins University (1973-1974) **MEM:** International Color Vision Society Secretary-Treasurer (1985-1994); Imaging and Perimetric Society; American Association for the Advancement of Science; Optical Society of America; The Association for Research in Vision and Ophthalmology **MH:** Albert Nelson Marquis Lifetime Achievement Award (2017); Distinguished Humanitarian (2017) **H:** Running; Singing; Piano; Gardening; Reading; Cooking; Astrophysics; Cosmology, Photography **PA:** Independent **ADD:** 4932 Pale Orchis Ct, Columbia, MD, 21044

DU MONT, NICOLAS, T: Psychiatrist **I:** Medicine & Health Care **CN:** St. Luke's Reserve Hospital **DOB:** 12/22/1954 **PB:** San Juan **SC:** Puerto Rico **PT:** Joseph Henri Du Mont; Isabel (Solano) Du Mont **ED:** Postgraduate Work, Public Community Psychiatry, Columbia University (1993); Postgraduate Work, Child and Adolescent Psychiatry, Columbia University (1992); Postgraduate Work, Adult Psychiatry, Columbia University (1990); MD, Universidad de Puerto Rico (1986); BS in Chemistry, Universidad de Puerto Rico, Magna Cum Laude (1982) **CT:** Certified Cognitive Behavior Therapist, National Association of Forensic Counselors (2008); Certified Hypnotherapist, International Association of Counselors & Therapists (1991); Certificate in History of Music, Puerto Rico (1978) **C:** Doctor, Private Practice, New York, NY

(2014-Present); Consulting Child, Adolescent and Adult Psychiatrist, Inwood Community Services, Inc. (1999-Present); Consulting Child, Adolescent and Adult Psychiatrist, PRFI, Inc. (1994-Present); Assistant Clinical Professor, NYP/Columbia University Medical Center, New York-Presbyterian Hospital (1997-2014); Attending Physician in Clinical Psychiatry, NYP/Columbia University Medical Center, New York-Presbyterian Hospital (1997-2014); Assistant Attending in Clinical Psychiatry, St. Luke's-Roosevelt Medical Center, Icahn School of Medicine at Mount Sinai (2009-2012); Research Psychiatrist, New York State Psychiatric Institute (2008-2012); Medical Director, Tavares' Hispanic Mental Health Clinic, New York-Presbyterian Hospital (1997-2009); Medical Director Tavares' Hispanic Mental Health Clinic, New York-Presbyterian Hospital (1997-2009); Consulting Child, Adolescent and Adult Psychiatrist, Leake and Watts Services, Inc. (1998-2000); Consulting Child, Adolescent and Adult Psychiatrist, Mental Health Providers of Western Queens Inc. (1993-1996); Assistant Attending Physician in Clinical Psychiatry, North Central Bronx Hospital, The City of New York (1991-1995); Consulting Child, Adolescent and Adult Psychiatrist, Westchester Jewish Community Services (1990-1995); Assistant Attending Physician in Clinical Psychiatry, Elmhurst Medical Center, The City of New York (1993-1994); Instructor in Human Anatomy, La Universidad Interamericana de Puerto Rico (1986-1987); Instructor in Basic Mathematics, School of Engineering, Polytechnic University, Puerto Rico (1985-1986) **CR:** Assistant Attending Physician, Medical Director, Tavares Hispanic Mental Health Clinical, New York-Presbyterian Hospital (1997-Present); Attending Physician, PRFI, INC. (1994-Present); Attending Physician, Montefiore Medical Center, New York City, NY (1991-1996); Attending Physician, Albert Einstein College of Medicine (1991-1996); Attending Physician, Westchester Jewish Community Services, Hartsdale, NY (1990-1995); Visiting Fellow, New York State Psychiatric Institute (1992-1993) **CW:** Editorial Board Member, "The International Journal of Pagan Studies, New York Edition" (1990-Present) **AW:** Recipient, Outstanding Service in Clinical Excellence Award in Child Psychiatry and Psychopharmacology, New York State Psychiatric Institute (1992); Recipient, Clinical Excellence Award, Universidad de Puerto Rico (1988); Recipient, Certificate, American Medical Society (1982) **MEM:** Senior Adviser, Association of Hispanic Mental Health Professionals (2003-Present); Membership Chair of Steering Committee, Gay and Lesbian Psychiatrists of New York, NY (2002-2010); Executive Committee, Association of Hispanic Mental Health Professionals (2001-2003); Treasurer, Board of Directors, Association of Hispanic Mental Health Professionals (2001-2003) **MH:** Albert Nelson Marquis Lifetime Achievement Award (2017) **ADD:** 200 W 70th St Ste 8F, New York, NY, 10023

DUBBS, THOMAS, T: Lawyer **I:** Law and Legal Services **CN:** Labaton Sucharow LLP **DOB:** 11/30/1947 **PB:** Chicago **SC:** IL/USA **PT:** Joseph Allan Dubbs; Martha Elaine (Moore) Dubbs **MS:** Married **SPN:** Elizabeth M.R. Brown (5/8/1982) **CH:** Alexander Joseph; Katherine Pearl; William Harrison **ED:** JD, University of Wisconsin-Madison (1974); MA in International Relations, Tufts University (1971); BA, University of Wisconsin-Madison (1970); Graduate, Culver Military Academy (Now Culver Education Foundation) (1965); MA, Fletcher School of Law Diplomacy, Tufts University **C:** Senior Partner, Labaton Sucharow LLP, New York, NY (1998-Present); Attorney, Kidder Peabody & Co., New York, NY

(1990-1998); Partner, Hall, McNicol, Hamilton & Clark, New York, NY (1985-1990); Associate, Chadbourne, Parke, Whiteside & Wolff (Now Chadbourne & Parke LLP), New York, NY (1974-1984) **CR:** Member, Board of Visitors, University of Wisconsin Law School (2016); Member, Board of Visitors, History Department, University of Wisconsin-Madison (2016) **CW:** Contributor, Articles to Professional Journals **MEM:** Litigation Section, ABA; The American Law Institute; Patron, The American Society of International Law; Association of the Bar of the City of New York; The Union Club Of the City Of New York; The University Club of New York; Reform Club; Down Town Association; New York Chapter, General Society of Mayflower Descendants; Chicago Chapter, The Cliff Dwellers; General Society Sons of the Revolution **BAR:** New York (1976); Supreme Court of the United States (1976); United States District Court for the Southern District of New York (1976); United States District Court Eastern District of New York (1976) **H:** Travel; Golf; Reading; History **BA:** 140 Broadway, Labaton Sucharow LLP, New York, NY, 10005 **ADD:** 140 Broadway, Suite 2300, Labaton Sucharow LLP, New York, NY, 10005

DUBOIS, JOHN P., T: President **I:** Engineering **CN:** Optimize, Inc. **PB:** Auburn **SC:** ME/USA **MS:** Married **CH:** Timothy; Jaime; Michael **ED:** BA, Industrial Engineering, University of Southern Maine (1988) **CT:** Six Sigma Black Belt **C:** President, Tandem Training Corporation, Tandem Training & Consulting, LLC, Portland, ME (2014-Present); Managing Agent, Innovation Transition Center, Inc., Optimize, Inc. (2010-Present); President, Optimize, Inc. (2007-Present); Director of Lean Services, Patrona Corporation, Dover NH (2007-2010); Vice President, Advanced Resource Development, MEP MSI, Time Wise Management Systems, Augusta, ME (1999-2007); Manager, Advanced Manufacturing Engineering, Formed Fiber Technologies (Now Conform Automotive) (1997-2000); Senior Project Engineer, Pactiv (1989-1997); Manager, Advanced Manufacturing Engineering, Auburn, ME (1985-1987); Bluegrass Automotive Manufacturing Association; Subject Matter Expert, Lean Special Projects Team, National Institute of Standards Technology (NIST); Developed, Focused Improvement Workshops; Facilitated Executive Planning Sessions (EPS); Submarine and Aircraft Carrier Overhaul and Repair Community **CIV:** Volunteer, Fundraising and Golf Tournament, Gary's House, Mercy Hospital, Portland, ME (2009-Present); Coaching Youth Sports Including Soccer and Hockey **H:** Skiing; Boating; Woodworking **ADD:** 5 Pemberly Dr, Windham, ME, 04062

DUMAS, BETHANY K., T: Linguist, Educator **I:** Education/Educational Services **CN:** University of Tennessee **PT:** John Wesley Dumas; Doris Ella (de Spain) Dumas **ED:** JD, College of Law, University of Tennessee, Knoxville, TN (1985); PhD, University of Arkansas, Fayetteville, AR (1971); MA, University of Arkansas, Fayetteville, AR (1961); BA, Lamar University, Beaumont, TX (1959) **C:** Professor Emeritus, University of Tennessee, Knoxville, TN (2012-Present); Professor, University of Tennessee, Knoxville, TN (1974-2012); Assistant Professor, Trinity University, San Antonio, TX (1973-1974); Assistant Professor, Southern University and A&M College, Baton Rouge, LA (1966-1973); Instructor, Missouri State University, Springfield, MO (1964-1966); Graduate Assistant, University of Arkansas, Fayetteville, AR (1959-1971) **CR:** Consultant, Expert Witness, Independent, Knoxville, TN (1983-Present) **CW:** Author, "E. E. Cummings: A Remembrance of Miracles"; Contributor, Book Chapters; Contributor, Articles,

Professional Journals **AW:** Grantee, National Endowment for the Humanities (1972-1973) **MEM:** American Bar Association; Law and Society Association; American Dialect Society; American Association for Applied Linguistics; New Ways of Analyzing Variation; International Association Forensic Linguists; Linguistic Society of America; Southeastern Conference on Linguistics **MH:** Albert Nelson Marquis Lifetime Achievement Award (2017) **H:** Horseback riding; Creative writing **PA:** Conservative **RE:** Episcopalian **ADD:** 1400 Kenesaw Avenue, Apt. 13G, Knoxville, TN, 37919 **URL:** https://english.utk.edu/people/bethany-dumas

DUNCAN, THOMAS WEBB, T: Media Executive (Retired) **I:** Media & Entertainment **DOB:** 11/03/1946 **PB:** Rhinebeck **SC:** NY/USA **ED:** BA in English, Wake Forest University (1968) **C:** Vice President, Penton Media Inc., Stamford, CT (2007-2014); Group Publisher, Primedia-Prism, Stamford, CT (1998-2007); Editor-in-chief, Intertec Publishing Corp., White Plains, NY (1992-1998); Publisher, Intertec Publishing Corp., White Plains, NY (1992-1998); Vice President, FM Business Publications, New York City, NY (1989-1991); Editor-in-chief, FM Business Publications, New York City, NY (1989-1991); Senior Editor, McGraw-Hill, San Francisco, CA (1979-1988); Regional Manager, McGraw-Hill, San Francisco, CA (1979-1988); Associate Editor, McGraw-Hill, New York City, NY (1976-1979); Editor-in-chief, Taconic Press, Millbrook, NY (1974-1976); Managing Editor, Dutchess Suburban Newspapers, Hyde Park, NY (1973-1974); Reporter, Poughkeepsie Journal (1968-1972); Copy Editor, Poughkeepsie Journal (1968-1972) **ADD:** 59 Daffodil Hill Rd, Garrison, NY, 10524

DUNKLE, LISA M., T: Clinical Program Team Leader for Respiratory Infections **I:** Medicine & Health Care **CN:** Sanofi Pasteur **DOB:** 10/31/1946 **PB:** Ann Arbor **SC:** MI/USA **PT:** Robert Henry Dunkle; Dorothy Rose (Heagstedt) Dunkle **MS:** Married **SPN:** Richard James Scheffler (12/28/1972) **CH:** Richard James Scheffler III; Margaret Dorothy Scheffler Heil, MD **ED:** Fellow, Infectious Diseases, Washington University in St. Louis (1974-1976); Resident in Pediatrics, Washington University in St. Louis (1973-1974); Intern, Washington University in St. Louis (1972-1973); MD, Johns Hopkins University (1972); AB, Wellesley College (1968) **CT:** Diplomate, National Board of Medical Examiners; Diplomate, American Board of Pediatrics; Pediatric Infectious Diseases Certification, American Board of Pediatrics; Diplomate, Pediatrics Infectious Disease Society **C:** Clinical Program Team Leader for Respiratory Infections, Sanofi Pasteur (2018-Present); Chief Medical Officer, Protein Sciences Corporation, Meriden, CT (2011-2017); Executive Director, ID Clinical Research (2009-2011); Executive Director, Global Clinical Research, Schering-Plough, New Jersey (2004-2011); Co-Founder, Achillion Pharmaceuticals, New Haven, CT (2000-2003); Senior Vice President of Drug Development, Achillion Pharmaceuticals, New Haven, CT (2000-2003); Executive Director, Antiviral Clinical Research, Bristol-Myers Squibb, Wallingford, CT (1997-2000); Executive Director, HIV Clinical Research, Bristol-Myers Squibb, Wallingford, CT (1995-1997); Director, Antiviral Clinical Research, Bristol-Myers Squibb, Wallingford, CT (1989-1995); Professor of Pediatrics, St. Louis University (1985-1989); Associate Professor of Microbiology, Associate Professor of Pediatrics, St. Louis University (1979-1985); Director, Infection Control Program, Cardinal Glennon Hospital, St. Louis, MO (1976-1989); Director, Infectious Diseases Laboratory, Cardinal Glennon Hospital,

St. Louis, MO (1976-1989); Director, Pediatrics Infectious Diseases, Cardinal Glennon Hospital, St. Louis, MO (1976-1989); Assistant Professor of Pediatrics, St. Louis University (1976-1979) **CIV:** Fundraiser, Episcopal Church of the Holy Advent, Clinton, CT (2012-Present); Fundraiser, Wellesley College (2010-Present); Class Representative, Class of 1972, Johns Hopkins University School of Medicine (2002-Present); Fundraiser, Episcopal Church of the Holy Advent, Clinton, CT (1998-2000); Fundraiser, Wellesley College (1997-1999); Fundraiser, The Forsyth School, St. Louis, MO (1988-1989); Fundraiser, Wellesley College (1975-1988) **CW:** Editorial Board, Pediatric Infectious Disease Journal (1989-1992); Contributor, Articles, Professional Journals **AW:** Distinguished Alumna Award, Johns Hopkins University (2011); Research Grantee, Cystic Fibrosis Foundation (1984); Scholar, John Hopkins University (1972) **MEM:** Program Committee, Interscience Conference on Antimicrobial Agents and Chemotherapy (1992-1996); President, Midwest Society for Pediatric Research (1989-1990); Secretary, Midwest Society for Pediatric Research (1983-1988); Fellow, Infectious Disease Society of America; Society for Pediatric Research; Midwest Society for Pediatric Research **MH:** Albert Nelson Lifetime Achievement Award (2018) **H:** Sailing; Piano **PA:** Independent **RE:** Episcopalian **ADD:** 12 Richborough Rd, Madison, CT, 06443

DUNSKY, ANNIE, I: Fine Art **DOB:** 04/11/1949 **PB:** Rochester **SC:** NY/USA **PT:** Arnold Philip Dunsky; Caroline (Weinstein) Dunsky **ED:** Postgraduate Coursework in Painting and Illustration, Rhode Island School of Design, 1984; BFA in illustration, Cleveland Institute of Art (1973) **CR:** Cultural Committee Rochester, NY (2012-Present); Member Roco Contemporary Art, Rochester (2013-2014) **CW:** Solo Exhibitions include Germanow Gallery (1986, 1988), Finger Lakes Exhibition, Philips Fine Art Gallery, Rochester, NY (1998), Knoll Internat (1998-2000), Caelum Gallery, New York (1999); Group Exhibitions include Rhode Island School of Design Waterman Exhibition Space (1984), Germanow Gallery (1986), Pyamid Arts Center (1988, 1993, 1996), Finger Lakes Exhibition (1989), Fire Angel Gallery (1993), Arts Reach (1995), Tea House Gallery (1994), Novotel, Seoul, Korea (1995), Village Gate Gallery (1996), Hallwalls, Buffalo (1996), Ward-Nasse Gallery, New York, NY (1997), Myung Sook Lee Gallery, New York, NY (1997), High Falls Invitational, Rochester (1997), Hallwalls, Buffalo, 1998, Warren Phillips Fine Arts, Rochester, Mill Gallery, New York (1998), Mushroom House Perinton New York (2001-2003), Albright Knox Museum, Buffalo, New York (2009), The Nest Gallery (2010), Warren Philips Fine Arts (1998), Gallery Mushroom House, The Time Tunned Sketches Perminet Collections, Rush Reese Rare Books and Manuscripts (2013); Artist in Residence, The Mushroom House; Paintings and Drawings, Megg Cook Design, Buffalo (2010-Present) **AW:** Creative Women, Germanow Gallery, Special Opportunities Stipend Award (1997); First Place Award, Germanow Gallery (1986) **MEM:** Member Pyramid Art Center **ACH:** null **H:** Travel; Collecting antiques; Gemology; Writing; Standard poodles

DUNSTAN, MARIE E., T: Chemistry Professor **I:** Education/Educational Services **CN:** York College of Pennsylvania **PT:** Dale Vernon Miller; Betty Jane (Kimmons) Miller **MS:** Widowed **SPN:** Isaac Dunstan (10/13/1979, Deceased) **CH:** Robyn; Wendy **ED:** MS in Medical Technology, University at Buffalo (1978); BS in Chemistry, Lebanon Valley College, Annville, PA (1975) **CT:** ACS Certified, Lebanon Valley College, Annville, PA (1975) **C:** York College of Pennsylvania (1981-Present);

Research Technologist, Milton S. Hershey Medical Center, PennState Health (1978-1981); Instructor Faculty Position, York College of Pennsylvania; Medical Laboratory Science, Coordinator, York College of Pennsylvania **CIV:** Advisory Council, Medical Laboratory of Science, York College of Pennsylvania; Advisory Council, Respiratory Therapy, York College of Pennsylvania; Sunday School Teacher, Lewisberry United Methodist Church **CW:** Author, "Principles of Chemistry and Organic Chemistry"; Contributor, Articles to Professional Journals **MEM:** Pennsylvania Academy of Sciences; American Chemical Society **MH:** Albert Nelson Marquis Lifetime Achievement Award (2017) **H:** Cooking Pennsylvania Dutch Food; Sewing **ADD:** 540 Garriston Rd, York Haven, PA, 17370 **URL:** http://www.marieedunstan.com

DUREN, PETER LARKIN, I: Education/Educational Services **DOB:** 04/30/1935 **PB:** New Orleans **SC:** LA/USA **PT:** William Duren; Mary (Hardesty) Duren **MS:** Married **SPN:** Grace Olcott Adkins (June 15, 1957) **CH:** Elizabeth Adkins, William Larkin III **ED:** PhD, Massachusetts Institute of Technology (1960); AB, Cum Laude, Harvard University (1956) **C:** Professor Emeritus, University of Michigan (2010-Present); Professor of Mathematics, University of Michigan (1969-2010); Chairman, Doctoral Committee, University of Michigan (1994-1996); Associate, Chairman Graduate Studies, University of Michigan (1987-1988); Associate Professor, University of Michigan (1966-1969); Assistant Professor, University of Michigan (1962-1966); Instructor, Stanford University (1960-1962) **CR:** Temporary Member, University Würzburg, Germany (2014); University Autonoma, Madrid (2000, 2005, 2013); Florida Analysis Seminar (2012); Modern Complex Analysis and Operator Theory, El Escorial, Spain (2009); Extremal Problems Complex and Real Analysis, Moscow (2007); Complex and Harmonic Analysis, Thessaloniki, Greece (2006); Universidad Catolica de Chile, Santiago (2004); Conference on Planar Harmonic Mappings, Technion, Haifa (1995, 2000); Visiting Scholar, Max-Planck Institute, Leipzig (2000); Conference on Analytic Functions, Lublin, Poland (1998); Visiting Scholar, Martin-Luther University, Halle, Germany (1998); Conference on Computational Methods and Function Theory, Nicosia, Cyprus (1997); Visiting Scholar, Norwegian University of Science and Technology (1996); Main Speaker, Southeastern Analysis Meeting, Atlanta (1995); Visiting Scholar, Bar-Ilan University, Ramat-Gan, Israel (1994); Visiting Scholar, University of Hawaii (1993); Ex-Students Association Lecturer, Texas Technical University (1992); Visiting Scholar, K.T.H., Stockholm (1990); Technical Alumni Fund and Lecturer, University of New Hampshire (1990); Visiting Scholar, Stanford University (1989); S.E.R.C. Visitor, University of York, England (1985); Visiting Scholar, Academia Sinica Conference, Xian, China (1984); Visiting Scholar, Mittag-Leffler Institute, Djursholm, Sweden (1983); Visiting Scholar, E.T.H., Zurich (1983); Visiting Scholar, University Paris-Sud (1965, 1982-1983); Visiting Scholar, Regional Conference Panel, Conference Board of Mathematics and Science (1979-1982); Visiting Professor, University of Maryland (1982); Visiting Scholar, Principal Lecturer, NATO Instructional Conference on Complex Analysis, Durham, England (1979); Visiting Scholar, Technion, Haifa, Israel (1975); Temporary Member, Institute of Advanced Study (1968-1969); Visiting Scholar, University of London (1964-1965) **CIV:** Board of Directors, Academy Freedom Lecture Fund (2000-Present) **CW:** Editor, "Menahem Max Schiffer: Selected Papers" (2013); Author, "Invitation to Classical Analysis" (2012); Editor, "New York Journal of Mathematics"

(2007-2011); Member, Editorial Board, "Complex Variables and Elliptic Equations" (1981-2008); Author, "Harmonic Mappings in the Plane" (2004); Co-author (with A. Schuster), Bergman Spaces (2004); Editor, "American Mathematics Monthly" (1996-2001); Editor, "Computational Methods and Function Theory" (2001); Editor, "Quasiconformal Mappings and Analysis" (1997); Editor, "Golden Years of Moscow Mathematics" (1993); Editor, "A Century of Mathematics in America" (1988-1989); Editor, "The Bieberbach Conjecture: Proceedings of the Symposium on the Occasion of the Proof" (1986); Author, "Univalent Functions" (1983); Managing Editor, "Michigan Mathematics Journal" (1976-1977); Author, "Theory of Hp Spaces" (1970); Contributor, Scientific Papers **AW:** Fellow, American Mathematical Society (2012); Special Issue Complex Variables and Elliptic Equations (2007); Honoree, Conference on Operator-Related Function Theory, El Escorial, Spain (2005); Fellow, Sloan Foundation (1964-1966) **MEM:** Governor, Mathematics Association of America (1979-1982); American Association of University Professors; American Mathematical Society; London Mathematical Society

DUTTA, SISIR K. PHD, T: Molecular Biologist **I:** Sciences **DOB:** 08/28/1928 **PB:** Rajshahi **SC:** India **PT:** Krishna K. Dutta; Satyabati Dutta **MS:** Married **SPN:** Minati Dutta (7/1/1955) **CH:** Mahasweta; Basabi Dipanla **ED:** PhD in Biochemical Genetics, Kansas State University (1960); MS in Biochemical Genetics, Kansas State University (1958); BS in Plant Genetics and Breeding, University of Dhaka (1949) **C:** Collaborator, U.S. Department of Agriculture, Beltsville, Maryland, (1985-Present); Professor, Department of Biology, Howard University, Washington, DC (1967-Present); Specialist in Biotechnology, United Nations (1981-1982); Faculty Fellow, Molecular Genetics Laboratory, National Institutes of Health, Bethesda, Maryland (1977-1978); Visiting Scientist, Institut Pasteur, Paris, France (1974-1975); Visiting Scientist, Biochemical Genetics Laboratory, The Rockefeller University (1968-1969); Chairman, Department of Science & Mathematics, Jarvis Christian College, Texas (1966-1967); Associate Professor of Biology, Jarvis Christian College, Texas (1966-1967); Assistant Professor of Biology, Texas Southern University, Houston (1965-1966); Director, Malaysian Pineapple Industry Board (1961-1964); Chief Resident Officer, Malaysian Pineapple Industry Board (1961-1964); Research Scientist, Department of Genetics & Breeding, Government of West Bengal, India (1949-1953); Research Scientist, Department of Agriculture, Government of West Bengal, India (1949-1953) **CR:** Speaker in Field **AW:** Eponym, The Dr. Sisir Dutta Center for Human Genomic Biomarker Medicine, Howard University (2017) **MEM:** American Association for the Advancement of Science; The Bioelectromagnetics Society; National Institute of Science; Mycological Society pf America; Texas Academy of Science; American Institute Biological of Sciences; American Horticultural Society; The American Phytopathological Society; Botanical Society of America; American Society of Environmental Mutagens (Now The Environmental Mutagenesis and Genomics Society); International Microwave Power Institute; The Genetics Society of America; Indian Science Congress Association; Beta Kappa Chi National Honor Society **MH:** Albert Nelson Marquis Lifetime Achievement Award (2017) **ADD:** 5505 Thornbush Ct, Bethesda, MD, 20814

DYKSTRA, KEVIN H., T: President, Chief Executive Officer **I:** Pharmaceuticals **CN:** qPharmetra **SC:** CO/USA **MS:** Married **ED:** Postdoctoral Fellowship, National Institutes of Health (1989-1992); PhD in Biochemical and Biomedical Engineering, University of Michigan (1989); MSE in Biochemical and Biomedical Engineering, University of Michigan (1985); Coursework in Biostatistics, Boston University (1984-1989); BS in German, University of Colorado, Boulder (1983); BSChemE, University of Colorado, Boulder (1983) **C:** President, qPharmetra (2010-Present); Chief Executive Officer, qPharmetra (2010-Present); Senior Vice President, Strategic Consulting, Pharsight Corporation (Now Certara, L.P.) (2009-2010); Vice President, Pharsight Corporation (Now Certara, L.P.) (2007-2009); Lead Scientist, Pharsight Corporation (Now Certara, L.P.) (2007-2009); Senior Scientist, Pharsight Corporation (Now Certara, L.P.) (2000-2007); Associate Director of Clinical Pharmacology, Wyeth Pharmaceuticals (1997-2000); Biostatistician, Genetics Institute (1995-1997) **CR:** Fellow, American College of Clinical Pharmacology **CW:** Contributor, Reporting Guidelines for Population H: Bicycling; Road riding; Mountain biking; Piano **ADD:** 9 Nollet Drive, Andover, MA, 01810 **URL:** http://www.qpharmetra.com

DYSON, TAMEARRA, T: Owner **I:** Food & Restaurant Services **CN:** Souley Vegan **PB:** Martinez Ca. **PT:** Catherine Williams; James Dyson **MS:** Single **CH:** Aquil Bey **ED:** Registered Nurse, Merritt College **CT:** Certified in Business **C:** Owner, Souley Vegan (2006-Present); Founder, Souley Vegan (2006-Present); President, Souley Vegan (2006-Present); Endoscopy Technician, Marin General Hospital (2001-2007); Certified Nursing Assistant, Marin General Hospital (1998-2001); **CIV:** Donor, PETA; Donor, SPCA International, Inc.; Donor, The Bread Project **CW:** Poet, Unpublished Works; Author, "Butterfly Kisses" **AW:** Honoree, Entrepreneur of the Month, Black Enterprise; Honoree, Top Ten Soul Food Restaurants in the Country, USA Today; Power Players 2018, Angeleno Magazine; Recipient, Several Local Awards **MEM:** National Restaurant Association **H:** Running; Writing poetry **BA:** 301 Broadway, Souley Vegan, Oakland, CA, 94607 **URL:** https://www.linkedin.com/in/tamearra-dyson-b7924835/

EASTLAND, S. STACY, T: Managing Director **I:** Financial Services **CN:** Goldman Sachs **DOB:** 10/27/1948 **PB:** Houston **SC:** TX/USA **PT:** Seaborn Eastland; Anne (Stacy) Eastland **MS:** Married **SPN:** Tara Gardner (3/24/1972) **CH:** Tara Doran; Seaborn Gardner **ED:** JD, The University of Texas, with Honors (1974); BS, Washington and Lee University, with Honors (1971) **C:** Managing Director, Goldman Sachs, Houston, TX (2000-Present); Partner, Baker Botts L.L.P., Houston, TX (1982-2000); Associate, Baker Botts L.L.P., Houston, TX (1974-1981) **CR:** Former Member, Board of Directors, Houston Estate and Financial Forum, Camp Mystic, Inc.; Member, Texas Board of Legal Specialization; Member, NAEPC **CIV:** Affiliate, Board of Directors, Oscar Neuhaus Foundation; Affiliate, St. John Memorial Endowment Fund; Member, Houston Chapter, Ortin Society; Affiliate, DePelchin Children's Center; Affiliate, Institute for Child & Family Health; Trustee, Kelsey Research Foundation **AW:** Named, Top Trust and Estate Lawyers, Best Lawyers in America **MEM:** Bylaws and Handbook Committee, ABA (1992-Present); Council, ABA (1990-Present); Secretary Advisor, Revision Uniform Partnership Act, ABA (1987-Present); Publications Coordinator, Probate and Trust Division, ABA (1992-1993); Publications Committee, ABA (1992-1993); Chairman, Transfer Tax Study Committee, The American College of Trust and Estate Counsel (1988-1993); Budget and Financial Committee, ABA (1991-1992); Chairman, Division Coordinator, Annual Meeting Programs, ABA (1987-1989); State Bar of Texas; Houston Bar Association; Houston Country Club; Texas Allegro Club; The International Academy of Estate and Trust Law; Fellow, The American College of Trust and Estate Counsel; Board of Regents, The American College of Trust and Estate Counsel **MH:** Albert Nelson Marquis Lifetime Achievement Award (2017) **H:** Tennis; Golf **RE:** Episcopalian **BA:** 1000 Louisiana Street, Suite 550, Goldman Sachs, Houston, TX, 77002 **ADD:** 232 Arborway St, Houston, TX, 77057

EASTMOND-ROBINSON, JUNE PATRICIA, T: Nursing Educator **I:** Education/Educational Services **DOB:** 06/21/1938 **PB:** New York **SC:** NY/USA **PT:** Claude T. Eastmond; Olivia G. Braithwaite-Eastmond **MS:** Married **SPN:** Arthur L. Robinson (5/16/1981); Maroa W. Gikuuri (1968, Divorced 1978) **CH:** Maroa L Gikuuri; Nyahiri Gikuuri-Dozier; Randall Robinson **ED:** EdD, Florida Atlantic University (1999); MS in Community Health, LIU Brooklyn (1974); BSN, New York University (1964); RN, Kings County Hospital Center School of Nursing, City of New York, NY (1958) **CT:** RN, Florida Board of Nursing (1978); Certified in Healing Touch, Healing Touch Wellness & Injury Center **C:** Part-Time Clinical Instructor, University of Central Florida, Orlando, FL (2005-2007); Part-Time Staff Member, Development and Education, Port St. Lucie Nursing and Restorative Care Center (2001-2003); Retired, Indian River State College, Fort Pierce, FL (2001); Associate Professor, Nursing, Indian River State College, Fort Pierce, FL (1980-2001); Director of Nursing, Florida Community Health Centers, Inc., West Palm Beach, FL (1978-1980); Director, Patient Relations, Kings County Hospital Center, City of New York, NY (1974-1978); In-Service Education Coordinator, Medgar Evers College, Brooklyn, NY (1972-1974); Public Health Nurse for Pregnant Teens, Project Teen Aid, Brooklyn, NY (1968-1972); Public Health Nurse, Department of Health, City of New York, NY (1961-1963); Staff Nurse, Kings County Hospital Center, City of New York, NY (1958-1959) **CR:** Test Consultant, National Council of State Boards of Nursing, Atlanta, GA (1997); Test Consultant, National Council of State Boards of Nursing, Atlanta, GA (1994); Co-chairperson, State of Florida Science Task Force (1980-1986) **CIV:** Member, Orlando Chapter, The Links, Incorporated (1996-Present); Supporter, Child Fund International (Formerly Christian Children's Fund) (1990-Present); Board of Directors, Herzing University (2013-2014); Volunteer Reader for Students, Bonneville Elementary School, Orange County, FL (2010-2015); Treasurer, Faces and Voices of St. Lucie County Inc. (2001-2003); Actor, Faces and Voices of St. Lucie County Inc. (2001-2003); Member, Board of Directors, Big Brothers Big Sisters of St. Lucie, Indian River, and Okeechobee Counties, Fort Pierce, FL (2001-2003); Vice President, Region III, Florida Special Needs Association (1986-1989); Publicity Chairperson, African-American Cultural Exposition for the Arts, Fort Pierce, FL (1983-2002); Past President, African-American Cultural Exposition for the Arts, Fort Pierce, FL; Supporter, Native American Child Health & Education; Supporter, Covenant House; Board Member, Central Florida Black Nurses Association of Orlando Inc. **CW:** Co-author, "Nursing Assistant Fundamentals" (1998) **AW:** Certificate for Serving as Committee Chair, Black Men's Health Summit (2015-2017); Award for Contributions in Public Health, Florida Department of Health, Seminole County, FL (2014); Outstanding School Volunteer of the Year, Bonneville Elementary School, Orange County Public Schools (2012); Certificate for General Education Specialist, High-tech Institute,

Inc., Orlando, FL (2009); Gratitude Award, Caribbean Nurses Association (2000); Certificate of Appreciation, National Council of State Boards of Nursing (1997); Academic Excellence Award, Florida Atlantic University (1997, 1995) **MEM:** NAACP (2010-Present); Central Florida Black Nurses Association of Orlando Inc. (2005-Present); National Black Nurses Association (2005-Present); Treasurer, District 24, Florida Nurses Association (2000-2003); Board of Directors, Caribbean Nurses Association (1999-2003); President, Association Practical Nurse Educators of Florida (1991-2000); Treasurer, Association Practical Nurse Educators of Florida (1991-2000); Board of Directors, Association Practical Nurse Educators of Florida (1991-2000) **H:** Reading; Exercise; Organizing community activities; Acting **PA:** Non-partisan **RE:** Baha'i Faith **ADD:** 14556 Lycastle Cir, Orlando, FL, 32826

EATON, LEONARD JAMES JR., T: President (Retired) **I:** Leisure, Travel & Tourism **CN:** World Travel **DOB:** 09/18/1934 **PB:** New York **SC:** NY/USA **PT:** Leonard James Eaton; Alice Edna (Leach) Eaton **MS:** Married **SPN:** Patricia Pride (11/30/1957) **CH:** Leslie; Pamela; Alexander **ED:** Postgraduate Coursework, Harvard University (1971); BA, Cornell University (1956) **C:** Retired (2007); President, World Travel, Tulsa, OK (2001-2007); Director of Finances, The NORDAM Group, Inc. (1993-2001); Chairman of the Board, Bank of Oklahoma (1978-1991); Chief Executive Officer, Bank of Oklahoma (1978-1991); President, Bank of Oklahoma (1973-1978); Executive Vice President, Bank of Oklahoma (1972-1973); With, First National City Bank, New York, NY (1956-1971); Director, Bank of Oklahoma **CIV:** Member, Advisory Council, Harry Ransom Center, The University of Texas at Austin; Regent, Oklahoma State Regents for Higher Education; Director, Oklahoma Chapter, The Nature Conservancy; Member, Board of Trustees, Meadville Lombard Theological School, The University of Chicago **MEM:** Board of Directors, Metropolitan Tulsa Chamber of Commerce (Now Tulsa Regional Chamber) **H:** Hiking; Walking **ADD:** 2617 E 26th Pl, Tulsa, OK, 74114 **URL:** https://www.worldtraveltoday.com/contact

EATON, MICHAEL CHRISTOPHER, T: Accounting Technician **I:** Financial Services **DOB:** 08/08/1959 **PB:** Columbus **SC:** OH/USA **PT:** Ronald Andrew Eaton; Rosaleen Ann (Murnane) Eaton **MS:** Married **SPN:** Charlene Ann (Guzmann) Eaton **ED:** AS, Burlington County College (Now Rowan College at Burlington County) (1984); Coursework, The Ohio State University (1978-1979); BBA, Air University **CT:** Diplomate, Officer Qualification Examination **C:** Contracting Specialist, Defense Supply Center, Defense Logistics Agency (1996-2002) **CIV:** Active Member, The Feinstein Foundation; Freshman Senate, The Ohio State University **MIL:** Staff Sergeant, U.S. Air Force (1980-1986); Squadron Leader, Squadron 3704, U.S. Air Force **AW:** 20th Century Award for Achievement (1990-2000); International Man of the Year (1996-1997); Purple Royalty Ribbon With Medallion; Good Conduct Ribbon, U.S. Air Force; Basic Training Ribbon, U.S. Air Force; Outstanding Unit Award, U.S. Air Force; Meritorious Achievement Medal With Ribbon; Longevity Ribbon, U.S. Air Force; Ten-Year Copper Pin, U.S. Air Force; Soccer Patch, President Jimmy Carter **MEM:** Chancellor, Knights of Columbus (1994-Present); Grand Knight, Knights of Columbus (2000-2001); Deputy Grand Knight, Knights of Columbus (1996-2000); Fourth Degree, Knights of Columbus (1994); Outside Guard, Saint Michael Church Council, Knights of Columbus; Saint Andrew's Parish Section, Columbian Martyr's Council, Knights of Columbus; Sir Knight,

Knights of Columbus; Catholic War Veterans & Auxiliary; Men's Auxiliary, Veterans of Foreign Wars; The American Legion; Ohio Chapter, AMVETS; Disabled American Veterans; American Foreign Service Association; Ohio Rickenbacker Chapter, Air Force Association **MH:** Albert Nelson Marquis Lifetime Achievement Award (2017) **PA:** Republican **RE:** Roman Catholic **ADD:** 2439 Loggers Run Court, Columbus, OH, 43235

ECHANDI, ROBERTO, T: Global Lead **I:** Financial Services **CN:** The World Bank Group **PB:** San Jose **SC:** Costa Rica **MS:** Married **CH:** One Child **ED:** Coursework, Strategic Negotiation Program, John F. Kennedy School of Government, Harvard Kennedy School, Cambridge, MA (1996); MPhil in Latin American Studies, St. Antony's College, University of Oxford, Oxford, United Kingdom (1995); LLM, The University of Michigan Law School, Ann Arbor, MI (1993); Doctoral Coursework, University of Michigan Law School, Ann Arbor, MI (1991-1993); Coursework, Introduction to the United States Legal System, International Law Institute, Georgetown University, Washington, DC (1991); Licenciado en Derecho Diploma, School of Law, University of Costa Rica, San Jose, Costa Rica (1991); Coursework, Legal Aspects of Trade with the United States, INCAE, San Jose, Costa Rica (1990) **C:** Global Lead, Investment Policy & Promotion, The World Bank Group, Washington, DC (2012-Present); Director, Program on International Investment, World Trade Institute, University of Bern, Bern, Switzerland (2010–2012); Faculty Member, Master in International Law and Economics, World Trade Institute, University of Bern, Bern Switzerland (2010–2012); Ambassador to the Kingdom of Belgium, the Grand Duchy of Luxembourg and the European Union, Government of Costa Rica, Brussels, Belgium (2007–2010); Chief Negotiator of Costa Rica for the Association Agreement between the European Union and Central America, Government of Costa Rica, Brussels, Belgium (2007–2010); Special Adjunct Ambassador for United States Trade Affairs, Ministry of Foreign Trade, San Jose, Costa Rica (2002–2005); Senior Special Advisor, Ministry of Foreign Trade, San Jose, Costa Rica (2000–2001); Director General for International Trade, Ministry of Foreign Trade, San Jose, Costa Rica (1998-2000); Legal Affairs Officer, Appellate Body Secretariat, World Trade Organization, Geneva, Switzerland (1997-1998); Advisor, Department of International Trade, Ministry of Foreign Trade, San Jose, Costa Rica (1995–1997); Advisor, Department of International Trade, Ministry of Foreign Trade, San Jose, Costa Rica (1993) **CR:** Faculty Member, Summer Academy, Module on Investment, World Trade Institute, University of Bern, Bern, Switzerland (2010–Present); Faculty Member, Course on Investment Protection, University of Barcelona (2009-Present); Designated Member, International Centre for Settlement of Investment Disputes Panel of Conciliators (2011-2017); Faculty Member, Courses on International Trade and Investment Law and Policy, Master's Program on Diplomatic Studies, Diplomatic Institute, Ministry of Foreign Affairs of Costa Rica, University of Costa Rica (2004-2006); Adjunct Professor of Law, Institute for International Economic Law, Georgetown University Law Center (2000-2001); Visiting Scholar, Institute for International Economic Law, Georgetown University Law Center (2000-2001); Fellow, Institute for International Economic Law, Georgetown University Law Center (2000-2001); Faculty Member, Courses on International Trade and Investment Law and Policy, Master's Program on Diplomatic Studies, Diplomatic Institute, Ministry of Foreign Affairs of Costa Rica, University of Costa Rica (1999); Faculty

Member, Courses on International Trade and Investment Law and Policy, Master's Program on Diplomatic Studies, Diplomatic Institute, Ministry of Foreign Affairs of Costa Rica, University of Costa Rica (1995-1996); Faculty Member, Courses on International Trade and Investment Law and Policy, Master's Program on Diplomatic Studies, Diplomatic Institute, Ministry of Foreign Affairs of Costa Rica, University of Costa Rica (1993); Contributing Expert, Latin America Initiative, Baker Institute for Public Policy, Rice University; Contributing Scholar, Latin America Initiative, Baker Institute for Public Policy, Rice University; Keynote Speaker, Multiple Conferences; Keynote Speaker, Multiple Seminars; Keynote Speaker, Training Activities; Instructor, International Trade & Investment Law and Policy **CW:** Author, "Be Careful with What You Wish: Saving Developing Countries from Development and the Risk of Overlooking the Importance of a Multilateral Rule-Based System on Investment in the Twenty-First Century," European Yearbook of International Economic Law, Euroyear, Volume Seven (2016); Editorial Board Member, "Journal of World Investment & Trade," Kluwer Law International (2012); Editorial Board Member, "Journal of International Economic Law," Oxford University Press; Author, Several Books; Author, Articles, Professional Journals **AW:** Mariano Montealegre Bustamante Excellence Award, President and the Minister of Foreign Affairs of Costa Rica to the Best Ambassador of the Administration (2006-2010); Ronaldo Falconer Scholarship, University of Oxford, Oxford, United Kingdom (1993-1995); Fulbright Scholar (1991-1992); Fellow, Academia de Centroamérica **MEM:** Honorary Member, Costa Rican Exporters Association (2010); Costa Rica Bar Association **MH:** Distinguished Humanitarian (2017) **ADD:** 713 E Custis Ave, Alexandria, VA, 22301 **URL:** http://www.worldbank.org/en/about/people/r/roberto-echandi

EDEIKEN-MONROE, BETH, T: Professor **I:** Education/Educational Services **CN:** University of Texas **MS:** Married **CH:** Two Sons **ED:** Clinical Fellowship, Oncology, MD Anderson Cancer Center, University of Texas, Houston, TX (1977-1978); Clinical Fellowship, American Cancer Society, Houston, TX (1976-1977); Clinical Residency, Diagnostic Radiology, University of Texas Combined Program, Houston, TX (1975-1977); Clinical Residency, Diagnostic Radiology, Jefferson Medical College, Philadelphia, PA (1974-1975); Clinical Internship, Jefferson Medical College, Philadelphia, PA (1973-1974); MD, Jefferson Medical College, Philadelphia, PA (1973); BS, Temple University, Philadelphia, PA (1969) **CT:** Board Certified, American Board of Radiology (1979); Texas Medical Board Physician's Permit (1978); License to Practice Medicine, State of Pennsylvania (1974-1978) **C:** Professor of Radiology, Department of Diagnostic Radiology, Division of Diagnostic Imaging, MD Anderson Cancer Center, University of Texas, Houston, TX (2004-Present); Cancer Information Service Consultant, MD Anderson Hospital & Tumor Institute, Houston, TX (1986-Present); Associate Professor, Department of Diagnostic Radiology, MD Anderson Cancer Center, University of Texas, Houston, TX (1989-2004); Assistant Chief, Emergency Radiology, Department of Radiology, Hermann Hospital, Houston, TX (1987-1989); Inter-Institutional Radiology Consultant, Hermann Hospital (1984-1986); Inter-Institutional Radiology Consultant, MD Anderson Cancer Center, University of Texas, Houston, TX (1984-1986); Chief, Diagnosis, Department of Radiology, MD Anderson Cancer Center, University of Texas, Houston, TX (1983-1987); Staff Physician, Department of Radiology,

Hermann Hospital, Houston, TX (1982-1989); Assistant Professor, Department of Radiology, University of Texas Medical School, Houston, TX (1982-1989); Assistant Professor, Volunteer Faculty, Department of Radiology, University of Texas Medical School, Houston, TX (1980-1982); Assistant Radiologist, Department of Diagnostic Radiology, MD Anderson Cancer Center, University of Texas, Houston, TX (1979-1988); Assistant Radiologist, The University of Texas System Cancer Center, Houston, TX, (1979-1982); Assistant Professor, Department of Radiology, MD Anderson Cancer Center, University of Texas, Houston, TX (1979-1982); Instructor, Department of Diagnostic Radiology, MD Anderson Cancer Center, University of Texas, Houston, TX (1978-1979) **CR:** Endocrine Program, CSAC Review (2008-Present); Fellow, American College of Radiology (1997); Radiological Practice Committee (1996); Cancer Prevention Breast QI Committee (1996); Scientific Program Committee (1994-1998); Communications Committee (1994-1995); Advisor, Diagnostic Radiology Residency, Houston, TX (1994); Interviewer, Medical School Admissions Committee, Houston, TX (1994); Panel Moderator, Local Arrangements Committee (1993-1998); Local Arrangements Committee (1993-1994); Chair, Committee on Teaching in Radiology (1992-1998); Resident Education Committee (1992); Medical Records Committee (1989-1991); Panelist, Image Interpretation Session, RSNA, Chicago, IL (1989); Written Boards Examination Committee (1989); Freshman Medical Student Advisor, The University of Texas Medical School (1988); Residency Policy Review Committee, Houston, TX (1986-1989); Examiner, MSRDP Quality Assurance Committee, Houston, TX (1986); Committee on Residency Training (1985-1989); Oncology Conference, Houston, TX (1985-1988); Advisor, Medical Students-Career Selections, Houston, TX (1985-1987); Medical School Admissions Committee, Houston, TX (1983-1988); Freshman Medical Student Advisor, University of Texas Medical School (1983-1986); Chief Proctor, Medical School Admissions Committee, Houston, TX (1983); Interviewer, Medical School Admissions Committee (1980-1989); Medical Quality Assurance Committee, MD Anderson Hospital & Tumor Institute (1980-1982) **CIV:** Mentoring; Teaching **CW:** Co-Author, "Ultrasound Characteristics and Ultrasound-Guided Fine-Needle Aspiration of Lymph Nodes in the Cervical Soft Tissues: A Radiology Perspective" Advanced Thyroid and Parathyroid Ultrasound (2017); Reviewer, Thyroid (2008); Reviewer, Academics Journal (1992); Co-Author, Co-Editor, "The Radiology of Acute Cervical Spine Trauma, 2nd Edition," Williams & Wilkins, Baltimore, MD (1987); Contributor, Over 50 Articles, Professional Journals; Contributor, Abstracts; Contributor, Editorials; Contributor, Chapters, Books; Invited Presenter, National and International Conferences **AW:** Best Doctors in America (2011-Present); Best Doctors in America (2007-2008); Distinguished Service Award, American Board of Radiology (2000); Finalist, Joseph E. Whitley, MD Award for "Excellence in Radiology Education" (1994); Nominee, American College of Radiology Fellowship (1993); Finalist, Joseph E. Whitley, MD Award for "Excellence in Radiology Education" (1992); Outstanding Clinical Teaching Recognition Award, University of Texas Medical School at Houston (1986-1988); Teaching Excellence List, University of Texas Medical School at Houston (1984-1988); Outstanding Clinical Teaching Recognition Award, University of Texas Medical School at Houston (1982-1983); Research Grants **MEM:** ASHNR (2015-Present); Corporate Relations Committee, ASHNR (2016-2017); Harris County Medical Society (1983-1994); TMA (1983-

1994); American College of Radiology; Association of University Radiologists; International Skeletal Society; Houston Radiological Society; Texas Radiological Society **H:** Writing **BA:** 1515 Holcombe Drive, Houston, TX, 77030 **ADD:** 62 E Bend Lane, Houston, TX, 77007

EDELSTEIN, MARTIN P., T: Family Practice Physician **I:** Medicine & Health Care **CN:** Office of Dr. Martin Edelstein **PB:** Montreal **SC:** QC/Canada **MS:** Married **SPN:** Judith Edelstein **CH:** Four Sons **ED:** Executive Certificate Program in Healthcare Delivery Management, Stern School of Business Management, New York University (2004); Executive Certificate Program in Healthcare Delivery Management, Cornell University (2004); Internship and Residency, Jewish General Hospital, Montreal (1971-1973); MDCM, Faculty of Medicine, McGill University (1971); Fellow, Cardio Respiratory Lab, The Montreal General Hospital (1966-1967); BS in Physiology and Psychology, McGill University (1965); Fellow, American Academy of Family Physicians **CT:** Board Certified in Family Medicine **C:** Vice-Chair, Department of Family Medicine, North Shore University Hospital, Northwell Health, Manhasset, NY (2014-Present); Clinical Assistant Professor, Department of Family Medicine, Donald and Barbara Zucker School of Medicine at Hofstra/Northwell Health (2012-Present); Executive Committee, DOFM, Donald and Barbara Zucker School of Medicine at Hofstra/Northwell Health (2012-Present); Clinical Assistant Professor, Albert Einstein College of Medicine (2009-Present); Senior Attending Physician, Department of Medicine, North Shore University Hospital (2006-Present); Lifetime Fellow, Royal Society of Medicine, London, England (2006-Present); Medical Board, North Shore University Hospital (2002-Present); Private Practice of Family Medicine, Great Neck, NY (1978-Present); Fellow, American Academy of Family Physicians (1976-Present); President of Medical Staff, North Shore University Hospital (2005-2006); Clinical Assistant Professor of Medicine, School of Medicine, New York University (1996-2009); Clinical Assistant Professor, Cornell University Medical College (1992-1996); Clinical Instructor, Cornell University Medical College (1981-1991); Deputy Medical Examiner, Nassau County (1981-1984); Director Department of Emergency Medicine, Misericordia Hospital Medical Center, Bronx, NY (1981-1982); Chief Emergency Room Physician, Central General Hospital, Plainview, NY (1980-1981); Chief of Emergency Room Physicians, St. Francis Hospital (1980); Emergency Room Physician, St. Francis Hospital, Roslyn, NY (1978-1980); Clinical Instructor, Department of Medicine, Division of Family Practice, Department of Medicine, University of California, Los Angeles (1978); Lecturer, Faculty of Medicine, McGill University (1977); Private Practice Family Medicine, Montreal, QC, Canada (1973-1977); Assistant Physician Jewish General Hospital, Montreal, QC, Canada (1973-1977) **CR:** North Shore University Hospital (NSUH), North Shore Long Island Jewish Health System (NS-LIJ), NorthWell Health (2016-Present); Standards of Care Committee, Department of Medicine/Family Medicine, Northwell Health System (2015-Present); Osler Society Advisory Board, Hofstra North Shore-LIJ School of Medicine (2014-Present); Medico-Legal Consulting as Expert Witness (1995-Present); Company Surgeon, Vigilant Hook & Ladder Fire Company (1988-Present); ePrescribing Provider/Clinical Work Group, Northwell (2014-2017); Physician Health Committee, NS-LIJ (2009-2011); Quality Assurance Committee, First Choice Home Care (2006-2013); Chair, Credentials, Committee of the

Medical Staff, NSUH (2006-2007); Pay-For-Performance Task Force, NS-LIJ Health System (2006); Medical Executive Council, NS-LIJ Health System (2005-2007); President, Medical Staff, NSUH (2005-2006); Co-Chair, Medical Staff Affairs Committee, NSUH (2005-2006); Chair, Professional Library Committee, NSUH (2004-2008); By-Laws Committee, NSUH (2003-2005); Osteoporosis Task Force, NSUH (2003-2004); Physician Advisory Committee, Oxford Health Plans (2002-2006); Geriatrics and Longevity Center Task Force, NS-LIJ (2002-2003); New York Medical Staff Leadership Council (2001-2005); Geriatrics Performance Improvement Coordinating Group, NS-LIJ (2001-2002); Quality Assurance Committee, Sterling Glen Home Care Program (2001-2002); Medical Staff Affairs Committee, NSUH (2000-2009); Geriatric and Longevity Steering Committee, NS-LIJ Health System (2000-2006); Medical Advisory Board, Ultrasound Diagnostic School, Carle Place, NY (1998-2003); Physician Leadership Council - NSUH/ LIJ Physicians (1997-1998); Chairman, Pharmacy and Therapeutics Committee, NMH/Informed Rx (1995-2008); New York State, Department of Health, Managed Care Quality and Information Committee (1995-1996); New York State Task Force on Clinical Guidelines and Medical Technology Assessment (1994-1996); State Legislation Committee, Medical Society of the State of New York (1993-2002); Federal Legislation Committee, Medical Society of the State of New York (1993-2002); Medical Ethics Committee, NSUH (1991-1996); Medical Consultant, Pre-employment Drug Screening Program, Long Island Savings Bank (50-Plus Branches) (1988-1998); Medical Consultant, Coca Cola Bottling Company of New York (1988-1990); Medical Consultant, Raytheon Company (1987-1991); Pre-employment Examiner, Garden City, NY (1986-1989); Medical Director, Corporate Head Office, Leviton Manufacturing (1985-2005); Quality Assurance Committee, Department of Medicine, NSUH (1984-1989); Director, Employee Health Services, St. Francis Hospital, Roslyn, NY (1979-1980); Division Chiefs/System Chairs Committee, Department of Medicine, Northwell Health System **CW:** Manuscript Reviewer, "The Strange Case of Dr. Doyle," Daniel Friedman, MD, Eugene Friedman, MD SquareOne Publishers (2015); Co-Chair, "Medicine, Art, Music and History", Osler Society of New York (2011); Chair, "Medicine in The Civil War" (2011); Co-Chair, "John Shaw Billings: From the Battle of Gettysburg to the Surgeon General's Office" (2010); Guest Speaker, Dr. John L. Cameron, Blalock Professor of Surgery, School of Medicine, Johns Hopkins University (2010); Guest Speaker, Dr. Jerome Lowenstein, Professor of Medicine, New York University (2010); Co-Chair, "A Combined Meeting of Oxford University Medical Alumni and The Osler Society of New York," Waldorf Astoria Hotel, New York, NY (2010); Guest Speaker: Dr. Rita Charon, Professor of Clinical Medicine, Columbia College of Physicians (2009); Manuscript Reviewer, "Patience Lost - Lines from a Hospital Trench," e-Journal, Dr. Lucien Nochomovitz (2008-2009); Chair, "Possible Connection between the Tuberculosis Epidemic in the 1800's and Our Present Epidemic of the Metabolic Syndrome," Guest Speaker, Dr. Jesse Roth, Professor of Medicine, Albert Einstein College of Medicine, and Past Professor of Medicine, Johns Hopkins Medical Center, Osler Society of New York (2008); Co-Chair, "The Doctor's Life" (2006); Manuscript Reviewer, "Family Practice Management" (2005-2010); Manuscript Reviewer, "Harvey Cushing: A Life in Surgery", Michael Bliss, Oxford University Press (2005); Conference Planning Committee, "Pay For Performance, the Promise and the Challenge of Improving the Quality of Health Care,"

NS-LIJ Health System (2005); Keynote Speaker, Commencement Ceremony, Ultrasound Diagnostic School (2004); Consultant Panel, "First Meals: The Complete Cookbook and Nutrition Guide," Annabel Karmel, DK Books, Penguin Putnam (2004); Consultant Panel, "Dr. Stoppard's Family Health Guide," DK Books, Penguin Putnam (2002); Program Chair, "Aging and Medicine of the Future-The Human Genome and Proteomics," The Mayfair of Great Neck (2002); Speaker, Colorectal Cancer Awareness Month, The Mayfair of Great Neck (2002); Speaker, National Health Care Day, Garden City, NY (2000); Several Others **AW:** Listee, "How to Find the Best Doctors," Castle Connolly Guide (1994-Present); Honoree, "The Art of Medicine" Annual Gala, DOFM, Donald and Barbara Zucker School of Medicine, Hofstra/Northwell (2015); Honoree, Hugs Across America (2015); Listee, Top Ten Family Physicians on Long Island, Newsday (2014-2015); Listee, Top Ten Family Physicians on Long Island, Newsday (2012); Listee, Top Ten Family Physicians on Long Island, Newsday (2008); Listee, "Guide to America's Top Family Doctors" (2002-2010); Listed in "The Best Doctors in NY", New York Magazine (2002-2003); Listee Top 55 Family Physicians in the United States, Ladies Home Journal (2002); Hartford Foundation Scholarship in Geriatrics (2001); "One of Top Doctors in his Field", Center for the Study of Services (2000); Featured, Town and Country Magazine's Guide to the Best Primary Care Physicians in the United States (2000); Listed in "The Best Doctors in NY", New York Magazine (2000); Nominee, "Family Physician of the Year", New York State Academy of Family Physicians (1987); Consumers Research Council of America **MEM:** Patron of The Osler Library, McGill University (2005-Present); The Osler Club of London (2003-Present); American Medical Association (1989-Present); Nassau County Medical Society (1989-Present); Medical Society of the State of New York (1989-Present); Founder and President, Osler Society of New York (2008-2012); The Gerontological Society of America (2003-2005); American Academy of Anti-Aging Medicine (1999-2002); The New York Alliance of Physicians and Surgeons (1988-2005); American College of Sports Medicine (1983-1995); American College of Occupational and Environmental Medicine (1980-1995); Canadian College of Family Physicians (1974-1999) **MH:** Albert Nelson Marquis Lifetime Achievement Award (2017) **H:** History of medicine; Collecting first editions, autographed books, and Victoriana; London and New York stage; Ice hockey; Spending time with his wife and family **ADD:** 11 Beverly Road, Great Neck, NY, 11021

EDMUNDS, JOHN SANFORD, T: Lawyer **I:** Law and Legal Services **CN:** John S. Edmunds, Attorney at Law, A Limited Liability Law Company **DOB:** 01/03/1943 **PB:** Los Angeles **SC:** CA/USA **PT:** Arthur Edmunds; Sarah Bernadine (Miles) Edmunds **MS:** Married **SPN:** Virginia Maejan Ching (11/30/1975) **CH:** Laura; Shauna **ED:** JD, University of Southern California Gould School of Law Moot Court Honors (1967); AB, Stanford University (1964) **C:** Managing Member, John S. Edmunds, Attorney at Law, A Limited Liability Law Company (2017-Present); Edmunds Verga & Omonaka, Attorneys at Law, A Law Corporation (2001-2017); Partner, Edmunds Maki Verga & Thorn, Honolulu, Hawaii (1997-2001); Acting Chief Justice, Supreme Court, Republic of Marshall Islands (1980-1981); Special Deputy Attorney General, State of Hawaii (1974-1975); Chief Deputy Public Defender, State of Hawaii (1970-1972) **CR:** Adjunct Professor, Law, University of Hawai'i (1976-1977, 1985-1989); Counsel, Hemmeter Investment Company; Counsel, Obayashi Corporation; Counsel, Shell

Oil Company; Counsel, Nestle USA; Counsel, Bank of America Corporation **CIV:** Vice-chair, Hawaii State Judicial Selection Commission (2000-2002); Board of Directors, Legal Aid Society of Hawai'i (1974-1975); Member, Federal Judicial Selection Commission (Under Presidents Carter and Reagan); Member, Federal Magistrate's Selection Commission **MEM:** Board of Governors, Hawaii Academy of Plaintiffs' Attorneys (1995-Present); National Committee, Legal Ethics and Professional Responsibility, American College of Trial Lawyers (1994); State Chairman, American College of Trial Lawyers (1991-1992); Advisory Council, ACLU (1974-1975); President, ACLU (1971-1973); Board of Directors, ACLU (1969-1973); Fellow, The International Academy of Trial Lawyers; American Bar Foundation; Lifetime Member, ABA; Hawaii State Bar Association; American Association for Justice; Master of Bench, American Inns of Court **BAR:** Hawaii State Bar Association (1968) **BA:** 841 Bishop St Ste 1715, Honolulu, HI, 96813 **ADD:** 841 Bishop St Ste 1715, John S. Edmunds, AAL ALLLC, Honolulu, HI, 96813

EDWARDS, CAROLYN MULLENAX, T: Public Relations Executive (Retired) **I:** Publishing **DOB:** 12/03/1943 **PB:** French Camp **SC:** CA/USA **PT:** Charles Harold Mullenax; Jessie Jewel Mullenax **MS:** Married **SPN:** Dennis D. Edwards (5/29/1993); Helton Pressley (Divorced) **ED:** MEd, Eastern New Mexico University (1976); BFA, University of Tulsa (1967) **C:** Retired (2014); Director, Publishing, Eastern New Mexico University, Portales, NM (2000-2014); Assistant Director, Alumni Affairs, Eastern New Mexico University, Portales, NM (1998-2000); Director of Marketing & Public Information, Clovis Community College (1990-1998); Director of Publishing, TV and Publishing Information, Eastern New Mexico University, Clovis, NM (1985-1990); Producer, Public Affairs Program, Station KMCC-TV, Clovis, NM (1981-1984); Development and Public Information Director, Mental Health Resources Inc., Portales, NM (1980-1985); Coordinator, Alumni Affairs and Publishing, Eastern New Mexico University, Portales, NM (1978-1980); Promotion and Art Director, Station KENW-TV, Portales, NM (1977-1978); News Editor, Clovis News Journal, Clovis, NM (1976-1977); Art Director, Station KMTY Radio, Clovis, NM (1976); Copywriter, Station KMTY Radio, Clovis, NM (1976); Advertising Coordinator, Crescent Department Store, Spokane, WA (1972-1973); Public Relations Director, Spokane Symphony Society (1970-1972); Artist, Wessels Agency, Spokane, WA (1968-1970); Adjunct Instructor in Art, Clovis Community College **CIV:** Organizer for Starting Alumnae Group, Tri Delta (2007-Present); Volunteer, Fundraising, Helping All-Volunteer Group, Staff Friends of Shuter Library (1995-Present); Volunteer, Music from Angel Fire, Annual Chamber Concert Series (1994-Present); Board of Directors, New Mexico Outdoor Drama Association, San Jon, CA (1986-1995); University Symphony League, Clovis, NM (1984-1988) **AW:** District IV Award, National Council for Marketing and Public Relations (1999); Women Communicator Of Achievement, New Mexico Press (1999); Design Award, Council for Advancement and Support Education (1999); Awards, National Association of Vocational and Technical Education (1995-1996); National Award, National Council for Marketing and Public Relations (1993-1998); District IV Award, National Council for Marketing and Public Relations (1993-1997); Design Award, Council for Advancement and Support Education (1991); District IV Award, National Council for Marketing and Public Relations (1989-1991) **MEM:** Panel Member, Zones 25 and 26, Rotary International (2006); Vice President, New Mexico

Press Women (2001-2002); Treasurer, New Mexico Press Women (2000-2001); Scholarship Chairman, New Mexico Press Women (1994-1999); Secretary-Editor, District IV, Council for Advancement and Support of Education (1990-1992); Communications Awards, National Federation Press Women (1984-1997); Communications Awards, New Mexico Press Women (1981-2002); American Women in Radio and TV, Spokane Junior League, Lubbock, TX; National Council for Marketing and Public Relations; Alliance Studying Paranormal Experiences; Moreno Valley Arts Council; Angel Fire Proud Committee; Altrusa Club; National Association of Vocational and Technical Education; Rotary Club Angel Fire; Garden Club; Former District Alumnae Officer, Delta Delta Delta; Chair, Delta Century Fund, Delta Delta Delta; Graphics Consultant, Delta Delta Delta **MH:** Albert Nelson Marquis Lifetime Achievement Award (2017) **H:** Reading; Classical music; Volunteer work; Dance; Photography **PA:** Republican **RE:** Episcopalian **ADD:** PO Box 2019, Angel Fire, NM, 87710

EDWARDS, STACY J.C., T: President, Chief Executive Officer **I:** Business Management/ Business Services **CN:** RealSource **MS:** Married **ED:** Master's Degree in Journalism and Accounting, University of Georgia; Bachelor's Degree in Accounting and Computer Systems, University of Georgia; AS in Business Administration, Abraham Baldwin Agricultural College (1967) **C:** President, RealSource (2010-Present); Chief Executive Officer, RealSource (2010-Present); Adjunct Faculty, Troy University (2001-2005); President, InFORMics, Inc. (1992-1995); Chief Executive Officer, InFORMics, Inc. (1992-1995) **CW:** Author, "Mind Your Business" **ADD:** 506 Forest Glen Dr, Albany, GA, 31707

EHLERS, KATHRYN, T: Physician **I:** Medicine & Health Care **CN:** Cornell University Medical College **DOB:** 12/22/1931 **PB:** Richmond Hill **SC:** NY/USA **PT:** Albert Ehlers; Edna (Hawes) Ehlers **MS:** Married **SPN:** James D. Gabler (12/5/1959) **CH:** Jennifer K.; Emily E. **ED:** Fellow in Pediatric Cardiology, Cornell University Medical College, New York City, NY (1960-1964); Assistant Resident of Pediatrics, New York Hospital (1958-1960); Intern, New York Hospital (1957-1958); AB, Bryn Mawr College (1953); MD, Cornell University **CT:** Diplomate, American Board of Pediatrics; Diplomate, American Board of Pediatric Cardiology **C:** Professor Emeritus, Cornell University Medical College (1996-Present); Vice Chairman of Pediatrics, Cornell University Medical College (1988-1996); Professor, Cornell University Medical College (1975-1996); Associate Professor of Pediatrics, Cornell University Medical College (1970-1975); Assistant Professor, Cornell University Medical College (1966-1970); Instructor of Pediatrics, Cornell University Medical College (1964-1966); Medical Practice Specializing in Pediatrics Cardiology, New York City, NY (1958-1964) **CIV:** American Heart Association (1962-1964); Research Trainee, New York Heart Association (1960-1962) **CW:** Contributor, Articles, Professional Journals **AW:** Hannah E. Longshore Memorial Medical Scholar (1953-1957) **MEM:** Fellow, American College of Cardiology; New York Heart Association; American Heart Association; Harvey Society; American Pediatric Society; American Academy Pediatrics; Alpha Omega Alpha **ADD:** 102 Wilderness Drive, Apartment 1117, Naples, FL, 34105

EICK, JOHN DAVID, T: Materials Engineer, Educator **I:** Education/Educational Services **CN:** University of Missouri School of Dentistry **MS:** Married **SPN:** Mary Elizabeth Warren (9/10/1960)

CH: Elizabeth Marion (Deceased); Cynthia Marie; Jennifer **ED:** PhD, State University of New York, Buffalo (1971); MS, George Washington University (1966); BS, University of Michigan (1963) **C:** Curators' Professor Emeritus, University of Missouri, School of Dentistry (2014); Fellow, University of Missouri (2002); Fellow, University of Missouri (1997); Chair, Department of Oral Biology, University of Missouri, School of Dentistry (1991-2014); Curators' Professor, Department of Oral Biology, University of Missouri, School of Dentistry (1989-2014); Professor, Department of Oral Biology, University of Missouri, School of Dentistry, Kansas City, MO (1986-1989); Associate Professor, Professor, Director of Dental Biomaterials, Oral Roberts University, Tulsa, OK (1977-1986); Instructor, Associate Professor, Department of Dental Materials, State University of New York, School of Dentistry, Buffalo, NY (1967-1977); Research Associate, American Dental Association, Chicago, IL (1963-1967); Laboratory Assistant, Department of Dental Materials, University of Michigan, Ann Arbor, MI (1960-1963) **CIV:** Active Member, Church (2014-Present); Episcopal Deacon, Diocese of Kansas and West Missouri, Kansas City, MO (1988-2005) **CW:** Contributor, Articles, Professional Journals **AW:** Grantee, NIH/NIDCR (2005-Present); Grantee, National Institutes of Health (2001-Present); Grantee, NIH/NIDCR (1996-Present); Sauder Distinguished Scientist Award, International Association Dental Research (2004); National Institutes of Health (1996-2001); Special Teaching Award, University of Missouri School of Dentistry (1992) **MEM:** Fellow, Associate, Academy of Dental Materials; Associate, Society of Biomaterials; Associate, American Dental Association; Associate, American Association of Dental Schools; Associate, International Association Dental Research; Honorary Member, Omicron Kappa Upsilon **MH:** Albert Nelson Marquis Lifetime Achievement Award (2017) **ADD:** 21 The Woodlands, Kansas City, MO, 64119

EIDEM, JON C., **T:** Maintenance Test Pilot (Retired) **I:** Military & Defense Services **CN:** United States Army **PB:** Minneapolis **SC:** MN/USA **ED:** BS in History, Regents College (Now Excelsior College) (1996); BS in Sociology, Regents College (Now Excelsior College) (1996) **CT:** Certified Maintenance Test Pilot, U.S. Army **C:** St. Paul Post Office Distribution, Minnesota **MEM:** Bloomington Business Men's Association; Association of the United States Army; Veterans of Foreign Wars of the United States; National Guard Association of the United States; American Legion; Army Aviation Association of America **H:** Spending time with his family and friends; Traveling **RE:** Lutheran **BA:** 206 Airport Road, Minnesota Army National Guard, Saint Paul, MN, 55107 **ADD:** 8144 5th Ave S, Minneapolis, MN, 55420

EINS, STEFAN, **T:** Artist, Science Research, Curator, Writer **I:** Fine Art **DOB:** 04/27/1941 **PB:** Prague **SC:** Czech Republic **PT:** Stefan Schmid; Daisy (Ganghofer) Schmid **ED:** BA in Sculpture, Akademie der Bildenden Künste, Vienna, Austria (1967); MA in Theology, University of Vienna (1965) **C:** Founder, Curator, Executive Director, Fashion Moda, New York, NY (1978-Present); Founder, Executive Director, Curator, 3 Mercer Street, New York, NY (1973-1978) **CIV:** Co-founder, New York City Chapter, National Audubon Society (1979) **CW:** Installation, Modernist, Istanbul (2006-Present); Installation, Lust/Pain-Pain/Lust, New York, NY (2004-Present); Installation, Trees, New York, NY (1998-Present); Installation, Project Vertebrae, Gresten, Austria (1994-Present); Exhibition Show, MoMA PS1, The Museum of Modern Art (2016); Exhibition, The Lodge Gallery, New York, NY (2014); Exhibition Show, Creon Gallery, NY (2014); Co-curator with Pawel Altwamer, New Museum of Contemporary Art (2014); Installation, Other Dimensions, New Museum of Contemporary Art, New York, NY (2014); Exhibition, ABC No Rio, NY (2014); Exhibition, New York City, Science & Religion & Kalksburger Club, Hofburg, Vienna (2013); Co-curator with Brooke McGowen, www.o-t-h-e-r-dimensions.info (since 2011); Exhibition Show, Creon Gallery, NY (2010); Exhibition, Refashioning: Fashion Moda (2009); Exhibition, Looking At Music, The Museum of Modern Art, New York, NY (2009); Exhibition, MoMA PS1, The Museum of Modern Art, New York, NY (2009); Exhibition, Picture Generation, The Metropolitan Museum of Art, New York, NY (2009); Installation, From Another Physics Reality, New York, NY (2008-2014); Installation, Portrait/Self, New York, NY (2007-2015); Curator, The Global Contemporary Artex, Bishkek and Artists Union, Osh, Kyrgyz Republic (2007); Exhibition, Kyrgyz National Fine Arts Museum, Bishkek, Kyrgyz Republic (2007); Exhibition, MoMa PS1, The Museum of Modern Art, New York, NY (2007); Installation, Hagia Sophia, Istanbul (2006); Exhibition, Grey Art Gallery, New York University, NY (2006); Exhibition, The Andy Warhol Museum, Pittsburgh, PA (2006); Exhibition, Haven Gallery, NY (2006); Co-curator with Shaarbek Amankul, OSH Artists Union (2006); Installation, President Clinton Spot, New York, NY (2003); Exhibition, Pfaffman Gallery, New York, NY (2001); Exhibition, Gallery X, New York, NY (2000); Installation, Gravity Needless, New York, NY (1996); Curator, Norbert Brunner Exhibition (1993); Installation, St. Ruprecht, St. Stefan, Vienna, Austria (1992); Exhibition, Fashion Moda (1991-1992); Exhibition, National Gallery, Vienna, Austria (1991); Exhibition, ABCNoRio, New York, NY (1989); Curator, Barbara Smith Exhibition (1988); Exhibition, Now Gallery, New York, NY (1987-1988); Curator, Ava Day Exhibition (1987-1988); Exhibition, Galerie Ariadne, Vienna, Austria (1987); Installation, Ave Juno, Thaon, Normandy, France (1987); Installation, Freedom, Centennial, Statue of Liberty (1986); Curator, Nancy Drew Exhibition (1986); Exhibition, ABCNoRio, New York, NY (1986); Exhibition, Fashion Moda (1985); Curator, Paolo Buggiani Exhibition (1984); Curator, Judy Glantzman Exhibition (1983); Curator, David Finn Exhibition (1983); Curator, Joy Walker Exhibition (1983); Curator, Dragan Ilic Exhibition (1983); Curator, Alyson Pou Exhibition (1983); Exhibition, Documenta 7 (1982); Co-curator with Jenny Holzer, Fashion Moda, Documenta 7 (1982); Curator, Dona McAdams Exhibition (1982); Curator, Tom Warren Exhibition (1982); Exhibition, Fashion Moda (1981); Curator, Keith Haring Exhibition (1981); Exhibition, New Museum, New York, NY (1980-1981); Co-curator with Joe Lewis, Fashion Moda, New Museum, New York, NY (1980-1981); Curator, David Reed Exhibition (1980); Curator, Jane Dickson Exhibition (1980); Curator, Wally Edwards Exhibition (1980); Curator, Haim Steinbach Exhibition (1980); Curator, Marianne Edwards Exhibition (1980); Curator, Elizabeth Clark Exhibition (1980); Curator, Ilona Granet Exhibition (1980); Curator, Paulette Nenner Exhibition (1980); Curator, California Billboards Exhibition, New York, NY (1980); Curator, Graffiti and the Arts, Graffiti Art Success for America (1980); Curator, Sophie Calle Exhibition (1980); Curator, Rebecca Howland Exhibition (1980); Curator, Justen Ladda Exhibition (1980); Curator, Paul Koenigsberg Exhibition (1980); Exhibition, Times Square Show, New York, NY (1980); Curator, Jenny Holzer Exhibition (1979); Curator, John Ahearn Exhibition (1979); Curator, David Wells Exhibition (1979); Curator, Christy Rupp Exhibition (1979); Exhibition, Fashion Moda (1978); Curator, Fashion Moda Inaugural Exhibition (1978); Curator, Robert Cooney Exhibition (1978); Curator, End of Modernism (1978); Curator, Art/Fashion Inter Mix Exhibition (1978); Exhibition, Multiculturalism (1978); Exhibition, Documenta 6 (1977); Curator, Sherrie Levine Exhibition (1977); Exhibition, MoMa PS1, The Museum of Modern Art (1976); Curator, Geoffrey Hendricks Exhibition (1976); Exhibition, 3 Mercer St., New York, NY (1973-1976); Installation, Liquid Steel/Life, New York, NY (1972); Exhibition, 112 Greene St., New York, NY (1971-1972) **AW:** Grantee, Adolph & Esther Gottlieb Foundation, Inc. (2004); New York Foundation for the Arts (2002); National Endowment for the Arts (1980); National Endowment for the Arts (1987) **MEM:** President, Collaborative Projects, Inc. (1988-1989, 2001-Present) **MH:** Albert Nelson Marquis Lifetime Achievement Award (2017) **ADD:** PO Box 33, New York, NY, 10013 **URL:** http://www.oneunoeins.com/

EL MEZYANI, TOURIA, **T:** Visiting Assistant Professor **I:** Education/Educational Services **CN:** University of West Florida **CH:** 1 Daughter **ED:** PhD, Universite des Sciences et Technologies de Lille, France (2005); MS in Physics, University of Science, Morocco **C:** Visiting Assistant Professor of Electrical and Computer Engineering, Center for Advanced Power Systems, University of West Florida (2016-Present); Research Faculty, Center for Advanced Power Systems (2014-2015); Research Associate, Center for Advanced Power Systems (2008-2013); Research Associates, School of Computational Science, Florida State University (2007-2008) **CW:** Author, "An Alternative Distributed Control Architecture for Improvement in the Transient Response of DC Microgrids," IEEE Transactions on Industrial Electronics (2016); Author, "Role of Power Hardware in the Loop in Modeling and Simulation for Experimentation in Power and Energy Systems," Proceeding of the IEEE (2015); Author, "Power flow control and network stability in an All-Electric Ship," Proceeding of the IEEE (2015); Author, "Complexity Quantification to enhance the Shipboard Power Systems design and Modeling," IET Electrical Systems in Transportation (2012) **AW:** Paper Award, IMCIC 2010 Conference Program (2010) **MEM:** IEEE Control Systems Society; IEEE Power and Energy; IEEE Women in Engineering **ADD:** 5034 Faircloth St, Milton, FL, 32571

EL-GENDY, AHMED ABOUD, **T:** Assistant Professor of Physics **I:** Education/Educational Services **CN:** The University of Texas at El Paso **DOB:** 07/11/1981 **PB:** Alexandria **SC:** Egypt **MS:** Exempt **ED:** PhD in Physics, Heidelberg University, Germany (2008-2011); Master's Degree, Alexandria University, Egypt; Bachelor's Degree, Alexandria University, Egypt **C:** Assistant Professor and Director of Nanomagnetism and Biomaterials Laboratory (Nanoland), Department of Physics, University of Texas at El Paso, El Paso, TX **CIV:** Treasurer, Richmond Chapter, Society of Magnetics, IEEE (2016-Present) **CW:** Editor, "Magnetic Nano structure materials from Lab to Fab" (2018); Contributor, Articles, Professional Journals **AW:** Recipient, International Young Scientists Award, National Natural Science Foundation of China (2018) **BA:** 500 West University Ave, Room No. 221D, University of Texas, Physical Science Building (PSCI), El Paso, TX, 79968 **ADD:** 7049 Westwind Dr. Apt 3022, El Paso, TX, 79912

EL-HADIDY, BAHAA, **T:** International Consultant **I:** Consulting **DOB:** 06/21/1931 **PB:** Cairo **SC:** Egypt **PT:** Sadek Ayoub El-Hadidy; Tafida Mostafa Fahmy El-Hadidy **MS:** Married **SPN:** Lily Ayad (3/27/1965)

ED: PhD in Information Science and Technology, University of Pittsburgh (1974); MLS, Rutgers, the State University of New Jersey, New Brunswick, NJ (1963); BS, Cairo University (1954) **CT:** Advanced Certificate, University of Pittsburgh (1966) **C:** International Consultant, Tampa, FL (1996-Present); Associate Professor, University South Florida, Tampa, FL (1987-1996); Assistant Senior Executive, Islamic International Bank, Cairo, Egypt (1984-1987); Vice President, Islamic International Bank, Cairo, Egypt (1984-1987); Assistant Professor, The Catholic University of America, Washington, DC (1974-1984); Librarian, University of Pittsburgh (1972-1974); Information Analyst, University Pittsburgh (1967-1972); Chemical Information Specialist, University Pittsburgh (1967-1972); Science Information Officer, National Research Centre, Cairo, Egypt (1955-1961) **CR:** Consultant, Academy of Scientific Research & Technology, Cairo, Egypt (1994-1998); Consultant, United Nations Industrial Development Organization, Vienna, Austria (1989-1995); Consultant, Academy of Sciences Ministry of Science Research, Manila, Philippines (1990); Consultant, Institute of Applied Science and Technology, Guyana (1989); Chairman, Training, Professional Management Services Center, Kuwait (1987); Visiting Professor, Cairo University (1985-1987); Principal Project Investigator, Information Facility, National Aeronautics and Space Administration Science, Baltimore, MD (1984); Consultant, Information Facility, National Aeronautics and Space Administration Science, Baltimore, MD (1984); Consultant, African Regional Center for Technology, Dakar, Senegal (1983-1984); Senior Consultant, Georgia Institute of Technology, Atlanta, GA (1979-1984); Consultant, The Franklin Institute, Philadelphia, PA (1977-1978); Consultant, National Science Foundation, Washington, DC (1975) **CIV:** Vice President, North Tampa Auxiliary, Children's Home Network, Tampa, FL (2000-2003); Chairman of the Board, SIG International Information Issues, Association for Information Science and Technology, Washington, DC (2001-2002); Board Member, Sertoma Club, University of South Florida, Tampa, FL (1997-1999); Chairman of the Board, South Florida Chapter, Association for Information Science and Technology, Tampa, FL (1992-1993); Chairman, U.S. Interim Committee, International Federation Documentation, Washington, DC (1982-1984); Board Member, U.S. National Committee, Educational General Information Program, United Nations, Washington, DC (1981-1984); Chairman, International Relations, Association for Information Science and Technology, Washington, DC (1981-1983); Representative, Friends Group, Bibliotheca Alexandria, Alexandria, Egypt **CW:** Editor, "Infrastructure of an Information Society" (1982); Author, "Approaches to the Economical Retrospective Machine-Searching of the Chemical Literature, in Computer-Based Chemical Information" (1973); Contributor, Articles, Professional Journals; Contributor, Technical Reports, Professional Journals; Contributor, Book Chapters **AW:** SIG Member of the Year, Association for Information Science and Technology (2000); Grantee, United Nations Industrial Development Organization (1989); Outstanding Service Information Science Profession, Information of Science and Technology Council (1984); Grantee, National Science Foundation (1979-1982) **MEM:** Board Member, Tampa Palms Golf & Country Club, ClubCorp. (2001-2003); Recognition Guidance, Teaching, and Advising, Beta Phi Mu - The International Library and Information Studies Honor Society (1996); Certified Appreciation and Recognition Outstanding Services, Association for Information Science and Technology (1984-2004); American Society for information and Technology; American Association of University Professors;

American Library Association; Suncoast Information Specialists; Association for Library and Information Science Education; Association of Egyptian-American Scholars; Special Libraries Association; ACM, Inc **H:** Classical music; Travel; Tennis **ADD:** 16104 Stowe Court, Tampa, FL, 33647 **URL:** http://prabook.com/web/person-view.html?-profileId=361029

ELIAS, JACK A., T: Senior Vice President of Health Affairs, Dean of Medicine and Biology **I:** Education/Educational Services **CN:** Brown University **PB:** Fayetteville **SC:** AR/USA **PT:** Gabriel Elias; Alma (Kowalsky) Elias **MS:** Married **SPN:** Sandra Gross Elias (1/3/1981) **CH:** Lauren Rachel **ED:** Fellow, Allergy and Immunology, Pulmonary and Critical Care Medicine, University of Pennsylvania Hospital, Philadelphia, PA (1979-1982); Senior Resident, Internal Medicine, University of Pennsylvania Hospital, Philadelphia, PA (1978-1979); Resident, Internal Medicine, Tufts- New England Medical Center, Boston, MA (1977-1978); Intern, Internal Medicine, Tufts- New England Medical Center, Boston, MA (1976-1977); MD, University of Pennsylvania (1973); Bachelor's Degree, University of Pennsylvania **CT:** Certified in Pulmonary and Critical Care Medicine; Diplomate, American Board of Allergy & Immunology; Diplomate, American Board of Internal Medicine **C:** Senior Vice President of Health Affairs, Brown University (2017-Present); Dean of Medicine and Biology, Brown University (2013-Present); Chair, Department of Internal Medicine, Yale University School of Medicine (2006-Present); Waldemar Von Zedtwitz Professor, Medicine, Yale University School of Medicine (2000-Present); Professor, Immunobiology, Yale University School of Medicine, (2007-2013); Professor, Medicine, Chief, Pulmonary and Critical Care Medicine, Yale University School of Medicine, New Haven, CT (1990-2006); Associate Professor, University of Pennsylvania School of Medicine, Philadelphia, PA (1988-1990); Director, Sarcoidosis & Interstitial Lung Disease Clinic, University of Pennsylvania Hospital (1982-1990); Assistant Professor, University of Pennsylvania School of Medicine, Philadelphia, PA (1982-1988) **CR:** Council Member, National Heart, Lung & Blood Institute, National Institutes of Health (2009-Present); Chief, Beeson Medical Service, Yale-New Haven Hospital (2006-Present); Physician-in-chief, Beeson Medical Service, Yale-New Haven Hospital (2006-Present); Herbert Y. & Anne L. Reynolds Grand Rounds Lecturer, Penn State Milton S. Hershey Medical Center (2010); Harold & Marilyn Menkes Memorial Lecturer, Bloomberg School of Public Health, Johns Hopkins University School of Medicine (2005); Pfizer Visiting Professor, Allergic Diseases and Asthma, University of Iowa (1998); Director, Medical Intensive Care Unit, Beeson Medical Service, Yale-New Haven Hospital (1991-1992); Chief, Pulmonary and Critical Care Medicine, Beeson Medical Service, Yale-New Haven Hospital (1990-2006); Director, Winchester Chest Clinic, New Haven, CT (1990-2006) **CIV:** Appointed Chair, Department of Medicine, Yale University (2006); Physician-in-chief, Yale-New Haven Hospital **CW:** Co-Editor, "Fishman's Pulmonary Diseases and Disorders, 5th Edition" (2015); Former Associate Editor, American Journal of Respiratory Cell & Molecular Biology; Former Editorial Board Member, Encyclopedia of Respiratory Medicine, Journal of Laboratory Investigation, Respiratory Research; Former Editorial Board Member, Journal Laboratory & Clinical Medicine; Former Editorial Board Member, American Journal Medicine; Contributor, Articles, Professional Journals **AW:** Honoree, Membership, National Academy of Medicine (2010) **MEM:** Vice President, American Thoracic Society (2010); Institute of Medicine;

Fellow, American College of Physicians; Fellow, American College of Chest Physicians; New Haven County Medical Association; Pennsylvania Thoracic Society; Connecticut Thoracic Society; Laennac Society; American Society of Clinical Investigation; Association of American Physicians; American Lung Association; Federation of American Societies for Experimental Biology; American Association of Immunologists; Reticuloendothelial Society; American Federation for Clinical Research; Institute of Medicine; The American Academy of Allergy, Asthma & Immunology; Interurban Clinical Club; Alpha Omega Alpha; Phi Beta Kappa **BA:** Dean Suite 222 Richmond St, Providence, RI, 02903

ELSTUN, ESTHER N., T: Foreign Language Educator **I:** Education/Educational Services **PB:** Berkshire Heights **SC:** PA/USA **PT:** Frank Emory Nies; Florence Mae (Sweigart) Nies **MS:** Married **SPN:** James Palmer Elstun (9/1/1956) **CH:** John Dudley **ED:** PhD, Rice University (1969); MA, Rice University (1964); BA, Colorado College, Magna Cum Laude (1960) **C:** Professor Emerita, German, George Mason University (2004); Assistant Professor, German, George Mason University (1969-2004) **CR:** Member, Executive Board, Virginia Conference of the American Association of University Professors (2002-2004, 1990-1992); Vice President, Faculty Senate, George Mason University (2001-2003); Member, Virginia Humanities Conference (1989-1990); President, Virginia Council for Study Abroad (1981-1982) **CIV:** Volunteer, Amnesty International (1978-Present) **CW:** Author, "The Life and Work of Richard Beer-Hofmann" (1983); Contributor, Articles, Professional Journals **AW:** Grantee, Houghton Library, Harvard University (1974); Grantee, The Leo Baeck Institute (1974); Amerika-Kreis Muenster Scholarship, University of Munster (1954-1955); Research Grant, George Mason University Foundation **MEM:** American Association of University Professors; American Association of Teachers of German; Modern Language Association of America; The Phi Beta Kappa Society; Delta Phi Alpha **MH:** Albert Nelson Marquis Lifetime Achievement Award (2017) **H:** Gardening; Piano; Travel **RE:** Presbyterian **ADD:** 10609 Elmont Ct, Fairfax, VA, 22030

EMCH-DERIAZ, ANTOINETTE SUZANNE, T: Historian **I:** Education/Educational Services **CN:** University of Florida **DOB:** 11/09/1935 **PB:** Geneva **SC:** Switzerland **PT:** Louis Georges Deriaz; Renee Gabrielle Deriaz **MS:** Married **SPN:** Gerard Gustav Emch (7/25/1959) **CH:** Florence Christiane; Rene-Didier Guillaume **ED:** PhD, University of Rochester **C:** Professor, Honors Program, University of Florida (2004-2008); Visiting Associate Professor, University of Florida (1992-2004); Assistant Professor, University of Mississippi (1985-1992); Research Associate, University of Rochester (1984); Visiting Scholar, University of Pennsylvania (1981); Technology Assistant, American Institute of Physics (1968-1970) **CR:** Visiting Scholar, Wellcome Collection (1994); Visiting Scholar, Universitat Wien (1994); Visiting Scholar, Georg-August-Universitat Gottingen (1985) **CW:** Author, "La Correspondance entre Tissot et Zimmermann 1754-1797" (2007); Co-Author, "Emilie du Chatelet (1706-1749)" (2006); Author, "Tissot: Physician of the Enlightenment" (1992); Author, "18th Century Concept of Health" (1984); Contributor, Book Chapters; Contributor, Articles, Professional Journals **MEM:** American Historical Association; American Association for the History of Medicine, Incorporated; American Society for Eighteenth-Century Studies **PA:** Democrat **RE:** Presbyterian **ADD:** 2911 SE Village Loop, Apt. 276, Vancouver, WA, 98683

ENGERRAND, DORIS DIESKOW, T: Business Educator (Retired) **I:** Education/Educational Services **DOB:** 08/07/1925 **PB:** Chicago **SC:** IL/USA **PT:** William Jacob Dieskow; Alma Louise Willhelmina (Cords) Dieskow **MS:** Single **SPN:** Gabriel H. Engerrand (October 26, 1946), Deceased (June 1987) **CH:** Steven; Kenneth; Jeannine **ED:** PhD, Georgia State University (1970); MEd in Business Education, Georgia State University (1966); BS in Elementary Education, University of North Georgia (1959); BS in Business Administration, University of North Georgia (1958) **C:** Retired (1990); Professor, Georgia College (1978-1990); Chairman, Department of Information Systems and Communications, Georgia College (1978-1989); Associate Professor, Georgia College (1974-1978); Assistant Business Professor, Georgia College (1971-1974); Assistant Professor, Troy University (1969-1971); Teacher, Lumpkin County High School, Dahlonega, GA (1960-1963, 1965-1968); Department Chairman, Lumpkin County High School (1960-1963, 1965-1968); Teacher, City of Gainesville, GA (1965) **CW:** Contributor, Articles on Business Education, Professional Publications **AW:** Recipient, Parker Liles Award, Georgia Vocational Association Inc. (1989); Recipient, Educator of the Year Award, Georgia Vocational Association Inc. (1984); Recipient, Postsecondary Teacher of the Year Award, Georgia Business Education Association (1984); Recipient, Postsecondary Teacher of the Year Award, Tenth District, Georgia Business Education Association (1983); Recipient, Executive of the Year Award (1983); Honoree, Outstanding Educator, Business Faculty, Georgia College (1975); Honoree, Pilot of the Year, Northern Georgia Chapter, The Ninety-Nines, Inc. (1973); Honoree, Outstanding Teacher, Lumpkin County School System (1963-1966); Fellow, Association for Business Communication **MEM:** President, Milledgeville Chapter, Professional Secretaries International (Now IAAP) (1996-1997); Vice President, Southeast Region, Association for Business Communication (1978-1984, 1989-1992); Georgia Vocational Association Inc.; Chairman, Northern Georgia Chapter, The Ninety-Nines, Inc. (1975-1976); Board of Directors, Association for Business Communication; National Business Education Association; Georgia Business Education Association; American Vocational Association (Now Association for Career & Technical Education) **MH:** Albert Nelson Marquis Lifetime Achievement Award (2017) **RE:** Methodist **ADD:** 1674 Pine Valley Rd, Milledgeville, GA, 31061

ENGINEER, CYRUS Y., T: Clinical Professor, Director, Healthcare Management **I:** Education/Educational Services **CN:** Towson University **ED:** PhD, Bloomberg School of Public Health, Johns Hopkins University (2007); MHS, Johns Hopkins University (2003); PGDWM, Worldwide Quality Council (2001); MHA, Tata Institute of Social Science (1996); BSc, St. Xavier's College, India (1990) **CT:** Auditor, ISO 9000 **C:** Clinical Professor, Towson University (2013-Present); Director, Health Management, Towson University (2013-Present); Adjunct Professor of Health Sciences, Johns Hopkins University; Consultant; Research **AW:** Knowledge for the World Award, Johns Hopkins University Alumni **MEM:** Board Member, American Society of Quality; Senior National Baldrige Examiner; American College of Health Care Executives; Association of University Programs in Health Administration **H:** Family; Cooking; Travel; Fitness **BA:** 8000 York Road, Towson University, Linthicum Hall 235 K, Towson, MD, 21252 **ADD:** 8210 Jeffers Cir, Towson, MD, 21204

ENTIN, ALVIN E., T: Partner **I:** Law and Legal Services **CN:** Entin Law Group **DOB:** 10/18/1945 **PB:** Brooklyn **SC:** NY/USA **MS:** Married **SPN:** Lois J. Entin **CH:** Keith; Marsha Kay; Amanda Sue; Seth David; Gary; Edmund **ED:** JD, University of Miami (1970); BA in Government, American University (1967) **C:** Senior Partner, Entin, Schwartz, Barbakoff & Schwartz, Miami, FL (1986-Present); Senior Partner, Entin, Schwartz, Dion & Sclafani, Miami, FL (1980-1986); Partner, Franklin, Entin, Kimler & Marks (1978-1980); Partner, Franklin, Ullman, Kimler & Entin (1976-1978); Partner, Ullman, Kimler & Entin (1972-1976); Partner, Becker, Kimler & Entin, Miami, Florida (1970-1972) **CIV:** Member, United Jewish Appeal 1984-1985; Member, Diamond Jubilee Committee, City of Miami (1972); Member, Young Leadership Cabinet, The Jewish Federations of North America **AW:** Recipient, Silver Palm, Jewish Federations of North America (2015); Recipient, Remy Award for Outstanding Contributions to Community Theater, South Florida Theater League (2015); Nominee, 13th Florida District, United States Congress (1980) **MEM:** Board of Directors, Dade County Bar Association (1983-1984, 1980-1981); American Association for Justice; Federal Bar Association; National Association of Criminal Defense Lawyers; Florida Justice Association; Florida Association of Criminal Defense Lawyers; Miami Optimist Club; North Miami Beach, Lions Clubs International **BAR:** United States District Court for the Southern District of Florida (1970) **MH:** Albert Nelson Marquis Lifetime Achievement Award (2017) **RE:** Jewish **BA:** 633 S Andrews Ave Ste 500, Entin & Della Fera, Ft Lauderdale, FL, 33301 **ADD:** 6002 Dogwood Cir, Tamarac, FL, 33319

EPSTEIN, NANCY ELLEN MD, T: Chief of Nuerosurgery, Clinical Professor of Neurosurgery **I:** Medicine & Health Care **CN:** NYU Winthrop Hospital, Stony Brook University **DOB:** 12/28/1950 **PB:** New York **SC:** NY/USA **PT:** Dr. Joseph A. Epstein; Ms. Natalie Epstein **MS:** Married **SPN:** Donald Charter Hood **ED:** MD, Columbia University (1976); BS, Barnard College (1972) **CT:** Diplomate, American Board of Neurological Surgeons (1984) **C:** Chief of Neurological Spine/Education, NYU Winthrop Hospital; Staff, Winthrop-University Hospital (Now NYU Winthrop Hospital), Mineola, NY (2014-Present); Chief of Neurosurgery, Winthrop-University Hospital (2005-Present); Resident in Neurosurgery, Bellevue Medical Center, NYU Langone Medical Center, New York City, NY (1977-1981); Intern, Bellevue Medical Center, NYU Langone Medical Center, New York City, NY (1976-1977) **CR:** Clinical Professor of Neurological Surgery, School of Medicine, Stony Brook University **CW:** Editor-in-chief, "Surgical Neurology International" (2017-Present); Member, Editorial Board, "Journal of Spinal Disorders/Techniques" (1990-2015); Editor, "The Spine Journal" (2000-2003); Contributing Editor, "Spine" (1990-1991); Member, Editorial Board, "Journal of Spinal Disorders" (1990); Member, Editorial Board, "Spine" (1990); Contributor, Over 300 Peer Reviewed Publications; Contributor, 49 Book Chapters **AW:** The Butterfly Awards (2015); Reviewer of the Year Award, Spine (2009); Clinical Research Award, Cervical Spine Research Society (2008); First Annual Reviewer's Award, The Spine Journal (2005); Achievers' Award in Medicine, Long Island Center for Business & Professional Women (1988) **MEM:** Fellow, American College of Surgeons (1985-Present); President, Cervical Spine Research Society (2001-2002); President-elect, Cervical Spine Research Society (2000-2001); Vice President-elect, Cervical Spine Research Society (1999-2000); Treasurer, Cervical Spine Research Society (1997-1998); Chair, Program Committee, Cervical Spine Research Society (1996); Fellow, International College of Surgeons (1984); AChairman, Scientific Program Committee, Joint Section on Disorders of the Spine and Peripheral Nerves, American Association of Neurological Surgeons (1993); American Medical Association; Congress of Neurological Surgeons; The International Society for the Study of the Lumbar Spine; North American Spine Society; New York State Neurosurgical Society; Nassau County Medical Society; American Medical Women's Association; Alpha Omega Alpha Honor Medical Society **MH:** Distinguished Humanitarian (2017) **ADD:** 450 Riverside Dr Apt 82, New York, NY, 10027

ERK, FRANK CHRIS, T: Biologist, Educator **I:** Sciences **DOB:** 12/17/1924 **PB:** Evansville **SC:** IN/USA **PT:** Carl Benjamin Erk; Matilda (Schumacher) Erk **MS:** Married **SPN:** Ruth Parker Hobgood (6/12/1948) **CH:** Susan Patricia Erk Tierney; Elisabeth Carlene Erk Smith; Stephanie Diane Erk Lutostanski **ED:** PhD in Genetics, Johns Hopkins University (1952); AB, University of Evansville, Magna Cum Laude (1948) **C:** Professor Emeritus, Stony Brook University (1990-Present); Professor, Biochemistry and Cell Biology, Stony Brook University (1981-1990); Chairman, Department of Biology, Stony Brook University (1962-1967, 1976-1978); Professor, Biological Sciences, Stony Brook University (1962-1981); Chairman, Department Biology, State University of New York, Long Island Center, Oyster Bay, NY (1958-1961); Director, University Choir, State University of New York, Long Island Center, Oyster Bay, NY (1957-1961); Chairman, Division of Science and Mathematics, State University of New York, Long Island Center, Oyster Bay, NY (1957-1960); Professor of Biology, State University of New York, Long Island Center, Oyster Bay, NY (1957-1961); Lalor Faculty Fellow, Johns Hopkins University, Baltimore, MD (1956); Director, College Choir, Washington College, Chestertown, MD (1952-1957); Associate Professor of Biology, Washington College, Chestertown, MD (1952-1957); Adam T. Bruce Fellow, Johns Hopkins University, Baltimore, MD (1951-1952); Junior Instructor, Johns Hopkins University, Baltimore, MD (1948-1951) **CR:** Director, Riderwood Women's Chorus (2007-2015); Director, Riderwood Balladeers, Silver Spring Maryland (2001-2012); Genealogy Chair, Three Village Historical Society, East Setauket, NY (1996-2000); Visiting Investigator, University Sussex (1971-1972, 1985-1986); Assistant Examiner, International Baccalaureate Program (1977-1982); Visiting Investigator, University of Edinburgh (1979); Visiting Investigator, Galton Laboratory, University College of London (1978-1979); Visiting Professor, University of Essex (1978-1979); Chairman, Advanced Placement Biology College Entrance Examination Board (1973-1977); President, Statewide State University of New York Faculty Senate (1969-1971); Research Collaborator, Masonic Medical Research Laboratory, Utica, NY (1968-1971); Director, Madrigal Singers, Stony Brook (1963-1971); Member, Examining Committee, Advanced Placement Biology College Entrance Examination Board (1967-1971); Senator, Statewide State University of New York Faculty Senate (1967-1969); Visiting Investigator, Genetics Institute, University of Milan, Italy (1965); Visiting Investigator, Poultry Research Center, Agricultural Research Council, University of Edinburgh (1964-1965); Visiting Associate Professor of Biology, Carnegie Intern in General Education, University of Chicago (1954-1955) **MIL:** 1st Lieutenant, U.S. Army Air Force (1943-1946) **CW:** Author, "It Seems Only Yesterday" (2013, 2017, 2018); Author, "William Sidney Mount: Family, Friends, and Ideas" (1999); Author, "Biological Science: An Ecological Approach" (1987); Editorial Board, Journal of Biological Education (1976-1990); Editor, "Evolution, Mammals and Southern Continents"

(1972); Author, "Biological Sciences: Interaction of Experiments and Ideas" (1965, 1970); Editor, Quarterly Review of Biology (1969-1999); Author, "Biological Science: Molecules to Man" (1963, 1968); Executive Editor, Quarterly Review of Biology (1966-1969) **AW:** Endowed Faculty Office, Washington College (2007); Chancellor's Award for Excellence in Teaching, SUNY (1982) **MEM:** American Association for the Advancement of Science; American Association of University Professors; American Genetics Association; Genetics Society of America; National Association of Biology Teachers; Society for Study Evolution; Human Biology Council; State University of New York Emeritus Faculty Association; Sigma Xi; Phi Beta Chi; Omicron Delta Kappa **ADD:** 3118 Gracefield Road, Apartment 310, Silver Spring, MD, 20904

ERNST, ERIK, T: Computer Scientist **I:** Engineering **CN:** Google **DOB:** 04/15/1961 **PB:** Sdr Omme **SC:** Denmark **PT:** Otto Ernst; Hedvig Irene Ernst **ED:** PhD, Aarhus University (1999); MSc, Aarhus University (1996); Diploma in Guitar, The Royal Academy of Music (1989) **C:** Software Engineer, Google (2014-Present); Associate Professor, Aarhus University (2005-2014); Assistant Professor, Aarhus University (2002-2005); Assistant Professor, Aalborg University (1999-2002) **CR:** Program Committee Chair, Modularity (2014); Program Committee Chair, The European Conference on Object-Oriented Programming (2007); Founding Member, Working Group on Programming Language Design, International Federation for Information Processing **AW:** Dahl Nygaard Junior Prize (2010) **MEM:** ACM, Inc **MH:** Albert Nelson Marquis Lifetime Achievement Award (2017) **ADD:** Bakkevej 41, Laasby, Denmark, 8670

ESPEY, LAWRENCE, T: Biology Professor **I:** Education/Educational Services **DOB:** 09/05/1935 **PB:** Mercedes **SC:** TX/USA **PT:** Harry Woods Espey; Evelyn Irene Espey **MS:** Married **SPN:** Doina Ionescu (9/18/1978) **CH:** Richard Andrew; Elaine Espey Allen; Annette Espey Dickerson; Alexandru Woods **ED:** Postdoctoral Fellow, University of Michigan Medical School, Ann Arbor, MI (1964-1966); PhD, Florida State University, Tallahassee, FL (1964); MA, The University of Texas at Austin (1961); BA, The University of Texas at Austin (1958) **C:** Professor Emeritus, Trinity University (2008-Present); Professor, Trinity University (1966-2008) **CR:** Visiting Professor, Department of Obstetrics-Gynecology, Graduate School of Medicine, Kyoto University (2001); Honorary Professor, Department of Obstetrics-Gynecology, School of Medicine, Shinshu University, Matsumoto, Japan (1996); Visiting Professor, Department of Cell Biology, Baylor College of Medicine, Houston, TX (1993); Guest Research Scholar, Department of Obstetrics-Gynecology, Graduate School of Medicine Kyoto University (1983); Rockefeller Foundation Fellow, Department of Obstetrics-Gynecology, UT Health San Antonio (1979); Fulbright-Hays Research Professor, Nicolae Balcescu Agronomic Institute, Bucharest, Romania (1977-1979); Visiting Professor, Department of Pharmacology, Medical University of South Carolina, Charleston, SC (1964); Speaker in Field **CIV:** Board of Directors, International Visitor's Alliance, San Antonio, TX (1990-2007); Board of Directors, Citizens for a Better Environment, San Antonio, TX (1973-1976) **CW:** Contributor, Articles to Professional Journals; Contributor, Chapters, Books **AW:** Recipient, Best Oral Presentation Award, GenHunter Corporation (2002); Grant, National Science Foundation (1998-2007); Recipient, Award, Japan Society of Obstetrics and Gynecology (1995); Grantee, National Institutes of Health (1994-1997); Grantee, The Lalor Foundation (1988-1989); Grantee, National Institutes of Health (1987-1992); Grantee, Trinity University (1983-1986); Grantee, National Institutes of Health (1980-1984); Recipient, Fulbright Hays Fellowship, United States Department of Education (1977-1979); Grantee, National Institutes of Health (1976-1978); Grantee, National Institutes of Health (1969-1972); Grantee, Morrison Trust (1967-1968); Recipient, Best Oral Presentation Award, GenHunter Corporation (1966) **MEM:** Endocrine Society; American Physiological Society; Society for the Study of Reproduction **MH:** Albert Nelson Marquis Lifetime Achievement Award (2017) **H:** Jogging; Travel **PA:** Conservative **RE:** Presbyterian **ADD:** 13422 Vista Del Rey, San Antonio, TX, 78216

ESPINO, ANA M., T: Associate Professor **I:** Education/Educational Services **CN:** University of Puerto Rico, Medical Sciences Campus **DOB:** 06/08/1959 **PB:** Havana **SC:** Cuba **PT:** Enrique A. Espino Perez; Fortuna J. Hernandez Rodriguez **MS:** Single **CH:** Jezabel Morera **ED:** Postdoctoral Fellow, Molecular Parasitology, Department of Pathology, School of Medicine, University of Puerto Rico (1998-2002); PhD in Medical Sciences, Institute of Tropical Medicine "Pedro Kouri," Havana, Cuba, Summa Cum Laude (1997); BS in Biochemistry, University of Havana, Summa Cum Laude (1982) **CW:** Editorial Board, Annals of Clinical and Medical Microbiology (2014-Present); Ad-Hoc Reviewer, PloS Neglected Tropical Diseases (2014-Present); Ad-Hoc Reviewer, Clinical and Vaccine Immunology (2012-Present); Ad-Hoc Reviewer, Experimental Parasitology (2004-Present); Editorial Board of Parasitaria, Spanish Association of Parasitology (2015); Editorial Board, Clinical and Vaccine Immunology (2013-2016); Ad-Hoc Reviewer, Veterinary Parasitology (2010); Ad-Hoc Reviewer, Acta Tropica (2010); Ad-Hoc Reviewer, Journal of Biomedicine and Biotechnology (2009); Ad-Hoc Reviewer, Parasitology Research (2008); Ad-Hoc Reviewer, Journal of Molecular Parasitology (2007); Ad-Hoc Reviewer, Vaccine Immunology (2006-2008); Ad-Hoc Reviewer, Journal of Microbes and Infection (2005); Ad-Hoc Reviewer, Pan American Journal of Public Health (1999-2002); Contributor, More Than 40 Articles, Professional Journals **AW:** Best Faculty Professor in the Department (2014-2017); Distinguished Professor of the Graduate Program, Deanship of Biomedical Sciences (2011-2017); National Institutes of Health Grant Award, MBRS-SCORE Program (2011); National Prize for Excellence in Teaching and Research, Havana, Cuba (1999); Prize for Excellence in Applied Research, Cuban Institute of Veterinary Medicine (1999); National Prize for Excellence in Applied Research, Havana, Cuba (1998); Award for the Best PhD Thesis in Medical Sciences, Havana, Cuba (1997) **MEM:** American Association of Immunologist (2015-Present); American Society of Parasitology (2010-Present); American Society of Microbiology (2006-Present); American Society of Tropical Medicine and Hygiene (2004-Present) **H:** Reading; Cycling; Traveling; Music **ADD:** 7000 Estancias del Boulevard, Carr 844, Apt. 166, San Juan, PR, 00926 **URL:** https://md.rcm.upr.edu/micro/dt_team/dr-ana-m-espino

EUFEMIA NELSON, PATRICIA ROSE MARIA, T: Lawyer, Principal **I:** Law and Legal Services **CN:** Nelson Family Law **PB:** Mississauga **SC:** ON/Canada **CH:** Three Children **ED:** BA in Philosophy and Political Science, University of Toronto, With Honors; LLB, Osgoode Hall Law School **C:** Lawyer/Principal, Nelson Family Law **CR:** Regular Guest, "Straight Talk Family Law Radio" **CIV:** Pro Bono Legal Services; Mentor, College Students; Advisor, Law Society of Upper Canada (Now Law Society of Ontario) **CW:** Ontario Bar Association (OBA) Conference Presenter, "Short Term Relationships, Paternity and Child Support," Fourth Annual Symposium on DNA Forensic Evidence (2002) **AW:** Award for Regional Family Law Firm, Corporate Livewire, Canada (2016); Super Lawyer, Corporate Livewire (2015); Honoree, Best Regional Family Law Firm, Acquisition International (2014) **MEM:** Peel Law Association **BAR:** Law Society of Upper Canada (Now Law Society of Ontario) **H:** Horseback riding; Book clubs; Gardening; Fitness training **BA:** 1470 Hurontario Street, Suite 201, Nelson Family Law, Mississauga, ON, Canada, L5G 3H4

EUFINGER, IRMA JEAN, T: Occupational Health Nurse **I:** Medicine & Health Care **CN:** Oklahoma City-County Health Department **ED:** BS in Nursing, University of Oklahoma (1959) **AW:** Lillian Wald Award for 25 Years of Exemplary Service in Nursing (2010); Award for Contributing to Field of Public Health, Oklahoma Public Health Association (2009); National Honor Society; Employee of the Year Award **MH:** Albert Nelson Marquis Lifetime Achievement Award (2017) **H:** Reading; Walking; Spending time with her friends; Caring for her dogs **BA:** 921 NE 23rd St, Oklahoma City-County Health Department, Oklahoma City, OK, 73105 **ADD:** 3716 Dow Dr, Oklahoma City, OK, 73116 **URL:** https://www.occhd.org

EURICH, DONALD A., T: Architect, Developer **I:** Architecture & Construction **PB:** New York City **SC:** NY/USA **PT:** Alvin Eurich; Nell (Plopper) Eurich **MS:** Married **SPN:** Jill Lazarus Eurich (4/11/1992); Valerie Quinn (11/12/1984, Divorced) **CH:** William **ED:** MArch, Rice University, with High Honors (1992); BA in Architecture, Art History, Wesleyan University (1976) **C:** Director, Various Real Estate LLCs (2015-Present); Chief Executive Officer, Daedalus Development, Newton, MA (2011-Present); Principal, Eurich & Associates (1992-Present); Principal, Kallmann, McKinnell & Wood Architects, Boston, MA (2009-2011); Associate Principal, Kallmann McKinnell & Wood Architects, Inc. (1998-2009); Architect Designer, Pei, Cobb, Freed & Partners, New York City, NY (1989-1990); Senior Project Manager, Carlin Contracting, Co. (1985-1996); President, DECCA Co. International, Newington, CT (1985-1988); Project Manager, Carlin Contracting Co., Waterford, CT (1983-1985); GM, Burlington Construction Co., Torrington, CT (1981-1983); Project Manager, District Manager, O&G Industries, Inc. (1980-1983); President, Contract Facilities, New York City, NY (1980-1982); General Manager, Bruce Woodworking, New York City, NY (1978-1981); Development Director, Raberg, Nusser & Raberg Construction Co., New York City, NY (1978-1981); President, HEK Building Contractors, Cromwell, CT (1976-1978) **CR:** Advisory Council, Rice School of Architecture **CW:** Architect, Faculty Housing, Dormitory Renovations, New Model Home Construction, Housing for the Elderly, Distribution and Warehouse Facilities, Graduate Housing Construction, High-Rise Office Towers, Office Buildings, Historic Building Restoration, High-End Custom Housing, Silver and Gold Certified Projects, Numerous Condominium Projects, Training Facilities, Classroom Buildings, Campus Centers, Manufacturing Facilities, Bank Buildings, Dining Facilities, Corporate Interiors, Hospital Facilities, Industrial Buildings and Pumping Stations, Executive Education Center, Hotels, Museums, Middle and High School Facilities, Theater Spaces, Broadway and University Facilities, Public Libraries, Courthouses and Affordable Housing **AW:** Academic Awards, Rice

University; I.M. Pei Finalist, Graduate Student Project, Rice University; First Place, Aerial Perspective Drawing Competition **MEM:** National Trust for Historic Preservation; United States Green Building Council; American Institute of Architects; American Concrete Institute; Boston Society of Architects; American Woodworking Institute; National Fire Prevention Association; Cape Cod Modern House Trust **PA:** Democrat **BA:** 7 Walnut St, Eurich & Assoc, Newtonville, MA, 02460

EVANS, LOUISE, T: Investor, Psychologist (Retired) **I:** Medicine & Health Care **PB:** San Antonio **SC:** TX/USA **PT:** Henry Daniel Evans; Adela (Pariser) Evans **MS:** Married **SPN:** Thomas Ross Gambrell (2/23/1960) **ED:** Fellow, Council of Sex Education and Parenthood (International) (1984); Postdoctoral Fellow, Clinical Child Psychology, The Menninger Clinic, Topeka, KS (1955-1956); PhD in Clinical Psychology, Purdue University (1955); Intern, Clinical Psychology, Menniger Foundation (1953); Intern, Clinical Psychology, Topeka State Hospital (1952-1953); MS in Clinical Psychology, Purdue University (1952); BS, Northwestern University (1949); Fellow, American University, Washington D.C. **CT:** Licensed Marriage, Family and Child Counselor, State of California; Registrant, National Register of Health Service Providers in Psychology; Licensed Psychologist, State of California; Licensed Psychologist, State of New York; Diplomate, Clinical Psychology, American Board of Professional Psychology **C:** Private Practice, Fullerton, CA (1960-1993); Clinical Research Consultant, Episcopalian City Diocese, St. Louis, MO (1959-1960); Instructor, Medical Psychology, Washington University School of Medicine in St. Louis (1959-1960); Head, Staff Psychologist, Child Guidance Clinic, Kings County Hospital, Brooklyn, NY (1957-1958); Staff Psychologist, Kankakee State Hospital (1954-1955); Director, Psychology Clinic, Barnes-Renard Hospital **CR:** Chair, Participant, Psychological Symposiums (1956-Present); Staff Consultant, Clinical Psychology, Martin Luther Hospital, Anaheim, CA (1963-1970); Psychological Consultant, Fullerton Community Hospital (1961-1981); Speaker in Field; Lecturer in Field **CW:** Contributor, Articles on Clinical Psychology, Professional Publications **AW:** IBC Medal, Outstanding Contributor to the Field of Psychology, Top 100 Health Professionals of 2012, International Biographical Centre (2012); Corann Okorodudu International Women's Advocacy Award, American Psychological Association and The Association for Women in Psychology (2009); Listed, International Profiles of Accomplished Leaders, Inaugural Edition, American Biographical Institute (2009); Listed, 2000 Outstanding Scientists of the 21st Century, American Biographical Institute (2009); Recognition for Pioneering Leadership in International Psychology, International Council of Psychologists (2003); Named, Ambassador for Life, International Council of Psychologists (2003); Recognition for Outstanding Leadership & Enduring Commitment Award, International Council of Psychologists (2003); International Psychology Recognition Award for Lifelong Contributions to the Advancement of Psychology Internationally, International Psychology Division, American Psychological Association (2002); College Arts and Sciences Merit Award, 1851 Society, Northwestern University (1997); Alumni Merit Award, Weinberg College of Arts and Sciences, Northwestern University (1997); Distinguished Alumni Award, Purdue Alumni Association (1993); Old Master, Purdue Alumni Association (1993); Statue of Victory Personality of the Year Award, Centro Studi E. Ricerche

Delle Nazioni, Italy (1985); Purdue University Citizenship Award, Purdue Alumni Association (1975); Service Award, Yuma County Head Start Program (1972); Distinguished Alumni Award, Central High School (1970); Named, Hall of Fame, Central High School, Evansville, IN (1966); Named, Miss Heritage, Heritage Publications (1965); Parent-Teacher Association Scholarship Award, Central High School (1945); Named, World Biographical Hall of Fame, Volume II, Historical Preservations of America **MEM:** Director, International Council of Psychologists (1977-1979); Director, Executive Board, Society of Consulting Psychology (1976-1979); Secretary, International Council of Psychologists (1973-1976); Executive Board, Los Angeles Society of Clinical Psychologists (1966-1967); Secretary, International Council of Psychologists (1962-1964); Lifetime Member, Insurance Committee, California Psychological Association (1961-1965); Charter Founder, Executive Board, Orange County Psychological Association (1961-1962); Emeritus Fellow, American Association for the Advancement of Science; Fellow, International Psychology Division, American Psychological Association; Fellow, The Association for Women in Psychology; Fellow, Society of Clinical Psychology; Fellow, Psychotherapy Division, American Psychological Association; Fellow, Academy of Psychological Clinical Science; Charter Fellow, American Association of Applied and Preventive Psychology; Emeritus Fellow, Royal Society for Public Health; Lifetime Fellow, American Orthopsychiatric Association; Lifetime Fellow, World Wide Academy of Scholars of New Zealand; Charter Fellow, Association for Psychological Science; Fellow, International Council of Psychologists; Fellow, Professional Organizations and Societies; Emeritus Member, American Association of University Professors; Emeritus Member, Los Angeles County Psychological Association; Emeritus Member, American Public Health Association; The International Platform Association; Emeritus Member, The New York Academy of Sciences; Lifetime Member, Purdue Alumni Association; Past President, Council, Purdue Alumni Association; Dean's Club, Purdue Alumni Association; 1851 Society, Northwestern University; Center for the Study of the Presidency & Congress; Charter Member, American Society of Jewelry Historians; The Alumni Association at The Menninger Clinic; Association for Women in Psychology; Emeritus Member, Sigma Xi; International Women's Review Board, Founding Member, Professional Women's Advisory Board, American Biographical Institute **MH:** Albert Nelson Marquis Lifetime Achievement Award (2017) **ADD:** 727 S Beverly Glen Blvd, Los Angeles, CA, 90024

EWBANK, THOMAS PETERS, I: Law and Legal Services **DOB:** 12/29/1943 **PB:** Indianapolis **SC:** IN/USA **PT:** William Curtis Ewbank; Maxine Stuart (Peters) Ewbank **ED:** JD, Indiana University (1969); AB, Indiana University (1965); Student, Stanford University (1961-1962) **CT:** Board Certified Estate Planner and Administrator, State of Indiana (2007); Certified Trust and Financial Advisor (1988) **C:** Consultant, Arc Ind. Master Trust (2012-Present); Partner, Krieg DeVault LLP, Indianapolis (1995-2011); From Probate Administrator to Senior Vice President and Senior Trust Officer, President, Merchants Capital Management, Inc., Ind. (1990-1993); With, Merchants National Bank & Trust Co. (now PNC Bank), Indianapolis (1972-1995); Assistant General Counsel, Everett I. Brown Co., Indianapolis (1971-1972); Associate, Hilgedag, Johnson, Secrest and Murphy, Indianapolis (1969-1971); Estate and Inheritance Tax Administrator, Merchants National Bank, Indianapolis (1967-

1969); Legislative Assistant, Indiana Legislative Council (1966-1967) **CIV:** Board Member, Forte Home Healthcare Inc. (2012-Present); Board Member, Forte Residential Inc. (2009-Present); Consultant Master Trust, American Red Cross (2012-Present); Board of Directors, Arthur Jordan Foundation (2002-Present); Board of Directors, Benjamin Harrison Home Foundation (2010-Present); Chairman, Advisory Committee, American Red Cross, Ind. (1987-2012); Secretary, Arthur Jordan Foundation (2010-2011); Chairman, Arthur Jordan Foundation (2006-2008); Vice Chairman, Arthur Jordan Foundation (2004-2006); Secretary, Benjamin Harrison Home Foundation (2003-2006); Board of Directors, Benjamin Harrison Home Foundation (1994-2006); Secretary, Arthur Jordan Foundation (2003-2004); Board of Directors, Center Philanthropy, Indiana University, Indianapolis (1998-2002); Board of Directors, Ruth Lilly Foundation (1997-2002); Board of Directors, Indianapolis Art Center (1997-2002); President, Benjamin Harrison Home Foundation (1998-2000); Board of Directors, Noble Foundation Ind. (1997-1999); Vice President, Benjamin Harrison Home Foundation (1996-1998); Board Member, American Red Cross (1989-1992); Retired, Candidate for Indiana Legislature (1974); Candidate for Indiana Legislature (1970); Assistant Treasurer, Ruckelshaus for U.S. Senator Committee (1968) **CW:** Contributor, Articles, Professional Journals **MEM:** Board Member, Kiwanis Foundation Indianapolis (1980-1982, 2007-Present); Board of Directors, Indiana Society of Pioneers (2004-2012); President, Estate Planning Council of Indianapolis (1982-1983); Treasurer, Indianapolis Bar Foundation (1976-1981); Fellow, American College Trust and Estate Counsel; Life Member, Indiana Bar Foundation; Indiana Landmarks Foundation and Indiana Historical Society; Hamilton County Bar Association; Indiana Bar Association; Indianapolis Bar Association; Blue Key Honor Society **BAR:** US Supreme Court (1974); Southern District of Indiana, US District Court (1969); US Tax Court (1969); Bar Association of Indiana (1969) **PA:** Republican **RE:** Baptist

EWIN, DABNEY MINOR, T: Surgeon **I:** Medicine & Health Care **CN:** Concentra Medical Centers **DOB:** 12/07/1925 **PB:** New Orleans **SC:** LA/USA **PT:** James Perkins Ewin; Lucille Havard (Scott) Ewin **MS:** Married **SPN:** Marilyn Allis; Ethelyn Alexander Sherrouse (6/6/1951, Divorced 1968) **CH:** Dabney, Jr.; Constance; Walton; Christopher; Leila **ED:** MD, Tulane University (1951) **C:** Staff Physician, Concentra Medical Centers (1999-Present); Private Practice (1957-1999); Chief Resident, Huey P. Long Charity Hospital, Pineville, LA (1956-1957); Resident, Ochsner Foundation Hospital, New Orleans, LA (1954-1956); Resident, Jefferson-Hillman Hospital, The University of Alabama, Birmingham, AL (1951-1954); Intern, Jefferson-Hillman Hospital University of Alabama, Birmingham, AL (1951) **CR:** Clinical Professor, Psychiatry, Louisiana State University; Clinical Professor, Surgery, Tulane Medical School; Clinical Professor, Psychiatry, Tulane Medical School; Staff Surgeon, Charity Hospital, Louisiana; Consultant Staff, Touro Infirmary Hospital, New Orleans, LA **CIV:** Board of Directors, Christ School (1979-1985); Sunday School Teacher, Senior Class, Trinity Episcopalian Church (1960-1966) **CW:** Contributor, Articles, Professional Journals **MEM:** Lifetime Member, American Medical Association; Director, American Trauma Society (1975-1979); Speaker, House of Delegates, American Burn Association; American College of Occupational and Environmental Medicine (1973-1975); Chairman, Industrial Medicine and Surgery Section, Southern Medical Association (1966-1967); Fellow, American

College of Surgeons; Past President, American Board of Medical Hypnosis; Past President, American Society of Clinical Hypnosis; Louisiana State Medical Society; Orleans Parish Medical Society; Surgical Association of Louisiana; New Orleans Surgical Society; Past Secretary, Alton Ochsner Surgical Society; Society for Clinical and Experimental Hypnosis, Louisiana Psychiatric Medical Association **MH:** Albert Nelson Marquis Lifetime Achievement Award (2017) **H:** Fishing; Tennis **PA:** Republican **BA:** 318 Baronne St, New Orleans, LA, 70112 **ADD:** 150 Broadway Apt 1208, New Orleans, LA, 70118

EWING, KY PEPPER JR., **T:** Lawyer **I:** Law and Legal Services **DOB:** 01/07/1935 **PB:** Victoria **SC:** TX/USA **PT:** Ky Pepper Ewing; Sallie (Dixon) Ewing **MS:** Married **SPN:** Almuth Rott (4/6/1963) **CH:** Kenneth Patrick; Kevin Andrew; Kathryn Diana **ED:** LLB, Harvard University, Cum Laude (1959); BA, Baylor University, Cum Laude (1956) **C:** Of Counsel, Vinson & Elkins, Washington, DC (2002-2003); Partner, Vinson & Elkins, Washington, DC (1980-2001); Deputy Assistant Attorney General, Antitrust Division, U.S. Department of Justice, Washington, DC (1978-1980); Partner, Prather, Seeger, Doolittle, Farmer & Ewing, Washington, DC (1964-1977); Associate, Covington & Burling, Washington, DC (1959-1964) **CR:** Co-chair, Ditchley Conference Competition Laws (2001); Secretary, Washington Institute of Foreign Affairs (1981-1999); Board of Directors, Washington Institute of Foreign Affairs (1971-2002); Assistant Secretary, Washington Institute of Foreign Affairs (1961-1981); Fellow, American Bar Foundation **CIV:** President, Potomac Valley League (1977); President, Carderock Springs Citizens Association (1975-1978) **CW:** Antitrust Advisory Board, Antitrust and Trade Regulation Report, Bureau of National Affairs (1990-Present); Author, "Competition Rules for the 21st Century: Principles from America's Experience" (2003); Editorial Board, Business Law International, International Bar Association (2000-2007); Editorial Board, Antitrust Report, Matthew Bender & Co. (1993-2007); Co-editor-in-chief, "State Antitrust Practice and Statutes," Three Volumes (1990) **MEM:** Chairman, Nominating Committee, Antitrust Section, American Bar Association (2002-2003); Chair, Antitrust Section, American Bar Association (2000-2001); Chair-elect, Antitrust Section, American Bar Association (1999-2000); Vice Chair, Antitrust Section, American Bar Association (1998-1999); House of Delegates, American Bar Association (1996-1998); Chairman, FTC/Department of Justice Working Group, American Bar Association (1994-1997); Finance Officer, Antitrust Section, American Bar Association (1994-1996); Council Antitrust Section, American Bar Association (1991-1994); Chairman, Legislative Committee, Antitrust Section, American Bar Association (1987-1991); Life District of Columbia Bar Association; Cosmos Club; Metropolitan Club **BAR:** U.S. Supreme Court (1963); District of Columbia (1959) **MH:** Albert Nelson Marquis Lifetime Achievement Award (2017) **PA:** Republican **RE:** Episcopalian **ADD:** 8317 Comanche Court, Bethesda, MD, 20817

EWING, JACK ROBERT, **T:** Certified Public Accountant (Retired) **I:** Financial Services **DOB:** 02/14/1947 **PB:** San Francisco **SC:** CA/USA **PT:** Robert Maxwell Ewing; Blanche Julia (Diak) Ewing **MS:** Married **SPN:** Joan Marie Coughlin Ewing (11/25/1967) **CH:** Tracy Marie Benjamin; Christina Ann Barnes **ED:** BS, University of Missouri (1969) **CT:** Certified Public Accountant **C:** Owner, Jack R. Ewing, CPA (1993-2007); Stockholder, Hunt, Spillman & Ewing, Professional Corporation, Fort Collins, CO (1982-1993); Audit Manager, Erickson,

Hunt & Spillman, Professional Corporation, Fort Collins, CO (1979-1982); Supervisor Auditor, Fox & Co., St. Louis, MO (1974-1979); Staff Accountant, Fox & Co., St. Louis, MO (1969-1970) **CR:** Lecturer, Writer on Mental Illness and Suicide Prevention (1986-Present) **CIV:** Member, Governor's Citizen Panel for Suicide Prevention, State of Colorado (1998-Present); President, Suicide Resource Center, Larimer County, Fort Collins, CO (1998-2000); Member, State of Colorado Indicators and Outcomes Committee (1998-2000); Co-Founder, Mental Health and Substance Abuse Partnership (1997-2012); Member, Steering Committee, Mental Health and Substance Abuse Partnership (1997-2012); President, Center for Diversity in Work Place (1996-1999); Member, Mental Health Pro Bono Project (1996-1997); Vice President, Colorado Behavioral Healthcare Council (1995-1997); Member, State of Colorado Mental Health Planning Council (1993-2000); Suicide Prevention Coalition of Colorado (1993-1996); Member, Board of Directors, Suicide Resource Center, Larimer County, Fort Collins, CO (1992-2008); President, Larimer County Mental Health Advisory Board (1992-1999); Member, Leadership, Fort Collins Class of 1992 (1992); Director Treasurer, Center for Diversity in Work Place (1991-1996); Director Treasurer, One West Contemporary Art Center (1989-1997); Member, Entrepreneur of Year Selection Committee, Fort Collins, CO (1989-1992); Member, Parent Advisory Board, Beattie Elementary School (1986-1987); President, Parent Advisory Board, Beattie Elementary School (1982-1983); President, Alpha Phi Omega Fraternity (1968-1969); Alpha Phi Omega Fraternity (1966-1969) **MIL:** Internal Auditor, US Air Force Audit Agency, Warren F.E. Warren Air Force Base, Cheyenne, WY (1972-1974); Radio Station Operator, US Air Force, Mountain Home Air Force Base, Idaho (1970-1972) **AW:** Recipient, Everyday Heroes and Heroines Award (2006) **MEM:** American Institute of Certified Public Accountants; Colorado Society of Certified Public Accountants **MH:** Albert Nelson Marquis Lifetime Achievement Award (2017); Marquis' Industry Leaders (2017) **H:** Writing; Hiking; Traveling **ADD:** 3112 Meadowlark Ave, Fort Collins, CO, 80526

EZOLD, JULIE, **T:** Californium-252 Program Manager **I:** Sciences **CN:** Oak Ridge National Laboratory **MS:** Single **CH:** Kyrsten **ED:** MS in Nuclear Engineering, North Carolina State University (1992); BS in Nuclear Engineering, Rensselaer Polytechnic Institute (1990) **C:** Californium-252 Program Manager, Research and Development Staff, Oak Ridge National Laboratory (1992-Present); Criticality Safety Engineer, B&W Y-12 (1995-2002) **CR:** Educational Outreach, Oak Ridge National Laboratory **CIV:** Board President, Ballet Gloria **AW:** Presidential Citation, American Nuclear Society (2009); Patricia Bryant Leadership Award, Women in Nuclear, Nuclear Energy Institute (2009); Honoree, UT-Battelle Awards Night for Exceptional Community Outreach (2007) **MEM:** American Chemical Society (2012-Present); Steering Committee, Women in Nuclear (2003-Present); Multiple National Committee Positions, American Nuclear Society (1988-Present); Nuclear Energy Institute **MH:** Albert Nelson Marquis Lifetime Achievement Award (2017) **H:** Tent camping with her daughter; Dancing ballet, tap, and jazz **BA:** 1 Bethel Valley Road, Oak Ridge, TN, 37831 **ADD:** 428 Russfield Drive, Knoxville, TN, 37934 **URL:** https://ornl.gov/staff-profile/julie-g-ezold

EZRATI, MILTON JOSEPH, **T:** Investment Company Executive **I:** Financial Services **CN:** Lord Abbett **DOB:** 05/22/1947 **PB:** New York **SC:** NY/USA **PT:** Al Ezrati; Edythe Ezrati **MS:** Married **SPN:**

Susan Arlene Graham (6/19/1976, Divorced 1999); Lynda Lamare (7/1970, Divorced) **CH:** Isabel Diana **ED:** Master of Social Science in Mathematics Economics, University of Birmingham, England (1973); BA in Economics, University at Buffalo (1969) **C:** Senior Economist, Strategist, Lord, Abbett & Co. (Now Lord Abbett), Jersey City, NJ (2000-2015); Chief Investment Officer, Nomura Asset Management Co., LTD, New York, NY (1987-1999); Senior Vice President, Manufacturers Hanover Investment Corporation, New York, NY(1985-1987); Director, Research, Manufacturers Hanover Investment Corporation, New York, NY (1985-1987); Chief Economist, Strategist, Manufacturers Hanover Investment Corporation, New York, NY (1983-1985); Chief Economist, Manufacturers Hanover Investment Corporation, New York, NY (1981-1983); Chief Economist, Lionel Edie & Co., New York, NY (1978-1981); Economist, Lionel Edie & Co., New York City, NY (1977-1978); Economist, JPMorgan Chase & Co., New York, NY (1973-1977); Economic Specialist, Citibank (Now Citigroup Inc.), New York, NY (1971-1973) **CIV:** Volunteer, Methodist Church **CW:** Author, "Thirty Tomorrows," Thomas Dunne Books, Saint Martin's Press (2014); Author, "Kawari: How Japan's Economic and Cultural Transformation Will Alter the Balance of Power Among Nations" (1999); Author, " Bite-Sized Investing"; Contributing Editor, "The National Interest"; Contributing Writer, "The City Journal," The Manhattan Institute; Contributor, Articles, Professional Journals; Author, "Investing for Beginners" **MEM:** American Economics Association; National Association of Scholars; Old Westbury Horsemen's Foundation **MH:** Albert Nelson Marquis Lifetime Achievement Award (2017) **H:** Riding horses; Training horses; Skiing **RE:** Methodist **ADD:** 400 E 54th St Apt 26B, New York, NY, 10022 **URL:** https://www.lordabbett.com/en/global/biographies/milton-ezrati.html

EZZO, DAVID ALBERT, **T:** Non-Profit Executive, Anthropologist, Educator **I:** Education/Educational Services **CN:** Erie Community College **DOB:** 06/09/1963 **PB:** Buffalo **SC:** NY/USA **PT:** Albert Ezzo; Ann Ezzo **MS:** Married **SPN:** Michelle Martin (8/13/2005) **ED:** PhD in Anthropology, Richardson University (2005); MPA, Hamilton University (2005); Coursework, New York University, New York, NY (1996); MA in Anthropology, University of Oklahoma, Norman, OK (1987); BA in Anthropology, State University of New York, Fredonia (1985) **CT:** Certified, Fundraising Executive (1997); Certified, Non-Profit Management, University South Florida, Tampa (1997); Certified, Personnel Management, State University of New York at Buffalo (1991) **C:** Adjunct Professor, Sociology and Anthropology, Erie Community College (2013-Present); Director, Endowment, Boy Scouts of America (2005-Present); Adjunct Professor of Anthropology, Villa Maria College, Buffalo, NY (2011); Director, Community Development, YMCA, Burbank, CA (2002); Director, Development and Public Relations, YMCA, St. Petersburg, FL (1996-1998); Staff Member to Director of Endowment, Boy Scouts of America, Buffalo, NY (1987-2005); Adjunct Teacher, Sociology, Niagara University; Lecturer, Anthropology, Villa Maria College; Adjunct Assistant Professor of Sociology and Anthropology, Genesee Community College **CR:** Lecturer in Field **CW:** Author, "Cannibalism & Cross-Cultural Perspective," Dog Ear Press (2008); Co-Author, "Papers on Historical Algonquin & Iroquois Topics," Dog Ear Press (2007); Contributor, Scientific Papers **AW:** Vigil Honor Award, Boy Scouts of America (1981); Eagle Scout Award, Boy Scouts of America (1977) **MH:** Albert Nelson Marquis Lifetime Achievement Award (2017) **H:** Fitness; Tennis; Music; Travel **ADD:** 52 Kenwood Road, Kenmore, NY, 14217

FAISON MCCLOUD, ANECE, T: Associate Dean of Students **I:** Education/Educational Services **CN:** Washington and Lee University **DOB:** 05/29/1937 **PB:** Dudley **SC:** NC/USA **PT:** J.D. Faison; Nancy Jane (Simmons) Faison-Cole **MS:** Married **SPN:** Verable Lancaster McCloud (6/1/1959) **CH:** Aja Siobhan; Carla Danette **ED:** Coursework, Basic Mediation Skills, Eastern Mennonite University (1994); MA, University of Nebraska, Omaha, NE (1989); BS, Bennette College, Greensboro, NC (1959) **C:** Associate Dean, Students, Washington and Lee University, Lexington, VA (1985-1999); First Director, Minority Student Affairs, University of Nebraska Medical Center (1976-1985); Assistant Registrar, Academy Records, University Nebraska Medical Center, Omaha, NE (1972-1976); Resident Adviser, Child Saving Institute, Omaha, NE (1967-1971); Educational Coordinator, Child Saving Institute, Omaha, NE (1967-1971); Teacher, Woodbridge Airforce Base, England (1961-1962); Teacher, Lincoln Junior High School, Greensboro, NC (1959-1960) **CR:** Consultant, Campus Alcohol Initiative, North Carolina Governor's Institute of Alcohol and Substance Abuse (1999); Consultant, Deans Forum on Revitalizing Health Professional Education, Department of Health and Human Services (1985); Peer Reviewer, Health Career Opportunity Program (1984); Peer Reviewer, Health Career Opportunity Program (1982); Consultant, Simulated Minority Admissions, Association of American Medical Colleges, Washington, D.C. (1979) **CIV:** Member, Virginia Advisory Committee, U.S. Commission on Civil Rights (1995-1999); Member, Virginia Identification Program for Advancement of Women in Higher Education (1995-1996); Board Member, Rockbridge Area Housing Corp., Lexington, VA (1988-1990); Vice President, Rockbridge Area Housing Corporation, Lexington, VA (1988-1990); Treasurer, Mayor's Commission on Status of Women, Omaha, NE (1977-1978); Congregational Church; Charity Work **AW:** Plaque for Outstanding Service to Washington and Lee Community (1994); Certificate, Acknowledgement of Contribution to Education, Omaha Public Schools (1984); Grantee, Health Career Opportunity, Disadvantaged Assistance Office, Department of Health and Human Services (1983); Grantee, Health Career Opportunity, Disadvantaged Assistance Office, Department of Health and Human Services (1980); Certificate, Black History Month Speaker, VA Hospital, Omaha, NE (1977); Grantee, Health Career Opportunity, Disadvantaged Assistance Office, Department of Health and Human Services (1976) **MEM:** Vice Coordinator, National Association of Medical Minority Educators (1982-1983); Chairperson, Subcommittee on Minority Affairs, Nebraska Association of Collegiate Registrars and Admissions Officers (1978-1984); American Association for Higher Education; National Association for Women in Education; American College Personnel Association; Association of American Medical Colleges; American Association of Counseling and Development; Nebraska Association for Non-White Concerns **MH:** Albert Nelson Marquis Lifetime Achievement Award (2017) **H:** Social research; Writing; Interior decorating **PA:** Democrat **ADD:** 2001 W. Rudasill Rd., Apt. 5208, Tucson, AZ, 85704

FAKUNLE, DAVID OLAWUYI, T: Co-Founder, Facilitator **I:** Health, Wellness and Fitness **CN:** DiscoverME/RecoverME **PT:** Taiwo Fakunle; Deborah Pierce-Fakunle **MS:** Married **SPN:** Doralee Calderon-Fakunle **CH:** Cruz-Matisse Fakunle **ED:** PhD in Mental Health, Johns Hopkins Bloomberg School of Public Health (2017); BA in Psychology, Criminology & Criminal Justice, University of Maryland, College Park (2009); Research Internship, National Institute of Mental Health (2008) **C:** Storytelling Workshop Facilitator, Red Bull Amaphiko, Baltimore, MD (2017-Present); Project Coordinator, Kaiser Permanente Social Innovation Challenge, Baltimore, MD (2016-Present); Staff Member, Office of Delegate Dan K. Morhaim, District 11, General Assembly of Maryland, Annapolis, MD (2015-Present); Applied Narrative Epidemiologist, DiscoverME/RecoverME, Baltimore, MD (2013-Present); Research Associate, Johns Hopkins University, Bloomberg School of Public Health, Departments of Mental Health and Health, Behavior & Society, Baltimore, MD (2013-Present); Thread Volunteer Training Facilitator, Thread's Circle Unbroken Project, Baltimore, MD (2016-2017); Policy, Community Engagement and Outreach Fellow, Baltimore City Health Department via Baltimore Corps, Baltimore, MD (2016-2017); Special Insurance Specialist, United States Social Security Administration, Office of Disability Operations, Woodlawn, MD (2010-2013); Research Analyst, Fors Marsh Group; Arlington, VA (2009-2010) **CR:** Presenter in Field **CW:** Ad Hoc Reviewer of Manuscripts, Journal of Epidemiology & Community Health, Journal of Neurosciences in Rural Practice, Net Journal of Social Sciences, Nicotine & Tobacco Research, PLOS One (2014-Present); Author, "How the Obama Presidency Changed the Political Landscape" (2017); Contributing Author, "Community Beacons: Making Waves" (2016) **AW:** Delegate, Centers for Disease Control and Prevention Millennial Health Leaders Summit (2016); Young Cultural Innovator, Salzburg Global Seminar (2015); Second Place, Dr. Donald O. Fedder Graduate Student Poster Competition, Maryland Public Health Association Annual Meeting (2014); Dean's List, University of Maryland, College Park (2009); Dean's List, University of Maryland, College Park (2008); President's List, University of Maryland, College Park (2008); Dean's List, University of Maryland, College Park (2007); Ida G. and L. Leonard Ruben Scholarship (2007); Maryland State Senatorial Scholarship (2007); East Baltimore Community Corporation College Scholarship (2005) **MEM:** Board President, WombWork Productions (2017-Present); Labs@LightCity Curator, Light City Baltimore (2017-Present); Board Member, Friends School of Baltimore Alumni Association (2016-Present); Co-Chair, Community Service Sub-Committee, Friends School of Baltimore Alumni Association (2016-Present); Member, Access to Wholistic and Productive Living Institute, Inc., Friends School of Baltimore Alumni Association (2016-Present); Board of Directors, Friends School of Baltimore Alumni Association (2016-Present); Board Member, African American Leadership Forum for Public Safety (2015-Present); Steering Committee Member, Light City Baltimore (2015-Present); Community Engagement Subcommittee, Light City Baltimore (2015-2016); LightCityU Subcommittee, Light City Baltimore (2015-2016); Member in Training, The College on Problems of Drug Dependence (2014-2017); National Association of Black Storytellers **H:** Performing arts; Fishing; Sports; Softball; Relaxing; Watching TV; Traveling; Being around family and friends; Trying new things **ADD:** 3512 Carriage Walk Ln, Laurel, MD, 20724 **URL:** http://discovermerecoverme.com

FALCO, MARIA J., T: Academic Administrator, Political Scientist (Retired) **I:** Education/Educational Services **CN:** DePauw University **DOB:** 07/07/1932 **PB:** Wildwood **SC:** NJ/USA **ED:** Student Management Program, Carnegie-Mellon University, Pittsburgh, PA (1993); Postdoctoral Research Fellow, Yale University (1965-1966); PhD in Political Science, Bryn Mawr College, Pennsylvania (1963); MA, Fordham University (1958); Fulbright Scholar, University of Florence, Italy (1954-1955); AB, Immaculata College, Pennsylvania (1954) **C:** Professor Emerita, DePauw University, Greencastle, IN (1993-Present); Professor, Political Science, DePauw University, Greencastle, IN (1988-1993); Academic Vice President, DePauw University, Greencastle, IN (1986-1988); Professor, Political Science, Loyola University, New Orleans, LA (1985-1986); Dean, College Arts and Sciences, Loyola University, New Orleans, LA (1979-1985); Chair, Faculty, Social and Behavioral Sciences, University of Tulsa, OK (1976-1979); Professor, Political Science, Stockton State College, Pomona, NJ (1973-1976); Chair, Department of Political Science, Le Moyne College, Syracuse, NY (1967-1973); Assistant Professor to Associate Professor, Political Science, Le Moyne College, Syracuse, NY (1966-1973); Research Assistant to Genevieve Blatt (1964-1965); Assistant Professor, Political Science, Washington College, Chestertown, MD (1963-1964); Instructor to Assistant Professor, History and Political Science, Immaculata College, Pennsylvania (1957-1963) **CIV:** Chairperson, New Parishioners Committee, St. An Church, Metairie, LA (2007-Present); Extraordinary Minister of Communion, St. An Church, Metairie, LA (2004-Present); President, Business and Professional Women, Jefferson Parish (2004-2005); 1st Vice President, Business and Professional Women, Jefferson Parish (2002-2004); President, Business and Professional Women's Association (2000-2004); Member, President's Council, Urban Partners, Institute of Human Relations, Loyola University, New Orleans, LA (1997-2000); President, Indiana Political Science Association (1992-1993); Chair, Indiana Political Science Association (1992-1993); Chair, Board of Directors, Personnel Management Committee, Institute for Human Understanding, New Orleans, LA (1985-1986); Board of Directors, Urban Partners, Institute of Human Relations, Loyola University, New Orleans, LA (1984-1986); Board of Directors, Committee for the Enhancement and support of Liberal Arts, American Conference of Academic Deans (1984-1985); Member, Mayor's Task Force on the Future of New Orleans (1983-1985); Vice President, Le Moyne College Chapter, American Association of University Professors (1971-1972); President, Syracuse Chapter, New Democratic Coalition (1970-1971) **AW:** Louisiana American Italian Woman of the Year Award, AIRF Sports Hall of Fame Banquet (2016); Panzeca Scholarship Presentation, Loyola, MD (2015); Named Mentor of Distinction, Women's Caucus for Political Science (1989); Grantee, Summer Research Grant National Science Foundation (1968); Faculty Fellow in State and Local Politics, National Center for Education in Politics (1964); Fulbright Scholar, University of Florence, Italy (1954-1955) **MEM:** Member, Advisory Committee, Women's Opera Guild (2013-Present); Board of Directors, Country Club Estates Civic Association (2008-Present); Webmaster, Country Club Estates Civic Association (2008-Present); Corresponding Secretary, American Italian Federation of the Southeast (2007-Present); Secretary, Women for a Better Louisiana (2007-Present); Recording Secretary, East Jefferson Italian-American Society (2005-Present); Women and Politics Research Section, American Political Science Association (1987-Present); President, Women for a Better Louisiana (2012-2013); Member, Advisory Council, New Orleans Opera Association (2010-2016); Webmaster, East Jefferson Italian-American Society (2008); Woman of the Year, East Jefferson Italian-American Society (2008); President, Jefferson Parish League of Women Voters (2001-

2004); Board of Directors, Jefferson Parish League of Women Voters (1999-2004); Chair, Committee for Outstanding Convention Paper Award, American Political Science Association (1990-1991); Computer Users Section, American Political Science Association (1987-1993); Dean's Council, Common Cause, Great Lakes College Association (1986-1988); Dean's Council, Association of Jesuit Colleges and Universities (1979-1985); Outstanding Convention Paper Committee, Southwest Political Science Association (1979-1980); Professional Ethics, American Political Science Association (1977-1980); Academy Freedom Committee, American Political Science Association (1977-1980); President, Women's Caucus for Political Science (1976-1977); Benjamin Evans Lippincott Award Committee, American Political Science Association (1976); Vice President, Women's Caucus for Political Science (1975-1976); Chair, Program Committee, Women's Caucus for Political Science (1975-1976); Program Chair, Epistemology and Methodology Section, American Political Science Association (1975); Program Section Chair, American Political Science Association (1975); Foundations Political Theory Group, American Political Science Association (1973-1993); Northeastern Political Science Association; Webmaster, American Italian Federation of the Southeast; Jefferson Beautification Inc.; New Orleans Opera Association; American Italian Digest, New Orleans, LA; Heritage Society, Loyola University; Committee Twenty-One; Volunteer, Country Club Estates Civic Association **RE:** Roman Catholic **ADD:** 4709 Tartan Dr, Metairie, LA, 70003 **URL:** http://www.falcosaerie.me

FALTER, ROBERT GARY, T: Real Estate Broker **I:** Real Estate **CN:** EXIT Real Estate Executives **DOB:** 09/14/1945 **PB:** New York **SC:** NY/USA **PT:** Lawrence Z. Falter; Helen (Smith) Falter **MS:** Divorced **ED:** PhD, Walden University (1993); MBA, Cornell University (1976); MA, Kean University (1973); BA, St. John's University (1967); AA, St. John's University (1965) **CT:** Certified Council of Residential Specialists; Certified Military Relocation Professional; Certified Negotiation Expert; Certified in Broker Opinion Resource, The Massachusetts Association of Realtors; Short Sale Foreclosure Resource Certificate, National Association of Realtors; Certified, Real Estate Buyer's Agent Council; Loss Mitigation Certificate, National Association of Realtors; Graduate, Realtor Institute; Certified in Loss Mitigation; Certified Accredited Buyer Representative; Certified e-Pro Internet Professional; Certified Seniors Real Estate Specialist; Certified Real Estate Instructor; Certified Realtor, Commonwealth of Massachusetts; Certified Realtor, State of Connecticut; Licensed Real Estate Broker **C:** Real Estate Executive, Exit Real Estate Executives, Brookfield, MA (2016-Present); Broker Associate, ERA Key Realty Services, Worcester, MA (2010-2016); Trainer, ERA Key Realty Services, Worcester, MA (2010-2016); Broker Associate, RE/MAX Advantage 1, Worcester, MA (2014); Trainer, RE/MAX Advantage 1, Worcester, MA (2014); Broker Associate, Gold Triangle, Shrewsbury, MA (2009-2010); Trainer, Gold Triangle, Shrewsbury, MA (2009-2010); Broker Associate, Keller Williams Realty, Worcester, MA (2008-2009); Trainer, Keller Williams Realty, Worcester, MA (2008-2009); Broker Associate, Weichert, Realtors, Auburn, MA (2007-2008); Trainer, Weichert, Realtors, Auburn, MA (2007-2008); Broker Associate, Home & Land Partners, Auburn, MA (2007-2008); Trainer, Home & Land Partners, Auburn, MA (2007-2008); Realtor, Coldwell Banker Residential Brokerage, Worcester, MA (2004-2007); Administrator, Linda Manor Extended Care Facility, Leeds, MA (2003-2004); Interim Administrator, Kindred Transitional Care and

Rehabilitation-Avery, Kindred Healthcare, Inc., Needham, MA (2003); Assistant Administrator, Kindred Nursing and Rehabilitation-Tower Hill, Kindred Healthcare, Inc., Canton, MA (2002-2003); Assistant Administrator, Kindred Nursing and Rehabilitation - Harborlights, Kindred Healthcare, Inc. (2002); Administrator-in-Training, Clark Manor Healthcare Center (2002); Health Care Administrator, Correctional Medical Services, Massachusetts Correctional Institution-Shirley, Shirley, MA (2000-2002); Quality Risk Manager, Federal Medical Center, Federal Bureau of Prisons, Devens, MA (2000); Quality Risk Manager, Federal Medical Center, Federal Bureau of Prisons, Ayer, MA (2000); Administrative Officer, Federal Medical Center, Federal Bureau of Prisons, Devens, MA (1999-2000); Administrative Officer, Federal Medical Center, Federal Bureau of Prisons, Ayer, MA (1999-2000); Chief Health Services Officer, Office of the Surgeon General, Public Health Service (1995-1999); Chief, Budget and Management Support Branch, U.S. Public Health Service, Rockville, MD (1993-1999); Chief, U.S. Public Health Service, Rockville, MD (1991-1993); Budget Officer BOP/HSD, U.S. Public Health Service, Rockville, MD (1991-1993); Chief, Program Liaison Unit, U.S. Public Health Service, Rockville, MD (1990-1991); Health Care Administrator, Individual Ready Research, U.S. Public Health Service, Rockville, MD (1989-1990); Material Management Officer (1989); Deputy Branch Chief (1989); Health and Services Administrator, Rockville, MD (1989); Resources and Services Administrator, Rockville, MD (1989); Associate Director, Administrative Services, Federal Employee Occupational Health, U.S. Public Health Service Region II, New York, NY (1988-1989); Associate Vice President of Operations, Staten Island University Hospital (1986-1987); Assistant Vice President, Customer Service, Empire Blue Cross Blue Shield, New York, NY (1982-1986); Assistant Vice President, Institutional Benefits, Empire Blue Cross Blue Shield, New York, NY (1982-1986); Administrator, Family Medicine, School of Medicine, The University of Tennessee Health Science Center, Memphis, TN (1981-1982); Associate Director, Ambulatory Care, U.S. Public Health Service Hospital, Boston, MA (1980-1981); Project Officer, Ambulatory Care Data Systems, Division of Hospitals and Clinics, U.S. Public Health Service, West Hyattsville, MD (1978-1980); Director, Out-Patient Clinic U.S. Public Health Service, Center for Disease Control, Atlanta, GA (1977-1978); Manager Ophthalmology, Hahnemann University Hospital, Philadelphia, PA (1976-1977); Administrative Resident, Weill Cornell Medicine, Cornell University, New York, NY (1975) **CR:** Instructor, Berkshire County Board of Realtors (2011-Present); Affiliate, North Central Massachusetts Association of Realtors (2010-Present); Affiliate, Real Estate Buyer's Agent Council, National Association of Realtors (2010-Present); Dean, Realtor Institute, Massachusetts Association of Realtors (2007-Present); Instructor, Center for Real Estate Studies & Training, REALTOR Association of Central MA (2007-Present); Real Estate Instructor, Massachusetts (2006-Present); Graduate, Realtor Institute, Massachusetts Association of Realtors (2009); Newsletter Proofreader, Massachusetts Rental Housing Association (2008); Adjunct Assistant, School of Nursing, Vanderbilt University, Nashville, TN (1999-2005); Senior Lecturer, Western New England College, Springfield, MA (2000-2002); Adjunct Assistant Professor, Preventive Medicine and Biometrics, Health Services Administration, Uniformed Services University of the Health Sciences, Bethesda, MD (1999-2001); Adjunct Assistant Professor, Division of Nursing Research, Graduate School of Nursing, Uniformed Services University of the Health Sciences,

Bethesda, MD (1996-2001); Lecturer, Health Economics Graduate Program, Health Services Administration, Salve Regina University, Newport, RI (1984); Lecturer of Fiscal Management, Christian Brothers University, Memphis, TN (1982) **CIV:** Member, Board of Assessors, Town Brookfield, MA (2016-Present); Member, Capital Improvement Committee, Town Brookfield (2017-Present); Member, Financial Advisory Committee, Town Brookfield, MA (2015-2016); Member, Worcester World Affairs Council (2014-2016); Member, Worcester Economic Club (2008-Present); Volunteer, UMass Memorial Health Care, Worcester, MA (2006-Present); Member, Lions Clubs International, Northborough, MA (2014-2016); Member, Board of Directors, Centro Las America's, Worcester, MA (2011-2012); Member, Council of Disabilities, Shrewsbury, MA (2010-2013); Usher Coordinator, St. Michael Catholic Church, Mount Airy, MD (1989-1991); Member, Board of Directors, Willowbrook Visiting Nurse Association (1982); Member, Community Advisory Board, Primary Health Care and Services, Allston Brighton Medical Care Coalition, Boston, MA (1981); Volunteers, Pastoral Care Department, Massachusetts Memorial Center **MIL:** Commissioned Corps. O-6, U.S. Public Health Service (1977-2001); U.S. Army (1968-1971) **CW:** Managing Editor, Journal of Correctional Health Care, National Commission on Correctional Health Care (1994-1997); Member, Editorial Board, Healthcare Executives, American College of Healthcare Executives (1986-1988); Book Reviewer, Hospital and Health Services Administration, American College of Healthcare Executives; Contributor, Articles, Federal Bureau of Prisons; Contributor, Articles, U.S. Public Health Service; Contributor, Chapters, Books **AW:** Named Educator of the Year, Worcester Regional Association of Realtors (2010); Named Rookie of the Year, Worcester Regional Association of Realtors (2006); Surgeon General's Exemplary Service Medal, U.S. Public Health Service (1999); Surgeon General's Exemplary Service Medal, U.S. Public Health Service (1996); Captain Stanley J. Kissel Junior Award, U.S. Public Health Service (1994); Five Year Service Award, Worcester Regional Association of Realtors **MEM:** Executive Committee, Military Officers Association of America (2004-Present); Reviewer, Military Medicine, AMSUS (1989-Present); Education Committee, Worcester Regional Association of Realtors (2010-2016); Membership Committee, Worcester Regional Association of Realtors (2009-2016); Professional Standards Committee, Worcester Regional Association of Realtors (2008-Present); Personal Affairs Officer, Military Officers Association of America (2007-2016); Professional Standards Committee, Massachusetts Association of Realtors (2007-2016); Director, Board of Directors, Massachusetts Association of Realtors (2009-2010); Alternate Director, Board of Directors, Worcester Regional Association of Realtors (2009); Forms Review Committee, Massachusetts Association of Realtors (2008); Education Committee, Worcester Regional Association of Realtors (2005-2008); Education and Events Committee, Massachusetts Association of Realtors (2006); Marketing Committee, Knights of Columbus (2005); President, Worcester County Chapter, Military Officers Association of America (2002-2004) **MH:** Albert Nelson Marquis Lifetime Achievement Award (2017) **H:** Travel; Writing; Consulting; Teaching; Coaching **PA:** Independent **RE:** Roman Catholic **BA:** 27 Fiskdale Road, Brookfield, MA, 01506 **ADD:** 10 Nanatomqua Drive, N56, Brookefield, MA, 01506 **URL:** https://www.linkedin.com/in/bobfalter

FANINI, OTTO NILSON, **T:** Principal Engineer, Electrical Oil Field Services **I:** Oil & Energy **CN:** Baker Hughes Incorporated **ED:** MBA in Finance, Houston Baptist University (1986); MSEE in Solid State, VLSI Micro Electronics, Laser Applications, Texas A&M University (1982); BSEE in Electronics, Federal University of Rio de Janeiro (1979) **CT:** Competent Communicator Program, Toastmasters International (2017); Certificate, Online Trading Academy (2014) **C:** Global Principal Engineer of Drilling and Evaluation, Baker Hughes Incorporated **AW:** Houston Technology Center Leadership Award (2017); High Temperature/ High Pressure Equipment Award, Baker Hughes Incorporated (2012) **MEM:** IEEE; Society of Petroleum Engineers; International Council on Systems Engineering; Houston Football Association; Brazil Press Association; Former Member, USA Triathlon **MH:** Albert Nelson Marquis Lifetime Achievement Award (2017) **H:** Music; Traveling; Soccer; Songwriting **ADD:** PO Box 79651, Houston, TX, 77279 **URL:** https://www.linkedin.com/pub/otto-fanini/b/b54/790

FARKAS, ANDREW, **T:** Library Director, Educator, Writer (Retired) **I:** Library Management/Library Services **DOB:** 04/07/1936 **PB:** Budapest **SC:** Hungary **PT:** Miklós Farkas; Renée (Schwartz) Farkas **MS:** Divorced **ED:** MLS, University of California, Berkeley (1962); BA, Occidental College, Los Angeles, CA (1959); Coursework, Eötvös Loránd University Faculty of Law, Budapest, Hungary (1954-1956) **C:** Library Director Emeritus, University of North Florida, Jacksonville, FL (2003); Director Emeritus, Program Committee Member, Florida Governor's Conference on Libraries, University of North Florida, Tallahassee, FL (1978); Director of Libraries, University of North Florida, Jacksonville, FL (1970-2003); Professor of Library Science, University of North Florida, Jacksonville, FL (1970-2003); Assistant Manager, Walter J. Johnson, Inc., New York City, NY (1967-1970); Chief Bibliographer, University of California (1966-1967); Assistant Head, Acquisitions Department, University of California (1965-1967); Gift and Exchange Libraries, University of California (1962-1965); Assistant Bibliographer, University of California, Davis (1962-1963) **CR:** IRS, Washington (1982); Expert Witness, IRS, Atlanta, GA (1981) **CIV:** Member, Council of Interinstitutional Planning, Jacksonville, FL (1983-1985) **MIL:** Quartermaster Corps, United States Army (1959-1961) **CW:** Contributing Editor, "Jussi Björling Society Journal" (1996-Present); Contributor Editor, The Opera Quarterly (1993-Present); Co-author, "Jussi" (1996); Co-author, "Enrico Caruso: My Father & My Family" (1990); Editor, "Lawrence Tibbett, Singing Actor" (1989); Author, "Opera and Concert Singers" (1985); Editor, "Librarians' Calendar" (1984-2005); Author, "Titta Ruffo: An Anthology" (1984); Editor, "Titta Ruffo: An Anthology" (1984) **AW:** Outstanding Faculty Scholarship Award, University of North Florida (2000); Distinguished Professor Award, University of North Florida (1991) **MEM:** American Library Association **MH:** Albert Nelson Marquis Lifetime Achievement Award (2017) **H:** Research; Creative Writing; Travel; Photography; Book and Record Collecting **PA:** Democrat **ADD:** 6970 Tonga Dr, Jacksonville, FL, 32216

FARMAKIDES, JOHN BASIL, **T:** Lawyer **I:** Law and Legal Services **PB:** Symi Island (Dodecanese) **SC:** Italy **PT:** Basil John Farmakides; Anna Maria (Zouroudis) Farmakides **MS:** Married **SPN:** Maria T. Kambanis (07/12/1964) **CH:** Basil J.; George S. **ED:** LLM, Georgetown University (1958); JD, The George Washington University, with Honors (1956); BS, Case Western Reserve University (1950) **C:** Attorney Neutral Arbitrator (1986-Present); Partner, Whitney & Dempsey, Washington, D.C. (1985-1988); Chairman, Board of Appeals, United States Department of Energy, Washington, D.C. (1975-1984); Appeals Board, Atomic Energy Commission, National Research Council, National Academy of Sciences (1972-1975); Assistant General Counsel, National Science Foundation (1970-1972); Board Contract Appeals, NASA (1968-1970); Attorney, NASA (1961-1970); Attorney, U.S. Air Force (1960-1961); Patent Examiner, United States Patent Office (1955-1959) **CR:** President Consultant, Department of Health, National Science Foundation; First United States Copyright Arbitration Panel, Library of Congress (1995); Chief Administrative Judge, City Council of New Orleans (1984-1999); United States Chinese Workshop on Computerized Information Systems, National Academy of Sciences (1972); United States Delegate, International Conference on Government Computer Experts, Geneva, Switzerland (1972); Chairman, Conference Legal Aspects Computerized Information Systems, National Academy of Sciences (1972); Commanding Officer, Joint Army, Navy, Air Force Special Analyst Division, United States Army Reserve (1971-1974); Director, Joint Army, Navy, Air Force Special Analyst Division, United States Army Reserve (1971-1974); Chairman, Subcommittee, Legal Aspects Computerized Info Systems, Federal Council for Science and Technology (1969-1972); Adjunct Professor in Intellectual Property Law, Patents and Copyrights and Computer and Law, American University Washington College of Law (1964-1972) **CIV:** President, Cosmos Club (1987) **MIL:** U.S. Army (1950-1954); Head of Military Committee for Censorship, Cold War **CW:** Contributor, Articles, Professional Journals **AW:** Letters of Appreciation, U.S. Army; Letters of Appreciation, United States Department of Health and Human Services; Letters of Appreciation, NASA; Letters of Appreciation, National Science Foundation; Apollo Achievement Award, NASA; Exceptional Service Medal, United States Department of Energy **MEM:** ABA; Federal Bar Association; IEEE; American Arbitration Association; The American Society for Public Administration; NASA Space League; The International Legal Honor Society of Phi Delta Phi; Cosmos Club; Washington Gold Club; National Lawyers Club **BAR:** The District of Columbia Bar (1957); United States Supreme Court (1958); Virginia State Bar (1986) **ADD:** 5835 Upton Street, McLean, VA, 22101

FARRIS, CAMISHA L., **T:** President **I:** Architecture & Construction **CN:** Anointed Flooring, Inc. **MS:** Married **CT:** Diplomate, Disadvantaged Business Enterprise (2012-2015); Certified in MSDBE, Durham, NC (2012-2014); Certified, Women's Business Enterprise National Council (WBENC) (2012-2013); Certified Small Business Enterprise, Charlotte, NC (2011-2014); Certified Historically Underutilized Businesses, North Carolina (2010-2014); Section III Certification, Charlotte Housing Authority (2010-2013); Certified, Economically Disadvantaged Women Owned Small Businesses (EDWOSB) **C:** President, Anointed Flooring, Inc. (2010-Present); Co-owner, Anointed Flooring, Inc. (2004-Present); Vice President, Anointed Flooring, Inc. (2004-2010) **CIV:** Small Business Advisory Board, Central Piedmont Community College (2017-Present); Commissioner Vilma Leake's Small Business Consortium Planning Committee (2015-Present); Treasurer, Metrolina Minority Contractors Association (MMCA) (2008-Present); Board of Directors, Metrolina Minority Contractors Association (MMCA) (2008-Present); Bank of America Trainer, DNC (Democratic National Convention) Volunteers, City of Charlotte Business Advisory Committee (2018); Disparity Study Advisory Committee, City of Charlotte (2017); Disparity Study Advisory Committee, City of Charlotte (2011) **AW:** Women of Color Achievement Award, 100 Black Men of Greater Charlotte & Women Presidents' Organization (2016); Future 50 Award, SmartCEO (2016); Client of the Year Award, Women Business Center of North Carolina (2016); Women in Business Award, Charlotte Business Journal (2015); Subcontractor Of The Year Award, Charlotte Construction Coalition (2015); Small Business Big Impact Award, Time Warner Cable Business Class (2014); Honoree, Goldman Sachs 10,000 Small Businesses Program Graduate (2014); Crowns of Enterprise Award, Rising Business of the Year, City of Charlotte and Mecklenburg County, NC (2012); Service Award, Metrolina Minority Contractors Association (MMCA) (2011); Small Business Advocacy Award, City of Charlotte (2011) **BA:** 2835 Jeff Adams Drive, Suite D, Anointed Flooring, Inc., Charlotte, NC, 28206 **URL:** https://www.linkedin.com/in/camisha-farris-a216053b

FAULKNER, JOHN SAMUEL, **T:** Physicist, Educator **I:** Education/Educational Services **CN:** Florida Atlantic University **DOB:** 09/30/1932 **PB:** Memphis **SC:** TN/USA **PT:** William Oliver Faulkner; Wilella (Aycock) Faulkner **MS:** Married **SPN:** Theodora Leventouri (8/6/1988) **CH:** Emily Koumeli; Lee Anne O'Brien **ED:** PhD, The Ohio State University (1959); Dupont Postgraduate Fellow, The Ohio State University (1958-1959); MS, Auburn University (1955); BS, Auburn University (1954) **C:** Professor Emeritus, Florida Atlantic University, Boca Raton, FL (2004-Present); Professor, Department of Physics, Florida Atlantic University, Boca Raton, FL (1986-2004); Head of Theory Group, Metals and Ceramics Division, Oak Ridge National Laboratory, Tennessee (1962-1986); Assistant Professor, University of Florida, Gainesville, FL (1959-1962) **CR:** Co-Director, Center for Biomedical and Materials Physics, Florida Atlantic University, Boca Raton, FL (1988-Present); Visiting Scientist, Der Kernforschungsanlange, Juelich, Federal Republic of Germany (1985-1986); Visiting Professor, University of Bristol, United Kingdom (1976-1977); Speaker in Field **CW:** Author, "The Sparrow" (2012); Contributor, Reviews to Professional Journals; Contributor, Articles to Professional Journals **AW:** Outstanding Referee, Editors of American Physical Society Journals (2008); Named, Best Sustained Research, United States Department of Energy (1982); Senior Fulbright Scholar, The University of Sheffield, United Kingdom (1968-1969) **MEM:** Fellow, American Physical Society; Fellow, American Association for the Advancement of Science **MH:** Albert Nelson Marquis Lifetime Achievement Award (2017) **H:** Squash; Boating **ADD:** 825 Walnut Terrace, Boca Raton, FL, 33486 **URL:** http://www.johnsamuelfaulkner.com

FEENEY, MATTHEW EDWARD, **T:** Linguist **I:** Education/Educational Services **DOB:** 12/24/1955 **PB:** Livermore **PT:** Martin Edward Feeney; Dorothy Ann Feeney **C:** Translator, Russian Articles on Literary Criticism, University of Wyoming, Laramie, WY (2004-Present); Participator, Crimea and Russia, Woodrow Wilson International Center of Scholars, Washington, DC (2014); Participator, Truth Briefings on the Crisis in Ukraine (2014); Researcher, Became a Friend, Smithsonian Institution (2012); Researcher, Laboratory of Internationalization, University of Wyoming, Laramie, WY (2012); Assistant Professor, Russian Language and Slavic Studies, Our Lady of Corpus Christi, Texas (2006-2007); Director, Summer Study Abroad Program in Croatia, University of Kansas,

Lawrence, KS (2002-2003); Teaching Assistant, Department of Slavic Language and Literature, University of Kansas, Lawrence, KS (1998-2003); Director, Study Abroad Program in Moscow, Russia, State University of New York, Albany (1992-1993); Graduate Assistant, State University of New York, Albany (1991-1993); Language Laboratory Assistant, University of Wyoming, Laramie, WY (1989-1991) **CR:** Participant, Readers Panel, Taking Surveys, National Geographic Magazine (2012-2016); Presenter in Field **CIV:** Volunteer Career Counselor, State University of New York (2012-2015) **CW:** Editor, English Translations of Russian Articles in Literary Criticism, University of Wyoming (2004-Present); Author, Presenter, Scholarly Paper, 20th Jubilee Conference of the Central Association of Russian Teachers in America, Pushkin State Russian Language Institute, Moscow, Russia (2018); Contributor, Slavic and East European Journal (2010); Contributor, Articles and Scholarly Papers, Professional Journals and Conferences; Contributor, Scholarly Papers, Numerous Conferences **AW:** Gold Medal, Central Association of Russian Teachers in America, Dallas, TX (2013) **MEM:** Annual Conference Member, American Association of Teachers of Slavic and East European Languages, San Francisco, CA (2008); Modern Language Association; Central Association of Russian Teachers in America; The Smithsonian Institution; Professional Association of Education; Pi Lambda Theta International Honor Society **ADD:** PO Box 2043, Laramie, WY, 82073

FEES, RUTH ANNA, **T:** Secondary School Educator **I:** Education/Educational Services **CN:** Kiowa County Plainview School **DOB:** 08/31/1952 **PB:** Sidney **SC:** NE/USA **PT:** Hugh Lawrence Fees; Verla Ellen Fees **ED:** MA, Colorado College (1980); BA, UNC (1972) **CT:** Certified Teacher, State of Colorado **C:** English Teacher, Kiowa County Plainview School, Sheridan Lake, CO; English Teacher, Holyoke Junior High School **CW:** Contributor, Articles, Professional Journals **MEM:** Colorado Education Association; National Education Association; UniServ Program, National Education Association; NCTE; Phi Lambda Theta; Kappa Delta Pi, International Honor Society in Education; The Phi Beta Kappa Society **MH:** Albert Nelson Marquis Lifetime Achievement Award (2017) **ADD:** 67170 Buffalo St, Sheridan Lake, CO, 81071

FEILD, JAMES RODNEY, **T:** Physician, Neurosurgeon **I:** Medicine & Health Care **DOB:** 03/12/1934 **PB:** Memphis **SC:** TN/USA **PT:** Roscoe A. Feild; Georgia (Bledsoe) Feild **MS:** Married **SPN:** Nancy Lee Tanner (2002) **CH:** Mary; Fred; Jamie; Alan; Glynn **ED:** Resident in Neurosurgery, Baptist Hospital, University of Tennessee, Memphis, TN (1960-1963); Private Practice, Albany, KY (1959); Intern, John Gaston Hospital, Memphis, TN (1958); MD, The University of Tennessee, Knoxville (1957); Coursework, Rhodes College (1952-1954) **CT:** American Board of Neurological Surgery **C:** Private Practice, Memphis, TN (1965-Present); Special Fellow in Neurology, Mayo Foundation for Medical Education and Research (MFMER), Rochester, MN (1964) **CW:** Author, "Unregulated Fees Drive the Use of CAM" (2005) **MEM:** Congress of Neurological Surgeons; International College of Surgeons; Fellow, American Association of Neurological Surgeons; Fellow, American College of Surgeons **MH:** Albert Nelson Marquis Lifetime Achievement Award (2017) **ADD:** 430 Whitehall Ct, Eads, TN, 38028 **URL:** https://www.doximity.com/pub/james-feild-md

FEINBERG, ROBERT S., **T:** Plastics Company Executive, Invention Development, Marketing Professional **I:** Manufacturing **CN:** LeMont Sales Company **DOB:** 05/14/1934 **PB:** Newark **SC:** NJ/USA **PT:** Clarence Jacob Feinberg; Sabina (Zorn) Feinberg **ED:** New York Institute of Advertising (1967); Diploma in Advertising, Association of Industrial Advertising (1967); MBA in Marketing, Fairleigh Dickinson University (1966); BA in English, BS in Chemistry, Trinity College, Hartford, CT (1955) **C:** Co-Chairman, Partner, Edgeroy Co., Inc., Ridgefield and Palisades Park, NJ (1973-Present); LeMont Sales Company, Teaneck, NJ (1973-Present); President, Trebor Associates and Trebor Plastics Company, Teaneck, NJ (1961-Present); Marketing Consultant, Computer Software, Zettler Software Company, Burroughs Corporation; Senior Council, Yankelovich, Skelly and White, Inc.; Consultant, Greenwich Associates; Consultant, Plastics Formulations W.R. Grace, Endicott Johnson, Brown Shoe Company, U.S. Shoe Co., Ciba, Uniroyal **CW:** Author, "Olympia Shoe Co. (Harvard Case Book Series)" **AW:** Bergen County Tennis League Hall of Honor (2009) **MEM:** U.S. Professional Tennis Association; Sell Overseas America; Sporting Goods Manufacturers Association; Senior Member, Society of Plastics Engineers; Vice President, Bergen County Tennis League; Vice President, Ahdeek Tennis Club **MH:** Albert Nelson Marquis Lifetime Achievement Award (2017) **BA:** PO Box 273, Teaneck, NJ, 07666-0273 **ADD:** PO Box 273, Teaneck, NJ, 07666

FELL, JAMES CARLTON, **T:** Principal Research Scientist **I:** Research **CN:** University of Chicago **CH:** Todd James; Brandon Paul; Donde Stephen **ED:** Master's Degree in Human Factors Engineering, State University of New York, Buffalo (1967); Bachelor's Degree in Human Factors Engineering, State University of New York, Buffalo **C:** Principal Research Scientist, National Opinion Research Center, University of Chicago, Bethesda, MD (2015-Present); Senior Research Scientist, Pacific Institute for Research & Evaluation, Calverton, MD (2001-2015); National Highway Traffic Safety Administration (1969-1999) **CW:** Contributor, Over 150 Publications in Book Chapters, Scientific Journals and Conference Proceedings **AW:** Donald F. Huelke Lifetime Membership Award, Association for the Advancement of Automotive Medicine (2016); James J. Howard Highway Safety Trailblazer Award, Governors Highway Safety Association (2015); Kevin Quinlan Advocacy Award, Maryland Highway Safety Office (2015); Erik Widmark Award, International Council on Alcohol, Drugs and Traffic Safety (2013); Ralph Hingson Research to Practice Award, MADD (2008); Distinguished Career Service Award, NHTSA (1999); Secretary of Transportations Silver Medal for Meritorious Achievement (1997) **BA:** 4350 E West Highway, NORC, University of Chicago, Bethesda, MD, 20814 **ADD:** 4313 Guinea Road, Annandale, VA, 22003

FELTER, JUNE, **T:** Artist **I:** Fine Art **DOB:** 10/19/1919 **PB:** Oakland **SC:** CA/USA **MS:** Married **SPN:** Richard Henry Felter (2/7/1943) **CH:** Susan; Tom **ED:** Coursework, San Francisco Art Institute (1960-1961); Coursework, Oakland Campus, California College of the Arts (1937-1940) **C:** Instructor, University of California, San Francisco (1984-1985); Instructor, Elaine Badgley-Arnoux School Art, San Francisco, CA (1982-1983); Instructor, Santa Rosa Junior College (1981); Instructor, University of California, San Francisco (1979-1980); Instructor, San Francisco Museum of Modern Art (1965-1978) **CW:** Painter, Permanent Collections, San Pablo Art Gallery, California (2013); Painter, Permanent Collections, 871 Fine Arts, San Francisco, CA (2013, 2009); Painter,

Permanent Collections, Grace Institute, New York (2011); Painter, Permanent Collections, de Young Museum, Fine Arts Museums of San Francisco (2008); Exhibitor, 10 Artists, George Krevsky Gallery, San Francisco, CA (2008); Exhibitor, June and Susan Felter 871 Fine Arts Gallery (2006); Exhibitor, Sanchez Art Center, Pacifica, CA (2006); Exhibitor, Kennedy Gallery (2001); Exhibitor, Holy Names University, Oakland, CA (2001); Exhibitor, 871 Fine Arts, San Francisco, CA (1999, 1992, 1990, 1987); Exhibitor, Dana Reich Gallery, San Francisco, CA (1980-1981, 1978); Exhibitor, Richmond Art Gallery (1971-1974); Exhibitor, Linda Ferris Gallery, Seattle, WA (1971); Exhibitor, Gumps Gallery, San Francisco, CA (1965-1966); Exhibitor, Permanent Collections, National Museum of Art, Washington D.C.; Exhibitor, Permanent Collections, Oakland Museum of California; Exhibitor, Permanent Collections, San Jose Museum of Art; Exhibitor, Permanent Collections, Achenbach Foundation for Graphic Arts, Fine Arts Museums of San Francisco; Exhibitor, Permanent Collections, Yale University Art Gallery, New Haven, CT **MH:** Albert Nelson Marquis Lifetime Achievement Award (2017) **ADD:** 6633 Mokelumne Ave, Oakland, CA, 94605

FERGUSON, JOHN PATRICK, **T:** Health Facility Administrator **I:** Health, Wellness and Fitness **DOB:** 01/22/1949 **PB:** Weehawken **SC:** NJ/USA **PT:** Donald George Ferguson; Margaret (Rienzo) Ferguson **MS:** Married **SPN:** Gene Marie Promersperger (1/16/1971) **CH:** Adam; David; Kate **ED:** Honorary LHD, Felician University (2005); MBA in Hospital Administration, The George Washington University (1973); BS in Economics, Saint Peter's University (1970) **C:** President, Hackensack University Medical Center (1986-2009); Chief Executive Officer, Hackensack University Medical Center (1986-2009); Acting President, Hackensack University Medical Center (1985-1986); Acting Chief Executive Officer, Hackensack University Medical Center (1985-1986); Senior Vice President, Hackensack University Medical Center (1985); Vice President, Operations, Hackensack University Medical Center (1981-1985); Senior Vice President, Vincent's Hospital Westchester (1972-1981); President, Blue Horizon Stem Cells; Chief Executive Officer, Blue Horizon Stem Cells; Chairman of the Board, Blue Horizon International LLC; Chief Executive Officer, Blue Horizon International LLC; President, Blue Horizon International LLC **CR:** Secretary, Board of Trustees, University of Medicine and Dentistry of New Jersey (2003-2005); Trustee, University of Medicine and Dentistry of New Jersey (2002-2005); Vice Chairman, University Health Systems (Now New Jersey Council of Teaching Hospitals), Trenton, NJ (2002-2003); Chairman, Board of Trustees, University Health Systems (Now New Jersey Council of Teaching Hospitals), Trenton, NJ (1999-2001); Adjunct Faculty, Graduate School for Management and Urban Professions, The New School, New York City, NY (1978-1984); President, Metropolitan Health Administrators, New York City, NY (1977-1978) **CIV:** Member, Diplomatic Council, United Nations (2015-Present); Board Member, Martha's Vineyard Community Services (2011-Present); Trustee, Molly Foundation for Diabetes Research (1995-Present); Chairman, Board, Martha's Vineyard Hospital (2000-2010); Member, Board of Governors, Greater New York Hospital Association (2000-2009); Chairman, Board of Directors, Martha's Vineyard Hospital (2002-2009); Trustee, Garden State Arts Foundation (2004-2007); Founding Commissioner, Economic Development Corporation, Bergen County (1996-2007); Trustee, St. Peter's College (2000-2006); Member, Jobs Growth and Economic Development Commission, State of New Jersey (2002); Commissioner,

Economic Development Commission, City of Hackensack (1996-2002); Co-Chairman, Health Transition Team, Governor-Elect Jim McGreevey (2001); Member, Executive Advisory Committee, Commission on Cancer Research, State of New Jersey (2000) **AW:** Leadership Award, New England Healthcare Assembly (2008); Named, One of 400 People Who Make a Difference, Cape Cod Life Publications (2007); Achievement Award, Modern Healthcare Magazine, Crain Communications, Inc. (2007); County of Bergen Significant Contributor Honor, Bergen Catholic (2006); Honoree, 100 Most Powerful People in Healthcare in the US, Modern Healthcare Magazine, Crain Communications, Inc. (2004-2006); Honoree, New Jersey 50 Most Influential Players in Political Healthcare Arena, Healthsense (2005); Regents Recognition Award, American College of Healthcare Executives (2004); Distinguished Alumni Award, School for Health Science Management and Policy, The George Washington University (2004); Humanitarian Award, NCCJ (2003); Distinguished Alumni Award for Professional Achievement, Saint Peter's University (2002); Named to Hall of Fame, Foundation for Free Enterprise (2002); Ellis Island Medal of Honor (2002); Good Scout Award, Northern New Jersey Council, Boy Scouts of America (2000); Medical Executive Award, Academy of Medicine of New Jersey (2000); President's Award, New Jersey State Nurses Association (1999); Named, Humanitarian of the Year, Boys' Towns of Italy (1999); Honoree, Distinguished Citizen of New Jersey, Ramapo College of New Jersey (1998); Distinction Award, Metropolitan Health Administration Association (1997); Chairman's Award for Outstanding Leadership, Commerce and Industry Association of New Jersey (1997); Distinguished Community Health Service Award, Board Of Chosen Freeholders, Bergen County (1996); Honoree, Humanitarian of the Year, Make-A-Wish Foundation of America (1996); Distinguished Citizen Award, The Hackensack Regional Chamber of Commerce (1995); Distinguished Community Service Award, Anti-Defamation League (1995); Man of the Year, Burn Foundation (1994); Honoree, Citizen of Year, Meadowlands Regional Chamber (1993); Medallion Award, Bergen Community College (1993); Honoree, One of 50 Business People to Watch for the 1990's, New Jersey Business Journal, BridgeTower Media (1990); Man of the Year Award, Tomorrows Children's Fund (1989); Honoree, One of the Top 12 Up and Coming Healthcare Executives, Modern Healthcare Magazine, Crain Communications, Inc. (1988) **MEM:** Commerce and Industry Association of New Jersey (1996-Present); Board of Directors, American Federation for Aging Research (1997-2000); Governor, District II, American College of Healthcare Executives (1994-1999); Member, Board of Directors, American Heart Association, Inc. (1993-1994); President, Mid-Bergen Division, American Heart Association, Inc. (1992-1993); Life Fellow, American College of Healthcare Executives; Regent, American College of Healthcare Executives; The Catholic Health Association of the United States; American Hospital Association; Metropolitan Health Administration Association **MH:** Albert Nelson Marquis Lifetime Achievement Award (2017) **BA:** 116 E 66th St Apt 9/10D, Apt 10, New York, NY, 10065 **ADD:** 255 Pond Road, Vineyard Haven, MA, 02568

FERGUSON, LLOYD "BUDDY", T: Partner **I:** Law and Legal Services **CN:** Strasburger & Price, LLP **C:** Partner, Strasburger & Price, LLP (1985-Present) **CIV:** Foundation Board, Children at Heart Ministries, Inc., Round Rock, TX **AW:** Honoree, Five Best Lawyers, Best Lawyers in America, U.S. News & World Report L.P. (2009-2018); Legal Eagle

Award, Franchise Times (2005) **BA:** 720 Brazos Street, Suite 700, Austin, TX, 78701 **ADD:** 15025 Sendero Lane, Waco, TX, 76712

FERGUSON, LEWIS, T: Lawyer **I:** Law and Legal Services **CN:** Public Company Accounting Oversight Board **DOB:** 10/22/1944 **PB:** Abilene **SC:** TX/USA **MS:** Married **SPN:** Molly M. Matthews (October 1, 2003) **ED:** MA, King's College (1972); JD, Harvard University (1971); BA, King's College (1968); BA, Yale University (1966) **CT:** Admitted to Practice, United States Tax Court (1972); Admitted to Practice, United States Court of Federal Claims (1972); Admitted to Practice, District of Columbia (1972); Admitted to Practice, State of Massachusetts (1971) **C:** Board Member, Public Company Accounting Oversight Board (2011-Present); Chairman, International Forum of Independent Audit Regulators (2013-2015); Partner, Gibson, Dunn & Crutcher LLP (2007-2010); General Counsel Public Company Accounting Oversight Board (2004-2007); Partner, Williams & Connolly LLP (1998-2004); Senior Vice President, Wright Medical Group N.V. (1994-1997); General Counsel, Wright Medical Group N.V. (1994-1997); Partner, Williams & Connolly LLP (1979-1993); Associate, Williams & Connolly LLP (1975-1979); Associate, Covington & Burling LLP (1972-1975); Law Clerk to Honorable Frank Murray, United States District Court District of Massachusetts (1971-1972) **CIV:** Treasurer, Board of Directors, Cambridge in America (1975-1988) **MEM:** Chairman, Independent Forum of Independent Audit Regulators (2013-Present); Vice-Chairman, Independent Forum of Independent Audit Regulators (2012-2013) **MH:** Albert Nelson Marquis Lifetime Achievement Award (2017) **ADD:** 6911 Radnor Road, Bethesda, MD, 20817

FERNANDEZ GONZALEZ, RICARDO, T: Pulmonary and Critical Care Physician **I:** Medicine & Health Care **CN:** San Juan City Hospital **PB:** San Juan **SC:** Puerto Rico **PT:** Ricardo; Celia **MS:** Married **SPN:** Sandra **CH:** Alejandra **ED:** Fellowship, American College of Physicians (2014); Fellowship, American College of Chest Physicians, FCCP (2009); Fellowship, Pulmonary and Critical Care Medicine, Pulmonary and CCM Section, San Juan VA Medical Center, San Juan, PR (2004-2007); Internal Medicine Residency, Medicine Service, San Juan VA Medical Center, San Juan, PR (2001-2004); Internship, Hospital Auxilio Mutuo, San Juan, PR (2000-2001); Bachelor's Degree, School of Medicine, Universidad Autonoma de Guadalajara, Jalisco, MX (2000); Pre-Internship, Hospital Regional de Aguadilla, Aguadilla, PR (1999-2000); Bachelor's Degree, University of Puerto Rico, Rio Piedras Campus, Cum Laude (1996) **CT:** Re-certified, American Board of Critical Care Medicine (2017); Re-certified, American Board of Pulmonary Diseases (2016); Certificate of Training, Bronchial Thermoplasty, Boston Scientific Company (2012); American Board of Critical Care Medicine (2007); American Board of Pulmonary Diseases (2006); American Board of Internal Medicine (2004); Step III, United States Medical License Examination (2003); Educational Commission of Foreign Medical Graduates (2003); Certified Course, Total Parenteral Nutrition, Puerto Rico (2002); Clinical Skills Assessment Examination, Philadelphia, PA (2001); Step II, United States Medical License Examination (2001); Parte III, Oral Examination, Reválida de Puerto Rico (2001); Step I, United States Medical License Examination (2000); Parte II, Clinic Skills, Reválida de Puerto Rico (2000); Parte I, Clinic Skills, Reválida de Puerto Rico (1998); Certified Course, Advanced Cardiac Life Support; Certified Course, Cardio-Respiratory Resuscitation; Medical License, Puerto Rico **C:**

Director, Pulmonary Division, Hospital Auxilio Mutuo (2013-Present); Assistant Professor, Internal Medicine and Pulmonary/Critical Care, San Juan Bautista School of Medicine (2012-Present); Adjunct Professor, Clinical Medicine, College of Medicine, American University of Antigua (2012-Present); Principal Investigator, Pulmonary/Critical Care Research Studies, Fundacion de Investigacion (2012-Present); Program Director, Pulmonary Fellowship, San Juan City Hospital, San Juan, PR (2012-Present); Faculty Physician, Pulmonary/ Critical Care Division, Hospital Auxilio Mutuo (2007-Present); Faculty Physician, Pulmonary/ Critical Care Division, San Juan City Hospital, San Juan, PR (2007-Present); Instructor, Intensive Care Unit Rotation, University of Pittsburgh Medical Center, Pittsburgh, PA (2007) **CW:** Co-Author, "An aggressive non small cell lung cancer in nonsmokers:a case report of an unusual presentation of a micropapillary lung adenocarcinoma," Respiratory Medicine Case Reports (2017); Co-Author, "A Rare but Malignant Cardiac Mass," Journal of Medical Cases (2016); Co-Author, "New Strain Multidrug Resistance Tuberculosis G24767 in Puerto Rico:Old disease a continuous Threat," Respiratory Medicine Case Reports (2016); Co-Author, "Diabetes Mellitus: An Important Risk Factor for Re Activation of Pulmonary Tuberculosis," Endocrinology, Diabetes and Metabolism Case Reports (2016); Co-Author, "Histoplasmosis capsulatum: A rare presentation in an immunocompromised host," ACP Hospitalist (2014); Co-Author, "Idiopathic Hypereosinophilic Syndrome," ACP Hospitalist (2014); Co-Author, "A Case of diffuse alveolar hemorrhage associated with hyaluronic acid dermal fillers," American Journal of Case Reports (2014); Co-Author, "The Effectiveness of the Polysaccharide Pneumococcal Vaccine for the Prevention of Hospitalizations Due to Streptococcus pneumoniae Pneumonia in the Elderly Differs Between the Sexes: Results From The Community-Acquired Pneumonia Organization (CAPO) International Cohort Study," Vaccine (2014); Co-Author, "An Unexpected Side Effect of a Commonly Used Drug," Boletin Asociacion Medica de Puerto Rico (2013); Co-Author, "Pulmonary Lymphangioleyomiomatosis: Literature Update," Boletin Asociacion Medica de Puerto Rico (2013); Co-Author, "Puerto Rico's Intensive Care Units: An Overview of Critical Care Medicine," Puerto Rico Health Science Journal (2013); Co-Author, "A very rare and aggressive lung tumor," International Journal of Medicine and Medical Services (2013); Co-Author, "Tracheobronchopatia osteochondroplastica: An underdiagnosed central airway disease," International Journal of Medicine and Medical Services (2012); Co-Author, "Pleural effusion as the initial extramedullary manifestation of Acute Myeloid Leukemia," F1000Research (2012); Co-Author, "A hematologic condition expressed as a lung disease," F1000Research (2012); Co-Author, "Secondary Biliary Cirrhosis due to a rare Choledocal Cyst Type II complicated with portal hypertension and pancytopenia in a young female patient," Boletin Asociacion Medica de Puerto Rico (2012); Co-Author, "Immunocompromised Patients: What a Challenge!" Boletin Asociacion Medica De Puerto Rico (2012); Co-Author, "uncommon hematologic disorder in an adult Puerto Rican patient," Critical Care and Shock (2012); Editor, "Severe Sepsis and Septic Shock: Understanding a Serious Killer," University of Dubrovnik School of Medicine, Intech Publishing Company, Croatia (2012); Co-Author, "Progressive dyspnea and a persistent wheeze: a subtle presentation of pulmonary embolism in a 64 year old woman," European Journal of General Medicine (2011); Co-Author, "An unusual case of dyspnea," Critical Care and Shock (2010); Co-Author, "An unusual presentation of idiopathic LIP in an immunocompetent 52 y/o patient," Clinical Respiratory Journal (2009); Co-Author, "An unusual presentation of alveolar hemorrhage," Primary Care Respiratory Journal (2009); Co-Author, "Compliance of Guidelines for Intensive Care Unit Admissions in San Juan City Hospital in a Three Months Period," Critical Care and Shock (2009); Co-Author, "Ventilator associated pneumonia:incidence,etiology and quality improvement," Critical Care and Shock (2009); Co-Author, "An Uncommon cause of Uncontrolled Asthma: Case report," Journal of Asthma (2008); Co-Author, "Benefits and Risks of Tight Glucose Control in Critically Ill Adults," JAMA (2008); Co-Author, "A study of Physician's Knowledge about the Surviving Sepsis Campaign in Puerto Rico," Critical Care and Shock (2007); Co-Author, "Abdominal Compartment Syndrome: case report," Critical Care and Shock (2007); Co-Author, "Early Diagnosis of Hyperinfection Syndrome in an Immunocompromised Patient: case report," Chest (2007); Author, "Sepsis: A study of physician's Knowledge in Puerto Rico," Critical Care (2006); Author, "Sepsis: A study of physician's knowledge in San Juan Veteran's Hospital," Critical Care Medicine (2005) **AW:** First Place, Poster Presentation, "Encephalopathy and Kidney Injury as Unexpected Complication of Recreational Drug Use: A Case Series," Clinical Vignettes and Research Competition, American College of Physicians, Intercontinental Hotel (2016); Second Place, Poster Presentation, "Aspergillus terreus: A New Threat for an Immunocompetent Patient?" American College of Physicians, Hotel La Concha (2015); First Place, Oral Presentation, "New Strain of MDR Tuberculosis G24767: Old Disease a Continuous Threat," Clinical Vignettes and Research Competition, American College of Physicians, Hotel San Juan (2014); Second Place, Poster Presentation, "A Case of Diffuse Alveolar Hemorrhage Associated with Hyaluronic Acid Dermal Filler," American College of Physicians, Hotel La Concha (2013); Third Place, Poster Presentation, "An Idiopathic Condition in a Healthy Young Man," American College of Physicians, Hotel La Concha (2013); Second Place, Poster Presentation, "Immunocompromised Patients: What a Challenge!" American College of Physicians, Embassy Suites, Dorado, PR (2010); Third Place, Resident's Research Presentation Award, "Insulin: Effect in mortality and renal failure in critically ill patients," Veteran's Hospital, San Juan, PR (2004); Fellow of the Year, Veteran's Hospital, San Juan, PR (2004-2007); Resident of the Year, Veteran's Hospital, San Juan, PR (2002-2004) **MEM:** Chairman, Scientific Committee, Puertorrican Chapter, American College of Physicians (2014-Present); Puertorrican Society of Pulmonologists (2007-Present); American College of Chest Physicians (2004-Present); American Thoracic Society (2004-Present); Society of Critical Care Medicine (2004-Present); Puertorrican Society of Critical Care Medicine (2004-Present); American College of Physicians (2003-Present); North American Student Association (1996-2000) **H:** Sports; Reading; Watching movies; Travel; Going to museums; History **RE:** Catholic **BA:** 100 Grand Paseo Blvd Ste 106, Galeria Paseos, San Juan, PR, 00926 **ADD:** 1 Calle Costa Azul, Paseo Las Brisas, San Juan, PR, 00926

FERNANDEZ, PATRICK H., I: Law and Legal Services **DOB:** 08/14/1948 **PB:** Baltimore **SC:** MD/USA **MS:** Married **SPN:** Glenda Harris **ED:** Postgraduate Coursework, Survey of Forensic Science, The George Washington University (1973); BS in Biology, Morgan State University (1971) **CT:** Certified Crime Scene Investigation Expert; Diplomate, Various Courses in Crime Scene Investigation Field **C:** Crime Lab Technician Supervisor, Mobile Unit, Baltimore Police Department (1980-2011); Crime Laboratory Technician, Mobile Unit, Baltimore Police Department (1971-1979); Substitute Teacher, Baltimore City Public Schools (1971) **AW:** Certificate for Service, Baltimore Police Department (2011); Special Service Commendation With Ribbon (1999, 2008); Two Letters of Commendation, Mobile Unit, Baltimore Police Department; Unit Citation With Ribbon **MEM:** Vanguard Justice Society, INC.; Lifetime Member, Morgan State University Alumni Association; Lifetime Member Baltimore City College High School Alumni Association; Lifetime Member, NAACP **MH:** Albert Nelson Marquis Lifetime Achievement Award (2017) **H:** Gardening; Wine and gourmet food; NFL football and music, doo wop especially **PA:** Independant **RE:** Christian **ADD:** 1937 Eutaw Pl, Baltimore, MD, 21217

FERRELL, RICHARD B., T: Psychiatrist **I:** Medicine & Health Care **CN:** Dartmouth College **DOB:** 08/13/1943 **PB:** South Bend **SC:** IN/USA **PT:** Rupert Tyler Ferrell; Beatrice Bradley Ferrell **MS:** Married **SPN:** Melanie A. Ferrell **CH:** Catherine Lynn; Elisabeth Jane Ferrell Horan; Anne Christine **ED:** MD, Indiana University (1969); AB, DePauw University (1965) **CT:** Diplomate in Behavioral Neurology and Neuropsychiatry, United Council for Neurologic Subspecialties (2006); Certified, Geriatric Psychiatric, American Board of Psychiatry and Neurology, Inc. (2001); Diplomate, American Board of Psychiatry and Neurology, Inc. (1975) **C:** Associate Professor, Psychiatry, Geisel School of Medicine, Dartmouth College, Hanover, NH (1981-Present); Assistant Professor, Psychiatry, Geisel School of Medicine, Dartmouth College, Hanover, NH (1975-1981) **CIV:** Girls Basketball Coach, Hanover Recreation Department, Hanover, NH (1982-2009); Board Member, Opera North, Lebanon, NH (1991-1997) **CW:** Contributor, Articles, Professional Journals **AW:** Honoree, Named Best Doctor **MEM:** Electrical Councilor, American Neuropsychiatric Association (2012); Electrical Fellow, American Neuropsychiatric Association (2010); Alpha Omega Alpha Honor Medical Society (1969); American Neuropsychiatric Association; Distinguished Life Fellow, American Psychiatric Association **MH:** Albert Nelson Marquis Lifetime Achievement Award (2017) **H:** Reading; Travel; Music; Opera singing **ADD:** 86 McKenna Rd, Norwich, VT, 05055

FETZER, RONALD C., T: Adjunct Faculty **I:** Education/Educational Services **CN:** Miami University **DOB:** 06/21/1943 **PB:** Tiffin **SC:** OH/USA **PT:** Charles Henry Fetzer; Marge (Beeler) Fetzer **MS:** Married **SPN:** Married Janice Marie Wilkenson (12/20/1962) **CH:** Rhonda Lynn; Charles Lee **ED:** PhD in Organizational Communication and Education and Employee Training & Development, The Ohio State University (1978); MA in Organizational Communication, Kent State University (1972); BA in Communication, English, & Latin Education, Heidelberg College (1966) **C:** Adjunct Faculty, Middletown Campus, Miami University; Visiting Professor, Department of Communication, Miami University (2002-Present); Owner, President, Fetzer Enterprises Inc. (1994-2006); Member, Adjunct Faculty Business College, Nova University, Fort Lauderdale, FL (1988-2005); National Doctorate Faculty, Nova Southeastern University (1988-2005); Owner, President, Fetzer Consulting & Training, Inc., Yellow Springs, OH (1981-1994); Member, Communications Faculty, Wright State University, Dayton, OH (1979-1994); Communications Faculty, University of Wisconsin, Superior, WI (1978); Adjunct Faculty, Miami University, Oxford, OH (1970-1975); Teacher, English, Latin, Speech, Middletown High School, Ohio (1967-1976); Teacher, English, Latin, Speech, New Riegel High School (1965-1966); Adjunct Communication Faculty, Miami University **CW:** Contributor, American Society for Training and Development Infoline Series (1987); Co-author,"Business Communication Practices and Principles" (1984); Author, "Designing Messages: A Guide for Creative Speakers" (1981); Co-author, "Business Communication: Careers" (1980); Contributor, Chapters, Books; Contributor, Articles, Numerous Professional Research Journals **AW:** Business Exchange Grant, China (2007, 2000, 1994, 1991); Research Exchange Grant (1989-1990); Contribution of Year Award, American Society for Training & Development (1989); Profession of Year Award, American Society for Training & Development (1987); National Excellence Award, American Society for Training & Development (1986-1987); Innovator of Year Award, American Society for Training & Development (1983) **MEM:** Officer, Speech Communication Association (1970-Present); National Task Force, American Society for Training & Development (1987-1991); Regional Leader of Ohio, West Virginia, New York, American Society for Training & Development (1986-1991); National Task Force, Speech Communication Association (1981-1989); President, Vice President, Board of Directors, Dayton Chapter, American Society for Training & Development (1980-1988); Society for Human Resource Management; National Conference Institute **MH:** Albert Nelson Marquis Lifetime Achievement Award (2017) **H:** Photography; Travel; Farming **ADD:** 7985 Preble County Line Rd, Germantown, OH, 45327

FIELD, REBECCA A., T: Psychologist, Educator **I:** Education/Educational Services **DOB:** 12/18/1934 **PB:** Denver **SC:** CO/USA **PT:** Herbert P. White Field; Marjorie (Sharp) Field **MS:** Widow **SPN:** Kenneth Gordon Field (9/5/1959) **CH:** David B.; Robert W. **ED:** PhD in Psychology and Eastern Philosophy, California Institute of Integral Studies (1990); PhD in Integral Psychology and Asian Philosophy, California Institute of Integral Studies (1981); MA, California Institute of Integral Studies (1977); BA, Northern Colorado State University (1957) **C:** Psychological Counselor, Los Gatos, CA (1981-1985); Senior Citizens Coordinator, West Valley College, Saratoga, CA (1977-1978); Teacher, Markham Illinois Public Schools (1959-1965); Teacher, Anchorage Public Schools (1957-1958); Camp Counselor, Flint, MI (1956); Camp Counselor, Girl Scouts of the United States of America, Colorado Springs, CO (1955); Consultant, Lecturer in Field **CR:** Active Member, Child Advocacy Council; Member, Speakers Bureau, Lupus Foundation of America, Inc.; Chairman of the Board, CONTACT Santa Clara County **CIV:** Symposium Facilitator, "Awaken the Dreamer"; Attendee, United Nations Summit on Social Development, Copenhagen. Denmark; Participant, United Nations Meetings, San Jose, CA; Participant, United Nations Meeting, Costa Rica; Participant, United Nations Meeting, New York, NY **CW:** Author, "Greatness 21 Compelling Stories That Moves The Heart"; Contributor, Articles, Professional Journals; Author, "To Choose the Fire of the Cosmos"; Co-author, "Unwavering Strength"; Co-author "The Great Invocation:A Hand Book" **AW:** Two Time New York Times Best-Selling Co-author **MEM:** San Jose Chamber of Commerce; American Society for Training and Development; American Futurist Association; The Association for Transpersonal Psychology;

President, Toastmasters; Alpha Psi Omega **MH:** Albert Nelson Marquis Lifetime Achievement Award (2017) **H:** Traveling; Workshops; Writing **PA:** Kern Foundation Grantee (1979-1981); Prize, Sri Aurobindo Centennial Essay Contest (1973); Area Governor of the Year Award, Toastmasters **ADD:** 110 Wood Road   D207, same, Los Gatos, CA, CA, 95030-6732 **URL:** http://www.rebeccaafield.com

FIERHELLER, GEORGE A., **T:** President **I:** Business Management/Business Services **CN:** Four Halls Inc. **DOB:** 04/26/1933 **PB:** Toronto **SC:** ON/Canada **PT:** Harold Parsons Fierheller; Ruth Hathaway (Bauld) Fierheller **MS:** Married **SPN:** Glenna E. Fletcher (4/17/1957) **CH:** Vicki Elaine; Lori Ann **ED:** DLitt, Trinity College, University of Toronto; LLD, Concordia University; BA, University of Toronto (1955) **C:** President, Four Halls Inc. (1997-Present); Vice Chair, Rogers Communications, Inc. (1993-1996); Chairman, Chief Executive Officer, Rogers Cantel Mobile, Inc. (1990-1993); President, Chief Executive Officer, Cantel Inc. (1985-1990); President, Chief Executive Officer, Premier Cable Systems (1979-1985); Founder, President, Systems Dimensions Ltd., Ottawa (1968-1979); Marketing Manager, IBM (1966-1968); Account Manager, IBM (1962-1965); With, IBM (1955-1958) **CR:** President, Board of Trade of Metropolitan Toronto (1996-1997); Board of Directors, Canadian Institute of Advanced Research **CIV:** Board Member, SOS Children's Villages Canada (2008-Present); Canadian Center for Advanced Research (2001-Present); Chair, Sunnybrook Health Sciences Center Campaign (1999-Present); Chair, Trinity College Campaign (1996-1999); Chair, United Way of Metropolitan Toronto (1994-1996); McMichael Canada Art Collection (1993-1999); Trustee, Sunnybrook Hospital Foundation (1993-1999); Chairman, General Campaign (1991); Vision 2000 (1990-1991); Member, Vancouver Centennial Commission (1983-1984); Vancouver General Hospital Foundation (1981-1985); Board of Governors, Simon Fraser University (1981-1984); Chairman, United Way Vancouver (1981); British Columbia Council of 80s (1980-1983); Trustee, Royal Ottawa Hospital (1978-1979); Chairman, Board of Governors (1977-1979); Board of Directors, Vice President, United Way Ottawa (1975-1979); Chairman, Campaign Carleton University (1975-1977); Trustee, Executive Committee, National Arts Center (1973-1979); General Chairman, United Appeal Campaign (1972); Opera Ottawa (1970-1971); Member, Advisory Committee, Norman Paterson School of International Affairs **CW:** Author, "Finnie's Family, Let Me Say This About That"; Contributor, Articles, Professional Journals **AW:** Queen's Diamond Jubilee Medal (2012); Computer World Lifetime Achievement Award (2011); Volunteer of the Year Award, Family Service Association (2008); Order of Constantine (2005); Queen's Golden Jubilee Medal (2002); Decorated Member, Order of Canada (2002); Salute to City Award, Toronto, Canada (2002); Outstanding Volunteer of the Year, Association of Fundraising Professionals (2001); Canadian Information Technology Hall of Fame (1998); Award, United Way of Canada (1998); Award of Excellence, Canada Wireless Industry Association (1996); Recipient, Award of Merit, City of Toronto (1991); Sigma Chi Hall of Fame **MEM:** 1812 Bicentennial Committee (2010-2012); Chairman, Toronto Adventurers Club (2003-2004); President, National Club (1998-1999); Chairman, Greater Toronto Marketing Alliance (1997-2003); Chairman, 1812 Bicentennial Committee, Smart Toronto (1996); Board of Directors, Canadian Center for Philanthropy (1987-1991); Board of Directors, Cellular Telecommunications Industry Association (1986-1994); President, Canadian

Information Processing Society (1970-1971); World President Organization; Chief Executives Organization; Canadian Association of Data Processing Service Organizations; Founding Committee, Canadian Information Processing Society; Honorary Director, Business Council on National Issues, Council for Business and the Arts in Canada; Toronto Club; York Club; Granite Club; Rosedale Golf Club; Arts & Letters Club **MH:** Albert Nelson Marquis Lifetime Achievement Award (2017); Distinguished Humanitarian (2017) **ADD:** 24 Pearwood Crescent, Toronto, ON, Canada, M3B 2C2

FILIPP-BESEDA, CAROLYN FRANCINE, **T:** Public School Educator, Private Music Teacher, Insurance Agent, Entertainer **I:** Education/ Educational Services **DOB:** 10/11/1950 **PB:** Houston **SC:** TX/USA **PT:** Emil Frank Filipp; Augustina Joyce (Klozik) Filipp **MS:** Widowed **SPN:** Rev. Henry Earnest Beseda (12/24/2005, Deceased) **ED:** Postgraduate Coursework, Houston Baptist University (1979-1980); Postgraduate Coursework, Houston Community College (1979-1980); MEd, Stephen F. Austin State University (1977); MusB, University of Houston (1973); Postgraduate Coursework, University of Houston **CT:** Certified Fraternal Insurance Counselor; Certified Music Educator (Pre-K Through 12); Professional Supervisor; Licensed General Lines Agent; Licensed Limited Lines Agent **C:** Piano and Woodwind Instructor, St. Mark Lutheran School Music Conservatory (2016-Present); Choral Director, Czech Chorus, SPJST (2015-Present); Lead Alto Saxophonist, Jazz Medics (2013-Present); Freelance Entertainer (2013-Present); Clarinetist, Jazz Medics (2013-Present); Vocalist, Jazz Medics (2013-Present); Performer, Slavic Heritage (2011-Present); Pianist, Westheimer Community Church (2003-Present); Assistant Band Director, SPJST (2000-Present); Pianist-Saxophonist, SPJST (2000-Present); Accompanist, SPJST (1990-Present); Insurance Agent, SPJST (1986-Present); Retired from Teaching (2013); Retired, RVOS Insruance (2010); Choral Director, Aldine Independent School District (1995-2013); Pianist, Cy-Fair Community Church (1989-2013); Band Director, Houston Independent School District (1985-1986); Clarinetist, Kovanda Orchestra (1984-1994); Chorister, Houston Symphony Chorale (1984-1986); Agent, RVOS Insurance (1982-2010); Saxophonist, Drabek Band (1980-1984); Lead Clarinetist, Drabek Band (1980-1984); Chorale Director, Houston Independent School District (1977-1995); Insurance Agent, Western Fraternal Life, Ltd., Cedar Rapids, IA (1977-1986); Band Director, Fort Bend ISD, Stafford, TX (1974-1977); Assistant Choral Director, Houston Brethren Church (1971-1973); Clerk/Typist, Dunn & Bradstreet (1968); Counter Saleswoman, North Main Theater (1967); Clarinetist, Space-City Dutchmen Orchestra (1965-1975); Saxophonist, Space-City Dutchmen Orchestra (1965-1975); Vocalist, Space-City Dutchmen Orchestra (1965-1975); Piano Teacher, Private Practice (1965-1975); Pianist, Houston Brethren Church (1965-1974); Clarinetist, SPJST (1964-1968); Clarinetist, Lad Pavelka Orchestra (1962-1965); Private Music Teacher, Houston, TX **CR:** Clarinetist, International Conventions, Alpha Delta Kappa; Past Pianist, Texas State Convention, Alpha Delta Kappa **CIV:** Trustee, Hus School (2016-Present); President, Christian Sisters Society of Westheimer Community Church (2017); President, Christian Sisters of Cy-Fair Community Church (2004-2013); Treasurer, Christian Sisters Society, Houston Brethren Church (1991-1994); Secretary, Board of Trustees, Hus School (1991-1994); Entertainer, Seven Acres Jewish Senior Care Services;

Entertainer, SPJST; Entertainer, Hermann Sons Life **CW:** Author, Curriculum Guide for General Music Eight; Author, "Unit for Sight-Singing Success"; Author, Various Music Teaching Unites; Composer, "Lend a Helping Hand"; Composer, "You, Lord, Are Merciful"; Composer, "A Tribute to Mother & Vigilance" **AW:** Service Award of Three Years of Service, Board of Trustees, Lodge 88, SPJST (2017); Service Award of Three Years of Service, Board of Trustees, Lodge 88, SPJST (2015); Service Award of Three Years of Service, Board of Trustees, Lodge 88, SPJST (2012); Outstanding Music Educator Award, American Classic Festivals (1999); Outstanding Student Band Conductor Award (1968); Music Scholarship, University of Houston (1968); Music Scholarship, Houston Baptist University (1968); Music Scholarship, Sam Houston State University (1968); Outstanding Assistant Drum Major Award (1967); Dance Scholarship, Mildred's School of Dance (1965); Numerous Superior I Medals for Performances on Clarinet & Piano (1964-1967); Bowling Trophy, Hermann Sons Bowling League; Dancing Trophies for Tap, Ballet & Jazz (1954-1966); Trophy, Baby Queen of Houston (1952); Perfect Attendance Awards, Houston Independent School District; Insurance and Performance Awards, SPJST; Service Award for Twelve Years of Service, SPJST; Service Award for Two Years of Service, Lodge 88, SPJST **MEM:** Assistant Chorus Director, Concert-Band, SPJST (2016-Present); Chorus Director, Lodge 88, SPJST (2015-Present); Chaplin, Lodge 88, SJST (2014-Present); Corresponding Secretary, Houston Tuesday Musical Club (2014-Present); Sapphire Sister, Alpha Delta Kappa (1980-Present); Hermann Sons Life (1980-Present); Houston Liederkranz (1973-Present); Texas Music Educators Association (1973-Present); Board of Trustees, SPJST (2017); Board of Trustees, SPJST (2015); Second Vice President, Lodge 88, SPJST (2006); First Vice President, Lodge 88, SPJST (2004-2005); Board of Trustees, SPJST (2004); Executive Vice President, Congress of Houston Teachers (1982-1984); Recording Secretary, Congress of Houston Teachers (1980-1982); Secretary, Lodge 289, WFLA (1977-1981); Secretary-Treasurer, Gamma Sigma Sigma (1971-1973); President, District V, Lodge 88, SPJST; Vice President, District V, SPJST; College Women's Club; Texas Band Masters' Association; American Choral Directors' Association; Past Secretary, Omicron Chapter, Alpha Delta Kappa; Past Chaplin, Omicron Chapter, Alpha Delta Kappa; Tau Beta Sigma National Band Fraternity; Alumni Association, University of Houston; Alumni Association, Stephen F. Austin State University; Tau Beta Sigma National Band Fraternity; Czech Center Museum of Houston; Czech Heritage Society **MH:** Albert Nelson Marquis Lifetime Achievement Award (2017) **H:** Travel; Reading; Golf; Bowling; Swimming **PA:** Republican **ADD:** 2515 Lazybrook Dr, Houston, TX, 77008

FILLIT, HOWARD MARTIN, **T:** Geriatrician **I:** Medicine & Health Care **CN:** Alzheimer's Drug Discovery Foundation **DOB:** 12/22/1948 **PB:** Bronx **SC:** NY/USA **ED:** Resident in Internal Medicine, Mount Sinai Beth Israel, Icahn School of Medicine at Mount Sinai, New York, NY (1974-1976); MD, SUNY Upstate Medical University (1974); BA, Cornell University, Cum Laude (1970) **CT:** Diplomate in Geriatrics, American Board of Internal Medicine; Diplomate in Laboratory Medical Immunology, American Board of Internal Medicine **C:** Founding Executive Director, Alzheimer's Drug Discovery Foundation (2004-Present); Chief Science Officer, Alzheimer's Drug Discovery Foundation (2004-Present); Founding Executive Director, Institute for Study of Aging (1998-Present); Professor of Geriatrics

Medicine and Neuroscience, Mount Sinai Medical Center (Now Icahn School of Medicine at Mount Sinai) (1992-Present); Corporate Medical Director for Medicare, New York Life Health Plans, New York (1995-1998); Associate Professor of Geriatrics, Mount Sinai Medical Center (Now Icahn School of Medicine at Mount Sinai) (1987-1992); Assistant Professor of Geriatrics and Immunology, Rockefeller University (1987-1989); Assistant Professor of Geriatrics and Immunology, Weill Cornell Medicine (1987-1989); Assistant Professor of Geriatrics, Stony Brook University (1980-1981); Fellow in Nephrology, Weill Cornell Medicine (1979-1980); Fellow in Immunology, Rockefeller University (1976-1979) **CR:** Executive Director, Foundation Ventures, LLC (2009); Advisory Board, Hadasit Medical Research Services and Development Inc.; Advisory Board, New York City Investment Fund Manager, Inc.; Scientific Advisory Board, Allon Therapeutics, Inc.; Advisory Board, Foundation Ventures, LLC; Scientific Advisory Board, Ablant Inc.; Fellow, American Geriatrics Society; Fellow, American College of Physicians; Fellow, Gerontological Society of America; Fellow, The New York Academy of Medicine **CW:** Editor, "Textbook of Geriatrics and Gerontology" (1992); Contributor, 300 Articles, Science Publications; Patentee in Field of Immunodiagnostics **AW:** Grantee in Field; Rita Hayworth Award, Alzheimer's Association **MH:** Albert Nelson Marquis Lifetime Achievement Award (2017) **H:** Tennis; Gardening; Squash **BA:** 57 W 57th Street, Suite 904, Alzheimer Drug Discovery Foundation, New York, NY, 10019

FINK, MATTHEW, T: Chair of Neurology **I:** Medicine & Health Care **CN:** Weill Cornell Medicine **ED:** MD, University of Pittsburgh (1976); BA, University of Pennsylvania (1972) **CT:** Internal Medicine; Critical Care Medicine; Neurology; Vascular Neurology **C:** Louis and Gertrude Feil Professor in Clinical Neurology, Weill Cornell Medical College (2012-Present); Chairman of Neurology, Weill Cornell Medical College (2012-Present); Professor of Clinical Neurology, Weill Cornell Medical College (2012-Present); Acting Chairman, Neurology and Neuroscience, Weill Cornell Medical College (2008-2012); Professor of Clinical Neurology and Neuroscience, Weill Cornell Medical College (2005-2012) **CR:** President, Chief Executive Officer, Beth Israel Medical Center; Chairman, Barbara and Alan Mirken Department of Neurology; Director, Comprehensive Stroke Center; Co-Director, Hyman-Newman Institute for Neurology and Neurosurgery; Professor of Clinical Neurology and Clinical Medicine, Albert Einstein College of Medicine, Yeshiva University **MEM:** Fellow, American Neurological Association; American Academy of Neurology; Stroke Council of the American Heart Association **MH:** Albert Nelson Marquis Lifetime Achievement Award (2017) **BA:** 525 East 68th St. Suite F-610, New York, NY, 10065 **ADD:** 215 E 68th St Apt 5L, New York, NY, 10065

FINNIGAN, ROBERT EMMET, T: Vice Chairman Emeritus **I:** Sciences **CN:** Finnigan Corp **DOB:** 05/27/1927 **PB:** Buffalo **SC:** NY/USA **PT:** Charles M. Finnigan; Marie F. (Jacobs) Finnigan **MS:** Married **SPN:** Bette E. Van Horn (4/1/1950) **CH:** Michael; Patrick; Robert E. Junior; Joan; Shawn; Thomas; Matthew **ED:** PhD, University of Illinois (1957); MS, University of Illinois (1954); BS, U.S. Naval Academy (1949) **C:** Vice Chairman Emeritus, Finnigan Corp, San Jose, CA (1992-2000); Consultant, Finnigan Corp, San Jose, CA (1992-2000); Co-founder, Finnigan Corp, San Jose, CA (1967-1992); Vice Chairman, Finnigan Corp, San Jose, CA (1967-1992); Senior Vice President, Finnigan Corp, San Jose, CA (1967-1992); Chief Strategy Officer, Finnigan Corp,

San Jose, CA (1967-1992); Director, Electronic Associates Inc., Palo Alto, CA (1963-1967); Senior Research Scientist, SRI International, Menlo Park, CA (1962-1963); Senior Scientist, Lawrence Livermore National Laboratory, University California (1957-1962) **CR:** Panel Member, National Academy of Sciences, Washington, DC (1986-1989), Co-founder, Organization International Metrological Legale (OIML) (1982-1987) **CIV:** Board Member, Overseers, Chemical Heritage Foundation, Philadelphia, PA (2005-Present); Member, President's Council, University of Illinois at Urbana–Champaign (2002-Present); Co-Founder, U.S. National Working Group on Pollution (OIML), Washington, DC (1982-1987); Chairman, International Organization for Legal Metrology, Washington, DC (1982-1987) **MIL:** Captain, U.S. Air Force (1954-1959); Commissioned Lieutenant, U.S. Air Force (1949) **CW:** Author, "Advances in Identification and Analysis of Organic Pollutants in Water" (1981); Author, "Identification and Analysis of Organic Pollutants in Water" (1976) **AW:** Named to Legend in Environmental Science, American Chemical Society (2008); Robert Finnigan Professorship Established, School of Applied Life Sciences, Keck Graduate Institute, Claremont, CA (2002); Named to Instrumentation Hall of Fame, Pittsburgh Conference on American Chemistry, Analytical Chemical Society (1999); Named Pioneer in Analytical Instrumentation-Mass Spectrometry, Society Analytical Chemists of Pittsburgh and Pittsburgh Conference on Analytical Chemistry (1994); Distinguished Service in Engineering,, College of Engineering, University of Illinois (1980); Distinguished Alumnus Award, Department Electrical and Computer Engineering Department, University of Illinois (1975); Honoree, "From Discovery to Precision Medicine: Mass Spectrometry Through the Years and Beyond", Pittcon 2017 **MEM:** President's Circle, United States Naval Academy Alumni Association & Foundation (1996-Present); Board of Overseers; Chemical Heritage Foundation (1990-Present); Board of Directors, American Electronic Association (1982-1984, 1987); ; Senior Member, IEEE; Board of Directors, American Society of Mass Spectrometry; Chairman, Co-Founder, Environmental and Occupational Health Committee, American Electronic Association; Sigma Xi **H:** Wine; Hiking; Snowshoeing **ADD:** 125 Los Altos Avenue, Los Altos, CA, 94022

FINOCCHIARO, ALFONSO, T: Bank Executive **I:** Financial Services **DOB:** 08/20/1932 **PB:** Catania **SC:** Italy **PT:** Giovanni Finocchiaro; Giuseppina (Cavalieri) Finocchiaro **MS:** Married **SPN:** Diana Louise Cavagnolo (1/19/1936) **CH:** John Paul; Carol Anne **ED:** Chemical Bank Management Course, Harvard Business School Faculty (1976-1977); MBA in International Finance, Pace University, New York, NY (1967); PhD in Political Science, University of Catania (1958) **C:** Chairman, BPD Bank, New York, NY (2005-2009); Chairman, FINAB International Corp. Service Ltd. (2000-2016); Advisor to Board of Directors, Banco Portugues do Atlantico, Lisbon, Portugal (1996-1997); Director, Banco Portugues do Atlantico Overseas Ltd. (1993-1996); Vice-Chairman, Banco Portugues do Atlantico, Brazil (1993-1996); Director, International Strategy Services (1990-1996); Director, BPA Futures Cayman (1989-1996); Director, Executive Vice President, Regional General Manager, Banco Portugues do Atlantico, New York, NY (1978-1995); President, General Manager, Connecticut Bank International, New York, NY (1977-1978); Vice President, Chemical Bank, New York, NY (1966-1977) **CR:** IMAG, New York, NY (2005-Present); Board of Directors, Alfie International, Inc. (1982-Present); Advisor to Board of Directors,

Banco International do Funchal, Lisbon, Portugal (1997-2007); BPD International Bank, New York, NY (1997-2005); Southern Financial Bank, VA (1997-2004); Fellow, International Management and Development Institute **CIV:** Chairman, Financial Committee; Trustee (1988-2001); Friends of Queen Catherine, Inc. **MIL:** Lieutenant, Carabinieri Corp, Italy **AW:** Decorated Commander, Order of Infante D. Henrique, Portugal; Leadership Award, International Management and Development Institute, Washington, DC **MEM:** Board of Directors, Portugal Chamber of Commerce (1978-Present); Board of Directors, European-American Chamber of Commerce in the U.S. (1997-1998); Board of Directors, Global Leadership Institute (1991-2001); President, Portugal-US Chamber of Commerce (1982-1983); Board of Directors, American Portuguese Society (1979-1998); Vice President, European-American Chamber of Commerce **MH:** Albert Nelson Marquis Lifetime Achievement Award (2017) **H:** Piano; Music; Travel; Foreign affairs **PA:** Republican **RE:** Roman Catholic **ADD:** 31 Four Seasons Drive, North Caldwell, NJ, 07006-6134

FISCHER, CORINNE ELEANOR, T: Doctor **I:** Medicine & Health Care **CN:** St. Michael's Hospital **PT:** Donald Fischer; Sheila Fischer **MS:** Married **SPN:** Bert Frankian **CH:** Mark **ED:** MD, University of Toronto (1989-1993) **CT:** Royal College Sub-Specialty Certification in Geriatric Psychiatry (2013); Royal College Specialty Certification in Psychiatry (1998) **C:** Associate Member, Psychiatry, Faculty of Medicine, Institute of Medical Science, University of Toronto (2015-Present); Associate Professor, Geriatric Psychiatry, Faculty of Medicine, University of Toronto (2014-Present); Associate Professor, Psychiatry, Faculty of Medicine, University of Toronto (2014-Present); Co-Director, Neurodegenerative Research, Keenan Research Centre, Li Ka Shing Knowledge Institute, Neuroscience, Faculty of Medicine, St. Michael's Hospital, Toronto, ON, Canada (2013-Present); Co-Director, Geriatric Psychiatry, St. Michael's Hospital, Toronto, ON, Canada (2013-Present); Co-Director, Neuroscience, Faculty of Medicine, St. Michael's Hospital, Toronto, ON, Canada (2013-Present); Adjunct Scientist, Keenan Research Centre, Li Ka Shing Knowledge Institute, St. Michael's Hospital, Toronto, ON, Canada (2007-Present); Director, Geriatric Mental Health Outreach Team, Mental Health Service, St. Michael's Hospital, Toronto, ON, Canada (2006-Present); Director, Geriatric Psychiatry, Mental Health Service, St. Michael's Hospital, Toronto, ON, Canada (2005-Present); Director, Memory Disorders Clinic, St. Michael's Hospital, Toronto, ON, Canada (2002-Present); Staff Member, Consultation Liaison Service, St. Michael's Hospital, Toronto, ON, Canada (1999-Present); Geriatric Psychiatrist, Consultation Liaison Service, St. Michael's Hospital, Toronto, ON, Canada (1999-Present); Staff Member, Mental Health Service, St. Michael's Hospital, Toronto, ON, Canada (1999-Present); Geriatric Psychiatrist, Mental Health Service, St. Michael's Hospital, Toronto, ON, Canada (1999-Present); Co-Director, Clinical Core, Toronto Dementia Research Alliance, Medicine, Behavioural Neurology, University of Toronto, Canada (2013-2015) **AW:** Certificate of Appreciation, Faculty of Medicine, University of Toronto Scarborough (2013-Present); Values in Action Award for Social Responsibility, St. Michael's Hospital, Toronto, ON, Canada (2013); Mental Health Service Award for Continuing Medical Education (2008-2009); Nominee, Department of Psychiatry Ivan Silver Award for Continuing Education (2008); Nominee, Ivan Silver Teaching Award (2008) **MEM:** International Society to Advance Alzheimer's Research and Treatment (2016-Present); Elder Care Task Force, St. Michael's Hospital, Toronto, ON, Canada (2011-Present); American Association of Geriatric Psychiatry (2005-Present); Canadian Association of Geriatric Psychiatry (2005-Present); Consortium of Canadian Centres for Clinical Cognitive Research (2005-Present); International Psychogeriatric Association (2005-Present); Canadian Medical Association (1998-Present); Mental Health Service Medical Advisory Committee (2005-2012); Pharmacy and Therapeutics Committee, St. Michael's Hospital, Toronto, ON, Canada (2005-2008); Delirium and Restraints Working Group, St. Michael's Hospital, Toronto, ON, Canada (2004-2007); Research Ethics Board, St. Michael's Hospital, Toronto, ON, Canada (2003-2005) **H:** Jogging; Swimming; Reading; Watching baseball; Listening to music **BA:** 30 Bond Street, St. Michael's Hospital, Toronto, ON, Canada, M5B 1W8 **ADD:** 114 Munro Boulevard, Toronto, ON, Canada, M2P 1C6 **URL:** http://stmichaelshospitalresearch.ca/researchers/corinne-e-fischer

FISH, ANDREW J., T: Professor of Electrical Engineering **I:** Education/Educational Services **CN:** University of New Haven **DOB:** 08/15/1944 **PT:** Andrew Joseph; Katherine Pauline (Frey) Fish **MS:** Married (6/21/1985) **SPN:** Paula Jean Bosiclaré **CH:** Ashley Marie **ED:** PhD, University of Connecticut (1980); MS in Mathematics, St. Mary University, San Antonio (1974); MSEE, University of Iowa (1973); BSEE, Worcester Polytechnic Institute (1966) **C:** Professor of Electrical Engineering, University of New Haven (1990-Present); Chairman, Department of Electrical and Computer Engineering, University of New Haven (1993-1995); Chairman, Department of Electrical Engineering, University of New Haven (1992-1994); Associate Professor of Electrical Engineering, University of New Haven (1987-1990); Associate Professor of Electrical Engineering, Western New England Colonel, Springfield, MA (1984-1987); Associate Professor of Electrical Engineering, University of Hartford, West Hartford, CT (1979-1984) **CR:** Co-Chairman, Nonlinear Systems Group, American Control Conference (1980); Executive Committee, Connecticut Micro-Electronics and Optics Conference **CIV:** Gate Keeper, Suffield Grange (1982) **MIL:** Captain, United States Air Force Reserve (1973-1977); Captain, United States Air Force Reserve, (1968-1973) **CW:** Contributor, Articles, Professional Journals and Publications **AW:** Fellowship, Yale University (1982-1983) **MEM:** American Association of University Professors; Lifetime Member, IEEE; Connecticut Farm Bureau; Sons of the American Revolution; Delegate at Large, Connecticut State Conference, American Association of University Professors **RE:** Roman Catholic **ADD:** 410 Taintor St, Suffield, CT, 06078

FISHER, ERIC O'NEILL, T: Economist **I:** Education/Educational Services **CN:** California Polytechnic State University **DOB:** 02/09/1954 **PB:** New York **SC:** NY/USA **PT:** Leonard Porter; Lora (Segall) Porter **MS:** Married **SPN:** Kathryn G. Marshall **CH:** Jane Marshall; Marshall Havard **ED:** PhD, University of California, Berkeley (1985); MA in International Relations, Johns Hopkins University, Washington, DC (1979); PhB, Princeton University, Princeton, NJ (1974) **C:** Professor, California Polytechnic State University, San Luis Obispo, CA (2006-Present); Director, Economics Laboratory, California Polytechnic State University, San Luis Obispo, CA (2006-Present); Assistant to Associate Professor, Ohio State University, Columbus, OH (1993-2006); Assistant Professor, Cornell University, Ithaca, NY (1987-1993); Economist, Federal Reserve System, Washington, DC (1984-1987); Board of

Governors, Federal Reserve System, Washington, DC (1984-1987) **CR:** Fellow, CESifo Research Network (2008-Present); Visiting Professor, Rice University (2015); Jon M. Huntsman Presidential Visiting Professor, Economics and Finance, Utah State University (2014); Visiting Professor, Cornell University (2012); Visiting Scholar, Federal Reserve Bank, San Francisco, CA (2007-2009); Visiting Professor, Chulalongkorn University (2007-2008); Visiting Professor, University of California, Santa Barbara (2005-2008); Visiting Professor, Virginia Polytechnic Institute (2004); Research Associate, Federal Reserve Bank, Cleveland, OH (2003-2006); Academic Fellow, Foundation for the Defense of Democracies (2003); Professor, Johns Hopkins University (2002-2003); Jean Monnet Fellow, European University Institute (2002-2003); COTA Legacy Council (2000-2004); Visiting Foreign Scholar, Institute of Social and Economic Research, University of Osaka, Japan (1998); Australian National University, Canberra, Australia (1994); Tinbergen Institute, Rotterdam, Sweden (1993); Visiting Assistant Professor, University of Chicago (1990-1991); Visiting Professor, University of Sao Paulo (1990); Visiting Fellow, Institute for International Economic Studies, Stockholm, Sweden (1987); Visiting Professor, Associazione Generale Italiana di Petrol **CIV:** Chair, Orfalea College of Business Senate Caucus (2013-Present); King David's Lodge #209 (2012-Present); Faculty Adviser, Cal Poly Economics Society (2009-Present); Legacy Council, COTA (2003-Present); Organizer, Southwest Economic Theory Meetings (2011); Chair, Cal Poly Senate Budget Committee (2009-2010); Vestry, St. Stephen's Church, San Luis Obispo, CA (2008-2011); Academic Senate, California Polytechnic State University (2007-2011); Appeared, "Viewpoint," WOSU Columbus Television (2005); Featured Interviewee, The Cleveland Plain Dealer (2004); Appeared, WVIZ Cleveland Television (2004); Speaker, WPTT Pittsburgh Radio (2004); Legacy Council, COTA (2001-2002); Council, Riverlea, OH (2000-2002); Village Council, Riverlea, OH (2000-2002); Appeared, Ohio News Network (2000-2001); Alternate, University Senate, Ohio State University (1998-2000); Organizer, Midwest Macroeconomics Meetings (1996); Coordinator, Economics Department Faculty, Ohio State University's Campus Campaign (1995); City of Ithaca Representative Committee (1991-1993); Faculty Council of Representatives, Cornell University (1989-1992); Speaker, National Public Radio (1988); Appeared, "Nightly Business Report" (1988); Staff, Amnesty International (1978); Volunteer, Peace Corps, Morocco (1975-1977); Speaker, "The American Entrepreneur" **CW:** Associate Editor, Review of International Economics (2013-Present); Associate Editor, Economics Bulletin (2011-Present); Associate Editor, Journal of Money, Credit and Banking (2005-2010); Associate Editor, Journal of International Economics (2004-2010); Editorial Council, Review of International Economics (1994-2013); Editorial Board, Journal of Economic Integration (1994-2000); Contributor, Over 30 Refereed Articles in Economics, Political Science, and Physics, Professional Journals; Contributor, American Economic Review; Contributor, Econometrica; Contributor, The Journal of Economic Theory **AW:** Seniors' Recognition of Outstanding Faculty, Sphinx and Mortar Board, Ohio State University (1995); Outstanding Teacher Award, Ohio State University (1993-1994); Best Article Award, Western Agricultural Economics Association (1993); Scholarship, Princeton University; Scholarship, Johns Hopkins University; Scholarship, University of California **MEM:** AGIP Professorship of International Economics, Bologna Center, Johns

Hopkins University; Sigma Chi **MH:** Albert Nelson Marquis Lifetime Achievement Award (2017) **H:** Fly fishing; Motorcycling **ADD:** 522 Stoneridge Drive, San Luis Obispo, CA, 93401

FISHER, LOUIS, T: Senior Specialist in Separation of Powers (Retired) **I:** Education/Educational Services **CN:** Library of Congress **DOB:** 08/17/1934 **PB:** Norfolk **SC:** VA/USA **CH:** Ellen; Joanna **ED:** PhD in Political Science, The New School (1967); MA, The New School (1966); Coursework in Physical Chemistry, The Johns Hopkins University (1956-1957); BS in Chemistry, College of William and Mary (1956) **C:** Professor, School of Law, College of William and Mary (1990-2015); Specialist in Constitutional Law, Law Library, Library of Congress (2006-2010); Professor, School of Law, The Catholic University of America (1990-1996); Professor, The Johns Hopkins University (1989); Professor, The Catholic University of America (1980-1989); Professor, Indiana University (1987); Professor, Georgetown University (1976-1977); Professor, American University (1975-1977); Senior Specialist in Separation of Powers, Congressional Research Service, Library of Congress (1970-2006); Professor, Queens College (1967-1970); Professor, Queens College (1967); Scholar-in-residence, The Constitution Project, Library of Congress **CR:** Assistant Editor, Plastics Technology (1962-1963); Writer, Miles-Samuelson, Inc. (1960-1962); Representative, Inside Sales, The Dow Chemical Company (1959-1960) **MIL:** First Lieutenant, U.S. Army (1957-1959) **CW:** Author, "President Obama: Constitutional Aspirations and Executive Actions" (2018); Author, "Supreme Court Expansion of Presidential Power: Unconstitutional Leanings" (2017); Author, "Congress: Protecting Individual Rights" (2016); Author, "Constitutional Conflicts Between Congress and the President, Sixth Edition" (2014); Author, "The Law of the Executive Branch: Presidential Power" (2014); Author, "Presidential War Power, Third Edition" (2014); Co-Author, "American Constitutional Law, 10th Edition" (2013); Author, "On the Supreme Court: Without Illusion and Idolatry" (2013); Author, "Defending Congress and the Constitution" (2011); Co-Author, "Political Dynamics of Constitutional Law, Fifth Edition" (2011); Author, "On Appreciating Congress; The People's Branch" (2010); Author, "The Supreme Court and Congress: Rival Interpretations" (2009); Author, "The Constitution and 9/11: Recurring Threats to America"s Freedoms" (2008); Author, "In the Name of National Security: Unchecked Presidential Power and the Reynolds Case" (2006); Author, "Military Tribunals and Presidential Power: American Revolution to the War on Terrorism" (2005); Author, "Nazi Saboteurs on Trial: A Military Tribunal & American Law, Second Edition" (2005); Author, "The Politics of Executive Privilege" (2004); Co-Author, "The Democratic Constitution" (2004); Author, "Nazi Saboteurs on Trial: A Military Tribunal & American Law" (2003); Author, "Congressional Abdication on War and Spending" (2000); Author, "The Politics of Shared Power, Fourth Edition" (1998); Author, Constitutional Dialogues" (1988); Author, "The Constitution Between Friends (1978); Author, "Presidential Spending Power" (1975); Author, "President and Congress" (1972); Author, 32 Books; Contributor, 174 Book Chapters; Contributor, More Than 400 Articles, Professional Publications; Invited Speaker in Field **AW:** The Career Service Award, American Political Science Association (2017); Honoree, Outstanding Academic Title (Choice) for "On the Supreme Court: Without Illusion and Idolatry" (2014); Hubert H. Humphrey Award, American Political Science Association (2012); Walter Beach Pi Sigma Alpha Award, National

Capital Area, Political Science Association (2011); Honoree, Outstanding Academic Title for "On Appreciating Congress" (2010); Richard Neustadt Book Award, Presidency Research Group, American Political Science Association (2006); Honoree, Outstanding Academic Title for "Nazi Saboteurs on Trial" (2004); Honoree, Outstanding Academic Title for "Congressional Abdication on War and Spending" (2001); Co-recipient, Pi Sigma Alpha Award, Western Political Science Association (1998); Aaron B. Wildavsky Award, Association for Budgeting & Financial Management (1995); Co-recipient, Dartmouth Medal, by the American Library Association (1995); Louis Brownlow Book Award, National Academy of Public Administration (1989); National Distinguished Service Award in the Academic Area, American Association for Budget & Program Analysis (1982); Louis Brownlow Book Award, National Academy of Public Administration (1976); Edith Henry Johnson Memorial Award for Outstanding Dissertation, The New School (1967) MEM: Fellow, National Academy of Public Administration (1992); Central and East European Law Initiative, ABA MH: Albert Nelson Marquis Lifetime Achievement Award (2017) ADD: 520 Ridgewell Way, Silver Spring, MD, 20902 URL: http://www.loufisher.org

FITCHETT STICK, THOMAS HOWARD, T: Corporate Architect, Construction Litigation Consultant I: Architecture & Construction DOB: 02/28/1938 PB: Baltimore SC: MD/USA PT: Gordon M.F. Stick; Anne Howard (Fitchett) Stick MS: Married SPN: Alyce C. Cushing (Married 1989); Joyce Yeargin Carr (Married 1982, Divorced 1989); Rosalie Wade Reynolds (Married 1959, Divorced 1982) CH: H. Edward M.; Alexander W.; David F. ED: Postgraduate Coursework, Graduate Architecture Program, University of Pennsylvania (1964); Postgraduate Coursework, Maryland Institute (1962); BA in Psychology, Yale University (1960) CT: Registered Architect, States of Pennsylvania, Maryland, Delaware, New Jersey, Virginia, Maine, New York, Washington, DC, Massachusetts, New Hampshire, North Carolina, Vermont, Tennessee, Oklahoma, Colorado, Indiana, Georgia, Illinois, Michigan, Kentucky, Kansas, Ohio; Registered Architect, Peoples Republic of China; Certified Recommendation, National Council of Architectural Registration Boards C: Director, Day & Zimmermann, Philadelphia, PA (2000-Present); Corporate Architect, Day & Zimmermann, Philadelphia, PA (1995-Present); Discipline Manager, Day & Zimmermann, Philadelphia, PA (1987-Present); Chief Architect, Day & Zimmermann, Philadelphia, PA (1985-Present); Senior Construction Claims Consultant, MDC Systems Corporation, Philadelphia, PA (1984-1985); Manager, Construction Administration, Ballinger Company Philadelphia, PA (1981-1983); Corporate Architect, Gino's Inc., King of Prussia, PA (1980-1981); Principal, Stick Associates, Gladwyne, PA (1977-1980); Founding Partner, Grim & Stick, Ardmore, PA (1975-1977); Architect, B.J. Hoffman & Associates, Berwyn, PA (1974); Architect, Vincent G. Kling & Partners, Philadelphia, PA (1964-1974) CIV: President, Fitchett Stick Inc. Foundation (2017-Present); Vice President, Fitchett Stick Inc. Foundation (1986-2017) CW: Photographer, Solo Exhibit, Eastern Camera Gallery (1972) AW: Listed, Architect of Best Food Plant of the Year, Food Engineering Magazine (1992) MEM: Secretary, General Society of the War of 1812 (1977-1982); American Institute of Architects; Pennsylvania Society of Architects; Building Officials and Code Administrators International; International Conference of Building Officials; Southern Building Code Congress International; Construction Specifications

Institute; National Fire Protection Association; Society of Cincinnati; Society of Colonial Wars; Sons of the Revolution; Descendants of Lords of the Maryland Manors; Military Order of the Loyal Legion of the United States; Huguenot Society; American Clan Gregor Society; St. Andrew's Society of Baltimore; St. George's Society of Baltimore; Merion Cricket Club, Haverford, PA; Yale Club, Commander, Sovereign Military Order of the Temple of Jerusalem; Knight of Justice, Sovereign Order of St. John of Jerusalem; Knights Malta; Zeta Psi MH: Albert Nelson Marquis Lifetime Achievement Award (2017) H: Photography ADD: 1501 Monticello Dr, Gladwyne, PA, 19713

FLAVELL, RICHARD, T: Professor I: Education/Educational Services CN: Yale University ED: PhD in Biochemistry, University of Hull (1970); BSc in Biochemistry, University of Hull, With Honors (1967) C: Investigator, Howard Hughes Medical Institute (1988-Present); Professor of Molecular, Cellular & Developmental Biology, Yale School of Medicine (1988-Present); Professor, Yale University School Medicine (1988-Present); Chairman of Immunobiology, Yale University School Medicine (1988-Present); Investigator, Yale University School Medicine (1988-Present); Sterling Professor of Immunobiology, Yale School of Medicine (2002); President, Biogen, Cambridge, Massachusetts (1984-1988); Chief Science Officer, Biogen, Cambridge, Massachusetts (1984-1988); Head Laboratory Gene Structure and Expression, National Institute for Medical Research, Medical Research Council, London, England (1979-1982); Assistant Professor of Biochemistry, UvA (1974-1979); EMBO Postdoctoral Fellow, Institute of Microbiology, Eidgenössische Technische Hochschule Zürich (1972-1973); Postdoctoral Fellow, UvA (1970-1972) CR: Member, Science Advisory Board, Curagen (1999-Present); Chairman, Science Advisory Board, Bionaut (2002); Darwin Trust Visiting Professor, Department of Cellular and Molecular Biology, University of Edinburgh (1995); Board of Directors, Conservation Law Foundation of New England; Lecturer in Field CIV: Member, Yale Stem Cell Center, Yale University; Member, Honors Degree Committee, Yale University; Member, Yale Comprehensive Cancer Center, Yale University CW: Editorial Board Member, Journal of Autoimmunity (2002-Present); Transmitting Editor, International Immunity (2001-Present); Associate Editor, Gene Screen (2000-Present); Associate Editor, Genes to Cells (1998-Present); Editor, Immunity (2000-2003); Member, Advisory Editorial Board, Molecular Medicine Today (1995-2000); Associate Editor, Immunity (1994-2000); Senior Editor, Genes and Function (1996-1998); Editor, EMBO Journal (1990-1993); Editor, Journal of Molecular and Applied Genetics (1983-1987); Managing Editor, Biochimica et Biophysica Acta (1980-1985); Editor, Nucleic Acids Research (1979-1982); Editor, Techniques in the Life Sciences (1981); Editor, Eukaryotic Genes (1980) AW: Recipient, Seymour & Vivian Milstein Award for Excellence in Interferon and Cytokine Research, International Cytokine & Interferon Society (2017); Recipient, The Rabbi Shai Shacknai Memorial Prize (2008); AAI-Invitrogen Meritorious Career Award (2008); Recipient, Distinguished Service Award, Miami Nature Biotechnology Winter Symposia (2001); Recipient, Darwin Trust Prize, University of Edinburgh (1995); Recipient, Colworth Medal (1980); Recipient, Anniversary Prize, Federation of European Biochemical Societies (1980) MEM: Fellow, American Association for the Advancement of Science; Royal Society of Chemistry; The National Academy of Sciences; European Research Institute for Integrated Cellular Pathology; Henry Kunkel

Society; Institute of Medicine; American Society for Microbiology; Connecticut Academy of Science and Engineering, Incorporated; International Conference on TNF; Science Committee, Super Family; The New York Academy of Sciences; The American Association of Immunologists, Inc.; Royal Institution; EMBO H: Horticulture BA: 300 Cedar St, Yale University, New Haven, CT, 06520

FLEMING, JOSEPH Z., T: Attorney I: Law and Legal Services CN: Greenberg Traurig P.A. DOB: 01/30/1941 PB: Miami SC: FL/USA PT: Richard Marion Fleming; Lenore C. Fleming MS: Married SPN: Betty Corcoran (2/12/1947) CH: Katherine Anne ED: LLM in Labor Law, New York University (1966); JD, University of Virginia (1965); Postgraduate, Hague Academy of International Law (1966); Postgraduate, University of Chicago (1959); BA in English, University of Florida (1958) CT: Certified Specialist in Labor and Employment Law, Florida Bar Association C: Attorney, Greenberg Traurig PA (2001-Present); Partner, Ford & Harrison (1996-2001); Partner, Fleming & Klink (1987-1988); Private Practice, Miami, FL (1986-1996); Partner, Fleming & Huck, Miami, FL (1981-1986); Partner, Fleming & Neuman (1974-1981); Partner, Paul & Thomson, Miami, FL (1972-1974); Associate, Paul & Thomson, Miami, FL (1966-1972) CR: Management Chair, International Labor & Employment Law Committee (2009-Present); Lecturer in Field; Fellow, College of Labor & Employment Lawyers CIV: Well Field Protection Advisory Committee, Dade County Task Force (1984-1987); Noguchi-Bayfront Park Trust, Miami, FL (1983-1989); Trustee, Metropolitan Dade County Center for Fine Arts (1982-1986); Biscayne Bay Environmental Task Force Subcommittee (1982-1983); President's Water Policy Implementation Workshops, Department of Interior Water Task Force (1979); President, Board of Directors, Florida Rural Legal Services (1967-1978); Board of Directors, Miami Chapter, American Jewish Committee CW: Editor, Contributing Author, Historic Preservation Law (2007-Present); Author, "Airline and Railroad Labor Law" (1981-Present); Editor, Contributing Author, Reporter's Handbook (1979-Present); Editor, Contributing Author, Entertainment, Arts, & Sports Law (2009-2012); Editor, Contributing Author, Entertainment, Arts, & Sports Law (2007); Editor, Contributing Author, Entertainment, Arts, & Sports Law (2005); Editor, Contributing Author, Historic Preservation Law (2004-2005); Editor, Contributing Author, Environmental Regulation and Litigation in Florida (2003-2012); Editor, Contributing Author, Entertainment, Arts, & Sports Law (2003); Editor, Contributing Author, Entertainment, Arts, & Sports Law (2001); Editor, Contributing Author, Historic Preservation Law (2001); Editor, Contributing Author, Environmental Regulation and Litigation in Florida (1999-2000); Editor, Contributing Author, Historic Preservation Law (1999); Editor, Contributing Author, Entertainment, Arts, & Sports Law (1997-1999); Editor, Contributing Author, Environmental Regulation and Litigation in Florida (1997); Editor, Contributing Author, Environmental Regulation and Litigation in Florida (1993-1995); Editor, Contributing Author, Environmental Regulation and Litigation in Florida (1990-1991); Editor, Contributing Author, Entertainment, Arts, & Sports Law (1989-1991); Editor, Contributing Author, Historic Preservation Law (1989); Editor, Contributing Author, Environmental Regulation and Litigation in Florida (1987-1988); Editor, Contributing Author, Historic Preservation Law (1984-1987); Editor, Contributing Author, Environmental Regulation and Litigation in Florida (1984-1985); Editor, Contributing Author, Environmental Regulation and Litigation in Florida (1982); Editor, Contributing Author, Environmental Regulation and Litigation in Florida (1980); Editor,

Contributing Author, Environmental Pollution and Individual Rights (1978) **AW:** Lawyer of the Year, Litigation - Land Use & Zoning, Miami, FL (2017); Labour, Employment & Benefits, Who's Who Legal (2016); Team Member, Law Firm of the Year, Environmental Law, Best Law Firms Edition, U.S. News - Best Lawyers (2016); Labour & Employment, Who's Who Legal (2016); Super Lawyers Magazine, Florida Super Lawyers (2015-2017); Top 100 Lawyers in Miami (2015-2016); Lawyer of the Year, Environmental Law, Miami, FL (2015); Senior Statesman, Chambers USA Guide (2014-2017); Labor and Employment - Labor-Management Relations, The Legal 500 United States (2014-2017); Top 100 Lawyers in Miami (2013); Team Member, Law360 Employment Practice Group of the Year, International Who's Who of Management Labor & Employment Lawyers (2011-2013); Team Member, Law Firm of the Year, Entertainment Law - Music, U.S. News - Best Lawyers (2011-2012); Top Lawyer, South Florida Legal Guide (2010-2016); Legal Elite, Employment Law, Florida Trend Magazine (2010); Super Lawyers Magazine, Florida Super Lawyers (2006-2013); Legal Elite, Employment Law, Florida Trend Magazine (2004-2008); Top Lawyer, South Florida Legal Guide (2004-2005); National - Employment Law, Chambers USA Guide (2003-2017); Employment Law - Management, Entertainment Law - Motion Pictures and Television, Environmental Law, Labor Law - Management, Land Use and Zoning Law, Litigation - Environmental, Litigation - Labor and Employment, Litigation - Land Use and Zoning, Sports Law, and Water Law, Best Lawyers in America (1983-2018); Honoree, Florida Audubon Society, Tropical Audubon Society, and 1,000 Friends of Florida (1981); Honoree, Miami Beach "Art Deco" Historic District Preservation Plan, Progressive Magazine **MEM:** Past Chairman, Environmental And Land Use Law Section, Labor Law and Employment Discrimination Law Section, Entertainment, Arts, and Sports Law Section, Chair, Entertainment Arts and Sports Law Section, Florida Bar Association (2011-Present); Chair, Entertainment Arts & Sports Law Section, Florida Bar Association (2011-2012); Board Trustee, New World Symphony (2009-2011); Continuing Professional Education Committee, American Law Institute, ALI-ABA (1985-2008) **BAR:** District of Columbia (1981); State of Florida (1965); U.S. Supreme Court; Fifth and 11th Circuits, U.S. Court of Appeals; U.S. District Courts, Middle and Southern Districts, State of Florida **MH:** Albert Nelson Marquis Lifetime Achievement Award (2017) **BA:** 333 SE 2nd Avenue, Suite 4400, Greenberg Traurig P.A., Miami, FL, 33131

FLINCHBAUGH, DAVID E., T: Physicist **I:** Medicine & Health Care **CN:** Advanced Medical Innovations, LLC **DOB:** 10/11/1934 **PB:** Poughkeepsie **SC:** NY/USA **PT:** Louis David Flinchbaugh; Lolita Mildred (Hook) Flinchbaugh **MS:** Married **SPN:** Heidi Maria Rose (6/15/1957) **CH:** William David; Laura Jean; Karen Marie; Karl Louis **ED:** Coursework, Computer Geodatabase Management, Harvard University (1979); PhD in Modern Physics, University of Connecticut (1964); MS in Physics, University of Connecticut (1960); Coursework, Atomic Physics, Case Institute of Technology (1957-1959); BS in Physics and Mathematics, Union College (1957) **CT:** Registered Professional Engineer, Commonwealth of Pennsylvania (1980); Registered Professional Engineer, State of Florida (1974); Certified Teacher, State of Florida; Federal Aviation Administration Certified Basic Ground Instructor; Federal Aviation Administration Certified Private Pilot Single Engine Land & Sea; Certified in American Red Cross Water Safety; Certified in CPR; Certified First Aid instructor; Certified EMT 1 **C:** President, Medtronic (2012-Present); Chief Executive Officer, Advanced Medical Innovations LLC,

Orlando, FL (2009-Present); Senior Executive Vice President, Global Medical Research LLC, Orlando, FL (2005-2008); Vice President, Director, Manufacturing, Chief Executive Officer, UroSolutions (Now Medtronic), Orlando, FL (2000-2005); Staff Consultant, Martin Marietta Aerospace Corp., Orlando, FL (1986-1987); Systems Engineering Manager, McDonnell Douglas Astronautics Company, Titusville, FL (1982-1986); Consultant, Team Leader, Westinghouse Electric Corporation, Pittsburgh, PA (1980-1981); Program Manager, P.I., Planning Research Corporation, Kennedy Space Center (1978-1980); Senior Staff Consultant, Sperry Microwave Electronics Corporation, Clearwater, FL (1977-1978); Staff Consultant, International Laser Corporation, Orlando, FL (1975); Staff Consultant, Martin Marietta Aerospace Corp., Orlando, FL (1971-1973); Vice President, Research & Development, Control Laser Corporation, Orlando, FL (1968-1971); Director, Research & Development, Orlando Research Corporation (1968-1969); Manager, Research & Development, Andersen Laboratories, Bloomfield, CT (1965-1968); Research Scientist, United Technologies Research Center, East Hartford, CT (1963-1965); Research Scientist, United Technologies Research Center, East Hartford, CT (1959-1960); Research Associate, Argonne National Laboratories, Lemont, IL (1958); Research Physicist, IBM Corporation, Poughkeepsie, NY (1956-1957); Executive Director, Foundation Fighting Fatal Infection & Disease, Inc. **CR:** Life Fellow, The Optical Society (1989-Present); Chief Consultant, Chief Executive Officer, Dr. David Flinchbaugh & Associate, P.A., Orlando, FL (1996-2005); Chief Consultant, Chief Executive Officer, Aerobeam Corporation, Orlando, FL (1971-2002); Life Fellow, IEEE (1954); Instructor, Union College; Instructor, University of Connecticut; Instructor, Case Institute of Technology; Instructor, University of Central Florida; Instructor, Florida Institute of Technology; Instructor, Valencia College; Instructor, Seminole State College of Florida; Instructor, Embry-Riddle Aeronautical University; Instructor, Orlando Youth Aviation Center; Tutor, Local District; Regional Merit Badge Counselor, Local District; Contractor, Training Systems, U.S. Navy Simulation Center, Orlando, FL; Life Fellow, Laser Institute of America; Fellow, SME; Fellow, American Society for Laser Medicine and Surgery; Associate Fellow, AIAA **CIV:** Choir Member, Deacon, Grace Covenant Presbyterian Church (1971-Present); Lead Counselor, Boy Scouts of America and Girl Scouts of the United States of America, Orlando, FL (1968-Present); Current President, Inventors Council of Central Florida (1986-2018); National Democratic Policy Committee (1984-1986); Founding Member, Inventors Council of Central Florida (1974); Volunteer Instructor, American Red Cross, Orlando, FL (1968-1990) **MIL:** U.S. Army Project Management, Training Devices (1969-1986); U.S. Air Force Reserve Officer Training (1953-1955); Stewart Air Force Base Summer Air Encampment (1952) **CW:** Contributor, 30 Articles, Technical Journals and Magazines; Author/Co-Author, Seven Books, Library of Congress; Six Church and Wedding Music Compositions **AW:** Florida Inventor of the Year, Palm Beach Society of American Inventors (1986-Present); SME Award of Merit for Engineering Professionalism in the Community (2018); Second Place Award, SCORE-sponsored "Pitchfest," National Entrepreneur Center, Orlando, FL (2017); George McClure Citation of Honor, IEEE (2016); Listee with Honorable Mention, NASA Tech Briefs and the Medical Design Tech Briefs (2014); Presidential Life Achievement Award, The Heritage Society (2008); Modern Marvels Invent Now National Challenge Semi-Finalist, Vanderbilt Hall, NY (2006); R&D 100 Best New Products Award Winner, Chicago Navy Pier (2004); Businessman of the Year Award, Con-

gressional Tax Summit, Washington, DC (2004); Design News Excellence in Design Grand Prize Winner, Chicago McCormick Place (2003); Medical Design Excellence Gold Award, MD&DI Magazine, Jacob Javits Center (2003); Albert M. Sargent International Progress Award, Society of Manufacturing Engineers (2003); Florida Professional Engineers in Industry Award (2002); DaVinci Award for Assistive Technology, Engineering Society of Detroit and The National MS Society (2002); Florida Governor's Best New Product Award (2002); Florida Institute of Consulting Engineers Award (2002); Environmental Excellence Award, Orange County, FL (1998); Entrepreneur of the Year, IEEE (1998); National Inventor of the Year, Inventor's Society of South Florida, Fort Lauderdale, FL (1988); Engineer of the Year, Florida Engineering Society, Tallahassee, FL (1984); Engineer of the Year, Orlando Section, IEEE (1982); Florida Governor A. W. Gilchrist Humanitarian Award; Florida Professional Engineering Society Award; IEEE-USA Professional Achievement Award; Laufmann-Greatbach Prize, Association for the Advancement of Medical Instrumentation; Best New Product Award, National Society of Professional Engineers, San Antonio,TX; Stevie Award, American Business Awards "Oscar," Times Square, NY; Congressional Gold Medal, Ronald Reagan Medal, Washington, DC; Cade Museum Foundation Innovation Competition Semi-Finalist, Gainesville, FL **MEM:** Ambassador, Orlando Section, International Council for Systems Engineering (2010-Present); President, Central Florida Association of Environmental Professionals (1993-1994); President, Florida Council of Engineering Societies (1985-1986); President, Inventors Council of Central Florida (1984-2018); Board of Directors, Executive Committee National Inventors Council (1982-1984); Board of Directors, Laser Institute of America (1975-1979); Executive Committee, IEEE; Life International Federation of Robotics; Past President, Florida Section, The Optical Society; National Society of Professional Engineers; Life Member, Florida Engineering Society **H:** Music; Photography; Aviation; Swimming; Boating **ADD:** 4855 Big Oaks Lane, Orlando, FL, 32806 **URL:** http://www.strathmoreworldwide.com/profoftheyear_bio.asp?id=303866&industry=Consulting/Inventing

FLORO, ALLAN ERNEST, T: Counsel **I:** Law and Legal Services **CN:** Nixon Peabody LLP **DOB:** 09/20/1956 **PB:** Wantagh **SC:** New York **PT:** Jack E. Floro; Jeanne Anne Floro **MS:** Married **SPN:** Beth Ann S. Floro **CH:** Christopher; Elizabeth **ED:** MA in Theology, Northeastern Seminary (2014); JD, Law School, Cornell University, Magna Cum Laude (1983); BA, Binghamton University, State University of New York, with Honors (1978) **C:** Associate, Partner, Counsel, Nixon Peabody LLP (1983-Present) **CIV:** Affiliate, Iron Sharpens Iron; Affiliate, Lifespan; Elder Board Member, Ridgeland Community Church **AW:** Listee, Best Lawyers in America (2012-Present); Listee, Super Lawyers (2011-Present); Named, Best Lawyer in Environmental Law in Rochester New York (2017); Honoree, Order of the Coif, Law School, Cornell University (1983); Honoree, Cornell Law Review (1982-1983); Honoree, Phi Beta Kappa, State University of New York at Binghamton (1978) **MEM:** ABA; New York State Bar Association; Monroe County Bar Association; Phi Beta Kappa; Order of the Coif **BAR:** New York; United States District Court Western District of New York **H:** Being involved in Ridgeland Community Church and local religious organizations **RE:** Protestant **BA:** 1300 Clinton Sq, Nixon Peabody LLP, Rochester, NY, 14604 **ADD:** 790 Pinnacle Road, Pittsford, NY, 14534 **URL:** https://www.nixonpeabody.com/en/team/floro-allan-e

FLUDD, ELISCHIA JANELLE, T: Founder, Executive Director **I:** Education/Educational Services **CN:** EOTO World **ED:** MBA in Nonprofit Leadership, New England College; BA in Forensic Psychology, John Jay College of Criminal Justice; AA in Liberal Arts, Borough of Manhattan Community College **C:** Educational Testing Service (2015-Present); Freelance Journalist (2013-Present); Founder, EOTO World (2009-Present); Executive Director, EOTO World (2009-Present); SafeHorizon (2009-2010) **CR:** Member, Board of Directors, Students Active for Ending Rape (SAFER) (2006-2009); Advocate, Sexual Assault Response Team Program (SATP), North Bronx Healthcare Network (2005-2010) **CIV:** Representative, EOTO World **CW:** Contributor, Articles, The Huffington Post, Oath Inc.; Contributor, 59 Articles, Professional Publications **AW:** Honoree, Top-Ranked United States Executive (2014); Recognition for Advocacy and Activism in the Community, Violence Against Women (VAW) (2010); Outstanding Service Award, Students Active for Ending Rape (SAFER) (2009); Outstanding Service to The City of New York (CUNY) Students, The City of New York (CUNY) Student Senate (2009); Congressional Recognition for Outstanding Service as a Sexual Assault Response Team Program (SATP) Advocate, Congressman Jose E. Serrano, 15th Congressional District, State of New York (2008); Sexual Assault Response Team Program (SATP) Advocate Adult Honoree for Excellence in Rape Crisis Counseling, North Bronx Health Care Network (2008) **MEM:** Women, Action & the Media (WAM!); National Association of Professional Women (NAPW) **ACH:** Co-led successful process that established the first system-wide policy for sexual assault, domestic violence and stalking for The City University of New York (CUNY) (2010); Participant of the internationally competitive human rights and leadership trainings hosted by the former UNESCO Chair at University of Connecicut and in Rwanda

FLYNN, BRIAN E., T: Consulting Engineer **I:** Consulting **CN:** Brian E. Flynn **ED:** Bachelor's Degree in Engineering, Pratt Institute (1981) **CT:** Certified Building Inspector **MEM:** Former President, Queens Chapter, New York State Society of Professional Engineers; Former Chairman, Professionals Design Center of New York Inc.; National Academy of Building Inspection Engineers; Practicing Institute of Engineering, Inc. **H:** Skiing; Canyon rafting; Volleyball; Hiking **ADD:** 7866 79th Pl, Glendale, NY, 11385 **URL:** http://www.beflynn.com

FOGEL, RICHARD, T: Lawyer **I:** Law and Legal Services **PB:** Brooklyn **SC:** NY/USA **MS:** Married **SPN:** Sheila Feldman **CH:** Bruce; Lori Ellen **ED:** JD, New York Law School (1974); BA, York College, City University of New York (1971) **C:** Private Practice (1988-Present); Private Practice (1985-1988); Private Practice (1981-1985); Senior Pension Consultant, Attorney, New York Life Insurance Company (1977-1981); Tax Law Specialist, IRS (1975-1977) **CR:** Lecturer, Institute for Continuing Legal Education, Newark, NJ (1977-Present); Presenter, 34th Annual Meeting, International Society for Systems Sciences, Portland State University (1990); Adjunct Faculty Member, Upsala College (1978-1988) **AW:** Founder's Day Award (1992); Distinguished Graduate Award, York College (1984); Certificate of Appreciation, Institute for Continuing Legal Education (1984); Certification in Recognition of Accomplishments, Cooperative Extension Cook College, Rutgers, the State University of New Jersey (1982); Certificate of Appreciation, Institute for Continuing Legal Education (1981-1982); Certificate of Appreciation, IRS (1977) **MEM:** Columbian Lawyers Association of the First Judicial Department **BAR:** U.S. District

Court, Southern District, State of New York (2000); U.S. District Court, State of New York (1981); U.S. Tax Court (1977); U.S. District Court, State of New Jersey (1976) **ADD:** PO Box 737, McAfee, NJ, 07428

FOLEY, GARY J., T: Chemical Engineer, Computer Scientist, Federal Agency Administrator, Researcher **I:** Engineering **CN:** United States Environmental Protection Agency **DOB:** 03/20/1943 **PB:** Staten Island **SC:** NY/USA **MS:** Married **SPN:** Barbara Ickes (1986) **CH:** Karen; Kevin; Ryan; Courtney **ED:** PhD in Chemical Engineering, University of Wisconsin (1968); MS, University of Wisconsin (1965); BChE, Manhattan College (1964) **C:** Rockefeller 100 RC Partnership Lead, United States Environmental Protection Agency (2014-Present); Acting Director, Robert S. Kerr Environmental Research Center, United States Environmental Protection Agency (2012-2014); Director, Office of Research and Development, United States Environmental Protection Agency (2011-2012); Executive, Office of Research and Development, United States Environmental Protection Agency (2011-2012); Director, United States Environmental Protection Agency (2007-2011); Executive, United States Environmental Protection Agency (2007-2011); Earth Observations Executive, United States Environmental Protection Agency (2007-2011); Office of Science Adviser, United States Environmental Protection Agency (2007-2011); Director, National Center for Environmental Research, United States Environmental Protection Agency (2005-2007); Director, National Exposure Research Laboratory, United States Environmental Protection Agency (1995-2005); Acting Assistant Administrator, Research and Development, National Exposure Research Laboratory, United States Environmental Protection Agency (1993-2005); Director, National Exposure Research Laboratory, United States Environmental Protection Agency (1987-1993); Engineer, United States Environmental Protection Agency (1979-1986); Engineer, United States Environmental Protection Agency (1973-1976); Engineer, American Oil Co. (1968-1973) **CR:** Member, Organization for Economic Co-operation and Development; Member, Air Quality Board, International Joint Commission; Member, Chemical Sciences Round Table, National Research Council, National Academies of Sciences, Engineering, and Medicine; Member, Advisory Board, IBM; Member, Intergovernmental Group on Earth Observations; United States Delegate, Various International Energy Summits, United Nations; Expert Witness in Field, United States Congress; Mentor to Younger Engineers and Scientists; **CW:** International Joint Commission-International Air Quality Advisory Board (1982-2012); First US UV-B Monitoring Network (1992); US Lead-US-Canada Partnership-Built First Great Lakes International Atmospheric Deposition Network (1990-1991); First International Workshop on Abandoned Waste Sites (1982); First Full Environmental Cost-Benefit Study of Sulfur Oxides & Acid Rain for 24 European Countries (1978) **AW:** Recipient, Award for Creating and being the 1st Chairman North American Public-Private Partnership on Air Pollution; Featured Listee, Who's Who in America (1995-2014, 2016); Featured Listee, Who's Who in Science and Engineering (1996-1997, 1999, 2001, 2003, 2010, 2016); Featured Listee, Who's Who in the World (2009-2014, 2016); Featured Listee, Who's Who in the South and Southwest (2000-2015); Recipient, Thank You Letter, President Bill Clinton (1995); Recipient, Presidential Meritorious Rank Award; Recipient, Bronze Medals for Research Excellence, United States Environmental Protection Agency; Recipient, Sustainability Award, Environmental

Protection Agency; Recipient, Award for Research Apprenticeship Program, Shaw University **MEM:** American Institute of Chemical Engineers **MH:** Albert Nelson Marquis Lifetime Achievement Award (2017) **H:** Movies; Reading; Crossword and Sudoku Puzzles; Vacations; Tennis **BA:** 109 TW Alexander Dr, US EPA, Research Triangle Park, NC, 27711 **ADD:** 5431 Regatta Way, Raleigh, NC, 27613

FONTANA, GREGORY P., T: Cardiac Surgeon, Hospital Administrator **I:** Medicine & Health Care **CN:** Hospital Corporation of America **ED:** MD, University of California, Los Angeles (1984); Bachelor's Degree, University of California, Riverside; Fellow, Pediatric Cardiac Surgery, Children's Hospital, Boston, MA; Fellow, Pediatric Cardiac Surgery, University of California, Los Angeles; Resident, Duke University Medical Center; Intern, Duke University Medical Center **CT:** Board Certified in Thoracic Surgery **C:** Cedars-Sinai Medical Center (1995-Present); Clinical Professor, Surgery, David Geffen School Medicine, University of California, Los Angeles; Attending Cardiac Surgeon, Heart Institute, Cedars-Sinai Medical Center; Fellow, American College of Surgeons; Vice Chair, Strategic Planning and Development, Department of Surgery, Cedars-Sinai Medical Center **CR:** National Principal Investigator, St. Jude Transcatheter Valve Trial; Principal Investigator, Partner, Trial of Transcatheter Aortic Valve Implantation **CW:** Contributor, Several Articles, Peer-reviewed Journals; Co-author, New England Journal of Medicine **AW:** Top Five Papers in Medicine (2010) **MEM:** Western Thoracic Surgical Association; International Academy of Cardiology; 21st Century Cardiac Surgical Society; California Society of Pediatric Cardiology; American Heart Association; Society of Pediatric Cardiovascular Surgery; David C. Sabiston Jr. Surgical Society; Society of Thoracic Surgeons; American Association for Thoracic Surgery; American College of Cardiology; Founding Member, International Society for Minimally Invasive Cardiac Surgery **MH:** Albert Nelson Marquis Lifetime Achievement Award (2017) **BA:** 227 W Janss Rd Ste 340, CardioVascular Institute of Los Robles Hospital & Medical Center, Thousand Oaks, CA, 91360

FORD, FREDERICK ROSS, T: Academic Administrator (Retired) **I:** Education/Educational Services **DOB:** 03/25/1936 **PB:** Kentland **SC:** IN/USA **PT:** Merl Jackson Ford; Marie Jeanne (Ross) Ford **MS:** Married **SPN:** Mary A. Harrison (5/31/1959) **CH:** Lynne Elizabeth; Steven Harrison; Katherine Jeannette **ED:** Honorary PhD in Management, Purdue University (1998); PhD, Purdue University (1963); MS, Purdue University (1959); BS in Mechanical Engineering, Purdue University (1958) **C:** Retired (1998); Executive Vice President, Purdue University (1974-1998); Treasurer, Purdue University (1974-1998); Business Manager, Purdue University (1969-1974); Assistant Treasurer, Purdue University (1969-1974); Assistant Business Manager, Purdue University (1965-1969); Assistant to Vice President, Purdue University (1961-1965); Assistant to Treasurer, Purdue University (1961-1965); Assistant to Business Manager, Purdue University (1959-1961) **CR:** Trustee, Teachers Insurance and Annuity Association of America - College Retirement Equities Fund, New York, NY (1982-2002) **CIV:** Investment Committee Chairman, Central Presbyterian Foundation, Central Presbyterian Church (2000-Present); Investment Committee, Westminster Village, West Lafayette, IN (2002-2014); Treasurer, Capital Funds Foundation, United Way of Greater Lafayette (1984-1985) **AW:** Distinguished Business Officer Award, National Association of College and University

Business Officers (1989) **MEM:** Management Board, COGR (1984-1990); Chairman, Education Relations Committee, Greater Lafayette Commerce (1984-1985); Secretary, National Association of College and University Business Officers (1982-1983); Board of Directors, National Association of College and University Business Officers (1980-1983); Executive Committee, CACUBO (1976-1981); President, CACUBO (1979-1980); President, Greater Lafayette Commerce (1978-1979); Rotary International; Delta Upsilon International Fraternity **MH:** Albert Nelson Marquis Lifetime Achievement Award (2017) **H:** Sailing; Fishing **PA:** Republican **RE:** Presbyterian **ADD:** 986 Westminster Cir Apt 313, West Lafayette, IN, 47906

FORD, IRENE ELAINE, T: Pastor **I:** Religious **DOB:** 10/06/1927 **PB:** West Union **SC:** WV/USA **PT:** Clurel Cecil Powell; Lillian Violet Gaskins **MS:** Widowed **SPN:** Claudius Arnold Ford (1/24/1946, Deceased 10/20/1997) **CH:** Richard Freeman; Michael Leroy **ED:** Coursework, Duke Divinity School (1984-1989); Coursework, West Virginia Wesleyan College (1984-1987); Coursework, West Virginia Northern Community College, Weirton, WV **CT:** Ordained Deacon, United Methodist Church (1992) **C:** Pastor, Nessly Chapel United Methodist Church, New Cumberland, WV (1997-2007); Pastor, Graysville United Methodist, Moundsville, WV (1994-1996); Associate, United Methodist Church (1992); Pastor, Christ-Owings Charge, United Methodist Church, Shinnston, WV (1989-1994); Pastor, Bristol Charge, United Methodist Church, Bristol, WV (1983-1989) **CR:** Council Member, Race Track Chaplaincy of America, Mountaineer Race Track (2005-Present); Parish Coordinator, United Methodist Church, Shinnston, WV (1989-1994); Parish Coordinator, United Methodist Church, Bristol, WV (1986-1989); President, Vice President, WHG District, United Methodist Women (1980) **CIV:** Member, WVARSE (2016-2018); School Board Member, Hancock County, WV (1979-1984); President, West Virginia Congress, Parent Teacher Organization (1975-1977) **MEM:** Associate, Deacon, West Virginia Annual Conference **MH:** Distinguished Humanitarian (2017) **RE:** Methodist **ADD:** PO Box 927, New Cumberland, WV, 26047

FORD, WILLIAM HERSCHEL, T: Science Educator **I:** Education/Educational Services **CN:** University of the Pacific **PB:** Ajo **SC:** AZ/USA **PT:** Harold Beecher Ford; Ernestine Theresa Gaskell **MS:** Widowed **SPN:** Shirley Griffin (12/19/1970, Deceased) **CH:** Bret Andrew; Bryce Merritt; Heather Louise **ED:** PhD, University of Illinois, Champaign, IL (1972); BS, Massachusetts Institute of Technology, Cambridge, MA (1967) **C:** Professor, Chair, Department of Computer Science, University of the Pacific, Stockton, CA (1974-2014); Assistant Professor, Clemson University, South Carolina (1972-1974) **CR:** Fellowship, National Science Foundation (1969-1972) **CW:** Author, "Introduction to Numerical Linear Algebra," Academic Press (2014); Author, "Data Structures with Java" (2005); Author, "Data Structures with C+ using STL" (2002); Author, "Introduction to Computing with C++ and Object Technology" (1999); Author, "Macintosh Assembly System, Version 2.0" (1992); Author, "Macintosh Assembly System BasePak," D.C. Heath Publishers (1990); Author, "The MC68000: Assembly Language and Systems Programming" (1988); Author, "Assembly Language Programming"; Author, "Data Structures with C+"; Author, "C+ Programming with Object Technology" **MEM:** SIGCSE; Phi Kappa Phi; Sigma Xi **MH:** Distinguished Humanitarian (2017) **H:** Astronomy **ADD:** 414 S Central Avenue, Stockton, CA, 95204

FORKAN, EVELEEN, T: Counselor **I:** Health, Wellness and Fitness **CN:** PRH International **DOB:** 01/08/1927 **PB:** Cloonmore **SC:** Ireland **PT:** Michael J. Forkan; Winnie Kate Sherlock **ED:** MA in Counseling, Saint Paul University, Ottawa, Canada (1980); MEd, Ottawa University, Canada (1963); BA, Ottawa University, Canada (1954); Coursework, Philosophy, Psychology, Marist Institute, Paris, France (1945-1948); Coursework, Anthropology, Spirituality, Marist Institute, England, U.K. (1944-1945) **C:** Healing Counselor, Personal Growth, PRH International, Detroit, MI (1982-Present); Facilitator, Personal Growth Workshops, PRH International, Detroit, MI (1982-Present); Teacher, Wheeling Catholic Schools, West Virginia (1972-1980); Teacher, St. Albert the Great Catholic School, Dearborn Heights, MI (1970-1972); Administrator, Children's Home, Edmundston, Canada (1964-1970); High School Teacher, New Brunswick Public Schools, Canada (1951-1964); Teacher, New Brunswick Public Schools, Canada (1948-1951) **AW:** Pepper Award (2004) **MEM:** Marist Sisters **MH:** Albert Nelson Marquis Lifetime Achievement Award (2017) **H:** Reading; Philosophy; Anthropology; Spirituality; Psychology **ADD:** 5280 Kreger St, Sterling Heights, MI, 48310

FORONDA, ELENA ISABEL, T: Secondary School Educator, Music Mentor and Vocal Coach **I:** Education/Educational Services **CN:** New York City Department of Education **DOB:** 01/15/1947 **PT:** Severino Deliso Foronda; LaVerne (Ibanez) Foronda **ED:** Graduate Coursework, American Field Studies, Saint Mary's College, Moraga, CA; MA in Music Education, Hunter College, City University of New York; BS in Music, Hunter College, City University of New York **CT:** Piano Adjudicator, Tottenville High School (2012-Present); Piano Adjudicator, New York University (2010-Present); Piano Adjudicator, The Mary Louis Academy, New York State School Music Association (2014); Piano Adjudicator, Marine Park Junior High School, New York State School Music Association (2013-2014); Piano Adjudicator, Tottenville High School, New York State School Music Association (2011-2012); Piano Adjudicator, Tottenville High School, New York State School Music Association (2011-2012); Piano Adjudicator, Bayside High School (2010-2011); Certified Piano Adjudicator, New York State School Music Association, Red Hook, NY (2010); Permanent Certified Teacher, State of New York **C:** Conductor, Choral Pieces, New York City Music Teachers Association, United Federation of Teachers, Music Educators Association of New York City (2012-Present); Vocal Coach, Stuyvesant High School (2007-Present); Music Substitute Teacher, Stuyvesant High School (2003-Present); Arts Matter Instrumental Music Mentor and Facilitator for Middle and High School, New York City Department of Education (2015-2016); Non-Certified NYSSMA Voice Adjudicator, La Guardia High School for Performing Arts (2013); NYSSMA Solo Piano Ajudicator, Solo Voice Adjudicator (2013); Adjudicator, Proctor, Arts Achieve, New York City Department of Education (2013); Non-Certified NYSSMA Piano Adjudicator, Marine Park Junior High School (2009); Choral Assistant, Stuyvesant High School (2006); Music Panelist, Auditor, Brooklyn Arts Council (2006); Assistant Conductor, Stuyvesant High School (2005); Music Panelist, Auditor, Brooklyn Arts Council (2005); Assistant Choral Conductor, Manhattan Arts Institute, FEMA at Stuyvesant High School (2003); Music Panelist, Auditor, Brooklyn Arts Council (2000-2003); Assistant Board of Examiner, New York City Public School System (1987-1989); Assistant Director, Teacher Placement, Hunter College, City University of New York (1971-1972)

CR: Mentor and Facilitator, Middle School, High School, Arts Matter Program (2015); Composer of Love Songs, Library of Congress (2006); Proctor, Arts Achieve Grant to New York City **CIV:** Cantor Zion Evangelical Lutheran Church, Brooklyn, NY (2005-2007); Board of Directors, Leif Ericson Day School, Brooklyn, NY (2002-2004); Lay Eucharistic Minister, Long Island Diocese Episcopal Church (1993-1999); Minister of Music, Church of the Holy Spirit, Brooklyn, NY (1988-1990); Delegate, Asian American Women's Caucus, PBS/WNET 13 Documentary "Ourselves" (1979); Sponsor, Children in World Vision International (1973-1997); Hunter College Choirs (1971); Hunter College Choirs (1968-1969) **CW:** Soprano Member, Distinguished Concerts International of New York, Carnegie Hall (2015-2016); Soprano Member, New York University Chorale (2013-2014); Soprano Member, Distinguished Concerts International of New York, David Geffen Hall, Lincoln Center for The Performing Arts (2013); Soprano Member, Kingsborough Music Society Inc., Goldstein Performing Arts Center (2010-2014) **AW:** Adjudicator Proctor Arts Achieved Grant (2011-2014); Music Educators Association of New York City Award (2013); Grantee, SPARC, Inc. (1999); District Winner, National Piano Playing Auditions, Carnegie Hall (1965) **MEM:** Recording Secretary, Executive Board, Music Educators Association of New York City (2005-Present); Advisory Member, Executive Board, Music Educators Association of New York City (1999-Present); Second Vice President, Executive Board, Music Educators Association of New York City (2003-2005); National Association for Music Education, Affiliate New York State School Music Association; Amateur Chamber Music Players **MH:** Albert Nelson Marquis Lifetime Achievement Award (2017); Distinguished Humanitarian (2017) **H:** Church Activities; Crocheting; British Theater; Traveling **PA:** Democrat **ADD:** 2650 Ocean Pkwy, Apt. 10A, Brooklyn, NY, 11235-7741

FORTENBERRY, MELANIE LEIGH, T: Director, Instructor **I:** Education/Educational Services **CN:** Mississippi College **ED:** MHS, Mississippi College (1990); Bachelor's, Science and Nursing, Mississippi College (1976) **C:** Director, Instructor, Master of Health Services Administration, Mississippi College (2008-Present); Education Coordinator, Mississippi Baptist Medical Center (2001-2008); Education Coordinator/Recruiter, Hinds General Hospital, Methodist Medical Center, Central Mississippi Medical Center (1986-2001) **CIV:** Board of Directors, Alzheimer's Mississippi, Inc. (2008-Present) **MEM:** Mississippi Hospital Association College of Hospital Executives; Organization of Nurse Executives; Mississippi Nurses Association; Board of Directors, Alzheimer's Mississippi; Trans-culture Nurse Society **BA:** 200 College Street, Clinton, MS, 39056 **ADD:** 150 Browning Dr, Flora, MS, 39071

FORTES, BRENDA JOYCE, T: High School Library Research Coordinator **I:** Education/Educational Services **CN:** Boyertown Area School District **DOB:** 08/27/1949 **PB:** Bryn Mawr **SC:** PA/USA **PT:** Laurence Antonio Fortes (Deceased 1959); Emma Hill Fortes Webb (Deceased 1969) **MS:** Divorced **SPN:** Divorced (1994) **CH:** Lauren Brenda Jenks, MPH; Angela Christine Jenks, PhD; Elita Joyce Fortes Jenks, MEd **ED:** MEd, Eastern University, St. Davids, PA (1998); BA, Eastern University, St. Davids, PA (1972); Diploma, Plymouth-Whitemarsh High School (1968) **CT:** Secondary English Teacher Certificate, State of Pennsylvania; Elementary Teacher Certificate, State of Pennsylvania **C:** High School Library Research Coordinator and English Language Learners Tutor, Boyertown Area School

District (2011-2016); Adjunct English Faculty, Montgomery County Community College, Pottstown, PA (1998-2005); High School English Teacher, Boyertown Area School District (1993-2011); Instructor in Basic Business English Communication and Keyboarding Skills, Opportunities Industrialization Center, Norristown, PA (1973-1976) **CR:** School Climate Committee, Boyertown Area Senior High School (2011-2016); Middle States Character Committee, Boyertown Area Senior High School (2007-2010); President's Advisory Board on Diversity, Montgomery County Community College, Blue Bell, PA (1997-2005) **CIV:** Researcher, Disability Ministry Sunday School Class (2016-Present); Volunteer, Pottstown Trauma Informed Community Connection (2016-Present); Member, No Place for Hate Committee, Police Department, Pottstown, PA (2003-2006); President's Advisory for Diversity, Montgomery County Community College (1997-2005); Committee Advisory Panel, Occidental Chemical, Pottstown, PA (1995-1998); Publicity Chairperson, NAACP, Pottstown, PA (1993-2015); Volunteer Researcher, Pastor's Sermon Illustrations, Coventry Church of the Brethren, Pottstown, PA; Volunteer Researcher, Children Church Materials, Music Education Materials and Resources for the Organist and Choir Director **AW:** Kappa Delta Pi National Honor Society in Education (1998-Present); Nominee, Disney America's Teacher Award (2002) **MEM:** Boyertown and Oley Retired Educators' Association (2016-Present); Kappa Delta Pi National Honor Society in Education (1998-Present); American Association of University Women; National Women's History Museum; Pennsylvania State Education Association; National Education Association; AARP; AAA **MH:** Marquis Who's Who in America; Marquis Who's Who Among American Women; Marquis Who's Who in the World; Who's Who Among America's Teachers **H:** Reading; Bread baking; Sewing; Piano lessons; Community service; Church volunteer **PA:** Democrat **RE:** Baptist **ADD:** 1133 Grandview Cir, Pottstown, PA, 19465

FOSSATI, SILVIA, T: Medical Educator, Director **I:** Education/Educational Services **CN:** New York University School of Medicine **PB:** Monteviale **SC:** Italy **ED:** Postdoctoral Training, Department of Pathology, New York University (2007-2012); PhD in Pharmacology and Toxicology, The University of Florence (2007); Research Fellow, Department of Pharmacology, The University of Florence (2003); BS in Molecular Biology, The University of Florence, Magna Cum Laude (2002); Student Fellow, Department of Experimental Pathology and Oncology, The University of Florence (2001-2002) **CT:** Certified in Essentials of Project Management, New York University, CCFL Training (2013); Certified in Leadership and Management Development, New York Academy of Science (2011) **C:** Director, Biofluid Biomarkers Core of the Cohen Veteran Center, Department of Psychiatry, New York University (2015-Present); Postdoctoral Fellow, Department of Pathology, New York University (2007-2012) **AW:** Leon Levy Fellowship in Neuroscience (2016); Chair, Jury to the 2015 Italian Scientists and Scholars of North America Award for Young Investigators (2015); Finalist, Finalist, Speaker, Young Investigator Award, Italian Scientists and Scholars of North America Foundation (2013) New Investigator Research Grant Award, Alzheimer's Association (2012); Postdoctoral Travel Award, Annual Meeting of the American Society for Biochemistry and Molecular Biology (2012); NYU Alzheimer's Disease Center Pilot Grant, Center of Excellence on Brain Aging, New York University Langone Medical Center (2010); Postdoctoral Travel Award, Alzheimer's Association International Conference on Alzheimer's Disease (2010);

Best Poster Presentation, Conference of the Italian Association of Research on Brain Aging (2006); Doctoral Fellowship, Pharmacology and Toxicology, The University of Florence (2004) **MEM:** Italian Scientists and Scholars in North America Foundation (ISSNAF) (2012-Present); American Heart Association (2012-Present); International Society to Advanced Alzheimer's Research and Treatment (2011-Present); Society for Neuroscience (2008-Present); New York Academy of Sciences (2007-Present); "Cohen Veteran Biosciences" Preclinical Program Committee (2016-Present); Research Alliance for PTSD Innovation and Discovery in Diagnostics (2016-Present); Director, Biofluid Biomaker Core of the Cohen Veteran Center (2015-Present); Committee Member, Alzheimer's Disease Center Pilot Grant Review (2014-Present); Chair, Jury for the ISSNAF Young Investigator Award in Biosciences and Cognitive Sciences (2015); New York Post Docs (2009-2012) **H:** Cooking; Baking; Latin dance; Theatre; Performances; The arts **ADD:** 4441 Purves Street, Apartment 809, Long Island City, NY, 11101 **URL:** http://www.med.nyu.edu/biosketch/fossas01

FOSTER, ELIZABETH CARROLL, T: Author (Retired) **I:** Writing and Editing **DOB:** 10/15/1928 **PB:** Lewisville, Arkansas **SC:** Arkansas/Lafayette **PT:** Benjamin F. Carroll; Era Mayfield Carroll **MS:** Widow **SPN:** John Kilby Foster (Deceased) **CH:** John K. Foster, Jr; Lindsey Foster Denton; Steven Carroll Foster; David Nielsen Foster **ED:** BA, University of Maryland (1974) **C:** Retired; Feature Writer, Editor, The Maryland Independent; Feature Writer, Editor, The St. Mary's Beacon; Freelance Writer, Maryland Magazine; Freelance Writer, Chesapeake; Freelance Writer, Various Magazines **CW:** Author, "Musings, Mutterings, and Aw Shucks: A Collection of Short Stories, Essays, and Features"(2011); Author, "Follow Me: The Life and Adventures of a Military Family" (2010); Author of novel, "Southern Winds A' Changing" (2008) **AW:** Author of the Month, Military Writers' Society of America (2011); First Honorable Mention, National Book Competition, Military Writers Society of America; Best Front Page Design, The Maryland Independent Newspaper **H:** Writing; Reading; Genealogy; Travel **RE:** Unitarianism **ADD:** 121 Cortez Rd Apt 426, Hot Springs, AR, 71909

FOTTLER, MYRON D., T: Professor, Executive Director **I:** Education/Educational Services **CN:** University of Central Florida **DOB:** 09/05/1939 **PB:** Boston **SC:** MA/USA **PT:** Myron Dustin Fottler; Anna Eileen Fottler **MS:** Widowed **SPN:** Carol Ann Fottler (8/11/1972, Deceased 6/2017) **ED:** PhD in Business, Columbia University (1970); MBA in Human Relations, Boston University, with Distinction (1963); BS in Industrial Relations, Northeastern University (1962); Coursework, Northeastern University **C:** Lecturer, "Health Services in Retail Outlets," University of Central Florida Public Television Station, Cocoa Beach Campus, Florida (2007); Lecturer, "Enhancing Customer Service in Oncology and Hematology," Michigan Society for Oncology and Hematology, University of Central Florida (2004); Lecturer, "Determinants of Medical Practice Organizational Performance," Physician Executive Program, College of Public Health, University of South Florida (1999); Lecturer, "Determining Your Strategic Web: Leadership Challenges and Choices," Strategic Leadership Institute, American College of Medical Practice Executives, MGMA Society for Physicians in Administration, Arthur D. Andersen Inc., San Antonio, TX (1998); Lecturer, "Navigating All Your Webs: Piloting Your Group's Future," Strategic Leadership Institute, American

College of Medical Practice Executives, MGMA Society for Physicians in Administration, Arthur D. Andersen Inc., Keystone, CO (1997); Lecturer, "Navigating Your Competitive Web: Making Strategy Work," Strategic Leadership Institute, American College of Medical Practice Executives, MGMA Society for Physicians in Administration, Arthur D. Andersen Inc., Keystone, CO (1997) **CR:** Senior Scholar, Lister Hill Center for Health Policy, School of Business and School of Health Related Professions, The University of Alabama at Birmingham (1983-1999); Adjunct Professor, Department of Sociology, The University of Alabama at Birmingham (1983-1999); Adjunct Professor, School of Public Health, The University of Alabama at Birmingham (1983-1999); Adjunct Professor, Community Health Sciences, College of Commerce and Business Administration, The University of Alabama, Tuscaloosa, AL (1979-1983); Visiting Associate Professor, Industrial Relations, College of Business Administration, The University of Iowa (1975-1976); Visiting Faculty Member, Industrial Relations Center, University of Minnesota (1975); Research Assistant, Graduate School of Business, Columbia University (1965-1966); Assistant to the Director, 28th Session, Executive Program in Business Administration, Arden House Campus, Columbia University, Harriman, NY (1965); Boston University Student Representative, United States Department of Labor, Washington, D.C. (1963) **CIV:** Associate Program Chairperson, Health Care and Public Sector Management, Southern Management Association (1994, 1990); Volunteer Radio Announcer, National Public Radio, WUAL 91.5 Tuscaloosa, AL (1989-1992); Associate Program Chairperson, Health Care and Public Sector Management, Southern Management Association (1987, 1983); Associate Program Chairperson, Health Care and Public Sector Management, Southern Management Association (1979); Judge, Institute for Administrative Research Proposal Award Contest, Academy of Management (1976-1977); United Way Citizens Advisory Committee, Volusia County, FL; Easterseals of Central Florida **CW:** Ad hoc Reviewer, "American Journal of Managed Care" (1999-Present); Editorial Board Member, International Journal of Applied Quality Management (1998-Present); Founding Editor, "Advances in Health Care Management" (1998-Present); Ad hoc Reviewer, "Journal of Labor Studies" (1994-Present); Member, Editorial Board Member, "Medical Care Research and Review" (1994-Present); Editorial Board Member, "Health Care Management Review" (1987-Present); Ad hoc Reviewer, "Hospital and Health Services Administration" (1987-Present); Co-Author, "Human Resources Management Applications: Cases, Exercises, Incidents, and Skill Builders," Seventh Edition, Southwestern College Publishing, Mason, OH (2011); Co-Author, "The Retail Revolution in Health Care," Praeger, Santa Barbara, CA (2010); Co-Author, "Essentials of Human Resources Management," Health Administration Press, Chicago, IL (2010); Co-Author, "Advances in Healthcare Management: Strategic Human Resource Management in Health Care, Volume Nine," Emerald Group Publishing Limited, Bingley, United Kingdom (2010); Co-Author, "Achieving Service Excellence, Strategies for Healthcare, Second Edition,"Health Administration Press, Chicago, IL (2010); Co-Editor, "Doctoral Education on Health Administration and Policy," Journal of Health Administration Education (2008); Co-Author, "Human Resources Management Applications: Cases, Exercises, Incidents, and Skill Builders, Sixth edition," Southwestern College Publishing, Cincinnati, OH (2008); Co-Author, "Human Resources in Healthcare Managing for

Success, Third Edition, "Health Administration Press, Chicago, IL (2008); Co-Author, "Advances in Health Care Management: Strategic Thinking and Entrepreneurial Action in Healthcare," Volume 6, JAI/Elsevier Science, Amsterdam, Netherlands (2007); Co-Author, "Applications in Human Resources Management, Fifth Edition," Southwestern College Publishing, Cincinnati, OH (2005) AW: Honoree, Fundamental of Human Resources Management (2018); Research Incentive Award, University of Central Florida (2007); Named, Best Paper, Healthcare Hospitality Management Track, Southern Management Association Meeting, Clearwater, FL (2006); Named, Best Paper, Healthcare/Hospitality Management Track, 2005 Southern Management Association Meeting, San Antonio, TX (2004); Named, Faculty Publication of the Year, American Association of Medical Administrators, Marriott Corporation Las Vegas, NV (2001); Recipient, Outstanding Service Award, Healthcare Management Division, Academy of Management (1999); Recipient, Second Place, Faculty Publication of the Year, American Association of Medical Administrators (1998); Southern Management Association Fellows Group (1998); Recipient, Edgar C. Hayhow Award for the Outstanding Article, "Hospital and Health Services Administration," American College of Healthcare Executives, Chicago, IL (1997); Recipient, Second Place, Faculty Publication of the Year, American Association of Medical Administrators (1997); Grant, Follow-Up and Evaluation of a Provider-Developed Report Card, St. Vincent's Hospital, Birmingham, AL (1997); Named, Best Paper Based on a Dissertation, Health Care Administration Division, Academy of Management, Cincinnati, OH (1996); Named, Best Theory to Practice Paper, Health Care Administration Division, Academy of Management, Vancouver, British Columbia (1995); Grantee, Medical Groups Face the Uncertain Future: Challenges, Opportunities, and Strategies, Abbott Laboratories, The Medical Management Association (1995); Recipient, Certificate of Appreciation, Administration-Health Services, University of Alabama at Birmingham (1994); Recipient, Second Place, Faculty Publication of the Year Award, American Association of Medical Administrators (1993); Named, Distinguished Lecturer, Army-Baylor Program, San Antonio, TX (1992); Named, Recommended Book, Best Books Committee, American College of Health Care Executives (1992); Finalist, George R. Terry Award, Academy of Management (1990-1991) MEM: Chair, Doctoral Education Faculty Forum, Association of University Programs in Health Administration (2007-Present); Chair, Research Committee, Healthcare Management Division, Academy of Management (2006-Present); Regents Advisory Committee for Central Florida, American College of Healthcare Executives (2000-Present); Site visitor, Accrediting Commission for Education in Health Administration, Association of University Programs in Health Administration (1989-Present); Invited speaker, Doctoral/Junior Faculty Consortium, Health Care Administration Division, Academy of Management (1986-Present); Member, Program Committee, Health Care Division, Academy of Management (1980-Present); Founder, Chairperson, Southern Industrial Relations Research Association (1980-Present); Chairperson, Sessions at national meetings, Academy of Management (1978-Present); Paper reviewer, Submissions to annual meetings, Academy of Management (1976-Present); Chair, Fund Raising Committee, Annual Meeting, Association of University Programs in Health Administration (2009); Member, Program Planning Committee, Annual Meeting, Association of University

Programs in Health Administration, Orlando, FL (2007); Member, Program Planning Committee, Annual Meeting, Association of University Programs in Health Administration, Washington, D.C. (2001); Member, Program Planning Committee, Annual Meeting, Association of University Programs in Health Administration, Los Angeles, CA (2000); Member, Task Force, Chief Executive Officer Evaluation, Association of University Programs in Health Administration (1997); Member, Program Planning Committee, Annual Meeting, Association of University Programs in Health Administration, Atlanta, GA (1996); Associate Program Chairperson, Health Care and Public Sector Management, Southern Management Association (1994) MH: Albert Nelson Marquis Lifetime Achievement Award (2017) H: Tennis; Jazz RE: Episcopalian BA: 4000 Central Florida Blvd, Department of Health Professions, University of Central Florida, Orlando, FL, 32816 ADD: 4670 Links Village Dr, unit A502, Ponce Inlet, FL, 32127-3008

FOURNIE, RAYMOND RICHARD, T: Equity Partner I: Law and Legal Services CN: Armstrong Teasdale, LLP DOB: 01/03/1951 PB: Belleville SC: IL/USA PT: Raymond Victor Fournie; Gladys M. (Muskopf) Fournie MS: Married SPN: Mary Lindeman (9/2/1978) CH: Sarah Dozier; John David; Anne Gerard; David Raymond ED: JD, School of Law, Saint Louis University (1979); BS, University of Illinois (1973) CT: United States District Court for the Eastern District of Missouri; United States District Court Southern District of Illinois; United States District Court for the Central District of Illinois; United States District Court for the Eastern District of Pennsylvania C: Partner, Armstrong Teasdale LLP, St. Louis, Missouri (1988-Present); Shareholder, Shepherd, Sandberg & Phoenix, St. Louis, Missouri (1986-1988); Associate, Shepherd, Sandberg & Phoenix, Professional Corporation, St. Louis, Missouri (1982-1986); Associate, Brown, James & Rabbitt, Professional Corporation, St. Louis, Missouri (1981-1982); Associate, Moser, Marsalek, et al., St. Louis, Missouri (1979-1980) CR: Executive Committee, Armstrong Teasdale LLP CIV: General Counsel, Board of Directors, Municipal Theatre Association of St. Louis; Chairman, Board of Directors, Municipal Theatre Association of St. Louis; Vice Chairman, Executive Board, Municipal Theatre Association of St. Louis CW: Performer, "Titanic," Municipal Theatre Association of St. Louis (2010) AW: Honoree, Best Lawyer in Mass Tort Litigation/Class Actions-Defendants, The Best Lawyers in America (2007-Present); Honoree, Lawyer of the Year in Mass Tort Litigation/Class Actions-Defendants, The Best Lawyers in America (2013); Honoree, Top-rated Lawyer in Health Care, Martindale-Hubbell (2013); Honoree, Top-rated Lawyer in Health Care, American Lawyer Media (2013); Honoree, Missouri/Kansas Region, Super Lawyers (2011-2015); Fellowship, University of Illinois (1974); AV Peer Review Rated Attorney, Martindale-Hubbell MEM: Chair, The Mini Opera (2014-2016); Chair, Board of Directors, Municipal Theatre Association of St. Louis (2014-2016); The Bar Association of Metropolitan St. Louis; Past President, Lawyer's Association of St. Louis; The St. Clair County Bar Association; DRI; IDC; Missouri Organization of Defense Lawyers BAR: Illinois State Bar (1980); The Missouri Bar (1979) MH: Albert Nelson Marquis Lifetime Achievement Award (2017) H: Singing; Baseball; Golf; Acting RE: Roman Catholic BA: 7700 Forsyth Blvd Ste 1800, Armstrong Teasdale, LLP, Saint Louis, MO, 63105 URL: https://www.armstrongteasdale.com/raymond-fournie/

FRAGNER, PAUL D., T: Orthopaedic Surgeon I: Medicine & Health Care CN: White Plains Hospital Physician Associates CH: Olivia; Ava; Isabella ED: Fellow in Hand and Upper Extremity Surgery, University of Pennsylvania, Philadelphia, PA (1991-1992); Resident in Orthopedic Surgery, SUNY Downstate Medical Center, Brooklyn, NY (1986-1991); MD, SUNY Upstate Medical University (1986) CT: Certified in Hand Surgery (1995-Present); Certified in Orthopedic Surgery (1994-Present) C: Physician, Orthopedic Hand Surgeon, White Plains Hospital, White Plains Physician Associates (1995-Present); Chief of Hand Surgery, Westchester Orthopedic Institute, White Plains Hospital; Chief, Division of Orthopedic Surgery, White Plains Hospital CR: Medical Consultant, New York Rangers; Clinical Instructor, Orthopaedic Surgery and Rehabilitation, Yale University School of Medicine AW: Named, Top Doctor in Hand Surgery, Westchester Magazine (2011-2017); Named, Top Doctor in Hand Surgery, Castle Connolly Medical Ltd. (2010-2017) MEM: American Academy of Orthopaedic Surgeons; American College of Surgeons; American Association for Hand Surgery; New York Society for Surgery of the Hand; New York State Society of Orthopaedic Surgeons; American Medical Association; The Medical Society of the State of New York; Westchester County Medical Society; International Society of Police Surgeons; The Phi Beta Kappa Society MH: Albert Nelson Marquis Lifetime Achievement Award (2017); Distinguished Humanitarian (2017) BA: 222 Westchester Ave Ste 101, WPHPA Orthopaedic Specialists, West Harrison, NY, 10604 URL: https://www.wphphysicianassociates.org/doctors/dr-paul-d-fragner-md

FRANCIS, TIMOTHY DUANE, T: Chiropractor I: Medicine & Health Care DOB: 03/01/1956 PB: Chicago SC: IL/USA PT: Joseph Duane Francis; Barbara Jane (Sigwalt) Francis ED: Postgraduate Work, Clark College (1986-Present); MS in Nutrition, University of Bridgeport (1990); MS in Biology, University of Bridgeport (1990); Doctorate of Chiropractics, Los Angeles College of Chiropractic, Southern California University Health Sciences, Magna Cum Laude (1984); BS, Los Angeles College of Chiropractic, Southern California University Health Sciences (1982); Coursework, University of Nevada, Reno (1974-1980); Coursework, Western Nevada College (1978) CT: Diplomate in Homeopathy, British Institute of Homeopathy International (1993); Diplomate, International College of Applied Kinesiology; Diplomate, American Academy of Pain Management; Diplomate, ANMCB; Certified Kinesiologist; Certified Applied Kinesiology Teacher; Licensed Chiropractor, State of California; Licensed Chiropractor, State of Nevada C: Chiropractor, Private Practice, Las Vegas, Nevada (1985-Present); Lead Instructor, Department of Principles & Practice, Los Angeles College of Chiropractic, Southern California University Health Science (1983-1985); Teaching Assistant, Department of Principles & Practice, Los Angeles College of Chiropractic, Southern California University Health Sciences (1983-1985); Instructor, Department of Recreation and Physical Education, University of Nevada, Reno (1976-1980) CR: Chairman, Syllabus Review Committee, International College of Applied Kinesiology (1994); Chairman, Exam Review Committee, International College of Applied Kinesiology (1993); Adjunct Faculty, The Union Institute College of Undergraduate Studies (Now Union Institute & University) (1993); Assistant Instructor, International College of Applied Kinesiology (1990); Joint Study Participant, National Olympic Training Center, Beijing, China (1990) CW:

Member, Editorial Review Board, "Alternative Medicine Review" (1996); Contributor, Articles, Professional Journals; Contributor, Publications, International College of Applied Kinesiology **AW:** Scholar of the Year Award, The Honor Society of Phi Kappa Phi (1980); Honoree, Charles F. Cutts Scholar (1980); Alan Beardall Memorial Award, International College of Applied Kinesiology **MEM:** Vice President, The Honor Society of Phi Kappa Phi (1979-1980); Fellow, International Academy of Medical Acupuncture, Inc.; Fellow, British Institute of Homeopathy International; Council on Sports Injuries, American Chiropractic Association; Council on Nutrition, American Chiropractic Association; Council on Roetgenology, American Chiropractic Association; Council on Technical Health, American Chiropractic Association; Council on Mental Health, American Chiropractic Association; Nevada Chiropractic Association; National Strength and Conditioning Association; Gonsted Clinical Studies Society; Foundation for Chiropractic Education; International Chiropractors Association; International College of Applied Kinesiology; International Federation of Practitioners of Natural Therapeutics; National Institute of Chiropractic Research; ANMA; The National Academy of Research Biochemists; The Phi Beta Kappa Society; Delta Sigma **MH:** Albert Nelson Marquis Lifetime Achievement Award (2017) **H:** Karate; Weightlifting **PA:** Republican **RE:** Roman Catholic **BA:** 7473 W Lake Mead Blvd Ste 100, Las Vegas, NV, 89128

FRANCISCO, RACQUEL RAMIREZ, I: Medicine & Health Care **ED:** BSN, St. Josephs Manila; Registered Nurse, Philippines **CT:** Certified Wound Care Nurse **C:** Registered Nurse, Windsor Care of Petaluma (2013); Psych Nurse, Crestwood (2008-2013) **CIV:** Volunteer, Local School **ACH:** Consistent honors student from elementary school through high school Class president, always an officer of the class

FRANK, STEVEN NEIL, T: Captain **I:** Infrastructure **CN:** Fairview Fire Rescue **DOB:** 02/15/1947 **PB:** Red Oak **SC:** IA/USA **PT:** Robert Joseph Frank; Joyce (Erickson) Frank **MS:** Married **SPN:** Carol Bert Femmer (1/4/1975) **ED:** ChD, California Institute of Technology (1974); BS, Colorado State University (1969) **C:** Captain, Fairview Fire Rescue (2009-Present); Vice President, Chief Technology Officer, L-3 Communications Infrared Products (2004-2008); Chief Technology Officer, Raytheon Commercial Infared, Dallas, TX (2002-2004); Chief Engineer, Raytheon Commercial Infrared, Dallas, TX (1999-2002); Manager, Uncooled IR Imaging, Texas Instruments Incorporated, Dallas, TX (1990-1999); Manager, Focal Plane Array Assembly and Testing, Texas Instruments Incorporated, Dallas, TX (1990-1991); Manufacturing Manager, Focal Plane Array, Texas Instruments Incorporated, Dallas, TX (1988-1990); Manager, Wafer Fabrication, Focal Plane Array, Texas Instruments Incorporated, Dallas, TX (1986-1988); Manager, Charge Coupled Imagers, Texas Instruments Incorporated, Dallas, TX (1983-1986); Manager, Fuel Cell Development, Texas Instruments Incorporated, Dallas, TX (1980-1983); Robert A. Welch Fellow, University of Texas (1974-1977); Senior Member, Technical Staff, Solar Energy Project, Texas Instruments Incorporated, Dallas, TX **CR:** Presenter in Field **CIV:** Volunteer Firefighter, Fairview Fire Rescue (1999-Present) **CW:** Referee, "Journal of Applied Physics" (1977-Present); Referee, "The Journal of Physical Chemistry A" (1977-Present); Co-Author, "Laboratory Techniques in Electroanalytical Chemistry" (1996); Contributor, Articles to Professional Journals **MEM:** American Association for the Advancement of Science; American

Chemical Society; The Electrochemical Society **MH:** Albert Nelson Marquis Lifetime Achievement Award (2017) **H:** Volunteer firefighting **ADD:** 471 Hackberry Drive, Mc Kinney, TX, 75069 **URL:** https://www.linkedin.com/in/steven-frank-00919712

FRANKEL, TAMAR, T: Law Educator **I:** Education/ Educational Services **CN:** Boston University School of Law **DOB:** 07/04/1925 **PB:** Tel Aviv **SC:** Israel **MS:** Married **SPN:** Raymond Clifford Atkins **CH:** Anat Bird; Michael Frankel **ED:** SJD, Harvard University (1972); LLM, Harvard University (1964); Diploma, Jerusalem Law Classes (1948) **C:** Professor of Law, Boston University School of Law (1971-Present); Assistant Professor of Law, Boston University School of Law (1968-1970); Lecturer, Boston University School of Law (1967); Special Assistant to Commissioner of Corps., State of California (1966-1967); Associate, Arnold & Porter, Washington (1965-1966); Associate, Ropes & Gray, Boston, MA (1964-1965); Legal Advisor, State of Israel Bonds Organization Europe, Paris (1962-1963); Private Practice, Tel Aviv (1951-1962); Assistant Attorney General, Legislative Department, Ministry of Justice, State of Israel (1948-1950) **CR:** Visiting Professor of Law, Harvard Law School (1979-1980, 2005); Harvard Business School (2006); Visiting Professor of Business Management (1980); Visiting Professor of Law, University of California, Berkeley (1982-1983); Faculty Member, Graduate School of Banking, Madison, WI (1985); Guest Scholar, Brookings Institute, Washington, DC (1986-1987); Attorney, Fellow, Securities and Exchange Commission, Washington, D.C. (1996-1997); Visiting Professor, Tokyo University Law School (1997); Chair, International Forum on the White Paper-Internet Organization (1998); Faculty Fellow, Berkman Klein Center for Internet & Society, Harvard Law School **CW:** Author, "Investment Management Regulation," Fathom Publishing (2015); Author, "The Ponzi Scheme Puzzle," Oxford University Press (2012); Author, "Fiduciary Law" (2010); Co-author, "Trust and Honesty in the Real World" (2009); Author, "Trust and Honesty, America's Business Culture at a Crossroads" (2006); Author, "Securitization: Structured Financing, Financial Assets Pools, and Asset-Backed Securities, 2nd Edition" (2006); Co-author, "The Regulation of Money Managers, 2nd Edition" (2001); Contributor, Chapters, Books; Contributor, Articles, Professional Journals and Newspapers **AW:** Visiting Fellow, Center for Socio-Legal Studies, St. Catherine's College, Oxford (2000); Women Trailblazers in the Law, American Bar Association; One of 500 Leading Lawyers in America, Lawdragon **MEM:** ABA; Committee on Federal Regulation of Securities, Banking Committee Section Corp. Banking and Business Law; Life Member, Administrative Committee, Restatement of Trusts, American Law Institute; Boston Bar Association; American Bar Foundation; Massachusetts Bar Association **BAR:** Massachusetts (1972) **ADD:** 61 Winston Rd, Newton, MA, 02459

FREEDMAN, RICHARD C., T: Vice President of Investments **I:** Business Management/Business Services **CN:** UBS **ED:** BBA in Accounting, Cleveland State University (1984) **C:** Vice President of Investments, UBS (2011-Present); Vice President of Wealth Management, Morgan Stanley Smith Barney LLC (1991-2011); Financial Adviser, Merrill Lynch (1987-1989) **CIV:** Board Member, Cleveland Baseball Federation; President, Board of Trustees, Temple Israel Ner Tamid **CW:** Guest, Radio Shows; Contributor, Articles to Professional Journals **AW:** Recipient, President's Award of Distinguished Service, Temple Israel Ner Tamid (2016) **BA:** 600 Superior Ave E Ste 2700, UBS Financial Services

Inc., Cleveland, OH, 44114 **ADD:** 6677 Silvermound Dr, Mentor, OH, 44060

FREEDMAN, JAY W., T: Lawyer (Retired) **I:** Law and Legal Services **CN:** Foley & Lardner LLP **DOB:** 05/19/1942 **PB:** Washington **SC:** DC/USA **PT:** Walter Freedman; Maxine (Weil) Freedman **MS:** Married **SPN:** Linda Newman (8/7/1966) **CH:** Courteney; Spencer **ED:** JD, Yale Law School, Yale University (1967); BA, Williams College (1964) **C:** Retired (2017); Partner, Foley & Lardner LLP, Washington D.C. (2001-2017); Managing Partner, Foley & Lardner LLP, Washington D.C. (2007-2010); Partner, Freedman, Levy, Kroll & Simonds, Washington D.C. (1972-2001); Associate, Freedman, Levy, Kroll & Simonds, Washington D.C. (1968-1972); Attorney, Office of General Counsel of the Federal Communications Commission (1967-1968) **CIV:** Board of Directors, Georgetown Business Improvement District (2012-Present); Secretary-Treasurer, Georgetown Business Improvement District (2012-Present); First Vice President, Georgetown Business Improvement District (2006-2008); Board of Directors, Heifetz International Music Institute (2003-2008); Board of Trustees, The Kreeger Museum (2002-2008); Board of Directors, Georgetown Business Improvement District (2002-2006); Board of Directors, Smithsonian Libraries (2001-2010); Past President, American Jewish Committee, Washington D.C. (1987-1989); Past President, Board of Trustees, Washington Hebrew Congregation (1982-1984); Co-head, Alumni Board, Smithsonian Libraries **MEM:** Secretary, Yale Law School Alumni Association (2003-2004); Executive Committee, Yale Law School Alumni Association (1999-2004); President, Woodmont Country Club (1997-1999); ABA; The District of Columbia Bar; The Economic Club of Washington, D.C.; The International Legal Honor Society of Phi Delta; Lifetime Member, Woodmont Country Club; Lifetime Member, American Jewish Committee, Washington D.C.; Lifetime Member, Washington Hebrew Congregation **BAR:** Supreme Court of the United States (1973); The District of Columbia Bar (1968) **BA:** 3000 K St NW Ste 600, Foley & Lardner Llp, Washington, DC, 20007 **ADD:** 7221 Hidden Creek Road, Bethesda, MD, 20817

FREEMAN, PETER S., T: Textile Executive **I:** Textiles **DOB:** 04/23/1944 **PB:** Brooklyn **SC:** NY/USA **PT:** Graydon Lavern Freeman; Ruth Crosby (Sunderlin) Freeman **MS:** Married **SPN:** Linda Raissa Blanco (9/23/1972) **CH:** Victoria Blanco **ED:** MBA in Finance, Syracuse University (1969); BS, Cornell University (1966) **CT:** Certification in Accounting, New York University (1979); Certified Public Accountant, State of Colorado **C:** Vice President, Financial Secretary, Charles Samelson, Inc., New York, NY (1995-2013); Consultant, Liberty Fabrics, Inc., New York, NY (1993); Corporate Controller, Liberty Fabrics, Inc., New York, NY (1986-1992); Vice President of Finance and Administration, Vitreous International Trading Company, Inc., Great Neck, NY (1986); Vice President of Finance, Toyobo Subsidiary, Rosewood Fabrics, New York, NY (1981-1985); Division Controller, Grace Textiles, New York, NY (1979-1981); Director of Financial Analysis and Reporting, Grace Textiles, New York, NY (1975-1979); Senior Financial Analyst, W.R. Grace Retail and Textiles, New York, NY (1973-1975); New Business Development and Product Manager, CBS Public Group, New York, NY (1970-1973) **CIV:** President, Freeman Family Foundation (2006-Present) **MIL:** U.S. Army, Vietnam (1968-1970) **MEM:** Secretary-Treasurer, American Life Federation (2000-2006); Board of Directors, American Life Federation (1997-2006); President, Cornell University Lambda Alumni (1985-1989); Board of Directors, Cornell University

Lambda Alumni (1982-1996); American Institute of Certified Public Accountants; Colorado Society of Certified Public Accountants **H:** Sports; Gardening **RE:** Presbyterian **ADD:** 3445 Kellys Corners Road, Interlaken, NY, 14847

FREEMAN, WALDEN SHANKLIN, T: History Educator (Retired) **I:** Education/Educational Services **DOB:** 08/31/1930 **PB:** Indianapolis **SC:** IN/USA **PT:** Harry Z. Freeman; Ellen (Shanklin) Freeman **MS:** Married **SPN:** Carolyn Louise Robertsdahl (8/19/1978) **ED:** PhD, Indiana University (1967); MA in History, Butler University (1959); BA in History, Butler University (1952) **C:** Retired (1994); Vice President, Academic Affairs, Schreiner University, Kerrville, TX (1986-1994); Professor of History, Schreiner University, Kerrville, TX (1986-1994); Chairman, Humanities Division, William Woods University, Fulton, MO (1983-1985); Professor, William Woods University, Fulton, MO (1983-1985); Associate Dean, Academic Affairs, William Woods University, Fulton, MO (1979-1983); Registrar, William Woods University, Fulton, MO (1979-1983); Professor of History, William Woods University, Fulton, MO (1979-1983); Associate Professor of History, William Woods University, Fulton, MO (1968-1972); Instructor in History, Gettysburg College (1963-1968) **CR:** Visiting Associate Professor of History, Indiana University Bloomington (1972-1973) **CIV:** Chapter Treasurer, American Red Cross, Kerrville, TX (1995-1998); Member, Board of Directors, American Red Cross, Kerrville, TX (1993-1997); Member, Steering Committee, Leadership Kerr County Alumni Association, Kerrville, TX (1988-1993); Chairman, Campaign Subcommittee, United Way (1982-1983); Former Chairman, Zion Lutheran Children's Center **MIL:** Commander, U.S. Naval Reserve (1954-1976) **CW:** Contributor, Articles, Professional Journals; Contributor, Book Reviews **MEM:** President, Kiwanis International, Kerrville, TX (1995-1996); National Secretary, Alpha Chi Honor Society (1991-1995); President, Kiwanis International, Fulton, TX (1981-1982); The Organization of American Historians; American Historical Association; Indiana Historical Society **MH:** Albert Nelson Marquis Lifetime Achievement Award (2017) **H:** Outside work in the yard **ADD:** 411 Coronado Dr, Kerrville, TX, 78028

FREITAS, JEFFREY ANTHONY, T: Textile Design Agency Executive **I:** Textiles **CN:** J. Anthony Group **DOB:** 09/29/1946 **PB:** Fall River **SC:** MA/USA **PT:** Antone Freitas; Belmira (Souza) Freitas **MS:** Married **SPN:** Donna Thayer Short **ED:** Coursework, Southeast Massachusetts University (Now University of Massachusetts Dartmouth) (1972-1973); BS, Roger Williams College (1972); AS, Franklin Institute (1967) **C:** President, J. Anthony Group, Pembroke, MA (1986-Present); Vice President, Kartex, Inc., Fall River, MA (1980-1984); Sweater Division Manager, Health-Tex, Inc., Central Falls, RI (1977-1980); Contractor, Manager, Garland Corp., Brockton, MA (1973-1977); Mechanical Designer, Raytheon Submarine Division, Portsmouth, RI (1967-1970) **CR:** Lecturer on Textiles, University of Massachusetts; Lecturer on Textiles, Dartmouth University **CIV:** Vice President, Pembroke Committee Kid's Fair (1990-Present); Chairman, Drug Awareness & Child Luring Prevention, Pembroke, MA (1989-Present) **MEM:** Chairman of Masonic Awareness, Freemasons (1989-Present); Board of Directors, Pembroke Chamber of Commerce, MA (1987-Present); President, Pembroke Chamber of Commerce, MA (1995-1997); President, Pembroke Chamber of Commerce, MA (1988-1989) **H:** Sailing; Golf; Skiing; Tae Kwon Do **RE:** Roman Catholic **ADD:** 65 Pattison Rd, Abington, MA, 02351

FRELOW, ROBERT DEAN SR., T: School System Administrator (Retired), Writer **I:** Education/Educational Services **DOB:** 08/01/1932 **PB:** Seminole **SC:** OK/USA **PT:** Jasper Wallace Frelow; Florine (Hamilton) Frelow **MS:** Married **SPN:** Rena Frelow (9/8/1983); Maxine Camille Gibbs (Divorced 5/1983) **CH:** Robert Frelow, Jr.; Frederick; Michael; Martin Hersh; Ruth Hersh **ED:** PhD, University of California, Berkeley (1970); MA, San Francisco State University (1960); BA, San Francisco State College (1954) **CT:** Certified Administrator, States of New York and California; Certified Teacher, States of New York and California **C:** Superintendent of Schools, Greenburgh Schools, Hartsdale, NY (1975-1990); Assistant Superintendent, Greenburgh Schools, Hartsdale, NY (1970-1975); Assistant to Superintendent, Berkeley Unified Schools (1967-1970); Teacher, Berkeley Unified Schools, California (1966-1967); Teacher, Oakland Unified Schools, California (1960-1966) **CR:** Consultant, Wise Services, White Plains, NY (1990-Present); Adjunct Professor, Pace University, New York, NY (1974-1990); Adjunct Professor, Columbia University, New York, NY (1970-1973); Coordinator, School Desegregation, Berkeley Schools (1967-1970); Consultant, School Desegregation, Berkeley Schools (1966-1970); Dance Instructor; Fellow, Board of Directors, Rotary International **CIV:** Board of Directors, Hartsdale Kiwanis (2003); Board of Directors, Westchester Cable Commission, White Plains, NY (1990); Board of Directors, Westchester Arts Council, White Plains, NY (1990); Board of Directors, California Synod, Presbyterian Church (1966) **MIL:** Captain, US Air Force (1954-1964) **CW:** Author, "Smoke And Mirrors" (2008); Author, "At the Rainbow's End" (2006); Author, "Blood Runs Deep" (2002); Co-Author, Editor, "I Am a Blade of Grass" (1989); Author, "The Berkeley Plan for Desegregation" (1968); Contributor, Articles to Professional Journals; Singer, San Francisco Opera; Singer, Chorus of Prisoners **AW:** Honoree, Greenburgh Central Seven Educational Foundation (2005); Eponym, Dr. Robert D. Frelow Cultural Center, Hartsdale, NY (1991); Recipient, Executive Leadership Award, Business Careers Club, Hartsdale, NY (1991); Recipient, Paul Harris Award, Rotary of America (1991); Recipient, Citizen of the Year Award, Kappa Alpha Psi (1984); Recipient, Citizen of the Year Award, Kappa Alpha Psi (1978); Urban Studies Grantee, University of California, Berkeley (1969) **MEM:** Kiwanis International **MH:** Albert Nelson Marquis Lifetime Achievement Award (2017) **H:** Writing; Reading; Travel; Photography; Theater; Musical performances; Singing; Sketching **PA:** Democrat **RE:** Presbyterian **BA:** 581 Old White Plains Road, Apt. 236, Tarrytown, NY, 10591

FRIEDBERG, AHRON, T: Psychiatrist **I:** Medicine & Health Care **PB:** New York City **SC:** NY/USA **ED:** MD, Jacobs School of Medicine and Biomedical Sciences, University at Buffalo (1985-1990); BA, Dartmouth College (1985) **CT:** Board Certified Psychiatrist; Licensed Psychoanalyst **C:** Psychiatrist/Psychoanalyst, Private Practice; Clinical Professor, Department of Psychiatry, Icahn School of Medicine at Mount Sinai; Co-Chair, Advisory Board, Department of Psychiatry, Icahn School of Medicine at Mount Sinai; Former Associate Director, Division of Psychotherapy, Icahn School of Medicine at Mount Sinai; Founding Director, Park Avenue Wellness Center **CIV:** Volunteer, United Jewish Appeal **CW:** Author, "Desire On and Off the Couch," The American Journal of Psychoanalysis (2013); Co-Author, "The Couch as Icon," The Psychoanalytic Review (2012); Co-Author, "Operationalizing a Bedside Pen Entry Notebook Clinical Database System in C-L Psychiatry," General Hospital Psychiatry (1995); Co-Author, "Gene Transfer for Therapy of Hematologic Diseases," Contemporary Issues in Pediatric Transfer Medicine (1988); Author, "A Hand and a Name," British Medical Journal (1984); Co-Author, "Psychotherapy for Schizophrenia: A Review of Modalities and Their Evidence Base," Psychodynamic Psychiatry; Co-Author, "Between Us: A Father and Son Speak"; Co-Author, "Flashing Seven: The Seven Essential Skills for Living and Leading"; Executive Editor, InternationalPsychoanalysis.net; Managing Editor, InternationalPsychoanalysis.net; Book Review Editor, Psychodynamic Psychiatry; Contributor, Articles to Professional Journals Including The Psychoanalytic Review, The American Journal of Psychoanalysis and Psychodynamic Psychiatry **AW:** Freud Award, American Society of Psychoanalytic Physicians (2017) **MEM:** Chair, International Council of Editors of Psychoanalytic Journals; Two-time National President, American Society of Psychoanalytic Physicians **BA:** 925 Park Ave # 1B, New York, NY, 10028 **URL:** http://www.ahronfriedbergmd.com

FRIEDMAN, C. MARSHALL, T: Owner, Attorney **I:** Law and Legal Services **CN:** C. Marshall Friedman, PC **CH:** Five Children **ED:** JD, Washington University in St. Louis (1964) **CT:** Certified Civil Trial Advocate, National Board of Trial Advocacy **C:** Owner, Attorney, C. Marshall Friedman, PC (1982-Present) **CR:** Adjunct Professor, School of Law, Washington University in St. Louis (1982-Present) **CIV:** Member, Railroad Safety Advisory Committee, Federal Railroad Administration; Former President, Missouri-Southern Illinois Chapter, American Board of Trial Advocates **CW:** Author, "Lung Damaged Caused by Exposure to TDI," Courtroom Medicine - Chest, Heart and Lungs (1986); Author, "Federal Employers' Liability Act, Jones Act and Longshoremen's and Harbor Workers' Compensation Act" **AW:** Honoree, Best Lawyers in St. Louis, The Wall Street Journal, Dow Jones & Company (2017); Outstanding Trial Lawyer Award, The Missouri Bar (1970); Honoree, The Best Lawyers in America **BAR:** The Missouri Bar **BA:** 1010 Market St Ste 1480, C. Marshall Friedman, PC, Saint Louis, MO, 63101

FROST, GLEN E., T: Attorney at Law **I:** Law and Legal Services **CN:** Frost & Associates, LLC **ED:** LLM in Taxation, University of Baltimore School of Law (2010); JD, University of Baltimore School of Law (2008); MS in Forensic Accounting, Villa Julie College (2006); BS in Accounting, Stevenson University (2006) **CT:** Certificate in Estate Planning Law, University of Baltimore School of Law (2010); Certified Public Accountant (2006) **C:** Owner, Attorney at Law, Frost and Associates (2011-Present); Owner, President, Glen E. Frost, Holdings (2002-Present); Attorney, Certified Public Accountant, Law Office of Gerald W. Kelly (2010-2011); Attorney, Thomas & Libowitz, P.A. (2009-2010); Certified Public Accountant, Law Office of Gerald W. Kelly (2007-2009); Auditor, Grant Thornton LLP (2004-2006) **AW:** Rising Stars, Super Lawyers (2013-Present) **MEM:** Board, American Systems Abroad; Board, Anarando County Bar Association; Board, Maryland State Bar Association Tax Section **H:** Boating; Fishing **BA:** 888 Bestgate Road, Suite 400, Annapolis, MD, 21491 **ADD:** 888 Bestgate RdÅ Ste 400, Frost & Associates, LLC, Annapolis, MD, 21401 **URL:** https://www.linkedin.com/in/irsattorney

FROST, BARRY WARREN, T: Attorney **I:** Law and Legal Services **CN:** Teich Groh & Frost **DOB:** 08/17/1947 **PB:** Glen Ridge **SC:** NJ/US **CH:** Benjamin; Alison; Max **ED:** JD, New York Law School

(1976); BS, Bradley University (1969) **C:** Partner, Teich, Groh & Frost, Trenton, NJ (1977-Present); Associate, Gladstein & Isaac, New York City, NY (1972-1977) **CW:** Author, "Recent Developments in the Area of Sex-Based Discrimination — The Courts, The Congress and The Constitution," 20 N.Y.L.F. 359 (1974) **AW:** American Jurisprudence Award **MEM:** Master, Bankruptcy American Inn of Court (2002-Present); Officer, State of New Jersey, Bankruptcy Law Section (1999); Member, Associate Editor, New York Law School Law Review (1973-1976); Green Acres Country Club; New York State Bar Association; ABA; Member, Panel of Trustees, U.S. Trustee for the District of New Jersey **BAR:** New Jersey State Bar Association; New York State Bar Association; United States District Court for the District of New Jersey; United States District Court for the Southern District of New York; United States Court of Appeals for the Third Circuit; Supreme Court of the United States **MH:** Albert Nelson Marquis Lifetime Achievement Award (2017) **BA:** 3131 Princeton Pike Bldg 110, Teich Groh & Frost, Lawrenceville, NJ, 08648 **ADD:** 3131 Princeton Pike Bldg 5 Ste 110, Teich Groh & Frost, Lawrenceville, NJ, 08648

FUENTES, YVONNE, T: Associate Professor of Spanish **I:** Education/Educational Services **CN:** University of West Georgia **PB:** New York **SC:** NY/USA **ED:** PhD, Universidad Complutense Madrid (1997); MA in Spanish Literature, New York University (1992); BA in Spanish, New York University (1978) **C:** Assistant Professor of Spanish, Department of Foreign Languages and Literature, University of West Georgia (2012-Present); Visiting Assistant Professor of Spanish, Department of Spanish and Portuguese, Emory University (2008-2009); Assistant Professor of Spanish, Department of Foreign Language and Literature, Louisiana State University (2001-2008); Visiting Assistant Professor of Spanish, Department of Romance Studies, Duke University (1995-1998); Visiting Lecturer, Duke University (1993-1998); Staff, Washington Academy of Languages (1985-1989); Staff, Spanish Branch, Marc Rich and Company (1982-1985); Staff, New York Branch, Marc Rich and Company (1980-1982); Staff, Morgan Stanley (1979-1980) **CR:** Standing Member, Bilingual Translation Review Committee, National Assessment of Educational Progress (2012-Present); Member, Women and Gender Studies Awards Committee for Best Dissertation, Louisiana State University (2003); Coordinator, Duke in Spain Summer Program, Duke University (1987-1995); Representative, Dissertations, Louisiana State University **CIV:** President. Ibero-American Society for Eighteenth Century Studies ; Executive Secretary, Ibero-American Society for Eighteenth Century Studies (2004-2011); Treasurer, Ibero-American Society for Eighteenth Century Studies (2004-2011); Speaker, Fifth Annual State Spanish Club Convention (2004) **CW:** Evaluator, "The People of Iberville Parish Series: The Spanish of Iberville," Iberville Museum Association (2008); Peer Reader, "Studies in Eighteenth-Century Culture" (2008); Peer Reader, "PORTAL: Journal of Multidisciplinary International Studies," UTS Press (2007); Author, " Martires y anticristos: Analisis bibliografico sobre la Revolucion francesa en Espana" Iberoamericana (2006); Editor, "Leading Ladies: Mujeres en la literatura hispana y en las artes," Louisiana State University Press (2006); Author, "El triangulo sentimental en el drama del siglo dieciocho (Inglaterra, Francia, Espana)," Reichenberger (1999); Contributor, Articles, Professional Journals; Contributor, Book Reviews; Contributor, Presentations, Professional Conferences **MEM:** Modern Languages Association; The American Association of Teachers of Spanish and Portuguese; Asociacion Internacional de Hispanistas;

American Society for Eighteenth-Century Studies; Ibero-American Society for Eighteenth Century Studies; AAUP; ATA **MH:** Albert Nelson Marquis Lifetime Achievement Award (2017) **H:** Reading; Travel **BA:** 1601 Maple Street, University Of West Georgia, Carrollton, GA, 30118 **ADD:** 517 N Lakeshore Dr, Carrollton, GA, 30117

FUKUCHI, KEN-ICHIRO, T: Medical Educator, Researcher **I:** Education/Educational Services **CN:** University of Illinois **PB:** Nagasaki **SC:** Japan **MS:** Married **ED:** PhD, Graduate School of Medicine, Osaka University (1985); MD, Graduate School of Medicine, Osaka University (1979) **C:** Professor, Department of Cancer Biology and Pharmacology, College of Medicine, University of Illinois (2005-Present); Associate Professor, Department of Cancer Biology and Pharmacology, College of Medicine, University of Illinois (2005-Present); Associate Professor, Department of Genetics, University of Alabama (2002-2005); Associate Professor, University of Alabama at Birmingham (1995-2002); Research Associate, Department of Medicine and Geriatrics, Osaka University (1981-1986); Intern, Department of Medicine and Geriatrics, Osaka University (1979-1980) **CR:** Zenith Fellow, Alzheimer's Association (2003); Chairman, Bio Safety Committee, "Frontiers in Bioscience"; Chairman, Chemical Safety Committee, "Frontiers in Bioscience" **CIV:** Board Member, Central Illinois Chapter, Alzheimer's Association **CW:** Managing Editor, "Frontiers in Bioscience" (2006-Present); Contributor, Articles, Professional Journals **AW:** Research Award, NIH (2017); Outstanding Research Award, University of Illinois College of Medicine (2007); Alzheimer Research Award, Fraternal Order of Eagles (1993); Mervin D. Peck Investigator Initiated Research Award, Alzheimer's Association (1990) **MEM:** American Associate for the Advancement of Science; Society for Neuroscience; Alzheimer's Association **MH:** Albert Nelson Marquis Lifetime Achievement Award (2017) **ADD:** 5130 W Ancient Oak Drive, Peoria, IL, 61615

FUKUSHIMA, GLEN S., T: Senior Fellow **I:** Government Administration/Government Relations/Government Services **CN:** Center for American Progress **PB:** Tokyo **SC:** Japan **MS:** Married **ED:** JD, Harvard University (1982); Master's Degree in Regional Studies, Harvard University (1976) **C:** Senior Fellow, Center for American Progress (2012-Present); Member, Board of Councilors, U.S.-Japan Council (2009-2014); Chairman, Japanese Division, Airbus S.A.S., Tokyo, Japan (2010-2012); Director, Japanese Division, Airbus S.A.S., Tokyo, Japan (2010-2012); President, Japanese Division, Airbus S.A.S. (2005-2010); Chief Executive Officer, Japanese Division, Airbus S.A.S. (2005-2010); Co-president, NCR Japan (2004-2005); President, Cadence Design Systems, Inc. (2000-2004); Chairman, Cadence Design Systems, Inc. (2000-2004); President, Arthur D. Little, Japan (1998-2000); Chief Executive Officer, Arthur D. Little, Japan (1998-2000); President, The American Chamber of Commerce in Japan (1997-1999); Vice President, Japanese Division, AT&T (1990-1998); Director for Japan & China, Office of the United States Trade Representative (1985-1990) **CR:** Member, Various Corporate Boards; Member, Various Government Advisory Councils; Board Member, Japan Association of Corporate Executives; Board Member, America-Japan Society; Board Member, Japan Center for International Exchange; Board Member, Japan Society of Boston; Board Member, Japan Society of Northern California; Board Member, Japan-America Society of Washington, DC; Board Member, International House of Japan; Board Member, Japanese American National Museum; Board Member, U.S.-Japan

Council; Board Member, Global Council of the Asia Society **CIV:** Global Advisory Committee, Tokyo Rotary Club, Rotary International; Director's Circle, San Francisco Museum of Modern Art; Board Member, Washington Bach Concert **AW:** Recipient, Leadership Award, Leadership Education for the Asian Pacific (2014); Honoree, Honorary Alumnus, Keio University (2012); Recipient, Person of the Year Award, National Japanese American Historical Society (2008); Recipient, Alumni Hall of Fame Award, Stanford University (2002); Recipient, Excellence 2000 Award, USPAACC (1999); Recipient, Masayoshi Ohira Memorial Prize, The Politics of U.S.-Japan Economic Friction (1993); Recipient, Fulbright Fellowship, National Science Foundation **BA:** 1111 23rd St NW Apt 5A, Center for American Progress, Washington, DC, 20037 **URL:** https://www.americanprogress.org/about/staff/fukushima-glen/bio/

FULLER, DAVID OTIS JR., T: Lawyer/Judge **I:** Law and Legal Services **CN:** Tuckahoe Village **DOB:** 05/28/1939 **PB:** Grand Rapids **SC:** MI/USA **PT:** David Otis Fuller; Virginia Chapin (Emery) Fuller **MS:** Married **SPN:** Isabelle Patrice Gigout (7/5/1968) **CH:** Thomas Andrew; Christian Scott; Pierre Emery; Margaret Isabelle **ED:** Postgraduate Coursework, University of Paris (1966); JD, Harvard Law School, Harvard University (1964); Postgraduate Coursework, The George Washington University (1963); BA, Wheaton College (1961) **C:** Partner, Bosworth, Gray & Fuller, Bronxville, NY (1994-Present); Justice, Tuckahoe Village, New York, (1986-Present); Partner, Baker, Nelson & Williams, New York City, NY (1987-1994); Private Practice, New York City, NY (1984-1987); Deputy, Reader's Digest Association, Inc., (1974-1984); General Counsel, Reader's Digest Association, Inc. (1974-1984); Corporate Attorney, Pan American World Airways, Inc. (1973-1974); Law Secretary to Justice, New York County (1972-1973); Assistant District Attorney, New York County (1966-1972); Associate, Amberg, Law & Fallon, Grand Rapids, MI (1964-1965); Law Clerk, U.S. House of Representatives Judiciary Committee (1963) **CIV:** Warden Episcopalian Church (1991-1997) **MIL:** Major, New York Guard (2001-2007) **CW:** Editor, Harvard Journal on Legislation (1962-1964) **AW:** Magistrate of Year Award, New York State Magistrates Association (2007) **MEM:** New York State Magistrates Association (2006-2007); President, Federal Bar Council, Westchester County Magistrates Association (1993-1994); Communications Law Committee, Association of the Bar of the City of New York (1984-1987); Arbitrator, American Arbitration Association (1983-1996); Chairman, Privacy Committee, New York State Bar Association (1982-1984); American Bar Association, Special Commission Future New York State Center; Westchester County Bar Association; Harvard Club, New York City **MH:** Albert Nelson Marquis Lifetime Achievement Award (2017) **H:** Coin Collecting/Numismatics; Fishing; Racquet Sports **BA:** 116 Kraft Ave Ste 11, Bosworth Gray & Fuller, Bronxville, NY, 10708

FULLER, JAMES W., T: Financial Planner **I:** Financial Services **CN:** Bridge Information Systems **DOB:** 04/03/1940 **PB:** Rochester **SC:** CA/USA **PT:** Raymond S.; Mildred (Osteimeier) F. **CH:** Kristen Anne; Glen William **ED:** MBA, California State University (1967); BS, San Jose State University, California (1962); AA, San Bernardino College, California (1960) **C:** Director, Bridge Information Systems, San Francisco, CA (1987-Present); President, Bull & Bear Corp., New York, NY (1985-1987); Senior Vice President, Charles Schwab & Co., San Francisco, CA (1981-1985); Senior Vice President, New York Stock Exchange, New York, NY (1977-1981); Director of Financial Programs, SRI International, Menlo Park, CA (1974-1977); Vice President, Shields & Co., San Francisco, CA (1971-1974); Vice President, Dean Witter, San Francisco, CA (1967-1971) **CR:** Cavitation Inc. (2009-Present); Chairman of Board Directors, Pacific Research Institute (1992-1997) **CIV:** California State Republican Party; San Francisco Republican Party; University of California, Santa Cruz (1999-2009); Director, Global Economic Action Institute, New York, NY (1989-2000); Director, Securities Industry Protection Corp., Washington (1981-1989) **MEM:** The Family Club; Olympic Club; Jonathon Club; University Club; The Lincoln Club; Political Committee for Economic Growth; Newcomen Society; World Affairs Council; San Francisco Committee, Council on Foreign Relations; Commonwealth Club **H:** Tennis; Politics; Public affairs **PA:** Republican **RE:** Presbyterian **ADD:** 2584 Filbert Street, San Francisco, CA, 94123

FULLER, ROBERT, T: Architect **I:** Architecture & Construction **CN:** Fuller Fuller & Associates **DOB:** 10/06/1942 **PB:** Denver **SC:** CO/USA **PT:** Kenneth Roller Fuller; Gertrude Ailene (Heid) Fuller **MS:** Married **SPN:** Virginia Louise Elkin (8/23/1969) **CH:** Kimberly Kirsten; Kelsey Christa **ED:** Masters of Architecture and Urban Design, Washington University in St. Louis (1974); Bachelor of Architecture, University of Colorado (1967) **CT:** Registered Professional Architect, State of Colorado; Certification, National Council of Architectural Registration Boards **C:** Principal, Fuller Fuller & Associates, Denver, CO (1975-Present); Urban Designer, Victor Gruen & Associates (1973-1975); Architect, Planner, Urban Research and Design Center, St. Louis, MO (1970-1972); Architectural Designer, Marvin Hatami Associates (1968-1969); Architectural Designer, Fuller & Fuller, Denver, CO **CIV:** Past President, Denver East Central Civic Association; Past President, Country Club Historic District Board of Directors; Cherry Creek Steering Committee; Treasurer, Cherry Creek Foundation; Past President, Horizon Adventures, Inc; Permanent Secretary-Treasurer, Architectural Education Foundation, AIA Colorado **MIL:** Sergeant, U.S. Marine Corps Reserve (1964-1970) **MEM:** Past President, Denver Chapter, American Institute of Architects; University Club, Denver; Rocky Mountain Vintage Racing Club; Past President, The Colorado Arlberg Club; Delta Phi Delta; Phi Gamma Delta **H:** Vintage car racing; Skiing; Fly fishing; Reading; Sketching **ADD:** 2244 E 4th Ave, Denver, CO, 80206 **URL:** http://fullerarch.com/Historical_Background.html

FUNDERBURK, RAYMOND, T: Circuit Court Judge **I:** Law and Legal Services **DOB:** 03/02/1944 **PB:** Philadelphia **SC:** PA/USA **PT:** Walter Funderburk; Inez (Prince) Funderburk **ED:** JD, University of Illinois (1978); MPA, Roosevelt University (1975); BA, University of Illinois (1974); AA, Olive-Harvey College (1972) **C:** Judge, Circuit Court of Cook County, Chicago, IL (1993-Present); Associate, Earl L. Neal and Associates, Chicago, IL (1988-1993); Associate, Jones, Ware & Grenard, Chicago, IL (1983-1988); Associate, O. Kenneth Thomas Ltd., Harvey, IL (1982-1983); Managing Attorney, Cook County Legal Assistance, Harvey, IL (1980-1982); Staff Attorney, Cook County Legal Assistance, Harvey, IL (1978-1980) **CR:** Legal Advisory Board, Thornton Community College, South Holland, IL (1982-Present); Chairman, Cook County Legal Assistance Foundation, Oak Park, IL (1985-1987); Aunt Martha's Service, Park Forest, IL (1981-1983); Board of Directors, Cook County Legal Assistance Foundation **CIV:** Chairman, Zoning Board of Appeals, Park Forest, IL (1988-1999); Housing Board of Appeals, Park Forest (1988-1999); Equal Employ-

ment Opportunity Board, Park Forest (1988-1999); Housing Review Board, Park Forest (1988-1999); Board of Directors, Park Forest Public Library (1982) **MIL:** U.S. Army (1965-1967) **AW:** Honoree, Distinguished Graduate, Olive-Harvey Junior College, City Colleges of Chicago (2001); Honoree, Distinguished Graduate, College of Law, University of Illinois at Urbana-Champaign (1998-1999); City Partner Award, The University of Illinois at Chicago (1995); Certificates of Appreciation, South Suburban YMCA (1986, 1987); Certificate of Appreciation Thornton Community College, now South Suburban College (1985); Certificate of Appreciation, Wendell Phillips Academy High School (1985); Certificate of Appreciation, Aunt Martha's Youth Service Center (1980) **MEM:** ABA; Chicago Bar Association; Cook County Bar Association; Illinois Judicial Council; Illinois Judges Association; Phi Alpha Delta; Alpha Phi Alpha **BAR:** Supreme Court of the United States (1983-Present); United States Court of Appeals for the Seventh Circuit (1983); United States Court of Appeals for the Federal Circuit (1983); Illinois (1979); United States District Court Northern District of Illinois (1979) **MH:** Albert Nelson Marquis Lifetime Achievement Award (2017) **H:** Running; Chess; Tennis; Golf; RV activities; Riding motorcycles **PA:** Democrat **BA:** 50 W Washington St Room 2600, Circuit Court, Cook County Illinois, Chicago, IL, 60466 **ADD:** 25 Monee Rd, Park Forest, IL, 60466

FURLOTTI, ALEXANDER AMATO, T: Real Estate and Investment Company Executive, Philanthropist **I:** Real Estate **CN:** Ae **DOB:** 04/21/1948 **PB:** Milan **SC:** Italy **PT:** Amato Furlotti; Polonia Concepcion (Lopez) Furlotti **MS:** Divorced **SPN:** Nancy Elizabeth Swift (6/27/1976, Divorced 2015) **CH:** Michael Alexander; Patrick Swift; Allison Nicole **ED:** JD, University of California, Los Angeles (1973); BA in Economics, University of California, Berkeley (1970) **C:** President, Aeneas Enterprises, LLC (2016-Present); President, Quorum Funds, Los Angeles, CA (2000-2015); President, Quorum Properties, Los Angeles, CA (1984-2015); Partner, Kravetz & Furlotti, Century City, CA (1981-1983); Partner, Alexander, Inman, Kravetz & Tanzer, Beverly Hills, CA (1978-1980); Associate, Alexander, Inman, Kravetz & Tanzer, Beverly Hills, CA (1973-1977) **CIV:** Founding Member, Director, Officer, The Alexander Furlotti Foundation (2016-Present); Director, Los Angeles Opera Company (2008-Present); Founding Member, Director, Officer, The Furrloti Family Foundation (2006-2013); Yosemite National Institute, San Francisco, CA (1990-1992); Trustee, Harvard-Westlake School, Los Angeles, CA (1989-1997) **AW:** Finalist, Pillars of Industry Award, National Association of Homebuilders (2004); Best Attached Housing Award (1998); Residential Project of the Year (1998); Golden Nugget Award (1998); Grand Award, Pacific Coast Builders Conference (1998); Platinum Award (1997); Grand Award, Pacific Coast Builders Conference (1993); Golden Nugget Award (1993); Grand Award, National Association of Home Builders (1993) **MEM:** American Bar Association; Urban Land Institute; The Beach Club; California Club; Bohemian Club; St. Francis Yacht Club **BAR:** California (1973); United States District Court for the Ninth Circuit (1973) **ADD:** 1080 Chestnut St Apt 11D, San Francisco, CA, 94109 **URL:** http://www.alexanderfurlotti.com

GAAR, MARILYN, T: Manager **I:** Business Management/Business Services **CN:** Ridgemar Group LLC **DOB:** 09/22/1946 **PB:** St. Louis **SC:** MO/USA **PT:** Arthur Wiegraffe; Marjorie Estelle (Miller) Wiegraffe **MS:** Married **SPN:** Norman E. Gaar (4/12/1986) **ED:** MS, Indiana University

(1973); MA, Indiana University (1970); AB, Indiana University (1968) **C:** Manager, Ridgemar Group LLC (1996-Present); Visiting Scholar, Moscow Symphony Orchestra, Russia (2003); Faculty, Johnson County Community College (1973-2014); Faculty, Stephens College, Columbia, MO (1971-1973) **CR:** Secretary, Central Slavic Conference (2000-2005); Admissions Criteria and Admissions Process Review Committee, School of Medicine, University of Kansas (1992); Governors Appointee, Admissions Panel, Congress Bundestag Youth Exchange Program (1991-1995); State Selection Committee Congress Bundestag Youth Exchange Program (1985); President, Faculty Delegate, Kansas Association of Community Colleges (1984-1985); Interviewer, Fellowship Candidates, Fulbright Hayes Teacher Exchange (1982-1992); Fellow, National Endowment of the Humanities (1980) **CIV:** Kansas City Friends of Chamber Music Volunteer (2014-2018); Kansas City Ballet Guild (2014-2018); Governing Board Member, International Relations Council, Kansas City (2001-2004); Executive Committee Member (2001-2003); Huntington Farms Homes Association, Leawood, Kansas (1994-1997); Women's Foundation of Greater Kansas City: Celebration of Woman (1994); Producer, Candidates Forum (1990); Johnson County Elder Net Coalition (1988); President, League of Women Voters Johnson County (1987-1989); Governing Board (1985-1989); Program Chairman, Kansas Federation of Republican Women (1984-1987); Alternate Member, Republican State Committee, Kansas (1984-1986); Board of Directors, Substance Abuse Center, Johnson County (1983-1985); Kansas City Chairman, Republican City Committee, Shawnee (1982-1986); Governing Board, Johnson County Mental Health Center (1981-1986); Volunteer Translator, Russian Refugee Resettlement Program, Jewish Family and Children Services, Kansas City (1979-1981); Treasurer, Heart of America, Japan American Society (1979); Honorary Director, Rockhurst College **CW:** Contributing Editor, "American Democracy" **AW:** Johnson County Community College Outcomes Assessments Grant (2011-2014); Teaching Excellence Award, Central Association of Russian Teachers of America (2010); Grant, Europaische Akademie, West Berlin, Germany (1997); Grant, Europaische Akademie, West Berlin, Germany (1994); Grant, Europaische Akademie, West Berlin, Germany (1992); Fulbright Hayes Grant, Netherlands (1982); Fulbright Hayes Grant, Japan (1975) **MEM:** Board of Directors, Central Association of Russian Teachers in America (2003-2004); Executive Committee, International Relations Council of Kansas City (2001-2004); Secretary, Russian and American International Studies Association (1999-2009); Secretary, Association of Russian and American Historians (1998-1999); Kansas Political Science Association; Community College Humanities Association; People to People; Phi Beta Kappa **MH:** Albert Nelson Marquis Lifetime Achievement Award (2017) **H:** Piano; Gardening **ADD:** 11126 Brookwood Avenue, Leawood, KS, 66211

GABRIEL, MICHAEL, T: Retired Psychology Professor **I:** Education/Educational Services **DOB:** 05/05/1940 **PB:** Philadelphia **SC:** PA/USA **PT:** Michael Gabriel; Josephine (Alesio) Gabriel **MS:** Married **SPN:** Sonda S. Walsh (1984); Linda Prinz (6/1967, Divorced) **CH:** Joseph Michael **ED:** PhD, University of Wisconsin (1967); MA, University of Wisconsin (1965); AB in Psychology, St. Joseph's College (1962) **C:** Professor, Department of Psychology, Beckman Institute for Advanced Science and Technology, University of Illinois at Urbana-Champaign (1982-2004); Appointee, Center for Advanced Study, University of Illinois at Urbana-Champaign (1990-1991); Associate Professor, University of Texas at Austin (1977-1982); Assistant Professor, University of Texas at Austin (1973-1977); Senior Postdoctoral Fellow, National Institute of Mental Health, University of California, Irvine (1970-1972); Staff Psychologist, Pacific State Hospital, Pomona, CA (1968-1970); Assistant Professor, Pomona College, Claremont, CA (1967-1970); Fellow, American Psychological Association; Fellow, International Behavioral Neuroscience Society **CR:** Neuroinformatics Review Panel, National Institutes of Health (2000-Present); Principal Investigator, Database System for Neuronal Pattern Analysis Project, National Science Foundation (1992-Present); Faculty, Beckman Institute for Advanced Science and Technology, University of Illinois (1989-Present); Ad Hoc Member, Biopsychology Review Panel, National Institute of Mental Health (1997-1998); Review Panel in Behavioral and Neural Sciences, National Science Foundation (1988-1991); Area Chairman, Biological Psychology Program, The University of Texas at Austin (1979-1982); Chairman, Neuronal Pattern Analysis Group, Beckman Institute for Advanced Science and Technology, University of Illinois **CW:** Co-Editor, With B. Vogt, "Neurobiology of Cingulate Cortex and Limbic Thalamus (1993); Co-Editor, "Learning and Computational Neuroscience: Foundations of Adaptive Networks" (1989); Editorial Board Member, Neural Plasticity, Neurobiology of Learning and Memory **AW:** Grantee, National Science Foundation (1992-2003); Grantee, National Institutes of Health (1988-2003); Grantee, National Institute of Mental Health (1998-2002); Grantee, National Institute on Drug Abuse (1996-2001); Grantee, Office of Scientific Research, United States Air Force (1988-1991); Grantee, National Institute of Mental Health (1978-1988) **MEM:** Sigma Chi **MH:** Albert Nelson Marquis Lifetime Achievement Award (2017) **H:** Jazz trombone **ADD:** 1016 Windward Way, Saint Augustine, FL, 32080 **URL:** https://www.reverbnation.com/gabrielshorn

GADUS, PEG, T: Pastoral Associate/Business Manager **I:** Religious **CN:** Archdiocese of Chicago **DOB:** 04/21/1935 **PB:** Chicago **SC:** IL/USA **PT:** Frank O'Brien; Katherine Alexander **CH:** Thomas J.; Timothy J.; Katherine M.; Kevin M. **ED:** BS in Education, Calumet College, Whiting, IN (1976) **CT:** Certified, Liturgical Institute, St. Anselmo, Rome, Italy (1999) **C:** Sacramental Preparation Coordinator, St. Florian Parish (2003-Present); RCIA Coordinator (2003-Present); Bereavement Minister (2001-Present); Archdiocesan Lay Minister (1997-Present); Director, Religious Education, Archdiocese of Chicago (1992-Present); Teacher, Elementary School, Archdiocese of Chicago (1959-2003); Teacher, Elementary School, Rockford Diocese (1957-1959); Teacher, Elementary School, Joliet Diocese (1955-1957) **CR:** Sacramental Preparation Coordinator, St. Florian School, with Marketing (2003-2005) **AW:** Christi Fideles Award, Archdiocese of Chicago (2013) **MH:** Albert Nelson Marquis Lifetime Achievement Award (2017) **RE:** Roman Catholic **ADD:** 12921 S Muskegon Ave, Chicago, IL, 60633

GAETA, ROSEMARIE, T: Psychotherapist **I:** Medicine & Health Care **DOB:** 04/15/1947 **PB:** Brooklyn **SC:** NY/USA **PT:** James Gaeta; Rose (Scorcia) Gaeta **ED:** MSW, Fordham University (1970); BS, Fordham University (1968) **CT:** Diplomate, National Association of Social Workers; Licensed Clinical Social Worker, State of New York; Board Certified Clinical Social Worker, American Board of Examiners in Clinical Social Work (1988); Board Certified in Clinical Social Work Psychoanalysis (2004) **C:** Private Clinical Practice, Staten Island, NY (1973-Present); Pri-

vate Practice **CR:** Co-Founder, Psychoanalytic Consortium (1991) **CIV:** Board Member, Accreditation Council for Psychoanalytic Education (2004-2008) **AW:** Distinguished Practitioner, National Academy Practice in Social Work **MEM:** First President, American Association for Psychoanalysis Clinical Social Work (1991-1993); Diplomate, Chair, State Committee on Psychoanalysis, New York State Society for Clinical Social Work Psychotherapists (1987-1991); Institute for Psychoanalytic Training and Research; International Psychoanalytical Association **ADD:** 416 Crown Avenue, Staten Island, NY, 10312

GAGEL, ROBERT FRANCIS, T: Endocrinologist, Educator **I:** Education/Educational Services **DOB:** 08/09/1946 **PB:** Celina **SC:** OH/USA **PT:** Aloys J. Gagel; Marguerite Hickey Gagel **MS:** Married **SPN:** Margo A. Cox (1977) **CH:** Elisabeth M. Anderson; Caroline K. Goodchild; Andrew C. **ED:** Fellow in Endocrinology, Tufts Medical Center, Boston, MA (1973-1975); Resident in Medicine, Tufts Medical Center, Boston, MA (1972-1973); Intern in Medicine, Tufts Medical Center, Boston, MA, (1971-1972); MD, Ohio State University, Columbus, OH (1971); BS, Ohio State University, Columbus, OH (1971) **CT:** Certified in Endocrinology and Metabolism; Certified in Internal Medicine **C:** Professor, Department of Endocrine Neoplasia and Hormonal Disorders (2017-Present); Head, Division of Internal Medicine, University of Texas MD Anderson Cancer Center, Houston, TX (2001-2014); Chairman, Department of Internal Medicine Specialties, University of Texas MD Anderson Cancer Center, Houston, TX (1995-2001); Chief, Section of Endocrine Neoplasia and Hormonal Disorders, MD Anderson Cancer Center (1991-2001); Head, Endocrinology Section, Veterans Administration Medical Center, Baylor College of Medicine, Houston, TX (1989-1991) **CR:** Adjunct Professor, Departments of Internal Medicine and Molecular and Cellular Biology, Baylor College of Medicine, Houston, TX **CIV:** Vice Chair, Paget & Bone & Cancer Foundations, New York, NY (2004-2017); Member, Board of Directors, National Osteoporosis Foundation, Washington, DC (2004-2017); President, National Osteoporosis Foundation (2013-2016); Director, Rolanette and Berdon Lawrence Bone Disease Program of Texas, Department of Endocrine Neoplasia and Hormonal Disorders, University of Texas MD Anderson Cancer Center, Houston, TX (2007-2012); Co-Founder, International Thyroid Oncology Group and Founding Chairman **MIL:** Lieutenant Commander, U.S. Navy, Great Lakes Naval Regional Medical Center (1975-1977) **AW:** Establishment of the Annual Robert F. Gagel International Thyroid Oncology Group Discovery Award (2015-Present); Recipient, Thyroid Cancer Survivors Association Award (2016); President's Recognition for Faculty Excellence, MD Anderson Cancer Center (2014); Grantee, National Institutes of Health (1982-2001); Winner of Boy Frame Award for Clinical Excellence (1987); Grantee, Veterans Administration (1982-1992) **MEM:** Board of Trustees, National Osteoporosis Foundation (2006-2016); President, National Osteoporosis Foundation (2013-2016); Associate Editor, Endocrine Reviews, Endocrine Society (2011-2015); Vice President, National Osteoporosis Foundation (2012-2013); Chairman, International Thyroid Oncology Group (2006-2011); Board of Directors, American Association of Clinical Endocrinology (2003-2006); External Advisory Board Member, University of Cincinnati Cancer Center, Cincinnati, OH (2004); Chair, Publication Committee, American Society of Bone & Mineral Research (1999-2003); Elected Master of American College of Endocrinology (2001); Chair, Annual Meeting, Pituitary Society (1998); President, Advances in Mineral Metabolism (1995-

1998); Chairman, Annual Meeting, American Society of Bone & Mineral Research (1995); Phi Beta Kappa (1966) **MH:** Albert Nelson Marquis Lifetime Achievement Award (2017) **H:** Skiing; Bicycling **BA:** PO Box 301402, MD Anderson Cancer Ctr, Houston, TX, 77230 **ADD:** PO Box 301402, MD Anderson Cancer Ctr, Houston, TX, 77230-1402

GAGELMAN, RITA, T: Parish Ministry Associate **I:** Religious **CN:** Garfield Lutheran Church **DOB:** 10/14/1945 **PB:** Great Bend, KS **PT:** Louis Oetken; Meta Rankin-Oetken **MS:** Single **CH:** Jerry; Krista (Deceased); Lance **ED:** MA in English, Fort Hays State University, Kansas (1992); MA in History, Fort Hays State University, Kansas (1987); BA in History, Fort Hays State University, Kansas (1968) **C:** Education and Training Assistant, Burns & McDonnell, Kansas City, KS (2004-2009); Adjunct Instructor, Kansas City Kansas Community College (1999-2015); Adjunct Instructor, Park University, Parkville, MO (1999-2014); Administrative Assistant, Lillenas Music Division, Nazarene Publishing House, Kansas City, MO (1998-2004); Adjunct to Instructor, Barton Community College, Great Bend, KS (1988-1998) **CIV:** Parish Ministry Associate, Garfield Lutheran Church; Parish Ministry Associate, Immanuel Lutheran in Kansas City, MO **CW:** Contributor, Articles, Publications **MH:** Albert Nelson Marquis Lifetime Achievement Award (2017); Distinguished Humanitarian (2017) **H:** Traveling **PA:** Democrat **RE:** Lutheran **ADD:** 1324 NW 20 Road, Albert, KS, 67511

GALATIANOS, GUS A., T: Computer Company Executive **I:** Information Technology and Services **CN:** ACCI Properties, Inc. **DOB:** 01/18/1947 **PB:** Hermoupolis **SC:** Greece **PT:** Athanssios Constantine Galatianos; Despina Athanssios (Stefanou) Galatianos **MS:** Married **SPN:** Katerina E. Saridis (September 29, 1974) **CH:** Athanssios; Deborah **ED:** PhD in Computer Science, Polytechnic University (Now NYU Tandon) (1986); MS in Computer Science, Stevens Institute of Technology (1977); MSEE, Columbia University (1977); BSEE, New York Institute of Technology (1974) **C:** Professor Emeritus, SUNY College at Old Westbury (2001-Present); President, ACCI Properties, Inc. (1988-Present); President, Computer Consultants International, Inc. (1988-2004); Manager of Financial Systems, Electronic Systems Division, Singer Sewing Co (1984-1987); Professor, SUNY College at Old Westbury (1993-2000); Chairman, Department of Computer Science, SUNY College at Old Westbury (1993-2000); Associate Professor, SUNY College at Old Westbury (1979-1993); Chairman, Department of Computer Science, SUNY College at Old Westbury (1979-1993); Technology Director, Computer Dynamics (1977-1979); Computer Consultant, Universal Computer Centers (1973-1977); Manager of Operations, Solomos Business Machines (1970-1973) **CR:** Consultant in Field **CIV:** Member, Police Athletic League of New York City (2010-Present); Representative, Presidential Task Force (1984-Present); Greater Whitestone Taxpayers Civic Association (1984-Present) **MIL:** Hellenic Air Force (1965-1967) **CW:** Author, "Principles of Software Engineering" (1986); Author, "Principles of Database Systems" (1986); Contributor, Articles, Professional Journals **MH:** Albert Nelson Marquis Lifetime Achievement Award (2017) **H:** Music; Hunting; Travel; Reading **PA:** Republican **RE:** Greek Orthodox **ADD:** 158-23 Riverside Dr, Whitestone, NY, 11357

GAMACHE, BERNADETTE , T: Vice President of Finance **I:** Financial Services **CN:** Emballage Classique Inc. **PT:** Emile Gamache; Mercedès Levert **ED:** Bachelors Degree, Psychology, HEC &

BIRLA Center (2016) **MH:** Albert Nelson Marquis Lifetime Achievement Award (2017) **H:** Drawing Portraits; Volunteering, Local Community and in Montreal

GAMPEL, ELAINE SUSAN, T: Investment Company Executive **I:** Financial Services **CN:** UBS **DOB:** 04/12/1950 **PB:** New Haven **SC:** CT/USA **PT:** Stanley Irwin Gampel; Marion (Levine) Gampel **MS:** Married **SPN:** Alan Joseph Tedeschi (9/9/1984) **CH:** Zachary Joseph Gampel Tedeschi; Matthew Samuel Gampel Tedeschi **ED:** MS in Counseling, Southern Connecticut State University (1975); BS in Special Education, Boston University (1972) **CT:** Certified Investment Management Analyst, The Wharton School, The University of Pennsylvania (1990) **C:** Senior Vice President, UBS (2007-Present); Senior Managed Accounts Consultant, UBS (2007-Present); Wealth Adviser, Dean Witter Reynolds (Now Morgan Stanley) (2000-2007); Senior Vice President in Investments, Dean Witter Reynolds (Now Morgan Stanley) (2000-2007); Senior Consultant, Dean Witter Reynolds (Now Morgan Stanley) (1993-2007); Vice President in Investments, Dean Witter Reynolds (Now Morgan Stanley) (1989-2000); Vice President, Paine Webber Inc. (1977-1989); Investment Management Consultant, Paine Webber Inc. (1977-1989); Special Education Teacher, Ansonia Public Schools (1972-1977) **CR:** Executive Committee Chair, Parent Association, University of Colorado Boulder (2013-2016) **CIV:** Member, Governance Committee, Jewish Family Service of Colorado (2008-Present); Member, Jewish Family Service of Colorado (2006-Present); Member, Investment Committee, Jewish Family Service of Colorado (2005-Present); Board of Directors, Project PAVE (2003-Present); Board Chair, Project PAVE (2008); Member, Judi's House (2004-2005); Chair, Women's Forum of Colorado, Inc. (2002); Chair, Board of Trustees, The Women's Foundation of Colorado (2002); Treasurer, The Women's Foundation of Colorado (1999); Treasurer, The Women's Foundation of Colorado (1998); Member, Women's Forum of Colorado, Inc. (1997-2003); Chair, Investment Committee, The Women's Foundation of Colorado (1995-1997); Community Board, Denver Nuggets (1992-1995); Outside Editorial Board, Denver Post, Digital First Media (1991-1994); Board of Directors, United Cerebral Palsy of Denver (Now Ability Connection) (1984-1993) **AW:** Women of Distinction Award, Girl Scouts of Colorado (2004); Women Leaders of Excellence Award, Colorado Women's Leadership Coalition (2003) **MEM:** Certified Committee, Investment Management Consultants Association, Inc. (1990-Present); Membership Committee, Investment Management Consultants Association, Inc.; Denver Society of Security Analysts **MH:** Albert Nelson Marquis Lifetime Achievement Award (2017) **H:** Tennis; Running; Biking **ADD:** 300 Dexter St, Denver, CO, 80220

GANT, DONALD, T: Investment Banker **I:** Financial Services **CN:** Goldman Sachs **DOB:** 10/05/1928 **PB:** Long Branch **SC:** NY/USA **PT:** Raymond LeRoy Gant; Evelyn (Ross) Gant **SPN:** Jane Harriet Taylor (9/12/1953) **CH:** Laura R.; Christopher T.; Sarah R.; Alison A. **ED:** MBA, Harvard University (1954); BS, University of Pennsylvania (1952) **C:** Senior Director, Goldman Sachs (1999-Present); Limited Partner, Goldman Sachs (1990-1999); Partner, Goldman Sachs (1965-1990); Associate, Goldman Sachs (1954-1964) **CR:** Visiting Committee Member, Harvard Business School (1991-1997) **MIL:** US Army (1946-1948) **PA:** Republican **RE:** Presbyterian **ADD:** 16 Sound Point Place, Fernandina Beach, FL, 32034

GARDNER, STEPHEN DAVID, T: Lawyer **I:** Law and Legal Services **CN:** Cooley LLP **DOB:** 12/03/1939 **PB:** Newark **SC:** NJ/USA **PT:** Henry Gardner; Florence (Temeles) Gardner **MS:** Married **SPN:** Mary Francis Voce (9/19/1973) **CH:** Benjamin Voce-Gardner; Daniel Voce-Gardner **ED:** LLM in Taxation, New York University (1965); LLB, University of Florida (1964); BA, University of Florida (1961) **C:** Partner, Cooley LLP, New York City, NY (1971-Present); Adjunct Professor of Law, New York University School of Law, New York City, NY (1969-Present); Managing Partner, Kronish Lieb Weiner & Hellman, LLP (Now Cooley LLP), New York City, NY (1980-1999); Associate, Hughes Hubbard & Reed LLP, New York City, NY (1968-1971); Associate Professor of Law, New York University School of Law, New York City, NY (1966-1968); Associate, Maguire Voorhis & Wells P.A., Orlando, FL (1965-1966) **CR:** Director, Safra National Bank of New York, New York City, NY (1987-Present); David Schwartz Foundation, New York City, NY (1980-Present) **MIL:** Sergeant, United States Army Reserve (1969-1972) **CW:** Contributor, Articles and Reviews to Professional Journals **MEM:** New York State Bar Association; The Florida Bar; Association of the Bar of the City of New York; Tax Club of New York; Order of the Coif **BAR:** Supreme Court of the United States (1980); New York State Bar Association (1967); The Florida Bar (1964) **H:** Skiing; Swimming; Gardening **RE:** Jewish **ADD:** 40 5th Ave , New York, NY, 10011-8843

GARFIELD, ERNEST, I: Financial Services **DOB:** 07/14/1932 **PB:** Colorado River Agency **SC:** AZ/USA **PT:** Emil Garfield; Carmen (Ybarra) Garfield **MS:** Married **SPN:** Betty Ann Redden (4/18/1953) **CH:** Laural; Jeffrey Alan **ED:** Master's Degree in International Business, American Graduate School (Now Thunderbird School of Global Management) (1976); Bachelor's Degree in International Business, American Graduate School (Now Thunderbird School of Global Management) (1975); BSBA, The University of Arizona (1975) **C:** President, Independent Bank Developers, LLC (1994-Present); Chairman, Independent Bank Developers, LLC (1994-Present); Chairman, United Bancorp Systems, Inc. (1979-Present); Commissioner, Arizona Corporation Commission (1974-1979); Treasurer, State of Arizona (1971-1974); Deputy Treasurer, State of Arizona (1970-1971); Owner, Garfield Insurance Agency, Tucson, Arizona (1962-1970); Senator, State of Arizona (1967-1968); Founder, Alliance of Business Banks **CR:** Appointed Member, Skill Standards Commission, State of Arizona (2007); Member, Board of Directors, Education Foundation, East Valley Institute of Technology (2004); Chairman, The White House Conference on Energy; Chairman, Committee on Energy Policy, National Association of Regulatory Utility Commissioners; President, Western Conference of Public Service Commissioners; Member Ad Hoc Committee on Regulatory Reform, Electric and Nuclear Energy Committee; Member, Financial Services Advisory Council to Congressman David Schweikert **CIV:** National Commission on Rape Prevention (1990-Present); Chairman, Financial Institutions Task Force, Arizona Department of Financial Institutions (2007); Commissioner, Governor's Commission on Violence Against Women, State of Arizona (1993-2003); Member, NRSC (1989); Member, President George H.W. Bush's Task Force (1989); Chairman, Governor's Commission on Rape Prevention, State of Arizona (1988); Member, National Kidney Foundation of Arizona; National Multiple Sclerosis Society; Member, Advisory Board, St. Joseph's Hospital and Medical Center, Dignity Health; Member, Establishment Committee, Pima Community College; Member,

Organization Committee, Pima County Halfway House; Active Member, Governor's Sexual Assault Task Force, State of Arizona; Director, Arizona Sexual Assault Network; Member, Men Against Violence Against Women; Member, Board of Directors, Arizona Cactus-Pine Council, Girl Scouts of the United States of America **MIL:** U.S. Army (1952-1955) **AW:** Sir C.V. Raman Award for Outstanding Contribution to Science (2009); Honoree, One of the Most Influential Business Leaders, The Phoenix Business Journal (2007); Named to United States Field Artillery Hall of Fame (1999); Outstanding Young Men in Arizona Award; Press Club Award; Recipient, Congressional Recognition for "Leadership and Dedication to Promoting Commerce Between the US and Asian Markets" **MEM:** Advisory Council, Thunderbird International Banking Institute (1990-Present); Arizona Hispanic Chamber of Commerce **MH:** Albert Nelson Marquis Lifetime Achievement Award (2017) **H:** Graphology **RE:** Roman Catholic **ADD:** 8442 N 72nd Pl, Scottsdale, AZ, 85258

GARLAND, CEDRIC FRANK, T: Epidemiologist, Educator **I:** Education/Educational Services **CN:** University of California **DOB:** 11/10/1946 **PB:** La Jolla **SC:** CA/USA **PT:** Cedric Garagliano; Eva (Caldwell) Garagliano **ED:** PhD, University of California, Los Angeles, CA (1974); MPH, University of California, Los Angeles, CA (1969); BA, University of Southern California (1967) **C:** Professor, UC San Diego School of Medicine (1981-Present); Assistant Professor, Johns Hopkins University, Baltimore, MD (1974-1981) **CW:** Contributor, Chapters, Books; Contributor, Articles, Professional Journals **AW:** Seeley Award, American College of Nutrition; Order of Merit of The Republic of Italy (2016); Environmental Health Coalition Distinguished Service Award (1984); Distinguished Achievement Award, Sierra Club (1984); National Institutes of Health Research Career Award (1982); Golden Apple Award for Teaching Excellence, Johns Hopkins University (1980); Aristotle Award for Academy Excellence, University of California, Los Angeles, CA (1974) **MEM:** Chairman, Save Our Shore, Sierra Club (1982-Present); Chairman, Information Resources, Physicians for Social Responsibility (1982-Present); Society for Epidemiologic Research; Fellow, American College of Epidemiology **RE:** Roman Catholic **ADD:** 2938 Renault St, San Diego, CA, 92122

GARNER, SHIRLEY IMOGENE, I: Education/Educational Services **DOB:** 06/08/1932 **PB:** Silverto **SC:** OR/USA **PT:** Julius Edgar Herr; Amelia Christine (Preszler) Herr **CH:** Mark Steven; Sheila Christine **ED:** MusB with Honors, University of Oregon, Eugene (1957) **C:** Vocal Music Teacher, San Jose USD, California (1968-1999); Retired, San Jose USD, California (1996); Part-Time Teacher, San Jose USD, California (1955-1968); Literature Teacher, Napa USD, California (1966-1967); Vocal Music Teacher, San Jose USD, California (1961-1966); Vocal Music Teacher, Berkeley USD, California (1958-1961); Elementary Teacher, Springfield USD, Oregon (1957-1958) **CR:** Choir Director, The Fun Time Singers, Campbell, CA (2000-2002); Choir Director, Pilgrim Haven Retired Home, Los Altos, CA (1975-1983); Choir Director, Various Churches (1969-1974) **CIV:** Education, Advisory Committee, Restoration of the Statue of Liberty and The Bicentennial of the Constitution, Washington, DC (1986); President, Women's Auxiliary; Volunteer Pianist, Chancel Choir; President, Sunnyvale-Mount View Salvation Army's Women's Auxiliary; Vocal Music Teacher, Castillero Music Performance; Volunteer, Salvation Army; Deacon, Chancel Choir; Volunteer, Menlo Park Presbyterian Church **AW:**

Certificate of Recognition, California State Senate (1993); Appreciation Certificate, California State Assembly (1993); Hall of Fame Award, Youth Focus, Inc. (1993); Hall of Fame Award California State Assembly (1993); Numerous Conference Awards, Booster Club (1996, 1989); Special Citation Award, Hawaii-California Elks Association; Service Public Education, Masonic Lodge **MEM:** Music Educators National Conference **ACH:** Achievements include instituted and directed annual music performances by over three hundred middle school students and professional musicians at the San Jose Centre for the Performing Arts. Choir Performances on the Carnation Stage in Disneyland, Disney Magic Music Days; **H:** Gardening; Flower arranging; Reading; Crossword puzzles; Walking **RE:** Presbyterian **ADD:** 485 Woodside Rd, Apt 3122, Redwood City, CA, 94061

GARRIS, CHARLES ALEXANDER JR., T: Professor of Engineering **I:** Education/Educational Services **CN:** George Washington University **DOB:** 02/02/1944 **PB:** Pomona **SC:** CA/USA **PT:** Charles Alexander Garris; Kathleen Ann (White) Garris **MS:** Married **SPN:** Eugenia Dolores Cardenas (9/11/1971) **CH:** Charles Alexander; Eugenia Catalina **ED:** PhD, Stony Brook University (1971); MS, Stony Brook University (1968); BEng, Maritime College, State University of New York (1965) **CT:** Registered Professional Engineer; Registered Patent Agent **C:** Professor of Engineering, George Washington University (1978-Present); Chairman of the Faculty Senate, George Washington University (2014-2017); Chief of Mechanical Engineering, Instituto Venezolano de Investigaciones Científicas (1976-1978); Research Associate, Massachusetts Institute of Technology (1973-1976); Virginia Research Chief, Mechanical Engineering Department, Instituto Venezolano de Investigaciones Científicas (1971-1973); Program Director, National Science Foundation **CR:** Consultant in Field **CW:** Contributor, Articles, Engineering Publications; Contributor, Informational Paper, National Academy of Inventors **AW:** Special Recognition of Service, Board of Trustees, George Washington University (2017); Special Recognition of Service, Faculty Senate, George Washington University (2017); Trachtenberg Prize, Pi Tau Sigma (2011); Thomas Edison Patent Award, The American Society of Mechanical Engineers (2006) **MEM:** Fellow, AIAA; The American Society of Mechanical Engineers; American Society for Engineering Education; Sigma Xi, The Scientific Research Honor Society; Pi Tau Sigma **MH:** Albert Nelson Marquis Lifetime Achievement Award (2017) **H:** Bicycling; Boating; Swimming **RE:** Roman Catholic **ADD:** 2125 Twin Mill Ln, Oakton, VA, 22124

GARTZ, ROLF, T: Foundation Administrator **I:** Nonprofit & Philanthropy **CN:** Eduard Rhein Foundation **DOB:** 12/23/1940 **PB:** Bonn **SC:** Germany **PT:** Fritz Gartz; Hildegard (Rhein) Gartz **MS:** Married **SPN:** Christel Anneliese Overgahr General Willebrand (8/7/1970) **CH:** Stephan **ED:** Honorary PhD, State University of Social Sciences, Moscow, Russia (2000); PhD in Cell Biology, Bonn University (1969); Coursework, Bonn University and Cologne University, Germany (1964-1969) **C:** Professor, Moscow Technological University (MIREA) (2005-2016); Managing Chairman, Eduard Rhein Foundation, Hamburg, Germany (1990-2016); Civil Servant and Government Director, Germany (1970-1990) **CR:** Member, Board of Directors, Professor Rhein Foundation, Koenigswinter, Germany (1987- Present); Honorary Professor, Russian New University (2008); Honorary Professor, Moscow International Business School- MIRBIS (2003); Academician, International Informatization Academy, United Nations (2000) **AW:** Decorated, Officer's Cross of the Order of Merit, Federal Republic of Germany (2013); Yuri Gagarin Medal, Russian Federation (2010); Highest Order of Merit, International Informatization Academy, UN (2001); Sputnik Medal, Russian Federation (2000) **MEM:** Elected Member, Board, German Technion Society (2008); American Association for the Advancement of Science; New York Academy of Sciences; Association of German Natural Scientists and Physicians; German Society of Cell Biology; Max Planck Society for the Advancement of Science; Society of Biochemistry and Molecular Biology **MH:** Albert Nelson Marquis Lifetime Achievement Award (2017) **H:** Hunting; Riding **ADD:** Alexander-von-Humboldt-Straße 6, Mayen, Germany, 56727

GELLER, ROBERT JAMES, T: Advertising Executive **I:** Advertising & Marketing **CN:** Charter Digital Media **DOB:** 05/05/1937 **PB:** New York **SC:** NY/USA **PT:** Jerome Geller; Pearl (Klein) Geller **MS:** Married **SPN:** Lois Dee Fromkin (June 9, 1968) **CH:** Richard Evan; Stephen Laurence **ED:** BS, The City College of New York (1958) **C:** Secretary-Treasurer, Charter Digital Media (2005-Present); Chief Financial Officer, Charter Digital Media (2005-Present); Chief Operating Officer, Charter Digital Media (2005-Present); Managing Director, Charter Digital Media (2002-Present); President, Robert J. Geller & Associates, Inc. (1993-2008); President, Reel America, Inc. (2000-2003); Chief Executive Officer, Reel America, Inc. (2000-2003); President, Adforce (1970-1992); Assistant Media Director, Foote, Cone & Belding (Now FCB Global) (1964-1969); Media Supervisor, Interpublic Group of Corporations (Now IPG) (1962-1964); Account Executive, Furman, Feiner & Company (Now Furman Feiner) (1958-1962) **CIV:** President, Robert J. and Lois F. Geller Foundation **CW:** Contributor, Articles, Professional Journals **MEM:** Assistant Secretary, American Advertising Federation (1992-Present); Plans Review Committee, American Advertising Federation (1990-Present); Board of Directors, Corporate Membership Committee, American Advertising Federation (1989-Present); Corporate Membership Committee, Association of National Advertisers (1990-1992); Management Policy Committee, Association of National Advertisers (1980-1992); The Advertising Club; The Royal Philatelic Society London **MH:** Albert Nelson Marquis Lifetime Achievement Award (2017) **H:** Stamp collecting **PA:** Republican **ADD:** 155 E. 76th Street, Apartment 6H, New York, NY, 10021

GENEROUS, WILLIAM THOMAS JR., T: Coach, Educator **I:** Education/Educational Services **CN:** The University of North Carolina at Chapel Hill **DOB:** 02/20/1939 **PB:** Pawtucket **SC:** RI/USA **PT:** William T. Generous; Marjorie Myette Generous Smith **MS:** Married **SPN:** Diane B. Kowalchuck (10/24/1964) **CH:** Michelle Elizabeth; Suzanne Felice **ED:** PhD in American History, Stanford University (1971); MA in American History, Stanford University (1968); AB in American Literature, Brown University, Cum Laude (1963) **C:** Squash Coach, The University of North Carolina at Chapel Hill (1999-Present); Coach, Wallingford Junior Squash (1992-1999); Boys Squash Coach, Choate Rosemary Hall, Wallingford, CT (1996-1999); Girls Squash Coach, Choate Rosemary Hall, Wallingford, CT (1975-1996); Charles T. Wilson Junior Teacher of History, Choate Rosemary Hall, Wallingford, CT (1971-1997) **CR:** Adjunct Associate Professor of Physical Education, St. Paul's School (1985, 1987); Squash Coach, St. Paul's School (1985, 1987); History Teacher, St. Paul's School (1985, 1987); Adjunct Professor of Peace, War and Defense, The University of North Carolina at Chapel Hill **MIL:** Lieutenant, U.S. Navy (1956-1967) **CW:** Author, "Sweet Pea at War: A History of U.S.S. Portland (CA-33) 1933-1946," University Press of Kentucky (2003); Author, "The School Upon the Hillside: Choate Rosemary Hall" (1997); Author, Article, "Over the River Jordan," California History (1984); Author, Article, "Advice to the Novice Debater," Cross-Currents: The Handbook for High School Debate (1980); Author, Article, "Hackhackhaaackhackkkkkk," The New York Times Company (1978); Author, "Swords and Scales: The Development of the Uniform Code of Military Justice, 1950-1969," Kennikat Press (1973) **MEM:** United States Squash Racquets Association **MH:** Albert Nelson Marquis Lifetime Achievement Award (2017) **H:** Flute; Ukulele; Piano **ADD:** 206 Wild Oak Ln, Carrboro, NC, 27510

GEORGE, JOHN S., T: Research Scientist, Deputy Group Leader **I:** Sciences **CN:** Los Alamos National Laboratory **DOB:** 11/01/1953 **SC:** AK/USA **PT:** Marlin E. George; Nel S. George **ED:** PhD, Vanderbilt University (1982) **C:** Research Scientist, Los Alamos National Laboratory; Deputy Group Leader, Los Alamos National Laboratory; Senior Research Scientist, New Mexico Consortium **CR:** Advisory Committees; Supervision of Graduate Students, Postdoctoral Fellows, Junior Researchers; Principal or Key Investigator on Over 30 Research Grants or Contracts from NIH, DARPA, NSF, DOE, LANL and Others **CW:** Author, Over 100 Articles, Scientific Journals and Books; Associate Editor, Editorial Committees, Professional Journals; Author or Associate, 4 Patents, and Over 12 Patent Disclosures; Organizer, Invited Speaker, Conferences, Workshops, Symposia, Public Lectures **AW:** R&D 100, R&D Magazine (2009); DOE 100 Award **MEM:** Professional organizations in Biophysics, Neuroscience, Functional Brain Mapping, Vision, Optics, and Computing; Scholastic Honararies in Journalism, Debate and Computing; Eagle Scout, National Camping School Instructor, Boy Scouts of America **H:** Flying; Skiing; Boating; Automobiles; Motorcycling; Architectural design and construction; Visual and graphics arts **BA:** PO Box 1663, Los Alamos National Laboratory, Los Alamos, NM, 87510 **ADD:** PO Box 1428, Abiquiu, NM, 87510

GERMAIN, PAMELA, T: Health Facility Administrator (Retired), Educator **I:** Medicine & Health Care **CN:** Roswell Park Cancer Institute **DOB:** 02/17/1952 **PB:** Buffalo **SC:** NY/USA **PT:** Philip William Germain; Alma Thering Germain **CH:** Constantine Skagias; Amelia Katerina Skagias **ED:** MBA, Harvard University, Boston (1985); BA in Economics, LeMoyne College, Syracuse, NY (1973) **C:** Vice President of Strategic Initiatives, Roswell Park Cancer Institute (2015-Present); Vice President of Managed Care and Outreach, Roswell Park Cancer Institute, Buffalo, NY (1998-2014); Director of Network Development and Operations, MFHS Managed Care, Inc., Millard Fillmore Health Systems, Buffalo, NY (1995-1997); Chief Operating Officer, MFHS Managed Care, Inc., Millard Fillmore Health Systems, Buffalo, NY (1995-1997); Vice President, Managed Care and Employee Benefits Operations Division, The Travelers Corp., Hartford, CT (1988-1993); Director, Corporate Strategy and Business Diversification Group, The Travelers, Hartford, CT (1987-1988); Associate Director, External Relations, Harvard Business School, Boston, MA (1985-1987); District Manager, Commercial Lines Casualty Property, The Travelers, Worcester, MA (1981-1983) **CR:** Lecturer Management, Development Programs, Harvard Business School Club, Buffalo, NY (1995-Present); Adjunct Faculty, D'Youville College, Buffalo, NY (2004-2005); Products and Services Committee Member, National Comprehensive Cancer Network, Philadelphia, PA (1998-2014); Presenter in Field **CIV:** Board Member, Mid-Erie Treatment and Counseling Services, Buffalo, NY (1996-Present); President, Mid-Erie Treatment and Counseling Services, Buffalo, NY (2005-2007) **MH:** Albert Nelson Marquis Lifetime Achievement Award (2017) **H:** Travel; Cultural Arts; Walking **RE:** Roman Catholic **ADD:** 485 Elmwood Ave Apt 4, Buffalo, NY, 14222

GERO, ANTHONY GEORGE, **T:** Securities And Commodities Trader **I:** Financial Services **CN:** RBC Capital Markets, RBC Dain Rauscher **DOB:** 05/31/1936 **PB:** London **SC:** England **PT:** Stephen Gero; Ilona (Braun) Von Rieger **MS:** Married **SPN:** Gale Gendason (2/14/1989); Joan Selinger (11/20/1969, Divorced 1980) **CH:** Danielle Joy **ED:** BS, New York University (1959) **CT:** Certified, National Defense University, ICAF (1990); Certified, Investment Bankers Institute, University of Pennsylvania (1965) **C:** Managing Director, RBC Capital Markets, RBC Dain Rauscher (2015-Present); Senior Vice President, RBC Capital Markets, RBC Dain Rauscher (2006-2015); Senior Vice President, Legg Mason Wood Walker Inc. (2003-2006); First Vice President, Prudential Securities (1981-2003); Vice President, Drexel Burnham & Co. (1971-1980); Vice President, Director, International First Hanover Corp. (1967-1969); Partner, Charles Plohn & Co. (1964-1967); Partner, Goodbody & Co. (1960-1964); Reporter, USIS Chilean Earthquake Relief, American Embassy (1959-1960) **CR:** Arbitrator, National Association Securities Dealers (FINRA), New York Stock Exchange (1992-Present); National Defense Executive Reserve (1989-2012); Board of Directors, Commodity Clearing Corp.; U.S. Department of Commerce **CIV:** Board of Member, COMEX Division CME (2006-Present); Commodity Floor Brokers and Traders Association (1990-Present); Director, Futures Options for Kids (1995-2016); Chairman, NYMEX Charitable Trust, New York (1990-1995); Director, Treasurer, Children's Fund Commodities Exchange Center, New York (1980-2016) **CW:** Author, "Precious Metals" (1985) **AW:** Certification, Holocaust Memorial (1991); 400 Top Advisors, The Financial Times Ltd. **MEM:** Hearing Board, National Futures Association (2006-Present); Director, International Precious Metals Institute (2000-Present); Chairman, Commodity Floor Brokers and Traders Association (1990-Present); Treasurer, New York City Chapter, New York Mercantile Exchange (1974-Present); President, International Precious Metals Institute (2008-2015); Board of Directors, Commodity Exchange (1995); New York Coffee, Sugar and Cocoa Exchange; Board of Directors, New York Cotton Exchange (1995); Investment Brokers Association; Retired Westchester County Police Revolver League; New York Police Reserve Association; Swaps and Derivatives Commission, Securities Industry Association; Police Reserve Association, New York; New York State Troopers Alumni Association; American Radio Relay League; New York Produce Exchange; Board of Directors, New York Mercantile Exchange **MH:** Albert Nelson Marquis Lifetime Achievement Award (2017) **H:** Photography; Amateur radio; Chess **PA:** Republican **ADD:** 180 East End Avenue, Apartment 9F, New York, NY, 10128 **URL:** http://www.rbcwmfa.com/gerovollmer

GEYMAN, JOHN PAYNE, **T:** Physician, Educator **I:** Education/Educational Services **CN:** University of Washington **DOB:** 02/09/1931 **PB:** Santa Barbara **SC:** CA/USA **PT:** Milton John Geyman; Betsy (Payne) Geyman **MS:** Married **SPN:** Eugenia Clark Deichler (6/9/1956) **CH:** John Matthew; James Caleb; William Sabin **ED:** Charter Fellow, American Academy of Family Physicians (1972); General Practice Residency, Sonoma County Hospital, Santa Rosa, CA (1961-1963); Rotating Internship, Los Angeles County General Hospital, Los Angeles, CA (1960-1961); MD, University of California, San Francisco (1960); Premedical Coursework, University of California, Berkeley (1955-1956); AB, Geology, Princeton University, Princeton, NJ (1952) **CT:** Diplomate, American Board of Family Practice (1996); Diplomate, American Board of Family Practice (1990); Diplomate, American Board of Family Practice (1983); Diplomate, American Board of Family Practice (1977); Diplomate, American Board of Family Practice (1971); Certified, American Board of Family Practice (1971) **C:** Publisher, Copernicus Healthcare (2010-Present); Publisher, Avian Ridge Books, Friday Harbor, WA (2000-Present); Professor Emeritus, Family Medicine, School of Medicine, University of Washington, Seattle, WA (1993-Present); Part-Time Group Practice, Inter-Island Medical Center, Friday Harbor, WA (1990-1997); Professor Emeritus of Family Medicine, Department of Family Medicine, School of Medicine, University of Washington, Seattle, WA (1990-1993); Professor, Department of Family Medicine, School of Medicine, University of Washington, Seattle, WA (1976-1990); Chairman, Department of Family Medicine, School of Medicine, University of Washington, Seattle, WA (1976-1990); Professor, Department of Family Practice, School of Medicine, University of California, Davis (1972-1976); Vice Chairman, Department of Family Practice, School of Medicine, University of California, Davis (1972-1976); Director, Family Practice Residency Network Program, University of California, Davis (1972-1976); Chairman, Division of Family Practice, College of Medicine, University of Utah, Salt Lake City, UT (1971-1972); Director, Family Practice Residency Program, Hospitals for Family Practice, University of Utah, Salt Lake City, UT (1971-1972); Director, Family Practice Program, Community Hospital of Sonoma County, Santa Rosa, CA (1969-1971); Project Coordinator, Sonoma County Demonstration Project, Regional Medical Programs (Area I), University of California, San Francisco (1969-1971); Director, Coronary Care Unit, Mercy Medical Center Mount Shasta, Mount Shasta, CA (1967-1969); Private Practice, Solo General Practice, Mount Shasta, CA (1963-1969) **CIV:** President, Physicians for a National Health Program (2005-2010); President, Healthcare Disconnects **MIL:** Lieutenant Junior Grade, U.S. Navy (1952-1955) **CW:** Author, "Trumpcare: Lies, Broken Promises, How It Is Failing, and What Should Be Done," Copernicus Healthcare, Friday Harbor, WA (2018); Author, "Flight as a Lifetime Passion: Adventures, Misadventures, and Lessons, Second Edition," Avian Ridge Books, Friday Harbor, WA (2017); Author, "Common Sense About Health Care Reform in America," Copernicus Healthcare, Friday Harbor, WA (2017); Author, "Crisis in U.S. Health Care: Corporate Power vs. the Common Good," Copernicus Healthcare, Friday Harbor, WA (2017); Author, "The Human Face of ObamaCare: Promises vs. Reality and What Comes Next," Copernicus Healthcare, Friday Harbor, WA (2016); Author, "How Obamacare Is Unsustainable: Why We Need a Single Payer Solution for All Americans," Copernicus Healthcare, Friday Harbor, WA (2015); Author, "Breaking Point: How the Primary Care Crisis Endangers the Lives of Americans, Spanish Translation" (2013); Author, "Breaking Point: How the Primary Care Crisis Endangers the Lives of Americans," Copernicus Healthcare, Friday Harbor, WA (2012); Author, "Health Care Wars: How Market Ideology and Corporate Power Are Killing Americans," Copernicus Healthcare, Friday Harbor, WA (2012); Author, "Souls on a Walk: An Enduring Love Story Unbroken by Alzheimer's," Copernicus Healthcare, Friday Harbor, WA (2012); Author, "The Cancer Generation: Baby Boomers Facing a Perfect Storm, Second Edition," Copernicus Healthcare, Friday Harbor, WA (2012); Author, "Hijacked: The Road to Single Payer in the Aftermath of Stolen Health Care Reform," Common Courage Press, Monroe, ME (2010); Author, "The Cancer Generation: Baby Boomers Facing a Perfect Storm," Common Courage Press, Monroe, ME (2009); Author, "Do Not Resuscitate: Why the Health Insurance Industry is Dying, and How We Must Replace It," Common Courage Press, Monroe, ME (2008); Author, "The Corrosion of Medicine: Can The Profession Regain Its Moral Legacy?" Common Courage Press, Monroe, ME (2007); Author, "Shredding the Social Contract: The Privatization of Medicine," Common Courage Press, Monroe, ME (2006); Author, "Falling Through the Safety Net: Americans Confront the Perils of Health Insurance," Common Courage Press, Monroe, ME (2005); Author, "An Open Cockpit Biplane Dream: Honey Bee III," Avian Ridge Books, Friday Harbor, WA (2005); Author, "Health Care in America: Can Our Ailing System Be Healed?" Butterworth-Heinemann, Woburn, MA (2002); Author, "The Corporate Transformation of Health Care: Can the Public Interest Still Be Served?" Springer Publishing Company, New York, NY (2002); Author, "Textbook of Rural Medicine," McGraw-Hill, New York, NY (2001); Author, "Evidence-based Clinical Practice: Concepts and Approaches," Butterworth-Heinemann, Woburn, MA (2000); Author, "Flight as a Lifetime Passion: Adventures, Misadventures, and Lessons," Avian Ridge Books, Friday Harbor, WA (2000); Editor, The Journal of the American Board of Family Practice (1990-2003); Author, "The Family Practice Drug Handbook," Mosby-Yearbook, Chicago, IL (1990); Author, "Family Practice: Foundation of Changing Health Care, Second Edition" (1985); Author, "Family Practice: An International Perspective in Developed Countries, Japanese Translation," Japan (1985); Author, "Family Practice: An International Perspective in Developed Countries," Appleton-Century-Crofts, East Norwalk (1983); Author, "Family Practice: Foundation of Changing Health Care," Appleton-Century-Crofts, New York, NY (1980); Author, "Behavioral Science in Family Practice," Appleton-Century-Crofts, New York, NY (1980); Founding Editor, "The Journal of Family Practice" (1973-1990); Author, "The Modern Family Doctor and Changing Medical Practice," Appleton-Century-Crofts, New York, NY (1971) **AW:** Citizen of the Year, San Juan Island Chamber of Commerce (2017); Wright Brothers Master Pilot Award (2010); Dr. Quentin Young Health Activist Award, Physicians for a National Health Program (2008); Marian Bishop Award, Society of Teachers of Family Medicine (2004); Alumnus of the Year, School of Medicine, University of California, San Francisco, CA (1998); Curtis B. Hames Research Award, North America Primary Care Research Group (1990); Curtis B. Hames Research Award, Society of Teachers in Family Medicine (1990); Alumnus of the Year, Community Hospital Alumni Association, Santa Rosa, CA (1988); Thomas W. Johnson Award for Contributions in Family Practice Education, American Academy of Family Physicians (1980); Certificate of Excellence, Society of Teachers of Family Medicine (1980); Gold Headed Cane Award, School of Medicine, University of California, San Francisco (1960) **MEM:** United Flying Octogenarians (2011-Present); Elected Member, National Academy of Social Insurance (2014); Elected Member, University of Washington Chapter, Alpha Omega Alpha (2010); President, Physicians for a National Health Program, Chicago, IL (2004-2005); National

Academy of Sciences (1985); Charter Member, American Board of Family Practice (1971) **MH:** Albert Nelson Marquis Lifetime Achievement Award (2017) **H:** Flying airplanes **RE:** Unitarian Universalist **ADD:** 34 Oak Hill Drive, Friday Harbor, WA, 98250

GHIRARDI, GIANCARLO, T: Professor (Retired) **I:** Education/Educational Services **CN:** Università degli studi di Trieste **DOB:** 10/28/1935 **PB:** Milan **SC:** Italy **PT:** Aldo Ghirardi; Dina (Bonfatti Sabbioni) Ghirardi **MS:** Married **SPN:** Laura Cottini (9/2/1961) **CH:** Monica; Barbara; Lucia **ED:** Doctor of Physics, University of Milan, Summa Cum Laude (1959); Diploma, Scientific Lyceum (1954) **C:** Consultant, International Centre for Theoretical Physics; Professor Emeritus, Università degli studi di Trieste; Professor, Theoretical Physics, Università degli studi di Trieste (1975-Present); Director, Department of Theoretical Physics, Università degli studi di Trieste (1984-1990, 1993-1999); Director, Institute of Theoretical Physics, Università degli studi di Trieste (1980-1984); Assistant Professor, to Associate Professor, Università degli studi di Trieste (1963-1975); Associate Professor, Università di Parma (1961-1963); Associate Professor, Università di Pavia (1961-1963); Researcher, Florence, Italy (1960-1961); Fellow, Rome, Italy (1959-1960); Fellow in Theoretical Physics, National Institute of Nuclear Physics **CR:** Member, Academic Board, Consultant, Physics, Italy (1975-Present); Member, Academic Board, Consultant in Physics, California (1975-Present); Member, Academic Board, Consultant in Physics, Turkey (1975-Present); Visiting Professor, University of Cincinnati, Ohio; Visiting Professor, Universidad de Santiago de Chile; Lecturer, Various Universities in Turkey; President, Consortium for Physics, Università degli studi di Trieste **CIV:** Member, Council Administration, Research Area (2007-Present); President, International Centre for Theoretical Physics, Università degli studi di Trieste (2002-Present); Director, International Centre for Theoretical Physics, Università degli studi di Trieste (1997-1998); Member, Standing Committee, International Colloquium on Group Theoretical Methods in Physics (1982-1996); Member, Council Administration, Research Area, Trieste, Italy (1989-1993); Member, Directory Committee, Gramsci Institute, Trieste, Italy (1980-1990) **CW:** Author, "Translation: Sneaking a Look at God's Cards: Unraveling the Mysteries of Quantum Mechanics" (2007); Editor, "Chance in Physics" (2001); Member, Editorial Board, European Journal of Philosophy of Science (1995-2001); Author, "Un Occhiata alle Carte di Dio" (1997); Editor, "Bridging the Gap: Philosophy and Physics" (1993); Editor, "Science in Europe" (1988); Editor, "Group Theoretical Methods in Physics" (1985); Co-Author, "Symmetry Principles in Quantum Theory" (1970); Co-Author, "Symmetry Principles in Quantum Physics" (1970); Member, Editorial Board, Foundations of Physics; Member, Editorial Board, Journal of Physics A: General Physics; Member, Editorial Board, Studies in History and Philosophy of Modern Science; Author, "The Ghirardi-Rimini-Weber Solution of the Quantum Measurement Problem" **AW:** Award, 2500 Citations (1986-Present); Member of Excellence, Italian Physics Society (2013); Prize, Italian Physical Society (1960); Spirit of Salam Prize; Primo Rovis Prize for Science Popularization; Medal of the Province of Trieste for Important Scientific Contributions **MEM:** Titulaire Académic International Philosophie Scis., Bruxelles (2007-Present); Member, Directory Committee, Italian Society of Logic and Philosophy of Science (1988-1996); Fellow, The World Academy of

Sciences; Italian Physical Society; The New York Academy of Sciences; President, Italian Society for the Foundations of Physics **MH:** Albert Nelson Marquis Lifetime Achievement Award (2017); Distinguished Humanitarian (2017) **H:** Listening to music; Playing music; Graphics; Photography **ADD:** Scala Santa 60/1, Trieste, Italy, 34135 **URL:** https://www.amazon.com/Sneaking-Look-Gods-Cards-Unraveling/dp/069113037X

GIAMBENE, GIOVANNI, T: Engineering Educator **I:** Education/Educational Services **CN:** University of Siena **DOB:** 08/16/1966 **PB:** Florence **SC:** Italy **PT:** Gianfranco Giambene; Marisa (Breschi) Giambene **MS:** Married **SPN:** Michela Nistri (2002) **CH:** Francesco **ED:** PhD in Telecommunications and Informatics, Italy (1997); Laurea Degree, University of Florence, Florence, Italy (1993) **C:** Associate Professor of Telecommunications, University of Siena, Siena, Italy (2015-Present); Adjunct Professor, University of Siena, Siena, Italy (2003-2015); Research Associate, University of Siena, Siena, Italy (1999-2001); GSM System Engineer, OTE, Florence, Italy (1997-1998); Affiliate, Electronic Engineering Department, University of Florence (1994-1997); Teacher, Telecommunications Networks **CR:** Member, SatNEx I, II, III, IV (2006-Present); EU FP7 Responsibility Project (2013-2016); National Representative, COST/IC906 EU Project (2010-2014); EU FP7 Radical Project (2008-2010); Vice-Chairman, COST 290 Project (2004-2008); School Assistant, University of Florence (1997-2003) **CW:** Author "Queuing Theory and Telecommunications: Networks and Applications, 2nd Edition" (2014); Editor, "Resource Management in Satellite Networks" (2007); Author "Queuing Theory and Telecommunications: Networks and Applications" (2005); Co-Author, "Protocols for High-Efficiency Wireless Networks" (2002); Contributor, Articles, Professional Journals; Contributor, Articles, Papers Publications **AW:** Best paper Award, 8th Advanced Satellite Multimedia Systems Conference and the 14th Signal Processing for Space Communications Workshop, Palma de Mallorca, Spain (2016) **MEM:** Technical Committee for Personal Communications, IEEE (2004-Present); Satellite and Space Communications Technical Committee, IEEE (2001-Present); IEICE Japan; IEEE Senior Member (2011-Present); Board of Directions, Europe, Middle East & Africa Region, IEEE Communications Society (2012-2016) **MH:** Albert Nelson Marquis Lifetime Achievement Award (2017) **H:** Football; Model-making **BA:** University of Siena, Via Roma 56, Siena, Italy, 53100 **ADD:** Via Pratese 297/A, Pistoia (PT), Italy, 51100 **URL:** http://www.dii.unisi.it/~giambene/index.html

GIBBS, LAWRENCE BLAIR, T: Lawyer **I:** Law and Legal Services **CN:** Miller & Chevalier **DOB:** 08/31/1938 **PB:** Hutchinson **SC:** KS/USA **MS:** Married **ED:** JD, University of Texas (1963); BA, Yale University (1960) **C:** Member, Miller & Chevalier, Washington, D.C. (1994-2017); Partner, Johnson & Gibbs, Washington, D.C. (1989-1994); Partner, Johnson & Gibbs, Dallas, TX (1989-1994); Commissioner, IRS, Washington, D.C. (1986-1989); Partner, Johnson & Swanson, Dallas, TX (1976-1986); Assistant Commissioner, IRS, Washington, D.C. (1973-1975); Acting Chief Counsel, IRS, Washington, D.C. (1973); Deputy Chief Counsel, IRS, Washington, D.C. (1972-1973); Associate to Partner, Branscomb, Gary, Thomasson & Hall, Corpus Christi, TX (1963-1972) **CIV:** Advisory Trustee, Southern Federal Tax Institute **MEM:** Vice Chairman, Administration Section, Taxation, ABA (1991-1992); Board of Regents, American College Trust and Estate Counsel (1990-1996); Chairman,

Taxation Section, State Bar of Texas (1978-1979); District of Columbia Bar; American Law Institute; Federal Bar Association; Board of Directors, Tax Analysts, American College Trust and Estate Counsel; Planning Committee, Tax Council Policy Institute, American College Trust and Estate Counsel **ADD:** 566 S Spoonbill Dr, Sarasota, FL, 34236

GILBERT, MARTHA JANE, T: Literature and Language Educator (Retired) **I:** Education/Educational Services **PB:** Jacksonville **SC:** AL/USA **PT:** William Troy Wilson; Eunice Margaret Wilson **MS:** Divorced **SPN:** Curtis Paul Gilbert, Jr. **CH:** Jennie LuAnne Gilbert Harper **ED:** MA, British Literature/English Education, Jacksonville State University, AL (1976); BS, Biology and English, Jacksonville State University, AL (1966) **CT:** Certified, Advanced Placement, Oglethorpe University, Atlanta, GA (1992); Certified in Gifted Education, Northwest Georgia Regional Education Service Association, Rome, GA (1996), Honors Certification; Certified Teacher, States of Georgia, Alabama **C:** Retired (2010); Teacher, English, East Paulding High School, Dallas,GA (1992-2010); Teacher, English, Paulding County High School, Dallas, Georgia (1990-1992); Teacher, English, Advanced Placement English Literature, Speech, Drama, Alexandria High School, Alexandria, AL (1966-1989); Teacher, AL English Composition and American Literature 201 & 202, Gadsden State Junior College, Gadsden, AL (1982- 1985); Teacher, AL English Composition, World Literature 331 & 332, Victorian Poetry, Eighteenth Century Literature, Jacksonville State University, Jacksonville, AL (1983-1989) **CR:** Adjunct Instructor, English Gadsden State Junior College, Gadsden AL (1982-1984); Instructor, Jacksonville State University (1983-1989); Instructor, American Institute of Banking (1978); Teacher, Drama; Director, Plays **AW:** Nominated Teacher of the Year (2004); Honoree, Yearbook Dedications in Alabama and Georgia **MH:** Albert Nelson Marquis Lifetime Achievement Award (2017) **H:** Travel; Church choir; Church activities **PA:** Republican Party **RE:** Protestant **ADD:** 75 Cambridge Dr, Covington, GA, 30014

GILL, JOAN COX, T: Professor **I:** Medicine & Health Care **CN:** Blood Center of Wisconsin **PB:** Los Angeles **SC:** CA/USA **MS:** Divorced **CH:** Gretchen **ED:** Fellowship, Pediatric Hematology Oncology, Medical College of Wisconsin and the Blood Center of Southeastern Wisconsin (1978-1981); Pediatric Residency, Milwaukee Children's Hospital, Medical College of Wisconsin (1977-1979); Pediatric Internship, Milwaukee Children's Hospital, Medical College of Wisconsin, Milwaukee, WI (1976-1977); MD, Medical College of Wisconsin, Milwaukee, WI (1976); BS, St. Norbert College, West De Pere, Wisconsin, Cum Laude (1965) **CT:** American Board of Pediatric Hematology/Oncology (1982); American Board of Pediatrics (1981) **C:** Chair, Regional Executive Council, Region V West, Great Lakes Hemophilia Foundation, MCHB Hemophilia Center Network (2005-Present); Chair, Medical and Scientific Advisory Committee, Great Lakes Hemophilia Foundation (2005-Present); Professor of Pediatrics, The Medical College of Wisconsin, Milwaukee, WI (1994-Present); Consultant, Regional Hemostasis Reference Laboratory, Blood Center of Southeastern Wisconsin, Milwaukee, WI (1981-Present); Medical Director, Hemophilia and Bleeding Disorders Center, Children's Hospital of Wisconsin, Milwaukee, WI (2003-2016); Director of Training Program, NIH funded General Clinical Research Center, Medical College of Wisconsin, Milwaukee, WI (2000-2002); Director, Comprehensive Center for Bleeding

Disorders, Blood Center of Wisconsin, Milwaukee, WI (1996-2013); Co-Director of Training Program, NIH funded General Clinical Research Center, Medical College of Wisconsin, Milwaukee, WI (1996-2000); Associate Program Director, NIH funded General Clinical Research Center, Medical College of Wisconsin, Milwaukee, WI (1996-2002); Director, Blood Center of Southeastern Wisconsin/ Children's Hospital of Wisconsin Satellite Unit, Medical College of Wisconsin, Milwaukee, WI (1992-2002); Consultant, Outpatient Transfusion Service, Children's Hospital of Wisconsin, Milwaukee, WI (1989-2009); Associate Professor of Pediatrics, Medical College of Wisconsin, Milwaukee, WI (1988-1994); Director, Milwaukee Hemophilia Comprehensive Treatment Center, Great Lakes Hemophilia Foundation, Milwaukee, WI (1984-1996); Consultant, Hemostasis Laboratory, Children's Hospital of Wisconsin, Milwaukee, WI (1984-1990); Medical Director, Great Lakes Hemophilia Foundation, Milwaukee, WI (1984-1996); Consultant, Wisconsin State Newborn Metabolic Screening Program (1983-1989); Assistant Professor of Pediatrics, The Medical College of Wisconsin, Milwaukee, WI (1982-1988); Director, Sickle Cell Comprehensive Care Center, Medical College of Wisconsin, Milwaukee, WI (1981 1989); Clinical Instructor, Pediatrics, The Medical College of Wisconsin, Milwaukee, WI (1981-1982); Assistant Medical Director, Great Lakes Hemophilia Foundation, Milwaukee, WI (1981-1984) **CR:** Senior Investigator, Blood Center of Southeastern Wisconsin, Milwaukee, WI (1991-2015) **CW:** Author or Co-author, 135 Peer-reviewed Publications; Author, 21 Book Chapters, Invited Reviews; Author, 171 Research Abstracts **AW:** Best Doctors in America (1996-Present); Distinguished Achievement Award in the Natural Sciences, St. Norbert College, DePere, WI (2017); Hemostasis and Thrombosis Research Society Joan Cox Gill Exemplary Service Award (2013); Visiting Professor, Detroit Children's Hospital, Detroit, MI (2005); Visiting Professor, University Medical Center, Jackson, MI (1997); Visiting Professor, Mayo Clinic, Rochester, MN (1995); Visiting Professor, Columbus Children's Hospital, Columbus, OH (1992); Clinical Fellowship, American Cancer Society (1979-1980) **MEM:** Co-founder, The Hemostasis and Thrombosis Research Society; American Society of Hematology; American Society of Pediatric Hematology/Oncology; International Society for Thrombosis and Haemostasis; Society for Pediatric Research **ADD:** 5891 Fulham Ct, Greenvale, WI, 53129 **URL:** https://www.bcw.edu/cs/groups/public/documents/documents/mdaw/mda0/~edisp/ccbd_newsletter_0514.pdf

GILLMAN, JOAN AVA, **T:** Elementary School Educator, Musician **I:** Education/Educational Services **CN:** Calhoun School **DOB:** 10/16/1958 **PB:** New York **SC:** NY/USA **PT:** Seymour Gillman; Pearl (Krauthamer) Gillman **ED:** MA in Education, New York University (1982); BA in Education, Felician College, Summa Cum Laude (1980) **CT:** Certified K-8 Elementary Educator; Certified in Hearing Impaired Education (K-12) **C:** Grade Five Science Teacher, Calhoun School, New York, NY (2008-Present); Grade Six Science Teacher, Calhoun School, New York, NY (2008-Present); Grade Five Mathematics Teacher, Yeshivat Noam, Paramus, NJ (2007-2008); Grade Six Mathematics Teacher, Yeshivat Noam, Paramus, NJ (2007-2008); Grade Five Science Teacher, Yeshivat Noam, Paramus, NJ (2007-2008); Grade Six Science Teacher, Yeshivat Noam, Paramus, NJ (2007-2008); Grade Four Science Teacher, Anna C. Scott Elementary School, Leonia, NJ (2006-2007); Grade Five Science Teacher, Anna C. Scott Elementary School, Leonia, NJ (2006-2007); Grades Four

Mathematics Teacher, Professional Children's School, New York, NY (1986-2006); Grades Five Mathematics Teacher, Professional Children's School, New York, NY (1986-2006); Grades Six Mathematics Teacher, Professional Children's School, New York, NY (1986-2006); Grades Four Science Teacher, Professional Children's School, New York, NY (1986-2006); Grades Five Science Teacher, Professional Children's School, New York, NY (1986-2006); Grades Six Science Teacher, Professional Children's School, New York, NY (1986-2006); Language Arts Teacher, Bede School, Englewood, NJ (1984-1986); Social Studies Teacher, Bede School, Englewood, NJ (1984-1986); Grades Four Teacher, Joytown Kent Elementary School, Bronx, NY (1983-1984); Grades Five Teacher, Joytown Kent Elementary School, Bronx, NY (1983-1984); Grade Five Teacher, Saint Angela Merici School, Bronx, NY (1982-1983) **CR:** Subject Area Representative, Elementary Level, Science Teachers Association of New York State (2016-Present) **CIV:** Member, Pitsco Teacher Advisory Group (2015-Present); Ambassador, Mars Atmosphere and Volatile Evolution Mission Program, National Aeronautics and Space Administration; Conference Workshop Leader, Science Council of New York City; Conference Workshop Leader, Science Teachers Association of New York State; Conference Workshop Leader, National Science Teachers Association; Conference Workshop Leader, National Science Teachers Association STEM **CW:** Author, "Straw Rockets are Out of This World" (2013); Violinist, Bergen Philharmonic Orchestra, Teaneck, NJ; Violinist, Calhoun Community Orchestra; Violinist, North Jersey Symphony Orchestra; Violinist, August Symphony Orchestra; Contributor, Articles to Newspapers **AW:** Named, National Dean's List, Urhy Thompson- Teacher of the Year Award, The Calhoun School (2017); Recipient, Young Teachers Incentive Award, Who's Who in American Universities (1980) **MEM:** Science Teachers Association of New York State; National Science Teachers Association; Kappa Delta Pi **MH:** Albert Nelson Marquis Lifetime Achievement Award (2017); Distinguished Humanitarian (2017) **H:** Classical piano; Violin; Macrame; Swimming; Beading **ADD:** 390 Briarcliffe Rd, Teaneck, NJ, 07666

GINTHER, DONNA, **I:** Education/Educational Services **PB:** , **ED:** PhD, University of Wisconsin-Madison (1995) **C:** Professor, Department of Economics, University of Kansas (2002-Present) **CW:** Lead Author, Articles **AW:** Byron Shutz Award, University of Kansas (2012) **MEM:** American Economics Association; Southern Economics Association; Association of Public Policy and Management; Population Association of America; American Association for the Advancement of Science

GIOVANELLI, JOHN, **T:** Research Chemist (Retired) **I:** Sciences **PT:** Grantel Elwin Giovanelli; Doris Eileen (Dennison) Giovanelli **MS:** Married **SPN:** Martha Masa Tsukiyama 4/15/1989); Edna Rosina Gankerseer (9/13/1959, Deceased 7/1988) **ED:** Postdoctoral Fellow in Plant Biochemistry, Johns Hopkins University, Baltimore, MD (1957-1959); PhD, University of California, Berkeley (1957); Honorary BSc in Agriculture, University of Sydney, Australia (1953) **C:** Visiting Scientist to Research Chemist, National Institute of Mental Health, Bethesda, MD (1965-2001); Research Scientist to Senior Research Scientist, Lecturer, Industrial Research Organization and University, Sydney, Australia (1959-1965) **CIV:** Special Volunteer, National Institute of Mental Health, Bethesda, MD (2001-Present) **CW:** Editorial

Board Member, Plant Physiology (1983-1992); Author, "Plant Biochemistry" (1964); Contributor, Articles to Professional Journals **AW:** Recipient, Peter Goldacre Award, Australian Society of Plant Physiologists, Sydney, Australia (1965); Pacific Scholar English Speaking Union, San Francisco, CA (1954) **MH:** Albert Nelson Marquis Lifetime Achievement Award (2017) **H:** Ballroom dancing; Hiking; Gardening **ADD:** 4409 Dresden St, Kensington, MD, 20895

GIROTTI, ALBERT W., **I:** Sciences **CN:** Medical College of Wisconsin **DOB:** 05/09/1905 **MS:** Single **SPN:** Deceased **CH:** Fr. John W. Girotti **ED:** Postdoctoral Coursework, Cornell University Medical College (1965-1969); PhD, University of Massachusetts, Amherst (1965) **C:** Professor of Biochemistry, Medical College Wisconsin, Milwaukee (1969) **CR:** Editorial Board, Photochemistry and Photobiology (2009-Present) **AW:** Research Grant, National Institutes of Health (1990-2017) **MEM:** President, American Society of Photobiology (1997-1998); American Society of Photobiology; Society of Free Radical Biology and Medicine; American Society of Biochemistry and Molecular Biology **ACH:** Achievements include research in role of lipid peroxides in cancer, role of nitric oxide in cancer progression, uregulation of cytoprotective nitric oxide in anti-tumor photodynamic therapy (PDT) **H:** Remote control model aircraft **PA:** Republican **RE:** Roman Catholic **ADD:** 8700 Watertown Plank, 8700 Watertown Plank, Milwaukee, WI, 53226

GIUFFRIDA, NADJA, **T:** Founder, Chief Executive Officer **I:** Business Management/Business Services **CN:** Dextro, LLC **ED:** Bachelors, Instituto Tecnológico y de Estudios Superiores de Monterrey (1990) **C:** Founder, Thinker, Inc. (2008-Present); Chair, Thinker, Inc. (2008-Present); Founder, Dextro, LLC (1996-Present); Chief Executive Officer, Dextro, LLC (1996-Present); Employment Adviser, U.S. Department of State (2000-2002) **CIV:** Chair, Thinkers, Inc. **AW:** Laureate Woman of the Year, National Association of Women Business Owners (2014); Professional of the Year Award, Pinnacle (2013); Laureate Woman of the Year, National Association of Women Business Owners (2012); Learning Leader Award in Knowledge Management, Bersin and Associates; Premier Honors Laureate, Computerworld; Honoree, Cambridge Who's Who; Honoris Causa Doctorate in Learning Management, HELP University of Malaysia **MEM:** Hispanic Scholarship Fund; White House Initiative for Hispanic Excellence; Thinkers. org; Mujeres en Plural; Consejo Coordinador Empresarial de Mujeres; Club de Industriales Mexicanos; National Association of Women Business Owners; AEM; Industrial Club, Mexico **H:** Spending time with her family; Outdoor activities; Reading **ADD:** PO Box 4472, Ashburn, VA, 20148

GLAHN, HARRY R., **T:** Scientist Emeritus (Retired) **I:** Sciences **CN:** National Weather Service **CH:** Robert Gale; Gary Lee **ED:** PhD in Meteorology, The Pennsylvania State University (1963); MS, Massachusetts Institute of Technology (1958); MS, Oklahoma A&M College (1958); BA, Truman State University (1953); Coursework in Statistics, American University **C:** National Weather Service (1958-2012); Director of the Meteorological Development Laboratory, National Weather Service (1976); Office of Meteorological Research (1960); School Teacher, MO (1947-1951); Forecaster, Air Force Alaskan Weather Center, Anchorage, AK **MIL:** Air Force **CW:** Contributor, More than 160 Scientific Papers, Professional Journals **AW:** Cleveland Abbe Award, American Meteorological Society (2005); Distinguished

Career Award, National Oceanic and Atmospheric Administration; Gold Medal Award, Department of Commerce; Silver Medal Award, Department of Commerce **MEM:** Fellow, American Meteorological Society; Probability and Statistics Committee, American Meteorological Society **ADD:** 3233 Holly Hill Dr, Falls Church, VA, 22042

GLASS, GLENDA JUNE, T: Clinical Microbiologist (Retired) **I:** Sciences **CN:** St. Joseph's Hospital **DOB:** 10/08/1950 **PB:** Boise **SC:** ID/USA **PT:** James Myron Glass; Elleen Grace (Heales) Glass **MS:** Divorced **SPN:** Tariq Khalidi (1972, Divorced 1998) **ED:** Graduate, Southwest School of Botanical Medicine (2003); BS in Medical Technology, University of Nevada, Reno (1973) **CT:** Certified Clinical Laboratory Technologist, State of California; Certified Medical Technologist **C:** Clinical Microbiologist, St. Joseph's Regional Health System, Stockton, CA (1992-2013); Quality Assurance Technologist, Fong Diagnostic Laboratory, Sacramento, CA (1991-1992); Supervisor, Microbiology, Fong Diagnostic Laboratory, Sacramento, CA (1981-1991); Clinical Microbiologist, M.D. Anderson Hospital, Houston, TX (1978-1980); Clinical Microbiologist, Biomedical Resources, Concord, CA (1976-1978) **CR:** Consultant in Field; Owner, Irish Hill Herbals; Lecturer, Prevention of Chronic Disease and Herbalism **CIV:** Member, Planned Parenthood **AW:** Doctor's Wives Scholar (1972); Fleischman Scholar (1969); Recognition of Appreciation at Retirement; Best in Show, Weaving Project, County Fair **MEM:** Planned Parenthood; National Organization of Women; American Society of Clinical Pathologists; American Herbalist Guild; California Association of Medical Laboratory Technologists; American Society for Clinical Pathology; American Civil Liberties Union **H:** Alternative energy; Herbal and alternative medicine; Crafts; Dog training; Flying; Weaving **BA:** United States, Ione, CA, 95640-9136 **ADD:** 2414 Irish Ridge Rd, Ione, CA, 95640

GLASS, RONALD BERNHARD JACOB, T: Attending Radiologist **I:** Medicine & Health Care **CN:** Icahn School of Medicine at Mount Sinai **DOB:** 12/20/1952 **PB:** Salisbury **SC:** Rhodesia **PT:** Joseph Glass; Inge Selma Glass **MS:** Single **ED:** Fellowship in Pediatric Radiology, Children's Memorial Hospital, Chicago, IL (1984-1986); Fellowship, Faculty of Diagnostic Radiology, the College of Medicine of South Africa (1984); Fellowship, Faculty of Radiology, the Royal College of Surgeons in Ireland (1983); Resident, Department of Radiology, Johannesburg Hospital, Johannesburg, South Africa (1980-1983); Intern, Addington Hospital, Durban, South Africa (1977); MB, University of the Witwatersrand, Johannesburg, South Africa (1976); BChir, University of the Witwatersrand, Johannesburg, South Africa (1976) **CT:** Licensed to Practice Medicine, State of New York (2017); Certified in Diagnostic Radiology with Added Qualifications in Pediatric Radiology, American Board of Radiology (2005, 1995); Licensed to Practice Medicine, State of Texas (1994); Licensed to Practice Medicine, State of Rhode Island (1993); Licensed to Practice Medicine, District of Columbia (1989); Licensed to Practice Medicine, State of Illinois (1984); Licensed to Practice Medicine, United Kingdom (1978); Licensed to Practice Medicine, South Africa (1977); Diplomate, Educational Commission for Foreign Medical Graduates (1976) **C:** Staff Radiologist, Elmhurst Hospital (2009-Present); Staff Radiologist, Mount Sinai Medical Center, Icahn School of Medicine at Mount Sinai (2009-Present); Associate Professor of Radiology, Icahn School of Medicine at Mount Sinai (2008-Present); Associate Professor of Radiology, Feinberg School of Medicine, Northwestern

University (2007-2009); Staff Radiologist, Children's Memorial Hospital, Chicago, Illinois (2006-2007); Staff Radiologist, Beth Israel Hospital, Icahn School of Medicine at Mount Sinai (2005-2006); Staff Radiologist, St Luke's Hospital, Icahn School of Medicine at Mount Sinai (2005-2006); Associate Professor of Clinical Radiology, Mount Sinai Medical Center, Icahn School of Medicine at Mount Sinai (2003-2005); Staff Radiologist, Mount Sinai Medical Center, Icahn School of Medicine at Mount Sinai (1997-2005); Assistant Professor of Radiology, Mount Sinai Medical Center, Icahn School of Medicine at Mount Sinai (1997-2003); Radiologist, Northern Metropolitan Radiology Associates, P.C. (1996-1997); Assistant Professor of Radiology, The University of Texas Health Science Center at Houston (1994-1996); Staff Radiologist, Department of Radiology, Hermann Hospital, Harris Health (1994-1996); Staff Radiologist, Department of Radiology, Lyndon Baines Johnson General Hospital, Harris Health (1994-1996); Clinical Assistant Professor of Radiology, Brown University (1993-1994); Staff Radiologist, Department of Diagnostic Imaging, Rhode Island Hospital (1993-1994); Assistant Professor of Radiology and Pediatrics, School of Medicine and Health Sciences, The George Washington University (1990-1993) Staff Radiologist, Department of Diagnostic Imaging and Radiology, Children's National Medical Center, Washington, D.C. (1990-1993); Special Radiology Fellow, Department of Diagnostic Imaging and Radiology, Children's National Medical Center, Washington, D.C. (1989-1990); Assistant Professor of Radiology and Pediatrics, Stritch School of Medicine, Loyola University Chicago (1987-1989); Director of Pediatric Radiology, Foster G. McGaw Hospital, Loyola University Chicago (1987-1989); Staff Radiologist, Foster G. McGaw Hospital, Loyola University Chicago (1987-1989); Assistant Professor of Pediatric Radiology, The University of Chicago (1986-1987); Staff Radiologist, Johannesburg Hospital, University of Witwatersrand, Johannesburg, South Africa (1984) **CR:** Consulting Radiologist, Shriners Hospital for Crippled Children, Houston, TX (1994-1995); Coordinator of Education, Department of Diagnostic Imaging and Radiology, Children's National Medical Center, Washington, D.C. (1990-1991); Guest Lecturer, Department of Radiology, National Navy Medical Center (1989-1993); Guest Lecturer, Department of Radiology, Walter Reed Army Medical Center, Washington, D.C. (1989-1993); Visiting Professor, Yale School of Medicine, New Haven, CT (1988); Visiting Professor, Children's Hospital Medical Center, Cincinnati, OH (1988); Visiting Professor, Rainbow Babies and Children's Hospital, Cleveland, OH (1988); Visiting Consultant, Department of Rheumatology, LaRabida Children's Hospital, Chicago, IL (1986-1989) **MIL:** Lieutenant, Medical Corps, South African Defense Force (1978-1979) **CW:** Consultant to the Editor, Radiology (2010-2017); Associate Editor, Radiology (2005-2010); Contributor, Articles to Professional Journals; Contributor, Scientific Exhibits; Contributor, Chapters to Books **AW:** Honoree, Fellow, American College of Radiology (2011) **MEM:** American Roentgen Ray Society (1998); New York State Radiological Society (1997); European Society of Pediatric Radiology (1994); American College of Radiology (1990); Radiological Society of North America (1986); Society for Pediatric Radiology (1986) **MH:** Albert Nelson Marquis Lifetime Achievement Award (2017) **H:** Attending performances at the Metropolitan Opera; Visiting the Metropolitan Museum of Art of New York **RE:** Jewish **ADD:** 75 E End Ave Apt 4L, Apt 4L, New York, NY, 10028

GOERGER, VIRGINIA FRANCES, T: Owner,

Photographer, Designer **I:** Other **CN:** Virginia's Photos and Flowers **DOB:** 07/29/1940 **PB:** Breckenridge **SC:** MN/USA **PT:** Conrad Vaplon; Irene Vaplon **MS:** Widowed **SPN:** David Goerger (Deceased) **CH:** Ida; Rosemary; Edmund **ED:** AA in Liberal Arts, North Dakota State College of Science; Coursework in Writing, Institute of Children's Literature **CT:** Certified in Dale Carnegie Program; Certified in Photo Workshops; Certified in N4C Camera Club **C:** Owner, Virginia's Photos & Flowers (1967-Present) **CIV:** Tour Guide, Bagg Bonanza Farm Historic Site (1990-Present); Lay Minister and Teacher of Faith Classes (1968-Present) **CW:** Author, "A Century of Life on the Bagg Farm and Red River Valley" (2016); Author, "Bonanza Farm Life and Beyond" (2015); Author, "Kulzer Family History Book" (2013); Author, "The Wyndmere Barney 125th Anniversary" (2008); Author, "Beyond the Snailhouse: History with Written and Used Photos between 1616-1993" (1993); Author, "Bagg Bonanza Farm Heirloom Cookbook" (1992); Author, "Fargo Catholic Diocese Cookbook" (1987); Author, "100 Years of Wyndmere History" (1982) **AW:** Outstanding Woman Owned Business of North Dakota (1994-1996); First Runner-Up, Mrs. North Dakota Contest (1962); International Scholar, Laureate Program; Family History Photo Contest Plaques; Volunteer Recognition, North Dakota Long Term Care Association; Community Leadership Award **MEM:** Phi Theta Kappa Honor Society; Professional Camera Shop; St. John the Baptist Catholic Church; St. Catherine's Living Center; Bagg Bonanza Farm Historic Preservation Society; AAUW; Southeast North Dakota Community Theater; Fargo Catholic Diocese Vocation; Wyndmere Community Club; Wyndmere Museum Foundation; Barney VFW Hall Foundation **H:** Sewing; Making quilts; Art; Painting; Cooking and decorating cakes; Flower gardening; Traveling **RE:** Catholic **BA:** 604 Elm Avenue, Virginia's Photos and Flowers, Wyndmere, ND, 58081

GOINES, LEONARD, T: Freelance Musician **I:** Fine Art **DOB:** 04/22/1934 **PB:** Jacksonville **SC:** FL/USA **PT:** Buford Goines; Willie Mae (Lamar) Goines **MS:** Divorced **SPN:** Margaretta Bobo (Divorced) **CH:** Lisan Lynette **ED:** Postdoctoral Fellow, Harvard University, Cambridge, MA (1982-1985); MA, New York University (1980); BA, The New School for Social Research (1980); EdD, Columbia University (1963); Professional Diploma, Columbia University (1961); MA, Columbia University (1960); MMus, Manhattan School of Music (1956); BMus, Manhattan School of Music (1955) **CT:** Certificate of Advanced Studies, Harvard University (1984); Certified in Clinical Counseling, Postgraduate Center for Mental Health, New York City, NY (1983); Certification, Music Program, Fontainebleau Associations, France (1959) **C:** Freelance Musician (1959-Present); Lecturer of Music, New York University (1970-1993); Professor, Borough of Manhattan Community College, City University of New York (1970-1992); Associate Professor of Music, Howard University, Washington, D.C. (1970-1972); Lecturer of Music, York College, City University of New York (1969); Lecturer of Music, Queens College, City University of New York (1969); Associate Professor of Music, Morgan State University, Baltimore, MD (1966-1968); Trumpeter, Symphony of the New World, New York City, NY (1965-1976) **CR:** Member, Preservation of Jazz Advisory Commission (1992-1993); Co-Executive Producer, "651," BAM Harvey Theater (1988-1996); District Visiting Professor, Lafayette College, Easton, PA (1986); Visiting Professor, Vassar College, Poughkeepsie, NY (1985); Visiting Professor, Williams College, Williamstown, MA (1984); Research Consultant, National Endowment for the Arts (1983); Partner, Organizational and

Educational Art, Shepard & Goines; Consultant, Jazz, Shepard & Goines; Appointee, United States Department of the Interior, Smithsonian Institute; Consultant in Field **CIV:** Music Panelist, Arts Connection, New York City, NY (1985); Trustee, National Guild for Community Arts Education, New York City, NY (1982-1985); Chairman, Special Arts Section Panel, New York State Council on the Arts, New York City, NY (1982-1985); Folklore Consultant, Field Researcher, African Diaspora, Smithsonian Institution (1972-1976); Field Researcher, Smithsonian and the National Endowment for the Humanities; Volunteer, Poverty Project **CW:** Contributor, Articles, Professional Journals **AW:** Scholar Incentive Award, The City University of New York (1983-1984); College Teachers Fellow, National Endowment of the Humanities (1982-1983); Public Service Award, United States Department of Labor (1980); Faculty Research Grantee, Howard University (1971-1973); Faculty Research Grantee, The City University of New York (1971-1973); Faculty Research Grantee, New York University (1971-1973); Named, Honorary Citizen, City of Winnipeg, Canada (1958) **MEM:** American Federation of Musicians Local 802; American Association of University Professors; National Academy of Recording Arts & Sciences, Inc.; Phi Delta Kappa International; Phi Mu Alpha Sinfonia Fraternity of America **MH:** Albert Nelson Marquis Lifetime Achievement Award (2017); Distinguished Humanitarian (2017) **H:** Running; Photography; Travel; Music; Walking; Meditating **PA:** Democrat **RE:** Episcopalian **ADD:** 221 W 131st St, New York, NY, 10027

GOLDBLATT, HAL MICHAEL, T: Chief Financial Officer, Photographer, Author **I:** Financial Services **CN:** Goldblatt, Inc. **DOB:** 02/06/1952 **PB:** Long Beach **SC:** CA/USA **PT:** Arnold Phillip Goldblatt; Molly (Stearns) Goldblatt **MS:** Married **SPN:** Shawn Naomi Doherty (8/27/1974) **CH:** Eliyahu Yonah; Tova Devorah; Raizel; Shoshana; Reuven Lev; Eliezer Noach; Esther Bayla; Rochel Leah; Zalman Ber; Perle Sara **ED:** MBA, Trinity University (2003); BA in Mathematics, California State University, Long Beach, CA (1975) **C:** Managing Partner, Glass IT (2014-Present); Special Agent, Goldblatt Security (2012-Present); Managing Partner, KHM Software (2012-Present); Director of Photography, Lightons Creations, Las Vegas, NV (2000-Present); Chief Financial Officer, Goldblatt, Inc. (1992-Present); President, SDG Computer Service, Las Vegas, NV (1985-Present); Owner, Star Publications, Las Vegas, NV (1975-Present); Senior Accountant, Cosmopolitan Resort (2009-2012); Document Control Manager, Turnberry West Construction (2007-2008); Manager, Fountainbleau Resorts (2006-2008); Budget Manager, Rhodes Homes (2004-2006); Executive MBA, Trinity Southern University (2003); Controller, Nevada Hand, Las Vegas, NV (2001-2004); Director Special Projects, Chabad Southern Nevada, Las Vegas, NV (1999-2000); Cost Accountant, Ameristar Casinos, Inc., Las Vegas, NV (1997-1999); Chief Executive Officer, Goldblatt, Inc., Las Vegas, NV (1996-1997); Chief Financial Officer, Stewart Construction, Las Vegas, NV (1995-1996); Controller, Amland Development, Las Vegas, NV (1993-1995); Chief Financial Officer, Martin & Mills Ltd., Las Vegas, NV (1992-1993) **CIV:** Security Director, Chabad of Southern Nevada (2012-Present); Vice President, Jews for Judaism, Long Beach, CA (1983-Present); Advisory Board, Actor's Repertory Theatre (1998-2003); Treasurer, Actor's Repertory Theatre (1995-1998); Board of Directors, Congregation of Lubavitch, Long Beach, CA (1991-1992); Board of Directors, Congregation of Lubavitch, Long Beach, CA (1987); Fundraising Chairman, Friends of Lubavitch, Long Beach, CA (1977); Founder, President, Jews for Judaism,

Long Beach, CA (1975-1982) **CW:** Author, "The Tis Bottle" (2014); Exhibited, Photo Gallery, Veteran Village Art Gallery (2013-2015); Author, "The Tis Bottle" (2012); Author, "Sarah: A Tormented Soul" (2009); Author, "Anger Management" (2008); Photographer, "Inspiration Through my Eyes" (2008); Exhibited, Photo Gallery, "Dinosaurs & Roses," Las Vagas, NV (2011-2013); Photographer, "Chanukah - Festival of Lights" (2006-2014); Photographer, "Care for Kids Telethon" (1999); Photographer, "Chanukah - Festival of Lights" (1998-2004); Photographer, "Garth Brooks World Tour" (1998); Photographer, "Care for Kids Telethon" (1998); Photographer, "Shavous Trek" (1997); Photographer, "A Day at Disneyland" (1985); Producer, Engineer, Audio Cassette, " Uforatzta Trio" (1982); Producer, Engineer, Audio Cassette, "Middle Class Dreams" (1981); Producer, Engineer, Audio Cassette, "From the Heart of My Dreams" (1980); Photographer, "Chassidic Fabrangen" (1979); Photographer, "Mikveh Yisorel" (1978) **AW:** Citizen of the Month, City of Las Vegas (2017); ART Distinguished Service Award (1996); Georgie Award, Actor's Repertory Theatre (1995); Floyd Durham Memorial Award for Outstanding Community Service (1973); Gold Press Card Award, Forty Niner Newspaper (1973-1974) **MEM:** Lifetime Member, American Locksmith Association; Lifetime Honorary Member, TUG **MH:** Albert Nelson Marquis Lifetime Achievement Award recipient **H:** Travel; Chess; Sailing **PA:** Republican **RE:** Jewish **ADD:** 4513 Del Monte Ave, Las Vegas, NV, 89102 **URL:** goldblattinc.com

GOLDEN, LEON, T: Classicist, Educator **I:** Education/Educational Services **DOB:** 12/25/1930 **PB:** Jersey City **SC:** NJ/USA **PT:** Nathan Golden; Regina (Okun) Golden **ED:** PhD, University of Chicago (1958); MA, University of Chicago (1953); BA, University of Chicago (1950) **C:** Program Director in Humanities, Florida State University, Tallahassee, FL (1976-2003); Professor, Florida State University, Tallahassee, FL (1968-2003); Chairman, Department of Classics, Florida State University, Tallahassee, FL (1986-1995); Associate Professor of Classical Languages, Florida State University, Tallahassee, FL (1965-1968); Assistant Professor of Ancient Languages, College of William and Mary (1960-1965); Instructor of Ancient Languages, College of William and Mary (1958-1960) **CR:** Board of Directors, Florida Endowment for Humanities (1983-1987) **MIL:** US Army (1953-1955) **AW:** Fellow, Cooperative Program Humanities Society for Religion in Higher Education (1971-1972); Fellow, Cooperative Program Humanities, U.N.C. and Duke (1964-1965) **MEM:** President, Southern Section, Classical Association Midwest and South (1972-1974); Archeological Institute of America; American Philological Association; Phi Beta Kappa **ADD:** 1526 Parchment Cove, Tallahassee, FL, 32308

GOLDFARB, HELENE DIANE, T: Counseling Administrator (Retired) **I:** Health, Wellness and Fitness **DOB:** 09/24/1929 **PB:** New York City **SC:** NY/USA **PT:** Joseph Goldfarb; Fay E. (Hirschhorn) Goldfarb **MS:** Single **ED:** MA, New York University (1953); BA, Hunter College (1951) **C:** Guidance Counselor, Albert Leonard Junior High School and Middle School, New Rochelle, NY (1968-1995); Science Teacher, Albert Leonard Junior High School, New Rochelle, NY (1960-1968); Assistant Producer, Tic Tac Dough, NBC, New York, NY (1956-1959); Science Teacher, Isaac E. Young Junior High School, New Rochelle, NY (1953-1956); Science and Social Studies Teacher, Hunter College High School, New York, NY (1951-1953) **CR:** Summer Administrator, O'Neill Critics Institute, Eugene O'Neill Theater Center, Waterford, CT (1994-Present); Summer Administrator, O'Neill

Critics Institute, Eugene O'Neill Theater Center, Waterford, CT (1981-1986); Secretary, Board of Directors, Westchester Arts and Science Program, Scarsdale, NY (1970-1997); Board of Directors, New Rochelle High School Scholarship Fund (1975-1995) **CIV:** Treasurer, Scholarship and Welfare Fund, Alumni Association of Hunter College (2017-Present); Treasurer, The Caring Neighbor (2003-2016), Member, Financial Committee, Board of Directors, Lenox Hill Neighborhood House, New York City, NY (1979-Present); Treasurer, President, Queens Chapter, Alumni Association of Hunter College (1953-2017); 1st Vice President, Scholarship and Welfare Fund, Alumni Association of Hunter College (2011-2016); Treasurer, Scholarship and Welfare Fund, Alumni Association of Hunter College (2011-2016); Treasurer, The Feminist Press, City University of New York (2005-2016); Board of Directors, Hunter College Foundation (2004-2007); President, Scholarship and Welfare Fund, Alumni Association of Hunter College (2004-2007); Chair, Subcommittee on Planned Giving, Hunter College Foundation (2003-2004); Board of Directors, Hunter College Hillel Foundation (2001-2004); Secretary, The Feminist Press, City University of New York (2001-2005); National Chair, Thomas Hunter Society (1999-2004); 1st Vice President, Scholarship and Welfare Fund, Alumni Association of Hunter College (1999-2004); Treasurer, Scholarship and Welfare Fund, Alumni Association of Hunter College (1999-2004); Board of Directors, Hunter College Foundation (1996-1999); President, Alumni Association of Hunter College, New York City, NY (1996-1999); Chair Board, The Feminist Press, City University of New York (1987-2002); President, Alumni Association of Hunter College, New York, NY (1979-1981) **AW:** Femmy Award, Feminist Press at the City University of New York (2004); President's Medal, Hunter College (1999); Femmy Award, Feminist Press at the City University of New York (1995); Alumni Recognition Award, Alumni Association of Hunter College (1984); Hall of Fame, Alumni Association of Hunter College (1978) **MH:** Albert Nelson Marquis Lifetime Achievement Award (2017) **ADD:** 500 E 85th St Apt 2L, New York, NY, 10028-7495

GOLDING, GREGORY S., T: Senior Vice President **I:** Business Management/Business Services **CN:** UBS **ED:** BA in Economics, Tulane University (1989) **CT:** Certified Investment Management Analyst; Certified Wealth Strategist; Certified Funds Specialist; Certified Divorce Financial Analyst **C:** Senior Vice President, UBS, Park City, UT (1989-Present) **CR:** President's Council, USB; IRA Rollover Advisory Council, USB; Advisory Council, Investment Consulting Services, USB **CIV:** Board Member, Youth Sports Alliance; Former Board Member, National Ability Center; Advisory Board, Mountain Trails Foundation **AW:** Named, Top 400 Financial Advisors, Financial Times (2015-2016); Named, Barron's Top 1,000 Financial Advisors (2010-2011); Named, Top 40 Advisors Under the Age of 40, Wall Street Magazine (2006) **BA:** PO Box 2879, UBS Financial, Park City, UT, 84060 **URL:** http://financialservicesinc.ubs.com/team/mogul/meetourteam.html

GOLDMAN, STANFORD M., T: Medical Educator **I:** Education/Educational Services **CN:** McGovern Medical School University of Texas at Houston **DOB:** 11/28/1940 **PB:** Salt Lake City **SC:** UT/USA **PT:** Osher Goldman; Miriam (Solomon) Goldman **MS:** Married **SPN:** Harriet Kaplow (4/2/1965) **CH:** Etan; Nava **ED:** Resident, Einstein College of Medicine, Bronx, NY (1966-1969) Intern, Jefferson University School of Medicine, Philadelphia, PA (1965-1966) MD, Einstein College of Medicine

(1965) BA, BRE, Yeshiva University (1961) **C:** Emeritus Professor, University of Texas Medical School (2012-Present); Professor of Radiology, The University of Texas MD Anderson Cancer Center (1995-Present); Professor of Radiology and Urology, Baylor College of Medicine (1995-Present); Professor of Urology, University of Texas Medical School, Houston, TX (1995-Present); Professor of Radiology, University of Texas Medical School (1993-2012); Professor, Chairman of Radiology, University of Texas Medical School, Houston, TX (1993-2000); Professor of Urology, Johns Hopkins University (1988-1993); Professor of Radiology, Johns Hopkins University (1986-1994); Clinical Professor, Uniformed Services University, Bethesda, MD (1981-1994); Associate Professor, Johns Hopkins University (1979-1986); Assistant Professor to Associate Professor, University of Maryland, Baltimore, MD (1975-1981); Instructor to Assistant Professor of Radiology, Johns Hopkins University School of Medicine, Baltimore, MD (1972-1979); Assistant Professor of Radiology, Einstein College of Medicine, Bronx, NY (1971-1972); Chairman, Department of Radiology, United States Public Health Service, Phoenix Indian Medical Center (1969-1971) **CR:** Professor Emeritus, Baylor College of Medicine, Houston, TX (2012-Present); Professor, The University of Texas MD Anderson Cancer Center (2007-Present); Medical Director, Ultrasound School of Technology (1999-2001); Professor of Radiology, The University of Texas MD Anderson Cancer Center (1995); Adjunct Professor of Radiology and Urology, Baylor College of Medicine, Houston, TX (1994-2012); Medical Director, Radiological School of Technology, Houston Community College (1994-2000) **CIV:** Chair, Board of Education, Beren Academy of Houston (2005-2008); Radiation Control Advisory Board, Maryland (1989-1993) **MIL:** Lieutenant, Commander, U.S. Public Health Service (1969-1971) **CW:** Editorial Board, Emergency Radiology (2006-Present); Consultant, Editor, Urology (1998-Present); Editor, Tc E Rm Del Trattos Genito-Urinario (1994); Associate Editor, European Urology (1993-2004); Editor, CT & MRI of the Genitourinary Tract (1990); Associate Editor, Radiology (1986-1994); Editor, Computed Tomography of Kidneys & Adrenals (1983); Associate Editor, Urologic Radiology (1982-1985) **AW:** Grantee, Royal College of Physicians (2006-Present); Fellow, Society Abdominal Radiology (2012); Gold Medal, Texas Radiological Society (2010); Lifetime Achievement Award, Society of Uroradiology (2008); Gold Medal, American Society of Emergency Radiology (2006); Distinguished Lifetime Achievement Award, American Society of Abdominal Radiology **MEM:** Committee on Emergency Radiology, American College of Radiology (2006-Present); Board of Directors, Albert Einstein Alumni Association (2003-Present); Counselor, American Society of Emergency Radiology (2009-2011); Joint Member, Bylaws Committee, SUR-SGR, American Society of Emergency Radiology (2009-2010); Joint Bylaws Committee, SUR-SGR, American Society of Emergency Radiology (2009-2010); Alternate Counselor, American Society of Emergency Radiology (2007-2009); Subcommittee on Radiation, Pregnancy Committee on Safety, American College of Radiology (2007-2008); Committee on Radiological and Nuclear Emergencies, American College of Radiology (2006-2015); Member, Board of Trustees, Texas Radiological Society (2005-2010); Chair, Organizational Structure Council, Texas Radiological Society (2005-2006); Board of Governors, Texas Radiological Society (2005-2006); Chair, Judicial Affairs Committee, Texas Radiological Society (2005-2006); Chair,

Nominating Society, Texas Radiological Society (2005-2006); Chairman, Bylaws Committee, Texas Radiological Society (2005-2006); Trustee, Texas Radiological Society (2005-2006); Chair, Board of Trustees, Texas Radiological Society (2005-2006); Liason to Committee on Trauma, American College of Surgeons, American College of Radiology (2004-2015); Chairman, Bylaws Committee, American Society of Emergency Radiology (2004-2008); President, Texas Radiological Society (2004-2005); Chairman, Legislation Committee, Texas Radiological Society (2003-2004); Ethics Committee, Society of Uroradiology (2003); Executive Committee, Texas Radiological Society (2002-2013); Alternate Counselor, American College of Radiology (2002-2011); Nominating Committee, American Society of Emergency Radiology (2002-2004); President, American Society of Emergency Radiology (2002-2004); Chair, Site Selection Committee, American Society of Emergency Radiology (2002-2004); Chairman, Program Committee, Texas Radiological Society (2002-2003); First Vice President, Texas Radiological Society (2002); First Vice President, Texas Radiological Society (2002); President, Houston Radiological Society (2002); Secretary-Treasurer, American Society of Emergency Radiology (2001); Vice President, Houston Radiological Society (2001); Second Vice President, Texas Radiological Society (2001); Treasurer, Houston Radiological Society (2000-2001); Medical Equipment Committee, Society of Uroradiology (2000-2001); Co-Chairman, Nominating Committee on Communications, American College of Radiology (2000-2001); Nominating Committee, American College of Radiology (1999); Executive Committee, American Society of Emergency Radiology (1998-2011); Secretary-Treasurer, American Society of Emergency Radiology (1998-2000); Fellowship, Nominating Committee, Texas Radiological Society (1998-2000); Hematuria Guidelines Panel, American Urological Association (1998-1999); Nominating Committee, Association of University Radiologists (1997-1998); Ethics Committee, Association of University Radiologists (1997); Board of Directors, Texas Radiological Society (1996-2010); Committee on Coding and Nomenclature of Commission on Economics, American College of Radiology (1996-2002); Counselor from Texas, American College of Radiology (1996-2002); Chairman, Program Committees, Subcommittee on Genitourinary Radiology (1996-1999); Financial Committee, American Society of Emergency Radiology (1996-1998); Site Committee, American Society of Emergency Radiology (1996-1998); Chairman, Long Range Planning Committee, Texas Radiological Society (1996-1997); Chairman, Science Program Committee, American Society of Emergency Radiology (1996-1997); Vice Chairman, Program Committee, American Society of Emergency Radiology (1996-1997); Distinguished Alumni Award, Albert Einstein Alumni Association (1996); Chair, Audit Committee, American Society of Emergency Radiology (1995-1999); Abstract Committee, American Society of Emergency Radiology (1995-1997); Board of Directors, American Society of Emergency Radiology (1994-2011); Industrial Committee, American Society of Emergency Radiology (1994-1998); Program Committee, Texas Radiological Society (1994-1996); Board of Directors, Society of Uroradiology (1992-1998); Board of Directors, Albert Einstein Alumni Association (1991-2002); Chairman, Scientific Exhibits Awards Committee, Radiological Society of North America (1988-1990); Associate, University of Maryland Alumni Association; American Roentgen Ray Society; Texas Medical

Society Liaison to Publication Subcommittee; Liaison to Performance Improvement and Patient Safety Subcommittee, American College of Radiology; American College of Surgeons; American Medical Association; Johns Hopkins Medical and Surgical Association; Houston Medical Society; Fellow, Society of Abdominal Radiology; Honorary Member, European Society of Urogenital Radiology; Honorary Member, Royal Belgian Radiological Society **MH:** Albert Nelson Marquis Lifetime Achievement Award (2017) **H:** Swimming; Music **RE:** Jewish **ADD:** 8877 Frankway Dr Apt 3323, Houston, TX, 77096

GOLDSTEIN, MARGARET ANN, T: 1) Professor Emeritus 2) Life Member **I:** Education/Educational Services **CN:** 1) Baylor College of Medicine 2) University of Cambridge **DOB:** 03/13/1939 **PB:** Sinton **SC:** TX/US **PT:** Daniel Archibald; Sarah Elizabeth (Tegg) McNeil **MS:** Widow **SPN:** Alexander Goldstein, Jr. (2/14/1959, Deceased) **CH:** David Neil Black **ED:** PhD, Rice University (1969); BA, Rice University, Magna Cum Laude (1965) **C:** Professor Emeritus, Baylor College of Medicine (2004-Present); Professor of Medicine and Molecular and Cellular Biology, Baylor College of Medicine (1989-2004); Associate Professor of Medicine and Molecular and Cellular Biology, Baylor College of Medicine (1979-1989); Assistant Professor of Medicine and Cell Biology, Baylor College of Medicine (1977-1979); Assistant Professor of Cell Biophysics and Medicine, Baylor College of Medicine (1973-1977); Assistant Professor of Biology, The University of Texas Health Science Center at Houston (1970-1977); Instructor in Cell Biophysics, Medicine and Anatomy, Baylor College of Medicine (1970-1973); Instructor in Biology, The University of Texas MD Anderson Cancer Center (1969-1970); Laboratory Instructor in Biology, Rice University (1965-1969) **CR:** Life Member, Clare Hall, University of Cambridge (2002-Present); Visiting Fellow, Clare Hall, University of Cambridge (2001-2002); National Research Council (1986-2000); Assembly Delegate (1995-1998); President, Microscopy Society of America (1995-1996); Chair, International Committee (1993-1995); Council Member, American Heart Association, Inc., Dallas, TX (1987-1994); Executive, Committee for Basic Sciences Council, American Heart Association, Inc., Dallas, TX (1987-1994); Consultant, National Heart, Lung, and Blood Institute, National Institutes of Health (1986-1994); Liaison, American Association for the Advancement of Science (1990-1995); Biological Director, Microscopy Society of America (1990-1992); President, Vice President, River Oaks Woman's Breakfast Club (1979-1984) **CIV:** Shepherd Society Governing Council, Rice University (1995-Present); Houston Friends of Music (1991-Present); Advisory Board Member, Houston Grand Opera (1995-1996); Award Committee, Young Women's Christian Association (1991-1996); Vice President, Board of Directors, Texas Chamber Orchestra, Houston (1982-1986); Board of Directors, River Oaks Women's Breakfast Club (1980-1985) **CW:** Contributor, 50 Articles, Professional Journals; Contributor, Chapters, Four Books; Newsletter Editor **AW:** Women On The Move Award (2002); Grantee, National Institutes of Health (1974-1998); Achievement Award For Cosmos 2G, National Aeronautics and Space Administration (1994); Achievement Award For Cosmos 2044, National Aeronautics and Space Administration (1991); Outstanding Houston Woman In Science And Technology Award, Young Women's Christian Association, Houston (1990); Order Of Silver Thistle, Scottish Heritage Foundation, Houston (1990) **MEM:** Executive Council, Council of Scientific Society Presidents

(1995-1998); President, Microscopy Society of America (1995-1997); Director, Microscopy Society of America (1990-1992); Vice President, Houston Chapter, Association of Women in Science (1979-1980); President, Executive Council, Texas Society for Electron Microscopy (1971-1983); American Association for the Advancement of Science; American Society for Cell Biology; Biophysical Society; American Heart Association **MH:** Albert Nelson Marquis Lifetime Achievement Award (2017) **H:** Music; Gardening; Physical fitness; Travel **ADD:** 5325 Dora St, Houston, TX, 77005

GOLUB, LORNE M., T: SUNY Distinguished Professor **I:** Education/Educational Services **CN:** Stony Brook University **DOB:** 01/13/1941 **PB:** Winnipeg **SC:** MN/Canada **PT:** Sydney Golub; Edith Golub **MS:** Married **SPN:** Bonny Golub (8/1964) **CH:** Marlo; Michael **ED:** Honorary DSc, Health Sciences Center, University of Connecticut (2018); Honorary MD, Faculty of Medicine, University of Helsinki (2000); Fellowship Certification in Periodontics, Harvard School of Dental Medicine (1968); MSc, University of Manitoba (1965); DMD, University of Manitoba (1963) **C:** SUNY Distinguished Professor, Department of Oral Biology and Pathology, Stony Brook University (1973-Present); Fellow, The National Academy of Inventors, Inc., Boston, MA (2017); Professor, Associate Dean for Research, and Acting Dean, School of Dental Medicine, Stony Brook University (1973-2000) **CW:** Guest Editor, "Pharmacological Research," Elsevier (2011); Editorial Board, Journal of Periodontology (1990); Editorial Board, Journal of Periodontal Research (1984); Editorial Board, Journal of Dental Research (1977); Contributor, More Than 300 Peer-Reviewed Papers, Professional Journals; Co-organizer of Scientific Conferences on "Matrix Metallo-Proteinase-Inhibitors," including The New York Academy of Sciences, Gordon Research Conferences, and Others **AW:** Chapter of the National Academy of Inventors, Stony Brook University (2016); Honoree, Research Paper Highlighted as Cover Story, The Journal of the American Dental Association (2011); Honoree, Distinguished Faculty, Center for Biotechnology, NYSTAR Center for Advanced Technology (2009); Gold Medal for Excellence in Research, American Dental Association (2006); Distinguished Alumnus Award, University of Manitoba (2002); Outstanding Inventors Award, SUNY Research Foundation (2002); Annual Norton M. Ross Award for Excellence in Clinical Research, American Dental Association (2001); Ramfjord Memorial Lectureship, University of Michigan (1999); Annual Distinguished Scientist Award in Oral Biology, International Association for Dental Research (1998); Annual Birnberg Research Award, Columbia University (1996); Rector's Medal, University of Helsinki (1991); Merit Award, National Institutes of Health (1988-1998); Honoree, Research Highlighted in "Technology Transfer Stories - 25 Innovations that Changed the World," Association of University Technology Managers **MEM:** National Academy of Inventors (2016); American Academy of Periodontology (1968) **H:** Medieval history; Travel; Vacationing in Florida; Hockey **PA:** Independent **RE:** Jewish **ADD:** 29 Whitney Gate, Smithtown, NY, 11787 **URL:** https://dentistry.stonybrookmedicine.edu/faculty/golub

GOMOLL, ANDREAS H., T: Associate Professor Of Orthopedic Surgery **I:** Medicine & Health Care **CN:** Hospital for Special Surgery **PB:** Munich **SC:** Germany **C:** Associate Professor of Orthopedic Surgery, Weill Cornell Medical School; Attending Orthopedic Surgeon, Department of Orthopedic Surgery Hospital for Special Surgery, NY **MEM:** International Society of Arthroscopy Knee Surgery and Orthopedic Sports Medicine; European Society for Sports Traumatology, Knee Surgery and Arthroscopy; Arthroscopy Association of North America; American Academy of Orthopedic Surgeon; American Orthopedic Society for Sports Medicine; International Cartilage Repair Society **MH:** Distinguished Humanitarian (2017) **BA:** 535 E 70th Street, Hospital for Special Surgery, New York, NY, 10021 **ADD:** 350 E 79th Street, #20A, New York, NY, 10075 **URL:** www.AndreasGomollMD.com

GOODMAN, MARTIN D., T: Surgeon **I:** Medicine & Health Care **CN:** Tufts Medical Center **ED:** MD, Rutgers New Jersey Medical School (1994); BA in Biology, Robert Wood Johnson Medical School (1990); Residency, Cooper Hospital; Fellowship, University of Pittsburgh Medical Center **C:** Surgeon, Tufts Medical Center, Boston, MA (2007-Present); Peninsula Surgical Specialists (2002-2007); Peritoneal Surface Malignancy Program; Assistant Professor, Tufts University School of Medicine **AW:** Top Doctor, Boston Magazine (2015); Top Cancer Doctors, Newsweek (2015); Top Doctor, Boston Magazine (2013); Top Doctor, Boston Magazine (2012); Top Doctor, Boston Magazine (2011); Top Doctor, Boston Magazine (2010); Schwartz Center Compassionate Caregiver Award **MH:** Albert Nelson Marquis Lifetime Achievement Award (2017) **BA:** 800 Washington St Fl 4, Tufts Medical Center, Boston, MA, 02111

GOODMAN, WILLA LOUISE, T: Women's Federal Program Manager (Retired) **I:** Government Administration/Government Relations/Government Services **CN:** United States Government **DOB:** 03/02/1934 **PB:** Shelby **SC:** NC/USA **PT:** Mable Baxter; James Baxter **MS:** Married **SPN:** Willie M. Goodman; Waldo Spears (Divorced) **CH:** Warren Spears; Angela Gaines; Ivonne Goodman **ED:** Associates Degree, Honolulu Business College (1957) **CT:** Plaque, Federal Employed Woman **C:** Women's Federal Program Manager, Equal Employment Opportunity Commission; Secretary, Vice President, President, American Federation of Government Employees **CR:** Data Processing **CIV:** Worthy Matron to Most Ancient Rose of Seven Seals, The Order of Eastern Stars **MIL:** U.S. Air Force, Korean War **AW:** Good Conduct Medal, Pentagon Duty, United States Air Force (1952-1954) **MH:** Who's Who in the World (1988); Who's Who in the West (1982-1983); Who's Who of American Women (1981-1982) **H:** Playing cards; Board games **PA:** Democrat **RE:** Protestant **ADD:** 39047 Hidden Creek Ln, Temecula, CA, 92591

GORDON, JOHN C., T: Laboratory Fellow **I:** Sciences **CN:** Los Alamos National Laboratory **ED:** ChD, University of Notre Dame, Notre Dame, IN (1990); BS in Chemistry, University of Glasgow, Glasgow, Scotland, With Honors (1985) **C:** Laboratory Fellow, Chemistry Division, LANS, LLC **CR:** Japanese Society for the Promotion of Science Invitation Fellowship (2017); Fellow, American Institute of Chemists (2015); Laboratory Fellow, Los Alamos National Laboratory (2014); Fellow, Royal Society of Chemistry (2014); Fellow, American Association for the Advancement of Science (2011); Fellows Prize, Los Alamos National Laboratory (2011) **CW:** Co-Author, "Metal Ligand Bifunctional Catalysis: The Accepted Mechanism, the Issue of Concertedness, and the Function of the Ligand in Catalytic Cycles Involving Hydrogen Atoms," ACS Catalysis (2017); Co-Author, "Why Does Alkylation of the NH functionality Within M/NH Bifunctional Noyori-Type Catalysts Lead to Turnover?" Journal of the American Chemical Society (2017); Co-Author, "The Effect of Functional Groups in Bioderived Fuel Candidates," ChemSusChem (2016); Co-Author, "The Mechanism of Enantioselective Ketone Reduction by the Noyori and Noyori-Ikariya Bifunctional Catalysts," Dalton Transactions (2016); Co-Author, "Air-Stable NNS (ENENES) Ligands and their Well Defined Ru and Ir Complexes for Outer-Sphere Molecular Catalysis," Organometallics (2015); Co-Author, "A New Spin on Cyclooctatetraene (COT) Redox-Activity: Comparing Triphos Chelates through their Support of Low-Spin Fe(I) Complexes Exhibiting Antiferromagnetic Coupling to a Singly Reduced eta 4-COT Ligand," Organometallics (2014); Co-Author, "Unravelling the Mechanism of the Asymmetric Hydrogenation of Acetophenone by [RuX2(diphosphine)(1,2-diamine)] Catalysts," Journal of the American Chemical Society (2014); Co-Author, "The Hydrodeoxygenation of Bioderived Furans into Alkanes," Nature Chemistry (2013); Co-Author, "Complexes Containing Multiple Bonding Interactions Between Rare Earth Metals and Main-Group Fragments," RSC Advances (2013); Co-Author, "Functional Group Dependence of the Acid Catalyzed Ring Opening of Biomass Derived Furan Rings: an Experimental and Theoretical Study," Catalysis Science and Technology (2013); Co-Author, "Iron Complex-Catalyzed Ammonia-Borane Dehydrogenation. A Potential Route Towards B-N Containing Polymer Motifs Using Earth Abundant Metal Catalysts," Journal of the American Chemical Society (2012); Co-Author, "Importance of Out-of-State Spin-Orbit Coupling for Slow Magnetic Relaxation in Mononuclear FeII complexes," Journal of the American Chemical Society (2011); Co-Author, "An Ionic Liquid-Mediated Route to Cerium(III) Bromide Solvates," Inorganic Chemistry (2011); Co-Author, "A Single Pot Approach to the Efficient Regeneration of Ammonia Borane Spent Fuel," Science (2011); Co-Author, "Mechanism of Alcohol Oxidation by Dipicolinate Vanadium(V): Unexpected Role of Pyridine," Journal of the American Chemical Society (2010); Co-Author, "Aerobic Oxidation of Lignin Models Using a Base Metal Vanadium Catalyst," Inorganic Chemistry (2010); Co-Author, "Efficient Regeneration of Partially Spent Ammonia Borane Fuel," Angewandte Chemie International Edition (2009) **AW:** Exceptional Mentor Award, Los Alamos Award Program, Chemistry, Life, and Earth Sciences Directorate, LANL (2010) **MEM:** American Institute of Chemists; American Association for the Advancement of Science; Inorganic Chemistry Division, American Chemical Society; Royal Society of Chemistry **MH:** Albert Nelson Marquis Lifetime Achievement Award (2017) **ADD:** 716 Jeffrey Place, White Rock, NM, 87547

GORDON, MALCOLM S., T: Professor of Biology **I:** Education/Educational Services **CN:** University of California, Los Angeles **DOB:** 11/13/1933 **PB:** Brooklyn **SC:** NY/USA **PT:** Abraham Gordon; Rose (Walters) Gordon **MS:** Married **SPN:** Carol A. Gordon (7/19/1992); Marjorie J. Weinzweig (1/28/1976, Deceased 3/1990); Diane M. Kestin (4/16/1959, Divorced 9/1973) **CH:** Dana Malcolm **ED:** PhD, Yale University (1958); BA, Cornell University, With High Honors (1954) **C:** Professor of Biology, Department of Ecology and Evolutionary Biology, University of California, Los Angeles (1968-Present); Chairman, Interdepartmental Committee, Environmental Science Engineering Program, University of California, Los Angeles (1984-1988); Director, Institute Evolutionary and Environmental Biology, University of California, Los Angeles (1971-1976); Assistant Director of Research, National Fisheries Center and Aquarium, U.S. Department of the Interior, Washington, DC (1968-1969); Associate Professor, University of California, Los Angeles (1965-1968); Assistant Professor, University of California, Los Angeles (1960-1965); Instructor,

University of California, Los Angeles (1958-1960) **CR:** Visiting Associate in Bioengineering and Aeronautics, California Institute of Technology (2003-2006); Co-founder, Institute for Environment and Sustainability, University of California, Los Angeles (1997); Chairman, Commission on Comparative Physiology, International Union for Physiological Science (1993-2009); Technology Advisory Committee, Santa Monica Bay Restoration Project, EPA (1988-2006); Technology Advisory Group on Milkfish Reproduction, Agency for International Development (1984-1992); Senior Queen's Fellow in Marine Science, Australia (1976); Visiting Professor of Zoology, Chinese University of Hong Kong (1971-1972); National Advisory Committee, R/V Alpha Helix, Scripps Institute of Oceanography (1969-1973); Committee on Latimeria, National Academy of Sciences (1969-1972); Guggenheim Fellow, Italy and Denmark (1961-1962); Fulbright Fellow (1957-1958); National Science Foundation Fellow, Yale University (1954-1957); Visiting Professor, University of California, Santa Cruz; Visiting Professor, Chinese University of Hong Kong; Fellow, American Association for the Advancement of Science **CIV:** Active, Community Organizations on Environmental and Civil Liberties **CW:** Joint Managing Board, Physiology Journal (2007-Present); Editorial Board, Journal Experimental Zoological (1990-1993); Editorial Board, Fish Physiological Biochemical Journal (1986-2008); Author, College Textbooks, Technical Books; Contributor, Articles, Professional Journals **AW:** Irving-Scholander Memorial Lecturer, University of Alaska-Fairbanks (2000) **MEM:** Treasurer, International Union of Physiological Sciences (2007-2013); Council Member, International Union of Physiological Sciences (2005-2013); International Physiological Committee, American Physiological Society (2002-2005); Executive Committee for Public Affairs, American Physiological Society (1989-1992); Chairman, Comparative Biochemical Physiology, Society for Integrative and Comparative Biology (1988-1989); Chairman, Ecology Division, Society for Integrative and Comparative Biology (1979-1980); American Physiological Society; Society for Integrative and Comparative Biology; Society for Experimental Biology; International Union of Physiological Sciences **MH:** Albert Nelson Marquis Lifetime Achievement Award (2017) **ADD:** 2801 Glendower Avenue, Los Angeles, CA, 90027

GORELICK, KENNETH J., **T:** Managing Director **I:** Medicine & Health Care **CN:** Zymo Consulting Group **ED:** Coursework in Medicine, Universite de Paris-Sud (1973-1986); MD, Weill Cornell Medicine (1978); BS in Biochemistry, University at Buffalo (1973) **CT:** Certified in Internal Medicine and Pulmonary Diseases **C:** Chief Medical Officer, PIN Pharma, Inc. (2012-Present); Managing Director, Zymo Consulting Group (2010-Present); Venture Partner, NGN Capital LLC (2004-Present); Director, Neurotrope (2016-2017); President, Enzybiotics Inc. (2002-2009); Chief Executive Officer, Enzybiotics Inc. (2002-2009); Consultant, Wyeth Research (2000-2009); Senior Vice President, Pharma Print Inc. (1998-2000); Chief Medical Officer, Pharma Print Inc. (1998-2000); Vice President, Global Clinical Research & Development, DuPont (1996-1998); Vice President, Global Clinical Research & Development, DuPont (1996-1998); Vice President, Drug Development, Genelabs Technologies, Inc. (1991-1996); Director, Clinical Research, XOMA (1987-1991); Associate Medical Director, Fisons PLC (1985-1987) **CW:** Author, 15-20 Peer-reviewed Papers and Book Chapters **MEM:** Fellow, American College of Chest Physicians; Fellow, American College of Physicians; Fellow, American Medical Association

H: Speaking French; Traveling to France; French theater; Eating **ADD:** 1 Maplewood Dr, Newtown Square, PA, 19073

GOUGH, HERBERT FREDERICK, **T:** Minister **I:** Religious **CN:** St. Barnabas Episcopal Church **DOB:** 05/03/1941 **PB:** Knoxville **SC:** TN/USA **PT:** Herbert Frederick Gough; Jessie (Post) Gough **MS:** Married **SPN:** Catherine Mauldin Hill (8/6/1986) **ED:** Student, Oxford University, Oxford, England (2012-2013); Certified, U.S. Army War College, Carlisle, PA (1990); Certified, St. George's College, Jerusalem, Israel (1980); MDiv, Virginia Theological Seminary, Alexandria, VA (1972); Bachelor's Degree, University of Chattanooga (1967) **C:** Rector, St. Barnabas Episcopal Church, Dillon, SC (2008-Present); Rector, St. Matthew's Episcopal Church, Darlington, SC (1996-2007); Council, Diocese of South Carolina, Charleston, SC (1988-1991); State Church Committee, Diocese of South Carolina, Charleston, SC (1987-1990); Rector, St. Barnabas Episcopal Church, Dillon, SC (1982-1996); Assistant Rector, Emmanuel Episcopal Church, Athens, GA (1980-1982); Rector, St. Paul's Episcopal Church, Clinton, NC (1976-1980); Vicar, St. Mark's Episcopal Church, Copperhill, TN (1973-1976); Curate, Holy Trinity Episcopal Church, Memphis, TN (1972-1973) **CR:** Chief Chaplain, South Carolina State Guard, Columbia, SC (1999-Present); Colonel, South Carolina Guard (1990-Present); Standing Committee, Diocese of South Carolina, Charleston, SC (2000-2003) **AW:** Parachutist Badge, Laos; Knight Grand Officer with the Order of the Star of Ethiopia; Knight Grand Cross with the Order of the White Eagle in Poland **MEM:** Board of Directors, South Carolina Military Heritage Foundation (2005-Present); Chaplain, Order of St. Lazarus (2000); South Carolina Foster Care Review Board, Columbia, SC (1993-1995); Chairman, Sampson County Association for Handicapped, Clinton, NC (1978-1979); Veterans Foreign Wars, American Legion; Sumter Guard of Charleston; Imperial Society of St. George of Lalibela; Darlington County History Society **MH:** Albert Nelson Marquis Lifetime Achievement Award (2017); Distinguished Humanitarian (2017) **H:** Reading; Skeet shooting; Travel; Archaeology **ADD:** 110 Circle Drive, Darlington, SC, 29532

GOULD, LISA, **T:** Associate Medical Director **I:** Medicine & Health Care **CN:** South Shore Hospital **ED:** MD, Medical Scholars Program, University of Illinois at Urbana-Champaign (1990); PhD, Medical Scholars Program, University of Illinois at Urbana-Champaign (1990); Fellowship, Hand Surgery and Microsurgery, Medical College of Wisconsin; Resident, General Surgery, Virginia Commonwealth University Health System; Resident, Plastic Surgery, Virginia Commonwealth University Health System **CT:** Medical License, State of Rhode Island (2018); Medical License, State of Texas (2018); Medical License, State of Florida (2017); Certified, American Board of Plastic Surgery; Certified, Hand Surgery **C:** Associate Medical Director, Wound Center, Southshore Hospital, Weymouth, MA (2017-Present); Chief of Plastic Surgery, James A. Haley Veterans Hospital (2001-2012) **CR:** Associate Professor Department of Medicine, Brown University (2017); Executive Board, Wound Healing Society; Clinical Research, Southshore Hospital; Lecturer, Family and Geriatric Medicine, Brown University; Lecturer, Wound Care, Wound Society **MEM:** American Society of Plastic Surgeons; Fellow, American College of Surgeons; Wound Healing Society **H:** Racing Sailboats; Hiking; Biking **BA:** 90 Libbey Industrial Parkway, Suite 100, Weymouth, MA, 02188 **ADD:** 118 Valentine Cir, Warwick, RI, 02886

GOULDEN, CLYDE EDWARD, **T:** Curator

Emeritus, Director **I:** Education/Educational Services **CN:** The Academy of Natural Sciences of Drexel University **PT:** Robert William Goulden; Gertrude Julia Sluss **MS:** Married **SPN:** Tuya Natsagdorj (5/20/1996) **CH:** Michael Lon; Marc Edward; Tslomon; Nomindari **ED:** PhD, Indiana University (1962); MS, Emporia State University Teachers College (1959); EdB, Emporia State University Teachers College (1958) **C:** Curator, Academy of Natural Sciences of Drexel University (1966-Present); Adjunct Professor, University of Pennsylvania (1966-2000); Exchange Scientist, Russian Academy of Sciences (1966); Research Scientist, Yale University (1962-1965) **CR:** Director, Asia Center, Academy of Natural Sciences of Drexel University (2007-Present); Visiting Professor, National University of Mongolia (2000-2007); Visiting Professor, International University of Ulaanbaatar (1999); Exchange Scientist, Russian Academy of Sciences; Director, Institute for Mongolian Biodiversity and Ecological Studies, Academy of Natural Sciences of Drexel University; Consultant in Field **CIV:** Member, World Heritage Nomination Committee, Government of Mongolia; Member, Eisenhower Exchange Fellows Selection Committee, Mongolia **CW:** Editor, "The Geology, Biodiversity and Ecology of Lake Hovsgol" (2006); Editor, "Changing Scenes in the Natural Sciences 1776-1976" (1977); Contributor, More than 100 Articles to Professional Journals **AW:** Honoree, Order of the Polar Star, Government of Mongolia (2013); Recipient, Friendship Medal, Government of Mongolia (2007); Honoree, Named Best Environment Worker, Ministry of Nature, Environment and Tourism, Government Of Mongolia (2006); Honoree, Honorary Professor, National University of Mongolia (2002); Honoree, Honorary Professor, International University of Ulaanbaatar (2001); Recipient, Ruth Patrick Honorary Curator Award, Academy of Natural Sciences of Drexel University (1980); Recipient, Equal Employment Opportunity Award, Academy of Natural Sciences of Drexel University (1978) **MEM:** Fellow, American Association for the Advancement of Science; Fellow, The Explorers Club; Association for the Sciences of Limnology and Oceanography; United States Permafrost Association; Union Concerned Scientist, American Geophysical Union **MH:** Albert Nelson Marquis Lifetime Achievement Award (2017) **H:** Travel; Cooking; Classical music **ADD:** PO Box 175, Morton, PA, 19070

GRABOWSKI, THEODORE C. PHD, **T:** Principal Electrical Engineer **I:** Engineering **CN:** Sandia National Laboratories **MS:** Married **ED:** PhD in Electrical Engineering, The University of New Mexico (1997); MSEE, The University of New Mexico (1990); BSEE, Texas Tech University (1988) **C:** Principal Electrical Engineer, Sandia National Laboratories (2016-Present); Senior Research Physicist, Air Force Research Laboratory (2010-2016); Senior Staff Engineer, SAIC (2000-2010) **CR:** Texas Tech University EECE Department, Industrial Advisory Board (2018-2020); Executive Committee of the IEEE NPSS Plasma Science and Applications Committee (2015-2017) **CW:** Author, "Parallel Triggering and Conduction of Rail-Gap Switches in a High-Current, Low-Inductance Crowbar Switch" (2016); Co-author, "Magneto-Inertial Fusion" (2016); Co-author, "Experimental Studies of an Ultrahigh-Speed Plasma Flow" (2014); Author, "Addressing Short Trapped-Flux Lifetime in High-Density Field-Reversed Configuration Plasmas in FRCHX" (2014); Author, "Recent Magneto Inertial Fusion Experiments on the Field Reversed Configuration Heating Experiment" (2013); Co-author, "Applied Magnetic Field Design for the FRC Compression Heating Experiment (FRCHX) at AFRL" (2013) **AW:** Laboratory Scientist of the Quarter Award, Directed Energy Directorate, Air Force Research Laboratory (2015) **MEM:** American Institute of Aeronautics and Astronautics (2017); Senior Member, IEEE (2017); IEEE (2010); American Physical Society (2010) **H:** Camping; Hiking **BA:** PO Box 5800 MS-1106, Albuquerque, NM, 87185-1106 **ADD:** 9621 Dona Marguerita Ave NE, Albuquerque, NM, 87111 **URL:** https://www.linkedin.com/in/chris-grabowski-2600a149/

GRACE, JOHN R. PHD, T: Professor Emeritus, Dean Emeritus **I:** Education/Educational Services **CN:** University of British Columbia **DOB:** 06/08/1943 **PB:** London **SC:** ON/Canada **MS:** Married **ED:** Honorary DSc, University of Western Ontario (Now Western University) (2003); PhD in Chemical Engineering, University of Cambridge (1968); BS in Engineering, University of Western Ontario (Now Western University) (1965) **C:** Professor Emeritus, University of British Columbia (2014-Present); Acting Director, Clean Energy Research Centre, University of British Columbia (2008-2009); Methanex Professor, University of British Columbia (2008-2009); Canada Research Chair, University of British Columbia (2001-2014); Dean of Graduate Studies, University of British Columbia (1990-1996); Professor, University of British Columbia (1979-2014); Head, Department of Chemical and Biological Engineering, University of British Columbia (1979-1987); Professor, McGill University (1978-1979); Senior Project Engineer, Sierra Nevada Corporation (1974-1975); Associate Professor, McGill University (1971-1978); Assistant Professor, McGill University (1968-1971) **CR:** Expertise in Fluidization, Reactor Design, Fluid-Particle Systems, Biomass, Coal, Combustion, Multi-Phase Flow, Contaminants; Supervisor, Graduate Students **CIV:** Former Canada Research Chair in Clean Energy Processes **CW:** Member, International Advisory Board, "Canadian Journal of Chemical Engineering" (2011-Present); Editorial Board Member, "Biomass Conversion and Biorefinery" (2010-Present); Member, International Advisory Board, "Particuology" (2004-Present); Editorial Board Member, "International Journal of Chemical Reactor Engineering" (2002-Present); Member, International Advisory Board, "Chinese Journal of Chemical Engineering" (2001-Present); Member, International Editorial Advisory Board, "Korean Journal of Chemical Engineering" (1999-Present); Editorial Board Member, "Engineering Chemistry and Metallurgy" (1996-Present); Editorial Board Member, "Biofuels and Biorefineries," Springer (2012-2015); Managing Guest Editor, "Special Issue of Fuel on Gasification and its Applications" (2013); Member, Editorial Advisory Board, "Industrial & Engineering Chemistry Research" (2009-2011); Editorial Board Member, "International Journal of Multiphase Flow" (1997-2010); Editorial Board Member, "Powder Technology" (1988-2012); Editorial Board Member, "Environmental and Waste Management World" (1987-1989); Regional Editor, "Chemical Engineering Science" (1984-1990); Editorial Board Member, "Canadian Journal of Chemical Engineering" (1978-1983); Editor, "Directory of Chemical Engineering Research in Canadian Universities" (1972-1974); Contributor, 650 Articles, Professional Journals **AW:** Dean of Applied Science Medal of Distinction, University of British Columbia (2016); Emeriti Faculty Award, University of British Columbia (2016); James Y. Oldshue Lecture Award, Inter-American Confederation of Chemical Engineering (2015); Eponym, Classroom, University of British Columbia (2015); Winner, John Grace Mentorship Award, Carbon Management Canada (2014); Canada's Clean16 Award (2014); Honoree, Officer

of the Order of Canada (2013); Montreal Medal, Chemical Institute of Canada (2012); Particle Technology Forum Award, American Institute of Chemical Engineers (2012); Meritorious Achievement Award, Engineers and Geoscientists BC (2010); Killam Award for Excellence in Mentoring, University of British Columbia (2009); Thomas Baron Award in Fluid-Particle Systems, American Institute of Chemical Engineers (2007); Award, Geo-environmental Division, Canadian Geotechnical (2006); Killam Teaching Award, University of British Columbia (2005); Dedication, Industrial & Engineering Chemistry Research Volume 43, Issue 18 (2004); Chairman's Award for Career Achievement, Science Council of British Columbia (2003); Western Alumni Association Award of Merit - Professional Achievement, Western University (2001); Killam Research Fellowship, National Research Council Canada (1999-2001); Century of Achievement Award, Canadian Society for Chemical Engineering (1999); International Fluidization Award of Achievement, Engineering Foundation (1998); Honorary Fellow, Green College, University of British Columbia (1997); FLOTU Award, Tsinghua University (1996); R.S. Jane Award, Canadian Society for Chemical Engineering (1995); Honoree, ICI Distinguished Lecturer, University of Alberta (1993); Fluor Daniel Award, American Institute of Chemical Engineers (1991); Best Paper Award, The American Society of Mechanical Engineers (1989); Killam Research Prize, University of British Columbia (1988); Killam Senior Research Fellowship, University of British Columbia (1984-1985); L.S. Lauchland Medal and Gzowski Lectureship, University of Western Ontario (Now Western University) (1984); ERCO Award, Canadian Society for Chemical Engineering (1983); Senior Industrial Fellowship, National Research Council Canada (1974-1975); Fellowship, National Research Council of Canada (1967-1968); Athlone Fellowship (1965-1967); General Motors Canadian Scholarship (1961-1965); J.H. Ferguson Award, University of Western Ontario (Now Western University) (1965); Board of Governors Medal, University of Western Ontario (Now Western University) (1965); Professional Engineers Medal, University of Western Ontario (Now Western University) (1965) **MEM:** Canadian Pulp and Paper Association (1985-Present); Fellow, Chemical Institute of Canada (1981-Present); Engineers and Geoscientists BC (1980-Present); Institution of Chemical Engineers (1980-Present); Canadian Society for Chemical Engineering (1968-Present); Fellowships Committee, Chemical Institute of Canada (2005-2009); Director, Applied Science and Engineering Division, The Royal Society of Canada (2004-2006); Chair, Selection Committee to Elect New Fellows, The Royal Society of Canada (2004-2006); Secretary, Applied Science and Engineering Division, The Royal Society of Canada (2002-2004); Past Chair, Chemical Institute of Canada (1996-1997); Chair, Chemical Institute of Canada (1995-1996); Vice-chair, Chemical Institute of Canada (1994-1995); Policies and Procedures Committee, Canadian Engineering Accreditation Board (1990-1992); Past President, The Chemical Institute of Canada (1990-1991); President, The Chemical Institute of Canada (1989-1990); Management Committee, Chemical Institute of Canada (1989-1990); CCPE Affairs Committee, Engineers and Geoscientists BC (1988-1992); Qualifications Committee, Engineers and Geoscientists BC (1988-1992); Canadian Engineering Accreditation Board (1988-1992); Vice President, Canadian Society for Chemical Engineering (1988-1989); Director, Canadian Society for Chemical Engineering (1982-1985); Publications Committee, Canadian Society for Chemical Engineering (1970-1972, 1977-1983); Chemical Institute of Canada (1968-

1981); Graduate Member, Institution of Chemical Engineers (1965-1980); Ordre des Ingénieurs de Québec (1969-1979) **BA:** Dept of Chemical & Biol Engng, 2360 East Mall, University of British Columbia, Vancouver, BC, Canada, V6T 1Z3 **ADD:** PH 3, 2350 West 39th Avenue, Vancouver, BC, Canada, V6M 1T9

GRADY, SANDRA, T: Founder, Director **I:** Religious **CN:** The Master's Keys **DOB:** 07/08/1941 **PB:** Kinston **SC:** NC/USA **PT:** William Devereaux Cobb; Nora Cathleen Davenport **MS:** Married **SPN:** Sanders W. Grady **CH:** Daniel; Dean **ED:** ThD, Wagner Leadership Institute, Colorado Springs, CO (2000); MS in Counseling and Education, East Carolina University, Greenville, NC (1971); BS in Business and English Education, East Carolina University, Greenville, NC (1963) **C:** Founder, Director, The Master's Keys, Fairfax, VA (2002-Present); Founder, Director, Virginia Prayer Network, Fairfax, VA (1990-Present); Owner, Instructor, Grady Studies, Fairfax, VA (1975-Present); School Teacher, Counselor, States of California, Connecticut, Arkansas (1965-1994) **CR:** International Speaker, Biblical Counselor (1990-Present); Instructor, The Citadel (2000-Present); Member, Advisory Board, International Leadership Embassy (2005-Present); National Council Government Intercessions (2005-Precent); Member, National Advisory Board, U.S. Strategic Prayer Network, Colorado Springs, CO (2003-Present); Intercessional Counselor, Eagles Team (1998-Present); Mid-Atlantic Director, Coordinator (1998-Present); Prayer Coordinator, Well Builders, Aledo, TX (1991-Present) **MEM:** National Federation of Music Teachers; International Coalition of Apostles **MH:** Distinguished Humanitarian (2017) **H:** Writing; Composition **PA:** Republican **ADD:** 9306 Ashmeade Drive, Fairfax, VA, 22032

GRANTNER, JANOS L. PHD, T: Professor **I:** Education/Educational Services **CN:** Western Michigan University **DOB:** 07/10/1947 **PB:** Budapest **SC:** Hungary **MS:** Married **SPN:** Ida Balazs **CH:** Rita E.; Janos A. **ED:** Degree in Technical Science, Hungarian Academy of Sciences, Budapest (1994); PhD in Computer Engineering, Budapest University of Technology and Economics (1979) **C:** Professor of Electrical & Computer Engineering, Western Michigan University, Kalamazoo, MI (2004-Present); Associate Professor, Western Michigan University, Kalamazoo, MI (1996-2004); Assistant Professor, Western Michigan University, Kalamazoo, MI (1993-1996); Senior Lecturer, Budapest University of Technology and Economics (1980-1993); Various Teaching Positions (1971-1980) **CR:** Member, Fuzzy Technical Committee, Computational Intelligence Society, IEE (2003-2009); Associate Editor, IEEE Transactions on Fuzzy Systems (1999-2007); Member, Technical Committee on Computational Cybernetics, SMC Society, IEEE **CW:** Contributor, Articles to Professional Journals; Patents in Hungary **MEM:** IEEE Computer Society; IEEE Systems, Man and Cybernetics Society; IEEE Computational Intelligence Society; American Society for Engineering Education **MH:** Albert Nelson Marquis Lifetime Achievement Award (2017) **BA:** 1903 W Michigan Ave, Department of Electrical and Computer Engineering, Kalamazoo, MI, 49008 **ADD:** 1903 W Michigan Ave, Western Michigan University, Kalamazoo, MI, 49008-5326 **URL:** http://wmich.edu/electrical-computer/directory/grantner

GREAVES, STANLEY JOSEPH, T: Artist, Educator **I:** Fine Art **DOB:** 11/23/1934 **PB:** Georgetown **SC:** Guyana **PT:** John Greaves; Priscilla Lydia (White) Greaves **CH:** André; Sonya; Fiona; Natasha **ED:** MFA, Howard University (1980); Diploma in Art Education, Newcastle University, England (1968);

BA in Fine Art, Newcastle University, with Honors, England (1967) **C:** Head, Division of Creative Arts, University of Guyana (1975-1987); Art Teacher, Secondary School, Queen's College, Georgetown, Guyana (1971-1975); Art Teacher, Berbice High School, New Amsterdam, Guyana (1968-1971); Art Teacher, Secondary School, St. Stanislaus College, Georgetown, Guyana (1957-1962); Teacher, Sacred Heart Primary, Georgetown, Guyana (1952-1957) **CR:** Instructor, The Barbados Community College (1990-2007); Assistant Chief Examiner, Arts and Crafts, Caribbean Examinations Council, Barbados (1977-1992); Tutor, The Barbados Community College **CIV:** Board of Trustees, National Art Collection, Guyana (1993); Past Member, Great Oak Youth Development Center, Fayetteville, NC **CW:** Exhibitor, Caribbean Culture Centre, New York (2017); Exhibitor, OAS Gallery Washington, D.C. (2016); Exhibitor, OAS Gallery Washington, D.C. (2015); Author, "Haiku" (2015); Exhibitor, Fayetteville Arts Council (2014); Exhibitor, University of North Carolina (2013); Exhibitor, Lisa' Gallery, Fayetteville, NC (2012); Exhibitor, Fayetteville State University, North Carolina (2012); Exhibitor, Maruka Gallery, Washington, D.C. (2011); Exhibitor, Claflin University, South Carolina (2011); Exhibitor, Fayetteville Museum of Art, North Carolina (2010); Author, "The Poems Man" (2008); Solo Exhibitor, The University of the West Indies, Cave Hill, Barbados (2007); Solo Exhibitor, Creative Arts Center, Martinique (2007); Exhibitor, Paris, France (2006); Exhibitor, Brussels, Belgium (2006); Exhibitor, Montreal, Canada (2006); Exhibitor, Ottawa, Canada (2006); Solo Exhibitor, Zemicon Gallery, Barbados (2006); Solo Exhibitor, National Gallery, Guyana (2005); Exhibitor, Cariforum Travelling Show, Caribbean (2004); Solo Exhibitor, Creative Arts Center, Martinique (2004); Solo Exhibitor, Castellani House, Guyana (2004); Solo Exhibitor, Islington Gallery, London, United Kingdom (2003); Author, "Horizons" (2002); Solo Exhibitor, Queen's Park Gallery, Bridgetown, Barbados (2002); Exhibitor, University of Florida (2001); Solo Exhibitor, Trinidad National Gallery (2001); Solo Exhibitor, South London Gallery (1999); Exhibitor, Cuenca Biennial, Ecuador (1998); Exhibitor, Santo Domingo Biennial (1996); Solo Exhibitor, Castellani House, Guyana (1994); Exhibitor, Santo Domingo Biennial (1994); Solo Exhibitor, Queen's Park Gallery, Bridgetown, Barbados (1993); Exhibitor, Santo Domingo Biennial (1992); Solo Exhibitor, Barbados Museum (1990); Solo Exhibitor, Barbados Museum (1989); Exhibitor, Wilfredo Lam Center, Havana, Cuba (1986); Exhibitor, Casa de Las Americas, Havana, Cuba (1977); Solo Exhibitor, Caribbean Festival of Creative Arts, Georgetown, Guyana (1972); Exhibitor, Coltejar Biennial, Colombia (1972); Exhibitor, San Paulo Biennial, Brazil (1971); Exhibitor, Inter-American Development Bank; Represented Artist, Guyana; Represented Artist, Barbados; Co-Author, "Art In The Caribbean"; Represented Artist, Casa de las Americas Havana, Cuba; Represented Artist, Numerous Private Collections **AW:** Recipient, Godfrey Chin Award, Heritage Journalism (2015); Recipient, Lifetime Achievement Award, Guyana (2014); Distinguished Fellow, The University of the West Indies, Cave Hill, Barbados (2003-2007); Recipient, Guyana Literature Prize (2002); Recipient, Gold Medal, Santo Domingo (1994); Recipient, Gold Medal, Barbados (1991); Recipient, Gold Medal, Barbados (1990); Recipient, Fulbright Scholarship (1979); Recipient, Golden Arrow Award, National Awards Committee, Government of Guyana (1975); Recipient, First Prize, Guyana (1970); Bridget Jones Bursary Fellow, Society for Caribbean Studies, United Kingdom; Recipient, Citation, Guyana Cultural Association of New York **MH:**

Albert Nelson Marquis Lifetime Achievement Award (2017) **H:** Reading; Music; Guitar; Writing; Woodworking; Cooking **ADD:** 390 Hilliard Dr, Fayetteville, NC, 28311

GREEN, MELISSA L., T: Chief Clinical Officer, Partner **I:** Health, Wellness and Fitness **CN:** Trio Healthcare **DOB:** 07/27/1966 **PB:** Fort Devens **SC:** MA/USA **PT:** June Higgins; Mary Higgins **MS:** Divorced **CH:** Heather Rae Martin; Corrie Ann Green **ED:** Coursework, Health Care Compliance Academy (2012); MS in Health Care Administration, Kennedy-Western University (2003) **CT:** Registered Nurse **C:** Multi-facility Management for Almost 30 Years as Senior VP of Clinical Services and Chief Clinical Officer for Various Companies **CR:** Member, Board of Directors, Virginia Health Care Association (2017-Present); Member, Quality Cabinet, American Health Care Association (2014-Present); Member, Advisor, Nurse Executive Council (2005-Present); Former Member, CMS Regulatory Committee **CIV:** Founder, L.I.L.Y (Ladies Inspiring Ladies and Youth) (2013) **AW:** Named, Top Ranked U.S. Executive, National Council of American Executives (2014) **MEM:** American Health Care Association; Virginia Health Care Association **RE:** Baptist **ADD:** 5100 Jackson River Rd, Hot Springs, VA, 24445-2209

GREENAPPLE, LAWRENCE, T: Law Partner **I:** Law and Legal Services **DOB:** 06/30/1929 **PB:** Brooklyn **SC:** NY/USA **PT:** Jack Greenapple; Pauline Greenapple **MS:** Widowed **SPN:** Emily Schneider (Deceased) **CH:** Beth Sara; Steven Bruce; David Marc **ED:** JD, Cornell University (1952); BA, Cornell University (1950) **C:** Partner, Cox Padmore Skolnik & Shakarchy LLP; Partner, Otterbourg, Steindler, Houston, & Rosen, P.C. (Now Otterbourg P.C.); Partner, Glass, Greenapple and Greenberg; Partner, Glass and Greenapple; Attorney, Berlack, Israels & Liberman, LLP; Bigelow Teaching Fellow, University of Chicago Law School **CR:** Assistant Editor, Cornell Law Review **MIL:** U.S. Army, Korean War (1952-1954) **AW:** A/V Preeminent Rating, Martindale-Hubbell **MEM:** Lecturer, Osher Lifelong Learning Institute, Berkshire County, Massachusetts **BAR:** State of New York (1952); U.S. District Court, Southern District, State of New York; U.S. Supreme Court **ADD:** 235 Walker Street, Apt. 275, Lenox, MA, 01240

GREENE-KARLAN, LYNNE JEANNETTE, T: Artist, Designer, Wellness Consultant **I:** Fine Art **CN:** Little Greene Apples Inc., Vital Advantage LLC **DOB:** 08/27/1938 **PB:** Albany **SC:** NY/USA **MS:** Married **SPN:** Michael Alan Karlan (9/29/1991); Stanley E. Greene (1/31/1962, Deceased 6/27/1987) **CH:** Stuart Nathaniel; Phillip; Peter **ED:** BA, Parsons School of Design, The New School, With Honors (1960); Coursework, Goucher College (1956-1957) **C:** Artist, Designer, Little Greene Apples Inc. (1999-Present); Designer, Little Greene Apples Inc. (1999-Present); Wellness Consultant, Vital Advantage LLC (1999-Present); Vice President, Design and Merchandising, The Intapp Group/Go Figure, New York, NY (1997-1999); Designer, Val Mode by Lynne Greene, New York, NY (1993-1997); Director of Marketing, Val Mode by Lynne Greene, New York, NY (1993-1997); Designer, Lady Lynne Lingerie, Guy Laroche Lingerie, Paris, France (1973-1993); Director of Marketing, Lady Lynne Lingerie, Guy Laroche Lingerie, Paris, France (1973-1993); Head Designer, Lynne Greene Designs Retail, Montclair, NJ (1972-1974); Owner, Lynne Greene Designs Retail, Montclair, NJ (1972-1974); Designer, Little Greene Apples Inc., Montville, NJ (1971-2005); President, Little Greene Apples Inc., Montville, NJ (1971-2005); Creative Director, Eye of the Peacock Sportswear, New Jersey (1968-

1972); Head Designer, Contessa/Monique/Fisher Lingerie, New York, NY (1967-1971); Designer, Kaleidoscope Lingerie, New York, NY (1966-1967); Owner, Kaleidoscope Lingerie, New York, NY (1966-1967); Designer, Flair Lingerie, New York, NY (1965-1967); Designer, Original Coats & Suits, New York, NY (1963-1965); Designer, IZOD Menswear; Designer, Divisions of David Crystal Inc.; Designer, Craig Craely Sportswear and Dresses, New York, NY (1961-1963); Assistant Designer, Haymaker Sportswear, New York, NY (1959-1961) **CR:** Master Class Instructor, Lingerie Critic, Pratt Institute (1990); Master Class Instructor, Lingerie Critic, Pratt Institute (1984) **CIV:** Stanley E. Greene Soccer Scholarship (1957-Present); Creator, Share Educated by the Book (SEBB) (1994-2000); Co-Founder and Active Participant, Montville Soccer Association (1972-1988); Fund Drives, American Heart Association, Inc.; Fund Drives, Cancer Inc.; Fund Drives, March of Dimes Foundation; Fund Drives, Special Olympics **CW:** Patentee, Multiple Patents in Field; Illustrator, Books; Illustrator, Pamphlets; Illustrator, Fashion; Illustrator, Packaging Fields; Commercial Illustrator, Home and Office **AW:** Legend Morris County Award, New Jersey State Legislature & Chamber of Commerce (2010-2011); Honors in Field, Humanitarian Award, Polar Bear Project, Nikken Inc. (2003); Kiwanian of the Year, Kiwanis International (2002-2003); Designer of the Year, French Lace Council (1980-1981); Designer of the Year, French Lace Council (1975) **MEM:** President, Kiwanis International (2004-2005); Powerful You! WXN; The Fashion Group International, Inc.; 200 Club of New Jersey **MH:** Albert Nelson Marquis Lifetime Achievement Award (2017) **H:** Sketching; Portraiture; Cooking; Sewing; Painting **PA:** Independent **RE:** Episcopalian **ADD:** 6718 Federal Drive, Bethlehem, PA, 18017

GREGORY-COLLURA, LEONORA, T: President **I:** Nonprofit & Philanthropy **CN:** ANCA World Autism Festival **ED:** TTC Diploma, Ballet Teachers Training, Royal Ballet School (1979); Coursework, Elmhurst Ballet School (1969-1974) **CT:** Certification in Professional Modelling & Makeup Art **C:** President, ANCA World Autism Fund (1995-Present); Consultant, Naturally Autistic ANCA (1985-2015) **CIV:** Board Member, Advisory Council, Sunny Hill Health Centre for Children, BC Children's Hospital (1996-1998); Playworks Instructor for Special Needs Teens, Community Living Association of Burnaby (1986); Volunteer Committee Member, Richmond Centre for Disability (1985); Parent Advisory Council, Vancouver School Board (1982-1992) **CW:** Co-Founder, Naturally Autistic Magazine; Author, "Anthony's Story: A Mother's Journey with Her Son," Naturally Autistic Magazine; Executive Producer, "CONNECTED," ANCA World Autism Film Festival; Choreographer; Writer **AW:** British Columbia Community Achievement Award (2013); Business of Distinction Award for Diversity (2009) **MEM:** Chamber Member, LOUD Business Association; Autistic Peoples Federation; Co-Founder, ANCA Consulting Inc.; Co-Founder, ANCA Foundation **BA:** PO Box 1658, Gibsons, BC, Canada, V0N 1V0 **URL:** https://www.linkedin.com/in/leonora-gregory-collura-a772b229

GRIFFIN, CATHY S., I: Real Estate **C:** Realtor/Broker, Century 21 Towne and Country (1991-Present); Owner and Operator, Winks S and W Fishcamp (1970-1992) **CIV:** Volunteer, Ministries **AW:** Double Centurion Award, Century 21 (2015-2017) **ACH:** number 1 Century 21 agent in the state in North Carolina for 5 years and 6th in the Nation in units. Last year she finished 2nd in commission **H:** Shagger (Dance)

GRIFFIN FARMER, CORNELIA, T: Lawyer **I:** Law and Legal Services **DOB:** 03/03/1945 **PB:** New York **SC:** NY/USA **PT:** John Bastin Griffin; Elizabeth McCue (Sussman) Griffin **MS:** Married **SPN:** William Paul Farmer (1/8/1972) **CH:** Suzanne Elizabeth; John Paul **ED:** JD, Marquette University (1978); Master's in Regional Planning, Cornell University (1970); BA, Mount Holyoke College (1967) **C:** Staff Attorney, Hearings Official, Lane Council Governments, Eugene, OR (1999-2001); Private Practice, Minneapolis, MN (1996-1999); Judicial Law Clerk, Commonwealth Court of Pennsylvania, Pittsburgh, PA (1992-1995); Adjunct Faculty, University of Pittsburgh (1986-1994); Consultant, County of Allegheny, Pittsburgh, PA (1983); Associate, Baskin & Sears, Pittsburgh, PA (1981-1982); Associate, Friebert & Finerty, Milwaukee, WI (1978-1980); Planner, State of Wisconsin and City of Milwaukee (1973-1975); Planner, Tri-State Regional Planning Committee, New York, NY (1971-1972); Planner, Frederick P. Clark Associate, Rye, NY (1970-1971) **CR:** Mediator, Dispute Resolution Center, St. Paul, MN (1998-1999); Child Advisor, Allegheny County Pro Bono Program, Pittsburgh, PA (1986-1992); Vice Chairman, Loan Monitoring Committee, Pittsburgh Countywide Corporation (1981-1987); Adjunct Faculty, University of Wisconsin, Milwaukee, WI (1978-1979) **CIV:** Chair, Reunion Gift Committee, Mount Holyoke College Annual Fund Committee (2008-Present); Volunteer, Cabrini Green Legal Aid Clinic, Chicago, IL (2005-Present); Lector, Holy Name Cathedral Parish, Chicago, IL (2004-Present); Head of Class, Fundraising. Gift Office, Mount Holyoke College (2002-Present); Volunteer, WITS Tutoring and Mentoring Program (2002-Present); Volunteer, Political Campaigns, Milwaukee, Pittsburgh, PA, Minneapolis, MN, Chicago, IL and Eugene, OR (1972-Present); Classes and Reunions Committee, Alumnae Association, Mount Holyoke College (2006-2009); Illinois Advisory Council, Midwest Eye-Banks (2004-2010); Court Monitor, Abuse Cases, WATCH, Minneapolis, MN (1996-1999); Vice President, PTA, Falk Laboratory School, University of Pittsburgh (1985-1989); Trustee, Falk School Fund; Volunteer, Start Making A Reader Today, Eugene, OR; Legal Aid, Barack Obama Senate Campaign; Tutor and Mentor, Education and Law, Witts Program **CW:** Reviewer, Reference Books and Book Articles **AW:** Alumni Medal of Honor, Mount Holyoke College (2007) **MEM:** APA; Silver Bay Association Council; Past President, Treasurer, Mount Holyoke Club of Pittsburgh **BAR:** State of Illinois (2002); State of Oregon (1999); State of Minnesota (1996); State of Pennsylvania (1981); State of Wisconsin (1978) **MH:** Albert Nelson Marquis Lifetime Achievement Award (2017) **H:** Lectures; Volunteering; Exercise; Taking French classes **ADD:** 100 E Bellevue Place, Apt. 22A, Chicago, IL, 60611

GRIFFITH, LAWRENCE S.C., T: Professor Emeritus **I:** Education/Educational Services **CN:** Johns Hopkins School of Medicine **DOB:** 09/16/1937 **PB:** Washington **SC:** DC/USA **PT:** Ernest Stacey Griffith; Margaret Dyckman (Davenport) Griffith **MS:** Married **SPN:** Anne Gorman Young (6/20/1959) **CH:** Lawrence; John (Deceased); Melinda; Gordon **ED:** Research Fellow in Cardiology, Johns Hopkins University, Baltimore, MD (1969-1971); Assistant and Associate Resident in Medicine, Strong Memorial Hospital, Rochester, NY (1967-1969); Assistant Resident in Surgery, Strong Memorial Hospital, Rochester, NY (1964-1965); Intern in Medicine and Surgery, Strong Memorial Hospital, Rochester, NY (1963-1964); MD, University Rochester, With Honors, New York (1963); BA, Haverford College, Pennsylvania (1959) **CT:** Diplomate, American Board of Internal Medicine;

Diplomate, American Board of Cardiovascular Disease **C:** Professor Emeritus, Johns Hopkins University (2014-Present); Clinical Director, Johns Hopkins Medicine International (1999-2008); Professor of Medicine, Johns Hopkins University, Baltimore, MD (1988-2013); Associate Professor of Medicine, Johns Hopkins University, Baltimore, MD (1976-1988); Assistant Professor, Radiology, Johns Hopkins University, Baltimore, MD (1974-1980); Assistant Professor, Medicine, School of Medicine, Johns Hopkins University, Baltimore, MD (1971-1976) **CR:** Consultant, VA Cooperative Study; Surgery for Coronary Artery Disease, Program on Surgical Control of Hyperlipidemias, University of Minnesota **CIV:** Board of Directors, Julia Dyckman Andrus Memorial, Inc., Yonkers, NY (1971-Present); Secretary, Treasurer, Surdna Foundation, New York, NY (2014-2016); Board of Directors, Surdna Foundation, New York, NY (1976-2016); Advisory Board, College of Medicine, American University of Antigua (2015); Vice President, Surdna Foundation, New York, NY (1988-1994); Chairman, Julia Dyckman Andrus Memorial, Inc., Yonkers, NY (1976-2007); Board of Directors, John E. Andrus Memorial Home for Aged, Hastings-on-Hudson, New York, (1974-1997); Chairman, Board of Directors, Baltimore Pastoral Counseling Service (1971-1980); United States Public Health Service (1965-1967) **CW:** Contributor, Articles to Professional Journals **MEM:** Fellow, American College of Physicians; Council on Clinical Cardiology of American Heart Association; American College of Cardiology; Alpha Omega Alpha **MH:** Albert Nelson Marquis Lifetime Achievement Award (2017) **PA:** Democrat **RE:** Methodist **ADD:** 802 W Saint Georges Rd, Baltimore, MD, 21210

GRIFFITH, ROBERTA JEAN, T: Artist, Educator **I:** Fine Art **DOB:** 05/14/1937 **PB:** Hillsdale **SC:** MI/USA **PT:** Robert Charles Griffith; Jane Marie (Randolph) Griffith Elliott **MS:** Widowed **SPN:** William Allen Woods (12/28/2006, Deceased 2/24/2016); Ray Schillmoeller (3/26/1966, Divorced 10/6/1995) **CH:** David Robert; Raymond Mark **ED:** MFA, Southern Illinois University, Carbondale, IL (1962); BFA, Chouinard Art Institute (1960); Coursework, Instituto Allende, Guanajuato, Mexico (1957-1958); University of Michigan, Ann Arbor, MI (1955-1957) **CT:** Certified Art Teacher, K-12, State of New York **C:** Professor Emerita, Hartwick College, Oneonta, NY (2008-Present); Arkell Hall Foundation Endowed Chair of Art, Hartwick College, Oneonta, NY (1976-2008); Chairperson, Art Department, Hartwick College (1973-1990); Art Professor, Hartwick College (1966-2008); Ceramic Designer, Design Technics, New York, NY (1965-1966); Art Teacher, American School of Barcelona, Spain (1964) **CR:** Juror, Pre-Columbian Art, Ninth Annual Vasefinder Nationals (2014); Lecturer in the Field, Ceramics and Ceramic History (1973-2008); Ceramic Workshops **CIV:** Board of Directors, Consultant in Field, Empire State Craft Alliance (2000-2003); President, Oneonta Chapter, American Association of University Professors (1989-1991); Vice President, Oneonta Chapter, American Association of University Professors (1986-1989); Delegate-at-Large, National Council on Education for the Ceramic Arts (NCECA) (1984-1986); Advisory Board Member, Oneonta Chapter, American Association of University Professors (1983-1986); President, Upper Catskill Community Council on the Arts (Now Community Arts Network of Oneonta) (1979-1980); Vice President, Upper Catskill Community Council on the Arts (Now Community Arts Network of Oneonta) (1978-1979); Executive Board Member, Oneonta Chapter, American Association of University Professors (1976-1977); Secretary, Upper Catskill Community

Council on the Arts (Now Community Arts Network of Oneonta) (1974-1978); Professor, Oneonta Chapter, American Association of University Professors (1966-1993) **CW:** Exhibitor, Solo Show, Holt Gallery, Honolulu Museum of Art (2017); Exhibitor, Group Show, Daum Museum of Contemporary Art, Sedalia, MO (2017); Exhibitor, Group Show, Galerie 103 (2015); Artist Presenter, Galerie 103, Kuku'ula, Hawaii (2014); Artist Presenter and Exhibitor, Group Show, Artists of Hawaii, Honolulu Museum of Art (2013); Exhibitor, Group Show, Grimmerhus Museum of International Ceramic Art (Now Clay Museum of Ceramic Art Denmark), Denmark (2012); Exhibitor, Group Show, Schaffer Portrait Challenge, Schaffer Gallery, Maui, HI (2012); Exhibitor, Group Show, Vasefinder Fifth Annual National (2012); Exhibitor, Group Show, Honolulu Museum of Art Contemporaries (2012); Exhibitor, Group Show, 75th Annual Cooperstown Art Association National Exhibition (2012); Exhibitor, Group Show, "Hawaii Craftsmen's 45th Annual Statewide Juried Exhibition (2012); Exhibitor, "What, larrain, larrain, reiner, emerson, griffith, britt," Galerie 103, Kukuiula, Kauai, HI (2011-2012); Exhibitor, Group Show, Honolulu Academy of Art, Honolulu, HI (2011); Exhibitor, "EXPOSED," American Museum of Ceramic Art (2011); Exhibitor, Solo Show, Kauai Museum, Kauai, HI (2010); Exhibitor, Group Show, Amy-Lauren's Gallery (2010); Exhibitor, Group Show, "Rhythms of Heart, Rhythms of Earth," Kaua'i Society of Artists, Lihue, HI (2010); Exhibitor, Group Show, Cooperstown National (2008); Exhibitor, Solo Show, Munson Williams Proctor Art Institute Museum, Utica, NY (2007); Public Presenter, "Tectonics," Hartwick College (2007); Exhibitor, Permanent Collection, Munson Williams Proctor Art Institute Museum (2007); Exhibitor, Group Show, Avenue Gallery, New York, NY (2005); Exhibitor, Solo Show, "50 Year Retrospective," Yager Museum of Art & Culture, Hartwick College, Oneonta, NY (2003); Exhibitor, Solo Show, Museo de Ceramica, Palau Reial de Pedralbes, Barcelona, Spain (1999); Exhibitor, Solo Exhibition, Warren Gallery, Yager Museum of Art & Culture, Hartwick College, Oneonta, NY (1994); Exhibitor, Solo Exhibition, Salem State College, Salem, MA (1992); Exhibitor, Solo Show, Museo de Ceramica, Barcelona, Spain (1984); Exhibitor, Group Show, "American Craftsmen 1966," Contemporary Crafts Museum (Now Museum of Arts and Design), New York, NY (1966); Exhibitor, Solo Show, DeMena Gallery, New York (1965); Exhibitor, Solo Show, Sala del Prado del Ateneo de Madrid, Spain (1964): Exhibitor, Group Show, "Young Americans 1962," Museum of Contemporary Crafts (Now Museum of Arts and Design), New York, NY (1962); Exhibitor, Solo Show, University Museum at University of Southern Illinois, Carbondale, IL (1961); Exhibitor, "Pottery Collective," Brooks Memorial Gallery (Now Memphis Brooks Museum of Art), Memphis, TN (1961); Exhibitor, Solo Show, Aspen Art Gallery, Aspen, CO (1958); Exhibitor, Group Show, "Battle Creek Youth Talent Exhibition", Enquirer & News, Battle Creek, MI (1948); Artist, Permanent Collection, American Museum of Ceramic Art, Pomona, CA, Arizona State University Art Museum, Tempe, AZ, Kutani Museum (Now Kutaniyaki Art Museum), Komatsu City, Ishikawa, Japan, Daum Museum of Contemporary Art, Sedalia, MO, East Stroudsburg State University Gallery, East Stroudsburg, PA, Everson Museum of Art, Syracuse, NY, First Albany Corporation, Albany, NY, Honolulu Museum of Art, Honolulu, Hawaii, Institute de Estudios Norte-Americanos Gallery, Barcelona, Spain, LaGrange Art Museum/Lamar Dodd Art Center, LaGrange, GA, L'Escola Massana, Barcelona, Spain, Museo de Ceramica, Barcelona, Spain, Munson Williams Proctor Art Institute

Museum, Utica, NY, Clay Museum of Ceramic Art, Grimmerhus, Denmark, Racine Art Museum, Racine, WI, Roberson Museum and Science Center, Binghamton, NY, University Museum at University of Southern Illinois, Carbondale, IL, University Art Museum, University at Albany, State University of New York, University of Michigan Museum of Art, Ann Arbor, MI, Yixing Teapot Museum, Yixing, China, and Yager Museum of Art & Culture, Hartwick College, Oneonta, NY; Artist, Private Collection, England, France, Germany, Japan, Mexico, Spain and United States; Contributor, Reviews and Photographs, Books, Newspapers, Magazines and Exhibition Catalogs, United States, Spain, France, Mexico, and Japan; Contributor, Articles to Professional Journals; Contributor, North American Correspondent, Ceramica Magazine, Madrid, Spain **AW:** Special Merit Award, LaGrange XVIII Biennial Competition, Lamar Dodd Art Center, LaGrange College, Grange, GA (2014); Jim Winters 3-D Design Award, Honolulu Museum of Art, Honolulu, HI (2013); Purchase Award for Porcelain Installation, Sharon and Thurston Twigg-Smith, Honolulu Museum of Art, Honolulu, HI (2011); First Prize, "The Mansion," Upper Catskill Community Council on the Arts (Now Community Arts Network of Oneonta), Oneonta, NY (2009); Inductee, Battle Creek Central High School Hall of Fame, Battle Creek, MI (2007); Special Merit Award, Cooperstown Art Association (2007); Lifetime Achievement Charles W. Hunt Award, Upper Catskill Community Council on the Arts (Now Community Arts Network of Oneonta), Oneonta, NY (2001); Research Grantee, 25 Grants, Hartwick College (1992-2005); Teacher-Scholar Award, Hartwick College (1995); Grantee, National Endowment for the Humanities (1991); First Prize, 54th Cooperstown National, New York (1989); First Prize, "Art '89," Norwich Fine Arts Guild, New York (1989); Purchase Prize, Hudson-Mohawk Regional, University Art Collections, University at Albany, State University of New York (1980); First Prize, Hudson-Mohawk Regional (1979); Museum of Contemporary Crafts (Now Museum of Arts and Design), Craftsmen USA (1966); Fulbright Grant, Spain (1962-1964); Award, Young Americans (1962); Best of Show, 12 and Under (10 Years) (1948); First Prize, Painting, "Battle Creek Youth Talent Show," Enquirer & News, Battle Creek, MI (1948); Purchase Award for Monoprint, Lamar Dodd Art Center, Lamar Dodd Art Center Collection, LaGrange, GA **MEM:** International Academy of Ceramics (AIC-IAC), Geneva, Switzerland (2017-Present); National Council on Education for the Ceramic Arts (NCECA); AAUW, Hartwick College; American Crafts Council; Cooperstown Art Association; The Smithy Gallery and Clay Studio, Cooperstown, NY; Kaua'i Society of Artists, Hawaii; Potters Council; Museum of Modern Art; Metropolitan Museum of Art **MH:** Albert Nelson Marquis Who's Who Lifetime Achievement Award (2017) **H:** Travel; Art; Ceramics **PA:** Democrat **RE:** Episcopalian **ADD:** PO Box 112, Otego, NY, 13825

GRIMES, MARY ANNE, T: Certified School Nurse **I:** Medicine & Health Care **DOB:** 06/19/1936 **PB:** Kansas City **SC:** KS/USA **PT:** John Andy Grimes; Bertha Helen Ball Grimes **CT:** Registered Nurse, St. Joseph School of Nursing; Certified School Nurse **C:** Nurse, South West School, Roosevelt School District (1996-2000); Health Service Coordinator, Catholic Coalition for Urban Schools, Diocese of Phoenix (1995-1996); School Nurse, Balsz School District #31 (1984-1994); School Nurse, Wilson School District Seven, Phoenix, AZ (1980-1984); Office Nurse, Phoenix Urological Clinic (1965-1979); Office Nurse, Manager, Phoenix Urological Clinic (1965-1979); Private Duty Nurse, Central Registry, Phoenix, AZ (1962-1965); Office Nurse, Phoenix Family Medical Clinic (1961-1962); Staff Nurse, St. Joseph's Hospital and Medical Center, Dignity Health, Phoenix, AZ (1957-1961) **CIV:** Secretary-Treasurer, Central Phoenix Council for Child Abuse Prevention (1991-1995); Cantemus Classical Chorus, Phoenix, AZ (1990); Campaign Worker, Secretary, Board of Directors, Republican Gubernatorial Election, Phoenix, AZ (1970); Campaign Worker, Secretary, Board of Directors, Republican Gubernatorial Election, Phoenix, AZ (1968); Volunteer, Senior Center; Primary Fundraiser, Classical Chorus Bach and Madrigal Society, Phoenix Chorale; Patron, Spreckels Organ Society, San Diego, CA **AW:** Woman of the Year, Metropolitan Chapter, ABWA Management, LLC. (1995) **MEM:** Vice President, ABWA Management, LLC. (1996-1997); Chapter President, ABWA Management, LLC. (1995-1996); President, ABWA Management, LLC. (1974-1975); National Association of School Nurses; School Nurses Organization of Arizona; Friend, Orpheus Male Chorus of Phoenix **MH:** Albert Nelson Marquis Lifetime Achievement Award (2017) **PA:** Republican **RE:** Roman Catholic **ADD:** 1805 N 21st Place, Phoenix, AZ, 85006

GROPP, WILLIAM D., T: Director, NCSA **I:** Education/Educational Services **CN:** University of Illinois at Urbana-Champaign **PB:** , **MS:** Married **SPN:** Patricia Davidson, June 24, 1987 **CH:** Christopher William **ED:** Stanford University, Stanford, CA; PhD in Computer Science (1982); MS in Computer Science (1980); University of Washington, Seattle, WA; MS in Physics (1978); Case Western Reserve University, Cleveland, OH; BS in Mathematics (1977) **C:** Professor of Computer Science, University of Illinois, Urbana-Champaign (2007-Present); Director, Parallel Computing Institute (2011-2017); Chief Scientist, National Center for Super Computing Applications; Associate Division Director, Argonne National Laboratory (2000-2006); Computer Scientist, Argonne National Laboratory (1990-1996); Senior Computer Scientist, Argonne National Laboratory (1996-2007); Associate Professor of Computer Science, Yale University, New Haven, CT (1988-1990); Assistant Professor of Computer Science, Yale University, New Haven, CT (1982-1988) **CW:** Author, "Using MPI"; Author, "Using MPI-2"; Author, "Domain Decomposition: Parallel Multilevel Methods for Elliptic Partial Differential Equations"; Author, "Using Advanced MPI" **AW:** Recipient, Ken Kennedy Award, ACM/IEEE-SC (2016); Recipient, Activity Group on Supercomputing Career Prize, Society of Industrial and Applied Mathematics (2014); Recipient, Prize in Computational Science and Engineering, SIAM/ACM (2014); Recipient, Sidney Fernbach Award, IEEE-CS (2008); Research and Development 100 Award, PETSc (2009); Recipient, MPICH2 (2006); Gordon Bell Award, Association for Computing Machinery (1999) **MEM:** Fellow, IEEE Computer Society; Fellow, Association for Computing Machinery; Fellow, Society Industrial and Applied Mathematics; National Academy Engineering **MH:** Albert Nelson Marquis Lifetime Achievement Award (2017) **H:** Reading history, science fiction and fantasy **ADD:** 404 W Pennsylvania Ave, Urbana, IL, 61801

GROSHOLZ, EMILY ROLFE, T: Philosopher, Educator, Poet **I:** Education/Educational Services **CN:** The Pennsylvania State University **DOB:** 10/17/1950 **PB:** Philadelphia **SC:** PA/USA **PT:** Edwin DeHaven Grosholz; Frances Skerrett Grosholz **MS:** Married **SPN:** Robert Roy Edwards (1/2/1987) **CH:** Benjamin; Robert; William; Mary-Frances **ED:** PhD, Philosophy, Yale University (1978); BA, The University of Chicago (1972) **C:** Edwin Erle Sparks Professor of Philosophy, African American Studies and English, The Pennsylvania State University (2017-Present); Liberal Arts Research Professor of Philosophy, African American Studies and English, The Pennsylvania State University (2011-2017); Associate, Center for Philosophy of Science, University of Pittsburgh (1992-Present); Associate, SPHERE, University of Paris 7 (2005-Present) **CR:** Advisory Editor, The Hudson Review (1984-Present); Instructor, Panelist, West Chester State University Poetry Conference (2016-2018); Instructor or Panelist, Writing the Rockies Creative Writing Workshop, Western State Colorado University (2015-2018); Instructor, Panelist, West Chester State University Poetry Conference (2013-2014); Instructor, Panelist, Writing the Rockies Creative Writing Workshop, Western State Colorado University (2012); Instructor, Panelist, West Chester State University Poetry Conference (2006, 2004, 2000-2001, 1995-1996) **CIV:** Supporter, Women's Resource Center, State College, PA; Supporter, Fundraiser, UNICEF **CW:** Author, "Great Circles: The Transits of Mathematics and Poetry" (2018); Author, "The Stars of Earth: New and Selected Poems" (2017); Poet, "Songs of Two Bellevilles" (2017); Author, Starry Reckoning: Reference and Analysis in Mathematics and Cosmology (2016); Poet, "Childhood Songs" (2016); Author, "Proportions of the Heart," Tessellations Publishing (2014); Author, "Childhood" (2014); Co-Author, "Feuilles/Leaves" (2007); Author, Representation and Productive Ambiguity in Mathematics and the Sciences (2007); Author, "The Abacus of Years" (2002); Co-Author, "Leibniz's Science of the Rational" (1998); Author, "Eden" (1992); Author, "Cartesian Method and the Problem of Reduction" (1991); Author, "Shores and Headlands" (1988); Author, "The River Painter" (1984) **AW:** Recipient, Fernando Gil Prize (2017); Recipient, Research in Paris Grant (2011); Fellow, National Endowment for the Humanities (2004-2005); Recipient, Transatlantic Cooperation Research Grant, Alexander Von Humboldt Foundation (1994-1997); Fellow, John Simon Guggenheim Memorial Foundation (1988-1989); Fellow, National Endowment for the Humanities (1985-1986) **MEM:** American Philosophical Association; Leibniz Society of North America; Leibniz Gesellschaft; History of Science Society; Association for the Philosophy of Mathematical Practice **PA:** Democrat **RE:** Episcopalian **BA:** 240 Sparks Bldg, Department of Philosophy, The Pennsylvania State University, University Park, PA, 16802 **ADD:** 116 Kennedy St, 116 Kennedy Street, State College PA 16801, State College, PA, 16801 **URL:** http://www.emilygrosholz.com

GROSS, PETER, T: Epidemiologist **I:** Medicine & Health Care **CN:** Rutgers, the State University of New Jersey **DOB:** 11/18/1938 **PB:** Newark **SC:** NJ/USA **PT:** Meyer P. Gross; Nathalie (Bass) (Denburg) Gross **MS:** Married **SPN:** Regina Teri Gittlin (5/30/1964) **CH:** Deborah Karen; Michael Philip; Daniel Brian **ED:** MD, Yale University (1964); BA, Amherst College, Cum Laude (1960) **CT:** Diplomate, American Board of Internal Medicine **C:** Chair, Board of Managers, Hackensack Alliance Accountable Care Organization (2012-present); Professor, New Jersey Medical School, Rutgers, the State University of New Jersey (2007-Present); Professor of Medicine, New Jersey Medical School, Rutgers, the State University of New Jersey (1981-Present); Executive Vice President, Hackensack University Medical Center (2010-2011); Executive Vice President, Chief Medical Officer, Hackensack University Medical Center (2006-2011); Vice Chairman, Department of Medicine, New Jersey Medical School, Rutgers, the State University of New Jersey (1994-2006);

Chairman, Medical Board, Hackensack University Medical Center (1986); Chairman, Department of Medicine, Hackensack University Medical Center (1980-2007); Chief, Infectious Disease Section, Hackensack University Medical Center (1974-2001); Chief, Infectious Disease Section, VA Hospital (1973-1974); Acting, Chief Infectious Disease Section, VA Hospital (1972-1973); Research and Education Associate, VA Hospital (1971-1973); Senior Resident, Peter Bent Brigham Hospital (1968-1969); Junior Resident, Yale-New Haven Hospital (1965-1966); Intern, Yale-New Haven Hospital (1964-1965) **CR:** Sentinel Event Advisory Group (2006-2011); Chairman, Sentinel Event Advisory Group (2004-2006); Chairman, Drug Safety and Risk Management Advisory Committee, Center for Drug Evaluation and Research Food and Drug Administration (2002-2006); Chairman, Pneumonia Clinical Advisory Panel, Joint Commission on Accreditation of Healthcare Organizations (1999-2001); Clinical Indicators Task Force (1987-1989); Associate Clinical Professor of Medicine, Columbia University College of Physicians and Surgeons (1977-1981); Investigator, Center for Biologic Evaluation and Research, Food and Drug Administration (1974-1995); Assistant Clinical Professor, Columbia University College of Physicians and Surgeons (1974-1977); Assistant Professor of Medicine, Yale University School of Medicine (1971-1974); National Institutes of Health Fellow, Yale University (1969-1971); Ad Hoc Reviewer of Research Grants, National Institutes of Health; Ad Hoc Reviewer of Research Grants, National Institute of Allergy and Infectious Diseases; Co-Chairman, New Jersey Quality Improvement Advisory Committee; Expert Panels on Community-Acquired Pneumonia, HCQIP; Project Director, Phase 112 Robert Wood Johnson Foundation and Institute for Healthcare Improvement; Fellow, Infectious Diseases Society of America **CIV:** Chairman, Board of Managers, ACO (2012-Present); Director, J.Infed (2011-Present); Lieutenant Commander, U.S. Public Health Service, CDC (1966-1968); Vice President, National Associate, ACO **CW:** Editorial Board Member, "Journal of Clinical Microbiology" (1980-Present); Editorial Board Member, "Managed Care" (1998-2009); Author, "Managing Your Health" (1991); Editorial Board Member, "Infection Control" (1980-1990); Author, "Gram Strain Recognition" Second Edition (1980); Author, "Gram Strain Recognition" (1975); Past Associate Editor, "Clinical Performance and Quality Health Care"; Former Editorial Advisory Board Member, "Joint Commission Journal of Quality Improvement" **MEM:** Chair, Practice Guidelines Committee, Infectious Diseases Society of America (2000-2002); Former President, Society of Healthcare Epidemiologists of America (1995); President, Society of Healthcare Epidemiologists of America (1994); President-Elect, Society of Healthcare Epidemiologists of America (1993); Vice President, Society of Healthcare Epidemiologists of America (1992); Councillor, Society of Healthcare Epidemiologists of America (1986-1988); Clinical Affairs Committee, Infectious Diseases Society of America; Task Force on Adult Immunization, American College of Physicians; American Academy of Microbiology; American Society of Virology; American Society of Microbiology **ADD:** 299 Chelsea Manor, Park Ridge, NJ, 07656

GROSS, JONATHAN L., T: Professor, Computer Scientist, Mathematician **I:** Education/Educational Services **CN:** Columbia University **DOB:** 06/11/1941 **PB:** Philadelphia **SC:** PA/USA **PT:** Nathan K. Gross; Henrietta E. (Light) Gross **MS:** Married **SPN:** Susan Fay Kodner (8/29/1976) **CH:** Aaron; Jessica; Joshua;

Rena Lea; Alisa Sharon **ED:** PhD, Dartmouth College (1968); MA, Dartmouth College (1966); BS, Massachusetts Institute of Technology (1964) **C:** Professor of Computer Science, Mathematics and Statistics, Columbia University (1978-Present); Director of Education, Center for Advanced Technology, Columbia University (1989-1993); Vice Chairman, Department of Computer Science, Columbia University (1982-1989); Associate Professor, Columbia University (1973-1978); Assistant Professor of Mathematical Statistics, Columbia University (1969-1972); Instructor of Mathematics, Princeton University (1968-1969) **CR:** Visiting Scientist, Carnegie Mellon University (1984-1985); Consultant, Russell Sage Foundation; Consultant, Institute for Defense Analyses; Consultant, AT&T Bell Laboratories; Consultant, Alfred P. Sloan Foundation; Consultant, IBM; Consultant, Oak Ridge National Laboratory **CIV:** Secretary, Executive Board, United Synagogue of the Mid-Atlantic Region (2008-Present); Executive Board Member, United Synagogue of the Mid-Atlantic Region (2005-Present); Executive Board Member, Jewish Federation of Princeton Mercer Bucks (2004-2008) **CW:** Editor, "Topics in Topological Graph Theory" (2009); Editor, "Methods with Computer Applications" (2008); Editor, "Handbook of Graph Theory" (2004); Editor, "Handbook of Discrete and Combinatorial Mathematics" (2000); Co-author, "Graph Theory and Its Applications" (1999); Co-author, "Topological Graph Theory" (1987); Co-author, "FORTRAN 77 Fundamentals and Style" (1985); Co-author, "WATFIV-S Fundamental Style" (1986); Co-author, "Measuring Culture" (1985); Co-author, "Pascal Programming" (1982); Co-author, "PASCAL" (1984); Co-author, "Introduction to Computer Programming" (1979); Co-Author, "FORTRAN 77 Programming" (1978); Co-Author, "Fundamental Programming Concepts" (1972); Advisory Editor, Columbia University Press; Advisory Editor, "Journal of Graph Theory, Computers and Electronics," CRC Press; Contributor, Articles, Professional Journals **AW:** Simons Research Grant, Simons Foundation (2014); Honoree, Sloan Fellow in Mathematics (1973-1975); Postdoctoral Fellowship, IBM (1972-1973); Research Grant, National Science Foundation; Research Grant, Office of Naval Research; Research Grant, Exxon Foundation, Exxon Mobil Corporation; Research Grant, ARCO Foundation, Atlantic-Richfield Corporation; Research Grant, The Andrew W. Mellon Foundation; Research Grant, Russell Sage Foundation; Research Grant, New York State Science and Technology Foundation; Research Grant, Citicorp **MEM:** President, Jewish Center of Princeton, New Jersey (2000-2002); Vice President, Jewish Center of Princeton, New Jersey (1997-1999); Secretary for Discrete Mathematics, Society for Industrial and Applied Mathematics (1994-1996); American Mathematical Society; ACM, Inc. **MH:** Albert Nelson Marquis Lifetime Achievement Award (2017) **RE:** Jewish **ADD:** 86 Rittenhouse Cir, Newtown, PA, 18940

GROTON, JAMES PURNELL, T: Retired Partner **I:** Law and Legal Services **CN:** Eversheds-Sutherland LLP **DOB:** 10/29/1927 **PB:** Newport News **SC:** VA/USA **PT:** Lafayette Watson; Mary (Skidmore) Groton **MS:** Married **SPN:** Ann Williams Platz (June 25, 2016); Eve Oxford (2006-2011), Deceased; Lora Frances Webster (1953-1999), Deceased **CH:** James Purnell; Hunter Webster; Molly Groton Urban; Lora Groton Rust **ED:** LLB, University of Virginia (1954); AB, Princeton University, Cum Laude (1949) **C:** Dispute Prevention Consultant (2001-Present); Partner, Sutherland, Asbill & Brennan (1961-2001); Associate, Sutherland, Asbill & Brennan, Atlanta, GA (1954-1961) **CR:** Author; Lecturer;

Researcher; Arbitrator; Mediator, Standing Neutral **CIV:** Trustee, Education Foundation, The National Association of Women in Construction (1993-1998); Chairman, Construction Industry Dispute Avoidance and Resolution Task Force (1991-1994); Board of Directors, Northwest Georgia Council, Girl Scouts of the United States of America (1973-1979); Treasurer, Northwest Georgia Council, Girl Scouts of the United States of America (1973-1979); Trustee, South Kent School (1973-1977); Board of Directors, Georgia Council for International Visitors (1968-1975) **MIL:** Active Duty, United States Marine Corps (1946-1948, 1952-1954) **CW:** Articles Editor, Virginia Law Review, University of Virginia; Author, More than 200 Articles on Construction, Dispute Prevention, and Alternative Dispute Resolution Subjects; Author, Various Professional Publications **AW:** Inductee, National Academy of Construction (2002); Recipient, Awards for Achievements in Alternative Dispute Resolution, International Institute Conflict Prevention and Resolution (1988, 1994); Recipient, Medal of Excellence, Engineering News-Record (1993); Honoree, Honorary Membership, American Institute of Architects (1985); Recipient, Bronze Medal, American Institute of Architects (1984); Recipient, Whitney North Seymour Medal, American Arbitration Association (1983); Fellow, Chartered Institute of Arbitrators; Fellow, College of Commercial Arbitrators; Fellow, American College of Construction Lawyers **MEM:** National Panel of Construction Arbitrators, American Arbitration Association (1970-2014); International Panel of Arbitrators, American Arbitration Association (2001-2014); National Construction Dispute Resolution Committee, American Arbitration Association (1992-2014); President, Georgia Arbitrators Forum (2011); Board of Directors, American Arbitration Association (1990-2002); President, American College of Construction Lawyers (2000-2001); Chairman, Construction Section, Atlanta Bar Association (1992-1993); Executive Committee, Georgia School Boards Association (1971-1978); Vice President, Princeton Club of Georgia, (1964-1977); National Academy of Construction; National Association of College and University Attorneys; Council of School Attorneys, National School Boards Association; Old War Horse Lawyers Club; Piedmont Driving Club; The Peachtree Club; International Legal Honor Society of Phi Delta Phi **BAR:** Admitted to Practice, Supreme Court of the United States (1964); State Bar of Georgia (1955); The District of Columbia Bar (1954); Atlanta Bar Association **MH:** Albert Nelson Marquis Lifetime Achievement Award (2017) **RE:** Christian **BA:** 999 Peachtree St NE Ste 2300, Eversheds Sutherland, Atlanta, GA, 30309 **ADD:** 999 Peachtree St NE Ste 2300, Atlanta, GA, 30309 **URL:** http://www.jimgroton.com

GRUBER, JOHN BALSBAUGH, T: Physics Professor (Retired) **I:** Education/Educational Services **DOB:** 02/10/1935 **PB:** Hershey **SC:** PA/USA **PT:** Irvin John Gruber; Erla R. (Balsbaugh) Gruber **MS:** Married **SPN:** Judith Anne Higer (6/20/1961) **CH:** David Powell; Karen Leigh; Mark Balsbaugh **ED:** NATO Postdoctoral Fellow, Institute of Technical Physics, Technical University Darmstadt, Germany (1961-1962); PhD, University of California, Berkeley, CA (1961); BS, Haverford College, Pennsylvania (1957) **C:** Professor of Research, Physics and Astronomy, University of Texas at San Antonio (2005-2013); Chairman, Department of Physics, San José State University (2001-2005); Director, Institute for Modern Optics, San José State University (1992-2005); Vice President of Development, San José State University (1986); Professor of Physics, San José State University (1984-2005); Academic Vice

President, San José State University (1984-1986); Vice President of Academic Affairs, Professor of Physics and Chemistry, Portland State University (1980-1984); Dean, Professor of Physics, College of Science and Mathematics, North Dakota State University, Fargo, ND (1975-1980); Professor of Chemical Physics, Washington State University (1971-1975); Associate Dean of Graduate School, Washington State University (1970-1972); Assistant Dean of Graduate School, Washington State University (1968-1970); Associate Professor of Physics, Washington State University, Pullman, WA (1966-1971); Assistant Professor of Physics, University of California, Los Angeles, CA (1962-1965); Gastdozent, Institute of Technical Physics, Technical University of Darmstadt, Germany (1961-1962) **CR:** President, The Gruber Group (2005-Present); Invited Lecturer, United States, Canada, Europe (1966-Present); Consultant, CACI International Inc (2004); Consultant, SAIC (2002-2006); Consultant, Newtec (2003-2004); PhD Examiner, Physics, The University of Texas at San Antonio (2000-2004); Consultant, Bicron Corporation (2000-2003); Consultant, Spectragen, Inc. (2000); Consultant, Laser Science and Technology Centre (1999-2014); Consultant, Raytech Corporation (1998-2002); Chairman, Scholarship Program, United States Department of Defense (1964-2001); Consultant, Lockheed Martin Aculight Corporation (1990-2000); Member, Battelle Science Board Selection, Graduate Scholarship Fellows (1964-1999); Chairman, Member, Program Review Board, American Society for Engineering Education, National Aeronautics and Space Administration (1994-1998); Consultant, United States Army Night Vision Laboratory, Fort Belvoir, VA (1993-2005); Chairman, International Conference on Novel Laser Sources and Applications, San José, CA (1993); General Conference Chairman, Novel Laser Sources and Materials (1992); Consultant, Adelphi Laboratory Center, United States Army Research Laboratory, United States Army (1991-2000); Member, Review Panel, Graduate Fellowship Program, United States Navy, American Society for Engineering Education (1990-2002); Consultant, Del-Tron Precision, Inc. (1990-1991); Chairman, Postdoctoral Selection Board, National Institute of Standards and Technology (1989-1991); Chairman of Selection Board, United States Naval Research Laboratory Postdoctoral Fellowship Program, American Society for Engineering Education (1988-2000); Consultant, LaserGenics, Inc. (1986-2005); Consultant, GTE Financial (1986-1989); Nominee, United States Assistant Secretary of Defense, Special Operations (1986-1987); Consultant, IBM (1985-1990); Distinguished Visiting Professor, Naval Air Weapons Station, China Lake, CA (1984-1993); Executive Secretary, Frank H. Spedding Award (1983); Secretary, Board of Directors, Rare Earth Research Conference Committee (1979-1984); Consultant, Battelle Memorial Institute (1964-1980); General Conference Chairman, 24th Rare Earth Research Conference (1979); Executive Secretary, Frank H. Spedding Award (1979); Executive Committee, Rare Earth Research Conference Committee (1977-1983); Member, Rare Earth Research Conference Committee (1976-1983); Visiting Professor, Ames Laboratory, United States Department of Energy, Iowa State University (1976-1980); Consultant, Battelle Memorial Institute (1964-1980); Consultant, Laser Physics and Spectroscopy, Los Alamos National Laboratory (1973-1974); Member, Task Force, Lunar Exploration, Apollo, National Aeronautics and Space Administration (1963-1973); Consultant, Laser Physics and Spectroscopy, Los Alamos National Laboratory (1969-1971); Member, Task Force, Lunar

Exploration, Apollo, National Aeronautics and Space Administration (1964-1969); Consultant, Laser Physics and Spectroscopy, Pacific Northwest National Laboratory, Battelle Memorial Institute, Richland, WA (1964-1969); Consultant, Laser Physics and Spectroscopy, North American Aviation, Space and Information Systems, Downey, CA (1964-1966); Visiting Professor, Joint Center for Graduate Study, Washington State University, Richland, WA (1964-1966); Consultant, Laser Physics and Spectroscopy, McDonnell Douglas Astronautics Company, Santa Monica, CA (1963-1969); Consultant, Laser Physics and Spectroscopy, The Aerospace Corporation, El Segundo, CA (1962-1965) **CIV:** Board of Directors, Westminster Foundation (1982-1984); Chairman, University, College and Public School Relations Boards (1979-1980); Trustee, Symphony Board, Fargo-Moorhead Symphony Orchestra (1978-1980); Trustee, North Dakota Symphony Orchestra Association (1978-1980); Trustee, Pullman Public Library (1973-1975); Member, Planning Commission, City of Pullman (1972-1975); Member, North Dakota Parent Teacher Association; Active, Boy Scouts of America **CW:** Co-Author, "Magnetooptical Spectrocopy of Rare Earth Compounds" (2012); Contributor, Articles, Professional Journals; Contributor, Chapters, Books; Co-Author, "Magnetooptical Spectrocopy of Rare Earth Compounds, Second Edition" **AW:** Award for Research into Night Vision Devices, United States Army (2001); Outstanding Achievement Award, United States Department of Defense (2001-2005); District Teacher Scholar Award (1999); Grantee, Defense Advanced Research Projects Agency, United States Department of Defense (1998-2006); Outstanding World Leadership in Science Award, Polish Academy of Sciences (1998); Outstanding Achievement Award, United States Department of Defense (1998); Award for Research into Night Vision Devices, United States Army (1997); District Teacher Scholar Award (1996-1997); Citation, Service and Achievement, United States Department of Defense (1996); Outstanding Achievement Award, United States Department of Defense (1995-1996); Award in the Field of Lasers And Electro-Optics; President's Scholarship, Frank H. Spedding Award (1994-1995); President's Scholarship, San José State University (1994-1995); Fellow, Ames Laboratory, United States Department of Energy, Iowa State University (1975-1980); Grantee, National Science Foundation (1972-1980); Outstanding Merit and Performance Award, San José State University (1990); Grantee, Office of Technology, Office of Naval Research (1988-1993); Grantee, Office of Naval Research (1987-2000); Grantee, United States Department of Defense (1984-2000); Grantee, United States Department of Energy (1979-1984); Grantee, Petroleum Research Funds, American Chemical Society (1979-1980); Grantee, Army Research Office, United States Army Research Laboratory, Durham, NC (1979-1980); Grantee, National Science Foundation (1976-1978); Grantee, National Science Foundation (1966-1972); Grantee, AEC-ERDA (1963-1975) **MEM:** Secretary, Lasers and Electro-Optics, IEEE (1995-1996); Program Committee National Meeting, IEEE Lasers and Electro-Optics Society (1995); Reviewer, Panel Member, Division of Material Science, National Science Foundation (1994-2003); Board of Directors, International Society for Optical Engineering (1993); President, Optical Society of Northern California (1993); Vice President, Optical Society of Northern California (1992); Distinguished Fellow, American Society for Engineering Education; Fellow, American Physical Society; Chairman, National Meeting Sessions,

American Physical Society; Fellow, American Academy of Spectral Sciences; American Association for the Advancement of Science; The New York Academy of Sciences; North Dakota Academy of Science; Oregon Academy of Science; National Academy of Sciences of Ukraine; Committee on Lasers and Electro-Optics, National Academies of Sciences, Engineering, and Medicine; Council of Colleges of Arts & Sciences; Phi Beta Kappa; Sigma Xi; Phi Kappa Phi; Sigma Pi Sigma; Phi Sigma Iota; Active Member, Various Committees **MH:** Albert Nelson Marquis Lifetime Achievement Award (2017) **H:** Amateur musician; Clarinet; Gardening; Service activities **ADD:** 5870 Meander Dr, San José, CA, 95120

GRUHL, ANDREA MORRIS, I: Library Management/Library Services **DOB:** 12/09/1939 **PB:** Ponca City **SC:** OK/USA **PT:** Luther Oscar Morris; Hazel Evangeline (Anderson) Morris **MS:** Married **SPN:** Werner Mann Gruhl (7/10/1965) **CH:** Sonja Krista; Diana Krista **ED:** Postgraduate Coursework, University of Oxford, England (1996); Postgraduate Coursework, University of Maryland, College Park, MD (1973); Postgraduate Coursework, Johns Hopkins University, Baltimore, MD (1970-1971); Postgraduate Coursework, University of Maryland, College Park, MD (1968); MLS, University of Maryland, College Park, MD (1968); BA, Wesleyan College, Macon, GA (1961) **C:** Supervisory Librarian, Government Printing Office, Washington D.C. (1993-2001); Cataloger, Federal Documents, Government Printing Office, Washington D.C. (1986-1993); European Exchange Staff, Library of Congress, Washington D.C. (1982-1986); Librarian, Prince Georges County Public Library (1981-1983); Librarian, Howard County Public Library (1974-1979); Art History Researcher, Joseph Alsop, Washington D.C. (1972-1974); Librarian, University of Maryland, College Park, MD (1970-1972); Librarian, Howard County Public Library, Columbia, MD (1969-1970); Librarian, Prince Georges County Public Library (1968); Librarian, Prince Georges County Public Library (1966); Teacher, U.S. Department of Defense, Heidelberg, Germany, Montgomery County, MD (1961-1966); Teacher, Broward County, Florida **CR:** State Delegate, White House Conference on Libraries (1978, 1990); Member, Official Library of Congress Delegation to International Federation, Library Association Annual Conference, Chicago, IL (1985); Women's Program Advisory Committee, Processing Department Representative, Library of Congress (1983-1986); Member, Official Library of Congress Delegation to International Federation, Library Association Annual Conference, Munich, Germany (1983) **CIV:** Trustee, Howard County Community College (1989-1995); Trustee, Howard County Public Library, Columbia, MD (1979-1987); Volunteer, National Gallery Art Library, Washington D.C. (1978-1980); Executive Board, Baltimore Regional Planning Council Library Committee (1976-1979); President, Friends of the Library, Howard County (1976); Citizens Representative, Howard County; Volunteer, League of Women Voters **CW:** Editor, "NCA News & Notes" (2003-2004); Editor, "Federal Librarian" (1994-1999); Editor, "LCPA Index to Library of Congress Information Bulletin" (1984); Indexer, Editor, "Learning Vacations, 3rd Edition" (1980) **AW:** Distinguished Service Award, Federal and Armed Forces Libraries Round Table (2001) **MEM:** Vice President, League of Women Voters National Capital Area (2013-Present); Director, League of Women Voters of Maryland (2009-Present); NCA Liaison, Howard County, League of Women Voters National Capital Area (2011-2013); Nominating Committee Chair, League of Women Voters National Capital Area (2010-2011); Vice President, Secretary, United Nations Association of the National Capital Area (2008-

2012); Civil Liberties, Homeland Security Director, League of Women Voters of Maryland (2007-2009); Vice President, League of Women Voters National Capital Area (2006-2010); Director, League of Women Voters of Howard County (2005-2014); President, Washington Area Chapter, Beta Phi Mu (2005-2006); Director, League of Women Voters of Maryland (2005-2006); Co-chair, Endowment Committee, United Nations Association of the National Capital Area (2004-2008); Co-president, League of Women Voters of Howard County (2004-2005); Task Force on Civil Liberties, LWVUS (2004-2005); Homeland Security Committee Chair, League of Women Voters National Capital Area (2003-2006); Director, League of Women Voters National Capital Area (2002-2006); Secretary, League of Women Voters of Howard County (2002-2004); President, District of Columbia Library Association (2002-2003); Chairman, Constitution and Bylaws Committee, Federal and Armed Forces Libraries Round Table (2001-2006); Vice President, District of Columbia Library Association (2001-2002); Co-chair, Council Caucus, American Library Association (2000-2001); President, Federal and Armed Forces Libraries Round Table (1998-1999); Liaison, Regional Council, League of Women Voters of Howard County; Councilor, American Library Association (1997-2001); Vice President, Federal and Armed Forces Libraries Round Table (1997-1998); IFLA Representative, Federal and Armed Forces Libraries Round Table (1996-2006); Co-chair, Management Interest Group, District of Columbia Library Association (1996-1997); Editor, Federal and Armed Forces Libraries Round Table (1994-1999); Board Director, Maryland Association of Community Colleges (1993-1995); Membership Committee, United Nations Association of the National Capital Area (1992-2009); Maryland Telephone Chair, United Nations Association of the National Capital Area (1992-1994); Board Director, Maryland Association of Community Colleges Trustees (1992-1993); Secretary, Maryland Association of Community Colleges Trustees (1991-1992); Chair, Library Science Interest Group, Library of Congress Professional Association (1985-1987); Program Chair, County and Municipal Employees Union (1984-1986); Coordinator, Annual Staff Art Shows, Library of Congress Professional Association (1982-1983); President, Trustee Division, Maryland Library Association (1982-1983); Coordinator, Members' Publication Exhibition, Art Libraries Society of North America (1980-1982); Board Member, League of Women Voters of Maryland; Government Documents Round Table; Library of Congress American Federation of State; Section on Cataloging, International Standard Bibliographical Description/Cartographic Materials Working Gro, International Federation Library Associations and Institutions; Oxford University Society; Board Chair, United Nations Association of the National Capital Area; Woman's National Democratic Club **PA:** Democrat **RE:** Lutheran

GUARINO, RICHARD A., T: Vice President **I:** Pharmaceuticals **CN:** Validus Pharmaceuticals LLC **ED:** MD, University of Siena, Italy; MS, New York University; BS, Fairleigh Dickinson University **C:** Consultant, Chief Medical Director, Validus Pharmaceuticals (2007-Present); Clinical and Regulatory Consultant, Amneal Pharmaceuticals, Paterson, NJ (2002-Present); President, Oxford Pharmaceutical Resources Inc.; Vice President, Medical Affairs, Validus Pharmaceuticals, Parsippany, NJ; Clinical and Regulatory Consultant, International Services Assistant Fund, Raleigh, NC; Medical Director, Oxford Pharmaceutical Services Inc.; Clinical and Regulatory Consultant, Vicus Therapeutics, Morristown, NJ; Director, Medical Education, EduNeering, Inc. (Now Kaplan EduNeering); Consultant, Wolf Haldenstein Adler Freeman & Hertz, LLP; Consultant, Schiffrin & Barroway, LLC; President, Chief Executive Officer, Oxford Research International Corp.; Vice President, Medical Director, Division of Revlon, Revlon Health Care; Director, Clinical Research, Sandoz, Inc.; Medical Staff, St. Barnabas Medical Center **CR:** Lecturer, Good Clinical Practices and ICH Regulations, Universities and Institutions Worldwide (1985-Present); Director, Center for Professional Advancement (1971-Present); Adjunct Professor, Fairleigh Dickinson University (1975-1977); Council of Presidential Advisors, Fairleigh Dickinson University; Advisory Board, Center for Radio Pharmaceutical Technology Management, Fairleigh Dickinson University; Fellow, Royal Society of Medicine; Fellow, Royal Society for the Encouragement of Arts, Manufactures and Commerce **CIV:** Board of Trustees, Family & Children's Services of North Essex; Board of Trustees, Columbus Hospital; Board of Trustees, New Community Foundation, Newark, NJ; Geriatric Neuropsychopharmacology Subcommittee, U.S. Food and Drug Administration; Board of Directors, East Orange General Hospital; Board of Directors, Cystic Fibrosis Foundation; Board of Directors, Lupus Erythematosus Foundation; Board of Directors, NorCrown Bank; Board of Directors, Ambassador South Development Corporation; Board of Directors, Republican Committee; Board of Trustees, Bloomfield College; Chairman, Board of Trustees, Board of New Community Foundation; Board of Trustees, Lacordaire Academy; Chairman, Board, Columbus Hospital Foundation **CW:** Scientific Exhibit Reviewer, Pharmaceutical Research and Manufacturers of America; Editorial Board, Journal of Geriatric Drug Therapy; Contributor, Articles, Professional Journals **AW:** Publishers Award (2010); Knight of Malta, American Association of the Sovereign Military Order of Malta (1990); Outstanding Young Man in America (1971); Humanitarian of the Year, Italian Tribune; Man of the Year, League for Family Service; Man of the Year, Federation of Italian-American Societies of New Jersey; Pinnacle Award, Fairleigh Dickinson University **MEM:** ACRP/APPI; BioScience Communications; National Association of Interns and Residents; Associates of Clinical Pharmacology; Association of Medical Directors; County of Essex American Heart Association; The New York Academy of Sciences; Drug Information Association; Advisory Committee, National Institutes of Health; American Academy of Clinical Toxicology; The Gerontological Society of America; American Geriatrics Society; National Institute on Aging; American Society of Geriatric Physicians; New Jersey Health Sciences Group; American Society of Angiology; The Center for Professional Advancement; American Society for Parenteral and Enteral Nutrition; Medical Advisors in the Pharmaceutical Industries; Pharmaceutical Manufacturing Association Committee on Guidelines for Monitoring Clinical Investigations; The Academy of Medicine of New Jersey; The New York Academy of Medicine; Kiwanis International; Co-Chairman, Glen Ridge Cultural Committee; President, Board Member, Glen Ridge Historical Society; Glen Ridge Public Library Expansion Committee; Science and Advisory Technology Council of New Jersey **MH:** Albert Nelson Marquis Lifetime Achievement Award (2017) **ADD:** 2 Claridge Drive, Apt. 3BE, Verona, NJ, 07044

GUDENZI-RUESS, IDA CARMEN, T: Piano Instructor **I:** Fine Art **DOB:** 11/04/1926 **PB:** Bronx **SC:** NY/USA **PT:** Hamlet G. Gudenzi; Dolores Gudenzi **MS:** Married **SPN:** Raymond Edmond Ruess (8/20/1965) **CH:** Raida **ED:** AA, Columbia-Greene Community College, Hudson, NY (1994); Student, Drawing and Sculpture, The Art Students League, New York, NY; Student, Concert Pianist Vladzia Mashke, New York, NY **CT:** Montessori Teaching Certificate, Bergamo, Italy (1973) **C:** Self-Employed Teacher, Piano and Sculpture, New York, NY **CW:** Sculptor, WWII Marine Corps Commandant General Holland Meade Smith (1966) **MEM:** National Organization for Women; Phi Theta Kappa **MH:** Albert Nelson Marquis Lifetime Achievement Award (2017) **ADD:** 12 Eldridge Lane, Red Hook, NY, 12571

GUHA, CHANDAN MBBS, PHD, T: Vice Chairman **I:** Medicine & Health Care **CN:** Montefiore Medical Center **ED:** Chief Resident, Department of Radiation Oncology, Montefiore Medical Center, Albert Einstein College of Medicine (1997-1998); Resident, Department of Radiation Oncology, Montefiore Medical Center, Albert Einstein College of Medicine (1996-1997); Research Fellow, Department of Radiation Oncology, Montefiore Medical Center, Albert Einstein College of Medicine (1995-1996); Resident, Department of Radiation Oncology, Washington University in St. Louis (1994-1995); Intern in Transitional Medicine, Temple University (1993-1994); PhD in Immunology, Medical University of South Carolina, Charleston, SC (1993); Intern, University of Calcutta (1987-1988); MBBS, N.R.S. Medical College, University of Calcutta, India (1987); BS, University of Calcutta (1987) **CT:** Diplomate, American Board of Radiology (1999); Licensed to Practice Medicine, State of New York (1998) **C:** Professor of Urology, Albert Einstein College of Medicine (2014-Present); Director, Einstein Institute of Onco-Physics, Albert Einstein College of Medicine (2013-Present); Professor of Pathology, Albert Einstein College of Medicine (2009-Present); Professor of Radiation Oncology, Albert Einstein College of Medicine (2008-Present); Vice Chairman, Department of Radiation Oncology, Montefiore Medical Center, Bronx, NY (2004-Present); Member, Experimental Therapeutics Program, Albert Einstein Cancer Center, Albert Einstein College of Medicine (2004-Present); Director of Translational Research, Department of Radiation Oncology, Albert Einstein College of Medicine (2000-Present); Active Medical Staff Attendee, Department of Radiation Oncology, Montefiore Medical Center (1998-Present); Member, Albert Einstein Cancer Center, Albert Einstein College of Medicine (1998-Present); Associate Professor of Radiation Oncology, Albert Einstein College of Medicine (2004-2008); Assistant Professor, Department of Radiation Oncology, Albert Einstein College of Medicine (1999-2004) **CR:** First Director of Translational Oncology and Radiation Medicine, Shanghai Proton and Heavy Ion Center, Shanghai, China (2014-Present); Visiting Professor, Institute of Liver and Biliary Sciences, Vasant Kunj, New Delhi (2012-Present); Senator, Albert Einstein College of Medicine (2003-Present); Member, Gene Therapy Core, Albert Einstein College of Medicine (2002-Present); Protocol Review Committee, Albert Einstein Cancer Center, Albert Einstein College of Medicine (1998-Present); Experimental Therapeutics Committee, Albert Einstein Cancer Center, Albert Einstein College of Medicine (1998-Present); Member, Marrion Bessin Liver Research Center, Albert Einstein College of Medicine (1998-Present); Senate Counsellor, Albert Einstein College of Medicine (2016); Member, Biosafety Committee, Albert Einstein College of Medicine (2005-2006); Faculty Coordinator, Introduction to Clinical Medicine Course (2005-2006); Consultant in Field; Lecturer in Field **CIV:** Member, Study Sections, National Institutes of Health **CW:** Associate Editor, "Radiation Research," Radiation Research Society

(2014-Present); Editorial Board Member, "Hepatic Medicine: Evidence and Research," Dove Medical Press Ltd." (2013-Present); Editorial Board Member, "Radiation Medicine Rounds," Demos Publishing (2012-Present); Ad Hoc Reviewer, Professional Journals; Contributor, Articles to Professional Journals; Contributor, Chapters to Books **AW:** Honoree, Top Doctors, Castle Connolly Medical Ltd. (2015-2016); Honoree, Top Doctors, New York Media LLC (2015-2016); Recipient, Research Grant, National Brain Tumor Foundation (2002); Honoree, President's Choice Poster, American Society of Liver Disease (1999); Recipient,, Methods in Clinical Cancer Research Fellowship, American Association of Cancer Research (1998); Recipient, Lalezari Award for Research Excellence, Montefiore Medical Center (1998); Recipient, Award for Excellence in Teaching, Leo Davidoff Society, Albert Einstein College of Medicine (1998); Recipient, Research Award, Radiological Society of North America (1997); Honoree, Jagadish Bose National Science Talent Search Scholar (1983-1987); Recipient, Silver Jubilee Medal, German Association of Fertility & Sterility (1985); Recipient, Jubilee Scholarship, TATA Motors (1982); Recipient, Merit Scholarship, Ministry of Education and Culture, Government of India (1980) **MEM:** Chair, Gastrointestinal Cancer Translational Research Program, American Society for Radiation Oncology (2006-Present); Translational Research Program, American Society for Radiation Oncology (2006-Present); Scientific Program Committee, American Society for Radiation Oncology (2014-2015); Session Discussant, American Society for Radiation Oncology (2007, 2013-2014); Session Chair, American Society for Radiation Oncology (2007); Reviewer, Radiobiology Abstracts, American Society for Radiation Oncology (2005-2007); Chair, Presentations, American Society for Radiation Oncology (2006); Radiation Biology Committee, American Society for Radiation Oncology (2004-2006); American Association of Cancer Research (2002); American Society of Clinical Oncology (2002); American College of Radiology (2001); American Brachytherapy Society (2001); American Society of Therapeutic Radiation Oncology (2001); American Society of Gene & Cell Therapy (1999); American Medical Association (1999) **ADD:** 350 Sprain Rd, Scarsdale, NY, 10583

GUINTO, RENZO R., **I:** Education/Educational Services **CN:** Harvard T.H. Chan School of Public Health **ED:** DPH Student, Harvard University (Pursuing); MD, University of the Philippines (2012) **CR:** Aspen New Voices Fellow, The Aspen Institute (2016) **MEM:** Health Systems Global; Planetary Health Alliance **H:** Travel; Singing; Reading; History; Art; Politics

GULA, KATHLEEN REILLY, **I:** Retail/Sales **PT:** Tom Reilly; Nancy (McFadden) Reilly **MS:** Married **SPN:** Jim Gula **CH:** Kaitlin; Kara; Kelsey **ED:** Diploma in Fashion Design and Merchandising, Marymount University, Summa Cum Laude; Diploma in Business-Marketing, Georgetown University **C:** Buyer, Woodward & Lothrop, Washington, DC; Buyer, Divisional Merchandise Manager, Gimbels, Philadelphia, PA, New York, NY; Buyer, Divisional Merchandise Manager, General Merchandise Manager, John Wanamaker Department Store, Philadelphia, PA; Vice President, Retailing, Eagle's Eye, Philadelphia, PA **CIV:** Chairperson, Various Fundraising Events **AW:** Recipient, Development Appreciation Award, Pan Florida Challenge (2017); Recipient, Don Guanella Challenger Award (2017) **MEM:** Women's Board, American Cancer Society, Inc.; Breastcancer.org; Friends of Field Hockey Board, Lafayette College; Challenge Board, Don Guanella

Village; Pan Florida Challenge Development Board; Barefoot Beach Social Committee Board; Union League of Philadelphia **MH:** Albert Nelson Marquis Lifetime Achievement Award (2017) **H:** Walking; Spinning; Tennis; Design **RE:** Catholic **ADD:** 180 Topanga Dr, Bonita Springs, FL, 34134

GUNDLACH, HEINZ LUDWIG, **T:** Principal, Chairman, Investment Banker **I:** Financial Services **CN:** Cardinal Capital Corp. **DOB:** 07/06/1937 **PB:** Dusseldorf **SC:** Germany **PT:** Heinrich Otto Gundlach; Ilse (Schuster) Gundlach **MS:** Married **SPN:** Cornelia T. Gundlach **CH:** Andrew; Annabelle; Julia Olivia **ED:** JUD, School of Law, University of University of Würzburg (1962); LLD, School of Law University of Heidelberg (1961) **C:** Principal, Cardinal Capital Corp., Palm Beach, FL (1991-Present); Chairman, Cardinal Capital Corp., Palm Beach, FL (1991-Present); Managing Director, Dean Witter Reynolds, Inc., New York, NY (1988-1991); Managing Director, Dean Witter Reynolds, Inc., London, United Kingdom (1988-1991); Chairman Successor Cos., Clearfoto, Inc. (1981-1988); Chairman Successor Cos., Trucolor Foto Inc. (1981-1988); Vice Chairman, Sunbelt Investment Holdings, Inc. (1981-1988); CEO Successor Cos., Sunbelt Investment Holdings, Inc. (1981-1988); Vice Chairman, Fed-Mart Corp., San Diego, CA (1975-1981); CEO, Fed-Mart Corp., San Diego, CA (1975-1981); Vice President, Loeb, Rhoades & Co., New York, NY (1969-1975); Partner, Loeb, Rhoades & Co., New York, NY (1969-1975); Vice President, Thyssen A.G. Dusseldorf (1964-1968) **MIL:** West Germany Army (1958-1959) **MEM:** Keswick Golf Club **MH:** Albert Nelson Marquis Lifetime Achievement Award (2017) **PA:** Republican **RE:** Protestant **ADD:** 3935 Fairway Dr, Keswick, VA, 22947

GUNN, LINDA SUE, **T:** Independent Author, Fine Artist and Illustrator **I:** Fine Art **DOB:** 01/28/1949 **PB:** Long Beach **SC:** CA/USA **PT:** John Lawrence Stewart; Barbara Winona Drake Stewart **MS:** Married **SPN:** Stephen Dennis Gunn (10/30/1970) **CH:** Heather Jean; Holly Elizabeth **ED:** Coursework, Studied Drawing and Watercolor with Mike Daniel, Long Beach City College (1981-1992) **C:** Trade Show Demonstrator, Art Materials Trade Association, Pasadena, CA (1987-2005; Instructor, Painting, Palos Verdes Art Center, Rancho Palos Verdes, CA (1997-2004); Program Director, Women Painters, West Burbank, CA (1996-1999); Founding Director, USA Chapter, National Acrylic Painters' Association (NAPA) (1995-2004); Instructor, Painting, Parks and Recreation, City of Long Beach, CA (1987-1992) **CR:** Guest Instructor, Theater Design Department, University of California, Los Angeles (2016); Faculty, Plein Air Convention (2014); Kanuga Watercolor Workshops, NC (2003); Kanuga Watercolor Workshops, NC (2001); Instructor, Sketchbook, Acrylic, Collage and Plein Air Watercolor Classes, Palos Verdes Art Center (1992-2000); Instructor, Watercolor Classes, Parks and Recreation, City of Long Beach, CA (1986-1991) **CW:** Exhibitor, Art Images Gallery, 2018, Exhibitor, Signature American Watermedia Exhibition, Fallbrook Art Center 2014, 2017, 2018.Exhibitor, Watercolor Exhibition, Forest and Ocean Gallery (2017); Exhibitor, Randy Higbee Gallery, 6" Squared Exhibition (2017); Exhibitor, Randy Higbee Gallery, 6" Squared Exhibition (2016); Exhibitor, "Art and Nature," LAPAPA (2016); Exhibitor, Millard Sheets Art Center at Fairplex (2016); Featured Artist, "Colour In Your Life" National TV Productions/Linda Gunn (2016); Exhibitor, "Fun at the Beach," LAPAPA (2016); Exhibitor, "California Light" with the CAC, Altadena Country Club (2016); Exhibitor, "Home for the Holidays," Forest and Ocean Gallery (2015); Exhibitor, Randy Higbee Gallery, 6" Squared Exhibition (2015); Exhibitor, "Last Days

of Summer," Forest and Ocean Gallery (2015); Exhibitor, LA County Fair, CAC at the Millard Sheets Art Center at Fairplex (2015); Exhibitor, Torrance Art Museum Auction (2015); Exhibitor, "Iconic Laguna," Forest and Ocean Gallery (2015); Exhibitor, "Best of Plein Air," Forest and Ocean Gallery (2015); Exhibitor, Long Beach Museum of Art Auction (2015); Illustrator, "Magic in the Mist," Knowonder Publications (2015); Exhibitor, Three Hour Painting Competition and Exhibition, LAPAPA (2014); Exhibitor, Three Paintings, Randy Higbee Gallery, 6" Squared Exhibition (2014); Exhibitor, Urban Beauty Exhibition, Randy Higbee Gallery (2014); Exhibitor, Artist of the Week, Catalina Island (2014); Exhibitor, "Best of America, Watermedia" (2010); Illustrator, "A Cedar Valley Christmas," ND Mansour (2004); Illustrator, "Floridan's Special Gift," ND Mansour (2003); Exhibitor, Cornell Museum of Art, FL (2003); Exhibitor, Cornell Museum of Art, FL (2001); Featured Artist, "Best of Watercolor - Painting Color" (2000); Featured Artist, "The Art of Paper Making"; Featured Artist, "The Artistic Touch"; Featured Artist, "Collected Best of Watercolor"; Exhibitor, Ronald Reagan UCLA Medical Center, UCLA Health; Exhibitor, UCLA Mattel Children's Hospital Emergency Room, UCLA Health; Exhibitor, Great Ormond Street Hospital Children's Charity, London, England; Exhibitor, San Pedro Visitor Center, Port of Los Angeles, CA; Contributor, Articles, Professional Journals; Artwork Published in Numerous Books and Publications, Including Sketchbook Journal, The Artist's Magazine, Watercolor Magic, Splash 6, Splash 9: Watercolor Secrets, and The Compiled Best of Watercolor; Featured Artist, Full Article plus Front and Back Cover, Ex'Corbet, Russia **AW:** International Artists Magazine Award, National Watercolor Society (2004); Named, Best Landscape Overall, London, England (2000) **MEM:** The International Society of Acrylic Painters; National Association of Women Artists, Inc.; Long Beach Museum of Art; Cornell Art Museum; California Art Club **MH:** Albert Nelson Marquis Lifetime Achievement Award (2017) **H:** Illustration; Painting; Writing **RE:** Protestant **ADD:** 5209 E Hanbury St, Long Beach, CA, 90808 **URL:** https://www.youtube.com/watch?v=E1j5UUMfa_U

GUPTA, INDRANIL, **T:** Pediatrician **I:** Medicine & Health Care **CN:** Pediatric Plus **ED:** MD, Calcutta National Medical College, University of Calcutta, West Bengal, India (1990); Fellowship, New York Medical College; Residency, Lincoln Medical and Mental Health Center **CT:** Medical License, State of New York (1997-2018); Certified Pediatrician, American Board of Pediatrics **AW:** Patient-Centered Medical Home Recognition Program, National Committee for Quality Assurance (2012-2014); Physician Practice Connections Recognition Program, National Committee for Quality Assurance (2012-2014) **BA:** 3187 Steinway Street, Suite 6, Pediatric Plus, Astoria, NY, 11103 **URL:** http://www.indranilguptamd.com

GURLEY, WILLIAM B. B., **I:** Education/Educational Services **ED:** PhD, University of Georgia (1976) **C:** Professor, University of Florida (1980-Present)

GUSSAKOVSKY, EUGENE EFIM, **T:** Biophysicist, Researcher, Educator **I:** Sciences **CN:** BL Photonics Inc. **DOB:** 11/29/1946 **PB:** Tashkent **SC:** Uzbekistan **PT:** Efim Micheal Gussakovsky; Valentina Nikolai Gussakovsky **MS:** Married **SPN:** Ludmila Abraham Shifer (7/8/1967) **CH:** Efim Eugene **ED:** DSc, Uzbek Academy of Science, Tashkent, Russia (1987); PhD, Uzbek Academy of Science, Tashkent, Russia (1976); MS, Novosibirsk State University, Russia (1970) **CT:** Certified Senior Scientist, The Volcani Center, Israel (1992); Certified Patentee, Highest

State Patent Courses, Union of Soviet Socialist Republic (1983); Certified Senior Scientist, Highest Certifying Committee, Union of Soviet Socialist Republic (1982) **C:** President, Chief Scientific/Technology Officer, BL Photonics Inc., Winnipeg, MB, Canada (2013-Present); Adjunct Professor, Instructor, Department of Chemistry, University of Winnipeg, Canada (2011-Present); Scientist/Consultant, Spectral Molecular Imaging Inc., Beverly Hills, CA (2011-2013); Research Officer, Institute of Biodiagnostics, National Research Council, Winnipeg, MB, Canada (2006-2011); Professor, Department of Botany, University of Manitoba, Winnipeg, MB, Canada (2005-2006); Senior Scientist, Institute of Horticulture Volcanic Center, Bet Dagan, Israel (1992-2004); Scientist, Bar Ilan University, Ramat Gan, Israel (1991-2004); Senior Scientist, Institute of Virology, Academy of Sciences of Uzbekistan (1986-1991); Leading Scientist, Institute of Biochemistry, Academy of Sciences of Uzbekistan (1970-1986) **CR:** Fellow, Wolfson Foundation, Israel and England (1992-1995); Lecturer, Tashkent State University (1989-1991); Consultant, Institute of Physiology, Academy of Sciences of Uzbekistan (1986-1991) **CW:** Author, "Iodinated Proteins and Amino Acids" (1985); Contributor, Articles, Professional Journals **AW:** Award, Kamea Foundation (1998-2004); Award, European Molecular Biology Organization (1998); Award, European Molecular Biology Organization (1997); Award, Rich Foundation and Giladi Foundation, Israel (1995); Award, European Molecular Biology Organization (1995); Certification for Outstanding Reviewer, Elsevier Scientific Journal **MEM:** American Biophysical Society; International Society of Photosynthesis; New York Academy of Science; American National Geographic Society; American Society of Photobiology; European Society of Photobiology; American Biophysical Society; International Society for Optical Engineering, Israel Society of Botany, Federation of European Societies of Plant Physiology, Federation of American Societies for Experimental Biology **H:** Music; Arts **RE:** Judaism **BA:** 870 Cambridge Street, Unit 909, Winnipeg, MB, Canada, R3M 3H5 **ADD:** 909-870 Cambridge Street, BL Photonics Inc., Winnipeg, MB, Canada, R3M 3H5

HABACHY, SUZAN SALWA SABA, T: Economist, Nonprofit Developer **I:** Nonprofit & Philanthropy **DOB:** 07/15/1933 **PB:** Cairo **SC:** Egypt **PT:** Saba Habachy; Gameela (Gindy) Habachy **ED:** MA, Harvard University, Cambridge, MA (1956); BA, Bryn Mawr College, Pennsylvania (1954) **C:** Executive Director, Trickle Up, New York, NY (1994-2001); Focal Point for Women, Office of Personnel, United Nations, New York, NY (1988-1993); Section Chief, United Nations, New York, NY (1975-1988); Program Officer, United Nations, New York, NY (1969-1975); Reporter, News Bureau, McGraw-Hill Education, London, England (1965-1968); Editor, News Bureau, McGraw-Hill Education, London, England (1965-1968); Reporter, Petroleum Intelligence Weekly, New York, NY (1964-1965); Editor, Petroleum Intelligence Weekly, New York, NY (1964-1965); Economist, Exxon Mobil Corporation, New York, NY (1959-1964); Teaching Fellow, Ohio University, Athens, OH (1957-1958) **MH:** Albert Nelson Marquis Lifetime Achievement Award (2017) **H:** Theater; Travel; Reading **ADD:** 1056 5th Avenue, Apt. 14B, New York, NY, 10028

HABACHY, SUZAN SALWA SABA, T: Economist, Not-for-profit Developer **I:** Nonprofit & Philanthropy **DOB:** 07/15/1933 **PB:** Cairo **SC:** Egypt **PT:** Saba Habachy; Gameela (Gindy) Habachy **ED:** MA, Harvard University, Cambridge, MA (1956); BA, Bryn Mawr College, PA (1954) **C:** Executive Director, Trickle Up, New York, NY (1994-

2001); Focal Point for Women, Office of Personnel, United Nations, New York City, NY (1988-1993); Section Chief, United Nations, New York City, NY (1975-1988); Program Officer, United Nations, New York City, NY (1969-1975); Reporter, News Bureau, McGraw-Hill Education, London, England (1965-1968); Editor, News Bureau, McGraw-Hill Education, London, England (1965-1968); Reporter, Petroleum Intelligence Weekly, New York City, NY (1964-1965); Editor, Petroleum Intelligence Weekly, New York City, NY (1964-1965); Economist, Exxon Mobil Corporation, New York City, NY (1959-1964); Teaching Fellow, Ohio University, Athens, Ohio (1957-1958) **H:** Theater; Travel; Reading **ADD:** 1056 5th Ave Apt 14B, New York, NY, 10028

HABER, WARREN H., T: Investment Company Executive **I:** Financial Services **CN:** Founders Equity Inc. **DOB:** 03/09/1941 **PB:** Brooklyn, NY **SC:** NY/USA **PT:** S. Jack Haber; Ruth (Kalish) Haber **MS:** Married **SPN:** Suellen Green (11/3/1964) **CH:** Warren Jr.; Kristin T. **ED:** BA in Finance, Baruch College, The City University of New York (1962) **C:** Chairman, Founders Property Management Company, Inc., New York, NY (1980-Present); Managing General Partner, Founders Property Management Company, Inc., New York, NY (1980-Present); Managing Partner, Founders Equity Inc., New York, NY (1969-Present); Chief Executive Officer, Founders Equity Inc., New York, NY (1967-Present); Chairman, Founders Equity Inc., New York, NY (1967-Present); Director, Batteries Inc. (1998-1999); Chairman, Batteries, Inc. (1995-1998); Chief Executive Officer, Batteries, Inc. (1995-1998); Director, International Power Machines Corporation, New York, NY (1986-1995); Chief Executive Officer, International Power Machines Corporation, New York, NY (1986-1992); Board Chairman, International Power Machines Corporation, New York, NY (1986-1992); Director, CoStar Group Inc.; Officer, Director Affiliates of Founders Equity Inc.; Director, Affiliates of Founders Equity Inc.; Founder, Former Chief Executive Officer, Ocilla Industries, Inc. Director - Building Intelligence Inc.; Director - COR Healthcare; Director - Source One Holdings **CR:** Member, Board of Directors, CoStar Group Inc.; Former Director, Gulf Resources Pacific Ltd; Former Chief Executive Officer, Vitamin Specialties Inc. (Medifast Inc.); Board Chairman, Vitamin Specialties Inc. (Medifast Inc.); Past Director, Metrocare Enterprises Inc.; Past Chairman, New America Industries, Inc.; Chief Executive Officer, New America Industries, Inc.; Past Chairman, Kenai Corporation; Chief Executive Officer, Kenai Corporation; Past Chairman, Watch Hill Group, Inc.; Chief Executive Officer, Watch Hill Group, Inc.; Past Chairman, Meadow Group Inc.; Chief Executive Officer, Meadow Group Inc. **CIV:** Trustee, Temple Emanu-El (2014-Present); Trustee, Leadership Enterprise for a Diverse America (2003-Present); Trustee, Mailman School of Public Health, Columbia University (2001-Present); Vice President, Baruch College Fund (1984-1990); Trustee, Board of Trustees, Baruch College Fund (1984-1990); Trustee, International Center for the Disabled (1984-1990); Member, Board of Trustees, The Allen-Stevenson School (1982-1985); Board Adviser, Mailman School of Public Health, Columbia University **MIL:** U.S. Army Reserve Medical Corps (1962) **AW:** Distinguished Alumni Award, Baruch College, The City University of New York (1984) **MEM:** Squadron A; City Athletic Club; Council Member, The University Club of New York; Council Member and Executive Committee, The University Club of New York; The Economic Club of New York **MH:** Albert Nelson Marquis Lifetime Achievement Award (2017) **H:** Bike riding; Tai Chi **ADD:** 545 5th Ave Ste 401, Founders Equity Inc., New York, NY, 10017 **URL:** fequity.com

HAGEN, RONALD J., I: Military & Defense Services **CN:** U.S. Air Force **ED:** Bachelor's Degree, Air Force Senior Noncommissioned Officer Academy; Associate Degree, Air Force Senior Noncommissioned Officer Academy **CT:** Certified Dietary Manager; Certified Food Protection Professional **AW:** Nutritional Medicine Team of the Year Award, Air Education and Training Command (2009); Nutritional Medicine Team of the Year Award, Air Education and Training Command (2008); Harvey A. Cain Diet Therapy Senior Noncommissioned Officer of the Year Award, Air Education and Training Command (2008); Award, Senior Non-Commissioned Officer Academy; Four-Time Recipient, Meritorious Service Medal **MH:** Distinguished Humanitarian (2017) **H:** Playing sports; Listening to music; Reading; Learning about history; Partaking in home improvements **ADD:** 1131B Century Oaks Drive, Gulfport, MS, 39507

HAGY HUMPHREYS, LOIS, T: Realtor **I:** Real Estate **DOB:** 09/25/1931 **PB:** Abingdon **SC:** VA/USA **PT:** Howard Barnett Hagy; Deltia Sylvia Caudill Hagy **MS:** Widowed **SPN:** Paul Everett Humphreys (4/15/1951, Deceased 2003) **CH:** Richard Everett; Jill Hagy Humphreys-Dalton **CT:** Certified in Floral Design **C:** Realtor, Virginia Realtors Association, Abingdon, VA (1976-1993); Retail Merchant, Humphrey's Flowers and Gifts, Abingdon, VA (1969-1987); Audio Visual Coordinator, Washington County Schools, Abingdon, VA (1968-1970); Secretary, Gentry's Furniture, Abingdon, VA (1966-1968); Sales Staff, Maxine's Fashions, Abingdon, VA (1955-1965); Dental Assistant, Dr. Loving and Buchanan, Bristol, Abingdon, VA (1949-1954) **CR:** Architectural Review Board (1988-Present); Mayor, Abingdon Town Council (1998-2009); Chairperson, Abingdon Town Council (1988-2009); Chairperson, Mount Rogers Planning, Commission Disabilities Board, Marion, VA (1988-1998) **CIV:** Mayor, Town of Abingdon (1998-Present); Tree Commission, Town of Abingdon (1998-2005); Council Member, Town of Abingdon (1988-2010); Architectural Review Board (1988-1998); Washington County Historical Society **AW:** Woman of the Year, Abingdon Business and Professional Women (1991-1992) **MEM:** Second Vice President, Johnson Memorial Hospital (2010-Present); Third Vice President, Johnson Memorial Hospital (2010); President, Abingdon United Methodist Women (1998-2002); Lifetime Member, Virginia PTA; Daughters of the American Revolution; William King Museum of Art; Chamber of Commerce, Arts Depot and Fairview Restoration, Abingdon, VA; Johnston Memorial Ladies Auxiliary; Creeper Trail Club; Business of Professional Women's Club **MH:** Albert Nelson Marquis Lifetime Achievement Award (2017) **H:** Doll collecting; Traveling **ADD:** 490 Court Street, Apt. 24, Abingdon, VA, 24210

HAINES, KATHLEEN N., T: Executive Director **I:** Business Management/Business Services **CN:** Kats Kitchen Without Borders **ED:** Master's Degree **CT:** Licensed Engineer in Computers; Licensed Broker **C:** Executive Director, Co-Founder, Kat's Kitchen Without Borders; Technology Support, Networking, Xerox, Brazil; Technology Support, Networking, Toshiba; Technology Support, Networking, Microsoft; Technology Support, Networking, MSI; Technology Support, Networking, Nortel Networks; Senior Underwriter, Mortgages; Senior Auditor **MEM:** American Society of Military Comptrollers (1992-Present); National Association of Professional Women; Phi Theta Kappa Honor Society; Eta Kappa Nu-Computer Engineering Honor Society; Rho Chapter, Alpha Omega; International Women's Leadership Association **ADD:** 3818 Blue Spring Dr, Houston, TX, 77068 **URL:** http://www.katskitchenwithoutborders.org/home.html

HAIS, SUSAN M., T: Partner **I:** Law and Legal Services **CN:** Hais Hais & Goldberger **MS:** Married **SPN:** Samuel J. Hais **CH:** Jessica; Jamie **ED:** JD, Law, School of Law, Saint Louis University (1974); MA in English, Saint Louis University (1971); BA, Washington University in St. Louis (1970) **CT:** Certified in Mediation **C:** Founding Partner, Hais, Hais, & Goldberger (2002-Present); Attorney, Private Practice (1979-2002) **CW:** Expert Speaker, Professional Conferences **AW:** Honoree, Highest Profile Attorney in St.Louis, Ladue News (2012); Honoree, Most High Profile Divorce Attorney in St. Louis, Ladue News (2009); Women of Substance Award **MEM:** ABA; Secretary, Lawyers Association, The Missouri Bar **BAR:** The Missouri Bar (1974); Supreme Court of the United States; United States Court of Federal Claims; United States Court of Appeals **BA:** 222 S Central Ave Ste 600, Hais, Hais & Goldberger, Clayton, MO, 63105 **URL:** http://hhg-law.com/our-attorneys

HALL, KENNETH RANDALL, T: Professor of History **I:** Education/Educational Services **CN:** Ball State University **ED:** Fulbright Coursework, Cambodia (2014); Fulbright Coursework, Cambodia (2003-2004); National Endowment for the Humanities Research Fellow, Oriental Institute, The University of Chicago (2000); Scholar-in-Residence, Williams College (1990); Mellon Fellow in Anthropology, New York University (1986); Junior Scholar-in-Residence, University of Hawai'i (1982); Postdoctoral Work in Comparative Medieval Studies, University of Michigan (1975-1976); PhD, University of Michigan (1975); MA, Northern Illinois University (1971); BA, Albion College (1969) **C:** Professor of History, Ball State University (1991-Present); Visiting Professor, The University of Chicago (2005); The University of Chicago (2002); The University of Chicago (2000); Brown Distinguished Visiting Professor, Williams College (1992); Professor of History and Political Science, Massachusetts College of Liberal Arts (1983-1991); Assistant Professor of History, Tufts University (1980-1983); Visiting Assistant Professor of History, Binghamton University, State University of New York (1979-1980); Assistant Professor of History and Economics, Elmira College (1976-1980); Lecturer in Asian Studies, University of Michigan (1975-1976) **CW:** Author, Books; Contributor, Articles, Professional Journals **AW:** Distinguished Visiting Professorship, ISEAS, Singapore (2015); Fulbright Senior Scholarship, U.S. Department of State (2013); Grantee, National Endowment for the Humanities (2005); Grantee, Japan Airlines Foundation (2005); Fulbright Senior Scholarship, U.S. Department of State (2003-2004); Grantee, Association of Southeast Asian Nations (2003); Grantee, National Endowment for the Humanities (2002); Focus Grant and Research Award, National Endowment for the Humanities (2001-2002); Grantee, Association of Southeast Asian Nations (2001); Grantee, National Endowment for the Humanities (2000); Grantee, Association of Southeast Asian Nations (1999); Grantee, Japan Airlines Foundation (1994); Archival Research/Travel Grantee, National Endowment for the Humanities (1993) **MEM:** Association for Asian Studies; Founder, The World History Association; International Economic History Association **H:** Tennis **BA:** 2000 W University Ave, Department of History, Ball State University, Muncie, IN, 47306

HALLBERG, BUDD JAYE, T: Retired Investment Banker and Management Consulting Firm Executive **I:** Consulting **DOB:** 10/02/1942 **PT:** Melvin Kenneth Hallberg; Janet Berina (Dowden) Hallberg **SPN:** Susan Lydia Jess (Life Partner);

Diana M. Pierce (Deceased January 23, 2011) **ED:** Coursework, Harvard University (2006); BS, State University of New York; MA, Goddard College; Diploma, U.S. Army Command and General Staff College (1981) **CT:** Pursuing Certificate of Higher Education, University of Oxford; Certificate, Wharton School, University of Pennsylvania; Certificate, Yale University **C:** President, SCAN Management Inc. (1985-2007); Vice President and Eastern Division Manager, Heinold Commodities Inc. (1983-1985); Director, U.S. Commodity Futures Trading Commission (1976-1983); Member, New York Mercantile Exchange (1974-1976); Vice President, Hornblower & Weeks, Hemphill-Noyes Inc.; Vice President, Dominick & Dominick Inc.; With, Francis I. duPont & Company since 1967 **CR:** Instructor of Philosophy and Logic, Harrisburg Area Community College (2004-2017); Board of Directors; Harrisburg Area Community College Foundation (2015-2017); Professor of Business and Finance, Graduate School of Business, Mount St. Marys University (2002-2007) **CIV:** Board of Directors, Adams County Office for Aging Inc., Gettysburg, PA (2016-2017); Citizen Advocate Team, AARP, Harrisburg, PA; Former Member, Zoning Hearing Board, Mount Joy Township; Former Commissioner, Township Planning Commission **MIL:** Commissioned Officer, United States of America. Retired honorably in 2002 at the rank of Lieutenant Colonel. **CW:** Author, "Alzheimers Disease: A Guide to Caregiving" (2016); Author, "Alzheimers Disease: A Potential $1.1 Trillion Call for Innovative Financial Products and Meaningful Tax Reform" (2015); Author, "Return to First Principles (2009, 2012); Author, How To Be An Effective Litigation Consultant and Expert Witness" (2010) **AW:** Recipient, US Federal Government Meritorious Service Award; Three-Time Recipient, Eric Hoffer Book Award for Excellence in Independent Publishing **MEM:** Society of the Cincinnati; St. Nicholas Society of the City of New York; Colonial Society of Pennsylvania; Pennsylvania Society of Sons of the Revolution; Society of Colonial Wars in the Commonwealth of Pennsylvania; Swedish Colonial Society; Army and Navy Club of Washington, DC; Racquet Club of Philadelphia **MH:** Albert Nelson Marquis Lifetime Achievement Award (2017) **ACH:** Certificate of Excellence, Harrisburg Area Community College **H:** Equestrian (hunter/jumper) competition; Ballroom dancing; Golf **PA:** Independent **RE:** Episcopalian **ADD:** 320 Spangler School Road, Gettysburg, PA, 17325

HALLQUIST, JOHN OSCAR PHD, T: Engineering Company Executive **I:** Engineering **CN:** LSTC **ED:** PhD in Mechanical Engineering and Engineering Mechanics, Michigan Technological University (1974); MS in Engineering Mechanics, Michigan Technological University (1972); BS in Industrial Engineering, Western Michigan University, Magna Cum Laude (1970) **C:** Founder, LSTC, California (1987-Present); President, LSTC, California (1987-Present); Employee, Weapons Laboratory, Lawrence Livermore National Laboratory (1974-1987) **AW:** Applied Mechanics Division Award, The American Society of Mechanical Engineers (2003); Department of Energy Award for Significant Contributions to Nuclear Weapons Progression (1986) **MEM:** National Academy of Engineering **MH:** Albert Nelson Marquis Lifetime Achievement Award (2017) **H:** Bicycling **BA:** 7374 Las Positas Rd, Livermore Software Tech Corp, Livermore, CA, 94551

HALVORSON, GARY ALFRED, T: Instructor **I:** Education/Educational Services **CN:** Sitting Bull College **DOB:** 07/18/1949 **PB:** Klamath Falls **SC:** OR/USA **PT:** Alfred Rueben Halvorson; Dorothy

Edna (Boxrud) Halvorson **MS:** Married **SPN:** Lynne Marie Lafer-Halvorson **CH:** Janet; Daniel; Anne; Clifford **ED:** PhD, Oregon State University (1979); MS, Oregon State University (1975); BA, St. Olaf College (1971) **C:** Agri-business/Science Instructor, Sitting Bull College, Fort Yates, ND (1997-Present); Soil Scientist, North Dakota State University (1989-Present); Director, Land Reclamation Research Center, North Dakota State University (1994-1996); Interim Superintendent, Land Reclamation Research Center, North Dakota State University (1991-1994); Associate Soil Scientist, North Dakota State University (1979-1988); Research Assistant, Oregon State University (1972-1978) **CR:** Timeryazov Agricultural Academy Research Fellow, Moscow, USSR (1978) **CIV:** President, Heart River Lutheran Church, Mandan, ND (1991-1993) **CW:** Contributor, Articles, Professional Journals **AW:** Honoree, Faculty of the Year, AIHEC (2006); Honoree, Researcher of Year Award, American Society of Mining and Reclamation (1995) **MEM:** President, Lions Club International (1995-1996); Secretary, Lions Club International (1988-1993); American Society of Agronomy; Soil Science Society of America; American Society of Mining and Reclamation; North Dakota Academy of Science **H:** Mountaineering; Canoeing; Skiing; Gardening **PA:** Democrat **RE:** Lutheran **BA:** 9299 Highway 24, Department of Environmental Science, Fort Yates, ND, 58538

HAMMON, JOHN W. JR., T: Professor Emeritus of Surgery **I:** Medicine & Health Care **CN:** Wake Forest School of Medicine **DOB:** 03/09/1942 **PB:** Springfield **SC:** MO/USA **PT:** John Hammon Sr.; Mary Ellen Hammon **MS:** Married **SPN:** Mary Lisa Hammon **CH:** Ian; Dudley; Daniel **ED:** Resident, General/Thoracic Surgery, Duke University Medical Center, Durham, NC (1972-1977); Resident, Duke University Medical Center, Durham, NC (1969-1970); Intern, Duke University Medical Center, Durham, NC (1968-1969); MD, Tulane University School of Medicine (1968); BA, Drury College (1964) **CT:** Diplomate, American Board of Thoracic Surgery (2008); Diplomate, American Board of Surgery (1978); Medical Certification, Board of Medical Examiners, State of North Carolina **C:** Professor Emeritus of Surgery, Wake Forest University School of Medicine, Winston-Salem, NC (2009-Present); Professor of Surgery School of Medicine, Wake Forest University, Winston-Salem, NC (1998-2009); Howard Holt Bradshaw Professor, Chairman, Bowman Gray School of Medicine, Winston-Salem, NC (1991-1995); Professor, Department of Cardiac and Thoracic Surgery, Vanderbilt University, Nashville, TN (1989-1991); Chief of Cardiac and Thoracic Surgery, Veterans Affairs Hospital, Nashville, TN (1987-1991); Associate Professor of Surgery, Vanderbilt University, Nashville, TN (1983-1989); Assistant Professor of Surgery, Vanderbilt University, Nashville, TN (1978-1983); Teaching Scholar of Cardiac Surgery, Duke University Medical Center, Durham, NC (1977-1978) **CR:** Cardiac Devices Panel, Federal Drug Administration (2009-Present); NIH Study Sections (1996-Present); President, Southern Thoracic Surgical Association (2008); Principal Investigator, National Institutes of Health Grants (1979-2008) **CIV:** Rotary Club of Winston Salem, NC (2016-Present) **MIL:** Lieutenant, Commander, U.S. Naval Hospital San Diego, CA (1970-1973) **CW:** Journal of Thoracic and Cardiovascular Surgery (2006-Present); Editorial Board Member, Journal of Cardiac Surgery (1993-2012); Editorial Board Member, Annals of Thoracic Surgery (1991-2002); Editorial Board Member, Cardiac Chronicle (1986-1991); Editorial Board Member, Journal of Surgical

Research (1986-1991); Editorial Board Member, European Journal of Cardio-Thoracic Surgery (1999-2017) **AW:** Lifetime Achievement Award, Tulane University School of Medicine (2018); Distinguished Alumni Award, Drury College (2001); Distinguished Alumni Award, Drury College (1989); President's Award for Best Scientific Paper, Southern Thoracic Surgical Association (1985); Scholarship, National Institutes of Health (1974); Teaching Scholar, Duke University Department of Surgery (1982-1983); **MEM:** Omicron Delta Kappa (1963-Present); Historian, Winston-Salem Surgical Association (2013-2015); Standard and Ethics Committee, Society of Thoracic Surgeons (2008-2012); Scientific and Governmental Affairs Committee, American Association for Thoracic Surgery (2007-2014); President, Southern Thoracic Surgical Association (2008); President, Southern Thoracic Surgical Association (2007-2008); President, North Carolina Surgical Association (2006-2007); Membership Committee, American Association for Thoracic Surgery (2002-2005); Membership Committee, American College of Surgeons (2002-2004); Governor, American College of Surgeons (2002); Residents Committee, American Association for Thoracic Surgery (1999-2003); Winston-Salem Surgical Association (1999-2000); Vice President, Southern Thoracic Surgical Association (1999-2000) **MH:** Albert Nelson Marquis Lifetime Achievement Award (2017) **H:** Golf; Fishing; Aircraft owner and pilot **PA:** Independent **RE:** Protestant **BA:** Department of Cardiothoracic Surgery, Wake Forest University School of Medicine, University School of Medicine, Winston- Salem, NC, 27157-27157 **ADD:** 1001 Dalton RD, Lewisville, NC, NC, 27023-8108

HAMMOND, CHARLES BESSELLIEU SR., T: Obstetrician, Gynecologist, Educator **I:** Medicine & Health Care **CN:** Duke University Health System **DOB:** 07/24/1936 **PB:** Fort Leavenworth **SC:** KS/USA **PT:** Claude G. Hammond; Alice (Sims) Hammond **MS:** Married **SPN:** Peggy A. Hammond (6/21/1958) **CH:** Sharon L. (Deceased); Charles B., Jr. **ED:** Resident in Obstetrics and Gynecology, Duke University (1966-1969); BS, Duke University (1964); Fellow in Reproductive Endocrinology, Duke University (1963-1964); Resident in Obstetrics and Gynecology, Duke University (1962-1963); Intern in Surgery, Duke University (1961-1962); MD, Duke University (1961); BS, The Citadel (1958) **CT:** Diplomate, American Board of Obstetrics and Gynecology; Diplomate in Reproductive Endocrinology **C:** E.C. Hamblen Professor of Obstetrics and Gynecology, Duke University (1980-2010); Chairman, Department of Obstetrics and Gynecology, Duke University (1980-2002); Professor, Duke University (1978-1980); Associate Professor, Duke University (1973-1978); Assistant Professor, Department of Obstetrics and Gynecology, Duke University (1969-1973); Fellow, Ad Eundem, Royal College of Obstetricians and Gynecologists **CR:** Fellow, Royal College of Obstetricians and Gynecologists **MIL:** Lieutenant Commander, U.S. Public Health Service, National Institutes of Health, Bethesda, MD (1964-1966) **CW:** Contributor, Over 400 Peer-reviewed Publications; Contributor, "Text Book of GYN"; Contributor, "Trophablastic Disease" **AW:** Lifetime Achievement, District IV, ACOG; Outstanding Teacher, Duke University Medical School **MEM:** President, American College of Obstetrics and Gynecology (2002); Chairman, District IV, American College of Obstetrics and Gynecology (1997-2000); President, American Association of Obstetrics and Gynecology Foundation (1996-2002); President, American Gynecological Club (1994); President, American Gynecological and Obstetrics Society (1993-1994); President, American Fertility Society (1985); President, North Carolina Society Obstetricians and Gynecologists (1985); Director, American Board of Obstetrics and Gynecology (1980-1988); Honorary Member, Society of Obstetrics and Gynecology of Canada; American Medical Association; Association of Professors in Obstetrics and Gynecology; Society of Gynecological Investigation; American Gynecological Society; American Association of Obstetrics and Gynecology; North Carolina Medical Society; National Academy of Medicine; Alpha Omega Alpha, Duke University Medical School **MH:** Albert Nelson Marquis Lifetime Achievement Award (2017) **H:** Gardening; Golf **PA:** Democrat **RE:** Presbyterian **ADD:** 2827 McDowell Road, Durham, NC, 27705

HANSON, VICTOR ARTHUR, T: Surgeon (Retired) **I:** Medicine & Health Care **CN:** Private Practice **DOB:** 05/05/1933 **PB:** Syracuse **SC:** NY/USA **PT:** Victor Arthur Hanson, Sr.; Dorothy (Burns) Hanson **MS:** Married **SPN:** Mary Diane Nadijcka (9/13/1985) **ED:** Fellow, American College of Surgeons (1975); Resident in General Surgery, University of Pennsylvania (1964-1969); Resident, School of Aviation Medicine, U.S.Navy (1961); Resident in Pathology, St. Joseph's Hospital, Syracuse, NY (1960-1961); Intern, University of Pennsylvania (1959-1960); MD, University of Pennsylvania (1959); AB, Princeton University (1955) **CT:** Certified Instructor in Advanced Trauma Life Support (1987); Diplomate, American Board of Surgery, Inc. (1971); Licensed to Practice Medicine, State of Georgia; Licensed to Practice Medicine, Commonwealth of Pennsylvania; Licensed to Practice Medicine, State of New Jersey; Licensed to Practice Medicine, State of New York; Pilot's License Single Engine Land **C:** Private Practice, Atlanta, GA (1996-Present); Staff Surgeon, Northside Hospital, Atlanta, GA (1991-Present); Staff Surgeon, Atlanta Outpatient Surgery Center, C-HCA, Inc. (1991-Present); Staff Surgeon, The Blood & Bone Marrow Group of Georgia (1998-2002); West Paces Hospital, Atlanta, GA (1996-1998); Staff Surgeon, Piedmont Healthcare (1993-1996); Staff Surgeon, The Southeast Permanente Medical Group, Inc., Atlanta, Georgia (1990-1996); Private Practice, Wilmington, DE (1988-1990); President, Pike Creek Enterprises, Inc. (1987-1994); Director of Research, Wilmington Veterans Affairs Medical Center, United States Department of Veterans Affairs (1983-1987); Assistant Professor of Surgery, Thomas Jefferson University (1980-1990); Staff Surgeon, Wilmington Veterans Affairs Medical Center, United States Department of Veterans Affairs (1980-1987); Clinical Assistant Professor of Surgery, SUNY Upstate Medical University (1979-1980); Assistant Professor of Surgery, SUNY Upstate Medical University (1971-1979); Assistant Attending General Surgeon, St. Joseph's Hospital Health Center (1971-1978); Private Practice, Syracuse, NY (1969-1980); Assistant Attending General Surgeon, SUNY Upstate Medical University (1969-1980); Staff Surgeon, Syracuse Veterans Affairs Medical Center, United States Department of Veterans Affairs (1969-1980); Assistant Attending General Surgeon, Crouse Hospital (1969-1980); Assistant Attending General Surgeon, Community Hospital of Greater Syracuse (1969-1971); Clinical Instructor, Department of Surgery, SUNY Upstate Medical University (1969-1971) **CR:** Chairman, Institution Review Board, Northside Hospital (2001); Board of Trustees, Brandon Hall School (2001); Member, Advisory Board on Surgical Technology, Georgia Medical Institute (Now Zenith Education Group, Inc.) (1999); Member, Board of Trustees, National Association of IRB Managers (Now NAIL) (1997-1998); Vice Chairman, Institutional Review Board, Northside Hospital (1995-2001); Member, Small & Large Bowel Pathway Committee, Northside Hospital (1995-1999); Vice Chairman, Education & Research Committee, Northside Hospital (1994-1997); Member, Clinical Advisory Committee, The Southeast Permanente Medical Group, Inc. (1993); Director, Diabetic Foot Surveillance Program, Georgia Region, The Southeast Permanente Medical Group, Inc. (1991-1995); Chairman, Institutional Review Board, Georgia Region, The Southeast Permanente Medical Group, Inc. (1991-1994); Breast Cancer Screening Committee, The Southeast Permanente Medical Group, Inc. (1991); Chairman, Guidelines for Mammography & Clinical Examination, The Southeast Permanente Medical Group, Inc. (1991); Member, Diabetic Task Force, The Southeast Permanente Medical Group, Inc. (1990-1995); Director, The Southeast Permanente Medical Group, Inc. (1990); President, Pike Creek Enterprises, Inc. (1987-1994); Member, Education Committee, Wilmington Veterans Affairs Medical Center, United States Department of Veterans Affairs (1987); Member, Library Committee, Wilmington Veterans Affairs Medical Center, United States Department of Veterans Affairs (1985-1987); Member, Veterans Benefits Committee, Wilmington Veterans Affairs Medical Center, United States Department of Veterans Affairs (1985-1987); Member, Antibiotic Audit Committee, Wilmington Veterans Affairs Medical Center, United States Department of Veterans Affairs (1984-1986); President, Veterans Affairs Medical Society, Wilmington, DE (1984-1985); Ex Officio Member, Research & Development Committee, Wilmington Veterans Affairs Medical Center, United States Department of Veterans Affairs (1983-1987); Ex Officio Member, Publications Subcommittee, Wilmington Veterans Affairs Medical Center, United States Department of Veterans Affairs (1983-1987); Ex Officio Member, Animal Studies Subcommittee, Wilmington Veterans Affairs Medical Center, United States Department of Veterans Affairs (1983-1987); Ex Officio Member, Human Studies Subcommittee, Wilmington Veterans Affairs Medical Center, United States Department of Veterans Affairs (1983-1987); Chairman, Research & Development Committee, Wilmington Veterans Affairs Medical Center, United States Department of Veterans Affairs (1982-1983); Presenter, 31 Presentations in Field **MIL:** Group Medical Officer, Third Marine Airwing, U.S. Marine Corps (1963-1964); Flight Surgeon, First Marine Airwing, U.S. Marine Corps (1962-1963); Flight Surgeon, Third Marine Airwing, U.S. Marine Corps (1961-1962) **CW:** Contributor, 28 Articles, Professional Journals **AW:** Citation, The Southeast Permanente Medical Group, Inc. (1995); Grantee, United States Food and Drug Administration (1988); Merit Review, Wilmington Veterans Affairs Medical Center, United States Department of Veterans Affairs (1985-1987); Grantee, Research Advisory Group Approval & Funding (1981-1985); Grantee, American Heart Association, Inc. (1975) **MEM:** Elected Vice Commander, Dunwoody Post, Veterans of Foreign Wars (2006); The American Legion (2005); Dunwoody Chapter, Veterans of Foreign Wars (2001); American Society of Bariatric Physicians (1997-2000); Society for Surgery of the Alimentary Tract (1996); Medical Association of Atlanta (1992); Medical Association of Georgia (1992); Delaware State Medical Society (1988-1989); New Castle County Medical Society (1988-1989); Delaware Academy of Medicine (1988-1989); American Medical Association (1988); The New York Academy of Sciences (1984-2000); American Association for the Advancement of Science (1984) **MH:** Albert Nelson Marquis Lifetime Achievement Award (2017) **H:** Tennis;

Model railroading **ADD:** 3875 W Nancy Creek Ct NE, Atlanta, GA, 30319 **URL:** https://doctor.webmd.com/doctor/victor-hanson-md-9c9fc0d0-d891-494f-8ea2-9849621d3664-overview

HAPKE, BRUCE W., T: Planetary Scientist, Educator **I:** Education/Educational Services **CN:** University of Pittsburgh **DOB:** 02/17/1931 **PB:** Racine **SC:** WI/USA **PT:** William E. Hapke; Blanche V. (Pulda) Hapke **MS:** Married **SPN:** Joyce Zellinger (6/18/1954) **CH:** Kevin; Jeffrey; Cheryl **ED:** PhD, Cornell University (1962); BS, University of Wisconsin (1953) **C:** Professor Emeritus, Department Geology and Planetary Science, University of Pittsburgh (2001-Present); Professor, Department of Geology and Planetary Science, University of Pittsburgh (1967-2001); Senior Research Associate, Center for Radiophysics and Space Research, Cornell University (1960-1967) **CR:** Member, Lunar Reconnaissance Orbiter Camera Science Team; Research Associate, Carnegie Museum of Natural History, Pittsburgh; Principal Investigator, Apollo Lunar Samples; Member, TV Science Team, National Aeronautics and Space Administration Mariner 10; Guest Scientist, TV Science Team, National Aeronautics and Space Administration Viking Lander; Consultant, National Aeronautics and Space Administration **MIL:** Lieutenant U.S. Naval Reserve (1953-1955) **CW:** Author, "Theory of Reflectance and Emittance Spectroscopy"; Contributor, Articles, Professional Journals **AW:** Kuiper Award for Outstanding Contributions to the Planetary Sciences, Division for Planetary Sciences, American Astronomical Society (2001); Eponym, Asteroid #3549 Hapke (1988); Eponym, Mineral Hapkeite; Eponym, Hapke Theory **MEM:** Chairman, Division of Planetary Sciences, American Astronomical Society (1988-1989); Fellow, American Geophysical Union; American Association for the Advancement of Science; International Astronomical Union **MH:** Albert Nelson Marquis Lifetime Achievement Award (2017) **ADD:** 5850 Meridian Rd Apt 510B, Gibsonia, PA, 15044 **URL:** http://www.geology.pitt.edu/person/bruce-hapke

HAQUE, MALIKA HAKIM, T: Pediatrician **I:** Education/Educational Services **CN:** Ohio State University **PB:** Madras **SC:** India **PT:** Syed Abdul Hakim; Rahimunisa (Hussain) Hakim **MS:** Married **SPN:** C. Azeez Haque (2/5/1967) **CH:** Kifi Zeba Haque; Masarath Haque Khan; Asim Zayd Haque **ED:** Fellow in Developmental Disabilities and Mental Retardation at Nisonger Center, Ohio State University and Columbus Children's Hospital(1970-1971); Resident in Pediatrics, New Jersey College of Medicine Babies and Children's Hospital (1968-1970); Rotating Intern, Miriam Hospital, Brown University, Providence, RI (1967-1968); MBBS equivalent to MD Madras Medical College (1967); **CT:** Fellow of American Academy of Pediatrics (1973); Diplomate, American Board of Pediatrics (May 21, 1972) **C:** Founder, Medical Director, NOOR Community Clinic/Muslim Clinic of Ohio Free Clinic Wexner Medical Center at Rardin Family Practice Center, Ohio State University, Columbus, OH (2010-Present); Clinical Professor of Pediatrics, College of Medicine, Ohio State University (1999-Present); Clinical Associate Professor, Department of Pediatrics and International, College of Medicine, Ohio State University (1981-1999); Clinical Assistant Professor of Pediatrics, Ohio State University (1974-1980); Staff Pediatrician, Children and Youth Project, Children's Hospital, Columbus, OH (1974-1980) Acting Chief of Pediatrics, Nisonger Center at the Ohio State University (1973-1974) **CR:** Founder, Medical Director, Noor Community Clinic - Muslim Clinic of Ohio (2010-Present); Medical Consultant to Bureau of Disabilities and

Social Securities and Rehabilitation Services State of Ohio (1991-2015); Pediatrician, Children's Hospital Physician Health Care Centers, Columbus, OH (1981-1999); Director, Pediatrics Academic Association (1992-2002); Consultant, Central Ohio Head Start Program (1974-1979) Has been an Expert Advisory Panelist to the Joint Commission of Hospitals which led to the formation of New Standards for management of Culturally Diverse population in Hospitals from (2008-2010) **CIV:** Board Member, International Women Coming Together, the Ohio State University (2013-Present); Board of Regents, Islamic Medical Association of North America (2007-2011); Board of Trustees, Islamic Foundation of Central Ohio (2006-2009); Trustee, Asian American Health Alliance Network, Columbus, OH (1994-2001); Charter Member, Ronald Reagan Republican Presidential Task Force (1982) **CW:** Contributor, Articles to Professional Journals and Newspapers on Pediatrics and on her Discoveries and Patents Related to her Research on Treatment for Human Papilloma Viral Tumors such as Warts and DNA Pox Viral Tumors such as Molluscum Contagiosum; Published Articles on Islamic Medical Ethics **AW:** APPNA-Ohio Chapter Foundering Member Award (2018); Deah's Award for Excellence In Community Service and Leadership by MY USA Project (2018); Letter Award by the State of Ohio Legislators and City Council Member Michael Stinziano for Excellence in Community Service and Leadership (2018); Named, One of America's Top Pediatrician, Consumer's Research Council America (2008-Present); 45 Years of Outstanding Service Award, Nationwide Children's Hospital (2017); APPNA-Ohio Award for outstanding community service; Lifetime Service Award, Islamic Medical Association North America (2016); Recipient, Health Care Heroes Award (2015) by Columbus Business First; Finalist, Jefferson Top Twenty Award, Community Service, State of Ohio (2014); Star Fish Award, International Women's Association (2014); 40 Years of Outstanding Service Award, Nationwide Children's Hospital (2012, 2013); Finalist, Jefferson Top Twenty Finalist Award, for Community Service, State of Ohio (2012); Sakinah Outstanding Leadership Award, Columbus Team (2012); Excellence Award, Asha-Ray of Hope (2011); Outstanding Community Service Award, Noor Islamic Cultural Center (2011); Community Service Award, CAIR, Ohio (2011); Outstanding Service and Contribution Award, Noor Islamic Cultural Center, Ohio (2008); Outstanding Service Award, Islamic Medical Association of North America (2005); Outstanding Service Award, CAIR, Ohio (2005); Physician of the Year Award, National Republican Congressional Committee (2003); Physician Recognition Award, American Medical Association (2002-2005); National Leadership Award (2001); Physician Recognition Award, American Medical Association (1988-1999); Presidential Medal of Merit, President Ronald Reagan (1982); Physician Recognition Award, American Medical Association (1971-1986); Gold Medals in Surgery, Radiology, Pediatrics and Obstetrics-Gynecology for outstanding performance in Medical School at Madras Medical College (1967) and University of Madras. Medal of Merit, President Ronald Reagan (1982) **MEM:** Expert Advisory Panelist, Joint Commission on Accreditation of Hospitals (2008-2010); Director, Pediatrics Academy Association (1992-2002); Ambulatory Pediatrics Association; Member COPS-Central Ohio Pediatric Society; Fellow, American Academy of Pediatrics; IIMANA-Islamic Medical Association of North America; APPNA Ohio -American Association of Physicians of Pakistani origin of North America; AAPI- American Association of Physicians of Indian Origin **MH:** Albert Nelson

Marquis Lifetime Achievement Award (2017) **H:** Spending time with family and friends; Reading; Traveling; Community service **ADD:** 5095 Noor Park Cir, Dublin, OH, 43205 **URL:** http://www.nationwidechildrens.org/malika-haque

HARBERT, CHARLES ARMON, T: Medicinal Chemist (Retired) **I:** Sciences **DOB:** 04/07/1940 **PB:** Indianapolis **SC:** IN/USA **PT:** Charles Homer Harbert; Ruth Laura (Griffey) Harbert **MS:** Married **SPN:** Kay Louise Strode (9/9/1961) **CH:** Kelle Harbert Moley; Jennifer Ruth **ED:** PhD, University of Missouri (1967); BS, University of Colorado (1962) **C:** Retired (1999); Vice President, Groton Research Site, Pfizer Inc., Connecticut (1993-1999); Senior Executive Director, Groton Research Site, Pfizer Inc., Connecticut (1991-1993); Executive Director, Groton Research Site, Pfizer Inc., Connecticut (1984-1991); Director, Groton Research Site, Pfizer Inc., Connecticut (1981-1984); Manager, Groton Research Site, Pfizer Inc., Connecticut (1976-1981); Project Leader, Groton Research Site, Pfizer Inc., Connecticut (1972-1976); Research Scientist, Groton Research Site, Pfizer Inc., Connecticut (1969-1972); National Institutes of Health Postdoctoral Fellow, Stanford University (1967-1969) **CR:** Member, Advisory Committee, Department of Chemistry, University of Missouri, Columbia, MO (1992-1999); Co-Chair, Keystone Symposium (1995); Member, Visiting Committee, Connecticut College, New London, CT (1993); Chair, Medicinal Chemistry Gordon Research Conference, New London, CT (1990); Member, Visiting Committee, Connecticut College, New London, CT (1986) **CIV:** Member, Board of Education, Waterford, CT (1979-1981); Member, Board of Finance, Waterford, CT (1977-1978); Member, Board Tax Review, Waterford, CT (1975-1977) **CW:** Author, "Bachelor Colorado: History of a San Juan Mining Ghost Town" (2017); Author, "Creede, Colorado History: Insights and Views Through Postcards" (2010); Author, "Colorado History: Insights and Views Through Postcards" (2006) **AW:** Team Innovation Award, American Chemical Society (2005); Distinguished Alumni Award, University of Missouri (1993) **MEM:** Awards Committee, Medical Chemical Division, American Chemical Society (1994-1999); Phi Lambda Upsilon **MH:** Albert Nelson Marquis Lifetime Achievement Award (2017) **BA:** 1035 West Dream Chaser Court, Oro Valley, AZ, 85737 **ADD:** PO Box 309, Creede, CO, 81130

HARE, JOHN L., T: Professor of American Studies and English **I:** Education/Educational Services **CN:** Montgomery College **DOB:** 03/10/1950 **PB:** Washington **SC:** DC/USA **PT:** Julian Matthew Hare; Grace Griffin Hare **MS:** Married **SPN:** Virginia Sue Derhaag (2/21/1976) **CH:** Derylyn Jennifer Stokes; James Julian; Matthew John **ED:** PhD in American Studies, University of Maryland (1997); MA in English, William & Mary, Williamsburg, VA (1977); BA in English, George Mason University, Fairfax, VA (1973) **C:** Professor of American Studies and English, Germantown Campus, Montgomery College (1987-Present); Administrative Associate to Vice President, Montgomery College (2006-2009) **CIV:** Pop Culture of America; Popular Culture Association in the South American Culture; American Culture Association in the South **CW:** Author, "Critical Reading, Writing, and Research" (2018); Author, "Will the Circle be Unbroken: Family and Sectionalism in the Virginia Novels of Kennedy, Caruthers, and Tucker 1830-1845" (2002) **MH:** Albert Nelson Marquis Lifetime Achievement Award (2017) **PA:** Democrat **RE:** Episcopalian **ADD:** 18300 Feathertree Way Apt 102, Montgomery Village, MD, 20886

HARKLEROAD, JO-ANN D., T: Director of Special Education **I:** Education/Educational Services **CN:** Highland County Schools **DOB:** 10/22/1936 **PB:** Wilkes-Barre **PT:** Leon Joseph Sr.; Beatrice Catherine (Wright) Decker **MS:** Married **SPN:** A. Dwayne Harkleroad **CH:** Leon Wade **ED:** Postgraduate Coursework, The George Washington University (1997-1999); MA in Special Education and Educational Diagnosis and Prescription, The George Washington University (1969); BS in Health, Physical Education and Recreation, Minor in Special Education, The George Washington University (1968); AS, The George Washington University (1960) **C:** Director of Special Education, Highland County Schools, Monterey, VA (1987-1990); Writer, Editor, Station WNVT-TV, Fairfax, VA (1980-1982); Supervisor Title I, Prince William County Schools, Manassas, VA (1971-1972); Educational Diagnostician, Prince William County Schools, Manassas, VA (1969-1971); Teacher, Bush Hill Day School, Franconia, VA (1961-1963); Instructor, Catholic University of America, Washington, D.C. (1960-1961) **CR:** Reviewer, Writers Readers **CIV:** Ruling Elder, Presbyterian Church, McDowell and Clifton, VA; Member Division of Faith in Action, Hunger Committee, Shenandoah Presbytery; Director, McDowell Presbyterian Church Choir; Rotating Director, Highland County Community Choir; Past President, Highland County Public Library Board; President, Vice President, Secretary, Bath Highland Retired Educators Association **CW:** Author, "Freezeout" (2008); Author, "Swep Culhane" (2007); Author, "Ketch Colt" (2005); Author, "Blood Atonement" (2004); Author, "Horse Thief Trail, Third Edition," (1986); Author, "Horse Thief Trail" (1981); Wyoming Valley Philharmonic Symphony Orchestra (1953-1954); Columnist, Op-ed Page, The Recorder; Radio Broadcaster, Station WVMR, Frost, WV **MEM:** Past President, Stonewall Women's Club (1990-1992); The International Women's Leadership Association; National Association of Professional Women; Women Writing the West; Western Writers of America; Life Member, Presbyterian Women in the Presbyterian Church (U.S.A.), Inc. **H:** Hiking; Camping; Rifle Shooting; Reading; Gardening **BA:** 218 Davis Run Road, Windy Ridge Farm, Mc Dowell, VA, 24458

HARMON, PHILLIP LOUIS, I: Law and Legal Services **DOB:** 09/08/1954 **PB:** Bourne **SC:** MA/USA **PT:** Russell Sanborn Harmon; Patsy (Bilger) Harmon **MS:** Married **SPN:** Kang Sung Ae (1997) **ED:** JD, Capital Law School, Columbus, OH (1980); BS in Business Management, Cornell University, Ithaca, NY (1976) **C:** Private Practice, Washington (1985-Present); General Counsel, USA Rugby (1989-1998); Assistant Vice President, Energy Department, Shawmut Bank, Boston (1983-1985); Manager International Loan Syndications, National Bank of Washington (1981-1982); Bank Officer, Huntington Bank, Columbus, OH (1978-1981); Law Clerk to Presiding Justice, Franklin County Probate Court, Columbus, OH (1976-1978); Chairman, General Counsel, Progress Economic and Environmental Responsibility, Inc; Private Practice, Columbus, Ohio **CIV:** Secretary, Franklin County Forum (2006-2008); Ohio City Council, Columbus (2005); Chairman, General Counsel, Progress with Economic and Environmental Responsibility, Inc. (2003-2005); Candidate, US House of Representatives (2000); Ohio 12th Congressional District (2000); Financial Advisor, Elliott Richardson for US Senate, Boston (1984) **MEM:** American Bar Association; Ohio State Bar Association; Columbus Bar Association **BAR:** US Supreme Court (1993); Sixth Circuit, US Court of Appeals (1986); US District Court of DC (1982); DC Circuit, US Court of Appeals (1982); DC Bar Association (1981); Southern District of Ohio, US District Court (1981); Ohio Bar Association (1980) **H:** Scuba diving; Swimming; Reading; Politics; Travel **PA:** Republican **RE:** Methodist

HARMON, MARY L., I: Financial Services **ED:** JD, University of Arkansas (1984); Degree in Accounting, University of Arkansas **C:** Managing Director, Goldman Sachs **AW:** Chief Counsel Award for Service as Special Counsel, Chief Counsel, IRS (1993) **MEM:** American Bar Association; Federal Bar Association

HARPER, CONRAD KENNETH, I: Law and Legal Services **DOB:** 12/02/1940 **PB:** Detroit **SC:** MI/USA **PT:** Archibald Leonard Harper; Georgia Florence (Hall) Harper **MS:** Married **SPN:** Marsha Louise Wilson (7/17/1965) **CH:** Warren Wilson; Adam Woodburn **ED:** Honorary LLD, Harvard University (2007); Honorary LLD, Vermont Law School (1994); Honorary LLD, The City University of New York (1990); LLB, Harvard University (1965); BA, Howard University (1962) **CT:** New York (1966) **C:** Retired Partner, Simpson Thacher & Bartlett (2010-Present); Of Counsel, Simpson Thacher & Bartlett, New York City, NY (2003-2009); Partner, Simpson Thacher & Bartlett, New York City, NY (1996-2002); Legal Adviser, U.S. Department of State, Washington D.C. (1993-1996); Partner, Simpson Thacher & Bartlett, New York City, NY (1974-1993); Associate, Simpson Thacher & Bartlett, New York City, NY (1971-1974); Staff Lawyer, NAACP Legal Defense and Educational Fund, New York City, NY (1966-1970); Law Clerk, NAACP Defense and Educational Fund, New York City, NY (1965-1966) **CR:** Member, Harvard Corp. (2000-2005); Member, Public Service Enterprise Group (1997-2012); Board of Directors, New York Life Insurance Co. (1992-1993, 1996-2013); Member, Permanent Court of Arbitration, The Hague, Netherlands (1993-1996, 1998-2004); Member, Administrative Conference U.S. (1993-1995); Chairman, Admissions and Grievances Committee, United States Court of Appeals for the Second Circuit (1987-1993); Co-chairman, Lawyers' Committee for Civil Rights Under Law (1987-1989); Visiting Lecturer, Law, Yale University (1977-1981); Consultant, Department of Health (1977); Lecturer, Law, Rutgers, The State University of New Jersey (1969-1970) **CIV:** Trustee, William Nelson Cromwell Foundation (1990-Present); Board of Trustees, Greenwall Foundation (2006-2012); Chairman, Board, William Nelson Cromwell Foundation (2005-2014); Board of Trustees, Metropolitan Museum of Art (1996-2013); Board of Directors, Phi Beta Kappa Associates (1992-1993); Board of Trustees, Institute of International Education (1992-1993); Vice-chairman, Board of Trustees, New York Public Library (1991-1993); Chairman, Executive Committee, New York Public Library (1990-1993); Board of Visitors, Fordham Law School (1990-1993); Board of Legal Advisors, Martindale-Hubbell (1990-1993); Board of Visitors, The City University of New York (1989-1993); Board of Managers, Lewis Walpole Library (1989-1993); Chancellor, The Episcopalian Diocese of New York (1987-1992); Vestryman, Church of St. Barnabas, Irvington, NY (1982-1985) **AW:** Named One of 50 Most Influential Minority Lawyers in America, National Law Journal (2008); Lifetime Achievement Award, The American Lawyer Magazine (2006); Alumni Achievement Award, Howard University (1994) **MEM:** Secretary, Academy of Political Science (2014-Present); Member, Council, American Philosophical Society (2010-Present); Senior Adviser, Academy of Political Science (2010-Present); Board of Directors, Academy of Political Science (1998-Present); Vice President, American Philosophical Society (2005-2010); Counselor, American Society of International Law (2000-2005); First Vice President, American Law Institute (2000-2004); Second Vice President, American Law Institute (1998-2000); Executive Committee, American Society of International Law (1998-2000); Council Member, Grolier Club (1993, 1997-2004); Executive Council, American Society of International Law (1997-2000); Board of Managers, Harvard Club (1993); President, Association of the Bar of the City of New York (1990-1992); Board of Directors, American Association for the International Commission of Jurists (1988-1993); Council, American Law Institute (1985-2011); Board of Editors, Journal, ABA (1980-1986); Chairman, Executive Committee, Association of the Bar of the City of New York (1979-1980); Fellow, American Bar Foundation; Fellow, New York Bar Foundation; Fellow, American College of Trial Lawyers; Fellow, American Academy of Arts & Sciences; National Bar Association; New York State Bar Association; Council on Foreign Relations; Century Association; Phi Beta Kappa **PA:** Democrat **RE:** Episcopalian

HARRELL, RAY, T: Performing Company Executive **I:** Media & Entertainment **CN:** Magic Circle Training **DOB:** 12/03/1941 **PB:** Ada **SC:** OK/USA **PT:** Ray E. Harrell; Cleo Mae Harrell; William O.A. Rockko **MS:** Married **SPN:** Stephanie Rose Weems (6/27/2005) **CH:** Jane Angela **ED:** MM, Manhattan School of Music (1973); BA, The University of Tulsa (1964) **CT:** Certified in Rubenfeld Synergy Method, Rubenfeld Center, New York, NY (1979) **C:** Artistic Director, American Masters Arts Festival Biennial, New York, NY (2003-Present); Producer, American Masters Arts Festival Biennial, New York, NY (2003-Present); Master Voice Teacher, Magic Circle Training, New York, NY (1978-Present); Founding Artistic Director, Magic Circle Opera Repertory Ensemble Inc., New York, NY (1978-Present); Summer Opera Director, Mannes School of Music, The New School, New York, NY (1987-1989); Teacher in Vocal Performance, Manhattan School of Music, New York, NY (1978-1986); Opera Teacher, Manhattan School of Music, New York, NY (1978-1986); Teacher in Vocal Anatomy, Manhattan School of Music, New York, NY (1978-1986); Vocal Soloist, The U.S. Army Chorus, Washington DC (1966-1970); Vocal Soloist, The United States Army Field Band, Fort Mead, MD (1964-1966); Commissioned Piano Teacher, The University of Tulsa (1962-1964) **CR:** Recording Producer, Magic Circle Opera Repertory Ensemble Inc., New York, NY (1990-Present); Co-Leader, MCORE Florentine Conference on Arts and Economics in America, Washington DC (2004); Lecturer on Donald Schoen, Teachers College, Columbia University, New York, NY (1988-1989); Director, Magic Circle Awards **CIV:** Lecturer, Panel Member, Non-Governmental Organizations, United Nations, New York, NY (2000); Cherokee Priest, Nuyagi Keetoowah Society, Inc, New York, NY (1988-2005) **MIL:** U.S. Army (1964-1970) **CW:** Singer, "Naqoyqatsi," Miramax, LLC (2001-2002); Singer, "Pocahontas" (1994); Author, "A Gypsy Carmen" **AW:** Recipient, Oscar Award for "Colors of the Wind," Academy of Motion Picture Arts and Sciences (1995); Recipient, Grammy Award for "Colors of the Wind," The Recording Academy (1995); Recipient, Golden Globe Award for "Colors of the Wind," Hollywood Foreign Press Association (1995); Regional Finalist, The Metropolitan Opera (1969) **MEM:** Lifetime Member, The Recording Academy; Phi Mu Alpha **MH:** Albert Nelson Marquis Lifetime Achievement Award (2017) **PA:** Liberal **RE:** Traditional Cherokee Keetoowah **ADD:** 200 W 70th St Apt 6C, New York, NY, 10023

HARRIS, CHRISTY FRANKLIN, **T:** Lawyer **I:** Law and Legal Services **CN:** Kinsey, Vincent, Pyle, P.L. **DOB:** 12/08/1945 **PB:** Greensboro **SC:** NC/USA **PT:** Luther Franklin Harris (Deceased); Rebecca Ann (Bluster) Harris (Deceased) **MS:** Married **SPN:** M. Dale Harris **CH:** Stacey Lynn; Aubrey Leigh **ED:** JD, Levin College of Law, University of Florida, with Honors (1970); BA, University of Florida (1967); AA, Oxford College of Emory University (1965) **C:** Of Counsel, Kinsey, Vincent, Pyle, P.L., Daytona Beach, FL (2003-Present); Shareholder, Peterson & Myers, Lakeland, FL (2003-2003); President, Harris, Midyette & Darby, P.A., Lakeland, FL (1998-2000); Senior Attorney, Harris, Midyette & Darby, P.A., Lakeland, FL (1998-2000); President, Harris, Midyette, Geary, Darby & Morrell, P.A., Lakeland, FL (1991-1998); Senior Attorney, Harris, Midyette, Geary, Darby & Morrell, P.A., Lakeland, FL (1991-1998); President, Harris & Midyette, P.A., Lakeland, FL (1989-1991); Senior Attorney, Harris & Midyette, P.A., Lakeland, FL (1989-1991); President, Harris, Midyette & Clements P.A., Lakeland, FL (1976-1989); Senior Attorney, Harris, Midyette & Clements P.A., Lakeland, FL (1976-1989); President, Canan & Harris P.A., Lakeland, FL (1974-1976); Associate, Holland & Knight LLP, Lakeland, FL (1973-1974); Associate, Holland & Knight LLP, Lakeland, FL (1970) **CR:** Board of Directors, International Speedway Corporation (1984-Present); Chairman, 10th Circle, Grievance Committee, Lakeland, FL (1986); Unauthorized Practice of Law Committee (1983-1986); Chairman, 10th Circuit Grievance Committee, Lakeland, FL (1983-1986); Vice Chairman, 10th Circle, Grievance Committee, Lakeland, FL (1980-1983); 10th Circle, Grievance Committee, Lakeland, FL (1976-1979); Board Member, Art League of Daytona Beach; Trustee, Art League of Daytona Beach **CIV:** Board of Directors, Campfire (1979-1985); Board of Directors, Program to Aid Drug Abusers, Lakeland, FL (1975-1976); Board of Directors, Automobile Competition Committee of the United States; Judge, International Tribunal & International Court of Appeals, FIA; Motorsports Judge, Court of Appeals, Automobile Competition Committee of the United States **MIL:** Military Judge, Judge Advocate, U.S. Marine Corps Reserve (1970-1973); Served to Captain, U.S. Marine Corps Reserve (1968-1977) **AW:** Honorable Kentucky Colonels (1974); The Key Collection, Phi Beta Kappa, Phi Kappa Phi, Alpha Epsilon Upsilon, Order of the Coif (Law School) **MEM:** Managing Board Member, AMA Pro Racing (2010-2013); Chairman, 10th Judicial Circuit Grievance Committee (1985-1986); 10th Judicial Circuit Grievance Committee (1983-1986); Vice-Chairman, 10th Judicial Circuit Grievance Committee (1979-1980); 10th Judicial Circuit Grievance Committee (1977-1980); Volusia County Bar Association; Attorneys' Title Fund Services, LLC; Founding Member, Grand American Road Racing Association; Order of the Coif; Trustee, Art League of Daytona Beach; Phi Beta Kappa; Phi Kappa Phi; Lakeland Bar Association; The Florida Bar; Volusia Manufacturers Association **BAR:** United States Court of Appeals for the 11th Circuit (1984); United States Court of Military Appeals (1971); Florida (1970); United States District Court Middle District of Florida (1970) **MH:** Albert Nelson Marquis Lifetime Achievement Award (2017) **H:** Art collecting; Fishing; Motor sports **PA:** Republican **BA:** 150 S Palmetto Ave Ste 300, Kinsey, Vincent, Pyle, P.L., Daytona Beach, FL, 32114 **ADD:** 6022 S Williamson Blvd, Port Orange, FL, 32128 **URL:** http://www.kvplaw.com/Christy-chris-F-Harris.shtml

HARRIS, JAN CAPLAN, **T:** Health Facility Administrator **I:** Health, Wellness and Fitness **CN:** University of Alaska Anchorage **DOB:** 01/15/1944 **PB:** Ithaca **SC:** NY/USA **PT:** Frank Caplan; Shirley Ellen (Rickard) Caplan **MS:** Married **SPN:** Sonny G. Harris (3/23/1990) **CH:** Josh; Greg; Ginger; Morgan; John **ED:** DHA, Central Michigan University (2015); MS in Healthcare Administration, University of Colorado (1989); MA in Liberal Studies, Dartmouth College (1974); BSN, Cornell University (1966) **CT:** Nursing Home Administrator, State of Alaska; Fellow, American College of Healthcare Executives **C:** Director, Alaska Center for Rural Health and Health Workforce, University of Alaska Anchorage (2015-Present); Vice Provost, Health Programs, University of Alaska Anchorage (2008-Present); Associate Dean, College of Health and Social Welfare, University of Alaska Anchorage (2005-2008); Director, Health Workforce Development, University of Alaska Anchorage (2003-2005); Senior Health System Specialist, Institute for Circumpolar Health Studies, University of Alaska Anchorage (2001-2003); Senior Health System Specialist, Alaska Center for Rural Health and Health Workforce, University of Alaska Anchorage (2001-2003); Manager, Medicare Operations, PRO-West, Anchorage, AK (1998-2001); Senior Healthcare Quality Improvement Coordinator, PRO-West, Anchorage, AK (1998-2001); Administrator, Health Services, Maniilaq Health Center, Kotzebue, AK (1993-1997); Vice President, Health Services, Maniilaq Health Center, Kotzebue, AK (1993-1997); Director, Planning and Development, Maniilaq Association, Kotzebue, AK (1985-1993); Interim President, Maniilaq Association, Kotzebue, AK (1985-1993); Operations Executive, Maniilaq Association, Kotzebue, AK (1985-1993); Coordinator, Federal Programs, Northwest Arctic School District, Kotzebue, AK (1976-1982); Director, Instruction, Northwest Arctic School District, Kotzebue, AK (1976-1982); Director, Tech. Center, Northwest Arctic School District, Kotzebue, AK (1976-1982) **CR:** Consultant, Harris Consulting (1986-2015); Consultant, Walrus Works, Anchorage, AK (1982-1985) **CIV:** Chair, Anchorage Neighborhood Health Center (2000-2002); Board of Directors, Anchorage Neighborhood Health Center (1999-2005) **AW:** Recipient, Chancellor's Award for Excellence, University of Alaska, Anchorage (2017); Recipient, Meritorious Service Award, Alaska Public Health Association (2009); Recipient, Service Award, American College Healthcare Executives (2009); Recipient, Regents Senior Level Executive Award, American College Healthcare Executives (2006); Service Award, Public Health Service & Indian Health Service **MEM:** President, Alaska Healthcare Executives Network (2001-2003); Fellow, American College Healthcare Executives; American Public Health Association; Alaska Public Health Association **MH:** Albert Nelson Marquis Lifetime Achievement Award (2017) **ADD:** 3409 Corvus Pl, Anchorage, AK, 99504

HARVEY, HAROLD A., **T:** Physician **I:** Medicine & Health Care **CN:** Penn State University College of Medicine **DOB:** 10/24/1944 **SC:** Barbados **MS:** Married **SPN:** Mary L. Goodfellow (4/28/1972) **CH:** William F.; Allison M. **ED:** Fellow, Medical Oncology, Tufts New England Medical Center, Boston, MA (1972-1974); Resident in Internal Medicine, Lemuell Shattuck & Faulkner Hospital, Boston, MA (1970-1972); Intern, Queen Elizabeth Hospital, Bridgetown, Barbados (1969-1970); MB, The University of the West Indies at Mona, Jamaica (1969); BS, The University of the West Indies at Mona, Jamaica (1969) **CT:** Diplomate in Medical Oncology, American Board of Internal Medicine (1973) **C:** Professor of Medicine, Penn State College of Medicine, Hershey, PA (1986-Present); Associate Professor of Medicine, Penn State College of Medicine, Hershey, PA (1980-1986); Assistant Professor of Medicine, Penn State College of Medicine, Hershey, PA (1974-1980) **CIV:** Board Member, American Society of Clinical Oncology (1976-2009); Board Member, American Cancer Society, Inc., Harrisburg, PA **CW:** Contributor, Articles, Professional Journals **MH:** Albert Nelson Marquis Lifetime Achievement Award (2017); Distinguished Humanitarian (2017) **BA:** 500 University Dr C046, Pennsylvania State College of Medicine, Hershey, PA, 17033 **ADD:** 8 Pheasant Dr, Hershey, PA, 17033

HASSAB ELNABY, HASSAN R., **T:** Associate Dean **I:** Education/Educational Services **CN:** The University of Toledo **PT:** Ramadan Ahmed HassabElnaby; Lilah Ahmed Mousa **MS:** Married **SPN:** Amal Said **CH:** Ahmed; Rahgad; Yusuf **ED:** PhD in Accounting, Cairo University (1998) **C:** Associate Professor, University of Toledo (2003-Present); Interim Dean, College of Business and Innovation, University of Toledo (2017-Present); Professor, University of Toledo (2015-Present); Associate Dean, Graduate Studies and Research, College of Business, University of Toledo (July 2017-October 2017); Chairman, Accounting Department, University of Toledo (2015-2017); Assistant Professor, Virginia State University (2000-2003) **CR:** Faculty Representative, Audit Committee Member, University of Toledo; Board of Trustees, University of Toledo; Financial Consultant **CW:** Contributor, Articles, Academic and Professional Journals **AW:** Outstanding Paper Award (2015); Emerald Literati Award (2015); College of Business Innovations Award, University of Toledo (2014); Best Paper Award, Ohio Region, American Accounting Association (2009); Outstanding Research Award, University of Toledo (2008) **BA:** University of Toledo, 2801 W Bancroft St, Toledo, OH, 43606 **ADD:** 2430 White Aspen Rd, Sylvania, OH, 43560

HAVNER, KERRY SHUFORD, **T:** Civil Engineering and Solid Mechanics Educator, Scientist **I:** Education/Educational Services **CN:** North Carolina State University **DOB:** 02/20/1934 **PB:** Huntington **SC:** WV/USA **PT:** Alfred Sidney Havner; Jessie May (Fowler) Havner **MS:** Widowed **SPN:** Roberta Lee Rider (8/28/1954, Deceased) **CH:** Karen Elese Smith; Clark Alan; Kris Sidney **ED:** PhD, Oklahoma State University, Stillwater, OK (1959); MS, Oklahoma State University, Stillwater, OK (1956); BSCE, Oklahoma State University, Stillwater, OK (1955) **CT:** Registered Professor of Engineer, State of Oklahoma **C:** Professor Emeritus, North Carolina State University, Raleigh, NC (1999-Present); Professor, Civil Engineering and Materials Science, North Carolina State University, Raleigh, NC (1982-1999); Professor, Civil Engineering, North Carolina State University, Raleigh, NC (1975-1982); Associate Professor, Civil Engineering, North Carolina State University, Raleigh, NC (1968-1975); Lecturer, Civil Engineering, University of Southern California, Los Angeles, CA (1965-1968); Section Chief, Solid Mechanics Research, Missile/Space Systems Division, McDonnell-Douglas Corporation (Now Boeing), Santa Monica, CA (1963-1968); Senior Stress and Vibration Engineer, Garrett Corporation (Now Honeywell International Inc.), Phoenix, AZ (1962-1963); Instructor to Assistant Professor of Civil Engineering, Oklahoma State University, Stillwater, OK (1957-1962); Stress Analyst, Douglas Aircraft Co., Tulsa, OK (1956) **CR:** Fellow, Engineering Mechanics Institute (2014); Senior Visiting Professor, Department of Applied Mathematics and Theoretical Physics, University of Cambridge (1989); Visiting Fellow, Clare Hall, Cambridge, University of Cambridge (1981); Senior Visiting Professor, Department of Applied Mathematics and Theoretical Physics, University of Cambridge (1981); Fellow, American Society of

Civil Engineers **MIL:** First Lieutenant, U.S. Army Reserve (1962); Second Lieutenant, U.S. Army (1961) **CW:** Author, "Finite Plastic Deformation of Crystalline Solids," Reissue (2008); Author, "Finite Plastic Deformation of Crystalline Solids" (1992); Editorial Advisory Board, International Journal of Plasticity (1986-2010); Contributing Author, "Mechanics of Solids, The Rodney Hill 60th Anniversary Volume" (1982); Board of Editors, Mechanics of Materials (1981-2006); Honorary Science Advisory Board, Mechanics of Materials (1981-2006); Contributor, Articles, Professional Journals; Contributor, Articles, Journal of Applied Mathematics and Physics; Contributor, Articles, Journal of Mechanics and Physics of Solids; Contributor, Articles, Acta Mechanica; Contributor, Articles, Proceedings and Philosophical Transactions of the Royal Society; Contributor, Articles, Philosophical Magazine **AW:** Hall of Fame, College of Engineering, Architecture & Technology, Oklahoma State University (2015); Teacher Link Fellow, North Carolina Science, Mathematics, and Technology Education Center (2003); Melvin R. Lohmann Medal, Oklahoma State University (1994); Research Grantee, National Science Foundation (1994); Research Grantee, National Science Foundation (1991); Research Grantee, National Science Foundation (1987); Outstanding Research Award, North Carolina State University Alumni Association (1987); Research Grantee, National Science Foundation (1983); Research Grantee, National Science Foundation (1981); Research Grantee, National Science Foundation (1978); Research Grantee, National Science Foundation (1976); Research Grantee, National Science Foundation (1974); Research Grantee, National Science Foundation (1971) **MEM:** Leroy Record Fund Committee, Sigma Xi (2008-2010); Education Committee, Sigma Xi (2004-2008); Associate Editor, Mechanics, American Academy of Mechanics (1991-1997); Chairman, ASCE-CERF Awards Committee (1991-1994); Chairman, Engineering Mechanics Advisory Board, Engineering Mechanics Division (1990-1991); Chairman, Engineering Mechanics Division (1987-1988); Secretary, Engineering Mechanics Division (1983-1985); Associate Editor, Journal of Engineering Mechanics (1981-1983); Engineering Mechanics Institute; Life Member, The American Society of Mechanical Engineers **MH:** Albert Nelson Marquis Lifetime Achievement Award (2017) **H:** Theater; Traveling **PA:** Democrat **RE:** Methodist **BA:** PO Box 7908, North Carolina State University, Department of Civil Engineering, Raleigh, NC, 27695

HAYES, DAN A., T: Former Mayor **I:** Government Administration/Government Relations/Government Services **CN:** Town of Tallulah Falls **ED:** Associate Degree, Georgia State University (1980) **C:** Former Mayor, Town of Tallulah Falls, Georgia; Owner, Dixie Eagle Enterprise Incorporated (1994-Present); President, Dixie Eagle Enterprise Incorporated (1994-Present); Chief Executive Officer, Dixie Eagle Enterprise Incorporated (1994-Present); Company Owner, Dan Hayers Enterprises Incorporated (1994-Present); Owner, Hayes Chrysler Dodge, Jeep, Chevrolet Buick Cadillac, GMC (1976-Present) **CIV:** Volunteer, National CASA Association **MEM:** Rabun County, Georgia Historical Society **BA:** PO Box 1, Tallulah Falls, GA, 30573 **URL:** https://www.linkedin.com/in/dan-a-hayes-8b4450125/

HAYNES, R. MICHAEL, T: Founder, Managing Partner **I:** Law and Legal Services **CN:** Law Offices of Michael Haynes **DOB:** 10/03/1940 **PB:** Safford **SC:** AZ/USA **PT:** Rodman Muluehill Haynes; Angeline Edna (Fragale) Haynes **MS:** Married **SPN:** Anne Marie de Almeida (8/15/1972) **CH:** Michelle Chloe **ED:** JD, Rutgers, The State University of New Jersey, With Honors (1968); BA, Rutgers, The State University of New Jersey (1963) **C:** Founder, Managing Partner, Law Offices of R. Michael Haynes (1990-Present); Principal/Shareholder, Semmes, Bowen & Semmes, Professional Corporation (2000-2018); General Counsel, National Association of Small Business Investment Companies (NASBIC) (1986-1990); Chief Counsel, Committee on Small Business & Entrepreneurship, U.S. Senate (1981-1986); Minority Counsel, Committee on Small Business & Entrepreneurship, U.S. Senate (1979-1981); Assistant U.S. Attorney, District of New Jersey, United States District Court (1976-1979); Executive Assistant District Attorney, Office of the Special Narcotics Prosecutor for the City of New York (1974-1976); Assistant District Attorney, The New York County District Attorney's Office (1969-1974); Deputy Chief, Rackets Bureau, The New York County District Attorney's Office (1969-1974); Associate, Cooper, Ostrin, DeVargo & Ackerman (1968-1969) **CR:** Counsel, White House Conference on Small Business (1980); Attorney General's Advisory Institute, U.S. Department of Justice (1978-1979); Adjunct Professor, Long Island University (1975-1976); Instructor, New York State Commission of Investigation (1974-1975) **CIV:** Chairman, Steering Committee, Rutgers Law School Class of 1968 50th Class Reunion (2017-Present); Adviser, Mock Trial Team, Washington International School (1991-1995) **MIL:** New Jersey Army National Guard (1958-1962) **AW:** AV Preeminent Rating in Both Legal Ability and Ethical Standards, The Bar and the Judiciary, Martindale-Hubbell (2015-2018); Honoree, Top Rated Lawyer, DC-Baltimore Edition (2015-2018); Special Achievement Award, Office of the Attorney General, U.S. Department of Justice (1977) **MEM:** Chairman, Small Business Committee, Financial Institutes and Economy Section, Federal Bar Association (1988-1989); Executive Committee, Government Business Forum on Capital Formation, U.S. Securities and Exchange Commission (1988-1989); Small Business Council, The U.S. Chamber of Commerce (1987-1989); Chairman, SBIC Subcommittee, Small Business Committee, ABA (1986-1989) **BAR:** The District of Columbia Bar (1992); United States District Court for the District of Columbia (1992); United States District Court for the District of New Jersey (1977); New Jersey (1977); United States District Court for the Southern District of New York (1973); United States District Court for the Eastern District of New York (1973); United States Court of Appeals for the Second Circuit (1973); Supreme Court of the United States (1973); New York (1969) **MH:** Albert Nelson Marquis Lifetime Achievement Award (2017) **PA:** Republican **RE:** Christian **ADD:** 3509 Idaho Ave NW, Washington, DC, 20016 **URL:** http://www.semmes.com

HECHTMAN, HOWARD R., T: Financial Analyst **I:** Financial Services **CN:** NYC Transit Authority **PB:** New York **SC:** NY/USA **PT:** Charles Hechtman; Pauline (Barmatz) Hechtman **MS:** Single **SPN:** Marsha Louise Garwin (12/19/1976, Divorced 1984) **ED:** MBA in Management, Adelphi University, with Distinction (1972); MS in Physics, Adelphi University (1970); BS, Brooklyn Polytechnic University (1968) **CT:** Advanced Certification in Labor Relations, Cornell University (2000); Certified in Labor Relations, Cornell University (1999) **C:** Assistant and Associate Analyst, New York City Transit Authority (1973-2016); Graduate Teaching Assistant, Physics Computer Center, Adelphi University, Garden City, NY (1970-1972) **CR:** Committee Member, Union; Delegate, Union **MIL:** Captain, New York Guard (NYS DMNA New York Guard) **AW:** Certificate of Merit, Republican National Committee (1990); Patron of the Arts, Society of Theater Arts Resources (1989-1990) **MEM:** Life Director, Polytechnic University Alumni Association (1996-Present); Delegate, Civil Service Technical Guild (1994-Present); Alumni Board of Directors, Polytechnic University Alumni Association (1978-Present); Gold Circle, Veterans of Foreign Wars of the US (Now Veterans of Foreign Wars (VFW)) (2010); Veterans of Foreign Wars of the US (Now Veterans of Foreign Wars (VFW)); Society of American Military Engineers; Polytechnic University Alumni Association **MH:** Albert Nelson Marquis Lifetime Achievement Award (2017) **BA:** 8345 Vietor Ave Apt 6X, Elmhurst, NY, 11373 **ADD:** PO Box 266, New York, NY, 10008 **URL:** https://www.linkedin.com/in/howard-hechtman-17832159

HEICHBERGER, ROBERT L., T: Professor Emeritus **I:** Education/Educational Services **CN:** State University of New York at Fredonia **DOB:** 01/19/1930 **PB:** Boston **SC:** MA/USA **PT:** Norman Allen Heichberger; Louise (Gross) Heichberger **MS:** Married **SPN:** Elaine Boldt (4/14/1956) **CH:** Lisa Elaine; Mark Robert **ED:** EdD, University at Buffalo (1970); EdM, University at Buffalo (1962); BS, Buffalo State University (1951) **CT:** Teacher; School Principal and Supervisor; School Superintendent **C:** Professor Emeritus, State University of New York at Fredonia (2006-Present); Distinguished Professor, Professor of Educational Administration, State University of New York at Fredonia (1977-2006); Executive Assistant to the President, State University of New York at Fredonia (1972-1977); Assistant Dean to Acting Dean of Professional Studies, State University of New York at Fredonia (1964-1972); Principal, East Aurora Public Schools (1951-1964) **CR:** Lecturer; Consultant-in-Field **CIV:** Founder, Graduate Educational Administration and Supervision Program, State University of New York at Fredonia (1992-2006); Director, Graduate Educational Administration and Supervision Program, State University of New York at Fredonia (1992-2006); Vice President, Tri-County Memorial Hospital, Gowanda, NY (1976-1979); Adjunct Faculty, University at Buffalo **MIL:** USMC (Honorable Discharge) **CW:** Author, "The Pleasant Family Abode" (2018); Author, "The Happy Pattern Road" (2017); Author, "We Will Be Friends Forever" (2017); Author, "The Land of Nature" (2015); Author, "Treasured Gilt-Edged Memories" (2014); Co-Author, "The Five Horses and the Friendship Tree" (2014); Author, "The Deer and the Pine Trees" (2013); Author, "Tell Me A Story Grandpa: For Our Grandchildren and For Children Everywhere" (2010); Co-Author, "Five Years on the Cutting Edge" (2008); Author, "Leadership Development: Theory and Practice" (1975); Radio Program Founder, "Focus on Education"; Radio Program Producer, "Focus on Education"; Radio Program Moderator, "Focus on Education"; Columnist, Observer Today; Independent Motivational Speaker **AW:** Recipient, Distinguished Service Award, Fredonia College Foundation (2015); Honoree, Educator of the Year, Phi Delta Kappa International (1979); Recipient, Distinguished Service Award, Phi Delta Kappa International (1975); Eponymous Honoree, Heichberger Family and Scholars Leadership Endowment **MEM:** Vice President, Fredonia Chamber of Commerce (1972-1980); President, Phi Delta Kappa International (1973-1976); National Association of Higher Education; National Association of Elementary School Principals; AASA; College Council, State University of New York at Fredonia; Gowanda Central School District Board of Education; Board Member, Tri-County Memorial Hospital **MH:** Albert Nelson Marquis Lifetime Achievement Award (2017) **RE:** Lutheran **ADD:** 110 Memorial Dr, Gowanda, NY, 14070

HEINLE, JEFFREY STEPHEN, T: Surgeon, Professor **I:** Medicine & Health Care **CN:** Texas Children's Hospital **ED:** Fellowship, Cardiovascular Surgery, Brigham and Women's Hospital (1996); Fellowship, Pediatric Cardiovascular Surgery, Boston Children's Hospital (1995); Residency in Thoracic Surgery, Duke University Medical Center (1994); Residency in Thoracic Surgery, Duke University Medical Center (1993); Internship in General Surgery, University of Pennsylvania Health System (1989); MD, University of Pittsburgh School of Medicine Medical School (1987); BS, Duke University (1982) **CT:** Subspecialty in Congenital Cardiac Surgery, American Board of Thoracic Surgery (2010); American Board of Thoracic Surgery (1997); Texas Board of Medical Examiners (1996); American Board of Surgery (1995); National Board of Examiners (1988) **C:** Pediatric Cardiovascular & Thoracic Surgeon, Children's Hospital of San Antonio, San Antonio, TX (2014-Present); Adult & Pediatric Cardiovascular & Thoracic Surgeon Covenant Children's Hospital, Lubbock, TX (2013-Present); Brad & Melissa Juneau Endowed Chair, Texas Children's Hospital (2012-Present); Associate Professor, Surgery & Pediatrics, Baylor College of Medicine (2011-Present); Associate Chief, Congenital Heart Surgery, Texas Children's Hospital (2009-Present); Associate Director, Residency Program, Texas Children's Hospital (2009-Present); Surgical Director, Heart & Lung Transplant Program, Texas Children's Hospital (2007-Present); Adult Congenital Heart Surgeon St. Luke's Episcopal Hospital (2006-Present); Associate Surgeon, Congenital Heart Surgery, Texas Children's Hospital (2002-Present); Associate Director, ACGME/CHS Fellowship Program, Texas Children's Hospital (2008-2010); Assistant Professor of Surgery, Texas Children's Hospital (2002-2010); Associate Medical Director, Cardiovascular Surgery, Cook Children's Medical Center (1999-2002); Pediatric Cardiovascular Surgeon, Cook Children's Medical Center (1996-2002) **CW:** Contributor, Articles to Professional Journals; Contributor, Chapters to Books **AW:** Named, America's Best Physicians (2017); Recipient, Star Award for Excellence in Patient Care, Baylor College of Medicine (2017); Named, Top Doctors, Castle Connolly Medical Ltd. (2016); Recipient, John A. Hawkins Top Scoring Abstract Award, Congenital Heart Surgeons' Society Annual Meeting (2015); Named, America's Best Physicians (2013); Named, Top Physician, United States News and World Report (2012); Listee, Top Doctors, Castle Connolly (2009); Listee, Top Doctors, Castle Connolly Medical Ltd. (2008); Named, America's Top Surgeons, Consumers' Research Council of America (2008); Listee, Best Doctors in America, Best Doctors, Inc. (2007); Inductee, Alpha Omega Alpha Medical Honorary Society (1987); Recipient, R. J. Behan Award (1987); Recipient, The Stanley J. Snarnoff Fellowship for Research in Cardiovascular Science (1985); Recipient, Medical Student Research Training Program Award (1984); Inductee, Phi Lambda Upsilon (1981) **MEM:** Texas Surgical Society (2014); American Association for Thoracic Surgery (2011); International Society for Heart & Lung Transplantation (2008); Congenital Heart Surgeons Society (2007); International Society for Minimally Invasive Cardiac Surgery (2003); Harris County Medical Society (2002); Society of Thoracic Surgeons (2001); Fellow, American College of Surgeons (2000); Fellow, American Academy of Pediatrics (1999); Texas Pediatric Society (1996); Brigham Surgical Society (1996); Sabiston Surgical Society (1995); Sabiston Surgical Society (1995) **BA:** 6621 Fannin St # WT19345H, Houston, TX, 77030 **ADD:** 6621 Fannin St # WT19345H, Texas Children's Hospital, Houston, TX, 77030 **URL:** https://www.texaschildrens.org/find-a-doctor/jeffrey-s-heinle-md

HEINLE, RICHARD, T: Lawyer **I:** Law and Legal Services **CN:** Pohl & Short, P.A. **DOB:** 05/13/1959 **PB:** New Kensington **SC:** PA/USA **PT:** Robert Alan Heinle; Barbara Jane (Klimeck) Heinle **MS:** Married **SPN:** Sharon Eileen Farrell (October 20, 1990) **CH:** Kelly; Kyra; Casey **ED:** JD, Georgetown University, Cum Laude (1984); AB, University of Chicago, Summa Cum Laude (1981) **C:** Shareholder, Gunster (2015-Present); Partner, Pohl & Short, P.A. (Now Gunster) (2003-2015); Partner, Foley & Lardner LLP (1994-2003); Associate, Foley & Lardner LLP (1989-1993); Associate, Arnstein & Lehr LLP (1984-1989) **CR:** Counsel, BBB Serving Central Florida (1996-2003) **CIV:** Board of Directors, BBB Serving Central Florida (2003-2009) **CW:** Author, Articles, Professional Journals **MEM:** Manufacturers Association of Central Florida (1995-2005); Board of Directors, Florida Chamber of Commerce (1999-2000); The Phi Beta Kappa Society **BAR:** The Florida Bar (1994); Illinois State Bar Association (1984) **H:** Golf; Running **RE:** Roman Catholic **ADD:** 8100 Vineland Oaks Boulevard, Orlando, FL, 32835

HELLER, MARY B., I: Medicine & Health Care

HELLSTROM, KARL ERIK, T: Professor Emeritus **I:** Education/Educational Services **CN:** University of Washington **PB:** Stockholm **SC:** Sweden **MS:** Married **SPN:** Ingegerd Hellstrom **CH:** Katarina Elisabet; Per Erik **ED:** PhD, Karolinska Institute Medical School, Stockholm, Sweden (1964); MD, Karolinska Institute Medical School, Stockholm, Sweden (1964); Candidate of Medicine, Karolinska Institute Medical School, Stockholm, Sweden (1955) **C:** Professor Emeritus, Department of Pathology, School of Medicine, University of Washington, Seattle, WA (2006-Present); Principal Investigator, Pacific Northwest Research Institute, Seattle, WA (1997-2004); Vice President of Immunotherapeutics Drug Discovery, Bristol-Myers Squibb Pharmaceutical Research Institute (1995-1997); Vice President of Oncology Drug Discovery, Bristol-Myers Squibb Pharmaceutical Research Institute (1990-1995); Vice President, Oncogen/Bristol-Myers (1986-1990); Laboratory Director, Oncogen, Seattle, WA (1985-1986); Adjunct Professor of Microbiology and Immunology, School of Medicine, University of Washington, Seattle, WA (1984-2005); Affiliate Professor of Pathology, School of Medicine, University of Washington, Seattle, WA (1984-2005); Senior Scientist, Oncogen, Seattle, WA (1983-1985); Head of Program on Tumor Immunology, Fred Hutchinson Cancer Research Center, Seattle, WA (1975-1983); Professor of Pathology, School of Medicine, University of Washington, Seattle, WA (1969-1983); Associate Professor of Pathology, School of Medicine, University of Washington, Seattle, WA (1966-1969); Investigator in Cell Biology, Swedish Medical Research Council (1964-1966); Assistant Professor, Department of Tumor Biology, Karolinska Institute Medical School, Stockholm, Sweden (1962-1966); Docent in Tumor Biology, Karolinska Institute Medical School, Stockholm, Sweden (1958-1962); Research Associate, Department of Histology, Karolinska Institute Medical School, Stockholm, Sweden (1957); Research Fellow, Department of Histology, Karolinska Institute Medical School, Stockholm, Sweden (1953-1957) **CR:** Scientific Advisory Council, Cancer Research Institute Inc.; Board of Directors, Seattle Genetics, Inc. **CIV:** Reviewer, Netherlands Cancer Foundation; Assessor, Anti-Cancer Council, Victoria, BC, Canada **CW:** Editorial Board, Cancer Immunology and Immunology; Contributor, Articles, 460 Scientific Publications **AW:** Humboldt Award for Senior United States Scientists, Humboldt Stiftung, Bonn, Germany (1980); Knight of the Northern Star, First Class, Swedish Order of Merit (1976); National Award for Cancer Research, American Cancer Society (1974); Pap Award for Outstanding Contribution in Cancer Research, Papanicolaou Cancer Research Institute, Miami, FL (1973); Parke Davis Award in Experimental Pathology (1972); Lucy Wortham James Award, Ewing Society (1971) **MEM:** Clinical Immunology Society; American Association for Clinical Research; American Association for the Advancement of Science; American Association of Immunologists; American Association of Experimental Pathology; American Association for Cancer Research; New York Academy of Sciences; Sigma XI; Alpha Omega Alpha **MH:** Albert Nelson Marquis Lifetime Achievement Award (2017) **H:** Boating; Gardening **ADD:** 3925 NE Surber Drive, Seattle, WA, 98105 **URL:** http://www.pathology.washington.edu/faculty/hellstromk

HELLY, DOROTHY O., T: Historian **I:** Research **DOB:** 02/02/1931 **PB:** Torrington **SC:** CT/USA **PT:** Benjamin Harrison Oxman; Sarah Rose Bernstein **MS:** Married **SPN:** Walter S. Helly (March 4, 1956) **CH:** Miranda Irene **ED:** PhD, Harvard University (1961); AM, Radcliffe College (1953); AB, Magna Cum Laude, Smith College (1952) **C:** Professor Emerita (1999-Present); Professor History, Hunter College, City University of New York (1987-1999); Associate Professor of History, Hunter College, City University of New York (1978-1986); Assistant Professor of History, Hunter College, City University of New York (1969-1977); Instructor, Hunter College, City University of New York (1963-1968) **CR:** Member, Women Writing Women's Lives Seminar, City University of New York Graduate Center (1993-Present); organizer and presenter Dorothy O. Helly Works-in-Progress Lecture (2012-Present); Member, Steering Committee WWWL(1999-Present); Program Chair, 25th Anniversary Conference (2015); Co-Facilitator University-Wide Faculty Development Seminar (1987-1990, 1991-1999); Faculty Member, PhD Program in History and Women's Studies Certification Program, City University of New York (1993-1999); Senior Associate Member, St. Antony's College, Oxford University (1990-1991); Visiting Research Fellow, International Gender Studies Center, Lady Margaret Hall (Formerly Queen Elizabeth House), Oxford University (1989; 1990-1991); Coordinator, Women's Studies Program, Hunter College (1984-1987); Associate Dean, Hunter College (1977-1983); Participant, Numerous Academic Committees and Workshops **CIV:** Board of Directors Feminist Press, City University of New York (1999-2007); Member, Statewide Advisory Council to Commissioner Education on Equal Opportunity for Women State of New York (1985-1994); Vice-Chair, Board of Directors, Institute Research History (1980-1986); Secretary, Board of Directors, Institute Research History (1977-1980) **CW:** Advisory Board, "Women's Studies Quarterly" (2005-Present); Co-Author, "Women's Realities, Women's Choices: An Introduction to Women's Studies" (1983, 1995, 2005, 2014); Editor, "Women's Studies Quarterly" (1985-2004); Founding Associate Editor, "Journal of Women's History" (1988-1998); Editor and Author, "Gendered Domains: Rethinking Public and Private in Women's History" (1992); Author,"Livingstone's Legacy: Horace Waller and Victorian Mythmaking" (1987); Editor and Author, "Family History" (1985); Consultant, Contributor, Numerous Articles, Professional Publications **MEM:** President, Program Committee, Mid-Atlantic Branch, North America Conference on British Studies (1996-

1999); Chair, Program Committee, Mid-Atlantic Branch, North America Conference on British Studies (1994-1996); Fellowships Committee, American Council of Learned Societies (1992-1994); Prescreener Fellowship Program, American Council of Learned Societies (1991-1992); Co-Chair, Program Committee, Fourth International Interdisciplinary Congress on Women (1987-1990); Co-Chair, Program Committee, Seventh Berkshire Conference of Women's History (1984-1987); Fellow, Royal Geographic Society; Member, American Historical Association; National Women's Studies Association; North American Victorian Studies Association; National Committee Curriculum Transformation Consultant; National Council for Research on Women (Now Re:Gender); Phi Beta Kappa **H:** Reading; Scrabble; Free Cell **ADD:** 91 Central Park W., Apartment 15D, New York, NY, 10023

HEMAMI, HOOSHANG, T: Engineering Educator **I:** Education/Educational Services **DOB:** 04/09/1936 **SC:** Iran **PT:** Hossein Hemami; Mohtaram Hodaii Hemami **CH:** Sheila Susann; Tara Lynn **ED:** PhD, The Ohio State University, Columbus, OH (1966); MS in Electrical Engineering, Massachusetts Institute of Technology (1962); Diplomate in Electrical and Mechanical Engineering, University of Tehran (1958) **C:** Professor, The Ohio State University (1966-2014); Senior Research Engineer, National Cash Register Company, Dayton, OH (1963-1964) **AW:** Distinguished Teacher Award, The Ohio State University Branch, Eta Kappa Nu, IEEE (2005-2007, 2009,2014); Fellowship, IEEE (1996); OSU College of Engineering Research Award (1984, 1996) **MEM:** IEEE **MH:** Albert Nelson Marquis Lifetime Achievement Award (2017) **H:** Oil paintings; Classical music; Soccer **ADD:** 6888 Downs St, Worthington, OH, 43085-2404

HENDLEY, COIT , I: Research **PT:** **ED:** PhD in Materials Science, Cornell University (2017); MA in Materials Science and Engineering, Cornell University (2012); BA in Materials Science and Engineering, University of Maryland, College Park **C:** Research Scientist, Department of the Navy (2017-Present) **CIV:** Volunteer, Boy Scouts of America **AW:** Teaching Assistant Award, Cornell University (2015) **MEM:** Eagle Scout, Boy Scouts of America

HENNESSY, DANIEL KRAFT, T: General Counsel, Principal **I:** Law and Legal Services **CN:** Garfield Public/Private LLC **DOB:** 01/04/1941 **PB:** Summit **SC:** NJ/USA **MS:** Married **SPN:** Susan Elizabeth (Bettina) Ware (6/17/1972) **CH:** Mary Elise; Daniel Joseph; Michael Ware; Catherine Anne **ED:** JD, Harvard University, Cum Laude (1970); BS, U.S. Naval Academy, with Highest Honors (1963) **C:** General Counsel Principal, Garfield Public/Private LLC, Dallas, TX (2007-Present); Partner, Garfield Traub Development LLC, Dallas, TX (2007-2016); Partner, Hughes & Luce, Dallas, TX (1973-2006) **CR:** Board of Regents, Ave Maria University (2005-2006) **CIV:** Catholic Pro-life Committee of North Texas (2001-Present); The Highlands School (1986-Present); Member, Board of Directors, Birth Choice Dallas (2011-2016); Chairman, Board of Visitors, College St. John Fisher & Thomas More (2006-2012); Dallas Chapter, Legatus International (2003-2012); Member, Board of Directors, Catholics United for Faith (1982-1999); Member, Board of Advisers, Jesuit College Preparatory School, Dallas, Texas (1975-1988); Greater Dallas Right to Life Educational Foundation (1974-1986); Member, Board of Directors, Dallas-North Texas Region, National Conference of Christians and Jews (Now National Conference for Community Justice) (1976-1983) **MIL:** U.S. Navy Lieutenant (1963-1967)

AW: Honoree, Decorated Knight Constantinian of the Order of St. George; Honoree, Knight of Malta; Honoree, Knight of the Grand Cross of the Equestrian Order of the Holy Sepulchre of Jerusalem **MEM:** Dallas Bar Association; State Bar of Texas; Knights of Columbus **BAR:** State of Texas (1970) **RE:** Roman Catholic **ADD:** 4405 Beverly Dr, Dallas, TX, 75205

HENRIKSON, DONALD MERLE, T: Forensic Pathologist **I:** Medicine & Health Care **CN:** Placer County Coroner's Office **DOB:** 05/02/1947 **PB:** Walla Walla **SC:** WA/USA **PT:** James Christan Henrikson; Carol Jean (DuBois) Henrikson **MS:** Married **SPN:** Eileen Ruth Mikita (10/12/1980) **ED:** MD, University of California, Davis (1981); BA, Harvard University (1969) **CT:** Diplomate, The American Board of Pathology **C:** Pathologist, Coroner's Office, County of Placer, California (2002-Present); Associate Pathologist, Northern California Forensic Pathology Medical Corps (1994-2002); Owner, Foothill Forensic Pathology Medical Group (1989-1994); Associate Pathologist, Foothill Forensic Pathology Medical Group (1987-1988); Associate Pathologist, Laboratory Medicine Consultants, Inc. (1986-1987) **CR:** Medical Staff, Sutter Auburn Faith Hospital, Sutter Health Sacramento Sierra Region (1986-2016); Assistant Clinical Professor, School of Medicine, University of California, Davis (1994-2002); Medical Staff, Sierra Valley District Hospital (1992-1995); Medical Staff, Oroville Hospital (1986-1995); Medical Staff, Sierra Nevada Memorial Hospitals, Dignity Health Sacramento (1986-1994); Fellow, College of American Pathologists **CIV:** Child Death Review Team, Placer County, California (1990-2017); Nevada County Child Death Review Team (1996-2017); Chair, Sacramento County Child Death Review Team (1994-2001) **MIL:** Sergeant, U.S. Army (1969-1971) **MEM:** American Medical Association; American Association for the Advancement of Science; American Academy of Forensic Sciences; American Society for Clinical Pathology **MH:** Albert Nelson Marquis Lifetime Achievement Award (2017) **H:** Hiking; Golf; Piano **ADD:** 11374 Marjon Drive, Nevada City, CA, 95959

HENRY, NICHOLAS L., T: Public Administration Educator **I:** Education/Educational Services **CN:** Georgia Southern University **DOB:** 05/22/1943 **PB:** Seattle **SC:** WA/USA **MS:** Married **SPN:** Muriel Bunney Henry **CH:** Adrienne Richardson Herrig; Miles Houston **ED:** PhD in Political Science, Indiana University (1971); MPA, Indiana University (1970); MA in Political Science, Pennsylvania State University (1967); BA in Government and English, Centre College (1965) **C:** Professor of Political Science, Georgia Southern University, Statesboro, GA (1998-2009); Professor, President, Georgia Southern University, Statesboro, GA (1987-1998); Dean, College of Public Programs, Arizona State University (1980-1987); Director, Center of Public Affairs, Arizona State University (1975-1980); Assistant Professor of Political Science, University of Georgia (1972-1975); Visiting Assistant Professor, University of New Mexico (1971-1972); Instructor, Indiana State University (1967-1969); Assistant to Dean, Instructor of Political Science, College of Arts and Sciences, Indiana State University (1967-1969); Director, Associate Professor, Arizona State University; Professor of Public Affairs, Center for Public Affairs, Arizona State University; Dean and Professor of Public Affairs, College of Public Programs, Arizona State University **CR:** Fellow, National Academy of Public Administration **CIV:** Savannah Downtown Neighborhood Association; Savannah Historic Board of Review; Chair, Savannah/Chatham County Historic Site and Monument Commission

CW: Co-Editor, "Managing Public Programs: Balancing Politics, Administration and Public Needs" (1989); Co-Author, "Reconsidering American Politics" (1985); Author, "Governing the Grassroots; State and Local Politics" (1980); Editor, "Copyright, Congress and Technology: The Public Record" (1980); Editor, "Doing Public Administration: Exercises, Essays and Cases" (1978); Author, Public Policy/Information Technology" (1976); Author, "Copyright/Public Policy" (1975); Author, "Public Administration and Public Affairs" (1975); Author, Public Administration and Public Affairs; Contributor, Journals and Chapters, Scholarly Books **AW:** Laverne Burchfield Award, Public Administration Review; Georgia Trend; Edwin O. Stene Award, American Review of Public Administration; Author of the Year Award, Association for Scientific Journals; Resolution of Commendation, Georgia State Senate; Special Commendation, Governor of Arizona; Centennial Award of Merit, Arizona State University **MEM:** Cosmos Club, Washington, DC; Omicron Delta Kappa; Various Honorary Societies **MH:** Albert Nelson Marquis Lifetime Achievement Award (2017) **ADD:** 407 E Hall Street, Savannah, GA, 31401

HEPTING, JACK B., T: Architect (Retired) **I:** Architecture & Construction **DOB:** 04/14/1941 **PB:** Asheville **SC:** NC/USA **MS:** Single **ED:** Master's Degree, Graduate School of Design, Harvard University (1972); Master's Degree in Architecture, Tulane University (1965); Bachelor's Degree in Architecture, Tulane University (1965); Coursework, The Architectural Association, University of London (1964); Coursework, Phillips Exeter Academy (1959) **CT:** National Architecture Certificate, NCARB; Registered Architect, State of Louisiana; Certified Inspector of Buildings, Commonwealth of Massachusetts (Retired); Former Registered Architect, State of Massachusetts; Former Official, Massachusetts Emergency Management Agency, Commonwealth of Massachusetts; Official's License, NASCAR **C:** Retired (2006); Inspector of Buildings, Sudbury, MA (1990-2006); Zoning Enforcement, Sudbury, MA (1990-2006); Special Constable, Sudbury, MA (1990-2006); Partner, Larson Associates, Inc., Arlington, MA (1986-1990); Senior Associate, The Architects Collaborative Inc., Cambridge, MA (1972-1986); Assistant Professor of Design, College of Architecture and Planning, Ball State University, Munice, IN (1968-1970); Partner, Hepting and Costello - Architects, Munice, IN (1968-1970); Chief Associate, Charles Colbert - Architect/Planner, New Orleans, LA (1965-1968) **CR:** Race Official, NASCAR (2007-2013); Technical Inspector, NASCAR (2007-2013); Tire Specialist, NASCAR (2007-2013 Chief Body Fabricator, NASCAR Busch North Series, Pelham, NH (2002-2006); Crew Member, NASCAR Busch North Series, Pelham, NH (2002-2006); Affiliate, Carolina Motorsports Tech Center, Conover, NC (2002); Car Owner, Mini Sprint Division, Sugar Hill Speedway, Weare, NH (2000-2001); Driver, Mini Sprint Division, Sugar Hill Speedway, Weare, NH (2000-2001); Shop Assistant, Banjo Mathews Racing, Asheville, NC (1960-1961) **AW:** Named to Top 101 Industry Experts, Cambridge Who's Who (2009); Second Place, Track Championship, Sugar Hill Speedway (2001); Fifth Place, Track Championship, Sugar Hill Speedway (2000); Honoree, Executive, Professional and Entrepreneurial Registry, Cambridge Who's Who; Janet Webel Memorial Scholarship, Harvard University; Honoree, Tau Sigma Delta; Henry Adams Fund Award for Excellence in Architecture; Citation Award, "Progressive Architecture Magazine" **H:** Racing; Tennis; Gemstone collecting/cutting/lapidary; Model building; Drumming;

Magic **ADD:** 8361 Timber Crest Drive, Apt 102, Raleigh, NC, 27617 **URL:** http://archive.boston.com/news/local/articles/2005/03/13/design_for_a_dictator/?page=full

HERARD, GILLES A. JR., T: President, Chief Executive Officer **I:** Financial Services **CN:** Capital Corp Merchant Banking **PB:** Montreal **SC:** QC/Canada **ED:** MBA in Administration, Canadian Bankers Institute, Montreal (1975); Fellow, Montreal University; Mastering Skills of International Trade, University of Central Florida **C:** President, Capital Corp Merchant Banking (1984-Present); Chief Executive Officer, Capital Corp Merchant Banking (1984-Present); Junior Credit Officer to Senior Credit Analyst, TD Bank, N.A. (1972); Manufacturers Hanover Corporation, New York **CIV:** Donor, Various Charities; Adviser, Senate Inner Circle; Chairman, President's Business Commission, President Barack Obama; Chairman, President's Business Commission, President George W. Bush **CW:** Contributor, Articles; Contributor, Blogs **AW:** Honoree, Best International Project Financing Firm, International Finance Magazine (2017); Honoree, Gamechanger of the Year, Acquisition Finance Magazine (2017); Honoree, Merchant Bank of the Year, Acquisition Finance Magazine (2017); Recipient, Best of Orlando Award for International Financial Consultants (2013-2017); Honoree, Premier Business Membership, U.S. Association of Accredited Businesses (2015); Recipient, Award in International Corporate Financing, Best of Orlando (2011); Recipient, Best of Orlando Award, International Financial Consultants **H:** Reading books on history; Reading books on religion; Traveling all over the world to meet religious leaders; Classical music; Swimming **BA:** 390 N Orange Ave Ste 1800, Capital Corp Merchant Banking, Orlando, FL, 32801 **URL:** https://www.capitalcorpmerchantbanking.com/

HERBERT, AMANDA KATHRYN, T: Special Education Educator **I:** Education/Educational Services **DOB:** 04/10/1948 **PB:** Cleveland **SC:** OH/USA **PT:** Ralph Earle Herbert; Nina Kathryn (Burkey) Herbert **SPN:** John Davis Reeves (6/26/1971, Divorced 1978) **ED:** MEd, Lynchburg College (1982); BA, Defiance College (1971); Coursework, The College of Wooster (1966-1968) **CT:** Certified Teacher, Commonwealth of Virginia **C:** Member, Wooster Symphony Orchestra, The College of Wooster (2014-Present); Member, Salem Evanelical Lutheran Church (2014-Present); Substitute Teacher, Campbell County Public Schools (2007-2013); Teacher in Elementary and Secondary Special Education, Amherst County Public Schools (1982-2007); Teacher of Fourth through Sixth Grade, District RE3, Platte Valley Schools (1978-1981); Teacher of Fourth Grade, Defiance City Schools (1976-1978); Title I Reading Teacher, Defiance City Schools (1973-1976); Substitute Teacher, Juvenile Detention Center, Lucas County (1972-1973); Elementary School Teacher, Napoleon Area City Schools (1970-1972) **CR:** Teacher, Camp Little Indian (1967-1977) **CIV:** Actor, Academy Center of the Arts, The Lynchburg, Virginia Regional Convention & Visitors Bureau (1983-Present); Singer, Academy Center of the Arts, The Lynchburg, Virginia Regional Convention & Visitors Bureau (1983-Present); Choir Member, Peakland United Methodist Church (1982-Present); Deacon, 1st Presbyterian Church (1973-1978); Elder, 1st Presbyterian Church (1973-1978); Singer, Defiance Community Choir, Definace College (1972-1977); Member, Wayne County Historical Society Community Band; Member, Salem Evangelical Lutheran Church **CW:** Contributor, Books **MEM:** National Education

Association; Virginia Education Association; People to People Citizen Ambassador Program to People's Republic of China; American Federation of Teachers, American Federation of Labor and Congress of Industrial Organizations; Alpha Chi Honor Society **MH:** Albert Nelson Marquis Lifetime Achievement Award (2017) **H:** Travel; Reading; Swimming; Acting; Instrumental performance; Vocal performance **RE:** Methodist **ADD:** 4424 Hunters Chase Ln, Wooster, OH, 44691

HERBST, ARTHUR L., T: Academic, Gynecologic Oncologist **I:** Education/Educational Services **CN:** University of Chicago **DOB:** 09/14/1931 **PB:** New York **SC:** NY/USA **PT:** Jerome Richard; Blanche (Vatz) Herbst **MS:** Married **SPN:** Lee Ginsburg (1958) **CH:** Elizabeth Herbst-Brady; Arthur L., Jr. **ED:** Honorary DSc, Northeast Ohio University (2001); MD, Harvard Medical School, Cum Laude (1959); AB, Harvard College, Magna Cum Laude (1953) **CT:** Diplomate, American Board of Obstetrics and Gynecology **C:** Joseph B. DeLee Distinguished Professor Emeritus, University of Chicago (2003-Present); Joseph B. DeLee Distinguished Service Professor, University of Chicago (1984-2002); Chairman, Department of Obstetrics and Gynecology, Chicago Lying in Hospital (1976-2001); Joseph B. DeLee Professor of Obstetrics and Gynecology, University of Chicago (1976-1983); Instructor, Associate Professor in Obstetrics and Gynecology, Massachusetts General Hospital and Harvard Medical School, Boston, MA (1965-1976); Resident in Obstetrics and Gynecology, Boston Hospital for Women (1962-1965); Resident, Massachusetts General Hospital (1960-1962); Intern, Massachusetts General Hospital, Boston, MA (1959-1960) **CR:** Honorary Fellow, Royal College of Obstetrics and Gynecology, Great Britain (1995) **CW:** Co-Editor, "Comprehensive Gynecology, 4th edition," Harcourt Health Sciences, Philadelphia, PA (2001); Co-Editor, "Yearbook of Obstetrics, Gynecology, and Women's Health," Mosby Year Book, St. Louis, MO (1998); Co-Editor, "Comprehensive Gynecology, 3rd edition," Mosby Year Book, St. Louis, MO (1997); Co-Editor, "Yearbook of Obstetrics, Gynecology, and Women's Health," Mosby Yearbook, Inc., St. Louis, MO (1997); Co-Editor, "Comprehensive Gynecology, 2nd edition," Mosby Yearbook, Inc., St. Louis, MO (1992); Co-Editor, "Comprehensive Gynecology," The C.V. Mosby Company, St. Louis, MO (1987); Co-Editor, "Developmental Effects of Diethylstilbestrol (DES) in Pregnancy," Thieme-Stratton Inc., New York, NY (1981); Contributor, 186 Publications, Professional Journals **AW:** Institute of Medicine of the National Academy of Sciences (1995) **MEM:** Board Member, Institute for the Advancement of Multicultural & Minority Medicine (2008-2012); President, American Gynecological and Obstetrical Society (1997-1998); Director of the Division of Gynecological Oncology, American Board of Obstetrics and Gynecology (1989-1991); Board of Directors, American Board of Obstetrics and Gynecology (1985-1993); American Association of Professors of Gynecology and Obstetrics; Chicago Gynecological Society; Society of Pelvic Surgeons; Society of Gynecologic Oncology; American College of Obstetricians and Gynecologists **MH:** Albert Nelson Marquis Lifetime Achievement Award (2017) **H:** Tennis; Swimming; Reading; Bridge **BA:** University of Chicago Medical Center, 5841 S Maryland Avenue, MC2050, Chicago, IL, 60637-1463 **ADD:** 1040 Lake Shore Drive, Unit 5C, Chicago, IL, 60611

HERMANN, DONALD HAROLD JAMES, T: Law Educator **I:** Education/Educational Services **CN:** DePaul University **DOB:** 04/06/1943 **PB:** Southgate

SC: KY/USA **PT:** Albert Joseph Hermann; Helen Marie (Snow) Hermann **ED:** Master's Degree in Liberal Studies, University of Chicago (2001); MA in Art History, School of the Art Institute of Chicago (1993); PhD, Northwestern University (1981); MA, Northwestern University (1979); LLM, Harvard University (1974); JD, Columbia University (1968); AB, Stanford University (1965) **C:** Professor of Law, DePaul University (1974-Present); Professor of Philosophy, DePaul University (1974-Present); Faculty Member, DePaul University (1972-Present); Director, Health Law Institute, DePaul University (1985-2000); Counsel, DeWolfe, Poynton & Stevens (1984-1989); Lecturer, Department of Philosophy, Northwestern University (1979-1981); Associate Dean, DePaul University (1975-1978); Director of Academic Programs and Interdisciplinary Study, DePaul University (1975-1976); Faculty Member, University of Kentucky, Lexington (1971-1972); Faculty Member, University of Washington, Seattle (1968-1971); Assistant Dean, Columbia University (1967-1968); Legislative Drafting Research Fund, Columbia University (1966-1968); Staff Member, Directorate Development Plans, U.S. Department of Defense (1964-1965) **CR:** Residential Scholar, Christ Church (1999); Visiting Professor, School of Law, Universidad de Puerto Rico (1993); Law and Medicine Fellow, Cleveland Clinic (1990); Bicentennial Fellow of the United States Constitution, The Claremont Colleges (1986); Honoree, Judicial Fellow, U.S. Supreme Court (1983-1984); Visiting Scholar, University of North Dakota (1983); Honoree, National Endowment of the Humanities Fellow, Cornell University (1982); Honoree, Criticism and Theory Fellow, Stanford University (1981); National Endowment of the Humanities Seminar on Property and Rights, Stanford University (1981); Lecturer, National and Kapodistrian University of Athens (1980); Faculty, Fondazione Istituto Superiore Internazionale di Scienze Criminali, Siracusa, Italy (1978-1982); Honoree, Law and Humanities Fellow, Northwestern University (1978-1982); Faculty Member, Summer Seminar in Law and Humanities, University of California, Los Angeles (1978); Center for Law-Focused Education, Chicago, IL (1977-1981); Board of Directors, Criminal Law Consortium, Cook County Government (1977-1980); Lecturer, Christ's College (1977); Visiting Professor, Universidade de Brasilia (1976); Consultant, Administrative Office, Illinois Courts (1975-1990); Board of Directors, Illinois Bar Automated Research Corporation (1975-1981); Lecturer in Law, American Society Foundation (1975-1978); Honoree, Law and Humanities Fellow, University of Chicago (1975-1976); Consultant, Federation of Commerce, Sao Paulo, Brazil (1975); Lecturer, School of Education, Northwestern University (1974-1976); Visiting Professor, Washington University in St. Louis (1974); Participant, Law and Economics Program, University of Rochester (1974); Honoree, Law and Humanities Fellow, Harvard University (1973-1974); Reporter, Illinois Judicial Conference, Illinois Courts (1972-1990); Consultant, Illinois Judicial Conference, Illinois Courts (1972-1990); Board of Directors, Council for Legal Education Opportunity, Ohio Valley Consortium (1972); Honoree, John Noble Fellow, Columbia University (1968); Honoree, International Fellow, National Endowment of the Humanities; Honoree, Medical Ethics Research Group Fellow, University of Illinois **CIV:** Contemporary Arts Council (1999-Present); Board of Visitors, Oriental Institute, University of Chicago (1995-Present); Board of Directors, Howard Brown Health (1994-Present); State's Attorney Task Force on Gay and Lesbian Issues, Cook County Government (1990-Present); Board of Directors, Chicago State University (1982-Present); Board of Directors, Mostly Music (1998-2001);

Director, Institute of Genetics, Law and Ethics, Illinois Masonic Hospital, Advocate Health Care, Downers Grove, IL (1993-2000); Vice President, Institute of Genetics, Law and Ethics, Illinois Masonic Hospital, Advocate Health Care, Downers Grove, IL (1993-2000); Trustee, 860 North Lakeshore Trust, Chicago, IL (1993-1995); Board of Directors, Chicago Area AIDS Task Force (1987-1990); Board of Directors, Horizons Community Services, Sentry Management, Inc. (1985-1988); Board of Directors, Gerber/Hart Library and Archives; Co-Chair, Parity and Inclusion Committee, Illinois HIV-Prevention Community Group, Illinois Department of Public Health; Scholars' Group on Ethics and Medical Research, College of Medicine, University of Illinois **CW:** Editor, "DePaul Journal of Healthcare Law" (1996-Present); Editor, "AIDS Monograph Series" (1987-Present); Editor, "Journal of Health and Hospital Law" (1986-1996) **AW:** Honoree, University Scholar, Northwestern University (1979); Honoree, Dean's Scholar Columbia University (1968); Honoree, George E. Gamble Honors Scholar, Stanford University **MEM:** Board of Directors, Renaissance Society (1995-Present); American Bar Association; Abraham Lincoln Marowitz Chapter, American Inns of Court Foundation; Chicago Council on Global Affairs; Illinois Association of Healthcare Attorneys; American Health Lawyers Association; Delegate, Association of American Law Schools; Section Chairman, Association of American Law Schools; Chairman, Section on Jurisprudence; SALTLAW; International Association of Penal Law; American Society of Writers on Legal Subjects; Society for Phenomenology and Existential Philosophy; Society for Business Ethics; American Philosophical Association; American Judicature Society; International Association for the Philosophy of Law and Social Philosophy; American Society for Political and Legal Philosophy; ASLME; American Law Institute; American Academy of Political and Social Science; Chicago Bar Association; SCA; Evanston History Center; Northwestern Alumni, Northwestern University; Chicago Literary Club; Quadrangle Club; Lawyers Club of Chicago; Arts Club of Chicago; Cliff Dwellers; Tavern Club; University Club of Chicago; Hasty Pudding Institute of 1770; Signet Society **BAR:** U.S. Supreme Court (1974); State of Illinois (1972); State of Kentucky (1971); State of Washington (1969); State of Arizona (1968) **MH:** Albert Nelson Marquis Lifetime Achievement Award (2017) **RE:** Episcopalian **ADD:** 880 North Lake Shore Drive, Apt. 15A, Chicago, IL, 60611

HERRMANN, ROLAND, T: Judge **I:** Law and Legal Services **DOB:** 07/06/1930 **PB:** Carroll **SC:** IA/USA **PT:** Rudolf Henry Herrmann; Louise Ida Herrmann **MS:** Married **SPN:** Fran Mary Herrmann (8/7/1954) **CH:** Mark; Karen; Paul **ED:** JD, Valparaiso University (1957); BA, Valparaiso University, IN (1957) **C:** Retired (1991); Circuit Judge, Woodstock, IL (1975-1991); Private Practice in Law, McHenry, IL (1959-1974) **CR:** Faculty National Judicial College, Reno, NV (1976) **MIL:** Corporal, United States Army (1952-1954) **AW:** Inductee, Worldwide Lifetime Achievement (2017); Featured Listee, Who's Who in America (2008, 2012-2013); Featured Listee, Who's Who in American Law (2007, 2009, 2011) **MEM:** Illinois Judges Association; Illinois State Bar Association; The American Legion (55 Years); Phi Alpha Delta Law Fraternity, International **BAR:** Supreme Court of the United States (1970); United States Court of Appeals for the Seventh Circuit (1966); United States District Court for the Northern District of Illinois (1960); Illinois State Bar Association (1958) **MH:** Albert Nelson Marquis

Lifetime Achievement Award (2017) **H:** Golf; Reading; Gardening; Exercise **PA:** Republican **RE:** Lutheran **ADD:** 635 S Park Centre Ave Apt 1225, Green Valley, AZ, 85614-6276

HERSH, BURTON DAVID, T: Author, Journalist **I:** Writing and Editing **DOB:** 09/18/1933 **PB:** Chicago **SC:** IL/USA **PT:** Maurice Henry Hersh; Florence Nita Hersh **MS:** Married **SPN:** Ellen Eiseman (8/3/1957) **CH:** Leo Joseph; Margery Clara **ED:** BA, Harvard College (1955); Fellow, Florida Studies Program, University of Southern Florida **C:** Consultant, Kennedy File Series, Reelz Network (Now REELZChannel) (2015-2016); Special Consultant, BBC 10-Part Series on J. Edgar Hoover (2008); Consultant, New York Times (Now The New York Times Company), Intelligence Affairs (2007); Faculty of the Sea, M.S. Westerdam (1998); Writers at Work, Major Workshop, Park City, Utah (1995); Consultant, Sundance Playwriters Workshop (1995); Consultant, Sundance Institute, Park City, Utah (1991) **CIV:** Director, New Hampshire Civil Liberties Union (Now ACLU of New Hampshire), Concord, NH (1983-1986); Founding Chairman, Bradford Conservation Committee, NH (1970); Finance Committee, New Hampshire Democratic Party (1970); Public Affairs Forum, St. Petersburg, FL; Contributor, Local Charities, Free Hospital Serving Indigent Community **MIL:** United States Army, Germany (1957-1959) **CW:** Author, "Edward Kennedy: An Intimate Biography," Counterpoint Press (2010); Author, "Trilogy of Novel" (2009); Author, "Bobby and J. Edgar," Carroll and Graf, Basic Books (2007); Author, "The Old Boys: The American Elite and the Origins of the CIA," Tree Farms (2002); Author, "The Nature of the Beast" (2002); Author, "The Shadow President: Ted Kennedy in Opposition," Steerforth Press (1997); Author, "The Old Boys: The American Elite and the Origins of the CIA," Scribner (1992); Author, "The Mellon Family: A Fortune in History," Morrow (1978); Author, "The Education of Edward Kennedy," Morrow (1972); Author, "The Ski People," McGraw Hill (1968); Author, "Comanche Country (The Landau Trilogy Book 3)," Tree Farm Books; Author, "Wet Work (The Landau Trilogy Book 2)," Tree Farm Books; Author, "The Hedge Fund: Where Blood Meets Money (The Landau Trilogy Book 1)," Tree Farm Books; Author, Memoir; Contributor, Articles to Periodicals Including Esquire (Now Hearst Communications), New York Times (Now The New York Times Company), The Washington Post, Huffington Post (Now Oath Inc.), Show, Horizon, Holiday, Venture (Now Venture Magazine), Ski (Now Active Interest Media), Town and Country (Now Hearst Communications, Inc.), Sports Illustrated (Time Inc., Sports Illustrated Group), The Transatlantic Review, Los Angeles Times, Newsday, Punch (Now Punch Ltd.), The Washingtonian (Now Washingtonian Media Inc.) and Newsweek (Now Newsweek LLC) **AW:** Writers Notes Award for Best Fiction, "The Nature of the Beast" (2003); Fortune Club Award (1978); Book Find Club Award (1972); Bread Loaf Fellow, Bread Loaf Writer's Workshop, Middlebury, VT (1964); Story on Martha Foley Distinguished Short Story List (1964); Fulbright Scholar, United States Government (1955-1956); Book of the Month Club Award; First Bowdoin Prize; History and Literature Prize, Harvard **MEM:** Elected, Academy of Senior Professionals at Eckerd College, St. Petersburg, FL (1993-Present); Board of Directors, New England Branch, Association of Former Intelligence Officers (1993-Present); Authors Guild; Writers Guild; American Society of Journalists and Authors; International Society for Comparative Literature and Theatre; PEN International; Phi Beta Kappa (Now The Phi Beta Kappa Society); Council on Foreign Relations; Fellow, Aspen Institute **MH:**

Albert Nelson Marquis Lifetime Achievement Award (2017) **H:** Print Collecting; Skiing; Tennis; Investing **PA:** Democrat **RE:** Jewish **ADD:** 6673 30th St S, Saint Petersburg, FL, 33712

HERZBERGER, EUGENE E., T: Neurosurgeon (Retired) **I:** Medicine & Health Care **DOB:** 06/07/1920 **PB:** Sotchi **SC:** Soviet Union **PT:** Eugene S. Herzberger; Mary P. Herzberger **MS:** Married **CH:** Henry; Monica **ED:** Resident in Neurosurgery, Beilinson Hospital, Tel Aviv, Israel (1949-1953); Resident in Surgery, University Hospital, Cluj, Romania (1947-1948); MD, University of King Ferdinand I, Cluj, Romania (1947); Intern, University Hospital, Cluj, Romania (1946-1947) **CT:** Diplomate, American Board of Neurological Surgery **C:** Attending Neurosurgeon, Mercy Hospital and Finley Hospital, Dubuque, IA (1976-1994); Attending Neurosurgeon, St. Clare Hospital, Monroe, WI (1960-1976); Instructor of Neurosurgery, Medical College of Georgia (1959-1960); Research Assistant, Yale University (1958-1959); Chief Neurosurgeon, Tel Hashomer Government Hospital, Tel Aviv, Israel (1953-1957) **CW:** Contributor, Articles to Medical Journals **MEM:** American Association of Neurological Surgeons; Iowa-Midwest Neurosurgical Society; Congress of Neurological Surgeons; American Academy of Neurology; Iowa State Medical Society **MH:** Albert Nelson Marquis Lifetime Achievement Award (2017) **ADD:** 15649 E El Lago Blvd, Fountain Hills, AZ, 85268

HEUERMANN-NOWIK, PATRICIA, T: Theater Director **I:** Fine Art **DOB:** 08/04/1933 **PB:** Atlanta **SC:** GA **PT:** William Royal Calhoun; Nancy Lee Griffitts **MS:** Widow **SPN:** Vete Nowik **CH:** Beryl Lee Heuermann; William Whitney Heuermann; Lana Amanda Heuermann; Dilwara Fletcher **ED:** Graduate, Curtis Institute of Music (1955) **C:** Director, Opera Theatre, Hofstra University, Hempstead, NY (2000-2006); Instructor, Stage Artistry, American Institute of Musical Studies, Graz, Austria (1994-2001); Founder, Artistic Director, Singers Theatre of New York, New York City, NY (1983-1992); Managing Director, Touring/Educational Program, Opera Carolina, Charlotte, NC (1980-1982); Founder, Artistic Director, Atlanta Opera (1975-1980); Director, Opera Theatre, Clark College (1972-1975); Director, Opera Theatre, Emory University, Atlanta, GA (1968-1975) **CR:** Chair, Artistic Advisory Board, Center for Contemporary Opera (1990-1996); Chair, International Opera Singers Competition (1990-1994) **MEM:** President, National Opera Association (2000-2002); Board of Directors, Opera for Youth (2000-2002); Vice President for Programs, National Opera Association (1998-2000); Board of Directors, New York Singing Teachers Association (1998-1999); Vice President for Resources, National Opera Association (1995-1998); Northeast Regional Governor, National Opera Association (1991-1994); Board Directors, National Opera Association (1991-1995); Opera for Youth; Program Chair National Conference; New York Singing Teachers Association; Opera America **MH:** Albert Nelson Marquis Lifetime Achievement Award (2017) **H:** Grandchildren; Cooking; Reading; Travel **PA:** Democrat **ADD:** 210 Crowfields Drive, Asheville, NC, 28803

HEYDERMAN, ARTHUR, T: Engineer, Civilian Military Employee **I:** Engineering **DOB:** 01/01/1946 **PB:** Brooklyn **SC:** NY/USA **YOP:** 2017-06-14 **PT:** Herbert Robert; Sally (Baron) H. **MS:** Married **SPN:** Renee Linda Pearlman (July 4, 1967) **CH:** Brian Douglas; Deborah Ann; Cathy Ruth **ED:** Postgraduate Work, The Wharton School of the University of Pennsylvania (1993); Postgraduate

Work, Brookings Institute (1992); Postgraduate Work, Stevens Institute of Technology (1982); MS in Applied Mathematics, Brooklyn Polytechnic (1973); BS in Applied Mathematics, Brooklyn Polytechnic (1966) **C:** Rock Island Site Manager, U.S. Army Armament Research, Development and Engineering Center (2006-2007); Associate Director, System Engineering, Analysis and Configuration Management, U.S. Army Armament Research, Development and Engineering Center, Rock Island, IL (2004-2006); Enterprise Manager, U.S. Army Armament Research, Development and Engineering Center (2003-2004); Chief Production and Logistics Engineering Support, U.S. Army Armament Research, Development and Engineering Center (1999-2003); Chief Artillery, System & Armor Division, U.S. Army Armament Research, Development and Engineering Center (1998-1999); Chief of Armor, Engineering, U.S. Army Armament Research, Development and Engineering Center (1996-1998); Chief of Improved Armor Engineering, U.S. Army Armament Research, Development and Engineering Center (1994-1996; Chief of Research Development, Test and Evaluation Integration, U.S. Army Armament Research, Development and Engineering Center (1993-1994); Armaments Research and Development Progressive Manager, U.S. Army Armament Research, Development and Engineering Center (1986-1993); Associate Technical Director, U.S. Army Armament Research, Development and Engineering Center, Picatinny Arsenal (1984-1986); Chief of Production Program Planning, U.S. Army Armament Research, Development and Engineering Center, Picatinny Arsenal, (1984); Assistant Technical Director, U.S. Army Armament Research, Development and Engineering Center, Picatinny Arsenal (1983-1984); Nuclear Weapons Engineer, U.S. Army Armament Research, Development and Engineering Center, Picatinny Arsenal, New Jersey (1971-1983) **CR:** President, OPICON, Bettendorf, IA (1989-2007); Scott Chamber of Commerce (1997); Lieutenant Colonel, Nuclear Weapons Officer U.S. Army Reserve, Fort Sheridan, IL (1989-1993); Adjunct Faculty, U.S. Army Command and General Staff College, Fort Leavenworth, KS (1981-1989); Board of Directors, Secretary, Treasurer, President, Iowa Chapter, American Defense Preparedness Association, Rock Island; National Council, American Defense Preparedness Association; Council Member, Quad-Cities Engineering and Science Council **CIV:** President, Board of Directors, Sussex County Jewish Center, Newton, NJ (1979-1986); Fundraiser, United Jewish Federation, Davenport, IA (1986-1999); Member, Rock Island Arsenal Committee for the Disabled (1987-1993); Quad Cities Coalition for Choice; Director of Intake, Quad City Chapter, American Civil Liberties Union; Member, Platform Committee, Scott County Democratic Central Committee (1994-Present), Veteran Caucus Chair (2011-Present); Member, Iowa First Congressional Democratic Central Committee (1994-2003, 2007); Co-Chair, 1st District Democratic Party (2008-Present); Member Platform Committee, Iowa State Democratic Party; Chair, Bettendorf, IA Democratic Party Presidential Caucuses (1992-Present); Chairman, Quad Cities World War II Commemoration Committee (1995); Quad Cities Vietnam Wall Committee (1997); Quad Cities Korean War Commemoration Committee (2003); Member, Iowa Sesquicentennial Commemoration Committee (1995); Rock Island County, Illinois Chamber of Commerce Speakers Bureau (1996); Board of Directors, Jewish Federation-Quad Cities (1996-1999); Funds Distribution Panelist, United Way of the Quad Cities (1999-2000, 2007); Board of Directors, Iowa Civil Liberties Union (1997-2003,

2007-2009), Secretary, Treasurer (2004-2005); Board of Directors, Iowa Civil Liberties Foundation (1997-2005); Member of the Board of Directors, ACLU Iowa Foundation (2009-Present), Vice President, Executive Committee Member, Board of Directors (2011-Present), President (2012-Present); Member, Scott County Foster Care Citizens Review Board (2000-2001) **MIL:** Major, Lieutenant Colonel, U.S. Army Reserve (1971-1993); Captain, U.S. Army, Vietnam (1968-1971) **CW:** Contributor, Column, Rock Island Argus/Moline Dispatch; Guest Editor, Quad Cities Times; Contributor, Technical Papers on Weapons and Weaponry Assessment to Professional Meetings **AW:** National Gold Medal, National Defense Industrial Association (2005); Award for Lifetime Contributions, National Defense Industrial Association (2005), LTG Lawrence Skibble Award for Lifetime Contribution to National Defense, National Defense Industrial Association (2005); National President's Award, Women in Defense (2003); Civilian of Year Award, Fifth Region, Association of the United States Army (1998); Decorated Bronze Star; Cross of Gallantry (Vietnam); Named to Honorable Order of Saint Barbara, U.S. Army Field Artillery Association **MEM:** American Legion; VFW, Vietnam Veterans of America (Chapter Director 2009-Present); Veterans Administration Voluntary Services Program Representative (2009-Present), American Civil Liberties Union (National Board of Directors (1998-2004); National Association for the Advancement of Colored People (Board of Directors, Quad Cities Chapter (1996-2001), U.S. Army Acquisitions Corps; Army Engineer Association; Association of the United States Army (Vice President, Fort Armstrong Chapter (1993-1996), Acting Chapter President (1996-1997), Vice President, Veterans 2010-Present); Society of American Military Engineers, Scholar (1966), Society of American Military Comptrollers; Federally Employed Women; Planned Parenthood, Member, Community Council; National Honor Society of Scabbard and Blade (Chapter Vice President (1965-1966); National Defense Industrial Association, President, Iowa-Illinois Chapter; Reserve Officers Association; Women in Defense; President, Quad City Chapter, Polytechnic Alumni Association (1989-Present); National Active and Retired Federal Employees Association, Mensa, Intertel **MH:** Albert Nelson Marquis Lifetime Achievement Award (2017) **H:** Horticulture; Art, Bonsai; Cooking; Photography **RE:** Jewish **ADD:** 9825 W. 57th Street, Countryside, IL, 60525

HEYDERMAN, ARTHUR, **I:** Other **PT:** Herbert Robert Heyderman; Sally (Baron) Heyderman **SPN:** Renee Linda Pearlman, (July 4, 1967) **CH:** Brian Douglas; Deborah Ann; Cathy Ruth **ED:** Postgraduate Coursework, Wharton School of Business, University of Pennsylvania (1993); Postgraduate Coursework, Brookings Institute (1992); Postgraduate Coursework, Stevens Institute of Technology (1982); MS in Applied Mathematics, Polytechnic Institute of Brooklyn (1973); BS in Applied Mathematics, Polytechnic Institute of Brooklyn **C:** Rock Island Site Manager, U.S. Army Armaments Research, Development and Engineering Center (2006-2007); Associate Director of System Engineering, Analysis and Configuration Management, U.S. Army Armaments Research, Development and Engineering Center, Rock Island **CR:** President OPICON, Bettendorf, IA (1989-2007); Lieutenant Colonel, Nuclear Weapons Officer, US Army Reserve, Fort Sheridan, IL (1989-1993); Board of Directors, Secretary/Treasurer, President Iowa-Illinois Chapter, American Defense Preparedness Association, Rock Island **CIV:** Fundraiser, United Jewish Federation, Davenport, IA (1986-1999); Member, Rock Island Arsenal

Committee for the Disabled (1987-1993); President, Board of Directors, Sussex County Jewish Center, Newton, NJ (1979-1986); Quad Cities Coalition for Choice **CW:** Contributor column to Rock Island Argus/Moline Dispatch; guest editor Quad Cities Times; contributor tech. papers on weapons and weaponry assessment to professional meetings. **AW:** Decorated Bronze Star; Cross of Gallantry (Vietnam); Honorary Order St. Barbara, U.S. Army Field Artillery Association; Civilian of the Year Award, Fifth Region Association of the U.S. Army (1998); National President's Award **MEM:** VFW; Chapter Director, Vietnam Veterans America (2009-Present); Voluntary Services Program Representative, Veterans Administration (2009-Present); National Board of Directors, ACLU (1998-2004); Board of Directors, Quad Cities Chapter, National Association for the Advancement of Colored People **H:** Horticulture; Art; Bonsai; Cooking; Photography **RE:** Jewish

HICKERSON, GLENN LINDSEY, **I:** Business Management/Business Services **CN:** Hickerson Associates **DOB:** 08/22/1937 **PB:** Burbank **SC:** CA/USA **PT:** Ralph M. Hickerson; Sarah Lawson (Lindsey) Hickerson **SPN:** Jane Fortune Hickerson (8/24/1973) **ED:** MBA, New York University (1960); BA in Business Administration, Claremont McKenna College, California (1959) **C:** President, Hickerson Associates (1998-Present); Chairman, SkyWorks Leasing, LLC (2006-2010); Chairman, Advisory Board, GATX Air Group, San Francisco, CA (1998-2006); President, GATX Air Group, San Francisco, CA (1995-1998); Executive Vice President, GATX Air Group, San Francisco, CA (1993-1995); Managing Director, GPA Asia Pacific, El Segundo, CA (1989-1993); Vice President, Commercial Marketing International, Douglas Aircraft Co., McDonnell Douglas Corporation (1983-1989); Vice President, International Sales, Lockheed California Co. (1981-1983); Director, Marketing International, Lockheed California Co. (1979-1981); Director, Marketing Americas, Lockheed California Co. (1978-1979); Director, Sales, Far East and Australia, Lockheed California Co. (1976-1978); Group Vice President, Marriott Hotels, Inc., Washington D.C. (1972-1976); President, Universal Airlines Co., Detroit, MI (1969-1972); Chairman, Board, Universal Aircraft Service, Inc., Detroit, MI (1969-1972); President, Universal Airlines, Inc., Detroit, MI (1969-1972); Vice President, Treasurer, Universal Airlines Co., Detroit, MI (1968-1969); Vice President, Treasurer, Assistant Secretary, Universal Aircraft Service, Inc., Detroit, MI (1968-1969); Vice President, Treasurer, Assistant Secretary, Universal Airlines, Inc., Detroit, MI (1968-1969); Executive Assistant to President, Universal Airlines, Inc., Detroit, MI (1967-1968); Regional Manager, Customer Financing, Douglas Financial Corp., Long Beach, CA (1967); Secretary, Treasurer, Douglas Financial Corp., Long Beach, CA (1964-1967); Executive Assistant, Douglas Aircraft Co., Santa Monica, CA (1963) **CR:** Executive Vice President, GATX Air Group, San Francisco, CA (1990-1995); Managing Director, GPA Asia Pacific, El Segundo, CA (1989-1990) **MIL:** Lieutenant (Junior Grade), U.S. Coast Guard Reserve (1960-1962) **AW:** H.B. Earhart Foundation Fellow (1962) **MEM:** Golden Eagle; Wings Club; St. Francis Yacht Club; Pacific Union Club; Honorary Trustee, Claremont McKenna College **H:** Sailing **PA:** Independent **RE:** Protestant **ADD:** Suite 115, Suite 115, San Francisco, CA, 94129

HICKMAN, ELIZABETH P., **T:** Placement Director, Career Counselor **I:** Education/Educational Services **CN:** Great Falls College Montana State University **DOB:** 09/30/1922 **PB:** Livingston **SC:** IL/USA **PT:** Louis Podesta; Della (Martin) Podesta

SPN: Franklin Jay Hickman (3/17/1944, Deceased) **CH:** Virginia Hickman Hellstern; Franklin **ED:** EdD, The George Washington University (1979); Postgraduate Coursework, Northeastern University (1967-1968); MA, The George Washington University (1966); Postgraduate Coursework, University of Virginia (1964-1966); Postgraduate Coursework, The University of Chicago (1945); BEd, Eastern Illinois State University, Summa Cum Laude **CT:** Licensed Counselor, State of Virginia **C:** Associate Dean of Counseling and Residence Life, Marymount University, Arlington, VA (1981-1984); Director of Counseling Center, Marymount University, Arlington, VA (1974-1981); Placement Director, Career Counselor, Great Falls College Montana State University, MT (1973-1974); Teacher, English Conversation, Fuchu, Japan (1969-1973); Community Counselor, Division of Massachusetts Employment Security, Newton, MA (1968-1969); Director of College Transfer Guidance, Maymount University, Arlington, VA (1964-1967); Teacher of Public Schools, Naples, Italy (1944-1964); Teacher of Public Schools, Virginia; Teacher of Public Schools, Illinois, Ohio **CR:** Member, Steering Committee, President's Committee on Employment of Handicapped (1974-1995); Special Advisor, International Ranger Camps, Denmark and Switzerland (1974-1981); Lecturer, Far East division University Maryland, Fuchu, Japan (1971-1973); Special Consultant International Quaker School, Werkhoven, Netherlands (1959-1963), Volunteer **CIV:** Volunteer, Office of White House Liaison (1986-Present); Volunteer, Kennedy Center Administration, Washington, D.C. (1984-Present); Volunteer, Judson Manor Library (2014); Volunteer, Arlington Free Clinic (2000-2002); Volunteer, The American National Red Cross (1967-1968); Volunteer, Family Services (1954-1975); Volunteer, WAVES (1943-1944) **AW:** Recipient, President's Volunteer Service Award, Washington, D.C. (2007-Present); Recipient, White House Volunteer Award (2008); Recipient, Distinguished Alumnus Award, Eastern Illinois University (1984); Grantee, Exxon Mobil Foundation; Grantee, Raskob Foundation **MEM:** Brent Society; Rose Society; Potomac Society, The George Washington University; Italian American Society; Marymount University Angels Society; The Women's Committee for the National Symphony Orchestra; Washington Concert Opera; Square Sigma Sigma; Pi Lambda Theta; American League **MH:** Albert Nelson Marquis Lifetime Achievement Award (2017) **H:** Travel; Exercise **RE:** Roman Catholic **ADD:** 1890 E 107th St, Apt 407, Cleveland, OH, 44106

HICKMAN, MAXINE VIOLA, T: President **I:** Business Management/Business Services **CN:** Trinity Foster Family Services of the Bay Area **DOB:** 12/24/1943 **PB:** Louisville **SC:** KY/USA **PT:** Everett Hickman; Ozella (Eichelberger) Hickman **MS:** Divorced **SPN:** William L. Malone (9/5/1965, Divorced 1969) **CH:** Gwendolyn **ED:** Postgraduate Coursework, California Coast University, (1991-Present); PhD, Northfield University (1994); MBA, Northfield University (1994); MS, Nova University (Now Nova Southeastern University) (1991); BA, San Francisco State University (1966) **CT:** License, California Department of Social Services **C:** President, Trinity Foster Family Services of the Bay Area (2010-Present); Chief Executive Officer, Hickman Homes, Inc., San Francisco, CA (1981-2015); Financial Planner, John Hancock Financial Services, San Mateo, CA (1977-1981); Administrator, Pine St. Guest House, San Francisco, CA (1969-1988); Department Manager, Sears Roebuck & Co. (Now Sears Brands, LLC), San Bruno, CA (1966-1977); IBM Professional Mechanic Operator, Wells Fargo Bank, San Francisco, CA (1961-1965) **CR:** Consultant, BeeBe Memorial Endowment Foundation, Oakland, CA (1990-1995); California Association of Children's Home, Sacramento, CA (1989-1995) **CIV:** President, San Francisco Chapter, National Coalition of 100 Black Women (2010-Present); National Association for the Advancement of Colored People, San Francisco, CA **AW:** Woman of the Year, Gamma Nu Chapter, Iota Phi Lambda Sorority, Inc. (1991); Named, Foster Mother of the Year, Children's Home Society of California (1985); Recognition, San Francisco Mayor's Office **MEM:** Former Member, Foster Parents United; Former Member, California Association of Children's Homes (Now California Alliance of Child & Family Services); National Business League, Inc.; Worthy Matron, Order of the Eastern Star, Masons; Alpha Kappa Alpha Sorority, Inc. **MH:** Albert Nelson Marquis Lifetime Achievement Award (2017) **H:** Singing; Walking; Interior design; Real estate; Community service **PA:** Democrat **RE:** Baptist **ADD:** 799 37th Ave, San Francisco, CA, 94121

HIGGINBOTHAM, KENNETH, T: Finance Company Executive **I:** Financial Services **CN:** Independent Retirement Planners, LLC **DOB:** 08/03/1942 **PB:** Philadelphia **SC:** PA/USA **PT:** James V. Higginbotham; Elizabeth R. (Roebus) Higginbotham **MS:** Married **SPN:** Ruth M. Schaffer (4/12/1969) **CH:** Jennifer K.; Scott G. **ED:** MBA, Drexel University (1973); BA, Rutgers, The State University of New Jersey (1971) **C:** Principal, Independent Retirement Planners, LLC, Richboro, PA (2000-Present); Regulation Representative, Lincoln Financial Advisors, Richboro, PA (1994-2000); District Representative, Aid Association for Lutherans, Appleton, WI (1984-1994); EFT Consultant, Control Data Corporation, Minneapolis, MN (1979-1984); Consultant, Corporate Cash Management, First Pennsylvania Bank, N.A., Philadelphia, PA (1977-1979); Financial Analyst, Discount Window, Federal Reserve Bank of Philadelphia (1972-1977); Founder, Owner, Independent Retirement Planners, LLC **CR:** Adjunct Faculty, La Salle University, Philadelphia, PA (1977-2006) **CIV:** Board of Directors, President, Mallard Creek Condominium Associates **MIL:** U.S. Navy (1963-1967) **AW:** Named, Five Star Wealth Manager (2011-2015, 2009) **MEM:** American Association of University Professors; Financial Planning Association; Officer, Bucks County Estate Planning Council; Past President, Bucks County Estate Planning Council; Board Director, Bucks County Estate Planning Council; NTBPA **MH:** Albert Nelson Marquis Lifetime Achievement Award (2017) **ADD:** 21 Holly Hill Rd, Richboro, PA, 18954

HILL, VALERIE CHARLOTTE, T: Nurse **I:** Health, Wellness and Fitness **DOB:** 12/02/1932 **PB:** Shaftsbury **SC:** VT/USA **PT:** William Henry Harrison; Angeline Margaret Estella (Fuller) Hill **MS:** Married **SPN:** Edward Joseph Klanit (Deceased July 1984) **CH:** Joyce Ellen Klanit **ED:** Mount Sinai Hospital School of Nursing (1955) **CT:** New York State Registered Nurse Certification **C:** Teacher, Technology for Creating, Albany, NY (1987-1995); Nurse, Albany Medical Center Hospital (1987-1995); Real Estate Sales Associate, Century-21 Home Towne Properties, Albany, NY (1989-1992); Real Estate Sales Associate, Century 21-Stanley Major Ltd., West Sand Lake, NY (1988); Nurse, Doctors Hospital, New York, NY (1984-1986); Teacher, Technology for Creating, New York, NY (1983-1986); Owner, Manager, Powers Fish Market, Inc., New York, NY (1977-1984); Nurse, Beth Israel Medical Center, New York, NY (1978-1979); Vice President, Chauffeurs Unlimited, New York, NY (1957-1977); Nurse, Rusk Institute, New York, NY (1957-1958); Nurse, Jack Martin Respiratory Center, Mount Sinai Hospital, New York, NY (1955-1957) **CIV:** Organizer, 55th Reunion, Mount Sinai Hospital School of Nursing, New York, NY (2010); Organizer, 50th Year Reunion, Mount Sinai Hospital School of Nursing (2005); Organizer, Class of 1955 Reunion, Mount Sinai Hospital School of Nursing (1956-1975); Member, National Committee to Preserve Social Security and Medicare **CW:** Author, Numerous Poems **AW:** Outstanding Service to the Community Award, Mayor Ed Koch, City of New York (1983) **MEM:** Alumnae Association of the Mount Sinai Hospital School of Nursing, Board of Directors (1968); League of Women Voters **MH:** Albert Nelson Marquis Lifetime Achievement Award (2017) **H:** Reading; Poetry; Home Videos; Piano; Still photography; Painting; Writing **PA:** Democrat **ADD:** 7618 129th Drive S.E., Snohomish, WA, 98290

HILLIARD-BRADLEY, YVONNE, T: Library Director (Retired) **I:** Library Management/Library Services **DOB:** 04/17/1949 **PB:** Jacksonville **SC:** FL/USA **PT:** James Ernest; Dorothy Amy Hilliard **MS:** Married (2/26/1983) **SPN:** Gregory Earl Bradley **CH:** Amanda Loren Bradley **ED:** MLS, Rutgers University (1976) **CT:** Certified Professional Librarian, Commonwealth of Virginia **C:** Retired Library Administrator; Director, Blackwater Regional Library System (2006-2015); Assistant Director for Public Services, Norfolk Public Library, Virginia (1999-2006); Acting Director, Norfolk Public Library, Virginia (2002-2003); From Youth Services Librarian to Extension Services Manager, Norfolk Public Library, Virginia (1976-1999) **CR:** Owner, Earth Offerings (2002-Present) **CIV:** Co-Founder, Financial Officer, Earth Weavers (2007-Present); Assistant Library Director, Norfolk After-School Initiative (2004-Present); Founding Member, Board of Directors, Police Historical Expansion Advisory Board, Norfolk (2002-2005); Founding Member, Regional Healthy Families Coalition, Norfolk (1999-2002); Founding member, Norfolk Healthy Families Coalition (1997-2002); British Isles Folk Dance Group **AW:** Grantee, Tidewater Children's Foundation (2000-2001); Grantee, Norfolk Foundation (1995); Fellow, Virginia State Library (1975-1976) **MEM:** Lifetime Member, Beta Phi Mu; Region Chair, Virginia Library Association (1977-1978); American Library Association; Public Library Association; Virginia Library Association; Mu Phi Epsilon **H:** Singing; Canoeing; Skiing **ADD:** 530 Washington Park, Norfolk, VA, 23517

HIRSCHMAN, ROBERT S., T: Psychologist **I:** Medicine & Health Care **CN:** Clement J. Zablocki Veteran's Affairs Medical Center **DOB:** 02/24/1955 **PB:** Brooklyn **SC:** NY/USA **PT:** Albert Hirschman; Mildred Hirschman **MS:** Married **SPN:** Aura Mollick Hirschman (09/05/1982) **CH:** Zachary; Benjamin; Ilan **ED:** PhD, University of Wisconsin (1985); MEd, University of Pennsylvania (1982); BS, University of Wisconsin (1977) **CT:** Registrant, National Register of Health Service Psychologists; Certified Psychologist, State of Wisconsin **C:** Psychologist, Clement J. Zablocki Veteran's Affairs Medical Center, Milwaukee, WI (2011-Present); Director of Psychology, Jackson Correctional Institution, Wisconsin Department of Corrections (2007-2011); Director of Psychology Services, Lakeview Rehabilitation Center, Waterford, WI (2001-2007); Senior Psychologist, Wisconsin Department of Corrections, Milwaukee, WI (1999-2000); Director of Psychology, Southern Wisconsin Center, Wisconsin Department of Health Services, Union Grove, WI (1997-1998); Director of Clinical Training, Wisconsin School Of Professional Psychology, Milwaukee, WI (1992-1996); Assistant Professor, University of Wisconsin School of Medicine and

Public Health (1985-1991) **CIV:** Member, Board of Trustees, Congregation Beth Israel Ner Tamid, Glendale, WI (1996-2003) **MEM:** The Association for Behavior Analysis International; National Academy of Neuropsychology; American Psychological Association **MH:** Albert Nelson Marquis Lifetime Achievement Award (2017) **H:** Chess; Bicycling; Writing **ADD:** 3343 N 53rd St, Milwaukee, WI, 53216

HIRSCHMANN, FRANZ GOTTFRIED, T: Director of Philanthropy, Entrepreneur, Air Transportation Executive (Retired) **I:** Aviation **CN:** ZPZ Foundation **DOB:** 10/04/1945 **PB:** Kempten **SC:** Germany **PT:** Kurt Rudolf Gottfried; Linda (Krieger) Hirchmann **MS:** Single **SPN:** Cindy Villarica (11/27/1992, Divorced 5/2005) **CH:** Dillon G.; Michael A. **ED:** MBA, Pepperdine University (1981); MA, University of Bonn, Germany (1973); BS, FWG College, Cologne, Germany (1965) **C:** Officer, NWI (2009-Present); Senior Research Analyst, Boeing Research & Technology (2007-Present); Director of Philanthropy, ZPZ Foundation (2018); Part Owner, Ecoloblue (2017); Part Owner, Can Am Heart Pump (2017); Co-Founder's Officer, Perfect Dry (2009); Manager of Business Development and Intellectual Property, Boeing Mathematics & Computing Technologies, Seattle (2004-2006); Manager, All Boeing Space Patents, Boeing, Anaheim, CA (2001-2004); Manager of Business Analysis, Boeing, Anaheim, CA (1999-2001); Manager of Strategic Planning, Hughes Aircraft Company, Canoga Park, CA (1993-1998); Manager of Business Development and Market Research, Hughes Aircraft Company, Canoga Park, CA (1989-1993); Manager of Special Projects, General Dynamics Corporation, Pomona, CA (1988-1989); Manager of Information Services, General Dynamics Corporation, Pomona, CA (1984-1988); Manager of International Marketing, General Dynamics Corporation, Pomona, CA (1983-1984); Marketing Manager, Western U.S. and Pacific Regions, Buehler Inc. (1981-1983); Marketing Manager Western U.S. and South American Regions, United Technologies, Ambac Industries (1978-1980) **CR:** Raising Venture Capital Start-Ups (2008); Owner, Hirschmann Industries Entertainment Co. (1992-2004); Contributor, E.I.A. 10-Year Forecast (1989-2004); Team Leader, E.I.A. 10-Year Forecast (1989-2004) **CIV:** Co-Lead, Environmental Campaigns (1996-Present); Chairman, North Orange County Cub Scouts (2000-2004); Fundraiser, Sierra Club (1996); Volunteer, Los Angeles County Lincoln Club (1981); Communications Member, Boy Scout Troop #553; Co-Founder, Retinitis Pigmentosa Foundation **CW:** Author, "Mandaic Inscription" (1970); Inventor, Deciphering Language Computer **MEM:** Chairman, North Orange County Cub Scouts (2000-Present); Co-Founder's President, Pepperdine University Alumni Seattle (2006-2010); Executive Board, Pepperdine University Alumni Affairs (1994-2004); Leader, Vice Chairman of the Council, Sierra Club (1990-1993); Co-Lead, Environmental Campaigns, North Orange County Cub Scouts **H:** Photography; Hiking; Sailing; Yoga **PA:** Democrat **RE:** Lutheran **ADD:** 14222 110 Ave Ct E, Puyallup, WA, 98374 **URL:** https://ecoloblue.com/

HIRVENSALO, EERO JOHANNES, I: Medicine & Health Care **DOB:** 06/06/1905 **PB:** Helsinki **SC:** Finland **PT:** Erkki Hirvensalo; Kaarina Johanna Hirvensalo **ED:** Coursework, Helsingin Normaalilyseo, Helsinki (1973) **CT:** Certified Orthopedic Surgeon, Helsinki University (1989) **C:** Chairman, Musculoskeletal Division of Surgery, Helsinki University Hospital, Finland (2000) **CR:** President, Finnish Orthopedic Association (2001-2003); Secretary, Finnish Surgical Society (1997-1999)

HODESS, ARTHUR B., T: Cardiologist **I:** Health, Wellness and Fitness **CN:** Brandywine Hospital **DOB:** 01/15/1950 **PB:** New York **SC:** NY/USA **PT:** Samuel Hodess; Dora (Rosenkrantz) Hodess **MS:** Married **SPN:** S. Christina Ellsworth (12/23/1987); Carol Yasuna (12/31/1969, Divorced 5/1985) **CH:** Joshua David; Jeremy Scott; Jonathan; Jason; Jordan **ED:** Resident in Medicine, Hospital of the University of Pennsylvania, Philadelphia, PA (1975-1977); Intern, Hospital of the University of Pennsylvania, Philadelphia (1974-1975); MD, Columbia University College of Physicians and Surgeons (1974); BA, Boston University, Magna Cum Laude (1970) **C:** Member, Board of Trustees, Brandywine Hospital, Coatesville, PA (2009-Present); Chief of Cardiology, Brandywine Hospital, Coatesville, PA (1990-Present); Director of Critical Care, Brandywine Hospital, Coatesville, PA (1989-Present); Attending Cardiologist, Brandywine Hospital, Coatesville, PA (1979-Present); President, Brandywine Valley Cardiology, Thorndale, PA (1991-2010); Chairman, Department of Medicine, Brandywine Hospital, Coatesville, PA (1991-1995); Clinical Associate, Department of Medicine, University of Pennsylvania, Philadelphia, PA (1979-1981); Fellow in Cardiology, Hospital of the University of Pennsylvania, Philadelphia, PA (1977-1979); Instructor of Physiology, Department of Animal Biology, University of Pennsylvania, School of Veterinary Medicine, Philadelphia, PA (1977-1978); Assistant Instructor, Department of Medicine, Hospital of the University of Pennsylvania, Philadelphia, PA (1974-1979) **CIV:** Board of Directors, Chestnut Hollow Homeowners Association, West Chester, PA (1995); Board of Directors, Beth Israel Congregation (1991-1996); Vice President, Chestnut Hollow Homeowners Association, West Chester, PA (1990-1994) **CW:** Contributor, Articles to Professional Journals **MEM:** Board of Directors, Brandywine Hospital (2009); Fellow, Council on Clinical Cardiology, American Heart Association, Inc.; Fellow, American College of Physicians; Fellow, American Society of Angiology; Fellow, American Society of Echocardiography; Fellow, American College of Chest Physicians; American College of Cardiology Foundation; Alpha Omega Alpha, Honor Medical Society; Society of Cardiovascular Computed Tomography; Society of Critical Care Medicine; Cardiac Electrophysiology Society **MH:** Albert Nelson Marquis Lifetime Achievement Award (2017) **H:** Music; Tennis; Fitness training; Theater; Opera **ADD:** 301 McFarland Dr, Downingtown, PA, 19335

HOFFMAN, LINDA M., T: Chemist, Professor Emeritus **I:** Education/Educational Services **CN:** Baruch College **DOB:** 12/18/1939 **PB:** New York **SC:** NY/USA **PT:** Theodore Weiss; Esther Weiss **MS:** Married **SPN:** Robert G. Hoffman (2/2/1958) **CH:** Samuel A. **ED:** Postdoctoral Fellow, Memorial Sloan Kettering Cancer Center, New York, NY (1972-1973); PhD in Organic Chemistry, New York University (1970); MS, New York University (1967); BS in Chemistry, Queens College, The City University of New York (1959) **C:** Professor Emeritus, Baruch College (2008-2018); Professor, Baruch College (1982-2008); Chairman, Department of Natural Sciences, Baruch College (1995-1998); Associate Professor, Baruch College (1979-1982); Assistant Professor, Baruch College (1977-1979); Research Associate, Kingsbrook Jewish Medical Center, NY (1973-1977) **CR:** Reviewer, Grant Proposals, National Institutes of Health **CIV:** Board of Directors, Forest Hills Gardens Corporation (1993-2000); Member, Education Committee, United Nations International School, New York, NY (1981-1984) **CW:** Contributor, Articles, Professional Journals

AW: 112th Precinct Community Council Award (1993); Moore Award, American Association of Neuropathologists (1984); Moore Award, American Association of Neuropathologists (1981); Founder's Day Award, New York University (1971) **MEM:** American Association for the Advancement of Science; American Chemical Society; Sigma Xi; Doctors without Borders; Sloan-Kettering Institute for Cancer Research; World Wildlife Foundation; Alley Cat Rescue **MH:** Albert Nelson Marquis Lifetime Achievement Award (2017) **BA:** One Bernard Baruch Way, Department of Natural Sciences, Baruch College, CUNY, New York, NY, 10010 **ADD:** 116 Whitson St, Forest Hills, NY, 11375

HOFFMAN, RONALD BRUCE, T: Biophysicist, Life Scientist, Consultant **I:** Sciences **DOB:** 03/29/1939 **PB:** Baltimore **SC:** MD/USA **PT:** Marvin Lionel Hoffman; Edna Mildred (Fillman) Hoffman **MS:** Married **SPN:** Carolyn Jean Phillips (7/6/1969) **CH:** Christine B.; David A.; Matthew T. **ED:** PhD in Biophysical Sciences, University of Houston (1974); MA in Psychology, University of Houston (1971); BS in Physics, University of Maryland (1962) **CT:** Certified Human Factors Engineering Professional **C:** President, Hoffman Science & Engineering (2012-Present); Senior Quality Engineer, The University of Texas MD Anderson Cancer Center (2009-2012); President, Hoffman Science & Engineering (2007-2009); Human Factors Engineer, MEI Technologies, Inc. (2005-2007); Discipline Coordinating Scientist, Neurosciences, Wyle Laboratory (Now KBR Inc.) (2004-2005); Senior Research Psychologist, SAIC (2001-2004); Lead Human Factors Engineer, Mitretek Systems (Now Noblis, Inc.) (1996-2001); Senior Human Factors Engineer, The MITRE Corporation (1995-1996); Lead Scientist, The MITRE Corporation (1987-1995); Manager of Biotechnology, Advanced Technologies, Inc. (1985-1987); Senior Project Manager, General Electric (1982-1985); Regional Manager, Technology Inc. (1980-1982); Science Manager, General Electric/Matsco (1977-1980); NRC-NASA Research Associate, National Research Council, National Academy of Sciences (1975-1977); Senior Research Analyst, Northrop Grumman Corporation (1974); Aerospace Engineer, Johnson Space Center, National Aeronautics and Space Administration (1964-1968); Associate Engineer, Douglas Aircraft Company, Inc. (Now Boeing) (1962-1964) **CR:** Government Industry Advisory Group, Man Systems Integrated Standards (1988); Life Science Consultant, Mitsui & Co. (U.S.A.), Inc. (1985-1986); Life Science Consultant, Bio-Systems International (1985-1986); Co-Investigator, Apollo-Soyuz Test Project Experimental Team, National Aeronautics and Space Administration (1974-1975); Research Fellow, Sigma Xi (1974); Associate Fellow, AIAA; Fellow, Aerospace Medical Association **CW:** Author, "One-Half C" (2009) **MEM:** President, Aerospace Human Factors Association, Aerospace Medical Association (2007); President, Potomac Chapter, Human Factors and Ergonomics Society (1997); Deputy Group Director, Space and Missiles Group, AIAA (1993-1996); Chairman, Human Factors Engineering Working Group, AIAA (1991-1996); Chairman, Life Sciences and System Technology Committee, AIAA (1989-1991); U.S. Air Force Space Operations Workshop, AIAA (1984-1985); Society for Neuroscience; Correspondent, International Academy of Astronautics **MH:** Albert Nelson Marquis Lifetime Achievement Award (2017) **H:** Photography; Scuba diving **ADD:** 7340 SE 63rd Avenue, Portland, OR, 97206

HOGAN, JAMES CARROLL JR., T: Public Health Administrator, Research Biologist **I:** Sciences **DOB:** 01/03/1939 **PB:** Milledgeville **SC:** GA/USA **PT:** James C. Hogan, Sr.; Leanna (Johnson) Hogan

MS: Married **SPN:** Izola Stinson (11/29/1959) **CH:** Pamela Renita; Gregory Karl; Jeffrey Darryl **ED:** Postdoctoral Fellowship, Ford Foundation, Marine Biological Laboratories (1980-1981); Postdoctoral Fellow, Department of Biology, Yale University, New Haven, CT (1972-1978); PhD in Biology, Brown University (1972); MS in Biology, University of Atlanta (1968); EdB in Science Education, Albany State University (1961) **C:** Division Director, Biomonitoring Biochemical and Chemical Terrorism, Department of Public Health Services, Hartford, CT (2003-2009); Chief, Director, Biochemistry and Environmental Chemistry, Department of Public Health, Hartford, CT (1997-2003); Chief, Clinical Chemistry and Hematology, Connecticut Department of Health Services, Hartford, CT (1991-1995); Director, Minority Student Affairs, University of Connecticut Health Center, Farmington, CT (1983-1987); Associate Professor, University of Connecticut, Storrs, CT (1978-1983); Assistant Anatomy Professor, Howard University College of Medicine, Washington, DC (1976-1979); Research Associate, Yale School of Medicine, New Haven, CT (1973-1976); Project Manager, Center for Disease Control and Prevention; Health Laboratory Section Manager, Environmental and Biochemistry Section, Division of Laboratory Services, Connecticut Department of Public Health **CR:** Connecticut Commission on Community Service, Office of Higher Education, New Haven, CT (1994-Present); Board of Directors, A Better Chance, Glastonbury, CT (1990-Present); Board of Selectmen, Community Services Commission, Town of North Haven (1989-Present); Board of Directors, Gateway Community College (1989-Present); Visiting Faculty Fellow, Yale University (1984-Present); Fellow, Josiah Macy, Jr. Foundation, Marine Biological Laboratories (1978-1980); Advisory Committee Member, Math Connections, Hartford Alliance for Science and Mathematics Education; Fellow, Ford Foundation; Fellow, University of Connecticut Research Foundation **CIV:** Board of Education, North Haven Public Schools (1993-Present); Active Member, Democratic Town Committee, North Haven, CT (1989-Present); Founder, President, North Haven Association of Black Citizens, Inc. (1988-Present); Chapter President, National Technical Association (1990); Coordinator, Martin Luther King Junior Annual Luncheon, Department of Public Health, Connecticut (1988-2009); Committee Chairman, Greater New Haven Chapter, NAACP; Founder, Black Health Professionals Network; President, Black Health Professionals Network; Chairman, Personal Committee, North Haven Board of Education; Chairman, North Haven Board of Education **CW:** Contributor, Articles, Professional Journals; Author, "Lead Poisoning in Young Children: A National Tragedy"; Presenter, Conferences **AW:** Frederick J. Adams Award, Department of Public Health, State of Connecticut (2001); Certificate of Recognition, Department of Public Health, State of Connecticut (2001); Eponym, Annual Dr. James C. Hogan Award, Department of Public Health, State of Connecticut; Honoree, 2000 Outstanding Scientists of the 20th Century, International Biographical Centre, Melrose Press Ltd. **MEM:** President, Men's Ministry, Immanuel Baptist (1998-Present); Lifetime Member, NAACP; American Public Health Association; Connecticut Public Health Association; Connecticut Academy of Science and Engineering, Incorporated; American Chemical Society; President, Connecticut Chapter, American Society for Cell Biology; Board of Directors, Connecticut Chapter, National Technical Association; New York Academy of Sciences; Planetary Society; Lifetime Member, Morehouse Alumni Association; Sigma Xi; Omega Psi Phi Fraternity Inc.; Chairman, Board of Directors, AIDS Interfaith Network; Minority Health Advisory Council Committee, Hos-

pital of St. Raphael; Founder, Academy of Math and Science, Immanuel Baptist **MH:** Albert Nelson Marquis Lifetime Achievement Award (2017) **RE:** Baptist **ADD:** PO Box 146, North Haven, GA, 06473 **URL:** http://www.drjameshogan.com

HOLBROOK-ROBINSON, MARLA, T: Registered Nurse **I:** Medicine & Health Care **DOB:** 09/15/1934 **PB:** Grass Valley **SC:** CA/USA **PT:** Hilmer Harrison Holbrook; Mable Lucille (Kline) Holbrook **MS:** Married **SPN:** Donald Wilson Robinson, Jr. (6/25/1961) **CH:** Jeffrey Brian; Jennifer Lee Villa **ED:** BSN, California State University, Chico, CA (1956); PHN Degree, California State University, Chico, CA (1956) **CT:** Registered Nurse; Certified Audiometer; Certified Teacher, K-8 Required Health Programs, State of California **C:** Community Care Nurse, Founder, Care Choice Health Systems (1994); School Nurse, All Saints' Day School, Carmel, CA (1969-1979); School Nurse, Public Health Nurse, San Francisco City and County (1960-1962); Supervisor Clinic, St. Luke's Hospital, San Francisco, CA (1959-1960); Nurse, UCSF Medical Center (1956-1959) **CIV:** The Carmel Foundation (2003) **AW:** Special Public Health Certification; 65-Year Member, Magnolia Chapter, Order of the Eastern Star **MEM:** President, Quota International of the Monterey Peninsula (1993); President, Jaycettes (1967); AAUW; Long Term Director, Nursing, Salinas, CA; Magnolia Chapter, Order of the Eastern Star; Delta Sigma Theta Sorority, Inc. **MH:** Albert Nelson Marquis Lifetime Achievement Award (2017); Distinguished Humanitarian (2017) **H:** Growing orchids; Crafts; Reading; Travel **RE:** Episcopalian **ADD:** 3739 Raymond Way, Carmel, CA, 93923

HOLDAWAY, CHARLES R., T: Chief Executive Officer **I:** Business Management/Business Services **CN:** Holatron Systems LLC **ED:** Coursework in Electrical Engineering, Massachusetts Institute of Technology (1962-1966) **CT:** Licensed Ham Radio Operator **C:** Chief Executive Officer, Holatron Systems, LLC (1999-Present); Principal Electronic Engineer, BAE Systems, Honolulu, HI (2000-2006) **CIV:** Member, Chamber of Commerce **CW:** Co-Author, "Amperometric Detection of Bacillus anthracis spores: A Portable, Low-Cost Approach to the ELISA" **AW:** Contributor Certificate, ASEPO, Inc (2017) **MEM:** ASEPO, Inc; Western Pyrotechnics Association; Pyrotechnics Guild International **BA:** 833 Ilaniwai St Ste 3, Holatron Systems LLC, Honolulu, HI, 96813 **URL:** https://www.linkedin.com/in/charlie-holdaway-a192507/

HOLDEN, KENTON, T: Professor of Neurology & Pediatrics **I:** Education/Educational Services **CN:** Medical University of South Carolina **DOB:** 04/28/1943 **PB:** Baltimore **SC:** MD/USA **PT:** Alfred Charles Holden; Alice Anita (Posadski) Holden **MS:** Married **SPN:** Patricia E. Chisholm (8/14/1965) **CH:** Kenton R., Jr.; W. Blake **ED:** Senior Assistant Resident, Department of Pediatrics, Johns Hopkins Hospital (1972-1973); Clinical Associate Fellow, Section on Child Neurology, National Institute of Neurological Diseases and Stroke, National Institutes of Health (1970-1972); Assistant Resident, Department of Pediatrics, Johns Hopkins Hospital (1969-1970); Intern, Department of Pediatrics, Johns Hopkins Hospital (1968-1969); MD, Medical College of Virginia, Richmond, VA (1968); BA, University of Virginia (1964) **CT:** Certified in CPR, Charleston Office, Greenwood Genetic Center (2011); Diplomate, Joint Subspecialty Board in Neurodevelopmental Disabilities, American Board of Pediatrics and American Board of Psychiatry and Neurology, Inc. (2011); Diplomate, Joint Subspecialty Board in Neurodevelopmental Disabilities, American Board of Pediatrics and American Board of Psychiatry

and Neurology, Inc. (2001); Diplomate, South Carolina Board of Medical Examiners (1990); Diplomate, Section on Neurology, American Board of Pediatrics (1978); Diplomate, American Board of Pediatrics (1973); Diplomate, Maryland State Board of Medical Examiners (Now Maryland Board of Physicians) (1969); Diplomate, National Board of Medical Examiners (1969); Diplomate, Virginia Board of Medicine (1968) **C:** Honorary Staff Consultant in Pediatric Neurology, Roper Hospital, Inc., Roper St. Francis Healthcare (2015-Present); Honorary Staff Consultant in Pediatric Neurology, Bon Secours St. Francis Hospital, Roper St. Francis Healthcare (2015-Present); Active Affiliate Staff, Department of Neurology, Medical University of South Carolina (2014-Present); Active Affiliate Staff, Department of Pediatrics, Medical University of South Carolina (2014-Present); Clinical Research Faculty, Comprehensive Epilepsy Program, Medical University of South Carolina College of Medicine (2009-Present); Director of Medical Student Clinical Neurogenetics Elective, Medical University of South Carolina (2006-Present); Visiting Professor of Child Neurology and Epilepsy, The National Medical School, Tegucigalpa, Honduras (2001-Present); Senior Clinical Research Neurologist, Greenwood Genetic Center (1999-Present); Chief, Clinical Neuroscience Section, Greenwood Genetic Center (1999-Present); Professor, Department of Pediatrics, Medical University of South Carolina (1996-Present); Professor, Department of Neurosciences, Medical University of South Carolina (1996-Present); Co-director, Topics in Global Health Introductory Course, Center for Global Health Instructor, Medical University of South Carolina (2012-2016); Staff Consultant in Pediatric Neurology, Roper St. Francis Mount Pleasant Hospital, Roper St. Francis Healthcare (2012-2015); Adjunct Professor of Global Health, Duke Global Health Institute, Duke University (2010-2011); Director of Medical Student Clinical Neurosciences Education, Department of Neurosciences Medical University of South Carolina (2002-2014); Chief Executive Officer, Pediatric Neurology Consultants, LLC (1997-1999); Associate Staff Physician in Pediatric Neurology, Roper Hospital, Inc., Roper St. Francis Healthcare (1991-2014); Staff Consultant in Pediatric Neurology, Bon Secours St. Francis Hospital, Roper St. Francis Healthcare (1990-2014); Staff Physician in Pediatric Neurology, Charleston Memorial Hospital, CAMC Health System, Inc (1990-2014); Clinical Director, Division of Pediatric Neurology, Medical University of South Carolina (1990-1998); Associate Professor, Department of Pediatrics, Medical University of South Carolina (1990-1996); Associate Professor, Department of Neurology, Medical University of South Carolina (1990-1996); Attending Physician, Pediatric Neurology Clinic, Johns Hopkins Hospital (1985-1990); Assistant Professor, Department of Pediatrics, Johns Hopkins Hospital (1976-1990); Assistant Professor, Department of Neurology, Johns Hopkins Hospital (1976-1990); Staff Consultant, Sinai Hospital (1975-1985); Clinic Director, Pediatric Neurology, Sinai Hospital (1975-1985); Nursery Staff Physician, Greater Baltimore Medical Center (1974-1990); Staff Consultant to Karin B. Nelson, MD, Perinatal Research Branch, National Institute of Neurological Diseases and Stroke, National Institutes of Health (1973-1990); Pediatrician, Private Practice, Baltimore, MD (1973-1990); Staff Physician, Department of Pediatrics, Sinai Hospital (1973-1990); Assistant Director, Pediatric Seizure Clinic, Johns Hopkins Hospital (1973-1985); Staff Physician, Department of Pediatrics, John F. Kennedy Institute (1973-1983); Instructor, Department of Pediatrics, Johns

Hopkins Hospital (1973-1976); Hospital Physician, Department of Pediatrics, Union Memorial Hospital, Medstar Health (1970-1972) **CR:** Fellow, American Academy of Pediatrics (1974-Present) **MIL:** Senior Assistant Surgeon, U.S. Public Health Service (1972-2007); Surgeon, U.S. Public Health Service (1970-1972) **CW:** Editorial Board Member, "Journal of Child Neurology" (2003-2017); Contributor, Over 200 Articles, Professional Publications; Ad Hoc Reviewer, Various Professional Journals; Editorial Consultant, Television Programs **AW:** Honoree, Humanism in Medicine Lecturer, Arnold P. Gold Foundation (2015); Global Health Grant, Medical University of South Carolina (2015); Arnold P. Gold Foundation Humanism in Medicine Award (2014); Distinguished Service Award, Colegio Medico de Honduras (2014); Community Service Award, Clinica Samaritana (2014); Honoree, Teacher of the Month, Medical University of South Carolina (2011); Honduran Medical Journal Annual Award (2008); Faculty Teaching Award, Medicos Residentes del Post-Grado de Neurologia, Hospital Escuela Materno–Infantil (2008); Article Award, London Dysmorphology & Neurogenetics Databases of Genetic Syndromes (2008); Honoree, America's Top Pediatricians, Consumers' Research Council of America (2003-2012); Honoree, Keynote Speaker, Second International Congress of Neurology, La Sociedad Hondurena de Neurologia, Tegucigalpa, Honduras (2001); Fritz E. Dreifuss International Travel Award, Epilepsy Foundation (2000); International Visiting Professor Award, Child Neurology Society (2000); Honoree, Best Doctors in America in Pediatric Neurology, Woodward-White, Inc./Best Doctors, Inc. (1999-2012); Humanism in Medicine Award, Medical University of South Carolina (1999); Honoree, Best Doctors in America in General Pediatrics, Woodward-White, Inc. (1999); Golden Apple Teaching Award, Medical College of Virginia (1998); Honoree, Presidential Marshal, Graduation Exercises, Medical University of South Carolina (1996); Honoree, Best Doctors in America, Southeast Region, Woodward-White, Inc. (1996); Golden Apple Teaching Award, Medical College of Virginia (1995); Nominee, National Distinguished Teachers Award, American Osteopathic Association (1995); Honoree, Educator/Mentor of the Year, Medical University of South Carolina (1995); Honoree, Pearl Lecturer, Senior Class, College of Medicine, Medical University of South Carolina (1994-1995); Honoree, Reader, Senior Class Oath Ceremony, Medical University of South Carolina (1993-1995); Nominee, Golden Apple Teaching Award, Medical College of Virginia (1993-1994); Lee Sutton Award in Pediatrics, Medical College of Virginia (1968); Lange Book Award in Obstetrics and Gynecology, Medical College of Virginia (1968); Mosby Book Award in Surgery, Medical College of Virginia (1968); SAMA-Alpha Omega Alpha Research Award, Medical College of Virginia (1968); SAMA-Research Award of Excellence, Annual Scientific Research Forum, Medical College of Virginia (1968); Inductee, Medical College of Virginia Chapter, Alpha Omega Alpha Honor Medical Society (1967); Inductee, Medical College of Virginia Chapter, Sigma Zeta National Science & Mathematics Honor Society (1967); Inductee, University of Virginia Chapter, Omicron Delta Kappa (1963) **MEM:** International Affairs Committee, Child Neurology Society (2009-Present); Southeastern Regional Genetics Group, Inc. (2008-Present); Developmental Neurogenetics Interest Group, Child Neurology Society (2002-Present); International Child Neurology Association (2002-Present); Child Neurology Society (1998-Present); South Carolina Chapter, American Academy of Pediatrics

(1990-Present); American Epilepsy Society (1978-Present); Section on Neurology, American Academy of Pediatrics (1974-Present); Johns Hopkins Medical and Surgical Association (1973-Present); Education Training Committee, Child Neurology Society (2009-2013); Charleston County Medical Society (2008-2016); Greenwood County Medical Society (2006-2008); International Affairs Committee, Child Neurology Society (2000-2006); Teaching Conference Symposium, Apple Tree Society (1994); Southern Medical Association (1991-2009); Maryland Neurological Society (1978-1990); Baltimore County Medical Association (1978-1990); Baltimore Neurological Society (1976-1978); Baltimore City Medical Society (1975-1978); Bradley Pediatric Society, University of Maryland (1974-2012); Maryland Chapter, American Academy of Pediatrics (1974-1990); President, Medical College of Virginia Chapter, Alpha Omega Alpha Honor Medical Society (1967-1968) **MH:** Albert Nelson Marquis Lifetime Achievement Award (2017) **H:** Missionary work; Youth assistance **BA:** PO Box 1047, Mount Pleasant, SC, 29465

HOLDER, ANTHONY W., T: Chief Executive Officer **I:** Financial Services **CN:** C&H Financial Services, Inc. **ED:** Diploma, The University of Illinois at Chicago; Diploma, Robert Morris Business College, Robert Morris University **C:** Founder, C&H Financial Services, Inc. (2008-Present); Chief Executive Officer, C&H Financial Services, Inc. (2008-Present); Chairman, Money Movers of America (2004-Present); Chief Executive Officer, Money Movers of America (2004-Present); President, Process Pink Payments, LLC (2010-2013); Divisional President, Unified Payments, Lodi, CA (2010-2013); National Sales Director, 1st National Processing (1998-2002) **CIV:** Affiliate, Kiwanis of Greater Lodi, Kiwanis International (2017-Present); Donor, Rotary Club of Chicago, Rotary International (2003) **AW:** Honoree, Number One Company in the State of Illinois, Inc. Magazine, Mansueto Ventures (2016); Honoree, Number One Company in Chicago, Inc. Magazine, Mansueto Ventures (2016); Honoree, Number Three Top Financial Services Company in the U.S., Inc. Magazine, Mansueto Ventures (2016); Honoree, One of the Fastest Growing Privately-Held Companies in America, Inc. Magazine, Mansueto Ventures (2015-2016); Paul Harris Fellowship, Rotary International (2013) **MEM:** Affiliate, Entrepreneurs' Organization, Sacramento, CA (2018-Present); Electronic Transactions Association; MidWest Acquirers Association; Western States Acquirers Association; Northeast Acquirers Association; Southeast Acquirers Association **MH:** Albert Nelson Marquis Lifetime Achievement Award (2017) **BA:** 1 Westbrook Corporate Ctr Ste 300, C&H Financial Services, Inc., Westchester, IL, 60154 **ADD:** 1949 W Kettleman Ln Ste 100, Lodi, CA, 95242 **URL:** https://www.linkedin.com/in/anthony-w-holder-1492487/

HOLGATE, STEPHEN TOWNLEY, T: Medical Research Council Clinical Professor **I:** Education/Educational Services **CN:** University of Southampton **DOB:** 05/02/1947 **PB:** Heywood **SC:** England **PT:** William Townley Holgate; Helen Margaret (Lancaster) Holgate **MS:** Married **SPN:** Elizabeth Karen Malkinson (10/28/1972) **CH:** Matthew; Edmund; Katharine; Michael **ED:** Honorary DSc, University of Exeter (2015); Honorary MD, Università degli Studi di Napoli Federico II (2012); Honorary MD, Jagiellonian University (1998); Honorary MD, University of Ferrara (1997); DSc, University of Southampton (1991); MD, University of London (1979); MB, University of London (1971); BChir, University of London (1971); BSc in Biochemistry, University

of London (1968) **CT:** Certified in Magnetic Resonance Cholangiopancreatography, URoyal College of Physicians, United Kingdom (1991) **C:** Medical Research Council Clinical Professor, University of Southampton (1987-Present); Senior Lecturer, Southampton General Hospital (1980-1987); Professor, University of Southampton (1980-1987); Southampton General Hospital (1980-1987); Lecturer, Southampton General Hospital (1975-1980); Honorary Senior Registrar, Southampton General Hospital (1975-1980); Registrar in General and Respiratory Medicine, Southampton & Salisbury Hospitals (1974-1975); Senior House Physician, National Hospital Nervous Disease & Brompton Hospitals (1972-1974); House Physician and Surgeon, Charing Cross Hospital, Imperial College Healthcare NHS Trust (1971-1972) **CR:** Chairman, Expert Panel on Air Quality Standards, Department for Environment Food & Rural Affairs (2003-Present); Member, Royal Commission on Environmental Pollution (2002-Present); Chairman, Science in Health Group, United Kingdom Science Council (1998-Present); Visiting Professor, School of Medicine and Public Health, University of Wisconsin (2016); The K. Frank Austen Visiting Professor, Women and Brigham Hospital (2014); Jeffrey Drazen Visiting Professor, Harvard Medical School (2010); Visiting Professor, Bloomberg School of Public Health, The Johns Hopkins University (2007); Visiting Professor, The Ohio State University (2007); Visiting Professor, Harvard University (1997, 2001, 2007); Visiting Professor, University of British Columbia (2005); Visiting Professor, University of California San Francisco (2005); Visiting Professor, University of Michigan (2004); Visiting Professor, Wake Forest University (2004); Visiting Professor, University of Cincinnati (2002); Visiting Professor, Thomas Jefferson Medical College (Now Sidney Kimmel Medical College) (2001); Chairman, Committee on the Medical Effects of Air Pollutants, Department of Health (1992-2001); Visiting Professor, University of Rochester (1998); Visiting Professor, Vanderbilt University (1996); Visiting Professor, Ontario Thoracic Society (1995); Member, System Board, Medical Research Council (1991-1995); Postdoctoral Research Fellow, Harvard Medical School (1978-1980); Co-founder, Synairgen; Lecturer in Field **CIV:** Chairman, Asthma, Allergy and Inflammation Research Trust, Southampton, England (1990, 2003); Trustee, Cancer Research UK; Trustee, Kennedy Trust; Trustee, Great Ormond Street Hospital Children's Charity; Chair, NC3Rs; Governing Board, Nuffield Council on Bioethics; Special Advisor, Air Quality, RCP; Chair, Various Research Committees and Councils; Member, National Environment Research Council **CW:** Chair, "Every Breath We Take: The Lifelong Impact of Air Pollution," Working Party on Air Pollution, Royal College of Physicians (2014); Co-chair, "Forward Look - Personalised Medicine," European Science Foundation (2010); Co-editor, "Asthma and Rhinitis" (2001); Co-editor, "Allergy: Principles and Practice" (2004); Associate Editor, "Clinical Science" (2002); Co-editor, "Clinical and Experimental Allergy" (1984-2009); Chair, "Allergy: The Unmet Need," Working Party on Allergy; Section Editor, Environment and Health, Faculty of 1000; Editorial Board Member, "Personalized Medicine," "Issues in Environmental Science and Technology," "BMC Proceedings," "American Journal of Respiratory Cell Molecular Biology," "Current Allergy & Asthma Reports," "Lancet Respiratory Medicine," and "European Respiratory Journal"; European Associate Editor, "World Allergy Journal"; Editor, "Allergy"; Contributor, 1025 Peer-reviewed Publications; Editor, 62 Books; Contributor, 472 Book Chapters and Reviews; Contributor, 59 Editorials; Contributor, 106 Official and Government Reports **AW:** William Busse Distinguished Lectureship,

American Academy of Allergy and Immunology (2016); Visiting Professorship, Universities of Mc-Master, Western Ontario and Toronto, Canada (2016); J. Allyn Taylor International Prize in Medicine, Robarts Research Institute, Canada (2016); The David Barker Lifetime Achievement Award, Southampton University Foundation Hospital Trust (2014); British Thoracic Society Medal (2013); Honoree, Included in Top 400 Most Highly Influential Biomedical Researchers 1996-2011 (2013); Miegunyah Distinguished Visiting Fellowship, University of Melbourne, Australia (2012); Recognition Award for Scientific Accomplishments (2012); William Frankland Award for Outstanding Services to Clinical Allergy, British Society for Allergy & Clinical Immunology (2012); Honoree, Commander of the Order of the British Empire for Contributions to Clinical Science (2011); Honoree, Second-most-cited European Author 1998-2009 in Respiratory Research (2011); David W. Talmage Lectureship, Aspen Allergy Jack Selner Conference (2010); Paul Ehrlich Award for Research, European Academy of Allergy, Asthma and Clinical Immunology (2008); Honoree, Overseas Member, American Association of Physicians (2005); Health and Life Sciences Gold Medal, Rijks University, Gent, Belgium (2004); Quintiles Prize in Immunopharmacology, British Pharmacological Society (2004); Hospital Doctor Academic Medicine Team of the Year Award (2004); Ellison-Cliffe Medal, Royal Society of Medicine (2003); Scientific Achievement Award, International Association of Asthmology (2003); Honoree, Highly Cited Researcher, ISI (2002); Honorary Fellow Award, American Academy of Allergy and Immunology (2001); Republic Medical Society Medal for Scientific Achievement, Prague (2001); Honoree, Most Highly Cited Researcher for Publications 1980-2000, Thompson ISI (2001); King Faisal International Prize in Medicine (1999); Medal for Scientific Achievement, Rijks University, Gent, Belgium (1999); Honoree, Ranked Eighth in UK Citations in Biomolecular Subjects, Thompson ISI (1999); Honoree, Robert Cooke Memorial Lecturer, American Academy of Allergy and Immunology (1995); World Health Award, Rhine-Poulenc Rorer (1995); Scientific Achievement Award, International Association of Allergy and Clinical Immunology, Stockholm, Sweden (1994); Thomas Young Medal, St George's Hospital, London (1993); Medical Book of the Year Award, British Medical Association (1993); Graham Bull Prize for Clinical Research (1993); Book Commendation, Royal Society of Medicine (1993); Hurst Brown Visiting Professorship, University of Toronto, Canada (1991) MEM: Honorary Fellow, Faculty of Public Health, Royal College of Physicians (2017); Honorary Fellow, inFlame Global Network, Global Network for Planetary Health (2017); Honorary Member, Società Italiana di Allergologia, Asme et Immunologia Clinica (2016); Fellow, European Respiratory Society (2015); Honorary Fellow, European Academy of Allergy and Clinical Immunology (2013); Lifetime Member, Primary Care Respiratory Society, United Kingdom (2011); Honorary Member, German Society of Allergy and Clinical Immunology (2006); Overseas Member, American Association of Physicians (2005); Honorary Member, Association of Physicians of Great Britain and Ireland (2004); Honorary Fellow, American College of Asthma, Allergy and Immunology (2004); Honorary Member, Biochemical Society (2004); Honorary Member, Germany Society for Pulmonology (2000) MH: Albert Nelson Marquis Lifetime Achievement Award (2017) H: Gardening; Running RE: Church of England ADD: 29 Cupernham Lane, Romsey, United Kingdom, so51 7JJ

HOLLOWAY BOLDRA, SUE ELLEN, T: Secondary School Educator **I:** Education/Educational Services **CN:** Fort Hays State University **DOB:** 09/09/1949 **PB:** McPherson **SC:** KS/USA **PT:** Herman Glenn Holloway; Betty Rose (Krehbiel) Holloway **MS:** Married **SPN:** Carl Sterling Boldra (12/19/1970) **CH:** Jeremy; Brandon; Amber; Chelsea **ED:** MS in Political Science, Fort Hays State University, Kansas (1977); BA in History and English, McPherson College, Kansas (1971) **CT:** Certified Teacher, National Board of Professional Teaching Standards **C:** Education Instructor, Fort Hays State University (1995-Present); Teacher, Social Studies, Hays High School (1990-2004); Teacher, English and Social Studies, Felten Middle School, Hays, KS (1972-1990); Teacher, English, Canton-Galva Middle School, Kansas (1971-1972) **CR:** Real Estate Agent, Bel Air Realty, Fort Hays, KS (2005-Present); Teacher, College of Education and Technology (2004-Present); Republican Member, Kansas House of Representatives (2013-2017); Adjunct Professor, Educational Administration and Counseling, Fort Hays State University, Hays, KS (1995-2004) **CIV:** Vice Chairman, Hays City-Ellis County Planning Commission, Hays, KS (1997-1998); Secretary, Hays City-Ellis County Planning Commission, Hays, KS (1996-1997); Hays City-Ellis County Planning Commission, Hays, KS (1995) **AW:** Kansas Teacher of the Year (2001) **MH:** Albert Nelson Marquis Lifetime Achievement Award (2017) **H:** Politics; Education **ADD:** 2405 General Custer Road, Hays, KS, 67601

HOLME, RICHARD "DICK" PHILLIPS, T: Lawyer **I:** Law and Legal Services **CN:** Davis, Graham & Stubbs **DOB:** 11/06/1941 **PB:** Denver **SC:** CO/USA **PT:** Peter Hagner Holme Jr.; Lena (Phillips) Holme **MS:** Married **SPN:** Barbara Friel Holme (6/17/1944) **CH:** Daniel Friel; Robert Muir **ED:** JD, University of Colorado (1966); BA, Williams College (1963) **C:** Senior Counsel, Davis, Graham & Stubbs, LLP (2011-Present); Partner, Davis, Graham & Stubbs, LLP (1991-2011); Managing Partner, District of Columbia Office, Davis, Graham & Stubbs, LLP (1987-1991); Partner, Denver Office, Davis, Graham & Stubbs, LLP (1972-1987); Deputy, Denver District Attorney (1969-1971); Associate, Denver Office, Davis, Graham & Stubbs, LLP (1966-1968) **CR:** Member, Civil Justice Committee, Colorado Supreme Court (1998-Present); Member, Civil Rules Committee, Colorado Supreme Court (1994-Present); Supreme Court Nomination Commission (2008-2013); Member, Grievance Committee Colorado Supreme Court (1979-1985) **CW:** Contributor, The Colorado Lawyer **MEM:** Board of Governors, Colorado Bar Association (2001-2003); Vice President, Denver Bar Association (1997-1998); Board of Governors, Colorado Bar Association (1995-1999); Board of Governors, Colorado Bar Association (1985-1987); Trustee, Denver Bar Association (1977-1980); Board of Governors, Colorado Bar Association (1974-1976); American Bar Foundation; Fellow, American College of Trial Lawyers; ABA; Colorado Bar Foundation; Order of the Coif **BAR:** United States Court of Appeals for the Federal Circuit (1995); United States Court of Federal Claims (1990); United States Court of Appeals for the Fourth Circuit (1989); United States District Court for the District of Columbia (1988); United States Court of Appeals District of Columbia Circuit (1988); United States Court of Appeals for the First Circuit (1980); Supreme Court of the United States (1975); United States Court of Appeals for the Tenth Circuit (1966); United States District Court for the District of Colorado (1966); Colorado (1966) **RE:** Presbyterian **ADD:** 3944 S Depew Way, Denver, CO, 80235

HOMBURGER, THOMAS C., T: Professor in the Practice **I:** Education/Educational Services **CN:** The University of Arizona **DOB:** 09/16/1941 **PB:** Buffalo **SC:** NY/USA **PT:** Adolf; Charlotte E. (Stern) Homburger **MS:** Married **SPN:** Louise Paula Shemin (6/6/1965) **CH:** Jennifer Anne; Richard Ephraim; Kathryn Lee **ED:** JD, Columbia University, New York City, NY (1966); BA, Columbia University, New York City, NY (1963) **C:** Expert Witness (1990-Present); Professor in the Practice, James E. Rogers College of Law, University of Arizona (2014-2018); Of Counsel, K&L Gates, LLP (2014-2016); Partner, K&L Gates LLP (2009-2013); Partner, Bell, Boyd & Lloyd LLP, Chicago (Now K&L Gates, LLP) (1986-2009); Chairman of Real Estate, Bell, Boyd & Lloyd (1986-2000); Associate and Partner Sonnenschein, Carlin, Nath & Rosenthal (Now Dentons), Chicago, IL (1966-1986) **CR:** Professor, in the Practice, James E. Rogers College of Law, University of Arizona (2014-Present); Adjunct Professor, The John Marshall Law School (1989-1997) **CIV:** Secretary, Anti-Defamation League (2012-Present); Chairman, National Executive Committee (2011, 1999-2003); Vice Chairman, Anti-Defamation League (2006-2012); President, Anti-Defamation Foundation (2003-2006); Member, Anti-Defamation League (2000-2003); Chairman. Chicago Regional Board, Anti-Defamation League (1986-1988); Member, Glencoe Board of Education, IL (1984-1989); The Standard Club; Director, Chicago Psychoanalytic Institute **CW:** Contributor, Articles, Professional Journals **AW:** Honoree, Best Lawyers in America in Real Estate Law (2010-2018); Honoree in Real Estate, Chambers USA (2008-2018); Honoree in Cross-border Corporation Real Estate, Illinois Super Lawyers (2005-2018); Barbara Balsen Lifetime of Achievement Award, Anti-Defamation League (2012); Decoration of Honor in Gold for Services for the Republic of Austria (1999); Honoree in Real Estate Financing, Leading Lawyers Network; Honoree in Business Consulting, Non-Profit Corporations **MEM:** Board Of Directors, Homeowners Association of Ventana Golf Villas, Tuscon, AZ; Real Property Division, ABA; Financial Subcommittee, Probate & Trust Law Section, ABA; Columbia University Club, NY; Chicago Mortgage Attorneys Association; American College of Real Estate Lawyers; Chicago Bar Association; Real Property Section, Illinois Bar Association; Ventana Canyon Golf & Racquet Club Tuscon, AZ; Standard Club; Law Club of Chicago; Lambda Alpha International **BAR:** Illinois State Bar Association (1966) **MH:** Albert Nelson Marquis Lifetime Achievement Award (2017) **ADD:** 20 E Cedar St Apt 2F, Chicago, IL, 60611

HONEA, F. FRANKLIN, T: Lawyer **I:** Law and Legal Services **CN:** Law Office of F. Franklin Honea **DOB:** 05/20/1950 **PB:** Dallas **SC:** TX/USA **PT:** Floyd Franklin Honea; Gloria Anne Honea **ED:** JD, The University of Texas at Austin, With Honors (1976); BS, University of North Texas, Magna Cum Laude (1973); Member, Alpha Chi National College Honor Society; Member, Pi Sigma Alpha National Political Science Honor Society **C:** Shareholder, Law Office of F. Franklin Honea (2003-Present); Shareholder, Winstead Sechrist & Minick, PC, Dallas, TX (1997-2003); Partner, Payne & Vendig, Dallas, TX (1976-1997) **CIV:** Sponsor, Buckner Foundation; Sponsor, Dallas Museum of Art; Member, Friends of Smithsonian Institute, Kimbell Art Museum; Sponsor, Dallas Symphony Association; Member, Baylor Health Care Systems Foundation; Chancellor's Counsel, University of Texas System; Sponsor, Dallas Arboretum; Keeton Fellow and Member, Dean's Council, University of Texas School of Law; Member, Dallas Historical Society; Member, Hayek Society of Americans for Prosperity; Life Member, National Rifle

Association; Life Member, University of Texas Alumni Association; Patriots Circle Member; Veterans of Foreign Wars; Life Changers Member of Salvation Army; Sponsor, St. Jude's Children's Research Hospital; Sponsor, PLAN International USA; Sponsor, American Bible Society; Sponsor, Blanton Museum; Sponsor, "Jesus Film Project" of Campus Crusade for Christ; Member, National Audubon Society; Supporter, Shriner's Hospitals for Children; member, National Geographic Society; Member, Children's Medical Center Foundation; Sponsor, Paralyzed Veterans of America; Associate Member, Sheriff's Association of Texas; Member, Southwestern Medical Foundation; Member UNT Foundation; Sponsor, Perot Museum of Nature and Science; Member, UT; Southwestern Circle of Friends **MIL:** Texas Air National Guard **AW:** America's Most Honored Professionals Award, Top 1%, Texas (2016); Martindale Hubbell Top Rated Lawyer in Litigation; Martindale Hubbell Top Rated Lawyer in Texas; Lifetime Member, Worldwide Registry of Executives and Professionals; 40th Year Anniversary Award, Martindale Hubbell for Highest Possible Peer Review Rating in Legal Ability and Ethical Standards; Personalities of America Awards, Contributions to Law; Personalities of the South Award **MEM:** American Bar Association; Dallas Bar Association; State Bar of Texas; Oil, Gas and Mineral Section, State Bar of Texas; Commercial Litigation Section, State Bar of Texas; Oil, Gas and Mineral Section, Dallas Bar Association **BAR:** State Bar of Texas (1976); U.S. Supreme Court; U.S. Court of Appeals for the Fifth and Tenth Circuits; U.S. District Court for the Northern, Eastern and Western Districts of Texas; U.S. Court of Claims **MH:** Albert Nelson Marquis Lifetime Achievement Award (2017) **PA:** Republican **RE:** Baptist **BA:** 4809 Cole Ave Ste 260, Law Office of F. Franklin Honea, Dallas, TX, 75205 **ADD:** 8865 Flint Falls Dr, Dallas, TX, 75243

HONG, YISEOK, T: Lecturer **I:** Education/Educational Services **CN:** Seo Kyeong University **SC:** Republic of Korea **ED:** PhD in Economics, University of Rochester (1992); MA in Economics, University of Rochester (1990); BA in Economics, Seoul National University (1980) **C:** Chairman, Department of Economics and Finance, Seokyeong University (2011-2017); Visiting Scholar, Department of Economics, University of Rochester (2010-2011); Chairman, Department of Economics, Seokyeong University (1997-2000); Associate Professor, Division of Business Administration, Seokyeong University (1996-2017); Research Fellow, Daewoo Economic Research Institute (1994-1996); Lecturer, Department of Economics, Hankuk University of Foreign Studies (1993-1994) **CW:** Editor, "Social Science Review," Social Science Research Institute, Seokyeong University (2015-2017); Abstract Reviewer, Global Trade Analysis Project Conference (2013-2017); Co-author, "Valuation of Han River Waterside Landscape with a Double-bound Dichotomous Choice Model and Policy Implications: Focused on the Exponential Willingness to Pay Model," Environmental and Resource Economics Review (2013); Editor, "Social Science Review," Social Science Research Institute, Seokyeong University (2002-2009); Author, "Nonparametric Estimation of a CES Production Function: A Simulation Study," Journal of Economic Theory and Econometrics (2000); Co-author, "Nonparametric Estimation and the Risk Premium," Cambridge University Press (1991); Co-author, "Some Simulation Studies of Nonparametric Estimators," Empirical Economics (1988); Referee, "Korean Economic Review"; Referee, "Journal of Economic Theory and Econometrics"; Referee, "Seoul Journal of Economics" **BA:** 124 Seogyeong-ro Seongbuk-gu, Seo Kyeong University, Division of Business Adminis-

tration, Seoul, Korea South, 02173 **ADD:** 304-101, Jeongreung Hillstate, 3rd Apt., 116 Bogukmunro, Sungbuk-Ku, Seoul, Korea South, 02702

HORN, ROBERT JACK (BOB), T: Partner **I:** Law and Legal Services **CN:** Husch Blackwell **ED:** JD, Fordham Univrsity (1967); BBA, City University of New York, Baruch School of Business and Public Administration and Economics (1964) **CT:** Certificate, Executive Training for Utility Executives, University of Michigan (1974) **C:** Legal Counsel, American Airmail Society (2012-Present); Outside Counsel, The Border Patrol Foundation (2011-Present); Shareholder, Jackson Lewis P.C. (2013-2016); Outside Counsel, Air Patrol (2012-2013); Partner, Patton Boggs LLP (2001-2013); Board Member, Executive Committee, United States Holocaust Memorial Council (1987-2000); Founder, Republicans National Lawyers Association (1984-2001); Chairman, Republicans National Lawyers Association (1984-2001); Vice President, Federal Affairs, DTE Energy (1978-2001); Director, Washington Office, State of Michigan (1975-1978); Executive Secretary, Presidential Clemency Board, President Gerald Ford (1974-1977); Special Assistant to the Secretary, United States Department of Housing and Urban Development; Energy & Natural Resources Group, Husch Blackwell's; Corporate Officer, Detroit Edison Co. **CIV:** Parliamentarian, Republican National Convention (1980-2012); Chairman, Washington Representatives of the Governors; Board of Directors, Michigan Energy and Resources Association; Executive Committee, United States Holocaust Memorial Museum; Chairman, Governance Committee, United States Holocaust Memorial Museum; Board of Directors, Republican National Lawyers Association; Founding Chair, Republican National Lawyers Association; Board of Directors, The Border Patrol Foundation; General Counsel, The Border Patrol Foundation; Board of Directors, The Friends of the Law Library of Congress; Board of Directors, National Council on Crime and Delinquency; American Air Mail Society **AW:** Inductee, Capital Pro Bono Honor Roll (2014); Named, Republican Lawyer of the Year, Republican National Lawyers Association (2005) **BAR:** United States Court of Federal Claims (1988); Washington, D.C. (1980); New York (1967) **BA:** 750 17th St NW Ste 900, Husch Blackwell, Washington, DC, 20006

HORNER, CARL MATTHEW, T: Chemistry Professor (Retired) **I:** Education/Educational Services **CN:** State University of New York College at Oneonta **DOB:** 06/04/1930 **PB:** Cicero **SC:** NY/USA **PT:** Oscar Wendell Horner; Gladys Cecilia Horner **ED:** PhD, Syracuse University (1965); MS, Syracuse University (1958); BS, LeMoyne College (1952) **C:** Professor Emeritus, State University of New York College at Oneonta (1998-Present); Professor, State University of New York College at Oneonta (1964-1997); Associate Professor, State University of New York College at Oneonta (1961-1964); Assistant Professor of Analytical Chemistry, State University of New York College at Oneonta (1958-1961) **CR:** Consultant, Edison Botanic Research Laboratory (2012-Present); Docent, Edison Botanic Research Laboratory, Fort Myers, FL (2006-Present); Volunteer Docent, Edison and Ford Winter Estate, Fort Myers, FL (2005-Present); Coordinator, Annual Instrumental Chemistry Workshops (1986-1995) **AW:** Grantee, CSIP, National Science Foundation (1986-1988); Grantee, Walter B. Ford Foundation (1983, 1980); Grantee, CAUSE, National Science Foundation (1979-1982) **MEM:** American Association for the Advancement of Science; American

Chemical Society **MH:** Albert Nelson Marquis Lifetime Achievement Award (2017) **H:** Scuba diving; Photography **ADD:** 24 Suncrest Ter, Oneonta, NY, 13820

HOROWITZ, EDWARD JAY, T: Attorney, President **I:** Law and Legal Services **CN:** Edward J. Horowitz, APC **DOB:** 02/13/1942 **PB:** Milwaukee **SC:** WI/USA **PT:** Aaron Horowitz; Sue Horowitz **MS:** Married **SPN:** Marcia Gold (4/29/1990) **CH:** Amy; Aaron **ED:** JD, Harvard University, Cambridge, MA (1966); BA, University of California, Los Angeles, Summa Cum Laude (1963) **CT:** Certified Specialist in Appellate Law, Board of Legal Specialization, The State Bar of California (1996) **C:** Lawyer, Edward J. Horowitz, A Professional Corporation, Los Angeles, CA (1978-Present); Partner, Horvitz, Greines & Horowitz, Encino, CA (1976-1978); Senior Attorney, Second Appellate District, California Court of Appeals, Los Angeles, CA (1972-1976); Partner, Goldhammer & Horowitz, Los Angeles, CA (1969-1972); Deputy Attorney General, California Department of Justice (1966-1969); Lead Counsel, More than 540 Appellate Cases, including 370 Civil and 170 Criminal Matters **CR:** Attorney Settlement Officer/Mediator, Second Appellate District, Judicial Council of California (1990-2015); Judge Pro Tem, Los Angeles Superior Court for Small Claims Appeals, Judicial Council of California (1985-1995); Lecturer, CEB (1982-1990); Judge Pro Tem, Los Angeles and Beverly Hills Municipal Courts, Judicial Council of California (1972-1997); Professor of Evidence, The San Fernando Valley College of Law (Now University of West Los Angeles) (1967-1970) **CIV:** Board of Directors, High School Alumni Association; Big Brothers of Greater Los Angeles **CW:** Co-Author, "Protecting the Record on Appeal," Los Angeles Lawyer (1990); Consultant, "California Civil Practice," Bancroft-Whitney (1990); Consultant, "California Civil Appellate Practice, Second Edition," CEB (1985); Co-Author, "The Proposed Panel to Resolve Intercircuit Conflicts: A Brief View from the Litigants' Perspective," Hastings (1984); Author, "Appellate Practice Handbook," Butterworth (1982); Author, "Reflections on Gun Control," Los Angeles Bar Journal (1976); Author, "Practitioners' Guide to California Habeas Corpus," Journal of the Beverly Hills Bar Association (1974); Author, "Excluding the Exclusionary Rule - Can There Be An Effective Alternative," Los Angeles Bar Journal (1972); Contributor, Articles to Professional Publications **AW:** Honoree, AV Rated Attorney, Martindale-Hubbell (1979-Present); Honoree, Best Lawyers in America, United States News & World Report, L.P. (2017); Honoree, California Lawyer of Year, California Journal Magazine (1999); Felix Frankfurter Scholarship Award, Student Legislative Research Bureau, Harvard University (1966); Featured Listee, Bar Register of Preeminent Lawyers, Martindale-Hubbell; Featured Listee, Best Lawyers in America **MEM:** Fellow, The American Academy of Appellate Lawyers (2000-Present); California Academy of Appellate Lawyers (1976-Present); Criminal Courts Bar Association - Los Angeles (1970-Present); Appellate Courts Section, Los Angeles County Bar Association (1980-2017); Los Angeles County Bar Association (1967-2017); Executive Committee, Senior Lawyers Section, Los Angeles County Bar Association (2009-2017); State Appellate Judicial Evaluation Committee, Los Angeles County Bar Association (2013-2015); Chairman, Senior Lawyers Section, Los Angeles County Bar Association (2013-2014); Chairman, State Appellate Judicial Evaluation Committee, Los Angeles County Bar Association (2001-2007); Appellate Advisory Committee, Judicial Council of California (2003-2006); Reporting of the Record

Task Force, Judicial Council of California (2002-2005); Appellate Process Task Force, Judicial Council of California (1997-2001); State Appellate Judicial Evaluation Committee, Los Angeles County Bar Association (1995-2011); Indigent Defense Oversight Advisory Committee, Judicial Council of California (1993-1995); Hearing Officer, Southern California Psychiatric Society (1990-1995); President, Criminal Courts Bar Association - Los Angeles (1987); Arbitrator, American Arbitration Association (1982-1995); President, California Academy of Appellate Lawyers (1982-1983); Chair, Appellate Courts Section, Los Angeles County Bar Association (1981-1982) **BAR:** United States Court of Appeals for the First Circuit (1999); Supreme Court of the United States (1970); California (1967); United States Court of Appeals for the Ninth Circuit (1967); United States District Court for the Central District of California (1967) **MH:** Albert Nelson Marquis Lifetime Achievement Award (2017) **H:** Swimming; Skiing; Backpacking; Writing humorous prose and poetry; Reading history and science **PA:** Democrat **ADD:** 1151 Bienveneda Ave, Pacific Palisades, CA, 90272

HOUCK, CARA M., T: Senior Principal **I:** Law and Legal Services **CN:** Miller Canfield Paddock & Stone PLC **ED:** MBA, Kellogg School of Management, Northwestern University (2012); JD, Western Michigan University Thomas M. Cooley Law School (1996); BS, Northwestern University (1990); Postgraduate Coursework, Northwestern University **C:** Senior Principal, Miller Canfield Paddock and Stone, P.L.C., Chicago, IL (2008-Present); Associate, McGuire Woods, LLP (Formerly Ross & Hardies), Chicago, IL (1998-2007) **CR:** Presenter in Field **CIV:** President, Awassa Children's Project, Ethiopia (2013-Present); Board Member, Awassa Children's Project, Ethiopia (2012); Volunteer, Awassa Children's Project, Ethiopia (2011); Board Member, The Chicago Challenge (2000-2005) **CW:** Contributor, Articles to Professional Journals **AW:** Listed, Illinois Super Lawyers, Business Litigation (2012-2016); Leading Lawyers (2018); Richard J. Seryak Pro Bono Award Winner (2018); Miller Canfield Award for Pro Bono Work (2011-Present) **MEM:** Chicago Bar Association; Illinois Bar Association; American Bar Association **BAR:** Illinois; Wisconsin **H:** Golf; Running; Cycling; Traveling **BA:** 225 W Washington St Ste 2600, Miller Canfield Paddock & Stone PLC, Chicago, IL, 60606 **URL:** https://www.millercanfield.com/offices-8.html

HOUGH, AUBREY JOHNSTON JR., T: Emeritus University Professor **I:** Education/Educational Services **CN:** University of Arkansas for Medical Sciences **DOB:** 07/20/1944 **PB:** Little Rock **SC:** AR/USA **PT:** Aubrey Johnston; Thelma Willeen (Miller) Hough **MS:** Single **CH:** Charles Prentiss; Robert Page **ED:** DSc, Hendrix College (2015); MD, Vanderbilt University (1970); BA, Hendrix College (1966); Resident, Vanderbilt University **CT:** Diplomate, American Board of Pathology **C:** Professor Emeritus, University of Arkansas for Medical Sciences (2017-Present); Distinguished Professor, University of Arkansas for Medical Sciences (2004-2017); Associate Dean of Translational Research, University of Arkansas for Medical Sciences (2002-2017); Professor of Medical Science, University of Arkansas for Medical Sciences (1980-2004); Associate Professor, Vanderbilt University (1970-1980) **CR:** Statewide Committee on Bio Terrorism (2002-Present); Special Assistant to the Chancellor of the University of Arkansas for Medical Sciences (2012-2016); Committee on Disaster Response, Arkansas Medical Society (2006-2007); Chief of Staff, University of Arkansas for Medical Sciences (1998-2000); Chairman, Pathology Test Committee, National Board of Medical Examiners (1993-1995); Comp II Committee, National Board of Medical Examiners (1992-1995); Residency Review Committee for Pathology Accreditation Council on Medical Education, National Board of Medical Examiners (1990-1996); Pathology Test Committee, National Board of Medical Examiners (1989-1992); Council of Department Chairman, University of Arkansas for Medical Sciences (1987-1988); Chief of Staff, University of Arkansas for Medical Sciences (1986-1988); President, Arkansas Academy of Science (1982-1986); Clinical Associate, National Institute of Arthritis and Musculoskeletal and Skin Diseases, Bethesda, MD (1972-1974); Fellow, American College of Pathologists **CIV:** Invited Keynote Lecturer, Odyssey Program Inauguration (2004); Vice-chair, Physicians Advisory Committee (1996); Chairman, Shideler Chemistry Education Endowment (1991-1997); Representative, Alumni Fund, Hendrix College, Conway, AR (1983-1986) **MIL:** Surgeon, U.S. Public Health Service Reserve (1974-1994); Surgeon, U.S. Public Health Service (1972-1974) **CW:** Editorial Board Member, "American Journal of Clinical Pathology" (2004-Present); Editorial Board Member, "Annals of Clinical Laboratory Science" (1989-2006); Associate Editor, "Human Pathology" (1988-1997); Author, "Tumors of the Adrenal Gland" (1987); Editorial Board Member, "American Journal of Pathology" (1986-1996); Contributor, Numerous Articles on Orthopedic Diseases, Professional Journals; Contributor, Book Chapters **AW:** Distinguished Service Award, University of Arkansas for Medical Sciences (2018); Honoree, Distinguished Alumni, Hendrix College (1999); Grantee, National Institute of Arthritis and Musculoskeletal and Skin Diseases (1988); Honoree, Brown Memorial Lecturer, Association of Clinical Scientists (1986); Distinguished Service Award, University of Arkansas for Medical Sciences (1985); Grantee, Altheimer Foundation (1984); Director's Commendation, U.S. Department for Veteran's Affairs (1980); Basic Science Grantee, National Institute of General Medical Studies (1978) **MEM:** Statewide Advisory Committee on Bioterrorism, AAMC (2002-Present); Publication Affairs Committee, Association of Pathology Chairs (1985-Present); Chairman, Publication Affairs Committee, Association of Pathology Chairs (1993-1996); Board of Directors, History of Medicine Associates (1986-1988); Council Academic Society, Washington Section, AAMC (1985-1989); Program Chair, Baptist Medical & Dental Mission International (1983-1984); Field Inspector, College of American Pathologists (1977-1988); American Medical Association, AAUP; USCAP; American Society for Clinical Pathology; American Society for Investigative Pathology; Association of Clinical Scientists; Arthur Purdy Stout Society; Orthopaedic Research Society **MH:** Albert Nelson Marquis Lifetime Achievement Award (2017) **H:** Fishing **BA:** 4301 West Markham Street, Little Rock, AR, 72205 **ADD:** 37 E. Ridge Road, Mayflower, AR, 72106

HOUSE, WILLIAM MICHAEL, T: Lawyer **I:** Law and Legal Services **CN:** Hogan Lovells US LLP **DOB:** 12/19/1945 **PB:** Birmingham **SC:** AL/USA **PT:** B. William House; Kathryn Regina (Cantrell) House **MS:** Married **SPN:** Gina Rigby **CH:** Tanner; Slade; Kate **ED:** JD, School of Law, The University of Alabama (1971); BS, Auburn University (1968) **C:** Partner, Hogan Lovells (1991-Present); Partner, Shaw, Pittman et al (1988-1991); Counsel, McNair Law Firm, P.A. (1986-1988); Administrative Assistant to Howell Helfin, United States Senate (1979-1986); Chief of Staff to Howell Helfin, United States Senate (1979-1986); Associate, Odom, Argo, Enslen, Montgomery (1976-1979); Administrative Assistant to Chief Justice, Supreme Court of Alabama, Alabama Judicial System (1973-1976); Legislative Assistant to James M. Collins, The United States House of Representatives (1971-1973); Chair, Legislative Group, Hogan Lovells **CIV:** Member, Board of Trustees, Shakespeare Theatre Company (2009-Present); Chair, Farrah Law Society, School of Law, The University of Alabama (2008-Present); Member, Advisory Board, Blackburn Institute, The University of Alabama (2006-Present); Member, President's Council, The University of Alabama (2000-Present); Co-Chair, Potomac Group, Democratic National Committee (1987-1993); Chair, Alabama Citizens Conference (1974-1975) **MIL:** Captain, U.S. Army (1971-1980) **AW:** Honoree, Ten Top Lobbyists, Washingtonian Media Inc. (2007); Honoree, Alabama's Outstanding Young Men, Alabama Jaycees (1979); Honoree, Named One Of Top Legislative Lawyers In Washington, Chambers USA, Chambers & Partners **MEM:** Board of Directors, Memorial Foundation, Pi Kappa Alpha (1980-1986); Alabama State Bar Association (1968); Society of International Business Fellows; American Judicature Society; Council for Excellence in Government **BAR:** The District of Columbia Bar (1992); Alabama (1968) **MH:** Albert Nelson Marquis Lifetime Achievement Award (2017) **H:** Cooking; Reading **BA:** Columbia Sq, 555 13th St NW, Washington, DC, 20004-1161 **ADD:** 1450 Emerson Ave Apt 505, McLean, VA, 22101

HOUSER, JAMES COWING, T: Artist **I:** Fine Art **DOB:** 11/12/1928 **PB:** Dade City **SC:** FL/USA **PT:** James C. Houser; Martha (Futch) Houser **MS:** Married **SPN:** Constance Woodward; **CH:** James Jackson; Katrina J. **ED:** MFA, University of Florida (1953); Postgraduate Coursework, Art Institute of Chicago (1952); BFA, Florida Southern College (1951); BS, Ringling School of Art (1949) **C:** Exhibitor, Sherry French Gallery (1985); Exhibitor, David Findlay Galleries, New York City, NY (1974-1984); Exhibitor, Gallery Camino Real, Boca Raton, FL (1972-2009); Exhibitor, Grand Central Moderns Gallery, New York City, NY (1966-1980); Exhibitor, Rudolph Galleries, Woodstock, NY (1964-1990); Exhibitor, Rudolph Galleries, Coral Gables, FL (1964-1990) **CR:** Director, Art Gallery, Kentucky Wesleyan College, Owensboro, KY (1974-1991); Art Chairman, Kentucky Wesleyan College, Owensboro, KY (1964-1970); Senior Instructor, Art, Kentucky Wesleyan College, Owensboro, KY (1954-1960); Art Instructor, Palm Beach State College; Judge, Local and National Art Competitions, Palm Beach State College; Lecturer in Field **CIV:** Certificate of Appreciation, The Society of the Four Arts (1996); Selection Committee, Palm Beach Council Arts (1987); Artist Review Board, Scholarship Awards, Palm Beach Post-Times (1982-1987) **CW:** Exhibitor, Group Show, Department State Special Exhibition, Washington D.C. (1967-Present); Exhibitor, Group Show, Martin County Art Center, Stuart, FL (2007); Solo Exhibitor, Gallery Camino Real, Boca Raton, FL (1972-1989, 1999, 2003, 2005-2007); Exhibitor, Group Show, Festival International Peinture, Cagnes-sur-Mer, France (2001); Exhibitor, Group Show, Fort Lauderdale Museum of Art, Men's Art, Northwood University, West Palm Beach, FL (1994); Exhibitor, Group Show, Southern Florida Invitational Exhibition (1991); Solo Exhibitor, Palm Beach State College (1988); Solo Exhibitor, Northwood Institute (1986); Exhibitor, Group Show, Northern Miami Museum Art Center, Northern Miami, FL (1985); Solo Exhibitor, David Findlay Galleries, New York City, NY (1976, 1978, 1981, 1983); Solo Exhibitor, Cocoa, Valencia College (1976, 1978, 1981, 1983); Exhibitor, Group Show, Major Florida Artist Invitational Exhibition, Sarasota, FL (1981-1992); Author, Video Texts, "Color for the Artist" (1975);

Solo Exhibitor, Brevard Community College, Orlando, FL (1974); Solo Exhibitor, Brevard Community College (1973); Exhibitor, Permanent Collection, Boca Raton Museum of Art; Exhibitor, Permanent Collection, Notre Dame University; Exhibitor, Permanent Collection, Cornell University; Exhibitor, Permanent Collection, New York University; Exhibitor, Permanent Collection, Palm Beach Society Four the Arts; Exhibitor, Permanent Collection, University of Miami; Exhibitor, Permanent Collection, Bethlehem Art Center, Pennsylvania; Exhibitor, Permanent Collection, Knoxville Museum of Art, Tennessee; Exhibitor, Permanent Collection, Syracuse University; Exhibitor, Permanent Collection, Owensboro Museum of Art, Kentucky; Exhibitor, Permanent Collection, Hunt Knight, Lousiana; Exhibitor, Permanent Collection, Florida Museum Fine of Arts; Co-author, "Anatomy of a Painting" **AW:** Established, Connie and Jim Houser Award, Contempary Exhibition Society Four Arts (1996-2002); Atwater Kent Award (1989, 1977); Philip Hulitar Award (1982); Akston Foundation Award (1977); Merit Award, Fort Lauderdale Museum (1974); Sixteen Major Arts Award (1966-1993) **MEM:** The Society of the Four Arts Certificate of Appreciation, The Society of the Four Arts (1996) **H:** Music; Photography; Computers **PA:** Republican **RE:** Methodist

HOVER, JOHN CALVIN II, T: Banker (Retired) **I:** Financial Services **DOB:** 05/13/1943 **PB:** Orange **SC:** NJ/USA **PT:** John Curry Hover; Edith Margaret (Hopkins) Hover **MS:** Married **SPN:** Jacqueline Whitley (9/4/1997) **CH:** Margaret Hover McCooey **ED:** The Aspen Institute (1988); MBA, The Wharton School, The University of Pennsylvania, Philadelphia, PA (1967); BA in English Literature, The University of Pennsylvania, Philadelphia, PA (1965) **C:** Retired (2000); Executive Vice President, Asset Management and Private Banking Group, United States Trust Company of New York, New York, NY (1991-1998); Senior Vice President, Division Manager, Private Banking, United States Trust Company of New York, New York, NY (1980-1991); Banker, Corporate Banking and Personal Banking, United States Trust Company of New York (1976-1980); Banker, Chemical Bank (1968-1976) **CR:** Director, Tweedy, Browne Fund Inc.; Former Director, Excelsior Funds **CIV:** Trustee, The University of Pennsylvania, Philadelphia, PA (1995-2005); Former Chairman, Penn Museum; Board of Overseers, Penn Museum; Member, Director's Council, Penn Museum **MIL:** First Troop Philadelphia City Cavalry **AW:** Alumni Award of Merit, The University of Pennsylvania (2006); Marian Angell Godfrey Boyer Medal, Penn Museum **MEM:** Saint Nicholas Society of the City of New York; General Society of Colonial Wars; St. Andrew's Society of Philadelphia; Most Venerable Order of the Hospital of Saint John of Jerusalem; The University Club of New York; Director, The Penn Club of New York; Former President, The Penn Club of New York; Psi Upsilon **MH:** Albert Nelson Marquis Lifetime Achievement Award (2017) **H:** Railroadiana **ADD:** 72 N Main St, New Hope, PA, 18938

HOWARD-JONES, DAVID, I: Financial Services **CW:** Author, Articles, Professional Publications **MEM:** CFA Institute; AICD

HOWE, DANIEL WALKER, T: Professor Emeritus **I:** Education/Educational Services **CN:** University of California, Los Angeles **DOB:** 01/10/1937 **PB:** Ogden **SC:** UT/USA **PT:** Maurice Langdon Howe; Lucie (Walker) Howe **MS:** Married **SPN:** Sandra Fay Shumway (9/3/1961) **CH:** Rebecca; Christopher; Stephen **ED:** Honorary PhD in Humanities, Weber State University (2014); PhD, University of California, Berkeley (1966); MA, University of Oxford, England (1965); AB, Harvard University, Magna Cum Laude (1959) **C:** Professor Emeritus, University of California, Los Angeles; Professor Emeritus, University of Oxford; Professor, University of California, Los Angeles (1977-1992); Chair, Department of History, University of California, Los Angeles (1983-1987); Associate Professor of History, University of California, Los Angeles (1973-1977); Associate Professor of History, Yale University (1966-1973); Instructor in History, Yale University (1966-1973) **CR:** Visiting Professor, Wofford College (2002); Rhodes Professor of Americna History, University of Oxford (1992-2002); Visiting Professor, Yale University (2001); Harmsworth Visiting Professor of American History, University of Oxford, England (1989-1990) **MIL:** Lieutenant, U.S. Army (1959-1960) **CW:** Author, "What Hath God Wrought: The Transformation of America, 1815-1848" (2007); Author, "Making the American Self" (1997); Author, "The Political Culture of the American Whigs" (1979); Author, "The Unitarian Conscience" (1970) **AW:** Winner, Pulitzer Prize for History, Columbia University (2008); Awarded Honorary Doctor of Humanities, Weber State University (2014); Elected Fellow of the American Academy of Arts and Sciences (2010); Fellowship, Huntington Library (1992, 1994, 2002-2003); Guggenheim Fellowship, John Simon Guggenheim Memorial Foundation (1984-1985); Fellowship, National Endowment for the Humanities (1975-1976); Fellowship, Charles Warren Center for Studies in American History, Harvard University (1970-1971); Kent Fellowship, Danforth Foundation (1964-1966); **MEM:** President, Society for Historians of the Early American Republic (2000-2001); Fellow, American Academy of Arts & Sciences, St. Catherine's College, Oxford, England; The Royal Historical Society; New-York Historical Society; America Historian Laureate; American Historical Association; Society of American Historians, Columbia University; Jonathan Club; Oxford and Cambridge Club **MH:** Albert Nelson Marquis Lifetime Achievement Award (2017) **H:** Classical music; Old movies; Spending time with his grandchildren **RE:** Episcopalian **ADD:** 3814 Cody Rd, Sherman Oaks, CA, 91403

HOWELL, JAMES BURT III, T: Agricultural Products Executive, US Army Reserve, Colonel (Retired) **I:** Agriculture **CN:** James B. Howell Family Farm, U.S. Army Reserve **DOB:** 12/11/1933 **PT:** James Burt Howell; Catharine Stanger (Sparks) Howell **MS:** Married **SPN:** Lorraine Marie Chanatry (2/18/1995) **ED:** MBA, University of Delaware (1980); BS, Rutgers, The State University of New Jersey, High Honors (1956) **C:** Sales Consultant, Asgrow Seed Company (Subsidiary of Upjohn Company), Vineland, NJ (1960-1999); Agricultural Sales Representative, Allied Chemical Corporation, Philadelphia, PA (1957-1959) **CR:** Member, Board of Directors, Advance Weight Systems, Inc., LaGrange, OH **CIV:** Admissions Liaison to Officer, United States Military Academy, West Point, NY (1973-Present); Member, Official Board, First Presbyterian Church of Cedarville, Cedarville, NJ (1960-Present); Chairman, Lawrence Township Zoning Board Adjustment, U.S. Army (1957) **MIL:** Colonel, U.S. Army Reserve **AW:** Heritage Award, New Jersey Agricultural Business Association (2003); Centennial Honor Roll, Alpha Zeta (1997); Burpee Horticultural Award, Rutgers University (1955); Brothers of the Century Award, Alpha Gamma Rho **MEM:** Reserve Officers Association, United States; New Jersey Agricultural Business Association; Vegetable Growers Association of New Jersey; National Defense Industrial Association, Alpha Zeta; Alpha Gamma Rho; The Phi Beta Kappa Society **MH:** Albert Nelson Marquis Lifetime Achievement Award (2017) **H:** Agriculture; Farming; Vegetable growing; Church activities **ADD:** 23 Shadow Brooke Dr, Bridgeton, NJ, 08302

HU, CHI YU, T: Physicist (Retired), Educator **I:** Education/Educational Services **CN:** California State University, Long Beach **DOB:** 02/12/1933 **PB:** Szechwan **SC:** China **PT:** T. C. Hu; P. S. (Yang) Hu **CH:** Marica; Mark; Albert; Han Chin **ED:** PhD, Massachusetts Institute of Technology (1962); BS, National Taiwan University (1955) **C:** Professor Emeritus, California State University, Long Beach, CA (2006-Present); Professor, California State University, Long Beach, CA (1972-2005); Associate Professor, California State University, Long Beach, CA (1968-1972); Assistant Professor of Physics, California State University, Long Beach, CA (1963-1969); Research Associate, St. John's University, Jamaica, NY (1962-1963) **CR:** National Science Foundation Visiting Professor, University of California, Los Angeles, CA (1988-1990) **CW:** Contributor, Articles to Professor Journals; Contributor, Scientific Papers **AW:** Grantee, National Science Foundation (1969-1970, 1986-2008); Grantee, Department of Energy (1986-1988); Fellow, National Science Foundation (1965, 1976); Grantee, California State University Long Beach Foundation (1965-1966, 1970, 1972) **MEM:** American Physical Society **MH:** Distinguished Humanitarian (2017) **ADD:** 21091 Inferno Ln, Huntington Beach, CA, 92646

HUBER, MELBA, I: Media & Entertainment **CN:** Melba's Inc. **DOB:** 10/01/1927 **SC:** TX/USA **PT:** Carl E. Stewart; Melba (Holt) Stewart **MS:** Married **SPN:** William C. Kinsolving, Jr.; James M. Huber (Deceased) **CH:** William Carey Kinsolving, III; Keith Brian Kinsolving; Melba Lauren **ED:** Master's Degree in History, Oklahoma City University (1999); AA, Lamar College (1946); Coursework, The University of Texas at Austin **C:** Establisher, Melba's Inc., McAllen, Texas (1958-Present); Owner, Melba's Inc., McAllen, Texas (1958-Present); Founder, McAllen Dance Theatre Company (1970); Teacher, Huston-Tillotson University (1948-1949) **CR:** Workshop Coordinator, Dance Department Oklahoma City University (2011); Panelist, New York Tap Festivals; Panelist, New York Tradition in Tap; Panelist, St. Louis Tap Festival; Member, Numerous Professional Panels **CW:** Columnist, "Tappin' In Dancer Magazine" (1998-2008); Columnist, "Dance and the Arts Magazine" (1988-1997); Columnist, "Tap Ambassador," International Tap Association; Columnist "Tap Talk"; Columnist, "New York Dance Pages"; Producer, "Jelly's Last Jam" **AW:** Recipient, Top Five Business Award, McAllen Chamber of Commerce (2014-2015); Recipient, Zonta Award, Hidalgo County, McAllen, Texas (2012); Recipient, Texas Tap Legend Award, Dance Council Honors (2007); Recipient, 50 Years In Business Celebration Award (2007); Recipient, Honor, Savion Glover (2006); Recipient, Tradition In Tap Historian, Educator, Writer Award (2005); Recipient, Women of Distinction Award, Detroit Tap Festival (2000); Recipient, Preservation of Our Heritage In American Dance Award, Oklahoma City University (1999); Recipient, Savion Glover Award, St. Louis Tap Festival (1998); Honoree, Presented Texas Flag, The Texas Senate (1997); Honoree, Texas Association of Teachers Dancing (1997); Recipient, Flo-Bert Award, New York Committee to Celebrate National Tap Dance Day (1996); Recipient, Teaching Award, Oklahoma City University (1994); Honoree, Member of the Year, South Texas Association of Dance Teachers, Inc. (1989); Recipient, Plaudit Award, National Dance Association (1970); Honoree, Named for Life Achievement in the Art of Dance and Gymnastics **MEM**: President, Texas Association of Teachers Dancing (1973-1974); South Texas Association of Dance Teachers, Inc. **ADD**: 605 N McColl Cir, McAllen, TX, 78501

HUCKMAN, MICHAEL S., **T**: Neuroradiologist, Educator **I**: Medicine & Health Care **DOB**: 08/20/1936 **PB**: Newark **SC**: NJ/USA **PT**: Louis Fillmore Huckman; Mollie (Lehman) Huckman **MS**: Married **SPN**: Beverly Joy Blachman (8/2/1964) **CH**: Andrew Garfield; Robert Steven **ED**: Resident in Radiology, Philadelphia General Hospital (1965-1968); Rotating Intern, Philadelphia General Hospital (1962-1963); MD, St. Louis University (1962); AB, Princeton University (1958); Fellow in Neuroradiology, Edward Mallinckrodt Institute of Radiology, Washington University in St. Louis **C**: Emeritus Professor, Rush Medical College (2012-Present); Faculty Member, Rush Medical College, Chicago, IL (1970-Present); Professor Emeritus, Rush Medical College (2012); Professor of Radiology, Rush Medical College (1978-2012); Faculty Member, Cook County Graduate School of Medicine (1972-1991); Director of Section on Neuroradiology, Rush University Medical Center (1970-2012); University Instructor of Radiology, Edward Mallinckrodt Institute of Radiology, Washington University (1968-1970) **CR**: Honorary President, XVI Symposium Neuroradiologicum (2014); Secretary-General, XVI Symposium Neuroradiologicum (1994-1998); Consultant, National Center for Health Care Technology (1980-1981); Special Fellow, National of Institute Neurological Diseases and Blindness (1968-1970); Fellow, American College of Radiology; Fellow, College Physicians of Philadelphia **MIL**: Lieutenant, Active Duty, U.S. Naval Reserve (1963-1965) **CW**: Consultant Editor, American Journal of Roentgenology (1990-1991); Editor-in-Chief, "American Journal of Neuroradiology" (1989-1997); Editorial Board Member, Applied Radiology (1987-1989); Editorial Board Member, Radiographics (1983-1987); Editorial Board Member, Journal of Computer Assisted Tomography (1976-1994); Contributor, Articles to Medical Journals **AW**: Alumni Merit Award, School of Medicine, St. Louis University (2012); Emil Grubbe Memorial Award, Chicago Radiological Society (2007-2008); Radiological Society of North America (2002); Gold Medal, American Society of Neuroradiology (1999) **MEM**: Editor Emeritus, American Society of Neuroradiology (1998-Present); Archivist, American Society of Neuroradiology (1998-Present); Vice President, World Federation Neuroradiology Societies (1997-Present); President, World Federation Neuroradiology Societies (2002-2006); President-elect, World Federation Neuroradiology Societies (1998); Historian, World Federation Neuroradiology Societies (1993-1997); President, American Society of Neuroradiology (1987-1988); President-elect, American Society of Neuroradiology (1986-1987); Trustee, Princeton Alumni of Chicago (1982-1984); Secretary, American Society of Neuroradiology (1980-1983); Radiological Society of North America; American Society of Head and Neck Radiology; American Roentgen Ray Society; Association of University Radiologists; American Society of Pediatric Neuroradiology; Honorary Member, European Society of Neuroradiology; Illinois Medical Society; Illinois Radiological Society; Chicago Medical Society; Blockley Radiological Society; Society for Scholarly Publication; Honorary Member, Japanese Society of Neuroradiology; Council of Biology Editors; Society of the Fifth Line; Honorary Lifetime Member, Indian Society of Neuroradiology; Honorary Member, Turkish Society of Neuroradiology; School of Medicine,

St. Louis University; Sigma Xi; Phi Delta Epsilon; American Medical Association **MH**: Albert Nelson Marquis Lifetime Achievement Award (2017) **RE**: Jewish **ADD**: 175 E Delaware Place, Apt. 7401, Chicago, IL, 60611 **URL**: https://www.doximity.com/pub/michael-huckman-md

HUDNUT, STEWART SKINNER, **T**: Manufacturing Executive, Lawyer **I**: Law and Legal Services **DOB**: 04/29/1939 **PB**: Cincinnati **SC**: OH/USA **PT**: William Herbert Hudnut; Elizabeth Allen (Kilborne) Hudnut **MS**: Married **SPN**: Vivian Leith (1993) **CH**: Alexander Putnam; Andrew Gerard; Nathaniel Parker **ED**: JD, Harvard University (1965); Postgraduate Coursework, Oxford University, England (1962); AB, Summa Cum Laude, Princeton University (1961) **CT**: Environmental Law Certification, Pace University (1991) **C**: Senior Vice President, General Counsel, Secretary, Illinois Tool Works Inc., Glenview, IL (1992-2005); Senior Vice President, General Counsel, Secretary, Municipal Bond Investors Assurance Corp., White Plains, NY (1987-1989); Vice President, General Counsel, Secretary, Scovill Manufacturing Company, Waterbury, CT (1977-1987); Vice President, Counsel, Bankers Trust Company (1973-1977); Associate, Davis Polk & Wardwell, Paris (1968-1970); Associate, Davis Polk & Wardwell, New York City, NY (1971-1973, 1965-1967) **CIV**: Kenilworth Union Church Instructor, Voyageur Outward Bound School (1989-1990); Board of Directors, Lyric Opera Guild of Chicago; Chicago Shakespeare Theater; Association for the Protection of the Adirondacks **AW**: Woodrow Wilson Fellow, Keasbey Fellow, Christ Church, Oxford University, England (1962) **MEM**: Woodrow Wilson Fellow, Keasbey Fellow, Christ Church Oxford University, England (1962); American Bar Association; Illinois Bar Association; Phi Beta Kappa **MH**: Albert Nelson Marquis Lifetime Achievement Award (2017) **PA**: Republican **RE**: Presbyterian **ADD**: 56 Indian Hill Rd, Winnetka, IL, 60093

HUDSON, DONALD JAMES, **T**: Stock Exchange Executive (Retired) **I**: Business Management/Business Services **DOB**: 09/26/1930 **PB**: British Columbia **SC**: Canada **PT**: John R. Hudson; Olive Hudson **MS**: Married **SPN**: Patricia Joan **CH**: Sharon; Susan **ED**: Honorary LLD, Simon Fraser University (1993); BA in Mathematics and Economics, The University of British Columbia (1952) **C**: President, Vancouver Stock Exchange (1982-1995); Senior Vice President, Pacific Division, Eaton's Department Store (1964-1981); Management in Marketing, Canadian Pacific Airlines (1953-1964); With, Shell Canada Limited (1952-1953) **CIV**: Chairman, Board of Governors, Simon Fraser University (1988-1990); Board of Governors, Simon Fraser University (1985-1990); Chairman, Board of Trustee, St. Paul's Hospital (1983-1985); Trustee, St. Paul's Hospital (1975-1985); President, Foundation Board, Simon Fraser University; Regional Director, The Canadian Council of Christians and Jews; Director, The Playhouse Theatre; Director, The Canadian Committee on the Pacific Basin Economic Council; President, Canadian Club of Vancouver **AW**: Recipient, Big Block Awards, The University of British Columbia Thunderbirds, The University of British Columbia; Recipient, University Medal in Arts and Science, The University of British Columbia **MEM**: General Campaign Chairman, United Way of Greater Vancouver (1974-Present); Board of Directors, Vancouver Club (1995-1999); Board of Directors, Canadian Club of Vancouver; Board of Directors, Vancouver Board of Trade; Board of Directors, Endowment Fund of YMCA of Greater Vancouver; Board of Governors, Duke of Edinburgh Award; Trustee, Schenley Awards, Canadian Football League; Corporate

Board Director, British Pacific Properties Limited; Corporate Board Director, Norwich Union Life Insurance Society; Commercial Board Director, Bird Construction; Commercial Board Director, Pacific Press; Voluntary Leader, The International Financial Centre; Voluntary Leader, YMCA; Voluntary Leader, The Niagara Institute; The Vancouver Club; The Vancouver Lawn and Tennis Club **MH**: Albert Nelson Marquis Lifetime Achievement Award (2017) **H**: Gardening; Sports; Hiking; Backpacking; Travelling; Golfing; Fishing; Trekking; Camping; Trail riding **RE**: The United Church of Canada **ADD**: 1603-5775 Hampton Pl, Vancouver, BC, Canada, V6T 2G6

HUFBAUER, GARY CLYDE, **T**: Economist **I**: Financial Services **CN**: Peterson Institute for International Economics **DOB**: 04/03/1939 **PB**: San Diego **ED**: JD, Georgetown Law, Georgetown University (1980); PhD, King's College, University of Cambridge, England (1963); AB, Harvard University (1960) **C**: Senior Fellow, Peterson Institute for International Economics, Washington, D.C. (1982-1985, 1992-1997, 1998-Present); Director of Studies, Council on Foreign Relations, New York City, NY (1997-1998); Wallenberg Professor of Finance, Georgetown University, Washington, D.C. (1985-1992); Deputy Director, International Law Institute, Georgetown Law Center, Washington, D.C. (1980-1982); Member, Rose, Schmidt, Chapman, Duff & Hasley, Washington, D.C. (1980-1985); Deputy Assistant, Secretary of the Treasury, International Trade and Investment Policy (1977-1980); Director, International Tax Staff, U.S. Department of the Treasury, Washington, D.C. (1974-1977); Professor, The University of New Mexico, Albuquerque, NM (1970-1974); Member of Faculty, Department of Economics, The University New Mexico, Albuquerque, NM (1963-1974) **MEM**: American Economic Association; The National Economics Club, Inc. **RE**: Episcopalian **BA**: 1750 Massachusetts Ave NW, Peterson Institute for International Economics, Washington, DC, 20036

HUGE, HARRY, **T**: Partner, Owner **I**: Law and Legal Services **CN**: The Huge Law Firm PLLC **DOB**: 09/16/1937 **PB**: Deshler **SC**: NE/USA **PT**: Arthur Huge; Dorothy (Vorderstrasse) Huge **MS**: Married **SPN**: Reba Kinne (7/2/1960) **CH**: Theodore **ED**: LLD, Nebraska Wesleyan University, With Honors (2005); JD, Georgetown University (1963); AB, Nebraska Wesleyan University (1959) **C**: Partner, The Huge Law Firm PLLC (2002-Present); Owner, The Huge Law Firm PLLC (2002-Present); Partner, Powell Goldstein Frazer & Murphy, Washington, DC (1995-2002); Senior Partner, Shea and Gould International, Washington, DC (1992-1994); Senior Partner, Donovan, Leisure, Rogovin, Huge & Schiller, Washington, DC (1976-1992); Partner, Arnold & Porter, Washington, DC (1965-1976); Associate, Arnold & Porter, Washington, DC (1965-1976); Associate, Chapman and Cutler LLP, Chicago, IL (1963-1965); Managing Trustee, AWI Licensing LLC **CR**: Affiliate, W.R. Grace Settlement Trust, Wilmington, DE (2014-Present); Chairman, Armstrong World Industries Settlement Trust, Wilmington, DE (2006-Present); Charleston Trustee, Shook & Fletcher Asbestos Settlement Trust, MFR Claims Processing Inc., Wilmington, DE (2002-Present); Affiliate, Owens Corning Asbestos Settlement Trust, Wilmington, DE (2006); Chairman, United Mine Workers Health and Retirement Fund (1973-1978); Trustee, UMWA H & R Funds (1973-1978); President, Voter Education Project, Atlanta, GA (1972-1977); Chairman, Board of Directors, Hollings Cancer Center, Medical University of South Carolina, Charleston, SC **CIV**: Member, Board of Governors, Nebraska Wesleyan University (1978-2015); Member, Task Force on

Local Government, The Greater Washington Research Center (1981-1982); Member, President's General Advisory Committee on Arms Control (1977-1981); President, Voter Education Project, Atlanta, GA (1974-1978); Special Master, Friends for All Children, Inc., United States District Court for the District of Columbia; Member, National Tobacco Settlement Arbitration Panel, Durham, NC **MIL:** Officer, U.S. National Guard (1960-1965); U.S. Army (1960) **CW:** Contributor, Articles, Professional Journals **AW:** Lifetime Achievement Award, Institute of Human Virology, School of Medicine, University of Maryland (2010); Order of the Cross, Terra Mariana, Estonia (2006) **MEM:** Honorary Consul, Estonia for South Carolina, Harry and Reba Huge Foundation (2006-Present); Chairman, Dorothy Vorderstrasse Huge Scholarship Fund for Women, Charleston, NC (2004-Present); Board of Directors, University of Maryland, Baltimore (1996); Co-chairman, Legislative Committee, Litigation Section, ABA (1981); Board of Professional Responsibility, The District of Columbia Bar (1976-1981); Governor, Nebraska Wesleyan University; Director, South Carolina Aquarium; Institute of Human Virology, School of Medicine, University of Maryland **BAR:** South Carolina Bar (1985); The District of Columbia Bar (1965); Illinois State Bar Association (1963) **MH:** Albert Nelson Marquis Lifetime Achievement Award (2017) **BA:** 25 East Battery St, The Huge Law Firm PLLC, Charleston, SC, 29401 **ADD:** 25 E Battery St, The Huge Law Firm PLLC, Charleston, SC, 29401

HUGHES, KEVIN PETER, **T:** Lawyer **I:** Law and Legal Services **DOB:** 09/08/1943 **PB:** New York **SC:** NY/USA **MS:** Married **SPN:** Margaret Ellen Comiskey (11/18/1967) **CH:** Erin; Cara; Deirdre **ED:** JD, St. John's University (1968); BA, Manhattan College (1965) **C:** Partner, Weil, Gotshal & Manges LLP, New York, NY (1977-Present); Associate, Weil, Gotshal & Manges LLP, New York, NY (1970-1977); Law Clerk to Justice, New York Court of Appeals, Albany, NY (1968-1970) **MEM:** Litigation Section, ABA; New York State Bar Association; Plandome Country Club, Manhasset, NY; Eagle Creek Country Club, Naples, FL **MH:** Albert Nelson Marquis Lifetime Achievement Award (2017) **H:** Skiing; Golf **RE:** Roman Catholic **ADD:** 47 Chester Drive, Manhasset, NY, 11030

HULL, KATHRYN B., **T:** Teacher of Piano and Music Theory **I:** Education/Educational Services **DOB:** 06/14/1928 **PB:** Sanders **SC:** ID/USA **PT:** Willett S. Blomquist; Ruby V. (Simons) Blomquist **CH:** Laurice; Craig; Eric **ED:** BA, Pasadena College (Now Point Loma University) (1949) **CT:** MTNA Certified Piano Teacher **C:** Arts Consultant (1986-Present); Independent Music Teacher and Composer (1949-Present); Teacher of Music Theory, College of the Desert, Palm Desert (1990-1992); Chief Development Officer, ArtScope, Palm Desert, CA (1987-1991); Public Delos Publications, Verdugo City, CA (1984-2005); Executive Director, Glendale Regional Arts Council, California (1982-1990); Managing Director, Guild Opera Company, Hollywood, CA (1981-1987); Music Teacher, Mount Olive Christian Elementary School, La Crescenta, CA (1971-1973); Statistical Analyst, Pacific Finance (1957-1959); Supervisor of Office Services, Stanford Research Institute (1951-1957) **CR:** California Piano Performance Workshop for Adults (2013-Present); Board of Directors, Encore! Musical Moments in Salon Settings (1994-Present); Steinway Society of Riverside County; Virginia Waring International Piano Competition **CIV:** Founder, President, Coachella Valley Arts Alliance (2005-2006); Founder, President, Coachella Valley Arts Alliance (2000-2003); Board of Directors, La Quinta Open

Air Museum (1996-2000); Commissioner, La Quinta Cultural Commission (1994-2000); Board of Directors, Glendale Youth Orchestra (1989-1990); Board of Directors, Glendale Chamber Orchestra (1983-1989); Member, Fine Arts Task Force, Glendale Unified School District (1983); Board of Directors, Pasadena Boys Choir (1982-1992) **CW:** Author, "Pure Luck"; Author, "Sarah's In-Line Skating Olympics"; Author, "Tory's Adventure With Johann Sebastian Bach"; Author, "Tory, the Time Traveler, An Adventure with Wolfgang Amadeus Mozart"; Author, "Tory Meets Ludwig van Beethoven"; Contributor, Articles, Professional Journals **AW:** Arts Award, Palm Desert Chamber of Commerce (1992); Dedication of Symphony No. 1, Brooke Halpin, Pasadena (1982); Service to the Arts Award, Glendale Regional Arts council (1979); Honorary Service Award, California Congress Parents and Teachers (1977) **MEM:** President, California Piano Performance Workshop for Adults (2017-Present); President, Music Teachers of the Desert (2014-2016, 2004); Board of Directors, California Association of Professional Music Teachers (2006-2008, 1968-2002); President, Steinway Society of Riverside County (2005-2006); Secretary, Steinway Society of Riverside County (2004-2005); Vice President, Music Teachers National Association (2001-2003); Treasurer, Music Teachers National Association (1993-1997); Board of Directors, Music Teachers National Association (1983-2003); American Society of Composers, Authors and Publishers; Judge, Virginia Waring International Piano Competition; Co-founder, Associates of the Brand Library and Art Center **MH:** Albert Nelson Marquis Lifetime Achievement Award (2017) **H:** Reading; Travel **PA:** Republican **RE:** Presbyterian **ADD:** PO Box 947, La Quinta, CA, 92247 **URL:** http://www.kathrynbhull.com

HUMMEL, KAY HETHERINGTON, **T:** Physical Therapist **I:** Medicine & Health Care **DOB:** 04/24/1943 **PB:** Cleveland **SC:** OH/USA **PT:** Lloyd Elmer Hetherington; Olive Agnes (Latou) Hetherington **MS:** Single **SPN:** Charles William Hummel, Divorced (2/1984) **CH:** Patrick H.; Robin E. **ED:** BA, Miami University (1965) **CT:** Certified in Physical Therapy, Columbia University (1966); Licensed Physical Therapist, State of Louisiana; Certified Official, Games Uniting Mind and Body **C:** Board Member, GUMBOINC (2008-Present); Physical Therapist, Private Practice, Shreveport (1985-2017); Part-Time Therapist, Little Works Pediatric Therapy (2009-2010); Itinerant Physical Therapist, Caddo Parish Public Schools (1976-2009); Board Member, GUMBOINC (1996-2002); Assistant Chief Physical Therapist, Community General Hospital (Now SUNY Upstate Medical University) (1970-1976); Staff Physical Therapist, Holy Cross Health (1969-1970); Staff Physical Therapist, Suburban Hospital, Johns Hopkins Health System (1969); Staff Physical Therapist, Wrightwood Extended Care Facility (1967-1968); Staff Physical Therapist, Saint Joseph Hospital, Presence Health (1966-1968) **CIV:** Elder, Presbyterian Church (USA) (2016-Present); Historian, Presbyterian Women Pines Presbytery (2016-Present); Moderator, Presbytery of the Pines (2009-2015) **AW:** Recipient, Albert Nelson Marquis Lifetime Achievement Award (2017); Honoree, Caddo/Bossier CEC Most Exceptional Resource Person (1986-1987); Recipient, Presbyterian Women's Life Member Award **MEM:** Presbyterian Women in the PC(USA), Inc; Team Coordinator, Presbytery of the Pines; North Louisiana Scottish Society of the Louisiana **MH:** Albert Nelson Marquis Lifetime Achievement Award (2017) **H:** Arts and crafts; Watching movies and plays **ADD:** 9437 Wardlow Dr, Shreveport, LA, 71106

HUMPHREY, DIANA, **T:** Volunteer, Fundraiser **I:** Nonprofit & Philanthropy **CN:** The Junior League of Boston, Inc., Boston Symphony Orchestra **DOB:** 02/07/1938 **PB:** Baltimore **SC:** MD/USA **PT:** Edwin Parson Young; Elizabeth Miller (Hoskins) Young **SPN:** George Lee Humphrey (5/22/1999); David Henry Carls (7/27/1963, Divorced 12/17/1997) **CH:** Peter Van Patten Carls; Elizabeth Roy Carls; Susan Montanye **ED:** AB, Smith College (1960); Diploma, The Wheeler School; Coursework, Roland Park Country School **CT:** Licensed Real Estate Broker, State of Massachusetts (1978) **C:** Events Fundraiser, Boston Symphony Orchestra (1975-Present); Volunteer Fundraiser, The Junior League of Boston, Inc. (1967-Present); Member, Board of Development, Center House, Inc. (Now Center Club Boston), Boston, MA (1981-1994); Volunteer Fundraiser, Smith College Club, Concord, MA (1976-1989); Foreign Rights Sales Representative, Little, Brown & Company, Hachette Book Group, Boston, MA (1960-1963); Volunteer Fundraiser, Bay Cove Human Services, Inc.; Co-Chair, 60th Reunion, Smith College; Director of Education, Hawthorne Partners Inc. **CR:** Honorary Member, Board of Events Fundraising, Massachusetts Society for the Prevention of Cruelty to Children, Boston, MA (1997-Present) **CIV:** Wayland Housing Partnership (1987-2004); Chairman, Wayland Planning Board, Wayland, MA (1976-1981); Advocate, John V. Lindsay for Mayor, New York, NY (1964-1965); Speechwriter, Nelson A. Rockefeller Presidential Campaign, New York, NY (1963-1964); Advisory Committee, REACH, Waltham, MA; Massachusetts Society for the Prevention of Cruelty to Children; Girl Scouts of Eastern Massachusetts; Former President, theseawayvillascondominium.com **CW:** Editor, Huntington Hartford Gallery of Modern Art, New York, NY (1963) **MEM:** The Junior League of Boston, Inc.; The Weston Golf Club **H:** Golfing; Traveling; Gardening; Singing; Discussing politics **RE:** Episcopalian **ADD:** 42 Cutting Cross Way, Wayland, MA, 01778

HUNDLEY, JOHN THOMAS, **T:** President, Lawyer **I:** Law and Legal Services **CN:** Sharp-Hundley, P.C. **DOB:** 10/13/1948 **PB:** Abilene **SC:** KS/USA **PT:** Thomas Woodrow Hundley; Hazel Annabelle (Masterson) Hundley **MS:** Married **SPN:** Judith Ann Hundley (2015) **CH:** Amy Frances; Joseph Andrew; Julia Hazel **ED:** JD, DePaul University College of Law, with Honors (1979); BS, University of Illinois, with Honors (1970) **C:** President, Lawyer, Sharp-Hundley, P.C. (2014-Present); Partner, The Sharp Law Firm, P.C. (2005-2014); Lawyer, The Sharp Law Firm, P.C. (2004); Owner, John T. Hundley Law Offices, Chicago, IL (1997-2004); Partner, Hundley & Brusslan, Chicago, IL (1994-1997); Owner, John T. Hundley Law Offices, Chicago, IL (1990-1994); Partner, Mayer, Brown & Platt, Chicago, IL (1986-1990); Associate, Mayer, Brown & Platt, Chicago, IL (1979-1986); Owner, President, Sharp-Hundley, P.C. **CR:** Cooperating Evaluator, Moot Court Competitions, Southern Illinois University School of Law (2004-Present); Consultant, Business Law Course, The American School (1997-1998); Adviser, Kenwood Academy Local School Council, Chicago, IL (1991-1997); Adjunct Instructor, Pretrial Civil Litigation, DePaul University College of Law (1990-1991); Adjunct Faculty, DuSable High School, Chicago Coalition for Law-Related Education (1989); School Reform Advisory Project, Chicago Lawyers' Committee for Civil Rights Under Law (1987-1991) **CIV:** Lecturer, Living Wills & the Alternatives, Grace United Protestant Church, Park Forest, IL (2004); Lecturer, Wills & the Alternatives, Grace United Protestant Church, Park Forest, IL (2004); Lay Leader, Grace United Church, Park Forest, IL (2002-2004); Treasurer, United Church of Hyde Park, Chicago,

IL (1993-1996); Secretary, United Church of Hyde Park, Chicago, IL (1989-1991) **CW:** Lecturer, Powers of Attorney and the Impaired Client, Franklin County Bar Association (2012); Speaker, "Advance Directives: Living Wills & The Alternatives," Mt. Vernon Rotary Club (2010); Lecturer, "Important Issues for Litigation Under the Bankruptcy Abuse Prevention & Consumer Protection Act," Southern Illinois Bankers Seminar (2005); Lecturer, Debt Collection in Illinois, National Business Institute (2004); Author, "Respondents in Discovery: A Beneficent Statute with Traps for the Unwary"; Contributor, Numerous Articles, Professional Journals **AW:** Litigation Council of America (2016); Lawyers of Distinction (2015-2016); District 6510 Rotarian of the Year, Rotary International District 6510 (2014); Chicago Bar Association Pro Bono Service Award (1997); Sigma Delta Chi College Newspaper Editorial Excellence Award (1970); Martindale-Hubbell Bar Register of Preeminent Lawyers; Super Lawyers of Illinois; Leading Lawyers Network of Illinois; Martindale-Hubbell AV Rating **MEM:** President, Mt. Vernon Rotary Club, IL (2011-2012); Board of Directors, DePaul University College of Law Alumni (1989-1994); ABA; Illinois State Bar Association; Jefferson County Bar Association; Illinois Creditors Bar Association **BAR:** United States District Court, Southern District of Illinois (2001); United States District Court, Central District of Illinois (1983); United States District Court, Northern District of California (1981); United States Court of Appeals for the Seventh Circuit (1980); Supreme Court of Illinois (1979); United States District Court, Northern District of Illinois (1979); Illinois (1979) **MH:** Albert Nelson Marquis Lifetime Achievement Award (2017) **PA:** Democrat **RE:** United Methodist **BA:** 1115 Harrison Street, Sharp-Hundley, PC, Mount Vernon, IL, 62864 **URL:** http://www.sharp-hundley.com

HUNSPERGER, ELIZABETH JANE, T: Educator **I:** Education/Educational Services **CN:** St. Joseph's University **DOB:** 08/30/1938 **PB:** Philadelphia **SC:** PA/USA **PT:** Francis Charles Thorpe; Elizabeth Julia Thorpe **MS:** Married **SPN:** Robert George Hunsperger (9/13/1958) **CH:** Lisa Marie **ED:** EdD in Educational Technology, University of Delaware, Newark, DE (2006); MA in Education, Delaware State College (1993); Postgraduate Studies, Rutgers, The State University of New Jersey (1978-1981); BA in Art History, University of Delaware, Newark, DE (1978); Student, University of California, Los Angeles (1975-1976); AA in Design, Santa Monica College, California (1974) **C:** Adjunct Professor of Education, St. Joseph's University, Philadelphia, PA (2011-Present); Art and Design Consultant, Lecturer, Art & Science Associates, Galena, MD (2001-Present); Art and Design Consultant, Lecturer, Art & Science Associates, Newark, DE (1980-2001); Freelance Designer, Malibu, CA (1967-1976); Designer, Cornell University, Ithaca, NY (1965-1967); Designer, Rothschild's, Ithaca, NY (1963-1965); Designer, Huntingdon Mills, Philadelphia, PA (1960-1963) **CR:** Art and Special Education Teacher, Dover High School, Capital School District (2006-Present); Art and Special Education Teacher, A.I. DuPont Institute, Wilmington, DE (1999-Present); Consultant, Educational and Design Services, Newark, DE (1995-Present); Educator, Kent County Public Schools, Maryland (2002-2004); Art Teacher, Kent County High School, Maryland (2002-2004); Art and Special Education Teacher, Shorehaven School, Chesapeake City, MD (1997-1999); Art and Special Education Teacher, A.I. DuPont High School, Red Clay Consolidated School District, Greenville, DE (1995-1997); Leech School (1994); Art Teacher, Catholic Diocese of Wilmington (1988-

1995); Consultant, Arts and Science Associates; Coordinator, Delmarva Education Action Learning Project **CIV:** President, Newark Housing Ministry, Inc. (1989-1991); Founding Member, Board of Directors, Vice President, Newark Housing Ministry, Inc. (1983-1994); Active, Council for Exceptional Children; Social Concerns Committee and Drug and Alcohol Task Force, Delaware **CW:** Exhibition, Newark Art Show (1987-1988); Exhibition, Malibu Art Association Show (1973-1974) **AW:** Governor's Volunteer of the Year Award, State of Delaware (1990); Award of Recognition Missionhurst (1982); Outstanding Service Award, YWCA, Santa Monica, CA (1972) **MEM:** National Art Education Association; American Craft Council; Board of Directors, President, Art Educators of Delaware; Soroptimist International; Debutante Assembly Club, New York City, NY **MH:** Albert Nelson Marquis Lifetime Achievement Award (2017) **H:** Painting; Boating; Gardening **PA:** Episcopal **ADD:** 3723 SE 18th Ave, Cape Coral, FL, 33904

HUNT, ROSEMARY, T: Language Educator **I:** Education/Educational Services **CN:** Technical College of the Lowcountry **DOB:** 04/24/1951 **PB:** Charleston **SC:** SC/USA **PT:** James Albert; Armine Kingsland Richardson **MS:** Married (8/13/1969) **SPN:** F. Nicholas Hunt **CH:** Tabitha Lynn **ED:** MA in Spanish, California State University, Sacramento (1995); BS in Secondary Education, College Charleston (1975); AA in Liberal Arts, Cape Cod Community College, Hyannis, MA (1972) **C:** Spanish instructor, Technical College of the Lowcountry, Beaufort (1993-Present); Spanish Teacher, Department Chairperson, Beaufort Academy, South Carolina (1976-1997) **CIV:** Host Mother, Rotary International Youth Exchange Program, Beaufort; Past President, Beaufort County Literacy Associate, Rotary District 7770 Rotary Youth Exchange Committee Member **H:** Travel; Animal Rescue, Watercolor **PA:** Democrat **RE:** Unitarian Universalist **ADD:** 12 Mises Road, Beaufort, SC, 29907

HYLAND, THOMAS W., T: Partner **I:** Law and Legal Services **CN:** Wilson Elser **DOB:** 05/25/1943 **PB:** New York **SC:** NY/USA **PT:** John Hyland; Anne (Dunleavey) Hyland **MS:** Married **SPN:** Coleen (2000); Francine Miles (10/1971, Deceased) **CH:** Jennifer; Thomas; Dylan (Stepchild); Conor (Stepchild); Carys (Stepchild) **ED:** LLM in Intellectual Property, New York University (1974); JD, Fordham University (1971); BA, Fordham University (1965) **C:** Partner, Wilson Elser (1977-2018); Chief Trial Counsel, New York Regional Office, Securities and Exchange Commission (1975-1977); Assistant District Attorney, The City of New York (1971-1975) **CR:** Adjunct Professor, Hunter College (1977-1982); Guest Lecturer, National College of District Attorneys (1975); Instructor, University of Houston; Instructor, Hunter College; Instructor, Maurice A. Deane School of Law, Hofstra University **MIL:** Captain, U.S. Army (1965-1971) **CW:** Co-author, Report on the Financial Collapse of the City of New York; Contributor, Articles, Professional Journals; Lecturer in Field **AW:** Honoree, Military and NYC Army Reserve Officer Corps Hall of Fame, Fordham University (2017); Featured Listee, Professional Liability: Defense Category, New York Super Lawyers (2008-2017); Named to "Irish Legal 100," Irish Voice (2011-2012); Child of Peace Award, Catholic Guardian Society (2007); Fellow, American College of Trial Lawyers; Honoree, AV Preeminent Attorney, Martindale-Hubbell; Recipient, 12 Military Decorations, U.S. Army **MEM:** Lawyers' Liability Review, Association of the Bar of the City of New York; Advisory

Board, DRI; Federal Bar Council; International Association of Defense Counsel; ABA; North Hempstead Country Club; New York Athletic Club **BAR:** Pennsylvania (1987); Supreme Court of the United States (1977); New York (1971); United States District Court Eastern District of New York (1972); United States Court of Appeals for the Second Circuit (1972); United States District Court Northern District of New York; United States District Court Southern District of New York; United States District Court Western District of New York; United States Court of Appeals for the Ninth Circuit **MH:** Albert Nelson Marquis Lifetime Achievement Award (2017) **H:** Golf; Tennis; Reading; New York Giants; Sports **BA:** 150 E 42nd St Bsmt 1, Elser Moskowitz Edelman & Dicker, LLP, New York, NY, 10017 **URL:** https://www.wilsonelser.com/attorneys/thomas_w_hyland

IDELCHIK, GARY M., T: Physician **I:** Medicine & Health Care **CN:** Dr. Gary M. Idelchik **MS:** Married **ED:** MD, University of Texas Southwestern Medical School, Dallas, TX (2002); Residency, University of Michigan Medical Center, Ann Arbor, MI; Internship, University of Michigan Medical Center, Ann Arbor, MI; Fellowship, Cardiology and Interventional Cardiology, Texas Heart Institute at St. Luke's Episcopal Hospital, Baylor College of Medicine, Houston, TX; Department of Cardiology Structural Heart Disease Fellowship, Chaim Sheba Medical Center at Tel HaShomer, Tel Aviv, Israel; Fellowship, Rambam Medical Center, Haifa, Israel **C:** Cardiology and Interventional Cardiology **AW:** Elite American Physicians (2015); Patient's Choice Award (2011-2015); Compassionate Doctor Recognition (2011-2015); Top Ten Doctors (2010-2015) **MEM:** American Board of Internal Medicine; Certified Cardiovascular Disease and Interventional Cardiology; Certification Board of Nuclear Cardiology; American Heart Association; American College of Cardiology Association; Texas Medical Association; Society of Coronary Angiography and Intervention **H:** Spending time with his wife; Race cars; Guitar; Cooking; Reading; Playing with his two miniature Schnauzers **ADD:** 5 Campion Lane, Saratoga Springs, NY, 12866

IMEL, ELIZABETH CARMEN CARMEN, T: Retired Physical Education Educator **I:** Education/Educational Services **DOB:** 05/22/1905 **PB:** Galesburg **SC:** IL/USA **PT:** Leo Henry Imel; Anna Imel **ED:** PhD, The University of Iowa, Iowa City, Iowa (1966); MA, The University of Iowa, Iowa City, Iowa (1964); BS in Education, Illinois State University, Normal, IL (1957) **C:** Retired (1995); Professor, Illinois State University, Normal, IL (1964-1995); Instructor, Research Methods, Dance, Physical Education, Kinesiology, The University of Iowa, Iowa City, Iowa (1962-1964) **CR:** President, Illinois Dance Association (1978-1980) **CIV:** Board Member, Hays County Historical Commission (2012); Board of Directors, Lyndon B. Johnson Museum (2006); Fundraising Advisory Board, Texas State University (2005-2006); Chairman, San Marcos Arts Commission (2003-2005); Active, Citizen's Review Commission, San Marcos, Texas (2000-2002); Active, Illinois Arts Commission (1981-1982); Regent, Daughters of the American Revolution (Now National Society Daughters of the American Revolution (NSDAR); President-elect, Friends of the San Marcos Cemetery, San Marcos, Texas; Secretary, Board Member, Lyndon B. Johnson Museum, San Marcos, Texas **CW:** Editor, Focus on Dance VIII Dance Heritage (1977); Editor, AAHPERED Periodical (1968-1970) **AW:** Named to Women's Hall of Fame, San Marcos, Texas (2005) **MEM:** Board of Directors, Heritage Association of San Marcos (2000-2006) **RE:** Lutheran

IMPELLIZERI, JOHN, T: Mathematics Educator **I:** Education/Educational Services **CN:** Uniondale School District **PT:** Jack Impellizeri; Catherine Impellizeri **MS:** Married **SPN:** Mary T. Blaney (8/28/1982) **CH:** Traci A.; Jack P.; Jeremy J. **ED:** MS in Education, New Paltz, State University of New York (1978); BA, New Paltz, State University of New York (1973) **CT:** Certified Teacher, New York State Education Department (1985) **C:** Mathematics Teacher, Uniondale School Teacher (1985) **CR:** Adjunct Associate Professor, Mathematics, Computers and Statistics Department, Nassau Community (1999-Present); Founding President, JMI Computer Services (1985-Present) **CIV:** Performer, Yesterday, Today & Tomorrow Entertainment Group (1978-2005); Director, Yesterday, Today & Tomorrow Entertainment Group (1978-2005); Founder, Yesterday, Today & Tomorrow Entertainment Group (1978-2005); Former Chief Timer, New York Region, SCCA; Former Scorer, New York Region, SCCA; Former Choral Member, The Cecilia Chorus of New York; Former Emergency Medical Technician Instructor, Franklin General Hospital; Former Choral Member, The Masterwork Chorus; Former Firefighter, Emergency Company Nine, Freeport Fire Department; Former Crew Chief, Port Jefferson EMS; Former First Aid Instructor, The American National Red Cross; Former Choir Member, Adult Choir, Our Holy Redeemer Roman Catholic Church; Former Co-Leader of Antioch Weekends, Our Holy Redeemer Roman Catholic Church; Former Leader of Folk Group, Our Holy Redeemer Roman Catholic Church; Former Vice President of School Board, Our Holy Redeemer Roman Catholic Church **CW:** Author, "Basic Mathematics Workbook"; Author, "Hyde Park Townsman," Anderson School; Author, "Archbishop Molloy Council Yearbook"; Editor, "Archbishop Molloy Council Yearbook"; Publisher, "Archbishop Molloy Council Yearbook"; Editor, "The Molloy Monitor"; Author, "The Molloy Monitor"; Publisher, "The Molloy Monitor"; Director, "RST Presents Lawrence Road JHS"; Producer, "RST Presents Lawrence Road JHS"; Contributor, Articles, Newspapers **AW:** Website of the Year, Knights of Columbus (2003); Third Place in Nassau County Bulletin Contest, Nassau/Suffolk Chapter, Knights of Columbus (1998); Top Website in the World, Knights of Columbus (1997); Featured Listee, #15 of Top 40 Catholic Websites in the World (19970 **MEM:** Grand Knight, Archbishop Molloy Council, Knights of Columbus (1998-2000); International Council of Webmasters; Nassau Reading Council; National PTA; Associate, Adjunct Faculty Association; Associate, Uniondale Teachers Association; Associate, Padre Pio Fourth Degree Assembly, Knights of Columbus; Friends for Long Island Heritage; Webmaster, Knights of Columbus; Supreme Council Internet Steering Committee, Knights of Columbus; Coordinator, Internet Workshop, Knights of Columbus; Associate, Archbishop Molloy Council, Knights of Columbus **MH:** Albert Nelson Marquis Lifetime Achievement Award (2017) **RE:** Roman Catholic **ADD:** 25 Lexington Ave, Freeport, NY, 11520

IMPELLIZZERI, ANNE ELMENDORF, T: Insurance Company Executive, Non-Profit Executive **I:** Insurance **DOB:** 01/26/1933 **PB:** Chicago **SC:** IL/USA **PT:** Armin Elmendorf; Laura (Gundlach) Elmendorf **MS:** Widowed **SPN:** Julius Simon Impellizzeri (10/12/1961, Deceased) **CH:** Laura Impellizzeri Wakeling; Theodore (Deceased); Julius Impellizzeri (Stepson); Robert Lee Walker (Stepson) **ED:** MA, Yale University (1957); BA, Smith College, Magna Cum Laude (1955) **CT:** Chartered Life Underwriter; Chartered Financial Consultant **C:** Executive Director, Russel Wright's Manitoga, Garrison, NY (1998-2001); President,

Chief Executive Officer, Blanton-Peale Institute, New York City, NY (1990-1998); Vice President, New York City Partnership, New York City, NY (1988-1990); Assistant Vice President, Vice President, Corporate Social Responsibility to Vice President of Group Insurance, Metropolitan Life Insurance Company, New York City, NY (1979-1988); Employee, Metropolitan Life Insurance Company, New York City, NY (1959-1988) **CR:** Trustee, Nuveen Mutual Funds (1994-2004); Trustee, Smith College (1991-1996); Board of Directors, Bard Music Festival (1990-2011); Business Urban Issues Council, The Conference Board (1981-1985) **CIV:** Treasurer, Board of Directors, Network 20/20 (2011-Present); Planning Board, Village of Cold Spring (2014-2015); Special Board for the Comprehensive Plan LWRP, Village of Cold Spring (2012); Special Board for the Comprehensive Plan LWRP, Village of Cold Spring (2011); Vice Chair, Village of Cold Spring (2009-2013); Special Board for the Comprehensive Plan LWRP, Village of Cold Spring (2006-2013); Secretary, Scenic Hudson (2004-2008); Treasurer, Scenic Hudson (1999-2002); Board of Directors, Scenic Hudson (1997-2009); Chair, American Association for Gifted Children (1985-1990); President, American Association for Gifted Children (1975-1985); Board of Directors, National Safety Council (1974-1980); President, Lakeland Board of Education, Westchester County, New York (1970-1971); Trustee, Lakeland Board of Education, Westchester County, New York (1967-1971) **AW:** Named, Academy of Women Achievers, YWCA of the City of New York (1978); Fulbright Grantee, Germany (1955-1956) **MEM:** Vice President, Women's City Club New York (2004-2006); Board Member, Women's City Club New York (2002-2006); Board of Governors, Association of Yale Alumni (1985-1988); Phi Beta Kappa; Yale Club of New York City; Smith College Club of New York City **MH:** Albert Nelson Marquis Lifetime Achievement Award (2017) **ADD:** 15 High St, Cold Spring, NY, 10516

INCHIOSA, MARIO A. JR., T: Professor **I:** Education/Educational Services **CN:** New York Medical College **PB:** Weehawken **SC:** NJ/USA **PT:** Mario Inchiosa; Christina Inchiosa **MS:** Married **SPN:** Elisabeth Harris Stamm (8/14/1977); Valerie Norma Stoppani (7/4/1955, Deceased 1/10/1972) **CH:** Maria Valerie Warburton; Mario Emil; Andrew Stamm **ED:** PhD, University of Illinois (1956); MS, Rutgers, The State University of New Jersey (1953); BS, Rutgers, The State University of New Jersey (1950) **C:** Professor of Pharmacology, New York Medical College, Valhalla, New York (1966-Present); Research Professor of Anesthesiology (1980-Present); Director, M.D./Ph.D. Program (1981-2007); Vice Chairman, Department of Pharmacology (1983-2010); Associate Dean for Academic Affairs (1985-1988) (all at New York Medical College); Research Associate, Harvard Medical School, Harvard University, Boston, Massachusetts (1960-1966); Senior Research Scientist, Department of Mental Hygiene, New York State, Staten Island, New York (1958-1960); Postdoctoral Fellow, Argonne National Laboratory, Argonne, Illinois (1956-1958) **CR:** Consultant, U.S. Food and Drug Administration, Washington (1996-Present) **CW:** Contributor, Articles, Professional Journals; Author, Books **AW:** Grantee, Berlex Laboratories, Inc. (1998-2001); Grantee, American Heart Association, Inc. (1987-1990); Grantee, National Heart and Lung Institute, National Institutes of Health (1970-1974); Grantee, U.S. Public Health Service (1974-1977); Grantee, National Heart Institute, National Institutes of Health (1963-1967) **MEM:** Society of Cardiovascular Anesthesiologists; International Anesthesia Research Society; The American

Society for Pharmacology and Experimental Therapeutics **MH:** Albert Nelson Marquis Lifetime Achievement Award (2017) **ADD:** 33 Clairmont Dr, Woodcliff Lake, NJ, 07677

INGERSOLL, JOHN, T: President & Founder **I:** Engineering **CN:** EcoCorp, Inc. **DOB:** 07/25/1948 **PB:** Athens **SC:** Greece **PT:** Gregory Ingersoll; Catherine (Asteris) Ingersoll **ED:** PhD, University of California, Berkeley (1978); MS, Syracuse University (1973); BS, National Technical University, Athens, Greece (1970) **C:** President & Founder & Founder, EcoCorp, Inc. (1999-Present); Founder, President, Helios International (Now EcoCorp, Inc.) (1991-2005); Staff Member, Advisor, United States Navy Energy Office, Washington, D.C. (1988-2011); Senior Staff Scientist, Hughes Aircraft Co., Los Angeles, CA (1983-1988); From Assistant Research Professor to Associate Research Professor, Lawrence Berkeley National Laboratory, University of California, Berkeley (1978-1982); Research Assistant, Lawrence Berkeley National Laboratory, University of California, Berkeley (1975-1977); Instructor of Physics, University of California, Berkeley (1974-1975) **CR:** Adjunct Associate Professor, Department of Industrial and System Engineering, University of Southern California (1996-Present); Building Industry, States of New York and California (1982-Present); Energy, Environmental and Technology Policy Advisor, USAID (2000-2002); Member, Technologies Team for Development of a Commercial Passenger Electric Vehicle, General Motors (1990-1993); Principal Investigator, Energy Technologies Group, Local Governments on Alternative Fuels, University of California, Los Angeles (1983-1993); U.S. Department Energy, Washington, D.C. (1981-1983); Consultant, California Energy Commission, Sacramento, CA (1981-1982) **CIV:** Member, Republican Presidential Task Force, CA (1981-1983) **MIL:** Commander, United States Naval Reserve (1982-2011) **CW:** Contributor, "Biomethane" (2011); Author, "Natural Gas Vehicles" (1996); Contributor, Over 100 Articles on Nuclear Science, Renewable Energy Sources, Indoor Air Quality, Efficient Utilization of Energy in Buildings, Passive Solar Systems, Solar Electrical Energy, Alternative Fuel Vehicle to Professional Journals; Author, One Book on Natural Gas Vehicles; Contributing Author, Three Books on Energy Management in Buildings; Patentee, Heat Pipe Developments, Non-freon Low Power Air Conditioner for Electric Vehicles and Buses **AW:** Honorary Membership, Cosmos Club (2015); First Place Award in Energy Efficient Design of Buildings, West-Side Cities (2000); First Place Award, Smithsonian Institute, American Institute of Architects (AIA) (1996); First Place Award, Smithsonian Institute/American Institute of Architects (AIA)/National Renewable Energy Laboratory, U.S. Department of Energy (1996); Second Place Award, Edison Electric Institute, General Motors, and U.S. Department of Energy (1993); Award, Rockefeller Foundation (1974); Award, Syracuse University (1972); Fellow, Democritus Nuclear Research Center, Athens, Greece (1970) **MEM:** General Motors Team (Tasked with Development, Production, Marketing of Passenger Electric Vehicle) **MH:** Albert Nelson Marquis Lifetime Achievement Award (2017) **H:** Walking; Hiking; Studying Archaeology and History of Greece and Egypt **ADD:** 1211 S Eads St Apt 803, Arlington, VA, 22202

INMAN, JAMES RUSSELL, T: Claims Consultant **I:** Consulting **DOB:** 05/24/1936 **PB:** Tucson **SC:** AZ/USA **PT:** Claude Colbert Inman; Myra Eugenia (Langdon) Inman **MS:** Widowed **SPN:** Patricia Ann Barham (6/20/2009, Deceased 11/22/2016); Margaret Williams Kendrick (4/26/1996, Deceased

2/2002); Charleen M. Bowman Inman (2/22/1964, Divorced 1977) **ED:** Coursework, Pomona College, Claremont, CA (1954-1960) **C:** President, Wilnor Corp., Los Angeles, CA (1984-2011); Board of Directors, Wilnor Corp. (1978-1984); Assistant Manager, Firemen's Fund, Beverly Hills, CA (1970-1983); Asbestos Specialist, Firemen's Fund, Beverly Hills, CA (1970-1983); Head, Entertainment Claims, Firemen's Fund, Beverly Hills, CA (1970-1983); Supervisor, Casualty Claims, CNA Insurance, Los Angeles, CA (1961-1970); Supervisor, Research Department, Honnold Library, Claremont College (1959-1960) **CR:** Litigation Senior Specialist, Reliance Insurance Co., Glendale, CA (1992-1994); Claims Consultant, Reliance Insurance Co., Glendale, CA (1992-1994); Assistant to President, American Multiline Corp., Los Angeles, CA (1988-1992); Claims Specialist, American Multiline Corp., Los Angeles, CA (1988-1992); Completion Bond Co., Century City, CA (1988); Claims Manager, Advent Management, Los Angeles, CA (1987); Claims, Auditor Directors and Officers Claims, Harbor/Continental Insurance, Los Angeles, CA (1984-1986); Expert Witness, Entertainment Claims Field **CIV:** Trustee, Woodbury University (2005-2012); President, Alcohol Information Center, Los Angeles, CA (1983-1985); Committee, Baldwin Hills Dam Disaster (1968-1972); First Century Families, California **MEM:** Los Angeles Athletic Club; Wilshire Country Club; Sloane Club, London, England; California Club; California Yacht Club; Jonathan Club; Rotary International **MH:** Albert Nelson Marquis Lifetime Achievement Award (2017) **H:** Classic cars; American and English silver **ADD:** 501 South Rossmore Avenue, Los Angeles, CA, 90020

INMAN, MITCHELL JR., T: Business Advisor **I:** Consulting **CN:** Infinite Health Care Academy **DOB:** 08/18/1951 **PB:** Waycross **SC:** GA/USA **PT:** James Inman; Alma Inman **MS:** Married **SPN:** Donna Gardner Inman **ED:** Coursework, Georgia Southern University (1986-1989); MA in Marketing and Distributive Education, Georgia State University (1982); MA in Business Education, Savannah State University (1975); BBA in Business, Savannah State University, Magna Cum Laude (1972) **C:** Business Advisor, Infinite Health Care Academy, Hinesville, GA (2015-Present); Board of Directors, Ware Inc. (2006-Present); Instructor of Marketing, Savannah Technical College (1986-2011); Director of Public Information, Savannah Technical College (1984-1986); Instructor of Marketing, Savannah Technical College (1974-1984); Purchasing Agent, Amoco Oil Co. (1973-1974) **CR:** President, Savannah Technical College Faculty Council (1998); Chairperson, Georgia Marketing Teacher's Consortium (1994-1997); Southeastern Georgia Marketing Teacher's Consortium (1994-1998) **CIV:** Board of Directors, Infinite Health Care Academy, Hinesville, GA (2014-Present); Board Member, Georgia Workforce Investment Board (1999-2004); Board Member, National Technology Honor Society (1988-1999); Board Member, Superintendent's Advisory Committee, Savannah-Chatham County Schools (1980-1982); Board Member, Garden City Planning Communications (1978-1984) **MIL:** Personnelman, Third Class, U.S. Naval Reserve (1986-1992) **AW:** Georgia Occupational Leadership Award (2007); Navy Meritorious Service Achievement Award, U.S. Naval Reserve (1990); Addy Award, Advertising Club of Savannah (1985-1986); Teacher of the Year, Savannah Technical College (1983); Georgia Occupational Leadership Award (1979) **MEM:** National Education Association; Alpha Kappa Mu National Honor Society; Savannah State University **H:** Restoring classic cars **PA:** Democrat **RE:** Baptist **ADD:** 1001 Riverside Avenue, Waycross, GA, 31501

INOUE, SUSUMU, T: Pediatric Hematologist/ Oncologist **I:** Medicine & Health Care **CN:** Hurley Medical Center **DOB:** 03/23/1940 **PB:** Kurashiki **SC:** Japan **SPN:** Mary Mitchell-Beren **CH:** Lisa; Hajime; Anne **ED:** Research Fellow, Cytogenetics, The Child Research Center of Michigan, Resident, Pediatrics Children's Hospital Michigan, Detroit, MI (1966-1968); Intern, Yokosuka Naval Hospital (1964-1965); MD, Okayama University (1964); BS, Okayama University (1960); Fellowship, Children's Hospital of Michigan **CT:** Certified in Pediatric Hematology-Oncology; Certified in Pediatrics **C:** Clinical Professor of Pediatrics, Wayne State University, Detroit, MI (1996-Present); Associate Director of Pediatrics Residency, Hurley Medical Center, Flint, MI (1987-2017); Director of Pediatric Hematology, Oncology, Hurley Medical Center, Flint, MI (1987-2015); Professor of Pediatrics, Michigan State University, East Lansing, MI (1987) **CIV:** Board of Directors, American Red Cross; Sickle Cell Support Group Board of Directors, Carriage Commons Condo Association **CW:** Contributed, Articles, Professional Journals; Contributor, Chapters, Books **AW:** William Weil Award, Michigan State University (2006) **MEM:** Society of Pediatrics Research; International Society of Experimental Hematology; American Society of Pediatric Hematology/Oncology; American Society of Clinical Oncology; American Society of Hematology **MH:** Albert Nelson Marquis Lifetime Achievement Award (2017) **H:** Travel; Zumba; Mystery books; Singing **PA:** Democrat **RE:** Christian **BA:** Hurley Medical Center, One Hurley Plaza, Flint, MI, 48503 **ADD:** 9140 Luea Ln, Swartz Creek, MI, 48473

ISAACS, ROGER DAVID, T: Public Relations Executive **I:** Corporate Communications & Public Relations **CN:** The Public Relations Board, Inc. **DOB:** 10/23/1925 **PB:** Boston **SC:** MA/USA **PT:** Raphael Isaacs; Agnes (Wolfstein) Isaacs **MS:** Married **SPN:** Joyce R. (Wexler) (5/26/1927) **CH:** Gillian; Jan **ED:** AB, Bard College (1949); Coursework, University of Wisconsin (1943) **C:** Senior Counselor, The Financial Relations Board, Inc., Chicago, IL; Public Relations Board, Inc., Chicago, IL (1948-1985); Senior Counselor, Porter/Novelli, Chicago, IL (1989-1991); Executive Vice President, General Manager, Doremus Porter Novelli, Chicago, IL (1986-1989); Chairman, PRB, a Needham Porter Novelli Co., Chicago, IL; Chairman, President, Public Relations Board, Inc., Chicago, IL (1975-1986); President, Public Relations Board, Inc., Chicago, IL (1966-1975); Executive Vice President, Public Relations Board, Inc., Chicago, IL (1960-1966); Partner, Public Relations Board, Inc., Chicago, IL (1951-1960); Account Supervisor, Public Relations Board, Inc., Chicago, IL (1948-1951) **CIV:** Board of Directors, Anti-Defamation League Chicago; Jewish Family and Community Service; Senior Centers Metropolitan Chicago; Highland Park Hospital; Metropolitan Crusade of Mercy; Suburban Fine Arts Center; Asthma and Allergy Foundation; Spertus College Community Advisory Board Station WBEZ; Board of Directors, Chicago Crime Commission; Life Board of Directors, North Shore University Health Systems; Advisory Council, Oriental Institute, The University of Chicago **MIL:** 345th Regiment, 87th Infantry, U.S. Army (1943-1945) **CW:** Author, "Talking with God: An Etymological Study of the Bible" (2010); Author, "The Golden Ark" (2016) **AW:** Decorated Purple Heart; Combat Infantryman Badge; French Legion of Honor; Bronze Star; Three Battle Stars, American Campaign, Army of Occupation Germany **MEM:** Accredited, Public Relations Society of America; Publicity Club of Chicago; Northmoor Country Club **ADD:** 1045 Hillcrest Rd, Glencoe, IL, 60022 **URL:** http://talkingwithgod.net/

ISACOFF, RICHARD I., T: Financial Planner **I:** Financial Services **CN:** MW Financial Group, Ltd. **DOB:** 09/07/1950 **PB:** New Haven **SC:** CT/USA **PT:** Paul Isacoff; Doris (Tashman) Isacoff **MS:** Married **SPN:** Bette Francesconi Isacoff (5/2/1970) **CH:** Kira Lyn Nash **ED:** JD, Western New England College (1977); BA, Western New England College (1972); Coursework, Clark University (1970) **CT:** Securities Licenses; Series 7 and 66 **C:** Financial Planner, MW Financial Group, Ltd., Farmington CT (2016-Present); Attorney, Richard I. Isacoff, P.C., Pittsfield, MA (1992-2016); Senior Vice President, Director of Trust Department, Bank of New England-West (1988-1992); CEO, Concord Savings Bank, FSB, Ellicott City, MD (1988-1988); Managing Officer, Universal Savings and Loan (1987-1988); Senior Vice President, Sharon Savings and Loan, Baltimore, MD (1986-1987); Director, Corporate Staff and Strategic Planning, In-House Counsel, Congressional Lobbying, Provident Bank of Maryland (1982-1986); Director of Human Resources and Corporate Secretary, Aspen Systems Corporation, Rockville, MD (1980-1982); Trust Officer, Third National Bank (1973-1977) **CR:** Financial Committee, PBS-WGBY TV, Springfield, MA; Allocations Committee, United Way of Pioneer Valley (1977-1980) **MIL:** 26th Infantry Division, Massachusetts National Guard SP5 (1970-1976); Senior Photographer, Massachusetts National Guard, Public Information Office (1973-1976) **AW:** ARCAM, U.S. Army for Performance in Massachusetts National Guard (1974); Pro Bono Award, Western Massachusetts Pro Bono Council **MEM:** ABA **BAR:** United States District Court, District of Massachusetts (1978); Northern District of New York (2012); Commonwealth of Massachusetts (1977) **MH:** Albert Nelson Marquis Lifetime Achievement Award (2017); Distinguished Humanitarian (2017) **H:** Photography; Dog Showing **BA:** MW Financial Group, Ltd, 197 Scott Swamp Road, Farmington, CT, 06032 **ADD:** Richard I. Isacoff, J.D., 494 Rldge Road, Orange, CT, 06477

ISRAEL, BARRY JOHN, T: Lawyer **I:** Law and Legal Services **DOB:** 03/14/1946 **PB:** Rockford **SC:** IL/USA **PT:** Robert John Israel; Bettie Jane (Erickson) Israel **MS:** Married **SPN:** Le Ngoc Khanh Tam **CH:** Alison; Ashley; Brenna **ED:** Honorary JD, The George Washington University (1974); Honorary BA in International Relations, University of Southern California, Los Angeles, CA (1968) **C:** Chief Executive Officer, Dai Phuc Development Co., Ltd (2014-Present); Chairman, Chief Executive Officer, Saigon Interiors, LLC. (2007-2014); Chairman, Chief Executive Officer, Danao International Holdings, Ltd (2000-2007); Private Law Practice (1995-2000); Partner, Stroock, Stroock & Lavan, Washington, D.C. (1992-1995); Partner, Dorsey & Whitney, Washington, D.C. (1985-1992); Partner, Stovall, Spradlin, Armstrong & Israel, Washington, D.C. (1982-1985); Associate, Clifford & Warnke, Washington, D.C. (1976-1982) **CR:** Board Chairman, Chief Executive Officer, Danao International Holdings Company, Ltd. (2000-2007); Special Assistant, Attorney General, Territory of Guam (1990-1995); Special Counsel, President, Federated States of Micronesia (1982-1984); Board Chairman, Chief Executive Officer, Gallo Ltd., Asia **CIV:** First Lieutenant, United States Army (1969-1972) **CW:** Author, "Investment Guides to the Federated States of Micronesia and the Republic of the Marshall Islands" (1989) **BAR:** United States District Court for the Northern Mariana Islands (1985); Supreme Court of the United States (1978); The District of Columbia Bar (1976); The State Bar of California (1975) **H:** Travel; Tennis **PA:** Democrat **BA:** 12/6 Khoi Nghia Bac Son, Villa 1A, Ward 10, Dalat, Vietnam, N/A

IVANOV, KOSTADIN NIKOLOV, **T:** Professor, Department Head **I:** Education/Educational Services **CN:** North Carolina State University **PB:** Dimitrovgrad **SC:** Bulgaria **PT:** Nikola Kostov Ivanov; Velichka Vangelova Ivanova **MS:** Married **SPN:** Maria N. Avramova **CH:** Mira Ivanova; Emil **ED:** PhD in Reactor Physics, Institute of Nuclear Research and Nuclear Energy, Bulgarian Academy of Sciences (1990); BS in Nuclear Engineering, Moscow Institute of Power Engineering, Russia; MEng in Nuclear Engineering, Moscow Institute of Power Engineering (1982) **CT:** Certified Nuclear Engineer, Bulgaria **C:** Professor of Nuclear Engineering, North Carolina State University (2015-Present); Department Head, Nuclear Engineering, North Carolina State University (2015-Present); Associate Professor, Pennsylvania State University, University Park, PA (1999-Present); Distinguished Professor, Pennsylvania State University (2007-2015); Visiting Professor of Nuclear System Dynamics, Karlsruhe Institute of Technology, University of Karlsruhe, Germany (2011-2012); Professor of Nuclear Engineering, Pennsylvania State University (1997-2007); Assistant Professor, Pennsylvania State University, University Park, PA (1997-1999); Research Associate, Pennsylvania State University, University Park, PA (1996-1997) **CR:** Member, Nuclear Energy Agency, OECD; Chairman, Scientific Board on Uncertainty Analysis in Modeling, Nuclear Energy Agency, OECD **CW:** Author, "Explicit Modeling of a VVER-1000 Radial Reflector by a Ring of Assembly-Size Nodes"; Author, "Genetic Algorithm Methodology for Determining UO2/Gd2O3 Fuel Pin Positions for a PWR Fuel Assembly Design"; Author, "Genetic Algorithm Application for Burnable Poison Placement in PWRs with Optimized UO2/Gd2O3 Fuel Pin Configuration"; Author, "Genetic Algorithm Methodology for Determining UO2/Gd2O3 Fuel Pin Positions for a PWR Fuel Assembly Design"; Author, "Genetic Algorithm Methodology for Determining UO2/Gd2O3 Fuel Pin Positions for a PWR Fuel Assembly Design"; Author, "Application of Genetic Algorithm to Optimize Burnable Poison Placement in PWRs Sensitivity"; Author, "Study on Determining Efficient Fuel Assembly Parameters in Training Data for Designing of Neural Networks in Hybrid Genetic Algorithms Optimum Discharge Burnup and Cycle Length For PWRs"; Author, "Analysis of the OECD/NRC Oskarshamn-2 BWR Stability Benchmark"; Author, "Development of an Iterative Diffusion-transport Method Based on MICROX-2 Cross-section Libraries" **AW:** Best Paper Award, Joint International Conference on Supercomputing in Nuclear Applications and Monte Carlo, Paris, France (2013); Innovations in Fuel Cycle Research Award, United States Department of Energy (2010); Best Paper Award, International ANS Conference PHYSOR, Pittsburgh, Pennsylvania (2010); Engineering Society Premier Research Award, The Pennsylvania State University (2009); Title of Distinguished Professor of Nuclear Engineering, The Pennsylvania State University (2007); Engineering Society Outstanding Research Award, The Pennsylvania State University (2003); Department Head Outstanding Faculty Award, MNE (2002-2003) **MEM:** American Nuclear Society **H:** Movies **RE:** Orthodox Christian **BA:** 230 Reber Building, Pennsylvania State University, University Park, PA, 16802 **ADD:** 540 Westview Ave, City College, PA, 16803

IVERSON, JANICE, **T:** Volunteer Exercise Physiologist **I:** Religious **CN:** Mother of God Monastery **DOB:** 03/03/1941 **PB:** Miranda **SC:** SD/USA **MS:** Single **ED:** MEd in Education and Exercise Physiology, Concentration in Cardiac Rehabilitation and Intervention, Virginia Polytechnic Institute and State University (1981); Master's Degree in Health, Physical Education, Recreation, and Dance, South Dakota State University (1972); EdB in Elementary Education, Mount Marty College (1968) **CT:** Certified in CPR **C:** Teacher, Professor **CR:** Presenter, Cardiac Rehab, Wellness, and Nutrition **CW:** Author, Research Article on Physiology, Cardiac Rehabilitation Education, Glucose Intolerance, Lipid Profiles, and Exercise **AW:** Certificate of Acknowledgement, Boys Town; Volunteer Award, South Dakota Police Department; Sister Janice Iverson Scholarship **H:** Reading; Basketball; Soccer; Biking; Woodworking; Tinkering with inventions **PA:** Democrat **RE:** Roman Catholic **ADD:** 110 28th Avenue SE, Apt. 308, Mother of God Monastery, Watertown, SD, 57201 **URL:** http://watertownbenedictines.org

JACKS, BLAKE BRICKEY, **T:** Radiology Resident **I:** Medicine & Health Care **CN:** University of Arkansas for Medical Sciences **ED:** MD, University of Arkansas for Medical Sciences (2015) **C:** Radiology Resident, University of Arkansas for Medical Sciences (2015-Present) **CW:** Contributor, Poster Publication, Medical Journal **AW:** Recipient, Professionalism Award, Department of Radiology, University of Arkansas for Medical Sciences (2017) **MEM:** Radiological Society of North America; American Medical Association; The Society of Interventional Radiology; Arkansas Medical Society **BA:** 4301 W Markham St Â– Slot 556, University of Arkansas for Medical Sciences, Little Rock, AR, 72205 **ADD:** 7626 Choctaw Rd, Little Rock, AR, 72205

JACKSON, JUANITA WALLACE, **T:** Educational Administrator (Retired) **I:** Education/Educational Services **DOB:** 03/07/1931 **PB:** Cincinnati **SC:** OH/USA **PT:** William J. Wallace; Viola D. (Shively) Wallace **MS:** Married **SPN:** John Arter Jackson (4/21/1967) **CH:** Karon Gibson-Mueller; Blaine Gibson **ED:** MEd, Miami University (1963); BS, University of Cincinnati (1955) **CT:** Certified Elementary Teacher, State of Maryland; Certified Elementary Principal, State of Massachusetts; Certified Teacher, State of Ohio; Certified Administrator, State of Ohio; Certified Lay Speaker, United Methodist Church **C:** Co-President, Interclub Council, Marvin Community House, Jamestown, NY; Director, Business Maintenance Organization, State University of New York Research Foundation; Executive Director, Schoharie County Child Development Council; Reading Coordinator, Cincinnati Public Schools; Director, Kindergarten Education, Wilmington Public Schools; Senior Supervisor, Massachusetts State Department of Elementary and Secondary Education **CR:** Founder, Chautauqua New York Chapter, National Society of Arts and Letters (2010); President, Chautauqua New York Chapter, National Society of Arts and Letters (2010); Consultant in Field **CIV:** Chairman, The NYS Forum, Inc. (1985-1986); Vice-Chairman, Board of Trustees, Chautauqua Institution; Former Vice Chairman, Board of Visitors, University of Maryland School of Music; Associate, Board of Trustees, Siena College; Advisory Board Member, Sphinx Organization; President, Womens Committee, National Symphony Orchestra; Albany Symphony Board; Vanguard Albany Symphony Orchestra; Vice President, Volunteer Council, American Symphony Orchestra League; Trustee Board, United Theological Seminary; Board Member, Board CASA; Court-Appointed Special Advocate, Board CASA; Special Advocate, Board CASA; President, National Capital Law Auxiliary; Chief Justice, Robert H. Jackson Center **CW:** Pianist, "Honoring the Legacy of the Spiritual" (1985); Contributor, Articles, Professional Journals; Contributor, Book Reviews, Professional Journals; Singer, Classical Concerts in English, German, Spanish, Latin and French **AW:** Honoree, East High School Hall of Fame, Akron, OH (2006); Distinguished Alumni Award, College of Education, University of Cincinnati (2005); Honoree, Declaration, Mayor Whalen, Juanita Wallace Jackson Day (1990); Certificate of Achievement, Schenectady County Republican Committee (1985); Certificate of Achievement, National Academy School Executives, AASA (1976); Tribute to Women Award, YWCA of the Greater Capital Region, Inc., Troy, NY **MEM:** President, Woman's Club of McLean (1994); President, Friday Morning Music Club, Incorporated (1990); President, Education Foundation, AAUW (1980); Washington Chapter, International Women's Forum; Washington Chapter, National Society of Arts & Letters; President, Albany Chapter, The Links, Incorporated; President, Association of Major Symphony Orchestra Volunteers; Board of Directors, Choral Arts Society Washington; Washington Chapter, National Capital Lawyers Auxiliary; Friend of the Arts, Delta Kappa Gamma; President, Alpha Kappa Chapter, Delta Kappa Gamma; Board Member, Sigma Alpha Iota **H:** Classical music; Singing; Playing the piano; Singing to individuals who are bed ridden, or terminally ill to uplift them **ADD:** PO Box 52, Chautauqua, NY, 14722

JAKUB, KATHLEEN ANN, **T:** Medical/Surgical Nurse **I:** Medicine & Health Care **CN:** Hillman Cancer Center **DOB:** 06/09/1947 **PB:** Pittsburgh **SC:** PA/USA **PT:** Michael E. Jakub; Mary Ellen (Kirchner) Jakub **ED:** MS in Professional Leadership, Carlow University (1996); BSN, University of Pittsburgh (1992); BA in Sociology, University of Pittsburgh (1979); BA in Administration Justice, University of Pittsburgh (1979); Diploma, St. Francis School of Nursing (1968) **CT:** Certified Intermediate Care Nurse; Certified Trauma Nurse; Certified Otorhinolaryngology and Head-Neck Nurse **C:** Collaborative Practice Nurse, Pain & Palliative Care Services, Hillman Cancer Center, UPMC (2009-Present); Nurse, Hillman Cancer Center, UPMC (2005-2006); Triage Nurse, Outpatient Department, Hillman Cancer Center, UPMC (2003-2005); Manager of Quality Improvement, Cancer Center, UPMC (2001-2003); Case Manager, Performance Improvement Department, UPMC (1999-2001); Case Manager, Neurosurgery Department, UPMC (1996-1999); Patient Care Manager, Medical and Surgical Unit, UPMC (1988-1996); Staff Nurse of Head/Neck and Ophthalmology, UPMC (1975-1988); Staff Nurse of Orthopedics-Plastics, UPMC (1970-1975); Staff Nurse of Physical Rehabilitation, St. Francis Medical Center (1968-1970) **MEM:** SOHN; American Trauma Society **MH:** Albert Nelson Marquis Lifetime Achievement Award (2017) **H:** Gardening; Reading; Spending time with family **ADD:** 4372 Winterburn Avenue, Pittsburgh, PA, 15207

JAMES, J.P., **T:** Assistant Professor of Marketing **I:** Education/Educational Services **CN:** Salem State University **ED:** PhD in Marketing, Rutgers Business School – Newark and New Brunswick, Rutgers, The State University of New Jersey (2017); MS in Integrated Marketing Communications, Northwestern University; Coursework in Business Administration, California State Polytechnic University, Pomona; Coursework in Marketing Management and Advertising, California State Polytechnic University, Pomona **CT:** Certification, AAAA, Chicago Institute of Advanced Advertising Studies Course; Certificate, Hispanic Marketing, Florida State University **C:** Assistant Professor of Marketing, Salem State University (2017-Present);

Marketing PhD Candidate, Rutgers Business School – Newark and New Brunswick, Rutgers, The State University of New Jersey (2013-2017); Marketing PhD Instructor, Rutgers Business School – Newark and New Brunswick, Rutgers, The State University of New Jersey (2013-2017); Adjunct Professor, New York University (2010-2016); Assistant Adjunct Professor, Hunter College (2011-2013); Director of Account Planning, Spike DDB (2009-2011); Brand Planning Director, GlobalHul (2007-2009); Director of Strategic Planning, UWG Inc. (2005-2007); Account Supervisor, Burrell (2002-2005); Account Executive, Y&R (1998-2002) **CW:** Author, Article, "Journal of Integrated Marketing Communications"; Author, Article, "Journal for Advertising Research"; Contributor, Book Chapter **AW:** Valuing Diversity Scholarship, American Marketing Association Foundation (2014); Commendations, National Student Advertising Competition; Finalist, Effie Award **MEM:** American Marketing Association; The Advertising Club; Former Member, Society of Consumer Practitioners **BA:** 342 LaFayette St, Salem, MA, 01970 **ADD:** 20 Berry St Unit 2116, North Andover, MA, 01845 **URL:** https://www.linkedin.com/in/jpjames/

JANSON, BARBARA JEAN, T: President **I:** Education/Educational Services **CN:** Janson Associates **DOB:** 03/07/1942 **PB:** Mason City **SC:** IA/USA **PT:** Harley Arnold Janson; Helen Victoria (Henrickson) Janson **MS:** Married **SPN:** Arthur R. Hilsinger (8/31/1997); John Batty Henderson (9/8/1984, Divorced 1990); W. John Shallenberger (2/24/1963, Divorced 9/1980) **CH:** Mona; Ann **ED:** MBA, University of Rhode Island (1982); MS in Mathematics, Trinity College (1970); BS in Mathematics, Iowa State University (1965); Coursework, Rhode Island School of Design **CT:** Certified Mathematics Teacher, States of Iowa, New York, and Connecticut **C:** President, Janson Associates, Dedham (1996-Present); Public Consultant, Everyday Learning/Tribune Education Group (1996-1998); President, Janson Publications, Inc., Dedham (1996-1998); Founder, President, Janson Publications, Inc. (Purchased by Tribune Education Group), Providence And Dedham, Massachusetts (1985-1996); Director of Publication, American Mathematical Society, Providence, RI (1982-1985); Assistant Director Editorial, American Mathematical Society, Providence, RI (1978-1981); Mathematics Instructor, Bristol County Community College, Fall River, MA (1977-1978); Mathematics Editor, Houghton Mifflin Company, Boston, MA (1974-1977); Mathematics Instructor, Ulster County Community College, Kingston (1973); Mathematics Teacher, Ulster Academy, Kingston, NY (1971-1973); Mathematics Teacher, Public High Schools, Avon, Farmington, Bloomfield, CT (1966-1968) **CR:** Massachusetts State Advisory Board, Mathematics & Science Education (2000-2008); Member, Expert Panel on Materials Development Reference, National Science Foundation (1996-1999); Member, Advisory Committee, Rhode Island State Systemic Initiative in Mathematics and Science (1993-1994); Member, Steering Committee, American Mathematics Project (1986-1992); Member, Rhode Island Legislative Commission for Mathematics and Science Education (1991); Representative, Science Publication Committee, American Heart Association (1986-1990); Member, Rhode Island State Advisory Commission on Libraries **CIV:** Member, Board of Directors, Iowa State University Foundation (2012-Present); Overseer, Boston Ballet (2003-Present); Overseer, Beth Israel Deaconess Medical Center (2013-Present); Member, Visiting Committee for American Art, Boston Museum of Fine Arts (2001-Present); Overseer, Boston (Massachusetts) Ballet (2003-Present); Investment Committee for University Endowment, Iowa State University Foundation (2009-2017); Chair, Investment Committee for University Endowment, Iowa State University (2002-2006); Governor, Iowa State University Foundation (2000); Member, Steering Committee, American Mathematics Project, Berkeley, CA (1986-1992); Board of Directors, Planned Parenthood of Rhode Island, Providence, RI (1986-1987); First Parish Unitarian Church, Beverly, MA (1975-1976); Member, Oversight Committee, Resources Mathematics Reform Educational Development Center, Newton, MA; Advisory Member, Rhode Island State Council on Libraries **CW:** Editor, "Scholarly Publishing: Managing Today, Planning for Tomorrow" (1986); Amateur Artist, Rhode Island School of Design **AW:** Distinguished Alumni Award, Iowa State University (2018); Outstanding Mathematics Department Alumni Award, College of Liberal Arts and Sciences, Iowa State University (2009); Entrepreneur of the Year Award, Ernst & Young (1987); Recipient, Mortar Board Award Iowa State University (1965) **MEM:** Board of Directors, Society for Scholarly Publishing (1986-1990); Chair, Annual Meeting, Society for Scholarly Publishing (1985); Journals Committee, Association of American Publishers (1982-1985); American Association for the Advancement of Science; League of Women Voters; The New York Academy of Science; American Mathematics Society; Mathematics Association of America; National Council of Teachers of Mathematics; NAWBO **MH:** Albert Nelson Marquis Lifetime Achievement Award (2018) **H:** Painting travel sketches; Studying piano; Studying plays; Reading; Investing **RE:** Unitarian Universalist **ADD:** 8 Jackson Pond Rd, Dedham, MA, 02026 **URL:** https://www.linkedin.com/in/barbara-janson-a5b861b/

JARMON, CHARLES, T: Social Sciences Professor **I:** Education/Educational Services **DOB:** 11/22/1938 **PB:** Kinston **SC:** NC/USA **PT:** John Baker Jarmon; Beatrice Jarmon **MS:** Single **SPN:** Faith Patricia Jarmon (8/15/1965, Deceased 3/4/1984) **CH:** Thad Patrick; Lee Eugene; Faith Kinsetta; Julius Morning **ED:** PhD, University at Buffalo (1972); MA, North Carolina Central University (1965); BS, North Carolina Central University (1964) **CT:** Certified Clinical Sociologist, Georgetown University (1990) **C:** Associate Dean of Arts and Sciences, Howard University (1992-2009); Professor, Department of Sociology and Anthropology, Howard University, Washington, D.C. (1988-1991); Chairman, Department of Sociology and Anthropology, Howard University, Washington, D.C. (1988-1991); Associate Professor, Howard University, Washington, D.C. (1978-1987); Assistant Professor, Virginia Commonwealth University, Richmond, VA (1972-1978); Instructor, University at Buffalo (1971-1972); Acting Department Chairman, Southern University and A&M College (1968-1969); Assistant Professor, Southern University and A&M College (1967-1968) **CR:** Consultant, U.S. African Development Foundation (1985-1986); Consultant, African Bureau, United States Agency for International Development (1982-1983) **CIV:** Founder, Student-Parent Support Group, Howard University (1999-Present); Public Member, Senior Service Selection Board, U.S. Department of State (2007); Advisor, Population Undercount, The USGenWeb Census Project (1999); Public Member, American Foreign Service Association **CW:** Contributing Author, "Blackwell Encyclopedia of Sociology" (2007); Editorial Board Member, "Canadian Review of Studies in Nationalism" (1985-2006); Book Review Editor, "Journal of African and Asian Studies" (1985-1993); Author, "Nigeria: Reorganization and Development since the Mid-Twentieth Century," E.J. Brill (1988); Contributing Author, "The Social and Political Implications of the 1984 Jesse Jackson Presidential Campaign," Praeger (1988); Co-Author, "African Americans: A Social Science Perspective," University Press of America (1976); Contributor, Articles, Professional Journals; Contributor, Chapters, Books **AW:** Service Award, Howard University, Army ROTC (1999-Present); Joseph S. Himes Lifetime Achievement Award, Association of Black Sociologists (2008); Grantee, Research and Travel, Reginald Lewis Research Fund (2006); Grantee, The Institute for Labor-Management Relations (1981-1982); James B. Duke Fellow, Duke University (1965-1966) **MEM:** President, Adkin High School Alumni and Friends (2014-Present); American Council of Academic Deans; American Sociological Association; Lifetime Member, Association of Black Sociologists **MH:** Albert Nelson Marquis Lifetime Achievement Award (2017) **H:** Billiards; Reading; Gardening **ADD:** 1789 Verbena St NW, Washington, DC, 20012

JAVITS, ERIC M., T: Ambassador **I:** Civil Service **CN:** Palm Beach Civic Association **DOB:** 05/24/1931 **PB:** New York **SC:** NY/USA **PT:** Benjamin A. Javits; Lily Javits **MS:** Married **SPN:** Margaretha Espersson Javits **CH:** Jocelyn Javits-Grajski; Eric M., Jr. **ED:** JD, Columbia University (1955); AB, Columbia University (1952); Freshman Student, Stanford University (1948-1949) **C:** Director, Palm Beach Civic Association (2013-Present); Chairman, Carver Scientific Inc. (2012-Present); Advisory Committee to Director General, Upon Future Chemical Weapons Convention (2010-2011); U.S. Permanent Representative and Ambassador, Organization of the Prohibition of Chemical Weapons, The Hague, Netherlands (2003-2009); U.S. Permanent Representative and Ambassador, UN Conference on Disarmament, Geneva, Switzerland (2001-2003); Senior Counsel, Robinson, Brog, Leinwand, Reich, Genovese & Gluck, Professional Corporation (1993-2001); Consultant to Department State, Ambassador-Designate to Venezuela (1989-1990); Senior Partner, Javits, Robinson, Brog, Leinwand & Reich, Professional Corporation (1984-1989); Firm to Senior Partner, Javits & Javits (1958-1982); Associate Firm, Javits & Javits, New York, NY (1955-1958); Temporary Consultant, Office of Defense Mobilization, Washington, DC (1951); Chairman, Calagen, Inc. **CR:** Board of Directors, New York State Convention Center Operating Corporation (1995-2001); New York City Commission for Protocol (1994-2001); Independent General Partner, ML Venture Partners (1982-1996); Counsel, New York Senate Committee on Affairs of the City of New York (1959); Special Deputy to New York Attorney, General Elections Frauds Bureau (1958-1959); Past Director, Companies Listed on New York Stock Exchange, American Stock Exchange, and Over the Counter Companies **CIV:** President, Eric Javits Family Foundation (2006-Present); Life Member, National Institute of the Society of Sciences (1958-Present); Chairman, Republican Eagles (1999-2001); Trustee, Cardozo Law School (1997-2001); Trustee, French Institute/Alliance Francaise (1995-2001); Board Member, Spain-USA Chamber of Commerce (1993-2001); Chairman Emeritus, Spanish Institute, New York, NY (1989-2001); Chairman, Spanish Institute, New York, NY (1987-1989); President, Spanish Institute, New York, NY (1981-1987); Board Member, Spanish Institute, New York, NY (1979-1989); President, Board Director, Fair Return League, Inc. (1975-2006); Board Member, Secretary, Counsel, American Health Foundation (1971-1985); Executive Secretary, U.S. Paper Exporters Council, Inc. (1964-1972); Executive Committee, National Republican Club (1962-1970); New York Republican County Committee (1960-1964); Board of Advisors, New York Young Republican

Club (1958-1964); Vice President, New York Young Republican Club (1957-1958); Numerous Charitable Committees, Board of Governors, New York Young Republican Club (1955-1958); Executive Committee, Jacob K. Javits Campaigns (1954-1980) **CW:** Author, "Twists and Turns" (2013); Author, "SOS New York" (1961) **AW:** Oxford Cup, Beta Theta Pi (2013); Superior Honor Award, U.S. Department of State (2009); Spanish Institute Gold Medal (1994); Decorated Order of Isabel La Catolica, Spain (1989); Decorated Order of Isabel La Catolica, Spain (1981) **MEM:** Nacoms; University Club of New York City; Phi Alpha Delta; Beta Theta Pi; Phi Beta Kappa **BAR:** U.S. Supreme Court (1959); State of New York (1955) **RE:** Jewish **ADD:** 150 Bradley Place, Unit 407, Palm Beach, FL, 33480

JENKINS, BRENDA GWENETTA, T: Pre-School Administrator, Special Education Educator, Fitness Instructor **I:** Education/Educational Services **DOB:** 08/11/1949 **PB:** Durham **SC:** NC/USA **PT:** Brinton Alfred Jenkins; Ophelia Arden (Eaton) Jenkins (Deceased) **MS:** Single **ED:** Postgraduate Coursework, Marymount College (1976); MEd, Howard University (1972); BS, Howard University (1971); Postgraduate Coursework, University of the District of Columbia; Postgraduate Coursework, American University; Postgraduate Coursework, Trinity College; Postgraduate Coursework, The Catholic University of America **CT:** Certificate, Advanced Graduate Studies, Special Education, Howard University (1975); Certified Teacher, Washington, DC; Certified Aerobics Instructor, National Dance Exercise Instructors Training Association; H2O Fitness Shallow Water Aerobics Training Certification, LG Total Fitness, LLC; H2O Deep Water Aerobics Instructor Training Certification, LG Total Fitness, LLC **C:** Adjunct Professor, Fitness Instructor, Prince George's Community College (2015-Present); Vice President, Nerdlihc Corporation, Washington DC (1985-Present); Aerobics Instructor, District of Columbia Public Schools, Washington DC (1982-Present); Fitness Instructor, Oxendine Music Academy, Prince George's County (1995-1996); Co-Chair, Program Committee, Maryvale Pom Pom/Cheerleaders, Montgomery County (1995-1996); Teacher, Collaborative Program, Goals 2000 English, Language Arts, History Writer, District of Columbia Public Schools, Washington, DC (1995-1996); Assistant Chairman, Teacher, Collaborative Program, Maryvale Pom Pom/Cheerleaders, Montgomery County (1992-1994); Instructor, Coach, YMCA of Metropolitan Washington, Washington DC (1992-1993); Instructor, Health, Nutrition Support, Rockville, MD (1992); Instructor, You Fit, Inc. National Children's Center, Washington, DC (1991-1993); Instructor, Aerobics, District of Columbia Department of Parks and Recreation, Washington, DC (1988-1993); Co-Owner, Fantasia Early Learning Academy, Washington, DC (1985-1998); Partner, Jenkins, Trapp-Dukes and Yates Partnership, Washington, DC (1984); Teacher, District of Columbia Public Schools, Washington, DC (1972-2008); Cheerleading Coach, Howard University, Washington, DC (1971-1986) **CR:** Advisory Board, Superintendent's Teacher Affairs (1999-Present); Aerobic Instructor, Regent Park Community Clubhouse, Prince George's County, Maryland (2006); Member, GAFSC (2005-2008); Assistant Building Representative, AFT Washington, AFL-CIO (2004-2005); Convention Delegate, American Federation of Teachers, AFL-CIO (2004); Superintendent Search Committee, District of Columbia Public Schools (2004); Pre-Test Participant, Corporation for National and Community Service (2004); Resident Mentor, Teacher, NABSE, Nashville, TN (1999-2004); Recruiter, NABSE, Nashville, TN (1999); Executive

Board of Directors, Assembly of Petworth (1998-2008); Member, Distinguished Educators Roundtable (1998-2004); Member, Special Education State Advisory Panel, Washington, D.C. (1998-2000); Convention Delegate, American Federation of Teachers, AFL-CIO (1998); Standards Specialist, Washington Teacher's Union (1997-2008); Building Representative, AFT Washington, AFL-CIO (1996-2004, 1991-1994,1987-1989); Assistant Building Representative, AFT Washington, AFL-CIO (1994-1995); Trainer, Substance Abuse Prevention Education (1995); Vice President, Special Education, Washington Teacher's Union (1994-2004); Coordinator, Curriculum Council, District of Columbia Public Schools (1994-1996); Developer, Learning Creations (1994); Master Teacher, Cooperative Teacher Corporation, District of Columbia Public Schools (1993); Curriculum Writer, District of Columbia Public Schools (1993); Member, Preschool Advisory Board, District of Columbia Public Schools (1992-1993); Trainer, Early Childhood Substance Abuse Project Training (1992-1993); Metro Foster Grandparent Program Advisory Board, Washington, D.C. (1992); Developer, BJ's Thinking Cap (1991); Trainer, AIDS in the Workplace (1990); Supervisor, Foster Grandparent Program, Sharpe Health School (1988-2008); Instructor, Recreation Services, City of Rockville, Maryland (1986-2005); Developer, My Special Friend Program (1984); Aerobic Instructor, Council for Exceptional Children, Washington, D.C. (1982); Member, Parent Training and Information Center; Member, American Red Cross, Inc. Advisory Panel; Executive Board of Directors, District of Columbia Public Schools; Presenter in Field, Speaker in Field **CIV:** District of Columbia Special Education State Advisor (1998-Present); Member, Martin Luther King Tribute Choir (2005-2009); Member, Leadership/Anchor Standards Team, District of Columbia Public Schools (2005-2008); Chairman, Professional Development Collaboration Team, District of Columbia Public Schools (2006-2007); Member, International Space Camp, Huntsville, AL (1998) **CW:** Singer, 2000 Voices, Lincoln Memorial (2000); Educational Games; Experimental Cook; Creator, Hand-Sewn Items; Developer, Educational Games; Singer, 2000 Voices, Washington Monument **AW:** Women of the Year, ABI (2008-2009); Grantee, Washington Post Grants in Arts (2006); Teacher of the Month, District of Columbia Public Schools (2006); Named, Cooperating Teacher, University of the District of Columbia (2004); State Winner, Elementary Level National Citizenship Education Teacher's Award, Ladies Auxiliary Veterans of Foreign Wars, Washington, D.C. (2002-2003); Educator Excellence Award, Masonic Scottish Rite (2001); Grantee, Washington Post Grants in Arts (1999-2004); Named, District of Columbia Teacher of the Year, Council Chief State School Officers (1998); Named to Hall of Fame, The Bison Foundation, Inc., Howard University (1995); Grantee, Citibank (1994); Grantee, District of Columbia Public Schools State Office (1993); Eponym, Brenda G. Jenkins Outstanding Cheerleader Award, Howard University's Alumni Cheerleaders' Association (1987); Citation, Washington Teachers Union (1985); Outstanding Service Award, Kappa Delta Pi (1984); Outstanding Recognition Award, Howard University's Alumni Cheerleaders' Association (1984); Outstanding Recognition Award, Howard University's Alumni Cheerleaders' Association (1984); Outstanding Service Award, Kappa Delta Pi (1981-1982, 1978-1979); Woman of the Year In Education; Listee, 500 Key Women, Two Hundred Years of Public Education in the Nation's Capital 1804-2014 **MEM:** Mentor, Center for Inspired Teaching (2008-2013); Vice President, Howard University's Alumni Cheerleaders' Association (1998-2009); District

of Columbia Public Schools Leadership/Anchor Standards Team Member, Math Specialist, DC Parents & Friends of Children with Special Needs (2005-2008); District of Columbia Public Schools Standards Facilitator, American Federation of Teachers, AFL-CIO (2005); Presiding Officer, Washington Special Educator and Service Provider, Forums, American Federation of Teachers, AFL-CIO (1998-2005); District of Columbia Public Schools New Teacher Orientation Trainer, American Federation of Teachers, AFL-CIO (2001-2004); Washington Teachers Union New Teacher Coordinator, American Federation of Teachers, AFL-CIO (2001-2004); Washington Teachers Union Positive Teacher Ad Campaign, American Federation of Teachers, AFL-CIO (2004); Critical Partners Group/Superintendents Task Force, DC Parents & Friends of Children with Special Needs (2003); School to Careers Teacher Extern, American Federation of Teachers, AFL-CIO (2001); President, Howard University's Alumni Cheerleaders' Association (2009-Present, 1990-1994); Co-Founder, Howard University's Alumni Cheerleaders' Association (1977); ASCD; Board of Directors, DC Parents & Friends of Children with Special Needs; Pi Lambda Theta; Executive Committee, Theta Alpha Chapter, Kappa Delta Pi **MH:** Albert Nelson Marquis Lifetime Achievement Award (2017) **H:** Cooking; Dance; Poetry; Sewing **PA:** Democrat **RE:** Baptist **ADD:** 6850 Farragut St, Hyattsville, MD, 20784

JENNINGS, BRUCE, T: Associate Professor **I:** Education/Educational Services **CN:** Vanderbilt University **DOB:** 04/27/1949 **PB:** Fort Wayne **SC:** IN/USA **PT:** Hugh Jack Jennings; Margaret Evangeline (Wisman) Jennings **MS:** Married **SPN:** Margaret Ann Machulis (5/26/1972) **CH:** Andrew **ED:** MA in Political Science, Princeton University (1973); BA in Political Science, Yale University, Magna Cum Laude (1971) **C:** Associate Professor, Vanderbilt University (2015-Present); Lecturer, Weill Cornell Medicine, Cornell University (2010-Present); Senior Adviser, The Hastings Center (2006-Present); Director of Bioethics, Center for Humans & Nature (2006-Present); Lecturer, Yale School of Medicine (1995-Present); Senior Lecturer, New York Medical College (2010-2015); Fellow, The Hastings Center (2007); Senior Research Scholar, The Hastings Center (1999-2006); Executive Vice President, The Hastings Center (1996-1999); Executive Director, The Hastings Center (1991-1996); Associate for Policy Studies, The Hastings Center (1983-1991); Research Associate, The Hastings Center (1980-1983); Assistant Professor of Political Science and Philosophy, Stockton University (1975-1980); Assistant Instructor, Department of Political Science, Princeton University (1973-1974); Senior Fellow, The Center for Humans and Nature **CR:** Member, Research Group, Rethinking Dependency Project, Montefiore Medical Center (2004-Present); Member, Education Committee, Huntington's Disease Society of America (2004-Present); Andrus-on-Hudson (2004-Present); Member, Genetic Counseling and Health Advocacy Programs, Sarah Lawrence College (2004-Present); Expert, Advisory Panel on Health Care Priorities, American Medical Association (1999-Present); Center for Urban Bioethics, The New York Academy of Medicine (1998-Present); VNA of Hudson Valley (1998-Present); Steering Committee, Partnership to Improve End of Life Care, NY (1998-Present); Aging in America (1998-Present); Member, Standards Committee, Last Acts Campaign, Robert Wood Johnson Foundation (1996-Present); Consultant, Ethics Committee, Sound Shore Medical Center (1996-Present); New York Citizens Committee on Health Care Decisions (1992-Present); Ethics Consultant Cabrini Eldercare (1990-Present);

Member, Ethics Committee, Weill Cornell Medicine (1989-Present); Hospital Ethics Committee, NewYork-Presbyterian Hospital (1989-Present); Treasurer, Board of Directors, American Health Decisions, Atlanta, Georgia (1988-Present); Member, Ethics Advisory Subcommittee, Centers for Disease Control and Prevention (2003-2009); Affiliate, Hospice and Palliative Care Association of New York State (1996-2004); Affiliate, National Hospice and Palliative Care Organization (1999-2003); Affiliate, Beth Abraham Center, Centers Health Care (2000-2001); Affiliate, Association for Politics and the Life Sciences (1998-2001); Consultant, Eli Lilly and Company (1996-1998); Member, Advisory Board, Health Advisory Program, Sarah Lawrence College (1996-1997); Member, Board of Directors, American Society for Bioethics and Humanities (1994-1997); Consultant, W.K. Kellogg Foundation (1993-1994); Adjunct Lecturer, School of Journalism, Columbia University (1984-1990); Adjunct Professor, Department of Political Science, Vassar College (1989); Adjunct Professor, Humanities Division, Purchase College State University of New York (1985); Consultant, Select Committee on Ethics, United States Senate (1980) **CIV:** Member, Ethics Advisory Board, March of Dimes Foundation, White Plains, NY (1995-Present); Adviser, Josephson Institute (1990-Present); Trustee, Hastings-on-Hudson, NY (2009-2015); Member, Board of Directors, YWAA (1995-2015); Chairman, Ethics Special Primary Interest Group, American Public Health Association (2010-2011); President, Yale Westchester Alumni Association (2007-2010); Trustee, Hastings-on-Hudson, NY (2000-2006); Member, Working Group on Science, Technology and Faith, The Domestic and Foreign Missionary Society (2000-2003); Member, Task Force on End-of-Life Care, The Domestic and Foreign Missionary Society (1998-2000); Police Commissioner, Hastings-on-Hudson, NY (1998-2000); Chairman, Task Force on Sexual Exploitation and the Clergy, Episcopal Diocese of New York (1997); Member, Bioethics Advisory Panel, American Hospital Association (1993-1994); Member, Task Force on Sexual Exploitation and the Clergy, Episcopal Diocese of New York (1992-1993); Chairman, Task Force on Sexual Exploitation and the Clergy, Episcopal Diocese of New York (1992); Chairman, Westchester County Fair Campaign Practices Committee (1991-2000) **CW:** Editor-in-Chief, "Bioethics: Fourth Edition" (2011-Present); Advisory Editor, "Journal of Health Politics and Law" (2002-Present); Advisory Editor, "Hastings Center Report" (1997-Present); Co-author, "Public Health Ethics: Theory, Policy and Practices" (2006); Co-author, "Access to Hospice Care: Expanding Boundaries, Overcoming Barriers" (2003); Co-author, "The Perversion of Autonomy: The Proper Uses of Coercion and Constraints in a Liberal Society, Second Edition" (2003); Co-author, "Faithful Living, Faithful Dying: Anglican Reflections on End of Life Care" (2000); Co-author, "The Perversion of Autonomy: The Proper Uses of Coercion and Constraints in a Liberal Society" (1996); Co-author, "Guidelines on the Termination of Life-Sustaining Treatment and the Care of the Dying" (1987); Co-author, "Congress and the Media: The Ethical Connection" (1985); Co-author, "Ethics of Legislative Life" (1985); Co-author, "On the Uses of the Humanities: Vision and Application" (1984); Co-editor, Books; Contributor, Over 150 Articles, Professional Journals; Contributor, Book Chapters **AW:** Mary Ann Quaranta Award for Palliative Care, Westchester, NY (2014); Elected Fellow, Hastings Center (2007); Community Service Award, Yale Westchester Alumni Association (2005); Special Recognition Award, National Hospice and Palliative Care Organization (2004); Andrew B. Weiss Visiting

Fellowship, Williams College (1987); Leadership Award, Prudential Foundation, Prudential Financial, Inc. (1987); University Fellowship, Princeton University (1971-1975); Honoree, Jack M. Griffin Memorial Scholar, Yale University (1967-1971); Honoree, International Merit Scholar (1967) **MEM:** President, Yale Westchester Alumni Association (2007-Present); Member, Ethics Advisory Committee, Chicago Chapter, Alzheimer's Association (1993-Present); APSA; Associate, Columbia Seminar on Social Thought; Association for Public Policy Analysis & Management; Conference on Political Thought; The Yale Club of New York City **MH:** Albert Nelson Marquis Lifetime Achievement Award (2017) **H:** Swimming; Bicycling; Poetry **PA:** Democrat **RE:** Episcopalian **BA:** 2525 W End Ave Ste 400, Center for Biomedical Ethics and Society, Nashville, TN, 37203 **ADD:** 9302 Grist Mill Ct, Brentwood, TN, 37027

JEPSON, HANS GODFREY, T: Investment Company Executive, Director **I:** Financial Services **DOB:** 07/24/1936 **PB:** Spencer **SC:** WV/USA **PT:** Hans G. Jepson; Juanita Imogene (Shears) Jepson **MS:** Married **SPN:** Barbara Gayle Keller (12/3/1966) **ED:** AB, Princeton University, Magna Cum Laude (1958) **C:** President, The Stanton Corporation, Delaware (1994-Present); President, Lafayette Enterprises, Inc., New York City, NY (1983-Present); President, Valquest Associates, Inc., New York City, NY (1980-Present); Executive Vice President, Chief Investment Officer, United States Trust Company of New York, New York City, NY (1976-1980); Director, Senior Vice President, Research Director, Alliance Capital Management Corp., New York City, NY (1970-1976); Vice President, Research Director, Dominick & Dominick, Inc., New York City, NY (1968-1970); Executive Editor, Arnold Bernhard & Co., Inc., New York City, NY (1961-1968) **CIV:** Board of Directors, J. Aron Charitable Foundation; Trustee, American Bible Society; Calvary Baptist Church, New York City, NY **MIL:** Captain, U.S. Army Reserve (1959-1966); Second Lieutenant, U.S. Army (1958-1959) **MEM:** Chartered Financial Analyst Institute; Cannon Dial Elm Club, Princeton, NJ; Princeton Club, New York City, NY; Economic Club of New York; La Boule New Yorkaise, New York City, NY; Federation Petanque United States of America, Inc.; New York Society of Security Analysts **H:** Reading; Movies; Pétanque **RE:** Protestant **ADD:** 100 Jericho Quadrangle Ste 214, Lafayette Enterprises Inc., Jericho, NY, 11753

JERDEE, SYLVIA A., T: Pastor (Retired) **I:** Religious **DOB:** 04/18/1941 **PB:** Alpine **SC:** TX/USA **PT:** Rolf Walter Kaasa; Marjorie O. Kaasa **MS:** Married **SPN:** Joseph C. Jerdee (6/15/1963) **CH:** Jonathan; Peter; Theodore **ED:** MDiv, Luther Seminary (1995); EdM, Boston University (1978); BA, Luther College (1963) **CT:** Ordained Minister, Evangelical Lutheran Church in America (1995) **C:** Retired (2005); Pastor, Little Norway Lutheran Church, Mentor, MN (1999-2005); Pastor, Calvary Lutheran Church, Orr, MN (1995-1999); Guidance Counselor, Frankfurt American High School, Germany (1985-1991); Teacher, Frankfurt American High School, Germany (1978-1985); Teacher, Army Education Center, Federal Ministry of Defence, Germany (1974-1978); Teacher, Washington High School, Sioux Falls, SD (1963-1964) **MH:** Albert Nelson Marquis Lifetime Achievement Award (2017) **H:** Travel; Reading **ADD:** 470 Hewitt Blvd Apt 119, Red Wing, MN, 55066

JERNIGAN, T. WATSON MD, MA, T: Vice Chair of Medical Education, OBGYN **I:** Education/Educational Services **CN:** East Tennessee State University **DOB:** 06/16/1949 **PB:** Fort Bragg **SC:** NC/

USA **PT:** Rupert Watson Jernigan, Jr (Deceased) Henrietta Marsh Hopkins Jernigan (Deceased) **MS:** Married **SPN:** Linda Wright Jernigan **CH:** April Jernigan Flanary Rachel Jernigan Acton Jessica Grace-Ann Jernigan-Johnson **ED:** MA in History, East Tennessee State University, Johnson City, TN (2005); Chief Resident in Obstetrics and Gynecology, Akron City Hospital, Akron, OH (1978-1979); Resident in Obstetrics and Gynecology, Akron City Hospital, Akron, OH (1975-1979); MD, West Virginia University, Morgantown, WV (1975); BA in History, Denison University, Granville, OH (1971) **CT:** National Certified Menopause Practitioner (2016); National Certified Menopause Practitioner (2013); National Certified Menopause Practitioner (2010); Diplomate, American Board of Obstetrics and Gynecology, Inc. (1981); Licensed to Practice Medicine, State of Tennessee (1979); Diplomate, National Board of Medical Examiners (1976) **C:** Vice Chair of Medical Education, James H. Quillen College of Medicine, East Tennessee State University (2018-Present); Residency Program Director, James H. Quillen College of Medicine, East Tennessee State University (2016-Present); Professor, Department of Obstetrics and Gynecology, James H. Quillen College of Medicine, East Tennessee State University (2009-Present); Clinical Adjunct Faculty Member, Department of Anatomy, James H. Quillen College of Medicine, East Tennessee State University (2000-Present); Clerkship Director, James H. Quillen College of Medicine, East Tennessee State University (2013-2017); Associate Dean of Clinical Affairs, James H. Quillen College of Medicine, East Tennessee State University (2011-2017); Chairman, Department of Obstetrics and Gynecology, James H. Quillen College of Medicine, East Tennessee State University (2011-2014); Interim Chairman, Department of Obstetrics and Gynecology, James H. Quillen College of Medicine, East Tennessee State University (2009-2011); Clinical Associate Professor, Department of Obstetrics and Gynecology, James H. Quillen College of Medicine, East Tennessee State University (2001-2009); OB/GYN, First Choice Health Care, P.C., State of Franklin Healthcare Associates (1997-2009); Clinical Associate Professor, Department of Obstetrics and Gynecology, James H. Quillen College of Medicine, East Tennessee State University (1997-1999); Interim Chairman, Department of Obstetrics and Gynecology, James H. Quillen College of Medicine, East Tennessee State University (1994-1995); Clerkship Director, James H. Quillen College of Medicine, East Tennessee State University (1992-1997); Assistant Professor, Department of Obstetrics and Gynecology, James H. Quillen College of Medicine, East Tennessee State University (1986-1997); OB/GYN, Clinical Practice, University Physicians Practice Group (1986-1997); Clinical Coordinator, University Physicians Practice Group (1986-1992); President, Thomas W. Jernigan, MD, P.C., Johnson City, TN (1981-1986); Clinical Assistant Professor, Department of Obstetrics and Gynecology, James H. Quillen College of Medicine, East Tennessee State University (1979-1986); Partner, Gordon-Ruffin-Hillman-Miller Clinic (1979-1981); Fellow, American Congress of Obstetricians and Gynecologists **CR:** ANEW Board of Directors, Physicians and Associates, East Tennessee State University (2016-Present); Graduate Medical Education Committee, James H. Quillen College of Medicine, East Tennessee State University (2016-Present); Anatomical Gift Oversight Committee, James H. Quillen College of Medicine, East Tennessee State University (2010-Present); Search Committee for Associate Dean of Finance and Administration, James H. Quillen College of Medicine, East

Tennessee State University (2017); Search Committee for Associate Dean of Graduate Medical Education, James H. Quillen College of Medicine, East Tennessee State University (2017); Electronic Record Upgrade Committee, James H. Quillen College of Medicine, East Tennessee State University (2015-2017); ISHN Credential Committee, Physicians and Associates, East Tennessee State University (2015); Provider Stakeholder Payment Reform Task Force, James H. Quillen College of Medicine, East Tennessee State University (2013-2017); Tennessee Payment Healthcare Reform Initiative, James H. Quillen College of Medicine, East Tennessee State University (2013-2017); Goals Task Force, Strategic Planning Committee, James H. Quillen College of Medicine, East Tennessee State University (2011); Task Force - LCME Self Study, James H. Quillen College of Medicine, East Tennessee State University (2011); CME Advisory Board, James H. Quillen College of Medicine, East Tennessee State University (2010-2017); Graduate Medical Education Committee, James H. Quillen College of Medicine, East Tennessee State University (2009-2014); Department of Athletics Committee, East Tennessee State University (1996-1998) **CIV:** First Christian Church (2003-Present); Foundation Board of Directors, Eastern Tennessee State University (1994-Present); Pirate Club, East Tennessee State University (1988-Present); President, Board of Directors, Pirate Club, East Tennessee State University (1998-2000); President, Board of Directors, Pirate Club, East Tennessee State University (1996-1998); Treasurer, Board of Directors, Pirate Club, East Tennessee State University (1994-1996) **CW:** Presenter, "Burnout and Depression Among Medical Profession," Department of OB/GYN Grand Rounds, Johnson City Medical Center Hospital (2017); Presenter, "Everything I wanted to know about Gynecology, but was afraid to ask," ABIM Certification Review Course (2017); Presenter, "MACRA: If you want to get paid in the future come to this lecture," "Why We Are Still on Probation," and "Residents as Teachers," Department of OB/GYN Grand Rounds, Johnson City Medical Center Hospital (2016); Presenter, "Everything I wanted to know about Gynecology, but was afraid to ask," ABIM Certification Review Course (2016); Presenter, "How Do I Manage Menopausal Patients in 2016," 20th Annual Louis Cancellaro Primary Care Conference, Millennium Centre (2016); Presenter, "Update on Hot Flashes," Department of OB/GYN Grand Rounds, Johnson City Medical Center Hospital (2015); Presenter, Evolution of Vasomotor Symptoms or "What's Up With Hot Flashes," 19th Annual Louis Cancellaro Primary Care Conference, Millennium Centre (2015); Presenter, "Episode of Care," Department of OB/GYN Grand Rounds, Johnson City Medical Center Hospital (2015); Presenter, "Everything I wanted to know about Gynecology, but was afraid to ask," ABIM Certification Review Course (2014); Presenter, "My Doctor Has Me On an Anabolic Steroid: Does He Think I am a Big League Baseball Player?" 18th Annual Louis Cancellaro Primary Care Conference, Millennium Centre (2014); Presenter, "The Future of Health Care is here: A new ACO and MEAC 2014," Transition to Residency Course, Keystone (2014); Presenter, "Fecal Microbiota Transplantation in Treatment of Relapsing C. Diff," "Healthcare Exchange: Obamacare and You – 2013," OB/GYN Grand Rounds, Johnson City Medical Center, Niswonger Children's Hospital (2013); Presenter, "Development of Accountable Care Organizations and Their Implementation," "How the H#%% Did we Get Here?: Government and Healthcare," Business in Medicine, Keystone Course (2013); Presenter, "Battle of the Titans:

W.H.I. versus K.E.E.P.S.," 17th Annual Primary Care Conference, Millennium Centre, Johnson City, TN (2013); Presenter, "Coming to Your Life....An ACO," Grand Rounds, Johnson City Medical Center, Niswonger Children's Hospital (2013); Presenter, "Development of Accountable Care Organizations Locally and Reimbursement in the Future," "How the H#%% Did We Get Here: Government and Health Care," Keystone Course, Votaw Auditorium, Clinical Education Building, Johnson City, TN (2012) **AW:** Honoree, Pearls of Wisdom For the Clinical Years, James H. Quillen School of Medicine, East Tennessee State University (2017); Nominee, Caduceus Award for Outstanding Attendee in Obstetrics and Gynecology (2015-2016); Excellence in Teaching Award, Association of Professors of Gynecology and Obstetrics (2013-2014); Excellence in Teaching Award, Council on Resident Education in Obstetrics and Gynecology, Association of Professors of Gynecology and Obstetrics (2013); Outstanding Private Physician Award, Department of Obstetrics and Gynecology, James H. Quillen College of Medicine, East Tennessee State University (2007); Outstanding Private Physician Award, Department of Obstetrics and Gynecology, James H. Quillen College of Medicine, East Tennessee State University (2005); Excellence in Teaching Award, Association of Professors of Gynecology and Obstetrics (1995-1996); Dean's Teaching Recognition Award (1993-1997); Dean's Excellence in Teaching Award (1992); Excellence in Teaching Award, Association of Professors of Gynecology and Obstetrics (1991-1992) **MEM:** Association of Professors of Gynecology and Obstetrics (2009-Present); American College of Physician Executives (2011-2017); Co-founder, The North American Menopause Society (1989); Co-founder, The North American Menopause Society; Washington-Carter-Unicoi County Medical Society; Tennessee Medical Association; Postgraduate Honor Society, Pi Gamma Mu; Postgraduate Honor Society, Gamma Beta Phi; Postgraduate Honor Society, Phi Kappa Phi **H:** Studying 19th Century History (Military and Medical); Golf **RE:** Christian (Restoration) **BA:** PO Box 70569, ETSU/Quillen College of Medicine, Johnson City, TN, 37614 **ADD:** PO Box 70569, Quillen College of Medicine, Johnson City, TN, 37614 **URL:** http://www.etsu.edu/com/obgyn/faculty/jernigan.php

JOHNSON, CLARENCE TRAYLOR JR., T: State Judge (Retired) **I:** Law and Legal Services **DOB:** 08/16/1929 **PB:** Trenton **SC:** FL/USA **PT:** Clarence Traylor Johnson; Jessie Granade (Wilson) Johnson **MS:** Married **SPN:** Shirley Ann Traxler (8/30/1957) **CH:** James Waring; Robert Dale; Douglas Earl; Jan Elizabeth **ED:** JD, University of Florida (1958); BSBA, University of Florida (1955) **C:** Retired (2002); Senior Judge, State of Florida (1992-2001); Circuit Court Judge, Eighteenth Judicial Circuit Court of Florida (1971-1992); Partner, Cone, Wagner, Nugent, Johnson, McKeown & Dell, West Palm Beach, FL (1958-1971) **CR:** Florida Bench Bar Commission, State of Florida (1990-1992); Chairman, Florida Conference of Circuit Judges (1990-1991); Florida Federal-State Judicial Council (1989-1991); Judicial Council of Florida (1989-1991); Faculty, Florida Judicial College (1988-1990) **CIV:** Charter President, The Vassar B. Carlton American Inn of Court (1992-1993); President, YMCA of Central Florida (1968-1971); President, Rotary Club of Cocoa (1965-1966); Chairman, Board, YMCA of Central Florida, Cocoa, FL (1965-1966); President, Cocoa Jaycees (1963-1964) **MIL:** U.S. Air Force (1950-1954) **AW:** Judicial Achievement Award, Academy of Florida Trial Lawyers (1987); Distinguished

Service Award, Cocoa Jaycees (1965); Clarence T. Johnson Ceremonial Courtroom, Courthouse, Viera, FL **MEM:** Board of Governors, The Florida Bar (1970-1971); President, Brevard County Bar Association (1969-1970) **BAR:** State of Florida (1958) **MH:** Albert Nelson Marquis Lifetime Achievement Award (2017) **H:** Fishing **RE:** Lutheran **ADD:** 1200 S Courtenay Parkway, Apt. 904, Merritt Island, FL, 32952

JOHNSON, DARRELL K., T: Regional Finance Manager **I:** Financial Services **CN:** Living Water International **PB:** Waukegan **SC:** IL/USA **PT:** Kurt Charles Johnson; Verna Naomi (Richards) Johnson **MS:** Married **SPN:** Rosa Gonzalez **CH:** Darrell; Mark; Mathew; Gabriel **ED:** PhD in Biblical Studies, Master's International University of Divinity (2014); PhD, California Coast University (1989); MA, Baptist Christian College (1986); BA, Baptist Christian College (1984); MBA, Southern Methodist University (1977); MA in International Management, American Graduate School of International Management - Thunderbird (1977); BA, Greenville College (1972) **C:** Regional Finance Manager, Living Water International, Stafford, TX (2015-Present); Partner and Treasurer, Lighthouse International School, Costa Rica (2008-Present); Regional Finance Manager, Habitat for Humanity International, Costa Rica (2009-2010); Regional Finance Manager for Latin America and the Caribbean, World Vision International, Costa Rica (1992-2008); Financial Manager for Southern Africa, World Vision International, Zimbabwe (1987-1992); Financial Executive, World Vision International, Monrovia, CA (1984-1986); Financial Associate for Asia, World Vision International, Philippines (1982-1984); Financial and Management Consultant, Agricultural Cooperative Development International, Bolivia (1980-1981); Management Consultant, Peace Corps, Guatemala (1978-1980); Financial Consultant, Peace Corps, Nicaragua (1977-1978); Management Consultant, Peace Corps, Colombia (1973-1975) **CIV:** Board Member, Crown Financial Ministries, Costa Rica (2010-2015); Partner, Crown Financial Ministries, Costa Rica (2010-2015) **AW:** Men of Achievement (1988); The International Who's Who of Intellectuals (1988); Outstanding Young Men in America (1985) **MEM:** Society for International Development; Evangelicals for Social Action **MH:** Who's Who in the West (1988); Who's Who in California (1987) **H:** Classical guitar; Tennis; Biking; Jogging; Foreign languages **RE:** Christian **BA:** 4001 Greenbriar Drive, Stafford, TX, 77477 **ADD:** 3228 Vista Lake Drive, Sugar Land, TX, 77478 **URL:** https://www.linkedin.com/in/darrell-johnson-1451b810

JOHNSON, KATHRYN, I: Education/Educational Services **PT:** Rudolph Erhard Johnson; Florence Anna (Reiner) Johnson **CR:** Coordinator, Environmental and Multicultural Theme Activities, Bel Air Elementary School, New Brighton, MN (1992-Present); Charter Member, Environmental Education Consortium (1995-1998); University of Minnesota Operation Pathfinder, Duluth (1997); Participant, Minnesota Humanities Commission Teacher, Institute of Native American Issues (1995) **CIV:** Political and Religious Activist for Women's Ordination, St. Joan of Arc Catholic Church, Minneapolis (1999-Present); Member, Planning Board, Life-long Learning, Coordinator-Facilitator and Teacher, Adult Educational Programs in Ecospirituality/Cosmology, St. Joan of Arc Catholic Church **MEM:** Adult Educator, Council of the Baptized (2013); Chair, Communications Council, Education Minnesota, Mounds View Education Association (1986-1988); National Education Association; Board Member, University of Minnesota Women's Club

JOHNSON, MADELINE MITCHELL, T: Administrative Assistant I: Financial Services CN: Federal Reserve Bank of Cleveland DOB: 10/24/1930 PB: Cleveland SC: OH/USA PT: Maidlon Mitchell; Katherine (Reynolds) Mitchell MS: Widowed SPN: Elvyn Frank Johnson (12/4/1954, Deceased 1982) ED: BS, Case Western Reserve University (1976) C: Coordinator, American Baptist Women Area White Cross (2008-2010); Ombudsman Representative, Federal Reserve Bank of Cleveland (1989-1992); Training Coordinator, Data Services, Federal Reserve Bank of Cleveland (1988-1992); Administrative Assistant, Federal Reserve Bank of Cleveland (1987-1992) CR: Adviser, Top Teens of America (1998-2005); Training Task Force, Federal Reserve System, Washington, DC (1987-1992); Board of Governors, Federal Reserve System, Washington, DC (1987-1992) CIV: Chair, Board of Trustees, Affinity Missionary Baptist Church (1990-1993); Volunteer, Cleveland Food Bank AW: Woman of the Year, Cleveland Chapter, Top Ladies of Distinction (1993-1994); Women of the Year Cleveland Chapter, American Business Women's Association (1987) MEM: Area White Cross Coordinator, American Baptist Women (2009-2015); Chairman, Status of Women, Top Ladies of Distinction (2003-2007); Treasurer, American Baptist Women (1998-2001); President, Top Ladies of Distinction (1995-1997); President, American Business Women's Association (1986-1988); National Council of Negro Women; Top Ladies of Distinction; Membership Chairman, American Baptist Women MH: Albert Nelson Marquis Lifetime Achievement Award (2017) H: Golf; Swimming; Reading ADD: 33705 Wellingford Court, Solon, OH, 44139

JOHNSON, RICHARD FRANK JR., T: Portfolio Manager I: Business Management/Business Services CN: Russell Investments Group, LLC ED: MBA in Finance and Marketing, The University of Chicago Booth School of Business (1992); BBA in Finance, Pacific Lutheran University School of Business, Cum Laude; Coursework in Value Investing, The Heilbrunn Center for Graham & Dodd Investing, Columbia University CT: Chartered Financial Analyst; Certificate of Completion, Continuing Studies, Stanford University C: Portfolio Manager, Russell Investments Group, LLC (2010-2017); Senior Portfolio Manager, Menta Capital (2007-2008); Co-Founder, Co-Portfolio Manager, Crescat Partners LLC (2005-2007); Director, Portfolio Manager, McMorgan & Company LLC (2000-2004); Principal, Barclays Global Investors (1994-2000) CW: Author, "Reflections on a Summer in Eastern Europe" (1992); Author, "A Summer in Eastern Europe" (1991) AW: Recipient, Team Award, Russell Investments Group, LLC (2011) MEM: CFA Institute; CFA Society of San Francisco; CQA ADD: 7406 27th street west, Suite 206, University place, WA, 98466 URL: https://www.linkedin.com/in/rich-johnson-cfa

JOHNSON, WAYNE R., T: Founder, President I: Law and Legal Services CN: Wayne R. Johnson & Associates CH: Meredith ED: LLM in Taxation Law, New York University School of Law (1995); JD, University of North Dakota School of Law (1994); BS in Accounting, Business, Finance, and Economics, North Dakota State University (1989) C: Shareholder, Founder, Wayne R. Johnson & Associates, PLC (2010-Present); Shareholder, Valensi Rose, PLC (1999-2010) CR: Adjunct Professor of Tax Law, Loyola Law School's Graduate Tax Program (2005-Present); Adjunct Professor of Law, Golden Gate University, Los Angeles Campus (1997-2002); Adjunct Professor of Law, Western State University College of Law (1997-2000); Speaker in Field CIV: Member, Board of Advisors, Graduate Tax Program, Loyola Law School; Former

Chair, Taxation Section, California State Bar; Chair, Make a Wish Foundation, Los Angeles, CA; Chair, Wise Senior Services; Committee Member, Reagan Foundation CW: Author, "Tax Collection Techniques: Money Still Talks," Journal of Tax Practice and Procedure (2007-2008); Author, "Is the Federal Offer-in-Compromise Program Still Viable," Journal of Tax Practice and Procedure (2005-2006); Author, "Current Developments in Individual Income Tax Planning," Major Tax Planning (2005); Author, "Reducing Debt Can Carry Tax Consequences," California Bar Journal (2002); Author, "At Tax Time, Modify Debt with Caution," California Bar Journal (2002); Author, "Qualifying Reverse Exchanges under Revenue Procedure 2000-37," Los Angeles Lawyer (2001); Author, "Estate Planning in Light of The Economic Growth and Tax Relief Reconciliation Act of 2001" (2001); Author, "North Dakota's New Contempt Law: Will it Mean Order in the Court?" North Dakota Law Review (1994); Author, Tax, Business and Estate Planning AW: V. Judson Klein Award, Taxation Section, State Bar of California (2011); Super Lawyer in the Field of Taxation Law (2009-2018); Rising Star Among Southern California Lawyers (2004-2006) MEM: Chair, Subcommittee on Individual Income Taxation, USC Tax Institute (2006-2009); State Bar of California; USC Tax Institute; Executive Committee, USC Tax Institute; Planning Committee, UCLA Tax Controversy Institute BAR: State Bar of California (1996); United States Tax Court; United States District Court for the Central District of California; United States Court of Appeals for the Ninth Circuit H: Hockey; Rugby; Travelling; Wine; Foreign languages BA: 5901 W Century Blvd Ste 650, Wayne R. Johnson & Assoc, Los Angeles, CA, 90045 ADD: 9595 Wilshire Blvd., Suite 900, Beverly Hills, CA, 90212

JONAS, ALAN BERNARD, T: Financial Planner I: Financial Services PB: Los Angeles SC: CA/USA PT: Leon Kerster Jonas; Mildred Miller Jonas MS: Married SPN: Felice Joyce Cohen (6/18/1957) CH: Mindy Cara; Lauren Kay; Corinne Merrill ED: MA in Dramatic Art, New York University (1958); BA in Dramatic Art, Brooklyn College (1957) CT: Former Certification in Financial Planning C: Independent Financial Planner (1981-Present); Registered Representative, Walnut St. Securities (2007-2008); Registered Representative, Contemporary Financial Solutions (2003-2006); Registered Representative, Royal Alliance Associates Inc., San Rafael, CA (1995-2003); Registered Representative, Financial Network Investment Corp., San Rafael, CA (1990-1995); Director, Marketing, Paul Revere Insurance Group, San Francisco, CA (1990-1995); Chairman, The Financial Store Inc., Santa Rosa, CA (1988-1989); President, The Financial Store Inc., Santa Rosa, CA (1983-1988); Registered Representative, Financial Planners Equity Corp., San Rafael, CA (1981-1988); President, Financial Associates Inc., San Rafael, Santa Rosa, CA (1981-1983); Investment Specialist, Sutro & Co., San Francisco, Santa Rosa, CA (1974-1981); Registered Representative, Royal Alliance Associates Inc., San Francisco, CA CR: Expert Member, Long-Term Care, Royal Alliance Associates, Inc. (1995-2003) CIV: President, Kiwanis Club of Oakland (1973-1974); Chairman, Membership Committee, Oakland Museum Association (1972-1976); Board of Directors, Oakland Museum Association (1972-1976); President, Meals for Millions Foundation, Marin County, CA (1966-1968) CW: Stock Market Reporter, KSFO Radio, San Francisco, CA (1975); Reporter, Writer, NBC News; Guest Appearances, Television Programs; Featured, Various Magazines; Author, Book about Facebook AW: Named, Nations Top Financial Planners MEM: Associate Member, Trusts and Estates Section, State Bar of

California; American Association for Long-Term Care Insurance ADD: 3711 Canyon Village Circle, San Ramon, CA, 94583

JONES, EVELYN GLORIA, T: Medical Technologist (Retired), Educator I: Sciences CN: Tennessee Department Health Laboratory Services DOB: 08/13/1940 PB: Roanoke SC: VA/USA PT: William Darnell Powell; Elizabeth (Harris) Powell MS: Married SPN: Theodore Joseph Jones (8/21/1965) ED: MEd in Administration and Supervision, Tennessee State University (1993); BS in Biology, Tennessee State University (1973) CT: Certified in Medical Technology, Vanderbilt University (1974) C: Microbiologist, Tennessee Department of Health Laboratory Services, Nashville, TN (1997-2007); Medical Technologist, Vanderbilt Medical Center, Nashville, TN (1978-1997); Medical Technologist, Metro General Hospital, Nashville, TN (1974-1978) CR: Technical Consultant, Vanderbilt Point of Care Program (1993-1996); Lecturer, St. Thomas Program of Medical Technology, Nashville, TN (1991-1994); Member, Advisory Board, Meharry Medical Technology Program, Tennessee State University, Nashville, TN; Instructor, Teaching Faculty, Public Health Laboratory Services, Nashville, TN CIV: Information Guide, Archive Section, Fisk University (2009-Present); Member, Docent Advisory Board, Frist Visual Arts Museum (2001-Present); Assistant Secretary, Henderville Area Chapter, The Links, Inc. (1997-2002); Nashville Board of Directors, Tennessee Valley Region American Red Cross Blood Services (1996-2002) MEM: American Association of University Women (AAUW); American Association for the Advancement of Science; Frist Center for the Visual Arts; Southern Association of Clinical Microbiology; Associate, American Society of Clinical Pathologists; Alpha Kappa Alpha Sorority, Incorporated; Phi Delta Kappa International H: Art; Travel; Reading RE: Roman Catholic ADD: 1003 Cross Bow Dr, Hendersonville, TN, 37075

JONES, HARRY EDWARD, T: Diplomat, Writer I: Writing and Editing DOB: 02/19/1938 PB: Philadelphia SC: PA/USA PT: Harry Edward Jones; Helen Jean (Spoon) Jones MS: Married SPN: Stephanie Cherubin (7/8/2016); Patricia Anne Pascoe (10/13/1964, Deceased 10/9/2009) CH: Michael Sumner; Christopher Steven; Anne Pelton ED: MPA, Pennsylvania State University (1975); Coursework, George Washington University (1960-1962); BS, Pennsylvania State University (1959) C: Senior Advisor, CIA, McLean, VA (2002-2014); Senior Foreign Service Officer, Minister Counselor, United States Department of State, Washington, D.C. (1965-2002) CR: Political Economic Minister; Consul General; Counselor of Embassy CIV: Volunteer, Food Bank; Officiant, St. George's Episcopal Church MIL: US Army Intelligence (1960-1962) CW: Author, "Shadow In a Weary Land"; Contributor, Articles to Professional Journals; Contributor, Op-ed Columns, Fredericksburg Free Lance-Star MEM: American Foreign Service Association; Diplomatic and Consular Officers Retired MH: Albert Nelson Marquis Lifetime Achievement Award (2017) H: Gardening; Painting; Book club RE: Episcopalian ADD: 208 Caroline St, Fredericksburg, VA, 22401

JONES, JAMES EDWARD, T: Registered Nurse I: Medicine & Health Care CN: Correct Care Solutions ED: Master's Degree, University of Arkansas (1982); Nursing Degree, University of Rochester (1968) CT: Registered Nurse, Correct Care Solutions C: Affiliate, Medical Department, Shelby County Jail, Memphis, TN (2000-Present); Director, Nursing and Care, Memphis VA Medical Center, Memphis, TN (1984-2005); Medic Hospital

Foreman (1964-1966) **CR:** Nurse Training, U.S. Navy, Rochester, NY (1966-1968) **MIL:** U.S. Navy (1964-1984) **AW:** Employee of the Quarter, Correct Care Solutions (2007) **MEM:** Secretary-Treasurer, Veterans Administration Nurse Alumni (VANA); School of Nursing Alumni Council, University of Rochester **BA:** 1045 Mullins Station Road, Correct Care Solutions, Memphis, TN, 38134 **ADD:** 2606 Union Avenue, Memphis, TN, 38112

JONES, LAWRENCE WILLIAM, T: Physics Professor Emeritus **I:** Sciences **CN:** University of Michigan **DOB:** 11/16/1925 **PB:** Evanston **SC:** IL/USA **PT:** Charles Herbert Jones; Fern (Storm) Jones **MS:** Widowed **SPN:** Ruth Reavley Drummond (6/24/1950, Deceased 2018) **CH:** Douglas Warren; Carol Anne; Ellen Louise **ED:** PhD in Physics, University of California, Berkeley (1952); MS in Physics, Northwestern University (1949); BS in Physics and Zoology, Northwestern University (1948) **C:** Professor Emeritus of Physics, University of Michigan, Ann Arbor, MI (1998-Present); Staff Associate, European Organization for Nuclear Research (1988-Present); Visiting Scientist, Faculty, University of Michigan, Ann Arbor, MI (1952-Present); Staff Member, Forward-Backward Lepton Jet Analyzer Group, European Organization for Nuclear Research (1988); Chairman, Department of Physics, University of Michigan, Ann Arbor, MI (1982-1987); Visiting Professor, Westfield College (Now Queen Mary University of London) (1977); Science Research Council Fellow, Westfield College (Now Queen Mary University of London) (1977); Visiting Professor, University of London (1977); Science Research Council Fellow, University of London (1977); Fellow, John Simon Guggenheim Memorial Foundation, European Organization for Nuclear Research (1965); Professor of Physics, University of Michigan, Ann Arbor, MI (1963-1998); Ford Foundation Fellow, European Organization for Nuclear Research (1961-1962); Associate Professor, Assistant Professor and Instructor, University of Michigan, Ann Arbor, MI (1952-1963); Research Assistant, Lawrence Berkeley National Laboratory, Berkeley, CA (1950-1952); Teaching Fellow, University of California, Berkeley (1949-1950); Teaching Fellow, Northwestern University (1948-1949); Scientist, United States Naval Ordnance Laboratory (1948) **CR:** Co-Chairman, Science Advisory Committee, Michigan Environmental Council (2000-Present); Visiting Scientist, European Organization of Nuclear Research, Geneva, Switzerland (1985-Present); Visiting Physicist, Fermi National Accelerator Laboratory, Batavia, IL (1971-Present); Visiting Physicist, Brookhaven National Laboratory, Upton, NY (1963-Present); Visiting Physicist, Lawrence Berkeley National Laboratory, Berkeley, CA (1959-Present); Consultant, National Aeronautics and Space Administration (2002); Member, International Advisory Committee, The Chacaltaya Observatory, Universidad Mayor de San Andreas (2001); Member, International Advisory Committee, Bolivian Observatory of Mount Chacaltaya (2001); Visiting Physicist, Superconducting Super Collider National Laboratory (1991-1994); Distinguished Visiting Scholar, The University of Adelaide (1991); Visiting Professor, Falkiner High Energy Physics Department (Now Particle Physics Group), The University of Sydney, Australia (1991); Visiting Scientist, Department of Physics, University of Auckland (1991); Consultant, Central Design Group, Superconducting Super Collider National Laboratory (1985-1987); Elementary Particle Physics Panel, Physics Survey Committee, National Research Council (1984); Trustee, Universities Research Association, Inc. (1982-1987); Visiting Professor, Tata Institute of Fundamental Research, Mumbai, India (1979); Consultant, National Aeronautics and Space Administration (1974-1981); Visiting Scientist, European Organization of Nuclear Research, Geneva, Switzerland (1965); Consultant, Lawrence Berkeley National Laboratory (1964-1966); Visiting Scientist, European Organization of Nuclear Research, Geneva, Switzerland (1961-1962); Physicist, Midwestern University Research Association (1956-1957); Visiting Physicist, European Organization for Nuclear Research Laboratory, Geneva, Switzerland **CIV:** President, Ecology Center, Ann Arbor, MI (1975); Treasurer, Ecology Center, Ann Arbor, MI (1974) **MIL:** US Army (1944-1946) **CW:** Member, Advisory Panel, Cosmic Rays, Journal of Physics G: Nuclear and Particle Physics (1991-1995); Speaker in the Field **AW:** Fellow, Science Research Council (1977); Fellow, John Simon Guggenheim Memorial Foundation (1965); Fellow, Ford Foundation, National Academy of Sciences (1961-1962) **MEM:** Friends of the History of Physics Group; Fellow, American Physical Society; American Association for the Advancement of Science **MH:** Albert Nelson Marquis Lifetime Achievement Award (2017) **H:** Amateur radio **RE:** Congregational (Christian-Protestant) **ADD:** 4001 Glacier Hills Dr Apt 127, Ann Arbor, MI, 48105 **URL:** https://en.wikipedia.org/wiki/Lawrence_W._Jones

JONES, MARK EVAN, T: Insurance Company Executive **I:** Insurance **CN:** Goosehead Insurance Agency, LLC **DOB:** 01/16/1962 **PB:** Edmonton **SC:** AB/CAN **MS:** Married **SPN:** Robyn Mary Elizabeth (08/16/1980) **CH:** Lanni Elaine Romney; Lindy Jean Langston; Camille LaVaun Peterson; Desiree Robyn Coleman; Adrienne Morgan; Mark Evan, Jr. **ED:** Master of Business Administration, Harvard Business School, Boston, MA (1991); Bachelor of Commerce, University of Alberta, Edmonton, AB, Canada (1985) **C:** Chairman, Goosehead Insurance Agency, LLC, Irving, TX (2004-Present); Chief Executive Officer, Goosehead Insurance Agency, LLC, Irving, TX (2004-Present); Co-founder, Goosehead Insurance Agency, LLC, Irving, TX (2004-Present); Director, Bain & Company, Boston, MA and Dallas, TX (1990-2004); Senior Partner, Bain & Company, Boston, MA and Dallas, TX (1990-2004); Staff Accountant, Clarkson Gordon (Now Ernst & Young Global Limited), Calgary, AB, Canada (1985-1989) **MH:** Albert Nelson Marquis Lifetime Achievement Award (2017) **H:** Reading; Boating; Spending time with family **ADD:** 1850 Post Oak Pl, Westlake, TX, 76262

JONES, ROGER C., T: Founding Partner & Managing Director **I:** Law and Legal Services **CN:** Huddles Jones Sorteberg & Dachille, PC **DOB:** 11/27/1959 **PB:** Ithaca **SC:** NY/USA **MS:** Married **SPN:** Janet E. Jones **CH:** R. Brennan Jones; Bradley C. Jones; Blake Marie Jones **ED:** JD, Washington University School of Law, St. Louis, MO (1985); BS in Architecture and Construction Management, The Catholic University of America (1982) **C:** Founding Partner, Principal, Managing Director, Huddles, Jones, Sorteberg & Dachille, PC (1995-2018); Principal, Braude & Margulies, P.C. (1985-1995) **CIV:** Mentor, Boy Scouts of America; Board Member, Officer, Villas at Corolla Bay Homeowner's Association **CW:** Author, "Construction Contract Changes," Lorman Education Services (2005); Author, "The Legal Implications of Construction Scheduling for Owners, Contractors & Subcontractors," Lorman Education Services (2004); Author, "Post Hoc Termination Justification: What Happened to the Logic?," Board of Contract Appeals, Judges Association Conference (1998) **AW:** Honoree, Named Top Attorney In Maryland (2013-2018); Honoree, Named Best Lawyer in America in Construction Law (2003-2018); Recipient, Recognition, U.S. News and World Report; Nominee, Maryland Super Lawyer; Recognition, Top 10% of America's Most Honored Professionals **MEM:** Public Contract Law Section, ABA; Construction Law Section, Maryland State Bar Association; Construction Law Section, Virginia State Bar **BAR:** Maryland; Virginia; Washington, D.C.; United States District Court for the District of Maryland; United States District Court for the Eastern District of Virginia; United States District Court for District of Columbia; United States Court of Appeals for the Fourth Circuit; United States Court of Appeals for the Eleventh Circuit; United States Court of Federal Claims; United States Court of Appeals for the Federal Circuit; Supreme Court of the United States **MH:** Lifetime Achievement Award (2018) **H:** Wilderness backpacking; Hiking; Camping; Vacationing in Corolla, North Carolina **BA:** 10211 Wincopin Cir Ste 200, Huddles Jones Sorteberg & Dachille, PC, Columbia, MD, 21044 **URL:** http://www.constructionlaw.com

JONES, TRACY L., T: Chief Executive Officer **I:** Financial Services **CN:** TLJ Professional Services, Inc. **PB:** San Francisco **SC:** CA/USA **MS:** Married **SPN:** Donald Jones **CH:** Domonic White; Brianna Cardoza; Deanna Jones; Jaianna Jones **ED:** MBA in Accounting, Keller Graduate School of Management, DeVry University (2016); MBA in Accounting and Public Administration, University of Phoenix (2007); BA in Business, University of Phoenix (2005); AA, Heald College (1991) **CT:** Preparer Tax Identification Number (PTIN), IRS; California Tax Education Council (CTEC); Certified Accounts Payable Management Certificate (APM), Institute of Finance and Management (IOFM) **C:** Chief Executive Officer, TLJ Professional Services, Inc. (2003-Present); Director, Accounts Payable, Digital Realty (2008-Present); Independent Associate, Legal Shield (2007-Present); Financial Accountant, Copy Central, Fairbanks Enterprises Corporate Office (2002-2017) **CIV:** Founder, President, Beat The Streets, Inc. (2005-Present) **AW:** Executive Woman of the Year, National Association of Professional Women (2014-2015) **MEM:** Oakland-Bay Area Chapter, NCBW (2015-Present); Volunteer Member, Finance Committee, Chair, Budget and Finance Committee; National Association of Professional Women; National Black MBA Association (NBMBAA); Landmark Worldwide **H:** Volunteering; Spa days **RE:** AME Church **ADD:** 157 Oriole Ct, Hercules, CA, 94547 **URL:** https://www.linkedin.com/in/tljprofessionalservices/

JONES-SMITH, LILLIAN LOUISE, T: Owner **I:** Leisure, Travel & Tourism **CN:** Smith Travel Agency LLC **DOB:** 02/14/1930 **PB:** Garner **SC:** NC/USA **PT:** Charlie Jones; Queen Esther Jones **MS:** Widowed **SPN:** Matthew Smith (Deceased) **CH:** Matthew L.; Ernest (Deceased) **ED:** MLS, Wayne State University, Detroit, MI (2001); MEd, Wayne State University, Detroit, MI (1971); BSc, Shaw University, Garner, NC (1954) **C:** President, Detroit Association of Retired School Personnel (2013-2014); Recording Secretary, Detroit Association of Retired School Personnel (2009-2012); Executive Director, Detroit Association of Women's Clubs (2002-2004); President, Detroit Association of Women's Clubs (1997-2004); Judge, Metropolitan Science Fair, Detroit (1991-2000); Biology Teacher, Detroit Public High School (1965-1991); Biology Teacher, Lillington Public High School, North Carolina (1962-1965); Insurance Agent, Diggs and Mammoth Insurance Co., Detroit, MI (1959-1962); Science Teacher, Speight High School, Fort Gaines, GA (1955-1957) **CR:** Distributor,

NEOLIFE (2015-Present); Owner, Concerned Parents and Citizens of Northwest Detroit (1980) **CIV:** Volunteer, Church Library, Ebenezer A.M.E. Church, Detroit, MI (2002-Present); President, Dorcas Society Club (1993-1995); President, Century of Progress Club (1983-1986); Director, Ebenezer Methodist Church Vacation Bible School (1982-1986); Treasurer, Pal Little Leaguers, Detroit, MI (1980) **AW:** Rosa L. Gragg Club Women of Year Award, Saginaw 21st Century Women's Club (2006); Community Service Award, National Association of Negro Business And Professional Women's Club (2004); Certificate of Appreciation, Michigan State Association of Colored Women's Clubs (1994); Worthy Matron Appreciation, International Free and Accepted Masons and Order of the Eastern Star (1991); Achievement Award, Wayne County Intermediate School District (1990); Professional Growth Award, State Board of Education (1990); Community Service Award, Wayne County Executive, Detroit, MI (1986) **MEM:** American Library Association; American Red Cross; CLIA; Saginaw 21st Century Women's Club **H:** Quilting; Golf; Reading; Computers **ADD:** 1300 E Lafayette Street, Apartment 812, Detroit, MI, 48207

KAGGEN, LOIS SHEILA, I: Nonprofit & Philanthropy **CN:** Resources for Artists with Disabilities **DOB:** 01/02/1944 **PB:** New York City **SC:** NY/USA **PT:** Elias Kaggen; Sylvia (Muntner) Kaggen **MS:** Divorced **SPN:** Michael Francis McCann (9/26/1984, Divorced 4/2007); Harold Jay Burns (6/26/1969, Deceased 1975) **CH:** David Henry (Deceased) **ED:** PhD, Department of Art and Art Professions, New York University, New York City, NY (1997); MA, Department of Art Education, The City College of New York, New York City, NY (1973); Coursework, Studio Art, The Cooper Union Evening School of Art and Architecture (Now The Cooper Union for the Advancement of Science and Art) (1967-1969); BS in Fine Arts, Skidmore College, Saratoga Springs, NY (1964) **C:** Founder, President, Resources for Artists with Disabilities, New York City, NY (1987-Present); Teacher of Fine Arts, Grades 7-9, Junior High School 149, Bronx, NY (1967-1974) **CR:** Board of Directors, Center for Independence of the Disabled of New York (CIDNY), New York City, NY (1996-Present); Traumatic Brain Injury Consumer Advisor (1977-Present); Search Committee for Director Tang, The Frances Young Tang Teaching Museum and Art Gallery at Skidmore College, Saratoga Springs, NY (2004); Gave Testimony, NYC Taxi & Limousine Commission, The City of New York, NY (2004); Information and Communications Committee, TBISEC (TBI Council), New York State Department of Health, Delmar, NY (2001); New York State Assembly Task Force on People with Disabilities, Public Hearing, The Graduate Center, CUNY (2001); American Council of Education Conference, "The Student with a Brain Injury: Achieving Goals for Higher Education," Washington, D.C. (2001); Presenter, National Institutes of Health, Consensus Development Conference on Rehabilitation of Persons with Traumatic Brain Injury, Bethesda, MD (1998); Fifth Annual Conference, Traumatic Brain Injury Program, New York State Department of Health, Albany, NY (1998); Panel Organizer, Moderator, Presenter, Institute for Research on Women's Health, 16th Anniversary Celebration of Our Work Conference, Douglass Residential College, Rutgers, The State University of New Jersey, New Brunswick, NJ (1998); Originator, Conference Committee, Co-organizer, Consumer Panelist, New York University Moses Center for Students with Disabilities and Center for Independence of the Disabled of New York, Loeb Student Center, New York University, New York City, NY (1998); Governor's Appointment to Traumatic Brain Injury Services Coordinating Council, Albany, NY (1997-2001); Steering committee, Annual Disability Independence Day March (1992-1993); Member, Media Outreach (1992); Consultant, Eastern Paralyzed Veterans Association, Guggenheim Museum of Art, The Solomon R. Guggenheim Foundation, New York City, NY (1990); Board of Advisors, Independent Arts Gallery, Queens Independent Living Center, Jamaica, NY (1987-1998); Advisory Board Committee, Art in Education Project, New York State Council on the Arts, Center for Safety in the Arts, New York City, NY (1987); Provider of Written and Oral Testimony in Field to Organizations; Art Presenter in Field **CIV:** Program Committee Member, Center for Independence of the Disabled, NY (2012-Present); Member, Disabilities Network of NYC, Inc. (2000-Present); Member, Information Subcommittee, New York City Council Planning Committee, Department of the Disabled (2000-Present); Access Subcommittee, 504 Democratic Club for Persons with Disabilities (2000-Present); Active Member, Manhattan Borough President Disability Advisory Council (1999-Present); Member, Peer Review Registry, U.S. Department of Education (1995-Present); Active Member, Disabled in Action of Greater New York (Now Disabled in Action of Metropolitan New York) (1989-Present); Patron, Village Independent Democrats Awards Gala (2011); Elected Judicial Delegate, 66th Assembly District, New York State Supreme Court Convention (2009); Member, Village Independent Democrats Turns 50 Committee, Village Independent Democrats 50th Anniversary Reception (2007); Vice President, Village Independent Democrats (2005-2007); Executive Committee, Village Independent Democrats, New York City, NY (2003-2009); Active in Assistive Signage Needs, New York City Council Planning Committee, Department of the Disabled (2000); Member, New York County Democratic Committee, 102ED/95 ED (1995-2007); Member, Citywide Coalition on Disability, New York City, NY (1994-1995); Member, Mayor's Advisory Committee on People with Disabilities, New York City, NY (1991-1993); Member, Executive Committee, 504 Democratic Club for Persons with Disabilities (1990-2002); Active Member, Manhattan Borough President Disability Advisory Council (1988-1998); Member, Disability Rights Steering Committee, 504 Democratic Club for Persons with Disabilities (1987-1988); Member, Office of Special Education and Rehabilitation Services, U.S. Department of Education, Washington, D.C.; Member, National Institute of Disability and Rehabilitation Research; Elected Judicial Delegate, First Judicial District, Supreme Court Convention, New York County **CW:** Photography Exhibition, Donnell Library Center Gallery, The New York Public Library (1981); Photography Exhibition, The Cathedral Church of Saint John the Divine Gallery, New York City, NY (1980); Photography Exhibition, Window Gallery, Metropolitan Savings Bank, New York City, NY (1980); Photography Exhibition, Leslie-Lohman Gallery, New York City, NY (1980, 1981); Photography Exhibition, 4th Street Photo Gallery, New York City, NY (1979); Photography Exhibition, Womanart Gallery, New York City, NY (1979); Photography Exhibition, Soho Photo Gallery, New York City, NY (1978); Photography Exhibition, 80 Washington Square East Galleries, New York University, New York City, NY (1977); Originator, Organizer, Various Exhibitions African-American Artists with Disabilities, Artists with Physical Disabilities; Contributor, Articles, Photographs to Professional Journals **AW:** Dean's Distinguished Alumni Achievement Award, New York University, New York City, NY (1998); Appreciation Certificate, Manhattan Borough President (1991); Grantee, Summer Film Institute, Stanford University (1968); The Cooper Union Scholar (Now The Cooper Union for the Advancement of Science and Art) (1967-1969); Grantee, Whitney Museum of American Art and the Smithsonian Institution, Summer (1967); New York State Regents College Scholarship (1960-1964) **MEM:** Committee Members with Disabilities for Accessible Programs and Places, College Art Association of America, Inc. (1990-Present); MADD (2018); New York City Council, Department for the Disabled; Life Member, MENSA **ADD:** 77 Seventh Avenue, PHG , 77 Seventh Avenue, PHH, New York, NY, 10011

KANG, Y. JAMES, T: President, Chief Executive Officer, Chief Scientist, Professor **I:** Education/Educational Services **ED:** Doctorate Degree, Iowa State University of Science and Technology (1989) **C:** China National One-Thousand-Talents Professor, Sichuan University; Director, Regenerative Medicine Research Center, Sichuan University; Director, Memphis Institute of Regenerative Medicine, The University of Tennessee Health Science Center; Chief Executive Officer, Revotek Co.; Chief Scientist, Revotek Co.; President, Sichuan 3D Bio-printing Institute; Director, Sichuan 3D Bio-printing Institute; Director, Sichuan Regenerative Medicine Engineering and Technology Center **CW:** Editor-in-Chief, "Cardiovascular Toxicology"; Editor-in-Chief, "Regenerative Medicine Research"; Editor, "Methods in Pharmacology and Toxicology" **AW:** Distinguished Scientist Award, Society for Experimental Biology and Medicine (2011) **BA:** Tianfu Financial District A Bldg 10, Innolife Co., LTD, Wuhouqu Chengdu, China, 610041

KAPLAN, ALAN L., T: Gynecologic Oncologist **I:** Medicine & Health Care **CN:** Houston Methodist Hospital **DOB:** 09/10/1930 **PB:** Atlanta **SC:** GA/USA **MS:** Married **SPN:** Cissie Rauch Kaplan (2/13/2004) **CH:** John; Robert; Gary; Janet **ED:** Fellow, Surgical Oncology, Columbia University Medical Center, NewYork-Presbyterian Hospital (1962-1963); Senior Resident, Obstetrics & Gynecology, Columbia University Medical Center, NewYork-Presbyterian Hospital (1961-1963); Assistant Resident, Obstetrics & Gynecology, Columbia University Medical Center, NewYork-Presbyterian Hospital (1956-1959); Intern, Jackson Memorial Hospital, Miami, FL (1955-1956); MD, Columbia University (1955); BA, Washington and Lee University (1951) **CT:** Diplomate in Gynecologic Oncology, American Board of Obstetrics and Gynecology, Inc. (2000, 1974); Diplomate, American Board of Obstetrics and Gynecology, Inc. (2000, 1966); Licensed to Practice Medicine, State of Texas (1963) **C:** Full Emeritus Member, Houston Methodist Research Institute, Houston, TX (2015-Present); Emeritus Professor, Obstetrics and Gynecology, Institute for Academic Medicine, Houston Methodist Hospital, Houston, TX (2015-Present); Clinical Professor, Obstetrics and Gynecology, Department of Obstetrics and Gynecology, Weill Cornell Medical College (2015-Present); Professor Emeritus, Department of Obstetrics and Gynecology, Baylor College of Medicine (2010-Present); Professor, Obstetrics and Gynecology, Institute for Academic Medicine, Houston Methodist Hospital, Houston, TX (2014-2015); Full Member, Houston Methodist Hospital, Houston, TX (2008-2015); Professor, Obstetrics and Gynecology, Department of Obstetrics and Gynecology, Weill Cornell Medicine (2005-2015); Professor, Director, Division of Gynecologic Oncology, Department of Obstetrics and Gynecology, Baylor College of Medicine (1979-2005); Associate Professor, Department of Obstetrics and Gynecology, Baylor College of Medicine (1968-1979); Assistant Professor, Department of Radiology,

Baylor College of Medicine (1963-2005); Assistant Professor, Department of Obstetrics and Gynecology, Baylor College of Medicine (1963-1968) **CR:** Advisory Committee, TMH Foundation Houston Methodist Hospital (2010-2015); Chairman, Houston Methodist Hospital Department of Obstetrics and Gynecology (2005-2015); Leadership Committee, Department of Obstetrics and Gynecology, Houston Methodist Hospital (2004-2015); Case Management and Performance Improvement Subcommittee Women's Services, Houston Methodist Hospital (2004-2015); Case Management and Performance Improvement Steering Committee, Houston Methodist Hospital (2004-2015); Medical Executive Committee, The Methodist Hospital (2004-2015); Cancer Governance Group, The Methodist Hospital (2001-2015); Medical Director, Gynecologic Oncology Program, Houston Methodist Hospital (1988-2015); The Methodist Hospital Abdominopelvic Utilization Review (1996-2000); St. Luke's Episcopal Hospital Cancer Research Committee (1995-1998); The Methodist Hospital Medical Staff Committee Council (1995-1997); Chairman The Methodist Hospital Cancer Committee (1995-1997); St. Luke's Episcopal Hospital Cancer Committee (1990-1994); Houston Methodist Hospital Cancer Committee (1985-2015); St. Luke's Episcopal Hospital OR Committee (1978-1987); Division Chief, Gynecologic Oncology, Baylor College of Medicine (1974-2005) **MIL:** Captain, Medical Corps, U.S. Army (1959-1961) **CW:** Author, "Vaginal Cancer: Stage I Bulky Squamous Cell Carcinoma," Gynecological Cancers (1996); Author, "Vulvar Cancer: Stage IV Squamous Cell Carcinoma," Gynecological Cancers (1996); Author, "Central Recurrence of Advanced Cervical Cancer 8 Months Following Surgery and Radiation Therapy," Gynecological Cancers (1996); Author, "Thrombophlebitis," Emergency Therapy (1984); Author, "Diagnosis and Treatment of Abscesses Associated with Gynecologic Diseases" (1971); Contributor, Articles, Professional Journals; Contributor, Chapters, Books; Presenter in Field; Lecturer in Field **AW:** Honoree, Houston's Top Doctors for Women (2006-Present); Honoree, Texas Super Doctors (2006-Present); Women's Health Event Award, Houston Methodist Hospital, Houston, TX (2015); Lifetime Achievement Award, Houston Methodist Hospital, Houston, TX (2014); Faculty of the Year Award, Houston Methodist Hospital, Houston, TX (2014); John W. Overstreet, MD Award, Houston Methodist Hospital, Houston TX (2007); Golden Forceps Award, Baylor College of Medicine (2003-2004); Honoree, Faculty Medical Student Educator of the Year, Baylor College of Medicine (1999-2001); Partners in Courage Award of Achievement, American Cancer Society, Inc. (1998); Honoree, Best Doctors in America (1995-2003); President's Award, Houston Gynecological & Obstetrical Foundation (1995); Resident Appreciation Award, Baylor College of Medicine (1994-1997); Honoree, Physician of the Quarter, CHI St. Luke's Health (1994); Faculty Recognition Award, Baylor College of Medicine (1989-1992); Honoree, Distinguished Faculty Member, Baylor College of Medicine (1978-1983) **MEM:** American Society of Clinical Oncology (1987-Present); Society of Gynecologic Surgeons (1983-Present); International Society for the Study of Vulvovaginal Disease (1983-Present); International Gynecologic Cancer Society (1980-Present); European Society of Gynaecological Oncology (1980-Present); American Urogynecologic Society (1979-Present); Houston Surgical Society (1971-Present); The International College of Surgeons (1970-Present); Founder, Society of Gynecologic Oncology (1969-Present); Texas Association of Obstetricians & Gynecologists (1966-Present); Central Association of Obstetricians and Gynecologists (1965-Present); American Cancer Society, Inc. (1964-Present); American College of Obstetricians and Gynecologists (1964-Present); American College of Surgeons (1964-Present); American Medical Association (1964-Present); Texas Medical Association (1964-Present); Harris County Medical Society (1964-Present); Houston Gynecological and Obstetrical Society (1964-Present) **MH:** Albert Nelson Marquis Lifetime Achievement Award (2017) **H:** Exercise; Reading **ADD:** 7 A South West Oak Dr, Houston, TX, 77056

KARIMYAN, ALTINA, T: Dentist **I:** Medicine & Health Care **CN:** Pasadena Family Cosmetic & Implant Dentistry **ED:** DDS, New York University (2005); Bachelor Degree, University of Southern California(2001) **CT:** Certified in Periodontal Disease, Perio Protect, LLC; Invisalign Certified **C:** Dentist, Pasadena Family Cosmetic & Implant Dentistry (2012-Present) **CR:** Expert Analyst, California Dental Board **CIV:** Volunteer Instructor, University of Southern California; Missionary, L.A. Care Health Plan **AW:** Pasadena Magazine Top Dentist Award (2010-2016) **MEM:** American Dental Association; San Gabriel Valley Dental Society; American Academy of Cosmetic Dentistry; Associate Member, American Academy of Implant Dentistry; California Dental Association **BA:** 800 Fairmount Ave Ste 100, Pasadena Family Cosmetic & Implant Dentistry, Pasadena, CA, 91105-3158 **URL:** http://pasadenadental.com/

KARMALI, RASHIDA A., T: Chief Executive Officer, Intellectual Property Lawyer, Cancer Research Scientist **I:** Law and Legal Services **CN:** Tactical Therapeutics, Inc. **DOB:** 05/12/1948 **SC:** Uganda **PT:** A. Karmali; S. Karmali **ED:** MBA, Rutgers, The State University of New Jersey (2007); JD, Rutgers, The State University of New Jersey (1993); PhD in Biochemistry, Newcastle University (1976); MSc, University of Aberdeen (1973); BSc, Makerere University (1971) **CT:** Certified Licensing Professional **C:** Founder, Chief Executive Officer, President, Tactical Therapeutics, Inc., New York City, NY (2005-Present); Intellectual Property Lawyer, Private Practice (2000-Present); Associate, Stroock, Stroock & Lavan LLP (1997); Associate, Bryan Cave (1995); Associate, Pennie & Edmonds (1994); Law Clerk to Hopgood Calimafde (1994); Judicial Clerk to Honorable Dickinson R. Debevoise, United States District Court District of New Jersey (1994); Adjunct Associate Professor, Cook College (Now School of Environmental and Biological Sciences, Rutgers, The State University of New Jersey) (1984-1990); Research Associate, Memorial Sloan Kettering Institute, Memorial Sloan Kettering Cancer Center, New York City, NY (1980-1984); Research Associate, East Carolina University, Greenville, NC (1978-1980); Fellow, Montreal Clinical Research Institute, Montreal, Canada (1976-1978) **CIV:** Mentor, Rutgers School of Law (2000-Present); Consultant, Seven Seas; Consultant, Bio-Oil; Consultant, The Upjohn Company; Consultant, F. Hoffmann-La Roche Ltd; Consultant, Nestle; Consultant, Nippon **CW:** Contributor, Articles, Medical Journals; Contributor, Book Chapters **AW:** Notable Alumni of Unversity of Newcastle Upon Tyne, United Kingdom (2017) **MEM:** ABA; Associate, American Society of Clinical Oncology (ASCO); AIPLA; Licensing Executives Society, Inc., Certified Licensing Professional **BAR:** New York (1994); United States Patent and Trademark Office; United States Court of Appeals for the Federal Circuit; United States District Court Southern District of New York; United States District Court Eastern District of New York **MH:** Albert Nelson Marquis Lifetime Achievement Award (2017) **H:** Sports; Traveling; Volunteering **RE:** Ismaili **BA:** 48 Wall St 12th Floor, New York, NY, 10005 **ADD:** 110 Livingston St Apt 10B, Brooklyn, NY, 11201 **URL:** www.tacticaltherapeutics.com

KASKINEN, BARBARA KAY, T: Author, Composer, Songwriter, Musician, Music Educator **I:** Media & Entertainment **PB:** , **PT:** Norman Ferdinand Kaskinen; Martha Agnes (Harju) Kaskinen **ED:** MusD in Musical Arts, University of Miami (2006); MAT, Florida Atlantic University (1995); BA, Florida Atlantic University, With Honors (1981); AA, Broward Community College, Coconut Creek, FL (1978) **C:** Studio Musician, Composer, Arranger, Electric Rize Productions, Margate, FL (1982-Present); Instructor, Private Music Studio, Margate, FL (1979-Present); Music Instructor, Guitar Center (2015-2016); Music Instructor; Autry Music Institute (2014-2015); Music Teacher, Sam Ash Music (2013-2014) **CR:** Adjunct Faculty, Broward Community College, Coconut Creek, FL (1996-Present); Adjunct Instructor, Accompanist, Palm Beach Atlantic University, West Palm Beach, FL (2003-2009); Adjunct Faculty, Miami Dade College (2003-2008); Adjunct Faculty, Florida Atlantic University (1995-1997); Assistant Director, TOPS Piano Camp (1994-1996); Co-Founder, Oasis Coffee House, Boca Raton, FL (1990-1992); Co-Owner, Electric Rize Publishing (1991) **CW:** Musician, Bass and Keyboard, Electric Rize Band (1982-Present); Doctoral Dissertation, "J.B. Floyd: A Multi-faceted Life in Music" (2006); Author, Books II and III, "Adult Electronic Keyboard Course" (1989); Author, Book I, "Adult Electronic Keyboard Course" (1988); Composer, Hansen House (1987-1988); Original Recordings, Electric Rize, Cdbaby **MEM:** Writer, American Society of Composers, Authors and Publishers (ASCAP); Treasurer, Composition Contest Chairman, Recording Secretary, Broward County Music Teachers Association; Florida State Music Teachers Association; National Guild of Piano Teachers; American Chamber Music Society **MH:** Albert Nelson Marquis Lifetime Achievement Award (2017) **BA:** 6601 NW 22nd Street, Margate, FL, 33063

KAVANAUGH, JAMES FRANCIS JR., T: Attorney **I:** Law and Legal Services **DOB:** 02/20/1949 **PB:** New Bedford **SC:** MA/USA **PT:** James Francis Kavanaugh; Catherine Mary (Loughlin) Kavanaugh **MS:** Married **SPN:** Cynthia Louise Ward (7/4/1968) **CH:** James F., III **ED:** JD, Boston College, Magna Cum Laude (1977); BA, College of the Holy Cross (1970) **C:** Partner, Conn Kavanaugh Rosenthal Peisch & Ford, LLP, Boston, MA (1988-Present); Partner, Burns & Levinson, Boston, MA(1983-1988); Associate, Burns & Levinson, Boston, MA (1978-1982); Law Clerk to Associate Justice, Massachusetts Supreme Judicial Court, Boston, MA(1977-1978) **CR:** Adjunct Lecturer, School of Law, Boston College (1994-1999); Litigation Specialist, School of Law, Boston College (1994-1999) **CIV:** Pro Bono Lawyer, Massachusetts Advocates for Children **CW:** Editor, Law Review, Boston College (1975-1977); Contributor, Law Review, Boston College (1975-1977) **MEM:** President, Alumni Association, School of Law, Boston College (1999-2001); ABA; Boston Bar Association **BAR:** Supreme Court of the United States (1990); United States District Court District of Massachusetts (1978); United States Court of Appeals for the First Circuit (1978); Massachusetts (1977) **MH:** Albert Nelson Marquis Lifetime Achievement Award (2017) **H:** Golf; Skiing; Reading fiction books; Reading American history books **BA:** 1 Federal St Fl 15, Conn Kavanaugh Rosenthal Peisch & Ford, Boston, MA, 02110 **ADD:** 49 Brookside Ave, Winchester, MA, 01890

KAYE, MARVIN NATHAN, T: Publishing Executive, Theatre Producer, Writer I: Writing and Editing DOB: 03/10/1938 PB: Philadelphia SC: PA/USA PT: Morris Kaye; Theresa (Baroski) Kaye MS: Married SPN: Saralee Bransdorf (8/4/1963) CH: Terry Ellen ED: MA in English Literature and Theater, The Pennsylvania State University (1962); Postgraduate Coursework, University of Denver (1960); BA in Liberal Arts, The Pennsylvania State University (1960); Upper Darby Senior High School (1956); Coursework in TV Writing, Columbia Pictures Writers Development Program; Coursework in Theater Directing, University of Denver; Coursework in Fundraising for the Arts, New York University; Coursework in Business Management, Cultural Council Foundation; Coursework in Music Theory, The New School for Social Research; Coursework in Comedy Improvisation, Chicago City Limits; Coursework in Producing, 14-week Seminar, Commercial Theater Institute; Coursework in Scene Study, HB Studio CT: Certified Reiki Master; Certified Craniosacral Therapist, The Upledger Institute International, Certified in Lymph Drainage, International Health Practitioners Alliance C: President, Nth Dimension Media, Inc. (2011-Present); Co-Publisher, Editor, "Weird Tales" (2011-Present); Editor, Sherlock Holmes Mystery Magazine (2008-Present); Artistic Director, The Open Book, New York, NY (1974-Present); Freelance Writer, New York City, NY (1970-Present); Editor, H. P. Lovecraft's Magazine of Horror (2004-2009); Co-Founder, The Open Book (1975); Senior Editor, Harcourt Brace Jovanovich, New York, NY (1966-1970); Assistant Managing Editor, Business Travel Magazine, New York, NY (1965); Reporter, Grit Publishing Company, Williamsport, PA (1963-1965) CR: Standardized Patient, Clinical Competence Center of New York (2008-Present); Standardized Patient, The Morchand Center, Mount Sinai Hospital (2006-Present); Adjunct Professor, Creative Writing, New York University, New York, NY (1976-Present); Improvisational Comic, The Jekyll and Hyde Club, New York, NY (2005-2008); Tutor, Coordinator, Manhattan Campus (2002-2006); Tutor Coordinator, Mercy College (2001-2006); Teacher, English Literature and Composition, Mercy College (2001-2002); Judge, World Fantasy Convention Awards (2000); Lecturer, New School for Social Research, New York City, NY (1975); Judge, Edgar Awards, Mystery Writers of America, International Thriller Writers; Guest Lecturer, Smithsonian Institute Travel Seminar, UK; New York Coordinator, Book PALS, SAG Foundation; Theater Correspondent, Grit Newspaper; Public Relations Writer, Questor Corporation; Public Relations Director, Light Opera of Manhattan CW: Author, Column, "Marvin Kaye's Nth Dimension," Nonfiction Articles and Essays, Space & Time Magazine (online) (2009-Present); Author, Fiction, "The Complete Incredible Umbrella" (2018); Author, Fiction, "The Passion of Frankenstein" (2015); Editor, Anthology, "A Book of Wizards" (2008); Editor, Anthology, "The Ghost Quartet" (2008); Editor, "Forbidden Planets" (2006); Publisher, "The Archie Goodwin Files" (2005); Editor, Anthology, "The Fair Folk" (2005); Publisher, "The Nero Wolfe Files," Marvin Kaye's Nth Dimension Books (2004); Publisher, "Mr. Justice Raffles," Marvin Kaye's Nth Dimension Books (2003); Publisher, "Sweeney Todd," Marvin Kaye's Nth Dimension Books (2002); Author, Fiction, "The Last Christmas of Ebenezer Scrooge" (2002); Editor, Anthology, "The Dragon Quintet" (2002); Editor, Anthology, "The Ultimate Halloween" (2001); Editor, Anthology, "The Vampire Sextette" (2001); Editor, Anthology, "Incisions" (2000); Publisher, "The Earth is Made of Stardust," Bleak House (2000); Author, Nonfiction Articles and Essays, Aboriginal SF Magazine (1999-2001); Editor, Anthology, "The Confidential Casebook of Sherlock Holmes (1998); Editor, Anthology, "Don't Open This Book" (1998); Editor, Publisher, "The Best of Weird Tales 1923," Bleak House (1997); Author, Introduction, Notes, and Appendices, "Dracula, The Definitive Edition," (1996); Editor, Anthology, "Page to Stage: Adapting Literature for Readers Theatre" (1996); Editor, Anthology, "The Resurrected Holmes" (1996); Author, Fiction, Short Story, "Too Many Stains," The Resurrected Holmes (1996); Editor, Anthology, "Readers Theatre" (1995); Editor, Anthology, "The Game is Afoot" (1994); Editor, Anthology, "Angels of Darkness" (1994); Editor, Anthology, "Masterpieces of Terror and the Unknown" (1993); Author, Fiction, Short Story, "Packaged Ogre" Fantasy Tales, UK (1993); Author, Fiction, Short Story, "Helping Hand," Fantasy Tales, UK (1993); Editor, Anthology, "Frantic Comedy" (1993); Author, Fiction, Short Story, "Soulmate," The Ultimate Witch (1993); Author, Fiction, Short Story, "Our Late Visitor," 100 Ghastly Little Ghost Stories (1993); Author, Fiction, "Fantastique" (1992); Editor, Anthology, "Sweet Revenge: 10 Plays of Bloody Murder" (1992); Editor, Anthology, "Lovers and Other Monsters" (1991); Editor, Anthology, "Haunted America" (1991); Author, Fiction, Short Story, "Happy Hour," Fantasy Tales, UK (1991); Editor, Anthology, "13 Plays of Ghosts and the Supernatural" (1990); Editor, Anthology, "Witches and Warlocks" (1989); Author, Fiction, Short Story, "Sindbad & the Midday Demon," Arabesques (1989); Editor, "Weird Tales, The Magazine That Never Dies" (1988); Author, Short Story, "Lovedeath," Fantasy Macabre (1988); Author, Fiction, "Ghosts of Night and Morning" (1987); Editor, Anthology, "Devils and Demons" (1987); Author, Column, Nonfiction Articles and Essays, Thrust Magazine (1985-1988); Editor, Anthology, "Masterpieces of Terror and the Supernatural" (1985); Author, Nonfiction Articles and Essays, Science Fiction Chronicle, New York (1984-2002); Co-Author, Fiction, "A Cold Blue Light" (1983); Co-Author, Fiction, "The Soap Opera Slaughters" (1982); Co-Author, Fiction, "Wintermind" (1982); Author, "The Possession of Immanuel Wolf" (1981); Author, Fiction, "The Amorous Umbrella" (1981); Author, Fiction, Short Story, "Grumblefritz," Amazing Stories (1981); Editor, Anthology, "Ghosts" (1981); Author, Fiction, Short Story, "A Smell of Sulphur," Amazing Stories (1981); Author, Fiction, Short Story, "Damned Funny," Fantastic Stories (1980); Author, Nonfiction Articles and Essays, The Gazette, The Wolfe Pack (1979-1986); Author, Nonfiction Articles and Essays, Long Life Magazine, Chicago, IL (1979-1980); Author, Fiction, "The Incredible Umbrella" (1979); Author, Fiction, "My Brother, The Druggist" (1979); Author, Fiction, Short Story, "Ms. Lipshutz & the Goblin," Fantastic Stories (1978); Co-Author, Fiction, "The Masters of Solitude" (1978); Author, Nonfiction, "Catalog of Magic" (1977); Author, Fiction, "The Laurel & Hardy Murders" (1977); Author, Fiction, "My Son, The Druggist" (1977); Author, Fiction, "Bullets for Macbeth" (1976); Author, Nonfiction, "The Handbook of Mental Magic" (1975); Editor, Anthology, "Brother Theodore's Chamber of Horrors" (1974); Editor, Anthology, "Fiends and Creatures" (1974); Author, Fiction, "The Grand Ole Opry Murders" (1974); Author, Nonfiction, "The Stein and Day Handbook of Magic" (1973); Author, Nonfiction, "A Toy is Born" (1973); Author, Fiction, "A Lively Game of Death" (1972); Author, Nonfiction, "The Histrionic Holmes" (1971); Author, More than 100 Nonfiction Articles, Grit (1970-1975) AW: World Fantasy Award, Best Anthologist, "The Fair Folk" (2006); International Thriller Award; Nero Award, Nero Wolfe Society; Honorary Member, The Mark Twain Circle of America MEM: President, The Sons of the Desert (1974-1976); Authors Guild (formerly the Authors League of America); Dramatists Guild of America, Inc.; Actors' Equity Association; The Broadway League (formerly the League of American Theatres and Producers); International Thriller Writers; Mystery Writers of America; The Wolfe Pack MH: Albert Nelson Marquis Lifetime Achievement Award (2017) H: Book collecting; DVD collecting ADD: 525 W End Ave Apt 12E, New York, NY, 10024 URL: http://www.marvinkaye.com

KEARNS, WILLIAM D. PHD, T: Associate Professor I: Education/Educational Services CN: University of South Florida ED: PhD in Philosophy in Experimental Psychology, University of South Florida (1989); MA in Experimental Psychology (1985); MA in Experimental Psychology, University of the Pacific, California (1979); BA in Psychology, Central College, Pella, IA (1976) C: Research Associate Professor, Department of Rehabilitation and Mental Health Counseling, College of Behavioral and Community Sciences, University of South Florida (2011-Present); Research Assistant Professor, Department of Rehabilitation and Mental Health Counseling, College of Behavioral and Community Sciences, University of South Florida (2008-2011); Research Assistant Professor, Department of Aging & Mental Health, Louis de la Parte Florida Mental Health Institute (2008-2011); Director, Office of Information Technology, FMHI Office of Information Technology (1992-2003); Assistant in Research, Department of Mental Health Law & Policy (1989-1995); Affiliate, Department of Psychiatry, Instructor, Department of Psychology, Rollins College (1987-1988); USF Health (1981-1987); Research Technician, Department of Psychiatry, Johns Hopkins Health System (1979-1981) CIV: Facilities Workgroup, Tims Presbyterian Church, Tampa, FL (2002-2014); Habitat for Humanity International (2010-2012); Deacon, Tims Presbyterian Church, Tampa, FL (2006-2009) AW: Third Place, National "Brain Trust" Competition, U.S. Department of Veterans Affairs (2016); Best Leading Edge Technologies Poster Paper Award, International Society for Gerontechnology (2014); Excellence in Innovation Award, Department of Research, University of South Florida (2011); Distinguished Keynote Speaker Award, International Conference and Master Class on Gerontechnology, Nan Kai University of Technology, Caotun, Taiwan (2008); USF Career Service Scholarship Award, Workshop on Intelligent Systems for Assisted Cognition, University of Rochester and Microsoft (1996); Numerous Grants MEM: President, North American Chapter, International Society for Gerontechnology (2014-Present); International Society for Gerontechnology (2004-Present); U.S. Department of Veterans Affairs (2013-2015); RFID in Healthcare Consortium (2013-2014); HIMSS 2014 Executive Committee (2013-2014); University Corporation for Advanced Internet Development (2005-2011); Human Factors and Ergonomics Society (2005-2007); University of South Florida Representative, Internet2 (1996-2006); Higher Education Telecommunications Consortium (1999-2003); National RTLS Implementation Team BA: 13301 N Bruce B Downs Blvd # MHC1601, University Of South Florida, Tampa, FL, 33612 URL: http://www.gerontechnology.org/

KEASTER, ARMON JOSEPH, T: Entomology Educator, Researcher I: Education/Educational Services DOB: 03/12/1933 PB: Lilbourn SC: MO/USA PT: John Powell Keaster; Nora L. (Cato) Keaster SPN: Mona Lee Scott Keaster (6/3/1956) ED: PhD in Entomology, University of Missouri (1985); MS in Entomology, University of Missouri (1961); BS in Agriculture, University of Missouri, Columbia, MO (1959); Coursework, Southeast Missouri State University, Cape Girardeau, MO (1955-1957) **C:** Professor, University of Missouri (1976-Present); Associate Professor, University of Missouri (1970-1976); Assistant Professor, University of Missouri Delta Center (1965-1970); Instructor, Entomology, University of Missouri, Columbia, MO (1962-1965); Instructor, University of Missouri Delta Center, Portageville, MO (1962-1965); Technologist Entomology, Southeast Missouri Research Station, University of Missouri, Sikeston, MO (1951-1961) **MIL:** U.S. Army Reserve, Republic of Korea (1953-1955) **CW:** Chairman, Editorial Board, Insecticide Acaricide News (1984-1985); Contributor, Articles, Professional Journals **AW:** C.V. Riley Merit Award, Entomological Society (1985-1986); NCB-ESA J.E. Bussart Memorial Award, Entomological Society of America (1984) **MEM:** Board of Directors, Entomological Society of America (1984-1986); Nominating Committee, Entomological Society of America (1979-1980); Membership Committee, Entomological Society of America (1979-1980); Chairman, Auditing Committee, North Central Branch, Entomological Society of America (1969-1970); Gamma Sigma Delta; Alpha Zeta; Sigma Xi; Kansas Entomological Society **MH:** Albert Nelson Marquis Lifetime Achievement Award (2017) **H:** Antiques; Jogging **RE:** Methodist **ADD:** 606 E Rockcreek Dr, Columbia, MO, 65203

KEENAN, CHARLES, T: Principal **I:** Law and Legal Services **CN:** Stark & Keenan A Professional Association **ED:** LLM in Taxation, University of Baltimore; JD, University of Michigan; AB, Brown University **C:** Attorney, Stark & Keenan A Professional Association (1987-Present) **CR:** Trial Magistrate, Maryland (1969-1972); Town Attorney, Bel Air, Maryland **CIV:** Active Member, Family Children Services, Maryland; Counsel, Ladew Topiary Gardens; Counsel, Harford Day School; Trustee, Close Foundation **AW:** Honoree, A/V Preeminent Attorney, Martindale-Hubbell **MEM:** Past President, Harford County Bar Association; Past Secretary, Harford County Bar Association; American Bar Association **BAR:** State of Maryland **H:** Mountain climbing **BA:** 30 Office Street, Stark & Keenan PA, Bel Air, MD, 21014

KEESING, AUDREY E., T: Agent **I:** Real Estate **CN:** Coast Pacific Properties **ED:** MA in Medical and Cultural Anthropology, University of Hawaii at Manoa (1999); MPH in International Health and Community Health Development, John A. Burns School of Medicine, University of Hawaii at Manoa (1995); BA in Anthropology, University of California, Berkeley (1988); Coursework, Pitzer College (1982-1984) **CT:** Diplomate, Sales Agent, Coldwell Banker Pacific Properties Real Estate School (2014); Private Pilot License, Flight School of Hawaii (2007-2008) **C:** Licensed Real Estate Salesperson, Coast Pacific Properties (2015-Present); Publisher, Diamond Head Studios (2014-Present); Sole Proprietor, Diamond Head Records (2007-Present); Academic Observer, United Nations (2006-Present); Owner, Keesing International (2004-Present); President, Keesing International (2004-Present); Chief Executive Officer, Keesing International (2004-Present) **H:** Singing **BA:** 1311 Kapiolani Blvd Ste 310, Coast Pacific Properties, Honolulu, HI, 96814 **ADD:** PO Box 15075, Honolulu, HI, 96830 **URL:** https://www.facebook.com/audrey.keesing?hc_ref=ART2UeHaI7Ja_7T41uQp5zuReqL-hPtA4xVvl–tOLaBVoimR0mNl

KEESOM, PIERRE HENRI MARIE, T: Principal **I:** Law and Legal Services **CN:** Keesom & Hendriks N.V. **DOB:** 08/21/1943 **PB:** Heerlen **SC:** Netherlands **PT:** Cornelis Hendrikus Anthonius Keesom

van Haringcarspel; Jeannetta Leonarda Catharina Pennarts, Lady of the Seigneurie of Haringcarspel **MS:** Married **SPN:** Xiaodu Liu, JDrs (4/9/1990) **CH:** Cor; Hans; Joseph **ED:** JDrs, Catholic University of Nijmegen, Netherlands (1988) **CT:** Chartered Linguist and Fellow, United Kingdom (2008); Translator and Interpreter, Practice Exams Association, Netherlands (2002); Certified Professional Representative, European Union Intellectual Property Office (1997); Sworn Interpreter and Translator of French (1981); Sworn Interpreter and Translator of English (1975); Certified, Sworn Trademark Broker, Court of Appeal (1973); Registered Trademark Attorney, Benelux Association forTrade Marks and Design Law **C:** Principal, Keesom & Hendriks N.V., The Hague, Netherlands (1973-Present); Trademark Attorney, Markgraaf, Amsterdam (1965-1975) **CIV:** Secretary, The Knighthood of Limburg, Corps Equestre du Limbourg (2010-Present); Trustee, ZerOrigIndia Trust (2015) **MIL:** National Service in the Telecommunication Regiment (Verbindingsdienst) (1963-1965) **CW:** Author, "The New Benelux Trademarks Act" (1986); Contributor, More than 100 Articles to Professional Publications **AW:** Named, Knight, Order of Saint Joseph of Tuscany, His Imperial and Royal Highness Archduke Sigismund, Titular Grand Duke of Tuscany (2016); Recipient, Medal of Saint John, Coadjutor and Chapter of the Order of Saint John in the Netherlands (2011); Named, Commander, Order Pro Merito Melitensi, Prince and Grand Master of the Sovereign Order of Malta, Fra' Matthew Festing (2011); Named, Commander, Most Venerable Order of the Hospital of St. John of Jerusalem, Her Majesty Queen Elizabeth II (2009); Named, Knight, Order of Orange-Nassau (2008); Named, Knight of the Blood (Grand Officer), Sacred Military Constantinian Order of Saint George, Spain, His Royal Highness the Infante don Carlos, Duke of Calabria (2007) **MEM:** Member, Netherlands Justice Department, Statutory Complaints Board Sworn Interpreters and Translators (2009-2011); President, Netherlands Society of Interpreters and Translators NGTV (2004-2005); Examiner, Chartered Institute of Linguists, London, England (2002); Treasurer, Royal Netherlands Society for Genealogy and Heraldry (1992-1997); Treasurer, Netherlands Society of Interpreters and Translators (1992-1993); Fellow, Chartered Institute of Linguists; Professional Representative, European Intellectual Property Office; Lifetime Fellow, Royal Society for the Encouragement of Arts, Manufactures and Commerce, London, England **MH:** Albert Nelson Marquis Lifetime Achievement Award (2017) **H:** Genealogy; History **RE:** Roman Catholic **ADD:** Mesdagstraat 120, Den Haag, Netherlands, NL2596 XZ **URL:** https://www.linkedin.com/in/pierre-keesom-70995012

KELLER, ARTHUR MICHAEL, T: Managing Partner **I:** Consulting **CN:** Minerva Consulting **DOB:** 01/14/1957 **SC:** New York **PT:** David Keller; Luba Keller **CH:** Sophie; Reta **ED:** PhD, Stanford University (1985); MS, Stanford University (1979); BS, Brooklyn College, Summa Cum Laude (1977) **C:** Chief Data Scientist, PSYCHeANALYTICS, Inc. (2011-Present); Chief Financial Officer, Psycheanalytics (2011-Present); Board Member, Psycheanalytics (2011-Present); Lecturer Researcher, University of California, Santa Cruz, CA (2003-Present); Co-Founder, Minerva Consulting, Palo Alto, CA (1981-Present); Managing Partner, Minerva Consulting, Palo Alto, CA (1981-Present); Co-Chairman, Citizens Advisory Committee, Comprehensive Plan Update, Palo Alto, CA (2015-2017); Standards Coordinator, Voting Systems Standards Committee, IEEE (2014-2017); Founder, Psycheanalytics (2011); Board Secretary, Open Voting Consortium (2005-2007); Co-Founder, Vice President of Operations and Finance,

Open Voting Consortium (2003-2005); Visiting Associate Professor, University of California, Santa Cruz (2001-2003); Chief Technical Advisor, Co-Founder, Target Mining Corporation, Los Altos, CA (1998-2003); Co-Founder, Chief Operating Officer, Mergent Systems Inc., Palo Alto, CA (1996-1999); Chief Financial Officer, Mergent Systems Inc., Palo Alto, CA (1996-1999); Senior Research Scientist, Stanford University (1992-1999); Chief Technical Adviser, Persistence Software, San Mateo, CA (1991-1999); Research Scientist, Stanford University (1991-1992); Senior Research Scientist, Advanced Decision Systems, Mountain, View, CA (1989-1992); Research Associate, Stanford University (1989-1991); Adjunct Assistant Professor, The University of Texas at Austin (1988-1989); Visiting Assistant Professor, Stanford University (1987-1989); Assistant Professor, The University of Texas at Austin (1985-1988); Research Associate, Stanford University (1985); Acting Assistant Chairman, Department of Computer Science, Stanford University (1982); Academy Associate, San Jose Research Laboratory, IBM (1981); Summer Research Assistant, Thomas J. Watson Research Center, IBM, Yorktown Heights, NY (1980); Instructor in Computer Science, Stanford University (1979-1981); Research Assistant, Stanford University (1977-1985); Instructor, Computer & Information Science, Brooklyn College (1977); Systems Analyst, Computer Center, Brooklyn College (1974-1977) **CR:** Adviser, Unspam Technology (2004-Present); Adviser, University Voting Systems Competition (Now VoComp), Portland, OR (2007); Board of Directors, Broader Minds Inc., Austin, TX (2001-2012); Adviser, Serus Corporation, Mountain View, CA (2001-2012); Interim Chief Executive Officer, Globallinx Network, Mountain View, CA (2000-2007); Co-Founder, Globallinx Network, Mountain View, CA (2000-2007); Board of Directors, Globallinx Network, Mountain View, CA (2000-2007); Board of Advisers, Propel Software Corporation, San Jose, CA (2000-2002); Chief Technology Adviser, Online HR Corporation, Mountain View, CA (1999-2004); Member, Program Committee, International Workshop on Advanced Transaction Models & Architectures, Goa, India (1996); International Conference on Very Large Data Bases, Amsterdam, The Netherlands (1989); Program Committee, International Conference on Data Engineering, Los Angeles, CA (1989); Program Committee, International Conference on Data Engineering, Los Angeles, CA (1986-1987); Graduate Fellowship, National Science Foundation (1977-1980); Adviser, Startups; Expert Witness on Patent Infringement Cases; Politically Active Environmentalist **CIV:** Voting Systems Performance Review Chair, Executive Committee (2005-Present); Environmental Affinity Group, Consult's Network Silicon Valley Social Venture Fund (2000-Present); Candidate, City Council of Palo Alto, CA (2016); Immediate Past Chair, P-1622, Standards Working Group on Voting Systems Electronic Data Interchange, IEEE (2013-2014); Vice Chair, Planning & Transportation Commission, Palo Alto, CA (2013-2014); Computer Society Standards Activities Board, IEEE (2010-2013); Chair, P-1622 Standards Working Group on Voting Systems Electronic Data Interchange, IEEE (2010-2013); Standards Working Group P1622 Voting Systems Electronic Data Interchange, IEEE (2009-2017); Facilities Steering Committee, Gunn High School, Palo Alto, CA (2009-2014); Board Member, Electrical Auto Association (2007-2010); National Science Foundation, Scientific Review Panel Member (2007); Planning & Transportation Commission, Palo Alto, CA (2006-2014); Founding Co-Chair, Environmental Affinity Group, Consult's Network Silicon Valley Social Venture Fund

(2006-2007); Board Member, Girls Middle School, Mountain View, CA (2005-2008); President, Adobe Meadow Neighborhood Association (2005-2006); Founder, Adobe Meadow Neighborhood Association (2005); National Science Foundation, Scientific Review Panel Member (2005); Site Council, Ohlone Middle School, Palo Alto, CA (2001-2003); Board of Directors, Congregation Kol Emeth, Palo Alto, CA (1996-2000); Finance Committee, TeX Users Group (1983-1985) **CW:** Author, "A First Course in Computer Programming Using Pascal, Japanese Language Version" (1988); Author, "A First Course in Computer Programming Using Pascal, French Language Version" (1985); Author, "A First Course in Computer Programming Using Pascal, Spanish Language Version" (1983); Author, "A First Course in Computer Programming Using Pascal, Italian Language Version" (1983); Author, "A First Course in Computer Programming Using Pascal" (1982); First Named Inventor, "Method and system for a reliable distributed category-specific do-not-contact list," US Patent 7,925,704, United States **AW:** Profesor, Extraordinario, Visitante, Universidad Vlas Pascal, Cordoba, Argentina (1994); Best Student Paper, Computer Data Engineering Conference, IEEE (1984); George Forsythe Memorial Award for Excellence in Student Teaching, Stanford University Computer Science Department (1981-1982); President Brooklyn College Chapter, Pi Nu Epsilon (1976-1977); Top Score, Brooklyn College on Putnam Exam (1976); Institutional Member Nominee, Brooklyn College, American Mathematical Society (1976); Scholarship, New York State Regents (1973-1977) **MEM:** Environmental & Water Resources Committee, Santa Clara Valley Water District (2015-Present); Forensic Expert Witness Association (2010-Present); Public Transit Coordinator, Gunn High School Parent Teacher Student Association Palo Alto, CA (2007-Present); ACM (1980-Present); Electrification Task Force, Palo Alto (2013-2014); Consultants Network, Silicon Valley, IEEE (2009-2017); Website Committee, City of Palo Alto, CA (2008-2009); National Popular Vote Study Committee, League of Women Voters of Santa Clara County, CA (2008-2009); Open Source Voting Systems Task Force, Security of State, CA (2007-2008); Post Issues Forum, League of Women Voters, Palo Alto, CA (2007); Program Committee, Collegiate Voting Systems Competition VoComp, Portland, OR (2007); Vice President of Publicity, Chai Society (1989-1990); Communications Officer, Chai Society (1987-1989); Questions Submission, Computer Science Graduate Record Exam, Educational Testing Service (1984); TeX Users Group (1983-1987) **MH:** Albert Nelson Marquis Lifetime Achievement Award (2017) **H:** Singing; Travel **ADD:** 3881 Corina Way, Palo Alto, CA, 94303 **URL:** http://www.minervaconsulting.com

KELLY, PATRICK M., **T:** Attorney **I:** Law and Legal Services **CN:** Wilson Elser **DOB:** 04/04/1943 **PB:** Pasadena **SC:** CA/USA **PT:** Ted John Kelly; Frances Ruth (Fudge) Swanson Kelly **MS:** Married **SPN:** Victoria Zinkand (8/25/1978) **CH:** Patrick; Laura **ED:** JD, Loyola Marymount University (1969); BA, Pomona College (1966) **C:** Partner, Wilson, Elser, Moskowitz, Edelman & Dicker LLP (Now Wilson Elser) (1980-Present); Associate, Jones, Day, Reavis & Pogue (1977-1980); Associate, Adams, Duque & Hazeltine (1975-1977); Associate, Yuson, Cassidy, Wyman & Bautzer (1973-1975); Associate, Bodle & Fogel, Beverly Hills, CA (1971-1973); Attorney, Southern Pacific (1969-1971); Regional Managing Partner, Wilson, Elser, Moskowitz, Edelman & Dicker LLP (Now Wilson Elser); Director of Litigation, Wilson, Elser, Moskowitz, Edelman & Dicker LLP (Now Wilson Elser) **CR:** Commissioner, Commission on Judicial Performance, State of California **CIV:** Delegate to Japan, U.S. Trade Representative (1991); Delegate to Vietnam, The State Bar of California **AW:** Honoree, Arbitration Area, The Best Lawyers in America (2013-2018); Honoree, Commercial Litigation Area, The Best Lawyers in America (2007-2018); Featured Listee, Southern California Super Lawyers (2006-2017); Lifetime Achievement Award, Association of Ski Defense Attorneys (2015); Leadership Award, Bench-Bar Coalition (2013); Honoree, Top 100 Lawyers in California, Daily Journal Corporation (2012-2013); Honoree, Southern California's Top Rated Lawyers (2012); Honoree, Named to "Irish Legal 100," Irish Voice (2012); Honoree, Southern California Super Lawyers (2004); Griffin Bell Volunteer Achievement Award, Dispute Resolution Services; Honoree, AV Preeminent Attorney, Martindale-Hubbell **MEM:** Board of Governors, Loyola Law School Alumni Association, Loyola Marymount University (1974-1980); ABA; Century City Bar Association; Wilshire Bar Association; Irish American Bar Association; National Ski Areas Association; American Arbitration Association; Association of Southern California Defense Counsel; National Association of Women Lawyers; The National Association of Railroad Trial Counsel; ASTM; Los Angeles County Bar Association; DRI; Board Member, Association of Ski Defense Attorneys; Association of Business Trial Lawyers; President, Coalition of Justice; Chair, Southern California Chapter, Professional Liability Underwriting Society; Vice-chair, Dispute Resolutions Services; The International Legal Honor Society of Phi Delta; Eagle Scout **BAR:** Admitted to Practice, Supreme Court of the United States (1973); Admitted to Practice, United States District Court for the Central District of California (1970); Admitted to Practice, Judicial Council of California; Admitted to Practice, United States District Court for the District of Nevada; Admitted to Practice, United States District Court for the Northern District of California; Admitted to Practice, United States District Court for the Eastern District of California; Admitted to Practice, United States District Court for the Southern District of California **MH:** Albert Nelson Marquis Lifetime Achievement Award (2017); Distinguished Humanitarian (2017) **H:** Music; Skiing **BA:** 555 S Flower St Ste 2900, Wilson Elser, Los Angeles, CA, 90071 **URL:** www.wilsonelser.com

KENNEDY, LINDA DALE, **T:** Musician, Educator **I:** Education/Educational Services **CN:** Studio of Linda Kennedy **PT:** William Lawrence; Jessie Merle Dale **MS:** Married **SPN:** Kurt Kennedy (6/7/1969) **CH:** Jennifer Tish; Terra Lee **ED:** MusM, Southeastern Louisiana University, Hammond, LA (1975); MusB, Southeastern Louisiana, Hammond, LA (1968) **CT:** Certified Professional Music Teacher, Arkansas State Music Teachers Association; National Professional Certification, Music Teachers National Association **C:** Organist, Accompanist, First United Methodist Church, North Little Rock, AR (2001-Present); Private Practice, Piano Studio of Linda Kennedy, Maumelle, AR (1987-Present); Organist, Accompanist, Winfield United Methodist Church, Little Rock, AR (1987-2001); Organist, Accompanist, Court Street, United Methodist Church, Hattiesburg, MS (1981-1985); Organist, Accompanist, Goodwood Baptist Church, Baton Rouge (1976-1979); Organist, Accompanist, Woodland Park Baptist Church, Hammond, LA (1972-1975); Organist, Accompanist, F.E. Warren Air Force Base, Cheyenne, WY (1969-1971); Instructor, Yamaha Music Program, New Orleans, LA (1968-1969) **CW:** Contributor, Articles, Professional Journals; Contributor, Articles, Magazines; Regular Columnist, Support of the Performing Arts, Maumelle Magazine **AW:** Named, Independent Teacher of the Year, Arkansas State Music Teachers Association (2001) **MEM:** State Junior Composers Chairperson, Arkansas Federation Music Clubs (2003-Present); Arkansas State Music Teachers Association (1994-2011); President, Music Teachers Association of Central Arkansas (1997-2001); Maumelle Performing Arts Council; Maumelle Music Teachers League; American Guild of Organists; Judge, National Guild of Piano Teachers; Music Teachers National Association; Little Rock Musical Coterie; National Federation of Music Clubs **MH:** Albert Nelson Marquis Lifetime Achievement Award (2017) **H:** Reading **RE:** Methodist **ADD:** 7 Pinecrest Ln, Maumelle, AR, 72113 **URL:** http://www.kennedypianostudio.com/

KENNEDY, X.J., **T:** Writer **I:** Writing and Editing **CN:** Self-Employed **DOB:** 08/21/1929 **PB:** Dover **SC:** NJ/USA **PT:** Joseph Francis Kennedy; Agnes (Rauter) Kennedy **MS:** Widowed **SPN:** Dorothy Mintzlaff-Kennedy (1962, Deceased 3/18/2018) **CH:** Kathleen; David; Matthew; Daniel; Joshua **ED:** Honorary DLitt, Westfield State College (2002); Honorary DFA, Adelphi University (1998); Honorary LHD, Lawrence University (1988); Certificate, University of Paris, France (1956); MA, Columbia University (1951); BSc, Seton Hall University (1950) **C:** Professor, Tufts University (1973-1979); Associate Professor, Tufts University (1967-1973); Assistant Professor of English, Tufts University, Medford, MA (1963-1967); Lecturer in English, Woman's College, University of North Carolina, Greensboro, NC (1962-1963); Instructor in English, University of Michigan (1960-1962); Teaching Fellow, University of Michigan, Ann Arbor, MI (1956-1960) **CR:** Visiting Lecturer, University of California, Irvine (1966-1967); Visiting Lecturer, Wellesley College (1964) **CIV:** Judge, Poetry Books Selections, National Council on Arts (1969-1970) **MIL:** U.S. Navy (1951-1955) **CW:** Author, "That Swing" (2017); Co-Author, "Literature," 13th edition (2016); Author, "A Hoarse Half-Human Cheer: An Entertainment" (2015); Author, "Fits of Concision: Collected Poems of Six or Fewer Lines" (2014); Co-Author, "The Bedford Guide for College Writers," 10th edition (2014); Co-Author, "The Bedford Reader," 12th edition (2014); Co-Author, "Literature for Life" (2012); Translator, "Guillaume Apollinaire, The Bestiary" (2011); Author, "City Kids" (2010); Co-Author, "Introduction to Fiction," 11th edition (2010); Author, "Introduction to Poetry," 13th edition (2010); Co-Author, "Handbook of Literary Terms," Second edition (2009); Poet-in-Residence, Walt Whitman Birthplace (2009); Author, "Poems" (2008-2016); Co-Author, "Writing and Revising" (2007); Author, "Peeping Tom's Cabin: Comic Verse" (2007); Author, "In a Prominent Bar in Secaucus: New and Selected Poems, 1955-2007" (2007); Co-Author, "Handbook of Literary Terms" (2005); Author, "The Seven Deadly Virtues" (2005); Author, "The Owlstone Crown," Second edition (2005); Co-Editor, "Knee-Deep in Blazing Snow: Poems by James Hayford" (2005); Co-Editor, "Pegasus Descending," Second edition (2003); Author, "The Lords of Misrule: Poems" (2002); Author, "Exploding Gravy" (2002); Author, "Elefantina's Dream" (2002); Editor, "Inside Man by George Fox" (2002); Author, "Elympics" (1999); Co-Author, "Knock at a Star: a Child's Introduction to Poetry," Revised edition (1999); Translator, "Lysistrata in Penn Greek Drama Series" (1999); Author, "The Eagle as Wide as the World" (1997); Author, "Uncle Switch" (1997); Author, "The Minimus Poems" (1996); Author, "Nude Descending a Staircase," Second edition (1994); Author, "Drat These Brats!" (1993); Author, "The Lords of Misrule: Poems" (1992-2001); Author, "Dark Horses: New Poems" (1992); Author, "The Beasts of Bethlehem" (1992);

Co-Author, "Talking Like the Rain" (1992); Author, "The Kite That Braved Old Orchard Beach" (1991); Author, "Winter Thunder" (1990); Author, "Fresh Brats" (1990); Author, "Ghastlies, Goops and Pincushions" (1989); Co-Author, "The Bedford Guide for College Writers" (1987); Author, "Brats" (1986); Author, "Cross Ties: Selected Poems" (1985); Author, "The Forgetful Wishing-Well" (1985); Author, "Hangover Mass" (1984); Author, "The Owlstone Crown" (1983); Author, "French Leave: Translations" (1983); Co-Author, "Knock at a Star: a Child's Introduction to Poetry" (1982); Author, "Did Adam Name the Vinegarroon?" (1982); Co-Author, "The Bedford Reader" (1982); Editor, "Tygers of Wrath: poems of hate, anger and invective" (1981); Author, "The Phantom Ice Cream Man" (1979); Author, "Literature" (1976); Author, "Introduction to Fiction" (1976); Author, "One Winter Night in August" (1975); Co-Author, "Three Tenors, One Vehicle" (1975); Author, "Celebrations After the Death of John Brennan" (1974); Author, "Emily Dickinson in Southern California" (1974); Editor, "Messages" (1973); Editor, Publisher, Counter/Measures Magazine (1971-1974); Author, "Breaking and Entering" (1971); Co-Editor, "Pegasus Descending" (1971); Co-Author, "Growing into Love" (1969); Author, "Introduction to Poetry" (1966); Co-Editor, "Mark Twain's Frontier" (1963); Poetry Editor, "Paris Review" (1961-1964); Author, "Nude Descending a Staircase" (1961) **AW:** Measure Parody Award (2013); Able Muse Book Award (2013); New Criterion Poetry Award (2008); X.J. Kennedy Poetry Award, Texas Review (2000); X.J. Kennedy Poetry Award, Texas Review (1990); X.J. Kennedy Poetry Award, Texas Review (1998); T.S. Eliot Prize, Thomas Jefferson University Press (1998) **MEM:** Council on New England, PEN (1996-Present); Association of Literary Scholars and Critics; John Barton Wolgamot Society; Modern Language Association; Poetry Society of America; National Council on Teachers of English; Authors Guild; Friends and Enemies of Wallace Stevens; Phi Beta Kappa; Honorary Member, Sigma Tau Delta **H:** Old movies **PA:** Independent **ADD:** 22 Revere Street, Lexington, MA, 02420

KENNEY, WILLIAM F., T: Lawyer **I:** Law and Legal Services **CN:** The Positive Edge **DOB:** 11/04/1935 **PB:** San Francisco **SC:** CA/USA **MS:** Married **SPN:** Susan Elizabeth Langfitt (1962) **CH:** Anne; Carol; James **ED:** JD, University of California, Berkeley (1960); BA, University of California, Berkeley (1957) **C:** General Partner, TK Storage (2014-Present); President, The Positive Edge (2000-Present); Partner, Marina Business Center (1998-Present); Partner, Cochrane Road Self Storage (1996-Present); General Partner, All American Self Storage (1985-Present); President, William F. Kenney Inc., San Mateo, CA (1968-Present); General Partner, Second Street Self Storage (1990-1996); Partner, Tormey, Kenney & Cotchett, San Mateo, CA (1965-1967); Associate, Miller, Osborne Miller & Bartlett, San Mateo, CA (1962-1964) **CIV:** Lesley Foundation (1992-2004); Samaritan House (1989-2006); Board of Directors, Boys & Girls Club of North San Mateo County (1972-1990); President, San Mateo-Foster City School District (1972-1974); President, March of Dimes (1972-1973); Trustee, San Mateo-Foster City School District (1971-1979) **AW:** Self Storage Association Hall of Fame (2010) **MEM:** Co-Chair, Self Storage Association (2015-Present); National Cabinet, Guideposts Foundation (2012-Present); Board of Governors, Self Storage Association (2009-Present); Co-Chair, Self Storage Association (2010-2012); President, Self Storage Association (1996); National Vice President, Self Storage Association (1994-1995); National Board of

Directors, Self Storage Association (1990-1997); Western Region President, Self Storage Association (1989-1990); Board of Directors, San Mateo County Chamber of Commerce (1987-1993); Legal Affairs Committee, California Association of Realtors (1978-2011); President, Local Rotary Club (1978-1979); Exalted Ruler, Local Lodge, BPO Elks (1974-1975); Taxation Committee, State Bar of California (1973-1976); Board of Directors, San Mateo County Bar Association (1973-1975) **RE:** Roman Catholic **BA:** 204 2nd Avenue, Suite 415, The Positive Edge, San Mateo, CA, 94401 **URL:** http://www.thepositiveedge.com/about.html

KERN, IRVING JOHN, T: Food Company Executive **I:** Food & Restaurant Services **DOB:** 02/10/1914 **PB:** New York **SC:** NY/USA **PT:** John Kleinberger; Minnie (Weitzner) Kleinberger **MS:** Married **SPN:** Beatrice Rubenfeld (6/22/1941) **CH:** John Alan; Arthur Harry; Robert Michael **ED:** DHL, Mercy College, Dobbs Ferry, NY (1980); Student Graduate, School of Art and Science, New York University (1960-1965); BS in Mathematics, New York University (1934) **C:** Consultant (1982-1985); Chairman and Chief Executive Officer, Dellwood Foods, Inc. (1977-1982); President, Dellwood Foods, Inc. (1966-1977); Dellwood Foods, Inc., Yonkers, NY (1945-1982); Assistant Buyer, Bloomingdale's Department Store, New York, NY (1934-1940) **CR:** Adjunct Professor, Political Science, San Diego State University (1989-1995); Director, Scarsdale National Bank **CIV:** Military Advisory Council Center for Defense Information (1986-1997); Board of Directors, Vice Chairman, Westchester Private Industry Council (1979-1982); National Dairy Council (1979-1981); Milk Industry Foundation (1976-1982); Board of Directors, Secretary, Westchester County Association (1976-1980); Westchester Minority Business Assistance Organization (1973-1975); Board of Directors, Westchester Coalition (1972-1980); Executive Board, Westchester County Better Business Bureau (1970-1973); County Mental Health Services Board of Westchester County (1954-1959); Board of Directors, Secretary, Westchester County Association (1950-1957) **MIL:** Lieutenant Colonel, U.S. Army (1940-1945) **AW:** Decorated Bronze Star **MEM:** President, Director, New York Milk Bottlers Federation; Executive Vice President, Director, Metropolitan Dairy Institute; Phi Beta Kappa; Tau Epsilon Phi **ADD:** Robert Kern, 45 Pondfield Road W, Apt. 4C, Bronxville, NY, 10708

KESSLER, JEFFREY THEODORE, T: Neurologist, President **I:** Medicine & Health Care **CN:** Neurological Associates of Long Island P.C. **DOB:** 09/04/1943 **PB:** Philadelphia **SC:** PA/USA **MS:** Married **SPN:** Ilana Camille Hercz (9/1/1983); Lauren Jane Goldberg (10/14/1973, Deceased 1980) **CH:** James; Andrew; Ian; Vi **ED:** Resident in Neurology, NewYork-Presbyterian Hospital, Weill Cornell Medicine (1971-1974); Resident in Medicine, NewYork-Presbyterian Hospital, Weill Cornell Medicine (1970-1971); Intern, NewYork-Presbyterian Hospital, Weill Cornell Medicine (1969-1970); MD, Weill Cornell Medicine (1969); BA, Wesleyan University (1965) **CT:** Diplomate, American Board of Psychiatry and Neurology, Inc. (1976); Diplomate, American Board of Internal Medicine (1974) **C:** Adjunct Neurologist, North Shore University Hospital, Northwell Health (2014-Present); Visiting Attendant, Mount Sinai Medical Center (Now Icahn School of Medicine at Mount Sinai) (2011-Present); Clinical Associate Professor of Neurology, Hofstra Northwell School of Medicine (2010-Present); Attending Neurologist, St. Francis Hospital, Catholic Health Services of Long Island (1976-Present); Private Practice in Neurology, Neurological Associates of Long

Island, P.C. (1976-Present); Assistant Attendant in Neurology, Long Island Jewish Medical Center, Northwell Health (1998-2014); Clinical Associate Professor Neurology, NYU School of Medicine (1996-2010); Attending Neurologist, North Shore University Hospital, Northwell Health (1976-2014); Clinical Associate Professor Neurology, Weill Cornell Medicine (1976-1996); Consultant, Deepdale General Hospital (1976-1980); Consultant, Manhasset Division, Long Island Jewish Medical Center, Northwell Health (1974-1986); Assistant Professor of Neurology, The New Jersey Medical School (Now Robert Wood Johnson Medical School, Rutgers, The State University of New Jersey) (1974-1976); Director of Resident Training, The New Jersey Medical School (Now Robert Wood Johnson Medical School, Rutgers, The State University of New Jersey) (1974-1976); Consultant, St. Michael's Medical Center, Prime Healthcare (1974-1976); Consultant, United Hospital (1974-1976); Staff Neurologist, East Orange Campus, VA New Jersey Health Care System, U.S. Department of Veterans Affairs (1974-1976); Staff Neurologist, Martland Medical Center (Now University Hospital Newark) (1974-1976) **CR:** Fellow, American Academy of Neurology; Fellow, Nassau Academy of Medicine **CIV:** Landmark Review Board, Kings Point, NY (2014-Present); Board of Zoning Appeals, Kings Point, NY (1993-1996); Architectural Review Board, Kings Point, NY (1988-1993) **AW:** Honoree, Long Island Top Doctors, Castle Connolly Medical Ltd (2008-Present); Honoree, NY Metro Area Top Doctors, Castle Connolly Medical Ltd (1998-Present); President's Award, North Shore University Hospital Staff, Northwell Health (2011); Honoree, New York Magazine Best Doctors, New York Media LLC (1999) **MEM:** American Medical Association; The Medical Society of the State of New York; Past Secretary, Nassau County Medical Society; Chairman, Peer Review Committee, Nassau County Medical Society; Multiple Sclerosis Club of the North Shore **MH:** Albert Nelson Marquis Lifetime Achievement Award (2017) **H:** Tennis; Golf; Skiing; Wine collecting **RE:** Jewish **BA:** 1991 Marcus Avenue, Suite 110, Neurological Associates of Long Island P.C., Lake Success, NY, 11042

KHAN, M. NISA, T: Founder and President **I:** Engineering **CN:** IEM LED Lighting Technologies **MS:** Married **ED:** PhD in Electrical Engineering, University of Minnesota Twin Cities, MN (1992); BA in Physics and Mathematics, Macalester College, MN (1986) **CT:** Licensed in Series 7 (Financial Brokerage); Licensed in Series 66 (Financial Advisor & Securities Law); Life and Health Insurance (Financial Protection) **C:** Founder, IEM Asset (2007-Present); President, IEM Asset (2007-Present); Managing Member, IEM ASSET (2007-Present); Founder, IEM LED (2007-Present); President, IEM LED (2007-Present); Managing Member, IEM LED (2007-Present); Founder, IEM LED Lighting Technologies (Now IEM LED) (2006-Present); President, IEM LED Lighting Technologies (Now IEM LED) (2006-Present); Managing Member, IEM LED Lighting Technologies (Now IEM LED) (2006-Present); Senior Financial Advisor and Asset Manager, American Express (Now American Express Company) (2002-2006); Advisory Board Member and Consultant, Qusion (Now Qusion.net) (2001-2002); (1999-2001); Manager, Advanced Technology, JDS Uniphase (Now VIAVI Solutions Inc.) (1999-2001); Member of Technology Staff and Principal Investigator, AT&T and Lucent Bell Laboratories (Now Nokia) (1993-1999); Research Associate, Honeywell (Now Honeywell International, Inc.) (1983-1993) **CW:** Author, College Textbook, "Understanding LED

Illumination," CRC Press (2013); Author, "Apple and Samsung: Litigation, Competition and Partnership are Just Business as Usual" (2013); Author, "Where the Money is: LED Display and Lighting" (2013); Author, "Outlook on Apple and Samsung Battle: Lighting to Lead the Way?" (2013); Author, "LEDs and OLEDs Light Up Markets" (2013); Author, "LED Update," Signs of the Times (2007-2016) **AW:** Research Award, Applied Optics Journal Paper, Optical Society of America (Now The Optical Society) (2017) **H:** Arts; Sports; Cooking; Music; Mentoring **BA:** 331 Newman Springs Rd Ste 143, IEM LED Lighting Technologies, Red Bank, NJ, 07701 **URL:** www.iem-asset.com

KHONG, THUAN H., **T:** Research Engineer **I:** Engineering **CN:** National Aeronautics and Space Administration **PB:** Saigon **SC:** Vietnam **PT:** Thanh Huu Khong; Phung Thi Nguyen **ED:** MS in Mechanical Engineering in Tracking Aerospace Engineering, The George Washington University, Washington, D.C. (1998); BS in Mechanical Engineering, California State University Fullerton, with Highest Honors (1996) **C:** Research Engineer, Langley Research Center, National Aeronautics and Space Administration (1999-Present); Research Assistant, Guidance and Control Branch, Langley Research Center, National Aeronautics and Space Administration, Hampton, VA (1996-1999) **MEM:** Graduate Research Scholar Assistant, Lockheed Martin (1999); Graduate Research Scholar Assistant, NASA's Joint Institute for Advancement Flight Sciences, Hampton, VA (1996); Graduate Research Scholar Assistant, The George Washington University **MH:** Albert Nelson Marquis Lifetime Achievement Award (2017) **H:** Reading; Watching television **BA:** 2 Fort Worth St, NASA Langley Research Center, Hampton, VA, 23669

KIESSLING, RONALD F., **T:** Deputy Chief (Retired), Federal Government Executive (Retired) **I:** Government Administration/Government Relations/Government Services **CN:** National Aeronautics and Space Administration **DOB:** 01/13/1934 **PB:** Cleveland **SC:** OH/USA **PT:** E. Oscar Kiessling; Carolina Martha (Goetz) Kiessling **MS:** Married **SPN:** Jeanette Metzger (4/5/1984); Lois L. Nimrichter (9/10/1955, Deceased 1981) **CH:** Tom, Bob, Elizabeth; Christopher; David **ED:** Diplomate, Lewis Research Center, National Aeronautics and Space Administration, Cleveland, OH (1990); Diploma, John Marshall High School, Cleveland, OH (1954-1990) **C:** Deputy Chief, Logistics Management Division, Lewis Research Center, National Aeronautics and Space Administration (1986-1989); Deputy Chief, Space Technology Operations, Lewis Research Center, National Aeronautics and Space Administration (1985-1986); Chief of Materials and Engine Components Branch, Lewis Research Center, National Aeronautics and Space Administration (1982-1985); Chief of Communications, Energy and Flight Hardware Branch, Lewis Research Center, National Aeronautics and Space Administration (1980-1982); Head, Advanced Systems/Spacecraft Testing Section, Lewis Research Center, National Aeronautics and Space Administration (1974-1980) **CIV:** President, Board of Trustees, Ohio Pythian Home (1999-Present); Trustee, Ohio Pythian Home, Springfield, OH (1998-Present); President, Congregation All Saints Lutheran Church (1997-Present); Retired Member, Senior Volunteer Program, Advisory Committee on Electronic Technology, Akron University (1973-1989) **MIL:** Sergeant, U.S. Marine Corps (1951-1954) **CW:** Author, Book on Computers **AW:** Supreme Chancellor Medal, Knights of Pythias (2016); Recipient Presidential Citation (1971); Medal, National Aeronautics and Space Administration **MEM:** Deputy Supreme Chancellor, K.P. (1998); Knight of the Golden Spur, K.P. (1997); Grand Chancellor, K.P., Ohio (1993); Chancellor Command, K.P. (1978); President, NASA Supervisors Club (1976); Department Commandant, Marine Corps League (1962-1964); American Legion Post 421; Marine Corp League for Veterans Affairs; Knights of Pythias; AQP; State and Local Officer, Marine Corps League **MH:** Albert Nelson Marquis Lifetime Achievement Award (2017) **H:** Teaching; Computers; Photography **RE:** Lutheran **ADD:** 19 Schuberts Aly, Olmsted Township, OH, 44138

KIM, BOE-HYUN, **T:** Instructor **I:** Education/Educational Services **CN:** Icahn School of Medicine at Mount Sinai **PB:** Seoul **SC:** Republic of Korea **ED:** Postdoctoral Research Fellow, Department of Medicine, Division of Infectious Diseases, Molecular Virology Laboratory, Icahn School of Medicine at Mount Sinai, New York, NY (2014-2015); PhD in Biomedical Gerontology (Interdepartmental Program), Hallym University, Republic of Korea (2006); Graduate Coursework in Biomedical Gerontology, Hallym University, Republic of Korea (2002-2006); MS in Biomedical Gerontology (Interdepartmental Program), Hallym University, Republic of Korea (2002); Graduate Coursework in Biomedical Gerontology, Hallym University, Republic of Korea (2000-2015); BS in Biology, Inha University, Republic of Korea (1999) **C:** Instructor, Department of Medicine, Division of Infectious Diseases, Volsky Laboratory, Icahn School of Medicine at Mount Sinai, New York, NY (2016-Present); Postdoctoral Research Scientist, Department of Pathology & Cell Biology and the Division of Molecular Virology, St. Luke's-Roosevelt Hospital Center, Columbia University Medical Center, New York, NY (2010-2013); Research Scientist, Ilsong Institute of Life Science, Hallym University, Republic of Korea (2006-2010); Postdoctoral Research Scientist, Neurobiology of Prion Disease in Human and Animal Models, Hallym University, Republic of Korea (2006-2010); Research Scientist, Virology, Institute for Basic Research in Developmental Disabilities, Staten Island, NY (2005); Research Scientist, Institute for Basic Research in Developmental Disabilities, Staten Island, NY (2005); Teaching Assistant, Department of Microbiology, Hallym University School of Medicine, Republic of Korea (2004); Research Assistant, Ilsong Institute of Life Science, Hallym University, Republic of Korea (2000-2004) **CW:** Editorial Board, Pandemics of Communicable Diseases (2017-Present); Editorial Board, Open Access Journal of Infectious Diseases (2017-Present); Editorial Board, Journal of Infectious Diseases Diagnosis & Treatment (2016-Present); Contributing Editor, American Journal of Virology (2014-Present); Co-Author, "HIV Infection Model of Chronic Obstructive Pulmonary Disease in Mice," American Journal of Physiology-Lung Cellular and Molecular Physiology (2017); Co-Author, "N-(Pivaloyloxy) Alkoxy-Carbonyl Prodrugs of the Glutamine Antagonist DON as a Potential Treatment for HIV Associated Neurocognitive Disorders," Journal of Medicinal Chemistry (2017); Co-Author, "The Vascular Pathology and Angiogenetic Factor VEGF in the Brains of Scrapie-Infected Mice" (2016); Co-Author, "Cellular Prion Protein Combined with Galectin-3 and -6 Affects the Infectivity Titer of an Endogenous Retrovirus Assayed in Hippocampal Neuronal Cells," PLOS One (2016); Co-Author, "Infectious HIV Model of Synaptodendritic Damage in Mouse Primary Brain Cell Cultures," Sixth Annual Neuroscience Retreat, The Friedman Brain Institute, Icahn School of Medicine at Mount Sinai, New York (2014); Co-Author, "Tropism of Chimeric HIV in Mouse Brain Cells," 11th International Symposium on NeuroVirology and 2012 Conference on HIV in the Nervous System, New York, NY, (2012); Co-Author, "Association of Endothelial Nitric Oxide Synthase and Mitochondrial Dysfunction in the Hippocampus of Scrapie-Infected Mice," Hippocampus (2011); Co-Author, "Spontaneous Immortalization of Oligodendroglial Cells Derived from an SV40 T Antigen-Positive Human Glioblastoma," Cancer Letters (2009); Co-Author, "Physiological Properties of Astroglial Cell Lines Derived from Mice with High (SAMP8) and Low (SAMR1, ICR) Levels of Endogenous Retrovirus," Retrovirology (2008); Co-Author, "The Involvement of Cellular Prion Protein in the Autophagy Pathway in Neuronal Cells," Molecular and Cellular Neuroscience (2008); Co-Author, "Physiological Properties of Astroglial Cell Lines Derived from Mice with High (SAMP8) and Low (SAMR1, ICR) Levels of Endogenous Retrovirus," International Conference on Alzheimer's Disease and Related Disorders, Chicago, IL (2008); Co-Author, "Alteration of Iron Regulatory Proteins (IRP1 and IRP2) and Ferritin in the Brains of Scrapie-Infected Mice," Neuroscience Letters (2007); Co-Author, "Spontaneous Immortalization of Oligodendroglial Cells Derived from an SV40 T Antigen-Positive Human Glioblastoma," FKMS International Meeting of the Federation of Korean Microbiological Societies, Seoul, Republic of Korea (2007); Co-Author, "Physiological Properties of Astroglial Cell Lines Derived from Mice with High (SAMP8) and Low (SAMR1, ICR) Levels of Endogenous Retrovirus," FKMS International Meeting of the Federation of Korean Microbiological Societies, Seoul, Republic of Korea (2006); Co-Author, Book Chapter, "Oxidative Stress and Mitochondrial Dysfunction in Neurodegeneration of Transmissible Spongiform Encephalopathies (TSEs)," in D.R. Brown Edition, "Neurodegeneration and Prion Disease," Springer Science Business Media, Inc., New York (2005); Co-Author, "A Neuronal Cell Line that Does Not Express Either Prion or Doppel Proteins," NeuroReport (2005); Co-Author, "Alteration of Rion Regulatory Proteins (IRP1 and IRP2) and Ferritin in the Brains of Scrapie-Infected Mice," Society of Neuroscience Meeting, Washington, D.C. (2005); Co-Author, "The Cellular Prion Protein (PrPC) Prevents Apoptotic Neuronal Cell Death and Mitochondrial Dysfunction Induced by Serum Deprivation," Molecular Brain Research (2004); Co-Author, "Detection of JC Virus in the Brains of Korean Glioblastoma Multiforme Patients," Journal of Korean Neurosurgical Society (2004); Co-Author, "A Neuronal Cell Line That Does Not Express Either Prion or Doppel Proteins," Federation Meeting of Korean Basic Medical Scientists, Seoul, Republic of Korea (2004); Co-Author, "A Neuronal Cell Line That Does Not Express Either Prion or Doppel Proteins," International Conference on Alzheimer's Disease and Related Disorders, Philadelphia, PA (2004); Co-Author, "The Cellular Prion Protein Prevents Apoptotic Neuronal Cell Death and Mitochondrial Dysfunction Induced by Serum Deprivation," Asia/Oceania Regional Congress of Gerontology Committee, Tokyo, Japan (2003); Co-Author, "The Cellular Prion Protein Prevents Apoptotic Neuronal Cell Death and Mitochondrial Dysfunction Induced by Serum Deprivation," Federation Meeting of Korean Basic Medical Scientists, Seoul, Republic of Korea (2002); Co-Author, "The Cellular Prion Protein Prevents Apoptotic Neuronal Cell Death and Mitochondrial Dysfunction Induced by Serum Deprivation," TSE Transmissible Spongiform Encephalopathies Conference Committee, Edinburgh, United Kinggdom (2002); Contributor, Articles to Professional Journals; Contributor,

Workshops, Meetings & Conferences **AW:** Recipient, Traineeship in "Training in Neurotherapeutics Discovery and Development: for Academic Scientists," National Institutes of Health, Bethesda, MD (2016); Recipient, Pioneer in NeuroVirology Lectureship Award, 13th International Symposium on NeuroVirology, International Society for NeuroVirology, San Diego, CA (2015); Recipient, Travel Award, 13th International Symposium on NeuroVirology, International Society for NeuroVirology, San Diego, CA (2015); Recipient, Grant Award, Principal Investigator, "Market Trends of Human and Animal Stem Cell Technology," Korea Institute of Science and Technology Information (2012-2013); Recipient, Grant Award, Principal Investigator, "The Role of Endogenous Retrovirus in Pathogenesis of Prion," Young Scientist of the Korea Healthcare Technology Research & Development Project, Ministry of Health, Welfare & Family Affairs (Now Ministry of Health and Welfare), Republic of Korea (2009-2010); Recipient, Award for a Travel Fellowship, 11th International Conference on Alzheimer's Disease and Related Disorders (2008); Recipient, Grant Award, Associate Research Scientist, "Mechanism of Cellular Aging and Development of Aging Suppressor Materials," Ministry of Health, Welfare & Family Affairs (Now Ministry of Health and Welfare), Republic of Korea (2006-2007); Recipient, Poster Session Award, International Meeting of the Federation of Korean Microbiological Societies, Seoul, Republic of Korea (2006); Recipient, Grant Award, Principal Investigator, "Analysis of Gene Expression Profile of Prion Protein-Deficient Neuronal Cell Line," International Research Internship Program, Korea Science and Engineering Foundation (Now National Research Foundation of Korea) (2005); Recipient, Travel Fellowship Award, Ninth International Conference on Alzheimer's Disease and Related Disorders (2004); Recipient, Award for Outstanding Research Poster Session Award, 10th Federal Meeting of Korean Basic Medical Scientists, Seoul, Republic of Korea (2002) **MEM:** Korean-American Scientists and Engineers Association (2016-Present); New York Korean Biologists (2016-Present); Ministry of Science, Republic of Korea (2010-Present); New York Academy of Sciences (2006-Present); International Society for NeuroVirology (2012-2015); Korean Society for Gerontology (2002-2010); The Korean Society for Virology (2000-2010); Expert Committee, Global Network of Korean Scientists and Engineers **ADD:** 6434 102nd St Apt 5U, Rego Park, NY, 11374 **URL:** https://www.linkedin.com/in/boe-hyun-kim-a8753930

KIM, MICHAEL KYONG-IL, T: Professor, Architect **I:** Education/Educational Services **CN:** College of Fine + Applied Arts, University of Illinois at Urbana-Champaign **DOB:** 03/05/1940 **PB:** Seoul **SC:** Republic of Korea **PT:** Sang-Hoo Kim; Hwa-Soon Chong **MS:** Married **SPN:** Samyoung Cho (4/4/1964) **CH:** Alexander Dojun; Andrew Dohyung; Susan K. Stevens **ED:** PhD, University of California, Berkeley (1977) **CT:** Registered Architect, NCARB - National Council of Architectural Registration Boards, State of California (1973) **C:** Professor of Architecture, University of Illinois at Urbana-Champaign (1984-Present); Associate Professor of Architecture, Harvard University, Cambridge, MA (1977-1984) **CW:** Design **AW:** Outstanding Faculty Award, College of Fine + Applied Arts, University of Illinois at Urbana-Champaign (1998) **MEM:** AIA **MH:** Albert Nelson Marquis Lifetime Achievement Award (2017) **BA:** 611 E Lorado Taft Drive, 212 Temple Hoyne Buell Hall, MC-621, Illinois School of Architecture, Champaign, IL, 61820-6921 **ADD:** 4 Grove St, Medford, MA, 02155

KIMBERLIN, RALPH DACE, T: Professor, Test Pilot **I:** Aviation **CN:** Florida Institute of Technology **DOB:** 01/06/1940 **PB:** Sullivan **SC:** MO/USA **MS:** Married **SPN:** Jean Kimberlin **CH:** Charles Anthony; Lisa **ED:** DEng, Aerospace, Aeronautical and Astronautical Engineering, Technical University of Aachen, Germany (1991); MS in Aerospace Engineering, University of Tennessee Space Institute (1975); BS, U.S. Naval Academy (1963) **CT:** Certified Pilot; Certified in Flight Testing, Certified Flight Instructor-Airplanes, Instruments and Multi Engine **C:** Professor, Florida Institute of Technology (2006-Present); Consultant (2006-Present); Test Pilot (1970-Present); Retired (2005); Professor, University of Tennessee Space Institute (1978-2005); Program Chairman, University of Tennessee Space Institute (1978-2005); Chief of Flight and Aerodynamics, Piper Aircraft, Inc. (1974-1978) **CR:** Fellow, Society of Experimental Test Pilots **MIL:** Colonel, U.S. Air Force Reserve **CW:** Author, "Flight Testing of Fixed Wing Aircraft" (2002) **MEM:** American Institute of Aeronautics and Astronautics; SAE International; Experimental Aircraft Association; Society of Experimental Test Pilots **ADD:** 205 Loma Drive, Winter Haven, FL, 33881 **URL:** https://www.bookdepository.com/Flight-Testing-Fixed-Wing-Aircraft-Ralph-D-Kimberlin/9781563475641

KIMEL, J. DANIEL, T: Physics Professor Emeritus **I:** Education/Educational Services **CN:** Florida State University **DOB:** 08/11/1937 **PB:** Winston-Salem **SC:** NC/USA **PT:** Jacob Daniel Kimel; Emily Nell (Davis) Kimel **MS:** Married **SPN:** Carol Ann Allen (2/27/1965, Divorced 2/1990); Laura G. **CH:** Leslie Ann; Kristine Lynn; Jacob Daniel III; Karen Elizabeth **ED:** PhD in Physics, University of Wisconsin (1965); MS in Physics, University of Wisconsin (1960); BS in Physics, The University of North Carolina at Chapel Hill (1959) **C:** Emeritus Professor, Florida State University (2003-Present); Professor, Florida State University, Tallahassee, FL (1988-2003); Associate Professor, Florida State University, Tallahassee, FL (1973-1988); Assistant Professor, Florida State University, Tallahassee, FL (1967-1973); Research Associate, Florida State University, Tallahassee, FL (1966-1967); Research Associate, University of Wisconsin-Madison (1965-1966) **CR:** Director, Graduate Affairs, Department of Physics, Florida State University (1989-1991) **CW:** Co-author, "Superconductivity Revisited" (2013); Contributor, Articles, Professional Journals **AW:** High Energy Physics Research Grantee, U.S. Department of Energy (1966-1990); Fellow, National Science Foundation (1960-1963); Fellow, Woodrow Wilson National Fellowship Foundation (1959) **MEM:** American Physical Society; Sigma Xi **MH:** Albert Nelson Marquis Lifetime Achievement Award (2017) **H:** Musician **RE:** Lutheran **ADD:** 2043 Owenby Dr, Tallahassee, FL, 32308

KIMM, MICHAEL S., I: Law and Legal Services **DOB:** 07/12/1963 **PB:** Seoul **SC:** Republic of Korea **PT:** Chun Teak Kimm; Chong Sim Kimm **ED:** JD, Boston University (1991); BA, Fordham University (1987) **C:** Private Practice, Hackensack, NJ **CIV:** General Counsel Korean-American Association for Rehabilitation of Disabled, Queens, NY (1992-1994) **CW:** Managing Editor, Boston University International Law Journal (1990-1991); Contributor, Articles, Professional Journals **MEM:** American Bar Association; New Jersey State Bar Association; New York State Bar Association **BAR:** US Supreme Court (1995); Second, Third and Federal Circuits, US Court of Appeals (1994); Southern and Eastern District, US District Court, New York (1993); New York Bar Association (1992); New Jersey Bar Association (1991); US District Court New Jersey (1991)

KING, RUFUS GUNN, T: Judge **I:** Law and Legal Services **DOB:** 06/16/1942 **PB:** New Haven **SC:** CT/USA **PT:** Rufus Gunn King; Janice Livingston (Chase) King **ED:** JD, Georgetown University (1971); AB, Princeton University (1966) **C:** Senior Judge, Superior Court of the District of Columbia (2008-Present); Chief Judge, Superior Court of the District of Columbia (2000-2008); Presiding Judge, Civil Division, Superior Court of the District of Columbia (1997-1998); Deputy Presiding Judge, Civil Division, Superior Court of the District of Columbia (1993-1996); Judge, Superior Court of the District of Columbia (1984-2008); Partner, Berliner and Maloney (1983-1984); Partner, King & Newmyer (1975-1983); Associate, Law Offices of Rufus King (1973-1975); Associate, Rollinson, Stein & Halpert (1973); Associate, Karr & Greensfelder (1971-1973); Law Clerk to Honorable Austin L. Fickling & Honorable William C. Pryor, Superior Court of the District of Columbia (1968-1971) **CIV:** Chair, Domestic Violence Coordinator Council (1991-1993); Member, Domestic Violence Coordinator Council (1989-1993); Chair, Committee of Technology and Automation (1986-2000) **MEM:** Dispute Resolution Division, ABA (2011-Present); Board Chair, National Conference of Metropolitan Courts (2005-Present); Board Director, National Center for State Courts (2006-2011); President, American Inns of Court (1988-1989); Counselor, American Inns of Court (1987-1988); Judicial Administrative Division, ABA (1985-1994); The Charles Fahy American Inn of Court (1985-1989); Chair, BADC (1982-1984); Fee Arbitration Board, BADC (1980-1984); Court System Study Horsky Committee, BADC (1980-1982); The American Law Institute; Counselors Club; Lawyers Club, The Barristers Club **BAR:** Maryland State Bar Association (1984); The District of Columbia Bar (1971)

KINGHAM, RICHARD FRANK, T: Lawyer **I:** Law and Legal Services **CN:** Covington & Burling LLP **DOB:** 08/02/1946 **PB:** Lafayette **SC:** IN/USA **PT:** James R. Kingham; Loretta C. Kingham **MS:** Married **SPN:** Justine Frances McClung (7/6/1968) **CH:** Richard Patterson **ED:** JD, University of Virginia (1973); BA, George Washington University (1968) **CT:** Registered Foreign Lawyer, Law Society of England and Wales (1994) **C:** Senior Counsel, Covington & Burling LLP (2016-Present); Co-Head, Life Sciences Industry Group, Covington & Burling LLP (2000-Present); Management Committee, Covington & Burling LLP (2000-2004); Managing Partner, London Office, Covington & Burling LLP (1996-2000); Partner, Covington & Burling LLP (1981-2016); Associate, Covington & Burling LLP, Washington, DC (1973-1981); Editorial Assistant, "Washington Star" (1964-1970) **CR:** Adjunct Professor, Georgetown University Law Center (2003-Present); Adviser, Working Group on Drug Regulation Reform, Indian Council for Research on International Economic Relations, New Delhi, India (2015-2017); Rapporteur, Working Group on Drug Regulation Reform, Pharmaceutical Law Institute, Tsinghua University Law School, Beijing, China (2013-2016); Working Group on Clinical Trials and Regulatory Pathways, Center for Global Development (2010-2011); Lecturer, Graduate Program of Pharmaceutical Medicine, Cardiff University (1999-2011); National Advisory Allergy and Infectious Diseases Council, National Institutes of Health (1988-1992); Adviser to Committees, Institute of Medicine, National Academy of Sciences (1983-2004); Lecturer, School of Law, University of Virginia (1977-1990) **CIV:** President, American Friends of St. Peter's Eaton Square (2001-2008); Treasurer, Parochial Church Council, St. Peter's Church, Eaton Square, London, England (1998-2001) **MIL:** U.S. Army (1968-1969) **CW:** Editor, Co-Author, "Life Sciences Law Review";

Contributor, Articles, Professional Journals **AW:** Food and Drug Law Institute Distinguished Service and Leadership Award (2013); LMG Life Sciences Hall of Fame (2013) **MEM:** American Bar Association; Society of Vertebrate Paleontology; Food Law Group, United Kingdom; Food and Drug Law Institute; Reform Club, London, England; Order of the Coif **BAR:** Fifth Circuit, U.S. Court of Appeals (1980); U.S. Supreme Court (1977); Eighth Circuit, U.S. Court of Appeals (1977); District of Columbia Circuit, U.S. District Court (1974); District of Columbia (1973) **H:** Vertebrate paleontology **RE:** Episcopalian **BA:** Covington & Burling LLP, One City Center, 850 Tenth Street NW, Washington, DC, 20001-4956 **ADD:** 616 Fort Williams Parkway, Alexandria, VA, 22304

KINTSCH, WALTER, I: Education/Educational Services **DOB:** 05/22/1905 **PB:** Temesvar **SC:** Romania **PT:** Christof Kintsch; Irene (Hollerbach) Kintsch **ED:** PhD, University of Kansas (1960) **C:** Retired (2004); Professor, University of Colorado, Boulder (1968-2004) **CW:** Editor, Psychology Review (1989-1994); Author, Books

KIRKPATRICK, RONALD CRECELIUS, T: Aerospace Engineer, Researcher **I:** Engineering **DOB:** 10/04/1937 **PB:** San Angelo **SC:** TX/USA **PT:** Frank Brown Kirkpatrick; Vida D. Kirkpatrick **MS:** Married **SPN:** Phyllis Abbie Furbeck **CH:** Abbie E.; Andrew W.; Ann M. Crider **ED:** NRC Postdoctoral Resident Research Associate, Theoretical Astrophysics Branch, Goddard Space Flight Center, National Aeronautics and Space Administration, Greenbelt, MD (1969-1971); PhD, The University of Texas at Austin (1969); MS, Texas A&M University, College Station, TX (1962); BS, Texas A&M University, College Station, TX (1959) **C:** Research Scientist, RAC, Los Alamos, NM (2008-2011); Senior Scientist, Otowi Technical Services, LLC, Los Alamos, NM (2007-2008); Retired (2005); Guest Scientist, Los Alamos National Laboratory, New Mexico (2004-2005); Staff Member, Los Alamos National Laboratory (1973-2004); Assistant Professor, Physics Department, Texas A&M University, College Station, TX (1971-1972); National Research Council Postdoctoral Resident Research Associate, NASA Goddard Space Flight Center (1969-1971); Research Scientist Assistant III, Astronomy Department, The University of Texas at Austin (1968-1969); Research Scientist Assistant III, Applied Research Lab, The University of Texas at Austin (1967-1968); National Aeronautics and Space Administration Trainee, Astronomy Department, The University of Texas at Austin (1964-1967); Research Engineer, Department of Mechanical Sciences, Southwest Research Institute, San Antonio, TX (1962-1964); Laboratory Assistant, Physics Department, Texas A&M University, College Station, TX (1961-1962); Instrumentation Engineer, Ames Research Center, National Aeronautics and Space Administration, Mountain View, CA (1959-1961); Gulf States Utilities, Port Arthur, TX (1958, 1957) **CR:** Chairman, Panel, Sciences & Engineers Symposia on Current Trends in International Fusion Research, Washington. DC (2007) **CW:** Creator, Hex Chess Board Game **MEM:** International Astronomical Union; American Astronomical Society **MH:** Albert Nelson Marquis Lifetime Achievement Award (2017) **H:** Track & field; Sprinter; Travel **RE:** Christian **ADD:** 716 Kris Ct, Los Alamos, NM, 87547

KITTLE BOYER RYAN, KAYE, T: Association Management Executive **I:** Business Management/Business Services **CN:** Boyer Management Services **DOB:** 07/05/1942 **PB:** Peoria **SC:** IL/USA **PT:** Keith Howard Kittle; Evelyn Pearl (Benson) Kittle **MS:** Married **SPN:** Michael Patrick Ryan (5/5/2011); Jon Frederick Boyer (3/20/1965,

Deceased 2009) **CH:** Tristan Boyer-Binns; Kristine Monique Hitchens **ED:** MA in Sociology, Rutgers, the State University of New Jersey, New Brunswick, NJ (1967); BS in Home Economics, Pennsylvania State University, University Park, PA (1964); Coursework, Merrill Palmer Institute, Detroit, MI (1964) **CT:** Certification, American Society of Association Executive (1988-2012); Certified in Family and Consumer Sciences (1987-2012) **C:** President, Boyer Management Services, Palm Coast, FL (2002-2013); President, Boyer Management Services, Earleville, MD (1986-2002); President, Boyer Management Services, Manalapan, NJ (1984-1986); Executive Director, New Jersey Home Economics Association, Manalapan, NJ (1975-1986); Feasibility Study Director, Ocean County College, Toms River, NJ (1975); Assistant to Chairman, 4-H Youth Development Department, Cook College (1973-1974); Coordinator, Instructor Pilot Project, Urban Coalition of Metropolitan Wilmington Inc. (1972); Instructor, Douglass College, Rutgers University, New Brunswick, NJ (1967-1970); Coordinator, Human Resources, New Jersey Cooperative Extension Service, New Brunswick, NJ (1966-1967); Extension Home Economist, Maryland Cooperative Extension Service, Westminster, MD (1964-1965); Creative Researcher, National Institute of Drycleaning, Silver Spring, MD (1963) **CR:** Meeting Manager, Costume Society of America, Palm Coast, FL (2011-2012); Executive Director, Costume Society of America, Palm Coast, FL (2006-2010); Textile Society of America (1998-2004); Maryland Academy of Family Physicians (1997); Baltimore County Medical Association (1995-1996); Maryland Academy of Family Physicians (1994); Board of Directors, Plumpton Park Zoological Gardens, Rising Sun, MD (1990-1992); Consultant, Plumpton Park Zoological Gardens, Rising Sun, MD (1988-1989); Manager, Costume Society of America, Palm Coast, FL (1984-2006); Consultant, New Jersey White House Conference, Trenton, NJ (1980); Advisory Committee, Department of Community Education, Rutgers University (1979-1984) **CIV:** Trustee, Cecil County Library Board (1998-2002); Soroptomist International of the Americas, Elkton, MD (1987-1994); Board of Directors, Community Library of Cecilton (1986-1992); Player, U.S. Amateur Public Links (1986) **CW:** Editor, Exchanges Newsletter; Resource Director, New Jersey Programs and Services Related to Adolescent Pregnancy **AW:** Super Senior Women's Club Champion, Grand Haven Golf Club (2014); Couples Net Champion, Grand Haven Golf Club (2011); Senior Women's Club Champion, Grand Haven Golf Club (2008); Couples Champion, Grand Haven Golf Club (2005); Senior Women's Club Champion, Grand Haven Golf Club (2005); Ruth O'Brien Project Grantee, American Association of Family and Consumer Sciences **MEM:** Board of Trustees, Costume Society of America (2012-Present); Board of Directors, Grand Haven Women's Golf Association (2010-2013); President, Grand Haven Women's Golf Association (2009-2010); Vice President, Grand Haven Women's Golf Association (2007-2009); Chair, Auction Committee, Daytona-Palm Coast Chapter, Pennsylvania State Alumni Association (2006-2007); Education Committee, Florida Society of Association Executives (2006); Chairman, Strategic Planning, Daytona-Palm Coast Chapter, Pennsylvania State Alumni Association (2003-2008); Educational and Professional Development Working Committee, PCMA (2002); Transition Team, Product Service, PCMA Education Foundation (2001); Trustee, PCMA Education Foundation (2000-2003); Learning Center Task Force, PCMA Education Foundation (2000-2001); Design Task Force, PCMA Education Foundation

(2000); Education and Professional Development Committee, PCMA (1996-2001); Chair, Constitution and Bylaws Committee, Kappa Omicron Nu (1994-1997); Vice President of Finance, Kappa Omicron Nu (1992-1993); Vice President, Program Development, New Jersey Division, American Association of University Women (1984-1986); Palm Coast Arts Foundation; Friends of the Library; Museum of Arts and Sciences; Renaissance Society; Endowment, Costume Society of America; Women's Golf Association; Florida Association of Family and Consumer Sciences; American Society of Association Executives; American Association of Family and Consumer Sciences **H:** Golf; Yoga; Tai chi **PA:** Democrat **ADD:** 107 Front Street, Palm Coast, FL, 32137

KLAGSBRUN, FRANCINE, T: Writer, Editor **I:** Writing and Editing **PB:** New York City **SC:** NY/USA **PT:** Benjamin Lifton; Anna Pike Lifton **MS:** Married **SPN:** Samuel Charles Klagsbrun **CH:** Sarah Devora **ED:** DHL in Hebrew Letters, Jewish Theological Seminary, New York City, NY (1999); MA, New York University (1959); Bachelor of Hebrew Literature, Jewish Theological Seminary, New York City, NY (1952); BA, Brooklyn College, Magna Cum Laude (1952) **C:** Editorial Director, Universal Education Co., New York City, NY (1969-1972); Executive Editor, Cowles Book Co., New York City, NY (1965-1968); Executive Editor, Encyclopedia Americana, New York City, NY (1963-1965); Managing Editor, World Book Encyclopedia, Chicago, IL (1962-1963); Senior Editor, World Book Encyclopedia, Chicago, IL (1957-1962) **CIV:** Founding Member, Congregation Or Zarua; Board of Directors, National Jewish Book Council; Founding Chair, Board of Overseers, Library, Jewish Theological Seminary; Trustee, Jewish Museum; Member, Academic Advisory Committee, Habassah Brandeis Institute; Member, Task Force, United Jewish Appeal Federation; Member, Women's Dialogue Group, American Jewish Committee **CW:** Columnist, Jewish Week (1993-Present); Author, "Lioness: Golda Meir and the Nation of Israel" (2017); Author, "The Fourth Commandment: Remember the Sabbath Day" (2002); Author, "Jewish Days: A Book of Jewish Life and Culture Around the Year" (1996); Author, "Mixed Feelings: Love, Hate, Rivalry and Reconciliation Among Brothers and Sisters" (1992); Columnist, Moment Magazine (1990-2010); Author, "Married People: Staying Together in the Age of Divorce" (1985); Author, "Voices of Wisdom: Jewish Ideals and Ethics for Everyday Living" (1980); Author, "Too Young to Die: Youth and Suicide" (1976); Editor, "Words of Women" (1975); Editor, "Free to Be... You and Me" (1974); Editor, "The First Ms. Reader" (1973); Author, "Freedom Now! The Story of the Abolitionists" (1972); Author, "Psychiatry: What It Is, What It Does" (1969); Author, "The First Book of Spices" (1968); Editor, "Assassination: Robert F. Kennedy" (1968); Author, "Sigmund Freud: A Biography" (1967); Contributor, Articles, Magazines and Newspapers; Board of Directors, Lilith Magazine; Editorial Board, Hadassah Magazine **AW:** National Jewish Book Award, Everett Family Foundation (2017); Founders Award, Congregation Or Zarua (2014); Vision in Leadership Award, Solomon Schechter School (2010); Alumna of the Year, Brooklyn College (2007); Honoree, Jewish Museum Purim Ball (2005); Woman Who Made a Difference, American Jewish Congress (2000); Stanley M. Isaacs Human Relations Award, American Jewish Committee (2000); Centennial Award, Rabbinical Assembly American (2000); Distinguished Alumna Award, Brooklyn College (2000); Outstanding Alumna Award, Jewish Theological Seminary (1996); Eternal Light Medal (1993); Book of the Year for

"Lioness: Golda Meir and the Nation of Israel" **MEM:** PEN American Center; Authors Guild; Phi Beta Kappa **H:** Collecting paintings; Furniture; Ceramics **PA:** Democrat **RE:** Jewish **ADD:** 941 Park Avenue, New York, NY, 10028

KLAGSBRUN, SAMUEL C., I: Medicine & Health Care **DOB:** 05/19/1905 **PB:** Antwerp, Belgium **SC:** Antwerp, Belgium **PT:** Son of Solomon and Rachel (Bodner) K.; **SPN:** Married Francine Lifton, January 21, 1955; **CH:** 1 child, Sarah Devora. **ED:** MD, Chicago Medical School, 1962; BRE, Jewish Theological Seminary, 1954; BA, City College of New York, 1955 **C:** Executive medical director, Four Winds Hospital, Katonah, New York, 1977-; Member faculty, Columbia University College Psychiatric Surgery, 1971-88; Associate clinical professor, Columbia University, New York City, 1971-88; Director, St. Lukes Psychiatric Consultation Service, New York City, 1971-74; Director, St. Lukes Psychiatric Day Hospital, New York City, 1969-71; Associate director, St. Lukes Hospital Psychiatric Walk-in-Clinic, New York City, 1968-69; Psychiatrist, private practice, New York City, 1968-80; Staff psychiatrist, New London Child Guidance Clinic, 1966-68; Clinical instructor, Yale University School of Medicine, New Haven, 1966-68; Chief of psychiatry, New London (Connecticut) Submarine Base, 1966-68; Resident in psychiatry, Yale University School Medicine, 1963-66 **CR:** Visitor St. Christopher's Hospital, London, England, 1975- faculty member Mount Sinai Hospital, School of Medicine, New York City, 1988-93 visiting professor, chairman in pastoral psychiatry Jewish Theological Seminary, New York City, 1973- lecturer in field professor clinical psychiatry Albert Einstein College Medicine, 1996-. **CW:** Contributor numerous articles to professional journals **AW:** Recipient Gittleson Scholarship award Jewish Theological Seminary, 1954. **MEM:** Fellow Am. Psychiatric Association; member American Medical Association, Westchester County Mental Health Association **H:** Sailing **RE:** Jewish

KLAUSS, KENNETH, T: Composer **I:** Fine Art **DOB:** 04/08/1923 **PB:** Parkston **SC:** SD/USA **PT:** Christian Klauss; Paulina (Engel) Klauss **ED:** MusB in Composition, University of Southern California (1946) **C:** Lecturer in Music History, SCI-Arc, Santa Monica, CA (1970-1976); Lecturer in Music for Dance, Idyllwild Arts, Idyllwild, CA (1967-1974); Composer, Los Angeles, CA (1961-1983); Educator, Los Angeles, CA (1961-1983); Music Teacher, San Francisco, CA (1950-1961); Composer, Lester Horton Theater, Los Angeles, CA (1949-1950); Composition and Piano Teacher, Los Angeles, CA (1946-1950) **CR:** Guest Lecturer, Milken Community Schools, Los Angeles, CA (2007-2008); Guest Lecturer, University of South Dakota, Vermillion, SD (2002-2008); Affiliate, Premieres, University of South Dakota, Vermillion, SD (2000-2013); Composer in Residence, Perry-Mansfield Performing Arts, Steamboat Springs, CO (1966); Guest Performer, Library of Congress, American University, Washington, DC (1996); Composer, Library of Congress, American University, Washington, DC (1996); Lecturer, Library of Congress, American University, Washington, DC (1996); Affiliate, Sonata Solo Violoncello (1956); Affiliate, Sonata Solo Contrabass (1956) **CIV:** Founder, Klauss-James Archive and Art Museum, Parkston, SD (1995); Patron, Klauss-James Archive and Art Museum, Parkston, SD (1995-Present) **CW:** Contributor, Violin Concerto, Played by John Thomson, Nelson Cathedral, Aukland, New Zealand (2016); Contributor, Solo, Sonata String Bass (2012); Contributor, "Making Music for Modern Dance" by Katherine Teck (2011); Contributor,

Los Angeles Youth Orchestra (2011); Contributor, Suite from Europe USD (2011); Contributor, Concert Music, Trombone & Strings, University of South Dakota (2009); Contributor, Performance, Sonata Orchestra, Vermillion, SD (2007); Contributor, Performance, Sonata Orchestra, Yankton, SD (2007); Contributor, Performance, Sonata Orchestra, Sioux Falls, SD (2007); Contributor, Performance, Sonata Orchestra, Brookings, SD (2007); Contributor, Performance, Performance, Sonata Orchestra, Worthington, MN (2007); Contributor, Performance, Rawlins Trio of University of South Dakota, Minneapolis, MN (2005); Contributor, Performance, Rawlins Trio of University of South Dakota, Omaha, NE (2005); Contributor, Performance, Rawlins Trio of University of South Dakota, Vermillion, SD (2005); Composer, Harpsichord/Violin Composition, Commissioned by University of South Dakota (2001); Composer, Music Composition, "Story of the World, Volumes I to VIII" (1952-1986); Author, Poetry, "Story of the World, Volumes I to VIII" (1952-1986); Composer, "Fall of the House of Russia (1952) **AW:** Honorable Mention, Opera Competition, Ohio University, Athens, OH (1954) **H:** History; Poetry **PA:** Democrat **BA:** PO Box 694, Parkston, SD, 57366 **ADD:** 440 Wren Dr, Los Angeles, CA, 90065

KLOSTERMAN, JAN, T: Nurse Life Care Planner **I:** Medicine & Health Care **CN:** Klosterman & Associates LLC **PB:** St. Louis, MO **MS:** Married **SPN:** Mark Klosterman **ED:** Diploma in Nursing, Goldfarb School of Nursing, Barnes-Jewish Hospital (1979) **CT:** Certified Nurse Life Care Planner, American Association of Nurse Life Care Planners; Certified Medicare Set Aside Consultant, Commission on Health Care; Certified Brain Injury Specialist **C:** Principal, Owner, Klosterman & Associates LLC (2006-Present) **CR:** Co-Owner Rodenbaugh & Klosterman Consulting (1999-2006) **CW:** Lecturer in Field **MEM:** American Association of Nurse Life Care Planners (1999-Present); AALNC (1998-Present); Past-President, American Association of Nurse Life Care Planners (2008); President, American Association of Nurse Life Care Planners (2007); President-Elect, American Association of Nurse Life Care Planners (2006) **BA:** 410 Sovereign Court, Suite 11, Klosterman & Associates LLC, Ballwin, MO, 63011 **URL:** http://www.klostermanandassociates.com/staff/jan-klosterman/

KNAPP, NANCY, I: Health, Wellness and Fitness **PT:** Henry Homer Hay; Aurore Louise (LaCroix) Hay **MS:** Married **SPN:** Richard Dominick Knapp (September 11, 1955) **CH:** Pamela Hay Burdett **CR:** Trainer, Pennsylvania Department of Health, Harrisburg, PA (1982-1985); Faculty Member, Main Line Night School, Ardmore, PA (1978-1980) **CIV:** Director, Chester Vocational/Educational Outreach (1982-1984); Coordinator, Chester Vocational/Educational Outreach (1978-1980); Board of Directors, Resources for Women, University of Pennsylvania, Philadelphia (1976-1980); Member, Steering Committee Coalition for Education/Placement of Women, Philadelphia (1976-1978) **CW:** Author, "Growing, Together" (1985); Author, "Prevention: Drug Misuse" (1983) **MEM:** American Counseling Association; American Psychological Association; Consultant, Association of Greater Philadelphia; Phi Delta Kappa

KOBAYASHI, HERBERT, T: Electrical Engineer **I:** Engineering **CN:** Kobayashi Inc. **DOB:** 02/06/1929 **PB:** Webster **SC:** TX/USA **PT:** Mitsutaro; Moto Kobayashi **MS:** Married **SPN:** Haruko Orita **CH:** June; Naomi; Ken **ED:** MS in Industrial Engineering, University of Michigan (1969); MSEE, University

of Michigan (1958); BSEE, University of Houston (1951) **C:** President, Kobayashi Inc., Webster, TX (1960-Present); Aerospace Technologist, NASA, Houston, TX (1963-2002); Design Engineer, Lockheed Electronics, Houston, TX (1963); Design Engineer, Boeing Aerospace, New Orleans, LA (1962); Design Engineer, Boeing Aerospace, Huntsville, AL (1961-1962); Design Engineer, SIE, Houston, TX (1960-1961) **CIV:** Planning and Zoning Commission, Webster, TX (1993-1994) **MIL:** U.S. Army (1954-1956) **MEM:** IEEE; American Institute of Aeronautics and Astronautics; Houston Inventors Association **H:** Research and development **ADD:** 1428 FM 528 Road, Webster, TX, 77598

KOEHLER-TRICKLER, SALLY JO, T: Illustrator (Retired) **I:** Other **CN:** Army & Atomic Energy **DOB:** 01/07/1948 **PB:** Burlington **SC:** IA/USA **PT:** Frank Joseph Koehler; Florence Christina (Hein) Koehler **MS:** Single **SPN:** James Edward Trickler (11/4/1967, Divorced) **CH:** Brenda Jo **ED:** BA, Western Illinois University (1988); AA, Southeastern Community College (1976) **CT:** Master Gardener, Department of Horticulture, Iowa State University (2008) **C:** Retired (1973); Draftsman, Iowa Army Ammunition Plant, Middletown (1967-1973); Draftsman, Army and Atomic Energy **CR:** Senior Technological Illustrator, JI Case Co., Burlington, IA (1973-Present); Representative, Technical Illustrating, Burlington Community HS Career Day Annual Event (1985-1991) **CIV:** Art Designer (1987); Chairman, Public Relations, United Way, Burlington, IA (1976-1977); Member, Public Relations Committee, United Way, Burlington, IA (1975) **CW:** Publisher, "History of Saints John and Paul Church (1839-2000)" (2000) **MEM:** The Good Samaritan Society, Iowa (1985-1987); Chairman, High School Counseling Committee on Career Days (1977-1980); Burlington Engineers Club (1974-1976); Allegro Motor Home Club; Phi Kappa Phi **MH:** Albert Nelson Marquis Lifetime Achievement Award (2017) **H:** Creative writing; Poetry; Fiction; Landscape design; Photography **RE:** Roman Catholic **ADD:** 11904 44th St, Burlington, IA, 52601

KOGER, RONNIE, T: Special Assistant to the President **I:** Education/Educational Services **CN:** Kennesaw State University **MS:** Married **ED:** EdD, University of Kansas (1975); MEd, University of Kansas (1964); BA, Pittsburg State University, Kansas (1961) **C:** Special Assistant to the President, Kennesaw State University (2015-Present); Vice President for Student and Enrollment Services, Southern Polytechnic State University; Vice President for Enrollment, University of Alabama, Huntsville; Director of Admissions, Indiana State University; Director of Admissions, Illinois Institute of Technology; Assistant Director of Admissions, Pittsburg State University, Kansas **CIV:** Past President, National Association for College Admissions Counselors, Washington, D.C. **H:** Community engagement **ADD:** PO Box 7686, Marietta, GA, 30065 **URL:** https://www.nacacnet.org/membership/member-spotlight/meet-ron-koger/

KOHL, JOHN PRESTON, I: Other **DOB:** 12/26/1942 **PB:** Allentown **SC:** PA/USA **PT:** Claude Evan Kohl; Edna Lenoir (Woodland) Kohl **ED:** PhD in Business Administration, Pennsylvania State University (1982); MS in Counseling, American Tech. University (1976); MS in Management, American Tech. University (1974); MDiv, Yale University (1967); BA, Moravian College (1964) **CT:** Ordained to Ministry, United Church of Christ (1967) **C:** Professor business administration, Lincoln University, Oakland, California (2009); Dean College Business and Econs., California State University-East Bay, Hayward (2005-2007);

Dean, Graduate School of International Trade & Business Administration, Texas Agricultural and Mechanical International University, Laredo (1999-2003); Interim Provost, Vice President of Academy Affairs, Texas Agricultural and Mechanical International University, Laredo (2002); Professor, Chairman, Department of Management, University of Nevada, Las Vegas (1988-1999); Associate Professor, San Jose State University (1985-1987); Assistant Professor Management, University Texas, El Paso (1982-1985); Instructor, Pennsylvania State University, University Park (1978-1982); Minister, First Congregational Church, Hutchinson, Minnesota (1971-1973); Minister, Christ Congregational Church, New Smyrna Beach, Florida (1968-1971) **CR:** Consultant in field **MIL:** Colonel, US Army Reserve (1993-1999); Captain, US Army (1973-1978) **CW:** Co-author, "Personnel Management" (1986); Contributor, Articles, Professional Journals **AW:** Decorated Army Commendation Medal; Meritorious Service Medal; National Defense Service Medal **MEM:** American Academy of Management

KONDRAK, BERTHA GENNA, T: Psychotherapist, Educator **I:** Social Work **CN:** Central Texas College **DOB:** 04/07/1949 **SC:** TX/USA **CH:** Three Children **ED:** MSW, University of Texas at Austin (1984); BA in Psychology, University of Texas at Austin (1971) **CT:** Licensed Clinical Social Worker, State of Texas (1985) **C:** Professor, Central Texas College, Killeen, TX (2003-Present); Private Practice, Austin, TX (1989-Present); Case Supervisor, Meridell Achievement Center, Austin, TX (1972-1989) **CR:** President, Central Texas College, Central Campus Faculty Senate (2011-2012); President-elect, Central Texas College, Central Campus Faculty Senate (2010-2011); Secretary, Central Texas College, Central Campus Faculty Senate (2009-2010); Faculty Senate Professional Development Committee **CIV:** President, Systems Centered Training and Research Institute, Austin, TX (2003-2010) **AW:** Professional Development Leadership Award, Central Texas College (2015-2016) **MEM:** Texas Community College Teachers Association **H:** Camping; Traveling **BA:** PO Box 1800, Killeen, TX, 76540 **ADD:** 14606 Alpha Collier Drive, Austin, TX, 78728

KOPPA, PATRICIA ANN, T: Lawyer **I:** Law and Legal Services **CN:** Manitowoc County **DOB:** 11/25/1960 **PB:** Wausau **SC:** WI/USA **PT:** Gerald Anthony Koppa; Beverly Helene (Boettcher) Writz **MS:** Married **SPN:** John Michael Bruce (6/17/1989) **CH:** Catherine Lynne; Carolyn Anne **ED:** JD, University of Wisconsin (1984); BS, University of Wisconsin-Stevens Point (1982) **CT:** State of Wisconsin (1985); United States District Court, Eastern District of Wisconsin (1985); United States District Court, Western District of Wisconsin (1985) **C:** Circuit Court Commissioner, Register in Probate, Manitowoc County, WI (1997-Present); Private Practice, Manitowoc, WI (1993-1997); Associate, Muchin, Muchin & Bruce, South Carolina (1985-1992); Associate, Muchin, Muchin & Bruce, Manitowoc, WI (1985-1992) **CR:** Wisconsin Register in Probate Association Forms Committee (2006-Present); President, Wisconsin Register in Probate Association (2017-2018); Secretary, Wisconsin Register in Probate Association (2015-2017); Chairman, Association Forms Committee (2008-2011); Member, Forms, Records Management Committee, The Wisconsin Supreme Court (2007-2011); Member, Board of Directors, Bankruptcy and Creditor Rights Section, State Bar of Wisconsin (1993-1994); Member, Chapter Seven Trustee Panel, Eastern District of Wisconsin (1991-1994) **CIV:** Leader, Girl Scouts of the United States of America

(1996-Present); Trainer, Girl Scouts of the United States of America (1996-Present); Volunteer, EAA AirVenture (1978-Present); Volunteer, Girl Scouts of Manitou; Former Member, Volunteer Thunder on the Lakeshore; Former Volunteer, MACS Home & School Association **MEM:** President, Wisconsin Register in Probate Association (2017-Present); Secretary, Wisconsin Register in Probate Association (2015-2017); Secretary, Manitowoc County Bar Association (1991-1997); State Bar of Wisconsin **MH:** Albert Nelson Marquis Lifetime Achievement Award (2017) **ADD:** 1108 Westwood Ln, Manitowoc, WI, 54220

KORNILOV, NIKOLAY , I: Sciences **DOB:** 06/01/1905 **PB:** Russia **ED:** DSc, Institute Physics and Power Engineering, Obninsk, Russia (1997); PhD, Khlopin Institute, Leningrad, Russia (1982) **C:** Science Researcher, IPPE-Russia, JRC-IRMM-Belgium, OU-USA (1969) **AW:** Best Peer-Reviewed Scientific Paper, JRC-IRMM (2008) **ACH:** Achievements include research in flight neutron spectrometer, neutron detector calibration; created Data Files for some fissile isotopes which were included in IAFA library.

KORNILOV, NIKOLAY VLADIMIROVICH, T: Research Scientist (Retired) **I:** Sciences **CN:** Ohio University **DOB:** 05/26/1946 **PB:** Ukraine **SC:** USSR **CH:** Anton Kornilov **ED:** DSc in Physics and Mathematics, Institute of Physics and Power Engineering, Obninsk, Russia (1997); PhD in Physics and Mathematics, V.G. Khlopin Radium Institute, Saint Petersburg, Russia (1982) **CT:** Diplomate, Moscow Physical Engineering Institute (1969) **C:** Researcher, Department of Physics and Astrophysics, Ohio University (2009-2013); Contract Agent, IRMM-JRC (2005-2008); Visiting Scientist, IRMM-JRC (2004-2005); Assistant Researcher to Leading Scientific Researcher, Institute for Physics and Power Engineering (IPPE) (1969-2004) **CR:** Invited Guest Professor, University L. Pasteur and Institut de Recherchers Subatomiques (2001); IAEA Consultant, Institute of Nuclear Physics and Nuclear Energy (1986); Lecturer, Training Courses, IAEA (1987, 1989, 1992) **CW:** Contributor, More than 150 Articles, Various Professional Journals **AW:** JRC-IRMM (EC) Excellence Award for Best Peer-Reviewed Scientific Paper (2007); Honoree, "Scientific Elite of Kaluga Region"; Honoree, "Great Men and Women of Science", 1st Edition, "Development of Neutron Experiments", IBC, Cambridge, England **MEM:** American Physical Society **ADD:** 9 Bolleana Pl, Athens, OH, 45701

KOROW, ELINORE MARIA, T: Artist, Educator **I:** Fine Art **CN:** Elinore Korow Potraits **DOB:** 07/31/1934 **PB:** Akron **SC:** OH/USA **PT:** Alexander Vigh; Elizabeth Helen (Doszpoly) Vigh **MS:** Single **SPN:** Harry Edward Bieber (8/1/1982, Deceased 1994); John Henry Korow (9/28/1957, Deceased 2008) **CH:** Christopher; David; Daniel **ED:** Diplomate, Cleveland Institute of Art (1957); Coursework, Siena Heights College (Now Siena Heights University) (1952-1953); Diplomate, Sawyer College of Business **C:** Owner, Elinore Korow: Portraits, Shaker Heights, Ohio (1973-1994); Artist, Portraits (1971-1980); Owner, Elinore Korow: Portraits, Akron, Ohio (1970-2018); Director, Special Corp, American Greetings Corporation, Cleveland, Ohio (1970-1973); Staff Artist, Designer, American Greetings Corporation, Cleveland, Ohio (1970-1973) **CR:** Instructor, Cleveland Institute of Art (2007-Present); Director, Special Exhibitions, Canton Museum of Art (2000-Present); Instructor, The University of Akron (1995-Present); Instructor, Painting, Cuyahoga Community College, Cleveland, Ohio

(1979-Present); Lecturer in Field; Director, Special Exhibitions, Massillon Museum; Chairman, Senior Excellence Art Exhibition, Cuyahoga Community College, Cleveland, Ohio **CIV:** Board of Directors, Faculty, Cleveland Institute of Art (2007-Present); Faculty, Cuyahoga Valley Art Center (2005-Present); Board of Directors, Akron Society of Artists (2001-Present); Board of Directors, Womens Art League of Akron Ohio (2001-Present); Judge, Akron Arts Expo, Ohio (2002-2008); Tutor, Fund Raising Benefit, American Diabetes Association (2006); Artist, Fund Raising Benefit, American Diabetes Association (2006); Board of Directors, Cuyahoga Valley Art Center (2005); Member, Women's Committee, Cleveland Orchestra (2002); Representative, Akron Area Arts Alliance (2001); President, Womens Art League of Akron Ohio (1999-2000); Charter Member, Visual Arts Alliance (1999-2000); Board of Directors, Akron Area Arts Alliance **CW:** Exhibitor, Stow-Munroe Falls Public Library, Ohio (2006); Exhibitor, Akron Woman's City Club (1996); Exhibitor, Cuyahoga Valley Art Center, Cuyahoga Falls, Ohio (1995); Exhibitor, Group Shows, Ohio Regional Painting Exhibition (1993); Exhibitor, Group Shows, Beck Center for the Arts, Lakewood, Ohio (1993); Exhibitor, Group Shows, Russell Art Exhibit, Novelty, Ohio (1992); Exhibitor, Group Shows, Canton Museum of Art (1988); Exhibitor, National Travelling Exhibition (1973-1974); Exhibitor, American Watercolor Society, Inc. (1973); Exhibitor, Group Shows, The Butler Institute of American Art, Youngstown, Ohio; Exhibitor, Group Shows, National Academy Museum and School, New York City, NY; Exhibitor, Group Shows, Lynn Kottler Galleries; Exhibitor, Group Shows, World Trade Center; Exhibitor, Group Shows, Other Exhibits; Solo Exhibits; Others Exhibits; Exhibitor, Permanent Collections, Blue Cross/Blue Shield Northeast Ohio; Exhibitor, Permanent Collections, American Greetings Corporation; Exhibitor, Permanent Collections, University of Akron Alumni Center; Exhibitor, Permanent Collections, Cleveland Play House; Exhibitor, Permanent Collections, Temple Emanu El, Cleveland Heights, Ohio; Exhibitor, Permanent Collections, The Fashion School, Kent State University; Exhibitor, Permanent Collections, First Congregational Church of Akron; Exhibitor, Permanent Collections, Sargent-Laessig Museum of Fine Arts, Hinckley, Ohio **AW:** First Place, Hyatt Regency Show, Cuyahoga Valley Art Center (2007); Best in Show, Stan Hywet Hall and Gardens, Akron, Ohio (2006); First Place Award, First Congregational Church of Akron (2005); First Place, Hyatt Regency Show, Lawrence Churski Gallery (2002); First Place, All Member Show (2001); First Prize, Cash Award, AIDS Benefit, Ohio (2000); First Place Award, 17th Annual Russell Show, Novelty, Ohio (1993); Merit Award, Arts Club of Washington (1980); Recipient, Numerous Best in Show Awards **MEM:** Founder, Sisters in Art (2008-Present); Womens Art League of Akron Ohio (1999-2000); Past President, Women's Art Club of Cleveland (1970-1971); Orange Branch of Cuyahoga County Public Library; Boardroom Advisory Group; Signature Member, Akron Society of Artists; Charter Member, Ohio Watercolor Society; Portrait Society of America; Associate, Pastel Society of America; Women Network **MH:** Lifetime Achievement Award (2017) **H:** Music; World Travel **PA:** Democrat **RE:** Catholic **ADD:** 923 Mayfair Rd, Akron, OH, 44303

KORTE, LEON, T: Accountant **I:** Education/Educational Services **CN:** University of South Dakota, Beacom School of Business **DOB:** 04/25/1952 **PB:** Hampton **SC:** IA/USA **PT:** Leuie Korte; Ruth (Westendorf) Korte **CH:** Kendra Marie; Kirsten Leigh **ED:** PhD, University of Nebraska

(1992); MBA, Ohio University (1979); BA, Northwestern College, Orange City, Iowa (1975) **CT:** CPA, Certified Management Accountant **C:** Associate Professor, Accounting, University of South Dakota, Vermillion, SD (1992-Present); Internal Auditor, Occidental/Nebraska Federal Savings Bank, Omaha, NE (1988-1990); Instructor, University of Nebraska, Omaha, NE (1983-1987); Instructor, Wayne State College (1979-1983); Revenue Auditor, Iowa Department of Revenue, Waterloo, Iowa (1975-1977) **CR:** Director, Institute of Rural Banking, Vermillion, SD **CIV:** Treasurer, Trinity Lutheran Church, Vermillion, SD (1999-2007); President, Trinity Lutheran Church, Vermillion, SD (1998); Vice President, Trinity Lutheran Church, Vermillion, SD (1997); Luther Center Campus Council, Vermillion, SD (1995-1997); Treasurer, Vermillion Area Arts Council (1994-1996) **MEM:** President, Institute of Management Accountants, Siouxland Chapter (1995-1996); Committee Member, American Accounting Association (1995-1996) **MH:** Albert Nelson Marquis Lifetime Achievement Award (2017) **H:** Genealogy; Photography **BA:** 414 E Clark St, USD, Beacom School of Business, Vermillion, SD, 57069

KOVACHY, EDWARD MIKLOS, I: Medicine & Health Care **DOB:** 12/03/1946 **PB:** Cleveland **SC:** OH/USA **PT:** Edward Miklos Kovachy; Evelyn Amelia (Palenscar) Kovachy **MS:** Married **SPN:** Susan Eileen Light (6/21/1981) **CH:** Timothy Light Kovachy; Benjamin Light Kovachy **ED:** MD, Case Western Reserve University (1977); MBA, Harvard University (1972); JD, Harvard University (1972); BA, Harvard University, Magna Cum Laude (1968) **CT:** Diplomate, National Board of Medical Examiners **C:** Private Practice in Psychiatry, Mediation, Executive Coaching, Menlo Park, CA (1981-Present); Chief Resident of Psychiatry, Stanford University Medical Center (1980-1981); Resident in Psychiatry, Stanford University Medical Center, Stanford, CA (1977-1981) **CR:** California Association of Marriage and Family Therapists (1999); Presenter, Annual Meeting, American Psychological Association (1998); Falk Fellow, American Psychiatric Association (1979-1981) **CIV:** National Co-Chairman Participation and Associates Giving, Harvard University (1999-Present); Co-Founder, Co-Producer, Harvard'68 Reunion Show (1983-Present); National Co-Chairman Participation, 50th Reunion, Harvard University (2018); 50th Reunion, Harvard University (2018); Alumni in Residence, Harvard Office of Career Services (2015); 45th Reunion, Harvard University (2013); National Co-Chairman Participation, 45th Reunion, Harvard University (2013); 40th Reunion, Harvard University (2008); National Co-Chairman Participation, 40th Reunion, Harvard University (2008); Harvard University Class of 1968 Reunion Program committee, 35th Reunion, Harvard University (2003); National Co-Chairman Participation, 35th Reunion, Harvard University (2003); Member, Board Advisors, Mid-Peninsula High School, Palo Alto, CA (2001-2012); Participation, 30th Reunion Chairman, West Coast, Harvard University (1998); Member, Gift Committee, Harvard University Class of 1968, 25th Reunion Chairman Participation, San Francisco, CA (1993); Trustee, Mid-Peninsula High School, Palo Alto, CA (1990-2001) **CW:** Co-Producer, Jolson and Company, Century Center for the Performing Arts, New York, NY (2002); Columnist, The Peninsula Times Tribune (1983-1985); Actor, Hasty Pudding Theatricals (1966) **AW:** Recipient, Richard T. Flood Award, Harvard University (2018); Recipient, Albert H. Gordon Award, Harvard University (2015); Recipient, Joseph R. Hamlen Award, Harvard University

(2013); Recipient, Albert H. Gordon Award, Harvard University (2011); Recipient, Joseph R. Hamlen Award, Harvard University (2008); Recipient, Albert H. Gordon Award, Harvard University (2007, 2005); Recipient, Joseph R. Hamlen Award, Harvard University (2003); Inductee, Hall of Fame, Shaker Heights High School Alumni Association (2003); Recipient, Albert H. Gordon Award, Harvard University (2000) **MEM:** Director, Harvard Alumni Association (2006-2009); Lifetime Member, Presenter of Annual Meeting, American Psychiatric Association (1998, 1984); Physicians for Social Responsibility; Association of Family and Conciliation Courts; Northern California Psychiatric Society **H:** Personal activism; Musical comedy; Athletics **RE:** Presbyterian **ADD:** 1187 University Drive, Menlo Park, CA, 94025

KRALLINGER, JOSEPH CHARLES, T: Certified Public Accoountant, Consultant, Entrepreneur, Writer **I:** Financial Services Member **DOB:** 05/29/1931 **PB:** Lancaster **SC:** PA/USA **PT:** Ferdinand Krallinger; Mathilde (Meyer) Krallinger **MS:** Married **SPN:** Hilde Eisenhauer Krallinger **CH:** Joanne Touchberry; Diane Schneider; Robert Krallinger **ED:** BS in Economics, Franklin & Marshall College, Cum Laude (1953) **CT:** Certified Public Accountant, Institute of Management Acconts **C:** Director, Business Advisor, Consultant, Investor, Various Industrial, Health Care, Mining, Oil and Gas Companies (1976-Present); Corporate Director (2006-Present); Author, (2006-Present); Consultant, Palm Desert, California (1988-2005); Consultant, Palm Desert, California (1988-2005); Vice President of Strategic Planning and Acquisitions, Berwind Corporation (1976-1988); Chief Financial Officer, Berwind Corporation (1976-1988); Partner, Arthur Andersen and Co. (Now split as Accenture) (1955-1976); Auditor, U.S. Army Audit Agency (1953-1955); Auditor, General Accounting Office (Now U.S. Government Accountability Office) (1953) **CR:** Director, Various Industries; Business Adviser, Various Industries; Consultant, Various Industries; Investor, Various Industries; Former Chairman of the Board, American Cancer Society **CIV:** President, Saint Genevieve Parish (1971-1976); Teacher of Religious Education, Saint Genevieve Parish (1971-1976); Board of Directors, Alumni Council, Franklin & Marshall College (1969-1975); Board of Directors, Citizens Council, Whitemarsh Township (1972-1975); Past Chairman, Board of Directors, Philadelphia Chapter, American Cancer Society, Inc. **MIL:** U.S. Army **CW:** Author, "Mergers and Acquisitions: Managing the Transaction," McGraw-Hill (1999); Author, "Fusiones y Adquisiciones De Enpresas," McGraw-Hill (1999); Author, "Mergers and Acquisitions: Managing the Transaction, Chinese Edition" (1997); Co-Author, "Strategic Planning Workbook," John Wiley & Sons (1989, 1993); Co-Author, "Planeacion Estrategica Practica," Compania Editorial Continental S.A. de C.V. (1991); Author, "How to Acquire the Perfect Business for Your Company," John Wiley & Sons (1991); Co-Author, "An Auditor's Approach to Statistical Sampling, Five Volumes" (1967-1972); Author, "Go From Piggy Bank To Millionaire — Save, Invest And Finance Wisely" **AW:** Honoree, Educators of the World (2008); Certificate of Merit, Institute of Management Accountants (1998); Crusade Award. American Cancer Society, Inc. (1985); Teaching Award, Saint Genevieve Parish (1985); National Volunteer Award, American Cancer Society, Inc. (1985); Honoree, Outstanding Intellectuals of the 21st Century; National Bronze Medal, American Cancer Society **MEM:** American Institute of CPAs; PICPA (Pennsylvania Institute Certified Public Accountants); Former President, Philadelphia Chapter, National Society of Accountants; Former President, Philadelphia

Chapter, Planning Forum (Now Professional Forums Ltd); Honorary Life Member, Philadelphia Chapter, American Cancer Society, Inc; Former President, Member, Institute of Management Accountants; Former President, Planning Executives Institute; Former Officer, Former Director, Ironwood Country Club, Palm Desert, CA; Communication Committee, McLendon Hills Property Owners Association **MH:** Albert Nelson Marquis Lifetime Achievement Award (2017) **H:** Golf; Racquet sports; Writing; Reading **ADD:** 636 McLendon Hills Dr, West End, NC, 27376

KREBS, WILLIAM H., T: Industrial Hygienist, Health Science Association Administrator. **I:** Medicine & Health Care **CN:** Industrial Health Sciences, Inc. **DOB:** 04/06/1938 **PT:** William Thomas; Mary Louise (Hoyt) K. **MS:** Married **SPN:** Jane Gerner Meikle (June 18); Susan Kathryn Bartholomew (August 8, 1964), (Divorced July 1976) **CH:** Elizabeth Louise; William Thomas II **ED:** PhD, University of Michigan (1970); MS, University of Michigan (1965); MPH, University of Michigan (1963); BS, University of Michigan (1960) **C:** President, Industrial Health Sciences, Inc. (2004-Present); Vice President, Industrial Health Sciences, Inc., Grosse Pointe Park, MI (1993-1994); Director, Industrial Hygiene Activity, GM Corp., Detroit, MI (1990-1993); Director, Toxic Materials Control Activity, GM Corp., Detroit, MI (1981-1990); Manager, Toxic Materials Control Activity, GM Corp., Detroit, MI (1977-1981); Industrial Hygienist, GM Corp., Detroit, MI (1970-1977); Industrial Hygienist, Lumbermens Mutual Casualty Co., Chicago, IL (1963-1964); Research Assistant, University of Michigan, Ann Arbor, MI (1962-1963) **CR:** Asbestos Advisory Committee, Michigan Occupational Health Standards Commission, Lansing, MI (1984-Present) **CIV:** Grosse Pointe Memorial Church; Grosse Pointe Farms (1954); Health and Safety Committee, Detroit Area Council; Boy Scouts of America (1980); Environment and Energy Committee, Detroit Regional Chamber **CW:** Contributor, Articles and Professional Journals **MEM:** President, International Occupational Hygiene Association (1992-1993); President, International Occupational Hygiene Association (1990-1991); Fellow, American Industrial Hygiene Association; President, American Industrial Hygiene Association (1988-1989); Board of Directors, American Industrial Hygiene Association (1986-1987); President, Michigan Industrial Hygiene Society (1980-1981); British Occupational Hygiene Society; Vice International Commission on Occupational Health; American Association for the Advancement of Science; American Public Health Association; Society of Automotive Engineers **RE:** Presbyterian **ADD:** 1014 Bishop Rd, Grosse Pointe Park, MI, 48230

KRISS, MICHAEL ALLEN, T: President **I:** Sciences **CN:** MAK Consultants **DOB:** 12/14/1940 **PB:** San Diego **SC:** CA/USA **PT:** Sidney Arthur Kriss; Bessy Leah (Talshinsky) Kriss **MS:** Married **SPN:** Gretchen Van Tries Renzel (6/23/1963) **CH:** Deborah; Aaron; Rebecca **ED:** PhD in Physics, University of California, Los Angeles (1969); MS in Physics, University of California, Los Angeles (1964); BA in Physics, University of California, Los Angeles (1962) **C:** President, MAK Consultants (2004-Present); Manager, Sharp Labs of America (1999-2003); Adjunct Professor, Executive Director, University of Rochester (1992-1999); Manager, Electronic Imaging Research Laboratories, Eastman Kodak Company, Rochester, NY (1988-1992); Manager, Research and Development, Kodak Japan, Tokyo, Japan (1985-1988); Laboratory Head, Research Laboratories, Eastman Kodak Company, Rochester, NY (1981-1985);

Senior Staff Member, Research Laboratories, Eastman Kodak Company, Rochester, NY (1974-1981); Senior Physicist, Research Laboratories, Eastman Kodak Company, Rochester, NY (1969-1974) **CR:** Adjunct Professor of Physics, Portland State University (2006-Present); Visitors Advisory Board to the Dean of the Physical Sciences, University of California at Los Angeles (2000-Present); Guest Professor, Department of Information and Computer Sciences, Chiba University (1994-1995); Member, West Irondequoit Board of Education (1990-1996); Guest Researcher, Mechanical Engineering Laboratory, National Institute of Advanced Industrial Science and Technology, Ministry of International Trade and Industry, Tsukuba, Japan (1990); Ad Hoc Committee, West Irondequoit School District (1988-1990); Member, West Irondequoit Board of Education (1982-1985) **CIV:** Member, West Irondoquoit School Board, Rochester, NY (1990-Present, 1983-1985); President, HOA Community **CW:** Editor-in-Chief, Three Volume Set, Wiley Handbook of Digital Imaging (2011-2015); Author, "Theory of Photographic Process" (1977); Contributor, Articles, Physical Review Letters; Contributor, Articles to the Journal of Low Temperature Physics; Contributor, Articles to the Journal of The Society of Photographic Science and Technology of Japan; Contributor, Articles to Professional Journals; Member, Editorial Review Board, Optics Encyclopedia, Wiley-VCH **AW:** Scientist of the Year, Society for Imaging Science and Technology Electronic Imaging Conference (2016); Honorary Member, Society for Imaging Science and Technology (2016); Named Electronic Imaging Scientist of the Year, Electronic Imaging Symposium, Society for Imaging Science and Technology (2016); Service Award, Electronic Imaging Conference (2009); Elected Fellow, Society of Imaging Science and Technology (2005); Davies Medal from Royal Photographic Society (1999); E.R. Davies Award for Scientific Merit, Royal Photographic Society of England (1999) **MEM:** IEEE; The Optical Society; Society for Imaging Sciences and Technology; Former Member, The New York Academy of Sciences; International Society for Optics and Photonics; Society of Motion Picture and Television Engineers; Society for Imaging Science and Technology; Sigma Xi; Sigma Pi Sigma **MH:** Albert Nelson Marquis Lifetime Achievement Award (2017) **H:** Softball; Taking good photos with good cameras **ADD:** 506 NE 193rd Ave, Camas, WA, 98607 **URL:** https://www.linkedin.com/in/michael-kriss-956b1214/

KROL, NANCY ANN, T: Nurse (Retired) **I:** Health, Wellness and Fitness **CN:** Kaleida Health **DOB:** 03/02/1949 **PB:** Buffalo **SC:** NY/USA **PT:** Walter S. Krol; Dorothy M. (Bojanek) Krol **ED:** Diploma in Nursing, Sisters of Charity Hospital, Catholic Health, Buffalo, NY (1970); RN, State of New York **CT:** Certified Critical Care Registered Nurse; Certified in Radiant Healing; Certified in Healing Touch for Animals; Certified Intuitive Healer, Spiritual Mentor, Holistic Healing Coach, Stillpoint Institute; Honorary Bachelor of Divinity, Universal Brotherhood **C:** Retired (2012); Charge Nurse, Preceptor, Staff Nurse, Surgical Intensive Care, VISICU, Transfer Center, Buffalo General Hospital, Kaleida Health (1980-2012); Staff Nurse, Neonatal ICU, Surgical Intensive Care Unit, OR, Recovery, Sisters of Charity Hospital, Catholic Health (1970-1980) **CR:** Appointed Panel Member, National Practitioner Data Bank (1997); Member, Nursing Education Study Group to Australia and New Zealand (1986); PA monitoring Study in Surgery During AAA Procedures; Created Patient Teaching Tools for Surgery,Recovery Room and Post-Op Care; Sisters of Charity Hospital, Catholic

Health (1970-1980) **CIV:** Supporter, Buffalo Zoo; Eucharistic Minister, Our Lady of Czestochowa Parish; Volunteer, SPCA Serving Erie County **CW:** Co-author, Play for International Critical Care Conference, Niagara Falls, New York (1994); Contributor, Articles, Nursing Newsletter, WNY-AACN **AW:** Margaret Driscoll Award in Obstetrics **MEM:** Publications Committee, Western New York Chapter, American Association of Critical Care Nurses (1989); Nominations Committee, American Association of Critical Care Nurses (1988); New York State Nurses Association; Buffalo Zoo; SPCA Erie County; Guiding Eyes for the Blind **H:** Intuitive healing; Healing touch for animals; Gardening; Travel **ADD:** 137 Pierce St., Buffalo, NY, 14206-3328

KROLICK, MERRILL A., T: Director of Cardiac Cath Lab and Interventional Cardiac Fellowship **I:** Medicine & Health Care **CN:** The Heart Institute at Largo **DOB:** 10/14/1959 **PB:** New York **SC:** NY/USA **PT:** Stanley David Krolick; Barbara Krolick **MS:** Single **CH:** Matthew; Alex **ED:** DO, College of Osteopathic Medicine, New York Institute of Technology (1985); BS, Rensselaer Polytechnic Institute (1981) **CT:** Board Certified, Internal Medicine, Cardiology, Interventional Cardiology, Endovascular Medicine **C:** Cardiologist, Heart Institute at Largo (1994-Present); Cardiologist, Prince William Cardiology, Manassas, VA (1992-1994) **CR:** Former Head, Pinellas County American Heart Association; Pinellas County Medical Society; Fellow, American College of Cardiology; Fellow, American College of Physicians; Fellow, American College of Osteopathic Internists; FASCAI; Fellow, American Board of Vascular Medicine **CIV:** President, American Heart Association, Pinellas County (1996) **CW:** Contributor, Articles, Medical Journals; Five-Minute Clinical Consultant, Southern Medical Journal **MEM:** American Medical Association; AKA **MH:** Albert Nelson Marquis Lifetime Achievement Award (2017) **H:** Collecting sports memorabilia **PA:** Republican **ADD:** 10316 Longwood Drive, Largo, FL, 33777

KRUESI, MARKUS JOHN POTTER MD, T: Professor Emeritus **I:** Medicine & Health Care **CN:** Medical University of South Carolina **ED:** Doctorate, University of Medicine and Dentistry of New Jersey (Now Rutgers, The State University of New Jersey) (1979); Resident, Medical College of Wisconsin; Resident in Psychiatry, Clinical Center, National Institutes of Health **CT:** Certified in Child & Adolescent Psychiatry, American Board of Psychiatry and Neurology, Inc.; Certified in Psychiatry, American Board of Psychiatry and Neurology, Inc.; Licensed to Practice Medicine, State of South Carolina **C:** Professor Emeritus, Medical University of South Carolina (2016-Present); Professor, Department of Psychiatry and Behavioral Sciences, Medical University of South Carolina; Training Director, Child and Adolescent Psychiatry Residency Training Program, Medical University of South Carolina; Director, Institute for Juvenile Research, University of Illinois; Head, Division of Child and Adolescent Psychiatry, University of Illinois; Researcher, Child Psychiatry Branch, The National Institute of Mental Health, National Institutes of Health **ADD:** 7 2nd Ave, Isle of Palms, SC, 29451

KRUMMEL, BRIAN, T: Visiting Assistant Researcher **I:** Education/Educational Services **CN:** University of California, Berkeley **ED:** PhD in Mathematics, Stanford University (2011); Coursework in Mathematics, University of Maryland, Baltimore County, Summa Cum Laude (2006) **C:** Visiting Assistant Researcher, University of California, Berkeley (2017-Present); Research Fellow, University of Texas at Austin (2015-2016);

Postdoctoral Research Fellow, University of Cambridge (2011-2015) **CIV:** Social and Networking Events Officer, Postdocs of Cambridge Society, University of Cambridge (2014-2015); Affiliate, Junior Warwick-Imperial-Cambridge Geometric Analysis Seminar (2013); Postdocs of Cambridge Society, University of Cambridge (2012-2014); Co-Organizer, Stanford Faculty Area Research Seminar (2007-2008); Affiliate, PCMI Summer Program, Park City, UT (2003) **CW:** Publisher, Papers, Professional Journals **AW:** Undergraduate Research Award, University of Maryland, Baltimore County (2006); Honoree, Meyerhoff Scholarship Program (2002-2006) **ADD:** 6401 Shellmound Street, Apt. 6314, Emeryville, CA, 94608 **URL:** https://math.berkeley.edu/~bkrummel/Curriculum%20Vitae%202017.pdf

KRUSE, CLEMENS SCOTT, T: Assistant Professor **I:** Education/Educational Services **CN:** Texas State University **MS:** Married **SPN:** Susan Hassell (5/1/1993) **CH:** Benjamin; Elizabeth **ED:** PhD, Health Related Sciences, Virginia Commonwealth University (2013); MS in Information Technology, University of Texas at San Antonio (2005); MHA in Healthcare Administration, Baylor University (2005); MBA in Management of Technology, University of Texas at San Antonio (2004); BS in Engineering Psychology, U.S. Military Academy, West Point, NY (2001) **CT:** Certified Six Sigma Green Belt; Certified Professional American College of Healthcare Executives; Certified Professional in Healthcare Information and Management Systems **C:** Assistant Professor, Texas State University (2013-Present); Healthcare IT Consultant, Kruse Consulting, Inc. (2011-Present); Adjunct Instructor, Capella University (2008-2013); Adjunct Instructor, Trinity University (2008-2009); Adjunct Instructor, Graduate Program, Health and Business Administration, Army-Baylor Department, Baylor University (2007-2017); Microsoft Certified Systems Engineer Fellow; Fellow, American College of Healthcare Executives **CIV:** Scoutmaster, Troop 90, Boy Scouts of America (2014-2017); Scoutmaster, Troop 475, Boy Scouts of America (2011-2014) **MIL:** Major, U.S. Army (1985-2011) **CW:** Author, "Telehealth and patient satisfaction: a systematic review and narrative analysis" (2017); Author, "Security Techniques for the Electronic Health Records" (2017); Author, "The effectiveness of telemedicine in the management of chronic heart disease – a systematic review" (2017); Author, "Challenges and Opportunities of Big Data in Health Care: A Systematic Review" (2016); Author, "Barriers to Electronic Health Record Adoption: a Systematic Literature Review" (2016); Author, "Cyber security in healthcare: A systematic review of modern threats and trends" (2016); Author, "Mobile health solutions for the aging population: A systematic narrative analysis" (2016); Author, "Telemedicine Use in Rural Native American Communities in the Era of the ACA: a Systematic Literature Review" (2016); Author, "Adoption factors of the EHR: A systematic review" (2016); Author, "The Effectiveness and Need for Facility Based Nurse Aide Training Competency Evaluation Programs" (2016); Contributor, Manuscripts **AW:** Presidential Distinction Award for Scholarly Activities, College of Health Professions (2016-2017) **MEM:** Healthcare Information and Management Systems Society (HIMSS); American Society for Quality **ADD:** 9006 Callaghan Road, San Antonio, TX, 78230 **URL:** https://www.linkedin.com/in/clemens-kruse-51a764b

KUDER, ARMIN, T: Lawyer **I:** Law and Legal Services **CN:** Kuder, Smollar, Friedman, & Mihalik, PC **DOB:** 11/14/1935 **PB:** Philadelphia **SC:** PA/USA **PT:** David Dennis Kuder; Ethel Rose (Strasburger) Kuder **MS:** Married **SPN:**

Margaret A. Trossen (7/26/2002); Patricia A. Hipple (6/28/1959, Divorced 3/1968) **CH:** Carlyn Elizabeth; Eric David; Keith Ulrich; Brendon Trossen (Stepson); Meghan Trossen (Stepdaughter) **ED:** LLB, Harvard University (1959); AB, Lafayette College (1956) **C:** Partner, Kuder, Smollar, Friedman, & Mihalik, PC, Washington D.C. (1978-Present); Partner, Kuder, Sherman Et Al., Washington D.C. (1968-1978); Partner, Smollar & Kuder, Washington D.C. (1967-1968); Associate, Mehler, Smollar Et Al., Washington D.C. (1965-1967); Associate, Coles & Goertner, Washington D.C. (1963-1965); Part-time Counsel, Kuder, Smollar, Friedman, & Mihalik, PC, Washington D.C. **CR:** Lecturer, Continuing Legal Education, Various Locations **CIV:** Member, International Steering Committee, The Bone and Joint Decade, Lund, Sweden (2000-Present); Treasurer, Arthritis and Rheumatism International (1998-Present); Member, Governor's Advisory Council on the Future of Nursing in Virginia (2002-2003); Board of Directors, Canadian Arthritis Network (2001-2002); President, Arthritis and Rheumatism International (1996-1998); Chairman, Arthritis Foundation, Atlanta, GA (1992-1994); Vice Chairman, Arthritis Foundation, Atlanta, GA (1990-1992); Chairman, New Art Association, Washington D.C. (1986-1987); Chairman, Hyde School, Bath, MI (1984-1987); Secretary, Combined Health Appeal, Washington D.C. (1984); Chairman, Center for Marine Conservation, Washington D.C. (1981-1983); Vice Chairman, Arthritis Foundation, Atlanta, GA (1979-1980); Chairman, National Institute of Mental Health Human Subjects Review Panel (1978-1983); Chairman, NCAC, National Health Agencies (1977-1978) **MIL:** United States Naval Reserve (1963-1966); Lieutenant Commander, Judge Advocate, General Corps, United States Navy (1959-1963) **AW:** Lifetime Service Award, Washington Psychiatric Society (2016) **MEM:** Chairman, Family Law Representation Committee, The District of Columbia Bar (2004-Present); Chairman, The District of Columbia Bar (1991-1992); Hearing Committee Chairman, Board on Professional Responsibility, The District of Columbia Bar (1985-1991); Trustee, Client Security Fund, The District of Columbia Bar (1984-1992); Fellow, American Academy of Matrimonial Lawyers; Fellow, IAFL; ABA; Maryland State Bar Association; Bar Association of Montgomery County; BADC **BAR:** Maryland State Bar Association (1987); United States District Court for the District of Maryland (1968); United States Court of Appeals for the Armed Forces (1962); The District of Columbia Bar (1959) **MH:** Albert Nelson Marquis Lifetime Achievement Award (2017) **H:** Traveling by Bus, Plane and Car; Golf **ADD:** 10317 Quarter Deck Ln, Berlin, MD, 21811

KUHLMAN, JAMES WELDON, T: County Extension Education Director (Retired) **I:** Education/Educational Services **DOB:** 02/13/1937 **PB:** Amarillo, TX **SC:** TX/USA **PT:** Herman Kuhlman; Alma Marie (Gerdsen) Kuhlman **MS:** Married **SPN:** Ann Bullock Davis (12/23/1967) **CH:** Lisa Ann; Jennifer Shawn **ED:** MS, University of Nebraska (1961); BS, West Texas State University (1959) **C:** Farmer, Randall County, TX (1955-Present); Education Director, Cerro Gordo County Extension, Iowa State University, Mason City, IA (1981-1997); Director, Worth County Extension, Iowa State University, Northwood, IA (1972-1981); Agent, Buffalo County Extension, University of Nebraska, Lincoln (1967-1972); Graduate Assistant, University of Nebraska, Lincoln (1959-1961); Teacher, West Texas State University,

Canyon, TX (1958-1959); Farmer, Buffalo County, NE (1955-1997) **CR:** Speaker, Various Civic Clubs (1980-Present); Flower Garden, Buchart Gardens, Victoria, Canada (1990-2001); Honorary Member, Texas State Historical Association, Randell County, TX **CIV:** Board of Directors, Central Gardens, Clear Lake, IA (2005-Present); Treasurer, Central Gardens, Clear Lake, IA (2005-Present); With, Congo Agriculture Project, North Central Office Presbytery (2006-2007); Treasurer, River City Trees (1998-2004); Chair Grants Committee, Mason City Iowa Convention and Visitors Bureau (1998-2000); Past President, Northern Iowa Figure Skating Club, Mason City, IA (1988-1989); Past Treasurer, Northern Iowa Figure Skating Club, Mason City, IA (1984-1987) **MIL:** U.S. Army Reserve (1961-1967) **CW:** Author, "When Herefords Were Supreme in Randall County, Texas" (2017); Author, "Seventy-Seven and going..." (2014); Author, "100 Year History of the Kuhlman Farm" (2012-2013); Author, "Reflections through a Milk Bottle: The Nebraska Years" (2004); Author, "From Kirchhatten to Canyon" (2001); Author, "The Block Pasture" (1998); Author, "The History of the Nance Hereford Ranch" (1996), Author, "This is Your Life - Holstein Queens" (1958) **AW:** Honorary Award, Randall County Texas Extension Service (2011); Hall of Fame, Iowa Hereford Breeders Association (2009); Named to Iowa's 4-H Hall of Fame (2005); Presentation Award, Rotary Club of Mason City (1995-2012); Distinguished Service Award, National Association County Agricultural Agents (1984); Top Award, Lions Club International, Northwood, IA (1979); Distinguished Presidential Award, Sertoma Club International, Kearney, NE (1966) **MEM:** Chair, Nominating Committee, Village Co-op Mason City (2011-2013); Nominating Committee, Village Co-op Mason City (2011-2018); Delegate, Annual Meeting, American Hereford Association (2011-2012); Past President, Rotary Club Mason City (2009-2010); Board of Directors, Rotary Club Mason City (2008-2010); President, Rotary Club Mason City (2008-2009); Leadership Excellence Award, Rotary Club Mason City (2008-2009); Chair, National Legislation Committee, Iowa Federation of National Association of Retired Federal Employees (2005-2008); Chair, Iowa PAC, Iowa Federation of National Association of Retired Federal Employees (2005-2008); Director, Iowa Hereford Breeders Association (2002-2008); Co-chair State Convention, National Association Retired Federal Employees (2001); Board of Directors, Rotary Club Mason City (2000-2003); Past, Vice Chair, North Central Iowa Geneology Club (1999-2000); President, North Central Iowa Geneology Club (1999-2000); Chair, Retiree Section, Iowa State University Council Ex Professionals (1999-2000); President, Local Chapter, National Association Retired Federal Employees (1998-1999); Committee Chair, Rotary Club Mason City (1997-2014); Director, Iowa Hereford Association (1991-1999); Voting Director, National Committee, National Association County Agricultural Agents (1990); Chairman, Regional Issues Committee, Mason City Chamber of Commerce (1990-1991); Committee Chair, Rotary Club Mason City (1988); Board of Directors, North Iowa Fair (1984-2009); Voting Director, National Committee, National Association County Agricultural Agents (1984); Agriculture Committee, Mason City Chamber of Commerce (1981-2004); Iowa Federation of National Association of Retired Federal Employees; Holstein Association of American; North Central Iowa Geneology Club; Rotary Club Mason City; Chair, Rotary Service, Rotary Club Mason City; Mason City Chamber of Commerce; Iowa State University Extension Association; Epsilon Sigma Phi; Honorary President, Sertoma Club **MH:** Marquis Who's Who Lifetime Achievement

Award (2017), Marquis Who's who Distinguished Humanitarian (2017) **H:** Genealogy; Writing; Gardening; Photography; Breeding cattle **RE:** Presbyterian **ADD:** 275 N Taft Ave Apt 118, Mason City, IA, 50401

KULLBERG, DUANE REUBEN, T: Managing Partner, Chief Executive Officer (Retired) **I:** Financial Services **CN:** Arthur Andersen & Co., S.C. **DOB:** 10/06/1932 **PB:** Red Wing **SC:** MN/USA **PT:** Carl Reuben Kullberg; Hazel Norma (Swanson) Kullberg **MS:** Married **SPN:** Susan Turley; Sina Nell Turner (10/19/1958, Deceased 9/1989) **CH:** Malissa Kullberg; Caroline Godellas **ED:** BBA, University of Minnesota (1954) **CT:** Certified Public Accountant **C:** Managing Partner, Chief Executive Officer, Arthur Andersen & Co., S.C. (1980-1989); Partner, Arthur Andersen & Co., S.C. (1967-1989); Vice Chairman, Accounting and Audit Practice Worldwide, Arthur Andersen & Co., S.C. (1978-1980); Deputy Managing Partner, Arthur Andersen & Co., S.C., Chicago, IL (1975-1978); Managing Partner, Arthur Andersen & Co., S.C., Minneapolis, MN (1970-1974); With, Arthur Andersen & Co., S.C. (1954-1989) **CIV:** Chair, Swedish Council of America (1999-2001); Chairman, Board of Trustees, University of Minnesota Foundation (1993-1995); United States Chair, New Sweden (1988); Leukemia and Lymphoma Society; Life Trustee, Art Institute of Chicago; Life Trustee, Northwestern University; Life Trustee, University of Minnesota Foundation **MIL:** U.S. Army (1956-1958) **AW:** Regents Award, University of Minnesota (1995); Legend in Leadership Award, Emory University (1992); Outstanding Achievement Award, University of Minnesota (1990); Decorated Commander, Royal Order of the Polar Star, Sweden (1989) **MEM:** Commercial Club of Chicago; Minneapolis Club **MH:** Albert Nelson Marquis Lifetime Achievement Award (2017) **H:** Reading; Plays; Art; Memoir writing **RE:** Protestant **ADD:** 1201 Yale Place, Apt. 1606, Minneapolis, MN, 55403

KUZMANIC, LILLIAN , I: Other **SC:** Denmark **C:** President, Palm Springs Womens Press Club (2014-Present); President, Homeowners Association (2015-2017); Board Member, Homeowners Association (2014-2015) **CR:** Sales in Electronics and Airlines; Domestic and International Marketing **H:** Walking; Meditation

KY, PAUL KUY-SEANG, T: Interventional Spine Specialist **I:** Health, Wellness and Fitness **CN:** 1)Advanced Pain Solutions 2) Ky Advanced Surgical Center **ED:** Fellowship, Department of Anesthesiology and Pain Medicine, School of Medicine, The Johns Hopkins University (2009); Resident, Department of Physical Medicine and Rehabilitation, School of Medicine, The Johns Hopkins University (2008); Family Medicine Intern, Downey Medical Center, Western University of Health Sciences (2005); DO, Touro College of Osteopathic Medicine, Vallejo, CA (2004); Coursework in Acupuncture Medicine, Xiamen University, Fujian, China (2000); Undergraduate Coursework, Business, California State University, Fresno (1990) **C:** Interventional Spine Specialist, Advanced Pain Solutions (2009-Present); Owner, Advanced Pain Solutions (2009-Present) **CW:** Co-Author, "Independent Medical Examinations: Facts and Fallacies" (2009); Co-Author, "Validation of ICD-9 code 787.2 for Identification of Individuals with Dysphagia from Administrative Databases" (2009); Co-Author, "Supratentorial Regions of Acute Ischemia Associated With Clinically Important Swallowing Disorders: A Pilot Study" (2008) **MEM:** American Osteopathic Association; Spine Interventional Society; American Academy of Physical Medicine and Rehabilitation; American

Society of Interventional Pain Physicians; **BA:** 6169 N Thesta St, Advanced Pain Solutions, Fresno, CA, 93710 **URL:** https://www.healthgrades.com/physician/dr-paul-ky-3h885

KYLMALA, MINNA MARGARETA, T: Cardiologist, Internist **I:** Medicine & Health Care **DOB:** 08/25/1971 **PB:** Helsinki **SC:** Finland **PT:** Jouko Juhani Kylmala; Karin Elisabeth Kylmala **SPN:** Mikko V. Haapio **ED:** PhD, Helsinki University, Finland (2014); Degree in Cardiology, Helsinki University, Finland (2014); Degree in Internal Medicine, Helsinki University, Finland (2007); MD, Helsinki University, Finland (1998) **CT:** EAE Certification in Echocardiography (2011) **C:** Cardiology Consultant, Helsinki University Hospital (2015-Present); Clinical Instructor, Helsinki University Hospital (2008-Present); Researcher, Division of Cardiology, Helsinki University Hospital (2005-Present); Fellow, Cardiology, Helsinki University Hospital (2007-2014); Fellow, Internal Medicine, Helsinki University Hospital, Finland (2001-2007); Resident, Internal Medicine, Selkameri Hospital, Kristiinankaupunki, Finland (1991-2001) **CR:** Junior House Officer, Necker-Enfants Malades Hospital, L'Universite Paris Descartes, France (1996-1997) **CW:** Contributor, Articles to Professional and Scientific Journals **AW:** Recipient, Kaj Tallroth's Award, Medical Society of Finland (2009); Recipient, Young Investigator's Award, Finnish Cardiac Society (2008) **MEM:** Chairman, Echocardiography Section, Finnish Cardiac Society (2015-Present); Editor, Medical Society of Finland (2011-Present); Secretary, Echocardiography Section, Finnish Cardiac Society (2013-2014); Board Member, Medical Society of Finland (2002-2008) **H:** Singing; Classical music; Golf; Boating **RE:** Evangelic Lutheran **BA:** Helsinki University Hospital, Heart-and Lung Center, Divsn Cardiology, PO Box 800, Helsinki HUS, Finland, 00029 **ADD:** Heinasuontie 2 A, Helsinki, Finland, 00430

LABIANCA, DOMINICK, I: Sciences **PT:** Dominick Leonard Labianca; Maria (Saulle) Labianca **MS:** Married **SPN:** Carol Ann Rudow (July 14, 1973) **CH:** Dominick Karl **CR:** Consultant and Expert Witness, DWI and Drug Cases **CW:** Member, Editorial Board, Forensic Toxicology & DWI Journal; Contributor, Articles, Various Scientific Journals **MEM:** American Association of University Professors; American Association for the Advancement of Science; National Science Teachers Association; New York Academy of Sciences; American Chemical Society; Sigma Xi

LANDIS, EDGAR DAVID, T: Corporate Executive (Retired) **I:** Business Management/Business Services **DOB:** 01/07/1932 **PB:** Myerstown **SC:** PA/USA **PT:** Edgar Michael Landis; Anna Irene (Dubble) Landis **MS:** Married **SPN:** Patricia Ann Leininger (6/13/1953) **CH:** Susan; Jean **ED:** MBA, Wharton School of the University of Pennsylvania (1957); BS, Lebanon Valley College (1953) **CT:** Certified Public Accountant (1959) **C:** Director, CDI Corp., Philadelphia, PA (1976-1998); Vice President, Senior Vice President, Executive Vice President, CDI Corp., Philadelphia, PA (1973-1997); Corporate Controller, Division Executive Vice President, Carlisle Corp., Pennsylvania (1964-1973); Accountant, Audit Supervisor, Peat, Marwick, Mitchell & Co. (Now KPMG), Philadelphia, PA (1957-1964) **CR:** Director, Sabal Palm Bank, Sarasota, FL (2006-2009); Director, Vice Chairman, Co-Chairman, Chairman, Allegiance Bank, Bala Cynwyd, PA (1998-2010); Consultant to CDI Corp., Philadelphia, PA (1998-2001) **CIV:** Director, YMCA, Sarasota, FL (1998-Present); Chairman, YMCA, Sarasota, FL (2008-2014);

Director, Branch Chairman, Vice Chairman, YMCA, Philadelphia, PA (1981-1997) **MIL:** First Cavalry Division, District Headquarters General's Staff, Hardy Barracks, US Army, Tokyo, Japan (1954-1956) **PA:** Republican **RE:** Methodist **ADD:** 988 Blvd of the Arts, Apt 511, Sarasota, FL, 34236

LANGBORT, POLLY, T: Advertising Executive **I:** Advertising & Marketing **PB:** New York **SC:** NY/USA **PT:** Julius Langbort; Nettie (Berman) Langbort **ED:** BA, Adelphi University **C:** Associate Publisher, Lear's Magazine (1990-1991); Executive Vice President of Marketing & Media Services, Y&R (1986-1990); Senior Vice President of Direct Marketing and Media Services, Wunderman Worldwide Division, Y&R (1985-1986); Senior Vice President of Communications Planning, Y&R (1980-1985); Vice President of Planning Development, Y&R (1975-1980); Vice President Group Supervisor, Y&R (1970-1975); Planning Supervisor, Y&R (1965-1970); Media Planner, Y&R (1960-1965); Media Buyer, Y&R; Secretary, Y&R **CIV:** Special Gifts Chairperson, American Cancer Society, Inc. (1985-1990) **CW:** Author, "DMA Factbook" (1986); Contributor, Articles to Professional Journals **MEM:** Boca Raton Resort and Club, Hilton Worldwide; The Club at Boca Pointe **H:** Classical music; Outdoor activities; Bridge **ADD:** 7614 La Corniche Circle, Boca Raton, FL, 33433

LANKFORD, GEORGE L., T: Attorney **I:** Law and Legal Services **CN:** Fanning, Harper, Martinson, Brandt & Kutchin, P.C. **MS:** Married **CH:** Two Sons **ED:** MBA, Texas Tech Graduate School of Business (1983); JD, Texas Tech School of Law (1983); BA in Economics, University of Texas at Austin (1979) **C:** Litigator, Fanning, Harper, Martinson, Brandt & Kutchin, PC (2016-Present); Partner, Martin, Disieri, Jefferson & Wisdom, LLP (2009-2016); Member, Fanning, Harper, Martinson, Brandt & Kutchin, PC (1991-2010) **CIV:** Active, Unit, District, and Council Levels, Boy Scouts of America; Active, Church **AW:** Robert E. Little Award for Outstanding Service to Scouting Movement, Circle 10 Council, Boy Scouts of America (2017); Section Chairman Rock Star" Award, State Bar of Texas (2015); Texas Super Lawyer, Thomson Reuters (2012-2016); Best Lawyers in America, Insurance Law, Woodward/White Inc. (2009-2016); Texas Super Lawyer, Thomson Reuters (2006-2007); Team Quarter Finalist, American Bar Association National Mock Trial Competition (1981); AV Preeminent Rating, Martindale-Hubbell **BAR:** Texas; United States Court of Appeals for the Fifth Circuit; United States District Court for the Northern District of Texas; United States District Court for the Southern District of Texas; United States District Court for the Eastern District of Texas; United States District Court for the Western District of Texas **BA:** 4849 Greenville Ave Ste 1300, Fanning, Harper, Martinson, Brandt & Kutchin, PC, Dallas, TX, 75206 **ADD:** 10372 White Rock Cir, Dallas, TX, 75238

LAPIDUS, ARNOLD, T: Engineer **I:** Engineering **CN:** Private Practice **DOB:** 11/06/1933 **PB:** Brooklyn **SC:** NY/USA **PT:** Morris Lapidus; Mollie Lapidus **MS:** Married **SPN:** Nancy Beatrice Latner (8/9/1952) **ED:** PhD, New York University (1967); MS, New York University (1967); BS, Brooklyn College (1956) **C:** Engineer, Private Practice, Englewood, New Jersey (1987-Present); Senior Engineer, Singer Electronic Systems Corporation (Now Singer Sewing Machine) (1986-1987); Professor, Fairleigh Dickinson University (1983-1985); Chair, Department of Computer and Decision Systems, Fairleigh Dickinson University (1983-1985); Associate Professor of Quantitative Analysis, Fairleigh Dickinson University (1973-

1983); Senior Member, Computer Sciences Technology Staff, Goddard Institute for Space Studies, National Aeronautics and Space Administration (1971-1973); Mathematics Analyst for Programming Methods, Goddard Institute for Space Studies, National Aeronautics and Space Administration (1970-1971); Mathematics Analyst for Computer Application, Goddard Institute for Space Studies, National Aeronautics and Space Administration (1968-1970); Research Scientist, Courant Institute of Mathematical Sciences, New York University (1956-1968) **CR:** Volunteer Mathematician, University of Medicine and Dentistry of New Jersey (Now Rowan University School of Osteopathic Medicine) (1998-2001); Owner, Advanced Mathematics Company (1987-2000) **CW:** Contributor, Articles, Professional Publications **MEM:** American Association for the Advancement of Science; American Association of University Professors; Mathematical Association of America; American Mathematical Society; Society for Industrial and Applied Mathematics **MH:** Albert Nelson Marquis Lifetime Achievement Award (2017) **ADD:** 5325 SW 76th Ter, Gainesville, FL, 32608

LARA, MARIA CECILIA, T: President **I:** Business Management/Business Services **CN:** Virtual Zone LLC **ED:** MBA, Nova University, Miami, FL (2017); BA, Business Administration and Management, Florida International University, Miami, FL (2013); AA, Business Administration, Miami Dade College, Miami, FL (2011); Coursework, Miami Dade College, Miami, FL (2000-2007); High School Diploma, Colegio Bethlemitas, Medellin, Colombia (1999) **CT:** Certified in Developing Management Skills, Eafit University, Medellin, Colombia (2017); Certified in Launching New Ventures, Harvard University (2017); Certified in Disruptive Innovation: Strategies for a Successful Enterprise, Harvard University (2017) **C:** Business Developer, Virtual Zone LLC (2009-Present); Chief Executive Officer, Virtual Zone LLC (2009-Present); Bartender, Mango's Tropical Cafe (2006-2009); Server, Mango's Tropical Cafe (2006-2009); Server, Hooter's Restaurant (2003-2006); Driver, Domino's Pizza (2002); Cashiers Supervisor, Chicken Kitchen (2001-2003) **BA:** 2350 NW 102nd Pl, Virtual Zone USA, Doral, FL, 33172

LAUERHASS, LUDWIG JR., T: History Professor **I:** Education/Educational Services **CN:** University of California, Los Angeles **DOB:** 01/06/1935 **PB:** Asheville **SC:** NC/USA **PT:** Ludwig Lauerhass, Sr.; Betty Bronson Lauerhass **ED:** MLS, University of California, Los Angeles (1976); PhD in History, University of California, Los Angeles (1972); MA in Latin American Studies, University of California, Los Angeles (1959); BA in Political Science, University of North Carolina, Chapel Hill, NC, With Honors (1957) **C:** Lecturer, Center for American Politics and Public Policy, University of California, Los Angeles, Washington, DC (1997-Present); Lecturer Emeritus, University of California, Los Angeles (1994-Present); Lecturer in History, University of California, Los Angeles (1973-Present); Professor, University of California, Los Angeles (2009-2014); History Department Recall, University of California, Los Angeles (2000); Director, Education Abroad Program, University of California, Los Angeles, Brazil (1995); History Department Recall, University of California, Los Angeles (1994-1996); Librarian Emeritus, University of California, Los Angeles (1994); Chair, Brazil Program, University of California, Los Angeles (1989-1994); Executive Director, Latin American Center, University of California, Los Angeles (1979-1984); Acting Director, Latin American Center, University of California, Los

Angeles (1978-1979); Assistant Director, Latin American Center, University of California, Los Angeles (1977-1978); Lecturer, Assistant Professor of History, University of California, Riverside (1975-1977); Latin American Bibliographer, University of California, Los Angeles (1968-1993); Teaching and Research Assistant, History and Latin American Studies, University of California, Los Angeles (1959-1963) **CR:** Visiting Professor, Washington, DC (1997-Present); Corresponding Member, Instituto Historico e Geografico Brasileiro (1997); Lecturer, Royal Viking Sun, Cunard Lines (1995) **CW:** Author, "American Memory, Monument and National Identity" (2016-Present); Principle Author, "Remember Hiroshima/Nagasaki: Compelling Images of the Atomic Experience" (2016); Co-Author, "Brazil in the Making" (2006); Editor, Reference and Special Studies Series, Latin American Center, University of California, Los Angeles; General Editor, Latin American Library Collection Guide Series, Latin American Center and University Library, University of California, Los Angeles; Contributor, Articles, Professional Journals **AW:** Hubert Herring Memorial Prize, Pacific Coast Council on Latin American Studies (1975) **MEM:** Various Committees, Seminar on Acquisition Latin American Library Materials (1970-Present); Projects and Publications Committee, Conference on Latin American History (1985-1987); Executive Board, Southern California Consortium on International Studies (1980-1981); President, Seminar on Acquisition Latin American Library Materials (1979-1980); President-Elect, Seminar on Acquisition Latin American Library Materials (1978-1979); Chair, Awards Committee, Pacific Coast Council on Latin American Studies (1977); Nominating Committee, Latin American Studies Association (1977); Governing Board, Pacific Coast Council on Latin American Studies (1975-1992); Vice President, Chair, Latin American Committee, Southern California Consortium on International Studies (1975-1984); American Historical Association; Cosmos Club **H:** Book collecting **ADD:** 11500 San Vicente Boulevard, Apartment 425, Los Angeles, CA, 90049

LAWRENCE, DAVID JR., T: Journalist, Early Childhood Advocate **I:** Publishing **CN:** The Children's Movement of Florida **DOB:** 03/05/1942 **PB:** New York City **SC:** NY/USA **PT:** David Lawrence Sr.; Wemple (Bissell) Lawrence **MS:** Married **SPN:** Roberta Phyllis Fleischman (12/21/1963) **CH:** David III; Jennifer Beth; Amanda Katherine; John Benjamin; Dana Victoria **ED:** LD, Johnson & Wales (2015); LD, St. Thomas University (2006); LD, Florida International University (2005); LD, Colgate University (1998); LD, Nova Southeastern University (1997); LD, University of Florida (1993); LD, Northwood University (1993); LD, Florida Memorial University (1992); LD, Barry University (1991); LHD, Northern Michigan University (1987); HHD, Lawrence Institute of Technology, Detroit, MI (1986); LHD, Siena Heights College (1985); Postgraduate Coursework, Advanced Management Program, Harvard University (1983); BS, University of Florida (1963) **C:** Founder, The Children's Trust (1999-Present); Publishing Chairman, The Miami Herald (1989-1999); Publishing Chairman, Detroit Free Press (1985-1989); Executive Editor, Detroit Free Press (1978-1985); Editor, Charlotte Observer (1976-1978); Executive Editor, Charlotte Observer, NC (1975-1976); Managing Editor, Philadelphia Daily News (1971-1975); Managing Editor, Palm Beach Post, FL (1969-1971); News Editor, Washington Post (1967-1969); Reporter, News Editor, St. Petersburg Times, FL (1963-1967) **CR:** Education and Communications Leadership Scholar, University of Miami **CIV:** Board of Trustees, Florida A&M

University; Former Member, Florida Children and Youth Cabinet; Founding Chair, The Children's Trust; Founding Chair, Miami-Dade/Monroe Early Learning Coalition **AW:** Humanitarian of the Year, The American National Red Cross (2009-Present); Spirit of Father Hall of Fame Inductees, National Partnership for Communications Leadership (2013); Living Legends, Miami Today (2013); Lewis Hine Award, Children and Youth (2002); Award of Excellence, American Public Health Association (2002); Lifetime Achievement Award, National Association of Minority Media Executives (2002); First Amendment Award, Scripps Howard (1993); Distinguished Service Award, National Association of Schools of Journalism and Mass Communications (1992); Silver Medallion Award, National Conference of Christians and Jews (1992); John S. Knight Gold Medal, Knight-Ridder (1988); Ida Wells National Award for the Advancement of Minorities, National Association of Black Journalists and National Conference of Editorial Writers (1988); First Amendment Freedoms Award, Anti-Defamation League (1988); National Human Rights Award, American Jewish Committee (1986); Distinguished Alumnus, University of Florida (1982) **MEM:** President, Inter-American Press Association (1995-1996); President, American Society of Newspaper Editors (1991-1992); Everglades Foundation; Americans for Immigrant Justice; The Children's Movement of Florida; Past Chair, New World School of the Arts; Miami Art Museum; Foundation for Child Development **BA:** 3250 SW 3rd Ave, The Children's Movement of Florida, Miami, FL, 33129 **URL:** http://childrensmovementflorida.org

LAWRENCE, E. JACK, T: Attorney **I:** Law and Legal Services **CN:** Jack Lawrence, Attorney at Law **DOB:** 09/23/1949 **PB:** Beaumont **SC:** TX/USA **PT:** Edward Jack Lawrence; Nelda Rae (McClure) Lawrence **ED:** JD, University of Houston (1988); Coursework in Legal Studies and Criminal Justice, University of Houston-Clear Lake (1983-1985); BA in Government, Lamar University (1971) **CT:** Certified Secondary Level Social Studies Teacher; Certified Secondary Level English Teacher **C:** Private Practice, Beaumont, TX (1990-Present); Attorney, East Texas Legal Services, Beaumont, TX (1989) **CIV:** Board Member, Progressive Democrats of Southeast Texas (2016-Present); Board of Directors, Clean Air and Water Organization (1996-Present); Board Directors, American Civil Liberties Union, Beaumont, TX (1978-2008); Southeast Texas Hike & Bike Coalition **CW:** Author, "Who Nullified Jury Nullification?" Lone Star Fully Informed Jury Association **MEM:** Jefferson County Bar Association; State Bar of Texas; Texas Bar College **BAR:** U.S. Supreme Court (1995); U.S. District Court, Eastern District, State of Texas (1993); State of Texas (1988) **MH:** Albert Nelson Marquis Lifetime Achievement Award (2017) **H:** Golf; Tennis; Poetry; Astronomy; Guitar **PA:** Democrat **RE:** Methodist-Unitarian **ADD:** 5570 Winfree Street, Beaumont, TX, 77705 **URL:** https://www.avvo.com/attorneys/77705-tx-jack-lawrence-173190.html

LAZOR, JOHN DENNIS, T: Operating Principal **I:** Business Management/Business Services **CN:** CapRock Pacific **ED:** BA in Finance, Kent State University (1976) **CT:** Certified Commercial Investment Member, CCIM Institute (1978) **C:** Partner, Operating Principal, CapRock Pacific (2017-Present); Chief Executive Officer, United Global Investments, LLC (2016-2017); Chief Executive Officer, Lion Investments Inc. (2000-2016) **AW:** Recipient, Award for CCIM, Commercial Real Estate Institute (1978); Named, Top Listing Broker in Ohio (1978); Recipient, Speaker Award on Complex

Leasing, International Council of Shopping Centers **MEM:** Advisory Board, President of United States (2017-Present); International Council of Shopping Centers; American Council of Real Estate; Realtors National Marketing Institute; American Apartment Owners Association **BA:** 445 Marine View Ave Ste 300, Caprock Pacific, Del Mar, CA, 92014 **ADD:** PO Box 2034, Rancho Santa Fe, CA, 92067

LE BON, JOËL, I: Advertising & Marketing **PT:** Luc Le Bon; Maisy Le Bon **CR:** Consultant in Marketing Strategy, Customer Relationship Management, Sales Strategy & Leadership (2001-Present); Founding Director, European Center of E-Business, Cergy-Pontoise, France (2001-Present); Visiting Research Scholar, Stephen Stagner Sales Excellence Institute, C. T. Bauer College of Business, University of Houston (2006-2007); Post-Doctoral Visiting Scholar, Institute for the Study of Business Market, Smeal College of Business, Pennsylvania State University (1998-1999); Lecturer in Marketing, University of Paris-Dauphine, France (1991-1998) **CW:** Editorial Board Member, Journal of Global Fashion Marketing, Korean Academy of Marketing Science (2009-Present); Editorial Board Member, Journal of Personal Selling and Sales Management (2009-Present); Editorial Board Member, Journal of Global Academy of Marketing Science, Korean Academy of Marketing Science (2009-Present); Co-Author, "Key Account Management: Strategies to Leverage Information, Technology, and Relationships to Deliver Value to Large Customers," Business Expert Press, New York City, NY (2015); Co-Author, "Competitive Intelligence and the Sales Force: How to Gain Market Leadership through Competitive Intelligence," Business Expert Press, New York City, NY (2014); Contributor, Articles to Professional Journals, Chapters to Books; Author, Books **MEM:** Co-Chair, Global Sales Science Institute Conference, Mauritius (2017); Workshop Facilitator, Faculty Sales Consortium, Marketing and Sales Interface Workshop, American Marketing Association, Fort Worth, TX (2013); Track Chair, Global Marketing Conference, Negotiation, Relationship Selling and Global Account Management Track, Tokyo, Japan (2010); Director, Observatory of Payment Policy in Asia, ESSEC Business School (2009-2010); SMRR Singapore Marketing Research Round Table, INSEAD, NUS, NTU, SMU/ESSEC (2009-2010); Track Chair, Academy of Marketing Science Conference, Electronic and Interactive Marketing Track, May, Vancouver, Canada (2008); Abstract Review Board, Journal of Personal Selling and Sales Management (2002-2005); Teaching & Pedagogical Committee Member, ESSEC Business School (2000-2006); Research Committee Delegate, Novancia Business School (1995-1997); Elected Member, Scientific Council, University of Paris-Dauphine, France (1991-1994); Elected Member, Post Graduate Council, University of Paris-Dauphine, France (1991-1992); American Marketing Association; Academy of Marketing Science; Society for Marketing Advances; Global Sales Science Institute; Chief Academic Researcher & Higher Education Representative, American Association of Inside Sales Professionals; Vice Chair of Digital Enablement & Development, Global Sales Science Institute; Vice Chair of the Africa Forum, Global Sales Science Institute; Vice Chair for Conference Programming, American Marketing Association Sales Special Interest Group; European Marketing Academy; French Marketing Association

LE QUÉRÉ, JEAN FRANÇOIS MARIE, T: Scientific Instrumentation Researcher **I:** Sciences **CN:** Paris Diderot University **DOB:** 04/07/1933 **PB:** Pabu **SC:** France **PT:** Yves Marie Le Quéré; Yvonne Marie Rose (Olivier) Le Quéré **MS:** Married **SPN:** Jacqueline Marie Le Colas (3/26/1964) **CH:** Anne Marie; Isabelle Marie; Jean-Yves Marie; Blandine Marie **ED:** DEng, University of Pierre and Marie Curie, Paris, France (1983); Engineer Physicist Graduate, National Conservatory of Arts and Industry (1968); Upper Technical Diploma, National Conservatory of Arts and Industry, Paris, France (1965) **C:** Engineering Researcher, Paris Diderot University (1972-Present); Engineering Researcher, Paris Diderot University (1972-1996); Member, Faculty, Paris Diderot University (1972-1994); Engineering Physicist, Paris Diderot University (1968-1972); Laboratory Upper Research Technician, Paris, France (1965-1968); Laboratory Technician, Paris, France (1961-1965); Electrician, Regie Renault, Paris, France (1950-1961) **MIL:** French Army (1953) **CW:** Contributor, Articles to Professional Journals **MEM:** President, Association of Teaching (1996) **MH:** Albert Nelson Marquis Lifetime Achievement Award (2017) **ADD:** 22 rue Pierre Brossolette, Noisy-le-Grand, France, 93160

LEE, SANG BAE, T: Senior Laboratory Scientist **I:** Sciences **CN:** Aramco Services Company **DOB:** 05/25/1973 **PB:** Youngdeok-gun **SC:** Republic of Korea **PT:** Lee, Sang Bae (Father); Kim, Young Ja (Mother) **ED:** PhD in Mining and Geological Engineering, The University of Arizona, Tucson, AZ (2007); MS in Earth System Sciences, Yonsei University, Seoul, Republic of Korea (2001); BS in Earth and Environmental Sciences, Andong National University, Andong, Republic of Korea (1999) **CT:** Certified Applied Geologist - First Level, Human Resources Development Service of Korea (1998); Certified Sales Manager - Second Level, Korea Chamber of Commerce and Industry (1996) **C:** Senior Laboratory Scientist, Aramco Research Center - Houston, Aramco Services Company (2018-present); Rock Mechanics Subject Matter Expert, Chesapeake Energy Corporation (2017-2018); Supervisor, Reservoir Technology Center, Chesapeake Energy Corporation (2014-2017); Rock Mechanics Team Lead, Chesapeake Energy Corporation (2012-2014); Senior Geomechanics Engineer, Baker Hughes (2008-2012); Geotechnical Engineer, Korea Infrastructure Safety and Technology Corporation (2002-2003); Geotechnical Engineering Intern, Korea Institute of Construction Technology (2000) **CR:** Rock Mechanics, Rock Fracture Mechanics, Geomechanics **MIL:** Korean Army (1993-1995) **CW:** Author, "Rock Mechanics for Unconventional Formations," Training Book, Chesapeake Energy Corporation, Oklahoma City, OK (2017); Author, "Ultrasonic Test Redesigns Sample Geometries, Identifies High-Resolution Anisotropy in Shale," Oil and Gas Journal (2016); First Author, "Comparison of Different Methods to Estimate Unconfined Compressive Strength in a Barnett Shale," Proceedings of the 50th United States Rock Mechanics/Geomechanics Symposium, American Rock Mechanics Association, Houston, TX (2016); Author, "Calibration of Rebound Hardness Numbers to UCS in Shale Formations," Journal of Petroleum Technology, Young Technology Showcase (2015); Primary Inventor, "New Application of Rebound Hardness Numbers to Generate Logging of Unconfined Compressive Strength in Laminated Shale Formations," Proceedings of the 48th United States Rock Mechanics/Geomechanics Symposium, American Rock Mechanics Association, Minneapolis, MN (2014); First Author, "Stress-Dependent Brittle-to-Ductile Deformation of Tuff in Geothermal Wells," Proceedings of the 46th United States Rock Mechanics/Geomechanics Symposium, American Rock Mechanics Association, Chicago, IL (2012); Author, "Rock Mechanics and Rock Mechanical Properties," Training Book Publication, Baker Hughes, Houston, TX (2011); First Author, "Modified PTS Test and Clump Modeling on Mixed Mode Crack Growth in Granite," Proceedings of Golden Rocks 2006, the 41st United States Symposium on Rock Mechanics, American Rock Mechanics Association, Golden, CO (2006); Co-Author, "Mode II Subcritical Crack Growth Parameters," Proceedings of Golden Rocks 2006, the 41st United States Symposium on Rock Mechanics, American Rock Mechanics Association, Golden, CO (2006); First Author, "Comparison Analysis of Factor of Safety on Rock Slope in Boeun Region Using Limit Equilibrium Method and Distinct Element Method," Journal of Geotechnical Engineering (2003); First Author, "Rock Cut Slope Stability Analysis in Sinpal-Ildong Region Using Distinct Element Method," Proceedings of the 10th Congress on Rock Mechanics: International Society for Rock Mechanics (2003); Technology Roadmap for Rock Mechanics, Gauteng, Johannesburg, Republic of South Africa (2003); First Author, "Comparison Analysis of Factor of Safety on Rock Slope in Boeun Region Using Limit Equilibrium Method and Distinct Element Method," Proceedings of the Korean Geotechnical Society, KGS Spring Conference, Seoul, Republic of Korea (2002); First Author, "Analysis of Factor of Safety on Rock Slope in Boeun Region Using Barton-Bandis Joint Model," Proceedings of the Korea Society of Economic and Environmental Geology, Spring Cooperation Scientific Conference, Seoul, Republic of Korea (2001); First Author, "Rock Slope Stability in Boeun Region Considering Properties of Discontinuities," Journal of Economic and Environmental Geology (2001); Author, Articles, Professional Journals; Contributor, Conference/Symposium Publications **AW:** Core Values Reward and Recognition, Baker Hughes (2011); Trade Secret Award, Baker Hughes (2011); Patent Award, Baker Hughes (2011) **MEM:** Society of Petroleum Engineers (2008-Present); International Society for Rock Mechanics (2007-Present); American Rock Mechanics Association (2006-Present) **H:** Go game, Movie **BA:** 16300 Park Row Drive, Houston, TX, 77084 **ADD:** 85-4, Deokgok-gil, Youngdeok-gun, Korea South, 36432 **URL:** https://www.linkedin.com/in/ji-soo-lee-41943431

LEE POWELL GEBHARD, JOY, T: Small Business Owner **I:** Education/Educational Services **CN:** Healing, Inc. **DOB:** 01/29/1936 **PT:** Yong Joon Lee; Chun Jal Lee **MS:** Married **SPN:** Karl Ten Eyck Gebhard (10/15/1995); Jimmy Wayne Powell (9/24/1960) **CH:** Chun Jal Lee; Miran Victoria; D. Gebhard **ED:** Postgraduate Coursework, Central State University, Oklahoma (1967-1968); BA, Wayland Baptist University, Plainview, TX (1966); Graduate Coursework, McMurry College, Abilene, TX (1956-1958); ·Graduate Coursework, National University of Pusan (1953-1955); Graduate Coursework, International Speech Academy, Pusan, Korea (1952) **CT:** Certified Antique Appraiser and Consultant **C:** Founder, Healing Inc. (1997-Present); Teacher, Spanish, Carl Albert High School (1969); Teacher, Oklahoma City School Systems (1968-1970); Head, Social Studies Department, Dunjee High School (1968); Special Study of Prejudice Among Children Grades 1-12, Public Opinion and Propaganda (1965-1966); Washington Post, U.S. Academy of Science (1960); Secretary, Retired Choir Organizer, Chaplain's Office, American University, Washington, DC (1958-1960); Secretary, Retired Choir Organizer, Chaplain's Office, U.S. A.S.C. Office, Ploydada, TX (1958); Secretary, Retired Choir Organizer, Chaplain's Office, Methodist Mission, Pusan, Korea (1955-1956); Secretary, Retired Choir Organizer, Chaplain's Office, UN Army Division 8069, Pusan, Korea (1954-1956); News Anchor, Pusan Radio Station (1953); Nurse, Rok Medical School, Pusan, Korea (1950-1953); Owner, International Antiques, Upperville, VA **CR:** Co-founder, Washington Korean Writers Association, Fairfax, VA (2008); Charter Member, Literary Magazine, Hiang **CIV:** Meadow Peace Park; Founder, Meadow Peace Park; Board Member, Washington Association for Korean School; Board Member, Korean American Culture Committee; Board Member, Korean Schools U.S.; Buchanan Hall, Upperville, VA **CW:** Author, Poetry, New Voices in American Poetry (1978); Contributor, Articles, Professional Journals; Contributor, Poems and Essays, Korean Periodicals **AW:** Writers Award, Sigma Tau Delta **MEM:** Sigma Tau Delta, McMurry College, Abilene, TX (1957); Fauquier County Chamber of Commerce; World Affairs Council of Washington; Yale Club of Washington; National History Preservation; Smithsonian Associates; President, Washington Jeonju Lee Chosun Dynasty Royal Family Association **MH:** Albert Nelson Marquis Lifetime Achievement Award (2017) **H:** Music; Writing; Swimming; Collecting; Travel **ADD:** PO Box 221, Upperville, VA, 20185

LEIBOVIC, K. NICHOLAS, T: Professor Emeritus, Biomedical Researcher **I:** Education/Educational Services **CN:** University at Buffalo **DOB:** 06/15/1921 **SC:** Lithuania **MS:** Single **SPN:** Vera Coppard (2005, Deceased 2017); Marianne Karpf (1944, Deceased 1998) **CH:** Three Sons **ED:** Degree in Engineering, Trinity College, University of Cambridge (1944); Degree in Mathematics, Birkbeck College, University of London (1943) **C:** Professor Emeritus, University at Buffalo (1996); Professor, University at Buffalo (1963-1996); Professor, Department of Biophysics and Physiology, University at Buffalo (1963); Adjunct Professor, Department of Ophthalmology, University at Buffalo; Assistant Director, Center for Theoretical Biology, University at Buffalo; Center for Cognitive Science, University at Buffalo; Numerous Committees, University at Buffalo; Researcher in Cybernetics, Westinghouse Research Laboratories, Pittsburgh, PA **CR:** Lecturer, Spain (2013); Lecturer, Italy (2012); Lecturer, United States and Abroad; Visiting Scholar, The Hebrew University of Jerusalem; Visiting Scholar, University of California, Berkeley; Visiting Scholar, Harvard University; Teacher, Courses on Human Behavior and Physics, Canterbury Woods, Episcopal Church Home & Affiliates, Inc., Buffalo, NY **CW:** Author, Numerous Scientific Papers, Professional Journals; Contributor, Book Chapters; Author, Books on Information Processing in the Nervous System, Nervous System Theory and Science of Vision **MEM:** Society for Neuroscience; Teaching Lessons of Holocaust, Adult and Student Groups, Holocaust Resource Center of Buffalo **H:** Drawing; Painting **ADD:** 735 Renaissance Drive, Apt. K-303, Buffalo, NY, 14221

LEIBOWITZ, HERMAN MAX, T: Attorney, Songwriter, Author **I:** Law and Legal Services **CN:** Herman Max Leibowitz **PB:** New York City **SC:** NY/USA **PT:** Sidney Leibowitz; Lillian (Pack) Leibowitz **MS:** Married **SPN:** Lorna (Ziprin) Leibowitz **CH:** Gabriel B. Leibowitz **ED:** JD, Rutgers Law School, Rutgers, The State University of New Jersey (1975); BS in English & American Literature, The City College of New York (CCNY) (1972) **CT:** Certified Law Guardian, New York State Supreme Court; Certified Article 81 Court Evaluator, New York State Supreme Court **C:** Attorney, Herman Max Leibowitz, Esq. (1976-Present); Songwriter and Author, Hank Fellows (Pen Name) (1972-Present) **CR:** Hundreds of Performances of His Patriotic and Inspirational Songs Across America by Schools, Churches and Civic Groups (2006-Present); Participant, More than 40 New York City and New

Jersey 9/11 Ceremonies Featuring His 9/11 Songs (2003-Present); Successful Oral Argument and Verdict, Case of Cia. Naviera Financiera Aries, S.A. v. 50 Sutton Place South Owners, Inc., United States Court of Appeals for the Second Circuit (2012); Author and Publisher, Children's Book, "Sirius, The Hero Dog of 9/11" (2009); Programs and Personal Performances across America as "Hank Fellows - America's Songwriter" CIV: Participant, Trial Judge and Presiding Judge, Annual Yale Mock Trial Tournament, Yale University, New Haven, CT (2007-Present) CW: Author and Publisher, Children's Book, "Sirius, The Hero Dog of 9/11" (2009); Speaker, Commencement Day, Rutgers Law School, Rutgers, The State University of New Jersey (1975); Composer of Approximately 100 Songs, Including "The Spirit of America," "Halfway to Heaven (A 9-11 Tribute)," "One Heart, One Voice," "The Men Who Built America," "The Tree of Life," "Take My Hand," "One Star," "Gloucester, Always Gloucester," and "6,000,000"; Composer, Lyricist and Producer, Cabaret Musical Revues, "An Open Stage," "Crosstown Rhythms," and "Late City Express," (1979-1984) Manhattan, NY; Associate Editor, Law Review, Rutgers, The State University of New Jersey AW: Citation of Merit for "Exceptional Songwriting Skills" in the Presentation of His Songs at 9-11 Ceremonies Honoring the 144 Bronx Residents Who Died on 9/11/01, Borough President of Bronx County, New York City, NY (2017); "Service Above Self" Community Service Award, Rotary Club of Jersey City, Rotary International (2008); Award for "Commitment and Dedication to Our Community," in Honoring the 38 Residents of Jersey City Killed in the Twin Towers on September 11, 2001, 9/11 Memorial Committee of Jersey City, Inc. (2007); Citation for "Continued Generosity and Devotion to the Remembrance of September 11th," New York City Council (2006); Five "Popular Music Awards," ASCAP; Special Achievement Award, Unisong International Song Contest MEM: Committee on Trusts & Estates, New York State Bar Association; Committee on Elder Law, New York State Bar Association; Senior Class President, Rutgers Law School, Rutgers, The State University of New Jersey; 9/11 Memorial Committee of Jersey City, Inc. BAR: Supreme Court of the United States (1982); New York State Bar Association (1976); New Jersey State Bar Association (1975); United States District Court for the Southern District of New York; United States District Court for the Eastern District of New York; United States Court of Appeals for the Second Circuit H: Photography; Gardening; Family Vacations BA: 56 W 45th St Ste 1004, Herman Max Leibowitz, New York, NY, 10036 URL: https://www.AmericasSongwriter.com

LEIGHTON, LAWRENCE W., T: Investment Banker, Managing Director **I:** Financial Services **CN:** Bentley Associates L.P. **DOB:** 07/01/1934 **PB:** New York City **SC:** NY/USA **PT:** Sidney Leighton; Florence (Ward) Leighton **MS:** Married **SPN:** Karen Chase (10/12/2013); Mariana Stoock (6/21/1959), Deceased 4/2008 **CH:** Michelle S.; Sandra L. Galvin **ED:** MBA, Harvard University (1962); BS in Engineering, Princeton University, New Jersey (1956) **CT:** Commercial Pilot License **C:** Managing Director, Bentley Associates L.P., New York (1997-Present); Managing Director, LM Capital Corp. (1994-1996); Vice-Chairman, 2I, Inc. (1993-1994); President, CEO, UI USA (subsidiary Credit Agricole) (1989-1993); Managing Director, Chase Investment Bank (1983-1988); Ltd. Partner, Bear, Stearns & Co. (1978-1982); Director of Strategic Planning, Mergers & Acquisitions, Norton-Simon, Inc. (1974-1978); Vice President, Co-Head, Corporate Finance Department, Clark, Dodge & Co., Inc. (1970-1974); Vice President,

Kuhn Loeb & Co., New York (1962-1969) **CR:** Board of Directors, China XD Plastics (2009) **CIV:** Trustee, Gillen Brewer School, Trustee, Waterford Institute (1985-Present); Member, National Finance Committee, Pete DuPont for President (1986-1988); Chairman, Harvard Business School Fund, New York (1964-1965) **MIL:** Lieutenant, U.S. Navy (1957-1960) **MEM:** Scholarship Committee, Princeton Club of New York (1970-Present); Board of Governors, Princeton Club of New York (1989-1996); Chairman, Princeton University Scholarship Committee (1964-1984); Stanwich Club, Greenwich, CT; Mid Ocean Club, Bermuda **H:** Flying; Golf; Photography **BA:** 250 Park Avenue, Suite 1101, Bentley Associates, LP, New York, NY, 10177 **ADD:** 1088 Park Avenue, New York, NY, 10128

LEIGHTON, SALLY BRIGGS, T: Attorney **I:** Law and Legal Services **CN:** Fitzer, Fitzer, Veal and McAmis **ED:** JD, Seattle University (1979); BS, Texas Tech University, Magna Cum Laude **C:** Of Counsel, Fitzer, Fitzer, Veal and McAmis PS (1981-Present) **CIV:** Past Chair, Mary Bridge Children's Hospital Foundation; Board of Directors, Carol Milgard Breast Center; Board of Directors, Multicare Health System; Past Chair Board of Trustees, Annie Wright School; Past Board of Trustees, Pierce County Bar Association; Greater Tacoma Community Foundation, past board member and Chair **MEM:** Associate, American Board of Trial Advocates (2008); Fellow, American Leadership Forum; Pierce County Bar; Washington State Bar; Washington Defense Trial Lawyers; Defense Research Institute; American Board of Trial Advocates; Washington Health Care Risk Management **BAR:** Texas; Washington **H:** Traveling **BA:** 1102 Broadway Ste 401, Fitzer, Fitzer, Veal and McAmis, Tacoma, WA, 98402 **ADD:** 5204 N Bennett St Apt 303, Ruston, WA, 98407 **URL:** http://f2vm.com/our-team/sally-leighton

LEMANN, THOMAS, T: Lawyer (Retired) **I:** Law and Legal Services **CN:** Liskow & Lewis **DOB:** 01/03/1926 **PB:** New Orleans **ED:** MCL, Tulane University (1953); LLB, Harvard University (1952); AB, Summa Cum Laude, Harvard University (1949) **C:** Of Counsel, Liskow & Lewis, New Orleans (1998-Present); Partner, Monroe & Lemann, New Orleans (1958-1998); Associate, Monroe & Lemann, New Orleans (1953-1958) **CIV:** Board of Directors, Zemurray Foundation, Hever Foundation, Hawkins Foundation, Parkside Foundation, Azby Fund, Azby Art Fund, Greater New Orleans Foundation (1996-2005); New Orleans Museum Art (1986-1992); President, Arts Council of Greater New Orleans (1975-1980); Board of Directors, Visiting Committee, Art Museums, Harvard University (1974-1980); Trustee, Metairie Park Country Day School (1956-1971); President, Metairie Park Country Day School (1967-1970); New Orleans Philharmonic Symphony Society (1956-1978); Flint-Goodridge Hospital (1960-1970); President, Louisiana Civil Service League (1974-1976); Secretary, Trust Advisory Committee, Chairman Mayor's Cultural Resources Committee (1970-1975); Arts Council of New Orleans, Musica da Camera; Member, Council of Louisiana State Law Institute; **MIL:** Served with Army of the United States, 1944-46, PTO **MEM:** American Law Institute; Society Bartolus; New Orleans Country Club; Wyvern Club (New Orleans); Phi Beta Kappa **BAR:** American Bar Association; Louisiana Bar Association; New Orleans Bar Association; New York City Bar Association **RE:** Jewish **ADD:** 6020 Garfield St, New Orleans, LA, 70118

LENFEST, HAROLD FITZGERALD, T: Philanthropist, Cable Television Executive, Lawyer **I:** Law and Legal Services **CN:** The Lenfest Group **DOB:** 05/29/1930 **PB:** Jacksonville **SC:** FL/USA **PT:** Harold Churchill Lenfest; Herrena (FitzGerald) Lenfest **MS:** Married **SPN:** Marguerite Brooks (7/9/1955) **CH:** Diane; H. Chase; Brook **ED:** DHL, Dickinson College (2014); DHL, Drexel University (2013); LLD, Webb Institute of Naval Architecture and Marine Engineering (2013); Honorary DHL, Columbia University (2009); Honorary DHL, Widener University (2006); Honorary DHL, Washington and Lee University (2004); Honorary DHL, Temple University (2002); Honorary DHL, Ursinus College (2000); LLB, Columbia University (1958); AB, Washington and Lee University (1953) **C:** President & CEO, Lenfest Group, Inc., West Conshohocken, PA (1974-Present); President, Suburban Cable TV Co. (1974-2000); Editorial Director, Seventeen Magazine, New York City, NY (1970-1974); Managing Director, Communications Division, Triangle Publications, New York City, NY (1970-1974); Associate Counsel, Triangle Publications, Philadelphia, PA (1965-1970); Associate, Davis Polk & Wardwell, New York City, NY (1958-1965) **CR:** Owner & Chairman, Philadelphia Inquirer, Daily News, Philly.com (2012-2015); Board of Directors, C-SPAN (1995-2000); Board of Directors, CAM Systems (1995-2001); Board of Directors, TelVue, Inc. (1990-2017); CEO, StarNet, Inc. (1989-2001); CEO, Cable AdNet, Inc. (1981-1992); Officer, Board of Directors, Pennsylvania Cable & Telecommunications Association (1976-1979); Chairman, Video JukeBox, Inc.; Board of Directors, Voice FX, Inc.; Board of Directors, Australis Media Ltd., Australia; Board of Directors, Videopole, France; Board of Directors, Cable Advertising Bureau; Board of Directors, Liberty Media Corp.; Board of Directors, TCI West, Inc.; President, Philadelphia Cable Club **CIV:** Chairman Emeritus, Lenfest Institute for Journalism (2017-Present); Chairman Emeritus, Museum of the American Revolution (2017-Present); Chair, Executive Committee, Temple University (2016-Present); Chairman Emeritus, Curtis Institute of Music (2014-Present); Chairman Emeritus, James Madison Council, The Library of Congress (2014-Present); Trustee, Temple University (2013-Present); Chairman Emeritus, Philadelphia Museum of Art (2010-Present); Board of Directors, Museum of the American Revolution (2005-Present); Fellow, Philadelphia College of Physicians (2004-Present); Trustee, Member of Executive Committee, Chesapeake Bay Foundation (1995-Present); Trustee, Philadelphia Museum of Art (1993-Present); Member, James Madison Council, Library of Congress (1989-Present); President, Permanent Class Council, Columbia University Law School (1956-Present); Chairman, Lenfest Institute for Journalism (2015-2017); Founding Chair, Advisory Council, Columbia University Global Policy Initiative (2013); Chairman, Philadelphia Inquirer, Philadelphia Daily News & Philly.com (2012-2015); Chairman, Interstate General Media LLC (2012-2015); Board of Directors, Bok Foundation (2012-2014); Honorary Board Founding Member, Opera Philadelphia (2012); Board of Governors, National Geographic Educational Foundation (2011-2013); Board of Directors, National Park Foundation (2007-2008); Chairman, James Madison Council, Library of Congress (2007-2014); Chairman, Curtis Institute of Music (2006-2014); Chairman, Museum of the American Revolution (2005-2016); Chairman, Business Leaders for Catholic Schools (2005-2007); Member, Board of Trustees, George C. Marshall Federation (2004-2007); Member, Philadelphia Children's Commission (2004-2008); Board of Directors, Smithsonian (2003-2004);

Chairman, Philadelphia Museum of Art (2001-2010); Trustee, Columbia University (2001-2013); National Campaign Chair, Washington and Lee University (2000-2004); President, Board of Regents, Mercersburg Academy (1994-1997); Trustee, Washington and Lee University (1989-1998); Board of Regents, Mercersburg Academy (1989-1997); Trustee, Walter Kaitz Foundation, Oakland, CA (1986-1988); Member, Board of Visitors, Columbia University Law School (1974-1978) **MIL:** Active Duty, U.S. Naval Reserve (1962); Captain, U.S. Naval Reserve (1953-1976); Active Duty, U.S. Naval Reserve (1953-1956) **AW:** Carnegie Medal of Philanthropy (2017); Publisher's Award for Service to Journalism, Poynter Institute (2016); Lafayette Prize, French-American Cultural Foundation (2016); Distinguished Service Award, National Maritime Historical Society (2015); Business Leader of the Year Award, LeBow College of Business, Drexel University (2015); Man of the Year, US Rowing (2014); Eagle Gold & Anchor Award, Philadelphia Chapter, Marine Corps/Scholarship Foundation (2013); Cable Hall of Fame, Cable Center (2012); Officier Legion d'honneur, Order National de France (2010); Gold Medal for Distinguished Achievement, Pennsylvania Society (2009); Citizen of Year Award, Children's Scholarship Fund Philadelphia (2009); Philadelphia Award (2008); Movers & Shakers Award, Philadelphia Ad Club (2008); William Penn Award, Greater Philadelphia Chamber of Commerce (2008); Crystal Award, Union League of Philadelphia (2008); Award of Philanthropy, Council of Independent Colleges (2008); Musser Excellence in Leadership Award, Fox School of Business, Temple University (2006); Joseph C. Donchess Distinguished Service Award, Wyoming Seminary (2006); Horatio Alger Award (2006); Robert P. Casey Medal, Association of Independent Colleges and Universities of Pennsylvania (2005); International Outstanding Philanthropist of the Year Award, Association of Fundraising Professionals (2005); Woodrow Wilson Award, International Center for Scholars, Smithsonian Institution (2005); Individual Philanthropist of Year, Greater Philadelphia Association of Fundraising Professionals (2004); Citizen of Year, PenJerDel Council (2004); Americanism Award, Anti-Defamation League (2004); Vision for Philadelphia Award, Philadelphia Hospitality, Inc. (2003); Russell H. Conwell Award, Temple University (2003); Patron of the Year Award, Governor of Pennsylvania (2002); Individual Leadership Award, Philadelphia Arts and Business Council (2002); Cable Operator of Year, Pennsylvania Cable & Telecommunications Association (1999); Order of the Coif, Washington & Lee University Law School (1999); Distinguished Alumnus Award, Columbia University School of Law (1997); Award of Excellence, Philadelphia Area Easter Seal Society (1993) **MEM:** Honorary Member, Society of the Cincinnati; Mayflower Society; Athenaeum of Philadelphia; Council on Foreign Relations; American Philosophical Society; American Antiquarian Society; American Society of the French Legion of Honor; Society of Colonial Wars; Phi Beta Kappa **BAR:** New York State Bar (1959) **MH:** Albert Nelson Marquis Lifetime Achievement Award (2017) **BA:** 300 Barr Harbor Drive, Suite 460, West Conshohocken, PA, 19428 **ADD:** 1400 Waverly Road, Gladwyne, PA, 19035 **URL:** https://www.medalofphilanthropy.org/lenfest-h-f-gerry-marguerite/

LEONARD, JERRY W., I: Internet **DOB:** 01/01/1900 **ED:** JD, University of North Carolina at Chapel Hill (1970) **CIV:** Board Member, American Society for the Prevention of Cruelty to Animals; Migrant Farm Workers Legal Defense Agency **AW:** Recipient, Legal Aid, National Legal Services (2005) **MEM:** Migrant Workers Legal Association; ACLU; White County Bar Association

LEONG, CAROL, T: Personal Care Industry Executive **I:** Health, Wellness and Fitness **CN:** Carol Leong Electrolysis **DOB:** 01/09/1942 **PB:** Sacramento **SC:** CA/USA **PT:** Walter Richard; Edith (Bond) Bloss **MS:** Single **SPN:** Oliver Arthur Fisk, III (1964-1973) **CH:** Victoria Kay **ED:** Degree in Esthetics, Zenzi's College (1998); Degree, Western Business College (1964); BA in Sociology, San Jose College (1963); Degree in Electrolysis, Bay Area of Electrolysis (1978) **CT:** Certified in Microdermabrasion (1998-Present); Certified Clinical Professional Electrologist (1984); Certification in Electrolysis, Bay Area College of Electrolysis (1978); Registered Electrologist **C:** Owner, Carol Leong Electrolysis, San Mateo, California (1978-Present); Model, Various Organizations (1951-2006); Director of Personnel, Kroger Food Corporation (1967-1968); Employment Counselor, Businessmen's Clearinghouse (1966-1967) **CR:** Neutraceutical Consultant, Market America Company (2008-Present); Member, Professional Women's Forum (1988-Present); Principal Designs by Carol (1987-Present) **CIV:** Indian SOS for Elephants (2015-Present); St. Joseph's Indian School (2012-Present); National Audubon Society (2015-Present); National Wildlife Federation (2007-Present); National Parks Conservation Association (2016-Present); The Nature Conservancy (1995-Present); Best Friends Animal Society (1992-Present); Volunteer, National Kidney Foundation of Northern California (1995-2012); Civic Garden Club (1995-2012); Business Network International (2008); President, Northern Chapter, Electrologists Association of California (2006-2008); President, Peninsula Auxiliary Lighthouse for the Blind (1984-1985, 1995-2002); National Federation of Republican Women (1996); First Vice President, Peninsula Auxiliary Lighthouse for the Blind (1993-1995) **MIL:** US Air Force-Military Wife 1964-1967 **CW:** Contributor, Articles, Professional Publications **AW:** Plaque, President of the Electrolysis Association of Northern California (2006-2008); Recipient, Certificate of Appreciation, San Francisco Lighthouse for the Blind (1981-1983); Miss San Jose, Miss America Pageant (1962); Who's Who of American Women, Who's Who in the West, Who's Who in Finance and Industry, Who's Who in America **MEM:** President, Electrologist Association of Northern California; Continuing Education Committee, International Guild of Professional Electrologists; National Association of Female Executives; Professional Women's Forum; Peninsula Humane Society; San Francisco Zoological Society; Friends of Filoli; American Electrologists Association; Electrologists Association of Northern California; International Platform Association; Order of the Eastern Star; Chi Omega **H:** Golf; Tennis; Ballet; Theater; Photography: Walking; Travel **PA:** Republican **RE:** Presbyterian **BA:** 11201 Gold Express Dr Ste 230, Carol Leong Electrolysis, Gold River, CA, 95670 **URL:** http://www.carolleongelectrolysis.com

LESTER, WILLIAM, I: Sciences **PT:** William Alexander Lester, Sr.; Elizabeth Frances (Clark) Lester **CR:** Board on Chemical Sciences and Technology, National Science Foundation Panel Theoretical & Computational Chemistry (2008); Board on Chemical Sciences and Technology, National Institutes of Health Molecular Structure & Function Study Section (2007-2010); Board of Trustees, Gordon Research Conferences (2006-2012); Board on Chemical Sciences and Technology, National Research Council (2004-2006); Selection and Scheduling Committee, Gordon Research Conferences (2000-2006); Department of Energy Advisory Committee on Advanced Science Computing, National Medal of Science (2000-2004); President, Committee National Medal of Science (2000-2002); External Visiting Committee, National Partnership for Advanced Computational Infrastructure (1999-2002); Advisory Board, Model Institutions for Excellence, Spelman College (1997-2004); Council Member, Gordon Research Conferences (1997-2000); Technical Assessment Board, U.S. Army Research Laboratory, National Research Council (1996-1999); Assistant to Director, Human Resource Development, Office of Advanced Science Computing Program (1995-1996); Committee on Mathematical Challenges from Theoretical Computational Chemistry, National Research Council (1994-1995); Committee on High Performance Computing and Communication: Status of a Major Initiative, National Research Council (1994-1995); Blue Ribbon Panel on High Performance Computing, National Science Foundation (1993); Federal Networking Council Advisory Committee (1991-1995); Steering Committee, National Research Council (1987-1988); Chairman, Office of Advanced Science Computing Program (1987); Advisory Committee, Office of Advanced Science Computing Program (1985-1987); Committee on Recommendations for U.S. Army Basic Science Research, National Research Council (1984-1987); Committee to Survey Chemical Sciences, National Research Council (1982-1984); Chemical Division Advisory Panel, National Science Foundation (1981-1983); Member, National Research Council Panel on Chemical Physics, National Bureau of Standards (1980-1983); Chairman, Gordon Conference Atomic and Molecular Interactions (1978); United States National Committee, International Union of Pure and Applied Chemistry (1976-1979); Consultant, National Science Foundation (1976-1977); Chemistry Research Evaluation Panel, Air Force Office of Scientific Research (1974-1978); Lecturer, Chemistry, University of Wisconsin (1966-1968); Senior Fellow, Science and Engineering, Office of Advanced Science Computing Program **CW:** Member, Advisory Board, Communications in Analysis and Geometry (1997-Present); Co-editor, "Advances in Quantum Monte Carlo" (2012); Member, Advisory Board, Autobiography of William A. Lester, Jr., The Journal of Physical Chemistry (2008); Member Advisory Board, A Symposium in Honor William A. Lester, University of California, Berkley (2007); Member, Advisory Board, Journal of Chemical Physics (2006-2008); Co-editor, "Recent Advances in Quantum Monte Carlo Methods, Part II" (2002); Co-editor, "Contemporary Problems in Mathematical Physics" (2000); Editor, "Recent Advances in Quantum Monte Carlo Methods" (1997); Co-author, "Monte Carlo Methods in Ab Initio Quantum Chemistry" (1994); Member, Advisory Board, Science (1989-1993); Member, Editorial Board, Computer Physics Communications (1981-1986); Member, Editorial Board, Journal of Computational Chemistry (1980-1987); Member, Editorial Board, Journal of Physical Chemistry (1979-1981); Editor, "Proceedings of Conference on Potential Energy Surfaces in Chemistry" (1971); Author, Over 200 Papers, Professional Journals **MEM:** President, Sigma Xi (2000-2001); Committee on Development, Sigma Xi (1999-2006); Chair, Sigma Xi (1998-2000); Vice President, University of California Berkeley Chapter, Sigma Xi (1998-2000); Board of Directors, Sigma Xi (1998-1999); Lectureships Committee, Sigma Xi (1993-2002); National Board of Directors, American Association for the Advancement of Science (1993-1997);

Committee on Nominations, American Association for the Advancement of Science (1988-1991); Chairman, Division of Chemical Physics, American Physical Society (1986); Executive Board, National Organization for the Professional Advancement of Black Chemists and Chemical Engineers (1984-1987); Chairman, Division of Physical Chemistry, American Chemical Society (1979); Treasurer, Division of Computers in Chemistry, American Chemical Society (1974-1977); Secretary-Treasurer, Wisconsin Section, American Chemical Society (1967-1968); Fellow, American Association for the Advancement of Science; Council Delegate, Chemistry Section, American Association for the Advancement of Science; California Academy of Sciences; Fellow, National Organization for the Professional Advancement of Black Chemists and Chemical Engineers; International Academy of Quantum Molecular Science

LEVIN, CHARLES LEONARD, I: Law and Legal Services **DOB:** 04/28/1926 **PB:** Detroit **SC:** MI/USA **PT:** Theodore and Rhoda (Katzin) L. **CH:** Arthur, Amy, Fredrick **ED:** Honorary LLD, Detroit College of Law (1980); LLB, University of Michigan (1947); BA, University of Michigan (1946) **C:** Associate Justice, Michigan Supreme Court (1973-1996); Judge, Michigan Court of Appeals, Detroit (1966-1973); Partner, Levin, Levin, Garvett & Dill, Detroit (1951-1966); Private Practice Lawyer, Detroit (1950-1966); Private Practice Lawyer, New York City (1948-1950) **CR:** Michigan Law Revision Commission (1966) **CIV:** Trustee, Marygrove College (1971-1977); Chairman, Marygrove College (1971-1974); Member, Visiting Committees to Law Schools, University of Michigan and University of Chicago (1977-1980); Wayne State University **MEM:** American Law Institute **BAR:** DC Bar Association (1954); US Supreme Court (1953); New York Bar Association (1949); Michigan Bar Association (1947)

LEVIN, GILBERT, T: Biotechnology Company Executive I: Biotechnology **CN:** Biospheres (Now Spherix) **DOB:** 04/23/1924 **PB:** Baltimore **SC:** MD/USA **PT:** Henry I. Levin; Lillian R. (Richman) Levin **MS:** Married **SPN:** Karen Bloomquist (10/25/1953) **CH:** Ron L.; Henry L.; Carol Y. **ED:** PhD, Johns Hopkins University (1963); MS, Johns Hopkins University (1948); EdB, Johns Hopkins University (1947) **CT:** Registered Professional Engineer, District of Columbia; Registered Professional Engineer, State of Maryland **C:** Co-investigator, European Habit Experiment Space Agency, Mars Express 2020, National Aeronautics and Space Administration (2008-Present); Executive Science Officer, Spherix Inc., Beltsville, MD (2003-2008); Board Chairman, Spherix Inc., Beltsville, MD (1967-2008); Chief Executive Officer, Spherix Inc., Beltsville, MD (1967-2003); Director, Life Systems Division, Hazleton Laboratories, Inc. (Now Covance Inc.) (1963-1967); Vice President, Resources Research, Inc., Washington, DC (1955-1963); Department of Health, District of Columbia (1951-1955); California Department of Public Health (1950-1951); Department of Health, State of Maryland (1948-1950) **CR:** Fellow, American Public Health Association **CIV:** Trustee, John Hopkins University (1982-1985) **MIL:** Merchant Marine, U.S. Coast Guard (1944-1946) **CW:** Editorial Board, BioScience (1960-1963); Contributor, 150 Articles, Professional Journals; Contributor, Over 100 Patents in Field **AW:** Distinguished Alumnus Award, Johns Hopkins University (1995); Whiting Medal, Johns Hopkins University (1987); Public Service Medal, National Aeronautics and Space Administration (1977); Newcomb Cleveland Prize, American Association for the Advancement of Science (1977) **MEM:** American Society of Civil Engineers; American Association

for the Advancement of Science; American Society for Microbiology; American Water Works Association; Water Pollution Control Federation; New York Academy of Sciences; Cosmos Club **MH:** Albert Nelson Marquis Lifetime Achievement Award (2017) **H:** Sailing; The discovery of life on Mars; Reading; Writing; Technical and scientific exchanges; Research **PA:** Independent **RE:** Humanist **ADD:** 8100 Connecticut Avenue, Apt. 314, Chevy Chase, MD, 20815

LEVIN, HARVEY JAY, T: Financial Institution Design and Construction Specialist, Developer, Auctioneer I: Consumer Goods and Services **CN:** Harv Levin, Inc. Auctioneers **DOB:** 04/27/1936 **PB:** Fitchburg **SC:** MA/USA **ED:** PhD in Philosophy of Business Management, La Salle University (1996); MA in Economics, University of New Hampshire (1970); BBA in Finance, University of Massachusetts, Amherst (1960); Coursework, Harvard University; Coursework, University of Maryland; Coursework, Boston University; Coursework, Brandeis University; Coursework, Auction Marketing Institute **CT:** Certified Auctioneer, Certified Auctioneers Institute at Indiana University, National Auctioneers Association (1993); Certified Accredited Auctioneer of Real Estate, AARE (1990); Licensed Auctioneer, State of Vermont; Licensed Auctioneer, State of Rhode Island; Licensed Auctioneer, State of New Hampshire; Licensed Auctioneer, State of Florida; Licensed Auctioneer, Commonwealth of Massachusetts; Licensed Auctioneer, State of Maine; Licensed Commercial Pilot, Federal Aviation Association (Now Federal Aviation Administration); Certified Real Estate Broker, State of Rhode Island; Certified Real Estate Broker, State of New Hampshire; Certified Real Estate Broker, Commonwealth of Massachusetts; Certified Real Estate Broker, State of Florida **C:** President, Harv Levin, Inc., Auctioneers (1986-Present); President, Wentworth By The Sea-Harborview Homeowners Association (2010); Vice President, Financial Concepts, Inc. (1980-1985); Consultant Service Manager, Bank Building Corporation (1974-1980); Director of Marketing and Sales, New England Homes (1973-1974); Vice President, Shelter Resources (1972-1973); Director of Marketing and Sales, Spacemakers (1970-1972); General Manager, Great Northern Homes (1966-1970); President, Central Tool Warehouse (1959-1966); President, American Bank Design, Inc.; President, Credit Union Building Corporation; Consultant, Personal Development Seminars **CR:** President, Hazel Dell Limited Partnership (1986-Present); Speaker in Field; Consultant, Republic Homes **CIV:** President-Elect, Parents Council, University of New Hampshire (1995); Chairperson, Parents Fund, University of New Hampshire (1993-1995); President, Pheasant Run Condominium Association (1993-1995); Chairman, School Building Committee, Kensington, NH (1985) **MIL:** U.S. Army (1955-1957) **CW:** Author, Personal Seminars; Lecturer, Personal Seminars; Author, Professional Seminars; Lecturer, Professional Seminars **AW:** Honorary Lieutenant Colonel, Aide-De-Camp, Governor of Alabama (1978); First Place Design Award, Bank Building Corporation of America (1977); Honor Award (1976); Best Marketing and Sales Plan Award, Automation In Housing Association (1972); National Housing Awards; Outstanding Sales Achievement Award; 50-Year Membership Award, Masons; Award For Best Elderly Housing Project, Farmers Home Administration **MEM:** Aircraft Owners and Pilots Association; Wentworth by the Sea Country Club; Hampton River Boat Club; Kennebunkport River Club (Now Kennebunk River Club); Portsmouth Power Squadron Club (Now United States Power Squadrons); Masons; Phi Sigma Kappa; Lifetime Member, National Auctioneers Association; New

Hampshire Auctioneers Association; Auction Marketing Institute (Now National Auctioneers Association); Lifetime Member, Florida Auctioneers Association; Associate, Massachusetts Auctioneers Association **MH:** Albert Nelson Marquis Lifetime Achievement Award (2017) **ADD:** PO Box 2114, New Castle, NH, 03854

LEVIN, JOSHUA Z., T: Computer Scientist I: Information Technology and Services **CN:** Levicar **DOB:** 02/05/1949 **PB:** Cambridge **SC:** MA/USA **PT:** Betty Louise Zimmermann; Herschel Levin **MS:** Married **SPN:** Susan Evelyn Goldsmith (1982), Divorced (2003) **CH:** David Reuven; Barry Naphtali **ED:** PhD in Computer and Systems Engineering, Rensselaer Polytechnic Institute (1980); MSEE, New York University (1974); BA in Physics, Queens College, With Honors (1971) **C:** Founder, Chief Creative Officer, LeviCar Unlimited, Marlton, NJ (2003-Present); Quality-Assurance Controller, Motorola Mobility LLC (1995-1998); Chief Computer Scientist, Epoch Engineering Inc. (1988-1994) **CIV:** Member, Metanexus Institute (2002-2003); Member, Beth Sholom Congregation (2000-2003) **MEM:** American Association for the Advancement of Science; IEEE; SAE International; The Phi Beta Kappa Society **MH:** Albert Nelson Marquis Lifetime Achievement Award (2017) **PA:** Democrat **RE:** Jewish **ADD:** 124 Arbor Ln, Marlton, NJ, 08053

LEVIN, MICHAEL JOSEPH, T: Lawyer I: Law and Legal Services **CN:** Wrobel Markham LLP **DOB:** 02/01/1943 **PB:** Detroit **SC:** MI/USA **PT:** Bayre Levin; Lydia Ruth (Kahn) Levin **MS:** Married **SPN:** Adah Hanson (8/3/1974) **CH:** Andrew; Stephen **ED:** JD, University of Michigan Law School (1967); Honorary BA, Johns Hopkins University (1964) **C:** Partner, Wrobel Markham LLP, New York, NY (2017-Present); Of Counsel, Simon & Partners LLP, New York, NY (2016-2017); Of Counsel, Barger & Wolen LLP (Now Hinshaw & Culbertson LLP), New York, NY (2000-2016); Of Counsel, Menaker & Herrmann LLP, New York, NY (1997-2000); Partner, Eversheds Sutherland LLP, New York, NY (1993-1997); Partner, Eversheds Sutherland LLP, Washington, D.C. (1993-1997); Partner, Boyle, Vogeler & Haimes, New York, NY (1986-1993); Associate, Milbank, Tweed, Hadley & McCloy LLP, New York, NY (1971-1986); Lawyer, Wrobel Markham LLP **CR:** Lecturer, "How to Try A Commercial Case"; Lecturer, "How to Try a Civil Case in Federal Court"; Counsel, New York Stock Exchange, Chapter 11 Case, Drexel Burnham Lambert; Appellate Defense Counsel, United States Court of Military Appeals **CIV:** Affiliate, Marine Corps Association; National Museum of the Marine Corps **MIL:** Lieutenant Colonel, U.S. Marine Corps (1963-1990); Marine Corps Officer, Prosecutor, Defense Counsel, Military Judge, U.S. Marine Corps **MEM:** State Bar of Michigan; New York State Bar Association; Association of the Bar of the City of New York; ABA **BAR:** New York (1973); Michigan (1969) **MH:** Albert Nelson Marquis Lifetime Achievement Award (2017) **BA:** 360 Lexington Ave Ste 1502, Wrobel Markham LLP, New York, NY, 10017 **ADD:** 1781 Fernwood Lane, Plainfield, NJ, 07060 **URL:** http://www.simonlawyers.com/michael_levin.html

LEVIN, S. MICHAEL, T: Owner I: Law and Legal Services **CN:** SMLevinLaw **DOB:** 07/31/1944 **PB:** New York City **SC:** NY/USA **ED:** JD, The George Washington University (1969); BA in Political Science, The George Washington University (1966) **C:** Principal, SMLevinLaw (2012-Present); Outside General Counsel, Japonica (1996-Present); Of Counsel, Winograd Shine Land & Finkle, PC (2005-2012); Partner, Chairman Litigation Department,

Edwards & Angell (1987-1995); Partner, McDermott Will and Emery (1984-1987); Attorney-in-Charge, Southeast Organized Crime Strike Force, U.S. Department of Justice (1980-1983); Deputy Chief Counsel, Senate Permanent Subcommittee on Investigations, United States Senate (1979-1980); Trial Attorney, Criminal Division, U.S. Department of Justice (1971-1979); Law Clerk to Honorable Edward A. Beard, Superior Court of the District of Columbia (1969-1970) **CR:** Adjunct Professor, Trial Advocacy Program, University of Miami School of Law (1984-1987); Member, Committee to Implement Standards Admission Practice, United States District Court Southern District of Florida **AW:** Albert Nelson Marquis Lifetime Achievement Award (2017); Named, Super Lawyers, Business Litigation (2013-2018); AV Preeminent Martindale-Hubbell Peer Review Rated **MEM:** President, South Florida Chapter, Federal Bar Association (1983-1984); ABA **BAR:** Rhode Island (1988); United States District Court Southern District of Florida (1982); Florida (1982); United States Court of Appeals for the Fifth Circuit (1981); United States Court of Appeals for the Eleventh Circuit (1981); Supreme Court of the United States (1980); United States Court of Appeals for the First Circuit (1975); United States District Court District of Rhode Island (1973); The District of Columbia (1970); Virginia (1970); United States Court of Appeals District of Columbia Circuit (1970); United States Court of Appeals for the District of Columbia Circuit (1970) **MH:** Albert Nelson Marquis Lifetime Achievement Award (2017) **ADD:** 33 Saddle Ridge, Bloomfield, CT, 06002 **URL:** https://www.linkedin.com/in/s-michael-levin-0b0ab94/

LEVINSON, KEN, T: Partner **I:** Law and Legal Services **CN:** Faegre Baker Daniels LLP **PB:** Mineola **SC:** NY/USA **PT:** Max Leonard Levinson; Eva (Klamen) Levinson **MS:** Married **SPN:** Laurel Lee Levinson (6/22/2013); Jerelyn E. Jarmacz (2/6/1982-2011, Divorced); Laura R. Levinson (9/14/1969, Divorced 1981) **CH:** Barbara Ann Schmidt; Alexander T. **ED:** LLM in Taxation, Georgetown University (1978); JD, The George Washington University, with Honors (1975); BA in Political Science, University of Wisconsin-Madison, with Distinction (1969) **C:** Partner, Faegre Baker Daniels, LLP (2005-Present); Managing Director, KPMG (2002-2004); Vice President, Tax, Risk Management and Insurance, Northwest Airlines, Inc. (1996-2001); From Vice President, Tax to Vice President, Tax, Risk Management & Insurance, Northwest Airlines, Inc., Eagan, MN (1990-1996); Vice President, International Project of Finance, Marriott International, Inc., Bethesda, MD (1985-1990); Vice President, Managing Tax Director, Marriott International, Inc., Bethesda, MD (1981-1985); Senior Tax Attorney, Pepper, Hamilton & Scheetz, Washington D.C. (1979-1981); Reviewer, Assistant Branch Office of the Chief Counsel, Interpretative Division IRS, Washington D.C. (1978-1979); Attorney, Advisor, Office of the Chief Counsel, Interpretative Division IRS, Washington D.C. (1975-1978) **CR:** Vice President, Wings Holdings, Inc., Northwest Airlines Corp. (1990-2001); Vice President, Tax, Northwest Airlines Corp. (1990-2001); Vice President, Various Subsidiary, Consultant, Chechhi Group, Beverly Hills, CA (1989-1990); Assistant Secretary, Vice President, Various Marriott International, Inc. Subsidiary, Bethesda, MD (1981-1990); Adjunct Professor, Georgetown University Law Center, Washington D.C. (1978-1986); Board of Directors, City Harbour Hotel, Ltd., London, England; Adjunct Professor, University of Minnesota Law School **CIV:** Volunteer Deputy Sheriff, Carver County Sheriff's Mounted Posse (2002-Present); Board of Directors, Minnesota Taxpayers Association, Minneapolis,

MN; Usher Captain, Temple Israel; Board Member, Search, Rescue, and Recovery Resources of Minnesota **MIL:** Lieutenant, U.S. Navy (1969-1972) **CW:** Contributor, Articles, Professional Journals; Presenter in Field **AW:** Named to the Pro Bono Honor Roll, Faegre Baker Daniels (2015-2016); Named, Best Lawyers in Litigation and Controversy Tax, Best Lawyers (2012-2017); Named, Top Lawyers in the State (2011-2015); Named, Best Lawyers in America in Tax Law, Best Lawyers (2010-2017); Named, The Legal 500 in Tax, Aviation and Captive Insurance; Listee, Who's Who in American Law; Listee, Who's Who International; Listee, Who's Who in Executives and Professionals **MEM:** Executive Committee, Minnesota Center for Fiscal Excellence (2006-Present); Nominating Committee, National Taxpayers Union (2003-Present); Board of Directors, Minnesota Center for Fiscal Excellence (1998-Present); Board President, Minnesota Center for Fiscal Excellence (2004-2006); Chairman, Air, International Air Transport Association (2002); Conference Chair, International Air Transport Association (2001); Board of Directors, Minnesota Chapter, Tax Executives Institute, Inc. (1999-2003); Board of Directors, National Taxpayers Union (1999-2002); Chair, Taxation Committee, International Air Transport Association (1999-2000); Vice Chairman, International Air Transport Association (1999); Chair, International Risk Managers Forum, International Air Transport Association (1998-2001); Chairman, Insurance Committee, International Air Transport Association (1997-1999); Chair, International Risk Managers Forum, International Air Transport Association (1995); Chairman, Insurance Committee, International Air Transport Association (1994); Chair Taxation Committee, International Air Transport Association (1991-1992); Subcommittee Chair, ABA (1978-1984); Airlines for America; Washington Tax & Public Policy Group LLC; Virginia State Bar; The District of Columbia Bar; Minnesota State Bar Association **BAR:** Supreme Court of the United States (1979); United States Court of Appeals District of Columbia Circuit (1976); United States Court of Federal Claims (1976); United States District Court for The District of Columbia (1976); United States Tax Court (1976); The District of Columbia (1975); Virginia (1975) **MH:** Albert Nelson Marquis Lifetime Achievement Award (2017) **H:** Golf; Art appreciation/collection; Boating; Equestrian show jumping; Skiing **BA:** 90 S 7th St Ste 2200, Faegre Baker Daniels LLP, Minneapolis, MN, 55402 **URL:** https://www.linkedin.com/in/ken-levinson-2b65635/

LEVY, BETTIE, T: Lawyer **I:** Law and Legal Services **CN:** BCL Entertainment **C:** Lawyer, BCL Entertainment

LEWIS MCDONALD, YVONNE, T: Manager, Legal Editorial **I:** Information Technology and Services **CN:** Thomson Reuters **PB:** , **ED:** Management Development Program (2005); JD, Law School, State University of New York, Buffalo (1997); MusB in Music Education, Nazareth College, Rochester, NY (1980) **CT:** Paralegal I and II, Saint John Fisher College **C:** Editorial Team Manager, Thomson Reuters, Rochester, NY (1997-Present); Owner, YLM Music Studio, Rochester, NY (1977-Present); Piano and Harp Instructor, Parkminster Music School, Rochester, NY (2000-2011); Paralegal, Legal Aid Society, Rochester, NY (1989-1994); Choir Director, Mt. Olivet Baptist Church Adult Choir, Office of Black Ministries Choir, Rochester, NY (1980-1985); Piano Accompanist, Rochester Ballet School, Rochester, NY (1978-1984); Accompanist, Rochester City School District, Rochester, NY (1980-1982) **AW:** Ignite Award,

Content Strategy & Editorial, Thomson Reuters (2017); Surge Award, Legal Editorial Operations, Thomson Reuters (2017); Emerging Women in Leadership (2015); Diversity and Inclusion Champion (2014); Management at Thomson Reuters Scholar (2013); Award of Excellence, Legal Editorial Operations, Thomson Reuters (2012); Above and Beyond Award, Legal Editorial Operations, Thomson Reuters (2011); Certificate of Appreciation, Diversity Committee, Monroe County Bar Association (2010); Certificate of Appreciation, Habitat for Humanity Award, Legal Editorial Operations, Thomson Reuters (2009); Faces of Leadership, Creating and Sharing Knowledge, Legal Editorial Operations, Thomson Reuters (2004); Diversity and Strategic Thinking, Harvard ManageMentor **MEM:** Black Law Students Association; Health and Well-Being Committee, Monroe County Bar Association **URL:** https://www.linkedin.com/in/yvonne-lewis-mcdonald-4a02a12b

LEZAK, CAROL SPIELMAN, T: Senior Manager, Executive Communications **I:** Business Management/Business Services **CN:** Walgreen Co. **DOB:** 10/24/1949 **PB:** New York City **SC:** NY/USA **PT:** Murray Spielman; Sylvia Zeena (Ruderman) Spielman **MS:** Married **SPN:** Jeffrey Mayer Lezak (3/2/1975) **CH:** Jessica Lilli Lezak Shlafrok **ED:** AMLS in Library Science, University of Michigan (1972); BA in Fine Arts and Art History, Boston University (1971) **C:** Senior Manager, Executive Communications, Walgreen Co. (2011-Present); Manager, Executive Communications, Walgreen Co. (2009-2011); Health Content Manager, Walgreens.com, E-Commerce Division, Walgreen Co. (2005-2009); Senior Medical Writer, Walgreens Health Services (2004-2005); Manager, Corporate Communications, Walgreens Health Services, Deerfield, IL (2001-2004); Editorial Director, Bounty SCA Worldwide, Chicago, IL (1999-2001); Editor, Eleven Magazine for WTTW Chicago, General Learning Communications, Northbrook, IL (1995-1999); Senior Editor, General Learning Communications, Northbrook, IL (1992-1999); Managing Editor, General Learning Communications, Highland Park, IL (1984-1992); Associate Editor, General Learning Communications, Highland Park, IL (1983-1984); Assistant Editor, General Learning Communications, Highland Park, IL (1982-1983); Head, Technical Services, Gilpin Library, Chicago Historical Society (1977-1979); Acting Head, Technical Services, Ryerson and Burnham Libraries, Art Institute Chicago, IL (1976-1977); Cataloger, Books, Ryerson and Burnham Libraries, Art Institute of Chicago (1972-1976) **CR:** Owner, Carol Spielman Lezak LLC (2017-Present); Editor, Writer, Campus Updates, People Matters, Chain Links, Walgreen Co. (2017-Present); Executive Writer, Walgreen Co. (2009-Present); Editor, Walgreen Weekly (2015-2017); Editor, Writer, Wasson's Weekly CEO Message (2009-2014); Editor, Writer, Walgreens.com Ask a Pharmacist Series (2005-2009); Editor, Walgreens.com Recipe File (2005-2009); Editor, Tobacco Free Clinical Care Management Program (2005); Editor, Walgreens Health Initiatives Outlook Trend Report (2005); Editor, "The Good Health Sourcebook" (1996); Editor, Writer, The Better Health Booklets (1995-1999); Editor, Writer, "Clara's Bakery Cookbook" (1995); Editor, Writer, Applegate's Boarding House Cookbook" (1995); Owner, North Woods Writing, Highland Park, IL (1994-2006); Editorial Consultant, "Breast Self-Exam Guide" (1993); Editor, Maturity Matters/Your Healthy Best (1992-1999); Editor, Your Health Report, Maturity Matters/Your Healthy Best (1992-1999); Editor, Your Health & Fitness (1984-1999); Design Consultant, Your

Health & Fitness (1984-1999); Editor, Writer, Index to Chicago History: The Magazine of the Chicago Historical Society, Chicago Historical Society (1977-1990) **CIV:** Volunteer Writing Laboratory Tutor, Highland Park Public Schools (1994-1996) **CW:** Poet, East on Central (2008-Present); Author, "Freelance Bookbinder," Highland Park, IL (1980-Present); Editor, East on Central (2012); Author, "Impostor" (2010); Author, "My Pal, Gal" (2009); Author, "At the End of the Earth" (2008); Author, "Leaves of Absence," North Shore Magazine (2008); Author, "Obituary" (2007); Author, Book Reviews, Elle Magazine (2005); Author, Other Works **AW:** Second Place, Highland Park Poetry Challenge (2018, 2011, 2009); First Place, Highland Park Poetry Challenge (2013); Third Place, Highland Park Poetry Challenge (2010); First Place, Highland Park Earth Day Poetry Challenge (2008); International Corporate SMART Award for Administrative Excellence (2000); Honorable Mention, Gardeners of the North Shore (1995); First Place, Logo Design, Sister Cities Foundation (1990); Various Awards, Educational Press Association (1988-1995) **MEM:** Member, Various Animal/Wildlife Charities **MH:** Albert Nelson Marquis Lifetime Achievement Award (2017) **H:** Writing; Editing; Reading; Gardening **BA:** 108 Wilmot Rd Ste 1845, Walgreen Company, Deerfield, IL, 60015

L'HEUREUX, RICHARD JOSEPH, T: Volunteer Advocate **I:** Civil Service **CN:** Senior Companion Program **DOB:** 04/05/1932 **PB:** Manchester **SC:** NH/USA **PT:** Arthur L'Heureux; Lilian Daigle L'Heureux **ED:** Coursework, North Hollywood College **CT:** Certified in CPR and First Aid, State of New Hampshire Community Emergency Response Team; Certification, Visiting Nurse Association, Hospice Senior Companion Program of New Hampshire **C:** Sales Specialist (1987); Employee, Moore's Center, New Hampshire; Companion, Senior Companion Program of New Hampshire, Manchester, NH; Hillsborough Nursing Home, Goffstown, NH; Visiting Hospice Patient Program, Visiting Nurse Association; Court-Appointed Special Advocate for Children, Elliott Hospital; Senior Program of New Hampshire; State of New Hampshire Community Emergency Response Team; Moore Center for the Handicap & Mental Clients; Neighborhood Watch **CR:** Owner, Extra Special Memories Creations **CIV:** Volunteer (1987-Present); Volunteer, Elliott Hospital, Manchester, NH; Volunteer, Hillsborough County Nursing Home, Goffstown, NH; Volunteer, Saint Anthony Church, Manchester **MIL:** Marine **CW:** Author, "Home Sweet Home Poem"; Author, "Lovingly Peace Poem"; Author, "Romancing Moon, Ladders of Bravery" **AW:** Spirit of New Hampshire Award; CYO Man of the Year **MEM:** The American Legion; International Society of Poets; Global Directory of Who's Who; Children Lobby, Remington, NY **MH:** Albert Nelson Marquis Lifetime Achievement Award (2017) **H:** Poetry; Bowling; Golf; Reading **PA:** Democrat **RE:** Catholic **ADD:** 159 Hall St Apt 1, Manchester, NH, 03103

LI, QING XIAO, T: Professor **I:** Education/Educational Services **CN:** University of Hawaii at Manoa **ED:** PhD in Agriculture and Environmental Chemistry, University of California, Davis (1990); BS in Agriculture, Shan Dong Agriculture University **C:** Professor, Department of Molecular Biosciences and Bioengineering, College of Tropical Agriculture and Human Resources, University of Hawaii at Manoa **CW:** Author, "Guanidination tryptic peptides without desalting for MALDI MS analysis," Analytical Chemistry PMID (2013); Author, "Diet-induced over-expression of flightless-I protein and its relation to flight dysfunction in Mediterranean

fruit fly, Ceratitis capitata," PLoS ONE (2013); Contributor, Over 300 Peer-reviewed Papers, Professional Journals; Published, Journal of American Chemical Society **AW:** AGRO Award for Innovation in Chemistry of Agriculture, American Chemical Society (2017) **MEM:** American Chemical Society **H:** Barbecuing; Hiking **BA:** 1955 East-West Rd, Rm 218, University of Hawaii at Manoa, Agricultural Science Building, Honolulu, HI, 96822 **LI, YU-TEH, T:** Professor **I:** Education/Educational Services **CN:** Tulane Medical School **MS:** Married **ED:** PhD, Biochemistry, University of Oklahoma (1963); MS, Biochemistry, National Taiwan University, Taiwan (1960); BS, Agricultural Chemistry, National Taiwan University, Taiwan (1957) **C:** Professor, Department of Biochemistry & Molecular Biology, Tulane University School of Medicine (1974-Present); Head, Department of Biochemistry, Tulane University National Primate Research Center (1975-1985); Associate Professor, Department of Biochemistry, Tulane University School of Medicine (1971-1974); Assistant Professor, Department of Biochemistry, Tulane University School of Medicine (1966-1971); Assistant Professor, Department of Biochemistry, University of Oklahoma School of Medicine (1965-1966); Postdoctoral Fellow, Department of Biochemistry, University of Oklahoma School of Medicine (1963-1965) **CR:** Scientific Advisory Board, International Conference on Biology and Chemistry of Sialic Acid (2002-Present); Member, Cellular and Molecular Biology of Glia Study Section, National Institutes of Health (2008); Editorial Board, Archives of Biochemistry and Biophysics (1994-1997); Editorial Board, Analytical Biochemistry (1992-1995); Board of Director, Society of Complex Carbohydrates (1986-1990); Editorial Board, Glycoconjugate Journal (1984-1990); Member, Biochemistry Study Section, National Institutes of Health (1983-1987); Editorial Board, Analytical Biochemistry (1981-1989) **AW:** Owl Club Award for Excellence in Teaching, Tulane University School of Medicine (2000); Fellow, Japan Society for the Promotion of Science Research (1996); Distinguished Lecturer Award for Outstanding Contributions to the Neuroscience, Neuroscience Center of Excellence, Louisiana State University School of Medicine (1994); Visiting Professor, Frontier Research Program, Institute of Physics & Chemistry Research, Japan (1992); Javits Neuroscience Investigator Award, National Institutes of Health (1991-1998); Sir C.V. Raman Visiting Professor, University of Madras, India (1987); Javits Neuroscience Investigator Award, National Institutes of Health (1984-1991); Visiting Professor, University of Milan, Italy (1984); Visiting Professor, Microbiology Institute, Chinese National Academy of Science, Beijing, China (1983); Japan Society for Promotion of Science Visiting Professor, University of Tokyo, Japan (1978); German Academic Exchange Visiting Professor, University of Kiel, Germany (1977); Guest Investigator, Department of Neurochemistry, University of Göteborg, Sweden (1973); Research Career Development Award, National Institutes of Health (1971-1976) **ADD:** 1717 Old Metairie St, Metairie, LA, 70001

LI, SHIOU-JIUAN, T: Heat Transfer Engineer **I:** Engineering **CN:** General Electric **ED:** PhD in Mechanical Engineering, Heat Transfer, Texas A&M University (2012); MS in Fluid Mechanics, Institute of Applied Mechanics, National Taiwan University (2006); BS in Mechanical Engineering, Fluid Mechanics, CCU (2004) **C:** Hot Gas Path Heat Transfer Engineer, GE Power, General Electric (2016-Present); Postdoctoral Research Associate, Texas A&M University (2013-Present); Teaching Assistant, Texas A&M University (2012); Research

Assistant, Turbine Heat Transfer Lab, Texas A&M University (2009-2012); Research Assistant, Energy and Environmental Fluid Dynamics Lab, National Taiwan University (2004-2006) **CR:** Invited Reviewer, Journals and International Conference **CW:** Author, "Turbine Platform Cooling and Blade Suction Surface Phantom Cooling from Simulated Swirl Purge Flow"; Author, "Influence of Mainstream Turbulence on Turbine Blade Platform Cooling from Simulated Swirl Purge Flow"; Author, "Turbine Blade Surface Phantom Cooling from Upstream Nozzle Trailing Edge Ejection"; Author, "Film Cooling for Cylindrical and Fan-Shaped Holes Using Pressure-Sensitive Paint Measurement Technique"; Author, "Experimental and Computational Film Cooling with Backward Injection for Cylindrical and Fan-Shaped Holes"; Author, "Effect of a Turning Vane on Heat Transfer in Rotating Multipass Rectangular Smooth Channel"; Author, "Effect of Coolant Density on Leading Edge Showerhead Film Cooling Using Pressure Sensitive Paint Measurement Technique"; Author, "Heat Transfer in Rotating Multipass Rectangular Ribbed Channel With and Without a Turning Vane"; Author, "Influence of Unsteady Wake with Trailing Edge Coolant Ejection on Turbine Blade Film Cooling"; Author, "Unsteady Wake and Coolant Density Effects on Turbine Blade Film Cooling Using PSP Technique" **AW:** Honorable Mentions for Outstanding Academic Performance, North America Taiwanese Engineering & Science Association (2011); Research Creativity Award; Certificate of Distinction for Fine Character and Excellent Scholastic Achievement; Leader Scholarship, Excellent Student Association **MEM:** Activity Section, Taiwanese Student Association, Texas A&M University (2010-2011); Documentation and Archives Leader, 42nd Graduate Committee, CCU (2003-2004); Leader, Mechanical Engineering Student Association, CCU (2002-2003); Financial Section, Sixth Taitung Student Association, CCU (2002-2003); American Society of Mechanical Engineering **ADD:** 434 Walden Creek Way, Greenville, SC, 29615 **URL:** https://www.linkedin.com/in/shiou-jiuan-anna-li-8584ab1a

LILES, CATHARINE, T: Painter, Marketing and Advertising Executive **I:** Advertising & Marketing **DOB:** 09/11/1944 **PB:** Macon **SC:** GA/USA **PT:** James Derry Burns; Hazel Blain (Holmes) Burns **MS:** Married **SPN:** Marion Harper Liles, Jr. (9/7/1963) **CH:** Mary Parker Liles-Johnson; Rebecca Holmes; Catharine Harper **ED:** Master in Liberal Studies, Mercer University (1989); BFA, Wesleyan College, Magna Cum Laude (1979) **C:** Owner, President, Liles & Associates Marketing and Advertising, Macon, GA (1982-Present); President, Liles & Associates Marketing and Advertising, Macon, FA (1982-Present); President, MarkWell, Inc. (1987-1994); Freelance Artist, Macon, GA (1971-1982); Office Manager, Sides & Pope Architects (1970-1971); Sales Coordinator, Burns Brick Company (1967-1970) **CR:** Adjunct Professor, Business Department, Wesleyan College (1988); Instructor, Department of Art, Mercer University (1983); Board of Directors, UGA Cortona; Board of Directors, University of Georgia; Board of Directors, Stratford Academy **CIV:** Active, Middle Georgia Military Affairs Committee, Warner Robins, GA (1990-Present); President, Board of Directors, Museum of Arts and Sciences (1991-1992); President, Macon Arts Alliance (1988-1989); Board of Directors, Leadership Macon (1985-1988) **CW:** Principal Painter, Collections, University of Texas Health Science Center, Houston, TX **AW:** Print Addy Award, Ad Club of Central Georgia (1992); Volunteer Award, Georgia Assembly of Community Arts Agencies (Now Georgia Arts Network) (1991); Service Award, Middle Georgia Council, Girl Scouts of America (1991); Distinguished Achievement Alumnae Award, Wesleyan College (1991); Women Business Owner of Year Award, Greater Macon Business Women (1989); Print Addy Award, Ad Club of Central Georgia (1987-1988); Alumni Service Award, Stratford Academy (1987) **MEM:** Board of Directors, Greater Macon Chamber of Commerce (1991-1994); Ad-Hoc Majors Committee, Georgia Council for the Arts (1990-1991); Vice President, Small Business Department, Greater Macon Chamber of Commerce (1987); Georgia Chamber of Commerce; Middle Georgia Art Association; Greater Macon Business Women; Kiwanis International **H:** Running; Travel; Art **RE:** Episcopalian **ADD:** 614 Rosa Taylor Drive, Macon, GA, 31204

LILLY-HERSLEY, JANE ANNE, T: Nursing Researcher **I:** Health, Wellness and Fitness **DOB:** 05/31/1947 **PB:** Palo Alto **SC:** CA/USA **PT:** Daniel Morris Feeley, Sr.; Suzanne (Agnew) Feeley **MS:** Married **SPN:** Dennis C. Hersley (January 16, 1993) **CH:** Cary Jane; Laura Blachree; Claire Foale **ED:** BSN, RN, Sacramento City College (1975); Student, University of Hawai'i (1970); BS, University of Oregon (1968) **CT:** Certified in Advanced Cardiovascular Life Support; Certified in Basic Cardiac Life Support **C:** Consultant, Self-Employed; Clinical Project Leader, Mycophenolate Mofetil Program Team, Syntex Research, Palo Alto, CA; Staff Nurse, Surgical ICU and Trauma Unit, Santa Clara Valley Medical Center, San Jose, CA; Staff and Charge Nurse, Acute Rehabilitation, Santa Clara Valley Medical Center, San Jose, CA **CR:** Nurse, Medevac, Japan (1969-1970); President, Research Consultation Inc., Santa Cruz, CA; Consultant, Medical Research, Research Consultation Inc., Santa Cruz, CA; Consultant, Pharmaceutical Research, Research Consultation Inc., Santa Cruz, CA; English Teacher, High School, Japan **CIV:** Co-founder, Citizens United For Responsible Environmentalism, Inc., (CURE); Chief Financial Officer, Citizens United For Responsible Environmentalism, Inc., (CURE); Director of Scientific Research, Citizens United For Responsible Environmentalism, Inc., (CURE); Wild Bird Rescue **CW:** Featured Participant, BBC Documentary; Appearances, National Television and Radio Broadcasts, Public Presentations; Contributor, Articles, Professional Publications **MEM:** American Association of Critical-Care Nurses; The Nature Conservancy; National Wildlife Federation; Monterey Bay Aquarium Foundation; World Wildlife Fund; Smithsonian Associates; Charter Member, The National WWII Museum; Legacy Sponsor, National Museum of the Pacific War; National Sludge Alliance, Inc. **MH:** Albert Nelson Marquis Lifetime Achievement Award (2017) **BA:** 2375 Benson Avenue, Almaden Consulting, Santa Cruz, CA, 95065

LINSTER, MICHELLE, I: Medicine & Health Care **PT:** John Bufer, Sr.; Susie Graves Linster **SPN:** George Thalma Glenn, October 19, 1985 (Divorced December 16, 2001) **CH:** George Thalma Glenn III; Mari-Michele Linster Glenn; Jonathan Maxwell Linster Glenn **ED:** Post-Graduate Degree, Academic Leadership Chicago School of Professional Psychology, Washington DC Campus (2014); PhD, University of North Carolina (1985); Master's Degree, University of North Carolina (1981) **CT:** Executive Coach (2010); Former, Practicing Psychologist North Carolina Psychology Board (1990) **C:** Adjunct Faculty, Center for Creative Leadership, Greensboro, NC (1994-Present); Dean, Division of Sciences and Mathematics, Bennett College (2016-Present); Interim Provos and Vice President for Academic and Student Affairs, Bennett College (2015); Dean of Natural and Behavioral Sciences and Mathematics, Bennett College (2011-2014); Associate Professor of Psychology, Bennett College (2008-2011) Visiting Professor, North Carolina A&T State University, Greensboro (2004-2006); Assistant Professor, Program Coordinator, Winston-Salem State University, North Carolina (1997-2004); Chair, Psychology Department, Bennett College (1990-1991); Assistant Professor, Greensboro, Bennett College, Greensboro, NC (1986-1991) **CR:** Career Coach (2010-Present); Advisor, Bennett College, Psi Chi (2009-Present); Advisor, WSSU Chapter, Psi Chi (2001-2004); Practicing Psychologist, Private Practice, Greensboro, NC (1992-1998) **CIV:** Co-Chair Outreach, Super Computing Conference (2002-2004); Member, Junior League, Greensboro, NC (1989-2003); Evaluation Specialists, Super Computing Global (2003); Co-Chair Outreach, Super Computing Conference (2003); American Psychological Association, Washington (1994-2000); Steering Committee Member, Committee of 100, Greensboro, NC (1994-1999); Board Member, Greensboro Montesorri School, Greensboro, NC (1996-1999); Member, North Carolina Psychological Association, Greensboro, North Carolina (1994-1998) **AW:** Fulbright Hayes Short Term Scholarship, Fulbright Foundation (1990); James Peterson Teacher Award, Winston-Salem State **MEM:** Executive Board Member, Greensboro Chapter, Jack and Jill, Inc. (2003-2013); Secretary, Jack and Jill, Inc. (2001-2004); Southeastern Psychological Association; American Psychological Society; Delta Sigma Theta Sorority **H:** Reading; Jogging; Volunteering **ADD:** 5305 Winterset Dr, Greensboro, NC, 27406

LIPMAN, IRA A., T: Founder, Chairman Emeritus **I:** Business Management/Business Services **CN:** Guardsmark, Inc. **DOB:** 11/15/1940 **PB:** Little Rock **SC:** AR/USA **PT:** Mark Lipman; Belle (Ackerman) Lipman **MS:** Married **SPN:** Barbara Ellen Kelly (7/5/1970) **CH:** Gustave K.; Joshua S; M Benjamin **ED:** Honorary LLD, Ohio Wesleyan University (2010); Honorary LLD, Northeastern University, Boston, MA (1996); Honorary LLD, Atlanta's John Marshall Law School (1970); Coursework, Ohio Wesleyan University (1958-1960) **CT:** Certified Protection Professional, American Society for Industrial Security (1978) **C:** Founder, Chairman Emeritus, Guardsmark, Inc. (2015-Present); Chairman of the Board, Guardsmark, Inc. (1968-2015); Chief Executive Officer, Guardsmark Inc. (1968-2015); President, Guardsmark, Inc. (1968-2015); Vice President, Guardsmark, Inc., Memphis, TN (1963-1966); Salesman, Executive, Mark Lipman Service, Inc., Memphis, TN (1960-1963) **CR:** Honorary Chairman, National Council on Crime and Delinquency (1997-Present); Chairman Emeritus, National Council on Crime and Delinquency (1993-Present); Board of Directors, National Council on Crime and Delinquency (1975-Present); Founding Co-Chairman, Memphis Shelby County Crime Commission (1997); National Chairman, National Council on Crime and Delinquency (1988-1992); Conference Planning Committee, 2nd National Law Enforcement Explorer Conference (1980); Board of Directors, Greater Memphis Council on Crime and Delinquency (1976-1978); Entrepreneurial Fellow, University of Memphis (1976); Member, Environmental Security Committee of Private Security Advisory Council, Law Enforcement Assistance Administration (1975-1976) **CIV:** Founder, The Ira A. Lipman Professorship In Journalism, Columbia University (2016); Founder, The Ira A. Lipman Chair in Emerging Technologies and National Security at the Council on Foreign Relations (2016); Guardsmark Professorship, The Wharton School at the University of Pennsylvania (2004); Founder, The Ira A. Lipman Professorship, The Wharton School at the University of Pennsylvania (2001); Founder, The Lipman Family Professorship of Criminology, Law and Public Policy, Northeastern University (1999); Founder, The John Chancellor Award for Excellence in Journalism (1995); Founder, Memphis Young Republicans Club (1960) **CW:** Author, "How To Be Safe, 5th Edition" (2012); Author, "How To Protect Yourself From Crime, 3rd Edition" (1998); Author, "How To Protect Yourself From Crime, 4th Edition" (1997); Special Editor, The Annals of the American Academy of Political and Social Sciences (1988); Author, "How To Protect Yourself From Crime, 2nd Edition" (1981); Author, "How To Protect Yourself From Crime" (1975); Contributor, Numerous Articles, Professional Journals; Contributor, Numerous Articles, Magazines; Contributor, Numerous Articles, Newspapers **AW:** Colonel Edgar B. Watson Award, National Association of Security Companies, New York (2014); Gershom Mendes Seixas Award, Columbia/Barnard Hillel (2006); The Wharton School Dean's Medal, University of Pennsylvania (2004); Stanley C. Pace Award for Leadership in Ethics, Ethics Resource Center (2002); Corporate Citizenship Award, Committee for Economic Development (2002); The Interfaith Medallion, International Council of Christians and Jews (1992); Security Person of the Year, Security Letter (1988); Sam Beber Distinguished Aleph Zadik Aleph Alumnus Award, B'nai B'rith Youth Organization (1988); Junior Achievement Master of Free Enterprise Award, Memphis, TN (1987); Outstanding Community Sales Award, Sales and Marketing Executives of Memphis (1987); Israel Freedom Award, The State of Israel Bonds Organization (1987); Humanitarian of the Year Award, National Conference of Christians and Jews, Memphis, TN (1985); Distinguished Service Award, NAACP (1983); Best Corporate Chief Executive of Achievement, Gallagher Presidents' Report (1974); Outstanding Young Men of America (1970) **MEM:** The Mount Sinai Surgery Advisory Board (2017-Present, 2009-2012); Chairman, Presidential Historical Commission, New-York Historical Society, Museum and Library (2017-Present); Board of Trustees, New-York Historical Society (2016-Present, 2007-2013); The Society of Entrepreneurs (2016-Present); Board, AlliedUniversal (2016-Present); Board of Trustees, Yeshiva University, New York (2016-Present); American Antiquarian Society (2016-Present); Founding Member, Homeland Security Project (2004-Present); The James Madison Council, Library of Congress (2004-Present); Committee on Corporate Affairs (2003-Present); The Grolier Club (2003-Present); Board of Directors, The Sherry Netherland, Inc. (2002-Present); Council on Foreign Relations (2002-Present); Member Emeritus, Alexis De Tocqueville Society National Leadership Council, United Way of America (1998-Present); Honorary Chair, National Council on Crime and Delinquency (1997-Present); Advisory Board, Center for Business Ethics, Bentley University (1996-Present); Past National Chairman, Chairman Emeritus, National Council on Crime and Delinquency (1993-Present); Honorary Chairman for Life, National Conference of Christians and Jews (1992-Present); Lifetime Member, Board of Trustees, United Way of the Mid-South (1985-Present); Shareholder, Board Member, Contemporary Media, Inc. (1985-Present); Board of Trustees, Simon Wiesenthal Center (1982-Present); Board, Universal Protection Services (2015-2016); Lifetime Member, American Society for Industrial Security (2015); Board of Overseers, The Wharton School, University of Pennsylvania (2005-2016, 2004, 1991); Past National Chairman, National Conference of Christians and Jews (1988-

1992); Board of Trustees, Yeshíva University of Los Angeles (1982-2011); American Society of Criminology (1979); International Society of Criminology (1979); International Association of Chiefs of Police (1968); Member, Academy of the University of Pennsylvania **PA:** Republican **RE:** Jewish **ADD:** 22 S 2nd St, Memphis, TN, 38103 **URL:** https://iraalipman.com/

LISS, MARK JAY, T: Lawyer **I:** Law and Legal Services **CN:** Leydig, Voit & Mayer, Ltd. **DOB:** 05/22/1956 **PB:** Chicago **SC:** IL/USA **PT:** Henry Liss; Ruth Edith (Greenburg) Liss **MS:** Married **SPN:** Lynne Marie Delterr (12/14/1986) **CH:** Jennifer **ED:** JD, Illinois Institute of Technology (1981); BA, University of Illinois (1978) **C:** Partner, Leydig, Voit & Mayer, Ltd., Chicago, IL (1989-Present); Partner, Alexander, Unikel, Zalewa & Tenenbaum, Ltd., Chicago, IL (1986-1989); Associate, Alexander & Zalewa (Now Alexander, Unikel, Zalewa & Tenenbaum, Ltd.), Chicago, IL (1981-1986) **AW:** Named to Illinois Super Lawyers, Intellectual Property Litigation (2012-2017); Named to Top Illinois Trademark Lawyer, World Trademark Review 1000 (2011-2017); Best Lawyers in America in the Area of Trademark Law (2013, 2014, 2015, 2016, 2017); Recognized as a Leading IP Practitioner, World IP Review's WIPR Leaders (2017); Client Choice Award for Intellectual Property, Trademarks; Selected by Peers as a Leading Lawyer in Intellectual Property Law – Leading Lawyers Network; Named One of Top Lawyers in Illinois in Intellectual Property Law, Chicago Lawyer; AV Preeminent Peer Review Rated, Martindale-Hubbell **MEM:** ABA; Illinois State Bar Association; The Chicago Bar Association; Associate Member, United State Trademark Association (Now International Trademark Association) **BAR:** United States Court of Appeals for the Ninth Circuit (1987); United States Court of Appeals for the Federal Circuit (1983); Illinois State Bar Association (1981); United States District Court for the Northern District of Illinois (1981); United States Court of Appeals for the Seventh Circuit (1981)

LIVINGSTON, CAROLYN H., T: Professor Emeritus **I:** Education/Educational Services **CN:** University of Rhode Island **DOB:** 01/07/1936 **PB:** Cookeville **SC:** TN/USA **PT:** Frazier Harris; Myrtle (Lee) Harris **MS:** Widow **SPN:** Burton Zitkin (5/29/2000, Deceased 5/2/2016); Jesse B. Livingston (9/1/1969); Frank W. Medley Jr. (6/28/1955, Deceased 12/1967) **CH:** Frank; Jane; Jennifer Medley Martin **ED:** PhD, University of Florida (1986); MEd, University of Florida (1981); BS, Tennessee Technological University (1959); Coursework, University of Maryland (1958-1959) **C:** Professor Emeritus, University of Rhode Island (2009-Present); Professor, University of Rhode Island, Kingston, RI (1999-2008); Director of Graduate Studies in Music, University of Rhode Island, Kingston, RI (1997-2006); Associate Professor, University of Rhode Island, Kingston, RI (1993-1999); Coordinator of Music Education, University of Rhode Island, Kingston, RI (1989-1997); Assistant Professor, University of Rhode Island, Kingston, RI (1987-1993); Music Specialist, Memphis City Schools (1986-1987); Music Specialist, Putnam County Schools, Cookeville, TN (1984-1986); Director of Choirs, First Lutheran Church, Gainesville, FL (1976-1983); Teacher Music, Private Practice, Gainesville, FL (1970-1980); Music Specialist, Prince Georges County Schools, Bowie, MD (1968-1969); Music Teacher, Private Practice, Bowie, MD (1960-1968) **CIV:** Founder, Director, University of Rhode Island Children's Chorus (1993-2000) **CW:** Editorial Committee Member, Journal of Historical Research on Music Education (2004-Present); Editorial Board Member, Bulletin Historical Research on Music Education (1990-Present); Author, "Charles Faulkner Bryan: His Life and Music" (2003); Co-Editor, "Rhode Islands Musical Heritage: An Exploration"; Contributor, Articles, Professional Journals **AW:** Humanities Fellowship, University of Rhode Island (2004) **MEM:** Chair, History Special Research Interest Group (1999-2001); Vice Chair, History Special Research Interest Group (1997-1999); President, Rhode Island Music Teachers Association (1992-1994); Sigma Alpha Iota; Pi Kappa Lambda; Kappa Delta Pi; The Honor Society of Phi Kappa Phi; Music Educators National Conference; Music Teachers National Association **MH:** Albert Nelson Marquis Lifetime Achievement Award (2017) **H:** Gardening; Traveling **RE:** Lutheran **ADD:** 6307 NW 37th Terrace, Gainesville, FL, 32653

LLINÁS, RODOLFO RIASCOS, T: Professor **I:** Education/Educational Services **CN:** New York University **DOB:** 12/16/1934 **PB:** Bogotá **SC:** Colombia **PT:** Jorge Enrique Llinás; Bertha (Riascos) Llinás **MS:** Married **SPN:** Gillian Kimber (12/24/1965) **CH:** Rafael Hugo; Alexander Jorge **ED:** Honorary Doctorate, Universidad Complutense Madrid (1997); Honorary PhD, Universidad Nacional de Colombia (1994); Honorary PhD, Universitat de Barcelona (1993); Honorary MD, Universidad de Salamanca (1985); PhD, The Australian National University (1965); MIH Postdoctoral Research Fellow, Department of Physiology, Univeristy of Minnesota, Minneapolis, MN (1961-1963); Postdoctoral Research Fellow, Department of Neurosurgery, Massachusetts General Hospital, Harvard Medical School (1960-1961); MD, Pontificia Universidad Javeriana (1959); BS, Gimnasio Moderno (1952) **C:** University Professor, New York University School of Medicine (2011-Present); Thomas and Suzanne Murphy Professor of Neuroscience, New York University (1985-Present); Professor, Department of Neuroscience and Physiology, New York University (1976-2011); Chairman, Department of Neuroscience and Physiology, New York University (1976-2011); Faculty Member, Summer Course in Neurobiology, Marine Biological Laboratory, Woods Hole, MA (1971-1974); Professor of Physiology, The University of Iowa (1970-1976); Head, Neurobiology Division, The University of Iowa (1970-1976); Clinical Professor, The University of Illinois at Chicago (1968-1972); Associate Professor, Department of Neurology and Psychiatry, Northwestern University (1967-1971); Head, Neurobiology Unit, Institute for Biomedical Research, American Medical Association (1967-1970); Associate Professor, University of Minnesota (1965-1966) **CR:** Executive Committee, U.S. National Committee, International Brain Research Organization (1985-Present); Board of Trustees, The Marine Biological Laboratory (1990-1992); Craythorne Lecturer, Miller School of Medicine, University of Miami (1988); Chairman, U.S. National Committee, International Brain Research Organization (1983-1989); Professorial Lecturer, College de France, Paris (1987); Ulf von Euler Lecturer, Karolinska Institutet (1987); Ralph Gerard Lecturer, University of California, Irvine (1987); McDowall Lecturer in Physiology, King's College, London (1984); Board of Trustees, The Marine Biological Laboratory (1983-1985); Lang Lecturer, The Marine Biological Laboratory (1982); Scientific Advisory Board, International Lecturer, International Brain Research Organization (1982); Acting Chairman U.S. National Committee, International Brain Research Organization (1982); Catedra Ramon y Cajal Inaugural Speaker, Instituto Politecnico Nacional (1981); Scientific Advisory Board, Instituto Politécnico Nacional (1981); Scientific Advisory Board, Max-Planck-Gesellschaft (1979-1983); Professorial Lecturer, College de France, Paris (1979); U.S. National Committee, International Brain Research Organization (1978-1981); Associate, Neurosciences Research Program, Massachusetts Institute of Technology (1974-1984); Neurology A Study Section, Division of Research Grants, NIH (1974-1978); Corporation Member, The Marine Biological Laboratory (1973-1982); Bowditch Lecturer, The American Physiological Society (1973); Consultant, School of Aerospace Medicine, United States Air Force (1972-1975); Neurological Science Research Training Committee, National Institute of Neurological Disorders and Stroke, NIH (1971-1973); Guest Professor in Physiology, Wayne State University (1967-1974); Professorial Lecturer in Pharmacology, The University of Illinois at Chicago (1967-1968) **CW:** Senior Editor, Thalamus & Related Systems (2001-Present); Editorial Board, Pflügers Archiv European Journal of Physiology (1981-Present); Editorial Board, Journal of Theoretical Neurobiology (1981-Present); Editorial Board, Journal of Neurobiology (1980-Present); Author, "El Cerebro y El Mito del Yo" (2017); Contributing Author, Science (2017); Contributing Author, Frontiers in Human Neuroscience (2017); Contributing Author, Alzheimer's & Dementia (2017); Contributing Author, Muscle & Nerve (2017); Contributing Author, Neuroscience (2016); Contributing Author, Proceedings of the National Academy of Sciences (2015-2016); Contributing Author, Neurocomputing (2015); Contributing Author, Physiological Reports (2015); Contributing Author, Frontiers in Neurology (2015); Contributing Author, Frontiers in Neuroscience (2015); Contributing Author, Robotics and Autonomous Systems (2014); Contributing Author, Frontiers in Synaptic Transmission (2014); Contributing Author, Frontiers in Neural Circuits (2014); Contributing Author, Mathematical Biology & Bioinformatics (2013); Contributing Author, Journal of Neuroscience (2012); Contributing Author, ITHEA ISS (2012); Contributing Author, The Cerebellum (2012); Contributing Author, Frontiers in Synaptic Neuroscience (2011); Contributing Author, "Science: Image in Action" (2011); Contributing Author, The Journal of Physiology (2010-2011); Contributing Author, Pain (2010); Contributing Author, "Translational Pain Research: From Mouse to Man" (2010); Contributing Author, Cell Calcium (2010); Contributing Author, Electronics and Communications in Japan (2009); Contributing Author, Comptes rendus de l'Académie des sciences (2009); Contributing Author, Biological Psychiatry (2009); Contributing Author, Biofizika (2009); Contributing Author, "Kaplan and Sadock's Comprehensive Textbook of Psychiatry" (2009); Contributing Author, Encyclopedia of Neuroscience (2009); Contributing Author, The Biological Bulletin (2009); Contributing Author, Philosophical Transactions of the Royal Society of London (2009); Contributing Author, Journal of Consciousness Studies (2008); Contributing Author, Clinical Neurophysiology (2008); Contributing Author, Physical Review E (2008) **AW:** Honoree, Scholar of the Year, Australian National University (2017); Nansen Neuroscience Lecture and Award, Norwegian Academy of Science (2016); Lecture and Award, Fundación Castilla de Pino (2015); Cajal Diploma, Queen Sophia of Spain (2013); Ragnar Granit Lecture and Award, The Norwegian Nobel Institute (2013); Gold Medal, CSIC (2012); The Miller Lecture and Award, CSHL (2011); Bernard Katz Award, Biophysical Society (2011); The Rovenstine Pain Research Award, NYU School of Medicine (2010); Santiago Grizolia Award and Medal, City of Valencia, Spain

(2004); Koetser Memorial Lecture and Prize, University of Zurich (2004); Breinin Lecture and Award, Emory University (2003); Morris Lecture and Award , Wright State University (2003); Signoret Award in Cognition, Fondation Ipsen La Salpâtrière (1994); Albert Einstein Gold Medal Award in Science, UNESCO (1991); F.O. Schmitt Lecture and Award in Neuroscience (1989); Luigi Galvani Lecture and Award, Georgetown University (1988); The John C. Krantz Award in Pharmacology and Experimental Therapeutics, University of Maryland School of Medicine (1976); Research Scholar, Department of Physiology, Institute of Advanced Studies, The Australian National University (1963-1965); Research Fellow in Physiology, NIH, University of Minnesota (1961-1963); Research Fellow, Massachusetts General Hospital, Harvard Medical School, Harvard University (1960-1961); Honoree, ISI Highly Cited Researcher, World Most Distinguished Scientists, ISIHighlyCited.com **MEM:** French Académie des Sciences (2002-Present); Real Academia Nacional de Medicina (1996-Present); The American Philosophical Society (1996-Present); American Academy of Arts and Sciences (1996-Present); European Neuroscience Association (1989-Present); National Academy of Sciences (1986-Present); National Academy of Medicine, National Academy of Sciences (1986-Present); Alpha Omega Alpha Honor Medical Society (1981-Present); Institute for Biomedical Research, American Medical Association (1970-Present); Scientific Advisory Board, The Roche Institute of Molecular Biology (1992-1994); Chairman, Neurolab Science Working Group, National Aeronautics and Space Administration (1991-1995); Scientific Advisory Board, Division for Basic Research, Max-Planck-Gesellschaft (1979-1983); Basic Neuroscience Research Task Force, National Academy of Sciences (1978-1982); National Research Council Committee, International Brain Research Organization (1978-1981); Council Member, Society for Neuroscience (1974-1978); Task Force on Neurophysiology, The American Physiological Society (1974-1978); Committee on Committees, The American Physiological Society (1974-1976); Neurological Science Research Training Committee A, National Institute of Neurological Disorders and Stroke, NIH (1971-1973); Associate Member, Institute for Biomedical Research, American Medical Association (1966-1968); Advisory Council, National Institute on Deafness and Other Communication Disorders, NIH; The American Society for Cell Biology; The Biophysical Society; The Harvey Society; International Brain Research Organization; The New York Academy of Sciences; Google Scholar **MH:** Albert Nelson Marquis Lifetime Achievement Award (2017) **H:** Astronomy **BA:** 550 1st Ave, NYU Medical School, New York, NY, 10016 **ADD:** 16 Sutton Pl Apt 7A, New York, NY, 10022 **URL:** https://es.wikipedia.org/wiki/Rodolfo_Llin%C3%A1s

LLOYD, JEAN, T: Primary School Educator (Retired) **I:** Education/Educational Services **DOB:** 03/03/1935 **PB:** Montgomery **SC:** AL/USA **YOP:** 2017-04-19 **PT:** James Jack Lloyd; Dorothy Gladys (Brown) Lloyd **CH:** Jamie Angelica **ED:** PhD, New York University (1976); MA, New York University (1960); BA, Queens College (1957) **C:** Kindergarten Teacher, New York City Board of Education (1984-2004); Instructor, Assistant Professor, University College Community, Rutgers, The State University of New Jersey, Newark, NJ (1969-1983); Director, Head Start Center, New York City Board of Education (1966-1967); Early Childhood Teacher, New York City Board of Education (1961-1969); Junior High School Teacher, New York City Board

of Education (1961) **CR:** Chairman, Board of Directors Your Family Inc., New York, NY (1989-2004); Consultant, Department of Personnel, New York, NY (1985); Research Consultant, Seymour Laskow CPA (1983); Consultant, Board of Examiners, New York, NY (1982) **CW:** Author, "Producing Brilliant Children" (2012); Producer, New Ventures Cable TV Show, New York, NY (1987-2004); Author, "Sociology and Social Life" (1979); Contributor, More than 10 Articles to Professional Journals **AW:** Recipient, Ed Press Award, Educational Press Association (1968) **MEM:** Oxford University Study Program (2009, 2007); Project Synergy Fellow, Teachers College, Columbia University (1991-1993); Christ Church College, Oxford University; Association for Supervision and Curriculum Development; United Federation of Teachers; Delta Kappa Gamma **MH:** Albert Nelson Marquis Lifetime Achievement Award (2017) **H:** Writing poetry and books; Painting; Singing in church choir **PA:** Democrat **RE:** Methodist **BA:** 180 W. End Avenue, Apt. 12H, New York, NY, 10023 **ADD:** Jaime Lloyd, 716 Fifth Avenue, Apt. 4, Brooklyn, NY, 11215

LOCASCIO, SALVADORE JOSEPH, T: Professor Emeritus **I:** Education/Educational Services **CN:** University of Florida **DOB:** 10/29/1933 **PB:** Hammond **SC:** LA/USA **PT:** John A. Locascio; Mary (Dantone) Locascio y **MS:** Married **SPN:** Carol Smith Riggall (12/29/1993); Sybil Olivette Johnson (11/21/1954, Deceased 5/1991) **CH:** John David; Judy Lynn; Paul Anthony; Heather Duque; Todd Riggall **ED:** PhD, Purdue University (1959); MS, Louisiana State University (1956); BS, Southeastern Louisiana University (1955) **C:** Professor Emeritus, University of Florida (2003-Present); Professor, University of Florida (1969-2003); Associate Professor, University of Florida (1965-1969); Assistant Horticulturist, University of Florida, Gainesville, FL (1959-1965); Graduate Assistant, Purdue University (1956-1959); Graduate Assistant, Louisiana State University (1955-1956) **CR:** Pioneer, Plastic Mulch Culture **CW:** Contributor, Articles to Professional Journals **AW:** Recipient, Pioneer Award, American Society for Plasticulture (2002); Recipient, Southern Region L. M. Ware Distinguished Research Award, American Society for Horticultural Sciences (1998); Recipient, Annual Research Award, Florida Fruit and Vegetable Association (1993); Recipient, Outstanding Weed Scientist of the Year Award, Florida Weed Science Society (1989); Recipient, Presidential Gold Medal Award, Florida State Horticultural Society (1978); Recipient, Junior Faculty Member Award, Gamma Sigma Delta (1969) **MEM:** Chairman, Board of Directors, Florida State Horticultural Society (1995); President, Florida State Horticultural Society (1994); President, Florida Weed Science Society (1990-1991); President-Elect, Florida Weed Science Society (1989-1990); Fellow, American Society for Horticultural Science (1989); Vice President of Vegetable Science, Florida State Horticultural Society (1975-1976) **MH:** Albert Nelson Marquis Lifetime Achievement Award (2017) **H:** Rooting for the Florida Gators; Enjoying football and basketball; Traveling with his wife; Visiting his five Children and nine grandchildren; Fishing; Tennis; Gardening **PA:** Independent **RE:** Roman Catholic **ADD:** 406 NW 32nd St, Gainesville, FL, 32607

LOEB, JOHN NICHOLS, T: Physician, Professor Emeritus **I:** Education/Educational Services **CN:** Columbia University **DOB:** 12/17/1935 **PB:** New York **SC:** NY/USA **PT:** Robert Frederick Loeb; Emily Guild (Nichols) Loeb **ED:** MD, Harvard Medical School, Summa Cum Laude (1961); AB, Harvard College, Summa Cum Laude (1957) **C:**

Special Lecturer in Medicine, Columbia University (2005-Present); Professor Emeritus of Medicine, Columbia University (2005-Present); Attending Physician, New York–Presbyterian Hospital (1998-Present); Vice Chairman for Academic Affairs, Columbia University (2003-2004); Associate Chairman for Research, Department of Medicine, Columbia University (1997-2003); Professor of Medicine, Columbia University (1979-2004); Attending Physician, Presbyterian Hospital (Now New York-Presbyterian Hospital), New York, NY (1979-1998); Associate Professor of Medicine, Columbia University (1973-1979); Associate Attending Physician, Presbyterian Hospital (Now New York-Presbyterian Hospital), New York, NY (1973-1979); Assistant Professor of Medicine, Columbia University (1967-1973); Assistant Attending Physician, Presbyterian Hospital (Now New York-Presbyterian Hospital), New York, NY (1967-1973); Assistant Physician, Presbyterian Hospital (Now New York-Presbyterian Hospital), New York, NY (1966-1967); National Institutes of Health Trainee in Metabolism, College of Physicians and Surgeons, Columbia University (1966-1967); Instructor in Medicine, Columbia University (1965-1966); Chief Resident in Medicine, Presbyterian Hospital (Now New York-Presbyterian Hospital), New York, NY (1965-1966); Research Associate, Laboratory of Molecular Biology, National Institute of Arthritis and Metabolic Diseases (Now National Institute of Arthritis and Musculoskeletal and Skin Diseases), National Institutes of Health, Bethesda, MD (1963-1965); Assistant Resident in Medicine, Presbyterian Hospital (Now New York-Presbyterian Hospital), New York, NY (1962-1963); Intern in Medicine, Massachusetts General Hospital, Boston, MA (1961-1962) **CR:** Praktikant, Friedrich Miescher Institute (FMI), Basel, Switzerland (1986); Board of Directors, Royal Society of Medicine Foundation, NY (1984-1995); Councillor, Harvard Medical Alumni Association (1982-1985); Visiting Professor, Department of Medicine, University of Cape Town, South Africa (1982); Visiting Professor, Department of Internal Medicine, Pahlavi University, Shiraz, Iran (1977); Secretary, Medical Board, Presbyterian Hospital (1976-1977); Adjunct Associate Professor, Rockefeller University, New York, NY (1975-1983); Medical Council of the Iran Foundation (1974-1975); Visiting Professor, Department of Internal Medicine, Pahlavi University (Now Shiraz University of Medical Sciences), Shiraz, Iran (1974); Adjunct Assistant Professor, The Rockefeller University, New York, NY (1970-1975); Assistant Visiting Physician, Harlem Hospital (Now NYC Health + Hospitals/Harlem), New York, NY (1968-1973); Visiting Chief Resident in Medicine, Massachusetts General Hospital, Boston, MA (1966); Fellow, American Association for the Advancement of Science; Fellow, American College of Physicians; Fellow, The New York Academy of Medicine; Fellow, Royal Society of Medicine **CIV:** Elder, Presbyterian Church (1982-Present); Advisory Council, Amateur Chamber Music Players, Inc. (1999-2006); Vice Chairman, Amateur Chamber Music Players, Inc. (1985-1999); Board of Directors, Amateur Chamber Music Players, Inc. (1984-1999); Ruling Elder, Madison Avenue Presbyterian Church, New York, NY (1983-1988); Surgeon, Lieutenant Commander Grade, U.S. Public Health Service, U.S. Department of Health and Human Services (1963-1965) **CW:** Contributor, Articles, Professional Journals **AW:** Distinguished Service Award, College of Physicians and Surgeons, Columbia University (2007); House Staff Recognition Award, Presbyterian Hospital (Now New York-Presbyterian Hospital) (2004); MERIT Award (1988-1999); Teaching Award Citation (1975); Distinguished Teacher Award,

College of Physicians and Surgeons, Columbia University (1974); Career Scientist Award, Irma T. Hirschl Charitable Trust (1973-1977); P&S Club Teaching Award (1969); Grantee, National Institutes Of Health (1967-1999); Boylston Medal, Harvard University (1961) **MEM:** Committee on Nomination of Officers, The American Philosophical Society (2008-Present); Councillor, The American Philosophical Society (2006-2012); Councillor, Peripatetic Club (1987-1994); President, Practitioners' Society of New York (1985-1986); President, Charaka Club (1984-1985); Secretary, Practitioners' Society of New York (1973-1974); Diplomate, American Board of Internal Medicine; Association of American Physicians; The American Society for Clinical Investigation; American Federation for Clinical Research; The Harvey Society; American Clinical and Climatological Association (Now ACCA Society); Century Association; Society for Experimental Biology and Medicine; Endocrine Society; Society of General Physiologists; Society for Endocrinology; Honorary Lifetime Member, Metabolism and Diabetes of Southern Africa (Now Endocrinology, Metabolism and Diabetes of South Africa); Interurban Clinical Club; Phi Beta Kappa (Now The Phi Beta Kappa Society); Alpha Omega Alpha (Now Alpha Omega Alpha Honor Medical Society) **RE:** Presbyterian **BA:** Department of Medicine; Columbia University, 630 West 168th Street, New York, NY, 10032-3702 **ADD:** 80 Haven Avenue, Apartment 3C, New York, NY, 10032

LOECHL, KEVIN J., **T:** Principal, Practice Group Head **I:** Law and Legal Services **CN:** Bird, Loechl, Brittain & McCants **DOB:** 12/17/1968 **PB:** Oak Park **SC:** Illinois **PT:** Richard E. Loechl, Jr.; Christine L. Loechl (Deceased) **MS:** Married **SPN:** Rebecca J. Loechl **ED:** JD, University of Chicago Law School (1994); BA in Political Science, Calvin College (1991) **C:** Principal, Head of Corporate and Securities Practice Group, Bird Loechl Brittain & McCants, LLC (2003-Present); General Outside Counsel, Ronald Blue & Co., LLC (2014-2017); Associate, Corporate and Securities Practice Group, Bird & Associates, P.C. (1997-2003); Associate, Banking and Finance Practice Group, Baker & McKenzie, LLP, Chicago, Illinois (1994-1997) **CR:** Student Body President, Calvin College Student Senate (1990-1991); Vice-President, Calvin College Student Senate (1989-1990); Senator, Calvin College Student Senate (1987-1989) **CIV:** Board of Trustees, Georgia Center for Opportunity, Atlanta, GA (2016-Present); Sunday School Teacher, East Cobb Presbyterian Church, Marietta, GA (2008-Present); Vice Chairman, Board, Georgia Center for Opportunity, Atlanta, GA (2014-2016); Board of Directors, Georgia Center for Opportunity, Atlanta, GA (2004-2016); President, Atlanta Leaders Group, Atlanta, GA (2009-2012); Elder, Hope Presbyterian Church, Marietta, GA (2001-2007) **CW:** "Kingdom-Minded Negotiation: A Strategy for Success", Speaker, Fellowship of Companies for Christ International Annual Conference, Fort Lauderdale, FL (2017) **AW:** Named, Georgia SuperLawyers Rising Star (2005); DeKruyer-Monsman Prize in Political Science, Calvin College (1991) **MEM:** Atlanta Leaders Group (2009-Present); President, Atlanta Leaders Group (2009-2012); Section of Business Law, ABA; Committee on LLCs, ABA; Partnerships and Unincorporated Business Entities, ABA; Section of Taxation, ABA; State Bar of Georgia; Illinois State Bar Association **BAR:** State of Georgia (1997); Illinois (1994) **H:** Gardening and horticulture; Hiking; Camping; Running **RE:** Presbyterian Church in America **BA:** 3414 Peachtree Rd NE Ste 1150, Bird Loechl Brittain & McCants, LLC, Atlanta, GA, 30326 **URL:** www.birdlawfirm.com

LOMBARD, JOHN JAMES JR., **T:** Lawyer (Retired) **I:** Law and Legal Services **DOB:** 12/27/1934 **PB:** Philadelphia **SC:** PA/USA **PT:** John James Lombard; Mary R. (O'Donnell) Lombard **MS:** Widowed **SPN:** Eugenia Smith (9/10/2010, Deceased 6/6/2016); Barbara Mallon (5/9/1964, Deceased, 7/20/2008) **CH:** John James, III; William M.; James G.; Laura K.; Barbara E. **ED:** JD, University of Pennsylvania (1959); BA, LaSalle University, Cum Laude (1956) **C:** Special Counsel, McCarter & English LLP, Philadelphia (2016); Partner, Morgan Lewis & Bockius LLP, Philadelphia (1984-2000); Vice-Chair, Personal Law Section, Morgan Lewis & Bockius LLP, Philadelphia (1990-2000); Manager, Personal Law Section, Morgan Lewis & Bockius LLP, Philadelphia (1985-1990); Managing Partner, Obermayer, Rebmann, Maxwell & Hippel, Philadelphia (1978-1984); Partner, Obermayer, Rebmann, Maxwell & Hippel, Philadelphia (1959-1984) **CR:** Member, Bioethics Committee, Medical Society of New Jersey (1985-Present); Member, Bioethics Committee, Hospital of the University of Pennsylvania (1995-2010); Chair, Subcommittee on Property and Health Care Powers of Attorney, Pennsylvania Joint State Commission (1993-2005); Co-founder and Member, Southern New Jersey Medical Ethics Alliance (1990-2000); Member, Pennsylvania Joint State Commission (1985-1993) **CIV:** Member and Legal Council, Cranaleith Spiritual Center, Philadelphia, PA (1994-Present); Board of Directors, LaSalle College High School, Wyndmoor, PA (1991-1997); Board of Directors, Gwynedd-Mercy College, Gwynedd Valley, PA (1980-1989); Board of Directors, Redevelopment Authority, Montgomery County, PA (1980-1987); Member and Chair, Planning Commission of Whitpain Township, Montgomery County, PA (1972-1980) **MIL:** Private First Class, Pennsylvania National Guard (1990-1998) **CW:** Co-Author, "Durable Powers of Attorney and Health Care Directives, First, Second and Third Editions," Shepards, McGraw-Hill (1980, 1994); Editor, Probate Notes, American College of Trust and Estate Counsel (1993) **AW:** William J. Whelan Alumni Service Award, La Salle College High School (2017); Distinguished Estate Planner Award, Philadelphia Estate Planning Council (2002); Treat Award, National College of Probate Judges (1992) **MEM:** Vice President, International Academy of Estate and Trust Law (2006-2014); Elder Law Committee, American College of Trust Counsel (1993-2010); Executive Committee, International Academy of Estate and Trust Law (1990-1994); Foundation President, American College of Trust and Estate Counsel (1990-1993); Chair, Real Property, Probate and Trust Law Section, ABA (1990-1991); Executive Committee, American College of Trust and Estate Counsel (1988-1991); Board of Regents, American College of Trust and Estate Counsel (1986-1991); Chair-Elect, ABA (1989-1990); Director, Probate Division, Real Property, Probate and Trust Law Section, ABA (1987-1989); Executive Committee, International Academy of Estate and Trust Law (1984-1988); Secretary, Real Property, Probate and Trust Law Section, ABA (1985-1987); Council, Real Property, Probate and Trust Law Section, ABA (1979-1985); Chairman, Membership Committee, Real Property, Probate and Trust Law Section, ABA (1972-1982); Chairman, Committee of Simplification Security Transfers, ABA (1972-1976); Chairman, Probate Section, Philadelphia Bar Association (1972); Philadelphia Bar Association; Pennsylvania Bar Association; The Union League of Philadelphia **BAR:** Pennsylvania (1960) **MH:** Albert Nelson Marquis Lifetime Achievement Award (2017) **H:** Art; Painting; Teaching; Painting **PA:** Republican **RE:** Roman Catholic **ADD:** 120 Mahogany Way, Upper Gwynedd, PA, 19446

LONDON, NORA, **I:** Nonprofit & Philanthropy **PT:** Jacob Schapiro; Jeanne Begagon **ED:** Student, Barnard College, New York, NY (1941-1943) **C:** President, George London Foundation for Singers, New York, NY (1991-Present); Founder, Honorary President, George London Stiftung, Vienna (1988) **CW:** Author, "George London, of Gods and Demons", German Edition (2009); Author, "George London, of Gods and Demons" (2005); Author, "Aria for George" (1986)

LONG, CHENGJIANG, **T:** Research Scientist **I:** Sciences **ED:** PhD, Stevens Institute of Technology, Hoboken, NJ (2015); MS, Wuhan University, Wuhan, Hubei, China (2011); BS, Wuhan University, Wuhan, Hubei, China (2009) **C:** Computer Vision Researcher, Kitware, Clifton Park, NY (2016); Research Intern, GE Global Research, General Electric, Niskayuna, NY (2015); Research Intern, NEC Labs America, Cupertino, CA (2013) **CW:** Contributor, Articles, Professional Journals **MEM:** IEEE

LONG, LINDA SUE, **T:** Special Education Teacher (Retired) **I:** Education/Educational Services **DOB:** 10/14/1947 **PB:** Marshall **SC:** MO/USA **PT:** Thomas Arnel Meads; Helen Louise (Ray) Meads **MS:** Married **SPN:** Mario Don Litch (9/27/2015); Robert Earl Long (8/7/1999) **CH:** Lisa Susanne Meads Casey; Paula Beth Waters; Gayla Brett Rountree **ED:** MS in Education (1996); BS in Education, University of Central Missouri, Cum Laude (1990); AA, Metropolitan Community College, Lee's Summit, MO (1987); Coursework, Missouri Valley College, Marshall, MO (1966-1967) **C:** Retired (2004); Special Education Teacher, Midway R1 School District, Cleveland, MO (1990-2004); Special Education Teacher, Lee's Summit R-7 School District (1990); Technician, AT&T, Lee's Summit, MO (1969-1987) **CR:** Program and District Coordinator for HIV/AIDS Education, Midway R1 School District; Guest Speaker for HIV/AIDS Education, Midway R1 School District **AW:** Crystal Apple Award for Teaching Excellence, Council for Advancement and Support of Education (1995) **MEM:** Council for Exceptional Children (CEC); Learning Disabilities Association of America; Kappa Delta Pi, International Honor Society in Education; The Honor Society of Phi Kappa Phi **MH:** Albert Nelson Marquis Lifetime Achievement Award (2017) **ADD:** 5613 NW Hutson Rd, Kansas City, MO, 64151

LOOMIS, HERSCHEL H. JR., **T:** Distinguished Professor Emeritus **I:** Education/Educational Services **CN:** Naval Postgraduate School **PB:** Wilmington **SC:** DE/USA **ED:** PhD, Massachusetts Institute of Technology (1963); MS in Electrical Engineering, University of Maryland (1959); BEE, Cornell University (1957) **CT:** Registered Electrical Engineer, State of California **C:** Distinguished Professor Emeritus, Department of Electrical and Computer Engineering, Naval Postgraduate School (2017-Present); Distinguished Professor of Electrical and Computer Engineering and Space Systems, Naval Postgraduate School (2010); Chairman, Electrical and Computer Engineering Department, Naval Postgraduate School (1995-1998); Naval Electronics Systems Command Chair Professor, Naval Postgraduate School, Monterey, CA (1981-1983); Department Chairman, University of California, Davis (1970-1975); Assistant Professor, Associate Professor, Professor of Electrical and Computer Engineering, University of California, Davis (1963-1981); Consultant, Lawrence Livermore Laboratory, Signal Science, Inc., Statistical Signal Processing, Inc., Hughes Space and Communications, Inc. **CR:** Director, The Carmel Pacific Repertory Theater

MIL: Electrical Engineer, National Security Agency, U.S. Navy (1957-1959); Retired Captain, U.S. Naval Reserve **CW:** Lighting Designer, 10 Gilbert & Sullivan Productions, Davis Comic Opera, Co.; Lighting Designer, "Twelfth Night," Pacific Repertory Theater; Contributor, More than 70 Articles, Professional Journals **AW:** Distinguished Performance Medal, United States National Reconnaissance Office (2017); Richard W. Hamming Excellence in Teaching Award (2007) **MEM:** Lifetime Senior Member, IEEE; Illuminating Engineering Society; Eta Kappa Nu; Phi Kappa Phi; Sigma Xi; Tau Beta Pi **BA:** 1 University Cir Rm M10, ECE Department, Naval Postgraduate School, Monterey, CA, 93943 **AD:** 999 Customs Road, Pebble Beach, CA, 93953 **URL:** http://faculty.nps.edu/vitae/cgi-bin/vita.cgi?p=display_vita&id=1023567768

LOONEY, DANIEL STEPHEN, I: Other

LOPEZ, PLACIDA RAMOS, T: Elementary School Educator (Retired) **I:** Education/Educational Services **DOB:** 10/11/1944 **PB:** Stafford **SC:** TX/USA **PT:** Urbano Zapata Ramos; Josefina (Saldaña) Arias Ramos **MS:** Widow **SPN:** Jose Jesus Lopez, Sr. (8/26/1969, Deceased) **CH:** Gabriel Elizalde **ED:** Postgraduate Coursework, University of St. Thomas, Minnesota (1987); BA in Elementary Education, Dominican College, Houston, TX (1975); Coursework, OLLU, San Antonio, TX (1966-1968); Coursework, Victoria College, Victoria, TX (1964-1966) **C:** Retired (2013); Consultant and tutor for Bilingual students for Alvin ISD from (2005-2013); Bilingual Teacher, Alvin Independent School District, Blackboard, Inc. (1994-2004); Fifth Grade Teacher, Alvin Independent School District, Blackboard, Inc. (1989-1994); First Grade Teacher, Alvin Independent School District, Blackboard Inc. (1984-1989); Bilingual Teacher, Pasadena Independent School District, Texas (1972-1982); Third Grade Teacher, Our Lady of Guadalupe School, Houston, TX (1966-1973); Volleyball Coach, Our Lady of Guadalupe School, Houston, TX (1966-1973) **CR:** Bilingual Consultant, Alvin Independent School District, Blackboard, Inc. (2005-2006); School based Supervisor for Student Teachers, University of Houston Main Campus; School based Supervisor for Student Teachers, University of Houston Clear Lake Campus; School based Supervisor for Student Teachers, Houston Baptist University; School based Supervisor for Student Teachers, Sam Houston State University **CIV:** Council Member, La Raza Southern Poverty Law Center; Translator, Local Community and Parish Members; Member, Texas Bilingual Textbook Committee, Pasadena Independent School District **CW:** Author, Poems; Author, Short Stories; Author, Daily Inspirational Thoughts; Author, Chapter, "The Adventures of Pipo & Pita" **AW:** Teacher of the Year Award (1990); Who's Who, Who's Who Among America's Teachers; Who's Who of American Women; Who's Who In America **MEM:** National PTA; National Education Association; HAABE; Alvin Teachers Association; United Teachers of Pasadena; Classroom Teachers Association; Bay Area Reading Council; Texas Association for Bilingual Education; TSTA; National Association for Bilingual Education; PTO; TRTA **MH:** Albert Nelson Marquis Lifetime Achievement Award (2017) **H:** Singing in public with various Mariachi groups; Writing; Reading; Playing guitar; Working in the garden **PA:** Democrat **RE:** Roman Catholic **ADD:** 9540 Ruth Rd, Rosharon, TX, 77583

JACK NORBECK LORBER, MORTIMER, T: Physiology Educator (Retired) **I:** Education/Educational Services **CN:** Georgetown University **DOB:** 08/30/1926 **PB:** New York City **SC:** NY/USA **PT:** Albert Lorber; Frieda (Levin) Lorber

MS: Married **SPN:** Eileen Segal (5/20/1956) **CH:** Kenneth; Stephanie **ED:** Assistant Resident, Medicine, Georgetown University Hospital, Washington D.C. (1958); Assistant Resident, Medicine, Mount Sinai Hospital, New York City, NY (1957); Resident, Hematology, Mount Sinai Hospital, New York City, NY (1953-1954); Rotating Intern, Albert Merritt Billings Hospital, University of Chicago (1952-1953); MD, Harvard University, Cum Laude (1952); DMD, Harvard University, Cum Laude (1950); BS, New York University (1945) **CT:** Diplomate, National Board of Medical Examiners **C:** Associate Professor, Georgetown University, Washington D.C. (1968-1997); Instructor, Department of Physiology and Biophysics, Georgetown University, Washington D.C. (1959-1968); Assistant Professor, Department of Physiology and Biophysics, Georgetown University, Washington D.C. (1959-1968) **CR:** Guest Scientist, Naval Medical Research Institute, Bethesda, MD (1978-1983); Lecturer, Physiology, Walter Reed Army Institute of Dental Research, Washington D.C. (1963-1970); Lecturer, Physiology, Navy Postgraduate Dental School, Walter Reed National Military Medical Center, Bethesda, MD (1962-1970) **MIL:** Lieutenant, U.S. Naval Reserve (1954-1956) **CW:** Contributor, "The Merck Manual, 17th Edition" (1999); Contributor, "The Merck Manual, 16th Edition" (1992); Contributor, "The Merck Manual, 15th Edition" (1987); Contributor, "The Merck Manual, 14th Edition" (1982); Contributor, Articles, Professional Journals **AW:** Distinguished Alumnus Award, Harvard School of Dental Medicine (2010); Distinguished Alumnus Award, Harvard School of Dental Medicine (2010); United States Public Health Service Research Career Development Award, National Institute of Dental Research, Bethesda, MD (1963-1970); Lederle Medical Faculty Award, Lederle Co., Pearl River, NY (1960-1963); Grant, American Cancer Society; Grant, United States Public Health Service **MEM:** American Physiological Society; American Society of Hematology; Association for Research in Vision and Ophthalmology; International Association for Dental Research **MH:** Albert Nelson Marquis Lifetime Achievement Award (2017) **RE:** Jewish **ADD:** 8100 Connecticut Ave Apt 1108, Chevy Chase, MD, 20815

LOURENCO, JULIA, T: Civil Engineer **I:** Engineering **CN:** University of Minho **DOB:** 08/19/1962 **PB:** Porto **SC:** Portugal **PT:** José Barbosa Lourenço; Júlia Adelaide Brandão de P. M. Lourenço **ED:** PhD in Civil Engineering, Institute Superior Técnico/UTL, Lisbon, Portugal (1997) **C:** Assistant Professor, University of Minho (2000-Present); Dean, Civil Engineering Studies, University of Minho (2000-2001) **CR:** Representative, Advisory Monitoring Committee Entrepreneurship Council, Minho and Lima, Braga, Portugal (2006-2015); National Delegate, Member, European Science Foundation, Sustainable Development Policies for Minor Deprived Urban Communities, Cost Action C27, Brussels, Belgium (2006-2010); Representative, Association of European Civil Engineering Faculties, Prague, Czech Republic (2000-2010); Expert Evaluators, European Community, Brussels, Belgium (1999-2003) **CIV:** Exhibition Curator, Prayer Beads, Casa Diocesana Vilar, Porto (2014-2015); Exhibition Curator, Prayer Beads, Santa Casa Misericórdia Guimarães (2013-2014); Honorary Member, Portuscale (2003-2015); President, Ludus, Porto, Portugal (1997-1999); Consultant, Portuscale, Porto, Portugal (1992-2002) **CW:** Contributor, Articles, Numerous Scientific Professional Publications **AW:** Gerd Albers Award, International Society of City and Regional Planners (2003) **MEM:** Bureau Member, International Society of City and Regional Planners

(2006-2012); President, Portuguese National Delegate, International Society of City and Regional Planners (2006-2012); Regional Science Association International; Board of Portuguese Engineers; Honorary Member, Associação dos Funcionários da CCDR-N **H:** Travel; Walking **RE:** Roman Catholic **ADD:** Rua dos Castelos, 369, 2, Porto, Portugal, 4250-118

LOVICH, RICHARD A. ESQUIRE, T: Senior Partner, Managing Litigation Attorney **I:** Law and Legal Services **CN:** Stephenson, Acquisto & Colman **DOB:** 10/03/1957 **PB:** Los Angeles **SC:** CA/USA **PT:** Howard Lovich; Marian Lovich **MS:** Married **SPN:** Michelle S. Lovich **CH:** Kristy L. Lovich; Jason Boles (Son-in-law); Alexandra J. Lovich-Murillo; Aaron Murillo (Son-in-law); Juliane H. Lovich; Kimberly E. Cormier-Lovich; Katherine R. Lovich; Penelope Blue Murillo (Granddaughter); Henry Bear Eugene Lovich-Boles (Grandson) **ED:** JD, Loyola Law School of Los Angeles (1983); BA in Political Science, California State University, Northridge, with Honors (1980) **CT:** Certified Trainer, National Association of Trial Advocacy **C:** Senior Partner, Managing Litigation Attorney, Stephenson, Acquisto & Colman (2005-Present); Managing Attorney, Lovich & Isaac (2002-2005); Managing Attorney, Lovich & Penn (1991-2002); Assistant Managing Attorney, Tucker & Lovich (1989-1991) **CR:** Speaker, "Hospital Service Contracting," Annual National Institute, American Association of Healthcare Administrative Management (2017); Speaker, "Litigating Reimbursement Denials," Stanford Health Care (2017); Speaker, "Current Issues on Healthcare Reimbursement," University of California, San Francisco (2017); Speaker, "Managed Care Contracts" and "Clinical Denials - Effective Strategies," HFMA Idaho-Winter Educational Meeting (2017); Speaker, "Managed Care Contracting Issues"⊠ and "Clinical Denials - The Legal Aspect," HFMA Educational Road Show, Tuscon, Prescott, and Kingman, AZ (2016); Speaker, "Increasing Your Success Rate on Clinical Denials," American Case Management Association (ACMA) Physician Advisory Conference, San Diego, CA (2016); Speaker, "Managed Care Contracting"⊠ and "Increasing Clinical Denial Success Rates," Santa Barbara Cottage Hospital (2016); Testimony before the United States Senate Committee on Commerce, Science, and Technology Regarding the Impact of the Telephone Consumer Protection Act on the Healthcare Industry (2016); Speaker in Field **CW:** Contributor, "The Dangers of Agreeing to an Independent Review Organization Requirement in a Hospital Services Agreement," The Journal of Healthcare Administrative Management (2014); Contributor, "A Rose is a Rose is a Rose... The Value of Authorization of Treatment and Verification of Benefits in Reimbursement Cases," The Journal of Healthcare Administrative Management (2013); Contributor, "The Good, the Bad and the Ugly of Managed Care Contracting," SAC Walnut Creek Seminar (2012); Contributor, "Escaping Co-pays and Deductibles by Abusing the Fair Debt Collection Practices Act," Southern California HFMA Newsbrief Newsletter (2012); Presenter, "The Development of the Case Theme," American International Group, National Trial Skills Seminar, IBM Conference Center, Palisades, NY (1999); Presenter, "The Examination and Cross Examination of Expert Witnesses," American International Group, National Trial Skills Seminar, IBM Conference Center, Palisades, NY (1998); Presenter, "Litigation and Trial of Employment Related Issues," American International Group, National Trial Skills Seminar, IBM Conference Center, Palisades, NY (1997); Presenter, "Compliance with Workplace Regulations Concerning the Physically Challenged," American

International Group, National Trial Skills Seminar, IBM Conference Center, Palisades, NY (1997); Presenter, "Civil Procedure for the Claims Professional," Hartford Insurance Group (1990) **AW:** Honoree, Nation's Top 1 Percent, National Association of Distinguished Counsel (2016-Present); Named, Southern California Super Lawyer (2011-Present); Preeminent AV Rating, Martindale-Hubbell (1995-Present); Named, Top Rated Lawyer in Healthcare, Corporate Counsel, The American Lawyer (2012) **MEM:** American Bar Association (ABA); Los Angeles County Bar Association; Chairman of Law and Ethics Committee, Western Regional Chapter, American Association of Healthcare Administrative Management (AAHAM); California Society for Healthcare Attorneys; Healthcare Financial Management Association **BAR:** Supreme Court of the United States (2013); United States Court of Appeals for the Ninth Circuit (2009); United States District Court for the Southern District of California (2009); United States District Court for the Northern District of California (2006); United States District Court for the Eastern District of California (2006); United States District Court for the Central District of California (1985); The State Bar of California (1984) **H:** Silent Movies; Sports Memorabilia; Los Angeles Dodgers **BA:** 303 N Glenoaks Blvd, Stephenson, Acquisto & Colman, Burbank, CA, 91502 **ADD:** 21054 Nashville St, Chatsworth, CA, 91311 **URL:** https://www.linkedin.com/in/richard-lovich-76875017

LOW, JAMES THOMAS, T: Emeritus Marketing Professor **I:** Advertising & Marketing **CN:** Wayne State University **DOB:** 03/31/1942 **PB:** Atlanta **SC:** GA/USA **PT:** Thomas Low; Pearl Louise Low **MS:** Married **SPN:** Louise Anderson (12/30/1967) **CH:** James William; Eric Linne; Kari Louise; Antony Anderson **ED:** PhD, University of Michigan, Ann Arbor, MI (1977); MBA, University of Michigan, Ann Arbor, MI (1971); BA, University of Michigan, Ann Arbor, MI (1965) **CT:** Jonah's Jonah Certification (1992); Avraham Y. Goldratt Institute, Jonah Certification (1989); CPIM Certification in Production and Inventory Management, APICS, Association for Operations Management **C:** Emeritus Professor, Wayne State University (2008-Present),Associate Professor of Marketing, Wayne State University (1998-2008); Consultant, i2 Technologies, Long Beach, CA (1998); Consultant, i2 Technologies, Naperville, IL (1998); Consultant, i2 Technologies (1998); Project Manager, i2 Technologies, Dallas, Texas (1996-1998); Software Engineer, i2 Technologies, Dallas, Texas (1996-1998); Associate Professor of Marketing, Wayne State University, Detroit, MI (1974-1996); Constraint Management Specialist, Arvin Meritor (Now Meritor, Inc.), Troy, MI (1994) **CR:** Consultant, MTU Detroit Diesel (Now Rolls-Royce Power Systems AG) (2008); Eastern Michigan University, Ypsilanti, MI (2006); Ford Motor Company, Wixom, MI (2002-2003); DaimlerChrysler, Indianapolis, IN (2002); DaimlerChrysler, Kenosha, WI (2001); DaimlerChrysler, Detroit, MI (2000-2001); DaimlerChrysler, Indianapolis, IN (2000); DaimlerChrysler, Auburn Hills, MI (2000) **CIV:** Director, Association of Manufacturing Excellence, Great Lakes Region, MI (1994-2001); Director, APICS, Association Operations Management, Detroit, MI (1991-1996); Director, Society of Manufacturing Engineers (Now SME), Ann Arbor, MI (1991-1993) **MIL:** United States Army, Fort Benning, GA (1966-1968) **CW:** Contributor, Numerous Scientific Papers; Contributor, Articles, Professional Journals **MEM:** Secretary and Treasurer, Beta Gamma Sigma Honor Society (Now Beta Gamma Sigma, Inc.) (1987-2008); Membership Committee, Travis Pointe Country Club (2004-2005); Secretary, University of Michigan, Alpha Kappa Psi Fraternity (1970-1971); Founder, Beta Gamma Sigma Honor Society (Now Beta Gamma Sigma, Inc.); Alumni Association of the University of Michigan; Theory of Constraints International Certification Organization (Now TOCICO) **ADD:** 3431 Surrey Dr, Saline, MI, 48176

LOW, MALCOLM, T: Professor of Physiology and Internal Medicine **I:** Education/Educational Services **CN:** University of Michigan **DOB:** 08/25/1955 **PB:** Edinburgh **PT:** George Duncan Low; Jessie Forbes Morton **MS:** Married **SPN:** Gaye Thomas (12/26/1981) **CH:** Nicholas Duncan Thomas-Low; Jacob Armon Thomas-Low **ED:** PhD, Tufts University (1987); Neuroendocrinology Fellow, New England Medical Center (Now Tufts Medical Center) (1982-1985); Resident in Internal Medicine, Michael Reese Hospital, Chicago, Illinois (1979-1982); Intern in Internal Medicine, Michael Reese Hospital, Chicago, Illinois (1979-1982); MD, Albany Medical Center (1979); BS, Rensselaer Polytechnic Institute (1975) **CT:** Diplomate in Endocrinology and Metabolism, American Board of Internal Medicine (1985); Diplomate, American Board of Internal Medicine (1982) **C:** David F. Bohr Collegiate Professor of Physiology, University of Michigan (2015-Present); Professor of Physiology and Internal Medicine, School of Medicine, University of Michigan (2009-Present); Senior Scientist, OHSU (2003-2009); Professor of Behavioral Neurosciences, OHSU (2002-2009); Scientist, OHSU (1995-2009); Associate Professor of Biochemistry and Molecular Biology, OHSU (1996-2002); Assistant Professor of Biochemistry and Molecular Biology, OHSU (1991-1995); Assistant Scientist, OHSU (1990-1994); Assistant Professor of Medicine, Tufts University (1986-1989) **CR:** Director, Systems and Integrative Biology Training Grant, University of Michigan (2013-Present); Director, Animal Phenotyping Core Laboratory, University of Michigan (2010-Present); Associate Director, Center for the Study of Weight Regulation & Associate Disorders (2005-2009); Member, Endocrinology and IPOD Study Section, Center pf Science Review, National Institutes of Health, Bethesda, Maryland (2001); Director, Mouse Metabolic Phenotypeing Center, University of Michigan **CW:** Associate Editor, "Gastroenterology" (2011-Present); Contributor, Articles, Professional Journals **AW:** Grantee, National Institutes of Health (1988-Present); The Rackham Graduate Distinguished Faculty Achievement Award, University of Michigan (2016); Honoree, University of Medical School League of Research Excellence (2011); Pfizer Scholar Award, Pfizer Inc. (1988-1990); Physician-Scientist Award, National Institutes of Health (1984-1989); Individual National Research Service Award (1983-1984) **MEM:** Fellow, American Association for the Advancement of Science (2011-Present); American Physicians Association; Pituitary Society, Society for Neuroscience; Endocrine Society; Alpha Omega Alpha Honor Medical Society **MH:** Albert Nelson Marquis Lifetime Achievement Award (2017) **H:** Travel; Model railroading **ADD:** 6 Haverhill Ct, Ann Arbor, MI, 48105

LOWRIE, YVONNE COLEMAN, T: Artist, Educator, Volunteer **I:** Education/Educational Services **DOB:** 03/04/1936 **PB:** Knoxville **SC:** TN/USA **PT:** Clarence F. Coleman; Helen Black Coleman **MS:** Married **SPN:** Max Lowrie (12/18/1962) **ED:** MEd, Southwestern Baptist Theological Seminary, Fort Worth, Texas (1962); BA, Carson-Newman College (Now Carson-Newman University), Jefferson City, TN (1959) **CT:** Certification, American Business Women's Association Leadership Conference (2010); Certified, Fund Development, Girl Scouts of the United States of America, Edith Macy Conference Center, NY (2010); Certified Teacher, S-T-R-E-T-C-H and Sew Teachers School, Eugene, OR (1975); Certified in Working with Adolescents, YWCA, Michigan State University, East Lansing, MI (1961); Training School Graduate Certificate, YWCA, Lake Erie College, Ohio (1959) **C:** Sales Consultant, Tole Etc., Fort Worth, Texas (1985-1988); Sewing Teacher and Sales, S-T-R-E-T-C-H and Sew Fabric Center, Arlington, Texas (1975-1977); Teen Program Director, YWCA, Fort Worth and Tarrant County, Texas (1959-1968); Assistant Executive Director, YWCA, Fort Worth and Tarrant County, Texas (1959-1968) **CIV:** Volunteer, World Association of Girl Guides and Girl Scouts of America; Volunteer, Girl Scouts of Texas Oklahoma Plains; Member, Highland Church of Christ **CW:** Exhibitor, Arlington Public Library, Arlington County Government (1989-Present); Exhibitor, Bob Duncan Community Center, Arlington CVB, Arlington, TX (1989-Present); Exhibitor, Fort Worth Regional Library, City of Fort Worth, TX (1986-Present); Exhibitor, Fort Worth Community Arts Center (2004); Artist, Painted Wall, Cancer Care Services, Children's Area, Fort Worth, TX; Artist, Painted Wall, Woman's Haven Children's School (Now Safehaven of Tarrant County), Fort Worth, TX; Artist, Painted Wall, Arlington Life Shelter; Artist, Painted Wall, Welcome House Youth Center, Mission Arlington ; Artist, Painted Wall, Dallas Outdoor Fence Enclosure, Family Gateway; Artist, Painted Wall, Fielder House Museum, Arlington Historical Society; Artist, Painted Wall, Thistle Hill House Museum; Exhibitor, Permanent Collection, White House; Exhibitor, Permanent Collection, Library of Congress; Exhibitor, Permanent Collection, Blair House; Exhibitor, Permanent Collection, Number One Observatory Circle; Exhibitor, Permanent Collection, Smithsonian Institute; Exhibitor, Permanent Collection, Anatole Hotel, Dallas, TX; Exhibitor, Permanent Collection, State Capitol of Texas, Austin, TX **AW:** Honor, 60-Year Pin, School Grades 2-11, Girl Scouts of the United States of America, Knoxville, TN (2018); Award, 50-Year Volunteer, Girl Scouts of the United States of America, Fort Worth, Texas (2018); Hall of Fame, Knoxville East High School Alumni Association (2016); Lifetime Achievement Award, Girl Scouts of Texas Oklahoma Plains (2015); Woman of District Award (2015); Appreciation Award, 100th Anniversary Task Group (2012); Centenary Appreciation Recognition Award, World Foundation for Girl Guides and Girl Scouts (2012); Volunteer Service Award, President's Council on Service and Civic Participation (2009); Lone Star Legend Award, Volunteer Center, Texas (2009); Council Award, Girl Scouts Alumnae Association (2008); Thanks Badge, Girl Scouts Circle T Council (2005); Outstanding Member Star Award, Fort Worth Decorative Painters (2005); Outstanding Chapter Service Award, Bluebonnet Tole and Decorative Painters, Inc. (2003); Dedicated Service Award, National Society of Tole and Decorative Painters (2003); Scholar, Funding Information Center, Fort Worth, Texas (2002); Outstanding Chapter Service Award, Fort Worth Decorative Painters (2001-2003); Juliette Low World Friendship Medal, Girl Scouts of the United States of America (1997); Outstanding Woman of the Year in the Arts, Fort Worth Mayor's Commission on the Status of Women (1996); Volunteer Service Award, Trinity Meadows Community, Girl Scouts Circle T Council (1992); Appreciation Pin (1986); Thanks Badge (1978); Inductee, Hall of Fame, Knoxville East High School Alumni Association (1952-1968); Grantee, Juliette Low World Friendship Fund, Girl Scouts of the United States, Sangam, India; Lifetime Achievement Award, World Foundation for Girl Guides and Girl Scouts **MEM:** National

Society Committee Member, Bluebonnet Tole and Decorative Painters, Inc. (1988-Present); Fundraiser, Sangam, World Centre, World Association of Girl Guides and Girl Scouts, India (1986-Present); Committee Member, Fort Worth Decorative Painters (1985-Present); Committee Member, National Society of Tole and Decorative Painters (1985-Present); Committee Member, American Business Women's Association (ABWA Management, LLC) (1961-Present); Instructor, Silk Scarf Painting, Girl Scout Alumnae Association (2018); Leadership, Gift Committee Member, World Foundation for Girl Guides and Girl Scouts (2014); Vice President, Tarrant County ABWA Friends Council (2011), Board Secretary, World Foundation for Girl Guides and Girl Scouts (2009-2013); Founding Chair, Girl Scouts Alumnae Association (2007); Invited, 32nd World Conference, World Foundation for Girl Guides and Girl Scouts (2005); National Division Board Director, National Society of Tole and Decorative Painters (1992-1994); Founding Chairman, Friends of Pax Lodge, World Foundation for Girl Guides and Girl Scouts (1991-2009); Committee Member, World Foundation for Girl Guides and Girl Scouts (1986); President-Elect, Forth Worth Charter - Six Flags Chapter, American Business Women's Association (ABWA Management, LLC); Chapter President, American Business Women's Association (ABWA Management, LLC); Vice President, American Business Women's Association (ABWA Management, LLC); Secretary, American Business Women's Association (ABWA Management, LLC); Treasurer, American Business Women's Association (ABWA Management, LLC); League of Women Voters of Tarrant County, Texas; Executive Board Member, Girl Scouts Alumnae Association; National Society of Tole and Decorative Painters; Founder, Fort Worth Decorative Painters; President, Fort Worth Decorative Painters; Vice President, Fort Worth Decorative Painters; Christmas Party Chair, Fort Worth Decorative Painters; SDP Chapter, Bluebonnet Tole and Decorative Painters, Inc; Olave Baden-Powell Society; Attendee, Annual Gathering of Girl Scout Committee Members, Edith Macy Conference Center, World Foundation for Girl Guides and Girl Scouts, NY; Founding Chair, PAX LODGE, World Centre in North London, World Association of Girl Guides and Girl Scouts, United Kingdom; Founding Chair, World Association of Girl Guides and Girl Scouts, United States **H:** Painting; Travel; Volunteering; Acting; Sewing **PA:** Independent **ADD:** 3250 Medina Ave, Fort Worth, TX, 76133

LOWTHER, FRANK EUGENE, **T:** Research Physicist **I:** Sciences **DOB:** 02/03/1929 **PB:** Orrville **SC:** OH/USA **PT:** John Finger Lowther; Mary Elizabeth (Mackey) Lowther **MS:** Married **SPN:** Elizabeth E. Koons (4/21/1951) **CH:** Cynthia E.; Victoria J.; James A.; Frank Eugene **ED:** Postgraduate Coursework, Boston University (1952-1954); BS in Engineering Physics, The Ohio State University, Columbus, OH (1952) **C:** Consultant, Atlantic Richfield Company, Plano, TX (1993-2001); Technical Adviser, Atlantic Richfield Company, Plano, TX (1993-2001); Research Adviser, Atlantic Richfield Company, Plano, TX (1988-1993); Scientific Adviser, Atlantic Richfield Company, Los Angeles, CA (1985-1988); Principal Scientist, Atlantic Richfield Company, Los Angeles, CA (1983-1985); Scientist, Energy Conversion and Materials Laboratory, Atlantic Richfield Company, Los Angeles, CA (1980-1983); Senior Engineering Associate, Linde Division, Union Carbide Corporation, Tonawanda, NY (1975-1980); Manager, Ozone Research and Development, W.R. Grace Co., Curtis Bay, MD (1972-1975); Chief Scientist, Purification Science, Inc. (1967-1972);

Adviser to President, General Railway Signal, Rochester, NY (1965-1967); Scientist, Missile Division, General Electric, Daytona Beach, FL (1957-1965); Scientist, Missile Division, General Electric, Syracuse, NY (1957-1965); Scientist, Missile Division, Raytheon Company, Boston, MA (1952-1957) **CR:** Adviser, Custom Technology Creations, Inc., Canandaigua, NY (1993-Present); Adviser, World Ecology Resources, Inc., Geneva, Switzerland (1999-2010); Adviser, Energy Science, Inc., Canandaigua, NY (1993-2010) **AW:** Wall of Honor, National Aviation and Space Exploration (2001) Inventor of the Year, AIPLA (1976) Inventor of the Year, Technical Societies Council (1976) **MEM:** Fellow, AIAA; American Association for the Advancement of Science; IEEE; Masons; The New York Academy of Sciences **MH:** Albert Nelson Marquis Lifetime Achievement Award (2017) **ADD:** 4965 Adams Dr, Canandaigua, NY, 14424

LU, MI, **T:** Computer Engineer **I:** Engineering **CN:** Texas A&M University **DOB:** 07/22/1949 **PB:** Chongqing **SC:** Sichuan/China **PT:** Chong Pu Lu; Shu Sheng Fan Lu **ED:** PhD, Rice University (1987); MS, Rice University (1984) **CT:** Registered Professional Engineer **C:** Professor, Texas A&M University (1998-Present); Associate Professor, Texas A&M University (1987-1998); Assistant Professor, Texas A&M University (1987-1998) **CR:** Conference Chairman, International Conference Computer Science and Informatics (2000, 2002-2003) **CW:** Associate Editor, Computer Science and Engineering (2011-Present); Associate Editor, Information Science (1996-1997, 2002-2003); Associate Editor, Journal of Computing and Information (1995-1997); Author, Arithmetic and Logic in Computer Systems; Contributor, Articles, Professional Journals **MEM:** Senior Member, Computer Society, IEEE **BA:** Department of Electric Co., Texas A&M University, College Station, TX, 77843 **ADD:** 12435 Shadycrest Drive, Houston, TX, 77082

LUDMERER, KENNETH MARC, **T:** Professor **I:** Education/Educational Services **CN:** Washington University School of Medicine **DOB:** 01/13/1947 **PB:** Long Beach **SC:** CA/USA **PT:** Sol Ludmerer; Norma (Helfer) Ludmerer **MS:** Married **SPN:** Loren Rae Starobin (8/9/1987) **CH:** Jordan Suzanne Ludmerer; Lindsey Francesca Ludmerer **ED:** Medical Resident, Fellow, Washington University, St. Louis, MO (1973-1978); MD, Johns Hopkins School of Medicine (1973); MA, Johns Hopkins University (1971); AB, Harvard University (1968) **C:** Mabel Dorn Reeder Distinguished Professor in the History of Medicine, Washington University in St. Louis (2010-Present); Professor of Medicine, Washington University in St. Louis (1992-present); Professor of History, Washington University, St. Louis (1992-present); Associate Professor of Medicine, Washington University in St. Louis (1986-1992); Associate Professor of History, Washington University in St. Louis (1986-1992); Assistant Professor of Medicine, Washington University in St. Louis (1979-1986); Assistant Professor of History, Faculty of Arts and Sciences, Washington University in St. Louis (1979-1986); Chief Resident, Internal Medicine, Barnes Hospital, St. Louis, MO (1978-1979) **CR:** Board Member, National Board of Medical Examiners (2011-Present); Board of Directors, Accreditation Council of Graduate Medical Education (2011-Present); North Shore LIJ Health System, Manhasset, NY (2003-Present); Medical Education Consultant, Various Schools, Hospitals, Professional Organizations, State Governments (2000-Present); Institute Medical Committee on Resident Duty Hours (2007-2008); Visiting Committee, Harvard Medical School, Boston, MA (2000-2002); Task Force on Medical

Education, Acadia University, Philadelphia, PA (1992-1996); Advisory Board, Culpeper Foundation Program in Medical Humanities, Stanford, CT (1992-1993); National Advisory Committee, Clinical Scholars Advisory Committee, Robert Wood Johnson Foundation, Princeton, NJ (1988-1992); New Pathway Program Evaluation Committee, Association of American Medical Colleges (1986-1988) **CIV:** Board Member, Saint Louis Symphony Orchestra (2016-Present); Board of Trustees, Accreditation Council for Graduate Medical Education (2012-Present); Member, Board of Trustees, National Board of Medical Examiners (2011-Present); Jewish Federation of St. Louis (2002-2009); Sommers Children's Welfare Bureau, St. Louis, MO (2000-2009); Chair, Community Research Peer Review Committee, St. Louis Heart Association (1988-1989); Trustee, Board of Directors, Missouri Historical Society, St. Louis, MO (1987-1993); Missouri History Museum (1987-1993); Medical Advisory Committee, St. Louis Science Center (1985-1987) **CW:** Member, Editorial Board, Annals of Internal Medicine (1993-Present); Member, Editorial Board, The Pharos (1986-Present); Author, "Let Me Heal: The Opportunity to Preserve Excellence in American Medicine" (2014); Author, "Time to Heal: American Medical Education from the Turn of the Century to the Era of Managed Care" (1999); Member, Editorial Board, History Education Quarterly (1993-1996); Member, Editorial Board, Journal for the History of Medicine (1988-1990); Author, "Learning to Heal: The Development of American Medical Education" (1985); Member, Editorial Board, American Journal of Medicine (1981-1996); Member, Editorial Board, Journal for the History of Medicine (1981-1983); Author, "Genetics and American Society: A Historical Appraisal" (1972) **AW:** Distinguished Faculty Award, Washington University School of Medicine (2018); Elected Fellow, Royal College of Physicians of London (2018); Lifetime Achievement Award, American Osler Society (2016); Distinguished Service Award, Washington University School of Medicine (2016); Distinguished Medical Alumnus Award, John Hopkins University School of Medicine (2015); Distinguished Alumnus Award, Johns Hopkins University Alumni Association (2001); Abraham Flexner Award for Distinguished Service to Medical Education, Association of American Medical Colleges (2003); Daniel Tosteson Award for Leadership in Medical Education, Harvard Medical School (2001); Nicholas Davies Award, American College of Physicians (1997); Research Award, Joseph Macy Junior Foundation (1989-1996); Faculty Scholar, General Internal Medicine, Henry Kaiser Family Foundation (1981-1986) **MEM:** Council, American Association for the History of Medicine (2000-2008); President, American Association for the History of Medicine (2002-2004); Vice President, American Association for the History of Medicine (2000-2002); President, American Osler Society (1994-1995); Vice President, American Osler Society (1992-1994); Committee on Publication Policy, Master, American College of Physicians (1988-1993); Board of Governors, American Osler Society (1988-1996); Council, American Association for the History of Medicine (1984-1987); Teaching and Research Scholar, American College of Physicians (1980-1983); Fellow, American Association for the Advancement of Science; Fellow, Midwest Council, American Academy of Arts and Sciences; Master, American College of Physicians; Association of American Physicians; American Clinical and Climatological Association; American Federation for Clinical Research; History of Science Society; American Association for the History of Medicine; American Osler Society; Phi Beta Kappa; Alpha

Omega Alpha; Sigma Xi; American Association for the History of Medicine **H:** Music; Running; Traveling **BA:** 660 S Euclid Ave, Campus Box 8066, Washington University, Dept of Medicine, Saint Louis, MO, 63110 **ADD:** 42 Rio Vista Dr, Saint Louis, MO, 63124

LUFF, RONALD, T: Director Anatomic Pathology for Clinical Trials **I:** Medicine & Health Care **CN:** Quest Diagnostics **DOB:** 05/21/1947 **PB:** Norman **SC:** OK/USA **MS:** Married **SPN:** Jean Beverly Sterner (7/7/1968) **CH:** Heather L.; Jennifer A.; Kimberly J. **ED:** Chief Resident, Department of Laboratory Medicine, Acting Assistant Medical Director, The Johns Hopkins Hospital, Baltimore, MD (1978-1979); Resident, Department of Laboratory Medicine, The Johns Hopkins Hospital, Baltimore, MD (1977-1978); Senior Resident in Anatomic Pathology, The Johns Hopkins Hospital, Baltimore, MD (1976-1977); Assistant Resident in Anatomic Pathology, Department of Pathology, The Johns Hopkins Hospital, Baltimore, MD (1974-1976); Rotating Intern, Malcolm Grow U.S. Air Force Medical Center, Andrews AFB, Washington D.C. (1973-1974); MD, Johns Hopkins University School of Medicine (1973); MPH, Johns Hopkins University (1972); BA, Lehigh University, Magna Cum Laude (1969) **CT:** Diplomate in Anatomic and Clinical Pathology, American Board of Pathology; Licensed Physician, States of Maryland, Pennsylvania **C:** Director, Anatomic Pathology for Clinical Trials, Quest Diagnostics (1995-Present); Vice President, Director, Anatomic Pathology, Corning Clinical Laboratory, Teterboro, NJ (1995-Present); Medical Director, Program in Cytotechnology, Thomas Jefferson University, Philadelphia, PA (1987-2014); Clinical Professor, College of Allied Health Sciences, Thomas Jefferson University, Philadelphia, PA (1983-2015); Associate Pathologist, Sacred Heart Hospital, Allentown, PA (1982-1994); Chief, Cytopathology, USAF/Wilford Hall, San Antonio, TX (1980-1982); Clinical Assistant Professor, Pathology, Instructor, School of Cytotechnology, The University of Texas Health Science Center at San Antonio (1979-1982); Assistant Chief, Anatomic Pathology, USAF/Wilford Hall, San Antonio, TX (1979-1980); Instructor, School of Cytotechnology, The Johns Hopkins Hospital, Baltimore, MD (1976-1977); Instructor, School of Public Health and Hygiene, The Johns Hopkins Hospital, Baltimore, MD (1974-1977); Instructor, Anatomic Pathology, School of Medicine, The Johns Hopkins Hospital, Baltimore, MD (1974-1979) **AW:** Certificate of Appreciation for Work as a Member and Chairman of Cytotechnology Programs Review Committee (1993-1994); Lovelace Award, Annual Air Force Society and Arnold Air Society National Meetings (1969) **MEM:** Medical Member, Executive Committee, American Society of Cytotechnology (1991-Present); Laboratory Inspector, College of American Pathologists (1984-Present); Co-chairman, Cytotechnology Programs Reviews Committee, American Society of Cytotechnology (1993-1994); Chairman, Cytotechnology Programs Review Committee, American Society of Cytotechnology (1990-1993); President, Alpha of Maryland Chapter, Alpha Omega Alpha (1975-1977); Fellow, American Society of Clinical Pathologists; Fellow, College of American Pathologists; American Medical Association; American Association for the Advancement of Science; American Society of Cytopathology; AABB; The New York Academy of Sciences; Lehigh County Medical Association; Delaware Valley Society of Cytology; Johns Hopkins Alumni and Faculty Association; Phi Beta Kappa **ADD:** 1377 Kelchner Rd, Bethlehem, NJ, 18018

LUMB, SANDRA J., T: Elementary School Educator **I:** Education/Educational Services **CN:** St. Monica School **DOB:** 06/01/1955 **PB:** Lawrence **SC:** MA/USA **PT:** William Taylor Lumb (Deceased); Virginia Ruth (Peate) Lumb **ED:** BS, University of Massachusetts Lowell (1977) **CT:** Certified Teacher, State of Massachusetts **C:** Middle School Teacher in English, Math, Social Studies, St. Monica School, Methuen, MA (2005-Present); Assistant Administrator, Our Lady of Mount Carmel School, Methuen, MA (1991-1992); Elementary School Teacher, Our Lady of Mount Carmel School, Methuen, MA (1980-2004); Instructional Assistant, Title I, Methuen, MA (1978-1980) **CIV:** Singer, Church Choir; Deliverer, Children's Message at Sunday Service, First Baptist Church, Methuen, MA **MEM:** Board of Directors, Children's Center, Methuen, MA (2007-Present); Methuen Community Chorus (1991-Present); National Catholic Educational Association **MH:** Albert Nelson Marquis Lifetime Achievement Award (2017) **H:** Bowling; Quilting; Stamp collecting **BA:** 212 Lawrence St, Methuen, MA, 01844 **ADD:** 895 Riverside Dr, Methuen, MA, 01844

LUND, JOHN W., T: Civil Engineering Educator, Geothermal Energy Researcher, Consultant **I:** Education/Educational Services **CN:** Self-Employed **DOB:** 07/07/1936 **PB:** Berkeley **SC:** CA/USA **PT:** John Jorgensen Lund; Lydia Marie (Olsen) Lund **MS:** Married **SPN:** Eva Odzganova (11/3/1990); Jacqueline Lee Urling (6/1962, Divorced 3/1985) **CH:** John David; Thomas Erik **ED:** PhD in Civil Engineering, University of Colorado, Boulder (1967); MS in Transportation Engineering, University of California, Berkeley (1962); BCE, University of Colorado, Boulder (1958) **CT:** Professional Engineer, Oregon and California **C:** Director Emeritus, Geo-Heat Center, Oregon Institute of Technology, Klamath Falls, OR (2010-Present); Professor Emeritus, Oregon Institute of Technology, Klamath Falls, OR (1999-Present); National Renewable Energy Lab (2010-2011); Director of Geo-Heat Center, Oregon Institute of Technology, Klamath Falls, OH (1997-2010); Dean of Engineering and Industrial Technology, Oregon Institute of Technology, Klamath Falls, OR (1996-1997); Institute of Technology, Klamath Falls, OR (1983-1987); Associate Dean, Division Chairman, Engineering Technology, Oregon Institute of Technology, Klamath Falls, OR (1980-1982); Chairman, Department of Civil Engineering Technology, Oregon Institute of Technology, Klamath Falls, OR (1977-1980); Research Associate, Geo-Heat Center, Oregon Institute of Technology, Klamath Falls, OR (1975-1997); Professor, Oregon Institute of Technology, Klamath Falls, OR (1973-1999); Associate Professor of Engineering, Engineering Technology, Oregon Institute of Technology, Klamath Falls OR (1967-1973); Assistant Professor of Civil Engineering, University of Alaska (1964-1965) **CR:** Invited Lecturer, Geothermal Training Program, United Nations University, Reykjavik, Iceland (1995); Invited Lecturer, Geothermal Training Program, United Nations University, Reykjavik, Iceland (1987); Chairman, National Council for Fundamentals of Engineering (1985-1999); Consultant, Zbinden Engineering, Klamath Falls, OR (1984-1995); Oregon State Board of Examiners for Engineering and Surveying, Salem, OR (1984-1993); Lecturer, Geothermal Institute; Consultant, Direct Utilization Geothermals, Kenya, Ethiopia, Canada, United States **CIV:** Treasurer, Ross Ragland Theater Guild, Klamath Falls, OR (1992-1994); Oregon Recreational Trails Advisory Committee, Salem, OR (1990-1999) **MIL:** First Lieutenant, U.S. Army (1959-1960) **CW:** Author, Editor, "Stories from a Heated Earth-our

Geothermal Heritage" (1999); Author, Editor, "Geothermal Direct-Use Engineering and Design Guidebook" (1998); Author, "Southern Oregon Cross Country Ski Trails" (1989); Contributor, Articles to Professional Journals **AW:** Medal of Honor, International Summer School (2002); Mitsubishi Fellow, University of Auckland, New Zealand (1995) **MEM:** Past President, International Geothermal Association (2007-Present); Past President, Geothermal Resources Council (2003-2004); President, Geothermal Resources Council (2001-2002); President-elect, Geothermal Resources Council (1999-2000); First Vice President, Geothermal Resources Council (1997-1998); Treasurer, International Geothermal Association (1995-1998); Honorary Member, Triaxial Institute of Asphalt Pavement Construction; National Council Examiners for Engineering and Surveying; American Society of Civil Engineers; American Society of Engineering Education **MH:** Albert Nelson Marquis Lifetime Achievement Award (2017) **H:** Cross country skiing; Hiking; Travel **PA:** Democrat **ADD:** 719 Hillside Avenue, Klamath Falls, OR, 97601

LUNDIN, SHIRLEY M., T: Consultant, Trainer, Principal **I:** Education/Educational Services **CN:** Lundin & Associates **DOB:** 02/06/1935 **PB:** Chicago **SC:** IL/USA **PT:** William Matcouff; Emma Martha (Graf) Matcouff **MS:** Married **SPN:** Roy Charles Lundin (9/1/1956) **CH:** Michael Roy; Laura Marie Lundin Simpkiss; Bethel Anne Lundin-Martinez **ED:** Master's Degree in Adult Continuing Education, National Louis University (1981); BA in Liberal Arts, Northwestern University (1957) **CT:** Certified Myers Briggs Type Indicator Interpreter, Association for Psychological Type (1995); Certified in Volunteer Administration (1991) **C:** Consultant, Lundin & Associates (1991-Present); Trainer, Lundin & Associates (1991-Present); Principal, Lundin & Associates (1991-Present); Adjunct Faculty, Harper College (1995-2001); Volunteer Management Curriculum Coordinator, Harper College (1995-2001); Coordinator of Volunteer Services, Frank Lloyd Wright Trust (1988-1991); Adult Development Program Consultant, Chicago Field Center, Girl Scouts of the United States of America (1983-1988); Trainer, HeadStart for Child Development (1981-1983); Field Adviser, HeadStart for Child Development (1981-1983); Community Economic Development Agent, HeadStart for Child Development (1981-1983); Assistant Program Coordinator, Parent Education Program, Triton College (1979-1980); Education Coordinator for HeadStart, CAPE (1976-1978); Director, HeadStart Center, CAPE (1974-1976) **CR:** Trainer, Heartland Alliance (1997-2003); Trainer in Volunteer Program Administration; Consultant in Field **CIV:** President, Senior Citizens Center of Oak Park and River Forest (1998-2001); Member, Board of Directors, Senior Citizens Center of Oak Park and River Forest (1996-2001); American Volunteer for International Development, National Forum Federation, Washington (1996-1997); Member, Committee Study of Infrastructure, Village of Oak Park (1996); Interim Director, Volunteer Center of Oak Park (1990-1995); Board President, Volunteer Center of Oak Park (1990-1995); Regional Chair, UUSC (1977-1980) **CW:** Newsletter Editor, Chicago Area Technology Assistance Providers (1992-1994); Co-Author, "How to Start a Parent Cooperative Preschool" (1980); Contributor, Articles, Professional Journals **MEM:** Conference Chair, Metro Chicago Region, Association for Volunteer Administration (1995); Bylaws Chair, SRA International (1995); Professional Development Committee, Metro Chicago Region, Association for Volunteer Administration (1993-1997); Regional Council, SRA International (1992-1995);

Association for Psychological Type International; Chicago Association for Psychological Type; Chicago Area Technology Assistance Providers; Board of Directors, Association for Volunteer Administration; Program Chair, Association for Volunteer Administration; Professional Development Committee, SRA International; Training Coordinator, SRA International **MH:** Albert Nelson Marquis Lifetime Achievement Award (2017) **H:** Archaeology; Choral singing; Dream work; Travel; Family **ADD:** 6489 Blackhawk Trl, Indian Head Park, IL, 60525

LUTTERODT, CLEMENT H., T: Educator **I:** Education/Educational Services **CN:** Howard University **DOB:** 08/17/1943 **PB:** Nsawam **SC:** Ghana **PT:** Samuel Augustus Christian Lutterodt; Olaonipekun Lutterodt **MS:** Married **SPN:** Sarah Anne French (9/25/1971) **CH:** Tobias; Isabelle; Justine **ED:** PhD, University of Birmingham (1974); MSc, University of Ghana (1972); BSc, University of Ghana (1967) **C:** Professor, Howard University, Washington, DC (1990-Present); Associate Professor, Howard University (1984-1990); Assistant Professor, Howard University (1980-1984); Visiting Assistant Professor, University of South Florida, Tampa, FL (1980); Senior Lecturer, University of Cape Coast (1978-1980); Lecturer, University of Cape Coast (1973-1978) **CR:** Fellow, Others, Miramare, Trieste, Italy (1999-2000); Fellow, Others, Miramare, Trieste, Italy (1988); Fellow, Others, Miramare, Trieste, Italy (1980); Fellow, Others, Miramare, Trieste, Italy (1977); Fellow, the Abdus Salam International Centre for Theoretical Physics (1975); Fellow, Others, Miramare, Trieste, Italy (1971) **CW:** Contributor, Articles, Professional Journals **MEM:** Abdus Salam International Centre for Theoretical Physics; Mathematical Association of America; New York Academy of Sciences; American Mathematical Society **H:** Ping pong/ table tennis; Walking; Reading **ADD:** 8732 Endless Ocean Way, Columbia, MD, 21045

LYMAN, GARY HERBERT, T: Executive Officer, Professor, Director **I:** Education/Educational Services **CN:** SWOG, University of Washington, Fred Hutchinson Cancer Research Center **DOB:** 02/24/1946 **PB:** Buffalo **SC:** NY/USA **PT:** Leonard Samuel Lyman; Beatrice Louise Lyman **CH:** Stephen Leonard; Christopher Henry **ED:** MPH, Harvard University (1982); Postdoctoral Fellow, Biostatistics, Harvard University (1981-1982); Fellowship in Oncology, Roswell Park Cancer Institute, Buffalo, NY (1974-1977); Special Clinical Fellow, Roswell Park Cancer Institute, Buffalo, NY (1975-1976); Resident, The University of North Carolina at Chapel Hill (1972-1974); MD, University at Buffalo (1972); BA, University at Buffalo (1968) **CT:** Diplomate, American Board of Internal Medicine; Diplomate, American Board of Oncology and Hematology **C:** Executive Officer, SWOG (2016-Present); Adjunct Professor, School of Pharmacy, University of Washington Seattle, WA (2014-Present); Adjunct Professor, School of Public Health, University of Washington, Seattle, WA (2014-Present); Director, Hutchinson Institute for Cancer Outcomes Research, Public Health Science Division, Fred Hutchinson Cancer Research Center, Seattle, WA (2014-Present); Member, Fred Hutchinson Cancer Research Center, Seattle, WA (2014-Present); Senior Fellow, Duke Clinical Research Institute, Duke University, Durham, NC (2007-2014); Director of Comparative Effectiveness and Outcomes Research, Duke Cancer Institute, Duke Health, Durham, NC (2007-2014); Professor of Medicine, Department of Medicine, Duke University, Durham, NC (2007-2014); Director, Duke University, Durham, NC (2002-2007); Professor of Medicine, Department

of Medicine, School of Medicine and Dentistry, University of Rochester (2002-2007); Professor of Biometry, School of Public Health, State University of New York (2000-2002); Professor of Statistics, School of Public Health, State University of New York (2000-2002); Director, Cancer Center, Albany Medical College (2000-2002); Director, Cancer Center, Union University (2000-2002); Thomas Ordway Professor, Medical Division of Hematology and Oncology, Albany Medical College (2000-2002); Thomas Ordway Professor, Medical Division of Hematology and Oncology, Union University (2000-2002); Professor of Epidemiology, College of Medicine, University of South Florida, Tampa, FL (1988-2000); Professor of Biostatistics, College of Medicine, University of South Florida, Tampa, FL (1988-2000); Professor of Medicine, College of Medicine, University of South Florida, Tampa, FL (1986-2000); Faculty Member, College of Medicine, University of South Florida, Tampa, FL (1977-2000); Chief of Medicine, Moffitt Cancer Center, College of Medicine, University of South Florida, Tampa, FL (1985-1993); Director, Division of Medical Oncology, College of Medicine, University of South Florida, Tampa, FL (1979-1993); Associate Professor of Medicine, College of Medicine, University of South Florida, Tampa, FL (1980-1986); Research Instructor in Medicine, Jacobs School of Medicine and Biomedical Sciences, University at Buffalo (1974-1977) **CR:** Visiting Professor in Medical Statistics, London School of Hygiene & Tropical Medicine (1997-1998) **CW:** Editor-in-Chief, "Cancer Investigation" (2006-Present); Editor, "Hematopoietic Growth Factors" (2011); Editor, "Cancer Supportive Care: Advances in Therapeutic Strategies" (2009); Editor, "Breast Cancer: Transitional Therapeutic Strategies" (2007); Editor, "Comprehensive Geriatric Oncology, Second Edition" (2004); Editor, "Geriatric Oncology" (1998); Editor, "Comprehensive Geriatric Oncology" (1997); Contributor, Articles, Professional Journals; Contributor, Book Chapters **AW:** Statesman Award, American Society of Clinical Oncology (2010) **MEM:** Statesman, American Society of Clinical Oncology (2012-Present); Board of Directors, American Society of Clinical Oncology (2012-Present); Special Fellow, The Leukemia & Lymphoma Society (1976-1977); Fellow, American College of Physicians; Fellow, American College of Preventive Medicine; Fellow, American College of Clinical Pharmacology; Fellow, Royal College Physicians **MH:** Albert Nelson Marquis Lifetime Achievement Award (2017) **BA:** 1100 Fairview Ave N, Fred Hutchinson Cancer Research Center, Seattle, WA, 98109 **ADD:** 210 Market St Apt 303, Kirkland, WA, 98033 **URL:** https://www.fredhutch. org/en/labs/profiles/lyman-gary.html

LYON, JAMES BURROUGHS, T: Lawyer (Retired) **I:** Law and Legal Services **CN:** Murtha Cullina LLP **DOB:** 05/11/1930 **PB:** New York **SC:** NY/USA **ED:** LLB, Yale University (1955); BA, Amherst College (1952); Graduate, Kingswood Oxford School, West Hartford, CT (1948) **CT:** Admitted to Practice, United States Court of Appeals for the Second Circuit; Admitted to Practice, United States Tax Court; Admitted to Practice, Supreme Court of the United States **C:** Retired (2016); Counsel, Murtha Cullina LLP, Hartford, CT (1996-2016); Partner, Murtha Cullina LLP, Hartford, CT (1961-1996); Associate, Murtha Cullina LLP, Hartford, CT (1956-1961); Assistant Football Coach, Yale University (1953-1955) **CIV:** Honorary Trustee, Horace Bushnell Memorial Hall (2013-Present); Honorary Trustee, Watkinson Library, Hartford, CT (2010-Present); Advisory Board, Tax Exempt Law Review (2007-Present); Honorary Trustee, Connecticut Historical Society (2006-Present); Honorary

Trustee, Old Sturbridge Village (2002-Present); Visiting Committee Member, Mortensen Library, University of Hartford (1996-Present); Honorary Trustee, Wadsworth Atheneum Museum of Art (1993-Present); Honorary Trustee, Kingswood Oxford School (1991-Present); Advisory Committee, Florence Griswold Museum, Old Lyme, CT (1981-Present); Corporator, Institute of Living (1981-Present); Corporator, Hartford Public Library (1979-Present); Corporator, Hartford Hospital (1975-Present); Secretary, Horace Bushnell Memorial Hall (1996-2013); Trustee, Horace Bushnell Memorial Hall (1993-2013); Trustee, Ellen Battell Stoeckel Trust, Norfolk, CT (1994-2010); Trustee, Watkinson Library, Hartford, CT (1990-2010); President, Watkinson Library, Hartford, CT (2001-2008); Trustee, Connecticut Junior Republic, Litchfield, CT (2000-2007); Trustee, St. Francis Hospital Foundation, Hartford, CT (1991-2007); Corporator, St. Francis Hospital Foundation, Hartford, CT (1976-2007); Trustee, Connecticut Historical Society (2000-2006); Secretary, Connecticut Historical Society (2002-2005); Trustee, YMCA of Greater Hartford (1985-1999); Trustee, Ellen Burr McManus Trust, Hartford, CT (1987-1998); Chairman, Board of Trustees, Old Sturbridge Village (1991-1993); Chairman, Austin House Committee, Wadsworth Atheneum Museum of Art (1988-1992); Trustee, Kingswood Oxford School (1961-1991); Trustee, Connecticut Public Broadcasting, Inc. (1979-1986); President, Wadsworth Atheneum Museum of Art (1981-1984); Chairman, 13th Conference Charitable Organization, Institute on Federal Taxation, New York University (1982); Chairman, Board of Trustees, Kingswood Oxford School (1975-1978); Trustee, Connecticut River Museum, Essex, CT (1971-1976); Alumni Trustee Candidate, Amherst College Alumni Council (1970); Trustee, Wadsworth Atheneum Museum of Art, Hartford, CT (1968-1993); Executive Committee, Amherst College Alumni Council (1963-1969); Chairman, Amherst College Alumni Council (1963-1969); Volunteer, Hartford Foundation for Public Giving; Board of Directors, YMCA of Greater Hartford **AW:** Recipient, Medal of Eminent Service, Amherst College; Recipient, Medals, Local Chapter, United Way **MEM:** President, Dauntless Club, Essex, CT (1989-1993); President, University Club of Hartford (1976-1977); Fellow, ABA; Fellow, American College of Tax Counsel; Fellow, The Phi Beta Kappa Society; The American Law Institute; The Yale Club of New York City; The Hartford Golf Club; The Union Club of the City of New York; Mory's Association, New Haven, CT; Phi Delta Phi; Theta Delta Chi; Co-Chair, Sub-Committee on Museums and Other Cultural Organizations, Section on Taxation Exempt Organization Committee, ABA; Exempt Organization Liaison Group, Northeast District, IRS; The American Law Institute **MH:** Albert Nelson Marquis Lifetime Achievement Award (2017) **ADD:** 40 Loeffler Rd Apt TN427, Bloomfield, CT, 06002

LYTTON, ROBERT LEONARD, T: Civil Engineering Educator **I:** Education/Educational Services **CN:** Texas A&M University **DOB:** 10/23/1937 **PB:** Port Arthur **SC:** TX/USA **PT:** Robert Odell Lytton; Nora Mae (Verrett) Lytton **MS:** Married **SPN:** Eleanor Marilyn Anderson (9/9/1961) **CH:** Lynn Elizabeth; Robert Douglas; John Kirby **ED:** PhD, The University of Texas at Austin (1967); MSCE, The University of Texas at Austin (1961); BSCE, The University of Texas at Austin (1960) **CT:** Diplomate, Geotechnical Engineering, Academy of Geo-Professionals (2009); Certified Land Surveyor, State of Louisiana; Registered Professional Engineer, State of Louisiana; Registered Professional Engineer, State of Texas **C:** Benson Chair Professor,

Texas A&M University (1995-Present); Director, Center for Infrastructure Renewal, Texas A&M Engineering Experiment Station, Texas A&M University (1995-2013); Head, Infrastructure and Transportation Division, Zachry Department of Civil Engineering, Texas A&M Transportation Institute (1993-1995); Wiley Chair Professor, Texas A&M University (1990-1995); Division Head, Texas A&M Transportation Institute (1982-1991); Professor, Texas A&M University (1976-1990); Associate Professor, Texas A&M University (1971-1976); Assistant Professor, The University of Texas at Austin (1967-1968); Associate, Dannenbaum and Associates, Consultant Engineers, Houston, TX (1963-1965); Cowhand, Slaughter Ranch (1963) **CR:** Keynote Speaker, Transportation Research Congress, Beijing, People's Republic of China (2017); Carl L. Monismith Lecturer on Pavement Engineering, The Geo-Institute, Transportation & Development Institute, American Society of Civil Engineers (2013); Keynote Address, First Pan American Conference on Unsaturated Soils, ISSMGE (2013); Keynote Lecturer, Seventh International Conference, RILEM, Delft, The Netherlands (2012); Keynote Speaker Fifth International Conference, RILEM, Limoges, France (2004); Distinguished Lecturer, TRB, National Academy of Sciences (2000); Keynote Address, First International Conference on Unsaturated Soils, ISSMGE (1995); Principal Investigator, A-005 Research Project, Strategic Highway Research Program (1990-1993); Keynote Address, Seventh International Conference on Expansive Soils, ISSMGE (1992); Vice President, Geostructural Tool Kit, Inc.; Board Director, Geostructural Tool Kit, Inc.; Board Director, MLAW Consultants, Inc. (Now MLAW Engineers); Board of Directors, MLA Labs, Inc. **CIV:** Active Member, Redemptorist Lay Community, Melbourne, Australia (1969-1970); Active Member, National Council of the US Society of St. Vincent de Paul (1963-1965) **MIL:** Captain, U.S. Army (1961-1963) **AW:** Francis C. Turner Award, American Society of Civil Engineers (2017); Distinguished Achievement in Teaching Award, College of Engineering, The Association of Former Students of Texas A&M University (2013-2014); Inductee, Academy of Distinguished Alumni, Department of Civil, Architectural and Environmental Engineering, Cockrell School of Engineering, The University of Texas at Austin (2010); Lifetime Achievement Award, GeoShanghai International Conference (2010); Dick and Joyce Birdwell Endowed Teaching Award (2006-2007); NOVA Award, Construction Innovation Forum, Construction Users Roundtable (2006); Honoree, Legend of Post-Tensioning, Post Tensioning Institute (2005); Honoree, Trendsetter, Public Works Magazine, Hanley Wood Media Inc. (2005); The TTI/Zachry Senior Researcher Award, Texas A&M Transportation Institute (1996); Distinguished Achievement in Research Award, The Association of Former Students of Texas A&M University (1996); Everite Bursary Award, CSIR, South Africa (1984); National Science Foundation Fellow, Commonwealth Scientific and Industrial Research Organisation, Melbourne, Australia (1969-1970); U.S. National Science Foundation Fellow, The University of Texas at Austin (1965-1967); John B. Hawley Award, Texas Section, American Society of Civil Engineers (1966); Hamilton Watch Award, Cockrell School of Engineering, The University of Texas at Austin (1960); Distinguished Military Graduate Award (1960); Honoree, Outstanding Senior Cadet, Society of American Military Engineers, The University of Texas at Austin (1959); Compatriot Medal of Honor, Sons of the American Revolution, St. Mary's University (1957); Fellow, American Society of Civil Engineers **MEM:** U.S. Representative, Technical Committee (TC-106), ISSMGE (1987-Present); Invited Lecturer, Congreso Internacional de Ingenieria , Queretaro, Mexico (2011); Elected Diplomate in Geotechnical Engineering, American Society of Civil Engineers (2009); Chairman, A2LO6 committee, TRB, National Academy of Sciences (1987-1993); AAPT; Honorary Lifetime Member, Foundation Performance Association, Houston,TX; Advisory Board, Post Tensioning Institute; American Society of Civil Engineers; Academy of Geo-Professionals; International Society for Asphalt Pavements; Texas Society of Professional Engineers; Sigma Xi, The Scientific Research Honor Society; The Honor Society of Phi Kappa Phi; The Tau Beta Pi Association, Inc.; Chi Epsilon, Inc.; Phi Delta Kappa International **MH:** Albert Nelson Marquis Lifetime Achievement Award (2017) **RE:** Roman Catholic **ADD:** 2108 Barak Ln, Bryan, TX, 77802

MACDONALD GAMBLIN, CYNTHIA, T: Mathematics Teacher Emerita, Lobbyist (Retired) **I:** Education/Educational Services **DOB:** 09/12/1946 **PB:** Chicago **SC:** IL/USA **PT:** Robert Eugene MacDonald; Janice (Billings) MacDonald **MS:** Divorced **SPN:** James Bradford Gamblin (9/6/1969, Divorced 6/1980) **ED:** MA in Teaching, Washington University, St. Louis, MO (1971); BS, Washington University, St. Louis, MO (1969) **CT:** Certified Teacher, State of Florida, State of Missouri; Licensed Basic Ground Instructor, FAA **C:** Mathematics Teacher, Dunedin High School, Florida (1973-2008); Office manager, Around the World Food Corp., St. Louis, MO (1972-1973); Executive Secretary, Coalition for the Environment, St. Louis, MO (1971-1972); Mathematics Teacher, Mary Institute, St. Louis, MO (1969-1970) **CR:** Advisor, DHS Sailing Club (2002-2003); Co-Chairman, Legislation Subcommittee (1989-1990); Member, Public Policy Committee, Juvenile Welfare Board, St. Petersburg, FL (1979-1998); Ground Instructor (1971-1973); Public Affairs Committee, Junior League of Clearwater-Dunedin; Storyteller for Children **MEM:** Volunteer, Lobbyist, Pinellas Classroom Teachers Association (1979-1992); Center for Florida's Children; Phi Delta Kappa International; Junior League of Clearwater-Dunedin **MH:** Albert Nelson Marquis Lifetime Achievement Award (2017) **H:** Flying planes; Sailing; Reading **PA:** Republican **RE:** Christian Science **ADD:** 1441 Fairway Dr, Dunedin, FL, 34698

MACDONALD, KAREN CRANE, T: Occupational Therapist **I:** Medicine & Health Care **DOB:** 02/24/1955 **PB:** Denville **SC:** NJ/USA **PT:** Robert William Macdonald; Jeanette Wilcox (Crane) Macdonald **MS:** Married (10/22/1993) **SPN:** Geno Piacentini **ED:** PhD, New York University (1998); MS, University of Bridgeport (1982); BS, Quinnipiac University (1977) **CT:** Certified Occupational Therapist **C:** Occupational Therapist, Rehabilitation Associates, Fairfield, CT (1993-1996); Occupational Therapist, Coordinator of the Special Care Unit, Jewish Home for the Elderly, Fairfield, CT (1977-1992); Private practice, Fairfield County, CT (1977-1988); Occupational Therapist, Day Treatment Center, New York Institute, New York City (1984-1986) **CR:** Lecturer, Consultant in Field, Adjunct Faculty, Sacred Heart University, Fairfield, CT (2007-Present); Instructor, Connecticut (2006-Present); Instructor, Housatonic Community College, Bridgeport, CT (2002-2015); Instructor, Quinnipiac College (1986-1992); Instructor, New York University (1985-1989) **CIV:** Deacon Southport Congregational Church (1992-1994); Chair, Consumer Committee, Alzheimer's Coalition of Connecticut (1991-1992); Youth Leader, Deacon, Union Memorial Church, Stamford, CT (1980-1988) **CW:** Co-Author, "Productive Aging: An Occupational Perspective," with Marli Cole (2015); Contributor, Articles, Professional Journals **AW:** Teaching Fellow, New York University (1983-1986) **MEM:** Daughters of the American Revolution; National Organization of Women; American Association of University Women; PEO; National Society United States Daughters of 1812; New York Academy of Sciences; Grange; Toastmasters International; Pi Lambda Theta; Council of Education, Scholar, American Occupational Therapy Association (1985); Gerontology Liaison, Connecticut Occupational Therapy Association (1980-1983) **H:** Writing poetry; Quilting **ADD:** 198 Glenbrook Road, Bridgeport, CT, 06610

MACFARLANE, ROBERT, T: Director, Chemist **I:** Sciences **CN:** THO Services **DOB:** 08/26/1930 **PT:** Robert MacFarlane; Mabel Edna Guile **MS:** Divorced **SPN:** Janet Ellen Burke **CH:** Joan Elizabeth MacFarlane; Susan Nancy Beckmann; Kurt MacFarlane; Beth Ellen Nigh; Laurie Ann Ornelas **ED:** PhD, Yale University (1956); BS, Brown University, Cum Laude (1952) **C:** Director, Sole Proprietor, THO Services, Madison, NJ (1993-Present); Manager, Technical Communications, AlliedSignal Corporation (1993); Manager, Quality Assurance, AlliedSignal Corporation (1978-1992); Group Leader, Engineering Plastics Research & Development, AlliedSignal Corporation (1974-1978); Senior Research Chemist, ExxonMobil Research and Engineering Company, Linden, NJ (1965-1974); Senior Research Chemist, Uniroyal Inc., Naugatuck, CT (1955-1965) **CR:** Chairman, Subcommittee on Thermoplastics, ASTM International (1986-Present) **CW:** Author, "Automotive Standards for Plastics - How Does Committee D-20 on Plastics Discover What's Needed?," Standardization News (1991); Co-Author, "Colloidal Skeleton Polymers", Journal of Polymer Science Part C (1966); Co-Author, "Polyelectrolytes. XII. Conductance of partially quaternized poly-4-vinyl pyridine in methanol -4-butanone mixtures," Journal of Polymer Science (1957); Co-Author, "Crosslinking of Polymers by Peroxides in Dioxane," Journal of the American Chemical Society (1955) **AW:** Committee D-20 on Plastics Outstanding Achievement Award, ASTM (2013); Technical Committee 61 Outstanding Service Award (2005); Committee D-20 on Plastics Award of Excellence, ASTM (1998); Award of Merit, ASTM (1993); Committee D-20 on Plastics Award of Recognition, ASTM (1990) **MEM:** Fellow, ASTM (1993); Chairman, ASTM (1984-2007); The Society of Rheology; The New York Academy of Sciences; American Chemical Society; SPE; Director, Palisades-New Jersey Section, SPE; Sigma Xi **MH:** Albert Nelson Marquis Lifetime Achievement Award (2017) **H:** Photography; Travel **ADD:** 24 Hillview Ave, Madison, NJ, 07940 **URL:** https://www.linkedin.com/in/robert-macfarlane-6916815/

MACK, LOUIS BARRY, T: Principal **I:** Law and Legal Services **CN:** The Mack Law Offices **ED:** JD, Washburn University School of Law (1976); BA, The University of Kansas (1973) **C:** Professor of Law, Desert Trial Academy of Law, (2016-present); Sole Practitioner, The Mack Law Offices (2004-Present); Principal, The Mack Law Offices (2004-Present); Superior Court Commissioner, Superior Court of California, County of Riverside (1995-2004); Private Practice (1976-1995) **AW:** AV Preeminent Rating, Martindale-Hubbell (2015) **BAR:** Admitted to Practice, United States District Court of the Central District of California (2007); Admitted to Practice, The State Bar of California (1976); Admitted to Practice, Kansas Bar Association (1976); Admitted to Practice, United States District Court of Kansas (1976); Admitted to Practice, Desert Bar Association **BA:** 74075 El Paseo Ste A3, The Mack Law Offices, Palm Desert,

CA, 92260 **URL:** http://www.louisbarrymack.com/Attorney-Profile/Louis-B-Mack.shtml

MACLEOD, ANTHONY MICHAEL, T: Partner **I:** Law and Legal Services **CN:** Whitman Breed Abbott & Morgan LLC **DOB:** 12/30/1947 **PB:** Manila **SC:** Philippines **PT:** Anthony Macaulay Macleod; Dorothy (Amend) Macleod **MS:** Married **SPN:** Carol Jeanne Silvani (8/5/1972) **CH:** Ryan Elissa; Anthony Matthew; Colin Macaulay **ED:** JD, School of Law, University of Virginia (1972); AB, University of Notre Dame, Magna Cum Laude (1969) **C:** Partner, Whitman Breed Abbott & Morgan LLC (1996-Present); Senior Vice President, Law and Administration, Bridgeport Hydraulic Company (1986-Present); Partner, Wiggin and Dana LLP, New Haven, CT (1992-1996); Secretary, Bridgeport Hydraulic Company (1988-1992); Vice President, Bridgeport Hydraulic Company (1984-1986); Of General Counsel, Bridgeport Hydraulic Company (1984-1986); Vice President, The Flintkote Company, Stamford, CT (1982-1984); Secretary, The Flintkote Company, Stamford, CT (1982-1984); Of Chief Counsel, The Flintkote Company, Stamford, CT (1982-1984); Secretary, The Flintkote Company, Stamford, CT (1980-1982); Of Chief Counsel, The Flintkote Company, Stamford, CT (1980-1982); Of Division Counsel, The Flintkote Company, Stamford, CT (1977-1980); Associate, Hirschberg, Pettengill, Strong & Nagle (Now Whitman Breed Abbott & Morgan LLC) (1973-1976); Law Clerk, Connecticut Judicial Branch, Hartford, CT (1972-1973) **CR:** Team Director, Management Decision Laboratory, Leonard N. Stern School of Business, New York University, New York, NY (1983-1984); Law Program Chairman, Connecticut Career Opportunities Program, Greenwich, CT (1975-1976) **CIV:** President, Greenwich Country Club (2014-Present); Board of Governors, Greenwich Country Club (2010-Present); Affiliate, Bridgeport Financial Review (1991-Present); Affiliate, Connecticut Forest & Park Association (1988-Present); Chairman, Flood & Erosion Control Board, Greenwich, CT (1988-Present); Affiliate, Economic Development, Bridgeport, CT (1988-1992); Flood & Erosion Control Board, Greenwich, CT (1987-2011); Trustee, Whitby School (1986-1989); Affiliate, Board Regents, Fairfield College Preparatory School (1985-1989); Board of Directors, Youth Center, Greenwich, CT (1984-1986); Representative, Town Meeting, Greenwich, CT (1984-1985); Executive Board, Greenwich Council, Boy Scouts of America (1975-1981); Chairman, Exploring Committee, Greenwich Council, Boy Scouts of America (1975-1979) **AW:** Super Lawyer, Connecticut; Super Lawyer, New England; A/V Preeminent Rating, Martindale-Hubbell **MEM:** Vice Chairman, Public Utility Law Committee, Connecticut Bar Association (1993-Present); Chairman, Regulatory Law Committee, National Association of Water Companies (1990-1993); Board of Directors, National Association of Water Companies (1990-1991); Board of Directors, Fairfield County Chapter, Notre Dame Alumni Club (1982-1990); American Bar Association; Connecticut Supreme Court Law Clerks Association; Association of Corporate Counsel; Corporate Bar; Greenwich Country Club; Southwestern Area Commerce & Industry Association of Connecticut Inc. **MH:** Albert Nelson Marquis Lifetime Achievement Award (2017) **BA:** 500 W Putnam Avenue, Suite 2, Whitman Breed Abbott & Morgan LLC, Greenwich, CT, 06830

MACPHERSON-SANCHEZ, ANN E., T: Professor (Retired) **I:** Education/Educational Services **CN:** University of Puerto Rico at Mayagüez **ED:** EdD, Universidad de Puerto Rico, Recinto de Rio Piedras (1993); MNS in Public Health Nutrition, Cornell University (1964); BS in Home Economics Education, University of California, Los Angeles (1957); Coursework in English and History, Pomona College (1953-1955) **CT:** Certified Teacher, University of California, Los Angeles (1958) **C:** Professor, Foods and Nutrition, Department of Agricultural Education, University of Puerto Rico at Mayagüez (2003-2011); Coordinator, Program to Improve Nutrition in Puerto Rico, Agricultural Extension Service, University of Puerto Rico at Mayagüez (1998-2003); Foods and Nutrition Specialist, Agricultural Extension Service, University of Puerto Rico at Mayagüez (1984-1998); Instructor, Education, Physical Education and Home Economics Department, Interamerican University, San Germain Campus, Puerto Rico (1984); Part-Time Instructor, Nursing Department, University of Puerto Rico at Mayagüez (1978-1984); Administrative and Clinical Dietitian, Mayagüez Medical Center, Puerto Rico (1978-1984); Instructor, Education, Physical Education and Home Economics Department, Interamerican University, San Germain Campus, Puerto Rico (1976); Science Teacher, Southwestern Educational Society, Mayagüez, Puerto Rico (1974-1977); Research Technical Associate, Department of Human Nutrition and Food, Cornell University, Ithaca, NY (1971-1973); Extension Associate, Department of Human Nutrition and Food, Cornell University, Ithaca, NY (1968-1970); Senior Research Aide, Graduate School of Nutrition, Cornell University, Ithaca, NY (1965-1967); Instructor, Food Chemistry, Hotel School, Cornell University, Ithaca, NY (1964-1965); Home Economics Teacher, James Monroe High School, Sepulveda, CA (1958-1962) **CR:** Society for Nutrition Education (1984-Present); Board Member, Nominating Committee, Society for Nutrition Education (2007-2009); Chair-elect, Weight Realities Division, Society for Nutrition Education (2006-2008); Member, Wellness Committee of the Department of Education, Government of Puerto Rico (2005-2009); Chair, School Food Policy Sub-Committee, Society for Nutrition Education (2005-2007); Chair, Sub-Committee to Establish the Scientific Basis of the Food Guide Pyramid for Puerto Rico of the Foods and Nutrition Commission and the Nutrition Committee of Puerto Rico (2005-2006); Advisory Committee on Public Policy, Society for Nutrition Education (2003-2007); Chair, Dietary Guidelines/Food Guide Pyramid Sub-Committee, Society for Nutrition Education (2003-2005); Chair, International Division, Society for Nutrition Education (2001-2002); Member, Foods and Nutrition Commission of Puerto Rico (2000-2003); Chair-elect, International Division, Society for Nutrition Education (2000-2001); Member, Chancellor's Advisory Committee for Research and Industrial Development (2000-2001); Member, Strategic Planning for Nutrition for Puerto Rico Committee, Food and Nutrition Service, San Juan Regional Office (2000-2001); Reviewer, Proposals for the Human Nutrition and Obesity Program of National Research Initiative (2000-2001); Member, Chancellor's Advisory Committee, Research and Industrial Development (2000-2001); President, Society for Nutrition Education (1999-2000); Reviewer, Proposals Received by the USDA for Development of Small Businesses (1999-2000); President-elect, Society for Nutrition Education (1998-1999); Chair, International Division, Society for Nutrition Education (1997-1998); Consultant, Training Materials for the Implementation of the New System for Designing Menus that they Planned to Adopt, Department of Education (1997); Co-Chair, Team Member, Nutrition Inter-Agency Committee, Department of Education, Agricultural Extension Service (1996-1998); Chair-elect, International Division, Society for Nutrition Education (1996-1997); Chair, Foods and Nutrition Inter-Campus Committee, University of Puerto Rico (1994-1999); Representative, International Division on the Partnerships Committee (1994-1996); Sub-Committee for Developing the Food Guide Pyramid for Puerto Rico, Society for Nutrition Education (1993-1995); Nutrition Committee of Puerto Rico, Society for Nutrition Education (1984-2009); Professional Association of Nutritionists and Dietitians of Puerto Rico, Colegio de Nutricionistas y Dietistas de Puerto Rico (1978-2009) **CW:** Member, Board of Reviewers, Journal of Nutrition Education (2000-Present); Author, "Integrating Fundamental Concepts of Obesity and Eating Disorders: Implications for the Obesity Epidemic," American Journal of Public Health (2015); Proposals Reviewer, Human Nutrition and Obesity Program, National Institute of Food and Agriculture, United States Department of Agriculture (2000-2001); Proposals Reviewer, Development of Small Businesses, United States Department of Agriculture (1999-2000); Author, "A Food Guide Pyramid for Puerto Rico," Nutrition Today (1998); Co-Author, "A Conspectus of Research on Iron Requirements of Man," Journal of Nutrition (1976); Author, "Trends in Fat Disappearance in the United States, 1909-1965," Journal of Nutrition (1967); Presenter in Field; Speaker in Field **AW:** Certificate of Recognition, University of Puerto Rico at Mayagüez (2006); Specialist of the Year, College of Agriculture, University of Puerto Rico at Mayagüez (2004); Statue of Don Quixote, Recognition for Conceptualizing and Implementing the Program MeNu (1999); Leadership Certificate in Recognition of Significant Volunteer Contributions, Society for Nutrition Education (1999); Plaque, Mayaguez Medical Center (1984); Public Health Service Assistantship for Pursuing Graduate Studies (1962-1963) **MEM:** American Dietetic Association (1978-2009); Puerto Rico Academy of Nutrition & Dietetics (1978-2009) **MH:** Distinguished Humanitarian (2017) **ADD:** 1307 Seagrape Cir, Weston, FL, 33326

MACRAE, CAMERON FARQUHAR III, T: Lawyer **I:** Law and Legal Services **CN:** Duane Morris LLP & Affiliates **DOB:** 03/21/1942 **PB:** New York **SC:** NY/USA **PT:** Cameron F. MacRae; Jane B. (Miller) MacRae **MS:** Married **SPN:** Ann Wooster Bedell (11/30/1974) **CH:** Catherine Fairfax; Ann Cameron **ED:** LLB, Yale University (1966); AB, Princeton University (1963) **C:** Partner of Counsel, Duane Morris LLP & Affiliates, New York, NY (2012-Present); Senior of Counsel, Dewey & LeBoeuf LLP, New York, NY (2008-2012); Senior of Counsel, LeBoeuf, Lamb, Greene & MacRae LLP, New York, NY 2005-2008); Vice Chairman, LeBoeuf, Lamb, Greene & MacRae LLP, New York, NY (1995-2000); Senior Partner, LeBoeuf, Lamb, Greene & MacRae LLP, New York, NY (1975-2004); Deputy Superintendent Counsel, New York State Banking Department (Now New York State Department of Financial Services), New York, NY (1972-1974); Associate, Davis Polk & Wardwell LLP, New York, NY (1970-1972); Attorney-Advisor, Office of General Counsel to Secretary of the Air Force, Washington, D.C. (1966-1969) **CR:** Director, National Integrity Life Insurance Company (2000-Present) **CIV:** Trustee, St. Andrew's Dune Church (1982-Present); Secretary, St. Andrew's Dune Church (1982-Present); Honorary Chairman, Clearpool Group (1990-1994); Captain, U.S. Air Force (1966-1969) **MIL:** Captain, U.S. Air Force Reserve (1966-1969); Office of General Counsel, Secretary of the Air Force **CW:** Note and Comment Editor, The Yale Law Journal (1965-1966) **MEM:** Association of the Bar of the City of New York; The District of Columbia Bar; President, The Meadow Club of Southampton;

Chairman, Executive Committee, The Meadow Club of Southampton; Board of Governors, The Meadow Club of Southampton; Shinnecock Hills Golf Club, Southampton, NY; Bathing Corporation of Southampton; Jupiter Island Club; Hobe Sound Yacht Club; Cottage Club, Princeton, NJ **BAR:** New York (1966); District of Columbia (1967); U.S. District Court for the Southern District of New York (1975) **PA:** Independent **RE:** Episcopalian **BA:** 14 Isle Ridge East, Hobe Sound, FL, 33455 **ADD:** 125 East 72nd Street, New York, NY, 10021

MADAD, SYRA S. DHSC, MSC, MCP, T: Director, System-wide Ebola and Special Pathogens Program **I:** Medicine & Health Care **CN:** NYC Health + Hospitals **MS:** Married **CH:** Two Sons **ED:** Doctorate of Health Science, Nova Southeastern University (2011-2014); Doctorate of Global Health, Nova Southeastern University (2011-2014); MS in Biotechnology, University of Maryland (2008-2010); BS in Psychology, University of Maryland (2006-2008); BS in Psychology, Howard University (2005-2006) **CT:** Certification, All Hazard Response Training, NYS Department of Health; Master Certification, Continuity Practitioner, Continuity or Operations, FEMA **C:** Director, System Wide Ebola and Special Pathogens Program, NYC Health + Hospitals (2015-Present); Fellow, Emerging Leaders in Bio Security, JHSPH Center for Health Security (2017-Present); Assistant Professor, Graduate Program of Biotechnology and Bio Defense, University of Maryland (2009-Present); Lead Continuity of Operations Planning Practitioner, Bio-threat and Chemical Threat Team, Texas Department of State Health Services (2012-2015); State Trainer, Biothreat and Chemical Threat Team, Texas Department of State Health Services (2012-2015); Senior Research Fellow, U.S. Department of Justice (2010-2014); Director of Education, CHCP (2012-2013); Deputy Chairman, BioScience Department, College of Health Sciences (2011-2012); Assistant Professor, Borough of Manhattan Community College (2010-2012); Visiting Scientist, U.S. Department of Agriculture (2008-2010) **CR:** Member, Core Faculty, NETEC **CIV:** Logistics Specialist, Sector 7, Texas Emergency Medical Task Force; Trauma Medical Responder, Sector 7, Texas Emergency Medical Task Force; Planning and Intelligence Specialist, Texas State Medical Operations Center **CW:** Content Editor, "Journal of Association of Interdisciplinary Doctors of Health Science"; Editor, "Journal of Medicine and Medical Sciences"; Co-Author, "Highly Pathogenic Infectious Disease Exercise Planning Tool (Webinar)"; Co-Author," Zika Response in New York State Hospitals"; Author, "Applying Conflict Analysis and Resolution Strategies to Assess Organizational Safety Culture in Accident Investigations"; Co-Author, "Clinical Laboratory Preparedness and Response Guide"; Author, "Bioterrorism: An Emerging Global Health Threat"; Author, "Standardized Protocol for Test Method Validations/Verifications"; Author, "Anatomy and Physiology Laboratory Manual"; Author, "Microbiology Case Study Manual for Allied Health Professionals" **AW:** Recognized as Emerging Leader, Special Pathogens Preparedness Pioneer; J. V. Irons Award for Scientific Excellence; Ebola Response Team Appreciation Award **MH:** Albert Nelson Marquis Lifetime Achievement Award (2017) **BA:** 125 Worth St, New York, NY, 10016 **ADD:** 52 Shaun Rdg, Rosyln Harbor, NY, 11576 **URL:** https://www.linkedin.com/in/syra-madad-dhsc-ms-mcp-5b9495/

MAESAKA, JOHN KAZUAKI, T: Nephrologist **I:** Medicine & Health Care **CN:** NYU Winthrop Hospital **DOB:** 06/23/1935 **PB:** Ewa **SC:** HI/USA **MS:** Married **SPN:** Martha Haruko Tanaka

(7/21/1963) **CH:** Alan Kazumi; Robert Kazuyuki **ED:** Postdoctoral Research Fellow in Renal Disease, Icahn School of Medicine at Mount Sinai (1967-1970); Medical Resident in Medicine, Icahn School of Medicine at Mount Sinai (1965-1967); Assistant Resident in Medicine, Barnes Hospital, Washington University in St. Louis (1962-1963); Intern in Medicine, Barnes Hospital, Washington University in St. Louis (1961-1962); MD, Boston University School of Medicine (1961); BA in Biology, Harvard University (1957) **CT:** Diplomate, Board of Internal Medicine, Subspecialty in Nephrology (1976); Diplomate, American Board of Internal Medicine (1968); Diplomate, National Board of Medicine Examiners (1961) **C:** Emeritus Chief, Division of Nephrology & Hypertension, Department of Medicine, NYU Winthrop Hospital (2005-Present); Professor, School of Medicine, Stony Brook University (1997-Present); Director of Research, NYU Winthrop Hospital (1996-2006); Chief, Division of Nephrology, NYU Winthrop Hospital, Mineola, NY (1994-2005); Associate Professor of Medicine, Albert Einstein College of Medicine, Bronx, NY (1994); Assistant Professor of Medicine, Albert Einstein College of Medicine (1990-1994); Chief, Division of Nephrology, Long Island Jewish Medical Center, New Hyde Park, NY (1985-1994); Associate Director of Nephrology Division and Fellowship Program, University of Medicine and Dentistry (Now Rutgers, The State University of New Jersey) (1982-1985); Associate Professor of Medicine, University of Medicine & Dentistry of New Jersey, Newark, NJ (1982-1985); Assistant Professor of Medicine, University of Medicine and Dentistry (Now Rutgers, The State University of New Jersey) (1973-1982); Assistant Director of Medicine, Jersey City Medical Center (1976-1978); Medical Consultant, Control Data Corporation (1974-1978); Medical Consultant, MRFIT Program, New York, NY (1973-1978); Associate Attending Physician, Jersey City Medical Center (1973-1978); Assistant in Medicine, Washington University in St. Louis (1961-1963) **MIL:** Captain, Medical Corps, U.S. Army (1963-1965) **CW:** Editorial Board Member, "Biomed Research International"; Editorial Board Member, "World Journal of Nephrology"; Editorial Board Member, "Conference Papers in Medicine"; Editorial Board Member, "Case Reports in Nephrology"; Editorial Board Member, "Journal of Translational Internal Medicine"; Editorial Board Member, "Journal of Nephrology and Urology"; Contributor, Articles, Professional Journals; Contributor, Chapters, Books; Contributor, Book Reviews; Contributor, Abstracts; Contributor, Essay, "Pearl Harbor, WWII and Experiences After" **AW:** Grantee, American Heart Association. Achievement Award, US Army, Fort Sill, OK (1965); Eponym, Howard and Shizuko Maesaka Endowed Scholarship, Punahou School, Honolulu, HI; Eponym, Howard and Shizuko Maesaka Award, Indiana University **MEM:** Research Committee for CTSA Grant Application, Stony Brook University (2007); National Advisory Board on Renal Diseases, Pfizer Inc. (2003-2005); Consultant Board of Cardiology Review (2002-2005); Grant Reviewer, Alzheimer Association (2002); Advisory Board, COX2 Inhibitors, Pfizer Inc. (1999); Advisory Board, Cardiovascular Diseases, Pfizer Inc. (1999); Research Committee, American Heart Council (1999); Medical Advisory Board, Long Island Nassau/Suffolk Chapter, JDRF (1997); Medical Advisory Board, National Kidney Foundation of New York (1992); Chairman, Subcommittee on Facilitating Bedside to Bench Research Recent Research Funding (2006); Chairman, Program Committee, Nephrology Society of New Jersey (1975-1976, 1979-1985); President, Nephrology Society of New Jersey (1977-1978); President-elect, Nephrology Society

of New Jersey (1976-1977); American Federation for Clinical Research; American Society of Nephrology; International Society of Nephrology; Academy of Medicine of New Jersey; American Geriatric Society **MH:** Albert Nelson Marquis Lifetime Achievement Award (2017) **ADD:** 1230 Park Ave Apt 17C, New York, NY, 10128

MAGEE, THOMAS HENRY, T: Radiologist, Educator **I:** Military & Defense Services **CN:** NSI Radiology **DOB:** 11/26/1958 **PB:** Newport **SC:** RI/USA **PT:** Francis Robert Magee; Anne Louise (Moriarty) Magee **MS:** Married **SPN:** Christina Marie (Lapolla) (6/7/1987) **ED:** MD, New York Medical College (1986); BA, Wesleyan University (1981) **CT:** Diplomate, American Board of Radiology **C:** Clinical Professor of Radiology, University of Miami (2006-Present); Staff Radiologist, Menorah Medical Park, Overland Park, KS (1994-Present); Assistant Professor of Medicine, Kansas University School of Medicine, Kansas City, KS (1994-Present); Assistant Professor of Radiology, University of Missouri, Kansas City, MO (1997-2006); Assistant Professor of Medicine, Uniformed Service School of Medicine, Bethesda, MD (1991-1994); Staff Radiologist, Bethesda Naval Hospital, Maryland (1991-1994) **CR:** President, Rockhill Radiology (1999); Board Examiner, American Board of Radiology; Reviewer, Professional Journals, American College of Radiology **MIL:** Lieutenant Commander, US Naval Reserve (1991-1994) **CW:** Contributor, Articles to Professional Journals; Contributor, Articles to the Journal of Computer Assisted Tomography; Contributor, Articles to the American Journal of Roentgenology **AW:** Recipient, National Institutes of Health Centers for Accelerated Innovations Award (2015); Recipient, Certificate of Merit, Radiological Society of North America (1990); Recipient, Jonas N. Muller Award, New York Medical College (1986) **MEM:** Board Examiner, American Board of Radiology (2005); Fellow, American College of Radiology; American Roentegen Ray Society; Moderator, Radiological Society of North America; President, Kansas City Roentegen Ray Society; International Skeletal Society **H:** Stamp collecting/philately; Tennis **ADD:** 235 Lansing Island Dr, Indian Harbor Beach, FL, 32937

MAHADEVEY, RAMUNLAL, T: Director **I:** Law and Legal Services **CN:** Mahadevey Maharaj Inc. **ED:** LLD, University of Columbiana (2015); Bachelor's Degree, University of KwaZulu-Natal (1983) **CIV:** Trustee, Bi-GocG Trust; Trustee, Black Lawyers Association **MEM:** Law Society of South Africa; National Association of Democratic Lawyers **BA:** 123A Wilton Avenue, Bryanston, Sandton, Johannesburg, South Africa, 2191

MAHALAWICH, ANNE, T: Mathematics Educator (Retired) **I:** Education/Educational Services **DOB:** 03/10/1922 **PB:** Norwich **SC:** CT/USA **PT:** Dimitry Pisarko; Emilia Pisarko **MS:** Married **SPN:** Nicholas Mahalawich (11/24/1945) **ED:** MS, Willimantis State Teachers College (1967); BS, Willimantis State Teachers College (1943) **CIV:** Member, RSVP (1980-2006); President, Taxpayer's Association; Board Member, Otis Library **AW:** Professional Woman of the Year, Beta Sigma Phi (1989) **MEM:** Norwich Teachers League (1972-1973); President, New London Retired Teachers; AARP; Phi Beta Kappa; Delta Kappa Gamma; Beta Sigma Phi **RE:** Eastern Orthodox **ADD:** 8 Harland Heights, Norwich, CT, 06360

MAHONEY, DENNIS MARTIN, T: Director **I:** Financial Services **CN:** Chimera Investment Corporation **DOB:** 12/04/1941 **PB:** Perth Amboy **SC:** NJ/USA **PT:** John "Jack" Mahoney; Clara S. (Ferretti) Mahoney

MS: Married **SPN:** Ellen Duschock (7/21/1973) **CH:** Susan A.; Dennis E.; Grandchildren: Victoria M.; Alexandra M.; Christopher T.; Lindsey T. **ED:** BA in Economics and Business Administration, Roanoke College, Salem, VA (1965); Graduate Diploma, American Savings and Loan Institute, Newark, NJ (1970); Coursework, Financial Management Program, US League of Savings Institutions, Boston, MA (1976); Postgraduate Coursework, ABA School of Bank Investments, Southern Methodist University, Dallas, Texas (1977); Postgraduate Coursework, ABA Graduate School of Bank Investments, University of Illinois at Urbana-Champaign, IL (1980); Coursework, Financial Planning Program, Fairleigh Dickinson University, Madison, NJ (1992-1993) **C:** Retired (2007); Senior Vice President, Investment Services, Columbia Bank, Fair Lawn, NJ (1994-2007); Director of Investment Research, Powell Financial Group, Watchung, NJ (1992-1993); Executive Vice President, Chief Operating Officer, and member of the Board of Directors, First Atlantic Federal Savings, South Plainfield, NJ (1988-1991); Executive Vice President, Treasurer, Carteret Savings Bank, Morristown, NJ (1965-1988) **CR:** Member of the Board of Directors, Chimera Investment Corporation and Chairman of the Audit Committee (2010-Present); Director, Cowger & Miller Mortgage Company, Louisville, KY; President, Board of Directors, Carteret Equity Corporation; Member, Asset/Liability, Pricing and Education Advisory Committee, Columbia Bank, Fair Lawn, NJ **MEM:** Former Member, Financial Managers Society, Inc.; Former Member, Bond Club of New Jersey; Former Member, New Jersey Chapter, National Association for Business Economics (Now Advanced Solutions International) **MH:** Albert Nelson Marquis Lifetime Achievement Award (2017) **H:** Golf; Traveling; Reading **RE:** Roman Catholic **BA:** 520 Madison Ave, Chimera Investment Corporation, New York, NY, 08840 **ADD:** 40 Clarendon Ct, Metuchen, NJ, 08840

MALINOWSKI, PATRICIA A., T: Professor **I:** Education/Educational Services **CN:** Finger Lakes Community College **DOB:** 01/19/1950 **PB:** Buffalo **SC:** NY/USA **PT:** Raymond J. Cybulski; Emily M. (Ferek) Cybulski **MS:** Married **SPN:** Leonard T. Malinowski (7/12/1975) **CH:** Adam; Christopher **ED:** MEd, Bowling Green State University (1972); BA, State University of New York at Fredonia (1971) **C:** Professor of Development Studies, Finger Lakes Community College, Canandaigua, NY (1996-Present); Chairperson, Development Studies Department, Finger Lakes Community College, Canandaigua, NY (1991-Present); Associate Professor, Finger Lakes Community College, Canandaigua, NY (1992-1996); Assistant Professor, Development Studies, Finger Lakes Community College, Canandaigua, NY (1987-1992) **CIV:** Member, Liturgy Committee, St. Benedict Parish, Canandaigua, NY (2002-2005); Member, Parish Council Youth Advisory Committee, St. Benedict Parish, Canandaigua, NY (2002-2005); Member, Youth Advisory Committee, St. Benedict Parish, Canandaigua, NY (2000-2005); Active Member, PTO, St. Mary's School, Canandaigua, NY (1998-2006); Active Member, Boy Scouts of America (1998-2005); Active Member, Literacy Volunteers, Canandaigua, NY (1994-2000); Member, School Board, St. Mary's School, Canandaigua, NY (1993-1999) **CW:** Editorial Board Member, International Reading Association (1994-Present); Editor, "Research and Teaching in Developmental Education" (1990-2006); Contributor, Articles to Professional Journals **AW:** Recipient, Excellence in Faculty Service Award, Chancellor's Office, New York State Education Department (2006); Nominee, Athena (2002); Recipient, Pelican Award, Boy Scouts of America (2002); Recipient, Distinguished Service Award, Finger Lakes Community College

(2000); Recipient, Outstanding Publication Award, The National Association for Developmental Education (1995); Recipient, Outstanding Professional Service Award, New York College Learning Skills Association (1995); Recipient, Excellence in Professional Service Award (1993); Recipient, Distinguished Service Award, Finger Lakes Community College (1988) **MEM:** Education Board, The National Association for Developmental Education, The National Association for Developmental Education (1994-Present); Chair of Academy, The National Association for Developmental Education (1992-2000); Conference Chairperson, New York College Learning Skills Association (1987-1990); Vice President, New York College Learning Skills Association; Secretary, New York College Learning Skills Association; New York State English Council; New York State Reading Association; National Council of Teachers of English; Phi Delta Kappa International **MH:** Albert Nelson Marquis Lifetime Achievement Award (2017) **H:** Reading; Traveling; Walking **BA:** 3325 Marvin Sands Dr, Finger Lakes Community College, Canandaigua, NY, 14424 **ADD:** 2616 East Street, Canandaigua, NY, 14424

MAMMIS, ANTONIOS, T: Physician, Assistant Professor **I:** Education/Educational Services **CN:** Rutgers New Jersey Medical School **ED:** Fellowship, Functional and Restorative Neurosurgery, North Shore University Hospital (2010-2011); Intern, Neurological Surgery, Rutgers New Jersey Medical School, Rutgers, The State University of New Jersey (2006-2013); MD, Columbia University (2006); BA, Biology, New York University, Summa Cum Laude (2002) **CT:** Certified Part 1: Pass, American Board of Neurological Surgery (2010); Certified STEP III: 211, USMLE (2007); Certified STEP II CK: 215, USMLE (2005); Certified CS: Pass, USMLE (2005); Certified STEP I: 248, USMLE (2004); Certified in Basic Life Support, American Heart Association; Certified in HeartCode ACLS, American Heart Association; Certified Medical Doctor, State of New Jersey; Certified Medical Doctor, State of New York; Certified Medical Doctor, State of Pennsylvania **C:** Assistant Professor, Anesthesiology, Rutgers New Jersey Medical School, Rutgers, The State University of New Jersey (2015-Present); Assistant Professor, Neurological Surgery, Rutgers New Jersey Medical School, Rutgers, The State University of New Jersey (2013-Present); Hospital Appointment, University Hospital, Newark, NJ; Hospital Appointment, Newark Beth Israel Medical Center; Hospital Appointment, Mountainside Hospital; Hospital Appointment, Robert Wood Johnson University Hospital; Hospital Appointment, St. Mary's Hospital, Passaic, NJ **CR:** Visiting Appointment, Robert Wood Johnson Gamma Knife Center; Visiting Appointment, Kessler Institute for Rehabilitation; Director, Center for Neuromodulation, Department of Neurological Surgery, Rutgers New Jersey Medical School, Rutgers, The State University of New Jersey; Director, Functional and Restorative Neurosurgery, Department of Neurological Surgery, Rutgers New Jersey Medical School, Rutgers, The State University of New Jersey; Surgical Director, Center for Headache, Orofacial and Neuropathic Pain, Department of Neurological Surgery, Rutgers New Jersey Medical School, Rutgers, The State University of New Jersey; Director, Nurse Practitioners and Physician Extender Staff, Neurological Institute **CW:** Editorial Board, AANS Neurosurgeon (2016-Present); Neurosurgeon Editorial Board, American Association of Neurological Surgeons (2006-Present); Editorial Board, Neurosurgery Times, Newark NJ (2014-2015) **AW:** Golden Apple Resident Teaching Award Nominee, Rutgers New Jersey Medical School, Rutgers, The State University of New

Jersey (2014-2017, 2012); Ronald Tasker Award, American Association of Neurological Surgeons Section on Pain (2011); Golden Apple Resident Teaching Award Nominee, Rutgers New Jersey Medical School, Rutgers, The State University of New Jersey (2009); Hellenic Medical Society of New York Medical Scholarship Award, Hellenic Medical Society of New York (2003-2005); Founder's Day Award, New York University (2002); Outstanding Performance in Biology Award, Beta Alpha Sigma (2002) **MEM:** University Hospital O.R. Committee, Rutgers New Jersey Medical School, Rutgers, The State University of New Jersey (2016-Present); University Hospital Skin Integrity Committee, Rutgers New Jersey Medical School, Rutgers, The State University of New Jersey (2016-Present); Clinical Practice Management Committee, Rutgers New Jersey Medical School, Rutgers, The State University of New Jersey (2016-Present); Neurological Surgery Chairperson Search Committee, Rutgers New Jersey Medical School, Rutgers, The State University of New Jersey (2016-Present); Clerkship Director, Third Year Medical Student Neurosurgery Rotation (2014-Present); Research and Scientific Oversight Committee, International Neuromodulation Society (2010-Present); Scientific Program Committee, North American Neuromodulation Society (2010-Present); American Society for Functional and Stereotactic Neurosurgery (2010-Present); World Society for Functional and Stereotactic Neurosurgery (2010-Present); Medical Society of the State of New York (2010-Present); Medical Society of the County of Queens (2010-Present); American Academy of Pain Medicine (2010-Present); American Hellenic Educational Progressive Association (2010-Present); Executive Board Member, Mytilenian Society of America (2010-Present); Congress of Neurological Surgeons (2006-Present); American Medical Association (2006-Present); Hellenic Medical Society of NY (2006-Present); Hellenic Professional Association (2006-Present); Phi Beta Kappa (2002-Present); Rutgers University Senate (2016-2017); University Structure and Governance Committee, Rutgers, The State University of New Jersey (2016-2017); Computerized Order Entry Committee, University of Medicine and Dentistry of New Jersey (2012-2013); Columbia University's Graduate Hellenic Association (2005-2006); Chairman, Health Sciences Campus (2005-2006) **BA:** 90 Bergen St Ste 8100, Rutgers New Jersey Medical School, Newark, NY, 07103 **ADD:** 4602 25th Ave, Astoria, NY, 11103

MANDERSCHEID, RONALD, T: Executive Director **I:** Nonprofit & Philanthropy **CN:** National Association of County Behavioral Health & Developmental Disability Directors **DOB:** 09/28/1943 **PB:** La Crosse **SC:** WI/USA **PT:** William Joseph; Norene Elsine Batteen **MS:** Married **SPN:** Frances Elizabeth Fedkiw (9/1/1973) **CH:** William Derrick; Kristen Elizabeth; Erika Marie **ED:** PhD, University of Maryland (1975); MA, Marquette University (1967); BA, Loras College, Maxima Cum Laude (1965) **CT:** Certified, Federal Executive Institute (1986) **C:** Executive Director, National Association of County Behavioral Health & Developmental Disability Directors (2009-Present); Senior Principal, Director of Mental Health and Substance Use Program, Global Health Sector/ SRA (2006-2011); Chief Survey & Analysis, Center for Mental Health Services (1992-2006); Acting Director, Division of State and Community System Development, Center for Mental Health Services (1992-1993); Chief, Statistic Research Branch, National Institute of Mental Health (1981-1992); Chief, Evaluation Research Section, National Institute of Mental Health (1975-1980); Research Associate, National Institute of Mental Health (1972-

1975); Research Assistant, University of Maryland (1970-1972) **CR:** University of Southern California (2016-Present); NASMHPD Research Institute (2011-Present); Council of Quality and Leadership (2011-Present); Danya Institute (2010-Present); Adjunct Professor, Department of Mental Health, Bloomberg School of Public Health, Johns Hopkins University (2006-Present); International Consortium of Mental Health Policy and Research (2000-Present); Pan American Health Organization (1995-Present); World Health Organization (1993-Present); Department of Health and Human Services Section Advisory Group Healthy People 2020 (2008-2011); Columbia University (1998-2001); Consultant, George Washington University (1978-1983); Fellow, Washington Academy of Sciences **CIV:** West Montgomery County Citizens Association, Potomac, MD (1983-Present) **MIL:** U.S. Army (1967-1969) **CW:** Co-Editor, "Outcome Measurement in the Human Service" (2011); Special Editor, "Journal of Washington Academy of Sciences" (2000); Producer, "Making the Numbers Work for You" (1987); Editor, "System Science and the Future of Health (1976); "International Journal of Mental Health"; Contributor of scientific articles to professional journals; Author, Editor, "Mental Health in the United States" **AW:** Lifetime Achievement Award, National Association for Rural Mental Health (2016); Public Policy Leadership Award, New York Association Psychosocial Rehabilitation Services (2014); Carl A. Taube Lifetime Achievement Award (2014); Stuart A. Rice Award, DC Sociological Society (2011); Secretary Distinguished Service Award, Department Health And Human Services (2008); Distinguished Service Award, American College of Mental Health Administrators (2006); Distinguished Service Tribute, National Association State Mental Health Program Directors (2006); Public Service Award, National Council of Community Behavioral Healthcare (2006); Secretary Distinguished Service Award, Department Health And Human Services (2004-2006); Consumer Leadership Award, American Public Heart Association (2003); Saul Feldman Lifetime Achievement Award, American College of Mental Health Administrators (2003); Irving Blumberg Humanitarian Award, American Association For Psychosocial Rehabilitation (2002); Mental Health Statistics Improvement Program Leadership Award, Department Health And Human Services (2001); Mental Health Chairperson's Distinguished Service Award, American Public Heart Association (2001); Mental Health Section Award, American Public Heart Association (2000); Meritorious Service Award, Federal Executive Institute Alumni Association (1999); Secretary Distinguished Service Award, Department Health And Human Services (1999); Distinguished Alumni Award, Loras College (1998); National Sociological Practice Award, Society of Applied Sociology (1995); Peter Gellman Award, Eastern Sociological Society (1984); Decorated Army Commendation Medal (1969) **MEM:** National Council of Community Behavioral Healthcare; Cosmos Club, Governing Board (2017-Present); President, American College of Mental Health Administrators (2011-2013); Executive Board, American College of Mental Health Administrators (2007-2015); President of the Foundation, Federal Executive Institute Alumni Association (2003-2011); President, Federal Executive Institute Alumni Association (2003); Executive Board, Federal Executive Institute Alumni Association (1997-2005); Chair of Mental Health, American Public Health Association (1997-1998); Chair, Policy Issues Committee (1995-2000); Chairman, Various Committees, Eastern Sociological Society; President, D.C. Sociological Society (1992-1993); President, Washington Academy of Sciences (1987-

1988); New York Academy of Sciences; Chairman, American Sociological Association (1983-1991); Chairman, Committee of Federal Standard of Sociologists, American Sociological Association (1983-1988); Executive Committee, Eastern Sociological Society (1979-1984); Chairman, Washington Chapter, Society for General Systems Research (1976-2010); President, Alpha Kappa Delta (1972-1973); World Academy of Art and Science; American Academy of Social Work & Social Welfare; Society of Applied Sociology; National Association State Mental Health Program Directors; Farmington Country Club; Delta Epsilon Sigma; Phi Kappa Phi **MH:** Albert Nelson Marquis Lifetime Achievement Award (2017) **H:** Coin collecting; Reading **BA:** 660 N Capitol Street NW, Suite 400, NACBHDD, Washington, DC, 20001 **URL:** http://www.nacbhdd.org

MANHEIM, MICHAEL PHILIP, T: Professional Photographer **I:** Fine Art **CN:** Michael Philip Manheim **PB:** Canton **SC:** OH/USA **PT:** Robert B. Manheim; Clara B. Manheim **MS:** Divorced **SPN:** Carolyn B. Olson (10/30/1965, Divorced 1/1995) **CH:** Jonathan; Allison **ED:** BS in Marketing, University of Pennsylvania (1962) **C:** Professional Photographer, State of Massachusetts (1969-Present); Manager, Clothing Retailer, Alliance, OH (1962-1969) **CR:** Graphic Art Judge, "Document Your Environment," EPA (2012); Artist-in-Residence, The Pahoa Village Museum (2010); Artist-in-Residence, Easton Mountain Retreat (2010); Artist-in-Residence, Bates College, Bates Dance Festival (2001-2004); Artist-in-Residence, Phillips Exeter Academy (2002) **CIV:** Contributor, University of Pennsylvania; Contributor, The Southern Poverty Law Center; Contributor, Planned Parenthood; Contributor, Oxfam America Inc.; Contributor, Project Bread; Contributor, Arlington Food Pantry; Contributor, Mass Audubon; Contributor, ACLU; Contributor, Public Radio Stations; Contributor, Dance Organizations **CW:** Author, "The Smoking Fifties: How Once We Looked: Photographs of the Past" (2017); Author, "See-Saw: A Sampler of How Once We Looked" (2016); Author, "Where My Spirit Guides Us: Ancient Hula on the Big Island of Hawai'i" (2015); Solo Exhibition, Hawaii Museum of Contemporary Art, East Hawaii Cultural Center, Hilo, HI (2013); Group Exhibition, "Creatives Rising," Digital Displays Here and Projected onto Manhattan Buildings, See | Exhibition Space, Long Island City, Queens, NY (2013); Group Exhibition, "Searching for the Seventies: The Documerica Photography Project," National Archives, Washington, DC (2013); Group Exhibition, "Shadows: Darkness and Light," Black Box Gallery, Portland, OR (2012); Group Exhibition, "Hawaiian Spirits," Kalani Oceanside Retreat+One Gallery, Big Island of Hawaii (2012); Solo Exhibition, Wailoa Center, Hilo, HI (2011); Solo Exhibition, Griffin Museum, DSI, Belmont, MA (2011); Solo Exhibition, National Museum of Dance, Saratoga Springs, NY (2010-2011); Group Exhibition, "30 Year Anniversary Show," Sylvia White Gallery, Ventura, CA (2009); Group Exhibition, "Introducing Moment Magazine," Safe-T-Gallery, Dumbo, Brooklyn, NY (2008); Group Exhibition, "Fifth Anniversary Show," Safe-T-Gallery, Dumbo, Brooklyn, NY (2007); Group Exhibition, "Contemporary/Vintage Works, LTD," The AIPAD Photography Show, Miami, FL (2007); Group Exhibition, Art Now Fair, Miami Beach, FL (2007); Solo Exhibition, Safe-T-Gallery, Dumbo, Brooklyn, NY (2007); Group Exhibition, "Edisa Weeks' Collaborations with Five Photographers," The Puffin Room, New York, NY (2006); Solo Exhibition, August Gallery, Santa Fe, NM (2006): Solo Exhibition, River City Silver, San Antonio, TX (2005); Group Exhibition,

"Growing Up Absurd," Radiant Light Gallery, Portland, ME (2004-2005); Group Exhibition, "Rhythms in Nature," Radiant Light Gallery, Portland, ME (2004); Group Exhibition, "Dance Photography," The Puffin Room, New York, NY (2003); Group Exhibition, "Winter Performance Project," The Puffin Room, New York, NY (2003); Solo Exhibition, International Photography Hall of Fame & Museum, Oklahoma City, OK (2003); Group Exhibition, "Multi-Exposures: Different Artists, Differing Images," Radiant Light Gallery, Portland, ME (2002); Solo Exhibition, Bates College Museum of Art, Lewiston, ME (2002); Group Exhibition, "Holiday Show," Panopticon Gallery, Waltham, MA (2001); Group Exhibition, "Terrors and Wonders: Monsters in Contemporary Art," DeCordova Museum and Sculpture Park, Lincoln, MA (2001); Group Exhibition, "Look Out: Photographing Dancers Outdoors," Jacob's Pillow Dance Festival, Becket, MA (2001); Group Exhibition, "Moving Images: Figures in Dynamic Tension," Radiant Light Gallery, Portland, ME (2000); Group Exhibition, "Seventh Annual Photography Show," Rice/Polak Gallery, Provincetown, MA (2000); Solo Exhibitions, National Museum of Dance, Saratoga Springs, NY (2000, 1999); Group Exhibition, "A Tenth Anniversary Celebration of Our Gallery Artists," Edward Carter Gallery, Gualala, CA (1999); Group Exhibition, "Group Show Curated by Pattee Stayrook," Mad River Post, Santa Monica, CA (1999); Group Exhibition, "Fall Collection 1998 Curated by Sadler Fine Arts," Mad River Post, Santa Monica, CA (1998); Group Exhibition, "The Painterly Photography," Lamont Gallery, Philips Exeter Academy, Exeter, NH (1998); Group Exhibition, "Selections from Surrealism & NeoNarrative," Public Corporation for the Arts, Long Beach CA (1998); Group Exhibition, "Surrealism & NeoNarrative," Long Beach Arts, Long Beach, CA (1998); Group Exhibition, "Earth, Sky and Sea," Ashwell Gallery, Beverly, MA (1998); Solo Exhibition, Renjeau Galleries, Concord, MA (1998); Group Exhibition, "Holiday Exhibit: Give Art," Cragin Fife Gallery, Brookline, MA (1997); Group Exhibition, "Holiday Exhibit," The Gallery at EverColor Fine Art, Worcester, MA (1997); Group Exhibition, "Holiday Exhibit," Ashwell Gallery, Beverly, MA (1997); Group Exhibition, "Simple/Multiple," INFES Gallery, Düsseldorf, Germany (1997); Group Exhibition, "Fall Show," Contemporary Artists' Services, New York, NY (1997); Group Exhibition, "Summer Show," Contemporary Artists' Services, New York, NY (1997); Group Exhibition, "Summer Show," Contemporary Artists' Services, Santa Monica, CA (1997); Solo Exhibition, John Callahan Gallery, Concord, MA (1996); Solo Exhibition, Panopticon Gallery, Boston, MA (1996); Solo Exhibition, Spazio Espositivo De Pellegrin, Riva del Garda, Italy (1996); Solo Exhibition, Pacifica Graduate Institute, Santa Barbara, CA (1996); Solo Exhibition, Terrakotta Gallery, Thessaloniki, Greece (1996); Solo Exhibition, Mythos Gallery, Burbank, CA (1995); Solo Exhibition, Arthur Griffin Center for Photographic Art, Winchester, MA (1994); Solo Exhibition, Fitchburg Art Museum, Fitchburg, MA (1993) **AW:** Honoree, Best of 2017 Award, American Society of Media Photographers (2017); Honoree, 3rd-6th-8th-9th-10th Annual Winners Gallery, International Color Awards and Master's Cup (2015-2017); Accepted Works, The Trienenberg Photography Competition and Salon (2015-2016); Honoree, 8th-9th-10th-11th-12th Annual Winners Gallery, Black & White Spider Awards (2013-2017); Certificate of Participation, The 7th Emirates Photography Competition (2012); Honorable Mention, Habitat Photo Competition, United Nations Habitat Conference, Vancouver, BC, Canada (1976) **MEM:** American Society of Media Photographers, Inc. (1969-Present); Photographic Resource Center, Inc. **MH:** Albert Nelson Marquis Lifetime Achievement Award (2017) **ADD:** 108 Palmer Street, Arlington, MA, 02474 **URL:** http://www.michaelphilipmanheim.com/MPM-portfolios.php

MANIS, PAULA KATHERINE, T: Of Counsel **I:** Law and Legal Services **CN:** Loomis, Ewert, Parsley, Davis & Gotting, PC **PB:** Dearborn **SC:** MI/USA **PT:** Edward T.; Jeanne Manis **MS:** Married **SPN:** Robin L. Omer **CH:** Taylor R. Omer; Alexis L. Omer **ED:** JD, Thomas M. Cooley Law School, Western Michigan University (1979); Postgraduate Studies, Michigan State University (1975); BA in Social Science, Multi-Discipline Program, Michigan State University (1973) **C:** Of Counsel, Lommis, Ewert, Parsley, Davis, & Gotting, P.C. (2012-Present); Attorney, Worman, Dixon & Manis, PLC (2000-2012) **CIV:** American Arbitration Association (2006-Present); Co-president, Dispute Resolution Center of Central Michigan (2005-2006); Member, ADR Oversight Committee, Ingham County Circuit Court (2003-2010); Board Member, Dispute Resolution Center of Central Michigan (2001-2010); Supporter, Mayo Clinic; Supporter, St. Jude's Children's Hospital; Hearing Panelist, Attorney Discipline Board, State of Michigan; Former Chair, Oil, Gas & Natural Resources Committee, Real Property Section, Dispute Resolution Center of Central Michigan **CW:** Author, "What is 'Reasonable Use'," Michigan Bar Journal (1999); Author, "Across the Great Divide: Surface Owners vs. Severed Mineral Owners" **AW:** Best Lawyer in America, Best Lawyers in America (2017); Leaders in the Law (2015-2018); Best Lawyers of America, Arbitration/Mediation (2014-2018); Bar Register of Preeminent Women Lawyers, LexisNexis and Martindale-Hubbell (2013); Best Lawyers of America, Alternative Dispute Resolution (2009-2013); Best Lawyers of America, Oil and Gas Law (2008-2018); AV Preeminent Peer Review Rating, Martindale-Hubbell **MEM:** Michigan Association of Petroleum Landmen (1981-Present); State Bar of Michigan; Real Property Law Section, State Bar of Michigan; Alternate Dispute Resolution Section, State Bar of Michigan; Former Member, Alternate Dispute Resolution Council, State Bar of Michigan; Ohio State Bar Association; Ingham County Bar Association; Former Chair Legislative Liaison Committee, Michigan Oil and Gas Association **BAR:** State Bar of Michigan; Ohio State Bar Association; Illinois State Bar Association (Inactive); Colorado Bar Association (Inactive) **BA:** 2400 Lake Lansing Rd Ste E, Loomis, Ewert, Parsley, Davis & Gotting, PC, Lansing, MI, 48912 **URL:** http://loomislaw.com/attorneys/paula-k-manis

MANKAMYER, CHARLES R., I: Insurance **C:** President of General Agents, First United American Insurance Co. (Now Globe Life Insurance Company of New York)

MANN, MARY ANNEETA, I: Writing and Editing **PB:** Rockhampton **SC:** QLD/Australia **PT:** Willie Augustus Mann; Dorothy Louisa Mann **ED:** PhD, University of Southern California (1982); MA, University of California, Berkeley (1970); BA, Sydney University, Australia (1964) **CW:** Author (2013-2015); Author, "Scenes From ANZAC" (2014); Author, "Anzac The Play" (2012); Author, "There Are No Enemies," Second Edition (2011); Author, "Mentoring Poems, Four Centuries Of Selected Poetry" (2010); Author, "Poems Of Woman" (2010); Author, "Anzac To Understanding" (2008); Author, "There Are No Enemies" (2007); Editor, "Science And Spirituality" (2004); Author, "Two Family Plays: Maria And The Comet The Round Table" (2004); Author, "Hubris, The Construction Of Tragedy," Review (2004); Author, "Thugun And Natasha" (2003); Author, "The Right Of The Womb-Post 911" (2003); Author, "The Round Table" (1995); Author, "Thugun And Natasha" (1993); Author, "The Construction Of Tragedy" (1985); Author, "Los Angeles Theatre Book" (1984); Author, "Anzac I And II" (1984); Author, "Maria And The Comet," (1983); Author, "Los Angeles Theatre Book" (1978); Author, "Tortoise Shell," "Diana Devereaux," "The Senator's Daughter," "The Tongue-Cut Sparrow"

MANOLAKAS, STANTON PETER, T: Artist **I:** Fine Art **CN:** Art Licensing International **DOB:** 07/25/1946 **PB:** Detroit **SC:** MI/USA **PT:** Constantine Stamatios Manolakas; Angela (Kaloyerpolous) Manolakas **MS:** Married **SPN:** Barbara Soldathos (July 25, 1971) **ED:** Postgraduate Studies, California State University, Long Beach (1969-1970); BA in Psychology, University Southern California, LA (1969); Student, Eastman School of Music (1964-1965); Gallery 131, Glendale, CA (1995-Present); Art Angle's Gallery, Orange, CA (1985-1994) **CIV:** Active, AFL-CIO County Federation of Labor (1982-1992); Member, Saint Sophia Cathedral Choir, L.A. (1970-1982); Glendale Symphony Orchestra (1975-1977); Burbank Symphony Orchestra (1973-1976) **CW:** Featured Artist, Ave Maria Fine Art Gallery, Ann Arbor, MI (2000-Present); Featured Artist, Thousand Oaks Community Gallery, Newbury Park, CA (2005); Featured Artist, By the Bay Gallery, Harbor Springs, MI (2001); Featured Artist, California Plaza Reopening Angels Flight, L.A. (1996); Featured Artist, Dossin Great Lakes Museum (1994); Featured Artist, L.A. Heritage Square Museum (1994); Demonstration Artist, City Art Exhibit, Millard Sheets Gallery, L.A. County Fair, Pomona, CA (1994); Featured Artist, Zantman Galleries, Carmel, CA (1989); Featured Artist, Ronald Reagan Presidential Library, Simi Valley, CA; Featured Artist, Lake Superior Maritime Museum, Duluth, MN; Featured Artist, Bechtel Industries, San Francisco, CA; Featured Artist, Marriott Hotel Corporation, Newton, MA; Featured Artist, Gallagher & Heffernan Inc., San Francisco, CA; Featured Artist, The Borovay Group, L.A.; Featured Artist, Datum Inc., Anaheim, CA; Featured Artist, Tarbell Realty Inc., Costa Mesa, CA; Featured Artist, Wolverine Bronze, Roseville, MI; Featured Artist, Dossin Great Lakes Museum; Featured Artist, Lake Superior Marine Museum; Featured Artist, Little Travis Bay Historical Society **MH:** Albert Nelson Marquis Lifetime Achievement Award (2017) **H:** Running; Swimming; Music **PA:** Republican **RE:** Eastern Orthodox **ADD:** 2029 Verdugo Blvd Apt 323, Montrose, CA, 91020

MARCALI, JEAN GREGORY, T: Chemist **I:** Sciences **DOB:** 05/29/1926 **PB:** Jermyn **SC:** PA/USA **PT:** John Robert; Anna Marie Gregory **MS:** Single **SPN:** Kalman Marcali (10/6/1956, Deceased 1996) **CH:** Coleman; Frederick **ED:** Coursework, University of Delaware (1971-1972); Coursework, University of Pennsylvania (1948-1952) **C:** Consultant, DuPont (1989-1992); Supervisor for Technology Information, DuPont (1985-1989); Supervisor for Administrative Services, Central Research Department, DuPont (1982-1985); Supervisor for Technology Information, DuPont (1970-1982); Senior Adviser, Technology Information, DuPont (1967-1970); Technology Information Analyst, Information Systems Department, DuPont (1964-1967); Technology Information Analyst, Organic Chemistry Department, DuPont (1960-1964); Microanalyst, DuPont (1943-1960) **CIV:** Winterthur Museum, Garden & Library (1996-2011); Wilmington District Republicans Committee (1976-2011); President, Parent-Teacher Association, Brandywine School District (1973); President, Parent-Teacher Association, Alfred I. DuPont Elementary School (1972); Secretary, Parent-Teacher Association, Alfred I. DuPont Elementary School (1971) **MEM:** Emeritus Member, American Chemical Society (2013); Committee on Chemical Abstracts Service, American Chemical Society (1983-1993); Division Councilor, American Chemical Society (1983-1990); Chairman, American Chemical Society (1982-1983); Chairman-elect, American Chemical Society (1981); Delegate Secretary, American Chemical Society (1979-1980); Treasurer, Chemical Information Division, American Chemical Society (1976-1981); American Chemical Society; American Chemical Society; Order of the Eastern Star; DuPont Country Club; Winterthur Museum Guild **MH:** Albert Nelson Marquis Lifetime Achievement Award (2017) **RE:** Lutheran **ADD:** 950 Willow Valley Lakes Drive, H-401, Willow Street, PA, 17584

MARCUS, EDWARD NEAL, T: Principal Research Software Application Engineer **I:** Engineering **CN:** Boston Children's Hospital **DOB:** 05/18/1959 **PB:** Boston **SC:** MA/USA **PT:** Louis Gerald Marcus; Judith Marcus **MS:** Married **SPN:** Cara Marcus **CH:** Two Stepchildren **ED:** MSc, Massachusetts Institute of Technology, Cambridge, MA (1982); BSc in Physics, Massachusetts Institute of Technology, Cambridge, MA (1981) **CT:** Training Program with the DICOM Imaging Standard, IEEE Course on FDA Software Development for Medical Device Manufacturers **C:** Principal Research Software Application Engineer, Boston Children's Hospital, Waltham, MA (1996-Present); Principal Application Development Specialist, Boston Children's Hospital, Boston, MA (1996-2012); Marcus Laboratories, Boston, MA (1995-2003); Boston Medical Technologies, Boston, MA (1992-1995); Beth Israel Hospital (Now Beth Israel Deaconess Medical Center), Boston, MA (1990-1992); Research Associate, Massachusetts Institute of Technology, Cambridge, MA (1986-1990); Technion-Israel Institute of Technology, Haifa, Israel (1982-1985); Endeco, Marion, MA (1981-1982) **CIV:** Big Brother Mentor, Waltham Public Schools; Volunteer Captain, Sailing Outings for Children with Asperger's Syndrome, Volunteer for Social Action Work for Persons with Disabilities **CW:** Co-author, "Ventricular Strain in Fetuses with Aortic Stenosis and Evolving Hypoplastic Left Heart Syndrome Before and After Prenatal Aortic Valvuloplasty," Fetal Diagnosis and Therapy (2014); Co-author, "Impact of Transcatheter Pulmonary Valve Replacement on Biventricular Strain and Synchrony Assessed by Cardiac Magnetic Resonance Feature Tracking," Circulation: Cardiovascular Interventions (2013); Co-author, "Echocardiographic Methods, Quality Review, and Measurement Accuracy in a Randomized Multicenter Clinical Trial of Marfan Syndrome," Journal of American Society of Echocardiography (2013); Co-author, "Comparison of Cardiac MRI Tissue Tracking and Myocardial Tagging for Assessment of Regional Ventricular Strain," The International Journal of Cardiovascular Imaging (2012); Co-author, "Circumferential and Longitudinal Ventricular Strain in the Normal Human Fetus," Journal of American Society of Echocardiography (2012); Co-author, "Significance and Outcome of Left Heart Hypoplasia in Fetal Congenital Diaphragmatic Hernia," Ultrasound in Obstetrics & Gynecology (2010); Co-author, "Comparison of Echocardiographic and Cardiac Magnetic Resonance Imaging Measurements of Functional Single Ventricular Volumes, Mass, and Ejection Fraction (from the Pediatric Heart Network Fontan Cross-Sectional Study)," American Journal of Cardiology (2009); Co-author, "Comparison of Echocardiographic and Cardiac Magnetic

Resonance Imaging Measurements of Functional Single Ventricular Volumes, Mass, and Ejection Fraction (from the Pediatric Heart Network Fontan Cross-Sectional Study)," American Journal of Cardiology (2009); Co-author, "Changes in Left Heart Hemodynamics After Technically Successful In-Utero Aortic Valvuloplasty," Ultrasound in Obstetrics & Gynecology (2007); Co-presenter, "Consistencies of Myocyte Flow Source and Developed Pressure Models of Cardiac Function," Proceedings of the International Conference on the Understanding of Complex Systems, Urbana, IL (2007); Co-presenter, "Methods of Motion Path Reconstruction with Uncertain Position Data," Proceedings of the International Conference on Complex Systems, New England Complex Systems Institute, Boston, MA (2007); Co-author, "Faster Flow Quantification Using Sensitivity Encoding for Velocity-Encoded Cine Magnetic Resonance Imaging: In Vitro and In Vivo Validation," Journal of Magnetic Resonance Imaging (2006); Co-presenter, "Manifestations of Cellular Contraction Patterns on the Cardiac Flow Output," Proceedings of the International Conference on Complex Systems, New England Complex Systems Institute, Boston, MA (2006); Co-author, "Fetal Aortic Valve Stenosis and the Evolution of Hypoplastic Left Heart Syndrome: Patient Selection for Fetal Intervention," Circulation (2006); Co-author, "Improving Outcomes in Fetuses and Neonates with Congenital Displacement (Ebstein's Malformation) or Dysplasia of the Tricuspid Valve," American Journal of Cardiology (2005); Co-author, "Magnetic Resonance Imaging Predictors of Coarctation Severity," Circulation (2005); Co-presenter, "Models of Right Ventricular Shape and Function," Proceedings of the International Conference on Complex Systems, New England Complex Systems Institute, Boston, MA (2004); Co-author, "Echocardiographic Assessment of the Right Ventricular Response to Hypertension in Neonates on the Basis of Average-Shaped Contraction Models," Journal of the American Society of Echocardiography (2002); Co-author, "A New Quantitative Method for the Diagnosis of Right Ventricular Hypertensive Disorders in 3 Dimensions," Journal of the American Society of Echocardiography (2000); Co-author, "Reconstruction of 3-Dimensional Right Ventricular Shape and Volume from 3 Orthogonal Planes," Journal of the American Society of Echocardiography (2000); Co-presenter, "Accuracy of Fourier Analysis in Describing Right Ventricular Shape," Journal of the American College of Cardiology, Abstract, American College of Cardiology Scientific Sessions (1999); Co-presenter, "Accurate Two-Dimensional Echocardiographic Evaluation of Right Ventricular Shape and Volume Using a Combination of Fourier Analysis and Simpson's Biplane Method: In Vitro Validation Study," Circulation, Abstract, American Heart Association Scientific Sessions (1997); Co-author, "Characterization of Regional Left Ventricular Contraction by Curvature Difference Analysis," Basic Research in Cardiology (1988); Co-author, "The Influence of Semicircular Canal Morphology on Endolymph Flow Dynamics. An Anatomically Descriptive Mathematical Model," Acta Oto-Laryngologica (1987); Co-presenter, "A Study of Quantitative Methods for Characterization of Left Ventricular Contraction," IEEE Conference on Computers in Cardiology, Stockholm, Sweden (1985); Co-presenter, "An Experimental Study of Windturbine Noise," Seventh Annual Conference on Aerodynamic Noise, Atlanta, GA (1982); Co-presenter, "Blade Passage Noise in Windturbines," Society for Noise Control Engineers (1981) **AW:** Male Scholar Athlete Award, Massachusetts Institute of Technology **MEM:** Sigma Xi, The Scientific Research Honor Society; Constitution Yacht Club; Greater Boston Chapter of the Acoustical Society of America; IEEE **H:** Swimming; Sailing; Golf; Home improvement **PA:** Democrat **RE:** Jewish **BA:** 9 Hope Avenue, Waltham, MA, 02453 **ADD:** 47 Morse Street, Watertown, MA, 02472

MARIANI, ANDREA, T: Surgeon **I:** Medicine & Health Care **CN:** Mayo Clinic **DOB:** 02/03/1968 **PB:** Carate Brianza **SC:** Italy **MS:** Married **SPN:** Raffaella Mariani **CH:** Letibia; Pietro; Giovanni; Giacomo **ED:** Honorary PhD in Gynecologic Oncology, University of Utrecht, Netherlands (2006); Gynecologic Oncology Fellowship Program, Mayo School of Graduate Medical Education, Mayo Clinic College of Medicine (2005); MS, Gynecologic Oncology, Mayo Clinic College of Medicine and Science, Rochester, MN (2005); Research Fellowship, Obstetrics & Gynecology Fellowship Program, Mayo School of Graduate Medical Education, Mayo Clinic College of Medicine (1998); Residency in Obstetrics and Gynecology, San Raffaele Hospital, Universita di Milano (1997); MD, Universita degli Studi Graduate School, Milano, Italy (1993) **C:** Gynecologic Oncology Surgeon, Mayo Clinic (2008-Present); Consultant, Department of Obstetrics & Gynecology, Mayo Clinic **CR:** Fellow, Society of Gynecologic Oncologists (2004-2005) **CIV:** Committee Member, Gynecologic Oncology Fellowship Clinical Competency Committee (2016-Present); Advisory Member, Minnesota Ovarian Cancer Alliance (2016-Present); Panel Member, National Comprehensive Cancer Network (2016-Present); Clinical Practice Executive Committee, Department of Obstetrics & Gynecology, Mayo Clinic (2015-Present); Clinical Practice Committee, Department of Obstetrics & Gynecology, Mayo Clinic (2015-Present); Gynecology Surgery Chair, Mayo Clinic Cancer Center Practice Committee (2014-Present); Mayo Clinic Cancer Care Advisory Council (2013-Present); Vice Chair, Molecular Analysis of Endometrial Cancer, Department of Obstetrics & Gynecology, Mayo Clinic (2012-Present); Vice Chair, Integrate Initiative, Department of Obstetrics & Gynecology (2011-Present); Conference Organizer, Gynecologic Oncology Conference, Department of Obstetrics & Gynecology, Mayo Clinic (2010-Present); Member-at-Large, Associazone Medicina & Persona (2010-Present); NCCN Guideline Panel, Mayo Clinic Cancer Care Advisory Council (2014); Associate Member, American College of Obstetricians and Gynecologists (2010-2012) **CW:** Contributor, Over 150 Peer Reviewed Publications, Medical Journals **AW:** J.G. Moore Award, Western Association of Gynecologic Oncologists Meeting, Lake Tahoe, CA (2006) **MEM:** Medical Advisory Committee, Minnesota Ovarian Cancer Alliance (2016-Present); Editorial Board Member, Turkish Journal of Gynecologic Oncology (2014-Present); Editorial Board Member, European Journal of Surgical Oncology (2013-Present); Invited Member Quality and Outcomes Committee, Society of Gynecologic Oncologists (2012-Present); American College of Obstetricians and Gynecologists (2012-Present); International Member, Society of Gynecologic Oncologists (2010-Present); Editorial Board Member, European Journal of Gynecologic Oncology (2010-Present); Editorial Board Member, Journal of Medicine and the Person (2010-Present); International Gynecologic Cancer Society (2009-Present); Minneapolis Surgical Society (2009-Present); Associate Fellow, American College of Surgeons (2008-Present); Mayo Clinic Alumni Association, Mayo Clinic College of Medicine and Science, Department of Education Administration (2005-Present); Candidate Member, Society of Gynecologic Oncologists (2005-2010); Resident Member, American College of Surgeons (2002-2005); Robotic Interest Group, Department of Surgery, Mayo Clinic; Gynecologic Oncology Specialty Interest Group, Obstetric & Gynecology Specialty Council, Mayo Clinic **H:** Traveling with family; Reading; Self-improvement **BA:** 200 First Street SW, Rochester, MN, 55905 **ADD:** 2022 Baihly Summit Drive SW, Rochester, MN, 55902 **URL:** http://www.mayo.edu/research/faculty/mariani-andrea-m-d/bio-00027348

MARION, MARJORIE A., T: Literature and Language Professor, Educational Consultant **I:** Education/Educational Services **CN:** University of St. Francis **DOB:** 05/06/1935 **PB:** Winterset **SC:** IA/USA **PT:** Virgil Arthur Hammon; Marilyn Ruth (Sandy) Hammon **MS:** Widowed **SPN:** Robert H. Marion (12/20/1964, Deceased) **CH:** Kathryn Ruth **ED:** Postgraduate, Institute for Management and Leadership in Education, Harvard University (1981); MA, Purdue University (1969); BA, Colorado College (1958) **C:** Professor Emeritus, University of St. Francis, Joliet, IL (1997-Present); Grant Writer, St. Paul Apostle School, Joliet, IL (2010-2011); Director of the Writing Center, University of St. Francis, Joliet, IL (1996); Director, Freshman Core Program, University of St. Francis, Joliet, IL (1993-1995); Associate Professor in English, University of St. Francis, Joliet, IL (1989-1997); Dean of Faculty, University of St. Francis, Joliet, IL (1985-1989); Acting Vice President of Academy Affairs, University of St. Francis, Joliet, IL (1984-1985); Director of Continuing Education, University of St. Francis, Joliet, IL (1980-1984); Coordinator of Instructional Development, University of St. Francis, Joliet, IL (1979-1980); Chairperson, Humanities and Fine Arts Division, University of St. Francis, Joliet, IL (1975-1979); Chairperson, English Department, University of St. Francis, Joliet, IL (1971-1975); Director of Public Relations, University of St. Francis, Joliet, IL (1968-1970); Chairperson, English Department, Lincoln-Way High School, New Lenox, IL (1964-1968) **CR:** Lecturer for Writing workshops, Literature Presenter (2004-2005); Consultant to Presidential Search, University of St. Francis (2001-2002); Conductor of Writing Workshops for Adults Returning to College (1995-1999); TV and Radio Appearances Regarding Lifelong Education, Chicago, IL, St. Louis, MO, Albuquerque, NM, and Phoenix, AZ (1982-1985); Lecturer for Educational Workshops and Institutions, Visiting Team, North Central Association, Joliet and Lockport, IL (1975-1979) **CIV:** Chairman, Catholic Franciscan Charism Council (2005-2006); Secretary, Preserve Condominium Homeowners Association Board **CW:** Author, "A Guide to Writing for the Faint at Heart" (1996); Drama Critic, "Joliet Herald News" (1970-1982); Author, "Monograph" **AW:** President's Award, University of St. Francis (1975) **RE:** Roman Catholic **ADD:** 2961 Covered Bridge Way, Joliet, IL, 60435

MAROVITZ, SANFORD EARL, T: Professor Emeritus **I:** Education/Educational Services **CN:** Kent State University **DOB:** 05/10/1933 **PB:** Chicago **SC:** IL/USA **PT:** Harold Marovitz; Gertrude (Luster) Marovitz **MS:** Married **SPN:** Eleonora Dimitsa (9/1/1964) **ED:** PhD, Duke University (1968); MA, Duke University (1961); BA, Lake Forest College, With Honors (1960) **C:** Professor Emeritus, Kent State University (1996-Present); Professor of English, Kent State University (1975-1996); Associate Professor of English, Kent State University (1970-1975); Assistant Professor of English, Kent State University (1967-1970); Fulbright Instructor, University of Athens, Greece (1965-1967); Instructor in English, Temple University (1963-1965) **CR:** Co-Director, Melville

Among the Nations, Greece (1997); National Trustee, Lake Forest College (1990-1998); Visiting Professor of English, Shimane University, Matsue, Japan (1976-1977); Woodrow Wilson Fellow (1960-1961); Chair, Graduate Studies, Kent State University **CIV:** Robert Miller Award for Best Article, Center for Educational Affairs Critic, College English Association (2000); **MIL:** U.S. Air Force (1953-1957) **CW:** Author, "Melville Among the Nations: Proceedings of an International Conference, Volos, Greece, July 2-6, 1997" (2001); Author, "Abraham Cahan," United States Authors Series (1996); Co-Author, "A Bibliographical Guide to the Study of the Literature of the U.S.A.," Fifth Edition (1984); Co-Editor, "Artful Thunder" (1975); Associate Editor, Studies in American Jewish Literature; Contributor, Articles, Professional Journals **AW:** Academic Quarter Research Awards, Kent State University (1977); Academic Quarter Research Awards, Kent State University (1974); Academic Quarter Research Awards, Kent State University (1971) **MEM:** Curator, Aldous Huxley Society (1998-Present); Editor, The Howellsian, W.D. Howells Society (2004-2007); President, W.D. Howells Society (2002-2003); Vice President, W.D. Howells Society (2000-2001); President, Melville Society (1998); Secretary, Melville Society (1994-1996); Modern Language Association; Jack London Society; College English Association; R.W. Emerson Society; Saul Bellow Society; Nathaniel Hawthorne Society; Phi Beta Kappa; Phi Beta Delta; Omicron Delta Kappa **H:** Jewish-American fiction, Western writing, and the literature of the American Renaissance **ADD:** 1155 Norwood Street, Kent, OH, 44240 **URL:** https://www.library.kent.edu/sanford-marovitz-papers-faculty-english

MARSHALL, DAVID FRANKLIN, T: Linguistics Educator, Consultant **I:** Education/Educational Services **DOB:** 01/06/1938 **PB:** Perry **SC:** OK/USA **PT:** Otto F. Marshall; Retta (Ritthaler) Marshall **MS:** Married **SPN:** Ruth Ann Brockert (3/5/1966) **CH:** Michael J.; Nathan N. **ED:** PhD in Linguistics, New York University (1975); MDiv, Union Theological Seminary (1964); BA, TCU (1960) **C:** Professor Emeritus, University of North Dakota, Grand Forks, ND (2009-Present); Professor, University of North Dakota, Grand Forks, ND (1994-2009); Associate Professor, University of North Dakota, Grand Forks, ND (1980-1993); Associate Professor, Barton College, Wilson, NC (1972-1980); Assistant Professor, Barton College, Wilson, NC (1972-1980) **CR:** Advisory Board Member, SLIA/A, San Diego, CA (1992-2000); Affiliate, Federal Language Project, The University of Arizona, Tucson, AZ (1988-2006); Consultant, C.G. Jung Foundation, New York, NY (1966-1972) **CIV:** Vice Chairman, Great River Shakespeare Festival (2015-2017); President, The Greater Grand Forks Symphony Orchestra (1985-1986) **MIL:** First Reconnaissance Battalion, U.S. Marine Corps Reserve **CW:** Contributor, "International Journal of the Sociology of Language," Berlin, Germany (1994-2004); Contributor, "New Language Planning Newsletter," Mysore, India (1992-2006); Editor, "Language Planning" (1991); Editor-in-Chief, "Pilgrim Press," Philadelphia, PA (1969-1972); Articles Editor, "U.C. Herald," New York, NY (1964-1969); Editor, Professional Journals; Co-Editor, Professional Journals **AW:** Fulbright Professor, University of Veliko Turnovo, Bulgaria; Fulbright Professor, Eatvos Lorand College of the Unversity of Hungary, Budapest (1993-1994); Summer Scholar, National Endowment for the Humanities, University of Wisconsin-Madison (1990); Fulbright Professor, Nanjing University, People's Republic Of China (1986-1987); Summer Scholar, National Endowment of the Humanities, Stanford University (1984); Summer Scholar, National Endowment of the Humanities, Stanford University

(1979); Lilly Visiting Scholar (1976-1977) **MEM:** Kiwanis Club, Grand Forks, ND (1981-2009); Winona Area Toys for Kids (2010-Present); Hiawatha Valley Marines (2010-2016) **MH:** Albert Nelson Marquis Lifetime Achievement Award (2017); Distinguished Humanitarian (2017) **H:** Fly fishing on the Whitewater and other local rivers **PA:** Democrat **RE:** Jewish **ADD:** 160 Janet Marie Ln, Winona, MN, 55987

MARSHALL, KENNETH LELAND, I: Other **ED:** Bachelor's Degree, Cleveland State University (1967-1971) **C:** Senior Research Engineer, Organic Optical Materials and Liquid Crystals, University of Rochester (2016-Present); Group Leader(Acting), Optical Materials Technologies, University of Rochester (2014-Present); Research Engineer, University of Rochester (1984-2016); TRP Energy Sensors (1983-1984); Chief Chemist, American Liquid Crystal Chemical Company (1975-1983); International Liquid Crystal Company (1973-1974) **CR:** High School Summer Research Program, University of Rochester (1997-Present) **CIV:** Chair, SPICE Conferences **CW:** Lecturer in field, Contributor to Professional Journals

MARTIN, DIANN , I: Medicine & Health Care **ED:** PhD in Nursing; MS, Nurse Practitioner **CR:** Attendee, Symposium, Ecuador (2016); Registered Nurse; Nurse Educator **CIV:** Children's Place Foundation **CW:** Contributor, Journal of Modern Poetry; Author, Nursing Textbook **H:** Writing; Biking; Watching movies

MARTIN, TERRENCE K., T: Lawyer, City Councilman **I:** Law and Legal Services **CN:** Terrence K. Martin & Associates **DOB:** 04/21/1939 **PB:** Lynchburg **SC:** VA/USA **PT:** Walter Worth Martin; Frances Louise (Keech) Martin **MS:** Single **SPN:** Cecilia Rudy (11/5/1983, Divorced 1999) **CH:** Theodore Worth; Timothy Francis **ED:** JD, University pf Virginia (1964); BA, University of Notre Dame (1961) **CT:** Virginia State Bar (1964) **C:** Lawyer, Private Practice, Newport News, Virginia (1970-1972, 1998-Present); Partner, Overman, Cowardin & Martin, PLC, Newport News, Virginia (1988-1998); Partner, Mason, Gibson, Cowardin & Martin, Newport News, Virginia (1983-1988); Attorney, Terrence K. Martin & Associates, Newport News, Virginia (1978-1983); Partner, Martin & Bensten, Newport News, Virginia (1974-1978); Partner, Martin & Rilee, Newport News, Virginia (1972-1974); Associate, Bert A. Nachman, Attorney, Newport News, Virginia (1969-1970); Assistant City Attorney, Newport News, Virginia (1967-1969) **CIV:** Treasurer, Board of Directors, Sister Cities of Newport News, Inc. (2011-Present); Member, Board of Directors, Sister Cities of Newport News, Inc. (1999-Present); Vice President, Board of Directors, Sister Cities of Newport News, Inc. (2005); President, Board of Directors, Sister Cities of Newport News, Inc. (2002-2003); Member, Board of Directors Virginia Living Museum (2001-2002); Community and Economic Development Steering Committee, National League of Cities (1999-2002); Council Member, Newport News, Virginia (1990-2002); Member, Transportation Safety Commission (1990-2002); Member, Youth Services Commission (1993-2000); Member, Board of Directors, Virginia Peninsula Economic Development Council (1996-1999); Member, Board of Directors, Sister Cities Commission, Newport News, Virginia (1992-1999); Member, Education Committee, Virginia Municipal League (1994-1995); Member, Task Force, City's Role in Education, National League of Cities **MIL:** Captain, Military Police Corps, U.S. Army (1965-1967) **MEM:** President, Kiwanis Club of the Peninsula at Oyster Point (2014-2015) **PA:** Republican **RE:** Roman Catholic **BA:** 727 J Clyde Morris Bou-

levard, Suite E, Terrence K. Martin & Associates, Newport News, VA, 23601 **ADD:** 727 J Clyde Morris Blvd Ste E, Terrence K. Martin & Associates, Newport News, VA, 23601

MARTIN-BOWEN, LINDSEY, T: Freelance Writer **I:** Writing and Editing **CN:** Metropolitan Community College-Longview; BkMk Press **SC:** KS/USA **PT:** Lawrence Richard Pickett; V. Marie Pickett **MS:** Partner **SPN:** Carl S. Rhoden (1999); Frederick E. Nicholson (Divorced); Edwin L. Martin (Divorced); Michael L. Bowen (Divorced) **CH:** Ki Elise; Aaron Frederick **ED:** JD, University of Missouri-Kansas City School of Law (2000); Postgraduate Coursework, University of Missouri-Kansas City (1991-1994); MA in English and Creative Writing, University of Missouri-Kansas City (1988); BA in English Literature, University of Missouri-Kansas City **C:** Preliminary Judge, Annual John Ciardi Poetry Contest, BkMk Press, University of Missouri-Kansas City (1995-Present); Editorial Assistant, New Letters (1985-Present); Features Writer, Columnist, The Squire, Prairie Village, KS (1990-1995); Copywriter, KXEO/KWWR Radio, Mexico, MO (1989); Consultant, Number One, Kansas City, MO (1988-1989); Writer, KC VIEW, Kansas City, MO (1988-1989); Editor, Number One, Kansas City, MO (1986-1988); Writer, College Boulevard News, Overland Park, KS (1985-1989); Associate Editor, Modern Jeweler, Overland Park, KS, New York City, NY (1984-1985); Reporter, Features Editor, Sun Newspapers, Overland Park, KS (1983-1984); Reporter, Photographer, Louisville Times (1982-1983); Technical Editor, Office of Hearings and Appeals, United States Department of the Interior, Washington, D.C. (1976-1977) **CR:** Teacher, English and Fiction, Metropolitan Community College-Longview, Missouri (2011-Present); Fiction Writer, Johnson County Community College (2002-Present); Judge, Poetry Contest BkMk Press, University of Missouri-Kansas City, MO (1998-Present); Instructor, Literature, Fiction Writing, Introduction to Journalism, Reporting, English, Cultural Studies, Technology Writing, Academy Writing and Literature, University of Missouri-Kansas City (1997-Present); Owner, Paladin Freelance Writing Service, Kansas City, MO (1988-Present); Writer, Paladin Freelance Writing Service, Kansas City, MO (1988-Present); Writing Contest Judge, New Letters (1987-Present); Writing Assessment Coordinator, University of Missouri-Kansas City (2005-2013); Teacher, English and Fiction, Metropolitan Community College-Longview, Missouri (2004-2005); Instructor, World Literature, Writing, Rockhurst University (2002-2003); Teacher, English and Fiction, Metropolitan Community Colleges, Missouri (1997-1998); Editor, National Paralegal Reporter, National Federation of Paralegal Associations, Inc. (1994-1997); Instructor, World Literature, American Literature, Women in Literature, Creative Writing, Metropolitan Community College-Penn Valley (1993-1998); Staff Writer, National Paralegal Reporter, National Federation of Paralegal Associations, Inc. (1992-2005); Columnist, National Paralegal Reporter, National Federation of Paralegal Associations, Inc. (1992-2005); Editor, National Paralegal Reporter, National Federation of Paralegal Associations, Inc. (1992-1995); Instructor, Writing and Mass Communications, Webster University (1990); Instructor, Johnson County Community College (1988-1995); Teacher, English and Fiction, Metropolitan Community Colleges, Missouri (1988-1995); Instructor, Literature, Fiction Writing, Introduction to Journalism, Reporting, English, Cultural Studies, Technology Writing, Academy Writing and Literature, University of Missouri–Kansas City (1986-1988); Faculty Sponsor, The Penn **CIV:** Campaigner, McGovern for President

Campaign, Kansas City, MO (1971-1972) **CW:** Author, "Where Water Meets the Rock" (2017); Author, "CROSSING KANSAS with Jim Morrison" (2016); Co-editor, "GIMME YOUR LUNCH MONEY: Heartland Poets Speak Out Against Bullies" (2016); Author, "Rapture Redux" (2014); Author, "Inside Virgil's Garage" (2011); Author, "Behind the Veil" (2009); Author, "Hamburger Haven" (2007); Author, "Standing on the Edge of the World" (2006); Author, "Let It Ride and Other Stories" (2006); Author, "Deep City" (2005); Author, "Denvie USA" (2003); Author, "Harvest" (2002); Staff Member, UMKC Law Review (1997-1999); Contributor, UMKC Law Review (1997-1999); Extra, "Truman," HBO Films (1995); Author, "Cicada Grove and Other Stories" (1992); Author, "Second Touch" (1990); Author, "The Dark Horse Waits in Boulder" (1985); Lead Actress, Productions Coach House Players (1969-1970); Author, Numerous Poems; Contributor, Articles, Professional Journals **AW:** Award for Book "CROSSING KANSAS with Jim Morrison," Looks Like a Million Contest, Kansas Authors Club (2017); Honorable Mention for Poem "Vegetable Linguistics," Non-Rhyming Poem Category, Writer's Digest, F+W, 85th Annual Writing Competition (2016); Semi-Finalist for Book "CROSSING KANSAS with Jim Morrison" in Chapbook Form, Quill Books Chapbook Contest (2015-2016); Runner-up for Book "Inside Virgil's Garage," Nelson Book Award, Kansas Authors Club (2015); Nominee, Pushcart Publishers Prize (2013); Top 10 Poetry Books for "Standing on the Edge of the World," McClatchy Newspapers (2008); Book Award, 10 Most Noteworthy Poetry Books (2008); Grand Prize for "Cicada Grove," Chapter One and Group of Poems, Barbara Storck Creative Writing Contest (1987); Nominated for a Fulbright Fellowship by the Fulbright Scholar Dr. James C. McKinley (1987); Grand Prize, Barbara Storck Creative Writing Contest (1986); GAF Fellow (1986); Regents Scholarship (1967) **MEM:** University of Missouri-Kansas City Alumni Association (1983-Present); Media Committee, University of Missouri-Kansas City (1983-1984); The Honor Society of Phi Kappa Phi **BAR:** The Missouri Bar (2001) **MH:** Albert Nelson Marquis Lifetime Achievement Award (2017) **H:** Music; Painting; Skiing; Cooking **PA:** Independent; Democrat **RE:** Roman Catholic **ADD:** 1104 SE 7th Street, Lees Summit, MO, 64063 **URL:** https://www.facebook.com/Lindsey-Martin-Bowen-Author-Poet-and-Writer-717398001615105/

MARTINEZ, DAVID R., T: Manager I: Sciences **CN:** Ramco Laboratories, Inc. **DOB:** 01/22/1954 **PB:** Toledo **SC:** OH/USA **PT:** Daniel Martinez; Herlinda (Ramirez) Martinez **MS:** Single **ED:** BS, The University of Toledo (1978) **C:** Manager of Quality Control, Ramco Laboratories, Inc. (2015-Present); Assistant Manager of Quality Control, Ramco Laboratories, Inc. (2013-2015); Extraction Chemist, PRACS Institute, Ltd. (2012); Extraction Chemist, Center for Research Institute (2010-2012); Associate Scientist II, Kelly Scientific (2009); Associate Scientist II, Cogenics, Beckman Coulter, Inc. (2007-2009); Research Associate II, University of Texas Medical Branch at Galveston (2005-2007); Research Assistant, The University of Texas Health Science Center at Houston (1996-2004); Research Technician, Howard Hughes Medical Institute (1997-1998); Research Technician, Howard Hughes Medical Institute (1993-1996); Research Assistant, Baylor College of Medicine (1991-1993); Research Assistant, The University of Texas Health Science Center at Houston (1987-1991); Quality Control Technician, Chardonol Division, Freeman Chemical Company (1985-1986); Quality Control Technician, Pepsico (1982-1983); Laboratory Technician, Shilstone

Engineering Testing Laboratory, Inc. (1981-1982); Research Chemist, Southwest Research Institute (1978-1980) **CIV:** Harris County Tejano Democrats **MEM:** American Chemical Society; American Association for the Advancement of Science **H:** Computers **PA:** Democrat **RE:** Roman Catholic **BA:** Ramco Laboratories, Inc., 4100 Greenbriar Drive, Suite 200, Stafford, TX, 77477 **ADD:** 8702 Ariel St, Houston, TX, 77074 **URL:** www.ramcolab.com/

MARTINEZ, ELIO F. JR., T: Attorney/ Partner I: Law and Legal Services **CN:** Espinosa Martinez, PL **ED:** JD, New York University School of Law (1985); BA, Fordham University, Summa Cum Laude, Cursu Honorum (1982) **C:** Attorney, Partner, Espinosa, Martinez PL **AW:** Named, Florida Super Lawyer, Year-2017 (Awarded by Super Lawyers magazine) Top Attorney Corporate and Business, South Florida Legal Guide (2015) **MEM:** NYU Alumni Association Board of Directors; Board of Directors, Casa Blanca Academy School for Autistic Children, Phi Beta Kappa **BAR:** Florida; The District of Columbia; United States District Court for the Southern District of Florida; United States District Court for the Middle District of Florida; United States Court of Appeals for the Eleventh Judicial Circuit; Supreme Court of the United States **H:** Reading; Sports; Baseball; Travels throughout the country attending baseball games **BA:** 1428 Brickell Ave Ste 100, Espinosa Martinez, Pl, Miami, FL, 33131 **URL:** http://etlaw.com/

MARX, GARY DEAN, T: Educational Consultant, Futurist, Think-Tank Executive I: Education/ Educational Services **CN:** Center for Public Outreach, Inc. **DOB:** 11/28/1938 **PB:** Manchester **SC:** SD/USA **PT:** Harvey Frederick Marx; Lucille (Stemple) Marx **MS:** Married **SPN:** Judy Rae Marx (6/18/1961) **CH:** John Fredrick; Daniel Winston **ED:** BA, University of South Dakota (1960) **CT:** Certificate, American Society of Association Executives (1979-Present); Certificate, National School Public Relations; Certificate, Public Relations Society of America, Inc. **C:** President, Center For Public Outreach, Inc., Vienna, VA (1998-Present); Executive Director, Leadership for Learning Foundation, AASA, Arlington, VA (1996-1998); Senior Associate Executive, AASA, Arlington, VA (1979-1996); Executive Director, Communications, Jeffco Public Schools, Denver, CO (1977-1979); Director, Communications, Westside Community Schools, Omaha, NE (1971-1977); Newscaster, Announcer, WOW Radio and Television Station, Omaha, NE (1961-1971); Newscaster, Announcer, Director, KSOO Radio and Television Station, Sioux Falls, SD (1958-1961) **CR:** Public Relations Consultant, National School of Public Relations Association, Rockville, MD (1972-Present); Evaluator, CIVITAS International Exchange Program, Calabasas, CA (2000-2011); Senior Research Fellow, Health, Energy and Productivity in Schools Project, Bethesda, MD (2000-2002); Vice President, Owner, Station KOAK Radio, Red Oak, IA (1977-1982); Vice President, Communications Development Inc., Denver, CO (1974-1976); Consultant, International Speaker, Six Continents, 81 Countries **CIV:** Member, Selection Committee, Apple Scholars, Apple FCU Education Foundation, Virginia (2012-Present); Board of Directors, Harvey Dunn Society, South Dakota (2009-Present); Judge, National History Day (2002-Present); Member, Selection Committee, Fulbright Scholars (1998-Present); Member, Steering Committee, Civitas International, Brussels, Belgium (1996-Present); International Consultant, Speaker, Center for Civic Education, Calabasas, CA (1996-Present); International Consultant, Speaker, United States Information Agency, U.S. Department of State, Washington D.C.

(1996-Present); Member, The Horace Mann League of the USA (1985-Present); Press, The Horace Mann League of the USA (2014); Twelve-Member Alternative Futures Panel, Future of Learning, Harvard Graduate School of Education (2012); Twelve-Member Alternative Futures Panel, Harvard University Think Tank on Global Education (2011); Board of Directors, Laura Ingalls Wilder Memorial Society (2007-2013); Twelve-Member Alternative Futures Panel, Washington Metro Area in 2025, The Washington Post (2007-2008); Board Director, Manchester Monument Advisory Council, South Dakota (2006-2007); Board of Directors, The Horace Mann League of the USA (2005-2015); Member, Steering Committee, Facilitator, National Center for Energy Management and Building Technicians (2004-2009); Member, Steering Committee, Goals (2000); Judge, All USA Academy Team, USA TODAY, Arlington, VA (1995-2000); Emmy Awards Judge, The National Academy of Television Arts & Sciences, New York City, NY (1995-1997); Announcer, Emcee, Presidential Scholars Program, Kennedy Center Alliance for Arts Education Network, John F. Kennedy Center for the Performing Arts, Washington D.C. (1994-2009); Member, Grants Selection Committee, Kennedy Center Alliance for Arts Education Network, John F. Kennedy Center for the Performing Arts, Washington D.C. (1993-1996); Member, Steering Committee, Arts Education Partnership, National Education Association, Washington D.C. (1993-1998); Member, Steering Committee, Disney Salute to the American Teacher, Burbank, CA (1993-1997); Member, Selection Committee, Disney Salute to the American Teacher, Burbank, CA (1993-1997); Judge, Disney Salute to the American Teacher, Burbank, CA (1993-1997); Board Director, US Coalition for Education for All (1993-1997); Member, Steering Committee, Design Arts Program, National Education Association, Washington D.C. (1993-1994); Member, Steering Committee, Library of Congress, Center for the Book, Washington D.C. (1992-1999); Founder, Coalition for America's Children, Washington D.C. (1992-1998); Member, Advisory Board, The More You Know Campaign, NBCUniversal, New York City, NY (1992-1998); Board Director, New Priorities Campaign, Washington D.C. (1992-1993); Member, National Advisory Board, Public Broadcasting Service (1990-1998); Founder, National Supervisor of the Year Program (1987); Member, Executive Committee, Education, Commission on the Bicentennial of the United States Constitution, Washington D.C. (1986-1992); Member, The National Press Club (1984-1998); Member, National Education Advisory Committee, Restoration, Statue of Liberty-Ellis Island Foundation, New York City, NY (1984-1986); Selection Committee Advisor, National Teacher of Year Program, Washington D.C. (1979-1999); Member, Urban Growth Policy Board, Omaha Parks and Recreation Board, City of Omaha (1976); Member, Omaha Parks and Recreation Board, City of Omaha (1975-1977); Founder, Chairman, Keystone Community Task Force, Omaha, NE (1970-1977); Member, Omaha Press Club (1962-2013) **CW:** Author, "Guide Version of Twenty-One Trends" (2015); Author, "Twenty-One Trends for the 21st Century: Out of the Trenches...Into the Future" (2014); Author, "Sixteen Trends...Their Profound Impact on Our Future" (2011, 2006); Author, "Future Focused Leadership... Preparing Schools, Students and Communities for Tomorrow's Realities" (2006); Author, "Ten Trends...Educating Children for a Profoundly Different Future" (2000); Author, "Preparing Students for the 21st Century" (1999, 1996); Author, "The Future of Community" (1999); Author, "Preparing Schools and School Systems for the 21st Century" (1999); Author, "Working with the News Media" (1993); Author, "Public Relations for Administrators" (1988); Author, "Excellence in Our Schools...Making it Happen" (1984); Author, "Radio...Get the Message" (1977); Author, "Radio... Your Publics are Listening" (1976); Contributor, Articles, Professional Journals **AW:** Albert Nelson Marquis Lifetime Achievement Award (2017); Marquis Who's Who Humanitarian Award (2017); Ambassadors Award, The Horace Mann League of the USA (2015); President Award, The Horace Mann League of the USA (2015); Ambassadors Award, The Horace Mann League of the USA (2009-2011); Distinguished Service Award, AASA (2000); President Award, National School Public Relations Association (1999); Radio Advertising Bureau Commercial Award (1967) **MEM:** Vice President, The Horace Mann League of the USA (2012-Present); Numerous Committees, National School Public Relations Association (1971-Present); President, The Horace Mann League of the USA (2014); Indicators Task Force, The Horace Mann League of the USA (2010-2015); Board of Directors, The Horace Mann League of the USA (2005-2015); Board Director, Education Writers Association (1983-1986); Public Relations Society of America, Inc.; American Society of Association Executives; AASA; Professional Member, World Future Society; ASCD; SAG-AFTRA **MH:** Albert Nelson Marquis Lifetime Achievement Award (2017); Distinguished Humanitarian (2017) **H:** Folk art; Travel; Reading; Writing; Photography: History **ADD:** 1831 Toyon Way, Vienna, VA, 22182

MASERITZ, GUY B., T: Business Lawyer (Retired) **I:** Law and Legal Services **CN:** Private Practice **DOB:** 06/05/1937 **PB:** Baltimore **SC:** MD/USA **PT:** Isadore H. Maseritz, MD; Gertude Miller Maseritz **MS:** Married **SPN:** Sally Jane Sugar Maseritz (3/30/1961) **CH:** Marjorie Ellen Norrholm; Michael Louis Maseritz **ED:** LLB, University of Maryland School of Law (1966); MA in Economics, Johns Hopkins University (1961); BA in Political Science, Johns Hopkins University (1959) **C:** Attorney, Private Practice, Columbia, MD (1978-2015); Special Assistant, United States Attorney, United States Department of Justice, Alexandria, VA (1978); Chief, Legislative Unit, Antitrust Division, United States Department of Justice (1977); Attorney, Evaluation Section, Antitrust Division, United States Department of Justice, Washington, D.C. (1974-1978); Assistant General Counsel of Securities, American Life Insurance Association, Washington, D.C. (1971-1974); Attorney, Securities and Exchange Commission, Washington, D.C. (1966-1970) **CIV:** Member, American Inns of Court (2005-2006); Distinguished Board Member Award, YMCA of Central Maryland, Howard County Branch (1998-1999); Member, Howard County Charter Revision Commission, Maryland (1979) **MIL:** Honorable Discharge, US Army Reserve (1960-1966) **CW:** Author, "No Inventions, No Innovations: Reassessing the Government's Antitrust Case Against United States Steel Corporation," Journal of Business & Technology Law (2012); Principal Contributor, "The Pricing and Marketing of Insurance", An Antitrust Report of the United States Department of Justice (1977); Author, "Fiduciary Duty and Implied Promises in Prospectus: United Funds, Inc. v. Carter Products, Inc.," 24 Maryland Law Review 204 (1964); Author, "The Relevant Market- A Case Study of the DuPont-General Motors Decision," The Antitrust Bulletin (1961) **AW:** Recipient, AV Preeminent Rating, Martindale-Hubbell (1985-2015); Recipient, Special Letter of Recognition for Work on the Insurance Study, Assistant Attorney General for Antitrust, Donald I. Baker (1977); Elected, Member of Maryland Law Review Editorial Board (1964) **MEM:** Board of Directors, Greater Howard County Chamber of

Commerce (1981-1984); General Counsel, Greater Howard County Chamber of Commerce (1981-1984); Maryland State Bar Association; The District of Columbia Bar Association **BAR:** United States District Court for the District of Maryland (1979); Supreme Court of the United States of America (1975); Washington, D.C. (1968); Maryland (1966) **MH:** Recipient, Albert Nelson Marquis Lifetime Achievement Award (2018) **PA:** Republican **RE:** Jewish **BA:** 5040 Rushlight Path, Guy B. Maseritz Law Office, Columbia, MD, 21044

MASLO, PAUL B., I: Law and Legal Services **CN:** Napoli Shkolnik PLLC **PB:** Marquette **SC:** MI/USA **PT:** Emil August Maslo; Corinne Ann Peters **MS:** Married **SPN:** Launa Maslo **CH:** Siah Corinne Kim Maslo; Emilia Alma August Maslo **ED:** AB in Biology, Cornell University; MS in Biology, Johns Hopkins University; JD, University of Pennsylvania Law School; Graduate Coursework in Finance, Wharton School of Business **C:** Partner, Class Actions and Commercial Litigation Department, Napoli Shkolnik, PLLC (2016-Present); Associate, Boies, Schiller, & Flexner LLP **CR:** Grant Funded Research Assistant, Harvard Medical School; Morgan Stanley **CW:** Sole Author, "Following the Letter of the Law into Absurdity: Why the Supreme Court's Severability Rule Does Not Preclude Determining an Arbitration Provision's Enforceability Under the Law Supplied by an Agreement's General Choice-of-Law Clause," 166 University of Pennsylvania Law Review Online 273 (2018); Sole Author, "Immunocompromised: A Call for Courts to Redefine the Boundaries of the Absolute Immunity Doctrine's Application to National Securities Exchanges," 11 New York University Journal of Law & Business 2 (2015); Sole Author, "2015 Amendments to the Federal Rules of Civil Procedure: Furthering Rule 1's Objectives of Expediency and Thrift," News for the Bar, Litigation Section of the State Bar of Texas (2015); Co-author, "A Complete View of the Cathedral: Claims of Tortious Interference and the Specific Performance Remedy in Mergers and Acquisitions Litigation," 3 University of Michigan Journal of Private Equity & Venture Capital Law 1 (2014); Sole Author, "Are the ICSID Rules Losing Their Appeal? Annulment Committee Decisions Make ICSID Rules a Less Attractive Choice for Resolving Treaty-Based Investor-State Disputes," 2 University of Virginia Journal of International Law Digest 54 (2014); Sole Author, "Amputating the Long Arm of the Law: An Analysis of the U.S. Supreme Court's Decision in Morrison and Why § 10(b) Still Reaches Issuers of ADRs," 89 Washington University Law Review 477 (2011); Sole Author, "Definition of Investment: Gatekeeper to Investment Treaty Arbitration," 8 Berkeley Journal of International Law Publicist (2011); Sole Author, "The Case for Semi-Strong-Form Corporate Scienter in Securities Fraud Actions," Covered in Nine Securities Class Action Reporter 22 (2011); Co-author, "Trends in International Investment Agreements, 2009/2010: Recent Steps in the Evolution of Bilateral Investment Treaties and the UNCITRAL Arbitration Rules," in Karl P. Sauvant, "Yearbook on International Law and Policy 2010/2011," Oxford University Press (2011); Sole Author, "The Case for Semi-Strong-Form Corporate Scienter in Securities Fraud Actions," 108 University of Michigan Law Review First Impressions 95 (2010); Co-author, "Protection of Work Product Shared with Outside Auditors," New York Law Journal (2010); Co-author, "Credit Default Swaps in the Crosshairs," Law360 (2009); Co-author, "2008 ARS Fallout: the Last Wave?," Law360 (2008) **AW:** New York Super Lawyer, Super Lawyers (2017-2018); Research Fellowship in Biology, Princeton University; Research Fellowship

in Biology, Rockefeller University **BAR:** New York State Bar Association; State Bar of Texas; United States Court of Appeals for the Third Circuit; United States Court of Appeals for the Sixth Circuit; United States Court of Appeals for the Seventh Circuit; United States Court of Appeals for the Ninth Circuit; United States District Court for the Eastern District of New York; United States District Court for the Southern District of New York; United States District Court for the Western District of Texas **H:** Reading and Academic Writing **ADD:** 1577 Edmondson Trl, Rockwall, TX, 75087-6021

MASSENGALE, MARTIN A., T: President, Chancellor Emeriti, Director, Foundation Distinguished Professor **I:** Education/Educational Services **CN:** University of Nebraska-Lincoln, University of Nebraska **DOB:** 10/25/1933 **PB:** Monticello **SC:** KY/USA **PT:** Elbert G. Massengale; Orpha (Conn) Massengale **MS:** Married **SPN:** Ruth Audrey Klingelhofer (7/11/1959) **CH:** Alan Ross; Jennifer Lynn **ED:** Honorary DSc, Senshu University (1995); Honorary LHD, Nebraska Wesleyan University (1987); PhD, University of Wisconsin-Madison (1956); MS, University of Wisconsin-Madison (1954); BS, Western Kentucky University (1952) **CT:** Certified Professional Agronomist; Certified Professional Crop Scientist **C:** President Emeritus, University of Nebraska (1994-Present); Chancellor Emeritus, University of Nebraska-Lincoln (2017-Present); Director Emeritus, Center for Grassland Studies, University of Nebraska-Lincoln (2017-Present); Foundation Distinguished Professor Emeritus (2017-Present); Director, Center for Grassland Studies, University of Nebraska-Lincoln (1994-2017); Foundation Distinguished Professor, University of Nebraska-Lincoln (1994-2017); President, University of Nebraska-Lincoln (1991-1994); Interim President, University of Nebraska-Lincoln (1989-1991); Chancellor, University of Nebraska-Lincoln (1981-1991); Vice Chancellor, Institute of Agriculture and Natural Resources, University of Nebraska-Lincoln (1976-1981); Associate Dean, College of Agriculture, The University of Arizona (1974-1976); Associate Director, Arizona Agricultural Experiment Station, The University of Arizona (1974-1976); Department Head, The University of Arizona (1966-1974); Professor, The University of Arizona (1965-1974); Agronomist, The University of Arizona (1965-1974); Associate Agronomist, The University of Arizona (1962-1965); Associate Professor, The University of Arizona (1962-1965); Assistant Professor, The University of Arizona (1958-1962); Assistant Agronomist, The University of Arizona (1958-1962); Research Assistant, University of Wisconsin-Madison (1952-1956); Teaching Assistant, Western Kentucky University (1951-1952) **CR:** Board of Directors, Nebraska Policy Institute (1999-Present); National Advisory Board, Center for the Study of Sport in Society (1989-Present); Committee for Selection of New Director, Center for Human Nutrition (2008); Panel Member, National Academy of Sciences (2006, 1972); Knight Foundation Commission on Intercollegiate Athletics (2004-2006, 2000-2001, 1989-1995); Mentoring Group, NCAA (2005-2008); Vice-chair and Member, Advisory Board, Trees America (2000-2009); Strategic Planning Committee, Council on Agricultural Science and Technology (1998-2002); Chair, Board of Directors, Agronomic Science Foundation (1997-2006); Chair, Executive Committee, Agronomic Science Foundation (1997-2006); Treasurer, Council on Agricultural Science and Technology (1997-2005); Chair, Selection Committee for Director of Development, Agronomic Science Foundation (1997-1999); Executive Committee, Council on Agricultural Science and Technology (1996-2005);

Accreditation Review Panel, NCAA (1996-2001); Advisory Committee, Nebraska Turfgrass Association (1995-2017); Board of Directors, Nebraska Technology Park (1995-2013); Executive Committee, Nebraska Technology Park (1995-2013); Member and Chair, Secretary of Agriculture National Advisory Board for Research, Extension, Education and Economics (1998-2010); Member, Outreach Committee, Council on Agricultural Science and Technology (1995-2005); New Initiatives Committee, Agronomic Science Foundation (1995-1997); Executive Committee, Economics America (1994-2008); Board of Directors, Agronomic Science Foundation (1994-2006); Board of Directors, Council on Agricultural Science and Technology (1994-2005, 1982-1985); Plant and Soil Science Work Group, Council on Agricultural Science and Technology (1994-2000); Board of Directors, The Association of Public and Land-grant Universities (1992-1994); Chair, Commission of Information Technology, The Association of Public and Land-grant Universities (1992-1994); Research Libraries Steering Committee, AAU (1992-1994); Committee on Policies and Purposes, American Association of State Colleges and Universities (1992-1994); Steering Committee, Systematic Initiative for Mathematics and Science, State of Nebraska (1991-1996); Task Force on Institutional Resource Allocation, American Association of State Colleges and Universities (1991-1994) **CIV:** Board of Directors, Historical Society Foundation, State of Nebraska (1999-Present); Board of Trustees, Historical Society Foundation, State of Nebraska (1989-Present); Audit Committee, Bryan Health (2009-2017); Board of Directors, Bryan Health (2008-2017); Corporate Compliance Committee, Bryan Health (2008-2009); President, Country Club of Lincoln (2005-2006); Chair, Planning Committee, Country Club of Lincoln (2002-2007); Board of Directors, Country Club of Lincoln (2002-2006); President, Country Club of Lincoln (2005-2006); Chair, Economics Committee, Advisory Board, Secretary of Agriculture (2001-2009); Board of Trustees, Historical Society, State of Nebraska (1999-2005); Chair, Executive Committee, Advisory Board, Secretary of Agriculture (1998-2010); Chair, Greens Committee, Country Club of Lincoln (1998-2002); Nominating Committee, Historical Society Foundation, State of Nebraska (1996-1997); Strategic Planning Committee, City of Lincoln, Nebraska (1986-1988); Chairman, United Way of Lincoln and Lancaster County (1985); Board of Directors, Industrial Development Corporation, Lincoln Chamber of Commerce (1983-1984); Cornhusker Boys State; Newcomer's Society of North America; Board of Directors, Nebraska Chapter, National Conference for Community and Justice; Board Member, Nine Corporate Boards **MIL:** Technical Adviser to Classified Project, U.S. Army (1956-1958) **CW:** Editorial Board Member, Council on Agricultural Science and Technology (1982-1985); Associate Editor, "Crop Science," Crop Science Society of America; Associate Editor, "Agronomy Journal," American Society of Agronomy; Contributor, Articles in Numerous Professional Journals and Popular Publications **AW:** Named, Nebraskan of the Year, Lincoln Rotary Club (2016); Legacy Award, College of Agriculture and Natural Resources Alumni Association (2016); Honoree, Selected as One of the Leading Scientists in the World (2015); Honoree, Top U.S. Executives (2014); Alumni Service Award, College of Agricultural Sciences and Natural Resources (2009); Distinguished Achievement in Agriculture Award, Gamma Sigma Delta (2008); Wagon Master Ward, Nebraskaland Foundation (2006); Brothers of the Century Award, Alpha Gamma Rho (2004); Honoree, Wayne County High School Hall of Fame

(2002); Outstanding President's Award, All-American Football Foundation (2001); Allen G. Blezerk Friend of LEAD Award (2001); Exemplary Service to Agriculture Award, Nebraska AgRelations Council (2000); Triumph of Agriculture "Agri-Award" (1999); Volunteer of the Year Award, Nebraska Company on Economic Education (1997); International Award of Merit, Gamma Sigma Delta (1997); Outstanding Service to Agriculture Award, Nebraska Crop Improvement Association (1997); Distinguished Career Award, Crop Science Society of America (1996); Distinguished Service Award, Alpha Pi Chapter, Alpha Gamma Rho (1995); Honoree, Most Admired Men of the Decade, ABI (1994); Service to Agriculture Award, Nebraska Rural Radio Services (1994); Clarence E. Swanson Award (1994); Honoree, Ambassador Plenipotentiary, State of Nebraska (1993); Honoree, Named to Nebraska Agricultural Hall of Achievement (1993); Ak-Sar-Ben Achievement Award (1986); Merit Certificate, American Forage and Grassland Council (1986); Outstanding Service Award, American Society of Agronomy (1984); Honoree, Midlands Man of the Year (1982); Public Service to Agriculture Award, Agribusiness Club, University of Nebraska-Lincoln; Presidential Award, Nebraska Turfgrass Foundation; Appreciation Award, Pacific Seedsman Association; Leadership Award, Marana Chapter, Arizona Future Farmers of America; Leadership Award, University of Nebraska-Lincoln; Browning Award, Crop Science Society of America; Recipient, Various Grants **MEM:** Chairperson, American Association for the Advancement of Science (1980-1981); Chairperson-elect, Section O, American Association for the Advancement of Science (1979-1980); President, Western Society of Crop Science (1964-1965); President-elect, Western Society of Crop Science (1962-1963); Program Chair, Western Society of Crop Science (1961-1962); President, Crop Science Society of America (1973); President-elect, Crop Science Society of America (1972-1973); Chairman, Division on Crop Physiology, Crop Science Society of America, Chairman of Organization and Policy Committee, Crop Science Society of America; Implementation of Strategic Plan Committee, Crop Science Society of America **H:** Reading; Golf; Being active in outdoor activities **BA:** 1400 R Street 203 Rm Keim Hall, University Nebraska, Lincoln, NE, 68588 **ADD:** Keim Hall Rm 203, University Nebraska, Lincoln, NE, 68588

MASSUCCI, LEEANN M., T: Principal **I:** Law and Legal Services **CN:** Massucci Law Group LLC **ED:** JD, Capital University Law School (2002); EdM, The Ohio State University (1985); BS, The University of Alabama (1983) **CT:** Divorce Mediation Certification, Capital University Law School (2004); Dispute Resolution Certification, Capital University Law School (2002); Pro Bono Honoree Certification, Capital University Law School (2002) **C:** Principal Owner, Massucci Law Group, LLC (2016-Present); Adjunct Professor, Capital University Law School (2006-2010) **CR:** Speaker in Field **CIV:** Founding Member, United Way PRIDE Council (2009-Present); Family Law Chair, Central Ohio Association for Justice (2014-2015); Past President, Capital University Law School Alumni Board (2011-2012); Board Member, Capital University Law School Alumni Board (2008-2015); Board Member, Tenth Appellate District Pro Bono Committee (2007-2016); Private Bar Liaison, Franklin County Domestic & Juvenile Court Community Advisory Board (2006-2011); Founding Member, Board of Trustees, Legacy Fund of the Columbus Foundation (2001-2006); Lambda Legal; National Center for Lesbian Rights; Founding Member, United Way of Central Ohio

Women's Leadership Council **CW:** Contributor, Articles, Professional Journals **AW:** Top 25 Female Attorneys in Columbus, Ohio, Super Lawyers (2017); Named, Ohio Super Lawyer (2014-2017); Named, Rising Star, Ohio Super Lawyer (2011-2013); Graduate of the Law Decade Award, Capital University Law School (2009); Outstanding Individual in Pro Bono Service, Columbus Bar Foundation (2009); Lambda Legal's National Pro Bono Advocate Honoree (2008); Barrister Leadership Graduate, Columbus Bar Association (2005); Dean's Award for Outstanding Female Graduate, Capital University Law School (2003) **MEM:** Chair, Family Law Committee, Columbus Bar Association (2007-Present); Board Member, Ohio State Bar Association's Council of Delegates (2014-2016); Board of Governors, Columbus Bar Association (2012-2016); Columbus Bar Association; Ohio State Bar Association; Family Law Committee, ABA; Franklin County Women Lawyers; Ohio Representative, National Family Law Advisory Counsel, National Center for Lesbian Rights; Founder, National LGBT Bar Association; Ohio State Bar Association Family Law Committee; Solo and Small Firm Committee, Columbus Bar Association **BAR:** Supreme Court of the United States (2006); Ohio (2003) **BA:** 250 Civic Center Dr Ste 500, Massucci Law Group LLC, Columbus, OH, 43215 **URL:** https://www.massuccilawgroup.com/attorneys/leeann-m-massucci

MASTERS, ROGER DAVIS, T: Political Scientist, Toxicologist, Educator **I:** Sciences **DOB:** 06/08/1933 **PB:** Boston **SC:** MA/USA **PT:** Maurice Masters; Grace (Davis) Masters **SPN:** Susanne R. Putnam (8/25/1984, Deceased 2006); Judith Ann Rubin (6/6/1956, Divorced 1984) **CH:** Seth J.; William A.; Katherine R. **ED:** Honorary MA, Dartmouth College, Hanover, NH (2015); PhD, University of Chicago (1961); MA in Political Science, University of Chicago (1958); BA, Harvard University, Cambridge, MA (1955) **C:** Professor Emeritus, Dartmouth College (1998-Present); Research Professor, Dartmouth College (1999-2013); Nelson A. Rockefeller Professor, Dartmouth College (1991-1998); Chairman, Department, Dartmouth College (1986-1989); John Sloan Dickey Third Century Professor, Dartmouth College (1980-1985); Professor, Dartmouth College (1973-1998); Associate Professor, Department of Government, Dartmouth College, Hanover, NH (1967-1973); Assistant Professor, Yale University (1962-1967); Instructor, Department of Political Science, Yale University (1961-1962) **CR:** Section Editor, Social Science, Information (1971-Present); Member, Get the Lead Out of Vermont Task Force (2006); Consultant, U.S. Department of Defense (2005-2009); Consultant, U.S. Department of Defense (1999-2003); Chairman, Executive Committee, Gruter Institute of Law and Behavioral Research (1995-1998); Visiting Lecturer, Vermont Law School (1993-1994); Visiting Lecturer, Yale University Law School (1988-1989); Director, D'etudes Associate, Ecole Hautes Etudes en Science Sociales (1986); Chairman, France-America Commission for Educational and Cultural Exchange (1969-1971); Cultural Attache, American Embassy, Paris, France (1969-1971) **CIV:** Chairman, Save the Park Committee, New Haven, CT (1965-1966) **MIL:** U.S. Army, Fort Bliss, TX (1955-1957) **CW:** Co-editor, "Collected Writings of J.J. Rousseau," 12 Volumes (1990-Present); Author, "Fortune is a River" (1998); Author, "Machiavelli, Leonardo, and the Science of Power" (1996); Co-editor, "The Neurotransmitter Revolution" (1994); Author, "Beyond Relativism" (1993); Editor, "Gruter Institute Reader in Biology, Law, and Human Social Behavior" (1992); Co-editor, "The Sense of Justice" (1992); Co-editor, "Primate Politics" (1991); Author, "The Nature of

Politics" (1989); Co-editor, "Ostracism: A Social and Biological Phenomenon" (1986); Editor, "Rousseau's Social Contract (1978); Author, "The Political Philosophy of Rousseau" (1968); Author, "The Nation Is Burdened" (1967); Editor, "Rousseau's Discourses" (1964) **AW:** Fellow, Hastings Center for Ethics and Life Sciences (1973-1978); Guggenheim Fellow (1967-1968); Fellow, Joint Yale University-Social Science Research Council (1964-1965); Fulbright Fellow, Institute D'Etudes Politiques, Paris, France (1958-1959) **MEM:** American Association for the Advancement of Science; American Political Science Association; Association of Political and Life Sciences; American Academy of Environmental Medicine **MH:** Albert Nelson Marquis Lifetime Achievement Award (2017) **H:** Studying toxins that harm people; Attending concerts; Going on walks **ADD:** 53 Lyme Rd Apt 21, Hanover, NH, 03755

MATHIS, RONALD F., T: Information Technology Specialist, Physicist, Computer Engineer **I:** Sciences **DOB:** 07/26/1942 **PB:** Los Angeles **SC:** CA/USA **PT:** Darrell Floyd Mathis; Gladys Mae (Buckles) Mathis **MS:** Married **SPN:** Charlotte Anne Gibson (6/5/1964) **CH:** Melanie Kay; Stephen Ronald; David Darrell; Michael Lee **ED:** PhD, Missouri University of Science and Technology, Rolla, MO (1973); MS, Missouri University of Science and Technology, Rolla, MO (1971); BA, California State University,Fullerton (1966) **C:** Civilian Physicist for U.S. Navy (2015-Present); Senior Scientist, SAIC (2009-Present); Chief Executive Officer, Photon Control Techs. Inc., Escondido, CA (1999-2001); President, Photonics Products, Inc., Murrieta, CA (1995-2015); Senior Scientist, SAIC, San Diego, CA (1992-1995); Engineering Staff Specialist, Electronics Division, General Dynamics, San Diego, CA (1978-1991); Senior Engineer, Cubic Corporation, San Diego, CA (1975-1978); Senior Physicist, IRT Corporation, San Diego, CA (1973-1975) **CW:** Contributor, Articles, Professional Publications **MEM:** American Physical Society; The Optical Society; IEEE; Creation Research Society **MH:** Albert Nelson Marquis Lifetime Achievement Award (2017) **H:** Backpacking **PA:** Republican **RE:** Baptist **ADD:** 23364 Caliente Springs Ave, Murrieta, CA, 92562

MATTHEWS, LISA ARNAZ, T: Program Director **I:** Business Management/Business Services **CN:** National Conference on Citizenship **PB:** Washington **SC:** DC/USA **ED:** BBA in Computer Information and System Science, University of the District of Columbia (1992) **CT:** Certificate, Program Management Analysis, U.S. Department of Agriculture (2005) **C:** Program Director, The National Conference on Citizenship, Washington, D.C. (2016-Present); Family and Community Advocate, Program Assistant, Office of Research and Evaluation, Corporation for National and Community Service (2015-2016); Senior Research Analyst, American Health Care Association (1996-2015); Recruiting Staff, Human Resources, Andersen Consulting/Arthur Andersen LLP (Now Andersen Tax LLC) (1992-1996); Personnel Clerk, Human Resources, Action, National Corporation for Community Service (1986-1992) **CR:** Policy Influence Strategist; Project Manager; Research Analyst; Database Manager; Graphic Designer **CIV:** Sibling Leadership Network, DC Chapter (2016-Present); Quality Trust, Program & Policy Committee (2016-Present); Co-founder, DC Sibs (2010-Present); Board Member, Associated Community Services (2009-Present); Advocate, Family and Community Support (Present); Chair, DC Developmental Disability Council (Present); Chair, Developmental Disabilities State Planning Council, Washington, D.C. (2016); DC Advocacy Partners (DCAP), Institute for Educational Lead-

ership (2014); Ward 7 Neighborhood Empowerment Program, Housing Counseling Services, Inc. (2010-2012); Volunteer, Project Coordinator, Greater DC Cares (2006-2013); Coach Committee, Program Coordinator, Kids Enjoy Exercise Now (KEEN) (2006-2011); Board Member, Group Home Organization; Panel Presentation, Lifespan Respite Caregiver Conference; AARP Caregiver Ambassador; Newsletter Co-Founder, Editor, District of Columbia Autism Society **CW:** Empower NOW; Write Choice Consulting; Co-founder, Co-editor, VOCAL Newsletter; Author, Poet, Published Online Articles, D-Mars Journal **MEM:** Chair, Board Member, Developmental Disabilities State Planning Council; Associated Community Services and Love by the Handles, Inc.; Washington DC Chapter, NBM-BAA; Quality Trust Program and Policy Committee, NBMBAA; Quality Trust Program and Policy Committee, DCASA; DC Chapter Representative, Sibling Leadership Network **H:** Reading; Writing poetry; Grant reviewing; Volunteering **BA:** 1900 L Street, NW - Suite 800, National Conference on Citizenship, Washington, DC, 20036 **ADD:** 1900 L Street, NW - Suite 800, National Conference on Citizenship, Washington, DC, 20036 **URL:** https://www.linkedin.com/in/lisamatthews1128/

MATTHEWS, TODD, T: Associate Professor, Department Chair **I:** Education/Educational Services **CN:** Cabrini University **ED:** PhD in Sociology, Mississippi State University (2008); MA in Sociology, University of Tennessee (1997); BA in Sociology, Salisbury University (1995) **C:** Associate Professor, Department of Leader and Organizational Development, Cabrini University (2015-Present); Chair, Department of Leader and Organizational Development, Cabrini University (2015-Present); Associate Professor, Department of Social Sciences, University of Maryland Eastern Shore (2012-2015); ORLD Doctoral Program Coordinator, Department of Social Sciences, University of Maryland Eastern Shore (2012-2015); Department Chair, Department of Sociology, University of West Georgia (2012); Assistant Professor, Department of Sociology, University of West Georgia (2008-2012); Interim Assistant Dean, College of Social Sciences, University of West Georgia (2010-2011); Assistant Professor, Department of Sociology and Anthropology, LaGrange College (2006-2008); Assistant Program Director, Delmarva Broad Casting (1999-2001); On-air Talent, Delmarva Broadcasting (1999-2001) **CIV:** Moveable Feast **CW:** Contributor, Research, Journals of Social Forces; Contributor, Research, Journal for the Scientific Study of Religion; Contributor, Research, Review of Religious Research; Contributor, Research, Religions; Contributor, Research, Sociological Inquiry; Contributor, Research, Sociological Spectrum; Contributor, Research, Professional Journals; Contributor, Research, Books **AW:** Phi Kappa Phi **MEM:** Organizational Development Network; Academy of Management; International Leadership Association **BA:** 610 King of Prussia Rd, Cabrini University, Radnor, PA, 19087 **ADD:** 205 Secretariat Dr Unit J, Havre De Grace, MD, 21078 **URL:** https://www.cabrini.edu/about/departments/academic-departments/school-of-business-arts-and-media/lea

MAUSNER, JEFFREY N., T: Lawyer **I:** Law and Legal Services **PT:** Howard Mausner; Ruth Mausner **MS:** Married **SPN:** Janet Mausner **CH:** Joshua; Jessica; Jasmine **ED:** JD, Cornell Law School, Magna Cum Laude (1976); BA in Political Science, Minor in Physics, Brown University (1972) **C:** Attorney, Intellectual Property Litigation, Law Offices of Jeffrey N. Mausner (2007-2012); Adjunct Professor, Southwestern Law School, teaching Advanced Copyright Law, Internet and

Computer Law, and Intellectual Property Law (1992-2016); Partner, Berman, Mausner & Resser, A Law Corporation (1986-2007); Special Assistant United States Attorney, Criminal Division, Eastern District of Virginia, United States Department of Justice (1982-1983); Special Assistant United States Attorney, District of Maryland (1982); Federal Prosecutor and Trial Attorney, United States Department of Justice, Criminal Division, Office of Special Investigations (Nazi War Crimes Unit) (1979-1985); Associate Attorney, Kaye, Scholer, Fierman, Hays & Handler (1976-1979) **CIV:** Volunteer, West Valley Animal Shelter; Board Member, Second Vice President, Tarzana Neighborhood Council; Chairman, Tarzana Neighborhood Council Animal Welfare Committee; Sub-Committee on No-Kill, Los Angeles Animal Services Department; Liaison from Valley Alliance of Neighborhood Councils to Los Angeles Animal Services Department **CW:** Author, "Apprehending and Prosecuting Nazi War Criminals in the United States," 15 Nova Law Review 747 (1991) **AW:** "Best of Award" for "Engaging the City to Save the Lives of Hundreds of Animals," Valley Alliance of Neighborhood Councils (2017); Southern California Super Lawyer (2006-2016); Adjunct Excellence in Teaching Award, Southwestern Law School (2001); U.S. Justice Department Outstanding Performance Rating (1985); Justice Department Special Achievement Award (1984); Justice Department Outstanding Performance Rating (1984); Outstanding Performance Rating (1983); U.S. Justice Department Meritorious Award for Superior Performance of Duties on a Continuous Basis (1982); Justice Department Exceptional Performance Rating (1982) **MEM:** President, Los Angeles Copyright Society (2003-2004); President-Elect, Los Angeles Copyright Society (2002-2003); Vice President, Los Angeles Copyright Society (2001-2002) **BAR:** State of New York; District of Columbia; State of California; State of Colorado; U.S. Supreme Court; U.S. Court of Appeals; U.S. District Courts **H:** Saving animals **ADD:** 6222 Amigo Avenue, Tarzana, CA, 91335 **URL:** http://www.mausnerlaw.com

MAZER, MIKE, T: Artist, Retired Cardiologist and Nephrologist **I:** Medicine & Health Care **DOB:** 05/17/1936 **PB:** Boston **SC:** MA/USA **PT:** Son of Louis and Belle Mazer **MS:** Married **SPN:** Marilyn Wood (February, 1987) **ED:** MD, University of Cincinnati (1962); BS, Cum Laude, Boston University (1958) **CT:** Diplomate in Cardiology, American Board of Cardiology (1979); Diplomate in Nephrology, American Board of Nephrology (1978); Diplomate in Internal Medicine, American Board Internal Medicine (1970) **C:** Artist (1997-Present); Private Practice, Bridgewater Goddard Park Medical Associates, Massachusetts (1968-1998); Chief, Echocardiography and Noninvasive Vascular Laboratory, Good Samaritan Medical Center (1994-1997); Chief of Cardiology, Good Samaritan Medical Center, Brockton (1994-1997); Co-Director, Brockton-Goddard Hemodialysis Unit, Brockton (1992-1997); Director, Cardiac Rehabilitation Center, Striar Jewish Community Center, Stoughton (1994-1997); Chief of Nephrology, Cardinal Cushing Hospital, Brockton, MA (1968-1994); Chief of Cardiology, Goddard Memorial Hospital (1986-1994); Chief Echocardiography and Noninvasive Vascular Lab, Goddard Memorial Hospital (1977-1994); Director of Acute Hemodialysis, Goddard Memorial Hospital, Stoughton, MA (1968-1990); Fellow of Cardiovascular Disease, West Roxbury VA Hospital, Boston (1967-1968); Fellow, Renal and Metabolic Studies Medical Center, Boston University (1964-1965); National Institutes of Health Junior Fellow in Gastroenterology and Hepatology, University of Cinncinati (1962-1964); Director,

Cardiac Ultrasonography and Transtelephonic Monitoring, National Medical Co, Taunton; Medical Director, Park Cardiographics, Taunton, MA **MIL:** LCDR US Navy (1962-1975); Volunteer Physician, Vietnam War (1965-1967) **CW:** Editor, "Journal of Diagnostic Medical Sonography" (1985-1987); Co-author, "Principles of Interpretation in Echocardiography" (1985); Artist, More than 700 Exhibitions; Featured Artist in Permanent Collections, US Coast Guard, Tabor Academy, New Bedford Free Public Library, Commonwealth of Massachusetts Department of Environmental Protection, Marion Art Center, Massachusetts Maritime Academy, Cape Cod Museum of Art and New Bedford Whaling Museum; Featured Artist in International Exhibitions, Zeeland Maritime Museum, Vlissingen, Holland; One-Man Show Performer, New Bedford Art Museum, Cape Cod Art Museum, New Bedford Whaling Museum, Coos Art Museum Marine Exhibition International Guild Realism, US Coast Guard Exhibition, Channel Islands Maritime Museum, California and Mystic Museum; Contributor, Articles to Professional Publications **AW:** Alpha Omega Alpha Art Honor Society; More Than 120 Major Art Awards **MEM:** American Society of Marine Artists, Rhode Island Watercolor Society, North Shore Arts Association, Philadelphia Watercolor Society, North East Watercolor Society, Texas Watercolor Society (Purple Sage Brush Society), Pennsylvania Watercolor Society, Missouri Watercolor Society, Mississippi Watercolor Society, Montana Watercolor Society, International Guild of Realism, International Society of Marine Painters, Hudson Valley Art Association, Georgia Watercolor Society, The Salmagundi Club, Watercolor Art Society-Houston, San Diego Watercolor Society, Red River Watercolor Society, Western Colorado Watercolor Society, Taos Watercolor Society, Society of Watercolor Artists, Louisiana Watercolor Society, Watercolor Society of Alabama and Kentucky Watercolor Society; Associate Member, the National Watercolor Society **MH:** Albert Nelson Marquis Lifetime Achievement Award (2017) **ADD:** 7 Holly Woods Rd, Mattapoisett, MA, 02739

MCALLISTER, FRANCIS R., T: Nonferrous Metal Company Executive **I:** Mining & Metals **CN:** Asarco Australia Ltd. **DOB:** 09/25/1942 **PB:** St. George **SC:** UT/USA **PT:** DeVere Richard McAllister; Ila (Cox) McAllister **MS:** Married **SPN:** Marcia Hutchinson (12/12/1963) **CH:** Christie; Trisha; Susanne; Francis Ralph; Amy; Elizabeth; Richard **ED:** Student, Advanced Management Program, Harvard University (1979); MBA, New York University (1971); BS in Finance, University of Utah (1966) **CT:** Certified Management Accountant, Institute of Management Accountants, Inc. **C:** Chairman, Asarco Australia Ltd. (1992-Present); Chairman, Stillwater Mining Company (Now Sibanye) (2001-2013); Chief Executive Officer, Stillwater Mining Company (Now Sibanye) (2001-2013); Chairman, ASARCO LLC (1999-2001); Chief Executive Officer, ASARCO LLC (1999-2001); Chief Operating Officer, ASARCO LLC (1998-1999); Executive Vice President, Copper Operations, ASARCO LLC (1993-1998); Executive Vice President, ASARCO LLC (1992-1999); Vice President, Finance & Administration, ASARCO LLC (1986-1992); Chief Financial Officer, ASARCO LLC (1982-1993); Vice President, ASARCO LLC (1982-1986); Comptroller, ASARCO LLC (1978-1982); Assistant Comptroller, ASARCO LLC (1975-1978); Staff Assistant to Comptroller, ASARCO LLC (1973-1975); Senior Accountant, Accounting Manager, ASARCO LLC (1968-1973); Systems Analyst, ASARCO LLC (1966-1968) **CR:** Board of Directors, Southern Peru Copper Corporation, Grupo Mexico S.A., Cliffs Natural Resources Inc. (1996-Present) **CIV:** President, Catalina Council,

Boy Scouts of America **MEM:** Trustee, Financial Executives International (1989-Present); Treasurer, Financial Executives International (1989-Present); Joint Council on Economic Education, Financial Executives International (1989-Present); Finance and Development Committee, Financial Executives International (1989-Present); Pension and Investment Committees, American Mining Congress (1989-Present); Financial Advisory Executive Committee Member, American Mining Congress (1983-Present); National Representative, Boy Scouts of America (1990); Chairman, Accounting Committee, American Mining Congress (1981-1982); Map Committee Member, National Association of Professional Accountants (1980-1982); American Institute of Mining, Metallurgical, and Petroleum Engineers; Board Member, Montana/Salt Lake City Chapter, Boy Scouts of America **MH:** Albert Nelson Marquis Lifetime Achievement Award (2017) **RE:** Latter-Day Saints **ADD:** 5565 S Walker Woods Lane, Salt Lake City, UT, 84117

MCAVOY, DAVID R., T: Chief Legal Counsel **I:** Law and Legal Services **CN:** Endocyte, Inc. **DOB:** 06/26/1962 **PB:** Anderson **SC:** IN/USA **PT:** Richard Lee McAvoy; Constance Vincent McAvoy **MS:** Married **SPN:** Karen Ohmart McAvoy **CH:** Alyson Lee; Ryan Edward; Kyle Ean **ED:** JD, Maurer School of Law, Indiana University, With Honors (1988); MS in Environmental Science, Indiana University, Bloomington, IN, With Highest Honors (1988); BA in Government, University of Notre Dame (1984) **C:** Chief Legal Counsel, Endocyte, Inc. (2018-Present); Business Leader, Strategic Alliances, Nutritional Health, Food Animal Production, Elanco Animal Health, Greenfield, IN (2016-2017); General Counsel, Emerging Markets, Eli Lilly and Company, Indianapolis, IN (2004-2016); Director, Office of Scientific & Regulatory Policy, Eli Lilly and Company, Indianapolis, IN (2002-2004); General Counsel, Latin America, Eli Lilly and Company, Indianapolis, IN (1998-2002); Senior FDA Counsel, U.S. Affiliate Pharmaceutical Operations, Eli Lilly and Company, Indianapolis, IN (1994-1998); Attorney, Environmental Affairs, U.S. Affiliate Manufacturing Operations, Eli Lilly and Company, Indianapolis, IN (1990-1994); Associate Counsel, Environmental and Public Sector Practice Groups, Squire, Sanders & Dempsey, Cleveland, OH (1988-1990) **CR:** Secretary, Board of Directors, The Villages, Inc. (2009-Present); Guest Lecturer, Liberty Fund; Co-Chair, Iran Health Committee, U.S. Chamber of Commerce; Pro Bono, Legal Aid Society of Cleveland **CIV:** Co-Chairman, High Adventure Committee, Troop 276, Boy Scouts of America (2000-Present); Ordained Stephen Minister (2008); Senior Member, Gubernatorial Campaign for Former Indiana Governor Mitch Daniels (2003-2005); Eagle Scout, Boy Scouts of America (1976) **CW:** Co-Author, A New Model for Communicating Risk Information in Direct-to-Consumer Print Advertisements, 41 Drug Inf J 111 - 120 (2007) **AW:** Lilly Research Labs' President's Recognition Award for Outstanding Scientific Achievement (2005); Hoosier Boys State (1979); Eagle Scout (1976) **MEM:** Association of Corporate Counsel (ACC) **BAR:** State of Indiana; Various U.S. Federal Courts **H:** Shōrei-ryū; Alpine climbing; Running in Desert Ultra Marathons **PA:** Libertarian **RE:** Episcopalian **BA:** 3000 Kent Avenue, Suite A1-100, Purdue Research Park, West Lafayette, IN, 47906-1075 **ADD:** 9326 Timber Crest Lane, Indianapolis, IN, 46256-8415 **URL:** https://www.linkedin.com/in/david-mcavoy-3b0116a7

MCCANN, JEAN FRIEDRICHS, T: Artist, Educator **I:** Fine Art **DOB:** 12/06/1937 **PB:** New York **SC:** NY/USA **PT:** Herbert Joseph Friedrichs; Catherine Brady (Ward) Friedrichs **MS:** Married **SPN:**

William Joseph McCann (5/14/1960) **CH:** Kevin; Brian; Maureen McCann Breslin; William; James; Denis Gerard; Kathleen **ED:** PhD, Nova College (1995); Completed Kellogg Leadership Program, School of Management, Binghamton University, State University of New York (1992); MFA in Art, Marywood University, Summa Cum Laude (1989); MA, Marywood University, Summa Cum Laude (1987); BS, Empire State College, Binghamton, NY (1986); AAS, Farmingdale State College (1959); Coursework, Caton-Rose Institute of Fine Arts (1955-1957) **C:** Tutor, Empire State College (1987-2016); Evaluator, Empire State College (1987-2016); Director, ArtSpace Gallery, Owego, NY (1992-1994); Substitute Art Teacher, Owego-Apalachin School District (1968-1988); Designer, Patton Corp., New York, NY (1959-1966) **CR:** President, Tioga County Council on the Arts (1992-1995); Vice President, Board of Directors, Tioga County Council on the Arts (1990-1991); Demonstrator, Various Schools, Educational TV Shows, County Museums **CIV:** Board of Directors, Birthright of Owego, NY (1993-2003) **CW:** Exhibitor, One-woman Shows, Wilson Gallery, Johnson City, NY (2003, 2001, 1994); Exhibitor, One-woman Shows, Krembs Gallery (2003, 2000, 1993); Exhibitor, Juried Show, Schwein Fourth Memorial Art Museum, Auburn, NY (2002); Exhibitor, One-woman Shows, Countryside Gallery, Owego, NY (2002, 1996); Exhibitor, One-woman Show, Memorial Gallery, Farmingdale State College (1998); Exhibitor, One-woman Show, Countryside Gallery, Owego, NY (1996); Exhibitor, One-woman Show, MacDonald Art Gallery, College Misericordia, Dallas, PA (1992); Exhibitor, One-woman Show, Plaza Gallery, Binghamton, NY (1992); Exhibitor, Juried Show, Arnot Art Museum, Elmira, NY (1992, 1989, 1974); Exhibitor, One-woman Show, ArtSpace, Owego, NY (1991); Exhibitor, One-woman Show, Visual Arts Center, Scranton, PA (1989-1990); Exhibitor, Juried Show, Grand Concourse Gallery, Albany, NY (1987); Exhibitor, One-woman Show, National Historical Court House (1982); Exhibitor, One-woman Show, Tioga Historical Society Museum (1975); Exhibitor, Juried Show, Arena National Exhibits, Binghamton, NY (1974-1976); Exhibitor, One-woman Show, IBM, Owego, NY (1972); Exhibitor, Juried Group Shows; Exhibitor, Numerous Private and Public Collections **AW:** First Place in Graphic Arts Award, Jericho Arts Council (1994); National Strathmore Award for Creative Excellence (1989); New York State Artisans Award (1982) **MEM:** President, Zeta Omicron Chapter, Kappa Pi (1987-1989); Charter Member, National Museum of Women in the Arts; Life, Kappa Pi; Artists Guild **MH:** Albert Nelson Marquis Lifetime Achievement Award (2017) **H:** Traveling; Reading **RE:** Christian **ADD:** 6431 Francis Dr, Victor, NY, 14564 **URL:** http://www.jeansbrush.com

MCCARTY, SHERIE, T: Chief Executive Officer **I:** Architecture & Construction **CN:** Mas Construction Services, LLC **PT:** Jerry Bender; Betty Catherine (Davis) Bender **MS:** Married **SPN:** William McCarty **CH:** Logan; Julie **ED:** BS, University of Delaware (1991); BS, Washington College **CT:** Certified Refrigeration Engineer; Society of Universal Refrigerants License; Certified Back Flow Device Inspector **C:** Owner, Mas Construction Services, LLC **CIV:** Habitat for Humanity **CW:** Author, "How to Reduce Energy Costs in Commercial and Industrial Buildings" (1992) **AW:** Distinguished Service Award, IFMA (2002) **MEM:** Board Member, ACE Mentoring Philadelphia Board (2017); Subcontractors Association of Delaware Valley; Executive Board, Vice President of the Board of Directors, United States Green Building Mechanical Contractor Association; Mechanical Service Contractor

Association; South Jersey Mechanical Contractors Association; General Building Council Association; National Association of Women in Construction; Refrigerant Service Engineer Society; Philadelphia Chapter, Professional Engineers Society; Women Construction Owners and Executives **H:** Golf **RE:** Catholic **BA:** 121 Market Street, Suite 316, MAS Construction Services, Camden, NJ, 08102 **URL:** https://www.masconstructionservices.com

MCCLENDON, WILLIAM HUTCHINSON III, T: Lawyer **I:** Law and Legal Services **CN:** Taylor, Porter, Brooks & Phillips **DOB:** 02/19/1933 **PB:** New Orleans **SC:** LA/USA **PT:** William H. McClendon, Jr.; Eleanor (Eaton) McClendon **MS:** Married **SPN:** Eugenia Mills Slaughter (2/6/1960) **CH:** William Hutchinson, IV; Virginia Morris; Eleanor Eaton; Bryan Slaughter **ED:** LLB, Tulane University (1958); BA, Tulane University (1956) **C:** Instructor, Osher Lifelong Learning Institute, Louisiana State University (2016-Present); Associate Mediator, Mediation Arbitration Professional Systems, Inc. (1999-2001); Executive Committee, Taylor, Porter, Brooks & Phillips L.L.P. (1987-2001); Partner, Taylor, Porter, Brooks & Phillips L.L.P. (1966-2001); Lawyer, Taylor, Porter, Brooks & Phillips L.L.P. (1960-2001); Attorney, Humble Oil & Refining Company (1958-1960) **CR:** Lecturer, Banking Seminar (2015); Adjunct Professor, Western Carolina University (2003-2010); Adjunct Professor, The University of Tennessee, Knoxville, TN (2003-2008); Real Estate Seminar Chairman, Lecturer, LSU Paul M. Hebert Law Center (1995); Lecturer, Banking Seminar (1995); Lecturer, Society of Louisiana Certified Public Accountants (1991); Lecturer, LSPS (1989); Real Estate Seminar Chairman, Lecturer, LSU Paul M. Hebert Law Center (1987); Real Estate Seminar Chairman, Lecturer, LSU Paul M. Hebert Law Center (1985); Adjunct Professor in Legal Negotiation and Professionalism, Louisiana State University (1983-2016); Real Estate Seminar Chairman, Lecturer, LSU Paul M. Hebert Law Center (1982); Real Estate Seminar Chairman, Lecturer, LSU Paul M. Hebert Law Center (1980); Real Estate Seminar Chairman, Lecturer, LSU Paul M. Hebert Law Center (1976); Real Estate Seminar Chairman, Lecturer, LSU Paul M. Hebert Law Center (1974); Real Estate Seminar Chairman, Lecturer, LSU Paul M. Hebert Law Center (1972); Lecturer in Movable Property, Bridging the Gap Institute, Louisiana State Bar Association (1965); Instructor of Commercial Law and Negotiable Instruments, American Institute of Banking, American Bankers Association (1963-1974); Lecturer, LSU Paul M. Hebert Law Center; Faculty Member, Professional Education Group, Inc.; Lecturer in Field **CIV:** Dean's Council, Tulane University Law School (1984-1988); Trustee, Episcopal High School (1976-1978); Board Director, Baton Rouge Chapter, American Cancer Society, Inc. (1968-1971) **MIL:** Captain, U.S. Army **CW:** Author, "Negotiations Seminar," Louisiana Bankers Association (2014); Author, "Professionalism Seminar," Louisiana State Legislature (2013); Author, "Deal Makers: Negotiating More Effectively Using Timeless Values" (2011); Contributor, Articles, Legal Journals **AW:** Preservation Award, Foundation for Historical Louisiana (Now Preserve Louisiana) (1997); Memorial Award, Louisiana State Bar Association (1987) **MEM:** Board Director, Baton Rouge Symphony Orchestra (2001-2002); Chairman, Baton Rouge Assembly (1999); Ball Chairman, Baton Rouge Assembly (1997); Board Director, Hilltop Arboretum (1993-1995); President, Louisiana Civil Service League (1992-1994); Board Director, Baton Rouge Green (1991-1993); Treasurer, Baton Rouge Assembly (1983); Board Director, Baton Rouge Club, Rotary International (1972); President, Toastmasters International (1970); Chairman, Trust Estates, Probate and Immovable Proper-

ty Law Section, Louisiana State Bar Association (1969-1970); Chairman, Title Standards Committee, Baton Rouge Bar Association (1968-1969); President, Tulane Alumni Association of Greater Baton Rouge, Tulane University (1968-1969); Vice President, Louisiana Tulane Law Alumni, Tulane University Law School (1964-1965); ABA; American Judicature Society; Feliciana Bar Association; Treasurer, Louisiana Tulane Law Alumni, Tulane University Law School; Pickwick Club; Kappa Alpha Order **BAR:** Supreme Court of the United States (1964); Louisiana (1958) **MH:** Albert Nelson Marquis Lifetime Achievement Award (2017) **PA:** Republican **RE:** Episcopalian **ADD:** 5844 Creekside Lane, Saint Francisville, LA, 70775

MCCONNELL, JAMES, T: Owner **I:** Law and Legal Services **CN:** Construction Law Services, LLC **DOB:** 09/24/1947 **PB:** Hinsdale, Illinois **SC:** United States **PT:** William F. McConnell; Virginia (Brown) McConnell **MS:** Married **SPN:** Linda Wold **CH:** Colin; Nicholas; Joanna; Cameron; Gabriel (Deceased) **ED:** JD, Northwestern University (1973); BS in Journalism, Iowa State University (1969) **C:** Owner, Construction Law Services, LLC (2009-Present); Partner, Goldstein, Fluxgold & McConnell, Chicago, IL (1996-2009); Partner, Freeborn & Peters, Chicago, IL (1990-1996); Partner, Bell, Boyd & Lloyd, Chicago, IL (1985-1988); Partner, Rooks, Pitts & Poust, Chicago, IL (1980-1985); Associate, Rooks, Pitts & Poust, Chicago, IL (1973-1980) **CR:** Adjunct Professor of Law, Chicago-Kent College of Law, Illinois Institute of Technology (1978-1984); Speaker in Field **CIV:** Chairman, McHenry County Historical Preservation Commission 2016-2018 **CW:** Editorial Board Member, "Hazardous Waste and Toxic Torts Law and Strategy" (1986-1993); Author, "Comparative Negligence Defense Tactics," John Wiley & Sons, Inc. (1985); Contributor, Book Chapters; Contributor, Articles, Professional Journals **MEM:** American Arbitration Association (1983-Present); Charter Fellow, Congress of Fellows, Center for International Legal Studies (2002); Environmental Law Committee, Chicago Bar Association (1987-1990); Tort Litigation Committee, Chicago Bar Association (1987-1990); Committee on Professional Liability, Litigation Section, ABA (1976-1990); Litigation Section, ABA (1975-1990); Tort and Insurance Practice Section, ABA (1973-1990); Civil Practice and Procedure Section, Illinois State Bar Association (1973-1990); Insurance Law Section, Illinois State Bar Association (1973-1990); Tort Law Section, Illinois State Bar Association (1973-1990); Vice-chair, Committee on Toxic and Hazardous Substances and Environmental Law, Tort and Insurance Practice Section, ABA (1987-1989); Special Committee on Lawyers' Interest Bearing Trust Accounts, Chicago Bar Association (1982-1984); Chairman, Professional Responsibility Committee, Young Lawyers Section, Chicago Bar Association (1979); Professional Responsibility Committee, Young Lawyers Section, Chicago Bar Association (1976-1979); Vice-chair, Professional Responsibility Committee, Young Lawyers Section, Chicago Bar Association (1978); Secretary, Standing Committee on Specialization, Illinois State Bar Association (1978); Standing Committee on Specialization, Illinois State Bar Association (1976-1978); Chairman, Economics of the Legal Profession Committee, Chicago Bar Association (1977); Economics of the Legal Profession Committee, Chicago Bar Association (1973-1977); Vice-chair, Economics of the Legal Profession Committee, Chicago Bar Association (1976) **BAR:** The Trial Bar for the Northern District of Illinois (1982); Supreme Court of the United States (1977); United States Court of Appeals for the Seventh Circuit (1973); United States District

Court Northern District of Illinois (1973); Illinois (1973) **MH:** Albert Nelson Marquis Lifetime Achievement Award (2017) **BA:** 101 N Virginia St Ste 120, Construction Law Services LLC, Crystal Lake, IL, 60014

MCCORD, LARRY J. III, T: Principal Attorney **I:** Law and Legal Services **CN:** Larry McCord and Associates, LLC **DOB:** 08/11/1946 **PB:** New Orleans **SC:** LA/USA **PT:** Alfred Sampson Smith; LaVerna Dorothy (Pembroke) Smith **MS:** Divorced **SPN:** Muriel Simmons McCord (8/3/1969, Divorced) **CH:** Larry J. McCord, IV; Tamkya; Tinysha; Daniel **ED:** JD, Touro College Jacob D. Fuchsberg Law Center (1997); MS in Administration and Human Services, Manhattan College (1993); BBA, Hofstra University (1975); AAS, Farmingdale State College (1972) **CT:** Ordained Pastor (2014); Certified Minister (1994); Certified Teacher, State of New York **C:** Managing Partner, Owner, Principle Attorney, Larry McCord and Associates, LLC (1999-Present); Project Manager, New York Life Insurance Company, New York City, NY (1986-Present); Project Manager, National Benefit Life, New York City, NY (1985-Present); Assistant Deputy Chief of Staff, Office of the Suffolk County Executive (1989-1991); Manager, Technical Support, Philipp Brothers, Inc., New York City, NY (1979-1985); Programming Supervisor, Metropolitan Life Insurance, New York City, NY (1977-1979); Financial Services Coordinator, J.C. Penney Comapny, New York City, NY (1976-1977); Project Manager, Teachers Insurance Company, New York City, NY (1972-1976); Director, Programming, Office Electronics Inc., Great Neck, NY (1972) **CR:** Chairman, OIC of America, Suffolk County, NY (1988-Present); Trustee, Board of Directors, Wyandanch Board of Education (1987-Present); President, Wyandanch Board of Education (1988-1989); Vice President, Wyandanch Midget Football League, New York (1978); Board of Directors, Wyandanch Midget Football League, New York (1977); Head Coach, Wyandanch Midget Football League, New York (1975); Elected Chairman, Liberal Candidate, Fourth District, The New York State Senate (1972); School Attorney; School Administrator **CIV:** Pastor, Local Church (2014-Present); Chairman, Personnel Committee, Local School District **MIL:** U.S. Army (1966-1968) **CW:** Author, "Victim of Vietnam" (1981); Author, "Poetry A to Z" (1980) **AW:** Top 100 Blacks American Business Award, Harlem YMCA (1984); Life Office Management Association Fellow (1975-1978); Leadership In Law Awards; Decorated Purple Heart; Bronze Star; Honoree, Named Top 10 Lawyer on Long Island **MEM:** Executive Committee, Cullinet Database User Group (1981-1985); Planning Chairman, Minority Interchange, Inc.; Suffolk County Bar Association; Amistad Long Island Black Bar Association; New York State Trial Lawyers Association; Touro Law Center Alumni Association **BAR:** Supreme Court of the United States (2013); United States District Court Eastern District of New York (2007); New York (1999); Second Judicial Department, Appellate Division, Supreme Court of the State of New York (1999) **PA:** Republican **RE:** Methodist **BA:** 1291 Straight Path, Larry McCord & Associates, LLC, West Babylon, NY, 11704 **URL:** http://longislandspecialeducationattorney.com/

MCCRAVEN, EVA PHD, T: Health Services Executive **I:** Health, Wellness and Fitness **DOB:** 09/26/1936 **SC:** CA/USA **PT:** Paul Melvin Stewart; Wilma Zech (Ziegler) Stewart **MS:** Widowed **SPN:** Carl Clarke McCraven (Deceased) **CH:** David Anthony; Lawrence James; Maria Mapes Stone **ED:** PhD, Cambridge Graduate School of Psychology (1991); MS, Cambridge Graduate School of Psychology (1987); BS, California State University,

Northridge, Summa Cum Laude (1974) **C:** Chief Executive Officer and President, Hillview Mental Health Center, Lake View Terrace, CA (2004-present); Los Angeles County Supervisors Commendation, Indigent Services (2011); Commendation LA County Board of Supervisors, Career Advocating Indigent Mentally Ill (2011); Former Member, Board of Directors, California Council of Community Mental Health Agencies; Member, Prevention & Early Intervention Steering Committee (2009); Executive Director, Hillview Community Mental Health Center, Lake View Terrace, CA (1999-2004); Assistant Executive Director, Vice President, Hillview Community Mental Health Center, Lake View Terrace, CA (1974-1999); Director, Health Education, Pacoima Memorial Hospital (1971-1974); Director, Special Projects, Pacoima Memorial Hospital (1969-1971) **CR:** Chief Executive Officer, President, Integrated Services Agency, Hillview Mental Health Center, Inc. (2005-Present); Executive Director, Integrated Services Agency, Hillview Mental Health Center, Inc. (1999-Present); Prevention and Early Intervention, Service Area Planning, LA County Service Area (2009); Director, Clinical Programs, Integrated Services Agency, Hillview Mental Health Center, Inc. (1996-1999); Director, Integrated Services Agency, Hillview Mental Health Center, Inc. (1993-1998); Developer, Manager, Long-term Residential Program (1986-1990); Past Director, Department of Consultation and Education, Hillview Center; Former Program Manager, Crisis Residential Program, Transitional Residential Program and Day Treatment Program for Mentally Ill Offenders; Past Director, Mentally Ill Offenders Services; Former Program Director, Valley Homeless Shelter Mental Health Counseling Program; Member, Steering Committee, Commendation Resolution LA County Board for Career Advocacy; Member at Large, Board of Directors, California Council of Community Mental Health Agencies; Board of Directors, California Council of Community Golden State; Board of Directors, California Council of Community for Behavioral Health Agencies; Chair, Adult Mental Health Agency **CIV:** Founder, Hillview Mental Health Center, Inc. (2014); Board of Directors, NE Valley Health Corp. (1970-1973); Board of Directors, Golden State Community Mental Health Center (1970-1973); Board of Advisors, Pacoima Senior Citizens Multi-Purpose Center; Former President, San Fernando Valley; Former President, Coordinating Council Area Association; Former President, Sunland-Tujunga Coordinating Council; Founder, NE San Fernando Valley Coalition **AW:** Commendation Award, County of Los Angeles Board of Supervisors (2011); Commendation Award, Sunland-Tujunga Business and Professional Women (2010); Women of Achievement Award, Sunland-Tujunga Business and Professional Women (1990); Community Services Commendation Award, City of Los Angeles (1989); Community Services Commendation Award, County of Los Angeles (1989); Community Services Commendation Award, California Assembly (1989); Community Services Commendation Award, California Senate (1989); Award, Sunland-Tujunga Police Support Council (1989); Resolution of Commendation, State of California (1988); Commendation Award (1988); Special Mayor's Plaque (1988) **MEM:** Past Vice President, Health Services Administration Alumni Association; Sunland-Tujunga Business and Professional Women; League of Women Voters, Valley Philharmonic **ADD:** 12450 Van Nuys Blvd Ste 200, Hillview Mental Health Center, Inc., Pacoima, CA, 91331

MCCUTCHEON, IAN MD, T: Professor of Neurosurgery **I:** Medicine & Health Care **CN:** The University of Texas MD Anderson Cancer Center **DOB:** 06/04/1959 **PB:** London **SC:** ON/Canada **PT:** Otty Earle McCutcheon; Selma Maureen (Burrows) McCutcheon **MS:** Married **SPN:** Melly Meadows (12/1/2004); Sylvie Bonnier (5/19/1984, Divorced 2001) **CH:** Noelle Tatiana; Nicolas Selss Mycroft **ED:** Chief Resident in Neurosurgery, McGill University Hospitals (1990-1991); Senior Assistant Resident in Neurosurgery, Montreal Neurological Institute (1989-1990); Medical Staff Fellow in Neurosurgery, Surgical Neurology Branch, National Institute of Neurological, Disorders and Stroke, National Institutes of Health, Bethesda, Maryland (1987-1989); Senior Assistant Resident, Montreal General Hospital, Montreal Children's Hospital (1986-1987); Junior Assistant Resident in Neurosurgery, Montreal Neurological Institute, Montreal General Hospital, Montreal Children's Hospital (1985-1986); Intern in General Surgery, Cedars-Sinai Medical Center, UCLA (1984-1985); MD, CM McGill University (1984); Research Fellow in Cardiology, Heart Research Laboratory, OHSU (1978-1980); BA, Yale University (1978) **CT:** Certified in Neurosurgery, Royal College of Surgeons of Canada **C:** Director, Neuroendocrine Program, Department of Neurosurgery, The University of Texas M D Anderson Cancer Center (2006-Present); Adjunct Professor of Neurosurgery, Baylor College of Medicine (2005-Present); Professor of Neurosurgery, The University of Texas M D Anderson Cancer Center (2003-Present); Clinical Assistant Professor of Neurosurgery, Department of Neurosurgery, Baylor College of Medicine (1991-2005); Associate Professor of Neurosurgery, The University of Texas M D Anderson Cancer Center (1997-2003); Consultant in Surgery, Michael E. DeBakey VA Medical Center, U.S. Department of Veterans Affairs (1995-2001); Assistant Professor of Neurosurgery, The University of Texas M D Anderson Cancer Center (1991-1997) **CR:** Board of Directors, NeurosurgeryPAC (2016-Present); Chairman, Executive Committee of the Medical Staff, The University of Texas M D Anderson Cancer Center (Present); Chairman, Credentials Committee of the Medical Staff, The University of Texas M D Anderson Cancer Center (2009-2012); Deputy Chair, Department of Neurosurgery, The University of Texas MD Anderson Cancer Center (1995-2000); Past President, Texas Association of Neurological Surgeons; Past President, Pituitary Network Association; President, Houston Neurological Society; Visiting Professor, 27 Different Universities and Institutes **CIV:** Board of Directors, Museum of Printing History, Houston, Texas (2015-Present); Vice President, Bridgeover, Inc. (2009-Present); Board of Directors, Greater Houston Youth Orchestra, Houston, TX (1999-2001); Board of Directors, Neartown Youth Baseball League, Houston, TX (1996-2001); Trustee, Alliance Francaise, Houston, TX (1992-1994) **MIL:** Retired, U.S. Naval Reserve (2005); Commander, U.S. Naval Reserve (1997); Lieutenant Commander, U.S. Naval Reserve (1990); Lieutenant, U.S. Naval Reserve (1988) **CW:** Editorial Board Member,"Frontiers in Endocrinology" (2014-Present); Editorial Board Member, Journal of Oncology (2009-Present); Editorial Board Member, Journal of Neuro-Oncology (2006-Present); Ad Hoc Editorial Reviewer, Various Professional Journals (1992-Present); Special Editor, Proceedings of the 7th meeting of the Asian Gamma Knife Academy, Acta Neurochirurgica (2017); Editorial Board Member, Pituitary (2010-2015); Special Editor, "Pituitary tumors," Current Problems in Cancer (2013); Editorial Board Member, Cancer.Net (2008-2015); Editorial Board Member, Neuro-Oncology (2010-2013); Editorial Board Member, Annals of Surgical Oncology (1995-2002); Member, Adult Treatment Advisory Editorial Board, National Cancer Institute, National Institutes of Health (1995-2000); Contributor, Over 150 Articles, Professional Journals; Contributor, 35 Book Chapters; Co-Editor of 3 Books **AW:** Featured Listee, Best Doctors in America (2003-Present); Named to Ashbel Smith Professorship, The University of Texas M D Anderson Cancer Center (2017); Recipient, Certificate of Teaching Excellence, Baylor College of Medicine (2010, 2017); Synthes Skull Base Lectureship, University of Utah (2016); Snodgrass Lectureship, University of Texas Medical Branch in Galveston (2015); Co-recipient, Certificate of Merit, Radiological Society of North America (2014); Honored Guest, Indian Skull Base Society (2012); Honored Guest, Indian Society of Neuro-Oncology (2011); Honored Guest, Dutch Society of Neurosurgery (2006); Honored Guest, Shanghai University (2004); Feindel Lectureship, Montreal Neurological Insitute, McGill University (1999); Recipient, Letter of Commendation, Naval Aviation Schools Command (1996); Recipient, Penfield-McNaughton Prize in Neurosurgery, Montreal Neurological Institute (1991); Recipient, First Prize, Poster Session Annual Meeting, American Association of Neurological Surgeons (1989); Recipient, Hill Scholarship, McGill University (1983-1984); Recipient, McNaghten Prize in Writing, McGill University (1983); Recipient, Friends of McGill Scholarship, McGill University (1980-1983); Recipient, Summer Research Fellowship, Oregon Heart Association (1981); Recipient, Honors Commendation in Russian History, Yale University (1977) **MEM:** Member-At-Large, Executive Committee, The Society of University Neurosurgeons (2018-); Membership Committee, The Society of University Neurosurgeons (2017-Present); Delegate to World Federation of Neurosurgical Societies, The Society of University Neurosurgeons (2017-Present); Bylaws Committee, The Society of University Neurosurgeons (2012-Present); Delegate to Joint Council of State Neurosurgical Societies, Secretary, Texas Association of Neurological Surgeons (2009-2012); Member, Committee on Applicants, South Texas District I, American College of Surgeons (2010-Present); Board of Directors, Houston Neurological Society (2007-Present); Board of Scientific Advisors, Pituitary Network Association (2006-Present); Organizer, Annual Meeting, The Society of University Neurosurgeons (2018); Member, Board of Directors, Texas Association of Neurological Surgeons (2015-2018); President, Houston Neurological Society (2006-2007, 2015-2017); President, Texas Association of Neurological Surgeons (2012-2013); Secretary, Texas Association of Neurological Surgeons (2009-2012); Member, Bylaws Committee, Society for Neuro-Oncology (2003-2010); Vice President, Texas Association of Neurological Surgeons (2006-2007); President, Pituitary Network Association (2003-2006); International Committee, Congress of Neurological Surgeons (1997-2001); Residents Committee, Congress of Neurological Surgeons (1997-2001); Publications Committee, American Association of Neurological Surgeons (1994-2001); Young Neurosurgeons' Committee, American Association of Neurological Surgeons (1994-1998); Liaison to Board of Trustees, American Association of Neurological Surgeons (1995-1996); Chairman, Young Neurosurgeons' Committee, American Association of Neurological Surgeons (1995-1996); Fellow, Royal College of Surgeons of Canada (1992); Fellow, American College of Surgeons (2008); President, Fellows' Society, Montreal Neurological Institute (1990-1991); Elected Member of American Academy of Neurological Surgery (2017) and of the Society of University Neurosurgeons (2012) **MH:** Albert Nelson Marquis Lifetime Achievement Award (2017) **H:** Travel; Art; Book Collecting; Theater **RE:** Methodist **BA:** 1400 Holcombe Blvd, FC7.2016, Houston, TX, 77030 **ADD:** 1128 Harvard St, Houston, TX, 77008

MCEVOY, SHARLENE ANN, T: Law Educator **I:** Education/Educational Services **DOB:** 07/06/1950 **PB:** Derby **SC:** CT/USA **PT:** Peter Henry McEvoy, Jr.; Madaline Elizabeth (McCabe) McEvoy **ED:** PhD, University of California, Los Angeles (1985); MA, University of California, Los Angeles (1982); MA, Trinity College, Hartford, CT (1980); JD, University of Connecticut, West Hartford, CT (1975); BA, Albertus Magnus College, Magna Cum Laude (1972) **C:** Professor of Business Law, Fairfield University (1998-Present); Director of Pre-Law Advising, Fairfield University (2012-2016); Associate Professor of Law, Fairfield University (1992-1998); Adjunct Professor of Business Law, Dolan School of Business, Fairfield University, CT (1986-1992); Private Practice, Derby, CT (1984-1999); Adjunct Professor of Business Law and Political Science, University of Connecticut, Stamford, CT (1984-1986); Acting Chairman, Political Science Department, Albertus Magnus College (1980); Adjunct Professor of Business Law and Political Science, Albertus Magnus College, New Haven, CT (1978-1980) **CR:** Chairman, Women's Resource Center, Fairfield University (1989-1991) **CIV:** Vice President, NEALSB (2006-Present); President, NEALSB (2008-2009); Program Chair, NEALSB (2007-2008); President, NEALSB (2003-2004); Vice President, NEALSB (2001-2002); Corresponding Secretary, Woodbury Democratic Town Committee (1996-1998); Alternate Member, Parks & Recreation Commission, Woodbury, CT (1995-1999); Treasurer, Woodbury Democratic Town Committee (1995-1996); Justice of the Peace, City of Derby Connecticut (1975-1983); Board of Directors, Valley Transit District, Derby, CT (1975-1977); Active, Derby Tercentenary Commission (1973-1974) **CW:** Editor-in-chief, North East Journal of Legal Studies (2003-Present); Staff Editor, American Business Law Journal (1995-1997); Senior Articles Editor, North East Journal of Legal Studies (1995-1996); Staff Editor, Journal of Legal Studies Education (1989-1994); Reviewer, American Business Law Journal (1988-1993) **AW:** Research Grantee, Fairfield University (1994); Research Grantee, Fairfield University School of Business (1991-1992); Best Paper Award, Tri-State Regional Business Law Association, ALSB (1991); Best Paper Award, Northeast Regional Business Law Association, ALSB (1990); Research Grantee, Fairfield University School of Business (1989) **MEM:** Coordinator, SINISTRAL Special Interest Group, Mensa International Limited (1977-Present); ABA; Connecticut Bar Association; ALSB **BAR:** Connecticut State Bar (1975) **MH:** Albert Nelson Marquis Lifetime Achievement Award (2017) **H:** Sailing; Swimming **PA:** Democrat **RE:** Roman Catholic **ADD:** 324 Church Hill Rd, Woodbury, CT, 06798

MCFADDEN, P. MICHAEL, T: Physician, Surgeon **I:** Medicine & Health Care **DOB:** 06/16/1946 **PB:** Hobbs **SC:** NM/USA **PT:** Paul Marion McFadden; Venita Lenora (Bowen) McFadden **MS:** Married **SPN:** Jennifer Marie James (4/8/1990) **CH:** Heather Anne; Jennifer Suzanne; Bryn Ellen; Callan Michael **ED:** Surgical Intern, Resident, Tulane University School of Medicine, New Orleans, LA (1974-1979); MD, Tulane University (1974); BS, Louisiana State University (1968) **CT:** Diplomate, American Board of Surgery, Inc.; Diplomate, The American Board of Thoracic Surgery **C:** Professor, Cardiothoracic Surgery, Surgical Director, Lung Transplantation, Keck School of Medicine of USC (2006-Present); Clinical Professor, Surgery, Tulane University School of Medicine (1991-Present); Director, Thoracic Surgery Program, Ochsner Clinic Foundation (1998-2006); Surgical Director, Lung Transplantation, Ochsner Clinic Foundation (1991-2006); Cardiovascular and Thoracic Surgeon, Ochsner Clinic Foundation (1991-2006); Chief, Cardiovascular Surgery, Palo Alto Medical Foundation Clinics, California (1983-1991); Cardiovascular and Thoracic Surgeon, Stanford University Medical Center, California (1981-1991); Resident, Thoracic Surgery, Ochsner Clinic Foundation, New Orleans, LA (1979-1981); Instructor, Surgery, Tulane University School of Medicine, New Orleans, LA (1974-1979); Thoracic Surgery Section Head Expert, Heart and Lungs Transplant; Thoracic Surgery Section Head, Huntington Hospital, Pasadena, CA **CIV:** Board of Governors, Tulane University School of Medicine (2010-Present); Board of Directors, Campus Health, Tulane University (2006-2010); Board of Directors, Palo Alto Family YMCA (1988-1991); Chairman, OneLegacy OPO, Los Angeles, CA; Thoracic Surgery Division Chair, Huntington Hospital **MIL:** Captain, U.S. Naval Reserve (1984-1994) **CW:** Member, Editorial Board, Chest Disease Reports (2010-Present); Member, Editorial Board, Journal of Thoracic and Cardiovascular Surgery (2011-Present); Contributor, Articles, Professional Journals **AW:** Berne Teaching Award (2014); Outstanding Alumnus Award, Tulane University School of Medicine (2012); Teaching Award, LAC+USC Medical Center (2010); Teaching Award, Keck School of Medicine of USC (2010); Hurst B. Hatch Memorial Teaching Award, Ochsner Clinic Foundation (1995); Tiki Award, Southern Surgical Associate (1994); Named One of the Top Doctors, Pasadena Magazines, New Orleans, LA; Named, Top Surgeons; Named, Best Doctors **MEM:** Fellow, American College of Surgeons; Fellow, American College of Cardiology Foundation; Fellow, American College of Chest Physicians; American Medical Association; Alton Ochsner Surgical Society; American Association for Thoracic Surgery; American Association for Vascular Surgery; Society for Vascular Surgery; American Society of Transplant Surgeons; Council on Cardiovascular Surgery, American Heart Association, Inc.; AMSUS, The Society of Federal Health Professionals; The International Society for Minimally Invasive Cardiothoracic Surgery; International Society for Heart & Lung Transplantation; Norman E. Shumway Surgical Society; Pacific Coast Surgical Association; Southern Surgical Association; STSA; The Thoracic Surgery Foundation; Tulane University Surgical Society; Tulane Medical Alumni Association; The Western Thoracic Surgical Association; Alpha Omega Alpha; Alpha Epsilon Delta; Nu Sigma Nu; Kappa Alpha **MH:** Albert Nelson Marquis Lifetime Achievement Award (2017) **H:** Hunting; Fishing; Weightlifting; Sailing; Golf **PA:** Republican **RE:** Presbyterian **ADD:** 5276 Gould Ave, La Canada Flintridge, CA, 91011

MCFEE, RICHARD, T: Electrical Engineer **I:** Engineering **DOB:** 01/24/1925 **PB:** Pittsburgh **SC:** PA/USA **PT:** William McFee; Beatrice (Allender) McFee **MS:** Married **SPN:** JoanEllen Lewis (December 31, 1974); Anne Stauffer, Divorced (1960) **ED:** Doctor of Philosophy in Electrical Engineering, University of Michigan (1955); MS in Physics, Syracuse University (1949); BEE, Yale University (1947) **C:** Independent Researcher, Hawi, HI (1986-2015); Independent Researcher, Union Springs, NY (1982-1986); Professor of Electrical Engineering, Syracuse University (1957-1982); Member, Technical Staff, Bell Telephone Laboratories, Whippany, NJ (1952-1957); Engineer, Electro-Mechanical Research Inc., Ridgefield, CT (1951-1952); Research Associate, University of Michigan Medical School (1949-1951); Instructor, Electrical Engineering Department Syracuse University (1948-1949); Research Assistant, Syracuse University Medical School (1947-1948) **MIL:** Sergeant, US Army (1943-1946) **CW:** Contributor, Articles on Electronics, Electrocardiography, Magnetocardiography, Superconductivity, Circuit Theory, Thermodynamics and Electrical Measurements; Patentee in Field; Contributor, Scientific Papers **AW:** Science Faculty Fellowship, National Science Foundation, Stanford University (1970) **MEM:** Emeritus Fellow, The Institute of Electrical and Electronics; American Association for the Advancement of Science; Sigma Xi **MH:** Marquis Who's Who Lifetime Achievement Award (2017) **H:** Hiking in the Adirondack mountains and the North Kohala coast on the Island of Hawaii **ADD:** P.O. Box 989, Kapaau, HI, 96755

MCGANN, LISA B. NAPOLI, T: English as a Second Language Teacher **I:** Education/Educational Services **CN:** LaGuardia Community College, City University of New York **SC:** CT/USA **PT:** James Lee Napoli **MS:** Married **SPN:** Edward Harrison McGann, Jr. **ED:** Postgraduate Coursework, Columbia University (1991-1995); MA, Middlebury College (1987); MA, Columbia University (1983); BA, Vassar College (1980) **CT:** Certified Teacher in French, English as a Second Language, and Italian, State of Connecticut **C:** English as a Second Language Instructor, LaGuardia Community College, City University of New York, Long Island City, NY (1983-Present); Assistant Director, English as a Second Language, Fordham University (1988-1989); English as a Second Language Instructor, Columbia University (1983-1996); Manager, English Teaching Committee, New York Junior League (1983-1984); Community English Program Coordinator, Teachers College, Columbia University (1982-1983) **CR:** Specialist, English as a Second Language Teacher, United Nations, New York, NY (1990); Instructor, English as a Second Language, Yale University (1988-1989) **CIV:** English as Second Language Teacher, Boys & Girls Club, Astoria, NY (1992); Big Sister, Highland Heights, New Haven, CT (1976-1977) **AW:** Awards and Scholarships **MEM:** TESOL International Association; Italian Historical Society of America; Council, National Italian American Foundation; The Statue of Liberty - Ellis Island Foundation, Inc. **MH:** Albert Nelson Marquis Lifetime Achievement Award (2017) **H:** Ballet; Reading; Travel; Real estate; Tennis **RE:** Roman Catholic **ADD:** 4122 42nd Street, Apt 1D, Long Island City, NY, 11104

MCGILL, SCOTT DOUGLAS, T: Information Services Executive, Consultant **I:** Consulting **DOB:** 09/24/1946 **PB:** Meadville **SC:** PA/USA **PT:** Gaylord Arthur McGill; Margaret Annetta (Kebert) McGill **MS:** Married **SPN:** Cathleen Ann Chaffin (11/28/1970) **CH:** Kelly Meghan; Kerry Shannon **ED:** MBA in Information Systems, University of Colorado (1985); MA in Computer Systems Management, University of Nebraska (1972); BS in Meteorology and Oceanography, New York University (1971); BS in Mathematics, Allegheny College (1968) **CT:** Certificate in Data Processing **C:** Director of Administrative Information Services, Michigan State University (1987-2012); Executive Director of Information Resources Management, Medical University of South Carolina, Charleston, SC (1986-1987); Director of Data Processing, City of Colorado Springs, Colorado (1975-1986); Manager of Programming and Design, City of Colorado Springs, Colorado (1975-1976); Senior Systems Analyst, Sperry Univac Company, Colorado Springs, Colorado (1973-1975); Systems Analyst, Sperry Univac Company, Washington (1972-1973); Systems Analyst, U.S. Air Force (1968-1972); Program Designer, U.S. Air Force (1968-1972) **CR:** Member, Executive Board, Medical Supercomputer Consortium (1986-1987); Member, Electronic Computing Health Oriented (1986-

1987); Member, Higher Education Computer Advisory Committee, South Carolina Commission (1986-1987) **CIV:** Children's Fund, Medical University of South Carolina (1987-1988); Business Advisory Council, Computer Training for Severely Handicapped, Denver, CO (1981-1988); Board of Directors, Goodwill Industries, Denver, CO (1981-1988); Colorado Commission on Children and their Families, Denver, CO (1983-1986); Trustee, Pikes Peak Library District, Colorado Springs, CO (1983-1986); Executive Board of Directors, Pikes Peak Council, Boy Scouts of America (1979-1986); Board of Directors, Goodwill Industries, Colorado Springs, CO (1982-1986); Chairman, Administrative Board, Calvary United Methodist Church, Colorado Springs, CO (1980-1983); Volunteer English Instructor, Poland; Volunteer English Instructor, Spain **MIL:** Captain, U.S. Air Force (1968-1972) **AW:** Frank Martin Service Award, CUMREC (1995); Recipient, Diamond Award, Data Processing Management Association (1989); Distinguished Greater Colorado Service Award, Denver Federal Executive Board (1980); Recipient, Outstanding Contributions to Data Processing Award (1978); Recipient, York Rite, Masons; Honoree, Kentucky Colonel; Honoree, Tennessee Squire **MEM:** Information Systems Advisory Committee, Lansing Community College (1998-Present); Lieutenant Governor, Michigan District 18, Kiwanis (1992-1993); Board of Directors, East Lansing Chapter, Kiwanis (1990-1992); Lifetime Member of Alpha Chapter, Board of Directors House Corp. Iota Chapter, Delta Tau Delta (1989-1990); Executive Board Member, MEDCOMP Medical Consortium (1986-1987); Executive Committee, South Carolina Association Data Processing Directors (1986-1987); International Director, Southern Colorado Chapter, Data Processing Management Association (1983-1986); Chairman, American Public Power Association (1985); Gold Individual Performance Award, Data Processing Management Association (1985); Former President, Pikes Peak Chapter, Kiwanis (1984); Chapter Chairman, Society for Information Management (1983); Chairman, Rocky Mountain Chapter, Society for Information Management (1983); Chairman, Rocky Mountain Association of Local Governmental Computer Users (1981-1982); Director, Colorado Information Management Council (1981-1982); Individual Silver Performance Award, Data Processing Management Association (1981); Board of Directors, Rocky Mountain Club (1981); President, Data Processing Management Association (1978); Individual Performance Award, Data Processing Management Association (1978); Outstanding Contributions to Data Processing in Local Government Award, Colorado Information Management Council (1978); Chapter Member of the Year, Data Processing Management Association (1977-1978); Chairman, Pikes Peak Chapter, Association for Computing Machinery (1977-1978); American Management Association; Charter Member, Association Institute for Certification Computer Profiles; Association for Systems Management; American Society for Public Administration; Univac Users' Association; Higher Education Network Association; Associate, IEEE; College and University Machine Records Conference, South Carolina Commission on Higher Education; Higher Education Network Association; James Island Yacht Club; Ducks Unlimited; Winter Night Club; Tuesday Afternoon Rest and Aspiration Club, Colorado Springs, CO; Elks; Board of Directors, Kiwanis International; Foundation Trustee, Kiwanis International; Master Mason; Board of Directors, Michigan Information Technology Network; Scholarship Chair, Michigan Information Technology Network; Board of Directors, Michigan Commanders Club; EAT; Breakfast Club Organizer, Retiree Association, Michigan State University; Division Vice President, Delta Tau Delta; Adviser to the Board of Directors, International Order of the Rocky Mountain Goats; Admiral, Nebraska Navy; Ducks Unlimited; Beaumont Tower Society; Ambassador, MakerMark; NAAG; American Council of Spotted Asses **MH:** Albert Nelson Marquis Lifetime Achievement Award (2017) **PA:** Republican **RE:** Methodist **ADD:** 524 Rosewood Ave, East Lansing, MI, 48823

MCGREGOR, MARGARET A., T: Independent Business Owner **I:** Business Management/Business Services **CN:** Elementary Success, LLC **ED:** Doctorate in Management, Concentration in Environmental and Social Sustainability, Colorado Technical University (2014); Master's Degree in Strategic Studies, Air War College (1999); Master's Degree in Logistics Business Systems Management, Colorado Technical University (1996); Master's Degree in International Relations, Troy University European Campus (1992) **MH:** Distinguished Humanitarian (2017) **H:** Spoiling her seven grandchildren; Travel **BA:** 16 Luxury Lane, Elementary Success, LLC, Colorado Springs, CO, 80921 **ADD:** 9321 Sibelius Home Drive, Vienna, VA, 22182 **URL:** http://myserenigy.com/elementarysuccess

MCGUIRE, SANDRA LYNN, T: Nursing Educator **I:** Medicine & Health Care **DOB:** 01/28/1947 **PB:** Flint **SC:** MI/USA **PT:** Donald Armstrong Johnson; Mary Lue (Harvey) Johnson **MS:** Widow **SPN:** Joseph L. McGuire (3/6/1976, Deceased) **CH:** Matthew; Kelly; Kerry **ED:** MSN, Emory University (1997); EdD, University of Tennessee (1988); MPH, University of Michigan (1973); BSN, University of Michigan (1969) **C:** Assistant Dean, Professor, Caylor School of Nursing, Lincoln Memorial University (2009-2014); Emeritus Professor, The University of Tennessee, Knoxville, TN (2009); Coordinator Gerontology, The University of Tennessee, Knoxville, TN (2008-2009); Professor, The University of Tennessee, Knoxville, TN (2007-2009); Chair, MSN Program, College of Nursing, The University of Tennessee, Knoxville, TN (2002-2009); Associate Professor, The University of Tennessee, Knoxville, TN (1990-2007); Coordinator Gerontological Nurse Practitioners Program, The University of Tennessee, Knoxville, TN (1998-2006); Assistant Professor, The University of Tennessee, Knoxville, TN (1983-1988); Assistant Professor, University of Michigan, Ann Arbor, MI (1975-1983); Public Health Coordinator, Plymouth Center for Human Development, Northville, MI (1974-1975); Instructor, Madonna University, Livonia, MI (1973); Public Health Nurse, Wayne County Health Department, Eloise, MI (1969-1972); Staff Nurse, University Hospital, Ann Arbor, MI (1969) **CR:** Director, Kids are Tomorrow's Seniors Program (1988-Present); Member, AARP National Policy Council (2006-2012); Member, Council on Accreditation, Nurse Anesthesia Educational Programs (2007-2010); Resource Person, Governor's Committee, Unification of Mental Health Services in Michigan; Speaker, Professional Associations; Speaker, Workshops **CIV:** Member, National Policy Council, AARP (2006-2012); Vice President, Paul F. Glenn Center for Aging Research (1995); Founder, Knoxville Intergenerational Network (1989); Board of Directors, Paul F. Glenn Center for Aging Research (1987-1993); Board of Directors, Knoxville Chapter, The American National Red Cross (1984-1985); Board of Directors, Michigan Chapter, The American National Red Cross (1980-1983) **CW:** Author, "Growing Up and Growing Older: Annotated Bibliography of Early Children's Literature" (2015); Contributor, "The Encyclopedia of Ageism" (2005); Co-Author, "Comprehensive Community Health Nursing, Sixth Edition" (2002); Co-Author, "Comprehensive Community Health Nursing, Fifth Edition" (1998); Contributor, "Violence, Neglect and the Elderly" (1996); Contributor, "A Multidisciplinary Treatment Program for the Preschool-aged Exceptional Child" (1986); Co-Author, "Comprehensive Community Health Nursing" (1981) **AW:** Mildred Selzer Service Award, Association for Gerontology in Higher Education (2018); Outstanding Service Award, Library Society, The University of Tennessee, Knoxville, TN (2004); John W. Runyan Jr. Community Health Nursing Award, The University of Tennessee Health Science Center (2002); Professional Development Award, The University of Tennessee, Knoxville, TN (1999-2000); Hewlett Innovative Technology Fellow, The University of Tennessee, Knoxville, TN (1999-2000); Robert Woodruff Fellow, Emory University (1996-1997); Professional Development Award, The University of Tennessee, Knoxville, TN (1996-1997); Book of the Year Award, American Journal of Nursing (1987, 1991); United States Public Health Service Fellow (1972-1973) **MEM:** Intergenerational Committee, Association for Gerontology in Higher Education (2010-Present); Board Member, Senior Citizens Home Assistance Service, Inc. (2009-Present); K12 Committee, Association for Gerontology in Higher Education (2008-Present); Book Awards Subcommittee, Association for Gerontology in Higher Education (2008-Present); Fellow, Association for Gerontology in Higher Education (2013); Chairman, Health Services, Michigan Public Health Association (1979-1982); Co-Chairman, Residential Services Committee, Michigan ARL (1976-1979); Plymouth ARC (1975-1977); Chairman, Mental Health Section, Michigan Public Health Association (1976); American Nurses Association, Inc.; Southern Gerontological Society; Tennessee Nurses Association; NGNA; The Arc; Michigan ARC; The Arc of Tennessee; ARC Knox County; ARC Detroit; Sigma Theta Tau; Pi Lambda Theta; Phi Kappa Phi **MH:** Albert Nelson Marquis Lifetime Achievement Award (2017) **ADD:** 11008 Crosswind Dr, Knoxville, TN, 37934 **URL:** http://www.sandralmcguire.com

MCKEEL, LILLIAN PHILLIPS, T: Retired Education Educator **I:** Education/Educational Services **DOB:** 08/23/1932 **PB:** Rocky Mount **SC:** NC/USA **PT:** Ellis Elma Phillips; Lillian Bonner (Archbell) Phillips **MS:** Widowed **SPN:** James Thomas McKeel, Jr. (07/23/1955, Deceased) **CH:** Sarah Lillian McKeel-Abbott; Mary Kathleen McKeel-Welch **ED:** EDd, Pennsylvania State University (1993); MEd, Pennsylvania State University (1978); Coursework, The Woman's College of North Carolina (Now University of North Carolina, Greensboro) (1954) **C:** Retired (2001); Assistant Professor, Shippensburg University, PA (1993-2001); Instructor, Pennsylvania State University, University Park, PA (1990-1993); Teacher, State College Area School District, Pennsylvania (1964-1990) **CR:** Faculty Sponsor, School Study Council, Shippensburg University (1993-1995); Book Review Panel, Outstanding Science Trade Books for Students K–12, NSTA (1992) **CW:** Contributor, Articles, Professional Journals; Writer, Curriculum **AW:** Achieving Women Award, Pennsylvania State University (1993); Distinguished Service Award, Phi Delta Kappa International (1992); Finalist, Teacher of the Year Program, Pennsylvania Department of Education, Harrisburg, PA (1991); Presidential Award for Excellence in Science and Mathematics Teaching, National Science Foundation (1990) **MEM:** NSTA; Society of Elementary Presidential Awardees; The Association for Science Teacher Education; Council for Elementary Science International; Phi Delta Kappa International; Pi Lambda Theta; The

Honor Society of Phi Kappa Phi **MH:** Albert Nelson Marquis Lifetime Achievement Award (2017) **H:** Photography; Collecting antique toys **ADD:** 300 Lion's Hill Road, State College, PA, 16803

MCKOWN, MARTHA, **T:** Minister (Retired), Writer **I:** Religious **DOB:** 05/29/1933 **PB:** Dixie **SC:** KY/USA **PT:** John William Powell; Dora Ellen (Melton) Powell **MS:** Married **SPN:** Leslie Henry McKown (6/22/1957) **CH:** Karen Marie McKown; Liana Jane McKown Edenfield **ED:** MDiv, Christian Theological Seminary School of Theology (1978); MA in Religious Education, Boston University (1957); AB in English, Evansville College (1955) **CT:** Ordained Elder, United Methodist Church (1979) **C:** Pastor, St. Paul United Methodist Church, Poseyville, IN (1985-1989); Pastor, Faith United Methodist Church, Princeton, IN, (1982-1985); Associate Pastor, Trinity United Methodist Church, Evansville, IN (1980-1982); Pastor, East Park United Methodist Church, Indianapolis, IN (1979-1980); Director, Christian Education, Maple Street United Methodist Church (1975-1976); Director, Christian Education, Temple United Methodist Church, Terre Haute, IN (1973-1975); Director, Christian Education, Maple Street Congregational Church, Danvers, MA (1957-1958) **CR:** Minister of Pastoral Care, First United Methodist Church, Henderson, KY (2003-2007); Teacher, North and South Indiana Conferences, DePauw University Pastor's School **CIV:** South Indiana Conference, United Methodist Historical Society (2000-2003); President, Joint Archives North and South Indiana Conferences (1998-1999); Archives and History Committee Member, Southern Insurance Conference (1996-2004); Representative, Red Bird Missionary Conference (1995-2002); Board of Directors, Evansville United Methodist Youth Home (1994-2002); Pastoral Counselor, Pike County Hospice, IN (1993-1996); Southern Indiana Conference Member, United Methodist Church **CW:** Author, "An Elephant Story for Alex" (2009); Author, "Palm Sunday Parade" (1995); Contributor, Articles to Various Publications **MEM:** President, Browning Club (1996-1997); President, Member Ohio Valley Writers Guild, Princeton Ministerial Association (1984); Tri-State Genealogical Society; Woman's Club **MH:** Albert Nelson Marquis Lifetime Achievement Award (2017) **H:** Gardening; Swimming; Walking; Reading; Genealogy **PA:** Democrat **ADD:** 425 Old Barn Ct, Henderson, KY, 42420

MCLAREN, ALFRED SCOTT, **T:** Captain (Retired) **I:** Military & Defense Services **CN:** U.S. Navy **DOB:** 08/09/1932 **PB:** Lake Arrowhead **SC:** CA/USA **PT:** Captain William Fleming McLaren (Deceased); Marta Antonia Brennan (Deceased) **MS:** Married **SPN:** Avery Battle Russell **CH:** Alfred Scott McLaren, Jr.; Margot Anne Scott McLaren; Erin Eisenhower McLaren; John Bandini McLaren **ED:** PhD, University of Colorado, Boulder (1986); MA, Cambridge University, England; MS, The George Washington University; BS, U.S. Naval Academy **CT:** Certified, Chief Pilot, Super Aviator, Deep-Diving Submersible; Certified, Instrument Rated Private Pilot; Certified in SCUBA **C:** U.S. Navy Submarine Officer, University of Colorado and Columbia University **CR:** Test Flew/Chief Pilot, Super Aviator (2015); Diver, Two Dives on the Titanic **CIV:** Rotary Club **MIL:** Diving Officer, Navigator, Chief Engineer, Executive Officer, Nuclear Attack Submarines; Commanding Officer, USS Queenfish (SSN 651); Commanding Officer, U.S. Naval Underwater Systems Center **CW:** Author, "Unknown Waters: A First-Hand Account of the Historic Under-Ice Survey of the Siberian Continental Shelf by USS Queenfish (SSN 651)"; Author, "Silent and Unseen, On Patrol in Three Cold War Attack Submarines"

AW: The Explorers Club Medal, The Explorers Club (2012); The Lowell Thomas Medal, The Explorers Club (2000); Distinguished Service Medal; Two Legions of Merit; Meritorious Service Medal; Navy Commendation Medal **MEM:** President Emeritus, American Polar Society; President Emeritus, The Explorers Club; Science News; Submarine Aviation Systems; University of Alabama Press; U.S. Naval Institute Press **MH:** Albert Nelson Marquis Lifetime Achievement Award (2017) **H:** Reading; Writing; Classical music; Traveling **PA:** Democrat **RE:** Roman Catholic **BA:** PO Box 3120, Nederland, CO, 80466 **ADD:** 73 Aspen Meadows Rd, P.O.Box 3120, Nederland, CO, 80466

MCLEAN, ROY LEE, **T:** Associate Professor **I:** Education/Educational Services **CN:** Ferris State University **DOB:** 07/15/1965 **PB:** Fayetteville **SC:** NC/USA **PT:** Houston McLean; Genevieve McLean (Stepmother) **ED:** PhD in Economics, University of South Carolina (1994); BA in Economics, University of South Carolina (1987) **C:** Associate Professor, Ferris State University, Big Rapids, MI (2001-Present); Assistant Professor, University of Central Arkansas, Conway, AR (1997-2001); Visiting Assistant Professor, University of Louisiana at Lafayette (1994-1997) **AW:** 15-Year Service Award, Ferris State University **MEM:** Alpha Sigma Phi; American Economics Association **ADD:** 318 Morrison Street, Apt. 10, Big Rapids, MI, 49307 **URL:** http://ferris.edu/business/faculty-staff/roy-mclean

MCNAIR, MARCIA L., **T:** Associate Professor, Writer, Editor **I:** Education/Educational Services **CN:** Nassau Community College **ED:** MA in Writing, New York University, New York City, NY (1989); BA in English, Dartmouth College, With Honors, Hanover, NH (1980) **C:** Associate Professor, English Department, Nassau Community College, Garden City, NY (1995-Present); Adjunct Lecturer, English Department, Molloy College, Rockville Center, NY (1998-2006); Adjunct Lecturer, English Department, York College (1994-1995); Program Coordinator, Instructor, LaGuardia Community College (1991-1993); Instructor, Basic Education, GED, York College Adult Learning Center (1989-1991); Instructor, Malcolm-King Harlem College Extension, Marymount Manhattan College (1988-1989); Assistant Program Coordinator, Institute of Afro-American Affairs, New York University (1984-1987) **CR:** Member, Women's Studies Project (2008-Present); Educational Consultant, African American Museum, Hempstead, NY (2005-Present); Member, Black History Month Committee (1998-Present); Lecturer, Nassau Community College (2006); Workshop Facilitator (2005); Chair, Scholarship Committee, African American Latino Asian American Native American Faculty Alliance (2000-2015); Co-Coordinator, African American Read-In, Nassau Community College (2000-2014); Women's Center Discussion Leader (1998-2008) **CIV:** Coordinator, Nassau Community College, National African American Read In, Garden City, New York (2002-2015) Executive Director and Founder, Long Island Girl Talk **CW:** Author, "The Incident-Black Lives Have Always Mattered" (2017); Co-Author, "Sistas on Fire! A Newsical," Shades of Truth Theatre Company, New York, NY (2008-2009); Arts and Entertainment Editor, "Lakeview Community News" (2006-2008); Co-Advisor, The Vignette (1998-2000); Chairperson, Monograph Series Editorial Committee, Institute of Afro-American Affairs, New York University (1987-1989); Assistant Editor, Essence Magazine, New York City, NY (1980-1983); Author, "E-Males"; Creative Director, "Diary of a Mad Black Feminist"; Contributor, Essays; Contributor, Articles, Professional Journals **AW:**

Finalist, New York International Theater Festival (2017); Grantee, AAUW (2016); Community Service Award, New Hempstead Democratic Club (2015); Women of Distinction Award, Learning Circle for Children (2015); Certificate of Recognition, Hempstead Township (2014); NCC Professional Development Award (2014); Grantee, Women's Fund of Long Island (2013-2014); Nassau County Legislature Citation, Women's History Month (2010); Finalist, Long Island Fringe Festival (2010); Semi-Finalist, Illuminating Artists New Works Festival, New York, NY (2010); NCCFT Certificate of Recognition, CARES (2008); Recognition, Nassau County Legislature (2007); Grantee, Long Island Arts Council at Freeport (2006-2007); Honorable Mention, The National New Millennium Writers Creative Nonfiction Contest (2003); Two Citations in Black Studies, Dartmouth College; Citation in Shakespearean Studies, Dartmouth College **MEM:** AAUW (1997-Present); African Latino Asian Faculty Association, Nassau Community College (1990-Present); Sigma Delta Chi (1985-Present); Schomburg Center for Research in Black Culture; Association of Black Women in Higher Education; Long Island Writers Guild **MH:** Albert Nelson Marquis Lifetime Achievement Award (2017) **ADD:** 1201 Birch St, Uniondale, NY, 11553

MCNELLY, FREDERICK W. JR., **T:** Psychologist **I:** Medicine & Health Care **CN:** Self-Employed **DOB:** 04/14/1947 **PB:** Bangor **SC:** ME/USA **PT:** Frederick Wright; E. Frances (Cutter) McNelly **MS:** Single **CH:** Roger; Joseph; Ronald; Michael; Jeffrey; Jeremy **ED:** PhD, University of Michigan (1973); MA, University of Michigan (1971); BA, University of Minnesota, Magna Cum Laude (1969) **CT:** Professional Qualification in Psychology; Registered Clinical Psychologist, State of Illinois **C:** Early Intervention Program Provider, Illinois (1995-2007); Consultant Psychologist (1986-2000); Program Director, Children's Development Center, Rockford, IL (1982-1986); Director of Psychological Services, Children's Development Center, Rockford, IL (1972-1982); Trainee, United States Public Health Service, University of Minnesota (1972); Educational Examiner, Ann Arbor Public Schools (1971); Teaching Fellow of Psychology, University of Michigan, Ann Arbor, MI (1970-1972); Trainee, United States Public Health Service, University of Minnesota (1969-1970); Laboratory Instructor, University of Minnesota (1969); Research Coordinator, National Science Foundation Project, University of Minnesota (1968-1969) **CR:** Mental Health Consultant, Access Services, Rockford, IL (2000-Present); Contractual Service Provider, St. Illinois Department of Children and Family Services (1995-Present); Rockford Head Start (1982-Present); Mental Health Consultant, Access Services, Mendota, IL (1992-2000); Blackhawk Region (1986-1992); Member, Health Services Advisory Committee, Human Resources Committee, City of Rockford (1985-2015); Full Time, Private Practice of Psychology, Beloit, WI (1985-1986); Part Time, Private Practice of Psychology (1980-1986); Lecturer, Rock Valley College (1974-1975); Presenter, State and Regional Workshops and Conferences; United Cerebral Palsy **CIV:** Big Brothers Big Sisters of America (2004-2009); Stronghold Renovation Session Committee, Presbytery Blackhawk (1985); Elder, Willow Creek United Presbyterian Church (1980-1983); Co-Chairman, Winnebago County Child Protection Association (1980); Boy Scouts of America (1978-1983); Chairman, Special Education Regional Advisory Committee, Bi-County Office of Education (1976-1978); Member, National and Illinois Committee of Child Abuse (1975-1985) **CW:** Contributor, Articles to Professional Journals **AW:** Recipient, 202nd Membership Grant, The

Association of State and Provincial Psychology Boards (1998); Recipient, Outstanding Young Man of the Year Award, United States Junior Chamber of Commerce (1977); Recipient, Certificate of Professional Qualifications in Psychology **MEM:** President, Northern Illinois Private Practice Mental Health Association (1994-1995); Vice President, Northern Illinois Private Practice Mental Health Association (1993); Illinois Association Infant Mental Health; National Alliance on Mentally Illness; National Association for the Mentally Ill; National Association for Disability Examiners; National Registry, Health Service Psychology; Northern Illinois Psychological Association; Illinois Psychological Association; Council for Exceptional Children **ADD:** 11591 Beverly Ln, Belvidere, IL, 61008-8708

MCNULTY, KATHLEEN, T: Private Practice **I:** Health, Wellness and Fitness **DOB:** 10/06/1958 **PB:** Hackensack **SC:** NJ/USA **PT:** Alfred Edward McNulty; Gertrude Natalie (Currie) McNulty **MS:** Married **SPN:** Henry Stanislaw Kowal (9/16/1988) **CH:** Eryn; Kelsey; Shawn **ED:** Postgraduate Coursework, Fielding Graduate Institute (2001-2009); MSW, Smith College (1984); BA, Rutgers, The State University of New Jersey (1980) **CT:** Lisensed Psychologist (1998-Present); Licensed Marriage and Family Therapist; Licensed Clinical Social Worker **C:** Private Practice, Teaching, Fairleigh Dickinson University Integrated Healthcare (2012-Present); Private Practice, Ridgewood, NJ (1999-Present); Private Practice, Rutherford, NJ (1987-1999); Clinical Social Worker, Cliffwood Mental Health Center, Englewood, New Jersey (1986-1987); Clinical Social Worker, Family Guidance Bergen, Hackensack, NJ (1986-1987); Clinical Social worker, Albert Einstein College of Medicine, Bronx, NY (1984-1986); Mental Health Aide, Belleville Mental Health Clinic, New Jersey (1980-1982); Director of Residential Program, St. Joseph Hospital Medical Center **CR:** Consultant, Meadowlands Weight Control, Rutherford, NJ (1988-Present); Consultant, St. Lukes-Roosevelt Hospital Center, New York, NY (1988) **CIV:** President, Ambulance Corp Emergency Medical Technician **CW:** Contributor, Articles to Professional Journals **MEM:** American Orthopsychiatric Association; Academy of Certified Social Workers; National Association of Social Workers; New Jersey Psychological Association **H:** Painting; Singing; Sports; Poetry **ADD:** 453 Wildwood Road, Northvale, NJ, 07647

MEDLIN, JEFFERY A., T: Project Assistant **I:** Engineering **CN:** United States Army Corp of Engineers **ED:** Pursuing Doctor of Public Administration Degree, University of La Verne, La Verne, CA (2016-Present); Pursuing Master's in Natural Resource Stewardship, Colorado State University, Fort Collins, CO (2016-Present); Intern, Construction Engineering Technician, NAVFAC SW, FEAD, Lemoore, CA (2014-2016); Master's in Public Administration, California State University, Fresno (2015); BS in Professional Aeronautics/Management, Embry-Ridale Aeronautical University, Daytona Beach, FL (2006); AA in Humanities, West Hills Community College, Lemoore, CA (2006) **CT:** General Radio and Telephone Operator License with RADAR Endorsement; Certified Journeyman Electronics Mechanic; Certified Journeyman Electronics Tester **C:** Project Assistant, United States Army Corps of Engineers (2016-Present); Engineering Technician, Naval Facilities Engineering Command (2014-2016) **CIV:** Merit Badge Counselor, Boy Scouts of America (2007-Present); Point-in-Time Count Tally Representative, Fresno Madera Continuum of Care, Fresno, CA (2016); District Commissioner's Staff, Kings River District, Sequoia

Council, Boy Scouts of America, Kings County, CA (2007-2013); Naturalist, Preserve Ranger, Sequoia Riverlands Trust, Tulare County, CA (2007-2013); Responder, Disaster Animal Response Team (2009-2011) **MIL:** Command Fitness Leader, U.S. Navy (2012-2014); Supervisor, Manager, Training Coordinator, U.S. Navy (1995-2014); Quality Assurance Specialist, Confined Space Program Entry Authority, U.S. Navy (2010-2014); Career Counselor, U.S. Navy (2004-2006); Avionics Technician, U.S. Navy (1994-2004); Auxiliary Security Force, U.S. Navy (1999-2001) **AW:** Junior White Collar Employee of the Quarter (2015); On the Spot Performance Award (2015); Third Place, Ralph Gates Memorial Day Salute to Veterans Memorial Day Shootout (2004); Commissioner's Arrowhead; Commissioner's Key; Community Organization Award; Military Outstanding Volunteer Award; Navy Achievement Medal; Navy Good Conduct Medals; Korean Defense Service Medal; Global War on Terrorism Expeditionary Medal; Global War on Terrorism Service Medal; Armed Forces Expeditionary Medal; Armed Forces Service Medal; Expert Marksmanship Medal; National Defense Service Medal; NATO Service Medal; Recipient, Six Letters of Commendation; Triple Crown Gold 1000 Award; UltraMarathon Cycling Association Platinum Year-Rounder Award; Larry Schwartz Award, UltraMarathon Cycling Association; R-12 Award, Randonneurs USA; 1000 Distance Award, Randonneurs USA **MEM:** Section on Environmental and Natural Resource Administration, American Society for Public Administration; Association of Pedestrian and Bicycle Professionals; League of American Bicyclists; Association of Natural Resource Professionals; Ultra-Marathon Cycling Association; Southern Sierra Cyclists; Kings County Cyclist; Fresno Cycling Club; Randonneurs USA; Central California Off-Road Cyclists **H:** Bicycling **ADD:** 1208 W Malone St, Hanford, CA, 93230

MEGRUE, GEORGE HENRY, T: Co-founder, Secretary **I:** Education/Educational Services **CN:** Foxglove School, Inc. **DOB:** 03/23/1936 **PB:** Jamaica **SC:** NY/USA **PT:** Enoch Gest Megrue; Mildred Katherine (Marker) Baehr **MS:** Married **SPN:** Suzanne Jacobsen (3/29/1958) **CH:** George Richard; Katherine Diane; Karen Lynn; Kevin Scott (Deceased 5/2013) **ED:** PhD, Geology, Columbia University (1962); MA, Columbia University (1960) AB, Amherst College (1957) **C:** Retired, Scientific Instrument Executive (2015); Co-founder, Foxglove School, Inc., New Canaan, CT (1975-Present); Secretary, Foxglove School, Inc., New Canaan, CT (1975-Present); Founder, Megrue Micro-analytical Systems Co., New Canaan, CT (1974-Present); Chief Executive Officer, Megrue Micro-analytical Systems Co., New Canaan, CT (1974-Present); Research Fellow, Harvard College Observatory, Cambridge, MA (1966-1973); Research Scientist, Smithsonian Astrophysical Observatory, Cambridge, MA (1966-1973); Research Chemist, Brookhaven National Laboratory, Upton, NY (1964-1966); Research Associate, Brookhaven National Laboratory (1962-1964) **CR:** Principal Investigator, NASA Apollo 12, 14, 15 Returned Lunar Samples, (1969-1973); Principal, Investigator, Ethiopian Rift Valley Expedition, National Geographic Society (1969) **CIV:** Co-founder, New Canaan Rotary Lobsterfest (1985); Co-founder, New Canaan Teen Center Inc. (1985); Trustee, New Canaan Historical Society (1985); Co-President, New Canaan High School PTA (1984-1985); Trustee, St. Luke's School, New Canaan, CT (1979-1985); Explorers Club (1974); Trustee, New York Academy Sciences **CW:** Co-Author, "Tectonic History of the Ethiopian Rift as deduced from Potassium - Argon Ages and Paleomagnetic Measurements," Journal of Geophysical Research (1972); Author, "Distribution and Origin

of Primordial Helium and Neon from the Fayetteville and Kapoeta Meteorites," International Symposium on Meteoritic Research, International Atomic Energy Agency, Vienna, Austria (1968); Author, "Age determination of the formation and thermal history of Achondrites and Palasite Meteorites," Journal of Geophysical Research (1965-1969); Co-Author, "Alteration of Sandstone Pipes in Laguna, New Mexico," Geological Society of America (1965, 1968); Author, Scientific Results, Journal of Geophysical Research **AW:** Carole Eisner Award for Sculpture for "Sunrise", 55th Annual Art of the Northeast Juried Exhibition (2004); Honoree, Apollo Lunar Analysis Group, NASA (1969-1973); Honoree, Ethiopian Rift Valley Expedition, National Geographic Society (1969) **MEM:** Local President, Rotary International (1985-1986); Founder, Austrian Summer Exchange, Rotary International (1983); Fellow, American Association for the Advancement of Science; American Geophysical Union; American Chemical Society; The Explorers Club **MH:** Albert Nelson Marquis Lifetime Achievement Award (2017); Distinguished Humanitarian (2017) **H:** Travel; Golf; Sailing; Photography **PA:** Republican **RE:** Presbyterian **ADD:** 140 Oenoke Ridge Rd, New Canaan, CT, 06840 **URL:** http://georgehmegrue.com/

MEHL, ROBERT , I: Machinery **ED:** Hands-on Training; Coursework, Raritan Valley Community College **C:** Chief Machine Mechanic, Bridgewater Wholesalers, Inc. (2012-Present) **CR:** General Repair Work **H:** Raising huskies

MEHTA, LINN CARY, T: Literature Educator **I:** Education/Educational Services **CN:** Gallatin School of Individualized Study, New York University **DOB:** 08/08/1955 **PB:** Chicago **SC:** IL/USA **PT:** William Lucius Cary; Katherine L.F. (Cooper) Cary **MS:** Married **SPN:** Ved Mehta (12/17/1983) **CH:** Alexandra Sage; Natasha Cary **ED:** PhD in Comparative Literature, Columbia University (2004); MPhil in Comparative Literature, Columbia University (1989); MA in English, University of Oxford (1979); BA in English, Yale University, New Haven, CT (1977); BA in French, Yale University, New Haven, CT (1977) **C:** Instructor, Gallatin School of Individualized Study, New York University (2012-Present); Lecturer, English Department, Barnard College, New York, NY (2000-Present); Fellow, The Heyman Center of the Humanities, Columbia University (2008); Instructor, Adjunct Assistant Professor, English Department, Vassar College, Poughkeepsie, NY (1994-1997); Instructor, Yale University, New Haven, CT (1993); Preceptor, Columbia University, New York, NY (1990-1991); Assistant Program Officer, Ford Foundation, New York, NY (1982-1985); Assistant to the President, Ford Foundation, New York, NY (1980-1982) **CR:** Board Secretary, Wrexham Foundation Inc, New Haven, CT (2010-Present); Literature Advisor, "Trilogy for Juan Rulfo," ID Studio Theater Performance and Research Group, Theater for the New City (2009-2014); President, "Allende," ID Studio Theater Performance and Research Group, Theater for the New City (2006); Board Chairperson, American Friends of St. Hilda's, Boston, MA (1995-2002); Board Secretary, Wrexham Foundation Inc, New Haven, CT (1988-1994) **CIV:** Library Associate, Yale University, New Haven, CT (2011-Present); Member, Board of Directors, American Friends of the National Portrait Gallery, London, England (2008-Present); Member, Board of Directors, Goddard Riverside Community Center (2007-Present); Member, Board of Directors, The New York Society Library (2002-Present); Vice President, Center for Traditional Music and Dance, New York, NY (2000-Present); President,

Lexington 79 Corporation, New York, NY (1993-1997); Member, Board of Directors, Norman Rockwell Museum, Stockbridge, MA (1991-1996); Member, Advisory Board, Appalshop, Inc, Whitesburg, KY (1990-1992); Board President, Center for Traditional Music and Dance, New York, NY (1989-1994) **CW:** Author, "Poetry and the Politics of Decolonization," LAP (2015); Translator, "Three Beggars and a Rich Man" (2014) **MEM:** President, Thursday Evening Club (1998-2001); America Comparative Literature Association; The Grolier Club of New York **H:** Music; Poetry; Languages; Theater **ADD:** 139 E 79th St Fl 12, New York, NY, 10075-0378

MELDER, KEITH E., T: Curator (Retired) **I:** Museums & Institutions **CN:** National Museum of American History, Smithsonian Institute **DOB:** 05/13/1932 **PB:** Seattle **SC:** WA/USA **YOP:** 2018-07-05 **PT:** F. Eugene Melder; Eleanor (Morrill) Melder **ED:** PhD, Yale University, New Haven, CT (1964); BA, Williams College, Williamstown, MA (1954) **C:** Curator Emeritus, National Museum of American History, Smithsonian Institute, Washington, D.C. (1995-Present); Curator of Political History, National Museum of American History, Smithsonian Institute, Washington, D.C. (1986-1994); Associate Curator, National Museum of American History, Smithsonian Institute, Washington (1964-1985); Assistant Curator, National Museum of American History, Smithsonian Institute, Washington, D.C. (1962-1963) **CW:** Author, "Hail to the Candidate: Presidential Campaigns from Banners to Broadcasts," Smithsonian Institute Press (1992); Author, "City of Magnificent Intentions: A History of Washington, District of Columbia," Intac Inc. (1983); Author, "Beginnings of Sisterhood: The American Woman's Rights Movement, 1800-1850," Schocken Books (1977) **AW:** Inductee, Centennial Honor Roll, American Association of Museums (2006) **MEM:** Capitol Hill Community Council, Washington, D.C. (1961-1968) **MH:** Albert Nelson Marquis Lifetime Achievement Award (2017) **ADD:** 330 Rainier Blvd N Apt 211, Issaquah, WA, 98027

MENEFEE, SAMUEL, T: Lawyer, Academic **I:** Law and Legal Services **CN:** University of Virginia **DOB:** 06/08/1950 **PB:** Denver **SC:** CO/USA **PT:** George Hardiman Menefee; Martha Elizabeth (Pyeatt) Menefee **MS:** Married **SPN:** Mary W. Menefee (4/21/2000) **CH:** Mary Elizabeth **ED:** MPhil in International Relations, University of Cambridge, England (1995); SJD, University of Virginia (1993); LLM in Oceans, University of Virginia (1982); JD, Harvard University (1981); LittB, Oxford University, England (1975); Diploma in Social Anthropology, Oxford University, England (1973); BA in Anthropology, Yale University, Summa Cum Laude (1972) **C:** Advisory Board, School of Law, University of Virginia (1997-Present); Maury Fellow, School of Law, University of Virginia (1989-Present); University of Virginia (2013-2017); Senior Associate, Center for National Security Law, School of Law, University of Virginia (1985-2017); Senior Fellow, Center for National Security Law, School of Law, University of Virginia (1985-2017); Senior Associate, Center for National Security Law, School of Law, University of Virginia (1985-1989); Of Counsel, Barham & Churchill PC, New Orleans, LA (1985-1988); Associate, Phelps, Dunbar, Marks, Claverie & Sims, New Orleans, LA (1983-1985); Fellow, Center for Oceans Law and Policy, School of Law, University of Virginia (1982-1983) **CR:** Interstate Commerce Commission, Consultative Task Force on Commercial Crime (1996-Present); Piracy Reporting Center Fellowship, Kuala Lumpur, Malaysia (1993-Present); IMB Fellowship, Interstate Commerce Commission, International Maritime Bureau, Interstate Commerce

Commission (1991-Present); Professor, Regent University (1998-2003); Scholar-at-Large, Regent University (1997-2003); Adviser, American Maritime Forum (1997-1999); Adviser, American Maritime Forum, The Mariners' Museum and Park (1997-1999); Huntington Fellowship, The Mariners' Museum and Park (1997); Visiting Professor, Regent University (1996-1997); Law Clerk, Honorable Pasco M. Bowman, Eighth Circuit, U.S. Court of Appeals (1994-1995); Cosmos Fellowship, School of Scottish Studies, University of Edinburgh (1991-1992); Visiting Assistant Professor, University of Missouri, Kansas City, MO (1990); Visiting Lecturer, University of Cape Town (1987); Scholar of the House Fellowship, Yale University (1972); Bates Traveling Fellowship, Yale University (1971); Lecturer, Various National and International Organizations; Fellow, Royal Anthropological Institute **CW:** National Editor, "Association Research on Peasant Diaries" (1996-Present); Editorial Board Member, "International Journal of Marine and Coastal Law" (1997-2003); Author, "Trends in Maritime Violence" (1996); Author, "Contemporary Piracy and International Law" (1995); Co-Editor, "Materials on Ocean Law" (1982); Author, "Wives for Sale: An Ethnographic Study of British Popular Divorce" (1981); Contributor, Various Articles to Professional Journals **AW:** Katharine Briggs Prize, American Folklore Society (1992); Rhodes Scholarship, Yale University (1972) **MEM:** United Nations Educational Study Group, Maritime Law Association of the United States (1998-Present); Chairman, Law of Sea Committee, Subcommittee on Naval Warfare, Maritime Terrorism and Piracy, ABA (1989-Present); Chairman, Committee of International Law of Sea, Maritime Law Association of the United States (1999-2003); Rapporteur, Joint International Working Group on Uniformity of Law of Piracy, International Law Association (1998-2001); Chairman, American Branch Committee on Law of Sea, International Law Association (1996-2001); Co-Chairman, American Branch Committee on Law of Sea, International Law Association (1996-2001); Law of Sea Steering Committee, ABA (1996-1999); Observer, Convention on Law of Sea Meeting of States Parties, United Nations (1996); Chair, Working Group of Piracy, Maritime Law Association of the United States (1992-2003); Rapporteur, American Branch Committee on Maritime Neutrality, International Law Association (1992); Chairman, Marine Security Committee, Marine Technology Society (1991-2004); Co-Chairman, Marine Security Committee, Marine Technology Society (1991-2004); Vice Chairman, Committee of International Law of Sea, Maritime Law Association of the United States (1991-1999); Chairman, Subcommittee on Law of Sea, Maritime Law Association of the United States (1988-1991); Proctor, Subcommittee on Law of Sea, Maritime Law Association of the United States (1988-1991); Committee Member, Subcommittee on Law of Sea, Maritime Law Association of the United States (1988-1991); Rapporteur, American Branch Committee EEZ, International Law Association (1988-1990); Vice Chairman, Marine Resources Committee, ABA (1987-1990); The American Anthropological Association; Royal Asiatic Society; RSAI; Society of Antiquaries of Scotland; Royal Geographic Society; Society of Antiquaries; Maritime International Committee, ASIS International; U.S. Naval Institute; Navy League of the United States; American Folklore Society; The Royal Celtic Society; International Studies Association; Royal Scottish Geographical Society; Royal African Society; Egypt Exploration Society; Arctic Institute of Northern America; The American Society of International Law; American Historical Society; Working Group on Terrorism,

ABA; Committee Member, Southeastern Admiralty Law Institute; The Society for the History of Discoveries; The Society for Nautical Research; International Association Research on Peasant Diaries; Christian Aid Mission; National Eagle Scout Association; Raven Society, The University of Virginia Alumni Association; The Jefferson Literary and Debating Society; Fence Club; Mory's Association; The Elizabethan Club; The Yale Political Union; Leander Club; The Cambridge Union; Oxford and Cambridge Club; Yale Club New York City; Paul Morphy Chess Club; Pendennis Club; Round Table Club of New Orleans; The Phi Beta Kappa Society; Omicron Delta Kappa The National Leadership Honor Society **BAR:** State of Maine (1986); State of Pennsylvania (1986); District of Columbia Circuit, U.S. Court of Appeals (1986); U.S. Supreme Court (1985); District of Columbia (1985); State of Nebraska (1985); State of Florida (1985); First, Third, Fourth, Fifth, Sixth, Seventh, Eighth and Ninth Circuits, U.S. Court of Appeals (1984); State of Virginia (1983); U.S. Court of Military Appeals (1983); U.S. Court of International Trade (1983); U.S. Court of Federal Claims (1983); Tenth Circuit, U.S. Court of Appeals (1983); State of Louisiana (1983); 11th Circuit, U.S. Court of Appeals (1982); State of Georgia (1981) **H:** Anthropology; Archaeology; Crew; Hiking **PA:** Republican **BA:** PO Box 5291, Charlottesville, VA, 22905

MENZEL, MARYBELLE PROCTOR, T: Volunteer, Community Activist **I:** Education/Educational Services **DOB:** 02/05/1940 **PB:** Milledgeville **SC:** GA/USA **PT:** Ennis Hall Proctor; Sara (Evans) McCarthy **MS:** Married **SPN:** Robert John Menzel (9/1/1961) **CH:** Blake; John; Craig **ED:** MA, University of Central Florida, Orlando, FL, with Highest Distinction (1986); BA, Wesleyan College, Macon, GA, Cum Laude (1962) **CT:** Certified Highest Level Teacher, State of Florida **C:** Adjunct Instructor, English and Humanities, Brevard Community College, Cocoa, FL (1985); Director, Brevard Community College Coop Preschool, Melbourne, FL (1982-1985); Director, Gerber Child Care Center, Indialantic, FL (1981); Teacher, Coral Gables High School (1965-1966); Teacher, East Syracuse Minoa High School (1964-1965); Teacher, Spaulding Junior High School, Griffin, GA (1962) **CIV:** Host, Denver Art Museum (2006-Present); Guide, Denver Art Museum (2006-Present); Ambassador, Denver Art Museum (2006-Present); Volunteer, American Association of University Women (1976-Present) **AW:** Million Dollar Woman, Wesleyan College (2005); National Award for Fundraising, American Association of University Women Educational Foundation (2001); Garden of Victories Award (1993) **MEM:** Women's Legislative Breakfast Committee, Colorado American Association of University Women (2005-Present); Public Policy Committee, Colorado American Association of University Women (2004-2014); Director, Colorado American Association of University Women (2004-2005); President, Colorado American Association of University Women (2002-2004); President-elect, Colorado American Association of University Women (2001-2002); Director, Colorado American Association of University Women (2000-2001); Melbourne Branch Legislative Chair, American Association of University Women (1981-1983); Committee, AAUW Interbranch Council to Enforce Title 9, American Association of University Women, California (1978-1979); State Executive Board, Colorado American Association of University Women; Women's Lobby, Colorado American Association of University Women; Wesleyan College Million Dollar Women; Charter, National Museum of Women's History; Friend, National Museum of Women in the Arts; Phi Kappa Phi; Sigma Tau Delta; PTA Groups,

Various; Principal's Advisory Committee; Officer, Boy Scouts of America; The Jamestown Society; American Association of University Women, Florida; American Association of University Women, Colorado; Lobby Corps, Equal Rights Amendment, American Association of University Women **MH:** Albert Nelson Marquis Lifetime Achievement Award (2017) **H:** Travel; Reading **PA:** Democrat **RE:** Methodist **ADD:** 6800 S Bemis Street, Littleton, CO, 80120

MENZER, ROBERT E., T: Toxicologist (Retired) **I:** Sciences **DOB:** 12/21/1938 **PB:** Washington **SC:** DC/USA **PT:** Russell Ernest Menzer; Ora Taylor (Oates) Menzer **MS:** Married **SPN:** Sara Lee Gribbon (12/29/1962) **CH:** R. Eric; Paul D.; Joan Coleraine **ED:** PhD, University of Wisconsin-Madison (1964); MS, University of Maryland (1962); BS in Chemistry, University of Pennsylvania (1960) **C:** Senior Science Adviser, National Center for Environmental Research, United States Environmental Protection Agency, Washington, D.C. (1995-2001); Director of Environmental Research Laboratory, United States Environmental Protection Agency, Gulf Breeze, FL (1989-1995); Director of Water Resources Research Center, University of Maryland (1981-1989); Chairman, Graduate Program, Marine-Estuarine-Environmental Sciences, University of Maryland (1978-1989); Acting Dean, University of Maryland (1977-1980); Associate Dean, Graduate Studies and Research, University of Maryland (1974-1977); Professor, University of Maryland (1973-1989); Associate Professor, University of Maryland (1969-1973); Member, Faculty, University of Maryland (1964-1989); Assistant Professor, Entomology, University of Maryland (1964-1969); Instructor, University of Wisconsin-Madison (1964) **CR:** Member, National Library of Medicine (2008-Present); Consultant in Field (2001-Present); National Library of Medicine (1998-Present); Professor Emeritus, University of Maryland (1990-Present); Chairman, Hazardous Substances Data Bank Science Review Panel, National Library of Medicine (1973-1997) **CW:** Contributor, Articles to Professional Journals **AW:** Recipient, Distinguished Alumnus Award, Department of Entomology, University of Maryland (2012); Recipient, Alumni Award, University of Maryland (1974) **MEM:** Fellow, Washington Academy of Sciences; American Association for the Advancement of Science; American Chemical Society; Society of Toxicology; Coastal & Estuarine Research Federation; Sigma Xi; Phi Kappa Phi; Cosmos Club **MH:** Albert Nelson Marquis Lifetime Achievement Award (2017) **PA:** Republican **RE:** Episcopalian **ADD:** 90 Highpoint Dr, Gulf Breeze, FL, 32561

MERAS, PHYLLIS LESLIE, I: Writing and Editing **DOB:** 05/01/1905 **PB:** Brooklyn **SC:** NY/USA **PT:** Edmond Albert Meras; Leslie Trousdale (Ross) Meras **ED:** MS in Journalism, Columbia University, New York City, NY (1954); BA, Wellesley College, Massachusetts (1953) **C:** Contributing Editor, Vineyard Gazette (1974-Present); Adjunct Instructor, Columbia University School of Journalism (1975-1976); Associate in Journalism, University of Rhode Island (1974-1975); Editor, Wellesley Alumnae Magazine (1979-1996); Travel Editor, Providence Journal (1976-1995); Associate Editor, Rhode Islander, Providence, RI (1970-1976); Managing Editor, Vineyard Gazette, Edgartown, MA (1970-1974); Copyeditor, Travel Section, New York Times (1962-1968); Editor, Weekly Tribune (1961-1962); Feature Writer, Ladies Home Journal Magazine (1957-1958); Reporter, Copy Editor, Providence Journal (1959-1961); Reporter, Copy Editor, Providence Journal (1954-1957); Swiss Government Exchange Fellow, Institute

for Higher International Studies, Geneva (1957) **CW:** Co-Author, "Rhode Island Explorer's Guide" (2012); Co-Author, "In Every Season: Memories of Mantha's Vineyard" (2012); Co-Author, "Martha's Vineyard: Quiet Pleasures" (2008); Co-Author, "The Historic Shops and Restaurants of Boston" (2007); Co-Author, "Country Editor: Henry Beetle Hough and the Vineyard Gazette" (2006); Author, "Eastern Europe: A Traveler's Companion" (1991); Author, "Castles, Keeps and Leprechauns: Tales, Myths and Legends of Historic Sites in Great Britain and Ireland" (1988); Author, "Exploring Rhode Island" (1984); Author, "Other Tales: An Anecdotal Guide to Europe" (1982); Co-Author, "Carry-out Cuisine" (1982); Co-Author, "Christmas Angels" (1979); Author, "Vacation Crafts" (1978); Author, "Miniatures: How to Make Them, Use Them, Sell Them" (1976); Author, "A Yankee Way With Wood" (1975); Author, "First Spring: Martha's Vineyard Journal" (1972); Author, "The Mermaids of Chenonceaux and 828" **AW:** Pulitzer Fellow (1967) **MEM:** Society of American Travel Writers **ADD:** PO Box 215, West Tisbury , MA, 02575-02115

MERRILL, GEORGE VANDERNETH, T: Lawyer, Investment Executive **I:** Law and Legal Services **CN:** M & R Capital Management, Inc. **DOB:** 07/02/1947 **PB:** New York City **SC:** NY/USA **PT:** James Edward Merrill; Claire (Leness) Merrill **MS:** Married **SPN:** Janice Anne Humes (5/11/1985) **CH:** Claire Georgina; Anne Stewart **ED:** MBA, Columbia University (1973); JD, Harvard University (1972); AB, Harvard University, Magna Cum Laude (1968); Coursework, Phillips Exeter Academy (1960-1964) **CT:** Series 65 License **C:** Senior Vice President, M & R Capital Management, Inc., New York City, NY (2012-Present); Investment Policy Committee Member, Bank of New York Mellon, New York City, NY (2004-2012); Vice President, Senior Personal Investment Officer, Sector Head, Bank of New York Mellon, New York City, NY (2000-2012); Vice President, Trust and Institutional Portfolio Management, Member of Florida Equity Committee, Northern Trust Corporation, Chicago, IL (1996-2000); Vice President of Institutional Portfolio Management, Fleet Investment Advisors (1995-1996); Vice President, Institutional Portfolio Management, Shawmut Investment Advisors (1993-1995); Board of Directors, Executive Vice President, Listowel, Inc., New York City, NY (1984-1993); Vice President, Listowel, Inc., New York City, NY (1982-1984); Vice President, Irving Trust Company, New York City, NY (1980-1982); Associate, Hawkins, Delafield & Wood, New York City, NY (1977-1979); Associate, Cleary, Gottlieb, Steen & Hamilton, New York City, NY (1974-1977); Co-Manager, Shawmut Growth & Income Equity Mutual Fund; Co-Manager, Galaxy Growth & Income Equity Mutual Fund, Fleet Investment Advisors **CR:** Senior Vice President, Secretary, Brougham Production Company, New York City, NY (1991-1993); Senior Vice President, Secretary, Brougham Production Company, New York City, NY (1990-1993); Executive Vice President, Scientific Design and Engineering Company, Inc., New York City, NY (1989-1993); Vice President, Secretary, Marinetics Inc., New York City, NY (1988-1990); Vice President, Scientific Design and Engineering Company, Inc., New York City, NY (1987-1988); President, Northfield Charitable Corporation, New York City, NY (1986-1993); Vice President, Secretary, Brougham Production Company, New York City, NY (1986-1989) **CIV:** Board of Directors, President, Arell Foundation, New York City, NY (1985-1993) **AW:** Recipient, Detur Award, Harvard University (1968); John Harvard Scholarship **MEM:** ABA; American Management Association; National Cum Laude Society; The Brook; Union Club, New York City, NY; Down Town Association;

Racquet and Tennis Club; Somerset Club, Boston, MA; Signet Society, Cambridge, MA; Pilgrims of the United States **BAR:** United States Court of Appeals for the Second Circuit (1974); United States District Court for the Southern and Eastern Districts of New York (1974); New York (1973) **H:** Art collector; Theatre **ADD:** 54 Loughlin Avenue, Cos Cob, CT, 06807

MERRITT, PHYLLIS J., T: Music Educator **I:** Education/Educational Services **DOB:** 03/28/1939 **PB:** Elizabethton **SC:** TN/USA **PT:** Earl H. Merritt; Willie Greene Merritt **ED:** MusM in Education, Florida State University (1972); BS in Music Education, East Tennessee State University (1960) **C:** Artistic Music Director, Phyllis Merritt Singers (2003-2014); Founder, Phyllis Merritt Singers, Pensacola (2003-2014); Director of Music, Trinity United Methodist Church, Fort Walton Beach, Florida (1991-1998); Director of Choral Music, Niceville High School (1980-1990); Director of Choral Music, Meigs Junior High School (1976-1980); Director of Choral Music, Escambia High School (1965-1976); Director of Choral Music, Brownsville Junior High School (1962-1965); Teacher of Music, Weis Elementary School (1961-1962); Teacher of Music, Kingsley Elementary School (1960-1961) **CW:** Singer, "Gloria" (2010); Singer, "The Promise of Living," Phyllis Merritt Singers (2008); Singer, Conductor, Big Apple Choral Festival (1986); Singer, Conductor, Young Americans National Choral Festival (1985); Singer, Conductor, International Association Cultural European Concert Tour (1973); Singer, Conductor, Institute of European Studies Concert Tour (1970) **AW:** FVA Hall of Fame (2010); Southern Division Excellence in Choral Art Award (2000); Wayne Hugoboom Distinguished Service Award (1989) **MEM:** Division President, Choral Directors Association (1979-1981); State President, American Choral Directors Association (1975-1977); President, Florida Vocal Association (1970-1973); District Chairman, Florida Vocal Association (1967-1969) **H:** Travel **ADD:** 431 Gregory Avenue, Valparaiso, FL, 32580

MESSINA, JOHN A. JR., T: Founding Partner **I:** Law and Legal Services **CN:** Messina Hankin LLC **CH:** Four Children **ED:** Certificate of Completion, The National Judicial College (2015); Juris Doctor in Law, Southwestern Law School (1993); BA in Business Management, University of Redlands, With Distinction (1982); Coursework in Manufacturing Technology, Don Bosco Technical Institute (1974) **CT:** Expert Network Distinguished Lawyer, Expert Network **C:** Founding Partner, Messina Hankin LLC (2016-Present); Associate Judge, Intertribal Court of Southern California (2009-Present); Reserve Captain, Investigative Reserve Unit, Orange County Sheriff's Department (2001-Present); Founding Partner, Kelly Lytton & Williams LLP (Now Messina Hankin LLC) (2012-2016); Partner, Kelly Lytton & Williams LLP (2008-2012) **CR:** Reserve Deputy Sheriff, Coroner Department, Orange County Sheriff's Department (2004-Present); Reserve Captain, Coroner Department, Orange County Sheriff's Department (2004-Present) **CW:** Author, "California Commercial Lease Option Purchase Agreements Line by Line: A Detailed Look at California Commercial Lease Option Purchase Agreements and How to Change Them to Meet Your Needs" (2009); Author, "Proposed Creation of an Orange County Real Estate Fraud Prosecution Unit" (2002); Author, "Obligations and Responsibilities of Officers and Directors of Nonprofit Organizations" (2000); Author, "Tribute to A Friend" (1998); Author, "Some Tax Consequences for Homeowners Seeking Financial

Relief, The Real Estate Professional" (1996); Author, "Collection of Fines Imposed in Felony Cases by Judges of the Los Angeles Superior Court" (1993); Author, "Cost Effective Maintenance within Bracket Field Airport: County vs. Private Sector" (1982); Author, "Business Formation; Addressing the 'What Ifs?'" **AW:** Named in Top Lawyers of California, The Legal Network (2015); Named in Inland Empire Top Lawyers, Inland Empire Magazine (2013); Named in Top Lawyers in San Diego, San Diego Magazine (2013); Honoree, Avvo Preeminent Peer Review Rating, Martindale-Hubbell (2013); Avvo Clients' Choice Award, Avvo Inc. (2013); Honoree, Avvo Rating 10.0, Avvo Inc. (2013); Named in Southern California's Top-Rated Lawyers, Los Angeles Times (2012) **MEM:** Private Sector, Federal Bar Association (2013-Present); Master of the Bench, Southwest Inn, American Inns of Court (2013-Present); President, Orange County Reserve Peace Officers Association (OCRPOA) (2009-Present); Board of Directors, Coastal Family Therapy (2004-Present); Board of Directors, Sheriff's Youth Foundation of Los Angeles County, Los Angeles, CA (1994-Present); Associate Member, Invest In the USA (IIUSA) (2012-2013); Of General Counsel, NLPOA (1994-2004) **BAR:** Federal Bar Association (2013-Present); The State Bar of California (1994) **BA:** 1400 Quail St Ste. 200, Messina Hankin LLC, Newport Beach, CA, 92660 **URL:** www.MessinaHankinLaw.com

MESSITTE, PETER J J., **T:** Federal Judge **I:** Law and Legal Services **PB:** Washington, D.C. **SC:** DC/USA **PT:** Jesse B. Messitte; Edith (Wechsler) Messitte **MS:** Married **SPN:** Susan P. Messitte (9/5/1965) **CH:** Zachariah; Abigail **ED:** JD, The University of Chicago (1966); BA, Amherst College, Cum Laude, MA (1963) **C:** Senior United States District Judge, United States District Court for the District of Maryland (2008-Present); Judge, United States District Court for the District of Maryland (1993-2008); Associate Judge, Montgomery County Circuit Court, Rockville, MD (1985-1993); Principal, Peter J. Messitte, P.A., Chevy Chase, MD (1981-1985); Member, Messitte & Rosenberg, P.A., Chevy Chase, MD (1975-1981); Solo Practice, Chevy Chase, MD (1971-1975); Associate, Zuckert, Scoutt & Rasenberger, L.L.P., Washington D.C. (1968-1971) **CR:** Adjunct Professor, Law, American University Washington College of Law (2012-Present); Special Advisor, American Bar Association Rule of Law Initiative, Latin America & Caribbean Division, ABA (2010-Present); Member, Advisory Board, World Justice Project, Levin College of Law, University of Florida (2009-Present); Lecturer, Law, Fulbright Senior Specialist, University of Lisbon School of Law, Porto, Portugal (2011); Member, International Judicial Relations Committee, Judicial Conference of the United States (1997-2003) **CIV:** Contributor, Mental Health Community Psychiatric Clinic (1986); Vice President, Community Psychiatric Clinic, Montgomery County, Maryland (1980-1985); Maryland Delegate, Democratic National Convention, New York City, NY (1980); Board of Directors, Community Psychiatric Clinic, Montgomery County, Maryland (1974-1985); Peace Corps Volunteer, Sao Paulo, Brazil (1966-1968) **AW:** Honoree, Order of the Southern Cross, Brazilian President Michel Temer (2017); Appreciation Award, National Association of Labor Court Judges, Brazil (2013); Diploma of Honor and Merit, Association of Sao Paulo Magistrates (2009, 2007); Named, Honorary Citizen of Riberao Preto, Brazil (2009, 2007); Medalha de Merito Academico, Academia Paulista de Magistrados (2009, 2002); Medal of Commendation, Sao Paulo Academy of Judges (2009); Jon Mills Award, University of Florida Levin College of Law (2009); Named, Honorary Citizen of the City of Sao Paulo (2008); Named, Honorary Citi-

zen of Uberlandia, Brazil (2007); Leadership in Law Award, Maryland Daily Record (2002); H. Vernon Eney Award for Contribution to Administration of Justice, Maryland Bar Foundation (2001); Gran Cruz da Ordem Sao Jose Operario, Brazilian Labor Tribunal, Mato Grosso, Brazil (2001); Century of Service Award, Bar Association of Montgomery County (1999); Elizabeth Scull Award for Outstanding Service to Montgomery County, MD (1993); Special Citation, The Montgomery County Divorce Roundtable (1993); Teaching Citations, FDIC Bank Examiner School (1979, 1975); Teaching Citations, American Institute of Banking (1978) **MEM:** Founder, The Montgomery County Maryland American Inn of Court (1989-Present); Board of Directors, Judicial Institute of Maryland (1989-1993); President, The Montgomery County Maryland American Inn of Court (1988-1990); Master, The Charles Fahy American Inn of Court (1987-1988); Fellow, Maryland Bar Foundation; ABA; Fourth Judicial Circuit, Federal Judges Association; The American Law Institute; Honorary Member, Instituto Paulista de Advogados; Bar Association of Montgomery County; Maryland State Bar Association; The District of Columbia Bar; Federal Bar Association **BAR:** United States Court of Appeals for the Fifth Circuit (1983); United States Court of Appeals for the District of Columbia (1982); United States Court of Appeals for the Fourth Circuit (1977); Supreme Court of the United States (1973); The District of Columbia (1969); Maryland State Bar Association (1969) **ACH:** Banned the use of the word ""Redskins"" in his courtroom and in court documents in a procedural order on July 15, 2014; Nominated by President Bill Clinton to a seat on the United States District Court for the District of Maryland vacated by Joseph C. Howard, Sr. **RE:** Jewish **URL:** https://en.wikipedia.org/wiki/Peter_Jo_Messitte

MIELCUSZNY, ALBERT JOHN, **I:** Business Management/Business Services **DOB:** 10/30/1941 **PB:** Pittsburgh **SC:** PA/USA **PT:** Joseph John Mielcuszny; Sophie (Krupa) Mielcuszny **MS:** Married **SPN:** Deborah Diamond (8/1/2017); Constance Lorraine Snyder (4/25/1964, Deceased 2015) **CH:** Alan; William **ED:** MBA in Finance, Duquesne University (1972); BS in Accounting, Duquesne University (1964) **CT:** Certified Second-Degree Black Belt, Tae Kwon Do (2013); Certified Public Accountant, Commonwealth of Pennsylvania; Certified Scuba Diver **C:** Senior Vice President, Servistar Corp. (1982-1995); Chief Finanace Officer, Servistar Corp. (1982-1995); Vice President of Finance Servistar Corp. (1979-1982); Treasurer, Servistar Corp. (1979-1982); Controller, Servistar Corp. (1974-1979); Assistant Controller, Servistar Corp. (1972-1974); Accountant, Touche Ross & Co. (1968-1972); Budget Analyst, Jones and Laughlin Steel Company (1967-1968); Management Trainee, Jones and Laughlin Steel Company (1964-1965) **CR:** Treasurer, The Community Development Corporation of Butler County (1974-Present); Owner, Viewpoints, Vail, Colorado (1995-2005); The Bank of New York Mellon Corporation (1980-1986); Teacher, Butler County Community College; Construction Manager, Warehouses; Construction Manager, Retail Hardware Locations **CIV:** Treasurer, Beaver Creek Metro District (2002-2006); Member, Board of Directors, Butler Region, The Salvation Army USA (1981-1984); Board Member, Coast to Coast; Board Member, Taylor Rental Co.; Board Member, Grand Rental Station; Board Member, Advocate Services, Inc.; Board Chair, Kurfee's Paint **MIL:** First Lieutenant, US Army (1965-1967) **MH:** Albert Nelson Marquis Lifetime Achievement Award (2017) **H:** Skiing; Water-skiing; Scuba diving; Tennis **PA:** Republican **RE:** Roman Catholic **ADD:** 320 Meadowbrook Country Club Est, Ballwin, MO, 63011

MIESS, ROBERT PHD, **T:** Chemistry Professor **I:** Education/Educational Services **CN:** Mayville State University **SC:** WI/USA **ED:** PhD, Texas A&M University (1992); BS, Viterbo University (1986) **C:** Chair, Division of Science and Mathematics, Mayville State University (1998-Present); Professor, Mayville State University (2006-Present); Associate Professor, Mayville State University (1998-2006); Assistant Professor, Mayville State University (1993-1998) **CIV:** Treasurer, Mayville Congregational United Church of Christ (1997-Present) **AW:** Recipient Teacher of Year, Student Senate, Mayville State University (2006-2007); Honoree, Named Outstanding Public Employee Of Year, North Dakota Public Employees Association, North Dakota United (1998) **MEM:** American Chemical Society **MH:** Albert Nelson Marquis Lifetime Achievement Award (2017) **ADD:** 810 Jahr Ave, Portland, ND, 58274

MILLER, BERTHA HAMPTON, **T:** History Professor **I:** Education/Educational Services **CN:** Fayetteville State University **DOB:** 10/03/1938 **PT:** James Robert Hampton; Millie Lucinda Lynch **MS:** Married **SPN:** Bobby Hugh Miller (6/12/1971) **ED:** PhD in American History, Duke University (1981); MA in American History, Case Western Reserve University (1970); BS in Sociology, Hampton University (1960) **C:** Executive Assistant, Chancellor for Strategic Initiative (2008-Present); Professor History, Fayetteville State University (2004-2008); Dean, College Arts and Sciences, Fayetteville State University, Fayetteville, NC (1996-2004); Vice Chancellor of Academy Affairs, Fayetteville State University (1994-1996); Dean, School of Education, Fayetteville State University, NC (1988-1994); Deputy Director, Bureau of History, Michigan Department of State, Lansing, MI (1985-1988); Instructor of History, A&T State University, Greensboro, NC (1971-1984); Department Chair, A&T State University, Greensboro, NC (1971-1984); History Teacher, Roanoke Public School (1967-1971); History Teacher, Portsmouth Public School, Portsmouth, VA (1960-1965) **CR:** Chair, Celebration Committee, Fayetteville State University's 150th Anniversary (2016-2018); Reviewer, Teacher Enhancement Grants, U.S. Department of Education (1999-2002); Member, Board of Examiners, NCATE, Washington, D.C. (1994-2003); Member, State Program Approval Team, North Carolina Department of Public Instruction, Raleigh, NC (1989-2000); Member, Michigan Council of Humanities, Lansing, MI (1986-1988); Member, Bicentennial of the Constitution Committee, Michigan Department of State, Lansing, MI (1985-1986); Presenter, Professional Conferences **CIV:** Speaker, Civic Clubs, Church, School, Cumberland County, NC (1988-2005) **CW:** Author, "Leisure and Popular Culture in the Gilded Age and Progressive Era," Encyclopedia of the Gilded Age and Progressive Era (2005); Creator, Historic Exhibits and PowerPoint Presentations (1988-1997); Editor, "Pathways to Michigan's Black History"; Author, "A History of Fayetteville State University, 1867-2003"; Contributor, Freshmen Studies Manual **AW:** Journeyman Award for Spirit of American Trails Video, Cumberland County (2014); Top 30 Educators for Diverse Issues in Higher Education (2012); Grantee, National Science Foundation (1996-2004); Grantee, North Carolina Department of Public Instruction (1994-2000); Grantee, Ford Foundation (1994-2000); Grantee, Sloan Foundation (1982-1983); Chancellor's Million Dollar Club Grantsmanship, North Carolina **MEM:** Association for the Study of African-American Life and History; AACTE; NAACP; Sigma Delta Phi; Delta Mu Delta; Kappa Delta Phi; Phi Alpha Theta; National Women's History Museum; Smithsonian **H:** Flower gardens;

Crossword puzzles; Collecting history books and brooches **PA:** Democrat **RE:** Methodist **ADD:** 6135 Lochview Dr, Fayetteville, NC, 28311

MILLER, DIANE WILMARTH, T: Human Resources Director (Retired) **I:** Human Resources **CN:** Aims Community College **DOB:** 03/12/1940 **PB:** Clarinda **SC:** IA/USA **PT:** Donald Wilmarth; Floy Pauline (Madden) Wilmarth **MS:** Married **SPN:** Robert Nolen Miller (8/21/1965) **CH:** Robert Wilmarth; Anne Elizabeth **ED:** MA, University of Northern Colorado, Greeley, CO (1994); BBA, University of Iowa, Iowa City, IA (1962); AA, Colorado Women's College, University of Denver (1960) **CT:** Certified Teacher, State of Colorado; Vocational Credential, State of Colorado; Certified Senior Professional in Human Resources; Licensed Insurance Producer, State of Colorado **C:** Director of Human Resources, Aims Community College, Greeley, CO (1984-2001); Instructor, Aims Community College, Greeley, CO (1972-1989); Travel Consultant, United Bank Travel Service, Greeley, CO (1972-1974); Business Teacher, Poudre School District R-1, Fort Collins, CO (1969-1971); Secretary-Counselor, Myrtle Beach Air Force Base, South Carolina (1968-1969); University of South Carolina Representative, Myrtle Beach Air Force Base, South Carolina (1968-1969); Instructor, Coastal Carolina Campus, University of South Carolina (Now Coastal Carolina University), Conway, SC (1967-1969); Business Teacher, Denver Public Schools, Denver, CO (1962-1966) **CR:** Chairperson, University of Northern Colorado Foundation, Inc., Greeley, CO (2007-2008); University of Northern Colorado Alumni Association, Greeley, CO (2004-2008); Member, Board of Directors, University of Northern Colorado Foundation, Inc., Greeley, CO (2003-2010) **CIV:** Member, Board of Directors, A Woman's Place (2017-Present); Member, Board of Directors, Greeley Philharmonic Orchestra (Now Greeley Philharmonic Orchestra Association, Inc.) (2017-Present); President, Board of Directors, Greeley Transitional House (2016); Chairperson, Museum Board, Greeley, CO (2013-2016); Member, Board of Directors, Greeley Transitional House (2011-2016); Member, Board of Directors, Museum Board, Greeley, CO (2010-2016); Member, Board of Trustees, First Congregational Church, Greeley, CO (2005-2010) **MEM:** President, Women's Investment Network (2007-2008); President, WTK Club (2006-2007); President, Questers (2002-2004); President, Philanthropic Educational Organization (Now P.E.O. Sisterhood) (1988-1989); President, Scroll and Fan Club (1985-1986); President, Women's Panhellenic Association (1983-1984) **MH:** Albert Nelson Marquis Lifetime Achievement Award (2017) **H:** Family activities; Traveling; Reading; Antiquing; Collecting for and decorating homes; Studying American history **ADD:** 3542 West Wagon Trail Rd, Greeley, CO, 80634

MILLER, HARVEY ALFRED, T: Botanist, Educator, Consultant Environmental Sciences, Writer **I:** Education/Educational Services **CN:** Miami University **DOB:** 10/19/1928 **PB:** Sturgis **SC:** MI/USA **PT:** Harry Clifton Miller; Carmen (Sager) Miller **MS:** Married **SPN:** Donna K. Hall (5/9/1992) **CH:** Valerie Yvonne; Harry Alfred; Timothy Merk; Tanya Merk; Jasper Adam **ED:** PhD, Stanford University (1957); MS, University of Hawaii (1952); BS, University of Michigan (1950) **C:** Adjunct Professor, Botany, Miami University, Oxford, OH (1985-Present); Vice President, D.H. Miller and Associates, Oxford, OH (1994-1997); Visiting Professor, Miami University, Oxford, OH (1994-1996); Research Specialist in Botany, Miami University, Oxford, OH (1985-2011); Associate, Natural Systems Analysts, Lotspeich & Associates, Inc., Winter Park, FL (1979-1994); Professor, University of Central Florida (1975-1994);

Professor, Department of Biological Sciences, University of Central Florida (1970-1975); Chairman, Department of Biological Sciences, University of Central Florida (1970-1975); Visiting Professor, Botany, University of Illinois (1969-1970); Professor, Program in Biology, Washington State University (1967-1969); Chairman, Program in Biology, Washington State University (1967-1969); Vice President, Marine Research Associates Ltd., Nassau, Bahamas (1962-1965); Associate Professor, Willard Sherman Turrell Herbarium, Miami University, Oxford, OH(1961-1967); Curator, Willard Sherman Turrell Herbarium, Miami University, Oxford, OH (1961-1967); Assistant Professor, Miami University, Oxford, OH (1957-1961); Instructor, Botany, Miami University, Oxford, OH (1956-1957); Instructor, Botany, University of Massachusetts (1955-1956) **CR:** Adjunct Professor, Environmental Science, Seminole State College of Florida (2002-2004); Adjunct Professor, The University of West Alabama (1997-2000); Consultant, Tropical Botany, Foliage Plant Patents, Designs for Science Buildings, Field Researcher on Alpine Meadows in Irian Jaya, Indonesia (1991-1992); Principal Investigator, Bryophytes of Melanesia, National Science Foundation (1983-1986); Research Associate, Orlando Science Center, Orlando Visiting Professor, University of Guam (1965); Director, Miami University Expedition to Micronesia and Philippines, National Science Foundation (1965); Principal Investigator, Miami University Expedition to Micronesia (1960); Principal Investigator, Systematic and Phytogeographical Studies of Bryophytes of the Pacific Islands, National Science Foundation (1959); Botanist, University of Michigan Expedition to Aleutian Islands (1949-1950) **CIV:** Trustee, Astronauts Scholarship Foundation (2011-Present); Board of Directors, Astronauts Scholarship Foundation (1985-2011); Chairman, Scholarship and Grant Selection Committee, Astronauts Scholarship Foundation (1985-2010) **CW:** Author, "Flora Hepaticarum Polynesiae, Hawaii" (2018); Co-author, "Field Guide, Florida Mosses and Liverworts" (1990); Co-author, "Prodromus Florae Hepaticarum Polynesiae" (1983); Co-author, "Prodromus Florae Muscorum Polynesiae" (1978); Editor, Florida Scientist (1973-1978); Author, "A Phytogeographical Study of Hawaiian Hepaticae" (1956); Contributor, Articles, Scientific Journals **AW:** Guggenheim Fellow (1958); Acacia Order of Pythagoras; Acacia National Award of Merit **MEM:** President, Florida Academy of Sciences, Florida Institute of Technology (1980); Executive Secretary, Florida Academy of Sciences, Florida Institute of Technology (1976-1983); Chairman, Science Committee for Botany, Pacific Science Association (1975-1983); President, American Bryological and Lichenological Society (1964-1965); Vice President, American Bryological and Lichenological Society (1962-1963); Fellow, American Association for the Advancement of Science; Fellow, The Linnean Society of London; Association for Tropical Biology and Conservation; American Institute of Biological Sciences; British Bryological Society; The Botanical Society of America; International Association for Plant Taxonomy; International Association of Bryologists (IAB); Michigan Academy of Science, Arts, and Letters, Alma College; American Society of Plant Taxonomists; Nordic Bryological Society; Acacia, Order Of Pythagoras; The Explorers Club; Sigma Xi, The Scientific Research Honor Society; Phi Sigma; Beta Beta Beta (TriBeta); Space Coast Writers' Guild **ADD:** 2053 Algeria St NE, Palm Bay, FL, 32905

MILLER, JAMES P., T: Professor **I:** Education/Educational Services **CN:** Boston University **ED:** Postdoctoral Fellow, Lawrence Berkeley Laboratory, U.S. Department of Energy (1976-1979); Postdoctoral Fellow, California Institute of Technology

(1974-1976); PhD, Carnegie Mellon University; MS, Carnegie Mellon University; BS, Carnegie Mellon University **C:** Professor of Physics, Boston University (1990-Present); Honoree, Fellow, American Physical Society (1996); Associate Professor of Physics, Boston University (1985-1990); Assistant Professor of Physics, Boston University (1979-1985); Physicist, Lawrence Berkeley Laboratory, U.S. Department of Energy (1976-1979); Physics Research Associate, California Institute of Technology (1974-1976) **BA:** 590 Commonwealth Avenue, Physics Department, Boston, MA, 02215 **URL:** https://edit.bu.edu/files/1/Miller-cv.pdf

MILLER, JAY J., T: Proprietor, Sole Member **I:** Law and Legal Services **CN:** Law Office of Jay J. Miller, Esq. **PT:** Murray Miller; Kitty Miller **MS:** Married **SPN:** Corinne Miller **CH:** Stephen Miller; Cindy Miller **ED:** JD, Columbia Law School (1955); BD, Syracuse University **C:** Proprietor, Law Office of Jay J. Miller, Esq. **CR:** Director, Numerous Public Companies; Director, Private Companies **MIL:** U.S. Coast Guard (1955-1958) **AW:** Honoree, AV Preeminent Attorney, Martindale-Hubbell **MEM:** ABA; New York State Bar Association; Former Director, AmTrust Financial Services; Former BOD, OneWest Bank, CIT Group Inc.; Newport Group, Inc. **BAR:** New York State Bar; Supreme Court of the United States **H:** Reading fiction and nonfiction; Tennis; Travel; Sports; Helping people **RE:** Jewish **ADD:** 430 E 57th St Apt 5D, New York, NY, 10022 **URL:** https://www.bloomberg.com/research/stocks/private/snapshot.asp?privcapid=3534610

MILLER, STEPHEN R., T: Lawyer **I:** Law and Legal Services **CN:** McDermott, Will & Emery **DOB:** 11/28/1950 **PB:** Chicago **SC:** IL/USA **PT:** Ralph Miller; Karin Ann (Olson) Miller **MS:** Married **SPN:** Sheila L. Krysiak (2/2/1998) **CH:** David Williams; Lindsay Christine **ED:** JD, Cornell University (1975); BA, Yale University, Cum Laude (1972) **C:** Counsel, McDermott, Will & Emery (2006-Present); Management Committee Member, McDermott, Will & Emery (1992-1995); Equity Partner, McDermott, Will & Emery (1986-2006); Income Partner, McDermott, Will & Emery (1981-1985); Associate, McDermott, Will & Emery (1975-1980) **CR:** Special Task Force on Post-Employment Benefits, Financial Accounting Standards Board, Norwalk, CT (1987-1991) **CIV:** Chicago Council on Global Affairs (1978-Present); President's Circle Steering Committee, Chicago Council on Foreign Relations (2005-2009); Member, Seabury Council (2004-2007); Chancellor, Seabury Western Theological Seminary, Evanston, IL (2004-2005); Member, External Relations Committee, Chicago on Council Foreign Relations (2002-2003); Chair, Trusteeship Committee, Seabury Western Theological Seminary, Evanston, IL (2000-2002); Chair, Development Committee, Chicago Council on Foreign Relations (1999-2002); Development Committee Member, Chicago Council on Foreign Relations (1997-2002); Chancellor, Seabury Western Theological Seminary, Evanston, IL (1996-1997); Trustee, Seabury Western Theological Seminary, Evanston, IL (1994-2002); Trustee, Police Pension Board, Wilmette, IL (1992-1998) **CW:** Contributor, Articles to Professional Journals **AW:** Honoree, Illinois Super Lawyers (2010-Present) **MEM:** Board of Directors, Center Companies That Care (2011-Present); Nordic Law Club; Worldwide Employee Benefits Network; Hundred Club Cook County; Cornell Club Chicago; Lawyers' Club Chicago; Yale Club of Chicago; Illinois State Bar Association; Associate, Chicago Bar Association; American Bar Association **BAR:** Illinois **H:** Sailing; Water skiing; Cross-country skiing **ADD:** 37 Lake Eden Dr, Boynton Beach, FL, 33435 **URL:** http://www.stephenralphmiller.com

MILLIGAN, JOHN , I: Law and Legal Services **ED:** JD, University of Michigan Law School (1949-1952) **C:** Judge, Ohio Court of Appeals (2005-Present)

MILLS SIMMONS, LYNDA MERRILL, T: Principal (Retired) **I:** Education/Educational Services **CN:** Hartvigsen School **DOB:** 08/31/1940 **PB:** Salt Lake City **SC:** UT/USA **PT:** Alanson Soper Mills; Madeline Helene (Merrill) Mills **MS:** Married **SPN:** Mark Carl Simmons **CH:** Lisa Lynn Simmons Morley; William Mark; Jennifer Louise; Robert Thomas **ED:** MS, University of Utah, Salt Lake City, UT (1983); BS, University of Utah, Salt Lake City, UT (1961) **CT:** Certification in Secondary Education, State of Utah (1988); Certified School Administrator, State of Utah; Certification in Special Education, State of Utah **C:** Alternative Teacher Preparation Council, Utah State University (2016-Present); Special Education Consultant, Academy for Math, Engineering and Science (2005-Present); Principal, Hartvigsen School, Salt Lake City, UT (1993-2002); Assistant Principal, Bennion Junior High School, Salt Lake City, UT (1990-1993); Teacher Specialist, Granite School District, Salt Lake City, UT (1985-1990); Resource Teacher, Eisenhower Junior High School, Salt Lake City, UT (1979-1988); Teacher, Special Education, Park City High School, Utah (1971-1973); Teacher, Altamont High School, Duchesne District, Utah (1964-1966); Teacher, Wasatch Junior High School, Granite District, Salt Lake City, UT (1961-1964) **CR:** Utah Principal Academy (1994-1995); Advisory Committee on Handicapped, Utah State Board of Education (1990-1993); Co-Chair, Utah Special Educators for Computer Technology, Salt Lake City, UT (1988-1990); Adjunct Professor, Special Education, University of Utah, Salt Lake City, UT (1987-1991); Consultant, Presenter in Field; Utah Mentor Academy **CIV:** Mission for Church of Latter-day Saints, Salt Lake City, UT (2013-Present); Mission for Church of Latter-day Saints, Blacksburg, VA (2003-2004); Community Board, Junior League, Salt Lake City, UT (1997-2000); District Chairman, March of Dimes (1982-2002); Cookie Chairman, Park City Area, Girl Scouts of the USA (1981); Board of Directors, Junior League, Salt Lake City, UT (1977-1980); Pack Leader, Park City Area Council, Boy Scouts of America (1976-1980); District Chairman, Heart Fund, Cancer Dr, Summit Park, UT (1970-1982) **CW:** Author, "Setting Up Effective Secondary Resource Program" (1985); Contributor, Articles to Professional Journals **AW:** Administrator of the Year, Utah Federation Council for Exceptional Children (2002); Business Woman of the Year, South Salt Lake City Chamber of Commerce (2001); Special Educator of the Year, Utah Federation Council for Exceptional Children (1995); Ambassador Award, Salt Lake Convention and Visiting Bureau (1993); Utah Honorary Battalion Chief, South Salt Lake City Fire Department **MEM:** State Treasurer, General Federation Women's Clubs (2017-Present); President, Seeley Genealogical Society (2015-Present); Newsletter Editor, General Federation Women's Clubs (2012-2018); Membership Chairperson, Seeley Genealogical Society (2010-2015); State Treasurer, General Federation Women's Clubs, Utah (2006-2008); President, Salt Lake City District, General Federation Women's Clubs (1998-2002); President, Women's Athanaeum (1994-2001); Chairperson, Woman of the Year, General Federation Women's Clubs, Utah (1998-2000); Community-Improvement Chairperson, General Federation Women's Clubs, Utah (1996-1998); Family History Consultant, Secretary-Treasurer, Granite Association School Administrators (1992-1994); President, Utah Federation (1991-1993); Vice President, Women's Athanaeum (1990-1993); President, Park City Young Women's Mutual (1989-1993); President, Salt Lake City Chapter, Council for Exceptional Children (1989-1990); Member, National Association of Secondary School Principals **MH:** Albert Nelson Marquis Lifetime Achievement Award (2017) **H:** Reading; Cooking; Writing; Sports; Handiwork; Knitting **RE:** Church of Jesus Christ of Latter Day Saints **ADD:** 125 Parkview Dr, Park City, UT, 84098

MINKOWITZ, MARTIN, I: Law and Legal Services **PT:** Jacob Minkowitz; Marion Minkowitz **CR:** Adjunct Professor, Law, Brooklyn Law School (2014-Present); Adjunct Professor, Law, New York Law School, New York City, NY (1982-Present); Advisory Board, College Insurance (1987-1990); Instructor, The City University of New York (1975); Hearing Officer, New York City Department of Transportation (1970-1975); Consultant, New York City Council (1969); Lecturer, ABA; Lecturer, Greater New York Chamber of Commerce; Lecturer, Practising Law Institute; Lecturer, New York State Bar Association; Lecturer, National Association of Insurance Commissioners; Lecturer, National Council of Insurance Legislators **CIV:** Honorary Member, Board of Directors, Met Council (2014-Present); Board Member, AMCOMP (2003-Present); Board Director, Met Council (1993-2014); Elected Director Emeritus, Kingsbay YM-YWHA, Brooklyn, New York (1999-2007); Chair, New York Division, National Conference for Community and Justice (1998-2001); Member, National Board of Trustees, National Conference for Community and Justice (1995-2001); Board Director, New York Division, National Conference for Community and Justice (1994-2001); Board Director, Kingsbay YM-YWHA, Brooklyn, New York (1978-1999); Secretary, Kingsbay YM-YWHA, Brooklyn, NY (1978-1999); Co-chairman, Executive Board, Metropolitan Council, American Jewish Congress, New York City (1983-1991); National Vice President, American Jewish Congress, New York, NY (1983-1991); President, Board of Directors, Shore Terrace Co-op, Brooklyn, NY (1982-1983) **CW:** Editor, "One on One," New York State Bar Association (2001-Present); Author, Commentaries, "McKinney's Consolidated Laws" (1982-Present); Author, "Labor, Employment and Worker's Compensation" (2015-2018); Co-Author, "Labor and Workers Compensation" (2013-2018); Member, Editorial Board, Journal of Occupational Rehabilitation, University of Rochester (1991-2015); Author, "West's New York Workers' Compensation, 2nd Edition" (2011); Co-Author, "The New York Rules of Professional Conduct" (2010); Author, "West's New York Workers' Compensation" (2003); Author, "Handling the Basic Workers' Compensation Law Case" (1996); Co-Author, "Workers Compensation, Insurance and Law Practice-The Next Generation" (1989); Co-Author, "Rent Stabilization and Control" (1973); Author, "West's New York General Practice"; Contributor, Articles, Professional Journals **MEM:** Board Director, New York County Lawyers Association (1997-2006, 2014-Present); Board of Directors, The New York Bar Foundation (2011-Present); House of Delegates, New York State Bar Association (1999-2007, 2009-Present); Committee on Access to Justice, New York State Bar Association (2008-2014); Committee for the Second Circuit, Federal Bar Council (1998-2014); Chair, General Practice Section, New York State Bar Association (2009-2010); Chair-elect General Practice Section, New York State Bar Association (2008-2009); Director, Executive Board, New York County Lawyers Association (2003-2005, 2006-2007); Chair, Professional Ethics Committee, New York County Lawyers Association (2001-2006); President, Board of Directors, Alumni Association, Brooklyn Law School (1995-1996); President-elect, Board of Directors, Alumni Association, Brooklyn Law School (1993-1994); Vice President, Board of Directors, Alumni Association, Brooklyn Law School (1984-1992); Chair, Worker's Compensation Committee, New York County Lawyers Association (1988-1991); Professional Ethics Committee, New York County Lawyers Association (1985-1991); Chairman, Unlawful Practice of Law Committee, New York County Lawyers Association (1982-1986); Committee on Professional Ethics, New York State Bar Association (1981-1984); Chairman, Unlawful Practice of Law Committee, New York State Bar Association (1981-1983); Fellow, The New York Bar Foundation; Chairman, Committee on Professional Discipline, New York State Bar Association; Committee on Judicial Nominations, New York State Bar Association **BAR:** United States Tax Court (1974); Supreme Court of the United States (1967); New York (1963); U.S. District Court - Eastern District of New York; United States District Court Northern District of New York; United States District Court Southern District of New York; United States District Court Western District of New York

MIRVIS, DAVID MARC MD, T: Professor Emeritus **I:** Education/Educational Services **CN:** University of Tennessee Health Science Center **DOB:** 12/20/1945 **PB:** Hampton **SC:** VA/USA **PT:** Allan Mirvis; Lena (Sear) Mirvis **MS:** Married **SPN:** Arlynn Shara Katz (6/30/1968) **CH:** Simcha Zev; Tova Aliza; Shoshana Fruma **ED:** Fellow in Cardiovascular Diseases, University of Tennessee (1975-1977); Chief Resident, Medicine, University of Tennessee (1973-1974); Assistant Resident, Medicine, University of Tennessee (1973-1974); Intern, University of Tennessee (1970-1971); MD, Albert Einstein College of Medicine (1970); Bachelor's Degree, Yeshiva University (1966) **CT:** Diplomate, American Board of Internal Medicine (1975); Diplomate, National Board of Medical Examiners (1972); Licensed to Practice Medicine, State of Tennessee **C:** Adjunct Professor, Department of Public Health, University of Tennessee, Knoxville (2010-Present); Professor Emeritus, College of Medicine, The University of Tennessee Health Science Center (2010-Present); Health Policy Fellow, Howard Baker Center for Applied Public Policy, University of Tennessee, Knoxville (2010-2011); Director, MD-MS Program in Health Systems Studies, College of Graduate Health Sciences, The University of Tennessee Health Science Center (2008-2009); Director, Health Policy Focus, Graduate Program in Health Science Administration, College of Graduate Health Sciences, The University of Tennessee Health Science Center (2000-2006); Graduate Faculty, Masters Program in Epidemiology, College of Graduate Health Sciences, The University of Tennessee Health Science Center (1999-2010); Graduate Faculty, Graduate Program in Health Science Administration, College of Graduate Health Sciences, The University of Tennessee Health Science Center (1999-2010); Director, The Center for Health Services Research, The University of Tennessee Health Science Center (1999-2006); Director, Division of Health Services and Health Policy Research, Department of Preventive Medicine, The University of Tennessee Health Science Center (1994-1999); Professor of Preventive Medicine, The University of Tennessee Health Science Center (1992-2010); Associate Dean for VA Medical Center Affairs, The University of Tennessee Health Science Center (1988-1997); Chief of Staff, Memphis VA Medical Center (1987-1997); Chief, Cardiology Section, Memphis VA Medical Center (1984-1988, 1997-2000); Professor of Medicine, The University of Tennessee Health Science Center (1983-2010); Cardiologist, UT Medical Group (Now University Clinical Health) (1978-1987); Associate Professor of Medicine, The

University of Tennessee Health Science Center (1978-1983); Chief, Section of Medical Physics, The University of Tennessee Health Science Center (1977-1988); Assistant Professor of Medicine, The University of Tennessee Health Science Center (1975-1978); Instructor of Medicine, The University of Tennessee Health Science Center (1974-1975) **CR:** Senior Research Fellow, Methodist LeBonheur Center for Health Care Economics, University of Memphis (2010-Present); Adjunct Professor, Faye Boozeman School of Public Health, University of Arkansas for Medical Sciences (2006-2014); Visiting Scientist, School of Public Health, Harvard University (2005-2016); Chair, NIH Research Resource Advisory Committee, Harvard University/Beth Israel Medical Center (2002-2006); Adjunct Professor, Fogelman College of Business and Economics, University of Memphis (1994-2006); Adjunct Graduate Faculty, Herff College of Engineering, University of Memphis (1989-2000); Founding President, Research, Incorporated **CIV:** Chair, Steering Committee, Consortium for Health and Economic Development in the Delta Region; Executive Director, Tennessee Consortium for Public Health Workforce Development; Pharmaceutical Economics and Policy Council, Pfizer, Inc.; Cardiovascular and Renal Study Section, National Institutes of Health; Special Review Committees, National Institutes of Health; Clinical Investigator Review Committees, National Institutes of Health **MIL:** Research Associate, Cardiovascular Physiology, U.S. Public Health Service (1971-1973) **CW:** Editorial Board Member, "American Journal of Cardiology" (1999-Present); Editorial Board Member, "American Journal of Noninvasive Cardiology" (1986-Present); Editorial Board Member, "Journal of Electrocardiology" (1984-Present); Author, Research Project Regarding Health Care Delivery Services (2018); Author, Editor, "Body Surface Electrocardiographic Mapping" (1988); Author, "Electrocardiography: A Physiologic Approach"; Associate Editor, Section on Electrocardiography, UpToDate, Inc.; Editor, Health Policy Series, "Tennessee Medicine"; Editorial Board Member, "Journal of Health and Human Resource Administration"; Abstract Review Committee, American Heart Association, Inc.; Abstract Review Committee, American College of Cardiology; Reviewer, "American Heart Journal"; Reviewer, "Chest"; Reviewer, "Circulation"; Reviewer, "Circulation Research"; Reviewer, "Journal of the American College of Cardiology"; Reviewer, "Journal of the American Geriatric Society"; Reviewer, "Journal of the American Medical Association"; Reviewer, "Journal of Cardiovascular Electrophysiology"; Reviewer, "Journal on Health Care for the Poor and Uninsured"; Reviewer, "Milbank Quarterly"; Reviewer, "Medical Care"; Reviewer, "Public Library of Science (Medicine)"; Associate Producer, "It Matters Series," WKNO TV; Contributor, 17 Book Chapters; Contributor, 164 Articles, Professional Journals; Contributor, 100 Abstracts in Field; Contributor, 38 Articles, Tennessee Medicine **AW:** Recipient, Special Recognition for Public Service, Tennessee General Assembly (2005); Research Career Development Award, National Heart, Lung and Blood Institute, National Institutes of Health (1979-1984); National Research Service Award, National Heart, Lung and Blood Institute, National Institutes of Health (1976-1977) **MEM:** Alpha Omega Alpha Honor Medical Society (1993-Present); American Society for Clinical Investigation (1982-Present); Fellow, Council on Circulation, American Heart Association, Inc. (1981-Present); Central Society for Clinical Investigation (1979-Present); Southern Society for Clinical Investigation (1979-Present); Sigma Xi (1979-Present); American Federation

for Clinical Research (1977-Present) **MH:** Albert Nelson Marquis Lifetime Achievement Award (2017); Distinguished Humanitarian (2017) **PA:** Democrat **ADD:** 5676 Redding Ave, Memphis, TN, 38120

MITCHELL, MADELEINE, T: Nutritionist (Retired) **I:** Health, Wellness and Fitness **DOB:** 12/14/1941 **SC:** Jamaica **PT:** William Keith Mitchell; Doris Christine (Levey) Mitchell **ED:** PhD in Nutrition, Cornell University, Ithaca, NY (1968); MS in Nutrition, Cornell University, Ithaca, NY (1965); BSc in Home Economics, McGill University, Montreal, Quebec, Canada (1963) **C:** Acting Chairman, Home Economics Research Center, Washington State University (1981-1983); Associate Professor, Washington State University (1978-2004); Assistant Professor, Washington State University (1969-1977) **CR:** Nutrition Scientist, United States Department of Agriculture (1980-1981) **CW:** Author, "Jamaican Ancestry: How to Find Out More" (2009); Contributor, Articles to Professional Journals **H:** Family history; Music; Reading **RE:** Episcopalian **ADD:** 5000 S.W. 25 Boulevard, Apartment 1111, Gainsville, FL, 32608 **URL:** www.mymynton.com/index.htm

MITCHELL, PAULA R., T: Dean **I:** Education/Educational Services **CN:** El Paso Community College **DOB:** 01/10/1951 **PB:** Independence **SC:** MO/USA **PT:** Millard Henry Gates; E. Lorene (Denton) Gates **MS:** Widow **SPN:** Ralph William Mitchell (5/24/1975) **CH:** Daniel Maher **ED:** EdD in Educational Administration, New Mexico State University (1996); MS in Nursing, The University of Texas (1976); BS in Nursing, Graceland University, Lamoni, IA (1973); Registered Nurse, State of Texas **CT:** Certification in Ambulatory Women's Healthcare, Nurses Association of the American College of Obstetricians and Gynecologists (1983-Present); Certified Childbirth Educator, American Society of Psychoprophylaxis Obstetrics (1978) **C:** Dean of Health Career & Technical Education, Math and Science, Rio Grade Campus, El Paso Community College, Texas (2008-Present); Dean of Health Occupations, Math and Science, Rio Grande Campus, El Paso Community College, Texas (2000-2008); Dean of Health Occupations, El Paso Community College, Texas (1999-2000); Division Dean, El Paso Community College, Texas (1998-1999); Director of Nursing, El Paso Community College, Texas (1985-2003); Acting Division Chairman, Health Occupations, El Paso Community College, Texas (1985-1986); Curriculum Facilitator, El Paso Community College, Texas (1984-1985); Instructor of Nursing, El Paso Community College, Texas (1979-1985) **CR:** Planned Parenthood, El Paso, TX (1986-1998); Nurse Practitioner in Obstetrics-Gynecology, Planned Parenthood, El Paso, TX (1981-1986); Consultant in Field **CIV:** Member, Steering Committee, El Paso Voluntary Organizations Active in Disaster (2014-Present); Chair, El Paso Voluntary Organizations Active in Disaster (2013-Present); Member, Health Care Council, Greater El Paso Chamber of Commerce (2002-Present); Member, Health Professional Shortage Task Force, Greater El Paso Chamber of Commerce (2001-Present); Coordinator, West Texas Medical Reserve Corps (2006-2014); Vice Chair, El Paso Voluntary Organizations Active in Disaster (2011-2013); Member Community Advisory Board, Victory Warriors Drill and Dance Academy, El Paso, TX (2001-2011); Chair, El Paso County Civil Service Commission (2009-2010); Member, El Paso County Civil Service Commission (2006-2010); Secretary-treasurer, Border Health Institute, El Paso, TX (2003-2008); Member, Star Advisory Committee, Canutillo Texas Independent

School District (2003-2005); Member, Governing Board, Mesa Hills Specialty Hospital (2002-2009); Board of Directors, Border Health Institute, El Paso, TX (2001-2008); Member, Advisory Committee, Center for Border Health Research, Paso del Norte Health Foundation (1998-2004); Member, Steering Committee, Unite El Paso Health, University Behavioral Health (1999-2000); Member, Leadership El Paso (1999); Co-chair, Health Taskforce, El Paso Community Legislative Agenda (1997-1999); Co-chair, Health and Human Services Task Force, Unite El Paso Health (1996-1998); Member, Collaborative Council, El Paso Magnet High School for Health Care Professions (1992-1994); Member, Professional Activities Committee, American Cancer Society, Inc., El Paso, TX (1992-1993); Member, Government Applications Review Committee, Rio Grande Council Governments (1989-1991); Member, El-Paso City-County Board of Health (1989-1991); Founder, Board of Directors, Health-CREST, El Paso, TX (1981-1985); Member, Public Education Committee, American Cancer Society, Inc., El Paso, TX (1983-1984) **MIL:** Captain, U.S. Army Reserve (1978-1998); Captain, U.S. Army (1972-1978); Officer, Medical Department, U.S. Army, Academy of Health Sciences **CW:** Co-author, "Nursing Perspectives and Issues" (1993, 1989); Contributor, Articles to Professional Journals **AW:** Excellence Award, NISOD (2014); Distinguished Service Award, Texas Society of Allied Health Professionals (2013); Outstanding Service Medal, Region 13 (2011); Outstanding Chapter Companion, Region 13 (2010); Silver Patrick Henry, Region 13 (2009); Merit Award, Region 13 (2008); Certificate of Appreciation (2006); Certificate of Appreciation for Community Responsibility (2005); Outstanding Community Service Award (2003); Merit and Service Certification, Victory Warriors Drill and Dance Academy (2003); Named Outstanding Alumni, Department of Education Management and Development, New Mexico State University (2002-2003); Named to Women's Hall of Fame, El Paso Commission (1999); Recipient, Unite El Paso Legacy Award (1997); Decorated Army Commendation Medal; Meritorious Service Medal **MEM:** Military Order of the World Wars National Vice Commander (2015-Present); Junior Vice Commander, Region 13 (2015-2017); Treasurer, El Paso Commission for Women (2007-Present); El Paso Chapter Commander, Military Order of the World Wars (2012-Present); Chair, Phoenician Award Committee (2009-2016; Commission on Accreditation, Site Visitor for Physical Therapist Assistant Programs, American Physical Therapist Association (1991-2015); Commander, Rio Grade Department, MOWW(2012-2015); Senior Vice Commander, Rio Grande Department, MOWW(2010-2012); Senior Vice Commander, El Paso Chapter, Military Order of the World Wars (2010-2012); Junior Vice Commander, Rio Grande Department, MOWW(2010-2011); Nomination Committee, District One, Texas Nurses Association (2009-2011); Past President, Texas Society of Allied Health Professionals (2009-2010); Junior Vice Commander, Military Order of the World Wars (2008-2010); Accreditation Site Visitor, Associates Degree Council, National League of Nursing (1990-2010); President, Texas Society of Allied Health Professionals (2008-2009); Board Member, District One, Texas Nurses Association (2008-2009); El Paso Chapter Staff Officer,Military Order of the World Wars (2007-2008); President-elect, Texas Society of Allied Health Professionals (2007-2008); Past President, District One, Texas Nurses Association (2005-2006); Secretary, National Council of Instructional Administrators, Texas Society of Allied Health Professionals (2004-2007); President, District One, Texas Nurses Association (2003-2005); President-elect, District One, Texas

Nurses Association (2002-2003); Healthcare Council, El Paso Chamber of Commerce (2001-2005); Nominating Committee, Associates Degree Council, National League of Nursing (1999-2000); Texas First Vice President, Associates Degree Council, National League of Nursing (1997-1999); Education Committee, American Society of Allied Health Professionals (1993-1996); Texas Third Vice President, Associates Degree Council, National League of Nursing (1992-1993); Program Standards Task Force, National Council for Workforce Education (1991-1993); Texas Education Committee, Associates Degree Council, National League of Nursing (1991-1992); National Bylaws Committee, Organization for Associate Degree Nursing (1990-1995); Chairman, Goals Committee, Organization for Associate Degree Nursing (1989-2004); Resolutions Committee, Associates Degree Council, National League of Nursing (1987-1989); Correspondent, Nurses Association of the American College of Obstetricians and Gynecologists (1987-1989); Articulation Task Force, National Council for Workforce Education (1986-1989); Texas Membership Chairman, Organization for Associate Degree Nursing (1985-1989); National Program Review Committee, Nurses Association of the American College of Obstetricians and Gynecologists (1984-1986); Legislative Committee, Advanced Nurse Practitioner Group El Paso (1984); Coordinator, Advanced Nurse Practitioner Group El Paso (1980-1983); Chapter Coordinator, Nurses Association of the American College of Obstetricians and Gynecologists (1979-1983); Sigma Theta Tau; Phi Kappa Phi; American Vocational Association; American Association for Women in Community and Junior Colleges; Texas Organization of Nurse Executives; American Legion **H:** Star Trek; Community service activities **PA:** Democrat **RE:** Christian **BA:** P.O. Box 20500, El Paso, TX, 79998 **ADD:** 4616 Cupid Dr, El Paso, TX, 79924 **URL:** www.epcc.edu

MITTLEBERG, ERIC M., T: Pharmaceutical Executive **I:** Pharmaceuticals **CN:** G&W Laboratories **DOB:** 11/07/1951 **PB:** New York **SC:** NY/USA **PT:** Irving Ralph Mittleberg; Rose (Schnieder) Mittleberg **MS:** Married **SPN:** Jane Susan Baumoehl (12/25/1977) **CH:** Scott; Alyson; Lauren **ED:** PhD in Pharmaceutics, St. Johns University, Jamaica, NY (1982); MS in IND Pharmaceutics, St. Johns University, Jamaica, NY (1978); BS in Pharmacy, St. Johns University, Jamaica, NY (1974) **CT:** Registered Pharmacist, State of New York **C:** Chief Strategy Officer, G&W Laboratories (2014-Present); Vice President, Pharmaceutical Division, G&W Laboratories (2014-Present); Chief Operating Officer, Nostrum Laboratories, New Brunswick, NJ (2013-2014); Executive Vice President, Pharmaceutical R&D, Sandoz Pharm, New Jersey (2009-2012); Executive Vice President, Pharmaceutical Research & Development, Par Pharmaceutical, Inc., Spring Valley, NY (2006-2009); Vice President, Science and Medical Affairs, Ivax Corp. (1997-2006); Senior Director, Pharmaceutical Development and Technical Services Worldwide, R.W. Johnson Pharmaceutical Research Institute, Raritan, NJ (1989-1997); Director, Production and Technical Services, Schering Labs, Miami, FL (1986-1989); Manager, Manufacturing Development, Key Pharmaceutical, Miami, FL (1983-1986); Department Head, Process Improvement, Lederle Labs, Pearl River, NY (1978-1983); Associate Scientist, Hoffmann-LaRoche Inc., Nutley, NJ (1974-1978) **MEM:** International Society Pharmaceutical Engineers; Academy of Pharmaceutical Science; American Pharmaceutical Association **MH:** Albert Nelson Marquis Lifetime Achievement Award (2017) **ADD:** 3 Horizon Dr, Wayne, NJ, 07470

MOCK, HELENA S. ESQ, T: Managing Attorney **I:** Law and Legal Services **CN:** The Peninsula Center for Estate and Lifelong Planning **DOB:** 10/30/1967 **PB:** Fairfax, VA **MS:** Married **SPN:** Michael D. Mock **CH:** Jordan A. Mock Allison L. Mock **ED:** JD, Marshall-Wythe School of Law, College of William & Mary (2000) MA in English Education & Literature, Old Dominion University (1996) BA in English, European Division, University of Maryland, Summa Cum Laude (1992) **CT:** Accredited Estate Planner, NAEPC (2016-Present); Accredited Attorney, U.S. Department of Veterans Affairs (2011-Present) **C:** Director, Elder & Disability Law Clinic, Marshall-Wythe School of Law, College of William & Mary (2011-Present); Attorney, The Peninsula Center for Estate and Lifelong Planning (2010-Present); Attorney, Jones, Blechman, Woltz & Kelly, P.C. (1999-2010) **CR:** St. George Tucker Adjunct Professor of Law, Marshall-Wythe School of Law, College of William & Mary (2014-Present); Director, Elder & Disability Law Clinic, Marshall-Wythe School of Law, College of William & Mary (2011-Present); Adjunct Professor of Law in Family Wealth Transactions, Marshall-Wythe School of Law, College of William & Mary (2005-2012); Adjunct Professor, Legal Skills Program, Marshall-Wythe School of Law, College of William & Mary (2004-2012) **CIV:** President, Peninsula Estate Planning Council (2017-Present); Life Planning Law Firms Association (2016-Present); Director, Williamsburg House of Mercy (2016-Present); Officer, Williamsburg House of Mercy (2016-Present); Advisory Board, Dream Catchers (2011-Present) NAELA (2009-Present); Peninsula Estate Planning Council (2001-Present) **MIL:** Legal Specialist, U.S. Army (1986-1989) **AW:** Honoree, Rating of 10.0 - Superb, AVVO (2010-Present); Honoree, Virginia's Exceptional Lawyers, Richmond Magazine (2017); Honoree, Virginia Super Lawyer, Super Lawyers (2013-2017); Honoree, Top Lawyer, Virginia Coastal Magazine (2015); Honoree, Legal Elite, Virginia Business Magazine (2004-2009, 2015); Client Distinction Award, Martindale-Hubbell (2013, 2015); Honoree, Expert Resource, Worldwide Registry (2014); Honoree, Rising Star, Super Lawyers (2007-2008) **MEM:** Williamsburg Bar Association (2000-Present); First Vice President, Peninsula Estate Planning Council (2016-2017); Secretary, Board of Directors, Mary Immaculate Hospital (2015-2017); Board of Directors, Mary Immaculate Hospital (2012-2017); Second Vice President, Peninsula Estate Planning Council (2015-2016); Treasurer, Peninsula Estate Planning Council (2014-2015); Secretary, Peninsula Estate Planning Council (2013-2014); Member, Newport News Bar Association (2002-2011); Treasurer, Newport News Bar Association (2002-2007); Secretary, Avalon: A Center for Women and Children (2002-2003) **BAR:** Virginia State Bar (2000); Supreme Court of Virginia; United States District Court Eastern District of Virginia; United States Court of Appeals for the Fourth Circuit **H:** Reading; Cooking; Yoga **BA:** 461 McLaws Circle, Suite 2, Williamsburg, VA, 23186 **ADD:** 461 McLaws Cir Ste 2, The Peninsula Center for Estate and Lifelong Planning, Williamsburg, VA, 23185

MOGIL, H. MICHAEL, T: Certified Consulting Meteorologist **I:** Sciences **CN:** How The Weatherworks **ED:** MS in Meteorology, Florida State University (1969); BS in Meteorology, Florida State University (1967) **CT:** Certified Consulting Meteorologist, American Meteorological Society; Certified Broadcast Meteorologist, American Meteorological Society; National Weather Association Digital Media Seal **C:** Content Producer, Northeast Weather Forum/Global Weather & Climate Center (2010-Present); Owner, Manager,

Tutor, Mathworks Tutoring, Inc. (2005-Present); Certified Consulting Meteorologist, How the Weatherworks (1993-Present); Certified Broadcast Meteorologist/Forensic Meteorologist, How the Weatherworks (1979-Present); Foot's Forecast, Foot's Forecast (2010-2013); Content Producer, Associated Content (2008-2013); Collaborator, Platypus Media (2006-2007); Forecaster, Branch Chief, Trainer, Researcher, National Oceanic and Atmospheric Administration (1972-1995); Meteorologist, National Weather Service (1972-1985) **CR:** Director, National Weather Camp Program (2008-Present); Independent Researcher **CIV:** Mentor; Board Member, Large Community Condo Association **CW:** Author, "Minding the Weather, How Expert Forecasters Think" (2017); Author, "Extreme Weather, Second Edition" (2009); Author, "Extreme Weather" (2007); Developer, Cloud Posters, Charts and Cards; Author, Weather Books; Blogger, Globalweatherclimatecenter. com; Contributor, Weather Wise Magazine **AW:** Digital Media Seal (2014) **MEM:** National Council of Industrial Meteorologists; American Meteorological Society; National Weather Association **MH:** Distinguished Humanitarian (2017) **BA:** 5644 Tavilla Cir Ste 201, How The Weatherworks, Naples, FL, 34110 **URL:** http://www.weatherworks.com

MOKRASCH, LEWIS CARL, T: Chemist **I:** Sciences **CN:** LSU Health New Orleans **DOB:** 05/09/1930 **PB:** St. Paul **SC:** MN/USA **YOP:** 2018-02-02 **PT:** Lewis Mokrasch; and Anna (Dvorak) Mokrasch **MS:** Married **SPN:** Jane Carolyn Church (4/20/1974) **ED:** PhD, University of Wisconsin (1955); BS, University of St. Thomas, Magna Cum Laude (1952) **C:** Professor Emeritus, Louisiana State University Medical Center (1992-Present); Acting Department Head, Louisiana State University Medical Center (1978-1979); Professor, Louisiana State University Medical Center, New Orleans (1976-1992); Associate Professor, Department of Biochemistry, Louisiana State University Medical Center, New Orleans (1971-1976); Research Associate, Department of Psychiatry and Neurology, Louisiana State University Medical Center, New Orleans (1956-1957) **CR:** Visiting Professor of neurology Duke University Medical Center (1981-1982); Staff Scientist, Neurosciences Research Programs, Brookline, MA (1970-1971); Grant Reviewer, Neurological Diseases and Blindness, National Institute of Mental Health (1969-1992); Adjunct Associate Professor of Biology, Hellenic College, Brookline, MA (1969-1971); Assistant Professor, Hellenic College, Brookline, MA (1967-1971); Associate Biochemist (1964-1971); Associate, Department of Biological Chemistry, Harvard Medical School (1964-1967); Assistant Biochemist, McLean Hospital, Belmont, MA (1960-1964); Associate in Medicine (1959-1962); Instructor of Medicine, University of Kansas Medical Center, Kansas City, MO (1957-1959); Fellow, American Association of Clinical Chemists **CIV:** Reynolda House Museum of American Art (2007-Present); Senior Services Program, Winston-Salem, NC (1992-Present); Senior Leader, Duke Long-Term Care Program Education Committee (1999); Education Committee Shepherd Center (1996); Citizens Quality Nursing Home Care, New Orleans, LA (1987-1992); President, Belmont Preservation Society (1969); Candidate Board Selectman, Belmont (1969); Inspector, Adult Care Home Community Advisory Committee, Forsyth County **CW:** Co-Author, "Myelin" (1971); Reviewer, Journal of Biological Chemistry (1956-1992); Contributor, Various Articles to Professional Journals (1952-1994) **AW:** Grantee, Louisiana Board of Regents (1986-1988); Grantee, Schlieder Foundation (1983-1984); Grantee, National

Institute of Mental Health (1973-1974); Grantee, Schlieder Foundation (1971-1972); Grantee, National Institute of Neurological Disability and Blindness (1957-1990) **MEM:** Vice President, Salemtowne Independent Resident Council (2014-2015); Chairman, Local Chapter, American Chemical Society (1976); Chairman, Local Chapter, American Society of Neurochemistry (1974); Founder, President, American Society of Biological Chemists; Membership Chairman, New England Section, Society of Research Administrators; National Citizens Coalition for Nursing Home Reform; Founder, American Association of Individual Investors; Secretary, Piedmont Chapter, American Association of Individual Investors; Former President, American Association of Individual Investors **PA:** Libertarian **ADD:** 3609 Bechler Lane, Winston Salem, NC, 27106

MOLTO, MAVIS BERTHA, T: Librarian (Retired) **I:** Library Management/Library Services **PB:** Ada **SC:** MN/USA **PT:** Martin Peter Molto; Hulda (Diegel) Molto **ED:** PhD, University of California, Los Angeles (1989); MS in Information Science, University of California, Los Angeles (1973); BS, Brigham Young University (1966) **C:** Librarian in Serials Cataloging, Merrill-Cazier Library, Utah State University (2000-2017); Interim Co-head, Cataloging Department, Merrill-Cazier Library, Utah State University (2014-2015); Co-librarian in Cataloging, Westridge School for Girls (1996-1999); Consultant, Various School and Special Libraries and Companies (1991-1999); Librarian Assistant in Cataloging, Westridge School for Girls (1994-1996); Lecturer, University of California, Los Angeles (1995); Contract Librarian, Various School and Special Libraries and Companies (1990-1995); Assistant/Adjunct Professor, San Jose State University, Fullerton (1991-1993); Research Assistant, University of California, Los Angeles (1982-1989); Technical Support Assistant, Systems Development Corporation (1982); Information Analyst, Union Oil Company of California (1976-1979); Librarian in Cataloging, TRW Defense and Space Systems (1973-1976); Caseworker, Garfield County, Utah (1966-1968) **CW:** Contributor, Articles, Peer-reviewed Journals; Contributor, Articles, Library Resources & Technical Services; Contributor, Articles, Cataloging & Classification Quarterly; Contributor, Article, Serials Review; Contributor, Article, Technical Services Quarterly; Contributor, Articles, Information Processing & Management; Contributor, Article, Journal of the American Society for Information Science; Author, "Genealogical Literature and its Users," Encyclopedia of Library and Information Sciences **AW:** Best of Cataloging & Classification Quarterly Award (1998); Inductee, The Honor Society of Phi Kappa Phi **MEM:** Genealogy Round Table, Utah Library Association (2007-Present); Technical Services Round Table, Utah Library Association (2000-Present); Utah Library Association (2000-Present); Association for Library Collections & Technical Services, American Library Association (1995-Present); American Library Association (1985-Present); Cataloging Forum Presenter, Continuing Resources Section, Association for Library Collections & Technical Services, American Library Association (2016); Continuing Resources Cataloging Committee, Continuing Resources Section, Association for Library Collections & Technical Services, American Library Association (2014-2016); CRS Liaison, Publications Committee, Association for Library Collections & Technical Services, American Library Association (2014-2016); Chair, Education, Research, and Publications Coordinating Committee, Continuing Resources Section, Association for Library Collections & Technical Services, American Library Association (2012-2014); RDA

Planning and Training Task Force, Cataloging and Metadata Management Section, Association for Library Collections & Technical Services, American Library Association (2012-2013); Publications Committee, Association for Library Collections & Technical Services, American Library Association (2009-2013); Research and Publications Committee, Continuing Resources Section, Association for Library Collections & Technical Services, American Library Association (2009-2011); Cataloging Committee, Utah Academic Library Consortium (2004-2009); North American Serials Interest Group (2000-2008); Secretary-treasurer, Technical Services Round Table, Utah Library Association (2006-2007); Chair, Cataloging Committee, Utah Academic Library Consortium (2004-2006); Cataloging Node Presenter, North American Serials Interest Group (2003); Cataloging Chair, Group Access Project, Independent School Library Exchange (1997-1999); Library Education and Recruitment Committee, California Library Association (1992-1994) **H:** Genealogy **RE:** Church of Jesus Christ of Latter-day Saints **ADD:** 2839 Van Buren Ave Apt 6, Ogden, UT, 84403 **URL:** https://scholar.google.com/citations?user=Hgs7vckAAAAJ&hl=en

MONK, DIANA C., T: Small Business Owner **I:** Business Management/Business Services **CN:** Longacre Training Stables **DOB:** 02/25/1927 **PB:** Visalia **SC:** CA/USA **PT:** Charles Edward Williams; Viola Genevieve (Shea) Williams **MS:** Married **SPN:** James Alfred Monk (8/11/1951) **CH:** Kiloran; Sydney; Geoffrey; Anne; Eric **ED:** Coursework, California College of the Arts, Oakland, CA (1972); Coursework, Academy of Art University - School of Fine Art, San Francisco, CA (1948-1951); Coursework, Sacramento City College (1947-1948); Coursework, University of the Pacific, Stockton, CA (1946-1947) **C:** Stable Owner, Manager, Longacre Training Stables, Santa Rosa, CA (1990-Present); Owner, Manager, Monk and Lee Associates, Lafayette, CA (1973-1980); Gallery Director, Jason Aver Gallery, San Francisco, CA (1970-1972); Private Art Teacher, Lafayette, CA (1963-1970); Art Teacher, Mount Diablo School District, Concord, CA (1958-1963); Oil Painter, Monk Fine Art **CIV:** Juror, Oakland California Art, A Street Gallery, Santa Rosa, CA (2000); Exhibit Chairman, Valley Art Gallery, Walnut Creek, CA (1977-1978); Chair, Board of Directors, Center for Community Arts, Walnut Creek CA (1972-1974); Juror, Women's Art Show, Walnut Creek, CA (1970); Advisor to Chairman, Center for Community Arts, Walnut Creek CA (1968-1972) **CW:** Exhibitor, Group Show, Lamorinda Arts Council Show, Orinda, CA (2017); Solo Exhibitor, John F. Kennedy University, Orinda, CA; Solo Exhibitor, Civic Arts Gallery, Walnut Creek, CA; Solo Exhibitor, Vallery Art Gallery, Walnut Creek, CA; Solo Exhibitor, Sea Ranch Gallery, Gualala, CA; Solo Exhibitor, Jason Aver Gallery, San Francisco, CA; Exhibitor, Group Show, Oakland Art Museum; Exhibitor, Group Show, Crocker National Art Gallery, Sacramento, CA; Exhibitor, Group Show, Le Salon des Nations, Paris, France **MH:** Albert Nelson Marquis Lifetime Achievement Award (2017) **BA:** 1702 Willowside Road, Longacre Training Stables, Santa Rosa, CA, 95401 **URL:** https://www.monkfineart.com

MONTGOMERY, JAMES D. SR., T: President, Lawyer **I:** Law and Legal Services **CN:** James D. Montgomery & Associates, Ltd. **MS:** Married **SPN:** Pauline M. Creightney (3/5/1971) **CH:** Linda; James, Jr.; Lisa; Michelle; Jewel; Jilian **ED:** JD, University of Illinois (1956); BA, University of Illinois (1953) **C:** Attorney, Sole Practice, Chicago, IL (1986-Present); Corporate Counsel, City of Chicago (1983-1986); Sole Practice, Chicago, IL (1981-1983); Partner, Law Offices of Montgomery and Holland, Chicago,

IL (1977-1981); Sole Practice, Chicago, IL (1970-1977); Partner, Newman, Kipnis and Montgomery, Chicago, IL (1966-1970); Partner, Montgomery, Holt and Bolden, Chicago, IL (1964-1966); Sole Practice, Chicago, IL (1960-1964); Assistant United States Attorney, Northern District of Illinois, Chicago, IL (1958-1960); President, James D. Montgomery & Associates **CR:** University of Chicago Law School (1996-1998); University of Chicago Law School (1994); Illinois Institute for Continuing Legal Education (1987); Corporate Counsel's Office, City of Chicago (1987); Teacher, DePaul College of Law, Chicago, IL (1982-1983); Hearing Board of Illinois Civil Service Systems, Illinois Parole and Pardon Board (Now Illinois Prison Review Board); Fellow, International Academy of Trial Lawyers **AW:** Edwin Bill C. Berry Award, Chicago Urban League (2017); Inductee, Trial Lawyers Hall of Fame (2017); Laureate, Academy of Illinois Lawyers, Illinois State Bar Association (1999); Earl Burrus Dickerson Award, Chicago Bar Association (1996); Hall of Fame Award, National Bar Association (1996); Hall of Fame Award, National Bar Association (1996); Edward H. Wright Award, Cook County Bar Association (1983) **MEM:** Board of Directors, National Association of Criminal Defense Lawyers (1980-1981); President, Cook County Bar Association (1974-1975); American Bar Association; American Board of Trial Advocates; National Bar Association; Trustee, National Institute Municipal Law Officers; Federal Bar Association; Illinois Association of Criminal Defense Lawyers; Illinois State Bar Association; Chicago Bar Association **BAR:** U.S. Supreme Court (1975); District of Columbia Circuit, U.S. Court of Appeals (1975); Seventh Circuit, U.S. Court of Appeals (1959); U.S. District Court, Northern District, State of Illinois (1957); State of Illinois (1956) **MH:** Albert Nelson Marquis Lifetime Achievement Award (2017) **H:** Golf **ADD:** 5026 S Greenwood Avenue, Chicago, IL, 60615 **URL:** http://www.jamesdmontgomery.com/About/James-D-Montgomery-2333349.shtml

MOODY OEHLER, JUDITH JANE, T: Counselor (Retired) **I:** Health, Wellness and Fitness **DOB:** 03/05/1942 **PB:** Farner **SC:** TN/USA **PT:** William Henry Moody; Peggy Pierce (Lindsey) Moody **MS:** Married **SPN:** Carl Bailey Oehler (6/1/1963) **CH:** David William Oehler; Paul Edwin Oehler **ED:** MEd, Texas Christian University (1976); BS in Elementary Education, The University of Texas at Austin (1963) **CT:** Certification in Library Science, The University of Texas at Austin (1963); Licensed Professional Counselor, State of Texas; National Board Certified Counselor **C:** Elementary School Counselor, Arlington Independent School District (1979-1996); Elementary School Teacher, Arlington Independent School District (1965-1978) **AW:** Recipient, Caring Award, North Central Texas Counseling Association (1995) **MEM:** Secretary, Daughters of the American Colonists Honorable Philip Livingston Chapter (2007-2008); Secretary, National Society Colonial Dames XVII Century Governor Thomas Hinckley Chapter (2007-2008); Club Photographer, Arlington Woman's Club (2005-2007); First Vice President, Encore Club (2004-2005); Secretary, Travel Department, Antique Department Chairman, Arlington Woman's Club (2003-2005); State President, Auxiliary Texas Society of Professional Engineers (1997-1998); Texas Association Counseling and Development; Secretary, North Central Texas Association of Counseling and Development (1995-1996); Vice President, Region V, Auxiliary Texas Society of Professional Engineers (1994-1995); Life Member, Texas State Teachers Association; Secretary, Arlington Association of Texas Professional Educators (1994-1995); Retired School Employees

Arlington; President, Mid-Cities Chapter, Auxiliary Texas Society of Professional Engineers (1992-1994); State Secretary, Auxiliary Texas Society of Professional Engineers (1993-1994); Treasurer and Chapter Regent, National Society Daughters of the American Revolution; National Society US Daughters 1812; United Daughter of the Confederacy; La Rochelle Chapter, National Huguenot Society; Life Member, National Society Magna Charta Dames and Barons; Life Member, Ligon Family and Kinsman Association; Life Member, Jamestowne Society Lone Star Company; National Society of the Sons and Daughters of the Pilgrims; National Society Dames of Court of Honor; Illinois State Society; The Plantagenet Society; The Order of Washington; Colonial Order of the Crown; Life Member, The Sovereign Colonial Society Americans Royal Descent; Guild Colonial Artisans and Tradesmen 1607-1783; The Society Descendants of Knights of the Most Noble Order of the Garter; Life Member, Society Descendants of Lady Godiva; Arlington Women Rotary; Phi Delta Kappa; Life Member, University of Texas at Austin Exes **MH:** Albert Nelson Marquis Lifetime Achievement Award (2017) **H:** Travel; Reading; Walking; Collecting recipes; Genealogy; Watching classic movies; Being a grandmother **RE:** Methodist **ADD:** 2408 Westwood Dr, Arlington, TX, 76012

MOON, LORETTA M., T: Recreation Therapist **I:** Social Work **CN:** Eastern State Hospital **DOB:** 01/22/1952 **PB:** Spokane **SC:** WA/USA **PT:** George Edmond Moon; Eva Louise Moon **ED:** BA in Recreation Administration, Eastern Washington University, Cheney, WA (1976); AA, Big Bend Community College, Moses Lake, WA (1974); AS, Big Bend Community College, Moses Lake, WA (1974) **CT:** Certified Recreation Therapist, National Council on Therapeutic Recreation (1989) **C:** Lifeguard Instructor, Waster Safety Instructor, YMCA, Spokane, WA (2009-Present); Recreation Therapist, Aquatic Therapy Specialist, Eastern State Hospital/Washington State Therapy Pool (1994-Present); Lifeguard Instructor, Lakeland Village, WA (2005-2009); Nurse Assistant, Carol's Adult Family Home, Nine Mile Falls, WA (2004-2006); Lifeguard, Instructor in Water Safety, YWCA (2002-2005); Recreation Therapist, Geriatric Unit, Eastern State Hospital, Medical Lake, WA (1992-1994); Coordinator, Adaptive Aquatic, YWCA (1992-1994); Instructor, Adult Swimming Class, YWCA, Spokane, WA (1990-1992); Recreation Leader 2, Interlake School of the Severe and Profound, Medical Lake, WA (1989-1992); Lifeguard, Spokane County Parks Department, Washington (1971-1976) **CIV:** Teacher, Latter Day Saints Church (1980-Present); President, Medical Lake Middle School (2001-2002); Leader, Outdoor Chairman, Inland North West Campfire, Spokane, WA (1983-1991) **AW:** Top Aquatic Therapy Center in the U.S., U.S. Water Fitness Association (2003-2009); Top 100 Aquatic Directors in the U.S., U.S. Water Fitness Association (1997-2009) **MEM:** Master Teacher, American Association of Physical Activity (2000-Present); U.S. Water Fitness Association; American Therapeutic Recreation Association **MH:** Albert Nelson Marquis Lifetime Achievement Award (2017) **H:** Swimming; Embroidery; Crocheting; Gardening **RE:** Latter-Day Saints **ADD:** 5732 N D Street, Spokane, WA, 99205

MOONEY, MARILYN, T: Lawyer **I:** Law and Legal Services **CN:** Norton Rose Fulbright US LLP **DOB:** 07/29/1952 **PB:** Pittsburgh **SC:** PA/USA **PT:** James Russell Mooney; Mary Elizabeth (Cartwright) Mooney **ED:** JD, University of Pennsylvania (1976); BA, University of Pennsylvania, Summa Cum Laude (1973) **C:** Chair, M & A Practice Group (2008-Present); Partner-in-Charge, Corporate and Securities Practice, Washington Office, Fulbright & Jaworski L.L.P. (2005-Present); Partner, Fulbright & Jaworski L.L.P., Washington, D.C. (1990-Present); Associate, Fulbright & Jaworski L.L.P., Washington, D.C. (1985-1989); Attorney, E. I. du Pont de Nemours & Co., Washington, D.C. (1985); Attorney, E. I. du Pont de Nemours & Co., Wilmington, DE (1976-1984) **CW:** Contributor, Articles, Professional Journals **MEM:** Federal Regulation Securities Committee, ABA; Corporate Finance and Securities Law and International Sections, The District of Columbia Bar; Issues and Trading in Securities Committee, International Bar Association; Securities Law Committee, Society of Corp Securities and Governance Profiles **BAR:** Pennsylvania (1990); United States Supreme Court (1986); United States District Court District of Columbia (1985); United States Court of Appeals for the District of Columbia (1985); The District of Columbia (1985); Massachusetts (1977) **MH:** Albert Nelson Marquis Lifetime Achievement Award (2017) **BA:** 799 9th Street N.W., Suite 1000, Norton Rose Fulbright Law Firm, Washington, DC, 20001 **ADD:** 799 9th St NW Ste 1000, Norton Rose Fulbright Law Firm, Washington, DC, 20001

MOORE, DERRICK LANIER, T: Minister, Community Leader, Military Officer **I:** Religious **DOB:** 01/06/1960 **PB:** Buffalo **SC:** NY/USA **PT:** Willis Carl Moore; Catherine Moore **MS:** Divorced **SPN:** Dorothy Powell (2006, Divorced); Jacquelee Lewis (1984, Divorced) **ED:** Graduate Certificate, Creativity and Change Leadership, University at Buffalo (2016); MBA, Project/Program Management, Keller Graduate School of Management, DeVry University, Washington, D.C. (2013); MS, Project Management, Keller Graduate School of Management, DeVry University, Washington, D.C. (2012); BS, Grambling State University, Grambling, LA (1983) **C:** Chairman, Executive Community Council, Buffalo Promise Neighborhood, Buffalo, NY (2013-Present); Ordained Pastor, Buffalo, NY (1998-Present); Ordained Minister, Buffalo, NY (1998-Present); Veterans Service Representative, U.S. Department of Veterans Affairs, Buffalo, NY (2016); Security Manager, Technical Services Division, Northrop Grumman, Panama City, FL (2008-2009); Security Management Lead, Northrop Grumman Technical Services Inc., Panama City, FL (2007-2008); Security Subject Matter Expert, Northrop Grumman Technical Services Inc., Panama City, FL (2007-2008) **CR:** Dispatched Military Working Dog and Explosive Ordnance Support, Presidential Inauguration (2009); Dispatched Military Working Dog and Explosive Ordnance Support, Olympic Games (2008); Program Management Support, United States Department of Defense Informational Security Program; Anti-Terrorism Planner, United States Department of Defense; Physical Security Planner, United States Department of Defense; Training Lead, United States Department of Defense; Functional Expert, United States Department of Defense; Security Management Support Lead, United States Air Force; Functional Expert, United States Department of Defense Very Important Persons Protection Support Agency; Dispatched Military Working Dog and Explosive Ordnance Support, Democratic National Conventions; Dispatched Military Working Dog and Explosive Ordnance Support, Republic National Conventions; Reception Manager, Air Force Aid; Reception Manager, Family Life Education; Reception Manager, Family/Personal Readiness; Reception Manager, Personal Financial Management; Reception Manager, Relocation Assistance; Reception Manager, Transition Assistance Program; Reception Manager, Crisis Intervention; Security Lead, Operation Enduring Freedom; Security Lead, Operation Iraqi Freedom **CIV:** Manager, Tops for Tots Program, RMHC; President, Atlas Booster Club; Choir Lead Vocalist, Traveling Musical Group; President, Wyoming Buffalo Soldier Association **MIL:** Management Analyst, United States Air Force (1984-2007); Security Specialist Manager, United States Air Force (1984-2007) **CW:** Actor, "The Sitting Place," United States Air Force **AW:** Six Air Force Commendation Medals; Military Outstanding Volunteer Service Medal; Non-Commissioned Officer of the Year; Key to the City, Biloxi, MS; NCO Academy, United States Air Force; Award for Best Antiterrorism Program, Tyndall Air Force Base, Air Education and Training Command, United States Air Force; Speaker's Award, Keynote; Community Service Award, ACURE; Tyndall Black Heritage Committee Legacy Award; Roy Wilkins Renown Service Award, NAACP; Principal Coordinator Juneteenth Heritage Award, Wyoming Buffalo Soldier Association; Martin Luther King Prayer Breakfast Keynote Speaker Award, NAACP, Bay County, FL; Numerous Quarterly Awards, United States Air Force **MEM:** The American Legion; Veterans of Foreign Affairs **PA:** Democrat **RE:** United Methodist **ADD:** 340 Highgate Ave, Buffalo, NY, 14215

MOORE, JOHN R., T: Professor Emeritus **I:** Education/Educational Services **CN:** University of Maryland **DOB:** 09/30/1929 **PB:** Columbus **SC:** OH/USA **PT:** Lawrence Levi Moore; Hazel Marie (Runyan) Moore **MS:** Married **SPN:** Marjorie Ann Coy (6/14/1953) **CH:** Lee; Andrew **ED:** PhD in Agricultural Economics, University of Wisconsin-Madison (1959); MSc in Agricultural Economics, Cornell University (1955); BSc in Agriculture, The Ohio State University (1951) **C:** Professor Emeritus, University of Maryland, College Park, MD (1995-Present); Assistant Dean, International Programs, University of Maryland, College Park, MD (1979-1994); Professor, World Food Situation and Food Marketing, University of Maryland, College Park, MD (1968-1995); Marketing Specialist, Economic Consultant, Ford Foundation, New Delhi, India (1968-1970); Associate Professor, University of Maryland, College Park, MD (1962-1968); Assistant Professor, Michigan State University, East Lansing, MI (1958-1962); Graduate Research Assistant, University of Wisconsin-Madison (1955-1958); Graduate Research Assistant, Cornell University, Ithaca, NY (1953-1955); County 4-H Club Agent, Ohio Cooperative Extension Service, Stuebenville, OH (1951) **CR:** Economic Consultant, The World Bank Group, Kyrgyz Republic (1997); Food and Agricultural Organization, Beijing, China (1990); Economic Consultant, The World Bank Group, Nigeria (1971-1974); Economic Consultant, The World Bank Group, India (1971-1974); Economic Consultant, Federal Trade Commission, Washington, D.C. (1963-1964); United States Agency for International Development, Indonesia; United States Agency for International Development, Malawi; United States Agency for International Development, Haiti; United States Agency for International Development, Liberia; United States Agency for International Development, Egypt **CIV:** Member, Board of Visitors, School of Music, University of Maryland, College Park, MD (2012-Present); Chairman, Board of Commissioners, College Park Housing Authority (1996-Present); Trustee, South-East Consortium for International Development (1978-1995) **MIL:** Lieutenant, Junior Grade, U.S. Naval Reserve (1951-1953) **CW:** Senior Author, "Indian Food Grain Market" (1972); Senior Author, "U.S. Investment In Latin American Food Processing" (1966); Senior Author, "Market Structure of Agriculture Industries" (1964) **AW:** Honoree, Meritorious

Intertiol Program, United States Department of Agriculture (1990); Certificate of Appreciation (1986); International Honor Award, United States Department of Agriculture, Washington, D.C. (1985); PhD Thesis Award **MEM:** Board of Visitors, University of Maryland School of Music, College Park, MD (2011-Present); Board Chairman, Trees for the Future (2007-Present); Chairman, Board of Trustees, Trees for the Future (1997-Present); President, Rotary International (1998-1999); Agricultural & Applied Economics Association; American Economic Association; International Association of Agricultural Economists **MH:** Albert Nelson Marquis Lifetime Achievement Award (2017) **H:** Photography; Travel; Gardening; Golf **BA:** Symons HI Rm 2213, University of Maryland, College Park, MD, 20742 **ADD:** 3616 De Pauw Pl, College Park, MD, 20740

MOORE, THOMAS E., **T:** Professor Emeritus **I:** Education/Educational Services **CN:** University of Michigan **DOB:** 01/10/1930 **PB:** Champaign **SC:** IL/USA **PT:** Gerald E. Moore; Velma (Lewis) Moore **MS:** Married, Widowed, 03/26/2016 **SPN:** E. Eleanor Sifferd (2/4/1951) **CH:** Deborah S.; Melinda S. **ED:** PhD, University of Illinois (1956); MS, University of Illinois (1952); BS, University of Illinois (1951) **C:** Professor Emeritus, University of Michigan (2000-Present); Curator of Insects, University of Michigan (1956-2000); Professor of Biology, University of Michigan (1966-2000); Director of Museum Exhibits, University of Michigan (1988-1993); Associate Professor of Zoology, University of Michigan (1963-1966); Assistant Professor of Zoology, University of Michigan (1959-1963); Instructor of Zoology, University of Michigan (1956-1959); Technology Assistant, Illinois Natural History Survey, University of Illinois (1950-1956) **CR:** Member, Grievance Committee, University of Michigan (1997-1998); Member, Faculty Handbook Committee, University of Michigan (1997-1998); Member, Steering Committee, University Colloquium on Environmental Research and Education (1991-1993); Member, Conference Planning Committee, National Institute of Environment Health Sciences, NIH (1991-1992); Board Director, Organization for Tropical Studies, San Jose, Costa Rica (1968-1979); Visiting Professor of Organization for Tropical Studies, San Jose, Costa Rica (1972); Member, Steering Committee, Tropical Biome, United States International Biological Program (1969-1972); Visiting Professor of Organization for Tropical Studies, San Jose, Costa Rica (1970) **CIV:** Board Member, Academy of Freedom Lecture Fund at the University of Michigan at the University of Michigan, Ann Arbor [501(c)(3)] (1995-Present); Member, Department of Public Safety Oversight Committee, University of Michigan (2010-2013); Board Member, Friends of Misery Bay (2007-2011); Consultant, Misery Bay Exhibits, Ontario Parks, Ontario, Canada (2005-2011); Member, Provost's Task Force on Grievance Policies, University of Michigan (2008); Treasurer, Academy of Freedom Lecture Fund, University of Michigan (1995-1998); Consultant on Visual Technology in Environmental Curricula, National Science Foundation (1994-1997); Vice Chairman, Senate Advisory Committee on University Affairs, University of Michigan (1995-1996); Member, Senate Advisory Committee on University Affairs, University of Michigan (1993-1996); County Representative, Huron River Watershed Council, Ann Arbor, MI (1987-1995); Member, Michigan High School Accreditation Advisory Committee, Ann Arbor, MI (1988-1992); Kempf House Museum, Ann Arbor, MI **CW:** Contributor, Article on 17-Year Cicadas in Michigan, Scientific Journal (2017); Co-Author, "Singing Insects of North America (SINA)" (2003-2014); Author, Television

Program on Cicadas (1998); Co-Editor, Lectures on Science Education (1991-1993); Co-Editor, "Cricket Behavior and Neurobiology" (1989); Author, "17-Year Cicadas" (1975) **AW:** Project Grantee, LAMBAC (2010); Research Grantee, Office of Naval Research, Defense Advanced Research Project Agency (1998-2001); District Faculty Governance Award, University of Michigan (1998); Research Grantee, National Science Foundation (1996-1997); Research Equipment Grantee, National Science Foundation (1984-1986); Research Grantee, National Science Foundation (1963-1969) **MEM:** Alvar Insect Reserve Project, Nature Conservancy of Canada (NCC) (2010-2011); Council, University of Michigan Chapter, Sigma Xi, The Scientific Research Honor Society (1993-1998); President, University of Michigan Chapter, Sigma Xi, The Scientific Research Honor Society (1994-1996); Fellow, The Linnean Society of London (1992); President, Association for Tropical Biology and Conservation (1973-1975); Fellow, American Association for the Advancement of Science; Fellow, Royal Entomological Society **MH:** Albert Nelson Marquis Lifetime Achievement Award (2017) **H:** Maintaining equipment and barn structures for small specialty horse farm **ADD:** 4243 N Delhi Rd, Ann Arbor, MI, 48103 **URL:** http://prabook.com/web/person-view.html?profileId=1667867

MOORE, THOMAS R., **T:** Attorney **I:** Law and Legal Services **CN:** Law Offices of Thomas R. Moore **DOB:** 03/27/1932 **PB:** Duluth **SC:** MN/USA **PT:** Ralph Henry Moore; Estelle Marguerite (Hero) Moore **MS:** Married **SPN:** Margaret C. King (9/10/1955 Deceased 5/10/2003) **CH:** Willard S.; Clarissa; Charles R.H. **ED:** JD, Harvard Law School, Harvard University (1957); BA, Yale University, Magna Cum Laude (1954) **C:** Partner, Law Offices of Thomas R. Moore, New York, NY; Partner, Breed, Abbott & Morgan (Now Whitman Breed Abbott & Morgan LLC), New York, NY; With, Dewey Ballantine (Now Dewey & LeBoeuf), New York, NY **CR:** Instructor, Harvard Law School, Harvard University (1956-1957); Lecturer, Harvard Law School, Harvard University; Lecturer, Cornell Law School, Cornell University; Lecturer, New York University School of Law; Lecturer, Practising Law Institute, New York, NY; Lecturer, Practising Law Institute, Las Vegas, NV; Lecturer, Practising Law Institute, New Orleans, LA; Lecturer, University of Oxford **CIV:** Board of Directors, Executive Committee, Citymeals on Wheels; President, Board of Directors, Prevent Blindness; Secretary-Treasurer, The A.D. Henderson Foundation; Trustee, The A.D. Henderson Foundation; Delegate, Phoenix Theatre; Trustee, Florida Board of Directors, Phoenix Theatre; Board of Directors, The Institute for Aegean Prehistory; Board of Directors, The Foundation for the Future of Man; Founder, AFV&A; London Conservator, The New York Public Library; Trustee, Foundation for the Renaissance of St. Petersburg-Leningrad; Trustee, Malcolm Hewitt Wiener Foundation; President, Laurence Levine Charitable Fund, Inc.; Board of Directors, Laurence Levine Charitable Fund, Inc.; Vice Chairman, New-York Historical Society; Honorary Chairman, Youth America Grand Prix; Board of Directors, Governor's Committee on Scholastic Achievement; Constitutional Advisor, President George H. W. Bush; Advisor, King Michael, Romania; Honorary Knight, Queen Elizabeth II **CW:** Author, "Plantagenet Descent: Thirty One Generations from William the Conqueror to Today" (1995); Co-author, "Estate Planning and the Close Corporation"; Editor-in-Chief, Gastronome; Board of Editors, "The Tax Lawyer"; Contributor, Articles, Professional Journals; Numerous Interviews, Popular Press;

Numerous Interviews, TV Commentaries **AW:** Clare College Scholar, University Cambridge; Scholar of the House Fellow, Yale University; Roscoe Pound First Prize, Moot Court Competition, Harvard Law School, Harvard University; Thomas R. Moore Distinguished Public Servant Award, Prevent Blindness; Inductee, Descendants of the Knights of the Garter; Inductee, The Baronial Order of Magna Charta; Recipient, Coat of Arms **MEM:** The Society of the Friends of Saint George's; National President, The Chaîne des Rôtisseurs; Director, The Chaîne des Rôtisseurs; Executive Committee, World Council, The Chaîne des Rôtisseurs, Paris, France; The Confrérie des Chevaliers du Tastevin; The Pilgrims of the United States; The University Club; Delta Sigma Rho; Prevent Blindness; Order of the Crown of Charlemagne; Order of Plantagenet; Order of Merovingian Dynasty **MH:** Albert Nelson Marquis Lifetime Achievement Award (2017) **PA:** Republican **RE:** Episcopalian **BA:** 1801 North Flagler Drive, West Palm Beach, FL, 33407 **ADD:** 785 Park Ave Apt 14E, New York, NY, 10021

MORGAN, ELISABETH J., **T:** Director of International Initiatives **I:** Education/Educational Services **CN:** Eastern Michigan University **DOB:** 04/19/1958 **PB:** Bay City **SC:** MI/USA **SPN:** Dave Woike **ED:** PhD in Foreign and Second Language Education, University at Buffalo (1991) **CT:** Certificate in French, Institut de Touraine, Tours, France **C:** Director of International Initiatives, College of Arts and Sciences, Eastern Michigan University (1991-Present); Coordinator of International Initiatives, College of Arts and Sciences, Eastern Michigan University (1991-Present); World Languages Department Head, College of Arts and Sciences, Eastern Michigan University (1991-Present); Undergraduate Studies Coordinator, College of Arts and Sciences, Eastern Michigan University (1991-Present); ESL Program Coordinator, College of Arts and Sciences, Eastern Michigan University (1991-Present); Professor, College of Arts and Sciences, Eastern Michigan University (1991-Present); Assistant Professor, College of Arts and Sciences, Eastern Michigan University (1991-Present); Curriculum Coordinator, Malaysian Program, University at Buffalo (1984-1990); Teaching Assistant, Malaysian Program, University at Buffalo (1984-1990); Instructor, Malaysian Program, University at Buffalo (1984-1990) **CIV:** Volunteer, American Cancer Society, Inc.; Volunteer, Susan G. Komen; Volunteer, Kumon North America, Inc. **AW:** Recipient, Teaching Excellence Award, NAFSA **MEM:** Association of International Education Administrators; NAFSA; Phi Beta Delta Honor Society for International Scholars **H:** Photography; Gardening; Traveling; Reading; Spending time with family **BA:** 103 Boone Hall, Eastern Michigan University, Ypsilanti, MI, 48197 **URL:** http://www.emich.edu/cas/international

MOROOKA, HIROSHI, **T:** President **I:** Medicine & Health Care **CN:** Morooka Neurosurgical and Pediatric Clinic **DOB:** 08/28/1946 **PB:** Kurashiki **SC:** Japan **PT:** Shigeru Morooka; Akiko (Kobayashi) Morooka **MS:** Married **SPN:** Michiko Ninomiya (6/6/1976) **CH:** Takatoshi; Hanako; Teruko **ED:** PhD, Okayama University (1978); MD, Okayama University (1971) **CT:** Diplomate, Japanese Board of Neurological Surgery **C:** Chief, Neurosurgery, Morooka Neurosurgery and Pediatrics Clinic, Okayama, Japan (2008-Present); Chief, Neurosurgery, Okayama Saidaiji Hospital (1996-2007); Chief, Neurosurgery, Bizen City Hospital (1993-1995); Chief, Neurosurgery, Okayama Rousai Hospital (1987-1992); Assistant Professor, Neurosurgery, Okayama University (1984-1986); Instructor, Neurosurgery, Okayama

University (1980-1983); Research Associate, Neurology, University of Miami (1977-1979); Clinical Assistant, Neurosurgery, Okayama University (1972-1977) **CW:** Author, "Cytoprotection & Cytobiology" (1995-1997); Author, "Brain Edema IX" (1993); Author, "Medical Biochemical & Chemical Aspects of Free Radicals" (1989); Author, "Intracranial Pressure VII" (1989) **AW:** Legion of Honor Award, United Cultural Convention, NC (2005); Distinguished Professor Award, BWW Society, Institute for the Advancement of Positive Global Solutions, CA (2003); National Research Grant (1981) **MEM:** American Association for the Advancement of Science; Japan Neurological Society; Societas Neurologica Japonica; The New York Academy of Sciences; American Heart Association, Inc.; American Chemical Society **MH:** Albert Nelson Marquis Lifetime Achievement Award (2017) **H:** Golf **PA:** Liberal Democrat **RE:** Christian **ADD:** 492-1 Kitajima Okucho, Morooka Neurosurgical & Pediatric Clinic, Setouchi, Okayama, Japan, 701-4232

MORRIS, JAMES MALACHY, T: Lawyer **I:** Law and Legal Services **CN:** FCS Insurance Corporation **DOB:** 06/05/1952 **PB:** Champaign **SC:** IL/USA **PT:** Walter Michael Morris; Ellen Frances (Solon) Morris **MS:** Married **SPN:** Mary Delilah Baker (10/17/1987) **CH:** James Malachy Jr.; Elliot Rice Baker; Walter Michael; Nicholas Aidan **ED:** JD, University of Pennsylvania (1977); BA, Brown University (1974); Coursework, Oxford University, England (1972) **C:** Counsel to FCA Banks Regulation (2018-Present); Sole Practice, FCS Insurance Corporation, McLean, VA (2013-2017); General Counsel, FCS Insurance Corporation, McLean, VA (2006-2013); Executive Assistant, Board Chairman, FCS Insurance Corporation, McLean, VA (2005-2006); Acting Secretary, General Counsel, FCS Insurance Corporation, McLean, VA (1990-1998); Counsel, Farm Credit Administration, Washington, DC (1987-2006); Sole Practice, New York, NY (1983-1987); Associate, Carter, Ledyard & Milburn, New York, NY (1981-1983); Senior Law Clerk, Supreme Court Illinois, Springfield, IL (1980-1981); Associate, Reid & Priest, New York, NY (1977-1980) **CR:** Consultant, Herbert Oppenheimer, Nathan & VanDyck, London, England (1985-2004); Pritzker Architecture Prize Foundation, New York, NY (1981-2002); International Awards Foundation, Zurich, Switzerland (1981-2002) **CW:** Contributor, Articles to Professional Journals **AW:** Albert Nelson Marquis Lifetime Achievement Award (2017); FCS Insurance Corporation Funding Award (2012); Farm Credit Administration Trust Award (2001) **MEM:** American Bar Association; Illinois Bar Association; New York State Bar Association; New York County Lawyers Association; Association of the Bar of the City of New York; British Institute of International and Comparative Law; American Institute of Parliamentarians; Brown University 1764 Society; Brown University Association Class Leaders; Lansdowne Club, London, England; Penn Club, New York, NY; Brown Club, Washington, DC; New York Athletic Club **BAR:** Barristers' Chambers, Manchester, England (1987); Supreme Court of the United States (1983); United States Tax Court (1982); Illinois (1980); New York (1978); United States District Court for the Southern and Eastern Districts of New York (1978) **MH:** Albert Nelson Marquis Lifetime Achievement Award (2017) **ADD:** PO Box 1407, Mc Lean, VA, 22101

MORRISON, RALPH R., T: Partner, Founder **I:** Law and Legal Services **CN:** Wallace Morrison & Casteel LLP **MS:** Married **ED:** JD, Georgia State University School of Law (1985) **C:** Partner, Wallace Morrison & Casteel, LLP; Founder, Wallace Morrison & Casteel, LLP **CIV:** Chair, Atlanta History Center; Pro Bono General Counsel, Historic Oakland Foundation; Chairman, Pitts Foundation; Board of Directors, Plan Giving Council, Emory University; Board of Directors, Atlanta Preservation Board **AW:** Lawyer of the Year, Best Lawyers (2016); Fellow, American Collage of Trust and Estates Counsel (1996); Legal Elite, Georgia Trend; AV Rated, Martindale-Hubbell; Chambers, HNW Individuals; Fellow, American College of Trust and Estate Counsel; Georgia Super Lawyer **MEM:** Georgia Bar Association; Past President, Fiduciary Section, Georgia Bar Association; Atlanta Bar Association **H:** Renovating his wife's old house **RE:** Episcopal Church of America **BA:** 1180 Peachtree St NE Ste 2010, Wallace Morrison & Casteel, Atlanta, GA, 30309 **URL:** http://wallacetrustlaw.com/attorneys/ralph-morrison/

MORROW, PATRICK C., T: Senior Partner **I:** Law and Legal Services **CN:** Morrow, Morrow, Ryan, Bassett & Haik **PB:** Plaquemine **SC:** LA/USA **PT:** Dr. Robert Morrow, Sr.; Ruth Wilbert Morrow **MS:** Married **SPN:** Mary Alice Palazzo (1967) **CH:** Patrick Craig Morrow, Jr.; Celeste Marcelle Morrow Lopez; Charlotte Grace Morrow Moreau **ED:** JD, Louisiana State University (1972); BA in Government, Louisiana State University (1969) **C:** Founding Partner, Senior Partner, Morrow, Morrow, Ryan, Bassett & Haik (1975-Present) **CIV:** Founder, Annual Scholarships for Local High School Seniors (2014-Present); Board of Trustees, Opelousas General Health System (2011-Present); Member, Hospital Service District No. 2, St. Landry Parish (2011-Present); Commissioner, Louisiana Department of Wildlife and Fisheries (2005-2011); Chairman, Louisiana Department of Wildlife and Fisheries (2008); Judge Pro Tempore, 27th Judicial District Court (1995); Advisory Committee, Crowne Parc Development District; Rules of Professional Conduct - Class Action Committee, Louisiana Supreme Court **CW:** Coauthor, "Images of America, St. Landry Parish" (2013) **AW:** Louisiana Super Lawyers, Law & Politics (2008-Present); Top Rated Lawyer in Mass Tort Law (2017); America's Top 100 High Stakes Litigators (2017); 10 Best Law Firms in Louisiana (2017); America's Top 100 Attorneys (2017); Stalwart Award, Louisiana Association for Justice (2016); Best Attorneys of America, Rue Ratings (2015); Leaders in Philanthropy Award, St. Landry Parish (2015); Best of the Best, Attorney, St. Landry Parish (2013); Citizen of the Year, Elks Club (2011); Distinguished Citizen Award, Evangeline Area Council of Boy Scouts (2003); Top 100 Trial Lawyers, National Trial Lawyers Association; Top Lawyers, Acadian Profile; AV Rating, Martindale-Hubbell; Nation's Top Attorneys, National Association of Distinguished Counsel; Top 25 Mass Tort Trial Lawyers; Lifetime Achievement Membership, America's Top 100 Attorneys **MEM:** Board of Governors, Louisiana Trial Lawyers Association (1987-Present); Secretary-Treasurer, St. Landry Parish Bar Association (1974); Lafayette Bar Association; ABA; Counsel of Directors, Louisiana Trial Lawyers Association; Counsel of Directors, Louisiana Association for Justice; American Association for Justice; The Louisiana City Attorneys Association; Fellow, American Board of Trial Advocates; Fellow, Louisiana Bar Foundation; Fellow, American Bar Foundation; Fellow, John M. Duhe, Jr., American Inn of Court; Fellow, International Academy of Trial Lawyers; Fellow, Litigation Counsel of America; Member, The Trial Lawyer Honorary Society; Member, Diversity Law Institute; Member, The Trial Law Institute; Member, Million Dollar Advocates Forum; District Advisory Committee, Crowne Parc Development **BAR:** Louisiana State Bar Association (1972); Admitted to Practice, Supreme Court of the United States; Admitted to Practice, Louisiana Supreme Court; Admitted to Practice, United States Court of Appeals for the Fifth Circuit; Admitted to Practice, United States Court of Appeals for the Eleventh Circuit; Admitted to Practice, United States District Court for the Eastern District of Louisiana; Admitted to Practice, United States District Court for the Western District of Louisiana; Admitted to Practice, United States District Court for the Middle District of Louisiana; Admitted to Practice, United States District Court for the Southern District of Texas **H:** Duck Hunting **BA:** 324 West Landry St, Morrow, Morrow, Ryan, Bassett & Haik, Opelousas, LA, 70570 **ADD:** PO Box 1787, Opelousas, LA, 70571 **URL:** http://www.mmrbhlawoffice.com

MORROW, WINSTON VAUGHAN, T: Business Executive **I:** Business Management/Business Services **DOB:** 03/22/1924 **PB:** Grand Rapids **SC:** MI/USA **PT:** Winston V. Morrow; Selma (Von Egloffstein) Morrow **MS:** Married **SPN:** Edith Burrows Ulrich (3/2/1990) **CH:** Thomas Christopher (Deceased); Mark Staples **ED:** JD, Harvard University (1950); AB, Williams College, Cum Laude (1946) **C:** Board of Directors, AECOM Technology Corp., Los Angeles, CA (1990-1999); Chairman, TRTS Data Services Inc. (1985-1991); Board of Directors, Westwood Equities Corp., Los Angeles, CA (1984-1995); CEO, Westwood Equities Corp., Los Angeles, CA (1984-1995); President, Westwood Equities Corp., Los Angeles, CA (1984-1995); Board of Directors, Ticor Title Insurance Co. (1982-1991); Chairman, Ticor Title Insurance Co. (1982-1991); President, Ticor Title Insurance Co. (1982-1991); Chief Executive Officer, Ticor Title Insurance Co. (1982-1991); Chairman, Teleflora Inc. and Subsidiary (1978-1980); President, Teleflora Inc. and Subsidiary (1978-1980); Board of Directors, Teleflora Inc. and Subsidiary (1978-1980); Chairman, Avis, Inc. and Avis Rent A Car System, Inc. (1965-1977); Chief Executive Officer, Avis, Inc. and Avis Rent A Car System, Inc. (1965-1977); Board of Directors, Avis, Inc. and Avis Rent A Car System, Inc. (1965-1977); President, Avis, Inc. (1964-1975); Vice President, Rent A Car Division, Avis, Inc. (1962-1964); General Manager, Rent A Car Division, Avis, Inc. (1962-1964); Executive Vice President, Avis, Inc. and Subsidiary (1957-1961); Assistant Treasurer, Avis, Inc. and Subsidiary (1957-1961); General Counsel, Avis, Inc. and Subsidiary (1957-1961); Board of Directors, Avis, Inc. and Subsidiary (1957-1961); Associate Attorney, Edwards & Angell, Providence, RI (1950-1957) **CR:** Co-chairman, Los Angeles Transportation Coalition (1985-1991); Los Angeles City-wide Airport Advisory Committee (1983-1985); Travel Advisory Board, U.S. Travel Services (1968-1976); President's Industry and Government Special Travel Task Force (1968); Fellow, The Huntington **CIV:** Chairman, Spring St. Foundation (1991-2006); President, Spring St. Foundation (1991-2006); Trustee, Committee Economic Development, Washington, DC (1987-1991); California Business Roundtable (1985-1990); Juvenile Delinquency Task Force, National Council on Crime and Delinquency (1985-1986); Board of Directors, Police Foundation, Washington, DC (1983-1991); Los Angeles Mayor's Business Council (1983-1986); Housing Roundtable, Washington, DC (1983-1985); Trustee, Adelphi University (1970-1975) **AW:** Two Battle Stars Award (1943-1945); Decorated Stella Della Solidarieta, Italy; Gold Tourism Medal, Austria **MEM:** Board of Governors, American Land Title Association (1989-1990); Board of Directors, Los Angeles Area Chamber of Commerce (1983-1990); National President, Car and Truck Rental Leasing Association (1961-1963); California Club; Los Angeles Tennis Club; Phi Beta Kappa; Kappa Alpha **BAR:** State of Rhode Island

(1950); U.S. District Court; U.S. Supreme Court **MH:** Albert Nelson Marquis Lifetime Achievement Award (2017) **ADD:** 4056 Farmouth Drive, Los Angeles, CA, 90027

MOSER, LOUISE, T: Professor **I:** Education/Educational Services **CN:** University of California, Santa Barbara **ED:** Doctorate, University of Wisconsin-Madison (1970) **CW:** Author, "A Distributed e-Healthcare System Based on the Service Oriented Architecture" (2007) **AW:** Recipient, Trustworthy Publication, Distribution and Retrieval Network, National Science Foundation (2010-2013); Recipient, First Prize, Services Computing Contest, IEEE (2007) **MH:** Albert Nelson Marquis Lifetime Achievement Award (2017) **BA:** University of California, Santa Barbara, Department of Electrical and Computer Engineering, Santa Barbara, CA, 93106 **ADD:** PO Box 13963, Santa Barbara, CA, 93106

MOSKOWITZ, MICHAEL ARTHUR, T: Professor of Neurology **I:** Education/Educational Services **CN:** Harvard Medical School **DOB:** 05/26/1942 **PB:** New York **SC:** NY/USA **PT:** Irving Lawrence Moskowitz, M.D.; Clara (Dranoff) Moskowitz **MS:** Married **SPN:** Mary Henderson, Ph.D. (Married; 5/18/1991) **CH:** Jenna Rachel **ED:** Honorary Degree, Jun Won University, Republic of Korea (2009); Honorary MSc, Harvard University (1992); Resident in Neurology, Peter Bent Brigham Children Hospital (1971-1974); Resident, Yale University (1969-1971); Intern, Department of Medicine, Yale University (1968-1969); MD, Tufts University (1968); AB, Johns Hopkins University (1964) **CT:** Diplomate, American Board of Psychiatry and Neurology; Diplomate, American Board of Internal Medicine; License to Practice Medicine, Commonwealth of Massachusetts **C:** Professor, Neurology, Harvard Medical School, Massachusetts General Hospital, (1992-Present); Associate Professor, Harvard Medical School, Boston, MA (1979-1992); Assistant Professor, Harvard Medical School, Boston, MA (1975-1979) **CR:** Neurophysiologist, Massachusetts General Hospital, Boston, MA (1981-Present); Science Advisory Board, Queen's Medical Center, Honolulu, HI (2008-2011; Chair 2009-2011); Charite Hospital, Berlin, Germany (2008-2018); Review Study Section Member, National Institutes of Health; Witter Lecturer, University of California, San Francisco (1994); Barraquer-LaFora Lecturer, Spanish Neurological Society, Barcelona, Spain (1994); H.J. Barnett Lecturer, Canadian Heart Association, Queens University, Canada (1993); Interagency Pain Coordinating Committee, National Institutes of Health (2011-2014); Seymour Diamond Lecturer (2007); Kenneth Carey Lecturer, University of Michigan (2006); Soriano Lecturer, American Neurological Association (2003); Dr. Chaim Mayman Lecturer, Beth Israel Hospital, Boston, MA (2003); John Graham Lecturer, American Association for the Study of Headaches (2000); Richardson Lecturer, Canadian Neurological Association (1998); 2nd International Honorary Lecturer, European Stroke Conference (1997); Decade of the Brain Lecturer, American Academy of Neurology (1995); Briggs Lecturer, Department of Pharmacology, The University of Texas at San Antonio (1995); Review Study Section Member, National Institutes of Health (1982-1985); Established Investigator, American Heart Association (1980-1985); Chairman, Science Advisory Board, Max Planck Institute; Consultant, Pharmaceutical Industry **CW:** Editor, Animal Models of Headache (1996); Editor, Neurobiological Basis of Migraine (Dalkara & Moskowitz 2017); Editorial Board, Stroke; Editorial Board, Acta Neurological Scandinavica Cephalalgia; Editorial Board, Journal of Cerebral

Blood Flow & Metabolism; Editorial Board, Cerebrovascular Disease; Science Editor, Stroke; Contributor, More Then 525 research articles in professional journals **AW:** Research Grantee, Bristol-Myers Squibb Neuroscience and Pain (1993-1998); Lifetime Achievement Award, International Society for the Study of Cerebral Blood Flow & Metabolism (2013); William Silen Lifetime Award for Mentoring, Harvard Medical School (2007); Director, MGH Interdepartmental Stroke Center, (1987-2012); Arnold Friedman Award, American Headache Society (2006); Thomas Willis Award (highest Award bestowed on a member), America Heart/Stroke Association (2006); Ottorini Rossi Award XVIII, Mondino Institute of Neurology, Pavia Italy 2007; C. Miller Fisher Award, American Stroke Association (2005); John Graham Award, AASH (1998); Zülch Prize from Reemstma Foundation, Max-Planck Society. Koln, Germany (1996); Enrico Greppi Award, Italian Neurology Society (1988, 1986); Mintz Lecturer, Mt Sinai Hospital, NYC 2010; Seymour A Solomon Award, American Headache Society, 2011; Fellow, Alfred Sloan Foundation (1978-1980); Teacher-Investigator Award, National Institute of Neurological Disease and Stroke (1975-1980); Postdoctoral Fellow, Massachusetts Institute of Technology (1974-1976); 2002,Top 200 Most Highly Cited in Neuroscience, Information Services Institute; Recipient, Research Grants, National Institute of Neurological Disorders and Stroke **MEM:** Scientific Advisory Board, Leducq Foundation (2012-2018); Board of Directors, American Headache Society (2010-2016); Co-chair, Program Committee, American Heart and Stroke Association (2002-2004); President, International Society for Cerebral Blood Flow and Metabolism (2001-3); Member, Interagency Pain Research Coordinator Committee (2011-2014); Soriano Lecturer, American Neurological Association (2003); Science Advisory Board, Max Planck Institute, Koln, Germany (1999-2008; Chair 1993-'98); National Research Committee, American Heart Association (1991-1996); Executive Committee, Stroke Council, American Heart Association (1991-1996); American Neurological Association; American Heart and Stroke Association; American Heart Association; American Academy of Neurology; American Pain Society; Society of Neuroscience; International Society for Cerebral Blood Flow and Metabolism; Board of Directors, International Society for Cerebral Blood Flow and Metabolism; Honorary Member, Canadian Neurological Society; Honorary Member, International Headache Society **MH:** Albert Nelson Marquis Lifetime Achievement Award (2017) **BA:** 149 13th St Rm 6403, Harvard Medical School, Charlestown, MA, 02129 **ADD:** 257 Prospect St, Belmont, MA, 02478 **URL:** https://www.linkedin.com/in/michael-moskowitz-a25a031b/

MOSS, BILL, T: Lawyer **I:** Law and Legal Services **DOB:** 09/27/1950 **PB:** Amarillo **SC:** TX/USA **PT:** Ralph Voniver Moss; Virginia May (Atkins) Moss **MS:** Single **CH:** Brandon Price **ED:** Certificate, Regulatory Studies Program, Michigan State University (1981); JD, Baylor University (1976); MA, West Texas A&M University (1974); BS, West Texas A&M University, With Honors (1972) **C:** Attorney at Law (2011-Present); Assistant Attorney General, Antitrust and Civil Medicaid Fraud Division, Office of the Attorney General, Texas (2004-2011); Assistant General Counsel, Texas Ethics Commission, Austin, TX (1997-2004); Founder, Owner, Price & Co. Publications, Austin, TX (1987-1997); Assistant General Counsel, State Bar of Texas, Austin, TX (1983-1987); Hearings Examiner, Public Utility Commission of Texas, Austin, TX (1981-1983); Associate, Culton,

Morgan, Britain & White, Amarillo, TX (1977-1980); Briefing Attorney, Court of Appeals for the Seventh Supreme Judicial District of Texas, Amarillo, TX (1976-1977) **CR:** Instructor, Lecturer, Eastern New Mexico University, Portales, NM (1977-1980); Instructor, Lecturer, West Texas State University, Canyon, TX; Speaker in Field **CIV:** Election Inspector, State of Texas (1998-Present) **MEM:** Panel Direction of ABA & Issues Facing Profession, American Bar Association; American Association of Individual Investors; Texas Bar Association; National Organization of Bar Counsel; National Council on Prescription Drug Programs; International Platform Association; Capitol of Texas Rotary Club; American Association of Individual Investors; Nature Conservancy; Alpha Chi; Lambda Chi Alpha; Omicron Delta Epsilon; Phi Alpha Delta; Sigma Tau Delta; Pi Gamma Mu **RE:** Episcopalian **ADD:** 506 Explorer Street, Lakeway, TX, 78734

MOSS, AMBLER HOLMES JR., T: Lawyer, Educator, Former Ambassador **I:** Education/Educational Services **CN:** University of Miami **DOB:** 09/01/1937 **PB:** Baltimore **SC:** MD/USA **PT:** Ambler Holmes Moss; Dorothea Dandridge (Williams) Moss **MS:** Married **SPN:** Serena Welles (5/6/1972) **CH:** Ambler H.; Benjamin Sumner; Serena Montserrat; Nicholas George Oliver **ED:** JD, George Washington University (1970); BA, Yale University (1960) **C:** Professor, University of Miami (1984-Present); Of Counsel, Greenberg, Traurig, LLP, Miami, FL (1995-2010); Dean, Graduate School of International Studies, University of Miami (1984-1994); Of Counsel, Greenberg, Traurig, LLP, Miami, FL (1982-1987); Ambassador to Panama, American Embassy, Panama City, Panama (1978-1982); Deputy Assistant, Secretary of State, Washington, DC (1977-1978); U.S. Negotiating Team for Panama Canal Treaties (1977); Resident Attorney, Coudert Brothers, Brussels, Belgium (1973-1976); Associate, Coudert Brothers, Washington, DC (1971-1973); Spanish Desk Officer, State Department, Washington, DC (1968-1970); Adviser, U.S. Delegate to Organization of American States (1966-1969); Vice Consul, Barcelona, Spain (1964-1966); Joined Foreign Service, State Department (1964) **CIV:** Panama Canal Consultative Committee (1995-2000) **MIL:** Lieutenant, Submarine Division, U.S. Navy (1960-1964) **AW:** Creu de Sant Jordi, Catalonia (Cross of Saint George), Orden del Merito Civil, Encomienda, Spain **MEM:** Governor, Greater Miami Chamber of Commerce (1983-1986); American Society of International Law; American Foreign Service Association; Council of Foreign Relations; American Legion; Inter-America Dialogue, Washington, DC; Navy League; Royal Institute of International Affairs, London, England; International Institute for Strategic Studies, London, England; Institute of Catalan Studies, Barcelona, Spain; Army and Navy Club **BAR:** District of Columbia; State of Florida **PA:** Democrat **RE:** Roman Catholic **ADD:** 5711 San Vicente Street, Coral Gables, FL, 33146

MOSSINGHOFF, GERALD JOSEPH, T: Lawyer, Educator **I:** Law and Legal Services **CN:** Oblon, McClelland, Maier & Neustadt, L.L.P., George Washington University **DOB:** 09/30/1935 **PB:** St. Louis **SC:** MO/USA **MS:** Married **SPN:** Jeanne Carole Jack (12/29/1958) **CH:** Pamela Ann Jennings; Gregory Joseph; Melissa M. Ronayne **ED:** JD, George Washington University, With Honors (1961); BEE, Saint Louis University (1957) **C:** Senior Counsel, Oblon, McClelland, Maier & Neustadt, L.L.P., Arlington, VA (1997-Present); Cifelli Professor, Intellectual Property Law, George Washington University, Washington, DC (1996-Present); President, Pharmaceutical Research and Manufacturers of America, Washington, DC (1985-1996); Assistant Secretary of Commerce, United States Patent and Trademark Office (1981-1985);

Commissioner, Patents and Trademarks, United States Patent and Trademark Office (1981-1985); Deputy General Counsel, National Aeronautics and Space Administration, Washington, DC (1976-1981); Director, National Aeronautics and Space Administration, Washington, DC (1967-1973); Congressional Liaison, National Aeronautics and Space Administration, Washington, DC (1967-1973); Project Engineer, Sachs Electric (1954-1957) **CR:** Ambassador, Paris Convention Diplomatic Conference; Fellow, National Academy of Public Administration **CW:** Contributor, "Reagan Remembered" (2011) **AW:** Jefferson Medal (2000); Honoree, Distinguished Alumnus, George Washington University (1996); Distinguished Public Service Award, Secretary of Commerce (1983); Outstanding Leadership Medal (1981); President Rank of Meritorious Executive (1980); Distinguished Service Medal (1980); Exceptional Service Medal, National Aeronautics and Space Administration (1971) **MEM:** Board of Directors, Reagan Alumni Association; Cosmos Club; Knights of Malta; Order of Coif; Pi Mu Epsilon; Eta Kappa Nu **BAR:** State of Virginia (1981); District of Columbia (1965); State of Missouri (1957) **MH:** Albert Nelson Marquis Lifetime Achievement Award (2017) **ADD:** 1530 Key Boulevard, Apt. 1328, Arlington, VA, 22209

MOTES, JOSEPH MARK, T: Travel Company Executive **I:** Leisure, Travel & Tourism **CN:** Trekruise & Seatrek, Trekon & Vulkon **DOB:** 10/12/1948 **PB:** Leesburg **SC:** FL/USA **PT:** Lewis Jackson Motes; Yolanda (Fernandez) Motes **ED:** AA in Computer Science, Miami-Dade Community College (1976) **C:** Convention Promoter, Trekon & Vulkon (1977-Present); Promoter, Trekruise & Seatrek (1975-Present); Vice President, Seatrek Enterprise, Inc., Cooper City, FL **CR:** President, Genesis Productions, Inc. (1992-Present) **MIL:** Sergeant, U.S. Marine Corps (1967-1974) **AW:** Honoree, Veteran of the Year, Broward County **MEM:** DAV; VFW; AMVETS; Sons of Confederate Veterans; Sons of the American Revolution; First Battalion, Ninth Marines Association; Third Marine Division Association; The American Legion, Marine Corps League **MH:** Albert Nelson Marquis Lifetime Achievement Award (2017) **H:** Water sports; Travel; Boating; Photography **PA:** Conservative **RE:** Roman Catholic **ADD:** 2133 NW 208th Terrace, Penbroke Pine, FL, 33029

MOURSALIAN, PATRICIA JEAN JEAN, I: Health, Wellness and Fitness **ED:** BS in Occupational Therapy, Loma Linda University (2001) **CT:** Certified Senior Strength Trainer **H:** Spending time with her children; Reading; Painting **RE:** Seventh Day Adventist

MUELLER, AMY LYNN, T: Insurance Company Executive **I:** Insurance **CN:** Marsh **DOB:** 03/06/1983 **ED:** Diploma, University of Mississippi (2005) **C:** Insurance Specialist, Marsh, Dallas, Texas (2015-Present); Accountant Tech, HUB International, Dallas, Texas (2010-2011); Executive Assistant, Community Liaison, Dallas County (2011-2014); Accountant Manager, Lockton Companies, Dallas, Texas (2011); Assistant Client Manager, Willis, Mobile, AL (2006-2010); Accountant Executive, International Assurance Inc., Mobile, AL (2005) **CR:** Board Member, Farmers Branch Chamber of Commerce (2014); Various Chamber of Commerces; Coppell Chamber of Commerce **AW:** Top Volunteer Award, Baylor University (2012); 100 Hours of Community Service, Junior League (2012); 75 Hours of Community Service, Junior League; Ambassador of the Month, Sachse Chamber of Commerce **MEM:** Vice President, Alpha Kappa Psi Fraternity (2004-2005); The Dallas

Arms Collectors Association, Inc.; Texas State Rifle Association; Dallas County Pioneers Association; The Daughters of the Republic of Texas; Daughters of the American Revolution (Now National Society Daughters of the American Revolution (NSDAR)); Women in Government; Founding Director, Passing the Hat; Dallas Safari Club; Kappa Alpha Theta **ADD:** 7310 Brennans Drive, Dallas, TX, 75214

MUELLER, GARY ALFRED, T: Software Engineer **I:** Engineering **ED:** MSEE, University of Colorado, Boulder, CO (1995); BSEE, Computer Science, University of Colorado, with Honors, Denver, CO (1975); BS in Mineral Engineering Mathematics, Colorado School of Mines (1973); BS in Mineral Engineering Physics, Colorado School of Mines (1972) **CT:** Registered Professional Engineer, State of Colorado **C:** Consultant (2017-Present); Principal Software Engineer, Oracle (2010-2016); Staff Software Engineer, Sun Microsystems (2007-2010); Consultant, Senior Staff Software Engineer, Sun Microsystems (2002-2007); Advisory Software Engineer, Storage Technology Corporation (1985-2001); Member, Technology Staff, AT&T Information Systems (1982-1984); Computer Programmer, Mathematician, United States Geological Survey (1977-1981); Research Assistant, University of Colorado Medical Center (1978-1980) **CR:** Adjunct Professor, University of Phoenix Online (2002-2016) **CW:** Co-Author, "An Industry Survey of Autonomic Infrastructure," The 6th International Conference on Autonomic Computing and Communications, Barcelona, Spain (2009); Co-Author, "Embedded Objects," Technical, Professional and Student Development Conference, Boulder, Colorado) (2005); Co-Author, "Extreme Embedded A Cautionary Tale," Embedded Workshop, XP Agile Universe Conference, Calgary, Canada (2004); Co-Author, "Extreme Embedded, A Report from the Front Line," Practitioner Report, OOPSLA, Seattle, WA (2002); Co-Author, "Java and Real Time Storage Applications," 19th IEEE Symposium on Mass Storage, Adelphi, MD (2002); Co-Author, "Embedded in the eXtreme," StorageTek Engineering Symposium (2001); Co-Author, "From Here to Java," StorageTek Engineering Symposium (2001); Co-Author, "Embedded Objects," StorageTek Engineering Symposium (2001); Author, "Policy Managed Storage," 18th IEEE Symposium on Mass Storage, San Diego, CA (2001); Author, "Jiro Management Applications," 18th IEEE Symposium on Mass Storage, San Diego, CA (2001); Co-Author, "Policy Based Storage Management," Workshop on Policies for Distributed Systems and Networks, Bristol, England (2001); Author, "Policy Based Management," StorageTek Engineering Symposium (2000); Author, "Building Jiro Management Applications," StorageTek Engineering Symposium (2000); Co-Author, "ACS Library Server," Tenth IEEE Symposium on Mass Storage Systems, Monterey, CA (1990) **AW:** StorageTek Bronze Level Technical Excellence Award (2000); StorageTek Cool Dog Award, Implementation and Presentation of StorageTek Jiro Prototype (1999); Honoree, Night on the Town, Callisto Architecture Paper (1996); StorageTek Key Employee Selection (1995); Outstanding Contribution, ACSLS Release 4.0 Beta Core Team (1993); Outstanding Contribution, ACSLS Release 4.0 Beta (1993); Operating Principles Excellence Award, (1993); Honoree, Night on the Town, Code Metrics Process and Procedures Team (1992) **MEM:** Senior Member, IEEE; Member, Association for Computing Machinery; Tau Beta Pi; Kappa Mu Epsilon; Eta Kappa Nu **MH:** Albert Nelson Marquis Lifetime Achievement Award (2017) **ADD:** 195 Garnet St, Broomfield, CO, 80020

MUELLER, PEGGY JEAN, T: Dancer **I:** Fine Art **CN:** Jean Mueller School of Dance **DOB:** 06/14/1952 **PB:** Austin **SC:** TX/USA **PT:** Rudolph George Mueller Jr.; Margaret Jean (Locke) Mueller **MS:** Divorced **SPN:** John Yerby Tarlton (6/24/1972, Divorced 6/1983) **ED:** BS in Home Economics, Child Development, University of Texas at Austin (1974) **C:** Dance teacher, Jean Mueller School of Dance, Austin, TX (1980-Present); Dance Teacher, University of Texas at Austin (1980-2010); Dance Teacher, Texas Agricultural and Mechanical University, College Station, TX (1977-1980); Dance Teacher, Jean Tarlton School of Dance, College Station, TX (1977-1980); Dance Teacher, Agricultural and Mechanical Consolidated Community Education, College Station, TX (1977-1978); Dance Teacher, Sul Ross State University, Alpine, TX (1975-1977); Dance Teacher, Jean Tarlton School of Dance, Alpine, TX (1975-1977); Dance teacher, Shirley McPhail School of Dance, Austin, TX (1972-1975) **CR:** Chairman, Trail Ride, Star of Texas Fair and PRCA Rodeo (2000-Present); Trail Boss, President, Austin Founders Trail Ride (1986-Present); Honorary Trial Boss, Grapevine/Houston Country Donkey, Mule and Horse Trail Ride (2000); Dance Teacher, Austin Club (1997-1998); Grapevine/Housgon Country Donkey, Mule and Horse Trail Ride (1997); Dream Catcher Ranch Trail Ride (1996); Honorary Trail Boss, Texas (1995); Contest Judge, Two-Stepping Across America, Austin, TX (1994); Head Contest Judge, America's Ultimate Dance Contest, Austin, TX (1994); Trail Boss, Bandera Longhorn Cattle Drive and Trail Ride (1990-1991); Dancer, Agent, George Strait/Bud Light Commercial Auditions (1990); Austin Ballroom Dancers (1988); Austin Travis County Livestock Show and Rodeo (1985-2005); Dancer, Contest Judge, Great Texas Dance-Off, Austin, TX (1985-1986); Choreographer, Head Cheerleader, Austin Texans Pro Football Team (1981); Member, Equestrian Committee (1980-1992) **CIV:** Settlement Club, Austin, TX (1987-Present); Recreation Chairman, St. Martin's Evangelical Lutheran Church, Austin, TX (1972-Present); Women's Symphony League of Austin (1972-Present); Honorary Trail Boss, St. Jude Children's Research Hospital Trail Ride, Austin, TX, Kyle, TX (1991) **CW:** Choreographer, "True Women" (1997); Choreographer, Lead Role Cabaret, Alpine, TX (1976); Dancer, Kiss Me Kate, Austin, TX (1970); Dancer, Oklahoma, Texas (1969) **AW:** Judge, Bill Aleshire, Travis County Commissioners (1989); Named, Texas First Lady Trail Boss, Governor Mark White, Mayor Frank Cooksey, Austin City Council (1986); Recipient, Outstanding Trail Rider of the Year Award, Wild Horse Trail Ride, OK (1984); Named, Outstanding Intramural Sports Team Manager-Player, Texas A&M University (1978-1979) **MEM:** Consultant, Llano Chamber of Commerce (2015-Present); President, Lone Grove Community Club (1999-Present); Player, Austin Country Club (1994-Present); Advisor, Austin Women's Tennis Association (1990-Present); Board of Directors, Llano Chamber of Commerce (2004-2009); Rodeo Chairman, Llano Chamber of Commerce (2002-2014); Executive Director, Lone Grove Community Club (1999-2000); Vice President, Lone Grove Community Club (1997-1999); Executive Trustee, Lone Grove Community Club (1997-1999); Treasurer, Lone Grove Community Club (1996-1997); Team Tennis Captain, Austin Country Club (1994-1995); Dance Teacher, Austin Country Club (1993-1996); President, Women's Team Tennis of Austin Association (1993-1994); Second Vice President, Zeta Tau Alpha (1993-1994); Yearbook Committee Member, Zeta Tau Alpha (1992-1994); President-elect, Women's Team Tennis of Austin Association (1992-1993); Nominating Chairman, Zeta Tau Alpha

(1992-1993); International Conference Official Delegate, Zeta Tau Alpha (1992); Parliamentarian, Austin Alumnae Panhellenic Associatio (1991-1992); President, Zeta Tau Alpha (1991-1992); Membership Comittee, Capital Area Tennis Association (1991-1992); Special Events Chairman, Austin Women's Tennis Association (1990-1992); President, Austin Alumnae Panhellenic Association (1990-1991); Historian, Junior Austin Woman's Club (1990-1991); Rush Forum Chairman, Austin Alumnae Panhellenic Association (1990); First Vice President, Austin Alumnae Panhellenic Association (1989-1990); Publicity Chairman, Zeta Tau Alpha (1989); International Conference Official Delegate, Zeta Tau Alpha (1988); Treasurer, Zeta Tau Alpha (1987-1989); President, Austin Women's Tennis Association (1986-1990); Vice President, Austin Women's Tennis Association (1985-1986); Austin Alumnae Chapter, Alumnae Photographer, Social Advisor, Zeta Tau Alpha (1982-1987); President, American Vetetrans Medical Association Auxiliary (1979-1980); Vice President, American Vetetrans Medical Association Auxiliary (1978-1979); Vice President, Omicron Nu (1973-1974); Texas Association of Teachers of Dancing, Inc.; Lifetime Member, United States Twirling and Gymnastics Association, University of Texas Ex-Students Association; Texas Executives in Home Economics; American Horse Shows Association; International Arabian Horse Association; Winner, Second Annual Harriet Crosson Outstanding Player & Community Service Award; Houston Salt Grass Trail Ride Association San Antonio Alamo Trail Ride Association; Fort Worth Chisholm Trail Ride Association; University of Texas Longhorn Alumni Band; Austin Chamber of Commerce; American Business Women's Association; Central Texas Arabian Horse; Capitol Area Quarter Horse Association; Junior Austin Women of Austin Country; Charter Member, Texas Equestrian Trail Riders Association; Austins Woman's Club; Women's Symphony League of Austin; Settlement Club of Austin; Settlement Home for Children; Texas and Southwestern Cattle Raisers Association; Hill Country Livestock Raisers Association; Texas Cattlewomen Association; Hill Country Cattle Women; The Austin Club; Easter Seals Fundraiser, Zeta Tau Alpha; **H:** Theater; Piano; Drums; Sports; Travel **PA:** Republican **ADD:** P.O. Box 5868, Austin, TX, 78763

MUJICA, BARBARA LOUISE, T: Professor of Spanish Literature **I:** Education/Educational Services **CN:** Georgetown University **PT:** Louis Kaminar; Frieda (Kline) Kaminar **MS:** Married **SPN:** Mauro E. Mujica (12/26/1996) **CH:** Lillian Louise; Mariana Ximena; Mauro Eduardo Ignacio **ED:** PhD, New York University (1974); MA, Middlebury College (1965); AB, University of California, Los Angeles (1964) **CT:** Certified in German Language, Advanced Level, German International School, Washington D.C. **C:** Professor of Spanish, Georgetown University (1974-2017); Instructor, The City University of New York (1973-1974); Assistant Professor of Romance Languages, The City University of New York (1973-1974); Associate Editor of Modern Languages, Harcourt Brace Jovanovich (Now Houghton Mifflin Harcourt) (1966-1973); Instructor of French, University of California, Los Angeles (1963-1964) **CR:** Faculty Member, Summer Institute, National Endowment for the Humanities (1980); President, Association for Hispanic Classical Theater, Inc.; Co-chair, Catholic Studies, Georgetown University; Faculty Adviser, Georgetown University Student Veterans Association; Co-director, Veterans Support Team; Lecturer, Dozens of Universities and Other Institutions Including the Smithsonian and Philadelphia Museum of Art **CIV:** Board of Directors, GALA Theatre; Judge, Helen Hayes Theater Awards; Judge, Gabriela Mistral Poetry Contest; ASAP Instructor; Workshops in Creative Writing for Veterans; Platoon Mom, AdoptaPlatoon; Education Unbound **CW:** Author, Editor, "A New Anthology of Early & Modern Spanish Theater" (2013); Editor, "Shakespeare and the Spanish Comedia" (2013); Author, "I am Venus: A Novel" (2013); Author, "Teresa de Avila: Lettered Woman" (2008); Author/Editor, "Women Writers of Early Modern Spain: Sophia's Daughters" (2004); Author/Editor, "Milenio" (2002); Author, "Frida: A Novel" (2001); Editor, "El Texto Puesto en Escena" (2000); Author, "Far From My Mother's Home: Short Stories" (1999); Author/Editor, "Siglos XVII y XIX" (1999); Author, "Sanchez Across the Street: Short Stories" (1997); Editor, "Premio Nobel" (1997); Author, "Books of the Americas" (1997); Editor, "Looking at the Comedia in the Year of the Quincentennial" (1993); Editor, "Texto y Vida: Introduccion a la Literatura Hispano-Americana" (1992); Author/Editor, "Antología de la Literatura Española: La Edad Media" (1991); Author/Editor, "Renacimiento y Siglo de Oro" (1991); Editor, "Texto y Vida: Introduccion a la Literatura Española" (1990); Author, "Et in Arcadia Ego" (1990); Author, "The Deaths of Don Bernardo: Novel" (1990); Author, "Texto y Espectáculo" (1987); Editor, "Verbena: Bilingual Review of the Arts" (1979-1985); Author, "Iberian Pastoral Characters" (1986); Author, "Pasaporte, Revised Edition" (1984); Author, "Entrevista" (1982); Author, "Calderon's Characters: An Existential Point of View" (1980); Author, "Pasaporte" (1980); Publisher, "Verbena: Bilingual Review of the Arts" (1979-1985); Author, "Aqui y Ahora" (1979); Author, "Readings in Spanish Literature" (1975); Author, "A-LM Spanish, Levels I-IV" (1969-1974); Author, "Teresa de Jesus: Espiritualidad y Feminismo"; Author, "Sister Teresa: A Novel"; Author, Short Story, "Imagining Iraq"; Author, Short Story, "Ahmed, the Tailor"; Author, Short Story, "Upside Down"; Author, Short Story, "Interrogating Calla"; Author, Short Story, "A Lucky Son-of-a Bitch"; Author, Short Story, "Jason's Cap"; Author, Short Story, "Judgment"; Author, Short Story, "Captain O'Reilly and the Professor"; Author, Short Story, "The Chaplain"; Author, Short Story, "Ox"; Author, Published in Hundreds of Magazines and Newspapers, Including The New York Times Company, The Washington Post, The Dallas Morning News Inc., Commonweal Magazine and Américas; Author, Articles, Academic Journals; Performer, Literary Readings, Universities, Bookstores, Book Clubs, Cultural Centers and Institutions Including United States Navy Memorial; Interviewee, Hundreds of Radio and Television Programs; Senior Associate Editor, "Washington Review"; Member, Board of Directors, "Washington Review"; Editorial Board Member, "Bulletin of Comediantes"; Editor, "Comedia Performance"; Editorial Board Member, "Hispania"; Book Review Editor, "Americas Magazine (OAS)"; Reviewer, "Washington Independent Review of Books"; Member, Board of Directors, "Washington Review" **AW:** Grantee, Georgetown University (2005-2006); Trailblazers Award (2004); Hoepner Award For Fiction (2002); Winner, E.L. Doctorow International Fiction Competition (1992); 50 Best Op-Eds of the Decade, The New York Times Company (1990); Pangolin Prize for Best Short Story (1998); Grantee, Poets And Writers Of New York, Spanish Government (1987); Penfield Fellow (1971); Distinguished Service Medal, Georgetown University; Best Professor Award, Georgetown University; Six-Time Recipient, Maryland Writers' Association Award; Five-Time Recipient, Short Stories Award **MEM:** President Emerita, Association for Hispanic Classical Theater, Inc.; Modern Language Association of America; The Renaissance Society of America; Sixteenth Century Society & Conference; GEMELA, Early Modern Women Writers Association; PEN America; The Writer's Center **MH:** Albert Nelson Marquis Lifetime Achievement Award (2017) **H:** Tennis; Yoga; Pilates **ADD:** 7601 Quintana Ct, Bethesda, MD, 20817 **URL:** http://www.barbaramujica.com

MUKERJEE, PASUPATI, T: Professor **I:** Education/Educational Services **CN:** University of Wisconsin **DOB:** 02/13/1932 **PB:** Calcutta **SC:** India **PT:** Nani Gopal Mukerjee; Probhabati (Ghosal) Mukerjee **MS:** Married **SPN:** Mina Maitra (11/14/1998); Lalita Sarkar (2/29/1964, Deceased) **ED:** PhD, University of Southern California (1957); MSc, University of Calcutta (1951); BSc, University of Calcutta (1949) **C:** Professor Emeritus, University of Wisconsin-Madison (1994-Present); Professor, School of Pharmacy, University of Wisconsin-Madison (1967-1994); Visiting Associate Professor, University of Wisconsin-Madison (1966-1967); Senior Scientist, Chemistry Department, University of Southern California (1964-1966); Guest Scientist, Utrecht University (1964); Reader in Physical Chemistry, IACS (1959-1964); Research Associate, Brookhaven National Laboratory (1957-1959); Lecturer, Visiting Assistant Professor, University of Southern California (1956-1957) **CR:** Visiting Professor, Indian Institute of Technology, Kharagpur, India (1971-1972); Commission on Colloid and Surface Chemistry, International Union Pure and Applied Chemistry; Fellow, American Association for the Advancement of Science **CW:** Editorial Board Member, "Journal of Colloid and Interface Science" (1987-1980); Editorial Board Member, "Langmuir," American Chemical Society (1985-1986); Editorial Board Member, "Colloids and Surfaces" (1980-1986); Editorial Board Member, "Asian Journal of Pharmaceutical Sciences" (1978-1985); Contributor, Articles, Professional Journals **AW:** Grantee, U.S. Public Health Service; Grantee, National Science Foundation; Grantee, National Bureau of Standards; Grantee, Petroleum Research Fund, American Chemical Society **MEM:** Academy of Pharmaceutical Sciences; American Institute of Chemists; American Chemical Society; American Pharmacists Association; Rho Chi Society **MH:** Albert Nelson Marquis Lifetime Achievement Award (2017) **ADD:** 5526 Varsity Hill, Madison, WI, 53705

MULASE, MOTOHICO, T: Associate Dean of the Faculty **I:** Education/Educational Services **CN:** University of California, Davis **DOB:** 10/11/1954 **PB:** Kanazawa **SC:** Japan **PT:** Ken-Ichi Mulase Mieko (Yamamoto) Mulase **MS:** Married **SPN:** Sayuri Kamiya (9/10/1982) **CH:** Kimihico Chris; Paul Norihico; Yurika **ED:** DSc, Kyoto University (1985); MS, Kyoto University (1980); BS, The University of Tokyo (1978) **C:** Associate Dean of the Faculty, University of California, Davis (2017-Present); Chairman, Department of Mathematics, University of California, Davis (2004-Present); Professor, University of California, Davis (1991-Present); Chairman, Department of Mathematics, University of California, Davis (1998-2001); Vice Chairman, Department of Mathematics, University of California, Davis (1995-1996); Associate Professor, University of California, Davis (1989-1991); Assistant Professor, Temple University, Philadelphia, PA (1988-1989); Hedrick Assistant Professor, University of California, Los Angeles (1985-1988); Visiting Assistant Professor, Stony Brook University (1984-1985); JMS Fellow, Harvard University, Cambridge, MA (1982-1983); Research Associate, Nagoya University, Nagoya, Japan (1980-1985) **CR:** Visiting Professor, Humboldt University, Berlin, Germany (2002);

Visiting Professor, Humboldt University, Berlin, Germany (1995-1996); Visiting Professor, Kyoto University (1993-1994); Visiting Professor, Max-Planck Institute for Mathematics, Bonn, Germany (1991-1992); Member, Institute for Advanced Study, Princeton, NJ (1988-1989); Member, Mathematical Sciences Research Institute, Berkeley, CA (1982-1984) **CIV:** Treasurer, Port of Sacramento Japanese School (1990-1991) **CW:** Contributor, Articles, Professional Journals **AW:** Distinguished Teaching Award, Academic Senate, University of California, Davis (2009) **MEM:** Committee on International Affairs, American Mathematical Society (1993-1996) **H:** Music **BA:** 1 Shields Ave, Davis, CA, 95616 **ADD:** 1716 Sapphire Ct, Davis, CA, 95618

MULVIHILL, JOHN EDWARD, T: Adjunct Judicial **I:** Law and Legal Services **CN:** Vicar Interdiocesan Appellate Tribunal **DOB:** 11/19/1939 **PB:** Chicago **SC:** IL/USA **PT:** Harry Hamilton Mulvihill; Marie Sylvia (Ryska) Mulvihill **ED:** EdD, University of Oxford (2008); PhD, University of Oxford (2008); PhD in Evolution, University of Oxford (2008); Diplomate in Spanish Language and Culture, Anahuac South University, Mexico City, Mexico (2003); Diplomate, New Orleans School of Cooking (1991); Diplomate in Christian Archaeology, Pontifical Institute of Christian Archaeology, Rome, Italy (1991); PhD in Ministry, San Francisco Theological Seminary, San Anselmo, CA (1990); STD, Pontifical Gregorian University, Rome, Italy (1971); Diplomate, Wine Advisory Board, California Department of Food and Agriculture (1970); Diplomate in Etruscology & Italic Antiquities, University of Perugia, Perugia, Italy (1970); MPhil, Aquinas Institute, River Forest, IL (1967) **CT:** Ordained Priest, Roman Catholic Church (1964) **C:** Professor, Graduate Theological Foundation (2012-Present); Judge, Interdiocesan Appellate Tribunal, Milwaukee, WI (2007-Present); Adjutant Judicial, Vicar Interdiocesan Appellate Tribunal, Chicago, IL (2006-Present); Pastor, St. John Bosco Parish, Chicago, IL (1992-1997); Judge, Interdiocesan Appellate Tribunal, Chicago, IL (1983-2009); Judge, Metropolitan Tribunal, Chicago, IL (1980-1989); Vicar for Men and Women Religious, Roman Catholic Archdiocese of Chicago, Chicago, IL (1971-1983); Curate, St. John Bosco Parish, Chicago, IL (1965-1992) **CR:** Holy Land Pilgrim Director, Vatican Commission for Christian Pilgrimages (1995); Lecturer, Clinical Pastoral Education, Presence Saint Joseph Hospital, Chicago, IL (1989); Lecturer, Institute of Spirituality, River Forest, IL (1976); Executive Board, National Association of Vicars for Religious (1974-1980); Lecturer, Institute for Continuing Theological Education, Pontifical North American College, Rome, Italy (1970); Web Master, Pontifical North American College, Rome, Italy (1965); Fellow, Roman Academy, Rome, Italy (1964) **CIV:** Lord, Abbas Hall, Suffolk, England; Hundred Lord, Blackbourn, Suffolk, England; Baron, Roscommon, Ireland **CW:** Author, "Place of Promise: Genius Loci of Israel" (1997); Author, "Life as Genius Loci" (1995); Author, "Natural Philosophy as Genius Loci" (1991); Author, "Liberty as Genius Loci" (1991); Author, "Genius Loci" (1990); Author, "Pastoral Symposium" (1989); Author, "Second Nuptials" (1988); Author, "Ministerial Priest" (1971) **AW:** Honoree, Knight Commander, Equestrian Order of the Holy Sepulchre of Jerusalem (1994); Decorated Knight, Equestrian Order of the Holy Sepulchre of Jerusalem (1991); Pilgrim Shell Award Patriarch of Jerusalem (1991); Cross of the Holy Land, Papal Custos, Jerusalem, Israel (1965) **MEM:** Catholic Theological Society of America; American Academy of Religion; Canon Law Society of America; The Manorial Society of Great Britain Ltd; Life Member, American Catholic

Philosophical Association; Tennessee Squire Association **MH:** Albert Nelson Marquis Lifetime Achievement Award (2017) **H:** Travel **ADD:** 3236 Lincoln Street, Franklin Park, IL, 60131

MUN, EUNMI, T: Assistant Professor **I:** Education/Educational Services **CN:** University of Illinois, Urbana-Champaign **SC:** South Korea **ED:** PhD, Economic Sociology,Harvard University (2011); MA in Sociology, Seoul National University (2004); BA in Sociology, Seoul National University, With Honors (2002) **C:** Assistant Professor of Sociology, University of Illinois, Urbana-Champaign (2016-Present); Assistant Professor of Sociology; Department of Anthropology and Sociology, Amherst College (2013-2016); Postdoctoral Fellow, Reischasuer Institute of Japanese Studies, Harvard University (2011-2012); Visiting Assistant Professor of Sociology, Amherst College **AW:** Project in Innovative Curriculum and Teaching Award, Amherst College (2013); Graduate Student Paper Award, Society for the Advancement of Socioeconomics (2010); Summer Research Grant, Reischauer Institute of Japanese Studies (2010); Research Grant, Weatherhead Center of International Affairs (2008); Ronals Burt Award for Outstanding Student Paper, ASA Economic Sociology Section (2007) **MEM:** American Sociological Association; Society for Advancement of Socioeconomics **BA:** 702 S Wright St, Lincoln Hall Rm 3098, University of Illinois, Urbana-Champaign, Urbana, IL, 61801 **ADD:** 702 S Wright St, Lincoln Hall Rm 3098, U of I Urbana-Champaign, Urbana, IL, 61801

MURPHY, BRUCE ALLEN, T: Law Educator **I:** Education/Educational Services **CN:** Lafayette College **DOB:** 09/30/1951 **PB:** Abington **SC:** MA/USA **MS:** Married **SPN:** Carol Lynn Wright (6/14/1975) **CH:** Emily; Geoffrey **ED:** PhD, University of Virginia (1978); BA, University of Massachusetts, Amherst, Summa Cum Laude (1973) **C:** Fred Morgan Kirby Professor of Civil Rights, Lafayette College (1998-Present); Professor of American History and Politics, Pennsylvania State University (1992-1998); Fellow, Institute for the Arts and Humanistic Studies, Pennsylvania State University (1989-1998); Professor of Political Science, Pennsylvania State University (1988-1992); Associate Professor of Political Science, Pennsylvania State University (1983-1988); Assistant Professor of Political Science, Pennsylvania State University (1978-1983) **CR:** Director, Mock Trial Team, Lafayette College (1999-2002); Director, Forensics Union, Lafayette College (1998-2002); Visiting Professor, School of Law, University of Texas at Austin (1990); Pre-law Adviser, Pennsylvania State University (1978-1987); Speaker, Graduation Address, Pennsylvania State University (1984); Speaker in Field; Committee Chair, Various University Committees **CIV:** Education Coordinator, Freedom's Foundation at Valley Forge (1987-Present); Educator, Freedom's Foundation at Valley Forge (1980-Present); Lecturer, Ed Rendell Center for Civics and Civic Engagement (2014); Web Developer, Constitution Center (2012); Director, Seminars, We the People; Lecturer, National Constitution Center **CW:** Author, "Scalia: A Court of One," Simon & Schuster (2014); Author, "Fifty-Two Weeks of Boot Camp," In Chambers: Stories of Supreme Court Law Clerks and Their Justices, University of Virginia (2012); Co-author, "Approaching Democracy: An Introduction to American Government," Seventh Edition, Prentice Hall (2011-2012); Co-author, "Approaching Democracy: An Introduction to American Government," Sixth Edition, Prentice Hall (2009); Co-author, "Justice Louis D. Brandeis, Professor Felix Frankfurter, and the Balfour

Declaration," Jordan Journal of International Affairs (2008); Co-author, "Extrajudicial Activities," Encyclopedia of the Supreme Court of the United States, Thomson Gale (2008); Author, "Seasons of Politics: Life-Mapping President George W. Bush," The International Journal of Humanities (2007); Author, "The Seasons of Justice: Life-Mapping the United States Supreme Court," Fifth International Conference on New Directions in Humanities Research, Paris, France (2007); Co-author, "Approaching Democracy: An Introduction to American Government," Fifth Edition, Prentice Hall (2006); Co-author, "Approaching Democracy: An Introduction to American Government: Portfolio Edition," Prentice Hall (2004); Co-author, "Approaching Democracy: An Introduction to American Government: Election Update Edition," Prentice Hall (2004); Co-author, "Approaching Democracy: An Introduction to American Government," Fourth Edition, Prentice Hall (2003); Author, "Wild Bill: The Legend and Life of William O. Douglas," Random House (2003); Author, "A Delicate Balance: Security and Civil Rights in Times of Crisis," World Book Focus on Terrorism , World Book Encyclopedia (2003); Co-author, "Felix Frankfurter," Great American Judges: An Encyclopedia, ABC-CLIO (2003); Co-author, "Louis D. Brandeis," Great American Judges: An Encyclopedia, ABC-CLIO (2003); Co-author, "Approaching Democracy: An Introduction to American Government," Third Edition, Prentice Hall (2001); Author, "Abe Fortas," Great American Lawyers: An Encyclopedia, Santa Barbara, CA: ABC-CLIO (2001); Author, "F. Lee Bailey," Great American Lawyers: An Encyclopedia, Santa Barbara, CA: ABC-CLIO (2001); Co-author, "Approaching Democracy: An Introduction to American Government," Second Edition, Prentice Hall (1999); Author, "Portraits of American Politics: A Reader," Third Edition Houghton Mifflin (1999); Author, "Justices and Presidents: Maintaining Judicial Independence in a Hostile Political World," Southern Political Science Association, Norfolk, Virginia (1997); Co-author, "Approaching Democracy: An Introduction to American Government," Prentice Hall (1996); Author, "Portraits of American Politics: A Reader," Second Edition, Houghton Mifflin (1994); Author, "The Impact of Abe Fortas on the Supreme Court," Jewish Justices of the Supreme Court, Supreme Court Historical Society (1994); "Uncovering a Life: Historical Research and the Biographer," American Political Science Association (1993); Author, "The Impact of Abe Fortas on the Supreme Court," Supreme Court Historical Society (1993); Author, "The Search for William O. Douglas," Maxwell School, Syracuse University (1993); Author, "Portraits of American Politics: A Reader," Houghton Mifflin (1991); Author, "Life-Mapping Justices: A Reassessment of Justice Abe Fortas," Southern Political Science Association (1991); Author, "At the Crossroads: The Elements and Propriety of Extrajudicial Politics," Ethics in the Courts: Policing Behavior in the Federal Judiciary, The National Legal Center for the Public Interest (1990); Author, "Abe Fortas: Presidential Advisor," The Lyndon Johnson Presidency, Greenwood Press (1989); Author, "Robert Bork and Abe Fortas: The Confirmation Process," The Pennsylvania Legal Society (1989); Author, "At the Crossroads: The Ethics of Extrajudicial Activities by the Supreme Court," American Political Science Association (1989); Author, "Fortas: The Rise and Ruin of a Supreme Court Justice," William Morrow (1988); Author, "Brandeis, F.D.R., and the Ethics of Judicial Advising," The Roosevelt New Deal: A Program Assessment Fifty Years After, Lyndon Baines Johnson Library, Lyndon Baines Johnson School of Public Affairs (1986); Author, "Abe

Fortas: The Justice and the Friend," Symposium on Lyndon Baines Johnson: A Texan in Washington (1986); Author, "Ethics and the Supreme Court," York County Bar Association (1984); Author, "Brandeis, Frankfurter, and the Supreme Court," School of Law, University of Pittsburgh (1983); Author, "Isaiah, his Scribe, and the Creation of the New Deal," Symposium on "The New Deal Fifty Years After: A Historical Assessment (1983); Author, "The Brandeis/Frankfurter Connection, The Bar Association of Baltimore City (1982); Co-author, "Ethical Considerations in the Practice of Law," Symposium on Legal Ethics, Harvard Law School, Harvard University (1982); Author, "The Brandeis/Frankfurter Connection: The Secret Political Activities of Two Supreme Court Justices," Oxford University Press (1982); Author, "Abe Fortas and Warren Burger as Judicial Politicians," Southwestern Political Science Association (1980); Author, "Elements of Extrajudicial Strategy: A Look at the Political Roles of Justices Louis D. Brandeis and Felix Frankfurter," Georgetown Law Journal (1980); Co-author, "Preserving the Progressive Spirit in a Conservative Time: The Joint Reform Efforts of Justice Louis Brandeis and Professor Felix Frankfurter, 1916-1933," Michigan Law Review (1980); Author, "The Extrajudicial Behavior of Justices Brandeis and Frankfurter," American Political Science Association (1978); Author, "A Supreme Court Justice as Politician: Felix Frankfurter and Federal Court Appointments," The American Journal of Legal History (1977) **AW:** Mary Louise Van Artsdalen Award, Lafayette College (2015); Marquis Award for Distinguished Teaching, Lafayette College (2011); Aaron O. Hoff Award for Organization Adviser of the Year (2000); Honoree, Recommended Course, New Improved College Book, Prentice Hall, (1994); Honoree, Best Professor, New Improved College Book, Prentice Hall, (1990); Harry S. Truman Library Presidential Research Grant (1990); Gerald R. Ford Library Presidential Research Grant (1990); Harry S. Truman Library Presidential Research Grant (1990); Gerald R. Ford Library Presidential Research Grant (1990); Honoree, "125 Alumni to Watch," University of Massachusetts at Amherst (1988); Institute for the Arts and Humanistic Studies Grant, Pennsylvania State University (1988); Christian R. and Mary F. Lindback Award for Distinguished Undergraduate Teaching (1987); Nominee, Charles A. Dana Award for Pioneering Achievements in Higher Education (1987); Citation Award, Council for Advancement and Support of Education (1984-1987); Finalist, Professor of the Year, Council for Advancement and Support of Education (1984-1987); Honoree, "Hot Prof," Pennsylvania State University, Philadelphia Magazine (1983); Research Grant, LBJ Foundation (1982-1983); Institute for the Arts and Humanistic Studies Grant, Pennsylvania State University (1982); Honoree, Alumni Association Faculty Adviser of the Year, College of the Liberal Arts, Pennsylvania State University (1981); Faculty Research Initiation Grant, Pennsylvania State University (1979-1980); Institute for the Arts and Humanistic Studies Grant, Pennsylvania State University (1979); Eleanor Roosevelt Foundation Research Grant (1977-1978) **MEM:** President, X-Club, Pennsylvania State University (1994); Vice President, X-Club, Pennsylvania State University (1993); Secretary, X-Club, Pennsylvania State University (1992); X-Club, Pennsylvania State University (1990-1998); The Phi Beta Kappa Society **MH:** Albert Nelson Marquis Lifetime Achievement Award (2017) **H:** Fishing; Reading; Sports **ADD:** 5651 Northwood Drive, Center Valley, PA, 18034 **URL:** https://en.wikipedia.org/wiki/Bruce_Allen_Murphy

MURPHY, DANIEL IGNATIUS, T: Lawyer **I:** Law and Legal Services **DOB:** 03/14/1927 **PB:** Philadelphia **SC:** PA/USA **PT:** John Anthony Murphy; Irene Cooper Thorn **MS:** Married **SPN:** Barbara Ann Uncles (1/1/1979); Jeanne B. Genetti (7/28/1956, Divorced 8/1978) **CH:** Jewel A.; Daniel Jr. **ED:** LLB, Yale University (1953); BS in Economics, University of Pennsylvania (1950) **C:** Of counsel, Stradley, Ronon, Stevens & Young, Philadelphia, PA (1993); Partner, Stradley, Ronon, Stevens & Young, Philadelphia, PA (1980-1992); Partner, Waters, Gallagher, Collins & Masterson, Philadelphia, PA (1972-1980); Partner, Takiff, Bolger & Murphy, Philadelphia, PA (1966-1972); Partner, Shapiro, Stalberg, Cook, Murphy & Kalodner, Philadelphia, PA (1964-1966); Partner, Cavanaugh, Murphy & Kalodner, Philadelphia, PA (1958-1964); Assistant City Solicitor, City of Philadelphia, PA (1956-1959); Associate, Evans, Bayard & Frick, Philadelphia, PA (1953-1955) **CR:** Judge Pro Tempore, Philadelphia County Court of Common Pleas (2000-Present); Lecturer, American Litigation University, Miskolc, Hungary (2009); Arbitrator, National Association of Securities Dealers (2001-2002); Appointed Special Master for Trial Management of Complex Litigation, Philadelphia County Court of Common Pleas (1994-2009); Pennsylvania College of Orphans Court Judges, Pittsburgh, PA (1991); Pennsylvania College of Orphans Court Judges, Harrisburg, PA (1978); Lecturer, Pennsylvania Bar Institute, Harrisburg, PA (1974-1992); Member, Executive Committee, Philadelphia Estate Planning Council (1958-1960); Teacher, American Society of CLUs, Villanova, PA (1956-1957) **CIV:** Board of Directors, Covenant House of Pennsylvania (2004-Present); Trustee, Easttown Library and Information Center, Pennsylvania (2004-2005); Trustee, Hahnemann University, Philadelphia, PA (1983-1986); Chairman, Committee of 70, Philadelphia, PA (1972-1974); Member, Committee of 70, Philadelphia, PA (1968-2003); Chairman, Philadelphia Chapter, American Cancer Society (1956-1963) **MIL:** U.S. Navy (1945-1946) **CW:** Editor, Philadelphia Bar Association Magazine, The Shingle (1958-1967); Contributor, Chapters, Manuals; Contributor, Articles, Professional Journals **MEM:** Board of Directors, Colonial Society of Pennsylvania (2001-2006); Vice Chairman, Committee Censors, Philadelphia Bar Association (1971); Life Fellow, Pennsylvania Bar Foundation; ABA; Pennsylvania Bar Association; Pennsylvania Society S.R.; Society of Colonial Wars; Union League of Philadelphia **BAR:** U.S. Supreme Court (1959); U.S. Tax Court (1956); State Bar of Pennsylvania (1954); U.S. District Court, Eastern District of Pennsylvania (1954); U.S. Court of Appeals for the 3rd Circuit (1954) **MH:** Albert Nelson Marquis Lifetime Achievement Award (2017) **H:** U.S. Civil War history **PA:** Democrat **RE:** Roman Catholic **ADD:** 1713 West Chester Pike Apt 217, West Chester, PA, 19382

MURRAY, JULIA KAORU, T: Occupational Therapist (Retired) **I:** Medicine & Health Care **DOB:** 11/18/1934 **PB:** Wahiawa, Oahu **SC:** HI/USA **PT:** Gijun Funakoshi; Edna Tsuruko (Taba) Funakoshi **MS:** Married **SPN:** Joseph Edward Murray (1961) **CH:** Michael Joseph Murray; Susan Kei Mallal; Leslie Ellen Heath; Bradley Heath **ED:** Certificate in Occupational Therapy, University of Puget Sound (1958); BA, University of Hawaii (1956) **C:** Occupational Therapist, Misawa AB Division, United States Naval Hospital, Yokosuka, Japan (2005-2009); Occupational Therapist, Yokota AB Division, United States Naval Hospital, Yokosuka, Japan (1999-2005); Occupational Therapist, United States Naval Hospital, Okinawa, Japan (1994-1999); Supervisor, Fairview Training Center, Marion County, Oregon (1984-1994); Occupational Therapist, Fairview

Training Center, Marion County, Oregon (1984-1994); Member, Oregon State Board of Examiners for Engineering and Land Surveying (1979-1987); Member, Advisory Committee, Oregon Higher Education Coordinating Commission (1979-1982); Vice President, Independent Living, Inc. (1976-1979); Vice Chairman, Advisory Board, Hospital Improvement Program, East Oregon State Hospital, Pendleton, OR (1974); Part-Time Therapist, Centre County Center for Crippled Children and Adults, State College, PA (1963); Senior Therapist, Hawaii State Hospital, Kaneohe, HI (1959); Therapist, Institute of Logopedics, Wichita, KS (1958); Instructor, Job Search **CIV:** Member, Executive Board, Liberty-Boone Neighborhood Association (1979-1983); Vice Chairman, Advisory Board, LINC (1978); Representative, Umatilla County Commissioners, Blue Mountain Economic Development Council (1976-1978); Member, Ashland, Wisconsin Park and Recreation Board (1972-1973) **AW:** Decorated, Meritorious Civilian Service Medal, United States Navy; Decorated, Meritorius Unit Citation, United States Naval Hospital Okinawa; Recipient, Numerous Letters of Commendations **MEM:** Oregon Board of Directors, League of Women Voters (1979-1981); Pendleton Board of Directors, League of Women Voters (1977-1978); President, League of Women Voters (1975-1977); Board of Directors Pendleton, League of Women Voters (1974); Wisconsin Vice President, League of Women Voters (1970); League of Women Voters, Ashland, WI (1967-1971); Secretary, OT Association of Hawaii (1960); American Occupational Therapy Association, Inc.; Occupational Therapy Association of Oregon **MH:** Albert Nelson Marquis Lifetime Achievement Award (2017) **H:** Chigiri-e with mountains, portraits, cards, art and decoration pieces; Reading and researching anthropology, archaeology, geology and astrophysics **ADD:** 760 Ironwood Dr SE, Salem, OR, 97306-1619

MYSLINSKI, MARY JANE, T: Associate Professor, Director of Human Performance Lab **I:** Education/Educational Services **CN:** Rutgers, The State University of New Jersey **ED:** EdM, EdD, Columbia University, New York City, NY (1995); MA in Cardiopulmonary Physical Therapy, New York University (1982); BS in Physical Therapy, Boston University (1977) **CT:** Physical Therapy License (1977-Present) **C:** Director, Human Performance Lab for the Doctoral Program of Physical Therapy, Rutgers, The State University of New Jersey (1995-Present); Associate Professor, Rutgers, The State University of New Jersey (1995-Present); Administrative Director of Rehab Services, St. Elizabeth Hospital (1993-1995); Various Capacities, JFK Medical Center **MEM:** American Physical Therapy Association; ACFM; American Association of Cardiovascular and Pulmonary Rehabilitation **H:** Fitness; Keeping up with politics **ADD:** 917 Manchester Dr, Branchburg, NJ, 08876 **URL:** https://www.linkedin.com/in/mary-jane-mary-myslinski-406b0726

NAIMI, LINDA L., T: 1) Professor 2) Attorney **I:** Education/Educational Services **CN:** 1) Purdue University 2) Naimi and Associates **PB:** Virginia **SC:** United States **PT:** David; Dorothy **MS:** Widowed **SPN:** Dr. M.T. Naimi (deceased) **ED:** Doctorate, Harvard University; JD, University of Connecticut School of Law **C:** Professor (2004-Present); Attorney at Law (1996-Present); Vice President of Information Resources (1997-2004); State Director of Computing and Educational Technology (1986-1997); Director of Computing (1983-1985); Systems Analyst (1981-1983); Elementary Teacher (1976-1981) **CIV:** Various Editorial and Advisory Boards; Ethics and Critical Thinking Journal;

Journal of Leadership & Organizational Studies; Global Journal of Business Research; International Journal of Business and Finance Research (IJBFR); Evaluation Panel, National Defense Science and Engineering Graduate Scholarship (NDSEG); Reviewer, Diversity Transformation Awards Program, American Society of Engineering Educators **CW:** Author, Darvish; Translator, Divine Act by MT Naimi; Translator, Persian Poetry; Author, 30 Journal Articles **AW:** Top 10% of Attorneys in USA; Lawyers of Distinction; Elite American Educators; Elite American Lawyer; Golden Key International Honor Society; Charles B. Murphy Award for Outstanding Undergraduate Teaching, Purdue University; Panhellenic Outstanding Professor Award, Purdue University; Dwyer Award for Outstanding Teaching, Department of Technology Leadership and Innovation, Purdue University; Induction, Teaching Academy, Purdue University **MEM:** CERIAS, Purdue University; National Association of Professional Women; American Society for Engineer Educators; AAUP; AUWP; ABA; American Association for the Advancement of Science; IEEE; International Leadership Association; International Women's Leadership Association **BAR:** Connecticut (1996) **H:** Travel; Gardening; Crocheting; Reading; Writing **PA:** Independent **RE:** Christian (Protestant) **BA:** 155 S Grant Str, Purdue University, Young Hall 311, West Lafayette, IN, 47907 **ADD:** 908 N. Grant Street, West Lafayette, IN, 47906 **URL:** http://tech.purdue.edu/profile/lnaimi

NANDA, VED, T: Law Educator, Director, Academic Administrator **I:** Education/Educational Services **CN:** University of Denver **DOB:** 11/20/1934 **PB:** Gujranwala **SC:** India **PT:** Jagan Nath Nanda; Attar (Kaur) Nanda **MS:** Married **SPN:** Katharine Kunz (12/19/1982) **CH:** Anjali Devi **ED:** LLD, Bundelkhand University, Jhansi, India (2000); Honorary LLD, Soka University, Tokyo, Japan (1997); Postgraduate Coursework, Yale University (1962-1965); LLM, Northwestern University (1962); LLM, University of Delhi (1958); LLB, University of Delhi (1955); MA, University of the Punjab (1952) **C:** Vice Provost, University of Denver (1994-Present); Evans University Professor, University of Denver (1992-Present); Thompson G. Marsh Professor, Law, University of Denver (1987-Present); Professor, Law, Director, International Legal Studies Program, University of Denver (1970-Present); Assistant Provost, University of Denver (1993-1994); Associate Professor, Law, University of Denver (1968-1970); Assistant Professor, Law, University of Denver (1965-1968) **CR:** Distinguished Visiting Scholar, The John Marshall Law School (2010); Visiting Professor, University of Colorado (1992); Distinguished Visiting Scholar, University of Hawaii, Honolulu, HI (1986-1987); Distinguished Visiting Professor, International Law, California Western School of Law, San Diego, CA (1983-1984); Distinguished Visiting Professor, Chicago-Kent College of Law (1981); Consultant, U.S. Department of Energy (1980-1981); Visiting Professor, University of San Diego (1979); Consultant, Solar Energy Research Institute (1978-1981); Visiting Professor, University of Iowa College of Law, Iowa City (1974-1975); Visiting Professor, Florida State University (1973); Visiting Professor, Numerous Summer Programs **CIV:** United Nations Day Chair, State of Colorado (2000-Present); Member, Governor's Commission on Public Telecommunications (1980-1982); Co-Chairman, Colorado Public Broadcasting Federation (1977-1978); Board Director, Various National and State Civic Organizations; Vice Chair, Executive Council, WFUNA, Geneva, Switzerland **CW:** Editor, "Climate Change & Environmental Ethics" (2011); Contributing Editor, "Climate Change and Environmental Ethics" (2010); Editor, "Law in the War Against International Terrorism" (2005); Co-Editor, "Law in the War Against International Terrorism" (2004); Co-Editor, "International Environmental Law and Policy for the 21st Century" (2003); Co-Editor, "Nuclear Weapons and the World Court" (1998); Co-Editor, "Hindu Law and Legal Theory" (1996); Co-Editor, "European Union Law After Maastricht" (1996); Co-Editor, "Nuclear Proliferation and the Legality of Nuclear Weapons" (1995); Co-Editor, "International Environmental Law and Policy" (1995); Co-Editor, "World Debt and Human Conditions" (1993); Co-Editor, "Europe Community Law After 1992" (1993); Co-Editor, "Breach and Adaption of International Contracts" (1992); Editor, Contributor, "Refugee Law and Policy" (1989); Co-Author, "Litigation of International Disputes in U.S. Courts" (1987); Co-Editor, "Human Rights and Third World Development" (1985); Co-Editor, "World Climate Change" (1983); Co-Editor, "Global Human Rights" (1981); Co-Editor, "The Law of Transnational Business Transactions" (1981); Co-Editor, "Water Needs for the Future" (1977); Co-Editor, "A Treatise on International Criminal Law" (1973); Member, Editorial Board, The American Journal of Comparative Law; Member, Editorial Board, Indian Journal of International Law; Member, Editorial Board, Transnational Weekly; Columnist, Denver Post **AW:** Pride India Award, The International Co-operative Alliance (2011); Distinguished Scholarly Achievement Award, International Academy of Law and Mental Health (2010); Lifetime Teaching Award, All India Law Teachers Congress (2009); Human Rights Award, India Canada Association (2006); Highest Order of Justice Award, World Jurist Association (2005); Community Peace Building Award, Gandhi King Ikeda (2004); Special Achievement Award, Indo-American Association (2002); Named, Ambassador for Peace, Interreligious and International Federation for World Peace (2001); Eponym, Gold Medal, Bundelkhand University (2000); Eponym, Rotary Fellowship, Denver Rotary (2000); Medal of Honor, World Congress of Ukranian Lawyers (1999); Pioneer Award, University of Denver (1997); Human Rights Award, United Nations Foundation (1997); Civil Right's Award, Anti-Defamation League (1996); India Development Association Award (1996); Arthur Goodman Leadership Award, United Nations Foundation (1995); Alumni Faculty Award, University of Denver Sturm College of Law (1994); Highest Honor Award, Soka University, Tokyo, Japan (1994); World Legal Scholar Award, World Peace Through Law Center, Beijing, China (1990); Burlington Northern Foundation Scholar Award, University of Denver (1990); International Excellence Award, Colorado Council of International Organizations (1985); University Gold Medal, Delhi University Faculty of Law; Graduate Fellow, Northwestern University Pritzker School of Law; Graduate Fellow, Yale Law School; Graduate Fellow, University of Delhi Faculty of Law; Co-Recipient, Hyde Prize in International Law, Northwestern University Pritzker School of Law **MEM:** Honorary President, International Law Association (2001-Present); Honorary President, World Jurist Association (2000-Present); Counselor, The American Society of International Law (2000-Present); Vice President, World Jurist Association (1991-Present); National Council, United Nations Foundation (1990-Present); Executive Committee, International Law Association (1986-Present); President, World Jurist Association (1998-2000); Member, Governing Board, United Nations Foundation (1995-2005); Vice-Chairman, WFUNA (1995-2001); Honorary Vice President, The American Society of International Law (1995-1996); President, United Nations Foundation (1993-1996); Board, Review and Development, The American Society of International Law (1988-1991); President, Colorado Council of International Organizations (1988-1990); President, World Association of Law Professors (1987-1993); Vice President, The American Society of International Law (1987-1988); President, United Nations Foundation (1986-1988); Executive Council, The American Society of International Law (1981-1984); Board of Directors, Executive Committee, United States Members, International Institute of Space Law (1980-1988); Vice President, Colorado Division, United Nations Foundation (1973-1976); Executive Council, The American Society of International Law (1969-1972); Board of Directors, American Society for Comparative Law; Association of American Law Schools; The United States Institute of Peace; Associate, International Academy of Comparative Law; International Academy of Commercial and Consumer Law; President, Order of St. Ives; Rotary International; Cactus Club; University Club **MH:** Albert Nelson Marquis Lifetime Achievement Award (2017) **BA:** 2255 E Evans Ave, Denver, CO, 80208 **ADD:** 1795 Glencoe St, Denver, CO, 80220

NASSTROM, ROY RICHARD, T: Educational Consultant **I:** Consulting **CN:** Roy R. Nasstrom, Consulting **DOB:** 10/28/1930 **PB:** Oakland **SC:** CA/USA **PT:** Roy Richard Nasstrom; Edith Dolores (Spilman) Nasstrom **MS:** Married **SPN:** Sally Louise Shaw (8/29/1964) **CH:** Karen; Eric **ED:** PhD, University of California, Berkeley (1971); MA, University of California, Berkeley (1964); BA, University of California, Berkeley (1956); AA, University of California, Berkeley (1955) **C:** Educational Political Consultant, Roy R. Nasstrom, Consulting (2002-Present); Professor Emeritus, Winona State University (2001-Present); Chairman, Educational Leadership Department, Winona State University (1998-2001); Professor, Winona State University (1976-2001); Chairman, Educational Administration Department, Winona State University (1976-1988); Assistant Graduate Dean, Winona State University (1976-1977); Mediator, Fact Finder, Indiana Education Employment Relations Board (1974-1976); Assistant Professor, Education, Purdue University, West Lafayette, IN (1971-1976); Assistant Professor, Educational Administration, University of Kentucky, Lexington, KY (1969-1970); Acting Instructor, Education, University of California, Berkeley (1965-1968); Assistant to Superintendent, Ravenswood City School District, East Palo Alto, CA (1964-1965); Delegate, Centers for Disease Control and Prevention, Alameda County, California (1962-1968) **CR:** Consultant, Various Organizations and Schools (1969-Present); Speaker in Field, Various Organizations and Schools (1969-Present); Director, Post-Masters Studies, Winona State University (1992-1999); Board of Abstractors, Educational Administration Abstracts (1976-1983) **CIV:** List Manager, Winona On-line Democracy (2005-2008); Steering Committee, Winona On-line Democracy (2003-2010); Delegate, Council of Democratic Clubs (1960-1968) **MIL:** U.S. Army (1952-1954) **CW:** Board of Editors, AASA Professor (1979-1982); Manuscript Reviewer, Various Journals and Publications (1973-1987); Editor, "School Education Newsletter," University of California, Berkeley (1965-1968); Editor, "Ravenswood Report" (1964-1965); Contributor, Articles, Professional Journals; Contributor, Book Chapters **AW:** Numerous Grants (1969-1998) **MEM:** Cal Alumni Association; Socrates Cafe; Pi Sigma Alpha **MH:** Albert Nelson Marquis Lifetime Achievement Award (2017) **H:** Reading; History; Politics; Travel **ADD:** 1702 Edgewood Road, Winona, MN, 55987

NAVARRA, TOVA, I: Fine Art **CN:** Independent Artist **DOB:** 07/10/1948 **PB:** Newark **SC:** NJ/USA **PT:** Joe Treihart; Rose Leslie Treihart **MS:** Single **SPN:** Robert B. Kern (7/10/2004, Divorced 2008); John G. Navarra, Jr. (8/26/1967, Divorced 1998) **CH:** Yolanda Navarra-Fleming, John G., III **ED:** AAS, Brookdale Community College (1984); BA, Seton Hall University, Magna Cum Laude (1974) **CT:** Registered Nurse, New Jersey **C:** Freelance, The New York Times (1994-2000); Contributing Editor, American Journal of Nursing (1990-1994); Feature Writer, Asbury Park Press (1985-1992); Art Critic, Art Columnist, Asbury Park Press (1985-1992); Asbury Park Press (1985-1992); Entertainment Writer, Asbury Park Press (1978-1985); Feature Writer, Asbury Park Press (1978-1985); Press Correspondent, Asbury Park Press (1978-1985); Teacher in Music, Seton Hall Preparatory School (1975-1978); Teacher in Humanities, Seton Hall Preparatory School (1975-1978); Teacher in German, Seton Hall Preparatory School (1975-1978); Teacher in Art, Seton Hall Preparatory School (1975-1978); Teacher in Art History, Seton Hall Preparatory School (1975-1978); Correspondent, Village Times, TBR News Media (1974-1975); Elementary School Teacher, Jersey City, NJ (1967-1969); Lifestyle Editor, The Two River Times; Art Columnist, The Two River Times; Syndicated Columnist, Feature Writer, Copley News Service **CR:** Sole Juror, 75th Anniversary, Audubon Artists Society (2017); Lecturer, "NJ Artists Through Time," Red Bank Public Library, Red Bank, NJ (2017); Lecturer, "NJ Artists Through Time," John F. Peto Museum, Island Heights, NJ (2017); Juror, Fine Arts and Sculpture, 43rd Monmouth Festival Arts, Monmouth Reform Temple (2013); Instructor, Bayshore Fitness and Wellness Center, Hackensack Meridian Health (2005); Lecturer, Writing Conferences; Art Coordinator, Monmouth Players **CIV:** Judge, Manasquan River Artists Art Show, Brielle, NJ (2017); Contributor, American Society for the Prevention of Cruelty to Animals; Contributor, PETA; Contributor, Monmouth SPCA **CW:** Author, "New Jersey Artists Through Time" (2015); Exhibitor, Monmouth University (2012-2013); Exhibitor, "Rechnitz Hall Inaugural Exhibition for Department of Art and Design," Monmouth University (2012-2013); Exhibitor, James Yarosh Associates Fine Arts Gallery (2010); Exhibitor, Window Summer Show (2010); Exhibitor, Germany (2010); Solo Exhibitor, New Jersey Resources (2010); Exhibitor, "Bayonet Farm Art Exhibition" (2010); Exhibitor, "Holiday Show" (2009); Exhibitor, Guild of Creative Art (2009); Exhibitor, "31st Ann. Juried Art Exhibition," Monmouth County Arts Council, Monmouth Museum (2008-2010); Contributor, "'d.' Magazine" (2007); Exhibitor, "Tova Navarra and Santo Pezzutti: Two Visions at 800 Gallery," Monmouth University (2007); Exhibitor, "Photographs in New York, New Jersey and Pennsylvania" Mid-Atlantic Riviera Magazine (2005); Associate Contributing Editor, "M.A.R. Magazine" (2005); Solo Exhibitor, Navesink Library Theater (Now Monmouth Players) (2004-2005); Author, "Encyclopedia of Vitamins, Minerals, and Supplements Second Edition" (2004); Author, "Encyclopedia of Allergies, Second Edition" (2004); Author, "Encyclopedia of Complementary and Alternative Medicine" (2004); Author, "Encyclopedia of Asthma and Respiratory Disorders" (2003); Author, "Young People/Tough Problems" (2003); Publisher, "On My Own: Helping Kids Help Themselves, A Kid's Guidebook: Great Advice to Help Kids Cope Second Edition" (2003); Author, "The Kids' Guidebook: Great Advice to Help Kids Cope, Second Edition" (2002); Author, "Monmouth University" (2001); Solo Exhibitor, M. Thomson Kravetz Gallery (2000); Lifestyle Editor, "The Two River Times" (1999-2000); Co-Author, "The American Century: Staten Island" (1999); Author, "Seton Hall University: A Photographic History" (1999); Author, "Staten Island II" (1998); Author, "Levittown II" (1998); Author, "Toward Painless Writing" (1998); Associate Editor, "The Courier" (1998); Co-Author, "Image of America: Levittown: The First Fifty Years" (1997); Author, "Staten Island" (1997); Author, "Images of America: Howell and Farmingdale" (1996); Publisher, "An Insider's Guide to Home Health Care: An Interdisciplinary Approach" (1995); Publisher, "Wisdom for Caregivers" (1995); Author, "Encyclopedia of Vitamins, Minerals, and Supplements" (1995); Publisher, "On My Own: Helping Kids Help Themselves, A Kid's Guidebook: Great Advice to Help Kids Cope" (1994); Co-Author, "Allergies A-Z" (1994); Exhibitor, Payne Gallery, Moravian College (1992); Solo Exhibitor, Gallery Axiom (1991); Solo Exhibitor, Millburn Free Public Library (1991); Solo Exhibitor, "Retrospective – 15 Years," Monmouth University (1991); Exhibitor, Art Forms (1991); Contributing Editor, "American Journal of Nursing" (1990-1994); Author, "Your Body: Highlights of Human Anatomy" (1990); Author, "Therapeutic Communication: A Guide to Effective Interpersonal Skills for Health Care Professionals" (1990); Solo Exhibitor, OK Harris Works of Art (1990); Health Trend Columnist, "Personal Fitness" (1989-1990); Author, "Playing It Smart: What to Do When You're on Your Own" (1989); Playwright, "Don't Cry, Pandora" (1989); Feature Writer, "Copley News Service" (1988-1993); Columnist, "Copley News Service" (1988-1993); Playwright, "Through the Kunai Grass with Dad" (1988); Author, "Jim Gary: His Life and Art" (1987); Author, Dog Star Poems, Iron Butterfly Press, (1987); Author, "The New Jersey Shore: A Vanishing Splendor" (1985); Copywriter, Jersey Shore Medical Center (1985); Photographer, Jersey Shore Medical Center (1985); Solo Exhibitor, Atlantic City Art Center (1982); Editor, Associated University Presses (1981-1982); Publisher, "Shore Affinity" (1979-1981); Editor-in-Chief, "Shore Affinity" (1979-1981); Staff Writer, "New Jersey Music and Arts" (1978-1981); Illustrator, "New Jersey Music and Arts" (1978-1981); Photographer, "New Jersey Music and Arts" (1978-1981); Solo Exhibitor, West Gallery, The New York Public Library (1978); Solo Exhibitor, County College of Morris (1975); Solo Exhibitor, Caldwell University (1975); Illustrator, "Drugs and Man" (1973); Contributor, "Nursing Spectrum Magazine"; Guest, Radio Programs; Guest, Television Programs; Contributor, Photographs in Books; Contributor, Book Illustrations; Contributor, Magazine Illustrations; Contributor, Newspaper Illustrations; Contributor, "Artvoices"; Contributor, Magazines **AW:** Winner, "This Changes Everything" First Prize in Sculpture, Monmouth County Senior Art Show (2017); First Prize, AAA World's Photo Contest (2006); AAA World's Photo Contest (2005) **MEM:** Monmouth Arts; Guild of Creative Art; The Humane Society of the United States; National Museum of Women in the Arts **ADD:** 1 Oakdale Drive, Apt. 4Q, Middletown, NJ, 07748

NEAL, DURWOOD E. JR., T: Professor **I:** Education/Educational Services **CN:** Augusta University **MS:** Married **SPN:** Katie Neal (1990) **CH:** Kalb **ED:** Resident, University of Texas Medical School (1987); Intern, University of Texas Medical School (1982); MD, UT Health Science Center San Antonio (1981); Fellow, University of Texas Health Science Center at Houston (1975); BS in Biology, Texas Christian University (1975) **CT:** Certified in Urology, American Board of Urology; Medical License, State of Texas; Medical License, State of Montana; Medical License, State of Oklahoma; Medical License, State of Georgia **C:** Chairman of Urology, Southern Illinois University; Chairman of Urology, University of Missouri, Columbia, MO; Chairman of Urology, University of Oklahoma, Tulsa, OK **CR:** Visiting Professor, Northern Mexico Urological Society (1997); Researcher, Urinary Tract Infections and Kidney Stones **CIV:** Volunteer, Bedlam Clinic, University of Oklahoma; Attending Physician, St. Vincent's Clinic, University of Texas Medical Branch at Galveston **CW:** Reviewer, 12 Journals **AW:** Crimson Apple Teaching Award, College of Medicine, University of Oklahoma (2013); Fellowship, RCEAS Emeritus Faculty, Lehigh University **MEM:** Jefferson Club, University of Missouri (2000); Study Section, National Institute of Diabetes and Digestive and Kidney Diseases (1997); President, Urology Section, SMA (1997); Secretary, Urology Section, SMA (1997); Grant Reviewer, National Institutes of Health; American Urological Association; American College of Sergeants **MH:** Albert Nelson Marquis Lifetime Achievement Award (2017); Distinguished Humanitarian (2017) **H:** Ice hockey **ADD:** 3 Eagle Pointe Drive, Augusta, GA, 30909

NEAL, MICHAEL B., T: Attorney at Law **I:** Law and Legal Services **CN:** Mcbb, Bragorgos, Burgess & Sorin, PLLC **ED:** JD, University of Memphis (1974); BA, Business Administration, Memphis State University (1967) **C:** Attorney, Member, Partner, McNabb, Bragorgos, Burgess & Sorin PLLC (2006-Present); Armstrong Allen PPLC (2006-Present); Assistant United States Attorney, District Attorney's Office **MIL:** Captain, Special Agent, Office of Special Investigations, U.S. Air Force (1967-1971) **AW:** AV Preminent, Martingdal Hubble (1987-2017) **MEM:** Memphis Bar Association; Tennessee Association of Professional Mediators; Tennessee Bar Association; Memphis Lawyers Journal Club; Tennessee Defense Lawyers Association; Transportation Lawyers Association; Defense Research Institute Trial Lawyers' Association **BAR:** Tennessee Supreme Court; United States Court of Appeals for the Sixth Circuit; United States District Court Western District of Tennessee; United States District Court Middle District of Tennessee; United States District Court Eastern District of Tennessee **BA:** 81 Monroe Ave Ste 600, Mcbb, Bragorgos, Burgess & Sorin, PLLC, Memphis, TN, 38103 **URL:** http://www.mbbslaw.com/attorneys/michael-b-neal

NELLIS, WILLIAM, T: Associate **I:** Education/Educational Services **CN:** Harvard University **PB:** Chicago **SC:** IL/USA **MS:** Married **SPN:** Carole Collins **CH:** William; Alicea; Jeffrey **ED:** PhD in Physics, Iowa State University (1968); MS in Physics, Iowa State University (1965); BS in Physics, Loyola University Chicago (1963) **C:** Associate, Department of Physics, Harvard University (2004-Present); Head, Center for High Pressure Sciences, Institute of Geophysics and Planetary Physics, Scripps Institution of Oceanography, University of California, San Diego (1984-1994); Associate Leader for Experiments, Division H, Lawrence Livermore National Laboratory (1981-1993); Leader, High-Dynamic-Pressure Experimental Group, Lawrence Livermore National Laboratory (1978-1993); Group Leader, Lawrence Livermore National Laboratory (1978-1981); Lab Employee, Lawrence Livermore National Laboratory (1976-2004); Computational Physicist, Lawrence Livermore National Laboratory (1973-1976); Assistant Professor of Physics, Monmouth College (1970-1973); Postdoctoral Research Associate, Materials Science Division, Argonne National Laboratory (1968-1970) **CR:** Chair, Ultracondensed Matter at High Pressures Symposium, March Meeting, American Physical Society, Minneapolis, MN (2000); Visiting Professor of Physics, University of California, San Diego (1989); Fellow, Division of Condensed Matter Physics, American Physical Society (1987); Chair, Topical Group on the Shock Compression of Condensed Matter, American Physical Society (1987); Co-chair, Topical Conference on Shock Compression of Condensed Matter, American Physical Society (1981); Speaker in Field; Visiting Speaker, American Physical Society; Fellow, Division of Condensed Matter Physics, American Physical Society **CW:** Author, "Ultra Condensed Matter By Dynamic Compression," Cambridge University Press (2017); Contributor, 300 Articles, Professional Journals; Patentee in Field **AW:** Bridgman Award, AIRAPT (2001); Shock Compression Science Award, American Physical Society (1997); Edward Teller Award, Lawrence Livermore National Laboratory; Duvall Award, American Physical Society **MEM:** American Geophysical Union (1986-Present); President, AIRAPT (2003-2007); Vice President, AIRAPT (1999-2003); Tutorial Lecturer, Shock Compression of Solids, American Physical Society (1990); American Association for the Advancement of Science; Executive Committee, AIRAPT (1987-1990); Chairman, Topical Group on Shock Compression of Condensed Matter, American Physical Society (1987); Materials Research Society; Hypervelocity Impact Society; Chair, American Physical Society Symposia **MH:** Albert Nelson Marquis Lifetime Achievement Award (2017) **BA:** 17 Oxford Street, Harvard University, Dept of Physics, Cambridge, MA, 02138 **ADD:** 249 Holly Point Road, Centerville, MA, 02632 **URL:** https://physics.aps.org/authors/william_nellis

NELSON, EDITH E., **T:** Consultant Dietitian **I:** Health, Wellness and Fitness **CN:** Private Practice **DOB:** 09/26/1940 **PB:** Vicksburg **SC:** MI/USA **PT:** Edward Kenneth Rolffs; Anna (McManus) Rolffs **MS:** Married **SPN:** Douglas Keith Nelson **CH:** Daniel Lee; Jennifer Lynn **ED:** MEd in Applied Nutrition, University of Cincinnati (1979); BS, Michigan State University (1962) **CT:** Licensed Dietitian, State of Florida **C:** Consultant Dietitian, Private Practice, Panama City, FL (1996-Present); Consultant Dietitian, Beverly Enterprises, Panama City Beach, FL (1994-1996); Consultant Dietitian, Northwest Florida Community Hospital, Chipley, FL (1993-1994); Renal Dietitian, Fresenius Kidney Care Fort Walton Beach, Fort Walton Beach, FL (1989-1992); Consultant Dietitian, Panama City Development Center, Panama City, FL (1988-1994); Consultant Dietitian, Fort Walton Beach Development Center, Fort Walton Beach, FL (1988-1994); Director, Nutrition Services, Dialysis Clinic, Inc., Cincinnati, OH (1979-1988); Graduate Teaching Assistant, University of Cincinnati (1978-1979); Clinical Dietitian, Spectrum Health Blodgett Hospital, Grand Rapids, MI; Clinical Dietitian, Macon County General Hospital, Macon County, GA **AW:** Grantee, National Kidney Foundation Grantee (1986); Michigan Education Association Scholar (1958) **MEM:** American Dietetic Association; Florida Dietetic Association; Panhandle District Dietetic Association; Omicron Nu **ADD:** 3522 Fox Run Blvd, Panama City Beach, FL, 32408

NELSON, KEVIN A., **T:** Public Health Analyst **I:** Health, Wellness and Fitness **CN:** Health Resources and Service Administration **DOB:** 12/29/1964 **PB:** New York **SC:** NY/USA **PT:** Phillip Jacob Nelson; Lucie Anne Nelson **ED:** PhD, Medical University of South Carolina, Charleston, SC (1998); MPH, The University of Alabama, Birmingham, AL (1993); MA, Wesleyan University, Middletown,

CT (1991); BA, The University of Chicago (1987) **C:** Public Health Analyst, United States Health Resources & Services Administration, Rockville, MD (2006-2007); Maternal and Child Health Epidemiologist, Michigan Department of Public Health, Lansing, MI (2005-2006); Employee, Penn State Health Milton S. Hershey Medical Center **CR:** Functional Analyst, Lockheed-Martin, Alexandria, VA (2003) **AW:** Fellow, National Cancer Institute (2000-2001); Fellow, National Heart, Lung, and Blood Institute (1998-2000) **MEM:** Associate, American Statistical Association; Associate, Mu Sigma Rho **ADD:** 404 Front St, Owego, NY, 13827

NEMIR, DONALD PHILIP, **I:** Law and Legal Services **DOB:** 10/31/1931 **PB:** Oakland **SC:** CA/USA **PT:** Philip F. Nemir; Mary (Shavor) Nemir **ED:** JD, University California, Berkeley (1960); AB, University California, Berkeley (1957) **C:** Private Practice, San Francisco (1961) **MEM:** Chairman, Committee on Discovery, San Francisco Bar Association; Committee on United Way, San Francisco Bar Association **BAR:** US Supreme Court (1980); Central District, US District Court of California (1975); California Bar Association (1961); Northern District, US District Court of California (1961); Ninth Circuit, US Court of Appeals (1961)

NERA, NENA M., **T:** President **I:** Business Management/Business Services **CN:** The "N" Company **DOB:** 05/18/1933 **SC:** Philippines **PT:** Benito D. Maneclang; Paz Maneclang **MS:** Married **SPN:** Dr. Eduardo A. Nera **CH:** Eduardo Gerard; Dorothy Lauren; Edmund Lawrence; Edwin Andres **ED:** Coursework, University of the Philippines (1959); MSW, University of Wisconsin **C:** Senior Health Policy Analyst, Health Canada (1995-2000) **AW:** Distinguished Toastmaster, Washington, DC (2010); Outstanding Filipino-Canadian Abroad **MEM:** Distinguished Toastmasters (2007); The International Society of Social Workers **ADD:** 1 Eleanor Drive, Ottawa, ON, Canada, K2E 6A3

NEUBAUER, DEAN V., **T:** Engineering Fellow, Chief Statistician, Data Analytics Leader **I:** Engineering **CN:** Corning Incorporated **SC:** IA/USA **PT:** Virgil Neubauer; Fanchon Neubauer **MS:** Married **SPN:** Kimberly **CH:** Jason; Bryan; Laura **ED:** MS in Applied and Mathematical Statistics, Rochester Institute of Technology (1988); BS in Statistics, Iowa State University of Science and Technology (1981) **CT:** Certified Quality Engineer; Certified Professional Accredited Statistician; Chartered Statistician **C:** Data Analytics Leader, Corning Incorporated, (2018-); Engineering Fellow/Chief Statistician (2011-Present); Senior Engineering Associate, Corning Incorporated (2003-2011); Engineering Associate, Corning Incorporated (1995-2003); Senior Project Engineer, Corning Incorporated (1991-1995); Project Engineer, Corning Incorporated (1989-1991); Senior Statistical Engineer II, Corning Glass Works, Corning Incorporated (1986-1989); Senior Statistical Engineer I, Corning Glass Works, Corning Incorporated (1983-1986); Statistical Engineer II, Corning Glass Works, Corning Incorporated (1981-1983); Mathematical Statistician, United States Census Bureau, Washington, D.C. (1979-1980) **CR:** Retired Adjunct Professor, Graduate Studies, Rochester Institute of Technology John R. Hromi Center for Quality & Applied Statistics **CIV:** Worship Committee, Methodist Church; Deacon Committee, Church of Christ **CW:** Co-author, "Acceptance Sampling in Quality Control, 2nd and 3rd Edition" (2017); Co-author, "Process Quality Control, 3rd and 4th Edition (2005)"; Past Editor, "Manual on Presentation of Data and Control Chart Analysis, 7th and 8th Edition (2010)"; Past

E11.90.03 Publication Chair; Past Coordinator, DataPoints Column, ASTM Standardization News (2008-2016) **AW:** Engineering Fellow, Corning Incorporated (2011-Present); Appreciation Award, E11 Committee on Quality & Statistics, ASTM (2013); Harold F. Dodge Award, ASTM (2011); Merit Award, ASTM (2010); Fellow, ASTM (2010); Appreciation Award, E11 Committee on Quality & Statistics, ASTM (2009-2013); Appreciation Award, E11 Committee on Quality & Statistics, ASTM (2007); Golden Quill Award, Quality Press, American Society for Quality (2006); Robert C. McDermond Medal for Excellence in Entrepreneurship, American Society for Quality (2005); Appreciation Award, E11 Committee on Quality & Statistics, ASTM (2005); Shewell Award, Chemical & Process Industries Division, American Society for Quality (2003); Appreciation Award, E11 Committee on Quality & Statistics, ASTM (2001); Fellow, American Society for Quality (2001); Fellow, The Royal Statistical Society (1993); Individual Outstanding Contributor Award, Corning Glass Works, Corning Incorporated (1986) **MEM:** E11 Committee Membership Secretary, ASTM (2014-Present); Vice Chairman, American Society for Quality (2010-Present); Past Member, E11 Committee on Quality & Statistics, ASTM (1993-Present); Committee on Standards, ASTM (2014-2016); Chair, E11 Committee on Quality & Statistics, ASTM (2012-2014); Vice Chair, E11 Committee on Quality & Statistics, ASTM (2009-2011); Chairman, E11.30 Statistical Quality Control, ASTM (2007-2011); Chairman, Chemical and Process Industries Division, American Society for Quality (2004-2005); Chairman-Elect, Chemical and Process Industries Division, American Society for Quality (2003-2004); Secretary, Chemical and Process Industries Division, American Society for Quality (2002-2003); Secretary, E11 Committee on Quality & Statistics, ASTM (2001-2003); Treasurer, Chemical and Process Industries Division, American Society for Quality (2001-2002); Chairman, E11 Sampling and Data Analysis, ASTM (1999-2003); Member-at-Large, ASTM (1999-2003); Examining Chairman, American Society for Quality (1994-2001); Section Chairman, American Society for Quality (1985-1986); Program Chairman, American Society for Quality (1983-1984); Chartered Statistician, The Royal Statistical Society; Certified Quality Engineer, American Society for Quality; Accredited Professional Statistician, American Statistical Association **MH:** Albert Nelson Marquis Lifetime Achievement Award (2017) **H:** Golfing; 3-D printing **PA:** Conservative **RE:** Methodist **BA:** HP-ME-02-53, Corning, NY, 14831 **ADD:** 15 Stoneybrook Rd E, Horseheads, NY, 14845 **URL:** http://www.deanvneubauer.com

NEUMAN, CLIFFORD, **T:** Computer Scientist, Educator **I:** Education/Educational Services **CN:** University of Southern California **DOB:** 09/27/1963 **PB:** New York **SC:** NY/USA **PT:** Peter H.X. Neuman; Barbara Diane (Allen) Gordon **MS:** Married **SPN:** Grace Ruth (Kwok) Neuman **ED:** PhD in Computer Science, University of Washington (1992); MS in Computer Science, University of Washington (1988); BS in Computer Science and Engineering, Massachusetts Institute of Technology (1985) **C:** Director, Center for Computer Systems Security, University of Southern California (2002-Present); Faculty, Department of Computer Science, Information Sciences Institute, University of Southern California, Los Angeles, CA (1992-Present); Chief Scientist, CyberSafe Corp., Issaquah, WA (1992-2001); Project Athena, Massachusetts Institute of Technology, Cambridge, MA (1985-1986) **CR:** Participant, Internet Research Task Force; Internet Engineering Task Force **CIV:**

President, Beth Shir Shalom (2010-2012); Board of Directors, Beth Shir Shalom (2006-2014); Ladera Heights Civic Association (2006-2014); King County Search and Rescue (1987-1991) **CW:** Co-designer, Kerberos Computer Security System; Designer, Prospero Distributed Computer System; Designer, NetCheque Electrical Payment System; Contributor, Articles, Professional Journals **AW:** Top Ten Technology Innovators, InfoWorld Magazine (2002) **MEM:** IEEE; Usenix Association; Internet Society; Association of Computer Machinery **MH:** Albert Nelson Marquis Lifetime Achievement Award (2017) **H:** Flying; Hiking; Skiing; Photography; Cooking; Amateur radio **BA:** 4676 Admiralty Way, Marina Del Rey, CA, 90292 **ADD:** PO Box 12232, Marina Del Rey, CA, 90295

NEUSTEIN, AMY PHD, I: Other

NEWLAN BOWER, JANET ESTHER, T: Freelance Writer, Educator (Retired) **I:** Education/Educational Services **DOB:** 04/14/1943 **PB:** National City **SC:** CA/USA **PT:** Murvel Newlan; Esther Eva (Clark) Newlan **MS:** Married **SPN:** Robert S. Bower Jr. (11/23/1968) **CH:** Llance Clark, Esther Elizabeth **ED:** Coursework, University of Cambridge, United Kingdom (1990); Coursework, UC San Diego (1989-1990); Coursework, UC San Diego (1980); MA in Education, United States International University (1970); MA in History, UCLA (1966); BA in History and Psychology, California Western University, San Diego, CA (1965) **CT:** Standard Junior College Credential, State of California; Elementary Credential, State of California **C:** Instructor, San Diego Community College District (1969-2012); Adjunct Faculty Member, San Diego Community College District (1969-2012); Instructor, Mira Costa College (2001-2007); Adjunct Faculty Member, Mira Costa College (2001-2007); Instructor, Palomar College District (1993, 1997-2007); Member, Adjunct Faculty, Palomar College District (1993, 1997-2007); Instructor, Grossmont/Cuyamaca College District (1973, 1997-2000); Member Adjunct Faculty, Grossmont/Cuyamaca College District (1973, 1997-2000); Instructor, Midlands Technical College, Columbia, SC (1995-1996); Adjunct Faculty Member, Midlands Technical College, Columbia, SC (1995-1996) **CR:** Historical Consultant, Horses of Tir Na Nog (2008-Present); Public Grant Writer, Horses of Tir Na Nog (2008-Present); Board of Directors, Horses of Tir Na Nog (2008-Present); Grant Writer, Lions, Tigers & Bears (2008); Adjunct Faculty Member, National University (1999-2005); Adjunct Faculty Member, Union Institute (2000-2004) **CIV:** Volunteer, Docent International Community Foundation (2008-2010); Board of Directors, Women of St. Paul's Episcopal Church, San Diego, CA (1983-1986); Oceanids, UC San Diego (1980-1985); St. Paul's Episcopal Cathedral; San Diego Historical Society **CW:** Blog Creator, Historyallaroud.com (2014); Contributing Author, "Women in the Biological Sciences" (1997); Editor, "Modernization of America, A Compilation of Selected Documents and Terms" (1993); Editor, "Formation of the Union, A Compilation of Selected Documents and Terms" (1990); Publisher, Friends of the International Center Newsletter, UC San Diego (1984-1985); Editor, Friends of the International Center Newsletter, UC San Diego (1984-1985); Contributing Author, "Chicken Soup for the Soul: Christian Living in Mature Years"; Contributor, Articles, Periodicals **AW:** Grantee, United States Department of Education (1968-1969) **MEM:** XO Chapter, PEO (2011-2014); EE Chapter, PEO (2008-2011); American Historical Association; California Historical Society; Honorary Lifetime Member, Project Wildlife; Globe Guilders of the Old Globe; San Diego History Center; Rancho Santa Fe Literary & Prologue Society **MH:** Albert

Nelson Marquis Lifetime Achievement Award (2017) **H:** Cooking; Traveling **PA:** Republican **RE:** Episcopalian **ADD:** 9046 Terrace Dr, La Mesa, CA, 91941 **URL:** newbower@gmail.com

NEWMAN, MICHAEL RODNEY, T: Lawyer **I:** Law and Legal Services **CN:** Daar & Newman a Professional Law Corporation **DOB:** 10/02/1945 **PB:** New York **SC:** NY/USA **PT:** Morris Newman; Helen Gloria (Hendler) Newman **MS:** Married **SPN:** Cheryl Jeanne Anker (6/11/1967) **CH:** Hillary Abra; Nicole Brooke **ED:** JD, John Marshall Law School/University of Chicago (1970); BA, University of Denver (1967); Student, NASA Institute for Space Physics, Columbia University (1964) **C:** Partner, Daar & Newman (1989-Present); Judge Pro Tempore, Los Angeles Municipal Court (1992-1998); Judge Pro Tempore, Los Angeles Superior Court (1988-1998); Partner, Miller, Daar & Newman (1988-1989); Partner, Miller & Daar (1978-1988); Partner, Daar & Newman (1976-1978); Associate, David Daar (1971-1976) **CR:** Chairman, Business Development Committee, Consulegis EEIG (1995-Present); Member, Business Development Committee, Consulegis EEIG (1995-Present); Co-Chair, California Lawyers Association International Law Section (2018-2019); Co-Chair, International Law Section, The State Bar of California (2017-2018); Speaker University of Southern California Law School (2018); Speaker UCLA Law School (2018); Speaker, Loyola Law School (2015, 2017); Advisory Board, Consulegis EEIG (1995-2015); Board of Directors, Consulegis EEIG (1995-2015); Speaker, Global California (2011); Speaker, California State Bar Convention (2009-2010); Guest Lecturer, UCLA Anderson School of Management (2009-2010); Guest Lecturer, International Law, California State University (2009, 2007); Guest Lecturer, California State University, Fullerton (2006); Vice Chairman, Board Directors, German American Chamber of Commerce, Inc. (2001-2002); Founder, Annual German-American Strategic Partnership Conferences (1992-2000); Facilitator, Annual German-American Strategic Partnership Conferences (1992-2000); Member, Board of Governors, Finance and Physical Development Committee University of Haifa, Israel **CIV:** Speaker, Relationship Foreign Bar Association, Marchilles Bar Association, France (2018); Speaker, Business Development of International Law Firms, Consulegis Bar Association, Dublin, Ireland (2018); Guest Lecturer, The State Bar of California (2009-2010); Guest Lecturer, UCLA Anderson School of Management (2009); Board of Directors, Center for the Study of Emerging Markets, California State University Fullerton Graduate School of Business and Economics (1997); Los Angeles Citizens Organizing Committee, Olympic Summer Games (1984); Governmental Liaison Advisory Commission (1984); Member, Southern California Committee for Olympic Summer Games (1984); Co-Chairman, Legal Committee, SPA-TAC; Certified Official, Athletics Congress of the United States; Trustee, Masada Lodge, B'nai Brith **AW:** Honoree, Super Lawyer (2015-2018); Distinguished Service Award, TAC (1988); Mathematics Award, U.S. Navy (1963); New York University Physics Medal (1962) **MEM:** Executive Committee, International Law Section (2013-Present); Chairman, External Relationship, Foreign Bar Relationship Committee (2011-Present); Consultant, Executive Committee, International Law Section, The State Bar of California (2010-2013); Executive Committee, International Law Section, Los Angeles County Bar Association (2008-2010); Chairman, Attorneys Errors and Omissions Prevention Committee, Los Angeles County Bar Association (1995-2005); International Committee, Rotary International; City Club; Breakfast Club; Porter Valley Country Club; Multi-District Litigation Subcommittee, Commit-

tee on Class Actions, ABA; Board of Directors, TAC; German American Business Association; Board Member, German American Lawyers Association of Southern California; Lawyers Professional Liability Bar Association; Conference of Insurance Counsel; Los Angeles World Affairs Council; Courts Committee, State Courts Coordinator Committee, Litigation Section, Los Angeles County Bar Association **BAR:** United States District Court Eastern District of California (1983); United States Tax Court (1979); United States District Court Southern District of California (1979); Supreme Court of the United States (1978); United States District Court Northern District of California (1975); United State Court of Appeals for the Ninth Circuit (1974); United States District Court Central District of California (1972); State of California (1971) **MH:** Albert Nelson Marquis Lifetime Achievement Award (2017) **H:** Sailing; Skiing; Tennis; Golf **BA:** 21700 Oxnard St Ste 350, Daar & Newman, Woodland Hills, CA, 91367 **ADD:** Suite 350, Daar & Newman, Woodland Hills, CA, 91367

NICHOLAS, NICKIE LEE, T: Industrial Hygienist (Retired) **I:** Other **CN:** USDOL-OSHA **DOB:** 01/19/1938 **PB:** Lake Charles **SC:** LA/USA **ED:** MS, University of Houston (1966); BS, University of Houston (1960) **C:** OSHA, Department of Labor, Austin, TX; Manager, OSHA, Department of Labor, Austin, TX (1982-1996); Area Director, OSHA, Department of Labor, Tulsa, OK (1979-1982); Industrial Hygienist, Compliance Officer, OSHA, Department of Labor, Houston, TX (1975-1979); Analytical Chemist, Tennessee Valley Authority, Muscle Shoals, AL (1973-1975); Chemist, NASA Johnson Spacecraft Center (1968-1973); Chief Biochemist, Baylor University College of Medicine (1966-1968); Chemist, VA Hospital, Houston, TX (1962-1966); Chemist, Food and Drug Administration, Dallas, TX (1961-1962); Science Teacher, Pasadena Independent School District (1960-1961) **CR:** Faculty, VA School of Medical Technology, Houston, TX (1963-1966) **AW:** Assistant Secretary Leadership Award, DOL-OSHA (1992, 1996); Certificate of Appreciation, OSHA (1991); Secretary's Exceptional Achievement Award, Department of Labor (1991); Distinguished Career Service Award (1991); Meritorious Performance Award (1990); Career Achievement Award, Federally Employed Women Inc. (1988); Personal Achievement Award, Department of Labor Federal Women's Program (1984); Group Achievement Award, Skylab Medical Team NASA (1974); Suggestion Award, VA (1968); Award For Outstanding Achievement, German Embassy (1958) **MEM:** President, Federal Executive Association (1984-1985); Chairman Elect, American Chemical Society (1973); Director of the Analytical Group, Southeastern Texas and Brazosport Sections, American Chemical Society (1971); American Harp Society; American Society of Safety Engineers; American Industrial Hygiene Association; American Conference of Governmental Industrial Hygienists; American Association of Clinical Chemists; Order of the Eastern Star; Kappa Epsilon **H:** Music; Playing the piano; Quilting; Singing in the choir **ADD:** 1603 Lcr 706, Kosse, TX, 76653

NIELSEN, GEORGE LEE, T: Senior Principal Architect **I:** Architecture & Construction **CN:** A.M. Kinney Inc. **DOB:** 12/12/1937 **PB:** Ames **SC:** IA/USA **PT:** Verner Henry Nielsen; Verba Lucile (Smith) Nielsen **MS:** Married **SPN:** Karen Wall (2/28/1959, Deceased) **CH:** David Stuart; Kristina; Melissa **ED:** MArch, Massachusetts Institute of Technology (1962); BArch, Iowa State University (1961) **CT:** Registered Architect, Commonwealths of Massachusetts and Kentucky; Registered Architect, States of Ohio, New York, Illinois; Registered Architect, National Council of Architectural Registration Boards **C:** Senior Principal, A.M. Kinney Inc. (1999-Present); Secretary, A.M. Kinney Inc., Illinois (1993-Present); Partner, A.M. Kinney Inc., Cincinnati, OH (1978-Present); Director, Project Manager, A.M. Kinney Inc., Cincinnati, OH (1970-Present); President, A.M. Kinney Inc., Cincinnati, OH (1994-1999); Director, Vice President, A.M. Kinney Inc., Cincinnati, OH (1992-1994); Project Architect, Pierce & Pierce, Boston, MA (1965-1970); Designer, F.A. Stahl & Associates, Cambridge, MA (1964-1965); Designer, Perry, Shaw, Hepburn & Dean, Boston, MA (1961-1964) **MIL:** U.S. Army (1962-1964) **CW:** Architect, Avco Research Laboratory, The American Institute of Physics; Architect, Cincinnati Children's Hospital Medical Center; Architect, Square D. Corporation; Architect, Nalco; Architect, Olin; Architect, Mead Johnson/Bristol Myers Squib; Architect, Cincinnati Gas and Electrical Holding Corporate Company (Now Duke Energy Corporation); Architect, Novartis Pharmaceutical Corporation; Architect, Celanese Corporation; Architect, Hoechst Marion Roussel; Architect, Martek Biosciences; Architect, Witco Corporation; Architect, Sotheby's; Architect, Shell Chemical Company; Architect, Bayer Corporation; Architect, Biomedical and Biological Sciences Research Laboratory, University of Kentucky; Architect, Chandler Medical Center Patient Care Facility, University of Kentucky; Architect, Wright Patterson Environmental Hazards Laboratory; Architect, Edwards Air Force Base Science Research Laboratory, U.S. Air Force; Architect, Glen Research Center, National Aeronautics and Space Administration **AW:** Design Awards, American Institute of Architects (2011, 2001-2002, 1994-1995, 1991, 1981, 1978, 1974, 1970-1971) **MEM:** American Institute of Architects **MH:** Albert Nelson Marquis Lifetime Achievement Award (2017) **RE:** Episcopalian **ADD:** 5680 Windridge View, Cincinnati, OH, 45243

NIELSEN, MICHAEL EDWARD, T: Professor, Chairman **I:** Education/Educational Services **CN:** Georgia Southern University **ED:** PhD in Social Organizational Psychology, Northern Illinois University, DeKalb, IL (1992); MA in Social Psychology, Northern Illinois University, DeKalb, IL (1990); BA in Psychology and Music, Southern Utah State University, Cedar City, UT (1986) **C:** Chair, Department of Psychology, Georgia Southern University, Statesboro, GA (2010-Present); Professor, Georgia Southern University (2007-Present); Interim Chair, Department of Psychology, Georgia Southern University, Statesboro, GA (2009-2010); Associate Professor, Georgia Southern University (2000-2007); Assistant Professor, Georgia Southern University (1993-2000); Adjunct Faculty, Columbia College at McHenry Community College, Crystal Lake, IL (1993); Visiting Lecturer, Department of Psychology, Lake Forest College, Lake Forest, IL (1993) **CR:** Lecturer in Field **CW:** Advisory Board, Journal of Pakistan Psychological Association (2011-Present); Co-Editor, Archive for the Psychology of Religion (2010-Present); Editorial Board, Journal for the Scientific Study of Religion (2010-Present); Advisory Board, Pakistan Journal of Psychology (2010-Present); Academic Review Board, Intermountain West Journal of Religious Studies (2009-Present); Editorial Board, Dialogue: A Journal of Mormon Thought (2004-Present); Advisory Board, Artha: Journal of Social Sciences, Christ College, Bangalore, India (2000-2004); Advisory Board, Wounded Healer e-Journal (1997-1998); Contributor, Articles, Professional Journals; Contributor, Book Chapters **AW:** SEPA Distinguished Lecture, Psi Chi, The International Honor Society in Psychology (2017); Ruffin Cup for Excellence in Scholarship and Teaching, College of Liberal Arts and Social Sciences, Georgia Southern University (2017); Nominee, Outstanding Adviser, Georgia Southern University (2016); Nominee, President-Elect, Division for the Psychology of Religion and Spirituality, American Psychological Association (2012-2014); Golden Anniversary Alumni Award, College of Liberal Arts & Sciences, Northern Illinois University (2009); Award for Excellence in Service, Georgia Southern University (2007); Success in University Faculty Appreciation Award, Georgia Southern University (1995); Golden Anniversary Alumni Award, College of Arts and Sciences, Northern Illinois University; Division 36 Award, American Psychological Association; Grantee in Field **MEM:** Faculty Mentor, Omicron Delta Kappa National Honor Society (2010); American Psychological Association; Society for the Scientific Study of Religion; International Association for the Psychology of Religion; Association for Psychological Science; President, Society for the Psychology of Religion and Spirituality; Georgia Psychological Society; Mormon Social Science Association **MH:** Albert Nelson Marquis Lifetime Achievement Award (2017) **H:** Volleyball; Reading; Movies; Kite flying **BA:** PO Box 8041, Georgia Southern University, Dept of Psychology, Statesboro, GA, 30460

NIEMONEN, JACK EDWIN, T: Sociologist **I:** Education/Educational Services **CN:** University of South Dakota **DOB:** 01/08/1952 **PB:** Duluth **SC:** MN/USA **PT:** Thury Niemonen; Lois Rhea; Lee Rhea (Stepfather) **MS:** Married **SPN:** Karen Engberg Brokenleg **CH:** Nicholas Brokenleg (Stepchild); Sarah Brokenleg (Stepchild); Anna Brokenleg (Stepchild) **ED:** PhD, Michigan State University (1982); MA, Michigan State University (1977); BA, Concordia College (1974) **C:** Sociology Program Director, University of South Dakota, Vermillion, SD (2006-2018); Sociology Professor, University of South Dakota (2002-2018); Associate Sociology Professor, University of South Dakota (1993-2002); Assistant Sociology Professor, University of South Dakota (1989-1993); Assistant Sociology Professor, Augustana College, Sioux Falls, SD (1986-1989); Visiting Assistant Sociology Professor, Cornell College, Mount Vernon, IA (1985-986); Assistant Sociology Professor, Augustana College (1983-1985) **CR:** Area Editor, Teaching Resources and Innovations Library for Sociology, American Sociological Association (2010-Present); Session Organizer, American Sociological Association (2000); Session Organizer, Midwest Sociological Society (1996-2014); State Director, Midwest Sociological Society (1997-1999) **CIV:** Member, Association for Humanist Sociology (1989-2010) **CW:** Reviewer, Referee, Sociology Journals (1989-Present); Editorial Consultant, Sociology Journals (1989-Present); Author, "Race, Class, and the State in Contemporary Sociology: The William Julius Wilson Debates," L. Rienner (2002); Associate Editor, Teaching Sociology (1996-1998); Editorial Advisory Board Member, Roxbury Publishing Company (1989-1996); Editorial Advisory Board Member, Collegiate Press (1989-1996); Contributor, The Sociological Quarterly, Taylor & Francis; Contributor, The American Sociologist, Springer; Contributor, Teaching Sociology, SAGE Publications; Contributor, Contemporary Sociology, SAGE Publications; Contributor, Sociological Spectrum, Taylor & Francis; Contributor, Humanity & Society, SAGE Publications; Contributor, Free Inquiry in Creative Sociology, Sociology Consortium of Oklahoma; Contributor, International Review of Modern Sociology, International Journals; Contributor, The Great Plains Sociologist, South Dakota State University; Contributor, Summation, Michigan State University; Contributor, The Encyclopedia of Race, Ethnicity, and Society, SAGE Publications; Contributor, 28 Professional Conference Presentations; Contributor, 17 Published Book Reviews; Contributor, 25 Sets of Teaching Materials Published by the American Sociological Association **AW:** 65th Annual Harrington Lecture, University of South Dakota (2017); Award, Gale Group (2004); Award, Gale Group (2002); Teaching Award, Great Plains Sociological Association (1999); Research Council Grantee, University of South Dakota (1999); Five Time Nominee, The Belbas Larson Award for Excellence in Teaching, University of South Dakota (1989-2017) **MEM:** American Sociological Association (1989-2017); Midwest Sociological Society (1989-2017); American Academy of Political & Social Science (1989-2017); Society for the Study of Social Problems (1989-2016); Mid-South Sociological Association (1989-2016); Great Plains Sociological Association (1989-2016); Alpha Kappa Delta, the International Sociology Honor Society; Pi Gamma Mu, the International Honor Society in Social Sciences; Psi Chi, the International Honor Society In Psychology **MH:** Albert Nelson Marquis Lifetime Achievement Award (2017) **H:** Cooking **PA:** Independent **ADD:** 4304 S Glenview Rd., Sioux Falls, SD, 57103

NIMETZ, MATTHEW, T: Lawyer & Investment Company Executive, Diplomat **I:** Law and Legal Services **CN:** General Atlantic LLC **DOB:** 06/17/1939 **PB:** Brooklyn **SC:** NY/USA **PT:** Joseph L. Nimetz; Elsie (Botwinik) Nimetz **MS:** Married **SPN:** Ann Nimetz **CH:** Alexandra Elise; Lloyd **ED:** Honorary LLD, Williams College (1979); MA, Oxford University, England (1966); LLB, Harvard University (1965); BA, Oxford University, England, Rhodes Scholar (1962); BA, Williams College (1960); Student, Balliol College **C:** Advisory Director, General Atlantic LLC, Greenwich, CT (2012-Present); Managing Director, COO, General Atlantic LLC, New York, NY (2000-2011); Partner, Paul, Weiss, Rifkind, Wharton & Garrison, New York, NY (1981-2000); Under Secretary of State for Security Assistance, Science and Technology, U.S. Department of State (1980); Acting Coordinator, Refugee Affairs, U.S. Department of State (1979-1980); Counselor, U.S. Department of State, Washington, DC (1977-1980); Partner, Simpson Thacher & Bartlett, LLP, New York, NY (1974-1977); Associate, Simpson Thacher & Bartlett, LLP, New York, NY (1969-1974); Staff Assistant to President Johnson (1967-1969); Law Clerk to Justice John M. Harlan, U.S. Supreme Court (1965-1967) **CR:** Personal Envoy of Secretary General for Greece-FYROM Talks, United Nations (1999-Present); Presidential Envoy, Greece-Macedonian Negotiations (1994-1995); New York State Advisory Council on State Productivity (1990-1992); Commissioner, Port Authority of New York and New Jersey (1975-1977); Director, Several Companies **CIV:** Director, Landesa (2017-Present); Trustee, American University of Central Asia (2010-Present); Chairman, Levin Institute, State University of New York (2010-Present); Co-Chair, Green City Force (2009-Present); Trustee, Central European University, Budapest, Hungary (2005-Present); Chairman, Founder, Center for Democracy and Reconciliation in Southeast Europe (1998-Present); Trustee, Levin Institute, State University of New York (2005-2012); New York State Nature Conservancy (1997-2005); Chairman, Carnegie Forum in the U.S., Greece and Turkey (1996-1998); Board Director, Charles H. Revson Foundation (1990-1998); Chairman, U.N. Development Corporation (1986-1994); Trustee, William College (1981-1996) **MEM:** New York City Bar Association; Council on Foreign Relations Clubs, Harvard, New York, NY **BAR:** District of

Columbia (1968); State of New York (1966) **MH:** Albert Nelson Marquis Lifetime Achievement Award (2017) **BA:** 55 E 52nd St., Floor 32, New York, NY, 10055 **ADD:** 1185 Park Ave., Apt. 7F, New York, NY, 10128

NORBECK, JACK CARL, T: President **I:** Research **CN:** Norbeck Research **DOB:** 12/08/1940 **PB:** Greensburg **SC:** PA/USA **PT:** Oscar E. Norbeck; Ann T. Norbeck **MS:** Single **CT:** Certificate, Opticians Institute (1971); Certified, Dale Carnegie (1967); Certificate in Dairy Manufacturing, Ratcliffe Hicks School of Agriculture, University of Connecticut (1964) **C:** Founder, Norbeck Research (1978-Present); President, Norbeck Research (1978-Present) **CIV:** Ambassador, International Order of Merit, International Biographical Centre (2015); Vice-Chancellor, World Academy of Letters, American Biographical Institute (2010) **MIL:** U.S. Army Corps. of Engineers **CW:** Author, "The Encyclopedia of American Steam Traction Engines"; Author, Article, "Clapp & Jones Steam Fire Engines"; Contributor, 114 Articles, Professional Journals; Exhibitor, 389 Photography Exhibits, 42 Countries, Seven Continents; Contributor, Photos, 118 Magazine Covers; Speaker, Steams Shows, United States and Canada; Contributor, Engineers and Engines; Contributor, Vintage Tractor Digest; Contributor, Draft Horse Journal; Contributor, Rural Heritage; Contributor, Contractors Market Center; Contributor, Ironman Album **AW:** Marquis Who's Who Lifetime Plaque for Achievement Career Longevity (2017); International Order of Merit Award, International Biographical Centre (2015); Honoree, Distinguished Accomplishment Hall of Fame, American Biographical Institute (2009); International Ambassadors Medal and Gold Record of Achievement (2001); Noble Prize (2001); American Medal of Honor (2001); Honoree, International Man of The Year (2000-2001); International Order of Merit Award, International Biographical Centre (1999); First Place Medal, U.S.A. and Canada Senior Men's AAU, Wisconsin Open Gymnastics Championships (1965); Third Place Medal, National Gymnastics Championships, Flint, MI (1964); Third Place, Merchant Marine Academy (1963); Medals, Intramural Sports Program, University of Connecticut (1963); Second Place Olympic Development Medal, University of Connecticut, University of Bridgeport (1962); Varsity Letters in Gymnastics (1958-960); 20th Century Award; Recipient, 78 Short Wave Radio Trophies, England, South Africa, France, Austria; Delhaas High School Varsity Letters in Gymnastics **MEM:** Former Member, Lower Bucks YMCA (1955-1961); Lower Bucks County Exhibition Gym Team (1955-1961); International Biographical Centre; Registered Athlete, YMCA of the USA; Registered Athlete, AAU; Registered Athlete, Allentown YMCA; American Legion; Union Historical Fire Society; Authors Guild; American Society of Agricultural and Biological Engineers; Historical Steam Associations; Faith Lutheran Church; International Biographical Centre; United States Gymnastics Federation **H:** Pictures; History **RE:** Lutheran **ADD:** 117 N Ruch St., Apt. 3, Coplay, PA, 18037

NORDSTRAND, NATHALIE, I: Fine Art **DOB:** 11/06/1932 **PB:** Woburn **SC:** MA/USA **PT:** Edward N. Johnson; Ruth (Peterson) Johnson **MS:** Married **SPN:** Robert I. Nordstrand (1/12/1962) **ED:** BA, Barnard College (1954); BA, Columbia University (1954); AA, Bradford College (1952); Coursework with Jay Connaway; Coursework with Don Stone; Coursework with Roger Curtis; Coursework with Paul Strisik; Coursework with Emile Gruppe **C:** Owner, Nordstrand Gallery (1970-1999); Clerk, Corporate Director, Johnson Brothers Greenhous-

es, Inc. (1958-1984); Research Associate, Gerontology Age Center of New England (1955-1964) **CIV:** Chair of Planned Giving, Athena Society, Barnard College (2003-2004); Planning Board, North Suburban Art Festival (1963-1968) **CW:** Featured Artist, Banks Gallery, St. Botolph Club (2008); Featured Artist, "Gallery of Marine Art" (1998); Featured Artist, "Landscape Inspirations" (1997); Solo Exhibitor, Reading Public Library Foundation (1997); Featured Artist, "Best of Oil Painting" (1996); Featured Artist, "Best of Watercolors" (1995); Featured Artist, Smithsonian American Art Museum (1994); Solo Exhibitor, Laura Knott Art Gallery, Bradford College (1982); Exhibitor, Silvermine Arts Center (1976); Exhibitor, American Chamber of Commerce, Hong Kong (1975-1976); Solo Exhibitor, Rockport Art Association (1969); Exhibitor, National Academy Museum; Exhibitor, Springfield Museums; Exhibitor, Hammond Museum & Japanese Stroll Garden, Inc.; Exhibitor, Bhulabhai Memorial Institute; Exhibitor, Copley Society; Exhibitor, Annual Copley Masters Exhibition, Copley Society; Exhibitor, Hermann Fine Arts Center, Marietta College; Featured Artist, "Best of Art Books" **AW:** Recipient, Regional Competition Awards (1960-Present); Recipient, National Competition Awards (1960-Present); Honorary Lifetime Member Grant, Concord Center for the Visual Arts (2012); Recipient, Women's Exhibition Award, Salmagundi Club (2012); Recipient, Honorary Award, The Reading Public Library Foundation (2009); Recipient, Citation Award, Massachusetts House Of Representatives, The General Court of the Commonwealth of Massachusetts (2009); Recipient, Award, Massachusetts Senate, The General Court of the Commonwealth of Massachusetts (2009); Recipient, Joseph C. Santoro Memorial Award, Rockport Art Association (2008); Recipient, Richard Ochs Memorial Award, Salmagundi Club (2008); Recipient, Robert Dunnelly Memorial Award, Rockport Art Association (2007); Recipient, Ogden Pleissner Memorial Award, Salmagundi Club (2006); Recipient, Joseph Santoro Memorial Award, Rockport Art Association (2005); Recipient, Thomas Moran Award, Salmagundi Club (2004); Recipient, Margery Saroka Memorial Award, Salmagundi Club (2003); Recipient, Joseph Hartley Award, Salmagundi Club (1989, 2001, 2002); Recipient, Rita Duis Memorial Award, Salmagundi Club (2001); Recipient, Lifetime Dedication to the Promotion of Art Award, Rockport Art Association (1999); Recipient, Excellence in Watercolor Award, Rockport Art Association (1997); Honoree, Wall of Fame, Baltimore Watercolor Society (1976); Recipient, Philip Isenberg Memorial Award (1997); Recipient, Bruce Crane Award, Salmagundi Club (1994); Recipient, New England Heritage Award, Academic Artists Association (1993); Recipient, A. Lassall Ripley Award, The Guild of Boston Artists (1993); Recipient, Mortimer Freehof Memorial Award, Salmagundi Club (1991); Recipient, Steven Blackman Award, Salmagundi Club (1988); Recipient, Elliot Liskin Memorial Award, Salmagundi Club (1988); Honoree, Citizen of the Year, Reading Chapter, American Cancer Society, Inc. (1983); Recipient, President's Awards, Reading Art Association Inc. (1973-1980); Recipient, Award, The American Artists Professional League (1978-1979); Recipient, MacGowin Tuttle Memorial Award, Salmagundi Club (1976, 1978-1979); Recipient, Watercolor Awards, Academic Artists Association (1973-1974, 1976-1977); Recipient, Award, New England Watercolor Society (1975); Recipient, Gold Medal, The American Artists Professional League (1971, 1975); Louis E. Seley Award (1974); Recipient, Gold Medal, Allied Artists of America (1973-1974) **MEM:** Member Emeritus, The Guild of Boston Artists (2012); Member Emeritus, Salmagundi Club (2010); Board of Directors, The Guild of Boston Artists (1986-

1999); Board of Directors, Hudson Valley North Shore (1964-1967, 1986-1995); Board of Directors, Reading Association of Fine New York City Arts (1993); Juror, International Exhibition, American Watercolor Society (1992); Vice President, New England Watercolor Society (1984-1990); Program Chairman, Reading Art Association Inc. (1960-1986); Vice President, Affiliated Art Association of Massachusetts (1980); Fellow, The American Artists Professional League; Academic Artists Association; Master Artist, Copley Society; Rockport Art Association; Concord Center for the Visual Arts; Allied Artists of America; National Museum of Women in the Arts **MH:** Albert Nelson Marquis Lifetime Achievement Award (2017) **RE:** Methodist **ADD:** 384 Franklin Street, Reading, MA, 01867

NORRIS, CHARLES RICHARD JR., T: Physician, Psychiatrist **I:** Medicine & Health Care **DOB:** 01/06/1949 **PB:** Danville **SC:** IL/USA **PT:** Charles Richard Norris; Elenor Joy (Bailey) Norris **MS:** Married **SPN:** Francesca Emanuele Norris (5/18/1979) **CH:** Charles III; Jacqueline L. **ED:** Resident, Institute of Living, Hartford HealthCare, Hartford, CT (1976-1979); Intern, Albany Medical Center, New York (1975-1976); MD, The University of Vermont, Burlington, VT; BS in Chemistry, Bates College, Lewiston, ME **CT:** Diplomate, American Board Psychiatry and Neurology, Inc. (1980); Certificate, National Board of Medical Examiners (1976) **C:** Physician, Private Practice, Boca Raton, FL (1996-Present); Director, MetLife Health Care, Miami, FL (1991-1995); Director of Addiction Treatment, Fair Oaks Hospital, Delray Beach, FL (1986-1991); Director of Ambulatory Services, Institute of Living, Hartford HealthCare, Hartford, CT (1985-1986); Director of Outpatient Services, Institute of Living, Hartford HealthCare, Hartford, CT (1983-1985); Director of Alcohol & Substance Abuse Service, Horizon Hospital, Clearwater, FL (1981-1982); Affiliate Clinical Assistant, Professor of Clinical Biomedical Sciences, Charles E. Schmidt College of Medicine, Florida Atlantic University **CR:** Consultant in Field **CW:** Author, "Family Addictions" (1990); Contributor, Articles to Professional Journals; Contributor, Chapters to Books **MEM:** Distinguished Lifetime Fellow, American Psychological Association; Florida Psychiatric Society; American Medical Association **MH:** Albert Nelson Marquis Lifetime Achievement Award (2017) **BA:** 1499 W palmetto Park Rd, Suite 216, Boca Raton, FL, 33486 **ADD:** 600 S Ocean Blvd Apt 404, Boca Raton, FL, 33432

NORTON, JENNY, T: Director **I:** Nonprofit & Philanthropy **CN:** Ramsey Social Justice Foundation **DOB:** 04/07/1945 **PB:** Waverly **SC:** NY/USA **PT:** Ralph Norton **MS:** Married **SPN:** Bob Ramsey (1971) **ED:** ThM, Fuller Theological Seminary (1997); BS in Justice Studies, Arizona State University (1993) **C:** Clinton Global Initiative (2012-Present); Director, Ramsey Social Justice Foundation (2006-Present); Senior Pastor, Tempe St. Luke's Hospital (2006-2016); Assistant Pastor, Desert Springs Foursquare Church (1990-2015); **CR:** Tempe Industrial Development Authority Board (1984-2015) **AW:** Alumnus Lifetime Achievement Award, Arizona State University (2014); Dr. Martin Luther King Service Award (2012); Lifetime Achievement Award, Tempe Chamber of Commerce (2010); Friend of Phoenix Union Award, Hall of Fame Award, College of Liberal Arts and Sciences, Arizona State University (2007); Service in Action Award, Tempe Community Action Agency (2006); Woman of the Year Award, National Criminal Justice Women's Association (2000); Woman of Distinction Award, Tempe St. Luke's Hospital (1987); All American Woman Award, City of Tempe (1984); Founders

Award **MH:** Albert Nelson Marquis Lifetime Achievement Award (2017); Distinguished Humanitarian (2017) **PA:** Republican **RE:** Christian **ADD:** 1318 E Commodore Place, Tempe, AZ, 85283

NOTTER, ROBERT H., I: Education/Educational Services **PT:** Dr. Harley A. Notter; Margaret T. Notter **ED:** MD, University Rochester (1980); PhD, University Washington (1969); MS, Stanford University (1965); BS, Stanford University (1964) **C:** Professor Emeritus of Pediatrics and Environmental Medicine, University of Rochester (2012-Present); Emeritus Professor, University of Rochester (2012); Professor of Pediatrics and Environmental Medicine, University of Rochester (2001-2011); Professor of Pediatrics, Environmental Medicine, and Chemical Engineering, University of Rochester (1989-2001); Associate Professor, Pediatrics, Chemical Engineering and Biophysics, University of Rochester (1983-1989); Assistant Professor of Pediatrics and Associate Professor of Chemical Engineering, University of Rochester (1980-1983) **CR:** Director of Neonatology Research, University of Rochester (1989-2000); Director, National Institutes of Health Special Center for Research in Lung Biology and Disease in Infants and Children, University of Rochester (1989-1997); Director, Biomedical Engineering Program, University of Rochester (1984-1995) **CW:** Editor, "Lung Injury: Mechanisms, Pathophysiology and Therapy" (2005); Author, "Lung Surfactants: Basic Science and Clinical Applications" (2000); Editor, "Lung Surfactant Replacement Therapy" (1989); Contributor, More Than 250 Articles and Abstracts, Professional Journals **AW:** Grantee, National Institutes of Health (1975-2015); Recipient Health Leadership Award, March of Dime (2005); Research Career Development Award, National Institutes of Health (1981); MD Research Award, University Rochester School Medicine (1980); Outstanding Teacher in College Engineering Award, Pennsylvania State University, (1976); Young Investigator Award, NHLBI, National Institutes of Health (1975); American Society of Testing Materials Award, Stanford University (1964); National Science Foundation Undergraduate Research Award (1962) **MEM:** American Institute of Chemists; American Institute of Chemical Engineers; Perinatal Research Society; Society Pediatric Research; Sigma Xi; Tau Beta Pi **ACH:** Achievements include research and development of surfactant-based therapies for lung disease and injury

NOVALES, RONALD RICHARDS, T: Zoologist, Educator **I:** Education/Educational Services **CN:** Northwestern University **DOB:** 04/24/1928 **PB:** San Francisco **SC:** CA/USA **PT:** William Henry Novales; Dorothy (Richards) Novales **MS:** Married **SPN:** Barbara Jean Martin (12/19/1953) **CH:** Nancy Ann; Mary Elizabeth **ED:** PhD, University of California, Berkeley, CA (1958); MA, University of California, Berkeley, CA (1953); Postgraduate Coursework, University of California, Los Angeles, CA (1951-1952); BA, University of California, Berkeley, CA (1950) **C:** Emeritus Professor, Neurobiology and Physiology, Northwestern University (1993-Present); Professor, Neurobiology and Physiology, Northwestern University (1981-1993); Professor, Northwestern University (1970-1980); Associate Professor, Northwestern University (1964-1970); Assistant Professor, Biological Sciences, Northwestern University, Evanston, IL (1958-1964); Professor, Biology, Six Year Medical Program, Northwestern University **CR:** Consultant, A.J. Nystrom Co. (1969) **MIL:** U.S. Army (1953-1955) **CW:** Member, Editorial Board, The American Zoologist (1969-1973); Contributor, Articles, Professional Journals; Contributor,

"Encyclopedia Britannica Book of the Year" **AW:** Research Grantee, National Science Foundation (1975-1978); Research Grantee, National Science Foundation (1959-1973) **MEM:** Fellow, American Association for the Advancement of Science **MH:** Albert Nelson Marquis Lifetime Achievement Award (2017) **RE:** Unitarian Universalist **ADD:** 2008 McDaniel Ave, Evanston, IL, 60201

NUWER, HENRY, T: Journalist **I:** Education/ Educational Services **CN:** Franklin College **DOB:** 08/19/1946 **PB:** Buffalo **SC:** NY/USA **MS:** Married **SPN:** Malgorzata Wroblewska (5/12/2017); Jenine (Howard) (4/9/1982, Divorced 2004) **CH:** Adam; Henry **ED:** Coursework, Hamline University (2014-Present); Postgraduate Coursework, University of Nevada (1975); Coursework, University of Bridgeport (1969) **C:** Professor of Journalism, Franklin College, Indiana (2002-Present); Freelance Author and Journalist (1969-Present); Adjunct Professor of Journalism, Anderson University (1998-2002); Adjunct Professor of Journalism, Indiana University School of Journalism, Indianapolis (1995-2008); Visiting Associate Professor of Journalism, University of Richmond (1995-1997); Editor in Chief, Arts Indiana Magazine, Indianapolis (1993-1995); Senior Editor, Rodale Press, Emmaus, PA (1990-1991); Associate Professor, Ball State University, Muncie, IN (1985-1989); Assistant Professor, Clemson University, SC (1982-1983); High School Teacher, New Mexico (1971-1972); Member, Editorial Staff, Reporter Dispatch (1969-1970); High School Teacher, New York (1968-1969) **CR:** Advisory Board, Security on Campus (2006-2017) **CIV:** Advisor, Alpha Lambda Delta Honorary Society **CW:** "Hazing: Destroying Young Lives" (2018); "Sons of Dawn: A Basque Odyssey" (2014); AARP Magazines (1976-1987); Contributor, Articles to Professional Journals **AW:** Hank Nuwer Hazing Education College State University of New York (2016); Anne Frank Fellow (2014); Third Place, Best Business Article, Indiana Competition (2002) **MEM:** Board Member, A-ha Foundation (2014-Present); Sons of the American Legion; Western Writers of America; Investigative Reporters and Editors, Society of Professional Journalists; Alpha Lambda Delta; Phi Kappa Phi **ADD:** PO Box 21, Waldron, IN, 46182

O'BRIEN, JAMES J., T: Construction Executive **I:** Architecture & Construction **CN:** James J. O'Brien, P.E. **DOB:** 10/20/1929 **PB:** Philadelphia **SC:** PA/USA **PT:** Sylvester Jerome O'Brien; Emma Belle Filer (Fulforth) O'Brien **MS:** Married **SPN:** Rita F. Gibson (11/1/1984); Carmen Hiester (6/10/1952, Divorced 8/1/1984) **CH:** Jessica; Michael; David **ED:** Postgraduate Coursework, University of Houston (1957-1958); BCE, Cornell University (1952) **CT:** Registered Professional Engineer, States of New York, New Jersey, Pennsylvania and Georgia; Certified Value Specialist **C:** Principal, James J. O'Brien P.E. (2003-Present); Consultant in Field (2002); Vice Chairman, O'Brien-Kreitzberg & Associates, New York City, NY, Pennsauken, NJ, San Francisco, CA (1993-2002); Chairman, Board of Directors, O'Brien-Kreitzberg & Associates, New York City, NY, Pennsauken, NJ, San Francisco, CA (1989-1993); Chief Executive Officer, O'Brien-Kreitzberg & Associates, New York City, NY, Pennsauken, NJ, San Francisco, CA (1980-1989); President, O'Brien-Kreitzberg & Associates, New York City, NY, Pennsauken, NJ, San Francisco, CA (1977-1980); Partner, James J. O'Brien P.E., Cherry Hill, NJ (1972-1977); President, MDC Systems, Cherry Hill, NJ (1968-1972); Founding Partner, Executive Vice President, Meridian Engineering Company, Philadelphia, PA (1965-1968); Consultant, Mauchly Associates, Fort Washington, PA (1962-1965); Project Engineer,

RCA Corp., Moorestown, NJ (1959-1962); Project Engineer, Rohm & Haas, Philadelphia, Texas (1955-1959) **MIL:** Lieutenant, United States Navy (1952-1955) **CW:** Co-Author, "CPM in Construction Management-Project Management with CPM, Seventh Edition" (2009); Author, "Construction Change Orders" (1998); Co-Author, "Construction Inspection Handbook, Fourth Edition" (1997); Author, "Standard Handbook of Heavy Construction, Third Edition" (1996); Co-Author, "Construction Documentation, Third Edition" (1995); Co-Author, "Preconstruction Estimating: Budget to Bid" (1994); Author, "Contractor's Management Handbook, Second Edition" (1990); Editor, "Recollections," L.D. Miles (1987); Co-Author, "Value Analysis in Design and Construction" (1976); Co-Author, "Construction Delay-Risks, Responsibilities and Litigation" (1976); Co-Author, "Construction Management: A Professional Approach" (1974); Co-Author, "Construction Inspection Handbook" (1974); Co-Author, "Management with Computers (1972); Author, "Contractor's Management Handbook" (1971); Co-Author, "Management Information Systems-Concepts, Techniques and Applications" (1970); Author, Editor, "Scheduling Handbook" (1969); Author, "CPM in Construction Management-Scheduling By the Critical Path Method" (1965); Author, "Critical Path Methods in Construction Management, Eighth Edition," McGraw Hill; Contributor, Articles to Professional Journals **AW:** First Jim O'Brien Achievement in Life Award (2005); Construction Manager of the Year Award, New York-New Jersey Chapter (1994); Fellow Award, Construction Management Association of America (1993); Board of Directors, Construction Management Association of America (1990-1992); Fellow Award, College Scheduling (1989); Award for Contribution to Project Management (1983); Construction Management Award, Committee on Quality in Civil Engineering Profession (1976); Recipient, Professional Manager Award, New York Chapter Society for Advancement Management (1969) **MEM:** National Academy of Engineering (2014); Vice President of Education, Project Management Institute (2004-2008); Editor, Time Management Chapter, PMBOK Third Edition (2004); Board of Directors, Miles Value Foundation (1999); Trustee, Miles Value Foundation (1990-1999); Committee on Quality in Civil Engineering Profession (1990-1997); Board of Directors, Construction Management Association of America (1990-1992); Board of Directors, Regional Alliance Small Contractors (1989-1995); Port Authority, Miles Value Foundation, New York and New Jersey (1987-1990); President, New Jersey Section, American Society of Civil Engineers (1987-1989); Dean's Advisory Committee, School Civil and Environmental Engineering, Cornell Society of Engineers (1986-1987); Vice President, New England Region, Society of American Value Engineers (1986-1987); Distinguished Engineer, South Jersey Branch, Committee on Quality in Civil Engineering Profession (1986); Vice President, Fellow, American Society of Civil Engineers (1985); President, South Jersey Branch, American Society of Civil Engineers (1985); Project Management Professional, Project Management Institute (1984); Board Chairman, Project Management Institute (1974-1975); President, Project Management Institute (1973); Vice President, Project Management Institute (1972); Secretary, Project Management Institute (1971); Chi Epsilon; Tau Beta Pi **MH:** Albert Nelson Marquis Lifetime Achievement Award (2017) **ADD:** 2 Linden Ave, Riverton, NJ, 08077

OCKUNZZI, KELLY, **T:** Principal Member of Technical Staff **I:** Manufacturing **CN:** GlobalFoundries **ED:** PhD in Computer Engineering, Case Western Reserve University (2001); MS in Computer Engineering, Case Western Reserve University (1996); BS in Computer Engineering, Case Western Reserve University (1994) **C:** Principal Member of Technical Staff, GlobalFoundries (2015-Present); Senior Member of Technical Staff, GlobalFoundries (2015); Advisory Engineer, IBM (2000-2015) **CR:** Graduate Research Fellowship, National Science Foundation (1996) **CW:** Author, "Optimizing Delay Tests at the Memory Boundary" **MEM:** IEEE; ACM; Society of Women Engineers **BA:** 1000 River Street, MS 863B, GlobalFoundries, Essex Junction, VT, 05452 **ADD:** 164 Chamberlin Lane, Williston, VT, 05495

O'CONNOR, KAREN, **T:** Political Science Professor **I:** Education/Educational Services **CN:** American University **DOB:** 02/15/1952 **PB:** Buffalo **SC:** NY/USA **PT:** Robert J. O'Connor; Norma (Wilton) O'Connor **MS:** Single **SPN:** Richard Cupitt (7/31/1992, Divorced 2011); Allen McDonough (6/7/1974, Divorced 1986) **CH:** Meghan **ED:** Degree in Political Science, Outstanding Graduate School (2010); PhD, University at Buffalo (1979); JD, University at Buffalo (1977); BA, University at Buffalo (1973) **C:** Jonathan N. Helfat Distinguished Professor, American University (2006-Present); Professor, American University (1995-2006); Professor, Emory University (1988-1995); Associate Professor, Emory University (1983-1988); Assistant Professor, Emory University (1978-1983); Instructor, Political Science, Emory University (1977-1978) **CR:** Director, Women & Politics Institute, American University (2009-Present); Director Emerita, Women & Politics Institute, American University (2009) **CW:** Editorial Board Member, Women & Politics Institute, American University (1980-Present); Co-Author, "American Government: Roots and Reform, 11th Edition" (2011); Co-Editor, "The Irish Legal 100" (2010-2012); Co-Author, "Women, Politics, and American Society (Longman Classics in Political Science), Fifth Edition" (2010); Co-Author, "Gender and Women's Leadership: A Reference Handbook, Volume II" (2010); Co-Author, "Gender and Women's Leadership: A Reference Handbook, Volume I" (2010); Co-Editor, "Gendering American Politics: Perspectives from the Literature" (2005); Editor, "Women and Congress: Running, Winning, and Ruling" (2002); Editor, Women & Politics Institute, American University (1999-2004); Editorial Board Member, "American Politics Quarterly" (1987-1990); Editorial Board Member, "The Journal of Politics" (1984-1987); Co-Author, "Women's Rights: The Struggle for Equality in the Nineteenth and Twentieth Centuries" (1983); Editorial Board Member, "Editorial Board Member, "Law & Policy" (1982-2005); Author, "Women's Organization's Use of the Courts" (1980); Editorial Board Member, "Journal of Women, Politics & Public Policy"; Contributor, Articles, Professional Journals **AW:** Diane Blair Award (2018); Times Top 100 Lawyers Award **MEM:** President, Organized Section, Women and Politics (2006-2007); President, The National Capitol Area Political Science Association (NCAPSA) (2001-2002); Southern Political Science Association (2000-2001); President, Organized Section, Law & Courts (1998); President, Organized Law & Courts Research Section, American Political Science Association (1987); Executive Council, American Political Science Association (1985-1987); Cosmos Club; The Garrett Club **BAR:** State of Georgia (1978) **MH:** Albert Nelson Marquis Lifetime Achievement Award (2017) **H:** Reading; Snorkeling; Yoga **BA:** 4400 Massachusetts Avenue NW, Kerwin Hall, American University, Washington, DC, 20016 **URL:** https://en.wikipedia.org/wiki/Karen_O%27Connor_(professor)

O'CONNOR, MARTIN PAUL, **T:** Economics Professor, Director **I:** Education/Educational Services **CN:** University of Versailles Saint-Quentin-en-Yvelines **DOB:** 01/25/1958 **PB:** Christchurch **SC:** New Zealand **PT:** Kevin Francis O'Connor; Margaret Mary Schmieg **SPN:** Sylvie Faucheux **CH:** Morgane Gwendoline Calypso **ED:** PhD in Economics, University of Auckland, New Zealand (1990); Diplôme d'Etudes Approfondies, Institute d'Etude Développement Economique Social, Paris, France (1988); MPhil in Economics, University of Auckland, New Zealand (1984); MA in Sociology, University of Canterbury, Christchurch, New Zealand (1981); BS in Physics, University of Canterbury, Christchurch, New Zealand, with Honors (1977) **C:** Professor of Economics, University of Versailles St-Quentin-en-Yvelines, Versailles, France (1995-Present); Team Leader, C3ED, Center d'Economie d'Ethique Pour l'Environnement Développement, Guyancourt, France (1995-2009); Lecturer of Economics, University of Auckland, New Zealand (1989-1995); Founder, Association ePLANETe Blue; President, Association ePLANETe Blue **CIV:** Science Director, Greater Western Paris RCE; Program Manager, REEDS International **AW:** Hayward Fellowship, New Zealand Foundation of Research Science and Technology (2005-2006) **ADD:** 10 Hameau du Mousseau, Dampierre-en-Yvelines, France, 78720

OELBERG, DAVID MD, **T:** Science Educator **I:** Education/Educational Services **PB:** Waukon **SC:** IA/USA **PT:** George Robert Oelberg; Elizabeth Abigail (Kepler) Oelberg **MS:** Married **SPN:** Debra Penuel (8/4/1979) **CH:** Anna Elizabeth; Benjamin George **ED:** Postdoctoral Gellow in Neonatal Medicine, University of Texas Medical School, Houston, TX (1981-1984); Intern, University Texas Medical Branch, Galveston, TX (1978-1979); MD, University Maryland (1978); BS, College William and Mary, with Highest Honors (1974) **CT:** Diplomate in Pediatrics and in Neonatal-Perinatal Medicine, American Board of Pediatrics **C:** Professor, Department of Pediatrics, Center for Pediatrics Research, Eastern Virginia Medical School (2001-Present); Interim Chairman, Department of Pediatrics, Center for Pediatrics Research, Eastern Virginia Medical School (2001-2002); Associate Professor of Pediatrics, Head of Perinatal Research Center, Pediatrics Research, Eastern Virginia Medical School (1993-2001); Associate Professor, University of Texas Medical School, Houston, TX (1990-1993); Assistant Professor, Department of Pediatrics, University of Texas Medical School, Houston, TX (1984-1990); Resident, University of Texas Medical Branch, Galveston, TX (1979-1981); House of Pediatrics Staff, University of Texas Medical Branch, Galveston, TX (1978-1981); Director, Division of Neonatal-Perinatal Medicine, Eastern Virginia Medical School **CR:** Medical Directors Office of Research, Sentara-Norfolk General Hospital (1993-Present); Medical Director, Office of Research, Children's Hospital of King's Daughters (1993-Present); Vice President for Academic Development, Children's Hospital of King's Daughters (2001-2002); Visiting Professor, Wyeth-Ayerst Laboratories (1992); Member, Hospital Staff, Lyndon B. Johnson County Hospital (1990-1993); Physician, Crippled Children's Services Program, Houston, TX (1985-1993); Member, Hospital Staff, Hermann Hospital, Houston, TX (1983-1993); President, Medical Staff, Sentara-Norfolk General Hospital **CIV:** Physician Consultant, Parents of Victims of Sudden Infant Death Syndrome, Houston, TX (1984); Chairman, Institutional Animal Care and Use Committee; Board Member, Fund for William Mary, United Methodist Volunteers in Mission, Missionary to Haiti, Nicaragua, Bolivia **CW:** Editorial Advisory

Board, Journal of Neonatal Intensive Care; Contributor, Articles to Professional Journals; Ad Hoc Reviewer, Professional Journals **AW:** Recipient, Founders' Award, SSPR (2012); Recipient, Clinical Investigator Award, National Institutes of Health, National Heart, Lung, and Blood Institute (1989-1994); Grantee, National Institutes of Health (1989-1994); Research Grantee, American Lung Association (1989-1990); Recipient, Award in Analytical Chemistry, American Chemical Society (1974); Recipient, Letter, Varsity Soccer (1971-1972) **MEM:** Phi Beta Kappa (1973); Fellow, American Academy of Pediatrics, New York Academy of Sciences; American Medical Association; National Academy of Sciences; Society for Experimental Biology and Medicine; Society for Pediatric Research; Phi Eta Sigma; Omicron Delta Kappa; Councilor, President, Secretary-Treasurer, Southern Society for Pediatric Research **MH:** Albert Nelson Marquis Lifetime Achievement Award (2017) **ADD:** 1624 W Little Neck Rd, Virginia Beach, VA, 23452

O'GEARY, DENNIS TRAYLOR, **T:** Vice President, Area Manager (Retired) **I:** Engineering **CN:** J.D. Abrams, L.P. **DOB:** 02/20/1925 **PB:** Waverly **SC:** VA/USA **PT:** King William O'Geary; Mary Virginia (Traylor) O'Geary **MS:** Married **SPN:** Alice Stuart Baum (8/3/1947) **CH:** Dennis Patrick; Mary Alice O'Geary Eisenbarth; Elizabeth Christina O'Geary Bernstorf **ED:** BS in Civil Engineering, Illinois Institute of Technology (1947); Degree in Surveying, Tri-State University (1943) **C:** Retired (1999); Vice President of Houston Operations, J.D. Abrams, L.P., Austin, TX (1985-1999); President, Peabody Southwest, Inc., Houston, TX (1984-1985); Vice President, S.J. Groves & Sons Co., Atlanta, GA (1982-1984); Assistant Division Manager, S.J. Groves & Sons Co., Atlanta, GA (1982-1984); Division Estimator, S.J. Groves & Sons Co., Atlanta, GA (1982-1984); Vice President, S.J. Groves & Sons Co., Springfield, IL (1978-1982); Area Manager, S.J. Groves & Sons Co., Springfield, IL (1978-1982); Engineer, S.J. Groves & Sons Co., Springfield, IL (1957-1977); Assistant Estimator, S.J. Groves & Sons Co., Springfield, IL (1957-1977); Project Manager, S.J. Groves & Sons Co., Springfield, IL (1957-1977); Vice President, S.J. Groves & Sons Co., Springfield, IL (1957-1977); Assistant to Area Manager, S.J. Groves & Sons Co., Springfield, IL (1957-1977); Civil Engineering Superintendent, Wiley Jackson Co., Roanoke, VA (1950-1957); Resident Engineering Trainee, Virginia Highway Department (Now VDOT), Richmond, VA (1947-1950) **CR:** Consultant, J.D. Abrams, L.P., Austin, TX; Consultant, Construction of Lynn Grove Bridge, Jasper Construction Company, North Carolina **CIV:** Member, Eagle Scouts, Boy Scouts of America **MIL:** U.S. Naval Reserve (1943-1958) **MEM:** American Society of Civil Engineers; American Concrete Institute; Society of American Military Engineers; National Maritime Historical Society **MH:** Albert Nelson Marquis Lifetime Achievement Award (2017) **H:** Gardening; Work around the house; Traveling **RE:** Christian (Disciples Of Christ) **ADD:** 15402 Cresent Oaks Ct, Houston, TX, 77068

O'HALLORAN, STACY PADULA, **T:** President, Author, College Counselor **I:** Education/Educational Services **CN:** South Shore College Consulting and Tutoring **PB:** Pembroke **SC:** MA/USA **PT:** Debra Fredette and Anthony Padula **MS:** Married **SPN:** Timothy O'Halloran **ED:** BS, Interior Design, Wentworth Institute of Technology, Boston, MA (2006) **CT:** Certified Tutor, International Tutor Association (2009) **C:** Founding President, South Shore College Consulting and Tutoring (2016-Present); Director of Operations,

JBG Educational Group (2008-2016); Associate in Architecture, Boston, MA (2006-2008) **CW:** Author, "The Forces Within" (2014); Author, "The Battle for Innocence" (2014); Author, "The Aftermath" (2013); Author, "When Darkness Tries to Hide" (2011); Author, "The Right Person" (2010) **AW:** Albert Nelson Marquis Lifetime Achievement Award, Who's Who in the World (2018); Honoree, Best-Seller Status, Amazon (2017); Academic Achievement Award, Miss Teen Southern New England (2000); Honoree, National Honor Society; Presidential Scholar, Dean's List, Wentworth Institute of Technology, Boston, MA **MH:** Who's Who in America (2018); Who's Who in the World (2018) **H:** Writing, skiing, attending Boston Bruins games, traveling **PA:** Republican **RE:** Christian **ADD:** 1 Chapel Hill Dr Apt 2, Plymouth, MA, 02360 **URL:** stacypadula.com

OLABISI, RONKE PHD, T: Assistant Professor **I:** Education/Educational Services **CN:** Rutgers, The State University of New Jersey **MS:** Married **ED:** Postdoctoral Research Fellow, City of Hope (2011-2012); NSBRI Postdoctoral Research Fellow, Rice University (2007-2011); Postdoctoral Research Associate, University of Wisconsin-Madison (2005-2006); PhD in Biomedical Engineering, University of Wisconsin-Madison (2005); MSc in Aerospace Engineering, University of Michigan (1999); MSc in Mechanical Engineering, University of Michigan (1994); BSc in Mechanical Engineering, Massachusetts Institute of Technology (1993); Diplomate in Aerospace Engineering (1991) **C:** Assistant Professor, Rutgers, The State University of New Jersey (2012-Present); Team Member, 100 Year Starship (2012-Present) **AW:** Best Poster Award, Frontiers in Bioengineering Symposium, University of Illinois (2014) **H:** Fencing; Jogging; Massage **BA:** 599 Taylor Rd, Piscataway, NJ, 08854 **ADD:** 830 26th St, Santa Monica, CA, 90403

OLDHAM, SALLY STARK, T: Attorney **I:** Law and Legal Services **CN:** Rutkin, Oldham & Griffin, LLC **MS:** Married **SPN:** Arnold Rutkin (2005) **CH:** Hannah S. Ross; Christopher E. Ross **ED:** JD, University of Connecticut, Cum Laude (1988); Degree, School of Psychology, Southern Connecticut State College (1975); MS, School of Psychology, Southern Connecticut State College (1974); BA in Psychology, Wesleyan University, Cum Laude (1972) **CT:** Certificate of Completion, Family Matters Comprehensive Guardian ad Litem/Attorney for Minor Child Training Program, State of Connecticut (2012) **C:** Partner, Rutkin, Oldham & Griffin, LLC (2011-Present); Partner, Arnold Rutkin (1994-Present); Partner, Day, Berry & Howard, Stamford, CT (1988-1994); Partner, Tyler, Cooper & Alcorn, New Haven, CT (1987); School Psychologist, Private Practice and Public Schools **CW:** "Alimony Recapture and Family Support", Connecticut Chapter of the American Academy of Matrimonial Lawyers Advanced Financial Issues Seminar (2016); "When Domestic Issues Result in Criminal Cases", Fairfield County Bar Association Criminal Law Committee Luncheon (2015); "Document Management", Connecticut Chapter of the American Academy of Matrimonial Lawyers Advanced Technology Seminar (2014); "The DSM-5 and Its Practical Application to the Family Lawyer", Connecticut Bar Association Annual Meeting (2013); "Substance Abuse Issues in Family Law Cases", Connecticut Chapter of the American Academy of Matrimonial Lawyers Advanced Custody Seminar (2012); "An Overview of Property Division and Spousal Support Regimes in the U.S.", International Academy of Matrimonial Lawyers Annual Meeting, Queenstown, New Zealand (2010); Moderator, Symposium on Professionalism, Regional Bar Association

(2004); "Inheritances, Gifts & Pre-Marital Assets", Connecticut Bar Association (2003); "Hot Topics, The Uniform Child Custody Jurisdiction and Enforcement Act (UCCJEA)", Connecticut Bar Association (2003); "How to Avoid the Pitfalls and Pratfalls of Dividing Pensions", Connecticut Bar Association (2002); "Effective Utilization of Mental Health Professionals in Family Cases", Connecticut Bar Association (2001); "Distributing Executive Compensation Benefits", The Family Advocate (2001); "Division of Stock Options in Divorce Cases", Mellon Bank, Hartford, Connecticut (1999); "Relocation Issues after Ireland v. Ireland", Connecticut Bar Association (1999); "Relocation of Minor Children", Stamford/Norwalk Regional Bar Association (1998); "Division of Stock Options: Wendt v. Wendt", Connecticut Bar Association (1998); "Appeals in Family Cases", Connecticut Bar Association (1998); "Evidentiary Issues in Family Law", Connecticut Bar Association (1997); "Recent Appellate Decisions", Connecticut Family Lawyer (1997); "Recent Appellate Developments", Connecticut Family Lawyer (1995); "Post Majority Support: The Statute Explained" Connecticut Family Lawyer (1993) **AW:** Best Lawyers in America, Woodward/White, Inc. (2007-Present); Super Lawyer, Connecticut Magazine (2006-Present); Top 25 Female Lawyers (2007-Present); New York Areas Best Lawyers, New York Magazine (2007-Present); Ten Leaders of Matrimonial & Divorce Law of Connecticut (2008-Present); Martindale-Hubbell Highest Possible Rating in Both Legal Ability and Ethical Standards, Martindale-Hubbell (2010-Present); The Bar Register of Preeminent Women Lawyers, Martindale-Hubbell (2012-Present); Honoree, AV Rated Preeminent Attorney, Martindale-Hubbell (2018); Female Lawyer of the Year for Westport, Family Law Experts (2015); New England Best Lawyers, The Wall Street Journal (2015) **MEM:** Association of Family and Conciliation Courts (2012-Present); Fellow, International Academy of Matrimonial Lawyers (2009-Present); Board of Managers, Connecticut Chapter, American Academy of Matrimonial Lawyers (2006-Present); Fellow, American Academy of Matrimonial Lawyers (2001-Present); Family Law Section, Connecticut Bar Association (1988-Present); Executive Committee, Connecticut Bar Association (1993-Present); Family Law Section, Fairfield County Bar Association (1988-Present); Family Law Section, American Bar Association (1988-Present); Board of Managers, USA Chapter, International Academy of Matrimonial Lawyers (2007-2015); President, Connecticut Chapter, American Academy of Matrimonial Lawyers (2013-2014); Chair, National Test Sub-Committee (2005-2010) **BA:** 5 Imperial Avenue, Rutkin, Oldham & Griffin, LLC, Westport, CT, 06880 **ADD:** 5 Imperial Ave, Rutkin, Oldham & Griffin, LLC, Westport, CT, 06880 **URL:** http://www.rutkinoldham.com/team/sarah-sally-stark-oldham/

OLIVER, NANCY LEBKICHER, T: Artist, Elementary School Educator (Retired) **I:** Education/Educational Services **PB:** Stockton **SC:** CA/USA **PT:** John B. Lebkicher; Marjorie Lebkicher **MS:** Married **SPN:** Douglas C. Oliver (1963) **CH:** Charles; Elaine **ED:** BA, San Jose State University, With Honors (1961) **CT:** California General Education Credential **C:** Associate Kindergarten Teacher, San Carlos School District (1976-1981); Kindergarten Teacher, Ukiah Unified School District (1963-1967); First Grade Teacher, Redwood City School District (1961-1963); Summer Playground Director, Recreation and Community Services, City of Redwood City (1956-1961) **CR:** Assistant, Historical Research (2000-Present); Department Store Shopper, Macy's, San Francisco, CA (1975-

1982) **CIV:** Membership Chair, Inter-Service Club Council (2017-Present); President, Inter-Service Club Council (2014-Present); Altar Guild, St. Peters Episcopal Church in Redwood City, CA (2009-Present); Chair, Historic Resources Advisory Board, San Mateo County (2009-Present); Board of Directors, Historic Resources Advisory Board, San Mateo County (2000-Present); Vestry Member, St. Peters Episcopal Church in Redwood City, CA (2013-2015); Secretary, Inter-Service Club Council (2008-2013); Secretary, Board of Directors, Sequoia High School Education Foundation (2005-2008); Sesquicentennial Committee Member, County of San Mateo (2005-2006); Co-Chairman, Board of Directors, Sequoia High School Education Foundation (2002-2005); Newsletter Editor, White Oaks Elementary School PTA, San Carlos School District (1978-1981); Leader, Girl Scouts of the United States of America, San Carlos, CA (1978-1981); Active Member, Parent Teacher Association, White Oaks Elementary School, San Carlos School District (1973-1981); Sunday School Director, St. Peters Episcopal Church in Redwood City, CA (1973-1978) **CW:** Newsletter Editor, Sequoia High School Alumni Association (2003-Present); Contributor, Article on the History of Sequoia High School, Climate Magazine (2017); Contributing Artist, Yearly SeriPrinters Silkscreened Calendars (1986-2014); Contributing Author, "Redwood City - A Hometown History," Star Publishing Company (2007); Editor, Historic Resources Booklet, AAUW (1989); Editor, Historic Tour Booklet, AAUW (1981); Newsletter Editor, San Carlos Branch, AAUW (1972-1974) **AW:** Purple Patriot Award, Sequoia High School Alumni Association (2010); Silver Second Place Award, Fine Arts Print Making Division, San Mateo County Fair (2001); Bronze Third Place Award, Fine Arts Print Making Division, San Mateo County Fair (2001); Unsung Hero Award, Sequoia High School Alumni Association (1998); Gift Honoree, AAUW (1976) **MEM:** President, Redwood City Inter-Service Club Coordinator Council (2014-Present); Parliamentarian, AAUW (2004-Present); Secretary, Sequoia High School Alumni Association (2002-Present); Founder, San Carlos Heritage Association (1995-Present); Director, San Carlos Heritage Association (1995-Present); Quilt Committee, The International Order of the Rainbow for Girls (1989-Present); Founding Secretary, Sequoia High School Alumni Association (1985-Present); Membership Chairman, Sequoia High School Alumni Association (1985-Present); Chairman, Historic Preservation Section, AAUW (1979-Present); Co-President, San Carlos Branch, AAUW (2011-2015); Serigrapher, SeriPrinters (1986-2014); Secretary, Redwood City Inter-Service Club Coordinator Council (2008-2013); Director-at-Large, AAUW (2004-2006); Co-President, San Carlos Branch, AAUW (2002-2004); President, Sequoia High School Alumni Association (1996-1998); Centennial Coordinator, Sequoia High School Alumni Association (1992-1995); Mother Adviser, The International Order of the Rainbow for Girls, Redwood City (1987-1989); President, AAUW, Willits Branch (1966-1967); Grand Officer, California Chapter, The International Order of the Rainbow for Girls (1957-1958); California State Parks Foundation; Historic Union Cemetery Association Inc.; San Carlos Friends of the Library; Friends of Redwood City Public Library; Archives Committee of the Redwood City Public Library, Inc.; National Trust for Historic Preservation; California Preservation Foundation; San Mateo County Historical Association; Various Conservation Groups **MH:** Albert Nelson Marquis Lifetime Achievement Award (2017) **H:** Needlecrafts; Historic preservation activities; Walking; Calligraphy; Classical music **PA:** Democrat **RE:** Episcopalian **ADD:** 147 Belvedere Ave, San Carlos, CA, 94070

OLSON, MYRNA RAYE, T: Chester Fritz Distinguished Professor in the College of Education and Human Development **I:** Cosmetics **CN:** University of North Dakota **DOB:** 03/11/1947 **PB:** Lakota **SC:** ND/USA **PT:** Merlin W. Munson; Ruby A. (Tufte) Munson **CH:** Nathan Olson; Austin Winger **ED:** EdD, University of North Dakota (1975); MEd, Montana State University (1971); BS in Education, Montana State University–Northern (1969); Postdoctoral Coursework in Visual Impairment and Blindness, San Francisco State University; Postdoctoral Coursework in Multiple Disabilities, Peabody Vanderbilt College **C:** Chester Fritz Distinguished Professor, College of Education and Human Development, University of North Dakota; Teacher, North Dakota School for the Blind, Grand Forks, ND; Teacher, Montana School for the Deaf and Blind, Great Falls, MT; Professor of Higher Education and Special Education, University of North Dakota **CR:** Speaker in Field **CW:** Author, "Collaboration Handbook for Educators" (1995); Author, "Women's Journeys Through Crisis" (1988); Author, Books **AW:** Named, Chester Fritz Distinguished Professor, University of North Dakota (2003); Recipient, Humanitarian Award, North Dakota Council for Exceptional Children (1999) **MH:** Albert Nelson Marquis Lifetime Achievement Award (2017) **ADD:** 3602 Chestnut St, Grand Forks, ND, 58201

OMMANNEY, C. SIMON L., T: Secretary General **I:** Sciences **CN:** International Glaciological Society **DOB:** 01/31/1942 **PB:** Farnham **SC:** England **PT:** Charles Lawrence Leslie; Violet Leslie **MS:** Married **SPN:** Edith Margaret Sutherland (12/7/1985) **CH:** John; Louise; Geordie; Janet; Ginny **ED:** MSc in Geography and Glaciology, McGill University, Montreal, Canada (1967); BA in Geography, McGill University, Montreal, Canada (1963); Diplomate, Outward Bound Sea School, Aberdovey, Wales (1958); Coursework, Wellington College, Crowthorne, Berkshire, England (1955-1960); Coursework, Heatherdown School, Ascot, Berkshire, England (1950-1955) **C:** Secretary, Canadian Committee on Antarctic Research, Canadian Polar Commission, Ottawa, Ontario (2005-2014); Secretary General, International Glaciological Society, Cambridge, England (1993-2003); Head, Climate and Hydrology Project, National Hydrology Research Centre, Saskatoon, Saskatchewan (1990-1993); Chief, Scientific Information Division, National Hydrology Research Centre, Saskatoon, Saskatchewan (1988-1990); Head, Cold Regions Section, National Hydrology Research Centre, Saskatoon, Saskatchewan (1986-1988); Section Head, Snow and Ice Division, Water Resources Branch, Environment Canada, Ottawa, Ontario (1972-1986); Section Head, Glaciology Subdivision, Inland Waters Branch, Energy, Mines and Resources, Ottawa, Ontario (1967-1972); Teacher, Nevill Holt Preparatory School, Northants, England (1963-1964); Assistant, Field Leader, McGill University Arctic Research Expedition to Axel Heiberg Island, Department of Geography, McGill University, Montreal (1961-1966) **CR:** Emeritus Associate, Scott Polar Research Institute, University of Cambridge, England (2003-Present); Explorer, Expedition to Arctic Sweden, British Exploring Society (1959) **CW:** Author, "Glacier Velocities and Dynamic Discharge from the Ice Masses of Baffin Island and Bylot Island, Nunavut, Canada" (2017); Co-Author, "Glacier Change on Axel Heiberg Island, Nunavut, Canada" (2011); Co-Author, "Women in Glaciology, a Historical Perspective" (2010); Author, "Canada and the World Glacier Inventory" (2009); Co-Author, "Recommendations for the Compilation of Glacier Inventory Data from Digital Sources" (2009); Co-Author, "World Glacier Inventory" (2009); Editor, Newsletter, Canadian Antarctic Research Network (2005-2012); Author, "Glaciers of Canada: Glaciers of the Canadian Rockies" (2002); Co-Author, "Quantitative Measurements of Tweedsmuir Glacier and Lowell Glacier Imagery" (2002); Author, "Glaciers of Canada: History of Glacier Investigations in Canada" (2002); Author, "Glaciers of Canada: Mapping Canada's Glaciers" (2002); Co-Author, "The Mass Balance of Circum-Arctic Glaciers and Recent Climate Change" (1997); Author, "Little Fish in Big Ponds: Fisheries and Community Development in Alaska and Greenland" (1997); Author, "100 Years of Glacier Observations in Canada 1890-1990" (1996); Co-Author, "Mass Balance of White Glacier, Axel Heiberg Island, N.W.T., Canada, 1960-1991" (1996); Co-Author, "Mass Balance of Axel Heiberg Island Glaciers, 1960-1991: A Reassessment and Discussion" (1995); Editor, ICE, News Bulletin of the International Glaciological Society (1994-2002); Co-Author, "Proceedings, Ninth International Northern Research Basins Symposium/Workshop" (1993); Author, "Geobotanical Dating in Alpine Carbonate Terrain: a Chronology for Little Ice Age Glacial Activity in Peter Lougheed and Elk Lakes Provincial Parks, Alberta and British Columbia" (1993); Co-Author, "Mackenzie Delta: Environmental Interactions and Implications of Development Proceedings of the Workshop on the Mackenzie Delta, 17-18 October 1989," Saskatoon, Saskatchewan (1991); Co-Author, "Northern Hydrology: Canadian Perspectives" (1990); Author, "Glacier Atlas of Canada, Limited Edition" (1989); Co-Author, "Characteristics of Surge-Type Glaciers" (1986); Co-Author, "Photo-Interpretation, Digital Mapping, and the Evolution of Glaciers in Glacier National Park, B.C." (1986); Author, "Mapping Canada's Glaciers Since 1965" (1986); Co-Author, "Evolution of the Illecillewaet Glacier, Glacier National Park, British Columbia, Using Historical Data, Aerial Photography and Satellite Image Analysis" (1986); Co-Author, "The Use of Landsat Digital Data for Glacier Inventories" (1986); Co-Author, "Snow in Strong or Weak Temperature Gradients. Part I: Experiments and Qualitative Observations" (1985); Author, "Repartition Spatiale, Evolution et Caractaristiques des Glaciers du parc National de Glacier, Colombie-Britannique" (1985); Co-Author, "Canadian Glacier Hydrology and Mass Balance Studies: a History of Accomplishments and Recommendations for Future Work" (1984); Co-Author, "Clef Pour la Photo-Interpretation des Glaciers Tempores" (1984); Co-Author, "Obituary. Fritz Muller 1926-1980" (1981); Author, "Inventory of Canadian Glaciers: Procedures, Techniques, Progress and Applications" (1980); Author, "The Role of Catastrophic Processes in the Evolution of Talus Derived Rock Glaciers" (1979); Author, "The Glacial Hydrology of an Ice-Dammed Lake, Ellesmere Island, N.W.T." (1976); Author, "An Inventory of the Perennial Ice Masses of Coburg Island, N.W.T.: a Case Study of Glacier Inventory Research Techniques" (1974); Co-Author, "The Contribution of Glacier Ice to the World Water Balance (a Status Report on the World Glacier Inventory)" (1972); Author, "A Study in Glacier Inventory: the Ice Masses of Axel Heiberg Island, Canadian Arctic Archipelago" (1969); Contributor, 350 Articles to Publications **AW:** Recipient, Queen Elizabeth II Diamond Jubilee Medal (2012); Recipient, Richardson Medal, IGS (2003); Recipient, Elton Geography Prize, Wellington College, Crowthorne, Berkshire, England **MEM:** Fellow, American Association for the Advancement of Science; Fellow, The Royal Canadian Geographical Society; Fellow, Royal Geographical Society; Board Member, The Royal Canadian Geographical Society; Committee Member, The Royal Canadian Geographical Society **H:** Reading; Sailing **ADD:** 56 Spinney Rd, Glenwood, NS, Canada, B0W 1W0

ONG, JOHN DOYLE, T: Manufacturing Executive, American Business Executive, Ambassador (Retired) **I:** Manufacturing **CN:** B.F. Goodrich Company **DOB:** 09/29/1933 **PB:** Uhrichsville **SC:** OH/USA **PT:** Louis Brosee Ong; Mary Ellen (Liggett) Ong **MS:** Married **SPN:** Mary Lee Schupp (7/20/1957) **CH:** John Francis Harlan; Richard Penn Blackburn; Mary Katherine Caine **ED:** Honorary Doctorate in Public Service, South Dakota State University (2002); Honorary LHD, The University of Akron (1996); Honorary HHD, The Ohio State University (1996); LHD, Kent State University (1982); LLB, Harvard University (1957); MA, The Ohio State University (1954); BA, The Ohio State University (1954) **C:** Chairman of the Board, Asurint (2013-Present); Chairman Emeritus, B.F. Goodrich Company, Akron, OH (1997-Present); Director, Asurint (2006-2012); Appointed by President George W. Bush, Ambassador Extraordinary and Plenipotentiary of the United States to the Kingdom of Norway (2001-2005); Chairman of the Board, B.F. Goodrich Company, Akron, OH (1979-1997); Chief Executive Officer, B.F. Goodrich Company, Akron, OH (1984-1996); President's Commission, Industrial Competitiveness, President Reagan Administration (1984); Co-chair, International Trade Committee, President's Commission, Industrial Competitiveness, President Reagan Administration (1984); Chief Operating Officer, B.F. Goodrich Company, Akron, OH (1978-1979); President, B.F. Goodrich Company, Akron, OH (1975-1984); Director, B.F. Goodrich Company, Akron, OH (1975-1977); Vice Chairman, B.F. Goodrich Company, Akron, OH (1974-1975); Executive Vice President, B.F. Goodrich Company, Akron, OH (1973-1974); Group Vice President, B.F. Goodrich Company, Akron, OH (1972-1973); Assistant Counsel, B.F. Goodrich Company, Akron, OH (1961-1966) **CR:** Chairman Emeritus, Ohio Business Roundtable; Member, Ohio Business Roundtable, Columbus, OH (1979-1997); Chairman, Business Roundtable, Washington, DC (1992-1994) **CIV:** Trustee Emeritus, The University of Chicago (2001-Present); Trustee, Musical Arts Association, Cleveland, OH (1975-2017); Trustee, Fort Ligonier (1997-2015); Trustee, The Ohio State University (2006-2010); The Business Council, Washington, D.C. (1989-2005); Trustee, Ohio History Society (1998-2002); Chairman, New American Schools (1998-2002); Chairman, Musical Arts Association, Cleveland, OH (1997-2001); National Trustee, John S. and James L. Knight Foundation (1995-2001); Trustee, The University of Chicago (1991-2001); President, Board of Trustees, Western Reserve Academy, Hudson, OH (1977-1995); Trustee, Western Reserve Academy, Hudson, OH (1975-1995); Board of Directors, National Alliance of Business (1981-1994); Trustee, Case Western Reserve University (1980-1992); Director, New American Schools (1991); Chairman, National Alliance of Business (1991); Chairman, National Alliance of Business (1984-1986); Trustee, Kenyon College (1983-1985); Trustee, Graduate School of Industrial Administration (Now Tepper Business School), Carnegie Mellon University (1978-1983); National Trustee, National Symphony Orchestra, The Kennedy Center (1975-1983); Trustee, Bexley Hall Seminary (1974-1981); Trustee, Hudson Library and Historical Society, OH (1967-1980); Business Advisory Committee, Transportation Center, Northwestern University (1975-1978); Vice President, Exploring Great Trail Council, Boy Scouts of America (1974-1977); President, Hudson Library and Historical Society, OH (1971-1972); Trustee, The Musical Arts Association of Cleveland, Cleveland Orchestra, OH; Former

Chairman, The Business Committee for the Arts **MIL:** Captain, JAG Corps, U.S. Army (1965); Ohio Army National Guard (1961-1965); U.S. Army (1957-1961) **AW:** Grand Cross, Royal Norwegian Order of Merit, King of Norway (2005); Humanities Award of Distinction; Alumni Medal, The Ohio State University **MEM:** Senior Visiting Policy Fellow, RTI International (2006-2012); Board of Directors, Chemical Manufacturers Association (Now American Chemistry Council) (1994-1997); Board of Directors, Chemical Manufacturers Association (Now American Chemistry Council) (1988-1991); Board of Directions, Rubber Manufacturers Association (1974-1984); Board of Governors, Corporate Counsel Section, Ohio State Bar Association (1962-1974); Chairman, Ohio State Bar Association (1970); Conference Board, Council of Retired Chief Executives; Council of American Ambassadors; Bohemian Club; Chagrin Valley Hunt Club; Portage Country Club; The Rowfant Club; Union Club; Links; Union League Club; Metropolitan Club; Rolling Rock Club; Castalia Trout Club; The Phi Beta Kappa Society; Phi Alpha Theta National History Honor Society **BAR:** Ohio (1958) **MH:** Albert Nelson Marquis Lifetime Achievement Award (2017) **H:** Fishing; Hunting **PA:** Republican **RE:** Episcopalian **BA:** 9 Uproar Street, Suite 2, Hudson, OH, 44236 **ADD:** 9 Aurora Street, Suite 2, Hudson, OH, 44236

ORFORD, ROBERT RAYMOND, T: Physician, Consultant **I:** Medicine & Health Care **CN:** Mayo Clinic **DOB:** 04/18/1948 **PB:** Winnipeg **SC:** MB/Canada **PT:** Robert Raymond Orford; Sarah Gloria L. (Gullden) Orford **MS:** Married **SPN:** Dale Laura Stuart (6/2/1972) **CH:** Carolyn Tiffany; Andrew Craig; Loren Brent **ED:** Special Clinical Fellow in Aerospace and Preventive Medicine, Mayo Clinic School of Graduate Medical Education, Mayo Foundation for Medical Education and Research (1988); MPH, Department of Environmental and Occupational Health Sciences, School of Public Health, University of Washington (1976); Resident, Preventive Medicine, School of Public Health, University of Washington (1976); MS in Medicine, Mayo Clinic School of Medicine, Mayo Foundation for Medical Education and Research (1975); Resident in Internal Medicine, Mayo Clinic School of Medicine, Mayo Foundation for Medical Education and Research (1975); Medical Internship, St. Joseph's Hospital London, London, ON, Canada (1972); MD, CM, McGill University (1971); BS, McGill University, With Great Distinction (1968) **CT:** Certification in Public Health and General Preventive Medicine, American Board of Preventive Medicine (1994); Certification in Aerospace Medicine, American Board of Preventive Medicine (1991); Certification in Occupational Medicine, American Board of Preventive Medicine (1979); Certification in Internal, Royal College of Physicians and Surgeons of Canada (1975); Certification in Internal Medicine, American Board of Internal Medicine (1974) **C:** Consultant, Department of Internal Medicine, Mayo Clinic, Scottsdale, AZ (1996-Present); Consultant, Preventive Medicine, Mayo Clinic, Rochester, MN (1991-1996); Senior Associate Consultant, Mayo Clinic, Rochester, MN (1988-1991); Medical Director of Employee Health, University of Alberta Hospital, Edmonton, AB, Canada (1988); Deputy Minister of Community Occupational Health, Government of Alberta, Edmonton, AB, Canada (1985-1987); Executive Director of Occupational Health Services, Government of Alberta, Edmonton, AB, Canada (1981-1985); Director of Medical Services, Government of Alberta, Edmonton, AB, Canada (1979-1981); Associate Professor of Community Medicine, University of Alberta, Edmonton, AB,

Canada (1978-1988) **CR:** Consultant, Executive Health Program, Mayo Clinic, Scottsdale, AZ (2008-Present); Assistant Professor, Mayo Medical School, Rochester, NY (1988-Present); Chairman of Preventive and Occupational Medicine Division, Director of Executive Health Program, Mayo Clinic, Scottsdale, AZ (1999-2007); Energy Resource Conservation Board, Government of Alberta, Canada (1988-1989); National Health Fellowship, Canada Awarding Organization (1975); Fellow, Royal College of Physicians and Surgeons of Canada **CIV:** Board Member, International Commission of Occupational Health (2014-Present); International Commission of Occupational Health (1980-Present); Appointed Delegate, American Medical Association, American College of Occupational and Environmental Medicine (ACOEM) **CW:** Contributor, Articles, Professional Journals **AW:** Award for Leadership and Service in Organized Medicine, Arizona Medical Association (2017); Award for Excellence in the Clinical Practice of Airline Medicine Boothby-Edwards (2008); President's Citation, Aerospace Medical Association (2003); Best Resident Presentation, Aerospace Medical Association (1975) **MEM:** Board Member, International Commission on Occupational Health (2015-Present); Delegate, American Medical Association (2012-Present); Parliamentarian, Aerospace Medical Association (2010-Present); Chairman, Section Council on Preventive Medicine, American Medical Association (2012-2014); President, Arizona Medical Association (2011-2012); President, American College of Occupational and Environmental Medicine (ACOEM) (2008-2009); National Secretary, International Commission on Occupational Health (2001-2012); American College of Preventive Medicine; President, Airlines Medical Directors Association; Council Member, International Academy of Aviation and Space Medicine **MH:** Albert Nelson Marquis Lifetime Achievement Award (2017) **H:** Languages; Fitness; Travel **RE:** Presbyterian **BA:** 13400 E Shea Boulevard, Mayo Clinic, Scottsdale, AZ, 58259 **ADD:** 15516 E Acacia Way, Fountain Hills, AZ, 85268 **URL:** https://www.mayoclinic.org/biographies/orford-robert-r-m-d/bio-20053863

OSAKWE, CHRISTOPHER, T: Partner, Lawyer, Educator **I:** Law and Legal Services **CN:** The Middleberg Riddle Group **DOB:** 05/08/1942 **PB:** Lagos **SC:** Nigeria **PT:** Simon Osakwe; Hannah (Morgan) Osakwe **MS:** Married **SPN:** Maria Elena Amador (8/19/1982) **CH:** Rebecca E. **ED:** JSD, University of Illinois (1974); PhD, Lomonosov Moscow State University (1970); LLB, Lomonosov Moscow State University, Summa Cum Laude (1967) **C:** Partner, Riddle and Brown (Now The Middleberg Riddle Group), New Orleans, LA (1989-Present); Eason Weinmann Professor of Comparative Law, Eason Weinmann Center for Comparative Law (Now Eason Weinmann Center for International and Comparative Law), Tulane University Law School, New Orleans, LA (1981-1986); Director, Eason Weinmann Center for Comparative Law (Now Eason Weinmann Center for International and Comparative Law), Tulane University Law School, New Orleans, LA (1981-1986); Professor, Tulane University Law School, New Orleans, LA (1972-1988) **CR:** Distinguished Visiting Professor of Comparative Private Law, National Research University Higher School of Economics (HSE), Moscow, Russia (2000-2013); Visiting Professor, Lomonosov Moscow State University (1999-2013); Visiting Fellow, Christ Church College, Oxford University (1988-1989); Consultant, U.S. Department of Commerce (1980-1985); Visiting Professor, Washington and Lee University (1986); Visiting Professor,

University of Michigan (1981); Visiting Fellow, St. Antony's College, University of Oxford (1980); Visiting Professor, University of Pennsylvania (1978) **CW:** Editor, Journal of Foreign Legislative and Comparative Law (2006-Present); Author, "Moral Harm In Anglo-American Law: Concept, Classification and Compensation" (2011); Author, "Canons Of a Learned Legal Translation: Reflections of a Comparative Law Scholar Drawing Upon Comparative Civil Law Scholarship" (2011); Author, "Comparative Law: Diagrammatic Commentary" (2008); Author, "Russian Civil Code: Text and Analysis" (2008); Author, "Comparative Law in Diagrams: General and Special Parts, Second Edition" (2002); Author, "The Russian Civil Code Annotated: Translation and Commentary" (2000); Author, "Comparative Law in Diagrams: General and Special Parts" (2000); Author, "Comparative Legal Traditions: Text, Materials and Cases, Second Edition" (1994); Author, "Soviet Business Law" (1991); Author, "Joint Ventures with the Soviet Union: Law and Practice" (1990); Author, "Comparative Legal Traditions: Text, Materials and Cases" (1985); Member, Editorial Board, American Journal of Legal Education (1983-1985); Co-author, "Comparative Legal Traditions in a Nutshell" (1982); Author, "The Foundations of Soviet Law" (1981); Editor, American Journal of Comparative Law (1978-1986); Author, "The Participation of the Soviet Union in Universal International Organizations" (1972) **AW:** Research Fellow, Kennan Institute for Advanced Russian Studies (1988); USSR Senior Research Exchange Fellow (1982); Russian Research Fellow, Harvard University (1972); Carnegie Fellow, The Hague Academy of International Law (1969) **MEM:** ABA; Société de législation comparée; Supreme Court Historical Society; The American Society of International Law; The American Law Institute; Order of the Coif **BAR:** Kazakhstan Bar Association (1997-Present); ABA (1974-Present); Moscow Bar Association (1967-Present) **MH:** Albert Nelson Marquis Lifetime Achievement Award (2017) **H:** Golf; Tennis; Classic Movies **PA:** Republican **RE:** Roman Catholic **ADD:** 339 Audubon Blvd, New Orleans, LA, 70125 **URL:** http://www.chrisosakwe.info/wp-content/uploads/2012/12/Full-Details-Resume-ENG.pdf

OSOFF, JEFFREY A., T: Chairman **I:** Media & Entertainment **DOB:** 06/05/1936 **PB:** Everett **SC:** MA/USA **PT:** Meyer Osoff; Minerva (Cogan) Osoff (Deceased) **MS:** Married **SPN:** Donna M. Peyre-Ferry (5/26/1990); Arlene Shuman (9/23/1962, Divorced 1988) **CH:** Judith Robin (Deceased); David Eric **ED:** MS, Columbia University (1959); BS, Bowling Green State University (1958) **C:** Chairman, D & J Enterprises, Ltd., Hudson, MA (1995-Present); Chairman, Dorian Enterprises, Ltd. (1992-Present); President, Chief Executive Officer, JAO Enterprises, Ltd., Hudson, MA (1987-Present); Chairman, Board, Concannon's Inc., Marlborough and Wellesley, MA (1990-1998); Chairman, Board, Jansson, Inc., Waltham, MA (1978-1987); Director, Public Affairs, Brandeis University (1969-1978); Assistant Director, Public Affairs, Brandeis University (1967-1969); Director News Bureau, Brandeis University, Waltham, MA (1964-1967); Acting Assistant City Editor, Boston Globe Media Partners, LLC (1963-1964); Reporter, Boston Globe Media Partners, LLC (1955-1964); Rewriteman, Boston Globe Media Partners, LLC (1962-1963); Reporter, Boston Globe Media Partners, LLC (1954-1955) **CR:** Lecturer in Journalism; Consultant, Public Relations **CIV:** President, Dysautonomia Foundation, Inc. (1973-1974); Board of Directors, Dysautonomia Foundation, Inc. (1965-1976); First Vice President, Dysautonomia Foundation, Inc., New York (1965-1966); Board of

Directors, New England Region, Anti-Defamation League **MIL:** U.S. Air Force (1961-1962) **AW:** Citation for Outstanding Journalistic Reporting, Massachusetts National Guard (1961); Several Awards for High Achievement in Graphics **MEM:** New England Newspaper & Press Association; International Academy of Clinical Thermology; Printing Industries of America; PINE; American College Public Relations Association; Jewish Council for Public Affairs; Public Relations Society of America, Inc.; Publicity Club of New England; Sigma Delta Chi; Zeta Beta Tau **MH:** Albert Nelson Marquis Lifetime Achievement Award (2017) **RE:** Jewish **ADD:** 3E Autumn Dr, Hudson, MA, 01749

OSSOFF, ROBERT H. DMD, MD, T: Otolaryngologist **I:** Medicine & Health Care **CN:** Vanderbilt Bill Wilkerson Center **DOB:** 03/25/1947 **PB:** Beverly **SC:** MA/USA **PT:** Michael Max Ossoff; Eve Joan (Kladky) Ossoff **MS:** Married **SPN:** Lynn Spilman (1984) **CH:** Leslin; Jacob **ED:** MS in Otolaryngology, Northwestern University, Chicago, IL (1981); American Cancer Society Clinical Fellow, Head and Neck Surgery, Department of Otolaryngology and Maxillofacial Surgery, Northwestern University Medical School, Chicago, IL (1980-1981); NIH Research Fellow, Medical Graduate Student, Otolaryngology, Northwestern University Medical School, Chicago, IL (1977-1978); Resident, Otolaryngology and Maxillofacial Surgery, Northwestern Memorial Hospital, Chicago, IL (1976-1980); Intern, General Surgery, Northwestern Memorial Hospital, Chicago, IL (1975-1976); MD, Tufts University School of Dental Medicine, Boston, MA (1975); DMD, Tufts University School of Medicine, Boston, MA (1973); BA, Bowdoin College, Brunswick, ME (1969) **CT:** Diplomate, American Board of Otolaryngology (1982); License to Practice Medicine, State of Tennessee **C:** Maness Professor, Laryngology and Voice, Department of Otolaryngology, Vanderbilt University School of Medicine (2008-Present); Otolaryngologist-in-Chief, Attending Surgeon, Vanderbilt University Hospital, Nashville, TN (1986-Present); Attending Surgeon, Veteran's Administration Hospital, Nashville, TN (1986-Present); Attending Surgeon, St. Thomas Hospital, Nashville, TN (2013); Attending Surgeon, Baptist Hospital, Nashville, TN (2010); Director, Vanderbilt Bill Wilkerson Center for Otolaryngology & Communication Sciences, Vanderbilt University Medical Center (1997-2008); Associate Vice Chancellor, Health Affairs, Vanderbilt University Medical Center (1995-2005); Chief of Staff, Vanderbilt University Hospital, Nashville, TN (1995-1997); Guy M. Maness Professor, Chairman, Department of Otolaryngology, Vanderbilt University School of Medicine (1986-2008); Associate Professor, Department of Otolaryngology-HNS, Northwestern University Medical School (1985-1986); Consultant, Cook County Hospital, Chicago, IL (1983-1986); Head, Division of Otolaryngology-HNS, Attending Surgeon, Evanston Hospital, Evanston, IL (1983-1986); Associate Attending, Northwestern Memorial Hospital, Chicago IL (1982-1986); Chief, Otolaryngology Service: Attending Surgeon, Veteran's Administration Lakeside Hospital, Chicago, IL (1982-1985); Attending, The Children's Memorial Hospital, Chicago, IL (1981-1986); Assistant Professor, Department of Oral Medicine, Northwestern University Dental School (1981-1986); Assistant Professor, Department of Otolaryngology-HNS, Northwestern University Medical School (1981-1985); Attending, Cook County Hospital, Chicago, IL (1981-1983); Adjunct Attending, Northwestern Memorial Hospital, Chicago, IL (1981-1982) **CR:** Special Assistant to Vice Chancellor, Vanderbilt Medical Center (2013-Present); Member, CME Advisory Committee (2005-Present); Chair, Vanderbilt Asthma Sinus and Allergy Program Operations Committee (1997-Present); President, Vanderbilt Asthma Sinus and Allergy Program Board of Directors (1997-Present); Executive Medical Director, The Vanderbilt Voice Center, Vanderbilt University (1996-Present); Member, Board of Directors, Vanderbilt Medical Group (1995-Present); Assistant Vice Chancellor, Compliance and Corporate Integrity, Vanderbilt Medical Center (2008-2013); Member, VMG Executive Committee (2005-2006); Member, Executive Faculty, Vanderbilt University School of Medicine (2001-2008, 1991-1993); Member, Ophthalmology Chair Search Committee (2001-2002); Chair, Self Insurance Trust Committee (1998-2005); Member, Clinical Chiefs Committee (1993-2008); Member, Executive Council of the Free Electron Laser Center, Vanderbilt University (1996); Associate Director, Free Electron Laser Program, Vanderbilt University (1994-1997); Member, Task Force on Administrative Infrastructure in Support of Clinical Practice (1993-1995); Member, Operations Improvement Task Force for Operation Services, Vanderbilt University Hospital (1992-1993); Member, Self-Insurance Committee, Vanderbilt University Medical Center (1991-1994); Member, Credentials Committee, Vanderbilt University Hospital (1991-1992); Member, Ad Hoc Committee on Conflict of Interest, Vanderbilt University School of Medicine (1991-1995) **CIV:** Member, Board of Directors, Nashville Academy of Medicine (2013- Present); Member, Board of Directors, Nashville Opera (2011-Present); Member, Advisory Board, W.O. Smith Nashville School of Music (1997-Present); Medical Advisory Board, The Ear Foundation (1986-Present); Member, Board of Directors, Tennessee Performing Arts Center (2010-2013); Member, Board of Director, Vanderbilt Employees' Credit Union (2009-2013); President, Nashville Academy of Otolaryngology-Head and Neck Surgery (1992-1993); Board of Directors, Bill Wilkerson Center for Hearing and Speech Sciences (1991-1997); Secretary-Treasurer, Tennessee Academy of Otolaryngology and Head and Neck Surgery (1988-1989); Leadership Nashville (1988-1989); Board of Directors, The Classic Chorale, Evanston, IL (1985-1986); Chairman, Membership Committee, The Midwest Bio-Laser Institute (1981-1986); Board of Trustees, The Midwest Bio-Laser Institute (1980-1986) **CW:** Editorial Board, Recent Advances in ENT (2011-Present); Advisory Board, Health Care Compliance (2010-Present); Editorial Board, Journal of Health Care Compliance (2010-Present); Editorial Board, International Journal of Otolaryngology (2008-Present); Editorial Board, Archives of Otolaryngology HNS (2006-Present); Editorial Board, The Journal of Voice (1987-Present); Editorial Advisory Board, Otolaryngology-Head and Neck Surgery (1985-Present); International Editor Board, Recent Advances in Otolaryngology, Head and Neck Surgery (2013); Editor-in-Chief, Lasers in Surgery and Medicine (1995-2005); Associate Editor, Diagnostic and Therapeutic Endoscopy (1992-2002); Editorial Advisory Board, General Surgery News (1990-1997); Editorial Board, Operative Techniques in Otolaryngology Head and Neck Surgery (1989-2004); Editorial Board, Journal of Laser Applications (1988-2005); Editorial Board, The Laryngoscope (1987-2006); Senior Editor, Lasers in Surgery and Medicine (1987-1994); Editorial Board, Clinical Laser Monthly (1984-1994); Contributor, Over 190 Articles, Professional Journals; Contributor, Over 60 Chapters, Books; Guest Speaker in Field; Guest Lecturer in Field **AW:** Honorary Member, Chicago Laryngological and Otological Society (1986-Present); American Laryngological Association Award (2015); Presidential Citation, American Laryngological Association (2015); President Citation, American Academy of Otolaryngology – Head & Neck Surgery, Vancouver, British Columbia, Canada (2013); Presidential Citation, Triological Society (2006, 2008); Presidential Citation, American Laryngological Association (2008); James Newcomb Award, American Laryngological Association (2007); Boehm Award for CME Excellence, Vanderbilt University School of Medicine (2007); Presidential Citation, ASLSM (2005); Lifetime Achievement Award, The Dedo Voice Center, UCSF (2004); Distinguished Service Award, AAO-HNS/F (2004); Presidential Citation, American Society of Laser Medicine and Surgery (2003); Presidential Citation, American Academy of Otolaryngology-Head and Neck Surgery (1999); Chevalier Jackson Award, ABEA (1997); Distinguished Service Award, American Academy of Otolaryngology-Head and Neck Surgery (1995) **MEM:** Secretary, SCCE/HCCA Board of Directors (2013-Present); HCCA Executive Committee (2013-Present); HCCA Board of Directors (2011-Present); Council, ALA (2010-Present, 1996-2008); Advisor, ALA Post-Graduate Member Committee (2010-Present); Historian, ALA (2010-Present); HCCA CHC Committee (2010-Present); Council, TRIO (2009-Present, 2002-2003); South Central Regional Conference Planning Committee (2009-Present); Chairman, ALA Post-Graduate Member Membership Committee (2007-Present); Senior Counselor, ABOto (2007-Present); Chairman, ALA Strategic Planning and Review Committee, ALA (2005-Present); Executive Council, TRIO (2005-Present); President, TRIO, (2011-2012); President-Elect, TRIO (2010-2011); Chairman, Continuing Medical Education (2005-2010); President, SUO-HNS (2005-2006); Executive Council (2004-2008); President, ALA (2004-2005); President-Elect, SUO-HNS (2004-2005); Vice-President, Southern Section, TRIO (2003); Vice-President, President-Elect, ALA (2003); Coordinator for Development, AAO-HNS (2001-2006); Ethics Committee, ABOto (2001-2004); Chairman, Maintenance of Certificates Committee, ABOto (2000-2006); President, AADO-HNS (2000-2002) **MH:** Albert Nelson Marquis Lifetime Achievement Award (2017) **H:** Boating; Skiing; Fly fishing; Golf; Photography; Pickle ball; Rving **BA:** 7302 MCE, South Tower, Vanderbilt University Medical Center, Dept of Otolaryngology, Nashville, TN, 37232 **ADD:** 5800 W State Road 80 Lot 76, RiverBend Motor Coach Resort, Fort Denaud, FL, 33935 **URL:** http://www.mc.vanderbilt. edu/reporter/index.html?ID=5806

OSTERLE, JOHN FLETCHER, T: Mechanical Engineering Educator **I:** Education/Educational Services **CN:** Carnegie Mellon University **DOB:** 07/31/1925 **PB:** Pittsburgh **SC:** PA/USA **MS:** Single **ED:** DSc in Mechanical Engineering, Carnegie Institute of Technology (Now Carnegie Mellon University) (1952); MS, Carnegie Institute of Technology (1949); BS, Carnegie Institute of Technology (1946) **C:** Acting Head, Mechanical Engineering Department, Carnegie Mellon University, Pittsburgh, PA (1985-1987); Chairman, Nuclear Science and Engineering Division (now Department of Materials Science and Engineering), Carnegie Mellon University, Pittsburgh, PA (1975-1985); Theodore Ahrens Professor of Mechanical Engineering, Carnegie Mellon University, Pittsburgh, PA (1958-1995); Instructor, Associate Professor, Carnegie Mellon University, Pittsburgh, PA (1946-1958) **CR:** Visiting Professor, University of Oxford, Oxford, England (1971); Visiting Professor, Delft University of Technology, Deft, Netherlands (1957-1958) **AW:** Walter D. Hodson Award, American Society of Lubrication Engineers (now Society of Tribologists and Lubrication Engineers) (1956) **MEM:** Fellow, The American Society of Mechanical Engineers **MH:** Albert Nelson Marquis Lifetime Achievement Award (2017) **ADD:** 5406 Kipling Rd, Pittsburgh, PA, 15217

OSTRZENSKI, ADAM, **T:** Professor, Emeritus Director **I:** Education/Educational Services **CN:** Howard University **DOB:** 08/29/1940 **PB:** Stanislawow **SC:** Poland **PT:** Pawel; Valery (Dzimira) **MS:** Married **SPN:** Maria Molenda, Attorney-at-Law (2/17/1967) **CH:** Katarzyna (Kasia) Ostrezenska, M.D.; Bartosz (Bart) Ostrzenski, Attorney-at-Law **ED:** Doctor Honoris Causa, Thomas More College, Rome, Italy (2017); Doctor Habilitant Degree, Jagiellonian University Medical College, Krakow, Poland (1998); Residency, Gynecology & Obstetrics, Buffalo State, The State University of New York (1982); PhD, Academy of Medicine, Wroclaw Medical University, Poland (1971); MD, Academy of Medicine, Wroclaw Medical University, Poland (1966); Residency, Gynecology & Obstetrics, Poland; Fellowship, Pelvic Surgery, Degree Specialist of Gynecology & Obstetrics, Poland **CT:** Diplomate, American Board of Obstetrics and Gynecology, Inc. **C:** Director Emeritus, Division of Operative Gynecology, Howard University, College of Medicine (1994-2001); Professor of Operative Gynecology, College of Medicine, Howard University (1994); Associate Professor, Clinical Obstetrics & Gynecology, The George Washington University (1987-1994); Surgeon, Gynecologic Surgery and Reproductive Endocrinology, Washington D.C. (1982-2001); Assistant Professor, Department of Obstetrics and Gynecology, The George Washington University (1982); Assistant Instructor, Gynecology & Obstetrics, Buffalo State, The State University of New York; Educational Coordinator, Gynecology & Obstetrics Residency Program, Howard University; Educational Coordinator, Medical Students, Department of Obstetrics and Gynecology, Howard University; Co-author, New Residency Program Curriculum, Residency Ruling Committee, Educational Program of OB/GYN for Students, Howard University **CR:** Visiting Professor, Universite degli Studi di Roma "La Sapienza"; Visiting Professor, Jagiellonian University Medical College, Krakow, Poland; Visiting Professor, Kuwait University Faculty of Medicine, Kuwait City, Kuwait; Visiting Professor, Arabian Gulf University, Manama, Bahrain (1991-2004); Co-Director, International Gynecological Endoscopy Workshop, Howard University College of Medicine; Co-Director, International Gynecological Endoscopy Workshop, Christian Albrechts Universitat zu Kiel, Kiel, Germany; Co-Director, International Gynecological Endoscopy Workshop, Universite degli Studi di Roma "La Sapienza," Rome, Italy; Moderator, Italian National Research Council Bio-ethical Aspect of Medical Experiments, Rome, Italy; Scientific Chairman, First World Congress of Reconstructive and Cosmetic Gynecology, Indian Reconstructive and Cosmetic Gynecology Society, New Delhi, India; Chairman, Women's Health Awareness Association, Washington D.C. **CIV:** Founder, Institute of Gynecology, Inc. **CW:** Author, "Total Laproscopic Hysterectomy" (1993); Author, "Gynecology: Integrating Conventional, Complementary, and Natural Alternative Therapy" (2002); Advisory Editorial Board, The Polish Journal of Medicine and Pharmacy (1988); Co-Editor-in-Chief, Journal of Prenatal and Perinatal Medicine and Psychology; Contributor, Over 250 Articles, Professional Publications; Author, 80 Abstracts; Contributor, Chapters, Books; Featured Guest, "The View" **AW:** Awarded Title of "The Father of Modern Cosmetic-Plastic Gynecology," India Cosmetic Gynecology Society (2017); Honoree, International Man of the Year for Contribution to Progressive Medicine (1995-1996); Outstanding Member of Metropolitan Washington D.C. Community; Honoree, "Doers Profile" Section, The Washington Times, LLC, Washington, D.C. (1995); Silver Medal, The Polish Patent Bureau (1973); Honorary Appointment, The Research Board of Advisers, American Biographical Institute; Medal, International Federation of Gynecology and Obstetrics; Medal, Falloppius International Society; Clinical Research Award, Turkish-German Gynecological Association; Medal, International Pelviscopy Society **MEM:** American Association of Professors of Gynecology and Obstetrics; Polish Gynecological Association **MH:** Albert Nelson Marquis Lifetime Achievement Award (2017) **H:** Outdoors **PA:** Independent **ADD:** 14808 Gulf Blvd, Madeira Beach, FL, 33708 **URL:** www.cosmetic-gyn.com

OSWALD, JAMES MARLIN, **T:** Educator, Researcher **I:** Education/Educational Services **DOB:** 08/17/1935 **PB:** Plainview **SC:** TX/USA **PT:** James Buchanan Oswald; Eula Bea (Marlin) Oswald **MS:** Married **SPN:** Dorothy Anne Veigel (12/27/1956) **CH:** Richard; Ramona; Roberta **ED:** EdD, Stanford University (1970); MA, West Texas State College (1958); BS, West Texas State College (1957) **C:** Energy Conservation Consultant (1959-Present); Instructional Development Specialist, Community College of Philadelphia (1980-1996); Field Coordinator, Pennsylvania, Delaware and New Jersey Citizen Education, Research for Better Schools, Philadelphia, PA (1978-1980); Assistant Superintendent, Instruction, East Pennsylvania School District, Emmaus, PA (1975-1978); Researcher, Global Cultural Studies Education Projects, American University Field Staff (1972-1975); Writer, Global Cultural Studies Education Projects, American University Field Staff (1972-1975); Director, Global Cultural Studies Education Projects, American University Field Staff (1972-1975); Assistant Professor, Social Studies and Social Science Education, Syracuse University, New York (1969-1972); Staff Associate, National Council of Social Studies (1968-1969); Washington Internship for Educational Leadership (1968-1969); Curriculum Specialist, American Institutes of Research (1966-1968); Teacher, Salt Lake City Public Schools (1958-1966); Supervisor, Salt Lake City Public Schools (1958-1966) **CR:** Career Mentor, Life Coach (2002-Present); Financial and Retirement Planning Consultant, DudeSpa (2002-Present); Nutrition Educator (1997-Present); Co-founder, Institute of Plant Based Nutrition (1996-Present); President, Institute of Plant Based Nutrition (1996-Present); Financial and Retirement Planning Consultant, Macro/Micro Agro (1992-Present); Financial and Retirement Planning Consultant (1980-Present); Proprietary Energy Consultant, Main Line Stoves (1972-Present); President, New York State Council of Social Studies (1971-1972); Physical Fitness Trainer; Consultant in Field **MIL:** Captain, Infantry, U.S. Army Reserve (1958-1968); U.S. Army (1957-1958) **CW:** Editor, Quarterly Newsletter, Plant Based Nutrition (1997-Present); Designer, "National Wildlife Foundation Dedication Site," Vine Creek Ecological Basin (1969-Present); Author, "Native Plants in Pennsylvania Today" (2018); Author, "Albert F.W. Vick, Native Plantsman" (2018); Author, "How Beautiful My Cynwyd" (2018); Author, "Plainview" (2018); Author, "Ranch Boy" (2018); Author, "Fort Elliot, Texas Frontier Post: 1874-1891" (1968, 2018); Author, "Zero Runoff Landscaping" (1959, 2018); Author, "Hollow Headed Zero Skill Schooling" (2017); Author, "Green Gourmet" (2006); Author, "Microagro" (2003); Author, "Plant Kingdom Gourmet" (2003); Author, "Ferdinand Magellan Vegan Cuisine" (2000); Author, "Christopher Columbus Vegan Cuisine" (1999); Author, "Criteria for Nutritional Guidelines for Century 21" (1999); Author, "Marco Polo Vegan Cuisine" (1998); Author, "Veganomics" (1998); Author, "Veganocracy" (1998); Author, "Veganagro" (1998); Author, "Our Home, the Earth" (1980); Author, "Planet Earth" (1976); Co-author, "Earthship" (1974); Author, "Research in Social Studies and Social Science Education" (1972); Author, "Global Cultural Studies" (1972); Author, "Humanself" (1972); Author, "The Monroe Doctrine: Does It Survive?" (1969); Author, "Commemoration of Heroic Produce Grower Sacrifices, Death and Survival on September 11, 2001"; Designer, "August 1777 Revolutionary War Memorial Monument," Saint John's Church Hill Sanctuary, Cynwyd, Pennsylvania; Contributor, Articles to Professional Journals; Educator, Career Archive, Library Special Collections, Stanford University **AW:** Fellow, Fulbright-Hays SEAsia, University Singapore Study Program (1967); Henry Newell Fellow, Stanford University (1966-1968); Sertoma Service to Mankind Award, Salt Lake City, UT (1966); Grantee, Stanford University; Grantee, National Science Foundation; Grantee, U.S. Office of Education; Grantee, Institute of International Studies **MEM:** Life Member, American Vegan Society; Institute of Plant Based Nutrition; Life Member, North American Vegetarian Society; Toronto Vegetarian Association; Founding President, Main Line Vegan Society; International Society of Kirsna Consciousness; Food for Life International; Archaeological Conservancy; Army Historical Foundation; Emeritus, Social Science Education Consortium; Life Member, Texas Panhandle-Plains Historical Society; Life Member, Utah Historical Society; Life Member, Descendants of the Founders of Ancient Windsor; Windsor Historical Society; St. Lawrence County Historical Society; Colonial Williamsburg Foundation; Ridley Park Colonial Plantation; Jenkins Arboretum; Marshall Steam Museum; Life Member, Lower Merion Historical Society; Montgomery Co. Historical Society; Pennsylvania Historical Society; Henry Foundation of Botanical Research; Pennsylvania Forestry Association; Pennsylvania Vegetable Growers Association; Lifer Member, Pennsylvania Nut Growers Association; Heritage Foundation; Life Member, Stanford University Alumni Association; Antique Automobile Association of America; Arbor Day Foundation Hazelnut Project; National Wildlife Foundation Demonstration Site Project; Emeritus, Phi Delta Kappa **MH:** Albert Nelson Marquis Lifetime Achievement Award (2017) **H:** Gardening; Writing; Photography **ADD:** 333 Bryn Mawr Ave, Bala Cynwyd, PA, 19004

OTT, ANDREW EDUARD, **T:** Attorney **I:** Law and Legal Services **CN:** Kamai, LLC **DOB:** 09/23/1962 **PB:** Vancouver **SC:** BC/Canada **PT:** Eduard Karl Ott; Elfriede Marie (Petryc) Ott **MS:** Single **CH:** Mehcila; Aiden **ED:** JD, School of Law, Seattle University, With Honors (1989); Honorary PhD, University of Graz, Austria (1986); BA in English, Seattle University, With Honors (1986) **C:** Contract Attorney, Jamin, Ebell, Schmitt & Mason, Kodiak, AK (1989-Present); Contract Attorney, Lieff Cabraser Heimann & Bernstein, San Francisco, CA; Contract Attorney, Keller Rohrback, Seattle, WA; Attorney, Kamai, LLC **CR:** Consultant, Omintech Engineering, Bothell, WA (1986-2000) **CIV:** Trustee, Kodiak Arts Council; Legal Advisor, Kodiak Team Court **CW:** Actor, Musicals and Theater (1998-2000); Actor, Musicals and Theater (1995-1996); Actor, Musicals and Theater (1992-1993); Musician Community Orchestra and Jazz (1990-2000) **AW:** Honoree, Marquis Who's Who (2000) **MEM:** Lions Club (1995-Present); American Bar Association **BAR:** State of Alaska (2003); U.S. District Court, District of Alaska (2003); U.S. District Court, Eastern District, State of Washington (1992); State of Washington (1990) **MH:** Albert Nelson Marquis Lifetime Achievement Award (2017) **H:** Skiing; Soccer; Bike riding; Running; Acting **BA:** 340 Mission Road, Kamai, LLC, Kodiak, AK, 96615 **URL:** http://kodiakattorney.com/profiles.php

OVERMIER, J. BRUCE, T: Professor of Psychology **I:** Education/Educational Services **CN:** University of Minnesota **ED:** PhD, University of Pennsylvania (1965); MA, Bowling Green State University (1962); AB, Kenyon College (1960) **C:** Professor, University of Minnesota (1965-2014) **CW:** Author, 5 Books; Contributor, Articles, Professional Journals **AW:** Distinguished Elder Citation, Minnesota Psychological Association (2015); John Paul Scott Distinguished Lecturer, Center for Neuroscience, Mind, & Behavior, Bowling Green, OH (2015); American Psychological Association BEA Outstanding Graduate Teaching of Psychology as a Core STEM Discipline Award (2014); Alan C Boneau Award for Outstanding Service to the Society for General Psychology (2012); Sigma Xi Distinguished Service Award, for Furthering Science and Research (2010); John P. Zubek Award Lecture, University of Manitoba (2006); American Psychological Association Inaugural Award for Distinguished Service to Psychological Science (2005); Outstanding Contributions to Psychology Award, Minnesota Psychological Association (2004); Neal E. Miller Distinguished Lecture Award, American Psychological Association Science Directorate (2004); President, International Union of Psychological Sciences (2004-2008); Outstanding Graduate Faculty Award, Minnesota Psychological Association (2003); W. Horseley Gantt Medal for Research, Pavlovian Society (2003); Outstanding Scholars of 20th Century Clifford T. Morgan Distinguished Service Award in Behavioral Neuroscience & Comparative Psychology (2001); Distinguished Lecturer, Society of the Sigma Xi National (1999-2001); President, Pavlovian Society (1995-1996); Distinguished Scholar Lecturer, Minnesota Psychological Association (1993); Elected Fellow, Society of Experimental Psychologists (1992); President, Society for Behavioral Neuroscience and Comparative Psychology (1990-1991); Doctor of Science Honoris Causa, Kenyon College (1990); Fellow, American Psychological Society (1989); Fogarty Senior International Fellowship for Advanced Study in the Health Sciences (1984); National Academy of Science Scientific Exchange Fellowship (1972); First Prize for Research, Pennsylvania Psychological Association (1965); NIH Predoctoral Fellowship, University of Pennsylvania (1963-1965); Research Fellowship in Perception and Choice Behavior, University of Pennsylvania (1962); Kenyon College Mathematics Prize (1956); Elected Fellow, American Psychology Association **MEM:** American Association for Applied & Preventative Psychology; American Association of University Professors; American Psychological Association; Board of Directors, American Psychological Association; Association for Psychological Science; Federation of Associations in Behavioral & Brain Sciences; International Association of Applied Psychology; International Brain-Gut Society; International Society for Comparative Psychology; International Behavioral Neuroscience; President, Society Midwestern Psychological Association; Charter Fellow, Minnesota Psychological Association; President, Pavlovian Society; Board of Directors, Psychology in Science Policy; Secretary-Treasurer, Psychonomic Society; Board of Governors, Psychonomic Society; Society for Comparative Cognition; Society of Experimental Psychologists; International Union of Psychological Science; International Council of Science **BA:** 75 East River Road, Psychology Department University of Minnesota, Minneapolis, MN, 55455

OWEN, CAROL THOMPSON, T: Artist **I:** Fine Art **CN:** Mount San Antonio College **DOB:** 05/10/1944 **PB:** Pasadena **SC:** CA/USA **PT:** Sumner Comer Thompson; Cordelia (Whittemore) Thompson **MS:** Married **SPN:** James Eugene Owen (7/19/1975) **CH:** Kevin Christopher; Christine Celese **ED:** MFA, Claremont Graduate University (1969); MA, California State University, Los Angeles (1967); BA, University of Redlands, With Distinction (1966); Coursework, Pasadena City College (1963) **CT:** Certified Community College Instructor, State of California **C:** Professor in Art, Mt. San Antonio College (1996-Present); Professor Emeritus, Mt. San Antonio College, Walnut, California, (1997); Director, College Art Gallery, Mt. San Antonio College (1972-1973); Instructor in Art, Mt. San Antonio College (1968-1996); Head Resident, Pitzer College (1967-1970) **CW:** Exhibitor, American Museum of Ceramic Art (2007); Solo Exhibitor, Redlands United Methodist Church (2006); Exhibitor, XIEM Clay Center (2005); Exhibitor, The Kellogg Gallery, California State Polytechnic University, Pomona (2005); Exhibitor, Multi-Media Mini Show, San Bernardino County Museum (2004); Exhibitor, Fine Arts Academy (2004); Exhibitor, City of Brea Gallery (2004); Exhibitor, The Kellogg Gallery, California State Polytechnic University, Pomona (2003); Exhibitor, "Feats of Clay XVI," Art League of Lincoln (2003); Exhibitor, Sanchez Art Center (2003); Exhibitor, Rocky Mount Arts Center, City of Rocky Mount, NC (2003); Exhibitor, "Containment," Sam Kasten Handweaver (2003); Exhibitor, Group International Exhibition, Internationale Wertbewerb Salzbrand Keramic (2002); Exhibitor, "der Handwerks Kammer Koblenz," Galerie Handwerk (2002); Exhibitor, National Juried Exhibition, Gallery 214 (Now Makeready Press Gallery) (2002); Exhibitor, Mia Tyson (2002); Exhibitor, Millard Sheets Art Center, Fairplex (2002); Exhibitor, "Abstraction," The Period Gallery in Omaha (2002); Exhibitor, "Mixed Media," The Period Gallery in Omaha (2002); Exhibitor, "Dysfunctional," Business of Art Center (Now The Manitou Art Center) (2001); Exhibitor, Esmay Fine Art Gallery (2001); Exhibitor, "Sequence 1" (2001); Exhibitor, Hillcrest Festival of Fine Arts (2001); Exhibitor, Alder Gallery (2001); Exhibitor, California State Polytechnic University, Pomona (2001); Exhibitor, Mt. San Antonio College (2001); Exhibitor, Rocky Mount Arts Center, City of Rocky Mount, North Carolina (2001); Exhibitor, TLD Design Center & Gallery (2000-2001); Exhibitor, North Tahoe Arts (2000); Exhibitor, Palos Verdes Art Center (2000); Exhibitor, Peck Gallery (2000); Exhibitor, Chiarosouro Galleries (2000); Exhibitor, San Angelo Museum of Fine Arts (2000); Exhibitor, Gallery 212 (2000); Exhibitor, Artists Unlimited, Inc. (2000); Exhibitor, UICA (2000); Exhibitor, TLCA (2000); Exhibitor, Santa Cruz Art League (2000); Exhibitor, Fine Arts Institute, San Bernardino County Museum (2000); Exhibitor, Vermont Artisan Designs (2000); Artist, "Collectible Teapots" (2000); Exhibitor, The American Ceramic Society (2000); Exhibitor Birger Sandzén Memorial Gallery (2000); Exhibitor, The Period Gallery in Omaha (1999-2003); Exhibitor, City of Brea Art Gallery (1999-2001); Exhibitor, "USA Craft" (1999); Exhibitor, Keith Gallery (1999); Exhibitor, The American Ceramic Society (1999); Exhibitor, Claremont Forum Gallery (1999); Exhibitor, Parham Gallery (1999); Exhibitor, "All Media Exhibit" (1999); Exhibitor, EarthenWorks Gallery (1999); Exhibitor, Missouri State University, Warrensburg (Now University of Central Missouri) (1999); Exhibitor, California State Polytechnic University, Pomona (1999); Exhibitor, Franklin Square Gallery (1999-2000); Exhibitor, The Judson Studios (1999-2000); Exhibitor, Festival, Art for Heaven's Sake (1998-1999); Exhibitor, Parham Gallery (1998-1999); Exhibitor, Westmoreland Arts & Heritage Festival (1998-1999); Exhibitor, Fine Art Institute Juried Show (1998-2000); Exhibitor, Riverside Art Museum (1998-2000); Exhibitor Birger Sandzén Memorial Gallery (1998); Exhibitor, Angels Gate Cultural Center (1998); Exhibitor, LA County Fair (1998); Exhibitor, Monrovia Arts Festival (1998); Exhibitor, "White & Gray," Artists Unlimited, Inc. (1998); Exhibitor, "Current Clay VII," La Jolla, California (1998); Exhibitor, The American Ceramic Society (1997); Exhibitor, San Bernardino County Museum (1996-1999); Exhibitor, "Separate Realities" (1995); Exhibitor, "The Aesthetic Process" (1993); Exhibitor, University of Redlands (1992); Exhibitor, Mt. San Antonio College (1991); Commissioned Artist, Ceramic Mural, University of Redlands (1991); Exhibitor, University of Redlands (1988); Exhibitor, University of Redlands (1978); Exhibitor, Covina Public Library, City of Covina California (1971); Exhibitor, University of Redlands (1970); Exhibitor, The American Ceramic Society (1969); Exhibitor, University of Redlands (1966); Exhibitor, University of Redlands (1965); Exhibitor, University of Redlands (1964); Collected Artist, Redlands Art Association; Exhibitor, Ink and Clay Exhibitions; Exhibitor, Tampa Florida Black Heritage Festival **AW:** Recipient, Honorable Mention, Millard Sheets Art Center, Fairplex (2002); Recipient, Third Place Monetary Award, City Of Brea Art Gallery (2000); Recipient, Honorarium For Teapots, UICA (2000); Recipient, Grand Prize, Parham Gallery (1999); Recipient, Chapter Monetary Award, The American Ceramic Society (1999); Recipient, Honorable Mention, San Bernardino County Museum (1999); Recipient, Honorable Mention, San Bernardino County Museum (1998); Recipient, Jack L. Conte Design Consultant Purchase Award, Westmoreland Arts & Heritage Festival (1998); Recipient, Past President Monetary Award (1997); Recipient, Honorable Mention, San Bernardino County Museum (1996) **MEM:** Design Division, The American Ceramic Society; California Scholarship Federation; Friends of Huntington Library, The Huntington Library, Art Collections, and Botanical Gardens; LACMA; Redlands Art Association; Sigma Tau Delta **MH:** Albert Nelson Marquis Lifetime Achievement Award (2017) **PA:** Republican **RE:** Presbyterian **ADD:** 534 S Hepner Ave, Covina, CA, 91723

OWEN, CYNTHIA CAROL, I: Oil & Energy **DOB:** 10/16/1943 **PB:** Fort Worth **SC:** TX/USA **PT:** Charlie Bounds Rhoads; Bernice Vera (Nunley) Rhoads **MS:** Married **SPN:** John Wayne Napier (11/26/2002); John Edward White (1/1/1988, Divorced 1991); Franklin Earl Owen (10/20/1961, Divorced 1987) **CH:** Jeffrey Wayne; Valeria Ann; Carol Darlena; Pamela Kay **ED:** Diplomate, Stratford Career Institute (2011); BBA in Management, University of Texas at Arlington (1981); Coursework, Tarrant County College (1974-1977) **CT:** Certified Keypuncher, Commercial College (1963) **C:** Project Manager, Square D, Schneider Electric, Carrollton, TX (1982-2009); Bookkeeper, Secretary, CB Service, Fort Worth, TX (1978-1982); Executive Secretary to Vice President, Sales, Pangburn Company, Inc., Fort Worth, TX (1972-1978); Secretary, Electro Tech Corporation, Mineral-Wells, TX (1967-1968); Keypunch Operator, Cantex Inc, Mineral-Wells, TX (1966-1967); Consultant, Natural Health Consultant **AW:** Marquis Who's Who Lifetime Achievement Award **MEM:** NAFE; National Organization for Women; AAUW **MH:** Albert Nelson Marquis Lifetime Achievement Award (2017) **H:** Collecting Barbie dolls; Collecting coins **RE:** Baptist **ADD:** 1221 Pine Ridge Road, Roanoke, TX, 76262-6441

PAKULA, HANNAH C., T: Writer **I:** Writing and Editing **DOB:** 07/23/1933 **PB:** Omaha **SC:** NE/USA **PT:** Mayer Louis Cohn; Gertrude (Marks) Cohn **MS:** Widow **SPN:** Alan J. Pakula (2/17/1973, Deceased);

Robert L. Boorstin (Deceased) **CH:** Anna; Robert O.; Louis C. **ED:** BA, Southern Methodist University (1956); Coursework, Université Paris-Sorbonne (1953-1954); Coursework, Wellesley College (1951-1953) **C:** Writer **CW:** Author, "The Last Empress: Madame Chiang Kai-shek and the Birth of Modern China" (2009); Author, "An Uncommon Woman: The Empress Frederick" (1995); Author, "The Last Romantic: A Biography of Queen Marie of Roumania" (1985) **AW:** Recipient, Eleanor Roosevelt Val-Kill Medal for Human Rights (1999) **MEM:** Human Rights Watch; Council on Foreign Relations; Former Chairman, Freedom to Write Committee, PEN America; The Century Association **MH:** Distinguished Humanitarian (2017) **PA:** Democrat **RE:** Jewish **ADD:** 160 E 72nd St Fl 6, New York, NY, 10021

PALMER, DONALD ALAN, T: Distinguished Research Scientist **I:** Research **CN:** Oak Ridge National Laboratories **DOB:** 08/12/1943 **PB:** Perth **SC:** WA/Australia **PT:** Alan George Palmer; Glynora Mary (Cooke) Palmer **MS:** Married **SPN:** Linda F. Barbier (2/2017); Maryann Carol Young (6/3/1972, Divorced 10/1996) **CH:** Christine Michelle; Carolyn Marie; David Andrew **ED:** PhD, University of Western Australia (1970); BS, University of Western Australia, With Honors (1966) **C:** Senior Research Scientist, Oak Ridge National Laboratory (1979-2007); Research Associate, Goethe-Universitat Frankfurt am Main (1972-1979); Postdoctoral Fellow, University at Buffalo (1971-1972); Research Assistant, Australian National University (1969-1970) **CR:** Fellow, The International Association for the Properties of Water and Steam (2008-Present); Chairman, Fifth International Symposium on Hydrothermal Reaction Symposium, Gatlinburg, TN (1997); Adjunct Professor of Geology, University of Nebraska–Lincoln (1997); Consultant TDB Working Group, National Education Association, Paris, France **CW:** Author, "Aqueous Chemistry at High Temperatures and Pressures" (2008); Editor-in-Chief, "Journal of Solution Chemistry" (2003-2009); Contributor, Journal of Chemical Engineering Data; Contributor, Geochimica et Cosmochimica Acta; Contributor, Journal of Solution Chemistry **AW:** Technology Achievement Award, Lockheed Martin Corporation (1995); Paul Cohen Memorial Award, International Water Conferences (1992) **MEM:** Chairman, Physical Chemical Working Group, International Association for the Properties of Water and Steam (1996-1999) **H:** Golf; Gardening; Travel; Reading **ADD:** 38 Deerfield Road, Hilton Head Island, SC, 29926

PANDEY, RAMESH C., T: Chemist **I:** Pharmaceuticals **CN:** Ramed Pharmaceuticals, Inc. **DOB:** 11/05/1938 **PB:** Nagaon **SC:** India **PT:** Gauri Dutt Pandey; Jivanti Pandey **ED:** PhD, University of Poona (1965); Junior Research Fellow, National Chemical Laboratory (1960-1964); MSc, Deen Dayal Upadhyaya Gorakhpur University (1960); BSc, University of Allahabad (1958) **C:** Chairman Director, Ramed Pharmaceuticals, Inc. (2009-Present); Chairman, G.D. Pandey Ayurvedic University (2001-Present); President, G.D. Pandey Ayurvedic University (2001-Present); Chairman, Xetapharm Inc. (1996-2007); Chief Executive Officer, Xetapharm Inc. (1996-2007); President, Xetapharm Inc. (1996-2007); Chairman, Xechem International Inc. (1994-2007); Chief Executive Officer, Xechem International Inc. (1994-2007); President, Xechem International Inc. (1994-2007); President, Xechem, Inc. (1990-2003); Chief Executive Officer, Xechem, Inc. (1990-2003); Director, Technology Development, Xechem, Inc. (1990-2003); President, Xechem, Inc. (1984-1990); Senior Scientist, Abbott

(1983-1984); Head, Chemical Section, Frederick Cancer Research Facility, National Cancer Institute (1982-1983); Senior Scientist, Fermentation Program, Frederick Cancer Research Facility, National Cancer Institute (1977-1982); Visiting Scientist, University of Illinois (1972-1977); Scientist, Organic Division, National Chemical Laboratory (1970-1972); Research Associate, Department of Chemistry, University of Illinois (1967-1970); Research Officer, National Chemical Laboratory (1965-1967) **CR:** Member, Life Science Advisory Board, NJ Tech Council (1999-Present); Member, Statewide Advisory Committee, Board of Managers, New Jersey Agricultural Experimental Station, Rutgers, The State University of New Jersey (2002-2010); Founder, G.D. Padney Ayurvedic University (2001); Consultant, LyphoMed, Inc. (1984-1990); Visiting Professor, Waksman Institute, Rutgers, The State University of New Jersey (1984-1986); Consultant, School of Medicine, Washington University in St. Louis (1976-1985) **CIV:** Member, Work Force Investment Board, Middlesex County (1999-2005); Member, Advisory Committee for Science Transfer and Science Technology Program, Middlesex County College (1999-2001); Vice Chairman, Republican Committeeman, Highland Park, NJ; Life Member, Republican Senator Inner Circle **CW:** Editorial Board Member, "International Journal of Antibiotics" (1986-Present); Presenter, Over 100 National and International, Conferences, Seminars; Contributor, Over 95 Scientific Papers; Contributor, Several Books **AW:** Honoree, Paul Harris Fellow, Rotary International (1996-Present); Lifetime Achievement Award, Republic of Mauritius (2009); Guest of Honor, All India Ayurvedic Congress – Centenary Celebrations, New Delhi, India (2009); UANA Lifetime Achievement Award for Outstanding Contributions to Development and Support of Uttarakhand Community (2008); Most Outstanding Asian American of Indian Community, Asian American Heritage Council (2008); Honoree, Named Readers Choice Chief Executive Officer of the Year, CBSMarketwatch.com (2006); Professor Priyadaranjan Ray Memorial Award, Indian Chemical Society (2006); Honoree, Vaidya Ratna (2004) **MEM:** President, New Brunswick Club, Rotary International (1999-2000); Fellow, Royal Society of Tropical Medicine and Hygiene; Fellow, American Society for Microbiology; Member Emeritus, American Chemical Society; Fellow Emeritus, American Institute of Chemists; American Society of Health-System Pharmacists; The American Society of Pharmacognosy; American Association for the Advancement of Science; New York Academy of Sciences; American Council for Medicinally Active Plants, Inc.; Indian Science Congress Association; Founder, National Ayurvedic Medical Association; Executive Trustee, National Ayurvedic Medical Association **MH:** Albert Nelson Marquis Lifetime Achievement Award (2017) **BA:** 30 S Adelaide Ave Unit 8M, Ramed Pharm. Inc, Highland Park, NJ, 08904 **ADD:** 30 S Adelaide Ave Apt 8M, Highland Park, NJ, 08904

PANT PAI, NITIKA, T: Associate Professor **I:** Education/Educational Services **CN:** McGill University **PB:** Allahabad **SC:** India **MS:** Married **SPN:** Madhukar Pai **CH:** One Child **ED:** Postdoctoral Fellowship, Clinical Trials, McGill University, Montreal, Canada (2006-2009); PhD, University of California, Berkeley, CA (2006); MPH, University of California, Berkeley, CA (2003); Graduate Research Assistant, Epidemiology, University of California, Berkeley, CA (2001-2006); Extern, Critical Care Medicine, Sundaram Medical Foundation Hospital, Madras, India (1999); Intern, Surgery, Obstetrics & Gynecology, Dermatology, Psychiatry, MLN Medical College, SRN Hospital, Affiliated Hospitals, Allahabad, India

(1998-1999); Bachelor of Medicine and Bachelor of Surgery, Motilal Nehru Medical College, University of Allahabad, Allahabad, India (1998) **CT:** Professional Certification and Licensure, Medical Council of India, India (1999-Present) **C:** Associate Professor, Medicine, McGill University, Montreal, Canada (2015-Present); Research Scientist, Division of Clinical Epidemiology, The Research Institute of the McGill University Health Centre (2009-Present); Associate Member, Division of Epidemiology, McGill University Health Centre (2009-Present); Coordinator, Departmental Seminar Series, Division of Clinical Epidemiology, McGill University Health Centre (2012-2014, 2010); Assistant Professor, Medicine, McGill University, Montreal, Canada (2009-2015); Registrar, General Surgery, Southern Railway Hospital, Madras, India (2000-2001) **CR:** Visiting Professor, Epidemiology, PHFI, New Delhi, India (2010-Present); Visiting Faculty, Obstetrics and Gynecology, Mahatma Gandhi Institute of Medical Sciences, Sevagram, India (2008-Present); Clinical Preceptorship, Prevention Training Center, STD Clinic, San Francisco, CA (2000-2001); Junior House Officer, Sundaram Medical Foundation, Madras, India (1999) **CIV:** Volunteer, Clinical Observation, Clinical Research in Incarcerated and Homeless Populations, Division of HIV/AIDS UCSF Positive Health Program, San Francisco General Hospital, San Francisco, CA (2001-2006) **CW:** Editorial Board Member, Journal of Evidence Based Medicine (2016-Present); HIV AIDS Clinical Section Reviewer, F1000 Research (2015-Present); Guest Editor, PLoS Medicine (2014-Present); Editorial Board Member, Annals of Medical and Health Sciences Research (2014-Present); Experts Board Member, Asian Pacific Journal of Tropical Diseases (2013-Present); Editorial Board Member, Science OPEN (2013-Present); Academic Editor, HIV Section, PLoS One (2008-Present); Invited Lead Guest Editor, AIDS Research and Treatment (2013); Lecturer in Field; Presenter in Field; Coordinator, Workshops; Ad Hoc Reviewer, Professional Journals; Reviewer, Grants; Invited Panelist in Field; Contributor, Conferences; Contributor, Numerous Articles, Professional Journals; Contributor, Chapters, Books **AW:** Canadian Stars in Global Health Award, Grand Challenges Canada, Canada (2013, 2011); MGH Foundation Award for Research Excellence, McGill University Health Centre (2013); Accelerating Science Award Program Award, Google, PLoS and Wellcome Trust, USA (2013); Maude Abbott Award for Excellence, McGill University, Canada (2013); Chanchalani Global Health Research Award, McMaster University, Canada (2012); Deanne Nesbitt Award - Distinction - Research Excellence, The Research Institute of the McGill University Health Centre, Canada (2009-2011); Young Investigator Award, Distinction for HIV/AIDS, Fifth IAS Conference, South Africa (2009); Recipient, Numerous Grants **MEM:** American Society For Microbiology (2016-Present); Canadian Chapter, International Union against Sexually Transmitted Infections (2015-Present); Innovations Committee, Department of Medicine, McGill University (2015-Present); American Association for Clinical Chemistry (2014-Present); Committee for Global Health Concentration, Department of Epidemiology, Occupational Health and Biostatistics (2013-Present); Canadian AIDS Society (2013-Present); European Society of Clinical Microbiology and Infectious Diseases (2013-Present); Research Institute of the MUHC Studentship Competition Committee (2010-Present); American Public Health Association (2010-Present); McGill Student Bursary Competition Committee, Faculty of Medicine (2010-Present); IEA (2007-Present);

Canadian Association for HIV Research (2006-Present); CSEB (2006-Present); CIHR Canadian HIV Trials Network (2006-Present); International Association of Providers of AIDS Care (2005-Present); International AIDS Society (2003-Present); Admissions Committee for MPH, Department of Epidemiology, Biostatistics & Occupational Health (2012-2014); IDSA (2010-2015); Canadian Public Health Association (2009-2011); Society for Clinical Trials (2006-2015); Society for Epidemiologic Research (2003-2012) **ADD:** 4685 Avenue Connaught, Montreal, QC, Canada, H4B 1X5 **URL:** http://nitikapantpai.com/

PAPE, PATRICIA ANN, T: Social Worker, Consultant **I:** Social Work **CN:** Pape & Associates **DOB:** 08/02/1940 **PB:** Aurora **SC:** IL/USA **PT:** Robert Frank Grover; Helen Louise (Hanks) Grover **CH:** Scott Allen; Debra Lynn **ED:** MSW, George Williams College (1979); BA in Sociology, Northwestern University (1962) **CT:** Certified Addictions Counselor, State of Illinois; Licensed Clinical Social Worker, State of Illinois; Licensed School Social Worker, State of Illinois; Employee Assistance Professional; Group Psychotherapist; Instructor, Minnesota Couple Communication Program; Instructor, Family Development **C:** Executive Director, Dupage Intergenerational Village, Wheaton, IL (1998-Present); Christian Counselor (1995-Present); Divorce Mediator (1993-Present); President, Pape & Associates, Wheaton, IL (1981-Present); Private Practice, Family Counseling (1979-Present); Instructor, National College of Education, Lombard, IL (1979-1998); Instructor, Introduction to Addictions (1979-1995); Program Director, College of Dupage, Glen Ellyn, IL (1979-1988); Director, Alcoholism Counselor Training Program, College of DuPage, Glen Ellyn, IL (1982-1987); Consultant, Lutheran Social Services of Illinois, Downers Grove, IL (1979-1982); Director, The Abbey Alcoholism Treatment Center, Winfield, IL (1980-1981); Coordinator, Community Resources, DuPage Probation Department, Wheaton, IL (1977-1980) **CR:** Chicago Affiliate, Employee Assistance Program (1982-Present); Consultant, Lutheran Society Services of Illinois (1979-1982) **CIV:** Member, Alcohol and Drug Task Force, Illinois Synod Lutheran Church of America, Chicago, IL (1985-Present); Active, St. Paul's Lutheran Church **CW:** Author, "Shedding Light on Domestic Violence" (1997); Author, "Divorce Mediation Supports Children's Rights" (1994); Author, "Issues in Assessment and Intervention with Alcohol and Drug-Abusing Women" (1993); Author, "Adult Children of Alcoholics: Uncovering Family Scripts and Other Barriers to Recovery" (1992); Author, "Does Gender Make a Difference?" (1992); "Author, "Making a Difference in Someone's Life: Children of Alcoholics in the Classroom" (1991); Author, "The Recovering Woman" (1990); Author, "Family Business" (1990); Author, "Your Boss is Not Really Your Parent!" (1989); Author, "CD/ACOA Women in Recovery, A Two-Year Treatment Model, Part II" (1989); Author, "CD/ACOA Women in Recovery, A Two-Year Treatment Model, Part I" (1989); Author, "Employee Assistance Programs and Chemically Dependent Women" (1988); Author, "Superwomen and Alcohol - The Unrecognized Link" (1988); Author, "Women and Alcohol: The Disgraceful Discrepancy" (1987); Author, "Removing the Shroud from Female Alcoholism" (1985); Contributor, Articles, Professional Journals, Workshops; Writer, Curriculum, Alcohol and Substance Abuse Program, College of DuPage; Author, "Relapse Prevention with Female Employee Assistance Program" **AW:** Social Worker of the Year, Fox Valley District (1998); Woman of the Year, Entrepreneur Women In Management, Oak Brook, IL (1986) **MEM:** Women's Issues Committee, Association of Labor Management Administrators and Consultants on

Alcoholism (1984-Present); Association of Labor Management Administrators and Consultants on Alcoholism; Academy of Certified Social Workers; American Association of Marriage and Family Therapists; National Association of Society Workers; Women in Management; Founder, Abby Alcoholism Treatment Center **MH:** Albert Nelson Marquis Lifetime Achievement Award (2017) **BA:** 618 S West St Ste A, Pape & Assocs, Wheaton, IL, 60187

PAPICH, MARK A., T: Director of Marketing & Development for Student Life and Athletics, Director of Food Service Contracts **I:** Education/Educational Services **CN:** University of the Incarnate Word **ED:** BS in Industrial Design, University of Cincinnati (1981) **C:** Director, Marketing and Development for Student Life and Athletics, University of the Incarnate Word; Food Services Contract Director, University of the Incarnate Word; Inner-Mathematics Director, University of the Incarnate Word **CR:** Volleyball Coach, U.S. Junior Olympic Program (1985-Present); Industrial Designer, John Frassinito and Associates, San Antonio, TX (1983); IBM (1980-1983); Private Consulting Practice; Director, Wellness Center, University of the Incarnate Word **CIV:** Director, Texas Junior Volleyball Club, United States Volleyball Association Group (1990-Present); Snackback; Volleyball Coach, U.S. Department of Defense **AW:** Outstanding Male Coach in Youth and Junior Division, United States Volleyball Association (1997); National Champion, Junior Olympic (1996); National Finalist, Junior Olympic (1995); Top Junior Olympic Team, United States Volleyball Association (1993); South West Regional Coach of the Year, United States Volleyball Association **MEM:** Board of Directors, Alamo Heights Rotary; Economic Develop Committee, Converse, TX **MH:** Albert Nelson Marquis Lifetime Achievement Award (2017) **BA:** 4301 Broadway, Campus Box 308, University of the Incarnate Word, San Antonio, TX, 78209 **ADD:** 5915 Woodridge Cove, San Antonio, TX, 78249

PARK, LEE CRANDALL, T: Psychiatrist (Retired) **I:** Medicine & Health Care **DOB:** 07/15/1926 **PB:** Washington, D.C. **SC:** DC/USA **PT:** Lee I. Park; Alice (Crandall) Park **MS:** Married **SPN:** Mary Woodfill Banerjee (4/27/1985); Barbara Ann Merrick (7/1/1953) **CH:** Thomas Joseph; Jeffrey Rawson; Stephen K. (Stepchild); Scott (Stepchild) **ED:** Resident in Psychiatry, Henry Phipps Psychiatric Clinic, The Johns Hopkins Hospital (1955-1959); Psychiatry Resident, U.S. Navy Hospital, Oakland, CA (1953-1954); Medicine Intern, The Johns Hopkins Hospital (1952-1953); MD, Johns Hopkins University (1952); BS in Zoology, Yale University (1948); Diploma, The Putney School (1944) **CT:** Diplomate, National Board of Medical Examiners; Diplomate, American Board of Psychiatry and Neurology, Inc. **C:** Honorary Staff, Department of Medicine, The Johns Hopkins Hospital (1991-2016); Staff, Department of Medicine, The Johns Hopkins Hospital (1970-1991); Member, Departmental Council, Henry Phipps Psychiatric Clinic, The Johns Hopkins Hospital (1972-1975); Director, Psychiatric Outpatient Services and Community Psychiatry Program, Henry Phipps Psychiatric Clinic, The Johns Hopkins Hospital (1972-1974); Assistant Psychiatrist, Henry Phipps Psychiatric Clinic, The Johns Hopkins Hospital (1955-1959) **CR:** Associate Professor Emeritus, Johns Hopkins University (2008-Present); Private Practice in Psychiatry (1964-2015); Faculty in Psychiatry, Johns Hopkins University (1959-2008); Treasurer, Maryland Interdisciplinary Council for Children and Adolescents (1980-1987); Member, Maryland Interdisciplinary Council for Children and Adolescents (1978-1998); Staff, Sheppard Pratt

Health System (1974-2000); Associate Professor, Johns Hopkins University (1971-2008); Executive Board, Seton Psychiatric Institute (1970-1973); Co-director, Time-Limited Psychotherapy Research Grant, National Institute of Mental Health (1969-1973); Attending Staff, Seton Psychiatric Institute (1966-1973); Physician in Charge of Psychiatric Services, Student Health Service, Johns Hopkins University (1961-1973); Co-principal Investigator, Outpatient Study of Drug-Set Interaction, Psychopharmacology Research Branch, National Institute of Mental Health (1960-1968); Principal Investigator, Outpatient Study of Drug-Set Interaction, Psychopharmacology Research Branch, National Institute of Mental Health (1960-1968) **MIL:** Lieutenant, Medical Corps, United States Naval Reserve (1953-1955); Staff Psychiatrist, Naval Hospital Camp Pendleton (1955); Division Psychiatrist, First Marine Division, Republic of Korea Navy **CW:** Co-author, "A Primer on Mental Disorders: A Guide for Educators, Families and Students" (2001); Contributor, Articles, Professional Journals; Contributor, Chapters, Books **AW:** Psychiatry Research Fellow, Johns Hopkins University (1955-1959); Fellow, American Association for the Advancement of Science; Distinguished Lifetime Fellow, American Psychiatric Association; Letter of Appreciation for Outstanding Performance of Duty, Commanding Officer, United States Navy; Distinguished Lifetime Fellow, American Psychiatric Association **MEM:** District Deputy President General, General Society War of 1812 (2017-Present); General Surgeon, The General Society Sons of the Revolution (2012-2015); Surgeon General, General Society War of 1812 (2011-2017); Surgeon General, Sons of the American Revolution (2009-2011); Governor, Maryland Section, National Society Sons and Daughters of the Pilgrims (2006-2008); Surgeon General, National Huguenot Society (2005-2008); President, Maryland Foundation for Psychiatry, Inc. (2000-2003); Board of Directors, Maryland Foundation for Psychiatry, Inc. (1995-2003); Psychiatric Research Network, American Psychiatric Association (1994-2002); Assembly Member, American Psychiatric Association (1983-1993); President, The Maryland Psychiatric Society, Inc. (1978-1979); American Association of University Professors; American Medical Association; The Saint Nicholas Society of the City of New York; The Ancient and Honorable Mechanical Company of Baltimore; Baltimore County Medical Association; Baltimore City Medical Society; MedChi, The Maryland State Medical Society; The Group Therapy Network; The New York Academy of Sciences; Society for Psychotherapy Research; Maryland Association of Private Practice Psychiatrists; American Association of Private Practice Psychiatrists; American College of Neuropsychopharmacology; American Society for Adolescent Psychiatry; International Society for the Study of Personality Disorders; American Psychosomatic Society; St. George's Society of Maryland; Sons of Union Veterans of the Civil War; Descendants of Mexican War Veterans; General Society of Colonial Wars; The Avery Memorial Association; The Denison Society, Denison Homestead Museum; Crandall Family Association; VanKouwenhoven-Conover Family Association; The Van Voorhees Association; The Parke Society; The Yale Club of New York City; Maryland Branch, Chevy Chase Country Club; The Metropolitan Club of The City of Washington; The Johns Hopkins Club; Farmington Country Club; Phi Beta Pi; Social Register Association **MH:** Albert Nelson Marquis Lifetime Achievement Award (2017) **H:** Hiking **RE:** Episcopalian **ADD:** 308 Tunbridge Rd, Baltimore, MD, 21212 **URL:** http://leecrandallparkmd.net/

PARK, MICHAEL JI SUNG, I: Business Management/Business Services **ED:** Bachelor's Degree, Leeward Community College (1983) **AW:** Recipient, Award for Dedication to Korean Community, Hawaii Korean Community Association

PARKER, KATHLEEN DAKOTA, T: Founder (Retired) **I:** Business Management/Business Services **CN:** Parker Communication **DOB:** 05/23/1948 **PB:** Ortonville **SC:** MN/USA **PT:** L. R. Parker; Barbara Severin (Deceased) **MS:** Single **SPN:** John B. Parker (Deceased) **CH:** One Daughter **ED:** Postgraduate Coursework, Harvard University (1990); MS in Journalism, Columbia University (1973); East Asia Fellow, Graduate School of Journalism (1972-1973); BA in East Asian Studies, Barnard College (1970) **C:** Founder, Parker Communications, Parker Pacific Communications (1999); Co-Founder, Endangered Species Recovery Council (1998-2009); Owner, Delta Communications, Station KHYL-FM and KAHI-AM, Sacramento, CA (1986-1994); Owner, Operator, Mountain Communications, Station KLZE-FM (Cumulus Media Inc.), Mountain View, CA (1986-1987); Owner, Operator, Desert Communications, Station KXTZ-FM, Las Vegas, NV (1984-1994); Owner, Operator, Parker Communications, Station KTCZ-FM and KTCJ-AM, Minneapolis, MN (1984-1994); Owner, Operator, Station KIKI Licensing Corporation, Tokyo, Japan (1981-1989); Owner, Operator, Island Communications, Station KIKI-AMand KpIG Fm Honolulu, Hawaii (1980-1989); Owner, Operator Station KOWL-AM, Inc. (D&H Broadcasting LLC), South Lake Tahoe, CA (1979-1983); Co-Founder, Parker Communications (1978-1993); President, Pacific Communications, South Lake Tahoe, CA (1979-1982); Reporter, Anchor woman, Station KFMB-TV (Midwest Television, Inc.), San Diego, CA (1975-1979); Journalist, CBS Network News (CBS Broadcasting Inc.), Los Angeles, CA (1974); Writer, Associated Press, New York, NY (1973-1974); Co-Founder, Global Nonprofit for Endangered Species; Co-Founder, Boutique Radio Station Group **CIV:** City 97 City Sampler, Radio Station Raised Over 50 Million Dollars for Charity; Past Board of Directors, Minnesota Zoological Society **CW:** Author, "LionessWithin" **AW:** East Asian Fellow, Columbia University School of Journalism **MEM:** Board Member, ChefsBest; Leadership Council, Barnard College; Board Member and Learning Officer for Young President Organization Gold, San Diego, CA; Explorers Club **H:** Collecting art; Writing; Walking **BA:** 7660 H Fay Avenue 803, La Jolla, CA, 92037 **ADD:** 7660 Fay Ave Ste H PMB 803, La Jolla, CA, 92037-4843

PARRON-RAGLAND, DELORES L., T: Federal Agency Administrator (Retired) **I:** Social Work **DOB:** 01/14/1944 **PB:** Red Bank **SC:** NJ/USA **PT:** James W. Parron (Deceased); Ruth Pitts Parron **MS:** Married **SPN:** Sherman L. Ragland **ED:** PhD in Philosophy, The Catholic University of America (1977); MSW, The Catholic University of America (1968); BA, Georgian Court College (Now Georgian Court University) (1966) **C:** Scientific Advisor for Capacity Development, National Institutes of Health, Bethesda, MD (2001-2007); Deputy Assistant Secretary for Planning and Evaluation, U.S. Department of Health & Human Services, Washington, D.C. (1999-2001); Associate Director, National Institute of Mental Health, National Institutes of Health, Rockville, MD (1983-1999); Senior Program Officer, Institute of Medicine (Now National Academy of Medicine), National Academy of Sciences, Washington, D.C. (1978-1983); Social Science Analyst, Presidential Commission on Mental Health, Washington, D.C. (1977-1978); Assistant Professor, Department of Psychiatry, Howard University College of Medicine, Washington, D.C. (1971-1978); Psychiatric Social Worker, Hillcrest Children's Center (Now Hillcrest Children and Family Center), Washington, D.C. (1969-1971) **CIV:** Trustee, Georgian Court College (Now Georgian Court University), Lakewood, NJ (1996-2001); Trustee, Center for the Advancement of Health, Washington, D.C. (1995-2001); Member, Walter Reed Society, Inc., Bethesda, MD **AW:** Distinguished Alumnae Award, Georgian Court University (2008); Award, American Psychological Association (2003); Distinguished Alumnae Award, The Catholic University of America (1978); National Association of Social Workers Foundation Honor as a NASW Social Work Pioneer in Recognition of Exceptional Contributions to the Profession and its Ability to Meet the Needs of All People **MEM:** Fellow, National Academy of Public Administration; National Association of Social Workers; American Psychological Association **MH:** Albert Nelson Marquis Lifetime Achievement Award (2017); Distinguished Humanitarian (2017) **RE:** Roman Catholic **ADD:** 1006 Heartfields Dr, Silver Spring, MD, 20904

PARTENHEIMER, DEBORAH DENSLOW, T: Primary School Educator (Retired) **I:** Education/Educational Services **DOB:** 05/02/1947 **PB:** Philadelphia **SC:** PA/USA **PT:** Merrill Tracy Denslow, Jr.; Margaret (Aiman) Denslow **MS:** Married **SPN:** Wayne Partenheimer (3/13/2010); James Tracy Grey, III (11/24/1972, Divorced 12/1980) **CH:** Sarah Elizabeth **ED:** MA in Educational Administration, Gwynedd Mercy University, Gwynedd, PA (2005); MA, Marygrove College, Detroit, MA (2000); BS, Gwynedd Mercy University, Gwynedd, PA (1971) **C:** Teacher, Willingsboro Township Public Schools (1971-2012) **CR:** Educational Adviser, National Constitution Center, Philadelphia, PA (2002-Present); Member, Horticulture Program, Barnes Foundation (2014); Board of Directors, Pennsylvania State South Jersey (2014); Master Gardener, Camden, NJ (2013); Member, Task Force for Reorganization, Morrisville School District (1991-1992); Union Representative, Burlington County Education Association, Willingboro, NJ (1981-1982) **CIV:** Judge, City Gardens Contest, Pennsylvania Horticultural Society, Philadelphia, PA (2002); Assistant Secretary, Treasurer, Morrisville Municipal Authority, Morrisville Borough, PA (2001); Member, Board of Directors, Morrisville Free Library, Morrisville Borough, PA (1988-2001); Chairman, Morrisville Municipal Authority, Morrisville Borough, PA (1996-2000); Assistant Secretary, Treasurer, Morrisville Municipal Authority, Morrisville Borough, PA (1995-1996); Chairman, Morrisville Municipal Authority, Morrisville Borough, PA (1994-1995); President, Borough Council, Morrisville Borough, PA (1992-1994); Member, Borough Council, Morrisville Borough, PA (1988-1994); Secretary, Board of Directors, Morrisville Free Library, Morrisville Borough, PA (1988-1990); Committeewoman, First Ward Morrisville Republican Committee, Morrisville Borough, PA (1986-1998); Borough Chairman, Morrisville Borough, American Cancer Society, Inc. (1986-1987); Republican Candidate, Borough Council, Morrisville Borough, PA (1986); Member, Morrisville Municipal Authority, Morrisville Borough, PA **CW:** Contributor, Articles, Magazines **MEM:** Board of Directors, Bucks County Boroughs Association (1989-Present); Professional Development Committee, Petroleum Marketers Association of America (2000-2001); President, Bucks County Boroughs Association (1992-1993); Vice President, Bucks County Boroughs Association (1990-1992); Alternate Union Representative, Willingboro Education Association (1988-1989); Secretary, Board of Directors, Mercer County Chapter, Parents Without Partners (1982-1984); Union Representative, Willingboro Education Association (1981-1982); Member, Board of Directors, Mercer County Chapter, Parents Without Partners (1981-1982); National Education Association, New Jersey Education Association **MH:** Albert Nelson Marquis Lifetime Achievement Award (2017) **H:** Swimming; Sailing **RE:** Presbyterian **ADD:** 244 Windsor Ave, Haddonfield, NJ, 08033

PARTRIDGE, MARK VAN BUREN, T: Managing Partner **I:** Law and Legal Services **CN:** Partridge Partners PC **DOB:** 10/16/1954 **PB:** Rochester **SC:** MN/USA **PT:** John V.B. Partridge; Constance (Brainerd) Partridge **MS:** Married **SPN:** Mary Roberta Moffitt (4/30/1983) **CH:** Caitlin; Lindsay; Christopher **ED:** JD, Harvard University (1981); BA, University of Nebraska (1978) **C:** Managing Partner, Partridge Partners, PC (2010-Present); Executive Committee, Pattishall, McAuliffe, Newbury, Hilliard & Geraldson, LLP (2003-2010); Partner, Pattishall, McAuliffe, Newbury, Hilliard & Geraldson, LLP (1988-2010); Associate, Pattishall, McAuliffe, Newbury, Hilliard & Geraldson, LLP, Chicago, IL (1981-1988) **CR:** Arbitrator, Mediator, American Arbitration Association (2008-Present); Mediator, International Trademark Association Panel of Neutrals (2005-Present); Neutral National Arbitration Forum, Intellectual Property Mediation and Arbitration Panel (2004-Present); Panelist, World Intellectual Property Organization, Domain Name Dispute Resolution Service (1999-Present); Mediator, Northern District if Illinois Voluntary Mediation Program (1997-Present); Adjunct Professor, John Marshall Law School, Chicago, IL (1987-Present); Adjunct Professor, University of New Hampshire (2012-2016); Arbitrator, Mediator, American Arbitration Associate (2007-2016); Cook County Mandatory Arbitration Program (1989-2003); Vice President, Harvard Legal Aid Bureau (1980-1981); Board Advisor, Northwest Law School, Journal of Technology and Intellectual Property **CW:** Advisory Board, IP Litigator (1995-Present); Author, Trademark and Copyright Litigation, Oxford University Press (2011); Author, "Alternate Dispute Resolution: An Essential Competency for Lawyers," Oxford University Press (2009); Author, Guiding Rights Trademarks, Copyright and the Internet, iUniverse (2003); Editorial Board Member, The Trademark Reporter (1994-1997); Contributor, Articles to Professional Journals **AW:** Listee, World Trademark Review 1000, World Trademark Review (1981) **BAR:** United States Court of Appeals for the First Circuit (2003); United States Court of Appeals for the Third Circuit (1998); United States Court of Appeals for the Fifth Circuit (1993); United States Court of Appeals for the Seventh Circuit (1992); United States Court of Appeals for the Fourth Circuit (1986); United States District Court for the Eastern District of Michigan (1983); Illinois (1981); United States District Court for the Northern District of Illinois (1981) **MH:** Albert Nelson Marquis Lifetime Achievement Award (2017) **H:** Writing; Music; Genealogy; Travel; Internet **BA:** 321 N Clark St Ste 720, Partridge Partners PC, Chicago, IL, 60654

PATEL, SHIL , I: Pharmaceuticals **ED:** PhD, Hertfordshire (1997) **C:** Senior Director, Eisai, Inc. (2016-Present) **CW:** 60+ First Author Publications

PATTILLO, MANNING MASON, T: President Emeritus **I:** Education/Educational Services **CN:** Oglethorpe University **DOB:** 10/11/1919 **PB:** Charlottesville **SC:** VA/USA **PT:** Manning Mason Pattillo; Margaret (Camblos) Pattillo **MS:** Single **SPN:** Martha A. Crawford (6/8/1946, Deceased) **CH:** Manning Mason, III (Deceased); Martha

Crawford; John Landrum **ED:** LLD, Oglethorpe University (1994); DCL, The University of the South (1993); LHD, Park University (1973); LHD, University of Detroit, Mercy (1968); LLD, St. John's University (1968); LittD, St. Norbert College (1967); LLD, LeMoyne College (1967); LHD, The College of New Rochelle (1967); PhD, University of Chicago (1949); AM, University of Chicago (1947); Graduate Student, University of California, Berkeley (1941-1942); BA, The University of the South, With Highest Honors (1941) **C:** Honorary Chancellor, Oglethorpe University (1988-Present); President, Oglethorpe University (1975-1988); Director of Special Projects, University of Rochester (1972-1975); Adjunct Professor, New York University (1968-1971); President, Foundation Center (1967-1971); Vice President, The Danforth Foundation (1966-1967); Associate Director, The Danforth Foundation (1964-1966); Director, Danforth Commission on Church Colleges and Universities (1962-1966); Executive Director for Education, Lilly Endowment Inc. (1961-1962); Associate Director, Lilly Endowment, Inc. (1956-1960); Associate Professor in Higher Education, University of Chicago (1949-1956) **CR:** Visiting Professor, Institute of Higher Education, University of Georgia (1988-1990); Chairman, Incentive Awards Committee, IBM (1970-1975); Consultant, Phillips Exeter Academy (1974); Advisory Committee, The Brookings Institution (1970-1971); Associate Secretary, Commission on Colleges and Universities, North Central Association of Colleges and Schools (1948-1956); Consultant, United States Air Force Academy (1952); Board of Directors, Fidelity National Bank; Consultant in Field **CIV:** Board of Visitors, Evangeline Booth College, The Salvation Army (1997-Present); Co-Director, College Consultant Network, SACS (1988-1996); Chairman, Atlanta College of Art (1984-1995); Interim President, Atlanta College of Art (1984-1995); Trustee, The University of the South (1984-1988); Executive Committee Association of Independent Colleges and Universities (1982-1986); Trustee, Independent College Funds of America (1982-1986); President, Georgia Independent College Association (1980-1981); Chairman, National Council on Philanthropy (1980); President, Georgia Independent College Association (1977); Trustee, Georgia Independent College Association (1977); President, Community Foundation of Greater Rochester (1975); Provost, St. Mary's College of Maryland (1975); Howard School Trustee, Community Foundation of Greater Rochester (1973-1975); Chairman, Board of Trustees, Park College (1972-1974); Trustee, LeMoyne College (1970-1983); Trustee, Seabury Press, ICU International Christian University (1970-1972); President's Advisory Council, Wellesley College (1969-1972); Trustee, National Council on Philanthropy (1968-1980); Trustee, Sacred Heart University (1968-1975); Board of Visitors, Kanuga Conferences Inc.; Trustee, Georgia Special Olympics; Trustee, National Association of Independent Colleges and Universities; Board of Directors, St. Martin's Episcopal School; Community Relations Commission, DeKalb County; Chairman, Community Council on the Aging, DeKalb County; Commission on Colleges, SACS; Steering Committee on Revision Accrediting Procedures, SACS; Vice-Chairman of Board, Woodruff Arts Center; Trustee, Woodruff Arts Center; Advisory Council, The American National Red Cross **MIL:** U.S. Army (1942-1946) **CW:** Author, "Oglethorpe University: A Historical Sketch" (2007); Author, "Private Higher Education in the United States" (1990); Author, "The Episcopal Church: Diagnosis and Reform" (1989); Co-Author, "Church Sponsored Higher Education in the United States" (1966); Co-Author, "Eight Hundred

Colleges Face the Future" (1965); Contributor, Articles, Professional Journals **MEM:** Director, President Branch, The English-Speaking Union; National Board of Directors, The English-Speaking Union; The Guild of Scholars of the Episcopal Church; Board of Directors, National Association of Independent Schools; National Association of Scholars; Honorary Member, Country Day School Headmasters' Association of The United States; Director, DeKalb Chamber of Commerce; Chairman, DeKalb Chamber of Commerce; Atlanta History Center; St. Andrew's Society of Atlanta; Chairman, Atlanta Chapter, American Anglican Council; President, Atlanta Chapter, The Phi Beta Kappa Society; Chairman, Atlanta Chapter, The Phi Beta Kappa Society; National Society Fellow, Atlanta Chapter, The Phi Beta Kappa Society; Kappa Sigma Fraternity; Omicron Delta Kappa; Federalist Society; President's Club, Heritage Foundation; Order of St. John **MH:** Albert Nelson Marquis Lifetime Achievement Award (2017) **RE:** Anglican **ADD:** 3747 Peachtree Road NE, Apt. 1407, Atlanta, GA, 30319

PAUL, J.J. III, T: Lawyer **I:** Law and Legal Services **CN:** Voyles Vaiana Lukemeyer Baldwin & Webb **DOB:** 10/27/1948 **PB:** New Albany **SC:** IN/USA **PT:** Jesse J. Paul, Jr.; Gyla J. Hottel Paul **ED:** JD, School of Law, Indiana University (1976); BA, Wabash College (1970) **CT:** Board Certified, DUI Defense Law **C:** Of Counsel, Voyles, Vaiana, Lukemeyer, Baldwin, & Webb (2016-Present); Principal, Voyles Zahn & Paul (1983-2016); Sole Practitioner (1980-1983); Deputy Prosecutor, Major Felony Narcotics and White Collar Crime (1979-1980); Karnowsky & Paul (1976-1978) **CR:** Lecturer, CLE Programs, Summer Sessions, Harvard Law School, NCDD (1983-Present); Dean, NCDD (2003-2004); Fellow, NCDD (2004); Founding Member and Regent, NCDD (1996-2003); Board Certification Committee, NCDD; Co-Chairman, DUI Advocacy Committee, National Association of Criminal Defense Lawyers **CW:** Author, Articles, "The Champion", National Association of Criminal Defense Lawyers; Author, Monographs, CLE Presentations in Criminal Defense, Appellate Practice, DUI Practice and Health Law **AW:** Erwin-Taylor Award, National College for DUI Defense (2006); Super Lawyers; Best Lawyers in America; Best Lawyers in Indiana; AV Rating, Martindale-Hubbell **MEM:** NCDD; National Association of Criminal Defense Lawyers; ABA; Indiana State Bar Association; Indianapolis Bar Association; NRA; American Motorcyclist Association; Porsche Club of America; Indiana Historical Society; BMW Motorcycle Owners of America; USA Table Tennis; ACLU; National Trust for Historic Preservation **BAR:** United States Court of Appeals for the Seventh Circuit (1986); Supreme Court of the United States (1980); United States District Court Northern District of Indiana (1978); United States District Court Southern District of Indiana (1976); Indiana (1976) **H:** Table tennis; Motorcycles; Photography; Travel; Gardening; Firearms; Art; Cooking **BA:** 141 E Washington St Ste 300, VZP Law, Indianapolis, IN, 46204 **URL:** https://www.facebook.com/voyleslegal/posts/10153300117318084

PAULEY, SHIRLEY STEWART, T: Vice President (Retired) **I:** Religious **CN:** Truth Alive Ministries **DOB:** 09/13/1938 **PB:** Boston **SC:** MA/USA **PT:** Charles Stewart; Nellie Stewart **MS:** Widowed **SPN:** Edward Pauley **CH:** David; Deborah **ED:** Postgraduate Studies, Boston University (1963); Postgraduate Studies, Arizona State University (1961); BA, Gordon College (1960) **C:** Vice President, Truth Alive Ministries, Dallas, TX (1995-Retirement); Secretary, Clerical Worker, GM, Westwood, MA (1962-1964); Assistant Office

Manager, Radiator Chemical Corp., Scottsdale, AZ (1960-1962); Secretary, Typist, Kelley Girl, Boston (1956-1960); Secretary, Receptionist, Atwell Co., Boston, MA (1956) **CIV:** Bible Study Leader, Prestonwood Baptist Church, Dallas Area (2006-2012); Messenger, Baptist General Convention of Texas, Fort Worth, TX (1996); Co-Youth Director, Blaney Memorial Baptist Church (1964-1966); Choir Director, Sherwood Baptist Church, Phoenix, AZ (1961-1962); Co-Youth Director, Blaney Memorial Baptist Church (1961); Speaker-at-Large, Boston, MA (1956-1960); Sunday School Teacher, Blaney Memorial Baptist Church (1956-1960) **AW:** Who's Who in America; Who's Who of American Women; Who's Who in the World **MH:** Albert Nelson Marquis Lifetime Achievement Award (2017); Distinguished Humanitarian (2017) **H:** Photography; Reading; Music **PA:** Republican **RE:** Baptist **ADD:** 1404 Auburn Pl, Plano, TX, 75093

PAULSON, BELDEN, T: Political Scientist **I:** Government Administration/Government Relations/Government Services **CN:** High Wind Association for Modeling Community for Sustainable Living **DOB:** 06/29/1927 **PB:** Oak Park **SC:** IL/USA **PT:** Henry Thomas Paulson; Evelina (Belden) Paulson **MS:** Married **SPN:** Louise D. Hill (1/9/1954) **CH:** Eric; Steven **ED:** PhD, The University of Chicago (1962); MA, The University of Chicago (1955); AB, Oberlin College (1950) **C:** Co-Founder, High Wind Association for Modeling Community for Sustainable Living (1980-Present); President, High Wind Association for Modeling Community for Sustainable Living (1980-Present); Member of Faculty, University of Wisconsin-Milwaukee (1962-Present); President, Plymouth Institute (1995-1998); Professor of Political Science, Extension Campus, University of Wisconsin (1969-1998); Founder, Center for Urban Community Development (1967-1990); Chairman, Center for Urban Community Development (1967-1990); Member, High Commission on Refugees, United Nations, Rome, Italy (1960-1961); Organizer, Homeless European Land Program, Sardinia, Italy (1957-1959); Member, Italian Service Mission, Naples, Italy (1950-1953) **CR:** Honorary Research Professor, International Technology and Economy Institute, Institute for Science of Sciences, Shanghai, China (1990-Present); Co-Founder, Global Learning Center (1998-2004); Member, Education Task Force, President's Council on Sustainable Development (1995-1998) **CIV:** Co-Organizer, Urban Waldorf School, Milwaukee Public Schools (1991); Trainer, Urban Waldorf School, Milwaukee Public Schools (1991); Co-Organizer, Peace Corps Training, University of Wisconsin-Milwaukee (1962-1963) **MIL:** US Naval Reserve (1945-1946) **CW:** Author, "The Odyssey Trail: From Dreams to Doing - Footprints Across the World" (2018); Author, "Against the Odds: Six Projects and Letters to the Six Intrepid Colleagues-in-arms Who Helped to Change Small Pieces of the World" (2018); Author, "Notes From The Field: Strategies Toward Cultural Transformation" (2014); Author, "Odyssey of a Practical Visionary, Eco-Communities, Sustainable Futures, Refugee Resettlement, Poverty and Racism, Dysfunctional Schools" (2009); Author, "Toward A New Kind of Think Tank," New Synthesis Think Tank Papers (1987); Co-Author, "A Reporting and Planning Model for Urban Community Development" (1976); Co-Author, "A Classe de Lideranca do Ceara, Brazil" (1968); Author, "The Searchers: Conflict and Communism in an Italian Town" (1966); Co-Author, "Local Political Patterns in Northeast Brazil," Community Case Study (1964); Author, "Development of Refugee Attitudes, Experiences of Sardinia Project," Research Group for European Migration Problems (1959); Contributor, Articles to Professional Journals **AW:**

Recipient, Lifetime Distinguished Achievement Award, Oberlin College (2004); Grantee, Social Science Research Council (1967-1968); Honoree, Findhorn Foundation Fellow **MEM:** Honorary Citizen, World Future Society, Simaxis, Sardinia **MH:** Albert Nelson Marquis Lifetime Achievement Award (2017) **BA:** W7122 County Road U, Plymouth, WI, 53073

PAULUS, BASIL MANTAS, T: Physician **I:** Medicine & Health Care **CN:** The Stern Cardiovascular Foundation **ED:** Interventional Cardiology Fellowship, Borgess Heart Institute/Michigan State University, Kalamazoo, MI (2009-2010); Cardiology Fellowship, University of Tennessee Health Science Center, Memphis, TN (2006-2009); Internal Medicine Residency, University of Tennessee Health Science Center, Memphis, TN (2003-2006); Medical Degree, Albany Medical College, Albany, NY (2003); BS in Biology, Rensselaer Polytechnic Institute, Troy, NY, Cum Laude (2001) **CT:** Interventional Cardiology, American Board of Internal Medicine (2011-Present); Cardiovascular Disease, American Board of Internal Medicine (2009-Present); Internal Medicine, American Board of Internal Medicine (2007-2017) **C:** Medical Director, Heart Valve Program, Baptist Memorial Hospital, Memphis, TN; Physician, The Stern Cardiovascular Foundation **CR:** Excellence in Teaching Fellow Award, "Best Teacher" by Internal Medicine Residents and Interns, Department of Internal Medicine, University of Tennessee Health Science Center, Memphis, TN (2008) **CIV:** Volunteer, Local Church **AW:** Top Ten Doctor, Voted One of the Top Ten Cardiologists in the State of Tennessee, Vitals.com (2014); America's Top Cardiologists, Consumers' Research Council of America (2013); Top 40 Under 40, Memphis Business Journal (2012); Patients' Choice Award, Vitals.com (2010-2014); Most Compassionate Doctor Award (2010-2012); Physician of the Month, St. Francis Hospital, Memphis, TN (2010); America's Top Cardiologists, Consumers' Research Council of America (2009); Cardiovascular Case Reports Scholar, SSCI Award for Outstanding Case Report, Southern Society for Clinical Investigation, New Orleans, LA (2008); Trainee Award, SSCI Research Award for Innovative Research Project, Southern Society for Clinical Investigation, New Orleans, LA (2007); American Hellenic Educational Progressive Association Scholarship, Rensselaer Polytechnic Institute, Troy, NY (1997-1999); Dean's List, Rensselaer Polytechnic Institute, Troy, NY (1997-1999); Dean's Award, Rensselaer Polytechnic Institute, Troy, NY (1997-1999) **MEM:** American Heart Association; American Medical Association; American College of Cardiology **H:** Basketball; Swimming; Reading; Traveling; Alto saxophone; Piano; Guitar **ADD:** 8596 The Island, Memphis, TN, 38125 **URL:** http://www.sterncardio.com/PaulusBasilM.aspx

PEARSON, CALVIN H. PHD, T: Professor Emeritus, Research Agronomist **I:** Education/Educational Services **CN:** Colorado State University **DOB:** 01/25/1954 **PB:** Ogden **SC:** UT/USA **PT:** Carmen Perry Pearson; Beth (Holbrook) Pearson **MS:** Married **SPN:** Heidi Williams (5/17/1979) **CH:** Kirk; Tyler; Candice; Travis **ED:** PhD, Oregon State University (1983); MS, Oklahoma State University (1979); BS, Brigham Young University (1978); AS, Ricks College (1976) **C:** Professor Emeritus, Colorado State University (2017-Present); Professor in Agronomy, Colorado State University, Fort Collins, CO (1995-2017); Associate Professor, Colorado State University, Fort Collins, CO (1989-1995); Assistant Professor in Agronomy, Colorado State University, Fort Collins, CO (1984-1989); Research Associate, Oregon State University, Corvallis, OR (1983-1984) **CR:** Expert

Witness/Consultant (2017-Present); Outreach Education, Irrigation in Afghanistan (2012); Fellow, American Society of Agronomy (2002); Agricultural Consultant, Bolivia (1992); Manager, Colorado State University Foundation Dry Bean Seed Project, Fruita, CO (1984-1996); DuPont Teaching Fellow, Oregon State University (1980-1981) **CIV:** Scientific Advisor, Start-Up Company, North Carolina (2016-Present); Expert Witness, Lawsuits, Arizona, Arkansas, and Wisconsin **CW:** Editor, Agronomy Journal (2002-2007); Technical Editor, Agronomy Journal (1995-1999); Associate Editor, Agronomy Journal (1990-1994); Contributor, Articles, Scientific Journals and Other Professional Publications **AW:** The Outstanding Young Alumni Award, Ricks College (1997); Faculty Research Grantee, Colorado State University, Fort Collins, CO (1984); Wimberly Small Grains Award, Oklahoma State University (1979) **MEM:** American Society of Agronomy; Crop Science Society of America; Soil and Water Conservation Society; Associate Member, Association of Official Seed Certifying Agencies; Council on Agricultural Science and Technology; Bean Improvement Cooperative; Sigma Xi; Gamma Sigma Delta; Alpha Zeta **MH:** Albert Nelson Marquis Lifetime Achievement Award (2017) **H:** Outdoor activities; Home maintenance; Making custom wood pens; Hobby work **RE:** Latter-Day Saints **ADD:** 371 W Carson Way, Salem, UT, 84653

PECKOL, JAMES KENNETH, T: President, Principal Lecturer **I:** Education/Educational Services **CN:** Oxford Consulting Ltd, University of Washington **DOB:** 10/24/1944 **PB:** Cleveland **SC:** OH/USA **PT:** William John Peckol; Elinor Elizabeth (Bustard) Peckol **CH:** Erin; Robyn **ED:** DEng in Electric Engineering, University of Washington (1985); MEE, University of Washington (1975); BS in Engineering, Case Western Reserve University (1966) **C:** Principal Lecturer, Department of Electrical Engineering, University of Washington (1995-Present); Founder, Oxford Consultant, Edmonds, Washington (1987-Present); President, Oxford Consultant, Edmonds, Washington (1987-Present); Senior Staff Engineer, MR&D Business Unit, John Fluke Manufacturing Company (Now Fluke Corporation), Seattle, Washington (1986-1993); Principal Lecturer, Department of Electrical Engineering, University of Washington (1984-1987); Senior Staff Engineer, Automated Systems Business Unit, John Fluke Manufacturing Company (Now Fluke Corporation), Seattle, Washington (1983-1986); Senior Staff Engineer, Industrial Products Business Unit, John Fluke Manufacturing Company (Now Fluke Corporation), Seattle, Washington (1972-1983); Consultant, General Electric (1966-1972); Consultant, Raytheon Company (1966-1972); Consultant, Ling Temco Vought (1966-1972); Consultant, RCA (1966-1972); Boeing (1966-1972) **CR:** Professor, Department of Electrical Engineering, Danang Technical University (Now University of Danang), Vietnam (1997-Present); Lecturer, Department of Computer Science, Edmonds Community College (1992-Present); Computer Science Embedded System and Electrical Engineering Curriculum Advisory Board, University of Washington Professional and Continuing Education (1990-Present); Lecturer, Department of Mathematics and Science, Shoreline Community College, Seattle, WA (1989-Present); Visiting Professor, Department of Electrical Engineering, Danang Technical University (Now University of Danang), Vietnam (2011); Visiting Professor, Department of Electrical Engineering, Danang Technical University (Now University of Danang), Vietnam (2008-2009); Associate Professor, Department of Engineering & Computer Science,

Universitae de Nantes (1996); Associate Professor, Department of Engineering & Computer Science, Universitae de Nantes (1993); Senior Lecturer, Department of Electrical Engineering, University of Aberdeen, Scotland (1987); Associate Professor, Department of Electrical Engineering, University of Aberdeen, Scotland (1987); Lecturer, Various Conferences and University Programs **CW:** Author, "Embedded Systems, A Contemporary Design Tool" (2008); Contributor, Articles, Professional Journals **MEM:** IEEE; Association for the Advancement of Artificial Intelligence; ACM, Inc.; The Tau Beta Pi Association, Inc. **MH:** Albert Nelson Marquis Lifetime Achievement Award (2017) **BA:** PO Box 461, Edmonds, WA, 98020

PEDLEY, TIMOTHY A., T: Henry and Lucy Moses Professor of Neurology **I:** Medicine & Health Care **CN:** Columbia University Medical Center **DOB:** 08/31/1943 **PB:** Phoenix **SC:** AZ/USA **PT:** Timothy Asbury Pedley III; Mary Adele (Newcomer) Melis **MS:** Married **SPN:** Barbara S. Koppel (3/17/1984) **ED:** Postdoctoral Fellow, Stanford University Hospital (1973-1975); Resident in Neurology, Stanford University Hospital (1970-1973); Intern, Stanford University Hospital (1969-1970); MD, Yale University (1969); BA, Pomona College (1965) **CT:** Certification in Neurology, Electroencephalography and Clinical Neurophysiology; Diplomate, American Board of Psychiatry and Neurology **C:** Henry and Lucy Moses Professor, Chairman of Neurology, Columbia University (1998-Present); Neurologist-in-Chief, Columbia University Medical Center, New York, NY (1998-2002); Associate Professor of Neurology to Professor, Vice Chairman, Columbia University (1979-1998); Assistant Professor of Neurology, Stanford University (1975-1979) **CR:** Member, National Advisory Neurological Disorders & Stroke Council, National Institutes of Health (2007-Present); Various Advisory Committees, National Advisory Neurological Disorders & Stroke Council (1990-1998); Professional Advisory Board, Epilepsy Foundation of America (1984-1998); Director of Comprehensive Epilepsy Center, Columbia University Medical Center (1983-1997); Chairman, Merit Review Board, Neurobiology Research, Virginia (1995-1996); Member, Merit Review Board, Neurobiology Research, Virginia (1992-1996); Chairman, Epilepsy Foundation of America (1993-1995); President, Board of Directors, Epilepsy Foundation of America (1991-1993); Chairman, National Institute of Neurological and Chronic Diseases and Strokes (1988-1989); Member, Review Committee, National Institutes of Health, National Institute of Neurological and Chronic Diseases and Strokes (1985-1989); Chairman, Professional Advisory Board, Epilepsy Foundation of America (1985-1987); Visiting Fellow in Experimental Neurology, Institute of Psychiatry, London, England (1978-1979); Visiting Professor, Various Universities, United States and Abroad **CW:** Editor-in-Chief, Epilepsia (1993-2001); Contributor, Articles to Professional Journals **AW:** Elected to Membership, National Academy of Medicine (2007); Fellow, American Association for the Advancement of Science, New York Academy of Medicine (2000); Recipient, Various Honors and Awards **MEM:** Board of Trustees, American Academy of Neurology (2001-Present); President, American Neurological Association (2007-2009); Secretary, American Academy of Neurology (2003-2007); First Vice President, American Neurological Association (2003-2004); Treasurer, American Neurological Association (1995-1998); Executive Committee, International League Against Epilepsy (1994-2002); Council, American Neurological Association (1992-1994);

President, American Epilepsy Society (1991-1992); President, American Electroencephalographic Society (1989-1990); Board of Directors, American Electroencephalographic Society (1981-1985); Treasurer, American Epilepsy Society (1980-1983); National Academies of Sciences, Engineering, and Medicine; Vidonian Club; Yale Club; New York Medical Surgical Society; Shenorock Shore Club; Alpha Omega Alpha; Fellow, American Academy of Neurology; Society of Neuroscience; The Royal Society of Medicine **BA:** 710 W 168th St, The Neurological Institute, New York, NY, 10032

PEREZ, JORGE LUIS, T: Manufacturing and Child Care Executive **I:** Manufacturing **CN:** IBM Corp. and Preschool Management, Inc. **DOB:** 11/29/1945 **PB:** Jaguey Grande **SC:** Cuba **PT:** Adalberto Aquileo Perez; Esther Mireya (Haedo) Perez **MS:** Divorced **CH:** Jorge Alejandro; Ricardo Javier; Ruben Luis **ED:** MBA, Drexel University (1981); BS in Commerce & Engineering Sciences, Drexel University (1969) **C:** Program Manager, IBM, Boca Raton, FL (1988-1992); Project Manager, IBM , Boca Raton, FL (1986-1988); Manager, Production Control, IBM, Boca Raton, FL (1983-1985); Finance Program Administrator, IBM, Franklin Lakes, NJ (1980-1982); Operations Research Analyst, IBM, Princeton, NJ (1977-1980); Staff Industrial Engineer, IBM, East Fishkill, NY (1976-1977); Senior Associate Industrial Engineer, IBM, East Fishkill, NY (1972-1975); Associate Industrial Engineer, IBM, East Fishkill, NY (1970-1971); Junior Industrial Engineer, IBM, East Fishkill, NY (1969-1970); Former Owner, Wee Bee Tots; Former Owner, Little Learners; Former Owner, Small World Preschools; Former Owner, Academy for Child Enrichment; Current Owner, Noah's Ark Academy **CR:** Consultant, Eclipse Group; Sponsor, Child Care Food Program of Florida **CIV:** Chair, Board of Directors, Transitions Elementary Charter School (2013); Executive Committee, Palm Beach County Republican Party (1989); President, Board of Directors, Palm Beach Farm Workers Coordinating Council (1989) **CW:** Author, "Machine Tooling"; Author, "Transportation Forecasting"; Author, "Workload Planning"; Author, "Measurement" **AW:** Excellence Award, Institute Industrial Engineers (1975) **MEM:** Board Member, Florida Association of Child Care Management (2010-2015); President, Palm Beach County Child Care Director's Association (2010); Vice President, Membership Committee, American Production and Inventory Control Society (1984-1985); President, Institute Industrial Engineers (1974-1975); American Production and Inventory Control Society; Senior Member, Institute Industrial Engineers **MH:** Albert Nelson Marquis Lifetime Achievement Award (2017) **H:** Boating; Fishing; Reading; Movies **PA:** Republican **RE:** Roman Catholic **ADD:** 17769 112th Dr N, Jupiter, FL, 33478

PERHACS, MARYLOUISE (MARYLOU) HELEN, T: Performer/Musician **I:** Media & Entertainment **DOB:** 06/15/1944 **PB:** Teaneck **SC:** NJ/USA **PT:** John Andrew Perhacs; Helen Audrey (Hosage) Perhacs **MS:** Divorced **SPN:** Robert Theodore Sirinek (1/27/1968) Divorced (1975) **ED:** Postgraduate Studies, Saint Peter's University (1977); Postgraduate Coursework, Hunter College (1976); MS, The Juilliard School (1968); BS, The Juilliard School (1967); Coursework, Ithaca College, New York (1962-1964), Singer Sage Chapel Choir, Cornell University (1963-1964) **CT:** Certified Music Teacher, State of New York; Certified Music Teacher, State of New Jersey **C:** Freelance Performer (1960-Present); Private Teacher, Cliffside Park, NJ (1976-2016); Vocal Music Teacher, West New York School District (1995-2016); Middle School Instrumental Teacher,

Paramus Public Schools (1993-1994); General Music Teacher, Little Ferry Public Schools (1991-1992); Music Teacher/Therapist, Bergen County Special Services School District (1990-1991); Adjunct Professor, Department of Education, St. Peter's University (1976-1991); Vocal Music Teacher, East Rutherford, New Jersey (1990); Teacher, New York City Department of Education TPD Special Needs (1980-1984); Trumpet Player, "Duke Ellington's Sophisticated Ladies" (1982); Trumpet Player, "Fiddler on the Roof" at Lincoln Center (1982); Trumpet Player, "Sarava" (1979); Trumpet Player, Westbury Music Fair (1974-1978); Schools (1976-1977); Brass Instruments Teacher, Jazz Program, Ramapo Indian Hills Regional High School District (1976); Trumpet Player, "The Debbie Reynolds Show" (1976); Vocal Soloist and Section Trumpeter, "Lee Castle and the Jimmy Dorsey Band (1976)"; Trumpet Player and Contractor, Madison Square Garden for McCall's Magazine (1975); Trumpet Player, "Sgt. Pepper's Lonely Heart's Club Band" at the Beacon Theater (1974-1975); Trumpet Player, "Jesus Christ Superstar" (1973); Performer, "Sugar" (1971-1972); Performer, "Lysistrata" (1972); Performer, "Promises, Promises" (1969-1971); Singer, Original Member, Peter Schickle's "P.D.Q. Bach Okay Chorale" (1965-1966); Singer, St. Louis Municipal Opera (1970); Singer, The Ed Sullivan Show (1970); Teacher, Jersey City Public Program Developer, Coordinator, Instructor, Urban Education Program, Newburgh Enlarged City School District (1968-1969); Instructor, Carabo Cone Carnegie Hall Corporation, New York, NY (1966-1969); Trumpet Player, St. Patrick's Cathedral; Trumpet Player, New Jersey Symphony (1965) **CR:** Vocal Music Teacher, West New York School District (1995-2016); Middle School Instrumental Teacher, Paramus Public Schools (1993-1994); General Music Teacher, Little Ferry Public Schools (1991-1992); Music Teacher & Therapy, Bergen County Special Services School District (1990-1991); Vocal Music Teacher, East Rutherford, New Jersey (1990); Teacher, New York City Department of Education TPD Special Needs (1980-1984); Private Teacher, Cliffside Park, NJ (1976-2016); Adjunct Professor, Department of Education, St. Peter's University (1976-1991); Teacher, Jersey City Public Schools (1976-1977); Brass Instruments Teacher Jazz Program, Ramapo Indian Hills Regional High School District (1976); Program Developer, Coordinator, Instructor, Urban Education Program, Newburgh Enlarged City School District (1968-1969); Instructor, Carabo Cone Carnegie Hall Corporation, New York, NY (1966-1969) **CIV:** Guest Artist, Brass Quintet, West Point Band (2010); Job Fair, Girl Scouts of the United States of America, Teaneck, NJ (1995); Consultant, Girl Scout Cadette Troops in Bergen County, NJ (1967-1968) **MIL:** None **CW:** Performer, Various Freelance Performances (1960-Present); Trumpeter, Sarah Lawrence College Orchestra New England Tour (1994); Writer, Host Series on Women in Music, Columbia Cable/United Artists (1984); Performer, "Duke Ellington's Sophisticated Ladies" (1982); Performer, "Fiddler on the Roof" at Lincoln Center (1982); Performer, "Sarava" (1979); Performer, "The Debbie Reynolds Show" (1976); Performer, "Sgt. Pepper's Lonely Heart's Club Band" (1974-1975); Performer, "Jesus Christ Superstar" (1973); Performer, "Sugar" (1971-1972); Performer, "Lysistrata" (1972); Performer, "Promises, Promises" (1969-1971); Trumpeter and Contractor, Madison Square Garden; Singer, St. Louis Municipal Opera (1970); Trumpeter, Westbury Music Fair; Singer, The Ed Sullivan Show (1970); Singer, Peter Schickle's "P.D.Q. Bach Okay Chorale" (1965-1966); Trumpeter, St. Patrick's Cathedral; Trumpeter, New Jersey Symphony (1965); Performer, with "Lee Castle and the Jimmy

Dorsey Band" **AW:** Senior Achievement Award, Epsilon Psi Chapter, Mu Phi Epsilon International Music Sorority (1969); Cliffside Park, NJ "Wall of Fame" plaque in Borough Hall (1985) Women of Achievement, organization of northern New Jersey women in various Who's Who editions (1993-2000) The World Who's Who of Women, 12th Edition, Cambridge, England **MEM:** American Federation of Musicians, Local 802 (1964-Present); Theater Committee Chairman, Local 802 (1973); Theater Committee Member, Local 802 (1972); Actors' Equity Association; SAG-AFTRA; Charter Member, International Women's Brass Conference; International Trumpet Guild; National Education Association; New Jersey School Music Association; New Jersey Education Association; Mu Phi Epsilon **MH:** Albert Nelson Marquis Lifetime Achievement Award (2017) **H:** Animal rescue, fostering and rehoming; Cake decorating; horticulture **PA:** Democrat **RE:** Episcopalian **ADD:** 23 Crescent Ave, Cliffside Park, NJ, 07010

PERKINS, NANCY, T: Industrial Designer **I:** Other **CN:** Perkins Design Ltd. **SC:** PA/USA **PT:** Gordon O. Perkins; Martha E. Perkins **ED:** BFA in Industrial Design, University of Illinois, Urbana-Champaign; Coursework, Ohio University **CT:** Certified Expert Witness in Design Patent Litigation **C:** Consultant in Industrial Design; President, Perkins Design Ltd.; President/CEO, Dallas Lighthouse for the Blind; Program Manager in Industrial Design, Jarden Consumer Solutions; Industrial Design Consultant, Sears Brands, LLC; Director of Graphic Design, Cameo Container Corporation; Industrial Designer, Deschamps Mills Associates; Industrial Designer, Peterson Bednar Associates **CR:** Lecturer, The City University of New York; Founder, Perkins Design Ltd.; Curator, Anna Wagner Keichline Gallery; Adjunct Professor, Graduate Design Seminar, Adjunct Instructor of Undergraduate Design, The University of Illinois at Chicago; Adjunct Instructor, Illinois Institute of Technology; Visiting Associate Professor, Carnegie Mellon University; Juror, Annual Design Review Industrial Design Magazine (Now Behance); Proposal Review Committee, Ben Franklin Technology Partners; Speaker in Field **CIV:** Cadette Troop Co-Leader, DuPage County Council, Girl Scouts of the United States of America **CW:** Featured Designer, "33 Plus 20 Chicago"; Featured Designer, Pratt Manhattan Gallery; Contributor, "Design and Feminism"; Contributor, "INNOVATION"; Featured Designer, Bard Graduate Center, New York, NY (2000); Contributor, Articles, Professional Journals; Featured Designer, Newspapers **AW:** Fellow, Industrial Designers Society of America (1993); Honoree, Industrial Designers Society of America 50 Notable Members of the Past 50 Years; Recipient, Outstanding Alumni Award, University of Illinois; Recipient, Goldsmith Award; Recipient, Profile, Industrial Design Magazine (Now Behance); Recipient, Profile, Feminine Ingenuity; Recipient, Profile, Dun & Bradstreet Reports, Inc.; Recipient, Profile, Philadelphia Media Network (Digital), LLC **MEM:** Design Patent Litigation Expert Witness; Board of Directors, National Industries for the Blind (2012-14); President, Design Foundation; Delegate, International Council of the Societies Industrial Design, Nagoya, Japan; Board of Directors, Industrial Designers Society of America; Industrial Designers Society of America: National Secretary-Treasurer, Co-Founder, Women's Section, Vice President Midwest District, Director-at-Large, Publications Committee, Annual Conference Committee, District Membership Committee, Chair, Vice Chair and Treasurer of the Chicago Chapter **MH:** Albert Nelson Marquis Lifetime Achievement Award (2017) **H:** Architectural Historic Preservation **BA:** P.O. Box 5263, Perkins

Design Ltd., Bellefonte, PA, 16823 **ADD:** P.O. Box 5263, Perkins Design Ltd, Bellefonte, PA, 16823

PESSERL, RICHARD, T: Autonomous Driving Cars Expert, Public Speaker **I:** Engineering **ED:** MA, Industrial Engineering, Instituto Tecnologico de Buenos Aires **AW:** Various Business Awards in the Areas of Radar, Video, Stability Control, Airbags, Boosters and Master Cylinders **H:** Traveling; Spending time with his grandson and family **ADD:** 30580 Crest Frst, Farmington Hills, MI, 48331 **URL:** https://www.linkedin.com/in/richardpesserl

PETRAITIS, KAREL, T: Lawyer **I:** Law and Legal Services **DOB:** 04/04/1945 **PB:** Chicago **SC:** IL/USA **PT:** Ferdinand John Petraitis; Dolores (Karroll) Petraitis **C:** Private Law Practice, College Park, MD (1980-Present); Real Estate Agent, Harloff & Perkins, Riverdale, MD (1978-1982); Attorney, Prince George's County Office of Law (1972-1980); Law Clerk, Prince George's County Office of Law (1971-1972); Past President, Vice President, Treasurer, Board of Directors, College Park Board of Trade **CIV:** President, Friends of Maryland Summer Institute for Creative & Performing Arts (1997-1998); Board of Trustees, Elizabeth Seton High School (1991-1995); Trustee, Friends of Maryland Summer Institute for Creative & Performing Arts (1986-2001); President, Friends of Maryland Summer Institute for Creative & Performing Arts (1983-1986); Director, Maryland Young Republicans (1979-1981); Legal Counsel, Maryland Young Republicans (1972-1979); National Committeewoman, Maryland Young Republicans (1971-1979); Youth Coordinator, Beall for Senate (1970); Youth Coordinator, Mathias for Senate (1968); Youth Coordinator, Agnew for Governor (1966) **MEM:** Advisory Council Member, Sports Legend Museum (2013-Present); President, Prince George's Chapter, University of Maryland Alumni Association (2007-Present); Treasurer, District of Columbia Chapter, Gamma Phi Beta Alumnae (2006-Present); Board of Directors, Gridiron Club (2006-Present); Board of Directors, Sports Legend Museum (2008-2012); Terrapin Club (2005-2012); Treasurer, University of Maryland Alumni Association (2004-2007); Legislative Committee of Advocacy, University of Maryland Alumni Association (2003-2009); Arts and Humanities Board, University of Maryland Alumni Association (1999-2004); Board of Directors, University of Maryland Alumni Association (1988-1996); President, Prince George's Chapter, University of Maryland Alumni Association (1986-1988); President, Maryland Chapter, George Washington Law Alumni Association (1985-1987); Secretary, George Washington Law Alumni Association (1982-1984); Board of Directors, George Washington Law Alumni Association (1979-1994); President, Young Alumni, University of Maryland Alumni Association (1978-1980); Social List of Washington; Prince George's County Bar Association; Maryland Bar Association; Honorary Member, Agriculture Alumni; Campus Club; FOMB; Fastbreakers; Rebounders **PA:** Republican **RE:** Roman Catholic **ADD:** 7307 Radcliffe Drive, College Park, MD, 20740

PETRAKIS, LAWRENCE THEODORE, T: Physician **I:** Medicine & Health Care **MS:** Married **CH:** Three Daughters **ED:** MD, Faculty of Medicine, University of British Columbia (1965); BS, University of British Columbia; Internship, St. Mary's Hospital, San Francisco, CA; Resident, University of Washington **CT:** Certified Practitioner, Canada; Certified Practitioner, United States **C:** Self-Employed Physician **CR:** Assistant Clinical Professor of Psychiatry, University of California, San Francisco; Consultant in Psychiatry, 30 Patient Inpatient Physical Medicine and Rehab,

St.Josephs Hospital in San Francisco; Private Practice, San Francisco, CA **MEM:** Fellow, Royal Society of Medicine, England; Fellow, Associated Board of the Royal Schools of Music; Fellow, Royal College of Physicians, Canada **BA:** 909 Hyde St Ste 330, San Francisco, CA, 94109

PETTAPIECE, BOB, T: Assistant Professor (Retired) **I:** Education/Educational Services **CN:** Wayne State University **PB:** Detroit **SC:** MI/USA **PT:** Alvy M. Pettapiece; Thelma M. (Fetterly) Mattson **CH:** Lori; Michelle Howe; Erin Howe **ED:** EdD, Wayne State University (1980); MEd, Wayne State University (1971); BA in Religion, Michigan State University (1967); BA in Humanities, Michigan State University (1963) **CT:** Certified Teacher in History, Humanities, Mathematics, Religion, State of Michigan **C:** Assistant Professor, Wayne State University, Detroit, MI (1996-2016); Associate Member, Graduate Faculty, Wayne State University, Detroit, MI (1990-2016); Instructor of Education, Wayne State University, Detroit, MI (1981-1996); Teacher, Detroit Public Schools (1967-1996); Program Coordinator for Middle Level Education and Social Studies Education, Wayne State University, Detroit, MI **CR:** Speaker in Field; Board of Directors, Population Connection **CIV:** Advisory Board Member, Sojourner Foundation; Member, State Board of Directors, American Civil Liberties Union of Michigan **CW:** Contributor, Articles, Professional Journals **AW:** Graduate Fellow, Wayne State University (1978) **MEM:** Associate Member, American Psychological Association; National Council for the Social Studies; Michigan Association for Computer Users in Learning; International Council for Computers in Education; Wayne State University Alumni Association; Phi Delta Kappa **H:** Squash; Photography; Computing; Travel **PA:** Progressive **ADD:** 1315 Nicolet Place, Detroit, MI, 48207 **URL:** http://pettapiece.6te.net

PETZ, LAWRENCE D., T: Medical Director **I:** Medicine & Health Care **CN:** StemCyte Cord Blood Bank **DOB:** 06/06/1931 **PB:** Chicago **SC:** IL/US **PT:** Earl Fred Petz; Louise A. Petz **MS:** Married **SPN:** Elizabeth Louise Petz (2/11) **ED:** Fellow in Hematology, Hammersmith Hospital and Royal Postgraduate Medical School, London, England, UK (1961-1963); Resident in Medicine, San Francisco Veterans Administration Hospital, San Francisco, CA (1960-1961); Resident in Medicine, San Francisco General Hospital, San Francisco, CA (1959-1960); Resident in Medicine, Cook County Hospital, Chicago, IL (1956-1957); Intern, Cook County Hospital, Chicago, IL (1955-1956); MD, University of Illinois College of Medicine (1955); BS, University of Illinois (1953) **CT:** Diplomate, Subspecialty of Hematology (1974); Re-certified, American Board of Internal Medicine (1974); Certified, American Board of Internal Medicine (1962); Medical License, State of California (1959); Medical License, State of Illinois (1956); Diplomate, National Board of Medical Examiners (1956) **C:** Medical Director, StemCyte International Cord Blood Center, Baldwin Park, CA (2001-Present); Emeritus Professor, Department of Pathology and Laboratory Medicine, UCLA Medical Center, Los Angeles, CA (2001-Present); Professor of Pathology, Director of Transfusion Medicine, UCLA Medical Center, Los Angeles, CA (1987-2000); Director, Department of Clinical and Experimental Immunology, City of Hope National Medical Center, Duarte, CA (1985-1986); Chairman, Division of Medicine, City of Hope National Medical Center, Duarte, CA (1981-1985); Section Head, Hematology and Blood Transfusion Services, Division of Clinical Pathology, City of Hope National Medical Center, Duarte, CA (1979-1981); Chief of Hematology Immunology Research Unit, Institutes

of Medical Sciences, Pacific Medical Center, San Francisco, CA (1974-1979); Associate Clinical Professor of Medicine, University of California, San Francisco, CA (1973-1979); Chief, Department of Medicine, Hematology Immunology Research Unit, Harkness Community Hospital and Medical Center, San Francisco, CA (1972-1974); Chief of Hematology, Harkness Community Hospital and Medical Center, San Francisco, CA (1969-1972); Assistant Clinical Professor of Medicine, University of California, San Francisco, CA (1966-1972); Dernham Senior Fellow in Oncology, San Francisco Veterans Administration Hospital, San Francisco, CA (1966-1968); Clinical Investigator, San Francisco Veterans Administration Hospital, San Francisco, CA (1963-1966); Chief, Department of Medicine, Walker Air Force Hospital (1957-1959) **MIL:** Air Force **CW:** Co-Author, "Effect of cord blood processing on transplantation outcomes after single myeloablative umbilical cord blood transplantation," Biology of Blood and Marrow Transplantation (2015); Co-Author, "Progress toward Curing HIV Infection with Hematopoietic Cell Transplantation," Stem Cells and Cloning: Advances and Applications (2015); Co-Author, "CCR5-/- homozygous cord blood allogeneic transplantation in a patient with HIV: a case report," Lancet HIV (2015); Co-Author, "Current thawing and infusion practice of cryopreserved cord blood: the impact on graft quality, recipient safety, and transplantation outcomes," Transfusion (2014); Author, "The cure of HIV with hematopoietic cell transplantation," Biology of Blood and Marrow Transplantation (2013); Author, "Cord blood transplantation for cure of HIV infections," StemCells Translational Medicine (2013); Co-Author, "Hematopoietic cell transplantation with cord blood for cure of HIV infections," Biology of Blood and Marrow Transplantation (2013); Co-Author, "Analysis of 120 pediatric patients with nonmalignant disorders transplanted using unrelated plasma-depleted or -reduced cord blood," Transfusion (2012); Co-Author, "Cell recovery comparison between plasma depletion/reduction and red cell reduction processing of umbilical cord blood," Cytotherapy (2011); Co-Author, "Selection of unrelated cord blood grafts," Blood Reviews (2011); Co-Author, "Eighth Annual International Umbilical Cord Blood Transplantation Symposium, San Francisco, California, June 3-5, 2010," Biology of Blood and Marrow Transplantation (2011); Co-Author, "The underutilization of cord blood Transplantation - Extent of the problem, causes and methods of improvement," Cord Blood Biology, Transplantation, Banking and Regulatory Considerations, AABB Press (2011); Co-Author, "Seventh Annual International Umbilical Cord Blood Transplantation Symposium, Los Angeles, California, June 5-6, 2009," Biology of Blood and Marrow Transplantation (2010); Author, "Diagnostic complexities in autoimmune hemolytic anemias," Transfusion (2009); Author, "Cold antibody autoimmune hemolytic anemias," Blood Reviews (2008); Co-Author, "Analysis of hematopoietic cell transplants using plasma-depleted cord blood products that are not red blood cell reduced," Biology of Blood and Marrow Transplantation (2007); Co-Author, "Direct antiglobulin test negative autoimmune haemolytic anaemia associated with fludarabine/cyclophosphamide/rituximab therapy," British Journal of Haematology (2007); Co-Author, "Fifth Annual International Umbilical Cord Blood Transplantation Symposium, Los Angeles, California, May 11-12, 2007," Biology of Blood and Marrow Transplantation (2007); Co-Author, "Analysis of hematopoietic cell transplants using plasma-depleted cord blood products that are not red blood cell reduced," Biology of Blood and Marrow Transplantation (2007); Author, "Bystander Immune Cytolysis," Blood Reviews (2007); Co-Author, "Fourth Annual International Umbilical Cord Blood Transplantation Symposium Los Angeles, California May 19-20, 2006," Biology of Blood and Marrow Transplantation (2006); Author, "Bystander Immune Cytolysis," Transfusion Medicine Reviews (2006); Co-Author, "Photochemically treated fresh frozen plasma for transfusion of patients with acquired coagulopathy of liver disease," Blood Reviews (2006); Co-Author, "Erythrocyte antigens and antibodies," Williams Hemotology, Seventh Edition, McGraw-Hill, NY (2005); Co-Author, "Third Annual International Umbilical Cord Blood Transplantation Symposium, Los Angeles, California, June 3-4, 2005," Biology of Blood and Marrow Transplantation (2005) **AW:** The Herbert Perkins and George Garratty Memorial Lectureship (2017); President's Award, American Association of Blood Banks (2017); International Cord Blood Symposium Leadership Award for Service from 2003-2014 (2015); Life Time Achievement Award, AABB (2011); Argencord Lectureship, Argentina (2007); Service and Leadership Award, California Blood Bank Society (1999); Owen Thomas Award, California Blood Bank Society (1997); The Tibor Greenwalt Scientific Memorial Award and Lectureship (1996); Morten Grove Rasmussen Memorial Award, American Association of Blood Banks (1994); Emily Cooley Award, American Association of Blood Banks (1991); Ruth Sanger Oration, Australasian Society of Blood Transfusion, Christchurch, NZ (1990); Transfusion Medicine Academic Award, NHLBI (1989); Jean Stubbins Annual Lecturer, University of Texas Medical Branch, Galveston, TX (1983); Frank Allende Memorial Lecture, University of California, San Francisco (1977); Elected Fellow, American College of Physicians (1966); Dernham Senior Fellowship in Oncology (1966) **MEM:** Board of Directors, California Blood Bank Society (1993-Present); Board of Directors, American Red Cross Blood Services, Southern California Region (1993-Present); Medical-Technical Advisory Committee, American Red Cross Blood Services, Southern California Region (1987-Present); Cord Blood Association (2016); Vice Chair, Clinical Transfusion Medicine Committee, American Association of Blood Banks (2001-2002); Chairman, Transfusion Practices Program Committee, American Association of Blood Banks (1998-2000); President, California Blood Bank Society (1998-1999); Editorial Board, AABB Press (1995-1999); Special Emphasis Panel, NHLBI (1995); Board of Trustees, National Blood Foundation (1994); Chairman, Grants Review Committee, National Blood Foundation (1993-1995); Committee for Review of Seed Grants, Jonsson Cancer Center (1992-1995); Operations Excellence Committee, University of California Los Angeles Medical Center (1992-1993); Academic Transfusion Medicine Committee, American Association of Blood Banks (1990-1993); Blood Diseases and Resources Advisory Committee, National Institutes of Health (1991-1992); Board of Trustees, National Blood Foundation (1990-1992); Liaison Member, Ad Hoc Annual Meeting Advisory Committee, American Association of Blood Banks (1990-1991); Liaison Member, Scientific Program Committee, American Association of Blood Banks (1990-1991); Chairman, Scientific Program Committee, California Blood Bank Society (1990-1991); Chairman, Abstract Selection Committee, American Association of Blood Banks (1988-1991); Chairman, Physician's Committee, California Blood Bank Society (1988-1989); Physician's Committee, California Blood Bank Society (1986-

1991); Western Association of Physicians (1985); Abstract Selection Committee, American Association of Blood Banks (1984-1991); Scientific Subcommittee of Transfusion Medicine, American Society of Hematology (1984-1986); Chairman, Scientific Advisory Committee, California Blood Bank Society (1980-1983); Scientific Advisory Committee, California Blood Bank Society (1978-1983) **H:** Classical music **RE:** Protestant **BA:** 13800 Live Oak Ave, StemCyte Cord Blood Bank, Baldwin Park, CA, 91706 **ADD:** 19633 Anadale Dr, Tarzana, CA, 91356 **URL:** o6/06/1931

PHILIPP, KARLA ANN, T: Musician, Educator, Conductor **I:** Education/Educational Services **CN:** Memphis Youth Symphony **DOB:** 09/12/1955 **PB:** Milwaukee **SC:** WI/USA **PT:** John William Philipp; Catherine Anne Philipp **ED:** MusM, Memphis State University (Now The University of Memphis) (1979); MusB, The University of Arizona (1977) **C:** Adjunct Instructor, The University of Memphis (2009-Present); Conductor, Youth Sinfonia, Memphis Youth Symphony Program (1997-Present); Conductor, Youth String Ensemble, Memphis Youth Symphony Program (1997-2017); Teacher, Itinerant Strings, Memphis City Schools (1979-2009) **CR:** Section Member, Jackson Symphony Orchestra (2011-Present); Orchestra Director, Intermountain Suzuki String Institute (2011); Note-Reading Teacher, Intermountain Suzuki String Institute (2011); Orchestra Director, Summer String Camp, The University of Memphis (2006-2008); Orchestra Director, Intermountain Suzuki String Institute (2001-2008); Note-Reading Teacher, Intermountain Suzuki String Institute (1993-2008); Principal Bass Player, Memphis Symphony Orchestra (1989-2007); Conductor, American Suzuki Institute, Suzuki Association of the Americas (1993-2005); Section Bass Player, Memphis Symphony Orchestra (1979-1989); Member, Tucson Symphony Orchestra (1977-1978); Presenter in Field **CIV:** Member, Integrity, Memphis, TN (2003-Present) **AW:** Honoree, Amro Music Educator's Walk (2015); West Tennessee School Band and Orchestra Associated Hall of Fame (2013); Outstanding Teacher Award, Tennessee Governor's School for the Arts (2009-2010); Award For Teacher Excellence, Rotary Club of Memphis (1998); Grantee, Rotary Club of Memphis (1997); Outstanding Teacher Award, Tennessee Governor's School for the Arts (1994-1995); Outstanding Teacher Award, Tennessee Governor's School for the Arts (1991); Grantee, Rotary Club of Memphis (1991); Haldeman Scholarship, School of Music, The University of Arizona (1974-1978) **MEM:** Vice President, West Tennessee Chapter, American String Teachers Association (1993-1995); International Society of Business Leaders; Tennessee Music Education Association; National Association for Music Education; Local 71, American Federation of Musicians **MH:** Albert Nelson Marquis Lifetime Achievement Award (2017) **H:** Reading; Travel **RE:** Episcopalian **BA:** 2009 Ridgeway Rd, Ridgeway High School, Memphis, TN, 38119 **ADD:** 4782 Verne Rd, Memphis, TN, 38117

PHILLIS, MARILYN HUGHEY, T: Artist **I:** Fine Art **CN:** Phillis Studio **PB:** Kent **SC:** OH/USA **PT:** Paul Hughey; Helen Hughey **MS:** Married **SPN:** Richard Waring Phillis (3/19/1949) **CH:** Diane E.; Hugh R.; Randall W. **ED:** BS, The Ohio State University (1949); Coursework, Kent State University (1945) **C:** Instructor of Watermedia, Springfield Museum of Art, Ohio (1976-1984); Instructor of Art, Edison State Community College, Piqua, OH (1976); Book Illustrator, American Association of University Women, Piqua, OH (1976); Periodical Illustrator, Western Reserve History Magazine,

Garrettsville, OH (1974-1979); Chemist, Battelle Memorial Institute, Columbus, OH (1949-1953) **CR:** Juror, Art Exhibitions, State and National Art Groups (1980-Present); Instructor of Painting, State and National Organizations (1980-Present); Lecturer of Art Healing, Wheeling Hospital (2009); Founder, Coordinator, National Creativity Seminar, Stretching Boundaries for Creative People (2007-2010); Founder, Coordinator, National Creativity Seminar, Stretching Boundaries for Creative People (2002); Founder, Coordinator, National Creativity Seminar, Stretching Boundaries for Creative People (1999); Founder, Coordinator, National Creativity Seminar, Stretching Boundaries for Creative People (1997); Founder, Coordinator, National Creativity Seminar, Stretching Boundaries for Creative People (1995); Lecturer of Art Healing, Wheeling Jesuit College, West Virgina (1994-1996); Founder, Coordinator, National Creativity Seminar, Stretching Boundaries for Creative People (1993) **CIV:** Co-Juror, Selections Allied Artists, West Virgina (2012); Art and Healing Workshop, International Society on the Study of Subtle Energies and Energy Medicine (1995); Co-Chairman, Community Health and Humor Program, Wheeling, WV (1992) **CW:** Newsletter Editor, American Watercolor Society (1992-Present); Exhibition, Watercolor Masters, Jiangsu Province Art Museum, Nanjing, China (2012); Exhibition, Watercolor Masters, Jiangsu Province Art Museum, Nanjing, China (2010); Exhibition, Taiwan Art Education Institute, Taipei (1994); Art Consultant, Science Journal, International Society Study Subtle Energies and Energy Medicine (1992-2006); Author, "Watermedia Techniques for Releasing the Creative Spirit" (1992); Contributor, Chapters to Books; Contributor, Articles and Illustrations to Professional Journals; One-Woman Show, Stifel Fine Art Center, Wheeling, WV; One-Woman Show, Springfield Art Museum; One-Woman Show, Zanesville Art Center, Ohio; One-Woman Show, Ohio University, Lancaster, OH; One-Woman Show, Ohio University, East St. Clairsville, OH; One-Woman Show, Cleveland Institute of Music; One-Woman Show, Columbus Museum of Art; One-Woman Show, Cheekwood Museum of Art; One-Woman Show, Botanical Hall, Nashville, TN; One-Woman Show, Idaho Falls Art Center; One-Woman Show, Monroe Community College, Monroe, MI; Exhibition, Butler Museum of American Art, Youngstown, OH; Permanent Collection, Heritage Hall Museum, Talladega, AL; Permanent Collections, Ohio University, Lancaster Campus, St. Clairsville Campus, Ohio; Permanent Collection, West Virginia Northern Community College; Permanent Collection, Leroy Springs & Company; Permanent Collection, Ohio Watercolor Society; Permanent Collection, West Virginia Women Artists; Permanent Collection, University of Charleston; Permanent Collection, Monroe Community College, Monroe, MI **AW:** Recipient, Lifetime Achievement Award, Ohio Watercolor Society (2012); Recipient, Church Jury Award, American Watercolor Society International Exhibition (2012); Lifetime Achievement Award, West Virginia Watercolor Society (2010); Hall of Fame Inductee, Kent, OH (2000); Hall of Fame Inductee, Wheeling, WV (2000); Recipient, Silver Award, Southern Watercolor Society (1999); Art Masters Award, American Artist Magazine (1996); Hudson Society Award, National Collage Society (1995); Gold Medal, Best of Show, Ohio Watercolor Society (1993); Recipient, First Place Award, Watercolor West, Riverside, CA (1990); Recipient, Second Place Award, Western Ohio Watercolor Society (1982); Recipient, Osborne Award, American Watercolor Society (1975) **MEM:** Chairman, Jury of Awards, American Watercolor Society (2012); Jury of Selection, American

Watercolor Society (2008); Chairman, Jury of Awards, American Watercolor Society (2003); Chairman, Selection Jury, National Watercolor Society (2001); President, Southern Watercolor Society (1997-1998); Director, American Watercolor Society (1991-1993); President, Ohio Watercolor Society (1990-1996); National Vice President, Society of Layerists in Multi-Media (1988-1993); Vice President, Ohio Watercolor Society (1982-1989); Secretary, Ohio Watercolor Society (1979-1982); President, Western Ohio Watercolor Society (1979-1980); Allied Artists New York; West Virginia Watercolor Society; Kentucky Watercolor Society; Georgia Watercolor Society; International Society Study Subtle Energies and Energy Medicine **H:** Hiking; Reading; Genealogy; Music; Travel **ADD:** 10 E Hawthorn Pkwy Apt 440, Vernon Hills, IL, 60061

PHILLIPS, TED, T: Advertising Executive **I:** Advertising & Marketing **CN:** Welti & Call Advertising **DOB:** 10/27/1948 **PB:** American Falls **SC:** ID/USA **PT:** Virn E. Phillips; Jessie N. (Aldous) Phillips **MS:** Married **SPN:** Dianne Jacqulynne Walker (5/28/1971) **CH:** Scott; Russell; Stephen; Michael **ED:** MA, Brigham Young University (1975); BA, Brigham Young University (1972) **C:** Vice President, Welti & Call Advertising (2010-Present); CEO, Virtual Ad Agency (2000-Present); CEO, Chairman, The Phillips Agency, Salt Lake City, UT (1994-2000); President, Hurst & Phillips, Salt Lake City, UT (1986-1994); President, Thomas/Phillips/Clawson Advertising, Inc., Salt Lake City, UT (1982-1986); Director of Advertising, O.C. Tanner, Salt Lake City, UT (1980-1982); President, CEO, David W. Evans/Atlanta, Inc., (1979-1980); Executive Vice President, Evans/Lowe & Stevens, Inc., Atlanta, GA (1979); Senior Vice President, Evans/Lowe & Stevens, Inc., Atlanta, GA (1978); Director, Advertising Division of Continuing Education, University of Utah, Salt Lake City, UT (1975-1978); Account Executive, David W. Evans, Inc., Salt Lake City, UT (1972-1975) **CR:** Advertising Instructor, Division of Continuing Education, Brigham Young University (1983-1985) **CIV:** Director, Communications, Salt Lake County Mayor's Office (2002-2004); Active Member, State Republican Party **AW:** Recipient, Distinguished James E. West Award (2012); Telly Award, American Advertising Federation (2002); Recipient, Spurgeon Award (1995); Recipient, Silver Beaver Award, Boy Scouts of America (1994); Telly Award, American Advertising Federation (1992); Telly Award, American Advertising Federation (1991); Clio Finalist, American Advertising Federation (1984); Best-in-West Awards, American Advertising Federation; National Addy Awards, American Advertising Federation **MEM:** Boy Scouts of America (1998-Present); President, American Advertising Federation (1984-1985); Board of Directors, American Advertising Federation (1980-1987); Board of Directors, American Advertising Federation (1976-1978); Marketing and Public Relations Committee; Great Salt Lake Council **H:** Fly fishing; Target shooting **RE:** The Church of Jesus Christ of Latter-Day Saints **ADD:** 110, So. Jordan, UT, 84009

PICKETT, STEPHEN WESLEY, T: Independent Consultant **I:** Consulting **CN:** Stephen W. Pickett **DOB:** 05/27/1956 **PB:** Billings **SC:** MT/USA **PT:** Wesley William Pickett; Carol Ann (Bollum) Pickett **ED:** MS, University of North Texas (1988); BA, Houston Baptist University (1980) **CT:** Graduate, Denton Chamber of Commerce, Leadership Program (1992); Certified Elementary Teacher, State of Texas; Certified Rehabilitation Counselor **C:** Director, Disability Services, University of Oregon, Eugene, OR (2002-2008); University Mentor, Advisor, University of North

Texas, Denton, Texas (1992-2001); Director, Office of Disability Accommodation, University of North Texas, Denton, Texas (1991-2001); Assistant Coordinator, Disabled Student Services, Office of Student Development, University of North Texas, Denton, Texas (1990-1991); Assistant to the Associate Dean of Students, University of North Texas, Denton, Texas (1988-1990); Hospital Teacher, Houston Independent School District (1981-1985) **CR:** Academic Access Consultant, University of Oregon, Eugene, OR (2008-Present); Elected Member, President's Advisory Committee, University of Oregon, Eugene, OR (2006-2008); Associate Director, Office of Academic Advising, University of Oregon (2002-2008); Member, Denton Chamber of Commerce (1992-1993) **CIV:** Member, Council-at-large, Sam Houston Area Council, Boy Scouts of America, Houston, Texas (1975-Present); Senior and Disabled Services Advisory Committee, Lane County, Eugene, OR (2010-2012); Board Member, Oregon Supported Living Program (2010-2012); Co-chair, University of North Texas American Dental Association Advisory Committee (2000-2001); Member, Budget Committee, United Way of Denton County (1998-2001); Executive Board, Service Provision for Aging Needs, United Way (1997-2001); Public Relations Chair, Leadership, Denton Steering Committee (1993-1994); Member, University of North Texas American Dental Association Access Advisory Board (1992-2001); Member, Advisory Board, Denton County Transportation Authority (1990-2001); Chair, Mayor's Committee on Employment of Persons with Disabilities, Denton, Texas (1990) **CW:** Co-author, Curriculum Guide, "The Newspaper as a Student Communicator" (1982) **AW:** Outstanding Alumnus Award, Center for Rehabilitation Studies, University of North Texas (1995); Distinguished Alumnus Award, Houston Baptist University (1994); Award for Services to Persons with Disabilities, North Texas Rehabilitation Association (1993); Community Service Award, University of North Texas (1992); Bronze Palm Eagle Scout (1973); Exxon Foundation's Impact Two Award **MEM:** Conference Co-chair, Association of Higher Education and Disability in Texas (1999); Secretary, Association of Higher Education and Disability in Texas (1998-1999); Co-chair, Endowment Foundation Committee, Texas Association of College and University Student Personnel Administrators (1996-1997); Vice President, Texas Association of College and University Student Personnel Administrators (1995-1996); Chair, Multicultural Committee, Texas Association of College and University Student Personnel Administrators (1994-1995); Association on Higher Education and Disability; NASPA; National Rehabilitation Association; American Rehabilitation Counseling Association (ARCA); Texas Rehabilitation Association; NACADA **MH:** Albert Nelson Marquis Lifetime Achievement Award (2017) **H:** Reading; Traveling; Stamp Collecting/Philately **RE:** Presbyterian **ADD:** 3725 Lake Country Dr, Denton, TX, 76210

PIECUCH, JIM, T: History Professor, Writer **I:** Education/Educational Services **CN:** Kennesaw State University **DOB:** 10/06/1959 **PB:** Manchester **SC:** NH/USA **PT:** Boleslaw Piecuch; Yvette Piecuch **MS:** Married **SPN:** Lori Warfield (3/28/1987) **CH:** Joseph **ED:** PhD in History, College of William & Mary (2005); MA in History, University of New Hampshire (1997); BA in History, University of New Hampshire (1994) **CT:** Certified Online Instructor (2016) **C:** Professor of History, Kennesaw State University (2017-Present); Associate Professor of History, Kennesaw State University (2011-2017); Assistant Professor of History, Kennesaw State

University (2006-2011); Visiting Lecturer in History, Clarion University of Pennsylvania (2004-2005); Instructor, Thomas Nelson Community College (2003-2004); Instructor, College of William & Mary (2003-2004); Writing Instructor, History Writing Resources Center, College of William & Mary (2000-2001); Instructor, College of William & Mary (1999-2000); Instructor, University of New Hampshire at Manchester (1998-1999); Teaching Assistant, College of William & Mary (1996-1997); Teaching Assistant, University of New Hampshire (1995-1996); Firefighter, City of Manchester, New Hampshire (1980-1993); Freelance Journalist (1978-1996); Tutor in History and English, University of New Hampshire (1992-1994) **CR:** Dissertation Reader, Stony Brook University (2016); Participant, Mentorship Program, The Organization of American Historians (2015); Member, Honors Internship Committee, Department of Anthropology, Kennesaw State University (2013); Examiner, Georgia State University (2011) **CIV:** Advisory Board Member, Southern Revolutionary War Institute (2006-Present); Chair, CHSS Scholarship Committee, Kennesaw State University (2016-2017); Summer Research Grants Awards Committee, College of Humanities and Social Sciences, Kennesaw State University (2015); American Studies MA Program Assessment Committee, Kennesaw State University (2015); American Studies Graduate Teaching Assistant Committee, Kennesaw State University (2012-2013); Dean Search Committee, College of Humanities and Social Sciences, Kennesaw State University (2011-2012); Pullen Prize Committee, Department of History and Philosophy, Kennesaw State University (2011); Moderator, American History Panel, Undergraduate Scholars Symposium, Kennesaw State University (2011); Moderator, American History Panel, Undergraduate Scholars Symposium, Kennesaw State University (2011); Tenure and Promotion Committee, Department of History and Philosophy, Kennesaw State University (2011); Public History Search Committee, Department of History and Philosophy, Kennesaw State University (2010-2011); College of Humanities and Social Sciences Faculty Awards Committee, Kennesaw State University (2010); Ad Hoc Committee on the Significance of Scholarship, Department of History and Philosophy, Kennesaw State University (2009-2011); College of Humanities and Social Sciences Search Committee for Director of the Center for the Study of the Civil War Era, Kennesaw State University (2009-2010); Committee on the Bartow County Land Gift, Kennesaw State University (2009); American Studies Ad Hoc Committee on Admissions and Graduate Research Assistantship Procedures, Kennesaw State University (2009); Member, Francis Marion Historic Trail Commission (2007-2009); Judge, National History Day Competition, Kennesaw State University (2007-2008); Judge in Nonfiction History, Georgia Author of the Year Awards (2007); Trip Coordinator, Alternative Spring Break Service, Kennesaw State University (2004); Graduate Student Representative, Search Committee for Dean of the Faculty of Arts and Sciences, College of William & Mary (2003-2004); Trip Leader, Alternative Spring Break Service (2000-2002) **CW:** Editorial Board Member, American Revolution Association (2008-Present); Co-Author, "Light Horse Harry Lee in the War for Independence," Nautical & Aviation Publishing Company (2013); Editor, "Cavalry of the American Revolution," Westholme Publishing (2012); Co-Editor, "General Nathanael Greene and the American Revolution in the South," University of South Carolina Press (2012); Author, "'The Blood Be Upon Your Head': Tarleton and the Myth of Buford's Massacre," Southern Campaigns of the American Revolution Press (2010); Co-Author, "'Cool, Deliberate Courage': John Eager Howard in the American Revolution," Nautical & Aviation Publishing Company (2009); Assistant Editor, "Encyclopedia of North American Colonial Conflict, 1607-1775" (2008); Author, "Three Peoples, One King: Loyalists, Indians, and Slaves in the Revolutionary South, 1775-1782," University of South Carolina Press (2008); Book Review Editor, "Southern Campaigns of the American Revolution" (2006-2009); Author, "The Battle of Camden: A Documentary History," The History Press (2006); Author, "Competence, Conflict, and Confusion: British and Loyalist Leadership in Revolutionary South Carolina, 1780-1782," University of Oklahoma Press; Author, Academic Articles; Associate Editor, Online Journal of the American Revolution; Author, Book Chapters; Contributor, Encyclopedia Entries; Editor, Books; Contributor, Conference Papers; Assistant Editor, Encyclopedia of the Wars of the Early Republic; Assistant Editor, "Encyclopedia of the North American Indian Wars, 1607-1890" **AW:** Nominee, CHSS Outstanding Engagement Award, Department of History and Philosophy, Kennesaw State University (2017); Recipient, Recognition for Excellence, Center for Excellence in Teaching and Learning, Kennesaw State University (2017, 2015); Recipient, Educator of the Year Award, South Carolina Society, Sons of the American Revolution (2016); Recipient, Recognition, Camden City Council (2015); Recipient, Historic Preservation Award, National Society Daughters of the American Revolution (2015); Recipient, Lectureship Award, Sons of the American Revolution (2013); Recipient, Summer Research Grant, College of Humanities and Social Sciences, Kennesaw State University (2013); Recipient, Research Fellowship, David Library of the American Revolution (2013); Recipient, Roundtable Lifetime Achievement Award for Scholarly Endeavors, Southern Campaigns of the American Revolution (2012); Recipient, Foundation Award, Historic Camden (2012); Recipient, Recognition for Excellence, College of Humanities and Social Sciences, Kennesaw State University (2011); Recipient, Recognition for Excellence, Center for Excellence in Teaching and Learning, Kennesaw State University (2010-2012); Recipient, Foundation Prize, Kennesaw State University (2009); Finalist, Roger's Prize, South Carolina Historical Society (2008); Finalist, Cox Prize, Society of the Cincinnati (2007-2009); Recipient, Price Visiting Research Fellowship, William L. Clements Library, University of Michigan (2002); Recipient, Research Fellowship, Institute for Southern Studies, University of South Carolina (2001-2002); Recipient, Research Fellowship, David Library of the American Revolution (2001) **MH:** Albert Nelson Marquis Lifetime Achievement Award (2017) **RE:** Roman Catholic **ADD:** 1074 Hermitage Pond Rd, Camden, SC, 29020

PIERARD, RICHARD VICTOR, T: History Educator **I:** Education/Educational Services **CN:** Indiana State University **DOB:** 05/29/1934 **PB:** Chicago **SC:** IL/USA **PT:** John Perkins Pierard; Diana Florence (Russell) Pierard **MS:** Married **SPN:** Charlene Burdett (6/15/1957) **CH:** David; Cynthia **ED:** PhD, University of Iowa (1964); MA, California State University, Los Angeles (1959); BA, California State University, Los Angeles (1958) **C:** Professor Emeritus, Indiana State University, Terre Haute, IN (2000-Present); History Professor, Indiana State University, Terre Haute, IN (1964-2000) **CR:** Member, Baptist Heritage and Identity Study Commission, Baptist World Alliance (1990-Present); Visiting Professor, South Asia Institute of Advanced Christian Studies, India (2007-2012); Visiting Professor, Scholar-in-Residence, Gordon College, Wenham, MA (2000-2007); Visiting Professor, Moscow Theological Seminary (2004); Visiting Professor, Moscow

Theological Seminary (2003); Visiting Professor, University of Otago, New Zealand (2002); Visiting Professor, Moscow Theological Seminary (2001); Visiting Professor, Moscow Theological Seminary (1999); Visiting Professor, Moscow Theological Seminary (1997); Visiting Professor, Fuller Theological Seminary, Pasadena, CA (1991); Fulbright Professor, Martin Luther University of Halle-Wittenberg, German Democratic Republic (1989-1990); Delegate, Lausanne II Congress on World Evangelical, Manila, Philippines (1989); Visiting Professor, Fuller Theological Seminary, Pasadena, CA (1988); President, Greater Terre Haute Church Federation Inc (1987-1988); Visiting Professor, New Orleans Baptist Theological Seminary, Lombard, IL (1987); Fulbright Professor, Goethe University Frankfurt, Federal Republic Germany (1984-1985); Visiting Professor, Trinity Evangelical Divinity School, Deerfield, IL (1982); Visiting Professor, Regent College, Vancouver, British Columbia, Canada (1975); Visiting Professor, Free Theological Academy, Seeheim, Federal Republic Germany (1978); Visiting Professor, Greenville College, IL (1972-1973); Visiting Professor, Free Theological Academy, Seeheim, Federal Republic Germany (1971) **CIV:** Precinct Committeeman, Democratic Party, Terre Haute, IN (1990-2000); Delegate, Indiana Democratic Party Convention, Indianapolis, IN (1988); Member, The Indiana Governor's Advisory Committee on Libraries and Information Services (1980-1981); Delegate, Indiana Democratic Party Convention, Indianapolis, IN (1980); Delegate, White House Conference on Library and Information Services, Washington, D. C. (1979); Precinct Committeeman, Democratic Party, Terre Haute, IN (1978-1980) **MIL:** U.S. Army (1954-1956) **CW:** Co-Author, "Global Evangelicalism: Theology, History and Culture in Regional Perspective" (2014); Co-Author, "Blues Music and Gospel Proclamation" (2008); Co-Author, "The American Church Experience" (2008); Author "The Unequal Yoke: Evangelical Christianity and Political Conservatism, New Edition" (2006); Co-Author, "Baptists Together in Christ" (2005); Co-Author, "The New Millennium Manual" (1999); Co-Author, "The Revolution of the Candles: Christians in the Revolution of the German Democratic Republic" (1996); Co-Author, "Two Kingdoms: The Church and Culture through the Ages" (1993); Co-Author, "Civil Religion and the Presidency" (1988); Author, "Bibliography on the Religious Right in America" (1986); Co-Author, "Twilight of the Saints: Biblical Christianity and Civil Religion" (1978); Author, "The Unequal Yoke: Evangelical Christianity and Political Conservatism" (1970); Contributor, Articles, Religious and History Publications **AW:** Lifetime Achievement Award, Conference on Faith and History (2014); W.O. Carver Distinguished Service Award, Baptist History and Heritage Society (2009); Recipient, Terra Award for Community Service, Terre Haute, IN (1991); Chavanne Scholar, Baylor University (1988); Research Fellow, The University of Aberdeen, Scotland (1978); Fulbright Scholar University of Hamburg, Federal Republic Germany (1962-1963) **MEM:** Board of Managers, American Baptist Historical Society (1993-2003); President, The Evangelical Theological Society (1985); Secretary, Treasurer, Conference on Faith and History (1967-2004); American History Association; American Society of Church History; American Society of Missiology; International Association for Mission Studies; Barbershop Harmony Society; Rotary International **H:** Coin collector **PA:** Democrat **RE:** Baptist **ADD:** 208 Aldersgate Cir, Asheville, NC, 28803

PIERCE, MICHAEL NORMAN, T: Medical Director **I:** Medicine & Health Care **CN:** Quik Clinic Medical Center **DOB:** 05/01/1955 **PB:** New York **SC:** NY/USA **PT:** Samuel Pierce; Ingeborg Pierce **ED:** Mini-Fellowship, Headache, Vagelos College of Physicians and Surgeons, Columbia University (2004); Preceptorship, HIV, The Johns Hopkins University School of Medicine (2001); Intern, Resident, Internal Medicine, California Pacific Medical Center, San Francisco, CA (1985-1988); Intern, General Surgical Resident, Los Angeles County+USC Medical Center, Los Angeles, CA (1982-1984); MD, The University of Vermont (1982); BA in Biology, Binghamton University, State University of New York (1977) **CT:** Certified Internal Medicine Specialist, Diplomate, American Board of Internal Medicine (2007); License to Practice Medicine, State of California; License to Practice Medicine, State of New York; License to Practice Medicine, State of Florida; HIV Specialist, American Academy of HIV Medicine **C:** Director, Internal Medicine Attending, Allmed Medical And Rehabilitation Center, New York (2006-Present); Director, HIV Medicine, Allmed Medical And Rehabilitation Center, New York (2006-Present); Associate Attending Physician, Mount Sinai St. Luke's-Roosevelt, New York, NY (2005); Assistant Attending Physician, Mount Sinai St. Luke's-Roosevelt, New York, NY (2002-2005); Attending Physician, Division of Correctional Health Services, HHC, St. Barnabas Hospital, East Elmhurst, NY (1998-2001); Attending Physician, Montefiore Medical Center, East Elmhurst, NY (1997-1998); Attending Physician, Saint Francis Memorial Hospital, San Francisco, CA (1989-1996) **CR:** Founder, Suboxone Program, Allmed Medical And Rehabilitation Center, Bronx, NY (2008-Present); Judge, Member, Abstract Review Board, Resident's Poster Competition, New York Downstate Medical University American College of Physicians-ASIM Science Meetings (1997-Present); Chair, Spring Conference, Mount Sinai St. Luke's-Roosevelt (2003); Assistant Clinical Professor, Medicine, Vagelos College of Physicians and Surgeons, Columbia University, New York, NY (2002-2005); Member, Continuing Medical Education Medical Board Committee (2002-2005); Principal Investigator, Pfizer Clinical Trial of Maravaroc HIV; Medical Specialist, State of New York; Member, Infectious Diseases Society of America; Member, HIV Medical Association; Key Faculty, Internal Medicine Residency Program, Mount Sinai St. Luke's-Roosevelt, New York, NY **CW:** Co-Author, "International HIV Controllers Study-Ragon Institute of MGH, Massachusetts Institute of Technology & Harvard" (2010); Member, Editorial Board, Johns Hopkins University School of Medicine Advanced Studies in Medicine (2002-2005); Contributor, Articles to Professional Publications **AW:** Recipient, Physician's Recognition Award with Commendation in Continuing Medical Education, American Medical Association (1991-2009); Inductee, Healthgrades Honor Roll (1991-2009); Fellow, American College of Physicians (1982); Grantee, Pharmaceutical Manufacturers Association (1979); Recipient, Patients' Choice Award; Recipient, Compassionate Doctor Recognition **MEM:** Surveyor, Reviewer, Hospital Continuing Medical Education Programs, Medical Society of the State of New York (1998-Present); Committee on Medical Students, American College of Physicians (2001-2005); Fellow, American College of Physicians; Fellow, Society of General Internal Medicine; American Medical Association; Accreditation Council for Pharmacy Education; American College of Occupational and Environmental Medicine; New York County Medical Society; Committee on Education, Medical Society of the State of

New York **MH:** Albert Nelson Marquis Lifetime Achievement Award (2017) **ADD:** 2609 NE 14th Ave Apt 106, Oakland Park, FL, 33334

PIESCHE, ANTOINETTE , I: Other **C:** Owner, La Bella Moda

PIIRTO, DOUGLAS DONALD, T: Owner, Consulting Forester **I:** Environmental Services **CN:** Crestline Forestry Inc. **DOB:** 09/25/1948 **PB:** Reno **SC:** NV/USA **PT:** Rueben Arvid Piirto; Martha Hilma (Giebel) Piirto **MS:** Married **SPN:** Mary Louise Cruz (10/28/1978) **CH:** Tom Cervantez (Stepchild); Henry Cervantez (Stepchild) **ED:** Certificate in Silviculture, University of California, Berkeley (1979); PhD in Wood Science, University of California, Berkeley (1977); MS in Forest/Wood Science, Colorado State University (1971); BS in Forestry, University of Nevada, Reno, NV (1970) **CT:** Professional Forester License, State of California (1984-Present); Archaeological Surveyor Certificate (2017); Diplomate, SAF Continuing Education Certificate (2011); Diplomate, SAF Continuing Education Certificate (2008); Diplomate, SAF Continuing Education Certificate (2005); Diplomate, SAF Continuing Education Certificate (2002); Re-Certified Silviculturist, U.S. Forest Service, United States Department of Agriculture (1991); Certified Silviculturist, U.S. Forest Service, United States Department of Agriculture (1982); Certified in Silviculture, University of California, Berkeley (1979); Certified California Community College Instructor (1979); Diplomate, SAF Continuing Education Certificate (1978-1985); Certified Forester, Society of American Foresters **C:** Professor Emeritus, California Polytechnic State University (2015-Present); Owner, Crestline Forestry (1997-Present); Consulting Forester (1977-Present); Board Director, Upper Salinas Las Tablas Resource Conservation District (2015); Head, Department of Natural Resources Management & Environmental Sciences, California Polytechnic State University (2001); Professor, Department of Natural Resources Management & Environmental Sciences, California Polytechnic State University (1985); Retired, California Polytechnic State University (2015); Consultant Forest Scientist, Sequoia National Forest, U.S. Forest Service, United States Department of Agriculture (1995-2003); Professional Forester, Sierra National Forest, U.S. Forest Service, United States Department of Agriculture (1990-1995); Interim Head, Department of Natural Resources Management & Environmental Sciences, California Polytechnic State University (1989-1990); Forest Project Director, Swanton Pacific Ranch (1987-2015); Timber Management Officer, Pineridge Ranger District, Sierra National Forest, U.S. Forest Service, United States Department of Agriculture (1980-1985); Silviculturist, Pineridge Ranger District, Sierra National Forest, U.S. Forest Service, United States Department of Agriculture (1980-1985); Forester, Kings River Ranger District, Sierra National Forest, U.S. Forest Service, United States Department of Agriculture (1979-1980); Inventory Forester, Shasta-Trinity National Forest, U.S. Forest Service, United States Department of Agriculture (1979); Presale Forester, Kings River Ranger District, Sierra National Forest, U.S. Forest Service, United States Department of Agriculture (1977-1979); Teaching Assistant, University of California, Berkeley (1974-1975); Graduate Research Assistant, University of California, Berkeley (1972-1977); Graduate Research Assistant, Colorado State University, Fort Collins, CO (1970-1971); Teaching Assistant, Colorado State University, Fort Collins, CO (1970-1971); Laboratory Assistant, College of Agriculture Soil and Water Testing Laboratory, University of Nevada, Reno, NV (1969-1970); Leader, Timber Stand Improvement Crew, Chiloquin Ranger District, Fremont-Winema National Forest, U.S. Forest Service, United States Department of Agriculture (1969); Engineering Aid, Milford Ranger District, Plumas National Forest, U.S. Forest Service, United States Department of Agriculture (1968); Fellow, Society of American Foresters **CR:** Chair, Southern California Society, Society of American Foresters (2004-2006); Graduate Student Advisor, College of Agriculture, Food and Environmental Sciences, California Polytechnic State University (1986-2015); Instructor, U.S. Forest Service, United States Department of Agriculture (1977-Present); Internal Reviewer, California Polytechnic Landscape Architecture Accreditation and Program Reviews (2014); Board of Forestry and Fire Protection, State of California (2007-2011); Chair, Forest Management Committee, California Board of Forestry and Fire Protection (2007-2011); Policy Committee, Board of Forestry and Fire Protection, State of California (2007-2011); Internal Reviewer, California Polytechnic Landscape Architecture Accreditation and Program Reviews (2007-2008); Chair, National Association of University Forest Resource Programs, Western Region (2006-2008); Instructor, California Department of Forestry and Fire Protection; Part-Time Instructor, Reedley College; Researcher; Consultant; Expert Witness in Field; Working Group, Society of American Foresters; Facilitator, Project Learning Tree, Teacher Preparation Workshops **CIV:** Volunteer, Local Community Organizations (1990-Present); FACA Science Advisory Board, Giant Sequoia National Monument, U.S. Forest Service, United States Department of Agriculture (2000-2003); State Forest Advisory Committee; State Pitch Canker Task Force **CW:** Co-Author, "Canopy Gap Characteristics in Two Giant Sequoia Groves with Differing Cultural Histories" (In preparation); Co-Author, "Young-Growth Giant Sequoia Responses to Management Strategies in the Southern Sierra Nevada. Forest Science" (In preparation); Co-Author, "Using FORSEE and Continuous Forest Inventory Information to Compare Volume Estimation methods in Santa Cruz County Coast Redwood Forest," Coast Redwood Symposium, USDA Forest Service General Technical Report (2016); Co-Author, "Science Consistency Review Report: Draft Environmental Impact Statement for Revision of the Inyo, Sequoia, and Sierra National Forests Land Management Plans," USDA Forest Service, Pacific Southwest Station, Redding, CA (2016); Co-Author, "Integrating Indigenous Knowledge and Western Science into Forestry, Natural Resources, and Environmental Programs," Journal of Forestry (2016); Co-Author, "Estimating Site Occupancy and Detection Probabilities for Cooper's and Sharp-shinned Hawks in the Southern Sierra Nevada," Journal of Raptor Research (2015); Co-Author, "Management Strategies for Pitch Canker Infected Ano Nuevo Stands of Monterey Pine," Forest Ecology and Management (2013); Co-Author, "First record of Serropalpus substriatus Haldeman, 1848 (Colepotera: Melandryidae) on giant sequoia Sequoiadendron giganteum (Lindl.) J. Buchholz (Cuppressaceae): New larval host," Pan-Pacific Entomologist (2012); Contributor, 43 Publications; Contributor, Articles, Science and Forestry Journals; Contributor, 44 Technical Reports; Contributor 17 Study Guides/Lab Manuals/Web Pages; Contributor, Seven Professional Reports; Contributor, 11 Opinion Editorials; Presenter, Over 84 Invited Papers; Consultant, 18 Projects; Featured Guest, Radio; Featured Guest, Television **AW:** Grantee, Annual Student Assistant Program, California Department of Forestry and Fire Protection (2001-2015); Grantee, NRES Department Administrator, McIntire-Stennis (2000-2015); Boswell Agricultural Education Foundation Grants (1988-2015); Francis Raymond Lifetime Forestry Achievement Award, California Board of Forestry and Fire Protection (2016); President's Diversity Award, California Polytechnic State University (2016); Grantee, USDA Forest Service (2015-2016); Eponym, Creation of the Dr. Douglas D. Piirto Endowment for Excellence in Forestry Education, California Polytechnic State University (2015); Swanton Pacific Award, California Polytechnic State University (2013-2014); Lifetime Achievement Fellow Award, Society of American Foresters (2011); Certificate of Appreciation, U.S. Forest Service, United States Department of Agriculture (2009); Certificate of Appreciation, Cooperative State Research, Education, and Extension Service, United States Department of Agriculture (2004); Plant Science Award for Outstanding Service, California Polytechnic State University (2000); Meritorious Performance Awards, California Polytechnic State University (1995-2000); Outstanding Teacher Award, Sponsored by Dole Food Company, California Polytechnic State University (1995); Meritorious Performance Awards, California Polytechnic State University (1988-1989) **MEM:** Past Chancellor, Nevada Chapter, Alpha Zeta (1970); Forest Products Research Society; Society of Wood Science and Technology; Elks Club (BPO Elks); Alpha Zeta; Past Advisor, Xi Sigma Pi, California Polytechnic State University; Sigma Xi; Beta Beta Beta; Advisor, Phi Sigma Kappa, California Polytechnic State University; California Licensed Foresters Association **MH:** Albert Nelson Marquis Lifetime Achievement Award (2017); Distinguished Humanitarian (2017) **H:** Woodworking; Exercise; Sports **PA:** Republican **RE:** Lutheran **ADD:** 626 Wooded Hills Trl, Hobart, WI, 54155 **URL:** http://www.crestlineforestry.com

PIKUS, DAVID H., T: A Principal **I:** Law and Legal Services **CN:** Bressler, Amery & Ross, P.C. **PB:** Newark **SC:** NJ/USA **PT:** Joseph D. Pikus; Lila R. Pikus **ED:** JD, School of Law, University of Virginia (1980); AB, Princeton University, Cum Laude (1977) **C:** Principal, Bressler, Amery & Ross, Morristown and New York, NY, New Jersey (1994-Present); Partner, Shea & Gould, New York, NY (1989-1994); Associate, Shea & Gould, New York, NY (1980-1988); Assistant to Governor, State of New Jersey, Trenton, NJ (1977) **CR:** Special Master, U.S. District Court, Southern District, State of New York (2010); Special Master, U.S. District Court, Southern District, State of New York (2006-2007); Assistant Counsel, Governor's Judicial Screening Committee, New York, NY (1986-1987); Adjunct Professor in Health Law, Jersey City State College (1985-1986) **CIV:** Director, Summer Youth Voter Registration, Democratic State Committee, Trenton, NJ (1977) **CW:** Author, "Class Action Counsel Fees: Will the Lodestar Ride Again," New Jersey Lawyer Magazine; Speaker in Field **AW:** New York Metro Super Lawyers (2007-Present); A/V Preeminent Rating, Martindale-Hubbell (2006-Present) **MEM:** Civil Court Committee, Association of the Bar of the City of New York (1991-1994); Administrative Law Committee, Association of the Bar of the City of New York (1988-1991); Nuclear Technology and Law Committee, Association of the Bar of the City of New York (1985-1988); American Bar Association; Princeton Club of New York **BAR:** U.S. District Court, Northern District, State of New York (2000); Third Circuit, U.S. Court of Appeals (1988); U.S. District Court, State of New Jersey (1982); State of New Jersey (1982); State of New York (1981); U.S. District Courts, Southern and Eastern Districts, State of New York (1981) **BA:** 325

Columbia Turnpike, Suite 301, Bressler, Amery & Ross, P.C., Florham Park, NJ, 07932 **URL:** http://www.bressler.com/attorneys/pikus-david-h

PILLERS, DE-ANN, T: Professor **I:** Education/Educational Services **CN:** University of Wisconsin-Madison **DOB:** 08/01/1957 **PB:** San Pedro **SC:** CA/USA **PT:** Lauritz Pillers; June Pillers **MS:** Married **SPN:** Robert Nourse (7/25/1981) **ED:** Fellow in Neonatal and Perinatal Medicine, Doernbecher Children's Hospital, Oregon Health & Science University, Portland, OR (1989-1991); Resident in Pediatrics, Doernbecher Children's Hospital, Oregon Health & Science University, Portland, OR (1986-1989); PhD, Oregon Health & Science University (1986); MD, Oregon Health & Science University (1984); BS in Chemical Engineering, Washington University in St. Louis (1979); AB in French, Washington University in St. Louis (1979) **CT:** Board Certification in Neonatal-Perinatal Medicine **C:** Assistant Program Director, Oregon Child Health Research Center (1996-Present); Chief of Neonatology, University of Illinois (2017); Associate Professor of Pediatrics, Associate Professor of Molecular and Medical Genetics, Oregon Health & Science University, Portland, OR (1996-2008); Assistant Professor of Molecular and Medical Genetics, Oregon Health & Science University, Portland, OR (1991-1996); Chief Resident in Pediatrics, Oregon Health & Science University, Portland, OR (1988-1989); Professor, University of Wisconsin **CR:** Professor of Neck and Head Surgery; Professor of Research in Otolaryngology **CW:** Contributor, Numerous Medical Research Articles to Professional Journals; Editorial Board, Journal of Perinatology **AW:** Named, Best Doctors, Best Doctors in America (2016); Ross Young Investigator Award, Western Society for Pediatric Research (1998); David Smith Pediatric Resident Research Award, Western Society for Pediatric Research (1991) **MEM:** Fellow, American Academy of Pediatrics; American Medical Association; The American Society of Human Genetics; American Institute of Chemical Engineers **H:** Travel; Walking; Leisure time in the woods/park; Needlecraft **BA:** 840 South Wood Street, MC 856, University of Wisconsin-Madison, Chicago, IL, 60612 **ADD:** 5735 Tuscany La, Waunakee, WI, 53597

PIRODSKY, DONALD MAX, T: Psychiatrist, Educator **I:** Education/Educational Services **DOB:** 02/02/1945 **PB:** Freeport **SC:** NY/USA **PT:** Son of; Max Pirodsky; Doris Geilhard (Biedermann) Pirodsky **MS:** Single **SPN:** Gail Giufre Pallotta (1/4/1997, Divorced) **CH:** Laura Anne; Jason Donald **ED:** Resident in Psychiatry, University Medical Center Tucson, Banner Health (1974-1976); Resident in Psychiatry, Strong Memorial Hospital, University of Rochester Medical Center, Rochester, NY (1973-1974); Intern, Northwestern Memorial Hospital, Northwestern Medicine, Chicago, IL (1970-1971); MD, SUNY Upstate Medical University, Syracuse, NY (1970); BA, Hofstra University, Hempstead, NY (1966) **CT:** Diplomate, National Board of Medical Examiners; Diplomate, American Board of Psychiatry and Neurology, Inc. **C:** Retired; Private Practice (1986-2007); Adjunct Attending Psychiatrist, SUNY Upstate Medical University, Syracuse, NY (1991-2006); Clinical Associate Professor, SUNY Upstate Medical University, Syracuse, NY (1985-2006); Psychiatrist, Private Practice, Syracuse, NY (1976-2006); Psychiatrist, Private Practice, Fayetteville, NY (1976-2006); Attending Psychiatrist, SUNY Upstate Medical University, Syracuse, NY (1976-1991); Chairman, Pharmacy Review and Therapeutic Agents Committee, Syracuse VA Medical Center, U.S. Department of Veterans Affairs (1980-1986); Staff Psychiatrist, Syracuse VA Medical Center,

U.S. Department of Veterans Affairs (1976-1987); Director, Consultation/Liaison Service, Syracuse VA Medical Center, U.S. Department of Veterans Affairs (1976-1987); Assistant Professor of Psychiatry, SUNY Upstate Medical University, Syracuse, NY (1978-1985); Member, Executive Committee of Medical College Assembly, SUNY Downstate Medical Center (1979-1982); Instructor, Psychiatry, SUNY Upstate Medical University, Syracuse, NY (1976-1978) **CR:** Adjunct Attending Psychiatrist, SUNY Upstate Medical University, Syracuse, NY (1991-2006) Psychiatric Consultant, Syracuse Developmental Center (1977-2006) Psychiatric Consultant, Rochester School for the Deaf (1978-1981) Psychiatric Consultant, Arizona State Schools for the Deaf and the Blind, Tucson, AZ (1975-1976) Ex-Official Member, Family Counseling Agency, Tucson, AZ (1975-1976) **MIL:** Lieutenant Commander, U.S. Public Health Service, U.S. Department of Health and Human Services (1971-1973) **CW:** Author, "Clinical Primer of Psychopharmacology: A Practical Guide, Second Edition" (1992); Co-Author, "Primer of Clinical Psychopharmacology: A Practical Guide" (1981); Contributor, Articles, Professional Journals; Contributor, Medical Book Chapters **AW:** Distinguished Fellow, American Psychiatric Association (2003) **MEM:** Fellow, American Psychiatric Association; Distinguished Member, Central New York District Branch, American Psychiatric Association; American Psychosomatic Society; American Association on Mental Retardation (Now AAIDD); The Medical Society of the State of New York; New York State Psychiatric Association; Onondaga County Medical Society; Association of American Physicians and Surgeons **MH:** Albert Nelson Marquis Lifetime Achievement Award (2018) **H:** Sports; Collecting baseball cards and other sports memorabilia **RE:** Episcopalian **ADD:** 5393 Cambiago St, Sarasota, FL, 34238 **URL:** https://www.linkedin.com/in/drdonaldpirodsky/

PIZZAMIGLIO, ALBERT THEODORE, T: Conductor, Band Leader **I:** Media & Entertainment **CN:** Al Pierson & Guy Lombardo's Royal Canadians **DOB:** 12/19/1931 **PB:** Spring Valley **SC:** IL/USA **PT:** Annibale Pizzamiglio; Sarah Pizzamiglio **MS:** Single **SPN:** Nancy Alice Gilman (3/27/1978, Deceased 5/8/2016) **CH:** Catherine Meddaugh; Gregory Pizzamiglio; Lisa Kay Forest; Lori Roberton; Randel Lovas **ED:** Coursework in Advanced Music Studies, University of Illinois; BA, Illinois State University; MA, Illinois State University **C:** Leader, Al Pierson & Guy Lombardo's Royal Canadians (1989-Present); Band Leader, Al Pierson Big Band (1954-1989); Conductor, Al Pierson Big Band USA (1975-1989); Owner, Dancing Horse Ranch, Aubrey, TX; With, Gilman, Inc. Artists Management; With, Al Pierson, Inc. **CR:** Leader, Guy Lombardo and His Royal Canadians (2000); Owner, Guy Lombardo and His Royal Canadians (2000); National Youth Music Director, American Institute of Cooperative Education; Teacher, Heyworth High School; Teacher, Illinois State University; Music Ambassador, Illinois State University; Teacher, Olympia Schools, Minier, IL (1970-1975) **CIV:** Musician, Presidential Inauguration of George W. Bush (2004); Musician, Presidential Inauguration of George W. Bush (2000); Musician, Presidential Inauguration of Bill Clinton (1992) **CW:** Conductor, Public Broadcasting Service (PBS) (1995-Present); Performer, "2000 Concert and Dance," Guy Lombardo's Royal Canadians with Al Pierson (2000); Ambassador, Music for World, Illinois State University (1998); President, Music for World, Illinois State University (1998); Contributing Performer, Television Specials, Public Broadcasting Service (PBS) (1994-1997); Founder, Al Pierson & Big Band USA; Musician; Lecturer; Composer; Arranger; Vocalist; Band

Leader; Performer, Shows, Riverboat Cruises; Performer, Numerous Famous Ballrooms and Private Parties; Performer, International Dance Tours, Europe; Performer, International Dance Tours, Asia; Performer, International Dance Tours, The Middle East; Performer, International Dance Tours, The Caribbean; Performer, International Dance Tours, Mexico; Performer, International Dance Tours, Alaska; Performer, International Dance Tours, Hawaii; Performer, International Dance Tours, Tahiti; Performer, Over 13 albums; Contributing Performer, New Year's Show, PBS **AW:** Honoree, Alumnus of the Year, Illinois State University (2004-Present); Silver Ring Master Award, Shriner's Circus Club (2017); Recipient, Distinguished Alumni Award, Illinois State University (2004); Recipient, Superman Award (1997); Honoree, America's Number One Dance Band (1977); Honoree, Ballroom Dancers' Hall of Fame (1976); Honoree, Best New Dance Band in the Country (1975); Honoree, Who's Who Among College and University Students (1954); Honoree, 2000 Outstanding Musicians of the 20th Century, International Biographical Center; Recipient, Men's Club Award, The Illinois Club; Who's Who in the World; Who's Who in America; Top 2000 Musicians in the 20th Century, International Biographical Centre **MEM:** The Grand Lodge of Texas; Shriners International **MH:** Albert Nelson Marquis Lifetime Achievement Award (2017) **PA:** Independent **RE:** Baptist **ADD:** 2469 Spring Hill Rd, Aubrey, TX, 76227

PLANT, JACKSON VAUGHN, T: Bishop **I:** Religious **CN:** Plant Ministries **DOB:** 03/09/1964 **PB:** Tallahassee **SC:** FL/USA **PT:** Harry Jackson; Caroline Plant **MS:** Married **SPN:** Julie M. Plant (2012) **ED:** Certificate in Computer Programming **CT:** Ordained Bishop, Church of God, Cleveland, TN (2010) **C:** Guitarist on Staff, Grace Point Fellowship, Harlingen, TX (2016-Present); Founder, Plant Ministires(2014-Present); Owner, Plant Designz (2004-Present); Senior Pastor, Kingdom Time Ministry (2013-2014); Senior Pastor, Hawaii MTTM Christian Servicemen's Center, Kapolei, HI (2014-2015); Youth Pastor, Hawaii MTTM Christian Servicemen's Center, Kapolei, HI (2013-2014); Associate Pastor, Kingdom Victory Church, Cumberland, MD (2007-2012); Associate Pastor, New Life Ministries, The Ark, Odenton, MD (2002-2007); Founder, For This Time Ministries, Glen Burnie, MD (1999-2014); Pastor, For This Time Ministries, Glen Burnie, MD (1999-2014); Senior Pastor, Yokosuka Ministry to the Military, Christian Servicemen Center, Yokosuka, Japan (1999-2002); Singles Pastor, Yokohama Ministry to the Military, Christian Servicemen Center, Yokohama, Japan (1998-1999); Minister, USS Kitty Hawk CV-63 (1998-1998); Guitarist, Pensacola First Assembly of God (1997-1998); Youth Pastor, First Assembly of God, Kings Bay, GA (1994-1997); Visitor Pastor, First Assembly of God, Kings Bay, GA (1994-1997) **CR:** Ordained Bishop, Church of God, Cleveland, TN **CIV:** Intelligence Analysis, Department of Defense (2008-2016) **MIL:** Cryptologic Technician Collection First Class (Surface Warfare) Petty Officer, First Class, U.S. Navy (1988-2008) **MEM:** Vice President, Eta Phi Chapter, Alpha Tau Omega Fraternity (1983); Life Member, Eta Phi Chapter, Alpha Tau Omega Fraternity **H:** Playing the guitar; Computers; Photography **PA:** Republican **RE:** Pentecostal Church of God **ADD:** 709 N 77 Sunshine Strip 140, Harlingen, TX, 78550 **URL:** http://www.jacksonplant.org

PLOTKIN, IRVING H., T: Economist, Consultant **I:** Consulting **DOB:** 07/19/1941 **PB:** Brooklyn **SC:** NY/USA **PT:** Samuel H. Plotkin; Dorothy (Falick) Plotkin **MS:** Married **SPN:** Janet V. Bufe (7/26/1969) **CH:** Aaron Jacob; Joshua Benjamin

ED: PhD in Mathematics and Economics, Massachusetts Institute of Technology (1968); BS in Economics, University of Pennsylvania (1963) **C:** Managing Director, PwC National Tax Services (2002-Present); Senior Economist, Director of Regulation and Economics, Vice President, ESOP Trustee, Arthur D. Little, Inc., Cambridge, MA (1968-2002); Independent Consultant, Economics and Operations Research to Banks, Mutual Funds, Insurance Companies, Government Agencies, Cambridge, MA (1965-1968); Corporation Planning Analyst, Mobil Oil Italiana, Genoa, Italy (1965); Corporation Planning Analyst, Mobil Oil Company, New York City NY (1962-1963) **CR:** Expert Witness, Unites States House of Representatives and Senate Committees, United States Court of Claims, United States Tax Court, International Criminal Court, Federal Trade Commission, Federal Maritime Commission, Federal District Courts, Federal Reserve Board, and Other Federal and State Courts and Government Agencies (1967-Present); Vice President, Arthur D. Little Valuation, Inc. (1979-2002); Instructor, Finance and Computer Sciences, Massachusetts Institute of Technology (1965-1968) **CIV:** Board and Finance Committee; Boston Symphony Orchestra; Boston Lyric Opera; American Repertory Theatre at Harvard; Rockport Music's Shalin Liu Performance Center **CW:** Editorial Reviewer, Journal of the American Statistical Association; Editorial Reviewer, Journal of Industrial Economics; Author, "Risk/Return: U.S. Industry Pattern," Harvard Business Review; Author, "Rates of Return in the Property and Liability Insurance Industry: A Comparative Analysis," Journal of Risk and Insurance; Author, "The Consequences of Industrial Regulation on Profitability, Risk Taking, and Innovation,"; Author, "Torrens in the United States,"; Author, "Economic Principles in Establishing Transfer Prices,"; Author, "Tax Management,"; Author, "Foreign Income Portfolio"; Contributor, Numerous Reports to Legislative, Regulatory, and Judicial Bodies **AW:** Fellow, American Bankers Association (1968); Fellow, National Science Foundation (1967); Fellow, NASA (1963-1966) **MEM:** Chapter President, Tau Delta Phi (1962-1963); American Economic Association, Econometric Society; American Finance Association; Beta Gamma Sigma; Pi Gamma Mu **H:** Classical Music; Opera; Collecting and viewing fine art; Travel; Reading **ADD:** 975 Memorial Dr Apt 910, Cambridge, MA, 02138

POGUE, JOHN MARSHALL, T: President **I:** Government Administration/Government Relations/Government Services **CN:** Governor William Bradford Compact **DOB:** 09/21/1945 **PB:** Washington **SC:** DC/USA **PT:** Lloyd Welch Pogue; Mary Ellen (Edgerton) Pogue **ED:** MD, Georgetown University; AB, Princeton University, With Honors **CT:** Diplomate, National Board of Medical Examiners **C:** President, Governor William Bradford Compact (GWBC) (2008-Present); Surgeon, GWBC (1999-Present); Historian, GWBC (1996-Present); Editor, Bradford Journal (1983-Present); Author, Bradford Journal (1983-Present); Vice President, GWBC (2005-2008); Intern, Medstar Georgetown University Hospital; Resident, Medstar Georgetown University Hospital **CR:** Speaker, Field of Cardiology; Lecturer, Field of Cardiology; Fellow, Royal Microscopy Society; Fellow, Royal Statistical Society; Fellow, Royal Geographical Society; Fellow, RSA; Fellow, ISHNE **CW:** Author, "Caldwell Blakeman Esselstyn, Junior, M.D. of the Cleveland Clinic, Defeater of Coronary Artery Heart Disease Through Low-Fat, Plant-Based Nutrition" (2008); Director, "Hugo Victor Rizzoli, Preeminent Neurosurgeon, A.B. and M.D., Johns Hopkins, Neurosurgery Training at Johns Hopkins Hospital" (2005); Designer, "Official Order of Descendants of

Colonial Physicians and Chirurgiens Flag" (2005); Author, "Sir William Osler, M.D., The Preeminent Physician: From McGill to the University of Pennsylvania, Johns Hopkins, and Oxford" (2004); Author, "Herbert Martin Giffin, M.D., A Role Model Physician and a Doctor's Doctor: From Princeton to Johns Hopkins, Mayo Clinic, US Navy, and Yater Clinic" (2000); Associate Editor, "Hereditary Society Blue Book" (1997); Editor, "Pogue/Pollock/Polk Genealogy as Mirrored in History, From Scotland to Northern Ireland/Ulster, Ohio, and Westward" (1990); Contributor, "Pogue/Pollock/Polk Genealogy as Mirrored in History, From Scotland to Northern Ireland/Ulster, Ohio, and Westward" (1990); Designer, "Official Governor William Bradford Flag" (1987); Contributor, Articles on Cardiology, Medical Journals **AW:** New Constellation Award, National Flag Foundation (1996); Genealogy Awards (1990); Meritorious History Awards (1990) **MEM:** Director, Order of Descendants Colonial Physicians and Chirurgiens (2015-Present); Flag Protector, Dutch Colonial Society (2015-Present); Surgeon General, Hereditary Order of Descendants of Colonial Governors (2011-Present); Honorary General President Emeritus, Order of Descendants Colonial Physicians and Chirurgiens (2006-Present); Surgeon General, Order of Descendants Colonial Physicians and Chirurgiens (2006-Present); Surgeon, District of Columbia Society of Mayflower Descendants (1998-Present); Honorary Chairman of Membership Committee, Order of Descendants Colonial Physicians and Chirurgiens (1994-Present); Patroon, Dutch Colonial Society (2012-2015); Colonial Member, Dutch Colonial Society (2010); Recording Secretary General, Hereditary Order of Descendants of Colonial Governors (2005-2013); President General, Order of Descendants Colonial Physicians and Chirurgiens (2003-2006); Vice President General, Order of Descendants Colonial Physicians and Chirurgiens (2000-2003); Surgeon General, Order of Descendants Colonial Physicians and Chirurgiens (1994-2000); Founder, Friends of the National Library of Medicine (1988); British Cardiovascular Society; Premium Professional Member, American Heart Association, Inc.; Gold Heart Member, American Heart Association, Inc.; Clinical Cardiology Council, American Heart Association, Inc.; Arteriosclerosis, Thrombosis & Vascular Biology Council, American Heart Association, Inc.; Basic Cardiovascular Sciences Council, American Heart Association, Inc.; American Medical Association; Cardiology Section, Royal Society of Medicine; Cardiothoracic Section, Royal Society of Medicine; European Society of Cardiology; Professional Member, Laennec Cardiovascular Sound Society; British Society of Echocardiography; Cardiac Sonography Council, American Society of Echocardiography; Intraoperative Echocardiography Council, American Society of Echocardiography; Pediatrics & Congenital Heart Disease Council, American Society of Echocardiography; Vascular Ultrasound Council, American Society of Echocardiography; International Society of Cardiovascular Ultrasound; International Society of Electrocardiology; International Academy of Cardiovascular Sciences; BSCMR; Society of Cardiovascular Magnetic Resonance; International Atherosclerosis Society; British Society for Heart Failure; Heart Failure Society of America; Cardiac Imaging Council, Heart Valve Society; International Society of Cardiovascular Pharmacotherapy; The British Society for Cardiovascular Research; Cardiac Metabolism Section, International Society for Heart Research; Stem Cell & Gene Therapy Section, International Society for Heart Research; Ischemia, Cardioprotection & Mitochondria Section, International Society for Heart Research; Cardiac Muscle Society; European Association for Cardiovascular Preven-

tion and Rehabilitation; EMS; Friends of the Osler Library, McGill University; Friends Organization, Museum of the History of Science; The Ashmolean Natural History Society; OUHS; Cambridge Bibliographical Society; Cambridge University Library, University of Cambridge; The International Shakespeare Association; Alumni Association of Princeton University; The Princeton Tigertones; National Gavel Society,; Hereditary Society of Community; Provincial Families of Maryland; Kenwood Park Citizens Association; Medical Art Society; Medical Music Society of London; Princeton Club of Washington; Oxford Bibliographical Society; Bodleian Libraries **H:** Classical music; Reading **ADD:** 5204 Kenwood Avenue, Chevy Chase, MD, 20815

POHOST, GERALD MICHAEL, T: 1) Cardiologist 2) Medical Educator **I:** Medicine & Health Care **CN:** 1) Salick Cardiovascular Centers 2) University of Alabama at Birmingham **DOB:** 10/27/1941 **PB:** Washington **SC:** DC/USA **MS:** Married **CH:** 3 Children **ED:** Senior Resident, Jacobi Medical Center, Department of Medicine, Albert Einstein College of Medicine, Bronx, NY (1969-1970); Assistant Resident, Montefiore Medical Center, Bronx, New York (1968-1969); Intern, Montefiore Medical Center, Bronx, New York (1967-1968); Cardiology Resident, Montefiore Medical Center; MD, University of Maryland (1967); BS, The George Washington University (1963) **CT:** Diplomate, American Board of Internal Medicine; Diplomate, American Board of Cardiovascular Disease; Diplomate, American Board of Nuclear Medicine **C:** Senior Vice President, Salick Cardiovascular Centers, Beverly Hills, CA (2006-Present); Medical Officer, Salick Cardiovascular Centers (2006-Present); Professor, Cardiovascular Medicine, University of Alabama at Birmingham (1991-Present); Mary Getrude Waters Chair, Cardiovascular Medicine Division, University of Alabama at Birmingham (1991-Present); Professor of Medicine and Radiology, University of Alabama at Birmingham (1983-Present); Head, Cardiovascular Medicine Division, Keck School of Medicine of University of Southern California (2002-2006); Department of Radiology, Massachusetts General Hospital, The General Hospital Corporation (1978-1983); Assistant, General Medical Services, General Hospital, The General Hospital Corporation, Boston, MA (1978-1982); Associate Medical Professor, Harvard Medical School, Harvard University (1977-1983); Assistant Medical Professor, Harvard Medical School, Harvard University (1977-1983); Medical Instructor, Harvard Medical School, Harvard University (1974-1977); Professor of Medicine, University of Southern California **CR:** Director, Center for Nuclear Magnetic Resonance Research and Development, University of Alabama at Birmingham (1986-Present); Consultant, Nuclear Medicine, Radiology Department, Massachusetts General Hospital, The General Hospital Corporation (1977-1983) **CW:** Editor-in-Chief, Journal of Cardiovascular Magnetic Resonance (1999-Present); Editor, Journal of Cardiovascular Magnetic Resonance, BioMed Central Ltd. (1998-Present); Senior Editor, "The Principles and Practice of Cardiovascular Imaging," Little, Brown & Co. (1991); Senior Editor, "New Concepts in Cardiac Imaging," Year Book Medical Publishers (1986-1989); Senior Editor, "New Concepts in Cardiac Imaging," G.K. Hall Medical Publishers (1985); Senior Editor, "Noninvasive Cardiac Imaging," Year Book Medical Publishers (1983); Contributor, Articles, Reviews, Editorials, Professional Journals; International Speaker in Field; Editorial Board, Circulation, Magnetic Resonance in Medicine, ISMRM; Editorial Board, The American Journal of Cardiology, Elsevier, Inc.; Editorial Board, International Journal of Cardiology, Elsevier B.V.; Editorial Board, NMR in BioMedicine, John Wiley & Sons Ltd.; Editorial Board, Coronary Artery Disease, Wolters Kluwer Health, Inc. **AW:** Training Grantee, National Institutes of Health, United States Department of Health and Human Services (1992-Present); Grantee, United States Department of Energy (1992-Present); Grantee, SCOR, National Institutes of Health, United States Department of Health and Human Services (1990-Present); National Center for Research Resources, National Institutes of Health, United States Department of Health and Human Services (1992-2011); Fellow, Research Committee, Subgroup A, American Heart Association, Inc. (1988-1991); Richard and Hinda Rosenthal Award for Excellence in Clinical Investigation, American Heart Association, Inc. (1985); Fellow, Research in Medicine, Harvard Medical School, Harvard College (1971-1973); Clinical Fellow, Research in Medicine, Massachusetts General Hospital (1971-1973); Fellow, American Heart Association, Inc.; Fellow, American College of Cardiology Foundation **MEM:** Executive Committee, ISMRM (1987-Present); Council on Clinical Cardiology, American Heart Association, Inc. (1975-Present); Council on Clinical Cardiology, American Heart Association, Inc. (1975-Present); Executive Committee, American Heart Association, Inc. (1998-2000); Executive Committee, Society for Cardiovascular Magnetic Resonance (1995-1999); President, Society for Cardiovascular Magnetic Resonance (1995-1998); Secretary Treasurer, Association of Professors of Cardiology (1995-1996); Trustee, Society for Cardiovascular Magnetic Resonance (1995); Founder, Society for Cardiovascular Magnetic Resonance (1995); Trustee, American College of Cardiology Foundation (1994-1999); Radiological Study Section, National Heart, Lung and Blood Institute, National Institutes of Health, United States Department of Health and Human Services (1994-1999); Immediate Past Chairman, American Heart Association, Inc. (1994); Chairman, Nominating Committee, American Heart Association, Inc. (1993-1995); Cardiovascular and Renal Study Section, National Heart, Lung and Blood Institute, National Institutes of Health, United States Department of Health and Human Services (1991-1994); Chairman, Executive Committee, American Heart Association, Inc. (1991-1993); Council on Nuclear Cardiology, Society of Nuclear Medicine and Molecular Imaging (1990-1992); Governor Relations Committee, American College of Cardiology Foundation (1989-1995); Vice Chairman, Executive Committee, Council on Clinical Cardiology, American Heart Association, Inc. (1989-1991); Budget Committee, American Heart Association, Inc. (1989-1991); Nominating Committee, American Heart Association, Inc. (1989-1991); Procedural Terminology Committee, American College of Cardiology Foundation (1988-1994); Chairman, American Heart Association, Inc. (1989-1991); Scientific Program Committee, ISMRM (1988-1989); Long Range Planning Committee, American Heart Association, Inc. (1986-1989); President, ISMRM (1986-1987); Chairman, Panel on Nuclear Magnetic Resonance and Imaging, American Medical Association (1985-1988); Advisory Committee, United States Nuclear Regulatory Commission (1984-1993); Program Project Review Committee, National Heart, Lung and Blood Institute, National Institutes of Health, United States Department of Health and Human Services (1984-1988); Alabama Affiliate, American Heart Association, Inc. (1983-2000); Journal Editorial Board, American College of Cardiology Foundation (1982-1988); Chairman, Cardiac Imaging Committee, American College

of Cardiology Foundation (1982-1988); Executive Committee, American Heart Association, Inc. (1981-1995); Chairman, Advanced Cardiac Technology Committee, Council on Clinical Cardiology, American Heart Association, Inc. (1981-1986); Established Investigator, American Heart Association, Inc. (1979-1984); Massachusetts Affiliate, American Heart Association, Inc. (1975-1983); American Federation for Medical Research; The American Society for Clinical Investigation; American Association of University Professors; Southern Medical Association; Reviewers Reserve, National Institutes of Health, United States Department of Health and Human Services; Association of University Cardiologists, Inc.; Sigma Xi **MH:** Albert Nelson Marquis Lifetime Achievement Award (2017) **ADD:** 4366 W 8th Street, Los Angeles, CA, 90005

POLK, HIRAM CAREY JR., T: Professor of Surgery **I:** Education/Educational Services **CN:** University of Louisville **DOB:** 03/23/1936 **PB:** Jackson **SC:** MS/USA **PT:** Hiram Carey Polk; Dorris (Hemby) Polk **MS:** Married **SPN:** Susan Galandiuk **CH:** Susan Elizabeth; Hiram Cary **ED:** Resident, Barnes Jewish Hospital (1961-1965); Intern, Barnes Jewish Hospital, St. Louis (1960-1961); MD, Harvard Medical School (1960); BS, Millsaps College (1956) **C:** Professor Emeritus, University of Louisville (2005-Present); Professor, University of Louisville (1971-2005); Chairman, Department of Surgery, University of Louisville (1971-2005); President, University Surgical Associates (1971-2005); Chairman of the Board, University Surgical Associates (1971-2005); Associate Professor, University of Miami (1969-1971); Assistant Professor of Surgery, University of Miami (1965-1969); Instructor in Surgery, Washington University in St. Louis (1964-1965); Chairman of the Board, Clinical Services Association, Inc. **CR:** Commissioner, State Department for Public Health, Kentucky (2015-2017); Member, Merit Review Board for Surgery, U.S. Department of Veterans Affairs (1983-1985) **CIV:** Senior Steward, Executive Committee, The Jockey Club (2011-Present); Founder, Safety Committee, The Jockey Club **CW:** Editorial Board Member, "Collected Letters in Surgery" (1978-Present); Editorial Board Member, "Current Surgery" (1977-Present); Editorial Board Member, "Current Surgical Techniques" (1977-Present); Editorial Board Member, "Emergency Surgery: A Weekly Update" (1977-Present); Editorial Board Member, "Current Problems in Surgery" (1973-Present); Chief Editor, "American Journal of Surgery" (1986-2004); Co-author, "Basic Surgery, Fifth Edition" (1995); Editorial Board Member, "British Journal of Surgery" (1981-1994); Co-author, "Basic Surgery, Fourth Edition" (1992); Co-author, "Basic Surgery," Third Edition (1987); Co-author, "Trauma: Clinical Care and Pathophysiology" (1987); Editorial Board Member, "Surgery" (1975-1985); Co-author, "Antibiotic Prophylaxis in Surgery: A Comprehensive Review" (1984); Co-author, "Basic Surgery, Second Edition" (1983); Co-author, "Trauma" (1982); Editorial Board Member, "Journal for Surgical Research" (1970-1972, 1975-1980); Co-author, "Basic Surgery" (1978); Author, Hospital-Acquired Infections in Surgery" (1977); Editorial Board Member, "Southern Medical Journal" (1970-1972); Co-author, "Contemporary Burn Management" (1971); Editor Emeritus, "American Journal of Surgery"; Contributor, Articles, Professional Journals **AW:** Research Initiative Initiation Award, National Science Foundation (2017) **MEM:** Vice President, James IV Association of Surgeons (2002-Present); President, American Surgical Association (2005); President, Southeastern Surgical Congress (1994-1995); National Delegation Director, American Cancer Society, Inc. (1989-1995); President, Kentucky Di-

vision, American Cancer Society, Inc. (1989-1990); President, Louisville Surgical Society (1989-1990); Executive Council for Kentucky, Southern Medical Association (1971-1977, 1989-1990); President, Southern Surgical Association (1988-1989); Secretary, American Surgical Association (1984-1989); President, Collegium International Chirurgiae Digestivae (1986-1987); President, Society for Surgery of the Alimentary Tract (1985-1986); Executive Council for Kentucky, Southeastern Surgical Congress (1985-1986); Secretary-treasurer, Collegium International Chirurgiae Digestivae (1981-1986); President, Society of Surgical Oncology (1984-1985); Chairman, Residency Review Committee for Surgery (1983-1985); President, Kentucky Surgical Society (1982-1983); Vice Chairman, Residency Review Committee for Surgery (1981-1983); President, Society of University Surgeons (1979-1980); Chairman, Ad Hoc Committee on Medicare and Medicaid, AAMC (1978-1979); Executive Council, Allen O. Whipple Society (1977-1980); Treasurer, Society for Surgery of the Alimentary Tract (1975-1978); President, Association for Academic Surgery (1975-1976); Governor, American College of Surgeons (1972-1980); Treasurer, Society of University Surgeons (1971-1974); Chairman, Section on Surgery, Southern Medical Association (1972-1973); Secretary, Southern Medical Association (1970-1972); Executive Council, American Association for Cancer Education (1968-1972); Vice Chairman, Section on Surgery, Southern Medical Association (1969-1970); Fellow, Royal College of Surgeons of Edinburgh; American Medical Association; The American Association for the Surgery of Trauma; American Burn Association; CSA; Task Group on Health Sciences, The Council on Public Higher Education; The Halsted Society; Jefferson County Medical Society; Kentucky Medical Association; International Society of Surgery; Society of Clinical Surgery; Society of Surgical Chairs, American College of Surgeons; Alpha Omega Alpha Honor Medical Society **MH:** Albert Nelson Marquis Lifetime Achievement Award (2017) **RE:** Presbyterian **BA:** 550 S Jackson St, Louisville, KY, 40202 **ADD:** 5609 River Knolls Dr, Louisville, KY, 40222

POLLACK, MARSHA, T: Secondary School Educator **I:** Education/Educational Services **CN:** New York City Department of Education **PT:** Harry Grunberg; Rose Grunberg **MS:** Married **SPN:** Bertram Pollack (7/15/1973) **CH:** Meredith Pollack-Richman **ED:** Specialist Diploma in Administration and Supervision, Queens College (2003); MS, Brooklyn College (1973); BA, Brooklyn College (1968) **CT:** Certified Teacher, National Board of Professional Teaching Standards (2001) **C:** Teacher, Private Religious School, Solomon Schechter School of Queens (2006-Present); Teacher, Coach, Staff Development, New York City Department of Education, Queens, NY (2003-2006); Assistant Principal, New York City Department of Education, Queens, NY (2002-2003); Teacher, New York City Department of Education, Brooklyn and Queens, NY (1968-2002) **CR:** Lesson Plan Abstract Evaluator, International Literacy Association (2003-2005); Professional Developer, Jericho Middle School (2003); National Staff Developer, New York City Department of Education (2000-2006); L.E.A.D. Teacher (1998-2002) **AW:** CAL Grantee, Chase Manhattan (2001) **MEM:** Former Member, American Federation of Teachers; Former Member, NCTE; Former Member, Phi Delta Kappa; Former Member, International Literacy Association; Former Member, ASCD **H:** Law; Educational research; Writing; Online classes **ADD:** 7850 221st St, Oakland Gardens, NY, 11364

POLLOCK, RICHARD A., **T:** Surgeon **I:** Medicine & Health Care **CN:** Lexington Medical Group **PB:** Wingham **SC:** ON/Canada **MS:** Married **CH:** Todd; Kerry; Leslie **ED:** MD in Plastic Surgery, University of Michigan (1984); Resident in Otolaryngology, School of Medicine, Emory University (1968); Fellowship, University of Toronto **CT:** Board Certified Otolayngologist **C:** Surgeon, Lexington Medical Group **AW:** Recipient, Bronze Star, U.S. Army (1971) **MEM:** North American Faculty, AO Foundation; American Academy of Otolaryngology — Head and Neck Surgery; Southeastern Society of Plastic and Reconstructive Surgeons; Reed Dingman Society, University of Michigan; American Society of Plastic Surgeons **H:** Exercise; Creative writing **BA:** 2160 Noll Dr Ste 200, Lexington Medical Group, Lancaster, PA, 17603

POMFRET, DAVID B., **T:** Physician **I:** Education/ Educational Services **CN:** TH Medical **DOB:** 11/22/1937 **PB:** Somerset **SC:** MA/USA **PT:** David B. Pomfret; Rhea Chouinard **MS:** Married **SPN:** Anna Rafferty (3/31/1964) **CH:** Mark; Bruce; Scott; Heidi **ED:** MD, University College Dublin, Ireland, Summa Cum Laude (1964); BS, Stonehill College (1959) **CT:** Diplomate, American Board of Internal Medicine **C:** Professor of Medicine, Tumaini University Makumira, Moshi, Tanzania (1996-2000); Clinical Professor, Tufts University, Boston, MA (1976-2001); Chief of Staff, Leonard Morse Hospital, TH Medical, Natick, MA (1976-1980); Chief of Medicine, Leonard Morse Hospital, TH Medical, Natick, MA (1968-1971) **CR:** Fellowship, American College of Physicians (1972) **CW:** Author, "Dispatches From Kilimanjaro" (2006); Author, "Computer Science" (1998); Contributor, Articles, Professional Journals; Lecturer in Field **AW:** Honoree, Outstanding Alumnus, Stonehill College (2003); Silver Medal in Medicine, School of Medicine, University College Dublin (1964); Gold Medal in Surgery (1964) **MH:** Albert Nelson Marquis Lifetime Achievement Award (2017) **H:** Skiing all over the world; Sailing; Offshore racing, but stopped racing in 2016 **ADD:** 20 Greygull Road, Jamestown, RI, 02535

PONDER, CATHERINE, **T:** Founding Minister **I:** Religious **CN:** Unity Church Worldwide **DOB:** 02/14/1927 **PB:** Hartsville **SC:** SC/USA **PT:** Roy Charles; Kathleen (Parrish) Cook **CH:** Richard **ED:** Honorary Doctorate, The Unity School of Christianity, Unity Worldwide Ministries (1976); BS in Education, Unity School of Ministerial Preparation, Unity Worldwide Ministries (1956); Coursework, Worth Business College (1948) **CT:** Ordained to Ministry, The Unity School of Christianity, Unity Worldwide Ministries (1958) **C:** Founding Minister, Unity Church, Unity Worldwide Ministries, Palm Desert, CA (1973-Present); Founding Minister, Unity Church of San Antonio, Unity Worldwide Ministries (1969-1973); Founding Minister, Unity Church of the Hills, Unity Worldwide Ministries (1961-1969); Minister, Unity of Birmingham, Unity Worldwide Ministries (1958-1961) **CW:** Contributing Author, "Keys to Prosperity" (1973-Present); Author, "Prosperity Love Story, From Rags to Enrichment" (2003); Author, "The Dynamic Laws of Prayer" (1987); Author, "Open Your Mind to Prosperity" (1984); Author, Â"The Prospering Power of Love" (1984); Author, "Dare To Prosper!: The Prospering Power of Prayer" (1983); Author, "Open Your Mind To Receive" (1983); Author, "The Secret of Unlimited Prosperity" (1981); Author, "The Millionaire from Nazareth" (1979); Author, "The Millionaire Joshua" (1978); Author, "The Millionaire Moses" (1977); Author, "The Millionaires of Genesis" (1976); Author, "Pray and Grow Rich" (1968); Author, "The Healing Secret of the Ages" (1967); Author, "The Dynamic Laws of Healing" (1966); Author, "The Prosperity Secret of the Ages" (1964); Author, "The Dynamic Laws of Prosperity" (1962) **MH:** Albert Nelson Marquis Lifetime Achievement Award (2017) **ADD:** 1697 Hillview Cv, c/o Karen French, Palm Springs, CA, 92264

PONSKY, JEFFREY, **T:** Surgeon **I:** Medicine & Health Care **CN:** Cleveland Clinic **DOB:** 09/23/1946 **PB:** Cleveland **SC:** OH/USA **PT:** Howard Ponsky; Esther Ponsky **MS:** Married **SPN:** Jacqueline Goldberg **CH:** Lee; Todd; Zac; Kimberly **ED:** MBA, Case Western Reserve University (1990); General Surgery Resident, University Hospitals, Cleveland, OH (1972-1976); General Surgery Intern, University Hospitals, Cleveland, OH (1971-1972); MD, Case Western Reserve University (1971); BA, Miami University (1967) **CT:** Diplomate, National Board Of Medical Examiners; Diplomate, American Board of Surgery; Licensed Physician, State of Ohio **C:** Oliver H. Payne Professor, Chairman, Department of Surgery, Case Western Reserve University School of Medicine (2005-2014); Chairman, Department of Surgery, University Hospitals, Cleveland, OH (2005-2014); Director, Graduate Medical Education, Cleveland Clinic Foundation (1999-2004); Director, Endoscopic Surgery, Cleveland Clinic Foundation (1997-2004); Executive Director, Minimally Invasive Surgery Center, Cleveland Clinic Foundation (1998-2000); Director, Department of Surgery, Mount Sinai Medical Center, Cleveland, OH (1979-1997); Assistant Surgeon, University Hospitals, Cleveland, OH (1976-1997); Director, Surgical Endoscopy, University Hospitals, Cleveland, OH (1977-1979); Professor, Surgery, Cleveland Clinic, Case Western Reserve University; Director, Developmental Endoscopy, Cleveland Clinic; Lynda & Marlin Yonker Chair, Developmental Endoscopy **CR:** Professor, Surgery, Case Western University (1991-Present); Associate Professor, Case Western University (1984-1991); Assistant Professor, Surgery, Case Western University (1977-1984); Senior Instructor, Surgery, Case Western Reserve University (1976-1977); Lecturer in Field **MIL:** Captain, U.S. Army Reserve (1972-1978) **CW:** Contributor, Over 300 Publications, Professional Journals; Editor, 10 Books **AW:** George Berci Lifetime Achievement Award, Society of American Gastrointestinal and Endoscopic Surgeons (2009); Rudolph Schindler Award, American Society for Gastrointestinal Endoscopy (2002) **MEM:** American Medical Association; Chairman, American Board of Surgery (2005-2006); President, Cleveland Surgical Society; President, Ohio Chapter, American College of Surgeons; President, Society of American Gastrointestinal and Endoscopic Surgeons; President, American Society for Gastrointestinal Endoscopy; Vice President, Society for Surgery of the Alimentary Tract; Vice President, American Surgical Association; Fellow, American College of Surgeons; Academy of Medicine of Cleveland & Northern Ohio; The Ohio State Medical Association; American Gastroenterological Association; American College of Gastroenterology; Collegium Internationale Chirurgia Digestivae; CSA; Society of University Surgeons; American Society for Parenteral and Enteral Nutrition; Association for Academy Surgery; The Ohio Gastroenterology Society **BA:** 9500 Euclid Ave, Cleveland Clinic Dept of Gen Surgery, Cleveland, OH, 44195

POOCHIGIAN, DONALD VAUGHN, **T:** Professor **I:** Education/Educational Services **DOB:** 10/07/1943 **PB:** Fresno **SC:** CA/USA **PT:** Vaughn Poochigian; Queenie Poochigian **SPN:** Toni Poochigian **CH:** Jennifer Howard; Aaron; Amy Cruz **ED:** Degree in Political Science, Fresno State University (1965); Diploma, Sanger High School (1961); PhD in Government and Political Theory, Claremont Graduate University; Graduate Student, Johns Hopkins University **C:** Professor Emeritus, University of North Dakota (2017); Professor, University of North Dakota (1971-2017); Teacher, University of Minnesota **CR:** Faculty Rights Committee, University of North Dakota; Presenter in Field **CW:** Reviewer, Annual Publication, ATINER **AW:** Outstanding Teaching Award, University of North Dakota (1974) **MEM:** American Philosophical Association; Board of Directors, ATINER, Athens, Greece **MH:** Albert Nelson Marquis Lifetime Achievement Award (2017) **H:** Research; Reading; Travel **BA:** 716 N 24th Street, Grand Forks, ND, 58203 **ADD:** 1484 Fall Brook Avenue, Clovis, CA, 93611

POON, PETER, **T:** Engineer **I:** Engineering **DOB:** 05/31/1944 **PB:** Hengyang **SC:** Hunan/China **PT:** Sam Chak-Kwong; Lai (Yiu) P **MS:** Married **SPN:** Mable Tsang (1974) **CH:** Amy Wei-Ling; Brian Wing-Yan **ED:** PhD, The University Southern California (1974); MA, California State University Long Beach (1969); BS, The University of Hong Kong (1965) **CT:** Certification, Advanced Project Management Program, Stanford University (2009) **C:** Telecommunications and Mission System Manager, Missions European Very Long Baseline Interferometry Network Project, Space Geodesy Program, Jet Propulsion Laboratory, NASA (2001-2009); Telecommunications and Mission System Manager, Voyager Interstellar Mission, Jet Propulsion Laboratory, NASA; Telecommunications and Mission System Manager, Mars Global Surveyor, Mars Odyssey Mission, Mars Exploration Rovers, Jet Propulsion Laboratory, NASA (2001-2009); From Multi-mission System Manager to Telecommunications and Mission System Manager, Cassini and Mars Missions, Jet Propulsion Laboratory, NASA (1988-2001); Software Management Standards, NASA (1986-1988); Task Leader, Software Management and Assurance Program, NASA; Advisor, Space Station, ADA Tasks, NASA (1984-1985); Technical Manager and Senior Engineer, Advanced Technology and Missions, Jet Propulsion Lab, California Institute of Technology, Pasadena, CA (1974-1983); Telecommunications and Mission System Manager, Ulysses Mission, Jet Propulsion Laboratory, NASA; Element Manager Software Information System, NASA **CR:** Member, Information Technology Subcommittee, International Organization for Standardization (1995-2007); Member, United States Technology Advisory Group,International Organization for Standardization (1995-2007); United States Panel Chair, Software Engineering Standards, International Symposium (2000-2009); England Panel Chair, Software Engineering Standards, International Symposium (1992-1999); Brazil Panel Chair, Software Engineering Standards, International Symposium (1992-1999); Canada Panel Chair, Software Engineering Standards, International Symposium (1992-2009); Delegate, Various Conferences; United States Chairman, Program and Management Committee, Software Engineering Standards, International Symposium **CIV:** President, HKUAASC (2013-2015); Director, American Counseling Association (2010-2014); Vice President, American Counseling Association (2009-2010); Active JPL Steering Committee, United Way, Pasadena, CA (1998-2005) **CW:** Member, Editorial Board, Software Quality Professional, American Society for Quality (1998-2009); Contributor, Articles to Professional Journals **AW:** Recipient, Congressional Recognition Award, United States House of Representatives (2015, 2013); Recipient, Recognition Award, California State Assembly (2013) ; Recipient, Distinguished

Chinese-American Award (2013); Recipient, Distinguished Science Alumni Award (2009); Recipient, Leadership Award, German Space Operations Center (2009); Recipient, Leadership Award, European Space Agency (2008); Recipient, Leadership Award, Mars Global Surveyor and Mars Odyssey (2002); Recipient, Achievement Awards, NASA (1977-2009); Recipient, Recognition for Inventions and Contributions **MEM:** President, Arcadia Music Club (1994-1995); Executive Committee, Software Engineering Standards, IEEE (1993-2000); Sigma Xi; Eta Kappa Nu; Phi Kappa Phi; The Athenaeum; IEEE **H:** Music; Hiking; Theater **ADD:** 77 Virginia Road, Arcadia, CA, 91006

POPE, BOB, T: Lawyer **I:** Law and Legal Services **CN:** White & Reasor **ED:** JD, University of Tennessee, Knoxville (1974) **C:** Lawyer, White & Reasor (2007-Present); Lawyer, Gullett Sanford (1980-2007); Trial Lawyer, Chief Counsel, Internal Revenue Service (1974-1980) **MIL:** U.S. Army (1968-1971) **AW:** Honoree, Best Tax Controversy and Litigation Lawyer, Nashville Section, Best Lawyers (2016, 2018); Super Lawyers (2017); Honoree, Elected Regent, The University of Tennessee, Knoxville (2016); Fellow, American College of Tax Counsel; Regent, American College of Tax Counsel **MH:** Albert Nelson Marquis Lifetime Achievement Award (2017) **BA:** 3100 West End Ave Ste 1100, White & Reasor, PLC, Nashville, TN, 37203

PORTE, MICHAEL SHELDON, T: Communications Educator (Retired) **I:** Education/Educational Services **CN:** University of Cincinnati **DOB:** 01/20/1932 **PB:** Chicago **SC:** IL/USA **PT:** Robert Harold Porte; Rose (Ellman) Porte **MS:** Married **SPN:** Barbara Alice Beers (12/20/1959) **CH:** Stephen; Eric; Alice **ED:** PhD, Northwestern University (1960); MS in Journalism, Northwestern University (1953); BS in Journalism, Northwestern University (1953) **CT:** Certification, Tai Chi for Arthritis **C:** Co-professor, Jews in American Film, University of Cincinnati (2005-2018); Adjunct Professor, University of Cincinnati (2010-2017); Professor Emeritus, University of Cincinnati (2003-Present); Co-professor, Italian Culture, University of Cincinnati (2003-2008); From Assistant Professor to Professor, University of Cincinnati (1960-2003); Instructor, Northwestern University, Evanston, IL (1956-1960); Instructor, Woodrow Wilson Junior College, Chicago, IL (1954-1955) **CR:** Instructor, Tai Chi, Clifton Cultural Arts Center (2008-Present); Adjunct Professor, Tai Chi and Meditation, Cincinnati State (2005-2015); Consultant, Loews Hotels & Resorts (1991); Consultant, General Electric, Cincinnati, OH (1990); Visiting Professor, Beijing Jiaotong University, Beijing, People's Republic of China (1986); Consultant, United States Department of Labor, Washington, DC (1973); Consultant, Procter & Gamble, Cincinnati, OH (1970-1974, 1980); Visiting Professor, The University of Southern California, Los Angeles, CA (1966); Consultant, Monsanto Research Corporation, Miamisburg, OH (1963) **CIV:** Tour Guide, New York Art Tours, New York, NY (1969-2017); Judge, Association of Community Theatre of Greater Cincinnati (1970-2014); Theater Reviewer, The Daily Northwestern; Reviewer, Choice Magazine, Middletown, CT (1982-1991); Film Adviser, Ohio Arts Council, Columbus, OH (1972-1976); Reviewer, Books, Chicago Sun Times; Reviewer, Films, 50 Plus **CW:** Translator, "Toa Te Ching" (2017); Co-editor, Cinema Now; Author, "The Servant in Restoration Comedy; " Co-editor, "Mei Guo Jing Ji" (1988); Author, "Media Coverage of Events Relating to the Swine Flu Program" (1981); Author, "Technical Writers" (1963); Author, Numerous Books, Film and Theater Reviews **MEM:** President, Association for Business Communication (1968);

Lifetime Member, Association for Business Communication; Modern Language Association of America; National Communication Association **MH:** Albert Nelson Marquis Lifetime Achievement Award (2017); Distinguished Humanitarian (2017) **H:** Tap dancing; Reading; Music; Travel; Piano **ADD:** 3344 Gano Ave, Cincinnati, OH, 45220

POULTON, ROBERTA DORIS, T: Nurse, Consultant **I:** Medicine & Health Care **DOB:** 10/19/1943 **PB:** Baltimore **SC:** MD/USA **PT:** Charles Robert Poulton; Mary Doris (Guercio) Poulton **MS:** Single **ED:** Nursing Diploma, Maryland General Hospital (1964); Coursework, Johns Hopkins University; Community College of Baltimore County **CT:** Certified in At-Home Infusion Instruction, ANA/ANCC American Nurses Center for Certification; Registered Nurse **C:** School Nurse, Mother Seton Academy, Baltimore, MD (2004-Present); Pediatrics Hemophilia Coordinator, Johns Hopkins Medical Institution (1996-2003); Pediatrics Hemophilia Coordinator, St. Agnes Hospital, Baltimore, MD (1993-2003); Pediatric Ambulatory Specialty Clinic Coordinator (1993-2003); Nurse Manager, Pediatric Emergency Room & Ambulatory Services, St. Agnes Hospital, Baltimore, MD (1988-1993); Staff Nurse-Preceptor, St. Agnes Hospital, Baltimore, MD (1983-1988); Camp Nurse, Baptist Convention of MD/DE (1976-1985); Team Leader, St. Agnes Hospital, Baltimore, MD (1972-1983); Staff Nurse, St. Agnes Hospital (1970-1972); Staff Nurse, Project Hope, Tunisia (1969-1970); Staff Nurse, St. Agnes Hospital, Baltimore, MD (1968-1969); Staff Nurse, Project Hope, Colombia (1967); Staff Nurse, Maryland General Hospital (1964-1967) **CR:** American Red Cross Nurse (1970-Present); Melvin Jones Fellow, Lions Club International (2006); Hemophilia Nurse, Johns Hopkins Medical Institution, Baltimore, MD (1998-2003); Board of Directors, Hemophilia Foundation of Maryland (1990-1993); Pediatrics Ambulatory Specialty Clinical Nurse; Consultant in Field **CIV:** Volunteer, Residential Counsel, Dining Service Committee; Moderator, Dietary Focus Group in Charlestown Retirement Community; Vestry Member and Lector, Charlestown United Protestant Church; Vice President, Baltimore 40 West Lions Club **CW:** Creator, "Learn About Hemophilia"; Contributor, "Emergency Care for Patients with Hemophilia"; Contributor, Articles, Newspapers; Contributors, Articles, Public Information Brochures **AW:** Maryland Senior Hall of Fame (2017); Founders Award, Mother Seton Academy (2015); Nurse of the Year, St. Agnes Health Care (1996); Honoree, Divisional Nurse of the Year in Maternal-Child Health (1996) **MEM:** Maryland General Nurses Alumni Association; Project Hope Alumni Association; W.A.R. Goodwin Society **MH:** Albert Nelson Marquis Lifetime Achievement Award (2017); Distinguished Humanitarian (2017) **H:** History (American and ancient); Travel; Photography; Model railroading **PA:** Independent **RE:** Baptist **ADD:** 707 Maiden Choice Lane, Apt. 8G16, Catonsville, MD, 21228

POWELL, RAYMOND WILLIAM, T: Financial Planner, School Administrator (Retired) **I:** Financial Services **DOB:** 06/17/1944 **PB:** Waterbury **SC:** CT/USA **PT:** Don C. Powell; Kathryn (Linhard) Powell **MS:** Married **SPN:** Janet Yasinski (6/24/1967) **CH:** Raymond Joseph **ED:** MS, Southern Connecticut State College, New Haven, CT (1969); BS, Southern Connecticut State College, New Haven, CT (1966); Postgraduate Coursework, University of Bridgeport, CT **CT:** Certified Financial Planner; Enrolled Agent **C:** Director, Owner, Powell's Financial Planning Service (1977-Present); Director, Owner, Powell's Accounting Service (1975-Present); Director, Owner, Powell's Income Tax Service, Watertown, CT (1972-Present);

Chief Executive Officer, R.W. Powell Enterprises, Inc., Prospect, CT (1972-Present); Finance and Tax Consultant, Prospect, CT (1972-Present); Superintendent of Schools, Winchester, CT (1995-2001) **CIV:** Vice Chairman, Watertown Town Council (1975-1976); Volunteer, YMCA; United Way **CW:** Contributor, Articles to Professional Journals **MEM:** National Association of Enrolled Agents; International Association of Financial Planners; American Society of Tax Consultants; Connecticut Association of Enrolled Agents; Rotary International **MH:** Albert Nelson Marquis Lifetime Achievement Award (2017) **H:** Tennis; Golf; Running **PA:** Democrat **ADD:** 417 Smith Pond Rd, Watertown, CT, 06795

POYDASHEFF, ROBERT STEPHEN, T: Lawyer **I:** Law and Legal Services **DOB:** 02/13/1930 **PB:** New York **SC:** NY/USA **PT:** Stephen Alexander Poydasheff; Pauline M. Miller Poydasheff **MS:** Married **SPN:** Anastasia Catherine Latto (8/29/1954) **CH:** Catherine Alexandra; Robert Stephen, Jr. **ED:** Honorary PhD, ITEP (2008); Diploma, U.S. Army War College (1976); Diploma, U.S. Army Command and General Staff College (1969); MA, Boston University (1966); JD, Tulane University (1957); BA in Political Science, The Citadel, The Military College of South Carolina (1954) **C:** Attorney, Private Practice, Columbus, GA (1995-Present); Mayor, Columbus, GA (2003-2007); City Council (1996-2002); Senior Vice President, SunTrust Bank of West Georgia, Columbus, GA (1979-1995) **CR:** Executive Vice President, Allied Technologies International, Inc., Columbus, OH (1995-2003); Adjunct Professor, Troy State University At Fort Benning, Fort Benning, GA (1976-2003); Adjunct Professor, International Law, Extension Division, University of Maryland, Berlin, Germany (1964-1967); Adjunct Professor, American Government, Extension Division, University of Maryland, Berlin, Germany (1964-1967); Adjunct Professor, Business Law, Extension Division, University of Maryland, Berlin, Germany (1964-1967); Instructor, Business Law, Extension Division, American University, Fort Benning, GA (1961-1963); Consultant, Strayer University; Former Legal Adviser to Secretary of the Army; Former Legal Adviser to Secretary of Defense on Military Dependent School and Labor Relations; Fellow, Leadership Morality Institute **CIV:** Board of Directors, Springer Opera House Association (1998-Present); Trustee, Georgia Council of Humanities, Executive Committee (1998-Present); City Councilor, City of Columbus (1996-2002); Board of Education, Fort Benning School (1976-1979); Chairman, Personnel Actions Committee, Fort Benning School (1976-1979); Trustee, Dr. Hospital; Board of Directors, Columbus United Way; River Center for the Performing Arts; Former President, Chattahoochee Council, Boy Scouts of America, Columbus, OH; Former President, Chattahoochee Valley, Association of the U.S. Army; Anne Elizabeth Shepherd Home; Columbus Symphony; American Red Cross; Chairman, Board of Directors, Leadership Morality Institute; Chairman, Civilian Military Council; Georgia Governors Commission on Transportation; Board of Trustees, Hughston Rehabilitation Hospital; Board of Visitors, Brookstone School; Notable Citadel Alumnus **MIL:** Colonel, United States Army (1979); Retired Colonel, United States Army, Vietnam War (1967-1968); Berlin Occupation (1964-1967); Second Lieutenant, United States Army (1955) **CW:** Contributor, Commentaries, Professional Journals; Contributor, Articles, Professional Journals; Contributor, Analyses, Professional Journals **AW:** Daniel Carter Beard Masonic Scouting Award (2015); Outstanding Alumnus Award, U.S. Army College (2010);

MLK Jr. Unity Award, Alpha Phi Alpha (2010); Outstanding Civilian Service Medal, U.S. Army (2004); Decorated Legion Of Merit with Two Oak Leaf Clusters; Bronze Star; Commendation Medal with Oak Leaf Cluster; Vietnam Service Medal with Four Bronze Stars; Honoree, Order Of St. George, Episcopal Church; Honoree, Infantry Order of St. Maurice; Honoree, Cavalry Armor, Order of Noble Patron of Armor; Paratrooper Badge; Badge of The Army Secretariat; Georgia Governors Humanities Medal; St. Michael the Archangel Medal, Greek Orthodox Archdiocese of America; Clara Barton Award, The American National Red Cross; CSM Robert McLoy Service Award; Service Mankind Award, Columbus Sertoma Club; Honoree, Army Ranger Hall of Fame; Georgia Military Veteran's Hall of Fame; Humanities Award, Sertoma Club, Columbus, GA **MEM:** Chairman of the Board, Leadership Morality Institute; Georgia Municipal Association; Columbus Bar Association; Board of Directors, Chamber of Commerce; Military Affairs Committee, Chamber of Commerce; Army Historical Foundation; Kiwanis International; 33rd Degree, Masons; Scottish Rite KCCH, Masons; Phi Delta Phi; Pi Sigma Alpha; Alpha Phi Alpha **BAR:** United States District Court for the Federal District of South Carolina (1988); United States District Court for the Federal District of Georgia (1987); United States District Court for the Middle District of Georgia (1987); State Bar of Georgia (1979); Supreme Court of the United States (1964); United States Court of Military Commission Review (1964); South Carolina Bar (1958); United States Court of Military Appeals (Now United States Court of Appeals for the Armed Forces) **H:** Walking; Reading **PA:** Republican **RE:** Orthodox Christian **ADD:** 6349 Mountainview Drive, Columbus, GA, 31904

PRADHAN, BASANT K., T: Associate Professor, Physician **I:** Medicine & Health Care **CN:** Cooper University Hospital **SC:** India **MS:** Married **SPN:** Madhusmita Sahoo, MD **CH:** Aarya **ED:** Fellowship in Child and Adolescent Psychiatry, Thomas Jefferson University, Philadelphia, PA (2010-2012); MD in Psychiatry, Albert Einstein Medical Center, Einstein Healthcare Network, Philadelphia, PA (2010); MD in Psychiatry, Postgraduate Institute of Medical Education and Research, With Distinction, Chandigarh, India (2006) **CT:** American Board of Psychiatry and Neurology; American Academy of Child & Adolescent Psychiatry **C:** Founding Director, Transcranial Magnetic Stimulation and Yoga and Mindfulness Based Cognitive Therapy, Department of Psychiatry and Pediatrics, Cooper University Health Care, Camden, Voorhees, NJ (2012); Assistant Professor, Psychiatry, Cooper University Health Care; Assistant Professor, Pediatrics, Cooper University Health Care **CR:** Guest Speaker, TIMBER Therapy for Adolescents with PTSD, American Academy of Child and Adolescent Psychiatry (2015); Invited Speaker, Caucus, American Psychiatric Association (2014); Plenary Speaker, Executive Member, Committees on Child and Publication, Group for the Advancement of Psychiatry (2013-2014) **CW:** Author, "Brief Interventions for Psychosis: A Clinical Compendium," Springer (2016); Author, "Yoga and Mindfulness Based Cognitive Therapy: A Clinical Guide," Springer (2014); Author, "Yoga and Mental Health: Demystification, Standardization, and Application"; Author, Books **AW:** NARSAD Young Investigator Award, The Brain & Behavior Research Foundation (2016-2017); Outstanding Achievement Award, New Jersey Psychiatric Association (2015); Kenneth Gordon Memorial Award, Regional Council of Child & Adolescent Psychiatry, NJ and PA (2012); Fellowship, Group for the Advancement of Psychiatry (2010);

Distinguished Laughlin Fellow (2010); Ginsburg Fellow, Group for the Advancement of Psychiatry (2010); National Quiz Championship, American Psychiatric Association (2009); Resident of the Year in Psychiatry, Philadelphia Psychiatric Society (Now Pennsylvania Psychiatric Society) (2009); Institutional Bronze Medal, Prime Minister of India and Postgraduate Institute of Medical Education & Research (2005) **MEM:** Executive Member, National Caucus of Integrative Medicine, American Psychiatric Association (2013); Executive Member, Group for the Advancement of Psychiatry (2011); Executive Member, Committee on Complementary and Alternative Medicine, American Academy of Child and Adolescent Psychiatry (2010); Fellow, American Psychiatric Association; Lifetime Member, American Psychiatric Association; Fellow, Group for the Advancement of Psychiatry; Honorary Member, Group for the Advancement of Psychiatry **H:** Scientific Writing; Meditation; Translational Research; Public Speaking **RE:** Hindu, Buddhism, Humanity **ADD:** 4031 Hermitage Dr, Voorhees, NJ, 08043 **URL:** https://www.linkedin.com/in/basant-pradhan-m-d-27415434

PRATT, GREGORY CARL, T: President **I:** Retail/Sales **CN:** Ornamental Products Tool & Supply Inc. **DOB:** 04/19/1947 **PB:** Fairview Park **SC:** OH/USA **ED:** Diploma, Tri-State College, Cleveland, Ohio (1968); Coursework, Radio School **C:** President, Ornamental Products, Tool & Supply, Inc. (2003) **CR:** Traveling Salesman (1970); Instructor, Workshops, Bowling Green State University; Instructor, Workshops, The Ohio State University; Instructor, Workshops, Kent University; Instructor, Workshops, Ohio Northern University; Ohio Department of Education; Advisory Committee, Grafton Correctional Institute, Ohio Department of Rehabilitation & Correction; Commercial Representative, OIAA Industrial Arts in Ohio **MIL:** United States Army, Vietnam **AW:** Award, Soccer Team, Parma, Ohio **MEM:** OIAA; Ohio Association for Career and Technical Education **H:** Train Collecting; Roller Dance Skating; Water Skiing; Snow Skiing; Boating; Fishing; Woodworking **RE:** Lutheran **BA:** 5105 Pearl Rd, Ornamental Products Tool & Supply Inc, Cleveland, OH, 44129 **ADD:** 5775 Fenn Rd, Medina, OH, 44256

PREMA, NITYA, T: Psychotherapist **I:** Medicine & Health Care **PB:** Los Angeles **SC:** CA/USA **PT:** James Nicholson; Phyllis Wickersham **ED:** MA, The Professional School of Psychology (1983); BA, Sonoma State University (1980); AS, Santa Rosa Junior College (1977) **CT:** Licensed Marriage and Family Therapist, Board of Behavioral Sciences, State of California (1982); Certified Psychiatric Technician, Board of Vocational Nursing, State of California (1979) **C:** Psychotherapist, Private Practice (2011-Present); Family Therapist, Private Practice (2000-2011); Military Consultant, Private Practice (2000-2011); Psychotherapist, County of Santa Clara (1998-2000); Therapist, O'Connor Hospital (1997-1999); Social Worker, O'Connor Hospital (1997-1999); Owner, Nitya Visionary Designs and Gallery (1982-1992); Designer, Nitya Visionary Designs and Gallery (1982-1992); Manufacturer, Nitya Visionary Designs and Gallery (1982-1992) **CR:** Presenter, William Faulkner Writer's Conference (2010, 2014); Speaker, International Journal for Mythological Studies (2008); Speaker, International Transpersonal Conference, International Transpersonal Association (1994) **CIV:** Activist, Rainbow Labyrinth Journey **CW:** Author, "The Spiral Labyrinth Journey: A Pilgrimage into Sacred Space" **MEM:** Ebbets Pass Forest Watch; Brewster Kaleidoscope Society **ACH:** Some of her achievements include providing the design of jeweled magic wands and kaleidoscopes.

PRIGMORE, JAY, T: Senior Engineer **I:** Engineering **CN:** Exponent **MS:** Married **CH:** Two Children **ED:** PhD, Electrical Engineering, Arizona State University (2013); Corporate Research Summer Intern, ABB (2012); MS, Electrical Engineering, Arizona State University (2012); BS, Electrical Engineering, Lamar University (2010); Coursework, Houston Baptist University (2005-2007) **CT:** Licensed Professional Engineer, State of California; Licensed Professional Engineer, State of Illinois; Licensed Professional Engineer, State of Kentucky; Licensed Professional Engineer, State of New Mexico; Licensed Professional Electrical Engineer, State of Texas; Licensed Professional Engineer, State of Wisconsin; Explosives License, Illinois Department of Natural Resources; Licensed PADI Open Water Diver; OSHA 10-hour Certification; Certified in First Aid; Certified in CPR; Certified, MISTREAS Ropeworks PDQ Competent User **C:** Senior Engineer, Exponent (2016-Present); Product Development Engineer, G&W Electric Co. (2013-2016); Teaching Assistant, Arizona State University (2012-2013); Graduate Research Associate, Arizona State University (2010-2013) **CR:** Founding Alternate Member, NFPA Technical Committee on Electrical Inspection Practices; Chair, IEEE IAS Early Career Development Executive Sub-Committee; Voting Member, IEEE Region 4 Power and Energy Society's Scholarship Committee; Voting Member, IEEE P1584 Guide for Performing Arc Flash Hazard Calculations **CW:** Co-Author, "Educating Students in Electrical Safety Practices and the Inclusion of Electrical Safety Material in Academic Curriculum" (2017); Co-Author, "Arc Flash Energy Underestimated" (2016); Author, "Protecting FPSO's from Arc Flash" (2016); Co-Author, "A Neodymium Hybrid Fault Current Limiter" (2015); Co-Author, "Comparison of Four Different Types of Ferromagnetic Materials for Fault Current Limiter Applications" (2013); Co-Author, "Modeling and Coordinated Controller Design of a Microgrid System in RTDS" (2013); Co-Author, "A Neodymium Permanent Magnet Fault Current Limiter for use in the FREEDM Project" (2012); Co-Author, "A Novel 7.2 kV Fault Current Limiter for use in the FREEDM Project" (2012); Co-Author, "An ETO-based AC Buck-type Fault Current Limiter for use in the FREEDM Project" (2012); Co-Author, "Autonomous Switch Fault Current Limiter" (2011); Co-Author, "An IGCT-based Electronic Circuit Breaker Design for a 12.47kv Distribution System" (2011); Presenter in Field; Contributor, Chapters, Books **AW:** Product of the Year Winner in Electrical Safety, Plant Engineering Magazine (2016); Arizona State Graduate Fellowship; National Science Foundation FREEDM Graduate Fellowship; Houston Endowment Scholarship **MEM:** IEEE Senior Member **BA:** 4580 Weaver Pkwy Ste 100, Exponent, Warrenville, IL, 60555 **ADD:** 3618 Fletcher Ln, Aurora, IL, 60506 **URL:** https://www.linkedin.com/in/jayprigmore/

PRISCO, FRANK J., I: Social Work **PB:** New York **SC:** NY/USA **PT:** Frank J. Prisco, Isabel (Gatano) Prisco **MS:** Married **SPN:** August Frances **CH:** Frank; Christian; Meredith **ED:** PhD in Psychoanalysis, New York University (1980); MA in History and Psychology, New York University (1972); BS in History, New York University (1964) **CT:** Diplomate, American Psychotherapy Association; Diplomate, American Board of Psychological Specialties, American College of Forensic Examiners; Certified Psychoanalyst; Certified Medical Hypnotherapist **C:** Instructor in Psychology, New York City Board of Education; Private Practice, Center for Modern Psychoanalytic Studies; Faculty, Psychanalytic Institute, Long Island, NY; Consultant, Staff Therapist, Creedmore Psychiatric Center **CR:** Trainer, Trainers Conflict Managers Program,

New York, NY; Discussion Leader, Great Books Foundation **CIV:** Eucharistic Minister, Catholic Church **AW:** Poet Merit Award, American Poetry Association (1988-1990); Society of Emil Award (1980) **MEM:** American Association for the Advancement of Science; American Psychological Society; American Association of Guidance and Counseling; New York Academy of Sciences; National Association for the Advancement of Psychoanalysis; Society of Modern Psychoanalysis

PRITYCHENKO, BORIS, T: Scientist **I:** Sciences **CN:** Brookhaven National Laboratory **DOB:** 04/07/1962 **PB:** Zabrama **SC:** Bryansk Region/Russian Federation **PT:** Vasily Alexeevich Pritychenko; Olga Dmitrievna (Tutunnick) Pritychenko **MS:** married **SPN:** Vickie L. Unferth **ED:** MS in Global Operations Management, Stony Brook University (2010); PhD in Physics, Michigan State University (2000); MS in Physics, Michigan State University (1996); MS in Engineering Physics, Karazin National University (1985). **CT:** Oracle Database Administration, UC Berkeley Extension (2003), Web Design, Stony Brook University (2005). **C:** Scientist, Brookhaven National Laboratory, Upton, NY (2003-Present); Solution Engineer, Plumtree Software, Inc., San Francisco, CA (2000-2003); Research Assistant, Cyclotron Laboratory, Michigan State University (1994-2000); Visiting Scientist, CFPA, Center for Particle Astrophysics, University of California, Berkeley (1991-1994); Staff Scientist, Baksan Neutrino Observatory, Russia (1985-1991); Staff Scientist, Institute for Nuclear Research, Troitsk, Russia (1985-1991) **MIL:** Lieutenant, Soviet Armed Forces (1986) **CW:** Editor-in-Chief, "Atomic Data and Nuclear Data Tables" (2014-Present) **MEM:** Lifelong Member, Division of Nuclear Physics, American Physical Society **BA:** National Nuclear Data Center, Bldg 817, Brookhaven National Laboratory, Upton, NY, 11973 **ADD:** 901 Skyline Drive, Coram, NY, 11727

PROCTOR, CONRAD ARNOLD, T: Member **I:** Medicine & Health Care **CN:** Proctor ENT, PLC **DOB:** 07/14/1934 **PB:** Ann Arbor **SC:** MI/USA **PT:** Bruce Proctor; Luena Marie Proctor **MS:** Married **SPN:** Phyllis Darlene Anderson (6/23/1956) **CH:** Sharon Heimbach-Pins; Barbara Jan Brown; David Conrad; Todd Bruce **ED:** Intern, St. Joseph Mercy Hospital (1959-1960); MS, University of Michigan (1964); MD, University of Michigan (1959) **CT:** Certificate, American Board of Otolaryngology **C:** Instructor, American Academy of Otolaryngology (1968-1982); Attending Staff, William Beaumont Hospital (1967-2012); Chief, Department of Otolaryngology, Munson Army Hospital (1965-1967); Senior Clinical Instructor, St. Joseph Mercy Hospital (1963-1965); Junior Clinical Instructor, St. Joseph Mercy Hospital (1961-1963) **CIV:** Sunday School Teacher, Bloomfield Hills Baptist Church (1967-Present); Financial Chairman, Bloomfield Hills Baptist Church (1975-1978); Director, Christian Education, Bloomfield Hills Baptist Church (1969-1972) **MIL:** Captain, Ready Reserves, U.S. Army (1967-1994); Captain, Ready Reserves, U.S. Army (1954-1965) **CW:** Author, "Etiology, Treatment of Fluid Retention in Meniere's Syndrome" (1992); Author, "Hyperinsulinemia and Tinnitus" (1988); Author, "Current Therapy in Otolayrngology" (1984-1985); Author, "Dietary Treatment of Meniere's Syndrome" (1983); Author, "Abnormal Insulin Levels and Vertigo" (1981); Author, "Hereditary Sensorineural Hearing Loss" (1978) **AW:** Merit Award, American Academy of Otolaryngology (1978); Commanding General's Achievement Award (1967); USA First Place Medical Research Award (1959); 12 World Records, Four Michigan Records, International Game and Fish Association; Ten World Records, National Fresh Water Fishing

Hall of Fame **MEM:** U.S. Fifth Army Basketball and Tennis Teams (1965-1967); American Medical Association; Michigan State Medical Association; Oakland County Medical Association; American Board of Otolaryngology; American College of Surgeons; Triological Society; Otosclerosis Study Group; International Game and Fish Association; American Legion; U.S. Tennis Association; Victors and Presidents Club; Phi Eta Sigma; Phi Kappa Phi; Phi Beta Kappa; American Rhinologic Society **MH:** Albert Nelson Marquis Lifetime Achievement Award (2017) **ADD:** 5793 Gark Road, Attica, MI, 48412

PROKASY, WILLIAM FREDERICK, T: Vice President (Retired) **I:** Education/Educational Services **CN:** University of Georgia **DOB:** 11/27/1930 **PB:** Cleveland **SC:** OH/USA **PT:** William Frederick Prokasy; Margaret Lovinia (Chapman) Prokasy **MS:** Married **SPN:** Pamela Pearson Prokasy **CH:** Kathi Lynn; Cheryl Anne; Lisa Wier Cauthen (Stepdaughter); Kevin Wier (Stepson) **ED:** PhD, University of Wisconsin (1957); MA, Kent State University (1954); BA, Baldwin-Wallace College (1952) **C:** Professor, Vice President for Academic Affairs, University of Georgia (1988-1998); Professor of Psychology Dean, College of Liberal Arts and Sciences, University of Illinois Urbana-Champaign (1980-1988); Acting Dean, Graduate School of Social Work, University of Utah (1979-1980); Distinguished Research Professor, University of Utah (1971-1972); Dean, College Social and Behavioral Sciences, University of Utah (1970-1979); Dean, Social and Behavioral Sciences, University of Utah (1968-1970); Professor of Psychology, Department Chairman, University of Utah (1966-1969); Assistant Professor, Associate Professor, Pennsylvania State University (1957-1966); Teaching Assistant, University of Wisconsin (1955-1957); W.A.R.F. Fellow, University of Wisconsin (1954-1955); Graduate Assistant, Kent State University (1953-1954) **CR:** Consultant in Field **CIV:** Member, Classic Center Cultural Foundation (2003-Present); Member, Board of Advisors, Georgia Museum of Art (1989-Present); Chairman, Athens Chapter, American Wine Society (2007-2010); Chairman, Athens Regional Library (2006-2008); Treasurer, Classic Center Cultural Foundation (2006-2007); Vice President, Athens-Clarke County Library Endowment Board (2003-2007); Advisory Board Member, Franklin College of Arts and Sciences (2003-2006); President, Friends of Dance (2003-2004); President, Athens-Clarke County Library Board (2003-2004); Member, Athens Regional Library (2002-2008); President, Friends of Georgia Museum of Art (2002-2003); Treasurer, Athens Opera Company Guild (2001-2006); Member, Athens-Clarke County Library Board (1999-2009); Member, Board Visitors, University of Georgia Libraries (1998-2007); Member, Board of Advisors, University of Georgia Performing Arts Center (1998-2003); Vice President, Board of Directors, Champaign-Urbana Symphony (1986-1988); Utah Board of Directors, American Civil Liberties Union (1978-1980); Trustee, Utah Planned Parenthood Association (1977-1980); Delegate, Utah Democratic Convention (1972-1974); Delegate, Utah Democratic Convention (1968-1970) **CW:** Co-Editor, With I. Gormezano and R. Thompson, Classical Conditioning III (1986); Editor, Psychophysiology (1974-1977); Editor, Electrodermal Responding in Psychological Research (1973); Co-Editor, With D. Raskin, Classical Conditioning II (1971); Associate Editor, Learning and Motivation (1969-1976); Consultant Editor, Journal of Experimental Psychology (1968-1980); Co-Editor, With A.H. Black, Classical Conditioning (1965) **AW:** Distinguished Alumni Award, Piedmont College (1998); University of Georgia Alumni Award of Excellence (1998);

Alumni Merit Award, Baldwin Wallace College (1992); Senior Postdoctoral Fellow, National Science Foundation (1963-1964) **MEM:** Executive Committee Council on Academy Affairs, NASULGC (1995-1996); Board of Educational Affairs, American Psychological Association (1993-1996); Board of Directors, Council of Research Librarians (1990-1996); Chairman, Council of Scientific Society Presidents (1990); Executive Board, Council of Scientific Society Presidents (1987-1991); President, Federation of Behavioral Psychological & Cognitive Sciences (1985-1987); Vice President, Federation of Behavioral Psychological & Cognitive Sciences (1984-1985); Board of Directors, American Psychological Association (1983-1986); President, Society for Psychophysiological Research (1982-1983); Board of Directorss, Association for the Advancement of Psychology (1982-1983); Council of Representatives, American Psychological Association (1980-1986); Board of Directors, Society for Psychophysiological Research (1978-1984); Chairman, Board of Scientific Affairs, American Psychological Association (1977-1978); President, University of Utah Chapter, Sigma Xi (1972-1973); President, Utah Psychological Association (1971-1972); Executive Board, Utah Psychological Association (1968-1970); Phi Kappa Phi; Fellow, American Association for the Advancement of Science; American Association for Higher Education; Psychonomic Society **MH:** Albert Nelson Marquis Lifetime Achievement Award (2017) **H:** Genealogy; Wine tasting; Reading; Photography **ADD:** 263 Wood Lake Dr, Athens, GA, 30606 **URL:** https://www.goodreads.com/author/show/3934634.William_F_Prokasy

PRUTER, MARGARET, T: Editor **I:** Writing and Editing **CN:** The Book Edit Group **PB:** Oak Park **SC:** IL/USA **PT:** Frederick G.; Margaret K. (Svoboda) Franson **MS:** Married **SPN:** Robert D. Pruter (July 22, 1972) **CH:** Robin **ED:** MA, Northwestern University, Evanston, IL (1965); AB, Dominican University, River Forest, IL (1961) **C:** Senior Editor, The Book Edit Group (2005-Present); Editorial Director, Elmhurst Editorial Services (1996-2005); Editor, McDougal Littell (1997-2004); Senior Editor, New Standard Encyclopedia (1975-1996); Associate Editor, New Standard Encyclopedia (1966-1975); Assistant Editor, New Standard Encyclopedia, Chicago (1964-1966); Research Associate, American Medical Association, Chicago (1962-1963); Assistant Editor, American People's Encyclopedia (1961-1962) **CR:** Executive Director, Militaria Archives (1972-Present) **CIV:** First Vice President, DuPage County Historical Society (2004-Present); Board of Directors, DuPage County Historical Society (1982-Present); Elmhurst Heritage Foundation (2007-Present); Member, Elmhurst Historical Commission (1981-2007); Member, Elmhurst Art Museum Foundation; Member, Friends of Elmhurst Public Library; President, Elmhurst Historical Commission (2000-2001); Vice President, Elmhurst Historical Commission (1995-2000); Executive Board Member, North Central College Parents Association (1995-1998); Board of Directors, DuPage County Sesquicentennial Committee (1988-1989) **CW:** Editor-in-Chief, 2018 Illinois Bicentennial Edition, DuPage Roots; Contributor, Encyclopedia of Chicago (2004); Co-Author, DuPage Roots (1985) **AW:** Historical Recognition Award, Elmhurst Heritage Foundation (2015); Illinois State Historical Publication Award (1986) **MEM:** Co-President, DuPage County Historical Society (2008-Present); President, Byrd's Nest Chapel Questers (1992-1994, 2003-2007); Board of Directors, American Association of University Women (1995-1999); Ocean Conservancy; Nature

Conservancy; Architect Conservancy; American Studies Association; National Women's History Museum; National Trust Historic Preservation; Organization of American Historians; American Philately Society; Illinois Historical Society; Elmhurst Historical Society; Chicago Historical Society; Chicago Architecture Foundation; National Parks and Conservation Association; World Wildlife Federation; Chicago Women in Publishing; Sisters in Crime; National Wildlife Federation; Sierra Club **ADD:** 576 Stratford Avenue, Elmhurst, IL, 60126

PUASCHUNDER, JULIA MARGARETE, **T:** Teaching Fellow **I:** Education/Educational Services **CN:** The New School **ED:** Coursework in Behavioral Law and Economics, University of Vienna (2009-Present); MS, The New School (2018); Postdoctoral Work, Department of Global Business and Trade, Vienna University of Economics and Business (2014); PhD in Philosophy, The New School (2014); Doctorate in Natural Sciences, University of Vienna (2006-2010); MPA, Maxwell School of Citizenship and Public Affairs, Syracuse University (2007-2008); MBA, Vienna University of Economics and Business (2000-2006); MPhil, University of Vienna (1998-2003) **C:** Teaching Fellow, Department of Economics, The New School (2017-Present); Teaching Assistant, Department of Economics, The New School (2017-Present); Co-Coordinator, The Schwartz Center for Economic Policy Analysis, The New School (2015-Present); Teaching Fellow, The New School (2018); Research Assistant to Dean, The New School (2016-2017); Research Assistant, Parsons School of Design, The New School (2016); Teaching Fellow, Parsons School of Design, The New School (2016); Teaching Assistant, Department of Politics, The New School (2016); Principal Investigator, Harvard University (2013); Associate, Center for the Environment, Faculty of Arts and Sciences, Harvard University (2010); Assistant, Research Institute for Managing Sustainability, Vienna University of Economics and Business (2008-2009); Policy Analyzer, U.S. Department of Education (2008); Management Assistant, Vienna University of Economics and Business (2003-2006); Affiliate, Human Resource Management, Consulting (2002-2003); Affiliate, Auditioning, Consulting (2002-2003) **AW:** Prize Fellowship, Inter-University Consortium of New York, The New School (2014); Max Kade Foundation Scholarship, Austrian Academy of Sciences (2011); Dean & HSBC Scholarship, Joint Study, Haskayne School of Business, University of Calgary (2005); Socrates Scholarship, Erasmus, LMU Munich (2002-2003); Joint Study Scholarship, The Australian National University, Canberra (2001); Named C2C Sustainability Leadership Fellow; The Fritz Thyssen Foundation Grantee; Merit-Based Dean Scholarship, Vienna University of Economics and Business **MEM:** ACUNS; Academy of Management; American Austrian Fulbright Association; AIRLEAP; The Association for Social Economics; Austrian Advertising Association; New York Representative, U.S. Austrian Chamber of Commerce; New York Invitee, Consulate General of Austria; ASCINA; ASNIE; European Finance Association; Founding Member, European Horizons; Observer, European Horizons; Department of European Law; International Law and Comparative Law Roundtable; Fulbright Women's Roundtable; Eastern Economic Association; Golden Key International Honour Society; Business Review Alumni Club, Harvard University; Business School Club of Boston, Harvard University; Club of Austria, Harvard University; Faculty Club, Harvard University; Law School Association for Law and Mind Sciences, Harvard University; Law School Law and Mind Sciences Board, Harvard University; International Leadership Association; Joseph von

Sonnenfels Center for the Study of Public Law and Economics; Institute for Humane Studies; Institute for New Economic Thinking; Alumni/ae Relations Leader, Kollegium Kalksburg Graduation, 1998 European Confederation of Jesuit; Liberty Fund Scholar, Maxwell School of Citizenship and Public Affairs, Syracuse University; Alumni Association, Maxwell School of Citizenship and Public Affairs, Syracuse University; International Student Association, Maxwell School of Citizenship and Public Affairs, Syracuse University; Society of Negotiations and Conflict Resolution, Maxwell School of Citizenship and Public Affairs, Syracuse University; Natural Sciences Forum, University of Vienna; New York Academy of Sciences; Board Member, Oxford Academic Research Network; Rotary Club of New York; Royal Economic Society; Society for Judgment and Decision Making; Society for International Development; The New York Academy of Sciences; The Situationist Project on Law and Mind Sciences, Harvard Law School; Department of European Law Roundtable, University of Vienna; National Honors Society; Viennese Opera Ball New York International Business Committee **BA:** 6 East 16th Street, 11 Floor, 1129F/99, Schwartz Center for Economic Policy Analysis, New York, NY, 10003 **ADD:** 6 East 16th Street, 11 Floor, 1129F/99, Schwartz Center for Economic Policy Analysis (SCEPA), New York, NY, 10003

PUGH, REVELLA BOOKER, **T:** Senior Pastor and Business Owner **I:** Religious **CN:** God's Anointed House **DOB:** 06/16/1947 **PB:** Clarksdale **SC:** MS/USA **PT:** Steve Booker; Louetta (Underwood) Booker **MS:** Divorced **SPN:** Lorenzo Pugh (Divorced) **CH:** Lorenzo, Jr.; Bethany Lynne **ED:** MBA, Cambridge College, Boston, MA (1998) **CT:** CPR, The American National Red Cross (1990); Certified Professional Secretary **C:** Senior Pastor, God's Anointed House (2013-Present); Owner, Visions From Above, Cleveland, OH (2004-Present); Assistant Manager, Richman Brothers, St. Louis, MO (1991-1993); Secretary, May Department Stores, St. Louis, MO (1980-1982); Payroll Department, Hercules Construction, St. Louis, MO (1979-1980); Secretary, Joseph T. Ryerson and Son (Now Ryerson Holding Corporation), St. Louis, MO (1967-1976) **CR:** Board of Directors, Ryerson Employees Credit Union, St. Louis, MO; National Association of Professional Women; International Women's Leadership Association; President, Board of Trustees, God's Anointed House; Board of Trustees, God's Anointed House **CIV:** Volunteer Speaker, Women's Self Help Center, St. Louis, MO (1990); Council Treasurer, Hazelwood PTA Council, St. Louis, MO (1986-1987); Cookie Chairman, Local Girl Scout Troop, Girl Scouts of America (1984-1985); President, Hazelwood PTA Council, St. Louis, MO (1982-1983); Treasurer, Christian Women Fellowship International (Now Church of God Mission International); School of Ministry Teacher; Ministry Leader; Adopted School Program with Cleveland Metro School District, Community Distribution of Spiritual Literature; Ministers at Local Shelter; Provide Supplies to Local Shelters; Counseling Services to Local Shelter **CW:** Discipleship Class Lessons, "God's Anointed House"; Healing Scriptures, "How To Stay Healed" **MEM:** Professional Secretary International **H:** Songwriting; Reading; Walking; Writing; Singing; Counseling; Traveling **ADD:** 632 Jefferson Drive, Highland Heights, OH, 44143 **URL:** http://www.godsanointedhouse.org

PUTTLITZ, KARL J. SR., **T:** Metallurgist **I:** Mining & Metals **CN:** Puttlitz Engineering Consultancy LLC **DOB:** 08/04/1941 **PB:** Kingston **SC:** NY/USA **PT:** Adalbert Puttlitz; Elizabeth Agnes (Barthel)

Puttlitz **MS:** Married **SPN:** Dianne Elizabeth Markle (9/16/1967) **CH:** Kirk; Christian; Karl Joseph, Jr.; Sara Ann **ED:** PhD, Michigan State University, East Lansing, MI (1971); MS, Michigan State University, East Lansing, MI (1967); BS, Michigan State University, East Lansing, MI (1965); AAS, Farmingdale State College, State University of New York (1961) **C:** President, Puttlitz Engineering Consultancy LLC, Wappingers Falls, NY (2004-Present); Senior Technical Staff Member, IBM (1999-2004); Senior Engineer, IBM, East Fishkill, NY (1984-1999); Advisory Metallurgist, IBM (1972-1984); Staff Metallurgist, IBM (1971-1972); Senior Associate Metallurgist (1967); Associate Metallurgist, IBM (1965-1966); Chemical Technician, IBM, Poughkeepsie, NY (1961-1962); Corporate Program Manager **CR:** Private Practice, Consultant, Wappingers Falls, NY (1975-Present); Fellow, IEEE (2003); Co-Chair, Inter-divisional Technical Liaison, Electronic Packaging Sciences, IBM Microelectronics Division (1994); Fellow, ASM International (1993); Publication Review Committee, IBM Microelectronics Division (1979-1991); Chair, Invention Disclosure Review Committee, IBM Microelectronics Division (1979); Chair, Inter-divisional Technical Liaison, Electronic Packaging Sciences, IBM Microelectronics Division (1979) **CIV:** SEMATECH Technical Advisory Board, Electronic Packaging Sciences (1994-1997); Manager, Senior League (1984-1988); Team Manager, Little League, Wappingers Falls, NY (1977-1981); President, Lake Oniad Lot Owners Association Inc, Wappingers Falls, NY (1974-1976) **CW:** Contributor, Over 50 Peer-Reviewed Articles, Professional Journals; Invited Speaker, Processes and Interconnections of Microelectronic Devices, 50 National and International Workshops and Tutorials; Co-Author, Co-Editor, Two 1,000-Page Engineering Handbooks; Author, Three Chapters, Books; Author, Fictional Suspense Novel **AW:** International IEEE Components, Packaging and Manufacturing Technology Medal and Award (2008); IEEE Distinguished Lecturer (2002); IBM Seventh-Level Invention Achievement Award (1998); SRC Outstanding Industrial Mentor Award in the Microelectronic Packaging Services (1996); Designated Master Inventor, IBM (1995); ISHM Outstanding Paper Award (1992); IBM Corporate Outstanding Innovation Award (1990); IEEE Transactions Outstanding Paper Award (1990); IBM Resident Scholar (1968-1971); National Indy Book Award for Fiction **MEM:** President, Michigan State University Chapter, ASM International (1964-1965); Phi Lambda Tau; Sigma Xi; NACE International; New York Academy of Sciences; American Welding Society; SAE International; SRC University Mentor Program; U.S. Information Technology Office **MH:** Albert Nelson Marquis Lifetime Achievement Award (2017) **H:** Travel; Stamp collecting **PA:** Republican **RE:** Roman Catholic **ADD:** 21 Central Avenue, Wappingers Falls, NY, 12590

PYLE, WALTER K., **T:** Lawyer **I:** Law and Legal Services **CN:** Walter K. Pyle & Associates **PB:** Chicago **SC:** IL/USA **PT:** Garland K.; Agnes G. (O'Connor) Pyle **MS:** Married **SPN:** Frances S. Kaminer **CH:** Michael K.; James B.; Isaac David **ED:** Postgraduate Work, New York University, New York, NY (1964-1965); JD, Loyola University, Chicago, IL (1964) **CT:** Certified Specialist, Appellate Law and Criminal Law, State Bar of California Board of Legal Specialization **C:** Private Law Practice, Berkeley, CA (1988-Present); Private Law Practice, San Francisco, CA (1981-1988); Private Practice, Chicago, IL (1978-1980); Assistant Attorney General of Illinois (1969-1978); Assistant State's Attorney, Criminal Division, Cook County State's Attorney's Office, Chicago (1967-1969); Private Practice, Chicago (1965-1967) **CR:** Arbitrator,

Alameda County Superior Court, Oakland, CA (1993-2012); Judge Pro Tempore, Alameda County Superior Court, Oakland, CA (1989-2011) **MEM:** President, California Appellate Defense Counsel (2009-Present); Secretary, California Appellate Defense Counsel (2002-2009); Director, Alameda County Bar Association (1992-1993), DuPage County Bar Association; Bar Association of San Francisco, Chicago Bar Association; California Association of Toxicologists; Irish-American Bar Association; American Bar Association; California State Bar; Illinois State Bar Association **BAR:** U.S. District Court, Central District of Illinois (2005); U.S. Court of Appeals for the Second Circuit (2004); U.S. Court of Appeals for the Seventh Circuit (1992); U.S. District Court, Southern District of California (1991); U.S. District Court, Central District of California (1989); U.S. District Court, Eastern District of California (1982); State of California (1981); U.S. District Court, Northern District of California (1981); U.S. Court of Appeals for the Ninth Circuit (1980); U.S. Court of Appeals for the First Circuit (1979); U.S. Court of Appeals for the Eighth Circuit (1977); U.S. Supreme Court (1972); U.S. District Court, Northern District of Illinois (1965); State of Illinois (1965) **MH:** Albert Nelson Marquis Lifetime Achievement Award (2017) **H:** Running; Cooking **PA:** Independent **BA:** 2039 Shattuck Avenue, Suite 202, Walter K Pyle & Assoc., Berkely, CA, 94704

PYSHER, ZANE KERMIT, T: Counselor **I:** Social Work **DOB:** 03/19/1943 **PB:** Pen Argyl **SC:** PA/USA **PT:** Kermit Joseph Pysher; Fern Elizabeth Pysher **MS:** Married **SPN:** Marcia Ann Cook (7/9/1966) **CH:** Erica Ann Draico; Zane-Alan **ED:** MA, Kean University (1970); BA, Albright College (1965) **CT:** Teacher, English and History, New Jersey, Pennsylvania, and Massachusetts; Student Personal Guidance Services, New Jersey and Pennsylvania **C:** Retired (2006); Counselor, Director, Guidance, Roxbury Public Schools, Succasunna, NJ (1969-2005); Teacher, English, Reading, Library Science, Warren Hills Regional School District, Washington, NJ (1965-1969) **CR:** Church Videographer (2000-Present); Church Photographer (2000-Present); Secretary, President, Board of Education Committee, Good Shepherd Nursery School, Easton, PA (1996-1998) **CIV:** Meals on Wheels Volunteer (2008-Present); Good Shepherd Lutheran Church, Easton, PA (2000-Present); Mutual Ministry Committee (2000-2012); Church Council, Good Shepherd Lutheran Church, Easton, PA (1992-1994); Chair, Church Stewardship Committee (1992-1994); Volunteer Counselor, Easton Hospital, Easton, PA (1976) **CW:** Author, "Pysher Family in America" **AW:** America's Registry of Outstanding Professionals (2003-2004); Morris County Teacher Recognition Award, Morris County Association of School Administrators (1999); Eisenhower School Teacher of the Year Award (1999); Who's Who Among Teachers (1994) **MEM:** School Test Coordinator, Roxbury Education Association (1987-2005); Scholarship Committee, Roxbury Education Association (1978-2005); School Building Representative, Roxbury Education Association (1972-1975); National Education Association; Morris County Council of Education Associations; Morris County Professional Counselor Association; New Jersey Education Association **H:** Photography; Golf; Bowling; Sports cards collecting; Coin collecting/numismatics **PA:** Democrat **RE:** Lutheran **ADD:** 2311 Ben Jon Road, Easton, PA, 18040

QUARLES, STEVEN P., T: Lawyer **I:** Law and Legal Services **CN:** Nossaman LLP **DOB:** 05/09/1942 **PB:** Kansas City **SC:** MO/USA **PT:** Samuel Princeton Quarles; Marianna (Platt) Quarles **MS:** Married

SPN: Suzanne Margaret-Mary Cleary (6/2/1970) **ED:** JD, Yale University (1968); AB, Princeton University (1964) **C:** Partner, Nossaman LLP (2015-Present); Partner, Sedgwick LLP (2013-2015); Partner, Crowell & Moring LLP (1983-2013); Partner, Nossaman, Guthner, Knox & Elliott (Now Nossaman LLP) (1981-1983); Deputy Under Secretary of the Interior, U.S. Department of the Interior (1979-1981); Director, Office of Coal Leasing, Planning, and Coordination, U.S. Department of the Interior (1978-1979); Counsel, U.S. Senate Committee on Energy & Natural Resources (1971-1978) **CR:** Trustee, NatureServe (2017-Present); Trustee, National Wildlife Refuge Association (2017-Present); Trustee, Bat Conservation International (2010-Present); Trustee, HJF (2008-Present); Binational Softwood Lumber Council (2007-Present); Trustee, Pacific Forest Trust, (2011-2017); Trustee, American Forest Foundation (2009-2016); Trustee, Catoctin Land Trust (2009-2012); Trustee, Maryland Environmental Trust (2008-2017); Oil and Gas Leasing Committee, National Academy of Sciences (1988-1989); Energy and Mineral Resources Board, National Academy of Sciences (1985-1988); Abandoned Mine Lands Committee, National Academy of Sciences (1985-1986); Advisor, Ford Foundation (1968-1971) **CIV:** President, Frederick County Civic Federation (1989-1994); Maryland Hazardous Waste Facilities Siting Board (1985-1987); Maryland Sewage Sludge Management Commission (1984); Chairman, Solid Waste Advisory Committee, Montgomery County Government (1980-1985); Chairman, Sugarloaf Citizens' Association (1977-1981) **AW:** Fulbright Scholarship, India (1964-1965) **MEM:** Advisory Committee, Federal Wind Turbine Guidelines (2008-2012); Advisory Board, National Agricultural Research, Extension, Education, and Economics (2008-2010); Environment, Energy and Resources Section, American Bar Association **BAR:** District of Columbia (1981); State of New York (1980) **MH:** Albert Nelson Marquis Lifetime Achievement Award (2017) **H:** Horse breeding **PA:** Independent **RE:** Episcopalian **BA:** 1666 K Street NW, Suite 500, Washington, DC, 20006

QURAESHI, ZAHIR, T: G.W. Haworth Chair of Global Business **I:** Education/Educational Services **CN:** Western Michigan University **PT:** Akila Quraeshi; Raschid Quraeshi **MS:** Married **SPN:** Nalini **CH:** Samir; Asim **ED:** PhD in Business Administration, Michigan State University (1978); MBA, Michigan State University, East Lansing, MI (1972); BS in Chemical Engineering, Indiana Institute of Technology, Cum Laude, Fort Wayne, IN (1970) **C:** G.W. Haworth Chair of Global Business, Haworth College of Business, Western Michigan University (2008-Present); Director Global Business Center, Haworth College of Business, Western Michigan University (2008-Present); Professor, Department of Marketing, Haworth College of Business, Western Michigan University (1989-Present); Tan Sri Noah Distinguished Chair of Business, Graduate College of Business, Universiti Kebangsaan Malaysia (1995-1996) **CW:** West Michigan District Export Council (2010); Chair, Global Marketing Committee, American Marketing Association (1988-1990); Board of Advisers, International Business Press, Haworth Publishing Company; Chair, International Business Education Committee, Haworth College of Business; Board of Directors, West Michigan Chapter, American Marketing Association; Adviser to the Chairman of the Board, Amigo Group, Karachi, Pakistan; Adviser to Chief Executive, Taxila Cotton Mills, Islamabad, Pakistan; Adviser to Founder, Chairman, International Textile Ltd. Karachi, Pakistan; Consultant in Field **CW:**

Author, "International Business 1979: A Selection of Current Readings," International Business and Economic Studies, Michigan State University (1979); Author, "International Business 1977: A Selection of Current Readings," International Business and Economic Studies, Michigan State University (1977); Author, "International Business 1975: A Selection of Current Readings," International Business and Economic Studies, Michigan State University (1975); Founding Editor, The Journal of Asia-Pacific Business; Contributor, Articles to Professional Journals **AW:** Recipient, Global Engagement Award, Western Michigan University (2017); Recipient, All University Teaching Excellence Award, Western Michigan University (1988) **MEM:** Academy of International Business; Academy of Marketing Science; American Marketing Association; West Michigan World Trade Association; World Future Society; American Society for Competitiveness; Kalamazoo International Trade Council; Association for Global Business; International Management Development Association **H:** Reading; Travel **ADD:** 1615 Old Deer Run, Kalamazoo, MI, 49009

RABB, DAVID, T: Co-Owner, Executive Vice President **I:** Business Management/Business Services **CN:** Leak Detection Technologies, Inc. **PT:** Robert Rabb; Georgia Rabb **MS:** Married **SPN:** Wendy Rabb **CH:** Jonathan; Samantha **CT:** 8 EPA Certified Leak Detection Methods **C:** Executive Vice President, Business Development, Leak Detection Technologies, Inc. (2007-Present); Business Development Manager, Research and Development Manager, Praxair (2003-2007); Business Development Manager, Research and Development Manager, Tracer Research Corporation (1997-2003) **MEM:** PEI **H:** Scuba diving; Sailing **BA:** 1889 N Oracle Rd, LeakDetection Technologies, Inc., Tucson, AZ, 85705 **URL:** http://www.leakdetect.net/

RAGAUSKAS, ARTHUR JONAS, T: Professor, Chair **I:** Education/Educational Services **CN:** The University of Tennessee, Knoxville **DOB:** 02/16/1957 **PB:** Sudbury **SC:** ON/Canada **PT:** Izidore Ragauskas; Marie (Lutzig) Ragauskas **MS:** Married **SPN:** Catherine Lyne (11/23/1984) **CH:** Emma; Alyse; Luke **ED:** Postdoctoral Fellow, Colorado State University, Fort Collins (1986-1987); Postdoctoral Fellow, University of Alberta (1985-1986); PhD, University of Western Ontario (Now Western University) (1985); BSc, University of Western Ontario (Now Western University) (1980) **C:** Professor, The University of Tennessee, Knoxville (2014-Present); Governor's Chair in Biorefining, The University of Tennessee, Knoxville (2014-Present); Faculty Member, Department of Chemistry, Georgia Institute of Technology (2003-2014); Professor, Institute for Paper Science & Technology, Georgia Institute of Technology (1989-2003); Assistant Professor, Institute for Paper Science & Technology, Georgia Institute of Technology (1989-2003); Research Associate, National Research Council of Canada, Ottawa, Ontario, Canada (1987-1989) **CW:** Author, Two Books; Contributor, 21 Articles to 434 Professional Journals **AW:** Honoree in Green Processing Engineering, American Institute of Chemical Engineers (2017); Recipient, Affordable Green Chemistry Award, American Chemical Society (2017); Recipient, Distinguished Service Award, University of California, Bourns College of Engineering, Center for Environmental Research and Technology (2017); Recipient, Gunnar Nicholson Gold Medal Award (2014); Named, Fulbright Distinguished Chair in Alternative Energy (2008-2009); Recipient, William H. Aiken Research Prize (2008) **MEM:** American Institute of Chemical

Engineers (2017-Present); American Society for Engineering Education (2014-Present); The Society of Chemical Industry (2011-Present); American Association of the Advancement of Science (2005-Present); International Academy of Wood Science (2003-Present); Technical Association of Pulp and Paper Industry (1993-Present); Cellulose, Paper and Textile Division, American Chemical Society (1991-Present); American Chemical Society (1985-Present); Assistant Program Chair, American Chemical Society (1996-1998); Student Activities Chair, American Chemical Society (1996-1998); Society for Industrial Microbiology and Biotechnology; American Society for Engineering Education; American Institute of Chemical Engineers **MH:** Albert Nelson Marquis Lifetime Achievement Award (2017) **H:** Hiking; Fishing; Biking; Golf; Chess **BA:** 1512 Middle Dr, Dept of Chemical & Biomolecular Engineering, Knoxville, TN, 37996 **ADD:** 1512 Middle Dr, UTK Dept of Chem & Biomolecular Engr, Knoxville, TN, 37996

RAMOS-CANO, HAZEL BALATERO, T: Caterer (Retired), Chef, Innkeeper (Retired), Entrepreneur, Culinary Instructor, Custom Framing Designer **I:** Business Management/Business Services **CN:** Innkeeper Victoria and Albert Inn **DOB:** 09/02/1936 **PB:** Davao City **SC:** Philippines **PT:** Mauricio C. Ramos; Felicidad (Balatero) Ramos **MS:** Married **SPN:** Nelson Allen Blue (5/30); William Harold Snyder (2/17/1964, Divorced 1981) **CH:** John Byron; Snyder; Jennifer Ruth **ED:** Postgraduate Coursework in Child Development and Family Relations, Pennsylvania State University (1966-1967); MA in Sociology, Pennsylvania State University (1963); BA in Social Work, University of Philippines, Quezon City, Philippines (1958) **CT:** Certified Executive Chef, American Culinary Federation; Certified Master Gardener **C:** Instructor, Culinary Cooking, Southeast Virginia Higher Educated Center, Abingdon, VA (2010-Present); Owner, The Frame Shop, Abingdon, VA (2004-Present); Innkeeper, Victoria and Albert Inn (2000-Present); President, Ramos-Cano Inc. (1996-Present); Innkeeper, Love House Bed and Breakfast (1996-Present); Caterer, The Eclectic Chef's Catering (1995-Present); Owner, The Eclectic Chef's Catering (1995-Present); Owner, Victoria and Albert Inn (2000-2013); Food Service Director, Southwest Virginia 4-H Educational Conference Center, Abingdon, VA (1994-1995); Manager, Child Nutrition Services, Wake County Public School Systems, Raleigh, NC (1993-1994); Assistant Food Service Manager, Granville Towers, Chapel Hill, NC (1990-1992); Regional Director, La Petite Academy, Raleigh, NC (1989-1990); Food Service Director, Brian Corp. Nursing Home, Raleigh, NC (1989-1990); Admissions Coordinator, Brian Corp. Nursing Home, Raleigh, NC (1986-1988); Social Worker, Brian Corp. Nursing Home, Raleigh, NC (1986-1988); Restaurant Owner, Hazel's on Hargett, Raleigh, NC (1985-1986); Manager, Hazel's on Hargett, Raleigh, NC (1985-1986); Loan Mortgage Specialist, Raleigh Savings & Loan (1983-1984); Early Childhood Educator, Learning Together, Inc., Raleigh, NC (1982-1983); Executive Director, Presbyterian Urban Council, Raleigh Halifax Court Child Care and Family Service Center (1973-1979); Research Assistant, Department of Child Development & Family Relations, Pennsylvania State University, University Park (1966-1967); Sociology Instructor, Albright College, Reading, PA (1963-1964); Faculty, Training Staff, Peace Corps Philippine Project, University Park, PA (1961-1963); Owner, Designer, The Flower Shop **CR:** Chair, International Cooking Demonstrations, Raleigh International Festival (1990-1993); Cooking Instructor, Wake Community Technical College, Raleigh, NC (1986-1992);

Freelance Caterer (1964-1995) **CIV:** Presbyterian Women, Sinking Spring Presbyterian Church, Abingdon, VA (1999-Present); Master Gardener, Virginia Tech Master Gardeners Program (1998-Present); Treasurer, Abingdon Newcomers Club (1997-Present); Elder Session Member, Sinking Spring Presbyterian Church (2008-2011); Elder Session Member, Sinking Spring Presbyterian Church (1997-1999); Board of Deacons, Elder Session Member, Sinking Spring Presbyterian Church (1993-1994); Chairman, Philippine Health and Medical Aid Committee, Phil-Am Association, Raleigh, NC (1985-1988); Publicity Chairman, Elder, Trinity Presbyterian Church, Raleigh, NC (1979-1981); Active, Pines of Carolina Council, Girl Scouts of America (1976-1985); Board of Directors, Project Enlightenment, Wake County Public Schools (1976-1977); Raleigh Chapter, North Carolina Association for the Education of Young Children (1975-1976); President, Wake County Day Care United Council (1974-1975) **AW:** Recipient, Award for Keeping Historical Abingdon Beautiful, Abingdon Kiwanis Club (1997); Recipient, Governor's Certificate of Appreciation, State of North Carolina (1990); Recipient, Raleigh Mayor's Award for Quality Childcare Services (1990); Recipient, Rockefeller Grant, Rockefeller Foundation (1958-1959); Recipient, Ramon Magsaysay Presidential Award, Philippine Leadership Youth Movement (1957); Recipient, Juliett Low Award, Girl Scouts of America (1953) **MEM:** Historian, American Culinary Federation, Presbyterian Women, Raleigh, NC (1975-1976); President, Penn State Dames (1968-1969) **H:** Playing Scrabble on the internet; Gardening; Creative cooking **PA:** Republican **RE:** Presbyterian **ADD:** 210 East Valley St, Abingdon, VA, 24210 **URL:** http://www.abingdonframeshop.com

RANGASWAMI, ARUN A., T: Associate Professor of Pediatrics **I:** Education/Educational Services **CN:** Stanford University **ED:** Fellow, Stanford University (1996); Resident, St. Louis Children's Hospital (1993); Intern, St. Louis Children's Hospital (1993); MD, Washington University in St.Louis (1990); BS, The Johns Hopkins University (1986) **C:** Clinical Associate Professor of Pediatrics, Stanford University (2006-Present); Assistant Professor, University of California, Davis (1996-2001) **CIV:** Mentorship Program, Stanford University **AW:** C. John Tupper Teaching Award for Excellence in Medical Education, University of California, Davis (1999) **MEM:** FIOP FIOPEL; The Children's Oncology Group; ACLOU **BA:** 1000 Welch Road Suite 300, Division of Pediatric, Division of Hematology Oncology, Palo Alto, CA, 94304 **ADD:** 324 Ridgewood Ave, San Francisco, CA, 94127 **URL:** https://www.linkedin.com/in/arunrangaswami/

RANSOM, LINWOOD H. JR., T: Chief Executive Officer **I:** Business Management/Business Services **CN:** Linwood H. Enterprises **ED:** PhD, South Carolina State University (1979); EdM, South Carolina State University (1972); Bachelor's Degree in Architectural Engineering, Hampton Institute in Virginia (Now Hampton University) **C:** Chief Executive Officer, Linwood H. Enterprises (2016-Present); Consultant, Ransom Group (1989-2016); Construction Division, Housing Authority, State of South Carolina (1976-1989) **CR:** Mortgage Banker **MIL:** Lieutenant Colonel, U.S. Army (1979); Second Lieutenant Field Officer, U.S. Army (1959) **MEM:** Disabled American Veterans **BA:** 1722 W Lombard St, Baltimore, MD, 21223

RASH, WAYNE JR., T: Journalist **I:** Writing and Editing **CN:** Infoworld **DOB:** 03/02/1948 **PB:** Erie **SC:** PA/USA **PT:** Wayne Rash; Elizabeth Rash **MS:**

Married **SPN:** Carolyn Louise Hall (11/25/1972) **CH:** Julia Leigh; Wayne III; Brittany Lynne **ED:** BA, Lynchburg College, Virginia (1980) **C:** Chief and Senior Columnist, Washington Bureau, eWEEK (2010-Present); Freelance Public Speaker, Computer Security, Information Technology (2001-Present); President, Wayne Rash & Associates (1970-Present); Senior Contributing Editor, Infoworld (2004-2006); Senior Analyst, Infoworld (2002-2004); Contributing Editor, South Dakota Times (2001-2002); Contributing Editor, CNet/ZDNet (2001-2002); Senior Contributing Editor, InternetWeek (2001-2002); Columnist, InternetWeek (1992-2002); Editor, Events, InternetWeek (2000-2001); Managing Editor, Technology, InternetWeek (1998-2000); Principal, America, Management Systems, Inc., Arlington, VA (1984-1992); Deputy Commissioner of Revenue, City of Lynchburg, VA (1976-1980) **CR:** Publishing (2009-Present); Contributing Editor, Information Week (2008-Present); Techweb Events (2008-Present); Ziff Davis Events and Custom Week (2008-Present); Contributing Editor, CABS (2008); Consultant, Synaxis Consulting, Seattle, WA (2008-2010); Executive Editor, Week Knowledge Center, CPA (2007-2009); Senior Technology Editor, Infoworld (2007); Senior Writer, Infoworld (2006); Washington Bureau Chief, Infoworld (2006-2008); Contributing Editor, Infoworld (2002); Member, Review Board, Infoworld (1990-1994) **CIV:** Board Member, U.S. Strategic Perspective Institute (2013-Present); Active Citizens Advisory Council on National Space Policy, Studio City, CA (1986-1995); President, Kings Park West Civic Association, Fairfax, VA (1986-1988); Director, Technology Policy, Commonwealth Policy Institute Network **MIL:** Lieutenant, U.S. Navy (1980-1984); U.S. Navy Supply Corps **CW:** Contributing Editor, Plane and Pilot (1995-Present); Contributor, The Washington Post (1994-Present); Editor, Byte Information Exchange (1984-2001); Senior Tech Editor, InternetWeek (1996-1998); Columnist, InternetWeek (1996-1998); Columnist, The Star Ledger, Newark, NJ (1996-1998); Author, "Politics on the Nets" (1997); Editor, Tech Report, The Washington Post (1996-1997); Columnist, Windows NT Magazine (1995-1996); Columnist, OS/2 Magazine (1994-1996); Consultant, Byte Magazine (1992-1995); Editor, Byte Magazine (1992-1995); Editor, The Washington Post Computer Showcase (1992-1993); Columnist, Byte Magazine (1988-1992); Consultant Editor, Byteweek (1988-1992); Consultant Editor, Computer Digest (1986-1991); Author, "WordPerfect Office 3.0: The Basics" (1991); Author, "The Novell Connection" (1989); Author, "The Executive Guide to Local Area Networks" (1989) **AW:** Albert Nelson Marquis Lifetime Achievement Award (2017); Bill Leonard Award for Professional Media Coverage of Amateur Radio (2016) **MEM:** Program Chairman, Brookville-Timberlake Chapter, National Press Club, Lions (1976-1980); Aircraft Owners and Pilots Association; American Flying Club; Experimental Aircraft Association; American Radio Relay League; Virginia Amateur Radio Emergency Service; Northern Virginia NTRAK; Plantation Hills HOA; NTRAK **MH:** Albert Nelson Marquis Lifetime Achievement Award (2017) **H:** Amateur radio; Scuba diving, Writing; Foreign travel; Flying; Wine; Cooking; Classical music **RE:** Episcopalian **ADD:** PO Box 332, Clifton, VA, 20124

RASKA, KAREL MD, PHD, T: Pathologist **I:** Medicine & Health Care **CN:** St. Peter's University Hospital **DOB:** 05/26/1939 **PB:** Prague, Czech Republic **SC:** Czech Republic **PT:** Karel Raska, MD,DSc; Helena Raskova, MD, DSc **SPN:** Jana Raskova, MD **CH:** Karel; Francis **ED:** PhD, Institute of Organic Chemistry and Biochemistry,

Czech Academy of Sciences (1965); MD, Charles University School of Medicine, Prague, Czech Republic (1962) **CT:** American Board of Pathology (Anatomic & Clinical); American Board of Pathology (Immunopathology) **C:** Rutgers University-Robert Wood Johnson Medical School (1968-Present); St.Peters University Hospital (1991-Present); Institute of Organic Chemistry and Biochemistry, Czech Academy of Sciences (1967-1968); Rutgers Medical School (1966-1967); Yale University School of Medicine (1965-1966) **CW:** 300 Publications **AW:** Comenius Medal, National Pedagogical Museum and Library of J.A. Comenius (2012); Medal of Merit First Class, Czech Republic (2010); Silver Medal of the Senate, Parliament of the Czech Republic (2010) **MEM:** American Association for Cancer Research; College of American Pathologists; American Association of Immunologists; American Society of Investigative Pathology; International Academy of Pathology; Pluto Club; Comenius Academic Club; American Society of Microbiology; American Society of Virology; American Society of Cell Biology **MH:** Albert Nelson Marquis Lifetime Achievement Award (2017) **H:** Skiing; Boating **RE:** Roman Catholic **ADD:** 400 Harrison Ave, Highland Park, NJ, 08904

RATNER, MARK A., T: Emeritus Professor of Chemistry **I:** Education/Educational Services **CN:** Northwestern University **DOB:** 12/08/1942 **PB:** Cleveland **SC:** OH/USA **PT:** Max Ratner; Betty (Wohlvert) Ratner **MS:** Married **SPN:** Nancy Ball (6/19/1969) **CH:** Stacy; Daniel **ED:** Honorary Akademischer Rat, Technical University of Munich, West Germany (1971); Honorary Amanuensis, Aarhus University, Denmark (1970); PhD, Northwestern University (1969); AB, Harvard University (1964) **C:** Professor of Chemistry, Northwestern University, Evanston, IL (1975-Present); Dow Research Professor, Northwestern University (1988-1990); Assistant Professor, New York University (1971-1975) **CR:** Visiting Professor, Rush Presbyterian School of Medicine (1990-Present); Director of Electrochemical Industries, Israel (1980–Present); Associate Dean, Arts and Sciences Northwestern University, Evanston (1980-1984); Consultant, U.S. Army, Huntsville, AL (1973-1975); Lecturer, IBM, Yorktown Heights, NY (1973) **CIV:** Board of Governors, Tel-Aviv University (1996-Present); Hebrew University Jerusalem (1996-Present); Board of Directors, Hillel Foundation, Evanston, IL (1984-Present) **MIL:** Consultant, U.S. Army, Huntsville, AL (1973-1975) **CW:** Contributor, Numerous Articles and Manuscripts, Professional Journals; Co-Author, "Introduction to Quantum Mechanics and Chemistry"; Co-Author, "Quantum Mechanics in Chemistry"; Co-Author, "Nanotechnology: A Gentle Introduction to the Next Bid Idea"; Co-Author, "Nanotechnology and Homeland Security: New Weapons for New Wars" **AW:** Fellow, A.P. Sloan Foundation (1973-1976); Recipient, Numerous Awards; Debye Award, American Chemical Society; Langmuir Award, American Chemical Society **MEM:** Institute for Advanced Study, Israel (1979); Fellow, American Association for the Advancement of Science; American Physical Society; American Chemical Society; Rumplestiltskin Society, Sigma Xi; Danish Academy; National Academy of Sciences **MH:** Albert Nelson Marquis Lifetime Achievement Award (2017) **H:** Scientific education; Canoeing; Conservation; Poetry; Piano; Fishing; Hiking **ADD:** 615 Greenleaf Ave, Glencoe, IL, 60022

RAUB, DONALD WILMER, T: Minister, Author **I:** Religious **DOB:** 12/24/1931 **PB:** Quakertown **SC:** PA/USA **PT:** Harvey Wilmer Raub; Estella Martha

(Bleam) Raub **MS:** Married **SPN:** Dolores Jean Kern (10/20/1951) **CH:** Diane; Donald; Deborah; Devlyn **ED:** ThD, Evangelical Bible Seminary, Lake Worth, FL (1999); DRE, Evangelical Bible Seminary, Lake Worth, FL (1987) **CT:** Ordained Minister, Evangelical Church Alliance (1951) **C:** Pastor, East Rockhill Chapel (1965-Present); Merck and Co., West Point, PA (1968-1994); Writer, Quakertown Free Press (1963-1973); Photographer, Quakertown Free Press (1963-1973); Pastor, Troy Gospel Tabernacle (1959-1960); Evangelist, Evangelical Church Alliance, Bradley, IL (1951-1958) **CR:** Adviser, Lebanon Gospel Association (1992-1994); Lecturer in Field **CIV:** Chairman, Board of Directors, Transylvania, Inc. (1997-2003); Vice President, Transylvania, Inc. (1994-1997); North Penn Symphony Orchestra Society, Lansdale, PA (1980-1990); Board of Directors, Transylvania Bible School (Now Biblical Life Institute), Freeport, PA (1957-2007) **CW:** Author, "Come and Reason," "Will the Christian Church Survive?" "Jesus, the Son of the Living God," Disciple Magazine, Chattanooga, TN (2015); Author, "Is OUr Lord's Return Closer Than We Think?" Biblical Life (2013); Author, "Just Call Me Brian," Biblical Life (2011); Author, "They Were Astonished" (2009); Author, "Five Roads to Walk With Jesus," "Evidences of the True God," PulpitHelps (2008); Author, "Affirming Christian Boundaries" (2005); Author, "Spiritual Missiles" (1997); Author, "The Value of Christian Holiness" (1992); Author, "Unusual Experiences and Special Moments," Fountain Press, Freeport, PA (1990); Author, "I, Being of Sound Mind, Second Edition," Fountain Press, Freeport, PA (1989); Author, "I, Being of Sound Mind," Fountain Press, Freeport, PA (1988); Inventor, "Independence" (1976); Author, "This Week's Sermonette," Perkasie News Herald; Author, "African Knife, a Gift of Love," Unpublished; Author, "The Story of 'Big Bear'"; Author, "Leadership Overload: Why Many Pastors are Frustrated"; Author, "Are We Preaching Things That Matter?" The Evangel; Patentee in Field; Contributor, Articles, Professional Journals **MEM:** Songwriters of North America **MH:** Albert Nelson Marquis Lifetime Achievement Award (2017) **H:** Horticulture **PA:** Republican **ADD:** PO Box 224, Tylersport, PA, 18971

RAVEN, RONALD J., T: Education Educator **I:** Education/Educational Services **CN:** University at Buffalo **DOB:** 01/07/1935 **PB:** San Francisco **SC:** CA/USA **PT:** Jacob Raven; Ella (O'Connor) Raven **MS:** Married **SPN:** Cynthia Opacinch Raven **CH:** Michael; Julie **ED:** EdD, University of California Berkeley (1965); MA, San Francisco State University (1960); BS, University of San Francisco (1952-1956) **C:** Professor Emeritus, University at Buffalo (1996-Present); Professor, University at Buffalo (1965-1996); Director of Graduate Studies, University at Buffalo (1972-1979); Member, Graduate School Executives Committee (1972-1979); Visiting Professor, Universidade Federal de Minas Gerais (1976); Visiting Professor, The University of Iowa (1973); Visiting Professor, Ontario Institute for Studies in Education, University of Toronto (1970); Visiting Professor, University of California Berkeley (1968); Lecturer of Biology, Fullerton College (1962-1963); Physics & Chemistry Teacher, Campbell Union High School District (1959-1962); Consultant, Science Curriculum Improvement Study, University of California Berkeley **CR:** Chairman, Editorial Review Board, The Association for Science Teacher Education (1975-1980) **MIL:** First Lieutenant, U.S. Army (1961-1964) **CW:** Editorial Board Member, "Science Education" (1970-1993); Editorial Board Member, "Journal of Research Science Teaching" (1970-1983); Author, "Raven Test of Sci. Reasoning" (1982); Author, "Tests: Raven Test of Logical

Operations" (1980); Section Editor, "Science Education" (1972-1975) **AW:** Recipient, 30-Year Service Award, University at Buffalo (1996) **MEM:** Executive Board, NARST (1976-1980); Board of Directors, NARST (1976-1980); Board of Directors, The Association for Science Teacher Education (1973-1976); Fellow, American Association for the Advancement of Science; American Educational Research Association; NSTA **MH:** Albert Nelson Marquis Lifetime Achievement Award (2017) **H:** Piano; Tennis **ADD:** 53 Wellingwood Drive, East Amherst, NY, 14051

RAYBURN, CAROLE ANN, T: Psychologist, Researcher, Writer, Consultant **I:** Medicine & Health Care **DOB:** 02/14/1938 **PB:** Washington **SC:** D.C./USA **PT:** Carl Frederick; Mary Helen (Milkie) Miller **MS:** Married **SPN:** Ronald Allen Rayburn (Deceased 4/1970) **CT:** Licensed Psychologist, State of Maryland **C:** Private practice (1971-Present); Psychometrician, Montgomery County Public Schools (1981-1985); Psychologist, Maryland Department Vocational Rehabilitation (1973-1974); Staff Clinical Psychologist, Institutional Care Services Division, D.C. Children's Center, Laurel, MD (1970-1978); Private practice (1969); Clinical Psychologist, Spring Grove State Hospital, Catonsville, MD (1966-1968); Psychometrician, Columbian Preparatory School, Washington, DC (1963) **CR:** Advisor, Graduate Psychological Students, Cardinal Stritch University, Milwaukee, WI (2005-Present); Consultant, Julia Brown Montessori School (1982-Present); Forensic Psychology, Expert Witness (1973-Present); Consultant, Veterans Affairs Center (1991-1993); Instructor, John Hopkins University (1988-1989); Adjunct Faculty, Professional School of Psychology Studies, San Diego, CA (1987); Adjunct Assistant Professor, Loyola College, Columbia, MD (1987); Guest Lecturer, Hood College, Frederick, MD (1986-1988); Instructor, Johns Hopkins University (1986); Guest Lecturer, Andrews University, Berrien Springs, MI (1979); Consultant, Julia Brown Montessori School (1978); Consultant, Veterans Affairs Center (1978); Consultant, Julia Brown Montessori Schools (1972); Lecturer, Strayer College, Washington, D.C. (1969-1970) **CIV:** Chair, Clinical Psychological Fellow Communications (2007-2012); President, Task Force Women's Spirituality (2007-2012); Treasurer, Mont County National Organization of Women (2005-2007); Speakers Task Force, Mont County National Organization of Women (2002-2007); Board of Directors, Psychologists for the Ethical Treatment of Animals (1998-2000); Chair, Task Force Women's Spirituality **CW:** Author, Member of Editorial Board, "International Journal of Ethics," Nova Science Publishers Inc., (2004-Present); Proposer, "Creative Personality Theory" (2011); Contributing Author, "Creative Personality Theory" (2011); Contributor, "Initiator of Task Force on Spirituality Creativity of Intuition," International Council of Psychologists (2011); Series, "Handbook for Women Mentors: Transcending Barriers of Stereotype, Race, and Ethnicity" (2010); Co-Editor, With Violet Franks, "Women & Psychology Series: Women of Vision is in this Series" (2010); Author, "Killers of the Spirit, Restores of the Soul" (2010); Co-Editor, With Lillian Comas-Diaz, "Woman Soul: Inner Life of Women's Spirituality" (2008); Co-Editor, With E. Gavin, A. Clamar, M.A. Sideritis, "Psychology of Women Series" (2008); Co-Editor, With Violet Franks, Florence Denmark, Mary Reuder, Asuncion Austria, Springer Focus on Women "Women of Vision" (2007); Co-Editor, With Violet Franks, "Focus on Women Series," Springer Publishing Company (2005); Author, "TEACH: Traumatic Experiences and Children's and Adolescents' Health" (2005); Author, "Creative Personality Inventory" (2005); Author, "Intuition Inventory"

(2005); Author, "Health and Traumatic Experiences in Adults" (2005); Co-Author, With Lee Richmond, "Inventory on Religiousness, Children's Version", (2005); Author, "Rayburn Creative Personality Theory" (2005); Author, "Creative Personality Inventory" (2005); Author, "Intuition Inventory" (2005); Author, "Inventory on Well-Being" (2004); Author, "Children's and Adolescents' Peace Inventory" (2002); Author, "Inventory on the Supreme and Work" (1999); Author, "Peacefulness Inventory" (1998); Co-Proposer, With Lee Richmond, "The Theory and Field of Theobiology: Interfacing of Theology and the Sciences"(1998); Author, "Life Choices Inventory" (1998); Author, "Sports, Exercise, Leadership and Friendship Questionnaire" (1997); Author, "Inventory on Religiousness" (1997); Author, "Inventory on Spirituality (IS)" (1996); Contributing Author, "Religion Personality and Mental Health" (1993); Author, "Body Awareness and Sexual Intimacy Comfort Scale (BASICS)" (1993); Contributing Author, "An Encyclopedic Dictionary of Pastoral Care and Counseling" (1990); Guest Editor, "Journal of Pastoral Counseling" (1988); Author, "Organizational Relationships Survey" (1987); Author, "Attitudes Toward Children Inventory" (1987); Author, "State-Trait Morality Inventory" (1987); Author, "Religious Occupational and Stress Questionnaire" (1986) ; Associate Editor, "Journal of Pastoral Counseling" (1985-1990); Co-Editor, With M.J. Meadow, "A Time to Weep and a Time to Sing" (1985); Contributing Author,"Clinical Handbook of Pastoral Counseling" (1985); Contributing Author, "The Other Side of the Couch: Faith of the Psychotherapist" (1981); Consultant Editor, "Professional Psychology" (1980-1983); Contributing Author, "Drugs, Alcohol and Women: A National Forum Source Book" (1975); Contributing Author, "Montessori: Her Method and the Movement (What You Need to Know)" (1973); Contributor, Numerous Articles to Professional Journals and Handbooks **AW:** William C. Bier Research Award, Psychology of Religion Division (2000); Mentoring Award, Division of Clinical Psychology, Section of Clinical Psychology of Women (1997); Mentoring Award, Psychology of Religion Division (1997); Certified Recognition, District of Columbia Psychological Association (1985); American Association of University Women Research Grantee (1983); Certified D.C. Department of Human Resources (1976); Certified Recognition, District of Columbia Psychological Association (1976); Service Award Council for Advancement Psychological Professions And Sciences (1975); Certified D.C. Department of Human Resources (1975) **MEM:** Liaison to Communications, International Relations, General Psychology Division, American Psychological Association (2004-Present); Newsletter Editor, International Society Political Psychology (1999-Present); Chair, Psychology Issues in Graduate Education and Clinical Training, American Psychological Association (1988-Present); Executive Advisory Committee, Maryland Psychological Association (1985-Present); Research Committee, Maryland Psychological Association (2015); Fellows Chair, Clinical Psychology Division, American Psychological Association (2010-2012); Association of Psychological Sciences (2011); President, Montgomery County National Organization of Women (2007-2009); Fellows Chair, Clinical Psychology Division, American Psychological Association (2007-2009); Treasurer, Montgomery County National Organization of Women (2005-2007); Fellow, Committee Member, Clinical Psychology Division, American Psychological Association (2006); President, Maryland Association of Measurement and Evaluation (2005-2007); Treasurer, American Psychological Association (1996-1998); President, Psychology of Religion Division, American Psychological

Association (1995-1996); Program Chair, American Psychological Association (1991-1994); Secretary, American Association of Applied and Preventive Psychology (1992-1993); Chair Fellows Committee, American Association of Applied and Preventive Psychology (1992-1993); Baltimore Association of Consultant Psychologists (1991-1992); Association of Practicing Psychologists, Montgomery-Prince George's Counties (1986-1988); Chair, Women's Section, Clinical Psychology, American Psychological Association (1984-1986); President, Maryland Psychological Association (1984-1985); Chair, Insurance Committee, Maryland Psychological Association (1981-1983); Fellow, Editorial Board, Journal Child Clinical Psychology, American Psychological Association (1978-1982); Chair, Equal Opportunity and Affirmative Action Division, Clinical Psychology, American Psychological Association (1980-1982); Chair, Women's Clinical Psychology Division, Task Force on Women and Religion, American Psychological Association (1980-1981); Chapter Recognition, Maryland Psychological Association (1978); Newsletter Editor, Maryland Psychological Association (1975-1976); Fellow, Division Evaluation Measurement and Statistics; American Orthopsychiatric Association; Member Committee, International Relations in Psychology, Society of Psychological Study Social Issues; Maryland Association of Counseling and Development; Honorary Member, Psi Chi; Fellow, International Psychology Division, Psychology of Religion Division, Psychology of Women Division, Clinical Psychology Division, Consultant Psychology Division, General Psychology Division, Psychotherapy Division, State Association of Affairs, Media Psychology Division, Family Psychology Division, Society and Social Issues Studies, Child Youth and Family Services Division, Health Psychology Division, Theoretical and Philological Psychology Division, Trauma Psychology Division, Psychology of Ethnic Minority Affairs Division, Educational Psychology Division, Evaluation, Measurement and Statistics Division, Society for the Psychology of Religion and Spirituality, American Psychological Association **MH:** Albert Nelson Marquis Lifetime Achievement Award (2017) **H:** Theater; Ballet; Opera; Collecting cat and dog figurines; Collecting rocks **PA:** Independent **ADD:** 1200 Morningside Dr, Silver Spring, MD, 20904

REAGAN, GARY, T: State Legislator, Lawyer **I:** Government Administration/Government Relations/Government Services **DOB:** 08/23/1941 **PB:** Amarillo **SC:** TX/USA **PT:** Hester Reagan; Lois Irene (Marcum) Reagan **MS:** Married **SPN:** Nedra Ann Nash (9/12/1964) **CH:** Marc; Kristi; Kari; Brent **ED:** JD, Stanford University (1965); BA, Stanford University (1963) **C:** Private Practice, Hobbs, NM (1982-Present); City Attorney, Hobbs, NM (1997-2004); New Mexico State Senate (1993-1997); City Attorney, City of Eunice, NM (1980-2004); City Attorney, Hobbs, NM (1978-1980); Partner, Williams, Johnson, Reagan, Porter & Love, Hobbs, NM (1977-1982); Partner, Williams, Johnson, Houston, Reagan & Porter, Hobbs, NM (1968-1977); Partner, Smith, Ransom, Deaton & Reagan, Albuquerque, NM (1967-1968); Associate, Smith & Ransom, Albuquerque, NM (1965-1967) **CR:** Co-Chair, Interim Legislative Ethics Committee (1993-1996); Vice-Chairman, Senate Judiciary Committee (1993-1996); New Mexico Commissioner, National Conference of Commissioners on Uniform State Laws (1993-1996); Advisory Member, New Mexico Constitutional Revision Commission (1993-1995); Instructor, New Mexico Junior College, Hobbs, NM (1978-1984); Instructor, University of the Southwest, Hobbs, NM (1978-1984) **CIV:** Trustee, New Mexico Conference, United Methodist Church (1988-Present); Mayor, Hobbs, NM (2008-2012);

Trustee, University of the Southwest, Hobbs, NM (1989-2001); Mayor, Hobbs, NM (1976-1977); President, Junior Achievement of Hobbs (1974-1985); Director, Junior Achievement of Hobbs (1974-1985); President, Landsun Homes, Carlsbad, NM (1972-1984); Trustee, Landsun Homes, Carlsbad, NM (1972-1984); Trustee, Lydia Patterson Institute, El Paso, TX (1972-1984); Mayor, Hobbs, NM (1972-1973); City Commissioner, Hobbs, NM (1970-1978) **CW:** Author, "CD-Roms in the Law Office," State Bar Bulletin (1990); Author, More Than 30 Articles on Computers and Software in the Law Office; Lecturer, "Law Office Management," New Mexico; Lecturer, "Law Office Management," Nevada; Lecturer, "New Mexico Oil and Gas Issues," Annual Oil and Gas Seminar, Midland, TX **AW:** Ten Best Estate Planning Attorneys in New Mexico, American Institute of Legal Counsel **MEM:** President, State Bar of New Mexico (1994-1995); Vice President, State Bar of New Mexico (1992-1993); Board of Bar Commissioners (1990-1997); Committees Member, State Bar of New Mexico (1989-1996); President, Hobbs Chamber of Commerce (1989-1990); President, Lea County Bar Association (1976-1977); President, Hobbs Tennis Club (1974-1975); American Bar Association **BAR:** U.S. Supreme Court (1986); State of New Mexico (1965); U.S. District Court, State of New Mexico (1965) **MH:** Albert Nelson Marquis Lifetime Achievement Award (2017) **BA:** 1819 N Turner Street, Suite G, Gary D Reagan PA, Hobbs, NM, 88240 **ADD:** 1819 N Turner Street, Suite G, Gary Don Reagan PA, Hobbs, NM, 88240

REDDITT, PAUL LEWIS, T: Religious Studies Educator (Retired) **I:** Education/Educational Services **DOB:** 08/08/1942 **PB:** Little Rock **SC:** AR/USA **PT:** Paul L. Redditt; Helen M. Redditt **MS:** Married **SPN:** Bonnie Louellen Redditt (12/18/1965) **CH:** Pamela Joyce Duenas; Alan B. **ED:** PhD, Vanderbilt University (1972) **C:** Adjunct Professor, Baptist Seminary of Kentucky (2008-2014); Professor, Georgetown College (1986-2008); Professor, Otterbein University (1972-1986) **CW:** Commentator, "Books of Chronicles"; Book Author; Book Editor; Contributor, Articles, Professional Journals; Contributor, Reference Books; Contributor, Church Educational Literature **MEM:** National Association of Baptist Professors of Religion; Catholic Biblical Association; Society of Biblical Literature **PA:** Democrat **RE:** Baptist **ADD:** 518 Estill Court, Georgetown, KY, 40324

REED, THOMAS JAMES, T: Law Educator **I:** Law and Legal Services **CN:** Veterans Law Clinic **DOB:** 01/01/1940 **PB:** Joliet **SC:** IL/USA **PT:** Thomas P. Reed; Bernardine M. (Dorsey) Reed **MS:** Married **SPN:** Emily A. Fabrycki (12/29/1962) **CH:** Martin; Valerie **ED:** JD, Notre Dame Law School, University of Notre Dame (1969); BA, Marquette University (1962) **C:** Professor Emeritus, Veterans Law Clinic, Widener University (2011-Present); Director, Veterans Law Clinic, Widener University (2006-Present); Professor of Law, Delaware School of Law, Widener University, Wilmington, DE (1993-Present); Professor, Delaware School of Law, Widener University, Wilmington, DE (1984-Present); Taishoff Professor of Law, Veterans Law Clinic, Widener University (2009-2011); Associate Dean, Delaware School of Law, Widener University, Wilmington, DE (1984-1993); Associate Professor, Delaware School of Law, Widener University, Wilmington, DE (1981-1984); Associate Professor, Western New England College School of Law, Springfield, MA (1979-1981); Assistant Professor of Law, Western New England College School of Law, Springfield, MA (1976-1979); Associate, Reller, Mendenhall, Kleinknecht & Milligan, Richmond, IN (1969-1976) **CR:** History Preservation Planner, Old Richmond, IN (1975-

1976); History Preservation Planner, History Centerville Inc., Indiana (1970-1976); History Preservation Planner, City Planning Association, Mishawaka, IN (1969-1971) **CIV:** Reporter, Delaware Appellate Handbook, Wilmington, DE (1984-Present) **CW:** Contributor, Articles to Professional Journals **AW:** Recipient, Governor's Lifetime Award for Pro Bono Service (2017) **MEM:** ABA; Federal Bar Association; Indiana State Bar Association **BAR:** Pennsylvania (1982); United States Court of Appeals for the Third Circuit (1982); United States District Court for the District of Massachusetts (1979); Massachusetts (1977); United States Court of Appeals for the Seventh Circuit (1974); United States District Court for the Southern District of Indiana (1969) **MH:** Albert Nelson Marquis Lifetime Achievement Award (2017) **H:** Civil War history; Genealogy; Historic preservation **RE:** Roman Catholic **BA:** 4601 Concord Pike, Widener University Law School, Wilmington, DE, 19803

REETZ, RUTH, **T:** Artist **I:** Fine Art **DOB:** 05/03/1938 **PB:** Parkers Prarie **SC:** MN/USA **PT:** Robert Paul Sanford; Charlotte Belle (Roberts) Sanford **MS:** Married **SPN:** Gary Engelbert Reetz (5/27/1960) **CH:** Randall Robert; Ryan Sanford **ED:** BSc, North Dakota State University (1960) **C:** Retired (2006); Owner, The Spirit of the Shell (1978-2006); Artist, The Spirit of the Shell (1978-2006); Teacher, The Spirit of the Shell (1978-2006); Owner, Creative Textiles, Minneapolis (1966-1983); Promotional Home Economist, Armo Company (1965-1972); Assistant Home Economist, Pillsbury, North Dakota (1962-1965); Textile Laboratory Technician, Munsingwear Inc. (1960-1962) **CW:** Author, "Flat Method of Sewing" (1976); Author, "Quality Dressmaking" (1968) **AW:** Winner in the Professional Division, Sana Bell Shelter (2015) **MEM:** President, COA (1980-1981); Cousteau Society; Angel Collectors Club of America; The Sanibel-Captiva Shell Club **H:** Travel; The shore; Russian pen pals; Angels; Music **ADD:** 40 Norman Ridge Dr, Minneapolis, MN, 55437

REGENSTREIF, HERBERT, **T:** Lawyer **I:** Law and Legal Services **DOB:** 05/13/1935 **PB:** New York **SC:** NY/USA **PT:** Max Regenstreif; Jeannette (Hacker) Regenstreif **MS:** Divorced **SPN:** Patricia Friedman (12/20/1980, Divorced 9/2002) **CH:** Cara Rachael **ED:** MLS, Pratt Institute (1985); JD, New York Law School (1960); BA, Hobart College (Now Hobart and William Smith Colleges) (1957) **C:** Reservist Attorney, Federal Emergency Management Agency (FEMA) (1998-1999); Partner, Fried & Regenstreif, Professional Corporation, Mineola, NY (1963-2012) **CR:** Secretary-treasurer, Station WAHY-FM, Inc. (1998-2000); Consultant in Field Arbitrator District Court, Nassau County, NY (1989-1991); New York City Civil Court (1984-1986) **CIV:** County Committeeman, Democratic Committee, Queens County, NY (1978-1979) **CW:** Contributor, Articles to Professional Journals **MEM:** Governor, Hobart Club of New York (Now HWS Club of New York City) (1968-1969); Bar Association of Nassau County (Now Nassaubar); Kentucky Bar Association; American Judges Association; The International Legal Honor Society of Phi Delta Phi; Beta Phi Mu - The International Library and Information Studies Honor Society **BAR:** United States District Court for the Eastern District of Kentucky (1998); Kentucky Bar Association (1985); United States Tax Court (1967); Supreme Court of the United States (1967); United States Court of Appeals for the Second Circuit (1962); United States District Court for the Southern District of New York (1962); United States District Court for the Eastern District of New York (1962); New York State Bar Association (1961) **ADD:** PO Box 22855, Lexington, KY, 40522-2855

REGES, MARIANNA, **T:** Marketing Executive (Retired) **I:** Advertising & Marketing **DOB:** 03/23/1947 **PB:** Budapest **SC:** Hungary **PT:** Otto H.; Alice M. Reges **MS:** Divorced **CH:** Rebecca; Charles III (Deceased) **ED:** MBA in Statistics, Baruch College, The City University of New York (1978); BBA, Baruch College, The City University of New York, Magna Cum Laude (1971); AAS, Fashion Institute of Technology, Summa Cum Laude, New York City, NY (1967) **C:** Media Manager, Procter & Gamble (2001-2012); Media Manager, Bristol-Myers Squibb Company (1984-2001); Senior Research Manager, Ziff Davis, New York, NY (1977-1984); Manager, Research and Sales Development, NBC Radio, New York, NY (1975-1977); Assistant Media Director, Benton & Bowles Advertising, New York, NY (1972-1975); Research Manager, Woman's Day Magazine, New York, NY (1971-1972); Research Supervisor, Station WCBS-TV, New York, NY (1970-1971); Media Research Analyst, Doyle, Dane, Bernbach Advertising, New York, NY (1967-1970) **CR:** Member, Pan European TV Audience Research Management Committee (1988-2012); Member, Spanish Radio Advisory Council, New York, NY (1986-1988) **CIV:** Member Advisor, Baruch College Advertising Society (1975-2012); Active Member, First Presbyterian Church, New York, NY **MEM:** Anthroposophical Society; Baruch Alumni Association **MH:** Albert Nelson Marquis Lifetime Achievement Award (2017) **RE:** Presbyterian **ADD:** 626 E 20th St Apt 11H, New York, NY, 10009

REGUEIRO, MIGUEL, **T:** Professor of Medicine **I:** Education/Educational Services **CN:** University of Pittsburgh School of Medicine **PT:** Jose Regueiro; Judy Regueiro **MS:** Married **SPN:** Carol Ronk (5/31/1995) **CH:** Matthew; Jack **ED:** Fellow in Hepatology, Beth Israel Hospital, Harvard Medical School (1994-1997); Medical Residency in Internal Medicine, Beth Israel Hospital, Harvard Medical School (1993-1994); Medical Internship in Internal Medicine, Beth Israel Hospital, Harvard Medical School (1992-1993); MD, Drexel University (1992); BA in American History, University of Pennsylvania (1988) **CT:** Medical License, State of Pennsylvania (1992) **C:** Associate Chief of Education, University of Pittsburgh Medical Center (2005-Present); Associate Professor of Medicine, Director of Gastrointestinal, Hepatology and Nutrition Fellowship Training Program, University of Pittsburgh Medical Center (2000-Present); Co-Director, Clinical Head, Inflammatory Bowel Disease Center, University of Pittsburgh Medical Center (2000); Senior Medical Lead of Specialty Medical Homes, University of Pittsburgh Medical Center **CIV:** Chair, Medical Advisory Committee, Crohn's & Colitis Foundation America, Pittsburgh, PA (2004-2008) **CW:** Contributor, Articles, Professional Journals **AW:** Top Doctor of the Award Year, Pittsburgh Magazine (2017); Physician of the Year Award, Crohn's & Colitis Foundation America (2002); Nominee, S. Robert Stone Teaching Award, Harvard Medical School (1996); Clinical Investigator Training Award, Harvard–MIT Program of Health Sciences and Technology (1996); Joan Komblum Memorial Prize, Hahnemann University (1992) **MEM:** Board Member, Patient Education Committee, Crohn's & Colitis Foundation America (2005-2009); Fellow, American College of Gastroenterology; American Gastroenterology Association; Alpha Omega Alpha **BA:** 200 Lothrop Street, Pittsburgh, PA, 15213 **ADD:** 624 Poia Rd, Sewickley, PA, 15143

REIFF, DANIEL DRAKE, **T:** Art Historian (Retired), Educator **I:** Education/Educational Services **DOB:** 08/17/1941 **PB:** Potsdam **SC:** NY/USA **PT:** Henry Reiff; Ione Drake Reiff **MS:** Married **SPN:** Janet Madej Reiff (6/28/1975) **CH:** Nicholas Andrew; Michael Christopher **ED:** PhD, Harvard University (1970); MA, Harvard University (1964); BA, Harvard College, Harvard University (1963); Coursework, The University of Liege, Belgium **C:** Distinguished Service Professor Emeritus, State University of New York at Fredonia (2003-Present); Distinguished Service Professor, State University of New York at Fredonia (2003-2004); Professor of Art History, State University of New York at Fredonia (1977-2003); Associate Professor of Art History, State University of New York at Fredonia (1972-1977); Assistant Professor of Art History, State University of New York at Fredonia (1970-1972); Acting Assistant Secretary, United States Commission of Fine Arts (1969-1970); Instructor of Art History, Baylor University (1964-1965, 1966-1967) **CIV:** President, Fredonia Preservation Society (1995-1998); Member, Fredonia Village Revitalization Committee (1994-1998); Member, Barker Commons Renovation Committee (1992-1994); Member, Chautauqua County Executive's Historic Preservation Task Force (1978-1983); Head, Chautauqua County Architectural Survey Steering Committee (1977); Member, Chautauqua County Bicentennial Committee (1975-1976); Head, Mayor's Historic District Committee, Fredonia, NY (1974-1975) **CW:** Co-Author, "Column Monuments: Commemorative and Memorial Column Monuments from Ancient Times to the 21st Century," Five Volumes (2017); Author, "Teacher, Scholar, Mentor: St. Lawrence University's Dr. Harry Reiff and His Family, 1938-1950" (2015); Author, "Teacher, Scholar, Mentor: Dr. Harry Reiff of St. Lawrence University" (2013); Contributor, Essay, "American Architects and their Books, 1940-1915" (2007); Contributor, Essays, "The Encyclopedia of the New York State" (2005); Author, "Houses from Books: Treaties, Pattern Books, and Catalogs in American Architecture, 1738-1950, A History and Guide" (2000); Author, "Architecture in Fredonia, New York, 1811-1997: From Log Cabin to I. M. Pei" (1997); Author, "Historic Camps of Mt. Arab and Eagle Crag Lakes" (1995); Author, "Small Georgian Houses in England and Virginia: Origins and Development Through the 1750s" (1986); Contributor, Essays, "The Macmillan Encyclopedia of Architects" (1982); Author, "Architecture in Fredonia, 1811-1972: Sources, Context, Development" (1972); Author, "Washington Architecture, 1791-1861: Problems in Development" (1971); Co-Author, "Georgetown Architecture - Selections from HABS No. 10" (1970); Co-Author, "Georgetown Architecture: The Waterfront - Selections from HABS No. 4" (1968); Contributor, Articles to Professional Journals **AW:** Historic Preservation Book Prize, Center For Historic Preservation, Mary Washington College (Now University of Mary Washington) (2001); Ruth Emery Award, Victorian Society in America (1999); Grantee, Graham Foundation (1991); Architectural Heritage Honor Award, Preservation League of New York State (1986); Fellow, National Endowment for the Humanities (1984); University of Delaware Press Award (1983); Grantee, American Council of Learned Societies (1980); Fellow, Rotary International, Evanston, IL (1965-1966) **MEM:** President, Fredonia Preservation Society (1995-1998); Preservation League of New York State; National Trust for Historic Preservation; Society of Architectural Historians; The Nature Conservancy; The Wilderness Society; Historic New England; Adirondack Architectural Heritage; Chair, SUNY Fredonia Art Department **MH:** Albert Nelson Marquis Lifetime Achievement Award (2017) **H:** Photography; Canoeing; Hiking; Camping; Travel; Family historical research **PA:** Democrat **ADD:** 38 Courier Blvd, Kenmore, NY, 14217

REIFFEL, ROBERT SISKIND, T: Plastic Surgeon **I:** Medicine & Health Care **CN:** Robert S. Reiffel, MD **DOB:** 06/01/1946 **PB:** New York City **SC:** NY/USA **PT:** Martin Lawrence Reiffel; Roslyn Anita (Siskind) Reiffel **MS:** Married **SPN:** Suzanne Mara Temkin (6/19/1977) **CH:** Lauren Kate; Alyssa Julie **ED:** Fellow in Hand Surgery, New York University Medical Center, New York City, NY (1979-1980); Resident in Plastic Surgery, New York University Medical Center, New York City, NY (1977-1979); Resident in General Surgery, Roosevelt Hospital, New York City, NY (1973-1977); Intern in General Surgery, Roosevelt Hospital, New York City, NY (1972-1973); MD, Columbia University (1972); BA, Yale University (1968) **CT:** Diplomate, American Board of Plastic Surgery; Diplomate, American Board of Surgery **C:** Private Practice, Plastic and Reconstructive Surgery, White Plains, NY (1980-Present) **CR:** White Plains Hospital Physicians Associates (2016-Present); Attending Physician, White Plains Hospital; Past President of Medical and Dental Staff, Plastic Surgery Section, White Plains Hospital **CW:** Contributor, Articles, Professional Publications **AW:** Best Original Photographic Exhibit Award, Greater New York Orchid Show (1993); 1st Prize, Senior Classification Scholarship Contest, Educational Foundation, American Society Plastic and Reconstructive Surgeons (1980); 1st Prize, Resident's Night, Plastic Surgery Section, New York Academy of Medicine and New York Regional Surgery (1979) **MEM:** Fellow, American College of Surgeons; Medical Society of the State of New York; New York Regional Society for Plastic and Reconstructive Surgery; New York Society for Surgery of the Hand; Westchester County Medical Society; American Burn Association; American Society for Surgery of the Hand; American Society Plastic and Reconstructive Surgeons **MH:** Albert Nelson Marquis Lifetime Achievement Award (2017) **H:** Golf; Tennis; Photography **BA:** 12 Greenridge Ave Ste 203, Artistic Plastic Surgery, White Plains, NY, 10605 **URL:** http://www.ArtisticPlasticSurgeryNY.com

REILLY, GEORGE AUGUSTINE, T: Attorney **I:** Law and Legal Services **CN:** Siegel Reilly & Kaufman, LLC **PB:** Norwalk **SC:** CT/USA **PT:** Lawrence H. Reilly; Katherine (McLachlan) Reilly **MS:** Married **SPN:** Lynn Reilly (10/17/1987) **CH:** Peter; Matthew; Christopher **ED:** JD, Fordham University (1984); BA, Union College (1977) **C:** Siegel Reilly & Kaufman, LLC (2016-Present); Partner, Rucci, Burnham, Carta & Edelberg, LLP (2004-2015); Counsel, Rucci, Burnham, Carta & Edelberg, LLP, Darien, CT (1994-2004); Partner, Pierson, Reilly & Seeley, Darien, CT (1993-1994); Bentley, Mosher & Babson, Professional Corporation, Stamford, CT (1991-1993); Associate, Jackson & Nash, New York, NY (1988-1991); Associate, McAnerney & Millar, Darien, CT (1984-1988) **CIV:** Darien Rowayton Bank (2007-Present); Board of Directors, Family Centers, Greenwich, CT (2005-Present); Board of Education, Darien, CT (2002-Present); Chairman, Center for Hope, Darien, CT (2003-2005); Member Board Selectman, Darien, CT (1999-2001); Charter Revision Commission, Darien, CT (1997-1999); President, Board of Trustees, King & Low-Heywood Thomas School, Stamford, CT (1990-1997); Executive Committee, United Way, Darien, CT (1986-1990); Chairman, Annual Campaign, United Way, Darien, CT (1986-1987); Norwalk Community College Foundation **AW:** Ray of Hope Award, Center for Hope, Darien, CT (2012); Top Lawyers in Connecticut, Connecticut Magazine (2007); Distinguished Alumnus Award, Connecticut Chapter, Fordham Law Alumni Association **MEM:** American Bar Association; Fairfield County Regional Bar Association; Connecticut Bar Association **BAR:** U.S. Supreme Court (1991); U.S. District Court, Southern District, State of New York

(1988); U.S. District Court, Eastern District, State of New York (1988); U.S. District Court, State of Connecticut (1986); State of New York (1985); State of Connecticut (1984) **H:** Golf; Skiing **BA:** 1266 East Main Street, Suite 3, Siegel Reilly & Kaufman LLC, Stamford, CT, 06902

REINISCH, JUNE MACHOVER, T: Psychologist **I:** Medicine & Health Care **CN:** Kinsey Institute **DOB:** 02/02/1943 **PB:** New York City **SC:** NY/USA **PT:** Mann Barnett Reinisch; Lillian (Machover) Reinisch **ED:** PhD, Columbia University, with Distinction (1976); MA, Columbia University (1970); BS, New York University, Cum Laude (1966) **CT:** Certified in Childhood Education, State of New York **C:** Director Emeritus, Kinsey Institute (1993-Present); Professor, Clinical Psychology, Indiana University School of Medicine (1983-1993); Director, The Kinsey Institute for Research in Sex, Gender, and Reproduction, Indiana University, Bloomington, IN (1982-1993); Professor, Psychology, Indiana University, Bloomington, IN (1982-1993); Adjunct Associate Professor, Psychiatry, Rutgers, The State University of New Jersey (1981-1982); Associate Professor, Psychology, Rutgers, The State University of New Jersey (1980-1982); Assistant Professor, Psychology, Rutgers, The State University of New Jersey (1975-1980) **CR:** Executive Director, Health and Science Advisory Board, Museum of Sex (2004-Present); Director, Acquisitions and new exhibitions, Museum of Sex (2003-Present); Visiting Senior Researcher, Institute of Preventive Medicine, Copenhagen Municipal Hospital, Copenhagen Health Services, Copenhagen, Denmark (1994-Present); Senior Research Fellow, Trustee, Kinsey Institute (1993-Present); President, R2 Science Communications Inc, New York (1985-Present); Director, Principal Investigator, Prenatal Development Projects, Copenhagen, Denmark (1976-Present); Vice President, Science Affairs, Museum of Sex (2003); Senior Consultant, Museum of Sex, New York City, NY (1998); Consultant, SUNY **CW:** Author, "The Kinsey Institute New Report on Sex" (1994, 1990); Editor, Contributor, Books, Kinsey Institute Series; Syndicated Newspaper Columnist, The Kinsey Report; Contributor, Research Reports, Professional Journals; Contributor, Reviews, Professional Journals; Contributor, Articles, Professional Journals; Featured Guest, Science Special, Public Broadcasting Service; Featured Guest, Science Special, BBC; Featured Guest, Science Special, ABC; Featured Guest, Science Special, NBCUniversal Media, LLC; Featured Guest, Discovery Communications, LLC; Featured Guest, A&E Television Networks, LLC; Featured Guest, 20/20, ABC; Featured Guest, The Oprah Winfrey Show; Featured Guest, The Geraldo Rivera Show; Featured Guest, The Charles Grodin Show; Featured Guest, The Montel Williams Show; Featured Guest, Sally; Featured Guest, Good Morning America; Featured Guest, The Today Show; Featured Guest, CBS This Morning; Guest Host, Real Personal, CNBC; Guest Host, Free Talk Live; Guest Host, Foreign Appearances **AW:** Named, Regents Lecturer, University of California, Los Angeles, CA (1999); Award for Contribution to Professional al Conocimiento dela Sexualidad Humana, Association Mexicana de Sexologia, Mexico City, Mexico (1996); Distinguished Alumnae Award, Teachers College, Columbia University (1992); Dr. Richard J. Cross Award, Robert Wood Johnson Medical School (1991); Award, First International Conference on Orgasm, New Delhi, India (1991); Grantee, National Institute on Drug Abuse (1989-1995); Medal for 9th Dr. S.T. Huang-Chan Memorial Lecturer in Anatomy, The University of Hong Kong (1988); Grantee, Eunice Kennedy Shriver National

Institute of Child Health and Human Development (1981-1988); Grantee, National Institute of Mental Health (1978-1980); Morton Prince Award, American Psychopathological Association (1976); Grantee, Ford Foundation (1973-1975); Grantee, National Institute of Education (1973-1974); Grantee, Erickson Educational Foundation (1973-1974); Founders Day Scholar, New York University (1966) **MEM:** Trainee, National Institute of Mental Health (1971-1974); Fellow, American Association for the Advancement of Science; Fellow, American Psychological Association; Fellow, Association for Psychological Science; Fellow, Society for the Scientific Study of Sexuality; Charter Member, International Academy of Sex Research; International Women's Forum; Women's Forum, Inc.; American Association of Sexuality Educators Counselors & Therapists; Sigma Xi **H:** Travel; Scuba diving; Flying; Skydiving **BA:** 3865 Ocean View Ave, Brooklyn, NY, 11224

REPACE, JAMES L., T: Secondhand Smoke Consultant, Physicist **I:** Sciences **CN:** Repace Associates, Inc. **DOB:** 11/01/1938 **PB:** Yonkers **SC:** NY/USA **PT:** Dominick Repace; Emma (Palladino) Repace **MS:** Married **SPN:** Hilarine M. Schultheis (6/8/1940) **ED:** Postgraduate Work, The Catholic University of America (1970-1972); Postgraduate Work, University of Maryland (1969); MSc in Physics, Polytechnic Institute of Brooklyn (Now NYU Tandon) (1968); BSc in Physics, Polytechnic Institute of Brooklyn (Now NYU Tandon) (1962) **C:** Scientific Consultant, Repace Associates, Inc. (1998-Present); Policy Analyst, Indoor Air Division, United States Environmental Protection Agency (1995-1997); Policy Analyst, Occupational Safety and Health Administration, United States Department of Labor (1994-1995); Physicist, Exposure Assessment Group, Office of Research and Development, United States Environmental Protection Agency (1993-1994); Policy Analyst, Indoor Air Division, United States Environmental Protection Agency (1986-1993); Policy Analyst, General Staff, Office of Air & Radiation, United States Environmental Protection Agency (1979-1986); Research Physicist, Electronics Division, U.S. Naval Research Laboratory (1971-1979); Research Physicist, Ocean Science Division, U.S. Naval Research Laboratory (1969-1971); Research Associate, Insulator Physics Group, RCA David Sarnoff Laboratory (1965-1968); Junior Physicist, Department of Physics, NYC Health + Hospitals (1964); Senior Laboratory Technician, Radioisotope Laboratory, Grasslands Hospital (Now Westchester Medical Center) (1963) **CR:** Visiting Assistant Clinical Professor, Tufts University (2003-2012); Consultant, Stanford University (2003-2012) **CIV:** Ad-hoc Consultant, Ontario Tobacco Control Unit (2000-Present); Consultant, Department of Civil and Environmental Engineering, Stanford University (2006-2012); Adviser, Tobacco Control Research & Policy Unit, Department of Community Medicine, The University of Hong Kong (2002-2012); Visiting Assistant Clinical Professor, Tufts University (2004-2011); Member, Scientific Peer-Review Panel, California Tobacco-Related Disease Program (1994-2001); Member, Expert Advisory Panel on Tobacco or Health, WHO (1987-1990); Member, Surgeon General's National Advisory Panel on Smoking & Health (1987-1989); Secretary, TT-7 Indoor Air Quality Committee, Air Pollution Control Association (1982); Founding Member, Ad-hoc Interagency Committee on Indoor Air Quality (1979); Ad-hoc Peer Reviewer in Cancer Epidemiology, National Cancer Institute; Ad-hoc Peer Reviewer, Epidemiology Panel, California Tobacco Related Disease Program; Ad-hoc Peer Reviewer, Epidemiology Panel, FAMRI **CW:** Author, "ENEMY NO. 1: Waging The War on Secondhand

Smoke," Repace Associates, Inc. (2018); Associate Editor, "Passive Smoking, Tobacco Control" (2000-2003); Contributor, 97 Articles, Professional Journals; Contributor, Conference Papers **AW:** Recipient, Constance L. Mehlman Award, International Society of Exposure Science (2015); Maryland GASP President's Award for International Tobacco Control Efforts (2006); Recipient, Certificate of Recognition for Excellence in Smoke Studies, National Cancer Institute of Milan (2003); Recipient, Distinguished Professor Award, FAMRI (2002); Flight Attendant Medical Research Institute Distinguished Professor Award (2002); Robert Wood Johnson Foundation Innovator Award (2002); Recipient, Innovators Combating Substance Abuse Award, The Robert Wood Johnson Foundation (2002); American Lung Association of Maryland Distinguished Service Award (2003); Natl. Cancer Institute of Milan (Italy), Recognition for Excellence in Smoke Studies (2003); Recipient, President's Award, Prince Georges' County, Maryland (1998); Recipient, Distinguished Service Award, Maryland Chapter, American Lung Association (1998); Recipient, Lifetime Achievement Award, American Public Health Association (1998); Recipient, Certificate of Appreciation, Action on Smoking and Health (1998); Recipient, Impact Award, Occupational Safety and Health Administration, United States Department of Labor (1994); Recipient, Certificate of Appreciation, U.S. Department of Health and Human Services (1990); Recipient, The Surgeon General's Medallion, Dr. C. Everett Koop (1989); Recipient, Certificate of Appreciation, U.S. Department of Transportation (1989); Recipient, Exceptional Performance Award, United States Environmental Protection Agency (1984); Recipient, Thomas Edison Fellowship, U.S. Naval Research Laboratory (1971-1972); Recipient, Graduate Assistantship Award, RCA David Sarnoff Laboratory (1967); Recipient, Certificate of Appreciation, American Nonsmokers' Rights Foundation **MEM:** American Society of Heating, Refrigerating and Air Conditioning Engineers (2003-Present); International Society of Indoor Air Quality and Climate (2002-Present); International Society for Exposure Science (1997-Present); American Public Health Association (1996-Present); American Association for the Advancement of Science (1976-1990); Air Pollution Control Association (1979-1986); American Physical Society (1964-1979) **MH:** Albert Nelson Marquis Lifetime Achievement Award (2017) **H:** Environmental tobacco smoke studies **ADD:** 3479 Monitor Ct, Davidsonville, MD, 21035

REPHAN, JACK, T: Lawyer **I:** Law and Legal Services **CN:** Pender and Coward, P.C. **DOB:** 03/16/1932 **PB:** Little Rock **SC:** AK/USA **PT:** Henry Rephan; Mildred (Frank) Rephan **MS:** Married **SPN:** Arlene Clark (6/23/1957) **CH:** Amy Carol; James Clark **ED:** LLB, University of Virginia School of Law (1959); BS in Commerce, The University of Virginia (1954) **C:** Shareholder, Pender and Coward, Professional Corporation, Virginia Beach, VA (2007-Present); Principal, Rephan Lassiter PLC, Norfolk, VA (2001-2007); Counsel, Hofheimer Nusbaum Professional Corporation, Norfolk, VA (1993-2000); Partner, Sadur, Pelland & Rubinstein, Washington, DC (1988-1993); Partner, Porter, Wright, Morris & Arthur, LLP, Washington, DC (1987-1988); Member, Braude, Margulies, Sacks & Rephan (Now Braude Law Group, P.C.), Washington, DC (1977-1987); Partner, Danzansky, Dickey, Tydings, Quint & Gordon, Washington, DC (1964-1977); Associate, Pierson, Ball & Dowd (Now Reed Smith, LLP), Washington, DC (1962-1964); Law Clerk to Judge Sam E. Whitaker, United States Court Claims (Now United States

Court of Federal Claims), Washington, DC (1960-1962); Associate, Kantor & Kantor, LLP, Norfolk, VA (1959-1960) **CR:** National Panel of Arbitrators, American Arbitration Association; National Panel of Mediators, American Arbitration Association; Board of Arbitrators, Financial Industry Regulatory Authority; Lecturer, Joint Committee on Continuing Legal Education, Virginia State Bar; Chair, Member, Board of Governors, Construction and Public Construction Law Section, Virginia State Bar; Guest Lecturer, Construction and Government Contract Law, Regent University School of Law; Guest Speaker, Seminars, Sponsored by Virginia Law Foundation, AGC of Virginia Inc., Associated Builders and Contractors, Inc., Hampton Roads Utility and Heavy Contractors Association, Other Construction Industry Organizations **CIV:** Linkhorn Bay Condominium Association (2000-2002); President, Seminary Ridge Citizens Association (1976-1977); Treasurer, John Adams Middle School PTA, Alexandria, VA (1970-1971); Democratic Candidate for Alexandria City Committee (1969); President, Patrick Henry PTA, Alexandria, VA (1968-1969) **MIL:** First Lieutenant, U.S. Army (1955-1957) **CW:** Contributor, Articles to Legal Journals **AW:** Listee, Virginia Super Lawyers (2017); Listee, Coastal Virginia's Top Lawyers, Arbitration & Mediation, Construction (2016-2018); Listee, Virginia's Legal Elite, Alternative Dispute Resolution, Virginia Business Magazine (2001-2017); President's Award, Hampton Roads Utility and Heavy Contractors Association (2016); Associate of the Year Award, Hampton Roads Utility and Heavy Contractors Association (2013); Associate of the Year Award, Hampton Roads Utility and Heavy Contractors Association (2006); President's Award, Hampton Roads Utility and Heavy Contractors Association (1996); Named, AV Preeminent, Martindale-Hubbell **MEM:** Government Section on Construction Law, The Virginia Bar Association (1999-Present); Chairman, The Virginia Bar Association (2007-2008); Vice Chairman, The Virginia Bar Association (2006-2007); Chairman, The Virginia Bar Association (1981-1982); Vice Chairman, The Virginia Bar Association (1980-1981); Government Section on Construction Law, The Virginia Bar Association (1979-1981); Chairman, Subcommittee on Procurement of Judicial Remedies, Public Contract Section, ABA (1973-1974); President, Landmark Club, Kiwanis International (1969); The District of Columbia Bar; The Associated General Contractors of America, Inc.; General Counsel, Hampton Roads Utility and Heavy Contractors Association **BAR:** United States Court of Appeals for the Fourth Circuit (1972); Supreme Court of the United States (1966); United States Court of Appeals for the Federal Circuit (1961); United States Court of Federal Claims (1961); United States Court of Appeals for the District of Columbia Circuit (1961); Supreme Court of Virginia (1959) **RE:** Jewish **BA:** 222 Central Park Ave Ste 400, Pender and Coward, P.C, Virginia Beach, VA, 23462

REYNOLDS, GENEVA, T: Special Education Educator **I:** Education/Educational Services **DOB:** 11/02/1953 **PB:** Saginaw **SC:** MI/USA **PT:** Roger Rucker; Alrine (Braddock) Rucker **MS:** Married **SPN:** Montie Reynolds (8/1/1981) **CH:** Monte; Marcus **ED:** MA, General Administration, Chicago State University; BS, Chicago State University (1986) **C:** Principal, South Central Community Services, Chicago (2006-Present); Information Superintendent, U.S. Air Force Reserve, Chicago, IL (1981-2006); Command and Control Specialist, U.S. Air Force (1977-1981); Administrative Specialist, U.S. Air Force (1973-1977); Director, Special Education, South Central Community Services **CIV:** U.S. Air Force Reserve

(1981-Present); SM Sergeant, U.S. Air Force (1973-1981) **AW:** Community Service Award, Chicago State University; Two Commendation Medals, U.S. Air Force; Longevity Medal, U.S. Air Force **MEM:** Council for Exceptional Children; Kappa Delta Pi **H:** Reading; Computers; Plays **PA:** Democrat **RE:** Baptist **ADD:** 162 W 74th St, Chicago, IL, 60621

RHIM, E. KIM MARSHALL, T: Founder, Executive Director **I:** Professional Training & Coaching **CN:** The Training Source, Inc. **MS:** Married **SPN:** Michael **CH:** Brittany, Justin **ED:** MBA in Finance, Corporate Relations and Management, Columbia University (1983); BBA in Business Administration and Insurance, Howard University (1981) **CT:** Certified Job Developer (2013); Certified Global Career Development Facilitator (2009); Certified "Who Moved my Cheese" Facilitator (2007); Certified Professional Resume Writer (2000) **C:** Founder, Executive Director, The Training Source, Inc. (1993-Present); Program Manager, IBM Corporation (1984-1993) **CR:** Member, Leadership Greater Washington (2002-Present); Former Board Member, Maryland Association of Nonprofit Organizations (2006-2011); Former Board Member, Human Services Coalition (2001-2010) **CIV:** United Way; Combined Federal Campaign; Maryland Charity Campaign; Truist; America's Charities **AW:** Prince George's Chamber of Commerce, Honorary Chair of Golf Tournament (2018); Community Youth Advocates, Outstanding Community Servant (2018); Prince George's Chamber of Commerce Woman Business Leader of the Year (2016); Outstanding Community Leader, Maryland Black Mayors, Inc. (2016); NAACP Hometown Champion, Radio One (2016); W3 Women's Empowerment Conference, Outstanding Community Leader (2014); Delta Sigma Theta Sorority, Inc., Fortitude Image Award (2014); Prince George's County Executive, Community Partner Award (2013-2014); US Congresswoman Donna F. Edwards, Outstanding Service to the Community Award (2013); Prince George's County Council, 20 Years of Excellence Award (2013); Town of Capitol Heights, Entrepreneurial Stewardship Award (2013); Community Foundation for Prince George's County, Bridge Builder Award (2011); National Award of Excellence, Women Work! (2007); International Who's Who in Business (1997) **MEM:** First Baptist Church of Glenarden; Maryland Association of Nonprofit Organizations; Nonprofit Prince George's County; Prince George's Chamber of Commerce; Leadership Greater Washington; Howard University Alumni Association; Sisters 4 Sisters Network **H:** Attending friend and family gatherings; Travel; Scrabble; The arts **RE:** Baptist **BA:** 59 Yost Place, The Training Source, Inc., Seat Pleasant, MD, 20743 **URL:** http://www.thetrainingsource.org

RHIM, JOHNG SIK, I: Medicine & Health Care **CN:** Uniformed Services University - Health **DOB:** 07/24/1930 **PB:** Kwang Ju **SC:** South Korea **CH:** 6 Children **ED:** MD, Seoul University, Republic of Korea (1957) **C:** Research Professor, Department of Surgery, Uniformed Services, University Health Sciences, Bethesda, MD (2000-Present); Associate Director, Professor, Surgery Center Prostate Disease Research, Uniformed Services University of the Health Science, Bethesda, MD (1999-Present); Senior Investigator, National Cancer Institute, National Institutes of Health, Bethesda, MD (1978-1998); Project Director, Cancer Research, Microbiology Associates, Bethesda, MD (1966-1978); Visiting Scientist, National Institute of Allergy and Infectious Diseases, National Institutes of Health, Bethesda, MD (1964-1966); Research Associate, Louisiana State University Academy of Medicine, New Orleans, LA (1962-1964); Research

Associate, Graduate School of Public Health, University of Pittsburgh (1962); Research Fellow, Baylor University College of Medicine, Houston, TX (1961); Research Fellow, Children's Hospital Research Foundation, Cincinnati, OH (1958-1960); Intern, Seoul National University Hospital (1958) **MEM:** American Association for the Advancement of Science; American Medical Association; American Association Cancer Research; American Society Virology; Society for Experimental Biology and Medicine; International Association of Leukemia Research **MH:** Albert Nelson Marquis Lifetime Achievement Award (2017) **ADD:** 11455 S Glen Rd, Potomac, MD, 20854

RICCIARDI, CYNTHIA BOOTH, I: Education/Educational Services **SC:** MA/USA **ED:** PhD, Brandeis University, Waltham, MA; MA, Boston College, Chestnut Hill, MA; BA, Bridgewater State College, Massachusetts **C:** Visiting Lecturer, Bridgewater State College (1984-2006) **CIV:** President, Old Colony Historical Society, Taunton, MA (2006-2012); President, Bridgewater State College Alumni Association (1997-1998) **CW:** Editor, Critic, "The Delicate Distress"; Contributor, Chapters to Books

RICHARDS, JAY CLAUDE, T: Owner/President **I:** Business Management/Business Services **CN:** J.C. Richards Associates **DOB:** 04/06/1954 **PB:** Glen Ridge **SC:** NJ/USA **PT:** Jacob Tilghman Richards; Joan Louise (Walsh) Richards **ED:** Coursework, Tennessee Wesleyan College, Athens, TN (1972-1973) **CT:** Certification in Assistance/Damage Assessment, State of New Jersey Department of Law & Public Safety Disaster (1989); New Jersey Radiological Monitoring Certification, Warren County, New Jersey (1987) **C:** Bread Baker, Walmart (2013-Present); President, J.C. Richards Associates, Harmony Township, New Jersey (1980-Present); Owner, Poor Richards' British Gun Shop, Harmony Township, New Jersey (1976-Present); Reporter, North Warren News (2002-2004); Reporter, The Knowlton News (1998-2002); New Jersey Superior Court Radio Correspondent, WRNJ-News (1991-2013); Freelance Court Reporter, The Morning Call, Allentown, PA (1986-2008); Reporter, Photographer, Press Publishing: The News, Belvidere, NJ (1977-1998); Various Positions, Armed Security Work (1973-1975) **CR:** Historian Consultant, Psychic Investigators Episode 39 - The Elizabeth Cornish Murder (2007); Photography Judge, Warren County 4-H, Belvidere, NJ (1990-2003); Press Officer, Warren County Office Emergency Management, Belvidere, NJ (1989-1998) **CIV:** Consultant, Harmony New Jersey Historical Preservation Commission (2000-Present); Trustee, Historian, Warren County War Memorial Corporation (1999-Present); Tailor of 1865 Haversacks Queen's, Own Rifle Regiment Canada (2014); Tailor of 1899 Haversacks, New Brunswick Military History Museum, Canada (2014); Historian, Researcher, Virginia Military Institute 1851-1864 Missing Clock Search Project (2011-2012); Participant of Foreign Policy Leadership, George Washington University (2005); Member, Glamour Photographers International (2003-2004); Participant of Foreign Policy Leadership, George Washington University (2003); Civil War Monument Project, Hackettstown, NJ (2001); Warren County Purple Heart Monument Construction Committee (2000); Participant of Foreign Policy Leadership, George Washington University (1999); Warren County War Memorial Committee (1997-1998); Member, Hazardous Materials Advisory County, Warren County, New Jersey (1989-1998); Member, Joint Emergency Management Council, Belvidere/White Township, New Jersey (1989-1998); Member, Warren County Arts Advisory Council; Statue

of Liberty - Ellis Island Foundation; History Consultant, Hoff-Vanatta Farmstead Restoration Project, Harmony, NJ **CW:** Author, "Civil War Warren County" (2011-Present); Author, "World War Two Veterans of Warren County, New Jersey - Expanded Edition" (2017); Author, "World War Two Veterans of Warren County, New Jersey - A Tribute to the Men & Women Who Defended Freedom" (2010); Author, "Just Another Dog Face Fighting Fascism for Freedom" (2007); Author, "Fighting Fascism for Freedom: Warren County, New Jersey in World War II" (2006); Author, "Officers and Men of Warren County in the Civil War, Expanded Edition" (2005); Author, "1903 Flood Centennial Souvenir Book" (2003); Author, "Warren, Warriors & The World: Warren County, New Jersey In the Plains Indians Wars & The Spanish-American War 1865-1902 (2002); Contributing Artist, New Jersey "Billy Yank" Civil War Monument, Hackettstown, NJ (2001); Author, "Following the Hand of Franklin: Warren County, New Jersey and the Search for the North Pole" (2000); Author, "More Bugles, Battles and Belvidere: Warren County, New Jersey Civil War Letters to Home" (1999); Author, "Officers and Men of Warren County, New Jersey Civil War" (1998); Author, "Bugles, Battles & Belvidere: The History of Warren County, New Jersey in the Civil War" (1997); Author, "Flames Along the Delaware" (1996); Author, "Penn, Patriots and the Pequest: The History of Pre-Victorian Belvidere, 1716-1845" (1995) **AW:** Recipient, Legion of Honor, Chapel of the Four Chaplains (2007); Recipient, Legion of Honor Award, Chapel of Four Chaplains (2007); Recipient, New Jersey Frontier Guard's Book Award (1997); Recipient, Outstanding Community Service Award, Am Legion Post 131 (1994); Named, Honorary Member, Boy Scout Troop 141, Belvidere, NJ (1993) **MEM:** National Indian Wars Association; Oxford New Jersey Historical Society; United States Naval Institute Senior Army Rescue Commodores Association; Rescue Officers Association of the United States; Society of Professional Journalists; National Press Photographers Association; Forks of the Delaware Historical Arms Society; Frederick A. Cook Society; Sigma Delta Chi **MH:** Albert Nelson Marquis Lifetime Achievement Award (2017) **H:** Gourmet cooking; Gardening; Herbal medicine; Military antiques; Making leather and canvas gear for re-enactors **ADD:** 3110 Belvidere Road, Philipsburg, NJ, 08865 **URL:** https://www.richardsreproductions.com

RICHARDS, LEONARD MARTIN, T: Principal **I:** Business Management/Business Services **CN:** Lenan Partners **DOB:** 06/04/1935 **PB:** Philadelphia **SC:** PA/USA **PT:** Leonard Martin Richards; Marion Clara (Lang) Richards **MS:** Divorced **SPN:** Phyllis Janelle Mowrey (8/26/1961), Divorced (1978) **CH:** Lisa; David Reed **ED:** ThD in Counseling, Universal Seminary, Denver CO (2000); MTh in Comparative Religions, Universal Seminary, Denver CO (1998); MBA in Finance, University of Pennsylvania Wharton School (1963); BS in Finance, Pennsylvania State University (1957) **CT:** Certified Technician, tCES, Nexalin Technologies (2010); Training Program, The Silva Method (2007); Certified Presenter, Succession Planning Workshops, Family Business Partners, LLC (2000); Certified Professional Trainer, PAIRS Foundation Relationships Courses (1999) **C:** Clinical Associate, Unique Mindcare, Houston, TX (2011-Present); Principal, Lenan Partners (2010-Present); Managing Director, The Enhancement Institute, Houston, TX (2003-2011); President, Lenan Holdings, Inc., Houston, TX (2005-2009); President, L.M. Richards & Company, Houston, TX (1982-2009); Member, Advisory Board, Trinity Life Services, Houston, TX (1996-2000); Vice President, Senior Investment Officer, American General Series

Portfolio Company (1977-1988); Vice President, Senior Investment Officer, Variable Annuity Life Insurance Company, Houston, TX (1977-1988); Member, Executive Committee, Variable Annuity Life Insurance Company, Houston, TX (1977-1988); Vice President, Manager, Institutional Funds Group, Republic National Bank of Dallas (1974-1977); Partner, G.H. Walker, Laird & Co., New York, NY (1972-1974); Vice President, Portfolio Manager, Bernstein-Macaulay, Inc., New York, NY (1968-1972); Assistant to Senior Partner, Van Cleef, Jordan and Wood, Inc., New York, NY (1963-1968) **CIV:** Trustee, PAIRS Foundation, Weston, FL (2004-2006); Trustee, Universal Seminary (1997-2000); Trustee, Post Oak School, Houston, TX (1997-1999); Board of Directors, Capital Institutional Services, Inc., Dallas, TX (1991-1999); Board of Directors, The Houston Choral Society (1988-1990); President, Board of Directors, Sand Dollar Youth Services, Houston, TX (1985-1996) **MIL:** Captain, U.S. Army (Artillery), Active Duty (1957-1960); USAR (1961-1965) **MEM:** ACFA Institute; CFA Society Houston; Wharton Club of Houston; The Houstonian Club **MH:** Albert Nelson Marquis Lifetime Achievement Award (2017) **H:** Skiing; Travel; Scuba, Art, Music and Theater **PA:** Independent **BA:** 1776 Yorktown St., Suite 500, Houston, TX, 77056 **ADD:** 9023 Briar Forest Dr, Houston, TX, 77024

RICHARDSON, PATRICIA JEAN, T: Librarian **I:** Library Management/Library Services **DOB:** 01/31/1943 **PB:** Walla Walla **SC:** WA/USA **PT:** Francis Hagel; Melba Lorraine (Bryant) Hagel **MS:** Married **SPN:** Michael E. Ovens **CH:** Shasha L.; Kathrine E.; Frances du Bruyeres; John E. du Bruyeres **ED:** MLS, University of Washington (1994); BA in English, University of Washington (1966); AA, Yakima Valley College, Yakima, WA (1963) **CT:** Certified Librarian, State of Washington **C:** Retired (2011); Library for Children's Services, King County Library Systems, Seattle, Washington (1993-2011); Library Assistant, Children's Department, Walla Walla Public Library (1984-1992); Library's Assistant, Microsoft, Redmond, Washington (1993-1994); Library's Assistant, Yakima Valley Libraries, Yakima, Washington (1956-1963) **MEM:** Board Member, CAYAS (1998-2000); Scholar, Walla Walla Chapter, AAUW (1992); Chairman, Membership Committee, AAUW (1971); American Library Association; Pacific Northwest Library Association; Washington Library Association **MH:** Albert Nelson Marquis Lifetime Achievement Award (2017) **H:** Gardening; Reading; Hiking; Collecting; Oil painting portraits and landscapes **PA:** Democrat **RE:** Catholic **ADD:** 4211 252nd Ave SE, Issaquah, WA, 98029

RICKEL, ANNETTE, T: Psychologist **I:** Social Work **CN:** Weill Cornell Medicine **PB:** Philadelphia **SC:** PA/USA **PT:** Ralph Francis Urso; Marguerite (Calcaterra) Urso **SPN:** John A. Leone **CH:** John Ralph **ED:** Fellow, American Council on Education, Princeton University (1990-1992); Fellow, American Council on Education, Rutgers, the State University of New Jersey (1990-1992); PhD, University of Michigan (1972); MD, University of Michigan (1972); BA, Michigan State University (1969) **CT:** Licensed Psychologist, State of Michigan; Licensed Marriage and Family Therapist, State of New York **C:** Involved, New York-Presbyterian Hospital (2010-Present); Professor, Weill Cornell Medicine (2005-Present); President, Annette Urso Rickel Foundation, Inc. (2003-Present); President, Memorial Sloan Kettering Cancer Center (2011-2013); Education Program Officer, The Rockefeller Foundation (2000-2003); Clinical Professor, Department of Psychiatry, Georgetown University (1995-2000); Assistant Provost, Wayne State University (1989-1991); Professor

Psychology, Wayne State University (1987-1992); Visiting Associate Professor, Columbia University (1982-1983); Associate Professor of Psychology, Wayne State University (1981-1987); Assistant Professor, Psychology, Wayne State University (1975-1981); Assistant Director, Northeast Guidance Center (1972-1975); Adjunct Faculty, University of Michigan (1969-1975); Faculty in Early Childhood Education, Merrill-Palmer Institute, Wayne State University (1967-1969); Psychotherapist, Private Practice; Visiting Professor, Princeton University **CR:** Museum of Modern Art, New York (2007-Present); Chairman, Bal Poudre, Flagler Museum, Palm Beach, FL (2015); President's National Health Care Reform Task Force (1992-1993); Congressional Science Fellow, Senate Finance Subcommittee on Health, American Psychological Association (1992-1993); Congressional Science Fellow, Senate Finance Subcommittee on Health, American Association for the Advancement of Science; Public Policy Staff, United States Senator Donald W. Riegle, Jr.; Fellow, American Psychological Association **CIV:** Vice President, Chamber Music Society of Lincoln Center (2002-Present); Board Member, Reading is Fundamental (2000-Present); Board Member, National Symphony Orchestra, The Kennedy Center (1997-Present); Board of Directors, The Children's Center (1989-Present); President, Society, Memorial Sloan Kettering Cancer Center (2002-2012); John D. and Catherine T. MacArthur Foundation (1998-1999); W.K. Kellogg Foundation (1996-1997); Epilepsy Center, Epilepsy Foundation of Michigan (1984-1992); Board Member, The Chamber Music Society of Lincoln Center; Board Member, Women's Forum **CW:** Author, "Chronic Illness in Children and Adolescents" (2007); Author, "Attention Deficit Hyperactivity Disorder in Children and Adults" (2006); Author, "Understanding Managed Care" (2000); Author, "High Risk Sexual Behavior" (1998); Author, "Keeping Children From Harm's Way" (1997); Author, "Teenage Pregnancy and Parenting" (1989); Co-Author, "Preventing Maladjustment" (1987); Co-Author, "Social and Psychological Problems of Women" (1984); Consulting Editor, Journal of Community Psychology; Consulting Editor, Journal of Primary Prevention; Contributor, Numerous Articles, Scientific Journals; Author, Eight Books **AW:** Distinguished Trustee Award, United Hospital Foundation (2013); Grantee, National Institutes of Health (2000); Grantee, The Catherine H. Tuck Foundation (1986-1990); Career Development Chair Award (1985-1986); Grantee, McGregor Fund (1982); Grantee, David M. Whitney Fund (1982); Grantee, The National Institute of Mental Health (1976-1986); Grantee, Eloise and Richard Webber Foundation (Now Hudson Webber Foundation) (1977-1980); Grantee, McGregor Fund (1977-1978) **MEM:** Division President, American Psychological Association (1984-1985); International Women's Forum; Society for Research in Child Development; The International Society for Research in Child and Adolescent Psychopathology; International Association of Applied Psychology, Inc.; Sigma Xi; Psi Chi, The International Honor Society in Psychology **MH:** Albert Nelson Marquis Lifetime Achievement Award (2017) **H:** Golf; Swimming; Piano; Horseback riding; Travel **RE:** Roman Catholic **ADD:** 700 Park Avenue, Apt. 2A, New York, NY, 10021

RIFKIN, BARRY R., T: Dean **I:** Education/Educational Services **CN:** Stony Brook University **DOB:** 03/30/1940 **PB:** Trenton **SC:** NJ/USA **PT:** Samuel H. Rifkin; Ida M. Rifkin **MS:** Married **SPN:** Linda Ruth Rosenberg (11/1993); Harriet Smith (3/1960, Divorced 9/1981) **CH:** Avery; Carl; Hannah **ED:** PhD, University of Rochester (1974);

DDS, Temple University (1968); MS, University of Illinois (1964); BS, Ohio State University (1961) **C:** Professor of Oral Biology and Pathology, Dean, School of Dental Medicine, Stony Brook University (1998-Present); Professor Emeritus, New York University (1998-Present); Head, Division of Basic Sciences, New York University (1991-1998); Chairman, Department of Oral Medicine and Pathology, New York University (1987-1991); Professor, New York University (1984-1991); Chairman, Department of Oral Medicine, New York University (1980-1987); Associate Professor, New York University (1980-1984); Associate Pathologist, Strong Memorial Hospital, University of Rochester Medical Center (1974-1980); Andrew Mellon Fellow, University of Rochester Medical Center (1974) **CR:** Board Member, Friends of the National Institute of Dental and Craniofacial Research (2005-Present); Researcher in Field; Fellow, American College of Dentists **CW:** Senior Editor, "Biology and Physiology of the Osteoclast" (1992); Editorial Board Member, "Journal of Dental Research"; Contributor, Articles, Professional Journals; Contributor, Abstracts, Professional Journals **MEM:** President, American Association of Oral Biologists (1992-1993); American Association for the Advancement of Science; American Society for Bone and Mineral Research; International Association for Dental Research; American Society for Cell Biology; New York Academy of Sciences; Sigma Xi, The Scientific Research Honor Society; Omicron Kappa Upsilon **BA:** 160 Rockland Hall, SUNY Stony Brook Health Sciences, Stony Brook, NY, 11794 **ADD:** 1 Washington Square Village, Apt. 7A, New York, NY, 10012

RILEY, ROBERT E., T: Financial Services Company Executive **I:** Financial Services **CN:** R. E. Riley Associates **DOB:** 02/19/1930 **PB:** Boston **SC:** MA/USA **PT:** Edward Gerard Riley; Nina Loretta (Wolfe) Riley **MS:** Married **SPN:** Carol Lee (Anthony) Riley (6/22/1974); Ann Elizabeth McCourt (11/10/1956, Divorced 1972) **CH:** Robert; David; Thomas; Michael; Brian **ED:** MBA, Harvard University (1953); AB, College of the Holy Cross (1951) **C:** Managing Director, J.W. Childs Associates, L.P. (2005-2009); President, Joseph P. Kennedy Enterprises (1998-2005); Chief Executive Officer, Joseph P. Kennedy Enterprises (1998-2005); President, Leggat McCall Properties (1995-1998); Chief Executive Officer, Leggat McCall Properties (1995-1998); President, Dreyfus Corporation (Now MBSC Securities Corporation) (1995); Chief Operating Officer, Dreyfus Corporation (Now MBSC Securities Corporation) (1995); Chairman, Prudential Reinsurance Company (Now Everest Re Group, Ltd) (1993-1994); Chief Executive Officer, Prudential Reinsurance Company (Now Everest Re Group, Ltd) (1993-1994); Chairman, Prudential Residential Services Company (1990-1993); Chief Executive Officer, Prudential Residential Services Company (1990-1993); Chairman, Prudential Realty Group (1986-1990); Executive Vice President, Prudential Investment Corporation (1986-1994); President, Prudential Asset Management Company (Now Prudential Financial, Inc.) (1985-1986); Senior Vice President, Group Pensions, Prudential Insurance Company of America (Now Prudential Financial, Inc.) (1984-1985); Senior Vice President, American Express Company (1981-1984); President, Marsh & McLennan Companies, Inc. (1974-1981); Chief Executive Officer, Marsh & McLennan Companies, Inc. (1974-1981); President, F.L. Putnam Investment Management Company (1970-1980); Chief Executive Officer, F.L. Putnam Investment Management Company (1970-1980) **CIV:** Associate Trustee, College of the Holy Cross; Board of Directors, John F. Kennedy Presidential Library and Museum; Finance Committee, Beth

Israel Deaconess Medical Center; Overseer, New England Deaconess Hospital, (Now Beth Israel Deaconess Medical Center); Trustee & Member, BC High; Chairman, Investment Advisory Committee, Cohasset Library Trust; Director & Member, Executive Committee, John F. Kennedy Presidential Library and Museum **MIL:** Lieutenant Commander, U.S. Navy (1953-1962) **CW:** Biographer, "Piercing the Irish Ceiling" (2011) **AW:** Chief Executive Officer of the Year, Financial World Magazine (1979); Chief Executive Officer of the Year, Financial World Magazine (1975); Silver Medal, Axiom Business Book Awards **MEM:** Union Club of Boston; The University Club of New York **MH:** Albert Nelson Marquis Lifetime Achievement Award (2017); Distinguished Humanitarian (2017) **H:** Boating; Skiing; Ice hockey **PA:** Republican **RE:** Roman Catholic **BA:** 50 Derby St Ste 240, Riley Associates, Hingham, MA, 02043

RINKENBERGER, PATRICIA JO, T: Music Educator **I:** Education/Educational Services **DOB:** 07/09/1947 **PB:** Leon **SC:** IA/USA **PT:** John Victor Hartnell; Margie Lurene Kendall **MS:** Married **SPN:** Stephen L. Rinkenberger (6/5/1977) **CH:** Michael Brandt; Geoffrey Marc **ED:** MS in Music Education, University of Illinois (1977); BM, DePaul University, With Highest Honors (1970); Coursework, Illinois Wesleyan University, St. John's University, Governor's State University, MS + 48 **CT:** Certification, VoiceCare Network **C:** Music Educator; Performer; Voice Teacher/Coach; Choral Director; Choral Coordinator; Music Minister; Guest Conductor; Program Builder; Clinician; Adjudicator; Former Senior Staff Vocal/Music Director, NightBlue Performing Arts Company **CR:** Musical Producer; Musical Director; Consultant, Music and Organizations, Illinois and Michigan; Volunteer Coordinator for multiple projects; Supervisor, Student Teachers in Music Education, University of Illinois; Teacher, Joliet Junior College; Teacher, High School; Teacher, Pre-School; Teacher, Grades K-8 **CW:** "Musical Concepts to Teach Preschoolers" Workshop in Parent Education (1985); Workshops on "Unplug the Christmas Machine" and "Half the Sky"; Singer; Arranger; Numerous Musical Projects and Workshops **AW:** Phi Delta Kappa; Alpha Lambda Delta National Honor Society, Illinois Wesleyan University; Full Tuition Waivers and Graduate Assistantship, University of Illinois **MEM:** Music Educators National Conference (Now National Association for Music Education); The Phi Beta Kappa Society; American Choral Directors Association; Beta Beta Chapter, Delta Kappa Gamma Society International; Local Service Organizations' Boards and Committees **MH:** Albert Nelson Marquis Lifetime Achievement Award (2017) **H:** Spending time with family; International and national travel; Gardening; Working at service organization; Attending Lyric & CSO, Reading; Walking; Museums **RE:** Protestant **ADD:** 2945 Birch Rd, Homewood, IL, 60430

RINO, BARBARA ELIZABETH, T: Orchestra Clinician, Conductor and Adjudicator for Solo and Group Festivals and Competitions, Private Studio Teacher for Violin/Viola **I:** Education/Educational Services **CN:** Barbara E. Rino, LLC **DOB:** 01/14/1945 **PB:** Lincoln **SC:** NE/USA **MS:** Widow **SPN:** Louis Stanislaus Rino (12/22/1974, Deceased 8/31/2004) **CH:** John Gaspare **ED:** MusB, Nebraska Wesleyan University, with Distinction, Lincoln, NE (1966) **CT:** Licensed Teacher, State of Colorado (1967) **C:** Orchestra Clinician, Guest Conductor, Adjudicator, Solo and Group Festivals and Competitions, (1973-Present); Private Studio Teacher, Self Employed, Westminster, CO (1971-Present); Colorado Adjudicator ASTA Certificate

Advancement Program, (2010-Present); Orchestra Director, Adams 12 Five Star Schools, Thornton, CO (1988-2001); Freelance Violinist, DMA, Denver, CO (1973-1995); Director of Orchestras, Denver Youth Musicians Inc. (1984-1989); Concertmaster, Rocky Mountain Chamber Orchestra (1985-1987); Director of Orchestras, Denver Youth Musicians Inc. (1973-1977); Concertmaster, Brico Symphony Orchestra, Denver, CO (1972-1974); Orchestra Director, Adams County School District 50, Westminster, CO (1969-1978); Music Educator, Denver Public Schools, Denver, CO (1966-1968); Violinist, LSO, Lincoln, NE (1962-1966) **CIV:** Stephen Minister, \Trinity United Methodist Church, Denver, CO (2017); Creator, The Barbara Cook Rino String Students Fund, Foundation for Lincoln Public Schools (2016); Music Activities, Westminster United Methodist Church, CO (1980-2005) **AW:** Recipient, Outstanding Music Alumni Award, Nebraska Wesleyan University (2006); Recipient, Outstanding Teacher of The Year Award, Colorado Chapter of The American String Teachers Association (2003) **MEM:** American String Teachers Association; Phi Kappa Phi; Kappa Delta Pi **MH:** Albert Nelson Marquis Lifetime Achievement Award (2017) **RE:** Methodist **ADD:** 3899 W 98th Ave, Westminster, CO, 80031

RITTER, WILLIAM, T: Professor Emeritus **I:** Education/Educational Services **CN:** University of Delaware **PB:** , **ED:** Doctorate, Iowa State University (1971) **C:** Core Faculty Member, Interdisciplinary Graduate Program in Environmental and Energy Policy, University of Delaware, Newark, DE (2003-2013); Core Faculty Member, Interdisciplinary Graduate Program in Environmental and Energy Policy, University of Delaware, Newark, DE (1993-1998); Professor, Chair, Bioresources Engineering Department, University of Delaware, Newark, DE (1992-1993); Assistant Professor, Bioresources Engineering Department, University of Delaware, Newark, DE (1992); Professor, Acting Chair, Bioresources Engineering Department, University of Delaware, Newark, DE (1982-1992); Professor, Bioresources Engineering Department, University of Delaware, Newark, DE (1977-1982); Summer Assistant Engineer in Extension, Ontario Department of Agriculture, Newmarket, Ontario, Canada (1973); Professor of Bioresources, Civil Engineering and Environmental Engineering, University of Delaware, Newark, DE (1971-2014); Associate Professor, Bioresources Engineering Department, University of Delaware, Newark, DE (1971-1977); Environmental Consultnat in Hazardous Waste Management and Sediment and Storm Water Management (1966-1971); Research Associate, Iowa State University, Ames, IA (1966); R. V. Anderson and Associates, Toronto, Ontario, Canada (1965); Project Manager, Wik Associates, Inc., New Castle, DE; Dairy Herdsman, Arnolds Dairy Farm, Moorefield, Ontario, Canada; Senior Policy Fellow, Center for Energy and Environmental Policy, University of Delaware, Newark, DE **AW:** Fellow, Environmental & Water Resources Institute, American Society of Association Executives (2013); Elected Diplomat, American Academy of Water Resources Engineers (2013); Recipient, Richard Torrence Award, American Society of Civil Engineers (2010); Recipient, Royce J. Tipton Award, American Society Of Civil Engineers (2004); Recipient, Distinguished Service Award, Northeast Agricultural and Biological Engineering Conference, American Society of Association Executives (2003); Recipient, Delaware Section Member of the Year Award, American Society Of Civil Engineers (1999); Lifetime Member, American Water Works Association (1998); Recipient, Outstanding News Correspondence Award, American Society of Civil Engineers

(1997); Fellow, American Society Of Civil Engineers (1997); Recipient, Water Resources Engineering Division Service Award, American Society of Association Executives (1995); Distinguished Lecturer, Northeast Agricultural and Biological Engineering Conference, American Society of Association Executives (1994-1995); Elected Fellow, American Society Of Civil Engineers (1994); Recipient, Irrigation and Drainage Division Outstanding Service Award, American Society Of Civil Engineers (1993); Recipient, F.D. Chester Outstanding Research Award, College of Agricultural Sciences (1990); Recipient, Gunlogson Countryside Engineering Award, American Society of Association Executives (1988); Recipient, University of Delaware Fellowship, Salzburg Seminar (1987); Recipient, North Atlantic Young Engineer of the Year, American Society of Association Executives (1984, 1981); Recipient, Superior Achievement Award, Environmental Protection Agency (1979); Recipient, Richard Torrence Award, American Society Of Civil Engineers; Recipient, New Castle County Water Resources Award **MEM:** American Society of Civil Engineers; Fellow, American Society of Agricultural Engineers; Fellow, American Water Works Association; Lifetime Member, Canadian Society of Agricultural Engineers; Water Environment Federation; Lifetime Member, American Academy of Environmental Engineers; Delaware Association of Professional Engineers; Tau Beta Pi; Gamma Sigma Delta; Sigma Xi; Alpha Epsilon **MH:** Albert Nelson Marquis Lifetime Achievement Award (2017) **ADD:** 63 Paper Mill Road, Elkton, MD, 21921

RIVIELLO, ROBERT, T: Physician, Surgeon **I:** Medicine & Health Care **CN:** Brigham and Women's Hospital, Harvard University **PB:** Burbank **SC:** CA/USA **MS:** Married **ED:** Fellow in Anesthesia Critical Care Medicine, Brigham and Women's Hospital (2008-2009); Fellow in Acute Care and Burn Surgery, Brigham and Women's Hospital (2007-2008); Research Fellow in Global Surgery, Center for Surgery and Public Health, Brigham and Women's Hospital (2007); Fulbright International Fellow in Global Surgery, CEML, Angola (2006-2007); Resident in General Surgery, Vanderbilt University Medical Center (2001-2006); MD, University of California, San Diego (2001); MPH in Population and International Health, Harvard University (2001); BA in Biology, Harvard University, Cum Laude (1995) **CT:** Board Certified, Surgical Critical Care (2009); Board Certified, General Surgery (2007) **C:** Assistant Professor of Surgery, Harvard Medical School, Harvard University (2015-Present); Assistant Professor of Global Health and Social Medicine, Harvard Medical School, Harvard University (2015-Present); Associate Surgeon, Brigham and Women's Hospital (2009-Present); Faculty Member, Center for Surgery and Public Health, Brigham and Women's Hospital (2009-Present); Consulting Staff in Surgery, Dana-Farber Cancer Institute (2009-Present); Affiliate in Global Health and Social Medicine, Harvard Medical School, Harvard University (2009-2015); Instructor in Surgery, Harvard Medical School, Harvard University (2007-2015); Assistant Surgeon, Brigham and Women's Hospital (2007-2008) **CR:** Program Co-director, U.S. Academic Consortium for the Rwanda Human Resources for Health (2014-Present); Fellow, American College of Surgeons (2014-Present); Director, Global Surgery Programs, Center for Surgery and Public Health, Brigham and Women's Hospital (2013-Present); Director, Global Health Equity Residency Program in General Surgery, Brigham and Women's Hospital (2012-Present); Surgical Program Director, U.S. Academic Consortium for the Rwanda Human Resources for Health (2011-Present); Associate to the Head of Department, De-

partment of Surgery, University of Rwanda (2015-2016); Junior Fellowship Award, Department of Surgery, Brigham and Women's University (2011); Surgical Program Adviser, Partners in Health, Rwanda (2010-2015); Scientific Adviser, Salud del Sol, Cincinnati, OH (2009-2010); Faculty Director, Academic Global Surgery Forum, Center for Surgery and Public Health, Brigham and Women's Hospital (2007-2015); Reader's Digest International Medical Fellowship, MAP International (2006); Carl and Lily Pforzheimer Public Service Fellowship, Harvard University (2000); Ford Fellowship in Physiology Research, Harvard University (1994) **CW:** Ad Hoc Reviewer, "PloS Medicine"; Ad Hoc Reviewer, "International Journal of Surgery"; Ad Hoc Reviewer, "World Journal of Surgery"; Ad Hoc Reviewer, "Annals of Surgery"; Ad Hoc Reviewer, "Lancet Global Health"; Ad Hoc Reviewer, "Surgery"; Ad Hoc Reviewer, "Journal of Surgical Education"; Ad Hoc Reviewer, "Injury" **AW:** Kletjian Foundation Research Endowment Award, Kletjian Foundation (2017); Joseph E. Murray and Simon J. Simonian Prize for Research Excellence in Surgery, Department of Surgery, Brigham and Women's University (2016); Minority Faculty Career Development Award, Center for Faculty Development and Diversity, Brigham and Women's University (2013); Nominee, Charles McCabe Faculty Prize for Excellence in Teaching, Harvard University (2012); Faculty Development Award, Center for Faculty Development and Diversity, Brigham and Women's University (2011); Faculty Teaching Award for Medical Student Teaching, Brigham and Women's University (2009); Honoree, Yale-Johnson & Johnson Physician Scholar in International Health, Yale School of Medicine (2006); Fulbright International Exchange Scholarship, African Division, U.S. Department of State (2006); Resident Educator Award Finalist, Vanderbilt University (2006); Joseph W. & Bonnie J. Graves Award for Excellence in Teaching, Vanderbilt University (2006); Hillman Award, Vanderbilt University (2006); Medical Student Housestaff Teaching Award, Vanderbilt University (2004-2005); Roderick K. Calverley Humanitarian Service Award, UC San Diego (2001); Outstanding Student-Leader Award, Student-Run Free Clinic, UC San Diego (2001); Health Education Award, International Medical Health Education Consortium (1999); Honoree, Dean's List, Harvard University (1995) **MEM:** Council Member, The G4 Alliance (2016-Present); Advisory Council, PAACS (2016-Present); International Surgical Society (2014-Present); New England Surgical Society (2014-Present); Massachusetts Chapter, American College of Surgeons (2014-Present); Rwanda Surgical Society (2013-Present); ASAP Today (2010-Present); American Burn Association (2009-Present); Association of Academic Surgeons (2008-Present); H. William Scott, Jr. Society, Vanderbilt University Medical Center (2007-Present); Fulbright Association (2007-Present); Alpha Omega Alpha Honor Medical Society (2005-Present); Christian Medical and Dental Association (1997-Present); Associate, American College of Surgeons (2006-2013); Committee on Global Affairs, Association of Academic Surgeons (2008-2010); Global Burden of Surgical Disease Working Group (2008-2010); Candidate Group, Society of American Gastrointestinal Endoscopic Surgeons (2006-2009); Physicians for Human Rights (2000-2009) **BA:** 75 Francis Street, Brigham And Women's Hospital, Boston, MA, 02115

ROACH, ROBERT M., T: 1) Lawyer 2) Entrepreneur 3) Educator 4) Legal Advocate **I:** Law and Legal Services **CN:** 1) Roach & Newton 2) Schrader Cellars 3) The University of Texas at Austin 4) University of Houston Law Center **DOB:** 05/27/1955 **PB:** Bronxville **SC:** NY/USA **PT:** Robert M. Roach; Mary Dee Roach **ED:** JD, The University of Texas at

Austin (1981); BA, Georgetown University (1977) **C:** Partner, RBS Napa Winery (Now Schrader Cellars) (2000-Present); Adjunct Professor, The University of Texas at Austin (2000-Present); Appellate Advocacy Director, University of Houston Law Center (1994-Present); Founding Partner, Roach & Newton (2008-Present); Founding Partner, Cook & Roach LLP (Now Roach & Newton) (1993-2008); ,Partner, Mayor, Day, Caldwell & Keeton (1989-1993); Associate, Mayor, Day & Caldwell (1983-1988); Associate, Ryan & Marshall (1983); Associate, Vinson & Elkins (1981-1983) **CR:** Adjunct Law Professor, University of Houston (1990-Present); Lecturer, Continuing Legal Education, University of Houston Law Center (1989-Present); Member, Texas Law Review (1979-1981); Researcher, United States Senate Select Committee on Nutrition and Human Needs (1975-1977); Editor United States Senate Select Committee on Nutrition and Human Needs (1975-1977); Researcher, Supreme Court of the United States (1977); Lecturer, Continuing Legal Education, State Bar of Texas; Lecturer, Continuing Legal Education, The University of Texas at Austin; Lecturer, Continuing Legal Education, University of Houston; Lecturer, Continuing Legal Education, South Texas College of Law Houston; Lecturer, Continuing Legal Education, Southern Methodist University; Lecturer, Continuing Legal Education, ABA **CW:** Editor, Defense Counsel Journal (1990-1993) **MEM:** Chairman, Appellate Section, State Bar of Texas (2006-2007); Chair of Council, State Bar of Texas (2007-2008); Product Liability Advisory Council; International Association of Defense Counsel; Federation of Defense & Corporate Counsel, Inc.; DRI; TADC, Inc.; Chair, Grievance Committee, State Bar of Texas; Chair, Insurance Section, State Bar of Texas; Judicial Liaison, State Bar of Texas; Former Chairman, Appellate Section, Houston Bar Association; Meadowood, Napa Valley; The Coronado Club; Houston Racquet Club **BAR:** United States District Court Northern District of Texas (1988); United States District Court Eastern District of Texas (1986); Supreme Court of the United States (1986); United States District Court Western District Of Texas (1984); United States District & Bankruptcy Courts of Southern District of Texas (1982); United States Court of Appeals for the Fifth Circuit (1982); State of Texas (1981) **MH:** Albert Nelson Marquis Lifetime Achievement Award (2017) **H:** Oenology; Music; Travel; Tennis **BA:** 10777 Westheimer Rd Ste 212, Roach & Newton LLP, Houston, TX, 77042

ROBERSON, ROBERT S., T: Investment Company Executive **I:** Financial Services **PB:** Mount Kisco **SC:** NY/USA **MS:** Married **SPN:** Barbara C. Drane (1967) **CH:** Elizabeth de V.; Merritt B.; Barbara D. **ED:** MBA, College of William and Mary (1973); Postgraduate Studies, Washington & Lee University Law School (1966); Postgraduate Studies, New York University Graduate School of Business Administration (1964); BS, New York University (1964) **C:** President, Director, Weaver Brothers, Inc., Newport News, VA (1967-Present); Board of Directors, First Peninsula Bank & Trust Company, Hampton, VA (1977-1978); Member, New York Produce Exchange (1965-1966); Various Positions in Financial and Building Industries (1964-1967) **CIV:** Former Member, Board of Directors, Peninsula Unit, American Cancer Society, Newport News, VA; Former Member, Board of Directors Heritage Council Girl Scouts USA, Hampton, VA; Former Member, Board of Trustees Newport News Public Library, Former Member, Board of Trustees, Virginia Living Museum, Newport News, VA; Former Member, Board of Trustees, Chairman, Committee on Development, Hampton Roads Academy, Newport News, VA; Former Member, Board of Visitors, George Washington's Mount Vernon National Shrine, Mount Vernon, VA; Former Member, Board of Trustees, President, Chief Curator, Golf Museum, Newport News, VA; Member, Board of Trustees, Randolph College/Randolph-Macon Woman's College, Lynchburg, VA; Former Commissioner, Chairman, Newport News Arts Commission, Virginia; Former Commissioner, Vice Chairman Williamsburg Area Arts Commission, Virginia; Former Member, Board of Directors, Muscarelle Museum of Art, Williamsburg, VA; Founding Member, Board of Trustees, Member, Executive Committee, Vice Chairman, Muscarelle Museum Art Foundation, Williamsburg, VA; Former Member, Board of Trustees, President, Virginia War Museum Foundation, Newport News, VA; Former Member, Governing Board of Visitors, Member, Executive Committee, Chairman, Committee on Development and Alumni Affairs, College of William and Mary, Williamsburg, VA; Member, Board of Trustees, Member, Executive Committee, Roberson Museum and Science Center/Planetarium, Binghamton, NY; Member, Board of Trustees, Chairman, The Roberson Foundation, Binghamton, NY; Member, Board of Trustees, Former Vice Chairman, Former Chairman Ad Hoc Institutional Transition Committee, Member, Executive Committee, Chairman Audit Committee, New York Genealogical and Biographical Society, New York, NY; Former Member, Governing Board of Visitors, Member, Executive Committee, Richard Bland College, Petersburg, VA; Member, Board of Trustees, Woodrow Wilson Presidential Library and Museum, Staunton, VA; Former Member, Museum Committee, Virginia State Golf Association Foundation, Midlothian VA; Former Member, Board of Visitors, Virginia Institute Marine of Science, Gloucester Point, VA; Former Member, Vet Corps Artillery of New York **AW:** Patrick Henry Award, Commonwealth of Virginia (2001); New York University Honorary Society (1964); Decorated Knight, Officer, Order of St. John, England; Knight, Order of Saints Maurice and Lazarus, Royal House Savoy, Italy; Honorary Deputy Chief, New York City Fire Department **MEM:** Newcomen Society US; US Golf Association, Far Hills, NJ; Former National Committeeman, Museum and Library, General Society Colonial Wars; St. Nicholas Society City New York; Colonial Order Acorn; Knight Commander, Sovereign Military Order Temple of Jerusalem; Squadron A Association; Pilgrims US/UK; Union Club; Down Town Association; Library and Arts Committee, The Brook Club; Church Club, New York, NY; Metropolitan Club, Washington, DC; Southampton Club, Long Island, NY; Farmington Country Club, Charlottesville, VA; Executive Committee, Vice President, Cypher Society of William and Mary; Former President, James River Country Club; Hampton Roads German Club; Hampton Roads Assembly; The Hundred Club, Newport News, VA; Williamsburg German Club; America's Cup Archives and Library Committee, New York Yacht Club; Fishers Island Yacht Club, New York; Former Member, Fishers Island Club, Long Island, NY; Social Register Association, New York, NY; The Blue Book of the Hamptons, Long Island, NY; Paul Harris Fellow, Rotary International; Blue Key Honor Society; Delta Sigma Pi **PA:** Republican **RE:** Episcopalian **ADD:** PO Box 3, Williamsburg, VA, 23187

ROBERTS HUNTER, BEVERLY CLAIRE, T: Research Scientist, Educator **I:** Research **CN:** Piedmont Research Institute **DOB:** 04/19/1941 **PB:** Pittsburgh **SC:** PA/USA **PT:** Eldon Clare Roberts; Ethel Mae (Kamer) Roberts **MS:** Married **SPN:** Harold G. Hunter (1/7/1966) **CH:** Cynthia Claire (Deceased); Gregory Shawn **ED:** Diploma, Education for Ministry, School of Theology, University of the South (2010); Diploma, Virginia Natural Resources Leadership Institute, University of Virginia (2007); BA, University of Pittsburgh, Cum Laude (1963) **CT:** Certification, Virginia Master Naturalist (2013); Certification, Geographic Information Systems, George Mason University (2003) **C:** President, Rappahannock Friends and Lovers of Our Watersheds (2004-Present); President, Piedmont Research Institute, Amissville, VA (1999-2011); Scientist, Boston College (1998-1999); Lead Scientist, BBN Corp. (1993-1998); National Science Foundation, Program Manager, Research on Teaching and Learning (1989-1993); Senior Staff Scientist, George Washington University, Human Resources Research Organization, Alexandria, VA (1970-1987); Staff Scientist, Matrix Research, Alexandria, VA (1969); Director, Instructional Programming, Human Resources Research Organization, Alexandria, VA (1966-1968); Systems Engineer, IBM Corp. (1965-1966) **CR:** Adjunct Professor, University of San Francisco (1985-1986); Apple Education Affairs Advisory Board (1984-1985); President, Targeted Learning Corp. (1983-1989); President, Piedmont Research Institute (1979-1980); Peer Reviewer, National Science Foundation, Apple Computer Inc., U.S. Office of Education; Consultant U.S. Congress, U.S. Office Education, Bell Laboratories, Telenet Communications **MIL:** Computer Programmer, U.S. Navy (1964-1965) **CW:** Co-Author, Discussion Organizer, "Pope Francis, Care for our Common Home" (2016-Present); Author, "Online Searching in the Curriculum" (1989); Author, "Working with the U.S. Congress" (1988); Author, "Guide to Learning Resources for Users of IBM Personal Computers," Scholastic Constitution Then and Now Data Files (1987); Author, "Guide to Learning Resources for Users of IBM Personal Computers," Scholastic Weather and Climate Data Files (1987); Author, "Guide to Learning Resources for Users of IBM Personal Computers," Scholastic Literature Databases (1986); Author, "Guide to Learning Resources for Users of IBM Personal Computers," Scholastic World Geography Data Bases (1986); Author, "Guide to Learning Resources for Users of IBM Personal Computers," Scholastic Poetry and Mythology Databases (1986); Author, "Guide to Learning Resources for Users of IBM Personal Computers," Scholastic, U.S. History Databases, (1985); Author, "Guide to Learning Resources for Users of IBM Personal Computers," Scholastic U.S. Government Databases (1985); Author, "Guide to Learning Resources for Users of IBM Personal Computers," Scholastic Life Science Databases (1985); Author, "Guide to Learning Resources for Users of IBM Personal Computers," Scholastic Physical Sciences Databases (1985); Author, "My Students Use Computers" (1984); Co-Author, "Computer Literacy" (1982); Co-Author, "Learning Alternatives in U.S. Education: Where Student and Computer Meet" (1975); Author, "Scientists at Work Hypermedia Database"; Editor, "Education and Computing International Journal"; Contributor, Articles to Publications **AW:** Lifetime Achievement Award, Rappahannock League for Environmental Protection (2007); Educator of the Year Award, Culpeper Soil and Water Conservation District (2005); Director's Award for Program Officer Excellence, National Science Foundation (1992); Grantee, National Science Foundation (1979-2003); National Merit Scholar, University of Pittsburgh **MEM:** Virginia Natural Resources Leadership Institute; Board Director, President, Rappahannock Friends and Lovers of Our Watershed; Rappahannock League for Environmental Protection; Nature Conservancy; Old Rag Master Naturalists; Trinity Episcopal Church **MH:** Albert Nelson Marquis Lifetime Achievement Award (2017) **ADD:** 130 Mossie Lane, Amissville, VA, 20106

ROBERTS, PAUL CRAIG III, **T:** Economics Professor, Writer, Columnist **I:** Education/Educational Services **CN:** Institute for Political Economy **DOB:** 04/03/1939 **PB:** Atlanta **SC:** GA/USA **PT:** Paul Craig Roberts; Ellen Lamar (Dryman) Roberts **MS:** Divorced **SPN:** Linda Jane Fisher (7/3/1969, Divorced 1994); Becky B. Bickerstaff (1959, Divorced 1968) **CH:** Becky Ellen; Stephanie Bradford; Pendaran **ED:** PhD, University of Virginia (1967); Postgraduate Coursework, Merton College, Oxford University, England (1964-1965); Postgraduate, University of California, Berkeley (1962-1963); BS, Georgia Institute of Technology (1961) **C:** Research Fellow, Independent Institute (1990-Present); Chairman, Institute for Political Economy (1985-Present); John M. Olin Fellow, Institute for Political Economy (1994-2004); William E. Simon Professor of Political Economy, Georgetown University Center for Strategic and International Studies, Washington, D.C. (1982-1993); Assistant Secretary of Treasury for Economic Policy, Department of Treasury, Washington, D.C (1981-1982); Senior Research Fellow, Hoover Institution, Stanford University (1978-2004); Member, United States Conglomerates Staff (1975-1978); Research Fellow, Hoover Institution, Stanford University (1971-1977); Associate Professor, University of New Mexico (1969-1971); Assistant Professor of Economics, Virginia Polytechnic Institute and State University (1965-1969) **CR:** Contributing Editor, Trends Journal (2011-Present); Investors Business Daily (1998-2005); Creators Syndicate (1997-2010); Contributing Editor, World Trade Magazine (1997-1998); Contributing Editor, National Review (1993-2003); Distinguished Adjunct Scholar, Center for Strategic and International Studies, Washington, D.C. (1993-1996); Distinguished Fellow, Cato Institute (1993-1996); Contributing Editor, Reason Magazine (1993-1995); Le Figaro, Paris (1992-1996); Nationally Syndicated Columnist, Scripps Howard News Service (1989-1997); San Diego Union (1988-1992); Liberation, Paris (1988-1989); Financial Post, Canada (1988-1989); Washington Times (1988-2002); Erfolg, Federal Representative of Germany (1988); Adjunct Scholar, Cato Institute (1987-1993); Member, Advisory Board, Marvin and Palmer (1986-1996); Columnist, Business Week (1983-1998); Lazard Freres Asset Management (1983-1997); Consultant, Department of Defense (1983-1984); Consultant, Department of Commerce (1983); Member, President-elect, Reagan's Task Force on Tax Policy (1980); Associate Editor, Columnist, Wall Street Journal, New York City, NY (1978-1980); Director, Value Line Investment Funds, New York City, NY; A. Schulman, Akron, Ohio Consultant Morgan Guaranty Trust Company; American Studies Program, Harding University; Member, Advisory Committee, Center for the American Founding Member Wright Investors' Service; International Board of Economic and Investment Advisors, Board of Directors, Committee on Present Danger; Trustee, Intercollegiate Studies Institute; Committee on Developing American Capitalism; Member Selection Committee; President, Economic and Communication Services Inc. **CIV:** Drafted Original Kemp-Roth Bill (1976) **CW:** Author, "How America Was Lost, French Edition" (2015); Author, "Amerikas Weltkriege" (2015); Author, "The Neoconservative Threat To World Order" (2015); Author, "The Failure of Laissez Faire Capitalism, Czech and Korean Editions" (2015); Author, "The Failure of Laissez Faire Capitalism, Chinese Edition" (2014); Author, "How America Was Lost" (2014); Author, "The Failure of Laissez Faire Capitalism" (2013); Author, "Amerikas Kriege" (2013); Author, "The Supply-Side Revolution: An Insider's Account of Policymaking in Washington, Chinese Edition (2012); Author, "Wirtschaft Am Abgrund" (2012); Author, "How The Economy Was Lost" (2010); Au-

thor, "The Tyranny of Good Intentions, New Edition (2008); Author, "The Tyranny of Good Intentions" (2000); Author, "Chile: Dos Visiones-la Era Allende-Pinochet" (2000); Author, "The Capitalist Revolution in Latin America, Oxford University Press (1997); Author, "The New Color Line: How Quotas and Privilege Destroy Democracy" (1995); Author, "Meltdown: Inside the Soviet Economy" (1990); Author, "Alienation and the Soviet Economy, New Edition" (1990); Author, "The Cost of Corporate Capital in the United States and Japan" (1985); Author, "The Supply-Side Revolution: An Insider's Account of Policymaking in Washington" (1984); Author, "Marx's Theory of Exchange, New Edition" (1983); Author, "Marx's Theory of Exchange" (1973); Author, "Alienation and the Soviet Economy" (1971); Member, Editorial Board, Modern Age, Intercollegiate Review; Contributing Editor, Harper's Magazine **AW:** International Journalism Award, Press Club of Mexico (2015); Frank E. Seidman Distinguished Award in Political Economy, President Inlet Beach Water Company (2000-2006); Warren Brookes Award for Excellence in Journalism (1992); Public Service Award, General Services Administration (1991); Chevalier De La Légion D'Honneur (1987); National Chamber Foundation Fellow (1984-1985); Meritorious Service Award, Department of Treasury (1982); American Philosophical Society Grantee (1968); Earhart Fellow, University of Virginia (1966-1967); Gridiron Secret Society, University of Georgia **MEM:** Beethoven Society; American Society French Legion of Honor; Taxation Policy Committee United States Chamber of Commerce; Polanyi Society; Sierra Club; Florida Wildlife Federation; American Civil Liberties Union; Union of Concerned Scientists; Audubon Society; Wilderness Society; Environmental Defense Fund **MH:** Albert Nelson Marquis Lifetime Achievement Award (2017) **BA:** 169 Pompano Street, Inlet Beach, FL, 32461 **ADD:** 11475 Big Canoe, Big Canoe, GA, 30143 **URL:** https://www.paulcraigroberts.org/

ROBERTSON, R.G. HAMISH, **T:** Physicist, Professor Emeritus **I:** Education/Educational Services **DOB:** 10/03/1943 **PB:** Ottawa **SC:** Canada **PT:** Hugh Douglas Robertson; Alice Madeleine (Bell) Robertson **MS:** Married **SPN:** Peggy Lynn Dyer (7/4/1980) **CH:** Ian **ED:** PhD, McMaster University (1971); MA, University of Oxford (1969); BA, University of Oxford (1965) **C:** Boeing Distinguished Professor, University of Washington, Center for Experimental Nuclear Physics and Astrophysics, (2008-Present); Science Director, Center for Experimental Nuclear Physics and Astrophysics, University of Washington (2000-Present); Professor, University of Washington (1994-2017); Fellow, LANS, LLC (1988-Present); Staff Member, LANS, LLC (1981-1994); Professor, Michigan State University (1981-1982); Associate Professor, Michigan State University (1978-1981); Assistant Professor, Michigan State University (1973-1978); Assistant Research Professor, Michigan State University (1972-1973); Research Associate, Michigan State University (1971-1972) **CR:** Director, Sudbury Neutrino Observatory (2003); Visiting Scientist, Chalk River Nuclear Laboratories, Ontario, Canada (1980); Scientist, Argonne National Laboratory, Illinois (1979); Research Associate, Princeton University (1975-1976) **CW:** Contributor, Over 120 Articles, Professional Journals **AW:** Boeing Distinguished Professorship (2008–2017); Honorary DSc, McMaster University (2017); Breakthrough Prize in Physics (2015); Washington State Academy of Sciences Founding Class (2008); Polanyi Prize (2006); Los Alamos National Laboratory Director's Colloquium (2005); Member of the National Academy of Sciences (2004);

Fellow, American Academy of Arts and Sciences (2003); Fellow of the Institute of Physics (London) (1998); Tom W. Bonner Prize, American Physical Society (1997); Fellow of the American Physical Society (1982); Recipient, Fellowship, Alfred P. Sloan Foundation, Michigan State University (1976); Recipient, Scholarship, National Research Council, McMaster University (1965-1969); Honoree, Trevelyan Scholar, England (1962-1965); Recipient, Scholarship, Oriel College (1962-1965) **MEM:** Chair, Division of Nuclear Physics, American Physical Society (2000); Fellow, American Physical Society; Institute of Physics; American Academy Arts and Sciences; National Academy of Sciences; Canadian Association of Physicists, IEEE **ADD:** 6605 136th Pl SW, Edmonds, WA, 98026 **URL:** https://en.wikipedia.org/wiki/Hamish_Robertson

ROBINSON, ANNETTMARIE, **T:** Entrepreneur **I:** Financial Services **DOB:** 01/31/1940 **PB:** Fayetteville **SC:** AR/USA **PT:** Christopher Jacy Simmons; Lorena (Johnson) Simmons **MS:** Married **SPN:** Roy Robinson (6/17/1966) **CH:** Steven (Deceased); Sammy; Pamela; Olen **ED:** BA in Business, Seattle Central College (1959); BA, Edison University of Technology (1958) **C:** Owner, Consulting Company, Reno, NV (1998-Present); Consultant, M'RAL, Inc. Retail Dry Goods, Anchorage, AK (1985); Consultant, Pioneer Investments, Anchorage, AK (1983-2009); Investor, Anchorage, AK (1971-2009); Director, Personnel, Country Kitchen Restaurants, Inc., Anchorage, AK (1966-1971) **CR:** Advocate for Victims of Incest; Advocate, Plea Bargains; Youth Radio Mentor **CIV:** Community Association Institute Condo/Coop/Townhouse Law (1999-Present); Director, Secretary, Radio (2000-2009); Director, Station, Reno, NV (1996-2009); Secretary, Station, Reno, NV (1996-2009); Director, Radio, Reno, NV (1996-2009); Secretary, Radio, Reno, NV (1996-2009); Director, Catholic Radio, Reno, NV (1996-2009); Secretary, Catholic Radio, Reno, NV (1996-2009); Republicans of Alaska, Anchorage, AK (1987); Chairman, Round Table YMCA, Anchorage, AK (1986-2009); Republican Presidential Task Force, Washington, DC (1984-2009); Active Member, Station, Reno, NV; Active, Child Abuse Issues and Prosecution; Director, Hunter Lake Townhouse Association, Reno, NV; Secretary, Hunter Lake Townhouse Association, Reno, NV **AW:** Honoree, Woman of the Year, Anchorage Lions Club (1989); Honoree, Marksman First Class, National Rifle Association of America (1953) **MEM:** Racing Team, Porsche Club of America (1998-Present); Chocktaw Tribe; Fair Sky Dawes Number Trail of Tears **MH:** Albert Nelson Marquis Lifetime Achievement Award (2017) **H:** Archaeology; Fishing **ADD:** 1407 Foster Drive, Reno, NV, 89509

ROBINSON, CHERYL ANITA JEFFREYS, **T:** Special Education Educator **I:** Education/Educational Services **CN:** Montgomery County Public Schools **DOB:** 01/02/1954 **PB:** Washington **SC:** DC/USA **PT:** William Charles Jeffreys; Dorothy Crawford Jeffreys **MS:** Married **SPN:** Norman Norris Robinson (June 21, 1975) **CH:** Nicole Lorraine; Natalie Lavonne **ED:** EdD, Nova Southeastern University (2003); MA, George Washington University (1977); BS, District of Columbia Teachers College (Now University of the District of Columbia), Summa Cum Laude (1976) **CT:** Diplomate, Administrative and Supervisory Certificate, Maryland State Department of Education (2005); Diplomate, Advanced Professional Certificate, Maryland State Department of Education **C:** Special Education Supervisor, Montgomery County Public Schools (2005-Present); Instructional Specialist for the Assistant Superintendent of Instruction, Charles County Public Schools, La Plata, MD (2006-2009);

Worked with Principal and Director of Special Education, Enhanced Special Education Program, Stethem Educational Center, Charles County Public Schools, La Plata, MD (2006-2009); Administrative Liaison, Stethem Educational Center, Charles County Public Schools, La Plata, MD (2006-2009); Organizer, Committee to Revise the Home and Hospital Procedures and Forms, Charles County Public Schools, La Plata, MD (2006-2009); Chair, Committee to Revise the Home and Hospital Procedures and Forms, Charles County Public Schools, La Plata, MD (2006-2009); Organizer, On-going Committee to Revise Home Instruction/Home Schooling Procedures and Forms, Charles County Public Schools, La Plata, MD (2006-2009); Chair, On-going Committee to Revise Home Instruction/Home Schooling Procedures and Forms, Charles County Public Schools, La Plata, MD (2006-2009); Networker with Central-Based Staff, Stethem Educational Center, Charles County Public Schools, La Plata, MD (2006-2009); Presenter, Initial information on International Baccalaureate Programs, Charles County Public Schools, La Plata, MD (2006-2009); Visitations Organizer, Local IB Programs, Charles County Public Schools, La Plata, MD (2006-2009); Regional Spelling Education Specialist, Maryland Public Schools, Maryland State Department of Education (1990-2005); Special Education Area Office Manager, Maryland Public Schools, Maryland State Department of Education (2001-2002); Special Education Resource Teacher, Maryland Public Schools, Maryland State Department of Education (1984-1990); Diagnostic-Prescriptive Teacher, Prince George's County, Maryland Public Schools, Maryland State Department of Education (1977-1983) **CR:** Member, School Chief Executive Officer's Faculty Support Team (2003-Present); Facilitator, School Staff/Parent Program for ADHD Students (2000-2001); Planned and Facilitated Teacher in ADHD Training (1998-2001); Advisory Committee Representative, Summer Institute, Nova Southeastern University (1997) **AW:** Recipient, Career Development Grant, AAUW (1997-1998) **MEM:** AAUW; Montgomery County Association of Administrators and Principals; National Education Association; Council for Exceptional Children; National Council of Negro Women, Inc.; Kappa Delta Pi, International Honor Society in Education; Alpha Kappa Alpha Sorority, Inc. **MH:** Albert Nelson Marquis Lifetime Achievement Award (2017) **H:** Art; Crafts; Antiques; Theater **PA:** Democrat **RE:** Baptist **ADD:** 11304 Brigadier Court, Fort Washington, MD, 20744

ROBINSON, JOSEPH, T: Geology Educator, Petroleum Engineer, Consultant **I:** Education/Educational Services **CN:** Syracuse University **DOB:** 06/25/1925 **PB:** Regina **SC:** SK/Canada **PT:** Webb Gabriel Wilton; Blanche Marion (Schiefner) R. **MS:** Divorced **SPN:** Mary Corrine Maclaughlin, November 1, 1952 (Divorced 1977) **CH:** Joseph Christopher; John Edward; Timothy Webb **ED:** PhD, University of Alberta (1968); MSc, McGill University (1951); BEng, McGill University (1950) **CT:** Registered Professional Engineer, Quebec, Canada **C:** Professor Emeritus, Syracuse University (1991-Present); Consultant Geologist, J.E. Robinson & Associates, Syracuse, NY (1976-Present); Professor of Geology, Syracuse University (1976-1991); Senior Geologist, Union Oil Company, Canada, Calgary, Alberta (1968-1976); Geophysicist, Imperial Oil Ltd., Canada (1951-1968) **CIV:** Electro-technical Officer, Canadian Navy (1943-1946) **CW:** Author, "Computer Applications in Petroleum Geology" (1982) **MEM:** American Association of Petroleum Geologists; Society of Exploration Geophysicists; Canadian Association of Petroleum Geologists; International Association for Mathematical Geology (Associate Editor 1976-1978) **ADD:** 837 Ackerman Avenue, Syracuse, NY, 13210

ROCKWELL, S. KAY, T: Professor **I:** Education/Educational Services **CN:** University of Nebraska, Lincoln **DOB:** 02/28/1940 **PB:** Columbus **SC:** NE/USA **PT:** Carrol Albert Becher; Lauretta Susan (Grossnicklaus) Becher (Deceased) **MS:** Married **SPN:** Leroy V. Rockwell (6/16/1962) **CH:** Kent Alan; Susan Kay Rockwell Downing; Keri Lynn **ED:** PhD in Community and Human Resources, University of Nebraska (1984); MA in Adult and Continuing Education, University of Nebraska (1975); BSN, University of Nebraska (1962); Graduate in Nursing, Lincoln General Hospital School of Nursing, Lincoln, NE (1960) **CT:** Former Registered Nurse, State of Nebraska **C:** Professor Emerita (2006-Present); Professor and Evaluation Specialist, University of Nebraska, Lincoln, NE (1997-2006); Associate Professor and Evaluation Specialist, University of Nebraska, Lincoln, NE (1990-1997); Assistant Professor, University of Nebraska, Lincoln, NE (1984-1990); Member, Advisory Board, Department of Adult Education and Social Foundation, University of Nebraska, Lincoln, NE (1984-1986); Evaluation Technologist, University of Nebraska, Lincoln, NE (1979-1984); Instructor, Lincoln General Hospital School of Nursing (1962-1967); Acting Assistant Director, Nursing Education, Lincoln General Hospital (1965-1966) **CR:** Consultant to Extension Specialists and Agents on Program Evaluation, Trainer on Program Evaluation, Nebraska Extension; Presenter, Workshops and Symposia in Field **CIV:** Volunteer, Farmer-to-Farmer Program, USDA (2002-Present); Partnered on Humanitarian Projects in Uganda and Kenya in Africa (2012-Present); Volunteer, Friendship Force International (FFI) in Kenya and Uganda (2013-Present); Member and Chairman, Social Ministry Committee, Nebraska Synod Evangelical Lutheran Church of America; Board Member, Advocacy Office, Evangelical Lutheran Church of America **CW:** Researcher-in-Brief, Editor, Journal Extension (1987-1990); Contributor, Articles, Professional Journals **AW:** Recognition of Exceptional Support to the Open World Program from the Open World Leadership Center at the Library of Congress, DC. (2006); Outstanding Adult Educator' from Adult and Continuing Education Association of Nebraska (2003); 'Team Award' from Epsilon Sigma (1996); Excellence in Evaluation Training Award, EEE-TIG, American Evaluation Association (1996); Sustained Excellence in Extension Evaluation, EEE-TIG, American Evaluation Association (1992); Certificate of Achievement, Epsilon Sigma Phi (1991) **MEM:** North Central Regional Representative, Extension Education Evaluation Topical Interest Group, American Evaluation Association (1990-Present); Nebraska Cooperative Extension Association; Adult and Continuing Education Association of Nebraska; Epsilon Sigma Phi; Gamma Sigma Delta; United States International Commission on Irrigation and Drainage **MH:** Albert Nelson Marquis Lifetime Achievement Award (2017); Distinguished Humanitarian (2017) **H:** Book club; Reading; Bridge; Traveling to 40 different countries **PA:** Democrat **RE:** Lutheran **ADD:** 2101 S 66th St, Lincoln, NE, 68506

RODRIGUES, HELENA, T: Library Administrator **I:** Library Management/Library Services **PT:** Edward Louis Rodrigues; Louise DeMello Rodrigues **ED:** ArtsD, Simmons College (1992); MS, Simmons College, Boston, MA (1986); MA, Emmanuel College, Boston, MA (1967); BA, Salve Regina University, Newport, RI (1964) **C:** University Dean of Libraries, Johnson & Wales University, Providence, RI (1993-Present); Bibliographic Control Librarian, Roger Williams University, RI (1989-1993); Rare Books Cataloger, The John Carter Brown Library, Brown University, Providence, RI (1985-1988); Technology Services Librarian, Rhode Island State Library, Providence, RI (1983-1985); Preliminary Cataloger, Library of Congress, Washington, D.C. (1979-1982) **CR:** Speaker and Lecturer in Field; Participant, International Conferences; President, Higher Education Library Information Network, Kingston, RI (2007-Present); Chairman of the Board, Higher Education Library Information Network, Kingston, RI (2007-Present); Advisory Board, Graduate School of Library and Information Studies, University of Rhode Island, Kingston, RI (1999-2002) **CW:** Contributor, Chapters, Books; Author, Scientific Papers in Field **AW:** Grantee, Research Foundation, Roger Williams University (1991-1992) **MEM:** American Library Association; NELA; Rhode Island Library Association; Beta Phi Mu; Sigma Phi Sigma; President, Association of College and Research Libraries, American Library Association **MH:** Albert Nelson Marquis Lifetime Achievement Award (2017) **H:** Researching the history of the wife of Christopher Columbus; Currently writing a book **ADD:** 101 Hathaway Rd, North Dartmouth, MA, 02747

ROOP, JOSEPH MCLEOD, T: Economist (Retired) **I:** Financial Services **CN:** Pacific Northwest National Laboratory **DOB:** 09/29/1941 **PB:** Montgomery **SC:** AL/USA **PT:** Joseph Ezra Roop; Mae Elizabeth (McLeod) Roop **MS:** Married **SPN:** Betty Jane Reed (9/4/1965) **CH:** Elizabeth Rachael **ED:** PhD, Washington State University, Pullman, WA (1973) BS, Central Missouri University, Warrensburg, MO (1963) **C:** Adjunct Professor, Department of Economics, Washington State University (1999-2011); Member, International Energy Agency, Paris, France (1990-1991); Staff Scientist/Economist, Pacific Northwest National Laboratory, Richland, WA (1981-2011); Senior Economist, Evans Economics, Inc., Washington (1979-1981); Economist, Economic Research Service, United States Department of Agriculture, Washington, D.C. (1975-1979) **MIL:** US Army (1966-1968) **CW:** Author, "The Maryland Descendants of Christian Rupp, 1732-1810" (2014); Contributor, Articles to Professional Journals **AW:** Retirement Honor, Pacific Northwest National Laboratory (2006); Research Grant, Cooperative State Research Service, United States Department of Agriculture (1971-1973) **MEM:** American Economic Association; Econometric Society; International Association for Energy Economics; American Statistical Association; Agricultural & Applied Economics Association **MH:** Albert Nelson Marquis Lifetime Achievement Award (2017) **H:** Genealogy **ADD:** 715 South Taft St, Kennewick, WA, 99336 **URL:** http://ieeexplore.ieee.org/abstract/document/1372914/?reload=true

ROSE, JOANNA SEMEL, I: Nonprofit & Philanthropy **DOB:** 11/22/1930 **PB:** Orange **SC:** NJ/USA **PT:** Philip Ephraim Semel; Lillian (Mindlin) Semel **MS:** Married **SPN:** Daniel Rose (9/16/1956) **CH:** David S.; Joseph B.; Emily, Gideon G. **ED:** Postgraduate Coursework, St. Hilda's College, Oxford University, with Honors (1953), BA, Bryn Mawr College, Summa Cum Laude, Pennsylvania (1952) **CT:** Certified, Shakespeare Institute, United Kingdom (1951) **C:** Board Member, New York Council for Humanities; Member, Advisory Council, National Dance Institute, New York City, NY; Former Chairman, Advisory Board, Partisan Review, New York City, NY; Former Board Director, Current Member, Advisory Council, Poets and Writers, Inc., New York City, NY; Board Director, Former President, Paper Bag Players, New York City, NY; Former Chairman,

American Friends of St. Hilda's College; Member, Executive Committee, American Friends of St. Hilda's College; Board Member, Harlemn Educational Activies Funds **CR:** Board of Directors, Center for Humanities, The City University of New York Graduate Center; Member, New York Institute for Humanities; Associate Fellow, Berkeley College; Associate Fellow, Yale University; Advisory Council, American Friends of the Jewish Museum, Greece; Former Board Director, Bay Street Theatre, Sag Harbor, NY **CIV:** Former Board of Directors, Eldridge St. Project, New York City, NY **AW:** Named Distinguished Friend, University of Oxford (2012); Honorary Fellow, St. Hilda's College, Oxford, England; Honorary Fellow, WEB Dubois Medal Hutchins Center, Harvard University **MEM:** American Academy of Arts & Sciences; Cosmopolitan Club; Bryn Mawr Club of New York; LVIS East Hampton **H:** Reading; Writing **PA:** Democrat **RE:** Jewish **ADD:** 895 Park Ave , #4A, New York, NY, 10075-0327

ROSE, JONATHAN CHAPMAN, T: Lawyer **I:** Law and Legal Services **CN:** Jones Day **DOB:** 06/08/1941 **PB:** Cleveland **SC:** OH/US **PT:** Horace Chapman; Katherine (Cast) Rose **MS:** Married **SPN:** Susan Ann Porter (1/26/1980) **CH:** Benjamin Chapman **ED:** LLB, Harvard University, Cum Laude (1967); AB, Yale University (1963) **C:** Retired (2015); Secretary, Standing Rules Committee, Jones Day (2011-2015); Partner, Jones Day (1977-1981, 1984-2015); Assistant Attorney General, Office of Legal Policy, Antitrust Division, U.S. Department of Justice (1981-1984); Department Assistant to Attorney General, Antitrust Division, U.S. Department of Justice (1975-1977); Associate, Department of Attorney General, U.S. Department of Justice (1974-1975); General Counsel, Council on International Economic Policy (1973-1974); Special Assistant to President Richard Nixon (1971-1973); Law Clerk, Justice R. Ammi Cutter, Massachusetts Supreme Judicial Court (1967-1968); General Counsel, The White House **CIV:** Yale Global Alumni Leadership Exchange (2009); Yale Inaugural Leadership Exchange (2008); Board of Governors, Yale Alumni Association (1996-1999); President, Yale Daily News Foundation; Principal, Center for Excellence in Government **MIL:** First Lieutenant, U.S. Army (1969-1971) **MEM:** ABA; Federal Bar Association; American Law Institute Clubs **BAR:** Ohio (1978); United States Court of Appeals (1977); Supreme Court of the United States (1976); The District of Columbia (1972); Massachusetts (1968) **PA:** Republican **RE:** Episcopalian **ADD:** 5955 Ranleigh Manor Dr, Mc Lean, VA, 22101

ROSEN, WILLIAM WARREN, T: Lawyer (Retired), Photographer **I:** Law and Legal Services **CN:** Litigation Consultation Services **DOB:** 07/22/1936 **PB:** New Orleans **SC:** LA/USA **PT:** Warren Leucht Rosen; Erma (Stich) Rosen **MS:** Married **SPN:** Eddy F. Kahn (11/26/1965) **CH:** Elizabeth K.; Victoria A. **ED:** JD, Tulane University (1964); Advanced Special Investigations Officer, United States Air Force Special Investigations Academy (1959); BA, Tulane University (1958); Fellow, Institute of Politics, Loyola University (1985) **CT:** Diplomate, United States Air Force Special Investigations Academy (1958) **C:** Founder and Director, Litigation Consultation Services, New Orleans, LA (1996-Present); Private Practice, New Orleans, LA (2002-2005); Partner, Rosen & Lundeen, LLP, New Orleans, LA (1999-2002); Of Counsel, Rittenberg & Samuel (Now Rittenberg, Samuel & Phillips, LLC), New Orleans, LA (1996-1999); Partner, Rosen and Samuel, New Orleans, LA (1989-1995); Private Practice, New Orleans, LA (1989-1990); Partner, Herman, Herman, Katz & Cotlar (Now Herman Herman & Katz, LLC), New Orleans, LA (1987-

1988); Partner, Lucas & Rosen, New Orleans, LA (1979-1987); Private Practice, New Orleans, LA (1970-1979); Associate, Law Office of J.R. Martzell (Now Martzell, Bickford & Centola), New Orleans, LA (1968-1970); Associate, Dodge & Friend, New Orleans, LA (1965-1968) **CR:** Lecturer, New Judges Seminar, Louisiana Judicial College (2000-2003); Chairman, Senior Council Committee, Louisiana State Bar Association (1995-1996); Lecturer, Real and Demonstrative Evidence, National Education Network (1993); Member, Advisory Committee, Paralegal Institute, The University of New Orleans (1990-2006); Adjunct Professor, Trial Advocacy, Tulane University Law School (1988-2006); Instructor, Legal Interviewing and Investigations (1986-1987); Assistant Bar Examiner for Ethics, Louisiana State Bar Association (1983-1985); Instructor, Legal Interviewing (1980-1981); Instructor, Various Business Organizations (1978); Member, Advisory Committee, Paralegal Studies Program (1977-1986); State Chairman, Youth Drug Abuse Education Committee (1970-1973); Lecturer, Legal and Paralegal Fields; Lecturer on Photography **CIV:** Tulane Hillel, New Orleans, LA (2003-2005); Member, Board of Directors, Planned Parenthood Federation of America Inc., LA (1994-2001); Member, Advisory Committee, University of New Orleans Paralegal Program (1990-2000); Member, Advisory Council, National Federation of Paralegal Associations, Inc. (1989-1999); Volunteer Lawyer for the Arts, Louisiana State Bar Association (1985-1998); President, Dad's Club, Isidore Newman School (1984-1985); Member, Professional Advisory Committee, Jewish Endowment Foundation of Louisiana (1982-2006); President, Uptown Flood Association (1982-1985); Member, Executive Committee, United States Olympic Committee, LA (1982-1984); Member, Advisory Committee, Tulane University Paralegal Studies Program (1977-1986); Member, Metropolitan Crime Commission, New Orleans, LA (1976-1982); Member, Board of Directors, Jewish Children's Home Service (1973-1976); Member, Advisory Council on Drug Education, Louisiana Department of Education (1973); Member, Budget and Planning Committee, Jewish Welfare Federation (1970-1973) **MIL:** Special Agent, Office of Special Investigations, U.S. Air Force (1958-1961) **CW:** Author, Book (Photography), "Four Feet, Fins & Feathers" (2017); Author, Book (Photography), "Natural Designs" (2016); Photographer, Magazine Cover, Louisiana Advocates (2016); Exhibitor, Photography, Bible Lands Museum, Jerusalem, Israel (2015); Photographer, CD Cover (2014); Photographer, Magazine Cover, Louisiana Advocates (2013); Photographer, Author, "Never Again - Inside Auschwitz Today," Nashville Arts Magazine (2012); Photographer, Miss Rodeo America Pageant (2010); Photographer, Miss Rodeo Tennessee Pageant (2009-2011); Photographer, Designer, "Immersion: A Katrina Room," Parthenon Museum, Nashville, TN (2009); Columnist, "Briefly Speaking," New Orleans Bar Association (1993-2000); Various Photographic Exhibits (1988-2017); Co-author, Trial Techniques and Trials, Louisiana Trial Lawyers Association (Now Louisiana Association for Justice) (1981); Author, Lecturer, "Photographing What You See; Seeing What You Photograph" **AW:** Honoree, The Best Lawyers In America (1983) **MEM:** Community Relations Committee, Jewish Federation of Nashville and Middle Tennessee (2014-2015); President, Miss Rodeo Tennessee Pageant (2012-2013); Public Advisory Committee, Nashville Public Television (2009-2014); Rotary Club of Franklin Noon (2006-2014); Vice President, Audubon Public Tennis Association, Inc. (2006-2011); Board of Directors, Rotary Club of New Orleans (2003-2005); Panel Moderator, New

Orleans Bar Association (1997); Chairman, Legal Committee, Rotary Club of New Orleans (1996-2005); Alternative Dispute Resolution Committee, New Orleans Bar Association (1996-2000); Board of Directors, Rotary Club of New Orleans (1996-1998); Chairman, Senior Counsel Committee, Louisiana State Bar Association (1995-1996); President, Louisiana Chapter, Association of Attorney-Mediators (1995); Lecturer, Legal Education, National Education Network (1993); Master, American Inns of Court Foundation (1992-2004); Legal Advisory Committee, National Choice of Dying (1992-1996); Chairman, Continuing Legal Education Committee, New Orleans Bar Association (1991-1992); Secretary, Family Law Section, American Association for Justice (1990-1991); Advisory Council, National Federation of Paralegal Associations, Inc. (1989-1998); Family Law Advisory Committee, American Association for Justice (1989-1990); Vice Chairman, Public Relations Committee, Louisiana State Bar Association (1988-1989); Lecturer, Legal Education, American Association for Justice (1988); Past Chairman, State Youth Drug Abuse Education Program, Volunteer Lawyers for Arts, Louisiana State Bar Association (1986-1996); Vice Chairman, Paralegal Committee, American Association for Justice (1986-1989); Keyperson Committee, American Association for Justice (1986-1989); Lecturer, Legal Education, American Association for Justice (1986); Lecturer, Legal Education, American Association for Justice (1983); Lecturer, Legal Education, American Association for Justice (1981); Lecturer, Legal Education, American Association for Justice (1979); Federal Bar Association (1970-1979); Board of Directors, Federal Bar Association (1970-1975); Vice Chairman, Public Relations Committee, Louisiana State Bar Association (1970-1973); Tennessee Association for Justice (Tennessee Trial Lawyers Association); American Arbitration Association; ABA; Fellow, Institute of Politics, Loyola University; Life Member, Louisiana Trial Lawyers Association (Now Louisiana Association for Justice); President's Advisory Council, Louisiana Trial Lawyers Association (Now Louisiana Association for Justice); Community Advisory Council, Rotary Club of New Orleans **BAR:** Colorado (1989); United States District Court Middle District (1985); Supreme Court of the United States (1984); United States Court of Appeals for the Fifth Circuit (1965); United States District Court for the Eastern District (1965); Louisiana (1964) **MH:** Albert Nelson Marquis Lifetime Achievement Award (2017) **H:** Photography; Music **ADD:** 704 Wild Timber Ct, Franklin, TN, 37069 **URL:** http://www.lcsno.com

ROSENBERG, BERNARD , I: Fine Art **PB:** , **ED:** Associate's Degree, City College of New York (1965) **C:** Owner, Olana Gallery; Private Jewelry Designer; Metromedia Advertising and Sales; Interior Design Magazine **AW:** Acknowledgement, National Gallery of Washington (2008) **ACH:** Two of his jewelry pieces are in a book named ""Collectable Silver Jewelry

ROSENKRANTZ, TED STEVEN, T: Neonatalogist **I:** Medicine & Health Care **CN:** UConn Health, Connecticut Children's Medical Center **DOB:** 04/09/1952 **PB:** Newark **SC:** NJ/USA **PT:** Sid Rosenkrantz; Joyce Claire (Wasserberg) Rosenkrantz **MS:** Married **SPN:** Vicki Lynn Hammer (7/29/1979) **CH:** Michael Andrew; April Hammer; Adam Matthew **ED:** Postgraduate Studies, T.H. Chan School of Public Health, Harvard University (2000); Resident in Pediatrics, UConn Health (1978-1980); Intern in Pediatrics, UConn Health (1977-1978); MD, Eastern Virginia Medical School (1977); BA in Biological Sciences, Rutgers, the

State University of New Jersey (1974) **CT:** Certified Regional Trainer for Neonatal Resuscitation, American Heart Association (1988-Present); Subspecialty Certification, Examination Preparation, Neonatal-Perinatal Medicine, American Board of Pediatrics (1990-1991); Diplomate, Neonatal-Perinatal Subspecialty Board, American Board of Pediatrics (1983); Diplomate, American Board of Pediatrics (1982); Licensed Medical Educator in Neonatology (1979); Diplomate, National Board of Medical Examiners (1978) **C:** Attending Neonatalogist, Connecticut Children's Medical Center (1998-Present); Medical Director, Neonatal Intensive Care Unit and Newborn Services, John Dempsey Hospital, UConn Health (1996-Present); Attending Neonatalogist, John Dempsey Hospital, UConn Health (1982-Present) **CR:** Health Center Faculty Review Board, School of Medicine, University of Connecticut (2016-Present); Academic Appeals Committee, School of Medicine, University of Connecticut (2016-Present); Co-director, Infant Breathing and Reflux Program, School of Medicine, University of Connecticut (2012-Present); Infant Breathing and Reflux Program, School of Medicine, University of Connecticut (2010-Present); Infant Feeding Team, School of Medicine, University of Connecticut (2010-Present); Director, Hypothermia Program, School of Medicine, University of Connecticut (2009-Present); Director, Transitional Clinic, School of Medicine, University of Connecticut (2007-Present); Co-chair, Infant Care Review Committee, John Dempsey Hospital, UConn Health (2007-Present); Chair, Infant Care Review Committee, School of Medicine, University of Connecticut (2007-Present); Pediatrics Professor, University of Connecticut (1996-Present); Obstetrics & Gynecology Professor, University of Connecticut (1996-Present); Infant Care Review Committee, School of Medicine, University of Connecticut (1985-Present); Lecturer in Field **MIL:** Fellow, National Library of Medicine (1997); Neonatology Fellow, Women and Infants Hospital of Rhode Island, Brown University (1980-1982) **CW:** Contributor, Articles, Professional Journals **AW:** Research Excellence Program Grantee, University of Connecticut (2016-2017); Grantee, Patient-Centered Outcomes Research Institute (2015-2017); Honoree, Best Abstract and Presentation, 14th Annual Neuroscience Retreat, University of Connecticut (2014); "Golden Paw" Award for Clinical Excellence, UConn Health (2011); Grantee, American SIDS Institute (2010-2013); Honoree, Leading Physicians of the World, International Association of Pediatricians (2010-2011); "Golden Paw" Award for Clinical Excellence, UConn Health (2009); Honoree, America's Best Pediatricians (2008); Community Grantee, Hartford FIMR Program, March of Dimes Foundation (2007-2008); Honoree, America's Best Pediatricians (2006); Featured Listee, Who's Who in Executive and Professionals (2005-2011); VEGF Observational Trial Grantee, Scios, Inc. (2005-2006); Best Research Award for Trainee, New England Perinatal Society (2005); "Golden Paw" Award for Clinical Excellence, UConn Health (2001); Poster Awards, Society of Perinatal Obstetricians (1994); Pediatric Research Grantee, Richard S. Reynolds Foundation (1990); Thomas Boggs Research Award, Philadelphia Perinatal Society (1990); Pediatric Research Award, American Academy of Pediatrics (1990); Research Foundation Grantee, Health Center Auxiliary University of Connecticut (1989); Research Foundation Grantee, Small Equipment, University of Connecticut (1989); Grantee, Ross Laboratories, Inc. (1988-1989); Grantee, University of Arizona (1988-1989); Research Foundation Grantee, Large Equipment, University of Connecticut (1988); Research Foundation Grantee, Clinical Research Center, University of Connecticut (1987-1988); Grantee, NIH (1986-1995); Research Foundation Grantee, University of Connecticut (1983-1986); Grantee, Charles H. Hood Foundation (1983-1984); Research Foundation Grantee, Small Equipment, University of Connecticut (1983) **MEM:** Case Fatality Review Committee, Office of the Child Advocate, State of Connecticut (2011-Present); Committee Member, Greater Hartford Fetal Infant Mortality Review Team, AHEC (2005-Present); Program Committee, District I Perinatal Section, American Academy of Pediatrics (2002-Present); Neonatal Coding Committee, American Academy of Pediatrics (1998-Present); Nominating Committee, Council of the District I Perinatal Section, American Academy of Pediatrics (1998-Present); Abstract Reviewer, APS-SPR (2015-2017); Chair, AHEC (2008–2009); Co-Chair, AHEC (2007-2008); President, New England Association of Neonatologists (2007-2008); Vice President, New England Association of Neonatologists (2006-2007); Secretary, New England Association of Neonatologists (2005-2006); Clinical Advisory Committee, HealthRight Management Medicaid, Inc. (1997-1999); Scientific Research Advisory Committee, National Neonatal Database (1993-2000); President, New England Perinatal Society (1989-1990); Vice President, New England Perinatal Society (1988-1989); Secretary Treasurer, New England Perinatal Society (1987-1988); Program Committee, New England Perinatal Society (1986-1992); Council Member, District I Perinatal Section, American Academy of Pediatrics; APS-SPR; Eastern Society for Pediatric Research; SPER, Inc; Hartford County Medical Association; Connecticut State Medical Society; American Medical Association; AHEC **MH:** Albert Nelson Marquis Lifetime Achievement Award (2017); Distinguished Humanitarian (2017) **H:** Music; Fly fishing **ADD:** 38 Sunnybrook Drive, Newington, CT, 06111

ROSKO, MARYANN RN, T: Nurse **I:** Medicine & Health Care **DOB:** 09/22/1930 **PB:** McKeesport **PT:** George Rosko; Anna Makar **ED:** Postgraduate Coursework in Nursing, Chicago Lying-In Hospital, Illinois (1952-1953); Graduate Coursework in Nursing, Homestead Hospital, Pennsylvania (1951) **C:** Registered Nurse Education, Magee Women's, Pittsburgh (1968-1985); RN Staff Development, McKeesport Hospital, Pennsylvania (1963-1968); RN Supervisor, McKeesport Hospital, Pennsylvania (1959-1962); RN Staff, Homestead Hospital, Pennsylvania (1951-1955) **ADD:** 2605 Sunset Dr, West Mifflin, PA, 15122

ROSS LEE, BARBARA, T: Academic Administrator **I:** Education/Educational Services **CN:** New York Institute of Technology **ED:** Honorary Diplomate, Wilmington University (2001); Diplomate, Michigan State University (1973); Honorary DSc, College of Osteopathic Medicine, New York Institute of Technology; BS, Wayne State University **C:** Vice President of Health Sciences and Medical Affairs, New York Institute of Technology (2001-Present); Dean, New York College of Osteopathic Medicine, New York Institute of Technology (2002-2006); Dean, School of Allied Health and Life Sciences, New York Institute of Technology (2001-2002); Dean, College of Osteopathic Medicine, Ohio University (1993-2001); Chairman, Department of Family Medicine, Michigan State University; Associate Dean of Health Policy, Michigan State University; Legislative Assistant to Senator Bill Bradley; Master Teacher of Special Populations, Wayne State University **CR:** Participant, Conferences; Trustee, Foundation for Appalachian Ohio; Member, Board of Directors, Association of Academic Health Centers; Member, Board of Directors, National Fund for Medical Education; Member, Board of Directors, National Health Services Corps' Association for Underserved Clinicians; Executive Director, Osteopathic Affiliate, National Medical Association; Affiliate, Institute for National Health Policy and Research; Director, Osteopathic Heritage Health Policy Fellowship Program, Ohio University; Lecturer in field **CW:** Contributor, More than 30 Articles to Medical Journals **AW:** Recipient, Walter F. Patenge Medal for Pubic Service, College of Osteopathic Medicine, Michigan State University (2001); Named, Ohio Women's Hall of Fame (1998); Recipient, Magnificent Seven Award, Business and Professional Women/USA (1993); Recipient, Distinguished Public Service Award, College of Osteopathic Medicine, Oklahoma State University; Recipient, Women's Health Award; Honoree, Blackboard African-American National Bestsellers **MH:** Albert Nelson Marquis Lifetime Achievement Award (2017) **H:** Being a grandmother; Traveling to visit her nine grandchildren **BA:** 18994 grande vista dr, northville, MI, 48168 **ADD:** 18994 Grande Vista Dr, Northville, MI, 48168

ROSSITER, BRYANT W., T: Emeritus Alumni **I:** Consulting **DOB:** 03/10/1931 **PB:** Ogden **SC:** UT/USA **PT:** Bryant B. Rossiter; Christine (Peterson) Rossiter **MS:** Married **SPN:** Betty Jean Anderson (4/16/1951) **CH:** Bryant Edwin (Deceased); Mark William; Diane; Steven Kent; Linda; Karen; Matthew James; Gregory Thomas **ED:** PhD in Chemistry, Minor in Physics, The University of Utah (1957); BA in Chemistry, The University of Utah (1954) **C:** Consultant, Editor and Author, Science and Technology Development (1990-Present): Senior Vice President, ICN Pharmaceuticals, Costa Mesa, CA (1989-1990); President, Viratek Inc., Costa Mesa, CA (1985-1989); Director, Science and Technology Development, Eastman Kodak Company, Rochester, NY (1984-1985); Director, Chemistry Division, Eastman Kodak Company, Rochester, NY (1970-1984); Head, Color Physical Chemical Laboratory, Eastman Kodak Company, Rochester, NY (1963-1970); Research Chemist, Eastman Kodak Company, Rochester, NY (1957-1963); Emeritus Alumni, The University of Utah **CR:** Member, Panel on President's Council of Advisors on Science and Technology, Washington D.C. (1991); Chairman, Research Advisory Committee, U.S. Agency for International Development (USAID), Washington D.C. (1989-1992); Chairman, Board, Nucleic Acid Research Institute, Costa Mesa, CA (1987-1988); Chairman, American Chemical Society Joint Board-Council Committee on International Activities, Washington D.C. (1984-1986); Board President, Eastman Dental Center, Rochester, NY (1982-1985); Editorial Advisory Boards, Science Magazine and Chemical and Engineering News (1982-1984); Chairman, CHEMRAWN II, "The International Conference on Chemistry and World Food Supplies," Manilla, Philippines (1982); Member, Advisory Committee, Cornell International Institute for Food, Agriculture and Development (1981-1987); Editor, Chemical Experimentation Under Extreme Conditions, John Wiley & Sons, Inc. (1979); Founder and Committee Chairman, IUPAC CHEMRAWN (Chemical Research Applied to World Needs) Program (1975-1987); Trustee, Eastman Dental Center, Rochester, NY (1973-1993); Senior Editor, John Wiley & Sons, Inc., New York City, NY (1970-1996); Physical Methods of Chemistry in 11 Volumes; Chairman, "United States National Committee of the International Union of Pure and Applied Chemistry (IUPAC)"; Chairman, International Activities Committee, American Chemical Society, Washington D.C. **MIL:** United States Air Force, Korean War (1953-

1955); First Lieutenant, United States Air Force Reserve (1951-1958) **CW:** Co-author, "The Art and Artistry of Dominic Man-Kit Lam: Chromoskedasic Painting," World Culture Organization, Won Chai Hong Kong (2017) **AW:** Distinguished Alumnus Award, The University of Utah (2017); Merit of Honor Award, The University of Utah (2012); Fellow, American Institute of Chemists (1988); Named Honorary Alumni, Brigham Young University, Provo, Utah (1982); Fellow, American Association for the Advancement of Science (1981); Will Judy Award, Juniata College (1978); American Institute of Chemists Fellows Lecture Award (1978) **MEM:** American Chemical Society; Sigma Xi, The Scientific Research Honor Society **MH:** Albert Nelson Marquis Lifetime Achievement Award (2017) **H:** Horseback Riding; Reading; Fishing **RE:** The Church of Jesus Christ of Latter Day Saints **ADD:** 25662 Dillon Rd, Laguna Hills, CA, 92653 **URL:** https://www.linkedin.com/in/bryant-rossiter-03110b54/

ROTHENBERG, ROBERT PHILIP, T: Public Relations Counselor **I:** Corporate Communications & Public Relations **CN:** Rothenberg Public Relations **DOB:** 06/05/1936 **PB:** New York **SC:** NY/USA **PT:** Robert Edward Rothenberg; Lillian Babette (Lustig) Rothenberg **ED:** MS, Boston University (1958); BA, Cornell University (1956) **C:** Chairman, President, Rothenberg Public Relations Communications Counsel, New York, NY (1988-Present); Director of Public Relations, BigChange Networks, LLC, Washington, D.C. (1998-2004); Vice President, Medbook Publications, Inc. (1995-2004); Senior Executive Vice President, Robert Marston and Associates, New York, NY (1978-1988); Partner, President, Marston and Rothenberg Public Affairs, Inc., New York, NY (1977-1988); Partner, Executive Vice President, Robert Marston and Associates, New York, NY (1970-1988); Senior Vice President, Rowland Co., New York, NY (1967-1970); Vice President, Rowland Co., New York, NY (1965-1967); With, Rowland Co., New York, NY (1963-1970); Press Secretary, Gubernatorial Candidate William R. Anderson, Tennessee (1962); Assistant to President, Harry N. Abrams Publishing Co., New York, NY (1960-1962); Public Relations Director, Harry N. Abrams Publishing Co., New York, NY (1960-1962); With, Publicity Department, Columbia Pictures, New York, NY (1959-1960); Senior Consultant, The Lund Group, Inc. **CIV:** Fellow, Metropolitan Museum of Art (1990-Present); Board of Directors, Amas Musical Theatre, Inc. (2002-2003); President, Chairman, Board of Trustees, St. Bartholomew's Preservation Foundation (1992-1995); Board of Directors, Foundation to Save African Endangered Wildlife, World Rehabilitation Fund, New York, NY (1982-1998); Trustee, Museum of Holography, New York, NY; Associate, National Park Foundation; Counselor, American Business Cancer Research Foundation, Southport, CT; Member, Blue Hill Troupe, Ltd.; Producer, Warner Theatre, Torrington, CT **MIL:** US Air Force Reserve (1959-1965) **MEM:** Elizabeth Hamilton Cullen Society, Memorial Sloan Kettering Cancer Society (2016); Clara Barton Society, American Red Cross (2015); International Society of Poets; Pride and Alarm Society; Christian Centurion Society; Harriman Society, American Red Cross; Trustee Media Research Center; English Speaking Union; Anchor Society; Morgan Library and Museum; DeWitt Clinton Society; Museum of the City of New York; Kent Historical Society; Kent Library Association; Blue Hill Troupe, Ltd.; Players Club; The Coffee House **RE:** Unitarian Universalist **ADD:** 400 E 54th St Apt 29C, New York, NY, 10022

ROTHROCK, MICHAEL S., T: Litigation Attorney **I:** Law and Legal Services **CN:** Hedrick Gardner Kincheloe & Garofalo **SC:** North Carolina **MS:** Married **CH:** One Son **ED:** JD, Norman Adrian Wiggins School of Law, Campbell University (2008); BA in Political Science, University of North Carolina Wilmington (2005) **C:** Associate Attorney, Hedrick Gardner, Raleigh, NC (2016-Present); Litigation Attorney, The Law Offices of James Scott Farrin (2014-2016); Litigation Attorney, Leone Noble & Seate (2008-2014) **CIV:** Member, Triangle Area Steering Committee, University of North Carolina Alumni Association (2015-Present); Mentor, Mentorship Program, Campbell Law Connections (2013-Present); Judge, Capital Area Teen Court (2010-2017); Mentor Attorney, Capital Area Teen Court (2010-2017); Attorney Adviser, Enloe High School Mock Trial (2009-2016); Assistant Coach, Campbell Law Buffalo-Niagara Trial Team (2014) **CW:** Author, "Soft Tissue Injury Case," Personal Injury Practice in North Carolina; Editor, "Blocker & Clifton 1st-3rd Edition"; Author, "MIST Cases: Maximize Your Client's Recovery Without Litigation Soft Tissue Injury Cases"; Author, "The Small Case is No Longer So Small to Me: Using the Abstract Absurd in the Soft Tissue Closing" **AW:** Honoree, AV Preeminent Attorney, Martindale-Hubbell (2017); Top 40 Lawyers Under 40 by American Society of Legal Advocates (2014-2018); Super Lawyers Rising Star (2018) **MEM:** North Carolina Association of Defense Attorneys; North Carolina Bar Association; Wake County Bar Association **BAR:** United States District Court Eastern District of North Carolina (2010); North Carolina (2008) **H:** Marathons and triathlons; Hiking; Running; Camping; Mountain biking **BA:** 4131 Parklake Ave Ste 300, Hedrick Gardner Kincheloe & Garofalo, Raleigh, NC, 27612 **ADD:** 7705 Highlandview Cir, Raleigh, NC, 27613 **URL:** https://www.linkedin.com/in/mikerothrock/

ROUMAN, JOHN, T: Classicist **I:** Education/Educational Services **CN:** University of New Hampshire **DOB:** 05/01/1926 **PB:** Tomahawk **SC:** WI/USA **PT:** Christ Rouman; Soteria (Dedes) Rouman **ED:** PhD in Classics, University of Wisconsin-Madison (1965); Coursework, University of Minnesota (1959-1960); Coursework, Christian-Albrechts-Universite zu Kiel (1956-1957); Coursework, Rutgers, The State University of New Jersey (1951-1953); MA in Greek, Columbia University (1951); BA in Greek, Carleton College (1950) **C:** Professor Emeritus of Classics, University of New Hampshire (1999-Present); Advisory Board Member, Professor John C. Rouman Classical Lecturer Series, University of New Hampshire (1997-Present); Professor, University of New Hampshire (1991-Present); Co-Chairman, Spanish and Classics Departments, University of New Hampshire; Associate Professor, University of New Hampshire (1971-1991); Assistant Professor of Classics, University of New Hampshire (1965-1971); Research Assistant in Greek Epigraphy, Institute for Advanced Study (1962-1963); Research Assistant in Ancient History, University Wisconsin-Madison (1961-1965); Teaching Assistant in Ancient History, University Wisconsin-Madison (1960-1961); Teacher in Ancient History, Malverne High School, Malverne Union Free School District (1957-1959); Teacher in German, Seton Hall Preparatory School (1954-1956) **CR:** Judge in Latin and Mythology, Warren H. Held Junior Exam-Contests (1988-Present); Executive Board Member, New Hampshire Section, Paideia, Inc. (2001); Advisory Board Member, Christos and Mary Papoutsy Distinguished Endowed Chair of Business Ethics, Southern New Hampshire University (2000-2003); Consultant, National Greek Examinations, American Classical League (1980);

Examiner in Latin and Greek, Department of Education, State of New Hampshire (1979-1980); Presenter in Field; Lecturer in Field **CIV:** Active Member, Colovos Road Committee (1981-1982) **MIL:** U.S. Navy (1944-1946) **CW:** Editor, "Tenth Anniversary Celebration of John C. Rouman" (2007); Editor, "Smart-Start Learning System" (2000) **AW:** Recipient, Archons of the Ecumenical Patriarchate in America (2011); Recipient, Chapter Adviser Award, Phi Kappa Theta (2002); Recipient, Profile of Service Award, University of New Hampshire (2000); Recipient, Man of Achievement Award, Phi Kappa Theta (2000); Recipient, Alumni Award for District Achievement, Alumni Association, Carleton College (2000); Recipient, Pericles Award, American Hellenic Educational Progressive Association (1993); National Excellence in Teaching Classics Award, American Philological Association (Now Society for Classical Studies) (1991); Recipient, Barlow-Beach Award, Classical Association of New England (1991); Recipient, Recipient, Distinguished Teaching Award, University of New Hampshire (1985); Recipient, Fulbright Scholarship, Christian-Albrechts-Universite zu Kiel (1956-1957) **MEM:** Contributing Editor to Newsletter, The American Classical League (2005-Present); Chairman of National Foundation, Phi Kappa Theta (1993-Present); Chair, Nominating Committee, New Hampshire Classical Association (1986-Present); Faculty Adviser, Phi Kappa Theta (1982-Present); President, Strafford County Greco-Roman Foundation (1978-Present); Executive Committee, New Hampshire Classical Association (1965-Present); Chairman of National Board, Phi Kappa Theta (1993-1994); Ad Hoc Committee on Elections and Appointments, Classical Association of New England (1991); President, Classical Association of New England (1987-1988); Nominating Committee, Classical Association of New England (1986-1987, 1983-1984); Treasurer, The American Classical League (1982-1983); Executive Committee-at-Large, Classical Association of New England (1981-1984); Finance Committee, American Classical League (1981-1982); Representative to TCNE at Annual Meeting, American Classical League (1978); Society for Classical Studies; Archaeological Institute of America; Classical Association of Canada; The Medieval Academy of America; Modern Greek Studies Association; National Association of Advisors for the Health Professions, Inc.; Vergilian Society, Inc.; Alumni Association, Carleton College **MH:** Albert Nelson Marquis Lifetime Achievement Award (2017) **PA:** Independent **RE:** Orthodox Christian **ADD:** 14 Cowell Drive, Durham, NH, 03824

ROVINE, ARTHUR W., T: Adjunct Professor of Law **I:** Education/Educational Services **CN:** Fordham Law School **DOB:** 04/29/1937 **PB:** Philadelphia **SC:** PA/USA **PT:** George Isaac Rovine; Rosanna (Lipsitz) Rovine **MS:** Widower **SPN:** Phyllis Ellen Hamburger (Deceased) **CH:** Joshua; Deborah **ED:** PhD, Columbia University (1966); LLB, Harvard University (1961); AB, University of Pennsylvania (1958) **C:** Adjunct Professor of Law, Fordham Law School (2005-Present); Partner, Baker & McKenzie, New York City, NY (1985-2005); Of Counsel, Baker & McKenzie, has New York City, NY (1983-1985); First Agent of United States Government to Iran-United States Claims Tribunal, United States Department of State, The Hague, Netherlands (1981-1983); Assistant Legal Adviser, United States Department of State, Washington, D.C. (1975-1981); Editor Digest of United States Practice in International Law, United States Department of State, Washington,

D.C. (1972-1975); Assistant Professor, Cornell University, Ithaca, NY (1966-1972); Associate, Curtis, Mallet-Prevost, Colt & Mosle, New York City, NY (1964-1966) **CR:** Visiting Lecturer of Law, Yale University (1998); Adjunct Professor of Law, Georgetown University, Washington, D.C. (1977-1981); Director of International Arbitration Conferences, Fordham Law School, 2006-2015; Arbitrator in International Disputes; Speaker and writer in Field **CIV:** Member, Panel on Settlement of Transnational Business Disputes, New York Panel Center for Public Resources; Chairman of Law Subcommittee of International Advisory Council on Professional Education Council on International Educational Exchange; Member, Council on Foreign Relations **CW:** Board of Editors, American Journal of International Law (1977-1987); Co-Editor, "The Case Law of the International Court of Justice" (1976); Co-Editor, "The Case Law of the International Court of Justice" (1974); Editor, "Digest of the United States Practice in International Law" (1973-1974); Co-Editor, "The Case Law of the International Court of Justice" (1972); Author, "The First Fifty Years: The Secretary-General in World Politics, 1920-1970" (1970); Co-Editor, "The Case Law of the International Court of Justice" (1968); Author of more than 40 Articles on International Law and Arbitration to Professional Journals **AW:** Certificate of Merit, American Society of International Law (1974) **MEM:** International Arbitration Committee, Chair, International Law Committee, Association of the Bar of the City of New York (2009-2011); President, American Society for International Law (2000-2002); Vice President, American Society for International Law (1998-1999); Delegate to House of Delegates, ABA (1988-1990); Chairman of International Law Section, ABA (1985-1986); Executive Council, American Society for International Law (1975-1977); London Court of International Arbitration; Fellow, American Bar Foundation; Panel of Arbitrators, International Center for Dispute Resolution; American Arbitration Association; Arbitration Committee, United States Council for International Business **BAR:** New York (1984); Washington, D.C. (1964) **MH:** Albert Nelson Marquis Lifetime Achievement Award (2017) **H:** Reading; Travelling **ADD:** 215 E 68th St Apt 12T, New York, NY, 10065

RUNKLE, BEATRIZ, T: Clinicial Educator, Neonatologist, Pediatrician (Retired) **I:** Medicine & Health Care **ED:** Fellow, Neonatal-Perinatal Medicine, University of Miami (1980-1983); Resident in Pediatrics, Georgetown University Medical Center (1975-1979); MD, Georgetown University (1975); AB, Radcliffe College, Cambridge, MA (1970) **CT:** Certified in Neonatal-Perinatal Medicine, American Board of Pediatrics; Licensed to Practice Medicine, Commonwealth of Virginia; Certified in Pediatrics, American Board of Pediatrics **C:** Neonatologist, Fairfax Neonatal Associates, PC (2013-2017); Medical Director of Nurseries, Virginia Hospital Center (1991-2004); Neonatologist, Virginia Hospital Center, Arlington, VA (1986-2013); Clinical Assistant Professor of Pediatrics, Georgetown University School of Medicine, Washington, D.C. (1986-2001); Assistant Professor of Pediatrics, Emory University School of Medicine, Atlanta, GA (1983-1986) **CW:** Co-Author, "Cardiovascular Changes in Group B Streptococcal Sepsis in the Piglet: Response to Indomethacin and Relationship to Prostacyclin and Thromboxane A2"; Co-Author, "Acute Cardiopulmonary Effects of Pancuronium Bromide in Mechanically Ventilated Newborn Infants"; Contributor, Articles to Professional Journals **MEM:** Fellow, American Academy of Pediatrics **H:** Learning about and exploring Medieval churches;

Traveling **ADD:** 11805 Foxclove Rd, Reston, VA, 20191 **URL:** https://health.usnews.com/doctors/beatriz-runkle-479234

RUSSELL, JAMES EDWARD, T: Physics Professor **I:** Education/Educational Services **CN:** University of Cincinnati **DOB:** 09/27/1931 **PB:** Fort Wayne **SC:** IN/USA **MS:** Married **SPN:** Mary Carol Schalk (9/17/1977) **ED:** PhD, Yale University (1958); Post-doctoral Fellow, University of Virginia (1957-1958); MS, Yale University; BS, Yale University **C:** Professor of Physics Emeritus, University of Cincinnati (2010-Present); Professor of Physics, University of Cincinnati (1974-2009); Associate Professor, University of Cincinnati (1965-1974); Senior Research Officer, University of Oxford, England (1963-1965); Visiting Assistant Professor, University of Padua, Italy (1962-1963); Research Physicist, Carnegie Mellon University (1960-1962); Research Associate, Indiana University, Bloomington (1958-1960) **CW:** Contributor, Scientific Papers, Professional Journals **MH:** Albert Nelson Marquis Lifetime Achievement Award (2017) **ADD:** 12 Cypress Garden, Cincinnati, OH, 45220

RUTKOWSKI, LAWRENCE, T: Lawyer, Partner **I:** Law and Legal Services **CN:** Seward & Kissel LLP **DOB:** 06/19/1953 **PB:** Fall River **SC:** MA/USA **ED:** JD, Columbia University (1978); BA, College of the Holy Cross, Magna Cum Laude (1975) **C:** Partner, Maritime, Aviation, Corporate Finance, Seward & Kissel, New York, NY (1992-Present); Co-Head, Hill, Betts & Nash (1982-1992); Co-Head, Cadwalader, Wickersham & Taft (1979-1982); Head, Transportation Finance Group, Seward & Kissel, New York, NY; Co-Head, Corporate Finance Department, Seward & Kissel **CR:** Adjunct Professor, Charleston School of Law **CIV:** Vice-Chair, New York Maritime Inc.; Advisory Committee, Seafarers International House, New York, NY; Director, President, College of the Holy Cross Lawyers Association **CW:** Managing Editor, Columbia Journal of Law and Social Problems (1977-1978) **MEM:** Chair, Maritime Law Committee, New York City Bar Association (1994-1997); American Bar Association; Maritime Law Association of the United States; Pi Sigma Alpha; Phi Beta Kappa **RE:** Roman Catholic **ADD:** 165 Duffy Drive, Allendale, NJ, 07401

SACHS, ADAM P., T: Partner **I:** Law and Legal Services **CN:** Husch Blackwell LLP **ED:** JD, Washington University School of Law (1992); BA, University of Virginia (1986); Diploma, Pembroke Country Day School (1982) **C:** Partner, Husch Blackwell LLP; Senior Legal and Legislative Positions, Capitol Hill; Advisor on Government Relations and Policy, Variety of Industries; Managing Federal and State Government Affairs Efforts, Midstream Energy Company Seeking to Construct a Propane Storage Facility, NY; Representing Competitive Energy Supplier on Prospective Wind Farm Development, Chase County, KS; Lobbying Congress for Federal $18 Million Alternative Fuel Cell Technology Tax Credit; Support and Guidance, Public-Private Partnership Attempting to Attract Utility-Scale Solar and Biofuel Projects to Remediated Brownfield Site; Public Relations and Government Affairs Guidance, Major Publicly Traded Hospitality Company; Chief Democratic Counsel, Oversight and Investigations, House Veterans' Affairs Subcommittee; Staff Director, Oversight and Investigations, House Veterans' Affairs Subcommittee; Chief Counsel to Former House Majority Whip and Assistant Democratic Leader James Clyburn; Staff Director to former House Majority Whip and Assistant Democratic Leader James Clyburn; Associate Counsel for Former Senator Paul Simon, IL; Senior Legislative

Assistant for Former Representative Lane Evans, IL **CR:** Sports Editor; Hilltop Newspaper; Layout Editor; Raider Yearbook **CIV:** Vice-Chair, Truman Library Institute (2016-Present); Co-Chair, Board of Directors, Truman Library Institute (2016-Present); Governance Committee, Truman Library Institute (2016-Present); School Board Member, Gordon Parks Charter School (2015-Present); Vice-Chair, Board of Directors, Negro Leagues Baseball Museum (2014-Present); Advisory Board, First Tee of Greater Kansas City (2009-Present); Board of Directors, Negro Leagues Baseball Museum (2006-Present); Vice-Chair, Board of Directors, Urban League of Greater Kansas City (2015-2016); Leadership Exchange, Greater Kansas City Chamber of Commerce (2014); President, University of Virginia Kansas City Area Alumni Association (2012-2013); Executive Committee, Pembroke Hill School Alumni Association (2010-2016); Co-Chair of Governance Committee, Negro Leagues Baseball Museum (2010-2014); Board of Directors, University of Virginia Kansas City Area Alumni Association (2009-2013); Advisory Board, Park University School of Business (2009-2012); Justice for All Campaign Committee, Legal Aid of Western Missouri (2009-2012); Executive Committee, Jewish Community Relations Bureau/American Jewish Committee (2009); Leadership Exchange, Greater Kansas City Chamber of Commerce (2007); Board of Directors, Jewish Community Relations Bureau/American Jewish Committee (2006-2008); Leadership Exchange, Greater Kansas City Chamber of Commerce (2005); Board Member, Urban League of Greater Kansas City (2004-2010); Advisory Board, Port Authority of Kansas City/Isle of Capri/Ameristar Foundation for Economic Advancement (2004-2010); Board Chair, Urban League of Greater Kansas City (2004-2007); Board Member, Urban League of Greater Kansas City (1993-1996) **AW:** Ferguson Award for Distinguished Board Service, Negro Leagues Baseball Museum (2016); Attorney of the Year in Missouri, Global International Magazine Global Award, Gaming Law (2015); Attorney of the Year in Missouri, Global International Magazine Global Award, Gaming Law (2014); Chairman's Service Award, Urban League of Greater Kansas City (2007); Veterans Service Award, Office of Inspector General, United States Department of Veterans Affairs (1998) **MEM:** ABA; International Masters of Gaming Law; Kansas City Metropolitan Bar Association; The Missouri Bar **BAR:** United States Court of Appeals for the Eighth Circuit (1994); Missouri (1992); United States Court, Western District of Missouri (1992) **H:** Architectural and portrait photography; Blogging for GolfDigest.com; Blogging for various golf related publications **PA:** Democrat **BA:** 4801 Main St Ste 1000, Husch Blackwell LLP, Kansas City, MO, 64112

SAENZ, NANCY ELIZABETH KING, T: Civic Worker **I:** Social Work **DOB:** 01/28/1930 **PB:** Greenville **SC:** TX/USA **PT:** Henry M. King; Vallie (Wheatley) King **MS:** Married **SPN:** Michael Saenz (7/28/1950) **CH:** Michael King; Cynthia Elizabeth Saenz Ward **ED:** Postgraduate Work, Lexington Theological Seminary (1953); Postgraduate Work, Escuela de Idiomas (1953); Postgraduate Work, Hartford Seminary (1952-1953); BS, TCU, Magna Cum Laude (1952); AB, Texas Christian University, With Honors (1950) **C:** Volunteer Coordinator, American Bible Society (1971-Present); Member, Quadrennial Committees, Women's Christian Fellowship (1974-1982); Member, General Board, Christian Church (Disciples of Christ) (1974-1978, 1980); President, CCSW (1976-1978); Chairman, Indiana District, State Christian Women Fellowship of Christian Churches (1968-1975); Chairman, Texas District, State Christian Women Fellowship of Christian Churches (1968-1975); Member, Administrative Committee of Texas, State Christian Women Fellowship of Christian Churches (1971-1974); Board of Directors, Administrative Board, Christian Church (Disciples of Christ), Puerto Rico (1950-1965); Missionary, United Christian Missionary Society, Puerto Rico (1954-1965); Chairman, Department of Christian Education, Christian Church (Disciples of Christ), Puerto Rico (1962-1964); Member, Department of Christian Education, Puerto Rico Section, World Council of Churches (1959-1964); State Director, Christian Church (Disciples of Christ) (1963); Secretary, State Christian Women Fellowship of Christian Churches (1955-1957, 1959-1963); Counselor, State Christian Women Fellowship of Christian Churches (1955-1957, 1959-1963); Secretary, Christian Church (Disciples of Christ) (1959-1961); Secretary, Puerto Rico Section, World Council of Churches (1959-1960); Missionary, United Christian Missionary Society, Indianapolis **CIV:** Member, Vocational-technology Advisory Council, Laredo Independent School District (1971-Present); Member, Women's Committee, Indiana State Symphony Society (1967-Present); Director, Tarrant County Volunteer Center (1982-1983); Board of Directors, Church Finance Council, Christian Church (Disciples of Christ) (1979-1983); President, Fort Worth Council of Churches (1981); Member, Advisory Committee, Tarrant County Volunteer Center (1976-1981); President, Fort Worth Chapter, Church Women United (1980); Chairman, Tarrant County Volunteer Center (1980); Interim Director, Fort Worth Council of Churches (1979); President-elect, Planned Parenthood Association of Webb County (1974-1975); President-elect, Mercy Hospital Auxiliary (1974-1975); Member, Mercy Hospital Auxiliary (1973-1975); Board of Directors, Civic Ballet Laredo (1972-1975); Board of Directors, Planned Parenthood Association of Webb County (1972-1974); Member, Women's Committee, ICU International Christian University (1962-1972); Board of Directors, Greater Indianapolis Federation of Churches (1970-1971); President, Indianapolis Chapter, ICU International Christian University (1967-1968); Member, State Committee, Home for Aged, United Church Women, Puerto Rico (1963); Secretary, Disciples of Christ Academy PTA, Bayamon, Puerto Rico (1962-1963) **CW:** Author, "Step by Step" (1984); Author, "Winds of Change" (1968) **MEM:** Executive Board, Irvington Union of Clubs (1966-Present); President, Association of Volunteer Centers (1990-1991); President, Irvington Women's Laredo Tuesday Music and Literature Club (1973-1974); Marion County Guardian Home Guild (1968-1970); Vice President, Irvington Union of Clubs (1968-1970); President, Irvington Chapter, Young Mom's Club (1967); Vice President, Irvington Chapter, Young Mom's Club (1965); Thistle Hill; Docent Guild of Texas; Laredo and Fort Worth Section, Pan American Round Tables of Texas; Civic Music Association of Laredo; Art League; Arts Council of Indianapolis; Texas Christian University Alumni Association; Women's City Club; Ann's Club, Rotary International; The Woman's Club of Fort Worth; Women's College Club; Phi Sigma Iota; Alpha Chi Honor Society **MH:** Distinguished Humanitarian (2017) **ADD:** 3201 River Park Dr Apt 803, Fort Worth, TX, 76116

SAENZ, MICHAEL, T: Academic Administrator (Retired) **I:** Education/Educational Services **DOB:** 10/25/1925 **PB:** Laredo **SC:** TX/USA **YOP:** 2016-11-03 **PT:** C.A. Saenz; Pola R. Saenz **MS:** Married **SPN:** Nancy Elizabeth King **CH:** Michael King; Cynthia Elizabeth **ED:** PhD in Economics, University of Pennsylvania (1961); MEd, Texas Christian University (1952); BS in Accounting,

Texas Christian University, With Honors (1949) **C:** President, Northwest Campus, Tarrant County College, Fort Worth, TX (1975-2006); Academy Dean, Laredo Junior College (1971-1974); Executive Secretary, United Christian Missionary Society, Indianapolis, IN (1965-1971); Administrator, United Christian Missionary Society, Bayamon, Puerto Rico (1954-1957); Administrator, United Christian Missionary Society, Bayamon, Puerto Rico (1959-1965); Deputy Collector, IRS, Fort Worth, TX (1949-1952) **CR:** Founder, National Hispanic Leadership Institute (1989-Present); Co-director, National Hispanic Leadership Institute (1989-Present); Board of Directors, National Communications College Hispanic Council (1985-Present); President, National Communications College Hispanic Council (1989-1991); Founder, National Communications College Hispanic Council (1985); Trustee, Texas Christian University, Brite Divinity School (1973-2001) **CIV:** Vice Moderator, General Board, Christian Church, Disciples of Christ (1991-1993); Trustee, Board of Directors, United Way Fort Worth (1979-1988); Chairman, Laredo's Bicentennial Committee (1973-1976); Director, Gulf Coast Council, Boy Scouts of America (1971-1975); Board of Directors, Civic Ballet of Laredo; Fort Worth Chapter, National Conference of Christians and Jews; Juliette Fowler Homes; Dallas Chairman, Aztec District; Governor, Career Development Center, Arlington, TX **MEM:** Board of Directors, American Association of Community Colleges (1991-1994); Commission on International Education; American Council on Education; Texas Junior College Teachers Association; Texas Association of Junior College Instructional Administrators; American Academy of Political and Social Sciences; Urban Ministries in Higher Education; Civic Music Association of Laredo; Rotary **ADD:** 3201 River Park Drive, Apt 803, Fort Worth, TX, 76116

SAGINI, MESHACK M., T: Associate Professor, Research Scientist **I:** Education/Educational Services **CN:** Langston University **DOB:** 11/30/1944 **PB:** Kisii **SC:** Kenya **PT:** Abraham Okemwa Mairura Sagini; Jelliah Kanika **MS:** Married **SPN:** Rachel Sagini **CH:** Paul M. Sagini; Dennis O. Sagini; Eileen M. Sagini **ED:** Postdoctoral Coursework in Public Policy, University of Central Oklahoma (2016-2018); Postdoctoral Coursework, Political Science, Oklahoma State University (1997); PhD in College and University Administration, Social Science Perspective, Michigan State University (1987); MA in Educational Leadership and History, Andrews University (1982); BEd in History, Education, and Religion, North Caribbean University (1979); Higher School Certificate IE Diploma in Social Sciences, University of Cambridge (1968) **C:** Professor, Langston University (1991-Present); Research Scientist, Langston University (1991-Present); Adjunct Assistant Professor, The University of Oklahoma (1994-1995); Adjunct Instructor, Michigan State University for Washtenow Community College and the University of Michigan (1990-1991); Adjunct Assistant Professor, Social Science, Lansing Community College (1989-1991); Swahili Tutor, Michigan State University (1985-1988); Lecturer, Northern Caribbean University Mandeville (1979-1980) **CR:** Visiting Scholar, Kisii University, Kenya (2014); Re-appointed to President Barack Obama's "Kitchen Cabinet" (2013); Appointed to President Barack Obama's "Kitchen Cabinet" (2009); Visiting Scholar, University of Michigan (2005) **CW:** Author, "Globalization: The Paradox of Organizational Behavior: Terrorism, Foreign Policy, & Governance" (2015); Author, "Comparative Perceptions of Planners of Four Michigan Community Colleges" (2011); Author,

"Strategic Planning & Management in Public Organizations: Behavior in Organizations" (2007); Author, "Organizational Behavior: The Challenges of the New Millennium" (2001); Author, "The African and the African American University: A Historical & Sociological Analysis" (1996); Author, Book Manuscript, "Poverty in Oklahoma and Its Implications on the National and Global Tableau" **AW:** Distinguished Super Professor of Faculty Row, Faculty Row Committee (2016-2018); Honoree, Oklahoma Political Science Association (2009); Recipient, 25 Awards for Teaching, Publications, Service **MEM:** Kenya Scholars & Studies Association; Nation Social Science Association; Association of American Foreign Policy; College of Education, Michigan State University; Phi Beta Delta; Gale, A Cengage Company: APSA **H:** Reading; Walking; Watching and listening to the news **PA:** Republican; Democrat **RE:** Seventh-day Adventist **BA:** PO Box 1500, Langston University, Langston, OK, 73050 **ADD:** 813 Richmond Rd, Edmond, OK, 73034 **URL:** https://www.linkedin.com/in/meshacksagini/

SAHAMI, SOHAILA , I: Law and Legal Services **ED:** JD, Thomas Jefferson School of Law (1994-1997) **MEM:** Board of Directors, OCIACC

SAHLEM, JAMES, T: Law Librarian (Retired) **I:** Library Management/Library Services **DOB:** 02/21/1948 **PB:** Buffalo **SC:** NY/USA **PT:** Lee M. Sahlem; Mildred A. (Hibschweiler) Sahlem **MS:** Married **SPN:** Susan Mary Schifferli **CH:** Steven; Andrea; Gregory **ED:** MS in Education, Canisius College, Buffalo, NY (1995); ASC, State University of New York, Buffalo (1985); MLS, State University of New York, Buffalo (1971); BS in Management, Canisius College, Buffalo, New York (1970) **CT:** State Certification for Addiction Counseling **C:** Principal Law Librarian, New York State Supreme Court Library (1981-2010); Librarian III, Director, North Park Crane Branches (1978-1981); Librarian II, Amherst Public Libraries, Williamsville, New York (1974-1978); Library I, Mobile Libraries, Buffalo-Erie County Public Library, Buffalo (1971-1974); Library Trainee, Business Labor Department, Buffalo-Erie County Public Library, Buffalo (1970-1971) **CR:** Visiting Professor, State University of New York at Buffalo (1986-2011); Consultant, Lippes, Silverstein et al, Buffalo (1985-2006) **CIV:** Treasurer, Western New York Library Resources Council; Former Co-President, Amherst Dance Club (2013-2014) **CW:** Co-Author with Jo Ann M. Wahl and Kevin Bauer, "Powers of the New York Court of Appeals" (1952-1994) **AW:** Inductee, The Phi Beta Kappa Society (2015) **MEM:** American Association of Law Libraries; President, New York State Unified Courts Law Libraries **H:** History; Gardening **ADD:** 1840 N. Forest Road, Williamsville, NY, 14221

SAILE, CATERINA GATTO, T: Attorney **I:** Law and Legal Services **CN:** Saile & Saile, LLP **DOB:** 07/06/1977 **PB:** Woodbury, NJ **MS:** Married **SPN:** Michael Saile Jr. **ED:** JD, Widener University School of Law (2003); BA in Criminal Justice and Political Science, University of Delaware (1999) **C:** Attorney, Saile & Saile, LLC (2017-Present); Criminal Prosecutor, Delaware Department of Justice, Wilmington, DE; Attorney, Lyons Law Firm **CR:** Head, Violent Criminal Enterprises Unit, Delaware Department of Justice, Wilmington, DE; Prosecutor, Operation Sun Son **CIV:** Supporter, Cancer Center, Children's Hospital of Philadelphia; Big Brothers, Big Sisters **AW:** Award, Delaware State Police (2014) **MEM:** American Association for Justice; New Jersey Association for Justice; National College for DUI Defense; Bucks County Bar Association; Alpha Chi Omega; Moe Levine

Trial Advocacy Honor Society; Widener Law Review **BAR:** Pennsylvania Bar Association (2004); New Jersey State Bar Association (2003); Delaware State Bar Association (2003); U.S. District Court for the District of Delaware; Supreme Court of Delaware; New Jersey Supreme Court; District Courts of New Jersey **H:** Spending time with family; Cooking; Reading; Traveling; Running **BA:** 403 Executive Dr, Saile & Saile, LLP, Langhorne, PA, 19047 **URL:** www.buckscountyduilawyers.com

SAINSBURY, R. MARK, T: Professor of Philosophy **I:** Education/Educational Services **CN:** The University of Texas at Austin **DOB:** 07/02/1943 **PB:** London **SC:** England **MS:** Married **SPN:** Victoria Goodman (2/2/2000) **CH:** Isabelle Miranda; William Edgar **ED:** DPhil, Corpus Christi College, Oxford (1970); MA, Corpus Christi College, Oxford (1970); BA, Corpus Christi College, Oxford (1964) **C:** Professor of Philosophy, The University of Texas at Austin (2002-Present); Susan Stebbing Professor of Philosophy, King's College London (1989-2008); Reader in Philosophy, King's College London (1987-1989); Lecturer in Philosophy, King's College London (1984-1987); Lecturer in Philosophy, Bedford College, University of London (1978-1984); Lecturer in Philosophy, University of Essex (1975-1978); Radcliffe Lecturer in Philosophy, Brasenose College, University of Oxford (1973-1975); Lecturer in Philosophy, St. Hilda's College, University of Oxford, England (1970-1973); Radcliffe Lecturer in Philosophy, Magdalen College, University of Oxford, England (1968-1970) **CR:** Visiting Professor, The University of Texas at Austin (1987); Editor, "Mind" (1990-2000); Editor, Aristotelian Society (1977-1982) **CW:** Author, "Thinking About Things," Oxford University Press (2018); Co-author, with Michael Tye, "Seven Puzzles of Thought and How to Solve Them: An Originalist Theory of Concepts" (2012); Author, "Fiction and Fictionalism" (2009); Author, "Paradoxes, Third Edition" (2009); Author, "Reference Without Referents" (2005); Author, "Departing from Frege" (2002); Author, "Logical Forms, Second Edition" (2000); Author, "Paradoxes, Third Edition" (2009); Editor, "Mind" (1990-2000); Author, "Logical Forms" (1988); Author, "Paradoxes" (1988); Author, "Russell" (1979); Contributor, Articles to Professional Journals **AW:** Honorary Fellow, Corpus Christi College, Oxford (2015); Erskine Visiting Fellow, University of ChristChurch (2000); Fellow, The British Academy (1998); Fellow, King's College London (1995); Leverhulme Fellow (1995); Radcliffe Fellow (1987-1988) **MEM:** Honorary Secretary, Editor, Aristotelian Society (1982-1986); Editor, "Mind, 1990" (2000); Fellow, British Academy **MH:** Albert Nelson Marquis Lifetime Achievement Award (2017) **H:** Baking Bread **ADD:** 4523 Avenue G, Austin, TX, 78751 **URL:** https://www.marksainsbury.net

SAITO, ROBERT SHUNICHI, T: Writer **I:** Fine Art **DOB:** 09/09/1933 **PB:** Alameda **SC:** CA/USA **PT:** Sam Shunji Saito; Yayeko Umegawa Saito **MS:** Married **SPN:** Naida Cervantes (12/07/1966) **ED:** Certification, Coronado School of the Arts (1980) **C:** Retired, United States Navy (1975); Personnel Officer, USS Camden, United States Navy (1972-1975); Advanced through Grades to Chief Petty Officer, United States Navy (1971); Enlisted, United States Navy (1955) **CR:** President, Mega Travel, Inc., La Mesa, CA (1983-1984) **CW:** Author, Poetry and Short Stories; Author, "My Life in Camps During the War and More" (2006) **AW:** First Place Award for Batik, Coronado Art Association (1977) **MH:** Albert Nelson Marquis Lifetime Achievement Award (2017) **H:** Batik art; Photography; Fishing; Walking; Tai chi **RE:** Roman Catholic **ADD:** 125 N U Avenue, National City, CA, 91950

SALAND, DEBORAH, T: Psychotherapist, Educator **I:** Social Work **CN:** Eating Disorder Texas Program **DOB:** 07/25/1954 **PB:** Val Dosta **SC:** GA/USA **PT:** Charles Gianniny; Audrey (Horan) Gianniny **ED:** PhD in Psychology, Southern California School for Professional Studies (Now California Southern University) (1996); MSW, Barry University (1992); Bachelor's Degree in Professional Studies, Barry University (1990) **CT:** Licensed Clinical Social Worker, State of Florida; Certified Addictions Professional; Certified Master Addiction Specialist; Diplomat, American Psychotherapy Association; Certified Forensic Sentence Mitigation Specialist; Certified Forensic Addictions Specialist; Certified Group Psychotherapist **C:** Founder, Eating Disorder Program, Texas (1997-Present); Private Practice, Institute for Human Potential, Miami, FL (1993-Present); Substance Abuse Counselor, Transitions Recovery Program, Miami, FL (1989-1991); Assistant Clinical Director, Interphase Recovery Center, Miami, FL (1988-1989); Owner, Obsessions in Time, Miami, FL (1984-1988); Substance Abuse Counselor, Spectrum Programs, Fort Lauderdale, FL (1974-1979); Clinical Director, Level II, Pathways Treatment Center, Miami, FL **CR:** Adjunct Faculty Member, New York Institute of Tech, Boca Raton, FL (1997-Present); Faculty Member, Addictions Training Institute, University of Miami (1993-Present); Clinical Supervisor, Transitions Recovery Program, Miami, FL (1993-Present); Director, American Family Eating Disorder Tract (1997-1998); Affiliate, Treatment Resources, Miami, FL (1993-1994); Lecturer, Addictions Training Institute, University of Miami (1992) **CW:** Contributor, Articles, Professional Journals **AW:** Special Alumni, Barry University (1996) **MEM:** National Association of Social Workers; American Psychological Association; Clinical Member, American Group Psychotherapy Association (AGPA); Clinical Associate, Medical Psychotherapists of America; Counselor, National Board for Certified Counselors, Inc.; Mental Health Association of Broward County **MH:** Albert Nelson Marquis Lifetime Achievement Award (2017) **ADD:** 4436 Cordia Circle, Coconut Creek, FL, 33066

SALIM, ABDULLAH, T: Attorney at Law **I:** Law and Legal Services **CN:** Law Office of Abdullah Salim, J.D., P.C. **PB:** Charlotte **SC:** NC/USA **PT:** Reginald Armistice Hawkins; Catherine Elizabeth (Richardson) Hawkins **MS:** Married **SPN:** Umme Salma Salim (6/2/1972) **CH:** Saladin; Abdul; Umme; Janna **ED:** JD, School of Law, George Mason University (1981); Postgraduate Coursework, University of Maryland (1976); Postgraduate Coursework in African History, Howard University (1970-1971); BA in Ancient History and Linguistics, The University of North Carolina at Chapel Hill (1970) **CT:** Certified Boat Crew, Instructor and Vessel Examiner (2009-Present); Admitted to Practice, United States District Court District of Maryland (1983) **C:** Ship Captain, Historic Tours of America (2014-Present); Adjunct Professor of Law, Hagerstown Community College, Maryland (1991-1992); History Consultant, Abdullah Salim & Associates, Silver Spring, MD (1983-2014); Private Practice, Silver Spring, MD (1983-2014); Material Damage Consultant, Crawford & Company, Fairfax, VA (1982-1984); Manager, E & S Consultant, Washington, D.C. (1981-1982); Public Transportation Manager, D.C. Barwood Cabs, Washington, D.C. (1977-1978); Manager, Associates IV Theaters, Oxon Hill, MD (1974-1975); Senior Appraiser, Claim Representative, Aetna Life & Casualty Company, McLean, VA (1971-1978); Teacher, District of Columbia Public Schools (1970-1971); Writer, Researcher, Pride Inc., Washington, D.C. (1970); Librarian Assistant, Smithsonian National Museum of Natural History, Washington, D.C. (1966); Morning News Carrier, Charlotte Observer Newspaper, Charlotte, NC (1964-1965) **CIV:** Trustee, A.L. Richardson Scholarship Fund (1984-Present); Guest Speaker, Numerous Nonprofit Organizations **MIL:** Civil Rights Coordinator, Fifth District, Southern Region, United States Coast Guard Auxiliary (2015-Present); Licensed Master Captain, U.S. Coast Guard (2011-Present); Flotilla Commander, United States Coast Guard Auxiliary (2009-Present) **AW:** Recipient, Outstanding Leadership Awards, United States Coast Guard Auxiliary (2015-2016); Recognition for Courageous and Visionary Efforts to Establish African & African American Studies, The University of North Carolina at Chapel Hill (2010); Recipient, Immigration Law Award, Ayuda Neighborhood Services (1981) **MEM:** Chairman, Black Law Students Association, George Mason University (1980-1981); Vice President, International Law Society, George Mason University (1980-1981); American Association for Justice; ABA; Alumni Association, George Mason University; Alumni Association, The University of North Carolina at Chapel Hill; International Platform Association; Maryland Trial Lawyers Association; National Bar Association; American Society of International Law; Phi Delta Phi **BAR:** Maryland State Bar Association, Inc. (1983) **MH:** Albert Nelson Marquis Lifetime Achievement Award (2017) **H:** Teaching; Golf **BA:** PO Box 183, Abdullah Salim Law Offices, Beltsville, MD, 20704 **ADD:** 4105 Taunton Dr, Beltsville, MD, 20705

SALTZMAN-SAVEKER, JUDY DEANE, T: Religious Studies Educator **I:** Education/Educational Services **DOB:** 02/02/1942 **PB:** San Jose **SC:** CA/USA **PT:** Kenneth E. Saltzman; Dorothy Deane Saltzman **MS:** Widow **SPN:** David R. Saveker (Deceased) **ED:** PhD, UC Santa Barbara (1977); MA in Religious Studies, UC Santa Barbara (1973); Fulbright Scholar, Freie Universität Berlin (1970-1971); Junior Fellow, Center for the Study of Democratic Institutions (1968-1969); MA, University of California, Berkeley (1965); BA in Philosophy, San Jose State University, Cum Laude (1963) **CT:** Certified Third Degree Black Belt, United Martial Arts Association (2015); Certified Second Degree Black Belt, Alemany Style Shaolin Kenpo (2003); Certified Water Safety Instructor (1960) **C:** Professor, California Polytechnic State University (1975-2004); Visiting Scholar, Stanford University (1983-1984); Instructor, Oxnard College (1973-1975); Instructor, Ventura College (1973-1975); Instructor of Philosophy and Sociology, Santa Barbara City College (1966-1967); Teaching Assistant, Social Science Integrated Course, University of California, Berkeley (1965-1966) **CR:** Martial Arts Instructor, United Martial Arts Association (2010-2017); Martial Arts Instructor, Craft Kenpo Karate (2010-2017); Leader, Girl Scouts of the United States of America (1959-1963); Waterfront Director, Girl Scouts of the United States of America (1959-1963) **CW:** Author, "Desire Nothing: Nirvana is Nowhere," Beijing: International Communication of Chinese Culture (2016); Author, "Himsa and Ahimsa in the Martial Arts," Comparative Philosophy in Times of Terror, Lexington Books (2006); Author, "Paul Natorp's Philosophy of Religion within the Marburg Neo-Kantian Tradition," Georg Olms Verlag (1980) **AW:** Meritorious Performance and Professional Progress Award, California Polytechnic State University (1980) **MEM:** Associate, Cosmos Cub; American Academy of Religion; Society for Asian and Comparative Philosophy; Society for Values in Higher Education **MH:** Albert Nelson Marquis Lifetime Achievement Award (2017) **H:** Swimming; Martial Arts; Creative Writing **BA:** 1459 7th St , Los Osos, VA, 93402-1617 **ADD:** 1459 7th St , Los Osos, VA, 93402-1617

SALVATI, EDUARDO, **T:** Surgeon **I:** Medicine & Health Care **CN:** Cornell University **DOB:** 11/11/1939 **PB:** Buenos Aires **SC:** Argentina **ED:** Fellow, Hospital of Special Surgery, New York City, NY (1969-1972); Resident, University of Florence, Italy (1963-1965); MD, La Platta Medical School, Buenos Aires, Argentina (1963); Intern, Hospital de Quilmes, Buenos Aires, Argentina (1962-1963); BS, Jose Manuel Estrada, Buenos Aires, Argentina (1957) **C:** Associate Scientist, Research Division, Hospital of Special Surgery, New York City, NY (1993-Present); Director, Hip and Knee Service, Hospital Special Surgery, New York City, NY (1991-Present); Professor, Cornell University, New York City, NY (1983-Present); Attending Orthopedic Surgeon, Hospital of Special Surgery, New York City, NY (1983-Present); Chief, Hip Service, Hospital of Special Surgery, New York City, NY (1975-1991); Assistant Attending Orthopedic Surgeon, Hospital of Special Surgery, New York City, NY (1972-1975); Instructor to Associate Professor, Clinical Orthopedic Surgery, Weil Medical College, Cornell University, New York City, NY (1969-1983) **MEM:** American Medical Association; Sociedad Medica Hispanoamericana; Venezuelan Society of Orthopaedic Surgery and Traumatology; Columbian Society of Orthopaedic Surgery and Traumatology; Argentine Medical Society; Argentine Society of Orthopaedic Surgery and Traumatology; New York State Society of Orthopaedic Surgeons; New York Academy of Medicine; New York County Medical Society; The Medical Society of the State of New York; Latinoamerican Society of Orthopaedic Surgery and Traumatology; International Hip Society; American Association of Hip and Knee Surgeons; American Hip Society; American Orthopaedic Association; American Academy of Orthopaedic Surgeons; Honorary Member, Association Medica Argentina **MH:** Albert Nelson Marquis Lifetime Achievement Award (2017) **ADD:** 25 Sutton Place South, PH G, New York, NY, 10022

SALYER, JEANNE, **T:** Associate Professor **I:** Education/Educational Services **CN:** Virginia Commonwealth University **DOB:** 08/02/1946 **PB:** Durham **SC:** NC/USA **PT:** Harry T. Salyer; Jeannette P. Salyer **MS:** Single **ED:** Postdoctoral Coursework in Interdisciplinary Outcomes Research, University of Minnesota (1998-1999); PhD in Nursing, Virginia Commonwealth University (1992); MSN, School of Nursing, The University of Alabama at Birmingham (1975); BSN, The University of Alabama at Birmingham (1972); Diploma in Nursing, UAB Hospital (1967) **C:** Associate Professor, School of Nursing, Virginia Commonwealth University, Richmond, VA (2001-Present); Interim Chair, Adult Health & Nursing Systems, Virginia Commonwealth University (2013-2016); Center Affiliate, Center of Excellence in Biobehavioral Approaches to Symptom Management, Virginia Commonwealth University (2009-2015); Center Affiliate, Center for Biobehavioral Clinical Research in Critical Health Experiences, Virginia Commonwealth University (2004-2009); Project Co-director, Outcomes Research in Nursing Administration, Virginia Commonwealth University (1995-2000); Assistant Professor, Department of Adult Health & Nursing Systems, Virginia Commonwealth University (1993-2001); Case Manager, Division of Medical/ Surgery-Trauma Nursing, School of Medicine, Virginia Commonwealth University (1992-1993); Research Nurse, Heart Failure/Heart Transplant Program, Division of Cardiology, School of Medicine, Richmond, VA (1989-1992); Staff Nurse, Nursing Relief Team, School of Medicine, Virginia Commonwealth University (1988-1989); Unit Coordinator, Cancer Rehabilitation & Continuing Care Program, School of Medicine, Virginia Commonwealth University (1987-1988); Clinical Nurse Specialist, Home Health Programs, Virginia Department of Health (1985-1987); Instructor, Critical Care Education Programs, VCU Medical College of Virginia Hospital (Now VCU Health) Richmond, VA (1982-1985); Nursing Education Coordinator, Critical Care Education Programs, VCU Medical College of Virginia Hospital (Now VCU Health) Richmond, VA (1982-1985); Unit Coordinator, Respiratory Intensive Care Unit, Division of Critical Care Nursing, School of Medicine, Virginia Commonwealth University (1979-1982); Pulmonary Clinical Nurse Specialist, Respiratory Intensive Care Unit, Division of Critical Care Nursing, School of Medicine, Virginia Commonwealth University (1979-1982); Instructor, Critical Care Staff Development Program, Department of Nursing Research and Development, Jackson Memorial Hospital, Jackson Health System, Miami, FL (1978-1979); Pulmonary Clinical Nurse Specialist, Department of Nursing, UAB Hospitals, UAB Health System, Birmingham, AL (1975-1978); Staff Nurse, Medical ICU, UAB Hospitals, UAB Health System, Birmingham, AL (1969-1972); Staff Nurse, Coronary Diseases Study Unit, UAB Hospitals, UAB Health System, Birmingham, AL (1969-1969); Staff Nurse, 48-Bed Surgical Specialties Unit, UAB Hospitals, UAB Health System, Birmingham, AL (1968-1969); Staff Nurse, Emergency Department, UAB Hospitals, UAB Health System, Birmingham, AL (1967-1968) **CW:** Author, More Than 50 Articles, Scientific Journals; Author, 5 Book Chapters **AW:** Nurse of the Year Award: Nursing Education, Research, and Author, Virginia Chapter, March of Dimes Foundation (2014); Outstanding Faculty Award, School of Nursing, Virginia Commonwealth University (2014); Elected Distinguished Scholar, National Academies of Practice in Nursing (2007); New Investigator Award, School of Nursing, Virginia Commonwealth University (2002); Grantee, "Correlates of HIV-Related Lipodystrophy," American Nurses Foundation (2000-2001); Grantee, "The Effects of Attending a Community-Based Weight Management Program on Weight Loss, Lipid Profile, and Blood Pressure in Long-Term Cardiac Transplant Recipients: A Pilot Feasibility Study," A.D. Williams Research Award (1999-2001); Nursing Research Award, Council on Nursing, Allied Health and Social Sciences, International Society for Heart & Lung Transplantation (1999); Grantee, "Health Promoting Lifestyle in Long-term Cardiac Transplant Recipients," School of Nursing Annual Fund (1995); Inductee, The Honor Society of Phi Kappa Phi (1992); Honoree, A.D. Williams Research Fellow (1989); Inductee, Nu Chapter, Sigma Theta Tau International (1975) **MEM:** Public Policy Committee (2012-Present); NAP Distinguished Scholar, Nursing Academy (2007-Present); NAP (2007-Present); American Heart Association, Inc. (2006-Present); American Society of Transplantation (2003-Present); Council on Nursing, Health Sciences and Allied Health, International Society for Heart and Lung Transplantation (1995-Present); Southern Nursing Research Society (1993-Present); Southern Nursing Research Society (1992-Present); Grants & Awards Committee (2011-2018); Membership Committee, American Society of Transplantation (2006-2010); Allied Health Professionals Community of Practice, American Society of Transplantation (2006-2010); Thoracic Organ Transplantation Community of Practice, American Society of Transplantation (2006-2010); Chairman, Awards Committee, Excellence in Research Award (2005-2006); Membership Committee, Gamma Omega Chapter, Sigma Theta Tau International (2001-2003); Treasurer, Gamma Omega Chapter, Sigma Theta Tau International (1998-2001); Research & Scholarship Committee, Gamma Omega Chapter, Sigma Theta Tau International (1996-2002); Council on Nursing, Health Sciences & Allied Health Research Committee, International Society for Heart and Lung Transplantation (1996-1997); Nominating Committee, Gamma Omega Chapter, Sigma Theta Tau International (1995-1998); American Association of Critical-Care Nurses **H:** Needlework; Photography; Traveling to historic sites **RE:** Episcopalian **BA:** 1100 E Leigh St, Richmond, VA, 23298 **ADD:** 1424 Camberly Ct, Midlothian, VA, 23113

SAMES, KLAUS, **T:** Anatomist, Gerontologist, Researcher, Educator (Retired) **I:** Sciences **CN:** University of Hamburg, University of Berlin **DOB:** 04/12/1939 **PB:** Kassel **SC:** HE/Germany **PT:** Ernst Sames; Margarete (Strack) Sames **MS:** Divorced **SPN:** Kornelia Steinecke (3/12/1968) **CH:** Almut **ED:** Habilitated Doctor, University of Erlangen, Germany (1981); MD, University of Muenster, Germany (1971) **CT:** Registered Medical Practitioner **C:** Personal Chair, Professor of Anatomy, University of Hamburg (1997-Present); Personal Chair, Professor of Anatomy, University of Berlin (1997-Present); Deputy Professor in Anatomy, University of Heidelberg, University of Freiburg, University of Zuerich, University of Hamburg (1988-1997); Professor of Anatomy and Experimental Gerontology, Free University Berlin (1987); Senior Lecturer in Anatomy, Free University Berlin (1985-1988); Lecturer in Anatomy, University of Heidelberg and University of Hamburg (1973-1985); Lecturer in Pathology, University of Heidelberg (1971-1973) **CW:** Editor, "Medizinische Regeneration und Tissue Engineering" (2000); Co-Editor, "Kompendium Der Gerontology" (1994); Co-editor, "Erfolgreiches Altern" (1989); Author, "The Role of Proteoglycans in Aging" (1994); "Sterblich Durch ein Fesetz der Natur" (2000); Contributor, Articles, Professional Journals **AW:** Grantee, German Forschunggsgemeinschaft **MEM:** Chairman, Section of Biology of Aging, German Society Gerontology and Geriatrics (2000), Anatomische Association; New York Academy of Sciences **H:** Writing Satiric Essays **ADD:** Brahmsstraße 7A, Senden, Germany, 89250

SAMMAN, JUAN M., **T:** President, Prosthodontist **I:** Sciences **CN:** JMSDDSPC **SC:** Syria **PT:** Moukhtar Samman; Souha Samman **MS:** Divorced **ED:** DDS, New York University, New York, NY (1984); MSc, London University (1983); BS, American University, Beirut (1976) **C:** Private Practice, JMSDDSPC, New York, NY (1988-Present); Clinical Assistant Professor, New York University, New York City, NY (1987-1993); Scientific Researcher, New York University, New York, NY (1984-1987); Honorary Clinical Assistant to the Dental Hospital, University College Hospital, London, UK (1983); Fellow, British Society for the Study of Prosthetic Dentistry **CR:** Sam Weber, DDS (1987-1988); Associate, New York Dental Implant Restorative and Cosmetic Dentistry Center (1985-1987); Lecturer, New York University **CW:** Contributor, Articles, Professional Publications **AW:** UNICEF Award (2017) **MEM:** International College of Prosthodontists; American College of Prosthdontists; European Prosthodontic Association; American Dental Association; International Association of Dental Research; Academy of Osseointegration **MH:** Albert Nelson Marquis Lifetime Achievement Award (2017) **H:** Music; Painting; Travel **ADD:** 355 S End Ave Apt 27J, New York, NY, 10280 **URL:** https://www.linkedin.com/in/juan-samman-4b243644

SAMPLE, JOSEPH, T: Foundation Administrator **I:** Media & Entertainment **CN:** Yellowstone Public Radio KEMC **DOB:** 03/15/1923 **PB:** Chicago **SC:** IL/USA **PT:** John Glen S.; Helen (Scanlon) S **SPN:** Miriam Tyler Willing (Deceased); Patricia M. Law (Divorced) **CH:** Michael Scanlon; David Forrest; Patrick Glen **ED:** BA, Yale University (1947) **C:** Director, Producer, Yellowstone Public Radio KEMC, Billings, MT (1993-Present); President, KPAX-TV, Missoula, MT (1955-1984); President, KRTV, Great Falls, MT; President, KXLF-AM-TV, Butte, MT; President, Montana Television Network KTVQ, Billings, MT; Vice President, Media Director, Dancer-Fitzgerald-Sample, Inc., Advertising Agency (1952-1953); Trainee, Media Analyst, Media Director, Dancer-Fitzgerald-Sample, Inc., Advertising Agency, Chicago, IL (1947-1950) **CIV:** Chairman, Wheeler Center, Montana State University **MIL:** U.S. Army (1950-1952); U.S. Army (1943-1946) **MEM:** Rotary International; Yellowstone Country Club; Port Royal Club; Hilands Golf Club **ADD:** 606 Highland Park Drive, Billings, MT, 59102

SANDERS, BARRY R., T: Chief Compliance Officer **I:** Financial Services **CN:** Balbec Capital LP **DOB:** 07/21/1957 **PB:** Oak Park **SC:** IL/USA **PT:** Eugene Haze Sanders; Muriel Efty Sanders **MS:** Married **SPN:** Diane Gaffney Sanders (12/28/1985) **CH:** Mattie Maria Murielle **ED:** MA in Law, University of Cambridge (1986); LLM, The University of Texas (1983); BA, University of Cambridge (1981); BA, The University of Virginia (1979) **C:** Chief Compliance Officer, Balbec Capital, LP (2016-Present); Member, Barry Sanders plc (2015-Present); Shareholder, Dickinson Wright PLLC (2013-2016); Shareholder, Mariscal Weeks McIntyre & Friedlander, P.A. (2005-2012); Shareholder, Allen, Price, Padden & Sanders PC, Phoenix, AZ (1999-2005); Shareholder, Ryley, Carlock & Applewhite, PA, Phoenix, AZ (1991-1999); Shareholder, Pohlman & Sanders, PA, Phoenix, AZ (1989-1991) **CIV:** Former Judge Pro Tempore, Superior Court of Arizona, Maricopa County **CW:** Contributor, "Arizona Attorney's Fee Manual" **AW:** Henry Prize in Advanced Moral Philosophy, University of Aberdeen, Scotland (1978) **MEM:** Chair, Antitrust Section, State Bar of Arizona (2002-2003, 1998-1999); Former Member, Civil Rules Committee, State Bar of Arizona **BAR:** United States Court of Appeals for the Eighth Circuit (2001); Supreme Court of the United States (1996); United States Court of Appeals for the Ninth Circuit (1989); United States District Court District of Arizona (1987); United States District Court Eastern District of California (1985); State of Arizona (1985); United States District Court Northern District of California (1984); State of California (1984) **MH:** Albert Nelson Marquis Lifetime Achievement Award (2017) **H:** Golf **ADD:** 5331 N 43rd Pl, Phoenix, AZ, 85018 **URL:** https://www.linkedin.com/in/barry-sanders-25a152b8/

SANDMAN, CURT A., I: Education/Educational Services **ED:** Doctoral Degree, Louisiana State University (1967-1971); BA, Fresno State University (1961-1967) **C:** Professor Emeritus, University of California, Irvine (1979-Present); Full Professor, Department of Psychology Ohio State University (1971-1979) **CR:** National Institute of Mental Health, National I **CW:** Published, More than 350 Papers **AW:** Research Award, National Institute of Mental Health (2013-2018) **H:** Expert skier; Bicycling; Hiking

SANSALONE, WILLIAM ROBERT, T: Biochemist, Educator, Biomedical Researcher (Retired) **I:** Education/Educational Services **CN:** Georgetown University **DOB:** 02/16/1931 **PB:** Vineland **SC:** NJ/USA **PT:** Fortunato Sansalone; Rosa (Pelle) Sansalone **MS:** Widowed **SPN:** Alice E. Koury (Deceased 2010) **CH:** Catherine Downs **ED:** PhD,

Rutgers, The State University of New Jersey (1961); MS, University of New Hampshire (1955); BS, Rutgers, The State University of New Jersey (1953) **C:** Associate Director for Research Development, Professor of Biochemistry, Georgetown University School of Medicine, Washington, D.C. (2002-2007); Senior Fellow, Georgetown University, Center for Food and Nutrition Policy (1996-2002); Director, Office of Scientific Planning and Evaluation, NIH, Bethesda, MD (1987-1996); Associate Director, Division of Lung Diseases, NIH, Bethesda, MD (1983-1987); Program Director, Scientific Evaluation, Cancer Research Centers, NIH, Bethesda, MD (1974-1983); Executive Secretary, Biochemistry Study Section, NIH, Bethesda, MD (1973-1974); Senior Project Scientist, NIH, Bethesda, MD (1972-1973); Project Scientist, NIH, Bethesda, MD (1971-1972); Associate Professor of Biochemistry, SUNY Downstate Medical Center, Brooklyn, NY (1970-1971); Assistant Professor of Biochemistry, SUNY Downstate Medical Center, Brooklyn, NY (1964-1970); Instructor of Biochemistry, SUNY Downstate Medical Center, Brooklyn, NY (1961-1964); Biochemistry Research Assistant, University of Connecticut, Storrs, CT (1955-1956) **CR:** Visiting Associate Professor of Physiology and Biophysics, Medical College of Pennsylvania, Philadelphia, PA (1970-1971) **MIL:** First Lieutenant, United States Air Force (1956-1958) **CW:** Author, Numerous Scientific Articles Published in Professional Journals; Edited and Published, Three Books on Contemporary Topics in Food and Nutrition; Published, Newspaper Articles and Monographs on the History of Southern New Jersey; Contributor, "Christmas in My Mind"; Author, "St. Mary's of Malaga 1922-1997"; Author, "The Grindstone at Betty Bajewicz Historical Center" **AW:** Named, Cavaliere Della Repubblica, Rome, Italy (1995); Outstanding Performance Award, National Institutes of Health (1980); Elected, Sigma XI (1965); University of New Hampshire Annual Research Award (1955); Garrett Scott Voorhee's Memorial Award (1953); William Danforth Fellowship Award (1952) **MEM:** American Association for the Advancement of Science; Society for Experimental Biology and Medicine; American Society for Nutritional Sciences; Biophysical Society; The Harvey Society; Alpha Gamma Rho; Sigma Xi, The Scientific Research Honor Society **H:** St. Jane Frances de Chantal Church Choir; Steierisch und Bairisch, a Bavarian Folk-dance Group **PA:** Independent **RE:** Roman Catholic **ADD:** 6835 Old Stage Road, Rockville, MD, 20852

SAROSIEK, JERZY, T: Professor, Vice Chair for Research **I:** Health, Wellness and Fitness **CN:** Texas Tech University Health Sciences Center, El Paso, Paul L. Foster School of Medicine **DOB:** 04/13/1945 **PB:** Pucilki **SC:** Poland **MS:** Married **SPN:** Irene Skiepko (8/27/1977) **CH:** Konrad Jerzy; Kris Andrew; Aleksandra Maria **ED:** Honorary Doctorate, Medical University of Bialystok (2016); PhD, School of Medicine, Biochemical Institute, The Medical University of Bialystok, Bialystok, Poland (1975); Senior Assistant Resident, Internal Medicine, Medical School, Department of Internal Medicine, University Hospital, Bialystok, Poland (1972-1975); Internship, Medical University of Bialystok, Poland (1969-1971); Residency in Medicine, Medical University of Bialystok, Poland (1969-1971); MD, School of Medicine, The Medical University of Bialystok, Bialystok, Poland (1969) **C:** Professor of Medicine, Associate Chairman for Research, Department of Internal Medicine, Internal Medicine Research Committee Chairman, Director, Molecular Medicine Research Laboratory, Texas Tech University Health Sciences Center, Paul L. Foster School of Medicine, El Paso, TX

(2009-Present); Research Professor of Medicine, Director of the Gastroenterology Research Laboratory, Kansas University Medical Center, Kansas City, KS (1997-2009); Research Associate Professor of Medicine, University of Virginia Health Science Center, Charlottesville, VA (1989-1997); Research Assistant Professor, University of Medicine and Dentistry of New Jersey (1988-1989); Research Associate, New York Medical College, Department of Medicine, Gastroenterology Research Laboratory, Westchester County Medical Center, Valhalla, NY (1986-1988); Assistant Professor, Medical University of Bialystok, Poland (1983-1986); Gastroenterology Research Fellow, New York Medical College, Metropolitan Hospital, New York, NY (1982-1983); Attending Physician, Internal Medicine, Medical University of Bialystok, Poland (1976-1982) **CR:** Visiting Professor, Jagiellonian University School of Medicine, Krakow, Poland (1999-Present) **CIV:** Board Member, Medical Exchange International, North Tarrytown, NY (1988-2007) **CW:** Invited Reviewer, Gastroenterology; Invited Reviewer, American Journal of Gastroenterology; Invited Reviewer, Digestive Diseases and Sciences; Invited Reviewer, American Journal of the Medical Sciences; Invited Reviewer, Digestion; Invited Reviewer, Digestive Diseases; Invited Reviewer, Gut; Invited Reviewer, Clinical Chemistry; Contributor, 130 Papers, Peer-Reviewed Journals; Contributor, 18 Chapters, Medical Books; Editorial Board, Polish Journal of Surgery; Invited Speaker, Symposiums **AW:** Tinsley Harrison Award for Senior Authorship Based on Innovative and Original Translational Research Concept, American Journal of the Medical Sciences (2018); Department of Internal Medicine Award of Excellence, Paul L. Foster School of Medicine, Texas Tech University Health Sciences Center El Paso (2018); AstraZeneca Senior Fellow Award, American College of Gastroenterology (2008); The World Medal of Freedom, American Biographical Institute (2005); Man of the Year, American Biographical Institute (2003); AstraZeneca Senior Fellow Award, American College of Gastroenterology (2003); Clinical Research Award, American College of Gastroenterology (1997); Astra Merck Award, American College of Gastroenterology (1996); Clinical Research Award, American College of Gastroenterology (1995); Clinical Research Award, American Gastroenterology Association (1993); SmithKline Beecham Clinical Research Award, American Gastroenterology Association (1993); Clinical Research Award, American College of Gastroenterology (1992); Special Award, Ministry of Health and Public Services, Warsaw, Poland (1979); International Scientific Award for Young Investigator, Sofia, Bulgaria (1972) **MEM:** Scientific Committee, World Organization for Specialized Studies on Diseases of the Esophagus (O.E.S.O.); Fellow, American Gastroenterological Association; Lifetime Fellow, American College of Gastroenterology; American Neurogastroenterology and Motility Society; Southern Society of Clinical Investigation; The New York Academy of Sciences; Polish Gastroenterological Association; Polish Society of Surgery; OESO Foundation, Paris, France **MH:** Albert Nelson Marquis Lifetime Achievement Award (2017) **H:** Swimming; Golf; Travel; Tennis **PA:** Conservative **RE:** Christian **BA:** 4800 Alberta Ave, TTUHSC, El Paso, TX, 79905 **ADD:** 6209 Pinehurst Drive, El Paso, TX, 79912

SARTAIN, JAMES EDWARD, T: Lawyer **I:** Law and Legal Services **DOB:** 02/09/1941 **PB:** Fort Worth **SC:** TX/USA **PT:** James F. Sartain; May Belle Sartain **MS:** Married **SPN:** Barbara Hardy (8/17/1962) **CH:** Bethany Sartain-McCann **ED:** LLB, Baylor

University (1966); BA, Texas Agricultural and Mechanical University (1963) **C:** Private Practice, Abilene, TX (2001-2012); Private Practice, Fort Worth, TX (1973-2001); Staff Attorney, U.S. Sen. William L. Scott, Fairfax, VA (1972); Staff Attorney, U.S. Department of Justice, Washington, DC (1970-1972) **CR:** Fellow, College of the State Bar of Texas **CIV:** Co-Administrator, W.J. Boaz Estate, Texas (2011-Present); Board of Directors, Fort Worth Boys Club (1980-1989); Board of Directors, Oakwood Cemetery, Fort Worth, TX (1979-1984); Advising Director, 12th Armored Division, Memorial Museum, Abilene, TX **MIL:** Captain, Artillery U.S. Army, Vietnam **MEM:** American Bar Association; National Rifle Association; VFW; Abilene Bar Association; Baylor Law Alumni Association; Masons; Phi Delta Phi **BAR:** U.S. District Court, Northern District, State of Texas (1974); U.S. Court of Military Appeals (1971); State of Texas (1966) **PA:** Republican **RE:** Presbyterian **ADD:** PO Box 450, Abilene, TX, 79604

SAVAGE, JOE C., T: Personal Injury Lawyer **I:** Law and Legal Services **CN:** The Joe C. Savage Law Firm **MS:** Married **SPN:** Christina Savage (1/19/2008) **CH:** Susan; Scott; Philip; Nicholas **ED:** LLM, Harvard Law School (1965); JD, University of Kentucky College of Law (1964) **CT:** Certified Civil Trial Advocate **C:** Personal Injury Lawyer, The Joe C. Savage Law Firm; Lecturer in Law and Medicine, Lecturer in Insurance, College of Law, University of Kentucky; Teacher, Continuing Legal Education Programs, Kentucky **CIV:** Trinity Hill United Methodist Church **AW:** Lawyer of the Year in Kentucky, Medical Malpractice Law (2011); Hall of Fame, University of Kentucky College of Law (2003); Justice Thomas B. Spain Award; Outstanding Lawyer, Kentucky; Best Lawyers in America, The American College of Trial Lawyers **MEM:** Former President, Kentucky Bar Association (1987-1988); Board of Directors, Trinity Hill Methodist Church; Florence Crittinden Home; Board of Governors, The Kidney Foundation; Former Chairman, Kentucky Judicial Conduct Commission; The International Society of Barristers; American Board of Trial Advocates **BA:** 271 W Short St Ste 300, The Joe Savage Law Firm, Lexington, KY, 40507 **ADD:** 501 Darby Creek Drive, Suite 53, The Joe Savage Law Firm, Lexington, KY, 40509

SAYEED, ZULFIQUAR, T: Quality Manager **I:** Business Management/Business Services **CN:** Nokia **SC:** Bangladesh **PT:** Abu Sayeed; Firoza Sayeed **MS:** Married **CH:** Rayyan; Umair **ED:** Doctorate in Electrical Engineering, University of Pennsylvania (1996); BS, California Institute of Technology, Pasadena, CA (1990); BA, Ohio Wesleyan University, Delaware, OH (1988) **C:** Quality Manager, Predictive Quality and Optimization, Nokia (2017-Present); Wireless Research Engineer, Nokia (1997-2017); Adjunct Professor, New Jersey Institute of Technology (2002); Instructor, Lucent Technologies, Bell Labs (Now Nokia) (2000-2001); Teaching Assistant, University of Pennsylvania (1993-1996); Intern, Bell Labs Area 11, AT&T (1994); Summer Intern, Jet Propulsion Laboratory, National Aeronautics and Space Administration (1989) **AW:** Recipient, Thomas Edison Patent Award, The Research & Development Council of New Jersey (2016) **MEM:** IEEE **ADD:** 7 Huber Ct, Hightstown, NJ, 08520 **URL:** https://www.linkedin.com/in/zulfiquar-sayeed-7003301/

SAYRE, LINDA DAMARIS, T: Career Coach Consultant **I:** Consulting **DOB:** 11/26/1945 **PB:** Washington **SC:** DC/USA **PT:** Wallace Stanley Sayre; Kathryn Louise (McKnight) Sayre **ED:**

EdD in Adult and Continuing Education, Rutgers, The State University of New Jersey (2002); MA in Sociology, University of Sussex, Brighton, England (1969); BA in English, Wells College (1967); Graduate Coursework, Columbia School of Social Work **C:** Collaborative Coach, University of South Florida, Tampa, FL (2016-Present); International Student Exchange Coordinator, Global Link, Inc., China (2013-2016); Visiting Instructor, Adult Education, University of South Florida (2011-2012); Training and Development Manager, BOC Gases, Murray Hill, NJ (1995-1999); Training and Human Resources Development Consultant (1991-1995); Director of Human Resources Development and Employment, Bronx-Lebanon Hospital Center (1988-1991); Adjunct Instructor, Marymount College; Adjunct Instructor, The New School; Adjunct Instructor, LaGuardia Community College **CIV:** Member, Steering Committee, Broadway Democrats, New York, NY (2006-2007); Member, Steering Committee, Broadway Democrats, New York, NY (1993-1996); Board Member, Westside Cares Food Voucher (1993-1995); Member, Steering Committee, Broadway Democrats, New York, NY (1974-1980); President, Broadway Democrats (1977); Coordinator, New York 20th Congressional District, Carter Presidential Campaign (1976); President, Broadway Democrats (1975) **MEM:** Nominating Committee, Board of Directors, New York City Chapter, ATD (2015); Director-at-Large, American Association for Adult & Continuing Education (2007-2013); Director, Commission for Workforce and Professional Development, American Association for Adult & Continuing Education (2004-2007); Secretary, Graduate School of Education Alumni Association, Rutgers, The State University of New Jersey (2002-2004); National Leadership Conference Design Team, ATD (1995-1998); Chapter President, New York Metro Chapter, ATD (1994); Vice President for Professional Development, New York Metro Chapter, ATD (1993); Director of Governmental Affairs, Atlanta Chapter, ATD (1989-1991); Director of Governmental Affairs, Atlanta Chapter, SHRM (1989-1991); Vice President for Programs, Northern New Jersey Chapter, ATD (1984-1986) **MH:** Albert Nelson Marquis Lifetime Achievement Award (2017) **H:** Writing; Community service **PA:** Democrat **ADD:** 423 W 120th St Apt 106, New York, NY, 10027

SCALIA, JOSEPH W., T: Attorney **I:** Law and Legal Services **CN:** Law Offices of Joseph W. Scalia, APC **PB:** Berkeley **SC:** CA/USA **ED:** JD, McGeorge School of Law, University of the Pacific (1976); BA, University of Notre Dame (1972) **AW:** AV Preeminent Rating, Martindale Hubbell (1998) **MEM:** Settlement Judge Pro Tempore, Sacramento County Superior Court (1988-Present); California Real Estate Brokers (1982-Present); Arbitrator, Sacramento County Judicial Arbitration Association (1979-Present); Board of Directors, National Multiple Sclerosis Mountain Valley California Chapter (1989); Governing Board Member, McGeorge Community Legal Services Center (1976); Pacific Law Journal (1975-1976); Sacramento County Bar Association; State Bar of California; Traynor Honor Society Law Review; Mediator, Alternative Dispute Resolution, El Dorado County, CA **BAR:** U.S. District Court for the Eastern District of California (1976); U.S. District Court for the Northern District of California (1976) **BA:** 3017 Douglas Blvd Ste 300, Law Offices of Joseph W. Scalia, APC, Roseville, CA, 95661

SCANLON, JANICE PARISH, T: Educator (Retired) **I:** Education/Educational Services **DOB:** 07/28/1940 **PB:** Goodland **SC:** KS/USA **PT:** Milton Parish Jr.; Bertha May Adams Parish **MS:**

Widowed **ED:** MA, University of Denver (1980); BS, Fort Hays State University (1962) **C:** Retired (1998); Teacher, Gifted Students, Washington Township Public Schools, Sewell, NJ (1983-1998); Kindergarten Teacher, Jefferson County Public Schools, Lakewood, CO (1963-1981); Kindergarten Teacher, Music, Brewster Public Schools, Kansas (1962-1963) **CR:** Secretary, New Jersey Teachers Gifted (1990-1992); Delegate, Gifted Teachers to Visit China, People to People International (1990); President, Jefferson County Kindergarten Teachers Association, Lakewood, CO (1964-1965) **CIV:** Active Member, Democratic Party, Southeast Manatee County, FL (2003-Present); Presenter, Indian History, St. Martha's School (2001-Present); Member, Palm Aire Nine Hole Women's Golf Association (2000-Present); President, Palm Aire Nine Hole Women's Golf Association (2002-2003); Vice President, Palm Aire Nine Hole Women's Golf Association (2001-2002); Member, St. Columbkille Catholic Church, Fort Myers, FL; Vice President, Home Owner's Association **CW:** Co-Author, "Ruleton and Its School" (2005); Co-Author, "Adams and Parrish Family" (2005); Author, "Guides for Washington Township Schools" (1983-1998); Author, "Jefferson County Kindergarten Curriculum" (1974); Contributing Author, "Teaching Children in Remote Areas" (1968); Actor, Films **AW:** Quilt Challenge First Prize, Columbine Quilt Guild (2013); Quilt Challenge Most Creative Award, Columbine Quilt Guild (2012); Co-recipient, Outstanding Volunteer Group Award, Haywood County, NC (2007); Presidential Award, Palm Aire Nine Hole Women's Golf Associate (2007); Tuition Grant, U.S. Department of Education, University of Denver (1978-1980); Scholar, Kiwanis Club, Goodland, KS (1958) **MEM:** Palm Aire Women's Club (1999-Present); Columbine Quilt Guild; New Jersey Retired Teachers Association; Alpha Delta Kappa; Treasurer, Alpha Delta Kappa; Devotions Leader, Alpha Delta Kappa **H:** Making quilts and teddy bears for the infirmary; Making handmade tote bags for veterans; Silk painting; Travel; Painting; Genealogy; Golf **PA:** Democrat **RE:** Roman Catholic **ADD:** 3831 Autumn Fern Ter, Sarasota, FL, 34243

SCHINDLER, THOMAS HELLMUT, T: Associate Professor of Radiology and Medicine **I:** Education/Educational Services **CN:** Washington University in St. Louis **DOB:** 10/26/1968 **PB:** Karlsruhe **SC:** Germany **MS:** Married **SPN:** Ines Valenta-Schindler **CH:** Laura Maria Schindler **ED:** Postdoctoral Fellowship in Nuclear Cardiology and Cardiac PET, University of California, Los Angeles (2002-2006); Cardiovascular Fellowship, University Hospitals of Basel, Switzerland (2000-2002); Postgraduate Coursework in Internal Medicine and Cardiovascular, Albert-Ludwigs University Hospital Freiburg, Germany (1996-2000); Doctor Medicinae in Radiological Science, University of Leipzig, Germany (1996); Diploma of Medicine, University of Leipzig, Germany (1995); Undergraduate Coursework, University of Leipzig, Cum Laude (1995); Pre-Diploma in Natural Science, University of Fribourg, Switzerland (1991) **CT:** Licensed to Practice Medicine, State of Missouri (2018-Present); Certified in Controlled Dangerous Substances, Division of Drug Control, State of Missouri (2018-Present); Medical License, State of Maryland (2013-Present); Diplomate, Certification Board of Nuclear Cardiology (2010); Privatdozent, University of Geneva, Switzerland (2009); Board Licensed Physician in Internal Medicine and Cardiology, Germany (2006) **C:** Associate Professor of Radiology and Medicine, Washington University in St. Louis (2018-Present); Adjunct Appointment as Associate Professor in Medicine, Johns Hopkins University

(2018-Present); Director of Cardiovascular Nuclear Medicine, Associate Professor in Radiology and Medicine, Johns Hopkins University (2013-2017); Deputy Head Physician in Cardiology, Johns Hopkins University (2010-2012); Private Docent, University of Geneva (2009); Head of Nuclear Cardiology, Johns Hopkins University (2006-2012); Head of Nuclear Cardiology, Geneva University Hospitals (2006-2012) CR: Section and Associate Editor, Circulation- Cardiovascular Imaging (2017-Present); Guest Editor, Journal of the American College of Cardiology - Cardiovascular Imaging (2015-Present); Editorial Board Member, Annals of Nuclear Cardiology (2012-Present); Editorial Board Member, Journal of Nuclear Cardiology (2011-Present); International Editorial Board Member, European Heart Journal (2010-2017); Consulting Editor, Current Cardiovascular Imaging Reports AW: Recipient, Hermann Blumgart-Award, Society of Nuclear Medicine and Molecular Imaging (2018); Recipient, Award, 65th Annual Meeting, Society of Nuclear Medicine and Molecular Imaging, Philadelphia, PA (2015); Recipient, Reviewer of the Year Award, European Heart Journal, European Society of Cardiology, Annual Meeting, London, England (2011-2012); Elite Reviewer Award, Journal of the American College of Cardiology (2006); Recipient, Young Investigator Award, Society of Nuclear Medicine (2005); Recipient, Young Investigator Award, American Society of Nuclear Cardiology (2004) MEM: Board Certification Committee for Nuclear Cardiology, European Society of Cardiology (2016-Present); Job Task Analysis, Certification Board of Nuclear Cardiology (2016-Present); Immediate Past President, Cardiovascular Council, Society of Nuclear Medicine and Molecular Imaging (2016-Present); Board Member, Certification Board of Nuclear Cardiology (2015-Present); Geriatric Cardiology Section, American College of Cardiology Foundation (2011-Present); Chair, Blumgart-Award Committee and Nomination Committee, Board of Directors, Cardiovascular Council, Society of Nuclear Medicine and Molecular Imaging (2016-2017); President, Board of Directors, Cardiovascular Council, Society of Nuclear Medicine and Molecular Imaging (2015-2016); European Association of Cardiovascular Imaging Representative, American Society of Nuclear Cardiology (2015-2016); Board Member, House of Delegates, Society of Nuclear Medicine and Molecular Imaging (2015-2016); Board of Directors, Center for Molecular Imaging Innovation & Translation, Society of Nuclear Medicine and Molecular Imaging (2015-2016); Board Member, Committee on Councils and Centers, Society of Nuclear Medicine and Molecular Imaging (2014-2016); Chair, Board Certification Committee, NC&CCT Section Committee, European Association of Cardiovascular Imaging, European Society of Cardiology (2014-2016); Membership Task Force, Society of Nuclear Medicine and Molecular Imaging (2014-2015); Vice President, Board of Directors, Cardiovascular Council, Society of Nuclear Medicine and Molecular Imaging (2014-2015); European Council of Nuclear Cardiology Member, Committee on Collaboration of Nuclear Cardiology (2013-2015); Committee for Practice Guidelines for the Diagnosis and Management of Acute Pulmonary Embolism, European Society of Cardiology (2012-2015); Certification Board Member, Integrated and Basic Course of Radioprotection and Nuclear Medicine, European University Viadrina Frankfurt (2012); Certification Board Member, Special Radioprotection Course for X-Ray Exams, European University Viadrina Frankfurt (2012); Certification Board Member, Application of Open Radioactive Substances in Nuclear Medicine, FH Aachen (2012); Chair, Basic and Clinical Young Investigator Award, Cardiovascular Council, Society of Nuclear Medicine and Molecular Imaging (2011-2014); Cardiology Technician, European Society of Cardiology (2009-2015); Board of Directors, Cardiovascular Council, Society of Nuclear Medicine and Molecular Imaging (2007-2012); Cardiology Technician, The American Physiological Society (2003-2013); Board of Directors, Cardiovascular Council, Society of Nuclear Medicine and Molecular Imaging (2007-2012); Council of Cardiovascular Radiology, American Heart Association, Inc.; Council of Arteriosclerosis, Thrombosis, and Vascular Biology, American Heart Association, Inc.; German Society of Cardiology, European Society of Cardiology; Swiss Society of Cardiology, European Society of Cardiology; Academy of Molecular Imaging; Society of Cardiovascular Magnetic Resonance; North American Society for Cardiovascular Imaging; Society of Cardiovascular Computed Tomography; International Society for Cardiovascular Translational Research; Scientific Advisory Board, World Congress on Heart Disease; Cardiovascular Council, European Association of Nuclear Medicine MH: Albert Nelson Marquis Lifetime Achievement Award (2017) BA: 510 S. Kinghshighway Boulevard, Campus Box 8223, St. Louis, MO, 63110 ADD: 15928 Wetherburn road, Chesterfield, MO, 63017

SCHLOSSMAN, JOHN I., T: Architect I: Architecture & Construction CN: Loebl Schlossman & Hackl DOB: 08/21/1931 PB: Chicago SC: IL/USA PT: Norman Joseph Schlossman; Carol (Rosenfeld) Schlossman MS: Married SPN: Shirley Goulding Rhodes (2/8/1959) CH: Marc N.; Gail S. Mewhort; Peter C. ED: MArch, Massachusetts Institute of Technology (1956); BArch, University of Minnesota (1955); BA, University of Minnesota (1953); Coursework, Grinnell College (1949-1950) CT: Registered Architect, State of Illinois (1998) C: Consultant Principal, Loebl Schlossman & Hackl, Chicago, IL (1998-Present); Principal, Loebl Schlossman & Hackl, Chicago, IL (1970-1998); Associate, Loebl Schlossman & Hackl, Chicago, IL (1965-1970); Architect, Loebl Schlossman & Hackl, Chicago, IL (1959-1965); Architectural Designer, The Architects Collaborative, Cambridge, MA (1956-1957) CR: Advisory Board, Department of Landscape Architecture, University of Minnesota (2003-2006); Board of Overseers, College Architecture, Illinois Institute of Technology, Chicago, IL (1994-2011); Founding Board of Directors, Chicago Architectural Assistance Center (1974-1979); Sustaining Fellow, Art Institute of Chicago; Fellow, AIA CIV: Life Trustee, Merit School of Music, Chicago, IL (2012); Village of Glencoe Contextual Design Review Commission (2005-2012); National Trust Council, National Trust for Historic Preservation, Washington, DC (2000-2013); Zoning and Planning Committee, The Magnificent Mile Association, Chicago, IL (2000-2001); President, Graham Foundation (1999-2001); Honorary Trustee, Merit School of Music, Chicago, IL (1996); Trustee, Graham Foundation (1995-1999); President, Merit School of Music, Chicago, IL (1988-1990); Advisory Board of Directors, Merit School of Music, Chicago, IL (1983-1993); Chairman, Glencoe Plan Commission, Illinois (1977-1982); Trustee, Chicago Architect Foundation (1971-1975); Trustee, Committee for Green Bay Trail, Glencoe, IL (1970-1977); Governing Member, Chicago Symphony Orchestra Association; Founders Council, The Field Museum, Chicago, IL AW: Director for Life, Young Men's Jewish Council, Chicago, IL (1971); Rotch Travelling Scholar (1957) MEM: Honorary Foundation Trustee, AIA (1995-Present); Chairman, Architects Liability Committee, AIA (1980-1982); Chairman, Architects Liability Committee, AIA (1976); Vice President, Chicago Chapter, AIA (1975); Chairman, Insurance Committee, AIA (1974-1975); Trustee, Insurance Trust, AIA (1971-1976); The Richard and Helen Thomas Club at Symphony Center; The Arts Club; The Sloane Club; Alpha Rho Chi MH: Albert Nelson Marquis Lifetime Achievement Award (2017) ADD: 232 Mary Street, Winnetka, IL, 60093

SCHMIDT, HELEN M., T: Medical Director I: Medicine & Health Care CN: Kindred at Home DOB: 11/16/1936 PB: Spokane SC: WA/USA MS: Single ED: Internship, Surgical Residency, Virginia Mason Medical Center, Seattle, WA (1968); MD, College of Medicine, Drexel University (1963); BA, University of Washington (1958) C: Medical Director, House Calls/Mobile Medical Clinic, Family Home Care & Hospice (2007-Present); Doctor, Mobile Medical Clinic (2005-2007) CR: Fellow, American College of Surgeons CIV: Missionary, North American Baptist Conference, Republic of Cameroon (1969-2004); Volunteer, Local Church AW: Medal of Honor, Republic of Cameroon; Physician of the Year, Home Care Association of Washington MEM: Spokane County Medical Society; Christian Medical & Dental Associations H: Reading; Helping seniors; Growing flowers; Offering facilitation services in Cameroon BA: 22820 E Appleway Avenue, House Calls Primary Care, Liberty Lake, WA, 99019 ADD: 10915 E 12th Avenue, Spokane Valley, WA, 99206

SCHNEIDER, CHRISTINE LYNN, T: Chief CBP Officer I: Government Administration/Government Relations/Government Services CN: Customs and Border Protection DOB: 02/03/1960 PB: Staten Island SC: NY/USA PT: Howard Thomas Schneider; Ina Elise (Beyer) Schneider ED: BS, State University of New York Maritime College, Bronx, NY (1984) CT: Licensed Third Mate, United States Merchant Marine; Certified United States Customs Firearms Instructor C: Chief CBP Officer, Customs and Border Protection, San Diego, CA (2003-Present); Chief Inspector, Customs and Border Protection, San Diego, CA (1989-2005) MIL: Lieutenant Commander, US Naval Reserve (1991-2006); Lieutenant Commander, US Naval Reserve (1984-1987) MH: Albert Nelson Marquis Lifetime Achievement Award (2017) H: Coin collecting/numismatics; Pistol shooting; Golf PA: Democrat RE: Lutheran ADD: 3505 Valley Rd Apt 3, Bonita, CA, 91902

SCHNEIDER, DAN W., T: International Partner I: Law and Legal Services CN: Baker McKenzie DOB: 04/28/1947 PB: Salem SC: OR/USA PT: Harold Otto Schneider; Frances Louis (Warner) Schneider MS: Married SPN: Nancy Merle Schmalzbauer (3/29/1945) CH: Mark Warner; Edward Michael ED: LLM, Columbia University (1975); JD, Willamette University (1974); BA, St. Olaf College, Cum Laude (1969) C: International Partner, Baker McKenzie (2000-Present); Partner, Hopkins & Sutter (1998-2000); Name Partner, Smith Lodge & Schneider (1995-1998); General Partner, Schiff Hardin LLP (1986-1995); Deputy Associate Director, Self-Regulatory Oversight and Market Structure Division in Market Regulation, U.S. Securities and Exchange Commission (1979-1986); Trial Attorney, Antitrust Division, The United States Department of Justice (1975-1979) CR: Board of Directors, NygaarArt CIV: President, Advisory Group, Arts in Education, Willamette University (2004-Present); Member, Advisory Board, Hallie Ford Museum of Art, Willamette University (1999-Present); Member, Advisory Board, Flaten Art Museum, St. Olaf College (1990-Present); Trustee, The American Academy of Art (1990-1998); Secretary, The American Academy of Art (1990-

1998) **CW:** Contributor, Articles, Professional Journals **AW:** Christie Award, Securities Transfer Association (1987); First Prize, Nathan Burkan Law Essay Competition, ASCAP (1974) **MEM:** The Metropolitan Club; Monroe Club; Plaza Club **BAR:** Illinois (1987); The District of Columbia (1979); Oregon (1974) **H:** Art Collecting; Art Writing; Music Composition **BA:** 300 E. Randolph Street, Suite 5000, Baker & McKenzie, Chicago, IL, 60601 **ADD:** 527 E Chicago Ave, Hinsdale, IL, 60521

SCHWARTZ, GERALD, I: Corporate Communications & Public Relations **DOB:** 06/22/1927 **PB:** New York **SC:** NY/USA **PT:** George Schwartz; Martha F. Schwartz **MS:** Married **SPN:** Felice P. Schwartz (June 25, 1950) **CH:** Gary R.; Gregg R.; Wendy L. **ED:** MS in Business Journalism and Mass Communications, Florida International University (2009); BS, University of Miami (1950); AB, University of Miami (1949); Student, North Carolina State University (1944-1945) **C:** Principal, Gerald Schwartz Agency, Miami, FL (1962-Present); Executive vice president, Bar-Ilan University, Ramat Gan, Israel (1960-1961); Press Secretary, Governor of Nebraska (1959-1960); Fund Raising and Public Relations Counselor, Miami, FL (1952-1958); Editor, Miami Beach Sun (1950-1951); Publicity Director, U.S. Army in Europe (1946-1948); Staff Writer, Miami Herald (1941-1944) **CIV:** Member, Executive Board, State of Israel Bonds Organization (1996-Present); Board of Directors, Temple Emanu-El of Greater Miami, President, B'nai Zion Chapter Florida (2009-2012); Board of Directors Administrative Committee, Jewish National Fund America (1995-2010); Vice President, Jewish National Fund, Florida (2000-2010); Board of Directors, Florida Chapter, Boys Town of Jerusalem (2006-2008); Vice Chairman, South Shore Medical Center Foundation (1989-2004); Executive Vice-Chairman, South Shore Hospital and Medical Center, Miami Beach (1989-2004); Trustee, South Shore Hospital and Medical Center, Miami (1987-2004); National Chairman, Friends of Pioneer Women/Na'amat (1984-1998); Vice President Greater Miami Region, Jewish National Fund of Am. (1996-1997); Chairman, City of Miami Beach Hurricane Defense Committee (1990-1997); Board of Directors, Crimestoppers of Dade County (1991-1994); National Vice President, American Zionist Federation (1991-1993); President, American Zionist Federation Southern Florida (1986-1992); Chairman, Economic Development Council, City of Miami Beach (1985-1991); Board of Directors, Miami Beach Taxpayers Association (1988-1989); National Vice President, American Zionist Federation (1985-1989); Board of Directors, Greater Miami Symphony (1982-1987); Vice Chairman, Urban League of Greater Miami (1983-1987); President, Civic League Miami Beach (1985-1987); Board of Governors, Barry University (1985-1986); Chairman, City of Miami Beach Hurricane Defense Committee (1978-1986); President Greater Miami chapter, Association Welfare of Soldiers in Israel (1983-1986); President President's council, Zionist Organization Am. (1983-1985); Board of Directors, Papanicolaou Cancer Research Institute, Miami (1962-1980); President, American Zionist Federation Southern Florida (1970-1973); Deputy Chairman, Democratic Midwest Conference (1958-1960); Vice Chairman, City of Miami Beach Planning Board (1953-1955) **MIL:** With, US Army (1944-1946) **CW:** Editor, Publisher Emeritus, Jewish Star-Times (2000-2003); Editor, Publisher, Jewish Herald Newspaper (1999-2000) **AW:** United Jerusalem Medal and National Honor Award, State of Israel Bonds (2012); Jerusalem 3000 Award, State of Israel (1996); Jerusalem Peace Award, State of Israel Bonds (1978) **MEM:** Greater Miami Chairman, Prime Minister's Club, State of Israel (1997-Present); Trustee, Miami Beach Chamber of Commerce

(1990-Present); Board of Directors, Miami Beach Taxpayers Association (1994-2000); Board of Directors, Miami International Press Club (1991-1999); President, Lead and Ink, Tiger Bay Club (1986-1988); Chapter President, National Association of Fund Raising Executives (1977-1978); President, Alpha Delta Sigma (1965-1967); Lodge President, B'nai B'rith (1964-1966); Chapter President, American Public Relations Association (1960-1961); Public Relations Society America; American Association of Political Consultants; Theta Omicron Pi; Omicron Delta Kappa; Zeta Beta Tau; Sigma Delta Chi; Society Professional Journalists; Investigative Reporters and Editors, Inc.; Jewish War Vets, USA

SCHNEIDER, THOMAS A., T: Surgeon (Retired) **I:** Health, Wellness and Fitness **DOB:** 12/22/1934 **PB:** St. Charles **SC:** MO/USA **PT:** Vincent Augustine Schneider; Anna Maria (Marheineke) Schneider **MS:** Married **SPN:** Joyce Elaine Diehr (June 7, 1958) **CH:** Lisa; Thomas; Dawn; Tracy **ED:** MD, Saint Louis University (1958); BS, Loras College (1954) **CT:** Diplomate, American Board of Surgery, Inc. **C:** Retired (2001); Surgeon, Private Practice, St. Charles (1963-2001); Resident in Surgery, City Hospital, City of St. Louis (1958-1963) **CR:** Medical Director, Vascular Laboratory (1991-Present); Assistant Clinical Professor, Saint Louis University (1991-Present); Director of Trauma Service, St. Joseph Hospital - St. Charles, SSM Health (1981-1991); Clinical Instructor, Saint Louis University (1966-1991) **MIL:** Major, U.S. Army (1962-1970) **MEM:** Vice President, St. Louis Surgical Society (1996-1997); President, St. Louis Vascular Society (1993-1995); Councilor, St. Louis Surgical Society (1988-1991); President, Hodgen Club (1988); Fellow, American College of Surgeons; Missouri Chapter, American College of Surgeons - Committee on Trauma; Alpha Omega Alpha Honor Medical Society **H:** Golf; Music; History **RE:** Roman Catholic **ADD:** 1793 Buckingham Green Ct, Saint Charles, MO, 63303

SCHONFELD, ESTHER, T: Attorney **I:** Law and Legal Services **CN:** Schonfeld and Goldring LLP **DOB:** 03/02/1960 **PB:** New York City **SC:** NY/USA **MS:** Married **SPN:** Benjamin Farkas (10/10/1999); Alan Seth Schonfeld (Divorced 1994) **CH:** Jeremy Adam; Alexandra; Judah Moritz Farkas; Esti Farkas (Stepchild); David Farkas (Stepchild); Paul Farka (Stepchild) **ED:** JD, Touro Law School, Summa Cum Laude (1999); BBA, The City University of New York (1981) **C:** Founding Partner, Schonfeld & Goldring LLP, Cedarhurst, NY (2007-Present); Founding Partner, Mosery & Schonfeld, PLLC, Cedarhurst, NY (2002-2007); Associate, Koopersmith & Brown, LLP, Lake Success, NY (1999-2002) **CW:** Author, "Malicious Prosecution As A Constitutional Tort: Continued Confusion And Uncertainty," Touro Law Review (1999); Editor-in-Chief, Touro Law Review (1998-1999); Author, "To Be Or Not To Be A Parent? The Search For A Solution To Custody Disputes Over Frozen Embryos," Touro Law Review (1998) **AW:** Scholarship Award, Jewish Lawyers Association of Nassau County (1997) **MEM:** Family Law Committee, Queens County Bar Association; Matrimonial Law Committee, Nassau County Bar Association; New York State Bar Association; Board Member, Jewish Lawyers Association of Nassau County **BAR:** United States Court of Federal Claims (2003); United States Court of Appeals for the District of Columbia Circuit (2003); United States Court of Appeals for the Armed Forces (2003); Supreme Court of the United States (2003); New York (2000) **H:** Travel; Piano; Cello; Literature; Art **BA:** 112 Spruce St Ste A, Schonfeld and Goldring LLP, Cedarhurst, NY, 11516 **URL:** http://www.schonfeldandgoldring.com/attorney-profiles/

SCHRAMM, JACK JOSEPH, T: Attorney **I:** Law and Legal Services **CN:** International Development Counsel, LLC **DOB:** 01/21/1932 **PB:** St. Louis **SC:** MO/USA **MS:** Married **SPN:** Dorian Meier Davis (12/29/1979) **CH:** Lori Geis; Adam Schramm; Justin Schramm; Taylor Schramm **ED:** JD, Washington University School of Law in St. Louis (1959); BA in Political Science, Colgate University, Cum Laude with Honors in Political Science (1953) **CT:** Admitted to Practice, Supreme Court of the United States (1974); Diplomate, Summer Study in Morelia, Mexico, World Learning **C:** Managing Director, International Development Counsel, LLC (2001-Present); Head, Institutional Strengthening Practice, PA Government Services, Inc. (1989-2001); Regional Administrator, United States Environmental Protection Agency (1977-1981); Lawyer, Private Practice, St. Louis, Missouri (1959-1977); Democratic Nominee, Lieutenant Governor of Missouri (1972); Member Executive Board, Missouri Governor's Advisory Council on Local Government Law (1967-1972); Chair, Municipal Corporations Committee, Missouri House of Representatives (1965-1972); Vice-chairman, Judiciary Committee, Missouri House of Representatives (1965-1972); Partner, Law Practice (1960-1977) **CR:** Senior Transboundary Water Rights Adviser to Government of Afghanistan, USAID (2011-2012); Team Leader, Assessment of U.S. Governance Assistance Program for Iraq Parliament, USAID (2011); Consultant, Formulation of Strategy to Operationalize the Reach and International Capacity of the Kansas City Port Authority to Improve the Economy of the Kansas City Region as an International Transportation Hub, Port KC (2010); Senior Legislative Adviser, Iraq International Development Counsel, USAID (2010); Legal Expert, Improvement of Legal Framework for Water Sector and Formulation of White Paper to Improve Economic Efficiency and Sub-National Management in Armenia, USAID (2005-2008); Lead Technical Specialist, Technical Assistance in the Development of Economic Incentives and Regulatory Standards, USAID, Peru (2003-2004); Team Leader, Strengthening Management Capacity in Industrial Parks, Asian Development Bank (2003-2004); Legal/Regulatory Specialist, Assessment of Regulatory Framework (Command-and-Control and Economic Incentives) for Turkmenistan, The World Bank Group (2002); Manager, Formulation of Environmental Management System for Two Cities in Lake Atitlan Bio-Region, USAID (2002); Legal Expert, Strengthening the Compliance Framework of the Pollution Levy System of Rostov Oblast, Organisation for Economic Co-operation and Development (2001-2002); Consultant, Formulation of Environmental Management System for Tarija, Bolivia, USAID (2001); Consultant, Formulation of Action Plan, Based on Economic Incentives, to Create an Urban EMS for Guatemala City, USAID (2000); Legal Expert, Formulation of Environmental Regulations and the Subsequent Design of an Integrated Command and Incentive-Based Management Pilot Program, Asian Development Bank (1996-1998); Team Leader, Development of Regulations for a National Program Integrating Command-and-Control and Incentive Mechanisms, USAID (1998-1999); Team Leader, Design of Integrated Environmental Management System, USAID, Egypt (1997-1999); Specialist, Design of Integrated Environmental Management System, USAID, Egypt (1997-1999); Consultant, Formulation of Concept Paper on the Adaptation of the "Environmental Management System" to Human Settlements in Developing Countries, USAID (1998); Team Leader, Improvements to Pollution Charge System, USAID (1997); Legal Specialist, Improvements to Pollution Charge System, USAID (1997); Legal Expert, Draft

Industrial Strategy for Egypt, USAID (1996-1997); Coordinator, Greater Rostov Environmental Strategic Action Plan, The World Bank Group (1996-1997); Concept Development Specialist, The World Bank Group, Egypt (1996); Legal Expert, Formulation of Integrated System of Pollution Control Laws, Asian Development Bank (1995-1996); Legal Expert, Integrating Environmental Control Strategies for Cities in Morocco, USAID (1994-1995); Team Leader, Team Leader, Design of Regulations to Operationalize the Philippines Management System for Urban Economic Zone (1993-1995); Legal and Institutional Expert, Legislative and Institutional Support Mission for Egypt, USAID (1992-1993); Speaker in Field **CIV:** Public Affairs Consultant, Arthur D. Little, Inc. (1973-1977); Board of Directors, Harris-Stowe College, St. Louis (1973-1976); Former President, Greater St. Louis Chapter, United Nations Association of the United States; Former President, Young Democrats of St. Louis County **MIL:** Paratrooper, 82nd Airborne Division, U.S. Army (1954-1956) **CW:** Author, "Passionate Purpose: A Global Governance Journey," New Insights Press (2016); Author, "What's Next for Afghanistan," Washington Magazine (2013); Author, "Former St. Louis Lawyer Seeks Solutions in Afghanistan," St. Louis Lawyer (2012); Author, "Election Laws that Coax Centrism Promote Political Stability," Washington University Law Magazine (2009); Author, "The Adaptation of Environmental Management Systems to Environmentally Impacted Urban Zones," Environmental Law Institute (2001); Author, "Ocean Incineration and Air Pollution," Environmental Law Institute; Contributor, Articles on Environmental Issues, Missouri Municipal Review; Member, Editorial Advisory Board, "The Environmental Forum," Environmental Law Institute **AW:** Recipient, Distinguished Law Graduate Award, Washington University in St. Louis (2017); Honoree, Professional of the Year, Cambridge Who's Who (2009); Recipient, Legislative Award, St. Louis Coalition for the Environment (1972); Recipient, Legislative Award, Sierra Club (1972); Recipient, Meritorious Public Service Award, St. Louis Globe-Democrat (1972); Recipient, Legislative Award, Missouri Conservation Federation (1971); Recipient, Special Services Award, The Missouri Bar (1968); Recipient, Certificate of Distinction for Outstanding Service in the Administration of Justice, The Bar Association of Metropolitan St. Louis (1965); Honoree, Outstanding Legislator, Eagleton Institute of Politics, Rutgers, The State University of New Jersey; Recipient, Speaker's Award for "The Outstanding First Term Democrat," Missouri House of Representatives; Recipient, Citation, President's Committee on Employment of the Handicapped, Easter Seal Society; Recipient, Citation, St. Louis County Suburban Teachers Association; Recipient, Pioneer of the Nuke Watch Award, United States Environmental Protection Agency; Honoree, AV-Rated Attorney, Martindale-Hubbell; Recipient, Carter-Tedrow Memorial Award, Washington University in St. Louis **MEM:** Missouri Bar Association, Bar Association of Metropolitan St. Louis; Associate, Environmental Law Institute; Charter Member, U.S. Senior Executive Service **BAR:** The Missouri Bar (1959) **MH:** Albert Nelson Marquis Lifetime Achievement Award (2017) **H:** Politics; Reading; Writing; Gardening **PA:** Democrat **ADD:** 9509 Mount Vernon Lndg, Alexandria, VA, 22309 **URL:** https://www.linkedin.com/in/jackschramm/

SCHRIBER, THOMAS JUDE, T: Professor Emeritus **I:** Education/Educational Services **CN:** University of Michigan **DOB:** 10/28/1935 **PB:** Flint **SC:** MI/USA **PT:** Francis Charles Schriber; Alma Marie (Jeannot) Schriber **MS:** Married **SPN:** Cornelia Ann (Sneed) Schriber (6/24/1967) **CH:** Sarah Elizabeth; John Cornelius; Maria Adams **ED:** PhD, University of Michigan (1964); Fulbright Fellow, Germany (1962-1963); National Science Foundation Fellow, University of Michigan (1959-1960, 1958-1959, 1957-1958); MA in Mathematics, University of Michigan (1959); MSE, University of Michigan (1958); BSE, Magna Cum Laude, University of Notre Dame (1957) **C:** Professor Emeritus, University of Michigan (2016-Present); Professor, Stephen M. Ross School of Business, University of Michigan, Ann Arbor, MI (1972-2016); Associate Professor, University of Michigan, Ann Arbor, MI (1969-1972); Assistant Professor, University of Michigan, Ann Arbor, MI (1966-1969); Assistant Professor and Director, Academic Computer Center, Eastern Michigan University, Ypsilanti, MI (1963-1966) **CR:** Visiting Scholar, National University of Singapore (1995); Visiting Scholar, Swiss Federal Technical University, Zurich, Switzerland (1987); Visiting Scholar, Stanford University, Palo Alto CA (1972-1973); Founder and Instructor, Two-Week Business Faculty Summer Programs in Computing, University of Michigan, Funded by IBM (1969-1973); Founder and Instructor, Discrete-Event Simulation Courses, Engineering Summer Conferences, University of Michigan (1969-1992); Various Consulting Engagements in Discrete-Event Simulation, Including General Motors, Ford Motor, Exxon Production Research, Occidental Petroleum, and the Wolverine Software Corporation; Participant, US-USSR Joint Science and Technology Exchange Agreement (1977-1980) **CW:** Author, "An Introduction to Simulation Using GPSS/H" (1991); Co-Editor, "Proceedings of the 1976 Bicentennial Winter Simulation Conference" (1976); Author, "Simulation Using GPSS" (1974); Editor, "FORTRAN Applications in Business Administration," Three-Volume Series (1969-1971); Author, "FORTRAN Case Studies for Business Applications" (1970); Author, "Fundamentals of Flowcharting" (1969); Many Articles Published Over the Years **AW:** Pioneer of Simulation, National Science Foundation (2013); Titan of Simulation, Winter Simulation Conference (2009); 40-Year Landmark Paper Award, Winter Simulation Conference (2007); Winter Simulation Conference Board of Directors Award for Distinguished Service (2007); Lifetime Professional Achievement Award, INFORMS College of Simulation (2001); Distinguished Service Award, College of Simulation, INFORMS (1996); Fellow of the Decision Sciences Institute (1979) **MH:** Albert Nelson Marquis Lifetime Achievement Award (2017) **H:** Travel; Grandchildren; Reading; Socializing; Continuing Developments in Computing **PA:** Independent **RE:** Roman Catholic **ADD:** 2116 Dorset Rd, Ann Arbor, MI, 48104-2604 **URL:** http://www.bus.umich.edu/FacultyBios/CV/schriber.pdf

SCHRIESHEIM, CHESTER ARTHUR, T: Distinguished Professor of Management **I:** Education/Educational Services **CN:** University of Miami **DOB:** 11/10/1946 **PB:** New York City **SC:** NY/USA **PT:** Frank Henry Schriesheim; Eugenia Sophia (Halley) Schriesheim **MS:** Married **SPN:** Linda Mary Shea (9/4/1982); Janet L. Fulk (12/26/1970, Divorced 1982) **CH:** Syle Richard; Joseph Frank **ED:** PhD, Ohio State University (1978); MBA, Michigan State University (1968); BS, Michigan State University (1967); AAS, State University of New York, Farmingdale (1965) **C:** Director, PhD Progressive Program in Business Administration, University of Miami (1988-Present); Distinguished Professor of Management, University of Miami (1986-Present); Professor of Management, University of Florida, Gainesville, FL (1982-1986); Associate Professor, University of Southern California, Los Angeles, CA (1978-1982); Assistant Professor, Kent State University (1976-1978) **CW:** Editorial Board, Journal of Organization Change Management (1987-Present); Editorial Board, Leadership Quarterly (1988-Present); Editorial Board, Technical Report Series (1980-Present); Editorial Board, Journal Business Research (1978-Present); Editorial Board, Journal of Management (1982-1985); Special Associate Editor, Journal of Business Research (1982-1983); Editorial Board, Management Science (1980); Editorial Board, Academy Management Journal (1979-1985); Co-Author, Orlando Behling, "Organizational Behavior: Theory, Research and Application" (1976); Contributing Author, Howard Wicker and John Minion, "Managing for Profit: A Simulation" (1974); Author, "The Introduction to Business Game" (1971); Contributor, Articles to Professional Journals **AW:** Lifetime Achievement Award, Research Methods Division, Academy of Management (2017); Fellow, American Psychological Association (1986); Fellow, Southern Management Association (1995) **MEM:** Academy of Management; American Psychological Association; American Sociological Association; Decision Sciences Institute; Institute of Management Sciences; Industrial Relations Research Association; Phi Kappa Phi; Beta Gamma Sigma; Alpha Zeta; Phi Theta Kappa **MH:** Albert Nelson Marquis Lifetime Achievement Award (2017) **H:** Swimming; Tennis; Computers **PA:** Independent **RE:** Catholic **BA:** 5250 University Drive, School of Business, Management Department, 414D Jenkins Building, Coral Gables, FL, 33146 **ADD:** 6200 SW 123rd Ter, Miami, FL, 33156

SCHRODER, WILLIAM HENRY, T: Member Manager **I:** Law and Legal Services **CN:** Schroder Partners LC **DOB:** 04/10/1941 **PB:** Atlanta, Georgia **SC:** United States of America **PT:** William Henry Schroder; Mary Elizabeth Barge Schroder **MS:** M **SPN:** Lynn Petters Cochran **CH:** Mary Catherine; Eileen Elizabeth; William Henry **ED:** JD, University of Virginia Law School (1966); BA in Economics, University of Notre Dame (1963) **C:** International Centre for Dispute Resolution's Standing National Panel of Mediators and Standing National Panel of Arbitrators, American Arbitration Association (1979-2018); Member-Manager, Schroder Partners, LLC (1995-2018); ADR Counsel for Florida and Georgia, Rogers Towers, P.A. (1993-1995); Senior Partner, Schroder and Murrell (1988-1993); Capital Partner for Southeast USA, Barnett and Alagia (1985-1988); Senior Partner, Killorin and Schroder (1978-1985); Principal, Law Offices of William H. Schroder (1976-1978); Senior Partner, Schroder Nicholson & Meals (1975-1976); Litigation Partner, Troutman Sanders (1969-1975); Associate, Troutman Sanders (1966-1969) **CR:** National Academy of Distinguished Neutrals (2009-2012); Georgia Academy of Mediators & Arbitrators (2008-2012); Georgia Office of Dispute Resolution for Court-Connected Arbitration, Early Neutral Evaluation, & Mediation (1995-2012); President, Georgia Arbitrators Forum (2004-2005); Internet Moderator, Lexis Counsel Connect, Law Journal, National ADR Forum (1994-1999); Board of Ethics, Fulton County (1985-1998); President, Atlanta Bar Foundation (1995-1998); President, Atlanta Dispute Resolution Lawyers (1994-1996); President, Atlanta Bar Association (1978-1979); President, Atlanta Council of Younger Lawyers (1974-1975) **CIV:** Life Member, Advisory Board, Winship Cancer Institute **MIL:** Georgia Army National Guard (1965-1971) **CW:** Internet ADR Forum Moderator, Lexis Counsel Connect/Law Journal EXTRA's National ADR Forum (1997-1999);

Internet ADR Forum Moderator, Lexis Counsel Connect/Law Journal EXTRA's Georgia ADR Forum (1994-1999); Speaker, "Effective and Ethical Mediation in the Courts," Atlanta Bar Association (1998); Speaker, State Bar of Georgia, ADR Institute (1996); Speaker, "ADR Veterans' Lawyering Strategies," Atlanta Bar Association (1995); Speaker, "ADR on Both Sides of the Atlantic," Palm Beach, FL (1994); Author, "Private ADR May Offer Increased Confidentiality," The National Law Journal (1994); Author, "Merlin is Replacing Sir Galahad," The Financial Times of London (1994); Speaker, "Private ADR in Florida," Jacksonville, FL (1993) **AW:** 42nd Consecutive Year of Highest AV-Preeminent Rating by Peers, Martindale-Hubbell (1977-2018); Recipient, Atlanta Bar Association's Distinguished and Sustained Service Award (1997); AV-Preeminent Rating, Martindale Judicial Edition; Top 1% of America's Most Honored Professionals; Best Lawyers in America; Best Law Firms **MEM:** Honorary Life Member, Piedmont Driving Club **BAR:** State Bar of Florida (1994); U.S. Supreme Court (1973); U.S. Court of Appeals for the Eleventh Circuit (1966); U.S. District Court for the Northern District of Georgia (1966); State Bar of Georgia (1965) **MH:** 2018 Albert Nelson Marquis Who's Who Lifetime Achievement Award **H:** Ocean Sailing; Woodworking; Woodturning **PA:** Independent **RE:** Catholic **BA:** 1201 Peachtree ST NE, Suite 200, Schroder Partners LC, Atlanta, GA, 30361 **URL:** https://www.martindale.com/atlanta/georgia/william-henry-schroder-856119-a/

SCHWARTZ, CHARLES WALTER, **T:** Lawyer **I:** Law and Legal Services **CN:** Skadden, Arps, Slate, Meagher & Flom LLP **DOB:** 12/27/1953 **PB:** Brenham **SC:** TX/USA **PT:** Walter C. Schwartz; Annie Schwartz **ED:** LLM, Harvard University, Cambridge, MA (1980); JD, University of Texas (1977); MA, University of Texas (1977); BS, University of Texas (1975) **CT:** Board Certified, Civil Appellate Law, Texas Board of Legal Specialization **C:** Partner, Skadden, Arps, Slate, Meagher & Flom LLP (2003-2016); Partner, Vinson & Elkins LLP (1986-2003); Associate, Vinson & Elkins LLP, Houston, TX (1980-1986); Law Clerk, Fifth Circuit, U.S. Court of Appeals, Austin, TX (1977-1979); Professor, University of Houston Law Center **CR:** Fellow, American College of Trial Lawyers; Life Benefactor Fellow, American Bar Foundation; Sustaining Life Fellow, Texas Bar Foundation; Fellow, College of the State Bar of Texas; Fellow, Houston Bar Foundation **CIV:** Regent, Texas A&M University Systems (2013-Present); Vice Chair, Board Lease, University Lands for the State of Texas (2013); Texas Committee for Lawyer Discipline (2008-2014) **CW:** Contributor, Articles, Law Review **AW:** A/V Preeminent Rating, Martindale-Hubbell; Recognition, Chambers and Partners **MEM:** Immediate Past Chairman, State Bar of Texas (2003-2004); Chairman, State Bar of Texas (2002-2003); Executive Committee, State Bar of Texas (2001-2004); Board of Directors, State Bar of Texas (2000-2004); Chairman, Grievance Committee, State Bar of Texas (1993-1999); ABA; Trustee, Center for American International Law; Texas Center for Legal Ethics and Professionals; Regent, Texas Agricultural and Mechanical University Systems; Director, Texas Law Review Association; Life Member, American Law Institute; The Bar Association of The Fifth Federal Circuit **BAR:** State of New York (2007); State of Texas (1977) **MH:** Albert Nelson Marquis Lifetime Achievement Award (2017) **ADD:** 2154 Chilton Road, Houston, TX, 77019

SCHWARTZ, SORELL L., **T:** Professor Emeritus **I:** Education/Educational Services **CN:** Georgetown University Medical Center **DOB:** 09/13/1937 **PB:** Buffalo **SC:** NY/USA **PT:** Jacob M. Schwartz; Rosalind (Greenberg) Schwartz **MS:** Married **SPN:** Marsha (Kohlenstein) Schwartz (6/9/1963) **CH:** Joanne Beth Gladden; Rebecca Lynn Perlman **ED:** PhD in Pharmacology, Medical College of Virginia (Now School of Medicine, Virginia Commonwealth University) (1963); BS in Pharmacy, University Medical (1959) **C:** Professor Emeritus, Pharmacology, School of Medicine, Georgetown University (1998-Present); Senior Pharmacology Advisor, Center for Biologics Evaluation and Research, Office of Biostatistic and Epidemiology, U.S. Food and Drug Administration (2011-2014); Head, Toxicology and Applied Pharmacokinetics Program, School of Medicine, Georgetown University (1988-1998); Professor, Pharmacology, School of Medicine, Georgetown University (1976-1998); Associate Professor, Pharmacology, School of Medicine, Georgetown University (1968-1976); Head, Pharmacology Division, School of Medicine, Georgetown University (1968); Pharmacologist, U.S. Naval Medical Research Institute, Bethesda, MD (1963-1966) **CR:** Chair, Institutional Review Board, Georgetown University Medical Center (1969-Present); Clinical Scholar, Center for Clinical Bioethics (1992-1998); Naval Investigational Drug Review Board (1964-1968); Chair, Public Information Committee, Federation of American Societies for Experimental Biology; Founding Secretary, Academy of Toxicological Sciences **CIV:** Montgomery County, Maryland Overdose and Substance Abuse Intervention team (2018-Present); Sexual Assault Response Team, Montgomery County, Maryland (2017-Present); Legislative Committee, Victim Service Committee, Maryland Human Trafficking Task Force, Montgomery County (2015-Present); Criminal Justice Coordinating Commission, Montgomery County, Maryland (2012-Present); Chair, Montgomery County, Maryland Victim Services Advisory Board (2011-Present); Victim Advocate, Domestic Violence Court, Maryland Victim Assistance and Sexual Assault Program, Montgomery County (2009-Present); Child Advocate, National CASA Association, Program of Montgomery County, Maryland (2000-Present); President, Congregation Har Shalom (2015-2017); Advocate for Homeless, Hand-to-Hand, Washington, DC (1990-2000) **MIL:** Lieutenant Commander, U.S. Navy, Vietnam (1963-1966) **CW:** Contributor, Chapters, Books; Contributor, More Than 150 scientific Papers, Professional Journals, Professional Meetings, Software **MEM:** American Society for Pharmacology and Experimental Therapeutics; Society of Toxicology; Society for Risk Analysis; International Society of Pharmacometrics **MH:** Albert Nelson Marquis Lifetime Achievement Award (2017) **H:** Still photography and photo artistry **RE:** Jewish **BA:** 3900 Reservoir Road NW, Georgetown University Medical Center, Washington, DC, 20007 **ADD:** 313 Oak Knoll Drive, Rockville, MD, 20850 **URL:** https://www.linkedin.com/in/sorell-l-schwartz-a4167a17

SCHWEGLER, NANCY, **T:** Librarian (Retired) **I:** Library Management/Library Services **DOB:** 01/22/1946 **PB:** Brooklyn **SC:** NY/USA **PT:** Richard Donald Newman; Beatrice Ella Stirba **MS:** Married **SPN:** Robert Andrew Schwegler (4/6/1968) **CH:** Brian Alexander; Christopher Robert; Ashley Marie **ED:** MLIS, University of Rhode Island (1991); BA, Hope College (1967) **C:** Children's Librarian, Bradley Hospital, Lifespan (1988-Present); Children's Librarian, East Greenwich Free Library (1984-1989); Cataloger, University of Cincinnati (1972-1973); Astronomy Librarian, University of Cincinnati (1972-1973); Children's Librarian, Watertown Free Public Library (1971-1972); Library Assistant, Art Library, The University of Chicago (1968-1971) **CW:** Author, "Rhode Island Parents' Paper, Writing in Depth" (2004); Author, "Choices: Voices Values and Writing Strategies" (2006); Contributor, Articles, Newspapers; Contributor, Articles, Professional Journals **MEM:** American Library Association, Delta Phi Delta Dance Fraternity, Inc.; Beta Phi Mu; The Honor Society of Phi Kappa Phi **MH:** Albert Nelson Marquis Lifetime Achievement Award (2017) **H:** Lighthouse preservation advocacy; International adoption advocacy; Watercolor painting **RE:** Reformed Church Of America **ADD:** 83 Darling Street, Warwick, RI, 02886

SCOTT, BONNIE, **T:** Transitional Senior Minister **I:** Religious **CN:** United Church on the Green **PB:** New York City **SC:** NY/USA **PT:** Prof. Robert C. L. Scott; Atty. Joan Keyes Scott **MS:** Single **CH:** Barton Allen; Josua Allen; Jenyu Allen; Scott Jeliaek, MD; Mark Jeliaek **ED:** Doctorate in Ministry, Andover-Newton Theological School, Newton, MA (1983); MA in Religion, Yale University (1969); BA, Lake Forest College (1967) **CT:** Ordained Minister, New Haven Association (2015-Present); Certified Supervisor, Andover Newton Theological School (1982-Present); Ordained Minister, Massachusetts Conference United Church of Christ (1979-2015); Certificate in Psychoanalytic Psychotherapy, Boston Institute for Psychotherapy (1989); Ordained Minister, The United Church of Christ (1977) **C:** Transitional Senior Minister, The United Church on the Green, New Haven, CT (2014-Present); Member, Yale Religious Ministries, Chaplains Office, Yale University, New Haven, CT (2014-Present); Counselor, Private Practice, Newton, MA (2010-Present); Psychotherapist, Private Practice, Newton, MA (2010-Present); Spiritual Director, Private Practice, Newton, MA (2010-Present); Pastoral Formation Guide, Metropolitan Boston Association, Massachusetts Conference United Church of Christ (2005-Present); Counselor, Private Practice, Wellesley, MA (2001-Present); Psychotherapist, Private Practice, Wellesley, MA (2001-Present); Spiritual Director, Private Practice, Wellesley, MA (2001-Present); Counselor, Private Practice, Spring Lake, MI (1986-Present); Psychotherapist, Private Practice, Spring Lake, MI (1986-Present); Spiritual Director, Private Practice, Spring Lake, MI (1986-Present); Interim Associate Pastor, Saint Pauls, Chicago, IL (2013-2014); Interim Minister, Youth Faith Formation, Saint Pauls, Chicago, IL (2013); Supervisor, Group and Individual Therapies, The Weaver Center - Metrowest Greater Boston Help for ADHD (2005-2010); Assistant Director, The Weaver Center - Metrowest Greater Boston Help for ADHD, Wayland, MA (2004-2010); Supervisor, The Weaver Center - Metrowest Greater Boston Help for ADHD, Wayland, MA (2004-2010); Minister-at-large, Wellesley Hills Congregational Church, Wellesley, MA (2001-2012); Interim Minister, West Stockbridge, MA (1994); Supervisor, Group and Individual Therapies, Massachusetts (1987-1997); Psychotherapist, Boston Institute for Psychotherapy (1986-1989); Senior Pastor, Newton Highlands Congregational Church, Newton, MA (1982-1986); Certified Supervisor, Newton Highlands Congregational Church, Newton, MA (1982-1986); Chaplain, Andover-Newton Theological School, Newton, MA (1981-1986); Counselor, Andover-Newton Theological School, Newton, MA (1981-1986); Adjunct Faculty, Andover-Newton Theological School, Newton, MA (1981-1986); Co-pastor, Newton Highlands Congregational Church, Newton, MA (1979-1982); Preacher, The United Church of Chester, Chester,

CT (1977-1979); Administrator, The United Church of Chester, Chester, CT (1977-1979); Counselor, The United Church of Chester, Chester, CT (1977-1979); Teacher, The United Church of Chester, Chester, CT(1977-1979); Associate Pastor, The United Church of Chester, Chester, CT (1974-1977) **CR:** Speaker, Conferences on Learning Disabilities (2006-Present); Teacher, The Great Books Program (1998-2001); Trainer, The Great Books Program (1998-2001); Vice President, Wellesley High School PTSO; Vice President, Parent-teacher Organization, Lake Hills Elementary School **CIV:** Board Member, Mary Wade Home; Board Member, Endowment for the Advancement of Psychotherapy, Harvard University; Executive Committee, Endowment for the Advancement of Psychotherapy, Harvard University; Head, Finance Committee, Endowment for the Advancement of Psychotherapy, Harvard University; Psychological Testing Task Force for Candidates for Ordination Pastoral Formation Guide, Massachusetts Conference United Church of Christ; The Metropolitan Boston Committee on Ministry, United Church of Christ; Registrar, Task Force on Spirituality, Boarding School Sector, Emma Willard School; Alumni Council, Emma Willard School; Board of Governors, Opportunity International **CW:** Co-author, "A new Model for Developing Psychologically Healthy Pastors; Pastoral Formation: A Pilot Project for In-Care Students in the United Church Of Christ in Massachusetts," Journal of Counseling Psychology (2008); Author, "The Pregnant Hour: the Psychological Effects of the Pregnant Therapist in the Holding Environment," How to work with Patients while pregnancy is 'in the room' (1989); Author, "One Co-Pastorate: A Viable Form of Ministry", Andover-Newton Theological School (1983); Author, "The Theological and Philosophical Assumptions of Martin Luther King, Jr's Ethics," Lake Forest College (1967) **AW:** Alumni Award for Outstanding Professional Achievement, Emma Willard School (2008); Scott Award in Religion and Philosophy, Lake Forest College (1967) **MEM:** Committee on Ministry, New Haven Association, The Connecticut Conference United Church of Christ; Development Committee, The Mary Wade Community; Committee on Ministry for United Church of Christ, New Haven Association; Junior League of Greater New Haven; American Psychological Association; American Group Psychotherapy Association; Massachusetts Mental Health Counselors Association, Inc. **MH:** Albert Nelson Marquis Lifetime Achievement Award (2017) **H:** Travel; Working out; Reading; Cooking **ADD:** 323 Temple St, The United Church on the Green, New Haven, CT, 06511

SCOTT, DAVID RODICK, T: Educator, Lawyer (Retired) **I:** Law and Legal Services **DOB:** 12/30/1938 **PB:** Philadelphia **SC:** PA/USA **PT:** Ernest Scott; Lydia Wister (Tunis) Scott **MS:** Married **SPN:** Ruth Erskine Wardle (8/20/1966) **CH:** Cintra W.; D. Rodman (Deceased 2005) **ED:** JD, Harvard University (1965); MA, Cambridge University (1962); AB, Harvard University, Magna Cum Laude (1960) **CT:** The District of Columbia (1977); United States Court of Appeals District of Columbia Circuit (1977); Supreme Court of the United States (1977); Pennsylvania (1966); United States District Court Eastern District of Pennsylvania (1966); United States Court of Appeals for the Third Circuit (1966) **C:** University Counsel, Rutgers, The State University of New Jersey, New Brunswick, NJ (1984-2004); Chief Counsel, Office of Government Ethics, Washington, D.C. (1980-1984); Acting Director, Office of Government Ethics, Washington, D.C. (1980-1984); Senior Trial Attorney, Criminal Division, U.S. Department of Justice, Washington, D.C. (1976-1980); Associate, Pepper, Hamilton & Scheetz, Philadelphia, PA (1972-1976); Assistant District Attorney, City of Philadelphia (1970-1972); Associate, Pepper, Hamilton & Scheetz, Philadelphia, PA (1966-1969); Law Clerk to Associate Justice, Supreme Court of Pennsylvania, Philadelphia, PA (1965-1966) **CR:** Instructor, Faculty of the Arts and Sciences, Rutgers, The State University of New Jersey (2004); Adjunct Professor, Rutgers Law School, Camden, NJ (2004); Acting Director, U.S. Office of Government Ethics (1982-1983); Lecturer in Law, Catholic University of America, Washington, D.C. (1977-1981); Lecturer, Institute of Paralegal Training, Philadelphia, PA (1970-1974); Lecturer in Field **CIV:** Princeton Day School (2006-Present); Trustee, Princeton Area Community Foundation, Inc. (2005-Present); Planned Parenthood Association of Mercer Area Inc. (2014-2015); International Tennis Club of the United States (2004-2012); Planned Parenthood Association of Mercer Area Inc. (2004-2012): Trustee, Princeton Area Community Foundation, Inc. (1991-2002); Trustee, United Way of Greater Mercer County (1990-2005); Board of Managers, Episcopalian Academy, Merion, PA (1970-1974); Board Member, Princeton Public Library Foundation **CW:** Contributor, Chapters, Textbooks; Contributor, Articles, Professional Journals **AW:** Keasbey Scholarship (1960-1962) **MEM:** Board of Directors, National Association of College and University Attorneys (1993-1996); Head, New Jersey Chapter, American Friends of Cambridge University (1987-1993); Pennsylvania Bar Association; The District of Columbia Bar **H:** Tennis; Skiing; Additional sports; Travel; Reading **ADD:** 8 Governors Ln, Princeton, NJ, 08540

SCOTT, ROSA M., T: Artist, Educator **I:** Education/Educational Services **CN:** Montauk School **DOB:** 04/12/1937 **PB:** East Hampton **SC:** NY/USA **PT:** James Alexander; Victoria (Square) Nicholson **MS:** Widowed **SPN:** Warner Bruce Scott (8/3/1985); Frank Albert Hanna (4/1/1957, Divorced 3/1985) **CH:** Frank Albert Hanna, III (Deceased) **ED:** BA, Mary Baldwin University (1992); AA, Dabney S. Lancaster Community College (1989) **C:** Teacher, After-School Program, Montauk School (2014-Present); Substitute Teacher, Lexington, VA Schools (1994-Present); Lead Teacher, After-School Program, Springs School (2011-2014); Substitute Teacher, East Hampton School (2000-2003); Lead Teacher, After-School Program, Springs School (2004-2005); Substitute Teacher, Springs School (2000-2003); Lead Teacher, After-School Program, Springs School (2000-2002); Lead Teacher, Suffolk Community College Child Care Center, Riverhead, NY (1999); Lead Teacher, East Hampton Day Care (1992-1994, 1997-1998); Cashier, Brook's Pharmacy, East Hampton, NY (1992); Clerk, Brook's Pharmacy, East Hampton, NY (1992); Secretary, Frank Hanna's Cleaning Company, East Hampton, NY (1962-1977); Cosmetologist, Rosa's Beauty Shop, East Hampton, NY (1962-1968) **CR:** Substitute Teacher, East Hampton School (1996-1997, 2000-2004); Secretary, Lylburn Downing Community Center, Inc., Lexington (1985-1992); Arts And Crafts Tutor, Supervisor East Hampton Town Youth After-School Program (1996-2011) **CIV:** President, Rockbridge Garden Club, Lexington, VA (1996); Co-Organizer, Virginia Cooperative Extension, Garden Clubs, Lexington, VA (1995); Member, Board of Directors, Rockbridge Area President Homes (1996); Fine Arts In Rockbridge (1985-1992); Friends of Lime Kiln Society (1985-1992) **AW:** Honorable Mention, Guild Hall, East Hampton, NY (2014) **MEM:** Co-Chair, East Hampton Town Anti-Bias Task Force (2013-2015); Board Member, East Hampton Artist Alliance (2012-Present); President, East Hampton Artist Alliance (2014-Present); Guild Hall; East End Arts Council; Receptionist, Montauk Artists Association (2003-Present); President, Montauk Artists Association (2010-Present); Artists Alliance of East Hampton (2014-2015); Vice President, Long Island Black Artist Association (2000-2005); President, Long Island Black Artist Association (2006-2011); Rockbridge Arts Guild **H:** Art; Reading; Theater; Tennis **ADD:** PO Box 1265, East Hampton, NY, 11937

SCOTT, STANLEY D., T: General Partner **I:** Business Management/Business Services **CN:** 145 Hudson Street Associates **DOB:** 11/02/1926 **PB:** Hudson County **SC:** NJ/USA **PT:** Stanley DeForest Scott; Anne Marie (Volk) Scott **MS:** Married **SPN:** Mary Elizabeth Forbes Hazard (12/30/1953) **ED:** BA, University of Southern California, Los Angeles, CA (1950) **C:** Chairman, President, S.D. Scott Printing Co., Inc., New York City, NY (1956-1992); General Manager, Alfred Scott Pubs., New York City, NY (1951-1956); General Partner, 145 Hudson St. Associates **CIV:** Co-Chairman, Museum and Art Committee, Fraunces Tavern Museum (1973-1987, 1998-2007); Former Member, Board of Directors, Business Relocation Committee; Former Member, Mayor's Industry Advisory Committee; Associate, The John Carter Brown Library **MIL:** U.S. Naval Reserve (1944-1946) **MEM:** Council, American Museum in Britain, Bath, England (1986-Present); National Trust for Scotland; French Heritage Society; The Frick Collection; The Friends of Canterbury Cathedral in the United States; Patron, Royal Academy of America; American Antiquarian Society; New-York Historical Society; The Morgan Library & Museum; The Metropolitan Museum of Art; The English-Speaking Union of the United States; The Royal Oak Foundation; Sir John Soane's Museum Foundation; The Museum of Modern Art; Advisory Committee, Mount Vernon Ladies' Association; The American-Scottish Foundation; International Council, World Monuments Fund; The American Trust For The British Library; Patron, New York Philharmonic; Honorary Past President, Sons of the Revolution in the State of New York; Former Trustee, American Numismatic Society; Patron, Carnegie Hall Society, Inc.; The Church Club of New York; The Union Club Of The City Of New York; Knickerbocker Club; The Grolier Club of New York; St. George's Society of New York; The Pilgrims of the United States; Council, General Society of Colonial Wars; The Society of Mayflower Descendants in the State of New York **MH:** Albert Nelson Marquis Lifetime Achievement Award (2017); Distinguished Humanitarian (2017) **H:** International travel; Photography; Rare ancient coin collector **PA:** Republican **RE:** Episcopalian **ADD:** 145 Hudson St Apt 10, New York, NY, 10013

SEABOLT, RICHARD, T: Lawyer **I:** Law and Legal Services **CN:** Duane Morris LLP **DOB:** 08/28/1949 **PB:** Chicago **SC:** IL/USA **ED:** JD, University California, Hastings (1975); BGS with distinction, University Michigan (1971) **C:** Partner, Duane Morris LLP, San Francisco (2006-Present); Co-head, Commercial Securities Antitrust Litigation Division Trial Group **CR:** Member, California Civil Jury Instructor Advisory Committee **CW:** Author, Matthew Bender Practice Guides, California Pretrial Civil Procedure and Civil Discovery (2004) **MEM:** President, Board of Governors, Association Business Trial Lawyers (2013); Chair, Litigation Section, State Bar of California (2006) **BA:** One Market Plaza, Suite 2200, San Francisco, CA, 94105-1127 **ADD:** One Market Plaza, Suite 2200, Duane Morris LLP, Spear Tower, San Francisco, CA, 94105-1127

SEAVER, ELIZABETH MARY, T: Music Educator (Retired) **I:** Education/Educational Services **DOB:** 11/19/1936 **SC:** IA/USA **PT:** Lewis Joseph

Novak; Annie Eva Novak **MS:** Widowed **SPN:** Robert Nicolson Seaver (3/22/1975, Deceased) **CH:** Shelly Ann; Shawn Keith **ED:** MA in Music Education, University of Michigan (1969); MusB, Alverna College, Milwaukee, WI (1967) **CT:** Certified Music Teacher, State of Florida; Certified in Music, State of Iowa **C:** Music Teacher, Orange County Schools, Orlando, FL (1974-2000); Adjunct Teacher, Cocoa Campus, Brevard Community College (Now Eastern Florida State College), Florida (1972-1974); Music Teacher, Tama Community Schools, Iowa (1970-1972); Music Teacher, North Winneshiek Community School, Decorah, IA (1969-1970); Adjunct Teacher, Luther College, Decorah, IA (1969-1970); Music Teacher, St. William School in Chicago, Chicago Catholic Diocese Schools (1964-1968); Music Teacher, Chicago Catholic Diocese Schools, Glenview, IL (1959-1964) **CR:** Accompanist, Brevard Community Chorale, Cocoa, FL (1972-1974); Supervisor, Music Education, Chicago Catholic Schools (1967-1968); Accompanist, Supervisor, Chicago Catholic Teachers Group (1965-1967) **CIV:** Member, Bell Choir, St. Mary Magdalen Church, Florida (2005-Present); Volunteer, Supporter, Special Olympics (1990-2006); Mentor, Piano **CW:** Compiler, Music Works, PTA School Programs (1983-2000) **AW:** Inductee, National Honorary Music Society, Chi Chapter, Pi Kappa Lambda, University of Michigan (1969); Fellowship for Music Administration and Supervision, University of Michigan (1968-1969) **MEM:** National Council of Catholic Women; Orange County Retired Educators Association; Pulashek Museum; National Down Syndrome Society; National Retired Teachers Association **MH:** Albert Nelson Marquis Lifetime Achievement Award (2017) **ADD:** 1206 Winterberry Ln Unit 147, Fern Park, FL, 32730

SEEFF, LEONARD B., T: Hepatology Consultant **I:** Medicine & Health Care **CN:** Einstein Healthcare Network **DOB:** 02/10/1936 **PB:** Johannesburg **SC:** South Africa **PT:** Harry Seeff; Hanny Seeff **MS:** Married **SPN:** Lynn Gerber; Adele F. Simler (12/20/1959, Divorced 7/1994) **CH:** Amanda Wynne Charny; Laura Claire Searles; Daniel Brian **ED:** MB, BChir, University of the Witwatersrand, Johannesburg (1961) **C:** Hepatology Consultant, Einstein Healthcare Network (2014-Present); Hepatology Consultant, U.S. Food and Drug Administration (2010-2013); Senior Scientist, Hepatitis C Research, The National Institute of Diabetes and Digestive and Kidney Diseases, NIH (1998-2009); Chief, Gastroenterology/Hepatology/ Nutrition Section, Washington DC VA Medical Center, U.S. Department of Veterans Affairs (1979-1998); Co-director, Washington DC VA Medical Center, U.S. Department of Veterans Affairs (1985-1998); Co-director, Gastroenterology and Hepatology Training Program, Georgetown University (1985-1998); Assistant Chief, Medical Service, Washington DC VA Medical Center, U.S. Department of Veterans Affairs (1971-1979); Resident, Washington DC VA Medical Center, U.S. Department of Veterans Affairs (1966-1977); Assistant Chief, Hepatology Section, VA Boston Healthcare System, U.S. Department of Veterans Affairs (1969-1971); Liver & Metabolic Research Associate, Washington DC VA Medical Center, U.S. Department of Veterans Affairs (1967-1968); Intern, Mount Sinai Hospital, Sinai Health System, Chicago, IL (1964-1965); Resident, The Coronation Hospital (Now Rahima Moosa Mother and Child Hospital), University of the Witwatersrand, Johannesburg (1963-1964); Resident, Johannesburg General Hospital (Now Charlotte Maxeke Johannesburg Academic Hospital), University of the Witwatersrand, Johannesburg (1963-1964); Intern, The Coronation Hospital (Now Rahima Moosa Mother and Child Hospital), University of the Witwatersrand, Johannesburg (1961-1963); Intern, Johannesburg General Hospital (Now Charlotte Maxeke Johannesburg Academic Hospital), University of the Witwatersrand, Johannesburg (1961-1963) **CIV:** Member, Abstract Review on Hepatitis C, Epidemiology, American Association for the Study of Liver Diseases (2010-Present); Data Quality Monitoring Board, Study on Validation of Serum Markers for the Early Detection of Hepatocellular Carcinoma, National Cancer Institute, NIH (2005-Present); Chair, Abstract Review on Hepatitis C, Epidemiology, American Association for the Study of Liver Diseases (2007-2009); External Advisory Board, Study on Functional Genomics and HCV-associated Liver Disease, National Institute on Drug Abuse, NIH (2003-2009); Advisor on Hepatitis, World Federation of Hemophilia, U.S. Food and Drug Administration (2001-2008); Consultant, Various Branches, U.S. Food and Drug Administration (1995-2009); Special Government Employee, U.S. Food and Drug Administration (1995-2009); Data Monitoring Committee, Nadolol for Prevention of Variceal Bleeding, The National Institute of Diabetes and Digestive and Kidney Diseases, NIH (1993-1996); Data Monitoring Committee, Thymosin Treatment for Chronic Hepatitis C, The National Institute of Diabetes and Digestive and Kidney Diseases, NIH (1991-1996); AIDS Protocol and Data Monitoring Policy Board, Liver Tissue Procurement and Distribution System, The National Institute of Diabetes and Digestive and Kidney Diseases, National Heart, Lung and Blood Institute, NIH (1987-1995); Ad Hoc Committee on Viral Hepatitis, Expert Group on Viral Hepatitis, Information Transfer Program, Lister Hill National Center for Biomedical Communications, U.S. National Library of Medicine (1986); Hepatology Consultant, NIH (1984-1998); Hepatology Consultant, District of Columbia General Hospital (1974-1984); Coordinator, Physical Diagnosis Course, Georgetown University (1975-1982); Policy Board, Post-Transfusion Hepatitis Reduction Study, The American National Red Cross (1975-1978) **AW:** Honoree, Best Doctors in America (2005-2006, 2009-Present); Grantee, Hoechst-Roussel Pharmaceuticals (Now Sanofi) (1993-Present); Distinguished Service Award, American Association for the Study of Liver Diseases (2005); Director's Group Award, NIH (2005); Lifetime Achievement Award, Vietnam Veterans of America (2002); Special Award for Outstanding Research and Contribution to Clinical Biochemistry, National Academy of Clinical Biochemistry, American Association of Clinical Chemistry (1999); Grantee, Natural History Study of Post Transfusion Non A, Non B Hepatitis, National Heart, Lung, and Blood Institute, NIH (1987-1998); Grantee, Long-term Follow-up of Air-Force Recruits with Hepatitis C Virus Infection, National Institutes of Allergy and Diseases, NIH (1995-1996); Grantee, Long-term Follow-up of Air-Force Recruits with Hepatitis C Virus Infection, National Cancer Institute, NIH (1994-1995); Grantee, ICN Pharmaceuticals, Inc. (1992-1993, 1995); Honoree, Teacher of the Year, George Washington University School of Medicine (1993); Vicennial Gold Medal, Georgetown University (1991); Grantee, Veterans Administration Merit Review, U.S. Department of Veterans Affairs (1984-1988); Gastroenterology Association of Jamaica Award, Wisconsin Gastroenterology Association (1987); Korean Society of Gastroenterology Award, Korean Gastroenterology Association (1986); Grantee, Yellow Fever Vaccine Study, National Cancer Institute, NIH (1984-1985); Elvehjem Memorial Award, Wisconsin Society of Internal Medicine (1980); Fellow, Mount Sinai Hospital, Sinai Health System, Chicago, IL (1965-1966); Fellow, Washington DC VA Medical Center, U.S. Department of Veterans Affairs (1965-1966); Fellow, American College of Gastroenterology; Fellow, American Association for the Study of Liver Diseases; Grantee, Lamivudine for Treatment of Chronic Hepatitis B, GlaxoSmithKline plc.; Grantee, Intron A Plus Ribavirin for Treatment of Chronic Hepatitis C, Schering-Plough Research Institute; Grantee, Long-term Follow-up of Parenteral Drug Abusers, National Institutes on Drug Abuse, NIH **MEM:** Liaison, American Association for the Study of Liver Diseases, NIH (2005-2009); Serum Repository Hepatitis C Advisory Panel Liaison, Kidney Disease: Improving Global Outcomes Organization, NIH (2005-2008); Nominations Committee, American Association for the Study of Liver Diseases (1988, 2000, 2005); Monitoring Committee, National Heart, Lung and Blood Institute, NIH (1997-2007); Councilor-At-Large, American College of Gastroenterology (1997-2000); Councilor-At-Large, American Association for the Study of Liver Diseases (1997-2000); Research and Development Committee, U.S. Department of Veterans Affairs (1976, 1979, 1981, 1997); Vice-President, Hepatitis Foundation International (1995-2005); Committee on Devices, Center for Drug Evaluation and Research, U.S. Food and Drug Administration (1995-2004); Advisory Council, National Hemophilia Foundation, Medical and Scientific, U.S. Food and Drug Administration (1995-2001); Nomenclature of Chronic Hepatitis (IASL), American Association for the Study of Liver Diseases (1993); Committee on Appointments and Promotions, Georgetown University (1992-1998); Research Planning and Operations Committee, Georgetown University (1992); Search Committee, Chief of Library Service, U.S. Department of Veterans Affairs (1991); Search Committee, Chief of Staff, U.S. Department of Veterans Affairs (1991); Member, American Registry of Pathology, American Association for the Study of Liver Diseases (1990-2004); Advisory Board, Gastroenterology Section, Children's Hospital National Medical Center (1989-1994); Committee for Dean's Prize for Biomedical Research, Georgetown University (1988, 1989); Alternate, American Registry of Pathology, American Association for the Study of Liver Diseases (1981 1989); Search Committee, Chief of Nephrology, U.S. Department of Veterans Affairs (1988); Chairman, Training and Education Committee, American Association for the Study of Liver Diseases (1988); VA Liver Transplant Committee U.S. Department of Veterans Affairs (1986-1990); AIDS Committee, U.S. Department of Veterans Affairs (1986); Chairman, Search Committee, Chief of GI, Georgetown University (1985); Advisory Committee, National Heart, Lung and Blood Institute, NIH (1983-1987); Training and Education Committee, American Association for the Study of Liver Diseases (1983); VA Ad Hoc Committee on Hepatitis Vaccine Use, U.S. Department of Veterans Affairs (1982-1983); VA Gastroenterology Advisory Group U.S. Department of Veterans Affairs (1982-1983); Executive Committee, VA Cooperative Study of Alcoholic Hepatitis, U.S. Department of Veterans Affairs (1978 1982); VA Representative, National Digestive Disease Advisory Board, U.S. Department of Veterans Affairs (1981-1994); Ad Hoc ALT screening Impact Assessment Committee, NIH (1981); Chairman, Research and Development Committee, U.S. Department of Veterans Affairs (1980); Library Committee, U.S. Department of Veterans Affairs (1976-1986); Medical and Chirurgical Society, State of Maryland (1976); Transfusion Task Force, American Blood Commission (1975-1979);

Chairman, Infectious Diseases Committee, U.S. Department of Veterans Affairs (1971); Associate Member, American College of Gastroenterology; American Association for the Study of Liver Diseases; International Association for the Study of the Liver; American Federation for Medical Research; Ad Hoc GAO Report Review Committee, American Blood Commission **MH:** Albert Nelson Marquis Lifetime Achievement Award (2017) **H:** Classical Music; Collecting Fountain Pens **ADD:** 6403 Hillmead Rd, Bethesda, MD, 20817

SEIDE, GEORGE N., **T:** Attorney **I:** Law and Legal Services **CN:** Law Office of George N. Seide, APLC **PB:** West Palm Beach **SC:** FL/USA **MS:** Married **CH:** One Child **ED:** JD, University of La Verne College of Law (1979) **CT:** Certified Specialist in Family Law, California Bar Board of Legal Specialization (2004-Present); Licensed Real Estate Broker (1990-Present) **C:** Attorney, Law Office of George N. Seide, APLC; Founding Partner, Adelman & Seide, LLP, Encino and Calabasas, CA **CR:** Merger in Judgments, California Bar Conference (2007-Present) **CIV:** Executive Committee, Law Practice Management and Technology Committee, The State Bar of California (2015-Present); Family Law Executive Committee, San Fernando Valley Bar Association (2007-Present); Chair, Family Law Executive Committee, The State Bar of California (2007); Pro Bono Legal Services, Harriett Buhai Center; Pro Bono Legal Services, Vincent Family Law Center; Co-chair, Counsel of Sections, Board of Governors Committee, The State Bar of California **CW:** Contributor, Numerous Articles, Family Law News, The State Bar of California **AW:** Honoree, Top 100 Attorneys in Southern California, Thompson-Reuters (2015-2017); Honoree, Top 100 Family Law Attorneys in California, American Academy of Trial Attorneys (2015); Inductee, Order of Distinguished Attorneys, Beverly Hills Bar Association (2013); Honoree, Super Lawyer, Los Angeles Magazine (2006-2016); Inductee, Omicron Delta Kappa (1972); Outstanding Law Enforcement Award, Florida Jaycees (1971); Inductee, Florida Blue Key, Leadership Honorary, University of Florida (1971); Honoree, Florida Student Leader of The Year, Florida Student Congress (1970-1971); Featured Listee, Who's Who in American Colleges & Universities (1970-1971); Honoree, Man of the Year, Theta Kappa Omega Fraternity (1969-1970) **MEM:** Association of Certified Specialists (2006-Present); Los Angeles County Bar Association (1996-Present); Co-vice-chairman, Council of State Bar Sections, The State Bar of California (2008-2009); Chair, Executive Committee, Family Law Section, The State Bar of California (2007-2008) **BAR:** Supreme Court of the United States (2004); United States District Court Central District of California (1993); United States Court of Appeals for the Ninth Circuit (1993); State of California (1992) **H:** His dogs; Reading; Travel; Volunteering with the state and local bar associations **BA:** 24025 Park Sorrento Ste 310, Law Office of George N. Seide, Calabasas, CA, 91302 **URL:** http://mayashulman.com/professionals/george-n-seide-esq-cfls/

SEIDEL, CARL WILLIAM, **T:** State Legislator **I:** Government Administration/Government Relations/Government Services **CN:** New Hampshire House of Representatives **DOB:** 08/18/1938 **PB:** Hempstead **SC:** NY/USA **PT:** Charles Francis Seidel; Wilma Marie Seidel **MS:** Widowed **SPN:** Lorraine C. Currier (5/29/2010, Deceased 2016); Suzanne Winslow Dana (Deceased 6/22/2005) **CH:** Lisa Marie; Michael Dana; Rebecca Suzanne; Elaine Marie **ED:** MS, University of Notre Dame; BS in Chemistry, University of Wisconsin **C:** Representative, Ward 1, Nashua, New Hampshire House

of Representatives (2014-Present); Hillsborough, District 28, New Hampshire House of Representatives, Concord, NH (2014-Present); Host, The People's View (2012-Present); President, Consultant, Carl W. Seidel & Associates (2000-Present); Hillsborough STET District 28 (2014); Vice Chair, Public Works & Highways Commission, New Hampshire (2010-2012); Chair, Hillsborough County Executive Committee (2010-2012); Hillsborough, District 28, New Hampshire House of Representatives, Concord, NH (2008-2012); President, International Isotopes, Denton, TX (1997-1999); CEO, International Isotopes, Denton, TX (1997-1999); Associate Director, DuPont Merck, Billerica, MA (1991-1997); Various Positions, Manufacturing Manager, Pharmaceutical Division, DuPont, Billerica, MA (1981-1991); General Manager, New Products, New England Nuclear, Billerica, MA (1979-1981); Assistant Division Manager, New England Nuclear, Billerica, MA (1973-1979); Product Manager, New England Nuclear, Billerica, MA (1969-1973); Chemist, Marketing manager, Nuclear Science and Engineering, Pittsburgh, PA (1962-1969) **CR:** Technology Adviser, U.S. Pharmacopoeia, Bethesda, MD (1995-2000); Consultant, Department of Energy, Washington, DC (1990-2001); Committee Member, American National Standards Institute, Gaithersburg, MD (1975) **CIV:** Chairman, Nashua Republican City Committee (2008); Treasurer, Nashua Republican City Committee (2007); Town Representative, Chelmsford, MA (1980-1997); Commission to Study the Legalization, Regulation, and Taxation of Marijuana, State of New Hampshire **MIL:** ROTC Corps, U.S. Air Force (1955-1957) **CW:** Co-Editor, "Mossbauer Effect Methodology," Volume Ten (1976); Co-Editor, "Mossbauer Effect Methodology," Volume Nine (1974); Co-Editor, "Mossbauer Effect Methodology," Volume Eight (1973); Editor, "The Mossbauer Effect and Its Application in Chemistry" (1967) **AW:** Regional Society of Nashua Public Access Channel Award **MEM:** International Isotope Society; American College of Nuclear Physicians; Legatus; Secretary-Treasurer, Therapy Council, Society of Nuclear Medicine; American Chemical Society; European Society of Nuclear Medicine **MH:** Albert Nelson Marquis Lifetime Achievement Award (2017) **H:** Tennis; Travel; Softball; Bicycling **PA:** Republican **RE:** Roman Catholic **ADD:** 39 Pilgrim Circle, Nashua, NH, 03063

SEIFERT, BETTY, **T:** Curator **I:** Museums & Institutions **CN:** Jefferson Patterson Park and Museum, State Museum of Archaeology **PT:** Marvin Leon Morris; Cleo Mae Bird **MS:** Married **SPN:** Walter Seifert (5/31/1970) **CH:** Eli; Sara Marguerite **ED:** MLS, Rutgers, The State University of New Jersey (1964); BS, Texas Woman's University (1962); BA, Texas Woman's University (1962) **C:** Curator, Jefferson Patterson Park and Museum, State Museum of Archaeology (2007-Present); Chief Conservator, Jefferson Patterson Park and Museum, State Museum of Archaeology (1989-Present); Deputy Director, Maryland Archaeological Conservation Laboratory, Jefferson Patterson Park and Museum, State Museum of Archaeology (1997-2007); Consultant, Various Organizations (1985-1989); Conservator, Various Organizations (1985-1989); Conservator, Professional Service Industries, Groton, MA (1982-1985); Conservation Technician, Maine State Museum, Augusta, ME (1976-1982); Exhibit Preparation Organizer, Maine State Museum (1975-1976); Librarian, James J. Peters VA Medical Center, U.S. Department of Veterans Affairs (1965-1968); Librarian, The New York Public Library (1962-1964) **CR:** Weaving Instructor, Arts and Crafts Program, The Riverside Church, New York, NY (1968-1973) **CIV:** Advisory Board Member for Conservation of the USS Monitor,

The Mariners' Museum and Park, Newport News, VA (2003-2006); Board Member, Advisory Council for Underwater Archaeology, The Society for Historical Archaeology (1990-2001); Master Gardener, Patterson Estate House, Jefferson Patterson Park and Museum, State Museum of Archaeology; Preservation Organizer, Jefferson Patterson Park and Museum, State Museum of Archaeology **CW:** Author, "Standards and Guidelines for Archaeological Investigations in Maryland: Technical Update No. 1: Collections and Conservation Standards"; Artist, Annual Woven Objects Exhibition, Annmarie Sculpture Garden & Arts Center, Koenig Private Foundation, Inc.; Author, "Untitled Patterson Family Biography" **AW:** Recipient, Special Recognition Award, Department of Housing and Community Development, State of Maryland (2004); Recipient, Distinguished Service Award, Governor Joseph Brennan, State of Maine (1978); Full Scholar, The New York Public Library (1962-1964) **MEM:** AIC; American Association for the Advancement of Science **MH:** Albert Nelson Marquis Lifetime Achievement Award (2017) **H:** Weaving; Spinning; Basketry; Master gardener; Art; Painting in water color **ADD:** 11532 Wolfhowl Ln, Lusby, MD, 20657

SELMAN, ALAN LOUIS, **T:** Computer Scientist **I:** Technology **DOB:** 04/02/1941 **PB:** New York **SC:** NY/USA **PT:** Dan Selman; Rose (Grass) Selman **MS:** Married **SPN:** Sharon Jevotovsky (7/7/1963) **CH:** Jeffrey; Heather **ED:** PhD, The Pennsylvania State University (1970); MA, University of California, Berkeley (1964); BS in Mathematics, The City College of New York, Cum Laude (1962) **C:** Professor Emeritus, Department of Computer Science and Engineering, University at Buffalo (2014-Present); Professor, Department of Computer Science and Engineering, University at Buffalo (1998-2014); Professor, Department of Computer Science, University at Buffalo (1990-1998); Professor, Chairman, Department of Computer Science, University at Buffalo (1990-1996); Acting Dean, Northeastern University, Boston, MA (1988-1989); Professor, Northeastern University, Boston, MA (1986-1990); Professor, Iowa State University of Science and Technology, Ames, IA (1982-1986); Associate Professor, Iowa State University of Science and Technology, Ames, IA (1977-1982); Assistant Professor, Computer Science, Florida State University, Tallahassee, FL (1972-1977) **CR:** Participant, Speaking Engagements; Participant, Presentations; Participant, Lectures **CW:** Author, "Computability and Complexity Theory" (2011); Co-Editor, "Complexity Theory Retrospective II" (1997); Editor, "Complexity Theory Retrospective" (1990); Co-Author, "Springer"; Member, Editorial Board, Chicago Journal of Theoretical Computer Science; Editor-in-Chief, "Theory Computing Systems" **AW:** Recipient, Humboldt Research Award (2005); Recipient, Distinguished Service Prize, Special Interest Group on Algorithms and Computation Theory, Association for Computing Machinery (2002); Recipient, Fulbright Award (1981-1982) **MEM:** Fellow, Association for Computing Machinery **MH:** Albert Nelson Marquis Lifetime Achievement Award (2017) **H:** Wine club; Traveling **ADD:** 10 Harlow Circle, Medford, NJ, 08055

SEMPLE, JANE FRANCES, **T:** Health Facility Director **I:** Medicine & Health Care **CN:** Alternative Healing Institute **DOB:** 02/14/1951 **PB:** Lakewood **SC:** OH/USA **PT:** Frank Joseph Semple; Margaret Eleanor (Carpenter) Semple **MS:** Divorced **SPN:** Nick N. Morana (6/24/1977, Divorced 1981) **ED:** Doctorate, Naturopathic Medicine, Trinity College of Natural Health (1999); Doctorate, Naturopathic Ministry, Trinity College of Natural Health (1999); MBA, Case Western Reserve University (1984);

BA, Baldwin-Wallace College, Summa Cum Laude (1980); AAB, Cuyahoga Community College, Summa Cum Laude, Cleveland, OH (1977) **CT:** Diplomate, American Board of Naturopaths **C:** Director, Alternative Healing Institute (1987-Present); Instructor, Baldwin-Wallace University, Berea, OH (1992-1993); Instructor, Cuyahoga Community College, Cleveland, OH (1986-1992); Market Research Manager, Sherwin-Williams Co., Cleveland, OH (1980-1985); Project Director, National Survey Research Center, Cleveland, OH (1977-1980); Administrative Assistant, DeVilbiss Co., Cleveland, OH (1969-1977) **CIV:** WomenSpace, Cleveland, OH (1980-1988); Family Homeless Shelter; Urban Hope Homeless Center; Member, Susan B. Anthony Society **CW:** Author, "Woodland Publishing Naturopathic Approach Series: Alzheimer's Disease"; Author, "Blood Pressure"; Author, "Cholesterol & Inflammation"; Author, "Fertility"; Author, "Healthy, Vibrant Skin"; Author, "HPV & Cervical Dysplasia"; Author, "Influenza and Parkinson's Disease"; Author, "Doctor's Guide to Breast Cancer Prevent and Treatment" **AW:** Ohio Woman of Achievement (2005) **MEM:** Sunshine Health Freedom Coalition; American Botanic Council; American Association of Nutritional Consultants; American Naturopathic Medical Association **MH:** Albert Nelson Marquis Lifetime Achievement Award (2017) **PA:** Democrat **RE:** Unitrian **ADD:** 4965 Dover Ctr Rd, North Olmsted, OH, 44070 **URL:** http://drjanesemple.mynsp.com

SEN, ABHIK, **T:** Research Scientist **I:** Research **CN:** Blanchette Rockefeller Neurosciences Institute, West Virginia University **ED:** PhD in Molecular Parasitology (2009); MA in Zoology, University of Calcutta (2002); BA in Zoology, University of Calcutta (2000); BA in Botany, University of Calcutta (2000); Doctorate, University of Calcutta **C:** Research Scientist, Center for Neurodegenerative Diseases, Blanchette Rockefeller Neurosciences Institute, West Virginia University (2017-Present); Assistant Professor, Blanchette Rockefeller Neurosciences Institute, West Virginia University (2013-2017); Postdoctoral Research Fellow, Blanchette Rockefeller Neurosciences Institute, West Virginia University (2009-2013) **MEM:** Society for Neuroscience; Sigma Xi Honor Society **ADD:** 8 Medical Center Drive, Morgantown, WV, 26505

SENNETT, MICHAEL, **T:** Lawyer **I:** Law and Legal Services **CN:** Jones Day **DOB:** 10/24/1951 **PB:** Chicago **SC:** IL/USA **ED:** JD, Loyola University Chicago, Cum Laude (1977); BA, Quincy University, with Honors (1973) **CT:** Supreme Court of the United States (1984); Illinois (1977) **C:** Partner, Antitrust and Competition law, Jones Day, Chicago, IL (2007-Present); Chair, Antitrust and Trade Regulation, Bell, Boyd & Lloyd LLP, Chicago, IL (1996-2007); Partner, Bell, Boyd & Lloyd, Chicago, IL (1984-2007); Associate, Bell, Boyd & Lloyd, Chicago, IL (1977-1983) **CR:** Board of Advisors, Institute for Consumer Antitrust Law Studies, Chicago, IL (1998-Present); Adjunct Law Faculty, Loyola University (1996-Present); Executive Editor, Loyola University Chicago Law Journal (1976-1977) **CIV:** Trustee, Children's Home and Aid Society of Illinois, Inc., Chicago, IL (2004-Present); Trustee, Quincy University (2006-2016) **CW:** Contributor, Chapters to Books **MEM:** International Bar Association; Chicago Bar Association; ABA; Lawyers Club of Chicago **H:** Spending time with his children and grandchildren; Traveling **ADD:** 1500 Maple Ave, Wilmette, IL, 60091 **URL:** msennett@jonesday.com

SERCHUK, IVAN, **T:** Partner, Chairman of Banking Practice Group **I:** Law and Legal Services **CN:** Pavia & Harcourt LLP **DOB:** 10/13/1935 **PB:** New York City **SC:** NY/USA **PT:** Israel Serchuk; Freda (Davis) Serchuk **CH:** Camille; Bruce Mead; Vance Foster **ED:** LLB, Columbia University (1960); BA, Columbia University (1957) **C:** Partner, Chairman, Banking Practice Group, Pavia & Harcourt LLP (2015-Present); Member, Spizz Cohen & Serchuk, P.C. New York City, NY (2003-2015); Partner, Serchuk & Zelermyer LLP, White Plains, NY (1976-2003); Partner, Berle & Berle (1972-1973); Special Counsel, New York State Senate, Banks Committee (1972); Deputy Superintendent, Counsel, New York State Banking Department, New York City, Albany, NY (1968-1971); Associate, Kaye, Scholer, Fierman, Hays and Handler (1963-1968); Law Clerk to Judge, United States District Court Southern District of New York (1961-1963) **CR:** Lecturer, Practicing Law Institute (1968-1971) **AW:** Harlan Fiske Stone Scholar, Columbia Law School (1960) **MEM:** Association of the Bar of the City of New York **BAR:** United States Court of Appeals for the Second Circuit (1964); United States District Court Southern District of New York (1963); New York State Bar (1961) **MH:** Albert Nelson Marquis Lifetime Achievement Award (2017) **H:** Art collecting **BA:** 230 Park Avenue, New York, NY, 11016 **ADD:** 100 United Nations Plz Ste 17B, New York, NY, 10017

SEYMOUR, JEFFREY ALAN, **T:** Government Relations Consultant **I:** Government Administration/Government Relations/Government Services **DOB:** 08/31/1950 **PB:** Los Angeles **SC:** CA/USA **PT:** Daniel Seymour; Evelyn (Schwartz) Seymour **MS:** Married **SPN:** Valerie Joan Parker (12/2/1973) **CH:** Jessica Lynn **ED:** MPA (1977); BA in Political Science, University of California, Los Angeles (1973); AA in Social Science, Santa Monica College (1971) **C:** Partner, Seymour Consulting Group (2002-Present); Adjunct Faculty, Occidental College (2014); Partner, Morey/Seymour & Associates (Now Seymour Consulting Group), Los Angeles, CA (1984-2002); Principal, Jeffrey Seymour & Associates, Los Angeles, CA (1983-1984); Vice President, Bank of LA, California (1982-1983); County Supreme's Senior Deputy, LA Board Supervisors, California (1974-1982); Councilman Aide, LA City Council, California (1972-1974) **CR:** Chair, West Hollywood Library Foundation (2013-Present); Advisory Board, UCLA Luskin School of Public Affairs; University of California, LA (2009); Board of Visitors, Department of Political Science (2008-2012); Member, Board of Overseers, Hebrew Union College-Jewish Institute of Religion (2008-2012); Member, Commercial Panel, American Arbitration Association (1984-1990) **CIV:** Chairperson, Audit Committee (2011-Present); Co-chairperson, Higher Education PAC (2011-Present); President, Higher Education Political Action Committee (2011-Present); Board of Directors, University of California, LA Foundation (2007-Present); Governmental Affairs Committee, Venice Family Clinical (2005-Present); Guardian of Justice (2015); Resolution City Council, City of West Hollywood (2015); Service Medal, UCLA Alumni Association (2008); Friends Committee, LA Free Clinical (2006-2007); Chair, University of California, LA Fund (2002-2004); Board of Regents, University of California (2001-2002); President Alumni Associations, University of California (2000-2002); President, University of California, LA Alumni Association (1998-2000); Vice President, Congregation N'Vay Shalom (1994-1995); Vice President, Congregation N'Vay Shalom (1990-1993); Board of Directors, Congregation N'Vay Shalom (1988-1993); Chairman, Social Action Committee, Temple Emanuel of Beverly Hills (1986-1989); Chairman, West Hollywood Parking Advisory Committee, Los Angeles, CA (1983-1984); Pan Pacific Park Citizens Advisory Committee, Los Angeles, CA (1982-1985); Board of Directors, William O'Douglas Outdoor Classroom, Los Angeles, CA (1981-1988) **AW:** Commendation LA County, Assessor (2015); Resolution City Council, City of West Hollywood (2015); Hebrew College Award (2008-2012); City Council of the City of LA, Advocate of the Year, UCLA Bruin Caucus (2014); Plaques for Services Rendered, UCLA Alumni Association (2002); Member, Board of Regents of the University of California (2000-2002); Plaques for Services Rendered, Santa Monica Mountains Conservancy (1999); Commendatory Resolutions, California State Assembly (1996); Commendatory Resolutions, County of LA (1987); Commendatory Resolutions, City of LA (1987); Plaques for Services Rendered, City of LA (1987); Commendatory Resolutions, Rules Committee California State Senate (1987); Commendatory Resolutions, California State Assembly (1987); Certificate of Appreciation, LA Olympic Organizing Committee (1984); Plaques for Services Rendered, County of LA (1984); Plaques for Services Rendered, Jewish Federation Council Greater LA (1983); Plaques for Services Rendered, Beverlywood Cheviot Hills Democratic Club, LA (1981) **MEM:** Co-chair, California Coalition for Public Higher Education (2012-Present); Board of Directors, UCLA Alumni Association (1995-Present); President, UCLA Alumni Association (1998-2000); Board of Directors, Century City Chamber of Commerce (1998-2000); Vice Chair, Jewish Community Relations Committee, Jewish Federation Council Greater LA (1998); Santa Monica Mountains Conservancy Advisory Committee (1996-1999); Board of Directors, UCLA Alumni Association (1995-2002); Chair, Governmental Relations Steering Committee, UCLA Alumni Association (1995-1997); Governmental Relations Commission (1995-1996); Chair, Campus Outreach Task Force (1994-1995); Cabinet, Jewish Community Relations Committee of Greater Los Angeles (1994); President, UCLA Jewish Alumni (1992-1995); Advisory Board, National Jewish Center for Immunology & Respiratory Medicine (1991-1993); Board of Directors, Hillel Council of LA (1991); Sub-Committee Chairman, Local Government Law and Legislation Commission (1990); Vice Chairman, Urban Affairs Commission (1989-1990); Trustee, University of California, Los Angeles Foundation (1989-1997); Co-chairman, Urban Affairs Commission (1987-1989); Co-chairman, UCLA Giving, Chancellor's Society (1986-1988); Vice President, Community Relations Metro Region, Jewish Federation Council of Greater Los Angeles (1985-1987); Liaison Advisory Commission, City and County Government, 1984 Olympics (1984); Arbitrator, Council of Better Business Bureaus (1984); Platform on World Peace and International Relations California Democrats (1983); Governmental Steering Committee, UCLA Alumni Association (1983-1997); California Democratic Party (1979-1982); President, Beverlywood-Cheviot Hills Democratic Club, LA (1978-1981); President, 43d Assembly District Democratic Council (1975-1979); Executive Section, California Young Democrats (1971); LA Olympic Citizens Advisory Committee; American Society for Public Administration; Associate of the Chancellor, University of California, Los Angeles; Valley Industry & Commerce Association; West Hollywood Chamber of Commerce **ADD:** 5803 Lubao Avenue, Woodland Hills, CA, 91362

SEYMOUR, RICHARD, **T:** Associate Professor **I:** Education/Educational Services **CN:** Ball State University **DOB:** 10/03/1955 **PB:** Shelby **SC:** OH/USA **PT:** G. Deming Seymour; Elizabeth (Peterson) Seymour **MS:** Married **SPN:** Vicki (Stebleton) Seymour **CH:** Ryan **ED:** EdD, West Virginia University (1990); MA, Ball State University (1982); BS in Education, The Ohio State University

(1978) **C:** Instructor to Associate Professor, Ball State University, Muncie, IN (1982-Present); Teacher, Crestview Senior High School, Ashland, OH (1978-1981) **CR:** Visiting Instructor, Oregon State University (1990-1991); Visiting Instructor, West Virginia University, Morgantown, WV (1985) **CIV:** Advisor, 4-H Clubs, Delaware County, IN (2012-Present); Director, Technology In-Service Workshops, Indiana Department of Education, Indianapolis, IN (1988-2000); Advisor, 4-H Clubs, Richland County, OH (1978-1981) **CW:** Co-Author, "Exploring Communications, Review Edition" (2000); Co-Editor, "Manufacturing in Technology Education" (1993); Co-Author, "Exploring Communications" (1987) **AW:** Outstanding Service Award, Teachers College at Ball State University (2018); Academy of Fellows, International Technology and Engineering Educators Association (2017); Award of Distinction, International Society for Technology in Education (1999); Named, Technology Teacher Educator of the Year, Council on Technology Teacher Education (1998) **MEM:** Board of Directors, International Technology and Engineering Educators Association (2010-2013); President, Council on Technology & Engineering Teacher Education (2007-2010); Vice President, Council on Technology & Engineering Teacher Education (2003-2005); Chairman, International Conference, International Society for Technology in Education (1999); President, Engineering/Technology Educators of Indiana (1995-1996); National Contest Coordinator, Technology and Engineering Education Collegiate Association (1992-2008); Board of Directors, International Technology Education Association (1992-1994); International Advisor, Technology and Engineering Education Collegiate Association (1990-1992); American Society for Engineering Education; Phi Delta Kappa; Epsilon Pi Tau **H:** Model railroading; Sports; Travel **RE:** United Methodist **ADD:** 8504 W Thorn Tree Rd, Muncie, IN, 47304

SHAINWALD, SYBIL, T: Lawyer **I:** Law and Legal Services **DOB:** 04/27/1928 **PB:** New York **SC:** NY/USA **PT:** Samuel Schwartz; Anne Schwartz **MS:** Widowed **SPN:** Sidney Shainwald (Deceased) **CH:** Robert; Louise; Laurie; Marsha **ED:** Honorary LLD, New York Law School (2000); JD, New York Law School (1976); MA, Columbia University (1972); BA, William and Mary (1948) **C:** Lawyer, Private Practice (1976), Women's Health Advocate **CR:** Chair, Sidney Shainwald Public Interest Lectures, New York Law School (2004-Present); Advisory Board of Southampton, The Hamptons Shakespeare Festival, Inc. (2000-Present); Trustee, New York Law School (2000-Present); Board of Directors, Friends of the Tel Aviv Museum, Tel Aviv Museum of Art (2000-Present); Board Member, School of Nursing, Northern Arizona University (1989-Present); Board Member, HERS Foundation (1985-Present); Board of Directors, Tel Aviv Museum's American Friends (2000-2010); Co-Chair, Take Home a Nude, New York Academy of Art (2001); Trustee, Civil Justice Foundation (1998-1999); Founding Board Member, Trial Lawyers for Public Justice (1982-1988); Founder, Kenneth R. Feinberg Scholarship, New York Law School; Member, Health Task Force, Office of the New York City Comptroller; Founder, Sybil Shainwald Charitable Foundation; Board of Directors, American Classical Orchestra; Fellow, The Morgan Library & Museum; Fellow, Pound Civil Justice Institute; Board of Directors, Consumer Interest Research Institute; Board of Advisors, Medical Legal Aspects of Breast Implants; Board Member, National Network to Prevent Birth Defects; Board Member, Dalkon Shield Information Network; Member, NARAL Pro-Choice America; Health Adviser, United Methodist Church **CW:** Co-Editor,

"Journal of Women and Health"; Contributor, Articles, Professional Journals **AW:** Recipient, Edith I. Spivak Award, New York County Lawyers Association (2010); Recipient, President's Medal, New York Law School (2007); Recipient, Susan B. Anthony Award, National Organization for Women; Recipient, Grant, Governor W. Averell Harriman; Recipient, Grant, The Rockefeller Foundation; Recipient, Grant, National Endowment for the Humanities; Recipient, Edward Coles Scholarship, William and Mary; Recipient, Judge Jack B. Weinstein Fellowship, University Graduate School of Arts and Sciences, Columbia University; Recipient, Center For Women Leadership Award; Recipient, Dean's Award For Distinguished Achievement, Graduate School of Arts and Sciences, Columbia University **MEM:** Judge, National Moot Court Competition, Association of the Bar of the City of New York (1988-2011); Co-Chair, Breast Implant Litigation Group, American Association for Justice (1992-2000); Contraceptive Implant Litigation Group, American Association for Justice (1995); Chair, Environmental and Toxic Tort Section, American Association for Justice (1988-1989); Chair, Health Law and Regulation, NWHN (1981-1988); Chairman, Board of Directors, NWHN (1982-1986); Board Member, NWHN (1980-1986); Chair, Litigation Service, NWHN (1980-1986); Dalkon Shield Litigation Group, American Association for Justice; Environmental Law Advisory Committee, American Association for Justice; Co-Chair, DES Litigation Group, American Association for Justice; Board Member, New York Academy of Art; Arts at MIT; Veteran Feminists of America, Inc.; Board of Governors, New York State Trial Lawyers; Society of Medical Jurisprudence; Co-Founder, Health Action International; Steering Committee, Health Action International; The Lawyers' Committee for Civil Rights Under Law; ASLME; President, U.S. Women's Health Alliance; Chair, U.S. Women's Health Alliance; Chair, New York State Affiliates, NWHN; The Phi Beta Kappa Society **BAR:** New York State (1976); U.S. Second Circuit of Appeals; U.S. Fourth Circuit of Appeals **MH:** Albert Nelson Marquis Lifetime Achievement Award (2017) **H:** Art; Music **ADD:** 15 Central Park W Apt 8B, New York, NY, 10023

SHALLCROSS, DORIS J., T: Education Educator **I:** Education/Educational Services **DOB:** 02/28/1933 **PB:** Cranford **SC:** NJ/USA **PT:** John William Shallcross; Ethel Belle (Ruth) Shallcross **MS:** Single **ED:** EdD, University of Massachusetts, Amherst (1973); MA, Wesleyan University (1962); BA, Montclair State University (1955) **C:** President, Shallcross Creativity Institute, Haydenville, MA (1995-2005); Professor, University of Massachusetts, Amherst (1982-1995); Director, Graduate Studies in Creativity, University of Massachusetts, Amherst (1982-1995); Assistant Professor of Education, Division of Home Economics, University of Massachusetts, Amherst (1978-1982); Program Development Specialist, Teacher Corps, State University of New York, Oneonta (1976-1978); Director of Humanistic Education, Montague Area Public Schools (1972-1975); Administrator, Cleveland Heights-University Heights City School District (1967-1969); Teacher, Cleveland Heights-University Heights City School District (1965-1967); Teacher, Roosevelt Junior High School (1961-1965); Teacher, Hunterdon Central Regional High School (1955-1961) **CR:** Trustee Emerita, Creative Education Foundation (2006); Professor, International Graduate Program in Creativity, University of Santiago de Compostela (1999); Board Director, Center for Critical and Creative Thinking (1995-1998); Co-Director, Global Odyssey (1992-1996); Board Director, Center for Critical and Creative Thinking (1989-1992); President, Board of Trustees, Creative Education

Foundation (1988-1994) **CIV:** Vice President, Enchanted Circle Theater (2010-Present); Enchanted Circle Theater (2007-Present); Commission for Creative & Innovative Education in Public Schools, Commonwealth of Massachusetts (2010); Board of Directors, Massachusetts Center for Charter Public School Excellence (2007-2011); Vice President, Massachusetts Charter Public School Association (2007-2010); Co-Chair, Creative Problem Solving Institute Council, Creative Education Foundation (2004-2005); President, Arts in Education Center (2002-2003); Board of Directors, Massachusetts Charter Public School Association (2001-2011); President, Pioneer Valley Performing Arts Charter Public School (1998-2010); Chair, Education Committee. Arts in Education Center (1997-2001); Vice President, Board of Directors, Pioneer Valley Performing Arts Charter Public School (1995-1998); Planning Board, Williamsburg, MA (1981-1989); Center Charter Public School of Excellence **CW:** Consultant Editor, "Journal of Creative Behavior" (1967-Present); Co-Author, "Celebrating the Soul of CPSI" (2004); Co-Author, "Intuition: An Inner Way of Knowing" (1989); Co-Author, "Leadership: Making Things Happen" (1987); Co-Author, "The Growing Person" (1985); Author, "Teaching Creative Behavior" (1981); Contributor, Articles, Professional Journals **AW:** Creativity Commonwealth Arts Educator Award (2013); Eponym, Shallcross Teaching Award, Pioneer Valley Performing Arts Charter Public School (2012); Honoree, Trustee Emeritus Creative Education Foundation (2010); Honoree, Massachusetts Commission (2010); Honoree, Creative Problem Solving Institute Hall of Fame (2004); Grantee, National Science Foundation (1987-1989); Grantee, University of Massachusetts Amherst (1987-1989); Distinguished Leader Award, Creative Education Foundation (1986) **MEM:** Treasurer, Hampshire Music Club (2011-Present); Massachusetts Commission for Education Creativity Measurement Index Developer in Pubic Schools (2010); Board of Directors, American Creativity Association (1990-1993); National Education Association; Massachusetts Society of Professors; IONS **MH:** Albert Nelson Marquis Lifetime Achievement Award (2017); Distinguished Humanitarian (2017) **H:** Music; Golf; Reading; Gardening **ADD:** 26 S Main Street, Haydenville, MA, 01039

SHALOWITZ, ERWIN, T: Civil Engineer **I:** Engineering **DOB:** 02/13/1924 **PB:** Washington **SC:** DC/USA **PT:** Aaron Louis Shalowitz; Pearl (Myer) Shalowitz **MS:** Widowed **SPN:** Elaine (Langerman) Shalowitz (Deceased 4/5/2009). "In memory of my dear, departed wife, Elaine, as a testimonial to her constant love, support and encouragement that became such a major factor in any success I may have achieved. Her efforts were greatly appreciated." - Erwin Shalowitz **CH:** Ann Janet; Aliza Beth; Jonathan Avram **ED:** Honorary PhD, International Biographical Centre, Cambridge, England (2017); Honorary LittD, International Biographical Centre, Cambridge, England (2015-2016); MPA, American University (1954); Graduate in Soil Mechanics, Catholic University of America (1951); Postgraduate Work, George Washington University (1948-1949); BCE, George Washington University (1947); Student, University of Notre Dame (1945); Student, University of Pennsylvania (1944-1945) **CT:** Registered Professional Engineer, Washington, DC **C:** Appointment as Honorary Director General, International Biographical Centre, Cambridge, England (2016-Present); Appointment as Vice President, World Congress of Arts, Sciences and Communications, Cambridge, England (2016-Present); Supervisory General Engineer, Special Assistant for Protective Construction Programs, Public Building Service, General Services Administration, Washington,

DC (1959-1998); Project Manager, Building Systems, Public Building Service, General Services Administration, Washington, DC (1959-1998); Chief, Research Branch, Public Building Service, General Services Administration, Washington, DC (1959-1998); Chief, Management Information, Public Building Service, General Services Administration, Washington, DC (1959-1998); Chief, Contracting Procedures and Support, Public Building Service, General Services Administration, Washington, DC (1959-1998); Chief, Contract Evaluation and Analysis, Deputy Director, Design Division, Director, Contract Management, Director, Liaison and Evaluation Division, Team Leader/Project Manager Electronic Acquisition Systems, Acquisition/Procurement Executive, Public Building Service, General Services Administration, Washington, DC (1959-1998); Chief, Structural Research Engineer, Bureau of Yards and Docks, U.S. Navy, Washington, DC (1948-1959); Head, Defense Research Section, Bureau of Yards and Docks, U.S. Navy, Washington, DC (1948-1959); Project Officer, Technical Adviser for Atomic Tests, Bureau of Yards and Docks, U.S. Navy, Washington, DC (1948-1959); Employee, Consultant Firm, Whitman, Requardt & Associates, Baltimore, MD (1947-1948); Engineer, Klemitt Engineering Company, New York, NY (1947) **CR:** Chairman, Federal Executive Training Program, United States Civil Service Commission (1950); Fellowship in Public Management, American University (1950); Fallout Shelter Analyst, Department of Defense, Served as Member of the Navy's Special Weapons Effects Test Planning Group; Chairman, Fire Safety Committee, General Services Administration; Chairman, Fallout Protection Committee, General Services Administration; Chairman, Building Evaluation Committee, General Services Administration; Interagency Committee on Housing Research and Building Technology; National Evaluation Board of Architect-Engineer Selections; Standing Committee on Procurement Policy, National Academy of Sciences; Building Research Advisory Board, Interagency Committee on Procurement Curriculum Review; Coordinator, Public Buildings Design and Construction, Small Business Program; Coordinator, Public Buildings Design and Construction, Minority Enterprise Program; Coordinator, Public Buildings Design and Construction, Minority Subcontracting Program; Vice President, World Congress on Arts, Sciences and Communications; Fellowship in Public Management, United States Civil Service Commission, American University; Fellowship, Patron of the International Biographical Association; Fellow, American Society of Civil Engineers; Fellow, American Biographical Institute **MIL:** Engineering Commanding Officer, U.S. Naval Reserve (1944-1946) **CW:** Contributor, Articles, Professional Journals **AW:** ADD: Lifetime Achievement Award, International Biographical Centre, Cambridge, England, (2017); Lifetime Achievement Award, World Congress on Arts, Sciences and Communications (2016); Cambridge Certificate for Outstanding Professional Achievement, International Biographical Centre, Cambridge, England (2015-2016); Honorary Professor of Engineering, International Biographical Centre, Cambridge, England (2015-2016); Honorary Director General, International Biographical Centre, Cambridge, England (2015-2016); Superior Accomplishment Award (1995); Outstanding Performance Recognition (1993-1996); Outstanding Performance Recognition (1987); Distinguished Engineer Alumni Achievement Award, School of Engineering and Applied Science, George Washington University (1985); Outstanding Performance Recognition (1983); Outstanding Performance Recognition

(1979); Outstanding Performance Recognition (1976-1977); Commendable Service Award, General Services Administration (1968) **MEM:** Society for Advancement Management; National Board of Advisors, American Biographical Institute; Society for American Military Engineers; Sigma Tau, National Engineering Honor Society; Pi Sigma Alpha, National Political Science Honor Society **MH:** Albert Nelson Marquis Lifetime Achievement Award (2017) **H:** Bible study; Ping pong/table tennis **RE:** Jewish **ADD:** 3122 Gracefield Road, Apartment 108, Silver Spring, MD, 20904

SHAMBAUGH, STEPHEN WARD, T: Lawyer (Retired) **I:** Law and Legal Services **DOB:** 08/04/1920 **PB:** South Bend **SC:** IN/USA **PT:** Marion Clyde Shambaugh; Anna Violet (Stephens) Shambaugh **MS:** Married **SPN:** Virginia; Marilyn Louise Pyle (Deceased 1993) **CH:** Susan Wynne; Shambaugh Hinkle (Deceased 1998); Kathleen Louise Shambaugh Thompson **ED:** LLB, University of Tulsa (1954); Coursework, University of Arkansas (1951); Coursework, San Jose State Teachers College (1938-1940) **C:** Sole Practice, Denver, CO (1981-1997); Senior Partner, Bowman, Shambaugh, Geissinger & Wright, Denver, CO (1964-1981); Vice President, Reading & Bates Drilling Company Ltd., Calgary, Canada (1954-1963); General Manager, Reading & Bates Drilling Company Ltd., Calgary, Canada (1954-1963); Of Legal Counsel, Reading & Bates Drilling Company Ltd., Calgary, Canada (1954-1963); Member Staff, Reading & Bates, Inc., Tulsa, OK (1951-1954); Member, Board of Governors, Oilmens Golf Tournament, Calgary, Canada; Former Chairman, Entertainment Committee; Former Member, Board of Governors, Canadian Petroleum Association; Former President, Board of Directors, Canadian Association of Oilwell Drilling Contractors; Member, Board of Directors, Canadian Association of Oilwell Drilling Contractors. Former Member of Board of Governors of Oilmen's Golf Tournament and Entertainment Chairman, Calgary **CR:** Director, Financial Counsel, Various Corporations **MIL:** Colonel, U.S. Air Force (Retired) **MEM:** Colorado Bar Association; Oklahoma Bar Association, P-51 Mustang Pilots Association; Lifetime Member, Military Officers Association of America; American Legion; Masons; Retired Member, Denver Bar Association, Retired Member, Federal Bar Associate; Elks; Organizer of Summers Hardy Law Fraternity Chapter, University of Tulsa,and member of Phi Alpha Delta **MH:** Albert Nelson Marquis Lifetime Achievement Award (2017) **ADD:** 926 Matador Dr SE, Albuquerque, NM, 87123

SHANDERA, WAYNE X., T: Faculty Physician, Educator **I:** Medicine & Health Care **CN:** Baylor College of Medicine **PB:** Fort Worth **SC:** TX/USA **PT:** Oscar E. Shandera; Augusta J. Shandera **ED:** MD, Johns Hopkins University, Baltimore, MD (1982); BA, Rice University, Houston, TX, Summa Cum Laude (1973) **CT:** Diplomate, American Board of Internal Medicine **C:** Faculty Physician, Baylor College of Medicine, Houston, TX (1988-Present); Assistant Professor, Baylor College of Medicine (1978) **CIV:** Organist, University of St. Thomas, Chapel of St. Basil **CW:** Contributor, Articles, Professional Journals **AW:** Jaworski Teaching Fellowship, Baylor College of Medicine (2017); Norton Rose Fulbright Teaching Award, Baylor College of Medicine (2016); San Martin de Porres, Annual Award (2011); Saint Nicholas Recognition, Houston Czech Center (2011); Certificate of Appreciation, Council of State and Territorial Epidemiologists (2006); First Prize, 7th Annual Methodist Hospital Oncology Research Symposium (1998); U.S. Public Health Service Commendation, Early Investigation of AIDS; Bradley Scott Award, Harris County Hospital District **MEM:** Houston Philosophical Society (2010-Present); Board of

Directors, Physicians for Social Responsibility, Houston, TX (1997-Present); Board of Directors, Physicians for Social Responsibility (1995-1998); Phi Beta Kappa (1968); American Association for the Advancement of Science; American College of Physicians; American Society of Tropical Medicine and Hygiene **H:** Music; Travel; Languages **RE:** Roman Catholic **ADD:** 2235 North Blvd, Houston, TX, 77098

SHANDRICK, REBECCA LYNN, T: Attorney at Law **I:** Law and Legal Services **CN:** Law Offices of Rebecca L. Shandrick, LLC **SC:** USA **PT:** Albert Joseph Shandrick , Wilma E. Shandrick **ED:** JD, University of Colorado School of Law (1982); BA in Biology, Magna Cum Laude, University of Colorado at Boulder (1978) **CT:** Teaching Certification, Colorado **C:** Principal, Law Offices of Rebecca L. Shandrick, LLC (1987-Present); Assistant City Attorney, Aurora, CO (1986-1987) **CR:** Instructor, Kaplan College (2002-2003) **CIV:** President, Augustana Foundation, Augustana Lutheran Church (2008-2011) **MEM:** Denver Senior Coalitions; Academy of Special Needs Planners; Northwest Denver Council for Seniors; National Academy of Elder Law Attorneys, Phi Delta Phi Legal Honor Society, Thomas Inn, University of Colorado **BAR:** Colorado **H:** Cooking; Painting; Piano **PA:** Democrat **BA:** 950 S Cherry St Ste 714, Rebecca L. Shandrick, LLC, Denver, CO, 80246 **URL:** https://www.elderlawdenver.com

SHARMA, SAMIN KUMAR, T: Director, Internist, Interventional Cardiologist, Educator **I:** Medicine & Health Care **CN:** The Mount Sinai Hospital **DOB:** 05/28/1955 **PB:** Alwar **SC:** India **ED:** Postdoctoral Studies, Mount Sinai Medical Center (1989-1990); Fellow, Cardiology, City Hospital Center at Elmhurst (1986); Resident, Internal Medicine, New York University Downtown Hospital (now New York-Presbyterian/Lower Manhattan Hospital) (1983-86); Resident, Internal Medicine, SMS Hospital, Jaipur, India (1979-1982); Intern, Internal Medicine, SMS Hospital, Jaipur, India (1978-1979); MD, SMS Medical College, Rajasthan University, Jaipur, India (1978); Undergraduate Degree, Maharaja College, India (1972) **CT:** Interventional Cardiology; Cardiovascular Disease; Internal Medicine **C:** Director of Clinical Cardiology, The Mount Sinai Hospital (2011-Present); Dean of International Clinical Affiliations, The Mount Sinai Hospital (2011-Present); Zena and Michael A. Wiener Professor of Medicine, Cardiology, The Mount Sinai Hospital (2002-Present); Director of Interventional Cardiology, Mount Sinai Medical Center, New York, NY (1996-Present); Professor of Medicine and Cardiology, Mount Sinai Medical School, New York, NY (Present) **CR:** President, Mount Sinai Heart Network (2011-Present); Cardiac Advisory Board, State of New York (2004-Present); Founder, Director, Live Symposium of Complex Coronary Cases (1998-Present); Angioplasty Instructor, India; Founder, Eternal Heart Care Center, Jaipur, India **CIV:** Vice President, Rajasthan Development Foundation, India; Contributor, Chief Minister Relief Fund, Rajasthan, India **CW:** Creator, Live Web Series, www.ccclivecases.org (2009); Contributor, Over 200 Articles, Professional Journals; Contributor, 15 Book Chapters; Author, Three Books; Featured, Today Show, New York Times, Wall Street Journal, New York Magazine, Barron's, Forbes, Newsweek, Washington Post, Crain's New York Business, Newsday, New York Post, New York Sun, Earthtimes, India Abroad, India Today **AW:** Honorary PhD, Honorary MS, Rajasthan University (2015); Honoree, Best Doctors, US News and World Report (2005-2008, 2011-2017); Honoree, Super Doctors (2008-2017); Physician Scientist Award,

AAPI-QLI (American Association of Physicians of Indian Origin of Queens and Long Island) (2014); Ellis Island Medal of Honor, The National Ethnic Coalition of Organizations (2011); Achievement in Cardiovascular Science & Medicine Award, American Heart Association (2011); Award, American Association of Physicians of Indian Origin (2011); Honoree, Excellence in Medicine, Association of Indians in America (AIA) (2010); Honoree, Academic Excellence, Tri-State Area Forum, American Association of Physicians of Indian Origin (AAPI) (2010); Cardiology Fellows Appreciation Award, The Mount Sinai Hospital (2009); Physician of the Year Award, The Mount Sinai Hospital (2007); Jacobi Medallion Award (2007); Governor's Award for Excellence, State of New York (2006); Honoree, Prestigious Jaipur, Rajasthan Government, Republic of India (2002); Simon Dack Award for Best Teacher, Cardiovascular Institute, The Mount Sinai Hospital (2000); Co-Recipient, Center of Excellence Award, Rotational Coronary Atherectomy (1996-2000); Honoree, Best Medical and Chief Resident, New York Infirmary-Beekman Downtown Hospital (now NewYork-Presbyterian/Lower Manhattan Hospital); Honoree, Top Physicians, Castle Connelly; Honoree, Top Physicians, Consumer Research Council America; Rajive Gandhi Memorial Award; Recipient, Rajasthan Gaurav, Sanskriti Organization of Rajasthan; Recipient, Bharat Gaurav, Sanskriti Organization of Rajasthan **MH:** Albert Nelson Marquis Lifetime Achievement Award (2017) **BA:** One Gustave L. Levy Place, Box 1030, The Mount Sinai Hospital, New York, NY, 10029 **ADD:** 1 Gustave L. Levy Place, Box 1030, The Mount Sinai Hospital, New York, NY, 10029 **URL:** samin.sharma@mountsinai.org

SHARP, DONALD EUGENE, T: Bank Consultant **I:** Consulting **DOB:** 11/04/1929 **PB:** Chicago **SC:** IL/USA **PT:** Arthur Eugene Sharp; Alma (Melchior) Sharp **MS:** Married **SPN:** Phyllis Stevens (9/11/1954) **CH:** John Stevens **ED:** MA in History, Columbia University (1959); BA in Political Science, Denison University (1952) **CT:** Certified, Economic Developer Emeritus **C:** Lending Consultant, Merchants Bank of New York, Valley National Bank (1996-2001); Lending Consultant, Community Mutual Savings Bank (1992-1996); Vice President, New York Job Development Authority (1986-1991); Vice President, Regular Credit Committee, Chemical Bank (1976-1986); Chemical Bank (1962-1986) **CIV:** Trustee, Bronxville, NY (1989-1991) **MIL:** Sergeant, U.S. Army, Korea (1952-1954) **CW:** Contributor, Articles, Professional Journals **MEM:** Academy of Political Science; Shenorock Shore Club; Skytop Club; Rotary; Omicron Delta Kappa **MH:** Albert Nelson Marquis Lifetime Achievement Award (2017) **PA:** Democrat **RE:** Episcopalian **ADD:** 66 Avon Road, Bronxville, NY, 10708

SHAW, NANCY RIVARD, T: Curator of American Art Emerita **I:** Education/Educational Services **CN:** Detroit Institute of Arts **PB:** Saginaw **SC:** MI/USA **MS:** Married **ED:** MA, Wayne State University (1973); BA, Oakland University, Magna Cum Laude (1969) **C:** Curator of American Art Emerita, Specialist in Late 19th Century and Early 20th Century American Art, Detroit Institute of Arts (1998-Present); Curator of American Art, Detroit Institute of Arts (1975-1998); Assistant Curator, American Art, Detroit Institute of Arts (1972-1975) **CR:** Adjunct Professor of Art and Art History, Wayne State University, Detroit, MI (1991-1998); Lecturer in Field; Organizer, Exhibitions **CW:** Contributing Author, "American Paintings in the Detroit Institute of Arts, Volume III: Forging A Modern Identity: Masters Of American Painting Born After 1847," Hudson Hills (2005); Contributing

Author, "American Paintings in the Detroit Institute of Arts, Volume II: Works by Artists Born Between 1816 and 1847," Hudson Hills (1998); Contributing Author, "American Paintings in the Detroit Institute of Arts, Volume I: Works by Artists Born Before 1816," Hudson Hills (1991); Contributor, Articles, Exhibition Catalogs; Contributor, Articles, Professional Journals; Contributor, Chapters, Books **MEM:** Wayne State University Alumni Association **MH:** Albert Nelson Marquis Lifetime Achievement Award (2017) **H:** Painting **BA:** Detroit Institute of Arts, 5200 Woodward Avenue, Detroit, MI, 48202 **ADD:** 9319 SE 137th Street Rd, Summerfield, FL, 34491

SHEFER, NERA GRISALES, I: Law and Legal Services **PT:** Ismenia Grisales; Oscar Grisales **ED:** JD, St. Thomas University School of Law (2003) Coursework, Universidad del Norte Law School, Barranquilla, Colombia **CW:** Contributor, Several Articles to the Huffington Post, Oath Inc. **AW:** Super Lawyers, Thomson Reuters (2015); Named to Top 50 Most Prominent Professionals, Colombia **ACH:** Listed, Top 50 Most Prominent Professionals, Colombia; Won a precedent case related to young adults that come from abroad when they are still children and face not having an immigration status; Won the first DACA benefit for an undocumented youth living in the United States, which set the precedence for the executive action that made DACA available for all undocumented youth who arrived to the United States while being minors

SHELLMAN-LUCAS, ELIZABETH C., T: Special Education Educator, Researcher **I:** Education/Educational Services **CN:** Bethel Gospel Assembly World Mission Outreach **DOB:** 02/05/1937 **PB:** Thomas County **SC:** GA/USA **PT:** Herbert Smith; Juanita (Coleman) Smith **MS:** Married **SPN:** John Lee Lucas, Jr. (Deceased); Eddie Joseph Shellman **CH:** Sandie Juanita Lucas-Boyce; Eddie Joseph Shellman, Jr. **ED:** MEd, City University of New York (1990) **CT:** Certified Teacher, State of New York (2011) **C:** Educational Consultant, Bethel Gospel Assembly World Mission Outreach (2013-Present); President-Elect, Missionary Ministry (2011-Present); Teacher, New York City High School District, Department of Education (1984-Present); Private Practice Cosmetologist, New York, NY (1959) **CIV:** President, Missionary-Ministry, Canaan Baptist Church of Christ, Harlem, NY (2011-2012); Recording Secretary, Missionary Ministry (2007-2011); Citizen Ambassador Delegate, People to People International (1994); Church School Teacher and Superintendent, Canaan Baptist Church of Christ, Harlem, NY (1990-2002); Volunteer, Various Community Organizations **AW:** New York City Church Women's Auxiliary (2011); Unsung Heroine Award (2007); Woman of Year (2000); Excellence in Scholarship & Career Development; Woman of Excellence Award, National Action Network **MEM:** Council for Exceptional Children **H:** Reading; Music; Dance; Jogging; Languages **ADD:** 330 Haven Avenue, Apartment 5D, New York, NY, 10033

SHEN, JENTA, I: Other **ED:** MD, National Taiwan University (1970) **CT:** Diplomate, American Board of Ob-Gyn-Gynecologic Oncology (1999); American Board of Ob-Gyn (1999); Licence to Practice, California (1976) **C:** Fellow, Gynecologic Oncology, LA County-University Southern California Medical Center (1979-1981); Resident Obstetrics-Gynecology Department, University California San Francisco Medical Center (1976-1979); Intern, University of California San Francisco Medical Center (1976); Affiliate, California Pacific Medical Center; Affiliate, St. Mary's Medical

Center; Affiliate, Seton Medical Center; Affiliate, Peninsula Hospital Center; Affiliate, Mills Health Center; Affiliate, Chinese Hospital; Affiliate, Herrick Campus, Alta Bates Summit Medical Center; Associate Clinical Professor, Obstetrics-Gynecology Department, University of California, San Francisco **MEM:** Fellow, American College of Surgeons; American College of Obstetrics and Gynocology

SHEPARD, CHRISTY J., T: Special Education Educator **I:** Education/Educational Services **CN:** Cypress-Fairbanks Independent School District **PB:** St. Louis **SC:** MO/USA **PT:** William E. Shepard; Shirley M. Shepard **ED:** MS in Occupational Education, University of Houston (1989); BS in Special Education, University of Houston (1974) **CT:** Certified in Braille (1974); Certified in Electronic Devices (1974); Certified in Interline From Braille to Print (1974); Certified in Deficient Vision; Certified in Elementary Education; Certified in Kindergarten Education; Certified in Mental Retardation Education; Certified in English Education **C:** University Supervisor, Texas Tech University (2012-Present); Facilitator for Braille Class, Stephen F. Austin State University (1999-Present); Teacher for Students with Visual Impairments, Cypress-Fairbanks Independent School District, Houston, TX (1976-2011); Teacher, Aldine Independent School District, Houston, TX (1974-1976); Secretary, Preston Exterminating Co., Houston, TX (1971-1974); Salesperson, Customer Service, Sears, Roebuck & Co., Houston, TX (1968-1993) **CR:** Facilitator, Region 4 Education Service Center, Houston, TX (1999-Present); Board Member, Harris County Municipal Utility District 23, Houston, TX (1989-Present); Assistant Secretary-Treasurer, Harris County Municipal Utility District 23, Houston, TX (1989-Present) **CIV:** Treasurer, Friends of the Fairbanks Library (2014-Present); Affiliate, Loving Arms Pet Placement (2010-Present); Vice President, Harris County Municipal Utility District 23, Houston, TX (1989-Present); Affiliate, People to People International (1995); Volunteer, Winant Clayton-Tea with Queen Mother of England (1973) **AW:** Recipient, Outstanding Member Award, Texas Association for Education of the Blind and Visually Impaired (2007) **MEM:** International Conference Program Chairperson, Association for Education and Rehabilitation of the Blind and Visually Impaired (2016-Present); President, Association for Education and Rehabilitation of the Blind and Visually Impaired (2014-2016); President-elect, Association for Education and Rehabilitation of the Blind and Visually Impaired (2012-2014); Treasurer, Texas Association for Education of the Blind and Visually Impaired (2000-2016); Former Member, Association of Texas Professional Educators **H:** Reading; Travel; Cross stitching **ADD:** 7415 Shady Mill Dr, Houston, TX, 77040

SHERROD, PHILIP LAWRENCE, T: Artist, Composer, Painter, Poet **I:** Fine Art **DOB:** 10/12/1935 **PB:** Pauls Valley **SC:** OK/USA **PT:** Jesse Lawrence Sherrod; Edrie Mae (Shumate) Sherrod **MS:** Single **SPN:** Helena Alicia Decastro (11/18/1961, Divorced); Peggy Anne Elledge (1/17/1959, Divorced 1959) **CH:** Sandro Arentino Mateos **ED:** Postgraduate Coursework, B. Carroll Reece Memorial Museum, East Tennessee State University (1968); Postgraduate Coursework, Jacques Seligmann & Co. (1968); Postgraduate Studies in Painting, The Art Students League, New York, NY (1961-1963); BA in Art, Oklahoma State University (1959); BA in Painting, Oklahoma State University (1959); BS in Zoology, Oklahoma State University (1957) **C:** Master Teacher, Baird Community Center, South Orange, NJ (2004-2008);

Teacher, The Art Students League, New York, NY (1984-2008); Master Teacher, School of Fine Arts, National Academy of Design (2005); Teacher, Visual Arts Center of New Jersey (1977-2003); Teacher, School of Fine Arts, National Academy of Design (1998); Teacher, School of Fine Arts, National Academy of Design (1996); Teacher, School of Fine Arts, National Academy of Design (1994); Teacher, Morris County Art Association, Morristown, NJ (1973-1974) **CR:** Founder, Street Painters, New York, NY (1977-Present) **CW:** Participant, Group Exhibition, National Academy of Design, New York, NY (2001-Present); Participant, Group Exhibition, National Academy of Design, New York, NY (1997-1999); Exhibitor, One-Man Show, Allan Stone Projects (1996-1997); Participant, Group Exhibition, Fordham University (1996); Participant, Group Exhibition, Galerie des Hamptons Antiques, TriLoca, Inc., Westhampton Beach (1994); Participant, Group Exhibition, National Academy of Design, New York, NY (1993-1995); Participant, Group Exhibition, Rita Dean Gallery, San Diego, CA (1993); Participant, Group Exhibition, New England Fine Arts Institute (Now New England School of Fine Art), Boston, MA (1993); Participant, Group Exhibition, National Academy of Design, New York, NY (1988-1990); Participant, Group Exhibition, Museum and Sculpture Garden, Smithsonian Institute, Washington, D.C. (1989); Poet, "Sex (I) Con" (1985); Poet, "Images Below the Belt" (1984); Poet, "Mr. Wigley Cums" (1983); Exhibitor, One-Man Show, Artists Choice Museum, New York, NY (1983); Participant, Group Exhibition, National Academy of Design, New York, NY (1982); Poet, "Black Truck" (1981); Exhibitor, One-Man Show, Allan Stone Projects (1981); Exhibitor, Group Exhibition, Cork Gallery, Visual Arts League, Lincoln Center, New York, NY (1981-2000); Poet, "30 Mental-Talia" (1980); Exhibitor, One-Man Show, Art Awareness Gallery, Lexington, NY (1980); Exhibitor, One-Man Show, 47 Bond St. Gallery, New York, NY (1979); Exhibitor, Group Exhibition, State University of New York (1979); Exhibitor, Group Exhibition, Boston University Gallery (1979); Participant, Group Exhibition, National Academy of Design, New York, NY (1978); Exhibitor, One-Man Show, JCC of Bayonne, NJ (1977); Exhibitor, Group Exhibition, New Jersey Center for the Arts (1977-2003); Exhibitor, One-Man Show, Bridgeport University, CT (1976); Exhibitor, One-Man Show, Cone Gallery (1976); Exhibitor, One-Man Show, Monique Knowlton Gallery (1976); Participant, Group Exhibition, National Academy of Design, New York, NY (1976); Participant, Group Exhibition, Allan Frumkin Gallery (1975); Exhibitor, One-Man Show, Gallery 100, Princeton, NJ (1975); Exhibitor, One-Man Show, Tower Art Gallery, Highland Falls, NY (1975); Exhibitor, One-Man Show, Allan Stone Projects (1975); Participant, Group Exhibition, National Academy of Design, New York, NY (1975); Exhibitor, One-Man Show, The Humanist Center (1974); Exhibitor, One-Man Show, The Humanist Center (1973); Exhibitor, One-Man Show, Grace Gallery (1973); Exhibitor, One-Man Show, Allan Stone Projects (1973); Participant, Group Exhibition, Allan Frumkin Gallery (1973); Exhibitor, One-Man Show, Pace University, New York, NY (1972); Exhibitor, One-Man Show, Artemis East Gallery (1972); Exhibitor, One-Man Show, Sonraed Gallery (1971); Exhibitor, One-Man Show, Allan Stone Projects (1971); Exhibitor, One-Man Show, East Rockaway Art Exhibition (1969); Exhibitor, One-Man Show, Allan Stone Projects (1969); Exhibitor, One-Man Show, Selected Artists Gallery (1968); Exhibitor, One-Man Show, Jacques Seligmann Gallery (1968); Exhibitor, One-Man Show, Gallery 9, Chatham, NJ (1967); Exhibitor, One-Man Show, Leonard Hutton Hutschnecker

Galleries (1966); Participant, Group Exhibition, National Academy of Design, New York, NY (1966); Exhibitor, Permanent Collection, Newcomb Art Museum, Tulane University, New Orleans, LA; Exhibitor, Permanent Collection, Michele and Donald D'Amour Museum of Fine Arts, Springfield, MA; Exhibitor, Permanent Collection, Everhart Museum, Scranton, PA; Exhibitor, Permanent Collection, Rose Art Museum, Brandeis University, Waltham, MA; Exhibitor Permanent Collection, Almsford House, Fine Arts Center, Anderson, IN; Exhibitor, Permanent Collection, Museum of the City of New York; Exhibitor, Permanent Collection, Hirshhorn Museum and Sculpture Garden, Smithsonian; Exhibitor, Permanent Collection, Hirshhorn Museum and Sculpture Garden, Smithsonian; Exhibitor, Permanent Collection, Phillips Exeter Academy, NH; Exhibitor, Permanent Collection, Worcester Art Museum; Exhibitor, Permanent Collection, Herbert F. Johnson Museum of Art, Cornell University; Exhibitor, Permanent Collection, Rhode Island School of Design; Exhibitor, Permanent Collection, Newark Museum, NJ; Exhibitor, Permanent Collection, National Academy of Design, NY; Exhibitor, Permanent Collection, American Broadcasting Company; Exhibitor, Permanent Collection, Paramount Pictures; Exhibitor, Permanent Collection, INA Corporation; Exhibitor, Permanent Collection, Montgomery Securities, San Francisco, CA; Exhibitor, Permanent Collection, Montgomery Securities, Boston, MA; Exhibitor, Permanent Collection, Montgomery Securities, New York, NY; Exhibitor, Permanent Collection, Allan Stone Projects; Exhibitor, Permanent Collection, Steven Paine; Exhibitor, Permanent Collection, Richard Brown Baker; Exhibitor, Permanent Collection, Tom and Mary Paxton; Exhibitor, Permanent Collection, Bill Paxton; Author, Poetry **AW:** International Prize Galileo Galilei, Salvatore Russo (2017); International Prize Tiepolo - Arte Milano (2016); The Canaletto Prize Artistic Career Award (2016); International Prize Leonardo Da Vinci, The Universal Artist (2016); International Prize Michelangelo, Artists at the Jubilee (2015); Marco Polo International Prize, Art Ambassador of Venice (2015); Prize International Rome Imperial (2015); Sandro Botticelli Prize of Artistic Merit (2015); Grantee, Adolph & Esther Gottlieb Foundation, Inc. (2006); Verbano Award, Accademia Internazionale (2004); Grantee, Adolph & Esther Gottlieb Foundation, Inc. (1996); Grantee, The Pollack-Krasner Foundation (1989); Grantee, Adolph & Esther Gottlieb Foundation, Inc. (1988); Prixe de Roma Fellowship, American Academy in Rome (1985-1986); Grantee, Young Artists Grant, National Endowment for the Arts (1982); Grantee, Adolph & Esther Gottlieb Foundation, Inc. (1981); Grantee, Creative Artists Public Service (1980); Childe Hassam Purchase Awards, American Academy of Arts and Letters (1974); Childe Hassam Purchase Awards, American Academy of Arts and Letters (1969); Childe Hassam Purchase Awards, American Academy of Arts and Letters (1967); Scholarship, Art Students League Federation of Arts and Letters (1963); First Award in Graphics, Ceramics, Etching, Oklahoma State University (1959) **MEM:** Fellow, American Academy in Rome; The Art Students League; Federation of Modern Painters and Sculptors; National Academy Museum (Now National Academy of Design); Treasured Poems of America **MH:** Albert Nelson Marquis Lifetime Achievement Award (2017) **H:** Fishing **ADD:** 41 W 24th St Apt 4F, New York, NY, 10010 **URL:** http://www.philipsherrod.com

SHIMKHADA, DEEPAK, T: Art Historian **I:** Education/Educational Services **DOB:** 09/05/1945 **PB:** Darkha **SC:** Nepal **PT:** Ratna Prasad; Kausalya

Shimkhada **MS:** Married **SPN:** Kanti Koirala (7/7/1970) **CH:** Leepi; Riti **ED:** PhD, Claremont Graduate University (2001); MA, University Of Southern California (1974); MFA, The Maharaja Sayajirao University of Baroda (1970); BFA, The Maharaja Sayajirao University of Baroda (1968) **C:** Professor, Claremont School of Theology (2012-Present); Assistant Professor, University of the West, Rosemead, CA (2010); Adjunct Professor, California State University, Northridge (2009); Adjunct Professor, Claremont Graduate University, Claremont, CA (2008-2012); Assistant Professor, Claremont Mckenna College, Claremont, CA (1999-2009); Professor, Mt. San Antonio College, Walnut, CA (1997-1998); Professor, Rio Hondo Community College, Whittier, CA (1995-1996); Adjunct Professor, Hindu Studies, Claremont School of Theology **CR:** President, Foundation for Indic Philosophy and Culture, Claremont, CA (2001-Present); Visiting Professor, Scripps College, Claremont, CA (1981-1982) **CIV:** Vice President, Asian Studies on the Pacific Coast (2005-Present); Founder, Himalayan Arts Council, Pacific Asia Museum, Pasadena, CA (1986-1994) **CW:** Co-Editor, "The Constant and Changing Faces of the Goddess: Goddess Traditions of Asia" (2008); Contributor, Woven Jewels (1992); Editor, "Himalayas At A Crossroads: The Portrait Of A Changing World" (1988); Editor, Compilation, "Original Buddhist Mantras In Sanskrit" (1985); Author, Exhibition Catalog, "Man, Woman, and Nature in Asian Art" (1982, 1973); Contributor, Exhibition Catalog, "USC Collects: A Sampling Of Taste" (1973); Author, Exhibition Catalog, "NEPALI ART"; Contributor, Articles, Professional Journals; Contributor, Chapters, Books; Exhibitor, Group Shows, Nepal, India, Japan, United States; Solo Exhibitor, Nepal, India, Japan, United States; Commentator, "Ancient Aliens," History Channel **AW:** Distinguished Alumni Service Award, President of Claremont Graduate University (2008); Grantee, Association for Asian Studies (1989); Grantee, North America Buddhist Foundation (1984); Graduate Students Alumni Research Award, The Ohio State University (1980); Grantee, Junior Research Fellow, American Institute of Indian Studies (1978-1979); Fellow, Tuition Fellowship, The University of Chicago (1974-1977); Fulbright Fellow, U.S. Department of State (1972-1974); Certificate Award, Nepal Association of Fine Arts (1969, 1966); Senior Cultural Fellow, Government of India (1968-1970) **MEM:** President, South Asian Studies Association (2017-Present); Vice President, Pacific Coast, Association for Asian Studies (2005-2007); Treasurer, South Asian Studies Association (2004-2010); President, America-Nepal Society of California (1998-2000); American Council for Southern Asian Art; American Academy of Religion; The Art Historians of Southern California; South Asia, Asia Society **MH:** Albert Nelson Marquis Lifetime Achievement Award (2017) **H:** Drawing; Reading **RE:** Hindu **ADD:** 1682 Lowell Ave, Claremont, CA, 91711 **URL:** https://en.wikipedia.org/wiki/Deepak_Shimkhada

SHOOK, JAMES, T: Real Estate Company Executive **I:** Real Estate **DOB:** 05/19/1931 **PB:** Lafayette **SC:** IN/USA **PT:** Charles Wheeler Shook; Jane Creighton (Peffer) Shook **MS:** Married **SPN:** Ruth Adams; Mary Weil (April 12, 1958), Deceased (January 1987) **CH:** James C. Jr.; Kathryn S. Bates; Stephen H.; Sara Sullivan **ED:** BS in Business, Indiana University (1952) **C:** President, The Shook Agency, Inc. (1986-2000); Partner, The Shook Agency (1954-1986) **CR:** Member, Board of Directors, Lafayette Union Railway Company; Director, The Indiana National Bank; Director, The Indiana Gas Company (Now Vectren Inc.) **CIV:** Chairman, North Central Health Services (1989-1991, 2003-2004); President, Lafayette Home

Hospital, Inc. (Now Franciscan Health, Inc.) (1973-1974); President, United Way of Greater Lafayette (1965-1966) **MIL:** First Lieutenant, U.S. Air Force (1952-1954) **MEM:** Board of Directors, Indiana Chamber of Commerce (1975-Present); President, Lafayette Country Club (1969-1970); The Indiana Academy; Crystal Downs Country Club **MH:** Albert Nelson Marquis Lifetime Achievement Award (2017) **H:** Golf; Community activities; Classic cars **PA:** Republican **ADD:** 4 Hitching Post Rd, West Lafayette, IN, 47906

SHULMAN, ABRAHAM, T: Professor Emeritus of Clinical Otolaryngology **I:** Medicine & Health Care **CN:** SUNY Downstate Medical Center **DOB:** 02/24/1929 **PB:** New York **SC:** NY/USA **PT:** Ben Shulman; Libby (Sarnoff) Shulman **MS:** Married **SPN:** Arlene P. (9/8/1957) **CH:** Rachel Dianne; Melanie Brenda **ED:** Fellow, Lempert Institute of Otology (1960); Resident, Division of Otolaryngology, Kings County Hospital Center (Now NYC Health + Hospitals/Kings County) (1957-1960); Internship, NYC Health + Hospitals/ Queens, New York, NY (1956); MD, University of Berne, Switzerland (1955); BS in Biology, City College of New York (1950) **CT:** Diplomate, American Board of Otolaryngology (1962) **C:** Professor Emeritus of Clinical Otolaryngology, SUNY Downstate Medical Center (1992-Present); Head & Neck Surgery Member, American Academy of Ophthalmology and Otolaryngology (Now American Academy of Otolaryngology - Head and Neck Surgery) (1962-Present); President, Board of Directors, Director of Otology Neurotology, Martha Entenmann Tinnitus Research Center, Inc. (1994-2016); Acting Director, Division of Otolaryngology, State University of New York (1975-1985, 1990-1991); Professor of Clinical Otolaryngology, SUNY Downstate Medical Center (1989-1992); Staff Attending Otolaryngologist (1985-2012); Chairman, International Tinnitus Forum (1982-2010); Director, Division of Otolaryngology, Center for Communicative Sciences Health Science Center, SUNY Downstate Medical Center (1980-1985); Brooklyn Veterans Affairs Medical Center (Now Brooklyn Campus of the Department of Veteran Affairs, New York Harbor Health Care System) (1977-1985); Associate Professor, SUNY Downstate Medical Center (1975-1989); Acting Director, Division of Otolaryngology, State University of New York (1975-1985); Assistant Clinical Professor of Otolaryngological Surgery, Albert Einstein College of Medicine (1968-1975); Clinical Instructor, Albert Einstein College of Medicine (1966-1968); Clinical Instructor, SUNY Downstate Medical Center (1962-1964); USNR Lieutenant Commander, Chief of ENT Clinic, Portsmouth Naval Hospital (Now Naval Medical Center Portsmouth), Portsmouth, NH (1960-1962) **CR:** Consultant, Clinical Trial of a Novel Neurobiological Treatment Approach to Tinnitus, Professional Translational Reorganization Training (2016); Moderator, Tinnitus Panel, International Federation Otolaryngology Societies (2005); Visiting Professor, Department of Otolaryngology, University of Wurzburg, Germany (1999); Guest Speaker, Visiting Professor, University of Pittsburgh (1988); Guest Speaker, Visiting Professor, University of Madrid, Spain (1988); Guest Speaker, Visiting Professor, 50th Annual Japan Society of Clinical ORL (1988); Guest Speaker, Department of Otolaryngology, Hellerup Hospital (Now Gentofte Hospital), Copenhagen, Denmark (1987); Chief of Otolaryngology, Brooklyn Veterans Affairs Medical Center (Now Brooklyn Campus Department of Veteran Affairs, New York Harbor Health Care System) (1977-1985); Attending Otolaryngologist, Director of Otolaryngology, Brookdale Medical Center (Now Brookdale University Hospital Medical Center) (1975-1992); Lecturer, Assistant Attending Otolaryngologist, Mount Sinai Hospital (1974); Attending Otolarnygologist, St. John's Queens Hospital (1969-1994); Chief of Otolaryngology, Catholic Medical Center, Brooklyn, NY (1969-1994); Chief of Otolaryngology, Catholic Medical Center, Queens, NY (1969-1994); Assistant Attending Otolaryngologist, Bronx Municipal Hospital (Now NYC Health + Hospitals/ Jacobi) (1967-1975); Chief of Otolaryngology, Lincoln Hospital (Now NYC Health + Hospitals/ Lincoln) (1967-1970); Assistant Surgeon, Brooklyn Eye & Ear Hospital (1966-1969); Assistant Attending Otolaryngologist, Kings County Hospital (Now NYC Health + Hospitals/Kings County) (1962-1964); Otology Consultant, College Point Nursing Home, New York (1962-1964) **CIV:** Medical Scientific Advisory Board, American Tinnitus Association (1980-2001); Consultant, Children's Development Center (1975); Medical Consultant, Office of Vocational Rehabilitation (1974); Director of Medical Service, Lexington School for the Deaf (1972-1974) **MIL:** Lieutenant Commander, U.S. Navy Reserve (1960-1962); Chief of Otolaryngology, Portsmouth Naval Hospital, Portsmouth, NH **CW:** Editor Emeritus, International Tinnitus Journal (2011-Present); Co-Chief Editor, International Tinnitus Journal (1994-2010); Author, Co-Editor, "Tinnitus Diagnosis and Treatment, First Edition," Lea and Febiger, Philadelphia, PA (1991); Editor, "Tinnitus Diagnosis and Treatment" (1991-2010); First Time Reported Application Nuclear Medicine Spect Brain Imaging in Tinnitus Patients, SUNY Downstate Medical Center/Kings County Hospital (1989); Honorary Editorial Board, Highlights, League for Hard of Hearing, New York (1972-2005); United States Patent, Neuroprotective Drug; United States Patent, US Provisional Patent Inner Ear Drug Delivery; Contributor, More than 250 Scientific Articles to Professional Journals; Contributor, Chapters to Textbooks; Reviewer, Several Scientific Journals **AW:** Sigma Xi, The Scientific Research Honor Society, SUNY Downstate Medical Center Section (1982-Present); Lifetime Achievement Award, Albert Nelson Marquis Who's Who (2017); for Exemplary Expertise and Knowledge in the Field of Tinnitus Research and Treatment, Expertscape (2013); Letter of Appreciation, Service Award for 35 Years of Dedicated Service to the United States Government, Department of Veterans Affairs, New York Harbor Health Care System (2012); Best Doctors, Castle Connolly (2010-2015); Neurotological Research Award, Neuroequilibrimetric Society (2010); Monograph, 150 Years of Medical Education Achievement Award, SUNY Downstate Medical Center (2010); Citation for 50 Years Devoted to the Service of the Public in the Practice of Medicine, Medical Society of the State of New York (2005); Honor Award, American Academy of Otolaryngology - Head & Neck Surgery (1994); Excellence In Teaching Resident Staff Award, Department of Otolaryngology, SUNY Downstate Medical Center (1994); Myrtle Reed Award, Hadassah Zion Organization of America (Now Hadassah, The Women's Zionist Organization of America, Inc.) (1993); Hocks Award, American Tinnitus Association (1990); Certificate of Appreciation, American Speech and Hearing Association (Now American Speech-Language-Hearing Association (1989); Letter of Achievement, Portsmouth Naval Hospital (Now Naval Medical Center Portsmouth), Portsmouth, NH (1962) **MEM:** Fellow, American College of Surgeons (1974-Present); The New York Academy of Sciences (1962-Present); Fellow, Head and Neck Surgery Member, American Academy of Ophthalmology and Otolaryngology (Now American Academy of Otolaryngology — Head and Neck Surgery) (1962-Present); Life Associate Fellow, American Society for Laser Medicine and Surgery, Inc. (2009); Consultant, American Academy of Otolaryngology — Head and Neck Surgery (1999-2005); Medical Scientific Advisory Board, American Tinnitus Association (1980-2001); Chairman, Geriatric Otolaryngology Committee, American Academy of Otolaryngology — Head and Neck Surgery (1995-1999); Emeritus, American Academy of Facial Plastic and Reconstructive Surgery (1997); First Chairman, International Tinnitus Study Group (1980-1995); Subcommittee on Hearing, American Academy of Otolaryngology — Head and Neck Surgery (1992-1995); Reappointment, Subcommittee on Hearing, American Academy of Otolaryngology — Head and Neck Surgery (1988-1990); First Chairman, International Tinnitus Study Group (1985-1988); Subcommittee on Hearing, American Academy of Otolaryngology — Head and Neck Surgery (1985-1987); Fellow, Politzer Society (1984); Fellow, American Audiology Society (Now The American Auditory Society) (1980); Working Group on Tinnitus, National Research Council (1980); Sigma Xi, The Scientific Research Honor Society, SUNY Downstate Medical Center Section (1978); Fellow, The American Neurotology Society (1974); American Council of Otolaryngology (1972) **MH:** Albert Nelson Marquis Lifetime Achievement Award (2017) **H:** Attending movies, ballet performances, theater productions and opera with his wife, family and friends; Science, including the neuroscience of brain function and space exploration; Baseball; Basketball **RE:** Hebrew **ADD:** 8508 210th St, Jamaica, NY, 11427 **URL:** http://www.expertscape.com/leaders/tinnitus

SHUMAN, EARL STANLEY, T: Music Publisher **I:** Publishing **CN:** ASCAP, Broadcast Music, Inc. **DOB:** 08/02/1923 **PB:** Boston **SC:** MA/USA **PT:** Benjamin Morris Schuman; Mildred Judith (Kaplan) Shuman **MS:** Married **SPN:** Margaret Stein (11/25/1956) **CH:** Cathy Elizabeth; Daniel James; Steven Lewis **ED:** BA, Yale University (1945) **C:** Publisher, ASCAP, New York, NY (1977-Present); Publisher, Broadcast Music, Inc., New York, NY (1977-Present); Owner, Earl Music Company (1957); Owner, Peg Music Company (1957); President, Earl Music Company (1957); President, Peg Music Company (1957) **MIL:** Captain, U.S. Marine Corps Reserve (1950-1951); Captain, U.S. Marine Corps Reserve (1943-1946) **CW:** Lyricist, "Not Now" (2014); Featured Soundtrack Artist, "Snow Flower and the Secret Fan" (2011); Featured Soundtrack Artist, "Persons Unknown" (2010); Featured Soundtrack Artist, "The Mighty Macs" (2009); Featured Soundtrack Artist, "Confetti" (2006); Featured Soundtrack Artist, "Must Love Dogs" (2005); Featured Soundtrack Artist, "Serving Sara" (2002); Featured Soundtrack Artist, "Nothing to Lose" (1997); Featured Soundtrack Artist, "Traveller" (1997); Featured Soundtrack Artist, "Shag" (1989); Featured Soundtrack Artist, "Sweet Dreams" (1985); Publisher, "Bat Out of Hell", Meat Loaf (1977); Co-lyricist, "The Young New Mexican Puppeteer" (1972); Co-lyricist, "Hey There Lonely Girl" (1970); Lyricist, "My Shy Violet" (1968); Lyricist, "Leaves are the Tears of Autumn" (1968); Composer, "Confidence," NFL on CBS (1967-1976); Lyricist, TV Theme, "Coronet Blue," ABC-TV (1967); Co-lyricist, "Time, Time" (1967); Lyricist, "Love Me Longer (Love Theme from Arrivederci, Baby!)" (1966); Lyricist, "Judith" (1966); Lyricist, "Situation Hopeless But Not Serious" (1965); Lyricist, "The River" (1965); Lyricist, Stage Musical, "The Secret Life of Walter Mitty" (1964); Co-lyricist, "Clinging Vine" (1964); Lyricist, "Robinson Crusoe on Mars" (1964); Lyricist, "Monica (Love Theme from The Carpetbaggers)" (1964); Lyricist, "The Disorderly Orderly" (1964); Co-lyricist, "Caterina" (1962);

Lyricist, "Close to Cathy" (1962); Lyricist, "Most People Get Married" (1962); Lyricist, "Theme for a Dream" (1961); Lyricist, "Meadow in the Sky" (1961); Lyricist, "Dondi" (1961); Lyricist, "Barabbas" (1961); Co-lyricist, "Hotel Happiness" (1960); Lyricist, "Starry Eyed" (1960); Lyricist, "Left Right Out of Your Heart" (1958); Co-lyricist, "The Banjo's Back in Town" (1955); Co-lyricist, "Seven Lonely Days (1953); Lyricist, "Let Children just Be Children" **AW:** Platinum Record, "Bat Out of Hell" (1977); Country and Western Award, "Seven Lonely Days" (1970); Gold Record, "Hey There Lonely Girl" (1970); Country and Western Award, "Leaves are the Tears of the Autumn" (1969); Award, "The Secret Life of Walter Mitty" (1965) **MEM:** ASCAP **MH:** Albert Nelson Marquis Lifetime Achievement Award (2017) **H:** Music; Baseball; Travel **ADD:** 111 E 88th Street, Apt. 3B, New York, NY, 10128

SICKING, RICHARD A., T: Lawyer, Shareholder **I:** Law and Legal Services **CN:** Touby, Chait & Sicking, PL **DOB:** 02/10/1938 **PT:** Joseph Edwin Sicking; Helen Sicking **MS:** Married **SPN:** Zoe Helmuth-Sicking (6/15/1963) **CH:** Elizabeth Ann; Rebecca Margaret **ED:** LLB, University of Miami (1963); AB, University of Miami (1960) **C:** Shareholder, Touby, Chait & Sicking, PL (2015-Present); Panel Lawyer, Worker's Compensation, National Football League Players Association, Tallahassee, FL (1983-1988); General Counsel, Congress of Industrial Organizations; General Counsel, American Federation Labor; General Counsel, Florida Professional Firefighters, International Association of Firefighters **CR:** Labor Member, The State of Florida Workers' Compensation Panel (1983-1987); Chairman, Special Disability Trust Fund Committee, Tallahassee, FL (1971-1975) **CW:** Editor, Journal Association Florida Compensation Attorneys (1963-1965) **AW:** Jon E. Krupnick Award for Perseverance, Florida Justice Association (2016); Compensation Institute Hall of Fame (2012); Recipient, Achievement Award, Friends of 440, Miami, FL (1979); Florida Workers **MEM:** Collectors Club, New York, NY; Workers' Compensation Section, Florida Bar **BAR:** Supreme Court of the United States (1968); Florida (1963) **MH:** Albert Nelson Marquis Lifetime Achievement Award (2017) **PA:** Democrat **RE:** Roman Catholic **BA:** 2030 S Douglas Rd Ste 217, Touby, Chait & Sicking, PL, Cora Gables, FL, 33134 **URL:** https://www.floridabar.org/directories/find-mbr/profile/?num=73747

SIEG, ALBERT, T: Manufacturing Executive **I:** Manufacturing **CN:** Albert L. Sieg Associates **DOB:** 03/25/1930 **PB:** Chicago **SC:** IL/USA **PT:** Albert Fredrick Sieg; Louise Augusta (Strege) Sieg **ED:** Professional Master's Degree, Harvard Business School (1971); PhD in Organic Chemistry, University of Rochester (1954); BS in Chemistry, University of Illinois (1951) **C:** Principal, Consultant, Albert L. Sieg Associates, Rochester, NY (1992-Present); Retired, Eastman Kodak Co., Rochester, NY (1992); Vice President, Director, Strategic Resources, Secretary, Imaging Board, Eastman Kodak Co., Rochester, NY (1991-1992); President, Representative Director, Eastman Chemicals Japan Ltd., Tokyo, Japan (1989-1991); President, Representative Director, Eastman Kodak Japan, Tokyo, Japan (1989-1991); President, Kodak Japan K.K., Tokyo, Japan (1984-1989); Vice President, Director, Eastman Kodak Co., Rochester, NY (1981-1984); Manager, Paper Management, Eastman Kodak Co., Rochester, NY (1976-1981); Corporate Manager Instant, Eastman Kodak Co., Rochester, NY (1972-1976); Supervisor of Emulsion, Eastman Kodak Co., Rochester, NY (1970-1972); Board of Directors, Eastman Kodak Japan, Tokyo, Japan **CR:** Advisory Board, World Scape, Inc. (2001-Present); Senior Lecturer, University of Rochester (1960-1969); American Cyanamide Fellow (1953-1954); Kiwanis Club of Chicago Fellow, University of Illinois (1947-1951); Board of Directors, XM Corporation, Kodak Japan Industries, Ltd.; Fellow, Photograph Society of America; Fellow, American Institute of Chemists **CIV:** Chair, Loop Ministries (2010-Present); Board of Directors, St. John's Foundation (2001-Present); Chairman-Elect, St. John's Foundation (2006-2007); Secretary, St. John's Foundation (2005-2006); Board of Directors, St. John's Home Foundation (2000-2008); Chair, St. John's Senior Services (1999-2001); Chairman, St. John's Nursing Home (1999-2001); President, St. John's Senior Services (1997-2001); Board of Directors, St. John's Senior Services (1997-2001); Chair Elect, St. John's Senior Services (1997-1999); Vice Chairman, Board of Directors, St. John's Nursing Home (1997-1999); Vice Chairman, Board of Directors, St. John's Home for Aging (1997-1999); Board of Directors, St. John's Home for Aging (1994-1999); Board of Directors, St. John's Nursing Home (1994-1999); Chairman, Corporate Gifts, International Museum of Photography at George Eastman House (1994); Chairman, Corporate Gifts, International Museum of Photography at George Eastman House (1993); Chairman, Corporate Gifts, Rochester Philharmonic Orchestra (1982-1984); President, Reformation Lutheran Church, Rochester, NY (1978-1983) **MIL:** Medical Service Corps, U.S. Army (1955-1957) **CW:** Co-Author, "Tokyo Chronicles" (1994); Co-Author, Eighth Here's How (1972); Inventor in Field **AW:** Lifetime Achievement Award, Photographic Society of America (2013); International Hall of Fame of Photography (2007); Progress Medal, Photograph Society of America (1995); George Eastman Medal, Kodak Camera Clubs (1980); Harold Lloyd Award, Photograph Society of America (1978) **MEM:** Chairman of the Board, Loop Ministries, Inc. (2010-Present); Board of Directors, National Steroscopic Association (2008-Present); National Steroscopic Association (2007-Present); Past President, North America Nature Photography Association (2007-Present); Board of Directors, Photograph Society of America (1992-Present); Elected President Emeritus, Photograph Society of America (2015); Elected Chairman of the Board, National Steroscopic Association (2009-2013); Board of Directors, International Photography Hall of Fame (2007-2011); President, North America Nature Photography Association (2006-2007); Board of Directors, North America Nature Photography Association (2005-2006); Board Directors, North America Nature Photography Association (2003-2007); President, Photograph Society of America (1999-2003); Executive Vice President, Photograph Society of America (1995-1999); President, International Stereoscopic Union (1993-1994); Vice President, American Chamber of Commerce, Japan (1989-1991); Board of Governors, American Chamber of Commerce, Japan (1988-1991); Vice President, Photograph Society of America (1969-1984); American Association for the Advancement of Science; Photographic Society of America; Society of Photograph Scientists and Engineers; American Chemical Society; Rochester Chamber of Commerce; Foreign Correspondents Club; American Club of Tokyo **H:** Skiing; Photography; Gardening **PA:** Republican **ADD:** 159 Hillhurst Lane, Rochester, NY, 14617

SIEGEL, DAVID A., T: Attorney **I:** Law and Legal Services **CN:** Nahon Saharovich and Trotz **SPN:** Dana Siegel **CH:** Josh; Stephanie **ED:** JD, The University of Tennessee, Knoxville (1985) **AW:** Admin Edmund Muskie Pro Bono Award, ABA, San Francisco, CA (2017); Named in Top 100 Lawyers in Tennessee (2015); Named in Top 50 Super Lawyers in Memphis (2015); Named in Top 100 Lawyers in Tennessee (2010-2011); Listed as Super Lawyer, "Law & Politics Magazine" (2008-2016); Named in Top 100 Trial Lawyers, American Trial Lawyers Association (2007-2011); Humanitarian Award, Greater Memphis United Chinese Association (2006); Special Recognition Award for Extraordinary Service (2004-2005) **MEM:** Phi Eta Sigma, Freshman National Honor Society **BA:** 488 S Mendenhall Rd, Memphis, TN, 38117 **ADD:** 3138 Heathstone Cv, Germantown, TN, 38138

SIEGEL, BIANCA, T: Pediatric Otolaryngologist, Assistant Professor **I:** Medicine & Health Care **CN:** Children's Hospital of Michigan **ED:** Pediatric Otolaryngology Fellowship, Children's Hospital of Pittsburgh of UPMC, Pittsburgh, PA (2014-2015); Otolaryngology Residency, Einstein-Montefiore Medical Center, Bronx, NY (2013-2014); MD, Wayne State University School of Medicine, Detroit MI, With High Distinction (2005-2009); BS in Biochemistry, University of Michigan, Ann Arbor, MI, With Honors (2001-2005) **CT:** American Board of Otolaryngology **C:** Assistant Professor, Department of Otolaryngology, Wayne State University School of Medicine, Detroit, MI (2015-Present); Pediatric Otolaryngologist, Children's Hospital of Michigan, Detroit, MI (2015-Present) **CR:** Board Member, Lions Hearing Club (2016-Present); Co-director, Multidisciplinary Aerodigestive Clinic, Children's Hospital of Michigan, Detroit, MI (2016-Present); Basic Science Course Director, WSUSOM Otolaryngology Residency Program (2016-Present); Administrative Chief Resident, Einstein-Montefiore Medical Center (2013-2014); ABOto Liaison, American Academy of Otolaryngology (2011-2013); Local Chair, World Health Student Organization, Wayne State University School of Medicine (2006-2007); Coordinator, Code Blue, Wayne State University School of Medicine (2006-2007) **CW:** Author, "Stridor and apnea as the initial presentation of primary hypoparathyroidism," International Journal of Pediatric Otorhinolaryngology (2016); Author, "The role of laryngotracheal reconstruction in the management of recurrent croup in patients with underlying subglottic stenosis," International Journal of Pediatric Otorhinolaryngology (2016); Author, "Comparative outcomes of severe obstructive sleep apnea in pediatric patients with trisomy," International Journal of Pediatric Otorhinolaryngology (2015); Author, "Open airway surgery for subglottic hemangioma in the era of propanolol: Is it sill indicated?" International Journal of Pediatric Otorhinolaryngology (2015); Author, "Securing stent for multi-stage laryngotracheoplasty: An evolved technique," International Journal of Pediatric Otorhinolaryngology (2015); Author, "Contemporary guidelines for tympanostomy tube placement," Current Treatment Options in Pediatrics (2015); Author, "Risk factors for perioperative airway difficulty and evaluation of intubation approaches among patients with benign goiter," Annals of Otology, Rhinology & Laryngology (2014); Author, "Tracheal rupture in complicated delivery: a case report and review of the literature," International Journal of Pediatric Otorhinolaryngology (2014); Author, "Adenoidectomy," Encyclopedia of Otolaryngology, Head and Neck Surgery, New York City, NY (2013); Author, "Gastroesophageal and Laryngopharyngeal Reflux," Pediatric Otolaryngology Head and Neck Surgery (2013); Author, "Hemispheric dominance and cell phone use," JAMA Otolaryngology – Head & Neck Surgery (2013); Author, "Endotracheal

Nitinol Stents: Lessons from the Learning Curve," Otolaryngology-Head and Neck Surgery (2013); Author, "Management of complex glottic stenosis in children with recurrent respiratory papillomatosis," International Journal of Pediatric Otorhinolaryngology (2013); Author, "Pectus excavatum in children with laryngomalacia," International Journal of Pediatric Otorhinolaryngology (2013); Author, "Laryngopyocoele: An unusual cause of a sore throat," American Journal of Emergency Medicine (2012); Author, "ENT-Head and Neck Surgery: Essential Procedures," Annals of Otology, Rhinology & Laryngology (2011); Author, "Otolaryngology Cases: The University of Cincinnati Clinical Portfolio," Annals of Otology, Rhinology & Laryngology (2010) **AW:** Teacher of the Year Award, Detroit Medical Center (2017); Difference Maker Award, Children's Hospital of Michigan (2016); Distinguished Service Award, Wayne State University School of Medicine (2009); Janet M. Glasgow Memorial Achievement Citation, Wayne State University School of Medicine (2009); Aesculapeans Honor Society, Wayne State University School of Medicine (2008); Deans List, University of Michigan (2001-2005); Phi Sigma Theta Honor Society, University of Michigan Chapter (2004) **MEM:** Fellow Member, American Society of Pediatric Otolaryngology (2015-Present); Fellow Member, American Academy of Pediatrics (2015-Present); Resident Member, American Academy of Otolaryngology (2009-Present); Vice President, Wayne State University School of Medicine Chapter, Alpha Omega Alpha (2008-2009) **BA:** 3901 Beaubien St, Children's Hospital of Michigan, Detroit, MI, 48201 **ADD:** 19365 Cumberland Way, Detroit, MI, 48203

SIEGEL, LAURENCE B., T: Director of Research **I:** Research **CN:** CFA Institute **PT:** Seymour Siegel; Atarah (Rosenthal) Siegel **MS:** Married **SPN:** Connie O'Hara (9/27/1980) **CH:** Joshua; Betsy **ED:** MBA, University of Chicago (1977); BA, University of Chicago (1975) **C:** Gary P. Brinson Director of Research, CFA Research Institute (2005-Present); Researcher, Marmon Holdings, Inc. (1977-Present); Director of Research, Ford Foundation (1994-2009); Managing Director, Ibbotson Associates (Now Morningstar, Inc.) (1984-1994); Consultant, Ibbotson Associates (Now Morningstar, Inc.) (1979-1984); Researcher, American Enterprise Institute (1975-1977); Board of Directors, Ibbotson Associates (Now Morningstar, Inc.) **CR:** Advisory Board, CFA Institute (2000-Present); Advisory Board, Commonfund, Westport, CT (1987-Present); Trustee, Emerging Growth Fund, Oberweis Asset Management (1993-1994); Moody's Investors Service, Inc. (1986-1988); Consultant in Field **CW:** Editorial Advisory Board, Journal of Portfolio Management (1986-Present); Author, "Benchmarks and Investment Management" (2003); Contributor, Articles, Professional Journals; Author, "Fewer, Richer, Greener" **AW:** Graham and Dodd Award, CFA Institute (2015); Edhec-Robeco Award (2009); Graham and Dodd Award, CFA Institute (1984) **MEM:** Class News Editor, Hawken School (1984-Present); Alumni Association of Metropolitan Chicago, University of Chicago; National Society of Rate Return Analysts; American Finance Association **MH:** Albert Nelson Marquis Lifetime Achievement Award (2017) **H:** Folk music; Rock music; Travel **RE:** Jewish **ADD:** 1229 Maple Avenue, Wilmette, IL, 60091

SIEW, SHIRLEY, T: Professor **I:** Education/Educational Services **CN:** Michigan State University **SC:** Republic of South Africa **ED:** PhD, MD, University of the Witwatersrand (1963) **CT:** License to Practice Medicine, State of Michigan; License to Practice Medicine, State of Indiana **C:** Professor, Pathology, College of Human Medicine, College of Osteopathic Medicine, Michigan State University (1977-Present) **CIV:** Member, Zonta International; Member, Lansing Dewitt Sunrise Rotary; Member, Greek Interpreters **CW:** Editorial Board, Group for Research and Pathology Education; Contributor, Chapters, Books; Contributor, 105 Articles, Professional Journals **AW:** Distinguished Service Award, College of Osteopathic Medicine, Michigan State University (2017); Distinguished Faculty Award, Michigan State University (2017, 1988); Recipient, 71 Teaching Awards **MEM:** United States & Canadian Academy of Pathology; Fellow, American College of Cardiology Foundation; American Heart Association, Inc.; American Society of Andrology; Microscopy Society of America; Michigan Chapter, American College of Cardiology; F.F.Path.(SA); FRCPath; FRSM **H:** Flying planes; Reading Scientific Journals; History; Reading biographies; Reading detective stories **BA:** 950 Fee St, East Lansing, MI, 48824 **ADD:** 2978 Crestwood Dr, East Lansing, MI, 48823 **URL:** https://www.doximity.com/pub/shirley-siew-md

SIFFERT, JOHN SAND, T: Partner **I:** Law and Legal Services **CN:** Lankler Siffert & Wohl LLP **DOB:** 03/26/1947 **PB:** New York **SC:** NY/USA **PT:** Robert Spencer Siffert; Miriam (Sand) Siffert **MS:** Married **SPN:** Goldie Alfasi-Siffert (6/1/1975) **CH:** David Alfasi; Matthew Alfasi **ED:** JD, Columbia University (1972); BA, Amherst College (1969) **C:** Partner, Lankler Siffert & Wohl LLP, New York, NY (1984-Present); Partner, Lankler & Siffert (Now Lankler Siffert & Wohl LLP), New York, NY (1983-1984); Partner, Fulop & Hardee, New York, NY (1979-1983); Assistant Attorney, United States District Court for the Southern District of New York (1974-1979); Law Clerk to the Honorable Murray I. Gurfein, United States District Court for the Southern District of New York (1972-1974) **CR:** Member, Committee on Admissions and Grievances, United States Court of Appeals for the Second Circuit (2015-Present); Vice Chairman of Projects & Initiatives, Historical Society of the New York Courts (2014-Present); Member, Grievance Committee Attorney Panel, United States District Court Southern District of New York (2014-Present); Member, Executive Committee, PLI Practising Law Institute (2012-Present); Member, Board of Directors, PLI Practising Law Institute (2010-Present); Member, Board of Directors, Historical Society of the New York Courts (2009-Present); Member, SDM (1992-Present); Adjunct Professor, School of Law, New York University (1979-Present); Member, Judicial Conference Advisory Committee on Criminal Rules (2012-2018); President, Northeast Region, American Friends of the Hebrew University (2014-2016); Member, Board of Directors, Northeast Region, American Friends of the Hebrew University (2010-2014); Special Master, First Department, Appellate Division, Departmental Disciplinary Committee, First Judicial Department (1999-2011); Member, Appellate Division, Departmental Disciplinary Committee, First Judicial Department (2005-2010); Member, Advisory Council, Procurement Policy Board, New York, NY (1991-1995) **CIV:** Emeritus Member, Board of Directors, New York Lawyers for the Public Interest (2011-Present); Member, Advisory Board, NYCRC (1995-Present); Member, Board of Directors, New York Lawyers for the Public Interest (1998-2011); Chair, New York Lawyers for the Public Interest (2006-2008); Secretary, New York Lawyers for the Public Interest (2003-2005) **CW:** Co-Author, "Business Crime" (1981); Co-Author, "Modern Federal Jury Instructions-Criminal"; Co-Author, "Modern Federal Jury Instructions-Civil" **AW:** Named to Top 100 Criminal Defense Lawyers, American Society of Legal Advocates (2013-2017); Named to Top 100 Trial Lawyers, The National Trial Lawyers (2010-2017); Health And Healing Award, Campaign for the Fair Sentencing of Youth (2014); Named to Top 100 Lawyers in New York City, Super Lawyers (2006-2010); Second Circuit Professionalism Award, American Institute of Law, Inc. (2009); Named to Top 10 Lawyers, Super Lawyers (2008) **MEM:** Foundation Trustee, American College of Trial Lawyers (2013-Present); American Society of Legal Advocates (2013-2017); Honors Committee, Association of the Bar of the City of New York (2011-2013); Nominating Committee, Association of the Bar of the City of New York (2011-2012); Executive Board Committee, Association of the Bar of the City of New York (2008-2010); Board of Regents, American College of Trial Lawyers (2006-2010); Board Member, New York Council of Defense Lawyers (2004-2008); Chairman, New York Downstate Committee, American College of Trial Lawyers (2004-2006); Chairman, Federal Legislative Committee, Association of the Bar of the City of New York (2003-2006); Chairman, Committee on Admission to Fellowship, American College of Trial Lawyers (2001-2004); President, American Inns of Court (2001-2002); Fellow, American Bar Foundation; Fellow, American College of Trial Lawyers; ABA; Super Lawyers; The National Trial Lawyers **BAR:** Admitted to Practice, Supreme Court of the United States (1979); Admitted to Practice, United States District Court for the Southern District of New York (1974); Admitted to Practice, United States District Court for the Eastern District of New York (1974); Admitted to Practice, United States Court of Appeals for the Second Circuit (1974); Admitted to Practice, New York State Bar Association (1973) **MH:** Albert Nelson Marquis Lifetime Achievement Award (2017) **PA:** Democrat **RE:** Jewish **BA:** 500 Fifth Avenue 34th floor, Lankler Siffert & Wohl LLP, New York, NY, 10110-3398 **URL:** http://www.lswlaw.com/attorney/john-s-siffert/

SILVA, CHRISTOPHER PATRICK, T: Electronics Engineer **I:** Engineering **CN:** The Aerospace Corporation **DOB:** 03/17/1960 **PB:** Fortuna **SC:** CA/USA **PT:** Joseph Sousa Silva; Maria Urania (Cabral) Silva **MS:** Single **ED:** PhD, University of California, Berkeley, CA (1993); MEE, University of California, Berkeley, CA (1985); Honorary BEE, University of California, Berkeley, CA, With Highest Honors (1982); AA, College of the Redwoods, Eureka, CA (1980) **C:** Senior Engineering Specialist, The Aerospace Corporation, El Segundo, CA (2003-Present); Engineering Specialist, The Aerospace Corporation, El Segundo, CA (1999-2003); Senior Technical Staff, The Aerospace Corporation, El Segundo, CA (1995-1999); Technical Staff, The Aerospace Corporation, El Segundo, CA (1989-1995) **CR:** Presenter to Professional Conferences, Dinner Meetings, Industries and Universities **CIV:** Project Judge, Aerospace 15th Anniversary Herndon Engineering and Science Fair (1992) **CW:** Contributor, Chapters to Books; Contributor, Articles to Professional Journals, Conference Proceedings, and Workshops at Professional Conferences **AW:** Associated Editor, IEEE Transactions on Microwave Theory and Techniques (2017-Present); Aerospace Corporate Achievement Award (2013-2014); Aerospace Corporate Team Achievement Award (2013); Aerospace Corporate Team Achievement Award (2009); Associate Editor, IEEE Transactions on Circuits and Systems (2002–2004); Aerospace Corporate Individual Achievement Award (2003); Fellow, IEEE (1999); Senior Member, AIAA (1999); Aerospace Corporate President's Award (1999);

Aerospace Corporate Team Achievement Award (1998); Lockheed Leadership Fellowship (1986-1988); National Science Foundation Fellowship (1983–1986); Alumni Scholar, University of California (1982); Physics Student of the Year, American Association of Physics Teachers (1979) **MEM:** IEEE; American Institute of Aeronautics and Astronautics; Society for Industrial and Applied Mathematics; American Mathematical Society; The Phi Beta Kappa Society; Eta Kappa Nu Electrical & Computer Engineering Honor Society; Tau Beta Pi Engineering Honor Society **MH:** Albert Nelson Marquis Lifetime Achievement Award (2017) **H:** Traveling; History; Religious reading; Home improvement; Desktop publishing; Photography **RE:** Roman Catholic **BA:** PO Box 92957 MS M1/111, The Aerospace Corporation, Los Angeles, CA, 90009 **ADD:** 26766 Menominee Place, Rancho Palos Verdes, CA, 90275

SIMMONDS, ROBERT MAURER, T: Educator, Operations Research Analyst (Retired) **I:** Education/Educational Services **DOB:** 04/16/1947 **PB:** Beaver Falls **SC:** PA/USA **MS:** Married **SPN:** Deborah Lynne Carawan (6/25/1977) **CH:** Stephen Maurer; Kent Hayes **ED:** MA, Naval War College (2008); Diplomate, Senior Executive Progressive, John F. Kennedy School of Government, Harvard University (2004); EdD, William & Mary (1985); MS, Youngstown State University (1975); BS, Youngstown State University (1973) **CT:** Advanced Certification in Education, William & Mary (1983) **C:** Retired (2013); Consultant, Applied Management Prosecuting, OEPM, MPP, OSD (2013); Deputy Director, Statistical Analysis, OEPM, MPP, OSD (2009-2012); Senior Army Fellow (2006-2009); Deputy Undersecretary (2006-2009); Senior Operations Researcher, Analyst, U.S. Army Human Resources Command, Washington, DC (2006); Department Chairman, System Engineering Department, U.S. Army Logistics Management College, Fort Lee, NJ (2001-2006); Associate Professor, St. Leo College, Fort Eustis, VA (1988-2001); Associate Professor, St. Leo College, Fort Eustis, VA (1985-1988) **MIL:** With, U.S. Navy (1965-1968) **CW:** Contributor, Articles, Professional Journals **MEM:** Treasurer, Combat Veterans Motorcycle Association (2016-Present); Webmaster, Combat Veterans Motorcycle Association (2015-Present) **MH:** Albert Nelson Marquis Lifetime Achievement Award (2017) **H:** Golf **ADD:** 16088 Dancing Leaf Pl, Dumfries, VA, 22025 **URL:** https://www.cvmavirginia27-2.org/

SIMMS, JAMES ROBERT, T: President (Retired) **I:** Engineering **CN:** Simms Industries Inc. **PB:** Vinita **SC:** OK/USA **PT:** Paul Otto Simms; Meda (Hall) Simms **MS:** Single **SPN:** Lanita Jayne Thiessen (11/30/1974, Deceased 1987); Pauline Sue Blackwell (8/12/1950, Deceased 1969) **CH:** Suzanne Marie **ED:** Bachelor's Degree, The University of Oklahoma (1950) **CT:** Registered Professional Engineer, State of Maryland **C:** President, Simms Industries Inc., Columbia, Maryland (1983-1997); Senior Associate, Booz, Allen & Hamilton, Bethesda, Maryland (1975-1983); Consultant, Private Practice, Clarksville, Maryland (1973-1975); Program Manager, General Electric, Beltsville, Maryland (1971-1973); Director of Operations, Systems Research Corporation (1970-1971); Program Manager, Systems Research Corporation, Washington, DC (1967-1970); Senior Technology Staff, ITT Intelcom, Baileys Cross, Virginia (1966-1967); Manager of Electronics and System Engineering, Fairchild, Hagerstown, Maryland (1961-1963); Systems Engineer, The Martin Company, Denver, Colorado (1956-1961); Electronic Engineer, The Martin Company, Baltimore, Maryland (1950-1956) **CIV:** Member, Board of Directors, Southern Howard County

Democrat's Club (1980-1983); County Coordinator, Committee to Elect Congresswoman Byron (1978, 1980, 1982); President, Southern Howard County Democrat's Club (1979) **MIL:** U.S. Navy (1943-1946) **CW:** Author, "Principles of Quantitative Living System Science" (2006); Author, "The Limits of Behavior: A Quantitative Social Theory" (1983); Author, "A Measure of Knowledge," Philosophical Library of Publishers (1971); Contributor, Articles, Professional Journals **AW:** Honoree, Cherokee Warrior, Cherokee Nation (2015) **MEM:** IEEE; Oklahoma Region, Cherokee Nation; World Future Society; American Society for Cybernetics; International Society for the Systems Sciences **MH:** Albert Nelson Marquis Lifetime Achievement Award (2017) **H:** Dancing with his lady **RE:** Methodist **ADD:** 9405 Elizabeth Ct, Fulton, MD, 20759

SIMONS, ANNEKE PRINS, T: Artist **I:** Education/Educational Services **DOB:** 02/15/1930 **PB:** Amsterdam **SC:** The Netherlands **PT:** Raphael Hugo; Charlotte Prins **ED:** MA in Social Science, Jersey City State College, Jersey City, NJ (1975); PhD, Pennsylvania State University, University Park, PA (1968); MAT, Harvard-Radcliffe, Cambridge, MA (1953); BA, Vassar College, Poughkeepsie, NY (1952) **C:** Professor Emeritus (2000-Present); Professor, New Jersey City University (1967-2000); Graduate Research Assistant, Teacher of Art Education, Pennsylvania State University, University Park, PA (1962-1964); Teacher, Art Director, Twin Pines, Oakland, CA (1961-1962); Metropolitan Museum Art (1957-1961); Part-Time Assistant Teacher, Boston Museum Children's Room, Boston, MA (1954-1956); Teacher, Originator Adult Art Education, South End House, Boston, MA (1953-1954) **CR:** Director, Art Program for Gifted High School Students, Jersey City State College; Personnel Committee Art Department; Senator-At-Large **CIV:** Co-Founder, Genesis Project, Jersey City, NJ (1986-2004) **CW:** One-Woman Show, The Courtney Gallery, Jersey City State College (1979); One-Woman Show, The Gallery, Jersey City, NJ (1981); One-Woman Show, Stevens Institute of Technology, Hoboken, NJ (1984); One-Woman Show, Jersey City Museum (1996); Exhibited in Group Show, Gallery Stendhal (1991); Exhibited in Group Show, Jersey City State College (1992); Juried Show, Exhibitions, Lemmerman Gallery, New Jersey City University (1999); Juried Show, Exhibitions, City Spirit Cultural Arts Festival, Jersey City, NJ (1981) (Best in Show, 1981); Juried Show, Exhibition, Visceglia Art Center Caldwell College, Caldwell, NJ (1994); Juried Show, Exhibitions, The Rotunda Gallery, City Hall, Jersey City, NJ (1995); Juried Show, Exhibitions, Viridian Gallery, New York City, NY (1997); Contributor to Articles and Professional Journals **AW:** Martin Luther King, Junior Community Service Award, Jersey City University (1999); Best in Show, Juried Show, Exhibitions, City Spirit Cultural Arts Festival, Jersey City, NJ (1981); Grantee, Chinese Art Historical College, Teachers Summer Seminar, National Endowment Humanities (1975); Graduate School Fellowship, Pennsylvania State University (1964-1965) **MEM:** Harvard Club of New York; Harvard Club of New Jersey **ADD:** 110 Manhattan Avenue, Jersey City, NJ, 07307

SIMONSEN BROWN, JACQUELINE, T: President, Head Coach **I:** Professional Training & Coaching **CN:** Northern Power WLC **DOB:** 08/08/1961 **PB:** Toronto **SC:** Canada **PT:** John Albert S.; Ina Fay S. **MS:** Widow **SPN:** Paul Gregory Brown (Deceased 12/2007); Joseph F. Caron (5/1/1988, Divorced 6/1993) **ED:** MEd, Health Sciences, Heat Thermal Physiology, University of Vermont (2013); BA in Physical Education, University of Toronto (1984) **CT:** Certified Strength and Conditioning

Specialist, NSCA, State of Oklahoma (1989) **C:** President, Northern Power WLC (2014); Head Coach, Northern Power WLC (2014); Strength Coach, Bellow Free Academy, Collins Perley Sports Center, St. Albans, VT (1989); Physical Education Teacher, Grades 6-8 (1984-1987) **CIV:** Fundraising Committee, Hardack; Advisory Board, VT Rise; Hard 'Ack Epi Center Committee, St. Albans, VT **CW:** Contributor, National Strength and Conditioning Association **AW:** Significant Community Contributor, Bellows Free Academy (2017); World Champion, 132-pound Class, World All-Round Weightlifting Championships, London, England (1995); World Champion, 139-pound Class, World Olympics-Style Weightlifting Championships, Perth, Australia (1995); World Champion, 143-pound Weight Class, World All-Round Weightlifting Championship, Boston, MA; Nominated, International All-Round Weightlifting Technical Committee **ADD:** PO Box 514, Saint Albans Bay, VT, 05481

SIMPSON, JOHN NOEL SR., T: Healthcare Administrator **I:** Medicine & Health Care **DOB:** 02/27/1936 **PB:** Durham **SC:** NC/USA **MS:** Married **SPN:** Virginia Marshall (June 27, 1959) **CH:** John Noel; William M. **C:** Divisional Consultant, Bon Secours Health System, Inc. (2000-Present); Regional Vice President, Bon Secours Health System, Inc. (1997-2000); Chief Executive Officer, Bon Secours Health System, Inc. (1997-2000); Chairman of Board, Bon Secours Health System, Inc. (1996-1997); President, Health Corp. of Virginia (1985-1996); President, Richmond Memorial Hospital, Bon Secours Health System, Inc. (1980-1985); Executive Vice President, Richmond Memorial Hospital, Bon Secours Health System, Inc. (1977-1980); Senior Vice President, Richmond Memorial Hospital, Bon Secours Health System, Inc. (1974-1977); Administrator, Richmond Memorial Hospital, Bon Secours Health System, Inc. (1974-1977); Associate Administrator, Richmond Memorial Hospital, Bon Secours Health System, Inc. (1970-1974); Associate Administrator, Riverside Health Systems (1965-1970); Assistant Administrator, Riverside Health Systems (1962-1965) **CR:** Preceptor, School Health Administration, Duke University; Preceptor, School Health Administration, Medical College of Virginia (Now School of Medicine, VCU); Preceptor, School Health Administration, Washington University of St. Louis; Participant, Leadership Metro Richmond; Member, Joint Subcommittee on Studying Virginia Medical Malpractice Laws, Division of Legal Chairman, Hanover Business Council (1994-1995); Member, Governor's Regional Economic Development Advisory Council (1994-1995); Member, Board of Directors, Sun Health (1979-1992); Chairman, Virginia Health Network (1989-1991); Chairman, Board of Directors, Sun Health (1985-1987); Vice-Chairman, Board of Directors, Sun Health (1984); Services, General Assembly of Communications, Commonwealth of Virginia (1984); Member, Virginia Board of Medical Assistance (1980-1984); Member, Board of Directors, Central Virginia Health Systems Agency (1980-1984); Vice-Chairman, Medical/Business Coalition (1981-1983); Member, Richmond Chapter, The American National Red Cross (1980-1983) **CIV:** Officer, Brooke General Hospital (Now Brooke Army Medical Center) **AW:** Recipient, Eva Tieg Hardy Service Award for Exceptional Corporate Support, Senior Connections of Capital-Area Agency on Aging (2009); Recipient, Distinguished Service Award, The Richmond Academy of Medicine, Inc (2000); Recipient, Distinguished Service Award, Virginia Hospital & Healthcare Association (1998); Recipient, Regents Award in the Senior Executive Level, American College of

Healthcare Executives (1995); Recipient, Edgar C. Hayhow Award American College of Healthcare Executives (1976) **MEM:** Chairman, RPBIII, American Hospital Association (1994-1997); Board of Trustees, American Hospital Association (1994-1997); Director, Virginia Hospital & Healthcare Association (1974-1997); Board of Governors, American College of Healthcare Executives (1990-1994); Delegate, American Hospital Association (1989-1993); Chairman-Elect, Virginia Hospital & Healthcare Association (1984-1985); Chairman, Virginia Hospital & Healthcare Association (1984-1985); Council of Regents, American College of Healthcare Executives (1976-1982); Chairman, Virginia Insurance Reciprocal (1977-1979); Fellow, American College of Healthcare Executives; Board of Directors, Virginia Peninsula Chamber of Commerce; The Richmond Academy of Medicine, Inc **MH:** Albert Nelson Marquis Lifetime Achievement Award (2017) **PA:** Republican **RE:** Presbyterian **ADD:** 9127 Carterham Rd, Richmond, VA, 23229

SINGH, UPENDRA, T: Principal Scientist **I:** Sciences **CN:** International Fertilizer Development Center **ED:** PhD, Soil Science, Department of Agronomy and Soil Science, University of Hawaii, Honolulu, HI (1985); MS, Soil Science/Chemistry, University of Hawaii, Honolulu, HI (1982); BSc, Chemistry and Biology, University of the South Pacific, Suva, Fiji (1979) **C:** Affiliate Professor, Department of Crop, Soil and Environmental Sciences, Auburn University, Auburn, AL (2017-Present); Adjunct Full Professor, Texas A&M AgriLife Research Center, Beaumont, TX (2014-Present); Principal Scientist, Soil Fertility/Systems Modeling, Fertilizer Research and Development Division, IFDC, Muscle Shoals, AL (2009-Present); Adjunct Associate Professor, Chemistry Department, University of Alabama-Huntsville, Huntsville, AL (2012-2013); Interim Science Officer, Virtual Fertilizer Research Center (VFRC), Washington, D.C. (2011-2013); Visiting Fellow, Cooperative Research Centre for Sustainable Rice Production, CSIRO-Land and Water, Griffith, Australia (2004); Visiting Scientist, Soil Management Collaborative Research Support Program and International Consortium for Application of System Analysis (ICASA), University of Hawaii, Honolulu, HI (2001-2002); Visiting Scientist, Department of Plant and Soil Sciences, Michigan State University, East Lansing, MI (2000); Senior Scientist, Soil Fertility/Systems Modeling, Research and Market Development Division, IFDC, Muscle Shoals, AL (1992-2009); Program Coordinator for IFDC-IRRI, International Rice Research Institute (IRRI), Los Baños, Philippines (1992-1997); Adjunct Associate Professor, University of the Philippines, Los Baños, Philippines (1992-1997); Systems Modeler, Agro-Economic Division, IFDC, Muscle Shoals, AL (1988-1991); Lecturer in Chemistry, University of the South Pacific, School of Pure and Applied Science, Suva, Fiji (1986-1988); Research Fellow, Department of Plant and Soil Sciences, Michigan State University, East Lansing, MI (1986); Demonstrator, Biology/Soil Science, University of the South Pacific, Suva, Fiji (1980) **CR:** Short-term Consultant, Catalyze Accelerated Agricultural Intensification for Social and Environmental Stability (CATALIST), Netherlands Government (2007-2010); Short-term Consultant, Agri-business Development and Development of Best Management Practices, USAID (2006); Short-term Consultant, Agricultural Productivity Enhancement Program, USAID (2004 -2008); Short-term Consultant, Agricultural Input and Markets Development Project, USAID (2003); Short-term Consultant, Emergency Fertilizer Development Project, USAID, Afghanistan (2003); Short-term

Consultant, Emergency Fertilizer Development Project, USAID, Afghanistan (2002); Coordinator/Consultant, BARC/IFDC International Training Program on Computer Simulation for Crop Growth and Resource Management, Agricultural Research Management Program-Bangladesh/World Bank Consultancy, Dhaka, Bangladesh (2002); Developer, SUBSTOR Taro Model, College of Tropical Agriculture, Department of Agronomy and Soil Science, University of Hawaii (1995); Consultant/instructor, Training Program on Crop Simulation Model Applications for Climate Change, Commonwealth Climate Change and Agricultural Monitoring (COMCIAM) Project, Australian International Development Assistance Board, ICRISAT Center, Patancheru, India (1993); Consultant, "Implications of Climate Change for International Agriculture: Global Food Production, Trade, and Vulnerable Regions," USAID, U.S. Environmental Protection Agency, Dhaka, Bangladesh (1990); Consultancy, "Crop Modelling: Principles and Uses," Center for Advanced Studies in Agricultural Meteorology, College of Agriculture, Mahatma Phule Agricultural University, Pune, India (1990); Conductor, Training Workshops, Development of DSSAT, Rice, Sorghum, and Millet Models, IBSNAT Project, University of Hawaii, Honolulu, HI (1986-1991); Prepared Report on Fertilizer Recommendations for Coffee Production on Taveuni, Fiji Islands, Carpenters Agriculture Ltd, Taveuni, Fiji (1986-1987); Training and Design of Multidisciplinary Research, Soil and Climate Evaluation Project (SCEP), South Pacific Commission (1986-1987); TropSoils Project, Sitiung, Indonesia (1986) **AW:** Board Chariman's Outstanding Professional Award, IFDC (2014); Visiting Fellow, Cooperative Research Centre for Sustainable Rice Production, CSIRO-Land and Water, Griffith, Australia (2004); Joint Doctoral Research Intern, East-West Center, Honolulu, HI (1984); East-West Center Award, East-West Center, Honolulu, HI (1980-1984); Gold Medal in Science, ICI (1979); Fiji Government Scholarship, University of the South Pacific, Suva, Fiji (1976-1979) **MEM:** Editorial Board Member, Nutrient Cycling in Agroecosystem and The Scientific World; Agricultural Model Intercomparison and Improvement Project; American Association for the Advancement of Science; American Society of Agronomy; Soil Science Society of America; International Society for Computer Simulation; International Society of Soil Science; International Consortium for Agricultural Systems Applications; Association for International Agriculture and Rural Development; International Geosphere-Biosphere Program; Honor Society of Phi Kappa Phi; Honor Society of Gamma Sigma Delta; Coordinator, Rice, Tropical Cereal and Millet Network, Agriculture and Production Systems Network, Global Change and Terrestrial Ecosystem Program **ADD:** 1802 Rosedale St, Muscle Shoals, AL, 35661

SINHA, KAUSHIK, T: Research Affiliate **I:** Research **CN:** Massachusetts Institute of Technology **DOB:** 02/11/1975 **ED:** Postdoctoral Associate, Massachusetts Institute of Technology (2014-2015); PhD in Engineering Systems and Aeronautics, Massachusetts Institute of Technology (2014); Research Intern, System Architecture Group, Xerox Corporation Research Center (2009); Master of Engineering in Aerospace Engineering, Indian Institute of Science, First Class with Honours (2000); Graduate Engineer Trainee, Gammon India Ltd (1997-1998); Bachelor of Engineering, Jadavpur University (1997) **CT:** Green Belt Certification (2004); Certified in Design for Six Sigma **C:** Research Affiliate, MIT (2017-Present); Co-founder, A FinTech StartUp (2015-Present); Scientist, Massachusetts Institute of Technology

(2015-2016); Manager, Daimler-Benz Research and Technology Centre (2001-2007); Software Engineer, Infosys (2000-2001) **CW:** Contributor, Articles, Professional Journals **MEM:** AIAA; The American Society of Mechanical Engineers; IEEE **ADD:** 37 Spring St, Lexington, MA, 02421

SIPPO, ARTHUR CARMINE, T: Medical Director **I:** Medicine & Health Care **CN:** Aetna Inc. **DOB:** 01/30/1953 **PT:** Carmine Constantine Sippo; Mildred Angela (Musto) Sippo **MS:** Married **SPN:** Katherine Velma Sager (1/8/1987) **CH:** Sean; Tiffany; Courtney **ED:** MPH, The Johns Hopkins University (1983); Resident, School for Aerospace Medicine, U.S. Air Force, Brooks Air Force Base, Texas (1981-1983); Intern in Obstetrics-Gynecology, Walter Reed National Military Medical Center (1978-1979); MD, Vanderbilt University (1978); BS in Chemistry, Saint Peter's University, Magna Cum Laude (1974) **CT:** Diplomate, American Board of Preventive Medicine **C:** Medical Director Etna INC (2016-Present); Emergency Room Physician, Shelbyville Hospital (Now HSHS Good Shepherd Hospital), IL (2012-Present); Emergency Room Physician, Pana Community Hospital (2005-Present); Occupational and Emergency Room Physician, HSHS St. Joseph's Hospital, Highland, IL (2001-Present); Medical Director, Express Medical, Fairview Heights, IL (2012-2016); Emergency Room Physician, John Cochran Division, VA St. Louis Health Care System, U.S. Department of Veterans Affairs (2008-2012); Emergency Physician, HSHS St. Francis Hospital, Litchfield, IL (2005-2007); Emergency Medicine Physician, HSHS St. Joseph's Hospital Breese (2003-2004); Emergency Medicine Physician, Utlaut Hospital (Now HSHS Holy Family Hospital) (2002-2004); Occupational Medicine Physician, Holland, Ohio (1990-2001); Occupational Care Consultant, Holland, Ohio (1990-2001); Medical Director, Aetna Inc. **CR:** Medical Director, Clyde, Ohio Division, Whirlpool Corporation (1990-2000); Medical Director, Libbey Inc., Toledo, OH (1990-2000) **MIL:** Assistant State Surgeon, Ohio National Guard, Columbus, OH (1995-2000); Deputy Commander for Clinical Services, 112th Medical Brigade, Ohio National Guard, Columbus, OH (1994-1995); Commander, 145th Mobile Army Surgical Hospital, Camp Perry, OH (1992-1994); Advanced through Grades to Lieutenant Colonel, U.S. Army (1992); Ohio National Guard (1990-2000); Exchange Officer, Royal Air Force Institute of Aviation Medicine, Farnborough, England (1986-1990); Director, Biodynamics Research Division, Aeromedical Research Laboratory, U.S. Army, Fort Rucker, AL (1983-1986); First Brigade Surgeon, 101st Airborne Division, U.S. Army, Fort Campbell, KY (1979-1981); Commissioned Second Lieutenant, U.S. Army (1978); Member, Aerospace Consultant Advisory Panel, Surgeon General's Office, U.S. Army **CW:** Author, "Sun Koh: Heir of Atlantis"; Contributor, Articles, Professional Journals **AW:** Echoes Award, Pulp Echoes (2010) **MEM:** Fellow, Aerospace Medical Association; Fellow, American College of Preventive Medicine; Fellow, American College Occupational and Environmental Medicine (ACOEM); American College of Emergency Physicians; United States Army Flight Surgeons Association; The Fellowship of Catholic Scholars **MH:** Albert Nelson Marquis Lifetime Achievement Award (2017) **H:** Theology; Philosophy; Biblical Studies; Patristics; Paleontology **RE:** Roman Catholic **BA:** 550 Maryville Centre Dr Ste 300, Aetna Insurance Company, St. Louis, MO, 63141 **ADD:** 300 Brentmoor Ct, Highland, IL, 62249

SIRJANI, DAVUD BARADARAN, T: Assistant Professor, Surgeon **I:** Medicine & Health Care **CN:** Stanford Medicine **ED:** Stanford Biodesign

Faculty Fellowship (2017); Fellow, American College of Surgeons (2013); Fellowship, University of Washington Medical Center (2009); Residency, Washington University School Of Medicine (2008); Internship, Washington University School Of Medicine (2002); MD, College of Medicine, The University of Arizona, Tucson, AZ (2001); Fellowship, University of Arizona College of Medicine, Pathology (1999); BS, The University of Arizona (1996) **CT:** Board Certification, Otolaryngology, American Board of Otolaryngology (2010) **C:** Director, Stanford Salivary Gland Program (2013-Present); Chief of Otolaryngology, VA Palo Alto (2012-Present); Clinical Assistant Professor, Department of Otolaryngology, Head and Neck Surgery, Stanford Medicine, Stanford, CA (2009-Present); Head and Neck Surgery Fellow, Department of Otolaryngology, University of Washington (2008-2009); Otolaryngology Resident, Department of Otolaryngology, Washington University (2001-2008) **CW:** Author, "Risk of Nodal Metastasis in Major Salivary Gland Adenoid Cystic Carcinoma," Official Journal of American Academy of Otolaryngology (2017); Author, "Association of Postoperative Radiotherapy With Survival in Patients With N1 Oral Cavity and Oropharyngeal Squamous Cell Carcinoma," JAMA Otolaryngology (2016); Author, "Ameloblastoma: a clinical review and trends in management," European Archives of Oto-Rhino-Laryngology (2016); Author, "Botulinum Toxin Confers Radioprotection in Murine Salivary Glands," International Journal of Radiation Oncology (2016); Author, "Consultation via telemedicine and access to operative care for patients with head and neck cancer in a Veterans Health Administration population," Journal for the Sciences and Specialties of the Head and Neck (2016); Author, "Contemporary mandibular reconstruction," Current Opinion in Otolaryngology & Head and Neck Surgery (2016); Author, "Anterolateral approach to the upper cervical spine: Case report and operative technique," Journal for the Sciences and Specialties of the Head and Neck (2015); Author, "Neurotrophic factor GDNF promotes survival of salivary stem cells," Journal of Clinical Investigation (2014); Author, "CD271 is a functional and targetable marker of tumor-initiating cells in head and neck squamous cell carcinoma," Oncotarget (2014); Author, "Cost-effectiveness landscape analysis of treatments addressing Xerostomia in patients receiving head and neck radiation therapy," Oral Surgery, Oral Medicine, Oral Pathology and Oral Radiology (2013); Author, "Impact of positron emission tomography/computed tomography surveillance at 12 and 24 months for detecting head and neck cancer recurrence," Cancer (2013); Author, "A Novel Aldehyde Dehydrogenase-3 Activator Leads to Adult Salivary Stem Cell Enrichment In Vivo," Clinical Cancer Research (2011); Author, "Osteotomy access to the Anterior Skull Base," Operative Techniques in Otolaryngology (2010) **AW:** Faculty Teaching Award, Stanford Department of Otolaryngology (2017); Faculty Teaching Award, Stanford Department of Otolaryngology (2013); Teacher of the Year, Department of Otolaryngology, Stanford University (2012-2013); "Surgery at the End of Life," American College of Surgeons, Issues Committee of Resident and Associate Society (2012); "Reconstructive Dilemma of a Rare Mandibular Tumor," Saint Louis ENT Club (2006); Resident Award, Association for Research in Otolaryngology (2004); Michael Paparella Award, Department of Otolaryngology, Washington University (2003); Young Investigator Award, Academy of Clinical Laboratory Physicians and Scientists (2000); Caldwell Research Award, University of Arizona College of Medicine (1999); Centennial Achievement Award, The University of Arizona (1996) **MEM:** Candidate for Fellowship, Triological Society (2016-Present); Medical Devices and Drugs Committee, American Academy of Otolaryngology (2013-Present); North American Skull Base Society (2012-Present); Association of Northern California Oncologist (2011-Present); American Telemedicine Association (2011-Present) **MH:** Distinguished Humanitarian (2017) **BA:** 875 Blake Wilbur Drive, Stanford University Cancer Center, CC-2223, MC5739, Palo Alto, CA, 94305 **ADD:** 875 Blake Wilbur Dr, Stanford University Cancer Center, CC-2223, MC5739, Palo Alto, CA, 94305

SIVASANKARAN, VELA, T: DMTS **I:** Telecommunications **CN:** Verizon **ED:** MBA in Global Management, University of Phoenix (2014); MS in Computer Science and Engineering, Indian Institute of Technology (1998); BS in Computer Science and Engineering, Thiagarajar College of Engineering (1996) **CT:** Certified Asterisk Professional; Sun Certified Enterprise Architect; Oracle Database Administrator; Certified in Six Sigma Design and Approaches for Requirements Development; Lean Six Sigma **C:** Distinguished Member, Technical Staff, Verizon (2013-2015); Solution Architect, Yoh Corporate Consultation (2012-2013); Chief Software Architect, Bayside Solutions (2011-2012); CTO, Verizon (1998-2016) **AW:** Recognized Professional, Strathmore Who's Who (2014); European Patent for Instant Messaging as a Communication Channel for a Contact Center (2009); Top Student Award, Indian Institute of Technology; Best Outgoing Student Award, Thiagarajar College of Engineering **MEM:** IEEE; ACM; AFCEA International **MH:** Albert Nelson Marquis Lifetime Achievement Award (2018) **H:** Spending time with her two daughters; Listening to music; Reading; Attending sporting events; Golf **BA:** 2298 Ruby Avenue, San Jose, CA, 95148 **ADD:** 232 Nellis Road, Bothell, WA, 98012

SKEEN, DAVID, T: Systems Engineer (Retired) **I:** Engineering **CN:** Enterprise Bus. Solutions **DOB:** 07/12/1942 **PB:** Bucklin **SC:** KS/USA **PT:** Claude E. Skeen; Velma A. (Birney) Skeen **MS:** Married **SPN:** Carol J. Stimpert, (8/23/1964) **CH:** Jeffrey Kent; Timothy Sean; Kimberly Dawn **ED:** DSc in Engineering Management, The George Washington University, Washington D.C. (1998); Graduate, Naval War College (1984); Graduate, Federal Executive Institute (1983); MS, American University, Washington D.C. (1972); BA in Mathematics, Emporia State University, Kansas (1964) **CT:** Certified, Office of Automation Professionals **C:** Consultant, Enterprise Business Solutions (2008-Present); Retired (2007); Systems Engineer, Consultant, GCI (2004-2007); Senior Engineering Manager, Consultant, Lockheed Martin, Washington D.C. (1998-2004); Deputy Director, Office of Operations, U.S. Department of Agriculture, Washington D.C. (1998); Director, Modernization of Administration Processes Program (1996-1998); Associate Director, Office of IRM, U.S. Department of Agriculture, Washington D.C. (1992-1996); Director, Manpower, Personnel Training Information Resource Management, Chief Naval Operations, Washington D.C. (1985-1991); Deputy Director, Manpower, Personnel Training Automated System, Department of Naval Military Personnel Command, Washington D.C. (1980-1985); Director, Management Information System, Naval Civilian Personnel Command, Washington D.C. (1978-1980); Director, Data Processing, Office of Naval Research, U.S. Navy Department, Arlington, VA (1973-1978); Computer System Analyst, Naval Command Systems Support Activity, Washington D.C. (1970-1973); Computer System Analyst to Commander-in-Chief, U.S. Naval Forces-Europe, London, England (1967-1970) **CR:** Adjunct Professor, Department of Public Administration, George Mason University (2005-Present); Adjunct Professor, School of Engineering and Applied Science, The George Washington University (1985-Present); Consultant, Electronic Data Processing Career Development Programs (1975-Present); Special, U.S. Department of Agriculture Field Structure Studies (1997); Special, USDA/Office of Management and Budget IRM (1993); Special, Navy IRM Studies, SECNAV (1991); Member, President's Federal Automated Data Processing Users Group, Washington D.C. (1978-1980); Detailed to President's Reorginization Project for Automated Data Processing (1978); Lecturer, The Institute of Science and Public Affairs (1973-1976) **MIL:** Captain, U.S. Naval Reserve (1960-1991) **CW:** Contributor, Articles, Professional Journals **AW:** Administrative Staff Performance Award (1998); Secretary's Certificate of Appreciation (1998); Outstanding Performance Award, Interagency Committee on Data Processing (1976) **MEM:** International Council on Systems Engineering; Senior Executive Association; Association for Federal IRM; Naval Reserve Association; President, Federal Automated Data Processing Users Group **H:** Traveling; Photography; Reading **ADD:** 544 Hidden Cove Lane, Lynch station, VA, 24571

SKILLMAN, WILLIAM A., T: Consultant, Engineering Executive (Retired) **I:** Engineering **CN:** Westinghouse Electric Corp. **DOB:** 01/22/1928 **PB:** Lakehurst **SC:** NJ/USA **PT:** Wilbur Newton Skillman; Greta Alfreda (Ekman) Skillman **MS:** Widowed **SPN:** Anne Marie Cavender (9/19/1948) **CH:** Thomas R.; Gregory A. (Deceased); Karen L. **ED:** MS in Physics, University of Rochester (1954); BS in Engineering Physics, Lehigh University (1952) **C:** Consultant, Electronic Systems Group, Westinghouse Electric Corp., Baltimore, MD (1993-Present); Consultant Engineer, Westinghouse Electric Corp., Baltimore, MD (1986-1993); Senior Advisory Engineer, Westinghouse Electric Corp., Baltimore, MD (1973-1985); Advisory Engineer, Westinghouse Electric Corp., Baltimore, MD (1964-1973); Supervisory Engineer, Westinghouse Electric Corp., Baltimore, MD (1961-1964); Senior Engineer, Westinghouse Electric Corp., Baltimore, MD (1958-1961); Engineer, Westinghouse Electric Corp., Baltimore, MD (1956-1958); Associate Engineer, Westinghouse Electric Corp., Baltimore, MD (1954-1956) **MIL:** U.S. Navy (1946-1948) **CW:** Author, "Radar Handbook," 2nd Edition (1990); Author, "Radar Calculations Using the TI-59 Programmable Calculator" (1983); Patentee in Field **AW:** Dennis J. Picard Medal for Radar Technologies and Applications, IEEE (2003); Pioneer Award, Aerospace and Electronic Systems Society (1995) **MEM:** Fellow, IEEE; Life Member, IEEE; Aerospace and Electronic Systems Society; Phi Beta Kappa **H:** Genealogy **PA:** Republican **RE:** Methodist **ADD:** 719 Maiden Choice Ln Apt BR630, Catonsville, MD, 21228

SKROUMBELOS, NICHOLAS, T: Management Consultant, President **I:** Consulting **CN:** PCMC, Inc. **DOB:** 02/08/1952 **PB:** Flemington **SC:** NJ/USA **PT:** George Athan; Georgia (Kannellis) S. **ED:** BS in Accounting, Fairleigh-Dickinson University, Madison, NJ (1976); AA, Mercer County College (1973) **CT:** CPA **C:** President, PCMC, Inc., Lawrenceville, NJ (1979-Present); Administrative Analyst to Executive Vice President, Beneficial Management, Morristown, NJ (1976-1978) **CR:** Charter Founder, 1st Constitution Bank, Cranbury (1989) **CIV:** Member, Committee to Celebrate 50th

Anniversary of War of the Worlds Broadcast, Grover's Mill and West Windsor, NJ (1986-Present); Co-Chairman, Host Committee, Ernie Kovacs 75th Birthday Commemoration (1994) **AW:** New Jersey Network Appreciation Award (1994); Merger Plaque, RT/Katek, Inc. (1983); Honorable Order of Kentucky Colonels **MEM:** Pennsylvania Society of CPAs; Friars Club **H:** Bicycling; Cross country skiing; Antique car collecting **RE:** Greek Orthodox **BA:** 1957 Lawrenceville Road, Lawrenceville, NJ, 08648

SKUTA, GREGORY L., T: Professor, Chair, President, Chief Executive Officer **I:** Education/Educational Services **CN:** The University of Oklahoma, Dean McGee Eye Institute **DOB:** 06/22/1956 **PB:** Benton **SC:** IL/USA **PT:** Richard Louis Skuta; Jacquelyn Gail (Weaver) Skuta **MS:** Married **SPN:** Anne Marie (Phelan) (May 26, 1984) **CH:** Jonathan Richard; Catherine Anne; Matthew Gregory **ED:** MD, University of Illinois (1981); BS, University of Illinois (1977); Diploma, Tuscola Community High School (1974) **CT:** Diplomate, American Board of Ophthalmology (1987, 2001, 2011); Licensed to Practice Medicine, Oklahoma (1992); Licensed to Practice Medicine, Michigan (1987); Diplomate, National Board of Medical Examiners (1982); Licensed to Practice Medicine, Wisconsin (1982) **C:** Edward L. Gaylord Professor, Department of Ophthalmology, College of Medicine, The University of Oklahoma (2009-Present); Chair, Department of Ophthalmology, College of Medicine, The University of Oklahoma (2009-Present); President, Dean McGee Eye Institute, Department of Ophthalmology, College of Medicine, The University of Oklahoma (2009-Present); Chief Executive Officer, Dean McGee Eye Institute, Department of Ophthalmology, College of Medicine, The University of Oklahoma (2009-Present); James P. Luton Clinical Professor, Department of Ophthalmology, College of Medicine, The University of Oklahoma (1998-2009); Deputy Dean, Dean McGee Eye Institute, Department of Ophthalmology, College of Medicine, The University of Oklahoma (1998-2009); Clinical Associate Professor, Department of Ophthalmology, College of Medicine, The University of Oklahoma (1992-1998); Dean, Dean McGee Eye Institute, Department of Ophthalmology, University of Oklahoma College of Medicine (1992-1998); Associate Professor, University of Michigan (1992); Assistant Professor, W.K. Kellogg Eye Center, Department of Ophthalmology, University of Michigan (1987-1992); Chief Resident, University of Wisconsin-Madison (1984-1985); Ophthalmology Resident, University of Wisconsin-Madison (1982-1985); Intern, St. Joseph Mercy Health System, Trinity Health (1981-1982) **CR:** Consultant, Oklahoma City VA Health Care System, U.S. Department of Veterans Affairs (1992-Present); Grant Reviewer, Clinical Applications, Special Emphasis Panel, National Eye Institute, NIH (2013, 2015); Ad-Hoc Grant Reviewer, Research to Prevent Blindness, Inc. (2010, 2012, 2015); Grant Reviewer, Dennis W. Jahnigen Career Development Awards Program, American Geriatrics Society (2008-2009); Fellowship Director, University of Oklahoma (1993-2009); Director, American Board of Ophthalmology (2001-2008); Board of Governors, World Glaucoma Association (2004-2007); Grant Reviewer, Fight for Sight (2007); Clinical Instructor, American Academy of Ophthalmology (1988-2001); Chair, Program Committee, Annual Meeting, American Glaucoma Society (1997, 1999-2000); Moderator, Glaucoma Session, Association for Research in Vision and Ophthalmology (1994-1999); Grant Reviewer, The Wellcome Trust (1994); Principal

Investigator, Collaborative Normal Tension Glaucoma Study, Clinical Center, University of Michigan, Foundation for Glaucoma Research (1988-1992); Consultant, VA Ann Arbor Healthcare System, U.S. Department of Veterans Affairs (1987-1992); Co-director, Glaucoma Service, W.K. Kellogg Eye Center, Department of Ophthalmology, University of Michigan (1990-1992); Director, Glaucoma Service, W.K. Kellogg Eye Center, Department of Ophthalmology, University of Michigan (1988-1990); Participant, Strategic Planning Retreat, Department of Ophthalmology, Medical School, University of Michigan (1990); Department Representative, Operating Room Conference on Total Quality Process, University of Michigan (1989); Department Representative, Referring Physician Advisory Council Dinner, University of Michigan (1988); Department Representative, Operating Room Management Conference, University of Michigan (1988); Invited Speaker, 60th Annual Ophthalmology Spring Conference, 10th Annual Midwest Glaucoma Symposium (1988); Moderator, Glaucoma Colloquium (1987); Invited Speaker, Various Conferences; Invited Lecturer, Various Conferences **CIV:** Member, United Methodist Church of the Servant (1993-Present); Charge Conference, United Methodist Church of the Servant (2006-2008); Invited Speaker, Neuro Night, Oklahoma Center for Neuroscience (2000); Mission Council, United Methodist Church of the Servant (1996-1997); Stewardship Campaign Worker, United Methodist Church of the Servant (1995); Member, First United Methodist Church of Ann Arbor (1988-1993) **CW:** Contributing Author, Articles, Journal of Neuro-Ophthalmology (2002-Present); Editorial Board, Journal of Glaucoma (1999-Present); Contributing Author, Articles, British Journal of Ophthalmology (1999-Present); Contributing Author, Articles, Survey of Ophthalmology (1998-Present); Contributing Author, Articles, Eye (1996-Present); Contributing Author, Articles, Cornea (1996-Present); Contributing Author, Articles, Ophthalmic Surgery and Lasers (1995-Present); Contributing Author, Articles, Current Eye Research (1994-Present); Contributing Author, Articles, Experimental Eye Research (1992-Present); Contributing Author, Articles, American Journal of Ophthalmology (1992-Present); Contributing Author, Articles, Journal of Glaucoma (1992-Present); Contributing Author, Articles, Archives of Ophthalmology (1991-Present); Contributing Author, Articles, Investigative Ophthalmology and Visual Science (1989-Present); Contributing Author, Articles, Ophthalmology (1988-Present); Editorial Board, EyeNet, American Academy of Ophthalmology (1997-2003); Contributing Author, Visual Sciences B, NIH (1991); Contributor, Articles, Professional Journals; Contributor, Chapters, Books **AW:** Honoree, America's Top Doctors, Castle Connolly Medical Ltd. (2013-Present); Honoree, Oklahoma Super Doctors (2013-Present); Honoree, America's Top Ophthalmologists, Consumers' Research Council of America (2002-Present); Honoree, Best Doctors in America (1994-Present); Grantee, Research to Prevent Blindness, Inc. (2010-Present); Honoree, Best Doctors in Oklahoma, Oklahoma Magazine (2002-Present); Honoree, Regents' Professorship, Board of Regents, University of Oklahoma (2017); Honoree, Hall of Fame, Tuscola Community High School (2014); Recipient, Lifetime Achievement Honor Award, American Academy of Ophthalmology (2013); Honoree, Guest of Honor, Meeting of the New England Ophthalmological Society (2004, 2013); Honoree, Shining Star Lecturer of the Month, Department of Ophthalmology, University of Oklahoma (2011);

Recipient, John W. Henderson Award, Louisiana State University Health Science Center (2007); Grantee, Alcon Laboratories (2006-2007); Grantee, GMP/Vision Solutions (2003-2006); Grantee, National Eye Institute (1987-2005); Grantee, Pharmacia & Upjohn Company (2002-2005); Grantee, Allergan Pharmaceuticals (2001, 2003-2004); Recipient, Senior Achievement Award, American Academy of Ophthalmology (2002); Recipient, Governor's Commendation, Oklahoma Governor Frank Keating (2000); Honoree, Outstanding Young Men of America (1996, 1998); Honoree, The Best Doctors in America: Central Region (1996-1997); Recipient, Honor Award, American Academy of Ophthalmology (1993); Grantee, Merck Sharp and Dohme Research Laboratories (1989-1993); Honoree, Two Thousand Notable American Men (1992); Honoree, Recognition for Outstanding Contributions to Resident Education, Resident Class of 1992, Department of Ophthalmology, University of Michigan (1992); Grantee, Michigan Eye Bank and Transplantation Center (1988-1989); Recipient, Resident Teaching Award, Resident Class of 1989, Department of Ophthalmology, University of Michigan (1989); Grantee, IOLAB Pharmaceuticals (1988); Glaucoma Service Fellow, Bascom Palmer Eye Institute (1985-1987); Recipient, National Research Service Award, National Eye Institute (1986); Recipient, Granville A. Bennett Award (1981); Child of a Korean Veteran Scholar, Douglas County Government (1979); Scholar, Illinois General Assembly (1978); Honoree, Honorary Membership, 100 Club (1977); Honoree, Premedical Honor Society, Alpha Epsilon Delta (1976); Honoree, Freshman Honor Society, Phi Eta Sigma (1975); Scholar, Central Illinois Light Company **MEM:** Board of Directors, Ophthalmic Mutual Insurance Company (2017-Present); Board of Directors, National Alliance for Eye and Vision Research/Alliance for Eye and Vision Research (2016-Present); Advisory Council, Truhlsen Eye Institute, University of Nebraska (2015-Present); American Glaucoma Society Foundation (2015-Present); Claims Committee, Ophthalmic Mutual Insurance Company (2012-Present); Finance Committee, Ophthalmic Mutual Insurance Company (2012-Present); Board of Directors, Regional Meetings of Arkansas and Oklahoma State Ophthalmological Societies (2009-Present); Voting Member, Board of Trustees, Dean McGee Eye Institute, Department of Ophthalmology, College of Medicine, The University of Oklahoma (2009-Present); Ophthalmic Clinical Education Council, American Academy of Ophthalmology (2002-Present); "Blue Ribbon" Committee, American Board of Ophthalmology (2002-Present) **MH:** Albert Nelson Marquis Lifetime Achievement Award (2017) **H:** Music; Theater; Tennis; Travel; American Presidential History **RE:** Methodist **BA:** 608 Stanton L Young Blvd, University of Oklahoma/Dean McGee Eye Institute, Oklahoma City, OK, 73104

SLOTTA, OLIVEANN DAVIS, T: Mathematics Educator, Curriculum Consultant **I:** Education/Educational Services **CN:** Metro State University **DOB:** 01/05/1942 **SC:** Ohio **MS:** Married **SPN:** James G. Slotta **CH:** Lizann; James D.; Jon; Karen Larson **ED:** PhD, University of Colorado Denver (1999); MA, University of Colorado Denver (1992); BA, Hiram College, Ohio (1963) **CT:** Licensed Professional Teacher, State of Colorado (2011); Certified Teacher (1991); Licensed Teacher, State of Ohio (1963) **C:** Adjunct Faculty, Metro State University (2010-Present); Coordinator, Denver Public Schools (2007-2010); Mathematics Program Specialist, Denver Public Schools (1994-1998); Mathematics Teacher, Denver Public Schools

(1986-1994); Executive Director, Cornerstone Center (1983-1985); Facilitator, Institute of Cultural Affairs (1979-1983); Facilitator, Montreal Catholic School Commission (1976-1979); Teacher of Secondary Mathematics, Painesville City Schools (1965-1969) **CR:** Initiating Committee, Accelerate Neighborhood Climate Action (2015-Present); Member, Selection Committee, American Teacher Awards (1993-2005); Charter Member, International Association Facilitators (1988-2000); Owner, Curriculum Design Consultant, Facilitator, Town Meeting Program, United States and Canada (1975-1980) **CIV:** Founding Member, Accelerate Neighborhood Climate Action Denver Program, Institute of Cultural Affairs-USA **AW:** Niles McKinley Hall of Fame (2009); Mayor's Award, City of Denver (2005); Fellow, University of Colorado Denver (1997); Alumni Award, University of Colorado Denver (1993); Outstanding Mathematics Teacher, Colorado Council Teachers of Math (1992); Named One of Mirabella's 1000 (1994); American Teacher Award, Disney Co. (1991) **MEM:** National Education Association; American Educational Research Association; National Council of Teachers of Mathematics; Colorado Education Association **MH:** Albert Nelson Marquis Lifetime Achievement Award (2017) **H:** Knitting; Skiing **RE:** United Methodist **ADD:** 1685 Steele St Apt 3, Denver, CO, 80206

SMART, JAMES ANTHONY, T: Music Educator **I:** Education/Educational Services **CN:** Cobb County School District **DOB:** 07/21/1959 **PB:** Marietta **SC:** GA/USA **PT:** James Bryant Smart; Patricia Morgan Williams **MS:** Single **CH:** Laurel Morgan; Andrew Forrest **ED:** Master's Degree in Music Education, Boston University (2013); MusM, Georgia State University (1985); MusB, Jacksonville State University (1982) **C:** Band Director, Cobb County School District, Marietta, GA (2014-Present); Orchestra Music Teacher, Cobb County School District, Marietta, GA (2014-Present); Adjunct Professor, University of West Georgia, Carrollton, GA (1995-2001); Teaching Assistant, Auburn University (1994-1996) **ADD:** 4318 Shiloh Trl, Powder Springs, GA, 30127

SMILEY, MARILYNN JEAN, T: Professor Emeritus **I:** Education/Educational Services **CN:** State University of New York at Oswego **DOB:** 06/05/1932 **PB:** Columbia City **SC:** IN/USA **PT:** Orla Raymond Smiley; Mary Jane (Bailey) Smiley **ED:** PhD, University of Illinois (1970); MusM, Northwestern University (1958); BS, Ball State University (1954) **CT:** Certification, Ecoles d'Art Americaines, Fontainebleau, France (1959) **C:** Professor Emeritus, State University of New York at Oswego (2014-Present); Department Chairperson, Music Department, State University of New York at Oswego (1976-1981); Distinguished Teaching Professor, State University of New York at Oswego (1974-2014); Faculty Member, Music Department, State University of New York at Oswego (1961-2014); Public School Music Teacher, Logansport, IN (1954-1961) **CR:** Presenter, Conference Papers, Oswego Opera Theater (2009-Present); President, Board of Directors, Oswego Opera Theater (2009-Present); Honorary Fellow, State University of New York Research Foundation (1974); Honorary Fellow, State University of New York Research Foundation (1972); Honorary Fellow, State University of New York Research Foundation (1971) **CIV:** Penfield Library Associates (1985-Present); Board of Directors, Oswego Opera Theater (1978-Present); Oswego Orchestra Society (1978-Present) **CW:** Co-Editor, "Remarkable Women in New York State History," History Press; Contributor, Articles, Professional Journals **AW:** National Endowment of the Humanities Grantee

(1990-1991); Grantee, AAUW (1984); Chancellor's Award for Excellence in Teaching (1973) **MEM:** Co-President, Oswego Branch, AAUW (2007-Present); Diversity Chairperson, Oswego Branch, AAUW (1995-Present); Historian, New York State Division, AAUW (2004-2013); Membership Committee, Society for American Music (2003-2004); Unofficial Historian, New York State Division, AAUW (2000-2004); Membership Chairperson, Society for American Music (1998-2003); Status of Women Committee, American Musical Society (1997-2000); Diversity Director, New York State Division, AAUW (1993-1996); Chapter Representative, Council, American Musical Society (1993-1996); Board of Directors, New York State-St. Lawrence Chapter, American Musical Society (1993-1996); New York Division Area Interest Representative, Cultural Interests, AAUW (1990-1992); Branch Council Coordinator, New York State Division, AAUW (1988-1990); Branch Council Representative, District III, New York State Division, AAUW (1986-1988); President, Oswego Branch, AAUW (1984-1986); Chairman, New York Chapter, American Musical Society (1975-1977); Music Chairperson, New York Chapter, Delta Kappa Gamma (1968); Music Chairperson, Indiana Chapter, Delta Kappa Gamma (1961); National Organization for Women; Oswego County Historical Society Safe Haven; Early Music America; American Recorder Society; The Renaissance Society of America; The College Music Society; Music Library Association; The Medieval Academy of America; Oswego Recorder Consort; Affiliate, Ontario Singers; Heritage Foundation of Oswego; Phi Kappa Phi; Kappa Delta Pi; Sigma Tau Delta; Sigma Alpha Iota; Pi Kappa Lambda; Delta Phi Alpha; Phi Delta Kappa **MH:** Albert Nelson Marquis Lifetime Achievement Award (2017) **H:** Traveling **RE:** Methodist **ADD:** 77 W 5th St, Oswego, NY, 13126

SMITH, CLARK MARSHALL II, T: Chief of Medicine **I:** Medicine & Health Care **CN:** Children's Minnesota **DOB:** 06/26/1947 **PB:** Madison **SC:** WI/USA **PT:** Clark M. Smith; Helen Smith **MS:** Married **SPN:** Natasha Zisson Smith **CH:** Scott; Craig Applebaum **ED:** Fellowship Pediatric Hematology Oncology, University of Minnesota (1976-1979): Residency Pediatrics, University of Minnesota (1973-1976); MD, University of Minnesota (1973) **CT:** Certified in Pediatric Hematology and Oncology, The American Board of Pediatrics (1978); Licensure, State of Minnesota (1974); Certification, National Board of Medical Examiners (1974) **C:** Chief of Medicine and Pediatrics, Children's Minnesota, Minneapolis, MN (2004-Present); Consultant in Hematology/Oncology, Children's Minnesota, Minneapolis, MN (1983-Present); Associate Professor, Departments of Pediatrics and Biomedical Engineering, University of Minnesota, Minneapolis, MN (1987-2012); Assistant Professor, Department of Pediatrics, Division of Hematology/Oncology, University of Minnesota, Minneapolis, MN (1980-1987); Assistant Professor, Biomedical Engineering, University of Minnesota, Minneapolis, MN (1986); Instructor, Department of Pediatrics, Division of Hematology/Oncology, University of Minnesota, Minneapolis, MN (1979) **CR:** Affiliate, Pediatric Hematology and Oncology (1995-Present); Medical Director of Ambulatory Operations, Children's Minnesota (2009-2013); Medical Director, System Wide Hematology Oncology Program, Children's Minnesota (2002-2004); Medical Director, C.H. Robinson Infusion Center, Children's Minnesota, Minneapolis, MN (2000-2004); Medical Director of Hematology/Oncology, Children's Minnesota, Minneapolis, MN (1999-2002) **CIV:** Member, Board of Directors, Memorial Blood Centers (1990-2017); Member, Advisory Committee on Newborn Screening, Minnesota Department of Health (1988-1999); Member,

American Red Cross, Saint Paul, MN (1992-1998); Chairperson, Subcommittee of Hemoglobinopathy, Minnesota Department of Health (1992-1996); Member, Executive Board, Minneapolis Metropolitan Pediatric Society (1988-1992); Member, Sickle-CellMN (1978-1984) **AW:** Best Doctors in America (2003-2008); Top Doctor, St.Paul Magazine, MSP Communications, Inc (2000-2006); Outstanding Teaching Award, Department of Pediatrics, University of Minnesota (1985, 1987, 1993); Philip P. Denegar Award (1984); Bausch and Lomb Science Award (1965); Named Valedictorian, De La Salle High School (1965) **MEM:** American Association for Physician Leadership (2005-Present); The American Society of Pediatric Hematology/Oncology (1981-Present); American Society of Hematology (1980-Present); Alpha Omega Alpha (1972-Present); Biomedical Engineering Society (1992-2013); The International Society of Biorheology - ISB (1986-2013); American Society for Investigative Pathology (ASIP) (1982-2013); American Heart Association Council on Hemostasis and Thrombosis (1983-2004) **H:** History; Philosophy; Boating; Kayaking; Travel **RE:** Catholic; Jewish **BA:** 2525 Chicago Ave So, Main Headquarters/Executive Suite, Minneapolis, MN, 55404 **ADD:** 1047 Fairmount Ave, Saint Paul, MN, 55105

SMITH, EARL, T: Nephrologist (Retired) **I:** Medicine & Health Care **DOB:** 03/01/1936 **PB:** Pittsburgh **SC:** PA/USA **PT:** Mose Smith; Irene Smith **ED:** Resident, Cleveland Clinic (1964-1968); Intern, Montefiore Hospital, UPMC, Pittsburgh, Pennsylvania (1961-1962); MD, University of Pittsburgh (1961); BS, Tufts University (1957) **C:** Professor of Medicine, Chicago Medical School (1995-Present); Chief, Nephrology Division, Mount Sinai Hospital, Sinai Health System, Chicago, Illinois (1971-Present); Vice Chair of Medicine, Mount Sinai Hospital, Sinai Health System, Chicago, Illinois (1987-2016); Chief, Nephrology Division, Chicago Medical School (1994-2014); Interim Program Director, Chicago Medical School (2007-2008); Interim Chair of Medicine, Mount Sinai Hospital, Sinai Health System, Chicago, Illinois (1994-1995, 2005-2006); President, Medical Staff, Mount Sinai Hospital, Sinai Health System, Chicago, Illinois (1985-1987); Physician, Cook County Health and Hospitals System, Chicago, Illinois (1968-1971) **CR:** Chair, Board of Directors, Hektoen Institute of Medicine **CIV:** Chair, Hypertension Committee, Chicago Heart Association (1973-1975) **MIL:** Captain, U.S. Air Force (1962-1964) **CW:** Associate Editor, "Kidney Journal" (1991-2011); Co-author, "Self Assessment in Internal Medicine" (1980); Co-author, "Medical Exam Book-Nephrology" (1976); Contributor, Articles, Professional Journals **MEM:** Fellow, American College of Physicians; Fellow, American Society of Nephrology; American Society for Artificial Internal Organs; American Society of Hypertension; Specialist in Clinical Hypertension; International Society for Nephrology; The Phi Beta Kappa Society; Alpha Omega Alpha Honor Medical Society; Sigma Xi **ADD:** 1355 N. Sandburg Terrace, Apartment 401, Chicago, IL, 60610 **URL:** DoB:01-03-1936

SMITH, ELDON, T: Cardiologist, Emeritus Professor **I:** Education/Educational Services **CN:** University of Calgary **ED:** Honorary LLD, Dalhousie University (2014); MD, Dalhousie University, Cum Laude (1967) **C:** Professor Emeritus, University of Calgary (2004-Present); Dean, Faculty of Medicine, University of Calgary (1992-1997); Associate Dean of Clinical Affairs, University of Calgary (1990-1992); Chair, Department of Medicine, University of Calgary (1985-1990); Professor of Medicine, Physiology and Biophysics, University of Calgary (1980-2004); Chief, Cardiology Division, University of Calgary (1980-1986); Associate Professor of

Medicine and Physiology, Dalhousie University (1973-1980) **CR:** Zenith Capital Corporation (2013-Present); Corporate Director, Resverlogix Corporation (2010-Present); Intellipharmaceutics International Ltd (2009-Present); LOGiQ Asset Management Inc. (2005-Present); Sernova Corporation (2000-2009); Vasogen, Inc. (1998-2009); Canadian Natural Resources, Ltd. (1997-2015); Fellow, Royal College of Physicians & Surgeons of Canada; Fellow, Canadian Academy of Health Sciences **CIV:** Alberta Health Services Board (2011-2014); Chair, Canadian Heart Health Strategy and Action Plan (2006-2009); Trustee, Alberta Heritage Foundation for Medical Research, Canada (2000-2007); Premier's Advisory Council for Health, Board of Directors, President, Peter Lougheed Medical Research Foundation (1999-2007); Health Professions Advisory Board **CW:** Editor-in-Chief, Canadian Journal of Cardiology (1997-2009); Contributor, 250 Papers and Books **AW:** Order of the University of Calgary; Officer, Order of Canada; Lifetime Achievement Award, City of Calgary **MEM:** American Heart Association; International Academy of Cardiovascular Sciences; Royal College of Physicians and Surgeons of Canada; Canadian Cardiovascular Society **MH:** Albert Nelson Marquis Lifetime Achievement Award (2017) **ADD:** 16-1901 Varsity Estates Drive NW, Calgary, AB, Canada, T3B 4T7

SMITH, G. LOUIS, T: Senior Research Scientist **I:** Sciences **CN:** Science Systems and Applications, Inc. **DOB:** 01/07/1938 **PB:** Raleigh **SC:** NC/USA **PT:** Louis Norman Smith; Viola Ruth (Rogerson) Smith **MS:** Married **SPN:** Olivia Parrilee (6/25/1960) **CH:** Joni Lynn; Diann Patsy; Laurie Ruth **ED:** PhD in Aerospace Engineering, Virginia Polytechnic Institute and State University (1968); MS in Aerospace Engineering, Virginia Polytechnic Institute and State University (1963); BS, Virginia Polytechnic Institute and State University, With Honors (1960); Coursework, The George Washington University **C:** Senior Scientist, Science Systems Applications, Inc. (2000-Present); Research Professor, Virginia Polytechnic Institute and State University (1997-Present); International Scanner, Radiation Science Working Group, Centre Nationale Etudes Spatiale, Paris, France (1995-Present); Research Scientist, Clouds and Earth Radiant Energy System, Langley Research Center, National Aeronautics and Space Administration (1991-2017); Research Scientist, Earth Radiation Budget Experiment, Langley Research Center, National Aeronautics and Space Administration (1975-1990); Research Scientist, Satellite Project Support and Planetary Reentry Analysis, Langley Research Center, National Aeronautics and Space Administration (1960-1974); Trainee, Langley Research Center, National Aeronautics and Space Administration (1956-1959) **CR:** Investigator, Clouds and Earth Radiation Energy Science Team, Langley Research Center, Hampton, VA (1990-Present); Investigator, Earth Radiation Budget Experiment Science Team, Langley Research Center, Hampton, VA (1979-1992); Investigator, Earth Radiation Budget Science Team, Goddard Space Flight Center, Beltsville, MD (1975-1983) **CW:** Contributor, Numerous Research Articles, Professional Journals **AW:** H.J.E. Reid Award for Best Publication, Langley Research Center, National Aeronautics and Space Administration (1981); Medal for Exceptional Scientific Achievement; Langley's Technical Excellence Award, National Aeronautics and Space Administration; Group Achievement Award, National Aeronautics and Space Administration; Group Achievement Award to CERES Team for Outstanding Group Achievement, National Aeronautics and Space

Administration **MEM:** American Meteorological Society; American Geophysical Union; Rotary Club of Yorktown Virginia **H:** Exercise; Gardening **ADD:** 955 Harpersville Road, Apartment 1029, Newport News, VA, 23681

SMITH, HAROLD HASKEN, T: President **I:** Nonprofit & Philanthropy **CN:** Governor's Scholar Program Foundation **DOB:** 03/16/1942 **PB:** Cincinnati **SC:** OH/USA **PT:** Harold C. Smith; Ruth V. (Hasken) Smith **MS:** Married **SPN:** Karen A. Willis (12/20/1969) **CH:** Amy Elizabeth; Andrew David; Anne Cameron **ED:** Honorary LHD, Centre College (2016); Honorary LHD, University of Pikeville (2014); Honorary LHD, University of Pikeville (2010); Honorary LLD, Cumberland College (2003); MBA in Business Administration, American University, Washington, DC (1968); AB, Centre College, Danville, KY (1964); Graduate, Newport Public High School, Newport, KY (1960) **C:** President, Governor's Scholar Program Foundation, Frankfort, KY (2009-Present); Senior Associate, Global Advancement LLC, Lexington, KY (2009-Present); President Emeritus, College of Osteopathic Medicine, University of Pikeville (2009-Present); President, College of Osteopathic Medicine, University of Pikeville (1997-2009); Vice President for Development, Muskingum University, New Concord, OH (1983-1997); Vice President, Centre College, Danville, KY (1980-1983); Dean of Students, Centre College, Danville, KY (1980-1983); Lecturer in Economics and Management, Dean of Admissions, Centre College, Danville, KY (1973-1980); Director of Admissions, Centre College, Danville, KY (1970-1972); Associate Director of Admissions, Centre College, Danville, KY (1968-1970); Area Representative, Centre College, Washington, DC (1966-1968); Resident Advisor, American University, Washington, DC (1966-1968); Admissions Counselor, Centre College, Danville, KY (1964-1966) **CR:** "Harvard Seminar for New Presidents," Harvard Graduate School of Education, Cambridge, MA (1997); "Institute for Educational Fundraising," Council for Advancement and Support of Education, Dartmouth College (1983); "Institute for Chief Student Affairs Officers," Student Affairs Administrators in Higher Education, Stowe, VA (1980); "College Board Admissions Institute," University of Chicago, Chicago, IL (1965); "Workshop on Liberal Arts Education," Danforth Foundation, Colorado College; Consultant in Education **CIV:** Director, Nativity Academy, Kentucky (2012-Present); Beargrass Christian Church, Louisville, KY (2010-Present); Vice-chair, Nativity Academy, Kentucky (2015-2016); Chairman, Presbyterian Homes and Services of Kentucky, Inc. (2013-2015); Chairman, St. James Group Foundation (2010); Trustee, Presbyterian Homes and Services of Kentucky, Inc. (2009-2015); Board of Directors, Leadership Kentucky (2002-2008); Leadership Kentucky (2000); First Presbyterian Church, Pikeville, KY (1997-2009); Vice Chair of Board, Southeast Ohio Regional Medical Center, Southeastern Medical Hospital, Cambridge, OH (1995-1996); Chair of Finance Committee, Southeast Ohio Regional Medical Center, Southeastern Med Hospital, Cambridge, OH (1993-1994); Board of Trustees, Southeast Ohio Regional Medical Center, Southeastern Med Hospital, Cambridge, OH (1987-1997); Board of Directors, Southeast Ohio Symphony Orchestra (1983-1997); Board of Directors, Renew Environment of New Concord (1983-1997); College Drive Presbyterian Church, New Concord, OH (1983-1997); Elder, Presbyterian Church, Danville, KY (1980-1983); Director, YMCA, Boyle County, KY (1979-1983); Director, Mercer County, Kentucky (1979-1983) **AW:** John A. Strosnider, DO Memorial

Lecturer Award (2015); Inductee, Athletic Hall of Fame, University of Pikeville (2009); Northern Kentucky Sports Legend (2009); Citizen of the Year, Kiwanis of Pikeville (2009); Lon B. & Mary Evelyn Rogers Lifetime Achievement Award, Pike County Chamber of Commerce (2009); Distinguished Alumnus Award, Centre College, Danville, KY (2006); Business Person of the Year, Pike County Chamber of Commerce (2001); Inductee, Centre College Athletic Hall of Fame, Centre College (1994); Distinguished Chairman Award, Rotary Foundation (Now Rotary International) (1981-1982) **MEM:** Director, Kentucky Athletic Hall of Fame (2009-Present); Kentucky Institute of Medicine (2007-2010); Chairman, Mid-South Athletic Conference of Presidents, Mid-South Conference Athletics (2007-2008); Chairman, Executive Committee, Association of Independent Kentucky Colleges & Universities (2006-2008); Commissioner, College Commission, Southern Association of Colleges and Schools (2005-2008); Council of Presidents, National Association of Intercollegiate Athletics (2003-2006); Chairman, Mid-South Athletic Conference of Presidents, Mid-South Conference Athletics (2002-2003); Pikeville Rotary Club, Kentucky (1997-2009); Chairman, Cambridge Chamber of Commerce (1994); Eastern Ohio Development Alliance (1990-1997); Muskingum Valley Council, Boy Scouts of America (1987-1992); Board of Directors, Rotary Club, Cambridge, OH (1985-1991); Board of Directors, Cambridge Chamber of Commerce (1984-1997); New Concord Area Board of Trade, Ohio (1983-1997); Rotary Club, Cambridge, OH (1983-1997); District Chairman, Educational Awards/Scholarship, Rotary International (1982-1983); Rotary District Governor's Representative (1981-1982); Policy Committee, Boyle-Mercer County YMCA, Kentucky (1980-1983); President, Rotary Club, Danville, KY (1979-1980); Council President, NASPA - Student Affairs Administrators in Higher Education; American College Personnel Association; National Association for College Admission Counseling; Zanesville Country Club; Green Meadow Country Club; Cardinal Club; Honorary Life Member, Southeastern Ohio Symphony Orchestra **ADD:** 4018 Saint Germaine Court, Louisville, KY, 40207

SMITH, HILARY CRANWELL BOWEN, T: Investment Banker **I:** Financial Services **CN:** United Stem Cell Technologies **DOB:** 11/01/1937 **PB:** Baltimore **SC:** MD/USA **PT:** Henry Bowen Smith; Clayton (Cranwell) Smith **MS:** Married **SPN:** Janet Simmons (06/09/1962) **CH:** Kent C.B.; Kendall S.; Hillary E. **ED:** MBA, University of Virginia (1967); BA, Colgate University (1960) **C:** CFO, USUB Medical, LLC; Board Member, USUB Medical, LLC; Senior Advisor, TAP Advisors LLC (2012-Present); CFO, United Stemcell Technologies (2011-2015); Board Member, United Stemcell Technologies (2011-2015); Senior Advisor, Houlihan Lokey (2009-2010); Senior Advisor, Greenhill & Co., Inc., New York, NY (2004-2008); Managing Director, UBS, New York, NY (1990-2004); Managing Director, Salomon Brothers, New York, NY (1979-1990); Senior Vice President, Blyth, Eastman Dillon & Co., New York, NY (1977-1979); Vice President, E. F. Hutton & Co., New York, NY (1974-1977); Vice President, Goldman Sachs, New York, NY (1969-1974); Vice President, Mercantile-Safe Deposit and Trust Company (1967-1969) **CIV:** Founder, SBUB (2014-Present); CFO, SBUB (2014-Present); Director, SBUB (2014-Present); Consultant, SBUB (2014-Present); Board of Directors, Forest2Market, INC. (2000-2015); Overseer, National Maritime Historical Society (2013); Riverside Theater (2007-2012); National Maritime Historical Society (2004-2012); Treasurer, National Maritime Historical

Society (2006-2010); Mystic Seaport (2005); Chesapeake Bay Maritime Museum (1998-2004); Trustee, Wheaton College (1997-2003); Greenwich Academy (1988-1994) **MIL:** Lieutenant, US Navy (1960-1963) **MH:** Albert Nelson Marquis Lifetime Achievement Award (2017) **ADD:** 398 Indies Dr, Vero Beach, FL, 32963

SMITH, J. ROY, T: Education Educator, Museum Director (Retired) **I:** Education/Educational Services **DOB:** 09/13/1936 **PB:** Washington **SC:** DC/USA **PT:** James Roy Smith; Nellie Irene (Mansfield) Smith **ED:** Certificate, Oxford University, England (1963); Postgraduate Coursework, Brown University (1957); BA, Mercer University (1956) **C:** Associate Director, Karpeles Manuscript Museum, Charleston, SC (2005-2015); Teacher, Berkeley County, Moncks Corner, SC (1979-1994); With, Charleston County, Charleston, SC (1976-1979); Teacher, Fulton County, Fairburn, GA (1965-1976); With, Charleston County, Charleston, SC (1962-1964); Teacher, City of Cranston, RI (1957-1959) **MIL:** Lieutenant Junior Grade, U.S. Navy (1959-1962) **AW:** English Speaking Union Scholar, Oxford University (1963); Fellow, Lowcountry Writing Project; Fellow, Newspaper Fund of the Wall Street Journal **MEM:** Honorary Governor, Sons and Daughters of the Pilgrims (1976-Present); Secretary-treasurer, South Carolina Society, Sons of the American Revolution (1977-1978); Governor, Georgia Branch, Sons and Daughters of the Pilgrims (1976); Georgia S.R.; The Society of the Second War with Great Britain; South Carolina Historical Society; Georgia Historical Society; Registered Tour Guide, Kappa Phi Kappa; Lecturer, Kappa Phi Kappa **ADD:** 108 Water St, Washington, GA, 30673

SMITH, KINNEAR KING, T: Sole Practitioner **I:** Law and Legal Services **CN:** Kinnear K. Smith, PA **PB:** Baltimore **SC:** MD/USA **MS:** Married **SPN:** Wayne **CH:** Blake **ED:** JD, Nova Southeastern University (1993); BA, University of Miami (1986) **C:** Family Law Attorney, Kinnear K. Smith, PA (1998-Present); Assistant State Attorney, Sixth Judicial Circuit, Clearwater, FL (1994) **AW:** Named, Ten Best Attorneys in Florida, American Institute of Family Law Attorneys (2016-2017); Named, America's Most Honored Professionals (2016); Named, Best Lawyers in America (2010-2011); Named Florida's Best Lawyers (2009-2010) **MEM:** Tampa Bay Academy of Collaborative Professionals; International Academy of Collaborative Professionals; Leadership Pinellas **BAR:** United States District Court Middle District of Florida (1998); Florida (1994) **H:** Going to restaurants; Watching movies **BA:** 1215 S Myrtle Ave, Kinnear K Smith PA, Clearwater, FL, 33756 **URL:** http://kinnearksmithpa.com/attorney-profile/

SMITH, NORMAN D., T: Emeritus Professor of Geology **I:** Education/Educational Services **CN:** University of Nebraska - Lincoln **DOB:** 01/26/1941 **PB:** Natural Bridge **SC:** NY/USA **PT:** Charles C. Smith; Doris E. Smith **MS:** Married **SPN:** Judith Ann Smith **CH:** Laurence Charles Smith; Daniel Graeme Smith **ED:** PhD in Geology, Brown University (1967); MS in Geology, Brown University (1964); BS in Geology, St. Lawrence University (1962) **C:** Professor Emeritus, University of Nebraska-Lincoln (2009-Present); Professor, University of Nebraska-Lincoln (1998-2009); Department Chair, University of Nebraska-Lincoln (1998-2004); Department Head, University of Illinois at Chicago (1986-1992); Professor, University of Illinois at Chicago (1967-1998) **CR:** Consultant, Migrate Mining Ltd., South Africa (2003); Visiting Scientist, University of Chile-Santiago (2003); Chair, Sedimenatary Geology Division, Geological Society of America (1993-1994); Visiting Scientist, New Zealand Institute of Oceanography (1988-1989); Editor, Journal of Sedimentary Geology (1983-1988); Geological Consultant, Council for Scientific & Industrial Research (CSIR) (1982); Visiting Scientist, Kananaskis Centre for Environmental Research, University of Calgary (1981); President, Great Lakes Section SEPM (1979-1980); Geological Consultant, Anglo-American Corp. of South Africa Ltd. (1978); Visiting Associate Professor, University of Alberta (1974-1975); Geological Consultant, Chamber of Mines, South Africa; Geological Consultant, Goldfields of South Africa; Geological Consultant, J.C.I. Ltd.; Geological Consultant, Anglo-Vaal Ltd. **CW:** Author, 75 Articles, Peer Reviewed Science Journals **AW:** Pettijohn Medal, Society for Sedimentary Geology (2012); FRD Fellow, University of Witwatersrand and Unviersity of Cape Town, South Africa (1995); CSIR Fellow, University of Cape Town (1989); Dedicated Service Award, Society for Sedimentary Geology (1988); Fulbright Scholar, University of Delhi, India (1982) **BA:** 1400 R Street, 126 Bessey Hall, UNL, Dept of Earth and Atmospheric Science, Lincoln, NE, 68558 **ADD:** UNL, Dept of Earth & Atmospheric Sciences, 126 Bessey Hall, Lincoln, NE, 68558-0340

SMITHERS, RAY J., T: Chief Executive Officer, Executive Director of Programming **I:** Nonprofit & Philanthropy **CN:** The Autism Channel **ED:** AA, The University of Fort Lauderdale (1972) **C:** Chief Executive Officer, The Autism Channel (2012-Present); Executive Director of Programming, Autism Channel (2012-Present); Partner, The Autism Channel (2012-Present); Partner, Flying Pig Ranch Studios (1983-Present); Partner, Touch-Map Systems (1983-Present); Creative Director, KMPC Radio, Gold West Broadcasting (1980-1983) **CW:** Producer, "Look Where I Stand," Flying Pig Ranch Studios **AW:** Award for Service to the Autism Community, Wings of Hope (2018); Award for "Look Where I Stand," AEGIS (2012); Gold Award for "Now is the Time," Hermes (2011); Award for "Look Where I Stand," Communitas (2010); News Documentary Award, Associated Press (1971); Best Radio Commercial Production, CLIO (1969) **MEM:** Co-Founder, Touch-Vote; Co-Founder, The Autism Channel; Co-Founder, Touch-MapSystems; Co-Founder, Flying Pig Ranch Studios **BA:** 5401 N Haverhill Rd Unit 119, The Autism Channel, West Palm Beach, FL, 33407 **ADD:** 699 Marginal Rd, West Palm Beach, FL, 33411 **URL:** http://www.theautismchannel.foundation/

SMITH, WANDA L., I: Business Management/Business Services **ED:** AS in Business Management, Harford Community College **CIV:** Advisory Board, Brightwood College; Advisory Board, Fortis Institute; Advisory Board, Casey Cares Foundation; Advisory Board, John W. Brick Mental Health Foundation **AW:** Listed, Inc. 5000, Inc. Magazine (2017) **H:** Golf; Travel; Entertaining Family and Friends at Her Home

SMOLEV, TERENCE ELLIOT, T: Lawyer, Educator **I:** Law and Legal Services **CN:** Berkman, Henoch, Peterson, Peddy & Fenchel **DOB:** 10/05/1944 **PB:** Brooklyn **SC:** NY/USA **PT:** Lawrence Smolev; Shirley (Lebowitz) Smolev **MS:** Married **SPN:** Phyllis C. Rudko (10/8/1995); Sherry Gale Rosen (11/24/1968, Divorced) **CH:** Cindy; Scott **ED:** LLM, New York University (1974); JD, American University Washington College of Law (1969); BBA, Hofstra University (1966) **C:** Of Counsel, Tax Controversies Department, Berkman, Henoch, Peterson, Peddy & Fenchel, PC (2016-Present); Adjunct Professor, American University Washington College of Law (2013-Present); Private Practice, Mineola, NY (2012-2016); Partner in Charge of Taxes, Trusts and Estates, Forchelli, Curto, Deegan, Schwartz, Mineo & Terrana, LLP (2000-2012); Private Practice, Mineola, NY (1992-2000); Partner, Naidich & Smolev (1972-1992); Director of Deferred Giving, Hofstra University, Hempstead, NY (1971-1974); Editor, Panel Publishers, Greenvale, NY (1970-1971); Accountant, Peat Marwick & Mitchell, New York, NY (1969-1970) **CR:** Board of Trustees, Dowling College (2007); Board of Trustees, Hofstra University (1992-2006); Adjunct Professor, Hofstra University, Hempstead, NY (1971-2006); District Counsel, North Merrick UFSD, NY (1975-1999); Vice President, Board of Directors, New York City Police Museum; Counsel, Board of Directors, New York City Police Museum; Board of Directors, Gurwin Geriatric Foundation, Alzheimer's Foundation of America **CIV:** Board of Directors, Audit Committee, Nassau County; Member, Israeli Bond Cabinet of Long Island, Development Corporation for Israel (1996-2004); Board of Directors, Long Island Chapter, Arthritis Foundation (1995-1997); Member, Nassau County Chapter, New York State Democratic Committee (1972-1980); Small Business Advisory Committee, Internal Revenue Service (1975-1977); Board of Directors, Long Island Chapter, Israeli Bond Cabinet of Long Island; Board of Directors, Economic Opportunity Commission of Nassau County, Inc.; Member, Judicial Screening Committee, New York State Democratic Party, Nassau County, NY **CW:** Contributor, Book Chapters; Contributor, Articles Professional Journals; New York Law Journal **AW:** Recipient, Community Service Award, Hebrew Academy of Nassau County (1997); Honoree, Alumnus of the Year, Hofstra University (1996); Recipient, Alumni Achievement Award, Hofstra University (1993); Recipient, George M. Estabrook Award, Hofstra University (1991); Honoree, Senator of the Year, Hofstra University (1985) **MEM:** Board of Directors, Hofstra University Club (1981-1995); President, Alumni Senate, Hofstra University (1987-1989); President, New York State Association of School Attorneys (1984); ABA; Nassau County Bar Association; New York State Bar Association **BAR:** New York State Bar (1970) **MH:** Albert Nelson Marquis Lifetime Achievement Award (2017) **H:** Photography; Golf **BA:** 100 Garden City Plaza, 3rd FL, Garden City, NY, 11530 **ADD:** 4175 NW 58th Lane, Boca Raton, FL, 33496 **URL:** http://www.smolevlaw.com

SMUKAL, MICHAEL WILLIAM, T: Music Educator (Retired) **I:** Education/Educational Services **PT:** Paul Herbert Smukal; Carol (Hannen) Smukal **CH:** Michael Adam; Stephen Andrew **ED:** MusM, UNLV (1985); BA, UNLV (1985) **C:** Retired (2015); Director, Bands, Charles Silvestri Junior High School, Clark County School District, Las Vegas, NV (1985-2015) **CR:** Musician, Independent Performances, Compositions and Lessons; Composer, Warner/Chappell Music, Inc., Las Vegas, NV; Music Arrangement, Warner/Chappell Music, Inc., Las Vegas, NV **CIV:** State President, National Association of Jazz Education (Now IAJE) (1984-1986) **MIL:** Technical Sergeant, United States Air Force, Washington, DC (1971-1975) **CW:** Trombonist, "Moody Blue," Elvis Presley, Sony Music Entertainment (2013); Trombonist, "Spring Tours '77," Elvis Presley, Sony Music Entertainment (2002); Trombonist, "Moody Blue," Elvis Presley, RCA Records (2000); Trombonist, "Elvis Aaron Presley: The Silver Box Set," Elvis Presley, RCA Records (1998); Trombonist, "Platinum: A Life in Music," Elvis Presley, RCA Records (1997); Trombonist, "Elvis in Concert," Elvis Presley,

RCA Records (1992); Trombonist, "This is Elvis," Elvis Presley, RCA Records (1981); Trombonist, "Elvis Aaron Presley: The Silver Box Set," Elvis Presley, RCA Records (1980); Trombonist, "Elvis: A Canadian Tribute," Elvis Presley, RCA Records (1978); Trombonist, "Elvis in Concert," CBS Television (1977); Trombonist, "Moody Blue," Elvis Presley, RCA Records (1977); Trombonist, "Elvis in Concert," Elvis Presley, RCA Records (1977); Trombonist, with Elvis Presley (1975-1977); Music Arranger, Educational Jazz Publications, "Now Rock, Ye Rested Gentlemen," Alfred Publishing Co., Inc.; Music Arranger, Educational Jazz Publications, "Song of the Volga Boatman," Alfred Publishing Co., Inc. **AW:** Honoree, Editor's Choice, "Now Rock, Ye Rested Gentlemen," Alfred Publishing Co., Inc. (2004); Southwest Region Distinguished Educator of the Year, Clark County School District (2003-2004) **MEM:** IAJE; Nevada Music Educators Association; National Conference, Music Teachers National Association **MH:** Albert Nelson Marquis Lifetime Achievement Award (2017) **ADD:** 2180 E Warm Springs Rd Unit 2179, Las Vegas, NV, 89119

SMUTNY, JOAN FRANKLIN, T: Director **I:** Education/Educational Services **CN:** The Center for Gifted/Midwest Torrance Center for Creativity **PB:** Chicago **SC:** IL/USA **PT:** Eugene Franklin; Mabel (Lind) Franklin **MS:** Married **SPN:** Herbert Paul Smutny **CH:** Cheryl Lind **ED:** MA, Northwestern University; BS, Northwestern University **C:** Director, Gifted Pre-K-Through Twelfth Grade, The Center for Gifted/Midwest Torrance Center for Creativity (1979-Present); Director, Right to Read Seminar (1973-1974); Director, Seminar for Gifted High School Students (1973); Executive Director, High School Workshops, National College of Education, Evanston, IL (1970-1978); Founder, Director, Woman Power Through Education Seminar (1969-1974); Faculty Member, Founder, Director, High School Workshop, National College of Education, Evanston, IL; Chairman, Communications Department, National College of Education, Evanston, IL; Founder, Director, Faculty Member, National High School Institute, Northwestern University School of Education, Evanston, IL; Teacher, New Trier High School, Winnetka, IL **CR:** Chairman, Board of Directors, Barbereux School, Evanston, IL (1992-Present); Assistant Editor, Editorial Board, Understanding Our Gifted (1994-2014); Member, Advisory Board, Educating Able Learners (1991-2001); Director, Project, National College of Education (1987-2008); Director, Summer Wonders, National College of Education (1986-2003); Director, Bright and Talented Project (1986); Director, The Center for Gifted (1982-2003); Director, North Shore Country Day School, Winnetka, IL (1982-1992); Board of Directors, Worlds of Wisdom and Wonder, Creative Children's Academy (1978-1988); Director, Job Creation Project (1980-1982); Director, Gifted Young Writers and Young Writers Conferences (1978-1979); Director, Humanities Program for Verbally Precocious Youth (1978-1979); State Team for Gifted Students, Illinois Office of Education, Office of Gifted, Springfield, IL (1977); Evaluation Consultant, DAVTE, IOE, Springfield, IL (1977); Director, Thinking for Action in Career Education Program (1976-1979); Coordinator, Career Education, National College of Education (1976-1978); Consultant, Research and Development, Illinois Department of Vocational Education (1973-1979); Director, New Dimensions for Women (1973-1978); Member, Leadership Training, Institute for the Gifted, United States Office of Education (Now United States Department of Education) (1973-1974); Co-Director, Instructor, Seminars in Critical Thinking, Illinois Family Service (1972-

1975); Writer, Educational Filmstrips in Language Arts and Literature, Society for Visual Education (1970-1978); Director, Future Teachers of America Seminar in College and Career (1970-1972); Advisory Committee, Education Professions Development Act, United States Office of Education (1969-1975); Writer, Consultant, Radiant Educational Corporation (1969-1971); Consultant, American Library Association (1969-1971); Speakers Bureau, Council on Foreign Relations (1968-1969); Director, TACE; The White House Conference on Children and Youth; Director, Workshops for High School Students; Consultant, United States Office of Education; Director, Gifted Programs, National Louis University, Evanston, IL; Speaker in Field **CW:** Editor, Illinois Association for Gifted Children Journal (1995-Present); Member, Advisory Board, Gifted Education Press Quarterly (1995-Present); Author, "Acceleration for Gifted Learners, K-5" (2007); Author, "Differentiation for the Young Child" (2004); Author, "Differentiation for the Young Child: Teaching Strategies Across the Content Areas" (2004); Author, "Gifted Education: Promising Practices" (2003); Author, "Stand Up for Your Gifted Child" (2001); Author, "Differentiated Instruction" (2003); Author, "Gifted Girls" (1998); Editor, "The Young Gifted Child: Potential and Promise: An Anthology" (1998); Author, "Teaching Gifted Young Children in the Regular Classroom" (1997); Assistant Editor, Understanding Our Gifted (1995-2007); Contributing Editor, Roeper Review (1994-1999); Author, Paperback, "Your Gifted Child - How to Recognize and Develop the Special Talents in your Child from Birth to Age Seven" (1991); Author, "Education of the Gifted: Programs and Perspectives" (1990); Author, "A Thoughtful Overview of Gifted Education" (1990); Editor, Creativity Series, "Ablex" (1988-1998); Author, "Your Gifted Child: How to Recognize and Develop the Special Talents in Your Child From Birth to Age Seven" (1987); Author, "Job Creation: Creative Materials, Activities and Strategies for the Classroom" (1982); Reviewer, Programs for Gifted and Talented, United States Office of Education (1976-1978); Editor & Contributor, "Maturity in Teaching"; Writer, Educational Filmstrips, "The Brothers Grimm"; Writer, Educational Filmstrips, "How the West Was Won"; Writer, Educational Filmstrips, "Mutiny on the Bounty"; Writer, Educational Filmstrips, "Dr. Zhivago"; Writer, Educational Filmstrips, "Christmas Around the World"; Writer, Educational Filmstrips, "Space Odyssey 2001"; Contributor, Numerous Books in Field; Editor, Numerous Books in Field; Contributor, Articles to Professional Journals; Contributor, Articles, Chicago Parent Magazine; Co-Editor, Newsletter, Early Childhood Division, National Association for Gifted Children **AW:** Legacy Book Award, Parents and Educators of Gifted and Talented Children (2011); E. Paul Torrance Award, Creativity Network, National Association for Gifted Children (2011); Past Presidents' Award for Significant Contributions to Gifted Education, California Association for the Gifted (2005); Outstanding Research Award, Phi Delta Kappa International (1996); Distinguished Service Award, National Association for Gifted Children (1996); Award for Outstanding Contributions to Education, Phi Delta Kappa International (1985) **MEM:** Co-Chairman, Schools and Programs, National Association for Gifted Children (1995-Present); Membership Chairman, National Association for Gifted Children (1991-1996); First Vice President, Evanston Chapter, National Society of Arts and Letters (1975-1995); Third Vice President, Evanston Chapter, National Society of Arts and Letters (1975-1995); President, Evanston Chapter, National Society of Arts and Letters (1975-1995); Vice President, Evanston

Chapter, Phi Delta Kappa International (1990-1992); Research Chairman, Evanston Chapter, Phi Delta Kappa International (1990-1992); Pi Lambda Theta; American Association of University Professors **H:** Reading; Playing piano **ADD:** 8184 Cielo Vista Dr, Whittier, CA, 90605

SNYDER, JAMES, T: Celebrity Tanning Expert, Visionary Inventor **I:** Cosmetics **CN:** Jimmy Jimmy Coco Corp **SC:** WA/USA **C:** Founder, Jimmy Jimmy Coco Corp (2003-Present); Chief Executive Officer, Jimmy Jimmy Coco Corp (2003-Present); Music Contract, Miami, FL; Bathing Suite Model, International Male **CR:** Celebrity Tan Expert, Victoria's Secret Fashion Shows **CIV:** Supporter, Best Friends Animal Society; Supporter, St. Jude Children's Research Hospital; Supporter, International Coastal Cleanup; Supporter, Sea Shepherd **AW:** Allure Best of Beauty Awards (2013); Allure Best of Beauty Awards (2011); Allure Best of Beauty Awards (2007-2009); Honoree, Pioneer of Tanning, New York Post; Honoree, Hollywood's Leading Man of Tan **BA:** 7095 Hollywood Boulevard, Suite 552, Jimmy Jimmy Coco Corp, Los Angeles, CA, 90028 **URL:** https://www.jimmycoco.com

SOLBERG, RINO , I: Business Management/Business Services **C:** Founder, Better Globe Forestry, Ltd. (2004-Present); Chairman, Better Globe Forestry, Ltd. (2004-Present); Sponsor, NGO Child Africa (1991-Present) **CW:** Author, Ten Books in Field **AW:** Winner, Award for Most Responsible Chief Executive Officer for the Forestry Industry, Business Worldwide Magazine (2017) **ACH:** Achievements include inventing and receiving patents in 12 countries on a grinding machine for gate and globe valves; Inventing machines that approximately 70% of all Nuclear Power Stations all over the world have used; Selling his company after running successfully for 13 years

SOLOMON MOORMAN, JOYCE ELAINE, T: Music Educator **I:** Education/Educational Services **CN:** Borough of Manhattan Community College **DOB:** 05/11/1946 **PB:** Tuskegee **SC:** AL/USA **PT:** Walker Emanuel Solomon; Mary Willie (Winkfield) Solomon (Deceased) **MS:** Widowed **SPN:** Wilson Moorman (10/3/2013, Deceased) **ED:** EdD, Columbia University (1982); MFA, Sarah Lawrence College (1975); MAT, Rutgers, The State University of New Jersey (1971); BA, Vassar College (1968) **C:** Professor, Borough Manhattan Community College (2017-Present); Associate Professor, Borough Manhattan Community College (2010-2017); Assistant Professor, Borough of Manhattan Community College (2003-2009); Teacher, Brooklyn College Preparatory Center Arts (1998-2003); Substitute Assistant Professor, LaGuardia Community College, Long Island City, NY (1994-1996); Teacher, Brooklyn Music School (1982-1993); Teacher, LEGAM Music School, Brooklyn, NY (1982-1990); Teacher, Manna House Workshops, New York, NY (1981-1983); Teacher, Harlem School of the Arts, New York, NY (1979-1980) **CR:** Adjunct Associate Professor, LaGuardia Community College, Long Island Community College, New York (1998-2003); Adjunct Associate Professor, New York City College of Technology (1998-2003); Panelist, New York State Council on Arts, New York, NY (1997-2000); Judge, National Association for the Advancement of Colored People, ACTSO Competition (1996-1999); Adjunct Assistant Professor, LaGuardia Community College, Long Island City, NY (1996-1998); Adjunct Assistant Professor, LaGuardia Community College, Long Island City, NY (1992-1994); Adjunct Assistant Professor, York College, Jamaica, NY (1991-1992); Adjunct Assistant Professor, Borough

Manhattan Community College, New York, NY (1983-1988) **CIV:** Financial Secretary, Psi Lambda Omega Chapter, Alpha Kappa Alpha Sorority (2009-2010); Former Secretary, Logan Condominium Association, Brooklyn, NY (1996-1998) **CW:** Composer, "Summer" (2018); Composer, "Cape Coast Castle" (2015); Composer, Jazz Concertino (2013); Composer, "The Snowstorm" (2012); Composer, Orchestral Suite from Elegies for the Fallen (2011); Composer, "Dream Variations" (2007); Composer, "Elegies for the Fallen" (2004); Composer, "Race Riot, 1964" (2000); Composer, "A Tone Poem for Victims of Racism and Hatred" (1998); Composer, "Remembrances'68" (1996); Composer, Trio for Flute, Guitar and Drumset (1991); Composer, "In Time of Silver Rain" (1990); Composer, "Sing My People" (1980); Composer, Fantasy for Violin and Piano (1979); Composer, "The Soul of Nature" (1975) **AW:** Recipient, Special Commendation, Nancy Van De Vate International Opera Competition (2004); Recipient, June Jordan Award, Pen and Brush, Inc. (2003); Recipient, Performance Award, Andy Warhol Composers' Competition, Pennsylvania Academy Fine of Arts (2000); Honorable Mention, Year 2000 Women of Color Composition Commission Competition; Winner, Vienna Modern Masters, Millennium Commission Competition (1998); Recipient, Standard Panel Award, American Society of Composers (1990-2012); Finalist, Detroit Symphony African American Symphonic Composers' Forum Award (1990) **MEM:** American Composers Forum (2013-Present); Black Music Research Center (1995-Present); American Society of Composers, Authors and Publishers (1980-Present); Pen and Brush, A Club for Women Artists (2003-2016); American Music Center (1981-2013) **H:** Tennis; Current events; Reading; Scrabble; Bridge **PA:** Democrat **RE:** Methodist **BA:** 199 Chambers Street, New York, NY, 10007 **ADD:** 104 St Marks Pl, Apt 1E, Brooklyn, NY, 11217

SOLOW, JOHN LEWIS, T: Economist, Educator **I:** Education/Educational Services **CN:** University of Iowa **DOB:** 02/27/1954 **PB:** Boston **SC:** MA/USA **PT:** Robert Merton Solow; Barbara (Lewis) Solow **MS:** Married **SPN:** Catherine Mary Mitiguy (8/21/1977) **CH:** Rebecca Marie; Benjamin Lewis **ED:** PhD, Stanford University (1983); MA, Stanford University (1981); BA, Yale University (1976) **C:** Professor of Economics, University of Iowa, Iowa City, IA (2012-Present); Associate Professor of Economics, University of Iowa, Iowa City, IA (1988-2012); Assistant Professor of Economics, University of Iowa, Iowa City, IA (1981-1987); Economist, Federal Energy Administration, Washington, DC (1976-1977) **MEM:** American Economic Association; North American Association of Sports Economists **H:** Sailing; Travel **ADD:** 607 Templin Rd, Iowa City, IL, 52246

SOMER, LAWRENCE E., T: Professor Emeritus of Mathematics **I:** Education/Educational Services **CN:** Catholic University of America **DOB:** 10/10/1948 **PB:** Brooklyn, New York, York, USA **SC:** New York/USA **PT:** Leon Somer; Dorothy Somer **MS:** Married **SPN:** Eva Feiglová **ED:** Doctorate, University of Illinois at Urbana-Champaign (1970-1985); BA in Mathematics, Cornell University, Cum Laude (1966-1970) **C:** Mathematician **CIV:** Arranger & Conductor, Religious Services and Classes, Roosevelt Hotel for Senior Citizens, Washington, D.C. (1981); Volunteer, Champaign County Nursing Home, IL (1971-1975, 1980) **CW:** 17 Lectures on Fermat Numbers, Springer-Verlag, NY (2001); Editorial Board, The Fibonacci Quarterly **AW:** Josef Hlavka Prize, Josef Hlavka Foundation (2010) **MEM:** Nominating Committee, Washington Section, Mathematical Association of America

(1983-1984); President, Pi Mu Epsilon, University of Illinois Chapter (1971-1972); American Statistical Association; American Mathematical Society; The Honor Society of Phi Kappa Phi **MH:** Albert Nelson Marquis Lifetime Achievement Award (2017) **PA:** Democratic **RE:** Jewish **BA:** 620 Michigan Ave NE, Catholic University of America, Department of Mathematics, Washington, DC, 20064 **ADD:** itná 25, c/o Michal Kr⬚ek, Institute of Mathematics CAS, Praha 1, Czech Republic, 115 67

SOMERVILLE, DAPHINE HOLMES, T: Elementary School Educator (Retired) **I:** Education/ Educational Services **DOB:** 01/19/1940 **PB:** Clinton **SC:** NC/USA **PT:** George Henry Holmes; Mamie Streeter Holmes **MS:** Single **SPN:** Kalford Burton Somerville (1970, Deceased 2014) **CH:** Daria Lynn **ED:** Postgraduate Coursework, State University of New York at Farmingdale (2000); Postgraduate Coursework, Columbia University (1971); MS in Education, Hofstra University (1967); BA, Blackburn College (1961); AA, Blackburn College (1959) **CT:** Certification in Elementary Teaching **C:** Field Supervisor, Department of Education, Dowling College (2006-2014); Teacher, Tutor, Computer Writing, Opportunities Industrialization Center (2009-2013); Teacher, East Islip School District (1961-1999) **CIV:** Contributor, Bay Shore Community Event, "Under the Big Tent" (2013-Present); By-Laws Revision Committee (2011-Present); Branch Historian, Islip Town National Association for the Advancement of Colored People (2008-Present); Chairperson, Meet and Greet Committee (2009-2013); Founding Member, National Dr. Martin L. King Junior Memorial (2005); Vice Chair Revitalization Committee, First Baptist Church, Bay Shore, NY (2000-2004); Chair, Partners in Education, First Baptist Church, Bay Shore, NY (1991-2001); Founder, Co-Author, Tutoring Program, Adopt-A-School Child/Family (1990); Director, Baptist Training Union (1974-1981); Trustee, First Baptist Church, Bay Shore, NY (1972-1990); Member, Bay Shore Civic Association and Bay Shore Public Schools Task Force for Advancement Equality Educational Opportunity (1967-1969); Secretary, Islip Town National Association for the Advancement of Colored People (1965-1990) **CW:** Contributor, Assistant Editor, The Colored Advancer, Islip Branch NAACP (2007-2013); Author, "Beamon Family Reunion Journal (2001); Founder, Co-Author, Tutoring Program, "Adopt-A-School Child/Family" (1990); Co-Author, "Baptist Training Union Study Guide, Committee on Christian Education" (1976) **AW:** Recipient, Trailblazer Award, First Baptist Church (2014); Recipient, Islip Town Founding Member Award, National Association for the Advanced of Colored People (2008); Recipient, Citation, Town of Islip (1999); Recipient, Editor's Choice Award, National Library of Poetry (1999); Recipient, African American Educators Award, Martin L. King Jr. Commission, Suffolk County, New York (1997); Recognition, Congressman Rick Lazio (1997); Grantee, Long Island School to Career Partnership for Proposed School/Bus Government Project (1996); Recipient, Dedicated Service Award, Partners in Education, First Baptist Church (1995-1996); Recipient, Distinguished Service Award, Long Island Region, NAACP (1993); Recipient, Lifetime Educational Involvement Award, National Council of Negro Women (1993); Recipient, Recognition Award, Islip Town, National Association for the Advancement of Colored (1987); Recipient, Community Service Award, Town Board, Town of Islip, Suffolk County, New York (1982) **MEM:** Founding Member, NAACP, Islip, NY (1958-Present); Silver Life Member, NAACP (2006); Financial Coordinator, Huntington Christian Women's Club (2003-2014); Past Building

Representative, New York State United Teachers; East Islip Teachers Association **MH:** Albert Nelson Marquis Lifetime Achievement Award (2017) **H:** Theater; Writing; Reading; Traveling; Yoga **ADD:** 130 Carman Road, Dix Hills, NY, 11746

SONMOR, MARILYN I., T: Music Educator (Retired) **I:** Writing and Editing **DOB:** 01/18/1933 **PB:** Wilson **SC:** WI/USA **PT:** John Reuben Haglund; Mary (Feldhahn) Haglund **MS:** Married **SPN:** Stephen Malcolm Sonmor (8/3/1957) **CH:** Tamara Lynn; Terri Lee; Stephen Mark **ED:** MA, Fuller Theological Seminary (1992); Postgraduate Music Studies, Arizona State University (1985-1986); MusB, University of Northwestern, Roseville, MN (1958) **C:** Author (2017-Present); Professor, Southwestern Conservative Baptist Bible College (Now Arizona Christian University) (1976-1995); Dean of Women, Southwestern Conservative Baptist Bible College (Now Arizona Christian University) (1976-1995); Professor, Conservative Baptist Bible College of the Philippines, Pasig City, Metro Manila, Philippines (1973-1975); Missionary, Conservative Baptist Foreign Mission Society, Manila, Philippines (1965-1975); Professor, Dallas Bible College (1960-1962); Teacher, Dallas Christian School (1960-1961); Teacher, Mesquite Independent School District (1959-1960) **CR:** Director, Women's Work, Campariza Association, Manila, Philippines (1973-1975); Director, Museum and Outreach Ministry, Conservative Baptist Bible College (1971-1975); Speaker, Conservative Baptist Association (1964-1975) **CW:** Author, "Led by an Unseen Hand: A Legacy for the Next Generation," West Bow Press (2017) **AW:** Honoree, First Place Winner, Voice Contest, Minnesota Music Teachers Association (1957) **MEM:** President, Southwestern Women's Auxiliary (1980-1982); American Association of Christian Counselors **MH:** Albert Nelson Marquis Lifetime Achievement Award (2017) **H:** Vocalist; Pianist; Needle crafts; Interior decorating; Writing **PA:** Republican **ADD:** 2305 N 127th Ave, Avondale, AZ, 85392 **URL:** http://www.marilynsonmorbook.com/

SOSHNICK, ANDREW Z., T: Partner **I:** Law and Legal Services **CN:** Faegre Baker Daniels LLP **MS:** Married **SPN:** Brenda Soshnick **CH:** Adam; Haley **ED:** JD, Northwestern University Pritzker School of Law, Cum Laude (1988); MA, Northwestern University Pritzker School of Law (1985); BA, Northwestern University Pritzker School of Law, With Distinction (1985) **CT:** State of Indiana Certified Family Law Specialist, Family Law Certification Board; Registered Family Law Mediator, State of Indiana **C:** Partner, Faegre Baker Daniels LLP **CIV:** Alumni Regent, Northwestern University Alumni Association; Member, Northwestern University Club of Indianapolis; President, Phi Chapter Educational Foundation, Fraternity of Phi Gamma Delta; Past President, Central Indiana Council, The American Israel Public Affairs Committee; Board of Directors Member, Indianapolis Public Library Foundation; Advisory Board Vice President, Borns Jewish Studies Program, Indiana University **AW:** Named Fellow, American Academy of Matrimonial Lawyers (1997); Named Fellow, International Academy of Family Lawyers (2017); Ranked in Indiana's Top 50, "Indiana Super Lawyers" (2004-2018); Ranked in Indiana's Top 10, "Indiana Super Lawyers" (2012-2014); Ranked Number Three in Indiana, "Indiana Super Lawyers" (2013); Ranked Number Two in Indiana, "Indiana Super Lawyers" (2012); Named Indianapolis Family Law Lawyer of the Year; "The Best Lawyers in America," Family Law; Ranked in Indiana's Top 10, "Indiana Super Lawyers" (2007-2010); Charles L. Whistler Pro Bono Award, Faegre Baker Daniels (2009); Gale M. Phelps Award, Indiana State Bar Association

(2006); Honoree, Forty Under 40, "Indianapolis Business Journal" (1998); Honoree, Best Divorce Lawyers in Indianapolis, "Indianapolis Monthly" **MEM:** Chairman, CLE Committee, Indiana State Bar Association; Past Member, Board of Governors, Indiana State Bar Association; Past Chairman, Family & Juvenile Law Section, Indiana State Bar Association; Past Chairman, Family Law Section, Indianapolis Bar Association; Past Member, Board of Directors, Indianapolis Bar Association; Family Law Section, American Bar Association; Litigation Section, American Bar Association; Past President, Indiana Continuing Legal Education Forum; Patron Life Fellow, Indiana Bar Foundation; Distinguished Senior Fellow, Indianapolis Bar Foundation; Fellow, American Bar Foundation; Phi Beta Kappa; Order of the Coif; Omicron Delta Epsilon; Phi Sigma Alpha; Mortar Board **BA:** 300 N Meridian St Ste 2700, Faegre Baker Daniels LLP, Indianapolis, IN, 46204 **ADD:** 9316 Irishmans Run Ln, Zionsville, IN, 46077

SOSTILIO, ROBERT FRANCIS, T: Office Equipment Marketing Consultant **I:** Advertising & Marketing **CN:** Sostilio and Associates International Inc. **YOP:** 2017-11-30 **PT:** Natale J. Sostilio; Louise Sostilio **MS:** Married **SPN:** Gail Marie McGuinness (4/17/1966) **ED:** Coursework, Miami-Dade Junior College (1979); Coursework, Broward Junior College, Fort Lauderdale (1967-1970); Coursework, University of Maine (1960-1961) **C:** President, Sostilio and Associates International Inc., Ocala, FL (2002-Present); Chief Executive Officer, Sostilio and Associates International Inc., Ocala, FL (2002-Present); Group Service Director of Converging Digital Peripherals, Cap Ventures (1996-2000); Director of Strategic Planning, Ricoh Corporation, West Caldwell, NJ (1994-1996); Director of Copier Marketing, Ricoh Corporation, West Caldwell, NJ (1990-1994); Associate Director of Copier Research, Dataquest, San Jose, CA (1987-1990); Manager of Product Program, Ricoh Corporation, West Caldwell, NJ (1986-1987); National OEM Manager, Panasonic Industrial Company, Secaucus, NJ (1982-1986); Manager, National Copier Service, Monroe Systems for Business, Morris Plains, NJ (1981-1982); National Service Manager, Cybernet International, Warren, NJ (1980-1981); International Service Manager, Saxon Export Corporation, Miami, FL (1977-1980); Product Assurance Engineer, Saxon Copystatics, Miami, FL (1970-1977) **CIV:** Sergeant-at-Arms, UNICO National, San Jose, CA (1990); Block Captain, Meadow Ridge Civic Association, Basking Ridge, NJ (1985-1987) **MIL:** U.S. Navy (1964-1967) **CW:** Editor, "SAI Digest" (2002-Present); Editor-in-Chief, Newsletter, Council 9649, Knights of Columbus (2006-2009); Editor, "Color Copiers" (1989); Editor, "Multifunctionality" (1987) **MH:** Albert Nelson Marquis Lifetime Achievement Award (2017) **H:** Woodworking; Home remodeling; Dog breeding; Travel; Cooking **RE:** Roman Catholic **BA:** 4425 SE 2nd Pl, Sostilio and Associates International Inc., Ocala, FL, 34471

SPANGLER, COLLEEN ANN, T: Marketing Professional **I:** Advertising & Marketing **DOB:** 08/14/1938 **PB:** Toledo **SC:** OH/USA **PT:** Irvin Fredrick Callahan; Eileen Rose Carey-Callahan **SPN:** Joseph Carl Spangler (12/12/1977, Deceased); Richard Leon Blass (1/14/1956, Deceased) **CH:** Edie Davenport; Vicki Schramm; Rick Blass; Tracy; Scott **C:** Marketing Specialist, SunCoast Blood Bank, Arcadia, FL (2000-2002); Past Chair, Democratic Executive Commission State Community Women, DeSoto County, FL (2000); Marketing Director, Arcadia Oaks Assisted Living (1997-2000); Marketing Specialist, SunCoast Blood Bank, Arcadia, FL (1995-1998); Promotion Director, Up River Adventures, Peace River Charters, Arcadia, FL (1995-1998); Ex-

ecutive Director, Arcadia Chamber of Commerce (1993-1995); Executive Director, Arcadia Main Street Program, FL (1991-1993); Volunteer Coordinator, Headquarters, Lucas County Democratic Party, Toledo, OH (1986-1989) **CR:** Board Member, DeSoto County Economic Development Council; Public Relations Officer, Arcadia-DeSoto County Habitat for Humanity **CIV:** Board Member, Team Arcadia; Chair, Board of Economic Development, Arcadia Main Street Advisory Council; Member, DNC; Board Member, Florida Notary; Board Member, Voluntary Organizations Active in Disaster; Advisory Council, DeSoto Friendship Center, The Friendship Centers; Member, DeSoto Home Health Professionals Advisory Committee; Eucharistic Minister, St. Paul's Catholic Church; Parish Council Member, St. Paul's Catholic Church **AW:** Award, Ladies of Moose; Democrat of the Year; Award, AMVETS National Ladies Auxiliary **MEM:** Family Advisory Council, Fawcett Hospital; AMVETS National Ladies Auxiliary **MH:** Albert Nelson Marquis Lifetime Achievement Award (2017); Distinguished Humanitarian (2017) **H:** Reading; Needle crafts; Cooking; Travel **PA:** Democrat **RE:** Roman Catholic **ADD:** 1269 SE Tangelo Dr, Arcadia, FL, 34266

SPECK, SAMUEL WALLACE JR., I: Education/Educational Services **DOB:** 01/31/1937 **PB:** Canton **SC:** OH/USA **PT:** Samuel Wallace Speck Senior; Lois Ione (Schneider) Speck **MS:** Widowed **SPN:** Sharon Jane Anderson (1/20/1962, Deceased 7/2017) **CH:** Samuel Wallace, III; Derek Charles **ED:** PhD, Harvard University (1968); MA, Harvard University (1963); Postgraduate Studies, University of Zimbabwe (1961); BA, Muskingum University (1959) **C:** Director, Department of Natural Resources, Governor's Cabinet, State of Ohio (1999-2007); President, Muskingum University (1988-1999); Acting President, Muskingum University (1987-1988); Executive Vice President, Muskingum University (1987); Assistant to President, Muskingum University (1986-1987); Associate Director, Federal Emergency Management Agency (1983-1986); 20th District, Ohio Senate (1977-1983); Ohio House of Representatives (1971-1976); Professor of Political Science, Muskingum University (1964-1983) **CR:** State Board of Nature Conservatory (2017); Chairman, FIPSE (1991); Board of Directors, Camco Financial Corporation (1990-2007); President, EODA (1990-1992); President, FIPSE (1990-1992) **CIV:** Commissioner, International Joint Commission (2008-Present); Ohio Higher Educational Facility Commission (2007-Present); Board Member, Battelle for Kids (2006-Present); Public Works Commission, State of Ohio (2003-2007); Chairman, Water Management Working Group, Council of Great Lakes Industries (2002-2005); Chairman, Great Lakes Commission (2002-2004); Board of Directors, Ohio Lake Erie Commission (1999-2007); Great Lakes Commission (1999-2007); Ohio Power Siting Board (1999-2007); Board of Directors, Ohio Water Resources Committee (1999-2005); Chairman, Ohio Water Resources Committee (1999-2005); Board of Directors, Ohio Tuition Trust Authority (1991-1993); Board of Directors, International Center for the Preservation Wild Animals, Inc. (1988-1999) **CW:** Contributor, Numerous Articles on African and American Government and Public Policy, Professional Journals **AW:** Distinguished Service Award, National Governors Association (2004); Outstanding Legislator Award, Veterans of Foreign Wars, Disabled American Veterans and The American Legion; Conservation Achievement Award, State of Ohio; Conservation Leadership Award, The Nature Conservancy **MH:** Albert Nelson Marquis Lifetime Achievement Award (2017) **H:** Dancing; Biking; Exercise **ADD:** 240 Greenbriar Court, Worthington, OH, 43085

SPENCE, GERALD LEONARD, T: Lawyer, Writer **I:** Law and Legal Services **CN:** The Spence Law Firm, LLC **DOB:** 01/08/2029 **PB:** Laramie **SC:** WY/USA **PT:** Gerald M. Spence; Esther Sophie (Pfleeger) Spence **MS:** Married **SPN:** LaNelle Hampton Peterson (11/18/1969); Anna Wilson (6/20/1947, Divorced) **CH:** Six Children **ED:** LLD, College of Law, University of Wyoming, with Honors (1990); JD, College of Law, University of Wyoming, Cum Laude (1952); BSL, University of Wyoming (1949) **C:** Senior Partner, The Spence Law Firm, LLC (2004-Present); Senior Partner, Spence Moriarity & Shockey, Jackson, WY (2002-2003); Senior Partner, Spence Moriarity & Schuster, Jackson, WY (1978-2002); Partner, Various Law Firms, Wyoming (1962-1978); Partner, Riverton and Casper, Wyoming (1962-1978); County and Prosecuting Attorney, Fremont County, WY (1954-1962); Sole Practice, Riverton, WY (1952-1954) **CR:** Founder, Trial Lawyer's College; Founder, Lawyers and Advocates for Wyoming; Commentator, Various Television Programs; Legal Consultant, NBCUniversal Media, LLC; Lecturer, Legal Organizations **CW:** Author, "A Small Pile of Feathers," Sastrugi Press (2017); Author, "Police State," St. Martin's Press (2015); Author, "The Lost Frontier," Gibbs Smith (2013); Author, "Bloodthirsty Bitches and Pious Pimps of Power," St. Martin's Press (2006); Author, "Win Your Case," St. Martin's Press (2005); Author, "The Smoking Gun," Scribner (2003); Author, "Seven Simple Steps to Personal Freedom," St. Martin's Press (2001); Author, "Half-Moon and Empty Stars," Scribner (2001); Author, "Gerry Spence's Wyoming," St. Martin's Press (2000); Author, "A Boy's Summer," St. Martin's Press (2000); Author, "Give Me Liberty!," St. Martin's Press (1998); Author, "O. J.: The Last Word," St. Martin's Press (1997); Author, "The Making of a Country Lawyer," St. Martin's Press (1996); Author, "How to Argue and Win Every Time," St. Martin's Press (1995); Author, "From Freedom to Slavery," St. Martin's Press (1993); Author, "With Justice For None," Penguin Group USA (1990); Author, "With Justice For None," Time (1989); Author, "Trial by Fire," HarperCollins Publishers (1986); Author, "Of Murder and Madness," Doubleday (1983); Author, "Gerry Spence: Gunning for Justice," Doubleday (1982); Host, "Larry King Live"; Guest, "Larry King Live"; Host, "The Rivera Show"; Guest, "The Rivera Show"; Host, Numerous National Television Shows; Guest, Numerous National Television Shows **AW:** Lifetime Achievement Award, American Association for Justice (2013); Inductee, Hall of Fame, American Associate of Justice (2009); Lifetime Achievement Award, Consumer Attorneys of California (2008); Honoree, Law and Letters, American Academy of Achievement **MEM:** ABA; Wyoming State Bar; Wyoming Trial Lawyers Association; American Associate of Justice; National Association of Criminal Defense Lawyers **BAR:** Admitted to Practice, Supreme Court of the United States (1982); Admitted to Practice, United States Court of Federal Claims (1952); Admitted to Practice, Wyoming State Bar (1952) **MH:** Albert Nelson Marquis Lifetime Achievement Award (2017) **BA:** PO Box 548, The Spence Law Firm, LLC, Jackson, WY, 83001 **URL:** http://www.spencelawyers.com/attorneys/gerry-l-spence/

SPROUL, HARVEY LEONARD ESQ, T: Attorney **I:** Law and Legal Services **CN:** The Law Offices of Harvey L. Sproul **DOB:** 10/08/1933 **PB:** Williamsburg **SC:** KY/USA **PT:** Harvey Lafayette Sproul; Ruth (Renfro) Sproul **MS:** Married **SPN:** Sylvia Ann Moulton (5/31/1958) **CH:** Daniel Harvey; Susan Rebecca Sproul Brown; Jane Anne Sproul Luttrell; Lyda Bentley Sproul Beane **ED:** JD, University of Tennessee (1957); BSBA, University of Tennessee (1955) **C:** Attorney, The Law Offices of Harvey L.

Sproul, Lenoir City, TN (Present); Partner, Sproul & Hinton (Now The Law Offices of Harvey L. Sproul), Lenoir City, TN (1988-2012); Affiliate, The Law Offices of Harvey L. Sproul (1982-1988); Partner, Sproul & Harvey (Now The Law Offices of Harvey L. Sproul), Lenoir City, TN (1979-1982); Affiliate, The Law Offices of Harvey L. Sproul (1974-1979); Judge, Loudoun County, TN (1966-1974); Mayor, Loudoun County, TN (1966-1974); Partner, Sproul & Bailey (1970-1972); Partner, Sproul & Russell (1969-1970); Partner, Dannel & Sproul, Lenoir City, TN (1962-65); Associate, Dannel & Fowler, Lenoir City, TN (1961-1962) **CR:** County Attorney, Loudoun County, TN (1982-2007); Attorney, Lenoir Board of Education (1980-1990); Staff Judge Advocate, 125th Army Reserve Command, U.S. Army Reserve, Nashville, TN (1986-1989); Commander, 194th Judge Advocate General, U.S. Army Reserve (1961-1980); Chairman, Board of Directors, Mid East CCA (1976-1978); Vice-Chairman, Tennessee Advisory Communications For Local Planning (1971-1974) **CIV:** President, Loudon County Economic Development Agency (2009-Present); Member, Board of Directors, Loudon County Education Foundation (2005-Present); Chairman, Board of Directors, Loudon County Chamber of Commerce (1988-Present); Organization Chairman, Board of Directors, Loudon County Economic Development Agency (1990-2013); Member, Board of Trustees, Roane State Community College (2001-2012); Affiliate, Loudon County United Way (2006-2011); Board Chairman, Roane State Community College (2008-2010); Member, Board of Directors, Good Samaritan Center (2003-2005); Affiliate, Nine Counties One Vision (2000-2005); Organizing President, Knoxville High School Alumni Association (1992-1995); Chairman, Loudon County Chamber of Commerce (1993); Organizing Chair, Loudon County Visitors Bureau (1988-1991); Lenoir City Chamber of Commerce (1980-1982); Chairman, Tellico Planning Council (1966-1974); Affiliate, Lenoir City Rotary (1970); Organizing Chairman, East Tennessee Developmental District (1966-1968); President, Lenoir City Jaycees (1966-1967) **MIL:** Colonel, Judge Advocate General's Corps, U.S. Army Reserve (Retired) **AW:** Named Outstanding Person of the Year, Loudon County (2015); Inductee, Loudon County Leadership Hall of Fame (2011); Robert E. Gonia E Tennessee Regional Leadership Award (2002); Named Man of the Year, Loudon County Chamber of Commerce (1989); Named Tennessee's Outstanding Young Man, Tennessee Jaycees (1967) **MEM:** President, Tennessee County Attorneys Association (1997-1998); Vice President, Tennessee Council School Board Attorneys (1995); Vice President, Tennessee County Judges Association (1972-1974); President, Loudon County Bar Association (1969); Tennessee Council School Board Attorneys; Loudon County Bar Association; ABA; Tennessee Bar Association; Tennessee County Judges Association; Tennessee County Attorneys Association; Omicron Delta Kappa; Kappa Sigma; Phi Delta Phi; Delta Sigma Phi **BAR:** Admitted to Practice, United States Court of Appeals for the Sixth Circuit (1972); Admitted to Practice, Supreme Court of the United States (1960); Admitted to Practice, Tennessee Board of Law Examiners (1957); Admitted to Practice, United States District Court, Eastern District of Tennessee (1957) **MH:** Albert Nelson Marquis Lifetime Achievement Award (2017) **H:** Tennis **PA:** Democrat **RE:** United Methodist **BA:** 205 E Broadway St, The Law Offices of Harvey L. Sproul, Lenoir City, TN, 37771

STACK, FRANK, T: Painter **I:** Education/Educational Services **CN:** University of Missouri **DOB:** 10/31/1937 **PB:** Houston **SC:** TX/USA **PT:** Maurice Z. Stack; Norma Rose (Huntington) Stack **MS:** Mar-

ried **SPN:** Mildred Roberta Powell (6/12/1959) **CH:** Jan Elaine; Robert Huntington **ED:** MA, University of Wyoming (1963); Postgraduate Work, School of the Art Institute of Chicago (1960-1961); BFA, The University of Texas at Austin (1959) **C:** Professor Emeritus, University of Missouri, Columbia (2000-Present); Catherine P. Middlebush Professor of Humanities, University of Missouri, Columbia (1995-2000); Professor of Art, University of Missouri, Columbia (1969-1995); Instructor, University of Missouri, Columbia (1963-1969); Associate Art Editor, Houston Chronicle (1959-1960) **CR:** Member, Executive Board, Art and Archaeology Museum, University of Missouri, Columbia (1981-1984); Visiting Artist, West Virginia Arts Council, Shepherd College, Shepherdstown, West Virginia (1983); Chairman, Art Department, University of Missouri, Columbia (1981-1983); Member, Regional Advisory Board, Missouri Arts Council, Columbia (1979-1980); Member, Personnel Committee, College of Arts and Sciences, University of Missouri, Columbia (1976-1980) **CIV:** Member, Museum Review Board, University of Missouri, Columbia (1989) **MIL:** U.S. Army (1960-1962) **CW:** Editor, "Alley Oop Magazine" (1997-Present); Contributing Writer, "The Comics Journal" (1989-Present); Advisory Board Member, "Journal of Cartoon and Comic Art" (1984-Present); Cartoonist, "Les Nouvelle Aventures De Jesus" (2008); Cartonist, "Les Aventures de Jesus" (2008); Cartoonist, "The New Adventures of Jesus: The Second Coming" (2007); Artist, "Naked Glory: Erotic Art of Frank Stack" (1997); Cartoonist, "The Bard Must Die" (1995); Editor, "Alley Oop, Volumes I-III" (1946-1949, 1990, 1993, 1995); Cartoonist, "The New Adventures of Jesus" (1963-1995); Artist, "Our Cancer Year" (1994); Cartoonist, "Dorman's Doggie" (1990); Artist, Traveling Exhibit, "Watercolors by Frank Stack" (1977-1979) **AW:** Recipient, Award, Missouri Watercolor Society (2003); Recipient, Research Grants, Research Council, University of Missouri Columbia (1969, 1985, 1993, 1998); Recipient, Awards, Kansas Watercolor Society (1992, 1996); Nominee, Best Reprint (1991, 1994, 1996); Recipient, Harvey Award for Best Graphic Story (1995); Recipient, Harvey Award for Best Graphic Novel (1995); Honoree, Artist Of Year, Governor's Arts Awards, Missouri Arts Council, St. Louis (1986) **MEM:** Advisory Board, Columbia Art League (1978-1982); Kansas Watercolor Society (1979-) **MH:** Albert Nelson Marquis Lifetime Achievement Award (2017) **H:** Historical research; Art history; Newspaper comics of the 1930s and 40s; Collecting master prints **ADD:** 409 Thilly Ave, Columbia, MO, 65203

STACK, PAUL FRANCIS, T: Lawyer **I:** Law and Legal Services **CN:** Stack & O'Connor Chartered **DOB:** 07/21/1946 **PB:** Chicago **SC:** IL/USA **PT:** Frank Louis Stack; Dorothy Louise Stack **MS:** Married **SPN:** Nea Waterman (7/8/1972) **CH:** Nea Elizabeth; Sera Waterman **ED:** JD, Georgetown University (1971); BS, The University of Arizona (1968) **C:** Managing Director, Stack & O'Connor Chartered, Riverside, IL (2016-Present); Managing Director, Stack & O'Connor Chartered, Chicago, IL (1976-2016); Assistant United States Attorney for the Northern District of Illinois (1972-1975); Law Clerk, United States District Court Northern District of Illinois (1971-1972) **CIV:** Member, Executive Committee, Chicago Area Transportation Study (1999-2001); President, Village of Riverside, IL (1997-2001); Member, Board of Education, Riverside-Brookfield High School, Riverside, IL(1989-1997); Member, Mayor's Ad Hoc Advisory Committee on Central Library, City of Chicago (1987-1988); Member, Board of Directors, Suburban Library Systems, Burr Ridge, IL (1979-1982); Member, Board of Directors Riverside Public Library, Riverside, IL (1977-1983) **CW:** Author, "The Leviathan" **MEM:**

Governing Member, Chicago Zoological Society, Brookfield, IL (1980-Present); Planned Giving Advisory Committee, Chicago Zoological Society (1996-1999); Board of Directors, Union League Club of Chicago (1986-1989); Illinois State Bar Association **BAR:** Admitted to Practice, United States Court of International Trade (1977); Admitted to Practice, United States Court of Claims (1975); Admitted to Practice, Supreme Court of the United States (1975); Admitted to Practice, United States Tax Court (1974); Admitted to Practice, Illinois Supreme Court (1971) **MH:** Albert Nelson Marquis Lifetime Achievement Award (2017) **BA:** 1 Riverside Rd, Stack & O'Connor Chtd, Riverside, IL, 60546 **ADD:** 238 N Delaplaine Rd, Riverside, IL, 60546

STADTLER, WALTER, T: American Diplomat **I:** Government Administration/Government Relations/Government Services **DOB:** 04/04/1936 **PB:** New York City **SC:** NY/USA **PT:** Walter Henry Stadtler; Paula (Nagl) Stadtler **MS:** Married **SPN:** Maida Maria Macdonald **CH:** Fiona; Walter Jr.; Catriona **ED:** Postgraduate Coursework, Columbia University (1957-1958); AB, Fordham University (1957); Coursework, Paris-Sorbonne University (1955-1956) **C:** Professor, Director, Program on Peacekeeping Policy, George Mason University, Fairfax, VA (1995-2000); United States Member, International Defense Advisory Board for the Baltic Republics (1995-2000); Senior Fellow, Office of the Secretary of Defense (1992-1994); Ambassador, United States Embassy, Cotonou, Benin (1986-1990); Member, Senior Seminar, Washington, D.C. (1985-1986); Charge' d'affaires, Deputy Chief, Mission, United States Embassy, Pretoria, Republic of South Africa (1982-1985); Counselor, United States Embassy, Bonn, Federal Republic of Germany (1980-1982); Member, Royal College of Defense Studies, London, United Kingdom (1979); European Affairs Advisor, United States Mission to the United Nations, New York City, NY (1978); First Secretary, United States Embassy, Stockholm, Sweden (1975-1978); First Secretary, United States Embassy, Addis Ababa, Ethiopia (1972-1975); Second Secretary, Consul, United States Embassy, Pretoria, South Africa (1969-1972); Personnel Officer, U.S. Department of State, Washington D.C. (1967-1969); Economic Officer, Second Secretary, United States Embassy, Bonn, Federal Republic of Germany (1966-1969); Third Secretary, United States Embassy, London, United Kingdom (1963-1964); Employee, U.S. Department of State (1962-1994); Vice Consul, American Consulate, Southampton, England (1962-1963); Vice President, National Defense University, Fort Lesley J. McNair, Washington D.C. **CR:** Senior Advisor, NDU Foundation (2011-Present); President, NDU Foundation (2008-2010); Board Member, Cooperative Housing Foundation (1994-2010); Councillor, Atlantic Council; Member, Council on Standards for International Educational Travel **MIL:** Captain, United States Army (1958-1962) **MEM:** American Foreign Service Association; The Army and Navy Club **H:** Music; Travel **RE:** Roman Catholic **ADD:** 7063 Wyndale St NW, Washington, DC, 20015

STALHEIM-SMITH, ANN, T: Professor Emeritus of Biology **I:** Education/Educational Services **CN:** Kansas State University **DOB:** 10/19/1936 **PB:** Garretson **SC:** SD/USA **YOP:** 2018-05-09 **PT:** Oliver Theodore Stalheim; O'dessa Beldina (Olson) Stalheim **MS:** Married **SPN:** Christopher Carlisle Smith (8/24/1960) **CH:** Heather; Andrea; Jamie **ED:** PhD, Northern Arizona University (1982); MS, University of Colorado (1960); BS, Augustana College, Sioux Falls, SD (1958) **C:** Professor Emeritus, Kansas State University (2003-Present); University Distinguished Teaching Scholar Chair,

Kansas State University (1997-1998); Associate Professor, Kansas State University, Manhattan, KS (1994-2003); Assistant Professor of Biology, Kansas State University, Manhattan, KS (1986-1994); Instructor, Kansas State University, Manhattan, KS (1970-1986); Instructor, Fisk University, Nashville, TN (1967); Instructor, Pacific Lutheran University, Tacoma, WA (1960-1961); Research Assistant, University of Colorado, Boulder (1959-1960); Teaching Fellow, University of Colorado, Boulder (1958-1959); Teaching Assistant, Augustana College (1955-1958) **CR:** Grant Review Panel, National Science Foundation, Washington, DC (1991); Grant Review Panel, National Science Foundation, Washington, DC (1982); Grant Review Panel, National Science Foundation, Washington, DC (1979); Textbook Reviewer, HarperCollins Publishers LLC (1975-1987); Textbook Reviewer, West Publishing (1975-1987); Textbook Reviewer, Saunders (1975-1987); Textbook Reviewer, Other Publishing Companies (1975-1987) **CIV:** Coordinator, First Christian Church of Mount Vernon; Family Promise Program, First Christian Church of Mount Vernon **CW:** Co-Author, Greg K. Fitch, "Understanding Human Anatomy and Physiology" (1993); Contributor, Articles, Professional Journals **AW:** Grantee, Howard Hughes Foundation (1992-Present); Grantee, National Science Foundation (1990-Present); Augustana College Alumnus Achievement Award (1994); Grantee, National Science Foundation (1979-1981) **MEM:** American Association for the Advancement of Science; American Society of Zoologists; Sigma Xi **MH:** Albert Nelson Marquis Lifetime Achievement Award (2017) **PA:** Democrat **RE:** Lutheran **ADD:** 1021 S 9th Street, Mount Vernon, WA, 98274

STAMM, JOSEPH B., **T:** President, Chief Executive Officer **I:** Medicine & Health Care **CN:** NYCHSRO/Med Review, Inc. **ED:** Doctorate, New York University (1972); MPA, New York University (1971) **C:** President, NYCHSRO/Med Review, Inc. (1985-Present); Chief Executive Officer, NYCHSRO/Med Review, Inc. (1985-Present) **CR:** Deputy Executive Director, Hospital Review, NYCHSRO/Med Review, Inc.; Deputy Executive Director, Ambulatory Care, NYCHSRO/Med Review, Inc.; Deputy Executive Director, Data Review, NYCHSRO/Med Review, Inc.; Deputy Executive Director, Medical Care Evaluation, NYCHSRO/Med Review, Inc.; Deputy Executive Director, Home Care Review, NYCHSRO/Med Review, Inc.; Associate Executive Director for Planning and Development, NYCHSRO/Med Review, Inc.; Director of Ambulatory Care Review, NYCHSRO/Med Review, Inc.; Faculty Member, Mailman School of Public Health, Columbia University; Director of Investigation and Enforcement, Department of Health, New York, NY; Director of Program Planning and Development, Department of Health, New York, NY; Assistant Director of Health Evaluation, Department of Health, New York, NY **CW:** Contributor, Articles, Professional Journals; Lecture, National Events; Lecture, International Events **AW:** Honoree, 9/11 Commemoration Heroes For Tolerance, Simon Wiesenthal Center (2017) **MEM:** Fellow, The New York Academy of Medicine **BA:** 199 Water St Fl 27, NYCHSRO/Med Review, Inc., New York, NY, 10038 **URL:** http://web.medreview.us/about-us/executive-staff/joseph-b-stamm-m-p-a-chief-executive-officerpreside

STAPELFELDT, WOLF H., **T:** Professor, Department Chairman **I:** Education/Educational Services **CN:** Saint Louis University **DOB:** 06/07/1958 **PB:** Bad Mergentheim **SC:** Germany **PT:** Bernhard Asmus Heinrich Stapelfeldt; Erika Maria Stapelfeldt Wagner **MS:** Married **SPN:** Nancy Marlene Jones **ED:** MD, School of Medicine, Ulm University, Summa Cum Laude (1983); Resident, Mayo Clinic, Mayo Foundation for Medical Education and Research; Resident in Internal Medicine, Klinikum Rechts der Isar; Resident, Mayo School of Graduate Medical Education **CT:** Medical License, State of Missouri (2013-2018); Medical License, State of Ohio (2008-2018); Medical License, State of Florida (1998-2018); Medical License, State of Minnesota (1990-2017); Certified Single-Engine Pilot **C:** Tenured Professor, Saint Louis University (2014-Present); Department Chairman, Saint Louis University (2014-Present); Chairman, Department of General Anesthesiology, Cleveland Clinic (2008-2013); Vice President of Surgical Operations, Department of General Anesthesiology, Cleveland Clinic (2008-2013); Vice Chairman of Information Systems and Technologies, Cleveland Clinic Anesthesiology Institute; Chairman of Transplantation and Anesthesiology, Mayo Clinic, Mayo Foundation for Medical Education and Research, Jacksonville, FL; Vice Chairman of Education, Department of Anesthesiology, Mayo Clinic, Mayo Foundation for Medical Education and Research, Jacksonville, FL; Co-Founder, Talis Clinical LLC; Chief Medical Officer, Talis Clinical LLC; Assistant Professor of Anesthesiology and Physiology, Mayo Clinic, Mayo Foundation for Medical Education and Research, Rochester, MN; Professor, School of Medicine, Saint Louis University **CR:** Director of Liver Transplant Anesthesiology, VA Pittsburgh Healthcare System, U.S. Department of Veterans Affairs; Assistant Professor of Anesthesiology, UPMC **CW:** Contributor, Journal of Physiology; Contributor, Mayo Clinic Proceedings; Contributor, Liver Transplantation; Contributor, Anesthesiology; Contributor, Anesthesia & Analgesia **AW:** Top Ten in Medicine Innovations Award, Cleveland Clinic Innovations (2014); Merit Review Award, U.S. Department of Veterans Affairs; Young Investigator Award, Foundation for Anesthesia Education and Research and Roche Laboratories; Named Resident of the Year, Mayo Clinic; Edward C. Kendall Award, Mayo Clinic **MEM:** Education Board Member, American Health Council; American Board of Anesthesiology; International Anesthesia Research Society; Healthcare Information and Management Systems Society; American Society of Anesthesiologists **H:** Flying sports; Animal rescue **BA:** 1 N Grand Blvd, Saint Louis University, St. Louis, MO, 63110 **ADD:** 3635 Vista Avenue, Saint Louis University, St. Louis, MO, 63110

STAPLES, DONALD EDWARD, **T:** Professor Emeritus of Film **I:** Education/Educational Services **CN:** University of North Texas **DOB:** 04/15/1934 **PB:** New York **SC:** NY/USA **PT:** Edward Daniel Staples; Ethlyne Babcock Staples **MS:** Married **SPN:** Kristen Petersen (11/26/1982); Diane Staunton (6/2/1956, Divorced 7/1980) **CH:** Douglas Arthur; Daniel Charles **ED:** PhD, Northwestern University (1967); MA in Cinema, University of Southern California (1959); BS in Speech, Northwestern University (1955) **C:** Professor Emeritus, University of North Texas (2004-Present); Professor, University of North Texas, Denton, TX (1979-2004); Professor, New York University, New York, NY (1969-1979); Professor, Vassar College, Poughkeepsie, NY (1972-1974); Associate Professor, The Ohio State University, Columbus, OH (1968-1969); Assistant Professor, The Ohio State University, Columbus, OH (1965-1968); Lecturer, Northwestern University, Evanston, IL (1963-1965); Instructor, Southern Illinois University, Carbondale, IL (1959-1963) **CIV:** Member, Denton Community Theatre (1980-Present); Juror, Film Festivals, National Museum of Communications, Irving, TX (1969-2004); Board of Directors, National Museum of Communications, Irving, TX (1983-1993); Member, Greater Denton Arts Council (1980-1987); Member, Advisory Board, Arts and Humanities Citation Index, Philadelphia, PA (1979-1985) **MIL:** Junior Grade Lieutenant, U.S. Navy (1955-1957) **CW:** Author, Editor, "American Cinema, 3rd Edition" (1991); Co-Author, "Film Encounter" (1973); Contributor, Articles, Professional Journals; Contributor, Film Reviews, Professional Journals **AW:** Danforth Foundation Associate (1968-1985); University Scholar, Northwestern University (1963-1965); University Scholar, University of Southern California (1957-1959) **MEM:** Lifetime Member, Dallas Corinthian Yacht Club (1980-Present); Vice President, International Association of Film and Television Schools (1982-1986); President, University Film & Video Association (1975-1977); President, Society for Cinema and Media Studies (1974-1975); Lifetime Member SAG-AFTRA; Lifetime Member, University Film & Video Association; Trustee Emeritus, University Film and Video Foundation **MH:** Albert Nelson Marquis Lifetime Achievement Award (2017) **H:** Sailing; Golf; Going on cruises; Watching films **RE:** Methodist **ADD:** 2901 Montecito Dr, Denton, TX, 76205

STARNES, SOFIA MOLINA, **T:** Writer, Editor, Literary Translator **I:** Writing and Editing **DOB:** 12/10/1952 **PB:** Manila **SC:** Philippines **MS:** Married **SPN:** William H. Starnes Jr. (3/04/1986) **ED:** Honorary LittD, Union College, Barbourville, KY (2013); MA in English Philology, Universidad Complutense Madrid (1976); BA in English Philology, Universidad Complutense Madrid (1975) **C:** Literary Translator, Williamsburg, VA (2015-Present); Freelance Writer, Williamsburg, VA (1986-Present); Manuscript Editor, Williamsburg, VA (1986-Present); English Instructor, Berlitz Languages, Inc. (1984-1986); Head of Studies, Centro Profesional Sopeña (1982-1984); English Teacher, Centro Profesional Sopeña (1980-1984); English Teacher, Instituto Dolores Rodriguez Sopeña (1973-1983); English Teacher, Colegio Manzanares (1970-1972) **CIV:** Liturgical Minister, St. Bede Catholic Church, Williamsburg, VA; Minister to the Homebound, St. Bede Catholic Church, Williamsburg, VA **CW:** Author, The Consequence of Moonlight, Poems (2018) (Available on Amazon and other booksellers); Fully Into Ashes (2011) (Available on Amazon and other book sellers); A Commerce of Moments (2003, 2013) (Available on Amazon and other booksellers); Corpus Homini: A Poem for Single Flesh (2008) (Available from Wings Press) **AW:** Recipient, Ellen Anderson Award, Poetry Society of Virginia (2018) Recipient, Vinnie Ream Award, Second Place in Letters, First in Poetry (2016); Nominee, Pushcart Prize (2015); Nominee, Pushcart Prize (1998, 2013); Honoree, Named Poet Laureate of Virginia (2012-2014); Nominee, Pushcart Prize (2011); Honoree, Distinguished Scholar, Union College (2009); Recipient, Whitebird Poetry Series Prize, Wings Press, San Antonio, Texas (2008); Recipient, Superior Poetry Achievement Award, Virginia Writers Club (2006); Recipient, Christianity and Literature Poetry Prize, Conference on Christianity and Literature, California (2004); Recipient, Honor Book Award, Library of Virginia, Richmond, VA (2003); Recipient, Editor's Choice, Marlboro Poetry Award, Marlboro Review, VT (2002); Recipient, Editor's Prize, Pavement Saw Press, Columbus, OH (2001); Recipient, Transcontinental Poetry Prize, Pavement Saw Press, Columbus, OH (2001); Recipient, Aldrich Poetry Award, Aldrich Museum, Ridgefield, CT (2001); Recipient, Poetry Fellowship, Virginia Commission for the Arts (2000); Recipient, Rainer Maria Rilke Poetry

Award, International Training Systems, CA (1997) **MEM:** Second Vice President, Virginia Writers Club (1997-1998); National League of American Pen Women; Honorable Member, Order of Kentucky Colonels; The Union College Legacy Society; Academy of American Poets; Poetry Society of Virginia; Chesapeake Bay Writers Club; Ut Prosim Society, Virginia Polytechnic Institute and State University **H:** Travel; Needlecrafts **RE:** Roman Catholic **ADD:** 4951 Burnley Dr, Williamsburg, VA, 23188 **URL:** www.sofiamstarnes.com

STEADMAN, STEPHEN GEOFFREY, T: Physicist **I:** Sciences **CN:** Massachusetts Institute of Technology **DOB:** 06/28/1942 **PB:** Rochester **SC:** NY/USA **PT:** Luville T. Steadman (Deceased); Elizabeth (Genung) Steadman (Deceased) **MS:** Married **SPN:** Brigitte M. Kreuzer (8/1/1975) **CH:** Claudia; Mark; William **ED:** PhD, Rutgers, The State University of New Jersey (1969); MS, Rutgers, The State University of New Jersey (1966); BS, University of Rochester (1964) **C:** Scientific Administrator and Lecturer, Massachusetts Institute of Technology (2011-2016); Associate Director, MIT Laboratory for Nuclear Science, Massachusetts Institute of Technology (2006-2011); Assistant Director, MIT Laboratory for Nuclear Science (2004-2006); Senior Nuclear Physics Advisor, U.S. Department of Energy Office of Science, Washington, DC (2002-2004); Program Manager, U.S. Department of Energy Office of Science (1998-2002) ; Senior Research Scientist, Massachusetts Institute of Technology (1982-1998); Associate Professor, Massachusetts Institute of Technology (1979-1982); Assistant Professor, Massachusetts Institute of Technology (1975-1979); Guest Scientist, Max Planck Institute for Nuclear Physics, Heidelberg, Germany (1974-1975); Senior Research Associate, Massachusetts Institute of Technology (1972-1974); Assistant, Albert Ludwig University of Freiburg, Freiburg im Breisgau, Germany (1971-1972); Visiting Scientist, Friedrich-Alexander University of Erlangen-Nuremberg, Erlangen, Germany (1969-1971) **CR:** E866 Co-Spokesman, Brookhaven National Laboratory, Upton, NY (1992-1998); Program Director, Nuclear Physics, National Science Foundation, Arlington, VA (1994-1997) **CIV:** Member, Watertown Provincial Guard (1998-Present); Member, Arsenal Reuse Committee, Watertown, MA (1992-1997) **CW:** Contributor, Articles, Professional Journals **AW:** Fellow of the American Physical Society **MEM:** American Physical Society; American Association for the Advancement of Science **MH:** Albert Nelson Marquis Lifetime Achievement Award (2017) **H:** Piano; Tropical fish **PA:** Democrat **RE:** Episcopalian **BA:** MIT Room 26-443, 77 Massachusetts Ave, Cambridge, MA, 02139 **ADD:** 91 Common St, Watertown, MA, 02472

STECKLER, LAWRENCE, T: Publishing Executive, Writer, Editor **I:** Writing and Editing **DOB:** 11/03/1933 **PB:** Brooklyn **SC:** NY/USA **PT:** Morris Steckler; Ida (Beekman) Steckler **MS:** Married **SPN:** Lorraine Mary Rubsamen (10/16/1999); Catherine Coccozza (6/6/1959, Divorced 1999) **CH:** Gail Denise; Glenn Eric; Kerri Lynn; Adria Lauren **ED:** Diploma, Graduate Realtor's Institute, Parkstate Institute (2007); Coursework, The City College of New York (1951) **CT:** Licensed Realtor, State of Arizona (2005); Certified E-Pro, National Association of Realtors **C:** President, Poptronix Inc., AZ (2005-2012); Realtor, Long Realty Company, Tucson, AZ (2005-2011); President, Poptronix Inc. (1997-2005); Publisher, Poptronix Handbook (1996-2003); Editor-in-Chief, Poptronix Handbook (1996-2003); Publisher, Radio Craft (1993-1996); Editor-in-Chief, Radio Craft (1993-1996); President, Silicon Chip (1993-1994); Publisher, Electronics Market Center (1991-1999); Editor-in-Chief, Electronics Market Center (1991-1999); Publisher, Editor-in-Chief, Electronics Shopper (1990-1999); Publisher, StoryMasters (1989-2001); Editor-in-Chief, StoryMasters (1989-2001); Publisher, Hobbyists Handbook (1989-1996); Editor-in-Chief, Hobbyists Handbook (1989-1996); Publisher, GIZMO (1988-1999); Editor-in-Chief, GIZMO (1988-1999); President, Science Probe Inc. (1989-1993); Publisher, Science Probe! Magazine (1989-1993); Editor-in-Chief, Science Probe! Magazine (1989-1993); Publisher, Video/ Stereo Digest (1989-1991); Editor-in-Chief, Video/ Stereo Digest (1989-1991); Publisher, Modern Short Stories (1987-1990); Editor-in-Chief, Modern Short Stories (1987-1990); President, Claggk, Inc. (1986-2003); Publisher, Experimenters Handbook (1986-1996); Editor-in-Chief, Experimenters Handbook (1986-1996); Publisher, Radio Electronics Magazine, New York, NY (1985-1992); Editor-in-Chief, Radio Electronics Magazine, New York, NY (1985-1992); Publisher, Computer Digest (1985-1990); Editor-in-Chief, Computer Digest (1985-1990); President, Gernsback Publications, New York, NY (1984-2003); Director, Gernsback Publications, New York, NY (1984-2003); Publisher, Hands-On Electronics (1984-1988); Editor-in-Chief, Hands-On Electronics (1984-1988); Publisher, Radio-Electronics Annual (1982-1984); Editorial Director, Radio-Electronics Annual (1982-1984); Publisher, Special Projects Magazine (1980-1984); Editorial Director, Special Projects Magazine (1980-1984); Vice President, Gernsback Publications, New York, NY (1975-1984); Director, Gernsback Publications, New York, NY (1975-1984); Editorial Director, Merchandising, 2-Way Radio Magazine, New York City, NY (1975-1977); Editor, Radio-Electronics Magazine, New York, NY (1967-1985); Associate Editor, Electro-Technology Magazine (1967); Associate Editor, Electronic Products Magazine, Garden City, NY (1965-1967); Electronics Editor, Popular Mechanics Magazine, New York, NY (1962-1965); Associate Editor, Radio-Electronics Magazine, New York, NY (1957-1962) **CR:** Board of Directors, Publishers Hall of Fame (1987-1989); President, National Electronics Industry Hall of Fame (1985-2001); Member, Board Cooperative Educational Services, Nassau County, NY (1975-1977); Member, Electronics Advisory Board **CIV:** Coordinator, Sylvia Wolens Daytimes (2014-Present); Vice Chairman, Appointed Board Adjusters, Marana, AZ (2011); Member, Advisory Commission, Dove Mountain Preserve (2008-2012); Appointed Advisory Board, Citizens Parks and Recreation Commission, Marana, AZ (2007-2012); Chairman, Citizens Parks and Recreation Commission, Marana, AZ (2007-2010); Appointed Board Adjusters, Marana, AZ (2005-2012); Appointed Secretary to Treasurer, Dove Mount Civic Association, Marana, AZ (2005-2012); President, Board of Directors, Temple Beth Am, Las Vegas, NV (2001-2002); First Vice President, Board of Directors, Temple Beth Am, Las Vegas, NV (1998-2002); Board of Directors, Nassau County Council, Camp Fire Girls (1971-1972); Board Member, Sylvia Wolens Daytimes; Member, HOA Advisory Communications, Dove Mountain **MIL:** Kentucky Colonel, United States Army (1993); With, United States Army (1953-1956) **CW:** Author, "French Humor" (2014); Author, "Flight" (2012); Author, "Hugo Gernsback, A Man Well Ahead of His Time" (2007); Publisher, "Poptronics Shopper" (2000-2003); Editor-in-Chief, "Poptronics Shopper" (2000-2003); Publisher, "PC Tech" (2000-2003); Editor-in-Chief, "PC Tech" (2000-2003); Co-Editor, The Shofar (1998-2002); Author, "Official Auto Radio Service Manual" (1993); Contributor, Articles, Professional Journals; Contributor, Articles, Magazines **AW:** ISCET Governor's Award (1998); FESA President Award (1998); M.L. Finneyberg Excellence Award (1994); Man of the Year Award, National Electronics Sales and Service Dealers Association (1985); Electronics Industry Hall of Fame (1985); Cooperative Award, National Alliance TV and Electronic Services Associations (1975); Man of the Year Award, National Electronics Sales and Service Dealers Association (1975); Cooperative Award, National Alliance TV and Electronic Services Associations (1974); PCA Color Television Pioneer Award (1974) **MEM:** Chairman, International Society of Certified Electronic Technicians (1999-2001); Region 9 Director, International Society of Certified Electronic Technicians (1995-1997); Chairman, International Society of Certified Electronic Technicians (1974-1996); Chairman, International Society of Certified Electronic Technicians (1993-1995); Treasurer, NESDA, The National Electronics Service Dealers Association, New York, NY (1991-1994); Director-at-large, International Society of Certified Electronic Technicians (1991-1993); Representative to NESDA Board, International Society of Certified Electronic Technicians (1991-1993); Recording Secretary, National Electronics Sales and Service Dealers Association, NY (1976-1978); IEEE; RTA; CART Committee; Graduate Realtor Institute; Marana Chamber of Commerce; Los Angeles Press; Society of Professional Journalists; Executive Director, International Performing Magicians; International Underwater Explorers Society; American Management Association; Senior Member, American Society of Business Press Editors; Radio Club of America **MH:** Albert Nelson Marquis Lifetime Achievement Award (2017) **ADD:** 2109 Pier Point Pl, Virginia Beach, VA, 23455

STEELE, HOWARD JOHN, I: Consulting **ED:** Diplomate, The University of Texas at El Paso (1962) **C:** Principal Audio-Visual Consulting Engineer, Howard Steele Consulting (2015-Present); Principal, Technology Plus, INC (2006-2015); Director, Shen Milsom & Wilke (2004)

STEENHUIS, HARM-JAN, T: Professor, International Business and MBA Chair **I:** Education/Educational Services **CN:** Hawaii Pacific University **MS:** Married **CH:** 2 Daughters **ED:** Postdoctoral coursework, Industry Technology Transfer, NC State University (2000-2002); PhD in Industrial Engineering and Management, International Technology Transfer, University of Twente, Netherlands (2000); MSc, Industrial Engineering and Management, University of Twente, Netherlands (1994); Propedeutic Degree, Applied Physics, University of Twente, Netherlands (1990) **C:** AACSB Accreditation Coordinator, Hawaii Pacific University College of Business Administration (2017-Present); Professor of Management, International Business, Hawaii Pacific University (2015-Present); Chair, MBA Program, Hawaii Pacific University (2015-Present); Professor of Management, Eastern Washington University (2010-2015); Researcher I, NIKOS, University of Twente, Netherlands (2007-2013); Chair Department of Management, Eastern Washington University (2006-2010); Associate Professor of Management, Eastern Washington University (2006-2010); Researcher II, NIKOS, University of Twente, Netherlands (2006); Researcher III, NIKOS, University of Twente, Netherlands (2005); Assistant Professor of Management, Eastern Washington University (2002-2006) **CR:** Editor in Chief, Journal of Manufacturing Technology Management (2014-Present); Editor in Chief, International Journal of Information and Operations Management Education (2014-Present) **CIV:** Executive Board Member, International Association of Management Technology (2012-Present) **CW:** Author, "International Operations: How Multiple International Environments Impact Productivity" (2015); Author, "The Global Commercial Aviation Industry" (2015); Author, "Project-based Learning: How to Approach, Report, Present and Learn from Course-long Project"; Author, Over 130 Refereed Articles; Contributor, Book Chapters and Conference Proceedings **AW:** Outstanding Faculty Awards in Scholarship, Eastern Washington University (2013); Professor of the Year Award, Eastern Washington University (2012); Outstanding Faculty Award, Eastern Washington University (2012); Professor of the Year Award, Eastern Washington University (2011); Outstanding Faculty Award in Service, Eastern Washington University (2011); Outstanding Faculty Award in Teaching, Eastern Washington University (2011); Outstanding Faculty Award in Scholarship/Creative Activity, Eastern Washington University (2011); Best Presenter Award, 3rd OSCM Conference, Bujang Valley, Malaysia (2009); Professor of the Year Award, Eastern Washington University (2008); Outstanding Faculty Award in Service, Eastern Washington University (2008); Outstanding Faculty Award in Teaching, Eastern Washington University (2008); Outstanding Faculty Award in Scholarship/Creative Activity, Eastern Washington University (2008); Professor of the Year Award, Eastern Washington University (2007); Outstanding Faculty Award in Service, Eastern Washington University (2007); Outstanding Faculty Award in Teaching, Eastern Washington University (2007); Outstanding Faculty Award in Scholarship/Creative Activity, Eastern Washington University (2007); Service Excellence Award, Eastern Washington University (2006); Publication and Teaching Innovation Faculty Achievement Award, Eastern Washington University (2004) **MEM:** International Association of Management of Technology; Portland International Center for Management of Engineering and Technology **BA:** 900 Fort St Mall Ste 600, Hawai'i Pacific University, Pioneer Plaza, Honolulu, HI, 96813 **ADD:** 1461 Honokahua St, Honolulu, HI, 96825 **URL:** https://www.linkedin.com/in/harm-jan-steenhuis-9b2132133/

STEER, IAN PATRICK, T: Curator, Writer **I:** Writing and Editing **PB:** Montreal **SC:** Canada **PT:** Christofer John Steer **MS:** Life Partner **SPN:** Lorna Catherine Stephenson **ED:** High School Education **C:** Curator, NASA/IPAC Extragalactic Database of Distances, Pasadena, CA (2006-Present); Freelance Writer (1999-Present); Freelance Photojounalist (1989-1994, 1999-Present); Head of Corporate Client Reactivations, MicroWarehouse Canada (1999); Developer, Advanced Computer Systems (1995-1998); Sales Associate, Canadian Telecommunications Group (Now British Telecom) (1986-1988); Sales Associate, Pitney Bowes Dictaphone (1985); Sales Associate, Telephone Clinic, Toronto (1983-1984); Sales Associate, WTT Communications (1974-1982) **CR:** Public Speaker, American Astronomical Society; Public Speaker, Royal Astronomical Society of Canada; Speaker, Idea Club; Speaker, Meetings, Royal Astronomical Society of Canada **CIV:** Former President, Toronto Chapter, Canada's Association of Competitive Telecommunications Suppliers (1985-1988); Author, ACTS Letter of Industry Support, Telco Bell Canada; Co-Author, Developer, ACTS Industry Code of Ethics **CW:** Contributing Author, "Galaxies: Brightest and Nearest," Royal Astronomical Society of Canada Observers Handbook (2012-2015); Contributor, "New Facts from the First Galaxy Distance Estimates," Journal of the Royal Astronomical Society of Canada (2011); Contributor, "Hubble Tuning Fork Shown to Scale Using NED-D," Journal of the Royal Astronomical Society of Canada

(2011); Contributor, Various Articles and Chapters to Peer-Reviewed Journals **AW:** Winner, Ostrander-Ramsay Award for Astronomical Writing, Royal Astronomical Society of Canada Toronto Centre (2012); Winner, Ostrander-Ramsay Award, Royal Astronomical Society of Canada (2010) **MEM:** Attendee, American Astronomical Society Annual Meetings (2011-Present); President, Toronto Chapter, Canada's Association of Competitive Telecommunications Suppliers (1985-1988); Royal Astronomical Society of Canada; American Astronomical Society **ADD:** 705-176 The Esplanade, Toronto, ON, Canada, M5A 4H2 **URL:** https://www.linkedin.com/in/ian-steer-72452446

STELLUTE, JOSEPH, T: Owner **I:** Law and Legal Services **CN:** The Stellute Law Firm **PB:** Hampton **SC:** VA/USA **ED:** JD, University of Memphis Law School (1972); BA, College of William and Mary (1968) **C:** Attorney (1975-Present); President, Hampton Bar Association (1996); Assistant City Attorney, Hampton, VA (1973-1975) **AW:** Best Law Firm, Coastal Magazine (2017) **BAR:** State of Virginia (1973) **BA:** 34 Wine Street, The Stellute Law Firm, Hampton, VA, 23669

STEPHENSON, MAX O. JR., T: Professor, Director **I:** Education/Educational Services **CN:** Virginia Tech Institute for Policy and Governance **ED:** PhD in Government, University of Virginia (1985); MA in Public Administration, University of Virginia (1979); BA in Government and Economics, University of Virginia, With High Distinction (1977) **C:** Affiliate, Faculty, Center for the Study of Rhetoric in Society, Virginia Polytechnic Institute and State University (2015-Present); Affiliate, Faculty, Institute for Creativity, Arts and Technology, Virginia Polytechnic Institute and State University (2012-Present); Affiliate, Faculty, Center for Peace Studies and Violence Prevention, Virginia Polytechnic Institute and State University (2012-Present); Affiliate, Faculty, Master of Public Health Program, Virginia Polytechnic Institute and State University (2012-Present); Professor, Social, Political, Ethical and Cultural Thought (ASPECT) Doctoral Program, College of Liberal Arts and Human Sciences, Virginia Polytechnic Institute and State University (2007-Present); Professor, Social, Political, Ethical and Cultural Thought (ASPECT) Doctoral Program, College of Architecture and Urban Studies, Virginia Polytechnic Institute and State University (2007-Present); Founding Director, School of Public and International Affairs, Virginia Tech Institute for Policy and Governance (2006-Present); Professor of Public and International Affairs, Virginia Polytechnic Institute and State University (1989-Present); Visiting Professor, University of Latvia (1995); Affiliate, Graduate Program and Political Science, West Virginia University (1984-1989) **CR:** Coordinator, School of Public and International Affairs, Virginia Polytechnic Institute and State University (2017-Present); Coordinator, Master's International Program, United States Peace Corps (2014-2017); Coordinator, Graduate Certificate in Nonprofit and Nongovernmental Organization Management, School of Public and International Affairs, Virginia Polytechnic Institute and State University (2005-2015); Co-Director, Institute for Governance and Accountabilities (IGA), School of Public and International Affairs, Virginia Polytechnic Institute and State University (2003-2006); Program Chairman, Urban Affairs and Planning, School of Public and International Affairs, Virginia Polytechnic Institute and State University (2003-2005); Co-Director, Institute for Innovative Governance (IIG), Department of Urban Affairs and Planning, Virginia Polytechnic Institute and State University (2002-2003); Associate Dean for Academic Affairs, College of Architec-

ture and Urban Studies, Virginia Polytechnic Institute and State University (1997-2002); Director, Doctoral Program in Environmental Design and Planning, College of Architecture and Urban Studies, Virginia Polytechnic Institute and State University (1997-2002) **CIV:** Member, International Advisory Committee, Cities of Peace (2014-Present); Member, Board of Trustees, Kimoyo Ghana (2010-Present); Chairman, Public Policy Committee (2009-Present); Member, National Advisory Group for Planning the Future of the Community Arts Network and Art in the Public Interest (2009-2010); Appointed Member, Advisory Board, Center for Peace Studies and Violence and Prevention, Virginia Polytechnic Institute and State University (2008-2010); Chairman, Board Development Committee (2008-2009); Member, Board of Directors, Virginia Network of Nonprofit Organizations (2006-2009); Member, Public Policy Committee (2006-2009); Member, Community Development and Outreach Advisory Board, Institute for Advanced Learning and Research, Danville, VA (2005-2008); Member, Board of Trustees, Visiting Homemakers Service of Monongalia County, West Virginia (1987-1989); Member, Board of Trustees, Monongalia County Easter Seals Society of West Virginia (1987-1989); Member, Governing Board, West Virginia Chapter, American Society for Public Administration, (1984-1989); Member, Governing Board, Charlottesville Housing Foundation (1980-1984) **CW:** Co-Editor, "RE: Reflections and Explorations: Essays on Public Policy and Governance," Institute for Policy and Governance, Virginia Polytechnic Institute and State University (2016); Co-Editor, "Arts and Community Change: Exploring Cultural Development Policies, Practices and Dilemmas," Routledge Publishers, Oxford, England (2015); Reviewer, "Blinded by Humanity: Inside the UN's Humanitarian Operations" (2015); Co-Editor, "Building Walls and Dissolving Borders: The Challenges of Alterity, Community and Securitizing Space," Ashgate Publishers (2013); Co-Editor, "Review of European Studies," The European Union and Peacebuilding (2013); Co-Author, "Peacebuilding through Community-Based NGOs: Paradoxes and Possibilities," Kumarian Press (2012); Reviewer, "Peacebuilding, Power, and Politics in Africa" (2012); Reviewer, "Advocacy Across Borders: NGOs, Anti-Sweatshop Activism, and the Global Garment Industry" (2011); Co-Editor, "Examining Disaster Dynamics in Networked Environments: Lessons from the Field," Journal of Emergency Management (2010); Reviewer, "Snakes in Paradise: NGOS and the Aid Industry in Africa" (2010); Co-Editor, "American Behavioral Scientist, Democracy in an Age of Networked Governance: Charting the Currents of Democratic Change and Democracy at a Crossroads: Acknowledging Deficiencies, Encouraging Engagement" (2009); Reviewer, "Taiwan, Humanitarianism and Global Governance" (2009); Reviewer, "Humanitarian Alert: NGO Information and its Impact on US Foreign Policy" (2006); Reviewer, "A Civil Republic: Beyond Capitalism and Nationalism" (2005); Reviewer, "Tales of the Once and Future City" (1996); Reviewer, "Rescuing ADR from its Advocates" (1990); Reviewer, "Intractable Conflicts and their Transformation" (1989); Reviewer, "The Deficit and the Public Interest: The Search for Responsible Budgeting n the 1980s" (1989); Reviewer, "Urban Politics and Administration: From Service Delivery to Economic Development" (1989); Reviewer, "Privatism and Urban Policy in Britain and the United States" (1989); Contributor, Articles, Professional Journals; Presenter, Various Conferences; Presenter, Various Panels **AW:** Excellence in Scholarship Award, College of Architecture and Urban Studies, Virginia Polytechnic Institute and State University (2017); Outstanding Faculty Award For Excellence,

Alliance for Social, Political, Ethical and Cultural Thought Doctoral Program, Virginia Polytechnic Institute and State University (2013); Summer Scholarship, Institute for Society, Culture and the Environment, Virginia Polytechnic Institute and State University (2011); University Relations Communications Excellence Award, Virginia Polytechnic Institute and State University (2010); Minority Academic Opportunities Program Award of Excellence, College of Architecture and Urban Studies, Virginia Polytechnic Institute and State University (2002); Teaching Excellence Award, College of Architecture and Urban Studies, Virginia Polytechnic Institute and State University (1993); Nominee for Best Dissertation, American Political Science Association, University of Virginia (1985-1986); Nominee, Leonard D. White Award, National Association of Schools of Public Affairs and Administration, University of Virginia (1985-1986) **MEM:** Virginia Tech Chapter, Society of International Scholars (1999-Present); Governing Board, West Virginia State Chapter, The American Society for Public Administration (1984-1989); President, West Virginia State Chapter, The American Society for Public Administration (1986-1987); Vice President, West Virginia State Chapter, The American Society for Public Administration (1985-1986); Secretary-Treasurer, West Virginia State Chapter, The American Society for Public Administration (1984-1985); Doctoral Research Fellow, United States General Accounting Office (1983-1984); Fellow in Politics, E.I. DuPont De Nemours, University of Virginia (1982-1983); Fellow in Politics, Thomas Jefferson Foundation, University of Virginia (1982-1983); Fellow in Politics, William Wiley Morton (1982-1983); ACUNS; Academy of Management; American Education Research Association; ARNOVA; Athens Institute for Education & Research; Imagining America; International Society for Third-Sector Research; IASNR; American Political Science Association; APA; The American Society for Public Administration; International Sociological Association (ISA); The International Studies Association; The Public Administration Theory Network; American Association for Policy Analysis and Management; Sustainable Agriculture Education Association **BA:** 201 West Roanoke Street, The Institute for Policy and Governance, Virginia Tech, Blacksburg, VA, 24061 **ADD:** 505 N Shanks St, Salem, VA, 24153 **URL:** http://www.ipg.vt.edu

STERN, GEOFFREY, T: Lawyer **I:** Law and Legal Services **CN:** Kegler Brown Hill + Ritter **DOB:** 11/29/1942 **PB:** Columbus **SC:** OH/USA **PT:** Justice Leonard J. Stern; Anastasia (Percin) Stern **MS:** Married **SPN:** Barbara Feuer **CH:** Emily Staheli; Elizabeth Leskowyak **ED:** JD, The Ohio State University, Summa Cum Laude (1968); BA, The Ohio State University, Cum Laude (1965); Coursework, Williams College (1960-1963) **C:** Director, Kegler Brown Hill + Ritter, Columbus, OH (2000-Present); Of Counsel, Kegler Brown Hill + Ritter, Columbus, OH (1997-2000); Of Disciplinary Counsel, The Supreme Court of Ohio (1993-1997); Partner, Arter & Hadden, Columbus, OH (1980-1993); Partner, Folkerth, Calhoun, Webster & O'Brien, Columbus, OH (1972-1980); Associate, Alexander, Ebinger, Holschuh & Fisher, Columbus, OH (1968-1972) **CR:** Of National Coordinating Counsel, Asbestos Litigation; Of National Coordinating Counsel, Combustion Engineering Inc.; Of National Coordinating Counsel, Basic, Inc.; Lecturer, Various Firms; Member, Special Commission to Review Ohio Ethics Rules; Member, Special Commission on Legal Education; Member, Symposium on Ethics and Chinese Legal System; Shanghai Keynote Speaker, Faith and Law Symposium; Of Counsel, Various Court Cases, The Supreme Court of Ohio; Special

Investigator, Board on Commissioners Character and Fitness, The Supreme Court of Ohio; Legal Educator, Presentations, Litigation Counsel of America; Legal Educator, CLE Presentations; Legal Educator, Various Presentations; Keynote Speaker, Addresses At Symposia, Columbus Bar Association; Member, Bell Commission of Disciplinary Rules **CIV:** President, City Council, Bexley, OH; Member, Civil Service Commission, Bexley, OH; Vice President, Creative Living, Columbus, OH; Trustee, Creative Living, Columbus, OH; Member, Ohio Citizens Committee for the Arts; Member, National Defense Committee on Asbestos in Buildings Litigation; Public Member, Ohio Optical Dispensers Board **CW:** Senior Editor, "Ohio State Law Journal," Moritz College of Law, The Ohio State University **AW:** Honoree, Top Ethics Lawyer of the Year, Columbus, OH (2017); Honoree, Top Ethics Lawyer of the Year, Columbus, OH (2014-2015); Weir Award for Statewide Distinction in Ethics and Professionalism, Ohio State Bar Association (2015); Honoree, Top Professional Malpractice Lawyer of the Year, Columbus, OH (2013); Honoree, Top Appellate Lawyer of the Year, Columbus, OH (2012); Liberty Bell Award for Community and Professional Service, Volunteer Honors, Ohio State Bar Association; American Jurisprudence Evidence Award, Moritz College of Law, The Ohio State University; Honoree, Top Attorneys, The Verdict; Honoree, Best Lawyers in America; Honoree, Ohio Super Lawyer; Lifetime Fellow, American Bar Foundation **MEM:** Committee on Legal Ethics and Professional Conduct, Ohio State Bar Association; Secretary, Ohio State Bar Association; Vice Chairman, Ohio State Bar Association; Chairman, Ohio State Bar Association; Fellow, Litigation Counsel of America; Fellow, Columbus Bar Foundation; Fellow, The Ohio State Bar Foundation; Professional Ethics Committee, Columbus Bar Association; The Order of the Coif; The Phi Beta Kappa Society; Pi Sigma Alpha **BAR:** Admitted to Practice, Ohio State Bar Association (1968); Admitted to Practice, The Supreme Court of Ohio **MH:** Albert Nelson Marquis Lifetime Achievement Award (2017) **BA:** 65 E State St Ste 1800, Kegler, Brown, Hill & Ritter, Columbus, OH, 43215

STERN, MARCUS A., T: Journalist, Investigator **I:** Media & Entertainment **CN:** Strategic Research **PB:** Washington **SC:** DC/USA **ED:** Diploma, University of California, Los Angeles **C:** News Editor, Washington Bureau, Copley News Service (2000-Present); Washington Bureau, Copley News Service (1983-Present); States News Service, Washington, D.C.; San Pedro News-Pilot, California **AW:** Recipient, Pulitzer Prize for National Reporting (2006); Recipient, News and Documentary Emmy Award (2017); Recipient, George Polk Award for Political Reporting (2006); Recipient, Edgar A. Poe Award, White House Correspondents Association (2006); Recipient, Eugene Katz Award, Center for Immigration Studies (1998) **MH:** Albert Nelson Marquis Lifetime Achievement Award (2017) **ADD:** 6010 NW 96th Way, Parkland, FL, 33076

STETLER, DIANNE L., T: Co-Owner **I:** Other **CN:** R-Bar-D Stables LLC, Tack + Village Store **DOB:** 03/28/1957 **PB:** Fremont **SC:** OH/USA **PT:** Harold Hufford; Judy Hufford **MS:** Married **SPN:** Richard Stetler **CH:** Mindy; Andrea **ED:** College Coursework; High School Diploma **C:** Co-Owner, R-Bar-D Stables, LLC; Co-Owner, Tack + Village Store **CIV:** Volunteer, Camp Fire USA; Fundraiser, Various Local Organizations **AW:** Hall of Fame Inductee, Northern Ohio Draft Pony Association (2014) **MEM:** Clyde Small Business Association; Northern Ohio Draft Pony Association **MH:** Albert Nelson Marquis Lifetime Achievement Award (2017) **H:** Flea markets; Antiquing; Crafting;

Travel; Horses; Bluegrass festivals; Cowboy shoot competitions **RE:** Methodist **BA:** 124 S. Broadway Street, Green Springs, OH, 44836 **ADD:** PO Box 134, R-Bar-D Stables LLC, Green Springs, OH, 44836 **URL:** http://www.diannestetler.com

STEWART, DAVID WAYNE, T: President's Professor of Marketing and Business Law **I:** Education/Educational Services **CN:** Loyola Marymount University **DOB:** 10/23/1951 **PB:** Baton Rouge **SC:** LA/USA **PT:** Wesley A. Stewart, Jr.; Edith L. (Richhart) Moore **MS:** Married **SPN:** Lenora Francois (6/6/1975) **CH:** Sarah Elizabeth; Rachel Dawn **ED:** PhD, Baylor University (1974); MA, Baylor University (1973); BA, Northeast Louisiana University (Now The University of Louisiana Monroe) (1972); Graduate, Leadership Riverside, Greater Riverside Chambers of Commerce; Graduate, Leadership Los Angeles, Los Angeles Area Chamber of Commerce **C:** President's Professor of Marketing and Law, Loyola Marymount University (2012-Present); Professor Emeritus, University of California, Riverside (2012-Present); Professor, Marketing & Law, University of California, Riverside (2012-Present); Professor, Management & Marketing, University of California, Riverside (2007-2012); Dean, The A. Gary Anderson Graduate School of Management, University of California, Riverside (2007-2011); Chairman, Department of Marketing, University of Southern California, Los Angeles, CA (2006-2007); Deputy Dean, Marshall School of Business, University of Southern California, Los Angeles, CA (1999-2001); Chairman, Department of Marketing, University of Southern California, Los Angeles, CA (1994-1999); Robert E. Brooker Professor of Marketing, University of Southern California, Los Angeles, CA (1991-2007); Ernest W. Hahn Professor of Marketing, University of Southern California, Los Angeles, CA (1990-1991); Professor, University of Southern California, Los Angeles, CA (1986-1990); Senior Associate Dean, Vanderbilt University, Nashville, TN (1984-1986); Associate Professor, Vanderbilt University, Nashville, TN (1980-1986); Associate Professor, Jacksonville State University, AL (1978-1980); Research Manager, Needham, Harper & Steers Advertising (Now DDB Worldwide), Chicago, IL (1976-1978); Research Psychologist, Department of Health and Human Services, LA (1974-1976) **CR:** Management Consultant (1978-Present) **CIV:** Member and Chair, United States Census Bureau Advisory Committee; Chair, City of Riverside Economic Development Planning Task Force ("Seizing Our Destiny") **CW:** Editor, Journal of Public Policy & Marketing (2012-2017); Editor-in-Chief, Oxford Online Bibliography in Marketing (2012-2015); Editor, Journal of the Academy of Marketing Science (2006-2009); Editor, Journal of Marketing (1999-2002); Author, "Secondary Research: Information Sources and Methods"; Co-author, "Effective Television Advertising: A Study of 1000 Commercials"; Co-author, "Consumer Behavior and the Practice of Marketing"; Co-author, "Focus Groups: Theory and Practice"; Co-author, "Attention, Attitude, and Affect in Response to Advertising"; Co-author, "Nonverbal Communication in Advertising"; Co-author, "Marketing Champions"; Author, "Handbook of Persuasion and Social Marketing"; Co-author, "Accountable Marketing: Linking Marketing Action to Financial Performance"; Author, "A Primer on Consumer Behavior"; Author, "Financial Dimensions of Marketing"; Co-author: "How to Get Published in the Best Marketing Journals"; Contributor, Articles to Professional Journals; Editorial Boards, Journal of Public Policy & Marketing, Journal of Marketing, Journal of Marketing Research, Journal of Advertising, The Journal of Advertising Research, Journal of

International Advertising, Journal of Interactive Marketing, Journal of Interactive Advertising, Journal of Promotion Management, Current Issues & Research in Advertising, Journal of International Consumer Marketing, Journal of Managerial Issues and Other Journals **AW:** American Marketing Association Award for Lifetime Contributions to Marketing and Public Policy (2015); Chairman's Award, Greater Riverside Chambers of Commerce (2010); Elsevier Distinguished Marketing Scholar Award, Society for Marketing Advances (2007); Cutco/Vector Distinguished Marketing Educator, Academy of Marketing Science (2006); Outstanding Contribution to Advertising Research Award, American Academy of Advertising (1998); Man of Merit Award, Omicron Delta Kappa **MEM:** Founding Chair, Marketing Accountability Standards Board (2004-Present); Vice President for Publications, American Marketing Association (2017-Present); Board of Governors, Academy of Marketing Science (2004-2010); Vice President of Finances, American Marketing Association (1998-1999); President, Academic Council, American Marketing Association (1997-1998); Chair, Section on Statistics in Marketing, American Statistical Association (1997); Past President, Policy Board, Journal of Consumer Research; Fellow, American Psychological Association; Council Representative, American Psychological Association; Charter Fellow, American Psychological Society (Now Association for Psychological Science); Past President, Society for Consumer Psychology; INFORMS; American Association for Public Opinion Research; Decision Sciences Institute; Association for Consumer Research; Academy of Management; Insights Association; The Psychometric Society **MH:** Albert Nelson Marquis Lifetime Achievement Award (2017) **H:** Traveling; Live Theatre **PA:** Republican **RE:** Baptist **ADD:** 13031 Villosa Pl Apt 121, Playa Vista, CA, 90094

STIFF NOVAK, RYNELL, T: Academic Administrator (Retired) **I:** Education/Educational Services **CN:** Texas A&M University **DOB:** 05/24/1929 **PB:** Collin County **SC:** TX/USA **PT:** Roy Odus Stiff; Wilma (Vermillion) Stiff **MS:** Married **SPN:** Joseph Robert Novak (5/11/1954) **CH:** Robert David; Daniel Allan; Timothy Criswell; Rebekah Proctor Knight; Elisabeth Richards **ED:** Postdoctoral Coursework, Texas A&M, College Station, TX (1987); Postdoctoral Coursework, University of North Texas, Denton, TX (1975-1978); PhD, University of North Texas, Denton, TX (1975); MA, University of North Texas, Denton, TX (1973); MRE, Southwestern Baptist Theological Seminary, Fort Worth, TX (1953); BA, University North Texas, Denton, TX (1949) **CT:** Certified Professional in Human Resources (1986); Certification in Library Studies, University of North Texas, Denton, TX (1965) **C:** Staff Associate, Texas A&M University, College Station, TX (1984-1994); Text Editor, Home Mission Board, Southern Baptist Convention, Atlanta, GA (1979-1983); Research Associate, University of North Texas, Denton, TX (1974-1979); Youth Director and Educational Secretary, University Baptist Church, Fort Worth, TX (1953-1954); Draftsman, Convair, Fort Worth, TX (1951-1952); Educational Secretary, College Avenue Baptist, Fort Worth, TX (1950-1951); Teacher, Plainview Independent School District, Texas (1949-1950) **CR:** Instructor in Speech, Blinn College, Brenham, TX (1988-1995) **CIV:** Trustee, Denton Baptist Association (2012-Present); Member, Denton Association of Christian Women (2003-present); Member, Director, Baptist Church Woman's Missionary Union (1996-Present); Member, Texas Baptist Missions Foundation Council (2015-2018); President, Denton Association of Christian Women (2007-2008, 2013-

2014); Member, Executive Board, Baptist General Convention of Texas (1974-1979; 2011-2018); Chairman, Denton County Historical Commission (2011-2012); Chairman, Denton County Historical Park Foundation (2005-2006); Member, Denton County Historical Park Foundation (2002-2008); Member and Officer, Denton County Historical Commission (1999-2016); District Officer, Texas Parent Teacher Association (1966-1971); Vice President, Texas Baptist Student Union (1948-1949); Member, Director, Baptist churches, Missions Council, 30 Missions Trips to Mexico, Guatemala, Costa Rica, Jamaica, Cuba, Brazil, Czech Republic, Portugal, Spain, England, Greece, China, and India **CW:** Author, "The Novak Connection" (1983); Author, Numerous Sets of Constitutions and Bylaws **MEM:** Texas State 1812 Honorary President (1998-Present); Society of the Descendants of Washington's Army at Valley Forge (1993-Present); National Society of United States Daughters of 1812 (1987-Present); Daughters of the American Revolution (1981-Present); DVF Bylaws Committee Chairman (2016-2018); Texas State Chairman (2006-2009); DVF Commander-in-Chief (2004-2006); Treasurer National 1812 (2003-2009); Regent, Benjamin Lyon Chapter DAR (2001-2002); Texas DVF Brigade Regimental Commander (1996-1999); Texas State 1812 President (1996-1998); DVF Officer and Chairman (1995-2013); Regent, la Villita Chapter DAR (1990-1992, 1994-1995); President, Stephen Williams Chapter 1812 (1992-1995); Texas DVF Brigade Commander, (1991-1995); Mensa; United Daughters of the Confederacy; Daughters of American Colonists; Officer, Dunn Family Reunion; Officer, Speaker, Vermillion Family Reunion; President, Altoga Cemetery Association; President, Stiff Chapel Cemetery Association; The Friends of Valley Forge Park; Lifetime Member, University of North Texas Alumni Association, Denton, TX; Lifetime Member, Baylor University Alumni Association, Waco, TX **MH:** Albert Nelson Marquis Lifetime Achievement Award (2017) **H:** Genealogy; Photography; Travel **ADD:** 2500 Hinkle Dr Apt 305, Denton, TX, 76201

STINCHCOMB, BRUCE L., T: Geology Educator, Paleontologist (Retired) **I:** Education/Educational Services **DOB:** 05/31/1938 **PB:** St. Louis **SC:** MO/USA **PT:** Lenord Henry Stinchcomb; Virginia May (Schlueter) Stinchcomb **MS:** Married **SPN:** Karoline Wachowee (3/25/1971) **CH:** Elizabeth **ED:** PhD in Geology, Missouri S&T, Rolla, MO (1978); MA in Geology, Washington University in St. Louis, St. Louis, MO (1966); BS in Geology, Missouri S&T, Rolla, MO (1961) **C:** Retired (2005); Professor of Geology, St. Louis Community College, St. Louis, MO (1975-2005); Associate Professor of Geology, St. Louis Community College, St. Louis, MO (1968-1975); Teacher, Earth Science, McCluer High School, Florissant, MO (1966-1968); Teacher, Chemistry, McCluer High School, Florissant, MO (1966-1968); Teacher, Fox C-6 School District, Arnold, MO (1962-1963); Geologist, Missouri Geological Survey, Rolla, MO (1962-1963) **CR:** Researcher, Extensive Summer Work in Geologic Exploration with a Focus on Uranium Exploration **CIV:** Gateway Antique Phonograph Society **CW:** Author, "Paleozoic Fossil Plants" (2013); Author, "Cenozoic Fossils 1: Paleogene" (2010); Author, "Cenozoic Fossils II The Neogene" (2010); Author, "Mesozoic Fossils II: The Cretaceous Period" (2009); Author, "Paleozoic Fossils" (2008); Author, "More Paleozoic Fossils" (2012); Author, "Mesozoic Fossils: Triassic and Jurassic" (2008); Author, "World's Oldest Fossils" (2007); Co-Author, "Stromatolites: Ancient, Beautiful, and Earth-Altering"; Author, "Meteorites"; Author, "Mineral Treasures of the Ozarks"; Author, "Jewels of the Early Earth: Minerals and Fossils of the

Precambrian" **AW:** Jacques O. L'Ecuyer Award, Eastern Missouri Society for Paleontology **MEM:** The Paleontological Society; Founder, EMSP **MH:** Albert Nelson Marquis Lifetime Achievement Award (2017) **H:** Early audio recording **PA:** Liberal **ADD:** 18 Patricia Ave, Ferguson, MO, 63135 **URL:** http://www.brucestinchcomb.com/about.html

STINNETT, TERRANCE LLOYD, T: Lawyer **I:** Financial Services **CN:** Fremont Bank, Fremont Bancorporation **DOB:** 07/22/1940 **PB:** Oakland **SC:** CA/USA **PT:** Lloyd Monroe Stinett; Gertrude (Hyman) Stinnett **MS:** Married **SPN:** Annette Taub Stinnett **ED:** JD, Santa Clara University, Magna Cum Laude (1969); BS, Stanford University (1962) **C:** Vice President, Fremont Bank, Fremont Bank Corporation (2013-Present); Vice President, General Counsel and Secretary, Fremont Bank, Fremont Bancorporation (2007-Present); Member, Goldberg, Stinnett Meyers & Davis, San Francisco, CA (1977-2006); Associate, Glicksberg, Kushner & Goldberg, San Francisco, CA (1972-1977); Associate, Hyman, Rhodes & Aylward, Fremont, CA (1970-1971); Law Clerk to Judge, California Court Appeals, San Francisco, CA (1969-1970); President, Member Board, Project Second Chance Inc., Adult Literary Program, Contra Costa Library **CR:** School Law Board, Visitors, Santa Clara University (1995-Present); Board of Directors, Fremont Bancorporation, Fremont Bank (1990-Present); Board Fellows, Santa Clara University (2009-2012); Vice-Chairman Board, Fremont Bancorporation, Fremont Bank (1998-2000) **MEM:** Chairman, Bench Car Liaison Committee, United States Bankruptcy Court, Northern District of California, Bar Association of San Francisco (1997); American Bar Association; California State Bar Association **BAR:** Supreme Court of the United States (1975); States District Court for the Eastern, Central and Southern Districts of California (1975); California State Bar (1970); United States District Court for the Northern District of California (1970); United States Court of Appeals for the Ninth Circuit (1970) **PA:** Republican **RE:** Roman Catholic **BA:** 39150 Fremont Blvd Fl 3, Freemont Bank, Freemont, CA, 94538

STITH, RANDY C., T: Chief Executive Officer **I:** Medicine & Health Care **CN:** Aurora Mental Health Center **PB:** Kansas City **SC:** MO/USA **CH:** Daniel D. Stith; Timothy V. Stith; Carolyn A. Timian; Kevin Diederichs; Tamara Diederichs; Keith Diederichs **ED:** PhD in Clinical Psychology, Saint Louis University (1972); Clinical Psychology Intern, Ft. Logan Mental Health Center (1970-1971); MS in Research, St. Louis University (1970); AB in Psychology, St. Louis University (1968); AA in Classical Education, St. Francis Junior College (1966) **CT:** Certified Psychologist, State of Colorado (1974) **C:** Chief Executive Officer, Aurora Mental Health Center (1978-Present); Executive Director, Aurora Mental Health Center (1978-Present); Chief Operating Officer, InNET, Inc. (1996-1998); Chief Executive Officer, Behavioral HealthCare, Inc. (1994-1996); Executive Director, Northwest Denver Community Mental Health Center Services (1985); Private Practice (1974-1978); Deputy Director, Weld County Mental Health (1971-1978); Family and Child Psychologist, Mental Health Center of Boulder County, Inc. (1971-1972); Psychologist, St. Louis State Hospital (1969-1970); Organizational Manager, Southwestern Company (1966-1968) **CR:** Consultant, 10 Countries **CIV:** Member, County Community Corrections Board **AW:** Recipient, Golden Light Bulb Award for Most Innovative Program, Aurora Youth Options, Colorado Behavioral Health Council (2011); Recipient, Community Partnership Award, Mutual of America (2011); Recipient, First Place Program Award, Aurora Center for Life Skills

Program, Eli Lilly (2010); Recipient, Honorable Mention, Golden Light Bulb Competition, Best New Program, Aurora Youth Options, Colorado Behavioral Healthcare Council (2010); Recipient, First Place in the Best Practices Category, Staff Leadership Program, Mountain States Employer's Council (2010); Recipient, Sloan Award for Workplace Flexibility, National Chambers of Commerce (2009-2012); Named, Number One Mental Health Center, State of Colorado Division of Mental Health (2005); Recipient, Lifetime Achievement Award for Excellence, National Council of Community Behavioral Health (2003); Recipient, Making it Happen Award, Intercept Center (2002); Recipient, Distinguished Service Award, Region VIII Mental Health Centers (2001); Recipient, Victim Advocacy Program Award, City of Aurora (2001); Recipient, Number One Mental Health Center, State of Colorado Division of Mental Health (1999); Recipient, Bronze Telly Award, National Educational Video Competition (1996); Named, Program of the Year, Colorado Mental Health Association (1993); Man of the Year, Aurora Chamber of Commerce (1993); Recipient, First Place Award for Mental Health Services, National Council of Community Mental Health Centers and Clinics (1985); Recipient, Program of the Year, Colorado Mental Health Association (1982); Named, Outstanding Young Men of America, Jaycees (1982); Recipient, Letter of Recognition, Arapahoe County Social Services (1981); Recipient, Letter of Appreciation, Colorado Division of Youth Services (1980); Recipient, Humanitarian Award, Greeley Headstart Corporation (1974); Graduate Fellow Award, St. Louis University (1969); Phi Beta Kappa, St. Louis University (1968) **MEM:** American Psychological Association; Colorado Psychological Association; Founding Member, International Initiative for Mental Health Leadership; Phi Beta Kappa; National Register of Health Providers; American College of Forensic Examiners **BA:** 11059 E. Bethany Drive #200, Aurora, CO, 80014

STOLL ARMSTRONG, RICHARD, T: Minister, Educator, Poet **I:** Education/Educational Services **CN:** Princeton Theological Seminary **DOB:** 03/29/1924 **PB:** Baltimore **SC:** MD/USA **PT:** Herbert Eustace Armstrong; Elsie Davis (Stoll) Armstrong **MS:** Married **SPN:** Margaret Childs (1/31/1948) **CH:** Ellen; Richard; Andrew; William; Elsie **ED:** DMin, Christian Theological Seminary-Indianapolis (1978); Doctorate, Temple University (1968); MDiv, Princeton Theological Seminary (1958); BA, Princeton University (1947) **CT:** Ordained to Ministry, Presbyterian Church (1958) **C:** Professor Emeritus, Princeton Theological Seminary, New Jersey (1990-Present); Professor of Ministry and Evangelism, Princeton Theological Seminary, New Jersey (1980-1990); Pastor, Second Presbyterian Church, Indianapolis, IN (1974-1980); Vice President of Development, Princeton Theological Seminary (1971-1974); Director of Development, Princeton Theological Seminary, New Jersey (1968-1971); Pastor, Oak Lane Presbyterian Church, Philadelphia, PA (1958-1968) **CR:** Life Trustee, Fellowship of Christian Athletes, Inc., Kansas City, MO (1979-Present); Member, Church Minister's Advisory Board, Christian Theological Seminary (1975-1980); Board of Directors, National Conference of Christians and Jews, Indianapolis, IN (1975-1980); Indianapolis Inter-Religious Commission on Human Equality (1975-1980) **CIV:** Trustee, American Boychoir School (1980-Present); Member, National Council of Presbyterian Men (1995-1998); Trustee, McDonogh School, Maryland (1980-1990); Board of Directors, Indianapolis Symphony Orchestra (1978-1980); Member, Advisory Committee, Center for Contextual Ministry, Pretoria University, South

Africa **MIL:** Lieutenant, Junior Grade, U.S. Navy (1942-1946) **CW:** Author, "A Sense of Being Called" (2011); Contributing Author, "A Faithful Witness" (2009); Author, "Being Buddies is Forever" (2009); Contributing Author, "The New Dictionary of Pastoral Studies" (2002); Author, "Captured Memories" (2006); Author, "Help! I'm a Pastor" (2005); Author, "Are you Really Free?" (2002); Author, "Faithful Witnesses MiniCourse" (1997); Author, "If I Do Say So Myself" (1997); Author, "Now, That's A Miracle!" (1996); Author, "Enough, Already!" (1993); Author, "The Pastor-Evangelist in the Parish" (1990); Author, "Faithful Witnesses" (1987); Author, "The Pastor-Evangelist in Worship" (1986); Author, "The Pastor as Evangelist" (1984); Contributing Author, "Westminster Dictionary of Christian Theology" (1983); Author, "Service Evangelism" (1979); Author, "The Oak Lane Story" (1971); Contributing Composer, Carmina Princetonia (1968) **AW:** Charles Grandison Finney Award (1997); Robert L. Peters Award, Princeton University (1990); Outstanding Service Award, National Conference Christians and Jews (1980); Branch Rickey Memorial Award (1974); Alumni Service Award, Princeton Theological Seminary (1974); Named, Man of the Week, Princeton Town Topics (1968); Distinguished Service Award Fellowship of Christian Athletes (1965); Named, Man of the Week, Princeton Town Topics (1957) **MEM:** Fellow, Gallup International Institute (1997-2002); Journal Editor, Academy for Evangelism Theological Education (1991-1997); President, Academy for Evangelism Theological Education (1989-1991); Philadelphia Athletics's Historical Society; Presbyterian Writers' Guild; Vice President, Presbytery of New Brunswick **MH:** Albert Nelson Marquis Lifetime Achievement Award (2017) **RE:** Presbyterian **ADD:** 2118 Windrow Dr, Princeton, NJ, 08540

STONE, MARVIN JULES MD, T: Physician, Educator **I:** Medicine & Health Care **CN:** Southwestern Medical Foundation **DOB:** 08/03/1937 **PB:** Columbus **SC:** OH/USA **PT:** Roy J. Stone; Lillian (Bedwinek) Stone **MS:** Married **SPN:** Kathleen Shannon (2010); Jill Feinstein (6/29/1958, Deceased) **CH:** Nancy Lillian; Robert Howard **ED:** MD, The University of Chicago, with Honors (1963); MS in Pathology, The University of Chicago (1962); Coursework, The Ohio State University (1955-1958) **CT:** Diplomate, Hematology, American Board of Internal Medicine; Diplomate, Medical Oncology, American Board of Internal Medicine **C:** Clinical Professor of Humanities, The University of Texas at Dallas (2014-Present); Professor of Internal Medicine, Texas A&M College of Medicine (2012-Present); Chief Emeritus of Hematology and Oncology, Baylor University Medical Center at Dallas, Baylor Scott & White Health (2013); Director of Oncology Medical Education, Quality & Safety, Charles A. Sammons Cancer Center at Dallas, Baylor Scott & White Health (2008-2013); Chairman, Bioethics Committee, The University of Texas Southwestern Medical Center (1979-1981); Co-Director, Hematology-Oncology, Department of Internal Medicine, Baylor University Medical Center at Dallas, Baylor Scott & White Health (1976-2013); Attending Physician, Departments of Internal Medicine and Oncology, Baylor University Medical Center at Dallas, Baylor Scott & White Health (1976-2013); Director of Immunology, Baylor University Medical Center at Dallas, Baylor Scott & White Health (1976-2010); Chief of Oncology, Charles A. Sammons Cancer Center at Dallas, Baylor Scott & White Health (1976-2008); Adjunct Member, Immunology Graduate Program, UT Health Science Center at Dallas (1976-1985); Faculty and Steering Committee, Immunology Graduate Program, UT Health Science Center Dallas

(1975); Associate Professor, Department of Internal Medicine, The University of Texas Southwestern Medical Center (1974-1976); Assistant Professor, Department of Internal Medicine, The University of Texas Southwestern Medical Center (1971-1973); Instructor, Department of Internal Medicine, The University of Texas Southwestern Medical Center (1970-1971); Fellow in Hematology-Oncology, Department of Internal Medicine, The University of Texas Southwestern Medical Center (1969-1970); Resident in Medicine, American College of Physicians Postgraduate Scholar (1968-1969); Clinical Associate, Arthritis and Rheumatism Branch, National Institute Arthritis and Metabolic Diseases, National Institutes of Health (1965-1968); Assistant Resident, Ward Medical Service, Barnes-Jewish Hospital (1964-1965); Intern, Ward Medical Service, Barnes-Jewish Hospital (1963-1964) **CR:** Member, Advisory Board, Baylor Research Institute (2012-2013); Chairman, Medical Advisory Committee, Leukemia Society of America Dallas Chapter (1978-1980); President, Dallas Chapter, American Cancer Society, Inc. (1978); Vice President, Dallas Chapter, American Cancer Society, Inc. (1977-1978); Board of Directors, Dallas Chapter, American Cancer Society, Inc. (1971-1980); Chairman, Patient-Aid Committee, Leukemia Society of America Dallas Chapter (1971-1976) **MIL:** United States Public Health Service, United States Department of Health and Human Services (1965-1968) **CW:** Contributor, Chapters, Various Books; Contributor, Articles to Professional Journals **AW:** Marvin J. Stone Annual Lectureship, Sammons Cancer Center and Department of Internal Medicine, Baylor University Medical Center at Dallas, Baylor Scott & White Health (2009-Present); Recipient, Lifetime Achievement Award, American Osler Society (2015); Recipient, Outstanding Faculty Member, Department of Internal Medicine, Texas A&M College of Medicine (2014); Eponym, Marvin J. Stone Oncology Education Center, Charles A. Sammons Cancer Center at Dallas, Baylor University Medical Center at Dallas (2013); Recipient, Ralph Tompsett Award for Excellence in Medical Education, Baylor University Medical Center at Dallas, Baylor Scott & White Health (2011); Recipient, Outstanding Volunteer Faculty, Alpha Omega Alpha, The University of Texas Southwestern Medical Center (2008); Recipient, Lifetime Achievement Award, International Workshop on Waldenstrom's Macroglobulinemia (2004); Recipient, Distinguished Service Award, The University of Chicago (2002); Recipient, Wings of Eagles Award, Baylor Health Care System Foundation (2001); Eponym, Marvin J. Stone Library, Baylor Institute for Immunology Research, Baylor Scott & White Health (1999); Recipient, Outstanding Full-time Faculty Member, Department of Internal Medicine, Baylor University Medical Center at Dallas (1986, 1977); Named, Established Investigator, American Heart Association (1970-1975) **MEM:** Board of Trustees, Southwestern Medical Foundation (2016-Present); Board of Governors, American Osler Society (2005-2008); President, American Osler Society (2003-2004); Chairman, Career Development Committee, American Society of Clinical Oncology (2002-2005); Education Committee, American Society of Clinical Oncology (2002-2005); Vice President, American Osler Society (2001-2003); Laureate, Texas Chapter, American College of Physicians (2000); Board of Governors, American Osler Society (1997-2000); Governor, North Texas, American College of Physicians (1993-1997); The Phi Beta Kappa Society; Sigma Xi, The Scientific Research Honor Society; Alpha Omega Alpha Honor Medical Society; Mastership, American College of Physicians; Overseas Fellow, Royal Society of

Medicine; American Medical Association; The American Association of Immunologists, Inc.; Distinguished Emeritus Member, American Society of Hematology; American Association for Cancer Research; Southern Society Clinical Investigation; Texas Medical Association; Dallas County Medical Society; Clinical Immunology Society **MH:** Albert Nelson Marquis Lifetime Achievement Award (2017) **H:** Medical history; Antique microscopes **ADD:** 6231 Prestonshire Lane, Dallas, TX, 75225

STONEBRAKER, DONALD, **T:** President **I:** Financial Services **CN:** Stonebraker Investments LLC **MS:** Widower **SPN:** Dorothy (Deceased) **ED:** MS, California Institute of Technology (1945) **C:** Meteorologist, Bermuda, Army Air Corps; Teacher, Air Force Academy, Colorado Springs, CO **MIL:** Pilot, U.S. Air Force **CW:** Author, "An Introduction To Engineering Systems," U.S. Air Force **BA:** 3361 Vista Dr, Boulder, CO, 80304 **ADD:** 95 Santa Barbara, Sedona, AZ, 86336

STORMES, JOHN M., **T:** Systems Analyst **I:** Research **CN:** Media Research Associate **DOB:** 10/07/1927 **PB:** Manila **SC:** Philippines **PT:** Max Clifford Stormes; Janet (Heldring) Stormes **MS:** Married **SPN:** Takako Sanae (July 29, 1955) **CH:** Janet Kazuko; Alan Osamu **ED:** MA, University of Southern California (1967); BA, University of Southern California (1957); BS, San Diego State University (1950) **CT:** Certified Secondary Education Teacher; Certified Community College Teacher; Certified Senior Professional in Human Resources **C:** Training and Communications Consultant, Media Research Associates Inc. (1973-Present); Adjunct Associate Professor, Alliant University (2001-2002); Instructional Design Supervisor, Southern California Gas Company, Sempra Energy (1985-2001); Project Director, General Behavioral Systems, Inc. (1969-1973); Publications Coordinator, Rockwell Automation, Inc. (1963-1968); Publications Director, Arthur D. Little (1962-1963); Proposals Supervisor, Rockwell Automation, Inc. (1961-1962); Editing Supervisor, Lockheed Propulsion Company (1957-1961) **CR:** Communications Consultant, Opinion Research of California (1974-2010); Lecturer, California State University, Northridge (1991-2003); Training Consultant National Educational Network (1966-1981) **CIV:** Curriculum Advisory Board, Communications Department. California State University Fullerton (1964-1978) **MIL:** Sergeant, U.S. Army (1953-1955) **CW:** Contributing Author, "ASTD's In Action Series of Casebooks" (1996-1999); Co-Author, "TV Communications Systems For Business and Industry" (1970) **MEM:** Chapter President, International Society for Performance Improvement (1990); Senior, Society for Technical Communication; Vice President, Los Angeles Chapter, International Society for Performance Improvement (1989); Vice President, Orange County Chapter, Society for Technical Communication (1962-1963) **H:** Photography; Sailing **PA:** Democrat **RE:** Episcopalian **ADD:** 3400 Paul Sweet Road Apt. A108, Santa Cruz, CA, 65065

STOTT, DON, **T:** Precious Metals Products Executive **I:** Mining & Metals **CN:** Colorado Gold **DOB:** 02/17/1934 **PB:** Washington **SC:** DC/USA **PT:** Marion McClelland Stott; Mabelle Louise (Maidem) Vanice **MS:** Married **SPN:** Bonnie Jean Peltoman (December 4, 2002); Dorothy Greene (Divorced) (June 21, 1962) **CH:** David Michael; Melissa Ann **C:** President, Colorado Gold, Montrose (1977-Present); Hotel Owner, Wyman, Alma House and Grand Imperial Hotels, Silverton, CO (1971-1994); Owner, Bijou Iced Creme Parlours, Philadelphia, PA (1967-1971); Owner, DS Theatres, DC and Philadelphia (1956-1967) **CW:** Author, "Where the Mountains

Meet the Sky, Three Feet to Silverton, Trails Among the Columbines, Consequences"; Contributor, Numerous Newspaper Columns **H:** Trains; Antiques; Architecture **RE:** Republican **ADD:** 222 S. 5th Street, Montrose, CO, 81401

STOUT, LANDON MD, **T:** Pathologist, Educator **I:** Education/Educational Services **CN:** University of Texas Medical Branch **DOB:** 02/20/1933 **PB:** Kansas City **SC:** MO/USA **PT:** Landon Clarke; Mildred Ann (Buckner) S. **MS:** Married **SPN:** Elaine Marie Farrell; Martha Ann McKone, May 1, 1954 (Divorced December 1975) **CH:** Lynn; Clinton; Karen; Sally; Edward Halsted **ED:** MD, University of Maryland (1957); BS, University of Maryland (1954) **CT:** Diplomate, American Board of Pathology **C:** Professor, University Texas Medical Branch, Galveston (1974-Present); Associate Professor of Pathology, University Texas Medical Branch, Galveston (1972-1974); Interim Chairman of Pathology, University of Oklahoma, Oklahoma City (1970-1972); Assistant Professor of Medicine, University of Oklahoma, Oklahoma City (1963-1972); Associate Professor, University of Oklahoma, Oklahoma City (1971-1972); Assistant Professor of Pathology, University of Oklahoma, Oklahoma City (1968-1971); Special Fellow in Pathology, University of Oklahoma, Oklahoma City (1967-1968); Resident in Pathology, University of Oklahoma, Oklahoma City (1966-1967); Resident in Internal Medicine, University of Oklahoma, Oklahoma City (1958-1961); Rotating Intern, University of Oklahoma, Oklahoma City (1957-1958) **CR:** Consultant, Oklahoma Medical Research Foundation, Oklahoma City (1970-1972); Pathologist **CW:** Contributor, Articles on Mitral Valve Disease and Diabetic Renal Disease, Professional Journals **AW:** Award, Texas Society of Pathologists; Grantee, National Institutes of Health; Grantee, John A. Hartford Foundation **MEM:** Fellow, American Heart Association; American College of Physicians; American Diabetes Association; United States and Canadian Academy of Pathology **BA:** 9th and Mechanic Street, U of T Med BR at Galveston, Galveston, TX, 77555 **ADD:** 3506 Princeton Street, Galveston, TX, 77554

STRASSER, JOEL A., **T:** Public Relations Executive, Engineer, Producer **I:** Corporate Communications & Public Relations **CN:** Strasser & Associates **DOB:** 08/08/1938 **PB:** New York **SC:** NY/USA **PT:** Albert Gerson Strasser; Nellie (Singer) Strasser **MS:** Married **SPN:** Isabel Strasser **CH:** Alison Debra; Andria Jocelyn; Jon Fredric **ED:** BS in English, City College of New York (1961) **CT:** Accredited, Public Relations Society of America, Inc. **C:** President, Strasser & Associates (2007-Present); Principal, Strasser & Associates (2007-Present); Vice President, Zlokower Company Public Relations (2000-2006); Executive Producer, Worldwide Corporate Network, Inc. (1998-2000); Director, Worldwide Corporate Network, Inc. (1998-2000); Vice President of Marketing and Corporate Communications, Digital Broadcast Corporation (1996-1998); Director of Corporate Communications, People's Choice Television Corporation (1993-1996); Principal, Joel A. Strasser & Associates (1991-1993); Senior Vice President, Shandwick / Dorf & Stanton Technology Communications (1985-1991); Managing Director, Shandwick / Dorf & Stanton Technology Communications (1985-1991); Executive Vice President, Thomas L. Richmond, Inc. (1983-1985); Vice President, Hill & Knowlton, Inc. (1968-1983); Syndicated Science Columnist, United Features Syndicate, North American Newspaper Alliance (1974-1980); Chief, New York Bureau, Aerospace Technology Magazine (1967-1968); Account Executive, Lescarboura Advertising, Inc. (1965-1967); Editor of Space Electronics, Electronics Magazine,

McGraw-Hill Education (1963-1965); News Editor, Electronic Design Magazine (1962) **CR:** Adjunct Instructor, Marymount College; Adjunct Assistant Professor, New York University; Adjunct Assistant Professor, L'École Française des Attaches de Presse; Organizer, Business Media Seminars; Session Organizer, Professional Conferences **CIV:** Member, Jewish Temple (1980-1983); Vice President, Citizens of Ramapo (1969-1970) **CW:** Co-author, "New Technology and Public Relations"; Contributor, Numerous Articles, Professional Journals **AW:** Recipient, Hermes Gold Creative Award (2014); Recipient, Communitas Award for Excellence in Community Service (2014); Recipient, Gold MarCom Awards (2013); Recipient, Technology Marketing Award, AdWeek Magazine (2003); Recipient, APEX Award of Excellence (2003); Honoree, Fellow, Public Relations Society of America, Inc. (1991); Recipient, John W. Hill Award, New York Chapter, Public Relations Society of America, Inc. (1989); Recipient, Silver Anvil Award, Public Relations Society of America, Inc. (1980) **MEM:** President, Hearing Loss Association of New Jersey New Jersey State Association (2015-Present); Trustee, Hearing Loss Association of New Jersey New Jersey State Association (2012-2014); The National Association of Science Writers, Inc. IEEE; Associate Fellow, AIAA; Public Relations Society of America, Inc.; College of Fellows, Public Relations Society of America, Inc.; Founding Chairman, National Technology Section, Public Relations Society of America, Inc.; Past President, New York Chapter, Public Relations Society of America, Inc.; Hearing Loss Association of America; Public Information Officer, Hearing Loss Association of New Jersey New Jersey State Association **MH:** Albert Nelson Marquis Lifetime Achievement Award (2017) **ADD:** 9 Melville Ln, Brick, NJ, 08724-1923 **URL:** 9 Melville Lane

STRAUB, PETER THORNTON, **I:** Law and Legal Services **DOB:** 03/27/1939 **PB:** St. Louis **SC:** MO/USA **PT:** Ralph H. Straub; Mary Louise (Thornton) Straub **MS:** Married **SPN:** Wendy B. Cubbage, (12/29/1964) **CH:** Karl Thornton; Philip Hamilton; Ellen Elizabeth **ED:** LLB, Washington and Lee University (1964); AB, Washington and Lee University (1961) **CT:** United States Bankruptcy Court (1991.); United States Tax Court (1971); United States Court of Appeals for the District of Columbia Circuit (1971); United States Court of Appeals for the Armed Forces (1970); Supreme Court of the United States (1970); United States Court of Appeals for the Eighth Circuit (1969); United States District Court Eastern District of Missouri (1967); Virginia (1964); Missouri (1964) **C:** Retired (2011); Of Counsel, Life & Estate Planning Law Center PLLC (2010-2011); Private Practice, Law Offices of Peter T. Straub, Alexandria, VA (1976-2010); General Counsel, Selective Service System, Washington D.C. (1974-1976); Minority Counsel, Committee on Judiciary, U.S. House of Representatives, Washington D.C. (1973-1974); Director, Office of Criminal Justice, Special Assistant to Attorney General, Department of Justice (1973); Attorney-adviser, Office of the Deputy Attorney General, Department of Justice (1972-1973); Trial Attorney, Internal Security Division, Department of Justice, Washington D.C. (1971-1972); Assistant U.S. Attorney, St. Louis, MO (1969-1971); Assistant Public Defender, St. Louis County, St. Louis, MO (1968-1969); Associate, Evans & Dixon, St. Louis, MO (1966-1968) **CIV:** Commander, Charter Judge Advocate General, American Legion Greenspring Post 123 (2012-Present); Member, Board of Directors, Greenspring Village Residents Advisory Council (2011-Present); Charter Member, Board of Directors, Charter Judge Advocate General, American Legion Greenspring Post 123 (2010-Present); Board of Directors, Friends of the Washington and Old Dominion Trail

(2002-Present); Advisory Board, Salvation Army, Alexandria, VA (1991-Present); Risk Management Committee, National Capital Area Council, Boy Scouts of America (2006-2011); Member, Economic Opportunity Commission, City of Alexandria, Virginia (2006-2010); Advisory Board, Hospice of Northern Virginia (2000-2009); Board of Directors, Sigma Nu Educational Foundation, Inc. (2000-2008); District Chairman, Boy Scouts of America (1998-2001); Chairman, Salvation Army, Alexandria, VA (1997-1999); Board Member, Salvation Army, Alexandria, VA (1997-1999); Chairman, Alexandria Community Shelter Advisory Board, Virginia (1995-1997); Virginia Escheat Attorney, City of Alexandria (1994-2002); Vice President, Salvation Army, Alexandria, VA (1994-1996); Secretary, Parc East Condominium (1992-2006); Advisory Board, American Heart Association, Alexandria, VA (1991-1992); Board of Directors, Parc East Condominium (1990-2009); Charter Member, Board of Directors, Alexandria Country Day School, Virginia (1983-1990); President, Governor Board, Alexandria Community Mental Health Center, Virginia (1982-1995); Member, Northern Virginia Estate Planning Council (1981-2011); President's Council, Trinity College, Washington D.C. (1980-1987) **MIL:** Captain, U.S. Army Reserve (1966-1972); U.S. Army (1964-1966) **AW:** Community Service Award, American Indian Alliance (1995); Collins Award, Alexandria Council for Persons with Disabilities (1993); Silver Beaver Award, Boy Scouts of America, Washington D.C. (1987); Certificate of Appreciation, Law Enforcement Assistance Administration, Department of Justice (1974); Certificate of Award, Department of Justice (1970) **MEM:** Treasurer, Optimists (1999-2001); Lieutenant Governor, National Capitol Virginia District, Optimists (1987-1989); Board of Directors, President, Alexandria Chapter, Optimists (1984); Federal Bar Association; ABA; National Academy of Elder Law Attorneys; Virginia Trial Lawyers Association; Alexandria Bar Association; Missouri Bar Association; The Bar Association of Metropolitan St. Louis; Virginia State Bar; National Eagle Scout Association; Sigma Nu **H:** Scouting; Reading; Bicycling **PA:** Republican **RE:** Congregationalist

STREETER, RICHARD HENRY, **T:** Attorney **I:** Law and Legal Services **CN:** Law Office of Richard H. Streeter **DOB:** 08/11/1943 **PB:** Paris **SC:** France **MS:** Married **SPN:** Lucille Clayton Anderson (8/28/1971) **CH:** Thomas Clayton Anderson Streeter **ED:** JD, The University of Texas at Austin (1970); MA,The University of Texas at Austin (1969); BA, The University of Texas at Austin (1965) **CT:** Admitted to Practice, United States Court of Appeals for the Eighth Circuit (1995); Admitted to Practice, United States Court of Federal Claims (1995); Admitted to Practice, Supreme Court of Texas (1995); Admitted to Practice, United States District Court District of Columbia (1995); Admitted to Practice, United States Court of International Trade (1995); Admitted to Practice, United States Court of Appeals for the Sixth Circuit (1988); Admitted to Practice, United States Court of Appeals for the Fifth Circuit (1986); Admitted to Practice, United States Court of Appeals for the Ninth Circuit (1986); Admitted to Practice, United States Court of Appeals for the 11th Circuits (1986); Admitted to Practice, United States Court of Appeals for the District of Columbia (1986); Admitted to Practice, United States Court of Claims (1986); Admitted to Practice, United States Court of Appeals for the Fourth Circuit (1976); Admitted to Practice, United States Court of Appeals for the Second Circuit (1975); Admitted to Practice, United States Court of Appeals for the Fifth Circuit (1974); Admitted to Practice, Supreme Court of the United States (1974); Admitted to Practice, United States District

Court Northern District of Texas (1973); Admitted to Practice, United States District Court Northern District of Ohio (1972); Admitted to Practice, United States District Court Western District of Texas (1972) **C:** Partner, Law Office of Richard H. Streeter (2011-Present); Partner, Barnes & Thornburg LLP, Washington, DC (1987-2010); Partner, Wheeler & Wheeler, Washington, DC (1978-1987); Associate, Wheeler & Wheeler, Washington, DC (1975-1978); Attorney, Office of General Counsel, Interstate Commerce Commission, Washington, DC (1971-1975); Managing Partner, Barnes & Thornburg LLP, Washington, DC **CR:** Managing Partner, DC Office, Barnes & Thornburg LLP (2001-2008) **CIV:** Vice Chairman, Washington, DC Rental Accommodations Commission (1979-1980); Member, Washington, DC Rental Accommodations Commission (1978-1980) **AW:** Named Super Lawyer in Transportation & Maritime Attorneys, Super Lawyers, Washington, DC (2012-2015) **MEM:** Vice President, Metropolitan Club, Washington, DC (2015-2016); Secretary, Board of Governors, Metropolitan Club, Washington, DC (2011-2016); House Committee, Metropolitan Club, Washington, DC (1986-1992); Chevy Chase Hillborough Club; Hillsboro Club; Director, Preservation Fund, Metropolitan Club; Georgetown Assembly **BAR:** State Bar of Texas (1970) **MH:** Albert Nelson Marquis Lifetime Achievement Award (2017) **RE:** Episcopalian **ADD:** 5255 Partridge Ln NW, Washington, DC, 20016 **URL:** http://www. richardstreeter.net

STROBER, MYRA H. PHD, T: Professor Emeritus **I:** Education/Educational Services **CN:** Stanford University **DOB:** 03/28/1941 **PB:** New York City **SC:** NY/USA **PT:** Julius William Hoffenberg; Regina Scharer **MS:** Married **SPN:** Jay M. Jackman (10/21/1990); Samuel Strober (3/23/1963, Divorced 12/1983) **CH:** Jason M.; Elizabeth A. **ED:** Doctorate, MIT (1969); PhD in Economics, Massachusetts Institute of Technology (1969); MA in Economics, Tufts University (1965); BS in Industrial Relations, Cornell University (1962) **C:** Emeritus Professor, Stanford University, CA (2007-Present); Program Officer in Higher Education, Atlantic Philanthropic Services, Ithaca, NY (1998-2000); Interim Dean, Stanford University, CA (1994); Associate Dean, Academy Affairs, Stanford University, CA (1993-1995); Professor of Education, Stanford University, CA (1990-2006); Associate Professor, School of Education, Stanford University, CA (1979-1990); Assistant Professor, Graduate School of Business, Stanford University, CA (1972-1986); Lecturer, University of California, Berkeley (1970-1972); Lecturer, Assistant Professor, Department of Economics, University of Maryland, College Park, MD (1967-1970) **CR:** Member, Policy and Planning Board (1992-1993); Chair, Provost's Committee, Recruitment and Retention of Women Faculty (1992-1993); Chair, Faculty Senate Committee on Committees (1992-1993); Dean, Alumni College (1992); Chair, Program Education Administration and Policy Analysis (1991-1993); Faculty Advisor, Women's Leadership Program, Rutgers, The State University of New Jersey (1991-1993); Member, College Board Committee to Develop Advanced Placement Examination of Economics (1987-1988); Director, Education Policy Institute (1984-1986); Founding Director, Center for Research on Women, Stanford University (1974-1976, 1979-1984); Member, Advisory Board, State of California, Office of Economic Policy Planning and Research (1978-1980); Organizer, Stanford Business Conference of Women in Management (1974) **CIV:** Member, Research Advisory Task Force, YWCA (1989-Present); Board of Trustees, Mills College (2004-2013); President, Board of Directors, Kaider Foundation, Mountain View,

CA (1990-1996); Chair, Executive Board, Stanford Hillel (1990-1992); Board of Directors, Resource Center for Women, Palo Alto, CA (1983-1984) **CW:** Member, Editorial Advisory Board, U.S.-Japan Women's Journal (1991-Present); Associate Editor, Journal of Economic Education (1991-Present); Member, Board of Editors, Sage Annual Review of Women and Work (1984-Present); Co-author, "Interdisciplinary Conversations: Challenging Habits of Thought" (2011); Co-author, "Interdisciplinary Conversations: Challenging Habits of Thought" (2010); Co-editor, "Faculty Salaries and Maximization of Prestige" (2007); Co-editor, "Habits of the Mind: Challenges for Multidisciplinarity" (2006); Co-editor, "Feminist Economics: Implications for Education" (2005); Co-editor, "Can Harvard Ever Play a Positive Role for Women in Higher Education" (2005); Co-author, "Can Harvard Ever Play a Positive Role for Women in Higher Education?" (2005); Co-author, "Children As a Public Good" (2004); Co-editor, "Children as a Public Good" (2004); Co-author, "Fear of Feedback" (2003); Co-editor, "Fear of Feedback" (2003); Co-editor, "Application of Mainstream Economics Constructs to Education: A Feminist Analysis" (2003); Co-editor, "The Road Winds Uphill All The Way: Gender, Work and Family in the U.S. and Japan" (1999); Co-editor, "Rethinking Economics Through a Feminist Lens" (1995); Co-editor, "Challenges to Human Capitol Theory: Implications for HR Managers" (1995); Co-author, "Challenge to Human Capital Theory: Implications for the HR Manager, American Economic Review" (1995); Co-author, "Rethinking Economics Through a Feminist Lens, Feminist Economics" (1995); Co-editor, "Industrial Relations" (1990); Co-author, Industrial Relations (1972, 1990); Co-editor, "Feminism, Children and the New Families" (1988); Co-author, "The New Palgrave: A Dictionary of Economic Theory and Doctrine" (1987); Co-author, "Computer Chips and Paper Clips: Technology and Women's Employment, Volume II" (1987); Co-author, "Gender in the Workplace" (1987); Co-editor, "Women and Poverty" (1986); Co-author, "Sex Segregation in the Workplace: Trends, Explanations, Remedies" (1984); Co-author, "Women in the Workplace" (1982); Associate Editor, Signs: Journal of Women in Culture and Society (1980-1985); Co-author, "Women in the Labor Market" (1979); Co-author, "Changing Roles of Men and Women" (1976); Member, Board of Editors, Signs: Journal of Women in Culture and Society (1975-1989); Co-editor, "Bringing Women Into Management" (1975); Co-author, "Sex, Discrimination and the Division of Labor" (1975); Contributor, Chapter to Book, Articles to Professional Journals **AW:** Schiff House Resident Fellow (1985-1987); Fellow, Stanford University (1975-1977) **MEM:** Board of Directors, Center of Gender Equality (2000-Present); Associate Editor, Feminist Economics, International Association for Feminist Economics (1994-Present); President, International Association for Feminist Economics (1997); Board of Directors, Legal Defense and Education Fund, National Organization of Women (1993-1998); Member, Committee on the Status of Women in the Economics Profession, American Economic Association (1972-1975); National Organization of Women; International Association for Feminist Economics; Industrial Relations Research Association; American Educational Research Association; American Economic Association **MH:** Albert Nelson Marquis Lifetime Achievement Award (2017) **ADD:** 892 Lathrop Drive, Stanford, CA, 94305

STRONG, JODI L., T: Diabetologist **I:** Medicine & Health Care **CN:** Ascension Health **MS:** Married **SPN:** Michael **CH:** Brett; Ellie; Garrett **ED:** DNP, University of Wisconsin-Eau Claire, Magna Cum Laude (2015); MSN, University of Wisconsin-Eau Claire, Summa Cum Laude (2010); BSN, University of Wisconsin-Eau Claire, Summa Cum Laude (2006); BSN in Genetics, University of Wisconsin-Madison **CT:** American Nurses Credentialing Center (2012-Present); Advanced Practice Nurse Prescriber (2010-Present); Drug Enforcement Agency (2010-Present); Certification, Wisconsin State Board of Nursing (2006-Present); National Certification-Board for Diabetes Educators (2004-Present); Board Certified-Advanced Diabetes Manager; Certified Diabetes Educator; Certified Product Trainer, Medtronic, Tandem, Dexcom, Animas, OmniPod, iPro, iPro2, AccuChek; Continuous Glucose Monitor Clinical Certification **C:** Adjunct Professor of Diabetes & Diabetes Pharmacology, Medical College of Wisconsin (2016-Present); Adjunct Professor of Diabetes, Department of Nursing, University of Wisconsin-Eau Claire (2011-Present); Diabetologist, Ascension Health (2010-Present) **CR:** Nominated Speaker for the 64th Postgraduate Course, National Speakers Bureau, American Diabetes Association (2017); National and International Speaker **CIV:** Diabetes Lions Camp, Rosholt, WI (2002-Present); Fundraising Advisor, Juvenile Diabetes Research Foundation Walk, Wisconsin; Medtronic Diabetes Insulin Pump Advocate and Educator; Senior Center Volunteer, Aging and Disability Resource Center of Portage County; Diabetes Support Group Facilitator, Ministry Medical Group **CW:** Contributor, Articles to Professional Journals **AW:** Grant Funding Application Recipient, Medication Assistance Program, Ministry Medical Group (2011-Present); Research Poster Accepted to European Association for the Study of Diabetes (2017); Highest Honors in Nursing Education Award, University of Wisconsin-Eau Claire, Eau Claire Student Nurses Association, Eau Claire, WI (2004-2006); Junior Professional Bowlers Association Scholarship, University of Wisconsin-Madison, Madison, WI (1998-2002); A1c Champion Nominee; Juvenile Diabetes Research Foundation Board Golden sneaker Fundraising Champion, Central Wisconsin Juvenile Diabetes Research Foundation Board One Walk **MEM:** Americans with Disabilities Act Leader and Presenter, Wisconsin State (2015-Present); Diabetes Advisory Group Board Member (2014-Present); YMCA Diabetes Management Program Board Member, Stevens Point, WI (2013-Present); American Diabetes Association, Wisconsin (2010-Present); Provider, Ascension Health, Diabetology Clinic (2010-Present); Wisconsin Nurses Association (2006-Present); American Diabetes Association (2006-Present); Board Member, Juvenile Diabetes Research Foundation Board (2006-Present); American Nurses Association (2006-Present); American Association of Diabetes Educators (2004-Present); Facilitator, Moderator, Ministry Medical Group Diabetes Support Group Advocate (2010-2013); Sigma Theta Tau—National Nursing Honor Fraternity (2002-2015); Evidence Based Diabetes Health Program Initiative Program Lead, Portage County Aging & Disability Resource Center; National Leader & Diabetes Expert, Wellness iNPractice Diabetes; Wisconsin State Legislation Work Group to Approve Wisconsin Truck Drivers the Ability to use Basal Insulin and Maintain Full Commercial Driver's Licensure; Core Curriculum Development CME Case Study Writer, American Diabetes Association; Core Curriculum Writer for Comprehensive Diabetes Education Programs, Marshfield Clinic, Ministry Medical Group; Faculty, American Diabetes Association **H:** Hockey; Football; Baseball; Tennis; Softball; Basketball; Swimming; Lacrosse **BA:** 824 Illinois Avenue, Ascension Health, Stevens Point, WI, 54481 **ADD:** 1941 Waterview Blvd, Plover, WI, 54467 **URL:** https://www.topnpi.com/wi1013234889/dr-jodi-strong

STUPAK, MARY JO, I: Medicine & Health Care **DOB:** 05/05/1905 **PT:** Carl Elmer Cross; Georgianna Viola Jones **ED:** MS in Community Counseling, University of Wisconsin (1985); Honorary BS, University of Wisconsin (1973) **CT:** Licensed Professional Counselor, State of Wisconsin **C:** Latch Key Lead Teacher, Cathedral School, Superior, WI (2000-Present); Psychotherapy, Human Resource Center, Superior, WI (1985-1995); Teacher, Rape and Incest Victim Organization, Superior, WI (1983-1985); Teacher, Douglas County Citizens, Superior, WI (1977-1982); Family Resource Coordinator, Head Start, Superior, WI (1974-1976); Intermediate Teacher, Cathedral School, Superior, WI (1972-1973) **CR:** Consultant, Head Start, Superior (1982-1983) **CIV:** Organist, St. Williams Church, Foxboro, WI (1952-Present); President, St. Williams Altar Society, Foxboro, WI (1952-Present) **CW:** Contributor, Articles to Professional Journals **H:** Painting; Folk art; Music; Reading **PA:** Democrat **RE:** Roman Catholic

STURCHIO, JEFFREY LOUIS, T: President & Chief Executive Officer **I:** Business Management/Business Services **CN:** Rabin Martin **DOB:** 09/28/1952 **PB:** Newark **SC:** NJ/USA **PT:** Malcolm Louis Sturchio (Deceased); Marianne Louise Delia (Deceased) **MS:** Married **SPN:** Rebecca Lynn Giles (1977) **CH:** Jeremy Giles Sturchio **ED:** PhD in History and Sociology of Science, University of Pennsylvania (1981); Postdoctoral Fellow, National Museum of American History, Smithsonian Institution (1980-1981); MA in History and Sociology of Science, University of Pennsylvania (1976); AB in History, Princeton University, Cum Laude (1973) **C:** Chairman, Corporate Council on Africa (2016-Present); President, Chief Executive Officer, Rabin Martin (2014-Present); Visiting Scholar, Institute for Applied Economics, Global Health, and the Study of Business Enterprise, The Johns Hopkins University (2009-Present); Senior Partner, Rabin Martin (2011-2014); President, Chief Executive Officer, Global Health Council (2009-2011); Chairman, Corporate Council on Africa (2008-2009); President, The Merck Company Foundation (2008); Vice President of Corporate Responsibility, Merck & Co., Inc. (2007-2008); Vice President of External Affairs, Human Health – Europe, Middle East, Africa, Canada, Merck & Co., Inc. (2006-2007); Vice President of External Affairs, Human Health Intercontinental, Merck & Co., Inc. (2005-2006); Vice President of External Affairs, Human Health – Europe, Middle East & Africa, Merck & Co., Inc. (2002-2005); Executive Director of Public Affairs, Human Health – Europe, Middle East & Africa, Merck & Co., Inc. (1997-2002); Executive Director of Public Affairs, Human Health – Europe, Merck & Co., Inc. (1995-1997); Director of Science & Technology Policy, Public Policy Management, Public Affairs, Merck & Co., Inc. (1993-1994); Associate Director, Information Resources and Publishing, Public Affairs, Merck & Co. Inc. (1992-1993); Manager, Public Affairs Information Center, Merck & Co., Inc. (1990-1992); Corporate Archivist, Merck & Co., Inc. (1989-1992) **CR:** Senior Associate, Global Health Policy Center, Center for Strategic and International Studies (2015-Present); Principal, JLS Consulting LLC (2009-Present); Senior Associate, Global Health Policy Center, Center for Strategic and International Studies (2011-2013); Visiting Research Fellow, Health and Social Care, London School of Economics (2004-2006); Senior Fellow and Consultant, National Museum of American History, Smithsonian Institution (1989-1994); Research Associate, Department of History & Sociology of Science, University of Pennsylvania (1989-1994); Senior Research Associate, AT&T Archives (1988-1989); Partner, Science History Consultants (1986-

1988); Acting Director, Center for the History of Chemistry, University of Pennsylvania (1986); Associate Director, Beckman Center for the History of Chemistry, University of Pennsylvania (1984-1988); Adjunct Assistant Professor, Department of History & Sociology of Science, University of Pennsylvania (1984-1987); Visiting Assistant Professor of History, Rutgers, The State University of New Jersey (1982-1983); Assistant Professor of History, Department of Humanities, New Jersey Institute of Technology (1981-1984); Archival Consultant, Division of Physical Sciences, National Museum of American History, Smithsonian Institution (1981-1982); Lecturer, Department of History & Sociology of Science, University of Pennsylvania (1976-1980); Research Associate, Chemical Indicators Project, Department of H&SS, University of Pennsylvania (1975-1980); Assistant Curator, Edgar Fahs Smith Memorial Collection in the History of Chemistry, Van Pelt Library, University of Pennsylvania (1973-1980) **CIV:** Expert Advisory Group, Health Security Commission, Center for Strategic & International Studies (2018-Present); Member, Working Group on HIV, Center for Strategic and International Studies (2017); Advisory Committee, No More Epidemics Campaign, Management Sciences for Health (2016-2017); Member, Task Force on Women's & Family Health, Center for Strategic and International Studies (2016-2017); Judge, Chronic Disease Challenge, SOLVE MIT (2016-2017); Member, Cardiovascular Disease Prevention Task Force, World Innovation Summit on Health, Doha, Qatar (2016); Advisor, United States Delegation, United Nations General Assembly High-Level Meeting on HIV/AIDS (2011); Council of Business Leaders, High Commissioner on Refugees, United Nations (2005-2008); Reference Group on HIV Prevention, Joint United Nations Program on HIV/AIDS (2005-2007); History Reference Group, Joint UN Program on HIV/AIDS (2005-2007); Global Steering Committee on Universal Access, Joint United Nations Program on HIV/AIDS (2005-2006); Task Force, "AIDS Scenarios for Africa" Project, Joint United Nations Program on HIV/AIDS (2003-2005); Millennium Project, Task Force on HIV/AIDS, Joint United Nations Program on HIV/AIDS (2003-2005); Resource Mobilization Committee, Global Fund to Fight HIV/AIDS, TB and Malaria (2003-2005) **CW:** Editorial Board, Globalization and Health (2010-Present); Co-Editor, "Noncommunicable Diseases in the Developing World: Addressing Gaps in Global Policy and Research," Johns Hopkins University Press (2014); Advisory Editor, "Eurohealth" (2001-2008); Advisory Editor, "The Patient's Network (International Alliance of Patients' Organizations)" (1996-1998); Co-Editor, "Health Care: The Patient's Perspective: Proceedings of the Patient's Charter Conference," Pharmaceutical Partners for Better Healthcare (1996); Editor, "Chemical Heritage Foundation History of Modern Chemical Sciences Series," American Chemical Society (1991-1995); Editor, "Values & Visions: A Merck Century," Merck & Co., Inc. (1991); Associate Editor, "American National Biography" (1989-1998); Editorial Advisory Board, "Chemical Sciences and Society Series," University of Pennsylvania Press (1989-1996); Editorial Board, "Bulletin for the History of Chemistry" (1989-1995); Contributing Editor, "Science, Technology, and Human Values" (1988-1990); Associate Editor, "Isis" (1986-1988); Co-Author, "Chemistry in America 1876-1976: Historical Indicators" (1985); Editor, "Corporate History and the Chemical Industries: A Resource Guide," CHOC (1985); Founding Editor, "Beckman Center News" (1982-1988); Visiting Assistant Editor, "Thomas A. Edison Papers," Rutgers, The State University of New Jersey (1982-1983); Editorial Assistant, "4S

Newsletter" (1977); Author, More than 70 Publications in Business, Public/Private Partnerships and Global Health Governance, Global Health, HIV/AIDS, Access to Medicines and the Pharmaceutical Industry and the History of Chemistry **AW:** Recipient, Social & Community Investment Award, Consulting Magazine (2017); Recipient, Powered by EF Leadership Award, Silicon Valley Community Foundation (2014); Co-Recipient, Harvard-Newcomen Award for Best Article in the Business History Review (1998); Recipient, Chairman's Award, Merck & Co., Inc. (1991); Recipient, Outstanding Paper Award, Division of the History of Chemistry, American Chemical Society (1988); Recipient, Summer Stipend, National Endowment for the Humanities (1984); Recipient, Postdoctoral Fellowship, Smithsonian Institution (1980-1981); Recipient, Grant-in-Aid, New Jersey Historical Commission (1974); Recipient, Shell Companies Foundation National Merit Scholarship (1970-1973) **MEM:** Board of Directors, Science History Institute (Formerly Chemical Heritage Foundation) (2017-Present); Advisory Council, The Partnership for Quality Medical Donations (2017-Present); Chair, Corporate Council on Africa (2016-Present); Program Technical Advisory Council, Intrahealth International, Inc. (2015-Present); Board of Directors, Friends of the Global Fight Against AIDS, TB and Malaria (2015-Present); Board of Directors, African Comprehensive HIV/AIDs Partnerships (2015-Present); Development Advisory Committee, Center for History of Medicine and Public Health, New York Academy of Medicine (2014-Present); Advisory Council, Center for Health and Wellbeing, Woodrow Wilson School of Public and International Affairs, Princeton University (2013-Present); Ambassador, Books for Africa (2013-Present); Advisory Board, Global Health Group, University of California San Francisco (2011-Present); Technical Advisory Committee, Global Task Force on Expanding Access to Cancer Care and Control in Developing Countries (2011-Present); Program Advisory Board, amfAR (2010-Present); Principal, Modernizing Foreign Assistance Network (2010-Present); Advisory Board, Global Health Frontline News Project (2009-Present); Health Initiative Advisory Committee, Corporate Council on Africa (2009-Present); Chairman, Board of Directors, BroadReach Institute for Training & Education (2009-Present); Steering Committee, Infectious Diseases Summit, Accordia Global Health Foundation (2008-Present); Board of Directors, Consortium for History of Science, Technology and Medicine (Formerly Philadelphia Area Center for History of Science) (2009-Present); Advisory Board, Digital Health Initiative: Technology for Equity (2009-2016); Chair, Development Committee, Philadelphia Area Center for History of Science (2009-2011) **H:** Book collecting; Reading; Playing with his grandchildren **RE:** Agnostic **BA:** 104 W 40th St Fl 3, Rabin Martin, New York, NY, 10018 **URL:** http://rabinmartin.com

SUBHAN, MOHAMMAD A., T: Clinical Assistant Professor **I:** Education/Educational Services **CN:** Kingman Regional Medical Center **MS:** Married **CH:** Four Children **ED:** MD, Dow University of Health Sciences, Karachi, Pakistan (1986); Internship, Internal Medicine, Advocate Illinois Masonic Medical Center, Advocate Health Care, Chicago, IL; Residency, Family Practice, Jackson Park Hospital Foundation, Chicago, IL **C:** Clinical Assistant Professor, Family Medicine Residency, Kingman Regional Medical Center **AW:** Honoree, America's Most Honored Professionals (2017) **BA:** 2202 N Stockton Hill Road, Suite 101, Kingman Regional Medical Center, Kingman, AZ, 86401

SULC, JEAN L.M., T: CIA (Support Staff), Lobbyist, Consultant **I:** Government Administration/ Government Relations/Government Services **DOB:** 03/17/1939 **PB:** Worcester **SC:** MA/USA **PT:** Emilio B. Beija; Julia B. Luena **MS:** Married **SPN:** Lawrence Bradley Sulc (11/4/1983, Deceased 2/1/2017); Lee Gwynne Mestres (10/9/1965, Divorced 1973) **ED:** Master in Urban and Regional Planning, University Colorado-Denver (1976); Intern, Adams County Planning Department, Brighton, CO (1974-1975); BS in Psychology, Tufts University (1961) **CT:** Licensed Realtor, State of Virginia; Licensed Private Pilot; Business Retention & Expansion Consultant; Community Emergency Response Team (CERT); **C:** President, EdgeSystem. XXI, Washington, D.C. (1996); Manager of Federal Relations, OXY USA Inc., Washington, D.C. (1990-1995); Government Affairs Representative, Cities Service, OXY USA Inc., Washington, D.C. (1982-1989); Assistant, International Director, Cities Service Oil and Gas Corporation, Washington D.C. (1980-1981); Program Director, International Urban Liaison Council, Washington D.C. (1976-1979); Office Policy Analysis Consultant, City and County of Denver (1976); Staff Member, CIA (Clandestine Service), Washington, D.C. (1962-1965) **CR:** Chairman, Government Affairs Committee, L.P. Gas Clean Fuel Coalition, Irvine, CA (1990-1992) **CIV:** National Panel of Arbitrators, Better Business Bureau, Virginia (1991-Present); Volunteer, Reagan/Bush and Bush/Quayle Presidential Campaigns and Inaugural Committees, Washington D.C. (1984-1989); President Hale Foundation, Nathan Hale Institute, Washington D.C. (1984-1985) **CW:** Newsletter Author, Editor, Dayton Climate Project (1979-1980); Public Introductions of U.S. Senators and Congressmen during Tenure; Vice President, American League of Lobbyists; Contributor, Articles **AW:** Presidential Citation, National Propane Gas Association (1992); Minority Intern Grant, Denver Regional Council of Governments (1974-1976); Two-Time Nominee, South Carolina Republican Woman of the Year (2003, 2007); Tobe Coburn, Honorable Mention, Fashion Career's Competition; Beaufort Gazette's Bouquet to the Angel Lady Series **MEM:** Emeritus, American League of Lobbyists (1999-Present); Eastern Regional Division, Association of Image Consultants International (1998-Present); Second Vice President, The American League of Lobbyists, Washington, DC (1996-1997); Board of Directors, The American League of Lobbyists (1994-1997); Associate, Arbitration Section, ABA; Greater Beaufort Chamber of Commerce; Psi Chi **MH:** Albert Nelson Marquis Lifetime Achievement Award (2017) **H:** Dance; Skiing; Sports; Shooting **PA:** Republican **RE:** Evangelical Christian **BA:** 1605 Village Market Blvd, Southeast Apt 313, Leesburg, VA, 20175-4687 **ADD:** 24 Harbor River Circle, St. Helena Island, SC, 29920

SUMIDA, GERALD AQUINAS, T: Partner **I:** Law and Legal Services **CN:** Carlsmith Ball LLP **DOB:** 06/19/1944 **PB:** Hilo **SC:** HI/USA **PT:** Sadamy Sumida; Kimiyo (Miyahara) Sumida **ED:** JD, Yale University (1969); AB, Princeton University, Summa Cum Laude (1966) **CT:** Supreme Court of the United States (1981); United States District Court District of Hawaii (1970); United States Courts for the Ninth Circuit (1970) **C:** Partner, Carlsmith Ball LLP (1976-1999, 2008-Present); General Counsel, Asian Development Bank (1999-2003); Associate, Carlsmith Ball LLP (1970-1976); Research Associate, Center for International Studies, Princeton University (1969) **CR:** Cameras in Courtroom Evaluation Committee, Supreme Court of the State of Hawaii, Hawaii State Judiciary (1984-1986) **CIV:** Chair, Strategic Planning Committee, University of Hawai'i Foundation

(2009-Present); President, Asia Pacific Center for Security Studies (2006-Present); Board of Trustees, University of Hawai'i Foundation (2004-Present); Director, Asia Pacific Center for Security Studies (2001-Present); Senior Adviser, Pacific and Asian Affairs Council (1996-Present); Founding Governor, Center for International Commercial Dispute Resolution (1987-Present); Executive Vice President, Center for International Commercial Dispute Resolution (1987-Present); Chairman of Rules and Procedures, Center for International Commercial Dispute Resolution (1987-Present); Vice Chairman, Honolulu Committee on Foreign Relations (1983-Present); Chair Emeritus, Steering Committee, Hawaii Clean Energy Initiative, State of Hawaii (2011); Secretary General, IPBA (2009-2011); Deputy Secretary, IPBA (2007-2011); Vice Chair, Steering Committee, Hawaii Clean Energy Initiative, State of Hawaii (2010); Chairman, Board of Directors, Hawaii Chapter, American Red Cross (1983-1999, 2003-2010); Deputy Secretary General, IPBA (2007-2009); Council Member, IPBA (2003-2005); Board of Directors, U.S. Chamber of Commerce (1998-2002); Chairman, Human Resources Committee, American Red Cross (1996-2000); Executive Committee, American Red Cross (1996-2000); Board of Governors, American Red Cross (1994-2000); Chairman, Hawaii Commission (1976-1979, 2000); Management Committee, PBEC (1994-1999); Member, PBEC (1993-1999); Executive Committee, Pacific Aviation Museum Pearl Harbor (1991-1999); Board of Directors, Chamber of Commerce Hawaii (1990-1999); Executive Committee, Pacific Islands Association (1988-1999); President, Hawaii Ocean Law Association (1978-1999); Director, Hawaii Ocean Law Association (1978-1999); Founding Member, Hawaii Ocean Law Association (1978-1999); Honolulu Community Media Council (Now Media Council Hawaii) (1976-1999); Science and Statistical Committee, Western Pacific Regional Fishery Management Council (1979-1999); Chairman, Chamber of Commerce Hawaii (1997-1998); Chairman, Pacific and Asian Affairs Council (1991-1996); Board of Governors, Pacific and Asian Affairs Council (1976-1996); Executive Committee, Asia-Pacific Center Reserve for International Business Disputes (1991-1995); Council Member, Asia-Pacific Center Reserve for International Business Disputes (1991-1995); President, Pacific and Asian Affairs Council (1982-1991); Vice Chairman, Board of Directors, Hawaii Chapter, American Red Cross (1990); Board of Directors, Hawaii Imin Centennial Corporation (1983-1990); Hawaii Public Radio-HPR2 (1983-1988); Director, Hawaii Council for the Legal Education of Youth (1983-1988); Director, Hawaii Institute for Continuing Legal Education (1976-1987); Hawaii Advisory Group, Law of Sea Institute, UC Berkeley School of Law (1977-1985); Executive Committee, Honolulu Community Media Council (Now Media Council Hawaii) (1976-1984); Member, Legal Aid Society of Hawai'i (1984); President, Hawaii Council for the Legal Education of Youth (1980-1983); Founding Member, Hawaii Council for the Legal Education of Youth (1980-1983); Legal Counsel, Honolulu Community Media Council (Now Media Council Hawaii) (1979-1983); President, Hawaii Institute for Continuing Legal Education (1979-1983) **MIL:** Study Group on Law of Armed Conflict and the Law of the Sea, Commander, U.S. Pacific Fleet, U.S. Navy (1979-1982) **CW:** Co-Author, "Alternative Approaches to the Legal, Institutional and Financial Aspects of Developing an Inter-Island, Electrical Transmission Cable System" (1986); Co-Author, "Legal, Institutional and Financial Aspects of An Inter-Island Electrical Transmission Cable" (1984); Editor, "Hawaii Bar News" (1972-1973); Contributor, Book Chapters **AW:** Co-Recipient,

C.T. Davide Junior Junior Judicial Reform Award, Supreme Court of the Philippines (2005); Recipient, Certificate of Appreciation, Governor George Ariyoshi (1979); Recipient, Resolutions of Appreciation, Hawaii State Legislature (1979); Recipient, Grant, Japan Foundation (1979) **MEM:** Secretary General, IPBA (2009-Present); Vice President, Hawaii State Bar Association (1984); President, Young Lawyers Section, Hawaii State Bar Association (1974); ABA; Japan-Hawaii Lawyers Association; The American Society of International Law; International Bar Association; American Judicature Society; International Law Association; The Plaza Club; The Colonial Club of Princeton University **BAR:** Hawaii State Bar Association (1970) **MH:** Albert Nelson Marquis Lifetime Achievement Award (2017) **PA:** Democrat **BA:** 1001 Bishop Street, Suite 2100, Carlsmith Ball LLP, Honolulu, HI, 96813

SUPPA-FRIEDMAN, JANICE, **T:** Secondary School Educator **I:** Education/Educational Services **DOB:** 04/27/1943 **PB:** Morristown **SC:** NJ/USA **YOP:** 2017-06-27 **PT:** Eugene Arthur DeStefano; Isabella Vienna (Bottiglia) DeStefano **MS:** Married **SPN:** Michael Jac Friedman (10/7/1995); Dennis Suppa (6/28/1964, Divorced 5/1994) **CH:** Julie Ann; Chad Dennis **ED:** Certificate, Advanced Graduate Study, Virginia Polytechnic Institute and State University (1990); MEd, Virginia Polytechnic Institute and State University (1977); EdB, Bowling Green State University (1964) **CT:** Certified Secondary Teacher, Commonwealth of Virginia **C:** Co-Teacher, Mentor, Fredericksburg City Schools (2004); Educational Consultant (2000-2017); Reading Specialist, Graham Park Middle School, Dumfries, VA (1999-2000); Lead Teacher, English and Reading, Brentsville District High School, Nokesville, VA (1975-1999); Language Arts Specialist, Department Head, Brentsville District High School, Nokesville, VA (1975-1999); Teacher, English, W.C. Taylor Middle School, Warrenton, VA (1973-1974); Teacher, English and Reading, Marsteller Middle School, Manassas, VA (1967-1972); Teacher, English and History, Canaseraga Central School District (1966-1967); Teacher, English and Reading, Northwood Junior High School (1964-1966) **CR:** Fellow, Central Virginia Writing Project, University of Virginia (2008); Educational Consultant, The College Board (2007-2017); Advanced Placement English Teacher, Mentor, The College Board (2004-2005); Adjunct Professor, George Mason University (2003-2004); Educational Consultant, Southern Region, The College Board (2001-2017); Adjunct Professor, Old Dominion University (1999); Reader, Advanced Placement Literature and Composition Exam, Old Dominion University (1998-2003); Reader, Advanced Placement Literature and Composition Exam, Old Dominion University (1996); Adjunct Professor, Northern Virginia Community College (1992-1994) **CIV:** Volunteer, Visitor Use Assistant and Survey Administration, Shenandoah National Park (2005-2017); Officer of Election, Stafford County, Virginia (2001-2004); Tour Guide, Kenmore Plantation, George Washington Foundation, Virginia (2001-2004); Tour Guide, George Washington's Ferry Farm, George Washington Foundation, Virginia (2001-2004) **CW:** Editor, Newsletter, Spinning Wheel (1991-1994); Contributor, Articles, Professional Journals; Contributor, Articles, Virginia English Bulletin **AW:** Frances Weimer Award, VATE (2007); Grantee, Virginia Communications of the Arts (2000); Grantee, Prince William County Public Schools Education Foundation (2000); Grantee, Virginia Opera Association, Inc. (2000); Grantee, Southern States Southland Corporation (2000); Grantee, Greater Washington Reading Council (1999-2000); Grantee, Prince William County Public Schools Education Foundation (1996); Grantee, Virginia Communications of the Arts (1994-1995); Service Award, VATE (1993) **MEM:** SCOA Region 2 Representative, NCTE (2009-2017); NCTE Liaison, VATE (2007-2017); President, VATE (2004-2005); President-Elect, VATE (2002-2003); Vice President, VATE (2001-2002); Judge, Virginia State Forensics Finals, NCTE (2000-2003); Judge, Virginia State Excellence in Literature Magazines, NCTE (1998-2002); Coordinator, Virginia State Achievement in Writing Awards, NCTE (1995-2001); Executive Board, VATE (1992-2017); President, NATE (1992-1994); Phi Delta Kappa **MH:** Albert Nelson Marquis Lifetime Achievement Award (2017) **H:** Reading; Music; Hiking; Swimming; Yoga; Snorkeling **ADD:** 171 Farmview Road, Stanardsville, VA, 22973

SUSSMAN, LAUREEN, **T:** Real Estate Agent **I:** Real Estate **CN:** Ramat Beit Shemesh **DOB:** 03/21/1953 **PB:** New York **SC:** NY/USA **PT:** Harry G.; Ruth (Goldstein) G. **SPN:** Alan Neil Sussman (5/30/1977) **CH:** David Efrem; Rachel Sarah Blima Simpser (Daughter-in-Law); Adam Jacob; Daniel Joshua; Annie Pesha Jacobs (Daughter-in-Law) **ED:** MSc, Hofstra University (1998); MS, Hofstra University (1998); BA, Brooklyn College (1974) **CT:** Certified Teacher, Nursery-6; Certified Special Education Teacher, All Grades; Licensed Israeli Real Estate Agent **C:** Licensed Real Estate Consultant, Ramat Beit Shemesh (2009-Present); Retired (2007); Junior High School Teacher, Torah Academy for Girls, Far Rockaway, NY (1997-2007); Kindergarten Teacher, Hebrew Academy of Long Beach (1996-1997); Administrative Assistant, Alan N. Sussman, CPA, Woodmere, NY (1978-1996); Administrative Assistant, Tour Operator, EasTours Division, Foreign Tours, New York, NY (1975-1978); Secretary, McCann-Erickson, Inc., New York, NY (1974-1975) **CR:** Trainer, Life Technology, Cedarhurst, NY (2004-2005); Participant, Instrumental Enrichment/IRI Skylight, New York, NY (1998); Dynamic Assessment Project, Touro College, New York, NY (1996); Participant, Instrumental Enrichment/IRI Skylight, New York, NY (1995); CSE Parent Representative, Advisor, Lawrence Public Schools (1992-1997); Real Estate Consultant, Ramat Beit Shemesh, Israel **CIV:** Advisory Board, Kulanu of the South Shore of Nassau County (2000-2007); Sisterhood Congregation of Bais Tefilah (1990-2003); Special Education PTA Lawrence Schools (1986-2003); Chair of Social Action, Israel Affairs, Sisterhood of East Meadow Jewish Center (1979-1981); Sisterhood Kehillah Aish Kodesh, Emunah of Am **CW:** Contributor, Articles, Professional Journals **MEM:** Founder, Nassau County Chapter, OTSAR (1987-Present); National Board of Directors, President, Nassau Chapter, OTSAR (1987-2002); Masada Chapter, AMIT Women **H:** Israeli and salsa dancing; Walking; Reading; Needlepoint; Jewelry making **PA:** Republican **RE:** Orthodox Jewish **ADD:** P.O. Box 353, Cedarhurst, NY, 11516

SWABY, CLEVELAND , **I:** Business Management/Business Services **PB:** , **ED:** Master's in Health Care Management, Collins University; Bachelor's in Health Care Management, Collins University **C:** Founder, Owner, Tradelink Network USA, LLC (2014-Present) **MEM:** Lauderhill, Florida Chamber of Commerce

SWAN, GEORGE STEVEN, **T:** Associate Professor **I:** Education/Educational Services **CN:** N.C. A&T **PB:** St. Louis **SC:** MO/USA **PT:** Raymond Albert Swan; Lorene Catherine (Kennedy) Swan **ED:** SJD, University of Toronto (1983); LLM, University of Toronto (1976); JD, University of Notre Dame (1974); BA, The Ohio State University (1970) **CT:** Investment Foundations Certificate (Chartered Financial Analyst Institute); Associate Professional Risk Manager (PRMIA); Certified Risk and Compliance Management Professional (IARCP); Certified Risk and Compliance Management Professional in Insurance and Reinsurance (IARCP); Certified Personal and Family Finance Educator (AAFCS); Certified Financial Planner; Chartered Financial Consultant, Chartered Life Underwriter; International Certificate in Banking Risk and Regulation (ICBRR) **C:** Associate Professor, N.C. A&T (1989-Present); Judicial Clerk, United States Court of Appeals for the Seventh Circuit (1988-1989); Professor of Law, St. Thomas University School of Law (1984-1988); Associate Professor, Delaware Law School (1983-1984); Assistant Professor, Delaware Law School (1980-1983); Judicial Clerk, Supreme Court of Ohio (1976-1978); Assistant Attorney General, State of Ohio (1974-1975) **CR:** Visiting Professor, The John Marshall Law School (2000-2001, 1996-1997) **CW:** Contributor, Professional Journals **MEM:** CFA Institute; International Association of Risk and Compliance Professionals; Professional Risk Managers' International Association; Global Association of Risk Professionals; American Association of University Professors; American Association of Family and Consumer Sciences; Academy of Management; Financial Planning Association; Society of Financial Service Professionals; The Honor Society of Phi Kappa Phi **BAR:** Louisiana (1999); Massachusetts (1999); Minnesota (1998); Nebraska (1998); United States Court of Appeals for the Seventh Circuit (1998); United States District Court Northern District of Georgia (1997); The District of Columbia (1997); Florida (1997); Georgia (1997); United States Court of Appeals for the Tenth Circuit (1994); United States Court of Appeals for the Sixth Circuit (1993); United States Court of Appeals for the Eleventh Circuit (1993); Supreme Court of the United States (1987); United States District Court Southern District of Ohio (1975); Ohio (1974) **ADD:** 1601 E Market St, Greensboro, NC, 27411

SWANEY WEHN, KAREN, **I:** Education/Educational Services **DOB:** 03/01/1950 **PB:** Chillicotne **SC:** OH/USA **PT:** Glenn Warren Swaney; Joyce Wood Swaney **MS:** Married **SPN:** David Carl Wehn (April 8, 1989) **CH:** Glenn Ian Taylor **ED:** MS, Kent State University (1986); BA, The Ohio State University (1980) **CT:** Certified Professional Geologist (1996) **C:** Assistant Professor, ECC (2000-Present); Lecturer, Buffalo State College (1997-Present); Project Geologist, Golder Associates (1997-Present); Project Geologist, Conestaga Rover 3 Associates (Now GHD) (1992-1997); Research Assistant, The Ohio State University (1976-1992) **CR:** President, Buffalo Association of Professional Geologists (1997-1998); Researcher, Antarctica (1980-1985) **CIV:** Lay Leader, Warrens Corners United Methodist Church (2004-2005) **CW:** Contributor, Articles, Professional Journals **AW:** Grantee, Travel and Work in Nigeria, Earthwatch Institute (1990-1991); Grantee, Travel to Australia, National Science Foundation (1982) **MEM:** Board Member, Air and Waste Management Association **MH:** Albert Nelson Marquis Lifetime Achievement Award (2017) **RE:** Methodist **ADD:** 5016 Ridge Rd, Lockport, NY, 14094

SWEIGART, LINDA INEZ, **T:** Nursing Educator **I:** Education/Educational Services **CN:** Ball State University **DOB:** 09/03/1947 **PB:** New Castle **SC:** IN/USA **PT:** Max Morris; Juanita F. (McKenzie) Temples **MS:** Married **SPN:** James Alonzo Sweigart (12/31/1966) **CH:** Michael Keith; Agenna Lynn **ED:** Postgraduate Certificate, Ball State University, Muncie, IN (2006); MS in Nursing, Indiana University, Indianapolis, IN (1986); BS in Nursing, Indiana University, with Highest

Distinction, Indianapolis, IN (1976) **CT:** Quality Matters Online Teaching Certificate (2015-2021); Adult Nurse Practitioner, American Academy of Nurse Practitioners (2016) **C:** Instructor, School of Nursing, Ball State University, Muncie, IN (2004-Present); Liaison, Breast Center, Ball Memorial Hospital (Now Indiana University Ball Memorial Hospital) (2004-2006); Women and Family Health Educator, Ball Memorial Hospital, Muncie, IN (1990-2004); Assistant Director, Nursing Department, Reid Memorial Hospital (Now Reid Health), Richmond, IN (1980-1988); Staff-Charge Nurse, ICU, Henry County Hospital (1979-1980); Head Nurse, Neonatal ICU, Lafayette Home Hospital, Lafayette, IN (1978-1979) **CR:** Presenter, Virtual Learning Environments in Nursing, Various State, National and International Organizations; Presentation, Virtual Learning Environments in Interprofessional Education, Global Forum on Innovation in Health Professional Education, Institute of Medicine (2015); Health Information Technology Scholar, Advancing Health Information Technologies Through Faculty Empowerment (2011) **CIV:** Member, First Church Nazarene (2004-Present); Board Secretary, Safe Sitter (2007-2008); Board Member, Safe Sitter (2002-2008); Delegate, Program Committee, Delaware County, Prevent Child Abuse Indiana (1997-2006); Volunteer Trainer, Reach Recovery, American Cancer Society (1995-2005); Board Member, Safe Kids Delaware County (2004); Founding Member, Safe Kids Delaware County (1995-2004); Member, New Hope Church (1979-2004) **CW:** Lead Author, Articles, Professional Journals; Contributing Author, Articles, Professional Journals; Lead Author, Interprofessional Education in a Virtual World, Journal of Nursing Education **AW:** Second Place, 15th International Meeting on Simulation in Healthcare (IMSH) (2015); SSH/IOM Global Forum on Innovation in Health Professional Education (IHPE) (2015); Healthcare Information Technology Scholar (2011); Indiana Section Award of Excellence in Education, Association of Women's Health, Obstetric and Neonatal Nurses (2000) **MEM:** National League for Nursing; Sigma Theta Tau International; Oncology Nursing Society; American Association of Nurse Practitioners; Coalition of Advanced Practice Nurses of Indiana; International Nursing Association for Clinical Simulation and Learning; Society for Simulation in Healthcare **MH:** Who's Who in Nursing, Who's Who in Education **PA:** Conservative **ADD:** 4235 S. Main Street, New Castle, IN, 47362

SWISHER, MICHAEL SCOTT, T: Chief Executive Officer, President **I:** Other **CN:** Bayport Printing House, Inc. **PT:** Donald Everett Swisher; Elizabeth Joy (McGee) Swisher **ED:** Degree, Vanderbilt University; Degree, University of Minnesota **C:** President, Bayport Printing House, Inc. (1991-Present); Bayport Printing House, Inc. (1973-Present) **CR:** Directorship, First State Bank and Trust; Directorship, Universal Financial Services; Directorship, Valley Agencies, Inc.; Chairman of the Board, Valley Agencies, Inc. **CIV:** Director, Chairman of the Board, Religion and Society Foundation, Stillwater, MN **AW:** Helen Keller Sight Award, Minnesota Lions Eye Bank; Officer of the Most Venerable Order of the Hospital of St. John of Jerusalem; Fellow, Society of Antiquaries of Scotland; Named, Kentucky Colonel **MEM:** Governor General, Sons and Daughters of the Pilgrims (2017-Present); University Club of St. Paul, Minnesota; University Club of San Francisco; Arts Club of Washington, D.C.; Stillwater, Minnesota Lions Club; St. John's Lodge No. 1, A.F. & A.M., Stillwater, MN; St. Paul Lodge No. 3, St. Paul, MN; Prometheus Lodge No. 851, F. & A. M., San Francisco, CA; The Morgan Lodge No. 9816, E.C., Malvern, England; St. Paul and Minneapolis, Minnesota York Rite Bodies; 32° Mason, Ancient & Accepted Scottish Rite, S.J., Valley of Minneapolis, Minnesota; Sons of the American Revolution; Sons of the Revolution; General Society of the War of 1812; Society of Colonial Wars; Order of Founders and Patriots of America; National Society, Sons of Confederate Veterans; Military Order of the Stars and Bars; National Order of the Blue and Grey; Hereditary Order of the Descendants of Loyalists and Patriots of the American Revolution; Order of the Crown of Charlemagne; Baronial Order of Magna Carta; Order of Americans of Armorial Ancestry; Order of Three Crusades; National Society of Americans of Royal Descent; St. Nicholas Society of the City of New York; Morgan Sports Car Club; Rolls Royce Owners' Club; Pyrotechnics Guild International; Flour City Lodge No. 118, I.O.O.F.; Oak Leaf Grange No. 569 **H:** Shooting; Fishing; Genealogy; Pyrotechny; Collecting antique guns; Pocket watches; Books; Automobiles **BA:** 102 Central Ave, Bayport Printing House, Inc., Bayport, MN, 55003 **URL:** http://www.bayportprinting.com

SWITZER, CAROLYN, T: Artist **I:** Fine Art **DOB:** 04/20/1931 **PB:** Petoskey **SC:** MI/USA **PT:** Eugene Constant Switzer; Burnis Hazel (Lower) Switzer **ED:** Coursework, St. John's College, Santa Fe, NM (1993); MA, Michigan State University (1964); Coursework, Wayne State University (1954-1955); BA, Michigan State University (1953) **CT:** Certified Teacher, State of Michigan **C:** Private Teacher, Drawing and Painting; Art Teacher, Birmingham Board of Education, Michigan (1956-1996); Art Teacher, Ferndale Board of Education (1953-1956) **CIV:** Consultant Girl Scouts of the United States of America, Birmingham, Petoskey, MI; Deacon, Northern Michigan Chorale Community Church; Member, Choir, First Presbyterian Church of Petoskey **AW:** Recognition Award, Birmingham Education Association Council (1967); Scholar, AAUW, Michigan State University (1962); Named, Outstanding Senior Woman, Lantern Night, Michigan State University (1953) **MEM:** AAUW; F.P. Chapter, PEO; National Art Education Association; Michigan Art Education Association; Michigan Education Association; Detroit Institute of Arts; National Museum of Women in the Arts; Zonta International; Crooked Tree Arts Center; Little Traverse Historical Museum; Life Member, Michigan State University Alumni Association; Friends of the Petoskey Public Library; Board, Friendship Centers, Emmet County, Petoskey, MI **H:** Music; Singing; Reading; Exercise class; Walking; Photography **ADD:** 805 Lindell Avenue, Petoskey, MI, 49770

SYDOW, MICHAEL DAVID SR., T: Attorney **I:** Law and Legal Services **CN:** Sydow Law Firm **DOB:** 12/12/1950 **PB:** Cuero **SC:** TX/USA **PT:** Vernon E. Sydow and Carolyn M. Rogas **MS:** Married **SPN:** Jody L. Sydow **CH:** Kristen; David **ED:** JD, The University of Texas at Austin, With Honors (1976); BA, Southwestern University (1973) **CT:** Certified in Civil Trial Law, Texas Board of Legal Specialization **C:** Owner, Sydow Law Firm, formerly Sydow & McDonald (1994-Present); Attorney, Sydow Law Firm (1994-Present); Chief Executive Officer, Texas Syngas (2008-2009); Shareholder, Verner, Liipfert, Bernhard, McPherson & Hand, Houston, Texas (1997-2002); Member of Firm, Reynolds & Sydow, LLP, Houston, Texas (1993-1994); Attorney, Private Practice (1990-1993); Member of Firm, Hagans & Sydow, LLP, Houston, TX (1985-1990); Member of Firm, Eastham, Watson, Dale & Forney, Houston, TX (1977-1984); Trial Attorney, Office of the General Counsel, United States Navy, Arlington, VA (1976-1977) **AW:** Recipient, President's Award, Houston Bar Association (1990) **MEM:** Practice and Procedures Committee, Maritime Law Association of the United States (1988-Present); Chairman, Judicial Liaison Committee, Houston Bar Association (1988-1990); Committee on General Average, Maritime Law Association of the United States (1977-1988); Fellow, Texas Bar Foundation; Fellow, Houston Bar Foundation; Phi Delta Phi **BAR:** United States District Court for the Western District of Texas (1986); United States District Court for the Northern District of Texas (1985); Supreme Court of the United States (1980); United States District Court for the Eastern District of Texas (1979); United States Court of Federal Claims (1977); United States Court of Appeals for the Fifth Circuit (1977); United States District Court for the Southern District of Texas (1977); Texas (1976) **MH:** Albert Nelson Marquis Lifetime Achievement Award (2017) **BA:** 5020 Montrose Blvd Ste 450, Sydow Law Firm, Houston, TX, 77006 **ADD:** 3355 W Alabama St Ste 444, Sydow Law Firm, Houston, TX, 77098

SYED, IBRAHIM BIJLI, T: Professor, Medical Educator, Medical Physicist **I:** Medicine & Health Care **CN:** University of Louisville **DOB:** 03/16/1939 **PB:** Bellary **SC:** India **PT:** Syed Ahmed Bijli Syed; Mumtaz Begum (Maniyar) Syed **MS:** Married **SPN:** Sajida Shariff (11/29/1964) **CH:** Mubin; Zafrin **ED:** DSc, Vijayanagara Sri Krishnadevaraya University, with Honors, Bellary, India (2013); PhD, University of Malta, with Honors, (1985); DSc, Johns Hopkins University, Baltimore, MD (1972); Diplomate in Radiological Physics, University of Bombay (Now University of Mumbai) (1964); MS, in Nuclear Physics, Central College of Bangalore, with Honors and Distinction (1962); MS, University of Mysore, with Honors and Distinction (1962); BS, Veerashaiva College Ballari, with Honors, Mysore, India (1960) **CT:** Certified Hazard Control Officer (1980); Certified International Health Care Safety Professional (1980); Diplomate, American Board of Radiology; Diplomate, American Board of Health Physics **C:** Commission on Human Relations, City Government of Louisville, Kentucky (2016-Present); Director, Nuclear Medical Sciences, School of Medicine, University of Louisville (1980-Present); Professor of Medicine, School of Medicine, University of Louisville (1979-Present); Member, Institutional Review Board, Louisville Veterans Affairs Medical Center (2000-2013); Executive Officer, Radiation Safety Committee, Louisville Veterans Affairs Medical Center (1979-2013); Medical Physicist, Radiation Safety Officer, Louisville Veterans Affairs Medical Center (1979-2013); Assistant Clinical Professor of Nuclear Medicine, School of Medicine, University of Connecticut, Farmington, CT (1975-1979); Consultant, Baystate Wingmemorial Hospital, Palmer, MA (1973-1979); Medical Physicist, Baystate Wing Hospital, Palmer, MA (1973-1979); Consultant, Medical Physicist, Mercy Hospital (1973-1979); Adjunct Professor, Radiology, Holyoke Community College (1973-1979); Director of Medical Physicis, Baystate Medical Center, Springfield, MA (1973-1979); Radiation Safety Officer, Baystate Medical Center, Springfield, MA (1973-1979); Chief Physicist, Halifax Infirmary, Canada (1967-1969); Consultant, Bangalore Nursing Home, India (1964-1967); Medical Physicist, Bangalore Nursing Home, India (1964-1967); Radiation Safety Officer, Bangalore Nursing Home, India (1964-1967); Consultant, Ministry of Health, Government of Karnataka, India (1964-1967); First Medical Physicist, Ministry of Health, Government of Karnataka, India (1964-1967); First Radiation Safety Officer, Ministry of Health, Government of Karnataka, India (1964-1967); Medical Physicist, Bowring and Lady Curzon Hospital, Bangalore Medical College and Research Institute, Bangalore,

India (1964-1967); Radiation Safety Officer, Bowring and Lady Curzon Hospital, Bangalore Medical College and Research Institute, Bangalore, India (1964-1967); First Medical Physicist, Victoria Hospital, India (1964-1967) **CR:** PhD Thesis Examiner, University of Allahabad (1996-Present); PhD Thesis Examiner, University of Delhi (1996-Present); Consultant, Radiopharmacology Division, Food and Drug Administration, United States Department of Health & Human Services (1989-Present); Founder, President, Islamic Research Foundation International, Louisville, KY (1988-Present); Consultant, Gastroenterology and Urology Division (1988-Present); Faculty Member, International Institute for Advanced Study, University of Delhi, Clayton, MO (1985-Present); Consultant, The American Council on Science and Health (1980-Present); Guest Lecturer, Religious Studies Program, University of Louisville (1979-Present); Course Director, Licensing for Nuclear Cardiologists (1980-Present); Speaker, Garden City College, Bangalore, India (2017); Speaker, Bellary Institute of Technology and Management, Bellary, India (2017); Speaker, Vijayanagara Institute of Medical Sciences, Ballari, India (2017); Speaker, Islamic Voice, Terrace Gardens Guest House, Bangalore, India (2013); Speaker, Raichur District Teachers Conferences, India (2013); Speaker, Vijayanagara Institute of Medical Sciences, Ballari, India (2013); Speaker, Sri Ram Mohan Lohia Institute of Medical Sciences, Lucknow, India (2013); Speaker, Integral University, Lucknow, India (2013); Speaker, Bellary Institute of Technology and Management, Bellary, India (2013); Speaker, Garden City College, Bangalore, India (2013); Speaker, Darus Salam, Bangalore, India (2005); Invited Faculty, Association of Muslim Social Scientists, Dallas, TX (2005); Member, Panel of Examiners, Radiological Physics, American Board of Radiology (1980-2010); Member, Admissions Committee, Nuclear Medicine Program, University of Louisville (1980-2002); Member, Panel of Examiners, Health Physics, American Board of Health Physics (1980-2000) **CIV:** Panel Member, Heavenly Culture, World Peace & Respiration of Light, Republic of Korea (2010-Present); Commissioner, Human Relations Commission, Metro Louisville Kentucky Government (2010-Present); Advisory Board, Partnership to Prevent Child Abuse, Louisville, KY (2007-Present); Founder, Bijli Foundation Charitable Trust, Bellary, India (2005-Present); Manager, Bijli Foundation Charitable Trust, Bellary, India (2005-Present); Trustee, Bijli Foundation Charitable Trust, Bellary, India (2005-Present); Board Director, American Muslim Association of North America, Louisville, KY (2003-Present); Board Director, Nur Islamic School, Louisville, KY (2003-Present); Board of Directors, The Louisville Islamic Center (1992-Present); Khatib, Islamic Center of Louisville, Louisville, KY (1992-Present); Speaker, Biotechnology Conference, Kuala Lumpur, Malaysia (2007); Speaker, Muslim Association of Cleveland East (2002); Moderator, Foreign Policy Workshop, United States Department of State, Louisville, KY (2000); Speaker, Muslim Student Association, University of Cincinnati (2000); Speaker, Dayton Islamic Center, Dayton, OH (2000); Speaker, Miami Valley Islamic Center, Springfield, OH (2000); Speaker, Muslim Community Center, Chicago, IL (1988-2008); President, Chairman, India Community Foundation of Louisville, Kentucky (1980-2010) **CW:** Freelance Writer, "The Message," London, England (1998-Present); Freelance Writer, "The Minaret," Botswana, South Africa (1998-Present); Associate Editor, AAlim (1998-Present); Freelance Writer, "Minaret Monthly Magazine," Los Angeles, CA (1995-Present); Freelance Writer, "Al-Balaagh," Lenasia, South Africa (1989-Present); Contributor, Health and Science Column, Muslim Journal

(1989-Present); Freelance Writer, "Islamic Voice," India (1988-Present); Contributing Editor, Islamic Food and Nutrition Council of America (1986-Present); Editorial Board, Journal of Islamic Medical Association (1981-Present); Freelance Writer, Minaret Biweekly, New York, NY (1975-Present); Author, Qur'anic Inspirations (2007); Author, Intellectual Achievements of Muslims (2002); Author, Knowledge Empowers You (2017); Freelance Writer, AL'FURQAN International, Norcross, GA (1990); Freelance Writer, Message International, Jamaica, NY (1990); Editor, Science and Technology for the Developing World (1988); Author, Radiation Safety Manual (1979); Manuscript Reviewer, Science Journals (1973); Manuscript Reviewer, Medical Journals (1973); Columnist, The Indian Muslim Observer; Science Editor, The Indian Muslim Observer; Contributor, President's Page; Author, Radiation Safety for Allied Health Professionals; Contributor, Articles to Scientific Journals; Contributor, Articles on Various Topics of Islam, Journals and Magazines; Managing Editor, Irfi.org **AW:** Distinguished Alumni Award, Veerashaiva College, Ballari, India (2017); Muslim Journal Muslim Civilization Advancement Award (2010); Diversity Award (2002), The American Board of Radiology (2008); Distinguished Service Award, The American Board of Radiology (2008); Hind Rattan Jewel of India Title Award, North Society of New Delhi (1984); Distinguished Community Service Award, India Community Foundation (1982); Public Health Service Fellow, Johns Hopkins University (1969-1972); Recipient, World Health Organization Fellowship **MEM:** Board of Directors, American Muslim Association of North America (2003-Present); Vice Chairman, Chairman, Islamic Cultural Association of Louisville Center (1999-Present); Chairman, Medical Health in Physics Committee, Health Physics Society (1989-Present); Secretary, Association of Muslim Scientists and Engineers of North America (1988-Present); Chairman, State Public Relations Committee, National Association of Americans of Asian Indian Descent (1982-Present); Faculty, Islamic Medical Association of North America (1998); Faculty, International Institute of Islamic Medicine, Birmingham, England (1998); Faculty, Islamic Society of Northern America, Chicago, IL (1998); Faculty, International Institute of Islamic Medicine, Orlando, FL (1996-1997); Speaker, Society of Nuclear Medicine India (1996); Speaker, Association of Medical Physicists of India (1996); Faculty, Islamic Medical Association of North America (1996); Convener, International Conference, Society of Nuclear Medicine and Molecular Imaging (1995); Faculty, Islamic Medical Association of North America (1994); Treasurer, Association of Muslim Scientists and Engineers (1987-1988); Program Chairman, Annual Conference, Association of Muslim Scientists and Engineers (1987); Faculty Member, Annual Meeting, Society of Nuclear Medicine and Molecular Imaging (1987) **H:** Chess; Public debating,; Evidence-based religion; Reading; Research; Critic; Public service; Mentor; Volunteer **PA:** Independent **RE:** Islamic **BA:** 3rd Fl ACB Bldg 710 S Jackson St, Louisville, KY, 40202 **ADD:** 7102 W Shefford Ln, Louisville, KY, 40242 **URL:** http://www.irfi.org

SYPHER, FRANCIS J., T: Writer, Editor, Educator **I:** Education/Educational Services **PT:** Francis J. Sypher; Mildred A. Sypher **SPN:** Eleanor C. Kramer (1970, Divorced 1983); Marie-Claire Cournand (1966, Divorced 1969) **CH:** Eleanor H. **ED:** PhD, Columbia University, New York City, NY (1968); AM, Columbia University, New York City, NY (1964); AB, Columbia University, New York City, NY (1963) **C:** Freelance Editor and Writer (1975-Present); Professor, University at Albany (1968-1975); Professor, Columbia University (1965-

1968) **CW:** Editor, "Society of Colonial Wars 125th Anniversary 1892-2017: 25 Year History" (2017); Editor, "Liber A of the Collegiate Churches of New York Part 2" (2017); Editor, L.E.L. Letitia Elizabeth Landon, The English Improvisatrice, Catalogue of a Collection of Manuscripts and Books Held by the Rare Book and Manuscript Library of Columbia University (2015); Author, "Charles Anthon: American Classicist" (2015); Author, "Saint Agnes Chapel of the Parish of Trinity Church, 2nd Edition" (2014); Editor, "New York State Society of the Cincinnati: The Institution of the Society of the Cincinnati" (2014); Editor, "Elizabeth Teft, Orinthia's Miscellanies, or a Complete Collection of Poems Never Before Published" (2013); Curator, Exhibitor, Author, "'Catalogue' The Collegiate Churches of New York 1628-2012" (2012); Author, "Strangers and Pilgrims: A Centennial History of The Laymen's Club of the Cathedral Church of Saint John the Divine" (2012); Curator, Author, Exhibitor, "The World of Letitia Elizabeth Landon: A Literary Celebrity of the 1830s" (2011); Author, "St. James' Church in the City of New York 1810-2010" (2010); Editor, "An Armory of American Families of Dutch Descent" (2010); Author, "Letitia Elizabeth Landon, 2nd Edition Revised" (2009); Author, "Eric Sams and the Real Shakespeare" (2009); Editor, "Chronicle of Society Colonial Wars New York" (2009); Editor, Translator, "Liber A 1628-1700 of Collegiate Churches" (2009); Author, "Histories of New York Regiments of the Continental Army" (2008); Editor, "St. Nicholas Society Genealogical Record (2007); Author, "The Donald M. Liddell Collection" (2007); Editor, "Landon's Works, 15th Volume" (2007); Author, "Landon Bibliography" (2005); Author, "New York Society of the Cincinnati: Biographies of Original Members and Other Continental Officers" (2004); Editor, "Minutes of Coroners Proceedings" (2004); Author, "Letitia Elizabeth Landon" (2004); Author, "Saint Agnes Chapel of the Parish of Trinity Church" (2002); Author, "Frederick L. Hoffman, His Life and Works" (2002); Editor, "Landon's Works" (1990); Contributor, Articles, Professional Journals; Editor, The Saint Nicholas Society of the City of New York **AW:** Lecturing Grant, Fulbright Senior Lectureship in American Literature (1986-1988, 1981-1983); Publishing Grant, The Andrew W. Mellon Foundation (1974); Research Grant, SUNY RF (1974); New York State Regents Fellowship (1963-1965) **MEM:** The Princeton Club of New York; Society of Colonial Wars; The Saint Nicholas Society of the City of New York; The Grolier Club of New York; The Huguenot Society of America; The New York State Society of the Cincinnati; Cosmos Club, Washington, DC **ADD:** 730 Fort Washington Ave Apt 1L, New York, NY, 10040

TABAKU, FLORIAN, T: Principal **I:** Law and Legal Services **CN:** The Law Offices of Florian Tabaku **ED:** JD, Cooley Law School, Western Michigan University (2011); Legal Intern, Sixty Plus, Inc. Elder Law Clinic, Cooley Law School, Western Michigan University (2010); BA in Political Science, Mount St. Mary's University (2008) **C:** Managing Partner, The Law Offices of Triantis & Tabaku (2013-Present); Owner, Tabaku Law Firm, LLC (2011-2013); Attorney, Tabaku Law Firm, LLC (2011-2013); Contractor, Walter Reed Army Institute of Research, U.S. Army Medical Research and Materiel Command (2007-2008) **CIV:** Former Volunteer, Montgomery Pro Bono Clinic; Affiliate, Occasional Pro Bono Work **AW:** Nationally Ranked in Top 10 Under 40, National Academy of Family Law Attorneys (2017); Named to Capital Region's Premier Lawyers; Client's Choice Award, Avvo Inc.; Honoree, 5 out of 5 Preeminent Rating, Martindale-Hubbell; Client Distinction Award, Martindale-Hubbell; Award for

Outstanding Lawyering, Board of Directors, Sixty Plus, Inc. Elder Law Clinic; Distinguished Student of Character and Integrity Award, Maher Inn, The International Legal Honor Society of Phi Delta Phi **MEM:** Bar Association of Montgomery County (2011-Present); Maryland State Bar Association, Inc. **BAR:** Maryland (2011-Present); United States District Court District of Maryland **H:** Soccer; Hiking **BA:** 4800 Hampden Ln Ste 200, Bethesda, MD, 20814 **ADD:** 4800 Hampden Ln Ste 200, The Law Offices of Florian Tabaku, Bethesda, MD, 20814 **URL:** https://tabakulaw.com/

TALPE, FERNAND P., T: Chief Executive Officer **I:** Financial Services **CN:** Fertagro Trading USA **SC:** Belgium **ED:** Diplomate in Psychology, Belgium; Diplomate, Business School, Belgium **C:** Owner, Fertagro Trading USA (2011-Present) Chief Executive Officer, Fertagro Trading USA (2011-Present) Owner, NV Fernand Talpe, Belgium (2008-Present) Director, NV Fernand Talpe, Belgium (2008-Present) Owner, Croenen En Carlier NV, Belgium (2008-Present) Chief Executive Officer, Croenen En Carlier NV, Belgium (2008-Present) Owner, Fertagro Trading EU, Belgium (2005-Present) Chief Executive Officer, Fertagro Trading EU, Belgium (2005-Present) Chief Executive Officer, Nordinvest (2004-2013) Merchandiser, Cargill, Incorporated (2002-2005) **BA:** 100 Biscayne Blvd Ste 3030, Fertagro Trading USA, Miami, FL, 33132

TAMBOLI, AKBAR R., T: Consultant **I:** Consulting **CN:** Thornton Tomasetti **DOB:** 07/20/1942 **PB:** Babhulgon **SC:** India **PT:** Rasul M. Tamboli; Chandbi Tamboli **MS:** Married **SPN:** Rounkbi A. Tamboli (5/21/1969) **CH:** Tahira; Ajim; Alamgir **ED:** MS, Stanford University (1967); BS, University of Poona (Now Savitribai Phule Pune University), Pune, India (1965) **C:** Consultant, Thornton Tomasetti, New York, NY (1999-Present); Principal, Thornton Tomasetti, New York, NY (1999-2014); Senior Vice President, Thornton Tomasetti, New York, NY (1999-2014); Consultant Engineer, CUH2A Inc. (Now HDR), Princeton, NJ (1992-1998); Vice President, Office of Irwin G. Cantor, PC, New York, NY (1981-1991); Senior Project Engineer, Engineers Inc., East Orange, NJ (1977-1980); Associate, Edwards & Hjorth, New York, NY (1970-1976); Senior Engineer, Miller Associates, Pottsville, PA (1967-1969) **CR:** Adjunct Professor, New York Polytechnic Institute (Now NYU Tandon School of Engineering), New York, NY; Lecturer, Stanford University, Stanford, CA; Lecturer, University of California, Berkeley; Lecturer, Massachusetts Institute of Technology, Cambridge, MA **CIV:** Volunteer, Cancer Fund Drive, NJ (1986) **CW:** Author, "Tall and Super Tall Buildings: Planning and Design" (2014); Author, "Handbook of Steel Connection Design and Details" (2009); Author, "Handbook of Structural Steel Connections: Design and Details" (1999); Author, "Steel Design Handbook: LRFD Method" (1996); Editor, "Steel Design Handbook: LRFD Method" (1996); Contributor, Structural Analysis Chapters, Building Design Handbook; Contributor, Structural Analysis Chapters, Civil Engineering Handbook **MEM:** Fellow, American Society of Civil Engineers; American Institute of Steel Construction; American Welding Society; ISPE; New York Society of Consulting Engineers; Professional and Scholarly Division, The Association of American Publishers **MH:** Albert Nelson Marquis Lifetime Achievement Award (2017) **H:** Golf; Boating **ADD:** 59 Murano Dr, Princeton Junction, NJ, 08550

TAMERLER, CANDAN, T: Wesley G. Cramer Professor **I:** Education/Educational Services **CN:** The University of Kansas **ED:** PhD in Chemical Engi-

neering, Bogazici University (1997); MSc in Chemical Engineering, Bogazici University (1991); BSc in Chemical Engineering, Bogazici University (1989) **CT:** "Design of Bioreactors," MED-CAMPUS, INETI-Portugal Engineering, Technology and Innovation Institute, Lisbon, Portugal; "Protein Structure, Function & Design," NATO/ASI: NATO Science Committee, Advanced Science Institute Series, Spetses, Greece; Downstream Processes in Biotechnology, MED-CAMPUS, Kusadasi, Turkey; Design and Operation Bioreactors, MED-CAMPUS, Kusadasi, Turkey; Purification of Biomolecules, MED-CAMPUS, Ege University, Izmir, Turkey; "Restriction Endonucleases and Modification, Methyltransferases," Federation of American Societies for Experimental Biology (FASEB), Vermont Academy; "Fermentation & Recovery of Biomolecules," MED-CAMPUS, Ege University, Izmir, Turkey; "Bacterial Genetics," International Centre for Genetic Engineering and Biotechnology (ICGEB), Trieste, Italy **C:** Associate Director, Bioengineering Program, The University of Kansas (2017-Present); Wesley G. Cramer Professor, Mechanical Engineering Department and Bioengineering Program, The University of Kansas (2016-Present); Core Director, Biomaterials & Tissue Engineering, Bioengineering Program, The University of Kansas (2014-Present); Director, Biomediated and Biomimetic Materials, Institute for Bioengineering, The University of Kansas (2013-Present); Affiliated Professor, Materials Science and Engineering Department, University of Washington, Seattle, WA (2013-Present); Wesley G. Cramer Associate Professor, Mechanical Engineering and Bioengineering, The University of Kansas (2013-2016); Research Professor, Materials Science and Engineering Department, University of Washington, Seattle, WA (2010-2013); Assistant Director, Genetically Engineered Materials Science (GEMSEC), an NSF/MRSEC, University of Washington, Seattle, WA (2010-2013); Associate Member, UNAM, National Nanotechnology Research Center, Bilkent University, Ankara, Turkey (2008-2010); Professor and Chair, Molecular Biology and Genetics Department, Istanbul Technical University, Istanbul, Turkey (2007-2010); TUBITAK National Expert, European Union Framework 7 on Nanoscience and Nanotechnology Area (TUBITAK: The Scientific and Technological Research Council of Turkey) (2006-2008); Founding and Executive Board Member, Genetically Engineered Materials Science (GEMSEC), an NSF/MRSEC, University of Washington, Seattle, WA (2005-2013); Executive Committee Member, TUBITAK-Genetic Engineering and Biotechnology Research Institute (2005-2006); Founding Director, Molecular Biology and Biotechnology Research Center, Istanbul Technical University, Istanbul, Turkey (2004-2010); Visiting Professor, Materials Science and Engineering Department, University of Washington, Seattle, WA (2002-2010); Associate Professor and Chair, Molecular Biology and Genetics Department, Istanbul, Turkey (2002-2007); Assistant Professor, Molecular Biology and Genetics Department, Istanbul Technical University (1999-2002); Postdoctoral Researcher, Molecular and Applied Biosciences, University of Westminster, London, England (1997-1999); Graduate Teaching Assistant, Chemical Engineering, Bogazici University, Istanbul, Turkey (1990-1997) **CR:** U.S. Delegation Member, The George C. Marshall Visit to Austria Program on "Advanced Materials," Vienna, Graz and Linz, Austria (2016); U.S. Delegation Member, USA-TR Joint Commission Meeting on Science & Technology Cooperation, Istanbul and Ankara, Turkey (2012); Visiting Scientist, Molecular & Applied Biosciences, University of Westminster, London, England; Visiting Professor, Green Mobility Research Center, Nagoya University, Japan; Served on Diverse Committees, Different Institutions Across Globe; Board of Trustees, Universi-

ty of Kansas Center for Research, Inc.; University Senate Ad-Hoc Committee on Gender Equity; Scientific Advisory Board, Center for Undergraduate Research; Search Committees for Associate Dean, Chair and Faculty Search at All Levels; Faculty Intellectual Property Committee; Bioengineering Program Leadership Committee, Bioengineering Program, The University of Kansas; Graduate Program Committees, Materials Science and Engineering, University of Washington; Molecular Biology & Biotechnology and Nanoscience and Nanotechnology, Istanbul Technical University; Co-chair, National Nanobiotechnology Network in Turkey; Deans Committee on "Improving Promotion and Tenure Criteria," Istanbul Technical University; Department Chair, Molecular Biology and Genetics, Istanbul Technical University; Founding Director, "Molecular Biology & Biotechnology Research Center (MOBGAM)," Istanbul Technical University; Accreditation and Continuous Improvement Committee, Istanbul Technical University **CW:** Author, More Than 140 Articles, Professional Journals; Author, Chapters; Author, Books; Patent in Field; National and International Plenaries, Keynote and Distinguished Seminars; Citations (>5900) and H-index (38) for Work; Editorial Board Member, Journals such as Advanced Engineering Materials, AIMS Bioengineering, Biomimetics, Surface Innovations, and Bioinspired, Biomimetic and Nanobiomaterials; Guest Editor on "Surfaces and Biointerfaces," "Surface Innovations," JOM: Journal of the Minerals, Metals and Materials Society, and "Biomaterials at Health Care"; Reviewer for Diverse Journals Including ACS Applied Materials and Interfaces, Acta Biomaterialia, Advanced Functional Materials, Annals of Biomedical Sciences, Applied Biochemistry and Biotechnology, Biochemistry, Biofabrication, Biomacromolecules, Biomaterials, Biopolymers, Biosensors, Biotechnology and Bioengineering, Biotechnology Journal, Biotechnology Letters, Colloids and Surfaces B: Biointerfaces, Enzyme and Microbial Technology, Journal of Biomedical Materials Research Part A, Journal of Chemical Technology and Biotechnology, Journal of Materials Research (JMR), Journal of the Royal Society Interface, Langmuir, Macromolecules, Macromolecular Biosciences, Macromolecular Materials and Engineering, Macromolecular Rapid Communications, Materials Science and Engineering C, Material Research Society Bulletin; Reviewer, Materials Research Society Proceedings, Nanomedicine and Nanobiotechnology Nanotechnology, RSC Advances, Science Advances, Trends in Biotechnology, and World Journal of Microbiology (WJM) **AW:** Grantee, Several Grants Supported by National and International Agencies including National Institutes of Health, National Science Foundation, European Union Framework Programs, TUBITAK: The Scientific and Technological Research Council of Turkey, Turkish State Planning Organization, Scientific Recognition Award, TUBITAK International Programs Office, Eureka Program, and University Research Awards (KU, UW and ITU) (2002-Present); Miller Professional Development & Recognition Award, School of Engineering, The University of Kansas (2016); Bellow Scholar Award, School of Engineering, The University of Kansas (2016); Cramer Award, Mechanical Engineering, The University of Kansas (2015); Miller Scholar Award, Mechanical Engineering, The University of Kansas (2014); Visiting Professor Fellowship Award, Green Mobility Collaborative Research Center-on Bioenabled Materials, Nagoya University, Japan (2013); Fellow, Turkish Academy of Sciences (2012); EU/MED-CAMPUS Fellowship, INETI-Portugal Engineering, Technology and Innovation Institute, Lisbon, Portugal (1996); NATO/ASI Fellowship, NATO Science Committee, Advanced Science Institute Series: Protein

Structure and Function, Spetses, Greece (1995); FASEB Fellowship, Federation of American Societies for Experimental Biology, Vermont Academy (1993); UNIDO/ICGEB Fellowship, International Centre for Genetic Engineering and Biotechnology (ICGEB), Trieste, Italy (1991); Fellowship, Chemical and Bioprocess Engineering, Hamburg Technical University (1989); Fellow, NATO/B1, European MED-CAMPUS Programs, Hamburg University of Technology, Hamburg, Germany; Scholar, Unilever Scholarship Program, Successful Engineering Undergraduate Students; Fellow, American Institute of Medical and Biological Engineering (AIMBE); Fellow, Turkish National Academy of Science **MEM:** Honorary Member, Pi Tau Sigma International ME Honors Society (2013); The Minerals, Metals & Materials Society (TMS); Materials Research Society (MRS); American Association for the Advancement of Science (AAAS); Society of Biomaterials; Turkish-American Scientists & Scholars Associations (TASSA) **MH:** Albert Nelson Marquis Lifetime Achievement Award (2017) **H:** Drawing; Photography; Birdwatching; Traveling **ADD:** 2712 Coralberry Ct, Lawrence, KS, 66047 **URL:** http://www.tamerlerlab.com/

TANESI, JUSSARA, T: Concrete Materials Researcher **I:** Research **CN:** SES Group & Associates, LLC **DOB:** 07/09/1970 **PB:** Sao Paulo **SC:** Brazil **MS:** Married **SPN:** Wael Tanesi (2000) **CH:** Rebecca **ED:** PhD in Civil Engineering, Universidade Estadual de Campinas, Brazil (2010); MSC, Sao Paulo University (1998); BSC, Universidade Estadual de Campinas (1995) **C:** Concrete Materials Researcher and Lab Manager, SES Group & Associates LLC (2002-Present); Consultant, Portland Cement Association, Illinois (2001-2002); Consultant, Brazilian Portland Cement Association, Sao Paulo, Brazil (1998-2001); Professor, Universidade Bandeirante, Sao Paulo, Brazil (1997-2001) **CR:** Organizer, Contractors Day, ACI Fall Convention (2014); ACI Sessions Organizer, Moderator; TRB Session Moderator; Technical Reviewer, National Science Foundation; Technical Reviewer, ACI Materials Journal, American Concrete Institute; Technical Reviewer, Journal of Materials in Civil Engineering, American Society of Civil Engineers; Technical Reviewer, Journal of Materials and Structures, Springer; Technical Reviewer, Advances in Civil Engineering Materials, ASTM; Technical Reviewer, Construction & Building Materials, Elsevier; Technical Reviewer, Journal of Cement and Concrete Composites, Elsevier; Technical Reviewer, Transportation Research Record, TRB; Technical Reviewer, Materials, MDPI; Technical Reviewer, International Journal of Pavement Engineering, Taylor and Francis; Technical Reviewer, International Society for Concrete Pavements Conferences; Technical Reviewer, Many Conferences; Judge, ACI Workability Competition **CIV:** Volunteer, Parent Liaison, Basis Independent McLean; Volunteer Sunday School Teacher, McLean Bible Church **CW:** Co-author, "Influence of Aggregate Characteristics on Concrete Performance," NIST Technical Note 1963, National Institute of Standards and Technology, Gaithersburg, MD (2017); Co-author, "Evaluation of the Specimen Saturation Criterion for the AASHTO T336 Test Method," Advances in Civil Engineering Materials (2017); Co-author, "Super Air Meter for Assessing Air-Void System of Fresh Concrete", ASTM Advances in Civil engineering Materials Journal (2016); Co-author, "The effect of nano materials on HVFA mixtures" Fifth International Symposium on Nanotechnology in Construction (NICOM-5), Springer International Publishing (2015); Co-author, "Multiscale investigation of the performance of limestone concrete", Construction and Building Materials (2015); Co-author, "Interlaboratory Study and Precision Statement for the AASHTO T 336 Test Method," Transportation Research Record, Journal of the Transportation Research Board, Transportation Research Board of National Academies, Washington, D.C. (2015); Co-author, "Effects of Nanomaterials on the Hydration Kinetics and Rheology of Portland Cement Pastes. Advances in Civil Engineering Materials", Journal of the American Society for Testing and Materials, ASTM (2014); Co-author, "Enhancing the Performance of High Volume Fly Ash Concretes Using Fine Limestone Powder," ACI SP 294 – Advances in Green Binder Systems, American Concrete Institute, Michigan (2013); Co-author, "Isothermal Calorimetry as a Tool to Evaluate Early Age Performance of Fly Ash Mixtures" Transportation Research Record, Journal of the Transportation Research Board, Transportation Research Board of National Academies, Washington, D.C. (2013); Co-author, "Ruggedness Study on the Coefficient of Thermal Expansion of Concrete Test Method (AASHTO T336)", Transportation Research Record, Journal of the Transportation Research Board, Transportation Research Board of National Academies, Washington, D.C. (2013); Co-author, "Reducing the Specimen Size of Concrete Flexural Strength Test (AASHTO T97) for Safety and Ease of Handling," Transportation Research Record, Journal of the Transportation Research Board, Transportation Research Board of National Academies, Washington, D.C. (2013); Co-author, "Guidelines for the development of concrete performance-based specifications in Brazil", IBRACON Structures and Materials Journal, Brazil (2012); Co-author, "Evaluation of High-Volume Fly Ash (HVFA) Mixtures (Paste And Mortar Components) Using a Dynamic Shear Rheometer (DSR) and an Isothermal Calorimeter", NTIS Report (2012); Co-author, "New AASHTO 336-09 Coefficient of thermal expansion test method: how will it affect you?," Transportation Research Record, Journal of the Transportation Research Board, Transportation Research Board of National Academies, Washington, D.C. (2010); Co-author, "Interlaboratory Study on Measuring Coefficient of Thermal Expansion of Concrete," Transportation Research Record, Journal of the Transportation Research Board, Transportation Research Board of National Academies, Washington, D.C. (2010); Co-author, "From prescription to performance: international trends on concrete specifications and the Brazilian Perspective", IBRACON Structures and Materials Journal, Brazil (2010); Editor, "SP 266 Modeling As a Solution to Concrete Problems", American Concrete Institute, Michigan (2009); Co-author, Durability of an Ultra high-Performance Concrete", ASCE Journal of Materials in Civil Engineering (2007); Co-author, "Freeze-Thaw Resistance of Concrete with Marginal Air Content", Transportation Research Record, Journal of the Transportation Research Board, Transportation Research Board of National Academies, Washington, D.C. (2007); Co-author, "Effect of CTE test variability on concrete pavement performance as predicted using the mechanistic-empirical pavement design guide," Transportation Research Record, Journal of the Transportation Research Board, Transportation Research Board of National Academies, Washington, D.C. (2007); Co-author, "Freeze-thaw resistance of concrete with marginal air content," Federal Highway Administration (2006); Contributor, "Central and South American Cement - Standards and Specifications", Portland Cement Association, Illinois (2004); Co-author, "Diseno y Control de Mezclas de Concreto", Portland Cement Association, Illinois (2004); Co-author, "Guia del albanil," Portland Cement Association. Spanish version of Cement Mason's Guide to Building Concrete Walls, Drives, Patios and Steps, Illinois (2003) **AW:** Fellow, American Concrete Institute (2015); Appreciation Award, ASTM (2014); Young Member Award for Professional Achievement, ACI (2009); CNPQ Graduate Scholarship (1996-1998) **MEM:** Transportation Research Board, TRB AFN30 and TRB AFH50; American Concrete Institute; ACI211; ACI231; ACI236; ACI238; ACI241; ACI325; ASTM Member-at-Large; International Society for Concrete Pavements **BA:** 6300 Georgetown Pike, SES Group and Associates, McLean, VA, 22101 **ADD:** 8380 Greensboro Dr Unit 1007, McLean, VA, 22102

TANGHERLINI, FRANK ROBERT, T: Physics Professor **I:** Education/Educational Services **DOB:** 03/14/1924 **PB:** Boston **SC:** MA/USA **PT:** Emiliano Francesco Tangherlini; Rosa (Robinson) Leclaire Tangherlini **MS:** Divorced **SPN:** Jane Kjaergaard Kjems (1/2/1960, Divorced 1979) **CH:** Arne E.(Deceased); Timothy R.; Daniel M.; Niels L. **ED:** PhD in Physics, Stanford University, California (1959); MS in Physics, The University of Chicago (1952); SB in Physics, Harvard University, Cum Laude, Cambridge, MA (1948) **C:** Emeritus, College of the Holy Cross, Worcester, MA (1994-Present); Associate Professor, College of the Holy Cross, Worcester, MA (1967-1994); Science Associate, Danish Space Research Institute, Lyngby, Denmark (1966-1967); Associate Professor, The George Washington University, Washington, D.C. (1964-1966); Assistant Professor, Duke University, Durham, NC (1961-1964); Research Associate, The University of North Carolina at Chapel Hill (1960-1961); Postdoctoral Fellow, National Science Foundation, Copenhagen, Naples (1958-1960); Research Engineer, Convair-Gen. Dynamics, San Diego, CA (1952-1955) **CR:** Visiting Scientist, International Center for Theoretical Physics, Trieste, Italy (1973-1974) **CIV:** Chairman, Cub Scouts of America, Auburn, MA (1975-1977) **MIL:** European Theater of Operations, U.S. Army (1944-1945); U.S. Army (1943-1946) **CW:** Contributor, "A Possible Alternative to the Accelerating Universe III," Journal of Modern Physics (2016); Contributor, "A Possible Alternative to the Accelerating Universe IV," Journal of Modern Physics (2016); Contributor, "Einstein and Gravitation," American Physical Society Newsletter (2016); Contributor, "A Possible Alternative to the Accelerating Universe," "A Possible Alternative to the Accelerating Universe II," Journal of Modern Physics (2015); Contributor, "Schr¶dinger's Radial Equation Letter," Physics Today (2015); Contributor, "Galilean-Like Transformation Allowed by General Covariance and Consistent with Special Relativity," Journal of Modern Physics (2014); Contributor, "Einstein's Pseudo-Tensor in Spatial Dimensions for Static Systems with Spherical Symmetry," Journal of Modern Physics (2013); Author, "The Velocity of Light in Uniformly Moving Frame" (2009); Contributor, "Maxwell's Equations and the Absolute Lorentz Transformation," The Abraham Zelmanov Journal (2009); Contributor, "A New Method of Fighting Wildfires," San Diego Union Tribune (2009); Contributor, "Canonical Commutation Relations and Special Relativity," Physica Scripta (2008); Author, "Little Katrina's Yellow Flower," "Thoughts on the Accelerating Universe," Dan River Anthology, Dan River Press, Thomaston, ME (2007); Author, "Love is Not Always Commutative" (2004); Author, "Introduction to the General Theory of Relativity, Chinese Translation" (1965); Author, "Introduction to the General Theory of Relativity" (1961); Author, "Catholic Girl and Atheist" (1947); Contributor, Articles, Professional Journals **AW:** Visiting Scholar, Harvard University (1988-1989); Travel Grantee, National Science Foundation (1984, 1980) **MEM:** American Association of University Professors; International Society on General Relativity and Gravitation; American Physical Society; Balboa Tennis Club; University of Chicago Club, San

Diego, CA; Harvard Club, San Diego, CA: Stanford Club, San Diego, CA; Sigma Xi **MH:** Albert Nelson Marquis Lifetime Achievement Award (2017) **H:** Poetry; History; Philosophy; Jogging; Dance; Tennis **BA:** PO Box 928211, San Diego, CA, 92192

TANNER, JIMMIE EUGENE, T: Dean (Retired) **I:** Education/Educational Services **DOB:** 09/27/1933 **PB:** Hartford **SC:** AR/USA **PT:** Alford C. Tanner; Hazel Ame (Anthony) Tanner **MS:** Married **SPN:** Carole Joy Yant (8/28/1958) **CH:** Leslie Allison; Kevin Don **ED:** PhD in English, The University of Oklahoma (1964); MA, The University of Oklahoma (1957); BA, Oklahoma Baptist University (1955) **C:** Professor, William Jewell College (1997-2003); Interim President, William Jewell College, Liberty, MO (1993-1994); Dean, William Jewell College, Liberty, MO (1980-1997); Vice President, Academic Affairs, Louisiana College, Pineville, LA (1978-1980); Vice President, Academic Affairs, Hardin-Simmons University, Abilene, TX (1972-1978); Professor, English, Oklahoma Baptist University, Shawnee, OK (1965-1972); Associate Professor, Franklin College, Franklin, IN (1964-1965); Professor, English, Oklahoma Baptist University, Shawnee, OK (1958-1964) **CIV:** Board of Directors, Missouri Council for Humanities (2003-2010); Member, Education Commission, Southern Baptist Convention (1967-1972); Member, Shawnee School Board (1966-1972) **MIL:** Captain, US Army Reserve **CW:** Contributing Author, "The Annotated Bibliography of D. H. Lawrence, Volume Two" (1985); Contributing Author, "The Annotated Bibliography of D. H. Lawrence, Volume One" (1982) **AW:** REcipient, Danforth Fellowship (1962-1963); Fellow, Southern Fellowships Fund (1960-1961) **MEM:** Sons of the American Revolution **MH:** Albert Nelson Marquis Lifetime Achievement Award (2017) **H:** Tennis; Photography **PA:** Democrat **RE:** Baptist **ADD:** 8559 N Line Creek Pkwy Apt 114, Kansas City, MO, 64154

TARDIFF-KOZLOWSKI, JILL A., T: Professional Cheesemonger, Customer-service Specialist **I:** Food & Restaurant Services **DOB:** 04/08/1953 **PB:** Morristown **SC:** NJ/USA **PT:** Howard James Tardiff; Jean Elizabeth (Cook) Tardiff **MS:** Single **SPN:** Paul Edward Kozlowski (February 11, 1984 - June 25, 2014) (Deceased) **ED:** Student, Institute of Culinary Education (2015-Present); Student, Training Program in Essential Foundations and Affinage, Academie Opus Caseus (2015, 2017); Student, The Cheese Course, Murray's Cheese (2007-2009, 2017); Cheese-Making Student, Artisanal Premium Cheese Center, Artisanal Premium Cheese (2007); Student, Language Center, Japan Society, New York, NY (1986-1997); Graduate Study in Film History, New York University (1981-1983); Graduate Study in Art History, Syracuse University (1975-1977); BA in Liberal Arts, College of Saint Elizabeth (1975) **CT:** Certification of Completion, Academie Opus Caseus (2015); Certified in Language Studies, Japan Society (2015); Certified Art Teacher, K-12, State of New Jersey (1975) **C:** Professional Cheesemonger, Customer-service Specialist (2017-Present); Saxelby Cheesemongers; Self-Proprietor, Bamboo River Associates, Hoboken, NJ; Manager, Lucy's Whey Artisanal Cheese, New York, NY (2016-2017); Lead Cheesemonger, Lucy's Whey Artisanal Cheese (2015-2016); Pre-flight Coordinator, "The Search for Meaning," Parabola Magazine (2010-2016); Cheesemonger, Lucy's Whey Artisanal Cheese (2012-2015); Cheesemonger, Beecher's (2011-2012); Advertising Manager, Guernica (2010-2011) Contributing Editor, PWxyz, LLC., New York, NY (1996-2011); Project Manager, PWxyz, LLC., New York, NY (1996-2011); Advertising Manager, "Where Spiritual Traditions Meet," Parabola Magazine (2006-2010); Customer Service Representative, Murray's Cheese (2007-2008); Advertising Manager, Persimmon: Asian Literature,

Arts and Culture (1999-2002); Associate Editor, R.R. Bowker LLC. (1995-1998); Managing Editor, Lintel Press, Inc. (1993-1994); Senior Researcher, Lintel Press, Inc. (1993-1994); Sales Manager, T&CO., New York, NY (1991-1993); General Manager, Doubleday Book Shops (1981-1991); Retail Manager, Hallmark, New York, NY (1976-1981) **CR:** Member-at-Large, Member Services Committee, American Cheese Society (2016-Present); Chair, National Reading Group Month, Women's National Book Association (2006-Present); Main Representative, United Nations Department of Public Information/NGO, Women's National Book Association (2000-Present); Social Media Administrator, American Cheese Society (2010-2014); Secretary, Board of Directors, Contemporary Asian Culture Inc. (1999-2013); Social Media Administrator, Beecher's (2011-2012); Professional Speaker, Bamboo River Associates (1991-2008); Tour Facilitator, Bamboo River Associates (1991-2008); Immediate Past National President, Women's National Book Association (2006-2008); National President, Women's National Book Association (2004-2006); President, New York City Chapter, Women's National Book Association (2000-2006); Participating Judge, New Hampshire Literary Award (2005); Advisory Board Member, Women's Ink, New York, NY (1999-2004); National Vice President, Women's National Book Association (2002-2004); President-Elect, Women's National Book Association (2002-2004); Newsletter Vice President, New York City Chapter, Women's National Book Association (1997-2000) **CW:** Columnist, Shinbunka Weekly (1995-2001); Contributing Editor, Kondasha Ltd. (1993-2000); Contributing Editor, Shueisha Inc. (1995-2000); Newsletter Publisher/Editor-in-Chief, Reading America (1993-1997); Contributor, Book Series, "Bob Vila's Guide to Historic Homes" **AW:** Recipient, The Albert Nelson Marquis Lifetime Achievement Award (2017) **MEM:** Extraordinary Women in Publishing; Honorary Member, International Women's Writing Guild; PEN America; PAMA; AAUW; American Cheese Society; Culinary Historians of NY; Food Tank; Japan Society; New York City Chapter, Slow Food USA; Women's National Book Association **MH:** Albert Nelson Marquis Lifetime Achievement Award (2017) **H:** Bird-watching and identification; Cheese making; Concerts; Gardening; Outdoor cycling; Hiking; Recreational travel; Recreational cooking; Reading group facilitation; Semi-professional photography **PA:** Independent **RE:** Roman Catholic **ADD:** 625 Madison St Apt 2, Hoboken, NJ, 07030

TAYLOR, STEPHEN MARL, T: Psychiatrist, Medical Director **I:** Medicine & Health Care **CN:** Stephen M. Taylor, MD, PC **ED:** Fellow, Division of Alcoholism and Drug Abuse, Department of Psychiatry, New York University Medical Center, Bellevue Hospital Center (1994-1996); Resident, Triple Board Residency Training Program in Pediatrics, General Psychiatry and Child Psychiatry, Albert Einstein College of Medicine, Bronx, NY (1989-1994); MPH, Harvard School of Public Health, Boston, MA (1989); MD, Howard University College of Medicine, Washington, DC (1988); BA in History and Science, Harvard University, Cambridge, MA, Cum Laude (1984) **CT:** Addiction Psychiatry, American Board of Psychiatry and Neurology (2010); Medical Review Officer, Medical Review Officer Certification Council (2003); Addiction Medicine, American Society of Addiction Medicine (2001); Child and Adolescent Psychiatry, American Board of Psychiatry and Neurology (1999); General Psychiatry, American Board of Psychiatry and Neurology (1998-2008); License to Practice Medicine, State of Alabama Medical Licensure Commission, State of Alabama (1996-2017);

Certified, Alabama Controlled Substances (1996-2017); License to Practice Medicine, Education Department, State University of New York, State of New York (1991); Registered, Drug Enforcement Administration (1991) **C:** Medical Director, National Basketball Players' Association Player Assistance/Anti-Drug Program (2007-Present); Private Solo Practice in General Psychiatry, Child/Adolescent Psychiatry and Addiction Psychiatry, Birmingham, AL (2007-Present); Private Group Practice in General Psychiatry, Child/Adolescent Psychiatry and Addiction Psychiatry with Child and Adolescent Associates, PC, Birmingham, AL (2005-2007); Private Solo Practice, General Psychiatry, Child/Adolescent Psychiatry and Addiction Psychiatry, Longwood Psychological Center (2003-2005); Private Group Practice, Alabama Psychiatric Services, P.C. (1999-2003); Private Group Practice, Valley Counseling Center, P.C (1999); Attending Psychiatrist, Huntsville Hospital, Huntsville, AL (1998-2004); Attending Psychiatrist, Huntsville Hospital, Huntsville, AL (1996-1998); Attending Psychiatrist, Crestwood Medical Center of Huntsville, Huntsville, AL (1996-2004); General Psychiatrist, Child/Adolescent Psychiatrist and Addiction Psychiatrist, North Alabama Psychiatric Services, Huntsville, AL (1996-1998); Medical Director, Alcohol Detoxification Unit, Bellevue Hospital Center, New York, NY (1995-1996); Attending Pediatrician and Child/Adolescent Psychiatrist, Bronx Children's Psychiatric Center (1995-1996); Private Practice in General Psychiatry, Child/Adolescent Psychiatry, and Addiction Psychiatry, Pelham, NY (1994-1996) **CR:** Assistant Professor of Psychiatry, School of Medicine, University of Alabama at Birmingham, Huntsville Campus (1998-2004); Fellow, American Society of Addiction Medicine **CIV:** Board of Directors, Pathway Healthcare, Dallas, TX (2017-Present); Board of Directors, All-In Mountain Brook (2014-Present); Board of Directors, Medical Review Officer Certification Council (2014-Present); Board of Directors, Mental Health Association, Madison County, AL (2002-2004); Board of Directors, Alcoholism Council/Fellowship Center of New York (1995-1996); Board of Directors, Partnership for a Drug-Free Community, Huntsville, AL (1994-2004) **AW:** Certificate for Academic Excellence, American Academic of Addiction Psychiatry (1996); American Academy of Addiction Psychiatrists Award for Excellence in Research and Teaching (1994); John Harvard Honorary Scholarship for Academic Excellence (1983-1984) **MEM:** American Academy of Child and Adolescent Psychiatry; American Academy of Addiction Psychiatry; National Medical Association; Alabama Regional Council of Child and Adolescent Psychiatry; International Society of Sports Psychiatry; Medical Association of the State of Alabama; Board of Trustees, Madison County Medical Society **BA:** 3500 Blue Lake Drive, Suite 260, Vestavia, AL, 35243

TEEM, PAUL LLOYD JR., T: Bank Executive (Retired) **I:** Financial Services **DOB:** 03/10/1948 **PB:** Gastonia **SC:** NC/USA **PT:** Paul Lloyd Teem Sr.; Ruth Elaine (Bennett) Teem **ED:** Degree of Distinction, Institute of Financial Education, Chicago, IL (1989); Diploma, Institute of Financial Education, Chicago, IL (1985); BA, University of North Carolina at Charlotte (1970) **CT:** Certificate, Institute of Financial Education, Chicago, IL (1984); Certified Teacher, States of North Carolina, Virginia and New Jersey; Certified Consumer Credit Executive; Licensed Real Estate Broker, State of North Carolina; Licensed Lay Reader and Lay Eucharistic Minister, Episcopal Church **C:** Executive Vice President, Secretary, Citizens South Banking Corporation, Gastonia, NC (1998-2012); Executive Vice President, Secretary, Citizens South Holdings, Mutual Holding Company, Gastonia, NC (1998-2002); Executive Vice President, Secretary, Board of Directors, Citizens South Financial Services Inc, Gastonia, NC (1988-2012); Executive Vice President, Secretary, Chief Administrative Officer, Citizens South Bank, Gastonia, NC (1983-2012) **CIV:** Board of Directors, Gastonia Masonic Temple Association, Inc. (1981-2018); Board of Directors, Gastonia Merchants Association, Inc. (1981-1983); Lay Reader, Lay Eucharistic Minister, Episcopal Church **AW:** Honoree, The Order of the Long Leaf Pine, The State of North Carolina (2016); Commissioned, Kentucky Colonel, The Commonwealth of Kentucky (1995); Honoree, Order of the Purple Cross of York, The York Rite Sovereign College (1990); Honoree, Legion of Honor, The Order of DeMolay International (1989); Recipient, Gold Honor Award, The York Rite Sovereign College (1988); Recipient, Distinguished Service Award, The York Rite Sovereign College (1987); Recipient, Excellence in Community Service Award, The National Society of the Daughters of the American Revolution (2015); Fellow, Society of Certified Credit Executives; Inductee, Freemason, The Grand Lodge of Ancient, Free and Accepted Masons; Inductee, Royal Order of Scotland; Inductee, Order of DeMolay International **MEM:** Order of the Purple Cross of York (1990); Legion of Honor (1989); Knights Templar (1973); 32nd Degree Ancient and Accepted Mason (1973); Freemason, The Grand Lodge of Ancient, Free and Accepted Masons (1973); Shriners International (1973); Royal Order of Scotland; National Society of Sons and Daughters of the Pilgrims; National Society of Sons and Daughters of Antebellum Planters; Sons of the American Revolution; Sons of Confederate Veterans; Military Order of Stars and Bars; National Order of the Blue and Gray; Honorable Order of Kentucky Colonels; Phi Alpha Theta; Gaston County Historical Society **MH:** Albert Nelson Marquis Lifetime Achievement Award (2017) **H:** Genealogy **PA:** Republican **RE:** Episcopalian **ADD:** 1208 Poston Circle, Gastonia, NC, 28054

TEMAM, ROGER M., T: Distinguished Professor, Mathematician **I:** Education/Educational Services **CN:** Indiana University **DOB:** 05/19/1940 **PB:** Tunis **SC:** Tunisia **PT:** Ange M. Temam; Elise (Ganem) Temam **MS:** Married **SPN:** Claudette Cukorja (8/21/1962) **CH:** David; Olivier; Emmanuel **ED:** DSc, University of Paris (1967); Master's Degree in Mathematics, University of Paris (1962) **C:** Distinguished Professor, Indiana University (2014-Present); Emeritus Professor, University of Paris (2003-Present); Director, Institute of Scientific Computing and Applied Mathematics, Indiana University, Bloomington, IN (1986-Present); Professor, University of Paris (1967-2003); Assistant Professor of Mathematics, University of Paris (1960-1967) **CR:** Honorary Professor, Lanzhou University (2012); Honorary Professor, Xi'an Jiaotang University (2010); Honorary Professor, Fudan University (1996); Professor, Ecole Polytechnique, Paris, France (1968-1985) **CW:** Author, "Mathematical Problems in Plasticity", Review Edition (2018); Co-author, "Navier-Stokes Equations and Turbulence" (2001); Author, "Numerical Analysis, Second Edition (2001); Author, "Navier-Stokes Equations, Review Edition" (2001); Co-author, "Dynamic Multilevel Methods and the Numerical Simulation of Turbulence" (1999); Co-author, "Convex Analysis and Variational Problems, Review Edition (1999); Author, "Infinite Dimensional Dynamical Systems in Mechanics and Physics, Second Edition" (1997); Author, "Infinite Dimensional Dynamical Systems in Mechanics and Physics" (1988); Author, "Mathematical Problems in Plasticity" (1983); Author, "Navier-Stokes Equations" (1977);

Co-author, "Convex Analysis and Variational Problems" (1976); Author, "Numerical Analysis" (1969); Associate Editor, Professional Journals; Contributor, Articles to Professional Journals **AW:** Elected Fellow, American Academy of Arts and Sciences (2014); Most Prolific Advisor in Mathematics, Mathematics Genealogy Project; Recipient, Several Prizes **MEM:** French Academy of Sciences (2007-Present); First President, French Chapter, Society for Industrial and Applied Mathematics (1983-1987); Fellow, American Association for the Advancement of Science; American Academy of Arts and Sciences; American Mathematical Society; New York Academy of Sciences **MH:** Albert Nelson Marquis Lifetime Achievement Award (2017) **BA:** 831 E 3rd Street, Indiana University, Math Department, Rawles Hall, Bloomington, IN, 47405

TETTERTON, HOLLI Y., T: Director of Human Resources and Accounts Payable **I:** Medicine & Health Care **CN:** Albemarle Eye Center/Precision Eye Care **ED:** Bachelor's Degree in Health Care Management, University of Mount Olive (2015); Coursework, Trust and Investment Management, Campbell University **CT:** Certificate in Human Resource Management, Continuing Studies, Duke University (2016); Ophthalmic Scribe Certificate (2015-2018); Certified Ophthalmic Assistant (2012-2015) **C:** Director of Human Resources and Accounts Payable, Albemarle Eye Center/Precision Eye Care (2015-Present); COA, Precision Eye Care (2009-2015); OSC, Precision Eye Care (2009-2015); Clinical Supervisor, Precision Eye Care (2009-2015) **ADD:** 1730 Carolina Ave, Washington, NC, 27889 **URL:** http://www.precisioneyecarenc.com

THEIS, POL, T: Founder **I:** Architecture & Construction **CN:** P&T Interiors **SC:** Luxembourg **ED:** Master's Degree in Business and Economic Law, Paris-Sorbonne University (1995); Master's Degree in Business and Tax Law, Pantheon-Assas University (1993) **C:** Founder, Principal, P&T Interiors (2002-Present); Attorney, Stibbe Simont Monahan Duhot; Attorney, Haarmann Hemmelrath; Attorney, Wildgen Spielmann & Ries, Luxembourg **CW:** Contributor, Interior Design Work, Over 50 Professional Journals (2006-Present); Featured Designer, "East Coast Modern: Contemporary Residential Architecture and Interiors" (2013); Featured Designer, "Luxury Interiors" (2013); Featured Designer, "Interiors New York" (2012-2013) **AW:** Top 50 Designers, New York Spaces (2017); Best Interior Design Apartment, American Property Awards (2015); Top 50 Designers, New York Spaces (2012-2014); International Property Awards, Bloomberg Television (2011); Profile, New York Home Magazine; Profile, The Wall Street Journal **BAR:** Luxembourg (1995) **H:** Travel; Cooking **BA:** 336 W 37th Street, Room 420, P&T Interiors, New York, NY, 10018 **URL:** http://www.pandtinteriors.com

THEON, JOHN S., T: Meteorologist **I:** Sciences **CN:** National Aeronautics and Space Administration **DOB:** 12/12/1934 **PB:** Washington **SC:** DC/USA **PT:** Lewis Theon; Merope Theon **MS:** Married **SPN:** Joanne Edens (7/31/1965) **CH:** Christopher James; Catherine **ED:** PhD in Engineering Science, Mechanics and Atmosphere Turbulence, The University of Tennessee, Knoxville (1985); MS, The Pennsylvania State University (1962); BS in Meteorology, The Pennsylvania State University (1959); BS in Aeronautical Engineering, University of Maryland (1957) **CT:** Aeronautical Engineering, University of Maryland (1957) **C:** Consultant, National Aeronautics and Space Administration (1995-2012); Executive Secretary Interagency Task Force on Observations and Data Management,

National Aeronautics and Space Administration (1984-1995); Program Scientist, Tropical Rainfall Measuring Mission (1984-1995); Chief of Climate Processes Research Program, National Aeronautics and Space Administration (1990-1994); Program Scientist, Spacelab Three Mission, National Aeronautics and Space Administration (1982-1990); Program Scientist, Global Weather Research Program, National Aeronautics and Space Administration (1978-1982); Nimbus Project Scientist, Atmospheric Sciences, National Aeronautics and Space Administration (1972-1978); Assistant Chief of Laboratory for Atmospheric Sciences, National Aeronautics and Space Administration (1977-1978); Head of Meteorology Branch, Goddard Space Flight Center, National Aeronautics and Space Administration (1974-1977); Research Meteorologist (1962-1974); Engineer, U.S. Naval Ordnance Laboratory (1962); Aeronautical Engineer, Douglas Aircraft Company (1957-1958); Chief of Atmospheric Dynamics and Radiation Program, National Aeronautics and Space Administration **CR:** Consultant, The George Washington University, Washington (2005-2014); Consultant, National Aeronautics and Space Administration (2005-2009); Consultant, Institute for Global Environmental Strategies (1995-2005); Consultant, Jet Propulsion Laboratory, California Institute of Technology (1997-1999); Orbital ATK, Inc (1995-1996); Federal Senior Executive Service, National Aeronautics and Space Administration (1982-1995) **CIV:** Northern Virginia Knights of the Round Table **MIL:** Weather Officer, U.S. Air Force (1958-1960) **CW:** Featured Interviewee, "Global Warming War" (2016); "Climate Hustle" (2017); Contributor, Articles, Professional Journals **AW:** Recipient, Radio Wave Award, Ministry Of Posts and Telecommunications, Japan (1995); Honoree, Named Distinguished Alumnus, The University of Tennessee, Knoxville (1989); Recipient,NASA Exceptional Performance Award, National Aeronautics and Space Administration (1986); Recipient, Goddard Exceptional Performance Award (1978) **MEM:** Fellow, American Meteorological Society; Associate Fellow, AIAA; American Geophysical Union **MH:** Albert Nelson Marquis Lifetime Achievement Award (2017) **H:** Educational trips to famous historical sites in the USA and Europe **RE:** Presbyterian **ADD:** 6801 Lupine Ln, McLean, VA, 22101

THEURER, BYRON W., T: Aerospace Engineer, Business Owner **I:** Engineering **DOB:** 07/01/1939 **PB:** Glendale **SC:** CA/USA **PT:** William Louis Theurer; Roberta Cecilia (Sturgiss) Theurer **MS:** Married **SPN:** Patricia Ann Pilcher (11/2002); Sue Ann McKay (9/15/1962, Divorced 1980) **CH:** Karen Marie; William Thomas; Allison Lee **ED:** MBA, University of Redlands (1991); MS in Aeronautical Science, University of California, Berkeley (1965); BS in Engineering Science, United States Air Force Academy (1961); Graduate, Industrial College of the Armed Forces (Now National Defense University) and the Systems Management College Department of Defense (Now Defense Acquisition University) **C:** Counselor, SCORE Association (2002-2007); Founder & Owner, The Princeton Review of Central California, TPR Education IP Holdings, LLC, San Luis Obispo, CA (1993-2001); Operator, The Princeton Review of Central California, TPR Education IP Holdings, LLC, San Luis Obispo, CA (1993-2001); Founder & Owner, The Princeton Review of Central California, TPR Education IP Holdings, LLC, Ridgecrest, CA (1989-1992); Operator, The Princeton Review of Central California, TPR Education IP Holdings, LLC, Ridgecrest, CA (1989-1992); Project Manager, CTA Inc. (Now Computer Technology Associates, Inc.), Ridgecrest, CA (1985-1989); Project Manager,

Support Systems Associates, Inc., Dayton, Ohio (1983-1984); Senior Engineer, Logicon Inc., Dayton, Ohio (1981-1983); Senior Engineer, Veda, Inc., Dayton, Ohio (1979-1981); Chief of Test, F-15 Systems Progressive Office, Wright-Patterson Air Force Base, Ohio (1976-1978); Project Officer, Space Shuttle Development Program, Houston, Texas (1971-1976) **CR:** Consultant in Field **CIV:** Member, Ivins Economic Development Committee (2009-Present) **MIL:** Lieutenant Colonel, United States Air Force (1978); Commissioned Officer, United States Air Force (1961); Interceptor Pilot, United States Air Force; Combat Forward Air Controller, United States Air Force, Southeast Asia; Instructor, USAF Test Pilot School (Now Edwards Air Force Base); Student, USAF Test Pilot School (Now Edwards Air Force Base) **AW:** Honoree, Named First-Ever Officer of The Year, Air Force Flight Test Center, Edwards Air Force Base (1970); Recipient, Decorated Silver Star; Recipient, Distinguished Flying Cross; Recipient 16 Air Medals **MEM:** Chapter President, Association of Graduates of the United States Air Force Academy (1981-1983); National Board of Directors, Association of Graduates of the United States Air Force Academy (1972-1975); Air Force Association; LVVSA; SCORE Association **MH:** Albert Nelson Marquis Lifetime Achievement Award (2017) **H:** Walking; Sports; Flying **ADD:** 387 E 800 S, Ivins, UT, 84738

THOMAS, JOYCE MARIE MARIE, I: Medicine & Health Care **CN:** Cleveland Medical Center **PT:** Joseph Kerritan; Laura Kerritan **ED:** MS, Grand Canyon University (2013) **C:** Nurse Manager, University Hospitals, Cleveland Medical Center (2006-Present) **AW:** Second Place for Research Presentation, Ohio Organization of Nurse Executives (2013)

THOMAS, LINDSEY KAY JR., T: Research Ecology Biologist, Educator, Consultant **I:** Education/Educational Services **DOB:** 04/16/1931 **PB:** Salt Lake City **SC:** UT/USA **PT:** Lindsey Kay Thomas; Naomi Lurie (Biesinger) Thomas **MS:** Married **SPN:** Nancy Ruth Van Dyke (8/24/1956, Deceased 2002) **CH:** Elizabeth Nan Thomas Reid; David Lindsey; Wayne Hal; Dorothy Ann Thomas Brown **ED:** Honorary PhD, University of Cambridge, England (2013); PhD, Duke University, Durham, NC (1974); MS in Genetics and Ecology, Brigham Young University, Provo, UT (1958); BS in Botany, Agricultural College of Utah (Now Utah State University), Logan, UT (1953) **C:** Research Ecologist Emeritus, Consultant, National Capital Region, National Park Service (1998-Present); Resource Management Specialist, National Capital Parks-East (1996-1998); Resource Management Specialist, Baltimore-Washington Parkway, Greenbelt, MD (1996); Research Biologist, Patuxent Environmental Science Center, National Biological Service, Triangle, VA (1995-1996); Research Biologist, Patuxent Environmental Science Center, National Biological Survey (1993-1994); Research Biologist, National Capital Region, Washington, D.C. (1985-1993); Research Biologist, National Capital Region, Triangle, VA (1974-1993); Research Biologist, National Capital Parks, Great Falls, MD (1971-1974); Research Biologist, Southeast Temperate Forest Park Areas, Great Falls, MD (1967-1971); Research Biologist, Southeast Temperate Forest Park Areas, Durham, NC (1966-1967); Research Biologist, Southeast Temperate Forest Park Areas, Washington D.C. (1966); Research Park Naturalist, National Capital Region, National Capital Parks, National Park Service, Washington, D.C. (1963-1966); Park Naturalist, Researcher, Region 6, National Capital Parks, National Park Service, Washington, D.C. (1962-1963); Park

Naturalist, National Capital Parks, National Park Service, Washington, D.C. (1957-1962); Research Biologist, Patuxent Environmental Science Center, National Biological Service, Washington, D.C. **CR:** Adjunct Professor, George Mason University, Fairfax, VA (1988-Present); Board of Directors, Prince William County Service Authority, Virginia (1996-2004); Adjunct Professor, The George Washington University, Washington, D.C. (1992-1998); Guest Lecturer, Washington Technical Institute (Now University of the District of Columbia) (1976); Aquatic Ecological Consultant, Fairfax County Federation Citizens Associations, Virginia (1970-1971); Instructor, United States Department of Agriculture Graduate School (1964-1966) **CIV:** Assistant Scoutmaster, Scoutmaster, Merit Badges Counselor, Boy Scouts of America (1958-Present); Preservation and Management Consultant, National Resources Division, Arlington County, Virginia (2004); Preservation and Management Consultant, Mattawoman and Mason Springs, Charles County, MD (2002-2006); Wildlife Management Consultant, Girl Scouts of the United States of America, Loudoun County, Virginia (1958); Preservation and Management Consultant, McAteean Magnolia Bogs; Preservation and Management Consultant, Save Araby; Active in Politics **CW:** Contributor, Articles, Professional Journals **AW:** Superior Performance Award (1989); Research Grantee, Washington Biologists' Field Club (1982, 1977); Recipient, Incentive Awards, National Park Service (1962); Scouters Training Award (1961) **MEM:** American Association for the Advancement of Science; The Book of Mormon Archaeological Digest; Maryland Native Plant Society; National Trust for Historic Preservation; Washington Biologists' Field Club; Southern Appalachian Botanical Society; The Nature Conservancy; The George Wright Society; Ecological Society of America; The Botanical Society of Washington; Sigma Xi **MH:** Albert Nelson Marquis Lifetime Achievement Award (2017) **RE:** The Church of Jesus Christ of Latter-day Saints **BA:** 13854 Delaney Rd, Woodbridge, VA, 22193 **ADD:** PO Box 2759, Woodbridge, VA, 22195

THOMAS, TOM, T: Manufacturing Executive **I:** Manufacturing **CN:** Canada Cup, Inc. **DOB:** 02/15/1932 **PB:** Malang **SC:** Indonesia **MS:** Married **SPN:** Jannie Chine Sneep (1/19/1956) **CH:** Gregory John; Renée Sonja Elfrieda; Michael Grant; Thomas **C:** Founder, Canada Cup, Inc. (1964-Present); Chief Executive Officer, Canada Cup, Inc. (1964-Present); Board of Directors, Canada Cup, Inc. (1964-1993); Senior Manager, Impac & Somerville Plastics (1960-1964); Junior Manager, Lever Brothers Ltd. (Now Unilever) (1954-1960) **CIV:** Chairman, Canadian Plastics Pioneers (1995-2010); Advisory Council, Toronto Symphony Orchestra (1995-2000); Council President, Canadian Opera Company (1980-1995); Trustee, Fraser Institute (1977-1993); Governor, The Corporation of Massey Hall & Roy Thomson Hall (1991-1992); Board of Directors, Toronto Symphony Orchestra (1986-1992); Member, Maestro's Club (1984); Member, President's Council, Canadian Opera Company (1980) **MH:** Albert Nelson Marquis Lifetime Achievement Award (2017) **H:** Sailing; History; Classical music; Chess **ADD:** 30-94 George Henry Boulevard, Toronto, ON, Canada, M2J 1E7

THOMASSON, DAN, T: Publishing Executive **I:** Publishing **DOB:** 12/22/1933 **PB:** Shelbyville **SC:** IN/USA **PT:** Hubert Lee Thomasson; Mary Margaret (King) Thomasson **MS:** Married **SPN:** Laqueta Fordurcey (9/7/1958) **CH:** Scot; Lisa; Sean; Patrick **ED:** LLB, Westfield State University (2012); Postgraduate Work, University of Colorado (1959); BS, Indiana University (1956) **C:** Vice President

of News, Scripps Howard Newspapers, The E.W. Scripps Company, Cincinnati, OH (1986-Present); Editor, Scripps Howard News Service, The E.W. Scripps Company, Washington, D.C. (1980-Present); Vice President, The E.W. Scripps Company (1996-1999); Managing Editor, Scripps Howard News Service, The E.W. Scripps Company, Washington, D.C. (1976-1980); Assistant Managing Editor, Scripps Howard Newspapers, The E.W. Scripps Company Washington, D.C. (1974-1976); Correspondent, Scripps Howard Newspapers, The E.W. Scripps Company, Washington, D.C. (1964-1974); Reporter, The Rocky Mountain News, Denver, CO (1959-1964); Reporter, The Lawton Constitution (1957-1958); Reporter, Indianapolis Star (1956); Editor, Indianapolis Star (1956) **CR:** Visiting Professor, Hampton University (2000); Weill Visiting Professor, Indiana University (1999) **CIV:** Trustee, Franklin College (1990-Present); President, Raymond Clapper Foundation, Washington, D.C. (1980-2004); Member, Board of Directors, Scripps Howard Foundation, Cincinnati, OH (1987-2003); Member, Board of Visitors, Institute for Political Journalism, Georgetown University (1990-1999); Vice President, Scripps Howard Foundation, Cincinnati, Ohio (1994); Member, National Advisory Committee, E.W. Scripps School Journalism, Ohio University (1990); Member, National Public Affairs Council, Indiana University (1990) **MIL:** U.S. Army (1956-1958) **AW:** Distinguished Alumni Award, Indiana University (2013); Franklin Junto Award, Franklin College (2013); Honoree, Media Fellow, Stanford University (2000, 2003, 2005); Honoree, Media Fellow, Hoover Institution, Leland Stanford Junior University (2001-2003); Honoree, Presidential Fellow, Trinity College (2000); Honoree, Named to the Indiana Journalism Hall Of Fame (1997); Honoree, Named Man of the Year, Washington Journalism Hall Of Fame (1993); Elected, The Indiana Academy (1993); Honoree, Named Man of Year, Shelby County Chamber of Commerce (1970) **MEM:** American Society of News Editors; White House Correspondent's Association; Gridiron Club of Washington; Overseas Press Club of America; The National Press Club; The University Club of Washington DC; Washington Golf and Country Club; Bohemian Club; Sigma Delta Chi **ADD:** 2355 King Place NW, Washington, DC, 20007

THOMPSON, HOWARD ELLIOTT, T: Professor Emeritus **I:** Education/Educational Services **CN:** University of Wisconsin-Madison **DOB:** 07/30/1934 **PB:** West Allis **SC:** WI/USA **PT:** Leonard Adolph Thompson; Hulda Axelina (Granstrom) Thompson **MS:** Married **SPN:** Judith M. Gram (6/30/1956) **CH:** Linda Kay; Karen Marie; James Howard; John Leonard; Ann Elizabeth **ED:** PhD in Commerce, University of Wisconsin-Madison (1964); MS in Mathematics, University of Wisconsin-Madison (1958); BS in Mathematics, University of Wisconsin-Madison (1956) **C:** Professor Emeritus, Department of Finance, Investment, and Banking, University of Wisconsin-Madison (2000-Present); Chair, Department of Finance, Investment, and Banking, School of Business, University of Wisconsin-Madison (1997-2001); Visiting Professor, Faculty of Management Science, The Ohio State University (1970-1971); Professor of Business, School of Business, University of Wisconsin-Madison (1969-2001); Associate Professor of Business, School of Business, University of Wisconsin-Madison (1967-1969); Chairman, Department of Quantitative Analysis, School of Business, University of Wisconsin-Madison (1966-1970); Assistant Professor of Business, School of Commerce, University of Wisconsin-Madison (1964-1967); Instructor of Business, School of Commerce, University of Wisconsin-Madison

(1963-1964); Project Assistant, School of Commerce, University of Wisconsin-Madison (1961-1963); Mathematician, Technical Computing Department, A. O. Smith (1957-1961); Operations Research Analyst, Economics and Marketing Research Department, A. O. Smith (1957-1961) **CR:** Consultant, U.S. Energy Information Administration, U.S. Department of Energy (1990-2001); Consultant, Read and Laniado, LLP (1994); Consultant, Lake Superior Band of Chippewa Indians (1990); Expert Witness, Lake Superior Band of Chippewa Indians (1990); Consultant, Universal Foods Corporation (1989); Consultant, American Public Power Association (1988); Consultant, Hospital-Rate Setting Commission, State of Wisconsin (1985); Consultant, The Institute for Health Planning (1982-1984); Consultant, Wisconsin Public Service Commission (1982); Consultant, The World Bank Group (1981-1984); Consultant, KPMG LLP (1979-1984); Consultant, WPPI Energy (1977); Consultant, Department of Natural Resources, State of Wisconsin (1976-1978); Consultant, Attorney General Robert W. Warren, State of Wisconsin (1972-1974); Expert Witness, Attorney General Robert W. Warren, State of Wisconsin (1972-1974); Consultant, Federal Energy Regulatory Commission, U.S. Department of Energy (1967-2000); Consultant, Kansas Public Service Commission, Public Service Commission of Washington, D.C., Michigan Public Service Commission, Missouri Public Service Commission (1967-2000); Consultant, CUNA Mutual Group (1966-1968) **CW:** Editorial Boards, Managerial and Decision Economics (1988-2000); Editorial Boards, Global Business and Finance Review (1997-2000); Editorial Boards, The Financial Review (1998-2000); Contributing Author, Articles, Journal of Economics and Finance (2015); Contributing Author, Articles, Wisconsin Magazine of History (2014); Author, "Laurence C. Gram: West Allis, Water and War" (2013); Contributing Author, Articles, Multinational Finance Journal (2011); Author, "Carl G. Koch: A 20th Century Success Story" (2010); Co-author, "Rev. Ebenezer Thompson: Sage of Glen Flora" (2009); Co-author, "Leonard A. Thompson of Glen Flora" (2007); Contributing Author, Articles, International Journal of Finance (2007); Contributing Author, Articles, Advances in Quantitative Finance and Accounting (2006); Contributing Author, Articles, Quarterly Review of Economics and Finance (2006); Author, "Reflections on My Life" (2006); Editorial Boards, Journal of Regulatory Economics (1988-2003); Editorial Boards, Decision Sciences (1993-2000); Contributing Author, Articles, Managerial and Decision Economics (1996, 1991-1992, 1987-1988, 1984-1985); Contributing Author, Articles, Review of Quantitative Finance and Accounting (1996, 1994, 1992); Contributing Author, Articles, The Engineering Economist (1996); Contributing Author, Articles, AREUEA (1994); Contributing Author, Articles, Fusion Technology (1992); Contributing Author, Articles, Economic Innovations in Public Utility Regulation (1992); Author, "Regulatory Finance: Financial Foundations of Rate of Return Regulation" (1991); Contributing Author, Articles, Journal of Regulatory Economics (1989-1990); Contributing Author, Articles, Journal of the American Statistical Association (1990); Contributing Author, Articles, Report of NASA Lunar Energy Enterprise Case Study Task Force (1989); Contributing Author, Articles, The Journal of Finance (1988, 1986, 1978, 1976, 1973); Contributing Author, Articles, Applied Economics (1988); Editorial Boards, Financial Management (1981-1988); Contributing Author, Articles, Policy Studies Journal (1987); Contributing Author,

Articles, Land Economics (1986-1987, 1984, 1973); Contributing Author, Articles, Regulating Utilities in an Era of Deregulation (1986); Contributing Author, Articles, The Quarterly Review of Economics and Business (1984, 1970); Contributing Author, Articles, Management Science (1984, 1981, 1975, 1968, 1966); Contributing Author, Articles, Regulation and Public Utilities (1984); Contributing Author, Articles, The Journal of Financial and Quantitative Analysis (1983, 1978); Contributing Author, Articles, The Financial Analysts Journal (1981, 1972); Co-author, "Management Science: Quantitative Methods in Context" (1981); Contributing Author, Articles, Naval Research Logistics Quarterly (1980); Contributing Author, Articles, The Bell Journal of Economics and Management Science (1979, 1975, 1971); Contributing Author, Articles, Journal of Risk and Insurance (1978, 1971, 1967-1968, 1964); Contributing Author, Articles, Decision Sciences (1978, 1975, 1972, 1970); Contributing Author, Articles, The Journal of the Operational Research Society (1978); Contributing Author, Articles, The Journal of Business (1977); Contributing Author, Articles, Omega (1977); Contributing Author, Articles, Perspectives in Business (1976-1978); Co-author, "A Brief Calculus with Applications to Business and Economics" (1976); Author, "Applications of Calculus in Business and Economics" (1973); Contributing Author, Articles, Journal of Bank Research, Operations Research, Management Science: Theory, Management Accounting, Journal of the Academy of Management, Management in Perspective, Communications of the Association for Computing Machinery; Founding Editor, Annals of Financial Economics **AW:** Honoree, Honorary Alumnus, The Applied Security Analysis Program, University of Wisconsin-Madison (2002); Larson Teaching Award, School of Business, University of Wisconsin-Madison (1995); E. A. Gaumnitz Outstanding Faculty Award, School of Business, University of Wisconsin-Madison (1990); Kuechenmeister-Bascom Professorship Grantee, University of Wisconsin-Madison (1985-2000); Mary Rennebohm Professorship Grantee, University of Wisconsin-Madison (1975-1980); Fellow, School of Commerce, University of Wisconsin-Madison (1961-1963) **MEM:** Chairman, Department of Finance, School of Business, University of Wisconsin-Madison (1997-2001, 1983-1984); Subcommittee of the Executive Committee, School of Business, University of Wisconsin-Madison (1996-1998, 1990-1991, 1985-1988, 1975-1983, 1969-1972); Chair, Institutional Advisory Committee on Outside Activities, University of Wisconsin-Madison (1995-1998); Laun Chair Search Committee, School of Business, University of Wisconsin-Madison (1994-1995); Research Committee, School of Business, University of Wisconsin-Madison (1993-1996); Executive MBA Committee, School of Business, University of Wisconsin-Madison (1992-1993); Chairman, Subcommittee of the Executive Committee, School of Business, University of Wisconsin-Madison (1991-1993, 1981-1982, 1972-1975); Search and Screen Committee for Dean of the School of Business, University of Wisconsin-Madison (1989-1990); Firstar Chair Search Committee, School of Business, University of Wisconsin-Madison (1989-1990); Schultz Chair Search Committee, School of Business, University of Wisconsin-Madison (1989-1990); Graduate Studies Committee, School of Business, University of Wisconsin-Madison (1987-1992, 1982-1983); Chairman, Search and Screen Committee for Dickson-Bascom Professor, University of Wisconsin-Madison (1987); Ad Hoc Committee on Search and Screen Policies, University of Wisconsin-Madison (1987); Ernst &

Young Chair Search Committee, School of Business, University of Wisconsin-Madison (1986-1989); National Issues Lecture Series Committee, School of Business, University of Wisconsin-Madison (1986-1988); Arthur Andersen Chair Search Committee, School of Business, University of Wisconsin-Madison (1986-1987); Awards Committee, School of Business, University of Wisconsin-Madison (1986-1987); University System Steering Committee for Strategic Planning in Business Administration, University of Wisconsin-Madison (1986-1987); Chairman, Search and Screen Committee for Dean of the School of Business, University of Wisconsin-Madison (1984-1985); Organization, Bylaws and Governance Review Committee, School of Business, University of Wisconsin-Madison (1980-1981); Faculty Senate, University of Wisconsin-Madison (1978-1980); Ad Hoc Committee to Evaluate the Department of Statistics, University of Wisconsin-Madison (1978); Tenure Density Committee, School of Business, University of Wisconsin-Madison (1977-1978) **MH:** Albert Nelson Marquis Lifetime Achievement Award (2017) **RE:** Presbyterian Church **ADD:** 7529 Fox Point Cir, Madison, WI, 53717

THOMPSON, JOHN A. JR., T: Dermatologist **I:** Education/Educational Services **CN:** University of North Carolina at Chapel Hill School of Medicine **DOB:** 06/05/1942 **PB:** Austin **SC:** TX/USA **PT:** J. Albert Thompson, Sr.; Elizabeth (Brady) Thompson **ED:** Resident in Dermatology, North Carolina Memorial Hospital, Chapel Hill, NC (1971-1973); Fellow in Dermatology, The University of North Carolina at Chapel Hill (1971-1973); Resident, Internal Medicine, Wake Forest Baptist Medical Center, Winston-Salem, NC (1967-1969); MD, Wake Forest School of Medicine (1967); BA, Georgetown University (1963) **CT:** Diplomate, American Board of Dermatology **C:** Private Practice, Charlotte, NC (1974-2013) **CR:** Clinical Professor, Department of Dermatology, University of North Carolina at Chapel Hill School of Medicine (1974-Present) **CIV:** Employee, Volunteer Headquarters, Penland School of Crafts **MIL:** Lieutenant Commander, U.S. Naval Reserve, Vietnam (1969-1971) **CW:** Author, Professional Papers **MEM:** Steering Committee, Southeastern Consortium for CME in Dermatology (1983-2003); Organizing Committee, South Central Dermatologic Congress (1982-1986); Advisory Board, Council Representative, Virginia-Carolinas Dermatological Society (1976-1979); Chairman, Subcommittee for School Health Education, American Academy of Dermatology (1976-1979); Task Force, National Health Insurance, American Academy of Dermatology; Charlotte Dermatology Association; Mecklenburg County Medical Society; North Carolina Medical Society; North American Clinical Dermatologic Society; Southern Medical Association; American Society for Dermatologic Surgery; American Academy of Allergy, Asthma & Immunology; American Society for Laser Medicine and Surgery, Inc. **MH:** Albert Nelson Marquis Lifetime Achievement Award (2017) **PA:** Democrat **RE:** Episcopalian **ADD:** 2633 Richardson Dr Apt 8A, Charlotte, NC, 28211

THOMPSON, JUDITH, T: Nursing Researcher **I:** Medicine & Health Care **CN:** University of Southern California **DOB:** 10/01/1933 **PB:** Marstal **SC:** Denmark **PT:** Edward Kastrup Pedersen; Anna Hansa (Knudsen) Pedersen **MS:** Single **SPN:** Richard Frederick Thompson (5/22/1960, Deceased 2014) **CH:** Kathryn Marr; Elizabeth Kastrup; Virginia St. Claire **ED:** MSN, University of Oregon (1963); BS, University of Oregon (1958); CT: RN, University of Oregon (1958); RN, State of Oregon; RN, State of California **C:** Research Associate, University of Southern California, Los Angeles, CA (1987-2010);

Research Associate, Stanford University (1982-1987); Research Assistant, Harvard University (1973-1974); Research Assistant, University of California, Irvine (1971-1972); Research Assistant, OHSU (1964-1965); Instructor in Psychiatric Nursing, OHSU (1963-1964); Head Staff Nurse, OHSU (1960-1961); Staff Nurse, OHSU (1958-1961); Staff Nurse, School of Medicine, University of Oregon (1957-1958) **CIV:** Scout Leader, Newport Beach Chapter, Girl Scouts of America (1970-1978); Treasurer, League of Women Voters of Orange Coast, California (1970-1974) **CW:** Contributing Author, "Behavioral Control and Role of Sensory Biofeedback" (1976); Contributor, Articles, Professional Journals **AW:** D.G. Marquis Behavioral Neuroscience Award (1999); Citizen of the Year, State of Oregon (1966) **MEM:** Society for Neuroscience; Charter, American Psychological Association; American Nurses Association, Inc.; Oregon Nurses Association **MH:** Albert Nelson Marquis Lifetime Achievement Award (2017) **H:** Bridge; Bocce ball; Attending lectures; Travel; Tennis **PA:** Republican **RE:** Lutheran **ADD:** 1373 Vicki Lane, Nipomo, CA, 93444

THORNTON, JONATHAN MILLS III, T: Professor Emeritus **I:** Education/Educational Services **CN:** University of Michigan **DOB:** 10/27/1943 **PB:** Montgomery **SC:** AL/USA **PT:** Jonathan Mills Thornton; Priscilla Marks Thornton **MS:** Married **SPN:** Brenda Booth (1/5/1985) **ED:** PhD in History, Yale University, New Haven, CT (1974); MPhil in History, Yale University, New Haven, CT (1969); BA in History, Princeton University, Princeton, NJ (1966) **C:** Professor Emeritus, University of Michigan (2010-Present); Professor, History, University of Michigan (1982-2010); Associate Professor, University of Michigan (1977-1982); Assistant Professor, University of Michigan (1974-1977); Instructor, The University of Illinois at Chicago (1971-1974) **CR:** Pitt Professor, American History, University of Cambridge (2007-2008); Fellow, Wilson Center (1994-1995) **CW:** Author, "Archipelagoes of My South, Episodes in The Shaping of A Region (1830-1965)," University of Alabama Press (2016); Author, "Dividing Lines: Municipal Politics and the Struggle for Civil Rights in Montgomery, Birmingham and Selma" (2003); Author, "Politics and Power in a Slave Society: Alabama, 1800-1860" (1978) **AW:** Liberty Legacy Foundation Prize, The Organization of American Historians (2003); Fellowship, John Simon Guggenheim Memorial Foundation (1978-1979); John H. Dunning Prize, American Historical Association (1978); Fellowship, Danforth Foundation (1966-1974) **MEM:** The Organization of American Historians; American Historical Association; Southern Historical Association; Society of Historians of the Early American Republic **MH:** Albert Nelson Marquis Lifetime Achievement Award (2017) **ADD:** 9524 Heathrow Dr, Montgomery, AL, 36117

THORP, JAMES, T: Professor Emeritus **I:** Education/Educational Services **CN:** Virginia Polytechnic Institute and State University **DOB:** 02/07/1937 **PB:** Kansas City **SC:** MO/USA **PT:** Joseph Chester Thorp; Ruth Vefe (McNamara) Thorp **MS:** Married **SPN:** Christine Annette Moore (8/10/1980); Barbara Anne Curit (6/27/1959, Divorced 7/1976) **CH:** Jeffrey Barton; Elizabeth Anne **ED:** Fellow, Churchill College, University of Cambridge (1988); Faculty Intern, American Electric Power (1976-1977); PhD, Cornell University (1962); MS, Cornell University (1961); BEE, Cornell University (1959) **C:** Department Head, Bradley Department of Electrical and Computer Engineering, Virginia Polytechnic and State University, Blacksburg, VA (2004-Present); Hugh

P. and Ethey C. Kelley Professor of Electrical and Computer Engineering, Virginia Polytechnic and State University, Blacksburg, VA (2004-Present); Charles N. Mellowes Professor of Engineering, Cornell University, Ithaca, NY (1994-2001); Director, School of Electrical Engineering, Cornell University, Ithaca, New York (1994); Associate Director, School of Electrical Engineering, Cornell University, Ithaca, NY (1991-1994); Professor, Cornell University, Ithaca, NY (1975-1994); Associate Professor, Cornell University, Ithaca, NY (1966-1975); Assistant Professor, Cornell University, Ithaca, NY (1962-1966) **CR:** Dowty Control Technologies, Boonton, NJ (1988-Present); Consultant, American Electric Power (1977-1983); Fellow, Power System Relaying Committee, IEEE **CW:** Editorial Board Member, Editor, "Transactions on Power Delivery," IEEE (1998-2001); Author, "Computer Relaying for Power Systems" (1988); Associate Editor, "Transactions on Circuits and Systems," IEEE (1985-1987); Contributor, Chapters to Books; Contributor, Articles, Professional Journals **AW:** Benjamin Franklin Medal in Electrical Engineering, Franklin Institute (2008); Outstanding Power Engineering Award, Power Engineering Society, IEEE; Career Service Award, IEEE **MEM:** National Academy of Engineering; Eta Kappa Nu, IEEE; The Tau Beta Pi Association, Inc.; Sigma Xi **MH:** Albert Nelson Marquis Lifetime Achievement Award (2017) **H:** Golf **ADD:** 1790 Lusters Gate Road, Blacksburg, VA, 24060 **URL:** http://news.cornell.edu/stories/2008/05/james-thorp-wins-benjamin-franklin-medal

TOBIAS, SHEILA, T: Higher Education Program Innovation **I:** Education/Educational Services **CN:** Self-Employed **PB:** New York **PT:** Paul Jay Tobias; Rose (Steinberger) Tobias **MS:** Widowed **SPN:** Carl T. Tomizuka (12/16/1987); Carlos Stern (10/11/1970, Divorced 1982) **ED:** Honorary PhD, Worcester Polytechnic Institute (2002); Honorary PhD, Michigan State University (2000); Honorary PhD, SUNY Potsdam (1996); Honorary PhD, Wheelock College (1995); Honorary PhD, Drury University (1994); Master of Philosophy in History, Columbia University (1974); MA in European History, Columbia University (1961); BA in History & Literature, Radcliffe Institute for Advanced Study, Harvard University, Magna Cum Laude (1957) **C:** Summer Lecturer, "Gender Issues in Education," Claremont Graduate University (1991-1997); Visiting Lecturer, "Gender and Politics," UC San Diego (1982-1992); Director, Math Anxiety Project, Washington School of Psychiatry (1978-1980); Summer Lecturer, "The Nuclear Predicament," University of California, Davis (1982-1989); Lecturer in War and Peace Studies, University of Southern California (1985-1988); Associate Provost, Wesleyan University (1970-1978); Assistant to Vice President, Academic Affairs, Cornell University (1967-1970); Lecturer in History, The City College of New York (1965-1967); Assistant Director, Upward Bound, College of Charleston (1966); Freelance Journalist, Germany (1957-1965); Freelance Radio Journalist, CBC/Radio-Canada (1964-1965); Reporter, The Army Times Publishing Company, Frankfurt, Germany; General Factotum, The Army Times Publishing Company, Frankfurt, Germany **CR:** Executive Director, Science-Enhanced General Education Project (2016-Present); Special Assignment, Teagle Foundation (2016-2017); Field Coordinator, Science Master's Initiative, (1997-2015); Sub-contractual Evaluator, Science Master's Program, National Science Foundation (2012-2014); Scientific Researcher, Research Corporation for Science Advancement (1989-1995, 2008-2010); Consultant, Science And Business, UvA (1995-1998); Visiting Professor, University of Leiden (1994-1997) **CIV:**

Executive Vice President, Veteran Feminists of America (2002-Present); Tucson Arizona Women's Commission (2010-2016) **CW:** Contributing Author, "Professional science degree may be 21st century MBA," Scientific American (2013); Co-author, "Banishing Math Anxiety," Kendall Hunt Publishing (2012); Co-author, "Science Teaching as a Profession: Why it isn't? How it Could Be?" (2009); Contributing Author, "Professional science degree may be 21st century MBA," Science News (2009); Co-author, "Faces of Feminism: An Activist's Reflections on the Women's Movement" (1997); Co-author, "The Hidden Curriculum" (1997); Author, "Science as a Career: Perceptions and Realities" (1995); Co-author, "Rethinking Science as a Career" (1995); Author, "Overcoming Math Anxiety: Revised Edition" (1994); Author, "Revitalizing Undergraduate Science: Why Some Things Work and Most Don't" (1992); Co-author, "Breaking the Science Barrier" (1992); Co-author, "They're Not Dumb, They're Different" (1990); Co-author, "Women, Militarism and War" (1987); Author, "Succeed with Math" (1987); Co-author, "The People's Guide to National Defense" (1982); Author, "Overcoming Math Anxiety" (1978); Researcher, "The Crucial Summer", ABC Inc. (1964); Advance Researcher, "Color in Britain" Intertel (1963); Co-author, "PSM mathematics professionals: where are they working? How are they employed?"; Co-author, "Targeting Grads through Social Media: A First-time Probe" **AW:** Consulting Grantee, Alfred P. Sloan Foundation (1997-2014); Fellow, American Association for the Advancement of Science; Math Anxiety Grantee, FIPSE; Women's Studies Grantee, Ford Foundation; Eight Honorary Doctorates **MEM:** Board Member, Association for Women in Science (2008); Board of Directors, MentoNet (2005-2007); Board of Directors, AAHEA (1993-1997); The Phi Beta Kappa Society **MH:** Albert Nelson Marquis Lifetime Achievement Award (2017) **H:** Hiking **PA:** Democrats Party **RE:** Jewish **ADD:** 724 N Campbell Ave, Tucson, AZ, 85719 **URL:** sheilatobias.com

TOIKKA, RICHARD S., T: Partner, Lawyer **I:** Law and Legal Services **CN:** Toikka Law Group, LLP **DOB:** 12/27/1944 **PB:** Gloucester **SC:** MA/USA **PT:** John H. Toikka; Pauline E. (Horton) Toikka **MS:** Single **ED:** JD, Georgetown University, Cum Laude (1988); PhD in Economics, University of Wisconsin (1971); MA, University of Wisconsin (1969); BA, Harvard University, Cum Laude (1966); AB, Harvard College, Cum Laude (1966) **CT:** Certification, U.S. Patent and Trademark Office **C:** Of Counsel, Farkas & Manelli, P.L.L.C., Washington, DC (1997-Present); Associate, Aviation and Product Liability Group, Graham & James, Washington, DC (1991-1996); Associate, Aviation Group, Washington Perito & Dubuc, Washington, DC (1989-1991); Associate, Aviation Group, Laxalt, Washington, Perito & Dubuc, Washington, DC (1988-1989); Deputy Area Manager, Applied Management Sciences, Silver Spring, MD (1983-1987); President, Toikka Enterprises, Arlington, VA (1981-1983); Senior Associate, Urban Institute, Washington, DC (1973-1981); Economist, Social Security Administration, Washington, DC (1971-1973); Partner, Toikka Law Group, LLP **CR:** Consultant, Equal Employment Opportunity Commission (1998); American Institutes for Research, Washington, DC (1982); Human Resource Organization, Alexandria, VA (1982); Ketron, Inc., Wayne, PA (1981-1982); National Center for Research in Vocational Education, Columbus, OH (1981); Westat, Inc., Rockville, MD (1981); Fellowship, U.S. Department of Labor (1969); Honoree, National Defense Education Act Fellow (1967) **CW:** Contributor, Articles,

Professional Journals and Legal Periodicals **AW:** Honoree, Lawyers of Distinction (2017) **MEM:** Chairman, Subcommittee on Damages, Aviation Committee, American Bar Association (1993-1996); The National Press Club; Harvard Club of Washington, DC **BAR:** U.S. District Court, State of Maryland (1997); U.S. Court of International Trade (1996); U.S. Supreme Court (1993); Federal Circuit, U.S. Court of Appeals (1993); U.S. District Court, District of Columbia (1992) **H:** Baseball; Golf; Participating in church and community activities **BA:** 1101 30th Street NW, Suite 500, Toikka Law Group, LLP, Washington, DC, 20007 **URL:** http://www.toikkalawgroup.com

TOKHEIM, ROBERT E., T: Physicist **I:** Sciences **CN:** SRI International **DOB:** 04/25/1936 **PB:** Eastport **SC:** ME/USA **PT:** Edward George; Ruth Lillian (Koenig) Tokheim **MS:** Married **SPN:** Diane Alice Green **CH:** Shirley Diane; William Robert; David Eric; Heidi Jean **ED:** PhD in Electrical Engineering with Physic Minor, Stanford University (1965); Degree in Engineering, Stanford University (1962); MSEE, California Institute of Technology (1959); BSEE, California Institute of Technology, with Honors (1958) **C:** Senior Physicist, SRI International, Menlo Park, CA (1973-Present); Head of Ferrimagnetic R&D Department, Watkins-Johnson Company, Palo Alto, CA (1966-1969); Microwave Engineer, Watkins-Johnson Company, Palo Alto, CA (1965-1973); Research Assistant, Hansen Physics Laboratories, Stanford University, California (1960-1965) **CR:** Associate Department Director, Poulter Laboratory, Physical Sciences Division, SRI International, Menlo Park (1998-2017) **CW:** Co-Author, Tutorial Handbook on X-ray Effects on Materials and Structures (1992); Contributor, Articles to Professional Journals; Contributor, Reports, Government Agencies and Companies; Past Presenter, Numerous Technical Conferences **MEM:** Life Member, IEEE; American Physical Society; Tau Beta Pi; Sigma Xi; Toastmasters International **H:** Extended family activities; Cultural and sports events; Financial investments; Writing poetry; Religious study; Church activities **RE:** Christian Scientist **BA:** 333 Ravenswood Ave, Menlo Park, CA, 94025 **ADD:** 5 Trinity Ct, Menlo Park, CA, 94025-6643

TOLLIVER, DOROTHY, T: Professor/Librarian **I:** Library Management/Library Services **DOB:** 04/10/1937 **PB:** New York **SC:** NY/USA **PT:** Morris and Rose (Poliner) Lamm **MS:** Widow **SPN:** Robert F. Tolliver (deceased 2008) **CH:** Craig Lee; Chana Rochel (Sulu) Tolliver; Marc Alan Tolliver; Adina Rose Tolliver (Grandchild) **ED:** MSLS, University Illinois, Champaign-Urbana (1973); BA, Indiana University (1958) **C:** Professor, University of Hawaii Maui College (1989-Present); Branch Manager, Kahului Public Library (1988); Head Librarian, Danville Area Community College Library (1968-1988); Reference and Youth Librarian, Burbank Public Library; Director, Temple City Library; Traveling Storyteller, Los Angeles County Library System; Reference Librarian, Los Angeles County System Headquarters **MEM:** Maui Friends of the Library; American Association of University Women - Maui Branch; Maui Library Ohana; Hawaii Library Association; American Library Association **MH:** Albert Nelson Marquis Lifetime Achievement Award (2017) **H:** Theater; Book clubs; Travel **BA:** 310 W. Kaahumanu Avenue, University Hawaii Maui College Library, Kahului, HI, 96732

TOLMAN, DAN E., T: Professor of Dentistry **I:** Medicine & Health Care **CN:** Mayo Clinic School of Medicine, Mayo Foundation for Medical Education and Research **DOB:** 08/09/1931 **PB:** Silver Creek **SC:** NE/USA **PT:** Nathaniel Edward Tolman; Virginia (West) Tolman **MS:** Married **SPN:** Suzanne Nelson (6/8/1957) **CH:** Kimberly Suzanne **ED:** MSD, University of Minnesota (1961); DDS, University of Nebraska (1957); BS in Dentistry, University of Nebraska (1957); BSBA, University of Nebraska (1953) **CT:** Diplomate, American Board Oral and Maxillofacial Surgery (ABOMS) (1965) **C:** Consultant, Nobel Biocare Services AG (1994-Present); Professor of Dentistry, Mayo Clinic School of Medicine, Mayo Foundation for Medical Education and Research (1993-Present); Consultant, Section of Dentistry and Oral and Maxillofacial Surgery, Mayo Foundation for Medical Education and Research (1965-1994); Associate Professor of Dentistry, Mayo Clinic School of Medicine, Mayo Foundation for Medical Education and Research (1978-1993); Assistant Professor of Dentistry, Mayo Clinic School of Medicine, Mayo Foundation for Medical Education and Research (1973-1978); Assistant Professor of Dentistry, Mayo Graduate School of Medicine, University of Minnesota (1970-1973); Instructor, Mayo Graduate School of Medicine, University of Minnesota (1966-1970); Resident, Mayo Graduate School of Medicine, University of Minnesota (1959-1962) **CR:** Panel Member, Division of Educational Resources and Programs, AAMC (1976); Member, Advisory Group, Northlands Regional Medical Program (1969-1971); Staff Member, Mayo Clinic School of Medicine, Mayo Foundation for Medical Education and Research **CIV:** Member, Benevolence Committee, First Presbyterian Church (1984-1985); Active Member, Olmsted County Republican Party (1968-1972); President-Elect, Jefferson PTA (1970-1971); Scholarship Committee, Rochester Council of PTA (1970-1971) **MIL:** Colonel, Dental Corps, U.S. Army Reserve (1983-1991); Lieutenant Colonel, U.S. Army Reserve (1979-1983); Instructor in Oral Surgery, U.S. Air Force, Scott Air Force Base, St. Clair County, IL (1964-1965); Chief of Oral Surgery, USAF Hospital, U.S. Air Force (1964-1965); Active Serviceman, U.S. Air Force (1956-1965); Chief of Oral Surgery, 836 TAC Hospital, U.S. Air Force (1962-1964) **CW:** Co-Editor, Proceedings, International Congress on Tissue Integrated Prosthesis (1990); Editor, Journal of Oral Surgery (1974-1981); Contributor, Articles, Professional Journals **AW:** Presidential Achievement Award, AAOMS (1998); Meritorious Service Medal (1993); The National Defense Service Medal (1991); Commendation Medal, U.S. Army (1990); Certificate of Recognition, Dental Corps, U.S. Army (1988); The Army Achievement Medal (1987); The St. George Medal, Minnesota Division, American Cancer Society, Inc. (1983); Meritorious Service Citation, Minnesota Dental Association (1981); Meritorious Service Citation, Minnesota Dental Association (1978); Honoree, Master, University of Nebraska (1970); Certificate of Merit, American Society of Dentistry for Children (1957); Named Honorary Administrator, Nebraska Navy (1953) **MEM:** Honorary Life Member, Board of Directors, Minnesota Division, American Cancer Society, Inc. (1996-Present); Organizing Committee, International Congress on Tissue Integrated Prosthesis (1996); Task Force on Paramaters on Care, AAOMS (1992-1994); Board of Directors, Minnesota Division, American Cancer Society, Inc. (1989-1993); Representative, American Dental Association Council on Geriatrics, AAOMS (1990-1992); Chairman, Legacy and Planned Giving Committee, Minnesota Division, American Cancer Society, Inc. (1990-1991); Representative to the Minnesota Dental Association, Minnesota Cancer Council (1978-1991); Chairman, Special Contracts Committee, Minnesota Division, American Cancer Society, Inc. (1988-1990); International Osseointegration Advisory Board (1990); Co-Chairman, International Congress on Tissue Integrated Prosthesis (1990); Legacy and Planned Giving Committee, Minnesota Division, American Cancer Society, Inc. (1988-1989); Vice Chairman, Legacy and Planned Giving Committee, Minnesota Division, American Cancer Society, Inc. (1988-1989); Chairman, Appeals Commission, AAOMS (1986-1987); Secretary-Treasurer, AAOMS (1985-1987); Board of Trustees, AAOMS (1985-1987); Chairman, Budget and Finance Committee, AAOMS (1985-1987); Professional Education Committee, Minnesota Division, American Cancer Society, Inc. (1973-1987); Board of Directors, Minnesota Division, American Cancer Society, Inc. (1973-1987); Chairman, Minnesota Cancer Council (1981-1986); International Consensus Committee on Tissue Integrated Implants (1985); Committee on Tissue Integrated Implants, International Congress on Tissue Integrated Prosthesis (1985); Chairman, Nominating Committee, Midwestern Society of Oral & Maxillofacial Surgeons (1984-1985); Constitutional and By-laws Committee, Minnesota Society of Oral & Maxillofacial Surgeons (1984-1985); Presidential Advisory Committee, AAOMS (1982-1983); Nominating Committee, Midwestern Society of Oral & Maxillofacial Surgeons (1981-1983); Executive Council, Midwestern Society of Oral & Maxillofacial Surgeons (1973-1983); Finance Committee, Minnesota Division, American Cancer Society, Inc. (1979-1982); Board of Trustees, AAOMS (1978-1982); Immediate Past President, Midwestern Society of Oral & Maxillofacial Surgeons (1981-1982); Chairman, Nominating Committee, Minnesota Division, American Cancer Society, Inc. (1980-1982); Board Liaison, Research Advisory Committee, AAOMS (1980-1981); President, Midwestern Society of Oral & Maxillofacial Surgeons (1980-1981); President, Minnesota Division, American Cancer Society, Inc. (1980-1981); Board Consultant, Committee on Hospital Affairs, AAOMS (1979-1981); Board of Directors, Olmsted County Unit, American Cancer Society, Inc. (1972-1981); Vice Chairman, Minnesota Cancer Council (1980); Chairman, Special Committee to Evaluate Unit Organization, Minnesota Division, American Cancer Society, Inc. (1980); President-Elect, Midwestern Society of Oral & Maxillofacial Surgeons (1979-1980); Chairman, Standing Crusade Committee, Olmsted County Unit, American Cancer Society, Inc. (1979-1980); Vice-Chairman, Minnesota Division, American Cancer Society, Inc. (1979-1980); President-Elect, Minnesota Division, American Cancer Society, Inc. (1979-1980); Personnel Committee, Minnesota Division, American Cancer Society, Inc. (1979-1980); Chairman, Professional Education Committee, Minnesota Division, American Cancer Society, Inc. (1977-1980); Executive Committee, Minnesota Division, American Cancer Society, Inc. (1977-1980); Board Consultant, Committee on Anesthesia, AAOMS (1978-1979); Chairman, Program Committee, Midwestern Society of Oral & Maxillofacial Surgeons (1978-1979); Standing Committee for Meeting Sites, Midwestern Society of Oral & Maxillofacial Surgeons (1978-1979); Nominating Committee, Minnesota Cancer Council (1978-1979); Chairman, Local Arrangements Committee, Midwestern Society of Oral & Maxillofacial Surgeons (1978-1979); Vice President, Midwestern Society of Oral & Maxillofacial Surgeons (1978-1979); Board Consultant, Committee on Residency Education and Training, AAOMS (1978-1979); Peer Review Committee, Minnesota Society of Oral & Maxillofacial Surgeons (1978-1979); Epidemiology Committee, Minnesota Division, American Cancer Society, Inc. (1975-1978); Advisory Committee. American Board of Oral and Maxillofacial Surgery

(1975-1978); Chairman, Special Oral Cancer Liaison Committee, Minnesota Dental Association (1974-1978); Secretary-Treasurer, Midwestern Society of Oral & Maxillofacial Surgeons (1973-1978); Special Oral Cancer Liaison Committee, Minnesota Dental Association (1972-1978); Vice Chairman, Professional Education Committee, Minnesota Division, American Cancer Society, Inc. (1976-1977); Chairman, Nominating Committee, Minnesota Division, American Cancer Society, Inc. (1976-1977); Professional Service Review Organization Committee, Minnesota Society of Oral & Maxillofacial Surgeons (1974-1977); Division of Educational Resources and Programs, AAMC (1976); Epidemiology Committee, Minnesota Division, American Cancer Society, Inc. (1975-1976); Research Committee, AAOMS (1971-1975); Chairman, Research Committee, AAOMS (1973-1974); Nominating Committee, Minnesota Society of Oral & Maxillofacial Surgeons (1973); International Association of Oral and Maxillofacial Surgeons (1973); Fellow, American College of Dentists (1973); Vice Chairman, Research Committee, AAOMS (1972-1973); Minnesota Alternate Delegate, AAOMS (1970-1972); Community Dental Health Committee, Zumbro Valley Dental Society (1970-1971); Northlands Regional Medical Program Advisory Group (1969-1971); Sigma Xi (1970); Committee on Credentials, AAOMS (1969-1970); Program Committee, Minnesota Society of Oral & Maxillofacial Surgeons (1960-1970); Minnesota Delegate, AAOMS (1967-1969); Olmsted County Welfare Committee, Zumbro Valley Dental Society (1967-1968); Milwaukee Dental Forum (1967); Mayo Alumni Association (1962) **MH:** Albert Nelson Marquis Lifetime Achievement Award (2017) **ADD:** PO Box 7155, Rochester, MN, 55903 **URL:** https://www.doximity.com/pub/dan-tolman-md

TOMAR, PAUL, T: Partner, Head of Family Law Department **I:** Law and Legal Services **CN:** Ashford & Wriston, LLP **ED:** JD, University of Miami (1973); BA, Lehigh University (1970) **C:** Partner, Ashford & Wriston, LLP (1999-Present); Head, Family Law Department, Ashford & Wriston, LLP (1999-Present) **CR:** Lecturer in Family Law, Legal Assistant Program, Kapiolani Community College **CIV:** Chair, Family Law Section, Hawaii State Bar Association (2000); Chairperson, Advisory Committee, Legal Assistant Program, Kapiolani Community College **CW:** Co-author, "Hawaii Divorce Manual, Fifth Edition" (1996); Featured Guest Speaker, Various Presentations in Field; Contributor, Articles, Professional Journals **AW:** Honoree, Honolulu's Best Lawyers, Best Lawyers in America (2017) **MEM:** Family Law Section, American Bar Association; Litigation Section, American Bar Association **BAR:** State of Hawaii **BA:** 999 Bishop Street, Suite 1400, Ashford & Wriston LLP, Honolulu, HI, 96813

TORRES, CYNTHIA ANN, T: Marketing Professional, Educational Consultant, Speaker **I:** Consulting **CN:** College Decisions, LLC **DOB:** 09/24/1958 **PB:** Glendale **SC:** CA/USA **PT:** Adolph Torres; Ruth Ann (Smith) Torres **MS:** Divorced **CH:** Spencer Williams Gisser; David Westfall Torres Gisser **ED:** MBA, Harvard Business School (1984); AB, Harvard College (1980) **C:** President, College Decisions, LLC, Los Angeles, CA (2010-Present); Director of Marketing and Client Service, Diamond Portfolio Advisors, LLC, Santa Monica, CA (2000-2010); President, Integrity Investments Consultants, Ltd. (1996-1999); Senior Vice President, Institutional Business Development, Fidelity Investments Management Ltd., Hong Kong, China (1993-1996); Vice President of Marketing, First Interstate Bancorp, Los Angeles,

CA (1989-1992); Vice President of Investment Banking, Goldman, Sachs & Co., New York, NY (1984-1988); Associate Consultant, Bain & Co., Boston, MA (1980-1982) **CIV:** Chair, Financial Oversight Committee, Santa Monica-Malibu Unified School District (2008-2010); Member, Judiciary Review Board, Harvard Business School, Boston, MA (1983-1984) **AW:** Recipient, Harvard Alumni Association Award (2018); Recipient, Outstanding Service Award, Financial Oversight Committee, Santa Monica-Malibu United School District (2014); Recipient, Fred Smith Outstanding Service Award, Harvard Club of Southern California (2013); Fellow, Council for Opportunity in Graduate Management Education (1982-1984); Recipient, Leadership Award, Johnson and Johnson (1980); Fellow, Harvard University Center for International Affairs (1979-1980); Recipient, Rockefeller Foundation Scholarship (1976) **MEM:** Director, Harvard Alumni Association Board (2004-Present); Executive Committee Member, Harvard Alumni Association (2009-Present); Vice Chair, West Coast Council, Harvard College Fund (2008-Present); Past President Director, Harvard Alumni Association Board (2015-2019; President, Harvard Alumni Association (2014-2015); First Vice President, Harvard Alumni Association (2013-2014); Vice President, Engagement & Marketing, Harvard Alumni Association (2012-2013); Co-Chair, Harvard Alumni Careers Task Force (2011-2014); Member-at-Large, Harvard Alumni Association Executive Committee (2009-2012); Committee to Nominate Overseers and Elected Directors, Harvard Alumni Association (2008-2011); Co-Chair, Clubs and Shared Interest Groups Committee, Harvard Alumni Association (2008-2009); Chair, Alumni Awards Committee, Harvard Alumni Association (2007-2008); President, Harvard Club of Southern California (2006-2008); Regional Director, Pacific Southwest, Harvard Alumni Association (2004-2007); President, Financial Women's Association, Hong Kong, China (1997-1998); Asia Society; Academy of Political Science **MH:** Albert Nelson Marquis Lifetime Achievement Award (2017) **ADD:** 788 Auburn Avenue, Sierra Madre, CA, 91024 **URL:** http://harvardmagazine.com/2014/09/embodying-access

TOUBY, MARK A., T: Managing Partner **I:** Law and Legal Services **CN:** Touby, Chait & Sicking, PL **ED:** JD, University of Miami (1995); BS in Finance, University of Florida (1992) **CT:** Board Certified in Workers' Compensation (2011) **C:** Managing Partner, Touby, Chait & Sicking, PL (2013-Present); Managing Partner, Touby, Grindal & Chait, PL (2012-2013); Litigation Attorney, Touby and Associates, P.A. (2010-2012); Litigation Attorney, Touby & Woodward, P.A. (1995-2009) **CR:** Chair, Workers' Compensation Rules Advisory Committee (2014-2015); Vice-Chair, Workers' Compensation Committee, Dade County Bar Association (2009-2013); President, Florida Workers' Advocates; Lecturer in Field; Member, Executive Council, Workers' Compensation Section, The Florida Bar **CIV:** Vice President of Fundraising, Friends of 440 Scholarship Fund (2012-Present); President, Friends of 440, Inc. (2009-2010) **CW:** Author, "Workers' Compensation Rules Annual Reports of Committees," The Florida Bar **AW:** Award and Recognition for Leadership, Florida Workers Advocates (2017); AV Preeminent Attorney, Martindale-Hubbell (2005-2017); Honoree, Super Lawyer (2015-2017); Honoree, Florida Legal Elite (2015, 2017); Jon E. Krupnick Award for Perseverance, Florida Justice Association (2016); Richard Sadow Award, Friends of 440 Scholarship Fund, Inc. (2016); Outstanding Claimant's Attorney Award, Friends of 440 Scholarship Fund, Inc. (2015); Rising Start in Florida, Super Lawyer

Magazine (2009); AVVO Rated Attorney **BAR:** United States District Court Southern District of Florida (2005); The Florida Bar (1995) **H:** Travel; Camping; Golf **BA:** 2030 S Douglas Rd Ste 217, Touby, Chait & Sicking, Pl, Coral Gables, FL, 33134

TOWE, THOMAS EDWARD, T: Lawyer **I:** Law and Legal Services **CN:** Towe, Ball, Mackey, Sommerfeld & Turner, P.L.L.P. **DOB:** 06/25/1937 **PB:** Cherokee **SC:** IA/USA **PT:** Edward Towe; Florence (Tow) Towe (Deceased) **MS:** Married **SPN:** Ruth James (8/21/1960) **CH:** James Thomas; Kristofer Edward **ED:** Coursework, University of Michigan, Ann Arbor, MI (1965-1967); LLM, Georgetown University (1965); LLB, University of Montana (1962); BA, Earlham College (1959); Coursework, University of Paris (1956) **C:** Chairman, Montana State Parks & Recreation Board (2013-2017); Partner, Towe, Ball, Mackey, Sommerfeld & Turner, P.L.L.P., Billings, MT (1967-Present); Lecturer, Institute of Law, Bashkir State University, Ufa, Russia (2010); Legislator, Montana State Senate, Billings, MT (1991-1994); Legislator, Montana State Senate, Billings, MT (1975-1987); Legislator, Montana House of Representatives, Billings, MT (1971-1975); Visiting Professor, Rajiv Gandhi National University Law School, Patiala, Punjab State, India (2018) **CR:** Member, Montana Coal Board (2013-2015) **CIV:** Treasurer, Our Montana Inc. (1993-Present); Board Member, Plains Justice (2014-2016); Board Member, The United States Institute of Peace (1993-2013); Board Member, Youth Dynamics (1989-1996); Board Member, ZooMontana (1985-2001); President, Alternatives, Inc., Billings, MT (1985-1986); Board Member, Volunteers of America, Billings, MT (1984-1989); Member, Advisory Committee, Youth Justice Council (1981-1983); Board Member, Alternatives, Inc., Billings, MT (1977-1999); Democratic Candidate for Congress (1976); Board of Directors, Rimrock Guidance Foundation (1975-1980); Board of Directors, Montana Consumer Affairs Council (1973-1977); Board Member, Community Services for the Developmentally Disabled (1975-1977); Member, Advisory Committee, Montana Crime Control Board (1973-1978); Member, State Democratic Executive Committee (1969-1973) **MIL:** Captain, Judge Advocate General Corps, U.S. Army (1962-1965) **CW:** Contributor, Articles, Law Reviews; Contributor, Articles, Guest Editorials **AW:** Jeanette Rankin Civil Liberties Award, ACLU (2008); Named One of 100 Most Influential Montanans in the 20th Century, Missoulian (1999); Named One of 12 State Officials in the United States as "Stars of the States," Washington Monthly Magazine; Named One of 10 Best State and Local Officials in the United States, Mother Jones Magazine; 50 Year Pin Award, State Bar of Montana **MEM:** Greater Yellowstone County Bar Association; State Bar of Montana; Yellowstone Area Bar Association; Billings Chamber of Commerce **BAR:** U.S. Court of Appeals, 2nd Circuit (2002); Crow Tribal Court (2002); U.S. Court of Appeals, 10th Circuit (1976); U.S. Court of Appeals, 9th Circuit (1974); U.S. District Court, District of Montana (1967); U.S. Claims Court (1965); U.S. Supreme Court (1965); U.S. Court of Military Appeals (1963); Montana Bar (1962) **H:** Outdoor recreation; Travel **PA:** Democrat **RE:** The Religious Society of Friends **BA:** 2525 6th Ave N, Towe, Ball, Mackey, Sommerfeld & Turner, P.L.L.P., Billings, MT, 59101 **ADD:** 2739 Gregory Dr S, Billings, MT, 59102

TOWNSEND, JOHN MICHAEL, T: Partner **I:** Law and Legal Services **CN:** Hughes Hubbard & Reed LLP **DOB:** 03/21/1947 **PB:** West Point **SC:** NY/USA **PT:** John D. Townsend; Vera (Nachman) Townsend **MS:** Married **SPN:** Frances M. Fragos

(10/8/1994) **CH:** James E.; Patrick M. **ED:** JD, Yale University (1971); BA, Yale University (1968) **C:** Partner, Hughes Hubbard & Reed LLP, Washington, DC (1990-Present); Partner, Hughes Hubbard & Reed LLP, New York, NY (1980-1990); Associate, Hughes Hubbard & Reed LLP, New York, NY (1975-1980); Associate, Hughes Hubbard & Reed LLP, Paris, France (1973-1974); Associate, Hughes Hubbard & Reed LLP, New York, NY (1971-1973) **CR:** Member, Panel of Arbitrators, International Center for Settlement Investment Disputes (2008-2016); Member, Board of Directors, American Arbitration Association (1995-2016); Trustee, United States Council for International Business (2000-2012); Chairman, Board of Directors, American Arbitration Association (2007-2010); Member, Chair, Mediation Committee, IBA (2005-2006); Chairman, Law Committee, American Arbitration Association; Vice President of Court, London Court of International Arbitration; Member, Council of the American Arbitration Association **MIL:** First Lieutenant, U.S. Army Reserve (1971-1975) **CW:** Author, "When the BIT hits the FAA: U.S. Courts Confront Conditions Precedent in Bilateral Investment Treaties," Contemporary Issues in International Arbitration and Mediation (2014); Author, "The Rise and Fall of Class Arbitration," AAA Yearbook on Arbitration & the Law, 23rd Edition, Juris Publishing Inc. (2011); Author, "The New Bahrain Arbitration Law and the Bahrain 'Free Arbitration Zone,'" Dispute Resolution Journal (2010); Author, "Drafting Arbitration Clauses: Avoiding the 7 Deadly Sins," Dispute Resolution Journal (2003); Co-Author, "Arbitration Across the Civil Law: Common Law Divide," Arbitration International (2002) **MEM:** ABA; The American Law Institute; College of Commercial Arbitrators; The University Club of Washington DC; The Yale Club of New York City; New York City Bar Association **BAR:** Admitted to Practice, United States Court of Appeals for the First Circuit (2003); Admitted to Practice, United States Court of Federal Claims (2000); Admitted to Practice, United States Court of Appeals for the 11th Circuit (2001); Admitted to Practice, United States Court of Appeals for the Federal Circuit (2000); Admitted to Practice, United States Court of Appeals for the Fourth Circuit (1991); Admitted to Practice, United States Court of Appeals District of Columbia Circuit (1990); Admitted to Practice, United States District Court District of Columbia (1990); Admitted to Practice, United States Court of Appeals for the Tenth Circuit (1986); Admitted to Practice, United States Court of Appeals for the Seventh Circuit (1986); Admitted to Practice, United States Court of Appeals for the Eighth Circuit (1982); Admitted to Practice, United States District Court Southern District of New York (1975); Admitted to Practice, U.S. District Court - Eastern New York (1975); Admitted to Practice, United States Court of Appeals for the Second Circuit (1975); Admitted to Practice, Supreme Court of the United States (1975); Admitted to Practice, The District of Columbia (1990); New York (1972) **MH:** Albert Nelson Marquis Lifetime Achievement Award (2017) **PA:** Democrat **RE:** Episcopalian **BA:** 1775 I St NW Ste 600, Hughes Hubbard & Reed LLP, Washington, DC, 20006 **ADD:** 4735 Woodway Ln NW, Washington, DC, 20016 **URL:** http://www.hugheshubbard.com

TRAVERS-SMITH, BRIAN J., T: Retired **I:** Fine Art **DOB:** 06/26/1931 **PB:** Tangshan **SC:** China **PT:** Iris Winifred; Auguste William Travers-Smith **MS:** Married **SPN:** Barbara Elizabeth **CH:** Diana Rochfort Travers-Smith; David Rochfort Travers-Smith; Edward Rochfort Travers-Smith **C:** Canada Trust, Estates Officer, Will Planner; Realtor; Professional Artist **CR:** President, Board

of Directors, Art Gallery of Greater Victoria **MIL:** High-speed Radio Operator, Instructor, Signal Corps, United States Army (1952-1954) **CW:** Artist, Various Painted Works, Collections; Featured Artist, Art Gallery of Greater Victoria; Artist, Collection of Watercolours, Royal Library, Windsor Castle, United Kingdom **AW:** Honoree, Honorary Citizen of Victoria, BC (1983); Queen Elizabeth II Silver Jubilee Medal (1977); First Prize, Annual Exhibition, Art Gallery of Greater Victoria **MEM:** Signature Member, American Watercolor Society, Inc.; Signature Member, Allied Artists of America; Past Member, Canadian Society of Painters in Water Colour; Past Member, Board of Directors, Victoria Symphony Canada; Past Member, Emily Carr College of Art + Design; Past President, Art Gallery of Greater Victoria **MH:** Distinguished Humanitarian (2017) **H:** Photography; Sports Fishing **RE:** Anglican **ADD:** 311-1725 Beach Dr, Victoria, BC, Canada, V8R 6H9

TREFRY, MARY G., T: Professor Emerita **I:** Education/Educational Services **CN:** Sacred Heart University **MS:** Married **SPN:** Robert (Bob) Tefry **CH:** Greg; Ginger Gary (Daughter-in-Law); Mike; Rebecca "Becca" Simpson (Daughter-in-Law) **ED:** PhD in Organizational and Social Psychology, Columbia University, New York, NY (1991); MA in Organizational and Social Psychology, Columbia University, New York, NY (1987); MLS in Library and Information Services, University of Maryland, College Park, MD (1974); BA in French, Agnes Scott College, Decatur, GA (1969) **C:** Professor Emerita, Sacred Heart University (2017-Present); Coordinator, Luxembourg MBA Programs, John F. Welch College of Business, Sacred Heart University (2011-2017); Associate Professor of Management, John F. Welch College of Business, Sacred Heart University (2006-2017); Chairperson, Department of Management, Sacred Heart University (2006-2010); Academic Graduate Programs, Sacred Heart University (2001-2002); Assistant Professor in Management, Sacred Heart University (2000-2006); Associate Professor, Sacred Heart University (1998-2017); Visiting Full-time Instructor, Sacred Heart University (1998-2000); Adjunct Instructor, Sacred Heart University (1994-1998); Principal, Trefry Resource Group (1983-2000); Public Services Coordinator, Kansas City Public Library (1979-1982); Branch Manager, Public Library System, Fairfax County Public Library (1974-1979) **CR:** Council on Internationalization, Jack Welch College of Business, Sacred Heart University (2015-2017); University Education Study Abroad Committee, Sacred Heart University (2013-2015); Internationalization Task Force, Sacred Heart University (2013-2014); Chairperson, Search Committee for Full-Time Faculty, Sacred Heart University, Luxembourg (2012-2013); Search Committee, Healthcare Informatics Faculty, Sacred Heart University (2012); Co-Chairperson, Faculty Assembly, Jack Welch College of Business, Sacred Heart University (2010-2016); Committee Member, Academic Affairs, Sacred Heart University (2010-2014); Chairperson, Future of Luxembourg Task Force, Sacred Heart University (2010-2011); Committee Member, Task Force on MBA Certificates, Sacred Heart University (2010); MBA Integrated Core Course Design Committee, Sacred Heart University (2009-2010); Search Committee for University Librarian, Sacred Heart University (2009-2010); Chairperson, Task Force on MBA Electives, Sacred Heart University (2009); Search Committee Member, Management Department, John F. Welch College of Business, Sacred Heart University (2008-2009); Committee to Review Non-Faculty Performance Appraisal Process, Sacred Heart University (2008); Chairperson, Search Committee, John F. Welch College of Business, Sacred Heart

University (2007-2009); Chairperson, Management Department, Sacred Heart University (2006-2010); Committee Member, University Core Curriculum Implementation Task Force, Sacred Heart University (2007-2008); Graduate Curriculum Subcommittee of Academic Affairs, Sacred Heart University (2006-2008); Task Force on Performance Appraisal Process for Non-Faculty Members, Sacred Heart University (2006-2007); Chairperson, Search Committee for Luxembourg Director, Sacred Heart University (2006); Participant, Experienced Leadership Retreats, Sacred Heart University (2005-2007) Committee to Select Recipient of Outstanding Teacher Award, Sacred Heart University (2005-2007); Chairperson, Undergraduate Advisement Task Force, Sacred Heart University (2005-2006); Search Committee for Associate University Librarian, Sacred Heart University (2005); Affiliate, Library Site Visit, Criteria Evaluation Team, Sacred Heart University (2005); Facilitator, "Work-Out" Session on Undergraduate Advisement, Sacred Heart University (2005); Affiliate, College of Business Governance Committee, Sacred Heart University (2005); Luxembourg Faculty Member, Sacred Heart University (2004); Search Committee, Sacred Heart University (2004); University Academic Governance Redesign Committee, Sacred Heart University (2003-2004); Chairperson, Search Committee for Luxembourg Academic Director, Sacred Heart University (2003-2004); AACSB Curriculum Standards of Self Evaluation Report Committee, Sacred Heart University (2003-2004); MBA Committee, AACSB (2003); Faculty Spokesperson, TV Advertisement, Sacred Heart University (2002-2008); Chairperson, Graduate Curriculum Committee, Sacred Heart University (2002-2006); Oral Communications Assessment Task Force, Sacred Heart University (2002-2003); Chairperson, MBA Director Search Committee, Sacred Heart University (2002); Strategic Planning Task Force, Sacred Heart University (2002); Administrative Affairs Committee, Jack Welch College of Business, Sacred Heart University (2001-2017); Co-Chairperson, Library and Information Services Standard Committee, Re-Accreditation Process, New England Association of Schools and Colleges (2001-2003); University Budget Committee, Sacred Heart University (2001-2002); Council of Graduate Directors, Sacred Heart University (2001-2002); Adult Services Task Force, Sacred Heart University (2001-2002); Chairperson, Ad Hoc Committee on Danbury MBA Program Closing, Sacred Heart University (2001); Faculty Institute Committee, Sacred Heart University (2001); Search Committee, Sacred Heart University (2001); Stamford Campus Director, Sacred Heart University (2001); Faculty Advisor, International Graduate Forum, Sacred Heart University (2000-2007); Search Committee Member, Management Department, John F. Welch College of Business, Sacred Heart University (2000-2003); Dean's Faculty Council, Sacred Heart University (1998-1999); Organization Development Consultant, White Plains, NY (1983-2000); Organization Development Consultant, Champaign, IL (1983-2000); Organization Development Consultant, Fairfield, CT (1983-2000); Management Trainer, White Plains, NY (1983-2000); Management Trainer, Champaign, IL (1983-2000); Management Trainer, Fairfield, CT (1983-2000); Adjunct Faculty Representative to Assistant Director, Public Library System, Kansas City, KS (1980-1983); Senior-Level Manager, Large Public Library Systems (1974-1983); Mid-Level Manager, Large Public Library Systems (1974-1983) **CIV:** Committee Chairperson, Strategic Planning Committee, Mercy Learning Center, Bridgeport, CT (2010-2012); Board Member, Mercy Learning Center, Bridgeport, CT (2006-2013); Facilitator, Staff Strategic Planning Process, Mercy

Learning Center, Bridgeport, CT (2006); Board of Directors, Bridgeport Hospital Auxiliary, Yale New Haven Health, Bridgeport, CT (2002-2010); Near & Far Aid Association Inc (2002-2005) **CW:** Co-Presenter, "Three Popes: Lessons in Leadership," Experiential Learning Association in Association with Eastern Academy of Management Annual Conference, New Haven, CT (2016); Co-Presenter, "Friendly and Fresh Foods Heads Off to China," Experiential Learning Association in Association with Eastern Academy Of Management, Annual Meeting, Philadelphia, PA (2015); Co-Author, "Windows on the World: An Experiential Exercise," Organization Management Journal (2014); Co-Presenter, "Aphorisms as Aids," Experiential Learning Association in Association with Eastern Academy of Management Annual Meeting, Newport, RI (2014); Co-Presenter, "Windows on the World: An Experiential Exercise," Experiential Learning Association in Association with Eastern Academy of Management Annual Meeting, Baltimore, MD (2013); Co-Author, "Culture Shock: Hiding in Plain Sight," Organization Management Journal, Volume Nine (2012); Presenter, "Hospital Headlines: Committed to Your Health and Keeping Your Trust," Case Association Annual Meeting in Association with the Eastern Academy of Management Annual Meeting, Philadelphia, PA (2012); Co-Presenter, "Critical Incidents: Catalyst for Team and Organizational Learning," Experiential Learning Association in Association with Eastern Academy of Management Annual Meeting, Boston, MA (2011); Co-Author, "Starting with Howard Gardner's Five Minds, Adding Elliott Jaque's Responsibility Time Span: Implications for Undergraduate Management Education," Organization Management Journal (2010); Co-Presenter, "Culture Shock: Hiding in Plain Sight - An Experiential Exercise," Experiential Learning Association in Association with Eastern Academy of Management Annual Meeting, Portland, ME (2010); Co-Presenter, "Designing Courses to Develop Minds for the Future," OBTC Teaching Conference for Management Educators, Babson College, Boston, MA (2008); Co-Presenter, "The Power of Five Minds: The Power of One Framework," Eastern Academy of Management Annual Meeting, Washington, DC (2008); Author, "A Double-Edged Sword: Organizational Culture in Multicultural Organizations," International Journal of Management (2006); Co-Author, "Dialogues and Decisions: Moral Dilemmas in the Workplace," Simulation and Gaming: An Interdisciplinary Journal of Theory, Practice and Research (2006); Others **AW:** Faculty Global Engagement Award, Sacred Heart University (2017); Distinguished Service Award, Alumni Organization, Sacred Heart University (2017); Bishop Walter J. Curtis Award, John F. Welch College of Business, Sacred Heart University (2013); Teaching Excellence Award, Sacred Heart University (2004); Leadership Award, Council of Graduate Students, Sacred Heart University (2003); Discovery Award, Sacred Heart University (1999) **MEM:** Eastern Academy of Management; ODN New York; Organizational Behavior and Teaching Society; North American Case Writers Association **MH:** Distinguished Humanitarian (2017) **RE:** Unitarian **ADD:** 190 Chatham Road, Fairfield, CT, 06825 **URL:** http://www.sacredheart.edu/academics/jackwelchcollegeofbusiness

TREFTS, JOAN, T: Principal **I:** Education/Educational Services **DOB:** 01/31/1930 **PB:** Pittsburgh **SC:** PA/USA **PT:** William Henry III Landenberger; Eleanore (Campbell) Landenberger; **MS:** Married **SPN:** Albert Sharpe Trefts, Sr. (June 20, 1952) **CH:** Dorothy; Albert, Jr.; William; Deborah; Elizabeth **ED:** Master's Degree, John Carroll University (1984); Master's Degree, John Carroll

University (1982); AB, Western College for Women (1952) **CT:** Licensed Home Economist; Principal, New York State Education Department; Principal, Ohio Department of Education; Supervisor; Biological Science Educator; Economics Educator; Vocational Educator; Pre-Kindergarten Educator **C:** Inner City Principal, John Adams High School (1996-2013); Inner City Principal, Collinwood High School (1996-2013); Inner City Principal, South High School (1996-2013); Science Teacher, John Adams High School (1996-2013); Science Teacher, Collinwood High School (1996-2013); Science Teacher, South High School (1996-2013); Summer School Principal, John Adams High School (1972-1995); Summer School Principal, Collinwood High School (1972-1995); Summer School Principal, South High School (1972-1995) **CR:** Consultant, Cleveland Partnership Program **CIV:** Trustee, Chautauqua Literacy and Science Circle; Trustee, Presbyterian Association of Chautauqua, New York **AW:** Recipient, Teacher of Year (1994) **MEM:** President General, The National Society of the Dames of the Court of Honor (2001-Present); State Officer, National Society Daughters of the American Revolution (2000-Present); National Society of Arts and Letters; Board of Directors, Ohio ACTE; National Committee Member, Association for Career & Technical Education; American Association of Family and Consumer Sciences; Trustee, Presbyterian Association of Chautauqua, New York; National Society Colonial Dames XVII Century; National Society United States Daughters of 1812; President, Chapter 18, The National Society of the Colonial Dames of America; Court Honor Officer, The National Society of the Colonial Dames of America; National Officer, National Officers Colonial Clergy; Chancellor, National Officers Colonial Clergy; State Officer, National Society Daughters of the American Colonists; National Officer, National Society Colonial Daughters of the Seventeenth Century; President, New England Society of Cleveland & The Western Reserve; Clearwater Country Club; Cleveland Skating Club; The Union Club of Cleveland **H:** Curling; Rug Hooking; Needlepoint **PA:** Republican **RE:** Presbyterian **BA:** 219 Park Circle S. PO Box 761, Chautauqua, NY, 14722 **ADD:** 219 Park Circle S., Dunedin, FL, 34698

TROW, ROBERT LEWIS, T: Chief Executive Officer, Owner **I:** Education/Educational Services **CN:** DermaConcepts USA **DOB:** 08/29/1945 **PB:** Atlantic City **SC:** NJ/USA **PT:** Henry A. Trow; Gertrude (Wortman) Trow **MS:** Married **SPN:** Jacqueline Rosemary Granger Boyden (11/22/1973); Carol Smira Trow **CH:** Amy Victoria; Abigail Boyden; Jon Sofro; Jill London **ED:** Degree, Institute for Educational Management, Harvard University (1985); MS, Long Island University (1970); BA, Hartwick College (1967) **C:** Vice President of Administration and Finance, Stockton State College, Pomona, NJ (1978-Present); Director, Planning and Development, Stockton State College, Pomona, NJ (1976-1978); Director of Administrative Operations, Staten Island Community College (1974-1976); Director of Financial Aid, Placement, Career Counseling, Staten Island Community College (1971-1974); Assistant Director, Staten Island Community College (1971); Counselor, Student Personnel, Staten Island Community College (1969-1971); Baseball Coach; Entrepreneur; Corporate Officer **CR:** Evaluator, Middle States Commission on Higher Education, Philadelphia, PA (1983-Present); Board of Directors, Southern New Jersey High Technology Consortium **CIV:** Budget Committee Member, Trustee, Federation of Jewish Agencies (1984-Present); Treasurer, Board of Directors, Family Services Association of New Jersey (1983-Present); Board of Directors,

Jewish Services of New Jersey (1983-Present); Chairman, Planning, Jewish Services of New Jersey (1983-Present); Board of Directors, Private Industry Council (1983-Present); Richard Stockton Foundation (1979-Present); New Jersey Natural Reserve Council (1979-1982); Trustee, Friends School, New Jersey (1979-1980) **CW:** Contributor, More than 100 Articles, Professional Trade Publications **MEM:** National Association of Governing Boards; National Association of College and University Business Officers; South Jersey Development Council; Mainland Chamber of Commerce **MH:** Albert Nelson Marquis Lifetime Achievement Award (2017) **H:** Reading; Writing; Golf; Supporting community arts and civic organizations **BA:** 168 Industrial Dr Unit 1, Dermacare USA, Mashpee, MA, 02649

TROZZOLO, ANTHONY MARION, T: Huisking Professor Emeritus of Chemistry **I:** Education/Educational Services **CN:** University of Notre Dame **DOB:** 01/11/1930 **PB:** Chicago **SC:** IL/USA **PT:** Pasquale Trozzolo; Francesca (Vercillo) Trozzolo **MS:** Widowed **SPN:** Doris C. Stoffregen (10/8/1955, Deceased 2011) **CH:** Thomas; Susan; Patricia; Michael; Lisa; Laura **ED:** PhD in Chemistry, The University of Chicago (1960); MS in Chemistry, The University of Chicago (1957); BS in Chemistry, Illinois Institute of Technology (1950) **C:** Charles L. Huisking Professor Emeritus of Chemistry, University of Notre Dame (1992-Present); Assistant Dean, College of Science, University of Notre Dame (1993-1998); Charles L. Huisking Professor of Chemistry, University of Notre Dame (1975-1992); Distinguished Lecturer of Science, University of Notre Dame (1986); Hesburgh Alumni Lecturer, University of Notre Dame (1986); Technical Staff, Bell Laboratories (Now Nokia), Murray Hill, NJ (1959-1975); Reilly Lecturer, University of Notre Dame (1972); Associate Chemist, Armour Research Foundation (Now IITRI), Chicago, IL (1953-1956); Assistant Chemist, Chicago Midway Laboratories (1952-1953) **CR:** Rocky Mountain Lecturer, American Chemical Society (2002); J. Crano Lecturer, The University of Akron (2000); Coronado Lecturer, American Chemical Society (1998); Osage Lecturer, American Chemical Society (1998); Southeast Texas Lecturer, American Chemical Society (1996); Rocky Mountain Lecturer, American Chemical Society (1996); Hoosier Lecturer, American Chemical Society (1995); Ozark Lecturer, American Chemical Society (1995); New York State Lecturer, American Chemical Society (1993); Coronado Lecturer, American Chemical Society (1993); Visiting Professor, Max Planck Institute für Strahlenchemie, Mülheim/Ruhr, Federal Republic of Germany (1990); Trustee, Gordon Research Conferences (1988-1992); Visiting Lecturer, Academia Sinica (1984-1985); Visiting Professor, Katholieke University, Leuven, Belgium (1983); Chevron Lecturer, University of Nevada, Reno, NV (1983); Pacific Coast Lecturer, American Chemical Society (1981); Visiting Professor, University of Colorado (1981); Coronado Lecturer, American Chemical Society (1980); Lecturer, Abbott Laboratories (Now Abbott) (1978); F.O. Butler Lecturer, South Dakota State University (1978); Sigma Xi Lecturer, Bowling Green State University (1976); Michael Faraday Lecturer, Northern Illinois University (1976); Texas Lecturer, American Chemical Society (1975); C.L. Brown Lecturer, Rutgers, The State University of New Jersey (1975); Visiting Professor, Columbia University, New York, NY (1971); Phillips Lecturer, The University of Oklahoma (1971); Founder, Gordon Research Conference on Organic Photochemistry (1964); Chairman, Gordon Research Conference on Organic Photochemistry (1964); Plenary Lecturer, Various International Conferences; Consultant in Field **CW:** Consultant Editor, Encyclopedia of Science and Technology (1982-1992); Editorial Advisory Board, Accounts of Chemical Research (1977-1985); Editor, Chemical Reviews (1977-1984); Associate Editor, Journal American Chemical Society (1975-1976); Contributor, Articles, Professional Journals; Patentee, 31 Patents in Field **AW:** Distinguished Alumnus Award, University of Chicago (2012); Elected Fellow, American Chemical Society (2012); Distinguished Alumnus Award, Illinois Institute of Technology (2009); UNICO National Marconi Science Award (2008); Elected Fellow, Inter-American Photochemical Society (2000); Pietro Bucci Prize, University of Calabria and Italian Chemical Society (1997); Named Honorary Citizen Of Castrolibero, Italy (1997); Halpern Award in Photochemistry, The New York Academy of Science (1980); Distinguished Service Award, Saint Joseph Valley Section, American Chemical Society (1979); Elected Fellow, American Association for the Advancement of Science (1963); Elected Fellow, American Institute of Chemists (1962); Fellow, National Science Foundation (1957-1959); Fellow, Atomic Energy Commission (Now Energy Research and Development Administration and the U.S. Nuclear Regulatory Commission) (1951); Student Award, American Institute of Chemists (1950) **MEM:** Chairman, Chemical Science Section, The New York Academy of Science (1969-1970); Life Fellow, American Association for the Advancement of Science; Inter-American Photochemical Society; American Chemical Society; American Institute of Chemists; Sigma Xi, The Scientific Research Honor Society **MH:** Albert Nelson Marquis Lifetime Achievement Award (2017) **RE:** Roman Catholic **ADD:** 53419 Hansel Ln, South Bend, IN, 46637 **URL:** https://chemistry.nd.edu/people/anthony-m-trozzolo/

TSAI, JAMES C., T: Ophthalmologist, Researcher, Educator, Healthcare Administrator **I:** Medicine & Health Care **CN:** New York Eye and Ear Infirmary of Mount Sinai **ED:** MBA, Vanderbilt University (1998); Resident in Ophthalmology, University of Southern California, Doheny Eye Institute, Los Angeles, CA (1990-1993); Intern in Medicine, Cedars-Sinai Medical Center, Los Angeles, CA (1989-1990); MD, Stanford University (1989); BA in Neuroscience, Amherst College (1985) **CT:** Diplomate, National Board of Medical Examiners; Diplomate, American Board of Ophthalmology **C:** President, New York Eye and Ear Infirmary of Mount Sinai, Mount Sinai Health System, New York, NY (2014-Present); System Chair, Icahn School of Medicine at Mount Sinai, New York, NY (2014-Present); Delafield-Rodgers Professor of Ophthalmology, Icahn School of Medicine at Mount Sinai, New York, NY (2014-Present); Robert Young Professor, Yale University School of Medicine, New Haven, CT (2006-2014); Chair, Department of Ophthalmology and Visual Science, Yale University School of Medicine, New Haven, CT (2006-2014); Chief of Ophthalmology, Yale-New Haven Hospital, New Haven, CT (2006-2014); Director, Glaucoma Division, Edward S. Harkness Eye Institute, Columbia University College of Physicians and Surgeons, New York, NY (2001-2006); Associate Professor of Ophthalmology, Edward S. Harkness Eye Institute, Columbia University College of Physicians and Surgeons, New York, NY (2001-2006); Assistant Professor of Ophthalmology and Visual Sciences, Vanderbilt University School of Medicine, Nashville, TN (1995-2001); Glaucoma Fellow, Moorfields Eye Hospital, London, England (1994-1995); Glaucoma Fellow, Bascom Palmer Eye Institute, Miami, FL (1993-1994) **CR:** Planning Committee, National Eye Institute, National Institutes of Health (2010-Present); Scientific Advisory Board, National Medical Research Council, Singapore (2010-Present);

Chair, Glaucoma Subcommittee, National Eye Health Education Program; Fellow, American College of Surgeons; Fellow, American Academy of Ophthalmology; Fellow, The New York Academy of Medicine **CIV:** Alumni Trustee, Amherst College (2011-2015) **AW:** Physician Scientist Award, Fight for Sight, Inc. (2015); Secretariat Award, American Academy of Ophthalmology (2015); Distinguished Alumnus Award, Doheny Eye Institute, University of Southern California (2013); Doheny Society of Scholars Medallion (2011); Senior Achievement Award, American Academy of Ophthalmology (2009); Visionary Award, Fight for Sight, Inc. (2007); Homer McK. Rees Glaucoma Scholar, Columbia University (2001-2004) **MEM:** Elected Member, American Ophthalmological Society; Elected Member, American Eye Study Club **BA:** 310 E 14th Street, New York Eye & Ear Infirmary of Mount Sinai, New York, NY, 10003

TSEYTLIN, YAKOV M., T: Doctor of Technical Sciences **I:** Engineering **CN:** International Society of Automation (ISA) **DOB:** 07/23/1933 **PB:** Leningrad **SC:** Russia **MS:** Widowed **CH:** Mark Tseytlin **ED:** Doctor of Technical Science, Mendeleev All Union Research Institute of Metrology, Russia (1991); PhD, Leningrad Polytechnic Institute (Now Peter the Great Sankt Petersburg Polytechnic University) (1965); MS in Mechanical Engineering, Leningrad Polytechnic Institute (Now Peter the Great Sankt Petersburg Polytechnic University) **C:** Project Engineer, Automatic Machine Co. (1999); Senior Designer, Federal Products Co. (1992); Senior Researcher, Federal Products Co. (1992); United States Adviser, Opponent Graduate Dissertations; Manager, Engineers, All Union Institute of Advanced Education Standardization & Metrology; Visiting Professor, Leningrad Institute of Fine Mechanics & Optics; Assistant to Associate Professor, Leningrad Polytechnic Institute (Now Peter the Great Sankt Petersburg Polytechnic University); Senior Designer, Leningrad Instrumental Plant, D.I. Mendeleev All-Russian Institute for Metrology; Senior Lead Researcher, Leningrad Instrumental Plant, D.I. Mendeleev All-Russian Institute for Metrology; Chief, Research Laboratory, Leningrad Instrumental Plant, D.I. Mendeleev All-Russian Institute for Metrology **CW:** Author, "Precision Elasticity in Micro-Nanomechanics" (2017); Author, "Advanced Mechanical Models of DNA Elasticity" (2016); Author, "Structural Synthesis in Precision Elasticity" (2006); Contributor, Numerous Articles, Professional Journals; Author, Five Monographs **AW:** Recognition Award, International Society of Automation; Gold Medal, School Graduation **MEM:** International Society of Automation (1998-2018); Life Member, International Society of Automation **MH:** Albert Nelson Marquis Lifetime Achievement Award (2017) **ADD:** 20 Randall St Apt 5G, Providence, RI, 02904

TUCKER, THOMAS, T: Mathematics Professor **I:** Education/Educational Services **CN:** Colgate University **DOB:** 07/15/1945 **PB:** Princeton **SC:** NJ/USA **PT:** Albert William Tucker; Alice Judson (Curtiss) Beckenbach **MS:** Married **SPN:** Mollie Dalton **CH:** Thomas John; Emily McDonnell **ED:** PhD, Dartmouth College (1971); AB, Harvard University, Magna Cum Laude (1967) **C:** Charles G. Hetherington Professor of Mathematics, Colgate University, Hamilton, NY (1994-Present); Professor, Colgate University, Hamilton, NY (1983-Present); Professor Emeritus, Colgate University (2013); Director, Division of National Science, Colgate University, Hamilton, NY (1993-1996); Acting Dean, Colgate University, Hamilton, NY (1991-1992); Chairman, Mathematics Department, Colgate University, Hamilton, NY (1982-1986); From Assistant Professor to Professor

of Mathematics, Colgate University, Hamilton, NY (1973-1983); Instructor, Princeton University (1971-1973) **CR:** Consultant, Educational Testing Service (1973-Present); President, Calculus Consortium for Higher Education, Inc. (1998-2005); Consultant, Institute for Defense Analyses, Princeton, NJ (1984-1985); Chairman, Advanced Placement Calculus Committee, College Board, New York City, NY (1983-1987); Visiting Associate Professor, Dartmouth College, Hanover, NH (1978-1979); Consultant, Institute for Defense Analyses, Princeton, NJ (1978-1979, 1974-1975) **CW:** Editor, "Priming the Calculus Pump" (1990); Co-author, "Topological Graph Theory" (1987); Contributor, Numerous Articles, Professional Journals **AW:** Grantee, National Science Foundation (1990-1997, 1989, 1986-1988, 1980-1982, 1976-1977) **MEM:** Vice President, Mathematical Association of America (1990-1992); American Mathematical Society; Society for Industrial and Applied Mathematics **ADD:** PO Box 163, Sagamore Beach, MA, 02562

TURNER, DEBORA , I: Law and Legal Services **ED:** JD, University of Miami **CT:** Certified Florida Public Pension Trustee, Florida Public Pension Trustees Association (2015)

TURNER, RALPH LAMAR, I: Education/Educational Services **CN:** Associate Professor **ED:** MEd, East Tennessee State University (2005); EdD, East Tennessee State University (1996); MPE, East Tennessee State University (1988); MA in Religion, Eastern Mennonite Seminary (1983); BA in Interdisciplinary Studies, Emory & Henry College (1978) **CT:** Apprentice Teacher License, State of Tennessee; Teaching License, State of Virginia; Kinesiotherapy Association License, United States **C:** Associate Professor, College of Education, Eastern Kentucky University (2014-Present); Library Science Program Coordinator, Eastern Kentucky University (2014-Present); Assistant Professor, College of Education, Eastern Kentucky University (2010-2014); Library Science Program Coordinator, Eastern Kentucky University (2010-2014); Assistant Professor, College of Library and Information Science, Southern Utah University (2008-2010); Adjunct Faculty, Clemmer College of Education, East Tennessee State University (2006-2010); Fulbright Professor, Department of Education, Istanbul, Turkey (2006); Librarian, Covington High School, Covington, VA (2005-2008); Media Specialist, Covington High School, Covington, VA (2005-2008); Graduate Assistant, Charles C. Sherrod Library, East Tennessee State University (2004-2005); Reference Librarian, Charles C. Sherrod Library, East Tennessee State University (2004-2005); English Language Instructor, EF International Schools (2003-2004); Fulbright Senior Professor, College of Padagogik und Sport Wissenschaft, Technical University of Munich (2002-2003); Registered Kinesiotherapist, James H. Quillen V.A. Medical Center, U.S. Department of Veterans Affairs, Johnson City, TN (2002); Exercise Physiologist, Johnson City Medical Center (1991-1993); Instructor, Department of Physical Education, King College (1986-1989) **CW:** Reviewer, "Smart Learning Contents Adaptation Engine for Learning Device," American Scientific Publishers (2017); Reviewer, "Dynamic FPGA Detection and Protection of Hardware Trojan: A Comparative Analysis," International Journal of Computing and Digital Systems (2016); Reviewer, "Applying the Humanistic Learning Theory: Effects on the Experience and Learning Pattern Related to the Prevention of Child Obesity," International Conference on Education, Jakarta, Indonesia (2016); Reviewer, "Process, Results, and Consequences of Madrasa Accreditation: A Case Study in Lampung, Indonesia," International

Conference on Education, Jakarta, Indonesia (2016); Reviewer, "Smart Learning Contents Adaptation Engine for Learning Devices Types and Learner's Property for Smart Learning," International Conference on Education, Jakarta, Indonesia (2016); Co-Author, "Speaking Without Tongues: Toward a More Humane Construct of the Online Learning Environment," National Social Science Association Proceedings (2016); Author, "'Why do you think I am paying you if not to have my way?' Genre complications in the free market critiques of fictional and filmed versions of True Grit," The Journal of Popular Culture (2015); Co-Author, "Trends and issues of the school librarianship curriculum," Journal of Education in Library and Information Science (JELIS) (2015); Author, "Taymor's tempests: Sea change, or seeing little change in responses to gender and leadership?" Journal of Gender Studies (2014); Author, "Collaborations beyond the Cave: A consideration of sacred architecture in the creation of collaborative library spaces," Journal of Learning Spaces (2013); Reviewer, "The Innovation of Biomaterial in Jewellery Design," IEEE Symposium on Business, Engineering and Industrial Applications (2013); Reviewer, "Myanmar Transformation: The American Perspective." IEEE Symposium on Humanities, Science & Engineering Research, Penong, Malaysia (2013); Peer-Reviewer, "International Journal of Sport and Society" (2012); Editor, "International Journal of Sport and Society" (2012); Peer-Reviewer, "International Journal of Sport and Society" (2011); Editor, "International Journal of Sport and Society" (2011); Reviewer, "The Study of Recovery in Rat Skeletal Muscles after Acute Contusion by Using Basic Fibroblast Growth Factor-Coated Magnetic Nanoparticles," The International Journal of Sport and Society (2011); Author, "Notes from the Noodle Factory: 21st-century leadership in search of new paradigms," School Libraries Worldwide (2011); Author, "'She's got game: The role of the female protagonist as mentor and muse in the sports films of Ron Shelton," The International Journal of Sport and Society (2010); Co-Author, "Trends in Print vs. Electronic Use in School Libraries," The Reference Librarian (2010); Author, "Review of Muscular Christianity: Manhood and sports in Protestant America, 1880-1920," The Journal of Popular Culture (2003); Co-Author, Book Chapter, "Handbook of American Popular Culture, Third Edition" (2002); Co-Editor, "Football as a war game: The annotated journals of General R.R. Neyland," Falcon Press (2002); Co-Author, "The cowboy way: The western leader in film," (2000); Author, "A comparative analysis of the effects of a 12-week exercise program on the met levels of anterior versus inferior myocardial infarct patients," Clinical Kinesiology (1996); Contributor, "God in the stadium," University Press of Kentucky (1995); Contributor, Papers, Presentations; Contributor, Papers, Meetings; Reviewer, Conferences AW: Provost's Faculty Development Grantee, Southern Utah University (2009); Provost's Faculty Development Grantee, Southern Utah University (2008); Grantee, Tech Prep Educational Consortium of Western Virginia (2006-2007); Grantee, Tech Prep Educational Consortium of Western Virginia (2005-2006); Emory & Henry I-Hey Scholar (1974-1978); National Chancellor's List; President's List, Emory & Henry College; ESTRAL Scholarship MEM: Tennessee Association of School Librarians; Kentucky Library Association; Kentucky Association of School Librarians; Utah Library Association; UELMA; Phi Kappa Phi; Kappa Delta Pi; Gamma Beta Phi; Kentucky Library Association; National Social Science Association; American Library Association; Popular Culture Association MH: Albert Nelson Marquis Lifetime Achievement Award (2017) ADD: 110 Elm Street, Berea, KY, 40403

TUROCK, BETTY, I: Consulting CN: Rock Information Associates Consulting DOB: 01/12/2018 PB: Scranton SC: PA/USA PT: David Argust; Ruth Carolyn (Sweetser) Argust MS: Married SPN: Gustav Friedrich (11/21/2010); Frank M. Turock, (6/16/1956, Deceased 10/2005) CH: David L.; B. Drew ED: PhD, Rutgers University (1981); MLS, Rutgers University (1970); Postgraduate Scholar), University of Pennsylvania (1956); BA, Syracuse University, Magna Cum Laude (1955) C: President, Rock Information Associates Consulting (2004); Associate Dean, School of Communications, Information, and Library Studies, Rutgers University (2004); Associate Dean, Department Chair, School of Communications, Information, and Library Studies, Rutgers University (2002-2003); Director, MLS Program, School of Communications, Information, and Library Studies, Rutgers University (2001-2002); Professor, School of Communications, Information, and Library Studies, Rutgers University (1994); Director, MLS Program, School of Communications, Information, and Library Studies, Rutgers University (1990-1995); Department Chair, School of Communications, Information, and Library Studies, Rutgers University (1989-1995); Associate Professor, School of Communications, Information, and Library Studies, Rutgers University (1987-1993); Assistant Professor, School of Communications, Information, and Library Studies, Rutgers University (1981-1987); Assistant Director, Monroe County Library System, Rochester, NY (1978-1981); Assistant Director, Director, Montclair Public Library, New Jersey (1973-1976); Branch Librarian, Area Librarian, Head of Extension Service, Forsyth County Public Library System, Winston-Salem, NC (1970-1973); Educational Media Specialist, Alhambra Public School, Phoenix, AZ (1967-1970); Storyteller, Wheaton Public Library, Illinois (1965-1967); Library and Materials Coordinator, Holmdel Public Schools, New Jersey (1963-1965); Professor Emerita, Associate Dean Emerita, School of Communications, Information, and Library Studies, Rutgers University CR: Adviser, Office of Librarian Programs, U.S. Department of Education (1988-1989); Visiting Professor, Graduate School of Library and Information Studies, Rutgers University (1980-1981) CIV: Advisory Council, Board of the American Librarian (2010-Present); Board of Advisors, Trejo Foundation (2009-Present); Trustee, Keystone College (2001-Present); National Library Council, Johns Hopkins University (2007); Trustee, Board of the American Librarian, Paris (1999-2009); Board Member, Trejo Foundation (1995-2013); Trustee, Fund for America's Librarians (1995); Trustee, Librarians for the Future (1994-1997); Trustee, Freedom to Read Foundation (1994-1997); Treasurer, Social Responsibilities Round Table (1978-1982); Coordinator, Task Force on Women (1978-1980); Board of Education, Raritan Township, NJ (1962-1966); Trustee, Raritan Township Public Library, New Jersey (1961-1962); Action Council, American Library Association; Chair, Academy Committee, Keystone College CW: Author, "Creating a Financial Plan" (1992); Editor, "The Bottom Line" (1984-1990); Author, "Serving Older Adults" (1983); Contributor, Articles, Professional Journals AW: Distinguished Alumni Award, Rutgers University Graduate School (2011); Lippincott Award, American Library Association (2006); Equality Award, American Library Association (1998); New Jersey Library Leadership Award (1994); Distinguished Alumni Award, Rutgers University Library and Information Studies Alumni Association (1994); Woman of the Year, Raritan-Holmdel Woman's Club (1975); Charles Weston Scholar, Syracuse University (1955) MEM: Honorary Life Member, American Library Association (2014-Present); President, American Library Association (1995-1996); President-Elect, American Library Association (1994-1995); Executive Board, American Library Association (1991-1997); Council, American Library Association (1988-1997); President, Rutgers University Library and Information Studies Alumni Association (1977-1978); Rutgers University Graduate School; Phi Theta Kappa; Psi Chi; Beta Phi Mu; Pi Beta Phi MH: Albert Nelson Marquis Lifetime Achievement Award (2017) RE: Unitarian Universalist ADD: 343 N 4th Avenue, Highland Park, NJ, 08904

TUROV, DANIEL, T: Writer I: Writing and Editing CN: Turov Investment Group Inc. DOB: 01/15/1947 PB: Brooklyn SC: NY/USA MS: Married SPN: Tasanee Boonchert (March 15, 2000); Rosalyn B. Kalishock (August 25, 1968) (Deceased) CH: Joshua Nathaniel; Steven Russell CT: Registered Investment Advisor; Registered Commodity Trading Advisor C: President, Turov Investment Group Inc. (1999-Present); President, Just Right Communications (1992-2002); Senior Vice President, Dean Witter Reynolds, Inc. (1983-1984); Vice President, Dean Witter Reynolds, Inc. (1982-1983); Director, Turov Investment Group Division, Moore & Schley, Cameron & Company (1980-1982); Senior Vice President, Cowen & Company (1977-1980); Senior Vice President, Faulkner Dawkins & Sullivan (1975-1977); Account Executive, Thomson McKinnon Securities (1972-1975); Account Executive, Walston & Company (1969-1972) CR: Interviewed, CNN (2000); Chairman, Philtrum Advertising Corporation (1982-1984); Faculty Member, New York Institute of Finance; New School Social Research; Panel Member, The Wall Street Transcripts Option Roundtable CW: Author, "Turov on Timing" (1993-Present); Editor, New Innovations Public Corporation (1979-1986); Monthly Investment Column, "Best Buys Magazine" (1982-1983); Author, "Turov on Investments and Hedging" (1972-1980); Contributor, Articles to Professional Journals and Newspapers AW: Supertrader of the Year Award, Stock Traders Almanac (1994, 2001) ADD: 9062 Rowlett Avenue, San Diego, CA, 92129

TURVEY, MICHAEL, T: Professor Emeritus I: Education/Educational Services CN: University of Connecticut ED: PhD, Ohio State University (1967) C: Board of Trustees, Center for the Ecological Study of Perception and Action, Department of Psychology, University of Connecticut; Distinguished Professor Emeritus, Department of Psychology, Center for the Ecological Study of Perception and Action, University of Connecticut; Senior Research Scientist, Haskins Laboratories AW: Lifetime Mentor Award, Association for Psychological Science (2013); Lifetime Achievement Award, Society of Experimental Psychologists (2011) MH: Albert Nelson Marquis Lifetime Achievement Award (2017) H: Sports; Writing ADD: 60 Sawmill Brook Lane, Mansfield Center, CT, 06250 URL: http://ione.psy.uconn.edu/mturvey

TUTTLE, HOWARD N., T: Philosopher I: Other DOB: 12/15/1935 PB: Salt Lake City SC: UT/USA PT: Howard Milton Tuttle; Emily Louise Nelson Tuttle MS: Married SPN: Carolyn Padelford (2/16/1963) CH: Carl Emerson; Laura ED: PhD, Brandeis University, Waltham, Massachusetts (1967); MA, Harvard University, Cambridge, Massachusetts (1963); MA, University of Utah, Salt

Lake City (1959); BA, University of Utah, Salt Lake City (1958) **CT**: Certificate, Universität Wien (1962) **C**: Adjunct Professor, University of Utah, Salt Lake City (2005-2015); Professor of Philosophy, The University of New Mexico, Albuquerque (1967-1996); Department Chair, The University of New Mexico, Albuquerque (1975-1982); Professor of Philosophy, Universität Duisburg-Essen (1978-1979); Instructor, Regis College, Weston (1965-1967); Teaching Fellow, Brandeis University (1964-1965); Instructor, Boston University (1963-1964); Instructor, Harvard University (1961-1963) **CR**: Member, Society for Iberian and Latin American Thought (1986-1996); President, New Mexico Texas Philosophical Society (1977) **MIL**: U.S. Air Force (1954-1959) **CW**: Advisory Board Member, "Journal of Environmental Ethics" (1980-1988); Author, "Wilhelm Dilthey's Philosophy of Historical Understanding: A Critical Analysis"; Author, "The Political in Hegel and Dewey"; Author, "The Dawn of Historical Reason: The Historicality of Human Existence in the Thought of Dilthey, Heideggerr, and Ortega y Gasset"; Author, "The Crowd is Untruth: The Existential Critique of Mass Society in the Thought of Kierkegaard, Nietzsche, Heidegger, and Ortega y Gasset"; Author, "Human Life is Radical Reality"; Author, "Fire Night: a Story about Pompeii"; Composer, "New York City Ground Zero Monument Remember Me"; Contributor, Articles, Professional Journals **AW**: Recipient, Distinguished Emeritus Service Award, University of Utah (2015); Recipient, Fellowship, Danforth Foundation (1968-1975) **MEM**: Society for Phenomenology and Existential Philosophy; American Philosophical Association; Alta Club **MH**: Albert Nelson Marquis Lifetime Achievement Award (2017) **ADD**: 939 S Donner Way Apt 108, Salt Lake City, UT, 84108

TYSON STROUD, PATRICIA, T: Writer **I**: Writing and Editing **PB**: Philadelphia **SC**: PA/USA **PT**: George Peterson; Jane Chapman **MS**: Married **SPN**: Alexander McCurdy, III **CH**: John Tyson, III; Peter H. Tyson; Lisa Tyson Ennis **ED**: AB, Smith College, Northampton, MA (1955) **C**: Writer, Private Practice, Philadelphia, PA (1982-Present); Adviser, A Bonaparte in America Exhibit, New Jersey State Museum (2003); Copywriter, Advertising and Public Relations Department, First Pennsylvania Bank **CR**: Lecturer in Field **CIV**: President, Board of Directors, Georgia Farm Foundation (1990-Present); Member, Board of Directors, University of Pennsylvania Press (2000-2003); Member, Board of Directors, Bartram's Garden (1994-1997); Chairman, Women's Committee, Academy of Natural Sciences of Philadelphia (1980-1982) **CW**: Author, "Bitterroot: The Life and Death of Meriwether Lewis (2018); Author, "'At what do you think the ladies will stop?' Women at the Academy," Proceedings of the Academy of Natural Sciences of Philadelphia (2013); Co-Author, "A Glorious Enterprise: The Academy of Natural Sciences of Philadelphia and the Making of American Science" (2012); Author, "The Man Who Had Been King: The American Exile of Napoleon's Brother Joseph" (2005); Author, "Point Breeze, Joseph Bonaparte's American Retreat, "The Magazine Antiques (2002); Author, "Napoleon's Most Brilliant Nephew," Smith College Alumnae Quarterly (2000-2001); Author, "Le neveu le plus brillant de Napoleon: Charles Lucien Bonaparte (1803-1857)," Études Napoléoniennes (2000); Author, "The Emperor of Nature: Charles Lucien Bonaparte and His World" (2000); Contributor, "American National Biography," Oxford University Press (1999); Author, "The Founding of the Academy of Natural Sciences in 1812 and its Journal in 1817," Proceedings of the Academy of Natural Sciences of Philadelphia: A Journal of Natural History and the Environment (1997); Author, "Forerunner of American Conservation: Naturalist Thomas Say," Forest and Conservation History (1995); Author, "The Founding of the Academy of Natural History of Philadelphia in 1812 and its Journal in 1817," The Natural History Museum (1995); Author, "Thomas Say: New World Naturalist" (1992); Editor, "Frontiers," National Academy of Sciences, Philadelphia, PA (1979-1982); Author, "Mary Sharples Schaffer: Explorer of the Canadian Rockies," The Academy of Natural Sciences (1981); Writer, Public Relations Releases, First Pennsylvania Bank, Philadelphia, PA (1968-1969); Contributor, Articles, Professional Journals **AW**: Albert Nelson Marquis Lifetime Achievement Award (2017); Literary Award, The Athenaeum of Philadelphia (2013); Special Citation for Outstanding Work of Non-Fiction by a Philadelphia Author, Athenaeum of Philadelphia (2012); Agnes Irwin School Willing Award (2011); Book Award, New Jersey Council for the Humanities (2006); Literary Award, International Napoleonic Society (2002, 2005); Literary Award, The Athenaeum of Philadelphia (2002); Honoree, Best Books of the Year 2000, Library Journal (2001) **MEM**: Authors' Guild; Études Napoléoniennes; Society for the History of Natural History; Fellow, International Napoleonic Society **H**: Reading; Gardening; Piano **ADD**: 613 Maplewood Rd, Wayne, PA, 19087 **URL**: https://www.amazon.com/Patricia-Tyson-Stroud/e/B001KHVP1A

UDEN, LAURA, T: President **I**: Engineering **CN**: NSI Engineering **MS**: Married **SPN**: Barry Uden **ED**: PhD, Salford University, Salford, England (2005); MS, Systems Engineering Management, San Jose State University (1996); BS, Industrial and Systems Engineering, San Jose State University (1993); Coursework in Physics, University of California, Berkeley (1987-1988); Coursework in Astronomy, University of California, Berkeley (1987-1988); Coursework in Physics, Diablo Valley College (1986-1987); Coursework in Physics, University of Washington (1980-1981) **CT**: Project Management Professional (PMP), Project Management Institute, Inc.; Certified Systems Engineering Professional, International Council on Systems Engineering (INCOSE); Certified Manager of Quality/Organizational Excellence (CMQ/OE), American Society for Quality **C**: Professor, School of Business Administration, Silicon Valley University (2010-Present); Partner, CLiM8 Consulting (2009-Present); Quality Assurance Manager, Quality Engineering, Inc. (1999-Present); Director, Organizational Learning Center (1992-Present); CFO, Organizational Learning Center (1992-Present); Change Management Consultant and Project Manager, Expressworks International (2006-2008); Professor, Industrial and Systems Engineering Department, San Jose State University (1990-2005) **CIV**: President, Bay Area Chapter, Disabled Veterans Business Alliance (2016); Professional Services Committee Secretary, Business Advisory Council, California High Speed Rail Authority, State of California (2015); Co-Chairperson, Infrastructure Working Group (IWG), International Council on Systems Engineering (INCOSE) (2014) **MIL**: Sergeant, U.S. Army (1981-1985) **CW**: Author, "Assessing innovation infrastructure in fossil power generation plants"; Author, "Optimizing the use of power generation assets: a process and people-based approach"; Author, "Work Culture and Process Improvement – Predictive Maintenance Case Study Report" **AW**: College Scholarship, American Society for Quality (1991) **MEM**: American Society for Quality; Institute of Industrial and Systems Engineers; International Council on Systems Engineering (INCOSE); Project Management Institute, Inc. **H**: Woodturning **BA**: 300 S 1st Street, Suite 300G, San Jose, CA, 95113 **ADD**: 18010 Olive Branch Lane, Morgan Hill, CA, 95037 **URL**: http://www.nsieng.com

UEDA, TETSUFUMI, T: Professor Emeritus, Neurochemist **I**: Education/Educational Services **CN**: University of Michigan **DOB**: 07/11/1940 **PB**: Osaka **SC**: Japan **PT**: Ryuji Ueda; Takao (Hamaguchi) Ueda **MS**: Married **SPN**: Yasuko Amano (1/11/1970) **CH**: Jane Kiyoko; Judy Yoshiko **ED**: Postdoctoral Fellowship, Department of Pharmacology, National Institute of Mental Health, Yale University, New Haven, CT (1974-1976); PhD in Biological Chemistry, University of Michigan (1971); BS in Chemistry, Kyoto University, Kyoto, Japan (1966) **C**: Professor of Pharmacology Emeritus, University of Michigan (2016-Present); Research Professor Emeritus, University of Michigan (2016-Present); Research Professor, Molecular and Behavioral Neuroscience Institute, University of Michigan (2003-2016); Professor of Pharmacology in Psychiatry and Pharmacology, University of Michigan, Ann Arbor, MI (1989-2016); Senior Research Scientist, Mental Health Research Institute, University of Michigan (1988-2003); Associate Professor of Pharmacology in Psychiatry and Pharmacology, University of Michigan (1982-1989); Associate Professor, Department of Pharmacology, University of Michigan, Ann Arbor, MI (1981-1988); Associate Research Scientist, Mental Health Research Institute, University of Michigan (1981-1988); Associate Professor of Pharmacology in Psychiatry, University of Michigan (1981-1982); Assistant Professor of Pharmacology in Pharmacology, University of Michigan (1981-1982); Assistant Research Scientist, Mental Health Research Institute, University of Michigan (1978-1981); Assistant Professor of Pharmacology in Psychiatry and Pharmacology, University of Michigan, Ann Arbor, MI (1978-1981); Research Associate, Department of Pharmacology, Yale University, New Haven, CT (1976-1978); Postdoctoral Associate, Department of Pharmacology, Yale University, New Haven, CT (1971-1974); Teaching Fellow, Department of Biological Chemistry, University of Michigan (1966-1970) **CR**: Research Professor, Molecular & Behavioral Neuroscience Institute, University of Michigan, Ann Arbor, MI (1988-Present); Member, Committee, Candidates for Pharmacology Faculty Positions, University of Michigan (2012); Member, Committee, Candidates for Molecular & Behavioral Neuroscience Institute Faculty Positions, University of Michigan (2011); Member, Committee, Candidates for Psychiatry Chairman, University of Michigan (2010); Committee on Departmental Operations, Department of Pharmacology, University of Michigan (2009); Member, Committee, Incoming Students for Programs in Biomedical Sciences, University of Michigan (2008); Member, Committee, Incoming Students for Neuroscience Program, University of Michigan (2008); Member, Committee, Candidates for Molecular & Behavioral Neuroscience Institute Faculty Positions, University of Michigan (2003-2004); Member, Committee, Incoming Students for Neuroscience Program, University of Michigan (2003-2004); Member, Committee, Incoming Students for Pharmacology, University of Michigan (2003-2004); Member, Committee, Candidates for Pharmacology Faculty Positions, University of Michigan (2003); Member, Committee, Candidates for Pharmacology Faculty Positions, University of Michigan (1999); Member, Committee, Incoming Students for Neuroscience Program, University of Michigan (1998-2000); Member, Committee, Candidates for Molecular & Behavioral Neuroscience Institute Faculty Positions, University of Michigan (1998); Member, Committee, Incoming

Students for Pharmacology, University of Michigan (1998); Grant Reviewer, Advanced Study Institute, NATO, Brussels, Belgium (1995); Faculty Search Committee, Pharmacology, University of Michigan (1995); Member, Neuroscience Council, University of Michigan (1994-1995); Review Committee, Discretionary Fund Programs, Office of Vice President for Research, University of Michigan (1994); Operating Committee, Medical Scientist Training Program, University of Michigan (1994); Member, Committee, Incoming Students for Medical Science Training Program, University of Michigan (1994); Member, Committee, Incoming Students for Neuroscience Program, University of Michigan (1994); Member, Committee, Candidates for Pharmacology Chairman, University of Michigan (1994); Appointments and Promotions Committee, Pharmacology, University of Michigan (1994); Member, Committee, Candidates for Pharmacology Faculty Positions, University of Michigan (1994); Grant Reviewer, Medical Research Council, London, England (1992-1993); Searle Scholars Selection Committee, University of Michigan (1992); Pew Scholars Selection Committee, University of Michigan (1992); Organizer of Departmental Seminar Series, Neurotransmitter Glutamate, Department of Pharmacology, University of Michigan (1992); Member, Committee, Incoming Students for Neuroscience Program, University of Michigan (1992); Review Committee, Discretionary Fund Programs, Office of Vice President for Research, University of Michigan (1992); Committee, Coon Symposium, University of Michigan (1989-1990); Member, Subcommittee I, Neurological Sciences Study Section, National Institutes of Health (1987-1991); Associate Research Scientist, Molecular & Behavioral Neuroscience Institute, University of Michigan, Ann Arbor, MI (1981-1988); Member, Committee, Incoming Students for Medical Science Training Program, University of Michigan (1980-1990); Committee, Smith, Kline & French Lectureship, University of Michigan (1980-1981); Member, Committee, Candidates for Pharmacology Chairman, University of Michigan (1980); Grant Reviewer, National Science Foundation (1978-1996); Assistant Research Scientist, Molecular & Behavioral Neuroscience Institute, University of Michigan, Ann Arbor, MI (1978-1981); Speaker in Field **CW:** Editorial Board, Neurochemical Research (2014-Present); Author, "Vesicular Glutamate Uptake," The Glutamate/GABA-Glutamine Cycle, Springer International (2016); Editorial Board, Journal of Medicine Neuroscience (1990-1993); Co-Author, "Characterization of Glutamate Uptake into Synaptic Vesicles," Journal of Neurochemistry, Raven Press (1985); Co-Author, "Adenosine Triphosphate-Dependent Uptake of Glutamate into Protein I-Associated Synaptic Vesicles," The Journal of Biological Chemistry (1983); Contributor, Articles to Professional Journals; Author, Chapters to Books **AW:** Grantee, National Institutes of Health (1999-2011); Grantee, Taisho Pharmaceutical Co., Ltd. (1997-2006); Recipient, Senior Research Scientist Lectureship Award, University of Michigan (1994); Recipient, Javits Neuroscience Investigator Award, National Institutes of Health (1988-1995); Grantee, American Diabetes Association (1988-1990); Listee, World Biographical Hall of Fame, Volume Two, Melrose Press Ltd. (1985-1986); Listee, The First Five Hundred (1985); Listee, The Biographical Roll of Honor, Third Edition (1985); Listee, Men of Achievement (1984-1985); Listee, Personalities of America (1984-1985); Grantee, National Science Foundation (1982-1988); Grantee, National Institutes of Health (1979-1996); Fellow, National Institute of Mental Health (1974-1976); Recipient, Osaka Prefectural

Board of Education Scholarship (1963-1966); Recipient, Japanese Ministry of Education (Now Ministry of Education, Culture, Sports, Science and Technology) Scholarship (1962-1966); Recipient, Japanese Ministry of Education (Now Ministry of Education, Culture, Sports, Science and Technology) Scholarship (1956-1959) **MEM:** American Chemical Society (1997-Present); American Society for Biochemistry and Molecular Biology (1982-Present); Society for Neuroscience (1979-Present); International Society for Neurochemistry (1979-Present); American Society for Neurochemistry (1979-Present); American Association of University Professors (1989-2016); The New York Academy of Sciences (1979-1997); American Association for the Advancement of Science (1970-2016) **MH:** Albert Nelson Marquis Lifetime Achievement Award (2017) **ADD:** 3474 Richmond Ct, Ann Arbor, MI, 48105

UNDERHILL, JOANNE, T: Attorney **I:** Law and Legal Services **CN:** Underhill Law, P.C. **DOB:** 10/06/1950 **PB:** Chicago **SC:** IL/USA **PT:** Charles Erwin Jr.; Justine Parsons **MS:** Married **SPN:** James C. Underhill, Jr. (June 20, 1981) **CH:** Maureen; James Charles **ED:** JD, Washington College of Law, The American University (1976-1979); BA, Cum Laude, Yale University (1973) **C:** Business, Tax, Government and Trial Attorney/Founder, Underhill Law, P.C. (2013-Present); Attorney, Shareholder, Underhill & Underhill, Professional Corporation, Greenwood Village, Colorado (1994-2013); Shareholder, Popham, Haik, Schnobrich & Kaufman, Ltd., Denver (1988-1994); Special Counsel, Gorsuch, Kirgis, Campbell, Walker & Grover, Denver, (1986-1987); Assistant General Counsel, Federal Home Loan Bank Board and FSLIC, Washington (1986); Trial Attorney, Federal Home Loan Bank Board, Washington (1983-1985); Associate, Howrey & Simon, Washington (1979-1983) **CR:** Member, Parks, Trails and Recreation Commission, Greenwood Village (1991-Present); Chair, Parks, Trails and Recreation Commission, Greenwood Village (1992-1995); Public Member, Colorado Board of Accountancy, Denver (1993-1999); Delegate, Statehouse Conference on Small Business, Denver, CO (1997) **CIV:** Board of Directors, Colorado Women's Chamber of Commerce, Denver, CO (1993-1996); Chair, Colorado Women's Leadership Coalition, Denver, CO (1996-1997) **AW:** Top Attorney, Global Directory of Who's Who (2017); Woman of Distinction Award, Girl Scouts Mile hi Council, Denver, CO (1997); The Power of One Award Colorado Woman (1998); National Honor Award, Girl Scouts of the USA **MEM:** Board of Directors, Colorado Women's Bar Association (1994-1995); Amicus Curaie Committee, Colorado Bar Association (1993-1995); Arapahoe County Bar Association; American Bar Association **BAR:** DC (1979); Colorado (1987); U.S. Court Appeals 10th Circuit (1985); U.S. District Court, Washington (1980); U.S. Court Appeals, DC Circuit (1980) **MH:** Albert Nelson Marquis Lifetime Achievement Award (2017) **BA:** 7350 E Progress Pl Ste 110, Underhill Law, PC, Greenwood Village, CO, 80111

UNGER YOUNG, ELIZABETH, T: Hospital Chaplain **I:** Religious **DOB:** 03/04/1936 **PB:** Manitoba **SC:** Canada **PT:** Johann Cornelius Unger; Ottillie (Hirsch) Unger **MS:** Married **SPN:** Alvin Young (1992) **ED:** MAT, Andrews University (1972); BA, Andrews University (1967) **CT:** Certified Fellow, College of Chaplains (1987) **C:** Pastor, Limon SDA Church, Limon, CO (1998-2003); Chaplain, Porter Hospice, Denver, CO (1991-1992); Chaplain, Hinsdale Hospital, Hinsdale, IL (1984-1990); Chaplain Services, Portland Adventist Medical Center and Portland Adventist Hospital, Portland,

OR (1971-1983); Secretary, Hewitt Research, Berrien Springs, MI (1970-1971); Secretary, Office Overload (1969-1970); Teacher, Andrews University (1969-1970); Administrative Secretary, Registrar and Teacher, Mount Pisgah Academy, Chandler, NC (1967-1969); Student Dean, Honor Dorms, Andrews University (1965-1966); Secretary, Chemistry Department, Andrews University (1964-1967); Assistant, Registrar's Office, Andrews University (1963-1964); Residence Hall Assistant, Women's Dormitory, Andrews University, Berrien Springs, MI (1962-1963); Insurance Claims Director, North York Branson Hospital, Toronto, ON, Canada (1960-1962); Assistant to Cost Accountant and Treasurer, Anthes-Imperial, St. Catherines, ON, Canada (1956-1960); Bookkeeper, G.A. Moggridge Printing Company, St. Catherines, ON, Canada (1955-1956); Office Clerk, Overland Express, St. Catherines, ON, Canada (1954-1955) **CR:** Teacher, Sabbath School Classes (1992-Present) **MH:** Albert Nelson Marquis Lifetime Achievement Award (2017) **H:** Decorating; Painting; Sewing; Designing; Gardening **RE:** Seventh-Day Adventist **BA:** 1103 S County Road 137, Bennett, CO, 80102

VALANIS, KIRK CHRISTIAN, T: Theoretical Mechanics Researcher, Educator **I:** Education/ Educational Services **CN:** Endochronics INC **DOB:** 03/06/1930 **PB:** Lefkara **SC:** Cyprus **PT:** Christakis Valanis; Panayota Valanis **MS:** Married **SPN:** Barbara G. Geesey (9/11/1978); Lilian E. Salisbury (9/10/1955, Divorced) **CH:** Christina; Paul; Catherine; Karen (Stepdaughter) **ED:** PhD, Purdue University (1963); MSc, Imperial College London (1957); BS, Imperial College London, with Honors (1955) **C:** Research Professor, University of Portland, Portland, OR (1998-Present); Owner, Endochronics Co., Vancouver, WA (1996-Present); President, Endochronics CO., Vancouver, WA (1986-1996); Professor, University of Cincinnati (1983-1986); Dean of Engineering, University of Cincinnati (1978-1983); Professor, The University of Iowa, Iowa City, IA (1968-1978); Head, The University of Iowa, Iowa City, IA (1968-1978); Professor, Iowa State University, Ames, IA (1964-1968) **CR:** Affiliate, BOD, University of Crete (1978-1986); Consultant, S-Cubed, Maxwell Technologies, Inc., La Jolla, CA (1976-1992); Affiliate, Jet Propulsion Laboratory, California Institute of Technology, National Aeronautics and Space Administration, Pasadena, CA (1966-1992) **CW:** Author, "Irreversible Thermodynamics" (1977); Author, "Constitutive Equations" (1976); Editor, "Constitutive Equations" (1976); Contributor, Articles, Professional Journals **AW:** Research Grantee, Waterways Experiment Station (1992); Research Grantee, U.S. Army Research Laboratory (1984); Research Grantee, National Science Foundation (1978); Research Grantee, Air Force Research Laboratory (1969); Honoree, The Hellenic Society of Rheology **MEM:** Fellow, The American Society of Mechanical Engineers; Society of Engineering Science Inc.; Mathematical Association of America; American Academy of Mechanics; The Hellenic Society of Rheology **MH:** Albert Nelson Marquis Lifetime Achievement Award (2017) **H:** Bridge; Chess; Tennis; Hiking; Stamp collecting; Philately; Research **RE:** Greek Orthodox **ADD:** 839 Carriage Hill Rd, Melbourne, FL, 32940

VAN HEERTUM, RONALD L., T: Radiologist **I:** Medicine & Health Care **CN:** 1) CAO Radiology 2) Columbia University 3) New York State Psychiatric Institute **DOB:** 11/23/1940 **PB:** Englewood **SC:** NJ/USA **PT:** Arnold Van Heertum; Irene Gladys (Ostheimer) Van Heertum **MS:** Married **SPN:** Elyse Ann Murphy (4/3/2004) **CH:** Richard Jonathan; Beth Jennifer; Jonathan Jason; Kristin Ashley

ED: Resident in Radiology, St. Vincent's Catholic Medical Center (1967-1970); Intern, Hackensack University Medical Center (1966-1967); MD, New Jersey Medical School, Rutgers, The State University of New Jersey (1966); BA, Gettysburg College (1962) **CT:** Diplomate, American Board of Nuclear Medicine (1973); Diplomate, American Board of Radiology (1971); Diplomate, National Board of Medical Examiners (1967) **C:** Vice President, Molecular Imaging, CAO Radiology (2012-Present); Radiology Professor, College of Physicians and Surgeons, Columbia University (2002-Present); Attending Physician, Department of Neuroscience, New York State Psychiatric Institute (1996-Present); Vice Chairman, Department of Radiology, College of Physicians and Surgeons, Columbia University (1993-Present); Attending Physician, Department of Brain Imaging, New York State Psychiatric Institute (1993-Present); Director, Nuclear Medicine Residency Training Program, New York-Presbyterian Hospital, Columbia University (1991-Present); Attending Physician, Department of Radiology, New York-Presbyterian Hospital, Columbia University (1991-Present); Executive Vice-Chair, CAO Radiology (2009-2012); Intern Chair of Radiology, College of Physicians and Surgeons, Columbia University (2008-2009); Professor of Clinical Radiology, College of Physicians and Surgeons, Columbia University (1991-2001); Director, Mini-Fellowship Program, Cerebral SPECT Learning Center, St. Vincent's Catholic Medical Center (1991-2001); Clinical Radiology Professor, New York Medical College (1988-1991); Associate Clinical Radiology Professor, New York Medical College (1983-1988); Medical Director, School of Nuclear Medicine Technology, St. Vincent's Catholic Medical Center (1982-1991); Assistant Director, Department of Radiology, St. Vincent's Catholic Medical Center (1981-1991); Director, Nuclear Medicine Residency Training Program, New York-Presbyterian Hospital, Columbia University (1980-1988); Director, Nuclear Radiology Residency Training Program, St. Vincent's Catholic Medical Center (1980-1991); Attending Physician, Departments of Radiology and Medicine, St. Vincent's Catholic Medical Center (1978-1991); Chief, Nuclear Medicine Section, St. Vincent's Catholic Medical Center (1977-1991); Clinical Assistant, Professor of Radiology, New York University School of Medicine (1977-1983); Associate Attending Physician, Departments of Radiology and Medicine, St. Vincent's Catholic Medical Center (1977-1978); Assistant Chief, Nuclear Medicine Section, St. Vincent's Catholic Medical Center (1975-1976); Assistant Attending Radiologist, St. Vincent's Catholic Medical Center (1975-1976); Adjunct Professor, School of Pharmacy, University of the Pacific, CA (1973-1974); Chief, Nuclear Medicine Service, Tripler Army Medical Center (1972-1974); Assistant Chief, Nuclear Medicine Service, Tripler Army Medical Center (1972); Clinical Assistant, Department of Radiology, St. Vincent's Catholic Medical Center (1971) **CR:** Board Member, American Board of Nuclear Medicine (1995-Present); Consultant, The Oxford Project to Investigate Memory and Aging, The John Radcliffe Infirmary and Department of Clinical Pharmacology, University of Oxford (1993-Present); Consultant, Biological Studies Unit, New York State Psychiatric Institute (1993-Present); Visiting Professor, Stony Brook Medicine (2005); Visiting Professor, University of Puerto Rico (2005); Chair, American Board of Nuclear Medicine (2000-2002); Vice Chair, American Board of Nuclear Medicine (1999-2000); Visiting Professor, Robert Wood Johnson Medical School, Rutgers, The State University of New Jersey (1999); Visiting Professor, Washington University in St. Louis (1998); Visiting Professor

of Medicine, University of Washington (1994); Director, Kreitchman PET Center, Columbia University (1993-2010); Visiting Professor, Veterans Affairs Caribbean Healthcare System, Medical Sciences Campus, University of Puerto Rico (1993); Consultant, Department of Radiology, St. Vincent's Catholic Medical Center (1991-1992); Core Member, DOE Sponsored Consensus Panel, Brain SPECT Perfusion Imaging: Optimizing Image Acquisition and Processing (1991); Visiting Professor, Eastern Virginia Medical School (1990); Visiting Professor, Saint Barnabas Medical Center (1989); Consultant, Long Island College Hospital (Now University Hospital of Brooklyn at Long Island College Hospital) (1980-1988); Visiting Professor, South Hills Health Systems, Pittsburgh, PA (1981); Alternate Delegate, American College of Neuropsychopharmacology (1980-1982); Visiting Professor, College of Medicine, Howard University (1980); Consultant, Nuclear Medicine, Catholic Medical Center of Brooklyn and Queens, Inc (1979-1988); Visiting Professor, Brooke Army Medical Center (1978) **MIL:** Major, United States Army Reserve (1971-1974) **CW:** Contributor, Articles to Professional Journals **AW:** Berson Yalow Award, Society of Nuclear Medicine and Molecular Imaging (2008); Physician Recognition Award, American Medical Association (1974-1993); Fellow in Nuclear Medicine, State University of New York (1974-1975); Fellow in Radiology and Nuclear Medicine, St. Vincent's Catholic Medical Center (1970-1971); Fellow, American College of Radiology; Recipient, Numerous Research Grants in Field **MEM:** Secretary, Nuclear Medicine Section, New York Academy of Medicine (1993-Present); Member, Brain Imaging Council, Society of Nuclear Medicine and Molecular Imaging (1988-Present); Vice Chairman, American College of Radiology (2002-2006); Chair, Accreditation Program, Chief's Committee, American College of Radiology (2002-2006); Chairman, Nuclear Medicine Accreditation Committee, American College of Radiology (2000-2006); Commission on Nuclear Medicine, American College of Radiology (1994-2000); Sub-chairman, Clinical Psychiatry, Science Program Committee, Society of Nuclear Medicine and Molecular Imaging (1993-1994); President, Society of Nuclear Medicine and Molecular Imaging (1992-1994); President-elect, Brain Imaging Council, Society of Nuclear Medicine and Molecular Imaging (1990-1992); Sub-chairman, Gastroenterology, Science Program Committee, Society of Nuclear Medicine and Molecular Imaging (1989-1990); Academy Council, Society of Nuclear Medicine and Molecular Imaging (1988); Board of Governors, Greater New York Chapter, Society of Nuclear Medicine and Molecular Imaging (1986-1989); Board of Governors, Greater New York Chapter, Society of Nuclear Medicine and Molecular Imaging (1982-1984); American Roentgen Ray Society; Radiological Society of North America; New York Roentgen Society; Senior Member, Society of Thoracic Radiology **MH:** Albert Nelson Marquis Lifetime Achievement Award (2017) **H:** Traveling; Reading; Spending Time with Children; Collecting Japanese Woodblock Prints **RE:** Presbyterian **BA:** 100 Overlook Center, Bioclinica, Inc, Princeton, NJ, 08540 **ADD:** 49 Heath Ct, Pennington, NJ, 08534 **URL:** http://www.ronaldlvanheertummd.com

VAN NORMAN, WILLIS, T: Biomedical Systems Analyst **I:** Medicine & Health Care **CN:** Mayo Clinic **DOB:** 06/17/1938 **PB:** Windom **SC:** MN/USA **ED:** MS, St. Thomas University (1991); BS, Mankato State College (1960); AA, Worthington Junior College (1958) **C:** Developer of Biomedical Computer System (1974-Present); Staff Analyst, Analyst International (1988-2002); With, Mayo Clinical, Rochester, (1962-1988); Instructor, Pilots

Ground School, Rochester Junior College (1968-1969); Teacher of Special Education, Rochester, MN (1963-1965); Teacher of Chemistry, Byron, MN (1962); Teacher of Chemistry, St. Peter, MN (1961) **CIV:** Woodland Advisor (1995-Present); Founding Member, Zumbro Valley Woodland Council (1996); Treasurer, United Methodist Church **AW:** River Friendly Farmer Award (1997); Farmer of the Year, Olmstead County Conservation (1992) **MEM:** National Education Association; Minnesota Education Association; Director, Mankato State Alumni Association; Vice President to President, Minnesota Flying Farmers; Director, International Flying Farmers; American Radio Relay League; Manager, Minnesota Secretary Traffic Net, KOJCF; President, Rochester Amateur Radio Club; Experimental Aircraft Association (EAA); Aircraft Owners & Operators Association (AOPA); American Medical Association; Academy Model Aeronautics **MH:** Albert Nelson Marquis Lifetime Achievement Award (2017) **H:** Flying **ADD:** 19230 26th Street NE, Saint Charles, MN, 55972

VAN NOY, TERRY, T: Health Facility Administrator, Founder **I:** Medicine & Health Care **CN:** Van Noy Consulting Group **DOB:** 08/31/1947 **PB:** Alhambra **SC:** CA/USA **PT:** Barney Willard; Cora Ellen (Simms) Van Noy **MS:** Married (12/27/1968) **SPN:** Betsy Helen Pothen **CH:** Bryan; Mark **ED:** MBA, Pepperdine University (1991); BS in Business Management, California State Polytechnic University (1970) **CT:** Chartered Life Underwriter **C:** Principal, Van Noy Consulting Group, Henderson, NV (1998-Present); President, Chief Executive Officer, Amil International, Las Vegas, NV (1995-1998); Division Director, Mutual of Omaha, Orange, CA (1987-1995); Vice President of Group Marketing, Mutual of Omaha, Omaha (1983-1987); National Sales Manager, Mutual of Omaha, Omaha, NE (1982-1983); Regional Manager, Mutual of Omaha, Dallas, TX (1977-1982); District Manager, Mutual of Omaha, Atlanta, GA (1974-1977); Group Sales Representative, Mutual of Omaha, Atlanta (1970-1974) **CR:** Presenter in Field; Member, Vice-Chairman, Division of Insurance Health Advisory Committee, State of Nevada Reinsurance Board **CIV:** Executive Committee, ABL Organization; Chairman, Board of Trustees, Desert Research Institute Foundation; Active, Good Samaritan Lutheran Church **MIL:** With, United States Army National Guard **MEM:** American Society of Chartered Life Underwriters; Orange County Employee Benefit Council; Western Pension & Benefits Council; Vice President, LVVSA; President, Great Basin Soaring Inc; International Foundation of Employee Benefit Plans **MH:** Albert Nelson Marquis Lifetime Achievement Award (2017) **H:** Skiing; Scuba diving; Soaring **PA:** Republican **RE:** Lutheran **ADD:** 2312 Prometheus Court, Henderson, NV, 89074

VARGUS, IONE D., T: Academic Administrator **I:** Education/Educational Services **DOB:** 07/19/1930 **PB:** Medford **SC:** MA/USA **PT:** Edward Dugger; Madeline (Kountze) Dugger-Kelley **MS:** Widow **SPN:** William H. Adams (8/26/1978, Deceased); William Vargus (3/27/1954, Divorced 1964) **CH:** Suzanne Holloman; William Vargus **ED:** PhD in Social Policy and Administration, Brandeis University, Waltham, MA (1971); MA in Social Service Administration, The University of Chicago (1954); AB, Tufts University, Medford, MA (1952) **C:** Professor Emeritus, Temple University, Philadelphia, PA (1995-Present); Director, Family Reunion Institute (1990-Present); Retired, Temple University, Philadelphia, PA (1995); Presidential Fellow, Temple University, Philadelphia, PA (1993-1995); Acting Vice Provost, Temple University, Philadelphia, PA (1991-1993); Dean, Professor,

Temple University, Philadelphia, PA (1978-1991); Associate Dean, Temple University, Philadelphia, PA (1974-1978); Assistant Professor, University of Illinois, Urbana, IL (1971-1974); Assistant Professor, Brandeis University, Waltham, MA (1970-1971); Project Director, Camp Fire Girls, Boston, MA (1964-1967); Family Worker, Boston Housing Authority (1961-1964) CIV: Trustee Emeritus, Tufts University (1991-Present); Founder, Family Reunion Institute, Temple University (1990-Present); Chair, The Multicultural Institute (1989-Present); Board of Directors, Unitarian Universalist Service Committee (1999-2003); Chair, Valentine Foundation (1994-2000); Chair, Juvenile Law Center (1991-2000); Vice President, Board of Directors, Tucker's House (1989-1995); Chair, The Philadelphia Foundation (1983-1988); Trustee, Tufts University (1981-1991) CW: Author, "Revival of Ideology: The Afro-American Society Movement" (1977); Contributor, Articles, Professional Journals AW: Apex Award, Black Meetings and Tourism Magazine (2015); History Makers Education Award (2006); Named, One of 498 Hardworking Women in Pennsylvania (1978) MEM: NAACP; National Association of Social Workers; National Urban League; The Association for the Study of African American Life and History; Alpha Kappa Alpha Sorority MH: Albert Nelson Marquis Lifetime Achievement Award (2017) H: Bowling; Crafts PA: Democrat RE: Unitarian Universalist ADD: 16115 Shannondell Dr, Audubon, PA, 19403 URL: https://www.familyreunioninstitute.net/

VASILAROS, STEVEN, T: Partner I: Law and Legal Services CN: Vasilaros Wagner DOB: 01/10/1951 PB: Pittsburgh SC: PA/USA PT: Thomas Vasilaros; Katerine Vasilaros MS: Married SPN: Jerilyn K. Vasilaros (12/7/1991) CH: Nicole ED: JD, Claude W. Pettit College of Law, Ohio Northern University (1978); BS, Franciscan University of Steubenville (1975) C: Attorney, Vasilaros Wagner (1988-Present); Attorney, Becks, Becks, & Wickersham, Daytona Beach, FL (1985-1988); Police Prosecutor, City of Steubenville (1980-1984); Attorney, Mascio, Blake, Hershey, & Vasilaros, Steubenville, OH (1978-1985) CR: Circuit Court Mediator, Florida Supreme Court (2007-Present) CIV: Florida Patient Protection Associate, Tallahassee, FL (2004-2006); Fundraiser, Democratic Party, Daytona Beach, FL (2000-2006) AW: Vanguard Award, Florida Lawyers Action Group (2006); Silver Eagle Award, Florida Justice Association (2006); Bronze Eagle Award, Florida Justice Association (2005); Tiger in the Bush Award, Floridians for Patient Protection, Academy of Florida Trial Lawyers (2005); Honoree, Wall of Fame, NAACP (2000) MEM: Multi Million Dollar Advocates Forum (2014-Present); Million Dollar Advocates Forum (2014-Present); American Association for Justice (2012-Present); Life Member, NAACP (1998-Present); Volusia County Trial Lawyers Association (1995-Present); Florida Justice Association (1990-Present); Flagler County Bar Association (1986-Present); The Florida Bar (1985-Present); Volusia County Bar Association (1985-Present); ABA (1979-Present); Dunn-Blount Inn, American Inns of Court (2007-2010); Board of Governors, Florida Justice Association (2005-2009) BAR: U.S. District Court, Middle District, State of Florida (1986-Present); State of Florida (1985-Present); U.S. District Court, Southern District, State of Ohio (1979-1985); State of Ohio (1978-2016) MH: Albert Nelson Marquis Lifetime Achievement Award (2017) H: Fishing PA: Democrat RE: Greek Orthodox ADD: 721 Beville Road, South Daytona, FL, 32119 URL: https://accidentfirm.com

VAUGHNDORF, BETTY RACHEL, T: Executive Secretary I: Business Management/Business Services DOB: 08/18/1924 PB: Savannah SC: Georgia/United States PT: Morris Vaughndorf; Lena Stanley MS: Single ED: Degree, Ryans Business College (1944); Student, Corcoran Art School (1948); Student, Abbott Art School (1950) C: Secretary to the Department of the Interior (1957-1963); United States Information Agency, Washington, DC (1951-1956); Smithsonian Institution, Washington, DC (1948-1950); Stenographer, United States Maritime Commission, Savannah, GA (1942-1947) CIV: Consultant, Republican National Committee, Savannah, GA (1997-2005) AW: Recipient, Outstanding Achievement in Amateur Photography Award, International Society of Photographers (2004-2005) MEM: Savannah Art Association; AARP H: Reading ADD: 322 E Taylor St Apt 1009, Savannah, GA, 31401

VENERABLE, GRANT DELBERT JR., T: Professor I: Education/Educational Services CN: California Polytechnic State University DOB: 08/31/1942 PB: Los Angeles SC: CA/USA PT: Grant Delbert Venerable; Thelma L. (Scott) Venerable MS: Single ED: U.S. Atomic Energy Commission Postdoctoral Certificate, UCLA Laboratory of Nuclear Medicine and Radiation Biology (1971); PhD in Physical Chemistry, University of Chicago (1970); MS in Physical Chemistry, University of Chicago (1967); BS in Chemistry, University of California, Los Angeles (1965) C: Adjunct Chemistry Instructor, Georgia Military College (2017-Present); Provost, Senior Vice President for Academic and Student Affairs, Lincoln University of Pennsylvania (2002-2011); Chair, Council of Chief Academic Officers, Atlanta University Center (2000-2001); Provost and Vice President for Academy Affairs, Morris Brown College (1999-2002); Associate Provost, Associate Vice President, Professor, Chemistry and African-American Studies, Chicago State University (1996-1999); President, Chief Executive Officer, Ventek Software, Inc. (1992-1999); History of Science Lecturer, College of Ethnic Studies, San Francisco State University (1989-1996); Executive Vice President, Omnitrom Associates, Coral Group and Courtland Group (1982-1989); Systems Scientist, Motorola Inc., Sloan Lecturer in Chemistry, Oakes College-University of California, Santa Cruz (1978-1980); Associate Professor of Chemistry, California Polytechnic State University, San Luis Obispo, CA (1972-1978); Chemistry and Biology Instructor, Duarte Unified School District (1971-1972) CR: Keynote Speaker, National Conference on Arts Education, John F. Kennedy Center for the Performing Arts (1987); Secretary, State Board, California Alliance for Arts Education (1985-1991); Keynote Speaker, National Conference on Arts Education, John F. Kennedy Center for the Performing Arts (1985); National Endowment for the Humanities (NEH) Faculty Fellowship, Michigan State University (1978); U.S. Atomic Energy Commission Postdoctoral Fellowship, University of California, Los Angeles (1970-1971); Argonne Universities Association Predoctoral Fellowship, University of Chicago and Argonne National Laboratory (1967-1970); Adjunct Professor, California Institute of Integral Studies; Chemistry Adjunct, Laney College; Pianist; Concert Organist; Oil Painter CIV: Board of Directors, City Quest, Chicago, IL (1998-2000); Secretary, State Board, California Alliance for Arts Education (1985-1991) CW: Artist, Molecular Art Oil Paintings (1963-Present); Author, "Human Footsteps in Art, Science, and the Chaotic Unknown-Oracles and Kinfolk" (2009-2018); Author, "Managing in a Five Dimension Economy" (1999); Author, "The Paradox of the

Silicon Savior" (1988); Author, "The Discovery of a Calculus of Transformations in Chemistry" (1974) AW: Albert Nelson Marquis Top Educator Award (2017); National Education Leadership Award, JGT Foundation of San Francisco (1996); "Step To" College Distinguished Teaching Award, San Francisco State University (1991); Outstanding Achievement Award, California Alliance for Arts Education (1990); Molecular Art Appreciation Award, Alpha Chi Sigma Chemistry Fraternity (1984); Outstanding Teaching Award for Chemistry, California Polytechnic State University (1977); Danforth Associate, The Danforth Foundation (1974) MEM: American Association for the Advancement of Science; American Chemical Society; National Organization for the Professional Advancement of Black Chemists and Chemical Engineers; Alpha Chi Sigma Chemical Fraternity MH: Albert Nelson Marquis Lifetime Achievement Award (2017) H: Piano and organ performance; Painting; Swimming; Bicycling ADD: 300 Gaelic Way, Tyrone, GA, 30290 URL: http://www.ArtMolecular.com

VER DUIN PALIT, HELEN MABEL, T: Founder, President I: Food & Restaurant Services CN: American Harvest, Inc. DOB: 05/12/1948 PB: Detroit SC: MI/USA PT: Cornelius Bos verDuin; Helen Estelle (Masenhimer) verDuin MS: Married SPN: Satyajit Joy Palit (May 17, 1980) ED: Honorary PhD, Iona College (1988); Postgraduate Studies in Sociology, Texas Tech University (1979); BA in Sociology, Psychology, Art, Texas Tech University (1978) C: Founder, President, American Harvest Inc., Rye Brook, NY (1990); Founder, City Harvest (1981); Founder, Soup Kitchen, Yale University CIV: President Bush's Fourth Point of Light (1989); Institute for Non-Profit Management, Columbia University (1988); Advisory Council, Select Committee on Hunger, U.S. House of Representatives (1985) AW: Recipient, Distinguished Alumna Award for Career Advancement, Texas Tech University (1991); Recipient, Eleanor Roosevelt Award, Presented by Mario Cuomo (1983-1989); Honoree, One of 10 Americans Who Made a Difference Better Health and Living (1987); Recipient, Second Award, Distinguished Alumna Award for Career Advancement, Texas Tech University MEM: Invested Dame, Imperial Russian Order of St. John of Jerusalem (1992) H: Travel; Reading; Making clothes; Artist; Sculptor; Architect BA: America Harvest Inc, 455 9th Pl, Vero Beach, FL, 32960-6822 ADD: 3840 E Robinson Rd, #416, W Amherst, NY, 14228

VIGLIOTTA, PEGGY D., T: Art Educator (Retired) I: Education/Educational Services ED: MLS, Wesleyan University, Middletown, CT (1984); BE in Art, LIU Post, Cum Laude, Brookville, NY (1979) CT: Permanent Certified Teacher, State of New York (1989) C: Retired (2007); Art Teacher, Sachem Central School District, Holbrook, NY (1985-2007); Art Teacher, Profoundly Deaf Students, Bishop McGann-Mercy Diocesan High School, Riverhead, NY (1979-1985) CR: Art Education Delegate, U.S.–Russia Educational Conference, Saint Petersburg, Russia (2006-2008); Representative, Art Education Delegation, Russian Joint Education Conference, Saint Petersburg, Russia (2006) CIV: Parish Council, Liturgy Committee, St Mark's Roman Catholic Church (1975-2000); Volunteer, Shoreham-Wading River Central School District (1968-1992); Religious Educator, St Mark's Roman Catholic Church (1968-1988); Parent Liaison Committee, Middle School Fundraiser, Boy Scouts of America CW: Sculptor, Advent Wreath; Sculptor, Ceramic Chalices MEM: Associate, National Art Education

Association **MH:** Albert Nelson Marquis Lifetime Achievement Award (2017) **H:** Travel; Crafts; Reading; Architecture; Opera **PA:** Independent **ADD:** 7 Sutton Pl, Islip, NY, 11751

VINCENT, K. MARK, T: Managing Shareholder **I:** Law and Legal Services **CN:** Vincent Serafino Geary Widdell Jenevein, P.C. **CH:** Two Sons **ED:** JD, Dedman School of Law, Southern Methodist University, Dallas, TX (1991); BA, Southern Methodist University (1988); Coursework, University of Georgia (1987) **C:** Vincent Serafino Geary Waddell Jenevein, P.C. **CW:** Co-Author, "The Ultimate Pretrial Notebook" (1992); Co-Author, "Production of Documents and Beyond" **AW:** Honoree, Texas Super Lawyer, Texas Monthly Magazine; Honoree, 40-and-Under Texas Super Lawyer, Texas Monthly Magazine **MEM:** Football Letterman's Club, University of Georgia; Dallas Association of Young Lawyers; Dallas Bar Association; State Bar of Texas; American Bar Association **BAR:** State of Texas (1991); U.S. District Court, Northern, Eastern, Southern, and Western Districts, State of Texas **H:** Spending time with his two boys; Baseball; Football **BA:** 1601 Elm Street, Suite 4100, Vincent Lopez Serafino Jenevein, P.C., Dallas, TX, 75201 **ADD:** 1601 Elm Street, Suite 4100, Vincent Serafino Waddell Geary and Jenevein, P.C., Dallas, TX, 75201 **URL:** http://www.vilolaw.com

VIOLA, MARY JO, T: 1) Art Educator 2) Artist **I:** Fine Art **CN:** 1) Bronx Community College 2) Self-Employed **DOB:** 07/25/1941 **PB:** Yonkers **SC:** NY/USA **PT:** William F. O'Connor; May (Cleary) O'Connor **MS:** Single **SPN:** Jerome Joseph Viola, (6/21/1967, Deceased 1990) **ED:** PhD in Art History, The City University of New York (1992); MPhil in Art History, The City University of New York (1983); MA in Art History, New York University (1966); BA in Fine Arts, College of Mount St. Vincent (1963) **C:** Teacher of Art History, Bronx Community College (1997-Present); Teacher of Art History, Brooklyn College (1990-1997); Teacher of Art History, Baruch College (1974-1997); Teacher of Art History, Rutgers University, The State University of New Jersey (1993-1995); Teacher of Art History, Parsons School of Design, The New School (1991-1993); Teacher of Art History, Marymount Manhattan College (1967-1971); Teacher of Art History, Hollins University (1966-1967); Teacher of Art History, Georgian Court University (1965-1966) **CR:** Gallery Guest Curator, Baruch College (1987-1988) **CIV:** Researcher, Ethnic Festivals, New York, NY (1993-2001) **CW:** Artist, Exhibitions, "Exhibiting artist with The New Rochelle Art Association' from 2009 to present; Dermot Gale Award 2018 for "Window" best 2D work; 94th Open Juried Exhibition," New Rochelle Public Library (2009); Artist, Exhibitions, "Of Earth & Sky: An Exhibition of Works by Curt Belshe, Mary Jo Ben-Nun, Elizabeth Ann Murphy and Mary Jo Viola" The Fitzgerald Gallery, Warner Library, Tarrytown, NY (2008); Artist, Exhibitions, "Faculty and Staff Exhibitions," Hall of Fame Gallery, Bronx Community College (1998-1999, 2004-2006, 2008); Artist, Group Show, Noel Fine Art, Bronxville, NY (2006); Artist, Exhibitions, Landscape & Travel Photos, Polaroid Transfer Exhibition, Omega Institute, Rhinebeck, NY (2004); Artist, Exhibitions, "Night & Day, Rye & Riverdale, Playland & Park," College of Mount Saint Vincent Library, Riverdale, NY (2002-2003); Artist, Exhibitions, "Celebrating Spirituality," Central Wyoming College (2002); Artist, Exhibitions, "Beauty Without Borders," York College (2002); Photographer, Production Stills, "Via Crucis," Riverdale Art Association, College of Mount Saint Vincent (2002); Artist,

Exhibitions, "Artists at Atria," Watercolor, Riverdale Art Association, College of Mount Saint Vincent (2002); Artist, One-Person Show, "Tunisian Fragments: Photographs and Collages," Riverdale Art Association, College of Mount Saint Vincent (2001); Artist, Exhibitions, Riverdale Art Association Art Exhibition, College of Mount Saint Vincent Library (2000); Artist, One-Person Show, "India: Photographs and Watercolors," Helen Hayes Hospital, West Haverstraw, NY (1999); Artist, One-Person Show, "Photographs of India," Organica Garden Restaurant, Mamaroneck, NY (1999); Exhibitor, Tribes Gallery (1996); Artist, Exhibitions, "Faculty and Staff Small Works III Exhibition," Parsons Exhibition Center (1992); Artist, Exhibitions, "Selected Works of the Baruch Faculty, Sidney Mishkin Gallery, Baruch College (1992); Editor, "A World View of Art History" (1985); Artist, Exhibitions, "Baruch College Art Department Faculty Exhibition," Baruch College (1981); Creator, Educational Videos **AW:** Grantee, President's Faculty and Staff Development, Bronx Community College (2005); Grantee, Teaching with Technology, "Wake Up to Graphic Design, Vol. 2," Bronx Community College (2003); PSC-CUNY Grantee, Editing "Via Crucis," Good Friday Liturgy, Saint Joseph's Church, Bronx, NY (2002); Grantee, President's Faculty and Staff Development, Student Visit to Fallingwater House, PA, Bronx Community College (2002); Fellow, The Henry Luce Foundation, Inc. (1990); Fellow, The City University of New York (1978); Fellow, Museum of Fine Arts, Boston, MA (1978); Fellow, Marymount Manhattan College (1970); Fellow, National Trust For Historic Preservation (1964) **MEM:** College Art Association; New Rochelle Art Association; National Trust for Historic Preservation **H:** Tai chi; Dance **ADD:** 37 Roosevelt St, Yonkers, NY, 10701 **URL:** www.drmaryjoviola.com

VOSBECK, WILLIAM FRERICK, T: Architect (Retired) **I:** Architecture & Construction **DOB:** 05/13/1924 **PB:** Mankato **SC:** MN/USA **PT:** William Frederick Vosbeck; Gladys (Anderson) Vosbeck **MS:** Married **SPN:** Elizabeth Just (8/2/1947) **CH:** Lee; William Frederick, III; Lynn; James Jon Scott **ED:** BArch, University of Minnesota (1947); Coursework, Cornell University (1945); Coursework, University of Notre Dame (1943) **CT:** National Council Architectural Registration **C:** Partner, Vosbeck Vosbeck Kendrick Redinger (1968-1990); Architect, VVKR Inc. Architects & Engineers (1962-1968); Partner, Vosbeck & Ward (1957-1962); Partner, Vosbeck & Vosbeck (1962-1968) **CR:** Board of Directors, Dominion Power; Board of Directors, Crestar Financial Corporation (Now SunTrust Banks, Inc.) **CIV:** Member, Virginia Board for People with Disabilities, Commonwealth of Virginia (1973); President of the Board, Alexandra Hospital (1970); Trustee, Virginia Foundation for Independent Colleges; Trustee, Virginia Museum of Fine Arts; Trustee, Virginia Chamber of Commerce; Visiting Design Critic, School of Architecture, University of Virginia **MIL:** U.S. Marine Corps Reserve (1943-1954) **CW:** Architect, Headquarters, National Automobile Dealers Association; Architect, Library, VPI Unix; Architect, Woodrow Wilson Rehabilitation Center; Architect, Alexandria Urban Renewal, NIH Cancer Clinic, Pentagon Operations Center, George Mason University Library **AW:** Outstanding Achievement Award, Engineering News-Record, BNP Media (1977); National Capital Award For Achievement In Architecture, Washington Academy of Sciences; Citation in Technology Services, National Rehabilitation Association; Gargoyle Award; T. David Fitz-Gibbon Architecture Firm Award, AIA Virginia; Numerous Awards, AIA Virginia; Numerous Awards, Virginia Museum of Fine

Arts **MEM:** President, Belle Haven Country Club (1994); President, Virginia Chapter, AIA (1971); Sigma Alpha Epsilon Foundation; Paul Harris Fellow, Rotary International; Cosmos Club; Fellow, AIA; Rotary **H:** Golf; Camping **RE:** Protestant-Presbyterian **ADD:** 9110 Belvoir Woods Parkway, Apartment 218, Fort Belvoir, VA, 22060

WAGGONER, SUSAN M., T: Electronics Engineer (Retired) **I:** Engineering **CN:** Naval Surface Warfare Center **DOB:** 09/01/1952 **PB:** East Chicago **SC:** IN/USA **PT:** Joseph John Vasilak; Elizabeth Vasilak **MS:** Married **SPN:** Steven Richard Waggoner (7/31/1976) **CH:** Kenneth David; Michael Christopher **ED:** Master's Degee in Public Affairs, Indiana University (1991); BS in Physics, Indiana University (1982); BA in Journalism, Indiana University (1976); AS, Indiana University (1975) **CT:** Certified, DAWIA Level III **C:** Electronics Engineer in Energy & Power, Naval Surface Warfare Center, Crane, Indiana (1991-2016); Electronics Engineer in Test and Measurement Equipment, Naval Surface Warfare Center, Crane, Indiana (1982-1991); Engineering Technician, Naval Surface Warfare Center, Crane, Indiana (1977-1982) **CR:** Member, Steering Committee, JT Service Power Exhibition (2015, 2017); Member, Steering Committee, Power Sources Conference (2010, 2012, 2014); Member, Steering Committee, Joint Service Power Exhibition (2005, 2007, 2011); Conference Chair, Joint Service Power Exhibition (2009); Conference Chair, Tri-Service Power Exhibition (2003) **AW:** Value Engineering Special Award, Department of Defense (2000) **MEM:** Federal Managers Association; FEW; American Rose Society; American Horticultural Society; Mensa International; Theatre Circle, Indiana University; National Defense Industrial Association; Sigma Pi Sigma, American Institute of Physics; Former Member, American Society of Naval Engineers; Former Member, AIAA; Former Member Women in Defense **MH:** Albert Nelson Marquis Lifetime Achievement Award (2017) **ADD:** 1257 Schuetter Rd, c/o Mike Waggoner, Jasper, IN, 47546

WAGLE, PRADEEP, T: Research Ecologist **I:** Research **CN:** United States Department of Agriculture **PB:** Gorkha **SC:** Nepal **PT:** Tikram Wagle; Kamala Wagle **MS:** Married **SPN:** Monika Ghimire **CH:** Anwesh Wagle **ED:** PhD in Crop Science, Oklahoma State University, Stillwater, OK (2013); MS in Horticulture, Oklahoma State University, Stillwater, OK (2010); BS in Agriculture, Tribhuvan University, Nepal (2004) **C:** Research Ecologist, USDA-ARS Grazinglands Research Laboratory (2016-Present); Research Scientist, USDA-ARS GRL/OU (Co-operative Agreement between USDA and The University of Oklahoma) (2015-2016); Postdoctoral Research Associate, The University of Oklahoma (2013-2015); Graduate Research Assistant, Oklahoma State University (2008-2013) **CR:** Graduate Faculty, Plant and Soil Science, Oklahoma State University (2016-2021); Instructor, Environmental Remote Sensing Course, The University of Oklahoma (2013-2014); Supervising/Mentoring MS and PhD Students, Oklahoma State University and The University of Oklahoma **CIV:** Secretary, Editorial Board, Global Journal of Agricultural and Allied Sciences Joint Secretary, Association of Nepalese Agricultural Professionals of Americas **CW:** Guests Editor, Special Issue, Remote Sensing of Evapotranspiration (ET), Remote Sensing (2018-2019); Guest Editor, Special Issue, Sustainability in the Mountains Region, Sustainability (2016-2017); Reviewer, Agricultural and Forest Meteorology; Reviewer, Agriculture, Ecosystems and Environment; Reviewer, Environmental Research Letters; Reviewer, Environmental Research; Reviewer, Global Change Biology Bioenergy;

Reviewer, Journal of Geophysical Research: Biogeosciences; Reviewer, Crop Science; Reviewer, ISPRS Journal of Photogrammetry and Remote Sensing; Reviewer, Remote Sensing; Reviewer, International Journal of Remote Sensing; Reviewer, PLOS ONE; Reviewer, Scientific Reports; Reviewer, Field Crops Research; Reviewer, Ecological Modelling; Reviewer, Ecological Indicators; Reviewer, Ecological Processes; Reviewer, Environmental Earth Sciences; Reviewer, Advances in Meteorology; Reviewer, Ecosystems; Reviewer, Journal of Climate; Reviewer, International Journal of Digital Earth; Reviewer, Biomass & Bioenergy; Contributor, Book Chapters; Contributor, Articles **AW:** Certificate of Merit, USDA (2017); Outstanding Performance Award, USDA (2017); Outstanding Reviewer Awards from several journals (Agricultural and Forest Meteorology Journal, ISPRS Photogrammetry and Remote Sensing Journal, and Environmental Research Letters) **MEM:** American Geophysical Union **H:** Playing and watching sports **BA:** 7207 W Cheyenne St, USDA, El Reno, OK, 73036 **ADD:** 11821 SW 9th St, Yukon, OK, 73099 **URL:** https://www.ars.usda.gov/plains-area/el-reno-ok/grazinglands-research-laboratory/forage-and-livestock-production-research/people/pradeep-wagle/

WAGNER, ANTONIN, T: Economics Professor **I:** Education/Educational Services **CN:** The New School **DOB:** 10/23/1937 **PB:** Lucerne **SC:** Switzerland **PT:** Anton Wagner; Cecile Wagner **MS:** Married **SPN:** Miriam Victory Spiegel (3/3/1984) **CH:** Ruth **ED:** PhD, University of Zurich, Switzerland (1972); ThM, University of Fribourg, Switzerland (1965) **C:** Professor Emeritus, The New School (2014-Present); Professor, The New School (2000-2014); Professor, University of Zurich (1975-2000) **CIV:** OneMarketing, Zurich, Switzerland (1999) **CW:** Contributor, Articles, Professional Journals **AW:** Scholarship, Swiss National Scientific Fund (1988-1998) **MEM:** Chair, International Society for Third-Sector Research (1997-2001); Verein fur Socialpolitik; Association for Research on Nonprofit Organizations and Voluntary Action **ADD:** 372 Central Park W, Apt. 17H, New York, NY, 10025

WAGNER, ELLYN SANTI, T: Mathematics Educator **I:** Education/Educational Services **ED:** Postgraduate Studies, George Mason University (1980-1982); MA, Northern Arizona University (1974); BS, Northern Arizona University (1971) **CT:** Certified Teacher, State of Virginia **C:** Assistant Professor of Mathematics, Northern Virginia Community College, Annandale, VA (1976-2004); Head, Mathematics Department, Flagstaff Public Schools, Arizona(1974-1976); Mathematics Teacher, Flagstaff Public Schools, Arizona (1972-1976) **CR:** Participant, Writing Across the Curriculum Workshops, Annandale, VA (1992-1993) **AW:** Recognition for Outstanding Contributions to Education, Northern Virginia Community College, Alumni Federation (1993) **MEM:** Coordinator, Spring Conference, Virginia Mathematical Association of Two-Year Colleges (1992); Regional Vice President, Virginia Mathematical Association of Two-Year Colleges (1989-1991); American Mathematical Association of Two-Year Colleges; Phi Kappa Phi **MH:** Albert Nelson Marquis Lifetime Achievement Award (2017) **H:** Classical piano; Ballroom dancing **ADD:** 9500 Grover Road, Gaithersburg, MD, 20877

WAGNER, MICHAEL F., T: Professor of Philosophy **I:** Education/Educational Services **CN:** University of San Diego **PT:** Anette C. Mueller; Victor V. Wagner **MS:** Single **ED:** PhD, The Ohio State University (1979); MA, The Ohio State University

(1976); BA in Philosophy and Mathematics, Texas A&M University (1974) **C:** Professor of Philosophy, University of San Diego (1989-Present); Director, Interdisciplinary Humanities Major Program, University of San Diego (1987-1993, 2001-2007); Chair, Department of Philosophy, University of San Diego (1988-1998); Acting Associate Dean, College of Arts and Science, University of San Diego (1988-1989); Associate Professor of Philosophy, University of San Diego (1984-1989); Assistant Professor of Philosophy, University of San Diego (1980-1984); Lecturer, The Ohio State University (1979-1980); Lecturer, Capital University (1979-1980); Graduate Teaching Assistant, The Ohio State University (1974-1979) **CR:** Integrated Teacher Preparation Program Advisory Council, University of San Diego (2017-Present); Liberal Studies Advisory Council, University of San Diego (2009-Present); Torero Athletic Council, University of San Diego (2007-Present); Interdisciplinary Humanities Major Advisory Committee, University of San Diego (1987-Present); University Core Planning Committee, University of San Diego (2013-2014); Vice-Chair, Academic Assembly Executive Committee, University of San Diego (2013-2014); Academic Assembly Executive Committee, University of San Diego (1982-1983, 1984-1987, 2013-2014); College Core Curriculum Committee, University of San Diego (2012-2014); Parliamentarian, Academic Assembly Executive Committee, University of San Diego (1984-1985, 2012-2013); College Undergraduate Curriculum Committee, University of San Diego (1981-1983, 1985-1986, 1988-1989, 2002-2005, 2012-2013); Adjunct and Advisory Member, Doctoral Dissertation Committee, Tbilisi State University (2011); Chair, Academic Assembly University Budget Procedures Task Force, University of San Diego (2005-2007); Chair, European Studies and Asian Studies Program Development Committee, University of San Diego (2002-2004); Chair, Interdisciplinary Humanities Major Advisory Committee, University of San Diego (1987-1993, 2001-2008); Ethics Across the Campus Assessment and Advisory Committee, University of San Diego (1996-2001); Weigand Foundation Ethics Across the Curriculum Grant Supervisory Committee, University of San Diego (1996-1998); Chair, Philosophy Program Assessment Committee, University of San Diego (1992-1998); Chair, Philosophy Library Acquisitions Committee, University of San Diego (1981-1985, 1988-1998); Adjunct and Advisory Member, Doctoral Dissertation Committee, The Hebrew University of Jerusalem (1997); Chair, University Senate Honorary Degrees Committee, University of San Diego (1996-1997); Faculty Representative for College of Arts & Sciences, University Senate, University of San Diego (1994-1997); Adjunct and Advisory Member, Doctoral Dissertation Committee, Union Institute & University (1996); Chair, Department Faculty Search Committee, University of San Diego (1989, 1990, 1992, 1996); Chair and Report Author, Department Strategic Long-Range Planning and W.A.S.C. Reaccreditation Committee, University of San Diego (1991, 1993, 1995); College Appointment, Reappointment, Rank, and Tenure Committee, University of San Diego (1991-1993); Adjunct and Advisory Member, Doctoral Dissertation Committee, University of California, Berkeley (1991); University Teaching Excellence Award Selection Committee, University of San Diego (1989-1991); University Grants & Contracts Officer, Search Committee, University of San Diego (1989-1990); Secretary, General Education Review Committee, University of San Diego (1988-1990); Arts & Sciences Faculty Research Grants Selection Committee, University of San Diego (1984-1986, 1988-1990); Convener, Gender Studies Program Planning Group, University of San Diego (1988-1989); Committee to Restruc-

ture the General Education Program, University of San Diego (1985-1988); Chair, Committee to Establish an Interdisciplinary Humanities Major, University of San Diego (1985-1987); Chair, Academic Assembly Executive Committee, University of San Diego (1985-1986); College Budget Committee, University of San Diego (1982-1984); Secretary, Academic Assembly Executive Committee, University of San Diego (1982-1983) **CW:** Editorial Board Member, Platonism and Neoplatonism Subseries, "Ancient Mediterranean and Medieval Texts and Contexts," Brill (2004-Present); Author, "The Enigmatic Reality of Time: Aristotle, Plotinus, and Today," Brill (2008); Editor, "Neoplatonism and Nature: Studies in Plotinus' Enneads," State University of New York Press (2002); Author, "Moral Philosophy: An Historical Introduction," Prentice Hall (1991); Contributor, Articles, Professional Journals; Contributor, Book Reviews **AW:** International Opportunity Grantee, University of San Diego (2017); Honoree, Distinguished Worldwide Humanitarian (2017); Industry Expert Honoree (2017) **MEM:** Treasurer, Board of Directors, ISNS (2004-Present); Board of Directors, ISNS (1998-Present); Secretary-Treasurer, United States Section, ISNS (1982-Present); Executive Council, American Catholic Philosophical Association (1997-2000); Chair, Constitution Revisions Committee, ISNS (1991-1993); Executive Council, Medieval Association of the Pacific (1987-1990) **MH:** Albert Nelson Marquis Lifetime Achievement Award (2017); Distinguished Humanitarian (2017) **H:** Science Fiction; Art (Charcoal Drawing & Painting); Model Car Racing; Chess **BA:** 5998 Alcala Park, University of San Diego, Dept of Philosophy, San Diego, CA, 92110 **ADD:** 5150 Balboa Arms Dr Apt G2, San Diego, CA, 92117

WAGNER, SAMUEL ALBIN MAR, I: Research **DOB:** 02/23/1942 **PB:** Brighton **SC:** CO/USA **PT:** Jacob Doer Wagner; Leota Garnet (Wilson) Wagner **MS:** Married **SPN:** Donna Dee Person (March 20, 1987) **CH:** Kurt; Andrea; Autumn; Jan; Arthur **ED:** STB (MTS) in History of World Religions, Harvard University, Cambridge, MA (1968); MA in History, University of Colorado (1965); BA in History, University of Colorado (1964) **CT:** Certification, Institute of Certified Records Managers (1983); Archivist, Academy of Certified Archivists (1994); Community College, Occupational Education Credential, Colorado State Board (1986); Certified Community College Teacher, State of California (1980); Certification in Archival Administration, University of Denver (1978) **C:** Deputy Director, Division Archives and Records Management, State New Jersey, Trenton (2007-Present); Chief, New Jersey Bureau Records Management, Trenton (1996-Present); President, Historic Research Services, Jefferson City, Trenton (1994-Present); President, Records Management Consultant International, Fort Collins, Vancouver, British Columbia, Trenton (1983-Present); Producer, Community Access, Station JCTV, Jefferson City, Missouri (1994-1996); Cataloging Editor, Electronic Records Analyst, Missouri State Archives, Jefferson City, (1993-1996); Assistant Professor, Master Archival Studies Program, University British Columbia, Vancouver, Canada (1990-1993); Public Records Administrator, State Rhode Island, Providence (1987-1990); Records Manager, Fort Collins Police Department, Colorado (1984-1987); State Records Analyst, Wyoming State Archives, Cheyenne (1979-1983); City Archivist, City of Providence (1978-1980); County Historian, Adams County, Colorado (1977-1978); Editor, Brighton Blade, Market Pl., Fort Lupton Press, Brighton Pub. (1973-1977); Senior Assistant Archivist, Regional History Collection, University Archives, Cornell

University, Ithaca, NY (1971-1973); Assistant Curator, Western History Collections, University Archives, University of Colorado, Boulder (1968-1970); Archival Assistant, Harvard University and Harvard Business School, Cambridge, MA (1965-1968) **CR:** Instructor, Professor, Lincoln University (1995-1996); Instructor, Professor, University British Columbia (1990-1993); Instructor, Professor, Colorado State University (1985-1987); Instructor, Professor, Chapman University (1981-1987); Instructor, Professor, Laramie County Community College (1982-1983); Instructor, Professor, LA Metropolitan College (1980-1982); Instructor, Professor, Boston Architectural Institute (1967-1968); Speaker in Field, National and International Conferences **CIV:** Chairman, Oral History Project, Cole County Historical Society (1996); Judge, National History Day, Missouri (1993-1996); Chairman, Information Profiles Legislation Task Force, Freedom of Information and Privacy Association (1991-1993); Rhode Island Public Records Advisory Council (1987-1990); Rhode Island Historical Records Advisory Board (1987-1990); Fort Lupton Bicentennial Committee (1975-1976); Rhode Island RSVP (1978-1980); County Historian, Adams County, CO (1977-1978); Member, Brighton Human Relations Commission (1977-1978); Officer, Board of Directors Adams County Historical Society (1973-1977); Board of Directors, Brighton Bicentennial Committee (1975-1976) **CW:** Author, "Images of America: Brighton", Colorado (2009); Author, "Brighton Reflections" (2006); Author, "Moving Archives" (2002); Author, "Adams County Colorado: A Centennial History" (2002); Editor, "Missouri State Archives", Jefferson City (1994-1996); Author, "Directory of Automated Records Management Systems" (1985-1991); Author, "Adams County: Crossroads of the West" (1977); Author, "Crossroads of the West: A History of Brighton and the Platte Valley" (1977); Author, "The Fort Lupton Story" (1977); "Editor, Brighton Blade", Fort Lupton Press, Colorado (1973-1977); Author, "Brighton Reflections" (1976); Contributor, Articles, Professional Journals; Contributor, Stories, Anthologies **AW:** Certificate of Special Congressional Recognition (2006); Award, Freedom of Information and Privacy Association (1993); Humanities and Social Sciences, University of British Columbia (1993); Grantee, National Historic Public and Records Commission (1988-1992); Historical Preservation Award, Adams County Historical Society (1978); Ethnic Heritage Project, Colorado Humanities Council (1977); Fellow, Ford Foundation (1964-1965) **MEM:** Program Committee, Mid-Atlantic Regional Archives Conference (1999-2000, 2002-Present); Exam Proctor and Grader, Institute of Certified Records Managers (1982-Present); President, Association Records Managers and Administrators (2002-2004); Mid-Year Seminar Program Committee, ISG (1998-2002); Commission on the Future of Archival Enterprise, Academy of Certified Archivists (1999-2000); Chairman, Archives, ISG (1997-1999); Committee for Automated Records and Techniques, Society of American Archivists (1990-1994); Freedom of Information and Privacy Legislative Committee, Archives Association of British Columbia (1990-1993); Electronic Records Select Committee, Association of Canadian Archivists (1991-1993); Editor, Software Director (1985-1991); Co-Chairman, Technology Applications Committee (1989-1990); Chairman, Microcomputer/PC Industry Action Committee (1984-1986); Records Management Standards and Glossary Task Forces (1985); Master Archives and Records Administration Advisory Committee, School of Library and Information Science, San Jose University; Public Sector Managers Association; ACLU; American Association for State and Local History, Nature Conservancy; Charter Member, American Historical Society of Germans from Russia; Lawrence Historical Society; Lawrence Arts Council; New Jersey Studies Academic Alliance Committee; Adams County Historical Society; South Plate Valley Historical Society; National Association Government Archivists and Records Administrators **H:** History, art, photography, filmmaking **PA:** Democrat **RE:** Unitarian Universalist

WAKIM, FAHD, T: Coordinator of Electrical Engineering **I:** Education/Educational Services **CN:** University of Massachusetts **DOB:** 08/06/1933 **PB:** Mieh-Mieh **SC:** Lebanon **PT:** George Hanna; Marriam (Semaan) Wakim **MS:** Married **SPN:** Bertha Villarreal **ED:** PhD in Solid State Physics, University of Texas, Austin (1964); MA in Solid State Physics, University of Texas, Austin (1960); BSc in Physics, American University, Beirut (1956) **C:** Coordinator of Electrical Engineering, University of Massachusetts, Lowell (1996-Present); Emeritus Professor, University of Massachusetts (2010); Associate Professor, Department of Electrical Engineering, University of Massachusetts, Lowell (1984-2010); Professor of Physics, Kuwait University, Kuwait (1973-1984); Associate Professor, American University, Cairo (1971-1973); Investigator, Texas Christian University, Fort Worth (1970-1971); Research Physicist, Itek Corp., Lexington, MA (1965-1970) **CR:** Presenter, Numerous Seminars **CW:** Contributor, Articles, Professional Journals **AW:** Grantee, Kuwait Institute For Science Research (1978, 1979, 1991); Grantee, Kuwait University (1979) **MEM:** American Physical Society **ADD:** 13 Stadium Road, Methuen, MA, 01844

WALBA, DAVID MARK, T: Professor **I:** Education/Educational Services **CN:** University of Colorado, Boulder **DOB:** 06/29/1949 **PB:** Oakland **SC:** CA/USA **PT:** Harold Walba; Beatrice (Alpert) Walba **MS:** Married **SPN:** Cassandra Geneson (10/30/1981) **CH:** Paul Geneson **ED:** Postdoctoral Work, University of California, Los Angeles (1977); PhD, California Institute of Technology (1975); BS, University of California, Berkeley (1971) **C:** Professor, University of Colorado, Boulder (1987-Present); Associate Professor, University of Colorado, Boulder (1983-1987); Assistant Professor of Chemistry, University of Colorado, Boulder (1977-1983) **CR:** Member, Board of Directors, Displaytech Inc., Boulder, CO (1995-2002); Founding Member, Interdisciplinary Liquid Crystal Materials Research Center **CW:** Contributor, Articles, Professional Journals; Patentee in Field **AW:** College Scholars Award (2012); Dreyfus Teacher Scholarship (1984-1986); Fellowship, Alfred P. Sloan Foundation (1982-1984) **MEM:** Fellow, American Association for the Advancement of Science (1999); American Chemical Society; Materials Research Society; Sigma Xi **MH:** Albert Nelson Marquis Lifetime Achievement Award (2017) **BA:** 215 UCB, UC, Dept of Chemistry and Biochemistry, Boulder, CO, 80309

WALDECK, JOHN WALTER, T: Lawyer **I:** Law and Legal Services **CN:** Walter & Haverfield LLP **DOB:** 05/03/1949 **PB:** Cleveland **SC:** OH/USA **PT:** John Walter, Sr.; Marjorie Ruth (Palenschat) Walter **MS:** Married **SPN:** Cheryl Gene Cutter (9/10/1977) **CH:** John III; Matthew; Rebecca **ED:** JD, Cleveland State University (1977); BS, John Carroll University (1973) **CT:** Certified in Business, Commercial, and Industrial Real Estate and Property Law, Ohio State Bar Association (2007) **C:** Executive Committee Member, Walter & Haverfield LLP (2003-Present); Partner, Walter & Haverfield LLP (1996-Present); Partner-in-Charge, Porter, Wright, Morris and Arthur (1990-1996); Partner, Porter, Wright, Morris and Arthur (1988-1990); Partner, Arter & Hadden (1986-1988); Associate, Arter & Hadden (1977-1985); Product Applications Chemist, Synthetic Products Company (1969-1976) **CR:** Secretary, Geauga Medical Center, University Hospitals (2015-Present); First Vice Chair, The Cleveland Music School Settlement (2014-Present); Director, Geauga Medical Center, University Hospitals (2013-Present); Ohio Trustee, The Cleveland Music School Settlement (2012-Present); Member, Leadership Council, Geauga Medical Center, University Hospitals (2011-Present); Board of Advisors Litigation Management, Inc. (2000-2004) **CIV:** Specialization Board, Real Property Law (2007-Present); Chairman, Real Property Law (2009-2014); Secretary, LeBlond Housing Corporation (1996); Chairman, Geauga County Board of Mental Health & Recovery Services (1995-1997); Section, Secretary, Fairmount Center for the Arts (1994-1995); Secretary, University Circle, Inc. (1993-1997); Secretary, Fairmount Center for the Arts (1993-1996); Vice Chairman, Geauga County Board of Mental Health & Recovery Services (1993-1995); Treasurer, Geauga County Board of Mental Health & Recovery Services (1991-1993); Trustee, LeBlond Housing Corporation, Cleveland, OH (1990-1996); Board of Advisors, Palliative & Supportive Oncology, Cleveland Clinic (1989-1991); Board of Directors, Geauga County Board of Mental Health & Recovery Services (1988-1997); Chairman, Board of Zoning Appeals, Bainbridge Township, Ohio (1984-1994); Secretary, Greater Cleveland Chapter, Lupus Foundation of America, Inc. (1979-1986); Trustee, Greater Cleveland Chapter, Lupus Foundation of America, Inc. (1978-1991) **AW:** Honoree, Best Lawyers in Real Estate (2013-Present); Honoree, Ohio Super Lawyer, Law & Politics Magazine (2007-Present) **MEM:** Vice Chair, Ohio State Bar Association (2015-Present); Board of Governors, Real Property Section, Ohio State Bar Association (2008-Present); Certification Board, Real Property Specialty, Ohio State Bar Association (2007-Present); Certified, Real Property Specialist, Ohio State Bar Association (2007-Present); Secretary, Ohio State Bar Association (2013-2014); Board of Governors, Real Property Section, Ohio State Bar Association (1992); Co-Chair of Real Property, Corporate Banking Section, Real Estate Law Institute, Bar Association of Greater Cleveland (1995-1996, 1990) **BAR:** Ohio (1977); Greater Cleveland, Ohio **MH:** Albert Nelson Marquis Lifetime Achievement Award (2017) **H:** Beekeeping; Gardening; Jogging **RE:** Roman Catholic **BA:** 1301 E 9th St Ste 3500, Walter & Haverfield LLP, Cleveland, OH, 44114

WALKER, RICHARD B., T: Chemistry Professor **I:** Sciences **CN:** University of Arkansas at Pine Bluff **DOB:** 05/14/1948 **PB:** Quincy **SC:** MA/USA **PT:** George Edgar Walker; Eva Mary (Taylor) Walker **ED:** PhD in Pharmaceutical Chemistry, University of California, San Francisco, CA (1975); BS in Biochemistry, University of Southern California (1970) **C:** Professor, Chemistry, University of Arkansas at Pine Bluff (1996-Present); Interim Chair, Department of Chemistry and Physics, University of Arkansas at Pine Bluff (2007-2009); Assistant to Associate Professor, Chemistry, University of Arkansas at Pine Bluff (1984-1996); Associate Professor, Chemistry, University of the Ozarks, Clarksville, AR (1983-1984); Research Scientist, Biophysical Foundation, San Diego, CA (1982-1983); Lecturer, School of Pharmaceutical Education And Research, Jamia Hamdard, New Delhi, India (1981-1982); Lecturer, Alliant International University, San Diego, CA (1978-1981); Research Associate, University of Washington, Seattle, WA (1976-1978); Research Associate, Oregon State University, Corvallis,

OR (1975-1976) **CR:** Project Director, Arkansas Systemic Science Initiative Chair, University of Arkansas at Pine Bluff Institutional Review Board (2003-Present); Principal Investigator, Minority Biomedical Research Support Program, National Institutes of Health, Bethesda, MD (1986-Present) **CIV:** Coordinator, Home Bible Fellowship, The Way International, North Little Rock, AR (2007-Present); Judge, Central Arkansas Science Fair, Little Rock, AR (1986-Present); Coordinator, Home Bible Fellowship, The Way International, Pine Bluff, AR (1984-1999) **CW:** Contributor, Articles, Professional Journals; Reviewer in Field **AW:** National Institutes of Health Research Grantee (2006, 1993, 1989, 1986) **MEM:** Secretary Treasurer, Central Arkansas Chapter, Sigma Xi (2005-2006); Vice President, Sigma Xi (2000-2007); American Chemical Society; Arkansas Academy of Science; American Association of Pharmaceutical Scientists **H:** Fishing; Golf; Skiing **BA:** 1200 Universtiy Dr, Mailbox 4941, University of Arkansas, Department of Chemistry & Physics at Pine Bluff, Pine Bluff, AR, 71601

WALKER, TIMOTHY BLAKE, T: Lawyer, Educator **I:** Law and Legal Services **CN:** Walker, Wright & Associates **DOB:** 05/21/1940 **PB:** Utica **SC:** NY/USA **PT:** Harold Blake Walker; Mary Alice (Corder) Walker **MS:** Married **SPN:** Sandra Blake **CH:** Janna Lynn; Stacey Anne; Kimberlee Corder; Tyler Blake; Kelley Loren **ED:** MA in Sociology, University of Denver (1969); JD, University of Denver, Magna Cum Laude (1967); AB, Princeton University, Magna Cum Laude (1962) **C:** Principal, Walker, Wright & Associates (2014-Present); Professor Emeritus, University of Denver (1999-Present); Principal, Walker & Associate Centennial (2010-2013); Partner, Cox, Mustain-Wood, Walker & Schumacher, Littleton, CO (1985-2010); Of Counsel, Cox, Mustain-Wood, Walker & Schumacher, Littleton, CO (1985-2010); Professor, University of Denver (1975-1999); Of Counsel, Robert T. Hinds, Junior & Associates PC, Littleton, CO (1980-1985); Lawyer, Private Practice, Denver, CO (1972-1979); Director, Administration of Justice Program, University of Denver (1971-1978); Associate Professor, University of Denver (1971-1975); Associate Professor, Indianapolis Law School, Indiana University (1970-1971); Visiting Associate Professor, The University of Toledo (1969-1970); Assistant Professor of Law, University of the Pacific (1968-1969) **CR:** Research on Lay Representation in Administrative Agencies, Colorado (1975-1976); Consultant in Field; Lecturer in Field **CIV:** President, Whisper Canyon Homeowners Association (2004-2010); President, Shawnee Water Consumers Association (1975-1984, 1993-1995); Delegate, Colorado Republican Convention (1978); Member, Indiana Child Support Commission (1970-1971) **CW:** Editor-in-chief, "Family Law Quarterly" (1983-1992); Editor, "Denver Law Journal" (1966-1967); Contributor, Articles, Professional Journals; Lecturer, Annual Presentations, Law Education Institute; Board of Editors, "Family Advocate," ABA **AW:** Grantee, Colorado Bar Association (1975-1976); Recipient, Awards for Merit, Family Law Section, ABA **MEM:** Board of Governors, ABA (2012-2015); Family Section Delegate, House of Delegates, ABA (2000-2015); House of Delegates, ABA (1999-2015); Chairman, Child Custody Task Force, ABA (2000-2001); Alimony, Maintenance and Support Committee, ABA (2000-2001); Chairman, Family Law Section, ABA (1995-1996); Chairman-elect, Family Law Section, ABA (1994-1995); Vice Chairman, Family Law Section, ABA (1993-1994); Secretary, Family Law Section, ABA (1992-1994); Fellow, American Bar Foundation; Fellow, International Academy of Matrimonial Lawyers; Fellow, American Sociological Association; Fellow, American Academy of Matrimonial Lawyers; Vice Chairman, Child Custody Subcommittee, ABA; Colorado Trial Lawyers Association **BAR:** Indiana (1971); State of California (1969); Colorado (1968) **MH:** Albert Nelson Marquis Lifetime Achievement Award (2017) **H:** Hunting; Fishing; Gardening **RE:** Presbyterian **BA:** 6601 S University Blvd, Centennial, CO, 80121 **ADD:** 13138 Whisper Canyon Rd, Castle Pines, CO, 80108 **URL:** https://www.walkerwrightlaw.com/

WALLANDER, WILLIAM L., T: Partner **I:** Law and Legal Services **CN:** Vinson & Elkins LLP **CH:** Two Daughters **ED:** MBA, University of Phoenix, Summa Cum Laude (2001); JD, School of Law, University of Texas (1984); BA in Political Science, University of Pittsburgh (1984) **CT:** Certified Microsoft User Specialist in Access Relational Database Software (2000) **C:** Partner, Vinson & Elkins, LLP **CR:** Head, Vinson & Elkins Restructuring and Reorganization Group **AW:** Best Lawyers in America, Bankruptcy and Creditor Debtor Rights/Insolvency and Reorganization Law (2005-Present); Chambers Global, Bankruptcy/Restructuring Law (2017); Corporate Restructuring: Including Bankruptcy (2015-2017); Best Lawyers in Dallas in Bankruptcy & Workouts, D Magazine (2014-2015); Legal Media Group's Guide to the World's Leading Insolvency & Restructuring Lawyers (2013); Legal 500 United States, Corporate Restructuring (2012–2014); Chambers Global, Bankruptcy/Restructuring Law (2012); Best Lawyers in Dallas in Bankruptcy & Workouts, D Magazine (2012); Legal Media Group's Guide to the World's Leading Insolvency & Restructuring Lawyers (2007-2011); Chambers USA, Bankruptcy/Restructuring Law (2004-2017); Texas Super Lawyers, Super Lawyers, Thomson Reuters (2004-2017) **BAR:** State of Texas; State of New York; Texas Supreme Court; U.S. Supreme Court; Fifth and Tenth Circuits, U.S. Court of Appeals; U.S. District Courts for the Northern, Eastern, Western, and Southern Districts, State of Texas; U.S. District Court, State of Arizona; U.S. District Court, Southern District, State of New York; U.S. District Court, State of Colorado **BA:** 2001 Ross Avenue, Suite 3700, Vinson & Elkins LLP, Dallas, TX, 75201 **URL:** https://www.velaw.com/Who-we-are/Find-a-lawyer/Wallander–William

WALSH, THOMAS J., T: Epidemiologist **I:** Medicine & Health Care **CN:** Weill Cornell Medicine, Cornell University; NewYork-Presbyterian **ED:** Honorary PhD in Microbiology, National and Kapodistrian University of Athens Greece (2011); MD, Johns Hopkins University School of Medicine (1978); BA, Assumption College, Summa Cum Laude (1974) **C:** Director, Transplantation-oncology Infectious Diseases Program, Weill Cornell Medical College, Cornell University and NewYork-Presbyterian (2010-Present); Chief, Immunocompromised Host Section, Pediatric Oncology Branch NCI, Bethesda, MD (1986-2009) **CR:** Adjunct Professor, Pathology, Johns Hopkins University School Medicine (2004-Present); Adjunct Professor, Medicine, University of Maryland School of Medicine (1998-Present); Councilor, American Society for Microbiology (2011-2012); Divisional Chair, American Society for Microbiology (2010-2011); President, Medical Mycological Society of the Americas (2003-2005); Councilor, International Immunocompromised Host Society (2002-2006); Professor, Medicine and Microbiology, Immunology, Cornell University **CIV:** Member, New York City Medical Reserve Corps **AW:** Lucille K. Georg Medal, The International Society for Human and Animal Mycology; Sanofi-Aventis Award, Interscience Conference on Antimicrobial Agents and Chemotherapy, American Society for Microbiology **MEM:** Fellow, American College of Physicians; Fellow, Infectious Diseases Society of America; Fellow, American Academy of Microbiology; Phi Beta Kappa; Alpha Omega Alpha **BA:** 1300 York Ave Room A421, Weill Cornell Medicine | Cornell University, New York, NY, 10065 **ADD:** 1300 York Avenue, Room A421, Weill Cornell Medicine, New York, NY, 10065

WALTER, HUGO G., T: Professor of English and Humanities, Poet **I:** Education/Educational Services **CN:** Berkeley College **DOB:** 03/12/1959 **PB:** Philadelphia **SC:** PA/USA **PT:** Elli R. Walter; Paul Walter **ED:** PhD in Interdisciplinary Humanities, Drew University (1996); MA in Humanities, Old Dominion University (1989); PhD in Literature, Yale University (1985); MPhil in Literature, Yale University (1984); MA in Literature, Yale University (1983); BA, Princeton University (1981) **C:** Professor, Berkeley College, Woodland Park, NJ (1999-Present); Assistant Professor, Kettering University, Flint, MI (1996-1999); Assistant Professor, Fairleigh Dickinson University, Madison, NJ (1992-1996); Assistant Professor, Washington & Jefferson College, Washington, PA (1989-1992); Adjunct Instructor, Old Dominion University, Norfolk, VA (1988-1989); Adjunct Instructor, Yale University, New Haven, CT (1981-1985) **CR:** Visiting Assistant Professor, University of Missouri, Columbia, MO (1987-1988); Visiting Assistant Professor, Rhodes College, Memphis, TN (1986-1987) **CW:** Author, "Sanctuaries in Washington Irving's The Sketch Book" (2014); Author, "Magnificent Houses in Twentieth Century European Literature" (2012); Author, "Beautiful Sanctuaries in Nineteenth and Early Twentieth Century European Literature" (2011); Author, "Sanctuaries of Light in Nineteenth Century European Literature" (2010); Author, "A Purple-Golden Renascence of Eden-Exalting Rainbows" (2001); Author, "Space and Time on the Magic Mountain: Studies in 19th and 20th Century European Literature" (1999); Author, "Amaranth-Sage Epiphanies of Dusk-Weaving Paradise, Second Edition" (1996); Author, "Amaranth-Sage Epiphanies of Dusk-Weaving Paradise" (1995); Author, "Dusk-Gloaming Mirrors and Castle-Winding Dreams" (1994); Author, "The Light of the Dance Is the Music of Eternity" (1993); Author, "Waiting for Babel Prophesies of Sunflower Dreams" (1992); Author, "Along the Maroon-Prismed Threshold of Bronze-Pealing Eternity" (1992); Author, "Golden Thorns of Light and Sterling Silhouettes" (1991); Author, "Amber Blossoms and Evening Shadows" (1990); Author, "Velvet Rhythms" (1989); Author, "The Fragile Edge" (1988); Author, "The Apostrophic Moment in 19th and 20th Century Lyric Poetry" (1988) **AW:** Recipient, Faculty of the Year Award, Berkeley College (2006) **MEM:** Academy of American Poets; International Society of Poets **MH:** Albert Nelson Marquis Lifetime Achievement Award (2017) **H:** Music; Painting **ADD:** 2130 Windrow Dr, Princeton, NJ, 08540

WALTERS, WILLIAM B., T: Professor **I:** Education/Educational Services **CN:** University of Maryland **DOB:** 04/26/1938 **PB:** Highland **SC:** KS/USA **PT:** Ben Guthrie; Dolly Varden (Shaw) W. **MS:** Married **SPN:** Barbara Lulu Sternaman (8/5/1962) **CH:** Katherine (Deceased, 2013); David **ED:** PhD in Physical Chemistry, University of Illinois, Urbana, IL (1964); BS in Chemistry and Education, Kansas State University, Manhattan, KS (1960); AS, Highland College, Highland, KS (1957) **C:** Professor of Chemistry, University of Maryland (1977-Present); Associate Professor of Chemistry, University of Maryland, College Park, MD (1970-1977); Assistant Professor of Chemistry, Massachusetts Institute of Technology (1965-1970); Research Associate, Massachusetts Institute of Technology (1964-1965) **CR:** University Athletic Council (2011-2016); Executive Committee Member, University Senate (2012-2013); Member, University Senate (2011-2014); Member, Physics Advisory Committee, Grand Accélérateur National d'Ions Lourds (2003-2006); Chair, University of Maryland College Park Senate (1999-2000); Chair, University Senate; Associate Chairman, Department of Chemistry (1982-1986); Visiting professor University Louvain, Belgium (1978) **AW:** Research Award, UMCP College Chem LFSC (2010); Research Award, University Maryland, College Chemical & Life Sciences (2010); Alexander von Humboldt Fellowship, University of Mainz (2001-2002, 2006); ACS Award in Nuclear Chemistry (2001); Recipient Nuclear Chemistry Award, American Chemical Society (2001); MCP Sigma Xi Award for Research (1998); Sigma Xi (1998); University of Maryland General Research Board Semester Awards (1982, 1990, 1997); Guggenheim Fellow, Oxford University (1986-1987); Phi Lambda Upsilon Senior Award, Kansas State University (1959); NSF Undergraduate Research Fellowship; NSF Graduate Fellowship; University of Illinois Fellowship **MEM:** Fellow, University Leuven, Belgium (2008); Chairman, Division of Nuclear Chemistry and Technology (1986); American Chemical Society; American Physical Society; European Physical Society; American Chemical Society; Rotary Club **MH:** Albert Nelson Marquis Lifetime Achievement Award (2017) **H:** Travel; Stamp Collecting **ADD:** 4612 Amherst Rd, College Park, MD, 20740

WALTERS, ARTHUR SCOTT, T: Neurologist, Educator, Clinical Research Scientist **I:** Education/Educational Services **CN:** Vanderbilt University School of Medicine **DOB:** 02/20/1943 **PB:** Baltimore **SC:** MD/USA **PT:** Charles Henry Walters; Jean Vivian (Scott) Walters **MS:** Married **SPN:** Lesley J. Gill (12/19/1992); Bokyun Kim (5/18/1985, Divorced 1992) **ED:** Movement Disorder Fellow, The Neurological Institute of New York, Columbia University (1982-1984); Resident, Neurology, SUNY Downstate Medical Center (1976-1979); Intern, Oakwood Hospital, Oakwood Health Care (Now Beaumont Health) (1972-1973); MD, School of Medicine, Wayne State University (1972); MS in Biological Sciences, Northwestern University (1967); BA, Kalamazoo College (1965) **CT:** Certification in Sleep, American Board of Medical Specialties (2011); Diplomate, American Board of Sleep Medicine (1995); Board Certified Neurologist, American Board of Psychiatry and Neurology, Inc. (1981) **C:** Professor, Neurology, Vanderbilt University School of Medicine, Nashville, TN (2008-Present); Visiting Professor, Department of Clinical Neurophysiology, Georg-August-Universität Göttingen, Goettingen, Germany (2013); Professor, Neuroscience, New Jersey Neuroscience Institute (Now JFK Neuroscience Institute), JFK Health (1999-2008); Professor, Neuroscience, Graduate School for Medical Education, Seton Hall University (1999-2008); Clinical Professor, Neurology, Robert Wood Johnson Medical School, University of Medicine and Dentistry of New Jersey (Now Rutgers New Jersey Medical School), Rutgers, The State University of New Jersey (1999-2008); Staff Neurologist, Lyons Campus, Veteran Affairs New Jersey Health Care System, U.S. Department of Veterans Affairs (1984-1999); Associate Professor, Neurology, Robert Wood Johnson Medical School, Rutgers, The State University of New Jersey (1991-1999); Assistant Professor, Neurology, Robert Wood Johnson Medical School, Rutgers, The State University of New Jersey (1984-1991); Assistant Chief, Division of Neurology, Lyons Campus, Veteran Affairs New Jersey Health Care System, U.S. Department of

Veterans Affairs (1985-1989) **CR:** Medical Advisory Board Member, International Restless Legs Syndrome Study Group (1992-Present); Founder, International Restless Legs Syndrome Study Group (1992-2007); First Chairman, International Restless Legs Syndrome Study Group (1992-2007); Consultant, Coney Island Hospital, Brooklyn, NY (1980-1981); Consultant, Brooklyn Jewish Hospital (1980-1981) **CW:** Committee Head, "International Classification of Sleep Disorders-3" (2014); Committee Head, "The AASM Manual for the Scoring of Sleep and Associated Events" (2007); Committee Head, "International Classification of Sleep Disorders-2" (2005); Contributor, Peer-reviewed Articles, Professional Journals; Contributor, Book Chapters; Contributor, Letters to the Editor; Contributor, Abstracts on Sleep-Related Movement Disorders; Contributor, Publications on the Cause and Treatment of Restless Legs Syndrome **AW:** Notable Alumni, School of Medicine, Wayne State University (2017); Collaborative Research Award, International Restless Legs Syndrome Study Group (2012); Senior Sleep Science Award, American Academy of Neurology for Excellence in Sleep Research (2010); Outstanding Teaching Award, Sleep Fellows and Community Sleep Physicians of New Jersey Neuroscience Institute (Now JFK Neuroscience Institute), JFK Health (2008); Distinguished Faculty Medical License, State of Tennessee (2008); Distinguished Service Award, International Restless Legs Syndrome Study Group (2007); Named Best Volunteer Neurology Faculty Member, Robert Wood Johnson Medical School, Rutgers, The State University of New Jersey (2007); Named Michael S. Aldrich Lecturer in Sleep Medicine for Outstanding Contributions to Patient Care, Education and Research, University of Michigan (2006); Named Researcher of the Year in Medicine, Seton Hall University (2003-2004); Distinguished Service Award, Restless Legs Syndrome Foundation, Inc. (1998); Bronze Oak Leaf Distinguished Service Award, Lyons Campus, VA New Jersey Health Care System, U.S. Department of Veterans Affairs (1998); Bronze Level, Ballroom Dance Championship, National United States Men's Pro Am Ballroom Dance (2013-2016); Research Grantee, NIH, U.S. Department of Veterans Affairs; Industry Grantee; Foundation Grantee; University Grantee **MEM:** Vice Chairperson, Specialty Committee on Sleep Medicine, World Federation of Chinese Medicine Societies (2011-Present); International Restless Legs Syndrome Study Group (1993-Present); Medical Advisory Board, Restless Legs Syndrome Foundation, Inc. (1992-Present); Vice President, New Jersey Sleep Society (1998-1999); Treasurer, New Jersey Sleep Society (1996-1997); Secretary, New Jersey Sleep Society (1995-1996); First Chairman, Medical Advisory Board, Restless Legs Syndrome Foundation, Inc. (1992-1998); Fellow, American Academy of Neurology; Fellow, American Academy of Sleep Medicine; Fellow, American Neurological Association; American Association for the Advancement of Science; Member, Sleep Research Society; Distinguished Member, International Parkinson and Movement Disorder Society; The New York Academy of Sciences; Named in "Leading Physicians of the World," IAHCP **MH:** Albert Nelson Marquis Lifetime Achievement Award (2017) **H:** Tennis; Competitive amateur ballroom dancing **BA:** MCN A-0118 1161 21st Ave S, Vanderbilt University School of Medicine, Nashville, TN, 37232

WARBERG, WILLETTA, T: Concert Pianist, Music Educator (Retired) **I:** Education/Educational Services **DOB:** 06/02/1932 **PB:** Twin Falls **SC:** ID/USA **PT:** George William Warber; Ethel Margaret Warberg-Chandler **MS:** Divorced **SPN:** David Jacob Bar-Illan (9/3/1954), Divorced **CH:** Daniela; Jeremy Oscar **ED:** BS, Mannes College The New School for

Music, New York, NY (1954); Mentorship, Rudolf Firkušný (1951-1953); Coursework, Aspen Music Camp (1951); Coursework, Colorado Women's College (1950-1951) **C:** Piano Coach, Saugerties and Woodstock, New York (2010-2014); Duo-Piano Partner, Composer Robert Starer, New York, Woodstock, NY (1991-2000); Syndicated Food Columnist, Music and Arts Critic, "Times News," (1978-1987); President, Owner, Willetta Enterprises, Advertising Agency, Twin Falls, ID (1976-1984); Freelance Writer, Photograph Stylist, "Gourmet" Magazine, New York, NY (1965-1975); Food Editor, "Ladies' Home Journal," New York, NY (1963-1966); Photograph Stylist, "Gourmet" Magazine, New York, NY (1961-1964); Food Editor, "Status" Magazine, New York, NY (1961-1962); Associate Food Editor, "Look" Magazine, New York, NY (1956-1961) **CR:** Artist-in-Residence, Holy Cross Concert Series, Kingston, NY (1994-2013); Restaurant Study in Israel, U.S. Department of State, International Cooperation Administration, Point 4 Program, Washington and Israel (1960) **CIV:** Board of Directors, Friends of the Maverick Concerts Inc., Woodstock, NY (2007-Present); Vice President, Board of Directors, Woodstock Chamber Orchestra (1993-Present); Chairman, Friends of the Maverick Concerts Inc., Woodstock, NY (1999-2014); President, Board of Directors, Woodstock Lyric Theatre (1994-2000); Board of Directors, Northwest Opera Association (1984-1987); Maverick Concert Association, Woodstock, NY **CW:** Concert Pianist, Idaho, Oregon, Utah, Washington, Colorado, New York (1940-Present); Syndicated Food Columnist, Hometown Market Basket (1978-1987); Author, "Space Age Cookery" (1977); Author, "Cooking from Scratch" (1976); Contributor, Food and Science Articles, "Cosmopolitan," "Modern Maturity," "Esquire," "Sun Valley," "Scientific Digest," "Redbook," "Food & Garden," "Girl Talk," "Flower & Garden" **AW:** Winner, Rocky Mountain Talent Search Contest, "Salt Lake Tribune," "Salt Lake Telegram" (1949) **MEM:** National Federation of Music Clubs; Certified Member, Music Teachers National Association; Kingston Music Society **H:** Swimming; Writing **ADD:** 10 Purdy Hollow Rd, Woodstock, NY, 12498 **URL:** http://www.willettawarberg.com/

WARMAN, LINDA K., T: English Instructor and Chair of English Department (Retired) **I:** Education/Educational Services **CN:** Easton Area School District **DOB:** 03/25/1942 **PB:** Indiana **SC:** PA/USA **PT:** James Edward Warman; Elizabeth Josephine (Hawk) Warman **MS:** Single **ED:** BA, Moravian College, Bethlehem, PA (1964); 64 Graduate Credits **CT:** Teaching Certification, Commonwealth of Pennsylvania; Masters Equivalency Certification, Commonwealth of State of Pennsylvania **C:** Retired (2001); Chair, English Department, Easton Area School District, PA (1986-2001); Teacher, Easton Area School District, PA (1964-2001) **CW:** Contributor, "Religious Literature of the West" (1970); The Bach Choir of Bethlehem (1963-1976); Member, College Choir, Moravian College, Bethlehem, PA; Soloist, Moravian College, Bethlehem, PA; Singer, Boston Symphony Hall; Singer, Carnegie Hall **AW:** Woman of the Year, National Association of Professional Women (2011-2012); Outstanding Instructor, University Honors Students, The Pennsylvania State University (1985); Named, Outstanding Secondary Educator, Association of Secondary School Principals (1975) **MEM:** National Association of Professional Women **H:** Travel; Reading; Home Decorating; Vegetable and Flower Gardening; Yard Work; Movies; Music **PA:** Democrat **RE:** Secular Humanist **ADD:** 152 El Do Lake Dr, Kunkletown, PA, 18058

WARNER, SUSAN M., **T:** Federal Agency Administrator **I:** Government Administration/Government Relations/Government Services **CN:** U.S. Department of Housing and Urban Development **DOB:** 07/20/1956 **PB:** Rochester **SC:** NY/USA **PT:** Harold J. Warner; Jeannette (Nichols) Warner **MS:** Divorced **CH:** Jennifer Lynn; Kathryn Alice **ED:** BA, Miami University, Oxford, OH (1978); Postgraduate Degree, Xavier University **C:** Resolution Specialist, U.S. Department of Housing and Urban Development (2013-Present); Underwriter, U.S. Department of Housing and Urban Development, St. Louis, MO (1987-2013); Underwriter, Shawmut Mortgage Corporation (1986-1987); Underwriter, Manufacturer's Hanover Mortgage Corporation (1986); Underwriter, Investors Diversified Services, Financial Services, Inc., Cincinnati, OH (1983-1986); Underwriter, U.S. Department of Housing and Urban Development, Cincinnati, OH (1979-1983); Loan Specialist, U.S. Department of Housing and Urban Development, Columbus, OH (1978-1979) **CR:** Housing Consultant, Cincinnati, OH (1985-Present) **CIV:** Member, Financial Committee, Community Land Cooperative, Cincinnati, OH (1985-Present); Adviser, Cincinnati State (1984-Present); March of Dimes (1996-2015); Volunteer, American Cancer Society (1981-2014); Conference Coordinator, Conference of Cincinnati Women (1987); Corporation Patrons Chair, Conference of Cincinnati Women (1986); Exhibits Chair, Conference of Cincinnati Women (1985); Leader, Girl Scouts **CW:** Author, "Community Land Cooperative Residents' Handbook" (1986) **AW:** Excellence in Government Award, Greater St. Louis Federal Executive Board (2003); Award for Superior Performance, United States Inspector, General Department of Housing and Urban Development (1990); Recipient, Mercury Awards IDS, Cincinnati, OH (1984) **MH:** Albert Nelson Marquis Lifetime Achievement Award (2017) **H:** Reading; Softball; Theater **PA:** Republican **RE:** Roman Catholic **ADD:** 771 Seven Hills Ln, Saint Charles, MO, 63304

WARREN, PETER GIGSTAD, **T:** Financial Planner **I:** Financial Services **DOB:** 09/29/1958 **PB:** Mankato **SC:** MN/USA **YOP:** 2017-12-04 **PT:** ValGene Lee Gigstad; Lynette Elizabeth (Grane) Gigstad **ED:** MBA, University of Dallas, with Highest Honors (2007); BS in Computer Science, Michigan Technological University, with Honors (1981) **CT:** Registered Investment Adviser; Certified Financial Planner Credentials; Certified Financial Manager **C:** Senior Investment Management Adviser, Wells Fargo Clearing Services, LLC (2007-Present); Vice President of Investments, Wells Fargo Clearing Services, LLC (2007-Present); PIM Portfolio Manager, Wells Fargo Clearing Services, LLC (2007-Present); Vice President of Finance, Merrill Lynch, Bank of America Corporation (1987-2007); Consultant, Merrill Lynch, Bank of America Corporation (1987-2007); Portfolio Manager, Personal Investment Advisory Program, Merrill Lynch, Bank of America Corporation (1987-2007); Systems Engineering Manager, COMPAQ Computer Corporation (1984-1987); Systems Programmer, Datapoint Corporation (Now Maintel) (1982-1984); Vice President, Intelligent Statements Inc. (1982); Chief Operating Officer, Intelligent Statements Inc. (1982); Staff Consultant, Duke University (1981-1982); Junior Programmer, IBM (1981) **CR:** Co-Owner, Soon Y. Warren, Warren's Art Studio (1999-Present) **CIV:** Member, Concert Choir International Tour to Kiev, Ukraine, Vilnius, Lithuania, Riga, Latvia, Tallinn, Estonia, Beijing, Xi'An, Nanjing, Guilin, Shanghai, Buenos Aires, Rosario, Mendoza Argentina, Santiago, Vina del Mar, Chile (1999-2009); Underwriter, Michigan

Technological University **CW:** Editor, "Painting Vibrant Flowers in Watercolor" (2014); Editor, "Painting Vibrant Watercolors: Discover the Magic of Light, Color and Contrast" (2009); Editor, "Vibrant Flowers in Watercolor" (2006); Artist, "States of Mind Exhibition" (2002); Exhibitor, "Nature Photography," Fort Worth Botanic Gardens (2001) **AW:** Honoree, Named Five-Star Wealth Manager, Texas Monthly (2010, 2012-2015); Honoree, Named One of America's Top 1000 Financial Planner (2005-2006) **MEM:** President, The Fort Worth Club (1993, 2000, 2008); Vice President, The Fort Worth Club (1992); Finance Committee, Lions Clubs International (1992); Secretary, The Fort Worth Club (1991); The International Platform Association; Board of Directors, Lions Clubs International; Sigma Iota Epsilon **MH:** Albert Nelson Marquis Lifetime Achievement Award (2017) **H:** Travel; Gourmet cooking; Public speaking; Photography; Choral performance; Candle-making **ADD:** 4062 Hildring Dr W, Fort Worth, TX, 76109

WARTHEN, HARRY JUSTICE III, **T:** Lawyer (Retired) **I:** Law and Legal Services **CN:** Hunton & Williams **DOB:** 07/08/1939 **PB:** Richmond **SC:** VA/USA **PT:** Harry Justice Warthen, Jr.; Martha Winston (Alsop) Warthen **MS:** Married **SPN:** Sally Berkeley Trapnell (9/7/1968) **CH:** Martha Alsop; William Trapnell **ED:** LLB, University of Virginia (1967); BA, University of Virginia (1961) **CT:** Admitted to Practice, United States District Court Eastern District of Virginia (1969); Admitted to Practice, United States Court of Appeals for the Fourth Circuit (1967) **C:** Retired (2016); Senior Counsel, Hunton & Williams, Richmond (2005-2016); Partner, Hunton & Williams, Richmond, VA (1976-2016); Associate, Hunton & Williams, Richmond (1968-2005); Attorney, Hunton & Williams, Richmond, VA (1968-1976); Law Clerk to Judge, United States Court of Appeals for the Fourth Circuit, Richmond, VA (1967-1968) **CR:** Lecturer in Field, School of Law, University of Virginia (1975-1977) **CIV:** Trustee, Woodrow Wilson Presidential Library (1997-2003, 2005-2011, 2014-Present); President, Woodrow Wilson Presidential Library (1997-2003, 2005-2011, 2014-Present); Vice President, Battersea Foundation, Petersburg, VA (2007-Present); Member, The National Trust for Historic Preservation (2003-2011); Trustee, Historical Richmond Foundation (1996-2008); Executive Committee, Historical Richmond Foundation (1996-2008); Director, Corporation for Jefferson's Poplar Forest (2005); Director, Executive Committee, Preservation Alliance of Virginia (Now Preservation of Virginia) (1991-1997); Trustee, Historical Richmond Foundation (1986-1995); Executive Committee, Historical Richmond Foundation (1986-1995); Moderator, Hanover Presbytery, The Reformed Presbyterian Church (1988); Elder, Grace Covenant Presbyterian Church; Trustee, Endowment Fund, Grace Covenant Presbyterian Church **MIL:** Lieutenant, U.S. Army (1962-1964) **MEM:** President, Antiquarian Society of Richmond (1998-1999); Chairman, Section on Wills, Trusts and Estates, The Virginia Bar Association (1981-1989); President, Antiquarian Society of Richmond (1977-1978); Fellow, American College of Trust and Estate Counsel; Fellow, Virginia Law Foundation; Country Club of Virginia; Deep Run Hunt Club **BAR:** Virginia State Bar (1967) **MH:** Albert Nelson Marquis Lifetime Achievement Award (2017); Distinguished Humanitarian (2017) **BA:** 951 East Byrd Street, Suite 200, Hunton & Williams LLP, Richmond, VA, 23219 **ADD:** 1319 Shallow Well Rd, Manakin-Sabot, VA, 23103

WATKINS, JOAN FRANCIS, **I:** Education/Educational Services **DOB:** 05/06/1905 **PB:** Linwood **SC:** NJ/USA **PT:** Francis Joseph Watkins; Alberta Catherine (Seabold) Watkins **ED:** BS, St. Bonaventure University, Saint Bonaventure, NY (1967) **CT:** Certfied Elementary Teacher, State of New Jersey **C:** Retired (2003); Teacher, Atlantic City Public Schools (1971-2003); Teacher, Various Parochial Schools (1961-1971) **MEM:** Atlantic City Education Association; New Jersey Education Association **H:** Working with children **RE:** Roman Catholic **ADD:** PO Box 714, Northfield, NJ, 08225-0714

WATSON, JO ANDREA, **T:** Director of Organizational Development and Learning **I:** Medicine & Health Care **CN:** St. Mary's Medical Center **MS:** Married **SPN:** Bill Watson (1979) **CH:** Drew; Corey **ED:** DNP, Walden University (2014); MSN, Walden University (2008); BSN, West Virginia University (1993); Nursing Diploma, St. Mary's Hospital School of Nursing (1979) **CT:** CPAN (1991-Present); CCRN (1990-Present); RN, West Virginia (1979) **C:** Director of Organizational Development and Learning, St. Mary's Medical Center, Huntington, WV (2016-Present); Training Center Coordinator, American Heart Association (2012-Present); Coordinator, American Heart Association Life Support Courses, St. Mary's Medical Center (2012-Present); Interim Director of Organizational Development and Learning, St. Mary's Medical Center, Huntington, WV (2015-2016); Coordinator, Emergency Management Plan, American Heart Association (1996-2015); Staff Nurse, Radiology Department, St. Mary's Medical Center (1993-1995); Staff Nurse, Post Anesthesia Care Unit/Outpatient Department, St. Mary's Medical Center (1990-1993); Staff Nurse, Open Heart Recovery Room, St. Mary's Medical Center (1980-1990) **CIV:** Local Emergency Planning Committee, Cabell Wayne (1998-Present); Lawrence County Emergency Planning Committee (2012-2015); Chair, Local Emergency Planning Committee, Cabell Wayne (2009-2016); Homeland Security Committee (2007-2015); Local Emergency Planning Committee, Phi Nu Chapter, Sigma Theta Tau (2006-2016); Regional Emergency Cardiovascular Care Committee, American Heart Association (2004-2007) **CW:** Author, "The Role of a Multimodal Educational Strategy on Healthcare Workers' Hand Washing," American Journal of Infection Control (2015) **AW:** Sigma Theta Tau, Nursing Honor Society (1996) **MEM:** Phi Nu Chapter, Sigma Theta Tau International Honor Society of Nursing (2013-Present); American Association of Critical Care Nurses; American Heart Association; Post Anesthesia Society of Nursing; West Virginia Voice of Nursing Leadership **MH:** Albert Nelson Marquis Lifetime Achievement Award (2017) **H:** Walking; Reading; Crochet; Animals **BA:** 2900 1st Avenue, Room 441, St. Mary's Medical Center, Huntington, WV, 25702 **ADD:** 44 Hickory Drive, Barboursville, WV, 25504

WATTS, RICHARD, **T:** Professor **I:** Education/Educational Services **CN:** Washington State University **DOB:** 05/22/1953 **PB:** Oxnard **SC:** CA/USA **PT:** William John Watts; Lillian Rose (Cink) Watts **MS:** Married **SPN:** Lennis Kay Boyer (5/19/1984) **ED:** PhD in Civil and Environmental Engineering, Utah State University (1984); MS, Utah State University (1979); BS, University of California, Davis, CA (1976) **CT:** Registered Professional Engineer, State of California **C:** Professor, Washington State University (1990-Present); Adjunct Professor, Center for Environmental Studies, Arizona State University, Tempe, AZ (1984-Present); Partner, Sun-Tech Engineering, Inc., Phoenix, AZ (1984-Present); Environmental

Engineer, Naval Energy and Environmental Support Activity, Port Hueneme, CA (1983-1984); Board Member, Research Council, Utah State University, Logan, UT (1982-1983); Research Associate, Utah Water Research Laboratory, Logan, UT (1977-1983); Teaching Assistant, Moorpark College, California (1976-1977); Laboratory Assistant, University of California, Davis, CA (1974-1976); Laboratory Assistant, National Cancer Institute, Bethesda, MD (1974) **AW:** Outstanding Research Faculty, Washington State University (2010); First Place Publication Award, Utah Water Pollution Control Association (1981-1982) **MEM:** Sargent-at-Arms, Toastmasters International (1983-1984); American Society of Civil Engineers; Arizona Water and Pollution Control Association; American Chemical Society; Water Pollution Control Federation; International Association on Water Pollution Research and Control **PA:** Democrat **RE:** Roman Catholic **BA:** 101 Sloan Hall, Washington State University, Dept of Civil & Environmental Engineering, Pullman, WA, 99164 **ADD:** 101 Sloan Hall, Washington State University, Dept of CEE, Pullman, WA, 99164 **URL:** http://www.richardwatts.com

WEAVER, ERIC JAMES EDD, T: Educational Administrator **I:** Education/Educational Services **DOB:** 05/14/1938 **PB:** Purley **SC:** England **PT:** Edward Arthur Weaver; Amelia Cecily (Ealden) Weaver **MS:** Married **SPN:** Joyce Lynn McKean (8/19/1973) **CH:** Stephanie Lynn; Heather Elizabeth; Jonathan Eric; Christopher James **ED:** EdD, Hofstra University (1980); Professional Diploma, Hofstra University (1973); MS, The City College of New York (1968); MDiv, The General Theological Seminary (1972); STB, The General Theological Seminary (1961); AB, Princeton University (1958) **CT:** Ordained Deacon (1961); Ordained Priest (1962) **C:** Director, Special Educational Services, Middle Country CSD, Suffolk County, NY (1981-1998); Director, Special Education, Middle Country CSD, Suffolk County, NY (1973-1981); Assistant Principal, Rosemary Kennedy School for Trainable Mentally Retarded, Wantagh, NY (1970-1973); Supervisor, Central Administration, Nassau BOCES (1967-1970); Special Education Teacher, Nassau BOCES (1963-1967); Vicar, St. Michael and All Angels Episcopal Church, Gordon Heights (1961-1963); Vicar, Church of the Messiah, Central Islip, NY (1961-1963); Director, Christian Education and Youth Work, Holy Cross Episcopal Church, Brooklyn, NY (1958-1961); Research Associate, Meadow Brook National Bank, West Hempstead, NY (1957-1961) **CR:** Educational Consultant (1998-2008); Member, Preschool Special Education Committee (1990-1998); Member, Special Education Administrative Leadership Training Academy (1989-1998); Chairman, Committee for Special Education Middle Country CSD (1973-1998); Instructor, Special Education Training Resource Center (1986-1998); Educational Consultant, Special Education Training Resource Center (1986-1998); Impartial Hearing Officer, State of New York (1982-1997); Vice Chairman, Project EQUALS (1983-1986); Adjunct Assistant Professor, Special Education, LIU Post (1979-1980) **CIV:** Rector Emeritus, Trinity Episcopal Church (2009-Present); Rector, Trinity Episcopal Church (1999-2009); Member, Trinity Episcopal Church (1966-1999); Honorary Member, Steering Committee, Annual Art Auction, Lake Grove Schools (1985-1990); Member, Board of Directors, Traffic Safety Board, Nassau County, NY (1969-1971); Captain, Auxiliary Police, Suffolk County, NY (1962-1969); Member, Robin Park Civic Association to Business Partnership (1963-1966); Assistant to Rector, Grace Gospel Church (1963-1966); Trustee, Police Hall of Fame **CW:** Author,

"Efforts of Special Education Administrators to Meet the Needs of Special Education Teachers by Inservice Training" (1980); Author, "Ocular, Manual and Podiatric Dominance in a Severely Retarded Older Adolescent Population" (1968); Author, "Rudolf Bultman and Entmythologisierung" (1961); Author, "Monographs: The Sources of the First Gospel" (1958) **MEM:** Treasurer, CASE (1985-1989); Executive Committee, Long Island Association of Special Education Administrators (1978-2008); President, Long Island Association of Special Education Administrators (1977-1978); Vice President, Long Island Association of Special Education Administrators (1976-1977); Secretary, Long Island Association of Special Education Administrators (1975-1976); President, Council for Exceptional Children (1973-1974); Director, Interagency Council on Recreation for Handicapped (1970-1973); Fellow, American Association for Mental Deficiency (Now American Association on Intellectual and Developmental Disabilities); Association to Help Retarded Children; American Educational Research Association; American Association of School Personnel Administrators; SAANYS; Phi Delta Kappa International; IASSIDD **MH:** Albert Nelson Marquis Lifetime Achievement Award (2017) **PA:** Republican **RE:** Episcopalian **ADD:** 8 Oceanside Ct, Northport, NY, 11768

WEBER, MARGARET LAURA JANE, T: Accountant **I:** Financial Services **DOB:** 01/04/1933 **PB:** Fairview **SC:** MO/USA **PT:** Mert James Joel; Margaret Orr (Mortensen) Joel **MS:** Married **SPN:** Albert H. Weber (6/1956); James E. Jennings (3/1953, Divorced) **CH:** James Edward Jennings; Janie Lea Franks; David Alan Jennings; Luhwanna Stonecipher; Margaret Anne **ED:** Postgraduate Work, Missouri Southern State University (1988); AA, Crowder College (1972) **C:** Accountant, Crowder College (1983-1998); Cashier, Crowder College (1968-1983); Clerk, Extension Department, University of Missouri (1967-1968); Clerk, Missouri License Department (1954-1957); First State Bank, Joplin, MO (1951-1953) **CIV:** Welfare Committee, Newton County, Missouri (1984-Present) **AW:** Business Associate of the Year, ABWA Management, LLC. (1987); Woman of the Year, ABWA Management, LLC. (1982) **MEM:** Board of Directors, Missouri Community College Association (1978-1982); NAFE; ABWA Management, LLC. **MH:** Albert Nelson Marquis Lifetime Achievement Award (2017) **PA:** Republican **RE:** Baptist **ADD:** 1205 Ozark Drive, Neosho, MO, 64850-1363

WEBSTER, DAVID MACPHERSON, T: Lawyer **I:** Law and Legal Services **CN:** Webster Law Office **DOB:** 06/22/1950 **PB:** Chicago **SC:** IL/USA **PT:** Robert Fielden Webster; Julia Orendorff (Macpherson) Webster **MS:** Married **SPN:** Lucia Maxwell Blair (10/3/1987) **CH:** Jessie Maxwell **ED:** Honorary DD, Seabury-Western Theological Seminary (2000); JD, University of Virginia (1975); BA in History, Williams College, Magna Cum Laude (1972) **C:** Private Practice, Webster Law Office, Wilmette, IL (2007-Present); Holy Family Ministries, Chicago, IL (2013-2016); Vice President, DeVry Inc., Oakbrook Terrace, IL (2005-2007); General Counsel, DeVry Inc., Oakbrook Terrace, IL (2005-2007); Secretary, DeVry Inc., Oakbrook Terrace, IL (2005-2007); Senior Vice President, Hawaiian Airlines, Honolulu, Hawaii (2003-2005); General Counsel, Hawaiian Airlines, Honolulu, Hawaii (2003-2005); Of Counsel, Butler Rubin Saltarelli & Boyd, Chicago, IL (2002-2003); Vice President, A.T. Kearney, Inc., Chicago, IL (1994-2002); General Counsel, A.T. Kearney, Inc., Chicago, IL (1994-2002); Assistant General Counsel

for Multilateral Negotiations, U.S. Arms Control and Disarmament Agency, Washington, D.C. (1989-1994); Special Assistant to Director, FBI, Washington, D.C. (1988-1989); White House Fellow, Washington, D.C. (1987-1988); Partner, Winston & Strawn, Chicago, IL (1981-1987); Associate, Winston & Strawn, Chicago, IL (1975-1981) **CR:** Member, Advisory Committee, Illinois Business Corporation Act, Illinois Secretary of State, Chicago, IL (1982-1987) **CIV:** Board of Directors, Illinois State Historical Society (2014-Present); Board of Directors, Holy Family Ministries, Chicago, IL (2013-2016); Advisory Board, Illinois State Historical Society, Springfield, IL (2012-2014); President, Orchard Village (2010-2011); Board of Directors, Orchard Village, Skokie, IL (2009-2012); Trustee, Village of Winnetka, IL (2003-2005); Trustee, Seabury-Western Theological Seminary, Evanston, IL (2002-2005); President, Illinois Society for the Prevention of Blindness, Chicago, IL (1999-2001); Board of Directors, Illinois Society for the Prevention of Blindness, Chicago, IL (1997-2004); Board of Directors, Better Government Association, Chicago, IL (1997-1999); Board of Directors, WBEZ Alliance, Inc., Chicago, IL (1996-2004); Chair, Board of Trustees, Seabury-Western Theological Seminary, Evanston, IL (1993-1996); Trustee, Seabury-Western Theological Seminary, Evanston, IL (1988-1996); Board of Directors, Illinois Society for the Prevention of Blindness, Chicago, IL (1980-1987); Trustee, Episcopalian Charities and Professional Services, Chicago, IL (1980-1987) **CW:** Contributor, Op-ed Articles, Newspapers **MEM:** Executive Committee, Chicago Chapter, The Phi Beta Kappa Society (1996-1998); The Manuscript Society; New England Historical Society; National Genealogical Society; Life Member, Illinois State Historical Society; White House Fellows Foundation and Association **BAR:** Illinois State Bar Association (1975) **H:** History; Writing **RE:** Episcopalian **BA:** 1443 N. Western Ave, Lake Forest, IL, 60045 **ADD:** 466 Central Avenue, Suite 12, Webster Law Office, Northfield, IL, 60093

WEINBERG, GERHARD L., T: History Professor, Writer **I:** Education/Educational Services **CN:** University of North Carolina **DOB:** 01/01/1928 **PB:** Hanover **SC:** Germany **PT:** Max Bendix Weinberg; Kate Sarah (Gruenebaum) Weinberg **MS:** Married **SPN:** Janet Kabler White (4/29/1989) **ED:** Honorary PhD, University of Hanover (2001); Honorary LHD, University at Albany, State University of New York (1989); PhD in History, University of Chicago (1951); MA, University of Chicago (1949); BA in Social Studies, University at Albany, State University of New York (1948) **C:** Professor Emeritus, University of North Carolina, Chapel Hill, NC (1999-Present); Acting Chairman of the History Department, University of North Carolina, Chapel Hill, NC (1989-1990); William Rand Kenan Jr. Professor of History, University of North Carolina, Chapel Hill, NC (1974-1999); Chairman of the History Department, University of Michigan (1972-1973); History Professor, University of Michigan (1963-1974); Associate Professor of History, University of Michigan, Ann Arbor, MI (1959-1974); Assistant Professor, University of Kentucky (1957-1959); Director, American Historical Association Project for Microfilming Captured German Documents (1956-1957); Visiting Lecturer in History, University of Kentucky, Lexington, KY (1955-1956); Visiting Lecturer in History, University of Chicago, Chicago, IL (1954-1955); Research Analyst, War Documentation Project, Columbia University, New York, NY (1951-1954) **CR:** Shapiro Senior Scholar-in-Residence, United States Holocaust Memorial Museum, Washington, DC (2001-2002); Visiting Professor, United States Air Force Academy (1990-1991); University of Bonn, Bonn, Germany (1983);

Fellow, National Endowment for the Humanities (1978-1979); Guggenheim Fellowship (1971-1972); Fellowship, ACLS (1965-1966); Fellowship, Rockefeller Foundation and SSRC (1962-1963) **CIV:** Michigan Democratic State Central Committee (1963-1967); Chairman, Ann Arbor Democratic Party Committee (1961-1963) **MIL:** U.S. Army (1946-1947) **CW:** Board of Editors, Journal of Intelligence History (2001-Present); Author, Korean Edition, "A World at Arms: A Global History of World War II" (2016); Author, "World War II: A Very Short Introduction" (2014); Consultant, "World War II Chronicle" (2007); Author, Italian Edition, "Il mundo in armi" (2007); Author, "Visions of Victory: The Hopes of Eight World War II Leaders" (2005); Editor, "Hitler's Second Book: The Unpublished Sequel to Mein Kampf" (2003); Author, Polish Edition, Part I, "A World at Arms: A Global History of World War II" (2001); Author, "Germany, Hitler, and World War II: Essays in Modern German and World History" (1995); Author, German Edition, "Die Welt in Waffen: Die globale Geschichte des Zweiten Weltkriegs" (1995); Author, Spanish Edition, "Un mundo en armas" (1995); Author, "A World at Arms: A Global History of World War II" (1994); Board of Editors, International History Review (1991-2000); Author, "World in the Balance: Behind the Scenes of World War II" (1981); Author, "The Foreign Policy of Hitler's Germany: Starting World War II 1937-1939" (1980); Editor, "Transformation of a Continent: Europe in the Twentieth Century" (1975); Author, Introductions, "The Trial of the Major War Criminals Before the International Military Tribunal, Nuremberg 1945-46" (1972); Author, Introductions, "Pearl Harbor Attack, Hearings before the Joint Committee on the Investigation of the Pearl Harbor Attack" (1972); Author, "The Foreign Policy of Hitler's Germany: Diplomatic Revolution in Europe, 1933-1936" (1970); Co-author, "Soviet Partisans in World War II" (1964); Editor, "Hitlers zweites Buch: Ein Dokument aus dem Jahr 1928" (1961); Author, "Germany and the Soviet Union, 1939-1941" (1954); Author, "Guide to Captured German Documents" (1952); Board of Editors, Central European History; Board of Editors, Journal of Modern History; Contributor, Articles, History Journals; Contributor, Chapters, Books **AW:** Lifetime Contribution to the Field Award, Holocaust Educational Foundation (2016); Spencer-Tucker Award for Publications in Military History, ABC-Clio (2012); Samuel Eliot Morison Award for Lifetime Achievement, Society for Military History (2011); Pritzker Military Library Literature Award for Lifetime Achievement in Military Writing, Tawani Foundation, Chicago, IL (2009); Order of Merit First Class, Federal Republic of Germany (1999); George Louis Beer Prize from American Historical Association (1995); Herbert Hoover Book Award, Herbert Hoover Presidential Library Association (1994-1995); Halverson Prize for "The Foreign Policy of Hitler's Germany: Starting World War II 1937-1939," German Studies Association (1981); George Louis Beer Prize from American Historical Association (1971); Distinguished Book Award, Society for Military History **MEM:** Counselor, National WWII Museum (2008-Present); American Academy of Arts & Sciences (1996-Present); Board of Directors, World War II Studies Association, American Historical Association (1968-Present); Chair, Moncado Prize Committee, Society for Military History (2012-2014); Convener of Presidential Counselors, National WWII Museum (2006-2008); Chairman, Historical Advisory Panel, Interagency Working Group Implementing the Nazi War Crimes Disclosure and Imperial Japanese Records Act (1999-2007); United States Army Training and Doctrine Command Military History Council (1999-

2001); Chairman, Advisory Committee, United States Army Historical (1998-2003); Advisory Committee, United States Army Historical (1996-1998); President, German Studies Association (1996-1998); Advisory Panel, Historical Records Declassification, United States Department of Defense (1995-2002); Vice President, German Studies Association (1994-1996); Consultant, United States Holocaust Memorial Council (1992); Executive Committee, German Studies Association (1989-1992); Chairman, European History Section, Southern Historical Association (1989); Vice Chairman, European History Section, Southern Historical Association (1988); Advisory Committee, United States Air Force Historical (1987-1990); Vice President of Research, American Historical Association (1982-1984); Chairman, Conference Group for Central European History, American Historical Association (1982-1983); Joint Committee on Historians and Archivists, American Historical Association, The Organization of American Historians and Society of American Archivists (1972-1976); Chairman, National Archives Liaison Committee, Conference Group for Central European History, American Historical Association (1969-1990); Consultant, Committee on War Documents, American Historical Association (1957-1959); American Historical Association Representative on the Joint **MH:** Albert Nelson Marquis Lifetime Achievement Award (2017) **RE:** Jewish **ADD:** 1416 Mount Willing Road, Efland, NC, 27243

WEINEL, PAMELA JEAN, T: General Health Scientist **I:** Sciences **CN:** U.S. Food and Drug Administration **DOB:** 12/14/1956 **PB:** Olney **SC:** MD/USA **PT:** Clarence Dawson Weinel; Jean Elizabeth (Woodward) Weinel **MS:** Married **SPN:** Nathan Richards (5/6/1995) **ED:** Coursework in Law, School of Law, University of Baltimore (2002); MBA, Merrick School of Business, University of Baltimore (2001); MS, Graduate School of Nursing, University of Maryland (1999); BSN, University of Maryland School of Nursing, Baltimore, MD (1986); Coursework in Nursing, University of Maryland, College Park, MD (1984); AA, Rockville Campus of Montgomery College (1976) **CT:** CPR/AED, Registered Nurse, State of Maryland; Registered Nurse, Washington, DC **C:** Regulatory Health Project Manager, Center for Tobacco Products, Office of Compliance & Enforcement, Division of Enforcement and Manufacturing, U.S. Food and Drug Administration (2018-Present); Regulatory Health Project Manager, Office of the Commissioner, Office of Special Medical Programs, Office of Pediatric Therapeutics, U.S. Food and Drug Administration (2010-2018); Regulatory Health Project Manager, Detail in Center for Drug Evaluation and Research (CDER), Office of Oncology Drug Products, Immediate Office, U.S. Food and Drug Administration (2009-2010); Faculty Associate, University of Maryland School of Nursing, Preceptor for Graduate Level Nursing Students (2006-2017); Associate Division Director for Program Operations, Office of Device Evaluation, Center for Devices and Radiological Health (CDHR), U.S. Food and Drug Administration (2006-2010); Project Manager for Medical Product Safety Network, Contract Position within U.S. Food and Drug Administration through Social & Scientific Systems Division of CODA, Center for Devices and Radiological Health (CDHR), Office of Surveillance and Biometrics (2004-2006); Infertility Nurse for Physician/Owner, Shady Grove Fertility (2002-2004); Research Program Manager, University of Maryland Medical Center, Marlene and Stewart Greenebaum Comprehensive Cancer Center (1998-2002); Part-Time Advice Line Triage Nurse/Strep Nurse, Kaiser Permanente/

Kensington Call Center, Kaiser Foundation Health Plan, Inc. (1991-1998); Coordinator/Administrator, Bone Marrow Transplant and Stem Cell Transplant Programs, Walter Reed Army Medical Center (Walter Reed National Military Medical Center) (1990-1998); Bone Marrow Transplant Coordinator, George Washington University Medical Center (Now George Washington University Hospital) (1987-1990); Oncology Nurse, George Washington University Medical Center (Now George Washington University Hospital) (1986-1987); Receptionist/Assistant to the Principal, Swanke Hayden Connell Architects, Washington, DC (1982-1983); Montgomery County School Bus Operator (1981-1982); Business Partner, Cherry Hill Exxon (1980-1982) **CR:** Lecturer, Contemporary Forums, San Francisco, CA (1994) **CIV:** Sponsor, International Student through Apex International Education Partners (AIEP) (2018-Present); Host, Family of Four from Cameroon (2018); CCD Instructor, Seventh Grade, Resurrection Roman Catholic Church (Now Church of the Resurrection), Burtonsville, MD (2001-2002); Sponsor for Adults, Resurrection Roman Catholic Church (Now Church of the Resurrection), Burtonsville, MD (1997-2000); Consultant, People to People International, Vietnam (1993); Roundtable Facilitator, International BMT Symposium, Omaha, NE (1992); Consultant, People to People International, Russia (1992); Lecturer in Oncology/Bone Marrow Transplantation **CW:** Co-author, "FDA's Pediatric Advisory Committee Post-Market Safety Monitoring of Drugs, Biologics and Vaccines," Pediatrics (2015); Contributor, "The Safety and Patterns of Use of Octreotide in the Treatment of Congenital Hyperinsulinism," Pediatric Endocrine Society Annual Meeting, Milan, Italy (2013); Contributor, "Analysis of Method to Capture Adverse Events in Children in Tertiary Care Pediatric Hospitals," International Society of Pharmecoepidemiology, Montreal, Canada (2013); Contributor, "Pediatric Therapies: Post-Marketing Safety Reviews," Pediatrics Academic Society (PAS) Meeting, Washington, DC (2013); Contributor, "Off Label Use of Octreotide in Infants," Annual Meeting of the International Society of Pharmacoepidemiology (ISPE), Barcelona, Spain (2012); Contributor, Articles, Professional Publications **AW:** Outstanding Service Award, Commissioner's Office, Office of Pediatric Therapeutics, U.S. Food and Drug Administration (2018); Community Service Award, Commissioner's Office, U.S. Food and Drug Administration (2014); Special Recognition Award, Center for Devices and Radiological Health (CDRH), U.S. Food and Drug Administration (2012); Leveraging/Collaboration Award, Office of the Commission, U.S. Food and Drug Administration (2012); Special Recognition Award, Center for Devices and Radiological Health (CDRH), U.S. Food and Drug Administration (2010); Employee of the Month, University of Maryland Medical System (2000); Outstanding Young Women of America (1997); Outstanding Achievement Award, Department of Medicine, Walter Reed Army Medical Center (Walter Reed National Military Medical Center) (1996); National Dean's List (1986) **MEM:** DIA Global Organization (2015); Society of Human Resource Management Scholar (SHRM) (2015); Equestrian Order of the Holy Sepulchre of Jerusalem (2002); Sigma Iota Epsilon (2001); Sigma Theta Tau International Honor Society of Nursing (1986); Phi Theta Kappa Honor Society (1976); The Honor Society of Phi Kappa Phi **H:** Travel; Photography; Writing; Reading **RE:** Catholic **BA:** 14721 Old Barn Court, Silver Spring, MD, 20905 **ADD:** 13 Tollgate Road, Owings Mills, MD, 21117

WEINTRAUB, BARRY M., **T:** Plastic Surgeon **I:** Medicine & Health Care **CN:** Dr. Barry M. Weintraub, MD, FACS **ED:** Residency, Plastic and Reconstructive Surgery, New York, NY (1980-1982); Residency, Straight General Surgery, Cedars-Sinai, Los Angeles, CA (1978-1980); Internship, Straight General Surgery, Harbor–UCLA Medical Center, Torrance, CA (1977-1978); Coursework, Weill Cornell Medicine, Cornell University, New York, NY (1977); MD, Brandeis University, Magna Cum Laude, Boston, MA (1973); BS in Biochemistry, Brandeis University, Boston, MA (1973); BS in Psychology, Brandeis University, Boston, MA (1973) **CT:** Certified Diplomat, American Board of Plastic Surgery (1983) **C:** Plastic Surgeon, Dr. Barry M. Weintraub, MD, FACS **CR:** National Spokesperson, American Society of Plastic Surgery; National Spokesperson, American Society of Aesthetic Plastic Surgery; Media Ambassador, American Society of Plastic Surgeons; Chief Resident, Burn Unit, Weill Cornell Medicine, Cornell University, New York, NY; Chief Resident, Cleft Lip and Palate Center, North Shore University Hospital, Northwell Health; Chief Resident, Memorial Sloan Kettering Cancer Center; Appointee, Lenox Hill Hospital, Northwell Health, New York, NY; Appointee, Manhattan Eye, Ear, and Throat Hospital, Northwell Health, New York, NY; Appointee, Center for Specialty Care, Weill Cornell Medicine, Cornell University, New York, NY **CW:** Contributor, "Expert Beacon" (2014); Contributor, "Fast Company" (2014); Contributor, "Glamour" (2014); Contributor, "USA Today" (2014); Contributor, "Smart Beauty Guide" (2014); Contributor, "Hollywood Life" (2014); Contributor, "El Diario La Prensa" (2014); Contributor, "In Touch Weekly" (2014); Contributor, "Daily Mail" (2014); Contributor, "StyleBlazer" (2014); Contributor, "Time Magazine" (2014); Contributor, "Plastic Surgery Practice" (2013-2014); Contributor, "ABC News" (2013); Contributor, "AARP" (2013); Contributor, "Hollywood Life" (2013); Contributor, "Life & Style Weekly" (2013); Contributor, "Fox News" (2013); Contributor, "Hamptons" (2011-2013); Speaker, Lecture on Post Partum Rejuvenative Surgery, The Ricky Haddad Memorial Foundation (2012); Contributor, "Sister to Sister" (2011); Contributor, "Plum Hamptons" (2011); Contributor, "Self" (2011); Contributor, "A.M. New York" (2011); Contributor, "In Touch Weekly" (2011); Contributor, "NY Daily News" (2011); Contributor, "Star" (2011); Speaker, Lecture on Psychological Impact of Aesthetics, The Ricky Haddad Memorial Foundation (2009); Speaker, Lecture on Facial Injectables, The Ricky Haddad Memorial Foundation (2009); Contributor, "The Fashion Daily" (2009); Contributor, "Scene" (2008); Contributor, "Image" (2008); Speaker, Topic-Slide Presentation on Current Concepts in Cosmetic Plastic Surgery of the Face and Body, Eagle Oaks Golf & Country Club (2007); Contributor, "The New York Times" (2007); Contributor, "Allure" (2004); Contributor, "Manhattan Magazine" (1998); Contributor, "Dan's Papers" (1997-1998); Contributor, "Departures" (1997); Contributor, "Marie Claire" (1997); Contributor, "React" (1997); Contributor, "Town & Country" (1996); Contributor, "The Observer" (1996); Contributor, "Cosmopolitan" (1996); Speaker, "Plastic and Reconstructive Surgery in the 90's - Where Are You Going?" New York State Medical Society (1995); Speaker, "Current Concepts in Plastic Surgery," The Princeton Club of New York (1995); Speaker, "New Trends and Concepts in Plastic and Reconstructive Surgery," The Medical Society of the State of New York (1995); Contributor, "Hamptons Magazine" (1995); Contributor, "Cosmopolitan" (1991-1993); Contributor, "Glamour" (1992); Contributor, "Allure" (1992); Co-Author, "How To Be Wrinkle Free" (1986); Contributor, "Time Magazine" (1986); Co-Author, "Mucoepidermoid Carcinoma of the Lacrimal Duct: A Rare Lesion," Plastic and Reconstructive Surgery (1982); Co-Author, "Extrusion of an Infected Orbital Floor Prosthesis After 15 Years," Plastic and Reconstructive Surgery (1981); Contributor, "Plastic and Reconstructive Surgery"; Contributor, "Annals of Plastic Surgery"; Contributor, "Plastic Surgery News"; Co-Author, "Bovine Cross-Linked Collagen as a Dermal Substitute," In Progress, Burn Unit, Weill Cornell Medicine, Cornell University, New York, NY **MEM:** American Society of Plastic Surgeons; American Society of Aesthetic Plastic Surgery; Fellow, American College of Surgeons; American Medical Association; New York Regional Society of Plastic Surgeons; The Rhinoplasty Society; Doctors Without Borders; Central Park Conservancy; The Metropolitan Museum of Art; The Nature Conservancy, East Hampton, NY; The Garden Club of East Hampton; The Skin Cancer Foundation; Cartier Grand Slam Benefitting the American Cancer Society **BA:** 800 5th Ave, Street Level, Dr. Barry M. Weintraub, MD, FACS, New York, NY, 10065 **URL:** http://www.drbarryweintraub.com

WEISS, ROBERT STEPHEN, **T:** Chief Executive Officer/President Health Products (Retired) **I:** Business Management/Business Services **CN:** The Cooper Companies Inc. **DOB:** 10/25/1946 **PT:** Stephen John Weiss; Anna Blanche (Lescinski) Weiss **MS:** Married **SPN:** Marilyn Annette Chesick (10/29/1970) **CH:** Christopher Robert; Kim Marie; Douglas Paul **ED:** BS in Accounting, University of Scranton, Cum Laude (1968) **CT:** CPA, New York **C:** President, The Cooper Companies, Inc., Pleasanton, CA (2008-2018); Chief Executive Officer, The Cooper Companies, Inc. (2007-2018); Chief Operating Officer, The Cooper Companies, Inc. (2005-2007); Executive Vice President , The Cooper Companies, Inc. (1995-2005); Chief Financial Officer, The Cooper Companies, Inc., Pleasanton, CA (1989-2005); Vice President, Treasurer, The Cooper Companies, Inc. (1989-2002); Senior Vice President, The Cooper Companies, Inc. (1992-1995); Vice President, Corporate Controller, The Cooper Companies, Inc. (Formerly CooperVision, Inc.), Palo Alto, California (1984-1989); Vice President, Corporate Controller, Cooper Laboratories, Palo Alto, CA (1981-1983); Group Controller, CooperVision, Inc. (1980); Assistant Corporate Controller, Cooper Laboratories, Inc., Parsippany, NJ (1977-1978); Supervisor, KPMG, New York, NY (1971-1976) **CR:** Board of Trustees, University of Scranton (2015-Present); Board of Directors, Accuray Inc., Sunnyvale, CA (2007-Present); Board of Directors, The Cooper Companies, Inc., Pleasanton, CA (1996-Present) **MIL:** U.S. Army (1969-1973) **AW:** Recipient, Frank J O'Hara Alumni Award, University of Scranton (2008); Recipient, Decorated Army Commendation Medal; Recipient, Bronze Star with Oak Leaf Cluster **MEM:** Past Member, American Institute of Certified Public Accountants; New York State Society of CPAs; Association of the United States Army **MH:** Albert Nelson Marquis Lifetime Achievement Award (2017); Distinguished Humanitarian (2017) **ADD:** 1775 Spumante Pl, Pleasanton, CA, 94566

WEITNAUER, MARY ANN, **T:** Professor, Senior Associate Chair **I:** Education/Educational Services **CN:** Georgia Institute of Technology, School of Electrical and Computer Engineering **ED:** PhD in Electrical and Computer Engineering, Georgia Institute of Technology (1989); BS in Electrical and Computer Engineering, Georgia Institute of Technology (1983) **C:** Senior Associate Chair, School of Electrical and Computer Engineering (2016-Present); Professor, Georgia Institute of Technology (2005-Present); Visiting Professor, Idaho National Laboratory, Idaho Falls, ID (2010); Visiting Professor, Aalborg University, Aalborg, Denmark (2006-2008); Associate Professor, Georgia Institute of Technology (1997-2005); Assistant Professor, Georgia Institute of Technology (1989-1997); Graduate Research Assistant, Georgia Institute of Technology (1986-1989); Research Engineer, Georgia Technical Research Institute (1983-1986) **CR:** Associate Editor, IEEE Transactions on Mobile Computing (2009-2013) **CIV:** Computer Lab, Decatur Cooperative Ministries (2011-2013); Volunteer, Helping Homeless Women Write Resumes and Find Affordable Housing **CW:** Contributor, 199 Peer-Reviewed Articles; Patent in field; Two patents pending **AW:** Recipient, Outstanding Service Award, Georgia Institute of Technology (2017); Recipient, Best Paper Award, First IEEE International Symposium on Wireless Vehicular Communications, Baltimore, MD (2007); Recipient, Best Paper Award, International Conference on Sensor Technologies and Applications, Valencia, Spain (2007); Recipient, Best Paper Award, IEEE INFOCOM, Hong Kong, China (2004); Named, Distinguished Lecturer, Symbol Technologies (2001); Recipient, Research Initiation Award, National Science Foundation (1991) **MEM:** Senior Member, IEEE **MH:** Albert Nelson Marquis Lifetime Achievement Award (2017) **BA:** 777 Atlantic Drive NW, Atlanta, GA, 30332-0250 **ADD:** 2208 Guinevere Way NE, Atlanta, GA, 30345 **URL:** http://sarl.ece.gatech.edu

WEITZ, KARL , **I:** Sciences **ED:** Associates Degree, Columbia Basin College (1991) **C:** Senior Research Scientist, Battelle Pacific Northwest National Labs (Now Pacific Northwest National Laboratory) (1992-Present) **CR:** Works, Seven Acre Farm **ACH:** 2 Patents 1 Provisional Patent, Year-2016 (Awarded by USPTO) **H:** Playing Basketball; Classic Car Collector

WELCH, JAMES DOUGLAS, **T:** Patent Attorney, Professional Engineer **I:** Law and Legal Services **DOB:** 12/04/1945 **PB:** Omaha **SC:** NE/USA **PT:** James J. Welch; Lois V. (Hibbs) Welch **MS:** Single **ED:** Postgraduate Studies, University of Nebraska (1993-Present); JD, University of Nebraska (1982); MASc in Electronic Engineering, University of Toronto (1974); BSEE, University of Nebraska (1969) **CT:** Registered Professional Engineer, State of Nebraska; License, Radio Federal Communications Commission; Notary Public, State of Nebraska **C:** Private Practice Lawyer And Engineer, Omaha, NE (1982-Present); Engineer, Omaha Public Power (1977-1978); Lab Technician, Nebraska Medical Center, Omaha, NE (1975-1976); Lab Instructor, Toronto University (1972-1974); Engineer, Federal Pacific Electric, Toronto, ON, Canada (1969-1972); Engineer, Public Service of Colorado, Denver, CO (1969); Technician, Communications Supply, Omaha, NE (1958-1966) **CW:** Holder, Patents **AW:** Grantee, U.S. Department of Energy (1993); Honoree, AV Rating, Martindale-Hubbell **BAR:** U.S. Patent and Trademark Office (1984); Judicial Branch, State of Nebraska (1982) **MH:** Albert Nelson Marquis Lifetime Achievement Award (2017) **H:** Auto restoration **PA:** Independent **RE:** Scientologist **ADD:** 10328 Pinehurst Ave, Omaha, NE, 68124

WELCH, OLIVER WENDELL, **T:** Pharmaceutical Executive **I:** Pharmaceuticals **DOB:** 01/09/1930 **PB:** Jacksonville **SC:** TX/USA **PT:** Jackson Andrew Welch; Annie Laura (Trapp) Welch **MS:** Widowed **SPN:** Wanda Virginia Urrey (11/14/1948, Deceased 6/30/2016) **ED:** MA, Columbia University (1958); BA, Texas Tech University (1952) **C:** Associate

Director, Regulatory Affairs, Sterling Winthrop Inc., New York, NY (1977-1994); Deputy Director, Regulatory Affairs, Sterling Winthrop Inc., New York, NY (1977-1994); Vice President, Biomedical Data Co., New York, NY (1975-1977); Manager, Corporate Development, Boehringer Mannheim Corp., New York, NY (1972-1975); Pharmaceutical Representative, Marketing Research, Manpower Development, Warner Lambert Co., Morris Plains, NJ (1962-1972); Supervisor, Marketing Research, Manpower Development, Warner Lambert Co., Morris Plains, NJ (1962-1972) **CR:** Consultant, Sanofi Winthrop, Inc., New York, NY (1995) **CIV:** Master of Ceremony, Saint Thomas Church, New York, NY (1982-2002) **MEM:** Regulatory Affairs Professionals Society; Drug Information Association; Order of St. John of Jerusalem **MH:** Albert Nelson Marquis Lifetime Achievement Award (2017); Distinguished Humanitarian (2017) **H:** Music; Travel; Theater **PA:** Republican **RE:** Episcopalian **ADD:** 3211 66th Street, Apt. B, Lubbock, TX, 79413

WELLS, NANCY , **I:** Medicine & Health Care **ED:** PhD, Boston University (1988); Postdoctoral Fellowship, Robert Wood Johnson University Hospital **C:** Director, Nursing Research, Vanderbilt University Medical Center **AW:** Early Scientist Award, University of Rochester; Facility Member of the Year

WELSH, JOHN BERESFORD, **I:** Law and Legal Services **DOB:** 02/16/1940 **PB:** Seattle **SC:** WA/USA **PT:** John B. Welsh; Rowena Morgan Welsh **ED:** LLB (1965); BA, University of Washington, Seattle (1962); Student, Georgetown University, Washington, DC (1960); Student, University of Hawaii (1960) **C:** Retired, House Committee on Health Care (2003); Counsel, House Committee on Health Care (1987-2003); Counsel, House Committee Human Services (1987-1991, 1993-1995); Attorney, Parliamentarian, Speaker, House of Representatives (1973); Senior Counsel, House Committee on Social and Health Services, Washington House of Representatives (1973-1986); Counsel, Public Health Committee, Labor Committee, Public Employees Collective Bargaining Committee, Committee on State Institutions and Youth Development, State of Washington (1967-1973); Attorney, Washington State Legislative Council (1967-1973); Assistant Attorney General, Department of Labor and Industries (1966-1967); Staff Counsel, Joint Committee on Governmental Cooperation (1965-1966) **CR:** With, Joint Conference of American and French Branches, Sons of the American Revolution Paris (2005, 2008, 2010-2014); Joint Select Committee Nurse Delegation (1995-1998); House Committee Trade and Economic Development (1995-1998); Council Licensure, Enforcement and Regulation, Norfolk (1997); Counsel Joint Select Committee on Oral Health (1996); Member, Suggested State Legislative Committee (1988-1995); Council Licensure, Enforcement and Regulation, San Antonio (1995); Council Licensure, Enforcement and Regulation, Boston (1994); Council Licensure, Enforcement and Regulation, Albuquerque (1992); Council Licensure, Enforcement and Regulation, Fort Lauderdale, Florida (1991); Member, Steering Committee (1986-1990); Council Licensure, Enforcement and Regulation, Seattle (1990); Council Licensure, Enforcement and Regulation, Indianapolis (1989); Legislative Issues Committee (1986-1988); Council Licensure, Enforcement and Regulation, Washington (1988); Council Licensure, Enforcement and Regulation, Kansas City, MO (1987); Council Licensure, Enforcement and Regulation, Denver (1986); Council Licensure, Enforcement and Regulation, Orlando, FL (1985);

Council Licensure, Enforcement and Regulation, San Francisco (1984); National Conference State Legislatures, New Orleans (1977); National Conference State Legislatures, Denver (1977); Envoy from Governor of Washington to Investiture Prince of Wales, London (1969); Legal Consultant, Governor's Commission on Youth Involvement (1969); Governor's Planning Commission on Vocational Rehabilitation (1968) **CIV:** Member, Governor's State Medal Merit Committee, Hampton Roads US Naval Museum (1986-2014); Volunteer, Hampton Roads, US Naval Museum **AW:** Medaille d'Or de la Renaissance Francaise, Brigade of the American Revolution (2011); French Renaissance Gold Medal, Brigade of the American Revolution (2011); Secretary of Health Award for Creating Meaningful Health Policy Change (2003); Secretary of State Award for Public Service to State Legislature and People of the State of Washington (2003); Speaker of House Award for Dedicated Public Service (2002); Governor's Award for Excellence in State Health Care Policy (2002); Outstanding Young Men in America Inc. (1974) **MEM:** Executive Vice President, Napoleonic Historic Society (2007, 2008-2010); President, Board, Northwest Historical Association (2003); Group Health HMO Foundation; Circle Des Amis De Lafaytte France; Brigade of the American Revolution; Washington Bar Association; Lieutenant General Board Member, Association of Washington Generals; Friends of Mount Vernon; Friends Willie and Joe; Colonial Williamsburg Foundation; Life Member, Society des Amis du Musee l'Armee; English Speaking Union, Custer Battlefield Historical and Museum Association; Board of Directors, Friends of Old Fort Stevens; National Washington Rochambeau Historical Revolutionary Route Association; Sons of the Union Veterans of the Civil War; National Society Sons of the American Revolution; Honorary Member, French Society Sons of the American Revolution **BAR:** Washington Bar Association (1965)

WERNER, FELIX-MARTIN, **I:** Sciences **DOB:** 05/28/1905 **PB:** Bonn **SC:** Germany **PT:** Anna Maria Edelhoff **ED:** MD, University of Bonn (1991); MD, Hardtberg-Gymnasium, Bonn, Germany (1983) **C:** Neuroscientist, Institute of Neuroscience, Castilla and Leon, Salamanca, Spain (2002-2015) **CR:** Team Leader, Formation Assistant, Elderly Care Euro Akademie, Germany (2014-Present) **CW:** Contributor, Articles, Professional Journals; Composer, Classical Music, Pop Music; Author, "Elegie zum Tod von Pinz Louis Ferdinand" **MEM:** Komponistenverband Thuringen e.V. **H:** Guitar; Piano

WEST, ALLEN BERNARD, **T:** Executive Director, Retired Lieutenant Colonel **I:** Government Administration/Government Relations/Government Services **CN:** National Center for Policy Analysis **DOB:** 02/07/1961 **PB:** Atlanta **SC:** GA/USA **MS:** Married **SPN:** Dr. Angela Graham-West **CH:** Aubrey; Austen **ED:** MS in Political Theory, Military History and Military Operations, Command & General Staff College, U.S. Army, Fort Leavenworth, KS (1997); MS in Political Science, Kansas State University, Manhattan, KS (1996); BS in Political Science, University of Tennessee, Knoxville, TN (1983) **C:** Executive Director, National Center for Policy Analysis (2015-Present); Contributor, FOX News Network LLC (2013-Present); Director of Programming, Next Generation Today (2013); Member, U.S. House Small Business Committee, Washington (2011-2013); Member, U.S. House Armed Services Committee, Washington (2011-2013); Representative, 22nd District of the State of Florida, U.S. House of Representatives, Wash-

ington (2011-2013); Senior Analyst, Chief Operations Planner, U.S. Army Installation Management Command (2007-2009); Senior Support Adviser, U.S. Central Command (2005-2007); Teacher, Track Coach, Deerfield Beach High School, FL (2004-2005) **CR:** Founder, Allen West Foundation; Vice Chairman, Board of Directors, National Center for Policy Analysis **MIL:** Lieutenant Colonel, U.S. Army (1982-2004) **CW:** Author, "Guardian of the Republic: An American Ronin's Journey to Family, Faith and Freedom" **AW:** Honoree, Instructor of the Year, Reserve Officers' Training Corps, U.S. Army (1993); Decorated, Three Army Commendation Medals with Three Oak Leaf Clusters and One Valor Device, U.S. Army; Decorated, Three Meritorious Service Medals with Two Oak Leaf Clusters, U.S. Army; Decorated, Bronze Star, U.S. Army; Decorated, Army Achievement Medal with One Oak Leaf Cluster, U.S. Army; Recipient, Valorous Unit Award, U.S. Army; Decorated, Air Assault Badge, U.S. Army; Decorated, Master Parachutist Badge, U.S. Army; Decorated, Parachutist Insignia, U.S. Navy, U.S. Marine Corps; Decorated, Parachutist Wings, Government of Italy; Decorated, Proficiency Badge with Bronze Award, Government of Germany; Inductee, ROTC Hall of Fame, University of Tennessee **MEM:** Senior Fellow, London Center for Policy Research; Legacy Life Member, Veterans of Foreign Wars; Life Member, Association of the United States Army; Life Member, National Rifle Association; Appointed, Texas Sunset Advisory Commission **MH:** Albert Nelson Marquis Lifetime Achievement Award (2017) **H:** Distance Runner; Master Scuba Diver; Motorcyclist; Fan of the Tennessee Volunteers **PA:** Republican **RE:** Christian **ADD:** 9925 Wood Forest Dr, Dallas, TX, 75243

WESTBERRY, JORY EDD, **T:** Principal **I:** Education/Educational Services **PT:** H. Everett Smith; Nadine Proctor Smith **MS:** Married **SPN:** Paul D. Westberry (8/4/1974) **CH:** Ryan Denev **ED:** EdD, University of Miami, FL (1996); MA in Educational Leadership, University of Wyoming, Laramie, WY (1985); BA in Elementary Education, Bethany College, West Virginia (1971) **CT:** Certified School Principal, State of Florida (1996) **C:** Principal, Collier County Public Schools, Marco Island, FL (2001) **CR:** Board Member, Education Foundation, Naples, FL (1998-1999); President, Board Member, Wyoming Association for Gifted Education (1984-1989) **CW:** Contributor, Articles, Professional Journals **AW:** Named, Assistant Principal of the Year, Collier County Schools (1998); Golden Apple Teacher Award, Education Foundation of Collier County (1994); Named, Wyoming Gifted Teacher of the Year, Wyoming Association for Gifted Education (1986) **MEM:** Florida Association of School Administrators, Inc.; ASCD **H:** Photography; Kayaking **ADD:** 147 San Salvador St, Naples, FL, 34113

WESTBIE, BARBARA J., **T:** Painter, Poet, Retired Graphic Designer **I:** Fine Art **DOB:** 11/03/1946 **PB:** Little Rock **SC:** AR/USA **PT:** Freeman Bryant Davis; Virginia Lee Thompson **CH:** Suzanne Michelle (Mikki); Derrek Christopher **ED:** Graduate Studies in Graphic Design, University of California, Davis (1992); Student, Chabot College, Hayward, CA (1974); Student, Miramar College, San Diego, CA (1976); **C:** Art Consultant, Reed Gallery, Tahoe City, CA (1988-1990); Director, Lake Gallery, Tahoe City, CA (1985-1987); Executive Director, Ambiance, Danville, CA (1980-1984); Painter; Poet; Graphic Designer **CR:** Art Director, Creative Consultant, Associated Students Re-Entry Center, Chico State University, CA (2001-2003) **CIV:** Oiled Wildlife Care Network (2015-Present); North Valley Animal Disaster Group, Chico, CA (2012-Present); University of California Davis (2013-Present);

Hazwhopper; Volunteer, Emergency Animal Rescue Services (2002-Present); Volunteer, American Red Cross, Butte County (2000-Present); Coordinator, New Volunteers, American Red Cross (2000-2001); Volunteer, Park Service, Washoe Lake State Park, Carson City, NV (1993-1994); Lead Counselor, Emotions Anonymous, 12-Step Program, North Lake Tahoe Area (1990-1993); Volunteer, Crisis Intervention Counselor; CIS/Tahoe Women's Services, Kings Beach, CA (1989-1991) **CW:** Brochure, Media Kit, Chocolate Festival (1989); Artist, Project Mana Fundraising Event (1988); Inventor, Fat Fuzzy/Ikonotrisc Family (1981) **AW:** Volunteer of the Year, Tahoe Women's Services (1989); Distinguished Service Award, CIS/Tahoe Women's Services (1989-1990) **MEM:** Associate, Smithsonian Institution; Southern Poverty Law Center; Red Rover; Distinguished Member, International Society of Poets; Poetry Nation **H:** Skiing; Reading; Gardening; Writing; Painting **RE:** Protestant **ADD:** 14816 Magalia Dr, Magalia, CA, 95954

WEYLAND, JACK, T: Physics Educator (Retired), Author **I:** Education/Educational Services **DOB:** 06/12/1940 **PB:** Butte **SC:** MT/USA **PT:** Arnold Clive Weyland; Lolita Teckla Weyland **MS:** Married **SPN:** Sheryl Raner (8/21/1965) **CH:** Barbara Dawn Yanish; Dan Auty; Bradley Jack; Jed Raner; Josie Marie **ED:** PhD in Physics, Brigham Young University, Provo, UT (1969); BS in Physics, Montana State University, Bozeman, MT (1962) **C:** Physics Professor, Ricks College, Brigham Young University Idaho, Rexburg, ID (1993-2005); Physics Professor, South Dakota School of Mines and Technology, Rapid City, SD (1968-1993); Campus Service Missionary, Brigham Young University Idaho, Rexburg, ID **CIV:** Missionary, Church Educational System, Long Island, NY; Missionary, Church Educational System, Philadelphia, PA **CW:** Author, "Hannah's Legacy," Create Space (2017); Author, "The Adventures of Don Croasmun," Create Space (2017); Author, "Mandy," Create Space (2016); Author, Illustrated by Becky Cowley, "Adventures of Benny the Dog," Create Space (2015); Author, "Be the Lion," Create Space (2014); Author, "Charly's Diary," Create Space (2013); Playwright, "Jack Weyland's Home Cooking" (2012); Author, "Favorites from Forever," Horizon Publishers (2012); Author, "Heather 101," Deseret Book (2012); Author, Illustrated by Natassia Scoresby, "Gerald Giraffe" (2012); Author, "Mackenzie for Congress, Amazon Services (2011); Author, "Cameron Meets Madison," Granite Publishers (2010); Author, "It All Started with Autumn Jones," Deseret Book (2010); Author, "Brianna, My Brother, and the Blog," Deseret Book (2009); Author, "As Always, Dave," Deseret Book (2008); Author, "Alone, Together," Deseret Book (2006); Author, "Saving Kristen," Deseret Book (2005); Author, "Everyone Gets Married in the End,"Horizon Publishers (2004); Author, "Cheyenne in New York," Deseret Book (2003); Author, "Adam's Story," Deseret Book (2003); Author, "Megan," Deseret Book (2001); Author, "Ashley & Jen," Deseret Book (2000); Author, "Emily," Deseret Book (1999); Author, "Jake," Deseret Book (1998); Author, "Brittany," Deseret Book (1997); Author, "Lean on Me," Deseret Book (1996); Author, "Night on Lone Wolf Mountain," Deseret Book (1996); Author, "On the Run," Deseret Book (1995); Contributor, "Science Goes to the Movies," World's Book Science Year (1994); Author, "Nicole," Deseret Book (1993); Author, "Kimberly," Deseret Book (1992); Author, "Michelle & Debra," Deseret Book (1990); Author, "Stephanie," Deseret Book (1989); Author, "Brenda at the Prom," Deseret Book (1988); Author, "A New Dawn," Deseret Book (1988); Author, "Sara, Whenever I Hear Your Name," Deseret Book (1987); Author, "Sam," Deseret Book (1987); Author, "If Talent Were Pizza, You'd be a Supreme," Deseret Book (1986); Author, "Last of the Big-Time Spenders," Deseret Book (1986); Author, "Megapowers: Science Fact vs. Science Fiction," Kids Can Press (1985); Author, "The Understudy," Deseret Book (1985); Author, "Pepper Tide," Deseret Book (1983); Author, "The Reunion," Deseret Book (1982); Author, "Charly," Deseret Book (1980); Author, "The Award" (1979); Author, Short Stories, The New Era (1973-2000); Author, "A Young Mormon's Guide to the Concert Band"; Playwright, "Home Cooking on the Wasatch Range"; Author, "The Phone Call"; Columnist, Science Topics, Rexburg Standard Journal **AW:** Outstanding Achievement Award for Fiction Writing, Whitney Award (2011); Presidential Award for Outstanding Professor of Physics, South Dakota School of Mines & Technology (1993) **RE:** The Church of Jesus Christ of Latter-day Saints **ADD:** 369 Yale Ave, Rexburg, ID, 83440 **URL:** https://www.linkedin.com/in/jack-weyland-50b3918/

WHAM, DAVID BUFFINGTON, T: Secondary School Educator **I:** Education/Educational Services **CN:** Chicago Public Schools **DOB:** 05/25/1937 **PB:** Evanston **SC:** IL/USA **PT:** Benjamin Wham; Virginia (Buffington) Wham **MS:** Single **SPN:** Joan Field Wilber (3/9/1968, Divorced 5/1972) **CH:** Benjamin; Rachel **ED:** MA, Southern Illinois University, Carbondale, IL (1967); BA, Harvard University, Cum Laude, Cambridge, MA (1959) **C:** Teacher, Chicago Public Schools (1994-Present); Freelance Writer, Chicago, IL (1980-1989); Legislative Assistant, U.S. Congress, Washington, D.C. (1969-1978); Instructor, Southern Illinois University, Carbondale, IL (1965-1967); Instructor, University of Wyoming, Powell, WY (1963-1965) **CR:** Speechwriter, Dawn Netsch Gubernatorial Campaign (1994); Speechwriter, Adlai Stevenson Gubernatorial Campaign (1986) **CIV:** Interviewer, Harvard Club of Chicago (1984-Present) **MIL:** U.S. Army (1959-1962) **CW:** Author, "A Wave of Bright Boys" (1994); Author, "The Comic Genuflection" (1984); Author, "My Farewell to Bohemia" (1968); Contributor, Think-tank Publication: Bureau of Social Science Research, Schomburg Center for Research in Black Culture, New York Public Library **AW:** Fiction Award, Columbia Pacific University (1994) **MEM:** Harvard Club of Chicago; Spee Club, Harvard University; Hasty Pudding Club, Harvard University **PA:** Democrat **RE:** Episcopalian **ADD:** 1001 Emerson St Apt 906, Evanston, IL, 60201

WHEELER, JOHN W., T: Lawyer **I:** Law and Legal Services **DOB:** 09/11/1938 **PB:** Murfreesboro **SC:** TN/USA **PT:** James William Wheeler; Grace (Fann) Wheeler **MS:** Married **SPN:** Dorothy Anita Pressgrove (8/5/1959) **CH:** Jeffrey William; John Harold **ED:** JD, University of Tennessee (1968); BS in Journalism, University of Tennessee (1960) **C:** Of Counsel, Hodges, Doughty & Carson, Knoxville, TN (2005-Present); Partner, Hodges, Doughty & Carson, Knoxville, TN (1972-2005); Associate, Hodges, Doughty & Carson, Knoxville, TN (1968-1972); Administrative Assistant to Laboratory Director, UT-AEC Research Laboratory, Oak Ridge, TN (1965-1968); Editor, The Covington Leader (1963-1965) **CR:** Chair, U.S. Magistrate Merit Selection Panel, U.S. District Court for the Eastern District of Tennessee (2002-2003, 1991); Founding Chairman, Historical Society, U.S. District Court for the Eastern District of Tennessee (1993-2004); Member, Bankruptcy Judge Merit Selection Panel (1992-1994); Member, Commission to Study Appellate Courts in Tennessee **CIV:** Member, Organizing Committee, Tennessee Supreme Court Historical Society **MIL:** Lieutenant, U.S. Army (1961-1963); Captain, Army Reserve **MEM:** Board of Directors, Fox Den Country Club (2001-2004); Tennessee Chair, American Bar Foundation (1999-2008); President, Tennessee Bar Association (1989-1990); House of Delegates, American Bar Association (1986-2000); Board of Governors, Tennessee Bar Association (1981-1991); Fellow, American Bar Foundation; Life Member, Tennessee Bar Foundation; Tennessee Bar Association; National Conference of Bar Examiners; President, American Inns of Court; International Association of Defense Counsel; Southern Conference of Bar Presidents; President, 6th Circuit Judicial Conference; Fox Hollow Golf Club **BAR:** U.S. Court of Appeals for the 6th Circuit (1975); U.S. District Court for the Middle District of Tennessee (1974); U.S. District Court for the Western District of Tennessee (1974); U.S. Supreme Court (1974); Tennessee State Bar (1968); U.S. District Court for the Eastern District of Tennessee (1968) **MH:** Albert Nelson Marquis Lifetime Achievement Award (2017) **H:** Golf; Travel **PA:** Republican **RE:** Lutheran **ADD:** 3476 Tarpon Woods Blvd, Palm Harbor, FL, 34685

WHELTLE, MARGARET MAIE, I: Law and Legal Services **DOB:** 10/19/1934 **PB:** Baltimore **SC:** MD/USA **PT:** Albert F. Wheltle, Sr.; Ruth (Morse) Wheltle **MS:** Single **ED:** STM, St. Mary's Seminary and University (1972); Postgraduate Coursework, The Catholic University of America (1967-1969); Postgraduate Coursework, Loyola Evening College (Now Loyola University Maryland) (1960-1961); JD, University of Maryland (1959); BA, Mount St. Agnes College (1956) **C:** Chair, Religion Department, Mount de Sales Academy (1979-1985); Trustee, Mount de Sales Academy (1979-1982); Lecturer in Theology, Mount de Sales Academy (1978-1985); Coordinator of Religious Education, St. Agnes Roman Catholic Congregation, Inc. (Now St. Agnes Catholic Church and St. William of York Catholic Church) (1971-1974); Assistant to the President, Mount St. Agnes College (1964-1967); Director of Development, Mount St. Agnes College (1964-1967); Television Production Coordinator, Mount St. Agnes College (1964-1967); Associate, Harley Wheltle Victor and Rosser (1959-1964) **CR:** Lecturer, St. Martin's Home for the Aged (1975); Instructor, Harmony Hill School (1969-1970); Director, Theology Department, Harmony Hill School (1969-1970); Director, Business Law Department, Harmony Hill School (1969-1970); Speaker's Bureau, Archdiocese of Baltimore; Birthright of Maryland; Howard County Right to Life **CIV:** Jeanne Jugan Association, Little Sisters of the Poor (2003-2005); School Board, Resurrection-St. Paul School (2001-2004); Chairperson of Development Committee, Resurrection-St. Paul School (2001-2004); Liaison, Board for Christian Formation (1987-1990); President, Parish Council, St. Mark Parish (1987-1988); West County Regional Council, Archdiocese of Baltimore (1986-1990); President, Corban Corporation (1986-1989); Vice President, Parish Council, St. Mark Parish (1986-1987); Advisor, Little Sisters of the Poor (1977-1980); Advisor, St. Martin's Home for the Aged (1977-1980); National Catechism Directory Committee, St. William of York (Now St. Agnes Catholic Church and St. William of York Catholic Church) (1977); Instructor of Adult Education, St. William of York (Now St. Agnes Catholic Church and St. William of York Catholic Church) (1976); Total Parish Education Committee, St. William of York (Now St. Agnes Catholic Church and St. William of York Catholic Church) (1975-1976); Vice-Chair, Birthright of Maryland (1975-1976); Public Relations Committee, Archdiocese of Baltimore (1975-1976); Co-Founder, St. Martin's Home for Aged Ladies Auxiliary (1973-1976);

Board President, St. Martin's Home for Aged Ladies Auxiliary (1973-1976); Parish Planning Team for Total Christian Education, St. William of York (Now St. Agnes Catholic Church and St. William of York Catholic Church) (1971); Sodality Prefect, St. William of York (Now St. Agnes Catholic Church and St. William of York Catholic Church) (1965-1967); President's Council, Mount St. Agnes College (1961-1967); President, National Alumnae, Mount St. Agnes College (1961-1965); Board of Directors, St. Martin's Home for Aged Ladies Auxiliary **CW:** Author, "The Notion of Presence in the Works of John of the Cross, " St.Mary's Seminary and University **AW:** Certificate of Appreciation, Mount de Sales Academy (1982); Certificate of Appreciation, Archdiocese of Baltimore (1981) **MEM:** Order of Malta **BAR:** Supreme Court of the United States (1969); Maryland (1959) **MH:** Albert Nelson Marquis Lifetime Achievement Award (2017); Distinguished Humanitarian (2017) **RE:** Roman Catholic **ADD:** 2823 Country Ln, Ellicott City, MD, 21042

WHISNAND, REX, T: Association Housing Executive **I:** Government Administration/Government Relations/Government Services **CN:** California Senior Legislature **DOB:** 01/02/1948 **PB:** Van Nuys **SC:** CA/USA **PT:** Harold Theodore Whisnand; Laura Fay Brigham Whisnand **MS:** Married **SPN:** Cathy Ladeane Bennett (4/01/1978) **CH:** Bryce James Whisnand **ED:** EdD in Organization and Leadership, University of San Francisco (2000); MPA in Housing Administration, University of San Francisco (1985); BSBA, California State University, Sacramento (1976); BS in Agricultural Business Management, California Polytechnic State University, San Luis Obispo (1970); Graduate, Naval Submarine School **CT:** Certified Basketball Coach, National Alliance for Youth Sports, Inc. (1994-1997); Certification, ASAE **C:** Member, Joint Rules Committee (2017-2018); Chairman, Senate Housing and Transportation Committee (2016-2018); Senior Senator, California Senior Legislature (2015-2018); Crew Member, New Melones Reservoir, Bureau of Reclamation, U.S. Department of Reclamation (2009-2010); Local Office Manager, United States Census Bureau (2008-2009); Executive Vice President, Calaveras County Association of Realtors, Angels Camp, CA (2005-2008); Executive Director, Housing Conservation and Development Corporation, San Francisco, CA (2002-2005); Field Representative, Westat Survey, U.S. Public Health Service (2000-2002); Crew Leader, American Housing Survey (2000); Field Operations Supervisor, Crew Leader Census 2000, American Housing Survey (1997-1998); Executive Vice President, Rental Housing Owners Association of Southern Alameda, Hayward, CA (1990-1996); Supervisor, Lumberjack Store, Lodi, CA (1988-1990); Executive Vice President, Pierce County, Building Industry Association of Washington, Tacoma, WA (1984-1986); Executive Vice President, West Bay Division, Northern California, Building Industry Association, Redwood City, CA (1980-1984); Director, Association Services, Building Industry Association of Superior California, Sacramento, CA (1976-1979); Executive Assistant, Construction Industry Legislative Council, Sacramento, CA (1974-1975); State Park Ranger, California Department of Parks and Recreation, Lompoc, CA (1969-1975); State Park Ranger, California Department of Parks and Recreation, Sacramento, CA (1969-1975); Generalist, W & W Hardware Store, Orcutt, CA (1964-1970) **CR:** Member, Executive Officers Council, Local Government Committee, California Apartment Association (1991-1996); Member, Alameda County Housing Research Advisory Board, Hayward, CA (1990-1993); Committee Member, California Building Industry Association, Sacramento,

CA (1976-1984) **CIV:** President, Movers & Shakers Inc. (2016-Present); Vice Chairman, Calaveras County Commission on Aging (2017); Chairman, Legislative Committee Chairman (2017); Board of Directors, Calaveras County Commission on Aging (2012-2017); Vice Chairman, Legislative Committee, Tuolumne County Commission on Aging (2014-2017); Foreman, Calaveras County Grand Jury (2014-2015); Chairman, Area 12 Agency on Aging (2014-2015); Graduate, Tuolumne County Senior Leadership Program (2012, 2015); Commission Chairman, Calaveras County Commission on Aging (2014); Foreman Pro Team, Calaveras County Grand Jury (2013-2014); Officer, Tuolumne County Commission on Aging (2012-2013); Pleasanton Housing Authority (2003-2006); Pleasanton Housing Commission (2003-2006); Council of Community Housing Organization, San Francisco, CA (2002-2005); Non-Profit Housing Association of Northern California (2002-2005); Homeless Taskforce, SPUR (2002-2004); Housing Committee, SPUR (2002-2004); Hayward Coalition for Healthy Youth (1995-1996); Bay Area Industrial Education Council (1995-1996); Board of Congregations, FESCO Family Emergency Shelter Coalition, Alameda County, CA (1995-1996); Fiscal Growth Committee, Pleasanton General Plan (1994-1996); Graduate, Pleasanton Leadership, Pleasanton Chamber of Commerce (1995); Chairman, Coastside Coalition for Safer Highways, Half Moon Bay, CA (1983-1984); Officer, Half Moon Bay Chamber of Commerce (1982-1984); Officer, Active 20-30 Sacramento No.1 (1981-1982); Officer, Active 20-30 Sacramento No.1 (1976-1980); Community Planning Advisory Board, South Sacramento Area, CA (1978-1979) **MIL:** Infantryman, Artillery Division, U.S. Army National Guard (1990-1992); Storekeeper, Nuclear Ballistic Missile Submarine, U.S. Naval Reserve (1970-1976) **AW:** Association Achievement Award, National Association of Home Builders (1984-1985); Outstanding Young Men in America, Junior Chamber of Commerce, Foster City, CA (1983) **MEM:** Government Affairs Director, California Association of Realtors (2006-2008); Executive Officers Council, California Association of Realtors (2006-2008); Affordable Strategy Committee, San Francisco Comprehensive Housing (2002-2004); Board of Directors, California Society of Association Executives (1995-1997); Committee, Conference of Association Executives (1995-1996); Committee Chairman, California Society of Association Executives (1993-1995); Economic Development Committee, Pleasanton Chamber of Commerce (1990-1996); Government Relations Council, Hayward Chamber of Commerce (1990-1995); President, Executive Officers' Council, Building Industry Association of Washington (1985); President, Peninsula Chapter, International Association of Business Communicators (1981); President, Sacramento Chapter, International Association of Business Communicators (1979); Board of Directors, California Vocational Industrial Clubs (1977-1980); Committee Chair, Alpha Gamma Rho (1969-1999); Charter Member, Alpha Gamma Rho; Cal Poly Alumni Association; Land Use and Environmental Committee, California Association of Realtors; Rural Forum Committee, California Association of Realtors **MH:** Albert Nelson Marquis Lifetime Achievement Award (2017) **H:** Dog training; Genealogy; Farming; Pigeon racing; Rock steady boxing **PA:** Republican **RE:** Episcopalian **ADD:** 2410 Buffalo Way, Copperopolis, CA, 95228

WHITE, ARTHUR L., T: Education Educator **I:** Education/Educational Services **DOB:** 03/07/1936 **PB:** Boulder **SC:** CO/USA **MS:** Married **SPN:** Louanne Reese (August 28, 1956) **CH:** Debra White, Terry Johnson, Mitzi Noland, Heather Cotterman **ED:** PhD, University of Colorado (1968); BS, Univer-

sity of Northern Colorado (1957) **CT:** Certified in Secondary Science and Mathematics Education, State of Colorado (1957) **C:** Professor, Ohio State University (1969-2013); Science Teacher, Fairview High School (1960-1968); Science Teacher, Sheridan Community Schools (1957-1960) **CR:** Member, International Consortium for the Research of Science and Mathematics Education (1984-2014); Co-Director, National Center for Science Teaching and Learning, Office of Education Research and Improvement (1990-1996); Consultant, United States Information Agency (1983-1987) **CIV:** Executive Director, NARST (1996-2000) **CW:** Contributor, Articles, Science and Mathematics Professional Journals **AW:** Recipient, Mallinson Distinguished Service Award, The School Science and Mathematics Association (2009) **MEM:** President, The School Science and Mathematics Association (2006-2008); Executive Director, The School Science and Mathematics Association (2003-2006) **MH:** Albert Nelson Marquis Lifetime Achievement Award (2017) **ADD:** 475 Riley Avenue, Worthington, OH, 43085

WHITE, JOE ELLIS JR., T: President **I:** Business Management/Business Services **CN:** White & Weddle, P.C. **PB:** Roswell **SC:** NM/USA **CH:** Joe, III; Jackson; Jade; Jule; Jilian **ED:** JD, College of Law, University of Oklahoma (1988); BA, Central State University **CT:** Diplomate, Central State University (Now University of Central Oklahoma) (1985) **C:** Founding Attorney, White & Weddle, P.C. (1997-Present); Founding Partner, White & Adams, Oklahoma City, OK (1995-Present); Partner, Hughes, White, Adams & Grant, Oklahoma City, OK (1993-1994); Associate, Hughes, White, Adams & Grant, Oklahoma City, OK (1985-1993) **CR:** Barrister, American Inns of Court, Oklahoma City, OK (1994-2000); Fellow, American College of Trial Lawyers; Fellow, International Academy of Trial Lawyers; Fellow, Litigation Counsel of America **CIV:** Board of Directors, University of Central Oklahoma Foundation, Edmond, OK (1992-2000); Trustee, Oklahoma Student Loan Authority, Oklahoma City, OK (1992-1996) **AW:** Listee, Oklahoma Super Lawyers, Oklahoma Magazine (2006-Present) **MEM:** American Board of Trial Advocates; American Association for Justice; Oklahoma Association for Justice; Society of Outstanding Lawyers of America; American College of Trial Lawyers **BAR:** United States Court of Appeals for the Eighth Circuit; United States Court of Appeals for the Tenth Circuit; United States District Court for the Eastern District of Oklahoma; United States District Court for the Western District of Oklahoma; United States District Court for the Northern District of Oklahoma; United States District Court for the Eastern District of Arkansas; United States District Court for the Western District of Arkansas; United States District Court for the District of Colorado **MH:** Albert Nelson Marquis Lifetime Achievement Award (2017) **PA:** Democrat **RE:** Baptist **BA:** 630 NE 63rd Street, White & Weddle, P.C., Oklahoma City, OK, 73105 **URL:** https://whiteandweddle.com/attorneys/joe-e-white-jr

WHITE, LETITIA H., T: Assistant General Council (Retired) **I:** Law and Legal Services **CN:** Total Petrochemicals & Refining USA, Inc. **DOB:** 04/12/1951 **PB:** Lafayette **SC:** IN/USA **PT:** Thomas Purcell White; Jean Holliday Phipps **ED:** JD, South Texas College of Law Houston (1986); BA in History, Indiana University (1974); BA in Archaeology, Indiana University (1974) **C:** Senior Attorney, Coastal Corporation, Houston, TX (1998-Present); Associate, Burlington Resources, Houston, TX (1986-1998) **CR:** Secretary-Treasurer, d-Zeiner, Inc., Houston, TX (1997-1998); Secretary-Treasurer, Norrant Enterprise, Houston, TX (1996-1998) **CIV:** United

Way Worldwide **AW:** AV-Rated Attorney, Martindale-Hubbell **MEM:** ABA; American Association of Corporate Council; Business Law Section, Texas Bar Association; Houston Bar Association **BAR:** Texas **MH:** Albert Nelson Marquis Lifetime Achievement Award (2017) **H:** Exercising; Attending the opera; Reading; Traveling **PA:** Republican **ADD:** 1112 Bering Dr Apt 55, Houston, TX, 77057

WHITE, SARAH ELIZABETH, T: Lawyer **I:** Law and Legal Services **CN:** Westmoreland, Patterson, Moseley, & Hinson, LLP **PB:** Douglas **SC:** GA/USA **ED:** JD, Walter F. George School of Law, Mercer University, Macon, GA (2005); BA in Political Science, Minor in Agribusiness, University of Georgia, Magna Cum Laude (2002) **CT:** Advanced Legal Writing Certificate, Walter F. George School of Law, Mercer University, Macon, GA **C:** Lawyer, Westmoreland, Patterson, Moseley, & Hinson, LLP (2011-Present) **AW:** Rising Star for Excellence in Practice, Super Lawyers Magazine (2017); AV Rating, Martindale-Hubbell (2017); Client Distinction Award (2016); Rising Star for Excellence in Practice, Super Lawyers Magazine (2016); Client Distinction Award (2015); Award of Achievement for Outstanding Service to the Public, Young Lawyers Division State Bar of Georgia (2012-2013); Leadership Macon Class of 2010; Order of the Barristers **BAR:** Georgia Court of Appeals (2011); Supreme Court of Georgia (2011); United States District Court Southern District of Georgia (2011); United States District Court Northern District of Georgia (2011); United States District Court Middle District of Georgia (2007); Georgia (2005) **MH:** Albert Nelson Marquis Lifetime Achievement Award (2017); Distinguished Humanitarian (2017) **BA:** 577 Mulberry St Ste 600, Westmoreland Patterson Moseley, Macon, GA, 31201

WHITEHAWK, ANN S., T: Secondary School Educator (Retired) **I:** Education/Educational Services **CN:** United High School **DOB:** 08/09/1951 **PB:** Sioux Falls **SC:** SD/USA **PT:** Shirley Christensen; Eunice Elthea Ugland **MS:** Married **SPN:** Ronald Mario Whitehawk (1/29/1971) **CH:** Jenine Nicole; Michael Christopher **ED:** BA in Communications, The University of Texas at Arlington (1973) **CT:** Certification in Speech; Certification in Theater Arts; Certification in English as a Second Language **C:** Teacher, United High School, Laredo, TX (1987-Present); Museum Director, Republic of the Rio Grande Museum, Laredo, TX (1984-1985); Teacher, St. George Catholic School, Fort Worth, TX (1973-1975) **CR:** Teacher, Speech, Debate, and English as Second Language, United Independent School District, Laredo, TX (1988-2002); Member, Liaison and Insurance Committee, United Independent School District, Laredo, TX (1988-2002); Member, District Education Improvement Council, United Independent School District, Laredo, TX (1992-1998); Member, Site Base Decision Making Committee, United High School, Laredo, TX (1991-1998); Sponsor, Laredo Youth Council (1985-1987) **CIV:** Co-Founder, Laredo Youth Council (1985-1987); Founder, El Paso Lupus Association (1979) **AW:** Woman of the Year, El Paso Lupus Association (1983) **MEM:** Southern Texas Writing Project; Texas Communications Association; Texas Forensic Association; National Forensic League; Retired Teachers Association; Texas Classroom Teachers; Texas Forensic Association; Former Member, National Forensic League **MH:** Albert Nelson Marquis Lifetime Achievement Award (2017) **H:** Painting; Furniture refinishing **PA:** Democrat **RE:** Roman Catholic **ADD:** 8786 Snow Falls Dr, Laredo, TX, 78045

WHITNEY, LORI, T: Legislative Staff Member **I:** Government Administration/Government Relations/Government Services **CN:** Wisconsin State Assembly **DOB:** 02/20/1968 **PB:** Rhinelander **SC:** WI/USA **PT:** Larry R. Whitney; Mary E. (Gaffney) Whitney **ED:** BA in Spanish and Political Science, University of Wisconsin-Eau Claire, Cum Laude, Eau Claire, WI (1990) **C:** Postmistress, Wisconsin State Assembly (2003-Present); Postal Clerk, Wisconsin State Assembly (1995-2003); Messenger, Wisconsin State Assembly, Madison, WI (1991-1995) **CIV:** Member, State Coordinating Committee, State Employees Combined Campaign, Madison, WI (1996-Present); Member, Donor, People for the American Way (1996-Present); Member, Donor, Southern Poverty Law Center (1994-Present); Fundraiser, State Employees Combined Campaign, Madison, WI (1992-Present); , Burke for Wisconsin (2014); Campaign Volunteer for America, Barack Obama (2012); Monthly Donor, Planned Parenthood National Leadership Council (1994-2012); Campaign Volunteer, Democratic Coordinated Campaign (2010); Member, Donor, Wisconsin Coalition Against the Death Penalty (1993-2009); Volunteer, Prevent Child Abuse, Wisconsin (1994-2008); Campaign Volunteer, Change Barack Obama (2008); Member, Hoop Troop Booster Club, University of Wisconsin Madison Women's Basketball (1993-2005); Fundraiser, Multiple Sclerosis Society (1993-2005); Member, Amnesty International (1991-2005); Fundraiser, Volunteer, American Diabetes Association (1993-2004); Campaign Volunteer, Fred Risser (2004); Campaign Volunteer, Russ Feingold (2004); Campaign Volunteer, Fred Risser (2000); Campaign Volunteer, State Representative Tammy Baldwin (1998); Campaign Volunteer, Russ Feingold (1998); Campaign Volunteer, Fred Risser (1996); Blood Donor, American Red Cross; Member, Donor, YWCA; Volunteer, Donor, Planned Parenthood Advocates of Wisconsin **AW:** Partners In Giving Excellence Award (2017); Bob Alesch Award, Partners in Giving, State Employees Combined Campaign (2005); Top Fundraiser Award, Madison Walk for Diabetes (2004); Know Your Wisconsin State Journal Award (2004); Backyard Hero Award, Prevent Child Abuse Wisconsin (2004); Hannah Needham Rogers Award, Planned Parenthood Advocates of Wisconsin (2002); Community Volunteer Award, United Way (2002); 10 SECC Fundraising Awards, Hopebuilder Habitat for Humanity Award (1995) **MEM:** National Organization For Women; Emily's List; South Central Wisconsin United To Amend **MH:** Albert Nelson Marquis Lifetime Achievement Award (2017) **H:** Reading; Sports; Rock music; Comedy movies; Travel **PA:** Democrat **ADD:** 4322 Melody Ln Apt 211, Madison, WI, 53704 **URL:** http://www.loriannwhitney.com

WHITTINGTON, LORIN DALE, T: Music Educator (Retired) **I:** Education/Educational Services **CN:** Owen Middle School **DOB:** 11/01/1951 **PB:** Baltimore **SC:** MD/USA **PT:** Cicero Edward Whittington; Dorothy Virginia Peters **MS:** Single **ED:** MusB, Appalachian State University (1979) **CT:** Certified Teacher in Music, Grades K-12, State of North Carolina **C:** Teacher, Charles D. Owen Middle School (1997-2006); Teacher, Charles D. Owen High (1981-1997); Teacher, Hill Street Middle School (1979-1981); Teacher, Hall Fletcher Middle School (Now Asheville Middle School) (1979-1981) **CR:** Chorus Master, MidAtlantic Opera Company (1985-1986) **CIV:** Member, Caldwell Men's Chorus, 2008 - present **CW:** Composer, "Rochelle" (1972) **AW:** Teacher of the Year, Owen Middle School (2005) **MEM:** National Association for Music Education **H:** Genealogy; Art; Computer graphics; Guitar; Travel **RE:** Christian **ADD:** 3964 Mountain View Cir, Lenoir, NC, 28645

WIERNIK, PETER, T: Oncologist **I:** Research **CN:** Cancer Research Foundation **DOB:** 06/16/1939 **PB:** Crocket **SC:** TX/USA **PT:** Harris Wiernik; Molly (Emmerman) Wiernik **MS:** Married **SPN:** Roberta Joan Fuller (9/6/1961) **CH:** Julie Anne; Lisa Britt; Peter Harrison **ED:** Doctorate Honoris Causa, Universidad de la República, Montevideo, Uruguay (1982); Resident, Osler Service, Johns Hopkins Hospital (1970-1971); Resident, Cleveland Metropolitan General Hospital (Now The MetroHealth System) (1969-1970); Intern, Cleveland Metropolitan General Hospital (Now The MetroHealth System) (1965-1966); MD, University of Virginia (1965); BA, University of Virginia, with Distinction (1961) **CT:** Diplomate, American Board of Medical Oncology, American Board of Internal Medicine **C:** President, Cancer Research Foundation (1998-Present); Director, Leukemia Program, St. Lukes Roosevelt Medical Center, Icahn School of Medicine at Mount Sinai (2010-2013); Professor of Radiation Oncology, Albert Einstein Cancer Center, Albert Einstein College of Medicine (1996-1998); Professor of Medicine, Albert Einstein Cancer Center, Albert Einstein College of Medicine (1983-1998); Associate Director, Albert Einstein Cancer Center, Albert Einstein College of Medicine (1982-1998); Associate Director, Cancer Treatment Division, National Cancer Institute, National Institutes of Health (1976-1982); Director, Baltimore Cancer Research Center (1976-1982); Chief, Clinical Oncology Branch, Baltimore Cancer Research Center (Now University of Maryland Medical Center) (1976-1982); Chief, Medical Oncology Section, Baltimore Cancer Research Center (Now University of Maryland Medical Center) (1971-1976); Senior Staff Associate, Baltimore Cancer Research Center (Now University of Maryland Medical Center) (1966-1971) **CR:** Chair, Eastern Division, American Federal Medical Research (2014-Present); Councillor-at-Large, National Council (2011-Present); Professor of Medicine and Radiation Oncology, New York Medical College (1998-Present); Principal Investigator, ECOG-ACRIN Cancer Research Group (1996-Present); Chairman, Medical Advisory Committee, Leukemia & Lymphoma Society (1989-Present); Council Member, Eastern Division, American Federal Medical Research (2010-2014); Director, Cancer Center, North Division, Montefiore Medical Center (2008-2010); Director, OLM Comprehensive Cancer Center, New York Medical College (1998-2008); Chairman, Leukemia Committee, ECOG-ACRIN Cancer Research Group (1988-1994); Science Consultant, Vermont Regional Cancer Center (1987-2008); Chairman Gynecological Oncology Committee, ECOG-ACRIN Cancer Research Group (1986-1988); Member, National Clinical Fellowship Committee, American Cancer Society, Inc. (1984-1996); Professional Education Grants Committee, New York City Division, American Cancer Society, Inc. (1983-1990); Principal Investigator, ECOG-ACRIN Cancer Research Group (1982-1994); Medical Advisory Committee, Leukemia & Lymphoma Society (1976-1988); Chairman, Adult Leukemia Committee, Cancer and Leukemia Group B (1976-1983); Professor, School of Medicine, University of Maryland (1976-1982); Associate Professor, School of Medicine, University of Maryland (1974-1976); Chairman, Patient Care Committee, American Cancer Society, Inc. (1972-1975); Member, Board of Directors, Baltimore City Unit, American Cancer Society, Inc. (1971-1978); Assistant Professor of Medicine, School of Medicine, University of Maryland (1971-1974); Consultant in Hematology and Medical Oncology, MedStar Union Memorial Hospital; Consultant in Hematology and Medical Oncology, GBMC; Consultant in Hematology and Medical Oncology, MedStar Franklin Square Medical Center **CIV:** Member, Secretary's Circle, The Phi Beta Kappa Society **MIL:** Medical Director, United States Public Health Service (1976); Senior Assistant Surgeon, United States Public Health Service (1966) **CW:** Editor, "Serbian Archives of Medicine" (2005-Present); Editor, "Journal of

Therapeutic Research" (1994-Present); Senior Editor, "Medical Oncology and Tumor Pharmacotherapy" (1991-Present); Editor, "Cancer Clinical Trials" (1977-Present); Editor, "Neoplastic Diseases of the Blood, Sixth Edition" (2018); Editor, "Neoplastic Diseases of the Blood, Fifth Edition" (2013); Consultant Editor, "Diagnosis in Oncology" (2010-2013); Consultant Editor, "Journal of Clinical Oncology" (2010-2013); Editor, "Neoplastic Diseases of the Blood, Fourth Edition" (2003); Editor, "Adult Leukemias" (2001); Editor, "Cancer Investigation" (1998-2007); Co-Editor, "Bone Marrow Transplantation" (1995); Associate Editor, "American Journal of Therapeutics" (1994-2013); Editorial Board Member, "Leukemia Research" (1991-2005); Editor, "Leukemia and Lymphoma" (1989-2007); Editor, "Journal of Clinical Oncology" (1989-1991); Co-Editor, "Handbook of Hematologic and Oncologic Emergencies" (1988-1998); Editor, "PDQ National Cancer Institute" (1987-1994); Associate Editor, "Medical Oncology and Tumor Pharmacotherapy" (1987-1991); Editor, "Journal of Cancer Research and Clinical Oncology" (1986-1989); Editor, "Leukemia" (1986-2003); Co-Editor, "Year Book of Hematology" (1986-1998); Editor, "Journal of Clinical Pharmacology" (1985-2014); Editor, "Neoplastic Diseases of the Blood" (1985); Editor, "Supportive Care of the Cancer Patient" (1983); Editor, "Controversies in Oncology" (1982); Editor, "Hospital Practice" (1979-2011); Editorial Board Member, "Leukemia Research" (1977-1986); Co-Editor, "American Journal of Medical Sciences" (1976-1981); Editorial Board Member, "Cancer Treatment Reports" (1972-1976); Contributor, Articles, Professional Journals; Contributor, Book Chapters; Contributor, More than 700 Peer-Reviewed Scientific Papers **AW:** Recipient, Distinguished Achievement Award, University of Virginia (2016); Recipient, Celgene Career Achievement Award, Faculty of 1000 Ltd (2009); Recipient, Statesman Award, American Society of Clinical Oncology (2008); Recipient, Gold Medal, First Polish Congress of Oncology (2002); Recipient, Osserman Award, Israel Cancer Research Fund (1998); Recipient, Janeway Gold Medal, American Radium Society (1996); Recipient, William F. Johnson Award, St. Joseph's Hospital and Medical Center (1990); Recipient, Byrd S. Leavell Hematology Award, School of Medicine, University of Virginia (1965); Recipient, Z Society Award, University of Virginia (1961); Recipient, Award, Phi Sigma (1961); Recipient, Gold Medal, Polish Society of Surgical Oncology **MEM:** Secretary-Treasurer, National American Federation for Medical Research (2018-Present); Public Member Polling Committee, American College of Clinical Pharmacology (2014-Present); Master Awards Committee, American College of Clinical Pharmacology (2014-Present); Board of Regents, American College of Clinical Pharmacology (2011-Present); Faculty in Biology, Faculty of 1000 Ltd (2007-Present); Credentials Committee, American College of Clinical Pharmacology (2005-Present); Awards Committee, American College of Clinical Pharmacology (1999-Present); President, Eastern Division Council, American Federation for Medical Research (2015); President-elect, Eastern Division Council, American Federation for Medical Research (2014); Board Director, The Association for Patient-Oriented Research (2010-2013); Health Services Research Committee, American Society of Clinical Oncology (2000-2003); Clinical Cancer Research Committee, American Association for Cancer Research (2002-2005); Founding Member, The Association for Patient-Oriented Research (1999-2014); Institutional Representative, The American Society for Clinical Investigation (1997-2001); Research Awards Committee, American Society of Clinical Oncology (1996-2000); President, American Radium Society (1993-1994) ; President-elect, American Radium Society (1992-1993); Public Issues Committee, American Society of Clinical Oncology (1990-1995); Secretary, American Radium Society (1990-1991); Program Committee, American Society of Clinical Oncology (1990); Executive Committee, American Radium Society (1988-1995); Publication Committee, American Radium Society (1988-1992); Program Committee, American Radium Society (1987-1993); Chairman, Education Training Committee, American Society of Clinical Oncology (1984); Writing Committee, American Board of Medical Oncology, American Board of Internal Medicine (1981-1987); Subcommittee for Clinical Investigation, American Society of Clinical Oncology (1980-1982); Chairman, Education Training Committee, American Society of Clinical Oncology (1976-1979); Fellow, American Association for the Advancement of Science; Fellow, American College of Physicians; Fellow, American Society of Clinical Oncology; Fellow, International Society of Hematology; Fellow, Royal Society of Medicine; Fellow, The New York Academy of Medicine; American Society of Hematology; National Board Council, American Academy of Clinical Toxicology; International Society for Experimental Hematology; The New York Academy of Sciences; Associate, The Phi Beta Kappa Society; Sigma Xi; Alpha Omega Alpha Honor Medical Society; Phi Sigma; American Society of Health-System Pharmacists; American Society for Clinical Pharmacology and Therapeutics; Polish Society of Surgical Oncology; The Harvey Society; Uruguayan Hematology Society; InterAmerican Network of Academies of Sciences; European Association for Cancer Research; European Hematology Association **MH:** Albert Nelson Marquis Lifetime Achievement Award (2017) **H:** Stamp collecting/philately; Amateur radio **ADD:** 43 Longview Ln, Chappaqua, NY, 10514

WILCOX, HELENA MARGUERITA, T: Music Educator **I:** Education/Educational Services **CN:** San Joaquin Delta College **DOB:** 02/16/1930 **PB:** Manhattan **SC:** KS/USA **PT:** Virgil Otis Jones; Helena Mary Viers-Jones **CH:** Charles E.; Marguerita E.; Patricia A. **ED:** MA, Iowa State University of Science and Technology (1959); Bachelor of Music, Iowa State University of Science and Technology (1952) **CT:** Certified Junior College Teacher, State of California (1972); Certified Music Teacher, State of California (1967); Certified Music Teacher, State of Arizona (1959) **C:** Suzuki Violin Teacher, San Joaquin Delta College, Stockton, CA (1972-Present); Musician, Stockton Symphony Association (1967-2012); String Instrument Teacher, Stockton Unified School District (1967-2002); Organizer, Yuma Orchestra Association (1962-1967); Violin Teacher, Arizona Western College (1965-1967); Art Supervisor, Yuma Elementary School District One (1960-1967); Private Kindergarten Teacher, Springerville, AZ (1959-1960); Summer Arts Teacher, Stockton Arts Commission, City of Stockton **CIV:** Founder, The Valley Community Orchestra, Stockton, CA (2012) **AW:** Recipient, Music Education Award, Stockton Arts Commission (2007); Production Grantee, Stockton Unified School District (1980) **MEM:** President, Stockton Branch, MTAC (2003-2017); American String Teachers Association (1975); MTNA; California Teachers Association; Suzuki Association of the Americas **PA:** Democrat **RE:** Unitarian **ADD:** 2348 W Alpine Ave, Stockton, CA, 95204

WILKEY, ELMIRA SMITH, T: Illustrator, Artist, Writer, Educator **I:** Education/Educational Services **DOB:** 12/13/1936 **PB:** Kankakee **SC:** IL/USA **PT:** Edmond Anthony Smith; Dorothy Agnes (Schilling) Smith **MS:** Single **SPN:** Lowell Gene Wilkey (Deceased 2013) **CH:** Anthony; Eric; Martin; Barry; Tad; Jeremy **ED:** BA, Loretto Heights College (Now Regis University), Cum Laude (1958) **C:** Founder, Studio Sans Serif Division, Bronte Press Ltd. (1977-Present); Co-Owner, Studio Sans Serif Division, Bronte Press Ltd. (1977-Present); Printer, Studio Sans Serif Division, Bronte Press Ltd. (1977-Present); English Teacher, Bishop McNamara High School (1994-2000); Art Instructor, Kankakee Community College (1988, 2000); Affiliate, Behavior Councils, Nutri-System (1987-1991); Substitute Teacher, Kankakee County Government (1965-1980); Manager, Duncan Associates (1960-1961); English/Drama Speech Teacher, Kankakee School District 111 (1958-1960); Professional Actor, Summer Stock Theater (1958) **CR:** Editorial Consultant, August 29 (2011); Instructor, Writers Workshops (1980-2007); Design Consultant, Histories Sisters, Servants of the Holy Heart of Mary (2002-2004); Treasurer, Chicago Branch, NLAPW (2002-2004); Editorial Consultant, Hoofbeats (2001); Advertising Consultant, MX-Tech Company (1987-2000); Art Adjunct, Olivet College (1993-1994); Writer, Kankakee Art League (1980-1990); Art Presenter, Kankakee Art League (1980-1990); Tour Leader-Instructor, Herbal-Wildflowers (1980-1990); Art and Letters Member, NLAPW (1979); Vice President, NLAPW (1979); President, DSP, Boston, MA (1965-1974); Illinois Textbook Art Consultant, DSP, Boston, MA (1965-1974); Illinois State President, Chicago Branch, NLAPW; Program Chairman, Chicago Branch, NLAPW; Programmer on Literature, Kankakee Chapter, General Federation of Womens Clubs; Programmer on Theatre, Kankakee Chapter, General Federation of Womens Clubs; Programmer on Costumes, Kankakee Chapter, General Federation of Womens Clubs; Liturgical Lector, Kankakee Chapter, General Federation of Womens Clubs; Book Reviewer, Kankakee Chapter, General Federation of Womens Clubs **CIV:** Art Exhibit Commentator, Merchant Street Gallery (2016-2017); Donor, Caldecott Awards, Manteno Public Library District (1982-2017); Member, CAC of Kankakee County; Member, Advisory Committee, Economic Alliance of Kankakee County **CW:** Exhibitor, One-Woman Show, ONU Brandenberg Gallery (1994-Present); Columnist, "Pat's Meanders" (1992-2015); Exhibitor, Group Show, Charlton Gallery (2012); Exhibitor, One-Woman Show, WI Gallery (2009); Exhibitor, Group Shows, Sanctuary Gallery (2005-2008); Exhibitor, Group Shows, Tall Grass Arts Association (2005-2008); Exhibitor, Group Shows, John Vanderpoel Humanities Academy (2004-2005); Exhibitor, Group Shows, Xavier University (2004-2005); Exhibitor, Group Show, Maison Lenoblet-au Plessis (2002); Illustrator, "Hoffbeats" (2001); Exhibitor, Group Shows, Tall Grass Arts Association (2001); Illustrator, "Herbal-Wildflowers," Village View Cable TV (1996-1999); Illustrator, "Early Materno and Rockville History," Village View Cable TV (1996-1999); Illustrator, Children's Book Program (1996-1999); Exhibitor, "Alumni Invitational," Regis University (1998); Exhibitor, "Miniature Book Competition," MBSociety (1991); Exhibitor, Group Show, Triton College (1991); Exhibitor, Group Show, Copley Society (1986); Exhibitor, Group Show, Elgin Community College (1987); Exhibitor, "First National Miniature Art Competition," NLAPW (1987); Exhibitor, One-Woman Show, Galesburg Civic Art Center (1984); Exhibitor, Group Show, Prairie State College (1980); Illustrator, "Come Spring"; Illustrator, "History of Rockville"; Illustrator, 15 Books on Various Subjects; Exhibitor, Western Michigan University; Exhibitor, Group Show, Illinois Women in the Arts Invitational **AW:** Honoree, Lucille Thies Personal Achievement Award, Manteno Historical Society (2015); Featured Listee, Twentieth Century United States Miniature Books (2000); Featured

Listee, Illinois Authors Cookbook, Bourbonnais Library (1985); Featured Listee, Illinois Authors, Read Illinois (1983-1985); Featured Listee, Illinois Artisans and Craftsmen, Barrett & Schuller (1984); Third Place Award, Tall Grass Arts Association; Purchase Award, Kankakee Community College; Purchase Award, Teachers' Retirement System of the State of Illinois; Purchase Award, Miniature Book Competition; Numerous Awards In Art; Honoree, Straw Series Signature Art Technique **MEM:** President, The Great Books Foundation (1980-1985); Charter, The Great Books Foundation (1980-1985); Charter, Illinois State Poetry Society; Transparent Watercolor Society of America; National Museum of Women in the Arts; Charter, The Great Books Foundation; Miniature Book Society; Kankakee Valley Historical Society; Bourbonnais Grove Historical Society; Manteno Historical Society **H:** Walking; Herb/plant identification; Music; Reading; Travel **PA:** Republican **RE:** Roman Catholic **BA:** 4136 W 6940N Rd, Studio Sans Serif Division, Bronte Press Ltd., Bourbonnais, IL, 60914

WILLETT, JAMES DELOS, T: Science Educator **I:** Sciences **CN:** George Mason University **DOB:** 01/16/1937 **PB:** Stockton **SC:** CA/USA **PT:** John Delos Willett; Marguerite Carmelia Willett **MS:** Married **SPN:** Marie Annette Costantino (8/18/1985); Genevieve Janet Stohler (Divorced) **CH:** Stephanie Renee; John Delos **ED:** Postdoctoral Work, Bio-organic Chemistry, Stanford University (1965-1968); PhD in Organic Chemistry, Massachusetts Institute of Technology (1965); BA in Chemistry, University of California, Berkeley (1959) **C:** Director, School of Systems Biology, College of Sciences, George Mason University (2011-Present); Professor, Department of Molecular and Microbiology, College of Sciences, George Mason University (2004-Present); Professor, Department of Bioinformatics and Computational Biology, College of Sciences, George Mason University (2004-Present); Chairman, Molecular Biology and Microbiology, College of Sciences, George Mason University (2006-2011); Professor, Biochemical Systematics, School of Computational Sciences, George Mason University (2001-2006); Professor, Biochemical Systematics, College of Arts and Sciences, George Mason University (2001-2006); Director of Operations, Biomedical Genomics and Informatics, College of Arts and Sciences, George Mason University (2001-2003); Assistant Director, Biodefense Center, College of Arts and Sciences, George Mason University (2001-2003); Director, Molecular Biosciences and Informatics, School of Computational Sciences, George Mason University (2000-2001); Professor, Molecular Biosciences Institute, School of Computational Sciences, George Mason University (1997-2000); Director, Cooperative Academic Enterprise Board, George Mason University (1997); Director, Molecular Biosciences and Technology Institute, George Mason University (1995-1997); Interim Director, Molecular Biosciences and Technology Institute, George Mason University (1995-1997); Executive Director, Biosciences Development, George Mason University (1995-1997); Acting Director, Computational Sciences and Informatics Institute, George Mason University (1993-1994); Vice-Provost, Research and Graduate Studies, George Mason University (1992-1994); Chairman, Biology Department, George Mason University (1989-1992); Chief, Biological Models and Materials Resources Section, Animal Resources Program, National Center of Research Resources, National Institutes of Health, Bethesda, MD (1985-1989); Health Science Administrator, Biomedical Research Models Development, Animal Resources

Program, Division of Research Resources, National Institutes of Health, Bethesda, MD (1984-1985); Special Assistant to Director, Division of Research Resources, National Institutes of Health, Bethesda, MD (1982-1984); Staff Assistant to Deputy Director, Division of Research Resources, National Institutes of Health, Bethesda, MD (1981-1982); Grants Associate, National Institutes of Health, Bethesda, MD (1980-1981); Professor, Chemistry and Biochemistry, University of Idaho, Moscow, ID (1977-1980) **CR:** Consultant, America Tomorrow Inc. (1997-1999); Research Collaborator, America Tomorrow Inc. (1997-1999); Research Collaborator, Environmental Science Associates (1996-2007); Research Consultant, BioSyn Corporation (1986-1989); Stockholder, BioSyn Corporation (1986-1989); President, Bio Concepts, Inc. (1979-1981); Chairman, Interdisciplinary Studies Program, College of Letters and Science, University of Idaho (1971-1974) **CIV:** Potomac Peddlers; Potomac Appalachian Trail Club; Moscow Road Runners **CW:** Co-Author, "Metabolic profiling in Caenorhanditis elegans provides an unbiased approach to investigations of dosage dependent lead toxicity," Metabolomics (2012); Co-Author, "The impact of lead toxicity on Caenorhabditis elegans Population," 90th Annual Meeting, Virginia Academy of Science, Norfolk, VA (2012); Co-Presenter, "The impact of lead toxicity on Caenorhabditis elegans Population," 90th Annual Meeting, Virginia Academy of Science, Norfolk, VA (2012); Co-Author, "Metabolic Profiling of Cold Stressed Caenorhabditis elegans," 90th Annual Meeting, Virginia Academy of Science, Norfolk, VA (2012); Co-presenter, "Metabolic Profiling of Cold Stressed Caenorhabditis elegans," 90th Annual Meeting, Virginia Academy of Science, Norfolk, VA (2012); Co-Author, "Applications of Cold Temperature Stress to Age Fractionate Caenorhabditis elegans: A Simple Inexpensive Technique," The Journals of Gerontology Series A: Biological Sciences and Medical Sciences (2010); Contributor, Peer-Reviewed Poster Presentation, "Lead's effect on purine metabolism in the nematode Caenorhabditis elegans," CE Aging, Stress, Pathogenesis, and Heterochrony: C. elegans Topic Meeting 4, University of Wisconsin (2008); Co-author, "Using C. elegans as a Tool for Identifying Environmental Lead Contamination: A New Endpoint for Relating Exposures to Lead Risk," Environmental Bioindicators (2008); Contributor, "Identification of an Exposure Based Biomarker for Lead using Caenorhabditis elegans," Environmental Science and Technology, Proceedings, Third International Conference on Environmental Science and Technology, Houston, TX (2007); Contributor, "The Use of Genomic Markers in Caenorhabditis elegans as Bioindicators for Environmental Lead Exposure: A Replacement for Current in-vivo and in-vitro Systems," International Society of Environmental Bioindicators and the International Union of Biological Sciences (IUBS) Commission on Bioindicators, The Conference Center at the Maritime Institute, Maryland (2006); Author, Invited Platform Presentation, "Probing Mechanisms of Toxicity through Metabolic Profiling-What can it reveal?," IBC's Inaugural International Conference on Metabolic Profiling: Using Metabolomics Technology to Accelerate Drug Discovery and Development, Hilton Durham Hotel, North Carolina (2005); Author, "Studies of Lead Toxicity through Metabolic Profiling in C. elegans," Gordan Research Conference on Toxicogenomics," Colby-Sawyer College, New London, NH (2005); Contributor, "Probing Mechanisms of Toxicity through Metabolic Profiling: Lead and Caenorhabditis elegans," Second International Conference on Pathways,

Networks and Systems: Theory and Experiments, Aldemar Knossos Royal, Crete, Greece (2004) **AW:** Merit Award, NIH/DRR (1987); Special Achievement Award, DHHS/PHS/NIH (1985); Phi Kappa Phi; NIH Career Development Award, University of Idaho (1975-1980); Faculty Research Fellowship, University of Idaho (1969); NIH Postdoctoral Fellowship, Stanford University (1965-1968); NIH Postdoctoral Fellowship, MIT (1964-1965); Schering Corp. E.B. Hershberg Predoctoral Fellowship, MIT (1963-1964); Chicle, Predoctoral Fellowship, MIT (1962-1963); Kooper's Predoctoral Fellowship, MIT (1962) **MEM:** Board of Directors, Pacel Corp. (1998-2000); Oak Ridge Associated Universities (1994-1995); Board of Trustees, Southeastern Universities Research Association (1991-1996); University Life Task Force (1990-1993); National Institutes of Health AIDS Database Committee (1985-1989); National Institutes of Health Liaison, Science Group, Office of Policy Planning and Evaluation, EPA (1984-1986); Co-Chairman, Biological Chemistry Session, Northwest Regional American Chemical Society Meeting (1978); Radiation Safety Committee, University of Idaho (1977-1980); Program Director, Biomedical Research Support Grant, University of Idaho (1977-1980); Treasurer, University of Idaho Chapter, American Federation of Teachers (1976-1977); President, Washington-Idaho Border Section, American Chemical Society (1976); Secretary, Washington-Idaho Border Section, American Chemical Society (1975); Treasurer, Washington-Idaho Border Section, American Chemical Society (1974); Treasurer, University of Idaho Chapter, American Federation of Teachers (1974); Vice Chairman, Chemistry-Physics Section, Northwest Scientific Association (1973); Radiation Safety Committee, University of Idaho (1971-1974); Ad-Hoc Committee to Study Potential Undergraduate and Graduate Curriculum in Environmental Sciences (1970); Campus Affairs Subcommittee on Drugs (1969-1970); Borah Foundation Committee, University of Idaho (1969-1971); Washington-Metropolitan Section, American Chemical Society; American Association for the Advancement of Science; Sigma Xi; American Institute of Chemists; American Association of Individual Investors; New York Academy of Sciences; Chairman, Senior Technical Advisory Research Team (START) **MH:** Albert Nelson Marquis Lifetime Achievement Award (2017) **BA:** 10910 University Blvd MSN4E3, Manassas, VA, 20110 **ADD:** 14502 Faraday Dr, Rockville, MD, 20853 **URL:** http://www.ib3.gmu.edu

WILLIAMS, JOHN P., T: Professor **I:** Education/Educational Services **CN:** University of Pittsburgh **DOB:** 12/29/1954 **PB:** Detroit **SC:** MI/USA **PT:** Dr. Edward T. Williams, II (Stepfather, Deceased); Marjorie Logan Williams (Mother, Deceased); Sidney Simpson (Father, Deceased) **MS:** Married **SPN:** Valerie **CH:** Brynna; Connor; Victoria **ED:** Fellowship, Guy's Hospital, London, United Kingdom (1982-1983); Residency in Anesthesiology, The University of Texas Medical School, Houston, Texas (1980-1982); Internship, St. Joseph Hospital, Houston, Texas (1979-1980); MD, Baylor College of Medicine (1979); BS in Zoology, Texas A&M University, Summa Cum Laude (1977) **CT:** Anesthesiology, Critical Care Medicine, Pain Medicine **C:** Anesthesiology and Critical Care Medicine **CR:** Current Member, Council on Medical Education, American Medical Association **CIV:** Board of Directors, Family House **AW:** National Registry of Who's Who in Executives and Professionals (2003-Present); Representative, American Medical Association to National Board of Medical Examiners (2016); Elected, Council on Medical Education, American Medical Association (2015); Inspirational Physician Mentor Award, American Medical Association's Women Physicians Congress (2010); Nominee, Secretary of Defense Employer Support Freedom Award (2008); Community Citation of Recognition, County of Allegheny, Office of the County Executive (2008); Health Sciences Ambassador Nominee, University of Pittsburgh School of Medicine (2007); Innovator Award, University of Pittsburgh (2007-2015); Strathmore's Who's Who (2005-2006); Peter and Eva Safar Professorship (2003-2014); Listee, Guide to America's Top Physicians (2002-2013); Inaugural Fellow, Council on Cardio-Thoracic and Vascular Surgery, American Heart Association, Inc. (2002); Life Member, National Registry of Who's Who (2001); Associate Examiner, American Board of Anesthesiology (1992-1995); Dean's Teaching Excellence Award, University of Texas, Houston (1989-1990); Dean's Teaching Excellence Award, University of Texas, Houston (1984-1986); Rink Prize in Anesthetics, Guy's Hospital, London, United Kingdom (1982); Elected Freshman Member, Phi Kappa Phi Honor Fraternity (1974) **MEM:** Executive Committee, Allegheny County Medical Society (2011-Present); Association of University Anesthesiologists (2009-Present); Board of Directors, Allegheny County Medical Society (2006-Present); Inaugural Fellow, American Heart Association, Inc. (2002-Present); Medical Group Management Association (2002-Present); Allegheny County Medical Society (2000-Present); Society for Education in Anesthesia (1998-Present); President of the Board, Allegheny County Medical Society (2016); President, Allegheny County Medical Society (2015); President-elect, Allegheny County Medical Society (2014); Vice President, Allegheny County Medical Society (2013); Secretary, Allegheny County Medical Society (2011); Orthopedic Anesthesia and Pain Rehabilitation Society (2010-2015); Residency Program Review Group, Society of Academic Anesthesiology Associations (2010-2014); Society of Academic Anesthesiology Associations (2010-2013); Committee on Simulation in Anesthesia in Education, Society for Education in Anesthesia (2010-2011); Board of Directors, The Pennsylvania Medical Political Action Committee (2009-2015); Executive Committee, Pennsylvania Delegation to the American Medical Association (2008-2013); Hospitality Committee, Pennsylvania Delegation to the American Medical Association (2008); Fundraising Committee, Society for Education in Anesthesia (2003); Chair, Research in Education, Society for Education in Anesthesia (2003-2004); Legislative Committee, Allegheny County Medical Society (2002); Communications Committee, Allegheny County Medical Society (1999-2001); Reference Committee, Pennsylvania Medical Society **H:** Travel **PA:** Unaligned to Libertarian **RE:** Episcopal to Catholic **ADD:** 5004 W Grove Ln, Gibsonia, PA, 15044 **URL:** www.anes.upmc.edu

WILLIAMS, THOMAS E., I: Medicine & Health Care **PB:** , **ED:** MD, University of Texas Southwestern Medical Center (1962); BA, Yale University (1958) **CT:** Board Certified in Pediatrics Hematology and Oncology **C:** Thistle Oncology Division of Thistle Advisors International (2007-Present); Staff Pediatrician, Children's Ward in Corpus Christi; Academic Medicine, San Antonio, Texas; Professor, University of North Carolina; Chief Executive Officer **CR:** Locums Doctor **CIV:** Volunteer Medical Missionary, Episcopal Medical Missions Foundations **MIL:** United States Navy **MH:** Albert Nelson Marquis Lifetime Achievement Award (2017) **RE:** Baptist **ADD:** 1174 Highland Terrace Drive, Canyon Lake, TX, 78133 **URL:** https://www.linkedin.com/in/tom-williams-57888415

WILLIAMSON, ALAN B., T: Literature Educator, Poet, Writer **I:** Education/Educational Services **CN:** University of California, Davis **DOB:** 01/24/1944 **PB:** Chicago **SC:** IL/USA **PT:** George Williamson; Jehanne (Bacher) Williamson **MS:** Married **SPN:** Geanne Foster (6/1/2010); Anne Winters (10/12/1968, Divorced 1988) **CH:** Elizabeth Kilner **ED:** PhD, Harvard University (1969); MA, Harvard University (1965); BA, Haverford College (1964) **C:** Teacher, Warren Wilson MFA Program for Writers (2013-Present); Professor of English, University of California, Davis (1982-2013); Fannie Hurst Lecturer, Brandeis University, Waltham, MA (1980-1982); Briggs-Copeland Lecturer, Harvard University, Cambridge, MA (1977-1980); Assistant Professor, University of Virginia (1969-1975) **CR:** Poetry Panelist, National Endowment for the Arts (1989) **CW:** Co-Translator, Geanne Foster, "The Living Theater, Selected Poems of Bianca Tarozzi" (2017); Author, "Westernness: A Meditation" (2006); Author, "The Pattern More Complicated: New and Selected Poems" (2004); Author, "Almost a Girl" (2001); Author, "Res Publica" (1998); Author, "Love and the Soul" (1995); Author, "Eloquence and Mere Life" (1994); Author, "The Muse of Distance" (1988); Author, "Introspection and Contemporary Poetry" (1984); Author, "Presence" (1983); Author, "Pity the Monsters" (1974) **AW:** Guggenheim Fellowship (1991); Poetry Fellowship, National Endowment for the Arts (1973) **MEM:** Executive Committee, Division on Poetry, Modern Language Association (1987-1991); Fellowship, Guggenheim Foundation; Fellowship, National Endowment for the Arts **MH:** Albert Nelson Marquis Lifetime Achievement Award (2017) **PA:** Democrat **RE:** Buddhist **ADD:** 1821 Vine St, Berkeley, CA, 94703

WILLIG, ROBERT PHD, T: Professor of Economics and Public Affairs emeritus **I:** Education/Educational Services **CN:** Princeton University **DOB:** 01/16/1947 **PB:** Brooklyn **SC:** NY/USA **PT:** Jack David Willig; Meg W. Willig **MS:** Married **SPN:** Virginia Mason (7/8/1973) **CH:** Jared Mason; Scott Mason; Brent Mason; Alexandra Mason **ED:** PhD in Economics, Stanford University (1973); MS in Operations Research, Stanford University (1968); BA, Harvard University (1967) **C:** Professor of Economics and Public Affairs, Princeton University (1978-Present); Deputy Assistant Attorney General, The United States Department of Justice (1989-1991); Member, Task Force on the Future of Postal Service, The Aspen Institute (1978-1980); Supervisor, Department of Economics Research, Bell Laboratories (Now Nokia) (1977-1978); Technology Staff, Bell Laboratories (Now Nokia) (1973-1977); Lecturer, Stanford University (1971-1973) **CR:** Senior Consultant, Compass Lexecon (2008-Present); Senior Consultant, Compass (2006-2008); Member, Competition Policy Associates, Inc. (Now FTI Consulting, Inc.) (2002-2005); Member, Board of Directors, Consultants in Industry Economists Incorporated (1992-2005); Adviser, Inter-American Development Bank (1997-2000); Member, Transportation Research Board Task Force (1995-1996); Member, Defense Science Board Task Force on Antitrust for the Defense Industry (1993-1994); Member, Research Advisory Board, American Enterprise Institute (1980-1988); Member, Governor's Task Force on Market-Based Pricing of Electricity, State of New Jersey (1987); Member, Organizing Committee, TPRC (1977-1978); Research Fellow, The University of Warwick (1977); Consultant in Field **CIV:** Member, Advisory Board, AJC (2010-2015); Member, Competition and Regulation Network Industries (2009-Present); Member, Advisory Board, B'nai B'rith Hillel Foundation, Princeton University (1978-1989) **CW:** Editor, "Second Generation Reforms in Infrastructure Services" (2002); Editorial Board Member, Utility Policy (1989-2001); Editorial Board Member, Journal of Industrial Economics (1985-1989); Editorial Board Member, Press Series on Government Regulation, Massachusetts Institute of Technology (1978-1989); Editor, "Can Privatization Deliver: Infrastructure for Latin America" (1999); Editor, "Handbook of Industrial Organization" (1986); Editorial Board Member, American Economic Review (1980-1983); Author, "Contestable Markets and the Theory of Industry Structure" (1982); Author, "Welfare Analysis of Policies Affecting Prices and Products" (1973); Contributor, Articles, Professional Journals **AW:** Grantee, National Science Foundation (1979-1985) **MEM:** Fellow, Program Committee, The Econometric Society (1978-1981); Nominating Committee, American Economic Association (1980-1981) **MH:** Albert Nelson Marquis Lifetime Achievement Award (2017) **ADD:** 220 Ridgeview Rd, Princeton, NJ, 08540-7665

WILLRICH, MASON, T: Energy Industry Executive **I:** Business Management/Business Services **DOB:** 05/30/1933 **PB:** Los Angeles **SC:** CA/USA **MS:** Married **SPN:** Wendy Webster (8/30/1997); Patricia Rowe (Married 6/11/1960, Deceased 7/1996) **CH:** Christopher; Stephen; Michael; Katharine **ED:** JD in Law Review, University of California, Berkeley (1960); BA, Yale University, Magna Cum Laude (1954) **C:** Chair, Governing Board, California Independent System Operator (2005-2011); Partner, Nth Power LLC (1996-2002); Chairman, EnergyWorks (1995-1998); Chief Executive Officer, PG&E Enterprises, San Francisco, CA (1989-1994); President, PG&E Enterprises, San Francisco, CA (1989-1994); Executive Vice President, Pacific Gas & Electric, San Francisco, CA (1988-1989); Senior Vice President, Pacific Gas & Electric, San Francisco, CA (1984-1988); Executive, Pacific Gas and Electric Company, San Francisco, CA (1979-1994); Vice President, Pacific Gas & Electric, San Francisco, CA (1979-1984); Director, International Relations, Rockefeller Foundation, New York, NY (1976-1979); John Stennis Professor of Law, University of Virginia (1975-1979); Professor of Law, University of Virginia (1968-1975); Associate Professor of Law, University of Virginia (1965-1968); Assistant General Council, United States Arms Control and Disarmament Agency (1962-1965); Attorney, Pillsbury Madison and Sutro, San Francisco, CA (1960-1962) **CR:** Member, Governing Board, California Clean Energy Fund (2004); Winrock International, Arlington, VA (1998-2007); Advisory Board Member, National Renewable Energy Laboratory, Golden, CO (1998-2006); Evergreen Solar Inc., Marlborough, MA (1998-2003); Electric Power Research Institute, Palo Alto, CA (1994-2003); Stanford University School Earth Sciences (1992-1998); Resources for the Future, Washington, D.C. (1990-1999); Nuclear Engineering, Massachusetts Institute of Technology (1978-1983) **CIV:** Director, California Clean Energy Fund (2007); Trustee, World Affairs Council of Northern California; Past Chairman, World Affairs Council of Northern California; Past Chairman, Midland School; Administration Board, Papers of Benjamin Franklin Committee, Yale University; California Independent System Service Operator, Light Up the State of California **MIL:** Pilot, Strategic Air Command, US Air Force (1955-1957) **CW:** Author, "Modernizing America's Electricity Infrastructure" (2017); Author, "Adventures Between History's Pages" (2007); Author, "Radioactive Waste Management and Regulation" (1977); Author, "Administration of Energy Shortages" (1976); Author, "Energy and World Politics" (1975); Author, "Nuclear Theft" (1974); Author, "Global Politics of Nuclear Energy" (1971); Author, "Non-Proliferation Treaty" (1969)

AW: Recipient, Dreyfuss Distinguished Alumnus Award, Midland School (2008); Recipient, John Simon Guggenheim Memorial Fellowship (1973) **MEM:** World Affairs Council of Northern California, San Francisco, CA; Commonwealth Club of California, San Francisco, CA; Council on Foreign Relations, New York, NY; Phi Beta Kappa; Order of the Coif; Captain, Yale Varsity Soccer Team **MH:** Albert Nelson Marquis Lifetime Achievement Award (2017) **PA:** Democrat **ADD:** 38 Dudley Ct, Piedmont, CA, 94611-3442

WILSON, AMANDA J., T: Director, Student and Alumni Affairs **I:** Education/Educational Services **CN:** American Public University System **DOB:** 02/03/1981 **PB:** Memphis **SC:** TN/USA **ED:** Pursuing DBA, Walden University; MBA, American Public University (2012); BS in English, Radford University (2004); Coursework, United Kingdom Study Abroad Program, Radford University (2002) **C:** Director, American Public University System (2014-Present); Senior Manager, Student and Alumni Affairs, American Public University System (2013-2014); Team Manager, Student and Alumni Affairs, American Public University System (2011-2013); Team Lead, Student and Alumni Affairs, American Public University System (2010-2011); Global Mentor Network Coordinator, American Public University System (2008-2010); English, Creative Writing, Multicultural Literature Teacher, Jefferson County Schools (2005-2008) **CIV:** Chapter Advisor, American Public University, American Military University, Golden Key International Honor Society (2009-Present); Chapter Advisor, Founder, West Virginia Students Alliance, American Public University System (2017); Coach, 9th Grade Girls Volleyball Team, Jefferson High School, Shenandoah Junction, WV (2007); Coach, JV Girls Softball Team, Jefferson High School, Shenandoah Junction, WV (2005) **AW:** Alumni University Service Award, American Public University System (2018); Nominated, Selected to Join Leadership, West Virginia's Class of 2017 (2017); Australian Travel Grant, Golden Key International Honour Society (2015); Inspire Leadership Award, American Public University System (2014); Winner, Provost Innovation Challenge, American Public University System (2014); South African Travel Grant, Golden Key International Honour Society (2013) **MEM:** Counsel Representation, United States Region 2, Golden Key International Honor Society (2016-Present); Honorary National Society for Collegiate Scholars; Student Affairs Administrators in Higher Education; International Mentoring Association; Honorary Member, The National Society of Collegiate Scholars **MH:** Albert Nelson Marquis Lifetime Achievement Award (2017) **H:** Reading; Writing; Listening to live music; Traveling **BA:** 111 W Congress St, American Public University System, Charles Town, WV, 25414 **URL:** https://www.leadershipwv.org/meet-the-class/?bio_id=1558

WILSON, BONNIE JEAN, T: Lawyer, Educator, Investor **I:** Law and Legal Services **PB:** Alameda County **SC:** CA/USA **PT:** August Ritzenthaler; Violet Adeline (Lockard) Ritzenthaler **MS:** Widowed **SPN:** Allan Nicholas Wilson (Deceased) **CH:** Albert Clyde; Bruce Allan **ED:** Intern, San Diego County District Attorney Office (1981); JD, Thomas Jefferson School of Law (1981); BA, University of California, Berkeley **CT:** Certified Teacher, State of California; Certified in Elementary Teaching, University of California, Berkeley **C:** Private Practice, La Jolla, CA (1982-Present); Elementary School Teacher, Contra Costa County; Elementary School Teacher, San Diego County **CIV:** Education Activist, San Diego Opera Association (1972-1976); La Jolla Presbyterian Church; San Diego Symphony Association; Friends of the La Jolla Library; Advisory Director, San Diego Opera Association **MEM:** Board of Directors, American Association of Individual Investors (1991-1997); Board of Directors, La Jolla Newcomer's Club (1968-1969); Board of Directors, San Diego Chapter, Cal Alumni Association (1961-1962); The State Bar of California; San Diego County Bar Association; Pi Lambda Theta; La Jolla Beach & Tennis Club; Prytanean Women's Honor Society, University of California, Berkeley; Club Altura, La Jolla, CA **BAR:** State of California **H:** Learning; Reading **RE:** Presbyterian **ADD:** 2235 Bahia Drive, La Jolla, CA, 92037

WILSON HARTMANN, ANN, T: Financial Planner **I:** Financial Services **CN:** Hartmann and Associates **DOB:** 03/05/1941 **PB:** Detroit **SC:** MI/USA **PT:** Robert Allan Wilson; Eunice Elizabeth (Seitz) Wilson **MS:** Single **SPN:** Frank Snug (9/11/2004, Deceased); Richard W. Brockmeyer (10/1/1994, Divorced 1999); James Cline Hartmann (7/18/1970, Deceased) **ED:** MBA in Finance, Rutgers, The State University of New Jersey (1975); BA, Montclair State College (1962) **CT:** Chartered Life Underwriter, The American College of Financial Services (1983); Chartered Financial Consultant, The American College of Financial Services **C:** Financial Planner, Hartmann & Associates (1980-Present); Senior Consultant, Health Systems Group, Ann Arbor, MI (1979-1980); Director, Finance and Field Personnel, Sycor, Inc. (1977-1979); Executive Director, YWCA Northwest Ohio (1972-1977); Administrator, YWCA, Summit, NJ (1972-1977); Administrator, Girl Scouts of the United States of America, Michigan (1963-1972); Administrator, Girl Scouts of the United States of America, Pennsylvania (1963-1972); Teacher, Bloomfield Board of Education, New Jersey (1962-1963) **CR:** Faculty, Cigna/Lincoln National Education Events (1984-Present); Adjunct Faculty, Lourdes College, Sylvania, OH (1987-1998); Adjunct Faculty, University of Toledo (1983-1987); Speaker in Field **CIV:** Chair, Affiliated Organizations Committee, Board of Trustees, West Ohio Conference of The United Methodist Church (2014-Present); Chair, Planned Giving Council, Montclair State University (2014-Present); Member, Development Committee, Toledo Museum of Art (2008-Present); Vice President, Western Ohio Region, Girl Scouts of the United States of America (2012-2018); President, Friendly Center (2009-2011); Board Member, Western Ohio Region, Girl Scouts of the United States of America (2009-2011); Trustee, Toledo Campus Ministry (2008-2011); Board Member, Toledo Campus Ministry (2008-2010); Vice President, Friendly Center (2008-2009); Trustee, Friendly Center (2005-2008); Treasurer, Zonta Foundation, Zonta International (2004-2006); President, Spiritual Counselling and Education Center (2004-2005); Trustee, Zonta Club Toldeo I Foundation Board, Zonta International (2003-2006); Trustee, Spiritual Counselling and Education Center (2002-2005); President, Maumee Valley Council, Girl Scouts of the United States of America (1990-1997); First Vice President, Girls Clubs of America, New York City, NY (1985-1987); Staff Instructor, National Aquatic School, The American National Red Cross (1974-1980); Trainer, National Aquatic School, The American National Red Cross (1974-1980) **CW:** Editor, "Money Talks" (1982-Present) **AW:** Inductee, Worldwide Lifetime Achievement (2017), Who's Who in America (2007-2008, 2002-2003, 1994-1998); Who's Who in Finance and Business (2007, 2005, 2002); Honoree, Distinguished Community Woman of the Year, Girl Scouts of Maumee Valley Council (2007); Kenneth Black Leadership Award, Society of FSP (2007); Honoree, Distinguished Accredited Estate Planner, NAEPC (2006); Who's Who of American Women (2002, 1997, 1995); Who's Who in the World (1999-2007); Who's Who in Finance and Industry (2001, 1997, 1995, 1993, 1991); Hines Award, National Board on Child Welfare (1986) **MEM:** Finance Committee, Epworth United Methodist Church (2016-Present); Art Alliance for Contemporary Glass (2015-Present); Nominations Committee, Epworth United Methodist Church (2011-Present); The Glass Art Society (2000-Present); Toledo Museum of Art Apollo Society (1997-Present); Chautauqua Literary and Scientific Circle (1992-Present); Mensa (1978-Present); President, Toledo Chapter, Society of FSP (2005-2006); Immediate Past President, National Nominating Committee, Society of FSP (2002-2003); President, Foundation, Society of FSP (2001-2003); President, National Nominating Committee, Society of FSP (2001-2002); President-Elect, National Nominating Committee, Society of FSP (2000-2001); Treasurer, National Nominating Committee, Society of FSP (1999-2000); Secretary, National Nominating Committee, Society of FSP (1998-1999); National Nominating Committee, Society of FSP (1996-1997); President, Toledo Association of Life Underwriters (1995); President-Elect, Toledo Association of Life Underwriters (1994); National Board of Directors, Society of FSP (1993-1996); Board of Directors, Toledo Estate Planning Council (1992-1998); Vice President, Toledo Association of Life Underwriters (1991-1994); President, Toledo Chapter, Society of FSP (1988-1990); Board of Directors, Zonta Club of Toledo (1987-1988); Commercial Panel, American Arbitration Association; Arbitrator, American Arbitration Association; Arbitrator, FINRA **MH:** Albert Nelson Marquis Lifetime Achievement Award (2017) **H:** Sailing; Bridge; Needle crafts **RE:** Methodist **ADD:** 7174 Twin Canyon Dr, Lambertville, MI, 48144 **URL:** https://wwlifetimeachievement.com/2017/09/11/ann-wilson-hartmann/

WINDSCHIEGL, MARILYN, T: Director of Clinical Research Contracts & Compliance **I:** Pharmaceuticals **CN:** PharmaSeek **ED:** JD, University of Wisconsin School of Law (1998); BS in Education, University of Wisconsin (1978) **C:** Director of Clinical Trials Contracts and Compliance, PharmaSeek (2015-Present); HIPAA Privacy Officer, Dean Health Plan, Inc. (2014-2015); Compliance Attorney, Dean Health Plan, Inc., Madison, WI (2013-2014); Board Member, Madison Civics Club (2012-2013); Council Member, Health Advisory Council, Wisconsin Commissioner of Insurance (2008-2010); Regulatory Compliance Director, Wisconsin Education Association Trust (2005-2013); Associate General Counsel, Wisconsin Education Association Trust (2001-2013); Legislative Counsel, Wisconsin Medical Society (2000-2001); Legal Counsel, Wisconsin Education Association Council (1999-2000); Manager, Field Service Operations and Electronic Claims, WPS Health Insurance (1983-1995); Presenter in Field **CIV:** World Wildlife Fund; National Defense Fund; National Park Foundation; St. Jude's Children's Research Hospital; American Players Theater, Chicago Art Institute, Madison Civics Club, Southern Poverty Law Center, American Civil Liberties Union **MEM:** HIPAA Collaborative of Wisconsin (2007-present); State Bar of Wisconsin (1999-Present); Planning Committee (2017, 2015) for The Mega Health Care Conference in Wisconsin **BA:** 8040 Excelsior Dr Ste 300, PharmaSeek, Madison, WI, 53717 **ADD:** 6004 Midwood Ave, Monona, WI, 53717 **URL:** https://www.linkedin.com/in/marilyn-windschiegl-15240326

WINEBRENNER, WILLIAM P., T: Writer **I:** Writing and Editing **DOB:** 09/26/1933 **PB:** West Columbia **SC:** WV/USA **PT:** Richard Arthur Winebrenner; Lucy Ethel Riley **MS:** Single **CH:** Rita Jean Hreha;

William Patrick, Jr.; Tonya Michelle Noel **ED:** High School Diploma, Mason, WV **C:** Journeyman, International Brotherhood of Electrical Workers (Now IBEW), Toledo, OH (1968-1995) **CR:** Advisory Board, Muskingum Area Technical College (Now Zane State College), Zanesville, OH (1998); Owner, Valley Enterprises Public, Stockport, OH (1993-1998) **CW:** Author, "The Last Deer Hunt" (2004); Author, "A Place of Evil" (1999); Author, "From Out of the Forest" (1998); Author, "Narrowbackin'" (1997); Author, "Smoke in the Valley" (1995); Author, "The Wood Walkers" (1993) **MEM:** Electrical Workers Retirement **MH:** Albert Nelson Marquis Lifetime Achievement Award (2017); Distinguished Humanitarian (2017) **H:** Hunting; Fishing; Writing; Promoting books **PA:** Democrat **ADD:** PO Box 535, Stockport, OH, 43787

WINFREY, JOHN CRAWFORD, T: Economist, Educator **I:** Education/Educational Services **CN:** Washington and Lee University **DOB:** 07/02/1935 **PB:** Somerville **SC:** TN/USA **PT:** Arthur Peter Winfrey; Frances (Crawford) Winfrey **MS:** Married **SPN:** Barbara Ann Strickland (7/20/1957) **CH:** Mae Millicent **ED:** PhD, Duke University (1965); AB, Davidson College (1957) **C:** Professor, Washington and Lee University, Lexington, VA (1974-Present); Associate Professor, Washington and Lee University, Lexington, VA (1969-1973); Assistant Professor of Economics, Washington and Lee University, Lexington, VA (1965-1968); Research Assistant in Economics, Duke University, Durham, NC (1963-1964); Assistant Director of Data Processing, Hanes Hosiery, Winston Salem, NC (1959-1962) **CR:** Adjunct Professor, Southern Virginia University (2009); Visiting Professor, Duke University (1995); Visiting Professor, Utrecht University, Netherlands (1995); Visiting Professor, University of California, Berkeley (1993); Visiting Professor, Duke University (1989); Visiting Professor, University of Virginia (1986); Visiting Professor, University of Illinois (1982); Visiting Professor, UCLA (1978); Visiting Professor, Tufts University, Boston, MA (1975); Visiting Professor, Vanderbilt University, Nashville, TN (1966) **CIV:** Candidate, House of Delegates, Virginia (2017); Board of Directors, Rockbridge Area Department of Social Services (2002-Present); Member, Behavioral Health Advisory Board, Rockbridge Area Community Services (2001-Present); President, Rockbridge Arts Guild (2001-2002); President, Rockbridge Arts Guild (1986-1988); Board of Directors, Rockbridge Area Conservation Council (1982-1984); Board of Directors, Lexington Tennis Clinic (1968-1972); Board of Directors, Lexington Family Mentoring Program; Member, Nelson Fine Art Gallery, Lexington, VA **CW:** Art Showcased in Nelson Gallery; Author, "Social Issues, The Ethics and Economics of Taxes and Public Programs" (1997); Author, "Public Finance, Public Choice and the Public Sector" (1973); Co-Author, "The Motion Commotion" (1972); Author, Articles, Professional Journals **AW:** Visiting Fellowship, University College, Oxford University (1979, 1995); Fellowship, National Endowment of the Humanities (1975, 1978, 1982, 1986, 1989, 1993); Community Service Award, Lexington Jaycees (1971) **MEM:** Fellow, Society for Values in Higher Education; American Economic Association; Southern Economic Association; History of Economics Society; Eastern Economic Association; High Wheelers Club, Lexington; Sunrise Rotary Club, Rotary International; Nelson Art Gallery **MH:** Albert Nelson Marquis Lifetime Achievement Award (2017) **H:** Artist **PA:** Democrat **RE:** Presbyterian **ADD:** 160 Kendal Dr Apt 1035, Lexington, VA, 24450

WIROSTKO, BARBARA M., T: Ophthalmologist **I:** Medicine & Health Care **CN:** University of Utah **MS:** Married **SPN:** Dr. Joseph Morelli (10/11/1990) **ED:** Glaucoma Fellow, Weill Cornell Medicine, Cornell University (1995-1996); Chief Resident, Columbia Presbyterian Medical Center, Edward S. Harkness Eye Institute, Columbia University (1994-1995); Ophthalmology Residency, Columbia Presbyterian Medical Center, Edward S. Harkness Eye Institute, Columbia University (1992-1994); Intern in Transitional Medicine, Hackensack University Medical Center, Hackensack Meridian Health (1991-1992); MD, Vagelos College of Physicians and Surgeons, Columbia University (1991); BA, The College of Arts & Sciences, Cornell University, with Distinction (1987) **CT:** Licensed Physician, State of Utah (2010-Present); Diplomate, American Board of Ophthalmology (1997-Present); Licensed Physician, State of New York (1992-2010); Diplomate, National Board of Medical Examiners (1992) **C:** Chief Medical Officer, EyeGate, Waltham, MA (2016-Present); Adjunct Associate Professor Department of Bioengineering, University of Utah, Salt Lake City, UT (2014-Present); Clinical Adjunct Associate Professor, Department of Ophthalmology, Moran Eye Center, University of Utah, Salt Lake City, UT (2010-Present); Senior Medical Director, Ophthalmology, Global Clinical Development Team & Medical Affairs Lead for Glaucoma, Pfizer Inc., New York, NY (2008-2010); Global Medical-Early Asset Medical Director of Ophthalmology, Pfizer Inc., New York, NY (2007-2008); Global Medical Director for Ophthalmology, Pfizer Inc., New York, NY (2006-2007); Chairperson of Ophthalmology, Huntington Medical Group PC, Huntington Station, NY (1996-2006) **CR:** Board of Directors, Glauconix L.L.C., Albany, NY (2015-Present); Appointed Grants Working Group Member, California Institute for Regenerative Medicine (2015-Present); Attending Physician, Department of Ophthalmology, Veterans Hospital, U.S. Department of Veterans Affairs, Salt Lake City, UT (2014-Present); Invited Scientific Advisory Member, The Glaucoma Foundation (2013-Present); Medical Monitor, Trial Runners, Dickinson, ND (2012-Present); Clinical Consultant, Trial Runners, Dickinson, ND (2012-Present); Entrepreneurial Faculty Scholars: University of Utah, Salt Lake City, UT (2011-Present); Advisor, Entrepreneurial Faculty Scholars: University of Utah, Salt Lake City, UT (2011-Present); Scientific Advisory Committee, Glaucoma Research Foundation (2011-Present); Professional Development and Education Committee, The Association for Research in Vision and Ophthalmology (2011-Present); Invited Speaker, World Ophthalmology Congress, Barcelona, Spain (2018); Session Chairperson, World Ophthalmology Congress, Barcelona, Spain (2018); Invited Speaker, World Glaucoma Congress, Helsinki, Finland (2017); President, Alumni Association, Edward S. Harkness Eye Institute, Columbia University (2017); Invited Guest Alumni and Speaker, Edward S Harkness Resident and Fellow Graduation and Research Day, Edward S. Harkness Eye Institute, Columbia University (2017); Invited Speaker, 23rd Annual Think Thank on XFS. New York, NY (2017); Moderator, MIT Annual Workshop, The Association for Research in Vision and Ophthalmology, Baltimore, MD (2017); Invited Guest Speaker, 121st Annual Meeting, Japanese Ophthalmologic Society, Tokyo, Japan (2017); Elected Member, Member in Training Committee, The Association for Research in Vision and Ophthalmology (2016-2018); Invited Guest Lecturer, Research Grant Administrators Program, Annual Meeting, The Association for Research in Vision and Ophthalmology, Seattle, WA (2016); Course Co-Moderator, The Association for Research in Vision and Ophthalmology, Seattle, WA (2016); Course Organizer, The Association for Research in Vision and Ophthalmology, Seattle, WA (2016); Appointed Member, Professional Development and Educational Committee, The Association for Research in Vision and Ophthalmology (2015-2018); Invited Speaker, New Horizons in Glaucoma Pharmaceuticals Session, Glaucoma Research Foundation New Horizons Meeting, San Francisco, CA (2013); Moderator, New Horizons in Glaucoma Pharmaceuticals Session, Glaucoma Research Foundation New Horizons Meeting, San Francisco, CA (2013); Program Committee Member, Annual GRF New Horizons Forum (2013); Invited Speaker, Meeting, American Glaucoma Society (AGS) (2012); Advisory Board Member, Fourth Ocular Diseases & Drug Discovery Conference, Las Vegas, NV (2012); Chairperson, Fourth Ocular Diseases & Drug Discovery Conference, Las Vegas, NV (2012); Moderator, Fourth Ocular Diseases & Drug Discovery Conference, Las Vegas, NV (2012); Co-Founder, Jade Therapeutics, Inc. (Now EyeGate) (2011-2016); Chief Scientific Officer, Jade Therapeutics, Inc. (Now EyeGate) (2011-2016); Advisory Board Member, Third Ocular Diseases & Drug Discovery Conference, Boston, MA (2011); Chairperson, Third Ocular Diseases & Drug Discovery Conference, Boston, MA (2011); Moderator, Third Ocular Diseases & Drug Discovery Conference, Boston, MA (2011); Chief Medical Officer, Altheos, San Francisco, CA (2010-2012); Retained Consultant, Altheos, San Francisco, CA (2010-2012); Advisory Board Member, Ocular Diseases & Drug Discovery Conference, Boston, MA (2010); Clinical Assistant Professor, Department of Ophthalmology, Stony Brook Medicine, Stony Brook, NY (2007-2010); Attending Volunteer, Department of Ophthalmology, Northport VA Medical Center, U.S. Department of Veterans Affairs, Northport, NY (2007-2010); Attending Physician, Department of Surgery, Huntington Hospital, Northwell Health, Huntington, NY (1996-2007); Clinical Instructor, Columbia Presbyterian Medical Center, Edward S. Harkness Eye Institute, Columbia University (1996-2003); Fellow, American Academy of Ophthalmology **CIV:** Founder, Joseph James Morelli Scholarship Foundation (2014-Present); Resident Research Director, Moran Eye Center, University of Utah, Salt Lake City, UT (2014-Present); Medical Consultant, Operation Hearts and Homes Inc, Cold Spring Harbor, NY (2001-2008); Mentor for Students; Sub-Committee, The Association for Research in Vision and Ophthalmology; Former Pdeck Committee Member, The Association for Research in Vision and Ophthalmology; TTF Grant Review Committee, The Glaucoma Foundation; Scientific Advisory Panel, The Glaucoma Foundation **CW:** Editorial Board, "Acta Ophthalmologica" (2010-Present); Peer Reviewer, "Journal of Glaucoma" (2010-Present); Peer Reviewer, "Journal of Ocular Pharmacology and Therapeutics" (2008-Present); Associate Editor, "Acta Ophthalmologica" (2007-Present); Peer Reviewer, "Acta Ophthalmologica" (2007-Present); Co-Author, "What does the literature indicate about rates of diabetic retinopathy progression?," Retinal Physician (2010); Co-Author, "The Role of the Vascular Endothelial Cell in Glaucoma," Glaucoma Today (2009); Manuscript Reviewer, "Ophthalmology" (1996-1999); Contributor, Articles, Professional Journals; Invited Lecturer, Numerous Presentations **AW:** America's Top Ophthalmologist (2009-Present); Grantee, The Glaucoma Foundation (2016-2017); SBIT Grantee, U.S. Department of Defense (2015-2017); SBIR Grantee, National Science Foundation (2015); Top

10 Percent of Nation's Clinicians (2015); Clinical Faculty of the Year Award, Moran Eye Center, University of Utah, Salt Lake City, UT (2014-2015); Clinician of the Year, Moran Eye Center, University of Utah, Salt Lake City, UT (2014); Grantee, National Science Foundation (2013-2014); Technology Commercialization & Innovation Program (TCIP) Grantee, USTAR (2012-2013); Scientific and Medical Research Grants Review Working Group, California Institute for Regenerative Medicine (2010-2015); Best Poster Award, American Academy of Ophthalmology, Chicago IL (2010); Third Annual Distinguished Alumni Award, Edward S. Harkness Eye Institute, Columbia University (2010); Pfizer La Jolla Team Award for Xalapeds Program, Pfizer Inc. (2010); Woman of the Year, National Association of Professional Women (2010); Honoree, Best Resident Presentation, The New York Academy of Medicine (1995); Upjohn Achievement Award for Excellence in Research (1991); Alvin Behrens Memorial Award in Ophthalmology (1991); Dean's Summer Research Scholarship, Vagelos College of Physicians and Surgeons, Columbia University (1988) **MEM:** American Glaucoma Society; The Association for Research in Vision and Ophthalmology; The Utah Ophthalmology Society; Glaucoma Research Foundation; Women in Ophthalmology **H:** Running; Sports; Tennis; Skiing; Mountain biking; Hiking; Piano; Oil painting; Horticulture **BA:** 201 Presidents Circle, Salt Lake City, UT, 84112 **ADD:** 7585 Ranch Club Trail, Park City, UT, 84098 **URL:** https://www.linkedin.com/in/barbarawirostko

WISE, KITTY, T: Writer, Composer, Artist, Designer, English Educator (Retired). **I:** Writing and Editing **PT:** Warren G. Wise **ED:** BA in English, University of Wyoming (1992) **CT:** Certified Educator, State of Wyoming **C:** Founder, Chief Executive Officer, Secretary-Treasurer, WiseWords Pub., Inc., Gillette, WY (1997-2004); Chief Executive Officer, Secretary, Vice President, Precision Well Service, Inc., Gillette, WY (1982-1989); Writer; Composer; Artist; Designer; Educator, English **CIV:** Leader, Camp Director, Girl Scouts of the United States of America **CW:** Author, "The Divine Miss Genevieve" (2004); Author, "Behold, The Power of the Wind" (2003); Co-author, Editor, Artist, "Teaching Parents to be Good Teachers: First, Do No Harm" (1999); Author, "Somewhere Beyond Tomorrow" (1997); Author, "Anywhere the Wind Blows" (1997); Co-author, Editor, Artist, "The Empowered Executive's Handbook for Life the Labyrinth: A Journey into Your Personal Power" (1997); Author, "Listen to the Wind" (1996); Author, "The Wind in My Hair" (1992); Author, "A Lost Soul" (1990); Author, Short Stories **AW:** Service Awards, American Legion and Gillette Jaycees (1976-1977) **MEM:** Senior Princess, International Order of Job's Daughters; Girl Scouts of the United States of America **MH:** Albert Nelson Marquis Lifetime Achievement Award (2018); Who's Who in the West; Who's Who of American Women **H:** Maintaining 15 Flower Gardens; Learning to Play the Violin **ADD:** 468 26th Ave, Greeley, CO, 80634

WISE, SHERWOOD WILLING JR., T: Professor of Geology **I:** Education/Educational Services **CN:** Florida State University **DOB:** 05/31/1941 **PB:** Jackson **SC:** MS/USA **PT:** Sherwood Willing Wise; Elizabeth (Powell) Wise **MS:** Married **SPN:** Cynthia Curtiss (8/21/1965) **CH:** Sarah Bliss; Sherwood Willing, III **ED:** PhD, University of Illinois (1970); MS, University of Illinois (1965); BS, Washington and Lee University (1963) **C:** Professor of Geology, Florida State University (1980-2016); Associate Professor, Florida State University (1975-1980); Assistant Professor, Florida State University (1971-1975); National Science Foundation

Postdoctoral Fellow, Eidgenossische Technische Hochschule Zurich (1970-1971) **CR:** Science Advisory Committee, United States (1991-1994); Information Handling Panel, Joint Oceanographic Institutes (1991-1994); Co-Chief Scientist, D/V Joides Resolution (1988); Southern Oceans Panel, Ocean Drilling Project (1987-1989); Scientist, Deep Sea Drilling Project, Glomar Challenger (1983); Chief Scientist, Ara Islas Orcadas (1978); Fellow, American Association for the Advancement of Science **CIV:** Chairman, School Board, Holy Comforter Episcopal School (1993-1995); Vice President, Parent-Teacher Organization, Sealey Elementary Math & Science Magnet School (1981-1982) **MIL:** Captain, U.S. Army (1965-1967) **CW:** Author, "Initial Reports of the Deep Sea Drilling Project" (1993); Author, "Initial Reports of the Deep Sea Drilling Project" (1983); Author, "Initial Reports of the Deep Sea Drilling Project" (1977) **AW:** Grantee, Petroleum Research Fund, American Chemical Society (1974-1981); Outstanding Paper Award, Gulf Coast Section, Society of Economic Paleontologists & Mineralogists (Now Society for Sedimentary Geology) (1971); Grantee, National Science Foundation **MEM:** President, Society of Economic Paleontologists & Mineralogists (Now Society for Sedimentary Geology) (1992-1995); President, North America Micropaleontology Section, Society of Economic Paleontologists & Mineralogists (Now Society for Sedimentary Geology) (1986-1987); Academie Suisse des Sciences Naturelles; Paleontology Society; Geological Society of America, Inc.; American Association of Petroleum Geologists **MH:** Albert Nelson Marquis Lifetime Achievement Award (2017) **RE:** Episcopalian **ADD:** 3318 Northshore Circle, Tallahassee, FL, 32312 **URL:** https://en.wikipedia.org/wiki/Sherwood_Wise

WISHENGRAD, MARCIA H., T: Lawyer **I:** Law and Legal Services **DOB:** 02/10/1936 **PB:** Hudson **SC:** NY/USA **PT:** Joseph Wishengrad; Jessie (Diamond) Wishengrad **MS:** Married **SPN:** Robert J. Metzger (9/3/1961) **CH:** Jocelyn M. **ED:** JD, Cornell University (1960); BA, Cornell University (1957) **C:** Deputy County Attorney, Monroe County (1974-1993); Senior Urban Renewal Attorney, Rochester, NY (1971-1974); Attorney, Monroe County, Legal Aid Society (1965-1967); Lawyer, Private Practice, Rochester, NY (1963-2013); Attorney, Monroe County Family Court (1963-1965) **CIV:** President, Board of Directors, Monroe County Chapter, ARC (1991-1993); President, Board of Visitors, State School Industry, Rochester, NY (1991-1998); Vice President, Arc Foundation of Monroe, Arc of Monroe County (1990-1999); Board of Directors, Monroe County Chapter, Association for Retarded Citizens (1983-2000); Board of Visitors, State School Industry, Rochester, NY (1983-1998) **AW:** Excellence in Law Award, The Daily Record (2012) **MEM:** Monroe County Bar Association; Judiciary Committee, Greater Rochester Association of Women Attorneys; Rochester/Monroe County Domestic Violence Consortium; World Affairs Council of Hilton Head; South Carolina Chapter, Women's National Republican Club, Inc.; Beaufort County Board of Disabilities and Special Needs **BAR:** U.S. Supreme Court (1964); U.S. District Court, Southern and Eastern Districts, State of New York (1962); State of New York (1960) **H:** Boating; Tennis; Reading **PA:** Republican **RE:** Jewish **ADD:** 44 Headlands Drive, Hilton Head, SC, 29926

WITHROW, JOHN R. JR., T: Statistical and Quantitative Ecologist **I:** Environmental Services **CN:** Cherokee Nation Businesses **DOB:** 08/28/1968 **PB:** Charlottesville **SC:** VA/USA **PT:** John R Withrow; Jo Ann McClure Withrow **MS:** Married **SPN:** Chrys K Withrow **CH:** Stuart Garver Remus

III; Bradley Justin Remus; Michael Gene Remus **ED:** PhD in Bio Agricultural and Pest Management, Colorado State University (2004); Master's Degree in Atmospheric Science, Colorado State University (1994); BA in Atmospheric Science, Carroll University (1990) **CT:** Secondary Education **C:** Statistical and Quantitative Ecologist, Cherokee Nation Technologies, Cherokee Nation Businesses (2013-Present) **CIV:** Member, Toastmasters International **AW:** Best Contest Speaker (2014); NRRC-A Green Team Honor Award **H:** Filmmaking; Saxophone playing; Climate activism **BA:** 2150 Centre Ave Bldg A, Ste 331, Cherokee Nation Technologies, Fort Collins, CO, 80526 **ADD:** 2518 Myrtle Court, Fort Collins, CO, 80521 **URL:** johnwithrow.com

WITTSTADT, THOMAS PETER, I: International Affairs/International Business **DOB:** 06/21/1905 **PB:** Muenster **SC:** Westphalia/Germany **PT:** Klaus Wittstadt; Brigitte (Effmert) Wittstadt **ED:** Coursework, University of Muenster (1987-1990) **C:** Vice President, German-North Korean Association (2002-Present); Partner, General Manager, Airgonomics GmbH (2000-2013); Partner, Pan Logon, Muenster (1993-2000) **CR:** Consultant, Pflueger International Consultant Berlin (2011-Present); Senior Partner, Skavica Project Initiative (2011-Present); Representative, Germany Robinco Mining (1998-Present); Initiator and Special Representative, Green Cross Germany (1997-Present); Partner, Resource Development International (1997-Present); CEO, Partner, Highlight GmbH, Muenster, Germany (1995-Present); Initiator Ecclesia Pro Albania (1993-Present); Partner, Kastrioti Co., Tirana, Albania (1993-Present); Initiator, Founding Member, Vice President, German Kosovar Economic Association (2009); Chairman, Supervisory Council, Foreign Trade Initiative of German Federal State, Northrine, Westphalia (2004); Founding Member, Global Business Factory (2003); General Manager, Hazy Investments GmbH (1998-2001); Managing Director, Universal Tolerance, Dusseldorf, Germany (1995-1996); Founding Member, Vice President, German-Albanian Economic Society (1995); Head, Task Force, Green African Bank, Johannesburg, South Afria (1995-2013); Teled International, Virginia Beach, VA (1994-1999); Media Forum, Munich, Germany (1994); Chief Advisor, International Hilfsfonds, Brussels, Belgium (1993-2000); Consultant, Chrome Industry, Government of Albania (1993); Various East European, African Governments **CW:** Writer, German TV; Australian TV; Contributor, Articles, Publications **H:** Travel; Reading **RE:** Roman Catholic

WOLF, SARA HEVIA, T: Art Librarian **I:** Library Management/Library Services **CN:** The Mint Museum **DOB:** 01/15/1936 **PB:** Havana **SC:** Cuba **PT:** Policarpo Hevia; Manuela (Ruiz) Hevia **MS:** Married **SPN:** Luis A. Wolf (9/23/1960) **CH:** Sara Caroline **ED:** BBA, Havana Business University (1956) **C:** Librarian, The Mint Museum, Charlotte, NC (1972-2007); Cataloguer, Central Piedmont Community College, Charlotte, NC (1970-1971); Librarian Assistant, North Carolina State University, Raleigh, NC (1963-1965) **CIV:** Steering Committee, Latin-American Week, Charlotte, NC (1993); Board of Directors, YMCA, Charlotte, NC (1985-1987); President, Catholic Hispanic Center, Charlotte, NC (1981-1982); Co-chair, All Nations Festival, Inc., Charlotte, NC (1977-1978); Chair, International Cultural Festival (1973-1976); Editor, Spanish Newsletter (1972-1975) **AW:** Art and Culture Award; Lifetime Achievement Award, Artsi; National Recognition, National Museum of Latin American Art; Latino Diamante Award for

Art and Culture; Eponym, Sara Wolf Scholarship Award **MEM:** President, Latin America Women's Association (1994-1996); George Wittenborn Memorial Book Awards Committee, Art Librarians Society of North America (1992); President, Southeast Chapter, Art Librarians Society of North America (1991); Vice President, Southeast Chapter, Art Librarians Society of North America (1990); Chair, Mary Ellen Lo Presti Publication Awards Committee, Art Librarians Society of North America (1989); Executive Board, Metrolina Librarian Association (1988); Chair, Nominating Committee, Southeast Chapter, Art Librarians Society of North America (1987); Art Librarians Society of North America; Latin America Coalition **MH:** Albert Nelson Marquis Lifetime Achievement Award (2017) **H:** Listening to music; Spending time with friends; Book clubs **ADD:** 9108 Four Acre Court, Charlotte, NC, 28210

WONNACOTT, RONALD PHD, T: Economics Professor **I:** Education/Educational Services **CN:** University of Western Ontario (Now Western University) **DOB:** 09/11/1930 **PB:** London **SC:** Canada **PT:** Gordon Wonnacott; Muriel (Johnston) Wonnacott **MS:** Married **SPN:** Eloise Howlett (9/11/1954) **CH:** Douglas; Robert; Cathy Anne **ED:** PhD, Harvard University (1959); AM, Harvard University (1957); BA, University of Western Ontario (Now Western University) (1955) **C:** Professor Emeritus, University of Western Ontario (Now Western University) (1996-Present); Department Chair, University of Western Ontario (Now Western University) (1969-1972); Professor of Economics, University of Western Ontario (Now Western University) (1964-1996); Member of Faculty, University of Western Ontario (Now Western University) (1958-1996) **CR:** Visiting Associate Professor, University of Minnesota (1961-1962); Consultant, Resources for the Future, Economic Council of Canada, Canada-America Committee, C.D. Howe Institute **CW:** Co-Author, "Trade Liberalization and the Canadian Furniture Industry," Heritage (2014); Co-Author, "The Nafta: Whats In, Whats Out, Whats Next" (1994); Author, "The Economics of Overlapping Free Trade Areas and the Mexican Challenge" (1991); Co-Author, "Economics Fourth Edition" (1990); Co-Author, "Introductory Statistics, Fifth Edition" (1990); Author, "Selected New Developments in International Trade Theory" (1984); Author, "Regression" (1981); Author, "Economics" (1979); Author, "Econometrics," Second Edition (1979); Author, "Canada's Trade Options" (1975); Author, "Econometrics" (1970); Co-Author, "Introductory Statistics" (1969); Co-Author, "Free Trade Between the U.S. and Canada" (1967); Author, "Canadian-American Dependence: An Interindustry Analysis of Production and Prices" (1961); Author, "The Cost of Capital in Canada" (1961); Author, "Canada's Great Free Trade Debate A Memoir" **AW:** Honoree, Officer, Order of Canada (2016) **MEM:** President, Canadian Economic Association (1981); Fellow, Royal Society of Canada; American Economic Association; London Hunt and Country Club; The Honourable Company of Edinburgh Golfers **MH:** Albert Nelson Marquis Lifetime Achievement Award (2017) **BA:** 1486 Richmond St Ste 510, University of Western Ontario, London, ON, Canada, N6G 2M3 **ADD:** 1486 Richmond St Ste 510, London, ON, Canada, N6G 2M3

WOOLSON, GLORIA MANUEL, T: Education Educator **I:** Education/Educational Services **CN:** Onondaga Community College **DOB:** 11/07/1941 **PB:** Syracuse **SC:** NY/USA **PT:** Glen James Manuel; Mattie Florence Turner **ED:** MA in Curriculum Development, State University of New York, Oswego (1985) BA, State University of New York, Oswego

(1965) **C:** Adjunct Teacher, English Course, Cayuga Community College, New York (2017); Tutor, Onondaga Community College, New York (2015); Adjunct Teacher, Onondaga Community College, New York (2007-2014); Adjunct Teacher, Cayuga Community College, Auburn, NY (2004-2014); Third-Grade Teacher, Jordan-Elbridge Central School District, Jordan, NY (1970-2002); Sixth-Grade Teacher, Jordan-Elbridge Central School District, Jordan, NY (1966-1970); Fifth-Grade Teacher, Auburn Enlarged City School District, New York (1965-1966) **CIV:** Director, One-room School Program, Spafford Area Historical Society; Deacon, Plainville United Church of Christ, New York; Choir Member, Plainville United Church of Christ, New York; Clerk Trustee, Plainville United Church of Christ, New York; Moderator, Plainville United Church of Christ, New York **AW:** Special Service Award, Onondaga County Teachers Association (1997); Excellence in Teaching Award, School of Education, Syracuse University (1996) **MEM:** NYSTRS; Secretary, Jordan-Elbridge Education Association; Building Representative, Jordan-Elbridge Education Association; Social Director, Jordan-Elbridge Education Association **MH:** Albert Nelson Marquis Lifetime Achievement Award (2017) **H:** Antiques; Exercise; Reading; Travel **ADD:** 7688 Tater Road, Memphis, NY, 13112

WRIGGINS RICHMOND, AIMEE MADELINE, T: Doctor **I:** Medicine & Health Care **CN:** Aimee M. Richmond, MD **DOB:** 02/22/1923 **PB:** Newark **SC:** NJ/USA **PT:** John Trevithick Wriggins; Madeline Esther (Ellerman) Wriggins **MS:** Divorced **CH:** L. Daniel Richmond; Julia Marie (Doerfler) Richmond; Eileen Claire Richmond **ED:** MA in Theology, Christian Life School of Theology (Now Beacon Institute of Ministry) (2003); Associate Degree in Theology (1992); Resident in General Surgery, University Hospital, Columbus, Ohio (1951); Resident in General Practice and Pathology, Grant Hospital, Columbus, Ohio (1950-1951); Rotating Intern, Easton Hospital, PA (1948-1949); MD, Woman's Medical College of Pennsylvania (Now Drexel University, College of Medicine) (1948); Postgraduate Coursework, Fordham University (1944); BS in Dietetics, Maryville College (1944) **CT:** Diplomate, American Board of Family Practice, American Board of Family Medicine, Inc. (1972-2006); Licensed to Practice Medicine, State of Ohio; Licensed to Practice Medicine, State of Indiana; Licensed to Practice Medicine, State of California; Licensed to Practice Medicine, State of Texas; Licensed to Practice Medicine, State of Florida; Licensed to Practice Medicine, State of Arizona **C:** Family Practice (1963-2003); Medical Doctor, Oak Hill, Ohio (1962-1963); Medical Doctor, The Ohio State University Student Health (1961-1962) **CR:** Medical Director, House of Hope for Alcoholics (1961) **CIV:** Medical Missionary to Nicaragua, Caring Partners International, Inc. (2005) **CW:** Author, "Dieting and Nutrition" (1997); Featured Guest, Praise the Lord Live TV Programs, TBN-TV, Richmond, IN (1997); Featured Guest, Praise the Lord Live TV Programs, TBN-TV, Richmond, IN (1992); Author, "Review and Questions and Answer, AIDS Not Bleeding the Number One Killer of Hemophiliac Men," Victory Press Publications (1992); Featured Guest, "An Ounce of Prevention" (1985-1989); Featured Guest, Praise the Lord Live TV Programs, TBN-TV, Richmond, IN (1985); Author, "Simply Nutrition"; Alto Singer, PROMISES; Performer, Recorder, PROMISES **AW:** Outstanding Achievement in Amateur Photography, The International Society of Photographers (2004); Honoree, America's Registry of Outstanding Professionals (2002); Honoree, Two Thousand Notable American Women, Fifth Illustrated Edition, American Biographical Institute (1992);

American Medical Association; Featured Listee, Personalities of the West and Midwest; Featured Listee, Dictionary of Medical Specialists; Featured Listee, Dictionary of International Biography **MEM:** The International Platform Association (1979); Charter Fellow, American Academy of Family Physicians (1973); American Medical Society on Alcoholism (1970); Delegate, National Meeting, Easterseals (1970); Delegate, National Council on Alcoholism and Drug Dependence, Inc. (1969-1971); Butler County, Easterseals (1969); National Council on Alcoholism and Drug Dependence, Inc. (1968-1973); Legislative Action Committee, Middletown Chamber of Commerce (1966-1974); Soroptimist International of the Americas (1964); American Medical Association; Ohio State Medical Association; Butler County Medical Society; American Association of Family Practice; Christian Medical Society (Now Christian Medical & Dental Associations); Hamilton Civil War Round Table; American Professional Practice Association **MH:** Albert Nelson Marquis Lifetime Achievement Award (2017) **H:** Travel; Photography; Swimming; Writing; Movies; Scrabble; Art **PA:** Repubican **RE:** Christian **ADD:** 4122 Dove Ct, Lebanon, OH, 45036

WRIGHT, DAVID L., T: Adjunct Faculty **I:** Education/Educational Services **DOB:** 03/12/1949 **PB:** Wenatchee **SC:** WA/USA **PT:** Franklin Sven Wright; Mary Elizabeth (Collins) Wright **MS:** Married **SPN:** Karen Sue Rice (3/28/1981) **CH:** Kara; Erin; Jonathan; Anna Catherine **ED:** PhD, Columbia University (2013); MPhil, Columbia University (2011); MA, Columbia University (2008); BA, University of California, Davis (1971) **CT:** Certification, Institutional Review Board Social and Behavioral Research (2012) **C:** Retired (2015); Adjunct Faculty, Columbia University (2010-2015); Vice President of Worldwide Government and Political Affairs, PepsiCo Inc., Purchase, NY (1987-2005); Director of Government Affairs, PepsiCo Inc., Purchase, NY (1984-1987); Special Assistant to the President for Legislative Affairs, The White House, Washington, D.C. (1981-1984); Administrative Assistant and Chief of Staff, Representative William C. Wampler, Washington, D.C. (1977-1981); Professional Staff Member, Committee on Agriculture, U.S. House of Representatives, Washington, D.C. (1975-1977); Chief of Research, Department of Benefit Payments, State of California, Sacramento (1972-1975) **CR:** Kearns Fellowship, Columbia University (2010); Weinberg Fellowship, Columbia University (2009); Board of Directors, Green Mountain Valley School (2007-2012); Vice Chair, Harvard Center on Media and Child Health (2004-2006); Board of Directors, United States Chamber of Commerce (2003-2005); Executive Committee, United States Council for International Business (1997-2005); Co-Founder, European Modern Restaurant Association; Founding Member, International Chamber of Commerce Commission on Corporate Responsibility **CIV:** Bush for President Campaign (1992); Bush for President Campaign (1988); Reagan for President Campaign (1984); Reagan for President Campaign (1980); Coordinator, Wampler for Congress Campaign, VA (1980); Coordinator, Wampler for Congress Campaign, VA (1978) **MIL:** U.S. Army Reserve (1971-1979); Captain, Armor Branch, U.S. Army **CW:** Author, "The Twenty-Sixth Amendment as a Teachable Moment: Young Adult Voter Turnout in US Elections, 1972-2006" (2013); Co-author, "Accuracy and Inaccuracy in Teachers' Perceptions of Young Children's Cognitive Abilities: The Role of Child Background and Classroom Context" (2011) **MH:** Albert Nelson Marquis Lifetime Achievement Award (2017) **ADD:** 2583 Five Points Road, Marshall, VA, 20115

WRIGHT, FRANCES JANE, **T:** Educational Psychologist **I:** Medicine & Health Care **DOB:** 12/22/1943 **PB:** Los Angeles **SC:** CA/USA **PT:** John David Brinegar (Stepfather); Evelyn Jane (Dale) Brinegar **ED:** Postdoctoral Coursework, Utah State University (1985-1986); EdD, Brigham Young University (1980); Postgraduate Coursework, University of Utah (1972-1973); Postgraduate Coursework, University of Nevada (1970); MA, Brigham Young University (1968); BA, Long Beach State University (1965) **CT:** Certified Secondary Teacher, State of Utah; Certified Administrator, State of Utah; License in Juvenile Justice **C:** Chief Educational Diagnostician, Center for the Evaluation of Learning and Development, Layton, UT (1989-1990); Resource Teacher, Junior High, Davis County Schools, Farmington, UT (1978-1990); Instructor, Brigham Young University, Salt Lake City, UT (1976-1983); Resource Elementary Teacher, Davis County Schools, Farmington, UT (1974-1978); Educational Consultant, Murray, UT (1973-1990); Diagnostician, Davis County Schools, Farmington, UT (1973-1974); Teacher of the Severely Handicapped, Davis County Schools, Farmington, UT (1971-1973); Vocational Counselor, Manpower, Salt Lake City, UT (1970-1971); State Specialist, Intellectually Handicapped, State Office of Education, Salt Lake City, UT (1969-1970); Teacher of the Mentally Handicapped, Santa Ana Unified Schools, California (1968-1969); Vocational Project Designer, Utah State Training School, American Fork, UT (1968); Self-Care Inservice Director, Utah State Training School, American Fork, UT (1968); Caseworker, Los Angeles County (1966-1967); Assistant Director, Teenpost Project, San Pedro, CA (1966) **CR:** Program Manager, Liberty Care Services Mental Health Clinic (2006-Present); Clinician, Adult Behavior Health, Department of Health and Welfare, Liberty Care Services (2006-Present); Clinician, Region 5 Behavioral Health (2006); District 5 Juvenile Justice Council (1997-Present); Member, Juvenile Justice Council (1996-Present); Program Director, Liberty Care Services (2002-2006); Clinical Program Manager, Liberty Care Services (2002-2006); Consultant, Address Issues with Youth and Families (2001-2006); Counselor, Address Issues with Youth and Families (2001-2006); Chairman, District 5 Juvenile Justice Council (1999-2001); Member, Idaho Juvenile Justice Commission (1999-2001); Advisory Board, Southern Central Learning Center (1999-2001); Parent Project Facilitator, District 5 (1998-2000); Acting Chairman, District 5 Juvenile Justice Council (1998-1999); Consultant, Northstar Family Preservation (1997-2001); Trainer, Detour Prison Prevention Program for Adolescents (1997-2000); Member, Oversight Board, Evaluator Status Offender Progressive (1997-2000); Consultant, Juvenile Correctional, District 5 (1996-2000); Member, Community Accountability Board, McNeil Association (1996-2000); Clinical Consultant, Magic Hot Springs Youth Camp (1996-1997); Co-Ranch Treatment Director, Idaho Youth Ranch (1995); Placement Officer, Idaho Youth Ranch (1995); Supervisor, Family Preservation Service/Aftercare Teams, Idaho Youth Ranch (1993-1995); Clinical Director, Intake Program, Idaho Youth Ranch (1992-1994); Clinical Director, Assessment and Observation Program, Idaho Youth Ranch (1990-1995); Lecturer in field; Private Consultant; Private Counselor **AW:** Named, Professional of the Year, Idaho Youth Ranch Treatment Centers (1993); Named, Professional of the Year, Idaho Youth Ranch Treatment Centers (1992); Named, Professional of the Year, Utah Association for Children with Learning Disabilities (1985) **MEM:** Coordinator, Leadership Development Activity Organization, Idaho (1991-2000); National Board of Directors, Association for Children and Adults with Learning Disabilities (1988-1991); Delegate, Association for Children and Adults with Learning Disabilities (1987); Professional Advisory Board, Utah Association for Children and Adults with Learning Disabilities (1985-1990); National Nominating Committee, Association for Children and Adults with Learning Disabilities (1985-1986); Delegate, Association for Children and Adults with Learning Disabilities (1979-1985); Executive Board, Utah Association for Children and Adults with Learning Disabilities (1978-1984); American Counseling Association; Idaho Mental Health Counselors Association; Council for Learning Disabilities; Regional Adviser, Association for Supervision and Curriculum Development; National Wildlife Foundation; World Wildlife Federation; Best Friends Animal Sanctuary; Job's Daughters **H:** Genealogy; Horseback riding; Sketching; Crafts; Reading **PA:** Democrat **RE:** The Church of Jesus Christ of Latter-day Saints **ADD:** 1358 W Forest Hill Dr, Saint George, UT, 84790

WU, HENVAI, **T:** Chief Executive Officer **I:** Business Management/Business Services **CN:** Somerset Hematology and Oncology Associates **ED:** MD, College of Medicine, National Taiwan University (1972) **AW:** Recipient, Lane Adam National Award, American Cancer Society Eastern Division (2006) **MEM:** Fellow, American College of Physicians **BA:** 30 Rehill Rd, Somerset Hematology/Oncology Assoc, Somerville, NJ, 08876 **ADD:** 2564 Beechwood Village Ct, Henderson, NV, 89052

WUBBENA, JAN HELMUT, **T:** Professor of Music (Retired) **I:** Education/Educational Services **CN:** John Brown University **DOB:** 07/11/1947 **PB:** Dover **SC:** DE/USA **PT:** Wyatt Jan Wubbena; Erika Luise Wubbena **MS:** Married **SPN:** Teresa Ch **CH:** Robert; Mary **ED:** Doctorate of Musical Arts, University of Colorado, Boulder (1975); MusM, University of Colorado, Boulder (1970); BA, Lebanon Valley College, Annville, PA (1969) **CT:** Fellow, American Guild of Organists **C:** Retired (2017); Professor, Music, John Brown University, Siloam Springs, AR (1977-2017); Assistant Professor, Music, Ferrum College, Virginia (1975-1977) **CR:** Organist, Choirmaster, Grace Episcopal Church, Siloam Springs, AR (1977-Present) **CW:** Choral Music **MEM:** District Convenor, Arkansas, American Guild of Organists (2006-2010); Chair, National Committee on Educational Resources, American Guild of Organists (1988-1990); Coordinator, Education in Region VII, American Guild of Organists (1984-1988); Chapter Dean, American Guild of Organists (1982-1984); Association of Anglican Musicians **RE:** Episcopalian **ADD:** 410 E Jefferson St, Siloam Springs, AR, 72761

WYLIE PRYOR, KAREN, **T:** Founder, Author **I:** Writing and Editing **CN:** KPCT **PT:** Philip Gordon Wylie; Sally Ondeck Wylie **MS:** Married **SPN:** Jon M. Lindbergh (5/14/1983); Taylor A. Pryor (6/25/1954, Divorced 1973) **CH:** Tedmund; Michael; Gale **ED:** Postgraduate Coursework, New York University (1977-1979); Coursework, University of Hawaii (1957-1959); Coursework, Rutgers, The State University of New Jersey (1950-1954); BA in English, Cornell University **C:** Marine Mammal Consultant (1970-Present); Freelance Writer (1963-Present); Copywriter, Fawcett-McDermott, Honolulu, HI (1973-1976); Drama Critic, Honolulu Advertiser (1971-1975); Founder, Curator, Sea Life Park Oceanarium, Honolulu, HI (1960-1971) **CR:** President, Sunshine Books, Inc. (1992-Present); Consultant, National Science Foundation, National Aeronautics and Space Administration, National Geographic Society (1976-Present); Public and Video Producer, Guest Faculty, The Ohio State University (1999); Public and Video Producer, Guest Faculty, The University of Kansas (1999); Public and Video Producer, Guest Faculty, Brown University (1996); Commissioner, Marine Mammal Commission, Washington, D.C. (1984-1987); Scientific Adviser, United States Tuna Foundation, Washington, D.C. (1976-1982) **CW:** Author, "Don't Shoot the Dog! The New Art of Teaching and Training, Review Edition" (1999); Editor, "Karen Pryor on Behavior" (1995); Co-author, With K.S. Norris, "Dolphin Societies: Discoveries and Puzzles" (1991); Co-editor, With Gale Pryor, "Crunch and Des: Classic Stories of Salt Water Fishing" (1991); Editor, "Nursing Your Baby" (1991); Author, "How to Teach Your Dog to Play Frisbee" (1985); Author, "Don't Shoot the Dog! The New Art of Teaching and Training" (1984); Author, Lads Before the Wind: Adventures in Porpoise Training" (1975); Author, "Nursing Your Baby, Review Edition" (1973); Author, "Nursing Your Baby" (1963); Contributor, Articles, Professional Journals **AW:** Award for Contributions to Science, University of North Texas Organization for Reinforcement Contingencies with Animals Association (2016); Excellence in Media Award, American Psychological Association (1984) **MEM:** International Marine Animal Trainers Association; Association for Behavior Analysis; Animal Behavior Society; Association of Zoos and Aquariums; Authors Guild; Charter Member, Marine Mammal Society; Society of Women Geographers; Cosmopolitan Club **MH:** Albert Nelson Marquis Lifetime Achievement Award (2017) **H:** Gardening; Bird watching **ADD:** 17 Commonwealth Rd, Watertown, MA, 02472

WYNNE, TERRY LYNNE, **I:** Professional Training & Coaching **DOB:** 03/28/1951 **PT:** Herbert Ray Wynne; Carolyne (Taylor) Wynne **ED:** EdS, Georgia State University (1977); MEd, Georgia State University, (1974); BA, Georgia State University (1972) **CT:** Licensed Professional Counselor, Georgia; National Certified Counselor; National Certified Career Counselor; Board Certified Coach; Master Career Counselor; Master Career Development Professional; Qualified to Administer Myers-Briggs Type Indicator; Certified Laughter Yoga Leader **C:** Career Coach (2013-Present); Freelance Writer (1980-Present); Owner, Sole Proprietor, Professional Edge, Tucker, Georgia (1990-Present); Trainer, Speaker, Writer, Atlanta (1980-Present); Career Counselor, Emory University, Atlanta (1997-2004); Career Counselor, Training Consultant Grad. School, USA, Atlanta (1996-2002); Career Counselor, Charter Behavioral Health Systems, Atlanta (1995-2000); Career Counselor, Emory University, Atlanta (1987-1996); Product Information Specialist, Unisys Corp., Atlanta (1984-1987); Various, Suntrust Bank (1977-1984); Instructor, Omni International Ice Skating (1980-1982); Assistant, Ernest L. Robinson, Phd, Atlanta (1976-1977) Various, Suntrust Bank, Atlanta (1971-1975); Radio Talk Show Host and Guest, Speaker, Trainer, National and State Conventions and on Cruise Ships **CIV:** Model for Fund Raising events (2005-2006) **CW:** Exhibitions include Ballroom Dance Competitor (Amateur and Pro-Am); Contributor, Articles, Professional Publications **AW:** Appreciation Award, US Department of Education Region IV, (1999); Third Place, Maupintour Travel Photography Contest (1991); Two Exemplary Action Awards, Unisys Corp. (1985); Sullivan Award Furman University (1969); Civil Rights Southern Division; Educational Opportunity Grantee, Furman University (1968) **MEM:** American Counseling Association; MENSA; National Career Development Association; Licensed Professional Counselors, Georgia Association; Georgia Career Development Association **ACH:** null **H:** Ballroom dance; Writing; Travel; Photography

XIANG, NING, T: Professor **I:** Education/Educational Services **CN:** Rensselaer Polytechnic Institute **PB:** Tianjin **SC:** China **PT:** Yang Xiang; Chongjie (Zhao) Xiang **MS:** Married **SPN:** Hong Zhou (6/12/1988) **ED:** DEng, Ruhr-Universitat Bochum, Germany (1990); Bachelor's Degree in Engineering, Tianjin University (1982) **C:** Professor, Rensselaer Polytechnic Institute, Troy, NY (2003-Present); Project Manager, Researcher, HEAD Acoustics GmbH, Herzogenrath, Germany (1991-Present); Research Assistant, Department of Electronic Engineering, Ruhr-Universitat Bochum, Germany (1984-1990); Technician, Fourth Telecommunication Factory, Tianjin, China (1974-1978) **CW:** Author, "A Mobile Universal Measuring System for the Binaural Room-Acoustic Modelling-Technique" (1991); Contributor, Articles, Professional Publications **AW:** Wallace Clement Sabine Award, Acoustical Society of America (2014) **MEM:** Acoustical Society of America **MH:** Albert Nelson Marquis Lifetime Achievement Award (2017) **BA:** 110 8th Street, Rensselaer Polytechnic Institute, Troy, NY, 12180 **URL:** https://www.researchgate.net/profile/Ning_Xiang

XUE, XIAOBO, T: Assistant Professor **I:** Education/Educational Services **CN:** University at Albany, SUNY **ED:** PhD in Environmental Engineering, University of Pittsburgh (2011); MS in Civil Engineering, Beijing Jiaotong University (2007); BS in Civil Engineering, Beijing Jiaotong University (2004) **CT:** FE in Environmental Engineering (2009); Forthcoming PE in Environmental Engineering **C:** Assistant Professor, Tenure Tack, Department of Environmental Health Sciences, School of Public Health, University at Albany, SUNY (2015-Present); ORISE Research Fellow, National Risk Management Research Laboratory, United States Environmental Protection Agency, Cincinnati, OH (2012-2015); Graduate Research Assistant, Department of Civil and Environmental Engineering, University of Pittsburgh, Pittsburgh, PA (2008-2011); Graduate Research Assistant, State Key Laboratory of Environmental Aquatic Chemistry, China Academy of Sciences, Beijing, China (2005-2007) **CIV:** Judge, High School Science Fairs, Pittsburgh, PA (2008-2016); Judge, High School Science Fairs, Cincinnati, OH (2008-2016); Judge, High School Science Fairs, Albany, NY (2008-2016); Judge, Middle School Science Fairs, Pittsburgh, PA (2008-2016); Judge, Middle School Science Fairs, Cincinnati, OH (2008-2016); Judge, Middle School Science Fairs, Albany, NY (2008-2016); Interpreter National Development and Reform Commission, China (2011-2014); Session Chairman, Academic Conferences; Organizing Committee Member, Academic Conferences; Grant Reviewer, Funding Programs. United States Environmental Protection Agency; Grant Reviewer, Funding Programs, Department of Energy **CW:** Co-Author, "Cost, Energy, Global Warming, Eutrophication and Local Human Health Impacts of Community Water and Sanitation Service Options," Water Research (2017); Co-Author, "Comparison of Production-phase Life Cycle Environmental Impacts Derived at the Farm and National Scale for United States Agricultural Commodities," Environmental Research Letters (2016); Co-Author, "Life Cycle Energy Consumption and Carbon Footprints of Water Systems," Water (2016); Co-Author, "Evaluating Ecotoxicity and Human Health Impacts of Pesticide Use in Midwest Corn Farming," International Journal of Life Cycle Assessment (2015); Co-Author, "Critical Insights for a Sustainability Framework to Address Community Water Services: Technical metrics and Approaches," Water Research (2015); Co-Author, "Sustainable Water Systems for City of Tomorrow," Sustainability (2015); Co-Author, "Comparing Life Cycle Environmental and Economic Impacts of Green and Gray Infrastructure: a Case Study of Rain Gardens in Cincinnati," Journal of the American Water Resources Association (2015); Co-Author, "Technologic Resilience Assessment of Coastal Community Water and Wastewater Service Options," Sustainability of Water Quality and Ecology (2015); Co-Author, "Life Cycle Economic and Nitrogen Flow Analysis of Alternative Wastewater Systems," Journal of Environmental Management (2015); Co-Author, "Comparative Human Health Risk Analysis of Coastal Community Water and Wastewater Service Options," Environmental Science & Technology (2014); Co-Author, "Evaluating Agricultural Management Practices to Improve the Environmental Footprints of Corn-derived Bioproducts," Renewable Energy (2014); Co-Author, "Environmental and Cost Life Cycle Assessment of Disinfection Options for Municipal Water Treatment" (2014); Co-Author, "Environmental and Cost Life Cycle Assessment of Disinfection Options for Municipal Wastewater Treatment" (2014); Co-Author, "Evaluation of Spatial Variability of Nitrogen and Phosphorus in Sewage-irrigated Soil in Tongliao, China," Transactions of Tianjin University (2013); Co-Author, "Regional Life Cycle Assessment of Soybean Derived Biodiesel for Transportation Fleet," Energy Policy (2012); Co-Author, "EPA Internal Progress Report on Environmental Assessment of Biofuel Options: Reference Supply Chains for Corn Ethanol and Gasoline and Preliminary Results for the Design of Sustainable Supply Chains" (2011); Co-Author, "Eutrophication Potential of Food Consumption Patterns," Environmental Science & Technology (2010); Co-Author, "A Comparative Analysis of Performance and Cost Metrics Associated with a Diesel to Biodiesel Fleet Transition," Energy Policy (2010); Contributor, "Biodiesel Feasibility Study," Department of Transportation, University of Pittsburgh, Pittsburgh, PA (2010); Co-Author, "Adsorption of a Nonionic Surfactant on Soils: Model Study," Adsorption Science and Technology (2006); Co-Author, "Experimental Study of Submerged Hollow Fiber Ultrafiltration Membrane on Reclaim of Sludge Water," Journal of Beijing Jiaotong University (2006); Contributor, Book Chapter, "Wastewater Treatment Design, Handbook for Certificated Environmental Engineer: Water and Wastewater Treatment," China Electricity Publish Press (2005); Co-Author, "Comparative life cycle assessments of crop production systems with wastewater and groundwater irrigation in China," Resources Conservation & Recycling; Co-Author, Life Cycle Environmental and Economic Assessment of the Water and Wastewater Systems in Cincinnati," Water Research; Co-Author, "Energy Assessment of the Water and Wastewater Systems in Cincinnati," Water Research; Co-Author, "Spatially Explicit Life Cycle Assessment of First Generation Biofuel Feedstock Production," Environmental Science & Technology; Co-Author, "The Influences of Allocation Mechanisms on Life Cycle Environmental Impacts of Agricultural Products," Agricultural Systems; Co-Author, "Life Cycle Energy, Greenhouse Gases and Costs of Aerobic and Anaerobic Membrane Bioreactor Systems: Influence of Scale, Population Density, Climate and Methane Recovery," Environmental Science & Technology; Invited Speaker, Numerous Conferences and Events; Reviewer, Submissions, Professional Journals **AW:** Grantee, NIH (2017-2019); Grantee, University at Albany, SUNY (2015-2018); Grantee, United States Environmental Protection Agency (2014-2018); Presidential Innovation Award, University at Albany, SUNY (2017); Grantee, Water Innovation Cluster (2013-2014); Grantee, Oak Ridge Institute of Science and Education, U.S. Department of Energy (2012-2014); Grantee, Industrial Ecology of Gordon Research Group, International Symposium on Sustainable Systems and Technology (2008-2014); Research Scholarship, University of Pittsburgh, Pittsburgh, PA (2008-2011); Grantee, Mascaro Center of Sustainability Innovation, University of Pittsburgh, Pittsburgh, PA (2009); Named Outstanding Graduate, Beijing Jiaotong University, Beijing, China (2006-2007) **MEM:** Industrial Society for Industrial Ecology; American Society of Civil Engineers; American Water Works Associations; Association of Environmental Engineering & Science Professors **BA:** 1 University Place, George Education Center Rm 155, University at Albany, SUNY, Rensselaer, NY, 12144 **URL:** https://sites.google.com/site/xiaoboxuealbany/

YAMADA, RYUJI, T: Scientist Emeritus, High Energy Physicist (Retired) **I:** Sciences **CN:** Fermilab **DOB:** 01/03/1932 **PB:** Hiroshima **SC:** Japan **PT:** Fukumatsu Yamada; Ayako (Imanaka) Yamada **MS:** Married **SPN:** Nanako (Narita) Yamada (12/4/1960) **CH:** Seiji; Kouji **ED:** Postdoctoral Researcher, Cornell University, Ithaca, NY (1965-1966); Postdoctoral Researcher, Brookhaven National Laboratory, Upton, NY (1963-1965); PhD in Physics, The University of Tokyo (1963); MS, The University of Tokyo (1956); BS in Physics, Hiroshima University (1954) **C:** Scientist Emeritus, Fermilab (2012-Present); Physicist, Fermi National Accelerator Laboratory, Batavia, IL (1968-2012); Tenured Research Associate, Institute for Nuclear Study, The University of Tokyo (1956-1968) **CR:** Consultant, KEK, Tsukuba, Japan (1982); Consultant, NAL, Oak Brook, IL (1967) **CW:** Original Determination of Top Quark Mass (1995); Unique Contributions for Successful Operation of 200 BeV Main Ring Accelerator Through Cryses (1972); Contributor, Accelerators; Magnets, Superconducting Accelerator Magnets, 3D Quench Calculation, Nb3Al Analysis; Contributor, Numerous Articles, Professional Journals **AW:** Superconductivity Technology Prize for Nb3A1 Work, Japanese Superconductivity Study Society (2010) **MEM:** American Physical Society **MH:** Albert Nelson Marquis Lifetime Achievement Award (2017) **H:** Photography; Personal Computers **ADD:** 1189 Waimanu St Apt 3705, Honolulu, HI, 96814 **URL:** http://www.ryujiyamada.com

YAMAMOTO, JANET K., T: Science Educator **I:** Education/Educational Services **CN:** University of Florida **PB:** Tokyo **SC:** Japan **PT:** Shunta Yamamoto; Chizuko Catherine Yamamoto **ED:** PhD, The University of Texas Medical Branch at Galveston (1981); BA, University of California, Davis (1976) **C:** Professor, College of Veterinary Medicine, University of Florida (2001-Present); Associate Professor, College of Veterinary Medicine, University of Florida (1993-2001); Adjunct Associate Professor, School of Veterinary Medicine, University of California, Davis (1991-1993); Assistant Research Immunologist, School of Veterinary Medicine, University of California, Davis (1985-1991); Researcher, University of California, Davis (1983-1985); Research Associate Scientist, Oklahoma Medical Research Foundation (1982-1983) **CR:** Consultant, Idexx Laboratories Westbrook, Maine (2010-2012); Consultant, Fort Dodge Animal Health, Iowa (2000-2002); Consultant, Clinical Division, BioRad, Hercules, California (1988-1989) **CIV:** Member, International House of Japan (2017-Present); Board of Directors, Afghanistan Projects, Creating Hope International, Michigan (1996-Present) **CW:** Developer, 17 United States Patents; Developer, 13 International Patents; Contributor, 88 Articles, Professional Publications **AW:** Honoree, Fellow, National Academy of Inventors (2015); Honoree, Florida

Inventors Hall of Fame (2015); Recipient, Pfizer Animal Health Award, University of Florida (1996, 2005); Honoree, Fellow, UC San Diego (1981-1982); Honoree, Fellow, The University of Texas Medical Branch at Galveston (1979-1981) **MEM:** Clinical Immunology Society; International AIDS Society; The American Association of Immunologists, Inc.; American Society for Microbiology; The New York Academy of Sciences; American Association for the Advancement of Science; Phi Zeta Upsilon **MH:** Albert Nelson Marquis Lifetime Achievement Award (2017) **H:** Music **PA:** Democrat **ADD:** 4309 SW 77th St, Gainesville, FL, 32608

YANG, LI-XIA, **T:** Biomedical Researcher **I:** Research **PT:** Chun Yang; Guizhen Yang **MS:** Married **SPN:** Lizhi Gu (8/4/1986) **CH:** Chunyang Gu **ED:** Intramural Research Fellow, Molecular Cellular Pathology, Molecular Imaging Lab Clinical Center National Institutes of Health (2002-2003); Postdoctoral Research Fellow, Molecular Cellular Development Neurobiology, National Institute of Child Health and Human Development, National Institutes of Health (1999-2002); Postdoctoral Researcher, Molecular Neurobiology, Institute for Physical Chemical Research (1996-1999); PhD in Biochemistry and Molecular Biology/ Genetics, Kochi Medical School (1996); MS in Pathophysiology, School of Medicine, Jiamusi University (1987); MD, School of Medicine, Jiamusi University, With Honors (1982) **C:** Senior Biological Scientist, University of Florida (2012-Present); Staff Scientist, The Foundation For Applied Molecular Evolution (2011-Present); Principal Scientist, Center for Innovative Research, Banyan Biomarkers, Inc. (2008-Present); Faculty Research Associate, Functional Genomics, University of Pittsburgh (2003-Present); Research Scientist, Hearing Research, Hough Ear Institute (2006-2008); Assistant Professor, Hough Ear Institute (2006-2008); Associate Professor, Medicine, School of Medicine, Jiamusi University (1994-1996); Principal Investigator, School of Medicine, Jiamusi University (1987-1994); Lecturer, Pathology, School of Medicine, Jiamusi University (1987-1994); Assistant Professor, Pathology, School of Medicine, Jiamusi University (1982-1986) **CR:** Science Judge, National Institutes of Health (2002) **CW:** Contributor, Articles, Professional Journals **AW:** Research Grant, Ministry of Education, Culture, Sports, Science and Technology, Japan (1990-1992) **MEM:** American Association for the Advancement of Science; International Society for Advancement of Cytometry; National Neurotrauma Society; Association for Research in Otolaryngology; Society for Neuroscience; Chinese Medical Association **MH:** Albert Nelson Marquis Lifetime Achievement Award (2017) **H:** Music; Art; Swimming; Dance; Yoga **ADD:** 813 Turkey Creek, Alachua, FL, 32615

YATES, CARL EUGENE, **I:** Law and Legal Services **DOB:** 11/11/1940 **PB:** Long Lane **SC:** MO/USA **PT:** Roma Earnest Yates; Mary Artimissi (Wing) Yates **MS:** Married **SPN:** Joy Lauranna Evertz (7/16/1965) **CH:** Steven B.; Julie C.; Nicole M. **ED:** JD, Washington University in St. Louis (1965); BA, Southwest Missouri State University (Now Missouri State University) (1962) **C:** Partner, Yates, Mauck, Bohrer, Elliff & Croessmann, Professional Corporation (Now Yates, Mauck, Bohrer, Elliff & Fels, P.C.) and Predecessor Firms, Springfield, MO (1971-Present); Partner, Lincoln, Forehand & Yates, Springfield, MO (1969-1971); Associate, Lincoln, Haseltine, Keet, Forehand & Springer, Springfield, MO (1965-1969) **CIV:** Vice Chairman, Missouri Highways and Transportation Commission, Missouri Department of Transportation, Jefferson City, MO (1984); Co-chairman, Governor's

Economic Development Advisory Committee, Springfield, MO (1979-1980); Chairman, Springfield Regional Airport Board (1979); Treasurer Missouri State Democratic Committee, Jefferson City, MO (1977-1979); Director Emeritus, Greater Ozarks Zoological Society **MIL:** Served, United States Army National Guard (1960-1966) **CW:** Author, "Lender Liability and How it Affects the Choice of Alternatives in the Workout" (1988); Author, "Regulation 2: A Dilemma for the Attorneys" (1967) **MEM:** President, Springfield Chamber of Commerce (1982); Treasurer, Greene County Bar Association (1968-1969); ABA; The Missouri Bar; National Association of Bond Lawyers **BAR:** United States Court of Appeals for the Eighth Circuit (1968); United States District Court for the Western District of Missouri (1965); The Missouri Bar (1965) **H:** Fishing; Gardening

YEAGER, MARK, **T:** Professor **I:** Education/ Educational Services **CN:** University of Virginia School of Medicine **PT:** Glen Yeager; Dorothy Yeager **MS:** Married **SPN:** Mary Roddy **ED:** MD, Yale University (1979); PhD, Yale University (1978); MPhil, Yale University (1973); Postdoctoral Fellow, Cell Biology **CT:** Certified in Cardiovascular Disease, American Board of Internal Medicine (1985); Certified in Internal Medicine, American Board of Internal Medicine (1983) **C:** Professor, Molecular Physiology and Biological Physics, University of Virginia School of Medicine (2007-Present); Professor, Cardiovascular Medicine, University of Virginia School of Medicine (2007-Present) **CR:** Training in Internal Medicine and Cardiology, Stanford Medicine **AW:** Fellow, American Association for the Advancement of Science (2015) **H:** Going to the beach; Swimming; Running; Skiing; Music; Playing guitar **ADD:** 645 Eight Woods Ln, Charlottesville, VA, 22903

YODER, ANNA A., **T:** Elementary School Teacher (Retired) **I:** Education/Educational Services **DOB:** 09/05/1934 **PB:** Beach City **SC:** OH/USA **PT:** Abram J. Yoder; Barbara D. (Miller) Yoder **ED:** MEd, Frostburg State University (1974); BS, Eastern Mennonite University (1966) **CT:** Certified Elementary Teacher, State of Ohio; Certified Recreational Leader, State of Ohio **C:** Retired (1998); Teacher, East Holmes Local Schools, Berlin, Ohio (1974-1998); Principal, Elementary School, Garrett County Public Schools, Oakland, MD (1970-1974); Teacher, Garrett County Public Schools, Oakland, MD (1966-1970) **CR:** Chairperson, Education Committee, German Culture Museum, Berlin, Ohio (1987-1990); Consultant in Bilingual Education, East Holmes Local Schools, Berlin, Ohio (1982-1998) **CIV:** Member, Holmes County Historical Society, Millersburg, Ohio (1989-Present); Member, Killbuck Valley Museum (1988-Present); Life Member, The Amish & Mennonite Heritage Center, Holmes County, Ohio (1985-Present); Supporting Member, German Culture Museum, Berlin, Ohio (1983-Present); Sustaining Member, The Wilderness Center, Wilmot, Ohio (1974-Present) **AW:** Silver Poet Award, World of Poetry (1986); Jennings Scholar, Martha Holden Jennings Foundation (1983-1984) **MEM:** Chapter Vice President, The Delta Kappa Gamma Society International (DKGSI) (2002-2004); President, The Delta Kappa Gamma Society International (DKGSI) (1998-2000); Ohio Retired Teachers Association (1998); Vice President, Holmes County Chapter, AAUW (1994); President, The Delta Kappa Gamma Society International (DKGSI) (1990-1992); Secretary, Beta Iota Chapter, The Delta Kappa Gamma Society International (DKGSI) (1987-1990); Secretary-Treasurer, Creative Arts Society (1987-1989); Education Committee, German Culture

Museum; Professional Teachers Group, The Delta Kappa Gamma Society International (DKGSI) **MH:** Albert Nelson Marquis Lifetime Achievement Award (2017) **H:** Nature Studies; Studying Birds; Studying Flowers; Handcrafts; Crocheting Doilies; Crocheting Hot Pads **RE:** Mennonite **ADD:** 5229 State Route 39, Millersburg, OH, 44654

YOUNG, JON NATHAN, **T:** Archaeologist **I:** Sciences **DOB:** 05/30/1938 **PB:** Hibbing **SC:** MN/ USA **PT:** Robert Nathan Young; Mary Elizabeth (Barrows) Roy **MS:** Divorced **SPN:** Tucker Heitman (1988, Divorced 1996); Karen Sue Johnson (1961, Divorced 1980) **CH:** Shawn Nathan; Kevin Leigh **ED:** PhD, University of Arizona (1967); MA, University of Kentucky (1962); BA, University of Arizona, Magna Cum Laude (1960) **C:** Archaeologist, Carson National Forest, Forest Service, United States Department of Agriculture, Taos, NM (1980-1999); Co-director, Las Palomas de Taos (1979); Assistant Director, Kit Carson Memorial Foundation Inc., Taos, NM (1978); Executive Camp Director, YMCA of Southern Arizona, Tucson, AZ (1976-1977); Archaeologist, Southwest Archaeological Center (Now Arizona Archaeological Center), Globe and Tucson, AZ (1967-1975) **CR:** Executive Order Consultant, United States Secretary of the Interior (1973-1975); Fellow, University of Kentucky Research Foundation (1960-1962); Fellow, Arizona Wilson Foundation; Fellow, National Science Foundation; Fellow, Baird Foundation; Fellow, Bausch and Lomb; Fellow, Elks National Foundation; Fellow, American Association for the Advancement of Science; Fellow, American Anthropological Association; Fellow, The Explorers Club; Fellow, Royal Anthropological Institute **CIV:** Active, White Rag Society, YMCA **CW:** Co-author, "The Gila Pueblo Salado" (2017); Co-author, "The Gila Pueblo Salado" (1997); Co-author, "First-Day Road Log in Tectonic Development of the Southern Sangre de Cristo Mountains" (1990); Co-author, "Excavation of Mound 7" (1981); Author, "The Salado Culture in Southwestern Prehistory" (1967) **AW:** Honorary Citizen, Taos County, NM (2013); Certificate of Merit, United States Department of Agriculture (1987); Grantee, National Endowment for the Humanities (1978) **MEM:** AAHS; Arizona Historical Society; The Couse Foundation, The Couse-Sharp Historic Site; Friends of the Taos Public Library; Kit Carson Home and Museum; New Mexico Museum of Natural History and Science; The Society for Historical Archaeology; Society for American Archaeology; Southwest Forest Service Amigos; Millicent Rogers Museum; Lifetime Member, Pinal County Historical Society; Taos County Historical Society; Taos Historic Museums; Sigma Xi; The Phi Beta Kappa Society; Alpha Kappa Delta; The Delta Chi Fraternity, Inc.; National Society of Pershing Rifles; Southwestern Mission Research Center **ADD:** 12 Mirlo Drive, El Prado, NM, 87529

YU, HYEON, **T:** Associate Professor **I:** Medicine & Health Care **CN:** University of North Carolina at Chapel Hill School of Medicine **DOB:** 10/18/1966 **PB:** Seoul **SC:** South Korea **MS:** Married **ED:** Clinical Fellowship, Radiology, Vascular and Interventional Radiology, University of North Carolina School of Medicine, Chapel Hill, NC, USA (2008-2010); Residency, Radiology, Chung-Ang University College of Medicine, Seoul, South Korea (1992-1996); Master's Degree, Radiology, Chung-Ang University College of Medicine (1994); Internship, Chung-Ang University College of Medicine, Seoul, South Korea (1991-1992); MD, Chung-Ang University College of Medicine (1991) **CT:** Interventional Radiology/Diagnostic Radiology, American Board of Radiology (2017);

Vascular and Interventional Radiology, American Board of Radiology (2014); Diagnostic Radiology, American Board of Radiology (2012); Education Commission for Foreign Medical Graduate Certification (2003); Korean Board Certification of Diagnostic Radiology (1996) **C:** Associate Professor of Radiology, Division of Vascular and Interventional Radiology, Department of Radiology, University of North Carolina School of Medicine, Chapel Hill, NC (2017-Present); Assistant Professor of Radiology, Division of Vascular and Interventional Radiology, Department of Radiology, University of North Carolina School of Medicine, Chapel Hill, NC (2010-2017); Assistant Professor, Division of Neuroradiology and Head & Neck Radiology, Department of Radiology, Chung-Ang University College of Medicine, Seoul, South Korea (2005-2008); Attending Physician, Section Chief, Division of Neuroradiology and Head & Neck Radiology, Department of Radiology, Seoul Veterans Hospital, Seoul, South Korea (1996-2005) **AW:** Best Presentation, Department of Radiology, University of North Carolina School of Medicine (2009) **MEM:** Southeastern Angiographic Society (2013-Present); American Medical Association (2011-Present); American College of Radiology (2011-Present); American Roentgen Ray Society (2011-Present); North Carolina Medical Society (2009-Present); Radiological Society of North America (2009-Present); Society of Interventional Radiology (2009-Present) **ADD:** 308 Pitch Pine Ln, Chapel Hill, NC, 27514

YUHASKI, STEVEN JOHN JR., T: Operations Research Analyst **I:** Military & Defense Services **CN:** U.S. Army **YOP:** 2018-06-06 **ED:** PhD, University of Massachusetts Amherst (1986); Fellow in Electrical Engineering and Computer Science (1983); MS in Industrial Engineering, University of Massachusetts (1982); Master's Degree of Mechanical Engineering, University of Florida (1979); BS in Aerospace Engineering, University of Massachusetts, Amherst (1973) **CT:** Certified in Level III Career Field of Engineering, U.S. Army (1999) **C:** Operations Research Analyst, Natick Soldier RD&E Center, U.S. Army (1987-Present) **CW:** Author, "Body Armor Load Analysis,"U.S. Army (1998); Author, "Analysis of Ballistic Protection Concepts Quantifying Operational Impacts and Design Criteria," U.S. Army (1998); Author, "Multi-Echelon Network Model and Heuristic for the Combat Service Support Supply System (CS4)," U.S. Army (1994); Author, "A New Production Scheduling Algorithm for Large Volume Multi-Product Bakery Operations Afloat," Natick Science Symposium, U.S. Army (1990); Author, "Modeling Circulation Systems in Buildings Using State Dependent Queueing Models," Queueing Systems (1989); Author, "Statistical Analysis of Concurrent and Exclusive Weibull Failure Populations" (1986); Author, "Maximum Likelihood Estimation Techniques for Concurrent Flaw Subpopulations," Journal of Material Science (1985) **AW:** Official Commendation, U.S. Army (1995); Award for Meritorious Achievement in Systems Analysis, U.S. Army (1994); Body Armor Configuration Optimization, AMC (1994) **MEM:** Alpha Pi Mu (1982); The Tau Beta Pi Association, Inc. (1973) **BA:** 15 General Greene Ave, Natick Soldier RD&E Center, Natick, MA, 01760

ZAHNER, MARY ANNE, T: Professor Emerita **I:** Education/Educational Services **CN:** University of Dayton **DOB:** 03/30/1938 **PB:** Dover **SC:** OH/USA **PT:** Alfred James Riggle; Anna Elizabeth (Stewart) Riggle **SPN:** John Charles Opalek (8/21/1982, Deceased 12/2012); Gordon Dean Zahner (8/27/1960, Deceased 3/1967) **CH:** Anne Colette Krach **ED:** PhD, The Ohio State University

(1987); MA, Ohio University (1969); BFA, Ohio University (1960) **C:** Professor Emerita, University of Dayton (2008-Present); Professor, University of Dayton (2000-2008); Associate Professor, University of Dayton (1991-2000); Assistant Professor, University of Dayton (1974-1991); Teaching Assistant, The Ohio State University, Columbus, OH (1980-1982); From Instructor, Art Education to Assistant Professor, University of Dayton (1971-1974); Chair, Art Department, Dover High School (1969-1971); Instructor, Art, Dover High School (1967-1968); Instructor, Art, Logan High School, Ohio (1961-1962); Instructor, Art, Springfield Township Schools, Akron, OH (1960-1961) **CR:** Executive Board, Oxford Round Table, England (2004); Member, Advisory Committee, Teacher Preparation Programs, Ohio Department of Education (1997); Board Member, Western Regional Professional Development Center (1996-2004); Reviewer, Prentice Hall, Inc. (1996-1998); Member, Arts Series Committee, University of Dayton (1995-1998); Member, Higher Education Steering Committee, Ohio Department of Education (1995); Reviewer, Harcourt Brace & Company (1993-1998); Member, Faculty Rights, Governance and Service Committee, University of Dayton (1992-1993) **CIV:** Member-at-Large, Education Committee, Culture Works: Arts and Culture Alliance Miami Valley (1996); Coordinator, 3D Congressional Art Contest, Sponsored by Tony P. Hall, Dayton, OH (1993-1995); Member, Discretionary Support Committee, Miami Valley Arts Council, Dayton, OH (1992); Secretary, Kettering Arts Council (1990); Member, Kettering Arts Council (1988-1993) **CW:** Exhibitor, Gallery Saint John, the Marianist Environmental Education Center, Dayton, OH (2013-2015, 2008-2011); Exhibitor, Open Air Painting, Massachusetts College of Art and Design (2011); Exhibitor, Pleiades Gallery of Contemporary Art, New York (2009, 2006-2007); Exhibitor, University Council of Art Educators, Pleiades Gallery Contemporary Art (2006); Author, "Barkan" (2003); Exhibitor, Group Shows, Westbeth Gallery, New York (1995); Editor, Newsletter Artline, Ohio Art Education Association (1988); Member, Editorial Board, Ohio Art Education Journal, Ohio Art Education Association (1986-2005); Contributor, Chapters, Books **AW:** Higher Education Division Award, Ohio Art Education Association (2007); Outstanding Art Teacher, Western District, Ohio Art Education Association (1996, 1992); Institute Faculty Award, Ohio Partnership for Visual Arts (1989); Best of Show Award, Canton Art Institute (1969) **MEM:** Workshop Coordinator, Ohio Art Education Association (1997, 1992); Consultant, Teacher Inservice for Dayton Public Schools, Ohio Art Education Association (1995); Organization of Educational Historians; Dayton Society of Artists; National Art Education Association; Fellow, Ohio Art Education Association **H:** Music; Theater; Physical fitness **PA:** Democrat **ADD:** 2649 Greystoke Ct, Xenia, OH, 45385

ZAKHEIM, DOV S., T: Economist **I:** Research **CN:** Center for Strategic and International Studies **DOB:** 12/18/1948 **PB:** Brooklyn **SC:** NY/USA **PT:** Zvi Hirsh Zakheim; Bella (Rabinowitz) Zakheim **MS:** Married **SPN:** Deborah Bing Lowy (May 26, 1991); Barbara Jane Portnoi (August 20, 1972), Divorced (1990) **CH:** Keith Samuel; Roger Israel; Scott Elisha **ED:** D.Phil. , University of Oxford (1974); BA, Columbia University, Summa Cum Laude (1970); Coursework, LSE (1968-1969) **C:** Senior Fellow, CNA (2010-Present); Senior Adviser, Center for Strategic & International Studies (2007-Present); Senior Vice President, Booz Allen Hamilton Inc. (2004-2010); Under-Secretary, U.S. Department of Defense (2001-

2004); Chief Financial Officer, U.S. Department of Defense (2001-2004); Chief Executive Officer, SPC International (1998-2001); Corporate Vice President, System Planning Corporation (1990-2001); Executive vice president, Systems Planning Corporation (1987-1990); Deputy under secretary for planning & resources, U.S. Department of Defense (1985-1987); Assistant under secretary for policy & resources, U.S. Department of Defense (1983-1985); Special assistant to under secretary, U.S. Department of Defense (1982-1983); Special Assistant to Assistant Secretary for International Security Policy, U.S. Department of Defense (1981-1982); Principal Analyst, Congressional Budget Office (1978-1981); Associate Analyst National Security and International Affairs, Congressional Budget Office (1975-1978); Assistant to Managing Director, United Kingdom Branch, International Credit Bank (1974-1975); Research Fellow St. Antony's College, University of Oxford (1974) **CR:** Commissioner, Military Compensation and Retired Modernization Commission (2013-Present); Consultant to Secretary of Defense (1987-2000, 2004-Present); Consultant to Undersecretary of Defense (1987-2000, 2004-Present); Adjunct Professor, Georgetown University (2012); Commissioner, Commission on Wartime Contracting (2009-2011); Adjunct Senior Fellow, Council on Foreign Relations (2000-2001); Adjunct Scholar, The Heritage Foundation (1988-2001); Adjunct Professor, Trinity College (1998); Presidential Fellow Trinity College (1998); Adjunct Professor, Yeshiva University (1995-1996); Adjunct Professor, Columbia University (1995-1996); Adjunct Professor, National Defense University (1992) **CIV:** Member, Defense Business Board (2004-2010, 2013-Present); Member, Executive Panel, Chief of Naval Operations (2004-Present); Member, Board of Directors, Friends of the Jewish Chapel at the United States Naval Academy (1997-Present); Member, Advisory Board, Secretary of the Navy (2008); Member, Board of Visitors, Overseas Regulatory Centers, U.S. Department of Defense (1998-2001); Member, Task Force on Defense Reform, U.S. Department of Defense (1997); Member, U.S Commission for the Preservation of America's Heritage Abroad (1991-1995); Chief, Rabbi's Chaplaincy Board, England (1971-1972); Member, Board of Deputies, British Jews (1971-1972) **CW:** Author, "A Vulcan's Tale: How the Bush Administration Mismanaged the Reconstruction of Afghanistan" (2011); Author, "Flight of the Lavi: Inside a U.S.-Israeli Crisis" (1996); "Nehemiah: Statesman and Sage" (2016) **AW:** Recipient, Medal For Outstanding Public Service, Secretary of the Navy (2004); Recipient, Distinguished Public Service Medal, U.S. Department of Defense (1986-1987, 2004); Recipient, Kellett Fellowship, Columbia University (1974); Recipient, Fellowship, National Science Foundation (1970-1973) **MEM:** Royal Swedish Academy of War Sciences; Royal Institute of International Affairs (Now Chatham House); IISS; Council for Foreign Relations; Cosmos Club; Oxford and Cambridge Club; The Columbia University Club; The Phi Beta Kappa Society **MH:** Albert Nelson Marquis Lifetime Achievement Award (2017) **H:** Stamp collecting/philately; Travel; Softball **ADD:** 11901 Viewcrest Ter, Silver Spring, MD, 20902

ZAPATA, TOMAS RAMON, T: Associate Professor **I:** Education/Educational Services **CN:** Universidad de Buenos Aires **DOB:** 02/09/1967 **PB:** Buenos Aires **SC:** Argentina **ED:** Executive MBA, Universidad Austral (2004); Postdoctoral Work in Geophysics, Cornell University (1996); PhD, Cornell University (1995); Special Master, Cornell University (1993); Licentiate in Geological

Sciences, Universidad de Buenos Aires (1990) **C:** Director of Geology, Repsol (2013-Present); Exploration Manager, Repsol (2013); Chief Reserve Officer, YPD (2012-2013); President, YPF (2011-2012); Vice President of Exploration and Production Services, YPF (2010-2011); Director of International Exploration, YPF (2009-2012); Vice President, Guyana Division, YPF (2009-2012); Onshore Exploration Manager, Repsol (2005-2008); Fold and Thurst Belt Exploration Manager, Repsol (2003-2005); Associate Professor, Universidad de Buenos Aires (2001-2011); Team Leader, Fold and Thrust Belt Team, Repsol (2001-2003); Exploration Geologist, Repsol (2000-2001); Internal Construction Manager, Repsol (1998-2010); Exploration Geologist, YPF (1996-2000); Junior Geologist, Marathon Petroleum Corporation (1991-1993) **MIL:** Armada Argentina (1979-1984) **CW:** Contributor, Articles, Professional Journals **AW:** Dr. Osvaldo Bracaccini Award, Geology Association of Argentina (2005); Grantee, National Science Foundation (1992-1994); Research Scholarship, Universidad de Buenos Aires (1990); Gold Medal, Universidad de Buenos Aires (1990); Young Band Achievement (1989) **MEM:** Spanish Association of Petroleum Geologist (2013-Present); IAPGH (2011-Present); Independent Petroleum American Association (2009-Present); Instituto Argentino del Petroleo (2006-Present); AAPG (1994-Present); Geology Association of Argentina (1992-Present); Geology Society of Spain **H:** Playing the bass **ADD:** 146 N Willow Point Circle, The Woodlands, TX, 77382

ZAREINIA, KOUROSH, T: Chief Engineer **I:** Engineering **CN:** Project neuroArm, University of Calgary **PB:** Stanford **SC:** CA/USA **ED:** PhD, University of Manitoba (2012); MSc, Electrical Engineering, Control Systems, University of Tehran (1997); BSc, Electrical Engineering, Ishafan University of Technology (1994) **C:** Adjunct Assistant Professor, University of Calgary (2015-Present); Project neuroArm, University of Calgary (2012-Present); Research Associate, Robotics, University of Calgary (2014-2015); Research Fellow, Robotics, University of Manitoba (2007-2011); Researcher, R&D Department, Mobarakeh Steel Complex, Isfahan, Iran (2007); Faculty member, Islamic Azad University (1999-2007); Design Engineer, RADAR and Communication, Iran Air Force, Tehran, Iran (1997-1999); President, Borhan Computer Institute, Isfahan, Iran (1994-2007); Founder, Borhan Computer Institute, Isfahan, Iran (1994-2007); Dean, Faculty of Engineering, Islamic Azad University **CIV:** University of Manitoba Iranian Students' Association (2010); University of Manitoba Graduate Students' Association (2008-2012) **CW:** Contributor, Articles, Peer Reviewed Journals; Reviewer, IEEE/ASME Transactions on Mechatronics; Reviewer, Journal of Mechatronics; Reviewer, ASME Journal of Dynamic Systems, Measurement and Control; Reviewer, Journal of Robotica, Cambridge University Press; Reviewer, IEEE Transactions on Cybernetics; Reviewer, Journal of Engineering in Medicine; Reviewer, International Journal of Advanced Robotic Systems; Reviewer, The International Journal of Medical Robotics and Computer Assisted Surgery; Reviewer, Sensors; Reviewer, Soft Computing and Automation Journal; Reviewer, International Journal of Computer Assisted Radiology and Surgery; Reviewer, World Neurosurgery; Reviewer, Neurosurgery; Reviewer, Control Engineering Practice **AW:** Grant, CHRP, CIHR-NSERC; Grant, CIHR; Grant, New Earth-Space Technologies, University of Calgary (2017); Grant, Alberta-Germany; International Graduate Student Scholarship, University of Manitoba (2009); University of Manitoba Graduate Fellowship (2008-2011); Man-

itoba Hydro Research Scholarship (2008-2010); Research Grant, IAU (2005); Research Grant, IAU (2003); Gold Medal in Olympiad of Vocational Skills (1999); Grant, CHRP, CIHR-NSERC **MEM:** Association of Professional Engineers and Geoscientists of Alberta APEGA; IEEE; ASME American Society of Mechanical Engineers **BA:** 1C70-HRIC, 3280 Hospital Dr NW, Project neuroArm, University of Calgary, Calgary, AB, Canada, T2N 4Z6 **URL:** http://www.neuroarm.org/people/

ZAROFF, CAROLYN REIN, T: Writer **I:** Writing and Editing **DOB:** 02/01/1936 **PB:** New York **SC:** NY/USA **PT:** Solomon Rein; Dorothy (Bloom) Rein **MS:** Single **SPN:** Lawrence I. Zaroff (11/4/1956, Deceased) **CH:** Susan Z. Breyer; Wendy Z. Davis, MD; Jonathon Gordon, MD **ED:** BA, George Washington University (1956) **C:** Freelance Writer, Aspen, CO (1990-Present); Advertising Manager, The Marlow Group, Inc., Aspen, CO (1986-1990); Advertising Manager, Rochester Institute of Technology (1980-1983); President, Zaroff Communications, Rochester, NY (1977-1980); Artist, Sausalito, CA **CR:** Trustee, RESPONSE, Aspen, CO (1987-Present) **CIV:** Delegate, Democratic National Convention, San Francisco, CA (1984); President, Rochester Merchants Association, Rochester, NY (1978-1980); Town Leader, Brighton Democratic Committee, Brighton, NY (1974-1977); New York State Democratic Committee, New York, NY (1974-1976); Volunteer Assistant Art Teacher, Arts Department, Bayside Martin Luther King Jr. Academy, Sausalito, CA; Retirement Community, Sausalito, CA **CW:** Editor, "Rochester Woman Magazines" (1983-1985); Contributor, Articles, Professional Journals **AW:** Honored Volunteer, Bayside Martin Luther King, Jr. Academy, Sausalito, CA **MEM:** Trustee, Aspen Writers' Foundation (Now Aspen Words) (1988-Present); President, Aspen Writers' Foundation (Now Aspen Words) (1989-1991); Chong-Moon Lee Center for Asian Art and Culture, Asian Art Museum; San Francisco Museum of Modern Art; De Young Museum, Fine Arts Museums of San Francisco; Aspen Women's Forum **MH:** Albert Nelson Marquis Lifetime Achievement Award (2017) **H:** Swimming; Hiking; Travel; Spending time with grandchildren **ADD:** 433 Bridgeway, Sausalito, CA, 94965 **URL:** https://www.saatchiart.com/czaroff

ZHAO, HUIJIE, T: Artist **I:** Fine Art **DOB:** 02/06/1981 **PB:** Shanghai **SC:** China **PT:** Hongbin Zhao; Meijun Gu **MS:** Married **SPN:** Zhigang Zhang **CH:** Jayden Zhang **ED:** MFA, RMIT University, Australia (2002-2003); BFA, Monash University, Australia (2000-2002) **C:** Vice President, Beijing Da You Qian Jing Painting and Calligraphy Institute, China (2014-Present); Art Director, HZ International Fine Arts, LLC (2009-Present); Freelance Artist, Warrandyte South, Australia (2003-Present) **CW:** Group Show, The 36th International Painting and Drawing Exhibition, Korea Gyeongbokgung Royal Palace (2016); Five Anniversary Spring Art Auction, Zhejiang Longan Auction Co., Ltd. (2016); Spring Art Auction, Beijing Zhongpai International Auction Limited Company (2015); Auction at Echo Lake, The Education Fund of Westfield, New Jersey (2014); Group Show, Imagine Gallery, New York (2012-2013); Auction at Echo Lake, The Education Fund of Westfield, New Jersey (2012); Solo Show, HZ Art Gallery (2011); Two-Man Show, Imagine Gallery, New York (2011); Two-Man Show, The 14th China Beijing International Art Expo (2011); Two-Man Show, The 6th ICCIE Expo, China International Exhibition Center (2011); Group Show, Riverside Gallery, New York (2010-2013);

Group Show, Century Fine Art, Georgia (2010-2012); Group Show, Reflection Gallery, New Mexico (2010-2011); Group Show, Royale Gallery, New York (2010); Solo Show, HZ Art Gallery (2010); Two-Man Show, The 14th Guangzhou International Art Fair (2010); Two-Man Show, New York International Expo (2009-2010); Group Show, Metro 5 Gallery, Melbourne, Australia (2006); Group Show, Victorian Exhibition, Crown Casino, Melbourne, Australia (2006); Group Show, Portia Geach Memorial Award Finalists Exhibition, S.H. Ervin Gallery, National Trust Centre (2005-2006); Solo Show, RMIT University (2003); Solo Show, Monash University (2002); Featured, New Chinese Art Chronicles (1949-2014); Spring Art Auction, Zhejiang International Commodity Auction Center Co., Ltd.; "Contemporary Famous Artist: Hui Jie Zhao Oil Painting" **AW:** Recipient, Best Display Award, The Sixth China Beijing International Cultural & Creative Industrial Exposition (2011); Recipient, The People's Choice Award, Ninth Freedom Art Prize Exhibition, Amnesty International, Australia (2006); Recipient, The People's Choice Award, The Hidden Faces of the Archbald Exhibition, Australia (2006); Recipient, Most Outstanding Artist Gold Medal, First Prize, Dandenong Festival (2001); Recipient, First Prize, Stoll Trust Award (1997); Recipient, First Prize, The Royal Overseas League (1996) **H:** Dance; Travel **ADD:** 125 Highland Ave, Basking Ridge, NJ, 07920

ZHOU, YUXUN, T: Quantitative Researcher **I:** Research **CN:** Citadel LLC **ED:** PhD, Electrical Engineering and Computer Sciences, University of California Berkeley (2017); Diplôme d'Ingénieur, École Centrale Paris, France (2012); BS in Electrical Engineering, Xi'an Jiaotong University, Xi'an, China (2009) **C:** Quantitative Researcher, Citadel LLC, Chicago, IL (2016-Present); Graduate Student Researcher, EECS, University of California, Berkeley (2012-Present); Data Scientist Intern, ASML Inc., San Jose, CA (2016); Graduate Student Instructor, EECS, University of California, Berkeley (2015-2016); Researcher Associate, Berkeley Education Alliance for Research in Singapore, Singapore (2015); Researcher Assistant, Lab of Applied Mathematics, ECP, Paris, France (2012); Internship, Electricity of France, Lille, France (2011) **CW:** Reviewer, NIPS; Reviewer, KDD; Reviewer, ICMLA; Reviewer, CASE; Reviewer, TSM; Reviewer, JNCA **AW:** Student Paper Award, Pacific-Asia Conference on Knowledge Discovery and Data Mining (2015); Hu BaoSheng Honor (2012); Fellowship, A&D SIMATICS (2011); Eiffel Excellence Scholarship (2009); First Prize, 6th National Advanced Mathematical Olympics (2008) **MEM:** American Association of Artificial Intelligence **ADD:** 25 W Randolph St Apt 1811, Chicago, IL, 60601 **URL:** https://www.linkedin.com/in/yuxun-zhou-2b8a1255/

ZIEGLER, JORDAN A., T: Senior Partner, Attorney **I:** Law and Legal Services **CN:** Pasternack Tilker Ziegler Walsh Stanton & Romano LLP **MS:** Married **SPN:** Wendy Ziegler **CH:** Zachary; Benjamin **ED:** JD, Touro College Jacob D. Fuchsberg Law Center (1992); Bachelor's Degree, The George Washington University (1988) **C:** Senior Partner, Pasternack Tilker Ziegler Walsh Stanton & Romano LLP (1997-Present); Attorney, Pasternack Tilker Ziegler Walsh Stanton & Romano LLP (1997-Present) **CR:** Adjunct Professor, Touro College Jacob D. Fuchsberg Law Center (2015-Present); Chair, Civil Service Disability Retirement Pension Department, Pasternack Tilker Ziegler Walsh Stanton & Romano LLP **CIV:** General Counsel, SCPBA; Counsel, Suffolk County Police Columbia Association; Counsel,

Suffolk County Police Asian Jade Society; Counsel, NYSFOP Suffolk County Lodge 124, Inc.; Disability Counsel, Port Authority Police Benevolent Association; Vice-chair, Advisory Board of Occupational & Environmental Medicine of Long Island, Northwell Health; Member, World Trade Center Council Advisory Commission; Lecturer, Workers Compensation Navigator Program, AFL-CIO **CW:** Contributor, Various Union Publications; Author, "The Little Textbook of Workers Comp" **AW:** The Stetson Award, The Police Benevolent Association of the New York State Troopers (2017); Honoree, Workers Compensation Area, Super Lawyers (2006-2016); Robert Briscoe Award, Emerald Isle Immigration Center; Honoree, Swing For Kids Program, Tilles Center for the Performing Arts; Honoree, EAC Network; Honoree, Sunrise Day Camp; Eastern Long Island Police Pipes and Drums Marching Band **MEM:** Board of Directors, Long Island Chapter, RMHC; National Association of Police Organizations; NYSTLA; N.Y.S. Association of PBAs; NYCOSH; ABA **BAR:** New York State Bar; U.S. District Courts for the Southern and Eastern Districts of New York; United States Supreme Court **H:** Golfing; Skiing **BA:** 551 5th Ave Rm 520, Pasternack Tilker Ziegler Walsh Stanton & Romano LLP, New York, NY, 10176 **ADD:** 15 Glenwood Dr, Great Neck, NY, 11021 **URL:** https://www.workerslaw.com/attorneys/jordan-a-ziegler-senior-partner/

ZILVETI, CARLOS B., **T:** Preventive Medicine, Physician, Pediatrician, Colonel **I:** Military & Defense Services **CN:** United States Air Force **DOB:** 06/14/1928 **PB:** Sucre **SC:** Bolivia **PT:** Carlos Zilveti; Marina (De La Reza) Zilveti **MS:** Married **SPN:** Vita Palazzolo (9/5/1987); Halina J. Daszewski (1957-1976) **CH:** Carlos Joseph, III **ED:** MPH, Yale University, New Haven, CT (1966); MD, University of San Francisco Xavier, Sucre, Bolivia (1954); BS, Sacred Heart College, Sucre, Bolivia (1946) **C:** Consultant, Aerospace and Preventive Medicine, Wilford Hall Medical Center, U.S. Air Force, Lackland Air Force Base, Texas (1984-1991); Consultant, Preventive and Occupational Medicine, U.S. Air Force, San Antonio, TX (1983-1991); Chief of Environmental Medicine, Wilford Hall Medical Center, U.S. Air Force, San Antonio, TX (1979-1983); Regional Medical Officer, Scientific Attache in West Africa, U.S. Department of State, Liberia, Ghana, Togo, Sierra Leone (1976-1979); Regional Medical Officer, South and Central America, Peace Corps, Bogota, Colombia (1975-1976); Director of Maternal-Child Health, New Haven Department of Health (1964-1974); Private Practice, New Haven and Branford, CT (1960-1963); Resident and Chief Resident in Pediatrics, Hospital of St. Raphael, New Haven, CT (1958-1959); Assistant Resident in Pediatrics, St. Luke's Hospital, Memorial Cancer Center, Woman's Hospital, New York, NY (1957-1958); Intern, Hospital Obrero Victor Paz Estenssoro, La Paz, Bolivia (1956); Physician in Rural Medicine, Bolivian Power Co., La Paz, Bolivia (1955) **CR:** Consultant, Headstart American Academy of Pediatrics, Stanford-Norwalk, CT (1968-1975); Consultant, Food and Drug Administration, U.S. Department of Health, Washington, DC (1966-1975); Regional Medical Officer, Science Attache, West Africa, U.S. State Department; Fellow Emeritus, American Academy of Pediatrics **CIV:** Chairman, Governor's Task Force, Connecticut State Department of Health (1969-1975) **MIL:** Colonel, U.S. Air Force, San Antonio, TX (1991); Reserve Appointment of Major, U.S. Air Force **CW:** Contributor, Articles, Professional Journals **MEM:** Emeritus Member, American College of Preventive Medicine; American Public Health Association; American Medical Association; New England Public Health Association; Connecticut Academy of Preventive Medicine; American Occupational Medical Association; Sons of Italy; San Antonio Chapter, American Legion **MH:** Distinguished Humanitarian (2017) **H:** Swimming; Tennis; Golf; Travel; Classical music **ADD:** 9222 Dover Ridge, San Antonio, TX, 78250

ZIMMERMANN, GERD A., **T:** Senior Attorney **I:** Law and Legal Services **CN:** Zimmermann & Colleagues **SC:** Germany **MS:** Married **ED:** JD, University of Tübingen (1970) **C:** Counselor at Law, Foreign Legal Consultant, Rechtesbeistand (1974-Present); Senior Attorney, Zimmermann and Colleagues (1970-Present) **MEM:** German American Chamber of Commerce; The Tempe Chamber of Commerce; American Chamber of Commerce in Germany; Life Member, Landsmannschaft Merovingia Giessen zu Mainz; Foreign Legal Consultant, State Bar of Arizona **BAR:** Germany; State of Arizona; Arizona Supreme Court **BA:** 1432 N Pasadena, Zimmermann & Colleagues, Mesa, AZ, 85201 **URL:** usgermanlawyers.com

ZUCCO, ROBERT A., **I:** Law and Legal Services **ED:** JD, University at Buffalo (1978) **C:** Assistant District Attorney, Office of the District Attorney, Niagara County **AW:** Distinguished Service Award, Office of the District Attorney, Niagara County (2017)

ZUK, CARMEN VEIGA MD, **T:** Psychiatrist (Retired) **I:** Medicine & Health Care **DOB:** 03/05/1939 **PB:** Buenos Aires **SC:** Argentina **MS:** Married (5/7/1974) **SPN:** Gerald Harvey **CH:** Cary Elizabeth; Gabrielle Anne **ED:** MD, University of Buenos Aires (1964) **CT:** Psychiatry Certification, University of Buenos Aires (1969); Diplomate, American Board of Psychiatry and Neurology **C:** Retired (2006); Staff Psychiatrist, Santa Clarita Child and Family Center (1999-2002); Partner, Southern California Permanente Medical Group, Van Nuys (1988-1998); Psychiatrist, Partner, Southern California Permanente Medical Group, Van Nuys (1988-1998); Mental Health Psychiatrist, L.A. County Department of Mental Health, San Fernando Mental Health Services (1986-1988); Associate, Psychiatry Medical Group, California (1985-1986); Director of Treatment Team, New Orleans Adolescent Hospital (1983-1985); Director of the Child and Adolescent Unit, Hospital of the Medical College of Georgia, Augusta (1981-1983); Child Psychiatry Fellowship, Medical College of Pennsylvania and Eastern Pennsylvania Psychiatric Institute, Philadelphia (1979-1981); Resident in Psychiatry, Norristown State Hospital, Norristown, PA (1977-1979); Intern, Medical College of Pennsylvania, Philadelphia (1974-1975) **CW:** Co-editor (with Gerald H. Zuk), "The Psychology of Delusion" **MEM:** American Medical Association; International Society for Adolescent Psychiatry **H:** Reading; Cooking; Gardening; Swimming; Music **PA:** Democrat **RE:** Catholic **BA:** 2140 Santa Cruz Ave Apt E-102, Menlo Park, CA, 94025 **URL:** carmenzuk@gmail.com

ZWASS, VLADIMIR, **T:** Inaugural Gregory Olsen Chair and Distinguished Professor **I:** Education/Educational Services **CN:** Fairleigh Dickinson University **PT:** Adam Zwass; Friderike (Getzler) Zwass **MS:** Marroed **SPN:** Alicia Kogut (4/24/1977) **CH:** Joshua Jonathan **ED:** PhD, Columbia University (1975); MPhil, Columbia University (1974); MS, Moscow Institute of Energetics (1969) **CW:** Editor-in-Chief, International Journal of Electronic Commerce (1996-Present); Editor-in-Chief, Journal Management Information Systems (1983-Present); Author, "Foundations of Information Systems" (1998); Author, "Management Information Systems" (1992); Author, "Programming in Basic" (1986); Author, "Programming in Pascal" (1985); Author, "Introduction to Computer Science" (1981); Author, "Programming in Fortran" (1981); Editor-in-Chief, Monographs Advances in Management Information Systems; Contributor, Articles to Professional Journals and Publications, Encyclopedia Britannica, New York Times, Chapters to Books **AW:** Helena Rubinstein Foundation Scholar (1971-1975); Columbia University Fellow (1970-1971); Grantee, U.S. Navy, Other Agencies **MEM:** IEEE; Association for Computer Machinery; Association for Information Systems; Sigma Xi; Eta Kappa Nu **MH:** Albert Nelson Marquis Lifetime Achievement Award (2017) **ADD:** 19 Warewoods Rd, Saddle River, NJ, 07458

NOTABLE LISTEES

71st Edition

Table of Abbreviations

The following abbreviations and symbols are frequently used in this section

A

A	Associate (used with academic degrees)
AA	Associate in Arts
AAAL	American Academy of Arts and Letters
AAAS	American Association for the Advancement of Science
AACD	American Association for Counseling and Development
AACN	American Association of Critical Care Nurses
AAHA	American Academy of Health Administrators
AAHP	American Association of Hospital Planners
AAHPERD	American Alliance for Health, Physical Education, Recreation, and Dance
AAS	Associate of Applied Science
AASL	American Association of School Librarians
AASPA	American Association of School Personnel Administrators
AAU	Amateur Athletic Union
AAUP	American Association of University Professors
AAUW	American Association of University Women
AB	Arts, Bachelor of
AB	Alberta
ABA	American Bar Association
AC	Air Corps
acad.	academy
acct.	accountant
acctg.	accounting
ACDA	Arms Control and Disarmament Agency
ACHA	American College of Hospital Administrators
ACLS	Advanced Cardiac Life Support
ACLU	American Civil Liberties Union
ACOG	American College of Ob-Gyn
ACP	American College of Physicians
ACS	American College of Surgeons
ADA	American Dental Association
adj.	adjunct, adjutant
adm.	admiral
administr.	administrator
administn.	administration
adminstrv.	administrative
ADN	Associate's Degree in Nursing
ADP	Automatic Data Processing
adv.	advocate, advisory
advt.	advertising
AE	Agricultural Engineer
AEC	Atomic Energy Commission

aero.	aeronautical, aeronautic
aerodyn.	aerodynamic
AFB	Air Force Base
AFTRA	American Federation of Television and Radio Artists
agr.	agriculture
agrl.	agricultural
agt.	agent
AGVA	American Guild of Variety Artists
agy.	agency
A&I	Agricultural and Industrial
AIA	American Institute of Architects
AIAA	American Institute of Aeronautics and Astronautics
AIChE	American Institute of Chemical Engineers
AICPA	American Institute of Certified Public Accountants
AID	Agency for International Development
AIDS	Acquired Immune Deficiency Syndrome
AIEE	American Institute of Electrical Engineers
AIME	American Institute of Mining, Metallurgy, and Petroleum Engineers
AK	Alaska
AL	Alabama
ALA	American Library Association
Ala.	Alabama
alt.	alternate
Alta.	Alberta
A&M	Agricultural and Mechanical
AM	Arts, Master of
Am.	American, America
AMA	American Medical Association
amb.	ambassador
AME	African Methodist Episcopal
Amtrak	National Railroad Passenger Corporation
AMVETS	American Veterans
ANA	American Nurses Association
anat.	anatomical
ANCC	American Nurses Credentialing Center
ann.	annual
anthrop.	anthropological
AP	Associated Press
APA	American Psychological Association
APHA	American Public Health Association
APO	Army Post Office
apptd.	appointed

Apr.	April
apt.	apartment
AR	Arkansas
ARC	American Red Cross
arch.	architect
archeol.	archeological
archtl.	architectural
Ariz.	Arizona
Ark.	Arkansas
ArtsD	Arts, Doctor of
arty.	artillery
AS	Associate of Science, American Samoa
ASCAP	American Society of Composers, Authors and Publishers
ASCD	Association for Supervision and Curriculum Development
ASCE	American Society of Civil Engineers
ASME	American Society of Mechanical Engineers
ASPA	American Society for Public Administration
ASPCA	American Society for the Prevention of Cruelty to Animals
assn.	association
assoc.	associate
asst.	assistant
ASTD	American Society for Training and Development
ASTM	American Society for Testing and Materials
astron.	astronomical
astrophys.	astrophysical
ATLA	Association of Trial Lawyers of America
ATSC	Air Technical Service Command
atty.	attorney
Aug.	August
aux.	auxiliary
Ave.	Avenue
AVMA	American Veterinary Medical Association
AZ	Arizona

B

B	Bachelor
b.	born
BA	Bachelor of Arts
BAgr	Bachelor of Agriculture
Balt.	Baltimore
Bapt.	Baptist
Barch	Bachelor of Architecture

BAS	Bachelor of Agricultural Science
BBA	Bachelor of Business Administration
BBB	Better Business Bureau
BC	British Columbia
BCE	Bachelor of Civil Engineering
Bchir	Bachelor of Surgery
BCL	Bachelor of Civil Law
BCS	Bachelor of Commercial Science
BD	Bachelor of Divinity
bd.	board
BE	Bachelor of Education
BEE	Bachelor of Electrical Engineering
BFA	Bachelor of Fine Arts
bibl.	biblical
bibliog.	bibliographical
biog.	biographical
biol.	biological
BJ	Bachelor of Journalism
Bklyn.	Brooklyn
BL	Bachelor of Letters
bldg.	building
BLS	Bachelor of Library Science
Blvd.	Boulevard
BMI	Broadcast Music, Inc.
bn.	battalion
bot.	botanical
BPE	Bachelor of Physical Education
BPhil	Bachelor of Philosophy
br.	branch
BRE	Bachelor of Religious Education
brig. gen.	brigadier general
Brit.	British
Bros.	Brothers
BS	Bachelor of Science
BSA	Bachelor of Agricultural Science
BSBA	Bachelor of Science in Business Administration
BSChemE	Bachelor of Science in Chemical Engineering
BSD	Bachelor of Didactic Science
BSEE	Bachelor of Science in Electrical Engineering
BSN	Bachelor of Science in Nursing
BST	Bachelor of Sacred Theology
BTh	Bachelor of Theology
bull.	bulletin
bur.	bureau
bus.	business
BWI	British West Indies

C

CA	California
CAD-CAM	Computer Aided Design - Computer Aided Model
Calif.	California
Can.	Canada, Canadian
CAP	Civil Air Patrol
capt.	captain
cardiol.	cardiological
cardiovasc.	cardiovascular
Cath.	Catholic
cav.	cavalry
CBI	China, Burma, India Theatre of Operations
CC	Community College
CCC	Commodity Credit Corporation
CCNY	City College of New York
CCRN	Critical Care Registered Nurse
CCU	Cardiac Care Unit
CD	Civil Defense
CE	Corps of Engineers, Civil Engineer
CEN	Certified Emergency Nurse
CENTO	Central Treaty Organization
CEO	chief executive officer
CERN	European Organization of Nuclear Research
cert.	certificate, certification, certified
CETA	Comprehensive Employment Training Act
CFA	Chartered Financial Analyst
CFL	Canadian Football League
CFO	chief financial officer
CFP	Certified Financial Planner
ch.	church
ChD	Doctor of Chemistry
chem.	chemical
ChemE	Chemical Engineer
ChFC	Chartered Financial Consultant
Chgo.	Chicago
chirurg., der	surgeon
chmn.	chairman
chpt.	chapter
CIA	Central Intelligence Agency
Cin.	Cincinnati
cir.	circle, circuit
CLE	Continuing Legal Education
Cleve.	Cleveland
climatol.	climatological
clin.	clinical
clk.	clerk
CLU	Chartered Life Underwriter
CM	Master in Surgery
CM	Northern Mariana Islands
cmty.	community
CO	Colorado
Co.	Company
COF	Catholic Order of Foresters
C. of C.	Chamber of Commerce
col.	colonel
coll.	college
Colo.	Colorado
com.	committee
comd.	commanded
comdg.	commanding
comdr.	commander
comdt.	commandant
comm.	communications
commd.	commissioned
comml.	commercial
commn.	commission
commr.	commissioner
compt.	comptroller

condr.	conductor
conf.	Conference
Congl.	Congregational, Congressional
Conglist.	Congregationalist
Conn.	Connecticut
cons.	consultant, consulting
consol.	consolidated
constl.	constitutional
constn.	constitution
constrn.	construction
contbd.	contributed
contbg.	contributing
contrbn.	contribution
contbr.	contributor
contr.	controller
Conv.	Convention
COO	chief operating officer
coop.	cooperative
coord.	coordinator
corp.	corporation, corporate
corr.	correspondent, corresponding, correspondence
coun.	council
CPA	Certified Public Accountant
CPCU	Chartered Property and Casualty Underwriter
CPH	Certificate of Public Health
cpl.	corporal
CPR	Cardio-Pulmonary Resuscitation
CS	Christian Science
CSB	Bachelor of Christian Science
CT	Connecticut
ct.	court
ctr.	center
ctrl.	central

D

D	Doctor of Chemistry
d.	daughter of
DAgr	Doctor of Agriculture
DAR	Daughters of the American Revolution
dau.	daughter
DAV	Disabled American Veterans
DC	District of Columbia
DCL	Doctor of Civil Law
DCS	Doctor of Commercial Science
DD	Doctor of Divinity
DDS	Doctor of Dental Surgery
DE	Delaware
Dec.	December
dec.	deceased
def.	defense
Del.	Delaware
del.	delegate, delegation
Dem.	Democrat, Democratic
DEng	Doctor of Engineering
denom.	denomination, denominational
dep.	deputy
dept.	department
dermatol.	dermatological
desc.	descendant
devel.	development, developmental
DFA	Doctor of Fine Arts

DHL	Doctor of Hebrew Literature	ency.	encyclopedia	FNP	Family Nurse Practitioner
dir.	director	Eng.	England	FOA	Foreign Operations
dist.	district	engr.	engineer		Administration
distbg.	distributing	engring.	engineering	found.	foundation
distbn.	distribution	entomol.	entomological	FPC	Federal Power Commission
distbr.	distributor	environ.	environmental	FPO	Fleet Post Office
disting.	distinguished	EPA	Environmental Protection	frat.	fraternity
div.	division, divinity, divorce		Agency	FRS	Federal Reserve System
dvsn.	division	epidemiol.	epidemiological	FSA	Federal Security Agency
DLitt	Doctor of Literature	Episc.	Episcopalian	Ft.	Fort
DMD	Doctor of Dental Medicine	ERA	Equal Rights Amendment	FTC	Federal Trade Commission
DMS	Doctor of Medical Science	ERDA	Elementary and Secondary	Fwy.	Freeway
DO	Doctor of Osteopathy		Education Act		
docs.	documents	ESL	English as a Second Language		
DON	Director of Nursing	ESSA	Environmental Science	**G**	
DPH	Diploma in Public Health		Services Administration		
DPhil.	Doctor of Philosophy	ethnol.	ethnological	GA, Ga.	Georgia
DR	Daughters of the Revolution	ETO	European Theatre of	GAO	General Accounting Office
Dr.	Drive, Doctor		Operations	gastroent.	gastroenterological
DRE	Doctor of Religious Education	EU	European Union	GATT	General Agreement on Tariffs
DrPH	Doctor of Public Health	Evang.	Evangelical		and Trade
DSc	Doctor of Science	exam.	examination, examining	GE	General Electric Company
DSChemE	Doctor of Science in Chemical	Exch.	Exchange	gen.	general
	Engineering	exec.	executive	geneal.	genealogical
DSM	Distinguished Service Medal	exhbn.	exhibition	geog.	geographic, geographical
DST	Doctor of Sacred Theology	expdn.	expedition	geol.	geological
DTM	Doctor of Tropical Medicine	expn.	exposition	geophys.	geophysical
DVM	Doctor of Veterinary Medicine	expt.	experiment	geriat.	geriatrics
DVS	Doctor of Veterinary Surgery	exptl.	experimental	gerontol.	gerontological
		Exly.	Expressway	GHQ	General Headquarters
		Ext.	Extension	gov.	governor
E				govt.	government
				govtl.	governmental
		F		GPO	Government Printing Office
E	East			grad.	graduate, graduated
ea.	eastern			GSA	General Services
Eccles.	Ecclesiastical	FAA	Federal Aviation		Administration
ecol.	ecological		Administration	Gt.	Great
econ.	economic	FAO UN	Food and Agriculture	GU	Guam
ECO SOC	UN Economic and Social		Organization	gynecol.	gynecological
	Council	FBA	Federal Bar Association		
ED	Doctor of Engineering	FBI	Federal Bureau of		
ed.	educated		Investigation	**H**	
EdB	Bachelor of Education	FCA	Farm Credit Administration		
EdD	Doctor of Education	FCC	Federal Communications		
edit.	edition		Commission	hdqs.	headquarters
editl.	editorial	FCDA	Federal Civil Defense	HEW	Department of health,
EdM	Master of Education		Administration		Education and Welfare
edn.	education	FDA	Food and Drug Administration	HHD	Doctor of Humanities
ednl.	educational	FDIA	Federal Deposit Insurance	HHFA	Housing and Home Finance
EDP	Electronic Data Processing		Administration		Agency
EdS	Specialist in Education	FDIC	Federal Deposit Insurance	HHS	Department of Health and
EE	Electrical Engineer		Commission		Human Services
EEC	European Economic	FEA	Federal Energy	HI	Hawaii
	Community		Administration	hist.	historical, historic
EEG	Electroencephalogram	Feb.	February	HM	Master of Humanities
EEO	Equal Employment	fed.	federal	homeo.	homeopathic
	Opportunity	fedn.	federation	hon.	honorary, honorable
EEOC	Equal Employment	FERC	Federal Energy Regulatory	House of Dels.	House of Delegates
	Opportunity Commission		Committee	House of Reps.	House of
EKG	electrocardiogram	fgn.	foreign		Representatives
elec.	electrical	FHA	Federal Housing	hort.	horticultural
electrochem.	electrochemical		Administration	hosp.	hospital
electrophys.	electrophysical	fin.	financial, finance	HS	High School
elem.	elementary	FL	Florida	HUD	Department of Housing and
EM	Engineer of Mines	Fl.	Floor		Urban Development
EMT	Emergency Medical	Fla.	Florida	Hwy.	Highway
	Technician	FMC	Federal Maritime Commission	hydrog.	hydrographic

I

IA — Iowa
IAEA — International Atomic Energy Association
IBRD — International Bank for Reconstruction and Development
ICA — International Cooperation Administration
ICC — Interstate Commerce Commission
ICCE — International Council for Computers in Education
ICU — Intensive Care Unit
ID — Idaho
IEEE — Institute of Electrical and Electronics Engineers
IFC — International Finance Corporation
IL, Ill. — Illinois
illus. — illustrated
ILO — International Labor Organization
IMF — International Monetary Fund
IN — Indiana
Inc. — Incorporated
Ind. — Indiana
ind. — independent
Indpls. — Indianapolis
indsl. — industrial
inf. — infantry
info. — information
ins. — insurance
insp. — inspector
inst. — institute
instl. — institutional
instn. — institution
instr. — instructor
instrn. — instruction
instrnl. — instructional
internat. — international
intro. — introduction
IRE — Institute of Radio Engineers
IRS — Internal Revenue Service

J

JAG — Judge Advocate General
JAGC — Judge Advocate General Corps
Jan. — January
Jaycees — Junior Chamber of Commerce
JB — Jurum Baccalaureus
JCB — Juris Canonici Doctor, Juris Civilian Doctor
JCL — Juris Canonici Licentiatus
JD — Juris Doctor
jg. — junior grade
jour. — journal
jr. — junior
JSD — Juris Scientiae Doctor
JUD — Juris Utriusque Doctor
jud. — judicial

K

Kans. — Kansas
KC — Knights of Columbus
KS — Kansas
KY, Ky. — Kentucky

L

LA, La. — Louisiana
LA — Los Angeles
lab. — laboratory
L.Am. — Latin America
lang. — language
laryngol. — laryngological
LB — Labrador
LDS — Latter Day Saints
lectr. — lecturer
legis. — legislation, legislative
LHD — Doctor of Humane Letters
LI — Long Island
libr. — librarian, library
lic. — licensed, license
lit. — literature
litig. — litigation
LittB — Bachelor of Letters
LittD — Doctor of Letters
LLB — Bachelor of Laws
LLD — Doctor of Laws
LLM — Master of Laws
Ln. — Lane
LPGA — Ladies Professional Golf Association
LPN — Licensed Practical Nurse
lt. — lieutenant
Ltd. — Limited
Luth. — Lutheran
LWV — League of Women Voters

M

M — Master
m. — married
MA — Master of Arts
MA — Massachusetts
MADD — Mothers Against Drunk Driving
mag. — magazine
MAgr — Master of Agriculture
maj. — major
Man. — Manitoba
Mar. — March
MArch — Master of Architecture
Mass. — Massachusetts
math. — mathematics, mathematical
MB — Bachelor of Medicine, Manitoba
MBA — Master of Business Administration
MC — Medical Corps
MCE — Master of Civil Engineering
mcht. — merchant
mcpl. — municipal
MCS — Master of Commercial Science
MD — Doctor of Medicine
MD, Md. — Maryland
MDiv — Master of Divinity

MDip — Master in Diplomacy
mdse. — merchandise
MDV — Doctor of Veterinary Medicine
ME — Mechanical Engineer
ME — Maine
M.E.Ch. — Methodist Episcopal Church
mech. — mechanical
MEd. — Master of Education
med. — medical
MEE — Master of Electrical Engineering
mem. — member
meml. — memorial
merc. — mercantile
met. — metropolitan
metall. — metallurgical
MetE — Metallurgical Engineer
meterorol. — meteorological
Meth. — Methodist
Mex. — Mexico
MF — Master of Forestry
MFA — Master of Fine Arts
mfg. — manufacturing
mfr. — manufacturer
mgmt. — management
mgr. — manager
MHA — Master of Hospital Administration
MI — Military Intelligence, Michigan
Mich. — Michigan
micros. — microscopic
mid. — middle
mil. — military
Milw. — Milwaukee
Min. — Minister
mineral. — mineralogical
Minn. — Minnesota
MIS — Management Information Systems
MIT — Massachusetts Institute of Technology
mktg. — marketing
ML — Master of Laws
MLA — Modern Language Association
MLitt — Master of Literature, Master of Letters
MLS — Master of Library Science
MME — Master of Mechanical Engineering
MN — Minnesota
mng. — managing
MO, Mo. — Missouri
moblzn. — mobilization
Mont. — Montana
MP — Member of Parliament
MPA — Master of Public Administration
MPE — Master of Physical Education
MPH — Master of Public Health
MPhil — Master of Philosophy
MPL — Master of Patent Law
Mpls. — Minneapolis
MRE — Master of Religious Education
MRI — Magnetic Resonance Imaging
MS — Master of Science
MS, Miss. — Mississippi
MSc — Master of Science
MSChemE — Master of Science in Chemical Engineering

MSEE	Master of Science in Electrical Engineering	**NC**	North Carolina	**OEO**	Office of Economic Opportunity
MSF	Master of Science in Forestry	**NCAA**	National College Athletic Association	**ofcl.**	official
MSN	Master of Science in Nursing			**OH**	Ohio
MST	Master of Sacred Theology	**NCCJ**	National Conference of Christians and Jews	**OK, Okla.**	Oklahoma
MSW	Master of Social Work			**ON, Ont.**	Ontario
MT	Montana	**ND**	North Dakota	**oper.**	operating
Mt.	Mount	**NDEA**	National Defense Education Act	**opthal.**	ophthalmological
mus.	museum, musical	**NE**	Nebraska	**ops.**	operations
MusB	Bachelor of Music	**NE**	Northeast	**OR**	Oregon
MusD	Doctor of Music	**NEA**	National Education Association	**orch.**	orchestra
MusM	Master of Music	**Nebr.**	Nebraska	**Oreg.**	Oregon
mut.	mutual	**NEH**	National Endowment for Humanities	**orgn.**	organization
MVP	Most Valuable Player			**orgnl.**	organizational
mycol.	mycological	**neurol.**	neurological	**ornithol.**	ornithological
		Nev.	Nevada	**orthop.**	orthopedic

N

		NF	Newfoundland	**OSHA**	Occupational Safety and Health Administration
N.	North	**NFL**	National Football League		
NAACOG	Nurses Association of the American College of Obstetricians and Gynecologists	**Nfld.**	Newfoundland	**OSRD**	Office of Scientific Research and Development
		NG	National Guard		
		NH	New Hampshire	**OSS**	Office of Strategic Services
		NHL	National Hockey League	**osteo.**	osteopathic
NAACP	National Association for the Advancement of Colored People	**NIH**	National Institutes of Health	**otol.**	otological
		NIMH	National Institute of Mental Health	**otolaryn.**	otolaryngological
NACA	National Advisory Committee for Aeronautics	**NJ**	New Jersey		
		NLRB	National Labor Relations Board		
NACDL	National Association of Criminal Defense Lawyers	**NM, N.Mex.**	New Mexico		
		No.	Northern	**PA, Pa.**	Pennsylvania
NACU	National Association of Colleges and Universities	**NOAA**	National Oceanographic and Atmospheric Administration	**paleontol.**	paleontological
				path.	pathological
NAD	National Academy of Design	**NORAD**	North America Air Defense	**pediat.**	pediatrics
NAE	National Academy of Engineering, National Association of Educators	**Nov.**	November	**PEI**	Prince Edward Island
		NOW	National Organization for Women	**PEN**	Poets, Playwrights, Editors, Essayists and Novelists
NAESP	National Association of Elementary School Principals	**nr.**	near	**penol.**	penological
		NRA	National Rifle Association	**pers.**	personnel
NAFE	National Association of Female Executives	**NRC**	National Research Council	**PGA**	Professional Golfers' Association of America
		NS	Nova Scotia		
N.Am.	North America	**NSC**	National Security Council	**PHA**	Public Housing Administration
NAM	National Association of Manufacturers	**NSF**	National Science Foundation	**pharm.**	pharmaceutical
		NSTA	National Science Teachers Association	**PharmD**	Doctor of Pharmacy
NAMH	National Association for Mental Health			**PharmM**	Master of Pharmacy
		NSW	New South Wales	**PhB**	Bachelor of Philosophy
NAPA	National Association of Performing Artists	**nuc.**	nuclear	**PhD**	Doctor of Philosophy
		numis.	numismatic	**PhDChemE**	Doctor of Science in Chemical Engineering
NARAS	National Academy of Recording Arts and Sciences	**NV**	Nevada		
		NW	Northwest	**PhM**	Master of Philosophy
NAREB	National Association of Real Estate Boards	**NWT**	Northwest Territories	**Phila.**	Philadelphia
		NY	New York	**philharm.**	philharmonic
NARS	National Archives and Record Service	**NYC**	New York City	**philol.**	philological
		NYU	New York University	**photog.**	photographic
NAS	National Academy of Sciences	**NZ**	New Zealand	**phys.**	physical
NASA	National Aeronautics and Space Administration			**physiol.**	physiological
				Pitts.	Pittsburgh

O

NASP	National Association of School Psychologists			**Pk.**	Park
				Pky.	Parkway
NASW	National Association of Social Workers	**ob-gyn**	obstetrics-gynecology	**Pl.**	Place
		obs.	observatory	**Plz.**	Plaza
nat.	national	**obstet.**	obstetrical	**PO**	Post Office
NATAS	National Academy of Television Arts and Science	**occupl.**	occupational	**polit.**	political
		oceanog.	oceanographic	**poly**	polytechnic, polytechnical
NATO	North Atlantic Treaty Organization	**Oct.**	October	**PQ**	Province of Quebec
		OD	Doctor of Optometry	**PR**	Puerto Rico
		OECD	Organization for Economic Cooperation and Development	**prep.**	preparatory
NBA	National Basketball Association			**pres.**	president
		OOEC	Organization of European Economic Cooperation	**Presbyn.**	Presbyterian
				presdl.	presidential

prin.	principal					

prin. principal
procs. proceedings
prod. produced
prodn. production
prodr. producer
prof. professor
profl. professional
prog. progressive
propr. proprietor
pros. prosecuting
pro tem. pro tempore
psychiat. psychiatric
psychol. psychological
PTA Parent-Teachers Association
ptnr. partner
PTO Pacific Theater of Operations, Parent Teacher Organization
pub. publisher, publishing, published, public
publ. publication
pvt. private

Q

quar. quarterly
qm. quartermaster
Que. Quebec

R

radiol. radiological
RAF Royal Air Force
RCA Radio Corporation of America
RCAF Royal Canadian Air Force
Rd. Road
R&D Research & Development
REA Rural Electrification Administration
rec. recording
ref. reformed
regt. regiment
regtl. regimental
rehab. rehabilitation
rels. relations
Rep. Republican
rep. representative
Res. Reserve
ret. retired
Rev. Reverend
rev. review, revised
RFC Reconstruction Finance Corporation
RI Rhode Island
Rlwy. Railway
Rm. Room
RN Registered Nurse
roentgenol. roentgenological
ROTC Reserve Officers Training Corps
RR rural route, railroad
rsch. research
rschr. researcher
Rt. Route

S

S. South
s. son of
SAC Strategic Air Command
SAG Screen Actors Guild
S.Am. South America
san. sanitary
SAR Sons of the American Revolution
Sask. Saskatchewan
savs. savings
SB Bachelor of Science
SBA Small Business Administration
SC South Carolina
ScB Bachelor of Science
SCD Doctor of Commercial Science
ScD Doctor of Science
sch. school
sci. science, scientific
SCV Sons of Confederate Veterans
SD South Dakota
SE Southeast
SEC Securities and Exchange Commission
sec. secretary
sect. section
seismol. seismological
sem. seminary
Sept. September
s.g. senior grade
sgt. sergeant
SI Staten Island
SJ Society of Jesus
SJD Scientiae Juridicae Doctor
SK Saskatchewan
SM Master of Science
SNP Society of Nursing Professionals
So. Southern
soc. society
sociol. sociological
spkr. speaker
spl. special
splty. specialty
Sq. Square
SR Sons of the Revolution
sr. senior
SS Steamship
St. Saint, Street
sta. station
stats. statistics
STB Bachelor of Sacred Theology
stblzn. stabilization
STD Doctor of Sacred Theology
std. standard
Ste. Suite
subs. subsidiary
SUNY State University of New York
supr. supervisor
supt. superintendent
surg. surgical
svc. service
SW Southwest
sys. system

T

Tb. tuberculosis
tchg. teaching
tchr. teacher
tech. technical, technology
technol. technological
tel. telephone
telecom. telecommunications
temp. temporary
Tenn. Tennessee
TESOL Teachers of English to Speakers of Other Languages
Tex. Texas
ThD Doctor of Theology
theol. theological
ThM Master of Theology
TN Tennessee
tng. training
topog. topographical
trans. transaction, transferred
transl. translation, translated
transp. transportation
treas. treasurer
TV television
twp. township
TX Texas
typog. typographical

U

U. University
UAW United Auto Workers
UCLA University of California at Los Angeles
UK United Kingdom
UN United Nations
UNESCO United Nations Educational, Scientific and Cultural Organization
UNICEF United Nations International Children's Emergency Fund
univ. university
UNRRA United Nations Relief and Rehabilitation Administration
UPI United Press International
urol. urological
US, USA U.S. of America
USAAF U.S. Army Air Force
USAF U.S. Air Force
USAFR U.S. Air Force Reserve
USAR U.S. Army Reserve
USCG U.S. Coast Guard
USCGR U.S. Coast Guard Reserve
USES U.S. Employment Service
USIA U.S. Information Agency
USMC U.S. Marine Corps
USMCR U.S. Marine Corps Reserve
USN U.S. Navy
USNG U.S. National Guard
USNR U.S. Naval Reserve
USO U.S. Organizations
USPHS U.S. Public Health Service
USS U.S. Ship
USSR Union of the Soviet Socialist Republics

USTA   U.S. Tennis Association
UT   Utah

V

VA   Veterans Administration
VA,Va.   Virginia
vet.   veteran, veterinary
VFW   Veterans of Foreign Wars
VI   Virgin Islands
vis.   visiting
VISTA   Volunteers in Service to America
vocat.   vocational
vol.   volunteer, volume
v.p.   vice president
vs   versus
VT, Vt.   Vermont

W

W   West
WA, Wash.   Washington (state)
WAC   Women's Army Corps
WAVES   Women's Reserve, US Naval Reserve
WCTU   Women's Christian Temperance Union
we.   western
WHO   World Health Organization
WI   Wisconsin, West Indies
Wis.   Wisconsin
WV, W.Va.   West Virginia
WY, Wyo.   Wyoming

Y

YK   Yukon Territory
YMCA   Young Men's Christian Association
YMHA   Young Men's Hebrew Association
YM&YWHA   Young Men's and Young Women's Hebrew Association
yr.   year
YT   Yukon Territory
YWCA   Young Women's Christian Association

Z

zool.   zoological

AARON, HANK, T: Retired MLB Player **I:** Athletics **DOB:** 02/05/1934 **PB:** Mobile, Alabama **PT:** Son of Herbert and Estella A. Aaron; **ED:** HHD (hon.), Princeton University, 2011 **C:** Founder, Chairman, 755 Restaurant Corp., Atlanta, 1995-; Senior Vice President, Assistant to President, Atlanta National League Baseball Club, Inc., 1989-; President, CEO, Hank Aaron Automotive Group, 1999-2007; Vice President Player Devel., Atlanta National League Baseball Club, Inc., 1976-89; Baseball Player, Milwaukee Brewers, 1975-76; Baseball Player, Atlanta Braves, 1966-75; Baseball Player, Milwaukee Braves, 1954-65; Former Semi-pro baseball player, **CR:** Board directors Medallion Fin. Corp., 2004-, Retail Ventures, Inc., 2000-, Turner Broadcasting Systems, Inc., 1980-96 member American League All-Star Team, 1975, National League All-Star Team, 1955-74 **CIV:** Organizer, Hank Aaron Scholarship Fund, Co-founder, Hank Aaron Chasing the Dream Foundation, Board advisors, Atlanta Tech. Institute, Board advisors, Atlanta Falcons Football Club, Member board governors, Boys & Girls Clubs America, **CW:** Author: (autobiography) I Had A Hammer: The Hank Aaron Story, 1991 **AW:** Named The National League's Most Valuable Player, 1957, Player of Year, The Sporting News, 1963, 1956; named one of The 100 Greatest Baseball Players, 1999; named to Major League Baseball's All-Century Team, 1999, The National Baseball Hall of Fame, 1982; recipient Presidential Medal of Freedom, The White House, 2002, Presidential Citizens Medal, 2001, Lou Gehrig Memorial award, 1970, National League Gold Glove award, 1958-60,Order of the Rising Sun, 2006, Lombardi Award of Excellence, 2006 **ACH:** Achievements include leading the National League in: doubles, 1955, 1956, 1961, 1965; batting average, hits, 1956, 1959; runs, 1957, 1963, 1967; home runs, 1957, 1963, 1966, 1967; runs batted in, 1957, 1960, 1963, 1966; member of World Series championship winning Milwaukee Braves, 1957; holding Major League Baseball's all-time record for: total bases (6856); runs batted in (2297); extra base hits (1477); breaking Babe Ruth's career home run record hitting his 715th home run, April 8, 1974 (total career home runs: 755); held record for most career home runs until 2007

ABBOTT, GREG, T: Governor of Texas **I:** Government Administration/Government Relations/Government Services **DOB:** 11/13/1957 **PT:** Son of Calvin Roger and Doris Lacristia (Jacks) Abbott; **ED:** JD, Vanderbilt University Law School, Nashville, 1984; BBA in Finance, University Texas, Austin, 1981 **CT:** Bar: US District Court (southern district) Texas 1985, Texas 1985 **C:** Governor, State of Texas, 2015-; Attorney general, State of Texas, 2002-15; Associate justice, Texas Supreme Court, Austin, 1996-2001; Trial judge, 129th State District Court, Houston, 1992-96; Attorney, Butler & Binion, Houston, 1984-92 **CR:** Member Gov.'s Committee Promote Adoption **CIV:** Member adv. board, Career & Recovery Resources Inc., Board trustees, Central Texas Goodwill Industries, Hon. state chairman, Big Brothers/Big Sisters Texas, 2004 Board directors, Maywood Children & Family Services, Board directors, Texas Institute Rehabilitation & Research Foundation, **AW:** Named Appellate Judge of Year, American Board Trial Advocates (Texas chapter), Jurist of Year, Texas Rev. Law & Politics, Outstanding Trial Judge, Texas Association Civil Trial & Appellate Specialists, 1995; named an Outstanding Young Texan, Texas Jaycees, 1995; recipient American Jurisprudence award, 1983 **MEM:** Mem.: Texas Association State Judges, Houston Young Lawyers Association, Houston Bar Association (Outstanding Young Lawyer 1994), State Bar Texas (Supreme Court liaison committee on judicial ethics) **PA:** Republican

ABDUL-JABBAR, KAREEM, T: Former Professional Basketball Player **I:** Athletics **DOB:** 04/16/1947 **PB:** New York **SC:** NY/USA **ED:** BA, UCLA, 1969 **C:** Global cultural ambassador, US Department State, 2012—; Founder, The Skyhook Foundation, 2009—; Cons., scout, New York Knicks, 2004—2005; Head coach, Oklahoma Storm, US Basketball League, 2002; Consultant, Ind. Pacers, 2001—2002; Assistant coach, L.A. Clippers, 2000—2001; Special assistant to head coach, L.A. Lakers, 2005—2011; Center, L.A. Lakers, 1975—1989; Center, Milwaukee Bucks, Milwaukee, Wisconsin, 1969—1975 **CW:** Actor: (films) Game of Death, 1978, The Fish that Saved Pittsburgh, 1979, Airplane, 1980, Fletch, 1985; (TV miniseries) The Stand, 1994, (TV appearances) Mannix, 1971, Emergency!, 1974, The Man from Atlantis, 1977, Dinah!, 1977, The Way It Was, 1977, Diff'rent Strokes, 1982, Pryor's Place, 1984, Tales from the Darkside, 1985, Stingray, 1987, 21 Jump Street, 1990, Good Sports, 1991, Uncle Buck, 1991, Amen, 1991, Matrix, 1993, The Critic, 1994, The Fresh Prince of Bel-Air, 1994, Full House, 1995, Martin, 1996, Everybody Loves Raymond, 1996, Living Single, 1997, Boston Common, 1997; author (with Peter Knobler): Giant Steps: An Autobiography of Kareem Abdul-Jabbar, 1983; author: (with Mignon McCarthy) Kareem, 1990; author: (with Stephen Singular) A Season on the Reservation: My Soujourn with the White Mountain Apaches, 2000; author: (with Alan Steinburg) Black Profiles in Courage: A Legacy of African-American Achievement, 2000; author: (with Anthony Walton) Brothers in Arms: The Epic Story of the 761st Tank Battalion, WWII's Forgotten Heroes, 2004; author: (with Raymond Obstfeld) On the Shoulders of Giants: My Personal Journey Through the Harlem Renaissance, 2007, What Color Is My World: The Lost History of African-American Inventors, 2012 (Outstanding Literary Work-Children, National Association for the Advancement of Colored People Image Awards, 2013) **AW:** Named NCAA Player of Year, Associated Press, 1967, 1969, 1st Team NCAA All-Am., 1967, 1968, 1969, NCAA Final Four Most Outstanding Player, 1967, 1968, 1969, NBA Rookie of Year, 1970, 1st Team All-NBA, 1971—74, 1976, 1977, 1980, 1981, 1984, 1986, NBA MVP, 1971, 1972, 1974, 1976, 1977, 1980, NBA Finals MVP, 1971, 1985, 1st Team All-Def., 1974, 1975, 1979, 1980, 1981; named to Eastern Conference All-Star Team, 1970—75, We. Conference All-Star Team, 1976, 1977, 1979—89, 35th Anniversary All-Time Team, NBA, 1980, NBA Hall of Fame, 1995; recipient NCAA Naismith Men's College Player of Year award, 1969, Lincoln Medal, Ford's Theatre Society, 2011, Presidential Medal of Freedom, The White House, 2016 **ACH:** Achievements include member of NCAA National Championship winning UCLA Bruins, 1967-69; being the first overall pick in the NBA Draft, 1969; leading the NBA in: field goals, 1970-72, 1974, 1977; points, 1970-72; field goal attempts, 1972; defensive & total rebounds, 1976, 1977; blocks, 1976, 1977, 1979, 1980; minutes, 1976; field goal percentage, 1977; member of NBA Championship winning Milwaukee Bucks, 1971; Los Angeles Lakers 1980, 1982, 1985, 1987, 1988; being the NBA career leader in: points scored (38,387), field goals attempted (28,307), field goals made (15,837) and minutes played (57,446) **H:** Jazz

ABNEY, DAVID PHILLIP, T: UPS CEO **I:** Business Management/Business Services **ED:** BBA in Marketing, Delta State University, 1976 **C:** CEO, United Parcel Service, Inc. (UPS), 2014-; President, UPS Airlines, 2007-08; President, UPS International, 2003-07; COO, United Parcel Service, Inc. (UPS), Atlanta, 2007-14; Senior vice president, United Parcel Service, Inc. (UPS), Atlanta, 2003-07; Fritz cos. integration manager, United Parcel Service, Inc. (UPS), Atlanta, 2001-02; Manager SonicAir, United Parcel Service, Inc. (UPS), Atlanta, 1995-2000; Various positions, United Parcel Service, Inc. (UPS), Atlanta, 1974-95 **CR:** Board of Directors United Parcel Service, Inc. (UPS), 2014-, Johnson Controls, Inc., 2009- **CIV:** Board member, Coalition Service Industries, Board member, Southern Center for International Studies, Board member, U.S. Japan Business Council, Trustee, UPS Foundation, Board member, Delta State Univ. Alumni Foundation

ABRAHAM, F. MURRAY, T: Actor **I:** Media & Entertainment **DOB:** 10/24/1939 **PB:** Pittsburgh **SC:** Pennsylvania **ED:** Student, University Texas, El Paso **C:** Professor, Brooklyn College, 1985—; Actor Broadway, Off-Broadway, children's theater, musicals, film, TV **CR:** Director No Smoking Please, New York City, Time & Space Ltd. Theatre, New York City; **CW:** Professional stage debut in The Wonderful Ice Cream Suit, Coronet Theatre, LA, 1965; Broadway debut in The Man in the Glass Booth, Royale Theatre, 1968; (Broadway plays) 6 Rms RivVu, 1972-73, Bad Habits, 1974, The Ritz, 1976, Teibele and Her Demon, 1979, It's Only a Play, 2014; (other stage appearances) Landscape of the Body, 1977, The Master and Margarita, 1978, The Golem, 1984, King Lear, 1981, Frankie and Johnny in the Claire de Lune, 1987, A Month in the Country, 1995, The Jew of Malta, 2007, Merchant of Venice, 2007, (films) They Might Be Giants, 1971, Serpico, 1974, The Sunshine Boys, 1975, All the President's Men, 1976, The Ritz, 1976, The Big Fix, 1979, Scarface, 1983, Amadeus, 1984 (Academy award for Best Actor 1984, Golden Globe award for Best Actor 1984), The Name of the Rose, 1986, Russicum, 1989, An Innocent Man, 1989, Bonfire of the Vanities, 1990, Cadence, 1991, Mobsters, 1991, National Lampoon's Loaded Weapon I, 1993, By the Sword, 1993, Last Action Hero, 1993, Surviving The Game, 1994, The Case, 1994, Nostradamus, 1994, Jamila, 1994, Fresh, 1994, Mighty Aphrodite, 1995, Dillinger and Capone, 1995, Baby Face Nelson, 1995, Looking for Richard, 1996, Children of the Revolution, 1996, Mimic, 1997, Eruption, 1997, Laurel and Hardy: For Love or Mummy, 1998, Star Trex IX, 1998, Falcone, 1999, Esther, 1999, Muppets From Space, 1999, Finding Forrester, 2000, The Knights of the Quest, 2001, Thir13en Ghosts, 2001, Joshua, 2002, Ticker, 2002, Five Moons Plaza, 2003, My Father, Rua Alguem 5555, 2003, Another Way of Seeing Things, 2004, Too Much Romance... It's Time for Stuffed Peppers, 2004, The Bridge of San Luis Rey, 2004, A House Divided, 2006, The Stone Merchant, 2006, Quiet Flows the Don, 2006, The Inquiry, 2006, Wine and Kisses, 2007, Carnera: The Walking Mountain, 2008, A House Divided, 2008, Perestroika, 2009, Sword of War, 2009, The Unseen World, 2010, The Day of the Siege: September Eleven 1683, 2012, Goltzius and the Pelican Company, 2012, Dead Man Down, 2013, Inside Llewyn Davis, 2013, The Gambler Who Wouldn't Die, 2013, The Grand Budapest Hotel, 2014, The Mystery of Dante, A Little Game, 2014, Isle of Dogs, 2018, How to Train Your Dragon 3, 2019; narrator Herman Melville, Damned in Paradise, PBS, 1985, (TV mini-series) Marco Polo, 1982-83, Larry McMurtry's Dead Man's Walk, 1996; TV special Einstein Revealed (voice), 1996, (TV films) Sex and the Married Woman, 1978, Silas Marner, 1987, Color of Justice, 1997, Noah's Ark, 1999, Esther, 1999, Noah's Ark, 1999, The Darkling, 2000, The Greatest Gift, 2000, Pompeii: The Last Day, 2003, Dead Lawyers, 2004, Shark Swarm, 2008, Beauty and the Beast, 2012, (TV series) Homeland, 2012-18, (TV appearances) Saving Grace, 2009, Bored to Death, 2010, The Good Wife, 2011-14, Blue Bloods, 2012, Elementary, 2013, Inside Amy Schumer, 2016, Curb Your Enthusiasm, 2017 **AW:**

Recipient Obie award for Uncle Vanya 1984; LA Film Critics award, 1985, The Gielgud Award, 2010,American Theater Hall of Fame, 2015; **MEM:** Member Actors Equity, American Federation of TV and Radio Artists, Screen Actors Guild; **BA:** Untitled Entertainment, 435 Hudson Street FL 9, New York, NY, 10014

ABRAHAM, RALPH, T: U.S. Representative from Louisiana **I:** Government Administration/Government Relations/Government Services **DOB:** 09/16/1954 **PB:** Monroe **SC:** LA/USA **ED:** M.D., Louisiana State University School of Medicine, 1994; D.V.M., Louisiana State University School of Veterinary Medicine,1980; B.A., Louisiana State University, 1980 **C:** Member, U.S. House of Representatives from Louisiana's 5th District, 2015-; Member, Committee on Agriculture; Member, Committee on Science, Space, and Technology; Member, Committee on Veterans Affair; Member, Veterans Affairs Committee, 2015-16 **BA:** 417 Cannon HOB, Washington, DC, 20515

ABRAMS, J.J., T: Television Producer, Scriptwriter **I:** Media & Entertainment **DOB:** 06/27/1966 **PB:** NYC **PT:** Son of Gerald W. and Carol Ann Abrams; **ED:** Attended, Sarah Lawrence College **CW:** (executive producer, director, writer): (TV series) Felicity, 1998-2002; Alias, 2001-06; Lost, 2004-10 (Emmy award for Outstanding Directing for a Drama Series, 2005, Producers Guild of America award for Best TV Series, Drama, 2006); executive prodr.: What About Brian, 2006, Six Degrees, 2006, Boundaries, 2008, Person of Interest, 2011-15, Alcatraz, 2012, Revolution, 2012-14, Almost Human, 2013-14, Believe, 2014; (TV films) Dead People, 2015; (executive producer, writer): (films) Forever Young, 1992; executive producer, writer (TV series) Fringe, 2008-13, Anatomy of Hope, 2009, Undercovers, 2010, Person of Interest, 2011, Alcatraz, 2012, Shelter, 2012,Revolution, 2012, Almost Human, 2013, Believe, 2014, Dead People, 2015, 11.22.63, 2016, Roadies, 2016, Westworld, 2016, Castle Rock, 2018; (producer, writer, actor): (films) Regarding Henry, 1991; prodr.: The Pallbearer, 1996, Cloverfield, 2008, Valencia, 2016, Mission: Impossible - Rogue Nation, 2015, Star Trek Beyond, 2016, Star Wars The Last Jedi, 2017, God Particle, 2018, Overlord, 2018, Mission Impossible 6, 2018, Star Wars Episode IX, 2019; (writer, producer) Joy Ride, 2001; (writer, director) Mission: Impossible III, 2006; Super 8, 2011; (writer) (screenplays) Gone Fishin', 1997; Armageddon, 1998; (producer, director): (films) Star Trek, 2009; Star Trek Into Darkness, 2013; producer, writer, director (films) Star Wars: The Force Awakens, 2015; actor: (films) Six Degrees of Separation, 1993, Diabolique, 1996, The Suburbans, 1999; featured in documentaries Showrunners: The Art of Running a TV Show, 2014, The Magic History of Cinema, 2014; co-author (with Doug Dorst): S., 2013 **AW:** Named one of The 100 Agents of Change, Rolling Stone magazine, 2009, 50 Smartest People in Hollywood, Entertainment Weekly, 2007, 100 Most Powerful Celebrities, Forbes.com, 2007, 100 Most Influential People, TIME magazine, 2006, 100 People in Hollywood You Need to Know, Fade In magazine, 2005; recipient Norman Lear Achievement award in TV, Producers Guild of America, 2013

ACOSTA, ALEX, T: U.S. Secretary of Labor, Former, Dean, Former Prosecutor **I:** Government Administration/Government Relations/Government Services **PB:** Miami **ED:** JD, Harvard University, 1994; BA, Harvard University **C:** Secretary,Department of Labor, Washington, DC, 2017—; Dean, Florida International University Law School, Miami, 2009-2017; US attorney (so. district) Florida, US Department Justice, Miami, 2006-09; Interim US

attorney (so. district) Florida, US Department Justice, Miami, 2005-06; Assistant attorney general civil rights division, US Department Justice, Washington, 2003-05; Principal deputy assistant attorney general civil rights division, US Department Justice, Washington, 2001-02; Senior fellow, Ethics & Pub. Policy Center, 1997-2000; Associate, Kirkland & Ellis, 1995-97; Law clerk, US Court Appeals (3rd cir.), Washington; **CR:** Member National Labor Relations Board, 2002-03 **AW:** Recipient Friend in Government award, American-Arab Anti-Discrimination Committee, 2005, Hugh A. Johnson, Junior Memorial award, DC Hispanic Bar Association, 2003, Excellence in Government Service award, Mex.-American Legal Defense and Education Fund, 2003, Distinguished Leadership award, Arab American Anti-Discrimination Committee Michigan, 2004 **BA:** US Department of Labor, 200 Constitution Ave NW, Washington, DC, 20210

ACTON, BRIAN, T: Co-founder **I:** Business Management/Business Services **CN:** WhatsApp Inc. **SC:** MI/USA **ED:** BS, Stanford University **C:** Founder, Signal Foundation (2017-Present); Co-founder, WhatsApp Inc. (2009-2017)

ADAMCZYK, DARIUS, T: CEO **I:** Manufacturing **CN:** Honeywell **SC:** Poland **ED:** B.A., Michigan State University; Masters, Syracuse University; M.B.A, Harvard University **C:** Chairman, Honeywell, 2018-; CEO, Honeywell, 2017-; President, Honeywell, 2016-

ADAMS, ALMA, T: U.S. Representative from North Carolina **I:** Government Administration/Government Relations/Government Services **C:** U.S. House of Representatives from North Carolina's 12 District, 2015-Present; State Representative District 58, North Carolina, 2003-2015; Former State Representative, District 26, North Carolina; Administrator, Professor in Arts **CR:** Chairman, Appropriations Committee; Vice Chairman, Commerce, Small Business And Entrepreneurship Committee; Health Committee; Education Subcommittee On Universities, Education Committee; Aging Committee **PA:** Democrat

ADAMS, AMY, T: Actress **I:** Media & Entertainment **DOB:** 08/20/1975 **PB:** Vicenza **SC:** Italy **PT:** Richard Adams; Kathryn (Hicken) Adams **CW:** Actress, Films, "Drop Dead Gorgeous" (1999), "Psycho Beach Party" (2000), "The Chromium Hook" (2000), "Cruel Intentions 2" (2000), "The Slaughter Rule" (2002), "Pumpkin" (2002), "Serving Sara" (2002), "Catch Me If You Can" (2002), "The Last Run" (2004), "Junebug" (2005), "Standing Still" (2005), "The Wedding Date" (2005), "Moonlight Serenade" (2006), "Talladega Nights: The Ballad of Ricky Bobby" (2006), "Tenacious D in The Pick of Destiny" (2006), "Fast Track" (2006), "Underdog" (2007), "Enchanted" (2007); "Charlie Wilson's War" (2007), "Sunshine Cleaning" (2008); "Miss Pettigrew Lives for a Day: (2008), "Doubt" (2008), "Night at the Museum: Battle of the Smithsonian" (2009), "Julie & Julia" (2009); "Moonlight Serenade" (2009); "Leap Year" (2010), "The Fighter" (2010), "The Muppets" (2011), "On the Road" (2012), "The Master" (2012), "Trouble with the Curve" (2012), "Man of Steel" (2013), "Her" (2013), "American Hustle" (2013), "Lullaby" (2014), "Big Eyes" (2014), "Batman v. Superman: Dawn of Justice" (2016), "Arrival" (2016), "Story of Your Life" (2016), "Nocturnal Animals" (2016), "Justice League" (2017), "Backseat" (2018); TV series, "Dr. Vegas" (2004-2005), "The Office" (2005-2006), "SNL" (2008, 2014), "Sharp Objects" (2018) **AW:** Named One of the 100 Most Influential People in the World, TIME Magazine (2014); Named One of

12 People to Watch, Newsweek Magazine (2008); Chanel Spotlight Award, Elle Magazine (2007); Best Supporting Actress, "Junebug," Critics' Choice Award (2006); Best Supporting Actress, "Junebug," National Society Film Critics Award (2006); Best Supporting Actress, "The Master," National Society Film Critics Award (2013); Best Performance by an Actress in a Motion Picture - Comedy or Musical, "American Hustle," Golden Globe Award (2014); Best Actress in a Comedy, "American Hustle," Critics' Choice Award (2014); Best Actress in a Motion Picture - Musical or Comedy, "Big Eyes," Golden Globe Award (2015) **BA:** Brillstein Entertainment Partners, 9150 Wilshire Blvd Suite 350, Beverly Hills, CA, 90212

ADAMS, JOHN COOLIDGE, T: Composer **I:** Fine Art **DOB:** 02/15/1947 **PB:** Worcester, Massachusetts **PT:** Son of Carl John and Elinore Mary (Coolidge) A. **ED:** MA, Harvard University, 1971; AB magna cum laude, Harvard University, 1969; Studied with Leon Kirchner, Earl Kim, Roger Sessions, Harvard University **C:** Former Composer-in-residence, Conductor, San Francisco Symphony Orchestra, 1979-85 **CW:** Artistic advisor, San Francisco Symphony Orchestra, from 1978, former composer-in-residence, San Francisco Symphony Orchestra; director, New Music Ensemble, from 1972-81; faculty member, San Francisco Conservatory, 1972-83; composer-in-residence, Marlboro Festival, 1970, Richard & Barbara Debs composer, Carnegie Hall, 2003-07; musical compositions include Electric Wake, 1968, Heavy Metal, 1971, American Standard, 1973, Kataadn, 1973, Onyx, 1976, Phrygian Gates, 1977, Shaker Loops, 1978; Onyx, Grounding, Sermon, Common Tones, 1979, Harmonium, 1980, Grand Pianola Music, 1982, Harmonielehre, 1985, Nixon in China, 1987 (Grammy for best contemporary composition, 1989), The Death of Klinghoffer, 1991, Chamber Symphony, 1993 (Royal Philharmonic Society Music award, 1994), Violin Concerto (Grawemeyer award for music, 1995), Naive and Sentimental Music, 1999, On The Transmigration of Souls, 2002 (Pulitzer prize for music, 2003), My Father Knew Charles Ives, 2003, Doctor Atomic, 2003, The Dharma at Big Sur, 2004, A Flowering Tree, 2006, Son of Chamber Symphony, 2007, String Quartet, 2008, First Quartet, 2008, City Noir, 2009, Absolute Jest, 2012, Saxophone Concerto, 2013, Scherazade.2, 2014, Second Quartet, 2014; author: Hallelujah Junction, 2008. **AW:** Named to rank of Chevalier dans l'Ordre des Artes et des Lettres, French Ministry of Culture; recipient Opera honor, National Endowment for the Arts, 2009, Distinguished Composer award, Am. Composers Orchestra, 2007, Nemmers prize in Music Composition, Northwestern University, 2004, Centennial medal, Harvard University Grad. School Arts & Sciences, 2004, California Gov's. Awd. for Lifetime Achievement in the Arts, Cyril Magnin Awd. for Outstanding Achievement in the Arts

ADELSON, SHELDON GARY, T: Hotel and Gaming Company Executive **I:** Leisure, Travel & Tourism **DOB:** 08/04/1933 **PB:** Dorchester **SC:** MA/USA **ED:** Student, City College of New York **C:** CEO, Sands China. Ltd., Macau, 2015-Present; Founder, Palazzo Resort Hotel Casino, 2008-Present; Founder, Venetian Macau, 2007-Present; Founder, Sands Macau, 2004-Present; Chairman, CEO, Las Vegas Sands Corp., 2004-Present; Founder, Venetian Resort Hotel Casino, 1991-Present; Founder, Sands Expo & Convention Center, 1990-Present; Chairman, CEO, Treasurer, Las Vegas Sands, Inc., 1989-Present; Founder, Comdex Trade Shows, 1991-1995; Chairman, CEO, Interface Group Inc., Needham, MA, 1974; Owner, Israel Hayom, Las Vegas Review-Journal; Financial Consultant;

Investment Advisor; Mortgage Broker; Paperboy **CR:** Guest Speaker, Babson College, Tel Aviv University, Columbia Business School, Harvard Business School, University of New Haven **CIV:** U.S. Holocaust Memorial Council, U.S. Holocaust Memorial Museum, Washington, DC **AW:** The 25 Most Influential Republicans, Newsmax Magazine, 2008, The World's Richest People, Forbes Magazine, 2005-Present, The Forbes 400: Richest Americans, 2006-Present **PA:** Republican **BA:** Venetian Resort Hotel Casino, 3355 Las Vegas Boulevard S, Las Vegas, NV, 89109

ADERHOLT, ROBERT BROWN, T: U.S. Representative from Alabama, Lawyer **I:** Government Administration/Government Relations/Government Services **DOB:** 07/22/1965 **PB:** Haleyville, Alabama **PT:** Son of Bobby Ray and Mary Frances Aderholt **ED:** JD, Samford University Cumberland School of Law, 1990; BA, Birmingham Southern University, 1987 **C:** Member, US Congress from 4th Alabama District, Washington, 1997-; Member, Committee on Foreign Affairs; Assistant Legal Advisor to Governor, State of Alabama, Montgomery, 1995-96; City Judge, Haleyville, Alabama, 1992-96 **CR:** Member Helsinki Commission on Security and Cooperation in Europe **PA:** Republican **BA:** US House of Representatives, 2369 Rayburn House Office Building, Washington, DC, 20515

ADICHIE, CHIMAMANDA NGOZI, T: Writer **I:** Writing and Editing **DOB:** 09/15/1977 **PB:** Enugu **SC:** Nigeria **PT:** Daughter of James Nwoye and Grace Ifeoma Adichie. **ED:** MA in Creative Writing, Johns Hopkins University, Baltimore; BA in Communications and Political Sci., summa cum laude, Eastern Connecticut State University, 2001; Educated, Drexel University, Philadelphia **CR:** Editor The Compass magazine, Nigeria **CW:** Author: (plays) For Love of Biafra, 1998, (collected poems) Decisions, 1998, (short story collection) The Thing Around Your Neck, 2009, (novels) Purple Hibiscus, 2003 (Hurston/Wright Legacy award best debut fiction, 2004, Commonwealth Writers' prize best first book (Africa), 2005, Commonwealth Writers' prize best first book (overall), 2005), Half of a Yellow Sun, 2006 (Anisfield-Wolf Book award fiction, 2007, PEN Beyond Margins award, 2007, Orange Broadband prize fiction, 2007), Americanah, 2013 **AW:** Named a MacArthur Fellow, The John D. and Catherine T. MacArthur Foundation, 2008; named one of The New Yorker's 20 Under 40, 2010; recipient International Nonino prize, 2009

ADJAYE, DAVID, T: Architect **I:** Architecture & Construction **PB:** Dar es Salaam **SC:** Tanzania **ED:** BA, London South Bank University; MA, Royal College of Art **C:** Adjaye Associates, 2000-Present; Owner/Creator, Adjaye and Russell, 1994-2000 **CW:** Author, (Book) David Adjaye Houses, 2005, David Adjaye: Making Public Buildings, 2006, (Buildings) National Museum of African American History, (Documentary) Building Africa: Architecture of a Continent, 2005 **AW:** RIBA Presidents Medal Students Award, 1993, Officer of the Order of the British Empire, 2007, TIME 100 Most Influential, 2017

ADKERSON, RICHARD C., T: Mining Company Executive **I:** Mining & Metals **CN:** Freeport McMoRan Copper & Gold Inc. **ED:** MBA, Mississippi State University, 1970; BA, Mississippi State University, With Honors, 1969 **C:** Co-Chairman, McMoran Exploration Co., 2004-Present; President, CEO And Director, Freeport-McMoran Copper & Gold, Inc., Phoenix, AZ, 2003-Present; President, CFO, Freeport-McMoran Copper & Gold, Inc., New Orleans, LA, 2000-2003; President, COO, CFO, Freeport-McMoran Copper & Gold, Inc.,

New Orleans, LA 1997-2000; CFO, Freeport-McMoran Copper & Gold, Inc., New Orleans, LA, 1992-1997; Financial Management Positions, Freeport-McMoran Copper & Gold, Inc., New Orleans, LA, 1989-1992; Partner, Managing Director, Head Worldwide Oil And Gas Practice, Arthur Anderson & Co., 1989; Professor, Accounting Fellow, Securities And Exchange Commission, Washington, DC, 1976-1978; Chairman, International Copper Association **CR:** Council On Foreign Relations; Advisory Council, Kissinger Institute On China And The U.S., Clinton Global Initiative; Board Of Directors, Arizona Commerce Authority, Greater Phoenix Leadership, And The Greater Phoenix Economic Council; Vice Chairman, National World War II Museum; Associate Fellow, Securities and Exchange Commission **CIV:** Trustee, National D-Day Museum, Board Directors, Alumni Association And Bulldog Club, Advisory Board, Crosby Arboretum, Board of Visitors, M.D. Anderson Cancer Center, President Council, Xavier University, Executive Board of Advisors, Ourso College, Louisiana State University, Development Board, Fellowship of Christian Athletes, New Orleans, LA, Business Council, New Orleans & River Region, Advisory Board, College of Business & Industry & Agribusiness Institute, Mississippi State University, Vice President, President, Board Director, Executive Committee, Mississippi State University Foundation **BA:** Freeport McMoRan Copper & Gold Inc., 333 N Central Avenue, Phoenix, AZ, 85004-4414

ADKINS, ADELE, T: Singer, Songwriter **I:** Media & Entertainment **DOB:** 05/05/1988 **PB:** London **SC:** England **ED:** Grad., BRIT School Performing Arts & Tech., London, 2006 **C:** Signed with, XL Recordings, 2006 **CW:** Singer: (albums) 19, 2008, 21, 2011 (Favorite Pop/Rock Album, American Music Awards, 2011, Album of Year, Best Pop Vocal Album, Grammy Awards, 2012, Top Billboard 200 Album, Billboard Music Awards, 2012, Top Pop Album, Billboard Music Awards, 2012, 2013), 25, 2015 (Top Billboard 200 Album, Billboard Music Awards, 2016), (songs) Hometown Glory, 2007, Chasing Pavements, 2008 (Best Female Pop Vocal Performance, Grammy Awards, 2009), Rolling in the Deep, 2010 (Record of Year, Song of Year, Best Short Form Music Video, Grammy Awards, 2012, Top Streaming Song (Audio), Top Alternative Song, Billboard Music Awards, 2012), Someone Like You, 2011 (Best Pop Solo Performance, Grammy Awards, 2012), Set Fire to the Rain, 2011 (Best Pop Solo Performance, Grammy Awards, 2013), Skyfall, 2012 (Best Song, Critics Choice Awards, 2013, Best Original Song-Motion Picture, Golden Globe award, Hollywood Foreign Press Association, 2013, Best Original Song, Academy Awards, 2013, Best Song Written for Visual Media, Grammy Awards, 2014), Hello, 2015 (Top Selling Song, Billboard Music Awards, 2016)(Television), SNL, 2008, Ugly Betty, 2009, Adele at the BBC, 2015, Ade **AW:** Named a member of the Most Excellent Order of the British Empire (MBE), Her Majesty Queen Elizabeth II, 2013; named Top Pop Artist, Billboard Music Awards, 2012 Top Digital Media Artist, 2012, Top Radio Songs Artist, 2012, Top Digital Songs Artist, 2012, Top Hot 100 Artist, 2012, Top Billboard 200 Artist, 2012, Top Female Artist, 2016, 2012, Top Artist, 2016, 2012, Favorite Pop/Rock Female Artist, American Music Awards, 2011, Favorite Adult Contemporary Artist, 2012, 2011, Best New Artist, Grammy Awards, 2009, Best Jazz Act, Urban Music Awards, 2008; named one of The 100 Most Influential People in the World, TIME magazine, 2016, 2012; recipient Women of Year award, Glamour magazine, 2011, 2009, BRIT Awards Critic's Choice, Brit. Phonographic Industry, 2008, Favorite Adult Contemporary Artist, Americana Music Awards, 2016, Billboard Top 100, Top Selling Song, 2016,

AFFLECK, BEN, T: Actor **I:** Media & Entertainment **DOB:** 08/15/1972 **PB:** Berkeley **SC:** CA/USA **PT:** Timothy Affleck, Chris Ann (Boldt) Affleck **MS:** Single **SPN:** Jennifer Garner, 6/29/2005, Divorced **ED:** Honorary DFA, Brown University, 2013 **CIV:** Founder, Eastern Congo Initiative, 2010-Present **CW:** Actor, (Films) School Ties, 1992, Dazed And Confused, 1993, Mallrats, 1995, Going All The Way, 1997, Chasing Amy, 1997, Armageddon, 1998, Phantoms, 1998, Reindeer Games, 1999, Forces Of Nature, 1999, Dogma, 1999, 200 Cigarettes, 1999, Daddy And Them, 1999, Boiler Room, 1999, Bounce, 2000, Jay And Silent Bob Strike Back, 2001, Pearl Harbor, 2001, The Sum Of All Fears, 2002, Changing Lanes, 2002, The Third Wheel, 2002, Daredevil, 2003, Gigli, 2003, Paycheck, 2003, Jersey Girl, 2004, Surviving Christmas, 2004, Man About Town, 2006, Clerks II, 2006, Hollywoodland, 2006, Smokin' Aces, 2006, He's Just Not That Into You, 2009, State Of Play, 2009, Extract, 2009, The Company Men, 2010, To The Wonder, 2012, Runner, Runner, 2013, Gone Girl, 2014, Batman V Superman: Dawn Of Justice, 2016, Suicide Squad, 2016, The Accountant, 2016, Live By Night, 2016, Bending The Arc, 2017, Justice League, 2017; Actor, Writer, (Films) Good Will Hunting, 1997; Writer, Director, Producer, (Films) Gone Baby Gone, 2007; Actor, Director, Writer, (Films) The Town, 2010; Actor, Director, Producer, (Films) Argo, 2012; Producer, (Films) Stolen Summer, 2002; Executive Producer, (Films) Crossing Cords, 2001, Speakeasy, 2002, The Battle Of Shaker Heights, 2003, (TV Series) Project Greenlight, 2001, Push, Nevada, 2002, Project Greenlight 2, 2003, Project Greenlight 3, 2005, Reporter, 2009, Curb Your Enthusiasm, 2009, The Leisure Class, 2015, The Runner, 2016, Incorporated, 2016, (TV Films) More Time With Family, 2014 **AW:** Favorite Humanitarian, People's Choice Awards, 2015, Critics Choice Awards For Best Director, Best Picture, Golden Globe Awards For Best Director, Best Picture, Screen Actors Guild Award For Outstanding Performance By A Cast In A Motion Picture, Darryl F. Zanuck Award For Outstanding Producer Of Theatrical Motion Pictures, Producers Guild Of America, Directors Guild Of America Award For Outstanding Directorial Achievement In Feature Film, BAFTA Awards For Best Film, Best Director, Academy Award For Best Picture, Argo, 2013, Special Achievement In Filmmaking Award, National Board Review, Argo, 2012, Entertainer of the Year, Entertainment Weekly, 2012, The Ten Most Fascinating People, Barbara Walters Special, 2012, National Board Review Award For Best Directorial Debut, Boston Society Film Critics Award For Best New Filmmaker, Gone Baby Gone, 2007, The 50 Smartest People in Hollywood, Entertainment Weekly, 2007, Academy Award For Best Original Screenplay, Good Will Hunting, 1998 **BA:** c/o Creative Artists Agency, 2000 Avenue of The Stars, Los Angeles, CA, 90067-4700

AFFLECK, CASEY, T: Actor **I:** Media & Entertainment **DOB:** 08/12/1975 **PB:** Falmouth **SC:** MA/USA **PT:** Timothy Affleck; Chris Ann (Boldt) Affleck **ED:** Attended, Columbia University **CW:** Actor, Films, "To Die For" (1995), "Race the Sun" (1996), "Chasing Amy" (1997), "Good Will Hunting" (1997), "Desert Blue" (1998), "200 Cigarettes" (1999), "American Pie" (1999), "Floating" (1999), "Drowning Mona" (2000), "Committed" (2000), "Hamlet" (2000), "Attention Shoppers" (2000), "American Pie 2" (2001), "Soul Survivors" (2001), "Ocean's Eleven" (2001), "Ocean's Twelve" (2004), "Lonesome Jim" (2005), "The Last Kiss" (2006), "Ocean's Thirteen" (2007), "The Assassination of Jesse James by the Coward Robert Ford" (2007), "Gone Baby Gone" (2007), "The Killer Inside Me" (2010), "Tower Heist" (2011), Voice, "ParaNorman"

(2012), "Ain't Them Bodies Saints" (2013), "Out of the Furnace" (2013), "Interstellar" (2014), "The Finest Hours" (2016), "Manchester by the Sea" (2016), "Triple 9" (2016), "A Ghost Story" (2017), "Light of My Life" (2018), "The Old Man and the Gun" (2018); TV Films, "Lemon Sky" (1988); TV Miniseries, "The Kennedys of Massachusetts" (1990), "WWII in HD: The Air War" (2010), "SNL" (2016); Actor, Writer, Films, "Gerry" (2002); Executive Producer, "All Grown Up" (2003); Director, Producer, Writer, Films, "I'm Still Here" (2010); Producer, Documentaries, "I Am Dying" (2010) **AW:** Academy Award for Best Actor for "Manchester by the Sea" (2016); Best Actor at the Golden Globes for "Manchester by the Sea" (2016); Best Supporting Actor Award, National Board of Review (2007)

AGASSI, ANDRE KIRK, T: Retired Professional Tennis Player **I:** Athletics **DOB:** 04/29/1970 **PB:** Las Vegas **PT:** Son of Mike and Elizabeth Agassi **C:** Professional Tennis player, ATP Tour, 1986-2006 **CR:** Member US Olympic Tennis Team, Atlanta, 1996, US Davis Cup Team, 1988- **CIV:** Founder, Andre Agassi College Prep Academy, 2001 Founder, Andre Agassi Boys & Girls Club, 1997 Founder, Andre Agassi Charitable Foundation, 1994 **CW:** Author: Open: An Autobiography, 2009 (#1 Publishers Weekly bestseller) **AW:** Named Champion of Champions, L'Equipe, 1999, Most Caring Athlete, USA Today, 2001, 1996, Player of Year, ATP, 1999, Most Improved Player of Year, 1998; named one of Most Influential People in the World of Sports, Business Week, 2008, The 100 Most Influential People in the World, TIME magazine, 2008, Barbara Walters 10 Most Fascinating People of 2006; named to The Tennis Hall of Fame, 2011; recipient ESPY award for Outstanding Men's Tennis Performance, 2000, Arthur Ashe Humanitarian award, ATP, 2001, 1995,ITF World Champion, 1999, BBC Overseas Sports Personality of the Year, 1992, 7th Greatest Male Player of All Time, 2010, International Tennis Hall of Fame, 2011 **ACH:** Achievements include being oldest player to be ranked no. 1 in the ATP entry system, 2003; winning Wimbledon, 1992, US Open, 1994, 1999, Australian Open, 1995, 2000, 2001, 2003, Roland Garros, 1999; winning gold medal, US Men's Singles, Atlanta Olympic Games, 1996; member of US Davis Cup Championship Teams, 1990, 1992, 1995; winner of 60 career singles titles, 1 doubles title, ATP Tour

AGEE, GEORGE "G." STEVEN, T: Federal Judge **I:** Law and Legal Services **DOB:** 11/12/1952 **PB:** Roanoke **SC:** VA/USA **ED:** LLM in Taxation, New York University, 1978; JD, University of Virginia, 1977; BA, Bridgewater College, 1974 **C:** Judge, U.S. Court of Appeals, Fourth Circuit, 2008-Present; Justice, Virginia Supreme Court, Richmond, VA, 2003-2008; Judge, Virginia Court of Appeals, Richmond, VA, 2001-2003; Virginia House of Delegates, 1982-1994; Shareholder, Director, Osterhoudt, Ferguson, Natt, Aheron, & Agee Professional Corporation, 1980-2001; Associate, Rocovich, Dechow, Parvin & Wilson, Professional Corporation, 1979-1980; Associate, Martin, Hopkins & Lemon, 1977-1979 **CR:** Virginia Criminal Sentencing Commission, 1997-2000 **CIV:** Trustee, Bridgewater College, Board Member, Bradley Free Clinic, Roanoke, VA **MIL:** Judge Advocate, General Corps, U.S. Army Reserve, 1985-1997 **MEM:** President, Roanoke County-Salem Bar Association, 1990-1991, Virginia Bar Association, DC Bar Association, Salem Rotary Club **BAR:** District of Columbia, 1979, Virginia, 1977 **BA:** 1100 E Main Street, #501, Richmond, VA, 23219

AGRAWAL, MIKI, T: Founder **I:** Apparel & Fashion **CN:** Tushy **ED:** BS, Business and Communication, Cornell, 2001; BS, Business, Marianopolis College, 1998 **C:** Founder, Tushy, 2016-; CEO/Co-Founder, THINZ, 2011-17; Founder, WILD, 2005- **CW:** (Book) Do Cool Shit, 2013

AGRE, PETER COURTLAND, T: Molecular Biologist, Educator **I:** Sciences **DOB:** 01/30/1949 **PB:** Northfield **ED:** MD, John Hopkins University School Medicine, Baltimore, 1974; BA in Chemistry, with honors, Augsburg College, Minneapolis, 1970 **CT:** Diplomate Am. Board Internal Medicine **C:** Director Malaria Research Institute, Univ. professor, Johns Hopkins University Bloomberg School Pub. Health, 2008-; Vice chancellor sci. and tech., Duke University Medical Center, Durham, North Carolina, 2005-08; Professor department cell biology and department medicine, Duke University Medical Center, Durham, North Carolina, 2005-08; Professor department biological chemistry and medicine, Johns Hopkins School Medicine, 1993-2005; Associate professor, Johns Hopkins School Medicine, 1988-93; Assistant professor, Johns Hopkins School Medicine, 1984-88; From research associate, then instructor department medicine and cell biology/anatomy, Johns Hopkins School Medicine, 1981-83; Clinical assistant professor medicine, University North Carolina, Chapel Hill, 1980-81; Postdoc. fellow hematology/oncology division, University North Carolina, Chapel Hill, 1978-80; Intern, resident internal medicine, Case Western Reserve University & Hospital, Cleveland, 1975-78 **CR:** Member sci. rev. board Howard Hughes Medical Institute member international sci. council Israeli-Palestinian Sci. Organization member adv. board Norwegian Research & Tech. Forum US/Can. visiting professor department embryology Carnegie Institution, Washington, 1988-89 senior clinical research scientist Wellcome Laboratories, Research Triangle Park, North Carolina, 1980-81 **CIV:** Hon. member, International Raoul Wallenberg Foundation, 2004- **CW:** Member editorial board Journal Clinical Investigation, 1993-, Blood, 1993-97, Journal Biological Chemistry, 2003-; contributor articles to professional journals **AW:** Co-recipient Biennial Spa Foundation prize, 2003; recipient Distinguished Eagle Scout award, Boy Scouts America, 2005, Karl Landsteiner award, Am. Association Blood Banks, 2005, Golden Plate award, Academy Achievement, 2004, Nobel prize for chemistry, 2003, Distinguished Alumnus award, Augsburg College, 1995, Young Investigator award, Am. Federation Clinical Research, 1991, Established Investigator award, Am. Heart Association, 1987-92, Basil O'Connor award, March of Dimes Birth Defects Foundation, 1986-88, Clinical Investigator award, National Heart, Lung & Blood Institute, 1981-85, Bloomberg Distinguished Professorships, 2014 **MEM:** Mem.: American Association for the Advancement of Science (president 2009-10), National Academy of Sciences (committee on human rights 2003-08), Am. Philosophical Society, Am. Academy Arts & Scis., Institute Medicine, Am. Society Nephrology (Homer Smith award 1999), Am. Society Biochemistry & Molecular Biology, Am. Physiological Society, Am. Society Clinical Investigation, Am. Society Cell Biology, Interurban Clinical Club (hon.) **ACH:** Achievements include patents in field

AGUILAR, PETE, T: U.S. Representative from California, Former Mayor **I:** Government Administration/Government Relations/Government Services **DOB:** 06/19/1979 **PB:** Fontana **ED:** BA in Government & Business Administration, University of Redlands, California (2001) **C:** U.S. Congressman, California 31st District, Washington, DC (2015-Present); Member, Committee on Energy and Commerce; Mayor, City of Redlands (2010-2014); Councilman, City of Redlands (2006-2010); From Deputy Director to Interim Director, Inland Empire Regional Office of Governor (2001-2006) **PA:** Democrat

AHMED, RIZ, T: Actor **I:** Media & Entertainment **DOB:** 12/01/1982 **PB:** Wembley **SC:** United Kingdom **C:** (Film) The Road to Guantanamo, 2006, Shifty, 2008, Baghdad Express, 2008, Rage, 2009, Four Lions, 2010, Centurion, 2010, Black Gold, 2011, Trishna, 2011, Ill Manors, 2012, The Reluctant Fundamentalist, 2012, Closed Circuit, 2013, Out of Darkness, 2013, Daytimer, 2014, Nightcrawler, 2014, Jason Bourne, 2016, Una, 2016, City of Tiny Lights, 2016, Rogue One, 2016, The Sisters Brothers, 2018, Venom,2018(Television) The Path to 9/11, 2006, Berry's Way, 2006, Britz, 2007, Wired, 2008, Dead Set, 2008, Freefall, 2009, The Fades, 2011, The Night of, 2016,(Primetime Emmy for Outstanding Limited Series 2016,Primetime Emmy Outstanding Lead Actor 2016) The OA, 2016, Girls, 2017(Album) Microscope, 2011, (Mixtape) Englistan, 2016

AKERLOF, GEORGE ARTHUR, T: Economics Professor **I:** Education/Educational Services **DOB:** 06/17/1940 **PB:** New Haven **PT:** Son of Gosta Carl and Rosalie C. Akerlof; **ED:** Doctor in Economics (hon.), University Zurich, Switzerland, 2000; PhD, Massachusetts Institute of Technology, 1966; BA, Yale University, New Haven, 1962 **C:** Professor, McCourt School of Public Policy at Georgetown, 2014-; Senior Fellow, Brookings Institution, Washington, 1994-; Professor, University California, Berkeley, 1980-; Professor, University California, Berkeley, 1977-78; Associate Professor, University California, Berkeley, 1970-77; Assistant Professor, University California, Berkeley, 1966-70 **CR:** Board directors National Bureau Economic Research, 1997- Cassel professor money & banking London School Economics, 1978-80 visiting research economist, special studies section Federal Reserve System, 1977-78 senior staff economist Council Economic Advisors, The White House, 1973-74 visiting professor Indian Statistical Institute, 1967-68 **CW:** Author: An Economic Theorist's Book of Tales, 1984; co-author: Efficiency Wage Models of the Labor Market, 1986, Looting: The Economic Underworld of Bankruptcy for Profit, 1993, Animal Spirits: How Human Psychology Drives the Economy, and Why It Matters for Global Capitalism, 2009, Identity Economics: How Our Identities Shape Our Work, Wages, and Well-Being, 2010; co-editor: Economics and Politics Journal, 1990-; associate editor Am. Economic Rev., Quarterly Journal Economics, Journal Economic Behavior and Organization; contributor articles to professional journals **AW:** Recipient Nobel prize in economics, 2001; grantee Fulbright fellowship, 1967-68, National Science Foundation Cooperative fellowship, 1963-66, Woodrow Wilson fellowship, 1962-63 **MEM:** Fellow: Econometric Society, Am. Academy Arts & Scis., Institute Policy Reform; mem.: Am. Economic Association (member executive committee 1988-91, vice president 1995), Can. Institute Advanced Research (associate) **BA:** Georgetown University, Intercultural Center 580 37th and O Streets, N.W.,, Washington, DC, 20057

AKINS, NICHOLAS K., T: Energy Company Executive **I:** Business Management/Business Services **PB:** 1960 **ED:** Master's Degree in Electrical Engineering, Louisiana Tech University, Ruston, 1986; Bachelor's Degree in Electrical Engineering, Louisiana Tech University, Ruston, 1982 **CT:** Registered professional engineer, Texas **C:** Director, president, CEO, American Electric Power Co., Inc., 2011-; President, American Electric Power Co., Inc., 2010-11; Executive vice president generation, American Electric Power Co., 2006-10; President, COO Southwestern Electric Power Co. subsidiary, American Electric Power Co., 2004-06; Vice president energy marketing services, American Electric Power Co., 2002-04; Vice president industry restructuring, American Electric Power Co.; Various director and manager positions including CSWS director restructuring readiness, CSWS director mergers and acquisitions, CSWS director solid fuels, WTU director fuels, Central and South West Corp. **CR:** Member Boards of American Coalition of Clean Coal Electricity, Edison Electric Institute, Nuclear Energy Institute, National Association of Manufacturers, Mid-Ohio Foodbank, Greater Columbus Arts Council, and the Wexner Center for the Arts **MEM:** Mem.: National Society of Professional Engineers, Texas Society Professional Engineers, Eta Kappa Nu, Tau Beta Pi

ALDA, ALAN, T: Actor **I:** Media & Entertainment **DOB:** 01/28/1936 **PB:** New York City **SC:** NY/USA **PT:** Son of Robert and Joan (Browne) A.; **SPN:** Arlene Weiss; **CH:** Eve, Elizabeth, Beatrice **ED:** Degree (hon.), Kenyon College, 1982; Degree (hon.), Connecticut College, 1980; Degree (hon.), Columbia University, 1979; Degree (hon.), Drew University, 1979; Degree (hon.), Fordham University, 1978; BS, Fordham University, 1956 **C:** Ind. Actor, Stage, Screen, TV, 1956 **CR:** Teacher Compass School Improvisation **CIV:** Presidential Appointee National Commission for Observance of International Women's Year, 1976 Co-chair National ERA Countdown Campaign, 1982 Trustee Museum of TV and Radio, 1985, Rockefeller Foundation, 1989 **CW:** Actor: (Broadway plays) Only in America, 1959, Purlie Victorious, 1961-1962, Fair Game for Lovers, 1964, Cafe Crown, 1964, The Owl and the Pussycat, 1964-1965, The Apple Tree, 1966-1967, Jake's Women, 1992, Art, 1998-1999, QED, 2001-2001, The Play What I Wrote, 2003, Glengarry Glen Ross, 2005, Love Letters, 2014; (films) Gone Are the Days, 1963, The Moonshine War, Paper Lion, 1968, The Extraordinary Seaman, 1968, Jenny, 1970, The Mephisto Waltz, 1971, To Kill a Clown, 1972, California Suite, 1978, Same Time, Next Year, 1978, The Seduction of Joe Tynan, 1979, Crimes and Misdemeanors, 1989 (D.W. Griffith Award, New York Film Critics award), Whispers in the Dark, 1992, Manhattan Murder Mystery, 1993, Canadian Bacon, 1995, Flirting With Disaster, 1996, Everyone Says I Love You, 1996, Murder at 1600, 1997, Mad City, 1997, The Object of My Affection, 1998, What Women Want, 2000, The Aviator, 2004, Resurrecting the Champ, 2007, Diminished Capacity, 2008, Flash of Genius, 2008, Nothing But the Truth, 2008, Tower Heist, 2011, Wanderlust, 2012, The Longest Ride, 2015, Bridge of Spies, 2015; (TV films) include The Glass House, 1972, Marlo Thomas and Friends in Free to be...You and Me, 1974, 6 Rms Riv Vu, 1974, Kill Me If You Can, And The Band Played On, 1993, White Mile, 1994, Club Land, 2001, The Killing Yard, 2001, (TV series) M*A*S*H, 1972-83 (also Writer of 17 Episodes, Director 30 Episodes, Emmy Award for Best Lead Actor in a Comedy Series, 1974, Outstanding Directing in a Comedy Series, 1977, Outstanding Writing in a Comedy or Comedy-Variety or Music Series, 1979, Outstanding Lead Actor in a Comedy Series, 1982, Golden Globe Award for Best Performance by an Actor in a TV Series Comedy/Musical, 1975, 1976, 1980, 1981, 1982, Humanitas Award for Writing), The West Wing, 2004-06 (Emmy award for Outstanding Supporting Actor in a Drama Series, 2006), 30 Rock, 2009-2010, The Big C, 2011-13, The Human Spark, 2012, Brain on Trial with Alan Alda, The Blacklist, 2013-14, Horace and Pete, 2016, Broad City, 2016; Creator: (TV series) We'll Get By, 1975, The Four Seasons; Writer, Narrator Scientific American Frontiers, 1993-; Actor, Writer, Dir.: (films) The Four Seasons, 1981, Sweet Liberty, 1986, A New Life, 1987, Betsy's Wedding, 1990; TV guest appearances include Route 66, 1963, The Nurses, 1963, The Carol Burnet Show, 1974, ER, 1999.; Author: Never Have Your Dog Stuffed - and Other Things I've Learned, 2005 **AW:** Recipient Theatre World award for Fair Game for Lovers, 7 People's Choice Awards; Elected to TV Academy Hall of Fame, 1994. **MEM:** Member American Federation of TV and Radio Artists, Directors Guild Am. (Awards 1977, 1982), Writers Guild Am. (Award 1977), Screen Actors Guild, Actors Equity Association; Fellow Am. Academy Arts & Sciences. **BA:** ICM Partners, 10250 Constellation Blvd 9th Fl, Los Angeles, CA, 90067

ALDEAN, JASON, T: Musician **I:** Media & Entertainment **PB:** Macon **SC:** GA/USA **PT:** Barry Aldean; Debbie Aldean **CW:** Musician: (albums) Jason Aldean, 2005 (Top New Male Vocalist, Academy Country Music Awards, 2006), Relentless, 2007, Wide Open, 2009, My Kinda Party, 2011 (Album of Year, Country Music Association Awards, 2011, Album of Year, Am. Country Awards, 2011, Top Country Album, Billboard Music Awards, 2012), Night Train, 2012, Old Boots, New Dirt, 2014 (Top Country Album, Billboard Music Awards, 2015), They Don't Know, 2016, Rearview Town,2018 (songs) (with Kelly Clarkson) Don't You Wanna Stay, 2010 (Musical Event of Year, Country Music Association Awards, 2011, Single of Yr.: Vocal Collaboration, Am. Country Awards, 2011, Music Video of Yr.: Group or Collaboration, Am. Country Awards, 2011, Vocal Event of Year, Acad Country Music Awards, 2012, Single Record of Year, Academy Country Music Awards, 2012), My Kinda Party, 2010 (Single of Yr.: Male, Am. Country Awards, 2011), Dirt Road Anthem, 2011 (Top Country Song, Billboard Music Awards, 2012), Tattoos on This Town, 2011 (Performance of Year, CMT Music Awards, 2012), The Only Way I Know (with Luke Bryan and Eric Church), 2012 (Vocal Event of Year, Academy Country Music Awards, 2013, Collaborative Video of Year, CMT Music Awards, 2013), Burnin' It Down, 2014 (Top Country Song, Billboard Music Awards, 2015), (with Bob Seger) Turn The Page (CMT Crossroads: Bob Seger and Jason Aldean), 2015 (Performance of Year, CMT Music Awards, 2015)(Film) Sweet Vengeance, 2013 **AW:** Named Entertainer of Year, Academy Country Music Awards, 2016, Male Vocalist of Year, 2015, 2014, 2013, Touring Artist of Year, Am. Country Awards, 2011, Artist of Year, 2011

ALEXANDER, LAMAR, T: U.S. Senator from Tennessee **I:** Government Administration/Government Relations/Government Services **DOB:** 07/03/1940 **PB:** Maryville **SC:** TN/USA **PT:** Andrew Lamar Alexander; Geneva Floreine (Rankin) Alexander **ED:** BA in Latin American History, Vanderbilt University, Nashville, TN (1962); JD, New York School of Law (1965) **C:** Chairman, US Senate Health, Education, Labor, & Pensions Committee (2015—Present); Partner, Dearborn & Ewing, Nashville, TN (1970-1976); Executive Assistant to Bryce Harlow, Office Congressional Liaison, The White House (1969-1970); Legislative Assistant to Senator Howard Baker, US Senate (1967-1968); Associate, Fowler, Rountree, Fowler & Robertson, Knoxville, TN (1965); Law Clerk to Honorable John Minor Wisdom, U.S. Court of Appeals for the Fifth Circuit, New Orleans, LA (1965—1966); US Senator from Tennessee (2003—Present); Chairman, US Senate Republican Conference (2007—2011); Private Practice Attorney, Nashville, TN (1999—2001); Counsel, Baker, Donelson, Bearman & Caldwell, Nashville, TN (1993-1998); Secretary, US Department Edu-cation, Washington, DC (1991-1993); President, University of Tennessee (1988-1991); Governor, State of Tennessee, Nashville, TN (1979—1987); Chairman, Leadership Institute, Belmont College, Nashville, TN (1987-1988) **CR:** Chairman, National Governors Association (1985—1986); President's Commission America's Outdoors (1985—1987); Co-director, Empower America (1994—1995); Goodman Visiting Professor, Practice of Public Service, Harvard University (2001—2002) **CIV:** Chairman, Republican Exchange Satellite Network (1993—1995); Republican Presidential Candidate (1995—1996, 2000); Campaign Manager, Winfield Dunn for Governor (1970); Chief Transition Team (1970—1971); Republican Nominee for Tennessee Governor (1974) **CW:** Author, "Steps Along the Way" (1986); Author, "Six Months Off" (1988); Author, "We Know What to Do" (1995); Co-editor, "Friends, Japanese and Tennesseans: A Model of U.S.-Japan Cooperation" (1986); Co-author, "The New Promise of American Life" (1995) "Lamar Alexander's Little Plaid Book" (1998) **AW:** James B. Conant Award, Education Commission of States (1988); Distinguished State Leadership Award, American Association State Colleges & Universities (1989); Teddy Roosevelt Award, National College Athletic Association (1993); Distinguished Congressional Award, National League Cities (2003); Krieble Freedom & Democracy Award, Free Congress Foundation (2004); National Congressional Award, National Recreation & Park Association (2005); Spirit of Enterprise Award, US Chamber of Commerce (2005, 2006, 2008, 2010); Congressional Leadership Award, Center for Study of Presidency (2005); Dale E. Kildee Civitas Award, We the People, Center for Civic Education (2005); Thomas Jefferson Award, International Foodservice Distributors Association (2006, 2010); Distinguished Friend of Science Award, Southwest Universities Research Association (2006); William Penn Mott Junior Park Leadership Award, National Parks Conservation Association (2007); George E. Brown Junior Science, Engineering and Technology Leadership Award, Science, Engineering and Technology Work Group (2007); Horst G. Denk Legislative Service Award (2007); Public Affairs Leadership Award, March of Dimes (2007); Gold Medallion Award, Tennessee Independent Colleges and Universities Association (2008); National Geographic Legislator Award (2008); Charles Dick Medal of Merit Award, US National Guard (2008) **MEM:** Phi Beta Kappa **BAR:** Tennessee Bar Association (1965) **PA:** Republican **BA:** Office of Lamar Alexander, US Senate 455 Dirksen Senate Office Bldg, Washington D.C., DC, 20510

ALI, MAHERSHALA, T: Actor **I:** Media & Entertainment **PB:** Oakland **SC:** CA/USA **CW:** (Films) Making Revolution, 2003, Umis Heart,2008, The Curious Case of Benjamin Button, 2008, Crossing Over, 2009, Predators, 2010, The Place Beyond the Pines, 2012, Go for Sisters, 2013, Supremacy, 2014, The Hunger Games: Mockingjay – Part 1, 2014, The Hunger Games: Mockingjay – Part 2, 2015, Kicks, 2016 Gubagude Ko, 2016, Free State of Jones, 2016, Moonlight, 2016, (Academy Award for Best Supporting Actor 2016) Hidden Figures, 2016, Roxanne Roxanne, 2017, Spider-Man: Into the Spider-Verse, 2018 (Television) Crossing Jordan, 2001, Haunted, 2002, NYPD Blue, 2002, CSI, 2003, The Handler, 2003, Threat Matrix, 2003-04, The 4400, 2004-07, Lie to Me, 2009, Law and Order, SVU, 2009, The Wronged Man, 2010, All Signs of Death, 2010, Lights Out, 2011, Treme, 2011, Alphas, 2011, Alcatra, 2012, House of Cards, 2013-16, Luke Cage, 2016, Comrade Detective, 2017, True Detective, 2019;;

ALITO, SAMUEL ANTHONY JR., **T:** Associate Justice **I:** Law and Legal Services **CN:** U.S. Supreme Court **DOB:** 04/01/1950 **PB:** Trenton **SC:** NJ/USA **PT:** Samuel Alito; Rose (Fradusco) Alito **ED:** JD, Yale University, 1975; BA, Woodrow Wilson School of Public and International Affairs, Princeton University, 1972 **C:** Associate Justice, U.S. Supreme Court, Washington, DC, 2006-Present; Judge, U.S. Court of Appeals, Third Circuit, Newark, NJ, 1990-2006; U.S. Attorney, U.S. Department of Justice, Newark, NJ, 1987-1990; Deputy Assistant to Attorney General Edwin Meese, Office of Legal Counsel, U.S. Department of Justice, Washington, DC, 1985-1987; Assistant to Solicitor General Rex E. Lee, U.S. Department of Justice, Washington, DC, 1981-1985; Assistant U.S. Attorney of New Jersey, U.S. Department of Justice, Newark, NJ, 1977-1981; Law Clerk, Hon. Leonard I. Garth, U.S. Court of Appeals, Third Circuit, Newark, NJ, 1976-1977 **CR:** Fellow, American Bar Foundation; Adjunct Professor, Seton Hall University; Editor, Yale Law Journal, 1974-1975 **MIL:** Captain, U.S. Army Reserve, 1972-1980 **AW:** St. Thomas More Award, Diocese of Trenton, St. Thomas More Society, 2006 **MEM:** Essex County Bar Association, American Judicature Society, Federalist Society for Law & Public Policy Studies, Association of the Federal Bar of New Jersey, American Law Institute, Advisory Committee on Appellate Rules **BAR:** State of New York, 1970; State of New Jersey, 1975 **BA:** U.S. Supreme Court, 1 First Street NE, Washington, DC, 20543 **ADD:** U.S. Courthouse, Federal Square & Walnut Street, PO Box 999, Newark, NJ, 07101-0999

ALLEN, PAUL GARDNER, **T:** Co-Founder **I:** Information Technology and Services **CN:** Microsoft **DOB:** 01/21/1953 **PB:** Seattle **SC:** WA/USA **PT:** Son of Kenneth S. and Faye G. Allen. **ED:** Docteur honoris causa (hon.), Ecole Polytechnique Federale de Lausanne, 2007; Student, Washington State University, 1971-73 **C:** Chairman, Charter Investment, Inc., 1998-; Chairman, Charter Communications Inc., 1998-; Owner, chairman, Seattle Seahawks, 1997-; Owner, chairman board, Portland Trail Blazers, 1988-; CEO, Vulcan Ventures, Bellevue, 1987-; Senior strategy adv., Microsoft Corp., 2000-; Founder, Allen Telescope Array, SETI Institute University California Berkeley, 2004; Sponsor, funder, SpaceShipOne Venture, Mojave, California, 2003; Owner, TechTV,; Founder, Starwave Corp., Bellevue, 1992; Co-founder, Interval Research Corp., Palo Alto, California, 1992; Founder, Vulcan Inc., Seattle, 1986; Founder, Asymetrix Corp., Bellevue, Washington, 1985; Executive vice president research & new product devel., Microsoft Corp., 1981-83; Vice president, Microsoft Corp., 1977-81; General partner, Microsoft Corp., 1975-77; Co-founder, Microsoft Corp. (formerly Micro-Soft), Albuquerque, 1975; Programmer, Honeywell International Inc., Waltham, 1974-75; Co-founder, Traf-O-Data Co., Seattle, 1972-73 **CR:** Founder Sci. Fiction Museum and Hall of Fame, Seattle, 2004-, Experience Music Project, Seattle, Allen Brain Atlas Initiative, Allen Institute for Brain Sci., 2003- board directors Darwin Molecular, Inc., Microsoft Corp., 1983-2000, Egghead Discount Software **CIV:** Co-founder, chairman board, Paul G. Allen Family Foundation, 1990- **CW:** Executive prodr.: (film series) The Blues; author: Idea Man: A Memoir by the Co-Founder of Microsoft, 2011 **AW:** Co-recipient Rave award for Sci., WIRED Magazine, 2007, Smithsonian's National Air & Space Museum Trophy, 2005; named one of The Most Influential People in the World of Sports, Business Week, 2008, 2007, The 100 Most Influential People in the World, TIME magazine, 2008, 2007, The Forbes 400: Richest Americans, 2006-, The World's Richest People, Forbes magazine, 1999-, The Top 200 Collectors, Artnews magazine, 2004-, The Top 15 Philanthropists in America; named to The Computer Museum Hall of Fame; recipient Herbie Hancock Humanitarian award, Thelonius Monk Institute Jazz, 2008, Vanguard award, National Cable & Telecommunications Association, 2008, Special Recognition award, Society Neurosci., 2007, Regents' Distinguished Alumnus award, Washington State University, 1999,Champion of Global Health Award, 2015, Andrew Carnegie Medal of Philanthropy, 2015 **MEM:** Mem.: NAE **ACH:** Achievements include sponsoring and funding the record flights for SpaceShipOne, which won the Ansari X prize on October 4, 2004; SpaceShipOne donated to Smithsonian Institution on October 6, 2005 **H:** Collecting impressionism, Old Masters, pop art, tribal art **BA:** Portland Trailblazers, One Center Court Suite 200, Portland, OR, 97227

ALLEN, RICK W., **T:** U.S. Representative from Georgia **I:** Government Administration/Government Relations/Government Services **PB:** Augusta **SC:** GA/USA **ED:** Degree in building construction, Auburn University **C:** Member, Committee on Agriculture, Committee on Education and the Workforce; Mem. US Congress from 12th Georgia District, 2014-; Founder, president, CEO, R.W. Allen & Associates, Inc., Augusta, 1976 **PA:** Republican

ALLEN, SAMUEL R., **T:** Farm Equipment Manufacturing Executive **I:** Manufacturing **PB:** Sumter **ED:** BS in Industrial Management, Purdue University, Ind., 1975 **C:** Chairman, CEO, Deere & Co., 2010-; President, CEO, Deere & Co., 2009-10; President COO, Deere & Co., 2009; President Worldwide Construction & Forestry Division, Deere & Co., 2005-09; President global operations, Deere Power Systems, 2003-05; President global. fin. services & corp. human resources, Deere & Co., 2003-05; Senior vice president, Deere & Co., 2001-09; Vice president region I (Latin America, Australia, Asia), Worldwide Agricultural Equipment Division, Deere & Co., 1999-2001; Manager worldwide engine manufacturing operations, Deere Power Systems, Deere & Co.,; Various management positions John Deere Horicon Works, Des Moines Works, Dubuque Works, Davenport Works, Waterloo Engine Works, Deere & Co.,; Various positions consumer products division, Deere & Co.,; Industrial engineer, Deere & Co., 1975 **CR:** Board directors Deere & Co., 2009-; Chairman of the U.S. Council on Competitiveness

ALLEN, WOODY, **T:** Filmmaker, Writer, Actor **I:** Media & Entertainment **DOB:** 12/01/1935 **PB:** New York **SC:** NY/USA **PT:** Son of Martin and Nettie (Cherry) Konigsberg; **SPN:** Partner Mia Farrow; Married Louise Lasser, February 2, 1966 (div. 1969); Married Harlene Rosen, March 15, 1956 (div. 1962) **CH:** Satchel **ED:** Student, City College of New York, 1953; Student, New York University, 1953 **CW:** Writer TV comedy for Sid Caesar, 1957, Art Carney, 1958-59, Herb Shriner, 1953; actor: (films) What's New Pussycat?, 1964, The Front, 1976, King Lear, 1988, Scenes From a Mall, 1990, Cannes...les 400 coups, 1997, Waiting for Woody, 1998, Impostors, 1998, (voice) Antz, 1998, Wild Man Blues, 1998, Stuck on You, 1998, Company Man, 1999, Picking Up the Pieces, 1999, Fading Gigolo, 2014; actor, writer: (films) Play It Again, Sam, 1972; actor, director, writer: (films) What's Up Tiger Lily?, 1966, Take the Money and Run, 1969, Bananas, 1971, Everything You Always Wanted to Know About Sex But Were Afraid to Ask, 1972, Sleeper, 1973, Love and Death, 1975, Annie Hall, 1977 (New York Film Critics Circle awards for Best Director, Best Screenplay 1977, Academy awards for Best Picture, Best Director, National Society Film Critics Screenwriting award) Manhattan, 1979 (New York Film Critics award for Best Director, 1979, BAFTA award for Best Screenplay, 1980), Stardust Memories, 1980, A Midsummer Night's Sex Comedy, 1982, Zelig, 1983, Broadway Danny Rose, 1984, Hannah and Her Sisters, 1986 (Academy award for Best Screenplay, D.W. Griffith award for Best Director, National Board Rev. Motion Pictures), Crimes and Misdemeanors, 1989, New York Stories (Oedipus Wrecks segment), 1989, Shadows and Fog, 1992, Husbands and Wives, 1992, Manhattan Murder Mystery, 1993, Mighty Aphrodite, 1995, Everyone Says I Love You, 1996, Deconstructing Harry, 1997, Count Mercury Goes to the Suburbs, 1997, Small Town Crooks, 2000, The Curse of the Jade Scorpion, 2001, Hollywood Ending, 2002, Anything Else, 2003, Scoop, 2006, To Rome with Love, 2012, Café Society (narrator), 2016, Wonder Wheel, 2017, A Rainy Day in New York, 2018; director, writer: (films) Interiors, 1978, Purple Rose of Cairo, 1985, Radio Days, 1987 September, 1987, Another Woman, 1988, Alice, 1990, Bullets Over Broadway, 1994, Celebrity, 1998, Sweet and Lowdown, 1999, Melinda and Melinda, 2004, Match Point, 2005, Cassandra's Dream, 2008, Vicky Cristina Barcelona, 2008 (Golden Globe award for Best Motion Picture-Musical or Comedy, 2009), Whatever Works, 2009, You Will Meet a Tall Dark Stranger, 2010, Midnight in Paris, 2011 (Critics' Choice Movie award for Best Original Screenplay, 2012, Writers Guild award for Best Original Screenplay, 2012, Golden Globe award for Best Screenplay-Motion Picture, 2012, Academy award for Best Original Screenplay, 2012), Blue Jasmine, 2013, Magic in the Moonlight, 2014, Irrational Man, 2015; appeared in: (documentaries) Woody Allen: A Documentary, 2011; author: Getting Even, 1971, Without Feathers, 1975, Side Effects, 1980, Mere Anarchy, 2007, The Insanity Defense: The Complete Prose, 2007; co-author: (with Stig Bjorkman) Woody Allen on Woody Allen: In Conversation With Stig Bjorkman, 2005; author: (plays) Don't Drink the Water, 1966, The Floating Lightbulb, 1981, Death Defying Acts, 1995; writer: (TV films) Sounds from a Town I Love, 2001; writer, dir.: (Off Broadway play) A Second Hand Memory, 2004; director (opera) Gianni Schicchi, 2008. **AW:** Sylvania Award, 1957, Special award Berlin Film Festival, 1975, Cecil B. DeMille Award, Hollywood Foreign Press Association, 2014. **PA:** Democrat **BA:** 42 West 600 3rd Avenue 23rd Floor, New York, NY, 10016

ALLES, MARK J., **T:** CEO **I:** Biotechnology **CN:** Celgene Corp. **ED:** Bachelor's Degree, Lock Haven University **C:** Chairman, Celgene Corp., 2018-Present; CEO, Celgene Corp., 2016-2018; President/COO, Celgene Corp., 2014-2016; Executive Vice President/Head of Hematology, Celgene Corp., 2012-2014; Vice President of Global Marketing, Celgene Corp., 2004-2009

ALLISON, JAMES PATRICK, **T:** Immunologist **I:** Medicine & Health Care **DOB:** 08/07/1948 **PB:** Alice **SC:** TX/USA **MS:** Married **SPN:** Malinda Bell **ED:** PhD in Biological Scis., University of Texas, 1973; BS in Microbiology, University of Texas, 1969 **C:** Director Ludwig Center Cancer Immunotherapy, Memorial Sloan-Kettering Cancer Center, New York City, 2007-; Professer and Chair of Immunology at the M.D. Anderson Cancer Center, 2012; Chairman Immunology Progressive, Memorial Sloan-Kettering Cancer Center, New York City, 2004-; Investigator, Howard Hughes Medical Institute, 1997-; David H. Koch Chair Immunologic Studies, Memorial Sloan-Kettering Cancer Center, New York City,; Co-chair and Howard Hughes Professor Immunology, University California, Berkeley,; Head Divsn Immunology, University California,

Berkeley, 1989-97; Interim Head Division Immunology, University California, Berkeley, 1987-89; Director Cancer Research Laboratory, University California, Berkeley, 1985-2004; Professor Immunology, University California, Berkeley, 1985-2004; Associate Biochemist and Associate Professor Biochemistry, Grad. School of Biomedical Scis., 1983-84; Assistant Professor Biochemistry, Grad. School of Biomedical Scis., 1981-84; Assistant Biochemist and Assistant Professor, University Texas, Smithville, 1977-83 CR: Adjunct Professor Zoology, University of Texas, 1979-84, Special Associate Member Grad. Faculty, 1980-84 Visiting Scholar Department of Pathology, Stanford University, 1983-84 Invited Participant, Dahlem Workshop on Leukemia, 1983 Faculty Advanced Course in Evolution of the Immune System Am. Association of Immunologists, 1985, Advanced Course in Regulation of the Immune System mem board Midwinter Conference of Immunologists, 1986-89 Convener Indo-U.S. Short Term Course on The Molecular and Cellular Biology of the T Lymphocyte All India Institute of Medical Scis., New Delhi, 1987 Editorial Board Devel. Immunology, 1989 Consultant Becton-Dickinson Immunocytometry Systems, Inc., 1984. CW: Reviewing Editor Science, 1985-87; Associate Editor Journal of Immunology, 1987; Transmitting Editor International Immunology, 1988; Several Articles to Professional Publications AW: Recipient Postdoctoral Fellowship National Institutes of Health, 1974-76, Department of Molecular Immunology Scripps Clinic and Research Foundation, 1974-77, O.B. Williams Award of the Texas Branch Am. Society Microbiology, 1971, Centeon Award for Innovative Breakthroughs in Immunology, 2001, William B. Coley Award for Distinguished Research, Cancer Research Institute, Richard V. Smalley, MD Memorial Lectureship Award, 2010, Roche Award for Cancer Immunology and Immunotherapy, 2011, Novartis Prize for Clinical Immunology, 2013, Szent-Gyorgyi Prize for Progress in Cancer Research, National Foundation for Cancer Research, 2014, Lasker-DeBakey Clinical Medical Research Award, 2015; Co-recipient 2014 Breakthrough Prize in Life Sciences, Canada Gairdner International Award, 2014, Time 100 Most Influential, 2017,Jacob Heskel Gabbay Award for Biotechnology and Medicine, 2011, Tang Prize in Biopharmaceutical Science, 2014, Breakthrough Prize in Life Sciences, 2014, Lasker Debakey Clinical Medical Research Award, 2015, Wolf Prize in Medicine, 2017, Balzan Prize, 2017 MEM: Fellow: American Association for the Advancement of Science, Am. Academy Microbiology; Mem.: National Academy of Sciences, Am. Association Immunologists (AAI-Dana Foundation Award in Human Immunology Research, 2008, Lifetime Achievement Award, 2011), Am. Association Cancer Rsch, Institute Medicine. BA: University of Texas Anderson Cancer Center, 1515 Holcombe Blvd, Houston, TX, 77030

ALLISON, ROBERT ARTHUR, T: Former Professional Stock Car Racing Driver I: Athletics DOB: 12/03/1937 PB: Miami SC: FL/USA PT: Edmond J. Allison; Katherine F. (Patton) Allison MS: Married SPN: Judith A. Bjorkman (2/20/1960) CH: David; Bonnie; Clifford; Caralene ED: Student, Parochial Schools, Miami C: President, Bobby Allison Racing, Inc.; With, Grand National Winston Cup, Division of National Association of Stock Car Auto Racing (1965-1988); Stock Car Racer (1955-1988) CIV: Member, Hueytown Industrial Development, AL; Board, Active Member, Boy Scouts of America AW: Named Driver of the Year, Martini & Rossi (1972); Driver of the Year National Motor Sport Press Association; Driver of the Year Olsenite (1983); Named Most Popular Driver, Motor Racing Network Poll (1971, 1972, 1973,

1981, 1982, 1983); Alabama Pro Athlete of 1978, Alabama Sportswriters Association (1978); Named to American Auto Racing, Writers and Broadcasters Association, All American Team (1978); Named Champion, Winston Cup (1983); Alabama Citizen of the Year (1985); Winner, Winston 500 NASCAR Event (1986); Winner, Firecracker 400 (1987); Winner, Daytona 500, (1978, 1982, 1988); Winner, Winston Cup Series, Most Popular Driver (1971-1973, 1980-1983); Named One of Nascars 50 Greatest Drivers (1998); Inductee, Nascar Hall of Fame (2011); Inductee, International Motorsports Hall of Fame (1993); Inductee, Motorsports Hall of Fame of America (1992); Most Popular Driver in Winston Cup Grand National Division (1971, 1972, 1973, 1981, 1982) MEM: National Association of Stock Car Auto Racing; Lions Club, Hueytown, AL

ALLRED, GLORIA RACHEL, T: Lawyer I: Law and Legal Services DOB: 07/03/1941 PB: Philadelphia PT: Daughter of Morris and Stella Bloom; SPN: Married William Allred, December 31, 1969 (div. October 1987); Married Peyton Bray, 1960 (div. 1962) CH: 1 child, Lisa; ED: LLD (hon.), University West L.A., 1981; JD, Loyola Law School, L.A., 1974; MA, New York University, 1966; BA, University Pennsylvania, 1963 CT: Bar: California 1975, US District Court (central district) California 1975, US Court Appeals (9th cir.) 1976, US Supreme Court 1979 C: Partner, Allred, Maroko, Goldberg & Ribakoff (now Allred, Maroko & Goldberg), LA, 1976 CR: Lecturer University Southern California Former Host KABC TalkRadio, LA CIV: President Women's Equal Rights Legal Defense and Education Fund, LA, 1978-, Women's Movement Inc., LA. CW: Co-author: (with Deborah Caulfield Rybak) Fight Back and Win: My Thirty-year Fight Against Injustice--and How You Can Win Your Own Battles, 2006; Contributor Articles to Professional Journals AW: Recipient Commendation award City of LA, 1986, Mayor of LA, 1986, Pub. Service award National Association Federal Investigators, 1986, Vol. Action award President of US, 1986, Women of Distinction award National Council on Aging, 1994, The Judy Jarvis Memorial award, 2001; named one of 50 Most Powerful Women in Law, 1998; named to Millennium Hall of Fame, National Association Women Business Owners, LA Chapter, 2000; named Southern California Super Lawyer Law and Politics and LA magazine, 2004, 2007, 2009, 2010, 2011 MEM: Member American Bar Association, California Bar Association, DC Bar Association, National Association Women Lawyers, California Women Lawyers Association, Women Lawyers LA Association, Friars Club (New York City), Magic Castle Club (Hollywood, California)

ALMANZAR (CARDI B), BELCALIS, T: Rapper I: Media & Entertainment DOB: 07/07/1905 PB: New York City SC: New York City, New York CW: (Album) Invasion of Privacy, 2018, (Television) Love & Hip Hop: New York, 2015-17, Uncommon Sense Charlamagne, 2015, Kocktails with Khloe, 2016, Being Mary Jane, 2017, Hip Hop Squares,2017, SNL, 2018, The Tonight Show Starring Jimmy Fallon, 2018 AW: Time 100 Most Influential, 2018

ALPERN, ROBERT J., T: Dean of Yale Medical School I: Education/Educational Services DOB: 11/03/1950 MS: Married SPN: Patricia Ann Preisig CH: Rachelle, Kyle ED: MD with honors, University Chicago, 1976; BA in Chemistry with honors and highest distinction, Northwestern University, 1972 CT: Diplomate Am. Board Internal Medicine; board cert in nephrology. C: Dean, Yale University School Medicine, New Haven, 2004-; Atticus James Gill Medical Corps Chair in Medical Sci., University Texas Southwestern Medical Center, Dallas, 2000-04; Dean, University Texas South-

western Medical Center, Dallas, 1998-2004; Ruth W. and Milton P. Levy, Senior chair in molecular nephrology, University Texas Southwestern Medical Center, Dallas, 1994-2004; Professor medicine, University Texas Southwestern Medical Center, Dallas, 1990-2004; Chief nephrology, University Texas Southwestern Medical Center, Dallas, 1987-98; Associate professor medicine, University Texas Southwestern Medical Center, Dallas, 1987-90; Assistant professor medicine division nephrology, University California Cardiovascular Research Institute, San Francisco, 1982-87; Fellow in nephrology and renal physiology, University California Cardiovascular Research Institute, San Francisco, 1979-82; Resident in internal medicine, Columbia University, New York City, 1977-79; Intern in internal medicine, Columbia University, New York City, 1976-77 CR: Max Martin Salick visiting professor, UCLA School Medicine, 1994 member Medical School Admissions committee University California San Francisco, 1985-87, general clinical research center adv. committee University Texas Southwestern Medical Center, 1987-91, search committee for chief of cardiology, 1989, search committee for chairman urology, 1993, search committee for chief of hematology/oncology, 1997, Medical School Admissions committee, 1994-96, chairman 1996-98 chairman general clinical research center adv. committee University Texas Southwestern Medical Center, 1988-90, search committee for chief of infectious diseases University Texas Southwestern Medical Center, 1994-96 adv. council National Institute Diabetes and Digestive and Kidney Diseases presenter, lecturer in field. CW: Editorial bd: Kidney International, 1989-90, Renal Physiology and Biochemistry, 1989-95, Am. Journal Physiology, 1992-94, International Yearbook of Nephrology, 1989-92, Seminars in Nephrology, 1990-, Am. Journal Kidney Diseases, 1991-96, Kidney and Blood Pressure Research, 1996-, Am. Journal Medical Scis., 1996-, Am. Journal Medicine, 1997-; consultant editor: Journal Clinical Investigation, 1993-99, Kidney International, 1990-; editorial committee Journal Clinical Investigation, 1988-93; associate editor Am. Journal Physiology, 1989-92, Hospital Practice: Physiology in Medicine, 1991-94; section editor: Annual Review of Physiology, 1993-97, Current Opinion in Nephrology and Hypertension, 1997-99; contributor papers, chaps., articles to professional pubs. AW: Recipient National Science Foundation award for research in developmental biology, 1971, National Institutes of Health Merit award, 1996-2003. MEM: Member Institute Medicine, Am. Society Nephrology (member council 1995-2002, pres.-elect 2000, president 2001), International Society Nephrology, Am. Physiological Society, Am. Heart Association, Am. Society Clinical Investigation, Association Am. Physicians, Alpha Omega Alpha, Sigma Xi, Phi Beta Kappa.

ALSOP, MARIN, T: Conductor, Violinist, Music Director I: Fine Art DOB: 10/16/1956 PB: NYC ED: MusD (hon.), Bournemouth University, England, 2007; MusM, Julliard School, New York City, 1978; MusB, Julliard School, New York City, 1977; Attended, Yale University, New Haven C: Director of Graduate Studies, Peabody Institute of John Hopkins,2015-; Music director, Baltimore Symphony Orchestra, 2007-; Conductor laureate, Colorado Symphony Orchestra, Denver, 2006-; Music director, Cabrillo Festival Contemporary Music, Santa Cruz, California, 1991-; Music director designate, Baltimore Symphony Orchestra, 2006-07; Principal conductor, Bournemouth Symphony Orchestra, Poole, England, 2002-08; Principal guest conductor, Royal Scottish National Orchestra,; Principal guest conductor, City of London Sinfonia,; Principal conductor, then music director, Colorado Symphony Orchestra, Denver, 1993-2005; Music director, Long Island Philharmonic, 1989-96; Music director, Eugene Symphony Orchestra, Oregon, 1989-96; Assistant conductor, Richmond Symphony, Virginia, 1987; Founder, artistic director, Concordia Chamber Orchestra, New York City, 1984; Debut with, Symphony Space, New York City, 1984 **CR:** Guest, conductor Royal Concertgebouw Orchestra, Zurich Tonhalle, Orchestre de Paris, Bavarian Radio Symphony, Boston Symphony, Pittsburgh Symphony, Tokyo Philharmonic, New York Philharmonic, Philadelphia Orchestra, LA Philharmonic **AW:** Named a MacArthur Fellow, John D. & Catherine T. MacArthur Foundation, 2005; named Artist of Year, Gramophone magazine, 2003; recipient European Woman of Achievement award, 2007, Conductor's award, Royal Philharmonic Society, 2003, American Society of Composers award, CSO's Contemporary Music Festival, 2002, Koussevitzky Conducting prize, Tanglewood Music Center, Massachusetts, 1988 **MEM:** Fellow: Am. Academy Arts & Scis **ACH:** Achievements include becoming the first woman to head a major American orchestra; becoming the first and only conductor to receive the prestigious MacArthur Fellowship **BA:** Meyeroff Symphony Hall, 1212 Cathedral St, Baltimore, MD, 21201

ALTUVE, JOSE, T: Professional Baseball Player **I:** Athletics **PB:** Maracay **SC:** Venezuela **C:** Second Baseman, Houston Astros, 2011-Present **AW:** All-Star, 2012, 2014, 2017, AL Stolen Base Leader, 2014-2015, AL Batting Champion, 2014, 2016-2017, Silver Slugger Award, 2014, 2017, Gold Glove Award, 2015, AL Hank Aaron Award, 2017, World Series Champion, 2017, AL MVP, 2017

AMASH, JUSTIN, T: U.S. Representative from Michigan, Former State Legislator **I:** Government Administration/Government Relations/Government Services **DOB:** 04/30/1980 **PB:** Grand Rapids **ED:** JD, University Michigan, 2005; BA in Economics magna cum laude, University Michigan, 2002 **C:** Member, US House Oversight & Government Reform Committee, 2011-; Member, US Congress from 3rd Michigan District, 2011-; Member, US House Budget Committee, 2011-12; Member District 72, Michigan House of Reps., 2009-10 **AW:** Named one of The Politics 40 Under 40, TIME magazine, 2010 **MEM:** Mem.: National Rifle Association, State Bar Michigan, Right to Life Michigan, Grand Rapids Bar Association, Economic Club of Grand Rapids **PA:** Republican

AMBRO, THOMAS L., T: Federal Judge **I:** Law and Legal Services **DOB:** 12/27/1949 **PB:** Cambridge **SC:** Ohio **ED:** JD, Georgetown University, 1975; BA, Georgetown University, 1971 **CT:** Bar: Del. 1976 **C:** Judge, US Court Appeals (3d cir.), 2000-; Partner, Richards, Layton and Finger, 1982-2000; Associate, Richards, Layton and Finger, 1976-82; Clerk Hon. Daniel L. Herrmann, Del. Supreme Court, 1975-76 **CR:** Member New York TriBar Opinion Committee, 1988- **CW:** Author: Third Party Legal Opinions in Asset Based Financing: A Transactional Guide, 1990; Contributor Articles to Professional Journals **MEM:** Mem.: American Bar Association (Vice-Chair Committee on Programs 1987-90, Chair Committee on Meetings 1988-90, participant Silverado Conference on Legal Opinions 1989, member drafting subcom. third-party legal opinion report 1989-91, chair subcom. on opinion letters 1989-95, member committee on commercial fin. services 1989-95, chair committee on meetings 1990-94, chair or co-chair committee on publications 1994-97, chair committee on legal opinions 1994-98, member council section business law 1994-98, editorial board The Business Lawyer

1998-99, editor The Business Lawyer 1999-2000, vice-chair section business law 1999-2000, chair elect business law 2000-01, chair secretary business law 2001-02, secretary section business law 1998-99, immediate past chairman 2002-03, member committee on uniform commercial code, member committee on negotiated acquisitions, member business bankruptcy committee), Am. Inns. Court Foundation (member board trustee 2004-), Am. Law Institute, Am. College Commercial Fin. Lawyers, Am. College Bankruptcy, Del. State Bar Association (chairman 1979-82, vice-chmn. 1982-83, commercial law section, chair subcom. on uniform commercial code 1983-2003), Phi Beta Kappa **BA:** 601 Market St, Philadelphia, PA, 19106

AMELIO, WILLIAM J., T: Electronic Components Company Executive **I:** Technology **ED:** MBA, Stanford University, 1989; BSChemE, Lehigh University, 1979 **C:** CEO Avnet, 2016-Present; CEO, CHC Helicopter Services AS, 2010-2015; President, CEO, Lenovo Group Ltd., Hong Kong, 2005-2009; Senior Vice President, Asia Pacific & Japan, Dell Inc., 2001-2005; Executive Vice President, COO, Retail & Finance Group, NCR Corp., 2000-2001; President, Transportation & Power Systems Divisions, Honeywell International Inc., 1997-2000; Management Positions Through General Manager Operations, Personal Computing Division, IBM Corp., 1979-1997 **BA:** Avnet, 2211 South 47th Street, Phoenix, AR, 85034

AMENT, JEFF, T: Musician **I:** Media & Entertainment **DOB:** 03/10/1963 **PB:** Havre, Montana **PT:** Son of George and Penny Ament **C:** Solo Artist, 2008-; Bassist, Member Band, Pearl Jam, 1991-; Co-founder, Ames Brothers, **CW:** Musician: (albums with Pearl Jam) Ten, 1991 (Jeremy - Video of Year, Best Group Video, Best Metal/Hard Rock Video, Best Direction, MTV Music Video Awards, 1993), Alive, 1991, Vs., 1993, Vitalogy, 1994 (Spin the Black Circle - Grammy award for Best Hard Rock Performance, 1996), No Code, 1996, Yield, 1998, Binaural, 2000, Riot Act, 2002, Pearl Jam, 2006, Backspacer, 2009, Lightning Bolt, 2013 (Grammy award for Best Recording Package, 2015), (albums with Temple of the Dog) Temple of the Dog, 1991, (albums with Mother Love Bone) Shine, 1989, Apple, 1990, Mother Love Bone, 1992, (albums with Three Fish) Three Fish, 1996, The Quiet Table, 1999, (solo albums) Tone, 2008, While My Heart Beats, 2012, (with Tres Mts.) Three Mountains, 2011, (Albums with Mother Love Bone), Thrash and Burn: The Metal Alternative, 1993, The Best of Grunge Rock, 1993, Alterno-Daze: Natural 90s Selection, 1995, Proud to Be Loud, 1997, Alternative Moments, 2001, The Road Mix: Music from the Television Series One Tree Hill, Volume 3, 2007,(Green River)Sub Pop 200, 1988, This House is Not a Motel, 1989, Sub Pop Rock City, 1989, Sub Pop Rock City, 1989, Another Pyrrhic Victory, 1989, Endangered Species, 1990, Dry As a Bone, 1990, Afternoon Delight, 1992, Hype!, 1996, Wild and Wooly: The Northwest Rock Collection, 2000, Sleepless in Seattle: The Birth of Grunge, 2006, 1984 Demos, 2016 **AW:** Named Favorite Pop/Rock New Artist, Favorite New Heavy Metal/Hard Rock Artist, American Music Awards, 1993, Favorite Alternative Artist, Favorite Heavy Metal/Hard Rock Artist, 1996, Favorite Alternative Artist, 1999. Grammy for Best Recording Package, 2015, Rock and Roll Hall of Fame Inductee, 2017. **BA:** Agricultural and Mechanical Records, 70 Universal City Plz, Universal City, CA, 91608

AMODEI, MARK EUGENE, T: U.S. Representative From Nevada **I:** Government Administration/Government Relations/Government Services **DOB:** 06/12/1958 **PB:** Carson City **SC:** NV/USA **ED:** JD,

University of the Pacific McGeorge School of Law, 1983; BA, University of Nevada, 1980 **C:** Committee on Appropriations, U.S. House of Natural Resources Committee, 2011-Present; U.S. House of Judiciary Committee, 2011-Present; U.S. House of Veterans' Affairs Committee, 2011-Present; U.S. Congress From Second Nevada District, Washington, DC, 2011-Present; Chairman, Nevada State Republican Party, Carson City, NV, 2010-2011; Chairman, Judiciary Committee, Nevada State Senate, Carson City, NV, 2003-2007; President, Pro Tempore, Nevada State Senate, Carson City, NV, 2003-2007; Nevada State Senate, Carson City, NV, 1999-2010; District 40, Nevada State Assembly, Carson City, NV, 1997-1998; Attorney, Allison McKenzie, Carson City, NV **MIL:** Captain, Judge Advocate, General Corps, U.S. Army, 1984-1987 **AW:** Outstanding Freshman Legislator, Nevada Assembly, 1997, Decorated Meritorious Service Medal, Army Commendation Medal, Army Achievement Medal **MEM:** American Bar Association, Clark County Bar Association, Nevada Bar Association, Reserve Officers Association, America & Washoe County Bar Associations **PA:** Republican **BA:** 5310 Kietzke Lane, Suite 103, Reno, NV, 89511-2043

AMOS, DANIEL PAUL, T: Chairman, President, and CEO **I:** Insurance **CN:** Aflac Incorporated **DOB:** 08/13/1951 **PB:** Pensacola **SC:** FL/USA **PT:** Paul Shelby Amos; Mary Jean (Roberts) Amos **MS:** Married **SPN:** Mary Shannon Landing (9/12/1972) **CH:** Paul Shelby; Lauren Alyse **ED:** BS in Risk and Insurance Management, University of Georgia, Athens, Greece (1973) **C:** President, Aflac Incorporated (2017-President); Chairman, Aflac Incorporated (2001-Present); Chief Executive Officer, Aflac Incorporated, Columbus, GA (1990-Present); Deputy Chief Executive Officer, American Family Corporate, Columbus, GA (1996); Chief Operating Officer, Aflac Incorporated, (American Family Life Assurance Co.) (1987-1990); President, Aflac Incorporated (American Family Life Assurance Co.), Columbus, GA (1983-1996); State Manager, Aflac Incorporated (American Family Life Assurance Co.), Columbus, GA (1978-1983); Co-state Manager, Aflac Incorporated (American Family Life Assurance Co.), Columbus, GA (1973-1978) **CR:** Director, Columbus Bank & Trust Company, Synovus Financial Corporation, Southern Company **CIV:** Board of Trustees, House of Mercy of Columbus; Board of Trustees, Children's Healthcare of Atlanta **AW:** Torch of Liberty Award, Anti-Defamation League; Dr. Martin Luther King Junior Unity Award **H:** Bridge **BA:** Aflac Inc, 1932 Wynnton Rd, Columbus, GA, USA, 31999

ANDERSON, JAMIE L., T: Professional Snowboarder **I:** Athletics **DOB:** 07/06/1905 **PB:** South Lake Tahoe, California **SC:** South Lake Tahoe, California **AW:** 6 Winter X Games Gold Medals,2007,08,12,13,17,18, 5 Winter X Games Silver Medals, 2010,14,15,16,17, 3 Winter X Games Bronze Medals, 2006,11,18, 2 Olympic Gold Medals,2014,18, 1 Olympic Silver Medal, 2018

ANDERSON, PAUL THOMAS, T: Film Director, Film Producer, Scriptwriter **I:** Media & Entertainment **PB:** Studio City **PT:** Ernie Anderson; Bonnie (Gough) Anderson; **CH:** Pearl Minnie; Lucille; Jack; Minnie Ida **ED:** Attended, New York University; Attended, Emerson College, Boston **CW:** Writer, director (films) The Dirk Diggler Story, 1988, Cigarettes & Coffee, 1993, Sydney, 1996, Flagpole Special, 1998, Mattress Man Commercial, 2003, Blossoms & Blood, 2003, writer, director, producer Boogie Nights, 1997 (Best New Filmmaker, Boston Society Film Critics, 1997), Magnolia, 1999, Punch-Drunk Love, 2002, There Will Be Blood, 2007 (Best Director, National Society Film

Critics, 2008), The Master, 2012, Inherent Vice, 2014, writer, director, Phantom Thread, 2017, Waterlily Jaguar, 2018 (TV films) SNL Fanatic, 2000; dir.: (TV films) Couch, 2003

ANDERSON, WES, T: Director **I:** Media & Entertainment **DOB:** 05/01/1969 **PB:** Houston **SC:** TX/ USA **ED:** PhB, University of Texas, 1991 **CW:** Writer, Director, (Films) Bottle Rocket, 1994; Writer, Producer, Director, Rushmore, 1998, The Royal Tenenbaums, 2001, The Life Aquatic With Steve Zissou, 2004, The Darjeeling Limited, 2007, Moonrise Kingdom, 2012, The Grand Budapest Hotel, 2014, Isle Of Dogs, 2017; Producer, She's Funny That Way, 2014, Escapes, 2017; Writer, Producer, Director, Voice, Fantastic Mr. Fox, 2009 **AW:** MTV Movie Award For Best New Filmmaker, Bottle Rocket, 1996, National Society Film Critics Award For Best Screenplay, Rushmore, 1999, Visionary Award, Stockholm Film Festival, 2007, National Board Review Special Filmmaking Achievement Award, Fantastic Mr. Fox, 2009, BAFTA Award For Best Original Screenplay, 2015, Golden Globe For Best Picture, The Grand Budapest Hotel, 2015 **BA:** United Talent Agency, 9336 Civic Center Drive, Beverly Hills, CA, 90210

ANDRÉS, JOSÉ, T: Chef **I:** Food & Restaurant Services **DOB:** 07/13/1969 **PB:** Mieres **ED:** Studied, Escola de Restauracio I Hostalatge de Barcelona, 1990 **C:** Executive chef, partner, Oyamel, 2004-; Executive chef, partner, Zaytinya, 2002-; Executive chef, partner, Jaleo, Crystal City, 2004-; Executive chef, partner, Jaleo, Washington, 1993-; Executive chef, Café Atlantico,; Executive chef, partner, Jaleo, Bethesda, Maryland,; Chef, El Dorado Petit, New York City, 1990-93 **CR:** Founder THINKfoodTANK, 2004- apprentice El Bullí, 1985-88 **CW:** Contributing editor Food Arts; featured in Gourmet magazine, Sunday Morning News with Chris Wallace, Food Network, USA Today, host, producer (TV series) Vamos a Cocinar, Television Española; author: Tapas: A Taste of Spain in America, How to Cook Everything: Bittman Takes on America's Chefs, Los fogones de José Andrés **AW:** Named Chef of Year, Restaurant Association of Metro. Washington, 2006, Bon Appetit, 2004; named one of The 100 Most Influential People in the World, TIME magazine, 2012, The Rising Stars of American Cuisine, Wine Spectator magazine, 1999; named to The Saveur 100 list, Saveur magazine, 2004, The 35 under 35 Tastemakers list, Food and Wine magazine, 2004; recipient Outstanding Chef award, James Beard Foundation, 2011, Order of Arts and Letters medallion, Spain, 2010, Best Chef of the Mid-Atlantic Region, James Beard Foundation, 2003 **MEM:** Mem.: D.C. Central Kitchen (chair of board, Chef/ Partner of Distinction 2001) **BA:** Jaleo, 480 7th St NW, Washington, DC, 20004

ANDRETTI, MARIO, T: Former Professional Racing Driver **I:** Athletics **DOB:** 02/28/1940 **PB:** Montona, Italy **PT:** Son of Alvise and Rina (Benvegnu) A.; Married Dee Ann Hoch, November 25, 1961; children: Michael, Jeffrey, Barbra **C:** Began racing career at age 19, Nazareth, Pennsylvania **AW:** Indy Car National Champion, 1965, 66, 69, 84; Daytona 500 winner, 1967; 12 Hrs. of Sebring winner, 1967, 70, 72; Indy 500 pole winner, 1966, 67, 87; USAC National Dirt Track Champion, 1974; Formula One World Champion, 1978; International Race of Champions titlist, 1979; Driver of the Year, 1967, 78, 84, Driver of the Quarter Century, 1992, Driver of the Century, 1999-00; all-time leader in Indy Car Pole Positions won (67); all-time Indy Car lap leader (7,587); all-time record holder for Indy Car starts (407); oldest race winner in recorded Indy Car history (53 years 34 days, Phoenix, 1993); only driver to win Indy Car races in four decades;

had 12 Formula One victories and captured 18 Formula One pole positions, International Motorsport Hall of Fame, 2001, National Sprint Car Hall of Fame, 1996, Motorsports Hall of Fame, 1990, Automotive Hall of Fame , 2005, Diecast Hall of Fame, 2012, Lombardi Award of Excellence, 2007 **BA:** Sports Management Network, 1301 West Long Lake Rd Suite 250, Troy, MI, 48098

ANDREWS, JULIE, T: Actress **I:** Media & Entertainment **DOB:** 10/01/1935 **PB:** Walton-on-Thames **SC:** England **ED:** Studied with Private Tutors; Studied Voice with Mme. Stiles-Allen **CW:** Debut as singer, Hippodrome, London, 1947; appeared in pantomime Cinderella, London, 1953; appearances include (Broadway productions) The Boy Friend; New York City, 1954, (& Connecticut, 2005), My Fair Lady, 1956-60 (New York Drama Critics award 1956), Camelot, 1960-62, Putting It Together, 1993, Victor/Victoria, 1995; (films) Mary Poppins, 1964 (Academy Award for Best Actress 1964), The Americanization of Emily, 1964, Torn Curtain, 1966, The Sound of Music, 1966, Hawaii, 1966, Thoroughly Modern Millie, 1967, Star!, 1968, Darling Lili, 1970, The Tamarind Seed, 1973, 1979, Little Miss Marker, 1980, S.O.B, 1981, Victor/ Victoria, 1982, The Man Who Loved Women, 1983, That's Life!, 1986, Duet For One, 1986, A Fine Romance, 1992, Relative Values, 2000, The Princess Diaries, 2001, Unconditional Love, 2002, (voice) Shrek 2, 2004, The Princess Diaries 2: The Royal Engagement, 2004, (voice) Enchanted, 2007, Tooth Fairy, 2010, (voice) Shrek Forever After, 2010, (voice) Despicable Me, 2010, Despicable Me 3, 2017; (TV series) The Julie Andrews Hour, 1972-73 (Emmy award for Best Variety Series), Julie, 1992; (TV films) Our Sons, 1991, One Special Night, 1999, Eloise at the Plaza, 2003, Eloise at Chrismastime, 2003, Broadway The American Musical, 2004, Great Performances: From Vienna The New Years Celebration 2009, 2009, Tudos Contra Juan, 2010, The Colbert Report, 2012, The Graham Norton Show, 2014, Julies Greenroom, 2017; author: (as Julie Edwards): Mandy, 1971, The Last of the Really Great Whangdoodles, 1974, Home: A Memoir of My Early Years, 2008, The Very Fairy Princess, 2010; recs.: The King and I, 1992; co-author The Very Fairy Princess Follows Her Heart, 2013 **AW:** Named World Film Favorite (female); 1967; Named to 100 Great Britons, 2002; Recipient Golden Globe Award, Hollywood Foreign Press Association, 1964, 1965, Lifetime Achievement Award, Kennedy Center, 2001, Screen Actors Guild, 2007, Golden Plate Award, Academy Achievement, 2004, Lifetime Achievement, Grammy Award, 2011, Spoken Word Album for Children: Julie Andrews' Collection of Poems. Songs and Lullabies-Julie Andrews & Emma Walton Hamilton, 2011 **ACH:** Achievements include knighted by Queen Elizabeth, 1999 **BA:** Greengage Productions, 11611 San Vicente Blvd Suite 840, Los Angeles, CA, 90049

ANISTON, JENNIFER, T: Actress **I:** Media & Entertainment **DOB:** 02/11/1969 **PB:** Sherman Oaks **SC:** CA/USA **PT:** Daughter of John and Nancy (Dow) Aniston; **ED:** Attended, Fiorello La Guardia School of Music, Art & Performing Arts, New York City **C:** Co-founder, Echo Films, 2008-; Co-founder, Plan B Entertainment, 2002-06 **CW:** Actress: (TV series) Ferris Bueller, 1990, Molloy, 1990, The Edge, 1992, Muddling Through, 1994, Friends, 1994-2004 (Screen Actors Guild Outstanding Ensemble Performance in Comedy Series, 1995, Emmy Award Best Actress, 2002, Golden Globe Award Best Actress, 2003, People's Choice Award Favorite Female Television Performer, 2001, 2002, 2003, 2004), (TV Appearances) Herman's Head, 1992-93, Quantum Leap, 1992, Burke's Law, 1994, Muddling Through, 1994, Partners, 1996, Hercules,

1998, Freedom: A History of Us, 2003, Dirt, 2007, 30 Rock, 2008, Cougar Town, 2010, Five, 2011, Burning Love, 2012, Call me Crazy a Five Film, 2013,; (TV Films) Camp Cucamonga, 1990, Sunday Funnies, 1993; (Films) Leprechaun, 1993, She's the One, 1996, Dream for an Insomniac, 1996, Til There Was You, 1997, Picture Perfect, 1997, The Thin Pink Line, 1998, The Object of My Affection, 1998, (Voice) The Iron Giant, 1999, Office Space, 1999, Rock Star, 2001, The Good Girl, 2002, Bruce Almighty, 2003, Along Came Polly, 2004, Derailed, 2005, Rumor Has It..., 2005, Friends With Money, 2006, The Break-Up, 2006, Marley & Me, 2008, He's Just Not That Into You, 2009, Love Happens, 2009, The Bounty Hunter, 2010, Just Go With It, 2011, Horrible Bosses, 2011, Wanderlust, 2012, We're the Millers, 2013, Life of Crime, 2013, She's Funny That Way, 2014, Horrible Bosses 2, 2014, Mother's Day, 2016, (Voice) Storks, 2016, Office Christmas Party, 2016, The Yellow Birds, 2018, Dumplin, 2018; actress, executive producer (Films) Management, 2008, The Switch, 2010, Cake, 2014; Executive Prodr.: (TV Films) Call Me Crazy: A Five Film, 2013; actress: (Off-broadway play) For Dear Life, Dancing on Checkers' Grave, (Music Videos) I'll Be There For You, 1995, Walls, 1996, I Want To Be In Love, 2001; host (Documentaries) Growing Up Grizzly 2, 2004 **AW:** Named Favorite Female Comedic Actress, People's Choice Awards, 2013, Favorite Female Star, 2007, World's Most Beautiful Woman, People Magazine, 2016; Named one of The 100 Most Powerful Celebrities, Forbes.com, 2008, 2007, The 50 Most Beautiful People, People magazine, 2005, 2004, 2003, 2002, The Most Beautiful People in the World, 1999, The Most Intriguing People, People Weekly, 1995; Recipient Crystal Award, Women in Film, 2009

ANSARI, AZIZ, T: Actor, Comedian **I:** Media & Entertainment **PB:** Columbia **SC:** SC/USA **PT:** Shoukath Ansari; Fatima Ansari **ED:** Degree in marketing, New York University, 2004 **C:** Comedian, Actor 2004- **CW:** Actor: (films) School for Scoundrels, 2006, The Rocker, 2008, Observe and Report, 2009, I Love You, Man, 2009, Funny People, 2009, Get Him to the Greek, 2010, 30 Minutes or Less, 2011, What's Your Number?, 2011, Ice Age: Continental Drift (voice), 2012, Epic (voice), 2013, This Is the End, 2013, Date and Switch, 2014; (TV series) Parks and Recreation, 2009-15; actor, executive producer, writer (TV series) Human Giant, 2007-08, TV appearances Uncle Morty's Dub Shack, 2004, New York Noise, 2005, Cheap Seats: Without Ron Parker, 2006, Flight of the Conchords, 2007, Human Giant, 2007-08, Water and Power, 2008; TV appearances Worst Week, 2008; TV appearances Scrubs: Interns, 2009, Scrubs, 2009, Reno 911!, 2009, The Life & Times of Tim, 2010, NTSF:SD:SUV, 2012, Ben 10:Omniverse, 2013-14, Kroll Show, 2015, voice Wander Over Yonder, 2013, Adventure Time, 2013, The Venture Brothers, 2013, Bob's Burgers, 2012-16, The League, 2013-15, Major Lazer, 2015, Animals, 2016, appearances, creator, writer, executive producer , SNL, 2017 (TV series) Shutterbugs, 2005-10, creator, writer, executive producer Master of None, 2015 (Emmy award for Outstanding Writing for a Comedy Series, 2016), performer, writer, executive producer Aziz Ansari: Intimate Moments for a Sensual Evening, 2010, Dangerously Delicious, 2012, performer, writer Who Is Aziz Ansari?, 2010, Aziz Ansari: Water Skiing Squirrel, 2010, Aziz Ansari: The Hurt Locker Date, 2010, Aziz Ansari: Let's Go to the Movies, 2010, Aziz Ansari: Hurt Locker 4-D, 2010, Aziz Ansari:Buried Alive, 2013, writer, executive producer Food Club, 2014, performer, writer, producer Aziz Ansari Live at Madison Square Garden, 2015, performer, creator, writer Raaaaaaaandy!, 2009, writer (blog) Aziz Is Bored; author: Modern

Romance, 2016 **AW:** Named one of The 100 Most Influential People in the World, TIME Magazine, 2016, Variety Power of Comedy Award, 2014

ANTHONY, CARMELO, T: Professional Basketball Player **I:** Athletics **DOB:** 05/29/1984 **PB:** NYC **ED:** Student, Syracuse University, 2003 **C:** Forward, Oklahoma City Thunder, 2017-; Forward, New York Knicks, 2011-2017; Forward, Denver Nuggets, 2003-11 **CR:** Founder Krossover Entertainment member US national team Summer Olympic Games, London, 2012, Beijing, 2008, Athens, Greece, 2004 **CIV:** Founder, Carmelo Anthony Youth and Devel. Center, Baltimore, 2006- Founder, Carmelo Anthony Foundation, Vol., Family Resource Center, Denver, **AW:** Named USA Basketball Male Athlete of Year, 2006, NBA Rookie of the Month (6 Times), 2003-04, NCAA Final Four Most Outstanding player, 2003; named one of All-NBA 3rd Team, 2006; named to Eastern Conference All-Star Team, NBA, 2013, 2012, Western Conference All-Star Team, 2011, 2010, 2008, 2007, 2005, All-Rookie 1st Team, 2004; recipient Gold medal, men's basketball, Summer Olympic Games, 2012, 2008 **ACH:** Achievements include member of the NCAA National Championship winning Syracuse Orangemen, 2003; tying the NBA record for points scored in one quarter (33), 2008; leading the NBA: scoring, 2013

ANYADIEGWU, KELECHI, T: CEO **I:** Information Technology and Services **CN:** Zuvaa **ED:** MHCI, Human Computer Interaction, Carnegie Mellon University, 2011-13; BS, Media and Communication Technology,African Studies, Michigan State University, 2007-11 **C:** Founder/CEO, Zuvaa, 2013-; Community Manager, Digitalundivided, 2013-14; Social Media Manager, Techiechic,2013-14; Web Design Consultant, MEMS Industry Group,2013 **AW:** 30 Under 30

APATOW, JUDD, T: Scriptwriter, Television and Film Producer **I:** Media & Entertainment **DOB:** 12/06/1967 **PB:** Syosset **PT:** Son of Maury and Tami; **CW:** Executive producer, writer (TV series) The Ben Stiller Show, 1992-93 (Emmy award for Best Writing, 1993), Freaks and Geeks, 1999-2000, executive producer, writer, director Undeclared, 2001-02, co-exec. producer, writer, director The Larry Sanders Show, 1992-98 (Cable ACE award, 1994, 1995); executive prodr.: (TV series) Girls, 2012-; prodr.: (films) The Cable Guy, 1996, Anchorman: The Legend of Ron Burgundy, 2004, Talladega Nights: The Ballad of Ricky Bobby, 2006; prodr.: (films) Forgetting Sarah Marshall, 2008; prodr.: (films) Step Brothers, 2008, Superbad, 2007, Get Him to the Greek, 2010, Bridesmaids, 2011, Wanderlust, 2012, The Five-Year Engagement, 2012; prodr.: (films) Anchorman: The Legend Continues, 2013; executive prodr.: (films) Kicking & Screaming, 2005, American Storage, 2006, The TV Set, 2006; executive prodr.: (films) Can a Song Save Your Life?, 2013; producer, writer (films) Knocked Up, 2007, Pineapple Express, 2008, producer, writer, director The 40 Year Old Virgin, 2005, Funny People, 2009, This Is 40, 2012, associate producer Crossing the Bridge, 1992, executive producer, writer Celtic Pride, 1996, executive producer, writer, actor Heavy Weights, 1995, producer, writer Walk Hard: The Dewey Cox Story, 2007, producer, director Trainwreck, 2015; actor: (films) Zookeeper (voice), 2011; producer, writer (TV films) Life on Parole, 2003, Sick in the Head, 2003, writer (screenplays) Fun with Dick and Jane, 2005; editor: (books) I Found This Funny: My Favorite Pieces of Humor and Some That May Not Be Funny At All, 2010; featured in documentary Salinger, 2013; author: Sick in the Head: Conversations About Life and Comedy, 2015 **AW:** Named one of The 100

Agents of Change, Rolling Stone magazine, 2009, The 100 Most Powerful Celebrities, Forbes.com, 2008, The 100 Most Influential People in the World, TIME magazine, 2008, The 50 Smartest People in Hollywood, Entertainment Weekly, 2007, The Top 25 Entertainers of Year (with Apatow Gang), 2007; recipient Louis XIII Genius award, Critics' Choice awards, 2013

ARMSTRONG, GREG L., I: Oil & Energy **ED:** BS, Southeastern Oklahoma State University, 1980 **CT:** CPA **C:** Chairman, CEO, Plains All American Pipeline, LP, Houston, 2001-; President, CEO, director, Plains Resources, Inc., 1992-2001; President, COO, Plains Resources, Inc., 1992; Executive vice president, CFO, Plains Resources, Inc., 1992; Senior vice president, CFO, Plains Resources, Inc., 1991-92; Vice president, CFO, Plains Resources, Inc., 1984-91; Treasurer, Plains Resources, Inc., 1984-87; Corp. secretary, Plains Resources, Inc., 1981-88; Formerly with, Price Waterhouse, **CR:** Board directors Varco International, 2004-, IPAA Texas Southeast Regional Board of Trustees, Petroleum Club of Houston

ARMSTRONG, RONALD E., T: Automotive Executive **I:** Automotive **C:** CEO, PACCAR, Inc., 2014-; President, PACCAR, Inc., Bellevue, Washington, 2011-2014; Executive vice president, PACCAR, Inc., Bellevue, Washington, 2010; Senior vice president, PACCAR, Inc., Bellevue, Washington, 2007-10; Vice president, controller, PACCAR, Inc., Bellevue, Washington, 2002-06; Operations controller, PACCAR, Inc., Bellevue, Washington, 1995-2002

ARONOV, MICHAEL, T: Actor and Playwright **I:** Media & Entertainment **CW:** Actor, Film, "Hedwig and the Angry Inch" (2001), "Law and Order: SVU" (2002), "Lbs" (2004), "Amexicano" (2007), "Without a Trace" (2008), "The Closer" (2010), "Blue Bloods" (2010), "White Collar" (2010), "Gun Hill" (2011), "Burn Notice" (2011), "Person of Interest" (2012), "Reign" (2013), "Elementary" (2013), "The Good Wife" (2013), "Madam Secretary" (2014, 2016), "The Americans" (2014-2016), "The Drop" (2014), "Quantico" (2015), "The Blacklist" (2017), "Half Magic" (2018); Actor, Theater, "King Lear" (1999), "The Bacheae 2.1" (2001), "Miss Julie" (2004), "A Streetcar Named Desire" (2009), "Manigma" (2010, 2006), "Golden Boy" (2012-2013), "Oslo" (2017) **AW:** Tony Award for Best Actor in a Play (2017)

ARRINGTON, JODEY, T: U.S. Representative from Texas **I:** Government Administration/Government Relations/Government Services **DOB:** 03/09/1972 **PB:** Kansas City **SC:** Missouri **ED:** M.A., Texas Tech University, 1997; B.A., Texas Tech University, 1994 **C:** Member, U.S. Representative from Texas' 19th District, 2017-; Member, Committee on Agriculture; Member, Committee on Budget; Member, Committee on Veterans Affairs; President, Scott Laboratories, 2014-17; Administrator, Texas Tech University, 2007-14; Deputy Federal Coordinator/ CEO, Office of the Federal Coordinator for Gulf Coast Rebuilding, 2005-06; Staff, Chairman of the Federal Deposit Insurance Corporation, 2001-05; Special Assistant, President George W. Bush, 2001 **AW:** Distinguished Public Service Award, 2003, Public Service Symposium in Lubbock **BA:** 1029 Longworth HOB, Washington, DC, 20515

ARROYO, MARTINA, T: Opera Singer **I:** Media & Entertainment **PB:** New York **SC:** NY/USA **PT:** Daughter of Demetrio and Lucille (Washington) Arroyo; **SPN:** Married Michel Maurel; Married Emilio Poggiono, 1961 (div.) **ED:** DHL (hon.), Hunter College City University of New York, 1987; BA in Romance Languages, Hunter College City University of New York, 1954; Student, Kathryn

Long Course Metropolitan Opera.; Studied successively with Marinka Gurevich, Joseph Turnau and Rose Landver **CR:** Distinguished professor emeritus music Ind. University, Bloomington other teaching credits include UCLA, University Del., Wilberforce University, Louisiana State University, International Sommerakademie-Mozarteum, Salzburg. **CIV:** Former member National Endowment of Arts, Washington trustee Carnegie Hall, New York City, Hunter College founder Martina Arroyo Foundation and Prelude to Performance Program. **CW:** Debut, Carnegie Hall, 1958, leading soprano, Metropolitan Opera, New York City; roles include: Trovatore, AIDA, Ballo, Forza, Chenier; performed opening night Metropolitan season, 1970-71, 1971-72, 1973-74, performed at La Scala, Milan, Munich Staatsoper, Berlin Deutsche Oper, Rome Opera, Vienna State Opera, Covent Garden, Teatro Colon, Buenos Aires, San Francisco, Chicago, and all major opera houses; soloist, New York, Vienna, Berlin, Royal (London), Paris philharmonics, San Francisco, Pittsburgh, Philadelphia, Chicago, Cleveland symphonies, Concertgebouw, other major orchestras; frequent performer Saratoga, Ravinia, Tanglewood festivals and festivals Vienna, Berlin, Edinburgh, Helsinki; recordings include I Vespri Siciliani, Un ballo in maschera, AIDA Verdi Requiem Don Giovanni, Missa solemnis, Ninth Symphony, Symphony of a Thousand, Gurre-Lieder, African Oratorio, Andromache's Farewell; recorded for Columbia, London, Angel, DGG, Philips, EMI, RCA. **AW:** recipient Verdi's medal, Amici di Verdi, London, Opera House award, National Endowment for the Arts, 2010, Kennedy Center Honors, John F. Kennedy Center Performing Arts, Washington, 2013,2010 Opera Honors Award from the National Endowment for the Arts **MEM:** Fellow: Am. Academy Arts and Scis. **BA:** The Martina Arroyo Foundation, Inc., 57 West 57th Street, 4th Floor, New York, NY, 10019

ATWOOD, MARGARET, T: Writer **I:** Writing and Editing **DOB:** 11/18/1939 **PB:** Ottawa **SC:** Ontario **PT:** Daughter of Carl Edmund and Margaret Dorothy (Killam) Atwood. **ED:** BA, University Toronto, 1961; AM, Radcliffe College, 1962; LittD (hon.), Trent University, 1973; LittD (hon.), Concordia University, 1980; LittD (hon.), Smith College, Northampton, Massachusetts, 1982; LittD (hon.), University Toronto, 1983; LittD (hon.), University Waterloo, 1985; LittD (hon.), University Guelph, 1985; LittD (hon.), Mount Holyoke College, 1985; LittD (hon.), Victoria College, 1987; LittD (hon.), University Montréal, 1991; LittD (hon.), University Leeds, 1994; LittD (hon.), McMaster University, 1996; LittD (hon.), Lakehead University, 1998; LittD (hon.), Oxford University, 1998; LittD (hon.), Cambridge University, 2001; LittD (hon.), Algoma University, 2001; LittD (hon.), Harvard University, 2004; LittD (hon.), Sorbonne Nouvelle, 2005; LittD (hon.), Literary and Historical Society, University College Dublin, 2005; LittD (hon.), Ontario College of Art and Design, 2009; LittD (hon.), National University of Ireland, 2011; LittD (hon.), Ryerson University, 2012; LittD (hon.), Royal Military College, 2012; LLD (hon.), Queen's University, 1974 **C:** Berg Chair, New York University, 1986; M.F.A. Honorary Chair, University Alabama, Tuscaloosa, 1985; Writer-in-residence, Trinity University, San Antonio, Texas, 1989; Writer-in-residence, Macquarie University, Australia, 1987; Writer-in-residence, University Toronto, 1972-73; Assistant Professor English, York University, Toronto, 1971-72; Lecturer in English, University Alberta, 1969-70; Lecturer in English, Sir George Williams University, 1967-68; Lecturer in English, University British Columbia, 1964-65 **CR:** President International P.E.N., Canadian Centre (English Speaking), 1984—1986; vice president

PEN International **CW:** Author: (novels) The Edible Woman, 1969, Surfacing, 1972, Lady Oracle, 1976, Life Before Man, 1979, Bodily Harm, 1981, The Handmaid's Tale, 1985 (Governor General's award, 1985, Arthur C. Clarke award, 1987), Cat's Eye, 1988 (Toronto Book award, 1989, Book of Year award, Foundation Advancement Can. Letters, 1989, Torgi Talking Book award, 1989, Foundation for the Advancement of Canadian Letters/Periodical Marketers of Canada Book of the Year, 1989), The Robber Bride, 1993 (Novel of the Year, Canadian Authors' Association, 1993, Trillium award for Excellence in Ontario Writing, 1994, Commonwealth Writers' prize for Canadian and Caribbean Region, 1994, Sunday Times award for Literary Excellence, London, 1994), Alias Grace, 1996 (Scotiabank Giller prize, 1996, Premio Mondello, Italy, 1997, Salon Magazine Best Fiction of the Year, 1997, Medal of Honor for Lit., National Arts Club, 1997), The Blind Assassin, 2000 (Man Booker prize for fiction, 2000, Dashiell Hammett prize, International Association Crime Writers, 2001), Oryx and Crake, 2003, The Penelopiad, 2005, The Year of the Flood, 2009, MaddAddam, 2013, Stone Mattress, 2014, (poetry collections) Double Persephone, 1961, The Circle Game, 1964 (Governor General's award, 1966), Expeditions, 1965, Speeches for Doctor Frankenstein, 1966, The Animals in That Country, 1968, The Journals of Susanna Moodie, 1970, Procedures for Underground, 1970, Power Politics, 1971, You Are Happy, 1974, Selected Poems, 1976, Two-Headed Poems, 1978, True Stories, 1981, Love Songs of a Terminator, 1983, Interlunar, 1984, Morning in the Burned House, 1995 (Trillium award for Excellence in Ontario Writing, 1995), Eating Fire: Selected Poems, 1965-1995, 1998, The Door, 2007 (Finalist, Governor General's Literary award, 2007), (short fiction collections) Dancing Girls, 1977 (St. Lawrence award for Fiction), Murder in the Dark, 1983, Bluebeard's Egg, 1983, Through the One-Way Mirror, 1986, Wilderness Tips, 1991 (Trillium award for Excellence in Ontario writing, 1992, Book of Year award, Periodical Marketers of Canada, 1992), Good Bones, 1992, Good Bones and Simple Murders, 1994, The Labrador Fiasco, 1996, The Tent, 2006, Moral Disorder, 2006, (nonfiction) Survival: A Thematic Guide to Canadian Literature, 1972, Days of the Rebels 1815-1840, 1977, Second Words: Selected Critical Prose, 1982, Strange Things: The Malevolent North in Canadian Literature, 1995, Negotiating with the Dead: A Writer on Writing, 2002, Moving Targets: Writing with Intent, 1982-2004, 2004, Curious Pursuits: Occasional Writing, 2005, Writing with Intent: Essays, Reviews, Personal Prose–1983-2005, 2005, Payback: Debt and the Shadow Side of Wealth, 2008, In Other Worlds: SF and the Human Imagination, 2011, (children's books) Up in the Tree, 1978; author: (with Joyce Barkhouse) Anna's Pet, 1980; author: For the Birds, 1990, Princess Prunella and the Purple Peanut, 1995, Rude Ramsay and the Roaring Radishes, 2003, Bashful Bob and Doleful Dorinda, 2006, Wandering Wenda and Widow Wallop's Wunderground Washery, 2011, (TV scripts) The Servant Girl, 1974, Snowbird, 1981—; Heaven on Earth, 1986; editor: (anthologies) The New Oxford Book of Canadian Verse in English, 1982, The Canlit Foodbook, 1987; co-editor (with Robert Weaver): The Oxford Book of Canadian Short Stories in English, 1986, The New Oxford Book of Canadian Short Stories in English, 1995; co-editor: (with Shannon Ravenel) The Best American Short Stories, 1989; editor: (plays) The Perelopiad: The Play, 2007, (Novels) The Heart Goes Last, 2015, Hag-Seed, 2016 **AW:** Decorated Officer, Order of Canada, Companion, Order of Canada, Chevalier dans l'Ordre des Arts et des Lettres, France; named Woman of Year, Ms. magazine, 1986, Author

of Year, Canadian Booksellers Association, 1989, 1996, Canadian Booksellers Association Author of the Year, 1989, Best Local Author, National Organization of Women Magazine Readers' Poll, 1995, 1997—2000; named one of Canada's Most Powerful woman, 2011; recipient E.J. Pratt medal, 1961, University Western Ontario President's medal, 1965, Union Poetry prize, Chicago, 1969, Bess Hoskins Poetry prize, 1974, The City of Toronto Book award, 1977, Canadian Bookseller's Association award, 1977, Periodical Distributors of Canada Short Fiction, 1977, St. Lawrence award for Fiction, 1978, Molson award, 1981, International Writer's prize, Welsh Arts Council, 1982, Ida Nudel Humanitarian award, 1986, Toronto Arts award, 1986, LA Times Fiction award, 1986, Arthur C. Clarke award for Best Sci. Fiction, 1987, National Magazine award, 1988, YWCA Women of Distinction award, 1988, Centennial medal, Harvard University, 1990, John Hughes prize, Welsh Devel. Board, 1992, Commemorative medal, Canadian Confederation 125th Anniversary, 1992, Swedish Humour Association International Humourous Writer award, 1995, Norwegian Order of Literary Merit, 1996, National Arts Club Medal of Honor for Lit., U.S.A., 1997, London Lit. award, 1999, International Crimewriters Association Dashiell Hammett award, 2001, Canadian Booksellers Association People's Choice award, 2001, Radcliffe medal, 2003, Harold Washington Literary award, 2003, Banff Centre's National Arts award, 2005, Edinburgh's International Book Festival Enlightenment award, 2005, Chicago Tribune Literary prize, 2005, Markets Initiative Order of the Forest, 2006, Blue Metropolis Literary Grand Prix, Montreal, 2007, Kenyon Review Literary Achievement award, U.S.A., 2007, Prince of Asturias award for Letters, Spain, 2008, Crystal award, World Economic Forum, Switzerland, 2010, Nelly Sachs, Dortmund, Germany, 2010, Sun Life Financial Arts & Communications award, 2011, Dan David prize for Literature, 2011, Governor General Canada's Golden Jubilee medal, 2012, Canadian Booksellers' Lifetime Achievement award, 2012, Nashville Public Library Foundation Literary award, 2012, Los Angeles Times Innovator award, 2012, Toronto United Church Council Heart and Vison award, 2012; fellow John Simon Guggenheim Memorial Foundation, 1981, Time 100 Most Influential, 2017, Gold Medal of the Royal Canadian Geographical Society, 2015, Golden Wreath of Struga Poetry Evening, 2016, Franz Kafka Prize, 2017, Peace Prize of the German Book Trade, 2017 **MEM:** Fellow: Royal Society Can., Royal Canadian Geographical Society (hon.); mem.: Writers' Union of Canada (president 1981—82), American Academy Arts & Sciences (foreign hon. member), Rare Bird Society (hon. president) **ACH:** Achievements include invention of LongPen, a remote-controlled pen that allows writers to sign books for fans from thousands of miles away **BA:** McClelland & Stewart Ltd, 320 Front Street West, Suite 1400, Toronto, ON, Canada, M5V 3A4

AULD, DAVID V., T: CEO **I:** Business Management/Business Services **CN:** D.R. Horton, Inc. **ED:** Bachelors in Accounting, Texas Tech University (1978) **C:** President/Chief Executive Officer, D.R. Horton, Inc. (2014-Present); Executive Vice President/Chief Operating Officer, D.R. Horton, Inc. (2013-2014); President, East Homebuilding, D.R. Horton, Inc. (2005-2013); President, D.R. Horton, Inc., Orlando, FL (1988-2005)

AUMANN, ROBERT JOHN, T: Mathmatician **I:** Education/Educational Services **DOB:** 06/08/1930 **PB:** Frankfurt am Main, Germany **PT:** Son of Siegmund and Miriam (Landau) Aumann; **ED:** PhD (hon.), Bar Ilan University, 2005; PhD (hon.), City University of New York, 2005; PhD (hon.),

University Chicago, 1992; PhD (hon.), Catholic University Louvain, Belgium, 1989; PhD (hon.), University Bonn., Germany, 1988; PhD in Math., Massachusetts Institute of Technology, 1955; SM in Math., Massachusetts Institute of Technology, 1952; BS in Math., City College of New York, 1950 **C:** Professor Emeritus, Hebrew University Jerusalem, 2001-; Member Center Rationality, Hebrew University Jerusalem, 1991-; Fellow Institute Advanced Studies, Hebrew University Jerusalem, 1979-80; Professor, Hebrew University Jerusalem, 1968-2001; Chairman Institute Math., Hebrew University Jerusalem, 1966-68; Associate Professor, Hebrew University Jerusalem, 1964-68; Senior Lecturer, Hebrew University Jerusalem, 1961-64; Lecturer, Hebrew University Jerusalem, 1958-61; Instructor, Hebrew University Jerusalem, 1956-58 **CR:** Oskar Morgenstern Visiting Professor Economics Northwestern University, 1999-2000, New York University, 1997 Member Math. Sci. Research Institute, Berkeley, 1985-86, Institute Math. & Applications, University Minnesota, 1984 Ford Visiting Research Professor Economics University California, 1985-86, Berkeley, 1971 Visiting Professor Center Game Theory, State University of New York, 1991-, Stony Brook, 1986-89, Stanford University, 1980-81, California, 1975-76, Tel Aviv University, 1969-93, Center Operations Research & Econometrics, Catholic University Louvain, 1984, 1978, 1972, Cowles Foundation Research in Economics, Yale University, New Haven, 1964-65 Seearch Associate Princeton University, New Jersey, 1960-61 **MIL:** Served in Israeli Army, 1969-84 **CW:** Author: Values of Non-Atomic Games, 1974, What Is Game Theory Trying to Accomplish?, 1985, Lectures on Game Theory, 1989, Repeated Games with Incomplete Information, 1995, Collected Papers, 2000; associate editor Journal Economic Theory, 1974-79, Econometrica, 1975-78, Journal European Math. Society, 2000-, Member Editorial Board International Journal Game Theory, 1971-, Games & Economic Behavior, 1989-; Contributor Articles to Professional Journals **AW:** Recipient Yakir Yerushalayim Award, City of Jerusalem, 2006, Nobel Prize in Economics, 1995, Bank of Sweden Prize in Economic Scis., 2005, John von Neumann prize, Institute Operations Research, 2005, Emet Prize for Economics, Israel, 2002, Erwin Plein Nemmers Prize in Economics, Northwestern University, 1998, Lanchester Prize, Operations Research Society America, 1995, Israel Prize in Economics, 1994, Harvey Prize in Sci. & Tech., Technion-Israel Institute Tech., 1983, Bank of Sweden Prize in Economic Sciences in Memory of Alfred Nobel, 2005 **MEM:** Fellow: Econometric Society (council member 1977-82, member executive committee 1982-85), British Academy (corr.); mem.: Israel Academy Scis. & Humanities, National Academy of Sciences, Am. Economic Association (hon.), American Association for the Advancement of Science (foreign hon.), Game Theory Society (founding president 1998-2003), Israel Math. Union (president 1990-92) **H:** Hiking, Climbing, Skiing, Cooking **ADD:** Hebrew U Jerusalem, Center For Rationality, Jerusalem, YT, Israel, 91999

AURIEMMA, GENO, T: College Basketball Coach **I:** Athletics **DOB:** 03/23/1954 **PB:** Montella **SC:** Italy **MS:** Married **SPN:** Kathy Auriemma **CH:** Jenna, Alysa, Michael **ED:** BA in Political Science, West Chester University, 1981 **C:** Head Coach, University of Connecticut Huskies, 1985-Present; Assistant Coach, St. Joseph's University Hawks, Philadelphia, PA, 1984; Assistant Coach, University of Virginia Cavaliers, 1981-1985; Coach Boys' Basketball, Bishop Kenrick High School, Norristown, PA, 1979-1981 **CR:** Chair, Kodak All-American Selection Committee, 1992, West Team U.S. Olympic Festival,

San Antonio, TX, 1993, Assistant Coach, USA World University Games Women's Basketball Team, 1995, Vice President, Board of Directors, Women's Basketball Coaches Association, 2007-2008, President, Board of Directors, Women's Basketball Coaches Association, 2009-2010, Voting Member, USA Today/Women's Basketball Coaches Association Top 25 Poll-In, Co-Head Coach, National Senior All-Stars, Coach, USA Basketball Select Team, Colorado Springs, CO, Head Coach, Speaker, National High School Coaches Association Convention, Connecticut, WNBA Analyst, ABC Sports, ESPN **CIV:** Honorary Chair, American Heart Association, Co-Chair, Connecticut Arthritis Foundation, Chair, Why-Me of New England **CW:** Co-Author, (Autobiography) Geno: In Pursuit of Perfection, 2006 **AW:** Big East Coach of the Year, 1989, 1995, 1997, 2000, 2002-2003, 2008-2011, Outstanding Contribution Award, UConn Club, 1992, Giant Steps Award, Center for the Study of Sport in Society, 1995, Victor Award, Women's Basketball Coaches Association, 1995-1996, 2000, Naismith National Coach of the Year, 1995, 1997, 2000, 2002, 2008-2010, Coach of the Year, Associated Press, 1995, 1997, 2000, 2003, 2008-2009, 2015, USBWA Women's National Coach of the Year, 1995, 2003, 2008-2009, 2016-2017, New England Basketball Hall Of Fame, 2002, NCAA Division I Coach of the Year, Women's Basketball Coaches Association, 2002, 2008-2009, Women's Basketball Hall Of Fame, 2006, Naismith Memorial Basketball Hall Of Fame, 2006, Italian-American Hall Of Fame, 2007, John R. Wooden Legend Of Coaching Award, 2012, Winged Foot Award, New York Athletic Club, 2013, American Athletic Conference Coach of the Year, 2014-2017, Naismith Coach of the Year, 2016-2017, AP Coach of the Year, 2016-2017, WBCA National Coach of the Year, 2016-2017 **MEM:** National Mortar Board **ACH:** Achievements include head coach of the NCAA Women's National Championship winning University of Connecticut Huskies, 1995, 2000, 2002-04, 2009, 2010, 2013, 2014, 2015, 2016 **BA:** University of Connecticut, Division of Athletics, Women's Basketball, 2095 Hillside Road, Unit 1173, Storrs-Mansfield, CT, 06269-1173

AXEL, RICHARD, T: Neuroscientist, Educator **I:** Education/Educational Services **DOB:** 07/02/1946 **PB:** NYC **ED:** MD, Johns Hopkins University School Medicine, Baltimore, 1970; AB magna cum laude, Columbia University, New York City, 1967 **C:** Howard Huges Medical Institute Investigator; Univ. professor, Columbia University, 1999-; Professor pathology and biochemistry, Columbia University, 1978-; Assistant professor department pathology, Columbia University, 1974-78; Research associate, US Public Health Service, National Institutes of Health, 1972-74; Visiting fellow department pathology, Columbia University College Physicians & Surgeons, 1971-72; Intern department pathology, Columbia University College Physicians & Surgeons, 1970-71 **CR:** Investigator Howard Hughes Medical Institute, 1984- **AW:** Recipient Nobel Prize in Physiology/Medicine, The Nobel Foundation, 2004, Gairdner Foundation International award, 2003, Medal for Distinguished Contribution in Biomed. Scis., New York Academy Medicine, 2001, Alexander Hamilton award, Columbia University, 1999, Bristol-Meyers Squibb award for distinguished achievement in neurosci. research, 1998, New York City Mayor's award for excellence in sci. & tech., 1997, Unilever Sci. award, New York Academy Scis. award in biological & medical scis., Ely Lilly award, 1983, Young Scientist award, Passano Foundation, 1979, Irma T. Hirschl Career Scientist award, 1976, Johns Hopkins Medical Society Research award, 1969,Fellow of the Royal Society, 2014 **MEM:** Mem.: National Academy of Sciences (Richard

Lounsbery award 1989), American Philosophical Society, American Academy Arts & Sciences, Phi Beta Kappa **ACH:** Achievements include discovery of odorant receptors and the organization of the olfactory system

AYOTTE, KELLY A., T: U.S. Senator from New Hampshire **I:** Government Administration/Government Relations/Government Services **DOB:** 06/27/1968 **PB:** Nashua **SC:** NH/USA **ED:** JD, Villanova University, 1993; BA with honors in Political Sci., The Pennsylvania State University, 1990 **CT:** Bar: Maine, New Hampshire **C:** U.S. Senator from New Hampshire, Washington, 2011-2017; Member, U.S. Senate Small Business & Entrepreneurship Committee, Washington, 2011-; Member, U.S. Senate Commerce, Science & Transportation Committee, Washington, 2011-; Member, U.S. Senate Budget Committee, Washington, 2011-; Member, U.S. Senate Armed Services Committee, Washington, 2011-; US Senator from New Hampshire, Washington, 2011-; Attorney general, State of New Hampshire, 2004-09; Deputy attorney general, State of New Hampshire, 2003-04; Legal counsel to Governor, State of New Hampshire, 2003; Senior assistant attorney general, chief, homicide unit, State of New Hampshire, 2000-02; Assistant attorney general, homicide unit, State of New Hampshire, 1998-2000; Associate, McLane, Graf, Raulerson and Middleton, Nashua, New Hampshire, 1994-98; Law clerk for Hon. Sherman Horton, New Hampshire Supreme Court, 1993-94 **AW:** Named Citizen of Year, New Hampshire Union Leader, 2008; recipient Kirby award, New Hampshire Bar Foundation, 2004 **MEM:** Mem.: New Hampshire Bar Association, Maine Bar Association **PA:** Republican

AZAR, ALEX MICHAEL II, T: Secretary of Health and Human Services **I:** Government Administration/Government Relations/Government Services **ED:** JD, Yale Law School, 1991; AB in Government & Economics, Dartmouth College, 1988 **CT:** Bar: DC 1995, Maryland 1993 **C:** Secretary designate, United State Department of Health and Human Services, Washington, DC, 2017—; President Eli Lilly USA, Eli Lilly & Co., Indianapolis, 2012-2017; Vice president U.S. managed care services & Puerto Rico, Eli Lilly & Co., Indianapolis, 2009-11; Senior vice president corporate affairs & communications, Eli Lilly & Co., Indianapolis, 2007-09; Deputy secretary, U.S. Department Health & Human Services, Washington, DC 2005-07; General counsel, U.S. Department Health & Human Services, Washington, DC 2001-05; Partner, Wiley, Rein & Fielding LLP, Washington, DC 1996-2001; Associate ind. counsel, Whitewater Investigation, Washington, DC 1994-96; Associate, Kirkland & Ellis LLP, Washington, DC 1993-94; Law clerk to Associate Justice Antonin Scalia, Supreme Court of the U.S., Washington, DC 1992-93; Law clerk to Hon. J. Michael Luttig, US Court Appeals (4th Cir.), 1991-92 **BA:** Health and Human Services Headquarters, 200 Independence Ave S.W., Washington, DC, 20201

BABIN, BRIAN, T: U.S. Representative from Texas **I:** Government Administration/Government Relations/Government Services **DOB:** 03/23/1948 **PB:** Port Arthur **SC:** TX/USA **ED:** DDS, University Texas, 1976; BS in Biology, Lamar University, Texas, 1975 **C:** Mem.-elect, US Congress from 36th Texas District, 2014-; Member, Committee on Science, Space and Technology; Member, Committee on Space; Dentist, Woodville, Texas, 1979-; Chairman, Tyler County Republican Party, Texas, 1990-95; Councilman, City of Woodville, 1984-89; Mayor, City of Woodville, 1982-84; County coordinator, regional coordinator, Ronald Reagan's Presidential Cam-

paign, 1980 **CR:** Member Lower Neches Valley Authority, 1999- board member Woodville Ind. School District, 1992-95, Texas Hist. Commission, 1989-95, Deep East Texas Council Governments, 1982-84 president Texas State Board Dental Examiners, 1981-87 **PA:** Republican

BACHARACH, ROBERT EDWIN, T: Federal Judge **I:** Law and Legal Services **DOB:** 05/20/1959 **PB:** Clarksdale **SC:** Mississippi **PT:** Son of Marvin Jerome & Norma Sarah (Pries) B.; **SPN:** Married Rhonda Diane Kinsey, October 15, 1994. **ED:** JD, Washington University, St. Louis, 1985; BA, University Oklahoma, 1981 **CT:** Bar: Oklahoma 1985, US District Court (western district) Oklahoma 1985, US Court Appeals (10th cir.) 1986, US Supreme Court 1989, US District Court (eastern district) Oklahoma 1990, US District Court (northern district) Oklahoma 1993. **C:** Judge, US Court Appeals (10th Cir.), 2013-; Magistrate Judge, US District Court (western district) Oklahoma, 1994-2013; Shareholder, Director, Crowe & Dunlevy, Oklahoma City, 1987-94; Law Clerk to Hon. William J. Holloway Junior, US Court Appeals (10th Cir.), Oklahoma City, 1985-87 **BA:** 1823 Stout St, Dearborn, CO, 80202

BACON, DON, T: U.S. Representative from Nebraska **I:** Government Administration/Government Relations/Government Services **DOB:** 08/16/1963 **PB:** Momence **SC:** Illinois **ED:** M.A., National War College, 2004; M.B.A, University of Phoenix,1996; B.A., Northern Illinois University, 1984 **C:** Member, U.S. Representative from Nebraska's 2nd District, 2017-; Member, Committee on Agriculture; Member, Committee on Armed Services; Member, Committee on Small Business; Assistant Professor, University of Bellevue, 2014-17; Staff, U.S. Representative Jeff Fortenberry of Nebraska, 2014-15; Director, ISR Strategy, Plans,Doctrine, and Force Development, 2012-2014 **MIL:** U.S. Air Force, 1985-2014 **AW:** Distinguished Service Medal, two Legion of Merits, and two Bronze Stars, Europe's Top Air Force Wing Commander, 2009 **BA:** 1516 Longworth HOB, Washington, DC, 20515

BACON, KEVIN, T: Actor **I:** Media & Entertainment **PT:** Edmund Bacon; Ruth Bacon **MS:** Married **SPN:** Kyra Sedgwick, (September 3, 1988) **CH:** Travis; Sosie Ruth **CW:** Actor: (off-Broadway debut) Getting Out, Marymount Manhattan Theatre, 1978, (Broadway debut) Slab Boys, Playhouse Theatre, 1983, other stage productions include Glad Tidyings, 1979-80, Mary Barnes, 1980, Album, 1980, Forty-Deuce, 1981, Flux, 1982, Poor Little Lambs, 1982, Men Without Dates, 1985, Loot, 1986; (films) National Lampoon's Animal House, 1978, Starting Over, 1979, Hero at Large, 1980, Friday the 13th, 1980, Only When I Laugh, 1981, Diner, 1982, Footloose, 1984, Quicksilver, 1985, White Water Summer, 1987, Planes, Trains and Automobiles, End of the Line, 1988, She's Having a Baby, 1988, Criminal Law, 1989, The Big Picture, 1989, Tremors, 1990, Flatliners, 1990, Queens Logic, 1991, He Said/She Said, 1991, Pyrates, 1991, JFK, 1992, A Few Good Men, 1992, The Air Up There, 1994, The River Wild, 1994, Murder in the First, 1995, Apollo 13, 1995, (voice) Balto, 1995, Sleepers, 1996, Destination Anywhere, 1997, Telling Lies in America, 1997, Picture Perfect, 1997, Digging to China, 1997, My Dog Skip, 1999, Stir of Echoes, 1999, Hollow Man, 2000, Novocaine, 2001, Trapped, 2002, Mystic River, 2003, In the Cut, 2003, Cavedweller, 2004, Beauty Shop, 2005, Where the Truth Lies, 2005, The Air That I Breath, 2007, Death Sentence, 2007, Rails & Ties, 2007, Saving Angelo, 2007, Frost/Nixon, 2008, Taking Chance, 2009 (Outstanding Performance by a Male Actor in a TV Movie or Miniseries, Screen Actors Guild, 2010),

My One and Only, 2009, (voice) Beyond All Boundaries, 2009, Super, 2010, X-Men: First Class, 2011, Elephant White, 2011, Crazy, Stupid, Love., 2011, Jayne Mansfield's Car, 2012, Skum Rocks!, 2013, R.I.P.D., 2013, Black Mass, 2015, The Darkness, 2016, Patriots Day, 2016; actor, executive prodr.: (films) Wild Things, 1998, The Woodsman, 2004, Cop Car, 2015; actor, director, prodr.: (films) Loverboy, 2005; actor: (TV films) The Gift, 1979, Enormous Changes at the Last Minute, 1982, The Demon Murder Case, 1983, Mister Roberts, 1984, The Little Sister, 1984, Lemon Sky, 1988, Taking Chance, 2009 (Best Performance by an Actor in a Mini-Series or Motion Picture Made for TV, Golden Globe Awards, 2010), The President's Gatekeepers, 2013; actor, dir: (TV films) Losing Chase, 1996; actor: (TV series) Search for Tomorrow, 1979, The Following, 2013-15; (TV appearances) Frasier (voice), 1994, Mad About You, 1996, Will & Grace, 2002, The Colbert Report, 2008, Taking Chance, 2009, Bored to Death, 2010, Robot Chicken, 2011, The Following, 2013, Comedy Bang Bang, 2016, I Love Dick, 2016, Tour De Pharmacy, 2017; dir.: (TV series) The Closer, 2006-09; musician: (albums with The Bacon Brothers) Forosoco, 1997, Getting There, 1997, Can't Complain, 2001, The Bacon Brothers Live - No Food Jokes Tour, 2003, White Knuckles, 2005, New Years Day, 2008, Philadelphia Road - Best of the Bacon Brothers, 2011. **AW:** Recipient Joel Siegel award, Broadcast Film Critics Association, 2010; Star, Hollywood Walk of Fame, 2003

BAEZ, JOAN CHANDOS, **T:** Vocalist **I:** Media & Entertainment **DOB:** 01/09/1941 **PB:** Staten Island, New York, January 9, 1941 **PT:** Daughter of Albert V. and Joan (Bridge) B.; **MS:** Married **SPN:** David Victor Harris, March 1968 (div. 1973); **CH:** Gabriel Earl **CIV:** Extensive TV appearances and speaking tours U.S. and Can. for anti-militarism, 1967-68 visit to Dem. Republic of Vietnam, 1972, visit to war torn Bosnia-Herzegovina, 1993 founder, vice president Institute for Study Nonviolence (now Resource Center for Nonviolence, Santa Cruz, California), Palo Alto, California, 1965 member national adv. council Amnesty International, 1974-92 founder, president Humanitas/Internat. Human Rights Committee, 1979-92 conductor fact-finding mission to refugee camps, Southeast Asia, October 1979 began refusing payment of war taxes, 1964 arrested for civil disobedience opposing draft, October, December, 1967. **CW:** Appeared in coffeehouses, Gate of Horn, Chicago, 1958, Ballad Room, Club 47, 1958-68, Newport (Rhode Island) Folk Festival, 1959-69, 85, 87, 90, 92, 93, 95, extended tours to colleges and concert halls, 1960s, appeared Town Hall and Carnegie Hall, 1962, 67, 68, U.S. tours, 1970-, concert tours in Japan, 1966, 82, Europe, 1970-73, 80, 83-84, 87-90, 93-, Australia, 1985; recording artist for Vanguard Records, 1960-72, Agricultural and Mechanical, 1973-76, Portrait Records, 1977-80, Gold Castle Records, 1986-89, Virgin Records, 1990-93, Grapevine Label Records (UK), 1995-97, Guardian Records, 1995-97, European record albums, 1981, 83, award 8 gold albums, 1 gold single; albums include Gone From Danger, 1997, Rare, Live & Classic (box set), 1993, Dark Chords on a Big Guitar, 2003, Bowery Songs, 2005, Day After Tomorrow,2008,Whistle Down the Wind, 2018; author: Joan Baez Songbook, 1964, (biography) Daybreak, 1968, (with David Harris) Coming Out, 1971, And a Voice to Sing With, 1987, (songbook) An Then I Wrote, 1979. **AW:** Rock and Roll Hall of Fame Inductee,2017, Grammy Lifetime Achievement Award, 2007,Grammy Hall of Fame, 2011, Independent Music Award for Best Song, 2016

BAKER, CHARLES DUANE JR., **T:** Governor of Massachusetts **I:** Government Administration/ Government Relations/Government Services **DOB:** 11/13/1956 **ED:** MBA, Northwestern University, 1986; BA in English, Harvard College, 1979 **C:** Governor, State of Massachusetts, 2015-; Entrepreneur-in-residence, General Catalyst Partners, Cambridge, Massachusetts, 2011-; Governor, State of Massachusetts, 2015-; Republican candidate for 2010 Massachusetts Gubernatorial race, 2009-10; President, CEO, Harvard Pilgrim Health Care (HPHC), Quincy, Massachusetts, 1999-2009; President, CEO, Harvard Vanguard Medical Associates, 1998; Secretary administration & finance, State of Massachusetts, 1994-98; Secretary health & human services, State of Massachusetts, 1991-94; Under secretary for health & human services, State of Massachusetts, Boston, 1991-92; Co-founder, The Pioneer Institute for Pub. Policy Research, 1988-91 **CR:** Board directors athenahealth, Inc., 2012, Med Venture Inc., 2010- board trustee Natixis Funds, 2005- **CIV:** Board member, Greater Boston C. of C., Board trustee, Rose Kennedy Greenway Conservancy, Board selectman, Swampscott, 2004-07 **AW:** Recipient Distinguished Service award, National Governor's Association, 1998 **MEM:** Mem.: Massachusetts Association of Health Plans (board chair) **PA:** Republican **BA:** State House, Office of the Governor Room 280, Boston, MA, 02133

BAKER, DOUGLAS M. JR., **T:** CEO of Ecolab **I:** Business Management/Business Services **DOB:** 12/05/1958 **ED:** English, College of the Holy Cross, 1981 **C:** Chairman/CEO, Ecolab, 2011-; Chairman, Ecolab, Inc., St. Paul, 2006-11; President, CEO, board director, Ecolab, Inc., St. Paul, 2004-; President, COO, Ecolab, Inc., St. Paul, 2002-04; Senior vice president institutional sector, Ecolab, Inc., 2001-02; Various positions including marketing director institutional division, European director institutional marketing and vice president & general manager of Kay, Ecolab, Inc., St. Paul, 1989-2001; Various marketing and management positions, Proctor & Gamble Co., **CR:** Board directors U.S. Bancorp, 2008-

BAKER, GERARD, **T:** Writer and Columnist **I:** Writing and Editing **ED:** MA, Corpus Christi College, Oxford University, 1983 **C:** Editor in Chief, Wall Street Journal, 2013-Present; Deputy Editor in Chief, Wall Street Journal, 2009-2012; U.S. Editor, The Times, 2004-2009; Washington Bureau Chief, Financial Times, 1998-2002; Tokyo Correspondent, Financial Times, 1994-1998; Producer, BBC, 1988-1994

BAKER, JIM, **T:** Former White House Chief of Staff **I:** Government Administration/Government Relations/Government Services **DOB:** 04/28/1930 **PB:** Houston **SC:** TX/USA **PT:** James Addison Baker; Ethel Bonner (Means) Baker **ED:** Honorary LLD, University Pennsylvania (2007); LLB, University of Texas (1957); BA, Princeton University (1952) **C:** Member, Iraq Study Group (2006-Present); Senior Partner, Baker & Botts, LLP, Washington, DC and Houston, Texas (1993-Present); Secretary, US Department of State (1989-1992); Chairman, George H.W. Bush Presidential Campaign (1988); Secretary, US Department of Treasury (1985-1988); Chief of Staff, Senior Counselor to President, The White House (1992-1993); Chief of Staff to President, The White House (1981-1985); Under Secretary, US Department of Commerce, Washington, DC (1975-1976); Attorney, Andrews Kurth Campbell & Jones, Houston, Texas (1957-1975) **CR:** Co-chair, Iraq Study Group (2006); Chairman, The B.P. Refineries Industry, Safety Review Panel (2005-2007); Special Presidential Envoy to Iraqi for Debt Reduction, The White House (2003); Personal Envoy of Secretary-General for Western Sahara,

United Nations (1997-2004); Board of Directors, Electronic Data Corporation (1996-2003); Senior Counselor, "The Carlyle Group" (1993-2005); Gulf Coast Regional Chairman, President Richard Nixon's Re-Election Campaign (1972); Finance Chairman, Republican Party (1971) **CIV:** Board of Trustees, Smithsonian Institution; Board of Trustees, Woodrow Wilson International Center of Scholars; Honorary Chairman, Rice University; James A. Baker III Institute Public Policy, Houston, Texas (1993-Present) **MIL:** Served, U.S. Marine Corps (1952-1954) **CW:** Author, "The Politics of Diplomacy: Revolution, War and Peace 1989-1992" (1995); Author, "Work Hard, Study...and Keep Out of Politics!: Adventures and Lessons from an Unexpected Political Life" (2006); Appearance, Documentary, "Reagan" (2011) **AW:** Named One of America's Best Leaders, US News & World Report (2007); George F. Kennan Award; Hans J. Morgenthau Award; Alexander Hamilton Award, US Department of the Treasury; Distinguished Service Award, US Department of State; Jefferson Award, American Institute Public Service; Lifetime Achievement Award, American Lawyer Magazine (2007); Woodrow Wilson Award for Public Service, Princeton University (2000); Presidential Medal of Freedom, The White House (1991); John Heinz Award for Greatest Public Service to an Elected or Appointed Official (1985) **MEM:** Fellow, American Academy of Arts & Sciences; ABA; American Judicature Society; Houston Bar Association; Texas Bar Association; Phi Delta Phi **H:** Hunting; Fishing; Tennis; Golf **PA:** Republican

BAKISH, ROBERT, **T:** CEO of Viacom **I:** Business Management/Business Services **DOB:** 01/01/1900 **ED:** MBA, Columbia Graduate School of Business, 1989; Bachelors Degree, The FU Foundation School of Engineering & Applied Science, 1985 **C:** President/CEO, Viacom Inc, 2016-; President/CEO, Viacom International Media Networks, 2011-16; President, MTV Networks Intl, 2007-11; Executive VP:Viacom Enterprises, Viacom Inc, 2005-07; Exec VP/COO, MTV Networks, 2001-05

BALDWIN, TAMMY SUZANNE GREEN, **T:** U.S. Senator from Wisconsin **I:** Government Administration/Government Relations/Government Services **DOB:** 02/11/1962 **PB:** Madison **PT:** Daughter of Joseph Edward and Pamela (Green) Baldwin. **ED:** JD, University Wisconsin Law School, Madison, 1989; AB in Government & Math., Smith College, Northampton, Massachusetts, 1984 **C:** Secretary, Senate Democratic Conference, 2017-; Member, US Senate Special Committee on Aging, 2013-; Member, US Senate Health, Education, Labor & Pensions Committee, 2013-; Member, US Senate Homeland Security & Governmental Affairs, 2013-; Member, US Senate Budget Committee, 2013-; US Senator from Wisconsin, 2013-; Member, US House Judiciary Committee, 2007-11; Member, US Congress from 2nd Wisconsin District, Washington, 1999-2013; Member District 78, Wisconsin State Assembly, 1993-99; Private law practice, Wisconsin, 1989-92; Supervisor, Dane County Board Supervisors, 1986-1994; Councilwoman, Madison City Council, 1986 **MEM:** Mem.: ACLU, National Organization of Women, Wisconsin State Bar Association, International Network Lesbian & Gay Officials **PA:** Democrat **BA:** Office of Tammy Baldwin, 709 Hart Senate Office Building, Washington, DC, 20510

BALE, CHRISTIAN, **T:** Actor **I:** Media & Entertainment **DOB:** 01/30/1974 **PB:** Haverfordwest Pembrokeshire **SC:** Wales **PT:** Son of David Bale and Gloria Steinem (Stepmother); **CIV:** Actively involved with various civic organizations including, Dian Fossey Gorilla Fund, Actively involved with various civic organizations including, World Wildlife Foundation, Actively involved with various civic organizations including, Greenpeace, Actively involved with various civic organizations including, Redwings Sanctuary, Actively involved with various civic organizations including, Ark Trust, Actively involved with various civic organizations including, Happy Child Mission, **CW:** Actor: (TV films) Anastasia: The Mystery of Anna, 1986, Treasure Island, 1990, A Murder of Quality, 1991, Mary, Mother of Jesus, 1999; (TV miniseries) Heart of the Country, 1987; (films) The Land of Faraway, 1987, Empire of the Sun, 1987, Henry V, 1989, Newsies, 1992, Swing Kids, 1993, Royal Deceit, 1994, Little Women, 1994, (voice) Pocahontas, 1995, The Secret Agent, 1996, Portrait of a Lady, 1996, Metroland, 1997, Velvet Goldmine, 1998, All the Little Animals, 1998, A Midsummer Night's Dream, 1999, American Psycho, 2000, Shaft, 2000, Captain Corelli's Mandolin, 2001, Laurel Canyon, 2002, Reign of Fire, 2002, Equilibrium, 2002, The Machinist, 2004, (voice) Howl's Moving Castle, 2004, Batman Begins, 2005 (MTV Movie Award for Best Hero, 2006), The New World, 2005, The Prestige, 2006, Rescue Dawn, 2006, 3:10 to Yuma, 2007, I'm Not There, 2007, The Dark Knight, 2008 (People's Choice award for Favorite On-Screen Matchup (with Heath Ledger), 2009, People's Choice award for Favorite Superhero, 2009), Terminator Salvation, 2009, Public Enemies, 2009, The Fighter, 2010 (Golden Globe award for Best Performance by an Actor in a Supporting Role in a Motion Picture, 2011, Screen Actors Guild award for Outstanding Performance by a Male Actor in a Supporting Role, 2011, Academy award for Best Actor in a Supporting Role, 2011, National Board Review award for Best Supporting Actor, 2010, Boston Society Film Critics award for Best Supporting Actor, 2010, Critics' Choice award for Best Supporting Actor, 2011), The Flowers of War, 2011, The Dark Knight Rises, 2012, Out of the Furnace, 2013, American Hustle, 2013, Exodus: Gods and Kings, 2014, Knight of Cups, 2015, The Big Short, 2015 (Critics' Choice award for Best Actor in a Comedy, 2016), The Promise, 2016, Hostiles, 2017, Jungle Book, 2018, Backseat, 2018; actor, executive producer (films) Harsh Times, 2005 **BA:** William Morris Endeavor Entertainment, 9601 Wilshire Blvd. 3rd Floor, Beverly Hills, CA, 90210

BALLMER, STEVE, T: Professional Sports Team Executive **I:** Business Management/Business Services **CN:** L.A. Clippers **DOB:** 03/24/1956 **PB:** Detroit **SC:** Michigan **PT:** Son of Frederick and Beatrice (Dworkin) Ballmer; **ED:** Attended, Stanford University Graduate School Business, 1980; AB in Applied Math. & Economics, Harvard University, 1977 **C:** Owner, L.A. Clippers, 2014-; CEO, Microsoft Corp., Redmond, Washington, 2000-14; Director, Accenture, 2001-06; President, Microsoft Corp., Redmond, Washington, 1998-2001; Executive vice president sales & support, Microsoft Corp., Redmond, Washington, 1992-98; Various positions including vice president marketing, vice president corporate staffs, senior vice president system software, Microsoft Corp., Redmond, Washington, 1980-92; Joined, Microsoft Corp., Redmond, Washington, 1980; Assistant product manager, Procter & Gamble Co., 1977-79 **CR:** Member advisory council Stanford Business School board overseers Harvard University board directors Accenture, 2001-06, Microsoft Corp., 2000-14 **CIV:** Launched USAFacts.org,2017 **AW:** Named one of The Forbes 400: Richest Americans, 2009-, The 100 Most Influential People in the World, TIME magazine, 2008, The World's Most Powerful People, Forbes magazine, 2012, The World's Richest People, 2006- **H:** Exercise, jogging, basketball **BA:** LA Clippers, 111 S Figueroa St, Los Angeles, CA, 90015

BALTIMORE, DAVID, T: Biologist **I:** Sciences **DOB:** 03/07/1938 **PB:** New York City **SC:** NY/USA **PT:** Richard I. Baltimore; Gertrude Baltimore **ED:** PhD, Rockefeller University, New York City, NY (1964); BA in Chemistry, Swarthmore College, with High Honors, PA (1960) **C:** Robert Andrews Millikan Professor of Biology, California Institute of Technology (2006-Present); President Emeritus, California Institute of Technology, Pasadena, CA (2006-Present); President, California Institute of Technology, Pasadena, CA (1997-2006); Professor, Rockefeller University, New York City, NY (1990-1994); President, Rockefeller University, New York City, NY (1990-1991); Founding Director, Whitehead Institute of Biomedical Research, Massachusetts Institute of Technology (1982-1990); Professor of Biology, Massachusetts Institute of Technology, Cambridge, MA (1972-1990); Associate Professor of Microbiology, Massachusetts Institute of Technology, Cambridge, MA (1968-1972); Research Associate, Salk Institute Biological Studies, La Jolla, CA (1965-1968); Postdoctorate Fellow, Albert Einstein College of Medicine, Bronx, NY (1964-1965) **CR:** Board of Directors Med-Immune, Inc. (2003-2007); Chair, Vaccine Advisory Committee, National Institutes of Health (1997-2002); Member, AIDS Research Advisory Council (1996); Co-chairman, Commission National Strategy of Aids (1986) **CIV:** Board of Governors, Weizmann Institute of Science, Israel; Board of Directors, Life Science Research Foundation **CW:** Member, Editorial Board, Journal of Molecular Biology (1971-1973); Member, Editorial Board, Journal of Virology (1969-1990); Member, Editorial Board, Science (1986-1998); Member, Editorial Board, New England Journal of Medicine (1989-1994); Contributor, Articles to Professional Journals **AW:** Warren Alpert Foundation Prize (2000); National Medal of Science (1999); Nobel Prize in Physiology/Medicine (1975); Gairdner Foundation International Award (1974); Eli Lilly and Company Award in Microbiology (1971); Warren Triennial Prize, Massachusetts General Hospital (1971); Gustav Stern Award in Virology (1970) **MEM:** Fellow, American Association for the Advancement of Science; President, American Association for the Advancement of Science (2007); Chairman, Board of Directors, American Association for the Advancement of Science (2008-2009); Fellow, American Academy of Mircobiology; Honorary Fellow, American Medical Writers Association; National Academy of Sciences; Foreign Associate, French Academy of Sciences; Foreign Associate, Royal Society; Pontifical Academy of Sciences; American Philosophical Society; Institute of Medicine; American Academy of Arts & Sciences **BA:** California Institute of Technology, 1200 E California Blvd, Pasadena, CA, 91125

BANDERAS, ANTONIO, T: Actor **I:** Media & Entertainment **DOB:** 08/10/1960 **PB:** Malaga **SC:** Spain **PT:** José Domínguez; Ana Banderas **CR:** Launched Signature Men's Fragrance, Spirit (2004); Launched Signature Women's Fragrance, Diavolo Donna (1999) **CW:** Actor, Films, "Labyrinth of Passion" (1982), "Pestanas Postizas" (1982), "Y del Sefuro...Ilbranos Señor!" (1983), "El Senor Galindez" (1983), "El Caso Almeria" (1983), "The Stilts" (1984), "La Corte de Faraon" (1985), "Requiem por un Campesino Espanol" (1985), "The Puzzle" (1986), "27 Hours" (1986), "Matador" (1986), "Delirios de Amor" (1986), "The Way They Were" (1987), "Law of Desire" (1987), "The Pleasure of Killing" (1988), "El Acto" (1987), "Baton Rouge" (1988), "Women on the Verge of a Nervous Breakdown" (1988), "Going South Shopping" (1988), "Si Que Dicen Que Cai" (1989), "The White Dove" (1989), "Tie Me Up! Tie Me Down!" (1990),

"Against the Wind" (1990), "New Land" (1991), "Woman in the Rain" (1991), "Madonna: Truth or Dare" (1991), "Borges Tales, Part I" (1991), "The Mambo Kings" (1992), "Shoot!" (1993), "Outrage" (1993), "Philadelphia" (1993), "The House of the Spirits" (1993), "Il Giovane Mussolini" (1993), "Of Love and Shadows" (1994), "Interview with the Vampire" (1994), "Never Talk to Strangers" (1995), "Miami Rhapsody" (1995), "Four Rooms" (1995), "Desperado" (1995), "Assassins" (1995), "Two Much" (1996), "Evita" (1996), "The Mask of Zorro" (1997), "Crazy in Alabama" (1998), "The 13th Warrior" (1999), "The White River Kid" (1999), "Play It to the Bone" (1999), "Dancing in the Dark" (2000), "The Body" (2000), "Spy Kids" (2001), "Original Sin" (2001), "Femme Fatale" (2002), "Spy Kids: Island of Lost Dreams" (2002), "Frida" (2002), "Ballistics: Ecks versus Sever" (2002), "Spy Kids 3-D: Game Over" (2003), "Imagining Argentina" (2003), "And Starring Pancho Villa as Himself" (2003), "Once Upon a Time in Mexico" (2003), Voice Actor, "Shrek 2" (2004), "The Legend of Zorro" (2005), "Take the Lead" (2006), "Bordertown" (2006), Voice Actor, "Shrek the Third" (2007), "My Mom's New Boyfriend" (2008), "The Other Man" (2008), "Thick as Thieves" (2009), Voice Actor, "Shrek Forever After" (2010), "You Will Meet a Tall Dark Stranger" (2010), "The Big Bang" (2011), "The Skin I Live In" (2011), Voice Actor, "Puss in Boots" (2012), "Haywire" (2011), "Ruby Sparks" (2012), "I'm So Excited" (2013), "Machete Kills" (2013), "The Expendables 3" (2014), "Knight of Cups" (2015), Voice Actor, "The SpongeBob Movie: Sponge Out of Water" (2015), "The 33" (2015), "Altamira" (2016), "Black Butterfly" (2017), "Gun Shy" (2017), "Security" (2017), "Acts of Vengeance" (2017), "Bullet Head" (2017), "Life Itself" (2018); Director, Films, "Crazy in Alabama" (1999), "Malaga Burning" (2000); Producer, Films, "White River Kid" (1999), "Forever Lulu" (2000), "Before the Fall" (2008), "The Missing Lynx" (2008); Director, Producer, Films, "Summer Rain" (2006); Actor, Producer, Films, Voice, "Justin and the Knights of Valour" (2013), "Autómata" (2014); TV Films, "La Otra Historia de Rosendo Juarez" (1990)

BANKS, JIM, T: U.S. Representative from Indiana **I:** Government Administration/Government Relations/Government Services **DOB:** 07/16/1979 **PB:** Columbia City **ED:** BA in Political Sci., Ind. University, Bloomington **C:** Member, U.S. House of Representatives from Indiana's 3rd District, 2017-; Member, Committee on Armed Services, Committee on Science, Space, and Technology, Committee on Veterans' Affairs; Member District 17, Ind. State Senate, 2010-2017; Councilman, Whitley County Council, 2009-10; Director business devel., The Hagerman Group, **PA:** Republican **BA:** 509 Cannon House Office Building, Washington, DC, 20515

BANNON, STEVE, T: Former Senior Counselor to the President **I:** Government Administration/Government Relations/Government Services **PB:** Norfolk **SC:** VA/USA **ED:** B.A., Urban Planning,Virginia Tech College of Architecture, 1976; M.A., National Security Studies, Georgetown University; M.A. Business Administration, Harvard Business School **C:** Senior Counselor to the President, 2017; White House Chief Strategist, 2017 **MIL:** Officer, U.S. Navy **CW:** (Films Produced) The Indian Runner, 1991, Titus, 1999, In the Face of Evil: Reagan's War in Word and Deed, 2004, Cochise County USA: Cries from the Border, 2005, Border War: The Battle over Illegal Immigration, 2006, The Chaos Experiment, 2009, Generation Zero, 2010, Battle for America, 2010, Fire from the Heartland, 2010, Still Point in a Turning World: Ronald Reagan and His Ranch, 2011, The Undefeated, 2011, Occupy Unmasked, 2012, The Hope and the Change 2012, District of Corruption, 2012, Sweetwater, 2012, Rickover: The Birth of Nuclear Power, 2014, Clinton Cash, 2016, Torchbearer, 2016 **AW:** Time 100 Most Influential, 2017

BAQUET, DEAN PAUL, T: Journalist **I:** Writing and Editing **DOB:** 09/21/1956 **PB:** New Orleans **SC:** LA/USA **PT:** Son of Edward Joseph and Myrtle (Romano) Baquet; **ED:** BA, Columbia University, 1978 **C:** Executive editor, The New York Times, 2014-; Executive vice president, editor, L.A. Times, 2005-06; Managing editor, L.A. Times, 2000-05; Managing editor for news, The New York Times, 2011-14; Assistant managing editor, DC bureau chief, The New York Times, 2007-11; National editor, The New York Times, 1995-2000; Deputy metropolitan editor, The New York Times, 1995; Special project editor office executive editor, The New York Times, 1994-95; Special projects editor business desk, The New York Times, 1992-94; Metropolitan reporter, The New York Times, 1990-92; Associate metropolitan editor for investigations, chief investigative reporter, Chicago Tribune, 1987-90; Investigative reporter, Chicago Tribune, 1984-87; Investigative reporter, The Times Picayune/The States Item, New Orleans, 1978-84 **AW:** Named Media Mensch of Year, New York Observer, 2006; recipient Pulitzer prize for investigative reporting, 1988,Peter Lisagor Award, 1988, William H Jones Award, 1987, 1988, 1989 **MEM:** Fellow: American Academy Arts & Scis. **ACH:** Achievements include first African-American editor to run the newsroom for the LA Times

BARBE, DAVID O., T: President of the American Medical Association **I:** Medicine & Health Care **ED:** Master in Health Administration, University of Missouri, Colombia, MO; MD, University of Missouri, Colombia, MO; Bachelor in Microbiology, University of Missouri, with Honors, Colombia, MO **CT:** Certified in Family Medicine **C:** President, American Medical Association (2017-Present); President, Regional Division, St. John's Clinic, Inc., Mountain Grove, MO (1999-Present); Private Practice in Traditional Family Medicine, Mountain Grove, MO (1984-Present); Medical Director, Department of Obstetrics, Texas County Memorial Hospital, Houston, MO (1986-2007); Chief, Medical Staff, Mercy Hospital, Mansfield, MO; Chief, Medical Staff, Texas County Memorial Hospital; Residency in Family Medicine, University of Kansas-St. Joseph's Hospital, Witchita, KS **CR:** Board Member, St. John's Health Plans; Member, Medical Executive Committee & Board of Directors, St. John's Hospital, MO **MEM:** Secretary, American Medical Association (2011-Present); Board of Trustees, American Medical Association (2009-Present); Chairman, Council on Medical Service, American Medical Association (2008-2009); President, Missouri State Medical Association (2005); Board of Directors, Missouri State Medical Association (2005); Chairman, Missouri State Medical Association (2003); Missouri Delegate, American Medical Association (1997-2009); Fellow, American Academy of Family Physicians; Missouri Academy of Family Physicians **BA:** American Medical Association, AMA Plaza, 330 N. Wabash Ave., Suite 39300, Chicago, IL, 60611

BARD, ALLEN JOSEPH, T: Chemist, Educator **I:** Sciences **DOB:** 12/18/1933 **PT:** Married Fran; children: Eddie, Sara **ED:** PhD (hon.), Weizmann Institute Sci., 2003; PhD (hon.), University Texas Agricultural and Mechanical University, 2000; PhD (hon.), University Paris-VII, 1986; PhD in Chemistry, Harvard University, 1958; MA in Chemistry, Harvard University, 1956; BSc in Chemistry summa cum laude, City College of New York, 1955 **C:** Director, Center for Electrochemistry, University

Texas, Austin, 2006-; Hackerman-Welch Regents Chair Chemistry, University Texas, Austin, 1985-; Professor chemistry, University Texas, Austin, 1967-; Norman Hackerman Professor Chemistry, University Texas, Austin, 1982-85; Jack S. Josey Professorship Energy Studies, University Texas, Austin, 1980-82; Associate professor, University Texas, Austin, 1962-67; Assistant professor, University Texas, Austin, 1960-62; Instructor chemistry, University Texas, Austin, 1958-60 **CR:** US national committee International Union Pure and Applied Chemistry-Nat. Research Council, 1983-93, chair, 1988-89, board energy and environmental system, 1983-86, 93-96, board chemical scis. tech., 1982-87, co-chair, 1985-87, national materials adv. board committee on electrochemical aspects of energy conservation and production, 1985, committee on chemical scis. and ad hoc panel on DOE research, 1980-84, National Academy of Sciences, National Research Council liaison committee on high temporary sci. and tech,. 1984 vice president, International Union Pure and Applied Chemistry, 1990-91, president, 1991-93 adv. board Department Energy and Energy Research, panel on Cold Fusion, 1989 chemical adv. committee National Science Foundation, 1981-84 external adv. committee Beckman Institute, 1989-97 board governors Weizmann Institute, 1995-2000, 2000-05, 2005-10, sci. & academy adv. committee, 1995-98, 2001- member scientific research evaluation panel, Air Force office, 1977-81 adv. board member, Bowling Green State University, Center for Photochemical Sciences, 2002-05 member energy research adv. board, panel on cold fusion, Department Energy, member low energy nuclear reactions review, 2004 Scientific adv. board, Biodesign Institute, Arizona State University, 2006-08 consultant SACHEM, BioVeris (was IGEN), Nucryst Pharma., Konarka Technologies Inc., Nanosys Inc. past consultant Orchid, Monsanto, CombiChem, Perkin-Elmer, Exxon Research and Engineering, ClearFlow, National Sci. Foundation, Phillips Petroleum, Rockwell International, Texas Instruments, Bell Northern, Radian Corp, E.I. DuPont, Electric Power Research Institute Woodward visiting professor, Harvard University, 1988 visiting professor, University of Tokyo, 1975 lecturer in field. **CW:** Author: Chemical Equilibrium, 1966, Integrated Chemical Systems, 1994; co-author: Electrochemical Methods, 1980; editor Electroanalytical Chemistry, 22 vols., 1966-, Encyclopedia of Electrochemistry, Encyclopedia of the Electrochemistry of the Elements, 16 vols., 1973-, Electrogeneral Chemiluminescence, 2004, (with others) Standard Potentials in Aqueous Solution, Scanning Electrochemical Microscopy; section editor Encyclopedia Physical Sci. & Tech., division editor, Journal Electrochemical Society, 1970-78, Electrochimica Acta, 1978-80; member editorial adv. board Analytical Letters, 1967-2004, Chemical Instrumentation, 1967-77, New Journals Chemistry, 1978-93, Journal Photoacoustics, 1982-84, Encyclopedia Physical Sci. and Tech., 1984-2004, Analytical Scis., 1985-99, Critical Revs. in Analytical Chemistry, 1985-91, Journal Supercritical Fluids, 1988-95, Catalysis Letters, 1988-94, Journal Supercritical Fluids, 1988-95, Academic Press Dictionary Sci. and Tech., 1989-92, Dictionary Modern Sci. and Tech., 1989-92, Encyclopedia Sci. Instrumentation, 1990-, Chemical Physics Letters, 1992-98, Organic Thin Films and Surfaces, 1991-, McGraw-Hill Encyclopedia Sci. and Tech., 1992-97, Heterogeneous Chemistry Revs., 1993-2007, Accounts of Chemical Research, 1993-97, Russian Chemical Bulletin, 1995-2008, Bulletin Chemical Society Japan, 1995-2004, Encyclopedia Analytical Chemistry: Instrumentation and Applications, 1996-2001, Structure and Bonding, 1996-2005, Nano Letters, 2005-06, NANO, 2007-08; contributor

over 750 articles to professional journals **AW:** Recipient Ward Medal in Chemistry, 1955, Analyst Year, Dallas Society Analystical Chemistry, 1976, Sherman Mills Fairchild scholar California Institute Tech., 1977, Scientific Achievement award City College New York, 1983, Bruno Breyer Memorial award Royal Australian Chemical Institute, 1984, Math. and Physical Scis. award New York Academy Scis., 1986, Townsend Harris medal City College New York, 1989, Charles N. Reilley award, Society Electroanalytical Chemistry, 1984, Edward Mack award Ohio State University, 1988, Outstanding Achievement in Fields of Analytical Chemistry award Eastern Analytical Symposium, 1990, G.M. Kosolapoff award, Auburn University, 1992, Luigi Galvani medal Societa Chimica Italiana, 1992, Sigillum Magnum di Bologna, 1996, Pittsburgh Analytical Chemistry award, 2001, Welch award in Chemistry, Welch Foundation, 2004, Distinguished Scientist award, Southeastern Universities Research award, 2009, National Medal of Science, 2012; co-recipient Wolf Foundation prize in Chemistry, Israel, 2008; National Science Foundation Predoctoral Fellowship, 1956-58, Fulbright Fellow, University Paris, 1973,Enrico Fermi Award, 2013, Wolf Prize, 2008, Priestley Medal, 2002 **MEM:** Fellow Electrochemical Society (Carl Wagner Memorial award 1981, Henry Linford award 1986, Olin-Palladium medal 1987, member committee education, 1968-70, vice-chmn., electro-organic division, 1968-70, division editor, Journal Electrochemical Society, 1970-78, member executive committee, S. Texas section, 1995-, Heinz Gerischer award-European Section, 2007), World Innovation Found.(fellow, 2004-2006, hon. member 2007); member American Association for the Advancement of Science (council del. 1992-95, chair-elect chemistry section 1996, chair, chemical section 1997-98, election panel, 2004), Am. Chemical Society (Harrison Howe award Rochester section 1980, Fisher award in Analytical Chemistry, 1984, Willard Gibbs award Chicago section 1987, Analytical Chemistry award in Electrochemistry, 1988, Oesper award Cincinnati section 1989, Linus Pauling award, Puget Sound and Portland Sections 1998, Priestley medal, 2002, William H. Nichols medal, New York, 2004, AdHoc task force to evaluate the Journal Am. Chemical Society, 1979, associate editor of journal, 1980-81, editor-in-chief, 1982-2001, committee to select editor for Analytical Chemistry, 1990, award committee, 1995-97, task force on ethics of the council policy committee, 2001, member governing board for publishing's task force on access and pricing for online journal backfiles, 2001, executive director 2010 committee, 2004), National Academy of Sciences (chairman chemistry section 1996-99, chair, selection committee, award in chemical sciences, 2002, member board on energy and environmental system, 1983-86, 1993-96, 2003-09, governing board member, 2004-05 Academy Medicine, Engineering and Sciences Texas, committee member award in chemical scis. 2006), Am. Academy Arts and Scis. (award 1990, Chemistry Section Election Panel, 2004, 2007), International Society Electrochemists (vice-chmn., chemical physics program, 1978-80), Am. Philosophical Society (award 2000), Association Harvard Chemists (Priestley medal 2002), Society Electroanalytical Chemistry, International Union of Pure and Applied Chemistry (member commission on electrochemistry, 1975-83, commission on chemical kinetics, 1983-87, co-chair CHEMRAWN IV: Conference on ocean resources, 1987, v.p./pres. elect, 1990-91, president, 1991-93), National Institute Standards and Tech. (member evaluation panel for Center for Analytical Chemistry, 1983-86), National Research Council (member National Materials Adv. Board (NAS/NRC Liaison: committee on high temperature sci. and tech., 1984, member, committee on chemical sciences and ad hoc panel on Department Energy research, 1980-84, member committee on electrochemical aspects of energy conservation and production, 1985), US National Committee for Biochemistry, 1985, ex-officio member US National Committee for Crystallography, 1985, Ad Hoc committee on the future of analytical chemistry, 1984, committee to survey opportunities in chemical sciences, 1984-86, member board on chemical sciences and tech., 1982-87, co-chair, 1985-87, member committee on potential applications of concentrated solar photons, 1990-91, member board energy and environmental system, 1983-86, 1993-96, 2003-2006, member chemical sciences roundtable, 1997-99 **ACH:** Achievements include research involving application of electrochemical methods to study of chemical problems and include investigations in electroanalytical chemistry, electron spin resonance, electro-organic chemistry, high resolution electrochemistry, electrogenerated chemiluminescence and photoelectrochemistry; patents in the field

BARDEM, JAVIER, T: Actor **I:** Media & Entertainment **PB:** Las Palmas de Gran Canaria, Gran Canaria, Canary Islands **SC:** Spain **PT:** Pilar Bardem **ED:** Attended, Escuela de Artes y Officios **CW:** Actor: (TV series) Segunda Ensenanza, 1986, El Dia por delante, 1989-90; (films) The Ages of Lulu, 1990, High Heels, 1991, Jamon, Jamon, 1992, Numbered Days, 1994, The Detective and Death, 1994, Mouth to Mouth, 1995, Not Love, Just Frenzy, 1996, Dance with the Devil, 1997, Airbag, 1997, Live Flesh, 1997, Torrente, the Stupid Arm of the Law, 1998, Between Your Legs, 1999, Sugunda piel, 1999, Before Night Falls, 2000 (National Board Review award for Best Actor, 2000), Without News From God, 2001, The Dancer Upstairs, 2002, Mondays in the Sun, 2002, Collateral, 2004, The Sea Inside, 2004, Goya's Ghosts, 2006, No Country for Old Men, 2007 (New York Film Critics Circle award for Best Supporting Actor, 2007, Boston Society Film Critics award for Best Supporting Actor, 2007, Critics Choice award, Broadcast Film Critics Association awards for Best Supporting Actor, 2008, Golden Globe award for Best Performance by an Actor in a Supporting Role in a Motion Picture, 2008, Screen Actors Guild award for Outstanding Performance by a Male Actor in a Supporting Role, 2008, Screen Actors Guild award for Outstanding Performance by a Cast in a Motion Picture, 2008, BAFTA award for Best Supporting Actor, 2008, Academy award for Best Actor in a Supporting Role, 2008), Love in the Time of Cholera, 2007, Vicky Cristina Barcelona, 2008, Biutiful, 2010, Eat Pray Love, 2010, To the Wonder, 2012, Skyfall, 2012, Alacrán enamorado, 2013, The Counselor, 2013, Autómata (voice), 2014, The Gunman, 2015,The Last Face, 2016, Pirates of the Caribbean: Dead Men Tell No Tales, 2017, Mother!, 2017, Loving Pablo, 2017, Everybody Knows, 2018; prodr.: (documentaries) Invisibles, 2007, Sons of the Clouds, 2012; actor, executive producer (films) Los lobos de Washington, 1999 **AW:** Recipient Star, Hollywood Walk of Fame, 2012, National Cinematography prize, Institute Cinematography and Audiovisual Art, 2008 **ACH:** Achievements include being the first Spanish actor nominated for an Academy Award

BARISH, BARRY C., T: Physics Professor, Researcher **I:** Sciences **PB:** Omaha **ED:** PhD in experimental high energy physics, Berkeley, 1962; BA in physics, University California, Berkeley, 1957 **C:** Linde Professor of Physics at California Institute of Technology, 2005-; Member, National Sci. Board, National Science Foundation, 2002-; Director,

Laser Interferometer Gravitational-Wave Observatory (LIGO) project, 1997-; Maxine and Ronald Linde professor physics, California Institute Tech., Pasadena, 1991-; Co-chair, High Energy Physics Adv. Panel subpanel,; Chairman US liaison committee, International Union Pure and Applied Physics (IUPAP),; Former chairman commission particles and fields, International Union Pure and Applied Physics (IUPAP),; Principal investigator, Laser Interferometer Gravitational-Wave Observatory (LIGO) project, 1994 **CR:** Speaker in field **AW:** Recipient Klopsteg award, Am. Association Physics Teachers, 2002, Nobel Prize in Physics 2017 **MEM:** Fellow: American Association for the Advancement of Science, Am. Physics Society; mem.: National Academy of Sciences **ACH:** Achievements include research in high-energy neutrinos important in demonstrating the quark substructure of the nucleon; research in search for magnetic monopole predicted in theories of Grand Unification,Fudan-Zhongzhi Science Award, 2017, Princess of Asturias Award, 2017, Cocconi Prize, 2017, Henry Draper Medal , 2017, American Ingenuity Award, 2016, Enrico Fermi Prize, 2016

BARKLEY, CHARLES WADE, T: Former NBA Player **I:** Athletics **DOB:** 02/20/1963 **PB:** Leeds **SC:** AL/USA **ED:** Student, Auburn University, Alabama, 1981-84 **C:** Host, Listen Up, TNT, 2002-; Co-host, Inside the NBA, TNT, 2001-; Forward, Houston Rockets, 1996-2000; Forward, Phoenix Suns, 1992-96; Forward, Philadelphia 76ers, 1984-92 **CR:** Member US Olympic team, 1996, 1992 **CIV:** Participant, Ante Up for Africa, Las Vegas, Nevada, 2008 **CW:** Co-author (with Roy S. Johnson): Outrageous! The Fine Life and Flagrant Good Times of Basketball's Irresistible Force, 1992; co-author: (with Rick Reilly) Sir Charles: The Wit and Wisdom of Charles Barkley, 1994; author: I May Be Wrong But I Doubt It, 2002, Who's Afraid of a Large Black Man, 2005; actor: (films) Forget Paris, 1995 **AW:** Named NBA MVP, 1993, NBA All-Star Game MVP, 1991; named to National Collegiate Basketball Hall of Fame, 2008, Naismith Memorial Basketball Hall of Fame, 2006, NBA All-Star team, 1988-93, All-Rookie team, 1985; recipient IBM award, 1986-88, Schick Pivotal Player award, 1986-88,Suns Ring of Honor, 2004, NBA All-Star team, 1987-97, All-NBA First team, 1988-1991, 1993 **ACH:** Achievements include leading the NBA in: offensive rebounds, 1987-89; free throw attempts, 1988

BARLETTA, LOU JAMES, T: U.S. Representative From Pennsylvania, Former Mayor **I:** Government Administration/Government Relations/Government Services **DOB:** 01/28/1956 **PB:** Hazleton **SC:** PA/USA **PT:** Rocky Barletta, Angeline Barletta **ED:** Student, Bloomsburg State College; Student, Luzerne County Community College, Nanticoke, PA **C:** U.S. House of Transportation & Infrastructure Committee, Washington, DC, 2011-Present; U.S. House of Education & the Workforce Committee, Washington, DC, 2011-Present; U.S. Congress From the 11th Pennsylvania District, Washington, DC, 2011-Present; Mayor, City of Hazleton, Hazleton City Council, 2000-2010; Councilman, Hazleton City Council, 1998-2000; Co-Founder, Interstate Road Marking Corp., Hazleton, PA, 1984; Committee on Homeland Security **CR:** Board of Directors, Northeast District, Pennsylvania League Cities & Municipalities; National Board of Advisors, Federation of American Immigration Reform **AW:** Mayor of the Year, Pennsylvania State Mayors Association, 2008 **MEM:** U.S. Conference of Mayors **PA:** Republican **BA:** U.S. House of Representatives, 115 Cannon House Office Building, Washington, DC, 20515 **ADD:** Lou Barletta for Congress, 8 W Broad Street, Suite M 1490 PO Box 128, Hazleton, PA, 18201

BARON, MARTY, T: Newspaper Editor **I:** Writing and Editing **PB:** Tampa, Florida, 1954 **ED:** MBA, Lehigh University, 1976; BA in Journalism, Lehigh University, Bethlehem, Pennsylvania, 1976 **C:** Executive Editor, The Washington Post, 2013-; Editor, The Boston Globe, 2001-12; Executive Editor, The Miami Herald, 2000-01; Associate Managing Editor Nighttime News Operations, The New York Times, 1997-99; Editorial Positions, The New York Times, 1996-97; Editor Orange County Edition, The L.A. Times, 1993-96; Assistant Managing Editor Page-one Special Reports, Pub. Opinion Polling & Special Projects, The L.A. Times, 1991-93; Business Editor, The L.A. Times, 1983-91; Various Editorial Positions, The L.A. Times, 1979-83; State Reporter, Business Writer, The Miami Herald, Florida, 1976-79 **CIV:** Chairman, Editor Journalism Adv. Committee, Knight Foundation; **AW:** Named Editor of Year, Editor & Pub. Magazine, 2001; Recipient Benjamin Bradlee Editor of Year Award, National Press Foundation, 2004 **MEM:** Mem.: Phi Beta Kappa

BARR, ANDY, T: U.S. Representative from Kentucky **I:** Government Administration/Government Relations/Government Services **DOB:** 07/24/1973 **PB:** Lexington **PT:** Son of Garland Hale and Donna R. (Faulconer) Barr; **ED:** JD, University Kentucky College Law, 2001; BA in Government & Philosophy, University Virginia, 1996 **C:** Member, US House Financial Services Committee, 2013-; Member, Republican Study Committee; Member, US Congress from 6th Kentucky District, Washington, 2013-; Associate, Kinkhead & Stilz, Lexington, Kentucky, 2008-12; Deputy general counsel to Governor Ernie Fletcher, State of Kentucky, Frankfort, 2007-08; General counsel Governor's Office Local Devel., State of Kentucky, Frankfort, 2004-07; Associate, Stites & Harbison, Lexington, Kentucky, 2002-04; Legislative assistant to Rep. Jim Talent, US House of Representatives, 1996-98 **CR:** Vice president Fayette County Republican Party part time instructor constitutional law Morehead State University, University Kentucky College Law member Gov.-Elect Ernie Fletcher's Transition Team, 2003-04 intern to Senator Mitch McConnell US Senate contributor The Virginia Advocate **CIV:** Board directors, Friends of the Isaac Murphy Memorial Art Garden, **MEM:** Mem.: Prevent Child Abuse in Kentucky (vice president 2007, president 2008-09), Fayette County Bar Association, Kentucky Bar Association **PA:** Republican

BARR, ROSEANNE, T: Actress, Comedienne, Television Producer, Writer **I:** Media & Entertainment **DOB:** 11/03/1952 **PB:** Salt Lake City **SC:** UT/USA **C:** Principal, Full Moon & High Tide Productions, Inc.; Former Window Dresser; Former Cocktail Waitress **CW:** Actress, (Films) She-Devil, 1989, (Voice Actress) Look Who's Talking Too, 199, Freddy's Dead: The Final Nightmare, 1991, Even Cowgirls Get The Blues, 1993, Blue In The Face, 1995, Meet Wally Sparks, 1997, Cecil B. Demented, 2000, Joe Dirt, 2001, (Voice Actress) Home On The Range, 2004, Master Of The Good Name, 2014, Roseanne For President!, 2016, (TV Shows) Roseanne, 1988-1997, 2018, Backfield In Motion, 1991, A Different World, 1992, The Rosey And Buddy Show, 1992, The Jackie Thomas Show, 1992, The Woman Who Loved Elvis, 1993, The Larry Sanders Show, 1993-1995, General Hospital, 1994, Woman Of The House, 1995, 3rd Rock From The Sun, 1997, The Nanny, 1997, My Name Is Earl, 2006, Downwardly Mobile, 2012, Portlandia, 2013, The Office, 2013, Teenage Mutant Ninja Turtles, 2013-2014, The Millers, 2014, Cristela, 2015; Appearance, Comedy Central Roast of Roseanne, 2012; Judge, Last Comic Standing, 2014-2015; Writer, Director, Executive Producer, Roseanne: Live from Trump Castle,

1990; Host, MTV Video Music Awards, 1994, Saturday Night Special, 1996, Momsters: When Moms Go Bad, 2014-2015; Host, Executive Producer, The Roseanne Show, 1998-2000, The Real Roseanne Show, 2003; Writer, Executive Producer, Roseanne Barr: Blonde and Bitchin, 2006; Host, Creator, Executive Producer, The Tipping Point, 2009; Executive Producer, Roseanne's Nuts, 2011 **AW:** TIME 100 Most Influential, 2018, Innovator Award, TV Land Award, Roseanne, 2008, Favorite Female TV Performer, People's Choice Awards, Roseanne, 1994-1995, Eleanor Roosevelt Award For Outstanding American Women, Funniest Female Performer in a TV Series, American Comedy Awards, Co-Recipient, (With Tom Arnold) Vanguard Award, GLAAD Media Awards, Outstanding Lead Actress in a Comedy Series, Emmy Awards, Best Actress – Television Series Musical or Comedy, Golden Globe Awards, Roseanne, 1993, Peabody Award, Humanitas Award, Favorite Female TV Performer, Favorite All-Around Female Entertainer, People's Choice Awards, Roseanne, 1990, Funniest Female Performer in a TV Series, American Comedy Awards, Favorite Female Performer in a New TV Program, People's Choice Awards, Roseanne, 1989, Funniest Female Performer in a TV Special, American Comedy Awards, On Location: The Roseanne Barr Show, 1988 **BA:** Full Moon & High Tide Productions Inc., 424 Main Street, El Segundo, CA, 90245-3002

BARRA, MARY, T: CEO **I:** Business Management/Business Services **CN:** General Motors Co. **DOB:** 12/24/1961 **PB:** Royal Oak **SC:** MI/USA **ED:** MBA, Stanford University (1990); BSEE, Kettering University, Flint, MI (1985) **C:** Chief Executive Officer, General Motors Co., Detroit, MI (2014-Present); Senior Vice President of Global Products Development, General Motors Co., Detroit, MI (2011-2014); Vice President of Human Resources, General Motors Co., Detroit, MI (2009-2011); Vice President of Global Manufacturing Engineering, General Motors Co., Detroit, MI (2008-2009); Executive Director of Vehicle Manufacturing Engineering, General Motors Co., Detroit, MI (2004-2008); Plant Manager, General Motors Co., Detroit, MI (2003-2004); Executive Director of Competitive Operations Engineering, North American Vehicle Operations, General Motors Co. (2001-2003); General Director of Internal Communications North America, General Motors Co. (1999-2001); Business Manager of Corporate Staffs, General Motors Co. (1996-1999); Senior Staff Engineer to Manager of Manufacturing Planning, General Motors Co., Warren, MI (1990-1996); Associate Plant Engineer to Senior Supervisor Maintenance, Tooling Fiero Assembly Plant, General Motors Co., Pontiac, MI (1985-1988) **CR:** Board of Directors, General Motors Co. (2014-Present); Board of Directors, General Dynamics Corp. (2011-Present) **CIV:** Board of Trustees, Kettering University; Board of Directors, Inforum Center for Leadership **AW:** Named, The 100 Most Influential People in the World, Time Magazine (2014); Named, The 50 Most Influential People in Global Finance, Bloomberg Markets (2014); Recipient, The World's Most Powerful People, Forbes Magazine (2014); Named, 50 Most Powerful Women in Business, Fortune Magazine (2012-2015); Named, 100 Most Powerful Women, Forbes Magazine (2011-2014); Recipient, Kettering Alumni Association Management Achievement Award (2010); Named, One of the 100 Leading Women in North American Auto Industry, Automotive News (2010); Named, One of the 100 Leading Women in North American Auto Industry, Automotive News (2005) **MEM:** Eta Kappa Nu; Tau Beta Pi **H:** Aerobics; Cooking; Skiing; Windsurfing **BA:** General Motors Co, 300 Renaissance Ctr PO Box 300, Detroit, MI, 48265

BARRAGAN, NANETTE, T: U.S. Representative from California **I:** Government Administration/Government Relations/Government Services **DOB:** 09/15/1976 **PB:** Harbor City, Los Angeles **SC:** C/USA **ED:** B.A. Political Science, Minor in Public Policy, University of California, 2000; Juris Doctor Degree, University of Southern California, 2005 **C:** Member, U.S. House of Representatives from California's 44th District, 2017-; Member, Committee on Homeland Security; Member, Committee on Natural Resources; Member, Hermosa Beach City Council, 2015-2017; Executive Director,Gillian S. Fuller Foundation, 2000-03 **BA:** 1320 Longworth HOB, Washington, DC, 20515

BARRASSO, JOHN ANTHONY, T: U.S. Senator From Wyoming **I:** Government Administration/Government Relations/Government Services **DOB:** 07/21/1952 **PB:** Reading **SC:** PA/USA **PT:** John A. Barrasso, Louise M. (DeCisco) Barrasso **ED:** MD, Georgetown University, Washington, DC, 1978; BS, Georgetown University, Washington, DC, 1974 **CT:** Diplomate, American Board of Orthopaedic Surgeons **C:** Chairman, U.S. Senate on Republican Policy Committee, 2013-Present; U.S. Senator From Wyoming, 2007-Present; Chairman, Senate Environment Committee, 2017; Chairman, U.S. Senate on Indian Affairs Committee, 2015-2017; Vice Chairman, U.S. Senate Republican Conference, 2010-2012; Vice Chairman, U.S. Senate on Indian Affairs Committee, 2009-2015; Chairman of Transportation, Highways & Military Affairs Committee, Wyoming State Senate, 2005-2007; District 27, Wyoming State Senate, 2003-2007; Minerals, Business & Economic Development Committee, Labor, Health & Social Services Committee, Wyoming State Senate, 2003-2005; Chief of Staff, Wyoming Medical Center, 2003-2005; Orthopedic Surgeon, Casper Orthopedic Associates, Wyoming, 1983-2007; Resident, Yale-New Haven Hospital, 1978-1983 **CR:** Leader, Delegation to Representative, China Republican National Convention, 1994, Delegate, China Republican National Convention, 1992, 2004, Treasurer, Republican National Committee, 1991-1992 **CIV:** Emcee, Jerry Lewis Labor Day Telethon, Wyoming's K-2 TV, President, Wyoming Health Fairs, President, United Way of Natrona County **AW:** One of the Ten Members to Watch in the 112th Congress, Roll Call, 2011, Friend of the Farm Bureau Award, Wyoming Farm Bureau Federation, 2010, Congressional Award, Small Business Council of America, 2010, Ken Alvord Community Service Award, National Association of Medical Communicators, 1992, Legislative Service Award, Veterans of Foreign Wars, Medal of Excellence, Wyoming National Guard, Wyoming Physician of the Year Award **MEM:** President, National Association of Physician Broadcasters, 1988-1989, Wyoming Medical Society **PA:** Republican **BA:** Office of John Barrasso, U.S. Senate 517 Hart Senate Office Building, Washington, DC, 20510

BARRETT, AMY C., T: Federal Judge **I:** Law and Legal Services **PB:** New Orleans **SC:** LA/USA **MS:** Married **SPN:** Jesse M. Barrett **ED:** BA, Rhodes College; JD, University of Notre Dame The Law School **C:** Judge, U.S. Court of Appeals for the Seventh Circuit (2017-Present)

BARRETT, GEORGE S., T: Chairman of Cardinal Health **I:** Medicine & Health Care **ED:** MBA, New York University, 1988; Bachelor's degree, Brown University, 1977 **C:** Chairman, Cardinal Health Inc, 2018-; Chairman, CEO, Cardinal Health, Inc., 2009-17; Vice-chmn., CEO healthcare supply chain services, Cardinal Health, Inc., Dublin, Ohio, 2008-; President, CEO, Teva North America, Teva Pharmaceuticals Industries, Ltd., 2006-08; Group vice president, North America, Teva Pharmaceuticals Industries, Ltd., 2005-06; President, Teva USA, Teva Pharmaceuticals Industries, Ltd., 1998-2005; Executive vice president, Global Pharmaceutical Markets, Teva Pharmaceuticals Industries, Ltd.,; Member, Office of CEO, Teva Pharmaceuticals Industries, Ltd.,; President, CEO, Teva North America, Teva Pharmaceuticals Industries, Ltd.,; Several positions, Teva Pharmaceuticals Industries, Ltd.,; Group vice president North America, CEO, Teva North America, 2005-08; President, CEO, Teva Pharmaceutical USA, 1999-2004; President, CEO, Diad Research, 1999; President, Barre National, subsidiary Alpharma Inc., 1991-94; President, Alpharma US Pharmaceutical group, 1994-97; President, NMC Laboratory (acquired by Alpharma Inc.), 1988-94; Various positions, NMC Laboratory, 1981-91 **CR:** Board directors Eaton Corp., 2011- **CIV:** Trustee, Healthcare Leadership Council, Member President Leadership Council, Brown Univ., Director, Nationwide Children's Hospital, Director, University Maryland School Pharmacy, Director, Am. Foundation for Pharmaceutical Education, Member board ambassadors, Project Restore, John Hopkins School Medical, **MEM:** Mem.: Generic Pharmaceutical Industry Association (past chairman, board director) **BA:** Cardinal Health Inc, 7000 Cardinal Pl, Dublin, OH, 43017

BARRINGTON, MARTIN J., T: Tobacco Products Company Executive **I:** Business Management/Business Services **DOB:** 07/16/1953 **PB:** Albany **SC:** NY/USA **ED:** JD, Albany University, 1980; BA, College St. Rose, 1977 **CT:** Bar: New York 1981, Virginia 1982. **C:** Chairman, CEO, Altria Group Inc., 2012-; President, Altria Group Inc. 2015-; Vice-chmn. innovation, pub. affairs, human resources & compliance, Altria Group Inc., 2011-12; Executive vice president, chief administrative officer, chief compliance officer, Altria Group Inc.,; Executive vice president corp. responsibility, Philip Morris USA,; Senior vice president, general counsel, Philip Morris USA & Philip Morris International, New York City,; Partner, Hunton & Williams, 1990-93; Associate, Hunton & Williams, 1982-89; Law clerk, U.S. Court Appeals (4th cir.), 1980-82 **CR:** Adj. assistant professor employment discrimination law University Richmond, 1988-89. Member, Board of Directors, Anheuser-Busch InBev. **CIV:** Past commissioner, Virginia Port Authority, Trustee, Virginia Museum Fine Arts, Trustee, College St. Rose, **CW:** Notes and comments editor Albany Law Rev., 1979-80. **MEM:** Member American Bar Association (member labor and employment section, committee for devel. of law under NLRA), Justinian Society

BARRON, DAVID JEREMIAH, T: Federal Judge, Law Educator **I:** Law and Legal Services **DOB:** 07/07/1967 **PB:** Washington **SC:** D.C. **PT:** Son of Jerome A. Barron. **ED:** JD, Harvard Law School, 1994; AB in History, Harvard University, 1989 **CT:** Bar: New York 1996 **C:** Judge, US Court Appeals (1st Cir.), Boston, 2014-; S. William Green professor public law, Harvard Law School, 2011-; Acting assistant attorney general, US Department Justice, Washington, 2009-10; Principal deputy attorney general Office Legal Counsel, US Department Justice, Washington, 2009-10; Professor, Harvard Law School, 2004-11; Assistant professor law, Harvard Law School, Cambridge, Massachusetts, 1999-2004; Atty.-advisor Office Legal Counsel, US Department Justice, 1996-99; Law clerk to Justice John Paul Stevens, US Supreme Court, 1995-96; Law clerk to Judge Stephen Reinhardt, US Court Appeals (9th Cir.), 1994-95; Reporter, News and Observer, Raleigh, North Carolina, 1989-91 **CR:** Member Massachusetts State College Building

Authority, 2012-, Massachusetts Board Higher Education, 2012- **AW:** Recipient Office Secretary Defense Medal for Exceptional Public Service, US Department Defense, National Intelligence Exceptional Achievement award, Office Director National Intelligence **BA:** 1 Courthouse Way, Boston, MA, 02210

BARTON, JOE, T: U.S. Representative from Texas **I:** Government Administration/Government Relations/Government Services **DOB:** 09/15/1949 **PB:** Waco **SC:** TX/USA **PT:** Larry Linus Barton, Bess Wynell (Buice) Barton **ED:** MS in Industrial Administration, Purdue University, West Lafayette, IN, 1973; BS in Industrial Engineering, Texas A&M University, College Station, TX, 1972 **C:** U.S. Congress From Sixth Texas District, 1985-Present; Chairman, U.S. House of Energy & Commerce Committee, 2004-2007; Natural Gas Decontrol Consultant, Atlantic Richfield Oil & Gas Co., Dallas, TX, 1982-1984; White House Fellow, Aide To Secretary James B. Edwards, U.S. Department of Energy, Washington, DC, 1981-1982; Various Positions To Vice President, Ennis Business Forms, Texas, 1973-1981 **MEM:** Association of Former Students, Texas A&M University **PA:** Republican **BA:** 2107 Rayburn House Office Building, Washington, DC, 20515

BARTSCH, JOEL A., T: President of the Houston Mus. of Natural Science **I:** Museums & Institutions **ED:** MA, Rice University, 2003; BA, Concordia University **C:** President, Houston Museum Natural Sci., 2004-; Curator Lester and Sue Smith Gem Vault, Houston Museum Natural Sci.,; Curator gems and minerals, Houston Museum Natural Sci.,; Director, California State Mining and Mineral Museum, Mariposa,; With, Lyman Museum, Hilo, Hawaii,; With, Texas Memorial Museum, Austin,; With, Colorado School Mines, Golden,

BARYSHNIKOV, MIKHAIL, T: Ballet dancer, actor **I:** Media & Entertainment **DOB:** 01/27/1948 **PB:** Riga **SC:** Latvian Soviet Socialist Republic **ED:** Doctorate (hon.), Montclair State University, 2008; Doctorate (hon.), Shenandoah University, 2008; Doctorate (hon.), New York University, 2007; Student, Kirov Ballet School, Leningrad, Russia; Student, Ballet School of Riga **C:** Artistic Director,White Oak Dance Project,1990-2002; Artistic Director,American Ballet Theater, 1980-89; Dancer, NYC Ballet, 1978-79 **CW:** (Film)Yuri Kopeikine, The Turning Point, 1977, When I Think of Russia, 1980, Narrator, That's Dancing!, 1985; Nikolai Rodchenko, White Nights, Columbia, 1985, Anton Sergeyev, Dancers, Golan-Globus/Cannon, 1987,; Pyotr Grushenko, 1991, Cesar, The Cabinet of Dr. Ramirez, 1991, Russian Holida, 1992, Le mystere Babilee, 2001 **AW:** Kennedy Center Honor, 2000 **BA:** Baryshnikov Arts Center, 450 West 37th Street Suite 501, New York, NY, 10018

BASINGER, KIM, T: Actress **I:** Media & Entertainment **DOB:** 05/28/1905 **PB:** Athens **SC:** GA/USA **PT:** Don Basinger; Ann Basinger **ED:** Student, Neighborhood Playhouse, New York City, NY **C:** Model, IMG Worldwide Inc. (2013-Present); Model, Eileen Ford Agency, New York City, NY (1972-1977) **CW:** Actress, Films, "Hard Country" (1981), "Mother Lode" (1982), "Never Say Never Again" (1983), "The Man Who Loved Women" (1983), "The Natural" (1984), "Fool for Love" (1985), "9½ Weeks" (1986), "No Mercy" (1986), "Blind Date" (1987), "Nadine" (1987), "My Stepmother is an Alien" (1988), "Batman" (1989), "The Marrying Man" (1991), "Final Analysis" (1992), "Cool World" (1992), "The Real McCoy" (1992), "Wayne's World 2" (1993), "The Getaway" (1994), "Ready to Wear (Prêt-à-Porter)" (1995), "L.A. Confidential" (1997), "I Dreamed of Africa" (2000), "Bless the

Child" (2000), "8 Mile" (2002), "People I Know" (2002), 'The Door in the Floor" (2004), "Elvis Has Left the Building" (2004), "Cellular" (2004), "The Sentinel" (2006), "Even Money" (2007), "The Informers" (2009), "Charlie St. Cloud" (2010), "Black November" (2012), "Third Person" (2013), "Grudge Match" (2013), "4 Minute Mile" (2014), "The 11th Hour" (2014), "The Nice Guys" (2016), "Fifty Shades Darker" (2017); TV Films, "Katie: Portrait of a Centerfold" (1978), "The Ghost of Flight 401" (1978), "Killjoy" (1981) "The Mermaid Chair" (2005); TV Miniseries, "From Here to Eternity" (1979); TV Series, "Dog and Cat" (1977), "From Here to Eternity" (1980), "Killjoy" (1981), Voice, "The Simpsons" (1998), "The Mermaid Chair" (2006); Music Video, "Mary Jane's Last Dance" by Tom Petty and the Heartbreakers (1993); Actress, Executive Producer, Film, "While She Was Out" (2008); TV Appearances include "Charlie's Angels" (1976), "Gemini Man" (1976), "The Six Million Dollar Man" (1977), "McMillan and Wife" (1977), "Vega$" (1978); Documentaries, "A Century of Cinema" (1994), "Sean Connery, an Intimate Portrait" (1997) **AW:** Academy Award for Best Supporting Actress; Golden Globe Award for Best Supporting Actress; Screen Actors Guild Award for Outstanding Performance by a Female Actor in a Supporting Role

BASS, HILARIE, T: lawyer **I:** Law and Legal Services **DOB:** 11/22/1954 **PB:** New York City **ED:** JD summa cum laude, Univ. Miami, 1981; BA magna cum laude, George Washington Univ., 1972 **CT:** President of the ABA, 2017-2018; US Supreme Court, US Court Appeals (11th cir.), US District Court (so., middle districts) Florida, bar: Florida 1981 **C:** Shareholder, chair national litigation practice group, Greenberg Traurig LLP, Miami, Florida, **CR:** Adjunct professor litigation Univ. Miami **CIV:** Board trustees, Univ. Miami, 2003-Chair, board director, United Way, Dade County, 1997-99 Member, executive committee, United Way, Dade County, 1995- **AW:** Named Business Woman of Year, Southern Florida Business Journal, 2001; named one of Legal Elite, Florida Trend Magazine, 2004, Best of the Best Rainmakers, Coral Gables Living Magazine, 2003, Southern Florida's Top Lawyers, Southern Florida Legal Guide, 2001-05; recipient Dorothy Shula award for volunteerism, United Way of Miami-Dade, 2000 **MEM:** Mem.: American Bar Association (board governor 1990-93, chair, council for fund for justice and education 2000-02, member, ho. of del. 1988-95, 2000-), Florida Bar Foundation (board director 1988-93, president)

BASS, KAREN RUTH, T: U.S. Representative from California, Former State Legislator **I:** Government Administration/Government Relations/Government Services **DOB:** 10/03/1953 **PB:** L.A. **SC:** CA/USA **ED:** BS in Health Services, California State University, Dominguez Hills, 1990; Attended, San Diego State University, 1971-73 **CT:** Cert. Physician Assistant University of Southern California **C:** Member of the U.S. House of Representatives from California's 35th District, 2015-, Member Committee on Foreign Affairs, Committee on Natural Resources; Member, U.S. House Judiciary Committee, 2013-; Member, U.S. House Foreign Affairs Committee, 2011-; Member, U.S. Congress from 37th California District, 2013-; Speaker emeritus, California State Assembly, 2010-; Clinical instructor, University Southern California School Medical, 1986-; Member, U.S. House Budget Committee, 2011-13; Member, U.S. Congress from 33rd California District, Washington, 2011-13; Speaker, California State Assembly, 2008-10; Majority floor leader, California State Assembly, 2007-08; Majority

whip, California State Assembly, 2005-06; Member District 47, California State Assembly, 2005-10 **CR:** Adj. instructor California State University, 1989-96 Project Director Health Careers Opportunity Program, 1986-90 **PA:** Democrat

BASSETT, ANGELA EVELYN, T: Actress **I:** Media & Entertainment **PB:** New York **SC:** NY/USA **PT:** Daniel Benjamin; Betty Jane Bassett **ED:** BA in African-Am. studies, Yale University, 1980; MFA, Yale School of Drama, 1983 **CW:** Actress: (plays) Colored People's Time, 1982, Ma Rainey's Black Bottom, 1984, The Mystery Plays, 1984-85, The Painful Adventures of Pericles, Prince of Tyre, 1986-87, Joe Turner's Come and Gone, 1986-87, King Henry IV Part I, 1987, His Girl Friday, 2005, Fences, 2006, The Mountaintop, 2011; (TV films) Line of Fire: The Morris Dees Story, 1991, The Jacksons: An American Dream, 1992, A Century of Women, 1994, Identity, 2011, Rogue, 2012, Betty and Coretta, 2013; guest appearances: (TV series) The Cosby Show, 1985, 1988, Spenser: For Hire, 1985, A Man Called Hawk, 1989, Tour of Duty, 1989, 227, 1989, thirtysomething, 1989, Alien Nation, 1990, The Flash, 1991, Nightmare Café, 1992, The Bernie Mac Show, 2003, Alias, 2005, ER, 2008-09 (National Association for the Advancement of Colored People Image award for Best Supporting Actress in a Drama Series, 2009), (films) F/X, 1986, Kindergarten Cop, 1990, Boyz N the Hood, 1991, City of Hope, 1991, Innocent Blood, 1992, Malcolm X, 1992, Passion Fish, 1992, What's Love Got to Do with It, 1993 (Golden Globe award for Best Actress in a Musical or Comedy 1994), Strange Days, 1995, Panther, 1995, Waiting to Exhale, 1995, A Vampire in Brooklyn, 1995, Contact, 1997, How Stella Got Her Groove Back, 1998, Wings Against the Wind, 1999, 50 Violins, 1999, Music of the Heart, 1999, Supernova, 2000, (voice) Whispers: An Elephant's Tale, 2000, Boesman and Lena, 2000, The Score, 2001, Sunshine State, 2002, Masked and Anonymous, 2003, The Lazarus Child, 2004, Mr. 3000, 2004, Akeelah and the Bee, 2006, Time Bomb, 2006, (voice) Meet the Robinsons, 2007, Gospel Hill, 2008, Meet the Browns, 2008, Nothing But the Truth, 2008, Jumping the Broom, 2011, Green Lantern, 2011, This Means War, 2012, Olympus Has Fallen, 2013, Black Nativity, 2013 (National Association for the Advancement of Colored People Image award for Outstanding Actress in a Motion Picture, 2014), White Bird in a Blizzard, 2014, Survivor, 2015, Curious George 3: Back to the Jungle, 2015, Chi-Raq, 2015, London Has Fallen, 2016, Black Panther,; 2018, Mission Impossible-Fallout, 2018,(TV series) American Horror Story, 2013-2016, Close to the Enemy, 2016, 9-1-1, 2018, (also executive producer),(TV mini-series) Close to the Enemy, 2016; actress, prodr.: (TV films) Ruby's Bucket of Blood, 2001; actress, executive prodr: (TV films) The Rosa Parks Story, 2002; executive prodr.: (TV films) Our America, 2002; dir.: (TV films) Whitney, 2015; co-author: (with Courtney B. Vance and Hilary Beard) Friends: A Love Story, 2007. **AW:** Recipient Lena Horne award for Outstanding Career Achievement in the Field of Entertainment, 2002, Star on Hollywood Walk of Fame, 2008 **MEM:** Mem.: Delta Sigma Theta (hon.)

BASTIAN, EDWARD H., T: CEO **I:** Business Management/Business Services **CN:** Delta Air Lines Inc. **ED:** BBA, St. Bonaventure University, New York, 1979 **CT:** CPA **C:** CEO, Delta Air Lines, Inc., Atlanta, 2016-; President, CEO, Northwest Airlines Corp., Eagan, Minnesota, 2008-09; Senior vice president, CFO, Acuity Brands, Inc., Atlanta, 2005; President, Delta Air Lines, Inc., Atlanta, 2008-16; President, CFO, Delta Air Lines, Inc., Atlanta, 2007-08; Executive vice president, CFO, Delta Air Lines, Inc., Atlanta, 2005-07; Senior vice president fin., controller, Delta Air Lines, Inc., Atlanta, 2000-05; Vice president fin., controller, Delta Air Lines, Inc., Atlanta, 1998-2000; Vice president business process reengineering Frito-Lay, PepsiCo, Inc.,; Vice president fin., controller Frito Lay International, PepsiCo, Inc., Dallas; Partner audit practice, Price Waterhouse; Strategic planning partner, Price Waterhouse, New York **CIV:** International board directors, Habitat for Humanity, Board directors, Woodruff Arts Center, Atlanta **H:** Golf, travel, reading **BA:** Delta Air Lines Inc, 1030 Delta Blvd, PO Box 20706, Atlanta, GA, 30320

BATALHA, NATALIE MARIE, T: Astronomer **I:** Sciences **ED:** PhD, University California, Santa Cruz, 1997; AB, University California, Berkeley, 1989 **C:** Assistant professor Physics and Astronomy, San Jose State University, California, 2002-; Co-investigator, Kepler mission, NASA Ames Research Center, Moffett Field, California, 2002-; Nrc research associate, NASA Ames Research Center, Moffett Field, California, 2000-02 **CR:** Director UARC Systems Teaching Institute, Moffett Field, California, 2006- **AW:** Postdoc. fellow, Observatorio Nacional, Rio de Janeiro, Brazil, 1998-2000,Time 100 Most Influential People, 2017 **MEM:** Mem.: Am. Astronomical Society **ACH:** Achievements include research in co-investigator for NASA's Kepler Mission to detect and characterize Earth-like planets in the habitable zone of Sun-like stars

BATCHELDER, ALICE MOORE, T: Federal Judge **I:** Law and Legal Services **DOB:** 08/15/1944 **PB:** Wilmington **SC:** DE/USA **MS:** Married **SPN:** William G. Batchelder, III **CH:** William G., IV, Elisabeth **ED:** Honorary LLD, University of Akron School of Law, 2001; Honorary LHD, Lake Erie College, 1993; LLM, University of Virginia, 1988; JD, Akron University, 1971; BA, Ohio Wesleyan University, 1964 **C:** Chief Judge, U.S. Court of Appeals, Sixth Circuit, Cleveland, OH, 2009-2014; Judge, U.S. Court of Appeals, Sixth Circuit, Cleveland, OH, 1991-2009; Judge, U.S. District Court, Northern District, Ohio, Cleveland, OH, 1985-1991; Judge, U.S. Bankruptcy Court, Northern District, Ohio, 1983-1985; Associate, Williams & Batchelder, Medina, OH, 1971-1983; Teacher, Buckeye High School, Medina County, 1967-1968; Teacher, Jones Junior High School, 1966-1967; Teacher, Plain Local School District, Franklin County, Ohio, 1965-1966 **CR:** Judicial Conference On U.S. Committee On Automation And Technology, 2000-2003, Judicial Conference Advisory Committee On Bankruptcy Rules, 1993-1996, Committee On Bankruptcy Education, Federal Judicial Center, 1988-1991 **CW:** Editor-in-Chief, University of Akron Law Review, 1971 **AW:** Women of Distinction Award, Medina County YWCA, 1997, Honorary Award, University of Akron School of Law, 1996, Outstanding Alumni Award, 1993 **MEM:** Federal Judge's Association, Federal Bar Association, Medina County Bar Association **BA:** 100 East Fifth Street, Cincinnati, OH, USA, 45202

BATES, KATHY, T: Actress **I:** Media & Entertainment **PB:** Memphis **SC:** TN/USA **PT:** Langdon Doyle Bates; Bertye Kathleen (Talbot) Bates **ED:** BFA, Southern Methodist University, 1969 **CW:** Actress: (plays) Vanities, 1976, Semmelweiss, Crimes of the Heart, The Art of Dining, Goodbye Fidel, 1980, Chocolate Cake and Final Placement, 1981, 5th of July, 'night, Mother, 1983, Two Masters: The Rain of Terror, 1985, Curse of the Starving Class, Frankie and Johnny in the Clair de Lune (OBIE award 1988), The Road to Mecca; (films) Taking Off, 1971, Straight Time, 1978, Come Back to the Five and Dime, Jimmy Dean, Jimmy Dean, 1982, Two of a Kind, 1983, Summer Heat, 1987, My Best Friend Is A Vampire, 1988, Arthur 2: On the Rocks, 1988, Signs of Life, 1989, High Stakes, 1989, Men Don't Leave, 1990, Dick Tracy, 1990, White Palace, Misery, 1990 (Academy award for Best Actress, 1991, Golden Globe award for Best Performance by an Actress in a Motion Picture - Drama, 1991), At Play in the Fields of the Lord, 1991, Fried Green Tomatoes, 1991, The Road to Mecca, 1992, Prelude to a Kiss, 1992, Used People, 1992, A Home of Our Own, 1993, North, 1994, Curse of the Starving Class, 1994, Dolores Claiborne, 1994, Angus, 1995, Diabolique, 1996, The War at Home, 1996, Primary Colors, 1998, Swept from the Sea, 1998, Titanic, 1998, The Waterboy, 1998, Baby Steps, 1999, Dash and Lilly, 1999, My Life as a Dog, 1999, Bruno, 2000, Rat Race, 2001, American Outlaws, 2001, About Schmidt, 2002, Love Liza, 2002, Dragonfly, 2002, Around the World in 80 Days, 2004, The Bridge of San Luis Rey, 2004, 3 & 3, 2005, Rumor Has It, 2005, Failure to Launch, 2006, Relative Strangers, 2006, Bonneville, 2006, (voice) Charlotte's Web, 2006, (voice) Bee Movie, 2007, Fred Claus, 2007, (voice) Christmas Is Here Again, 2007, P.S., I Love You, 2007, The Golden Compass, 2007, The Family That Preys, 2008, The Day the Earth Stood Still, 2008, Revolutionary Road, 2008, Chéri, 2009, The Blind Side, 2009, Valentine's Day, 2010, A Little Bit of Heaven, 2011, Midnight in Paris, 2011, Tammy, 2014, (voice) When Marnie Was There, 2014, Hear My Song, 2014, Complete Unknown, 2016, The Great Gilly Hopkins, 2016, The Boss, 2016, Bad Santa 2, 2016, Krystal, 2017, The Death and Life of John F. Donovan, 2018, On the Basis of Sex, 2018; (TV films) Johnny Bull, 1986, Murder Ordained, 1987, Roe versus Wade, 1989, No Place Like Home, 1989, Hostages, 1993, Talking with, 1995, The West Side Waltz, 1995, The Late Shift, 1996 (Golden Globe award for Best Performance by an Actress in a Supporting Role in a Series, Mini-Series or Motion Picture Made for TV, 1997), Annie, 1999, My Sister's Keeper, 2002, Warm Springs, 2005; (TV series) American Horror Story, 2013- (Emmy award for Outstanding Supporting Actress in a Mini-Series or a Movie, 2014), American Horror Story: Freak Show, 2014, Mike and Molly, 2014, American Horror Story: Hotel, 2015, American Dad!, 2015, American Horror Story: Roanoke, 2016, Feud: Bette and Joan, 2017, Disjointed, 2017; (TV appearances) The Doctors, 1977, The Love Boat, 1978, All My Children, 1984, St. Elsewhere, 1986-87, China Beach, 1989, LA Law, 1989, 3rd Rock from the Sun, 1999, (voice) King of the Hill, 2001, Six Feet Under, 2003-05, The Office, 2010-11, Harry's Law, 2011-12, Two and a Half Men, 2012 (Emmy award for Outstanding Guest Actress in a Comedy Series, 2012), Mike & Molly, 2014-15; dir.: (TV films) Fargo, 2003, (films) Have Mercy, 2006; actress, executive prodr.: (films) The Ingrate, 2004; actress, dir.: (TV films) Ambulance Girl, 2005. **AW:** Recipient Mary Pickford award, International Press. Academy, 2007

BATES, MASON, T: Composer **I:** Media & Entertainment **DOB:** 01/23/1977 **ED:** Student, University California, Berkeley; Degrees in music composition and English lit., Juilliard School **C:** Young Am. composer-in-residence, California Symphony, 2007-; Music Alive resident, Mobile Symphony,; Composer-in-residence, Young Concert Artists, Inc., 2000-02; Member, Young Concert Artists, Inc., **CW:** Composer: Everywhere West, 1995 (inaugural Jacob Druckman memorial prize, Aspen Music Festival, 1997), Sounds for His Animation, 1999 (Leo Kaplan award, American Society of Composers, 1999), Elements, 2000, Ode, 2002 (Morton Gould award, American Society of Composers, 2002), Mercury Soul, 2002, String Band, 2002, Icarian Rhapsody, 2003, Omnivorous Furniture, 2004, From Amber Frozen, 2004, Digital Loom, 2006, Rusty Air in Carolina, 2006, Liquid Interface, 2007, Music from Underground Spaces, 2008, , White Lies for Lomax, 2009, Omnivorous Furniture, 2004, Ode, 2001, Icarian Rhapsody,1999, California Fictions, (theatrical works) Trout Fishing in America, 1997, In Bed, String Band, 2002, Mercury Soul, 2002, Scrapyard Exotica, 2015, Works for Orchestra,2016, Anthology of Fantastic Zoology,2016 **AW:** Recipient Academy award in Music, Am. Academy Arts and Letters, 2007, Rome prize, Am. Academy Rome, 2004; fellow John Simon Guggenheim Memorial Foundation, 2008, Tanglewood Music Center; Anna-Maria Kellen fellow, Am. Academy Berlin, 2005, Charles Ives fellow, Am. Academy Arts and Letters, 2002 **MEM:** Mem.: Young Concert Artists, Inc.

BEA, CARLOS TIBURCIO, T: Federal Judge **I:** Law and Legal Services **DOB:** 04/18/1934 **PB:** San Sebastian **SC:** Spain **ED:** JD, Stanford University, 1958; BA, Stanford University, 1956; Student, Menlo Junior College, 1950-51 **CT:** Bar: California 1959 **C:** Judge, US Court Appeals, (9th cir.), San Francisco, 2003-; Judge, San Francisco (California) Superior Court, 1990-2003; Principal, owner, Carlos Bea Law Corp., 1975-90; Partner, Dunne, Phelps & Mills, 1967-75; Associate, Dunne, Phelps & Mills, 1959-66 **BA:** US Ct Appeals, 95 Seventh St, San Francisco, CA, 94103

BEAMON, BOB, T: Retired Professional Track and Field Athlete **I:** Athletics **DOB:** 08/29/1946 **PB:** Bronx **SC:** NY/USA **C:** Olympic athlete **CIV:** Fund raiser U.S. Olympic Committee, 1984 **AW:** Named to Olympic Hall of Fame, 1983; National Track and Field Hall of Fame **ACH:** Achievements include setting of long jump world record Olympic Games, 1968; first long jumper to surpass 28 and 29 ft.

BEATTY, JOYCE, T: U.S. Representative from Ohio **I:** Government Administration/Government Relations/Government Services **DOB:** 03/12/1950 **PB:** Dayton **SC:** OH/USA **ED:** PhD; PhD (hon.), Ohio Dominican University, 2003; PhD, University Cincinnati, 1997; MS in Counseling Psychology, Wright State University, Dayton, 1974; BA in Speech, Central State University, Wilberforce, Ohio, 1972 **C:** Member, U.S. House Financial Services Committee, Washington, 2013-; Member, U.S. Congress from 3rd Ohio District, Washington, 2013-; Senior Vice President Outreach & Engagement, The Ohio State University, Columbus, 2008-12; Assistant Minority Leader, Ohio House of Reps., Columbus, 2007-09; Member District 27, Ohio House of Reps., Columbus, 1999-2008 **CR:** Delegate Democratic National Convention, 2012, 2008, 2004, 2000, 1996 **AW:** Named Linden Pride Grand Marshall, 2000, Legislator of Year, Ohio Credit Union Association, Ohio Nurses Association, Pub. Children Services Association of Ohio; Named to The Power 150, Ebony Magazine, 2008; Recipient Women of Achievement Award, YWCA, 2002 **MEM:** Mem.: National Association for the Advancement of Colored People, American Society Training & Devel., Columbus Urban League (Chairman Board of Directors), Ohio Legislative Black Caucus (Service award), Democratic Women's Caucus, The Links, Inc. (National Endowment Chair), United Negro College Fund, Delta Sigma Theta (Life) **H:** Writing, Boating, Travel **PA:** Democrat **BA:** 133 Cannon House Office Building, Washington, DC, 20515

BECKER, BORIS, T: Retired Professional Tennis Player **I:** Athletics **DOB:** 11/22/1967 **PB:** Leimen **SC:** Germany **PT:** Son of Karl-Hinez and Elvira Becker; **C:** Commentator, BBC,; Owner, Mercedes dealerships,; Co-owner, Völkl,; Professional tennis player, ATP, 1985-99 **CR:** Member Federal Republic Germany championship team Davis Cup Tournament, Goteborg, Sweden, 1988. **CW:** Author:

(autobiography) Boris Becker - The Player: An Autobiography, 2004 **AW:** Winner numerous tennis tournaments, including West German Junior Championship, 1983, Young Masters Tournament, Birmingham, England, 1985, Grand Prix Tournament, Queen's, 1985, Men's Singles Championship, Wimbledon, England, 1985, 86, 89, US Open Singles Tournament, New York, 1989, Australian Open, 1991, 96, ATP World Championship, 1995; (with Michael Stich) Men's Doubles Gold Medal, Olympics, 1992. Named to Tennis Hall of Fame, 2003,ITF World Champion, 1989, ATP Player of the Year, 1989, ATP Most Improved Player, 1985 **MEM:** Mem.: Laureus World Sports Academy **ACH:** Achievements include winning 49 career singles titles, 15 career doubles titles, ATP

BECKHAM, ODELL CORNELIUS, T: Professional Football Player **I:** Athletics **DOB:** 11/05/1992 **PB:** New Orleans **SC:** LA/USA **PT:** Son of Odell Cornelius and Heather (Van Norman) Beckham. **ED:** Attended, Louisiana State University, 2011-13 **C:** Wide receiver, New York Giants, East Rutherford, 2014-Present **AW:** Named Bridgestone Performance Play of the Yr.-amazing one-handed 43-yard touchdown catch, NFL, 2015, Offensive Rookie of the Year, Associated Press, 2015; named to The National Football Conference Pro Bowl Team, 2014; recipient Paul Hornung award, Louisville Sports Commission, 2013,First- Team All-Sec, 2013, First Team All American, 2013, SEC Champion, 2011, PFWA All-Rookie Team, 2014, Second-Team All-Pro, 2015-16, Pro Bowl, 2014-16 **ACH:** Pro Bowl, 2014-, All Pro, 2015, 2017

BEE, SAMANTHA, T: Comedian, Actress **I:** Media & Entertainment **PB:** Toronto **SC:** ON/Canada **ED:** Graduate, University of Ottawa; Student, McGill University **C:** Correspondent, The Daily Show with Jon Stewart, 2003-2015; Sketch Comedy Troupe, The Atomic Fireballs **CW:** Actress, (Films) Ham & Cheese, 2004, Underdog, 2007, The Love Guru, 2008, Motherhood, 2009, Whatever Works, 2009, Learning To Drive, 2014, Get Squirrely (Voice), 2015, Sisters, 2015, (TV Films) Ham I Am, 2001, Jasper, Texas, 2003, Two Families, 2007, Love Letters, 2010, (TV Series) Good God, 2012, Bounty Hunters, 2013, Creative Galaxy (Voice), 2013-2014, Game On, 2015; TV Appearances, Rescue Me, 2007, Bored To Death, 2009-2011, Deadbeat, 2014, Numerous Others; Author, I Know I Am, But What Are You?, 2010

BELAFONTE, HARRY, T: singer, concert artist, actor **I:** Media & Entertainment **DOB:** 03/01/1927 **PB:** Harlem **SC:** New York **PT:** Son of Harold George and Melvine (Love) B.; Married Margurite Byrd, 1948 (div. 1957); children: Adrienne, Shari; Married Julie Robinson, March 8, 1957; children: David, Gina; Married Pamela Frank **ED:** LLD (hon.), Princeton University, 2015; LHD (hon.), Brooklyn College, 1998; Doctor in Civil Law (hon.), University Newcastle, Britain, 1998; LLD (hon.), McMaster University, Hamilton, Ontario, Can., 1996; Degree (hon.), University Massachusetts, 1996; DLitt (hon.), University West Indies, Kingston, Jamaica, 1996; DA (hon.), Bard College, 1993; DHL (hon.), Columbia University, 1993; DSc (hon.), Long Island University, 1991; DSc (hon.), Brandeis University, 1991; DSc (hon.), Tufts University, 1991; DFA, City College of New York, 1990; DFA (hon.), Spelman College, 1990; DFA (hon.), State University of New York, Purchase, 1987; MusD (hon.), Morehouse College, 1987; Doctorate Liberal Arts, Arts (hon.), New School Social Research; HHD (hon.), Park College; LHD (hon.), Park College, Missouri, 1968 **C:** President, Belafonte Enterprises, Inc., New York City **CR:** Participant, Voices of the Arts Kennedy Center for Performing Arts, Washington, 2006 **CIV:**

Chairman Martin Luther King., Junior Holiday Commission, 1987; goodwill ambassador UNICEF, 1987; board directors New York State Martin Luther King, Junior Institute for Nonviolence, 1989-; New York State Employees Brotherhood committee (Benjamin Potocker brotherhood award 1993); served with US Navy **CW:** Singer, actor in Broadway shows John Murray Anderson's Almanac (Tony award 1953), Three for Tonight, 1955; (films) Bright Road, 1952, Carmen Jones, 1954, Island in the Sun, 1957, The World, the Flesh and the Devil, 1958, Odds Against Tomorrow, 1959, The Angel Levine, 1969, Buck and the Preacher, 1971, Uptown Saturday Night, 1974, White Man's Burden, 1995, Kansas City, 1996, Bobby, 2006 (documentaries) Fidel, 2001, XXI Century, 2003, Conakry Kas, 2003, Ladders (narrator), 2004, Mo & Me, 2006, Motherland, 2009, Sing Your Song, 2011, Hava Nagila: The Movie, 2013; prodr.: (stage play) To Be Young Gifted and Black, 1969; (TV films) Grambling's White Tiger, 1981, Swing Vote, 1999; prodr.: (TV spls.) A Time for Laughter, 1967, Harry and Lena, 1969; TV program Tonight with Belafonte, 1960 (Emmy award); appeared on German TV special I Sing What I See, 1980; concert performances in Cuba, Jamaica, Europe, 1980, Australia, NZ, US, Europe, 1981, Can., 1982, US, Europe and with Can. symphony orchestras, 1983, US, 1985, US, Can., Japan, Europe, 1986; prodr.: Strolling Twenties-TV, Parting the Waters, (miniseries), 2000; co-prodr. Beat Street, 1984; appeared at Golden Nugget, Atlantic City and Las Vegas, 1985, 1986; initiator, performer recording We Are the World, 1985 (Grammy award 1985); performer concert tours, US, Can. and Europe including 60 city tour, 1988, concerts in US, Europe, Can., 1989, 90, 93, concerts in US, Japan and Can., 1991, concert tour US, 1992, concerts US, Can. and Europe, 1995, US, Can., Europe and Far East, 1996, 50-city European tour, 1998; 1st New York appearance in 30 years Avery Fisher Hall, Lincoln Center, 1993; albums: Mark Twain and Other Folk Favorites, 1954, Belafonte, 1956, Calypso, 1956, An Evening with Belafonte, 1957, Belafonte Sings the Caribbean, 1957, To Wish You a Merry Christmas, 1958, Swing Dat Hammer, 1960, Jump Up Calypso, 1961, Midnight Special, 1962, Streets I Have Walked, 1963, Ballads, Blues and Boasters, 1964, Calypso in Brass, 1966, Belafonte Sings of Love, 1968, Homeward Bound, 1970, The Warm Touch, 1971, Play Me, 1973, Turn the World Around, 1977, Loving You is Where I Belong, 1981, Paradise in Gazankulu, 1988, The Long Road to Freedom, 2001, Island in the Sun: The Complete Recordings 1949-1957, 2002, The Essential Harry Belafonte, 2005, many others.; **AW:** Recipient award of appreciation for initiation of and work for USA for Africa, Am. Music, 1986, Leader for Peace award Peace Corps, 1988, Danny Kaye award US Committee for UNICEF, 1989, Africa's Future award, 1994, Whitney M. Young Junior Service award Boy Scouts Am., 1989, Golden Acorn award Bronx Community College, 1989, Kennedy Center Honors, 1989, Mandela Courage award (inaugural presentation), 1990, Tribute to a Black Am. award National Conference Black Mayors, Inc., 1991, Bill of Rights award ACLU Southern California, 1991, International House Berkeley award, 1994, Food and Hunger Hotline award, 1994, Humanitarian award New York Association New Americans, 1994, Brotherhood award 100 Black Men, 1994, Children's Champion award UNICEF Committee Greater Boston-joint award with Julie Belafonte, 1994, National Medal of the Arts, 1994, Letelier-Moffitt Human Rights award, 1994, Best Supporting Actor (Kansas City), 1996, New York Film Critics Cir., Jesse Owens Humanitarian award, 1996, Man of the Year award New York chapter Hadassah, 1996, Hadassah International First Citizen of the World award, 1996,

Medal of Distinction, Lenox Hill Hospital, New York City, 1996, South African-Am. Organization Leadership award, 1996, Florinda Lasker Civil Liberties award, 1997, Living Landmark award New York Landmarks Conservancy, 1997, Humanitarian of Year award WLIW/21, 1997, William Moses Kunstler Racial Justice award, 1997, New York Arts & Business Council award, 1997, Chmn.'s award National Association for the Advancement of Colored People Image Awards, 1999, Ronald H. Brown award National Child Labor Committee, 1999, Grammy Lifetime Achievement award, 2000, Humanitarian award, Black Entertainment TV, 2006, Spingarn Medal, National Association for the Advancement of Colored People Image Awards, 2013; inducted into Miami Children's Hospital International Pediatrics Hall of Fame, 1996,Jean Hersholt Humanitarian Award, 2014 **BA:** The Random House Publishing Group, 1745 Broadway 18th Fl, New York, NY, 10019

BELICHICK, BILL, T: Professional Football Coach **I:** Professional Training & Coaching **DOB:** 04/16/1952 **PB:** Nashville **SC:** TN/USA **PT:** Stephen Belichick; Jeannette (Munn) Belichick **MS:** Married **SPN:** Debbie Belichick (4/30/1977) **CH:** Amanda; Stephen; Brian **ED:** LHD, New England Institute of Technology (2004); LHD, Boston University (2004); BS in Economic, Wesleyan University (1975) **C:** Head Coach, New England Patriots, Foxboro, MA (2000-Present); Assistant Head Coach, Defensive Backs Coach, New York Jets (1997-1999); Assistant Head Coach, Defensive Backs Coach, New England Patriots, Foxboro, MA (1996-1997); Head Coach, Cleveland Browns (1991-1995); Defensive Backs Coach, New York Giants (1989-1991); Defensive Coordinator, New York Giants (1985-1991); Linebackers Coach, New York Giants (1983-1985); Special Teams & Linebackers Coach, New York Giants (1981-1983); Special Teams Coach, New York Giants (1979-1981); Assistant Special Teams Coach & Assistant to Defensive Coordinator, Denver Broncos (1978-1979); Tight Ends & Receivers Coach, Detroit Lions (1977-1978); Assistant Special Teams Coach, Detroit Lions (1976-1977); Special Assistant to the Coaching Staff, Baltimore Colts (1975) **CW:** Author, "The Little Black Book of Coaching" (2001) **AW:** Named NFL Coach of the Year, Pro Football Weekly (2003); Named NFL Coach of the Year, The Sporting News (2003); Named NFL Coach of the Year, NFL.com (2003); Named NFL Coach of the Year, NFL Alumni (2003); Named NFL Coach of the Year, Associated Press (2003, 2007, 2010); Coach of the Year, Dallas Morning News (2002,2003); Named One of TIME's 100 Most Powerful & Influential People in the World, TIME Magazine (2004); Amos Alonzo Stagg Coaching Award, U.S. Sports Academy (2004); Tom Landry Award: AFC Coach of the Year, USA Today (2002); Baldwin Medal, Wesleyan University (2002) **ACH:** Achievements include being a member of the Super Bowl Championship winning: New York Giants, 1986, 1990, New England Patriots, 2002, 2004, 2005, 2015

BELL, LEVEON, T: Professional Football Player **I:** Athletics **PB:** Reynoldsburg **SC:** OH/USA **ED:** Student, Michigan State University **C:** Running Back, Pittsburgh Steelers, 2013-Present **AW:** Big Ten Champion, 2010, First-Team All-American, 2012, First-Team All-Big Ten, 2012, Pro Bowl, 2014, 2016-2017, First-Team All-Pro, 2014, 2017, Second-Team All-Pro, 2016

BENCH, JOHNNY LEE, T: Former MLB Player **I:** Athletics **DOB:** 12/07/1947 **PB:** Oklahoma City **PT:** Son of Ted Bench. **ED:** Grad. high school **C:** Color Commentator, CBS, 1989-1993; Speaker, Keppler Associates Inc., Arlington, Virginia, 1998-; Broadcaster,; Special consultant to general manager, Cincinnati Reds, 1997-98; Catcher, Cincinnati Reds, National League, 1967-83 **CR:** Propr. bowling alley, Cincinnati spokesman, board directors Interactive Marketing Tech., Inc., Tarzana, California, 1999-. **CW:** Professional nightclub singer, from 1970; host TV interview show MVP-Johnny Bench, until 1976; baseball instructional show The Baseball Bunch, 1981, 82, 83; toured Vietnam with Bob Hope Christmas Show, 1970, 71; co-author: (with Paul Brashler) Catch You Later: The Autobiography of Johnny Bench, 1979, (with Paul Daugherty) Catch Every Ball: How to Handle Life's Pitches, 2008 **AW:** Named Minor League Player of Year, Sporting News, 1967, National League Rookie of Year, Sporting News, 1968, National League Rookie of Year, Baseball Writers Association Am., 1968, National League MVP, 1970, 72, Major League Player of Year, Sporting News, 1970, National League Player of Year, Sporting News, 1970, MVP, 1976 World Series; player National League All-Star Fielding Team, 1968-77, 79-80, National League All-Star Team, Sporting News, 1968-70, 72, 73-77; inducted into Baseball Hall of Fame, 1989; recipient Gold Glove award 10 times; named to All-Time Rawlings Gold Glove Team, 2007,Sporting News 100 Greatest Baseball Players, 1999 **ACH:** Achievements include catching over 100 games a year for 13 consecutive seasons. **BA:** 138 Royal Saint Georges Way, Rancho Mirage, CA, 92270

BENING, ANNETTE, T: Actress **I:** Media & Entertainment **PB:** Topeka **SC:** KS/USA **PT:** Arnett Grant; Bening; Shirley (Ashley) Bening **MS:** Married **SPN:** Warren Beatty (March 3, 1992); J. Steven White (May 26, 1984) (div. 1991) **CH:** Kathlyn Bening; Benjamin; Isabel Ashley Ira; Ella **ED:** Student, American Conservatory Theatre; Degree in theatre, San Francisco State University; Student, Mesa College **CR:** Board governors Academy Motion Picture Arts & Sciences, 2008- **CW:** Actress: (films) The Great Outdoors, 1988, Valmont, 1989, The Grifters, 1990, Postcards from the Edge, 1990, Guilty by Suspicion, 1991, Regarding Henry, 1991, Bugsy, 1991, Love Affair, 1994, Richard III, 1995, The American President, 1995, Mars Attacks!, 1996, The Siege, 1998, American Beauty, 1999, In Dreams, 1999, What Planet Are You From?, 2000, Open Range, 2003, Being Julia, 2004 (Named Best Actress National Board Rev. Motion Pictures 2004, Golden Globe for Best Actress, 2005), Running with Scissors, 2006, The Women, 2008, Mother and Child, 2009, The Kids Are All Right, 2010 (New York Film Critics Cir. award for Best Actress, 2010, Golden Globe award for Best Performance by an Actress in a Motion Picture-Comedy or Musical, 2011), Ruby Sparks, 2012, Ginger and Rosa, 2012, Girl Most Likely, 2012, The Face of Love, 2013, The Search, 2014, Danny Collins, 2015, 20th Century Women, 2016, Rules Don't Apply, 2016, Film Stars Don't Die in Liverpool, 2017, The Seagull, 2018, Life Itself, 2018, Georgetown, 2018; (TV films) Manhunt for Claude Dallas, 1986, Hostage, 1988, Mrs. Harris, 2005; (TV appearances) Miami Vice, 1987, Wiseguy, 1987, Sagwa, The Chinese Siamese Cat 2001-03, Liberty Kids, 2002-03 The Sopranos, 2004, Mrs Harris, 2005, Saturday Night Live, 2006; (TV series) Liberty's Kids: Est. 1776, 2002; (stage appearances) Coastal Disturbances, 1986, (Clarence Derwin award 1987, Theatre World award 1987), Spoils of War, 1988, Hedda Gabler, 1999, Euripides, 2009, The Female of the Species, 2010 **AW:** Recipient Board of Governors award, Am. Society Cinematographers, 2008, Star, Hollywood Walk of Fame, 2006

BENIOFF, MARC, T: CEO of Saleforce **I:** Business Management/Business Services **DOB:** 09/25/1964 **PB:** San Francisco **SC:** California **ED:** BS in Business Admin., University Southern California, 1986; Doctorate. 2014 **C:** Chairman/CEO/Co-Founder, Salesforce.com, 2001-; Co-Chairman,Presidents IT Advisory Committee,2003-05; Founder, chairman, CEO, Salesforce.com, Inc., San Francisco, 1999-; Senior vice president marketing, Oracle Corp., 1996-99; Senior vice president web/workgroup systems div., Oracle Corp., 1995-96; Various leadership positions in sales, marketing and prod. devel., Oracle Corp., Santa Clara, California, 1986-95; Assembly language programmer Macintosh division, Apple Computer, Inc., Cupertino, California, 1984; Founder, Liberty Software, 1979 **CR:** Member Citizens to Achieve Reform in Education, 2003- co-chmn. President's Information Technology Advisory Committee (PITAC), 2003-05 board directors Cisco Systems, Inc., 2012-, Salesforce.com, Inc., 1999-, DW Data, Inc., 1999- **CIV:** Founder, salesforce.com Foundation, 2000- **CW:** Co-author (with Karen Southwick): Compassionate Capitalism: How Corporations Can Make Doing Good an Integral Part of Doing Well, 2004; co-author: (with Carlye Adler) The Business of Changing the World: 20 Great Leaders on Strategic Corporate Philanthropy, 2006, Behind the Cloud: The Untold Story of How Salesforce.com Went from Idea to Billion Dollar Company and Revolutionized an Industry, 2009 **AW:** Named Executive of Year, San Francisco Business Times, 2009, CEO of Year, CRO magazine, 2008, Ernst & Young Entrepreneur of Year, 2007, International CEO of Year, Selling Power, World Class Innovator, DEMO, 2005, Entrepreneur of Year, SunBridge, Alumni Entrepreneur of Year, University Southern California Marshall School Business, 2004, Northern California Entrepreneur of Year, Ernst & Young, 2003; named one of The 25 Most Effective Philanthropists, Barron's, 2010, The Forbes 400: Richest Americans, Forbes magazine, 2009-, The Top 100 Most Influential People in IT, eWEEK, 2007, The 50 Who Matter Now, CNNMoney.com Business 2.0, 2006, The Agenda Setters, Silicon.com, The 20 Most Influential People in the Industry, CRM Magazine, The 25 People Responsible for Turning E-Business Around, BusinessWeek, The Business People of Year, Fortune magazine, 2010, Top 10 Entrepreneurs to Watch, 2003; recipient David Packard Medal of Achievement, 2010, Excellence in Corp. Philanthropy award, Committee Encouraging Corp. Philanthropy, 2007, Bridge award, HEAVEN (Helping Educate, Activate, Volunteer, and Empower via the Net), Promise of Peace award, Prime Minister of Israel Benjamin Netanyahu **ACH:** Created an on-demand hosted Customer Relationship Management (CRM) solution that would replace traditional enterprise software technology which went public in June, 2004.

BENNET, CHANCELLOR J., T: Rapper **I:** Media & Entertainment **PB:** Chicago **SC:** IL/USA **CW:** (Mixtapes) 10 Day, 2012, Acid Rap, 2013, Coloring Book, 2016(Grammy for Best Rap Album 2017)(with the Social Experiment) Surf, 2015 **AW:** Grammy for Best New Artist, 2017, Grammy for Best Rap Performance, 2017

BENNET, MICHAEL FARRAND, T: U.S. Senator From Colorado **I:** Government Administration/Government Relations/Government Services **DOB:** 11/28/1964 **PB:** New Delhi **SC:** India **PT:** Douglas Joseph Bennet, Susanne (Klejman) Bennet **ED:** JD, Yale Law School, New Haven, CT, 1993; BA in History, Wesleyan University, Connecticut, 1987 **C:** U.S. Senate Finance Committee, 2013-Present; U.S. Senate Health, Education, Labor & Pensions Committee, Washington, DC, 2009-Present; U.S.

Senate Agricultural, Nutrition & Forestry Committee, Washington, DC, 2009-Present; U.S. Senator From Colorado, 2009-Present; U.S. Senate Banking, Housing & Urban Affairs Committee, Washington, DC, 2009-2013; U.S. Senate Special Committee on Aging, Washington, DC, 2009-2013; Superintendent, Denver Public Schools, 2005-2009; Chief of Staff to Mayor John Hickenlooper, City of Denver, 2003-2005; Managing Director, Anschutz Investment Co., Denver, CO, 1997-2003; Counsel to Deputy Attorney General, U.S. Department of Justice, Washington, DC, 1995-1997; Law Clerk, Hon. Francis D. Murnaghan, U.S. Court of Appeals, Fourth Circuit, 1993-1994 **CR:** Board of Visitors, U.S. Air Force Academy, 2011-Present; Chairman, Democratic Senatorial Campaign Committee (DSCC), 2013-2015; National Campaign Co-Chair, Obama for America, 2012 **PA:** Democrat **BA:** The Office of Michael Bennet, 261 Russell Senate Office Building, Washington, DC, 201510

BENNETT, TONY, T: Entertainer **I:** Media & Entertainment **DOB:** 08/03/1926 **PB:** Astoria **SC:** NY/USA **ED:** Student, Am. Theatre Wing, New York City; MusD, University Berkeley **CR:** Official Artist, Kentucky Derby, 2001; **CIV:** Raised millions of dollars for Juvenile Diabetes Foundation; co-founder (with Susan Crow) Frank Sinatra School for Arts HS, Queens, New York, 2001 **MIL:** Served with infantry Army of the U.S., World War II **CW:** Classic pop vocalist, entertainer (frequent appearances on TV, in concert); singer: (albums) Treasure Chest of Songs, 1955, Tony, 1957, Count Basie Swings, Tony Bennett Sings, 1958, Blue Velvet, 1959, To My Wonderful One, 1960, Bennett and Basie Strike Up the Band, 1961, I Left My Heart in San Francisco, 1963 (Album of Year, Grammy Awards, 1962), I Wanna Be Around, 1963, Love Story, 1971, Summer of '42, 1972, Sunrise, Sunset, 1973, 16 Most Requested Songs, 1986, The Art of Excellence, 1986, Bennett/Berlin, 1987, The Movie Song Album, 1989, Astoria, 1990, Forty Years: The Artistry of Tony Bennett, 1991, Perfectly Frank, 1992 (Best Traditional Vocal Performance, Grammy Awards, 1992), Steppin' Out, 1993 (Best Traditional Pop Vocal, Grammy Awards, 1993, 2003), The Essence of Tony Bennett, 1993, In Person! With Count Basie and His Orchestra, 1994, MTV Unplugged, 1994 (Album of Year, Best Traditional Pop Vocal, Grammy Awards), Here's to the Ladies, 1995, Tony Bennett on Holiday, 1997, Tribute to Billie Holiday, Bennett Sings Ellington-Hot and Cool, 1999, The Ultimate Tony, 2000, Playin' With My Friends: Bennett Sings The Blues, 2001, The Essential Tony Bennett, 2002, A Wonderful World, 2002, The Art of Romance, 2005 (Best Traditional Pop Vocal, Grammy Awards, 2006), Duets: An American Classic, 2006 (Best Pop Collaboration with Vocals for Once in My Life, Best Traditional Pop Vocal Album, Grammy Awards, 2007), Tony Bennett Sings the Ultimate American Songbook, Vol. 1, 2007, Duets II, 2011 (Best Pop Performance by a Duo or Group, with Amy Winehouse for Body and Soul, Grammy Awards, 2012), Viva Duets, 2012, (with Lady Gaga) Cheek to Cheek, 2014 (Best Traditional Pop Vocal Album, Grammy Awards, 2015), (with Bill Charlap) The Silver Lining: The Songs of Jerome Kern, 2015 (Best Traditional Pop Vocal Album, Grammy Awards, 2016); appeared in : The Scout, 1994; appeared in (TV films) Men, Movies & Carol, 1994, The Scout, 1994, Sinatra: 80 Years My Way, 1995, (TV series) The Simpsons, 1989, Muppets Tonight, 1996, (TV special) Tony Bennett on Holiday: A Tribute to Billy Holiday, 1997, Analyze This, 1999, Tony Bennett: An American Classic, 2006 (Primetime Emmy for Outstanding Individual Performance in a Variety or Music Progressive, Academy TV Arts and Scis., 2007), TV guest appearances The Andy Williams Show, 1966, The Jackie Gleason Show, 1969, Space

Ghost Coast to Coast, 1994, Suddenly Susan, 1997; painting, Homage to Hockney, hangs permanently in Butler Institute Am. Art, exhibitions include Butler Institute of Am. Art, Youngstown, Ohio, 1994, National Arts Club, New York City; author: Tony Bennett: What My Heart Has Seen, 1996, Life is a Gift: The Zen of Bennett, 2012; co-author: The Good Life: The Autobiography of Tony Bennett., 1998, Tony Bennett in the Studio: A Life of Art & Music, 2007 **AW:** Named to Big Band and Jazz Hall of Fame, 1997, Long Island Music Hall of Fame, New Jersey Hall of Fame, 2011; recipient Gold records for recs., Because of You, I Left My Heart in San Francisco, Best Male Vocalist award, Cash Box magazine, 1951, Grammy lifetime achievement award, Salute to Greatness award Martin Luther King Center, Atlanta, Lifetime Achievement award, American Society of Composers, Authors, and Publishers, 2002, Kennedy Center Honor, John F. Kennedy Center for Performing Arts, 2005, Billboard Century award, 2006, UN High Commissioner for Refugees Humanitarian award, 2006, National Endowment for the Arts Jazz Masters award, 2006, of Star on Hollywood Walk of Fame

BENSOUDA, FATOU, **T:** Prosecutor **I:** Law and Legal Services **DOB:** 01/31/1961 **PB:** Banjul **ED:** LLM, UN/IMO International Maritime Law Institute, Malta; LLB, University Ife, Nigeria **CT:** Barrister-at-law: Nigeria Law School, Lagos **C:** Chief prosecutor, International Criminal Court (Interstate Commerce Commission), 2012-; Deputy prosecutor, International Criminal Court (Interstate Commerce Commission), The Hague, Netherlands, 2004-12; Legal advisor, trial attorney, International Criminal Tribunal for Rwanda, Arusha, Tanzania, 2001-04; General manager, International Bank Commerce, Ltd., The Gambia, 2002; Private practice attorney, Ya Sadi, Bensouda and Co., Banjul, The Gambia, 2000-02; Attorney general, secretary state for justice, Government of Gambia, 1998-2000; Solicitor general and legal secretary of republic, Government of Gambia, 1997-98; Various positions including senior state counsel, deputy director pub. prosecutions, Government of Gambia, 1987-97 **CW:** Contributor articles to professional journals **AW:** Named one of The 100 Most Influential People in the World, TIME magazine, 2012; recipient World Peace Through Law award, The Whitney Harris World Law Institute, 2011, International Jurists award, International Court Justice, 2009,Time 100 Most Influential, 2017, International Jurists Awards, 2009, World Peace Through Law Award, 2011, **ADD:** International Criminal Court, PO Box 19519, The Hague, YT, Netherlands, 2500

BENTON, WILLIAM DUANE, T: Federal Judge **I:** Law and Legal Services **DOB:** 09/08/1950 **PB:** Springfield **SC:** MO/USA **PT:** Son of William Max and Patricia F. (Nicholson) B. **MS:** Married **SPN:** Sandra Snyder (1980) **CH:** Megan Blair, William Grant **ED:** LLD (hon.), Westminster College, 1999; LLM, University of Virginia, 1995; LLD (hon.), Central Missouri State University, 1994; Student, Institute Judicial Administration, New York University, 1992; MBA in Accounting, Memphis State University, 1979; JD, Yale University, 1975; BA in Political Science, summa cum laude, Northwestern University, 1972 **CT:** CPA, Missouri **C:** Judge, US Court Appeals (8th cir.), Kansas City, Missouri, 2004-; Chief justice, Missouri Supreme Court, Jefferson City, 1997-99; Judge, Missouri Supreme Court, Jefferson City, 1991-2004; Director revenue, Missouri Department of Revenue, Jefferson City, 1989-91; Private practice, Jefferson City, Missouri, 1983-89; Chief of staff, Congressman Wendell Bailey, Washington, 1980-82; Judge advocate, US Navy, Memphis, 1975-79; Advanced through

grades to captain, 1993; Ensign, US Navy, 1972 **CR:** Adjunct Professor Westminster College, 1998-, University Mo.-Columbia School Law, 1998- **CIV:** Chairman, Multistate Tax Commission Washington, 1990-91, Chairman, Missouri State Employees Retirement System, Jefferson City, 1989-93, Regent, Central Missouri State University, 1987-89, Director Council for Drug Free Youth, Jefferson City, 1989-97, Member Missouri Military Adv. Committee, 1989-91, Member, Missouri Commission Intergovernmental Cooperative, Jefferson City, 1989-91, Trustee, Deacon 1st Baptist Church, Jefferson City **MIL:** Lieutenant, US Navy, 1975-80 **CW:** Contributor Articles, Professional Journals; Managing Editor, Yale Law Journal, 1974-75 **AW:** Danforth Fellow, JFK School Government, Harvard University, 1990 **MEM:** Member American Institute of Certified Public Accountants (tax committee 1983-), Missouri Bar Association (tax committee 1975-), Missouri Society CPA's (tax committee 1983-), Navy League, Military Order of World Wars, Vietnam Vets of Am., VFW, Am. Legion, Phi Beta Kappa, Beta Gamma Sigma, Rotary **BAR:** Bar: Missouri 1975 **RE:** Baptist **BA:** Thomas F. Eagleton Courthouse, 111 South 10th Street, St. Louis, MO, 63102

BERA, AMI, T: U.S. Representative from California, physician **I:** Government Administration/Government Relations/Government Services **DOB:** 03/02/1965 **PB:** Hollywood **ED:** MD, University California Irvine, 1991; BS in Biological Sciences, University California Irvine, 1983 **C:** Member, US House Space, Sci., & Technology Committee, 2013-; Member, Committee on Ways and Means; Member, US House Foreign Affairs Committee, 2013-; Member, US Congress from 7th California District, Washington, 2013-; Clinical professor medicine, University California Davis School Medicine, 2004-; Associate dean for admissions, University California Davis School Medicine, 2004-07; Chief medical officer, Sacramento County Department Health & Human Services, 1999-2004; Director care management, Mercy Healthcare, 1998-99; Assistant medical director, MedClinic Medical Group, 1997-98; Chief internal medicine department, MedClinic Medical Group, 1996-97 **PA:** Democrat

BERGMAN, JOHN W., T: U.S. Representative from Michigan, Former Marine Corps Lieutenant General **I:** Government Administration/Government Relations/Government Services **DOB:** 02/02/1947 **PB:** Savage **SC:** MN/USA **ED:** MBA, University of West Florida, 1975; BA in Business Administration, Gustavus Adolphus College, 1969 **CT:;** **C:** Member, U.S. House of Representatives from Michigan's 1st District, 2017-;; Member, Committee on the Budget, Committee on Natural Resources, Committee on Veterans' Affairs; Commander, Marine Forces Reserve/Marine Forces North, 2005-2009; Director, Reserve Affairs, Quantico, Virginia, 2003-2005; Commander, 4th Marine Aircraft Wing, New Orleans, Louisiana in August 2000-2002; Commander, II Marine Expeditionary Force Augmentation Command Element, Camp Lejeune, 2000;; Chief of Staff, Marine Expeditionary Force Augmentation Command Element, Camp Pendleton, California, 1996-99; Commander, Marine Corps Mobilization Station, Chicago, 1991-95; Commanding Officer, Stewart ANGB, Newburgh, New York, 1988-90; Logistics Officer, Marine Corps Mobilization Station, Chicago, 1988; Pilot Training Officer, National Academy of Sciences Glenview, US Marine Corps Reserve, 1978-81; Released from Active Duty, 1975; Flight Instructor, National Academy of Sciences Whiting Field, Milton, Florida, 1972-75; Squadron Pilot, Marine Corps Air Station, New River, North Carolina, 1970-72; Advanced through Grades to Brigadier General, US

Marine Corps; Commissioned 2d Lieutenant, US Marine Corps, 1969 **BA:** 414 Cannon House Office Building, Washington, DC, 20515

BERGMAN, STANLEY M., T: CEO **I:** Consumer Goods and Services **CN:** Henry Schein **ED:** Certificate in the Theory of Accounting, University of the Witwatersrand, 1973; Bachelor of Commerce, University of the Witwatersrand, 1972 **CT:** CPA, New York **C:** Chairman, CEO, Henry Schein, Inc., Melville, NY, 2005-Present; Board Director, Henry Schein, Inc., Melville, NY, 1982-Present; Chairman, CEO, President, Henry Schein, Inc., Melville, NY, 1989-2005; Vice President, Finance And Administration, Henry Schein, Inc., Melville, NY, 1980-1985; Executive Vice President, Henry Schein, Inc., Melville, NY, 1985-1989 **MEM:** Forsyth Institute, American Institute of CPAs, Honorary Member, American Dental Association **BA:** Henry Schein Inc., 135 Duryea Road, Melville, NY, 11747-0000

BERMAN, WAYNE L., T: Businessman, Former Lobbyist **I:** Business Management/Business Services **ED:** BA, University Buffalo **C:** Senior Advisor for Global Government Affairs The Blackstone Group; Managing director, Ogilvy Government Relations (merged with Berman Enterprises), 2004-; Vice chairman, JLT Am.,; Founder, Berman Enterprises; Managing partner, Am. Mercantile Group,; Assistant secretary, US Department Commerce, Washington, 1989 **CR:** Senior advisor Bush/Cheney transition, 2001 vice presidential campaign director Dole/Kemp deputy director Rep. National Convention, 1996 director Congl. relations Bush/Quayle campaign, 1988 deputy director Bush/Reagan transition team, 1981 **CIV:** Board trustees, Center for Study of Presidency, Board trustees, Center for Strategic and International Studies, Board trustees, Libr. of Congress, **AW:** Named one of 50 Top Lobbyists, Washingtonian magazine, 2007

BERNSTEIN, CARL, T: Writer **I:** Writing and Editing **DOB:** 12/11/1930 **PB:** Botosani **SC:** Romania **PT:** Son of Shalom and Deborah B. **MS:** Married **SPN:** Sylvia Dorfman, August 10, 1983; Lena Goldstein, November 12, 1951 (div. June 1978) **CH:** Shlomo, Selma, Rony **ED:** Student, art school, Bat Yam, Israel, 1965-70; Student, Laurian, Romania, 1948 **C:** Owner, Gold Styles Inc., New York City, 1982-; Teacher arts, art history, art school, Bat Yam, 1972-75 **CR:** Chairman Jewelers Organization Tel-Aviv (Israel), 1970-75, Art Students Association **CW:** Exhibited in shows at World Art Gallery, New York City, 1998, New York Tech. Institute Show, 1999, Arts Forum, New York City, 1999-2000, Flecher Gallery, Woodstock, New York, 2000, 4 West Gallery, Piermont, New York, 2000,(Book) The Secret Man, 2005 **AW:** Recipient Zahal award, Israeli Army, 1953-58 **H:** Painting, travel, camping, archaeology **PA:** Democrat

BERNSTEIN, CARL, T: Investigative Journalist **I:** Media & Entertainment **DOB:** 02/14/1944 **PB:** Washington, February 14, 1944 **PT:** Son of Alfred David and Sylvia (Walker) B.; **SPN:** Married Christine; Married Carol Ann Honsa, April 28, 1968 (div. 1972); Married Nora Ephron, April 14, 1976 (div. 1980) **CH:** children: Jacob Walker, Max Ephron; **ED:** LLD, Boston University, 1975; Student, University Maryland, 1961-64 **C:** Political Commentator, CNN; Guest Lecturer, Stony Brook University, Long Island, New York, 2013-; Contributing Editor, Vanity Fair, 1997-; Corr., Contributor, TIME magazine, 1990-91; Corr., ABC News, New York City, 1981-84; Washington Bureau Chief, ABC, 1979-81; Reporter, The Washington Post, 1966-76; Reporter, Elizabeth (New Jersey) Journal, 1965-66; From Copyboy to Reporter, Washington Star, 1960-65

CR: Visiting Professor New York University, 1992 Executive Editor voter.com **CIV:** Served with Army of the U.S., 1968. **CW:** Co-author: (with Bob Woodward) All The President's Men, 1974, The Final Days, 1976; (with Marco Politi) His Holiness: John Paul II and the History of Our Time, 1996; author: Loyalties: A Son's Memoir, 1989, A Woman in Charge: The Life of Hillary Rodham Clinton, 2007 **AW:** Recipient 1st Prize Feature Writing, 1966, 1st Prize General Reporting New Jersey Press Association, 1966, 1st Prize Investigative Reporting, 1966; Drew Pearson Prize for Investigative Reporting of Watergate, 1972; George Polk Memorial Award; Worth Bingham Prize; Heywood Broun Award International Newspaper Guild; Sigma Delta Chi Distinguished Service Award; Sidney Hillman Foundation Award; Gold Medal University Missouri School Journalism, 1972; Pulitzer Prize Citation, 1972 **BA:** Greater Talent Agency, 437 Fifth Ave, New York, NY, 10016

BERRY, HALLE MARIA, T: Actress **I:** Media & Entertainment **DOB:** 08/14/1966 **PB:** Cleveland **SC:** OH/USA **PT:** Jerome Berry; Judith (Hawkins) Berry **MS:** Divorced **SPN:** Olivier Martinez (2013, Divorced 2016); Eric Benét (1/24/2001, Divorced 1/3/2005); David Christopher Justice (12/31/1992, Divorced 6/24/1997) **CH:** Two Children **ED:** BA, Cuyahoga Community College, Cleveland, Ohio (1986) **CR:** Spokeswoman, Revlon Cosmetics (1996-Present) **CW:** Actress, Films, "Jungle Fever" (1991), "The Last Boy Scout" (1991), "Strictly Business" (1991), "Boomerang" (1992), "Father Hood" (1993), "The Program" (1993), "The Flintstones" (1994), "Losing Isaiah" (1995), "The Rich Man's Wife" (1996), "Executive Decision" (1996), "Race The Sun" (1996), "Girl 6" (1996); "B*A*P*S" (1997), "Bulworth" (1998), "Why Do Fools Fall in Love" (1998), "Victims of Fashion" (1999), "Ringside" (1999), "X-Men" (2000), "Swordfish" (2001), "Monster's Ball" (2001), "Die Another Day" (2002), "X2: X-Men United" (2003), "Gothika" (2003), "Catwoman" (2004), Voice Actor, "Robots" (2005), "X-Men: The Last Stand" (2006), "Perfect Stranger" (2007), "Things We Lost in the Fire" (2007), "Dark Tide" (2011), "New Year's Eve" (2011), "Dark Tide" (2012), "Cloud Atlas" (2012), "The Hive" (2013), "Movie 43" (2013), "The Call" (2013), "X-Men: Days of Future Past" (2014), "Kevin Hart: What Now?" (2016), "Kidnap" (2017), "Kings" (2017), "Kingsman: The Golden Circle" (2017); Actress, Producer, "Frankie & Alice (2010); Actress, TV Films, Solomon & Sheba (1995), "The Wedding" (1998), "Oprah Winfrey Presents: Their Eyes Were Watching God" (2005), "Extant" (2014); Actress, TV Series, "Living Dolls" (1989), "Knots Landing" (1992), "Extant" (2014-Present); Actress, TV Miniseries, "Queen: The Story of an American Family" (1992); Actress, Executive Producer, TV Films, "Introducing Dorothy Dandridge" (1999); Actress, Films, "Kidnap" (2016), Executive Producer, TV Films, "Lackawanna Blues" (2005); TV Appearances Include "Amen" (1991), "A Different World" (1991), "They Came from Outer Space" (1991), "Martin" (1996), "Frasier" (1998), "The Bernie Mac Show" (2002) **AW:** Named Favorite Female Action Star, People's Choice Award (2007); Woman of the Year, Hasty Pudding Theatrical Society (2006); Female Star of the Year, ShoWest (2004); Miss USA (1987); First-runner Up, Miss USA (1986); Miss Teen All-America (1985); Named to the Power 150, Ebony Magazine (2008); Sherry Lansing Leadership Award, The Hollywood Reporter (2009); Women in Hollywood Tribute Award, ELLE Magazine (2008); Star on Hollywood Walk of Fame (2007); Outstanding Lead Actress in a Miniseries or a Movie, "Introducing Dorothy Dandridge," Emmy Award (2000); Best Performance by an Actress in a Mini-Series or Motion Picture

Made for TV, "Introducing Dorothy Dandridge," Golden Globe Award (2000); Outstanding Actress in a TV Movie, Miniseries, or Dramatic Special, "Introducing Dorothy Dandridge," National Association for the Advancement of Colored People Image Award (2000); Outstanding Performance by a Female Actor in a TV Movie or Miniseries, "Introducing Dorothy Dandridge," Screen Actors Guild Award (2000); Outstanding Actress in a Motion Picture, "Boomerang," National Association for the Advancement of Colored People Image Award (1993); Best Actress in a Leading Role, "Monster's Ball," Academy Award (2002); Best Actress, "Monster's Ball," National Board Review Award (2001); Outstanding Performance by a Female Actor in a Leading Role, "Monster's Ball," Screen Actors Guild Award (2002); Best Actress, "Monster's Ball," BAFTA Award; Outstanding Supporting Actress in a Motion Picture, "Die Another Day," National Association for the Advancement of Colored People Image Award (2003); Outstanding Lead Actress in a TV Movie or Mini-Series, "Queen: The Story of an American Family," National Association for the Advancement of Colored People Image Award (1995) **ACH:** Achievements include becoming the first African American actress to win Academy Award for Best Actress for the film Monsters Ball, 2002 **BA:** international Creative Management, 10250 Constellation Boulevard, Los Angeles, CA, 90067

BERTOLINI, MARK T., T: Aetna CEO **I:** Business Management/Business Services **ED:** MBA in Fin., Cornell University; BS in Business Administration, Wayne State University **C:** Chairman, president, CEO, Aetna, Inc., Hartford, Connecticut, 2011-; President, CEO, Aetna, Inc., Hartford, Connecticut, 2010-11; President, Aetna, Inc., Hartford, Connecticut, 2007-10; Executive vice president business operations, Aetna, Inc., Hartford, Connecticut, 2007; Executive vice president regional business, Aetna, Inc., Hartford, Connecticut, 2006-07; Senior vice president regional business, Aetna, Inc., Hartford, Connecticut, 2005-06; Senior vice president specialty group, Aetna, Inc., Hartford, Connecticut, 2005; Senior vice president, specialty products, Aetna, Inc., Hartford, Connecticut, 2003-05; Senior vice president, regional & middle market, Cigna Corp., 2002-03; Senior vice president, national sales & delivery, Cigna Corp., 2000-02; Executive vice president, NYLCare Health Plans,; CEO, previously COO, SelectCare, 1992-95 **CR:** Board directors Aetna Inc., 2010- **CIV:** Member advisory board, Cornell University School Human Ecology, Chairman operations committee, Association Health Insurance Plans, Board directors, Connecticut Business & Ind. Association, Board directors, University Connecticut Health Center,

BERZON, MARSHA S., T: Federal Judge **I:** Law and Legal Services **DOB:** 04/17/1945 **PB:** Cincinnati **SC:** Ohio **ED:** JD, Boalt Hall School Law, 1973; BA, Radcliffe College, 1966 **CT:** Bar: DC 1975, California 1973 **C:** Judge, US Court Appeals (9th cir.), 2000-; James Madison Lecturer, New York University Law School, 2008; Associate General Counsel, AFL-CIO, 1987-99; Attorney, Altshuler, Berzon, Nussbaum, Berzon & Rubin, San Francisco, 1978-2000; Attorney, Woll & Mayer, Washington, 1975-77; Clerk, Justice William Brennan, 1974-75; Clerk, Judge James Browning, 9th Cir., 1973-74 **CR:** Practitioner-in-residence Ind. University Law School, 1998, Cornell School of Law, New York, 1994 Lecturer Louisiana State University School of Law, 2003, University California School Social Welfare, Berkeley, California, 1992 **AW:** Named Margaret Brent Award, American Bar Association, 2007 **MEM:** Mem.: Federal Bar

Association, State Bar of California, DC Bar Association, Am. Law Institute, Am. Bar Foundation **BA:** US Ct Appeals 9th Cir, 95 7th St, San Francisco, CA, 94103-1526

BETTMAN, GARY BRUCE, T: National Hockey League Commissioner **I:** Business Management/Business Services **DOB:** 06/02/1952 **PB:** NYC **PT:** Son of Howard G. and Gretel J. (Pollack) B.; **SPN:** Michelle Weiner, August 24, 1975; **CH:** Lauren, Jordan, Brittany **ED:** JD, New York University, 1977; BS, Cornell University, 1974 **CT:** Bar: New York 1978, New Jersey 1978, U.S. District Court (so. and eastern dists.) New York 1979. **C:** Commissioner, NHL, New York City, 1993-; Senior vice president, general counsel, NBA, New York City, 1989-93; Vice president, general counsel, NBA, New York City, 1984-89; Assistant general counsel, NBA, New York City, 1981-84; Associate, Gutkin, Miller et al, Milburn, New Jersey, 1980-81; Associate, Proskauer Rose, New York City, 1977-80 **AW:** Named one of The Most Influential People in the World of Sports, Business Week, 2008, 2007, 50 Most Influential People in Sports Business, Street & Smith's SportsBus. Journal, 2007-09 **MEM:** Member New York State Bar Association, Association of Bar of City of New York (chairman committee on sports law), New Jersey Bar Association, Sports Lawyers Association (board directors 1985-93, entertainment and sports law committee 1990-93), Phi Kappa Phi. **H:** Skiing, golf

BETZIG, ERIC, T: Physicist **I:** Sciences **CN:** Howard Hughes Medical Inst. Janelia Farms Research Campus **DOB:** 01/13/1960 **PB:** Ann Arbor **PT:** Son of Robert Betzig **ED:** PhD in Applied & Engineering Physics, Cornell University, 1988; MS in Applied & Engineering Physics, Cornell University, 1985; BS in Physics, California Institute Technology, 1983 **C:** UC Berkeley, Lawrence Berkely National Laboratory, 2017-; Group leader Janelis Research Campus, Howard Hughes Medical Institute, Ashburn, Virginia, 2005-; Owner, New Millenium Research, Okemos, Michigan, 2002-05; Vice president research & development, Ann Arbor Machine Co., Chelsea, Michigan, 1996-2002; Owner, NSOM Enterprises, Berkeley Heights, New Jersey, 1994-96; Member technical staff Semiconductor Research Department, AT&T Bell Labs, Murray Hill, New Jersey, 1988-94; Grad. research assistant, Cornell University Department Applied & Engineering Physics, Ithaca, New York, 1983-88; Undergraduate research assistant, Graduate Aeronautical Laboratories California Institute Technology, Pasadena, California, 1980; Undergraduate research assistant, Graduate Aeronautical Laboratories California Institute Technology, Pasadena, California, 1979 **AW:** Nobel Prize in Chemistry, 2014

BEUTLER, BRUCE A., T: Geneticist, Immunologist **I:** Sciences **DOB:** 12/29/1957 **PB:** Chgo. **PT:** Son of Ernest and Brondelle May Beutler; **ED:** MD (hon.), Tech. University Munich, 2007; MD, University Chicago Pritzker School Medicine, 1981; BA, University California, San Diego, 1976 **C:** Founding director, Center Genetics of Host Defense, University Texas Southwester Medical Center, 2011-; Chairman department genetics, Scripps Research Institute, 2007-11; Professor department immunology, Scripps Research Institute, La Jolla, California, 2000-11; Associate physician, Rockefeller University Hospital, 1984-86; Assistant professor, Rockefeller U, 1985; Fellow, Rockefeller U, New York, 1983-85; Professor, University Texas Southwester Medical Center, 1996-2000; Associate professor, University Texas Southwester Medical Center, 1990-96; Assistant professor, University Texas Southwester Medical Center, Dallas, 1986-90;

Medical training, University Texas Southwester Medical Center, Dallas, 1981-83 **CR:** Investigator Howard Hughes Medical Institute, 1986-2000 **AW:** Co-recipient Shaw Foundation prize for Life Sci./ Medicine, Hong Kong, 2011, Nobel Prize in Physiology or Medicine, 2011, Albany Medical Center prize, 2009, International Balzan Foundation prize, 2007, Robert Koch prize, Germany, 2004; recipient Will Rogers Institute Ann. prize for research, 2009, William B. Coley award, Cancer Research Institute, 2006, Charles-Léopold Mayer prize, French Academy Scis., 2006, Young Investigator award, American Federation Clinical Research, 1994 **MEM:** Mem.: National Academy of Sciences, Institute Medicine, Association American Physicians, American Society Clinical Investigation, European Molecular Biology Organization (assoc.; foreign associate) **ACH:** Achievements include first to isolate mouse tumor necrosis factor-alpha (TNF) and to demonstrate the inflammatory potential of this cytokine, proving its important role in endotoxin-induced shock; invention of recombinant molecules expressly designed to neutralize TNF used extensively in the treatment of rheumatoid arthritis, Crohn's disease, psoriasis, and other forms of inflammation

BEVAN, BEV, **T:** Drummer **I:** Media & Entertainment **PB:** Sparkhill **SC:** England **CW:** (Solo) Let There Be Drums, 1976,(The Move) The Move, 1968, Shazam, 1970, Looking On, 1970, Message from the Country, 1971,(With ELO) The Electric Light Orchestra, 1971, ELO 2, 1973, On the Third Day, 1973, The Night the Light Went On, 1974, El Dorado, 1974, Face the Music, 1975, A New World Record, 1976, Out of the Blue, 1977, Discovery, 1979,Time,1981 Secret Messages, 1983, Balance of Power, 1986, The Eternal Idol, 1987, ELO Part 2, 1990, Moment of Truth, 1994 **AW:** Rock and Roll Hall of Fame, 2017

BEVIN, MATTHEW GRISWOLD, **T:** Governor of Kentucky **I:** Government Administration/Government Relations/Government Services **DOB:** 01/09/1967 **PB:** Denver **PT:** Son of Avery and Louise Bevin; **ED:** BA, Washington and Lee University, 1989 **C:** Governor, State of Kentucky, 2015-; President, Bevin Brothers Manufacturing Co., 2011-; Partner, Waycross Partners, Kentucky,; Took over management, Bevin Brothers Manufacturing Co., 2008; Co-founder, Integrity Asset Management (sold to Munder Capital Management), 2003-11; With, National Asset Management, 1999-2003; Vice president, Putnam Investments,; Fin. consultant, SEI Investments Co., Boston,; Fin. consultant, SEI Investments Co., Pennsylvania, **PA:** Republican

BEWKES, JEFFREY LAWRENCE, **T:** Former Chairman and CEO of Time Warner Inc. **I:** Media & Entertainment **DOB:** 05/25/1952 **PB:** Paterson **PT:** Son of Eugene Garrett Bewkes Junior; **ED:** MBA, Stanford University, 1977; BA in Philosophy, Yale University, 1974 **C:** Chairman, CEO, Time Warner, Inc., New York City, 2009-18; President, CEO, Time Warner, Inc., New York City, 2008; President, COO, Time Warner, Inc., New York City, 2005-07; Chairman entertainment. & networks grp., Time Warner, Inc., New York City, 2002-05; Chairman, CEO, HBO, Inc., New York City, 1995-2002; President, COO, HBO, Inc., New York City, 1991-95; Executive vice president, CFO, HBO, Inc., New York City, 1987-91; Accountant officer, Citibank, NA, New York City,; Operations director, Sonoma Vineyards, Inc., Healdsburg, California, **CR:** Board directors Time Warner Cable Inc., 2008-09, Time Warner Inc., 2007-, Council Foreign Relations, 2002- **CIV:** Member adv. board, Museum TV & Radio, Member adv. board, Creative Coalition, Member adv. council, Am. Museum National

Hist., Member adv. council, Stanford University Grad. School Business, Member adv. council, Yale School Management, Trustee, Museum Moving Image, Trustee, Yale University, **AW:** Named one of Business People of Year, Fortune magazine, 2010, 25 Leaders Reshaping New York, Crain's New York magazine, 2008

BEYER, DON, **T:** U.S. Representative from Virginia **I:** Government Administration/Government Relations/Government Services **DOB:** 06/20/1950 **PB:** Trieste, Free Territory of Trieste **PT:** Son of Donald Sternoff Senior and Nancy Prew (McDonald) B.; **SPN:** Married Megan Carroll, September 19, 1987; Married Carolyn Anne (McInerney), July 15, 1972 (div.); **CH:** Children: Donald III, Stephanie **ED:** BA in Economics, Magna Cum Laude, Williams College, 1972 **C:** Member, U.S. House of Representatives from Virginia's 8th District, 2015-; Member, Committee on Natural Resources; Member, Committee on Science, Space and Technology; Member, Joint Economic Committee; Owner, Don Beyer Volvo, Falls Church, Virginia, 1974-; US Ambassador to Switzerland & Liechtenstein, US Department State, Bern, 2009-13; Lieutenant Governor, Commonwealth of Virginia, Richmond, 1990-98 **CR:** Urban at Large Member Commonwealth Transportation Board, Virginia, 1987-90 Chairman Virginia Poverty & Welfare Reform Commission, 1994-95, Transportation & Land Use Group, Virginia Commission on Climate Change, 2008 **CIV:** Chairman Baliles for Governor, Northern Virginia, 1985 Paul Simon for President, Virginia, 1988 Bill Clinton for President, Virginia, 1992 member 11th District Democratic Committee, Vienna, Virginia, 1992 Dem. nominee Governor of Virginia, 1998. **AW:** Named TIME Magazine Quality Dealer of Year, Virginia, 1991; Dealer of Excellence Award; Grand Award for Highway Safety, National Safety Federation; James Wheat Award for Service to Virginians with Disabilities; Earl Williams Leadership in Tech. Award. **MEM:** Member Land Rover Alexandria (president 1997); Northern Virginia Business Roundtable; Northern Virginia HighTech. Council (co-founder), American International Automobile Dealers Association, 2006-07; Board Member Youth for Tom morrow; Washington Community Foundation & the Red Cross. **H:** Golf, Skiing, Climbing **PA:** Democrat. **RE:** Epsicopalian.

BEZOS, JEFF, **T:** CEO of Amazon **I:** Retail/Sales **CN:** Amazon **DOB:** 01/12/1964 **PB:** Albuquerque **SC:** NM/USA **PT:** Miguel Bezos, Jacklyn (Gise) Bezos **ED:** Honorary Doctorate in Science & Technology, Carnegie Mellon University, Pittsburgh, PA, 2008; BSEE in Electrical Engineering & Computer Science, Princeton University, New Jersey, Summa Cum Laude, 1986 **C:** Owner, The Washington Post, 2013-Present; Founder, Blue Origin, Seattle, WA, 2000-Present; President, Amazon.com, Inc., Seattle, WA, 2000-Present; CEO, Amazon.com, Inc., Seattle, WA, 1996-Present; Founder, Chairman, Amazon.com, Inc., Seattle, WA, 1994-Present; Treasurer, Secretary, Amazon. com, Inc., Seattle, WA, 1996-1997; President, Amazon.com, Inc., Seattle, WA, 1994-1999; Senior Vice President, D.E. Shaw & Co., New York, NY, 1992-1994; Vice President, D.E. Shaw & Co., New York, NY, 1990-1992; Bankers Trust Co., New York, NY, 1988-1990; Fitel, New York, NY, 1986-1988 **CR:** Chairman, The Business Council, 2014-Present; Board of Directors, Drugstore.com, 1998-2004, Amazon.com Inc., 1994-Present **AW:** The World's Richest People, 2006-Present, The Forbes 400: Richest Americans, 2005-Present, The Ten Most Fascinating People, Barbara Walters Special, 2015, The 50 Most Influential People In Global Finance, Bloomberg Markets, 2013, Business Person of the Year, Fortune Magazine, 2012, The 40 Under

40, 2003, Innovation Award, The Economist, 2011, The World's Most Powerful People, Forbes Magazine, 2010-2014, The Business People of the Year, Fortune Magazine, 2010, The 100 Agents Of Change, Rolling Stone Magazine, 2009, The 100 Most Influential People In The World, TIME Magazine, 2008-2009, 2014, Person of the Year, Publishers Weekly, 2008, America's Best Leaders, U.S. News & World Report, 2008, The Global Elite, Newsweek Magazine, 2008, The 50 Most Important People On The Web, PC World, 2007, The 50 Who Matter Now, Cnnmoney.Com Business 2.0, 2006-2007, TIME Magazine, 1999 **MEM:** Tau Beta Pi, Phi Beta Kappa **ACH:** Achievements include funding Blue Origin, builders of low cost vehicles that would send passengers into space on short flights; launching and landing Goddard, a first development vehicle in the New Shepard program at Blue Origin **BA:** Amazon Headquarters, 410 Terry Avenue N, Seattle, WA, 98109

BIBAS, STEPHANOS, **T:** Federal Judge **I:** Law and Legal Services **PB:** Queens **SC:** NY/USA **MS:** Married **SPN:** Juliana Denise Bibas **ED:** BA, Columbia University; BA, University of Oxford; MA, University of Oxford; JD, Yale Law School **C:** Judge, U.S. Court of Appeals for the Third Circuit (2017-Present); Professor, University of Pennsylvania Law School (2006-2017)

BIDEN, JOE, **T:** Former Vice President of the U.S. **I:** Government Administration/Government Relations/Government Services **DOB:** 11/20/1942 **PB:** Scranton **SC:** PA **PT:** Joseph Robinette Biden, Sr.; Catherine Eugenia (Finnegan) Biden **ED:** JD, Syracuse University College of Law (1968); BA in History & Political Science, University of Delaware (1965) **C:** Benjamin Franklin Presidential Practice Professor, University of Pennsylvania (2017-Present); Chairman, Middle Class Working Families Task Force (MCWFTF), The White House (2009-2017); Vice President of the U.S. (2009-2017); US Representative to General Assembly, United Nations (2000); Chairman, International Narcotics Caucus (2007-2009); Chairman, US Senate, Foreign Relations Committee (2007-2009); Chairman, US Senate, Foreign Relations Committee (2001-2003); Chairman, US Senate, Foreign Relations Committee (2001); Chairman, US Senate Judiciary Committee (1987); US Senator from Delaware (1973-2009); Private Law Practice, Wilmington, DE (1968-1972) **CR:** US Democratic Vice Presidential Nominee (2008); Adjunct Professor, Widener University School of Law, Wilmington, DC (1991-Present); Member, New Castle County Council, DE (1970-1972) **CW:** Author, "Promises to Keep: On Life and Politics" (2007) **AW:** Named Senator of the Year, National Association of Police Organizations (2000); Named One of the 100 Most Influential People in the World, TIME Magazine (2011, 2013); Named to the Peter J. McGovern Little League Hall of Excellence (2009); Harry S. Truman Award, Democratic Leadership Council (2005); National Leadership Award, Coalition of Juvenile Justice (2004); Rail Spike Award, Delmarva Rail Passenger Association (2003); Balkan Peace Award, Albanian American Civic League (2002); Charles Dick Medal of Merit, US National Guard Association, Delaware Chapter (2002); Silver Medal of Appreciation, Czech Republic (1999); Spirit of Enterprise Award, US Chamber of Commerce (1998); Friend of Zion Tribute Award, Jerusalem Fund (1998) **BAR:** Delaware State Bar Association (1968) **PA:** Democrat **BA:** University of Pennsylvania, 3451 Walnut Street, Franklin Building Room 150, Philadelphia, PA, USA, 19104

BIEBER, JUSTIN DREW, T: Singer **I:** Media & Entertainment **DOB:** 03/01/1994 **PB:** Stratford **SC:** Ontario Canada **PT:** Son of Jeremy Jack Bieber and Patricia Lynn Mallette. **CIV:** Spokesman, manager Guatemala campaign, Pencils of Promise, Schools4All, **CW:** Singer: (albums) My World, 2009, My World 2.0, 2010 (Choice Music: Pop Album, Teen Choice Awards, 2010, Favorite Pop/Rock Album, American Music Awards, 2010, Top Pop Album, Billboard Music Awards, 2011), Under the Mistletoe, 2011, Believe, 2012 (Favorite Pop/Rock Album, American Music Awards, 2012), Believe Acoustic, 2013, Journals, 2013, Purpose, 2015, (songs) (featuring Ludacris) Baby, 2010 (Favorite Song, Nickelodeon Kids' Choice Awards, 2011), (featuring Rascal Flatts) That Should Be Me, 2010 (Collaborative Video of Year, CMT Music Awards, 2011), Boyfriend, 2012 (Choice Single by a Male Artist, Teen Choice Awards, 2012), (featuring Skrillex and Diplo) Where Are Ü Now, 2015 (Collaboration of Year, American Music Awards, 2015, Best Dance Recording, Grammy Awards, 2016), What Do You Mean?, 2015 (Favorite Song, People's Choice Awards, 2016); TV appearances True Jackson, VP, 2009, School Gyrls, 2010, CSI: Crime Scene Investigation, 2010-11, The Simpsons (voice), 2013, Repeat After Me, 2015; author: First Step 2 Forever: My Story, 2010; featured in (documentaries) Justin Bieber: Never Say Never, 2011, Justin Bieber's Believe, 2013, Behaving Badly, 2014, Zoolander, 2, Killing Hasselhoff, 2017 **AW:** Named Top Male Artist, Billboard Music Awards, 2016, 2013, Top Social Artist, 2016, 2015, 2014, 2013, 2012, Top New Artist, 2011, Favorite Male Singer, Nickelodeon Kids' Choice Awards, 2011, Best New Artist, MTV Video Music Awards, 2010, T-Mobile Breakthrough Artist, American Music Awards, 2010, Favorite Pop/Rock Male Artist, 2012, 2010, Artist of Year, 2012, 2010, Choice Male Music Star of the Summer, Teen Choice Awards, 2012, Choice Male Fashion Icon, 2012, Choice Music: Breakout Artist Male, 2010, Choice Male Artist, 2012, 2010; named one of The 10 Most Fascinating People of 2010, Barbara Walters Special; recipient Milestone award, Billboard Music Awards, 2013, The 100 Most Influential People in the World, TIME magazine, 2011, Best Male Video, MTV Video Music Awards, 2011, American Music Awards, Favorite Pop Song, 2016, Video of the Year, 2016, Favorite Pop Album, 2016, Favorite Rap Song, 2017, Favorite Pop Song, 2017

BIGELOW, KATHRYN, T: Director **I:** Media & Entertainment **DOB:** 06/13/1905 **PB:** San Carlos, California **SC:** San Carlos, California **PT:** Daughter of Ronald Elliot and Gertrude Kathryn (Larson) Bigelow; **ED:** Student, Columbia University School Film; Student, Whitney Museum Ind. Study Program; Student, San Francisco Art Institute **C:** Former Gap model, **CW:** Director, writer (films) The Loveless, 1982, Near Dark, 1987, Blue Steel, 1990, director, producer K-19: The Widowmaker, 2002, The Hurt Locker, 2008 (Best Director, Boston Society Film Critics, 2009, Best Director, New York Film Critics Cir., 2009, Best Director, National Society Film Critics, 2010, Critics' Choice award for Best Directing, Broadcast Film Critics Association, 2010, Critics' Choice award for Best Picture, 2010, Darryl F. Zanuck Producer of Year award in Theatrical Motion Pictures, Producers Guild America, 2010, Outstanding Directorial Achievement in Feature Film, Directors Guild America, 2010, Best Film, Brit. Academy Film & TV Arts, 2010, Academy award for Best Picture, 2010, Academy award for Best Director, 2010), Zero Dark Thirty, 2012 (Best Director, Best Picture, New York Film Critics Cir., 2012, Best Director, Best Picture, National Board Review, 2012, Best

Director, Best Picture, Boston Society Film Critics, 2012, Best Picture, African American Film Critics Association, 2012), Last Days, 2014, Detroit, 2017; dir.: (films) Point Break, 1991, Strange Days, 1995, The Set Up, 1998, The Weight of Water, 2003; (TV series) Homicide Life on the Street, 1998, Karen Sisco, 2004; (TV miniseries) Wild Palms, 1993; writer (TV films) Undertow, 1996, (TV series) The Equalizer, 1985, director, executive producer (TV films) The Miraculous Year, 2011; actress: (films) Born in Flames, 1983 **AW:** Named one of The 100 Most Influential People in the World, TIME magazine, 2010

BIGGS, ANDY, T: U.S. Representative from Arizona **I:** Government Administration/Government Relations/Government Services **ED:** JD, University of Arizona; MA in Political Sci., Arizona State University; Bachelor in Asian Studies, Brigham Young University **C:** Member U.S. House of Representatives from Arizona's 5th District, 2017-; Member District 22, Arizona State Senate, 2011-2017; Member ways & means committee, Arizona House of Reps.; Vice chair appropriations committee, Arizona House of Reps.; Chair transportation & infrastructure committee, Arizona House of Reps.; Member District 22, Arizona House of Reps., 2003-11; Retired attorney **AW:** Named a Friend of Liberty, Goldwater Institute; named #1 Friend of Taxpayer, Arizona Federation Taxpayers **BAR:** Bar: Arizona, Washington, New Mexico **PA:** Republican **BA:** 1626 Longworth House Office Building, Washington, DC, 20515

BILES, SIMONE, T: Professional Gymnast **I:** Athletics **PB:** Columbus **SC:** OH/USA **CW:** (Books) The Simone Biles Story: Courage to Soar **AW:** (Rio Olympics) 4 Gold Medals And One Bronze Gymnastics, 2016, (World Championships), 10 Gold Medals, 2 Silver Medals, 2 Bronze Medals, (Pacific Rim Championships) 2 Gold Medals(National Championships)11 Gold Medals, 6 Silvers Medals, Time 100 Most Influential, 2017 **ACH:** Three-Time World Champion, 2013-15; Three-Time World Floor Champion, 2013-15; Two-Time World Balance Beam Champion, 2013-16

BILIRAKIS, GUS MICHAEL, T: U.S. Representative from Florida, lawyer **I:** Government Administration/Government Relations/Government Services **DOB:** 02/08/1963 **PB:** Gainesville **PT:** Son of Michael Bilirakis; **ED:** JD, Stetson University College Law, DeLand, Florida, 1989; BA, University Florida, 1986 **C:** Member, US Congress from 12th Florida District, 2013-; Member, Committee on Energy and Commerce, Committee on Veterans' Affairs; Senior whip, US Congress from 9th Florida District, 2006-08; Member, US Congress from 9th Florida District, Washington, 2007-13; Member District 48, Florida House of Reps, 1999-2006; Attorney, Bilirakis Law Group, Holiday, Florida, **CR:** Member Pinellas County Republican Executive Committee, 1996- adjunct professor St. Petersburg Junior College, 1997 staff member, Rep. Don Sundquist US House of Representatives intern to President Ronald Reagan The White House **MEM:** Mem.: West Pasco Chamber of Commerce, Tarpon Springs Chamber of Commerce, Palm Harbor Chamber of Commerce, Clearwater Bar Association, American Hellenic Education Progressive Association, Tarpon Springs Rotary, Masons, Elks, Moose Lodge **PA:** Republican

BIRD, LARRY JOE, T: Professional Sports Team Executive, Retired Professional Basketball Player **I:** Athletics **DOB:** 12/07/1956 **PB:** West Baden **PT:** Son of Joe and Georgia B; Married Dinah Mattingly October 1, 1989; children: Corrie, Connor. **ED:** LittD (hon.), Boston University, 2009; BS, Ind. State

University, 1979; Student, Northwood Institute, West Baden, Ind., 1974; Student, Ind. University, 1974 **C:** President basketball operations, Ind. Pacers, 2013-17; President basketball operations, Ind. Pacers, 2003-12; Head coach, Ind. Pacers, Indianapolis, 1997-2000; Special assistant to executive vice president, Boston Celtics, 1992-97; Forward, Boston Celtics, 1979-92 **CR:** Member US men's basketball team Summer Olympic Games, Barcelona, 1992, World Univ. Games, Sophia, Bulgaria, 1977 **CW:** Co-author: (with Bob Ryan) Drive, 1989, (with Magic Johnson and J. MacMullan) When the Game Was Ours, 2009; actor (film) Blue Chips, 1994. **AW:** Recipient Gold medal, men's basketball World Univ. Games, 1977, Summer Olympic Games, 1992, John R. Wooden award, 1979; named 1st Team All-Am. Associated Press, 1978, 1979, Naismith Men's College Player of Year, 1979, NCAA Player of Year, Associated Press, United Press International, National Association Coaches, 1979, NBA Rookie of Year, 1980, 1st Team All-NBA, 1980-88, NBA All-Star Game MVP, 1982, NBA Finals MVP, 1984, 1986, NBA MVP, 1984-86, NBA Coach of Year, 1998, NBA Executive of Year, 2012; named to NBA All-Rookie Team, 1980, Eastern Conference All-Star Team, 1980-88, 1990-92, Naismith Memorial Basketball Hall of Fame, 1998, National Collegiate Basketball Hall of Fame, 2009; named one of 50 Greatest Players in NBA History, 1996. **ACH:** Achievements include member of NBA Championship winning Boston Celtics, 1981, 1984, 1986; leading the NBA in: free throw percentage, 1984, 1986, 1987, 1990; 3-point field goal attempts, 1986; 3-point field goals made, 1986, 1987

BISCIOTTI, STEPHEN J., T: Staffing Company Executive, Professional Sports Team Executive **I:** Staffing and Recruiting **DOB:** 04/10/1960 **PB:** Philadelphia **SC:** PA/USA **PT:** Bernard Bisciotti, Patricia Bisciotti **ED:** BA, Salisbury State University, MD (1982) **C:** Owner, Baltimore Ravens (2004-Present); Minority Owner, Baltimore Ravens (2000-2004); Chairman, Allegis Group, Inc. (Formerly Aerotek); Co-founder (with Jim Davis), Allegis Group, Inc. (Formerly Aerotek) **CIV:** Board of Directors, Mother Seton Academy, Baltimore, MD; Board of Directors, Catholic Charities **AW:** Named one of Forbes 400: Richest Americans (2006-Present) **H:** Golf; Boating

BISHOP, MICHAEL D., T: U.S. Representative from Michigan **I:** Government Administration/Government Relations/Government Services **DOB:** 03/18/1967 **PB:** March 18, 1967 **ED:** JD, Detroit College Law, 1993; BA, University Michigan, 1989 **CT:** Bar: US Supreme Court, DC, Michigan; lic. real estate broker **C:** Member, U.S. House of Representatives Michigan's 8th District,2015-; Member, Committee on Education and the Workforce; Member, Committee on the Judiciary; Member, Committee on Ways and Means,; Member, Republican Study Committee; Senior counsel, Clark Hill PLC, Birmingham, Michigan, 2011-; Attorney, Booth Patterson, PC, 1995-; President, owner, Freedom Realty, Inc., 1995-; President, owner, Pro Management, Inc., 1994-; Majority leader, Michigan State Senate, 2006-11; Member District 12, Michigan State Senate, 2003-11; Member District 45, Michigan House of Reps., Lansing, 1999-2002; Private practice attorney, 1993-95; Teacher, constitutional law, Detroit Cooley HS, 1992; Congressional campaign treasurer, Republican Party, 1993-95; Precinct del., Republican Party, 1991-94; Congressional campaign manager, Republican Party, 1991-92; Judicial externship, Oakland County 6th Cir. Court, 1991-92; Judicial clerk, Hon. Richard Kuhn, Oakland County 6th Cir. Court, 1991; Legal research & writing assistant, Oakland County 6th Cir. Court, 1990-92; Friend of court, Oakland County 6th Cir. Court, 1990; Law clerk, Oakland County 6th Cir. Court, 1989; Football recruiter, University Michigan Wolverines, 1987-88;

Legis. aide, Senator Richard Fessler, Michigan State Senate, Lansing, 1985-86 **CIV:** Member, Michigan Republican State Committee, 1995- **AW:** Named one of The 40 Under 40, Crain's Detroit Business, 2006 **MEM:** Mem.: American Bar Association, Macomb County Bar Association, Oakland County Bar Association, tate Bar Michigan, Michigan Association Realtors, Sports Lawyers Association **PA:** Republican

BISHOP, ROB, T: Chairman of the US House Natural Resources Committee **I:** Government Administration/Government Relations/Government Services **DOB:** 07/31/1951 **PB:** Kaysville **SC:** UT/USA **ED:** BA in Political Science, University of Utah, Salt Lake City, Utah (1974) **C:** Chairman, US House Natural Resources Committee (2015-Present); Member, US Congress from the First Utah District (2003-Present); Chairman, Utah Republican Party (1997-2001); Speaker, Utah House of Representatives (1992-1994); Minority Leader, Utah House of Representatives (1990-1992); Member, District 2, Utah House of Representatives (1982-1994); Member, District 61, Utah House of Representatives (1978-1982); Teacher, Debate Coach, Ben Lomond High School, Orden, Utah (1980-1985); Teacher, Box Elder High School (1985-2002); Teacher, Box Elder High School, Brigham City, Utah (1974-1980) **CR:** Co-founder, Member, Executive Board, Western States Coalition (1994); Chair, Utah State Convention (1990); Chairman, Utah Speech Arts Association (1981-1984); Member, Utah Speech Arts Association (1975-1987) **CIV:** Chairman, Brigham City Community Theater; Member, Brigham City Heritage Alliance Committee; Member, Brigham City Historical Preservation Committee **PA:** Republican **BA:** Office of Rob Bishop, 123 Cannon Building, Washington, DC, 20515

BISHOP, SANFORD DIXON JR., T: U.S. Representative from Georgia **I:** Government Administration/Government Relations/Government Services **DOB:** 02/04/1947 **PB:** Mobile **SC:** AL/USA **PT:** Sanford Bishop; Minnie Bishop **ED:** JD, Emory University (1971); BA in Political Science, Morehouse College (1968) **C:** Member, US Congress from the Second Georgia District (1993-Present); Member Appropriations Committee, US Congress from the Second Georgia District; Member, Georgia State Senate (1991-1992); Member, Georgia House of Representatives from the 94th District (1977-1990); Partner, Bishop & Buckner, Professional Corporation, Columbus, GA (1972-1992) **CR:** Delegate, Democratic National Convention (1980, 1984, 1988) **AW:** Named Man of the Year, Men's Progressive Club Columbus, GA (1977); Black Georgian of the Year (1983); Named One of the Most Influential Black Men in Georgia; Outstanding Legislator Award, Georgia National Organization of Women (1983-1984); Legislator Service Award, Georgia Municipal Association (1984, 1986); Friend of the Children Award, Child Advocate Coalition; Distinguished Eagle Scout Award; Earl Warren Fellow (1971-1972); Named One of the Most Influential Black Americans, Ebony Magazine (2006); Named to Power 150, Ebony Magazine (2008) **MEM:** ABA; National Bar Association; Georgia Bar Association; Alabama Bar Association; American Judicature Society; Shriners; 32nd Degree, Masons; Phi Delta Phi; Pi Sigma Alpha; Kappa Alpha Psi; Sigma Pi Phi **PA:** Democrat **BA:** Albany Towers Ste 114, 235 Roosevelt Ave, Albany, GA, 31701

BISIGNANO, FRANK, T: CEO **I:** Business Management/Business Services **CN:** First Data Corp. **PB:** Brooklyn **SC:** NY/USA **ED:** Newport University; University of Kansas **C:** Chairman, First Data Holdings Inc, 2014-; CEO, First Data Holdings Inc, 2013-14; Co-Chief Operating Officer, JP Morgan

Chase & Co, 2012-13; CAO/CEO: Mortgage Banking, JP Morgan Chase & Co, 2011-12; CAO, JPMorgan Chase & Co, 2005-11

BITZER, MARC R., T: Appliance Company Executive **I:** Business Management/Business Services **ED:** MBA, St. Gallen Grad. School Business, Economics and Law; PhD, St. Gallen Grad. School Business, Economics and Law **C:** CEO, Whirlpool Corp., 2017-; President, COO, Whirlpool Corp., 2015-2017;; Executive vice president, president, North America, Whirlpool Corp., 2010-2015; President, US Operations, Whirlpool Corp., 2008-10; President, Whirlpool Europe, 2006-08; Senior vice president, marketing sales and services, Whirlpool Europe, 2000-06; Vice president, Bauknecht Brand Group, Whirlpool Europe, 1999; Manager, vice president, Boston Consulting Group, Inc., 1999; With, Boston Consulting Group, Inc., Munich, 1991; With, W.L. Gore & Associates, Munich,; With, Institute Management, St. Gallen, Switzerland,; With, Simex Trading Air Corps, Gais, Switzerland,

BLACK, CLINT, T: Country Singer, Musician **I:** Media & Entertainment **DOB:** 02/04/1962 **PB:** Long Branch **SC:** NJ/USA **MS:** Married **SPN:** Lisa Hartman, (1991) **CH:** 1 daughter **CW:** Singles include Nobody's Home, A Better Man, Killin' Time, Put Yourself in my Shoes; albums: Killin' Time, 1989, Put Yourself in My Shoes, 1990, The Hard Way, 1992, No Time to Kill, 1993, One Emotion, 1994, Looking for Christmas, 1995, Nothin' but the Taillights, 1997, D'Lectrified, 1999, Spend My Time, 2004, Christmas with You, 2004, Drinkin Songs and Other Logic, 2005, On Purpose, 2015,(Film) Flicka: Country Pride, 2012, Flicka 2, 2010, Anger Management, 2003, Going Home 2000 **AW:** Recipient Country Music Association awards: Horizon award, 1989, Best Male Vocalist, 1990, Best New Touring Artist, 1990; recipient Academy of Country Music awards: Best Album (Killin'Time) 1990, Best Single (Nobody's Home) 1990, Best New Male Vocalist, 1990, Best Male Vocalist, 1990, Vocal Event of the Year, 1993, 1999; Grammy nomination, Best Country Vocal Collaboration for "A Bad Goodbye" (with Wynonna Judd), Grammy award, Best Country Collaboration With Vocals for song "Same Old Train", 1998.

BLACK, DIANE LYNN, T: Chair of the House Budget Committee **I:** Government Administration/Government Relations/Government Services **DOB:** 01/16/1951 **PB:** Baltimore **ED:** BSN, Belmont University, Nashville, 1991; Associate Degree in Nursing, Anne Arundel College, Annapolis, Maryland, 1971 **CT:** RN **C:** Chair, US House Budget Committee, 2017-2018; Member, US House Ways & Means Committee, Washington, 2011-; Member, US House Budget Committee, Washington, 2011-; Member, US Congress from 6th Tennessee District, Washington, 2011-; Republican Caucus chairman, Tennessee State Senate, Nashville, 2008-11; Member District 18, Tennessee State Senate, Nashville, 2005-10; Member District 45, Tennessee House of Reps., Nashville, 1999-2005; Executive director, Summer Regional Health Systems Foundation, Gallatin, Tennessee, 1993-98; Assistant professor allied health, Vol. State Community College, Gallatin, Tennessee, 1988-93 **CIV:** Past chair, Sumner County United Way, Past vice president, Sumner County Habitat for Humanity, President, Hendersonville Rotary Foundation, Past board directors, Sumner County chapter Am. Heart Association, Past board directors, Sumner County chapter American Red Cross, Past board directors, Sumner County YMCA, Board directors, Children Are People, Inc., Board directors, Vol. State Community College Foundation, Board of directors, Tennessee Center Nursing **AW:**

Named Legislator of Year, Tennessee Association Assessing Officers, 2008, American Heart Association, 2008, Junior Leagues Tennessee, 2008, Tennessee Devel. District Association, 2008, Tennessee Nurse Association, 2005, Tennessee Right to Life, 2004, American Cancer Society, 2003, Vol. of Year, Sumner County YMCA, 2001; named an Outstanding State Senator, County Officials Association Tennessee, 2005; recipient Guardian of Small Business award, National Federation Ind. Business, 2008, Hon. Chair award, Tennessee Association Homes & Services for Aging, 2008, Champions for Seniors in Assisted Living award, Assisted Living Federation America, 2008, Statesman award, Tennessee Home Education Association, 2008, State Pub. Policy Leadership award, American Diabetes Association, 2007 **MEM:** Mem.: Hendersonville League Women Voters, Leadership Sumner Alumni Association (past president, Distinguished Alumni award 1998), Gallatin Toastmasters, Hendersonville Rotary Club (Rotarian of Year 1993) **PA:** Republican

BLACK, JACK, T: Actor, Singer **I:** Media & Entertainment **PB:** Santa Monica **SC:** CA/USA **PT:** Thomas Black; Judith Cohen **ED:** Student, UCLA **C:** Member, The Actors Gang, LA **CW:** Actor: (films) Bob Roberts, 1992, Airborne, 1993, Demolition Man, 1993, The Never Ending Story III, 1994, Blind Justice, 1994, Dead Man Walking, 1995, Bye Bye Love, 1995, Waterworld, 1995, Crossworlds, 1996, Bio-Dome, 1996, The Cable Guy, 1996, The Fan, 1996, Mars Attacks!, 1996, The Jackal, 1997, Johnny Skidmarks, 1998, I Still Know What You Did Last Summer, 1998, Bongwater, 1998, Enemy of the State, 1998, Cradle Will Rock, 1999, The Love Letter, 1999, Jesus' Son, 1999, High Fidelity, 2000, Frank's Book, 2001, Saving Silverman, 2001, Shallow Hal, 2001, Ron Ronnie Run, 2002, Orange County, 2002, (voice) Ice Age, 2002, Tenacious D: The Complete Masterworks, 2003, Melvin Goes to Dinner, 2003, The School of Rock, 2003, Envy, 2004, Anchorman: The Legend of Ron Burgundy, 2004, (voice) Shark Tale, 2004, King Kong, 2005, Danny Roane: First Time Director, 2006, Nacho Libre, 2006, The Holiday, 2006, Margot at the Wedding, 2007, Be Kind Rewind, 2008, (voice) Kung Fu Panda, 2008, Tropic Thunder, 2008, Year One, 2009, (voice) Kung Fu Panda 2, 2011, Bernie, 2011, The Big Year, 2011, (voice) Goosebumps, 2015, Kung Fu Panda 3, 2016, Kung Fu Panda: Secrets of the Scroll, 2016, The Polka King, 2017, Jumanji: Welcome to the Jungle, 2017, Don't Worry, He Won't Get Far on Foot, 2018, Unexpected Race, 2018, The House with a Clock in Its Walls, 2018; actor, writer (films) Tenacious D: The Pick of Destiny, 2006, actor, producer Gulliver's Travels, 2010, The D Train, 2015; executive prodr.: (films) Wizard's Way, 2013, Entertainment, 2015; actor: (TV films) Our Shining Moment, 1991, Marked for Murder, 1993, The Innocent, 1994, Heat Vision and Jack, 1999, Lord of the Piercing, 2002, Jack Black: Spider-Man, 2002; actor, executive producer (TV films) Shredd, 2011, actor, producer My Life as an Experiment, 2011; actor: (TV series) Tenacious D, 1999, Computerman, 2003, (voice) Crank Yankers, 2002; actor, producer (TV series) The Brink, 2015; actor: (TV appearances) The Golden Palace, 1991, Life Goes On, 1993, Northern Exposure, 1993, All-American Girl, 1995, Pride & Joy, 1995, The X Files, 1995, Touched By an Angel, 1995, The Single Guy, 1995, Picket Fences, 1995, Mr. Show with Bob and David, 1996, Clone High, 2002, Will & Grace, 2003, Player$, 2003, Cracking Up, 2004, Tom Goes to the Mayor, 2004, Acceptable TV, 2007, The Naked Trucker and T-Bones Show, 2007, The Simpsons, 2007, Sesame Street, 2008, The Office, 2009, Yo Gabba Gabba, 2009, Community, 2010, ICarly, 2010, Comedy Bang! Bang!, 2012, Drunk History, 2013, Metalocalypse: The Doomstar Requiem, 2013, Workaholics, 2015, The Brink, 2015, Documentary

Now!, 2015, Panda Republic,2016, Great Minds with Dan Harmon, 2017, The Last Man on Earth, 2017; singer, songwriter with Tenacious D: albums Tenacious D, 2001; singer, songwriter with Tenacious D (albums) The Pick of Destiny, 2006, Rize of the Fenix, 2012 (Grammy award for Best Metal Performance for The Last In Line, 2015); actor((voice)): (video game) Brutal Legend, 2009

BLACK, LEWIS, **T:** Comedian **I:** Media & Entertainment **PB:** Silver Spring **SC:** MD/USA **PT:** Sam Black; Jeannette Black **ED:** MFA in Drama, Yale University, 1977; BA, University North Carolina, Chapel Hill, 1970 **C:** Comedian, Actor, 1986- **CW:** Actor: (films) Hannah and Her Sisters, 1986, Jacob's Ladder, 1990, The Hard Way, 1991, Joey Breaker, 1993, The Night We Never Met, 1993, Sidesplitters: The Burt & Dick Story, 2000, American Dummy, 2002, The Gynecologists, 2003, Accepted, 2006, Man of the Year, 2006, Unaccompanied Minors, 2006, Peep World (narrator), 2010, Inside Out (voice), 2015, Stereotypically You, 2015; (TV series) Scooby-Doo! Mystery Incorporated (voice), 2010-13; writer, producer (films) The Deal, 1998, contributor (TV series) The Daily Show, 1996-, comedian, writer (TV specials) Comedy Central Presents: Lewis Black, 2000, 2002, comedian, writer, producer Lewis Black: Taxed Beyond Belief, 2002, Lewis Black: Black on Broadway, 2004, Lewis Black: Red, White and Screwed, 2006, comedian, writer, executive producer In God We Rust, 2012, Lewis Black: Old Yeller - Live at the Borgata, 2014, host (TV series) Root of All Evil, 2008; author: (autobiography) Nothing's Sacred, 2005, Me of Little Faith, 2008, I'm Dreaming of a Black Christmas, 2010; performer: (comedy albums) The White Album, 2000, The End of the Universe, 2002, Rules of Enragement, 2003, Luther Burbank Performing Arts Center Blues, 2005, The Carnegie Hall Performance, 2006 (Grammy award for Best Comedy Album, 2007), Anticipation, 2008, Stark Raving Black, 2010 (Grammy award for Best Comedy Album, 2011), The Prophet, 2011, (Film) Rock Dog, 2016, The Last Laugh, 2018,(Television) Robotomy, 2011, The Penguins of Madagascar, 2011, Teenage Mutant Ninja Turtles, 2012, Madoff, 2016, Crisis in Six Scenes, 2016 **AW:** Named Funniest Male Stand-Up Comic, American Comedy Awards, 2001

BLACKBURN, ELIZABETH HELEN, **T:** Molecular Biologist **I:** Sciences **DOB:** 11/26/1948 **PB:** Hobart **SC:** Tasmania, Australia **PT:** Harold; Marcia **ED:** PhD in Molecular and Cellular Biology, Yale University, New Haven, CT (1977); PhD in Molecular Biology, University of Cambridge, England (1975); MSc in Biochemistry, University of Melbourne, Australia (1972); BSc in Biochemistry, University of Melbourne, Australia (1970) **C:** President, Salk Institute (2016-Present); Professor, Department of Microbiology and Immunology, Department of Biochemistry and Biophysics, University of California, San Francisco (1990-Present); Chair, Department of Microbiology and Immunology, University of California, San Francisco (1993-1999); Professor, University of California, Berkeley (1986-1990); Associate Professor, University of California, Berkeley (1983-1986); Assistant Professor, Department of Molecular Biology, University of California, Berkeley (1978-1983); Postdoctorate Fellow, Biochemistry, University of California, San Francisco (1977-1978); Postdoctorate Fellow, Department of Biology, Yale University (1975-1977); Researcher, Medical Research Council, Laboratory Molecular Biology, Cambridge, England (1971-1974); Morris Herzstein Endowed Chair of Biology and Physiology, University of California, San Francisco **CR:** Member, Science Advisory Board, Huntsman Cancer Research Institute,

University of Utah (2003-Present); Non-resident Fellow, Salk Institute of Biological Studies, La Jolla, CA (2001-Present); Fred Hutchinson Cancer Research Center (2001-Present); Walter & Eliza Hall Institute of Medical Research (1998-Present); Member, National Institutes of Health, National Advisory Council on Aging (2003-2006); Presidential Council of Bioethics (2002-2004); Member, Advisory Panel on Cell Biology, National Science Foundation (1982-1985) **CW:** Member, Editorial Board, Molecular & Cellular Biology (1988-Present); Member, Editorial Board, Nucleic Acids Research (2003-2005); Associate Editor, Molecular Biology of the Cell (1992-2004); Member, Editorial Board, Journal of Eukaryotic Microbiology (1992-1998); Associate Editor, Journal of Protozoology (1988-1991); Member, Editorial Board, Journal of Cell Biology (1985-1988); Member, Editorial Board, Science (1985-1988); Contributor, Articles to Professional Journals **AW:** Eli Lilly Research Award (1988); AIC Gold Medal (2012); Paul Ehrlich & Ludwig Darmstaedler Prize, Germany (2009); Pearl Meister Greengard Prize (2009); Nobel Prize in Physiology/Medicine (2009); Medicine & Biomedical Research Prize, Albany Medical Center (2008); L'Oréal-UNESCO Award for Women in Science (2008); Women & Science Award, Weizmann Institute of Science (2008); Louisa Gross Horwitz Prize, Columbia University (2007); Named One of the 100 Most Influential People in the World, TIME Magazine (2007); Vanderbilt Prize in Biomedical Science (2007); Albert Lasker Award for Basic Medical Research (2006); Genetics Prize, Peter Gruber Foundation (2006); Benjamin Franklin Medal for Life Sciences, Franklin Institute (2005); Dr. A.H. Heineken Prize for Medicine (2004); Robert J. & Claire Pasarow Foundation Medical Research Award (2003); Bristol-Myers Squibb Award for Distinguished Achievement in Cancer Research (2003); Alfred P. Sloan Junior Prize, GM Cancer Research Foundation (2001); International Award for Cancer Research, Pezcoller Foundation/ American Association for Cancer Research (2001); E.B. Wilson Medal, American Society of Cell Biology (2001); G.H.A. Clowes Memorial Award, American Association for Cancer Research (2000); American Cancer Society Medal of Honor (2000); Dickson Prize for Medicine (2000); Feodor Lynen Award (2000); Rosenstiel Award, Brandeis University (1999); Named California Scientist of the Year (1999); Novartis-Drew Award for Biomedical Science (1999); Passano Foundation Award (1999); Baxter Award, Association of American Medical Colleges (1999); Harvey Prize, Technion-Israel Institute of Technology (1999); Keio University of Medical Science Fund Prize (1999); Australia Prize (1998); Gairdner Foundation International Award (1998); Molecular Biology Award, National Academy of Sciences (1990) **MEM:** Board of Directors, Genetic Society of America (2000-2002); President, American Society of Cell Biology (1998); Fellow, American Association for the Advancement of Science; Fellow, American Academy of Arts & Sciences; Fellow, Royal Society of London; Foreign Associate, National Academy of Sciences; Institute of Medicine; American Academy of Microbiology; Harvey Society of New York **ACH:** Achievements include discovery of structures called telomeres on the tips of chromosomes which hold them together; discovery of an enzyme called telomerase, the enzyme that restores the ends of chromosomes by replenishing telomeres, which are the protective caps that seal off these chromosome ends

BLACKBURN, MARSHA, **T:** U.S. Representative from Tennessee **I:** Government Administration/ Government Relations/Government Services **DOB:** 06/06/1952 **PB:** Laurel **SC:** MS/USA **ED:** BS,

Mississippi State University (1973) **C:** Member, US Congress from the Seventh Tennessee District (2003-Present); Member, Committee on Energy and Commerce; Republican Study Committee; Republican Congressional Committee; Owner, Marketing Strategies, Williamson County, TN (1978-Present); Member, District 23, Tennessee State Senate, Nashville, TN (1998-2002); Director, Retail Fashion, Caster Knott Co., Nashville, TN (1975-1978) **CR:** Executive Director, Tennessee Film, Entertainment & Music Commission (1995-1997) **CIV:** Board of Directors, Arthritis Foundation; Board of Directors, Nashville Symphony Guild **AW:** Spirit of Enterprise Award, US Chamber of Commerce (2004) **MEM:** American Council of Young Political Leaders; National Association of Retail Merchants; Foundation of Women Legislators; Country Music Association **PA:** Republican

BLAIR, BONNIE KATHLEEN, **T:** Former Professional Speedskater, Olympic athlete **I:** Athletics **DOB:** 03/18/1964 **PB:** Cornwall **PT:** Daughter of Charlie and Eleanor Blair; Married David Cruikshank; 1 child, Grant B. Cruikshank **ED:** Student, Montana Tech. Univ. **C:** Motivational speaker, 1995-; Retired from competitive speedskating, 1995; Pro tour speedskater, 1994-95; Gold medalist, 1000m Speedskating, Lillehammer Olympic Games, 1994; Gold medalist, 500m Speedskating, Lillehammer Olympic Games, 1994; Gold medalist, 1000m Speedskating, Albertville Olympic Games, 1992; Gold medalist, 500m Speedskating, Albertville Olympic Games, 1992; Gold medalist, 500m Speedskating, Bronze medalist 1,000m, Calgary Olympic Games, 1988; Member, U.S. Olympic Team, Sarajevo, Yugoslavia, 1984 **CR:** Active fundraiser Am. Brain Tumor Association founder Bonnie Blair Charitable Fund motivational speaker ABC sports commentator **CW:** Author: Bonnie Blair: A Winning Edge **AW:** Recipient James E. Sullivan award for Outstanding U.S. amateur athlete, 1993, Sportwoman of the Year, Sports Illustrated, 1994; named Female Athlete of Year, Associated Press, 1994; inducted into National Speedskating Hall of Fame, International Women's Sports Hall of Fame, US Olympic Hall of Fame,Chicagoland Sports Hall of Fame, Wisconsin Athletic Hall of Fame. Oscar Mathisen Award, 1992 **ACH:** Achievements include 1st American woman in any sport to win gold medals in consecutive Winter Olympics; 1st American speedskater to win a gold medal in more than one Olympics. Most decorated female Olympian of all time – five gold medals, six total.

BLANCHETT, CATE, **T:** Actress **I:** Media & Entertainment **DOB:** 05/14/1969 **PB:** Victoria **SC:** Australia **PT:** Robert Blanchett; June Blanchett **ED:** Coursework, National Institute of Dramatic Art, Australia (1992) **C:** Joint Artistic Director, Australia's Sydney Theatre Company (2006-Present); Performer, Belvoir St. Theatre Company; Performer, Sydney Theatre Company **CW:** Actress, "Where's You Go, Bernadette" (2018); Actress, "Ocean's 8" (2018); Actress, "The House with a Clock in its Walls" (2018); Actress, "Mowgli" (2018); Actress, "Thor Ragnarok" (2017); Actress, "Song to Song" (2017); Actress, "Manifesto" (2016); Actress, "Voyage of Time" (2016); Actress, Executive Producer, "Carol" (2015); Actress, "Cinderella" (2015); Actress, "Knight of Cups" (2015); Actress, "Truth" (2015); Voice Actress, "How to Train Your Dragon 2" (2014); Actress, "The Hobbit: The Battle of the Five Armies" (2014); Actress, "Rake" (2014); Actress, "Blue Jasmine" (2013); Actress, Director, "The Turning" (2013); Actress, "The Turning" (2013); Actress, "The Hobbit: The Desolation of Smaug" (2013); Actress, "The Hobbit: An Unexpected Journey" (2012); Actress, "Uncle Vanya" (2011); Actress, "Hanna" (2011); Actress, "The Last Tiem I

Saw Michael Gregg" (2011); Actress, "Robin Hood" (2010); Actress, "A Streetcar Named Desire" (2009); Actress, "Indiana Jones and the Kingdom of the Crystal Skull" (2008); Actress, "The Curious Case of Benjamin Button" (2008); Actress, "Hot Fuzz" (2007); Actress, "I'm Not There" (2007); Actress, "Elizabeth: The Golden Age" (2007); Actress, "Hedda Gabler" (2006); Actress,"Babel" (2006); Actress, "Notes on a Scandal" (2006); Actress, "The Good German" (2006); Actress, "The Life Aquatic with Steve Zissou" (2004); Actress, "The Aviator" (2004); Actress, "Little Fish" (2004); Actress, "The Lord of the Rings: The Return of the King" (2003); Actress, "The Missing" (2003); Actress, "Coffee and Cigarettes" (2003); Actress, "Veronica Guerin" (2003); Actress, "The Lord of the Rings: The Two Towers" (2002); Actress, "Heaven" (2002); Actress, "Bandits" (2001); Actress, "Charlotte Gray" (2001); Actress, "The Shipping News" (2001); Actress, "Galadriel" (2001); Actress, "The Lord of the Rings: The Fellowship of the Ring" (2001); Actress, "The Gift" (2000); Actress, "The Man Who Cried" (2000); Actress, "The Talented Mr. Ripley" (1999); Actress, "An Ideal Husband" (1999); Actress, "Pushing Tin" (1999); Actress, Producer, "Bangers" (1999); Actress, "Plenty" (1999); Actress, "Elizabeth" (1998); Actress, "Paradise Road" (1997); Actress, "Thank God He Met Lizzie" (1997); Actress, "Oscar and Lucinda" (1997); Actress, "Parklands" (1996); Actress, "Bordertown" (1995); Actress, "Hamlet" (1995); Actress, "Heartland" (1994); Actress, "Police Rescue" (1994); Actress, "Oleanna" (1993); Actress, "Kafka Dances" (1993); Actress, "Sweet Phoebe"; Actress, "The Tempest"; Actress, "The Seagull"; Actress, "The Blind Giant is Dancing"; Actress, "Top Girls" **AW:** Recipient, Golden Globe Award for Best Performance by an Actress in a Motion Picture - Drama (2014); Recipient, Critics' Choice Award for Best Actress (2014); Recipient, Award for Outstanding Performance by a Female Actor in a Leading Role, Screen Actors Guild (2014); Recipient, British Academy of Film and TV Arts Award for Best Leading Actress (2014); Recipient, Academy Award for Best Actress in a Leading Role (2014); Recipient, Golden Globe Award for Best Performance by an Actress in a Supporting Role in a Motion Picture (2008); Inductee, Hollywood Walk of Fame (2008); Named, One of the 100 Most Powerful Celebrities, Forbes. com (2007-2008); Recipient, Career Achievement Award, Palm Springs International Film Society, Palm Springs International Film Festival (2007); Named, One of the World's Most Influential People, Time Magazine (2007); Named, One of the 50 Smartest People in Hollywood, Entertainment Weekly (2007); Recipient, Academy Award for Best Performance by an Actress in a Supporting Role (2005); Recipient, British Academy Film and TV Association Award (2005); Recipient, Award for Outstanding Performance by a Female Actor in a Supporting Role, Screen Actors Guild (2005); Recipient, Outstanding Performance by a Cast in a Motion Picture, Screen Actors Guild (2004); Recipient, Award for Best Supporting Actress, National Board of Review (2001); Recipient, Golden Globe Award for Best Performance by an Actress in a Motion Picture - Drama (1999); Recipient, British Academy Film and TV Arts Award for Best Actress in Leading Role (1999); Recipient, Prestigious Helpmann Award for Best Female Actor in a Play; Recipient, Best Actress Award, Rosemont and Sydney Theater Critics Circle; Recipient, Newcomer Sydney Theatre Critics Circle Award **BA:** c/o Wolf-Kasteler Public Relations, 335 North Maple Dr Ste 351, Beverly Hills, CA, 90210-3857

BLAND, BOB, T: Activist and Fashion Designer **I:** Apparel & Fashion **ED:** Savannah College of Art and Design, Fashion Design **C:** Creator/Owner, Manu- facturing Innovation Hub for Apparel, Textiles+ Wearable Tech, 2014-; Owner, Brooklyn Royalty, 2006-13 **AW:** Time 2017 Most Influential, Fortune 50 Worlds Greatest Leaders, Glamour Women of the Year **MEM:** Co-Chair Women's March, 2017

BLANK, ARTHUR M., T: Professional Sports Team Executive, Retired Retail Executive **I:** Athletics **PB:** Queens, New York **ED:** LLD (hon.), Babson College, 1998; BS, Babson College **C:** Owner, CEO, Atlanta Falcons Football Club, 2002-; Chairman, president, CEO, AMB Group LLC, 2001-; Chairman, Arthur M. Blank Family Foundation, 1995-; Co-chmn., Home Depot Inc., Atlanta, 2000-01; President, CEO, Home Depot Inc., Atlanta, 1997-2000; President, COO, Home Depot Inc., Atlanta, 1978-97; Co-founder, Home Depot Inc., Atlanta, 1978; Vice president, treasurer, Handy Dan Home Improvement Ctrs. Inc., Los Angeles, 1974-78; With, Daylin Inc., Los Angeles, 1967-74; Accountant, Arthur Young & Co., New York City, 1963-67 **CR:** Distinguished executive in residence Goizueta Business School, Emory Univ., 2001; board directors Staples Inc., Cox Enterprises **CIV:** Board member, North Carolina Outward Bound School, Trustee, Cooper Institute, Trustee, Emory Univ., Trustee, Carter Center **AW:** Co-recipient Abe Goldstein Human Relations award, Anti-Defamation League, 2001, Georgia Philanthropist of the Year, National Society Fundraising Executive, 2000; named Georgia Most Respected CEO, Georgia Trend magazine, 2003, 2001; named one of Forbes 400: Richest Americans, 2006-, 50 Most Generous Philanthropists, BusinessWeek, 2005; named to Business Hall of Fame, Georgia State Univ., 2002, Junior Achievement Atlanta, 2001, Academy Distinguished Entrepreneurs, Babson College, 1995; recipient Brotherhood / Sisterhood award, National Conference of Christians & Jews, 1994 **MEM:** Mem.: Commerce Club

BLANKENSHIP, CHARLES P. JR., T: CEO **I:** Business Management/Business Services **CN:** Arconic Inc **ED:** PhD in Materials Sci. & Engineering, University of Virginia, 1992; BS in Materials Sci. & Engineering, Virginia Poly Institute & State University, 1988 **C:** CEO, Arconic Inc, 2018-; President, CEO, GE Appliances & Lighting, 2013-; President, CEO, GE Appliances, Louisville, 2012-13; Vice president, general manager commercial engines, GE Aviation, 2008-11; General manager Aero Energy, GE Energy, Houston, 2006-08; Staff scientist, corporate research & devel, GE Aviation, Schenectady, New York; Program manager, GE Aviation; Leader, CF6 Airline Support Engineering team, Commercial Engines, GE Aviation; Manager, CF34 EMBRAER programs, Commercial Engines, GE Aviation, GE Co.; General manager, Small Commercial Engine Operation, GE Aviation, GE Co.; General manager, Aero Energy business, GE Co. **BA:** 1 Corporate Drive, Kingston, NY, 12401

BLANKFEIN, LLOYD CRAIG, T: Goldman Sachs CEO **I:** Financial Services **DOB:** 09/20/1954 **PB:** Bronx **ED:** JD, Harvard Law School, 1978; BA, Harvard University, 1975 **C:** Chairman, CEO, Goldman Sachs Group, Inc., New York City, 2006-; President, COO, Goldman Sachs Group, Inc., New York City, 2004-06; Vice chairman, Goldman Sachs Group, Inc., New York City, 2002-04; Co-head fixed income, currency & commodities division, Goldman Sachs Group, Inc., New York City, 1997-2004; Co-head, currency & commodities division, J. Aron & Co. (subsidiary Goldman Sachs Co.), New York City, 1994-97; Gold salesman, currency & commodities division, J. Aron & Co. (subsidiary Goldman Sachs Co.), New York City, 1982; Corporate tax lawyer, Donovan, Leisure, Newton & Irvine, 1978-81 **CR:** Board of directors, Goldman Sachs Group, Inc., 2003- **CIV:** Board directors, Robin Hood Foundation, Board directors, Partnership New York City, Board overseers, Cornell University Weill Medical College, Board trustees, New York Hist. Society, Member executive committee com. on univ. resources, Harvard University, Co-chair financial aid task force, Harvard University, **AW:** Named one of The 50 Most Influential People in Global Finance, Bloomberg Markets, 2011-14, The World's Most Powerful People, Forbes magazine, 2009-14, The 25 Leaders Reshaping New York, Crain's New York magazine, 2008, The 100 Most Influential People in the World, TIME magazine, 2008, The 25 Most Powerful People in Business, Fortune Magazine, 2007 **PA:** Democrat

BLASER, MARTIN JACK, I: Medicine & Health Care **DOB:** 12/18/1948 **PB:** New York City **PT:** Son of Frederick S. and Irene J. Blaser; **SPN:** Married Ronna Wineberg, September 3, 1979 (div. 2012); Married Maria Gloria Dominguez Bello, March 1, 2013; **CH:** children: Daniel (Wineberg), Genia (Wineberg), Simo **ED:** MD, New York University, 1973; BA, University Pennsylvania, 1969 **CT:** Cert. National Board Medical Examiners **C:** Muriel and George Singer Professor, Medicine and Director, Human Microbiome Program, New York University, 2012-; Professor Department Microbiology, New York University, 2000-; Frederick H. King Professor and Chairman Department Medicine, New York University, New York City, 2000-12; Scoville Professor, Vanderbilt University, Nashville, 1989-2000; Epidemic Intelligence Service Officer, Ctrs. for Disease Control, Atlanta, 1979-81; From Assistant Professor Medicine to Associate Professor Medicine, University Colorado, Denver, 1981-89; Fellow in Infectious Diseases, University Colorado, Denver, 1977-79; Resident in Medicine, University Colorado, Denver, 1974-77; Intern in Medicine, University Colorado, Denver, 1973-74 **CR:** Chair Bacteriology Study Section National Institutes of Health, Bethesda, 1994 Guest Investigator Rockefeller University, New York City, 1987-88 Invited Professor Institute Pasteur, Paris, 1991, 92, 94, 96 Vice President Enteric Research Laboratory Inc., New York, 1988- Board Sci. Counselors, National Cancer Institute, 2005-2010 Adv. Board Clinical Research, National Institutes Health, 2009-2013 Chair 2012-2013 Speaker in Field **CW:** Editor: (book) Infections of the GI Tract, 1995, 2003; Co-editor: (book) Principles and Practice of Infectious Disease 8th Edition, 2014; Holder 25 US Patents for Bacterial Products **AW:** Recipient Young Investigator award West Society Clinical Investigation, 1989, Am. Association Cancer Research American College of Surgeons Award Cancer Epidemiology, 2003, Institute Medicine, 2011, Am. Academy Arts and Scis., 2013, Infectious Diseases Society America Alexander Fleming Award, 2014. **MEM:** Master American College of Physicians, American Public Health Association (Wade Hampton Frost award 2001); fellow Infectious Disease Society Am. (councillor 1993-96, vice president 2003, pres.-elect 2004, president 2005, Squibb award 1992), Am. Epidemiological Society, Am. Academy Microbiology (board governors, 2013-16); member Am. Board Internal Medicine (member subsplty. board infectious disease 1996-02), Association Am. Physicians, Am. Society Clinical Investigation, Am. Clinical Climate Association **H:** Hiking

BLECHARCZYK, NATHAN, T: Chief Strategy Officer of Airbnb **I:** Business Management/Business Services **PB:** U.S. **SC:** U.S. **SPN:** Elizabeth Morey Blecharczyk **ED:** B.S., Harvard University **C:** CSO, Airbnb, 2017-; CTO/Co-Founder, Airbnb, 2008-2017; Lead Developer, Batiq, 2007-08; Engineer, OPNET Technologies, 2005-07

BLIGE, MARY JAY, T: Singer, Actress **I:** Media & Entertainment **DOB:** 01/11/1971 **PB:** Yonkers, New York **PT:** Daughter of Thomas and Cora Blige; **CW:** Singer: (albums) What's the 411?, 1992, (New York Music award for Best R&B Album, 1993), My Life, 1994 (Billboard Music award for R&B Album of Year, 1995), Mary Jane, 1995, Share My World, 1997 (American Music award for Favorite R&B Album, 1998), Mary, 1999, The Tour, 1999, No More Drama, 2001, Dance For Me, 2002, Love & Life, 2003, The Breakthrough, 2005 (Favorite Album, Am. Music Awards, 2006, Billboard R&B Album of Year, 2006, Grammy awards for Best R&B Album, 2007), Reflections: A Retrospective, 2006, Mary J. Blige and Friends, 2006, Growing Pains, 2007 (Grammy award for Best Contemporary R&B Album, 2009), Stronger With Each Tear, 2009, My Life II...The Journey Continues (Act 1), 2011, A Mary Christmas, 2013, The London Sessions, 2014, Strength of a Woman, 2017; (songs) I'll Be There for You/ You're All I Need (with Method Man), 1995 (Grammy award for Best Rap Duo Performance, 1996, named one of 100 Greatest Videos Ever Made, MTV, 1999), No More Drama, 2001 (MTV Video Music award for Best R&B Video, 2002), He Think I Don't Know, 2001 (Grammy award for Best Female R&B Vocal Performance, 2003), Whenever I Say Your Name (with Sting), 2003 (Grammy award for Best Pop Collaboration With Vocals 2004), Be Without You, 2005 (BET Video of Year award, 2006, Billboard R&B Song of Year, Hot 100 Airplay Song of Year, R&B Song Airplay of Year, Videoclip of Year, 2006, Grammy awards for Best Female R&B Vocal Performance, Best R&B Song, 2007, National Association for the Advancement of Colored People Image award for Music Video, 2007), (with Chaka Khan) Disrespectful, 2007 (Grammy award for Best Duo R&B Performance with Vocals, 2008), (with Aretha Franklin) Never Gonna Break My Faith, 2007 (Grammy award for Best Gospel Performance, 2008), (with Ludacris) Runaway Love, (BET award for Best Collaboration, 2007), (with Sam Smith) Stay with Me, 2014 (National Association for the Advancement of Colored People Image award for Outstanding Duo, Group or Collaboration, 2015); (featured in album by Kendrick Lamar), Good Kid, M.A.A.D. City, 2012, actress: (films) Angel, 2001, Prison Song, 2001, I Can Do Bad All by Myself, 2009, Rock of Ages, 2012, Black Nativity, 2013,Mudbound, 2017, Sherlock Gnomes, 2018 (TV films) The Wiz Live!, 2015; actress, executive prodr.: (TV films) Betty and Coretta, 2013; guest appearances (TV series) The Jamie Foxx Show, 1998, Strong Medicine, 2001, Ghost Whisperer, 2007, Entourage, 2007, 30 Rock, 2009, Empire, 2015, Black-ish, 2015, The Wiz Live, 2015, How to Get Away with Murder, 2016; guest mentor, American Idol, 2012. **AW:** Recipient Heroes Award, RIAA, 1999, Patrick Lippert Award, Rock the Vote, 2001, Best Female R&B Award, Black Entertainment TV (BET), 2001, 2006, Favorite R&B Female Artist, Am. Music Awards, 2003, 2006, Legend Award, Vibe magazine, 2005, 9 Billboard Music Awards, including R&B Artist of Year, Female R&B Artist of Year, R&B Songs Artist & Album Artist of Year, 2006, Female Artist Award, National Association for the Advancement of Colored People Image Awards, 2007, Voice of Music Award, ACAP Rhythm & Soul Music Awards, 2007.

BLISS, CORWIN "CORRY" ALBERT, T: Campaign Manager **I:** Government Administration/ Government Relations/Government Services **PB:** Westchester County **SC:** NY/USA **MS:** Married **SPN:** Kim (Fanok) Bliss **CH:** One Son **ED:** JD, CUNY School of Law; Undergraduate Degree, Boston University **C:** Executive Director, Congressional Leadership Fund, 2016-Present; Executive

Director, American Action Network, 2016-Present; Campaign Manager, 2010-Present; Campaign Manager, Re-Election of Rob Portman to the U.S. Senate, Ohio, 2016; Campaign Manager, Pat Roberts in Kansas, 2014; Campaign Manager, Georgia Secretary of State Karen Handel Campaign, U.S. Senate, 2013; Campaign Manager, Linda McMahon Campaign, U.S. Senate in Connecticut, 2012; Campaign Manager, Gov. Brian Dubie for Governor of Vermont, 2010

BLOBEL, GÜNTER, T: Cell Biologist, Educator **I:** Education/Educational Services **DOB:** 05/21/1936 **PB:** Waltersdorf **SC:** Silesia/Germany **ED:** PhD in Oncology, University of Wisconsin, Madison, 1967; MD, University Tübingen, Germany, 1960 **C:** John D Rockefeller, Junior professor, Rockefeller University, New York City, 1992-; Professor, Rockefeller University, New York City, 1976-; Associate professor, Rockefeller University, New York City, 1973-76; Assistant professor cell biology, Rockefeller University, New York City, 1969-73; Fellow laboratory cellular biology, Rockefeller University, New York City, 1967-69 **CR:** Investigator Howard Hughes Medical Institute, Chevy Chase, Maryland, 1986- **CW:** Contributor articles to professional journals, chapters to books **AW:** Recipient Ellis Island Medal of Honor, 2000, Nobel prize in physiology/medicine, 1999, King Faisal International prize for sci., 1996, Ciba Drew award in biomed. research, 1995, Albert Lasker award for basic medical research, 1993, Max-Planck Research award, Alexander von Humboldt-Found., 1992, Waterford Bio-Med. Sci. award, 1989, Louisa Gross Horwitz prize, Columbia University, 1987, VD Mattia award, Roche Institute Molecular Biology, 1986, Warburg medal, German Biochem. Society, 1983, Gairdner Foundation International award, 1982,AACR Academy, 2014, Pour Le Merite, 2001 **MEM:** Mem.: National Academy of Sciences (US Steel award in molecular biology 1978, Richard Lounsbery award 1983), Am. Philosophical Society, Am. Society Cell Biology (president 1990, Wilson medal 1986), Am. Academy Arts & Scis., German Society Cell Biology (hon.), Japan Biochem. Society (hon.), European Molecular Biological Organization (associate)

BLOUNT, SALLY E., T: Dean **I:** Education/Educational Services **CN:** Northwestern Business School **ED:** PhD, Kellogg School of Management, Northwestern University, 1992; MS, Kellogg School of Management, Northwestern University, 1991; BS, School of Engineering & Applied Sciences, Woodrow Wilson School of International & Public Affairs, Princeton University, 1983 **C:** Michael L. Nemmers Professor of Management & Organizations, Kellogg School of Management, Northwestern University, Evanston, IL, 2010-Present; Dean, Kellogg School of Management, Northwestern University, Evanston, IL, 2010-Present; Special Advisor, President & Provost for Global Academy Integration, New York University, 2007-2010; Vice Dean, Stern School of Business, New York University, 2004-2010; Abraham L. Gitlow Professor of Management & Organization., Stern School of Business, New York University, 2004-2010; Professor of Management, Stern School of Business, New York University, 2001-2004; Associate Professor of Behavioral Science, Booth School of Business, University of Chicago, 1996-2001; Assistant Professor of Behavioral Science, Booth School of Business, University of Chicago, 1992-1996; Instructor, Research Assistant, Kellogg School of Management, Northwestern University, Evanston, IL, 1988-1992; Director of Finance & Planning, Eva Maddox Associate, Inc., Chicago, IL, 1985-1988; Associate Consultant, Boston Consulting Group, Inc., Chicago, IL, 1983-1985 **CR:**

Board of Directors, Abbott Laboratories, 2011-Present; Advisory Review Panel, Risk & Management Sciences Program, National Science Foundation, 2003-2005 **CW:** Editorial Board, International Journal of Conflict Management, 2003-2005; Contributor, Articles to Professional Journals, Chapters to Books **MEM:** Executive Board, Economic Science Association, 1997-2000; Society of Judgment & Decision Making; International Association of Conflict Management; American Psychological Society; American Psychological Association; Academy of Management **BA:** Kellogg School of Management, 2001 Sheridan Road, Evanston, IL, 60208

BLUM, JASON, T: CEO **I:** Business Management/ Business Services **CN:** Blumhouse Productions **PB:** Los Angeles **SC:** CA/USA **C:** Founder, Blumhouse Productions, 2000 **CW:** (Films) Kicking and Screaming, 1995, Hamlet, 2000, The Adventures of Tom Thumb and Thumbelina, 2002, The Fever, 2004, Griffin and Phoenix, 2006, The Darwin Awards, 2006, Graduation, 2006, Paranormal Activity, 2007, The Accidental Husband, 2008, The Reader, 2008, Tooth Fairy, 2010, Insidious, 2010, Paranormal Activity 2, 2010, Paranormal Activity 3, The FP, 2011, The Babymakers, 2012, Sinister, 2012, Lawless, 2012, The Lords of Salem, 2012, The Bay, 2012, Paranormal Activity 3, 2011, The FP, 2011, The Babymakers, 2012, Sinister, 2012, Lawless, 2012, The Lords of Salem, 2012, The Bay, 2012, Paranormal Activity 4, Dark Skies, 2013, The Purge, 2013, The Green Inferno, 2013, Insidious: Chapter 2, 2013, Plush, 2013, Best Night Ever, 2013, Paranormal Activity: The Marked Ones, 2014, Whiplash, 2014, 13 Sins, 2014, Creep, 2014, Not Safe for Work, 2014, Oculus, 2014, The Purge Anarchy, 2014, Unfriended, 2014, The Town that Dreaded Sundown, 2014, Jessabelle, 2014, Ouika, 2014, Mockingbird, 2014, Mercy, 2014, Stretch, 2014, The Boy Next Door, 2015, The Lazarus Effect, 2015, Exeter, 2015, The Gift, 2015, Sinister 2, 2015, Visions, 2015, The Visit, 2015, Curve, 2015, Martyrs, 2015(Television)Hysterical Blindness, 2002, Washingtonieene, 2009, The River,2012, Stranded, 2013, The Normal Heart, 2014,(Primetime Emmy for Outstanding Television Movie) Ascension, 2014, Eye Candy, 2015, The Jinx, 2015, Hellevator, 2015, Tremors, 2016 **AW:** Time 100 Most Influential, 2017

BLUM, ROD, T: U.S. Representative from Iowa **I:** Government Administration/Government Relations/Government Services **DOB:** 04/26/1955 **PB:** Dubuque **SC:** IA/USA **ED:** M.B.A., University of Dubuque, 1989; B.A., Loras College, 1977 **C:** Member, U.S. Representative from Iowa's 1st Congressional District, 2015-; Member, Committee on Oversight and Government Reform; Member, Committee on Small Business; Former Member, Budget Committee; Owner, Digital Canal, 2000-; CEO, Eagle Print Software, 1990-2000 **BA:** 1108 Longworth HOB, Washington, DC, 20515

BLUMENAUER, EARL, T: U.S. Representative from Oregon **I:** Government Administration/ Government Relations/Government Services **DOB:** 08/16/1948 **PB:** Portland **SC:** OR/USA **ED:** JD, Lewis & Clark College Northwestern School Law, Portland, 1976; BA in Political Sci., Lewis & Clark College, Portland, 1970 **C:** Member, US Congress from 3rd Oregon district, 1996-; Member, Committee on Ways and Means; Commissioner pub. works, Portland City Council, 1987-96; Commissioner, member governor board, Multnomah County Board Commissioners, 1979-87; Member District 11, Oregon House of Reps., 1973-79; Assistant to president, Portland State University, 1971-77 **CR:** Member Gov.'s Commission Higher Education, 1990-91 board directors Portland

Community College, 1975-81 **AW:** Named Humane Legislator of Year, Am. Humane Society, 2008, Legislator of Year, Am. Planning Association, 1999; named one of Top 25 Change Agents in Bicycling History, League Am. Bicyclists, 2005; recipient Public Ofcl.'s award, Water Environment Federation, 2006, Global Sustainability award, Institute Transportation & Devel. Policy, 2005, Pub. Radio Leadership award, National Pub. Radio, 2005, National Distinguished Service award, Am. Pub. Transit Association, 2004, Community Health Super Hero award, National Association Community Health Centers, 2002, Apgar award, National Building Museum, Washington, 2000; grantee German Marshall Fund, 1995 **MEM:** Mem.: Am. Society Consulting Engineers (hon.), Am. Institute Architects (hon.), Am. Society Landscape Architects (hon.), Amalgamated Transit Union (hon.) **H:** Bicycling, running **PA:** Democrat **BA:** 1111 Longworth HOB, Washington, DC, 20515

BLUMENTHAL, RICHARD, T: U.S. Senator from Connecticut **I:** Government Administration/Government Relations/Government Services **DOB:** 02/13/1946 **PB:** New York City **SC:** NY/USA **ED:** JD, Yale Law School, 1973; BA, Harvard College, 1967 **C:** Member, U.S. Senate Veterans' Affairs Committee, Washington, 2013-; Member, U.S. Senate Commerce, Sci. & Transportation Committee, Washington, 2013-; Member, U.S. Senate Armed Services Committee, Washington, 2011-; Member, U.S. Senate Judiciary Committee, Washington, 2011-; Member, U.S. Senate Special Committee on Aging, Washington, 2011-; U.S. Senator from Connecticut, Washington, 2011-; Member, U.S. Senate Health, Education, Labor & Pensions, Washington, 2011-13; Attorney general, State of Connecticut, Hartford, Connecticut, 1991-2011; Member District 27, Connecticut State Senate, Hartford, Connecticut, 1987-90; Member District 145, Connecticut House of Reps., Hartford, Connecticut, 1984-87; Partner, Silver Golub & Teitell LLP, Stamford, Connecticut, 1984-90; Partner, Cummings & Lockwood LLC, 1981-84; US attorney District Connecticut, US Department Justice, Hartford, Connecticut, 1977-81; Administrator assistant to Rep. Abraham Ribicoff, US Senate, Washington, 1975-76; Law clerk to Justice Harry A. Blackmun, US Supreme Court, Washington, 1974-75; Law clerk to Hon. Jon O. Newman, US District Court Connecticut, 1973-74 **CR:** Founder Citizens Crime Commission Connecticut, 1982 vol. counsel National Association for the Advancement of Colored People Legal Defense Fund, 1981-86 **MIL:** Sergeant US Marine Corps Reserve **AW:** Recipient Raymond E. Baldwin award for Pub. Service, Quinnipiac University School Law, 2002 **PA:** Democrat

BLUNT, EMILY, T: Actress **I:** Media & Entertainment **PB:** London **SC:** England **PT:** Oliver Simon Peter Blunt; Joanna Blunt **CW:** Actress: (plays) The Royal Family, 2001, Romeo & Juliet, 2002; (films) Boudica, 2003, My Summer of Love, 2004, Irresistible, 2006, The Devil Wears Prada, 2006, The Jane Austen Book Club, 2007, Windchill, 2007, Dan in Real Life, 2007, Charlie Wilson's War, 2007, Sunshine Cleaning, 2008, The Great Buck Howard, 2008, Curiosity, 2009, The Young Victoria, 2009, The Wolfman, 2010, Gulliver's Travels, 2010, (voice) Gnomeo & Juliet, 2011, The Adjustment Bureau, 2011, (voice) The Muppets, 2011, Salmon Fishing in the Yemen, 2012, The Five-Year Engagement, 2012, Your Sister's Sister, 2012, Looper, 2012, Arthur Newman, 2012, (voice) The Wind Rises, 2013, Edge of Tomorrow, 2014 (Critics' Choice award for Best Actress in an Action Movie, 2015), Into the Woods, 2014, Sicario, 2015, The Huntsman: Winter's War, 2016, The Girl on the Train, 2016, (voice) Animal Crackers, 2016, (voice)

Animal Crackers, 2017, (voice) My Little Pony: The Movie, 2017, A Quiet Place, 2018, Mary Poppins, 2018: (TV films) Henry VIII, 2003, The Strange Case of Sherlock Holmes & Arthur Conan Doyle, 2005, Gideon's Daughter, 2005 (Golden Globe award for Best Supporting Actress, 2007); (TV miniseries) Empire, 2005, (TV appearances) Foyle's War, 2003, Agatha Christie: Poirot, 2004, (voice) The Simpsons, 2009

BLUNT, ROY DEAN, T: U.S. Senator from Missouri **I:** Government Administration/Government Relations/Government Services **DOB:** 01/10/1950 **PB:** Niangua **SC:** MO/USA **PT:** Son of Leroy and Neva (Letterman) B.; **MS:** Married **SPN:** Abigail Perlman, 2003; Roseann Blunt (div. 2003) **CH:** Matthew Roy, Amy Roseann, Andrew Benjamin **ED:** MA in Hist. & Government, Southwest Missouri State University, 1972; BA in Hist., Southwest Baptist University, Missouri, 1970 **C:** Chair, Senate Rules Committee, 2015-17; Vice chairman, US Senate Republican Conference, 2012-; Member, US Senate Rules & Administration Committee, Washington, 2011-; Member, US Senate Commerce, Science & Transportation, Washington, 2011-; Member, US Senate Select Committee on Intelligence, Washington, 2011-; Member, US Senate Appropriations Committee, Washington, 2011-; US Senator from Missouri, Washington, 2011-; Interim majority leader, US Congress from 7th Missouri District, 2005-06; Assistant minority leader (minority whip), US Congress from 7th Missouri District, 2007-09; Assistant majority leader (majority whip), US Congress from 7th Missouri District, 2002-07; Chief deputy majority whip, US Congress from 7th Missouri District, 1999-2002; Member, US Congress from 7th Missouri District, 1997-2011; President, Southwest Baptist University, 1993-96; Secretary state, State of Missouri, 1985-93; Clerk, Greene County, Missouri, 1973-85; Instructor, Drury College, Springfield, Missouri, 1973-82; Teacher, Marshfield HS, Missouri, 1970-73 **CR:** Del. Atlantic Treaty Association Conference, 1987 **CIV:** member Missouri Mental Health Advocacy Council, 1998-99 member executive board American Council of Young Political Leaders, 1998-99 chairman Missouri Housing Devel. Commission, Kansas City, 1981, Rep. State Convention, Springfield, 1980 chairman Governor's Advisory Council on Literacy co-chmn. Missouri Opportunity 2000 Commission, 1985-87 Republican candidate for Lieutenant Governor of Missouri, 1980 **CW:** Co-author: Missouri Election Procedures: A Layman's Guide, 1977, Jobs Without People: The Coming Crisis for Missouri's Workforce, 1989 **AW:** Named one of The 10 Outstanding Young Americans US Jaycees, 1986, Springfield's Outstanding Young Man Jaycees, 1980, Missouri's Outstanding Young Civic Leader, 1981, Missouri Republican of Year 2002; Recipient Distinguished Member of Congress award, American Wire Producers Association, 2002, Health Leadership award American Association of Nurse Anesthetists, 2003, Arthur T. Marix Congressional Leadership award Military Officers Association America, 2004, Community Health Defender award National Association Community Health Ctrs. Inc., 2005. **MEM:** Member National Association Secretaries of State (vice president 1990), American Council Young Political Leaders, Kiwanis, Masons. **PA:** Republican

BLUNT ROCHESTER, LISA, T: U.S. Representative from Delaware **I:** Government Administration/Government Relations/Government Services **DOB:** 02/10/1962 **PB:** Philadelphia **SC:** PA/USA **ED:** B.A., International Relations, Farleigh Dickinson University; Master's Degree, Urban Affairs and Public Policy, University of Delaware **C:** Member,U.S. House of Representatives from Delaware at Large District, 2017-; Member,Committee on Agriculture;

Member, Committee on Education and the Workforce; CEO, Metropolitan Wilmington Urban League, 2004-2007; State Personal Director, California, 2001-04; Secretary, Department of Labor, 1998-01; Deputy Secretary, Department of Health and Social Services, 1993-98 **BA:** 1123 Longworth HOB, Washington, DC, 20515

BOCHCO, STEVEN, T: Screenwriter, Television Producer **I:** Media & Entertainment **DOB:** 12/16/1943 **PB:** New York **SC:** NY/USA **YOP:** 2018-04-02 **PT:** Son of Rudolph and Mimi B. **MS:** Married **SPN:** Dayna Kalins August 12, 2000; Barbara Bosson, 1969 (div. 1997; **ED:** BA, Carnegie Mellon University, 1996 **C:** Chairman CEO, Steven Bocho Productions, LA, 1987-; Writer, producer, Disney Touchstone TV, 2005-; Writer, producer, Paramount Network TV, 1999-2004; Writer, producer, Twentieth Century Fox, LA, 1985-87; Writer, producer, MTM Enterprises, Studio City, 1978-85; Scriptwriter, editor, producer, Universal Studios, LA, 1966-78 **CW:** Writer: (films) (with Michael Cimino and Deric Washburn) Silent Running, 1972, (TV series) Ironside, 1967-75, Columbo, 1971-78, McMillan and Wife, 1971-76, Griff, 1973-74, Delvecchio, 1976-77, McMillan, 1977, Turnabout, 1979, (TV films) (with Harold Clements) The Counterfeit Killer, 1968, Double Indemnity, 1973, Uneasy Lies the Crown, 1990; writer, prodr.: (TV series) Bay City Blues, 1983-84, Griff, 1973-74, (TV mini series) Over There, 2005; (TV films) The Invisible Man, 1975, Richie Brockelman: Missing Twenty-four Hours, 1976, Lieutenant Schuster's Wife, 1972, Columbo: Uneasy Lies the Crown, 1990; writer, executive prodr.: (TV series) Paris, 1979-80, (TV films) Vampire, 1979, prodr: (TV series) Capitol Critters, 1992, The Byrds of Paradise, 1994; co-creator, executive producer, writer: (TV series) Hill Street Blues, 1981-86 (Emmy award best drama series 1981, 82, 83, 84, Emmy award best writing in drama series 1981, 82, Golden Globe award best drama series 1982, 83), L.A. Law, 1986-87 (Emmy award best drama series 1987, 89, Emmy award best writing in drama series 1987, Golden Globe award best drama series 1987, 88), Hooperman, 1987-89, Doogie Howser, M.D., 1989-93, Cop Rock, 1990, Civil Wars, 1991-93, NYPD Blue, 1993-2005 (Golden Globe award best drama series 1994, Outstanding Drama Series Emmy award, 1995), Murder One 1995-96, Total Security, 1997, Philly, 2001; executive prodr.: (TV series) Public Morals, 1996, Brooklyn South, 1997-98, City of Angels, 2000, Commander in Chief, 2005-, F*ck, 2006, Murder in the First, 2014. **BA:** Variety Magazine, 11175 Santa Monica Blvd, Los Angeles, CA, 90025

BOCHY, BRUCE DOUGLAS, T: Professional Baseball Manager **I:** Athletics **DOB:** 04/16/1955 **PB:** Landes de Boussac **SC:** France **MS:** Married **SPN:** Kim Bochy **CH:** Greg, Brett **ED:** Attended, Florida State University, Tallahassee; Attended, Brevard Community College, Cocoa Beach, Florida **C:** Manager, San Francisco Giants, 2006-; Manager, Double-A Wichita, Texas League, 1992; Manager, High Desert, California League, 1991; Manager, Single-A Riverside, 1990; Manager, Spokane, Northwest League, 1989; Minor league player, coach, Triple-A Las Vegas, 1988; Manager, San Diego Padres, 1994-2005; Third base coach, San Diego Padres, 1993-94; Catcher, San Diego Padres, 1983-87; Catcher, New York Mets, 1982; Catcher, Houston Astros, 1978-80 **CW:** (Books) A Book of Walks, 2015 **AW:** Named National League Manager of Year, The Sporting News, 1998, 1996, MLB, 1996; recipient Ronald L. Jensen award for Lifetime Achievement, Positive Coaching Alliance, 2011,Ronald L Jensen Award, 2011 **ACH:** Achievements include managing the San Fracisco Giants to 3 World Series Championships (2010, 2012, 2014)

BOEHEIM, JIM, T: College Basketball Coach **I:** Athletics **DOB:** 11/17/1944 **PB:** Lyons **SC:** NY/USA **ED:** Master in Social Sci., Syracuse University; BA in Social Sci., Syracuse University, 1966 **C:** Head Basketball Coach, Syracuse University Orange, 1976-; Full-time Assistant Basketball Coach, Syracuse University Orange, New York, 1972-76 **CR:** Member Coaching Staff US National Team World University Games, 1989, FIBA World Championships, 1990, 2006, 2010, Goodwill Games, 1991, FIBA Americas Championship, 2007, Summer Olympic Games, Beijing, 2008, London, 2012 **CIV:** Hon. Chairman Kidney Foundation Active Organizations Multiple Sclerosis, Cystic Fibrosis, Children's Miracle Network, Make-A-Wish, Pioneer Center for Blind and Disabled, Lighthouse, People in Wheelchairs, Easter Seals, Special Olympics, Coaches versus Cancer **AW:** Recipient Arents Award Syracuse University, 2000, Claire Bee Award, 2000, James P. Wilmot Cancer Center Inspiration Award University Rochester Medical Center, 2005, John R. Wooden Legends of Coaching Award, 2006, Henry Iba Award US Basketball Writers Association, 2010, Metropolitan Award National Association Basketball Coaches, 2010; Named Coach of Year U.S. Basketball Writers Association, 1979, 1980, 1991, District II Coach of Year, 2010, 2012, National Association Basketball Coaches, 1979, 1980, 1984, 1987, 1989, 1992, 2000, 2003; Big East Conference Coach of Year, 1984, 1991, 2000, 2010, National Coach of Year USA Basketball, 2001, Associated Press, 2010; Naismith Men's College Coach of Year Atlanta Tipoff Club, 2010; Named to Naismith Memorial Basketball Hall of Fame, 2006,John R. Wooden Legends of Coaching Award, 2006, Sporting News National Coach of the Year, 2010, NABC Coach of the Year, 2010, Basketball Hall of Fame, 2005 **ACH:** Achievements include having the basketball court at the Carrier Dome named in his honor, "Jim Boeheim Court" 2002; head coach of the NCAA National Championship winning Syracuse Orange, 2003; recording his 800th career win as a head coach, November 9, 2009

BOITANO, BRIAN, T: Olympic Athlete **I:** Athletics **DOB:** 10/22/1963 **PB:** Mountain View **C:** U.S. Olympic Figure Skating Gold medallist, 1988; U.S. Olympics 6th place, 1994; Silver medallist, U.S. National Figure Skating Championships, 1994; Gold medallist, World Figure Skating Championships, 1988; Gold medallist, U.S. National Figure Skating Championships, 1988; Silver medallist, World Figure Skating Championships, 1987; Gold medallist, World Figure Skating Championships, 1986; Gold medallist, U.S. National Figure Skating Championships, 1985; Bronze medallist, World Figure Skating Championships, 1985; Competitive in amateur ice-skating events, 1978-88 **CR:** Owner White Canvas Productions **CW:** Author (with Suzanne Harper): Boitano's Edge: Inside the Real World of Figure Skating, 1997; (performer): (TV films) Carmen on Ice, 1990 (Emmy award, 1990); Nutcracker on Ice, 1995; Skating Romance II, 1996; Skating Spectacular, 2003; Blades of Glory, 2007; featured on cover: Sports Illustrated; host (TV series) What Would Brian Boitano Make?, 2009-,(Television) The Brian Boitano Project, 2014 **AW:** Named Role Model of the Year, Professional Skaters' Cooperative, 1998; named to World Figure Skating Hall of Fame, 1996, U.S. Figure Skating Hall of Fame, 1996; recipient Gustav Lussi award, Professional Skaters Association, 1999

BOLLINGER, LEE CARROLL, T: President of Columbia University **I:** Education/Educational Services **DOB:** 04/30/1946 **PB:** Santa Rosa **SC:** CA/USA **ED:** JD, Columbia University, 1971; BS, University Oregon, 1968 **C:** President, trustee, Columbia University, 2002-; Provost, professor government,

Dartmouth College, 1994-96; President, professor law, University Michigan, 1997-2002; Professor, University Michigan, 1978-94; Associate professor, University Michigan, 1976-78; Assistant professor law, University Michigan, 1973-76; Dean, University Michigan, Ann Arbor, 1987-94; Law clerk to Chief Justice Warren Burger, US Supreme Court, 1972-73; Law clerk to Judge Wilfred Feinberg, US Court Appeals (2nd cir.), 1971-72 **CR:** Board directors The Washington Post Co., 2007- chairman Federal Reserve Bank New York, 2011-, board directors, 2007- research associate Clare Hall, Cambridge University, 1983 trustee Institute of International Education, Kresge Foundation **CIV:** Trustee, Kresge Foundation, Board directors, Gerald R. Ford Foundation, Royal Shakespeare Co., **CW:** Co-author (with Jackson): Contract Law in Modern Society, 1980; author: The Tolerant Society: Freedom of Speech and Extremist Speech in America, 1986, Images of a Free Press, 1991; co-editor (with Geoffrey Stone): (essay collection) Eternally Vigilant: Free Speech in the Modern Era, 2001 **AW:** Recipient National Humanitarian award, National Conference Community and Justice, Medal Excellence, Columbia Law School Association, 2002; fellow, Am. Rockefeller Humanities **MEM:** Fellow: American Academy Arts & Sciences, Clare Hall, Cambridge University (hon.); mem.: Institute International Education **BA:** Office of the President Columbia University, 202 Low Library, 535 W. 116 St., New York, NY, USA, 10027

BOLT, USAIN, T: Professional Runner **I:** Athletics **DOB:** 08/21/1986 **PB:** Trelawny **SC:** Jamaica **PT:** Wellesley Bolt; Jennifer Bolt **C:** Professional Sprinter (2004) **CR:** Member, Jamaica Track & Field Team, IAAF World Athletics Final, Thessaloniki, Greece (2009); Member, Jamaica Track & Field Team, IAAF World Athletics Final, Stuttgart, Germany (2006); IAAF World Championships in Athletics, Moscow, Russia (2013); IAAF World Championships in Athletics, Daegu, Republic of Korea (2011); IAAF World Championships in Athletics, Berlin, Germany (2009); IAAF World Championships in Athletics, Osaka, Japan (2007); IAAF World Championships in Athletics, Helsinki, Finland (2005); IAAF World Championships in Athletics, Summer Olympic Games, Rio de Janeiro, Brazil (2016); IAAF World Championships in Athletics, London, England (2012); IAAF World Championships in Athletics, Beijing, China (2008); IAAF World Championships in Athletics, Athens, Greece (2004) **AW:** Named a Champion for Sport, United Nations Educational (2008); Named Laureus World Sportsman of the Year (2009, 2010); Track & Field Athlete of the Year, Track & Field News Magazine (2008, 2009); IAAF World Athlete of the Year (2008, 2009, 2011); Named One of the 100 Most Influential People in the World, TIME Magazine (2016); Gold Medal, 200m, IAAF World Athletics Final (2009); Gold Medal, 100m, 200m, 4x100m Relay, Summer Olympic Games (2008, 2012, 2016); Gold Medal, 100m, Reebok Grand Prix (2008); Gold Medal, 200m, 4x100m, IAAF World Championships in Athletics (2011); Gold Medal, 100m, 200m, 4x100m (2009, 2013); Silver Medal, 200m, 4x100m (2007); Gold Medal, 200m, Central America and Caribbean Championships (2005); Gold Medal, 200m, 4x100m Relay, 4x400m Relay, CARIFTA Games (2004); Austin Seal Trophy (2003-2004); Order of Jamaica (2009) **ACH:** Achievements include first sprinter to break world records in both the 100 meters and 200 meters in the same Olympics, 2008; first sprinter in history to win gold medals in the 100 and 200 meters in three consecutive Summer Olympic Games, 2008, 2012, 2016; setting individual world records in: 100 meters (9.58 seconds), 2009; 200 meters (19.19 seconds), 2009; member of the world record breaking 4x100 meter Jamaican relay team

(36.84 seconds), 2012; receiving three sprinting gold medals in three consecutive Olympics 2008, 2012, 2016 **ADD:** c/o Jamaica Olympic Assn, 9 Cunningham Ave, Kingston, YT, Jamaica, 00000

BOLTON, JOHN R., T: Director **I:** Government Administration/Government Relations/Government Services **CN:** National Security Advisor **DOB:** 11/20/1948 **PB:** Baltimore **SC:** MD/USA **PT:** Edward Jackson Bolton, Virginia (Godfrey) Bolton **MS:** Married **SPN:** Gretchen Louise Brainerd, 1/1986; Christine Bolton, 1972, Divorced 1983 **CH:** Jennifer Sarah **ED:** JD, Yale University, 1974; BA, Yale University, Summa Cum Laude, 1970 **C:** Director, National Security Advisor, 2018-Present; Of Counsel, Kirkland & Ellis LLP, Washington, DC, 2008-Present; Senior Fellow, American Enterprise Institute (AEI), Washington, DC, 2007-Present; Permanent U.S. Representative To UN, U.S. Department of State, New York, NY, 2005-2006; Under Secretary For Arms Control & International Security Affairs, U.S. Department of State, Washington, DC, 2001-2005; Of Counsel, Kutak Rock LLP, Washington, DC, 1999-2001; Senior Vice President, American Enterprise Institute (AEI), Washington, DC, 1997-2001; Partner, Lerner, Reed, Bolton & McManus (And Predecessor Firms), Washington, DC, 1993-1999; Assistant Secretary For International Organization Affairs, U.S. Department of State, Washington, DC, 1989-1993; Assistant Attorney General (Civil Division), U.S. Department of Justice, Washington, DC, 1988-1989; Assistant Attorney General For Legislative Affairs, U.S. Department of Justice, Washington, DC, 1985-1988; Partner, Covington & Burling LLP, Washington, DC, 1983-1985; Executive Director Committee On Resolutions, Republican National Committee, Washington, DC, 1983-1984; Assistant Administrator For Progressive & Policy Coordination, U.S. Agency For International Development (USAID), Washington, DC, 1982-1983; General Counsel, U.S. Agency For International Development (USAID), Washington, DC, 1981-1982; Legal Consultant, The White House, Washington, DC, 1981; Associate, Covington & Burling LLP, Washington, DC, 1974-1981; **CR:** Board of Directors, Project For A New American Century, 1989-2001; Senior Fellow,, Manhattan Institute, 1993; Adjunct Professor, George Mason University Law School, 1994-1996; President, National Policy Forum, Washington, DC, 1995-1996; Commissioner, U.S. Commission On International Religious Freedom, 1999-2001; Subcommittee On International Law, Federalist Society, 1999-2001; Board of Directors, Diamond Offshore Drilling, Inc., 2007-Present; Board of Directors, EMS Technologies, Inc., 2009-Present **MIL:** U.S. Army Reserve, 1974-1976; U.S. Army National Guard, 1970-1974 **CW:** Author, (Books) Surrender Is Not an Option: Defending America at the United Nations, 2007; Contributor, Articles, Professional Journals **AW:** Tree of Life Award, Northern & Southern New England Regions of Hadassah, 1990, Distinguished Service Award, U.S. Department of State, Edmund J. Randolph Award, U.S. Department of Justice, 1998 **MEM:** Pi Sigma Alpha, Phi Beta Kappa **BAR:** District of Columbia, 1975, U.S. District Court, District of Columbia, 1975, U.S. Court of Appeals, District of Columbia Circuit, 1975, U.S. Court of Appeals, Fourth Circuit, 1977, U.S. Court of Appeals, Third Circuit, 1978, U.S. Supreme Court, 1978, U.S. Court of Appeals, Fifth and 11th Circuits, 1981, U.S. Court of Appeals, Tenth Circuit, 1983, U.S. Court of Appeals, First, Sixth, Seventh, Eighth, and Ninth Circuits, 1988, U.S. Court of Appeals, Second Circuit, 1989 **PA:** Republican **BA:** 9107 Fernwood Road, Bethesda, MA, 20817-3019

BONAMICI, SUZANNE MARIE, T: U.S. Representative from Oregon **I:** Government Administration/ Government Relations/Government Services **DOB:** 10/14/1954 **PB:** Detroit, October 14, 1954 **ED:** JD, University Oregon School Law, 1983; BA in Journalism, University Oregon, 1980; AA, Lane Community College, 1978 **C:** Member, US Congress from 1st Oregon District, 2012-; Member, Committee on Science, Space and Technology,; Committee on Education and the Workforce; Member District 17, Oregon State Senate, 2008-11; Member District 34, Oregon House of Reps., 2007-08; Legis. assistant, Oregon House of Reps., 2001-06; Attorney, Stoll & Stoll, Portland, Oregon,; Legal assistant , law clerk, Lane Co. Legal Aid Service,; Attorney Bureau Consumer Protection, Federal Trade Commission, **CIV:** Board directors, Northwest Children's Theatre & School, **MEM:** Mem.: Citizens for Beaverton Schools, Beaverton Education Foundation **PA:** Democrat

BONDS, BARRY LAMAR, T: Professional Baseball Player **I:** Athletics **DOB:** 07/24/1964 **PB:** Riverside **PT:** Son of Bobby and Pat Bonds; **ED:** BA in Criminal Justice, Arizona State University, 1986 **C:** Hitting Coach, Miami Marlins, 2016,; Special Advisor, Giants, 2017-; Outfielder, San Francisco Giants, 1992-2007; Outfielder, Pittsburgh Pirates, 1986-92 **PT:** Founder, Barry Bonds Family Foundation, 1993- **CW:** (star): (Reality TV show) Bonds on Bonds, 2006 **AW:** Named Male Athlete of Year, 2001, MLB Athlete of Decade, 1990's, The Sporting News, 1999, National League Player of Year, 1991, 1990, MLB Player of Year, 2004, 2001, 1990, National League MVP, Baseball Writers' Association of Am., 2001-04, 1992-93, 1990; named one of The Most Influential People in the World of Sports, Business Week, 2007; named to National League All-Star Team, Major League Baseball, 2007, 2000-04, 1992-98, 1990, All-Am. Team, Sporting News College, 1985; recipient Hank Aaron award, Major League Baseball, 2004, 2002, 2001, Philanthropist of Year award, National Conference Black Philanthropy, 1999, Espy award, Best Male Athlete, ESPN, 1994, Espy award, Best Baseball Player, 2004, 2002, 1994, Silver Slugger award, Major League Baseball, 2000-04, 1990-97, Gold Glove award, 1996-98, 1990-94 **ACH:** Achievements include holds the record for most home runs in a single season (73), 2001; became third player in MLB to hit 700 career home runs on September 17, 2004; only member in 500/500 Club (HR/Steals); became MLB all-time leader in walks with 2,191 on July 4, 2004; led National League in batting average, 2002 (.370), 2004 (.362); oldest player to win National League MVP Award at 40 years old, 2004; holds MLB record with 7 league MVP awards; holds MLB record for consecutive seasons with 30+ Home Runs, 1992-2004; passing Hank Aaron for the all-time home run record by hitting his 756th on August 7, 2007, against the Washington Nationals **H:** Golf, photography, music **BA:** Barry Bonds Family Foundation, 3 Lagoon Dr, Redwood City, CA, 94065

BON-JOVI, JON, T: Musician, Actor, Former Sports Team Executive **I:** Media & Entertainment **DOB:** 03/02/1962 **PB:** Perth Amboy **SC:** NJ **PT:** John Bongiovi; Carol Bongiovi **MS:** Married **SPN:** Dorothea Hurley (5/1989) **CH:** Stephanie Rose; Jesse James Louis; Jacob Hurley; Romeo Jon **ED:** Diploma, High School, Sayreville, NJ **C:** Singer, Songwriter, Band, Bon Jovi (1984-Present) **CR:** Co-owner, Philadelphia Soul Arena Football League Team (2004—2011) **CIV:** Restaurant Owner, Soul Kitchen, Red Bank, NJ (2011—Present); Campaigned Heavily for Al Gore (2000), John Kerry (2004) and Barack Obama (2008, 2012) **CW:** Member, Various Local Bands Including The Rest, The Wild Ones, Johnny and the Lechers, The Raze, Atlantic City Expressway; Singer, Albums with Bon Jovi, "Bon Jovi" (1984), "7800 Fahrenheit" (1985), "Slippery When Wet" (1986), "Bon Jovi Live" (1987), "New Jersey" (1988), "Keep the Faith" (1992), "Crossroad" (1994), "These Days" (1995), "Bon Jovi" (1999), "Crush" (2000), "Bounce" (2002), "Distance" (2003), "This Left Feels Right" (2003), "100,000,000 Bon Jovi Fans Can't Be Wrong" (2004), "Have a Nice Day" (2005), "Lost Highway" (2007), "Circle" (2009), "Bon Jovi: The Ultimate Collection" (2010), "What About Now" (2013), "Burning Bridges" (2015), "This House is Not for Sale" (2016), "This House is Not for Sale- Live from the London Palladium" (2016); Singer, Solo Albums, "Blaze of Glory" (1990), "Destination Anywhere" (1997); Singer, Songs, with Jennifer Nettles, "Who Says You Can't Go Home" (2005), With LeAnn Rimes, "Nothin' Better to Do" (2007); Actor, Films, "The Return of Bruno" (1988), "Moonlight and Valentino" (1995), "The Leading Man" (1996), "Long Time Nothing New" (1997), "Little City" (1997), "Homegrown" (1997), "Row Your Boat" (1998), "U-571" (2000), "Pay It Forward" (2000), "Vampires: Los Muertos" (2002), "Cry Wolf" (2005), "Pucked" (2006), "New Year's Eve" (2011); Guest Appearances include "Top of the Pops" (1986-2002), "Unsolved Mysteries" (1998), "Sex and the City" (1999), "Ally McBeal" (2002), "The West Wing" (2006), "30 Rock" (2010) **AW:** Co-recipient, Award of Merit, American Music Awards (2004); Named Top Touring Artist, Billboard Music Award (2014); Named One of the 100 Most Powerful Celebrities, Forbes.com (2008); Named to New Jersey Hall of Fame (2009); Named to Songwriters Hall of Fame (2009); Diamond Award, World Music Awards (2005); Collaborative Video of the Year, Country Music TV (2006); Grammy Award, Best Country Collaboration with Vocals (2007); People's Choice Award, Favorite Rock Song (2007); Collaborative Video of the Year, Country Music TV (2008); Inducted, Rock & Roll Hall of Fame (2018) **BA:** The Gersh Agency, 232 North Canon Drive, Beverly Hills, CA, 90210

BONNER, JOHN TYLER, T: College Professor **I:** Education/Educational Services **CN:** Princeton University **DOB:** 05/12/1920 **PB:** New York **SC:** NY/ USA **PT:** Paul Hyde Bonner, Lilly Marguerite (Stehli) Bonner **ED:** DLitt, University College of Cape Breton, 2005; LLD, Concordia University, 2003; DSc, Princeton University, 2006; DSc, Middlebury College, 1970; PhD, Harvard University, 1947; MA, Harvard University, 1942; BSc, Harvard University, 1941; Graduate, Phillips Exeter Academy, 1937 **C:** Emeritus Professor, Princeton University, 1990-Present; Chairman, Department of Biology, Princeton University, 1965-1977, 1983-1984, 1987-1988; Professor, Princeton University, 1958-1990; Assistant To Associate Professor, Princeton University, 1947-1958; Junior Fellow, Harvard University, 1942, 1946-1947 **CR:** Raman Professor, Indian Academy of Sciences, 1990, Arnold Bernhard Visiting Professor, Williams College, 1989, Special Lecturer, Brooklyn College, 1966, National Science Foundation Senior Postdoctoral Fellow, 1963, Guggenheim Fellow, Scotland, 1958, 1971-1972, Trustee, Biological Abstracts, 1958-1963, University of London, 1957, Rockefeller Travelling Fellow, France, 1953, Lecturer, Embryology, Marine Biological Lab, Woods Hole, MA, 1951-1952, Fellow, American Academy of Arts and Sciences **CIV:** Staff, Aeronautical Medical Laboratory, Wright Field, OH **MIL:** First Lieutenant, USAC, 1942-1946 **CW:** Author, Morphogenesis, 1952, Cells And Societies, 1955, The Evolution Of Development, 1958, The Cellular Slime Molds, 1959, The Cellular Slime Molds, Review Edition, 1967, The Ideas Of Biology, 1962, Size And Cycle, 1965, The Scale Of Nature, 1969, On Development, 1974, The Evolution Of Culture In Animals, 1980, The Evolution Of Complexity, 1988, Researches On Cellular Slime Molds, 1991, Life Cycles, 1993, Sixty Years Of Biology, 1996, First Signals, 2000, Lives Of A Biologist, 2002, Why Size Matters, 2006, The Social Amoebae, 2009, Randomness In Evolution, 2013, Randomness In Evaluation, 2013; Co-Author, (With T.A. McMahon) On Life And Size, 1983; Editor, Growth And Form, 1961, Evolution And Development, 1981; Associate Editor, American Scientist, 1961-1969; Editorial Board, Growth, 1955-1989, American Naturalist, 1958-1960, 1966-1968, Journal of General Physiology, 1962-1969, Differentiation, 1976-1990, Oxford Surveys In Evolutionary Biology, 1982-1993; Board of Editors, Princeton University Press, 1965-1968, 1971; Trustee, Princeton University Press, 1976-1982 **AW:** Selman A. Waksman Award for Contributions to Microbiology, Theobold Smith Society **MEM:** Honorary Member, Indian Academy of Sciences, National Academy of Sciences, American Philosophical Society, Society of Growth and Development, American Society of Naturalists, Sigma Xi, Phi Beta Kappa **BA:** Princeton University, Princeton, NJ, 08544

BOOKER, CORY ANTHONY, T: U.S. Senator from New Jersey **I:** Government Administration/Government Relations/Government Services **DOB:** 04/27/1969 **PB:** Washington **PT:** Son of Cary Alfred and Carolyn Rose (Jordan) Booker. **ED:** Doctor (hon.), Fairleigh Dickinson University, 2012; LLD (hon.), Bard College, 2012; LLD (hon.), Washington University, 2013; LHD (hon.), Williams College, 2011; LHD (hon.), Yeshiva University, 2010; LHD (hon.), New Jersey Institute of Technology, 2009; JD, Yale Law School, 1997; BA with Honors, University Oxford, 1994; MA in Sociology, Stanford University, 1992; BA with Honors, Stanford University, 1991 **CT:** Bar: New Jersey 1998 **C:** Member, US Senate Small Business Committee, 2013-; Member, US Senate Environment & Public Works Committee, 2013-; Member, US Senate Commerce Committee, 2013-; US Senator from New Jersey, 2013-; Mayor, City of Newark, 2006-13; Councilman Central Ward, City of Newark, New Jersey, 1998-2002; Partner, Booker, Rabinowitz, Trenk, Lubetkin, Tully, DiPasquale & Webster, PC, West Orange, New Jersey, 2002-13; Program coordinator, Newark Youth Project, 1998; Staff attorney, Urban Justice Center, 1997 **CR:** Board member International Longevity Center, Integrity Inc., North Star Academy, Black Alliance for Educational Options, Stanford University Board Trustees, Columbia University Tchr.'s College Board Trustees, Bloomberg Family Foundation, 2010- member executive committee Yale Law School **CIV:** Founder, director, Newark Now, **CW:** Contributor articles to law journals; appeared in (documentaries) The Lottery, 2010; author: United: Thoughts on Finding Common Ground and Advancing the Common Good, 2016 **AW:** Named The Savior of Newark, TIME magazine, 2000; named one of The 100 Most Influential People in the World, 2011, America's Best Leaders, US News & World Report, 2009, America's Most Powerful Players Under 40, Black Enterprise, 2005, The New Jersey Top 40 Under 40, New Jersey Monthly, The Country's 40 Best and Brightest, Esquire magazine, 2002; named to The Power 150, Ebony magazine, 2008; recipient John Heinz award for Greatest Public Service by an Elected or Appointed Official, 2010; Honorary Public Interest Fellow, University Pennsylvania Law School, Senior Fellow, Rutgers University School Public Policy & Planning, Skadden fellow, University Oxford, 1997 **PA:** Democrat **BA:** Office of Corey Booker, 359 Dirksen Senate Office Building, Washington, DC, 20510

BOOZMAN, JOHN NICHOLS, **T:** U.S. Senator from Arkansas **I:** Government Administration/Government Relations/Government Services **DOB:** 12/10/1950 **PB:** Shreveport **SC:** LA/USA **ED:** OD, Southern College of Optometry (1977); Coursework, University of Arkansas, Fayetteville, AK (1969-1972) **C:** Member, U.S. Senate on Veterans Affairs Committee, Washington, DC (2011-Present); Member, U.S. Senate on Agricultural, Nutrition & Forestry Committee, Washington, DC (2011-Present); Member, U.S. Senate on Environment & Public Works Committee, Washington, DC (2011-Present); Member, U.S. Senate on Commerce, Science & Transportation Committee, Washington, DC (2011-Present); U.S. Senator from Arkansas, Washington, DC (2011-Present); Member, U.S. Congress from the Third Arkansas District, Washington, DC (2001-2011); Private Practice, Eye Clinic (1977) **CR:** Co-Founder, Boozman-Hof Regional Eye Clinic, P.A., Rogers, AK (1977) **CIV:** Member, Rogers Board of Education, Arkansas (1994-2001); Establisher, Low-Vision Program, Arkansas School for Blind for Little Rock **AW:** Recipient, A in English Award, US English, Inc. (2010); Recipient, Award for Manufacturing Legislative Excellence, National Association Manufacturers (2010); Recipient, Brighter Vision Award, Age-Related Macular Degeneration Alliance International (2006); Recipient, Small Business Advocate Award, Small Business Survival Committee (2004); Recipient, Hero of the Taxpayer Award, Americans for Tax Reform (2003); Recipient, Spirit of Enterprise Award, U.S. Chamber of Commerce (2001-2003); Recipient, Hero of the Taxpayer Award, Americans for Tax Reform (2001-2002); Recipient, Distinguished Advocate Award, Arkansas Chapter, Association of Education & Rehabilitation of the Blind & Visually Impaired **MEM:** International Academy of Sports Vision; Arkansas Optometric Association; American Optometric Association; Fellowship of Christian Athletes **PA:** Republican **BA:** Office of John Boozman, 141 Hart Senate Office Building, Washington, DC, 20510

BORAS, SCOTT D., **T:** Professional Sports Agent **I:** Media & Entertainment **DOB:** 11/02/1952 **ED:** JD, McGeorge School Law Pacific University, 1982; PhD in Indus. Pharmacology, University Pacific, 1976; BS in Chemistry, University Pacific, 1974 **CT:** Bar: Washington **C:** Sports agent, 1981-; Founder, president, CEO, Impact Marketing,; Founder, owner, talent evaluator, The Boras Corp., Newport Beach, California,; Former infielder outfielder, St. Louis Cardinals Minor League Org.,; Former infielder outfielder, Chicago Cubs Minor League Org., **AW:** Named one of The Most Influential People in the World of Sports, Business Week, 2008, 2007, 50 Most Influential People in Sports Business, Street & Smith's SportsBus. Journal, 2007-09 **ACH:** Achievements include representing major clients including Barry Bonds, Alex Rodriguez, Bernie Williams, JD Drew, Johnny Damon, and Daisuke Matsuzaka

BORG, BJORN, **T:** Retired Professional Tennis Player **I:** Athletics **DOB:** 06/06/1956 **PB:** Sodertlage **SC:** Sweden **PT:** Son of Rune and Margaretha Borg; **MS:** Single **SPN:** Loredana Berte, September 4, 1989 (div. 1992) **CH:** Robin **C:** Returned to professional tennis, 1991-; Retired from professional tennis, 1983; Joined, World Championship Tennis circuit, 1974; Member, Sweden's Davis Cup Team, **AW:** Named World Champion of Men's Tennis International Tennis Federation, 1978,ITF World Champion, 1978-80, ATP Player of the Year, 1976-1980, Sweden's Top Sportsperson of all time by Dagens Nyheter, 2014, British Broadcasting Corporation Lifetime Achievement Award, 2006, BBC Sports Personality of the Year overseas Personality, 1979 **ACH:** Won Italian Open, 1974, Swedish Open, 1974, 78, French Open, 1974, 75, 78, 79, 80, 81, U.S. Professional Tennis championship, 1974, 75, 76, Wimbledon championship, 1976, 77, 78, 79, 80, U.S. National Indoor Tennis championship, 1977, World Championship Tennis, 1976, Can. Open, 1979, Colgate Grand Prix Masters, 1980, ATP Senior Tour, 1992, Champions Tour, 1992-99.

BOSEMAN, CHADWICK, **T:** Actor **I:** Media & Entertainment **PB:** Anderson **SC:** SC/USA **CW:** Actor, (Films) The Express: The Ernie Davis Story, 2008, The Kill Hole, 2013, 42, 2013, Draft Day, 2014, Get on up, 2014, Gods of Egypt, 2016, Captain America: Civil War, 2016, Message from the King, 2016, Marshall, 2017, Black Panther, 2018, Avengers: Infinity War, 2018, (Television) Third Watch, 2003, All My Children, 2003, Law and Order, 2004, CSI:NY, 2006, ER, Cold Case, 2008, Lincoln Heights, 2009, Lie to Me, 2009, Persons Unknown, 2010, The Glades, 2010, Castle, 2011, Fringe, 2011, Detroit 1-8-7, 2011, Justified, 2011

BOSSY, MICHAEL, **T:** Retired Professional Hockey Player **I:** Athletics **DOB:** 01/22/1957 **PB:** Montreal, Quebec, Can. **SC:** Montreal Que. Can. **PT:** Married Lucie Bossy; children: Josieane, Tanya. **C:** MSG Network Analyst, 2014,; TVA Sports Broadcaster, 2015; Executive Director Corp. Relations, New York Islanders, 2006-; TV Broadcaster, Quebec Nordiques, 1987-90; Right Wing, New York Islanders, 1977-87; Right Wing, Laval National Hockey Club, 1973-77 **AW:** Recipient Calder Memorial trophy, 1978, Conn Smythe trophy, 1982, Lady Byng Trophy, 1983, 100 Greatest NHL Players in History, 2017 **ACH:** Achievements include being a member of Stanley Cup Champion New York Islanders, 1980-83; NHL single season record for most point and assists by right wing for 1981-82 season; NHL record 9 consecutive 50+ goal seasons 1977-85

BOST, MIKE, **T:** U.S. Representative from Illinois **I:** Government Administration/Government Relations/Government Services **DOB:** 12/30/1960 **PB:** December 30, 1960 **ED:** Attended, University Illinois **CT:** Cert. firefighter Murphysboro Fire Department, 1992 **C:** Member, U.S. House of Representatives from Illinois 12th District,2015-, Member, Committee on Agriculture, Committee on Small Business, Committee on Veterans' Affairs, Republican Study Committee; Co-owner, White House Salon, 1993-; Member District 115, Illinois House of Reps., 1999-2015; Township trustee, Murphysboro, 1993-; Deacon,; Treasurer, Murphysboro, 1989-92; Member, Jackson Country Super Max Prison,; Member, Patriots Bravo Country,; Member, Transportation & Motor Vehicles & Vet. Affairs Committees,; Member, Steering Committee,; Member, Local Government Committee,; Member, Elementary & Secondary Education Higher Education,; Member, Jackson Country Board, 1984-88; Committeeman Precinct 4, Murphysboro, 1985-89; Truck manager, 1982-92; Driver, Bost Trucking Service, 1979 **CIV:** Youth minister, Elm St Baptist Church, 1985-91 **MEM:** Mem.: Jackson Co Young Rep. (treasurer 1986), Jackson Country Rep. Boosters (president 1986), Mason (32 degree), Murphysboro Rotary Club 1986 **PA:** Republican **BA:** 1440 Longworth House Office Building, Washington, DC, 20515

BOURDAIN, ANTHONY MICHAEL, **T:** Chef, Writer, Television Personality **I:** Food & Restaurant Services **DOB:** 06/25/1956 **PB:** New York **SC:** NY/USA **YOP:** 2018-06-08 **PT:** Pierre Bourdain, Gladys Bourdain **ED:** Graduate, Culinary Institute of America, Hyde Park, NY, 1978; Student, Vassar College **C:** Executive Chef, Brasserie Les Halles; Chef, Sullivan's; Chef, One Fifth Avenue; Chef, Supper Club, New York, NY **CR:** Food Book Of Year, Brit. Guild Food Writers, Cook's Tour: In Search of the Perfect Meal, 2002, Creative Arts Emmy Award For Outstanding Cinematography For Nonfiction Programming, Anthony Bourdain: No Reservations, 2009, 2011; Emmy Award For Outstanding Informational Series Or Special, 2013, Producers Guild Of America Award For Outstanding Producer Of Non-Fiction TV, 2014, Peabody Award, 2014, Critic's Choice Award For Best Unstructured Reality Show, Anthony Bourdain: Parts Unknown, 2016 **CW:** Author, Kitchen Confidential: Adventures in the Culinary Underbelly, 2000, Typhoid Mary: An Urban Historical, 2001, Cook's Tour: In Search of the Perfect Meal, 2001, Cook's Tour: Global Adventures in Extreme Cuisines, 2002, Anthony Bourdain's Les Halles Cookbook: Strategies, Recipes, and Techniques of Classic Bistro Cooking, 2004, La Cocina De Les Halles: Strategies, Recipes and Techniques of Classic Bistro Cooking, 2005, The Nasty Bits: Collected Varietal Cuts, Usable Trim, Scraps, and Bones, 2006, No Reservations: Around the World on An Empty Stomach, 2007, Medium Raw: A Bloody Valentine to the World of Food and the People Who Cook, 2010, (Fiction Novels) Bone in the Throat, 1995, Gone Bamboo, 1997, The Bobby Gold Stories, 2003; Host, (TV Series) A Cook's Tour, 2002, Anthony Bourdain: No Reservations, 2005-2012, The Layover, 2011-2013, Anthony Bourdain: Parts Unknown, 2013-2018; Narrator, Executive Producer, The Mind of a Chef, 2012-2015; Guest Judge, Bravo's Top Chef, Host the Taste, 2013-2015; Guest Appearance, Miami Ink, 2006, Bizarre Foods With Andrew Zimmern, 2007; Contributor and Authority, Food Arts Magazine; Featured, The Times, The New York Times, Observer, Face, and Scotland on Sunday **AW:** Food Writer of the Year, Bon Appétit Magazine, 2001, James Beard Foundation Who's Who of Food and Beverage in America, 2008, Honorary CLIO Award, 2010

BOURQUE, RAY, **T:** Retired Professional Hockey Player **I:** Athletics **DOB:** 12/28/1960 **PB:** Montreal, Quebec **SC:** Canada **C:** Consultant, Boston Bruins (2005-Present); Co-owner, Tresca, Boston, MA; Defenseman, Colorado Avalanche (2000-2001); Captain, Boston Bruins, MA (1988-2000); Co-captain, Boston Bruins, MA (1985-1988); Defenseman, Boston Bruins, MA (1979-2000) **AW:** Named NHL Rookie of the Year, Sporting News (1980); Named to NHL All-Star Game (1981-1986, 1988-1994); Named to Second All-Star Team, NHL (1981, 1985, 1986, 1989); Named to First All-Star Team (1980, 1982, 1984, 1985, 1987, 1990, 1994); Named to Sporting News All-Star First Team (1982, 1984, 1987, 1988, 1990); Named to Sporting News All-Star Second Team (1981, 1983, 1986, 1989); Named to Sporting News All-Star First Team (1994); King Clancy Memorial Trophy (1992); James Norris Memorial Trophy (1987, 1988, 1990, 1991, 1994); Calder Memorial Trophy (1980); Named One of the 100 Greatest NHL Players (2017); Lester Patrick Trophy (2003); Named to NHL First Team All-Star (2001); NHL All-Star Game Shooting Accuracy Competition (2000-2001); Stanley Cup Champion (2001) **ACH:** Achievements include being a member of Stanley Cup Champion Colorado Avalanche, 2001; holding NHL record for most goals, assists and points scored by a defenceman; having his number, 77, retired by Colorado Avalanche, 2001, Boston Bruins, 2001; being inducted into the Hockey Hall of Fame, 2004

BOWMAN, SCOTTY, **T:** Former Professional Hockey Coach **I:** Athletics **DOB:** 09/18/1933 **PB:** Montreal, Can **PT:** Son of John and Jane (Scott) Bowman **ED:** Doctor in Pedagogy (hon.), Niagara University, Niagra Falls, New York, 2009; LHD (hon.), Canisius College, Buffalo, 2003; Student, Sir George Williams Business School, 1954 **C:** Senior advisor hockey operations, Chicago Blackhawks Hockey Operations, 2008-; Consultant, Detroit Red Wings Stanley Cup Champions, 2002-08; Director player personnel, Detroit Red Wings, 1993-2002; Head coach, Detroit Red Wings, 1993-2002; Head coach, Pittsburgh Penguins, 1992-93; Interim head coach, Pittsburgh Penguins, 1991-92; Director player devel., Pittsburgh Penguins, 1990-91; TV analyst, Hockey Night in Can., 1987-90; Head coach, general manager, director hockey operations, Buffalo Sabres, 1979-86; Head coach, general manager, St. Louis Blues, 1966-71; Head coach, Montreal Canadiens, 1971-79; Scout executive, Montreal Canadiens, 1956-66 **CR:** Head coach Team Can.; 1976 member Hockey Hall of Fame Selection Committee **AW:** Named NHL Executive of Year, Hockey News, 1997, NHL Coach of Year, 1993-97, 1977, Sporting News, 1996, NHL Executive of Yr, 1980; named to St. Louis Sports Hall of Fame, 2011, Quebec Sports Hall of Fame, 2005, Can.'s Sports Hall of Fame, 2004, Can. Walk of Fame, 2003, Buffalo Sports Hall of Fame, 2000, Michigan Sports Hall of Fame, 1999; recipient Wayne Gretzky Award of Excellence, US Hockey Hall of Fame, 2002, Award, Can. Society New York, 2001, Lester Patrick Trophy, 2001, Victor award for NHL Coach of Year, 2002, 1996, 1993, Jack Adams Award, 1996, 1977, Officer of the Order of Canada, 2012, Order of Hockey in Canada, 2017 **ACH:** Achievements include being the head coach of Stanely Cup Champion, Montreal Canadiens, 1973, 1976, 1977, 1978, 1979, Pittsburgh Penguins, 1992, Detroit Red Wings, 1997, 1998, 2002; being the only head coach in NHL history to win Stanley Cup with 3 different teams; being inducted into the Hockey Hall of Fame, 1991; holding NHL career regular season records for wins (1,244) and winning percentage (.670); holding NHL career playoffs records for wins (223) and games (353)

BOXER, BARBARA, T: U.S. Senator from California **I:** Government Administration/Government Relations/Government Services **DOB:** 11/11/1940 **PB:** Brooklyn **SC:** NY/USA **PT:** Daughter of Ira and Sophie (Silvershein) Levy; **ED:** BA in Economics, Brooklyn College, 1962 **C:** Ranking Member ,Senate Enviroment Committee, 2015-2017; Chair, U.S. Senate Select Committee on Ethics, 2007—15; Chair, U.S. Senate Environment & Public Works Committee, 2007—15; U.S. Senator from California, 1993—2017; Chair, U.S. House Subcommittee on Government Activities & Transportation, 1990-93; Member, U.S. Congress from 6th California District, 1983—1993; Journalist, Associate Editor, Pacific Sun, 1972-74; Stockbroker, Economic Researcher, New York City, New York, 1962-65; Congressional Aide to Rep. John L. Burton, U.S. House of Representatives, 1974—1976 **CIV:** Member Marin County Board Supervisors, 1976-82, President 1980-81; Member Bay Area Air Quality Management Board, San Francisco, 1977-82, President, 1979-81; Board Directors Golden Gate Bridge Hwy. & Transport District, San Francisco, 1978-82; President Dem. New Members Caucus, 1983 **CW:** Author (with Nicole Boxer): Strangers in the Senate: Politics and the New Revolution of Women in America, 1993; (with Catherine Whitney) Nine and Counting: The Women of the Senate, 2000, (with Mary-Rose Hayes) (novels) A Time to Run, 2005, Blind Trust, 2009 **AW:** Recipient Rep. of Year Award, National Multiple Sclerosis Society, 1990, Margaret Sanger Award, Planned Parenthood, 1990, 2003, Women of Achievement Award, Anti-Defamation League, 1990, Star Legis. Award, LA Women's Legis. Coalition, 1991, Edgar Wayburn Award, Sierra Club, 1997, Demetris Bouhoutsos Award, Hellenic-American Council Southern California,

1998, President's Award for the Advancement of Women, National Association Women Lawyers, 1998, Alumnae of Year Award, Brooklyn College, 1999, Elected Official of Year Award, Sacramento Area Council Governments, 1999, Vision Award, Highwood Online Girlsite, 1999, Pub. Servant Award, National Organization Fetal Alcohol Syndrome, 1999, Every Action Counts Congl. Award, Hadassah, 1999, Dorothy Donahoe Women of Year Award, 1999, Spirit of Achievement Award, Albert Einstein Medical College, 2000, Paul E. Tsongas Award, Lymphoma Research Foundation America, 2000, Peter H. Behr Award, Friends of River, 2000, Environmental Leadership Award, California League Conservation Voters, 2003, Star Award, Women's Campaign Fund, 2003, Julian C. Dixon Award, Mobility 21, 2004, Leadership Award, National Foundation Women Legislators, 2005, Community Action Hero Award, No Drugs America Association, 2006, Woman of Year Award, Women's Image Network, 2006, National Champion Families Award, Parents Anonymous, 2007, Dr. Jane Evans Pursuit of Justice Award, Women of Reform Judaism, 2007, Native American Hertiage Association Award, 2007, John H. Chafee Congl. Environmental Award, Association American Railroads, 2008, Legislator of Year Award, American Planning Association, 2009, California Primary Care Association, 2009, Air Quality Management District, 2009, Information & Tech. Industry Council, 2009, Legis. Leader Award, Humane Society of US, 2010, Phil Burton Badge of Courage Award, Sierra Club San Francisco Bay Chapter, 2010 **MEM:** Mem.: Marin Community Video, Marin National Women's Political Caucus, Marin Education Corps. **PA:** Democrat **BA:** Office of Barbara Boxer, 112 Hart Senate Office Building, Washington D.C., DC, 20510

BOYLE, BRENDAN F., T: U.S. Represerive from Pennsylvania **I:** Government Administration/Government Relations/Government Services **PB:** Phila. **SC:** PA/USA **ED:** MPP, Harvard University, John F. Kennedy School of Government, Cambridge, Massachusetts, 2005; BA in Government, completed Hesburgh Program in Pub. Service, University of Notre Dame, Notre Dame, Ind., 1999 **C:** U.S. House of Representatives from Pennsylvania's 13th District, 2015-,; Member, Committee on Foreign Affairs,; Committee on Oversight and Government Reform; Member District 170, Pennsylvania House of Representatives, 2009-15; Former sportscaster, 640 WVFI-AM, South Bend, Ind., **AW:** Named one of Top 10 Rising Stars, Philadelphia Daily News, 2008 **PA:** Democrat **BA:** 1133 Longworth HOB, Washington, DC, 20515

BRADFORD, SAM, T: Professional Football Player **I:** Athletics **DOB:** 11/08/1987 **PB:** Oklahoma City **SC:** OK/USA **PT:** Son of Kent and Martha Bradford. **ED:** BS in Finance, University Oklahoma, Norman, 2010 **C:** Quaterback, Arizona Cardinals, 2018-; Quarterback, Minnesota Vikings, 2016-2018; Quarterback, Philadelphia Eagles, 2015; Quarterback, St. Louis Rams, 2010-2015; Quarterback, University of Oklahoma Sooners, 2007-09; **CIV:** Registered member, Cherokee Nation, Oklahoma, **AW:** Named NFL Offensive Rookie of Year, Associated Press, 2010, Offensive Player of Year, Big 12 Conference, 2008, First Team All-Conf., 2008, First Team All-American, The Sporting News, 2008, Associated Press, 2008, National Player of Year, 2008, College Football Player of Year, The Sporting News, 2008, Freshman of Year, 2007; recipient Heisman Memorial Trophy award, Heisman Trophy Trust, 2008, Sammy Baugh award, Touchdown Club of Columbus, 2008, Davey O'Brien award, Davey O'Brien Foundation, 2008 **ACH:** Achievements include being the first overall pick in the NFL Draft, 2010 **BA:** Arizona Cardinals, PO Box 888, Phoenix, AZ, 85001-0888

BRADWAY, ROBERT, T: President, CEO **I:** Biotechnology **CN:** Amgen, Inc. **ED:** MBA, Harvard University; BA in Biology, Amherst College, Massachusetts **C:** President, CEO, Amgen, Inc., Thousand Oaks, CA, 2012-Present; Board of Directors, Amgen, Inc., Thousand Oaks, CA, 2011-Present; President, COO, Amgen, Inc., Thousand Oaks, CA, 2010-2012; Executive Vice President, CFO, Amgen, Inc., Thousand Oaks, CA, 2007-2010; Vice President, Operations Strategy, Amgen, Inc., Thousand Oaks, CA, 2006-2007; Positions Through Managing Director, Morgan Stanley, New York, NY, London, England, 1988-2006 **BA:** Amgen Inc., 1 Amgen Center Drive, Thousand Oaks, CA, 91320-1799

BRADY, KEVIN PATRICK, T: U.S. Representative from Texas **I:** Government Administration/Government Relations/Government Services **DOB:** 04/11/1955 **PB:** Vermillion, South Dakota, April 11, 1955 **ED:** BS in Mass Communications, University South Dakota, Vermillion, 1990 **C:** Chairmen, House Ways and Means Committee, 2015-; Member, US Congress from 8th Texas district, 1997-; Deputy whip, US Congress from 8th Texas district; Member from District 15, Texas House of Reps., 1991-97; President, South Montgomery County-Woodlands C. of C., 1985-96 **CIV:** Active, Saints Simon and Jude Catholic Church **AW:** Named Legis. Standout, Dallas Morning News, Outstanding Young Texan, Texas Jaycees; named one of 10 Best Legislators for Families and Children, State Bar Texas; recipient Victims Rights Equalizer award, Texans for Equal Justice Center, Support for Family Issues award, Texas Extension Homemakers Association, Scholars Achievement award, Excellence in Pub. Service, North Harris Montgomery Community College District, Achievement award, Texas Conservative Coalition **MEM:** Mem.: Rotary **PA:** Republican

BRADY, ROBERT A., T: U.S. Representative from Pennsylvania **I:** Government Administration/Government Relations/Government Services **DOB:** 04/07/1945 **PB:** Philadelphia **C:** Ranking Member, U.S. Committee on House Administration, 2007-; Member, US Congress from 1st Pennsylvania District, Washington, 1998-; Democratic leader 34th ward, Metropolitan Regional Council Carpenters & Joiners, 1980-; Chairman, US House Administration Committee, Washington, 2007-11; Commissioner, Philadelphia Turnpike Commission, 1991-98; Union official, Metropolitan Regional Council Carpenters & Joiners, Philadelphia,; Carpenter, Philadelphia, 1963-65 **CR:** Board directors Philadelphia Redevelopment Authority lecturer University Pennsylvania, 1997-; chairman, Philadelphia Democratic Party, 1986-; deputy mayor for labor, City of Philadelphia, 1984-87; sgt.-at-arms, Philadelphia City Council, 1975-83 **AW:** Named Friend of National Parks, National Parks Conservation Association **PA:** Democrat

BRADY, TOM, T: Professional Football Player **I:** Athletics **DOB:** 08/03/1977 **PB:** San Mateo, California, August 3, 1977 **PT:** Son of Thomas and Galynn (Johnson) Brady; **SPN:** Married Gisele Bündchen, February 26, 2009; **CH:** children: Benjamin Rein, Vivian Lake; 1 child, John Edward Moynahan (with Bridget Moynahan) **ED:** BA in Organizational Studies, University Michigan, 2000 **C:** Quarterback, New England Patriots, 2000 **CW:** Appeared in (TV series) Entourage, 2009 **AW:** Named NFL Comeback Player of Year, Associated Press, 2009, NFL Player of Year, The Sporting News, 2007, 1st Team All-Pro, Associated Press, 2010, 2007, NFL MVP, 2010, 2007, NFL Offensive Player of Year, 2010, 2007, Male Athlete of Year, 2007, Sportsman of Year, Sports Illus., 2005, The Sporting News, 2007, 2004, Super

Bowl XLIX MVP, 2015, Super Bowl XXXVIII MVP, 2004, Super Bowl XXXVI MVP, 2002; named one of The Most Influential People in the World of Sports, Business Week, 2008, 2007; named to Junipero Serra HS Hall of Fame, 2003, American Football Conference Pro Bowl Team, NFL, 2009-14, 2007, 2005, 2004, 2001, Time 100 Most Influential, 2017, Pro Bowl 2017,recipient Ed Block Courage award, New England Patriots, 2010, ESPY award, Best NFL Player, ESPN, 2008, ESPY award, Best Breakthrough Athlete, 2002 **ACH:** Achievements include leading the NFL in: passing touchdowns, 2002, 2007, 2010; passing yards, 2005, 2007; passer rating, 2007, 2010; being a member of Super Bowl Championship winning New England Patriots, 2002, 2004, 2005, 2015; setting the NFL record for: touchdown passes in a single-season (50), 2007; consecutive pass attempts without an interception (340), 2010-11

BRANAGH, KENNETH, T: Actor, Film Director **I:** Media & Entertainment **PB:** Belfast **SC:** Ireland **PT:** William Branagh; Frances (Harper) Branagh **ED:** LittD (hon.), Queens University, Belfast, 1990; Grad., Royal Academy of Dramatic Art, 1981 **C:** Co-founder, Renaissance Theater Co., England, to 1994 **CW:** Actor: (films) Coming Through, 1985, A Month in the Country, 1987, High Season, 1987, Dead Again, 1991, Swing Kids, 1993, Othello, 1995, The Gingerbread Man, 1998, The Proposition, 1998, Celebrity, 1998, The Theory of Flight, 1998, The Dance of Shiva, 1998, The Periwig-Maker (voice), 1999, Wild Wild West, 1999, How to Kill Your Neighbor's Dog, 2000, The Road to El Dorado (voice), 2000, Schneider's 2nd Stage, 2001, Alien Love Triangle, 2002, Rabbit-Proof Fence, 2002, Harry Potter and the Chamber of Secrets, 2002, Five Children and It, 2004, Valkyrie, 2008, Pirate Radio, 2009, My Week with Marilyn, 2011, Stars in Shorts, 2012, Jack Ryan: Shadow Recruit, 2014, Mindhorn, 2016, Dunkirk, 2017, Murder on the Orient Express 2017; (TV films) Too Late to Talk to Billy, 1982, Easter 2016, 1982, A Matter of Choice for Billy, 1983, To the Lighthouse, 1983, A Coming to Terms for Billy, 1984, Ghosts, 1986, The Lady's Not for Burning, 1987, Strange Interlude, 1988, Look Back in Anger, 1989, Shadow of a Gunman, 1995, Big Al Uncovered, 2000, Conspiracy, 2001 (Emmy award for Outstanding Lead Actor in a Miniseries or a Movie, 2001), Shackleton, 2002, Warm Springs, 2005; (TV miniseries) Maybury, 1981, Boy in the Bush, 1984, Fortunes of War, 1987; (TV series) Thompson, 1988; actor, producer (TV series) Wallander, 2008-12, director (films) Dead Again, 1991, Swan Song, 1992, Thor, 2011, Cinderella, 2015, (TV films) Twelfth Night, or What You Will, 1988, director, writer (films) In the Bleak Midwinter, 1995, Listening, 2003, actor, director, writer Henry V, 1989 (BAFTA award for Best Direction, 1989), Hamlet, 1996, actor, director, producer Peter's Friends, 1992, actor, director, co-prodr. Frankenstein, 1994, actor, director, producer, writer Much Ado About Nothing, 1993, Love's Labour's Lost, 2000; (actor, director): (films) Jack Ryan: Shadow Recruit, 2014; (director, producer, writer) As You Like It, 2006; (director, producer) The Magic Flute, 2006; Sleuth, 2007; (actor, director): (Broadway plays) The Play What I Wrote, 2003; (actor, co-dir. with Rob Ashford): (plays) Macbeth, 2013; narrator (documentaries) Anne Frank Remembered, 1995, The Tramp and the Dictator, 2002, World War 1 in Colour, 2005, IMAX: Galapagos, 2005, Goebbels-Experiment, Das, 2005, Great Composers, 1997 **AW:** Named a Commander of the Order of the British Empire, Queen Elizabeth II, 2012; Recipient Decorated Order of Arts and Letters, France

BRANCH, ELIZABETH L., T: Federal Judge **I:** Law and Legal Services **DOB:** 06/25/1905 **PB:** Atlanta, Georgia **SC:** Atlanta, Georgia **ED:** B.A., Davidson College; J.D., Emory University School of Law **C:** Judge, U.S. Court of Appeals for the Eleventh Circuit (2018-Present); Judge, Georgia Court of Appeals (2012-2018); Senior Official, Administration of President George W. Bush (2004-2008)

BRAT, DAVE, T: U.S. Representative from Virginia **I:** Government Administration/Government Relations/Government Services **CN:** Randolph-Macon Coll. Randolph-Macon College **PT:** Son of Paul Brat and Nancy Bray; **ED:** PhD in Economics, American University, 1995; MDiv., Princeton Theological Seminary, 1990; BBA, Hope College, 1986 **C:** Member, U.S. House of Representatives from Virginia's 7th District, 2014-; Member, Committee on the Budget; Member, Committee on Education and the Workforce,; Member, Committee on Small Business **CR:** Republican nominee for Virginia's 7th Congressional District, 2014 director BB&T Moral Foundations of Capitalism Randolph-Macon College, 2010-12 member Governor's Advisory Board Economists, 2006- **PA:** Republican **RE:** Christian

BREEN, EDWARD DEVEAUX, T: Chemical Company Executive **I:** Manufacturing **DOB:** 03/14/1956 **ED:** BS in Business Administration and Economics, Grove City College **C:** Chairman, Chief Executive Officer, DowDuPont (2017-Present); Chief Executive Officer, DuPont, Co. (2015-Present); Chairman, Tyco International, Portsmouth, NH (2012-2015); Chairman, Chief Executive Officer, Tyco International, Portsmouth, NH (2002-2012); Board of Directors, Motorola; President, Chief Operating Officer, Motorola, Schaumburg, IL (2002); Executive Vice President, President Networks Sector, Motorola (2001-2002); Executive Vice President, President, Broadband Communications Sector, Motorola (2000-2001); Chairman, President, Chief Executive Officer, General Instrument (1997-2000); Senior Vice President, Sales Broadband Networks Group, General Instrument (1996-1997); Executive Vice President, Terrestrial System, General Instrument (1994-1996); Senior Vice President, Sales Terrestrial Products Worldwide Sales Organization, General Instrument (1988-1994); With, General Instrument (1978-1988) **CR:** Advisory Board Member, New Mountain Capital, LLC; Independent Director, DuPont USA (2015-Present); Board of Directors, Comcast Corporation (2005-2011, 2014-Present); Board of Directors, Tyco International Ltd.; Board of Directors, McLeod USA Inc. (2001-2005) **AW:** Named One of Top 15 CableFAX Magazine's 100 Most Influential People in Cable (1999); Vanguard Award, National Cable TV Association (1998) **BA:** DuPont Co, 1007 Market St, Wilmington, DE, 19898

BREYER, JAMES WILLIAM, T: Venture Capitalist **I:** Business Management/Business Services **DOB:** 07/26/1961 **PB:** New Haven **SC:** CT/USA **PT:** Son of John Paul and Eva Breyer **MS:** Married **SPN:** Susan Zaroff (6/20/1987) **ED:** MBA, Harvard University, 1987; BS, Stanford University, 1983 **C:** Founder, FWD.us, 2013-; Founder/CEO, Breyer Capital, 2006-; Managing General Partner, Accel Partners, San Francisco, 1995-; Chairman, Stanford Engineering Venture Fund; General Partner, Accel Partners, San Francisco, 1990-95; Associate, Accel Partners, San Francisco, 1987-90; Joined, Accel Partners, 1985; Consultant, Management, McKinsey & Co.; Senior Business Analyst, McKinsey & Co., New York City, 1983-85; Worked, Product Marketing and Management, Apple Computer; Worked, Product Marketing and Management, Hewlett-Packard Co. **CR:** Honorary Professor

Yuelu Academy, Hunan University, 2005-, Board of Directors, Ubermedia, 2011-, Booyah! Inc., 2010-, Dell Inc., 2009-, Facebook, Inc., 2006-, Marvel Entertainment, Inc., 2006-09, Wal-Mart Stores, Inc., 2001-, RealNetworks, Inc., 1995-2008 **CIV:** Board of Trustees, Menlo School, Board of Trustees, San Francisco Museum Modern Art, Board Associates, Technet, Board Associates, Chairman, Stanford Tech. Ventures Program, Board Associates, Pacific Community Ventures, Board Associates, Harvard Business School **AW:** Named One of The 10 Smartest People in Tech, Forbes magazine, 2010; Baker Scholar, Harvard University, 1987 **MEM:** Member, National Association Venture Capitalists (board directors), Western Association Venture Capitalists (board directors), Harvard Business School Club of No. California **H:** Art, Films **BA:** Breyer Capital, 2500 Sand Hill Road, Suite 300, Menlo Park, CA, 94025

BREYER, STEPHEN GERALD, T: Associate Justice of the U.S. Supreme Court **I:** Government Administration/Government Relations/Government Services **DOB:** 08/15/1938 **PB:** San Francisco **SC:** CA/USA **PT:** Son of Irving G. and Anne R. Breyer; **ED:** LLD (hon.), University Rochester, 1983; LLB, Harvard University, 1964; BA (Marshall scholar), Oxford University, 1961; AB, Stanford University, 1959 **CT:** Bar: Massachusetts 1971, D.C. 1966, California 1966 **C:** Associate justice, US Supreme Court, Washington, 1994-; Oliver Wendell Holmes lecturer, Harvard Law School, Cambridge, Massachusetts, 1992; Chief judge, US Court Appeals (1st cir.), Boston, 1990-94; Judge, US Court Appeals (1st cir.), Boston, 1980-90; Chief counsel, US Senate Judiciary Committee, 1979-81; Special counsel, US Senate Judiciary Committee, 1974-75; Assistant special prosecutor, Watergate Special Prosecution Force, 1973; Professor John F. Kennedy School Government, Harvard University, 1978-81; Lecturer, Harvard University, 1981-94; Professor, Harvard University, 1970-81; Assistant professor law, Harvard University, 1967-70; Special assistant to assistant attorney general (antitrust) Donald Turner, US Department Justice, Washington, 1965-67; Law clerk to Hon. Arthur J. Goldberg, US Supreme Court, Washington, 1964-65 **CR:** Judicial Conference representative to Administrative Conference US, 1981-94 visiting professor University Rome, 1993 visiting lecturer Salzburg (Austria) Seminar, 1993, 1978, College Law, Sydney, 1975 member board directors Dia Art Found, 1985-86 member Judicial Conference of US, 1990-94, US Sentencing Commission, 1985-89 **CIV:** Board overseers, Dana Farber Cancer Institute, Boston, 1977-94 Trustee, University Massachusetts, 1974-81 **MIL:** US Army, 1957 **CW:** Author (with Paul MacAvoy): The Federal Power Commission and the Regulation of Energy, 1974; author (with Richard Stewart) Administrative Law and Regulatory Policy, 1979, Administrative Law and Regulatory Policy, 3rd edition, 1992; author: Regulation and its Reform, 1982, Breaking the Vicious Circle, 1993, Active Liberty: Interpreting Our Democratic Constitution, 2005, Making Our Democracy Work: A Judge's View, 2010; contributor articles to professional journals **AW:** Recipient Fordham-Stein Ethics prize, Fordham University, 2008, Distinguished Eagle Scout award, Boy Scouts of America, 2007, Annual award for Scholarship in Administrative Law, American Bar Association, 1987 **MEM:** Mem.: American Bar Association, Council Foreign Relations, American Academy Arts & Sciences, American Law Institute, American Bar Foundation, Academie des Sciences Morales et Politiques (foreign) **BA:** US Supreme Court, One First St St NE, Washington, DC, USA, 20543-0001

BRIDENSTINE, JIM, **T:** U.S. Representative from Oklahoma **I:** Government Administration/Government Relations/Government Services **DOB:** 06/15/1975 **PB:** Ann Arbor **SC:** MI/USA **ED:** MBA, Cornell University (2009); BS in Economics, Business & Psychology, Rice University (1998) **C:** Member, U.S. House of Science, Space & Technology Committee (2013-Present); Member, U.S. House Armed Services Committee (2013-Present); Member, U.S. Congress from the First Oklahoma District, Washington, DC (2013-Present); Executive Director, Tulsa Air & Space Museum & Planetarium (2008-2010); Defense Consultant, Wyle Laboratories (2007-2008) **AW:** Decorated, Battle Efficiency Ribbon; Recipient, Expert Pistol Medal; Recipient, Naval Sea Service Deployment Ribbon; Recipient, Global War on Terrorism Expeditionary Medal; Recipient, Iraq Campaign Medal; Recipient, Armed Forces Expeditionary Medal; Recipient, National Defense Service Medal; Recipient, Navy & Marine Corps Achievement Medal; Recipient, Navy Commendation Medal with V Medal; Recipient, Air Medal **PA:** Republican

BRIDGES, JEFF, **T:** Actor **I:** Media & Entertainment **DOB:** 12/04/1949 **PB:** Los Angeles **SC:** CA/USA **CIV:** Co-Founder, End Hunger Network, 1983, National Spokesperson, No Kid Hungry Campaign, Share Our Strength Organization, 2010—Present **CW:** Actor, (Films) Silent Night, Lonely Night, 1969, Halls Of Anger, 1970, The Last Picture Show, 1971, The Yin And Yang Of Mr. Go, 1971, In Search Of America, 1971, Fat City, 1972, Bad Company, 1972, Lolly-Madonna XXX, 1973, The Last American Hero, 1973, The Iceman Cometh, 1973, Thunderbolt And Lightfoot, 1974, Rancho Deluxe, 1975, Hearts Of The West, 1975, Stay Hungry, 1976, King Kong, 1976, Somebody Killed Her Husband, 1978, Winter Kills, 1979, The American Success Company, 1979, Heaven's Gate, 1980, Cutter's Way, 1981, Tron, 1982, Kiss Me Goodbye, 1982, (Voice Actor) The Last Unicorn, 1982, Against All Odds, 1984, Starman, 1984, Jagged Edge, 1985, 8 Million Ways To Die, 1986, The Morning After, 1986, Nadine, 1987, Tucker: The Man And His Dream, 1988, See You In The Morning, 1989, The Fabulous Baker Boys, 1989, Texasville, 1990, The Fisher King, 1991, American Heart, 1992, The Vanishing, 1993, Fearless, 1993, Blown Away, 1994, Wild Bill, 1995, White Squall, 1996, The Mirror Has Two Faces, 1996, The Big Lebowski, 1998, Arlington Road, 1999, The Muse, 1999, Simpatico, 1999, The Contender, 2000, Scenes Of The Crime, 2001, K-PAX, 2001, Masked And Anonymous, 2003, Seabiscuit, 2003, The Door In The Floor, 2004, The Amateurs, 2005, Tideland, 2005, Stick It, 2006, (Voice Actor) Surf's Up, 2007, A Dog Year, 2008, Iron Man, 2008, How To Lose Friends & Alienate People, 2008, The Open Road, 2009, The Men Who Stare At Goats, 2009, Crazy Heart, 2009, Tron: Legacy, 2010, True Grit, 2010, (Voice Actor) Pablo, 2012, A Place At The Table, 2012, R.I.P.D., 2013, Seventh Son, 2014, (Voice Actor) The Little Prince, 2015, Hell Or High Water, 2016, The Only Living Boy In New York, 2017, Kingsman: The Golden Circle, 2017, Only The Brave, 2017; Narrator, (Documentaries) The Heroes Of Rock And Roll, 1979, Raising The Mammoth, 2000, Lost In La Mancha, 2002, Lewis & Clark: Great Journey West, 2002; Actor, Executive Producer, (TV Films) Hidden In America, 1996, A Dog Year, 2008, SNL, 2010, The Jonathan Ross Show, 2017; Actor, Producer, The Giver, 2014; Musician, (Albums) Be Here Soon, 2000, Jeff Bridges, 2011; Author, Photographer, Pictures: Photographs By Jeff Bridges, 2003; Co-Author, (With Bernie Glassman): The Dude And The Zen Master, 2013 **AW:** Desert Palm Achievement Award, Palm Springs International Film Festival, 2010, Screen Actors Guild Award For Outstanding Performance By A Male Actor In A Leading Role, Golden Globe Award For Best Actor In A Motion Picture Drama, Hollywood Foreign Press Association, Academy Award For Best Actor, Academy Motion Picture Arts & Sciences, Award For Best Actor, Broadcast Film Critics Association, Denver Film Critics Society, LA Film Critics Association, Crazy Heart, 2009 **BA:** Creative Artists Agency, 2000 Avenue of the Stars, Los Angeles, CA, 90067

BRIN, SERGEY MIHAILOVICH, **T:** Computer Scientist **I:** Technology **CN:** Google Inc. **DOB:** 08/21/1973 **PB:** Moscow **SC:** Russia **PT:** Michael Brin, Eugenia Brin **ED:** Honorary MBA, IE Business School, Madrid, Spain, 2003; MS, Stanford University, California, 1995; BS in Mathematics & Computer Science, University of Maryland, College Park, With Honors, 1993 **C:** CEO, Alphabet, 2017-Present; Director of Special Projects, Google, Inc., Mountain View, CA, 2011-Present; President of Technology, Google, Inc., Mountain View, CA, 2001-2011; Co-President, Google, Inc., Mountain View, CA, 1998-2001; Co-Founder, Google, Inc., Mountain View, CA, 1998 **CR:** Fellow, American Academy of Arts & Sciences; Speaker, Technological, Entertainment & Design Conference, World Economic Forum; National Science Foundation Graduate Fellowship, 1993-1995; Board Directors, Google, Inc., 1998-Present **CIV:** Co-Founder, The Brin Wojcicki Foundation **CW:** Author, (Public Academic Papers) Dynamic Itemset Counting and Implication Rules for Market Basket Data, 1997, Beyond Market Baskets: Generalizing Association Rules to Correlations, 1997, Extracting Patterns and Relations From the World Wide Web, 1998, Scalable Techniques for Mining Causal Structures, 1998; Co-Author, (With Larry Page) Dynamic Data Mining: A New Architecture for Data With High Dimensionality, 1998; Guest Appearance, Charlie Rose Show, CNBC, CNNFN **AW:** Marconi Prize, 2004, Persons of the Week (With Larry Page), ABC World News Tonight, 2004, Business Leader of the Year, Science American Magazine, 2005, The 100 Most Influential People in the World, TIME Magazine, 2005, The 50 Who Matter Now, Cnnmoney. Com Business 2.0, 2006-2007, The 25 Most Powerful People in Business, Fortune Magazine, 2007, The 50 Most Important People on the Web, PC World, 2007, Power Player, Advertising Age, 2009, The 100 Agents of Change, Rolling Stone Magazine, 2009, The 40 Under 40, Fortune Magazine, 2009-2012, The World's Most Powerful People, Forbes Magazine, 2009-2014, The Forbes 400: Richest Americans, 2006-Present, The World's Richest People, 2007-Present **BA:** Google Inc., 1600 Amphitheatre Parkway, Mountain View, CA, 94043-1351

BRISCOE, MARY BECK, **T:** Federal Judge **I:** Law and Legal Services **DOB:** 04/04/1947 **PB:** Council Grove **SC:** KS/USA **ED:** LLM, University of Virginia, 1990; JD, University of Kansas, 1973; BA, University of Kansas, 1969 **C:** Judge, U.S. Court of Appeals, Tenth Circuit, Topeka, KS, 1995-Present; Chief Judge, U.S. Court of Appeals, Tenth Circuit, 2010-2015; Chief Judge, Kansas Court of Appeals, 1990-1995; Judge, Kansas Court of Appeals, 1984-1995; Assistant U.S. Attorney For Wichita And Topeka, Kansas, Department of Justice, 1974-1984; Attorney-Examiner, Financial Division, Interstate Commerce Commission, 1973-1974; Research Assistant, Harold L. Haun, Esq., 1973 **CR:** Fellow, Kansas Bar Foundation, Fellow, American Bar Foundation **AW:** Women's Hall of Fame, University of Kansas, 2001; University of Kansas Law Society Distinguished Alumnus Award, 2000; Outstanding Service Award, Kansas Bar Association, 1992 **MEM:** American Bar Association, Women Attorneys Association of Topeka, Kansas Bar Association, Topeka Bar Association, National Association of Women Judges, American Judicature Society, University of Kansas Law Society, Kansas Historical Society, Honorary Member, Washburn Law School Association **BA:** U.S. Court of Appeals, Tenth Circuit, Byron White U.S. Courthouse, 1823 Stout Street, Denver, CO, 80257

BROAD, ELI, **T:** Philanthropist **I:** Nonprofit & Philanthropy **DOB:** 06/06/1993 **PB:** New York City **SC:** NY/USA **ED:** HHD (hon.), Michigan State University, 2002; LLD (hon.), Southwestern University, 2000; BA in Accounting, cum laude, Michigan State University, 1954 **CT:** CPA, Michigan, 1956 **C:** Founder, Chairman, Kaufman and Broad Home Corp. (now KB Home), LA, 1993-; Chairman, Executive Committee, Kaufman and Broad Home Corp., LA, 1993-95; Chairman, Kaufman and Broad Home Corp., LA, 1989-93; Chairman, SunAmerica Inc. (formerly Kaufman & Broad, Inc., now AIG Retirement Services Inc.), 2001-05; Co-founder, Chairman, President, CEO, SunAmerica Inc. (formerly Kaufman & Broad, Inc.), LA, 1957-2001; Assistant Professor, Detroit Institute Tech., 1956; Certified Public Accountant, 1954-56 **CR:** Member, Executive Committee, Advisory Board, Federal National Mortgage Association, 1972-73, Active, California Business Roundtable, 1986-2000, Co-owner, Sacramento Kings and Arco Arena, 1992-99, Trustee, Committee for Economic Development, 1993-95, Member, Real Estate Advisory Board, Citibank, New York City, 1976-81, Board of Directors, Sacramento Kings and ARCO Arena **CIV:** Member, Board of Directors, LA World Affairs Council, 1988-2003, Chairman, 1994-97, DARE Am., 1989-95, Honorary Member, Board of Directors 1995-, Founding Trustee, Windward School, Santa Monica, California, 1972-77, Board of Trustees, Pitzer College, Claremont, California, 1970-82, Chairman, Board of Trustees, 1973-79, Life Trustee, 1982-, Haifa University, Israel, 1972-80, California State University, 1978-82, Vice Chairman, Board of Trustees, 1979-80, Trustee Emeritus, 1982-, Museum Contemporary Art, LA, 1980-93, Founding Chairman, 1980, Archives Am. Art, Smithsonian Institution, Washington, 1985-98, Am. Federation Arts, 1988-91, Leland Stanford Mansion Foundation, 1992-2000, California Institute Tech., 1993-, Armand Hammer Museum Art and Cultural Center UCLA, 1994-99, President, California Non-Partisan Vote Registration Foundation, 1971-72, Chancellor's Associate, UCLA, 1971-, Member, Visiting Committee, Grad. School Management, 1972-90, Trustee, UCLA Foundation, 1986-96, Executive Committee Board of Visitors School of the Arts & Architecture, 1997-, Associate Chairman, United Crusade, LA, 1973-76, Chairman, Mayor's Housing Policy Committee, LA, 1974-75, Delegate, Speaker Federal Economic Summit Conference, 1974, State Economic Summit Conference, 1974, Member, Contemporary Council, LA County Museum Art, 1973-79, Board of Trustees, Acquisitions Committee, 1978-81, Trustee, 1995- Board of Fellows, Member, Executive Committee, The Claremont (California) Colleges, 1974-79, National Trustee, Baltimore Museum Art, 1985-91, Member, Advisory Board, Boy Scouts Am., 1982-85, LA Business Journal, 1986-88, Member, Advisory Council, Town Hall of California, 1985-87, Trustee Dem. National Committee Victory Fund, 1988, 1992, 1996, Member, Painting and Sculpture Committee, Whitney Museum, New York City, 1987-89, Chairman, Advisory Board ART/LA, 1989, Board of Overseers, The Music Center of LA County, 1991-92, Member, Board of Governors, 1996-98, Hon. Governor, 1998-, Member, Contemporary Art Committee, Harvard University Art Museum,

Cambridge, Massachusetts, 1992-2004, Member, International Directors Council, Guggenheim Museum, New York City, 1993-98, Trustee, Museum Modern Art, New York City, 2004-, Active National Industrial Pollution Control Council, 1970-73, Maeght Foundation, St. Paul de Vence, France, 1975-80, Mayor's Special Adv. Committee on Fiscal Administration, LA, 1993-94, Board of Directors, UCLA/Armand Hammer Museum Art And Cultural Center, 1994-1999, Co-founder, Broad Foundation, 1999-, Board of Regents, Smithsonian Institute, 2004- **CW:** Author: (book) The Art of Being Unreasonable: Lessons in Unconventional Thinking, 2012 **AW:** Recipient, Man of Year Award, City of Hope, 1965, Golden Plate Award, Am. Academy Achievement, 1971, Housing Man of Year Award, National Housing Council, 1979, Humanitarian Award, National Conference of Christians and Jews, 1977, Am. Heritage Award, Anti Defamation League, 1984, Pub. Affairs Award Coro Foundation, 1987, Honors Award, Visual Arts, L.A. Arts Council, 1989, Lifetime Achievement Award, LA C. of C., 1999, Visionary Award, Harvard Business School Association, Southern California, 1999, Visionary Award, KCET, 1999, Julius Award, University Southern California School Policy, Planning and Devel., 2001, Chmn.'s Award, Asia Society Southern California, 2000, Teach for Am. Educational Leadership Award, 2001, Exemplary Leadership in Management Award, UCLA, The Anderson School, 2002, Alexis de Tocqueville Award, United Way, 2002, Brass Ring Award, United Friends the Children, 2003, Civic Medal Hon. LA C. of C., 2004, Earl Warren Outstanding Pub. Service Award, Am. Society Pub. Administration LA Metro. Chapter, 2004, Frederick R. Weisman Award, Ams. for the Arts, 2005, Service to Community Award, Am. Institute to Architects LA Chapter, 2005, Louise T. Blouin Foundation Award, 2006; Named One of Top 200 Collectors, ARTnews Magazine, 2004-12, World's Richest People, Forbes Magazine, 1999-, Forbes 400: Richest Americans, 1999-; Eli Broad College Business and Eli Broad Grad. School Business Named in his Honor, Michigan State University, 1991; Edythe and Eli Broad Art Center Named in his Honor, UCLA; Knighted Chevalier in National Order Legion of Honor, France, 1994, TIME's 100 Most Influential, 2018 **MEM:** Fellow: American Association for the Advancement of Science; mem.: California Club, Hillcrest Country Club (LA), Regency Club, Beta Alpha Psi **H:** Collecting contemporary art **BA:** 75 Oakmont St, Los Angeles, CA, 90049

BROADUS JR., CALVIN(SNOOP DOG), T: Rap Artist, Actor **I:** Media & Entertainment **PB:** Long Beach **SC:** CA/USA **PT:** Beverly Tate **C:** Founder, owner, Doggy Style Records, Inc. (formerly Dogg-House Records), 1999 **CIV:** Founder, Snoop Youth Football League, California, 2005 **CW:** Musician: (albums) Doggystyle, 1993, Tha Doggfather, 1996, Da Game Is To Be Sold Not To Be Told, 1998, No Limit Top Dogg, 1999, Tha Last Meal, 2000, Doggy Style Allstars: Welcome to Tha House, 2002, Paid Tha Cost to Be da Bo$$, 2002, Soundtrack Raw N Uncut, Vol. 1, 2002, Welcome to Church: Mix Tape, Vol. 1, 2003, R&G - Rhythm and Gangster: The Masterpiece, 2004, Dogg Pound Mix, 2005, Me & My Homies, 2005, Tha Blue Carpet Treatment, 2006, The Chronicalz, Vol. 1: The Mixed Up Album, 2006, Ego Trippin', 2008, Malice N Wonderland, 2009, More Malice, 2010, Doggumentary, 2011, Reincarnated, 2013, Coffee from Colombia, 2014, Bush, 2015, Coolaid, 2016, Cuzznz, 2016, Neva Left, 2017; actor: (films) Half Baked, 1998, I Got the Hook Up, 1998, Ride, 1998, Caught Up, 1998, Urban Menace, 1999, The Wrecking Crew, 1999, Hot Boyz, 1999, Tha Eastsidaz, 2000, Baby Boy, 2001, Training Day, 2001, Bones, 2001, The Wash, 2001, Crime

Partners, 2001, Malibu's Most Wanted, 2003, Old School, 2003, Starsky & Hutch, 2004, Soul Plane, 2004, Racing Stripes (voice), 2005, The Tenants, 2005, Boss'n Up, 2005, Hood of Horror, 2006, Down for Life, 2009, Falling Up, 2009, The Big Bang, 2011, We the Party, 2012, Mac & Devin Go to High School, 2012, Turbo (voice), 2013; actor: (films) Scary Movie 5, 2013, Pitch Perfect 2, 2015, Dispensary, 2015, (Himself): (documentaries) Reincarnated, 2013, Scary Movie 5, 2013, The Distortion of Sound, 2014, Pitch Perfect 2, 2015, Dispensary, 2015, The Culture High, 2015, Popstar: Never Stop Never Stopping, 2016, Grow House, 2017 : (TV appearances) King of the Hill (voice), 2001, MADtv, 2004, The L Word, 2004, The Bernie Mac Show, 2004, The Boondocks, 2007-08, Monk, 2007, One Life to Live, 2008, Dog After Dark, 2009, Xavier: Renegade Angel, 2009, Brothers, 2009, The Boondocks, 2010, Big Time Rush, 2010, 90210, 2011, The Cleveland Show, 2011, Love and Hip Hop: Atlanta, 2014, Love and Hip Hop Hollywood, 2014, Snoop and Son A Dads Dream, 2015, Sanjay and Craig, 2015, Show Me the Money 4, 2015, Trailer Park Boys, 2016, Marth & Snoops Potluck Dinner Party, 2016, The Simpsons, 2017, Growing Up Hip Hop:Atlanta, 2017, The Joker's Wild Presented by Snoop Dogg, 2017 (reality TV series) Snoop Dogg's Father Hood, 2007-09; co-author (with David Seay): Tha Doggfather: The Times, Trials, and Hardcore Truths of Snoop Dogg, 1999; co-author: (with David E. talbert) Love Don't Live Here No More: Book One of Doggy Tales, 2006 **AW:** Best Art Direction, MTV Video Music Awards, 2015

BRODERICK, MATTHEW, T: Actor **I:** Media & Entertainment **PB:** New York **SC:** NY **PT:** James Broderick; Patricia (Biow) Broderick **MS:** Married **SPN:** Sarah Jessica Parker, (May 19, 1997) **CH:** James Wilkie Broderick; Marion Loretta Elwell Broderick; Tabitha Hodge Broderick **ED:** Student high school, New York City **C:** Actor, 1981- **CW:** Actor: (stage productions) Valentine's Day, 1980, Torch Song Trilogy, 1982 (Villager award 1982, Outer Critics Circle award 1982), Brighton Beach Memoirs, 1983 (Los Angeles Critics award 1983, Drama League award 1983, Theatre World award 1983, Antoinette Perry award 1983), Biloxi Blues, 1985, The Widow Claire, 1986-87, How to Succeed in Business Without Really Trying, 1995 (Tony award Lead Actor in a Musical, Outer Critics Cir. award, Drama Desk award), The Producers, 2001-02, 2003, The Odd Couple, 2005, The Philanthropist, 2009, Nice Work If You Can Get It, 2012, It's Only a Play, 2014; (films) Max Dugan Returns, 1983, WarGames, 1983, Ladyhawke, 1985, 1918, 1985, Ferris Bueller's Day Off, 1986, On Valentine's Day, 1986, Project X, 1987, Courtship, 1987, Biloxi Blues, 1988, Torch Song Trilogy, 1988, Glory, 1989, Family Business, 1989, The Freshman, 1990, Out on a Limb, 1992, The Night We Never Met, 1993, (voice) The Lion King, 1994, The Road to Wellville, 1994, Mrs. Parker and the Vicious Circle, 1994, (voice) Arabian Night, 1995, The Cable Guy, 1996, Addicted to Love, 1997, Godzilla, 1998, Walking to the Waterline, 1998, Election, 1999, Inspector Gadget, 1999, You Can Count on Me, 2000, (voice) Good Boy!, 2003, Marie and Bruce, 2004, The Stepford Wives, 2004, The Last Shot, 2004, The Producers, 2005 (Hollywood Supporting Actor of Year, Hollywood Film Festival Board Adv., 2005), Deck the Halls, 2006, Then She Found Me, 2007, (voice) Bee Movie, 2007, Diminished Capacity, 2008, Finding Amanda, 2008, (voice) The Tale of Despereaux, 2008, Wonderful World, 2010, Margaret, 2011, Tower Heist, 2011; (TV movies) Master Harold...and the Boys, 1985, A Life in the Theater, 1993 (Emmy nomination for best supporting actor miniseries or special, 1994), The Music Man, 2003, Beach Lane, 2010, Will Ferrell: Mark Twain Prize, 2011; producer, director,

actor: (film) Infinity, 1996.(Films) New Year's Eve, 2011, Skum Rocks!, 2013, Dirty Weekend, 2015, Trainwreck, 2015, Manchester by the Sea, 2016, The American Side, 2016, Rules Don't Apply, 2016, Spider-Man Homecoming, 2017, The Gettysburg Address, 2018, Look Away, 2018, Amusement Park,2019(Television) Adventure Time, 2012, Modern Family, 2012, Untitled Tad Quill Project, 2013, The Jim Gaffigan Show, 2015, Adventure Time, 2016, Bojack Horseman, 2017, A Christmas Story Live!, 2017(Theatre) Sylvia, 2015, Oh Hello on Broadway, 2016, Shining City, 2016, Evening at the Talk House, 2017 **AW:** Named to Hollywood Walk of Fame, 2006 **MEM:** Member Actors' Equity Association, Screen Actors Guild

BRODEUR, MARTIN, T: Professional Hockey Player (Retired) **I:** Athletics **DOB:** 05/06/1972 **PB:** Quebec **SC:** Canada **PT:** Denis Brodeur; Mireille Brodeur **C:** Assistant General Manager, St. Louis Blues (2015-Present); Management Team, Canada's Men's Hockey Team (2017); Senior Advisor to General Manager, St. Louis Blues (2015); Goaltender, St. Louis Blues (2014-2015); Goaltender, New Jersey Devils (1991-2014); Selected, First Round NHL Entry Draft, New Jersey Devils (1990) **CR:** Co-Owner, La Pizzeria; Montreal Member, Team Canada, Olympic Games, Vancouver, Canada (2010); Montreal Member, Team Canada, Olympic Games, Torino, Italy (2006); Member, Team Canada, World Cup of Hockey (2004); Montreal Member, Team Canada, Olympic Games, Salt Lake City, UT (2002); Montreal Member, Team Canada, Olympic Games, Nagano, Japan (1998); Member, Team Canada, World Cup of Hockey (1996) **CW:** Co-Author, "Brodeur: Beyond the Crease" (2006) **AW:** Named, Forty Under 40, NJBIZ (2010); Recipient, William M. Jennings Trophy (2010); Named, Second All-Star Team, NHL (2008); Named, NHL All-Star Game (2007-2008); Recipient, Vezina Trophy (2007-2008); Named, First All-Star Team, NHL (2007); Named, Second All-Star Team, NHL (2006); Recipient, William M. Jennings Trophy (2003-2004); Recipient, Vezina Trophy (2003-2004); Named, First All-Star Team, NHL (2003-2004); Recipient, William M. Jennings Trophy (1998); Named, Second All-Star Team, NHL (1997-1998); Named, NHL All-Star Game (1996-2004); Named, All-Rookie Team (1994); Recipient, Calder Memorial Trophy (1994) **ACH:** Achievements include being a member of Stanley Cup Champion New Jersey Devils, 1995, 2000, 2003; being a member of gold medal winning Canadian Hockey Team, Salt Lake City Olympics, 2002, Vancouver Olympics, 2010; being a member of World Cup Champion Team Canada, 2004; being the first goaltender in NHL history to record 12 consecutive 30 win seasons; holds NHL record with eight 40 win seasons; setting NHL record with 7 playoff shutouts, 2003; setting NHL record for most wins in a single season with 48, 2007; being the second goaltender to record 500 NHL victories, 2007; setting NHL record for career wins by a goaltender, 2009; becoming the NHL's all-time minutes leader, 2009; setting NHL record for regular-season appearances by a goaltender, 2009; becoming the all-time shutout leader in NHL history, 2009; being the first goaltender to record 600 NHL victories, 2010; having jersey #30 retired by the New Jersey Devils, 2016 **BA:** St Louis Blues Hockey Club Scotttrade Center, 1401 Clark Ave at Brett Hull Way, Saint Louis, MO, 63103

BRODY, ADRIEN, T: Actor **I:** Media & Entertainment **DOB:** 04/14/1973 **PB:** New York **SC:** NY/USA **PT:** Elliot Brody; Sylvia Plachy **ED:** Student, HS for the Performing Arts, New York City; Student, American Academy of Dramatic Arts, New York City **CW:** Actor: (plays, off-Broadway) Family Pride in the '50s, 1986; (TV series) Annie McGuire, 1988; (TV films) Home at Last, 1988, Jailbreakers, 1994; (films) New York Stories, 1989, The Boy Who Cried Bitch, 1991, King of the Hill, 1993, Angels in the Outfield, 1994, Solo, 1996, Bullet, 1996, The Last Time I Committed Suicide, 1997, Nothing to Lose/ Ten Benny, 1998, Six Ways to Sunday, 1997, The Undertaker's Wedding, 1997, Restaurant, 1998, The Thin Red Line, 1998, Oxygen, 1999, Summer of Sam, 1999, Liberty Heights, 1999, Bread and Roses, 2000, Harrison's Flowers, 2000, Love the Hard Way, 2001, The Affair of the Necklace, 2001, Dummy, 2002, The Pianist, 2002 (Academy award for Best Actor, 2003), The Singing Detective, 2003, The Village, 2004, The Jacket, 2005, King Kong, 2005, Hollywoodland, 2006, (narrator) The Tehuacan Project, 2007, The Darjeeling Limited, 2007, Cadillac Records, 2008, The Brothers Bloom, 2009, Splice, 2009, Predators, 2010, The Experiment, 2010, Midnight in Paris, 2011, InAPPropriate Comedy, 2012, Back to 1942, 2012, Third Person, 2013, The Grand Budapest Hotel, 2014, American Heist, 2014, Backtrack, 2014, Septembers of Shiraz, 2015, Manhattan Night, 2015, Stone Barn Castle, 2015, Bullethead, 2017, Emperor, 2017; (TV) Houdini, 2014; prodr.Breakthrough, 2015, Dice, 2016, Peaky Blinders,2017: (films) Giallo, 2009; actor, executive producer (films) Detachment, 2011, Wrecked, 2011

BROOKS, GARTH, T: Musician **I:** Media & Entertainment **DOB:** 02/07/1962 **PB:** Tulsa **PT:** Son of Troyal Raymond and Colleen McElroy (Carroll) Brooks; **ED:** BS in Advertising and Journalism, Oklahoma State University, Stillwater, 1984 **CIV:** Founder, Teammates for Kids Foundation, 1999 **CW:** Recording artist (albums) Garth Brooks, 1989, No Fences, 1990 (Academy Country Music award for Album of Year, 1991), Ropin' The Wind, 1991, Beyond the Season, 1992, The Chase, 1992, In Pieces, 1993, The Hits, 1994, Fresh Horses, 1995, Sevens, 1997, The Limited Series, Double Live, 1998 (American Music award for Favorite Country Album, 2000), In the Life of Chris Gaines, 1999, Scarecrow, 2001, The Lost Sessions, 2005, The Ultimate Hits, 2007, Blame It All On My Roots: Five Decades of Influences, 2013, Man Against Machine, 2014, Christmas Together, 2016, Gunslinger, 2016 (songs) The Dance (Country Music Association award for Video of Year, 1991, Academy Country Music awards for Song of Year, Video of Year, 1991), Friends in Low Places (Academy Country Music award for Single Record of Year, 1991), If Tomorrow Never Comes (American Music award for Country Song of Year, 1991), The Thunder Rolls, We Shall Be Free (Academy Country Music award for Video of Year), Somewhere Other Than The Night, Learning to Live Again, (TV spls.) This is Garth Brooks, 1992, This is Garth Brooks, Too, 1994, Garth Brooks: The Hits, 1995, Garth Brooks Live in Central Park, 1997; performer: Encore Hotel and Casino. Las Vegas, 1999-2014, (Television) The Voice, 2016 **AW:** Named Favorite Country Artist, American Music Awards, 2000, Best Male Musical Performer, People's Choice Awards, 1992, Best Male Country Music Performer, 1993, 1992, Artist of Decade, Academy Country Music Awards, 1999, Best County Collaboration with Vocals, Grammy Awards, 1998, Best Male Country Vocalist, 1992, Entertainer of Year, Country Music Association, 1992, 1991; named to Country Music Hall of Fame, 2012, Grand Ole Opry; recipient Horizon award, Crystal Milestone award, Academy Country Music Awards, 2015, 2008, Male Vocalist of Year award, Academy Country Music, 1991, Entertainer of Year award, 1991, Entertainer of the Year, Country Music Association, 2016-2017

BROOKS, JAMES, T: Film Producer, Director, Screenwriter **I:** Media & Entertainment **DOB:** 05/09/1940 **PB:** North Bergen **SC:** NJ/USA **PT:** Edward M. Brooks; Dorothy Helen (Sheinheit) Brooks **MS:** Married **SPN:** Holly Beth Holmberg (7/23/1978); Catherine Morrissey (7/7/1964, Divorced) **CH:** Amy Lorraine; Chloe: Cooper **ED:** Student, New York University (1958-1960) **C:** Founder & Owner, Gracie Films (1984); Writer-producer, Documentaries, Wolper Productions, Los Angeles, CA (1966-1967); Writer, CBS News, New York City, NY (1964-1966) **CR:** Guest Lecturer, Stanford Graduate School of Communications **CW:** Creator, TV Series, "Room 222" (1968-1969); Co-creator, Producer, TV Series, "Lou Grant"; Executive Producer, Co-creator, TV Series, "Mary Tyler Moore Show" (1970-1977); Writer, Producer, TV Series, "Paul Sand in Friends and Lovers" (1974); Co-creator, Co-executive Producer, TV Series, "Rhoda Show" (1974-1975); Writer, TV Show, "The New Lorenzo Music Show" (1976); Co-writer, Co-producer, TV Film, "Thursday Game" (1971); Co-creator, Executive Producer, TV Series, "Taxi" (1978-1980); Co-executive, Producer, Co-writer, TV Series, "Cindy" (1978); Co-creator, Executive Producer, TV Series, "The Associates" (1979); Executive Producer, Co-executive Producer, Co-creator, "The Tracey Ullman Show" (1986-1990), "The Simpsons" (1990-Present); Writer, Co-producer, Film, "Starting Over"; Actor, Film, "Modern Romance" (1981); Producer, Writer, Director, Film, "Terms of Endearment" (1983), "Broadcast News" (1987), "How Do You Know" (2010), "The Longest Daycare" (2012), "The Edge of Seventeen" (2016); Executive Producer, Film, "Big" (1988), "The War of the Roses" (1989), "Say Anything" (1989); Executive Producer, TV Series, "The Critic" (1994), "What About Joan" (2001); Writer, Co-producer, "I'll Do Anything" (1994); Director, Play, "Brooklyn Laundry"; Producer, Films, "Bottle Rocket" (1996), "Jerry Maguire" (1996), "As Good As It Gets" (1997), "Riding in Cars with Boys" (2001); Writer, Director, Films, "Spanglish" (2004); Writer, Producer, Film, "The Simpsons Movie" (2007) **AW:** Emmy Award for Outstanding New Series (1969); Peabody Award (1978); Emmy Award for Comedy Writing (1971, 1974-1977); Outstanding Comedy Series (1975-1977); Peabody Award (1977); Writers Guild of America Best Teleplay The Last Show; TV Critics Achievement in Comedy Award (1977); Achievement in Series Award (1977); Humanitas (1977); Emmy Award for Outstanding Writing in Drama (1978-1980); Emmy Awards, Outstanding Drama (1979, 1980), Humanitas Awards (1977, 1982); Emmy Award for Best Show, Best Writing (1978-1979, 1979-1980, 1980-1981); TV Film Critics Circle Award for Achievement in Comedy and in a Series (1976-1977); Golden Globe Awards for Best Comedy Series (1978, 1979, 1980); Humanitas Prize for Episode Entitled Blind Date (1979); Emmy Awards, Outstanding Variety or Comedy Series (1987, 1988, 1990); Emmy Awards, Outstanding Writing Variety or Music Show (1988-1989); Emmy Awards, Outstanding Animated Special, Outstanding Animated Program, Outstanding Animated Program; Golden Globe, Best Screenplay Award (1983); Academy Awards for Best Film, Best Director, Best Screenplay (1984); Best Director Award, Directors' Guild of America (1983); Comedy Based on Material from Another Medium (1983); National Board of Review, Best Picture (1983); Golden Globe Award, Best Picture (1983); New York Film Critics Best Picture; Best Picture, Best Director, Best Screenplay, New York Film Critics Awards; Peoples Choice Award for Favorite Comedy Motion Picture **MEM:** Directors Guild of America; TV Academy of Arts and Sciences; Screen Actors' Guild; Academy of Motion Picture Arts and Sciences **BA:** Gracie Films/ Columbia Pictures/Sony Pictures Ent Poitier Bldg, 10202 Washington Blvd, Culver City, CA, 90232

BROOKS, MORRIS J., T: U.S. Representative From Alabama, Lawyer **I:** Government Administration/ Government Relations/Government Services **DOB:** 04/29/1954 **PB:** Charleston **PT:** Jack Brooks; Betty Brooks **ED:** JD, University of Alabama, 1978; BA, Duke University **C:** Committee on the Budget, Committee on Oversight and Government Reform, Committee on Science, Space and Technology, Republican Study Committee; U.S. Congress, Fifth Alabama District, Washington, DC, 2011-Present; Private Law Practice, 2002-Present; Commissioner, Madison County Commission, 1996-2010; Special Assistant Attorney General, State of Alabama, 1995-2002; District Attorney, Madison County, Alabama, 1991-1992; District 10, Alabama House of Representatives, 1984-1992; District 18, Alabama House of Representatives, 1982-1984; Law Clerk, Circuit Court Judge John David Snodgrass, 1980-1982; Attorney, Tuscaloosa District Attorney Office, 1980 **PA:** Republican **BA:** U.S. House of Representatives, 1230 Longworth House Office Building, Washington, DC, 20515

BROOKS, SUSAN WIANT, T: Chairwoman of the House Ethics Committee **I:** Government Administration/Government Relations/Government Services **DOB:** 08/25/1960 **PB:** Fort Wayne **SC:** IN/USA **PT:** Daughter of Robert and Marilyn Wiant; **ED:** JD, Ind. University Indianapolis School Law, 1985; BA, Miami University, 1982 **C:** Chairwoman of the House Ethics Committee, 2017-; Member, U.S. House Select Committee on the Events Surrounding the 2012 Terrorist Attack in Benghazi, 2014-; Member, U.S. House Homeland Security Committee, 2013-; Member, U.S. House Ethics Committee, 2013-; Member, U.S. House Education & the Workforce Committee, 2013-; Member, U.S. Congress from 5th Ind. District, Washington, 2013-; Senior vice president workforce & economic devel., general counsel, Ivy Tech Community College, 2007-11; U.S. attorney Southern District of Indiana, U.S. Department Justice, 2001-07; Of counsel, Ice Miller Law Firm, Indianapolis, 2000-01; Deputy mayor, City of Indianapolis, 1998-99; Partner, McClure, McClure & Kammen, 1985-97 **CIV:** Chair, United Way's Violence and Safety Impact Council, Board member, Network of Women in Business, Board member, Marion County Commission on Youth, Board member, Little Red Door Cancer Agency, Board member, Junior League of Indianapolis, Member, Ind. Federal Community Defender Board, Adv. board, Marion County Commission on Youth, Nominating committee, Hoosier Capitol Girl Scouts Council, Protocol chair, World Police & Fire Games, Indianapolis, 2001 Board member, Greater Indianapolis Progress Committee, **AW:** Named Alumnae of Year, Ind. University School Law, 2006, Influential Woman of Indpls, Indianapolis Business Journal, 1999; named one of The Who's Who in Law, 2002 **PA:** Republican **BA:** Office fo Susan Brooks, 1030 Longworth House Office Building, Washington, DC, 20515

BROSNAHAN, RACHEL, T: Actress **I:** Media & Entertainment **PB:** Milwaukee **SC:** WI/USA **CW:** (Film) The Unborn, 2009, The Truth About Average Guys, 2009, Coming Up Roses, 2011, NorEaster, 2012, Beautiful Creatures, 2013, Care, 2013, A New York Heartbeat,2013, Munchausen, 2013, Adrift, 2013, Basically, 2013, The Smut Locker, 2014, I'm Obsessed with You(But You've Got to Leave Me Alone, 2014, Louder than Bombs, 2015, James White, 2015, The Finest Hours, 2016, Burn Country, 2016, Patriots Day, 2016, (Television)Mercy, 2010, Gossip Girl, 2010, The Good Wife, 2010, In Treatment, 2010, CSI:Miami, 2011, House of Cards,

2013, Greys Anatomy, 2013, Orange is the New Black, 2013, Olive Kitteridge, 2014, The Blacklist, 2014, Black Box, 2014, Manhattan, 2014, The Dovekeepers, 2015, Crisis in Six Scenes, 2016, The Marvelous Mrs. Maisel, 2017 (Golden Globe for Best Actress in a Television Musical or Comedy 2017)

BROUSSARD, BRUCE D., **T:** CEO of Humana **I:** Business Management/Business Services **ED:** MBA, University Houston, 1989; Bachelors, Texas A&M **C:** President, CEO, Humana, 2013-; President, Humana, Louisville, 2011-12; CEO, US Oncology (division McKesson Corp.), 2010-11; Chairman, US Oncology, Inc., 2009-10; President, CEO, US Oncology, Inc., Houston, 2008-10; Executive vice president, pharmaceutical services, US Oncology, Inc., Houston, 2003-06; President, US Oncology, Inc., Houston, 2006-08; CFO, US Oncology, Inc., Houston, 2000-06; CEO, Harbor Dental Inc., 1997-2000; Executive vice president, CFO, Regency Health Services, Inc., 1996-97; CFO, board directors, Sun Healthcare Group, Inc., 1993-96 **CR:** Board directors U.S. Physical Therapy Inc. **BA:** Humana Headquarters, 500 West Main Street, Louisville, KY, 40202

BROWN, ANTHONY GREGORY, **T:** U.S. Representative from Maryland **I:** Government Administration/Government Relations/Government Services **DOB:** 11/21/1961 **PB:** Huntington **SC:** NY/USA **PT:** Son of Roy Hershel and Lilly Ida Brown **ED:** JD, Harvard Law School, 1992; AB cum laude, Harvard College, Cambridge, Massachusetts, 1984 **C:** Member, U.S. House of Representatives from Maryland's 4th District; Member, Committee on Armed Services, Committee on Ethics, Committee on Natural Resources; Lieutenant Governor, State of Maryland, 2007-15; Majority Whip, Maryland House of Delegates, 2004; Rep. from District 25, Maryland House of Delegates, 1999-2004; Attorney, Gibbs & Haller, Lanham, Maryland, 1998-2007; Attorney, Wilmer, Cutler & Pickering, Washington, 1994-98; Law Clerk, US Court Appeals Armed Forces, Washington, 1992-94 **CR:** Member Gov.'s Task Force Medical Malpractice & Health Care Access, 2004, Member, Committee Higher Education Affordability & Accessibility, Maryland House of Delegates, 2003-04, Co-chair, Judiciary Committee, 2003-04, Member Article 27 Revision Committee, 2003-04, Member, Joint Committee Administrative, Executive & Legislative Review, 2003-04, Member, Tech. & Bus. Division Task Force, 2000, Member, Economic Matters Committee, 1999-2003, Member, Law Enforcement & State-appointed Board Committee, 1999-2002, Member Legis. Black Caucus Maryland, 1999-, lecturer Legal Assistant Program, Georgetown University, Washington, 1996-97 **CIV:** Chairman, Prince George's Community College, 1998-99, Member, Board of Trustees, Prince George's Community College, Largo, 1995-99 Board of Directors, Adoptions Together, Inc., Silver Spring, Maryland, 2001, Board of Directors, Prince George's County Law Foundation, Hyattsville, 2000 **MIL:** Senior Consultant to Iraqi Ministry of Displacement and Migration 353rd Civil Affairs Command, 2004-05, Colonel Judge Adc. General's Corps **AW:** Decorated Armed Forces Reserve Medal, Military Outstanding Vol. Service Medal, Global War on Terrorism Service Medal, National Defense Service Medal, Army Reserve Component Achievement Medal, Army Commendation Medal, Meritorious Service Medal, Bronze Star; Recipient, Distinguished Community Service Award, Prince George's County Educators' Association, 2005, Medal of Civic Honor, National Conference State Legislators, 2005, Leadership Award, Maryland Justice Coalition, 2004, Adoption Visionary Award, Maryland Society Services Administration, 2003, Legis. Award, Medical & Chirurgical Faculty Maryland, 2003, Army Achievement Medal **MEM:** Mem.: Lake Pointe Home Owners' Association (president 1996-98), J. Franklyn Bourne Bar Association, Maryland State Bar Association (real property, planning & zoning section) **BAR:** Bar: DC 1994, Maryland 1994, New York 1993 **PA:** Democrat **BA:** 1505 Longworth House Office Building, Washington, DC, 20515

BROWN, ANTONIO, **T:** Professional Football Player **I:** Athletics **DOB:** 07/10/1988 **PB:** Miami **SC:** FL/USA **ED:** Central Michigan University **C:** Pittsburgh Steelers, Wide Receiver, 2010- **AW:** Pro Bowl,2011, 2013–2017,First-team All-Pro,2014–2017,; Second-team All-Pro,2013,NFL receiving yards leader,2014, 2017, NFL receptions leader,2014, 2015, First-team All-American,2008, 2009,First-team All-MAC,2008,; 2009,Second-team All-MAC,2007,MAC Freshman of the Year,2007

BROWN, CARRIE B., **T:** Editor **I:** Writing and Editing **CN:** Politico **C:** Editor, Politico, 2016-Present; White House Correspondent, Politico, 2009-2014 **AW:** Merriman Smith Award, 2012

BROWN, DAN, **T:** Writer **I:** Writing and Editing **DOB:** 06/22/1964 **PB:** Exeter **PT:** Son of Richard G. and Constance Brown **ED:** BA in English and Spanish, Amherst College, Massachusetts, 1986 **C:** Spanish teacher, Lincoln Akerman School, Hampton Falls, New Hampshire; English teacher, Phillips Exeter Academy, New Hampshire; Teacher, Beverly Hills Preparatory School, California; Founder record co. Dalliance **CW:** Author: (novels) Digital Fortress, 1998, Angels & Demons, 2000, Deception Point, 2001, The Da Vinci Code, 2003 (#1 New York Times bestseller, 2003), The Lost Symbol, 2009 (#1 Publishers Weekly bestseller), Inferno, 2013; co-author: (humor) 187 Men to Avoid: A Survival Guide for the Romantically Frustrated Woman, 1995, The Bald Book, 1998; musician (producer): (children's album) Synth-Animals, (albums) Perspective, 1990, Dan Brown, 1993, Angels & Demons, 1994, (charity album) Musica Animalia, 2003; executive prodr.: (films) The Da Vinci Code, 2006, (Books) Origin, 2017 **AW:** Named one of 100 Most Influential People, TIME magazine, 2005; named to Celebrity 100, Forbes magazine, 2005 **ACH:** Achievements include having novels translated into more than 40 languages; all four of his novels named to New York Times bestseller list in the same week in 2004 **H:** Tennis

BROWN, JERRY, **T:** Governor of California **I:** Government Administration/Government Relations/Government Services **DOB:** 04/07/1938 **PB:** San Francisco **SC:** CA/USA **PT:** Son of Edmund Gerald and Bernice (Layne) Brown; **ED:** JD, Yale Law School, New Haven, 1964; BA in Classics, University California, Berkeley, 1961 **CT:** Bar: California 1965 **C:** Governor, State of California, Sacramento, 2011-; Mayor, City of Oakland, California, 1998-2006; Chairman, California Dem. Party, Sacramento, 1989-91; Attorney general, State of California, Sacramento, 2007-11; Governor, State of California, Sacramento, 1975-83; Secretary state, State of California, Sacramento, 1971-75; Board trustees, L.A. Community College, 1969-71; Attorney, Tuttle & Taylor, L.A., 1966-69; Law clerk to Justice Mathew Tobriner, California Supreme Court, 1964-65 **CIV:** Democratic candidate for President, 1992 Democratic candidate for President, 1980 Democratic candidate for President, 1976 **AW:** Named one of The 100 Most Influential People in the World, TIME magazine, 2014 **PA:** Democrat **BA:** Office of Jerry Brown, State Capitol, Suite 1173, Sacramento, CA, 95814

BROWN, JIM, **T:** Former NFL Player **I:** Athletics **DOB:** 02/17/1936 **PB:** St. Simon's Island **SC:** GA/USA **PT:** Son of Swinton and Theresa B. **MS:** Married **SPN:** Monique Gunthrop, 1997; Sue Jones, 1958 (div. 1972); **CH:** Kim and Kevin (twins), Jim, Aris, Morgan **ED:** BA, Syracuse University, New York, 1957 **C:** Special Advisor, Cleveland Browns, 2013-; Part-owner, Long Island Lizards, Major League Lacrosse, 2012-; Special consultant, Cleveland Browns, 1993-2010; Founder, Amer-I-Can Program, 1988; Founder, Vital Issues, 1986; Founder, Negro Industrial Economic Union (now Black Economic Union), 1965; Retired, NFL, 1966; Fullback, Cleveland Browns, 1957-65 **CR:** Member Commission on the Status of African Am. Males, 1994 **CW:** Actor: (films) Rio Conchos, 1964, The Dirty Dozen, 1967, The Mercenaries, 1968, Ice Station Zebra, 1969, The Split, 1968, Riot, 1969, 100 Rifles, 1969, ...tick...tick...tick..., 1970, The Grasshopper, 1970, El Condor, 1970, Kenner, 1971, Superbug, 1971, Slaughter, 1972, Black Gunn, 1972, Slaughter's Big Rip-off, 1973, I Escaped from Devil's Island, 1973, The Slams, 1973, Three the Hard Way, 1974, Take a Hard Ride, 1975, Adios Amigo, 1976, Gus, 1976, I Will, I Will . . . For Now, 1976, Kid Vengeance, 1977, Fingers, 1977, The Wild One, 1977, One Down, Two to Go, 1982, The Running Man, 1987, I'm Gonna Git You Sucka, 1988, L.A. Heat, 1989, Crack House, 1989, Killing American Style, 1990, Twisted Justice, 1990, The Divine Enforcer, 1991, Original Gangstas, 1996, Mars Attacks!, 1996, He Got Game, 1998, Small Soldiers (voice), 1998, Any Given Sunday, 1999, On the Edge, 2002, She Hate Me, 2004, Animal, 2005; (TV movies) Lady Blue, 1985, Hammer, Slammer & Slade, 1990, Sucker Free City, 2004; (TV appearances) I Spy, 1967, Police Story, 1977, CHiPs, 1979, 1983, T.J. Hooker, 1983, 1984, Knight Rider, 1984, The A-Team, 1986, Highway to Heaven, 1988, Good Sports, 1991, Between Brothers, 1998, Arli$$, 2000, Soul Food, 2004; actor, producer Pacific Inferno, 1979; executive producer Richard Pryor Here and Now, 1983; author: Off My Chest, 1964, Out of Bounds, 1989,(Films)Sideliners, 2006, Dream Street, 2010, Draft Day 2014 **AW:** Recipient Jim Thorpe Trophy, 1959, Bert Bell Memorial award, 1964, NFL Rookie of Year award Associated Press, 1957, NFL MVP award, 1957, 1958, 1965, Hickock Belt as Professional Athlete of Year, 1964, Blanton Collier award NFL Players Association, 2010; named to NFL Pro Bowl 1958-65, Pro Football Hall of Fame, 1971, Lacrosse Hall of Fame, 1983, College Football Hall of Fame, 1995, 1960s All-Decade Team, NFL 75th Anniversary Team, All-Time NFL Team, 2000; named 1st Team NFL All-Pro, 1957-65, Pro Bowl MVP, 1961, 62, 65, Player of Century, Sports Illus., 1999. **ACH:** Achievements include member of NFL championship winning Cleveland Browns, 1964 **BA:** The Amer-I-Can Program, 269 S. Beverly Drive, Suite 1048, Beverly Hills, CA, 90212

BROWN, KATE, **T:** Governor of Oregon, former state legislator **I:** Government Administration/Government Relations/Government Services **DOB:** 06/21/1960 **PB:** Torrejon de Ardoth **ED:** JD, Lewis & Clark College; BA in Environmental Conservation, University Colorado, Boulder **C:** Governor, State of Oregon, 2015-; Secretary of state, State of Oregon, Salem, 2009-15; Majority leader, Oregon State Senate, 2004-09; Member District 21, Oregon State Senate, 1997-2009; Member District 13, Oregon House of Reps., 1991-97; Attorney, Tennyson, Winemiller & Lavalle, 1991-94 **CR:** Adjunct professor administration justice Portland State University, 1994 **AW:** Named one of 24 Rising Stars in American Politics, Rodel Fellowship, 2009; recipient Profiles in Courage award, Basic Rights Oregon, 2012, President's award of Merit, Oregon State Bar, 2007, National Pub. & Community

Service award, American Mental Health Counselors Association, 2004, Woman of Achievement award, Oregon Commission Women, 1995, Outstanding Young Oregonian award, Oregon Jaycees, 1993 **MEM:** Mem.: Multnomah Bar Association, Oregon Trial Lawyers Association **ACH:** Achievements include making history being the first openly bisexual governor in the country **PA:** Democrat

BROWN, LARRY, T: College Basketball Coach **I:** Athletics **DOB:** 09/14/1940 **PB:** Bklyn. **ED:** Student, University North Carolina, Chapel Hill, 1959-63 **C:** Head coach, Southern Methodist University Mustangs, Dallas, 2012-; Head coach, Charlotte Bobcats, 2008-10; Head coach, New York Knicks, 2005-06; Head coach, Detroit Pistons, 2003-05; Executive vice president, Philadelphia 76ers, 2007-08; Head coach, Philadelphia 76ers, 1997-2003; Head coach, Ind. Pacers, 1993-97; Head coach, LA Clippers, 1992-93; Head coach, San Antonio Spurs, 1988-92; Head coach, University Kansas Jayhawks, Lawrence, 1983-88; Head coach, New Jersey Nets, 1981-83; Head coach, UCLA Bruins, 1979-81; Head coach, Denver Nuggets, 1976-79; Head coach, Denver Rockets, 1974-76; Head coach, Carolina Cougars, 1972-74; Professional basketball player, Denver Rockets, 1971-72; Professional basketball player, Virginia Squires, 1970-71; Professional basketball player, Washington Caps, 1969-70; Professional basketball player, Oakland Oaks, 1968-69; Professional basketball player, New Orleans Buccanneers, 1967-68; Assistant coach, University North Carolina Tar Heels, Chapel Hill, 1965-67; Amateur basketball player, Akron Goodyears, Ohio, 1963-65 **CR:** Head coach US national team Summer Olympic Games, Athens, Greece, 2004, assistant coach US national team, Sydney, 2000, member US national team, Tokyo, 1964 **AW:** Named Coach of Year, NBA, 2001, American Basketball Association, 1976, 1975, 1973, All-Star Game MVP, 1968; named to The Naismith Memorial Basketball Hall of Fame, 2002, American Basketball Association All-Star Team, 1968-70; recipient Espy Award for Best Coach/Mgr., ESPN, 2004, Gold medal, men's basketball, Summer Olympic Games, 1964,All-ABA Second Team, 1968,NBA All-Star Game Head Coach, 1977, 2001, NCAA Champion, 1988, Naismith College Coach of the Year, 1988, Basketball Hall of Fame, 2002 **ACH:** Achievements include member of the American Basketball Association championship winning Oakland Oaks, 1969; head coach of the NCAA Final Four men's national championship winning University of Kansas Jayhawks, 1988; head coach of the NBA Finals championship winning Detroit Pistons, 2004; being the only coach in history to win both NCAA and NBA titles

BROWN, SHERROD CAMPBELL, T: U.S. Senator from Ohio **I:** Government Administration/Government Relations/Government Services **DOB:** 11/09/1952 **PB:** Mansfield, Ohio **PT:** Son of Charles G. and Emily (Campbell) Brown; **ED:** MPA, Ohio State University, 1981; MEd, Ohio State University, 1979; BA in Russian Studies, Yale University, New Haven, 1974 **C:** Ranking Member, Senate Banking Committee, 2015-; US Senator from Ohio, Washington, 2007-; Member, US Congress from 13th Ohio District, Washington, 1993-2007; Secretary of State, State of Ohio, Columbus, 1983-91; Member, Ohio House of Reps., Columbus, 1975-82 **CR:** Faculty Associate Mershon Center Ohio State University, 1991-93, Political Sci. Instructor, 1979-80 **CW:** Author: Congress from the Inside: Observations from the Majority and the Minority, 1999, Myths of Free Trade, 2004 **AW:** Named Distinguished Pub. Health Legislator of Year, American Public Health Association, 2002; recipient Friend

of Education award, 1978 **MEM:** Mem.: National Association Sec.'s of State **PA:** Democrat **BA:** Office of Sherrod Brown, 713 Hart Senate Office Bldg, Washington, DC, 20510

BROWN, STERLING K., T: Actor **I:** Media & Entertainment **PB:** Los Angeles **SC:** CA/USA **ED:** B.A., Stanford University; M.F.A., NYU **CW:** (Film) Brown Sugar, 2002, Trust the Man, 2005 ,Stay, 2005, Righteous Kill, 2008, Out Idiot Brother, 2011, The Suspect, 2013, Mojave, 2015, Whiskey Tango Foxtrot, 2016,Spaceman, 2016, Marshall, 2017, Black Panther, 2018, The Predator, 2018,(Television) Third Watch, 2002-04, Hack , 2003, Tarzan, 2003, ER, 2004, NYPD Blue, 2004, JAG, 2004, Boston Legal, 2005, Starved, 2005, Supernatural , 2006, Alias, 2006, Smith, 2006, Without A Trace, 2006, Army Wives, 2007, Shark, 2007, Standoff, 2007, Eli Stone, 2008, Medium, 2010, Detroit 187, 2011,The Good Wife, 2011, Harry's Law, 2011, Nikita, 2012, Person of Interest, 2012, NCIS, 2013, The Mentalist, 2014, Masters of Sex, 2014, Castle, 2015, Criminal Minds, 2015, The People v. O.J. Simpson: American Crime Story, 2016(Primetime Emmy for Outstanding Support Actor 2016), This is Us, 2016(Golden Globe Outstanding Lead Actor in a Drama Series 2018, Primetime Emmy for Outstanding Lead Actor), Insecure, 2017, Running Wild with Bear Grylls, 2017

BROWNBACK, SAM, T: U.S. Ambassador at Large for Religious Freedom **I:** Government Administration/Government Relations/Government Services **DOB:** 06/12/1956 **PB:** Parker **SC:** KS/USA **ED:** JD, University of Kansas, 1982; BS in Agricultural Economics, Kansas State University, With Honors, 1979 **C:** Ambassador At-Large For Religious Freedom, U.S., 2018-Present; Governor, State Of Kansas, Topeka, KS, 2011-2018; U.S. Senator From Kansas, 1996-2011; U.S. Congress From Second Kansas District, Washington, DC, 1995-1996; Secretary of Agriculture, State Of Kansas, Topeka, KS, 1986-1993; City Attorney, Ogden & Leonardville, KS; Law Instructor, Kansas State University; Farm Broadcaster, Station-KKSU **CR:** Commissioner, U.S. Helsinki Commission; Vice Chairman, Riley County Republican Committee **CIV:** President, Kansas Prayer Breakfast **CW:** Co-Author, (With Jim Nelson Black) From Power To Purpose: A Remarkable Journey Of Faith And Compassion, 2007 **AW:** Pro Deo et Patria Medal, Christendom College, Virginia, 2005, U.S. Oncology Medal of Honor, 2002, Honor Award, Oncology Nursing Society, 2002, Manufacturing Excellence Award, National Association of Manufacturers, 2001, Kansan of Distinction, 1988 **MEM:** Vice President, National Future Farmers of America, 1977, American Bar Association, American Judicature Society, American Agricultural Law Association, Riley County Bar Association, Kansas Bar Association **BAR:** State of Kansas, 1982 **PA:** Republican

BROWNLEY, JULIA, T: U.S. Representative from California, former state legislator **I:** Government Administration/Government Relations/Government Services **DOB:** 08/28/1952 **PB:** Aiken **ED:** MBA, American University, 1979; BA in Political Sci., George Washington University, 1975 **C:** Member, US House Veterans' Affairs Committee, 2013-; Member, US House Sci., Space, & Technology Committee, 2013-; Member, US Congress from 26th California District, Washington, 2013-; Member District 41, California State Assembly, 2006-12; Member, Santa Monica-Malibu School Board, 1994-2006 **AW:** Named YWCA Woman of Year, 2005 **PA:** Democrat

BRYAN, LUKE, T: Musician **I:** Media & Entertainment **DOB:** 07/17/1976 **PB:** Leesburg **SC:** VA/USA **PT:** Tommy Bryan; LeClaire Bryan **ED:** Coursework, Georgia Southern University **CW:** Musician, "What Makes You Country" (2017); Musician, "Spring Break...Checkin Out" (2015); Musician, "Kill the Lights" (2015); Musician, "Play It Again" (2014); Contributing Performer, with Lionel Richie, "Oh No/All Night Long" (2014); Contributing Musician, with Florida Georgia Line, "This Is How We Roll" (2013); Musician, "Crash My Party" (2013); Musician, "Spring Break...Here to Party" (2013); Contributing Musician, with Jason Aldean and Eric Church, "The Only Way I Know" (2012); Musician, "I Don't Want This Night to End" (2011); Musician, "Tailgates & Tanlines" (2011); Musician, "Do I" (2009); Musician, "Doin' My Thing" (2009); Musician, "I'll Stay Me" (2007) **AW:** Named, Top Country Artist, Billboard Music Awards (2016); Named, Vocal Event of the Year, Academy Country Music Awards (2015); Named, Male Video of the Year, CMT Music Awards (2015); Named, Entertainer of the Year, Academy Country Music Awards (2015); Named, Entertainer of the Year, Country Music Association Awards (2014-2015); Named, Performance of the Year, CMT Music Awards (2014); Named, Top Country Artist, Billboard Music Awards (2014); Named, Collaborative Video of Year, CMT Music Awards (2014); Inductee, Grammy Hall of Fame (2014); Named, Top Country Album, Billboard Music Awards (2014); Named, Collaborative Video of the Year, CMT Music Awards (2013); Named, Vocal Event of the Year, Academy Country Music Awards (2013); Named, Entertainer of the Year, Academy Country Music Awards (2013); Named, Favorite Country Male Artist, American Music Awards (2012-2015); Named, Male Video of the Year, CMT Music Awards (2012); Named, USA Weekend Breakthrough Video of Year, CMT Music Awards (2010); Named, Top New Artist (2010); Named, Top New Solo Vocalist of Year (2010); Inductee, Country Music Hall of Fame (1999)

BRYANT, KOBE, T: Former NBA Player **I:** Athletics **CN:** Los Angeles Lakers **DOB:** 08/23/1978 **PB:** Philadelphia **SC:** PA/USA **PT:** Joe Bryant, Pamela (Cox) Bryant **C:** Guard, Los Angeles Lakers, 1996-2016 **CR:** U.S. National Team, Summer Olympic Games, London, England, 2012, U.S. National Team, Summer Olympic Games, Beijing, China, 2008, FIBA Americas Championship, 2007 **CIV:** Founder, Kobe Bryant China Fund, Ambassador, After-School All-Stars **AW:** NBA Finals MVP, 2009-2010, NBA Athlete Of Decade, 2000's, The Sporting News, 2009, NBA All-Star Game Co-MVP, 2009, Gold Medal, Men's Basketball, Summer Olympic Games, 2008, 2012, NBA Player of the Year, 2008, NBA MVP, 2008, The 100 Most Powerful Celebrities, Forbes.com, 2008, The Most Influential People In The World Of Sports, Business Week, 2007-2008, NBA All-Star Game MVP, 2002, 2007, All-NBA First Team, NBA, 2002-2004, 2006-2013, NBA All-Defensive First Team, 2000, 2003-2004, 2006-2008, 2010-2011, Western Conference All-Star Team, 1998, 2000-2013, NBA All-Star Slam Dunk Champion, 1997, National HS Player of the Year (Lower Merion High School), 1996 **ACH:** Achievements include being the youngest player ever (19 years of age) to appear in an NBA All-Star game, 1998; member of the NBA Championship winning LA Lakers, 2000, 2001, 2002, 2009, 2010; leading the NBA in: field goals, 2003, 2006, 2007; scoring, 2003, 2006-08; points per game, 2006, 2007; field goal attempts, 2006-08; scoring a career high 81 points in a single game (second-highest total in NBA history), 2006; becoming the youngest player in NBA history to reach 25,000 career points (31 years, 151 days), 2010; setting a record for playing the most seasons with the same team (20 seasons) **BA:** Los Angeles Lakers, 555 N Nash Street, El Segundo, CA, 90245-2818

BRYANT, KRIS, T: Former Professional Baseball Player **I:** Athletics **PB:** Las Vegas **SC:** NV/USA **C:** Third Baseman, Chicago Cubs, 2015-Present **AW:** NL Hank Aaron Award, 2016, World Series Champion, 2016, NL MVP, 2016, All-Star, 2015-2016, NL Rookie of the Year, 2015, Golden Spikes Award, 2013, Dick Howser Trophy, 2013

BRYANT, PHIL, T: Governor from Mississippi **I:** Government Administration/Government Relations/Government Services **DOB:** 12/09/1954 **PB:** Moorhead **SC:** MS/USA **ED:** MS in Political Sci., Mississippi College, Clinton, 1988; BS in Criminal Justice, University of Southern Mississippi, Hattiesburg, 1977; AA, Hinds Community College, Raymond, Mississippi **C:** Governor, State of Mississippi, Jackson, 2012-; President, Mississippi State Senate, Jackson, 2007-12; Lieutenant governor, State of Mississippi, Jackson, 2008-12; Auditor, State of Mississippi, Jackson, 1996-2008; Member, Mississippi House of Reps., Jackson, 1991-96; Insurance fraud investigator, 1981-91; Deputy sheriff, Hinds County, Mississippi, 1976-81 **CR:** Part-time faculty Mississippi College, 2008- **CIV:** Member, Law Enforcement & Fire Fighter Relief Fund, Member, Gov.'s Commission Recovery & Renewal, Active, Mission Mississippi, Active, Mississippi Mentoring Network, Active, Habitat for Humanity, Active, St. Marks United Methodist Church **CW:** Contributing author 21st Century Government: Digital Promise, Digital Reality, Leadership Secrets of Government Financial Officials, Best Case Practices **AW:** Named Statesman of Year, American Family Radio, 2004, Crime Victims Advocate of the Year award, 2003; named to The Southern Mississippi Alumni Association Hall of Fame, 1999; recipient In the Arena award, Center for Digital Government, Kirk Fordice Freedom award, Central Mississippi National Rifle Association, 2005, Mississippian of the Year award, Association Information Tech. Professionals (AITP), 2003, Distinguished Alumnus award, Mississippi College Department Hist & Political Sci., 1997; Henry Toll fellow, 1998 **MEM:** Mem.: National Rifle Association, Mississippi Rep. Elected Officials Association (past president), National Association State Auditors (chairman bylaws committee, executive committee), Mississippi Fire Investigators Association, International Association Arson Investigators, Leadership 2000, Ducks Unlimited, Greater Jackson Law Enforcement Officers Association (president), Jaycees, Reservoir Lions Club **PA:** Republican

BRYSON, BILL, T: Writer Academic Administrator **I:** Writing and Editing **DOB:** 12/08/1951 **PB:** Des Moines **PT:** Son of William and Mary Bryson; **ED:** DCL (hon.), Durham University, England, 2004; Doctor (hon.), Bournemouth University; Doctor (hon.), Open University, UK, 2002; Attended, Drake University, Des Moines **C:** Chancellor, Durham University, 2005-11; Deputy national news editor, business section, The Independent, London,; Journalist, chief copy editor, The Times, London, **CR:** Schwartz visiting fellow Pomfret School, Connecticut, 2007 appointed commissioner for English heritage Hist. Buildings & Monuments Commission England, 2003-07 **CIV:** President, Campaign to Protect Rural England, 2007- **CW:** Author: (books on travel) The Palace Under the Alps and Over 200 Other Unusual, Unspoiled, and Infrequently Visited Spots in 16 European Countries, 1985, The Lost Continent: Travels in Small-Town America, 1989, Neither Here Nor There: Travels in Europe, 1992, Notes from a Small Island, 1996,

A Walk in the Woods: Rediscovering America on the Appalachian Trail, 1999, I'm a Stranger Here Myself/ Notes from a Big Country, 2000, In a Sunburned Country/Down Under, 2001, Bill Bryson's African Diary, 2002, (books on science) A Short History of Nearly Everything, 2003 (Aventis prize for sci. books, 2004, Descartes prize for sci. communications, European Union, 2005), A Really Short History of Nearly Everything, 2008, Seeing Further: The Story of Science, Discovery, and the Genius of the Royal Society, 2010, (books on the English language) The Penguin Dictionary of Troublesome Words, 1984, The Mother Tongue: English and How it Got That Way, 1990, Made in America: An Informal History of the English Language in the U.S., 1998, Bill Bryson's Dictionary of Troublesome Words, 2004, Bryson's Dictionary for Writers and Editors, 2008, (memoir) The Life and Times of the Thunderbolt Kid, 2006, (biography) Shakespeare: The World as Stage, 2007, (history) At Home: A Short History of Private Life, 2010, One Summer: America, 1927, 2013,(Book) The Road to Little Dribbling: More Notes From A Small Island, 2015 **AW:** Named an Hon. Freeman of Durham City, 2009; recipient James Joyce award, Lit. & Hist. Society, Univ. College Dublin, 2007, Key to the City, Des Moines, 2006, Honorary Fellow of the Royal Society, 2013

BRZEZINSKI, MIKA, I: Media & Entertainment **DOB:** 05/02/1967 **PB:** New York **SC:** NY/USA **ED:** Bachelor of English, Williams College, 1989 **C:** Co-host, reader Morning Joe, MSNBC, 2007-; Correspondent, CBS-TV News, New York City, 2001-07; Anchor, Up To The Minute, MSNBC, 2007; Anchor, reporter, co-anchor host Home Page, MSNBC,; Co-anchor Up To The Minute, CBS-TV News, New York City, 1997-2000; Anchor Eyewitness News This Morning, At Noon, At Six, WFSB-TV, Hartford, 1995-97; New Haven bureau chief, substitute anchor, WFSB-TV, Hartford, 1993-95; General assignment reporter, Station WTIC-TV, Hartford, 1991-92; Assignment editor, futures editor, Station WTIC-TV, Hartford, 1990-91; Desk assistant World News This Morning, ABC-News, 1990 **CW:** Author: All Things Once, 2010, Knowing Your Value: Women, Money and Getting What You're Worth, 2011, Obsessed: America's Food Addiction and My Own, 2013; writer (monthly column, Getting What You Want) Cosmopolitan **AW:** Recipient Excellence in Journalism award Society Professional Journalists, 1996. **MEM:** Mem.: Council of Foreign Relations

BUCHANAN, VERN, T: U.S. Representative From Florida **I:** Government Administration/Government Relations/Government Services **DOB:** 05/08/1951 **PB:** Detroit **SC:** MI/USA **ED:** MBA, University of Denver, 1986; BBA, Cleary University, Michigan, 1975 **C:** Way and Means Committee, U.S. Congress from 16th Florida District, 2013-Present; Chairman, Buchanan Enterprises, 1994-Present; U.S. Congress from 13th Florida District, Washington, DC, 2007-2013; Founder, Chairman, American Speedy Printing, 1976-1991 **CR:** State Finance Chair, Mel Martinez's Election Campaign, 2004 **CIV:** Active, Community Foundation of Sarasota; Active, Boys and Girls Club **MEM:** Board of Directors, Executive Committee, U.S. Chamber of Commerce, Past Chairman, Sarasota Chamber of Commerce, Chairman, Board of Directors, Florida Chamber of Commerce **PA:** Republican **BA:** 2104 Rayburn HOB, Washington, DC, 20515

BUCK, KEN, T: U.S. Representative from Colorado **I:** Government Administration/Government Relations/Government Services **DOB:** 02/16/1959 **PB:** Ossining **SC:** NY/USA **ED:** JD, University Wyoming, 1985; Grad., Yale University, 1981 **C:** Member, U.S.

Congress from 4th. Colorado District, 2014-; District attorney, Weld County, Colorado, 2005-; Construction executive, Hensel Phelps Construction Co., Greeley, Colorado, 2002-05; Prosecutor, U.S. Attorney's Office, 1990-2002; Trial attorney, U.S. Justice Department, 1987-90; Staff attorney, Iran-Contra Investigation, 1986-87 **PA:** Republican

BUCK, LINDA B., T: Biologist **I:** Education/Educational Services **DOB:** 01/29/1947 **PB:** Seattle **SC:** WA/USA **ED:** PhD in Immunology, University of Texas Southwestern Medical Center, Dallas, 1980; BS in Microbiology, University of Washington, Seattle, 1975; BS in Psychology, University of Washington, Seattle, 1975 **C:** Affiliate Professor Department of Physiology & Biophysics, University of Washington School Medicine, Seattle, 2003-; Staff Member Division of Basic Scis., Fred Hutchinson Cancer Research Center, Seattle, 2002-; Professor, Harvard University, 2001-02; Associate Professor, Harvard University, Boston, 1996-2001; Assistant Professor Neurobiology, Harvard University, Boston, 1991-96; Postdoc. Fellow, Columbia University, New York City, 1980-84 **CR:** Board of Directors International Flavors & Fragrances Inc., 2007-, DeCode Genetics Inc., 2005-09 Investigator Howard Hughes Medical Institute, 2001-, Associate Investigator, Sweden, 1997-2000, Assistant Investigator, 1994-97, Associate, 1984-91 **CW:** Contributor Articles to Professional Journals **AW:** Co-recipient Nobel Prize in Physiology/Medicine, The Nobel Foundation, 2004; Recipient Gairdner Foundation International Award, 2003, Lewis S. Rosenstiel Award, Brandeis University, 1997, R.H. Wright Award in Olfactory Research, 1996, Unilever Sci. Award, 1996, Distinguished Alumnus Award, University of Texas Southwestern Medical Center, 1995, Takasago Award for Research in Olfaction, 1992, Scholar Award, McKnight Endowment Fund for Neurosci., 1992, Fellow of the Royal Society, 2015 **MEM:** Fellow: American Association for the Advancement of Science, Am. Academy Arts & Scis.; Mem.: National Academy of Sciences, Institute Medicine **ACH:** Achievements include discovery of odorant receptors and the organization of the olfactory system **BA:** Basic Scis Divsn Fred Hutchinson Cancer Rsch Ctr A3-020, 1100 Fairview Ave N PO Box 19024, Seattle, WA, 98109

BUCSHON, LARRY DEAN, T: U.S. Representative from Indiana, surgeon **I:** Government Administration/Government Relations/Government Services **DOB:** 05/31/1962 **PB:** Kincaid **ED:** MD, University Illinois, Chicago, 1988; Bachelor, University Illinois, Urbana-Champaign, 1984 **CT:** Cert. in cardiothoracic surgery American Board Thoracic Surgery **C:** Member, US House Transportation & the Workforce Committee, Washington, 2011-; Member, Committee on Energy and Commerce, Republican Study Committee; Member, US House Education & the Workforce Committee, Washington, 2011-; Member, US Congress from 8th Ind. District, Washington, 2011-; Chief of cardiothoracic surgery and medical director open heart recovery intensive care unit, St. Mary's Hospital, Evansville,; Cardiothoracic surgeon, president, Ohio Valley HeartCare, Evansville, Ind., 2003-10; Fellow in cardiothoracic surgery, Medical College Wisconsin,; Chief resident in surgery, Medical College Wisconsin, Milwaukee, **CIV:** Youth hockey coach, Member, Our Redeemer Lutheran Church, Evansville, **MIL:** Lieutenant Commander medical corps US Naval Reserve, 1994-98, lieutenant medical corps US Naval Reserve, 1989-94 **AW:** Named Physician of Year, St. Mary's Medical Staff, 2007 **PA:** Republican

BUDD, TED, **T:** U.S. Representative from North Carolina **I:** Government Administration/Government Relations/Government Services **PB:** Winston-Salem **SC:** NC/USA **ED:** M.B.A, Wake Forest University; M.A., Dallas Theological Seminary; B.S., Appalachian State University, 1994 **C:** Member, U.S. Representative from North Carolinas 13th District, 2017-; Member, Committee on Financial Services

BUFFETT, WARREN EDWARD, **T:** CEO **I:** Other **CN:** Berkshire Hathaway, Inc. **DOB:** 08/30/1930 **PB:** Omaha **SC:** NE/USA **PT:** Howard Homan Buffett; Leila (Stahl) Buffett **ED:** MS in Economics, Columbia Business School (1951); BS in Economics, University of Nebraska (1950); Student, University of Pennsylvania **C:** Chairman, Chief Executive Officer, Berkshire Hathaway, Inc., Omaha, NE (1970-Present); General Partner, Buffett Partnership, Ltd., Omaha, NE (1956-1969); Security Analyst, Graham-Newman Corporation, New York City, NY (1954-1956); Investment Salesman, Buffett-Falk & Co., Omaha, NE (1951-1954) **CR:** Board of Directors, The Kraft Heinz Co. (2015-Present); Board of Directors, H. J. Heinz Co. (2013-2015); Board of Directors, The Lubrizol Corp. (2012-Present); Board of Directors, MidAmerican Energy Holdings Co. (2011-Present); Board of Directors, Graham Holdings Co. (1968-2011); Board of Directors, The Coca-Cola Co. (1989-2006); Board of Directors, The Washington Post Co. (1974-1986, 1996-2011); Board of Directors, Berkshire Hathaway, Inc. (1965-Present) **CIV:** Life Trustee, Grinnell College, Iowa (1968-Present); Life Trustee, Urban Institute **CW:** Actor, TV Series, "All My Children" (One Episode) (2008); Author, Several Books; Author, "The Essays of Warren Buffett: Lessons for Corporate America" (2008); Author, "The Essays of Warren Buffett" (2001); Author, "The Essays of Warren Buffet, Second Edition" (2008) **AW:** Named One of the 50 Most Influential People in Global Finance, Bloomberg Markets (2011-2014); Named One of the Top 25 Market Movers, US News & World Report (2009); Named One of the Global Elite, Newsweek Magazine (2008); Business People of the Year, Fortune Magazine (2010); Named One of the 25 Most Powerful People in Business (2007); Named One of the 100 Most Influential People in the World, TIME Magazine (2007, 2012); Named One of the Forbes 400 Richest Americans, Forbes Magazine (1982-Present); Named One of the World's Most Powerful People (2009-2015); Lifetime Philanthropy Award (2013); Presidential Medal of Freedom, The White House (2010) **MEM:** American Academy of Arts & Sciences **PA:** Democrat **BA:** Berkshire Hathaway Headquarters, 3555 Farnam St, Omaha, NB, 68131

BUFORD, R.C., **T:** Professional Sports Team Executive **I:** Business Management/Business Services **ED:** Grad., Friends University; Student, Oklahoma State University; Student, Texas A&M University **C:** President sports franchises, general manager, San Antonio Spurs, 2008-; Assistant coach, University Florida, 1993-94; Assistant coach, LA Clippers, 1992-93; Senior vice president, general manager, San Antonio Spurs, 2004-08; General manager, San Antonio Spurs, 2002-04; Vice president, assistant general manager, San Antonio Spurs, 1999-2002; Director scouting, San Antonio Spurs, 1997-99; Head scout, San Antonio Spurs, 1994-97; Assistant coach, San Antonio Spurs, 1988-92; Head coach, University of Kansas, 1983-88 **CIV:** Hon. board member, Juvenile Diabetes Foundation, Board directors, Playing for Peace, Board member, Roy Maas' Youth Alternatives, **AW:** Named NBA Executive of the Year, 2014

BULLOCK, SANDRA, **T:** Actress **I:** Media & Entertainment **DOB:** 07/26/1964 **PB:** Arlington **SC:** VA/USA **PT:** John Bullock, Helga Bullock **ED:** Student, East Carolina University **CW:** Actress, (Films) Hangmen, 1987, Fire On The Amazon, 1991, Religion Inc., 1989, Love Potion #9, 1992, When The Party's Over, 1992, Who Do I Gotta Kill, 1992, The Vanishing, 1993, Demolition Man, 1993, The Thing Called Love, 1993 (Also Composer For Song Heaven Knocking On My Door), Wrestling Ernest Hemingway, 1993, Speed, 1994, While You Were Sleeping, 1995, The Net, 1995, Two If By Sea, 1996, A Time To Kill, 1996, In Love And War, 1996, Speed 2: Cruise Control, 1997, Practical Magic, 1998, Forces Of Nature, 1999, Exactly 3:30, 1999, 28 Days, 2000, Divine Secrets Of The Ya-Ya Sisterhood, 2002, Crash, 2004, Loverboy, 2005, Infamous, 2006, Premonition, 2007, The Proposal, 2009, All About Steve, 2009, The Blind Side, 2009, Extremely Loud And Incredibly Close, 2011, The Heat, 2013, Gravity, 2013, (Voice Actress) Minions, 2015, Our Brain Is Crisis, 2015, Ocean's 8, 2018, (TV Films) Bionic Showdown: The Six-Million Dollar Man And The Bionic Woman, 1989, Who Shot Patakango, 1989, The Preppie Murder, 1989, (TV Series) Working Girl, 1990, (TV Mini-Series) Lucky/Chances, 1990; Actress, Director, Writer, (Films) Making Sandwiches, 1998; Actress, Producer, (Films) Gun Shy, 1999, Miss Congeniality, 2000, Two Weeks Notice, 2002, Miss Congeniality 2: Armed And Fabulous, 2005, The Lake House, 2006; Actress, Executive Producer, (Films) Hope Floats, 1998, Murder By Numbers, 2002, Our Brand Is Crisis, 2015; Producer, (Films) Our Father, 1996, Trespasses, 1999; Executive Producer, (TV Series) George Lopez, 2002 **AW:** World's Most Beautiful Woman, People Magazine, 2015, Critics' Choice Award For Best Actress In An Action Movie, Gravity, 2014, Favorite Comedic Movie Actress, 2014, Favorite Dramatic Movie Actress, 2014, Humanitarian Award, People's Choice Awards, 2013, The Most Entertaining Person of the Year, Entertainment Weekly, 2013, The 100 Most Powerful Women in Entertainment, Hollywood Reporter, 2013, Favorite Movie Actress, 2010, 2014, 2016, Golden Globe Award For Best Performance By An Actress In A Motion Picture-Drama, Critics' Choice Award For Best Actress, Screen Actors Guild Award For Outstanding Performance By A Female Actor In A Leading Role, Academy Award For Best Actress In A Leading Role, Teen Choice Award For Choice Movie Actress: Drama, The Blind Side, 2010, MTV Generation Award, 2010, Ten Most Fascinating People, Barbara Walters Special, 2010, The 100 Most Influential People in the World, TIME Magazine, 2010, New Orleans, Louisiana High School Hall of Fame, 2009, The 100 Most Powerful Celebrities, Forbes.com, 2007, Favorite Female Movie Star, 2006, Outstanding Performance by a Cast in a Motion Picture, Screen Actors Guild Awards, 2006, Woman of the Year, Glamour Magazine, 2006, Star, Hollywood Walk of Fame, 2005, American Comedy Award for Funniest Female Performer in a Motion Picture, 2001, Favorite Actress, People's Choice Awards, 1997, 1999, The 50 Most Beautiful People, People Magazine, 1996, 1999, People's Choice Award For Favorite Actress In A Motion Picture, While You Were Sleeping, 1996, Best Actress, US Magazine, 1995, Best Actress, MTV's Big Picture, 1994-1995, MTV Movie Awards For Best Female Performance, Most Desirable Female, Speed, 1994 **BA:** c/o Kevin Huvane Creative Artists Agency, 9830 Wilshire Boulevard, Beverly Hills, CA, 90212-1825

BULLOCK, STEVE, **T:** Governor of Montana, former state attorney general **I:** Government Administration/Government Relations/Government Services **DOB:** 04/11/1966 **PB:** Missoula **ED:** JD with honors, Columbia Law School, New York City, 1994; BA, Claremont McKenna College, California, 1988 **C:** Governor, State of Montana, Helena, 2013-; Private law practice, Helena, Montana, 2004-08; Attorney, Steptoe & Johnson LLP, Washington, 2001-04; Attorney general, State of Montana, Helena, 2009-13; Executive assistant attorney general, then acting chief deputy, State of Montana, Helena, 1997-2001; Chief legal counsel to secretary of state, State of Montana, Helena, 1996 **CR:** Adjunct professor George Washington University School Law, 2001-04 **PA:** Democrat

BURDICK, KENNETH, **T:** CEO **I:** Health, Wellness and Fitness **CN:** Wellcare Health Plans **ED:** J.D., University of Connecticut School of Law, 1981-85; B.A, Amherst College, 1976-80 **C:** CEO, Wellcare Health Plans Inc, 2015-; President/COO, Wellcare Health Plans Inc, 2014-2015; President National Health Plans, Wellcare Health Plans Inc, 2014 **MEM:** Board Member, Preferred Homecare of America

BURGESS, MICHAEL CLIFTON, **T:** U.S. Representative from Texas **I:** Government Administration/Government Relations/Government Services **DOB:** 12/23/1950 **PB:** Rochester, Minnesota **PT:** Son of Harry Meredith Burgess and Norma Crowhurst; **ED:** Doctor of Pub. Service (hon.), University North Texas Health Scis. Center, 2009; MA in Medical Management, University Texas, Dallas, 2000; MD, University Texas Medical Center, Houston, 1977; MS, North Texas State University, 1976; BS, North Texas State University, 1972 **C:** Chair Congl. Health Care Caucus, US Congress from 26th Texas District, 2009-; Member, Committee on Energy and Commerce; Member, US Congress from 26th Texas District, 2003-; Chief Obstetrics, Chief of Staff, Lewisville Medical Center,; Private Practice, Ob-Gyn. Associates, Lewisville, Texas,; Resident, Parkland Memorial Hospital, Dallas, **AW:** Named House Legislator of Year, Multiple Sclerosis Society, 2008, Legislator of Year, Am. Academy Nurse Practitioners, 2005; Recipient Taxpayer Hero Award, Council Citizens Against Government Waste, Guardian of Small Business Award, National Federation Ind. Business **MEM:** Mem.: Denton County Medical Society (Past President) **PA:** Republican

BURGUM, DOUGLAS J., **T:** Governor from North Dakota **I:** Government Administration/Government Relations/Government Services **PB:** Arthur **ED:** PhD (hon.), University Mary, 2006; PhD (hon.), North Dakota State University, 2000; BA, North Dakota State University, 1978; MBA, Stanford University, 1980 **C:** Governor, State of North Dakota, 2016-; Senior vice president, Microsoft Business Solutions Group, Microsoft Business Division, Microsoft Corp., 2005-07; Joined, Microsoft Corp., 2001; Chairman, CEO, Great Plains Software Inc. (acquired by Microsoft Corp.), 1984-2001; Consultant, McKinsey & Co., 1980-83 **CR:** Board directors SuccessFactors, Inc. 2007- **CIV:** Board member, Stanford Grad. School Business, Founder, Doug Burgum Family Fund,

BURKE, MICHAEL, **T:** Engineering Company Executive **I:** Engineering **CN:** AECOM Technology Corp. **ED:** BS in Accounting, University of Scranton; JD, Southwestern University **CT:** CPA **C:** Chairman, AECOM, 2015-Present; CEO, AECOM, 2014-Present; President, AECOM Technology Corp., 2011—Present; Executive Vice President, CFO, AECOM Technology Corp., 2006—2011; Chief Corporate Officer, AECOM Technology Corp., 2006—2009; Senior Vice President, Corporate Strategy, AECOM Technology Corp., 2005; Managing Partner, Western Area, KPMG LLP, 2002—2005; Joined, KPMG LLP, 1990; Worked, Arthur Andersen And Co., Los Angeles, CA, 1986—1990 **CR:** Board of Directors, KPMG LLP, 2000—2005; Rentech Inc., 2007—Present **CIV:** Board of Directors, Children's Bureau; Trustee, Neighborhood Youth Association **MEM:** American Institute of Certified Public Accountants, California Society of CPAs, California Bar Association **BA:** AECOM Technology Corp., 555 S Flower Street, Suite 3700, Los Angeles, CA, 90071

BURKE, TARANA, T: Activist **I:** Nonprofit & Philanthropy **PB:** Bronx **SC:** NY/USA **ED:** Coursework, Alabama State University; Coursework, Auburn University **C:** Founder, Just Be Inc. (2006-Present); Senior Director, Girls for Gender Equity **AW:** Named One of TIME's 100 Most Influential, TIME Magazine (2018); Ridenhour Prize for Courage (2018)

BURNETT, MARK, T: Television Producer **I:** Media & Entertainment **DOB:** 07/17/1960 **PB:** London **PT:** Son of Archie and Jean Burnett; **C:** Founder, president, Mark Burnett Productions, **CIV:** Ambassador, Operation Smile, Board directors, Elizabeth Glaser Pediatric Aids Foundation, **CW:** Creator (televised natural adventure race) Eco-Challenge, 1995- (Sports Emmy award for Outstanding Program Achievement for Eco-Challenge: Morocco, 2000, Banff Rockie award in the Sports Program Category, Banff Rockie Awards Festival, 2000), creator, writer (TV series) Diili, 2005-13, O Aprendiz, 2004-11, Bully Beatdown, 2009-12, creator, executive producer Survivor, 2000- (People's Choice award for Favorite Reality Based Television Program, 2001, 2002, 2003, 2004, Special Recognition award, Gay & Lesbian Alliance Against Defamation, Emmy award for Outstanding Non-Fiction Program, 2001), The Apprentice, 2003-11, Celebrity Apprentice Australia, 2011-12; executive prodr.: (TV series) Combat Missions, 2002, Boarding House: North Shore, 2003, The Restaurant, 2003-04, The Casino, 2004, Rock Star: INXS, 2005, Apprentice: Martha Stewart, 2005, The Contender, 2006-09, On the Lot, 2007, Are You Smarter Than a 5th Grader?, 2007-15, Expedition Africa, 2009, Wedding Day, 2009, How'd You Get So Rich?, 2009, StarMaker, 2009, Shark Tank, 2009-15, The Voice, 2011-12 (Outstanding Producer of Competition TV award, Producers Guild of America, 2014, 2016), Stars Earn Stripes, 2012, A.D. The Bible Continues, 2015, Coupled, 2016, Beat Shazam, 2017, Steve Harveys Funderdome, 2017; (TV films) Are We There Yet?, 2003; (TV miniseries) The Bible, 2013, The Dovekeepers, 2015; (films) Son of God, 2014, Little Boy, 2014, Woodlawn, 2015, Ben Hur 2016; author: Dare to Succeed: How to Survive and Thrive in the Game of Life, 2002, Jump In! Even if You Don't Know How to Swim, 2005 **AW:** Named a Maverick, Details magazine, 2007; named Philanthropist of Year, Reality Cares Foundation; named to 100 Most Influential People list, Time magazine, 2004; recipient Norman Lear Achievement award in TV, Producers Guild of America, 2010, Star, Hollywood Walk of Fame, 2009 **MEM:** Mem.: National Academy TV Arts & Scis., British Academy Film & TV Arts (two elected terms, board directors) **H:** Scuba diving, skydiving

BURR, RICHARD MAUZE, T: U.S. Senator From North Carolina **I:** Government Administration/Government Relations/Government Services **DOB:** 11/30/1955 **PB:** Charlottesville **SC:** VA/USA **ED:** BA in Communications, Wake Forest University, Winston-Salem, NC, 1978 **C:** Chairman, U.S. Senate Select Committee On Intelligence, 2015-Present; U.S. Senator From North Carolina,

2005-Present; U.S. Congress From Fifth North Carolina District, 1995-2005; State Co-Chairman, North Carolina Taxpayers United, 1993-1998; National Sales Manager, Carswell Distributing, Winston-Salem, NC, 1978-1994 **CIV:** Co-Chairman, Partnership Drug Free North Carolina, Forsyth County Earning By Learning, Board of Directors, Brenner Children's Hospital, Winston-Salem, NC **AW:** Legislator of the Year, Biotechnology Industry Organization, 2002, Jefferson Award, Citizens For Sound Economics, 2001, Ground Water Protector Award, National Ground Water Association, 2000, Manufacturing Legislative Excellence Award, National Association of Manufacturers, 1999, Alfred & Alma Hitchcock Tribute Award, Cystic Fibrosis Foundation, 1999 **MEM:** Optimist Soccer League, Rotary Club **PA:** Republican **BA:** Office of Richard Burr, 217 Russell Senate Office Building, Washington, DC, 20510

BURSTYN, ELLEN, T: Actress **I:** Media & Entertainment **DOB:** 12/07/1932 **PB:** Detroit **SC:** Michigan **PT:** Daughter of John Austin Gillooly and Correine Marie Hamel; **SPN:** Married William Alexander, 1950 (div. September 1955); Married Paul Roberts, September 14, 1958 (div. 1962), **CH:** 1 Adopted Child, Jefferson **ED:** LHD (hon.), Dowling College; DFA (hon.), School Visual Arts **C:** Artistic Director, The Actor's Studio, New York City, 1982-88 **CIV:** Member Individual Artists Grants and Policy Overview Panels National Endowment for the Arts, Theater Adv. Council City of New York. **CW:** Actress: (films) Gunfight in Black Horse Canyon, 1961, Alex in Wonderland, 1970, Tropic of Cancer, 1970, The Last Picture Show, 1971, The King of Marvin Gardens, 1972, The Exorcist, 1973, Harry and Tonto, 1974, Alice Dosen't Live Here Anymore, 1974 (Academy award for Best Actress, 1975), Same Time, Next Year, 1978, Resurrection, 1980, Silence of the North, 1981, In Our Hands, 1984, The Ambassador, 1984, Twice in a Lifetime, 1985, Hanna's War, 1988, Grand Isle, 1991, Dying Young, 1991, The Cemetery Club, 1993, The Color of Evening, 1994, Choosing One's Way: Resistance in Auschwitz/Birkenau (narrator, presenter), 1994, When a Man Loves a Woman, 1994, Roommates, 1995, The Baby-Sitters Club, 1995, How to Make an American Quilt, 1995, The Spitfire Grill, 1996, Deceiver, 1997, You Can Thank Me Later, 1998, Playing by Heart, 1998, Walking Across Egypt, 1999, Requiem for a Dream, 1999, The Yards, 1999, Divine Secrets of the Ya-Ya Sisterhood, 2002, Distance, 2002, (voice) Red Dragon, 2002, Down in the Valley, 2005, The Elephant King, 2006, The Wicker Man, 2006, 30 Days, 2006, The Fountain, 2006, The Loss of a Teardrop Diamond, 2008, Lovely, Still, 2008, W., 2008, The Velveteen Rabbit, 2009, According to Greta, 2009, The Mighty Macs, 2009, Main Street, 2010, Another Happy Day, 2011, Someday This Pain Will Be Useful to You, 2011, Wish You Well, 2013, The Calling, 2014, Interstellar, 2014, The Age of Adaline, 2015, About Scout, 2015, Wiener-Dog, 2016, Custody, 2016, The House of Tomorrow, 2017, A Little Something for Your Birthday, 2017, Nostalgia, 2018 (TV films) Thursday's Game, 1974, The People versus Jean Harris, 1981, Acting: Lee Strasberg and the Actos Studio, 1981, Surviving, 1985, Into Thin Air, 1985, Something in Common, 1986, Act of Vengeance, 1986, Hellow Actors Studio, 1987, (voice) Dear America: Letters Home from Vietnam, 1987, Pack of Lies, 1987, When You Remember Me, 1990, Mrs. Lambers Remembers Love, 1991, Taking Back My Life: The Nacy Ziegenmeyer Story, 1992, Shattered Trust: The Shary Karney Story, 1993, Getting Out, 1994, Getting Gotti, 1994, Trick of the Eye, 1994, My Brother's Keeper, 1995, Follow the River, 1995, Timepiece, 1995, Our Son, The

Matchmaker, 1996, Murder in the Mind, 1996, A Deadly Vision, 1997, Flash, 1998, The Patron Saint of Liars, 1998, Night Ride Home, 1999, Mermaid, 2000, Within These Walls, 2001, Dodson's Journey, 2001, Brush with Fate, 2003, The Madam's Family: The Truth About the Canal Street Brothel, 2004, The Five People You Meet in Heaven, 2004, Our Fathers, 2005, Mrs. Harris, 2005, Mitch Albom's For One More Day, 2007, Possible Side Effects, 2009, Old Soul, 2014, Flowers in the Attic, 2014, Petals on the Wind, 2014, (TV series) The Ellen Burstyn Show, 1986-87, (mini-series) A Will of Their Own, 1998, Big Love, 2007-11, Political Animals, 2012 (Emmy award for Outstanding Supporting Actress in a Miniseries or Movie, 2013), Coma, 2012, House of Cards, 2016, (TV appearances) Cheyenne, 1955, Gunsmoke, 1955, Maverick, 1957, The Big Valley, 1965, The Time Tunnel, 1966, The Bold Ones: The Lawyers, 1969, Law & Order: Special Victims Unit: Swing, 2009 (Emmy Award for Outstanding Guest Actress in a Drama Series, 2009), Mom, 2015, (Plays) The Little Flower of East Orange, 2008, (Broadway plays) Fair Game, 1957-1958, Same Time, Next Year, 1975-1978, (Drama Desk Award for Outstanding Actress in a Play, 1975, Tony award for Best Actress in a Play, 1975), 84 Charing Cross Road, 1982-1983, Shirley Valentine, 1989, Shimada, 1992, Sacrilege, 1995, Oldest Living Confederate Widow Tells All, 2003, Picnic, 2013; Author: (autobiography) Lessons in Becoming Myself, 2006. **AW:** Named to, The Michigan Women's Hall of Fame, 1997, Am. Theatre Hall of Fame, 2013 **MEM:** Member Actors Equity Association (President 1982-85) **PA:** Democrat **BA:** Classic Stage Company, 136 E 13th Street, New York, NY, 10003

BURTON, TIM, T: Director **I:** Media & Entertainment **DOB:** 08/25/1958 **PB:** Burbank **SC:** CA/USA **PT:** Bill Burton, Jean (Erickson) Burton **SPN:** Helena Bonham Carter, Partner; Lena Gieseke, 2/24/1989, Divorced 12/31/1991 **CH:** Billy Ray, Indiana Rose **ED:** Student, California Institute of the Arts, 1979-1980 **C:** Apprentice Animator, Disney Productions; Cartoon Artist, Disney Productions **CR:** Disney Fellowship, California Institute of the Arts **CW:** Director, (Films) Vincent, 1982, Pee-Wee's Big Adventure, 1984, Beetlejuice, 1988, Batman, 1989, Sleepy Hollow, 1999, Planet Of The Apes, 2001, Big Fish, 2003, Charlie And The Chocolate Factory, 2005, Corpse Bride, 2005, Sweeney Todd: The Demon Barber Of Fleet Street, 2007, Alice In Wonderland, 2010, Frankenweenie, 2012, Dark Shadows, 2012, Miss Peregrine's Home For Peculiar Children, 2016, Dumbo, (TV Films) Hansel And Gretel, 1982; Producer, Production Designer, (Films) The Nightmare Before Christmas, 1993; Producer, (Films) Cabin Boy, 1994, Batman Forever, 1995, James And The Giant Peach, 1996, Abraham Lincoln: Vampire Hunter, 2012, Alice Through The Looking Glass, 2016; Director, Producer, (Films) Stalk Of The Celery, 1979, Edward Scissorhands, 1990, Batman Returns, 1992, Ed Wood, 1994, Mars Attacks!, 1996, The World Of Stainboy, 2000, Frankenweenie, 2012, Big Eyes, 2014; Executive Producer, (TV Films) Lost In Oz, 2000, (TV Series) Beetlejuice, 1989-1991, Family Dog, 1992; Author, My Art & Films, 1993, The Melancholy Death Of Oyster Boy And Other Stories, 1997 **AW:** Best Animated Film, New York Film Critics Circle, Boston Society Film Critics, Frankenweenie, 2012, Officier, Ordre des Arts et de Lettres, Government of France, 2010, Best Director Award, National Board Review, Sweeney Todd: The Demon Barber Of Fleet Street, 2007, Golden Lion Award, Venice International Film Festival, 2007, Tropopkin's Top 25 Most Intriguing People, 50 Greatest Directors of All Time, Entertainment Weekly **BA:** Tim Burton Productions, 8033 Sunset Boulevard, Suite 7500, West Hollywood, CA, 90046

BUSH, BARBARA, **T:** Former First Lady **I:** Government Administration/Government Relations/Government Services **DOB:** 06/08/1925 **PB:** NYC **SC:** NY/USA **YOP:** 2018-04-18 **ED:** Student, Smith College, 1944; Degree (hon.), Stritch College, Milwaukee, 1981; Degree (hon.), Mount Vernon College, Washington, 1981; Degree (hon.), Hood College, Frederick, Maryland, 1983; Degree (hon.), Howard University, Washington, 1987; Degree (hon.), Judson College, Marion, Alabama, 1988; Degree (hon.), Bennett College, Greensboro, North Carolina, 1989; Degree (hon.), Smith College, 1989; Degree (hon.), Morehouse School Medicine, 1989 **C:** Operating & Facilities Division, Department Administration, Washington, DC, 1992; First Lady of the U.S., Washington, DC, 1989—1993 **CIV:** Hon. Chair Adv. Board Reading is Fundamental; Hon. Member Business Council for Effective Literacy; Member Adv. Council Society of Memorial Sloan-Kettering Cancer Center; Hon. Member Board of Directors Children's Oncology Services of Metropolitan Washington, The Washington Home, The Kingsbury Center; Hon. Chairman National Adv. Council Literacy Vols. of America, National School Vols. Program; Sponsor Laubach Literacy International; National Hon. Chairman Leukemia Society of America; Hon. Member Board of Trustees Morehouse School of Medicine; Hon. National Chairman National Organ Donor Awareness Week, 1982-86; President Ladies of the Senate, 1981-88; Member Women's Committee Smithsonian Associates, Texas Federation of Rep. Women, Life Member, Hon. Member; Hon. Chairperson National Committee on Literacy and Education United Way, Washington Parent Group Fund, Girls Clubs of America, 10th Anniversary Harvest National Food Bank Network, National Committee for the Prevention of Child Abuse, Childhelp USA, Leukemia Society Am., Children's Literacy Initiative, Read Am., Boarder Baby Project, Barbara Bush Foundation for Family Literacy, 1989-, Hon. Member; Hon. President Girl Scouts U.S; Hon. Chair National Committee for Adoption; Member Board of Trustees Mayo Clinic Foundation; Member Board of Visitors M. D. Anderson Cancer Center; Hon. Member Reading is Fundamental; Ambassador-at-large Americares. **CW:** Author: C. Fred Story, 1984, Millie's Book, 1990, Barbara Bush: A Memoir, 1994, Reflections: Life After the White House, 2003. **AW:** Recipient National Outstanding Mother of Year Award, 1984, Woman of Year Award United Service Organizations, 1986, Distinguished Leadership Award United Negro College Fund 1986, Distinguished Am. Woman Award Mount St. Joseph College, 1987, Free Spirit Award Freedom Forum, 1995 **MEM:** Member Texas Federation Republican Women (life), International II Club (Washington), Magic Circle Rep. Women's Club (Houston), YWCA. **H:** Reading, Gardening, Needlepoint **BA:** Office of Former President George Bush 243 Ocean Ave, Kennebunkport, ME, 040046

BUSH, GEORGE HERBERT WALKER, **T:** 41st President of the U.S. **I:** Government Administration/Government Relations/Government Services **DOB:** 06/12/1924 **PB:** Milton, Massachusetts **PT:** Son of Prescott Sheldon and Dorothy (Walker) B.; **SPN:** Married Barbara Pierce, January 6, 1945; **CH:** Children: George Walker, Pauline Robinson (Robin) (deceased October 11, 1953), John Ellis (Jeb), Neil Mallon, **ED:** LLD (hon.), Harvard University, 2014; LHD (hon.), University New Hampshire, 2007; BA in Economics, Yale University, 1948 **C:** Senior Adv., Carlyle Group, 1998-2003; President of the US, 1989-93; Vice President of the US, 1981-89; Chairman, First International Bank, Houston, 1977-80; Director, CIA, Washington, 1976-77; Chief US Liaison Office, People's Republic of China, US Department State, Peking,

1974-76; Chairman, Republican National Committee (RNC), Washington, 1973-74; US ambassador to UN, US Department State, New York City, 1971-73; Member, US Congress from 7th District Texas, 1967-71; Chairman Board, Zapata Off Shore Co., 1964-66; President, Zapata Off Shore Co., Houston, 1956-64; Co-founder, Director, Zapata Petroleum Corp., Midland, 1953-59; Co-founder, Bush-Overbey Oil Devel. Co., 1951 **CR:** Chairman National Constitution Center, Philadelphia, 2007-08 Board Visitors M.D. Anderson Cancer Center, Houston Adjunct Professor Administrative Sci. Rice University Jones School Business, Houston, 1978 **CIV:** Co-founder (with Bill Clinton), Fundraiser, Bush-Clinton Tsunami partnership, 2005- Co-founder (with Bill Clinton), fundraiser, Bush-Clinton Katrina Fund, 2005- Del., Republican National Convention, Miami Beach, Florida, 1968 Del., Republican National Convention, San Francisco, 1964 Republican candidate, US Senate, 1970 Republican candidate, US Senate, Texas, 1964 **MIL:** Served in US Navy, 1942-45, WWII **CW:** Co-author (with Victor Gold): Looking Forward, 1987; Co-author: (with Brent Scowcroft) A World Transformed, 1998; Author: All The Best, George Bush: My Life and Other Writings, 1999, All The Best, George Bush: My Life and Other Writings, Revised Edition, 2013; Appeared in (documentaries) 41, 2012 **AW:** Decorated 3 Air Medals, Distinguished Flying Cross; Co-recipient Liberty Medal, National Constitution Center, 2006; Named a Knight Commander of the British Empire (KBE), Her Majesty Queen Elizabeth II, 1993; Named Man of Year, TIME Magazine, 1990; Named one of The 100 Most Influential People in the World, 2006; Recipient Profile in Courage Award, John F. Kennedy Library Foundation, 2014, 5,000th Daily Point of Light Award, Points of Light Foundation, 2013, Presidential Medal of Freedom, The White House, 2010, Ronald Reagan Freedom Award, 2007, Dwight D. Eisenhower Medal, 2003, George C. Marshall Award, 2002, Albert Schweitzer Gold Medal for Humanitarianism, 1997, International Security Leadership Award, 1993 **MEM:** Fellow: American Academy Arts & Sciences **PA:** Republican

BUSH, GEORGE WALKER, **T:** 43rd President of the U.S. **I:** Government Administration/Government Relations/Government Services **DOB:** 07/06/1946 **PB:** New Haven **SC:** CT/USA **PT:** George Herbert Walker; Barbara (Pierce) Bush **ED:** MBA, Harvard Business School, Harvard University (1975); BA in History, Yale University (1968) **C:** President, U.S., Washington, DC (2001-2009); Governor, State of Texas, Austin, TX (1994-2000); Managing General Partner, Texas Rangers (1989-1994); Senior Advisor, George Herbert Walker Bush Presidential Campaign (1988); Board of Directors, Harken Energy Corp. (Formerly Spectrum 7 Energy Corp.), Midland, TX (1986-1999); Chairman, Spectrum 7 Energy Corp. (Formerly Bush Exploration), Midland, TX (1984-1986); Founder, Chief Executive Officer, Bush Exploration (Formerly Arbusto Energy Inc.), Midland, TX (1982-1984); Founder, Chief Executive Officer, Arbusto Energy Inc., Midland, TX (1977-1982) **CR:** Board of Directors, Caterair International, Inc. (1990-1994) **CIV:** Pilot, Texas Air National Guard (1968-1970) **CW:** Author, "41: A Portrait of My Father" (2014); Author, "Decision Points" (2010); Co-Author, with Karen Hughes, "A Charge to Keep" (1999) **AW:** Named, One of the 50 Highest-Earning Political Figures, Newsweek (2010); Named, The 100 Most Influential People in the World, Time Magazine (2008); Named, The 100 Most Influential People in the World, Time Magazine (2004-2006); Named, Person of the Year, Time Magazine (2004); Recipient, Big D Award, Dallas All Sports Association (1989); Named,

#1 New York Times Bestseller **MEM:** President, Delta Kappa Epsilon (1965-1968) **ACH:** Achievements include becoming the first governor in the history of Texas to be elected to two consecutive four-year terms **PA:** Republican **BA:** George W Bush Presidential Center, 2943 SMU Boulevard, Dallas, TX, 75205

BUSH, JEB, **I:** Government Administration/Government Relations/Government Services **DOB:** 02/11/1953 **PB:** Midland **SC:** TX/USA **PT:** Son of George Herbert Walker and Barbara Pierce Bush; Married Columba Garnica Gallo, February 23, 1974; children: George, Noelle, John Junior **ED:** BA in Latin American Affairs, University of Texas, 1974 **C:** Founder, President, Jeb Bush & Associates LLC, Miami, 2007-; Senior Advisor, Barclay's PLC, 2008-14; Governor, State of Florida, Tallahassee, 1999-2007; Secretary of Commerce, State of Florida, Tallahassee, 1987-88; President, COO, Codina Group, Miami, Florida, 1995-98; Co-founder, Codina Bush Group, Miami, Florida, 1981-93; Vice President, Texas Commerce Bank, Caracas, Venezuela, 1974-79 **CR:** Chairman, Dade County Republican Party, 1984-86, National Constitution Center, 2013-, Board of Directors, Safecard Services, 1995-96, Tenet Healthcare Corp., 2007-14, CNL Bancshares, Inc., 2007-14, Rayonier, Inc., 2008-14, Angelica Corp., 2008-14, CorMatrix Cardiovascular, Inc., 2010-14, Swisher Hygiene, Inc., 2010-13, Board Member, Bloomberg Family Foundation, 2010-14 **CIV:** Chairman, Miami-Dade County Beacon Council, 1990-91, Volunteer, Miami Children's Hospital, United Way of Dade County, Dade County Homeless Trust, Founder, Foundation for Florida's Future, 1995, Co-founder, Liberty City Charter School, 1995, Trustee, Heritage Foundation, 1995 **CW:** Co-author (with Brian Yablonski): Profiles in Character, 1996 **PA:** Republican

BUSH, JOHN K., **T:** Federal Judge **I:** Law and Legal Services **PB:** Hot Springs **SC:** AR/USA **ED:** BA, Vanderbilt University; JD, Harvard Law School **C:** Judge, U.S. Court of Appeals for the Sixth Circuit (2017-Present)

BUSH, LAURA WELCH, **T:** Former First Lady **I:** Government Administration/Government Relations/Government Services **DOB:** 11/04/1946 **PB:** Midland, Texas, November 4, 1946 **PT:** Daughter of Harold Bruch and Jenna Louise (Hawkins) Welch; **ED:** MLS, University Texas, Austin, 1973; BS in Education, Southern Methodist University, 1968 **C:** First Lady of the U.S., 2001-09; First Lady of Texas, 1995-2001; Libr., Dawson Elementary School, Austin, 1974-77; Libr., Houston Pub. Lib., 1973-74; Teacher, John F. Kennedy Elementary School, Houston, 1969-72; Teacher, Longfellow Elementary School, Dallas, 1968-69 **CR:** Speaker Republican National Convention, New York City, 2004 launched National Book Festival, 2001 established Rainbow Rooms, Texas, Adopt-A-Caseworker programs, Texas **CIV:** Vol., Hurricane Help for Schools **CW:** Co-author (with Jenna Bush): (children's books) Read All About It!, 2008; author: ((memoirs)) Spoken from the Heart, 2010 (#1 New York Times bestseller) **AW:** Named one of The 100 Most Powerful Women, Forbes magazine, 2004-08; recipient President's Crystal Apple award, American Association School Librarians, 2006 **PA:** Republican **BA:** Prairie Chapel Ranch, McLennan County, TX, 0

BUSH, WESLEY G., **T:** Aerospace Transportation Executive **I:** Aviation **ED:** MSEE, Massachusetts Institute of Technology; BS in Elect. Engineering, Massachusetts Institute of Technology, 1983 **C:** President, CEO, Chairman, Northrop Grumman

Corp., L.A., 2017-; President, CEO, Northrop Grumman Corp., L.A., 2010-2017; President, COO, Northrop Grumman Corp., L.A., 2007-09; President, CFO, Northrop Grumman Corp., L.A., 2006-07; Corp. vice president, CFO, Northrop Grumman Corp., L.A., 2005-06; Corp. vice president, president space tech., Northrop Grumman Corp., L.A., 2003-05; President, CEO, global aeronautical system, TRW-United Kingdom, 2001-03; Vice president, general manager, TRW Ventures, 2000-01; President, CEO, TRW Aeronautical Systems, 2001-03; From. system engineer to vice president, general manager telecomm. programs division, TRW Aeronautical Systems, 1987-99; Corp. vice president, president space tech., Comsat Labs,; With engineering staff, Serospace Corp., **CR:** Member National Infrastructure Advisory Council, 2008- board directors Northrop Grumman Corp., 2009- **CIV:** Board member, Conservation International, Board member, Smithsonian Air & Space Museum, Board member, Bus.-Higher Education Forum, Board director, National Action Council for Minorities in Engineering

BUSTOS, CHERIE, **T:** U.S. Representative from Illinois **I:** Government Administration/Government Relations/Government Services **DOB:** 10/17/1961 **PB:** Springfield **PT:** Gene; Ann Callahan **ED:** MA in Journalism, University of Illinois (1985); BS in Political Science & History, University of Maryland (1983); Coursework, Illinois College (1981) **C:** Chair, Democratic Policy and Communications Committee (2017-Present); Member, U.S. House Agricultural Committee (2013-Present); Member, U.S. House of Transportation Infrastructure Committee (2013-Present); Member, U.S. Congress from 17th Illinois District, Washington, DC (2013-Present); Vice President, Public Relations & Communications, Iowa Health System (2008-2010); Alderman City Council, City of East Moline, IL (2007-2011); Senior Director of Corporate Communications, Trinity Regional Health System (2001-2007); Reporter, Editor, Quad-City Times, Davenport, Iowa (1985-2001) **AW:** Athena Business Women's Award (2009); Named to Illinois College Sports Hall of Fame (1994) **MEM:** Blue Dog Coalition **PA:** Democrat

BUTKUS, DICK, **T:** Former NFL Player **I:** Athletics **DOB:** 12/09/1942 **PB:** Chicago **SC:** IL/USA **MS:** Married **SPN:** Helen Butkus **CH:** Nicole; Richard; Matthew **ED:** Student, University of Illinois **C:** Broadcaster, Station WGN-Radio, Chicago, 1986-; Broadcaster, CBS NFL Today broadcasts, New York City, 1988-89; With professional football team, Chicago Bears, 1965-73 **CW:** Appeared in TV movies including Brian's Song, 1971, The Legend of Sleepy Hollow, 1980, TV miniseries Rich Man, Poor Man, 1977, Blue Thunder, 1984, motion picture Johnny Dangerously, 1984, numerous TV commls. **AW:** Named to Pro-Football Hall of Fame, 1979

BUTTERFIELD, GEORGE KENNETH JR., **T:** U.S. Representative from North Carolina **I:** Government Administration/Government Relations/Government Services **DOB:** 04/27/1947 **PB:** Wilson, North Carolina **PT:** Son of G. K. and Addie (Davis) Butterfield; **ED:** JD, North Carolina Central University School Law, 1974; BS in Political Sci. and Sociology, North Carolina Central University, 1971 **CT:** Bar: North Carolina 1975 **C:** 2nd vice chair, Congressional Black Caucus, 2011-; Member, Committee on Energy and Commerce; Member, US Congress from 1st North Carolina District, 2004-; Judge, North Carolina Special Superior Court, 2002-04; Justice, North Carolina Supreme Court, 2001-02; Judge, North Carolina Resident Superior Court District 7B, 1989-2001; Senior partner, Butterfield, Fitch & Wynn, 1974-88 **MIL:** Specialist US

Army, 1968-70 **AW:** Named one of Most Influential Black Americans, Ebony magazine, 2006; named to Power 150, 2008; recipient Lawyer of Year award, North Carolina Association Black Lawyers **MEM:** Mem.: North Carolina Bar Association (vice president 2003-) **PA:** Democrat

BUTZ, NORBERT LEO, **T:** Actor **I:** Media & Entertainment **PB:** St. Louis **SC:** MO/USA **PT:** Elaine Butz; Norbert Butz **ED:** MFA, Alabama Shakespeare Theatre; BFA, Webster University **CW:** Actor: (Broadway plays) Rent, 1996; (Broadway plays, national tour) Cabaret (Helen Hayes award, outstanding actor in a musical); (Broadway plays) Thou Shalt Not, 2001-02, Wicked, 2003, Dirty Rotten Scoundrels, 2005 (Tony award for Best Performance by an Actor in a Leading Role in a Musical, 2005, Drama League award, distinguished performance, 2005, Outer Critics Circle award, outstanding actor in a musical, 2005, Drama Desk award, outstanding actor in a musical, 2005), Is He Dead?, 2007-08, Speed-the-Plow, 2008-09, Enron, 2010, Catch Me If You Can, 2011 (Tony award for Best Performance by an Actor in a Leading Role in a Musical, 2011), Dead Accounts, 2012-13, Big Fish, 2013-; (plays, off-Broadway) Buicks, The Last Five Years, 2002 (Drama League award, outstanding actor in a musical), Juno and the Paycock; (plays) Saved; (films) Went to Coney Island on a Mission from God...Be Back by Five, 1998, (voice) Looking for an Echo, 2000, Noon Blue Apples, 2002, West of Here, 2002, Fair Game, 2011, Higher Ground, 2011, Disconnect, 2012, Greetings from Tim Buckley, 2012, The English Teacher, 2013; (TV series) The Deep End, 2010; (TV films) The Miraculous Year, 2011, County, 2012

BYRNE, BRADLEY, **T:** U.S. Representative from Alabama **I:** Government Administration/Government Relations/Government Services **DOB:** 02/16/1955 **PB:** Mobile **SC:** AL/USA **PT:** Arthur LaCoste Byrne, Elizabeth Patricia (Langsdale) Byrne **MS:** Married **SPN:** Rebecca Dow Dukes, 5/16/1981 **CH:** Patrick McGuire, Kathleen Roberts, Laura Ann, Colin Arthur **ED:** BA, Duke University, 1977; JD, University of Alabama School of Law, 1980 **C:** U.S. House of Natural Resources Committee, 2014—Present; U.S. House of Armed Services Committee, 2014—Present; U.S. Congress From First Alabama District, Washington, DC, 2014—Present; Chancellor, Alabama Department of Postsecondary Education, 2007—2009; District 32, Alabama State Senate, 2003—2007; Jackson Myrick Chambers & Byrne, Mobile, AL, 1995—2013; Partner, Management Committee, Miller, Hamilton, Snider & Odom, Mobile, AL, 1989-1995; Partner, Miller, Hamilton, Snider & Odom, Mobile, AL, 1985-1995; Associate, Miller, Hamilton, Snider & Odom, Mobile, AL, 1980-1985 **CIV:** Active, Alabama State Board Of Education, 1994-2002; Secretary, Mobile City Planning Commission, 1990-1994; Honorary Life Member, Alabama PTA **AW:** Outstanding Young Men Of America, 1981-1982, Phi Delta Phi Outstanding Lay Person Award, 1998, Alabama Association of School Boards' Champion For Children Award, 2004, Council For Leaders In Alabama Schools Legislative Leadership Award, 2004, Legislator of the Year Award, Alabama Wildlife Federation, 2005, South Alabama Literacy Champion Award, 2006, Leadership Award, Alabama Civil Justice Reform Committee, 2007 **MEM:** Vice Chairman, Mobile Area Chamber of Commerce, 1989-1991, Litigation Section, American Bar Association, Alabama Bar Association, Alabama State Bar, Mobile Bar Association, Leadership Alabama **BAR:** State of Alabama, 1980, U.S. District Court, Southern District, State of Alabama, 1980, U.S. Court of Appeals, Fifth and 11th Circuits, 1981, U.S. District Court, Middle

District, State of Alabama, 1985, U.S. Court of Appeals, Eighth Circuit, 1985, U.S. District Court, Northern District, State of Alabama, 1986, U.S. Supreme Court, 1987 **BA:** U.S. House of Representatives, 2236 Rayburn HOB, Washington, DC, 20515

CABRANES, JOSE ALBERTO, **T:** Federal Judge **I:** Law and Legal Services **DOB:** 12/22/1940 **PB:** Mayaguez **SC:** Puerto Rico **PT:** Manuel Cabranes, Carmen Lopez Cabranes **ED:** Honorary LLD, Colgate University, 1988; MLitt in International Law, Cambridge University, England, 1967; JD, Yale University, 1965 AB, Columbia University, 1961; Honorary LLD, Other Universities **CT:** U.S. District Court, Connecticut, 1976, District of Columbia, 1975, New York, 1968 **C:** Judge, U.S. Foreign Intelligence Surveillance Court Review, (FISCR), 2013-Present; Judge, U.S. Court Appeals, Second Circuit, 1994-Present; Chief Judge, U.S. District Court, Connecticut, New Haven, CT, 1992-1994; Judge, U.S. District Court Connecticut, New Haven, CT, 1979-1994; General Counsel, Yale University, New Haven, CT, 1975-1979; Special Counsel To Governor Puerto Rico, Head, Office of the Commonwealth of Puerto Rico, Washington, DC, 1973-1975; Associate Professor, Law School, Rutgers University, Newark, NJ, 1971-1973; Associate, Casey, Lane & Mittendorf, New York, NY, 1967-1971 **CR:** President's Commission on White House Fellowships, 1993-1996, Federal Courts Study Committee, 1988-1990, Consultant To Secretary, Department of State, 1978, Chairman of the Board, Puerto Rico Legal Defense And Education Fund, 1977-1980, U.S. Delegate, Conference on Security And Cooperative In Europe, Belgrade, Serbia, 1977-1978, President's Commission on Mental Health, 1977-1978, Founding Member, Puerto Rico Legal Defense And Education Fund, 1972, Supervisor In International Law Queens' College, Cambridge University, 1966-1967, Kellett Research Fellow, Columbia College At Cambridge University, 1965-1967, Instructor of History, Puerto Rico Colegio San Ignacio De Loyola, Rio Piedras, Puerto Rico, 1962, Fellow, American Bar Association Foundation; Fellow, Mexican-American Lawyers Association **CIV:** Trustee, Columbia University, 2000-Present, Board of Directors, James Madison Memorial Fellowship Foundation, 1995-2003, Special Recognition Award, Mexican-American Lawyers Association, 1994, Naruk Judicial Award, Connecticut Bar Association, 1993, Trustee, Yale University, 1987-1999, Trustee, Federal Judicial Center, 1986-1990, Trustee, Yale-New Haven Hospital, 1984-1987, Trustee, Century Foundation, New York, NY, 1983-2000, Trustee, Colgate University, 1981-1990, Trustee, Yale-New Haven Hospital, 1978-1980, Chairman, Aspira Of New York, 1971-1973, Board of Directors, Aspira Of New York, Elected Member, Council On Foreign Relations **CW:** Author, Citizenship and the American Empire, 1979; Co-Author, (with Kate Stith) Fear of Judging: Sentencing Guidelines in the Federal Courts, 1998; Contributor, Articles on Law and International Affairs **AW:** Learned Hand Medal For Excellence In Federal Jurisprudence, Federal Bar Council, 2000, Certificate Of Merit, Fear Of Judging: Sentencing Guidelines In The Federal Courts, American Bar Association, 1998, Life Achievement Award, Student Division, National Hispanic Bar Association, 1991, John Jay Award, Columbia College, 1991, Life Achievement Award, National Puerto Rico Coalition, 1987 **MEM:** Life Member, American Bar Association Foundation, National Hispanic Bar Association, American Law Institute, Connecticut Bar Association **BA:** 40 Foley Square, New York, NY, 10007

CAFORIO, GIOVANNI, **T:** CEO **I:** Pharmaceuticals **CN:** Bristol-Myers **ED:** M.D., Universita Degli Studi Di Roma LA Sapienza **C:** Chairman/CEO, Bristol-Myers, 2017-; CEO, Bristol-Myers,2015-17; COO, Bristol-Myers, 2014-15; Exec VP/Chief Commercial, Bristol-Myers, 2013-14; President of Pharmaceuticals, Bristol-Myers, 2011-13

CAGE, NICOLAS, **T:** Actor **I:** Media & Entertainment **DOB:** 05/27/1905 **PB:** Long Beach, California **SC:** Long Beach, California **PT:** Son of August Coppola and Joy Vogelsang; **CH:** Married Patricia Arquette, April 8, 1995 (div. May 18, 2001); Married Lisa Marie Presley, August 10, 2002 (div. May 16, 2004); Married Alice Kim, July 30, 2004 **ED:** Grad., UCLA; DFA (hon.), California State Fullerton, 2001 **CW:** Actor: (films) Fast Times At Ridgemont High, 1982, Valley Girl, 1983, Rumble Fish, 1983, Racing with the Moon, 1984, Birdy, 1984, The Boy in Blue, 1986, The Cotton Club, 1984, Peggy Sue Got Married, 1986, Raising Arizona, 1986, Moonstruck, 1988, Vampire's Kiss, 1989, Never on a Tuesday, 1989, Tempo di Uccidere, 1989, Fire Birds, 1990, Wild at Heart, 1990, Zandalee, 1991, Honeymoon in Vegas, 1992, Time to Kill, 1992, Amos & Andrew, 1993, Red Rock West, 1993, Deadfall, 1993, Guarding Tess, 1994, It Could Happen to You, 1994, Trapped in Paradise, 1994, Kiss of Death, 1995, Leaving Las Vegas, 1995 (LA Film Critics award for Best Actor, 1995, New York Film Critics award for Best Actor, 1995, Golden Globe award for Best Actor 1996, Academy award for Best Actor 1996), The Rock, 1996, The Funeral, 1996, Con Air, 1997, Face Off, 1997, Welcome to Hollywood, 1998, Snake Eyes, 1998, City of Angels, 1998, 8MM, 1999, Bringing Out the Dead, 1999, Gone in 60 Seconds, 2000, Family Man, 2000, Captain Corelli's Mandolin, 2001, Windtalkers, 2002, Adaptation, 2002, Matchstick Men, 2003, National Treasure, 2004, The Weather Man, 2005, (voice) The Ant Bully, 2006, World Trade Center, 2006, Ghost Rider, 2007, Grindhouse, 2007, National Treasure: Book of Secrets, 2007, Bangkok Dangerous, 2008, Knowing, 2009, (voice) Astro Boy, 2009, Bad Lieutenant: Port of Call New Orleans, 2009, Season of the Witch, 2010, Drive Angry 3D, 2011, Seeking Justice, 2011, Trespass, 2011, Ghost Rider: Spirit of Vengeance, 2011, Stolen, 2012, The Frozen Ground, 2013, The Croods (voice), 2013, Joe, 2013, Tokarev, 2014, Outcast, 2014, Left Behind, 2014, Dying of the Light, 2014, The Runner, 2015, Pay the Ghost, 2015, The Trust, 2016, Dog Eat Dog, 2016, Snowden, 2016, Army of One, 2016, US Ship Indianapolis: Men of Courage, 2016, Arsenal, 2017, Vengeance A Love Story, 2017, Inconceivable, 2017, Mom and Dad, 2017, The Humanity Bureau, 2017,Looking Glass, 2017, Between Worlds, 2017, Mandy, 2018, #211, 2018, Primal, 2018, The Croods 2, 2020; actor, prodr.: (films) Lord of War, 2005, The Wicker Man, 2006, Next, 2007; actor, producer, dir.: (films) Sonny, 2002; actor, executive prodr.: (films) The Sorcerer's Apprentice, 2010; prodr.: (films) Shadow of the Vampire, 2000, The Life of David Gale, 2003, A Thousand Words, 2012, Cant Stop Losing You: Surviving the Police, 2012 **AW:** Named one of The 100 Most Powerful Celebrities, Forbes.com, 2008;

CAHILLANE, STEVEN A A., **T:** CEO of Kellogg Co **I:** Food & Restaurant Services **DOB:** 01/01/1900 **ED:** Bachelors,Northwestern University **C:** Chairman, Kellogg, 2018-; CEO, Kellogg, 2017-; Exec VP, Coca Cola, 2013-14; President of the Americas, Coca-Cola, 2013; Executive Officer, Coca-Cola, 2010-13; Exec VP/President North America,Coca-Cola,2008-10; Exec VP/President Europe Group, Coca-Cola,2007-08; CMO, Inbev NV, 2005-07

CAIN, JONATHAN, **T:** Singer, Songwriter **I:** Media & Entertainment **PB:** Chicago **SC:** IL/USA **CW:** (Solo) Windy City Breakdown, 1977, Back to the Innocence, 1995, Piano with a View, 1995, Body Language, 1997, For A Lifetime, 1998, Namaste,

2001, Anthology, 2001, Animated Movie Love Songs, 2002, Bare Bones, 2004, Where I Live, 2006, What God Wants to Hear, 2016, Unsung Noel, 2017 **AW:** Rock and Roll Hall of Fame, 2017

CAINE, MICHAEL, **T:** Actor **I:** Media & Entertainment **DOB:** 03/14/1933 **PB:** London **SC:** United Kingdom **C:** Actor, Theatre Workshop, London, 1955; Actor, Lowestoft Repertory, 1953-55; Assistant Stage Manager, Westminster Repertory, Horsham, England, 1953 **CW:** Actor: (plays) Next Time I'll Sing for You, 1963; (films) A Hill in Korea, 1956, How to Murder a Rich Uncle, 1958, Zulu, 1964, The Ipcress File, 1965, Alfie, 1966, The Wrong Box, 1966, Gambit, 1966, Hurry Sundown, 1967, Woman Times Seven, 1967, Deadfall, 1967, The Magus, 1968, Battle of Britain, 1968, Play Dirty, 1968, The Italian Job, 1969, Too Late the Hero, 1970, The Last Valley, 1971, Zee & Co., 1972, Kidnapped, 1972, Pulp, 1972; Actor, (films) Sleuth, 1971, The Black Windmill, 1974, Marseilles Contract, 1974, The Wilby Conspiracy, 1974, Peeper, 1975, The Romantic Englishwoman, 1975, The Man Who Would Be King, 1975, Harry and Walter Go to New York, 1975, The Eagle Has Landed, 1976, A Bridge Too Far, 1976, Silver Bears, 1976, The Swarm, 1977, California Suite, 1978, Beyond the Poseidon Adventure, 1979, Dressed to Kill, 1980, The Island, 1980, The Hand, 1981, Victory, 1981, Deathtrap, 1982, Educating Rita, 1983, Beyond the Limit, 1983, The Jigsaw Man, 1984, The Holcroft Covenant, 1984, Blame It On Rio, 1984, The Whistle Blower, 1985, Water, 1985, Hannah and Her Sisters, 1986 (Academy Award for Best Supporting Actor, 1987), Sweet Liberty, 1986, Mona Lisa, 1986, Half Moon Street, 1986, Jaws: The Revenge, 1987, Surrender, 1987, The Fourth Protocol, 1987, Without a Clue, 1988, Dirty Rotten Scoundrels, 1988, A Shock to the System, 1989, Bullseye!, 1990, Mr. Destiny, 1990, Noises Off, 1991, The Muppets Christmas Carol, 1992, On Deadly Ground, 1994, Bullet to Beijing, 1995, Blood and Wine, 1996, Curtain Call, 1997, Blue Ice, 1993, Little Voice, 1998 (Golden Globe Award for Best Performance by an Actor in a Motion Picture - Comedy or Musical), Debtors, 1999, Cider House Rules, 1999 (Academy Award for Best Supporting Actor), Quills, 1999, Shiner, 2000, Miss Congeniality, 2000, Last Orders, 2001, Quicksand, 2001, The Quiet American, 2002, Austin Powers 3, 2002, The Actor, 2003, Secondhand Lions, 2003, The Statement, 2003, Around the Bend, 2004, The Weatherman, 2005, Batman Begins, 2005, Bewitched, 2005, Children of Men, 2006, Sleuth, 2000, The Prestige, 2007, Flawless, 2008, The Dark Knight, 2008, Is Anybody There?, 2008, Inception, 2010, (voice) Gnomeo & Juliet, 2011, Cars 2, 2011, Journey 2: The Mysterious Island, 2012, The Dark Knight Rises, 2012, Now You See Me, 2013, Last Love, 2013, Stonehearst Asylum, 2014, Interstellar, 2014, Kingsman: The Secret Service, 2014, Youth, 2015, The Last Witch Hunter, 2015, Going in Style, 2016, Now You See Me 2, 2016, Going in Style, 2017, Dunkirk, 2017, Dear Dictator, 2018, Sherlock Gnomes, 2018; (TV films) Jekyll and Hyde, 1990; (TV miniseries) Jack the Ripper, 1988, World War II: When Lions Roared, 1994, Mandela and De Kleerk, 1997, 20,000 Leagues Under the Sea, 1997, Freedom: A History of Us, 2003; Executive Prodr.: (films) The Fourth Protocol, 1987, Forever After, 2001, The Double, 2013; author: What's It All About?: An Autobiography, 1993, The Elephant to Hollywood, 2010 **AW:** Named Commander Most Excellent Order of Brit. Empire, Her Majesty Queen Elizabeth II, 1993; Named an Hon. Knight Commander Most Excellent Order of Brit. Empire, 2000; Recipient Variety Club Award for Outstanding Contribution to Show Business, 2008 **BA:** Pam Puerto Rico Inc, 4401 Wilshire Blvd, Los Angeles, CA, 90010

CALAGIONE, SAM, **T:** Owner **I:** Business Management/Business Services **CN:** Dogfish Head Brewery **C:** Founder and CEO of Dogfish Head Craft Brewing, Milton, Delaware, 1995-; **AW:** Recipient James Beard Award, 2017 for Outstanding Wine, Spirits or Beer Professional of the Year;

CALANTZOPOULOS, ANDRÉ, **T:** tobacco company executive **I:** Business Management/ Business Services **ED:** MBA, INSEAD; Degree in Electrical Engineering, Swiss Federal Institute Tech. **C:** CEO, Philip Morris International, Inc., 2013-; COO, Philip Morris International, Inc., Lausanne, Switzerland, 2008-13; President, CEO, Philip Morris International (subsidiary Altria Group), Lausanne, Switzerland, 2002-08; President, Eastern European region, Philip Morris, 1999-2002; Managing director, Philip Morris, Poland, 1996-99; Manager, PMI affiliate, Philip Morris, 1993-96; Area director, Central Europe, Philip Morris, 1992-93; General manager, Philip Morris, Czech Republic, 1991-92; General manager, Philip Morris, Finland, 1990-91; With area operations department, Philip Morris, 1987-90; Business devel. analyst, Philip Morris, 1985-87

CALATRAVA, SANTIAGO, **T:** Architect **I:** Architecture & Construction **DOB:** 07/28/1951 **ED:** Doctor (hon.), Technion, Israel, 2004; Doctor of Tech. (hon.), Lund University, Sweden, 1999; Doctor of Civil Engineering (hon.), University degli Stugi di Cassino, Italy, 1999; Doctor (hon.), Milwaukee School Engineering, Wisconsin, 1995-97; DSc (hon.), University Tech., Delft, The Netherlands, 1995; DSc (hon.), University Strathclyde, Glasgow, Scotland, 1995-97; DSc (hon.), University College Salford, England, 1995; LittD in Environmental Studies (hon.), Heriot-Watt University, Edinburgh, Scotland, 1994; Doctor (hon.), University Seville, Spain, 1994; Doctor (hon.), Poly University, Valencia, 1993; Doctor of Tech. Sci., Federal Institute Tech., 1981; Degree, Federal Institute Tech., Zürich, 1979; Degree, Institute Architecture, Valencia, 1974 **CT:** Lic. professional engineer, California, structural engineer, Illinois **C:** Private practice, Valencia, Spain, 1991-; Private practice, Paris, 1989-; Private practice, Zurich, 1981 **CW:** Principal works include Stadelhofen Railway Station, Zürich, Switzerland, 1983-84 (City of Zürich award, 1991, Brunel award, 1992), Alamillo Bridge and La Cartuja Viaduct, Seville, Spain, 1987-92, Campo Volantin Footbridge, Bilbao, Spain, 1990-98, Sondica Airport, Bilbao, 1990-99, Alameda Bridge and Underground Station, Valencia, 1991-95, Palace of the Arts, Valencia, Spain, 2001, City of Arts and Sci. Valencia, Valencia, Oriente Station, Lisbon, Portugal, 1993-98, Lyon Airport Station, Lyon, Turning Torso Tower, Malmö, World Trade Center Transportation Hub, New York City, Milwaukee Art Museum expansion, Milwaukee, 2001, Tenerife Auditorium, Canary Islands, The Chicago Spire, 2007, exhibitions include Jamileh Weber Gallery, Zürich, 1985, Museum of Architecture, Basel, Switzerland, 1985, traveling exhibition, New York, St. Louis, Chicago, LA, Toronto, Montreal, 1985, Suomen Rakennustaiteen Museum, Helsinki, Finland, 1991, Museum of Design, Zürich, Switzerland, 1991, Dutch Institute Architecture, Rotterdam, Holland, 1992, Royal Institute Brit. Architects, London, England, 1992, ArkitekturMuseet, Stockholm, Sweden, 1992, Deutsches Museum, Munich, Germany, 1993, Museum Modern Art, New York City, New York, 1993, La Lonja Museum, Valencia, Italy, 1993, Pavilion Overbeck Society, Lübeck, Germany, 1993, Architecture Center, Gammel Dok, Copenhagen, Sweden, 1993, Bruton St. Gallery, London, England, 1994, Museum Applied and Folk Art, Moscow, Russia, 1994, Ma Gallery, Tokyo, Japan, 1994, Arqueria de los

Nuevos Ministerios, Madrid, Spain, 1994, Sala de Arte La Recova, Santa Cruz de Tenerife, 1994, Museum of Design, Zürich, Switzerland, 1995, Center Cultural de Belem, Lisbon, Portugal, 1995, Navarra Museum Pamplona, 1995, Archivo Floral, Bilbao, 1995, Palazzo della Raggione, Padova, Italy, 1995, Department of Building, Basel, Switzerland, 1995, Milwaukee Art Museum, 1995, Britannic Tower, London, 1995, Israel National Museum of Sci., Haifa, 1995, Palazzo Strozzi, Florence, 2000-01, Metropolitan Museum Art, New York City, 2005,(Principal Works) Liege-Guillemins Railway Station, 2009, Oviedo Conference Center, 2000-2011, Margarat Hunt/ Peace Bridge, 2007-2012, Florida Polytechnic University, 2009-2014, Museum of Tomorrow, 2010-15, WTC Hub,2003-2016 **AW:** Named Gold Master of the High Direction Forum, Madrid, 1995, Global Leader for Tomorrow, World Economic Forum, Davos, Switzerland, 1993; named one of Time Magazine 100 Most Influential People, 2005; recipient Golden Plate award, Academy Achievement, 2004, Gold Medal, Am. Institute Architects, 2005, Eugene McDermott award in the arts, Massachusetts Institute of Technology, 2005, Gold medal, American Institute of Architects, 2005, Principe de ASTURIAS award for the arts, 1999, art prize, Louis Vuitton-Moet Hennessy, Paris, 1995, European award for steel structures, Berlin, 1995, Gold medal, Ministry of Culture, Granada, Spain, 1995, award for good building, Canton of Lucerne, Switzerland, 1995, medal of honor, Fundaci?n Garcia Cabrerizo, Madrid, 1993, Urban Design award, City of Toronto, 1993, II Honor prize, City of Pedreguer, 1993, Gold medal, Institute Structural Engineers, London, 1992, European Glulam award, Munich, 1991, Silver medal for research and technique, Foundation Academy Architecture, Paris, 1990, Fritz Schumacher prize for urbanism, architecture and engineering, Hamburg, Germany, 1985, prize, Fomento de las Artes y del Dise?o, Spain, 1985, International Association Bridge and Structural Engineering, 1985, Press Association award, Valencia, 1985, Art prize, City of Barcelona, 1985, Auguste Perret prize, International Union Architects, 1979; fellow Fazlur Rahman Khan International for architecture and engineering, 1985 **MEM:** Fellow: Royal Incorporation of Architects (Scotland) (hon.); mem.: Royal Swedish Academy Engineering Scis., Order of Arts and Letters (Paris), European Academy (Cologne, Germany), Real Academy Bellas Artes de San Carlos, International Academy Architecture, Union of Swiss Architects, Real Academy Bellas Artes de San Fernando (hon.), College Architects Mexico City (hon.), Royal Institute Brit. Architects (hon.), Union of German Architects (hon.) **BA:** Santiago Calatrava Inc, 713 Park Ave, New York, NY, 10021

CALDWELL, ZOE, **T:** Actress, Film Director **I:** Media & Entertainment **DOB:** 09/14/1933 **PB:** Hawthorn **SC:** VIC/Australia **MS:** Married **SPN:** Robert Whitehead, 1968 **CH:** Sam, Charlie **ED:** Student, Methodist Ladies College, Melbourne, VIC, Australia **C:** Actress, 1952-Present **CR:** Dorothy F. Schmidt Visiting Eminent Scholar in Theatre, Florida Atlantic University, 1989-1993 **CW:** Theater Debut, Union Theatre Repertory Co., Melbourne, VIC, Australia, 1953; Actress, (Other Appearances) The Way of the World, The Caucasian Chalk Circle, Minneapolis, MN, Slapstick Tragedy, New York, NY, Madwoman Of Chaillot, Goodman Theatre, Chicago, IL, 1964, Antony and Cleopatra, Richard III, The Merry Wives of Windsor, Shakespeare Festival, Stratford, ON, Canada, 1967, The Prime of Miss Jean Brodie, 1967, Colette, New York, NY, 1970, A Bequest to the Nation, London, England, 1970, The Creation of the World and Other Business, New York, NY, 1972, Love and Master Will, Washington, DC, 1973, The Dance of Death,

New York, NY, 1974, Long Day's Journey Into Night, New York, NY, Washington, DC, 1976, Medea, New York, NY, 1982, Lillian, 1986, Come A-Waltzing With Me, A Perfect Ganesh, 1993, Master Class, 1995, A Little Night Music, 2004, A Spanish Play, 2007; Director, (Plays) An Almost Perfect Person, New York, NY, 1977, Richard II, Stratford, ON, Canada, 1979, These Men, Off-Broadway, 1980, The Taming of the Shrew, Hamlet, American Shakespeare Theatre, 1985, Vita and Virginia, New York, NY, 1995, Limonade Tours Les Jours, Bay St. Theatre, Sag Harbor, NY, 2004; Voice Actress, (Films) Lilo & Stitch!, 2002, Stitch! The Movie, 2003, Elective Affinities, 2011; Actress, (Films) Extremely Loud and Incredibly Close, 2011 **AW:** Decorated Order of the British Empire; Best Supporting Actress, Slapstick Tragedy, Tony Awards, 1966; Theatre World Award, 1966; Best Actress, The Prime of Miss Brodie, Tony Awards, 1968; Best Actress, Medea, Tony Awards, 1982; Best Actress, Master Class, Tony Awards, 1996; John Gielgud Award, Shakespeare Guild/ Folger Shakespeare Library, 1998; Linda Wilson Lifetime Achievement Award, Excellence in the Theatre, University of Florida, 1998; Bernard B. Jacobs Excellence in the Theatre Award/U.J.A. Federation of New York, 1999; Medal of Distinction, Barnard College, 1999 **BA:** White Head Stevens, 1501 Broadway, New York, NY, 10036

CALIFANO, JOSEPH ANTHONY JR., **T:** Chairman of the National Center on Addiction and Substance Abuse **I:** Government Administration/Government Relations/Government Services **DOB:** 05/15/1931 **PB:** Brooklyn **SC:** New York **PT:** Son of Joseph Anthony and Katherine (Gill) C.; **SPN:** Married Hilary Paley Byers, 1983; **CH:** children by previous marriage: Mark Gerard, Joseph Anthony III, Claudia Frances; stepchildren: Brooke A. Byers, John Fr **ED:** LLB, Harvard University, 1955; BA, Holy Cross College, 1952 **CT:** Bar: New York 1955, US Supreme Court 1966, DC 1969. **C:** Chairman emeritus, National Center on Addiction & Substance Abuse, Columbia University, New York City, 2012-; Professor public health policy, Columbia University School Medicine & Public Health, New York City, 1992-; Chairman, National Center on Addiction & Substance Abuse, Columbia University, New York City, 1992-2012; Senior partner, Dewey Ballantine LLP, Washington, 1983-92; Partner, Califano, Ross & Heineman, Washington, 1980-82; Secretary, US Department Health, Education, & Welfare (Department of Health), Washington, 1977-79; Partner, Williams, Connolly & Califano, Washington, 1971-77; General counsel, Democratic National Committee, 1971-72; Partner, Arnold & Porter LLP, Washington, 1969-71; Special assistant to President, The White House, 1965-69; General counsel, US Department Army, 1963-64; Special assistant to secretary, US Department Army, 1962-63; Special assistant to secretary & deputy secretary, US Department Defense, 1964-65; Special assistant to general counsel, US Department Defense, 1961-62; Attorney, Dewey Ballantine LLP, New York City, 1958-61 **CR:** Board directors CBS Corp., 2006-, Midway Games Inc., 2004-09, Willis Group Holdings, Ltd., 2004-13, Viacom Inc., 2003-05, Automatic Data Processsing, Inc., 1982-2005 **CIV:** Trustee Urban Institute, American Ditchley Foundation, Century Fund, LBJ Foundation, National Health Museum board governors New York and Presbyterian Hospital Inc. chairman Institute Social and Economic Policy in Mid. East, Harvard University, 1983-98. **CW:** Author: The Student Revolution: A Global Confrontation, 1969, A Presidential Nation, 1975, Governing America: An Insiders Report from the White House and the Cabinet, 1981, The 1982 Report on Drug Abuse and Alcoholism, America's Health Care Revolution: Who Lives, Who Dies, Who Pays, 1986,

The Triumph and Tragedy of Lyndon Johnson: The White House Years, 1991, Radical Surgery: What's Next for America's Health Care, 1995, (memoir) Inside: A Public and Private Life, 2004, High Society: How Substance Abuse Ravages America and What to Do About It, 2007, How to Raise a Drug-Free Kid-The Straight Dope for Parents, 2009; co-author: (with Howard Simons) The Media and the Law, 1976, The Media and Business, 1978. **AW:** Recipient Distinguished Civilian Service award Department Army, 1964; Man of Year award Justinian Society Lawyers, 1966; Distinguished Public Service medal US Department Defense, 1965; named One of The Ten Outstanding Young Men of America, 1966, Gustav O. Lienhard award, Institute Medicine National Academy Sciences, 2010. **MEM:** Member New York State Bar Association, D.C. Bar Association, Metropolitan Club (Washington), Century Association, Univ. Club. **PA:** Democrat **BA:** Columbia University, 16th St & Broadway, New York, NY, 10027

CALIPARI, JOHN VINCENT, **T:** College Basketball Coach **I:** Athletics **DOB:** 02/10/1959 **PB:** Moon Township, Pennsylvania **SPN:** Married Ellen Calipari; **CH:** children: Erin Sue, Megan Rae, Bradley Vincent. **ED:** Bachelor, Clarion State University, Pennsylvania, 1982; Attended, University North Carolina, Wilmington **C:** Head Coach, University Kentucky Wildcats, 2009-; Head Coach, University Memphis Tigers, 2000-09; Assistant Coach, Philadelphia 76ers, 1999; Head Coach, Executive Vice President Basketball Operations, New Jersey Nets, East Rutherford, 1996-99; Head Coach, University Massachusetts Minutemen, Amherst, 1988-96; Assistant Coach, University Pittsburgh Panthers, 1985-88; Recruiting Coordinator, University Vermont Catamounts, 1983; Assistant Coach, University Kansas Jayhawks, 1982-85 **CR:** Assistant Buckler Challenge All-Star Team, 1993, Head Coach, 1994 Coach East Squad US Olympic Festival, Denver **CIV:** Vol. Camp Good Days and Special Times Chairman Children's Miracle Network Telethon, Springfield. **CW:** Author: Players First, 2014 **AW:** Named Eastern Basketball Coach of Year, 1992, Atlantic 10 Coach of Year, 1993, 1994, 1996, District I Coach of Year US Basketball Writers Association, 1993, District IV Coach of Year, 2009, The Sporting News National Coach of Year, 1996, Naismith National Coach of Year Atlanta Tip-off Club, 1996, 2008, East Region Coach of Year Basketball Times, 1996, South Region Coach of Yr, 2007, District VII Coach of Year National Association Basketball Coaches, 2004, Co-Coach of Year, 2009, Conference USA Coach of Year, 2006, 2008, 2009, Sports Illus. National Coach of Year, 2009, Jim Phelan National Coach of Year, 2009, Southeastern Conference Coach of Year, 2012; recipient Lombardi award UNICO National, 2003, Adolph Rupp Cup Commonwealth Athletic Club Kentucky, 2010; named to National Italian Am. Sports Hall of Fame, 2004, University Massachusetts Athletic Hall of Fame, 2004, Naismith College Coach of the Year, 2015, Associated Press Coach of the Year, 2015, Basketball Times Coach of the Year, 2015, Adolph Rupp Cup, 2015, SEC Coach of the Year, 2015 **ACH:** Achievements include head coach of the NCAA Final Four Division I National Championship winning University of Kentucky Wildcats, 2012

CALLAHAN, CONSUELO MARIA, **T:** Federal Judge **I:** Law and Legal Services **DOB:** 06/09/1950 **PB:** Palo Alto **SC:** CA/USA **ED:** LLM, Univ. Virginia, 2004-; JD, McGeorge School of Law, Univ. Pacific, 1975; BA, Leland Stanford Junior Univ., 1972 **C:** Judge, US Court of Appeals (9th cir.), 2003-; Associate Judge, Court of Appeals, State of California, 1996-2003; Judge, San Joaquin County Superior Court, San

Joaquin, California, 1992-96; Court Communications, Municipal Court of Stockton, Stockton, California, 1986-92; Sup. District Attorney, District Attorney's Office, San Joaquin County, California, 1982-86; Deputy District Attorney, District Attorney's Office, San Joaquin County, California, 1976-82; Deputy City Attorney, City of Stockton, Stockton, California, 1975-76 **AW:** Recipient Mexican-Am. Hall of Fame, San Joaquin County, 1999, Stockton Peacemaker of the Year, 1997, Susan B. Anthony Award for Women of Achievement, Award for Criminal Justice Programs, Governor **BAR:** Bar: California 1975 **ACH:** Achievements include first hispanic, first woman named to San Joaquin Co. Superior Ct **BA:** 95 7th St, San Francisco, CA, 94013

CALVERT, KEN, T: U.S. Representative from California **I:** Government Administration/Government Relations/Government Services **DOB:** 06/08/1953 **PB:** Corona **ED:** BS in Economics, San Diego State University, 1975; AA, Chaffey College, 1973 **C:** Member, US Congress from 42nd California District, 2013-; Member, Committee on Appropriations; Member, US Congress from 44th California District, 2003-13; Member, US Congress from 43rd California district, Washington, 1992-2003; President, general manager, Ken Calvert Real Properties, Corona, California, 1980-91; General manager, Marcus W. Meairs Co., Corona, California, 1979-81; General manager, Jolly Fox Restaurant, Corona, California, 1975-79; Congressional aide to Rep. Vitor Veysey, US House of Representatives, California, 1975-79 **CR:** Reagan-Bush campaign worker, 1980 Corona/Norco youth chairman for Nixon, 1968 **MEM:** Mem.: Corona C. of C. (president 1990), Monday Morning Group, Elks, Riverside County Lincoln Club (founder, chair), Corona Rotary Club (president 1991) **PA:** Republican **BA:** 2269 Rayburn House Office Bldg, Washington, DC, 20515

CAMERON, JAMES, T: Film Director, Screenwriter, Producer **I:** Media & Entertainment **DOB:** 08/16/1954 **PB:** Kapuskasing **SC:** Ont. Canada **PT:** Son of Philip and Shirley Cameron **ED:** Attended, California State University, Fullerton **C:** Founder, head, Lightstorm Entertainment, Burbank, California, 1992-; Board directors, Digital Domain, LA, 1993-98 **CIV:** Member adv. board, Sci. Fiction Museum & Hall of Fame **CW:** Art director (films) Battle Beyond the Stars, 1980, production designer Galaxy of Terror, 1981, creator special effects Escape from New York, 1981, director, screenwriter Xenogenesis, 1978, The Terminator, 1984, Aliens, 1986, The Abyss, 1989, director Piranha II: The Spawning, 1981, Terminator 2 3-D, 1996, (TV films) Earthship, 2001, screenwriter (films) Rambo: First Blood Part II, 1985, Strange Days, 1995, Terminator 3: Rise of the Machines, 2003, executive producer Point Break, 1991, Sanctum, 2011, director, producer, screenwriter Terminator II: Judgement Day, 1991(6 Academy award nominations, Ray Bradbury award for dramatic screenwriting, 5 Saturn awards Academy Sci. Fiction, 5 MTV Movie awards, People's Choice award), True Lies, 1994, Avatar, 2009 (Best Motion Picture-Drama, Golden Globe award, Hollywood Foreign Press Association, 2010, Best Dir.-Motion Picture, Golden Globe award, Hollywood Foreign Press Association, 2010, Critics' Choice award for Best Editing, Broadcast Film Critics Association, 2010, Critics' Choice award for Best Action, Broadcast Film Critics Association, 2010) Alita Battle Angel, 2018, Avatar 2, 2021, Avatar 3, 2021, director, producer, editor Titanic, 1997 (Academy award for Best Picture and Best Director, 9 others, 1997), director, producer Ghosts of the Abyss, 2002, (TV films) Expedition Bismarck, 2002; prodr.: (films) Volcanos of the Deep Sea, 2003, Aliens of the Deep, 2005; (TV

films) Titanic Adventure, 2005, Last Mysteries of the Titanic, 2005; (documentaries) The Lost Tomb of Jesus, 2007; writer, executive producer (TV series) Dark Angel, 2000-02, writer Terminator: The Sarah Connor Chronicles, 2008-09, executive producer (TV films) The Exodus Decoded, 2006, (documentaries) The Lost Tomb of Jesus, 2007, actor-appeared as himself, James Cameron Voyage to the Bottom of the Earth, 2012, A New Age of Exploration, National Geographic at 125, 2013, Years of Living Dangerously, 2014 (TV series) Entourage, 2005-06 **AW:** Named one of The Ten Smartest People in Tech, Forbes magazine, 2010, The 100 Most Influential People in the World, TIME magazine, 2010, The 100 Agents of Change, Rolling Stone magazine, 2009, The 50 Smartest People in Hollywood, Entertainment Weekly, 2007; recipient Milestone award, Producers Guild of America, 2011 **MEM:** Mem.: Am. Cinema Editors **ACH:** Achievements include performing the deepest solo dive in a Deepsea Challenger submersible to the bottom of the Mariana Trench (nearly 7 miles, an area 200 miles southwest of the Pacific Island of Guam) on March 26, 2012

CAMERON, MATTHEW DAVID, T: Musician **I:** Law and Legal Services **DOB:** 06/25/1905 **PB:** San Diego **SC:** San Diego **C:** Pearl Jam, 1998- **CW:** Drummer: (bands) BamBam, Feedback, Skin Yard; drummer, songwriter Soundgarden, 1986-1997, 2010-, Pearl Jam 1998-; recording artist (with Chris Cornell and others) Temple of the Dog tribute to Andrew Wood, 1990; formed band Hater with Ben Shepherd, 1993; formed half of M.A.C.C. with Chris Cornell; formed band Tone Dogs; (albums with Skin Yard) Deep Six, 1986, Start at the Top, 2001, (albums with Tone Dogs) Ankety Low Day, 1990, (albums with Temple of the Dog) Temple of the Dog, 1991, (albums with Hater) Hater, 1993, Hempilation: Freedom is NORML, 1995, the 2nd, 2005, (albums with Wellwater Conspiracy Succour) The Terrascope Benefit Album, 1995, Declaration of Conformity, 1997, Brotherhood of Electric: Operational Directives, 1999, The Scroll and Its Combinations, 2001, Wellwater Conspiracy, 2003, (albums with Pearl Jam) Binaural, 2000, Riot Act, 2002, Pearl Jam, 2006, Backspacer, 2009, Lightning Bolt, 2013, (albums with Soundgarden) Ultramega OK, 1988, Louder Than Love, 1989, Badmotorfinger, 1991, Superunknown, 1994, Down on the Upside, 1996, Telephantasm, released through video game series Guitar Hero: Warriors of Rock, 2010, King Animal, 2012, numerous collaborations,(Solo Album) Cavedweller, 2017 **AW:** Named Favorite Alternative Artist, American Music Awards, 1999; Rock and Roll Hall of Fame Inductee, 2017

CAMPION, JANE, T: Film Director **I:** Fine Art **DOB:** 04/30/1954 **PB:** Wellington **SC:** New Zealand **PT:** Richard Campion; Edith Campion **ED:** Honorary DLitt, Victoria University (1999); Diploma in Direction, Australian Film, Television and Radio School, Sydney, Australia (1984); Degree, Sydney College of the Arts (1979); Diploma of Fine Arts, Chelsea School of Arts, London, England (1979); BA in Anthropology, Victoria University, Wellington, New Zealand (1975) **CR:** Adjunct Professor, Sydney College of the Arts (2000) **CW:** Executive Producer, "Abduction: The Megumi Yokota Story" (2008); Director, "8-The Water Diary" (2005); Director, "In the Cut" (2002-2003); Co-Writer, Director, "Holy Smoke" (1998-1999); Producer, "The Portrait of a Lady" (1996); Writer, Director, "The Piano" (1993); Director, "An Angel at my Table" (1990); Co-Writer, Director, "Sweetie" (1988); Director, "Two Friends" (1986); Director, "Un Certain Regard" (1986); Writer, Director, "Mishaps of Seduction and Conquest" (1984-1985); Director, "After Hours" (1984); Composer, "Feel the Cold"

(1983); Director, Screenwriter, "A Girl's Own Story" (1983); Director, Screenwriter, "Peel: An Exercise in Discipline" (1982); Director, "Dancing Daze"; Co-Producer, Co-Director, Co-Writer, "Passionless Moments" **AW:** Recipient, Alfred I. duPont Award, Columbia University (2009); Recipient, Wimfemme Film Festival Women's Image Network (2000); Recipient, Francesco Pasinetti Award for Best Film, President of the International Jury, Mostra International Art Cinematography Festival, Venice Film Festival (1997); Nominee, Best Costume, Academy Awards (1997); Nominee, Best Supporting Actress, Academy Awards (1997); Recipient, Academy Award for Best Original Screenplay (1994); Named, Best Director, Best Actress, Best Film, Australian Critics Awards (1990); Recipient, New Generation Award, Los Angeles Film Critics (1990); Recipient, Best Foreign Film Award, Spirit of Independence Awards (1990); Recipient, Otto Debelius Prize, Berlin Film Festival; Recipient, Best Foreign Film, Spirit of Independence Awards, Venice Film Festival, World Premiere (1990); Recipient, Byron Kennedy Award, Australian Cinema (1990); Recipient, Golden Plaque for TV Category, Chicago International Film Festival (1987); Named, Best Director, Best Telemovie, Best Screenplay, Australian Film Institute Awards (1987); Recipient, First Prize, Cinestud Amsterdam Film Festival (1985); Named, Best Film, Cinestud (1985); Recipient, XL Elders Award for Best Short Fiction, Melbourne International Film Festival (1985); Named, Most Popular Short Film, Sydney Film Festival (1985); Recipient, Rouben Mamoulian Award (1984); Named, Best Overall Short Film, Sydney Film Festival (1984); Recipient, Unique Artist Merit, Melbourne Film Festival (1984); Recipient, Awards for Best Direction, Best Screenplay, Best Cinematography, Australian Film Institute (1984); Recipient, Best Experimental Film Award, Australian Film Institute (1984); Finalist, Greater Union Awards, Australian Film Institute Awards (1983-1984); Recipient, Diploma of Merit, Melbourne Film Festival (1983); Recipient, First Prize Festival and Press Prize; Recipient, George Sadoul Prize for Best Foreign Film; Recipient, Special Jury Prize, Elvira Notari Award for Best Woman Director, Agia Scuola Italian Minister of Culture; Recipient, Best Film Si Presci Award, Panel of International Critics; Recipient, Best Film O.C.I.C. Award for Christian Journalists, Best Film for Young Audiences, Cinema e Ragazzi Italian Film Critics Prize; Recipient, Critics Award, Toronto Film Festival; Named, Most Popular Film in the Forum; Nominee, Awards for Best Picture, Best Director, Best Cinematography, Academy Awards; Recipient, Australian Film Institute Awards, Australia Film Critics, Southeastern Film Critics Association; Named, Best Foreign Film, Chicago Film Critics; Recipient, Caesar Award **ADD:** HLA Mgmt Pty Ltd, 87 Pitt St, Redfern, YT, Australia, -NSW 2016

CANORA, MARCO, T: Chef, Restaurateur **I:** Food & Restaurant Services **PB:** Elizabeth **SC:** NJ/USA **C:** Chef/Founder, Brodo, 2014-Present; Chef/Founder, Terroir, 2008-Present; Chef/Founder, Hearth, 2003-Present **CW:** Author, (Books) Salt to Taste: The Key to Confident Cooking, 2009, A Good Food Day: Reboot Your Health With Food That Tastes Great, 2014, Brodo: A Bone Broth Cookbook, 2015 **AW:** James Beard Award for Best Chef, 2017

CANTWELL, MARIA E., T: U.S. Senator from Washington **I:** Government Administration/Government Relations/Government Services **DOB:** 10/13/1958 **PB:** Indianapolis, October 13, 1958 **PT:** Daughter of Rose and Paul Cantwell. **ED:** BA in Pub. Administration, Miami University, Ohio, 1981 **C:** Ranking Member, Senate Energy Committee, 2015-,; Chairman, Senate Small Business

Committee, 2014-2015, Chairman, Senate Indian Affairs Committee, 2013-; Chair, US Senate Small Business & Entrepreneurship Committee, 2014-; US Senator from Washington, 2001-; Chair, US Senate Indian Affairs Committee, 2013-14; Senior vice president consumer & e-commerce, Real Networks (formerly Progressive Networks), Seattle, 1997-2000; Vice president marketing, Progressive Networks, Seattle, 1995-97; Member, US Congress from 1st Washington District, Washington, 1993-95; Member District 44, Washington House of Reps., Olympia, Washington, 1987-92; Public relations consultant, Cantwell & Associates, 1981-87 CIV: Board directors, Washington Economic Develop. Financial Authority, AW: Named Woman of Year, KING-TV Evening Magazine, 2001; recipient Friend of Blues award, Experience Music Project-Vulcan, Inc., 2003, Cyber Champion award, Business Software Alliance, 2003 PA: Democrat

CAPECCHI, MARIO RENATO, T: Geneticist, Educator I: Sciences DOB: 10/06/1937 PB: Verona SC: Italy ED: MD (hon.), University Florence, Italy, 2004; PhD in Biophysics, Harvard University, Cambridge, Massachusetts, 1967; BS in Chemistry and Physics, Antioch College, Yellow Springs, Ohio, 1961 C: Co-chair department human genetics, University Utah School Medicine, 2002-; Distinguished professor human genetics & biology, University Utah School Medicine, 1993-; Professor human genetics, University Utah School Medicine, 1989-; Adjunct professor oncological scis., University Utah School Medicine, 1982-; Professor biology, University Utah School Medicine, Salt Lake City, 1973-; Associate professor, Harvard Medical School, 1971-73; Assistant professor department biochemistry, Harvard Medical School, 1969-71 CR: Chairman Banbury Conference Devel. Genetics, Cold Spring Harbor, New York, 1989, Gordon Conference Molecular Genetics, 1986 investigator Howard Hughes Medical Institute, 1988-, Am. Heart Association, 1969-72 CW: Member editorial board Cell & Molecular Biology, 1982-, DNA, 1982-, Molecular & Cellular Biology, 1985-, Mechanisms of Devel., 1990-, Molecular Medicine, 1994-, Cell Structure & Function, 1994-, Neurobiology of Disease, 1994-2000, Devel. Biology, 1995-2001; contributor articles to professional journals AW: Recipient Jacob Heskel Gabbay award in biotech. & medicine, Brandeis University, 2007, Nobel prize in physiology/medicine, 2007, March of Dimes prize in devel. biology, 2005, Wolf prize in medicine, Israel, 2003, International Cancer Research award, Pezcollar Found./Am. Association Cancer Research, 2003, Gov.'s Sci. & Tech. award, Utah, 2002, Massry prize, 2002, John Scott Medal award, 2002, Albert Lasker award for basic medical research, 2001, National Medal Sci., 2001, Jiménez-Díaz prize, Spain, 2001, Pioneers of Progress award, 2001, Phoenix-Anni Verdi award for genetics research, Italy, 2000, Horace Mann Distinguished Alumni award, Antioch College, 2000, Baxter award for distinguished research in biomed. scis., Association Am. Medical Colleges, 1998, Rosenblatt prize for excellence, University Utah, 1998, Franklin medal for advancing knowledge of physical scis., 1997, Kyoto prize, Inamori Foundation, Japan, 1996, Molecular Bioanalytics prize, Germany, 1996, Alfred P. Sloan Junior prize, GM Cancer Research Foundation, 1994, Gairdner Foundation Inernat. award, 1993, Bristol-Myers Squibb award for distinguished achievement in neurosci. research, 1992, Faculty Research award, Am. Cancer Society, 1974-79, Career Devel. award, National Institutes of Health, 1972-74, Am. Chemical Society Biochemistry award, 1969,American Heart Association Distinguished Scientist Award,2008, Mike Hogg Award, 2011, American Association of Cancer Research

Lifetime Achievement Award, 2015 MEM: Fellow: American Association for the Advancement of Science, Am. Academy Microbiology, Molecular Medical Society; mem.: National Academy of Sciences, European Academy Scis., Am. Society Hematology (hon. life), Am. Academy Arts & Scis., European Academy Scis., Genetics Society America, International Genome Society, Society Devel. Biology, Am. Society Biochemistry & Molecular Biology, Am. Society Microbiology, Am. Society Biological Chemistry, Am. Biochem. Society, Phi Kappa Phi ACH: Achievements include pioneering work in gene targeting of the mouse embryo-derived stem cells BA: U Utah Sch Medicine, 15 N 2030 E Rm 5440, Salt Lake City, UT, 84112

CAPITO, SHELLEY MOORE, T: U.S. Senator from West Virginia I: Government Administration/ Government Relations/Government Services DOB: 11/26/1953 PB: Glen Dale, West Virginia PT: Daughter of Arch Alfred and Shelley (Riley) Moore; ED: MEd, University Virginia Curley School Education, 1976; BS in Zoology, Duke University, Durham, North Carolina, 1975 C: Member, US Senate Rules & Administration Committee, 2015-; Member, US Senate Appropriations Committee, 2015-; Member, US Senate Environment & Public Works Committee, 2015-; Member, US Senate Energy & Natural Resources Committee, 2015-; US Senator from West Virginia, 2015-; Member, US Congress from 2nd West Virginia District, 2001-15; Member District 30, West Virginia House of Delegates, 1996-2000; Director Educational Information Center, West Virginia Board Regents, 1978-81; Career Counselor, West Virginia State College, 1976-78 PA: Republican BA: Office of Shelley Capito, 172 Russell Senate Office Building, Washington, DC, 20510

CAPUANO, MICHAEL EVERETT, T: U.S. Representatives From Massachusetts I: Government Administration/Government Relations/Government Services DOB: 01/09/1952 PB: Somerville SC: MA/USA PT: Andrew Capuano, Rita (Garvey) Capuano MS: Married SPN: Barbara Teebagy, 1974 CH: Michael, Joseph ED: Honorary LLD, Boston University, 2009; JD, Boston College, 1977; BA in Psychology, Dartmouth College, 1973; Postgraduate, Boston University C: Ethics Committee, Financial Services Committee, Transportation And Infrastructure Committee, U.S. Congress for the Seventh Massachusetts District, 2013-Present; U.S. Congress for the Eighth Massachusetts District, Washington, DC, 1999-2013; Mayor, Somerville, MA, 1990-1999; Alderman-At-Large, Somerville, MA, 1985-1989; Alderman Ward 5, Somerville, MA, 1977-1979; Private Law Practice, 1978-1984; Chief Legal Counsel, Mass Legislature Joint Economic Committee CR: President, Massachusetts Municipal Association, 1998 BAR: Massachusetts, 1977 PA: Democrat

CARBAJAL, SALUD, T: U.S. Representative from California I: Government Administration/Government Relations/Government Services PB: Moroleon SC: Mexico ED: Master's Degree in Organizational Management, University of California C: Member, U.S. House of Representatives from California's 24th District, 2017; Member, Committee on Armed Services; Member, Committee on the Budget; Member, Board of Supervisors, Santa Barbara County,2004-16

CÁRDENAS, TONY, T: U.S. Representative from California, former city councilman I: Government Administration/Government Relations/Government Services DOB: 03/31/1963 PB: Pacoima PT: Son of Andres and Maria (Quezada)

Cárdenas; ED: BEE, University California, Santa Barbara, 1986 C: Member, US House Oversight & Government Reform Committee, 2013-; Member, US House Natural Resources Committee, 2013-; Member, US House Budget Committee, 2013-;; Member, Committee on the Judiciary, Committee on Small Business; Member, US Congress from 29th District, Washington, 2013-; Councilman District 6, LA City Council, 2003-13; Owner, president, Our Community Real Estate Co.,; Member District 39, California State Assembly, 1996-2002; Engineering specialist, Hewlett Packard Co., CIV: Commissioner, El Pueblo de LA Hist. Monument, Member, Coalition Against Pipeline, Member, LA Business Advisor Committee MEM: Mem.: San Fernando Valley Association Realtors PA: Democrat BA: 2423 Rayburn HOB, Washington, DC, 20515

CARDER, DAN, T: Director for Center for Alternative Fuels Engines and Emissions I: Engineering ED: M.S. Mechanical Engineering, West Virginia University, 1999; B.S. Mechanical Engineering, West Virginia University, 1992 C: Researcher, West Virginia University AW: Time 100 Most Influential, 2016

CARDIN, BEN, T: U.S. Senator from Maryland I: Government Administration/Government Relations/Government Services DOB: 10/05/1943 PB: Baltimore SC: MD/USA ED: BA, cum laude, University of Pittsburgh, 1964,; JD, University of Maryland, 1967,; LLD (hon.), University of Baltimore, 1990,; LLD (hon.), University of Maryland, Baltimore, 1993,; LLD (hon.), Baltimore Hebrew University, 1994,; LLD (hon.), Goucher College, Baltimore, 1996,; LLD, Villa Julie College, Stevenson, Maryland, 2007 C: Ranking Member, Senate Foreign Relations Committee, 2015-18,; US Senator from Maryland, 2006—,; Member, Maryland House of Delegates, 1967-86,; Chairman, US House Organization & Study Review Committee, 1997—2006,; Member, US House Ways & Means Committee, Washington, DC, 1999—2005,; Member, US House Human Resources & Social Security Subcommittee, Washington, DC, 1991—2006,; Member, US House Standards & Official Conduct Committee, Washington, DC, 1991-97,; Member, US Congress from 3rd Maryland District, Washington, DC, 1987—2006,; Private Practice Attorney, Baltimore, Maryland, 1967-87,; Speaker, Maryland House of Delegates, 1979-86,; Chairman, Ways & Means Committee, Maryland House of Delegates, 1974-79 CR: Commissioner, Commission on Security and Cooperation in Europe (US Helsinki Commission) 1993—, chairman, 2009—; vice president Organization Security and Cooperation in Europe Parliamentary Assembly; Member, National Security Working Group CIV: Chairman MD Legal Service Corp., 1988-95; Trustee St. Mary's College, 1988-99, Goucher College, 1999-2008, Baltimore Council on Foreign Affairs, 1999—; Board of Visitors University Maryland School Law, 1991—, University of Maryland Baltimore County, 1998—, US Naval Academy, 2007—; Member, National Advisory Board Johns Hopkins University Institute Policy Studies, 2003—. CW: Contributor, Articles to Professional Journals AW: Recipient, Common Cause of Maryland Ann Hogan Memorial Award, 1987, Maryland Psychiatric Society Friend of Psychiatry Award, 1988, University of Maryland Law School Alumni Association Cardin Pro Bono Award, 1990, Israel Freedom Award, 1992, National Multiple Sclerosis Society Rep. of Year Award, 1993, Small Business Council Am. Congl. award, 1993, 1999, 2005, H. John Heinz III National Leadership Award, Coalition for a Lead Safe Environment, Alliance to End Childhood Lead Poisoning, 1994, Hunting S. Williams Award, 1995, Maryland Bar Foundation Vernon Eney Award, 1996, Maryland Save Our

Streams' Living Stream Award, 1996, Digestive Disease National Coalition Pub. Policy Leadership Award, 1996, Rep. of Year Award National Association Police Organization, 1998, Jacob K. Javits Award Am Psychiatric Association, 1999, American Medical Association Dr. Nathan Davis Award for Pub. Service, 1999, Congl. Advocate of Year Award, Child Welfare League America, 2000, National Leadership award for Service to Children and Families, Casey Family Service, 2000, Congl. Leadership Award, Am. College Emergency Physicians, 2001, Congl. Champion Award, National Coalition Cancer Research, 2002, Legislator of Year, Am. Associate Health Plans, 2003, Daily Record Leadership Law award, 2008; Elizabeth & David Scull Metropolitan Pub. Service Award, Metropolitan Council Government, 2008, Congl. Champion Award, National Association Psychiatric Health Systems, 2008, Congl. Voice Children Award, National PTA, 2009, Maryland Affordable Housing Coalition Leadership Award, 2009; Named to Concord Coalition's Deficit Hawk Honor Roll, 1998, 1999, Welfare Advocates Wall of Fame, 2005 **MEM:** Mem.: Maryland Bar Association, American Bar Association (Pro Bono Pub. Award 1989), Baltimore City Bar Association; **BAR:** Bar: Maryland 1967 **PA:** Democrat **BA:** Office of Ben Cardin, 509 Hart Senate Office Building, Washington D.C., DC, 20510

CARELL, STEVE, T: Actor, Comedian **I:** Media & Entertainment **DOB:** 08/16/1962 **PB:** Concord **SC:** MA/USA **PT:** Edwin A. Carell; Harriet T. (Koch) Carell **ED:** BA in History, Denison University, 1984 **CR:** Performed with theater groups including Wisdom Bridge, The Goodman, Second City, Chicago **CW:** Actor: (films) Curley Sue, 1991, Over the Top, 1997, Tomorrow Night, 1998, Suits, 1999, Street of Pain, 2002, Bruce Almighty, 2003, Sleepover, 2004, Anchorman, 2004, Melinda and Melinda, 2004, Bewitched, 2005, Little Miss Sunshine, 2006 (Screen Actors Guild award for Outstanding Performance by a Cast in a Motion Picture, 2007), Evan Almighty, 2007, Dan in Real Life, 2007, Over the Hedge (voice), 2006, Horton Hears a Who (voice), 2008, Get Smart, 2008, Date Night, 2010, Despicable Me (voice), 2010, Dinner for Schmucks, 2010, Seeking a Friend for the End of the World, 2012, Hope Springs, 2012, The Way, Way Back, 2013, Despicable Me 2 (voice), 2013, Anchorman 2: The Legend Continues, 2013, Foxcatcher, 2014, Alexander and the Terrible, Horrible, No Good, Very Bad Day, 2014, Minions (voice), 2015, Freeheld, 2015, The Big Short, 2015, Café Society, 2016, Despicable Me 3, 2017, Battle of the Sexes, 2017, Too Funny to Fail, 2017, Last Flag Flying, 2017, Beautiful Boy,2018, The Women of Marwen, 2018, Backseat, 2018; (TV films) Life As We Know It!, 1991, H.U.D., 2000; (TV series) Saturday Night Live, 1996-2002, Over the Top, 1997, The Daily Show with Jon Stewart, 1999-2004, Watching Ellie, 2002-03, Come to Papa, 2004, The Office, 2005-11 (Golden Globe award for Best Performance by an Actor in TV Series-Musical or Comedy, 2006, Screen Actors Guild award for Outstanding Performance by an Ensemble in a Comedy Series, 2007, 2008, Writers Guild America award for Episodic Comedy (Casino Night), 2007, Teen Choice award for Choice TV Actor: Comedy, 2007, 2008), SNL , 2005, The Naked Trucker and T-Bones Show, 2007, Life's Too Short, 2011, The Simpsons, 2012, Web Therapy, 2013, The Tonight Show Starring Jimmy Fallon, 2014,Angie Tribeca, 2016; actor, writer (TV series) The Dana Carvey Show, 1996; (actor, writer, producer): (films) The 40-Year-Old Virgin, 2005 (MTV Movie award for Best Comedic Performance, 2006); actor, producer (films) Crazy, Stupid, Love, 2011, The Incredible Burt Wonderstone, 2013; executive prodr.: (TV

series) Riot, 2014; executive producer, writer (TV series) Angie Tribeca, 2016-, TV appearances Web Therapy, 2013 **AW:** Named Favorite TV Comedy Actor, People's Choice Awards, 2010; named one of The 100 Most Powerful Celebrities, Forbes.com, 2008, The 50 Most Powerful People in Hollywood, Premiere magazine, 2006

CAREY, MARIAH, T: Singer **I:** Media & Entertainment **DOB:** 03/27/1970 **PB:** Huntington **PT:** Daughter of Alfred Roy and Patricia Carey **CR:** Global ambassador Jenny Craig, 2011-; Debuted collection of jewelry, fragrances and shoes for HSN, 2010; Launched fragrance, Mariah Carey's Luscious Pink, 2008; Launched M by Mariah Carey Gold Deluxe Edition, 2008; Launched first fragrance, M by Mariah Carey, 2007; Launched jewelry line, Glamorized by Mariah Carey, 2006 **CW:** Singer: (albums) Mariah Carey, 1990, Emotions, 1991, Mariah Carey MTV Unplugged, 1992, Music Box, 1993, Merry Christmas, 1994, Daydream, 1995, Butterfly, 1997, #1's, 1998, Rainbow, 1999, Greatest Hits, 2001, Charmbracelet, 2002, Through the Rain, 2003, The Remixes, 2003, Emancipation of Mimi, 2005 (Grammy award for Best Contemporary R&B Album, 2006, National Association for the Advancement of Colored People Image award for Outstanding Album, 2006), E-MC2, 2008, Memoirs of an Imperfect Angel, 2009, Merry Christmas II You, 2010, Me. I Am Mariah... The Elusive Chanteuse, 2014, #1 to Infinity, 2015, (shows) The Colosseum, Caesars Palace, 2015-; actress: (films) Glitter, 1998, The Bachelor, 1999, WiseGirls, 2002, State Property 2, 2005, Tennessee, 2008, Precious, 2009, The Butler, 2013, Popstar: Never Stop Never Stopping, 2016, The Lego Batman Movie, 2017, Girls Trip, 2017, The Star, 2017, Mariah Carey's All I Want for Christmas Is You, 2017; (TV films) A Christmas Melody, 2015; TV appearances Ally McBeal, 2002, American Dad! (voice), 2013, Empire, 2016, judge American Idol, 2013, reality TV personality Mariah's World, 2016-; author: (children's book) All I Want for Christmas Is You, 2015 **AW:** Angel for Animals Award, PETA, 2017, Named Favorite R&B Artist, People's Choice Awards, 2010, Female Entertainer of Year, World Music Awards, 2005, Best-Selling R&B Artist, 2005, Best-Selling Pop Female Artist, 2005, Female Billboard 200 Album Artist of Year, Billboard Music Awards, 2005, Female R&B/Hip-Hop Artist of Year, 2005, Favorite Female R&B Artist, Am. Music Awards, 2005, Best R&B Song for We Belong Together, Grammy Awards, 2006, Best Female R&B Vocal Performance award for We Belong Together, 2006, Best Pop Vocal Performance by Female, 1990, Best New Artist, 1990; named one of The 50 Most Powerful Women in New York City, New York Post, 2008, The 100 Most Influential People in the World, TIME magazine, 2008; recipient Star, Hollywood Walk of Fame, 2015, Special Achievement award, World Music Awards, 2008, Song of Year award for We Belong Together, Radio Music Awards, 2005, Hot 100 Song of Year award, Rhythmic Top 40 Title of Year award and Hot 100 Airplay of Year award for the song We Belong Together, Billboard Music Awards, 2005, Hon. award, Am. Music Awards, 2008, Horizon award, Congressional Foundation awards, 1999 **ACH:** Achievements include surpassing Elvis Presley's Record for Most No. 1 Singles on the Billboard Singles Chart, 2008, #1 Album for 2010, Merry Christmas II You, Billboard Top 100, Star on the Hollywood Walk of Fame, 2015

CARLISLE, RICK, T: Professional Basketball Coach **I:** Athletics **DOB:** 10/27/1959 **PB:** Ogdensburg **SC:** NY/USA **ED:** BA in Psych., University of Virginia, 1984; Student, University of Maine **C:** Head Coach, Dallas Mavericks, 2008-; Executive Vice President Basketball Operations, Ind. Pacers,

2006-07; Head Coach, Ind. Pacers, 2003-07; Head Coach, Detroit Pistons, 2001-03; Assistant Coach, Ind. Pacers, 1997-2000; Assistant Coach, Portland Trail Blazers, 1994-97; Assistant Coach, New Jersey Nets, 1989-94; Professional Basketball Player, New Jersey Nets, 1989; Professional Basketball Player, New York Knicks, 1987-88; Professional Basketball Player, Boston Celtics, 1984-87 **AW:** Named Coach of Year, NBA, 2002, NBA Champion, 2011, NBA All-Star Game Head Coach, 2004 **ACH:** Achievements include member of the NBA Finals Championship winning a Boston Celtics, 1986; head coach of the NBA Finals Championship winning Dallas Mavericks, 2011 **H:** Golf, Piano **BA:** American Airlines Stadium, 2500 Victory Ave, Dallas, TX, 75219

CARLOS, WENDY, T: Composer **I:** Fine Art **DOB:** 05/19/1905 **PB:** Pawtuckeet, Rhode Island **SC:** Pawtuckeet, Rhode Island **CW:** (Album)Switched-On Bach, 1968, The Well-Tempered Synthesizer 1969, Sonic Seasonings, 1972, Wendy Carloss Clockwork Orange, 1972, Switched-On Bach II, 1973, By Request, 1975, Switched-On Brandenburgs, 1979, Digital Moonscapes, 1984, Beauty in the Beast, 1986, Secrets of Synthesis, 1987, Peter and the Wolf, 1988; Switched-On Bach 2000, 1992, Tales of Heaven and Hell, 1998, (Soundtracks) A Clockwork Orange, The Shining, 1980, Tron, 1982 **AW:** Grammy for Album of the Year, 1969, Grammy for Best Classical Performance, 1969, Grammy for Best Engineered Recording, 1969

CARLSON, ERIK, T: CEO **I:** Telecommunications **CN:** Dish **ED:** BA, Bradley University **C:** President/ CEO, Dish Network Corp., 2017-Present; President/ COO/Head of Sling, TV Dish Network Corp., 2017; President/COO, Dish Network Corp., 2015-2017

CARLSON, GRETCHEN ELIZABETH, T: Television Personality **I:** Media & Entertainment **DOB:** 06/21/1966 **PB:** Anoka **ED:** Attended, Oxford University; BA in Sociology, Stanford University, 1990 **C:** Anchor, Fox News Channel, 2005-; Co-host Fox & Friends, Fox News Channel, 2006-13; Co-anchor Saturday Early Show, CBS TV, 2002-05; CBS Newspath correspondent, CBS TV, 2000-02; Weekend anchor, reporter, KXAS-TV, Dallas, 1998-2000; Anchor, reporter, WOIO-TV, Cleveland, 1996-98; Anchor, reporter, WUAB-TV, Cleveland, 1995-96; Anchor, reporter, WCPO-TV, Cinn., 1992-94; Anchor, political reporter, WRIC-TV, Richmond, Virginia, 1990-92 **CIV:** National celebrity spokesperson, March of Dimes, **AW:** Named Miss America, 1989, Miss Minnesota, 1988; recipient First Place citation for pub. service reporting, 1997, Emmy award, 1996, 1994, award for Best Newscast in Ohio, two Ohio Press Club awards, 3 Am. Women in Radio and TV National awards,Time 100 Most Influential, 2017

CARLSON, TUCKER, T: News Correspondent **I:** Media & Entertainment **DOB:** 05/16/1969 **PB:** San Francisco **SC:** CA/USA **PT:** Son of Richard Warner Carlson and Patricia Caroline Swanson; **ED:** Degree in history, Trinity College, Hartford, Connecticut **C:** Co-founder, editor-in-chief, The Daily Caller, Washington, 2010-; Co-host, weekend edition, Fox & Friends, Fox News Channel, 2013-; Political news corr., Fox News Channel, 2009-; Host The Situation With Tucker Carlson, anchor, MSNBC, 2005-08; Host, managing editor Tucker Carlson: Unfiltered,, PBS, 2004-05; Co-host Crossfire, Cable News Network (CNN), 2001-05; Co-host The Spin Room,, Cable News Network (CNN), 2000-01; Political analyst Washington bureau, Cable News Network (CNN),; Staff writer, Arkansas Democrat-Gazette, Little Rock,; Writer, Policy Rev., Washington, **CW:** Author: Politician, Partisans and Parasites: My Adventures in Cable News, 2003; regular contributor The Weekly Standard, Esquire magazine, regular panelist Verdict with Dan Abrams **BA:** Fox News, 1211 Avenue of the Americas, New York City, NY, 10036

CARLTON, STEVEN NORMAN, T: Former Professional Baseball Player **I:** Athletics **DOB:** 12/22/1944 **PB:** Miami, Florida **ED:** Student, Miami Dade Junior College **C:** Pitcher, Minnesota Twins, 1987-88; Pitcher, Cleveland Indians, 1987; Pitcher, Chicago White Sox, 1986; Pitcher, San Francisco Giants, 1986; Pitcher, Philadelphia Phillies, 1972-86; Pitcher, St. Louis Cardinals, 1965-71 **AW:** Recipient National League Cy Young Memorial award, 1972, 77, 80, 82; named lefthanded pitcher National League All-Star Team, Sporting News, 1968, 69, 71, 72, 74, 77, 79, 80, 81, 82, Pitcher of Year Sporting News, 1972, 77, 80, 82; inducted into Baseball Hall of Fame, 1994. **BA:** Game Winner Sports Management, 555 S Camino del Rio b2, Durango, CO, 81303

CARNES, EDWARD EARL, T: Federal Judge **I:** Law and Legal Services **DOB:** 06/03/1950 **PB:** Albertville **SC:** AL/USA **ED:** JD cum laude, Harvard Law School, 1975; BS, The University of Alabama, Tuscaloosa, 1972 **C:** Chief judge, U.S. Court of Appeals for the Eleventh Circuit 2013-; Judge, U.S. Court of Appeals for the Eleventh Circuit 1992-2013; Chief capital punishment & post-conviction litigation division, State of Alabama, 1981-92; Assistant attorney general, State of Alabama, Montgomery, 1975-92 **MEM:** Mem.: Judicial Conference Adv. Com Criminal Rules (chairman 2001-04) **BA:** 56 Forsyth St NW, Atlanta, GA, 30303

CARNES, JULIE ELIZABETH, T: Federal Judge **I:** Law and Legal Services **DOB:** 10/31/1950 **PB:** Atlanta **SC:** Georgia **PT:** Married Stephen S. Cowen. **ED:** JD magna cum laude, University Georgia, 1975; BA summa cum laude, University Georgia, 1972 **CT:** Bar: Georgia 1975. **C:** Judge, US Court Appeals (11th Cir.), Atlanta, 2014-; Chief judge, US District Court (northern district) Georgia, 2009-14; Judge, US District Court (northern district) Georgia, Atlanta, 1992-2014; Commissioner, US Sentencing Commission, 1990-96; Special counsel, US Sentencing Commission, 1989; Appellate chief criminal division, US Department Justice, 1987-89; Assistant US attorney (northern district) Georgia, US Department Justice, Atlanta, 1978-90; Law clerk to Hon. Lewis R. Morgan, US Court Appeals (5th cir.), 1975-77 **CR:** Member US Attorney General's Advisory Committee on Sentencing Guidelines, 1988-90 **BA:** US Court Appeals, 56 Forsyth St NW, Atlanta, GA, 30303

CARNEY, JOHN C. JR., T: Governor of Delaware **I:** Government Administration/Government Relations/Government Services **DOB:** 05/20/1956 **PB:** Claymont, Del. **ED:** MPA, University Del.; BA in English, Dartmouth College, 1978 **C:** Governor, State of Delaware,2017-; Member, US House Financial Services Committee, Washington, 2011-; Member at-large, US Congress from Del., Washington, 2011-; Lieutenant Governor, State of Del., Dover, 2001-09; Secretary Fin., State of Del., Dover, 1997-2000; Deputy Chief of staff to Governor, State of Del., 1994-97; Acting Director Pub. Works, New Castle County,; Deputy Chief Administrative Officer, New Castle County, 1989-94; Staff Assistant to Senator Joseph R. Biden, US Senate, 1986-89; Associate Director, Catholic Youth Organization, Wilmington, **CIV:** Board Directors, Catholic Youth Organization **PA:** Democrat **BA:** Carvel State Office Building, 820 N. French Street, 12th Floor, Wilmington, DE, 19801

CARNEY, SUSAN LAURA, T: Federal Judge **I:** Law and Legal Services **DOB:** 09/16/1951 **PB:** Waltham **SC:** MA/USA **ED:** JD magna cum laude, Harvard University, 1977; AB in Russian History & Lit. cum laude, Harvard University, 1973 **CT:** Bar: Connecticut, DC, Massachusetts **C:** Judge, U.S. Court Appeals (2nd cir.), New York City, 2011-; Acting general counsel, Yale University, New Haven, 2008; Deputy general counsel, Yale University, New Haven, 2001-11; Associate general counsel, Yale University, New Haven, 1998-2001; Associate general counsel, Peace Corps, Washington, 1996-98; Of counsel, Bredhoff & Kaiser, Washington, 1994-96; Founding partner D.C. Office, Tuttle & Taylor, Washington, 1988-93; Associate then partner, Rogovin, Huge & Lenzner, Washington, 1979-88; Associate, Ropes & Gray, Boston, 1979; Law clerk to Hon. Levin Hicks Campbell, U.S. Court Appeals (1st cir.), Boston, 1977-78 **CIV:** Vol. tutor, New Haven Reads, Board member, Women Organizing Women Political Action Committee, Board member, New Haven Youth Soccer, **AW:** Fellow Silliman College **MEM:** Mem.: Connecticut Bar Association, National Association College & Univ. Attorneys (board directors) **BA:** US Court of Appeals Thurgood Marshall US Courthouse, 40 Foley Square, New York, NY, 10007

CARO, ROBERT ALLAN, T: Historian, Writer **I:** Writing and Editing **DOB:** 10/30/1935 **PB:** New York City **SC:** NY/USA **PT:** Son of Benjamin and Cele (Mendelow) Caro **ED:** MFA (hon.), School Visual Arts, 2009; DLitt (hon.) New School for Social Research, 1997; DLitt (hon.), Long Island University, 2003; DLitt (hon.), Merrimack College, 1983; AB cum laude, Princeton University, 1957 **C:** Nieman fellow, Harvard University, Cambridge, Massachusetts, 1965-66; Reporter, Newsday, Garden City, New York, 1960-66; Reporter, New Brunswick Home News, New Jersey, 1957-59 **CIV:** Board directors, John Simon Guggenheim Memorial Found, Board directors, Theatre for New Audience, Board directors, New York Society Libr. **CW:** Author: The Power Broker: Robert Moses and the Fall of New York, 1974 (Pulitzer prize for biography, 1975, Francis Parkman prize, 1975), The Years of Lyndon Johnson: The Path to Power, 1982 (National Book Critics award for biography, 1983, Texas Institute Arts and Letters award for non-fiction, 1983), The Years of Lyndon Johnson: Means of Ascent, 1990 (National Book Critics Cir. award for biography, 1991), The Years of Lyndon Johnson: Master of the Senate, 2002 (National Book award for nonfiction, 2002, Pulitzer prize for biography, 2003, LA Times Book prize for biography, 2003, Carl Sandburg award in Lit., 2004, Chicago Pub. Libr. Foundation award, 2003), The Years of Lyndon Johnson: The Passage of Power, 2012, (Book) Extraordinary Lives: The Art and Craft of American Biography, 1988 **AW:** Co-recipient Ann. Political Book award, Washington Monthly, 1975, 1983, 1991; recipient National Humanities medal, US President, 2009, numerous awards, Plutarch award, The Passage of Power, 2013, Mark Lynton History prize, 2013, LA Times Book prize, 2013, National Book Critics Cir. award, 2013, Norman Mailer prize, 2012, Writing award, 2009, New York Hist. Society History Makers award, 2008, Texas Book Festival Book End award, 2008, New York Hist. Society History Makers award, 2008, Distinguished Achievement award, English-Speaking Union, 2004, John Steinbeck award, Southampton College, 2004, Lifetime Achievement in Arts award, Guild Hall Academy Arts, 1992, H.L. Mencken prize, Free Press Association, 1983, Special citation New York chapter American Institute of Architects, 1975, Deadline Club award, Society Professional Journalists 1964, 1965, Society of the Silurians

award, 1964, National Book Award, 2016 **MEM:** Fellow: Society American Historians (Francis Parkman prize 1975); mem.: American Academy of Arts and Letters (Lit. award 1986, Gold medal in biography 2006), American Academy Arts & Sciences, Century Club, PEN American Center (member executive board 1986-88, vice president 1989-92), Authors Guild America (board director 1976—, president 1980-82) **BA:** Robert A Caro Inc, 250 W 57th St Ste 2215, New York, NY, 10107

CARPENTER, JOHN HOWARD HOWARD, T: Film Director, producer, writer, and composer **I:** Media & Entertainment **DOB:** 05/20/1905 **PB:** Carthage, New York **SC:** Carthage, New York **PT:** Son of Howard Ralph and Milton Jean (Carter) C; **SPN:** Married Adrienne Barbeau, January 1, 1979 (div. 1984); Married Sandra Ann King, December 1, 1990; **CH:** 1 child, John Cody **ED:** Student, University Southern California, 1972 **CW:** Co-writer, editor, composer: (short film) The Resurrection of Bronco Billy, 1970 (Academy award best live action short subject 1970); writer, producer, director, composer: (films) Dark Star, 1974; writer, director, composer: (films) Assault on Precinct 13, 1976, Halloween, 1978, The Fog, 1980, Escape from New York, 1981, Prince of Darkness, 1987, They Live, 1988, Escape from L.A., 1996, Ghosts of Mars, 2001; writer, producer, composer: (films) Halloween II, 1981; producer, composer: (films) Halloween III: Season of the Witch, 1982; writer, prodr.: (films) The Fog, 2005; dir.: (films) The Thing, 1982, Starman, 1984, Memoirs of an Invisible Man, 1992, In the Mouth of Madness, 1994, Escape from L.A., 1996, Vampires, 1998, Halloween H2O, 1998; The Ward, 2010, Halloween, 2018 (writer, composer); (TV movies) Elvis, 1979; director, composer: (films) Christine, 1983, Big Trouble in Little China, 1986; executive prodr.: (films) The Philadelphia Experiment, 1984, (TV movies) John Carpenter Presents Body Bags, 1993; writer: (films) The Eyes of Laura Mars, 1978, Black Moon Rising, 1986, (TV movies) Zuma Beach, 1978, Better Late Than Never, 1979, El Diablo, 1990, Blood River, 1991; writer, dir.: (TV movies) Someone's Watching Me!, 1978; (TV Series) Zoo 2015-2017; composer: (films) Halloween V: The Revenge of Michael Myers, 1989. **MEM:** Member American Society of Composers, Directors Guild Am. West, Writers Guild Am. West. **H:** Music, helicopter piloting

CARPER, TOM, T: U.S. Senator from Delaware **I:** Government Administration/Government Relations/Government Services **DOB:** 01/23/1947 **PB:** Beckley, West Virginia **PT:** Son of Wallace Richard and Mary Jean (Patton) Carper; **ED:** MBA, University Del., 1975; BA in Economics, Ohio State University, 1968 **C:** Ranking Member, Senate Environment Committee, 2017; Chairman, US Senate Homeland Security & Governmental Affairs Committee, 2013-; Member, US Senate Finance Committee, 2009-; US Senator from Del., 2001-; Member, US Senate Commerce, Sci. & Transportation Committee, 2007-09; Member, US Congress from Del., Washington, 1983-93; Governor, State of Del., 1993-2001; State Treasurer, State of Del., Dover, 1977-83; Industrial Devel. Specialist, Del. Division Economic Devel., Dover, 1975-76 **CR:** Board Directors AMTRAK (National Railroad Passenger Corp.), 1994-97 **CIV:** Hon. Chair, Del. Special Olympics, 1987- Fundraising Chairman, Big Brothers/Big Sisters Del., 1993 Fundraising Chairman, Big Brothers/Big Sisters Del., 1985 **MIL:** Commander US Navy Reserve, 1973-91, Lieutenant US Navy, 1968-73 **AW:** Decorated Commendation medal, Air medal; recipient George Falcon Golden Spike award, National Association Railroad Passengers, 2004, Early Stage East Founders' award, 2003, Rook of Year award, Rehoboth Beach-Dewey

Beach, Del. C. of C., 2002, Magnificent Mentor award, Del. Mentoring Council, 2002, American Financial Leadership award, Financial Services Roundtable, 2002 **MEM:** Mem.: National Gov.'s Association (vice chairman 1997-98, chairman 1998-99) **PA:** Democrat

CARRERAS, JOSE, T: Tenor **I:** Media & Entertainment **DOB:** 12/05/1947 **PB:** Barcelona **SC:** Spain **PT:** Son of Jose and Antonio C.; **MS:** Married **CH:** Alberto, Julia **ED:** Doctor honoris causa, University Camerino, Italy; Doctor honoris causa, University Mendeleyev, Russia; Doctor honoris causa, University Sheffield and Loughborough, UK; Doctor honoris causa, University Barcelona, Spain **CR:** Museum director opening ceremonies Barcelona Olympics, 1992. **CIV:** Founder José Carreras Medical Research Foundation president José Carreras International Leukemia Foundation hon. member Leukemia Support Group grand official Republic Italy Goodwill Ambassador United Nations Educational. **CW:** Author: Singing from the Soul, 1991; professional opera debut as Gennaro in Lucrezia Borgia, Liceo Opera House, Barcelona, 1970-71 season; appeared in La Bohème, Un Ballo In Maschera and I Lombardi alla Prima Crociata in Teatro Regio, Parma, Italy, 1972 season; Am. debut as Pinkerton in Madame Butterfly with New York City Opera, 1972; Metropolitan Opera debut as Cavaradossi, Vienna Staatsoper with rigoletto at London's Royal Opera House with Traviata and at the New York Metropolitan Opera House, Opera of Munich with Tosca, 1974, La Scala debut as Riccardo in Un Ballo In Maschera, 1975; appeared in film Don Carlos, 1980, TV Great Performances: West Side Story, 1985; other appearances throughout the world include Carnegie Hall, New York, Barbican and Royal Albert Hall, London, Salle Pleyel, Paris, Teatro Colón, Buenos Aires, Argentina, Covent Garden, London, Vienna Staatsoper, Easter Festival, Summer Festival, Salzburg, Aix en Provence, Edimburgh, Verona, Austria, Lyric Opera of Chicago, La Bohème San Francisco Opera, Musikverein and Konzerthaus, Vienna, Suntory Hall and NHK Hall Tokyo, others; recs. include Otello (Rossini), Un Ballo in Maschera, La Battaglia di Legnano, Il Corsaro, Un Giorno, I Due Fuscari, Simone Boccanegra, Macbeth, Don Carlo, Tosca, Thais, Aida, Cavalleria, Turandot, Pagliacci, Lucia di Lammermoor, Elisabetta d'Inghilterra, Amigos Para Siempre, Cabellé and Carreras in Paris, Hollywood Golden Classics, My Barcelona, With a Song in My Heart, Tenorissimi with Placido Domingo and Luciano Pavarotti, The Three Tenors, L.A. (also a PBS special and videotape); repertoire of over 60 operas include Andrea Chenier, La Bohème, Tosca, Werther, carmen, la Forza del Destino, I Pagliacci, L'Elisir d'Amore, Un Ballo in Maschera; leading role in operatic films for TV, Cinema, Video include La Bohème, I Lombardi, Andrea chnier, Turandot, Carmen, requiem (Verdi), Don Carlo, La Forza del Destino, Stiffelio, Fedora and Jerusalem. **AW:** Recipient Emmy Academy TV, Grand Prix du Disque Academy Paris, Luigi Illica prize, Grammy award, 1991, Sir Lawrence Olivier award, Gold medal New York Spanish Institute, City Vienna, Fine Arts His Majesty the King of Spain, City of Barcelona, Autonomous Government Catalonia, Prince of Asturias award, 1991, Golden Plate award, Academy Achievement, 2004; honorary awardee Austrian Republic. **MEM:** Member Royal Academy Music (hon.), European Society Medicine (hon.), Vienna Staatsoper (Kammersänger and lifetime hon. member) European Society Med. oncology (hon. patron); Commander des Arts et des Lettres and Chevalier dans l'Ordre de la Légion d'Honneur de la République Française, Gran Croce di Cavaliere, Albert Schweizer Music award ,1996, International award St. Boniface General Hospital

Research Foundation, 1996. **BA:** William Morris Agency, 151 El Camino Dr, Beverly Hills, CA, 90212

CARREY, JIM, T: Actor **I:** Media & Entertainment **DOB:** 01/17/1962 **PB:** Newmarket **SC:** ON/Canada **PT:** Percy Carrey, Kathleen (Oram) Carrey **SPN:** Lauren Holly, 9/23/1996, Divorced 7/29/1997; Melissa Womer, 3/28/1987, Divorced 12/11/1995 **CH:** Jane Erin **ED:** Honorary DFA, Maharishi University of Management, 2014 **C:** Actor, 1983-Present **CW:** Actor, (Films) Finders Keepers, 1984, Once Bitten, 1985, Peggy Sue Got Married, 1986, The Dead Pool, 1988, Earth Girls Are Easy, 1989, Pink Cadillac, 1989, High Strung, 1991, The Mask, 1994, Dumb and Dumber, 1994, Batman Forever, 1995, Ace Ventura: When Nature Calls, 1995, The Mask's Revenge, 1996, Liar, Liar, 1996, The Cable Guy, 1996, The Truman Show, 1997, Simon Birch, 1998, Man on the Moon, 1999, Me, Myself, and Irene, 2000, How the Grinch Stole Christmas, 2000, The Majestic, 2001, Eternal Sunshine of the Spotless Mind, 2004, Lemony Snicket's a Series of Unfortunate Events, 2004, The Number 23, 2007, (Voice Actor) Horton Hears a Who!, 2008, Yes Man, 2008, I Love You Phillip Morris, 2009, (Voice Actor) A Christmas Carol, 2009, Mr. Popper's Penguins, 2011, The Incredible Burt Wonderstone, 2013, Kick-Ass 2, 2013, Anchorman 2: The Legend Continues, 2013, Dumb and Dumber To, 2014, The Bad Batch, 2016, True Crimes, 2016, (TV Series) The Duck Factory, 1984, In Living Color, 1990-1994, (TV Films) Mike Hammer: Murder Takes All, 1989, Doing Time on Maple Drive, 1992; Actor, Writer, (Films) Ace Ventura: Pet Detective, 1994; Actor, Producer, (Films) Bruce Almighty, 2003, Fun with Dick and Jane, 2005 **AW:** Webby Best Celebrity or Fan Website, International Academy of Digital Arts and Sciences, 2010, Favorite Comedic Star, People's Choice Awards, 2010, Best Comedic Performance, MTV Movie Awards, Yes Man, 2009, People's Choice Award for Favorite Funny Male Star, 2008, Muhammad Ali Celebrity Entertainer Award, 2006, 50 Most Powerful People in Hollywood, 2004-2006, Golden Globe Award for Best Performance by an Actor in a Motion Picture, The Truman Show, 2000, Golden Globe Award for Best Performance by an Actor in a Motion Picture, Man on the Moon, 2000, Star, Hollywood Walk of Fame, 2000 **BA:** c/o Creative Artists Agency, 2000 Avenue of the Stars, Los Angeles, CA, 90067-4700

CARROLL, DIAHANN, T: Actress **I:** Media & Entertainment **DOB:** 05/14/1905 **PB:** New York, **SC:** New York, **PT:** Daughter of John and Mabel (Faulk) Johnson; **SPN:** Married Monte Kay, February 26, 1956 (div. January 14, 1963); Married Fredde Glusman, February 21, 1973 (div. July 20, 1973) **CH:** 1 child, Suzanne Kay; **ED:** Student, New York University **CW:** Began career as model; actress: (films) Carmen Jones, 1954, Porgy and Bess, 1959, Paris Blues, 1961, Hurry Sundown, 1967, The Split, 1968, Claudine, 1974, The Five Heartbeats, 1991, Eve's Bayou, 1997, Peeples, 2013, The Masked Saint, 2014; (Broadway) House of Flowers, 1954, No Strings, 1962, (recipient Tony Award, Best Actress in a Musical), Same Time, Next Year, 1977, Agnes of God, 1983, Love Letters, 1990, Sunset Boulevard, 1995, Bubbling Brown Sugar, 2004, A Raisin in the Sun, 2014; (plays) Same Time, Next Year; (TV series) Julia, 1968-1971, (recipient Golden Globe Award for Best TV Star, 1969), Dynasty, 1984-87, The Colbys, 1986, Lonesome Dove, 1994-95, White Collar, 2009-2013; (TV films) Death Scream, 1975, I Know Why the Caged Bird Sings, 1979, Sister, Sister, 1982, Murder in Black and White, 1990, Sunday in Paris, 1991, A Perry Mason Mystery: The Case of the Lethal Lifestyle, 1994, The Sweetest Gift, 1998, Motown 40: The Music is Forever, 1998, Having Our Say: The Delany Sisters' First 100

Years, 1999; (TV miniseries) Roots: The Next Generations, 1979, Motown 40: The Music is Forever, 1998, Jackie's Back!, 1999, The Courage to Love, 2000, Sally Hemmings: An American Scandal, 2000, Livin' for Love: the Natalie Cole Story, 2000, At Risk, 2010, The Front, 2010; (guest appearances) Julia, 1970-71, Different World, 1991-93, Evening Shade, 1994, Touched By An Angel, 1995, Strong Medicine, 2003, Whoopi, 2003, Soul Food, 2004, The 4th Annual TV Land Awards: A Celebration of Classic TV, 2006, Grey's Anatomy, 2006-07, Diary of a Single Mom, 2010-11, and others; host Diahann Carroll Show, 1976; singer: (albums) Diahann Carroll Sings Harold Arlen Songs, 1957, Best Beat Forward, 1958, The Persian Room Presents Diahann Carroll, 1959, Diahann Carroll and the Andre Previn Trio, 1960, Fun Life, 1961, Modern Jazz Quartet - The Comedy, 1962, Showstopper!, 1962, The Fabulous Diahann Carroll, 1963, A You're Adorable: Love Songs for Children, 1967, Nobody Sees Me Cry, 1967, Diahann Carroll, 1974, A Tribute to Ethel Waters, 1978, The Time of My Life, 1997.

CARROLL, PETE, T: Professional Football Coach **I:** Athletics **DOB:** 09/15/1951 **PB:** San Francisco **ED:** MS in Physical Education, Univ. Pacific, 1976; BS in Business Administration, Univ. Pacific, 1973 **C:** Head football coach, Seattle Seahawks, 2010-; Head football coach, defensive coordinator, Univ. Southern California Trojans, L.A., 2001-10; Head football coach, New England Patriots, 1997-99; Defensive coordinator, San Francisco 49ers, 1995-97; Head football coach, New York Jets, 1994; Defense coordinator, New York Jets, 1990-94; Defense backs coach, Minnesota Vikings, 1985-90; Defense backs coach, Buffalo Bills, 1984-85; Assistant head coach, offensive coordinator, Univ. Pacific Tigers, 1983; Defense coordinator, secondary coach, North Carolina St. Wolfpack, 1980-82; Secondary coach, Ohio St. Univ. Buckeyes, 1979; Secondary coach, Iowa St. Univ. Cyclones, 1978; Grad. assistant, secondary, Univ. Arkansas Razorbacks, 1977-78; Grad. assistant, secondary coach, Univ. Pacific Tigers, 1975-77; Grad. assistant, wide receivers coach, Univ. Pacific Tigers, 1974-75 **CW:** Co-author (with Yogi Roth): Win Forever: Live, Work, and Play Like A Champion, 2010 **AW:** Named National Coach of Year, ESPN.com, 2003, Maxwell Club College Coach of Year, 2003, Home Depot National Coach of Year, 2003, Coach of Year, American Football Coaches Association, 2003; recipient Eddie Robinson award, Football Writers Association America, 2003, Munger award, Maxwell Football Club, 2003 **ACH:** Achievements include head coach of the BCS National Championship winning University of Southern California Trojans, 2003; head coach of Super Bowl XLVIII Championship winning Seattle Seahawks, 2013 **BA:** Seattle Seahawks, 12 Seahawks Way, Renton, WA, 98056

CARSON, ANDRÉ D., T: U.S. Representative from Indiana **I:** Government Administration/Government Relations/Government Services **DOB:** 10/16/1974 **PB:** Indianapolis, October 16, 1974 **ED:** MA in Business Management, Ind. Wesleyan University; BA in Criminal Justice Management, Concordia University **C:** Member, US House Intelligence Committee, 2015-; Member, Armed Services Committee, Committee on Transportation and Infrastructure; Whip, Congressional Black Caucus, 2011-; Member, US Congress from 7th Ind. District, 2008-; Member, Indianapolis City-County Council from 15th district, 2007-08; Committeeperson, Center Township of Marion County, Ind.,; Marketing specialist, Cripe Architects & Engineers,; Local board officer, investigator, Ind. State Excise Police, **CR:** Board member Citizens Neighborhood Coalition member IndyParks Kennedy/King Park

Adv. Board **AW:** Named to Power 150, Ebony magazine, 2008 **PA:** Democrat **BA:** 2135 Rayburn House Office Building, Washington, DC, 20515

CARSON, BENJAMIN, T: Secretary of Housing and Urban Development, Retired Neurosurgeon **I:** Government Administration/Government Relations/Government Services **CN:** Vaccinogen, Inc. USA **DOB:** 09/18/1951 **PB:** Detroit **SC:** MI/USA **MS:** Married **SPN:** Lacena "Candy" Carson **CH:** Rhoeyce Carson; Murray Carson; Ben Carson Jr. **ED:** BA, Yale University, New Haven, 1973; MD, University Michigan School Medicine, Ann Arbor, 1977; DSc (hon.), Gettysburg College, 1988; DSc (hon.), Andrews University, 1989; DSc (hon.), Sojourner-Douglas College, 1989; DSc (hon.), Shippenburg University, 1990; DSc (hon.), Jersey City State College, 1990; DSc (hon.), Southwestern Adventist College, 1992; DSc (hon.), University Massachusetts, Boston, 1992; DSc (hon.), Marygrove College, 1993; DSc (hon.), University Detroit Mercy, 1994; DSc (hon.), Spalding University, 1994; DSc (hon.), Western Maryland College, 1994; DSc (hon.), Morgan State University, 1994; DSc (hon.), Long Island University, 1994; DSc (hon.), North Carolina State University, 1994; DSc (hon.), Tuskegee University, 1995; DSc (hon.), Yale University, 1996; DSc (hon.), Del. State University, 1996; DSc (hon.), Medical University South Africa, 1997; DSc (hon.), University Del., 1997; DSc (hon.), College William & Mary, 1998; Numerous other hon. degrees **CT:** Diplomate American Board Neurological Surgery, American Board Pediatrics Neurological Surgery, National Board Medical Examiners **C:** Secretary, Department of Housing and Urban Development, Washington, DC, 2017—; Chairman, Vaccinogen, Inc., 2014—2017; Surgical intern, Johns Hopkins Hospital, Baltimore, Maryland, 1977-78; Professor neurological surgery. oncology, plastic surgery and pediatrics, Johns Hopkins School Medicine, 1999—2013; Associate professor neurological surgery. oncology, plastic surgery and pediatrics, Johns Hopkins School Medicine, 1991—1999; Assistant professor pediatrics, Johns Hopkins School Medicine, Baltimore, Maryland, 1987—1996; Assistant professor neurological surgery , assistant professor oncology, Johns Hopkins School Medicine, Baltimore, Maryland, 1984—1991; Senior registrar, Sir Charles Gairdner Hospital, Perth, Western Australia, 1983-84; Director division pediatric neurosurgery, Johns Hopkins Hospital, 1984—2013; Chief resident, fellow neurological surgery, Johns Hopkins Hospital, Baltimore, Maryland, 1982-83; Neurosurg. resident, Johns Hopkins Hospital, Baltimore, Maryland, 1978-82 **CR:** Senior neurosurgical resident Loch Raven VA Hospital, Baltimore, 1980, Baltimore City Hospitals, 1981; co-dir. Johns Hopkins Cleft & Craniofacial Center, 1991—2013; board directors Kellogg Co., 1997—, Costco Wholesale Corp., 1999—; served on President's Council on Bioethics, 2004; member advisory board Vaccinogen, Inc., 2014—; weekly opinion columnist The Washington Times, 2013—; contributor FOX News, 2013—2014; candidate for the 2016 Republican Party presidential nomination **CIV:** Hon. chair Maryland Red Cross, 1987; member medical adv. board Children's Cancer Foundation, 1987—; emeritus fellow Yale Corp. **CW:** Author: Gifted Hands, 1989, Think Big, 1996, The Big Picture, 1999, Take the Risk: Learning to Identify, Choose, and Live with Acceptable Risk, 2008, America the Beautiful: Rediscovering What Made This Nation Great, 2011, One Nation: What We Can All Do to Save America's Future, 2014, A More Perfect Union: What We the People Can Do to Reclaim Our Constitutional Liberties, 2015; contributor articles to professional journals, chapters to books **AW:** Named a Living Legend award, Libr. Congress, 2000; named one

of Top 100 Black Physicians in America, Black Enterprise Magazine, 2001, America's Top 20 Physicians & Scientists, CNN/TIME Magazine, 2001, America's Best Leaders, US News & World Report, 2008; named to Society of World Changers, Ind. Wesleyan University, 2007; recipient Cum Laude award, Radiological Society North America, 1982, Howard L. Cornish Humanitarian award, Omega Psi Phi, 1987, Memorial award for outstanding service to underprivileged children, Continental Societies, Inc., 1987, Achievement award, Detroit Medical Society, 1987, Maryland State Department Health & Mental Hygiene, 1989, Liberty Bell award, Philadelphia, 1987, George Washington Carver award, 1993, Citation for Excellence, Detroit City Council, 1987, Philadelphia City Council, 1987, Michigan State Senate, 1987, Partner in Health award, Maryland Health Convocation, 1988, Outstanding Achievements in Medicine award, Howard University, Baltimore, 1988, American Black Achievement award, Ebony magazine, 1988, Dr. Daniel Hale Williams award, Jefferson Medical College, Philadelphia, 1989, Outstanding Service & Excellence in Medicine award, Medical Society Eastern Pennsylvania, 1989, Andrew White Medal, Loyola College, Baltimore, 1989, Leonard F. Swain Esteemed Alumni award, University Michigan, 1989, Booker T. Washington award, Business League Baltimore, 1990, Benjamin E. Mays Memorial award, North Carolina State University, 1991, Special Recognition award, National Council Negro Women, 1991, Appreciation award, National Association Equal Opportunity & Higher Education, 1991, Essence award, 1993, Horatio Alger award, 1994, Martin Luther King, Junior award for community service, Johns Hopkins Hospital, 1994, Golden Plate award, American Academy Achievement, 1995, Outstanding Achievement award, Anheuser-Busch Co., 1996, Congress Racial Equality, 1996, Making A Difference award, National Association for the Advancement of Colored People Baltimore chapter, 1998, Tree of Life award, Jewish National Fund, 1998, Public Service award, American Institute Pub. Service, 2000, Distinguished Service to Children award, National Association Elementary School Principals, 2002, Ralph Metcalfe award, Congressional Black Caucus, 2003, Medical award of Excellence, Ronald McDonald House Charities, 2003, Spingarn award, National Association for the Advancement of Colored People, 2006, Ford's Theatre Lincoln Medal, The White House, 2008, Presidential Medal of Freedom, 2008; Paul Harris fellow, Rotary International, 1988, John Conley Scholar, American Academy Otolaryngology Head & Neck Surgeons, 1993 **MEM:** Mem.: American Medical Association, American Association for the Advancement of Science, Institute Medicine, American Cleft Palate-Craniofacial Association, Maryland Neurological Society, Congress Neurological Surgeons, American Association Neurological Surgeons, National Medical Association (Clinical Practitioner of Year award 1988, Living Legend award 1992, William E. Matory award 1992, Excellence in Medicine award 1994), National Pediatric Oncology Group, Monumental Medical Society, Maryland Congress Parents & Teachers (hon. life), Alpha Omega Alpha **ACH:** Achievements include first to successfully separate a pair of Siamese twins joined at the head in 1987, leading a 70-member surgical team working for 22 hours; conducted the first intrauterine procedure to relieve pressure on the brain of a hydrocephalic fetal twin, and a hemispherectomy, in which an infant suffering from uncontrollable seizures has half of its brain removed **BA:** U.S. Department of Housing and Urban Development, 451 7th Street, Washington, DC, 20410

CARTER, EARL, T: U.S. Representative from Georgia **I:** Government Administration/Government Relations/Government Services **PB:** Savannah, Georgia, **C:** Member, U.S. House of Representatives from Georgia's 1st District, 2015-; Member, Committee on Energy and Commerce, Republican Study Committee; State senator District 1, Georgia, 2009-2015; Secretary, Health & Human Services Committee,; Member, Appropriations, Economic Devel. & Tourism Committees,; State rep. District 159, Georgia, 2004-09; Mayor, Pooler, 1996-2004 **PA:** Republican **BA:** 432 Cannon House Office Building Washington, DC 20515, Washington, DC, 20515

CARTER, JIMMY, T: 39th President of the U.S. **I:** Government Administration/Government Relations/Government Services **DOB:** 10/01/1924 **PB:** Plains **SC:** GA/USA **PT:** Son of James Earl and Lillian (Gordy) Carter; **ED:** Attended, Georgia Southwestern College; Attended, Georgia Institute Tech.; BS, US Naval Academy, 1947; LLD (hon.), Morris Brown College, 1972; LLD (hon.), Morehouse College, 1972; LLD (hon.), University Notre Dame, 1977; LLD (hon.), Emory University, 1979; LLD (hon.), Kwansei Gakuin University, Japan, 1981; LLD (hon.), Georgia Southwestern College, 1981; LLD (hon.), New York Law School, 1985; LLD (hon.), Bates College, 1985; LLD (hon.), Centre College, 1987; LLD (hon.), Creighton University, 1987; PhD (hon.), Weizmann Institute Sci., 1980; PhD (hon.), Tel Aviv University, 1983; PhD (hon.), Haifa University, 1987; DHL (hon.), Central Connecticut State University, 1985; DEng (hon.), Georgia Institute Tech., 1979 **C:** Univ. Distinguished Professor, Founder Carter Presidential Center, Emory University, Atlanta, Georgia, 1982—; Founder, Jimmy Carter Libr. & Museum, Atlanta, Georgia; President of the U.S., Washington, DC, 1977-81; Governor, State of Georgia, Atlanta, Georgia, 1971-75; Member District 14, Georgia State Senate, 1963-67; Farmer, Warehouseman, Plains, Georgia, 1953-77 **CR:** Chairman Congressional Campaign Committee Democratic National Committee, 1974 **CIV:** Active Vol. Habitat for Humanity, Board of Directors, 1984—1987; Member Sumter County School Board, Georgia, 1955—1962, Chairman, 1960—1962; Member Sumter County Libr. Board, 1961; Founding Member The Elders, 2007—; Sunday School Teacher Maranatha Baptist Church, Plains; Trustee Mercer University, 2012— **MIL:** Service to Lieutenant U.S. Navy, 1946—53 **CW:** Author: Why Not the Best?, 1975, A Government as Good as Its People, 1977, Keeping Faith: Memoirs of a President, 1982, Negotiation: The Alternative to Hostility, 1984, The Blood of Abraham, 1985, Everything to Gain: Making the Most of the Rest of Your Life, 1987, An Outdoor Journal, 1988, Turning Point: A Candidate, a State, and a Nation Come of Age, 1992, Talking Peace: A Vision for the Next Generation, 1993, Always a Reckoning, 1995, Living Faith, 1996, Sources of Strength: Meditations on Scripture for a Living Faith, 1997, The Virtues of Aging, 1998, An Hour Before Daylight: Memories of a Rural Boyhood, 2001, Christmas in Plains: Memories, 2001, The Nobel Peace Prize Lecture, 2002, The Hornet's Nest: A Novel of the Revolutionary War, 2003, Sharing Good Times, 2004, Our Endangered Values: America's Moral Crisis, 2005 (Grammy Award for Best Spoken Word Album, 2007), Palestine Peace Not Apartheid, 2006, Beyond the White House: Waging Peace, Fighting Disease, Building Hope, 2007, A Remarkable Mother, 2008, We Can Have Peace in the Holy Land: A Plan That Will Work, 2009, White House Diary, 2010, Through the Year with Jimmy Carter: 366 Daily Meditations from the 39th President, 2011, NIV Lessons from Life Bible: Personal Reflections with Jimmy Carter, 2012, A Call to Action: Women, Religion,

Violence, and Power, 2014, A Full Life: Reflections at Ninety, 2015 (Grammy Award for Best Spoken Word Album, 2016) **AW:** Named Humanitarian of Year, GQ Magazine, 1996; Recipient Silver Buffalo Award, Boy Scouts America, 1978, Gold Medal, International Institute Human Rights, 1979, International Mediation Medal, American Arbitration Association, 1979, Martin Luther King, Junior Peace Prize, 1979, International Human Rights Award, Synagogue Council America, 1979, Harry S. Truman Pub. Service Award, 1981, Ansel Adams Conservation Award, Wilderness Society, 1982, Human Rights Award, International League Human Rights, 1983, World Methodist Peace Award, 1985, Albert Schweitzer Prize for Humanitarianism, 1987, Edwin C. Whitehead Award, National Center Health Education, 1989, Jefferson Award, American Institute Pub. Service, 1990, Liberty Medal, National Constitution Center, 1990, Spirit of America Award, National Council Social Studies, 1990, Physicians for Social Responsibility Award, 1991, Aristotle Prize, Alexander S. Onassis Foundation, 1991, W. Averell Harriman Democracy Award, National Dem. Institute International Affairs, 1992, Spark M. Matsunaga Medal of Peace, U.S. Institute Peace, 1993, Humanitarian Award, CARE International, 1993, Conservationist of Year Medal, National Wildlife Federation, 1993, Freedom Award, National Civil Rights Museum, 1994, Félix Houphouët-Boigny Peace Prize, United Nations Educational, 1994, Bishop John T. Walker Distinguished Humanitarian Award, Africare, 1996, Indira Gandhi Prize for Peace, Disarmament & Devel., 1997, UN Human Rights Award, 1998, Hoover Medal, 1998, International Child Survival Award, UNICEF Atlanta, 1999, William Penn Mott, Junior, Park Leadership Award, National Parks Conservation Association, 2000, Zayed International Prize for the Environment, 2001, Herbert Hoover Humanitarian Award, Boys & Girls Clubs America, 2001, Nobel Peace Prize, Norwegian Nobel Committee, 2002, Berkeley Medal, University California, 2007, Mahatma Gandhi Global Nonviolence Award, Mahatma Gandhi Center Global Nonviolence, James Madison University, 2009, American Peace Award, 2009, International Catalonia Award, 2010, International Advocate for Peace Award, Yeshiva University Benjamin N. Cardozo School Law, 2013 **PA:** Democrat

CARTER, JOHN RICE, T: U.S. Representative from Texas **I:** Athletics **DOB:** 11/06/1941 **PB:** Houston **PT:** Son of John James and Elizabeth (Rice) Carter; **ED:** JD, University Texas School Law, Austin, 1969; BA in History, Texas Tech University, 1965 **CT:** Bar: Texas 1969 **C:** Member, US Congress from 31st Texas District, Washington, 2003-; Member, Committee on Appropriations; Secretary, US House Republican Conference, Washington, 2007-13; District Judge, 277th District Court Williamson County, 1982-2002; Judge, 277th District Court Williamson County, Texas, 1981-82; Municipal Judge, Round Rock, 1978-80; Private Practice Attorney, Round Rock, Texas, 1973-81; Counsel, Texas House of Reps., Austin, 1969-72 **CR:** Chairman Round Rock Planning Committee, 1975-78 **MEM:** Mem.: Williamson County Bar Association (president 1976), Round Rock Jaycees 1975, (Jaycee of Year 1975) **PA:** Republican

CARTER, ROSALYNN, T: Former First Lady **I:** Government Administration/Government Relations/Government Services **DOB:** 08/18/1927 **PB:** Plains **SC:** Georgia **PT:** Daughter of Edgar and Allie (Murray) Smith; **SPN:** Married James Earl Carter, Junior, July 7, 1946; **CH:** Children: John William, James Earl III, Donnel Jeffrey, Amy Lynn **ED:** Attended, Georgia Southwestern College, 1944—1946; DHL (hon.), Morehouse College, 1980; LLD

(hon.), University Notre Dame, 1987 **C:** Co-Creater of The Carter Center, 1982-; Distinguished fellow, Women's Studies Department, Emory University, Atlanta, Georgia, 1990—; Distinguished Centennial Lecturer, Agnes Scott College, Decatur, Georgia, 1988—1992; First Lady of U.S., Washington, DC, 1977—1981 **CIV:** Co-founder Every Child by Two Campaign for Early Immunization; Co-founder (with Jimmy Carter) The Carter Center, 1982, Trustee, Creator and Chair Mental Health Task Force; Annual Host Rosalynn Carter Symposium on Mental Health Policy; Founder Rosalynn Carter Fellowships for Mental Health Journalism, 1996; Chair International Committee of Women Leaders for Mental Health; Adv. Board Member Habitat for Humanity; Member Georgia Gov.'s Commission to Improve Services for Mentally and Emotionally Handicapped, 1971; President Board Director, Rosalynn Carter Institute for Caregiving Georgia Southwestern State University; Hon. Chair Pres.'s Commission on Mental Health, 1977—1978; Deacon Maranatha Baptist Church, Plains, Georgia, 2006— **CW:** Author: First Lady from Plains, 1984; Co-author (with Jimmy Carter) Everything to Gain: Making the Most of the Rest of Your Life, 1987, (with Susan Golant) Helping Yourself Help Others: A Book for Caregivers, 1994, (with Susan Golant) Helping Someone With Mental Illness: A Compassionate Guide for Family, Friends and Caregivers, 1998, (with Susan Golant & Kathryn E. Cade) Within Our Reach: Ending the Mental Health Crisis, 2010; Appeared in (documentaries) Jimmy Carter Man from Plains, 2007 **AW:** Recipient Vol. of Decade Award National Mental Health Association, 1980, Presidential Citation American Psychological Association, 1982, Nathan S. Kline Medal of Merit International Committee Against Mental Illness, 1984, Distinguished Alumnus Award Am. Association State Colleges and Univs., 1987, Dorothea Dix Award Mental Illness Foundation, 1988, Dean's Award Columbia University College Physicians and Surgeons, 1991, Notre Dame Award for international Humanitarian Service, 1992, Eleanor Roosevelt Living World Award Peace Links, 1992, National Caring Award The Caring Institute, 1995, Kiwanis World Service Medal Kiwanis International Foundation, 1995, Jefferson Award Am. Institute for Pub. Service, 1996, Georgia Woman of Year Award Georgia Commission Women, Rhoda and Bernard Sarnat International Prize in Mental Health, Institute Medicine, US Surgeon General's Medallion, Presidential Medal of Freedom, 1999; Named to National Women's Hall of Fame, 2001. **MEM:** Fellow: Am. Psychiatric Association (hon.); **H:** Fly fishing, birdwatching, swimming, bicycling **PA:** Democrat **BA:** The Carter Ctr One, Copenhill 453 Freedom Pkwy NE, Atlanta, GA, 30307

CARTER, SHAWN "JAY-Z", T: Rapper **I:** Media & Entertainment **DOB:** 12/04/1969 **PB:** Brooklyn **SC:** NY/USA **C:** Licensed Agent, Roc Nation Sports, 2013-Present; Founder, Roc Nation, LLC, 2008-Present; Principal, Owner, 40/40 Club, Atlantic City, NJ, 2005-Present; Principal, Owner, 40/40 Club, New York, NY, 2003-Present; Co-Founder, CEO, Rocawear, 1999-Present; Co-Founder, StarRoc, 2008; President, Def Jam Recordings, 2005-2007; Part-Owner, New Jersey Nets (Now Brooklyn Nets), 2004-2013; Co-Founder, Roc-A-Fella Records, New York, NY, 1996 **CIV:** Founder, Shawn Carter Scholarship Fund, 2002-Present, Founder, Annual Jay-Z Santa Claus Toy Drive, Founder, Team Roc **CW:** Rapper, (Albums) Reasonable Doubt, 1996, In My Lifetime, Vol. I, 1997, Vol. 2: Hard Knock Life, 1998, Vol. 3: Life and Times of S. Carter, 1999, The Dynasty: Roc La Familia, 2000, MTV Unplugged, 2001, The Blueprint, 2001, The Blueprint, Vol. 2: The Gift & the Curse, 2002, Blueprint 2.1, 2003, The Black Album, 2003, Kingdom Come, 2006,

American Gangster, 2007, The Blueprint 3, 2009, Magna Carta...Holy Grail, 2013, (Collaboration Albums) (With R. Kelly) Best of Both Worlds, 2002, (With R. Kelly) Unfinished Business, 2004, (With Linkin Park) Collision Course, 2004, (With Kanye West) Watch the Throne, 2011, Magna Carta Holy Grail, 2013, 4:44, 2017, (Songs) Hard Knock Life (Ghetto Anthem), 1998, I Just Wanna Love U (Give It 2 Me), 2000, Excuse Me Miss, 2002, (With Beyoncé) Crazy in Love, 2003, 99 Problems, 2004, (With Linkin Park) Numb/Encore, 2004, (With Rihanna) Umbrella, 2007, (With T.I., Kanye West, & Lil Wayne) Swagga Like Us, 2008, D.O.A. (Death of Auto-Tune), 2009, (With Rihanna & Kanye West) Run This Town, 2009, (With Alicia Keys) Empire State of Mind, 2009, (With Swizz Beatz) On to the Next One, 2009, (With Kanye West) Otis, 2011, Niggas in Paris, 2011, (With Kanye West, Frank Ocean, & The-Dream) No Church in the Wild, 2011, (With Justin Timberlake) Holy Grail, 2014; Actor, Producer, Writer, Streets is Watching, 1998; Actor, (Films) State Property, 2002, Paper Soldiers, 2002, Fade to Black, 2004, Made in America, 2013, Annie, 2014; Producer, Paid in Full, 2002, Fade to Black, 2004; Author, (Memoir) Decoded, 2010; Executive Producer, (Video Games) NBA2K13, 2012 **AW:** Best Rap Album, Grammy Awards, Vol. 2: Hard Knock Life, 1999, Sammy Davis Junior Entertainer of the Year, Soul Train Music Awards, 2001, Best Male Hip Hop Artist, 2001, 2004, Favorite Rap/Hip Hop Artist, American Music Awards, 2004, 2009, Favorite Rap/Hip Hop Album, American Music Awards, The Blueprint 3, 2009, CD of the Year, BET Hip Hop Awards, The Blueprint 3, 2010, Best Rap/Sung Collaboration, Best R&B Song, Grammy Awards, Best Collaboration, BET Awards, Crazy in Love, 2004, Best Rap Solo Performance, Grammy Awards, 99 Problems, 2005, The 100 Most Influential People in the World, TIME Magazine, 2005, 2013, Best Rap/Sung Collaboration, Grammy Awards, Numb/Encore, 2006, Ten Most Fascinating People, Barbara Walters, 2006, Best Rap/Sung Collaboration, Grammy Awards, Umbrella, 2008, The 100 Most Powerful Celebrities, Forbes.com, 2008, The Power 150, Ebony Magazine, 2008, Best Rap Performance By a Duo or a Group, Grammy Awards, Swagga Like Us, 2009, The 40 Under 40 Rising Stars, Fortune Magazine, 2009, Best Rap Solo Performance, Grammy Awards, D.O.A. (Death of Auto-Tune), 2010, Best Rap/Sung Collaboration, Best Rap Song, Grammy Awards, Run This Town, 2010, New York Times Bestseller, Decoded, 2010, Best Collaboration, BET Awards, Empire State of Mind, 2010, Favorite Male Singer, Nickelodeon Kids' Choice Awards, 2010, Best Rap/Sung Collaboration, Best Rap Song, Grammy Awards, Empire State of Mind, 2011, Best Rap Performance By a Duo or a Group, Grammy Awards, On to the Next One, 2011, Best Rap Performance, Grammy Awards, Video of the Year, BET Awards, Otis, 2012, Best Group, The Throne, (With Kanye West), BET Awards, 2012, Best Rap Performance, Best Rap Song, Grammy Awards, Niggas in Paris, 2013, Best Rap/Sung Collaboration, Grammy Awards, No Church in the Wild, 2013, Best Rap/Sung Collaboration, Grammy Awards, Holy Grail 2014 **BA:** c/o Island Records, 825 Eighth Avenue, 28th Floor, New York, NY, 10019

CARTER JR., DWAYNE (LIL WAYNE), T: Rap Artist **I:** Media & Entertainment **DOB:** 09/27/1982 **PB:** New Orleans **PT:** Son of Jacida Carter and Dwayne Michael Turner; **ED:** Attended, University Houston **C:** Solo artist, 1999-; Founder, CEO, Young Money Entertainment, 2005-07; Founding member rap group, Hot Boys, 1997-2001 **CW:** Singer: (albums with Hot Boys) Get It How U Live, 1997, Guerilla Warfare, 1998, Let Em Burn, 2003, (solo albums) Tha Block is Hot, 1999, Lights Out, 2000,

500 Degreez, 2002, Tha Carter, 2004, Tha Carter II, 2005, Tha Carter III, 2008 (Best Rap Album, Grammy Awards, 2009), Rebirth, 2010, I Am Not a Human Being, 2010, Tha Carter IV, 2011 (Top Rap Album, Billboard Music Awards, 2012), I Am Not a Human Being II, 2013, Free Weezy Album, 2015, Tha Carter V, 2015,(Extended Plays) The Leak, 2007, In Tune We Trust, 2017 (collaboration albums) (with Birdman) Like Father, Like Son, 2006, (with Young Money Entertainment) We Are Young Money, 2009, (songs) A Milli, 2008 (Track of Year, BET Hip-Hop Awards, 2008, Best Rap Solo Performance, Grammy Awards, 2009), (featuring Static Major) Lollipop, 2008 (Best Hip-Hop Video, MTV Video Music Awards, 2008, BET Viewer's Choice award, 2008, Best Rap Song, Grammy Awards, 2009), (with Jay-Z, T.I. and Kanye West) Swagga Like Us, 2008 (Best Rap Performance By A Duo Or Group, Grammy Awards, 2009), (with Keri Hilson) Turnin' Me On, 2008 (Best Collaboration, BET Awards, 2009), (with Young Money featuring Lloyd) Bedrock, 2009; actor: (films) Baller Blockin', 2000, Who's Your Caddy?, 2007, Hurricane Season, 2010, Freaknik:The Movie, 2010; regular contributor ESPN The Magazine **AW:** Named Top Rap Artist, Billboard Music Awards, 2012, Top Male Artist, 2012, Best Male Hip-Hop Artist, BET Awards, 2009, Lyricist of Year, BET Hip-Hop Awards, 2008, Choice Rap Artist, Teen Choice Awards, 2008, Hottest MC in the Game, MTV, 2007, Best Rapper, Vibe Music awards, 2007; named one of The 100 Agents of Change, Rolling Stone magazine, 2009 **BA:** The Coalition, 9100 Wilshire Boulevard Suite 520 E, Beverly Hills, CA, 90212

CARTWRIGHT, MATT, T: U.S. Representative From Pennsylvania **I:** Government Administration/Government Relations/Government Services **DOB:** 05/01/1961 **SC:** PA/USA **PT:** Alton Cartwright; Adelaide Cartwright **ED:** JD, School of Law, University of Pennsylvania, 1986; BA in History, Hamilton College, 1983; Student, London School of Economics, 1981 **C:** U.S. House Oversight & Government Reform Committee, 2013-Present; U.S. House Natural Resources Committee, 2013-Present; U.S. Congress From 17th Pennsylvania District, Washington, DC, 2013-Present; On-Air Legal Analyst, The Law & You, WBRE-TV, Nexstar Broadcasting Group, 2005-2011; Partner, Munley, Munley & Cartwright, Scranton, PA, 1988-2012; Associate, Montgomery, McCracken, Walker & Rhoads LLP, 1986-1989; Committee on Appropriations; Committee on Steering and Policy **CR:** Delegate, Democratic National Convention, 1992 **MEM:** Board of Governors, American Association for Justice, 2009-2011; International Society of Barristers; Bar of the State of New York; Pennsylvania Bar Association **PA:** Democrat

CASEY, ROBERT PATRICK JR., T: U.S. Senator from Pennsylvania **I:** Government Administration/Government Relations/Government Services **DOB:** 04/13/1960 **PB:** Scranton **SC:** PA/USA **PT:** Robert Patrick Casey; Ellen Theresa (Harding) Casey **ED:** JD, Catholic University, Washington, DC (1998); BA, College of the Holy Cross, Springfield, MA (1982) **C:** Ranking Member, Senate on Aging Committee (2017-Present); Chairman, U.S. Congressional Joint Economic Committee (2011-Present); Member, U.S. Congressional Joint Economic Committee (2007-Present); U.S. Senator from Pennsylvania (2007-Present); State Treasurer, State of Pennsylvania, Harrisburg, PA (2005-2006); Auditor General, State of Pennsylvania, Harrisburg, PA (1996-2005); Private practice attorney, Scranton, PA (1991-1996) **BAR:** Pennsylvania (1991) **PA:** Democrat **BA:** Office of Robert Casey, 393 Russell Senate Office Building, Washington, DC, 20510

CASPER, MARC NOLAN, I: Sciences **DOB:** 03/10/1968 **PB:** New York **SC:** NY/USA **PT:** Son of Herman and Betty Casper. **ED:** MBA, Harvard University, 1995; BA, Wesleyan University, 1990 **C:** President, CEO, Thermo Fisher Scientific, Inc., Waltham, Massachusetts, 2009-; Executive vice president, COO, Thermo Fisher Scientific, Inc., Waltham, Massachusetts, 2008-09; Executive vice president, Thermo Fisher Scientific, Inc., Waltham, Massachusetts, 2007-08; President, Analytical Technologies Group (subsidiary of Thermo Fisher Scientific Inc.), 2007-09; Executive vice president, Thermo Electron Corp. (subsidiary of Thermo Fisher Scientific Inc.), 2006-07; Senior vice president, Thermo Electron Corp. (subsidiary of Thermo Fisher Scientific Inc.), 2003; President, life & laboratory sciences, Thermo Electron Corp. (subsidiary of Thermo Fisher Scientific Inc.), 2001-05; President, CEO, Kendro Laboratory Products, Newton, Connecticut, 2000-01; President, Americas, Dade Behring Inc., Deerfield, Illinois, 1997-2000; Associate, Bain Capital, Boston, 1995-96; Strategy consultant, Bain & Co., Inc., Boston, 1992-93; Associate consultant, Bain & Co., Inc., Boston, 1990-92 **CR:** Board directors Zimmer, Inc., 2009- **MEM:** Member Phi Beta Kappa.

CASSIDY, BILL, T: U.S. Senator from Louisiana **I:** Government Administration/Government Relations/Government Services **DOB:** 09/28/1957 **PB:** Highland Park **ED:** MD, Louisiana State University, 1983; BS in Biochemistry, Louisiana State University, 1979 **C:** US Senator from Louisiana, 2015-; Member, US Congress from 6th Louisiana District, 2009-15; Member District 16, Louisiana State Senate, 2006-09; Associate professor medicine, Louisiana State University Health Sci. Center, **CIV:** Sunday school teacher, Chapel on the Campus, **MEM:** Mem.: American College Physicians, Louisiana State Medical Society (board directors), East Baton Rouge Parish Medical Society (president 1998), American Association Study of Liver Diseases, Gastroenterology Society, Rotary Club Baton Rouge **PA:** Republican

CASTOR, KATHY, T: U.S. Representative from Florida **I:** Government Administration/Government Relations/Government Services **DOB:** 08/20/1966 **PB:** Miami **SC:** FL/USA **PT:** Daughter of Don and Betty (Bowe) Castor **ED:** JD, Florida State University College Law, 1991; BA, Emory University, Atlanta, 1988 **C:** Member, US Congress from 14th Florida District, 2013-;; Member, Committee on the Budget, Committee on Energy and Commerce; Member, US Congress from 11th Florida District, Washington, 2007-13; Member, Hillsborough County Board Commissioners, Florida, 2002-06; Practicing attorney, Florida, 1994-2000; Assistant general counsel, Florida Department Community Affairs, 1991-94 **MEM:** Mem.: Florida Association Women Lawyers (past president) **PA:** Democrat **BA:** 2052 Rayburn House Office Building Washington, DC 20515, Washington, DC, 20515

CASTRO, JOAQUÍN, T: U.S. Representative from Texas, Former State Legislator **I:** Government Administration/Government Relations/Government Services **DOB:** 09/16/1974 **PB:** San Antonio **SC:** TX/USA **PT:** Son of Jesse Guzman and Maria Castro; **ED:** JD, Harvard University Law School, Massachusetts, 2000; BA in Communications & Political Sci. with honors, Stanford University, California, 1996 **C:** Member, U.S. House Foreign Affairs Committee, 2013-; Member, Permanent Select Committee on Intelligence; Member, U.S. House Armed Services Committee, 2013-; Member, U.S. Congress from 20th Texas District, Washington, 2013-; Member District 125, Texas House of Representatives, Austin, 2003-13; Co-founder, Law

Offices of Julián Castro, PLLC, San Antonio, 2005-13; Associate, Akin Gump Strauss Hauer & Feld LLP, San Antonio, 2001-05 **CR:** Adjunct professor Trinity University, San Antonio visiting professor law, St. Mary's University **PA:** Democrat

CATENA, TOM, T: Physician **I:** Medicine & Health Care **DOB:** 01/01/1900 **SC:** U.S. **ED:** Bachelors Degree, Brown University; Medical Degree, Duke University **C:** Physician, Mother of Mercy Hospital, 2008- **AW:** Aurora Prize for Awakening Humanity, 2017, Time 100 Most Influential 2015

CERERE, ANDREW, T: CEO **I:** Financial Services **CN:** U.S. Bancorp **ED:** BA, University of Saint Thomas; MBA, Finance, University of Minnesota **C:** CEO, Bancorp, 2017-Present; Vice Chairman, US Bank, 2015-Present; Independent Director, Donaldson Company, 2013-Present

CERVERIS, MICHAEL, T: Actor **I:** Media & Entertainment **PB:** Bethesda **SC:** MD/USA **ED:** Educated, Yale University (1983); Educated, Phillips Exeter Academy (1979) **C:** Actor (1983-Present) **CW:** Actor, Broadway Plays, "The Who's Tommy" (1993-1995), "Titanic" (1997-1999), "Assassins" (2004), "Passion" (2004), "Children and Art" (2005), "Sweeney Todd" (2005-2006), "Lovemusik" (2007), "Evita" (2011-2013), "Fun Home" (2015); Off-Broadway, "MacBeth" (1983), "Life is a Dream" (1984), "The Games" (1984), "Green Fields" (1985), "Total Eclipse" (1985), "Blood Sports" (1986), "Abingdon Square" (1986), "Hedwig and the Angry Inch" (2000), "Fifth of July" (2003), "The Apple Tree" (2005), "King Lear' (2007), "Road Show" (2008), "Nikolai and the Others" (2013); TV Series, "Fame" (1986), "Fringe" (2008-2013), "Treme" (2011-2012), "The Good Wife" (2014-2015); Films, "Tokyo Pop" (1988), "Rock 'n' Roll High School Forever" (1990", "Steel and Lace" (1991), "A Woman, Her Men, and Her Futon" (1992), "Lulu on the Bridge" (1998), "The Mexican" (2001), "The Temptation" (2004), "Brief Interviews with Hideous Men" (2007), "Cirque du Freak: The Vampire's Assistant" (2009), "Meskada" (2010), "Stake Land" (2010), "Leaving Circadia" (2014), "Detours" (2015), "The Good Wife" (2013), "The Tick" (2017), "Gotham" (2017), "Mosaic" (2017); Off Broadway, "Fun Home" (2013); Performer, Album, "Dog Eared" (2004) **AW:** Theatre World Award (1993); Tony Award for Best Featured Actor in a Musical (2004); Tony Award for Best Performance by an Actor in a Leading Role in a Musical (2015)

CHABON, MICHAEL, T: Writer **I:** Writing and Editing **PB:** Washington **SC:** DC/USA **ED:** MFA in Creative Writing, Univ. California, Irvine; BA, Univ. Pittsburgh **C:** Writer, 1988- **CIV:** Board chairman, MacDowell Colony, 2010- **CW:** Author: (novels) The Mysteries of Pittsburgh, 1988, Wonder Boys, 1995 (made into feature film), The Amazing Adventures of Kavalier & Clay, 2000 (Pulitzer Prize for Fiction, 2001, Notable Book of Year Am. Libr. Association, 2000), The Final Solution, 2004 (National Jewish Book award, 2005, Aga Khan prize for fiction Paris Rev., 2004), The Yiddish Policemen's Union, 2007, Gentlemen of the Road, 2007, Telegraph Avenue, 2012, (Young Adult Fiction) Summerland, 2002 (Mythopoeic Fantasy award for children's lit., 2003), (Children's Book) The Astonishing Secret of Awesome Man, 2011, (short stories) Son of the Wolfman (O. Henry Prize collection, 1999, National Magazine award), (collections) A Model World and Other Stories, 1991, Werewolves in Their Youth, 1999, (Essay Collections) Maps and Legends, 2008, Manhood for Amateurs, 2009; columnist Details magazine, 2005-,(Book) Moonglow, 2016 **AW:** Fernanda Pivano Award, 2014, IMPAC Literary Award, 2014, National Book Critics Circle Award, 2017,

California Book Awards Gold Prize, 2017, IMPAC Literary Award, 2018 **MEM:** Academy of American Letters

CHABOT, STEVE, T: Chairman of the US House Small Business Committee **I:** Government Administration/Government Relations/Government Services **DOB:** 01/22/1953 **PB:** Cincinnati **PT:** Son of Gerard Joseph and Doris Leona (Tilly) Chabot; **ED:** JD, Northern Kentucky University Salmon P. Chase College Law, Highland Heights, 1978; BA in History, College William & Mary, Williamsburg, Virginia, 1975 **C:** Chairman, US House Small Business Committee, 2015-; Member, US House Small Business Committee, Washington, 2011-; Member, US House Foreign Affairs Committee, Washington, 2011-; Member, US House Judiciary Committee, Washington, 2011-; Member, US Congress from 1st Ohio District, Washington, 2011-; Member, US Congress from 1st Ohio District, Washington, 1995-2009; Private law practice, Westwood, Ohio, 1978-94; Teacher, St. Joseph School, Cincinnati, 1975-76 **CR:** Commissioner Hamilton County, Ohio, 1990-94 member Cincinnati City Council, 1985-90 **H:** Reading **PA:** Republican

CHAFFETZ, JASON E., T: U.S. Representative from Utah **I:** Government Administration/Government Relations/Government Services **DOB:** 03/26/1967 **PB:** Los Gatos **SC:** CA/USA **PT:** Son of John and Katherine Chaffetz; **ED:** BA in Communications, Brigham Young University, Provo, Utah, 1989 **C:** Chairman, U.S. House Oversight & Government Reform Committee, 2015-2017; Member, U.S. Congress from 3rd Utah district, 2009-; Campaign manager, Jon Huntsman's Gubernatorial Campaign,; Founder, president, Maxtera, Inc., Alpine, Utah, 2005-08; Chief of staff to Governor Jon Huntsman, Junior, State of Utah, Salt Lake City, 2005 **CR:** Chairman Utah NG Adjutant General Rev.; commissioner, Highland City Planning Commission **CIV:** Trustee, Utah Valley State College, **MEM:** Mem.: BYU Utah County Cougar Club (president), Cougar Club (member board directors) **PA:** Republican

CHAGARES, MICHAEL ARTHUR, T: Federal Judge **I:** Law and Legal Services **DOB:** 05/01/1962 **PB:** Pittsburgh **SC:** Pennsylvania **ED:** JD, Seton Hall University, 1987; BA, Gettysburg College, 1984 **CT:** Bar: New Jersey 1987 **C:** Judge, US Court Appeals (3rd Cir.), 2006-; Partner, Cole, Schotz, Meisel, Forman & Leonard, P.A., Hackensack, New Jersey, 2004-06; Chief civil division, US Department Justice, 1999-2004; Director affirmative civil enforcement unit, US Department Justice, 1996-99; Assistant US attorney Dist New Jersey, US Department Justice, 1990-2004; Attorney, McCarter & English, 1988-90; Law clerk to Hon. Morton I. Greenberg, US Court Appeals (3rd Cir.), 1987-88 **CR:** Hearing officer 9/11 Compensation Fund adjunct professor law Seton Hall University, 1991- **CIV:** Trustee, Federal Bar State New Jersey, **MEM:** Mem.: Lawyers Adv. Committee, US District Court, New Jersey, New Jersey State Bar Association (chair, Federal Practice & Procedure Section 1998-2000) **BA:** 601 Market St, Philadelphia, PA, 19106

CHALFIE, MARTIN, T: Biology Professor **I:** Education/Educational Services **DOB:** 01/15/1947 **PB:** Chgo. **PT:** Son of Eli and Vivian Chalfie; **ED:** PhD in Physiology, Harvard University, Cambridge, Massachusetts, 1977; BS in Biochemistry, Harvard University, Cambridge, Massachusetts, 1969 **C:** Faculty member, Columbia University, New York City, 1982-; William R. Kenan, Junior professor, chairman department biological sciences, Columbia University, New York City,; Researcher, Laboratory Molecular Biology, Cambridge, England, 1977-82; Teacher, Hamden Hall Country

Day School, Connecticut, 1970-71 **CW:** Co-editor (with Steven Kain): Green Fluorescent Protein: Properties, Applications and Protocols, 1998; mem.editl. board Genome Biology, Molecular Biology of the Cell; contributor articles to professional journals **AW:** Recipient Nobel prize in chemistry, 2008,National Academy of Sciences, 2004, Golden Goose Award, 2012, E.B. Wilson Medal, 2008 **MEM:** Mem.: National Academy of Sciences **ACH:** Achievements include being credited (with others) with popularization of green fluorescent protein (GFP) found in jellyfish as a genetic marker

CHAN, JACKIE, T: Actor **I:** Media & Entertainment **DOB:** 04/07/1954 **PB:** Hong Kong **PT:** Chi-Ping Chan; Lee-Lee Chan **MS:** Married **SPN:** Lin Fong Chiao (12/1/1982) **CH:** Jaycee **ED:** Honorary PhD, University of Cambodia; PhD in Social Science, Hong Kong Baptist University (1996); Trained, Peking Opera School **C:** Dean, Jackie Chan Film and TV Academy; Owner/Co-owner, Jackie & JJ Productions; Owner/Co-owner, Jackie and Willie Productions; Owner/Co-owner, JC Group China; Owner, Founder, Film Company, JCE Movies Ltd. **CIV:** Founder, Jackie Chan Charitable Foundation (1988); Goodwill Ambassador, UNICEF; Founder, Dragon's Heart Foundation (2005) **CW:** Actor, Films, "Little Tiger of Guangdong, Little Tiger from Canton, Hand of Death" (1975), "New Fist of Fury" (1976), "Shaolin Wooden Men" (1976), "To Kill with Intrigue" (1977), "Snake in the Eagle's Shadow, Snake and Crane Arts of Shaolin, Magnificent Bodyguards" (1978), "Drunken Master" (1978), "Spiritual Kung Fu" (1978), "Dragon Fist" (1979), "The Young Master" (1980), "Half a Loaf of King Fu, Battle Creek Brawl" (1980), "The Cannonball Run" (1981), "Marvelous Fists" (1982), "Winners and Sinners" (1983), "The Fearless Hyena Part 2, Cannonball Run II" (1984), "Wheels on Meals" (1984), "My Lucky Stars" (1985), "The Protector" (1985), "Twinkle Twinkle Lucky Stars" (1985), "Heart of the Dragon" (1985), "Armour of God" (1987), "Project A Part 2" (1987), "Dragons Forever" (1987), "Police Story II" (1987), "Mr. Canton and Lady Rose" (1989), "Amour of God II: Operation Condor" (1991), "Island of Fire" (1991), "Twin Dragons" (1992), "City Hunter" (1993), "Crime Story" (1993), "Drunken Master II" (1994), "Rumble in the Bronx" (1994), "Police Story IV: First Strike" (1996), "Mr. Nice Guy" (1997), "Rush Hour" (1998), "Who Am I?" (1998), "The King of Comedy" (1999), "Gen-X Cops" (1999), "Shanghai Noon" (2000), "Rush Hour 2" (2001), "The Tuxedo" (2002), "Shanghai Knights" (2003), "Vampire Effect" (2003), "The Medallion" (2003), "Around the World in 80 Days" (2004), "Fa Dou Daai Jin" (2004), "San Gin Chaat Goo Si" (2004), "San Wa" (2005), "Rush Hour 3" (2007), "The Forbidden Kingdom" (2008), Voice Actor, "Kung Fu Panda" (2008), "Looking for Jackie" (2009), "The Spy Next Door" (2010), "The Karate Kid" (2010), "The Legend of Silk Boy" (2010), Voice Actor, "Kung Fu Panda 2" (2011), "Shaolin" (2011), "1911" (2011), "Personal Tailor" (2013), "Police Story: Lockdown" (2013), "As the Light Goes Out" (2014), Voice Actor, "Kung Fu Panda 3" (2016), "Skiptrace" (2016), "The Master, A Lego Ninjago Short" (2016), "Railroad Tigers" (2016), "Kung Fu Yoga" (2017), "The Nut Job 2: Nutty by Nature" (2017), "The Lego Ninjago Movie" (2017), "The Foreigner" (2017), "Bleeding Steel" (2017), "Namiya" (2017), "Viy 2" (2018), "Knights of Shadows, Walker Between Halfworlds (2019), Many Other Films; Actor, Director, Executive Producer, Writer, Films, "The Fearless Hyena" (1979), "Dragon Strike" (1982), "Police Story" (1985), "Chinese Zodiac" (2012); Actor, Director, Writer, Films, "Project A" (1983), "Police Story" (1985); Actor, Producer, Writer, Films, "Gorgeous" (1999); Actor, Producer, Films, "The Accidental

Spy" (2001); Actor, Executive Producer, Films, "Police Story 3: Supercop" (1992), "Thunderbolt" (1995), "The Shinjuku Incident" (2009), "Dragon Blade" (2015); Producer, Films, "Center Stage" (1991), "Legendary Amazons" (2011), "Skiptrace" (2016), Documentary, "Gambling on Extinction" (2015) **AW:** Lifetime Achievement Award, MTV (1995); PETA Humanitarian Award (1999); International Lifetime Achievement Award, International Leadership Foundation (2000); Taurus Honorary Award; Outstanding Achievement for Acting in Actions Film, World Stunt Award (2002); Star, Hollywood Walk of Fame (2002); Named Favorite Action Star, People's Choice Award (2011) **ACH:** Named Goodwill Ambassador, 2004. **BA:** Jackie& Willie Productions Ltd., 70 Pak To Ave, Clear Water Bay, Kowloon, 0

CHAN, PRISCILLA, T: Philanthropist **I:** Nonprofit & Philanthropy **PB:** Braintree **SC:** MA/USA **C:** Founder, The Chan Zuckerberg Initiative (2015-Present) **AW:** Named One of TIME's 100 Most Influential People, TIME Magazine (2016)

CHAO, ELAINE L., T: Secretary of Transportation, Former U.S. Secretary of Labor **I:** Government Administration/Government Relations/Government Services **DOB:** 03/26/1953 **PB:** Taipei **SC:** Taiwan **PT:** Daughter of James South Carolina and Ruth M.L. (Chu) Chao; **ED:** LittD (hon.), Shanghai Jiaotong University, 2012; LittD (hon.), St. Catharine College, 2011; LittD (hon.), NYACK College, 2008; DHL (hon.), Murray State University, 2008; Doctor in Organizational Leadership (hon.), Regent University, 2003; Doctor in Public Service (hon.), Western Kentucky University, 2011; Doctor in Public Service (hon.), Sweet Briar College, 2007; Doctor in Public Service (hon.), DePauw University, 2002; DPA (hon.), Northern Kentucky University, 2004; DPA (hon.), Campbellsville University, 2002; D Arts & Letters (hon.), Miami-Dade C.C., 2001; DHum (hon.), Kentucky Wesleyan College, 1998; DHum (hon.), Thomas More College, 1994; DHum (hon.), Drexel University, 1992; DHL (hon.), Wingate University, 2004; DHL (hon.), Centre College, 2003; DHL (hon.), Northern Alabama University, 2003; DHL (hon.), University South Carolina, 2001; DHL (hon.), University Louisville, 1996; DHL (hon.), Goucher College, 1996; DHL (hon.), University Toledo, 1995; DHL (hon.), Bellarmine College, 1995; DHL (hon.), Niagara University, 1992; LLD (hon.), Marquette University, 2006; LLD (hon.), Elmira College, 2006; LLD (hon.), Agnes Scott College, 2006; LLD (hon.), Catholic University America, 2004; LLD (hon.), Fu-Jen Catholic University, 2003; LLD (hon.), St. Marys College, 2002; LLD (hon.), University Notre Dame, 1998; LLD (hon.), Sacred Heart University, 1991; LLD (hon.), St. John's University, 1991; LLD (hon.), Villanova University, 1989; MBA, Harvard Business School, 1979; AB in Economics, Mount Holyoke College, 1975 **C:** Secretary of Transportation, Washington, DC, 2017—; Distinguished fellow, Heritage Foundation, Washington, DC 2009-2017; Secretary, US Department Labor, Washington, DC 2001-09; Distinguished fellow, Heritage Foundation, Washington, DC 1996-2001; President, United Way of America, Alexandria, Virginia, 1992-96; Director, Peace Corps., 1991-92; Chairman, Federal Maritime Commission, Washington, DC 1988; Deputy secretary, U.S. Department Transportation, Washington, DC 1989-91; Deputy maritime administrator, US Department Transportation, Washington, DC 1986-88; Vice president, capital markets group, Bank of America Corp., San Francisco, 1984-86; Senior lending officer, Citicorp, NA, New York City, 1979-83; Associate, Gulf Oil Corp., Pittsburgh, 1978 **CR:** Board directors News Corp., 2012-, Protective Life Corp., 2011-, Wells Fargo & Co., 2011-, Dole

Food Co., Inc., 2009-13 adj. assistant professor St. John's University Grad. School Business Administration, New York, 1984 White House fellow, 1983-84 **CIV:** Board member, National World War II Museum, Board member, Harvard Kennedy School, Ford's Theatre, **AW:** Recipient Woodrow Wilson award for Public Service, 2011, Outstanding Alumni award, Harvard Business School, 1993, Young Achiever award, National Council Women US, Inc., 1986; fellow Eisenhower Association, 1984 **MEM:** Mem.: Council Foreign Relations, Harvard Club **PA:** Republican **BA:** US Department of Transportation, 1200 New Jersey Ave, S.E., Washington, DC, 20590

CHAPPELLE, DAVE, T: Actor, Comedian **I:** Media & Entertainment **PB:** Washington **SC:** DC/USA **PT:** William David Chappelle III; Yvonne Reed **C:** Actor 1982- **CW:** Actor: (films) Robin Hood: Men in Tights, 1993, Undercover Blues, 1993, Getting In, 1994, The Nutty Professor, 1996, Joe's Apartment, 1996, Con Air, 1997, The Real Blonde, 1997, Bowl of Pork, 1997, Woo, 1998, You've Got Mail, 1998, 200 Cigarettes, 1999, Blue Streak, 1999, Screwed, 2000, Undercover Brother, 2002, Chi-Raq, 2015; (TV series) Buddies, 1996, Comedy: Coast to Coast, 1994, (voice) Crank Yankers, 2002; actor, writer, executive producer (TV series) Chappelle's Show, 2003-06, actor, co-writer, and producer (films) Half Baked, 1998, writer and executive producer (TV special) The Dave Chappelle Project, 1997, Dave Chappelle: Killin' Them Softly, 2000, writer, producer (films) Dave Chappelle's Block Party, 2006,(Film) Dave Chappelle: For What It's Worth, 2004, Deep in the Heart of Texas: Dave Chappelle Live at Austin City Limits, 2017, The Age of Spin: Dave Chappelle Live at the Hollywood Palladium,2017, A Star is Born,2018, Dave Chappelle: Equanimity, Dave Chappelle: The Bird Revelation, 2017(Television) SNL, 2017(Emmy Award for Outstanding Guest Actor 2017)

CHARLES, RUPAUL ANDRE, T: Actor, Television Personality **I:** Media & Entertainment **DOB:** 11/17/1960 **PB:** San Diego **SC:** CA/USA **C:** Actor, 1987-, Singer, 1993- **CR:** Driver luxury car business, 1978-82 on-air reporter Manhattan Cable, England first face of M.A.C., M.A.C. Cosmetics, 1995 **CW:** Albums include: Freak Sex, 1985, RuPaul is Supermodel of the World, 1993, Foxy Lady, 1996, Star Booty, 1997, Ho Ho Ho, 1997, Red Hot, 2004, Workout, 2005, Champion, 2009, Glamazon, 2011, Born Naked, 2014, Realness, 2015, Slay Belles, 2015; formed groups RuPaul and the U-Hauls, Wee Wee Pole; (TV appearances) The Am. Music Show, (TV films) A Mother's Prayer, 1995, An Unexpected Life, 1998, The Truth About Jane, 2000; (films) Crooklyn, 1994, Wigstock: The Movie, 1995, To Wong Foo, Thanks for Everything! Julie Newmar, 1995, Smoke, 1995, Red Ribbon Blues, 1995, The Brady Bunch Movie, 1995, Blue in the Face, 1995, A Very Brady Sequel, 1996, Fled, 1996, An Unexpected Life, 1998, EDtv, 1999, But I'm a Cheerleader, 1999, Rick & Steve the Happiest Gay Couple in the World, 2000, The Eyes of Tammy Jane, 2000, The Truth About Jane, 2000, For the Love of May, 2000, Who is Cletis Tout?, 2001, Skin Walker, 2004, Whitepaddy, 2006, Starrbooty, 2007, How We Got Over (voice), 2008, Another gay Sequel: Gays Gone Wild!, 2008; (video) B-52's Love Shack; co-host (with Michelle Visage) WKTU morning radio show, New York City, 1996; host, The RuPaul Show, 1997, RuPaul's Drag Race, 2009-, Drag Race: Untucked!, 2010-11, RuPaul's Drag U, 2010-12, Good Work, 2015-; author: Lettin' It All Hang Out, 1995, Workin' It! RuPaul's Guide to Life, Liberty, and the Pursuit of Style, 2010,(Music) Butch Queen, 2016, American, 2017 (Movies) Hurricane Bianca, 2016 (Television) Bubble Guppies, 2015, The Muppets, 2016, Gay for Play Game Show

Starring RuPaul, 2016, The Real O'Neals, 2016, 2 Broke Girls, 2017 Animals, 2017, Girlboss, 2017, Then and Now with Andy Cohen, 2017, Bojack Horseman, 2017, Broad City, 2017, Adam Ruins Everything, 2017 **AW:** Recipient Vito Russo Entertainer Year, Gay and Lesbian Alliance Against Defamation, 1999,Time 100 Most Influential, 2017, Primetime Emmy for Outstanding Host for a Reality or Reality- Competition Program, 2016-17

CHARPENTIER, EMMANUELLE MARIE, T: Microbiologist, Educator, researcher **I:** Sciences **DOB:** 12/11/1968 **PB:** Juvisy-sur-orge **PT:** Daughter of Pierre Rene and Jacqueline Raymonde Charpentier. **ED:** PhD (hon.), University Pierre and Marie Curie, Paris, 1995; MA in Microbiology, University Pierre and Marie Curie, Paris, 1992; BS in Biochemistry, University Pierre and Marie Curie, Paris, 1991 **C:** Guest professor Max F. Perutz Laboratories Department Microbiology and Immunobiology, University Vienna, 2002-; Research associate, Skirball Institute Biomolecular Medicine, New York City, 1999-2002; Visiting scientist, St. Jude Children's Research Hospital, Memphis, 1999; Assistant research scientist, New York University Medical Center, New York City, 1997-99; Postdoctoral associate, Rockefeller University, New York City, 1996-97; Postdoctoral assistant, Pasteur Institute, Paris, 1995-96 **CR:** Consultant Biovertis AG, Vienna, 2003-, Sandoz GmbH, Vienna, 2005 reviewer sci. journals in field, 2002- **CW:** Contributor articles to professional publications **AW:** Recipient Equivalent University Assistant award, French Government, 1993-95; grantee, Austrian Research Promotion Co., 2007-, Life Sci., Vienna Sci. and Tech. Fund, 2006-, Research, European Community, 2006-, Austrian National Bank, 2004-, University Anniversary Donation City of Vienna, 2004-05, Austrian Sci. Fund, 2004-; scholar, French Government, 1992-95; Marie Curie research fellow, European Community, 2002-04, Pasteur-Weizmann fellow, 1996 **MEM:** Mem.: Am. Society Microbiology **ADD:** Max F Perutz Labs U Vienna Dept Microbiology and Immunobio, Dr Bohrgasse 9/4, Vienna, YT, Austria, 00000

CHASE, CHEVY, T: Actor **I:** Media & Entertainment **DOB:** 10/08/1943 **PB:** New York **SC:** NY/USA **ED:** CCS, Institute Audio Research, 1970; BA in English, Bard College, 1967 **CT:** Sports Car Club of America (Certified Technology Inspector, Accredited Driving Instructor, 11-Time Conference/Division Champion, Three-Time Regional Driver of the Year) **CW:** Arista MGM Records, 1968; Writer, MAD Magazine, 1969; Director, Writer, Actor, National Lampoon Theatre Company, 1972-1974; Performer, Off Broadway and National Tour, "National Lampoon's Lemmings," 1973; Actor, (TV Series) The Great American Dream Machine, 1971, Saturday Night Live, 1975-1976, Community, 2009-2014; Actor, (Films) Walk... Don't Walk, 1968, The Groove Tube, 1974, Foul Play, 1978, Oh Heavenly Dog, 1980, Caddyshack, 1980, Seems Like Old Times, 1981, Under the Rainbow, 1981, Modern Problems, 1981, National Lampoon's Vacation, 1983, Deal of the Century, 1983, Fletch, 1984, National Lampoon's European Vacation, 1985, Spies Like Us, 1985, Sesame Street Presents: Follow That Bird, 1985, Three Amigos, 1986, Funny Farm, 1988, The Couch Trip, 1988, Caddyshack II, 1988, Fletch Lives, 1989, National Lampoon's Christmas Vacation, 1989, Nothing but Trouble, 1991, L.A. Story, 1991, Memoirs of an Invisible Man, 1992, Hero, 1992, Last Action Hero, 1993, Cops and Robbersons, 1994, Man of the House, 1995, National Lampoon's Vegas Vacation, 1997, Dirty Work, 1998, The One Armed Bandit, 2000, Snow Day, 2000, (Narrator) Pete's a Pizza, 2001, Vacuums, 2002, Orange County, 2002, Bad Meat, 2003, Our Italian

Husband, 2004, (Voice Actor) The Karate Dog, 2004, Ellie Parker, 2004, Goose On the Loose, 2006, (Voice Actor) Doogal, 2006, Funny Money, 2006, Zoom, 2006, Cutlass, 2007, Hot Tub Time Machine, 2010, Not Another Not Another Movie, 2011, Before I Sleep, 2013, Lovesick, 2014, Hot Tub Time Machine 2, 2015, Vacation, 2015, The Last Movie Star, 2017, Hedgehogs, 2017, The Last Laugh, 2018; Actor, (TV Films) America's Most Terrible Things, 2002, The Secret Policeman's Ball, 2006; Actor, (TV Appearances) Will Rogers: Look Back in Laughter, 1987, The Dave Thomas Comedy Show, 1990, Law & Order, 2006, Brothers & Sisters, 2007, Hjalp, 2009, Chuck, 2009, Community, 2009, (Voice Actor) Family Guy, 2009, Hot in Cleveland, 2014, Wishin and Hopin, 2014, Chevy, 2015, A Christmas in Vermont, 2016; Host, Producer, Writer, The Chevy Chase Show, 1993 **AW:** Award for Best Script in a Comedy Variety Special, Writers Guild; Award for Best Supporting Actor in a Comedy Variety Series, National Academy of TV Arts And Science; Two Emmy Awards, Saturday Night Live; Emmy Award, Co-Writer, The Paul Simon Special; Harvard Lampoon Lifetime Achievement Award, 1996; Honor, Harvard University Hasty Pudding Theatrical Group, 1992; Time 100 Most Influential, 2018 **MEM:** American Federation of Musicians, Stage Actors Guild, Actors' Equity Association, American Federation of TV and Radio Artists **PA:** Democrat **BA:** Cornelius Productions, PO Box 257, Bedford, NY, 10506-0257

CHASE, DAVID, I: Media & Entertainment **DOB:** 05/30/1905 **PB:** Mount Vernon, New York **SC:** Mount Vernon, New York **ED:** MA in Film, Stanford University, California; Degree, New York University; Student in Filmmaking, School Visual Arts, New York **CW:** Dir.: (TV series) Alfred Hitchcock Presents, 1985; writer, director (TV series) Almost Grown, 1988, writer Kolchak: The Night Stalker, 1974, (TV films) Grave of the Vampire, 1972, Moonlight, 1982, (TV series) Northern Exposure, 1993-95, writer, producer The Rockford Files, 1976-80 (Emmy award, 1977), writer, executive producer I'll Fly Away, 1991 (Norman Felton award Producers Guild Am., 1993), writer, producer (TV films) Off the Minnesota Strip, 1980 (Writers Guild Am. award, 1980, Emmy award, 1979), writer, producer, director (TV series) The Sopranos, 1999-2007 (Emmy award for College episode, 1998, Golden Globe award, 1999, Norman Felton award Producers Guild Am., 2000, Outstanding Directorial Achievement award Directors Guild Am., 1999, Peabody award, 2000, Drama Series of Year award Am. Film Institute, 2001, Primetime Emmy for Outstanding Writing for a Drama Series (Made in America) & Outstanding Drama Series, Academy TV Arts and Scis., 2007, Best Episodic TV-Drama, Producers Guild Am., 2008); prodr.: (TV films) The Rockford Files: A Blessing in Disguise, 1995; writer, producer, director (TV films) The Rockford Files: The Punishment and Crime, 1996, (films) Not Fade Away, 2012 **AW:** Recipient Norman Lear Achievement award in TV, Producers Guild America, 2009, Paddy Chayefsky Laurel award for TV, Writers Guild America West, 2008

CHASTAIN, JESSICA, T: Actress **I:** Media & Entertainment **PT:** Jerri Chastain **ED:** BFA, Juilliard School, New York City, 2003 **CW:** Actress: (TV films) Dark Shadows, 2005, Blackbeard, 2006; (TV series) Law & Order: Trial by Jury, 2005-06; (films) Jolene, 2008, Stolen, 2009, The Debt, 2010, Take Shelter, 2011 (Best Supporting Actress, National Society Film Critics, New York Film Critics Cir., 2011), Coriolanus, 2011, The Tree of Life, 2011 (Best Supporting Actress, National Society Film Critics, New York Film Critics Cir., 2011), The Help, 2011 (Best Supporting Actress, National Society

Film Critics, New York Film Critics Cir., 2011), Wilde Salome, 2011, Texas Killing Fields, 2011, Madagascar 3: Europe's Most Wanted (voice), 2012, Lawless, 2012, Tar, 2012, To the Wonder, 2012, Zero Dark Thirty, 2012 (Best Actress, National Board Review, 2012, Best Actress, Critics Choice Awards, 2013, Best Performance by an Actress in a Motion Picture-Drama, Golden Globe award, Hollywood Foreign Press Association, 2013), Mama, 2013, Salomé, 2013, Miss Julie, 2014, Interstellar, 2014, A Most Violent Year, 2014 (Best Supporting Actress, National Board Review, 2014), The Martian, 2015, Crimson Peak, 2015, The Huntsman: Winter's War, 2016, The Zookeeper's Wife, 2016, Molly's Game, 2017, Woman Walks Ahead, 2017, X-Men: Dark Phoenix, 2018; (Broadway plays) The Heiress, 2012; guest appearances (TV series) ER, 2004, Veronica Mars, 2004, Close to Home, 2006, Journeyman, 2007, Agatha Christie's Poirot, 2010, Animals, 2016, SNL, 2018 actress, producer (films) The Disappearance of Eleanor Rigby: Him, 2013, The Disappearance of Eleanor Rigby: Her, 2013, The Disappearance of Eleanor Rigby: Them, 2014 **AW:** Named one of The 100 Most Influential People in the World, TIME Magazine, 2012

CHAZELLE, DAMIEN, T: Director, Screenwriter, Producer **I:** Media & Entertainment **PB:** Providence **SC:** RI **CW:** Producer, Guy and Madeline on a Park Bench, 2009, First Man, 2018, Writer, The Last Exorcism Part II, 2013, Gran Piano, 2013, 10 Cloverfield Lane, 2016,Director, Whiplash, 2014, La La Land, 2016(Academy Award for Best Director, 2017)

CHEADLE, DONALD FRANK, T: Actor **I:** Media & Entertainment **DOB:** 11/29/1964 **PB:** Kansas City **SC:** MO/USA **PT:** Donald Frank Cheadle, Sr., Bettye North **ED:** BA in Fine Arts, California Institute of the Arts **CIV:** Goodwill Ambassador, UN Environmental Programme, 2010 **CW:** Actor, (Films) 3 Days, 1984, Moving Violations, 1985, Punk, 1986, Hamburger Hill, 1987, Colors, 1988, Roadside Prophets, 1992, The Meteor Man, 1993, Things To Do In Denver When You're Dead, 1995, Devil In A Blue Dress, 1995, Rosewood, 1997, Volcano, 1997, Boogie Nights, 1997, Bulworth, 1998, Out Of Sight, 1998, Mission To Mars, 2000, The Family Man, 2000, Traffic, 2000, Things Behind The Sun, 2000, Manic, 2001, Swordfish, 2001, Rush Hour 2, 2001, Ocean's Eleven, 2001, The Hire: Ticker, 2002, The U.S. Of Leland, 2003, The Assassination Of Richard Nixon, 2004, Hotel Rwanda, 2004, Ocean's Twelve, 2004, The Other Side Of Simple, 2006, The Dog Problem, 2006, Reign Over Me, 2007, Ocean's Thirteen, 2007, Talk To Me, 2007, Traitor, 2008, Hotel For Dogs, 2009, Brooklyn's Finest, 2009, Iron Man 2, 2010, Flight, 2012, Iron Man 3, 2013, Avengers: Age Of Ultron, 2015, Captain America: Civil War, 2016, Kevin Hart: What Now?, 2016, Avengers: Infinity War, 2018, (TV Films) Lush Life, 1993, Rebound: The Legend Of Earl The Goat Manigault, 1996, The Rat Pack, 1998, A Lesson Before Dying, 1999, Fail Safe, 2000, (TV Appearances) Hill Street Blues, 1981, Fame, 1982, L.A. Law, 1986, The Bronx Zoo, 1987, Hooperman, 1988, Night Court, 1984, Booker, 1989, China Beach, 1988, The Simpsons, 1989, The Fresh Prince Of Bel-Air, 1990, Picket Fences, 1992, The Golden Palace, 1992, Hangin' With Mr. Cooper, 1992, The Bernie Mac Show, 2001, ER, 2002, (TV Series) House Of Lies, 2012-Present; Actor, Producer, (Films) Crash, 2004; Actor, Executive Producer, The Guard, 2011; Actor, Producer, Director, Writer Miles Ahead, 2015; Co-Author, (With John Prendergast) Not On Our Watch: The Mission To End Genocide In Darfur And Beyond, 2007; Producer, (TV Series) Crash, 2008 **AW:** Golden Globe Award For Best Performance In A Supporting Role, The Rat Pack, 1999, Screen Actors Guild Award

For Outstanding Performance By A Cast In Motion Picture, Crash, 2006, African American Film Critics Association Award For Best Actor, Talk to Me, 2007, BET Humanitarian of Year Award, 2007, Summit Peace Award, 2007, National Association For The Advancement Of Colored People Image Award For Outstanding Literary Work-Non-Fiction, Not On Our Watch: The Mission To End Genocide In Darfur And Beyond, 2008, Power 150, Ebony Magazine, 2008, Golden Globe Award For Best Performance By An Actress In A TV Series-Comedy Or Musical, National Association For The Advancement Of Colored People Image Award For Outstanding Actor In A Comedy Series, House of Lies, 2013, National Association For The Advancement Of Colored People Image Award For Outstanding Directing In A Comedy Series, House of Lies, 2016 **BA:** c/o Liberman-Zerman Management, 252 North Larchmont Boulevard, Los Angeles, CA, 90004

CHEEK, JULIA TAYLOR TAYLOR, T: CEO of Everlywell **I:** Business Management/Business Services **DOB:** 01/01/1900 **ED:** MBA, Harvard Business School, 2011; B.A., Vanderbilt University, 2002-05 **C:** CEO and Founder, EverlyWell,2015-; Venture Partner, NextGen Venture Partners, 2016-; Vice President, Moneygram International, 2013-15; Director of Strategy and Operations, George W. Bush Presidential Center,2011-13

CHENAULT, KENNETH IRVINE, T: CEO **I:** Financial Services **CN:** American Express **DOB:** 06/02/1951 **PB:** New York **SC:** NY/USA **PT:** Son of Hortenius and Anne N. (Quick) C. **MS:** Married **SPN:** Kathryn Cassell, August 20, 1977 **CH:** Kenneth I. Junior, Kevin A. **ED:** LLD, Iona College, 1996; PhD (hon.), University Notre Dame, 1998; PhD (hon.), Howard University, 1998; PhD (hon.), South Carolina State University, 1997; PhD (hon.), Xavier University, 1997; PhD (hon.), Bowdoin College, 1996; PhD (hon.), Adelphi University, 1995; PhD (hon.), Stony Brook University, 1996; PhD (hon.), Morgan State University, 1990; JD, Harvard University, 1977; BA, Bowdoin College, 1973 **CT:** Bar: Massachusetts 1981. **C:** Chairman, CEO, American Express Co., New York City, 2001-; President, COO, American Express Co., New York City, 1997-2000; Vice-chmn., American Express Co., New York City, 1995-97; President U.S.A., American Express Travel Related Services Co., Inc., New York City, 1993-95; President consumer card and fin. services group, American Express Travel Related Services Co., Inc., New York City, 1990-93; Executive vice president personal card division, American Express Travel Related Services Co., Inc., New York City, 1988-89; Executive vice president platinum card/gold, American Express Travel Related Services Co., Inc., New York City, 1986-88; From vice president to senior vice president, American Express Travel Related Services Co., Inc., New York City, 1983-96; Director strategic planning, American Express Co., New York City, 1981-83; Consultant, Bain & Co., Inc., Boston, 1979-81; Associate, Rogers & Wells, New York City, 1977-79 **CR:** Board directors American Express Co., 1997-, IBM Corp., 1998-, The Procter & Gamble Co., 2008- board member Bloomberg Family Foundation, 2010- member President's Council on Jobs & Competitiveness, 2011- **CIV:** member Dean's Advisory Board Harvard Law School **AW:** Named one of America's Best Leaders, US News & World Report, 2007; named to Power 150, Ebony magazine, 2008; recipient National Equal Justice award, National Association for the Advancement of Colored People Legal Defense & Educational Fund, Inc., 2008, Most Influential Black Americans, Ebony magazine, 2006 **MEM:** Member American Bar Association; fellow American Academy Arts & Sciences, Council Foreign Relations,

CHENEY, DICK, T: 46th Vice President of the U.S. **I:** Government Administration/Government Relations/Government Services **DOB:** 01/30/1941 **PB:** Lincoln **SC:** NE/USA **PT:** Richard Herbert Cheney; Marjorie Lauraine (Dickey) Cheney **ED:** Student, University of Wisconsin (1966-1968); MA in Political Science, University of Wyoming (1966); BA in Political Science, University of Wyoming (1965); Student, Casper Community College (1963); Student, Yale University (1959-1962) **C:** Vice President of the U.S., Washington, DC (2001-2009); Chairman, Chief Executive, Halliburton Co., Dallas, Texas (1995-2000); Senior Fellow, American Enterprise Institute, Washington, DC (1993-1995); Secretary, US Department of Defense, Washington, DC (1989-1993); Chairman, US House Republican Policy Committee, Washington, DC (1981-1988); Minority Whip, US Congress from Wyoming, Washington, DC (1988-1989); Member, US Congress from Wyoming, Washington, DC (1979-1989); Chief of Staff to President, The White House, Washington, DC (1975-1977); Deputy Assistant to President for Operations, The White House, Washington, DC (1974-1975); Partner, Bradley, Woods & Co. (1977-1978); Partner, Bradley, Woods & Co. (1973-1974); Assistant Director for Operations, Cost of Living Council, The White House, Washington, DC (1971-1973); Deputy to Presidential Counselor, The White House, Washington, DC (1970-1971); Special Assistant to Director, Office of Economic Opportunity, The White House, Washington, DC (1969-1970); Congressional Fellow, Staff Member to Representative William A. Steiger, US House of Representatives, Washington, DC (1968-1969); Staff Aide to Governor Warren Knowles, State of Wisconsin, Madison, WI (1966); Intern, Wyoming State Legislature, Cheyenne, WY (1965) **CIV:** Member, University of Wyoming Alumni Association **CW:** Co-author, "Kings of the Hill: Power and Personality in the House of Representatives" (1983); Co-author, "In My Time: A Personal and Political Memoir" (2011); Author, "Exceptional: Why the World Needs a Powerful America" (2015); Co-author, "An American Medical Odyssey" (2013); Appearance, Documentary, "The World According to Dick Cheney" (2013) **AW:** Named Conservative of the Year, Human Events Magazine (2009); Named One of the 50 Highest-Earning Political Figures, Newsweek (2010); Named One of the 50 Most Powerful People in D.C., GQ Magazine (2009); Reagan Award, National Republican Congressional Committee (2011); Presidential Medal of Freedom, The White House (1991); J.E. Davies Congressional Fellowship Award (1968) **PA:** Republican

CHENEY, LIZ, T: U.S. Representative from Wyoming **I:** Government Administration/Government Relations/Government Services **DOB:** 07/28/1966 **PT:** Daughter of Richard Bruce and Lynne Anne (Vincent) Cheney; **ED:** JD, University of Chicago Law School, 1996; BA, Colorado College, 1988 **C:** Member, U.S. House of Representatives from Wyoming's at Large District,2017-; Member, Committee on Natural Resources; Member, Committee on Armed Services; Member, Committee on Rules; Co-founder, board member, KeepAmericaSafe.com, 2009-; Principal deputy assistant secretary, US Department State, 2005-06; Deputy assistant secretary, Bureau Near Eastern Affairs, US Department State, Washington, 2002-04; International law attorney, consultant, International Finance Corp., 1999-2002; Associate, White & Case LLP, 1996-99; Associate, Armitage Associates LLP, 1993-96; With, U.S. Agency International Devel. (USAID),; Special assistant to deputy secretary for assistance to former Soviet Union, U.S. Department State, **CR:** Contributor FOX News, 2012- **CIV:** Senior foreign policy adv., Mitt Romney presidential campaign, 2008 National co-chair, Fred Thompson presidential campaign, 2007-08 Member W Stands for Women initiative,, Bush-Cheney re-election campaign, 2003-04 Member international board visitors, University Wyoming, **CW:** Co-author (with Dick Cheney): In My Time: A Personal and Political Memoir, 2011 **PA:** Republican

CHENOWETH, KRISTIN, T: Actress **I:** Media & Entertainment **PB:** Broken Arrow **SC:** OK/USA **PT:** Jerry Morris Chenoweth; Junie (Smith) Chenoweth **ED:** MA in Opera, Oklahoma City University **CW:** Actress: (Broadway plays) Steel Pier, 1999 (Theatre World award), You're a Good Man, Charlie Brown, 1999 (Tony award for Best Featured Actress, 1999, Drama Desk award, 1999, Clarence Derwent award, 1999, Outer Critics Circle award, 1999), Epic Proportions, 1999-2000, Funny Girl, 2002, Wicked, 2003-04, Promises Promises, 2010, On the Twentieth Century, 2015 (Drama desk award outstanding actress in a musical, 2015_ My Love Letter to Broadway,2016; (plays) Box Office of the Damned, 1994, Dames at Sea, 1994, Phantom, 1994, The Fantasticks, 1995, Scapin, 1997, A New Brain, 1998, Strike Up the Band, 1998, The Apple Tree, 2005, Stairway to Paradise, 2007, Love, Loss, and What I Wore, 2009, The Dames of Broadway...All of 'Em!, 2013; (TV series) LateLine, 1998, Kristin, 2001, Baby Bob, 2002, Sesame Street, 2003, The West Wing, 2004-06, Pushing Daisies, 2007-09 (Primetime Emmy for Outstanding Supporting Actress in a Comedy Series, Academy TV Arts & Scis., 2009), Sit Down Shut Up, 2009, GCB, 2012, (TV appearances) Ugly Betty, 2007, Frasier, 1993, Glee, 2009-14, Hot in Cleveland, 2012, The Good Wife, 2012, BoJack Horseman (voice, The Muppets, 2015, 2014-15,American Gods, 2017, Younger,2017, Mom, 2018 , Rupaul's Drag Race All Stars,2018; (TV miniseries) Paramour, 1999, Lovin' Lakin, 2012; (TV films) Annie, 1999, The Music Man, 2003, 12 Men of Christmas, 2009, Legally Mad, 2010, Descendants, 2015; (films) Topa Topa Bluffs, 2002, Bewitched, 2005, The Pink Panther, 2006, RV, 2006, Stranger than Fiction, 2006, Running with Scissors, 2006, Deck the Halls, 2006, Space Chimps (voice), 2008, Four Christmases, 2008, You Again, 2010, Hit and Run, 2012, Family Weekend, 2013,; actress: (films) Family Weekend, 2012, Rio 2 (voice), 2014, The Opposite Sex, 2014, The Boy Next Door, 2015, Strange Magic (voice), 2015, The Peanuts Movie (voice), 2015, Hard Sell, 2015, Class Rank,2017, My Little Pony:The Movie, 2017, The Star, 2017; guest soloist: West Side Story Suite of Dances; singer: (albums) Let Yourself Go, 2001, As I Am, 2005, A Lovely Way to Spend Christmas, 2008, Some Lessons Learned, 2011, Coming Home, 2014; author: A Little Bit Wicked: Life, Love, and Faith in Stages, 2009, The Art of Elegance, 2016 **AW:** Metropolitan Opera Award **ACH:** Performed leading roles at Goodspeed Opera House, Guthrie Theatre, Paper Mill Playhouse, North Shore Music Theatre; guest soloist with National Symphony Orchestra, New York Philharmonic, London's Divas at Donmar series, Carnegie Hall, Lincoln Center and the Kennedy Center, and has performed with Placido Domingo, Paul Newman, Joshua Bell and Harvey Fierstein.

CHESKY, BRIAN JOSEPH, I: Business Management/Business Services **DOB:** 08/29/1981 **PB:** Niskayuna **SC:** NY/USA **ED:** BFA in Industrial Design, Rhode Island School Design, 2004 **C:** Co-founder, CEO, Airbnb, San Francisco, 2007-; Principal, Brian Chesky, Inc., 2007; Industrial designer, 3DID, LA, 2005-07 **AW:** Named one of The 40 Under 40, Fortune magazine, 2012-14

CHESNEY, KENNY, T: Musician **I:** Media & Entertainment **DOB:** 03/26/1968 **PB:** Knoxville **SC:** TN/USA **PT:** Son of David Chesney and Karen Chandler; **ED:** Degree in advertising, E. Tennessee State University, 1991 **C:** Creator, owner, Blue Chair Bay Rum, 2013-; With, RCA, Subsidiary BNA, Tennessee,; Record contract, with Capricorn, Tennessee, 1993; Publication deal, with Acuff-Rose, 1992; Resident performer, The Turf, Nashville,; Performer, Chuckie's Trading Post and Quarterback's Barbecue, Johnson City, Tennessee, **CW:** Musician: (albums) In My Wildest Dreams, 1993, All I Need To Know, 1995, Me & You, 1996, I Will Stand, 1997, Everywhere We Go, 1999, No Shirt, No Shoes, No Problem, 2002, All I Want For Christmas is a Real Good Tan, 2003, When the Sun Goes Down, 2004 (Album of Year, Country Music. Association, 2004), The Road & the Radio, 2005, Just Who I Am: Poets & Pirates, 2007, Lucky Old Sun, 2008, Hemingway's Whiskey, 2010, Welcome to the Fishbowl, 2012, Life on a Rock, 2013, The Big Revival, 2014, Some Town Somewhere, 2016, (songs) The Good Stuff, 2002 (Single of Year, Academy Country Music, 2003), You Save Me, 2005 (Male Video of Year, Country Music TV, 2007), Cosmic Hallelujah, 2016, Live in No Shoes Nation, 2017, I Go Back, 2004 (Male Video of Year, Country Music TV, 2005), (with Tracy Lawrence & Tim McGraw) Find Out Who Your Friends Are, 2007 (Musical Event of Year, Country Music Association, 2007, Vocal Event of Year, Academy Country Music, 2008), (with Grace Potter) You and Tequila, 2011 (Music Video of Year, Country Mussic Association, 2011), (with Tim McGraw) Feel Like a Rock Star, 2012 (Musical Event of Year, Country Music Association Awards, 2012); musician: (guest appearance with Willie Nelson and Leon Russell) Last Thing I Needed First Thing This Morning, 2003; producer, co-dir. (TV films) Boys of Fall, 2010 **AW:** Named Favorite Male Singer, People's Choice Awards, 2007, Country Songs Artist of Year, Billboard Music Awards, 2006, Entertainer of Year, Country Music Association Awards, 2006-08, 2004, Academy Country Music Awards, 2005-08, Top Male Vocalist, 2002, Top New Male Vocalist, 1997; recipient Milestone award, 2015, Touring award, Billboard Music Awards, 2005-08

CHICAGO, JUDY, T: Artist **I:** Fine Art **PB:** Chicago **SC:** IL/USA **PT:** Arthur M. Cohen; May (Levenson) Cohen **ED:** Doctorate (hon.), Duke University, 2003; Doctorate (hon.), Smith College, 2000; Doctorate (hon.), Lehigh University, 2000; Doctorate (hon.), Russell Sage College, 1992; MA, UCLA, 1964; BA, UCLA, 1962 **CR:** Co-founder Feminist Studio Workshop, L.A., 1973, Through the Flower Corp., 1977 prof. in residence We. Kentucky University, 2001 visiting artist Ind. University, 1999, Duke University, 2000, University North Carolina, 2000, California Poly. Institute, Pomona, 2003. **CW:** Author: Through the Flower: My Struggle as a Woman Artist, 1975, The Dinner Party: A Symbol of Our Heritage, 1979, Embroidering Our Heritage: The Dinner Party Needlework, 1980, The Birth Project, 1985, Holocaust Project: From Darkness Into Light, 1993, Beyond the Flower: The Autobiography of a Feminist Artist, 1996, The Dinner Party, 1996, Women and Art: Contested Territory, 1999, Fragments from the Delta of Venus, 2004, Kitty City: A Feline Book of Hours, 2005 Through the Flower: My Struggle as a Woman Artist. Lincoln: Authors Choice Press,2006, Frida Kahlo: Face to Face,2010,. Institutional Time: A Critique of Studio Art Education,2014, one-woman shows include, Pasadena (California) Museum Art, 1969, Jack Glenn Gallery, Corona del Mar, California, 1972, JPL Fine Arts, London, 1975, Quay Ceramics, San Francisco, 1976, San Francisco Museum Modern Art, 1979, Brooklyn Museum, 1980, 2002, Parco

Galleries, Japan, 1980, Fine Arts Gallery, Irvine, California, 1981, Musee d'Art Contemporain, Montreal, 1982, American Counseling Association Galleries, New York City, 1984, 85, 86, 2004, 05, National Museum of Women in the Arts, 2002; group exhibitions include Jewish Museum, New York City, 1966, 67, Whitney Museum, 1972, Winnipeg Art Gallery, 1975; represented in permanent collections Brooklyn Museum, San Francisco Museum Modern Art, Oakland Museum Art, Pennsylvania Academy Fine Arts, L.A. County Museum Art, also numerous private collections. **AW:** Time 100 Most Influential, 2018

CHIN, DENNY, T: Federal Judge **I:** Law and Legal Services **PB:** Kowloon **SC:** Hong Kong **ED:** JD, Fordham University, 1978; BA, Princeton University, Magna Cum Laude, 1975 **C:** Judge, U.S. Court of Appeals, Second Circuit, New York, NY, 2010-Present; Judge, U.S. District Court, Southern District of New York, New York, NY, 1994-2010; Attorney, Vladeck, Waldman, Elias & Engelhard, New York, NY, 1990-1994; Attorney, Campbell, Patrick & Chin, New York, NY, 1986-1990; Assistant U.S. Attorney, U.S. District Court, Southern District of New York, New York, NY, 1982-1986; Attorney, Davis, Polk & Wardwell, New York, NY, 1980-1982; Law Clerk To Hon. Henry F. Werker, U.S. District Court, Southern District of New York, New York, NY, 1978-1980 **CR:** Adjunct Professor, Fordham Law School, 1986-1994 **MEM:** American Bar Association, Association of the Bar of New York City, Fordham Law Review Alumni Association, New York County Lawyers Association, President, Asian American Bar Association of New York, 1992-1994 **BA:** U.S. Court of Appeals, 40 Foley Square, New York, NY, 10007

CHOI, ROY, T: Chef **I:** Food & Restaurant Services **PB:** Seoul **ED:** Bachelor in Philosophical, California State University, Fullerton; Attended, Culinary Institute America, Hyde Park **C:** Owner, executive chef, Kogi, 2008-; Owner, executive chef, Chego, LA, 2010-; Chef de cuisine, Beverly Hilton, LA, 2007; With, Embassy Suites, Lake Tahoe, California,; With, Le Bernardin, New York City, **AW:** Named one of America's Best New Chefs, Food & Wine Magazine, 2010

CHOMSKY, AVRAM NOAM, T: Philosopher, Political Activist, Historian **I:** Education/Educational Services **DOB:** 12/07/1928 **PB:** Philadelphia **SC:** PA/USA **PT:** Son of William and Elsie (Simonofsky) C.; **SPN:** Carol Doris Schatz, December 24, 1949 (deceased December 19, 2008); **CH:** Aviva, Diane, Harry Alan **ED:** DHL (hon.), Uppsala University, Sweden, 2007; DHL (hon.), University de la Frontera, Temuco, Chila, 2006; DHL (hon.), University de Chile, 2006; Doctorate (hon.), others; Doctorate (hon.), Bologna, 2005; Doctorate (hon.), Ljubljana, 2005; Doctorate (hon.), Scuola Normale Superiore, Pisa, Italy, 1999; LLD, Harvard University, 2000; LLD (hon.), University Buenos Aires, 1996; LittD (hon.), University Calcutta, 2001; LittD (hon.), Cambridge University, England, 1995; LittD (hon.), Visva-Bharati University, Santiniketan, West Bengal, 1980; LittD (hon.), Delhi University, India, 1972; DHL (hon.), University Athens, 2004; DHL (hon.), Central Connecticut State University, 2004; DHL (hon.), University Florence, 2004; DHL (hon.), Central Connecticut State University, 2003; DHL (hon.), Vrije University, Brussels, 2003; DHL (hon.), University National Bogota, Colombia, 2002; LittD (hon.), University London, 1967; DHL (hon.), University National Comahue, Argentina, 2001; DHL (hon.), University Western Ontario, 2000; DHL (hon.), University Toronto, 2000; DHL (hon.), University Connecticut, 1999; DHL (hon.), Columbia University, 1999; DHL (hon.), University Guelph, Can., 1999; DHL (hon.), McGill University, 1998; DHL (hon.), University Rovira i Virgili, Catalonia, 1998; DHL (hon.), Amherst College, 1995; DHL (hon.), Gettysburg College, 1992; DHL (hon.), University Maine, 1992; DHL (hon.), University Massachusetts, 1973; DHL (hon.), Bard College, 1971; DHL (hon.), Swarthmore College, 1970; DHL (hon.), Loyola University, Chicago, 1970; DHL (hon.), The University of Chicago, 1967; DHL (hon.), University of Pennsylvania, 1984; PhD, University of Pennsylvania, 1955; MA, University of Pennsylvania, 1951; BA, University of Pennsylvania, 1949 **C:** Institute Professor, Massachusetts Institute of Technology, 1976-; Ferrari P. Ward Professor Modern Language and Linguistics, Massachusetts Institute of Technology, 1966-76; Professor Modern Languages, Massachusetts Institute of Technology, 1961-76; Faculty Member, Massachusetts Institute of Technology, 1955-61 **CR:** Visiting Professor Columbia University, New York City, 1957-58 Member Institute Advanced Study Princeton University, 1958-59 Linguistic Society Am. Professor UCLA, Summer 1966 Beckman Professor University of Calif.-Berkeley, 1966-67 John Locke Lecturer Oxford University, 1969 Bertrand Russell Memorial Lecturer, Cambridge, 1971 Nehru Memorial Lecturer, New Delhi, 1972 Huizinga Lecturer University Leiden, 1977 Woodbridge Lecturer Columbia University, 1978 Kant Lecturer Stanford University, 1979 Jeanette K. Watson Distinguished Visiting Professor Syracuse University, 1982 Pauling Memorial Lecturer Oregon State University, 1995. **CW:** Author: Syntactic Structures, 1957, Current Issues in Linguistic Theory, 1964, Aspects of the Theory of Syntax, 1965, Cartesian Linguistics, 1966, Topics in the Theory of Generative Grammar, 1966, (with Morris Halle) Sound Pattern of English, 1968, Language and Mind, 1968, American Power and the New Mandarins, 1969, At War with Asia, 1970, Problems of Knowledge and Freedom, 1971, Studies on Semantics in Generative Grammar, 1972, For Reasons of State, 1973, (with Edward Herman) Counterrevolutionary Violence, 1973, Peace in the Middle East, 1974, Logical Structure of Linguistic Theory, 1975, Reflections on Language, 1975, Essays on Form and Interpretation, 1977, Human Rights and American Foreign Policy, 1978, (with Edward Herman) The Political Economy of Human Rights, 2 vols., 1979, Language and Responsibility, 1979, Rules and Representations, 1980, Lectures on Government and Binding, 1981, Concepts and Consequences of the Theory of Government and Binding, 1982, Towards a New Cold War, 1982, Radical Priorities, 1982, Fateful Triangle, 1983, Turning the Tide, 1985, Barriers, 1986, Knowledge of Language, 1986, Pirates and Emperors, 1986, On Power and Ideology, 1987, Language and Problems of Knowledge, 1987, Language in a Psychological Setting, 1987, Generative Grammar, 1987, Culture of Terrorism, 1988, (with Edward Herman) Manufacturing Consent, 1988, Language and Politics, 1988, Necessary Illusions, 1989, Deterring Democracy, 1991, Chronicles of Dissent, 1992, What Uncle Sam Really Wants, 1992, Year 501, 1993, Rethinking Camelot, 1993, Letters from Lexington, 1993, The Prosperous Few and the Restless Many, 1993, Language and Thought, 1994, World Orders, Old and New, 1994, The Minimalist Program, 1995, Powers and Prospects, 1996, The Common Good, 1998, Profits Over People, 1998, The New Military Humanism, 1999, New Horizons in the Study of Language and Mind, 2000, Rogue States, 2000, A New Generation Draws the Line, 2000, Architecture of Language, 2000, 9-11, 2001, Propaganda and the Public Mind, 2001, Understanding Power: The Indispensable Chomsky, 2002, On Nature and Language, 2002, Pirates and Emperors, Old and New, 2002, Middle East Illu-

sions, 2003, Hegemony or Survival: America's Quest for Global Dominance (The American Empire Project), 2003, Imperial Ambitions: Conversations with Noam Chomsky on the Post-9/11 World, 2005, Failed States: The Abuse of Power and the Assault on Democracy, 2006, (with Gilbert Achcar) Perilous Power: The Middle East and U.S. Foreigh Policy, 2006, Interventions, 2007, What We Say Goes: Conversations on U.S. Power in a Changing World, 2007, Inside Lebanon: Journey to a Shatterred Land with Noan and Carol Chomsky, 2007, The Essential Chomsky, 2008, Hopes and Prospects, 2010, New Worlds of Indigenous Resistance, 2010, Making the Future: The Unipolar Imperial Moment, 2010, (with Ilan Pappe) Gaza in Crisis: Reflections on Israel's War Against the Palestinians, 2010, 9-11: Was There an Alternative?, 2011, Making the Future: Occupations, Interventions, Empire and Resistance, 2012, Power Systems: Conversationms on Global Democratic Uprisings and the New Challenges to the U.S. Empire, 2012, Masters of Mankind: Essays and Lectures, 1969-2013, 2015,(Book)The Science of Language, 2012, Occupy: Reflections on Class War, Rebellion and Solidarity 2013,Nuclear War and Environmental Catastrophe, 2013, On Anarchism, 2013, On Western Terrorism: From Hiroshima to Drone Warfare, 2013, Masters of Mankind: Essays and Lectures, 2014, Democracy and Power: The Delhi Lectures, 2014, The Quotable Chomsky, 2014, What Kind of Creatures Are We?, 2015,Because We Say So, 2015, Who Rules the World, 2016, Requiem for the American Dream, 2017, Globel Discontents: Conversation on the Rising Threats to Democracy, 2017 **AW:** Recipient Carl-von-Ossietzky Prize, Oldenburg, Germany, 2004, Society Writers and Artists Award, UN, 2004, Award, Kurdish Human Rights Association, Dyarbakir, 2002, Peace Award, Turkish Publishers' Association, Istanbul, 2002, Adela Dwyer St. Thomas Villanova Peace Award, Villanova University, Philadelphia, 2002, Rising Sun of Mehgarh Award, Dawn Islamabad, 2001, Rabindranath Tagore Centenary Award, Asiatic Society Calcutta, 2000, Benjamin Franklin Institute Award, 1999, Helmholtz Medal, Berlin-Brandenburgische Akad. Wissenschaften, 1996, Loyola Mellon Humanities Award, Loyola University Chicago, 1994, Homer Smith Award, New York University School of Medicine, 1994, Joel Seldin Peace Award, Psychologists for Social Responsibility, 1993, Lannan Lit. Award for Nonfiction, 1992, James Killian Faculty Award, Massachusetts Institute of Technology, 1992, George Orwell Award, National Council Teachers English, 1989, 1987, Kyoto Prize, Kyocera Foundation, 2001, 1988, Distinguished Sci. Contribution Award, American Psychological Association, 1984; Junior Fellow Society Fellows Harvard University, 1951-55,Sean Macbride Peace Prize, 2017, Neil and Saras Smith Medal for Linguistics, 2014, Sydney Peace Prize, 2011, **MEM:** Fellow American Association for the Advancement of Science, Brit. Academy (Corr.), Brit. Psychological Society (Hon.), Royal Anthropological Institute Great Britain, Royal Anthropological Institute Ireland, Utrecht Society Arts & Sciences (Hon.), Gesellschaft für Sprachwissenschaft (Hon.), American Academy Sciences, American Academy Philosophy, Royal Society Can. (foreign), American Philosophical Society; Member American Psychological Association (William James Fellow 1990), National Academy of Sciences, American Academy Arts & Scis., Linguistic Society America, Deutsche Akademie der Naturforscher Leopoldina, Association for Education in Journalism and Mass Communications (Professional Excellence Award 1991). **ACH:** Achievements include development of theory of generative grammar **BA:** Massachusetts Institute of Technology Linguistics and Phi-

losophy 32-D808, 77 Massachusetts Ave, Cambridge, MA, 02139

CHOPRA, PRIYANKA, I: Media & Entertainment **DOB:** 07/18/1982 **PB:** Jamshedpur, Bihar **SC:** India **PT:** Ashok Chopra; Madhu Chopra **CW:** Actor: (films) Thamizhan, 2002, The Hero: Love Story of a Spy, 2003, Andaaz, 2003 (Best Debut - Female, Filmfare Awards, 2004), Plan, 2004, Kismat, 2004, Asambhav, 2004, Mujhse Shaadi Karogi, 2004, Aitraaz, 2004 (Best Performance in a Negative Role, Screen Weekly Awards, 2005, Best Actor in a Villainous Role, Filmfare Awards, 2005), Blackmail, 2005, Karam, 2005, Wagt: The Race Against Time, 2005, Yakeen, 2005, A Sublime Love Story: Barsaat, 2005, Taxi No. 9 2 11: Nau Do Gyarah, 2006, 36 China Town, 2006, Alag: He Is Different...He Is Alone..., 2006, Krrish, 2006, Don, 2006, Salaam-E-Ishq, 2007, Big Brother, 2007, Love Story 2050, 2008, God Tussi Great Ho, 2008, Chamku, 2008, Drona, 2008, Fashion, 2008 (Best Actress, Screen Weekly Awards, 2009, Best Actress, Filmfare Awards, 2009), Dostana, 2008, Kaminey: The Scoundrels, 2009, What's Your Raashee, 2009, Pyaar Impossible!, 2010, Anjaana Anjaani, 2010, 7 Khoon Maaf, 2011 **AW:** Recipient Neilsen Box Office Star of Asia award, Asian Film Awards, 2009

CHRISTEN, MORGAN BRENDA, T: Federal Judge, Former State Supreme Court Justice **I:** Law and Legal Services **DOB:** 12/05/1961 **PB:** Chehalis **SC:** WA/USA **ED:** JD, Golden Gate University School of Law, 1986; BA, University of Washington, 1983 **C:** Judge, U.S. Court of Appeals, Ninth Circuit, 2011-Present; Associate Justice, Alaska Supreme Court, 2009-2011; Presiding Judge, Alaska Superior Court, 2005-2009; Judge, Alaska Superior Court, Anchorage, AK, 2001-2009; Partner, Preston, Gates & Ellis, 1992-2001; Associate, Preston, Gates & Ellis, 1987-1992; Law Clerk, Hon. Brian Shortell, Alaska Superior Court, 1986-1987 **CIV:** Board Director, Rasmuson Foundation, Alaska Community Foundation **AW:** Community Outreach Award, Alaska Supreme Court, 2008, Athena Society Award, Anchorage Chamber of Commerce, 2004, Light of Hope Award, 2004 **BAR:** State of Alaska, 1987 **BA:** 95 7th Street, Los Angeles, CA, 94103

CHRISTIE, JULIE, T: Actress **I:** Media & Entertainment **PB:** Chukua **SC:** India **PT:** Frank St. John; Rosemary Ramsden Christie **MS:** Married **SPN:** Duncan Campbell (Jan, 26, 2008) **ED:** Student, Central School Dramatic Art, London; Student, Brighton College Tech. Professional **CW:** Debut in Brit. TV series, A is for Andromeda, 1962; (TV films) Dadah is Death, 1988, The Railway Station Man, 1992; (TV miniseries) Karaoke, 1996; (films) Crooks Anonymous, 1962, The Fast Lady, 1963, Billy Liar, 1963, Young Cassidy, 1964, Darling, 1965 (New York Film Critics Cir. award for Best Actress, 1965, Best Actress in a Leading Role, Academy Motion Picture Arts and Sciences, 1966, Best Brit. Actress, Brit. Academy Film and TV Awards, 1966, Golden Laurel award, 1966, Best Actress, National Board Review, 1966), Dr. Zhivago, 1965, Fahrenheit 451, 1966, Far From the Madding Crowd, 1967, Petulia, 1968, In Search of Gregory, 1969, The Go-Between, 1971, McCabe and Mrs. Miller, 1971, Don't Look Now, 1974, Shampoo, 1975, Demon Seed, 1977, Heaven Can Wait, 1978, The Return of the Soldier, 1981, Memoirs of a Survivor, 1981, Heat and Dust, 1983, The Gold Diggers, 1984, The Tattooed Memory, 1986, Fathers and Sons, 1988, Power, 1986, Miss Mary, 1987, (La Mémoire Tatouée, Fools of Fortune, 1990, The Railway Station, 1991, Hamlet, 1996, Dragonheart, 1996, Afterglow, 1997 (New York Film Critics Cir. award for Best Actress 1997, National Society Film Critics award for Best Actress 1997, Best Ensemble Cast, Fort Lauderdale

International Film Festival, 1997, Best Female Lead, Ind. Spirit Awards, 1998), Belphegor-Le fantome du Louvre, 2001, No Such Thing, 2001, Snapshots, 2002, I'm with Lucy, 2002, Troy, 2004, Harry Potter and the Prisoner of Azkaban, 2004, Finding Neverland, 2004, The Secret Life of Words, 2005, Away from Her, 2006 (Best Actress award, National Board Review, 2007, New York Film Critics Circle, 2007, Best Performance by an Actress in a Leading Role, Phoenix Film Critics Society, 2007, 2007 Best Actress, Critics Choice award, Broadcast Film Critics Association, 2008, Best Performance by an Actress in a Motion Picture-Drama, Golden Globe award, Hollywood Foreign Press Association, 2008, Outstanding Performance by a Female in a Leading Role, Screen Actors Guild, 2008, Best Actress, Online Film Critics Society, 2008), Glorious 39, 2009, Red Riding Hood, 2011, The Company You Keep, 2012; appeared with Birmingham Repertory Co., 1963, Royal Shakespeare Co., 1964; appeared in plays Old Times, Wyndham's, 1995.

CHU, JUDY MAY, T: U.S. Representative from California, former state agency administrator **I:** Government Administration/Government Relations/Government Services **DOB:** 07/07/1955 **PB:** L.A. **PT:** Daughter of Judson and May Chu; **ED:** PhD, California School Professional Psychology, 1979; MA in Clinical Psychology, California School Professional Psychology, 1977; BA in Math., UCLA, 1974 **C:** Member, US House Education & Labor Committee, 2009-; Member, US Congress from 27th California District, 2013-; Member, Committee on Armed Services, Committee on Science, Shape and Technology, Committee on Small Business; Member, US Congress from 32nd California District, 2009-13; Vice chair, California State Board Equalization, 2009; Chair, California State Board Equalization, 2008; Member, District 4, California State Board Equalization, 2007-09; Member District 49, California State Assembly, 2001-06; Mayor, Monterey Park City Council, 1995-95; Mayor, Monterey Park City Council, 1990-91; Member, Monterey Park City Council, 1988-2001; Professor, East L.A. College, Monterey Park, 1988-2001; Associate professor, L.A. City College, 1981-88; Lecturer, UCLA, 1980-86 **CIV:** Board directors, Garvey School District, 1985-88 Chair, LA Unified School District, 1984-85 Chair, Commission for Sex Equity, **CW:** Author, editor Linking Our Lives: Chinese American Women in Los Angeles, 1984; contributor articles to professional journals **AW:** Named L.A. Outstanding Founder, 1995, Vol. of Year, San Gabriel Valley Chapter United Way, 1989, Democrat of Year, 59th Assembly District Democratic Committee, 1989; named one of The 88 Leaders for 1988, L.A. Times, 1988; recipient Leadership award, West San Gabriel Valley chapter American Red Cross, Award for Excellence in Public Service, UCLA Alumni, 1991, Public Service award, Pacific Legal Center, 1989, Achievement award, Asian Pacific Family Center, 1980 **MEM:** Mem.: Soroptimists **PA:** Democrat **BA:** 1023 Longworth House Office Building, Washington, DC, 20515

CHURCH, GEORGE MCDONALD, T: Geneticist, Educator, Researcher **I:** Sciences **DOB:** 08/28/1954 **PB:** MacDill AFB **SC:** FL/USA **PT:** Henry Stewart McDonald, III; Virginia Anne Strong **ED:** PhD in Biochemistry & Molecular Biology, Harvard University, Cambridge, MA (1984); BA in Zoology & Chemistry, Duke University, Durham, NC (1974) **C:** Robert Winthrop Professor of Genetics, Harvard Medical School (2015-Present); Director, National Human Genome Research Institute, Centers of Excellence in Genomic Science, Harvard Medical School/Washington University (2004-Present); Senior Associate, Broad Institute, Harvard Medical School/Massachusetts Institute of Technology

(2006-Present); Director, DOE Genomes to Life Center, Harvard Medical School/Massachusetts Institute of Technology (2002-Present); Director, Lipper Center for Computational Genetics, Harvard Medical School (1997-Present); Professor of Genetics, Harvard Medical School (1998-Present); Co-founder, Genome Center (1990); Member, Wyss Institute; Director, National Institutes of Health, Center for Excellence in Genomic Science, Harvard Medical School; Assistant Professor to Associate Professor of Genetics, Harvard Medical School (1986-1998); Research Fellow of Anatomy, University of California, San Francisco (1985-1986); Scientist, Biogen Research Corporation, Cambridge, MA (1984); Life Sciences Research Foundation Fellow (1985-1986); National Science Foundation Predoctoral Fellow (1974-1975) **CR:** Scientific Board Advisor, Cellular Dynamics International, Inc.; Science Advisor, PharmoRx Medical Advisor, DNAdirect; Member, Scientific Advisory Board, Codon Devices, Genomatica; Helicos Senior Associate, Broad Institute of Harvard & Massachusetts Institute of Technology (2006-Present); Director, Harvard/MIT DOE Genomes-to-Life Center (2002-Present); Lipper Center Computational Genetics (1997-Present); With Howard Hughes Medical Institute (1986-1997) **CW:** Member, Editorial Board, Nature/European Molecular Biology Organization - MSB; Member, Editorial Board, Genome Biology; Member, Editorial Board, Omics; Member, Editorial Board, BioMedNet; Contributor, Articles to Science Journals **AW:** Bower Award & Prize for Achievement in Science, Franklin Institute (2011); American Society for Microbiology Biotechnology Research Award (2009); World Economic Forum Technology Pioneer Award (2008); Named Time's 100 Most Influential, TIME Magazine (2017) **MEM:** National Academy of Sciences **ACH:** Achievements include developing, with Walter Gilbert, the first direct genomic sequencing method, 1984; founder Personal Genome Project **H:** Water-skiing; Swimming; Sailing; Tennis; Skiing; Bicycling; Scuba Diving; Camping; Rock Climbing

CICILLINE, DAVID NICOLA, T: U.S. Representative from Rhode Island **I:** Government Administration/Government Relations/Government Services **DOB:** 07/15/1961 **PB:** Providence **SC:** RI/USA **ED:** JD Cum Laude, Georgetown University Law Center, Washington, 1986; BA in Political Sci., Magna Cum Laude, Brown University, Providence, 1983 **C:** Member, U.S. House Small Business Committee, 2011-; Chair, Democratic Policy and Communications Committee, 2017-,Member, Committee on Judiciary; Member, U.S. House Foreign Affairs Committee, 2011-; Member, U.S. Congress from 1st Rhode Island District, 2011-; Private Practice, Providence, 1987-; Mayor, City of Providence, 2003-11; Member District 4, Rhode Island House of Reps., 1995-2003; Staff Attorney, Pub. Defender Service, Washington, 1986-87 **CR:** President National Conference Democratic Mayors, 2008 Adjunct Professor Law Roger Williams University School of Law, Bristol, Rhode Island **CIV:** Member, Rhode Island Criminal Justice Commission, Board of Directors, Nickerson Community Center, Board of Directors, Mount Hope Neighborhood Association, Board of Directors, Langston Hughes Center for Arts, Board of Directors, Rhode Island Project AIDS, Board of Directors, Center Individualized Teaching & Education, Chairman Board of Directors, Very Special Arts Rhode Island, Vol. Attorney, ACLU, Providence, 1990- **CW:** Author (contributing): Criminal Practice Institute Trial Manual, 1987 **MEM:** Mem.: Rhode Island Association Criminal Defense Lawyers, Rhode Island Bar Association, DC Bar Association, Pub. Defender Alumni Association, National Association Criminal Defense Lawyers **PA:** Democrat

CLAPTON, ERIC, T: Guitarist, Singer **I:** Media & Entertainment **DOB:** 03/30/1945 **PB:** Ripley, Surrey **SC:** England **PT:** Edward Fryer Clapton; Patricia Molly Clapton **MS:** Married **SPN:** Melia McEnery (January 1, 2002); Patricia Anne Boyd, March 27, 1979 (div. 1988) **CH:** Julie Rose, Ella May, Sophie; Conor (Deceased) **ED:** Student, Kingston Art School **C:** Solo artist, 1970—; Guitarist, The Roosters, 1963; Guitarist, singer, Derek and the Dominos, 1970—1971; Guitarist, Delaney and Bonnie & Friends, 1969—1970; Guitarist, singer, Blind Faith, 1969; Guitarist, singer, Cream, 1966—1968; Guitarist, Powerhouse, 1966; Guitarist, singer, John Mayall's Bluesbreakers, 1965—1966; Guitarist, The Yardbirds, 1963—1965; Guitarist, Casey Jones & the Engineers, 1963 **CIV:** Founder Crossroads Centre, 1997— **CW:** Guitarist (albums with The Yardbirds) Five Live Yardbirds, 1964, For Your Love, 1965, Having A Rave Up, 1965, guitarist, singer (albums with John Mayall's Bluesbreakers) Bluesbreakers with Eric Clapton, 1966, (albums with Cream) Fresh Cream, 1966, Disraeli Gears, 1967, Wheels of Fire, 1968, Goodbye, 1969, Live Cream, 1970, Live Cream Volume II, 1972, Strange Brew: The Very Best of Cream, 1983, Those Were the Days, 1997, BBC Sessions, 2003, Cream Gold, 2005, Royal Albert Hall London 2-6 May 2005, 2005, guitarist (albums with Blind Faith) Blind Faith, 1969; guitarist (albums with Delaney and Bonnie & Friends) On Tour with Eric Clapton, 1970; singer, guitarist (albums with Derek and the Dominos) Layla And Other Assorted Love Songs, 1970, In Concert, 1973, The Layla Sessions: The 20th Anniversary Edition, 1990, Live at the Fillmore, 1994, (solo albums) Eric Clapton, 1970, 461 Ocean Boulevard, 1974, There's One in Every Crowd, 1975, E.C. Was Here, 1975, No Reason to Cry, 1976, Slowhand, 1977, Backless, 1978, Just One Night, 1980, Another Ticket, 1981, Time Pieces: Best of Eric Clapton, 1982, Money and Cigarettes, 1983, Behind the Sun, 1985, Time Pieces Vol. II 'Live' in the 70's, 1985, August, 1987, Crossroads, 1988, One Moment in Time, 1988, Journeyman, 1989, 24 Nights, 1991, Unplugged, 1992 (Grammy awards for Album of Year, Best Rock Vocal Performance, 1993), From the Cradle, 1994 (Grammy award for Best Traditional Blues Album), The Cream of Clapton, 1995, Crossroads II: Live in the Seventies, 1996, Retail Therapy, 1997, Pilgrim, 1998, Clapton Chronicles: The Best of Eric Clapton 1981-1999, 1999, The Blues, 1999, Reptile, 2001 (Grammy award for Best Pop Instrumental Perf.), One More Car, One More Rider, 2002, Me and Mr. Johnson, 2004, Sessions for Robert J., 2004, Back Home, 2005, Complete Clapton, 2007, Clapton, 2010, Old Sock, 2013, The Breeze: An Appreciation of JJ Cale, 2014, I Still Do, 2016, (soundtracks) Rush, 1992, (soundtracks with The Band & others) The Last Waltz, 1976, (albums with others) A Concert for Bangladesh, 1972 (Grammy award for Album of Year), Rainbow Concert, 1973, Bob Dylan 30th Anniversary Concert Celebration, 1993, (albums with B.B. King) Riding with the King, 2000 (Grammy award for Best Trad. Blues Album), (albums with J.J. Cale) The Road to Escondido, 2006, (albums with Steve Winwood) Live From Madison Square Garden, 2009, (songs) Tears in Heaven, 1993 (Grammy awards for Song of Year, Record of Year, Male Pop Vocal Performance, 1993), Change the World, 1997 (Grammy award for Song of Year, 1997), My Father's Eyes, 1999 (Grammy award for Best Male Pop Vocal Performance, 1999); producer (with Rod Stewart): (albums) Beginnings, 2004; composer: (songs) BBC miniseries Edge of Darkness, 1986, (film score) Lethal Weapon, 1986, Homeboy, 1988, Lethal Weapon 2, 1989, The Van, 1996, Nil by Mouth, 1997; co-composer (film score) Lethal Weapon 3, 1992; performer: (films) The Concert for Bangladesh, 1972, The Last

Waltz, 1978, Bob Dylan 30th Anniversary Concert Celebration, 1993, The Rolling Stones Rock 'N' Roll Circus, 1996, numerous songs written for films throughout the years; author: Clapton: The Autobiography, 2007 **AW:** Named one of The 100 Greatest Guitarists of All-Time, Rolling Stone magazine; named to The Rock & Roll Hall of Fame, (as member of The Yardbirds, 1992, as member of Cream, 1993, as solo artist, 2000); recipient Silver Clef Award Outstanding Achievement in World of British Music, presented by Princess Michael of Kent, 1983, Lifetime Achievement Award, British Phonographic Institute, 1987, presented with silver model of a Fender Stratocaster by Prince Charles to commemorate 25th year in music industry, 1988, Best Guitarist Award, International Rock Awards, 1989, Living Legend Award, 1990, W.C. Handy Award For Blues, 16th Annual Ceremony, 1995, Man of Year Award music: solo artist, GQ Magazine, 1999, Stevie Ray Vaughan, Music Assistance Program, 1999, Commander of the British Empire, Her Majesty Queen Elizabeth II, 2003, Grammy Lifetime Achievement award, (as member of Cream), 2006, Commandeur of the Ordre des Artes et des Lettres, 2017 **ACH:** Achievements include minor planet named "(4305) Clapton" in his honor, 1990; first triple inductee into Rock & Roll Hall of Fame **BA:** Warner Brothers Records, 3300 Warner Blvd, Burbank, CA, 91505

CLARK, KATHERINE MARLEA, T: U.S. Representative from Massachusetts, Former State Legislator **I:** Government Administration/Government Relations/Government Services **DOB:** 07/17/1963 **PB:** New Haven **SC:** CT/USA **PT:** Daughter of Harrison C. Clark; **ED:** MPA, Harvard University John F. Kennedy School Government, Massachusetts; JD, Cornell University Law School, Ithaca, New York, 1989; BA, St. Lawrence University, Canton, New York, 1985 **C:** Member, U.S. House Natural Resources Committee, 2014-; Member, House Appropriations Committee; Member, U.S. Congress from 5th Massachusetts District, Washington, 2013-; Member Middlesex & Essex District, Massachusetts State Senate, 2011-13; Member 32nd Middlesex District, Massachusetts House of Reps., 2008-11; Chief policy division, Office of Massachusetts Attorney General,; General counsel, Massachusetts Office of Childcare Services,; Private practice attorney,; Attorney, Colorado District Attorney's Council,; Prosecutor, Colorado Attorney General's Office, 1991-93; Clerk, Federal Court, 1990-91 **CR:** Chair Melrose School Committee, Massachusetts, 2001-03, member, 2001-07 **AW:** Named Legislator of Year, Citizens Public Schools, 2010 **PA:** Democrat

CLARK, MARCIA RACHEL, T: Lawyer **I:** Law and Legal Services **DOB:** 08/31/1953 **PB:** Berkeley **SC:** CA/USA **PT:** Abraham I. Kleks **ED:** JD, Southwestern University, 1979; BA in Political Sci., UCLA, 1974 **C:** Prosecutor, LA County District Atty.'s Office, LA, 1981-97; Attorney, Brodey and Price, LA, 1979-81 **CR:** Host Judge and Jury for MSNBC, Equal Time for CNBC substitute host Rivera Live legal corr. Entertainment Tonight legal analyst, expert commentator NBC, CNBC, MSNBC, 1998-2000 **CW:** Co-author (with Teresa Carpenter): Without a Doubt, 1997; author: Guilt By Association, 2011, Guilt By Degrees, 2012, Killer Ambition, 2013, The Competition, 2014, Blood Defense, 2016, (short stories) If I'm Dead, 2013, Trouble In Paradise, 2013; executive consultant, co-writer (TV series) For the People, Lifetime TV, 2002, host Lie Detector, FOX, 1998, contributor The Daily Beast, guest appearances Oprah Winfrey Show, Larry King Show, the Today Show, The Early Show, Good Morning America, and others, provides legal commentary on Anderson Cooper 360 and Issues with Jane Velez Mitchell,(Books) Blood Defense, 2016, Moral Defense, 2016, Snap Judgement, 2017 **BAR:** California 1979

CLARKE, YVETTE DIANE, T: U.S. Representative from New York **I:** Government Administration/Government Relations/Government Services **DOB:** 11/21/1964 **PB:** Brooklyn **SC:** NY/USA **PT:** Daughter of Una S.T. Clarke. **ED:** Attended, Medgar Evers College; Attended, Oberlin College, 1982-86 **C:** Secretary, Congressional Black Caucus, 2011-; Member, Committee on Energy and Commerce, Committee on Small Business; Member, US Congress from 9th New York District, 2013-; Member, US Congress from 11th New York District, Washington, 2007-13; Councilwoman District 40, New York City Council, 2002-07; Director business develop., Bronx Empowerment Zone,; Director youth programs, Hospital League / 1199 Training & Upgrading Fund, 1991; Executive assistant to Assemblywoman Barbara Clark, New York State Assembly,; Legis. aide to Senator Velmanette Montgomery, New York State Senate, 1986; Child care specialist, Erasmus Neighborhood Federation, 1985 **AW:** Named to Power 150, Ebony magazine, 2008 **PA:** Democrat

CLAY, ERIC L., T: Federal Judge **I:** Law and Legal Services **DOB:** 01/18/1948 **PB:** Durham **SC:** NC/USA **ED:** JD, Yale University, 1972; BA, University of North Carolina, 1969 **CT:** Bar: US Court Appeals (DC cir.) 1994, US District Court (we. District) Michigan 1987, US Court Appeals (6th cir.) 1978, US Supreme Court 1977, US District Court (eastern district) Michigan 1972, Michigan 1972 **C:** Judge, U.S. Court Appeals (6th cir.), Detroit, 1997-; Attorney, Shareholder, Director, Lewis, White & Clay, Professional Corporation, Detroit, 1973-97; Law clerk to Judge Damon J. Keith, U.S. District Court (eastern district) Michigan, 1972-73 **CR:** Hearing Panelist Attorney Discipline Board, State of Michigan, 1985-97 **AW:** Fellow John Hay Whitney, Yale University **MEM:** Mem.: American Bar Association, Wolverine Bar Association, Detroit Bar Association, National Association Railroad Trial Counsel, National Bar Association, U.S. Sixth Judicial Conference (Life), Phi Beta Kappa **BA:** Potter Stewart US Courthouse, 100 E 5th St, Cincinnati, OH, 45202-3988

CLAY, WILLIAM LACY JR., T: U.S. Representative from Missouri **I:** Government Administration/Government Relations/Government Services **DOB:** 07/27/1956 **PB:** St. Louis, July 27, 1956 **PT:** Son of William Lacy and Carol Ann (Johnson) C.; **MS:** Married **SPN:** Ivie Lewellen, January 24, 1992 **ED:** LLD (hon.), Harris-Stowe State University; LLD (hon.), Lincoln University; Student, Harvard University John F. Kennedy School Government; BS in Government & Politics, University Maryland, College Park, 1983 **CT:** Cert. paralegal; lic. real estate salesman, Missouri **C:** Member, US Congress from 1st Missouri District, 2001-; Member,- Committee on Financial Services, Committee on Oversight and Government Reform; Member District 4, Missouri State Senate, 1991-2001; Member District 59, Missouri House of Reps., Jefferson City, 1983-91; Assistant doorman, US House of Representatives, 1978-83 **CIV:** Chairman Missouri Jesse Jackson 1988 Presidential Campaign Jackson del. to 1988 Democratic National Convention committeeman to Democratic National Committee board directors William L. Clay Scholarship & Research Fund., Congressional Black Caucus Foundation **AW:** Recipient Award for Political Leadership, National Newspapers Publishers Association Foundation, 2011, Health Care Advocate award, Missourians for Single Payer, 2006 **MEM:** Member Americans for Democratic Action (Outstanding Legis. Missouri chapter 1985, 86). **PA:** Democrat **BA:** 2428 Rayburn House Office Building, Washington, DC, 20515

CLEAVER, EMANUEL JR., T: U.S. Representative from Missouri, Former Mayor, Minister **I:** Government Administration/Government Relations/Government Services **DOB:** 10/26/1944 **PB:** Waxahachie **SC:** TX/USA **PT:** Lucky Cleaver, Marie (McKnight) Cleaver **MS:** Married **SPN:** Dianne Donaldson, 6/1970 **CH:** Evan Donaldson, Emanuel, III, Emiel, Marissa Dianne **ED:** Honorary DD, Baker University, 1988; MDiv, St. Paul School of Theology, Kansas City, MO, 1974; BS in Sociology, Prairie View Agricultural and Mechanical University, Texas, 1968 **CT:** Ordained to Ministry, United Methodist Church **C:** U.S. Congress From Fifth Missouri District, 2005-Present; Senior Pastor, St. James United Methodist Church, Kansas City, MO, 1969-Present; Chairman, Congressional Black Caucus (Canadian Broadcasting Co.), 2011-2013; Host, Under the Clock, KCUR-FM Public Radio, Kansas City, MO, 2000-2004; Special Advisor, Secretary Andrew Cuomo, U.S. Department of Housing & Urban Development (HUD), 1999-2000; Mayor, City of Kansas City, 1991-1999; Mayor Pro-Tem, City of Kansas City, 1987-1991; Council Member, City of Kansas City, 1979-1991; Committee on Financial Services **CR:** Lecturer to Churches, Schools, Civic and Social Organizations Nationwide **CIV:** Mid-Central Regional Vice President, Southern Christian Leadership Conference; Founder, Co-Chair, Kansas City Harmony in a World of Difference; Chairman, Kansas City Council on Plans and Zoning Committee, 1984-1987; Policy and Rules Committee, 1987-1991 **AW:** Centurions Leadership Award, Greater Kansas City Chamber of Commerce, 1987, William Yates Distinguished Service Medallion, William Jewel College, 1987, Public Service Award, American-Jewish Committee, 1991, Juneteenth Man of the Year Award, Black Archives of Mid-America Inc., 1991, Distinguished Citizen Award, Greater Kansas City Urban Affairs Council, 1991, Community Service/Leadership Award, Webster University, 1991, Distinguished Service Award, Park College, 1991, Friend of the Youth Award, Boys & Girls Clubs, 1991, Drum Major for Justice Award, Southern Christian Leadership Conference, 1991, Outstanding Contributions to Black Community Award, Concerned Citizens Black Clergy of Atlanta, 1991, 100 Most Influential Kansas Citizens Award, Kansas City Globe, 1991-1993, Rainbow Award, 1992, Bridge Builders Award, Kansas City Globe, 1992, Harold L. Holiday Senior Civil Rights Award, National Association for the Advancement of Colored People, 1992, Distinguished Graduate Award, St. Paul School of Theology, 1993, Kansas City Anti-Apartheid Award, 1993, James C. Kirkpatrick Excellence for Government Award, 1993, Distinguished Citizen of the Midwest Award, National Conference of Christians and Jews, 1993, Governor Award for Local Elected Official of the Year, State of Missouri, 1994, Most Influential Black Americans, Ebony Magazine, 2006, Power 150, Ebony Magazine, 2008 **MEM:** National Association for the Advancement of Colored People, Greater Kansas City Chamber of Commerce, Alpha Phi Alpha **PA:** Democrat **BA:** U.S. House of Representatives, 2335 Rayburn House Office Bldg, Washington, DC, 20515

CLEMENS, ROGER, T: Retired Baseball Pitcher **I:** Athletics **DOB:** 08/04/1962 **PB:** Dayton **SC:** OH/USA **PT:** Son of Bess Clemens and Woody Booher (Stepfather); **ED:** Attended, University of Texas at Austin, 1982-83; Attended, San Jacinto Junior College, Pasadena, Texas, 1981 **C:** Pitcher, Sugar Land Skeeters, Atlantic League, Texas, 2012; Pitcher, Houston Astros, 2004-06; Pitcher, New

York Yankees, 2007; Pitcher, New York Yankees, 1999-2003; Pitcher, Toronto Blue Jays, 1997-98; Pitcher, Boston Red Sox, 1984-96 **CR:** Pitcher Team USA, World Baseball Classic, 2006 **CIV:** Co-founder, Roger Clemens Foundation, 1992 **AW:** Named Sportsman of Year, March of Dimes, 2001, Pitcher of Year, 2001, 1997-98, 1991, 1986, Major League Player of Year, Sporting News, 1986, All-Star Game MVP, 1986, Am. League MVP, 1986, Boston Red Sox Rookie of Year, 1984; Named to MLB All-Century Team, 1999, National League All-Star Team, 2004-05, Am. League All-Star Team, 2003, 2001, 1997-98, 1990-92, 1988, 1986; Recipient Cy Young Award, National League, 2004, Cy Young award, Am. League, 2001, 1997-98, 1991, 1986-87, Thomas A. Yawkey Award, Boston Red Sox, 1986,World Series Champion, 1999, 2000, Triple Crown, 1997-98, ERA Leader, 1986, 1990-1992, 1997, 1998, 2005, AL Strikeout Leader, 1988, 1991,1996-1998 **ACH:** Achievements include holds MLB record for strikeouts in a single game (20); recorded 300th career win and 4,000 career strikeouts, June 13, 2003; being a member of World Series Champion New York Yankees, 1999, 2000; holds MLB record for Cy Young Awards (7), 2004; holds MLB record for oldest player to win Cy Young Award (age 42), 2004; became 8th pitcher to reach 350 career wins, July 2, 2007

CLEMENT, EDITH BROWN, T: Federal Judge **I:** Law and Legal Services **DOB:** 04/29/1948 **PB:** Birmingham **SC:** AL/USA **PT:** Erskine John Brown; Edith (Burrus) Brown **MS:** Married **SPN:** Rutledge Carter Clement Jr. (9/3/1972) **CH:** Rutledge Carter III, Catherine Lanier **ED:** JD, Tulane University (1972); BA, University of Alabama (1969) **C:** Judge, U.S. Court of Appeals for the Fifth Circuit, New Orleans, LA (2001-Present); Chief Judge, U.S. Court of Appeals for the Fifth Circuit (2001); Judge, U.S. District Court for the Eastern District of Louisiana, New Orleans, LA (1991-2001); Partner, Jones, Walker, Waechter, Poitevent, Carrere & Denegre, New Orleans, LA (1975-1991); Law Clerk to Honorable Herbert W. Christenberry, U.S. District Court, New Orleans, LA (1973-1975) **MEM:** Fellow, Louisiana Bar Foundation; Life Member, Louisiana Bar Foundation; American Law Institute; Louisiana Bar Association; Federalist Society Advisory Board, Louisiana Chapter; Maritime Law Association of the U.S.; Federal Bar Association; American Inn of Court; Committee Administration Office of the Judicial Conference of the U.S., Fifth Circuit Judicial Council; Tulane Law School American Inn of Court **BAR:** Louisiana State Bar Association (1973) **BA:** US Ct Appeals 5th Cir, 600 Camp Street Rm 200, New Orleans, LA, 70130-3313

CLINTON, BILL, T: 42nd President of the U.S. **I:** Government Administration/Government Relations/Government Services **DOB:** 08/19/1946 **PB:** Hope **SC:** AR/USA **PT:** Son of Virginia Dell Cassidy and William Jefferson Blythe IV **MS:** Married **SPN:** Hillary Diane Rodham (10/11/1975) **CH:** Chelsea Victoria **ED:** BS in International Affairs, Georgetown University, 1968; Postgrad., Oxford University, 1970; JD, Yale Law School, 1973; Doctor in Public Service (hon.), Northeastern University, 1993; LHD (hon.), Pace University, 2006; LHD (hon.), University of New Hampshire, 2007; LHD (hon.), West Virginia University, 2010; LLD (hon.), University of Hong Kong, 2008; LLD (hon.), McGill University, 2009; LHD (hon.), Mount Sinai School of Medicine, 2010; LHD (hon.), University of Central Missouri, 2011; Doctor (hon.), Mediterranean University, 2011; LHD (hon.), University of Central Florida, 2013; Doctor (hon.), University of Edinburgh, 2013 **C:** Co-chmn., Interim Haiti Recovery Commission, 2010—2011; Special Envoy to Haiti, UN, 2009—2013; Special Envoy

for Tsunami Recovery, UN, 2005—2007; President, US, Washington, DC, 1993-2001; Of Counsel, Wright, Lindsey & Jennings, Little Rock, Arkansas, 1981-82; Governor, State of Arkansas, Little Rock, Arkansas, 1979-81, 83-92; Attorney General, State of Arkansas, Little Rock, Arkansas, 1977-79; Private Law Practice, 1973-76; Professor of Law, University of Arkansas School Law, Fayetteville, 1973-76 **CR:** Chairman Southern Growth Policies Board, 1985-86; Chairman, National Constitution Center, Philadelphia, 2009-13, Chairman, Advisory Board Teneo Holdings, LLC, 2011- **CIV:** Chairman, Education Commission of the States, 1986-87; Member, Task Force on Adolescent Education, Carnegie Foundation; Chairman Dem. Leadership Council, 1990-91; Honorary Co-chair, Club of Madrid; Co-chair, Families of Freedom Fund; Chairman Global Fairness Initiative; Founder, American India Foundation, 2001; Advisory Board, Co-chair, International AIDS Trust **CW:** Author: Between Hope and History: Meeting America's Challenges for the 21st Century, 1996, My Life, 2004 (Grammy Award for Spoken Word Album, 2005, Publishers Weekly Bestseller, New York Times Bestseller, Biography of Year, Brit. Book Awards, 2005, Audiobook of Year, Audio Publication Association, 2005), Giving: How Each of Us Can Change the World, 2007, Back to Work: Why We Need Smart Government for a Strong Economy, 2011 **AW:** Rhodes Scholar, University College, Oxford University, 1968-70; Named Knight Commander of the Most Courteous Order of Lesotho, 2005, Fellow World Tech. Network, 2006, Person of Year, People for the Ethical Treatment of Animals, 2010, Father of Year, National Father's Day Council, 2013; Named One of The 100 Most Influential People in the World, TIME magazine, 2004-06, 2010, The Global Elite, Newsweek magazine, 2008, The 50 Highest-Earning Political Figures, 2010, The World's Most Powerful People, Forbes magazine, 2009, 2011-14; Recipient, James Madison Award for Distinguished Public Service Princeton University American Whig-Cliosophic Society, 2000, Medal for Distg. Public Service US Department Defense, 2001, Jimmy & Rosalynn Carter Award for Humanitarian Contributions to the Health of Humankind, National Foundation Infectious Diseases, 2005, Pasteur Foundation Award, 2005, Citizen of World Award, UN Correspondents Association, 2006, Distinguished International Leadership Award, The Atlantic Council, 2010, Advocate for Change GLAAD Media Award, 2013, Presidential Medal of Freedom, The White House, 2013, Happy Heart Fund Lifetime Achievement Award, 2014; Co-recipient Liberty Medal, National Constitution Center, 2006 **MEM:** Member American Bar Association, Arkansas Bar Association, National Governors Association (vice chairman 1986, chairman 1986-87, co-chmn. task force for education 1990-92); Fellow American Association for the Advancement of Science **ACH:** Established the William J. Clinton Foundation, which includes the Clinton Presidential Center (library, foundation offices, and Clinton School of Public Service at the University of Arkansas) on November 18, 2004. The foundation's purpose is to focus on four major areas: health security; economic empowerment; leadership development and citizen service; and racial, ethnic and religious reconciliation. **PA:** Democrat **BA:** William J Clinton Foundation, 55 W 125th St, New York, NY, 10027

CLINTON, HILLARY, T: 67th U.S. Secretary of State, Former First Lady **I:** Government Administration/Government Relations/Government Services **DOB:** 10/26/1947 **PB:** Chicago **SC:** IL/USA **PT:** Hugh Ellsworth Rodham, Dorothy (Howell) Rodham **MS:** Married **SPN:** Bill Clinton, 10/11/1975 **CH:** Chelsea **ED:** Honorary LLD, University of St. Andrews, 2013; Honorary LLD, Yale University,

2009; Honorary LLD, Rensselaer Polytechnic Institute, 2005; Honorary LLD, Marymount Manhattan College, 2005; Honorary LLD, University of Ulster, 2004; Honorary DHL, Manhattanville College, 2004; Honorary DHL, Pace University, 2003; Honorary DHL, Ohio University, 1997; Honorary Doctorate in Public Service, University of Maryland, College Park, MD, 1996; Honorary DHL, Drew University, 1996; Honorary LLD, San Francisco State University, 1995; Honorary LLD, University of Minnesota, 1995; Honorary LLD, University of Illinois, 1994; Honorary Doctorate in Public Service, George Washington University, 1994; Honorary LLD, University of Michigan, 1993; Honorary LLD, University of Pennsylvania, 1993; Honorary LLD, University of Sunderland, 1993; Honorary LLD, Hendrix College, 1992; Honorary LLD, Arkansas College, 1988; Honorary LLD, University of Arkansas, Little Rock, AR, 1985; JD, Yale Law School, 1973; BA in Political Science, Wellesley College, With High Honors, 1969 **C:** Creator, Onward Together, 2017-Present; Secretary, U.S. Department of State, Washington, DC, 2009—2013; U.S. Senate Armed Services Committee, 2003—2011; U.S. Senate Health, Education, Labor & Pensions Committee, 2001—2011; U.S. Senate Environment & Public Works Committee, 2001—2011; U.S. Senator From New York, 2001—2009; U.S. Senate Budget Committee, 2001—2002; First Lady Of The U.S., Washington, DC, 1993—2001; Chair, Presidential Task Force On National Health Care Reform, 1993; First Lady Of Arkansas, Little Rock, AR, 1983—1992; First Lady Of Arkansas, Little Rock, AR, 1979—1981; Assistant Professor of Law, University of Arkansas School of Law, Little Rock, AR, 1979-1980; Partner, Rose Law Firm, Little Rock, AR, 1977-1992; Assistant Professor of Law, Director of Legal Aid Clinic, University of Arkansas School of Law, Fayetteville, AR, 1974-1977; Counsel, Impeachment Inquiry Staff, U.S. House Judiciary Committee, Washington, DC, 1974; Legal Consultant, Carnegie Council On Children, New Haven, CT, 1973-1974; Attorney, Children's Defense Fund, Cambridge, MA, Washington, DC, 1973-1974 **CR:** Democratic Party Nominee, President Of The U.S., 2016; Candidate, Democratic Party Nomination, 2008; Paul Harris Fellow, Rotary Foundation, 1996; Fellow, American Academy of Arts & Sciences; Fellow, American Bar Foundation **CIV:** Board of Directors, Children's Defense Fund, Washington, DC, 1976-1992, Legal Services Corporation, 1977-1981, Founder, President, Board of Directors, Arkansas Advisors For Children And Families, 1977-1984, Chair, Legal Services Corporation, 1978-1980, Chairman, Arkansas Education Standards Committee, 1983-1984, Commission On Quality Education, Southern Regional Education Board, 1984-1992, Chair, Children's Defense Fund, Washington, DC, 1986-1991, Chair, American Bar Association Commission On Women In The Profession, 1987-1991, Advisory Board, HIPPY, 1988-1992, Honorary Chair, New York Academy of Sciences Gala, 2005, Honorary Member, The Pen And Brush, 1996—Present, (Board of Directors) New World Foundation, 1982-1988, Wal-Mart Stores, Inc., 1986-1992, TCBY, 1986-1992, La5arge, 1990-1992, Child Care Action Campaign, 1986-1992, National Center On Education & The Economy, 1987-1992, Arkansas Children's Hospital, 1988-1992, Franklin And Eleanor Roosevelt Institute, 1988-1992, Children's TV Workshop, 1989-1992, Public/Private Ventures, 1990-1992 **CW:** Author, (Books) Handbook on Legal Rights for Arkansas Women, 1977, 1987, It Takes a Village: And Other Lessons Children Teach Us, 1996, Dear Socks, Dear Buddy: Kids' Letters to the First Pets, 1998, An Invitation to the White House: At Home with History, 2000, (Autobiographies) Living History, 2003, Hard Choices, 2014; Syndicated Columnist, Talking It

Over, 1995—2000; Contributor, Articles, Professional Journals **AW:** Outstanding Layman of the Year, Phi Delta Kappa, 1984, Health Educator of the Year, Ryan White Foundation, 1995; Lewis Hine Award, National Child Labor Law Committee, 1993, Albert Schweitzer Leadership Award, Hugh O'Brian Youth Foundation, 1993, Iris Cantor Humanitarian Award, UCLA Medical Center, 1993, Friend of the Family Award, American Home Economics Association, 1993, Charles Wilson Lee Citizen Service Award, Committee For Education Funding, 1993, Claude D. Pepper Award, National Association For Home Care, 1993, Commitment To Life Award, AIDS Project, Los Angeles, CA, 1994, Distinguished Service, Health Education, & Prevention Award, National Center For Health Education, 1994, First Annual Eleanor Roosevelt Freedom Fighter Award, 1994, Brandeis Award, University of Louisville School Of Law, 1994, Social Justice Award, United Auto Workers, 1994, Ernie Banks Positivism Trophy, Emil Verban Memorial Society, 1994, Humanitarian Award, Alzheimer's Association, 1994, Elie Wiesel Foundation, 1994, International Broadcasting Award, Hollywood Radio & TV Society, 1994, Ellen Browning Scripps Medal, Scripps College, 1994, Distinguished Pro Bono Service Award, San Diego Volunteer Lawyer Program, 1994, HIPPY USA Award, 1994, C. Everett Koop Medal, American Diabetes Association, 1994, Women's Legal Defense Fund Award, 1994, Martin Luther King, Jr. Award, Progressive National Baptist Convention, 1994, 30th Anniversary Women At Work Award, In Public Policy, National Commission On Working Women, 1994, Greater Washington Urban League Award, 1995, Servant Of Justice Award, New York Legal Aid Society, 1995, Presidential Award, Brooklyn College, 1995, Outstanding Mother Award, National Mother's Day Committee, 1995, Dedication, Annual Survey of American Law, New York University, 1995, National Breast Cancer Coalition Leadership Award, 1995, Faith In Humanity Award, National Council on Jewish Women, 1996, NICHE Humanitarian Award, 1996, National Association of Elementary School Principals District Service Award, 1996, Grammy Award, 1997, Bully Pulpit Award, National Council For Adoption, 1997, National Family Advocate Award, Parents' Plus Newspaper, 1997, Distinguished Service To Education Award, College Board, 1997, Distinguished Service Award, Columbia University Center Of Addiction And Substance Abuse, 1997, Commitment To Children Award, The Elizabeth Glaser Pediatrics AIDS Foundation, 1997, Eleanor Roosevelt Living World Award, Peace Links, 1997, Humanitarian Award, American Foundation for Suicide Prevention, 1999, Lifetime Humanitarian Achievement Award, Children of the Chernobyl Relief Fund And Ukrainian Institute of America, 1999, Mother Teresa Award, Government of Albania, 1999, Shalom Chaver Award, International Leadership, Yitzhak Rabin Center for Israel Studies, 1999, Distinguished American Award, John F. Kennedy Library Foundation, 2004, Woman of the Year Award, Metropolitan Council On Jewish Poverty, New York, NY, 2004, German Media Prize, 2004, The 100 Most Influential People In The World, TIME Magazine, 2004, 2006-2012, 2014, Health Quality Award, National Committee for Quality Assurance, 2005, Intrepid Freedom Award, Intrepid Sea, Air, And Space Museum, 2005, President's Vision And Voice Award, American Medical Women's Association, 2005, President's Award, Reserve Officers Association, 2005, National Women's Hall Of Fame, New York, NY, 2005, 2007, The World's 100 Most Powerful Women, Forbes Magazine, 2005-2014, Remembrance Award, Alzheimer's Association, 2006, Life-Sized Figure, Madame Tussauds' Wax Museum, Times Square,

New York, NY, 2006, Energy Leadership Award, U.S. Energy Association, 2006, The 50 Most Powerful Women In New York City, New York Post, 2007-2008, The 50 Most Powerful People In DC, GQ, 2007, 2009, 2012, Ten People Who Mattered, Newsweek, 2008, The Global Elite, Newsweek, 2008, Alice Award, Sewall-Belmont House & Museum, 2009, The Ten Most Powerful Women In Washington, Fortune Magazine, 2009-2010, The 100 Most Powerful Women In DC, Washingtonian Magazine, 2009, 2011, The World's Most Powerful People, 2009-2013, The Ten Most Fascinating People, Barbara Walters Special, 2012, Medal For Distinguished Public Service, U.S. Department of Defense, 2013, Liberty Medal, National Constitution Center, 2013, The Most Fascinating Person, Barbara Walters Special, 2013, Award Of Merit, Yale Law School, 2013, Champion Of Peace Award, Women For Women International, 2013 **MEM:** Association of Trial Lawyers of America, Pulaski County Bar Association, Arkansas Women Lawyers Association, Arkansas Trial Lawyers Association, Arkansas Bar Association, Chair, Commission On Women In The Profession, American Bar Association **BAR:** U.S. Supreme Court, 1975, State of Arkansas, 1973, U.S. District Court, Eastern District, State of Arkansas, 1973, U.S. District Court, Western District, State of Arkansas, 1973, U.S. Court of Appeals, Eighth Circuit, 1973 **ACH:** Achievements include First First Lady elected to the US Senate and the first woman elected statewide in New York **PA:** Democrat **BA:** 15 Old House Lane, Chappaqua, NY, 10514

CLOONEY, GEORGE, T: Actor I: Media & Entertainment **DOB:** 05/06/1961 **PB:** Lexington, Kentucky, May 6, 1961 **PT:** Son of Nick and Nina Clooney; **ED:** Student, Northern Ky University, 1979-81 **C:** Messenger of Peace, UN, 2008-; Co-founder, Not On Our Watch, 2007 **CIV:** Organizer, Hope for Haiti Telethon, 2010 **CW:** Actor: (TV series) E/R, 1984-85, The Facts of Life, 1985-86, Roseanne, 1988-89, Sunset Beat, 1990, Baby Talk, 1991, Bodies of Evidence, 1992-93, Sisters, 1993-94, ER, 1994-99, Friends, 1995, South Parkm 1997, Murphy Brown, 1998, Fail Safe, 2000, 2010, Hope for Haiti Now, 2010, Text Santa 4, 2014; (films) Grizzly II: The Predator, 1987, Return to Horror High, 1987, Return of the Killer Tomatoes, 1988, Red Surf, 1990, Unbecoming Age, 1992, One Fine Day, 1996, From Dusk Till Dawn, 1996, Batman & Robin, 1997, The Peacemaker, 1997, The Thin Red Line, 1998, Out of Sight, 1998, Three Kings, 1999, South Park: Bigger, Longer and Uncut (voice), 1999, O Brother, Where Art Thou, 2000 (Golden Globe award for Best Performance by an Actor in a Motion Picture, 2001), The Perfect Storm, 2000, Ocean's Eleven, 2001, Spy Kids, 2001, Solaris, 2002, Spy Kids 3-D: Game Over, 2003, Intolerable Cruelty, 2003, Ocean's Thirteen, 2007, Burn After Reading, 2008, The Men Who Stare at Goats, 2009, Fantastic Mr. Fox (voice), 2009, Up in the Air, 2009 (National Board Review award for Best Actor, 2009, New York Film Critics Cir. award for Best Actor, 2009), The American, 2010, The Descendants, 2011 (National Board Review award for Best Actor, 2011, Critics' Choice award for Best Actor, 2012, Golden Globe award for Best Performance by an Actor in a Motion Picture-Drama, 2012), Gravity, 2013, Tomorrowland, 2015, A Very Murray Christmas, 2015, Hail, Caesar!, 2016, Money Monster, 2016, Suburbicon, 2017; (TV films) Combat High, 1986, Bennett Brothers, 1987, Knights of the Kitchen Table, 1990, Rewrite for Murder, 1991, Without Warning: Terror in the Towers, 1993; actor, director (films) Confessions of a Dangerous Mind, 2002, Leatherheads, 2008, The Ides of March, 2011, actor, director, writer Good Night and Good Luck, 2005 (National Board Review award for Best Film, 2005, George Selvin

award, Writer Guild of America, 2006), actor, executive producer Ocean's Twelve, 2004, Syriana, 2005 (Golden Globe award for Best Performance by an Actor in a Supporting Role in a Motion Picture, 2006, Academy award for Best Supporting Actor, Academy Motion Picture Arts & Sciences, 2006), Michael Clayton, 2007 (National Board Review award for Best Actor, 2007), (TV films) Fail Safe, 2000, producer, writer (films) Kilroy, 1999; executive prodr.: (films) Rock Star, 2001, Insomnia, 2002, Welcome to Colinwood, 2002, Far From Heaven, 2002, The Jacket, 2005; prodr.: Criminal, 2004, Argo, 2012 (Darryl F. Zanuck award for Outstanding Producer of Theatrical Motion Pictures, Producers Guild of America, 2013), Our Brand Is Crisis, 2015; actor, producer, director, writer (films) The Monuments Men, 2014, actor, producer Money Monster, 2016; executive prodr.: (TV series) K Street, 2003; dir.: Unscripted, 2005; actor: (TV appearances) Riptide, 1984, Street Hawk, 1985, Crazy Like A Fox, 1985, Hotel, 1986, Throb, 1986, Hunter, 1987, Murder, She Wrote, 1987, The Golden Girls, 1987, The Building, 1993, South Park (voice), 1997, Murphy Brown, 1998 **AW:** Named a WIRED Renegade, WIRED Rave Awards, 2006; named Favorite On Screen Match-Up (with Brad Pitt), People's Choice Awards, 2008, Sexiest Man Alive, People magazine, 2006, 1997; named one of 50 Smartest People in Hollywood, 2007, Top 25 Entertainers of Year, Entertainment Weekly, 2007, 100 Most Powerful Celebrities, Forbes.com, 2007, The 100 Most Influential People in the World, TIME magazine, 2009, 2008, 2007, 2006; recipient Cecil B. DeMille award, Hollywood Foreign Press, 2015, Chairman award, Palm Springs International Film Festival, 2011, Hope Humanitarian award, Primetime Emmy awards, Academy of TV Arts and Sciences, 2010, Chevalier des Arts et Lettres medal, Government of France, 2007, American Cinematheque award, 2006, Freedom award, Broadcasting Film Critics Association, 2006, SAE award, 1999, 1998

CLOSE, GLENN, T: Actress I: Media & Entertainment **DOB:** 03/19/1947 **PB:** Greenwich **SC:** CT/USA **PT:** Daughter of William Taliaferro and Bettine (Moore) C; **SPN:** David Shaw, February 3, 2006 (divorced); James Marlas, 1984 (div. 1987); Cabot Wade 1969 (div. 1971); **CH:** Annie Maude Starke; **ED:** BA in Drama and Anthropology, College William and Mary, 1974 **C:** Joined, New Phoenix Repertory Co., 1974 **CR:** Co-owner The Leaf and Bean Coffee House, Bozeman, Montana, 1993-94. **CIV:** Founder, Chairman BringChange2Mind **CW:** Actress: (Broadway debut) Love for Love, 1974; (Broadway plays) The Rules of the Game, 1974, The Member of the Wedding, 1975, Rex, 1976, Barnum, 1980—81, The Real Thing, 1984—85 (Tony Award for Best Actress in a Play, 1984), Benefactors, 1985—86, Death and the Maiden, 1992 (Tony Award for Best Actress in a Play, 1992), Sunset Boulevard, 1994—95 (Tony Award for Best Actress in a Musical, 1995), A Delicate Balance, 2014, (Other Theatre Appearances Include) Uncommon Women and Others, The Singular Life of Albert Nobbs, 1982, Childhood, 1985, Joan of Arc at the Stake, 1985, Sunset Boulevard (LA), 1993—94, The Vagina Monologues, 1998; (films) The World According to Garp, 1982, The Big Chill, 1983, Greystoke: The Legend of Tarzan, Lord of the Apes (voice), 1984, The Natural, 1984, The Stone Boy, 1984, Jagged Edge, 1985, Maxie, 1985, Fatal Attraction, 1987, (voice) Gandahar, 1988, Dangerous Liaisons, 1988, Immediate Family, 1989, Reversal of Fortune, 1990, Hamlet, 1990, Meeting Venus, 1991, Hook, 1991, The House of the Spirits, 1993, The Paper, 1994, Mary Reilly, 1996, 101 Dalmations, 1996, Mars Attacks!, 1996, Paradise Road, 1997, Air Force One, 1997, Cookie's Fortune, 1999, (voice) Tarzan, 1999, Things You Can't Tell Just by Looking at Her, 2000, 102 Dalmations, 2000, The Safety of Objects, 2001, (voice) Pinocchio, 2002, Le Divorce, 2003, The Stepford Wives, 2004, Nine Lives, 2005, Heights, 2005, The Chumscrubber, 2005, (voice) Hoodwinked, 2005, Tarzan II, 2005, Evening, 2007, (voice) Hoodwinked Too! Hood VS. Evil, 2010, Low Down, 2014, 5 to 7, 2014, Guardians of the Galaxy, 2014, Anesthesia, 2015, The Great Gilly Hopkins, 2015, Warcraft, 2016, What Happened to Monday?, 2017, The Girl with All the Gifts, 2016, The Wilde Wedding, 2017, The Wife, 2017 Crooked House, 2017, Father Figures; (TV Series) Damages, 2007—12 (Golden Globe Award for Best Performance by an Actress in a TV Series - Drama, 2008, Emmy Award for Outstanding Lead Actress in a Drama Series, 2008, 2009) Louie, 2015, Family Guy, 2016, Sea Oak, 2017; (TV films) The Rules of the Game, 1975, Too Far to Go, 1979, Orphan Train, 1979, The Elephant Man, 1982, Something About Amelia, 1984, Stones for Ibarra, 1988, She'll Take Romance, 1990, In the Gloaming, 1997, The Lion in Winter, 2003 (Golden Globe Award for Best Actress in a Mini-series or TV Movie, 2005, Screen Actors Guild Award for Best Actress in a TV Movie or Mini-series, 2005), Strip Search, 2004; (TV series) The Shield, 2005; actress, executive producer (TV films) Sarah, Plain and Tall, 1991, Skylark, 1993, Serving in Silence: The Margarethe Cammermeyer Story, 1995 (Emmy Award for Best Actress in a Mini-series or Special, 1995), Sarah, Plain and Tall: Winter's End, 1999, Baby, 2000, The Ballad of Lucy Whipple, 2001, South Pacific, 2001, Actress, Producer, Writer (films) Albert Nobbs, 2011; Executive Prodr.: (TV films) Journey, 1995; Contributor AW: Recipient Woman of Year Award Hasty Pudding Theatricals, Harvard University, 1990, Dartmouth Film Award, 1990, Sherry Lansing Leadership Award Sherry Lansing Foundation, 2008; Named One of Top 25 Entertainers of Year, Entertainment Weekly, 2007 MEM: Member Phi Beta Kappa. BA: Trillium Productions, 2nd Fl PO Box 1560, New Canaan, CT, 06840

CLYBURN, JAMES ENOS, T: U.S. Representative from South Carolina **I:** Government Administration/Government Relations/Government Services **DOB:** 07/21/1940 **PB:** Sumter **PT:** Son of Enos Lloyd and Almeta (Dizzley) Clyburn **ED:** LLD (hon.), Voorhees College, 1996; LHD (hon.), South Carolina State University, 1995; LLD (hon.), Claflin College, 1995; LHD (hon.), St. Augustine College, 1994; DSc (hon.), Medical University South Carolina, 1993; DSc (hon.), College Charleston, 1992; LHD (hon.), Winthrop College, 1987; BA in History, South Carolina State College, Orangeburg, 1962 **C:** Assistant minority leader (minority whip), US Congress from 6th South Carolina District, 2011-; Member, US Congress from 6th South Carolina district, 1993-; Member, Joint Select Committee on Deficit Reduction, 2011; Chairman, US House Democratic Caucus, 2006-07; Assistant majority leader (majority whip), US Congress from 6th South Carolina District, 2007-11; Commissioner, South Carolina Human Affairs Commission, 1974-92; Staff member, Governor John C. West, Charleston, 1971-74; Executive director, South Carolina Commission Farmworkers Inc., 1968-71; Director, Charleston County Neighborhood Youth Corps/New Careers Projects, 1966-68; Employment counselor, South Carolina Employment Security Commission, 1965-66; Teacher, Charleston County Pub. School Systems, South Carolina **CIV:** President, International Association Official Human Rights Agencies, 1985-87 President, National Association Human Rights Workers, 1980-81 Board directors, South Carolina Literacy Association, Board directors, James R. Clark Sickle Cell Anemia Foundation, **AW:** Named one of the Most Influential

Black Americans, Ebony magazine, 2006; recipient Pub. Administrator of Year award, Am. Society Pub. Administration **MEM:** Mem.: National Association for the Advancement of Colored People (life), Shriners, Masons, Omega Psi Phi **PA:** Democrat

COATES, TA-NEHISI, T: Author **I:** Writing and Editing **PB:** Baltimore **SC:** MD/USA **CW:** Author, Monograph, "We Were Eight Years in Power: An American Tragedy. One World" (2017); Author, Comics, "Black Panther and the Crew" (2017); Author, Comics, "Black Panther#1" (2016); Author, Comics, "Black Panther: World of Wakanda" (2016); Author, Monograph, "Between the World and Me: Notes on the First 150 Years in America" (2015); Author, Novel, "Between the World and Me" (2014); Author, Novel, "The Beautiful Struggle" (2008); Author, Monograph, "The Beautiful Struggle: A Father, Two Sons, and an Unlikely Road to Manhood" (2008); Author, Monograph, "Asphalt Sketches" (1990) **AW:** Named One of TIME's 100 Most Influential People, TIME Magazine (2016)

COATS, DANIEL, T: Director of National Intelligence **I:** Government Administration/Government Relations/Government Services **DOB:** 05/16/1943 **PB:** Jackson **SC:** MI/USA **PT:** Son of Edward R. and Vera E. C.; **MS:** Married **SPN:** Marcia Ann Crawford, September 4, 1965; **CH:** Laura, Lisa, Andrew **ED:** JD cum laude, Ind. University, 1971; BA in Government & Economics, Wheaton College, Illinois, 1965 **CT:** Bar: Ind. 1972 **C:** Director, National Intelligence of the U.S., Washington DC, 2017-; U.S. Senator from Indiana, 2011-2017; Member, Congressional Joint Economic Committee, Washington, 2011-2017; Member, US Senate Select Committee on Intelligence, Washington, 2011-; Member, US Senate Energy & Natural Resources Committee, Washington, 2011-; Member, US Senate Appropriations Committee, Washington, 2011-; US Senator from Ind., Washington, 2011-; Senior counsel, co-chmn. government relations group, King & Spaulding LLP, Washington, 2005-09; US ambassador to Germany, US Department State, Berlin, 2001-05; Special counsel, Verner, Liipfert, Bernhard, McPherson & Hand, 1999-2001; US Senator from Ind., Washington, 1989-99; Member, US Congress from 4th Ind. District, Washington, 1981-89; District rep. for Rep. Dan Quayle, 1976-80; Assistant vice president, counsel, Mutual Security Life Insurance Co., Fort Wayne, Ind., 1969-75 **CIV:** President, Big Brothers/Big Sisters of America, Ind. Served with U.S. Army, 1966-68. **PA:** Republican **BA:** Office of the Director of National Intelligence, 1500 Tysons Mclean Drive, Mclean, VA, USA, 22102

COCHRAN, THAD, T: U.S. Senator from Arizona **I:** Government Administration/Government Relations/Government Services **DOB:** 12/07/1937 **PB:** Pontotoc **SC:** MI/USA **PT:** Son of William Holmes and Emma Grace (Berry) Cochran; **ED:** JD cum laude, University Mississippi, 1965; BA in Psychology, University Mississippi, 1959 **CT:** Bar: Mississippi 1965 **C:** Chairman, US Senate Appropriations Committee, 2015-; US Senator from Mississippi, 1978-2018; Chairman, US Senate Republican Conference, 1991-97; Vice chairman, US Senate Republican Conference, 1985-91; Chairman, US Senate Appropriations Committee, 2005-07; Ranking member, US Senate Agricultural Committee, 2013-15; Chairman, US Senate Agricultural Committee, 2003-05; Member, US Congress from 4th Mississippi District, 1973-78; Associate, Watkins & Eager, 1965-72; Attorney, Jackson, Mississippi, 1965-72 **MIL:** Served as lieutenant US Naval Reserve, 1959-61 **AW:** Named Conservationist of Year, Dicks Unlimited, 1994, Outstanding Young Man of Jackson, 1971; named one of Three Outstanding Young Men of Mississippi,

1971; recipient Conservation Achievement award, National Wildlife Federation, Congressional Leadership award, Airports Council International North America, 2004 **MEM:** Mem.: American Bar Association, Mississippi Bar Association (president young lawyers section 1972-73), Rotary, Pi Kappa Alpha, Phi Kappa Phi, Omicron Delta Kappa **PA:** Republican **BA:** Office of Thad Cochran, 113 Dirksen Senate Office Building, Washington, DC, USA, 20510

COEN, ETHAN, T: Filmmaker **I:** Media & Entertainment **DOB:** 09/21/1957 **PB:** Saint Louis Park **SC:** MN/USA **ED:** Coursework in Philosophy, Princeton University **C:** Former Statistical Typist, Macy's, New York, NY **CW:** Producer, Fargo (2014-Present); Producer, "The Ballad of Buster Scruggs" (2018); Producer, "Suburbicon" (2017); Producer, "Hail, Caesar!" (2016); Producer, "Inside Llewyn Davis" (2013); Producer, "Gambit" (2012); Producer, "True Grit" (2010); Producer, "A Serious Man" (2009); Producer, "Burn After Reading" (2008); Producer, "No Country for Old Men" (2007); Writer, Director, "Paris, I Love You" (2006); Producer, "Romance & Cigarettes" (2005); Producer, "The Ladykillers" (2004); Producer, "Intolerable Cruelty" (2003); Producer, "Bad Santa" (2003); Producer, "A Fever in the Blood" (2002); Producer, "The Man Who Wasn't There" (2001); Writer, Director, Producer, "O Brother, Where Art Thou?" (2000); Executive Producer, "Down From the Mountain" (2000); Producer, "The Naked Man" (1998); Producer, "The Big Lebowski" (1998); Producer, "Fargo" (1996); Producer, "The Hudsucker Proxy" (1994); Producer, "Barton Fink" (1991); Producer, "Miller's Crossing" (1990); Writer, "Crime Wave (formerly XYZ Murders)" (1985); Producer, "Raising Arizona" (1987); Producer, "Blood Simple" (1984) **AW:** Recipient, David L. Wolper Award for Outstanding Producer of Long-Form TV, Producers Guild of America (2016); Recipient, Award for Best Original Screenplay, National Board Review (2013); Recipient, National Society Film Critics Award for Best Screenplay (2010); Recipient, Award for Best Screenplay, Boston Society of Film Critics (2009); Recipient, National Board Review Award for Best Original Screenplay (2009); Named, One of the 100 Most Influential People in the World, Time Magazine (2008); Recipient, Critics Choice Award, Broadcast Film Critics Association (2008); Recipient, Golden Globe Award for Best Screenplay/Motion Picture (2008); Recipient, Directors Guild of America Award for Outstanding Directorial Achievement in Feature Film (2008); Recipient, Award for Best Feature Film, Producers Guild of America (2008); Recipient, Award for Best Director, British Academy of Film and TV Arts (2008); Recipient, Award for Best Adapted Screenplay, Writers Guild of America (2008); Recipient, Academy Award for Best Adapted Screenplay, Best Directing and Best Picture (2008); Recipient, Award for Best Picture, Boston Society of Film Critics (2007); Recipient, National Board Review Award for Best Adapted Screenplay (2007); Recipient, Award for Best Screenplay, Best Director, Best Picture, New York Film Critics Circle (2007); Recipient, Academy Award for Best Screenplay (1997); Recipient, Palme D'Or Award for Best Director Award, Cannes International Film Festival (1996); Recipient, Cannes International Film Festival Award for Best Director (1996) **MEM:** Fellow, American Academy of Arts & Sciences **BA:** United Talent Agency, 9336 Civic Center Drive, Beverly Hills, CA, 90210

COEN, JOEL, T: Filmmaker **I:** Media & Entertainment **DOB:** 11/29/1954 **PB:** Saint Louis Park **SC:** MN/USA **ED:** Student in Film, New York University; Student, Simon's Rock College **CR:** Fellow,

American Academy of Arts & Sciences **CW:** Writer, Director, (Films) Blood Simple, 1984, Raising Arizona, 1987, Miller's Crossing, 1990, Barton Fink, 1991, The Hudsucker Proxy, 1994, Fargo, 1996, The Big Lebowski, 1998, O Brother, Where Art Thou?, 2000, The Man Who Wasn't There, 2001, Intolerable Cruelty, 2003, Paris, I Love You, 2006; Executive Producer, (Films) Down From The Mountain, 2000, Bad Santa, 2003, Romance & Cigarettes, 2005, (TV Series) Fargo, 2014-Present, (Television) The Ballad Of Buster Scruggs, 2018; Writer, Producer, Director, (Films) The Ladykillers, 2004, No Country For Old Men, 2007, Burn After Reading, 2008, A Serious Man, 2009, True Grit, 2010, Inside Llewyn Davis, 2013, Hail, Caesar!, 2016, Suburbicon, 2017; Writer, XYZ Murders (Now Crime Wave), 1985, Gambit, 2012, Bridge Of Spies, 2015 **AW:** The David L. Wolper Award For Outstanding Producer Of Long-Form TV, Producers Guild Of America, Fargo, 2016, National Board Review Award For Best Original Screenplay, Inside Llewyn Davis, 2013, National Society of Film Critics Award For Best Screenplay, A Serious Man, 2010, National Board Review Award For Best Original Screenplay, Boston Society of Film Critics Award For Best Screenplay, A Serious Man, 2009, Critics Choice Award, Broadcast Film Critics Association, Golden Globe Award For Best Screenplay/Motion Picture, Directors Guild Of America Award For Outstanding Directorial Achievement In Feature Film, Producers Guild Of America Award For Best Feature Film, British Academy of Film And TV Arts Award For Best Director, Writers Guild Of America Award For Best Adapted Screenplay, Academy Awards For Best Adapted Screenplay, Best Directing, Best Picture, No Country For Old Men, 2008, The 100 Most Influential People in the World, TIME Magazine, 2008, National Board Review Award For Best Adapted Screenplay, New York Film Critics Circle Awards For Best Screenplay, Best Director, Best Picture, Boston Society of Film Critics Award For Best Picture, No Country For Old Men, 2007, Academy Award For Best Screenplay, Fargo, 1997, Cannes International Film Festival Award For Best Director, Fargo, 1996, Palme D'Or Award For Best Director, Cannes International Film Festival, Barton Fink, 1991 **BA:** United Talent Agency, 9336 Civic Center Drive, Beverly Hills, CA, 90210

COFFMAN, MIKE, T: U.S. Representative from Colorado, former state official **I:** Government Administration/Government Relations/Government Services **DOB:** 03/19/1955 **PB:** Ft. Leonard Wood **PT:** Son of Harold and Dorothy Coffman; **ED:** Grad. Senior Executive Progressive State/Local Government, Harvard University John F. Kennedy School Government, 1995; Student, University Veracruz, Mexico; Student, Vaishnav College, India; Bachelor, University Colorado, 1979 **C:** Member, US Congress from 6th Colorado District, 2009-; Member, Committee on Armed Services, Committee on Veterans Affairs; Secretary state, State of Colorado, Denver, 2007-08; Treasurer, State of Colorado, Denver, 1998-2006; Chairman fin. committee, Colorado State Senate,; Member, Colorado State Senate, 1994-98; Member, Colorado State House of Reps., 1988-94; Founder, president, Colorado Property Management Grp., Inc., Aurora, 1983 **CIV:** Member, Univ. Park United Methodist Church, **MIL:** Civil officer US Marine Corps, 2005-06, major US Marine Corps, 1994, served in US Marine Corps Reserve, 1983-94, major US Marine Corps, 1979-82 US Arm **MEM:** Mem.: South Metro C. of C., Aurora C. of C., Am. Legion, Vets. of Foreign Wars **PA:** Republican **BA:** 2443 Rayburn House Office Bldg, Washington, DC, 20515

COHEN, STEVE, T: U.S. Representative from Tennessee **I:** Government Administration/Government Relations/Government Services **DOB:** 05/24/1949 **PB:** Memphis **SC:** TN/USA **PT:** Son of Morris David and Genevieve (Goldsand) Cohen. **ED:** JD, University Memphis, 1973; BA, Vanderbilt University, Nashville, 1971 **CT:** Bar: Tennessee 1974 **C:** Member, US Congress from 9th Tennessee district, 2007-; Member, Committee on the Judiciary, Committee on Transportation and Infrastructure; Deputy speaker, Tennessee State Senate, 2000-07; Member District 30, Tennessee State Senate, 1983-2007; Commissioner, Shelby County Board Commissioners, 1978-80; Legal advisor, Memphis Police Department, 1975-78 **CR:** Member executive committee National Conference State Legislatures, 1998-2005 member Shelby County Charter Commission, 1984 interim judge Shelby County General Sessions Court, 1980 **CIV:** Board trustees, Memphis College Art, 1988-2002 Del., Am. Council Young Political Leaders USA/Japan Study Mission, 1986 Del., Dem. National Convention, 2008 Del., Dem. National Convention, 2004 Del., Dem. National Convention, 1992 Del., Dem. National Convention, 1980 Chairman, Shelby County Legis. Del., 1988-90 Vice president, Tennessee Constitutional Convention, 1977 **AW:** Recipient Pub. Leadership award, Tennessee Human Rights Campaign, 2002, Legislator of the Year, Boys & Girls Clubs of Tennessee, 2003 **MEM:** Mem.: Memphis Bar Association **PA:** Democrat **BA:** 2404 Rayburn House Office Bldg, Washington, DC, USA, 20515

COHN, GARY D., T: Former Government Official, Former Diversified Financial Services Company Executive **I:** Government Administration/Government Relations/Government Services **DOB:** 08/27/1960 **PB:** Cleve. **ED:** BSBA in Finance, American University Kogod School Business, 1982 **C:** Chief Economic Adviser to President Trump, 2017-2018; Director of the National Economic Council, Office of the White House, 2017-2018;; President, COO, Goldman Sachs Group, Inc. (formerly Goldman, Sachs & Co.), 2009-2017; Member management committee, Goldman Sachs & Co., 2002-; Managing director, Goldman Sachs & Co., 1996-; President, co-COO, The Goldman Sachs Group, Inc, 2006-09; Co-head global securities, The Goldman Sachs Group, Inc, 2004-06; Co-head equities division, The Goldman Sachs Group, Inc, 2003-04; Head fixed income, currency & commodities division, Goldman Sachs & Co., 2002-06; Co-COO fixed income, currency & commodities division, Goldman Sachs & Co., 2002; Co-head commodities division, Goldman Sachs & Co., 1996-99; Partner, Goldman Sachs & Co., 1994-96; Senior trader J. Aron Futures unit, Goldman Sachs & Co., London, 1990; Silver trader,; Salesman home products division, US Steel Corp. **CR:** Board directors The Goldman Sachs Group, Inc., 2006-, New York Mercantile Exchange, 1998-2000, London Medal Exchange, 1994 treasurer Commodity Exchange Inc., 1990 **CIV:** Trustee, New York University School Medicine Foundation, Trustee, American University, Trustee, Gilmour Academy, Cleveland, Trustee, New York University Child Study Center, Trustee, New York University Hospital, Trustee, Harlem's Children Zone **AW:** Recipient Effecting Change award, 100 Women in Hedge Funds, 2005

COLBERT, STEPHEN, T: Talk Show Host, Comedian, Actor **I:** Media & Entertainment **DOB:** 05/13/1964 **PB:** Washington **SC:** DC/USA **PT:** Son of James and Lorna (Tuck) Colbert; **ED:** DFA (hon.), Knox College, 2006; Grad., Northeastern University, 1986 **C:** Performer, Annoyance Theatre, Chicago,; Performer, Second City, Chicago, **CW:** Actor: (films) Snow Days, 1999, Nobody Knows Anything, 2003, Bewitched, 2005, The Love Guru, 2008, (voice) Monsters versus Aliens, 2009, Company, 2011, (voice) Mr. Peabody & Sherman, 2014; actor, writer (TV series) Exit 57, 1995-96, The Dana Carvey Show, 1996, Saturday Night Live (co-creator and voice of Ace, The Ambiguously Gay Duo), 1996, (TV films) Strangers with Candy: Retardation, a Celebration, 1998; (actor, writer, co-prodr.): (TV series) Strangers with Candy, 1999-2000; voice (TV series) Harvey Birdman, Attorney at Law, 2001-05, Crank Yankers, 2002, news corr. The Daily Show with Jon Stewart, 1997-2005, writer, 2003-06 (co-recipient, Emmy award for Outstanding Writing for a Variety, Music or Comedy Program, 2004, 2005, 2006, 2008, 2010, 2013,2014), host, writer The Colbert Report, 2005-14 (Best Comedy/Variety - Series, Writers Guild America, 2008, Emmy award for Outstanding Writing for a Variety, Music or Comedy Program, Academy TV Arts & Scis., 2008, Producers Guild of America award for Live Entertainment/Competition, 2009, 2010, Producers Guild of America award for Outstanding Producer of Live Entertainment & Talk TV, 2013, 2014, Emmy award for Outstanding Variety Series, 2013,114 Emmy award for Outstanding Writing for a Variety Series, 2013, People's Choice award for Favorite Late-Night Talk Show Host, 2014), host, writer, executive producer Late Show with Stephen Colbert, 2015-, featured entertainer White House Correspondents' Association Dinner, 2006; co-author (with Amy Sedaris and Paul Dinello): Wigfield: The Can Do Town That Just May Not, 2003; author: I Am America (And So Can You!), 2007 (New York Times bestseller, Publishers Weekly bestseller), America Again: Re-becoming the Greatness We Never Weren't, 2012 (Grammy award for Best Spoken Word Album, 2014), I Am a Pole (And So Can You!), 2012; performer: (songs) A Colbert Christmas: The Greatest Gift of All!, 2008 (Grammy award for Best Comedy Album, 2010),Host of the 69th Primetime Emmy Awards,2017 **AW:** Co-recipient Peabody awards for work on The Daily Show: Indecision 2000 and Indecision 2004; named Webby Person of Year, International Academy Digital Arts & Sciences, 2008, Celebrity of Year, Associated Press, 2007, Person of Year, US Comedy Arts Festival, 2007; named one of The 100 Agents of Change, Rolling Stone magazine, 2009, The 50 Highest-Earning Political Figures, Newsweek, 2010, The 100 Most Influential People in the World, TIME magazine, 2012, 2006, The Men of Year, GQ, 2006; recipient 2007 Peabody award-The Colbert Report Hello Doggie Inc., Busboy Productions, and Spartina Productions,Producers Guild Outstanding Producer of live Entertainment and Competition Television, 2008-2015 **BA:** The Ed Sullivan Theater, 1697 Broadway, New York, NY, 10019

COLE, RANSEY GUY JR., T: Federal Judge **I:** Law and Legal Services **DOB:** 05/23/1951 **PB:** Birmingham **SC:** AL/USA **PT:** Ransey Guy Cole; Sarah Nell (Coker) Cole **ED:** JD, Yale University (1975); BA, Tufts University (1972) **C:** Chief Judge, U.S. Court of Appeals for the Sixth Circuit (2014-Present); Judge, U.S. Court of Appeals for the Sixth Circuit, Cinncinatti, OH (1995-Present); Partner, Vorys, Sater, Seymour and Pease, Columbus, OH (1993-1995); Judge, U.S. Bankruptcy Court, Columbus, OH (1987-1993); Partner, Vorys, Sater, Seymour and Pease, Columbus, OH (1980-1986); Trial Attorney, U.S. Department of Justice, Washington, DC (1978-1980); Associate, Vorys, Sater, Seymour and Pease, Columbus, OH (1975-1978) **CIV:** Board of Trustees, Children's Hospital (1990-Present); Board of Trustees, Columbus Area International

Progressive (1986-1994); Board of Trustees, March of Dimes, Ohio (1985-1988); Board Trustee, Neighborhood House (1985-1988); Board Trustee, YMCA (1984-1988) **MEM:** ABA; Columbus Bar Association; National Bar Association **BAR:** Washington, DC (1982); Ohio (1975) **BA:** 100 East Fifth Street, Cincinnati, OH, 45202

COLE, TOM, T: U.S. Representative from Oklahoma **I:** Government Administration/Government Relations/Government Services **DOB:** 04/28/1949 **PB:** Shreveport **SC:** LA/USA **PT:** John D. Cole, Helen Gale Cole **ED:** PhD in British History, University of Oklahoma, Norman, OK, 1984; MA in British History, Yale University, New Haven, CT, 1974; BA in History, Grinnell College, Iowa, 1971 **C:** U.S. Congress From Fourth Oklahoma District, 2003-Present; Founding Partner, President, Cole, Hargrave, Snodgrass & Associates, Oklahoma City, OK, 1989-Present; Secretary Of State, State Of Oklahoma, Oklahoma City, OK, 1995-1999; Oklahoma State Senate, 1988-1991; Instructor, Oklahoma Baptist University, 1981; Lecturer, Grinnell College, 1977-1979; Instructor, University of Oklahoma, 1975-1978; Committee On Appropriations, Committee On The Budget, Committee On Rules **CR:** Chairman, National Republican Congressional Committee, 2006-2008, Executive Director, National Republican Congressional Committee, 1999-2000, Thomas J. Watson Fellow, Fulbright Fellow, 1977-1978 **CIV:** Chairman, Oklahoma Republican Party, 1985-1989, Executive Director, Reagan-Bush Presidential Campaign, Oklahoma, 1984, Executive Director, Oklahoma Republican Committee, 1980-1981, National Board of Directors, Fulbright Association, Enrolled Member, Chickasaw Nation, Oklahoma **AW:** Congressional Lifetime Achievement Award, National Center for American Indian Enterprise Development, 2009, Chickasaw Nation Hall Of Fame, 2004, Guardian Small Business Award, National Federation of Independent Business, Robert A. Taft Award, Oklahoma Republican Party **MEM:** Oklahoma Chamber Of Commerce, Society of the Study of Labor History, American Historical Association, Institute of Historical Research, Phi Alpha Theta **PA:** Republican **BA:** 2467 Rayburn HOB, Washington, DC, 20515

COLLINS, CHRISTOPHER, T: U.S. Representative from New York **I:** Government Administration/Government Relations/Government Services **CN:** Bloch Industries LLC **DOB:** 05/20/1950 **PB:** Schenectady **SC:** New York **PT:** Son of Gerald Edward and Constance (Messier) Collins; **ED:** BSME, North Carolina State University, 1972; MBA, University Alabama, 1975 **C:** Member, US House Agricultural Committee, 2013—; Vice President Corporate Devel., Wilson Greatbatch Ltd., Clarence, New York, 1999; President, Nuttall Gear, LLC, Niagara Falls, 1997-98; Chmn., President, CEO, Nuttall Gear Corp., Niagara Falls, New York, 1983-97; Manager Gearing Division, Westinghouse Electrical Corp., Buffalo, New York, 1980-82; Manager Market Planning, Westinghouse Electrical Corp., Buffalo, New York, 1978-79; Market Research Analyst, Westinghouse Electrical Corp., Buffalo, New York, 1976-77; Sales Engineer, Westinghouse Electrical Corp., Birmingham, Alabama, 1972-76; Member, US House Small Business Committee, 2013—; Member, US Congress from 27th New York District, 2013—; Vice President, Easom Automation Systems, Detroit, Michigan, 2003—; Treasurer, Volland Electric Equipment Corp., Buffalo, New York, 2001—; Chairman Board, Zepto Metrix Corp., Buffalo, New York, 1999—; Chairman Board, CEO, Bloch Industries LLC, Rochester, New York, 1999—; Member, US House Sci. Space and Tech. Committee, 2013; County Executive, Erie County, 2007—2011 **CR:** Treasurer Frontier Industrial Supply, Buffalo, 2001—, Mead Supply, Buffalo, 2002—; Chairman Niagara Machinery Corp., Wilson, New York, 2003—2004; Chairman and CEO Audubon Machinery Corp., Buffalo, 2004—; Treasurer Niagara Ceramics Corp., Buffalo, 2004—2012; Chairman Bio Clinical Partners, Boston, 2004—; Chairman, CEO Oxygen Generating Systems International, Buffalo, 2004—; Treasurer Lang & Washburn Electric, Buffalo, 2004—; President, CEO Buckler Biodefense Corp., Buffalo, 2006—; Vice President, Board of Directors Innate Therapeutics Ltd., Auckland, New Zealand, 2006—; Chairman Starboard Sun Corp., Buffalo, 2007—2008; County Executive Erie, Buffalo, 2008—2011 **CIV:** Board directors Kenmore Mercy Hospital, 1986-93; member ho. of dels. United Way, Buffalo, 1986-2003; member small business adv. council Federal Reserve Bank, New York, 1992?1995; treasurer; member Buffalo Financial Planning Committee, 1994; vice president administration, executive board directors Greater Niagara Frontier council Boy Scouts America, 1998—; Republican & Conservative candidate for US Congress, 1998; mentor Center for Entrepreneurial Leadership, State University of New York, 1999— **MEM:** Member Chief Executives Organization, World President's Organization, Young President Organization (chairman education committee 1988-89, chapter chairman 1989-90, chairman membership 1990-91, chairman executive committee 1991-96), Brookfield Country Club, Holimont Ski Club. **H:** Golf, skiing, aviation **PA:** Republican **BA:** 1117 Longworth House Office Building, Washington, DC, 20515

COLLINS, DOUG, T: U.S. Representative from Georgia **I:** Government Administration/Government Relations/Government Services **DOB:** 08/16/1966 **PB:** Gainesville **SC:** GA/USA **ED:** Grad., Georgia Legislative Leadership Institute; JD, John Marshall Law School, 2007; MDiv, New Orleans Baptist Theological Seminary, 1996; BA in Political Sci. & Criminal Law, North Georgia College & State University, 1988 **C:** Vice Chairman of the House Republican Conference, 2017, Member, Committee on Rules; Member, US House Oversight & Government Reform Committee, 2013-; Member, US House Judiciary Committee, 2013-; Member, US House Foreign Affairs Committee, 2013-; Member, US Congress from 9th GA District, Washington, 2013-; Managing partner, Collins & Csider Law Firm, 2010-; Member District 27, Georgia House of Reps., 2007-13; Senior pastor, Chicopee Baptist Church, 1994-2005 **MIL:** Major-chaplain 94th Airlift Wing US Air Force Reserve, 2002-, Iraq War, chaplain US Navy **AW:** Named one of Georgia's Most Influential Citizens, James magazine **PA:** Republican

COLLINS, PHIL, T: Drummer **I:** Media & Entertainment **DOB:** 01/30/1951 **PB:** London **SC:** England **PT:** Son of Greville and June Collins **SPN:** Orianne Cevey (1999, Divorced 2008); Jill Collins (1984, Divorced 1996); Andrea Collins (1975, Divorced 1982) **CH:** Simon, Lily Jane, Nicholas; Matthew; Joely (Stepchild) **C:** Lead Singer, Songwriter, Rock Band, Genesis, 1975-; Drummer, Rock Band Genesis, 1971-75 **CW:** Albums with Genesis include: Nursery Cryme, 1971, Foxtrot, 1972, Selling England by the Pound, 1973, Genesis Live, 1973, The Lamb Lies Down on Broadway, 1974, Trick of the Tail, 1976, Wind and Wuthering, 1977, Seconds Out, 1977, Spot the Pigeon, 1977, And Then There Were Three, 1978, Duke, 1980, Abacab, 1981, Three Sides Live, 1982, Genesis, 1983, Invisible Touch, 1986, We Can't Dance, 1991, The Way That We Walk Volume One: The Shorts, 1992, The Way That We Walk Volume Two: The Longs, 1993; Solo albums include: Face Value, 1981, (Remastered deluxe edition), 2016, Hello, I Must be Going, 1982, (Remastered deluxe edition), 2016, No Jacket Required (Grammy Award 1986), 1985, 12"Ers, 1987, ...But Seriously, 1989, Serious Hits-Live, 1990, Both Sides, 1993, (Remastered deluxe edition), 2016, Dance into the Light, 1996, (Remastered deluxe edition), 2016, Hits, 1998, Big Band-A Hot Night in Paris, 1999, Testify, 2002, The Platinum Collection, 2004, Love Songs: A Compilation...Old and New, 2004, Take A Look At Me Now Collector's Edition, 2016; Composer, Film: Against All Odds (Academy award nomination), 1984, White Nights, 1985, Buster, 1988, Going Back, 2010 (voice) Balto, 1995, Tarzan, 1999, Moulin Rouge!, 2001, Brother Bear, 2003, The Jungle Book 2, 2003; TV movie, Hook, 1991, Frauds, 1993, Calliope, 1993, And the Band Played On, 1993; Composer, Lyricist (Broadway) Tarzan, 2006 **AW:** Winner, Grammy Award for Best Song (Against All Odds), 1985, Grammy Award for Two Hearts, 1989, 5 others, 2 Silver Clef Awards, 2 Awards Variety Club of Great Britain, 1 Elvis Award, Golden Globe for the song Two Hearts from the movie Buster, 1989, Oscar and Golden Globe for the song You'll be in My Heart from the movie Tarzan, 2000, numerous others, Star on the Hollywood Walk of Fame, 1999, Diamond Award RIAA, 1999, City of Life Award, 2002, Named to Rock and Roll Hall of Fame (with Genesis), 2010, Johnny Mercer Award, Songwriters Hall of Fame, 2010

COLLINS, SUSAN MARGARET, T: U.S. Senator from Maine **I:** Government Administration/Government Relations/Government Services **DOB:** 12/07/1952 **PB:** Caribou **SC:** ME/USA **ED:** BA in Government magna cum laude, St. Lawrence University, Canton, New York, 1975 **C:** Chairwoman, Senate Aging Committee, 2015-; Member, US Senate Appropriations Committee, 2009-; Member, US Senate Homeland Security & Governmental Affairs Committee, 1997-; US Senator from Maine, 1997-; Chairman, US Senate Homeland Security & Governmental Affairs Committee, 2003-07; Executive director, Center Family Business, Husson College, Bangor, Maine, 1993-96; Director New England operations, US Small Business Administration (Small Business Administration), 1992-93; Commissioner, Maine Department Professional & Fin. Regulation, 1987-92; Staff director, US Senate Subcommittee on Oversight Government Management, 1981-87; Principal adv. business affairs to Rep. William S. Cohen, US House of Representatives, 1975-78 **CR:** Special inspector general to handle Hurricane Katrina Relief, 2005- **CIV:** Rep. candidate for Governor, Maine, 1994 **CW:** Author ((with Catherine Whitney)): Nine and Counting: The Women of the Senate, 2000 **AW:** Named Port Person of Year, American Association Port Authorities, 2006; named one of The 10 Most Powerful Women in DC, Elle magazine, 2014, The 10 Most Powerful Women in Washington, Fortune magazine, 2010, 2009; recipient National Public Policy Leadership award, American Diabetes Association, Congl. Leadership award, National Urban League, 2006, Outstanding Legislative award, Triangle Coalition Sci. & Tech. Education, 2005, Public Service award, Emergency Nurses Association, 2004, Teacher Leader award, Reading Recovery Council North America, 2004, Outstanding Alumni award, St. Lawrence University, 1992 **MEM:** Bangor Rotary Club, Phi Beta Kappa **PA:** Republican **BA:** Office of Susan Collins, 413 Dirksen Senate Office Bldg, Washington, DC, 20510

COLLIS, STEVEN H., T: CEO **I:** Pharmaceuticals **CN:** AmerisourceBergen **SC:** South Africa **ED:** Bachelor in Commerce, University of the Witwatersrand, Johannesburg, South Africa, With Honors **CT:** Licensed in Charter Accountancy,

1986 **C:** President, CEO, AmerisourceBergen Corp., Valley Forge, PA, 2011-Present; President, COO, AmerisourceBergen Corp., Valley Forge, PA, 2010-2011; President, AmerisourceBergen Drug Corp., 2009-2010; Executive Vice President, AmerisourceBergen Corp., Valley Forge, PA, 2007-2010; President, AmerisourceBergen Specialty Group, Dallas, TX, 2001-2009; Senior Executive Vice President, President, ASD Specialty Healthcare, Inc., 2000-2001; Executive Vice President, ASD Specialty Healthcare, Inc., 1996-2000; General Manager, ASD Specialty Healthcare, Inc., 1994-1996; Principal and General Manager, Sterling Medical, Irvine, CA; Johannesburg Stock Exchange **CR:** Board of Directors, Thoratec Corp., 2008-Present **CIV:** Active, American Cancer Society **BA:** AmerisourceBergen Corp., 1300 Morris Drive, Chesterbrook, PA, 19087-5594

COLLOTON, STEVEN, T: Federal Judge **I:** Law and Legal Services **CN:** US Ct. Appeals (8th cir.) **DOB:** 01/09/1953 **PB:** Iowa City **SC:** Iowa **ED:** JD, Yale Law School, 1988; AB, Princeton University, 1985 **C:** Judge, US Court Appeals (8th cir.), Des Moines, 2003-; U.S. Attorney, Southern District Iowa, 2001-03; Partner, Belin Lamson McCormick Zumbach Flynn, Des Moines, 1999-2001; Associate counsel, Office Ind. Counsel Kenneth W. Starr, 1995-96; Assistant U.S. Attorney, No. District Iowa, 1991-99; Special assistant to Assistant Attorney General, Department Justice Office Legal Counsel, 1990-91; Law clerk to Hon. William H. Rehnquist, US Supreme Court, Washington, 1989-90; Law clk to Hon. Laurence H. Silberman, US Court Appeals, DC cir., Washington, 1988-89 **BA:** Thomas F. Eagleton Courthouse, 111 South 10th Street, St. Louis, MO, 63102

COMANECI, NADIA, T: Professional Gymnast **I:** Athletics **DOB:** 06/08/1905 **PB:** Onesti, Romania **SC:** Onesti, Romania **ED:** Student, College Physical Education and Sports, Bucharest, Romania **C:** Junior team coach,, from 1984 **CR:** Overall European champion, Skien, 1975, Prague, Czechoslovakia, 1977, Copenhagen, 1979, Olympic champion, Montreal, Quebec, Can., 1976, World Univ. Games champion, Bucharest, 1981 gold medal for vault, asymmetric bars and beam European Championships, Skien, 1975, for bars, Prague, 1977, for vault and floor exercises, Copenhagen, 1979, for beam World Championships, Strasbourg, France, 1978, team title, Fort Worth, 1979, for bars and beam Olympic Games, Montreal, 1976, for beam and floor, Moscow **CW:** 1980, for vault and floor World Cup, Tokyo, 1979, for vault, bars, floor and team title World Univ. Games, Bucharest, 1981; silver medals for floor European Championships, Skien, 1975, for vault, Prague, 1977, for vault World Championships, Strasbourg, 1978, team title Olympic Games, Montreal, 1976, individual all-round and team title, Moscow, 1980, for beam World Coup, Tokyo, 1979; bronze medal for floor Olympic Games, Montreal, 1976; retired, 1984. **AW:** Great Immigrant Honoree, Carnegie Corporation, 2016, The Olympic Order, 2004, Flo Hyman Award, 1998, Marca Leyen, International Gymnastics Hall of Fame, 1993

COMBS, SEAN, T: Record Company Executive, Producer, Actor, Entrepreneur **I:** Media & Entertainment **DOB:** 11/04/1969 **PB:** Harlem **SC:** NY/USA **PT:** Son of Melvin and Janice Combs **CH:** Justin; Christian; D'Lila Star; Jessie James **ED:** Attended, Howard University, Washington, DC, 1988-90 **C:** Launched clothing line, Sean John, 1998-; Founder, CEO, Bad Boy Entertainment, 1993-; Launched fragrance, Unforgivable, I Am King, 2008; Launched fragrance, Unforgivable, 2006; Acquired, Enyce, 2008; Owner, Justin (restaurant), Atlanta, 1997-

2012; Various positions including intern, head A&R department, Uptown Records, 1990-93 **CW:** Prodr.: Forever My Lady (Jodeci), 1991, Diary of a Mad Band (Jodeci), 1993, What's the 411? (Mary J. Blige), 1993, My Life (Mary J. Blige), 1994, Project: Funk Da World (Craig Mack), 1994, Ready to Die (The Notorious B.I.G.), 1994, Think of You (Raymond Usher), 1994, Faith (Faith Evans), 1995; also producer records by Supercat, 1996, Keith Sweat, Caron Wheeler, Mix Tape Volume 2, 1997, Money Talks, 1997, Diana, Princess of Wales: Tribute, 1997, Chef Aid: The South Park Album, 1998; performer: (albums) In Tha Beginning... There Was Rap, 1997, No Way Out, 1997 (Grammy Award, Best Rap Album); performer, producer (albums) Forever, 1999, The Saga Continues, 2001, Press Play, 2006, Last Train to Paris, 2010, MMM, 2014, No Way Out 2; executive prodr.: (TV series) Making the Band II, 2002, Making the Band III, 2005-06, Run's House, 2005, Making the Band 4, 2007, Taquita & Kaui, 2007, StarMaker, 2009, I Want to Work for Diddy, 2010; (TV films) The Making of 'Press Play', 2006, Diddy Makes an Album, 2006; (documentaries) Undefeated, 2012 (Academy award for Best Documentary Feature, 2012); actor: (films) Made, 2000, Monster's Ball, 2001, Death of a Dynasty, 2003, Get Him to the Greek, 2010, Draft Day, 2014, Muppets Most Wanted, 2014, Can't Stop Won't Stop: A Bad Boy Story, 2017; appeared in (TV series) CSI: Miami (2 episodes), 2009, Entourage, 2010, Hawaii Five-0, 2011, It's Always Sunny in Philadelphia, 2012; executive producer, actor: (TV films) A Raisin in the Sun, 2008 (Best Actor in a TV Movie, Mini-Series or Dramatic Special, National Association for the Advancement of Colored People Image award, 2009) (executive soundtrack producer): (films) Bad Boys II, 2003; actor: (Broadway plays) A Raisin in the Sun, 2004 **AW:** Named Menwear Designer of Year, Council of Fashion Designers of Am., 2004, Songwriter of Year, American Society of Composers, 1996; named one of The 100 Most Powerful Celebrities, Forbes.com, 2008, 2007, The 100 Most Influential People in the World, TIME magazine, 2006, The Most Influential Black Americans, Ebony magazine, 2006, The 50 Most Influential African-Americans, 2004; named to The Power 150, 2008; recipient Alumni award for Distinguished Postgraduate Achievement, Howard University, 1999, BET Best Male Hip Hop Artist, 2007,Outstanding Actor in a Television Movie, 2009

COMER, JAMES R., T: U.S. Representative from Kentucky **I:** Government Administration/Government Relations/Government Services **DOB:** 08/19/1972 **ED:** BA in Agricultural magna cum laude, Western Kentucky University, Bowling Green **C:** Member, U.S. House of Representatives from Kentucky's 1st District, 2016-; Commissioner, Kentucky Department Agricultural, 2012-2016; Member District 53, Kentucky House of Reps., 2001-12; Director, South Central Bank, Monroe County, Kentucky,; Co-owner, Land & Cattle Co., Kentucky,; Founder, owner, James Comer, Junior Farms, Monroe County, Kentucky, **CR:** President Monroe County C. of C., 1999-2000 **MEM:** Mem.: Monroe County Farm Bureau, Monroe County C. of C. (former president) **PA:** Republican **BA:** 1513 Longworth HOB, Washington, DC, 20515

COMEY, JAMES BRIEN JR., T: Former FBI Director **I:** Government Administration/Government Relations/Government Services **DOB:** 12/14/1960 **PB:** Yonkers **SC:** NY/USA **ED:** JD, University of Chicago Law School (1985); BS in Chemistry & Religion, College of William & Mary (1982) **C:** Director, FBI, US Department of Justice, Washington, DC (2013-2017); Senior Research Fellow, Hertog Fellow in National Security Law, Columbia Law School, New York City, NY (2013); General

Counsel, Bridgewater Associates, Westport, CT (2010-2013); Senior Vice President, General Counsel, Lockheed Martin Corporation, Bethesda, MD (2005-2010); Deputy Attorney General, US Department of Justice, Washington, DC (2003-2005); US Attorney, Southern District of New York, US Department of Justice, New York City, NY (2002-2003); Managing Assistant US Attorney, Eastern District of Virginia, US Department of Justice, Richmond, VA (1996-2002); Partner, McGuire Woods, LLP, Richmond, VA (1993-1996); Assistant US Attorney, Southern District of New York, US Department of Justice, New York City, NY (1987-1993); Associate, Gibson, Dunn & Crutcher LLP, New York City, NY (1986-1987); Law Clerk to Honorary John M. Walker, US District Court for the Southern District of New York, New York City, NY (1985-1986) **CR:** Board of Directors, HSBC Holdings Plc (2013); Member, Defense Legal Policy Board (2012-2013); Carter O. Lowance Fellow, College of William & Mary Law School (2011-2012); Chairman, National Chamber Litigation Center, US Chamber of Commerce (2009-2013) **CW:** Author, "A Higher Loyalty: Truth, Lies and Leadership" (2018) **AW:** Henry L. Stimson Medal, Association of the Bar of the City of New York (1993); Named One of TIME's 100 Most Influential People, TIMES Magazine (2017) **H:** Squash; Bicycling; New York Giants and Knicks; Teaching Sunday School **PA:** Republican

COMSTOCK, BARBARA J., T: U.S. Representative from Virginia **I:** Government Administration/Government Relations/Government Services **DOB:** 06/30/1959 **PB:** Springfield **SC:** VA/USA **ED:** JD, Georgetown University Law Center, Washington, DC 1986; BA, Middlebury College, Vermont, 1981 **C:** Member, U.S. House of Representatives from Virginia's 10th District, 2015-; Member, Committee on House Administration; Member, Committee on Science, Space, and Technology; Member, Committee on Transportation and Infrastructure; Member District 34, Virginia House of Dels., Richmond, 2010-2014; Owner, partner pub. affairs firm., Corallo Comstock, Alexandria, Virginia,; Partner, senior principal government relations, Blank Rome, LLP, 2003-07; Chief spokesperson, communications strategist to Attorney General john Ashcroft, U.S. Department Justice, Washington, 2002-03; Director research & strategic planning, Rep. National Committee, 1999-2001; Chief investigative counsel, chief counsel, US House of Reps. Committee on Government Reform and Oversight, Washington; Senior aide to Rep. Frank Wolf, U.S. House of Representatives, Washington, **CR:** Legal & political commentator CNN, FOX News, MSNBC; senior consultant Romney for President, 2006-08 **CIV:** Member, McLean Community Center Governing Board, 1993-96 Board member, Childhelp, Board member, Support Our Aging Religious, **MEM:** Mem.: Northern Virginia Tech. Council, Fairfax County C. of C., Federalist Society **PA:** Republican

CONAWAY, MIKE, T: Leader **I:** Government Administration/Government Relations/Government Services **CN:** House Intelligence Committee **DOB:** 06/11/1948 **PB:** Borger **SC:** TX/USA **ED:** BBA, Texas Agricultural and Mechanical University, 1970 **CT:** CPA **C:** Leader, House Intelligence Committee, 2017-Present; Chairman, U.S. House Agricultural Committee, 2015-Present; U.S. Congress From 11th Texas District, 2005-Present; Chairman, House Standards of Official Conduct Committee (Now U.S. House Ethics Committee), 2013-2015; CFO, Arbusto Energy Inc., Midland, TX, 1981-1986; Accountant, Price Waterhouse, Midland, TX **CIV:** Chairman, Texas State Board of Public Accountancy, 1997-2005, Texas State Board of Public Accountancy, 1995-2002, Midland Independent School District, 1985-1988 **AW:** Volunteer of the Decade, Midland YMCA, 1990 **PA:** Republican **BA:** Washington DC Office of Mike Conaway, 2430 Rayburn House Office Building, Washington, DC, 20515

CONNELLY, MICHAEL, T: Writer **I:** Writing and Editing **DOB:** 07/21/1956 **PB:** Phila. **ED:** BA in Journalism, University Florida, 1980 **C:** President of the Mystery Writers of America, 2003-2004, Writer, 1992-; Crime reporter, LA Times, 1987-95; Crime beat reporter, Fort Lauderdale News & Sun-Sentinel, Florida, 1981-86; Crime beat reporter, Daytona Beach News Journal, Florida, 1980-81 **CW:** Author: (novels) (Harry Bosch Series) The Black Echo, 1992 (Edgar Allen Poe award for Best First Novel, 1992), The Black Ice, 1993, The Concrete Blonde, 1994, The Last Coyote, 1995, Trunk Music, 1997, Angels Flight, 1999, A Darkness More Than Night, 2001, City of Bones, 2002 (New York Times Notable Book of Year, 2002, Anthony award for Best Novel, 2003), Lost Light, 2003, The Narrows, 2004, The Closers, 2005 (New York Times bestseller), Echo Park, 2006, The Overlook, 2007, The Drop, 2011, The Black Box, 2012, The Burning Room, 2014, (Mickey Haller series) The Lincoln Lawyer, 2005 (Macavity award for Best Mystery Novel, 2006, Shamus award, 2006), (Harry Bosch/Mickey Haller Series) The Brass Verdict, 2008 (#1 Publishers Weekly bestseller), Nine Dragons, 2009, The Reversal, 2010 (#1 Publishers Weekly bestseller), The Fifth Witness, 2011 (Harper Lee Prize for Legal Fiction, 2012), The Gods of Guilt, 2013, The Crossing, 2015, (other novels) The Poet, 1996 (Anthony award for Best Novel, 1997, Dilys award, 1997, Nero award, 1997), Blood Work, 1998 (Anthony award for Best Novel, 1999, Macavity award for Best Mystery Novel, 1999), Void Moon, 2000, Chasing The Dime, 2002, The Scarecrow, 2009 (#1 Publishers Weekly bestseller), (nonfiction) Crime Beat: A Decade of Covering Cops and Killers, 2006, (short stories) Two-Bagger, 2001, Cahoots, 2002, After Midnight, 2003, Christmas Even, 2004, Cielo Azul, 2005, Angle of Investigation, 2005, Mulholland Drive, 2007, Suicide Run, 2007, One Dollar Jackpot, 2007, Father's Day, 2008, Short Cut, 2009, Blue on Black, 2010, The Perfect Triangle, 2010, Blood Washes Off, 2011, The Safe Man, 2012; writer, creator (TV series) Level 9, 2001, guest editor (collected short stories) Best American Mystery Stories, 2003, Murder In Vegas, 2005, The Blue Religion, 2008, In the Shadow of the Master, 2009,(Film) The Wrong Side of Goodbye, 2016, The Late Show, 2017, Two Kinds of Truth, 2017(Television) Castle, 2009, Bosch, 2015 **AW:** Recipient Grand Prix award, France, 38 Caliber award, Premio Bancarella award, Italy, Maltese Falcon award, Japan,Time 100 Most Influential, 2017 **MEM:** Mem.: Mystery Writers America (president 2003-04)

CONNERY, SEAN, T: Actor **I:** Media & Entertainment **DOB:** 08/25/1930 **PB:** Edinburgh **SC:** Scotland **PT:** Son of Joseph and Euphamia C.; **MS:** Married **SPN:** Micheline Roquebrune, 1975; Diane Cilento, December 6, 1962 (div. September 6, 1973); **CH:** Jason **ED:** PhD (hon.), Edinburgh Napier University, 2009; DLitt (hon.), St. Andrews University, 1988; DLitt (hon.), Heriot-Watt University, 1981 **C:** Founder, Fountainbridge Films, Los Angeles, 1992-2002 **MIL:** With Brit. Royal Navy **CW:** First theater appearance in road show co. of South Pacific, England, 1953, also in Macbeth, Judith; actor: (films) Let's Make Up,1955, Lilacs in the Spring, 1954, No Road Back, 1956, Action of the Tiger, 1957, Hell Drivers, 1957, Time Lock, 1957, Another Time, Another Place, 1958, Tarzan's Greatest Adventure, 1959, Darby O'Gill and the Little People, 1959, The Frightened City, 1961, Operation Snafu, 1961, The Longest Day, 1962, Dr. No., 1962, From Russia With Love, 1963, Marnie, 1964, Woman of Straw, 1964, Goldfinger, 1964, The Hill, 1965, Thunderball, 1965, A Fine Madness, 1966, You Only Live Twice, 1967, Shalako, 1968, The Molly Maguires, 1970, The Red Tent, 1971, The Anderson Tapes, 1971, Diamonds are Forever, 1971, The Offence, 1973, Zardoz, 1974, The Terrorists, 1974, Murder on the Orient Express, 1974, The Wind and the Lion, 1975, The Man Who Would be King, 1975, Robin and Marian, 1976, The Next Man, 1976, A Bridge Too Far, 1977, The Great Train Robbery, 1979, Cuba, 1979, Meteor, 1979, Outland, 1981, Time Bandits, 1981, Sword of the Valiant, 1982, Wrong is Right, 1982, Five Days One Summer, 1982, Never Say Never Again, 1983, Highlander, 1986, The Name of the Rose, 1986, The Untouchables, 1987 (Academy award for Best Supporting Actor), The Presidio, 1988, Indiana Jones and the Last Crusade, 1989, Family Business, 1989, The Hunt for Red October, 1990, The Russia House, 1990, Highlander 2: The Quickening, 1991, Robin Hood: Prince of Thieves, 1991, Rising Sun, 1993, A Good Man in Africa, 1994, Just Cause, 1995, First Knight, 1995, The Rock, 1996, (voice only) Dragon Heart, 1996, Playing By Heart, 1998; actor, prodr.: Entrapment, 1999, Finding Forrester, 2000, Sir Billi, 2012; actor, executive producer.: The Avengers, 1998, The League of Extraordinary Gentlemen, 2003; actor, co-exec. prodr.: Medicine Man, 1992; (TV films) Requiem For a Heavyweight, 1957, Women in Love, 1957, The Square Ring, 1959, The Crucible, 1959, Colombe, 1960, Without the Grail, 1961, MacBeth, 1961, Anna Karenina, 1961, Male of the Species, 1969, Blitz, 2006; producer, dir.: The Bowler and the Bonnet (film documentary), I've Seen You Cut Lemons (London stage); prodr.: Something Like the Truth, Playing by Heart, 1998, (narrator) Macbeth, 1999; actor: (video games) James Bond 007: From Russia with Love (voice only), 2005; author: (autobiography) Being a Scot, 2008. **AW:** Named Star of the Year, National Association Theater Owners, 1987, Commander of Arts, France, Knight Commander of the Most Excellent Order of the Brit. Empire, Queen Elizabeth II, 2000; recipient Tribute award Brit. Academy Film and Television Arts, 1990, Career Achievement award National Board Rev., 1993, Cecil B. DeMille Golden Globe award Hollywood Foreign Press Association, 1996, Lifetime Achievement award ShoWest Convention, 1999, Life Achievement award Am. Film Institute, 2005, Campidoglia prize, 2006.

CONNOLLY, GERALD E., T: U.S. Representative from Virginia **I:** Government Administration/Government Relations/Government Services **DOB:** 10/20/1950 **PB:** Boston **SC:** MA/USA **ED:** MPA, Harvard University, 1979; BA in Lit., Maryknoll College, Glen Ellyn, Illinois, 1971 **C:** Member, US Congress from 11th Virginia district, 2009-; Member, Committee on Foreign Affairs; Member, Committee on Oversight and Government Reform; Director community relations, Sci. Applications International Corp. (SAIC),; Vice president, SRI International, Washington, 1989-97; Senior professional staff member, US Senate Committee Foreign Relations, Washington, 1979-89; Executive director, US Committee Refugees, Arlington, Virginia, 1975-78; Associate executive director, American Freedom From Hunger Foundation, 1972-74; Devel. associate, Heifer Project International, Little Rock, 1971-72 **CR:** Chairman Fairfax County Board Supervisors, 2003-08 **CIV:** Past president, Mantua Citizens Association, Past president, Fairfax County Federation Citizens Associations, Board trustees, Greater Washington Initiative, Member, US del. to 14th Ann. Conference Soviet Academy Sci., Moscow, 1990 Del., Dem. National Convention, 1988 Del., Dem. National Convention, 1984 Congl. advisor, UN Conference New and Renewable Energy Resources, 1981 Member, US del. to World Population Conference, Bucharest, Romania, 1974 Member, Fairfax County Dem. Committee, 1984 Board directors, Virginia Institute Government, Board directors, Institute Regional Excellence, Board directors, Medical Care for Children Partnership, Board directors, Fairfax County C. of C., Board directors, American Red Cross National Capital Area, Board directors, Fairfax Partnership for Youth, **MEM:** Mem.: Virginia Association Counties, Washington Trade Association **PA:** Democrat

CONNOLLY, SEAN, T: Food Products Executive **I:** Food & Restaurant Services **ED:** MBA, University Texas, Austin; BA in Economics, Vanderbilt University **C:** CEO, Conagra Brands, Chicago, 2015-; CEO, The Hillshire Brands Company, 2012-2014; CEO Sara Lee North American Retail; from 2012.; President North America soup, sauces & beverages division, Campbell Soup Co., Camden, New Jersey, 2010-2012; President, Campbell USA, Camden, New Jersey, 2008-10; President North American foodservice, Campbell Soup Co., Camden, New Jersey, 2007-08; Vice president, general manager U.S. soup, Campbell Soup Co., Camden, New Jersey, 2004-06; Vice president, general manager beverages & Mexico-Latin Am., Campbell Soup Co., Camden, New Jersey, 2003-04; Vice president food brands, Campbell Soup Co., Camden, New Jersey, 2002-03; Food & beverage brand management positions, Procter & Gamble Co., 1992-2002 **BA:** Conagra, Merchandise Mart, Chicago, IL, 60654

CONNORS, JIMMY, T: Retired Professional Tennis Player **I:** Athletics **DOB:** 09/02/1952 **PB:** East St. Louis **SC:** IL/USA **PT:** Son of James and Gloria (Thompson) C. (deceased); **MS:** Married **SPN:** Patti McGuire **CH:** Brett David, Aubree Leigh **ED:** Student, UCLA **C:** Now in Men's Seniors' Circuit,; Joined, World Championship Tennis, Inc., 1972 **CW:** Author: The Outsider: A Memoir, 2013 **AW:** ITF World Champion, 1982, ATP Player of the Year, 1982, ATP Comeback Player of the Year, 1991Recipient Player of Year award, 1974; named All-Am., 1971; ranked number 1 male tennis player in U.S. and World, 1976; ranked number 1 in world, 1978; elected to Tennis Hall of Fame, 1998. **ACH:** Achievements include winning Australian Men's Singles, 1974, Wimbledon Men's Singles, 1974, 82, Wimbledon Men's Doubles (with Ilie Nastase), 1973, U.S. Pro Championship Men's Singles, 1973, Cologne Cup, 1976, U.S. Clay Court Championship-Men's Singles, 1974, 76, 78, 79, U.S. Open Men's Singles, 1974, 76, 78,82, 83, U.S. Indoor Open Men's Singles, 1973, 74, 75, 78, 79, 83, 84, Pro Indoor Men's Singles, 1976, 78, 79, 80, U.S. Open Men's Doubles (with Ilie Nastase), 1975, U.S. Indoor Men's Doubles (with Frew McMillan), 1974, (with Ilie Nastase), 1975, U.S. Clay Court Men's Doubles (with Ilie Nastase), 1974, S.African Men's Singles, 1973, 74, World Championship Tennis Singles, 1977, Grand Prix Masters Championship, 1978, U.S. National Indoor Men's Singles, 1978, Australian Indoor Men's Singles, 1978, Suntory Cup, 1986, D.C. Tennis Classic, 1987, Olympia Open, Toulouse, France, 1987, Toulouse Grand Prix, 1989; member Davis Cup Team, 1976, 81, World Cup Team, 1976, 85(winning team). **BA:** Harpercollins Publishers, 195 Broadway, New York, NY, 10007

CONWAY, KELLYANNE, T: Counselor to the President **I:** Government Administration/Government Relations/Government Services **DOB:** 01/20/1967 **ED:** JD, George Washington University, With Honors; Student, Oxford University; BA, Trinity

College, Magna Cum Laude **C:** Counselor to the President, U.S., 2017-Present; President, CEO, The Polling Co., Inc., Washington, DC, 1995 **CR:** Board Member, National Journalism Center; Adjunct Professor, George Washington University Law Center **CIV:** Board Member, Men Against Breast Cancer and National Women's History Museum **CW:** Co-Author, What Women Really Want: How American Women Are Quietly Erasing Political, Racial, Class, and Religious Lines to Change the Way We Live, 2005, Editor, Public Womantrends **MEM:** Qualitative Research Consultants Association (QRCA), American Association of Public Opinion Research (AAPOR), Phi Beta Kappa **BAR:** District of Columbia, State of Pennsylvania, State of New Jersey, State of Maryland **BA:** Suite 790, 400 N Capitol Street NW, Washington, DC, 20001-1560

CONYERS, JOHN JR., **T:** Former U.S. Representative from Michigan **I:** Government Administration/Government Relations/Government Services **DOB:** 05/16/1929 **PB:** Detroit **SC:** MI/USA **PT:** Son of John and Lucille (Simpson) C.; **MS:** Married **SPN:** Monica Estes; **CH:** John Junior, Carl Edward **ED:** LLD, Wilberforce University, 1969; JD, Wayne State University, 1958; BA, Wayne State University, 1957 **CT:** Bar: Michigan 1959 **C:** Ranking member, US House Judiciary Committee, 1997-2017; Member, US Congress from 13th Michigan District, 2013-2017; Chairman, US House Government Operations Committee, 1989-95; Chairman, US House Judiciary Committee, 2007-11; Member, US Congress from 14th Michigan District, 1993-2013; Member, US Congress from 1st Michigan District, 1965-92; Referee, Michigan Workman's Compensation Department, 1961-64; Senior partner, Conyers, Bell & Townsend, 1959-61; Legis. assistant to Rep. John Dingell, US House of Representatives, 1959-61 **CR:** Past director education Local 900, United Auto Workers member adv. council Michigan Liberties Union general counsel Detroit Trade Union Leadership Council vice chairman national board Ams. for Democratic Action vice chairman adv. council ACLU an organizer Members Congress for Peace through Law board directors numerous other organizations including African-Am. Institute, Commission Racial Justice, Detroit Institute Arts, National Alliance Against Racist and Political Repression, National League Cities. co-founder Congressional Black Caucus, 1969-. **CIV:** Trustee Martin Luther King Junior Center for Non-Violent Social Change. Served to 2nd lieutenant U.S. Army, 1950-54, Korea. **CW:** Sponsor, contributing author: American Militarism, 1970, War Crimes and the American Conscience, 1970, Anatomy of an Undeclared War, 1972; Contributor articles to professional journals **AW:** Recipient Rosa Parks award Southern Christian Leadership Conference, National Association for the Advancement of Colored People National Voter Fund Pioneer award, Frederick Douglass Men of Strength award, Congressional Black Caucus Foundation Lifetime Achievement award, Council on American-Islamic Relations Leadership award for Civil Rights, Justice for All Disability Rights award, American Association of People with Disabilities, Black Broadcasters Alliance Golden Mike, National Jazz Heritage award, Spingarn medal, National Association for the Advancement of Colored People, 2008; named one of The Most Influential Black Americans, Ebony magazine 2006; named to The International Jazz Hall of Fame, Power 150 Ebony magazine, 2008. **MEM:** Member National Association for the Advancement of Colored People (executive board Detroit), Kappa Alpha Psi. **PA:** Democrat **BA:** Office of John Conyers, 2426 Rayburn HOB, Washington, DC, 20515

COOGLER, RYAN, **T:** Film Director, Screenwriter **I:** Media & Entertainment **DOB:** 05/23/1986 **PB:** Oakland **SC:** CA/USA **PT:** Ira Coogler, Joselyn (Thomas) Coogler **MS:** Married **SPN:** Zinzi Evans, 2016 **ED:** Student, USC School of Cinematic Arts, University of Southern California, Los Angeles, CA; Graduate, Finance, California State University, Sacramento; Student, Saint Mary's College of California, Moraga, CA **CIV:** Counselor, Juvenile Hall, San Francisco, CA, 2007-Present; Founding Member, Supporter, Blackout for Human Rights Campaign **CW:** Director, Writer, Actor, Sound Editor, (Short Films) Locks, 2009; Director, Writer, (Short Films) The Sculptor, 2011, (Films) Fruitvale Station, 2013, Creed, 2015, Black Panther, 2018; Director, Producer, (Films) Wrong Answer; Director, (Short Films) Fig, 2011, Gap, 2011; Executive Producer, (Films) The Day the Series Stopped, ESPN 30 for 30, 2014, Creed II, 2018; Co-Producer, (With LeBron James) Space Jam 2; Camera Operator, (Documentary) On the Grind, 2009; Camera Operator, Grip, (Short Films) It's Just Art, Baby, 2012; Boom Operator, Sound Editor, Sound Mixer, (Short Films) Get Some, 2010; Author, Graphic Novel and Young Adult Novel **AW:** Best Director, 44th Saturn Awards, Black Panther, 2018, Outstanding Directing in a Motion Picture, Outstanding Writing in a Motion Picture, NAACP Image Awards, Best or Top Ten Films of the Year Awards, National Board of Review, Boston Online Film Critics Association, African-American Film Critics Association, New Generation Award, Los Angeles Film Critics Association, Best Director Award, African-American Film Critics Association, Creed, 2015, Best First Film, Austin Film Critics Association, Best New Filmmaker, Boston Online Film Critics Association, Prix de l'Avenir d'Un Certain Regard, Cannes Film Festival, Bingham Ray Breakthrough Director Award, Gotham Awards, Breakout Filmmaker of the Year, Las Vegas Film Critics Society, Vimeo Award for Best Writer/Director, Nantucket Film Festival, Best Directorial Debut, National Board of Review, Best Debut Director, New York Film Critics Online, Marlon Riggs Award, San Francisco Film Critics Circle, Audience Award: U.S. Dramatic, Grand Jury Prize: U.S. Dramatic, Sundance Film Festival, Best First Feature, Independent Spirit Awards, Honorary Satellite Award, Satellite Awards, Fruitvale Station, 2013, Jack Nicholson Award for Achievement in Directing, Gap, 2011, HBO Short Film Competition, American Black Film Festival, DGA Student Film Award, Nominee, Outstanding Independent Short Film, Black Reel Awards, Fig, 2011, Dana and Albert Broccoli Award for Filmmaking Excellence, Tribeca Film Festival, Locks, 2009

COOK, DEBORAH L., **T:** Federal Judge **I:** Law and Legal Services **DOB:** 02/08/1952 **PB:** Pittsburgh **SC:** PA/USA **ED:** LLD (hon.), University of Akron, Ohio, 1996; JD, University of Akron, Ohio, 1978; BA in English, University of Akron, Ohio, 1974 **C:** Judge, US Court Appeals, (6th cir.), Cincinnati, 2003-; Justice, Ohio Supreme Court, 1995-2003; Judge, 9th district, Ohio Court Appeals, 1991-94; Partner, Roderick & Linton, Akron, 1976-91 **CIV:** Board of Trustees, Summit County United Way, Vol. Center, Stan Hywet Hall and Gardens, Akron School Law, College Scholars, Inc. Board of Directors Women's Network vol. Mobile Meals, Safe Landing Shelter **AW:** Named Woman of Year, Women's Network, 1991; National Shield Award, Delta Gamma **MEM:** Fellow, Am. Bar Foundation; Member, Omicron Delta Kappa, Delta Gamma (president) **BA:** 532 Potter Stewart US Courthouse, 100 E Fifth St, Cincinnati, OH, 45202-3988

COOK, IAN M., **T:** Chairman, CEO **I:** Consumer Goods and Services **CN:** Colgate-Palmolive Co. **ED:** University of London **C:** Chairman, President, CEO, Colgate-Palmolive Co., 2009-Present; Director, Colgate Holdings, 2003-Present; President, CEO, Colgate-Palmolive Co., 2007-2008; President, COO, Colgate-Palmolive Co., 2005-2007; COO, Colgate-Palmolive Co., 2004-2005; Executive Vice President, Colgate-Palmolive Co., 2000-2004; President, Colgate-North America, Colgate-Palmolive Co., 1997-2002; Executive Vice President, Marketing, Colgate North America, Colgate-Palmolive Co., New York, NY, 1994-1997; Colgate, United Kingdom, 1976; General Manager, Colgate's Nordic Group, Copenhagen, Denmark; General Manager, Colgate, Dominican Republic; Marketing Director, Colgate, Philippines **CR:** Board of Directors, PepsiCo, Inc., 2008-Present; Colgate-Palmolive Co., 2007-Present; Director, Catalyst; Director, The Consumer Goods Forum **BA:** Colgate-Palmolive Co, 300 Park Avenue, New York, NY, 10022-0000

COOK, PAUL J. JR., **T:** U.S. Representative from California **I:** Government Administration/Government Relations/Government Services **DOB:** 03/03/1943 **PB:** Meriden, Connecticut **ED:** MA in Political Sci., University California, Riverside, 2000; MPA, California State University, San Bernadino, 1996; BS in Teaching, Southern Connecticut State University, 1966 **C:** Member, US House Foreign Affairs Committee, 2013-; Member, Committee on Energy and Commerce; Member, US House Veterans' Affairs Committee, 2013-; Member, US House Armed Services Committee, 2013-; Member, US Congress from 8th California District, Washington, 2013-; Member District 65, California State Assembly, 2006-12; City councilman, City of Yucca Valley, 1998-2006 **CR:** Instructor political violence & terrorism University California Riverside, 2002- professor Copper Mountain College, 1998-2002 director Yucca Valley Chamber of Commerce, 1993-94 **MIL:** Served in US Marine Corps, 1966-92, Vietnam **AW:** Decorated Purple Hearts (2), Bronze Star **MEM:** Mem.: Disabled American Vets., Yucca Valley Chamber of Commerce, United Way and Red Cross local chapter, Vets. Foreign Wars, American Legion **PA:** Republican

COOK, SCOTT DAVID, **T:** Co-Founder of Intuit **I:** Business Management/Business Services **DOB:** 07/26/1952 **PB:** Glendale **SC:** California **ED:** MBA, Harvard University; BA in Economics & Math., University Southern California **C:** Founder, Center for Brand and Product Management at the University of Wisconsin–Madison School of Business, 2002; Independent Director, The Proctor and Gamble Company, 2000-; Independent Director, Ebay, 1998-2015; Board directors, Intuit, Inc., Menlo Park, California, 1984-; Co-founder, Intuit, Inc., Menlo Park, California, 1983-; Chairman, Intuit, Inc., Menlo Park, California, 1993-98; President, CEO, Intuit, Inc., Menlo Park, California, 1984-94; Consultant, Bain & Co., Inc., **CR:** Board of Directors The Procter & Gamble Co., 2000-, Various Marketing Positions, Including Brand Manager Board of Directors eBay, 1998- **CIV:** Board Visitors, Intuit Scholarship Foundation, Board Visitors, Center Brand and Product Management, University Wisconsin, Board Visitors, Harvard Business School, Board Trustees, Asia Foundation **AW:** Named one of Forbes 400: Richest Americans, 2006-; Recipient Lifetime Achievement Award, PC magazine, 2003, Software Publishers Association, 1994 **MEM:** Mem.: Phi Beta Kappa **BA:** 2700 Coast Avenue, Mountain View, CA, 94043

COOK, TIM, T: CEO of Apple **I:** Technology **CN:** Apple **DOB:** 11/01/1960 **PB:** Mobile **SC:** AL/USA **PT:** Son of Donald D. and Geraldine Cook **ED:** MBA, Duke University Fuqua School Business, 1988; BS in Industrial Engineering, Auburn University Samuel Ginn College Engineering, 1982 **C:** CEO, Apple, Inc. (formerly Apple Computer, Inc.), 2011-; COO, Apple, Inc. (formerly Apple Computer, Inc.), Cupertino, 2005-11; Interim CEO, Apple Computer Inc., 2009; Executive vice president worldwide sales and operations, Apple Computer Inc., 2002-05; Senior vice president worldwide operations sales and support, Apple Computer Inc., 2000-02; Senior vice president worldwide operations, Apple Computer Inc., Cupertino, California, 1998-2000; Vice president corporate materials, Compaq Computer Corp., Harris County, Texas, 1997-98; COO, Reseller division, Intelligent Electronics Inc., 1996-97; Senior vice president fulfillment, Intelligent Electronics Inc., 1994-96; With, IBM Corp., Research Triangle Park, North Carolina, 1982-94 **CR:** Board directors National Football Foundation, Apple Inc., 2011-, Nike Inc., 2005- **CIV:** Board trustees, Duke University, 2015- **AW:** Named one of The 50 Most Influential People in Global Finance, Bloomberg Markets, 2015, 2014, 2012, The 100 Most Influential People in the World, TIME magazine, 2016, 2015, 2012, The World's Most Powerful People, Forbes magazine, 2011-15; Fuqua scholar, Duke University; Alabama Academy of Honor Inductee 2015; Fortune Magazine's World's Greatest Leader, 2015; Ripple of Change Award. 2015; Financial Times Person of the Year, 2014,Human Rights Campaign Visibility Award, 2015

COONS, CHRISTOPHER ANDREW, T: U.S. Senator from Delaware **I:** Government Administration/Government Relations/Government Services **DOB:** 09/09/1963 **PB:** Greenwich **SC:** CT/USA **PT:** Son of Ken Coon and Sally Coons; **ED:** Studies abroad, University Kenya, Nairobi; MA in Ethics, Yale Div. School, Connecticut, 1992; JD, Yale Law School, Connecticut, 1992; BA in Chemistry & Political Sci., Amherst College, Massachusetts, 1985 **C:** Vice Chair, Senate Ethics Committee, 2017-; Member, U.S. Senate Appropriations Committee, 2013-; Member, U.S. Senate Judiciary Committee, 2010-; Member, U.S. Senate Foreign Relations Committee, 2010-; Member, U.S. Senate Budget Committee, 2010-; U.S. Senator from Del., 2010-; Member, U.S. Senate Energy & Natural Resources, 2010-13; County executive, New Castle County, 2004-10; President, New Castle County Council, Del., 2000-04; In-house counsel, W.L. Gore & Associates, 1996-2004 **CIV:** Active, South African Council Churches, Active, Council for Homeless, Hon. life member, Minquadale Fire Co., Del., Member adv. board, Hearts and Minds Film Organization, Member adv. board, Del. College Art & Design, Member adv. board, First State Innovation, Member adv. board, Better Business Bureau Del., Member adv. board, Wilmington Riverfront Devel. Corp., Del., Member adv. board, Bear/Glasgow Boys & Girls Club, Board directors, National "I Have a Dream" Foundation, **AW:** Named Hon. Life Member, Minquadale Fire Co., Hon. Commander, 166th Air Wing of Del. Air National Guard; recipient Governor's Outstanding Volunteer award, 1999; Aspen-Rodel fellow, Aspen Institute Rodel Fellowships in Pub. Leadership, 2009 **MEM:** Mem.: Kiwanis Club Wilmington **PA:** Democrat **BA:** The Office of Christopher Coons, 127A Russell Senate Office Building, Washington, DC, 20510

COOPER, ANDERSON HAYS, T: Broadcast Journalist, News Correspondent **I:** Media & Entertainment **DOB:** 06/03/1967 **PB:** NYC **PT:** Son of Wyatt Emory Cooper and Gloria Vanderbilt. **ED:** Attended, Vietnam National University, Hanoi; BA in Political Sci., Yale University, New Haven, 1989 **C:** Corr. 60 Minutes, CBS News, 2007-; Anchor, host Anderson Cooper 360, Cable News Network (CNN), 2003-; Host, Anderson Live, 2011-13; Co-anchor NewsNight, Cable News Network (CNN), 2005; Weekend prime-time anchor CNN, Cable News Network (CNN), 2002-03; Co-anchor American Morning,, Cable News Network (CNN), 2002; Host The Mole,, ABC, 2001-02; Co-anchor World News Now, ABC News, 1999-2000; Corr., ABC News, 1995-99; Producer, chief international corr., Channel One News, **CR:** Contributing editor Details magazine host CNN's New Year's Eve special from Times Square, 2002- **CW:** Author: Dispatches From the Edge: A Memoir of War, Disasters and Survival, 2006 (#1 New York Times bestseller, #1 Publishers Weekly bestseller); co-author (with Gloria Vanderbilt): The Rainbow Comes and Goes: A Mother and Son on Life, Love, and Loss, 2016; host (annual TV special) CNN Heroes: An All-Star Tribute, 2007-, co-host (documentaries) Planet in Peril, 2007, Planet in Peril: Battle Lines, 2008, narrator (Broadway plays) How to Succeed in Business Without Really Trying, 2011, appearances in numerous films and documentaries **AW:** Named one of The 100 Agents of Change, Rolling Stone magazine, 2009; recipient Vito Russo award, Gay & Lesbian Alliance Against Defamation, 2013, Emmy award for Outstanding Live Coverage of a Current News Story - Long Form, 2011, Emmy award for Outstanding Coverage of a Breaking News Story in a Regularly Scheduled Newscast, 2011, Bronze award, National Education Film & Video Festival, Silver Plaque, Chicago International Film Festival, National Order Honour & Merit, Government Haiti, 2010, Action Against Hunger Humanitarian award, 2008, Emmy award Outstanding Feature Story in a Regularly Scheduled Newscast, 2006, Emmy award for Outstanding Live Coverage of Breaking News Story - Long Form, 2006, National Headliners award, Press Club Atlantic City, 2005, Peabody award, Henry W. Grady College Journalism & Mass Communications, University Georgia, 2005, GLAAD Media award, Gay & Lesbian Alliance Against Defamation, 2001, Emmy award for contribution to ABC's coverage of Princess Diana's funeral, 1997

COOPER, BRADLEY, I: Media & Entertainment **DOB:** 06/05/1905 **PB:** Philadelphia **SC:** PA **PT:** Son of Charles J. and Gloria (Campano) Cooper; **ED:** MFA, Actors Studio Drama School, New York City; BA in English, Georgetown University, 1997 **CW:** Host (TV series) Treks in a Wild World, 2000; actor: (TV series) The Street, 2000-01, Alias, 2001-06, Touching Evil, 2004, Jack & Bobby, 2004-05, Kitchen Confidential, 2005-06, Nip/Tuck, 2007-08, Wet Hot American Summer: First Day of Camp, 2015-; (films) Wet Hot American Summer, 2001, My Little Eye, 2002, Carnival Knowledge, 2002, Stella Shorts 1998-2002, 2002, Wedding Crashers, 2005, Failure to Launch, 2006, The Comebacks, 2007, Older Than America, 2008, The Rocker, 2008, The Midnight Meat Train, 2008, New York, I Love You, 2008, Yes Man, 2008, He's Just Not That Into You, 2009, The Hangover, 2009, All About Steve, 2009, Case 39, 2009, Valentine's Day, 2010, The A-Team, 2010, The Hangover Part II, 2011, Hit and Run, 2012, The Place Beyond the Pines, 2012, The Hangover Part III, 2013, Guardians of the Galaxy (voice), 2014, Serena, 2014, Aloha, 2015, Adam Jones, 2015, Burnt, 2015, Joy, 2015, 10 Cloverfield Lane, 2016; (TV films) The Last Cowboy, 2003, I Want to Marry Ryan Banks, 2004; (Broadway plays) Three Days of Rain, 2006, The Elephant Man, 2014; (plays) The Understudy, 2008; actor, executive producer (films) Limitless, 2011, Silver Linings Playbook, 2012 (National Board Review award for Best Actor,

2012, Critics' Choice award for Best Actor in a Comedy Movie, 2013), The Words, 2012, American Hustle, 2013, actor, producer American Sniper, 2014 (Critics' Choice award for Best Actor in an Action Movie, 2015, MTV Movie award for Best Male Performance, 2015); prodr.: (films) War Dogs, 2016 **AW:** Named Sexiest Man Alive, People magazine, 2011; named one of The 10 Most Fascinating People of 2015, Barbara Walters Special; recipient International Man of Year award, GQ, 2011

COOPER, JAMES HAYES SHOFNER, T: U.S. Representative from Tennessee **I:** Government Administration/Government Relations/Government Services **DOB:** 06/19/1954 **PB:** Nashville **PT:** Son of William Prentice Junior and Hortense (Powell) Cooper; **ED:** JD, Harvard Law School, 1980; BA, MA in Politics and Economics, Oxford University, 1977; BA in History and Economics, University North Carolina, Chapel Hill, 1975 **C:** Member, US Congress from 5th Tennessee District, 2003-; Member, Committee on Armed Services,; Committee on Oversight and Government Reform; Co-founder, Partner, Chairman Board Directors, Brentwood Capital Advs. LLC, Nashville, 1999-2002; Managing Director, Equitable Securities Corp., Nashville, 1995-99; Member, US Congress from 4th Tennessee District, 1983-95; Attorney, Waller, Lansden, Dortch & Davis, Nashville, 1980-82 **CR:** Adjunct Professor Vanderbilt University Owen School Management, Nashville, 1995- **AW:** Rhodes Scholar, 1975, Morehead-Cain Scholar, 1972 **MEM:** Mem.: Phi Beta Kappa **PA:** Democrat **BA:** 1536 Longworth HOB, Washington, DC, 20515

COOPER, ROY ASBERRY III, T: Governor of North Carolina **I:** Government Administration/Government Relations/Government Services **DOB:** 06/13/1957 **PB:** Rocky Mount, North Carolina **PT:** Son of Roy Asberry Junior and Beverly (Batchelor) Cooper; **ED:** JD, University North Carolina School Law, 1982; BA, University North Carolina, Chapel Hill, 1979 **CT:** Bar: North Carolina 1982 **C:** Governor, State of North Carolina, 2017-,; Attorney General, State of North Carolina, 2001-2017; Attorney General, State of North Carolina, 2001-; Dem. Majority Leader, North Carolina Senate, 1997-2001; Member, North Carolina Senate, 1991-2001; Chairman Judicial Committee, North Carolina House of Reps., 1989-91; Member, North Carolina House of Reps., 1987-91; Partner, Fields and Cooper, Rocky Mount, 1982-2001 **AW:** Recipient Morehead Scholar, University North Carolina, 1975-79 **MEM:** Mem.: National Association Attorneys General (President 2010-11, Kelley-Wyman award 2013) **PA:** Democrat **BA:** Office of Roy Cooper, 20301 Mail Service Center, Raleigh, NC, 27699-0301

COPELAND, MISTY DANIELLE, T: Dancer **I:** Media & Entertainment **DOB:** 09/10/1982 **PB:** Kansas City **PT:** Daughter of Doug Copeland and Sylvia DelaCerna; **C:** Principal dancer, Am. Ballet Theatre, New York City, 2015-; Soloist, Am. Ballet Theatre, New York City, 2007-15; Corps de ballet, Am. Ballet Theatre, New York City, 2001-07; Studio co., Am. Ballet Theatre, New York City, 2000; Summer intensive program, Am. Ballet Theatre, New York City, 1998-2000 **CR:** Sponsored athlete Under Armour, 2014- guest judge So You Think You Can Dance, 2014 **CIV:** Spokesperson, Project Plie, 2013- **CW:** Author: (autobiography) Life in Motion: An Unlikely Ballerina, 2014,Firebird,2014, Ballerina Body, 2017; (appeared in): (Broadway plays) On the Town, 2015 **AW:** Named one of The 10 Most Fascinating People of 2015, Barbara Walters Special, The Most Influential People in the World, Time Magazine, 2015, 25 to Watch, Dance Magazine, 2003 **ACH:** Achievements include becoming the first African-American woman to be promoted to principal dancer in American Ballet Theatre's 75 year history **BA:** American Ballet Theatre, 890 Broadway, New York, NY, 10003

COPPOLA, FRANCIS, T: Film Producer, Director, Screenwriter **I:** Media & Entertainment **DOB:** 04/07/1939 **PB:** Detroit **SC:** MI/USA **ED:** MFA, UCLA, 1968; BA, Hofstra University, 1958 **C:** Founder, Blancaneaux Turtle Inn, 2000-; Founder, Zoetrope All-Story, 1997-; Owner, Niebaum Coppola Estate Winery, Napa Valley, 1995-; Founder, Am. Zoetrope, Ltd., San Francisco, 1968-; Pub., City Magazine, San Francisco, 1975-76 **CW:** (director, producer, writer): (films) Tonight for Sure, 1962; The Godfather, 1972 (Academy Award for Best Adapted Screenplay, 1973, Director Guild Am. award for Best Director, 1973, Golden Globe award for Best Director, Hollywood Foreign Press., 1973, Golden Globe award for Best Screenplay, Hollywood Foreign Press., 1973, Writer Guild Am. award for Best Screenplay, 1973); The Conversation, 1974 (Golden Palm award, Cannes Film Festival, 1974, National Board Review award for Best Director, 1974); The Godfather: Part II, 1974 (Academy Award for Best Picture, 1975, Academy Award for Best Adapted Screenplay, 1975, Academy Award for Best Director, 1975, Director Guild Am. award for Best Director, 1975, National Society Film Critics award for Best Director, 1975, Writer Guild Am. award for Best Screenplay, 1975); Apocalypse Now, 1979 (BAFTA award for Best Director, 1979, Golden Palm award, Cannes Film Festival, 1979, Golden Globe award for Best Director, Hollywood Foreign Press., 1979); The Godfather: Part III, 1990; Tetro, 2009; director, producer, writer (films) Twixt, 2011, Distant Vision, 2015; (director, executive producer, writer): (films) Rumble Fish, 1983; (director, producer) The Terror, 1963; Gardens of Stone, 1987; Bram Stoker's Dracula, 1992; Jack, 1996; (director, writer) Dementia 13, 1963; You're a Big Boy Now, 1966; The Rain People, 1969; One From the Heart, 1982; Captain EO, 1986; New York Stories (Life Without Zoe segment), 1989; The Rainmaker, 1997; (director, writer): (films) Youth Without Youth, 2007; dir.: Nebo zovyot, 1960, The Bellboy and the Playgirls, 1962, Finian's Rainbow, 1968, The Outsiders, 1983, The Cotton Club, 1984, Peggy Sue Got Married, 1986, Tucker: The Man and His Dream, 1988; (TV series) Faerie Tale Theatre, 1987; prodr.: (films) American Graffiti, 1973, The Junky's Christmas, 1993, Frankenstein, 1994, Don Juan DeMarco, 1995, Lanai-Loa, 1998, The Florentine, 1999; executive prodr.: THX 1138, 1971, Kagemusha, 1980, The Escape Artist, 1982, Hammett, 1982, The Black Stallion, 1979, Koyaanisqatsi, 1982, The Black Stallion Returns, 1983, Mishima: A Life in Four Chapters, 1985, Lionheart, 1987, Tough Guys Don't Dance, 1987, Powaqqatsi, 1988, Wait Until Spring, Bandini, 1989, Wind, 1992, The Secret Garden, 1993, My Family, 1995, Haunted, 1995, Buddy, 1997, The Virgin Suicides, 1999, The Third Miracles, 1999, Goosed, 1999, Sleepy Hollow, 1999, CQ, 2001, No Such Thing, 2001, Jeepers Creepers, 2001, Suriyothai, 2001, Pumpkin, 2002, Assassination Tango, 2002, Jeepers Creepers II, 2003, Lost in Translation, 2003, Kinsey, 2004, Marie Antoinette, 2006, The Good Shepherd, 2006, Somewhere, 2010, On the Road, 2012; (TV films) The People, 1972, Dark Angel, 1996, White Dwarf, 1995, Tecumseh: The Last Warrior, 1995, Kidnapped, 1995, Survival on the Mountain, 1997, The Odyssey, 1997, Outrage, 1998, Moby Dick, 1998, Dr. Jekyll and Mr Hyde, 1999, In My Life, 2002; (TV series) The Outsiders, 1990, First Wave, 1998, Platinum, 2003, The 4400, 2007; (writer): (films) Is Paris Burning?, 1966; This Property Is Condemned, 1966; author: (screenplays) The Great Gatsby, 1974, Patton, 1970 (Academy Award

for Best Original Screenplay, 1971); appeared in (documentaries) Hearts of Darkness: A Filmmaker's Apocalypse, 1991, I Knew It Was You: Rediscovering John Cazale, 2010 **AW:** Recipient Mary Pickford award, 2001, Lifetime Achievement award, Director Guild Am., 1998, Bill Wilder award, National Board Review, 1997, Career Golden Lion award, Venice Film Festival, 1992 **MEM:** Directors Guild Am. Inc. **BA:** American Zoetrope, 916 Kearny St, San Francisco, CA, 94133

COPPOLA, SOFIA CARMINA, T: Film Director, Film Producer, Scriptwriter **I:** Media & Entertainment **PB:** New York **SC:** NY/USA **PT:** Francis Ford Coppola; Eleanor Coppola **C:** Designer, Milk Fed; Intern with Karl Lagerfield, Chanel, **CW:** Actor: (films) The Godfather, 1972, The Godfather: Part II, 1974, The Outsiders, 1983, Rumble Fish, 1983, The Cotton Club, 1984, Frankenweenie, 1984, Peggy Sue Got Married, 1986, Anna, 1987, The Godfather: Part III, 1990, Inside Monkey Zetterland, 1992, Star Wars: Episode I-The Phantom Menace, 1999, CQ, 2001; director, producer, screenwriter (films) Lick the Star, 1998, Lost in Translation, 2003 (Boston Society of Film Critics award for Best Director, 2003, National Board Review award for Special Achievement, 2003, New York Film Critics Circle award for Best Director, 2003, Golden Globe for Best Screenplay, 2004, Academy award for Best Screenplay, 2004), Marie Antoinette, 2006, Somewhere, 2010 (NAt. Board Review award for Special Filmmaking Achievement, 2010), The Bling Ring, 2013, A Very Murray Christmas, 2015, The Beguiled, 2017 director, screenwriter The Virgin Suicides, 1999, host (TV series) Hi-Octane, 1994, segment writer New York Stories, 1989, costume designer, 1989, series creator Platinum, 2003, writer, 2003; executive prodr.: (TV series) Platinum, 2003; costume designer (plays) The Spirit of '76, 1990

CORBAT, MICHAEL LOUIS, T: CEO **I:** Financial Services **CN:** Citigroup, Inc. **DOB:** 05/02/1960 **PB:** Bristol **SC:** CT/USA **PT:** Deanne Corbat **ED:** BA in Economics, Harvard University, Cambridge, MA (1983) **C:** Chief Executive Officer, Citigroup, Inc. (2012-Present); Chief Executive Officer, Citi Holdings (2009-2012); Interim Chief Executive Officer, Citi Holdings (2009); Chief Executive Officer, Citi Global Wealth Management (2008-2009); Chief Executive Officer, Europe, Middle East & Africa, Citigroup, Inc. (2012); Managing Director, Head, Global Corporation/Global Commercial Banks, Citigroup, Inc.; Head, Global Emerging Markets, Citigroup, Inc.; Various Advisory/Structuring Positions, Citigroup, Inc., London, England, New York City, NY; Managing Director, Head, Fixed Income Sales Department, Salomon Brothers (1993-1998); With Fixed Income Sales Department, Salomon Brothers, Atlanta, GA (1983-1993) **CR:** Board of Directors, Citigroup, Inc. (2012-Present) **CIV:** Board of Trustees, Salisbury School, CT **MEM:** Board of Directors, Swedish American Chamber of Commerce **H:** Fly Fishing; Golf; Skiing

CORDANI, DAVID M., T: President and CEO **I:** Health, Wellness and Fitness **CN:** Cigna Corp. **ED:** MBA in Marketing, University of Hartford, CT (1994); BS, Texas Agricultural and Mechanical University, College Station, Texas (1988) **CT:** CPA, Chartered Financial Consultant **C:** President, Chief Executive Officer, Cigna Corp. (2010-Present); President, Chief Operating Officer, Cigna Corp. (2008-2009); President, Cigna HealthCare (2005-2008); President, Health Segments, Cigna HealthCare (2004-2005); Senior Vice President, Chief Financial Officer, Cigna HealthCare (2002-2004); Senior Vice President, Transformation and Progressive Management, Cigna HealthCare (2002); Chief Financial

Officer, Field of Operations, Cigna HealthCare; President, Southeast Region, Cigna HealthCare; Vice President, Corporate Accounting and Planning, Cigna Corp. (2000-2002); Controller, Cigna Corp.; With, Coopers & Lybrand **CR:** Board of Directors, National Association of Manufacturers **BA:** CIGNA HealthCare, 900 Cottage Grove Rd, Bloomfield, CT, 06002

CORDEN, JAMES, T: Actor, Television Personality **I:** Media & Entertainment **PB:** Buckinghamshire **SC:** England **PT:** Malcolm Corden; Margaret (Collins) Corden **C:** Television Personality, Actor, Comedian, 1996- **CW:** Actor: (Broadway plays) The History Boys, 2006, One Man, Two Guvnors, 2012 (Tony award for Best Performance by an Actor in a Leading Role in a Play, 2012); (TV series) Boyz Unlimited, 1999, Teachers, 2001-03, Fat Friends, 2000-05, Horne & Corden, 2009; TV appearances Beast Hunters, 2010, National Theatre Live, 2011, Stella, 2012; actor: (TV films) Jack and the Beanstalk: The Real Story, 2001, Cruise of the Gods, 2002, The One Ronnie, 2010, The Gruffalo (voice), 2009, The Gruffalo's Child (voice), 2011, Ronald Dahl's Esio Trot, 2014; (films) Whatever Happened to Harold Smith, 1999, Heartlands, 2002, Pierrepoint: The Last Hangman, 2005, Starter for 10, 2006, The History Boys, 2006, Heroes and Villains, 2006, How to Lose Friends & Alienate People, 2008, Telstar: The Joe Meek Story, 2008, Vampire Killers, 2009, Gulliver's Travels, 2010, The Three Musketeers, 2011, Can a Song Save Your Life?, 2013, One Chance, 2013, Into the Woods, 2014, Roald Dahl's Esio Trot (narrator), 2014, Kill Your Friends, 2015, The Lady in the Van, 2015, Norm of the North (voice), 2016, Trolls (voice), 2016; actor, writer, associate producer (TV series) Gavin & Stacey, 2007-10, actor, writer The Wrong Mans, 2013-14, , (TV special) ,(Film) The Emoji Movie, 2017, Ralph Breaks the Internet: Wreck-It Ralph 2, 2018, Peter Rabbit, 2018, Ocean's 8, 2018, Smallfoot, 2018 (Television) The Wrong Mans, 2013, The Guess List, 2014, The Late Late Show with James Corden, 2015 (Primetime Emmy for Outstanding Interactive Program, 2016, Primetime Emmy Award for Outstanding Variety, Music, or Comedy Special, 2016-17) Very British Problems, 2015, 70th Tony Awards, 2016, Matilda and the Ramsay Bunch, 2016, John Bishop: In Conversation With..., 2016, 59th Annual Grammy Awards, 2017,(Outstanding Special Class Program, 2017)

COREA, CHICK, T: Musician, Composer **I:** Media & Entertainment **DOB:** 06/12/1941 **PB:** Chelsea **SC:** MA/USA **PT:** Son of Armando John and Anna (Zaccone) **C:**; **MS:** Married **SPN:** Gayle Moran; **CH:** Thaddeus, Liana **ED:** Student, Columbia, 1960; Student, Juilliard School Music, 1961 **C:** Founder, Stretch Records, LA, 1992— **CW:** Pianist with Mongo Santamaria, 1962; Pianist, Composer with Blue Mitchell, 1965, Stan Getz, 1966-68; Pianist with Miles Davis, 1969-71, Sarah Vaughan, 1970; Founder, Leader, Pianist with Group Return to Forever, 1971—; Author: The Jazz Style of Chick Corea, 1972; Founder Group The Elektric Band, 1986; Over 100 Recs. Including Piano Improvisations 1 & 2, 1971, The Leprechaun, 1976, My Spanish Heart, 1976, Mad Hatter, Delphi 1, 2, & 3, Light as a Feather, Romantic Warrior, Hymn of the Seventh Galaxy, 1973, Music Magic, 1977, (with Steve Kujala) Voyage, 1984; Toured, Recorded The Chick Corea Elektric Band, 1986, Light Years, 1987, (Grammy Award for Best R&B Instrumental Performance, 1989), Eye of the Beholder, 1988 (Best Keyboard Album 1988), Chick Corea Akoustic Band, 1989; Record with Elektric Band Inside Out, 1990, Chick Corea Akoustic Band Alive!, 1991, Elektric Band Beneath the Mask, 1991; Album Early Circle, 1992, Solo Album Expressions, 1994,

Paint the World, 1993, Time Warp, 1995, From Nothing, 1996, Remembering Bud Powell, 1997, Native Sense, 1997 (Grammy Award for Best Jazz Instrumental Performance), Origin, 1998, Change, 1998, Corea Concerto, 1999 (Grammy Award for Best Instrumental Arrangement, 2000), Come Rain or Shine, 1999, Past, Present & Futures, 2001, Sea Breeze, 2002, Rendezvous in New York, 2003 (Grammy Award for Best Jazz Instrumental Solo: Matrix, 2003), To the Stars, 2004, I Ain't Mad at You, 2005, Fiesta Gillespie & Milhaud Jazz, 2005, The Ultimate Adventure, 2006 (Best Jazz Instrumental Album, Best Instrumental Arrangement, Grammy Awards, 2007), The Enchantment, 2007 (Best Instrumental Album, Latin Grammy Awards, 2007), Chillin' in Chelan, 2007, From Miles, 2007, The New Crystal Silence, 2008 (Best Jazz Instrumental Album, Grammy Awards, 2009) Five Peace Band Live, 2009, Duet, 2009, Forever, 2011 (Best Instrumental Album, Latin Grammy Awards, 2011, Best Jazz Instrumental Album, Grammy Awards, 2012), Hot House, 2012 (Grammy Awards for Best Improvised Jazz Solo, Best Instrumental Composition for Mozart Goes Dancing (with Gary Burton), 2013); numerous collaborations and appearances on albums with other groups, The Continents: Concerto for Jazz Quintet & Chamber Orchestra, 2012, The Mothership Returns, 2012, The Vigil, 2013, Trilogy, 2013, Solo-piano-Portraits, 2014, Two, 2015, The Musician, 2017. **AW:** Recipient Grammy Award for Best Jazz Group Performance, 1975, 1976, for Best Jazz Group Instrumental Peformance, 1978, 1979, 1981, 1989, 1999, for Best Instrumental Arrangement, 1976, 2000, 2007, for Best R&B Instrumental Performance, 1988, for Best Jazz Instrumental Solo, 1998, 2003, for Best Jazz Instrumental Album, 2007, 2012, Grammy for Best Jazz Instrumental Album, 2015; 6 Playboy Music Poll awards; 19 Downbeat awards including Best Electric Pianist, 1987, Best Electric Group, 1988, Best Electric Piano, 1988, 17 Keyboard Magazine Readers Poll awards, Best Overall Keyboardist, 1988, 89, Best Jazz Piano, 1989, Best Jazz Keyboards, 1988, 89, Other Awards; Named Jazz Life Musician of World, Jazz Forum Music Poll, Europe, 1974, Jazzman of Year, Swing Journal, Japan, 1978, Swing Journal Critics Poll, 1980, Best Electric Jazz Group Downbeat Readers Poll, 1990, Best Acoustic Pianist Jazz Times Reader Poll, 1990, Best Jazz Piano, 1990, Keyboard Sythesist, 1990, Overall Best Keyboardist Keyboard Magazine Readers Poll, 1990, Top Jazz Keyboardist, 1990, Top Jazz Pianist, 1990, #1 in Field of Jazz, 1990, Best Keyboard Player Swing Journal Magazine, 1990, Doctor Honoris Causa Norwegian University Science and Tech., 2010. **PA:** Member Church of Scientology **BA:** Chick Corea Productions, 10400 Samoa Ave, Tujunga, CA, 91042

CORIGLIANO, JOHN PAUL, T: Composer **I:** Media & Entertainment **DOB:** 02/16/1938 **PB:** NYC **PT:** Son of John and Rose (Buzen) C. **ED:** BA cum laude, Columbia University, 1959 **C:** Member faculty, Juilliard School of Music, New York City, 1991-; Distinguished professor music, Lehman College, New York City **CW:** Composer: Violin Sonata, 1963, Tournaments Overture, 1965, The Cloisters for Voice and Orchestra, 1965, Concerto for Piano and Orchestra, 1988, A Dylan Thomas Trilogy: A Choral Symphony, 1961-76, Concerto for Oboe and Orchestra, 1975, Etude Fantasy for Piano, 1976, Concerto for Clarinet and Orchestra, 1977, Promenade Overture, 1981, Summer Fanfare, 1982, Pied Piper Fantasy: Concerto for Flute and Orchestra, 1982, Fantasia on an Ostinato for Orchestra, 1985, The Ghosts of Versailles, 1987, Symphony # 1, 1991 (Grawemeyer award 1991), Troubadours (Variations for Guitar and Chamber Orchestra), 1993, Fanfares to Music, 1993, Phan-

tasmagoria for Cello and Piano, 1993, String Quartet, 1996, The Red Violin (chaconne for violin and orchestra, Academy award for best original score 1999), 1997 (Genie award Best Original Score 1998), A Dylan Thomas Trilogy, rev. edition, 1998, Vocalise for Soprano, Orchestra and Electronics, 1999, Phantasmagoria for Orchestra, 2000, Mr. Tambourine Man: Seven Poems by Bob Dylan, 2000; film scores Altered States, 1981, Revolution, 1985, The Red Violin, 1998; commns. from New York Philharmonic, Boston Symphony Orchestra, James Galway, Van Cliburn Foundation, Inc., Metropolitan Opera Association **AW:** Guggenheim fellow, 1968; nominee Academy award and Grammy award for film score Altered States, 1981; recipient Anthony Asquith award for Best Film Score, Brit. Film Institute, 1985, Academy Institute Arts and Letters award, 1989, Grawemeyer award for Symphony Number 1, 1991, 2 Grammy awards for Symphony No. 1, 1992, International Classical Music award Composition of Year The Ghosts of Versailles (opera), 1992; named Composer of Year, Musical America, 1992, 2 Grammy awards for string quartet, 1996, Grammy for Symphony No. 1, 1996 (Classical CD of Year). **MEM:** Fellow: Am. Academy Arts and Scis.; mem.: American Society of Composers, Bohemian, Academy Institute Arts and Letters, Association Classical Music

CORKER, BOB, T: U.S. Senator from Tennessee **I:** Government Administration/Government Relations/Government Services **DOB:** 08/24/1952 **PB:** Orangeburg **PT:** Son of Robert Phillips Corker; **ED:** BS in Industrial Management, University Tennessee, 1974 **C:** Chairman, Senate Foreign Relations Committee, 2015-; US Senator from Tennessee, 2007-; Owner, Osborne Building Corp. & Stone Fort Land Co., 1999-; Founder, Chattanooga Neighborhood Enterprise, 1986-; Mayor, City of Chattanooga, Tennessee, 2001-05; Finance & administration commissioner, State of Tennessee, 1995-96; Founder, Bencor Corp., 1978-2001 **CIV:** Member executive committee, United Way, Board directors, Southside Devel. Corp., Board directors, Creative Discovery Museum, Board directors, Chattanooga Housing Authority, Board directors, University Chattanooga Foundation, **MEM:** Mem.: Urban League, Rotary Club **PA:** Republican **BA:** Office of Bob Corker, Dirksen Senate Office Building SD-425, Washington, DC, 20510

CORNELL, BRIAN CHRISTIAN, T: CEO of Target **I:** Business Management/Business Services **PB:** 1959 **ED:** Attended, UCLA Anderson Grad. School Management; BA, UCLA, 1981 **C:** Chairman, CEO, Target Corp., Minneapolis, 2014-; President, CEO Sam's Club Division, Wal-Mart Stores, Inc., Bentonville, Arkansas, 2009-12; CEO, Michaels Stores, Inc., Irving, Texas, 2007-09; Executive vice president, chief marketing officer, Safeway, Inc., Pleasanton, California, 2004-07; Senior vice president sales & president North American food service division, PepsiCo, Inc., 2002-04; Senior vice president marketing, European regional president, PepsiCo Beverages International, 2001-02; President Tropicana International, Tropicana Products, 1999-2001; Senior vice president, general manager Tropicana North America, Tropicana Products, 1998-99; Management positions, Joseph E. Seagram Co., 1984-91; Management positions, Gallo Wine Co., 1981-84 **CR:** Board directors Target Corp., 2014-, Polaris Industries, Inc., 2012-, Centerplate, Inc., 2010-, The Home Depot, Inc., 2008-09, OfficeMax Inc., 2004-07 **CIV:** Board visitors, UCLA Anderson Grad. School Management, **AW:** Named Retailer of Year, Grocery Headquarters magazine, 2006, Marketer of the Year, Supermarket News, 2005 **BA:** Target Headquarters, 1000 Nicollet Mall, Minneapolis, MN, 55403

CORNELL, ERIC ALLIN, T: Physics Professor **I:** Education/Educational Services **PB:** Palo Alto **SC:** CA/USA **PT:** Allin Cornell; Elizabeth (Greenberg) Cornell **ED:** Postdoctoral Fellow, Joint Institute for Laboratory Astrophysics, Boulder, CO (1990-1992); Postdoctoral Fellow, Rowland Institute, Cambridge, MA (1990); PhD in Physics, Massachusetts Institute of Technology (1990); BS in Physics, Stanford University, with Honors (1985) **C:** Professor, University Colorado Boulder (1995-Present); Assistant Professor, Adjunct Department of Physics, University of Colorado Boulder (1992-1995); Teaching Fellow, Harvard Extension School, Cambridge, MA (1989); Research Assistant, Stanford University, California (1982-1985) **CR:** Senior Scientist, National Institute of Standards and Technology, Boulder, CO (1992-Present) **CW:** Contributor, Articles to Professional Journals **AW:** Recipient, Nobel Prize in Physics (2001); Recipient, Benjamin Franklin Medal in Physics (1999); Recipient, R.W. Wood Prize (1999); Recipient, Lorentz Medal (1998); Recipient, Alan T. Waterman Award, National Science Foundation (1997); Recipient, King Faisal International Prize in Science (1997); I.I. Rabi Prize in Atomic, Molecular and Optical Physics, American Physical Society (1997); Recipient, Presidential Early Career Award in Science and Engineering (1996); Recipient, Gold Medal, U.S. Department of Commerce (1996); Recipient, Fritz London Prize in Low Temperature Physics (1996); Recipient, Carl Zeiss Award, Ernst Abbe Fund (1996); Recipient, Newcomb-Cleveland Prize, American Association for the Advancement of Science (1995-1996); Recipient, Samuel Wesley Stratton Award, National Institute of Science & Technology (1995) **MEM:** Fellow, American Academy of Arts & Sciences, American Physical Society, Optical Society of America; National Academy of Sciences; Royal Netherlands Academy of Arts & Science **BA:** Joint Inst Lab Astrophysics U Colo, Campus Box 440, Boulder, CO, 80309-0440

CORNYN, JOHN, T: U.S. Senator from Texas **I:** Government Administration/Government Relations/Government Services **DOB:** 02/02/1952 **PB:** Houston **SC:** Texas **PT:** Son of John and Gale Cornyn; **ED:** BA in Journalism, Trinity University, San Antonio, 1973; JD, St. Mary's University, 1977; LLM, University Virginia, 1995 **CT:** Bar: Texas 1977, US District Court We. District Texas 1980, cert.: Texas Board Legal Specialization (in personal injury trial law) **C:** Senate Majority Whip, 2015-; Member, US Senate Finance Committee, 2009—; Attorney General, State of Texas, Austin, Texas, 1999—2002; Partner, Thompson & Knight, 1997—1999; Justice, Supreme Court Texas, Austin, 1991—1997; Presiding Judge, 4th Administrative Judicial Region, 1989—1992; Judge, 37th District Court, Bexer County, 1985—1990; Attorney, Groce, Locke & Hebdon, San Antonio, Texas, 1977—1984; Assistant Majority Leader (Majority Whip), 2015—; US Senator from Texas, 2002—; Chairman, National Republican Senatorial Committee (NRSC), 2009—2013; Vice Chairman, US Senate Republican Conference, 2007—2009; Vice Chairman, US Senate Select Committee on Ethics, 2007—2009; Member, US Senate Armed Services Committee, 2011—2013; Member, US Senate Agricultural, Nutrition & Forestry Committee, 2009—2011; Assistant Minority Leader (Minority Whip), 2013—2015 **CR:** Texas Supreme Court Liaison Gender Bias Task Force, 1993—1995; Chairman James Madison Memorial Foundation, 2009— **AW:** Named a Champion for Healthcare in Rio Grande Valley, Valley Baptist Medical Center, Texas, 2004; Recipient Outstanding Texas Leader Award, John Ben Shepperd Pub. Leadership Forum, 2000, James Madison Award, Freedom Information Foundation Texas, 2001, Distinguished Alumnus Award, Trinity University, 2001, Manufacturing Legis. Excellence

Award, National Association Manufacturers, 2004, Congl. Partnership Award, National Association Devel. Organization, 2004, Friend of Farm Bureau Award, American Farm Bureau Federation, 2004, Friend of Rural Water Award, Texas Rural Water Association, 2004, Hero of Taxpayer Award, American Tax Reform, 2004, Statesman of Year Award, Texas Asian Rep. Conference, 2004, Border Texan of Year Award, 2005, Children's Champion Award, National Child Support Enforcement Association, Fighter of Free Enterprise Award, Texas Association Business, Guardian of Small Business Award, National Federation Independent Business, Latino Leadership Award, National Coalition Latino Clergy & Christian, International Leadership Legislative Award, Mexico American Chamber of Commerce **MEM:** Fellow: San Antonio Bar Foundation, Texas Bar Foundation; mem.: American Bar Association, Texas Bar Association, Robert W. Calvent Inn of Court (president 1994—95), William Sessions Inn of Court (master bencher 1988—90, president 1989—90), American Law Institute **PA:** Republican **BA:** Office of John Cornyn, US Senate 517 Hart Senate Office Bldg, Washington D.C., DC, 20510

CORREA, LOU, T: U.S. Representative from California **I:** Government Administration/Government Relations/Government Services **ED:** JD, University of California, Los Angeles; MBA, University of California, Los Angeles; BA in Economics, California State University, Fullerton **C:** Member, U.S. House of Representatives from California's 46th District (2017-Present); Member, District 34, California State Senate (2006-2017); Board Member, Orange City Boy Scouts; Board Member, California Small Business; Board Member, Orange City Community Development Council; Member, Banking, Finance and Insurance Committee, Business, Professions and Economic Development Committee, California State Senate; Vice Chair, Veterans Affairs Committee, California State Senate; Chair, Public Employees and Retirement Committee, California State Senate; Member, District 69, California State Assembly (1998-2004); Board Member, Orange County Community Development Council; Former Board Supervisor, District 1, Orange City, CA **AW:** Named Legislator of the Year, Orange County Area Council, California Hispanic Chamber of Commerce & Boys & Girls Clubs of America, California Optometric Association, Crime Victims of United California, California Sexual Assault Investigators Association, California Coalition Nurse Practitioners, Golden State Mobile Home Owners League, Peace Officers Research Association of California; High Tech. Legislator of the Year, America Electronics Association; Superintendent's Bravo! Award, Santa Ana Unified School District; Hunger Fighter Award, California Hunger Coalition **MEM:** California Real Estate Board, The State Bar of California **PA:** Democrat

COSTA, GREGG JEFFREY, T: Federal Judge **I:** Law and Legal Services **DOB:** 06/19/1972 **PB:** Baltimore **SC:** MD/USA **ED:** JD, School of Law, University of Texas, 1999; BA, Dartmouth College, 1994 **C:** Judge, U.S. Court Appeals, Fifth Circuit, Austin, TX, 2014-Present; Judge, U.S. District Court, Southern District, Texas, Galveston, TX, 2012-2014; Assistant U.S. Attorney, Southern District, Texas, U.S. Department of Justice, Houston, TX 2005-2012; Associate, Weil, Gotshal & Manges, Houston, TX, 2002-2005; Law Clerk to Chief Justice William Rehnquist, U.S. Supreme Court, Washington, DC, 2001-2002; Bristow Fellow, Office of the Solicitor General, U.S. Department of Justice, Washington, DC, 2000-2001; Law Clerk, Hon. A. Raymond Randolph, U.S. Court of Appeals, District of Columbia Circuit, Washington, DC, 1999-

2000; Elementary School Teacher, Sunflower, MS, 1994-1996 **BA:** John Minor Wisdom U.S. Court of Appeals Building, Fifth Circuit, 600 Camp Street, New Orleans, LA, 70130

COSTA, JIM, T: U.S. Representative from California **I:** Government Administration/Government Relations/Government Services **DOB:** 04/13/1952 **PB:** Fresno **SC:** CA/USA **ED:** BA Political Sci., California State University, Fresno, 1974 **C:** Member, US Congress from 16th California District, 2013-; Member, Committee on Intelligence, Committee on Armed Services;; Member, US Congress from 20th California District, Washington, 2005-13; CEO, Costa Group, 2002-04; Member District 16, California State Senate, 1994-2002; Member District 30, California State Assembly, 1978-94; Administrative assistant to Rep. Richard Lehman, California State Assembly, 1976-78; Special assistant to Rep. John Krebs, US House of Representatives, 1975-76 **CR:** President National Conference State Legislatures, 2000-01 senate rep. California World Trade Commission, 1995-2004 co-founder, co-chair Congressional Victims' Rights Caucus co-founder Congressional Water Caucus member Blue Dog Coalition **CIV:** Board member, Fresno-Madera Agency on Aging **MEM:** Mem.: Fresno Historical Society (board directors), Fresno County Farm Bureau (member steering committee), Fresno Cabrillo Club **PA:** Democrat

COSTELLO, RYAN A., T: U.S. Representative from Pennsylvania, county commissioner **I:** Government Administration/Government Relations/Government Services **DOB:** 09/07/1976 **ED:** JD, Villanova University, 2002; BA, Ursinus College, 1999 **C:** Mem.-elect, US Congress from 6th Pennsylvania District, 2014-; Member, Committee on Energy and Commerce; Chairman, Chester County Board Commissioners, 2013-; Member, Chester County Board Commissioners, 2011-; Attorney, O'Donnell, Weiss & Mattei, Professional Corporation, Phoenixville, Pennsylvania, 2002-; Chairman board supersivors, East Vincent Township, 2004-07; Member board supervisors, East Vincent Township, Pennsylvania, 2002-07 **CR:** Member board directors West Chester Business Improvement District member board trustees Phoenixville Hospital member adv. committee County Commissioners Association of Pennsylvania Deferred Compensation member Chester County Economic Devel. Council, Chester County Industrial Devel. Auth. **PA:** Republican **BA:** 326 Cannon HOB, Washington, DC, 20515

COSTNER, KEVIN, I: Media & Entertainment **DOB:** 01/18/1955 **PB:** Lynwood **SC:** CA/USA **PT:** Bill Costner; Sharon Costner **MS:** Married **SPN:** Christine Baumgartner (September 25, 2004); Cindy Silva, March 5, 1978 (div. December 12, 1994) **CH:** Annie; Lily; Joe; Liam; Cayden; Wyatt **ED:** BA in Marketing, California State University, Fullerton (1978) **C:** Owner, Midnight Star Casino, Deadwood, South Dakota; Singer, guitarist, Modern West; Owner production co., TIG Productions **CW:** Actor: (films) Sizzle Beach U.S.A., 1974, Shadows Run Black, 1981, Chasing Dreams, 1981, Frances, 1982, Night Shift, 1982, Testament, 1983, Table for Five, 1983, Stacy's Knights 1983, The Gunrunner, 1983, The Big Chill, 1983, American Flyers, 1985, Fandango, 1985, Silverado, 1985, The Untouchables, 1987, No Way Out, 1987, Bull Durham, 1988, Field of Dreams, 1989, JFK, 1991, The Bodyguard, 1992, A Perfect World, 1993, The War, 1994, Tin Cup, 1996, For Love of the Game, 1999, Play It to the Bone, 1999, 3000 Miles to Graceland, 2001, Dragonfly, 2002, The Upside of Anger, 2005, Rumor Has It..., 2005, The Guardian, 2006, Mr. Brooks, 2007, Swing Vote, 2008, The New Daughter, 2009, The Company Men, 2010, Man of Steel, 2013, Three

Days to Kill, 2013, Jack Ryan: Shadow Recruit, 2014, Draft Day, 2014, 3 Days to Kill, 2014, McFarland, USA, 2015, Batman v Superman: Dawn of Justice, 2016, Criminal, 2016, (TV mini-series) Hatfields & McCoys, 2012 (Emmy award for Outstanding Lead Actor in a Mini-series or Movie, 2012, Golden Globe award for Best Performance by an Actor in a Mini-series or Motion Picture Made for TV 2013, Screen Actors Guild award for Outstanding Performance by a Male Actor in a TV Movie or Miniseries, 2013); actor, director, prodr.: (films) Dances with Wolves, 1990 (Academy award for Best Director 1991, Academy award for Best Picture, 1991, Directors Guild of America award for Best Director Feature Film, 1991), The Postman, 1997, Open Range, 2003; actor, prodr.: (films) Revenge, 1990, Robin Hood: Prince of Thieves, 1991, Wyatt Earp, 1994, Waterworld, 1995, Message in a Bottle, 1999, Thirteen Days, 2000, Black or White, 2014; (TV appearances), Amazing Stories, 1985; host, executive prodr.: (TV series) 500 Nations; co-prodr.: China Moon, 1993; executive prodr.: Rapa Nui, 1994; singer, guitarist: (albums with Modern West) Untold Truths, 2008. **AW:** Named Hasty Pudding Man of Year, Harvard University, 1990; recipient Star of Tomorrow award, National Association Theatre Owners, 1987

COTILLARD, MARION, T: Actress **I:** Media & Entertainment **PB:** Paris **SC:** France **PT:** Jean-Claude Cotillard; Niseema Theillaud **CH:** Marcel **CR:** Spokesperson, Greenpeace **CW:** Actress (films) The Story of a Boy Who Wanted to Be Kissed, 1994, Snuff Movie, 1995, My Sex Life...Or How I Got Into an Argument, 1996, La Belle Verte, 1996, Taxi, 1998, War in the Highlands, 1999, Furia, 1999, L'Appel de la cave, 1999, Blue Away to America, 1999, Quelques jours de trop, 2000, Le Marquis, 2000, Taxi 2, 2000, Heureuse, 2001, Boomer, 2001, Lisa, 2001, Pretty Things, 2001, A Private Affair, 2002, Taxi 3, 2003, Love Me If You Dare, 2003, Big Fish, 2003, Innocence, 2004, A Very Long Engagement, 2004, Cavalcade, 2005, Edy, 2005, Ma vie en l'air, 2005, Mary, 2005, Burnt Out, 2005, La Boîte noire, 2005, Toi et moi, 2006, Dikkenek, 2006, Fair Play, 2006, A Good Year, 2006, La Vie en rose, 2007 (Best Actress, LA Film Critics Association, 2007, Best Actress, Boston Society Film Critics, 2007, Best Actress, African Am. Film Critics Association, 2007, Best Performance by an Actress in a Motion Picture - Musical or Comedy, Golden Globe Awards, 2008, Best Leading Actress, Brit. Academy Film and TV Awards, 2008, Best Actress in a Leading Role, Academy Awards, 2008), Nine, 2009, Inception, 2010, Little White Lies, 2010, Midnight in Paris, 2011, Contagion, 2011, Rust & Bone, 2012, The Dark Knight Rises, 2012, Blood Ties, 2013, The Immigrant, 2013, Anchorman 2: The Legend Continues, 2013, Two Days, One Night, 2014, The Little Prince (voice), 2015, Macbeth, 2015, April and the Extraordinary World (voice), 2015, It's Only the End of the World, 2016, From the Land of the Moon, 2016, Allied, 2016, Assassin's Creed, 2016, Ismael's Ghosts, 2017, Rock'n Roll, (TV films) Interdit de vieillir, 1998, Une femme piégée, 2001, Jeanne d'Arc au bûcher, 2012, Le Debarquement, 2013, Comedy Central's All- Star Non-Denominational Christmas Special, 2014, Castings, 2015 **AW:** Named chevalier Order of Arts and Letters, French government, 2010; Recipient Chopard Trophy, Cannes Film Festival, 2004

COTTON, TOM, T: U.S. Senator from Arkansas **I:** Government Administration/Government Relations/Government Services **DOB:** 05/13/1977 **PB:** Russellville **PT:** Son of Thomas Leonard and Avis (Bryant) Cotton; **ED:** JD, Harvard Law School, 2002; BA in Government, Harvard College, 1999

C: US Senator from Arkansas, 2015-; Member, Committee on Foreign Affairs; Member, US House Foreign Services Committee, 2013-15; Member, US House Financial Services Committee, 2013-15; Member, US Congress from 4th Arkansas District, Washington, 2013-15; Management consultant, McKinsey & Co., 2010-11; Associate, Gibson Dunn & Crutcher LLP, 2003-05; Law clerk to Hon. Jerry Edwin Smith, US Court Appeals (5th Cir.), 2002-03 **MIL:** Served in 101st Airborne Division US Army, 2005-09, Iraq, Afghanistan **AW:** Decorated Army Commendation medal, Combat Infantryman Badge, Ranger Tab, Bronze star **PA:** Republican

COULTER, ANN HART, T: Writer, Political Columnist, Lawyer **I:** Writing and Editing **DOB:** 12/08/1961 **PB:** New Caanan **PT:** Daughter of John Vincent and Nell Husabands (Martin) Coulter. **ED:** JD, University Michigan Law School, 1988; BA in History cum laude, Cornell University, 1985 **C:** Legal affairs corr., Human Events,; Litigator, Center Individual Rights, Washington, DC,; Political commentator, MSNBC, 1996; Handled crime and immigration issues for Senator Spencer Abraham, US Senate Judiciary Committee, Michigan, 1994-96; Corp. lawyer, private practice, New York City,; Attorney, US Department Justice Honors Program for outstanding law school grads.,; Law clerk to Hon. Pasco Bowman II, US Court Appeals (8th cir.), Kansas City, 1989 **CR:** Contributing editor, syndicated columnist National Review Online, 2001 writer, weekly to occasional columns Human Events, 1998-2003 regular columnist George Magazine, 1999 guest appearances The Today Show, Piers Morgan, The Early Show, The Tonight Show with Jay Leno, Entertainment Tonight, Hannity, The O'Reilly Factor, Fox & Friends, Dr. Drew, The Glen Beck Show, & Real Time with Bill Maher, The Leeza Show, Good Morning America, "This Week", ABC, Crossfire, American Morning with Paula Zahn, The O'Reilly Factor, Hannity and Colmes, Larry King Live, Politically Incorrect legal correspondent for human events, syndicated column writer Universal Press Syndicate **CW:** Author: High Crimes and Misdemeanors: The Case Against Bill Clinton, 1998, Slander: Liberal Lies About the American Right, 2002, Treason: Liberal Treachery From the Cold War to the War on Terrorism, 2003, How to Talk to a Liberal (If You Must): The World According to Ann Coulter, 2004, Godless: The Church of Liberalism, 2006, If Democrats Had Any Brains, They'd Be Republicans, 2007, Guilty: Liberal 'Victims' and Their Assault on America, 2009, Demonic: How the Liberal Mob is Endangering America, 2011, Mugged: Racial Demagoguery from the Seventies to Obama, 2012, Never Trust a Liberal Over Three-Especially a Republican, 2013, Adios America: The Left's Plan to Turn Our Country into a Third World Hellhole, 2015 **AW:** Named one of The 50 Highest-Earning Political Figures, Newsweek, 2010, The 100 Most Influential People in the World, TIME magazine, 2005, the Top 100 Public Intellectuals, 2001 **PA:** Republican

COURIC, KATIE, T: Broadcast Journalist **I:** Media & Entertainment **DOB:** 01/07/1957 **PB:** Arlington **SC:** VA/USA **ED:** BA in American Studies, University Virginia, 1979; DSc (hon.), Case Western Reserve University, Cleveland, 2010; LHD (hon.), Boston University, 2011 **C:** Founder, Katie Couric Media, 2015-; Global anchor, Yahoo News, Sunnyvale, California, 2014—; Reporter, WRC-TV, Washington, DC, 1987—1989; General assignment reporter, WTVJ, Miami, Florida, 1984—1986; Assignment editor, Cable News Network (CNN), Atlanta, Georgia; Desk assistant, ABC News, Washington, DC, 1979; Host, Katie, 2012—2014; Guest co-host, Good Morning America, 2012; Special corr., ABC News, 2011—2013; Corr. 60 Minutes, CBS Evening News,

2006—2011; Anchor, managing editor, CBS Evening News, New York City, New York, 2006—2011; Co-host Today, NBC News, 1991—2006; National political corr., substitute anchor Today (The Today Show), NBC News, 1989—1991; Deputy Pentagon corr., NBC News, Washington, DC, 1989 **CR:** Substitute anchor Sunday edition NBC Nightly News, 1989—1993; co-host NBC's live coverage Macy's Thanksgiving Day Parade, 1991—2005; contributing anchor Dateline NBC, 1994—2006 **CIV:** Co-founder National Colorectal Cancer Research Alliance (NCCRA), 1999; UNICEF Goodwill Ambassador for US; **CW:** Author: The Best Advice I Ever Got: Lessons from Extraordinary Lives, 2011, (children's books) The Brand New Kid, 2000, The Blue Ribbon Day, 2004; cameo appearances (films) Austin Powers in Goldmember, 2002, Shark Tale (voice), 2004, TV guest appearances Murphy Brown, 1992, Cheers, 1993, Will & Grace, 2002, Glee, 2011, General Hospital, 2013; executive prodr.: (documentaries) Fed Up, 2014, Gender Revolution, 2017, Flint, 2017; **AW:** Named News Person of Year, TV Guide, 2001, Wow Woman of Year, Glamour magazine, 2002; named one of The 25 Most Intriguing People, People magazine, 2001, The 100 Most Powerful Women, Forbes magazine, 2005—08, 2010, The 100 Most Influential People in the World, TIME magazine, 2006, The 100 Most Powerful Women in Entertainment, The Hollywood Reporter, 2012; recipient Emmy award, National Academy TV Arts & Scis., 1999, 2000, 2004, Emmy Governor's award, 2009, Peabody award, 2001, Julius B. Richmond award, Harvard School Pub. Health, 2003, Golden Plate award, Academy Achievement, 2006, Walter Cronkite award for Journalism Excellence, 2009, Gracie Allen award, American Women in Radio & TV, 2009, Sigma Delta Chi award, National Society Professional Journalists, Associated Press award, Matrix award, National Headliner award, Television Hall of Fame, 2005 **BA:** Creative Artists Agency, 2000 Avenue of the Stars, Los Angeles, CA, 90067

COURTNEY, JOE, T: U.S. Representative from Connecticut **I:** Government Administration/Government Relations/Government Services **DOB:** 04/16/1953 **PB:** Hartford **SC:** CT/USA **PT:** Son of Robert Edward and Dorothy (Kane) Courtney; **ED:** JD, University Connecticut, 1978; BA, Tufts University, 1975 **C:** Member, US Congress from 2nd Connecticut district, 2006-; Member armed services committee, energy & labor committee, US Congress from 2nd Connecticut district,; Town attorney, Vernon, Connecticut,; Partner, Courtney, Boyan & Foran, LLC.,; Member, Connecticut General Assembly from 56th district, 1987-94; Assistant pub. defender, Rockville Superior Court, 1979-81 **CR:** Connecticut coordinator John Edwards campaign, 2004 **AW:** Named Dem. Most Admired by Republicans, Connecticut Magazine, 1994 **PA:** Democrat

COX, BOBBY, T: Retired Professional Baseball Manager **I:** Athletics **DOB:** 05/21/1941 **PB:** Tulsa **PT:** Married Pamela Cox; **CH:** Kami, Keisha, Skyla **ED:** Student, Reedley Junior College, California **C:** Manager, Toronto Blue Jays, 1982-85; Manager, Atlanta Braves, 1990-2010; Manager, Atlanta Braves, 1978-81; Manager, Eastern League, West Haven, Connecticut, 1972; Manager, Florida State League, Fort Lauderdale, 1971; Player, Florida State League, Fort Lauderdale, 1971; 1st base coach, New York Yankees, New York City, 1977; Player, New York Yankees, New York City, 1968-69; Manager, International League, Syracuse, 1973-76; Player, International League, Syracuse, New York, 1970; Player, International League, Richmond, Virginia, 1967; Player, Pacific Coast League, Tacoma, 1966; Player, Pacific Coast League, Salt Lake City,

1965; Player, Texas League, Albuquerque, 1963-64; Player, Northwest League, Salem, Oregon, 1961-62; Player, California League, Reno, 1960 **AW:** Named Am. League Manager Year, 1985, Major League Baseball Writers Association; National League Manager Year, 1991, 2004-05,Atlanta Braves Hall of Fame, 2011, Baseball Hall of Fame, 2014 **ACH:** Achievements include being the manager of the World Series Champion Atlanta Braves, 1995; being the ninth manager in Major League Baseball history to win 2,000 games, 2004; winning his 2,000th career game as manager of the Atlanta Braves, 2009 **BA:** National Baseball Hall of Fame, 25 Main Street, Cooperstown, NY, 13326

COX, LAVERNE, T: Actress **I:** Media & Entertainment **DOB:** 01/01/1900 **PB:** Mobile, Alabama **SC:** Mobile, Alabama **ED:** Alabama School of Fine Arts; Marymount Manhattan College(**CW:** (Film) Betty Anderson, 2000, The Kings of Brooklyn, 2004, All Night, 2008, Uncle Stephanie, 2009, Bronx Paradise, 2010, Carla, 2011, Musical Chairs, 2011, Migraine, 2012, The Exhibitionists,2012, 36 Saints, 2013, Grand Street, 2014, Laverne Cox Presents: The T Word, 2014,(Daytime Emmy for Outstanding Special Class Special,2015) Grandma, 2015, Freak Show,2017(Television) Law & Order: Special Victims Unit, 2008, I Want to Work for Diddy, 2008, Law and Order, 2008, Bored to Death, 2009, TRANSform Me,2010, Orange is the New Black,2013, Faking It,2014, Girlfriends Guide to Divorce, 2014, The Mindy Project, 2015, The Rocky Horror Picture Show: Lets Do the Time Warp Again, 2016, Lip Sync Battle, 2016, Doubt, 2017 **AW:** Time 100 Most Influential, 2015

CRACCHIOLO, JAMES M., T: CEO of Ameriprise Financial **I:** Financial Services **ED:** MBA, New York University; BS, New York University **CT:** CPA **C:** Chairman, CEO, Ameriprise Financial, Inc., Minneapolis, 2005-; Chairman, CEO, Am. Express Fin. Advisors, 2001-05; President, CEO, Am. Express Financial, 2000-05; Chairman, Am. Express Bank Ltd., 2000-05; Group president, Am. Express Global Fin. Services, 2000-05; President, Am. Express Travel Related Services International, 1998-2003; With, American Express Co., 1982-2005 **CR:** Board directors Tech Data Corp., 1999- **CIV:** Member board adv., March of Dimes, **BA-** 55 Ameriprise Financial Center, Minneapolis, MN, 55474

CRAMER, KEVIN, T: U.S. Representative from North Dakota **I:** Government Administration/ Government Relations/Government Services **DOB:** 01/21/1961 **PB:** Rolla, North Dakota, January 21, 1961 **PT:** Son of Richard & Clarice Cramer: Married Kris Cramer; children: Ian, Isaac, Rachel, Annie. **ED:** MA in Management, University Mary, 2003; BA in Social Work, Concordia College, 1983 **C:** Member, U.S. house of Representative from North Dakota's At Large District, 2013-; Member, Committee on Energy and Commerce; Member, US House Sci., Space, & Technology Committee, 2013-; Member, US House Natural Resources Committee, 2013-; Member at-large, US Congress from South Dakota, Washington, 2013-; Commnr., North Dakota Public Service Commission, 2003-12; Director, Harold Schafer Leadership Foundation, Bismarck, North Dakota, 2001-03; State economic devel. director, State of North Dakota, 1997-2000; State tourism director, State of North Dakota, 1993-97 **CR:** Supporter, member Growing North Dakota Programs committee member Growing North Dakota III, 1994. **CIV:** Chairman, executive director North Dakota Republican Party, 1991-93 **PA:** Republican **BA:** 1717 Longworth House Office Building, Washington, DC, 20515

CRANDALL, ROGER W., **T:** Massachusetts Mutual CEO **I:** Business Management/Business Services **ED:** MBA, University Pennsylvania, Philadelphia; BA in Econs., University Vermont, Burlington **CT:** Chartered Financial Analyst **C:** Chairman, president, CEO, MassMutual Financial Group, 2010-; President, CEO, MassMutual Financial Group, 2010; President, COO, MassMutual Financial Group, 2008-09; Co-COO Massachusetts Mutual Life Insurance Co., MassMutual Financial Group, 2007-08; Executive vice president, chief investment officer Massachusetts Mutual Life Insurance Co., MassMutual Financial Group, 2005-07; President, CEO, Babson Capital Management LLC (subsidiary of MassMutual Fin. Group), 2006-08; Chairman, Babson Capital Management LLC (subsidiary of MassMutual Fin. Group), 2005-08; Head corp. bond management, pub. bond trading and institutional fixed income units, Babson Capital Management LLC (subsidiary of MassMutual Fin. Group),; Vice chairman, managing director, head corp. securities, Babson Capital Management LLC (subsidiary of MassMutual Fin. Group), 2000; Joined, MassMutual Financial Group, 1988

CRANE, CHRISTOPHER MARK, **T:** President and CEO of Exelon Corp, **I:** Oil & Energy **ED:** Student, New Hampshire Tech. College **CT:** Cert. senior reactor operator **C:** President, CEO, Exelon Corp., 2012-; President, COO, Exelon Corp., 2008-12; President, Exelon Generation Co., LLC, 2008-12; Executive vice president, COO, Exelon Generation Co., LLC, 2007-08; President, CEO AmerGen, Exelon Corp.,; President, chief nuclear officer, Exelon Nuclear, 2004-07; COO, Exelon Nuclear, 2003-07; Senior vice president nuclear operations, Exelon Corp., 1999-2003; Vice president boiling water reactor operations, Exelon Corp., 1998-99; Site vice president, Tennessee Valley Authority Browns Ferry Nuclear Plant, Athens, Arizona, 1997-98 **CR:** Board of Directors Exelon Corp., 2012- **BA:** Exelon Corp 10 S Dearborn St 37th Fl, PO Box 805398, Chicago, IL, 60680-5398

CRANSTON, BRYAN LEE LEE, **T:** Actor **I:** Media & Entertainment **DOB:** 03/07/1956 **PB:** San Fernando Valley **SC:** CA/USA **PT:** Joe Cranston **CW:** Actor: (TV series) Loving, 1983, One Life to Live, 1985, Raising Miranda, 1988, Mighty Morphin' Power Rangers (voice), 1993, Teknoman, 1994, Seinfeld, 1994-97, Eagle Riders, 1996, The King of Queens, 1999-2001, Malcolm in the Middle, 2000-06, Fallen, 2007, The Cleveland Show, 2012-13; (TV miniseries) North and South, Book II, 1986, From the Earth to the Moon, 1998; (films) Wings of Honneamise, 1987, Amazon Women on the Moon, 1987, The Big Turnaround, 1988, Corporate Affairs, 1990, Dead Space, 1991, Moldiver, 1993, Clean Slate, 1994, Erotique, 1994, Time Under Fire, 1996, That Thing You Do!, 1996, Street Corner Justice, 1996, Strategic Command, 1997, Saving Private Ryan, 1998, The Big Thing, 2000, The Prince of Light, 2000, Terror Tract, 2000, Seeing Other People, 2004, Illusion, 2004, Magnificent Desolation: Walking on the Moon 3D (voice), 2005, Intellectual Property, 2006, Little Miss Sunshine, 2006, Hard Four, 2007, Love Ranch, 2010, The Lincoln Lawyer, 2011, Detachment, 2011, Contagion, 2011, Larry Crowne, 2011, Drive, 2011, Red Tails, 2012, John Carter, 2012, Madagascar 3: Europe's Most Wanted (voice), 2012, Rock of Ages, 2012, Argo, 2012, Total Recall, 2012; actor, (films) Get a Job, 2008, Cold Comes the Night, 2013, Godzilla, 2014, Trumbo, 2015, Kung Fu Panda 3 (voice), 2016, The Masterpiece, 2016, In Dubious Battle, 2016, Why Him?, 2016, Wakefield, 2016 The Disaster Artist, 2017, Power Rangers, 2017, The Upside, 2017, Last Flag Flying, 2017, Isle of Dogs,2018; (TV films) The Return of the Six-Million-Dollar Man and the Bionic Woman, 1987, I Know My First Name Is Steven, 1989, Dead Silence, 1991, The Disappearance of Nora, 1993, Prophet of Evil: The Ervil LeBaron Story, 1993, Men Who Hate Women & the Women Who Love Them, 1994, Days Like This, 1994, The Companion, 1994, Extreme Blue, 1995, Kissing Miranda, 1995, The Rockford Files: Punishment and Crime, 1996, 'Twas the Night, 2001, The Santa Claus Brothers, 2001, Thanksgiving Family Reunion, 2003; (Broadway plays) All the Way, 2014 (Drama Desk award for Outstanding Actor in a Play, 2014, Tony award for Best Leading Actor in a Play, 2014); actor, prodr.: (TV series) Breaking Bad, 2016, (video) KidSmartz; actor, writer, director producer (films) Last Chance, 1999, actor, executive producer (TV series) SuperMansion, 2015, All the Way, 2016, Philip K Dicks Electric Dreams, 2017, Curb Your Enthusiasm, 2017 (films) The Infiltrator, 2016, (TV films) All the Way, 2016 **AW:** Named one of The 100 Most Influential People in the World, TIME magazine, 2013

CRAPO, MICHAEL, **T:** U.S. Senator from Idaho **I:** Government Administration/Government Relations/Government Services **DOB:** 05/20/1951 **PB:** Idaho Falls **SC:** ID/USA **PT:** George Lavelle Crapo; Melba (Olsen) Crapo **ED:** BA in Political Science, Brigham Young University, Summa Cum Laude, Provo, Utah (1973); Student, University of Utah; JD, Harvard University, Cum Laude (1977) **C:** Chairman, Senate Banking Committee (2017); US Senator from Idaho (1999—Present); Member, US Congress from the Second Idaho District, Washington, DC (1993—1999); President Pro-tempore, Idaho State Senate (1989-1992); Assistant Majority Leader, Idaho State Senate (1987—1989); Member, District 32A, Idaho State Senate (1985—1993); Partner, Holden, Kidwell, Hahn & Crapo, Idaho Falls, Idaho (1983-1992); Attorney, Holden, Kidwell, Hahn & Crapo, Idaho Falls, Idaho (1979-1992); Associate, Gibson, Dunn & Crutcher, Los Angeles, CA (1978-1979); Law Clerk to Honorable James M. Carter, U.S. Court of Appeals for the Ninth Circuit, San Diego, CA (1977-1978) **CR:** Precinct Committeeman, District 29 (1980-1985); Vice Chairman, Legislative District 29 (1984-1985); Member, Health & Welfare Committee (1985-1989); Resources and Environmental Committee (1985-1990); State Affairs Committee (1987-1992); Republican President Task Force (1989) **CIV:** Active Member, Boy Scouts of America, CA, ID (1977—1992) **AW:** Named One of the Outstanding Young Men of America (1985); Named One of the 10 Members to Watch in the 112th Congress, Roll Call (2011); Certificate of Merit, Republican National Committee (1990); Guardian of Small Business Award, National Federation of Independent Business (1990, 1994); Certificate of Recognition, American Cancer Society (1990); Idaho Housing Agency (1990); Idaho Lung Association (1985, 1986, 1989); Friend of Agricultural Award, Idaho Farm Bureau (1989-1990); Medal of Merit, Republican Presidential Task Force (1989); National Legislator of the Year Award, National Republican Legislators Association (1991); Golden Bulldog Award, Watchdogs of the Treasurer (1996); Thomas Jefferson Award, National American Wholesale Grocers Association-Independent Food Distributors Association (1996); Spirit of Enterprise Award, US Chamber of Commerce (1993, 1994, 1995, 1996); Watchdogs of Treasury Golden Bulldog Award, American Frozen Food Institute (2000); Ground Water Protector Award, National Ground Water Association (2002); Best and Brightest Award, American Conservative Union (2003) **MEM:** ABA; Idaho Bar Association; Rotary International **BAR:** The State Bar of California (1977); Idaho State Bar (1979) **H:** Sports; Backpacking; Hunting; Skiing **PA:** Republican **BA:** Office of Michael Crapo, US Senate 239 Dirksen Senate Office Building, Washington D.C., DC, 20510

CRAWFORD, RICK, **T:** U.S. Representative from Arkansas **I:** Government Administration/Government Relations/Government Services **DOB:** 01/22/1966 **PB:** Homestead AFB **ED:** BA in Agriculture Business & Economics, Arkansas State University, Jonesboro, 1996 **C:** Member, US House Transportation & Infrastructure Committee, 2011-; Member, US House Agricultural Committee, 2011-; Member, US Congress from 1st Arkansas District, 2011-; Owner, operator, AgWatch Network, Arkansas,; John Deere dealer group marketing manager,; Syndicated producer, anchor, Delta Farm Roundup TV, Greenville, Mississippi,; Syndicated producer, anchor, Delta Farm Roundup TV, Jonesboro,; Syndicated producer, anchor, Delta Farm Roundup TV, Cape Girardeau, Missouri,; Farm director, Station KFIN-FM, Jonesboro,; Agri-reporter, news anchor, Station WKAIT, Jonesboro, **CIV:** First vice-chmn., Craighead County GOP Committee, Member, 4-H Foundation Board Arkansas, **CW:** Features columnist NE Arkansas Business Today **AW:** Named Announcer of Year, National Federation Professional Bullriders, 1996-98 **MEM:** Mem.: National Association Farm Broadcasting (Newscast award 2006, 2008) **PA:** Republican

CREEL, GAVIN, **T:** Actor and Singer **I:** Media & Entertainment **PB:** Findlay **SC:** OH/USA **ED:** BA, University of Michigan School of Music, Theatre & Dance **CW:** Actor, Theater, "Spring Awakening" (2001), "Thoroughly Modern Millie" (2002), "Hair" (2004), "La Cage Aux Folles" (2004), "Mary Poppins" (2006), "Hair" (2009-2010), "The Book of Mormon" (2012-2015), "She Loves Me" (2016), "Hello,Dolly!" (2017); Actor, Film, The Ceiling Fan" (2016); Actor, Television, "Eloise at the Plaza" (2003), "Eloise at Christmastime" (2003), "She Loves Me" (2016); Singer, Albums, "Goodtimenation" (2006), "Quiet" (2010), "Get Out" (2012) **AW:** Tony Award for Best Featured Actor in a Musical (2017)

CRENN, DOMINIQUE, **T:** Chef **I:** Food & Restaurant Services **C:** Chef/Owner, Bar Crenn, 2016-; Chef/Owner, Petit Crenn,2015-; Chef/Owner,Atelier Crenn,2011-; Luce, 2009-11 **AW:** 2 Michelin Stars,2009,2010, Best Female Chef 2016, by Worlds 50 Best Restaurant Awards

CRENSHAW, BEN, **T:** Professional Golfer **I:** Athletics **DOB:** 01/11/1952 **PB:** Austin **SC:** Texas **MS:** Married **SPN:** Julie Ann **CH:** Katherine Vail, Claire Susan, Anna Riley **ED:** Grad., University Texas **C:** Professional golfer, 1973-; Team captain, Ryder Cup Team, 1999; U.S. team captain, Kirin Cup, 1988; Member, U.S. Ryder Cup, 1981, 83, 87, 95,; Member, U.S. World Amateur Cup Team, 1972 **AW:** Winner San Antonio Open, 1973, Western Amateur open match and medal plan champion, 1973, Bing Crosby National Pro-Am., Ohio Kings Island Open, Hawaiian Open, 1976, Colonial National Invitational, 1977, NCAA Championship, 1971, 72, 73, Irish Open, 1976, Phoenix Open, 1979, Walt Disney World Team Championship, 1980, Anheuser-Busch Classic, 1980, Texas State Open winner, 1980, Ryder Cup, 1981, 83, 87, Byron Nelson Classic, 1983, Masters tournament, 1984, PGA Senior Event Jeremy Ranch Shoot-Out teamed with Miller Barber, 1985, Buick Open, 1986, Vantage Championship, 1986, USF&G, 1987, Doral Ryder Open, 1988, World Cup, 1988, Western Open, 1992, Masters winner Augusta National Golf Club, 1995, Masters Tournament, 1995, Ryder Cup, 1999, admitted to World Golf Hall of Fame, 2002, Winner of the Wendy's Champions Skins Game, 2009 **MEM:** Member Professional Golfers Association Am.

CREW, DEBRA ANN, **T:** Farmers Group CEO **I:** Business Management/Business Services **DOB:** 12/20/1970 **ED:** MBA, University Chicago, 2000; BA, University Denver **C:** CEO, Reynolds American, 2017-; COO, R.J. Reynolds Tobacco Co.,2015-17; President, chief commercial officer, R.J. Reynolds Tobacco Co., Winston-Salem, North Carolina, 2014-; President, general manager, PepsiCo North America Nutrition, 2014; President, PepsiCo Americas Beverage, 2012-14; President Western Europe region, PepsiCo Europe, 2010-12; Chief marketing officer, general manager PetCare US, Mars, Inc., 2008-10; Senior vice president marketing frozen snacks, Dreyer's Grand Ice Cream, 2004; Category business director foodservice division, Kraft Foods, Inc., 1997-2004 **CR:** Board directors Stanley Black & Decker, Inc., 2012- **AW:** Named one of The 50 Most Powerful Women in Business, Fortune magazine, 2014-15 **MEM:** Board of directors,Stanley Black and Decker,2013

CRIST, CHARLIE, **T:** U.S. Representative From Florida **I:** Government Administration/Government Relations/Government Services **DOB:** 07/24/1956 **PB:** Altoona **SC:** PA/USA **PT:** Charles Joseph Crist, Nancy (Lee) Crist **ED:** JD, Samford University Cumberland School of Law, Birmingham, AL, 1981; BA in Government, Florida State University, 1978; Student, Wake Forest University, Winston-Salem, NC **C:** Partner, Morgan & Morgan, St. Petersburg, FL, 2011-Present; U.S. House of Representatives From Florida's 13th District, 2017; Governor, State Of Florida, 2007-2011; Attorney General, State Of Florida, 2003-2007; Education Commissioner, State Of Florida, 2000-2002; Deputy Secretary, Florida Department of Business & Professional Regulation, 1999-2000; Florida State Senate, Tallahassee, FL, 1992-1998; Attorney, Wood & Crist, 1987-1999; General Counsel, National Association of Professional Baseball Leagues, 1982-1987 **CR:** Fellow, American Swiss Association **CIV:** Advisory Committee, Tampa Bay MDA, Pinellas County Republican Executive Committee, Administrative Board, First United Methodist Church, Board of Directors, Police Athletic League, Board of Directors, Foundation of Florida's Future **AW:** Legislative Conservation Award, Florida Conservation Association, 1996, Phil Piton Award For Service To MLB, Leadership St. Petersburg, Distinguished Legislator Award, Florida Police Benevolent Association, 1996, Honorary Sheriff, Police Benevolent Association, 1995, Conservationist Legislator of the Year, Florida Wildlife Federation, 1995, Senatorial Leadership Award, Florida Professional Attorneys Association, 1995, Government Award, Urban League, 1995, Legislation Award, Florida Sheriffs Association, 1994, 1996, Florida Association School Administrators, 1993, Pinellas School Administrators, 1993, Roll Call Award, Florida Chamber of Commerce, 1993, True Grit Award, Suncoast Tiger Bay Club **MEM:** American Bar Association, Board of Governors, Republican National Lawyers Association, St. Petersburg Bar Association, Hillsborough Bar Association, Pinellas Park Chamber of Commerce, St. Petersburg Chamber of Commerce, Florida Conservation Association, Pinellas County President's Council, American Lung Association, Rotary, Board of Directors, Suncoast Tiger Bay Club, Suncoaster Civic Club **H:** Water-skiing, Reading, Jogging **PA:** Democrat **BA:** 427 Cannon HOB, Washington, DC, 20515

CROSBY, SIDNEY, **T:** Professional Hockey Player **I:** Athletics **DOB:** 08/07/1987 **PB:** Cole Harbor **SC:** Nova Scotia Canada **PT:** Troy Crosby; Trina (Forbes) Crosby **C:** Captain, Pittsburgh Penguins (2007-Present); Center, Pittsburgh Penguins (2005-Present); Center, Rimouski Oceanic (QMJHL), Canada (2003-2005) **CR:** Member, Captain, Team Canada, Olympic Games, Sochi, Russia (2014); Member, Team Canada, Olympic Games, Vancouver, Canada (2010); Team Canada, World Junior Championships, Grand Forks, ND (2005); Team Canada, World Junior Championships, Helsinki, Finland (2004) **AW:** Co-recipient, Maurice Richard Trophy (2010); Named NHL Player of the Year, Sporting News (2007); Player of the Year, Canadian Hockey League (2004, 2005); Rookie of the Year (2004); Named One of the Most Influential People in the World of Sports, Business Week (2007, 2008); Named to Second All-Star Team, NHL (2010); Named to All-NHL Team, Sporting News (2010); Named to First All-Star Team, NHL (2007); Named to NHL All-Star Game (2007, 2008, 2009, 2015); Recipient, Conn Smythe Trophy, NHL (2016); Ted Lindsay Award (2013, 2014); ESPY Award, Best NHL Player, ESPN (2007, 2008, 2009, 2010); Lou Marsh Award, Toronto Star (2007); Mark Messier Leadership Award (2007, 2010); Lester B. Pearson Award (2007); Art Ross Trophy (2007, 2014); Hart Memorial Trophy (2007, 2014); Stanley Cup Champion (2016, 2017); Conn Smythe Trophy (2016, 2017); Art Ross Trophy (2014); Maurice Rocket Richard Trophy (2017); Ten Lindsay Awards (2013, 2014); Hart Memorial Trophy (2014); Named to NHL First All-Star Team (2013-2014, 2016); Named to NHL Second All-Star Team (2015, 2017); Named to NHL All Star Selection (2011, 2015, 2017); Pittsburgh Penguin MVP (2010, 2013, 2014, 2016, 2017); A.T. Caggiano Memorial Booster Club Award (2010, 2013, 2014); Aldege Bastien Memorial Good Guy Award (2010); The Edward J. Debatolo Community Service Award (2010, 2016, 2017); Named to ESPN Top 20 Athletes (1995-2015); Named ESPN Top Ten NHL Players of the Decade (2009) **ACH:** Achievements include being the only player under the age of 18 to play for the Canadian Junior Hockey Team, 2004; being the first overall draft pick in NHL entry draft, 2005; being a member of the gold medal winning Canadian Hockey Team, World Junior Championships, 2005; being a member of the Stanley Cup Champion Pittsburgh Penguins, 2009, 2016, 2017; being the youngest NHL captain to win the Stanley Cup, 2009; being a member of the gold medal winning Canadian Hockey Team, Vancouver Olympics, 2010, Sochi Olympics, 2014 **BA:** CAA Sports, 2000 Avenue of the Stars, Los Angeles, CA, 90067

CROWE, RUSSELL, **T:** Actor **I:** Media & Entertainment **DOB:** 04/07/1964 **PB:** Wellington **SC:** New Zealand **PT:** John Alexander Crowe; Jocelyn Yvonne (Wemyss) Crowe **CW:** Actor: (plays) Grease, Rocky Horror Picture Show; (films) The Crossing, 1993, The Quick and the Dead, 1995, Proof, 1995, Romper Stomper, 1995, Rough Magic, 1995, Virtuosity, 1995, Under the Gun, 1995, Heaven's Burning, 1997, Breaking Up, 1997, L.A. Confidential, 1997, Mystery Alaska, 1999, The Insider, 1999 (National Society Film Critics award for Best Actor, 2000), Gladiator, 2000 (Academy award for Best Actor, 2001), Proof of Life, 2000, A Beautiful Mind, 2001 (Golden Globe award for Best Actor in a Drama, 2002, Screen Actors Guild award for Best Actor, 2002, BAFTA Film award for Best Actor, 2002), Master and Commander: The Far Side of the World, 2003, Cinderella Man, 2005, 3:10 to Yuma, 2007, American Gangster, 2007, Tenderness, 2008, Body of Lies, 2008, State of Play, 2009, The Next Three Days, 2010, The Man With the Iron Fists, 2012, Les Miserables, 2012, Broken City, 2013, Man of Steel, 2013, Winter's Tale, 2014, Noah, 2014, The Nice Guys, 2016, War Machine, 2017, The Mummy, 2017, Boy Erased,2018; dir.: 60 Odd Hours in Italy, 2002, Sydney Unplugged, 2013; actor, producer (films) Robin Hood, 2010, actor, director The Water Diviner, 2014, actor, executive producer Fathers and Daughters, 2015; (director,

producer): (documentaries) Texas, 2002; singer: 30 Odd Foot of Grunts(Television) Neighbors, 1987, Brides of Christ, 1991, Republic of Doyle, 2012; **AW:** Named one of 50 Most Powerful People in Hollywood, Premiere magazine, 2004-06; recipient Global Achievement award, Australian Film Institute, 2001

CROWLEY, JOSEPH, **T:** U.S. Representative from New York **I:** Government Administration/Government Relations/Government Services **DOB:** 03/16/1962 **PB:** Elmhurst **ED:** BA in Political Sci. & Communications, Queens College, 1985 **C:** Chair of the House Democratic Conference, 2017-; Vice chairman, US House Democratic Caucus, 2013-2017; Member, US Congress from 14th New York District, 2013-; Member, US Congress from 7th New York District, Washington, 1999-2013; Member District 30, New York State Assembly, 1987-98 **CR:** Del. American Institute Free Labor Devel. Observers of Nicaragua Election, 1990 **AW:** Recipient YMCA Congl. Champion award, YMCA of U.S.A., 2003 **MEM:** Member Armagh Association, Cavan Men's Association, Hudson Council, VFW, Knights of Columbus **PA:** Democrat

CRUISE, TOM, **T:** Actor **I:** Media & Entertainment **DOB:** 07/03/1962 **PB:** Syracuse, New York **PT:** Son of Thomas C. III and Mary Lee Mapother; **SPN:** Married Mimi Rogers, May 9, 1987 (div. February 4, 1990); Married Nicole Kidman, December 24, 1990 (div. August 8, 2001); **CH:** Adopted Children: Isabella Jane Ki **C:** Co-owner (with Paula Wagner), United Artists Entertainment, LLC, 2006-; Producer, Partner, Cruise/Wagner Productions,; Co-founder (with Paula Wagner), Cruise/Wagner Productions, 1993-2006 **CW:** Actor: (films) Endless Love, 1981, Taps, 1981, The Outsiders, 1983, Losin' It, 1983, Risky Business, 1983, All the Right Moves, 1983, Legend, 1985, Top Gun, 1986, The Color of Money, 1986, Cocktail, 1988, Rain Man, 1988, Born on the Fourth of July, 1989 (Golden Globe award for Best Actor in a Motion Picture Drama, 1990), Far and Away, 1992, A Few Good Men, 1992, The Firm, 1993, Interview with the Vampire, 1994, Jerry McGuire, 1996 (Golden Globe award for Best Actor, 1997), Eyes Wide Shut, 1998, Magnolia, 1999 (Golden Globe award for Best Supporting Actor in a Motion Picture, 2000), Minority Report, 2002, Collateral, 2004, War of the Worlds, 2005, Knight and Day, 2010, Rock of Ages, 2012, Oblivion, 2013, Edge of Tomorrow, 2014, Mission Impossible Rogue Nation 2015, Jack Reacher Never go Back 2016, The Mummy, 2017, American Made, 2017, Mission Impossible 6, 2018 The; actor, prodr.: (films) Mission: Impossible, 1996, Mission: Impossible II, 2000, Vanilla Sky, 2001, The Last Samurai, 2003, Mission: Impossible III, 2006, Valkyrie, 2008, Mission: Impossible-Ghost Protocol, 2011, Jack Reacher, 2012, Mission: Impossible-Rogue Nation, 2015, Jack Reacher: Never Go Back, 2016; Actor, Writer: (films) Days of Thunder, 1990; Prodr.: (films) Without Limits, 1998; Executive Prodr.: (films) The Others, 2001, Narc, 2002, Shattered Glass, 2003; Prodr.: (films) Elizabethtown, 2005, Ask the Dusk, 2006; Actor, Executive Prodr.: (films) Lions for Lambs, 2007. **AW:** Co-recipient Nova award for Outstanding Achievement by New or Emerging Producer in Theatrical Motion Pictures, Producer's Guild, 1997; named one of The Ten Most Fascinating People of 2008, Barbara Walters, The 100 Most Powerful Celebrities, Forbes.com, 2008, 2007, 2006-07, The 10 Most Fascinating People of 2005, Barbara Walters Special, 50 Most Powerful People in Hollywood, Premiere magazine, 2004-06; recipient Museum Moving Image Salute, 2007, John Huston Award for Artists Rights, The Artists Rights Foundation, 1998, Star on the Hollywood Walk of Fame

CRUTCHER, BRIAN, T: CEO I: Business Management/Business Services CN: Texas Instruments Incorporated ED: Bachelors, University of Central Florida; MBA, University of California, Irvine C: President/Chief Executive Officer, Texas Instruments Incorporated (2018-Present); Executive Vice President/Chief Operating Officer, Texas Instruments Incorporated (2017-2018); Executive Vice President, Business Operations, Texas Instruments Incorporated (2014-2017); Senior Vice President/General Manager, Texas Instruments (2012-2014)

CRUZ, PENÉLOPE, T: Actress I: Media & Entertainment DOB: 04/28/1974 PB: Madrid SC: Spain PT: Eduardo Cruz; Encarna Cruz ED: Coursework in Classical Ballet, National Conservatory, Madrid, Spain CIV: Founder, Sabera Foundation CW: Actress, "Everybody Knows" (2018); Actress, "The Assassination of Gianni Versace" (2018); Actress, "Loving Pablo" (2017); Actress, "Murder on the Orient Express" (2017); Actress, "The Queen of Spain" (2016); Actress, "Layover" (2016); Actress, "Zoolander 2" (2016); Actress, "The Brothers Grimsby" (2016); Actress, "The Queen of Spain" (2016); Actress, Producer, "Ma Ma" (2015); Actress, "I'm So Excited" (2013); Actress, "The Counselor" (2013); Actress, "To Rome with Love" (2012); Actress, "Venuto al Mondo (2012); Co-Producer, "Twice Born" (2012); Actress, "Pirates of the Caribbean: On Stranger Tides" (2011); Actress, "Sex and the City 2" (2010); Actress, "Nine" (2009); Actress, "Los Abrazoz Rotos" (2009); Actress, "Elegy" (2008); Actress, "Vicky Cristina Barcelona" (2008); Actress, "The Good Night" (2007); Actress, "Bandidas" (2006); Actress, "Volver" (2006); Actress, "Sahara" (2005); Actress, "Chromophobia" (2005); Actress, "Noel" (2004); Actress, "Head in the Clouds" (2004); Actress, "Masked and Anonymous" (2003); Actress, "Fanfan la Tulipe (2003); Actress, "Gothika" (2003); Actress, "Waking Up in Reno" (2002); Actress, "Blow" (2001); Actress, "Captain Corelli's Mandolin" (2001); Actress, "Sin Noticias de Dios" (2001); Actress, "Vanilla Sky" (2001); Actress, "Woman on Top" (2000); Actress, "All the Pretty Horses" (2000) Actress, "Todo Sobre Mi Madre (1999); Actress, "Volavèrunt" (1999); Actress, "Don Juan" (1998); Actress, "The Man with Rain in His Shoes" (1998); Actress, "Talk of Angels" (1998); Actress, "La Niña de Tus Ojos (1998); Actress, "The Hi-Lo Country" (1998); Actress, "Et Hjørne af Paradis" (1997); Actress, "Carne Trémula" (1997); Actress, "Abre Los Ojos" (1997); Actress, "La Celestina" (1996); Actress, "Más Que Amor, Frenesí" (1996); Actress, "La Ribelle" (1993); Actress, "Framed" (1992); Actress, "Belle Époque" (1992); Actress, "Jamón, Jamón" (1992); Actress, "El Laberinto Griego" (1991) AW: Named, Sexiest Woman Alive, Esquire Magazine (2014); Named, One of the World's Most Influential People, Time Magazine (2009); Named, Best Supporting Actress, Britain Academy of Film and TV Arts (2009); Named, Best Actress in a Supporting Role, Academy Awards (2009); Named, Outstanding Actress - Motion Picture, American Latino Media Arts Awards (2009); Named, Best Supporting Actress, National Board Review (2008); Named, Best Supporting Actress, New York Film Critics Circuit (2008); Named, Best Supporting Actress, Boston Society of Film Critics (2008); Recipient, Best Film Award, Elle Magazine (2007); Named, Knight in the Order of Arts and Letters, France (2006) BA: Untitled Entertainment, 350 S. Beverly Drive, Suite 200, Beverly Hills, CA, 90212

CRUZ, TED, T: U.S. Senator from Texas I: Government Administration/Government Relations/Government Services DOB: 12/22/1970 PT: Son of Rafael Bienvenido and Eleanor Elizabeth (Darragh) Cruz; ED: JD magna cum laude, Havard Law School, Cambridge, Massachusetts, 1995; AB cum laude, Princeton University, Princeton, New Jersey, 1992 CT: Bar: US District Court (Texas), US Court Appeals (4th, 5th, DC, Federal cirs.), US Supreme Court, DC 1998, Texas 1997 C: Vice Chairman Grass Roots Outreach, National Republican Senatorial Committee (NRSC), 2013-; Member, US Senate Special Committee on Aging, 2013-; Member, US Senate Judiciary Committee, 2013-; Member, US Senate Rules & Administration Committee, 2013-; Member, US Senate Commerce, Sci. & Transportation Committee, 2013-; Member, US Senate Armed Services Committee, 2013-; US Senator from Texas, 2013-; Partner, Morgan, Lewis & Bockius LLP, Houston, 2008-12; Solicitor General, State of Texas, Austin, 2003-08; Director Office Policy Planning, Federal Trade Commission, Washington, 2001-03; Associate Deputy attorney General, US Department Justice, Washington, 2001; Domestic Policy Advisor, Bush-Cheney 2000, Austin, Texas, 1999-2000; Associate, Cooper, Carvin, & Rosenthal PLLC, Washington, 1997-99; Law Clerk to Justice William Rehnquist, US Supreme Court, Washington, 1996-97; Law Clerk to Hon. J. Michael Luttig, US Court Appeals (4th Cir.), Washington, 1995-96 CR: Candidate for the 2016 Republican Party presidential nomination Adjunct Professor US Supreme Court Litigation University Texas School Law, 2004-09 US Department Justice Coordinator Bush-Cheney Transition Advisory Committee, 2000-01 Team Member Bush-Cheney 2000, Inc., 1999-2000 CIV: US Department Justice coordinator, Bush-Cheney Transition Team, Washington, 2001 Attorney, Bush-Cheney Presidential Recount, Florida, 2000 Foundation director, Texas Mavericks, Board advisors, Hispanic Alliance for Progress, Board advisors, Texas Rev. Law & Politics, CW: Editor: (primary) Harvard Law Rev., 1995, (executive) Harvard Journal of Law and Pub. Policy, 1995, (co founding) Harvard Latino Law Rev.; Author: A Time for Truth: Reigniting the Promise of America, 2015 AW: Named Traphagen Distinguished Alumnus, Harvard Law School; named one of The 100 Most Influential People in the World, TIME Magazine, 2016, America's Leading Lawyers for Business, Chambers USA, 2010, 2009, The 25 Greatest Texas Lawyers of the Past Quarter Century, Texas Lawyer, 2010, The 50 Most Influential Minority Lawyers in America, The National Law Journal, 2008, Litigation's Rising Stars, The American Lawyer, 2007, The 50 Most Influential People in Politics, George magazine, 2001, The 100 Most Influential Hispanics, Hispanic Business Magazine, 2000, Hispanic Business magazine, 1999, The 20 Young Hispanics to Watch, Newsweek magazine, 1999; named to The Appellate Hot List, The National Law Journal, 2010; recipient Best US Supreme Court Merits Brief award, National Association Attorney Generals, 2003-07; John M. Olin Fellow, Harvard Law School MEM: Mem.: American Law Institute, Texas Philosophical Society, Texas Lyceum (past vice president, director) PA: Republican

CRYSTAL, BILLY, T: Actor I: Media & Entertainment PB: Long Beach SC: NY/USA PT: Jack Crystal; Helen Crystal MS: Married SPN: Janice Goldfinger, June 4, 1970 CH: Jennifer; Lindsay ED: BFA in TV & Film Direction, New York University, 1970; Student, Nassau Community College; Student, Marshall University, Huntington, West Virginia CW: House manager for play You're a Good Man Charlie Brown, 1971; member group 3's Company; later solo appearances as stand-up comedian; executive producer, writer Midnight Train to Moscow, 1989 (Emmy award for Outstanding Writing, 1989), Sessions, 1991; actor: (films) Rabbit Test, 1978, (voice) Animalympics, 1979, This Is Spinal Tap, 1984, Running Scared, 1986, The Princess Bride, 1987, Goodnight Moon, 1987, Throw Momma from the Train, 1987, (also producer, co-screenwriter) Memories of Me, 1988, When Harry Met Sally..., 1989, Forget Paris, 1995, Hamlet, 1996, Father's Day, 1997, Deconstructing Harry, 1997, My Giant, 1998, Analyze This, 1999, The Adventures of Rocky & Bullwinkle, 2000, America's Sweethearts, 2001, (voice) Monsters, Inc., Mike's New Car, 2002, Analyze That, 2002, (voice) Howl's Moving Castle, 2004, (voice) Cars, 2006, Small Apartments, 2012, (voice) Monsters University, 2013, Party Central, 2014, The Comedian, 2016, Untogether, 2017; actor, director, prodr, writer: (films) City Slickers (Am. Comedy award 1991), 1991, Mr. Saturday Night, 1992, City Slickers II: The Legend of Curley's Gold, 1994; actor, prodr.: (films) Parental Guidance, 2012; (TV films) SST-Death Flight, 1977, Human Feelings, 1978, Breaking Up Is Hard to Do, 1979, Enola Gay, The Men, The Mission, The Atomic Bomb, 1980; director, prodr.: (TV films) 61, 2001; (TV series) Soap, 1977-81, The Billy Crystal Comedy Hour, 1982, Saturday Night Live, 1984-85; (theatre performances) 700 Sundays, 2005, 2013, (Outer Critics Cir. award, Outstanding Solo Performance, 2005, Tony award for Best Special Theatrical Event, 2005, Drama Desk award, Outstanding Solo Performance, 2005),(Television) SNL, 2015, The Comedians, 2015, Modern Family, 2017; host (HBO) Comic Relief, 1986, (TV host) Grammy Awards, 1988, 1989, Academy Awards, 1990-93, 1996-98, 2000, 2004, 2012 (Emmy award for Outstanding Performance in Special Events, 1989, Emmy award for Outstanding Writing, 1991, Emmy award for Outstanding Individual Performance, 1991, 1998), Saturday Night Live: 25th Anniversary, 1999, AFI's 100 Years, 100 Laughs: America's Funniest Movies, 2000; author: I Already Know I Love You, 2004, 700 Sundays, 2005, Grandpa's Little One, 2006, 65: Where I've Been, Where I'm Going, and Where the Hell Are My Keys?, 2013, Still Foolin' 'Em, 2013; co-author: (with Dick Schaap) Absolutely Mahvelous, 1986; recordings You Look Mahvelous, 1985. AW: Recipient Mark Twain prize for Am. Humor, Kennedy Center, 2007

CUBAN, MARK, I: Business Management/Business Services DOB: 07/31/1958 PB: Pittsburgh SC: PA/USA ED: BA in Business Administration, Ind. University, 1981 C: Co-founder, president, chairman, HDNet and HDTV Cable Network, 2001-; Owner, managing partner, Dallas Mavericks, 2000-; Co-owner, 2929 Entertainment,; Chairman, majority owner, Rysher Entertainment,; Chairman, co-owner, Landmark Theaters,; Chairman, co-owner, Magnolia Pictures,; Co-founder, Audionet (became broadcast.com in 1998 (acquired by Yahoo!), 1995-99; President, Radical Computing,; Founder, MicroSolutions (sold to CompuServe), 1983-90 CR: Speaker in field investor Goowy Media Inc., Brondell, Inc., Weblogs, Inc. partner RedSwoosh owner IceRocket CIV: Founder, The Fallen Patriot Fund, 2003- Founder, Mark Cuban Foundation, CW: Executive prodr.: (films) Godsend, 2004; executive prodr.: (films) Criminal, 2004, The War Within, 2005, One Last Thing..., 2005, Bubble, 2005, Good Night and Good Luck, 2005, The Jacket, 2005, Akeelah and the Bee, 2006, The Architect, 2006, Diggers, 2006, Fay Grim, 2006, Turistas, 2006, Black Christmas, 2006, Fast Track, 2006; executive prodr.: (films) Broken English, 2007; executive prodr.: (films) We Own the Night, 2007, Redacted, 2007, The Life Before Her Eyes, 2007, What Just Happened, 2008, Quid Pro Quo, 2008, Two Lovers, 2008, The Burning Plain, 2008, The Girlfriend Experience, 2009, The Road, 2009, Rejoice and Shout, 2010, Tim and Eric's Billion Dollar Movie, 2012; (documentaries) Searching for Debra Winger, 2002, Enron: The Smartest Guys in the Room, 2005, Herbie Hancock: Possibilities, 2006, Gonzo: The Life and Work of Dr. Hunter S. Thompson, 2008, Conquering Kilimanjaro with Angie Everhart, 2009, Casino Jack and the U.S. of Money, 2010; (TV series) The Mark Cuban Show, 2002; executive prodr.: (TV series) Geek to Freek with Dennis Rodman, 2007; co-exec. producer (TV series) Star Search, 2002-04; actor: (films) Talkin About Sex, 1994, Lost at Sea, 1995; (TV series) Walker, Texas Ranger, 2000, Entourage (3 episodes), 2010, (video) Like Mike 2: Streetball, 2006; (TV films) 20 on 20, 2007; (host, producer): (TV series) The Benefactor, 2004; panel member (TV series) Shark Tank, 2011-; maintains (blog site, Blogmaverick.com); performer: Dancing With the Stars, 2007 **AW:** Named a WIRED Renegade, WIRED Rave Awards, 2006; nominee WIRED Rave award-Blogs, 2005; named one of The Most Influential People in the World of Sports, Business Week, 2008, 2007, 50 Most Influential People in Sports Business, Street & Smith's SportsBus. Journal, 2008, 2007, Forbes 400: Richest Americans, 2000-; recipient Webby Entrepreneur of Year, International Academy Digital Arts and Scis., 2006

CUELLAR, HENRY ROBERTO, T: U.S. Representative From Texas, Lawyer **I:** Government Administration/Government Relations/Government Services **DOB:** 09/19/1955 **PB:** Laredo **SC:** TX/USA **PT:** Martin Cuellar, Odilia (Perez) Cuellar **ED:** PhD in Government, University of Texas, Austin, TX, 1998; MA in International Trade, Texas A&M International University, Laredo, TX, 1982; JD, University of Texas, Austin, TX, 1981; BS in Foreign Service, Georgetown University, Washington, DC, Cum Laude, 1978; AA, Laredo Community College, 1976 **CT:** Licensed Customs Broker, 1983 **C:** U.S. Congress From 28th Texas District, 2005-Present; Secretary of State, Texas, 2001; District 42, Texas House of Representatives, 1993-2001; District 43, Texas House of Representatives, 1987-1993; Committee on Appropriations; Committee on Homeland Security; Private Practice Attorney, Laredo, TX **CR:** Adjunct Professor, International Commercial Law, Texas A&M International University, 1984-1986; Instructor, Laredo Community College, 1982-1986 **CIV:** State Legal Advisor, American GI Forum Texas, 1986-1988, President, Board of Directors, International Good Neighbor Council, 1984-1985, President, Board of Directors, Laredo Legal Aid Society Inc., 1982-1984, Board of Directors, Treasurer, Stop Child Abuse & Neglect (SCAN), 1982-1983, President, Board of Directors, Laredo Volunteer Lawyers Program Inc., 1982-1983 **AW:** Laredo Pro Bono Attorney of the Year, 1985 **MEM:** American Bar Association, Inter-American Bar Association, Texas Bar Association, President, Laredo Young Lawyers Association, 1982-1983, Board of Directors, Kiwanis, 1982-1983 **BAR:** U.S. Court of International Trade; U.S. Court of Appeals, Fifth Circuit; U.S. District Court, Southern District, Texas; State of Texas **PA:** Democrat

CULBERSON, JOHN ABNEY, T: U.S. Representative from Texas **I:** Government Administration/Government Relations/Government Services **DOB:** 06/24/1956 **PB:** Houston **SC:** TX/USA **ED:** JD, South Texas College Law, 1988; BA in History, Southern Methodist University, Dallas, 1981 **C:** Member, US Congress from 7th Texas district, 2001-; Member, Committee on Appropriations; Minority whip, Texas House of Reps., 1999-2001; Member from District 130, Texas House of Reps., 1993-2001; Member from District 125, Texas House of Reps., 1987-93; Senior associate civil defense attorney, Lorance & Thompson, Houston, 1985; Political advertising agency employee, 1981-85; Oil rig mud logger, 1978-81 **AW:** Recipient Brighter Vision award, Seniors Coalition, 2005, Manufac-

turing Legis. Excellence award, National Assn Manufacturers, 2005, Spirit of Enterprise award, US C. of C., 2002, Hero of Taxpayer award, Americans for Tax Reform, 2002, Friend of Taxpayer award, Texas Citizens for Sound Economy, 2000, Outstanding Young Houstonian award, Houston Jaycees, 1994, Leader of Excellence award, Free Market Association, 1993 **PA:** Republican **BA:** 2352 Rayburn House Office Bldg, Washington, DC, 20515

CULLUM, JOHN, T: Actor and Singer **I:** Media & Entertainment **PB:** Knoxville **SC:** TN/USA **MS:** Married **SPN:** Emily Frankel **CH:** John David **ED:** BA, University of Tennessee **C:** Former tennis player and real estate salesman; Actor 1960- **MIL:** With, US Army **CW:** New York debut with Shakespearewrights, 1957; joined New York Shakespeare Festival, 1960; Broadway debut in Camelot, 1962; played Laertes in Hamlet, 1964; other Broadway appearances include On A Clear Day You Can See Forever, 1965 (Theatre World award 1965), Man of La Mancha, 1966, 1776, 1969, Vivat! Vivat Regina, 1972, Shenendoah, 1975 (Tony award as best actor 1975), The Trip Back Down, 1977, On the Twentieth Century, 1978 (Tony award as best actor in musical 1978), Deathtrap, 1979, Whistler, 1981 (Drama Desk award), Private Lives (with Richard Burton and Elizabeth Taylor), 1983, Doubles, 1985, The Boys in Autumn (with George C. Scott), 1986, Urinetown, 2002, Purlie, 2005, The Other Side, 2005, 110 in the Shade, 2007, Cymbeline, 2007; other leading roles include plays Hamlet, Cyrano de Bergerac, The Conscientious Objector, 2008; film appearances include: All the Way Home, 1963, Hawaii, 1966, 1776, 1972, The Prodigal, 1982, Sweet Country, 1985, Marie, 1985, The Boys in Autumn (with George C. Scott), 1986, Ricochet River, 1998, Held Up, 1999, Blackwater Elegy, 2003, The Notorious Bettie Page, 2005, The Night Listener, 2006; concert readings include The Golden Apple, 2005; appeared in TV films A Man Without a Country, 1973, The Day After, 1984, Shootdown, 1988, With a Vengeance, 1992, Inherit the Wind, 1999; TV films include Summer, 1980, Carl Sandburg, 1981; TV series include Buck James, 1987-88, Northern Exposure, 1990-95 (Emmy nomination, Supporting Actor, Comedy, 1993), ER, 1997-2000, To Have & To Hold, 1998, Law & Order: Special Victims Unit, 2003-07; TV appearance in All My Children, 1997; spokesman for arts and entertainment cable TV, Victorian Days.(Theatre) August: Osage County, 2009, The Scootsboro Boys, 2010, Measure for Measure, 2011, All's Well That Ends Well, 2011, Casa Valentina, 2014, Waitress, 2016 (Television) Mad Men, 2007, The Middle, 2009, 30 Rock, 2012, Nurse Jackie, 2013, Unbreakable Kimmy Schmidt, 2015, Thanksgiving, 2016, Madam Secretary, 2017(Film) The Conspirator, 2011, Kill Your Darlings, 2013, Adult World, 2013, Love is Strange, 2014, Christine, 2016

CUMBERBATCH, BENEDICT, T: Actor **I:** Media & Entertainment **DOB:** 07/19/1976 **PB:** London **SC:** England **PT:** Timothy Carlton Cumberbatch; Wanda Ventham **ED:** MA in Classical Acting, London Academy of Music and Dramatic Art; BA in Drama, University of Manchester **C:** Co-founder, Production Co., SunnyMarch Ltd. (2013) **CIV:** Ambassador, Motor Neurone Disease Association **CW:** Actor, TV Series, "Sherlock" (2010-Present); Actor, Film, "Magik" (2018); Actor, Film, "Avengers Infinity War" (2018); Actor, Film, "Mowgli" (2018); Actor (Voice), Film, "Dr. Seuss How the Grinch Stole Christmas" (2018); Actor, Film, "The Current War" (2017); Actor, Film, "Thor Raganrok" (2017); Actor, TV Miniseries, "The Child in Time" (2017); Actor, TV Miniseries, "The Hollow Crown" (2016); Actor, TV Miniseries, "SNL" (2016); Actor, Film, "Zoolander 2" (2016); Actor, Film, "Doctor Strange"

(2016); Actor, Film, "Black Mass" (2015); Narrator, "Cristiano Ronaldo: World at His Feet" (2014); Actor, Film, "The Imitation Game" (2014); Actor (Voice), Film, "Penguins of Madagascar" (2014); Actor, Film, "The Hobbit: The Battle of the Five Armies" (2014); Actor, Play, "Hamlet" (2014); Actor, Film, "Star Trek into Darkness" (2013); Actor, Film, "12 Years a Slave" (2013); Actor, Film, "The Fifth Estate" (2013); Actor, Film, "August: Osage County" (2013); Actor, Film, "The Hobbit: The Desolation of Smaug" (2013); Radio Work, "Cabin Pressure, Neverwhere" (2013); Radio Work, "Copenhagen" (2013); Actor, Play, "50 Years on Stage" (2013); Actor, Film, "The Hobbit: An Unexpected Journey" (2012); Actor, TV Series, "Parade's End" (2012); Narrator, Documentary, "Girlfriend in a Coma" (2012); Actor, Film, "Tinker Tailor Soldier Spy" (2011); Actor, Film, "War Horse" (2011); Actor, Film, "Wreckers" (2011); Actor, Play, "Frankenstein" (2011); Actor, Film, "Four Lions" (2010); Actor, Film, "Third Star" (2010); Actor, Film, "The Whistleblower" (2010); Actor, TV Film, "Van Gogh: Painted with Words" (2010); Actor, Play, "Hedda Gabler, The Children's Monologues" (2010); Actor, TV Film, "Small Island" (2009); Actor, Film, "Burlesque Fairytales" (2009); Radio Work, "Rumpole and the Penge Bungalow Murders" (2009); Actor, Film, "Creation" (2009); Actor, TV Miniseries, "The Last Enemy" (2008); Actor, Film, "The Other Boleyn Girl" (2008); Actor, TV Film, "Stuart: A Life Backwards" (2007); Actor, Film, "Atonement" (2007); Actor, Film, "Starter for 10" (2006); Actor, Film, "Amazing Grace" (2006); Actor, TV Miniseries, "To the End of the Earth" (2005); Actor, TV Film, "Hawking" (2004); Actor, TV Miniseries, "Cambridge Spies" (2003); Actor, Film, "To Kill a King" (2003); Actor, TV Series, "Fortysomething" (2003); Actor, TV Miniseries, "Tipping the Velvet" (2002); Actor, TV Film, "Fields of Gold" (2002); Voice for Audiobooks Casanova, "The Tempest," "The Making of Music," "Death in a White Tie," "Artists in Crime," "Sherlock Holmes: The Rediscovered Railway Mysteries and Other Stories"; Voice-overs for Commercials, Jaguar, Sony, Pimms, Google **AW:** Emmy Award for Outstanding Lead Actor in a Miniseries or a Movie, "Sherlock" (2014); Named Hollywood's Hottest Star, Critics' Choice Awards (2013); Laurence Olivier Award for Best Actor, "Frankenstein" (2011)

CUMMINGS, ELIJAH EUGENE, T: U.S. Representative from Maryland, Ranking Minority Member of the Oversight Committee **I:** Government Administration/Government Relations/Government Services **DOB:** 01/18/1951 **PB:** Balt. **ED:** JD, University Maryland, 1976; BS, Howard University, 1973 **CT:** Bar: Maryland 1976 **C:** Ranking Democrat, US House Select Committee on the Events Surrounding the 2012 Terrorist Attack in Benghazi, 2014-; Ranking member, US House Oversight & Government Reform Committee, Washington, 2011-; Member, US Congress from 7th Maryland District, Washington, 1996-; Chairman, Congressional Black Caucus, Washington, 2003-05; Speaker pro tempore, Maryland House of Dels., Annapolis, 1995-96; Vice chairman house economic matters committee, Maryland House of Dels., Annapolis, 1994-96; Chairman committee economic devel., Maryland House of Dels., Annapolis, 1996; Vice chairman constitutional and administrative law committee, Maryland House of Dels., Annapolis, 1987-96; Member, Maryland House of Dels., Annapolis, 1983-96; Attorney, Maryland General Assembly, 1982; Private law practice, 1980-96 **CIV:** Chairman Maryland Legis. Black Caucus chairman Gov.'s Commission on Black Males, 1990- president Bancroft Lit. Society, Congressional Black Caucus Foundation (first vice chairman, board directors, now chair) 1998, chairman, 2003-. **AW:** Named

Outstanding US Student Government Leader Royal Arts Society of London; named one of The Most Influential Black Americans Ebony magazine, 2006, The 10 Members to Watch in the 112th Congress, Roll Call, 2011; named to Power 150 Ebony magazine, 2008. **MEM:** Mem.: Maryland Bar Association **PA:** Democrat

CUNNINGHAM, BILLY, T: Former Professional Basketball Coach **I:** Athletics **DOB:** 06/03/1943 **PB:** Brooklyn **SC:** NY/USA **MS:** Married **SPN:** Sondra Cunningham, 1966; **CH:** Stephanie, Heather **ED:** Bachelor, University North Carolina, Chapel Hill **C:** Partner, Miami Heat, Florida, 1988-94; Lead NBA color commentator, CBS Sports, 1985-89; Small forward, Carolina Cougars, American Bar Association, 1972-74; Head coach, Philadelphia 76ers, 1977-85; Small forward, Philadelphia 76ers, 1965-72, 74-76 **CR:** Owner Billy Cunningham's Court, West Conshohocken, Pennsylvania, 1987-2005 **AW:** Named American Bar Association MVP, 1973; named to New York City Basketball Hall of Fame, 1996, Naismith Memorial Basketball Hall of Fame, 1986, American Bar Association All-Star Team, 1973, NBA All-Star Team, 1969-73,NBA All-Star Game Head Coach, 1978, 1980, 1981,1983, ACC Player of the Year, 1965, NBA All-Star, 1969-1972, ABA MVP, 1973 **ACH:** Achievements include member of NBA championship winning Philadelphia 76ers, 1967; head coach of NBA championship winning Philadelphia 76ers, 1983

CUOMO, ANDREW MARK, T: Governor of New York, former state attorney general **I:** Government Administration/Government Relations/Government Services **DOB:** 12/06/1957 **PB:** Queens **PT:** Son of Mario Matthew and Matilda (Raffa) Cuomo **ED:** JD, Albany Law School, 1982; BA, Fordham University, Bronx, New York, 1979 **C:** Governor, State of New York, Albany, 2011-; Attorney general, State of New York, Albany, 2007-10; Secretary, US Department Housing & Urban Devel. (HUD), Washington, 1997-2001; Assistant secretary for community planning & devel., US Department Housing & Urban Devel. (HUD), Washington, 1993-97; Chairman, New York City Commission on Homeless, 1991-93; Partner, Blutrich, Falcone & Miller, New York City, 1985-88; Assistant district attorney, Manhattan District Attorney's Office, New York City, 1984-85; Special assistant to Governor Mario Cuomo, State of New York, Albany, 1983; Campaign manager, Mario Cuomo Gubernatorial Campaign, New York, 1982 **CR:** Visiting fellow Harvard University Institute Politics, pub. speaker, The Allen Agency **CIV:** Founder, Housing Enterprise for Less Privileged (HELP), 1986 Candidate for Governor, New York, 2002 Manager gubernatorial campaign, Mario M. Cuomo, New York, 1982 **CW:** Editor: Crossroads: The Future of American Politics, 2003; author: (memoir) All Things Possible: Setbacks and Success in Politics and Life, 2014 **AW:** Named one of The 100 Most Influential People in the World, TIME magazine, 2012; recipient Innovation award, Harvard University John F. Kennedy School Government, 1998, Distinguished Community Service award, New York University, 1991, Pub. Service award, Council Jewish Organizations, 1989, Ed Sulzberger award, Our Town - Manhattan Media LLC, 1989, Man of Year award, Coalition Italian Am. Organizations, 1988 **PA:** Democrat **BA:** Office of Andrew Cuomo, State Capitol Building, Albany, NY, 12224

CUOMO, CHRISTOPHER, T: News Correspondent **I:** Media & Entertainment **DOB:** 08/09/1970 **PB:** Queens **SC:** NY/USA **PT:** Mario Cuomo, Matilda Raffa Cuomo **ED:** JD, Fordham University, Bronx, NY, 1995; BA, Yale University, New Haven, CT, 1992 **C:** Field Anchor, Co-Host of New Day, CNN,

2013-Present; Co-Anchor, 20/20, ABC News, 2009-2013; Chief Law And Justice Correspondent, ABC News, 2009-2013; News Anchor, Good Morning America, ABC News, 2006-2009; Senior Legal Correspondent, ABC News, 2005-2007; Co-Anchor, Primetime, ABC News, 2004-2006; Correspondent, Co-Anchor, 20/20 Downtown, ABC News, 2002; Correspondent, ABC News, 1999-2002; Reporter, Fox Files, Fox Broadcast Network, 1998-1999; Political Policy Analyst, Correspondent, Fox News Channel; Political Policy Analyst, CNN, MSNBC, CNBC **AW:** Peabody Award, 2013, Gerald Loeb Award, 2005, News Emmy Award, Silver Gavel Award, American Bar Association, Edward R. Murrow Award for Breaking News Coverage **BA:** CNN, 1221 Avenue of the Americas, New York, NY, 10020

CUPICH, BLASE JOSEPH, T: Cardinal **I:** Religious **DOB:** 03/19/1949 **PB:** Omaha, March 19, 1949 **PT:** Son of Blase and Mary Mayhan Cupich. **ED:** STD in Sacramental Theology, Catholic University of America, 1987; STL in Sacramental Theology, Catholic University of America, 1979; MA in Theology, North American College & Gregorian University, Rome, 1975; STB, North American College & Gregorian University, Rome, 1974; BA in Philosophy, University Saint Thomas, 1971 **C:** Archbishop, of Chicago, 2014-; Archbishop-designate, of Chicago, 2014; Bishop, of Spokane, Washington, 2010-14; Ordained bishop, of Rapid City, South Dakota, 1998; Bishop, of Rapid City, South Dakota, 1998-2010; Pastor, Saint Robert Bellarmine Parish, Omaha, 1997-98; Pres.-rector, Pontifical College Josephinum, Columbus, Ohio, 1989-96; Pastor, Saint Mary Parish, Bellevue, 1987-89; Secretary, Apostolic Nunciature, Washington, 1981-87; Instructor, Continuing Education of Priests Program & Diaconate Formation, Creighton University, Omaha, 1980-81; Instructor, Paul VI HS, Omaha, 1975-78; Associate pastor, Saint Margaret Mary Parish,; Chair Commission on Youth, of Omaha, 1978-81; Director Office Divine Worship, of Omaha, 1978-81; Ordained priest, of Omaha, 1975 **CR:** Chair Subcommittee for the Church in Central and Eastern Europe US Conference of Catholic Bishops, 2013-, At-large rep. Task Force on Priestly and Religious Vocations, 2008, chair Committee on Protection of Children and Young People, 2008-11, member Committee on Protection of Children and Young People, 2005-06, chair Committee on Vocations, 2004-07, member adv. committee, 2004-06, member Committee on Domestic Policy, 2003-04, member Ad Hoc Committee on Sexual Abuse, 2002-05, member Ad Hoc Committee on Scripture Translation, 2002-, member Ad Hoc Committee for the 2004 Assembly, 2001-02, member Committee on the Liturgy Task Force on Liturgy with Children, 2000-05, member Bishops' Committee for Young Adults, 2000-03, member Committee on the Liturgy, 1999-2007, consultant Ad Hoc Committee to Oversee the Use of the Catechism, 1999-, member Ad Hoc Committee on Native American Catholics, 1999-2003, member Communications Committee, 1999-2003 **CIV:** Board trustee, Saint Paul Seminary, University Saint Thomas, 1999-2009 Board directors, National Pastoral Life Center, 2006- Board member, Crazy Horse Memorial Foundation, South Dakota, 2014 Apostolic visitator to Seminaries, 2005-06 Episcopal advisor, Serra Club, 2004-08 **CW:** Contributor of articles to In America magazine; author: The "I" of Priestly Identity in the Priest, 1994, The Priest as Administrator: Rediscovering Our Tradition of Pastoral Leadership in Priests for a New Millennium, 2000 **MEM:** Mem.: National Catholic Education Association (chairman 2013-), Catholic Mutual Relief Society (trustee 2002-, board member), Catholic Extension Society (board governor 2009-, chair mission committee 2011)

CURBELO, CARLOS, T: U.S. Representative-elect from Florida **I:** Government Administration/Government Relations/Government Services **DOB:** 03/01/1980 **PB:** Miami **SC:** FL/USA **PT:** Son of Teresita and Carlos Curbelo; **ED:** MPA, University of Miami; BBA, University of Miami **C:** Member, U.S. Congress from 26th Florida District, 2014-; Member, Committee on Ways and Means; Administrator, Miami Dade County Public School District, 2010-; Board, Miami-Dade Metropolitan Planning Organization, 2010; State director, U.S. Senator George LeMieux, 2009-10; Founder, Capitol Gains, 2002 **PA:** Republican

CURRY, STEPHEN, T: Professional Basketball Player **I:** Athletics **DOB:** 03/15/1988 **PB:** Akron **PT:** Son of Dell and Sonya Curry **ED:** Student in sociology, Davidson College, North Carolina, 2006-09 **C:** Guard, Golden State Warriors, 2009-present **CR:** Member US national team FIBA World Championships, Turkey, 2010 **AW:** Named NBA Most Valuable Player, 2016, 2015, 1st Team NBA All-Rookie, 2010, 1st Team All-American, Associated Press, The Sporting News. National Association Basketball Coaches, 2009; recipient Gold medal, FIBA World Championship, 2014, 2010,NBA Champion, 2015, 2017, NBA All-Star, 2014-17, All-NBA First Team, 2015, 2016, All-NBA Second Team, 2014-2017, NBA Scoring Champion, 2016, NBA Steals Leader, 2016, 50-40-90 Club, 2016, NBA Three-Point Contest Champion, 2015, NBA Sportsmanship Award, 2011 **ACH:** Achievements include winner of the NBA All-Star Weekend Skills Challenge, 2011; leading the NBA in free throw percentage (.934), 2011, 2015; leading the NBA in three-point field goals, 2013, 2014, 2015; being a member of the NBA champion Golden State Warriors, 2015; the first unanimous MVP winner in NBA history in 2016

CURTIS, JAMIE LEE, T: Actress **I:** Media & Entertainment **PB:** LA **SC:** CA/USA **PT:** Tony Curtis; Janet Leigh **MS:** Married **SPN:** Christopher Guest (December 18, 1984) **CH:** Annie, Thomas **ED:** Student, University Pacific, Stockton, California, 1976 **CW:** Actress: (films) Halloween, 1978, The Fog, 1980, Prom Night, 1980, Terror Train, 1980, Halloween II, 1981, Road Games, 1981, Trading Places, 1983, Love Letters, 1984, Grandview USA, 1984, The Adventures of Buckaroo Banzai: Across the 8th Dimension, 1984, Perfect, 1985, Welcome Home, 1986, A Man in Love, 1987, Amazing Grace and Chuck, 1987, Dominick and Eugene, 1988, A Fish Called Wanda, 1988, Blue Steel, 1990, Queens Logic, 1991, My Girl, 1991, Forever Young, 1992, My Girl 2, 1994, Mother's Boys, 1994 True Lies, 1994 (Golden Globe award for Best Actress - Musical or Comedy), House Arrest, 1996, Ellen's Energy Adventure, 1996, Fierce Creatures, 1997, Homegrown, 1998, Halloween H2O, 1998, Virus, 1999, Drowning Mona, 2000, The Tailor of Panama, 2001, Daddy and Them, 2001, Rudolf the Red-Nosed Reindeer and the Island of Misfit Toys (voice), 2001, Halloween: Resurrection, 2002, Freaky Friday, 2003, Christmas with the Kranks, 2004, The Kid and I, 2005, Beverly Hills Chihuahua, 2008, You Again, 2010, From Up on Poppy Hill (voice), 2011, The Little Engine That Could (voice), 2011, Veronica Mars, 2014, Spare Parts, 2015; Halloween, 2018 (TV films) Colombo: Bye-Bye Sky-High I.Q. Murder Case, 1977, Death of a Centerfold: The Dorothy Stratten Story, 1981, Money on the Side, 1982, As Summers Die, 1986, The Heidi Chronicles, 1995, Nicolas' Gift, 1998, Only Human, 2014; (TV series) Operation Petticoat, 1977-78, She's in the Army Now, 1981, Anything but Love, 1989-92, (Recipient Golden Globe Award, 1989) Scream Queens, 2015-2016; (TV appearances) Quincy, 1977, Hardy Boys/Nancy Drew Mysteries, 1977, Charlie's Angels,

1978, The Love Boat, 1978, Buck Rogers in the 25th Century, 1979, The Drew Carey Show, 1996, Pigs Next Door, 2000 (voice), NCIS, 2012, New Girl, 2012-15; dir.: Anything But Love, 1990; author: (children's books): When I Was Little: A Four-Year-Old's Memoir of Her Youth, 1993, Tell Me Again About the Night I Was Born, 1996, Today I Feel Silly and Other Moods That Make My Day, 1998, Where Do Balloons Go? An Uplifting Mystery, 2000, I'm Gonna Like Me: Letting Off a Little Self-Esteem, 2002, It's Hard to Be Five: Learning How to Work My Control Panel, 2004, Is There Really a Human Race?, 2006, Big Words for Little People, 2008, My Mommy Hung the Moon: A Love Story, 2010.

CURTIS, JOHN R., T: U.S. Representative from Utah I: Government Administration/Government Relations/Government Services PB: Salt Lake City SC: UT/USA ED: BS, Brigham Young University C: U.S. House of Representatives Utah's Third District, 2017-Present; Mayor, Provo, UT, 2010-2017

CYRUS, MILEY, T: Singer, Actress I: Media & Entertainment DOB: 11/23/1992 PB: Franklin PT: Daughter of Billy Ray and Leticia Cyrus CW: Actress: (films) Big Fish, 2003, (voice) Bolt, 2008, Hannah Montana: The Movie, 2009 (Best Song from a Movie (The Climb), MTV Movie Awards, 2009, Choice Movie Actress Music/Dance, Teen Choice Awards, 2009), The Last Song, 2010, LOL, 2012, So Undercover, 2012, The Night Before, 2015, A Very Murray Christmas, 2016, Crisis in Six Scenes, 2016, Guardians of the Galaxy Vol. 2, 2017; (TV series) Hannah Montana, 2006-11 (Choice TV Actress: Comedy, Teen Choice Awards, 2007, 2008, 2009), Crisis in Six Scenes, 2016; performer: (concert films) Hannah Montana/Miley Cyrus: Best of Both Worlds Concert Tour, 2008, (video) Hannah Montana: One in a Million, 2008; singer: (albums) Hannah Montana, 2006, Hannah Montana, Vol. 2: Meet Miley Cyrus, 2007, Breakout, 2008, The Time of Our Lives, 2009, Can't Be Tamed, 2010, Bangerz, 2013, Miley Cyrus and Her Dead Petz, 2015, Younger Now, 2017 (albums with Billy Ray Cyrus) Wanna Be Your Joe, 2006, Home at Last, 2007, (soundtracks) Hannah Montana: The Movie, 2009 (Choice Music: Single, Teen Choice Awards, 2009), Hannah Montana Forever, 2010, (songs) Wrecking Ball, 2013 (Top Streaming Song (Video), Billboard Music Awards, 2014, Video of Year, MTV Video Music Awards, 2014); guest appearances Doc, 2003, The Suite Life of Zack and Cody, 2006, High School Musical 2, 2007, The Emperor's New School, 2007, Two and a Half Men, 2012, host MTV Video Music Awards, 2015, judge (reality singing competition) The Voice, 2016-2017 AW: Named Top Streaming Artist, Billboard Music Awards, 2014, Favorite Breakout Movie Actress, People's Choice Awards, 2010, Favorite Female Singer, Kids Choice Awards, 2008, Favorite TV Actress, 2008, Choice Music Female Artist, Teen Choice Awards, 2008, Choice Summer Artist, 2007, Favorite TV Actress, Nickelodeon Kids' Choice Awards, 2007; Named One of The 10 Most Fascinating People of 2013, Barbara Walters Special, The 10 Most Fascinating People of 2008, The 100 Most Powerful Women in Entertainment, Hollywood Reporter, 2013, 2008, The 100 Most Powerful Celebrities, Forbes.com, 2008, The 100 Most Influential People in the World, TIME magazine, 2014, 2008, The Top 25 Entertainers of Year, Entertainment Weekly, 2007 BA: Cunningham Escott Slevin & Doherty, 10635 Santa Monica Boulevard, Los Angeles, CA, 90025

DAFOE, WILLEM, T: Actor I: Media & Entertainment PB: Appleton SC: WI/USA PT: William Dafoe, Muriel (Sprissler) Isabel MS: Married SPN: Giada Colagrande, 3/25/2005; Elizabeth LeCompte CH: Jack ED: Student, University of Wisconsin CR: Theatre X Theatrical Co., 1975; Co-Founder, The Wooster Group Theatrical Co., New York, NY, 1977-Present CW: Actor, (Films) The Loveless, 1982, The Hunger, 1983, New York Nights, 1984, Roadhouse 66, 1984, Streets Of Fire, 1984, To Live And Die In LA, 1985, Platoon, 1986, The Last Temptation Of Christ, 1988, Off Limits, 1988, Mississippi Burning, 1988, Triumph Of The Spirit, 1989, Born On The Fourth Of July, 1989, Cry-Baby, 1990, Wild At Heart, 1990, Flight Of The Intruder, 1991, White Sands, 1992, Light Sleeper, 1992, Body Of Evidence, 1992, Far Away So Close!, 1993, The Night And The Moment, 1994, Clear And Present Danger, 1994, Tom And Viv, 1995, Victory, 1995, The English Patient, 1996, Basquiat, 1996, Speed 2: Cruise Control, 1997, Affliction, 1997, Lulu On The Bridge, 1998, Existen Z, 1998, American Psycho, 1999, The Boondock Saints, 1999, Bullfighter, 2000, The Animal Factory, 2000, Shadow Of The Vampire, 2000, The Gangs Of New York, 2000, Pavilion Of Women, 2001, Edges Of The Lord, 2001, Spider-Man, 2002, Auto-Focus, 2002, Finding Nemo (Voice), 2003, Once Upon A Time In Mexico, 2003, Camel Cricket City (Voice), 2003, The Reckoning, 2004, The Clearing, 2004, Spider-Man 2, 2004, The Life Aquatic With Steve Zissou, 2004, The Aviator, 2004, Ripley Under Ground, 2005, Control, 2005, Xxx: State Of The Union, 2005, Inside Man, 2006, American Dreamz, 2006, (Voice) Fantastic Mr. Fox, 2009, Farewell, 2010, Daybreakers, 2010, A Woman, 2010, Miral, 2011, Fireflies In The Garden, 2011, 4:44 Last Day On Earth, 2011, The Hunter, 2011, John Carter, 2012, Tomorrow You're Gone, 2012, Odd Thomas, 2013, Out Of The Furnace, 2013, Nymphomaniac: Vol. 1, 2013, Nymphomaniac: Vol. 2, 2013, The Grand Budapest Hotel, 2014, A Most Wanted Man, 2014, Bad Country, 2014, The Fault In Our Stars, 2014, Pasolini, 2014, John Wick, 2014, My Hindu Friend, 2015, Dog Eat Dog, 2016, Finding Dory, 2016, The Headhunter's Calling, 2016, Sculpt, 2016, The Great Wall, 2016, Do Donkeys Act?, 2017, The Florida Project, 2017, What Happened To Monday, 2017, Mountain, 2017, Death Note, 2017, Justice League, 2017, Murder On The Orient Express, 2017, Opus Zero, 2017, Aquaman, 2018, At Eternity's Gate, 2018, Motherless Brooklyn, (Plays) The Hairy Ape, 1997, North Atlantic, 1999, Idiot Savant, 2009, The Old Women, 2014, (TV Appearances) The Hitchhiker, 1985, The Simpsons (Voice), 1997, 2014, Family Guy, 2007, American Experience, 2010, The Simpsons, 2014, Piigs, 2017; Actor, Co-Producer, (Films) New Rose Hotel, 1998; Actor, Writer, (Films) Before It Had A Name, 2005 AW: Karlovy Vary International Film Festival, Crystal Globe for Outstanding Contribution to World Cinema, 2016

DAILEY, JEFFREY J., T: CEO I: Insurance CN: Farmers Group ED: Bachelors in Economics, University of Wisconsin-Madison; MBA, University of Wisconsin-Madison C: Chief Executive Officer, Farmers Group (2012-Present); President/Chief Operating Officer, Farmers Group (2011-2012)

DAINES, STEVE, T: U.S. Senator from Montana I: Government Administration/Government Relations/Government Services DOB: 08/20/1962 PB: Van Nuys ED: BS in Chemical Engineering, Montana State University, 1984 C: US Senator from Montana, 2015-; Member, US House Transportation & Infrastructure Committee, 2013-15; Member, US House Natural Resources Committee, 2013-15; Member, US House Homeland Security Committee, 2013-15; Member at-large, US Congress from Montana, Washington, 2013-15; Various positions including vice president customer service, vice president Asia-Pacific, & vice president North American sales, RightNow Technologies, Bozeman, Montana, 2000-12; Private construction business, Bozeman, Montana, 1997-2000; Management roles, The Procter & Gamble Co., Hong Kong China, 1991-97; Management roles, The Procter & Gamble Co., 1984-91 CR: Montana chairman Governor Mike Huckabee for President, 2008 co-founder Giveitback.com delegate Republican National Convention, 1984 PA: Republican BA: Office of Steve Daines, 320 Hart Senate Office Building, Washington, DC, 20510

DALEY, GEORGE QUENTIN, T: Hematologist, Bio-Medical Research Scientist I: Medicine & Health Care DOB: 11/13/1960 PB: Catskill PT: Son of Frank Leonard and Natalie Alcine (Evans) Daley; ED: MD summa cum laude, Harvard University, 1991; PhD in Biology, Massachusetts Institute of Technology, 1989; AB, Harvard University, 1982 CT: Diplomate Am. Board Internal Medicine C: Dean of the Harvard Medical School,2017-; With division hematology/oncology, Children's Hospital, Boston, 2003-; Associate professor, biological chemistry and molecular pharmacology, Harvard Medical School, 2002-; Associate professor, pediatrics, Children's Hospital, Boston,; Associate director stem cell/devel. biology research, Children's Hospital, Boston,; Clinical research fellow hematology/oncology, Children's, Brigham, Women's and Dana Farber Cancer Center Institute,; Fellow, Whitehead Institute for Biomedical Research, Massachusetts Institute of Technology, Cambridge, Massachusetts, 1995; Chief resident in internal medicine, Massachusetts General Hospital, Boston, 1994-95 CR: Chairman pre-med. adv. committee Quincy House, Harvard University, Cambridge, 1987-95. CW: Contributor articles to sci. journals AW: Recipient research award for Clinical Trainees National Institutes of Health, 1992, Burroughs-Wellcome Fund Career award, Scholar award, Leukemia and Lymphoma Society Am., Pioneer award, National Institutes of Health, 2004; national scholar Harvard University, 1978-91. MEM: Member American Association for the Advancement of Science, Am. Society Clinical Investigation. ACH: Achievements include creation of mouse model for chronic myelogenous leukemia; research in stem cells of the blood to define the molecular basis for human leukemia; self-renewal and differentiation of human ES cells, target directed chemotherapy for chronic myelogenous leukemia (CML); first creation of functional sperm cells from embryonic stem cells (cited a "Top Ten" breakthrough for 2003 by Science magazine).

DALTREY, ROGER, T: Singer I: Media & Entertainment DOB: 03/01/1944 PB: London SC: England PT: Son of Harry and Irene D.; MS: Married SPN: Heather Taylor (July 19, 1971); Jacqueline January 29, 1964 (div. 1968); CH: Simon, Rosie Lea, Willow Amber, Jaimie ED: Degree (hon.), Middlesex University,2012 C: Lead Singer, The Who,(formerly The Detours, The High Numbers), 1964— CW: Singer: (albums with The Who) The Who Sings My Generation, 1965, Happy Jack, 1966, The Who Sell Out, 1967, The Magic Bus: The Who on Tour, 1968, Tommy, 1969, Live At Leeds, 1970, Meaty Beaty Big & Bouncy, 1971, Who's Next, 1971, Quadrophenia, 1973, Odds & Sods, 1974, The Who By Numbers, 1975, Who Are You, 1978, Face Dances, 1981, Hooligans, 1981, It's Hard, 1982, Who's Greatest Hits, 1983, Who's Last, 1983, Who's Missing, 1985, Two's Missing, 1987, Who's Better, Who's Best, 1988, Join Together, 1990, Thirty Years of Maximum R&B, 1994, Live at the Isle of Wight Festival 1970, 1996, My Generation: The Very Best of The Who, 1996, The BBC Sessions, 1999, The Blues to the Bush,

1999, The Ultimate Colllection, 2002, Live at the Royal Albert Hall, 2003, The Who: Then & Now, 2004, Live from Toronto, 2006, Endless Wire, 2006; (soundtracks) The Kids Are Alright, 1979, Quadrophenia, 1979; (solo albums) Daltrey, 1973, Ride A Rock Horse, 1975, One of the Boys, 1977, Parting Should Be Painless, 1984, Under a Raging Moon, 1985, Can't Wait to See the Movie, 1987, Rocks in the Head, 1992, Martyrs & Madmen: The Best of Roger Daltrey, 1997; (sountracks) McVicar, 1980; performer (films) Monterrey Pop, 1968, Woodstock, 1970, The Kids Are Alright, 1979, The Who Rocks America, 1982, The Rolling Stones Rock 'N' Roll Circus, 1996, Message to Love: The Isle of Wight Festival, 1997, Amazing Journey: The Story of The Who, 2007; Actor: (films) Tommy, 1975, Lisztomania, 1975, The Legacy, 1979, Bitter Cherry, 1983, Pop Pirates, 1984, Murder: Ultimate Grounds for Divorce, 1984, The Hunting of the Snark, 1987, The Little Match Girl, 1987, Gentry, 1987, Three Penny Opera, 1988, Cold Justice, 1989, Mack the Knife, 1989, Buddy's Song, 1990, If Looks Could Kill, 1991, Lightning Jack, 1994, Bad English I: Tales of a Son of a Brit, 1995, 1996, Like It Is, 1998, Best, 2000, Chasing Destiny, 2001, .com for Murder, 2002, Johnny Was, 2006, The Last Detective, 2007, Once Upon a Time, 2012, Going Back Home, 2014,; (TV movies) The Beggar's Opera, 1983, The Comedy of Errors, 1983, Forgotten Prisoners: The Amnesty Files, 1990, (voice) The Real Story of Happy Birthday to You, 1992, The Wizard of Oz in Concert: Dreams Come True, 1995, The Magical Legend of the Leprechauns, 1999, Dark Prince: The True Story of Dracula, 2000, Strange Frequency 2, 2001, Chasing Destiny, 2001, Trafalgar's Battle Surgeon, 2005; (TV mini-series) Pirate Tales, 1997; (TV appearances) One of the Boys, 1977, Buddy, 1986, Crossbow, 1987, How to Be Cool, 1988, Midnight Caller, 1991, Tales from the Crypt, 1993, Lois & Clark: The New Adventures of Superman, 1996, Sliders, 1997, Fitzcairn, 1997-98, Highlander, 1998, The Bill, 1999, Rude Awakening, 1999-2000, That 70's Show, 2002, Witchblade, 2001-02, Once Upon a Time on the Westway, 2006, CSI: Crime Scene Investigation 2006, Pawn Stars, 2013; (stage appearances) The Wizard of Oz in Concert: Dreams Come True, 1995, Scrooge, 1998; actor, prodr.: (films) McVicar, 1980; Executive Prodr.: (films) Quadrophenia, 1979; (voice) (educational films) Wheels on the Bus Series: Mango & Papaya's Animal Adventure, 2005, Mango Helps the Moon Mouse, 2005, Mango's Big Dog Parade, 2008; Featured in Numerous Documentaries. **AW:** Named an Honorary Knight Commander of the Most Excellent Order of the British Empire, 2005; Named to Rock & Roll Hall of Fame (as member of The Who), 1990, UK Music Hall of Fame, 2005; Recipient Ivor Novello Award for Contribution to British Music, 1982, BRIT Award for Outstanding Contribution to British Music, 1988, Grammy Lifetime Achievement Award, 2001, Kennedy Center Honors, John F. Kennedy Center for the Performing Arts, 2008, James Joyce Award, 2009, Steiger Award, 2012, Best Blues Award, British Blues Awards **BA:** WEA/ Atlantic, 75 Rockefeller Plz, New York, NY, 10019

DAMON, MATT, T: Actor **I:** Media & Entertainment **DOB:** 10/08/1970 **PB:** Cambridge **SC:** MA/USA **PT:** Son of Kent Telfer Damon and Nancy Carlsson-Paige **CR:** Member, One X One Foundation **CW:** Actor: (films) Mystic Pizza, 1988, School Ties, 1992, Geronimo: An American Legend, 1993, Courage Under Fire, 1996, Glory Daze, 1996, Chasing Amy, 1997, The Rainmaker, 1997, Rounders, 1998, Saving Private Ryan, 1998, The Talented Mr. Ripley, 1999, Dogma, 1999, All the Pretty Horses, 1999, Titan A.E. (voice), 2000, The Legend of Bagger Vance, 2000, Jay and Silent Bob Strike Back, 2001, The Majestic (voice), 2001, Ocean's

Eleven, 2001, Gerry, 2002, The Bourne Identity, 2002, Spirit: Stallion of the Cimarron (voice), 2002, Confessions of a Dangerous Mind, 2002, Stuck on You, 2003, Eurotrip, 2004, The Bourne Supremacy, 2004, Ocean's Twelve, 2004, The Brothers Grimm, 2005, Syriana, 2005, The Departed, 2006, The Good Shepherd, 2006, Ocean's Thirteen, 2007, The Bourne Ultimatum, 2007, Invictus, 2009, The Informant!, 2009, Green Zone, 2010, Hereafter, 2010, True Grit, 2010, The Adjustment Bureau, 2011, Contagion, 2011, Margaret, 2011, Happy Feet Two (voice), 2011, We Bought a Zoo, 2011, Elysium, 2013, The Zero Theorem, 2013, The Monuments Men, 2014, Interstellar, 2014, The Martian, 2015 (National Board Review Award for Best Actor, 2015, Golden Globe Award for Best Performance by an Actor in a Motion Picture - Musical or Comedy, 2016), The Great Wall, 2016, Bending the Arc, 2017, Downsizing, 2017, Suburbicon, 2017, Thor: Ragnarok, 2017, Ocean's 8, 2018; (TV films) Behind the Candelabra, 2013; actor, writer (films) Good Will Hunting, 1997 (Golden Globe Award for Best Screenplay-Motion Picture, 1998, Academy Award for Best Writing, Screenplay Written Directly for Screen, 1998), actor, writer, producer Promised Land, 2012, actor, executive producer The Third Wheel, 2002, actor, producer Jason Bourne, 2016, narrator (documentaries) Inside Job, 2010; actor: (TV appearances) Entourage, 2009; executive prodr.: (films) Speakeasy, 2002, The Battle of Shaker Heights, 2003, Feast, 2005; prodr.: Stolen Summer, 2002, Manchester-by-the-Sea, 2016; (TV series) Project Greenlight, 2001-05, Push, Nevada, 2002, SNL, 2002, The Bernie Mac Show, 2002, Will and Grace, 2002, Journey to Planet Earth, 2003-14, Arthur, 2007, Entourage, 2009, The People Speak, 2009, Cubed, 2010, 30 Rock, 2010-11, House of Lies, 2013, Years of Living Dangerously, 2014, The Leisure Class, 2015, The Runner, 2016, Incorporated, 2016; executive prodr.: (TV films) More Time with Family, 2014, The Leisure Class, 2015; (TV series) The Runner, 2016; guest appearances (TV series) 30 Rock, 2010-11 **AW:** Named Favorite Male Action Star, People's Choice Awards, 2008, Sexiest Man Alive, People magazine, 2007; named one of The 100 Most Influential People in the World, TIME magazine, 2011, Top 25 Entertainers of Year, Entertainment Weekly, 2007, The 100 Most Powerful Celebrities, Forbes.com, 2008, 2007, 50 Most Powerful People in Hollywood, Premiere magazine, 2005-06; Recipient, Star on the Hollywood Walk of Fame, 2007 **BA:** Endeavor Agency, 9601 Wilshire Boulevard, 3rd Floor, Beverly Hills, CA, 90210

DANGERMOND, JACK, T: Co-Founder of the Environmental Systems Research Institute **I:** Sciences **ED:** Grad., Harvard University; Masters, University Minnesota; Bachelors, California Polytech. College, Pomona **C:** Founder, president, Environmental Systems Research Institute, Redlands, California, 1969- **CR:** Adv. committee NASA, EPA, National Academy of Sciences, NCGIA **AW:** Recipient Horward award Urban and Regional Information Systems Association, Anderson medal Association Am. Geographers, John Wesley Powell award U.S. Geological Survey, Cullum Geog. Medal Am. Geographical Society, 1999, named one of Forbes 400: Richest Americans, 2009, Alexander Graham Bell Medal, 2010, Audubon Medal, 2015 **MEM:** Member Eurasian Academy Society, Numerous Organizations

DANGERMOND, LAURA, T: Co-founder **I:** Sciences **CN:** Environmental Systems Research Institute (ESRI) **C:** Co-founder, Environmental Systems Research Institute (ESRI) (1969-Present) **DANIELS, JEFF, T:** Actor **I:** Media & Entertainment **PB:** Clarke County **SC:** GA/USA **PT:** Robert Lee Daniels; Marjorie J. (Ferguson) Daniels **ED:**

DFA (hon.), University Michigan, 2009; Student, Central Michigan University **C:** Founder, Purple Rose Theatre Co., Chelsea, Michigan, 1991-; Executive director, Purple Rose Theatre Co.,; Apprentice, Circle Repertory Co., New York City, **CW:** Actor: (plays) The Farm, 1976, My Life, 1977, Brontosaurus, 1977, Feedlot, 1977, Lulu, 1978, Slugger, 1978, Johnny Got His Gun, 1982 (Obie award), Three Sisters, 1982-83, Short-Changed Review, Blackbird, 2007, Turn of the Century, 2008, (Broadway plays) The Fifth of July, 1978, 1979, 1980-81, The Golden Age, 1984, Redwood Curtain, 1993, God of Carnage, 2009, Blackbird, 2016, (films) Ragtime, 1981, Terms of Endearment, 1983, The Purple Rose of Cairo, 1985, Marie, 1985, Heartburn, 1986, Something Wild, 1986, Radio Days, 1987, The House on Carroll Street, 1988, Sweet Hearts Dance, 1988, Grand Tour, 1989, Checking Out, 1989, Arachnophobia, 1990, Welcome Home, Roxy Carmichael, 1990, Love Hurts, 1990, The Butcher's Wife, 1992, Gettysburg, 1993, Speed, 1994, Dumb and Dumber, 1994, Fly Away Home, 1996, 2 Days in the Valley, 1996, 101 Dalmatians, 1996, Trial and Error, 1997, Pleasantville, 1998, My Favorite Martian, 1999, All the Rage, 1999, Chasing Sleep, 2000, Blood Work, 2002, The Hours, 2002, Gods and Generals, 2003, I Witness, 2003, Imaginary Heroes, 2004, Because of Winn-Dixie, 2005, The Squid and the Whale, 2005, Good Night, and Good Luck, 2005, RV, 2006, Infamous, 2006, The Lookout, 2007, (voice) Space Chimps, 2008, Traitor, 2008, State of Play, 2009, Paper Man, 2009, Away We Go, 2009, Howl, 2010, Quad, 2011, Looper, 2012, Quad, 2013, Dumb and Dumber To, 2014, Steve Jobs, 2015, The Martian, 2015, The Divergent Series: Allegiant - Part 1, 2016,The Catcher Was A Spy,2018 (TV films) A Rumor of War, 1980, An Invasion of Privacy, 1983, The Caine Mutiny Court Marshall, 1988, No Place Like Home, 1989, Disaster in Time, 1992, Redwood Curtain, 1995, The Crossing, 2000, Cheaters, 2000, The Goodbye Girl, 2004, The Five People You Meet in Heaven, 2004, (TV series) The Newsroom, 2012-14 (Outstanding Lead Actor in a Drama Series, Emmy Awards, 2013)Godless, 2017, The Looming Tower, 2018; actor, director, writer: (films) Escanaba in da Moonlight, 2001, Super Sucker, 2002; playwright: Shoeman, 1991, The Tropical Pickle, 1992, The Vast Difference, 1993, Thy Kingdom's Coming, 1994, Escanaba in da Moonlight, 1995, Across the Way, 2002; singer: (albums) Grandfather's Hat, Jeff Daniels Live and Unplugged.

DANIELS, LEE, T: Producer, Director **I:** Media & Entertainment **PB:** Manhattan **SC:** NY/USA **CW:** (Television) (Co-Creator), Empire, 2015, Star, 2016, (Film Produced) Monsters Ball, 2001, The Woodsman, 2004, Shadowboxer, 2005, Tennessee, 2008, Precious, 2009, The Paperboy, 2012, Lee Daniels The Butler, 2013 (Actor,) A Little Off Mark, 1986, Agnes und Seine bruder, 2004

DANSON, TED, T: Actor **I:** Media & Entertainment **DOB:** 06/12/1905 **PB:** San Diego, **SC:** San Diego, **ED:** Student, The Kent School, Connecticut, 1966; Student, Stanford University, 1968; Student, Carnegie-Mellon University, 1972 **CW:** Teacher The Actors' Institute, LA, 1978. **CW:** Actor: (Off Broadway) The Real Inspector Hound, 1972, Comedy of Errors, Comedians, (TV films) The Women's Room, 1980, Once Upon a Spy, 1980, Dear Teacher, 1981, Our Family Business, 1981, Allison Sydney Harrison, 1983, Cowboy, 1983, Something About Amelia, 1984, Gulliver's Travels, 1996, Thanks of a Grateful Nation, 1998, Living with the Dead, 2004, It Must Be Love, 2004, Our Fathers, 2005, Knights of the South Bronx, 2005, (films) The Onion Field, 1979, Body Heat, 1981, Creepshow, 1983, A Little Treasure, 1985, A Fine Mess, 1986,

Just Between Friends, 1986, Three Men and a Baby, 1987, Cousins, 1989, Dad, 1989, Three Men and A Little Lady, 1990, Made in America, 1993, Getting Even With Dad, 1994, Loch Ness, 1996, Jerry & Tom, 1998, Homegrown, 1998, Saving Private Ryan, 1998, Mumford, 1999, Fronterz, 2004, The Moguls, 2005, Nobel Son, 2007, Mad Money, 2008, The Human Contract, 2008, The Open Road, 2009, (voice) Jock, Big Miracle, 2012, The One I Love, 2014, Hearts Beat Loud, 2018, (TV series) Somerset 1975-76, Cheers, 1982-1993 (Emmy award for Outstanding Lead Actor in a Comedy Series, 1990, 1993, Golden Globe award for Best Performance by an Actor in a Mini-Series or Motion Picture Made for TV, 1985, 1990, 1991), Becker, 1998-2004, Curb Your Enthusiasm, 2000-09, Help Me Help You, 2006-07, Damages, 2007-10, Bored to Death, 2009-11, CSI: Crime Scence Investigation 2011-15, Fargo, 2015, CSI: Cyber, 2015-, The Good Place, 2016-(Critics Choice Award, Best Actor in a Comedy Series 2018); co-prodr.: (TV series) Down Home, 1990; (TV appearances) B.J. and the Bear, 1979, Laverne & Shirley, 1980, Family, 1980, Tucker's Witch, 1982, Benson, 1981, Magnum P.I., 1981, Taxi, 1982, Frasier, 1995, Diagnosis Murder, 1999, Veronica's Closet, 1998, Heist, 2006, Help Me Help You, 2006, Tim and Eric Awesome Show, Great Job! 2010, CSI: New York, 2013; (voice) The Simpsons, 1994, Grosse Pointe, 2000, Gary the Rat, 2003, The Magic 7, 2006; actor, exec prodr.: (TV films) When The Bough Breaks, 1986, We Are The Children, 1987, (films) Pontiac Moon, 1994, Bye Bye Benjamin, 2006, (TV series) Ink, 1996; author: Oceana: Our Endangered Oceans and What We Can Do to Save Them, 2011. **AW:** Recipient Presidential End Hunger award Agency for International Development, 1989, Am. Comedy Award, 1991, The Peoples Choice Award for Favorite Male TV Performer, 1992, Star on Walk of Fame, 1999.

DAUGAARD, DENNIS MARTIN, T: Governor of South Dakota **I:** Government Administration/Government Relations/Government Services **DOB:** 06/11/1953 **PB:** Sioux Falls **SC:** SD/USA **ED:** JD, Northwestern University School of Law, Chicago, IL, 1978; BS in Political Science, University of South Dakota, 1975 **C:** Governor, State Of South Dakota, 2011-Present; Lieutenant Governor, State Of South Dakota, 2003-2011; Executive Director, Children's Home Society of South Dakota, 2003-2009; District 9, South Dakota State Senate, 1997-2003; Development Director, Children's Home Society of South Dakota, 1990-2002; Vice President & Trust Officer, First Bank of South Dakota, 1981-1990; Attorney, Shand Morahan & Co., 1980-1981; Attorney, Supena & Nyman, 1978-1979 **CR:** Sioux Falls Estate Planning Council, South Dakota Planned Giving Council **MEM:** South Dakota Bar Association, National Society of Fund Raising Executives, Rotary **BAR:** South Dakota **PA:** Republican **BA:** Office of the Governor, 500 E Capitol Avenue, Pierre, SD, 57501-5070

DAVID, LARRY, T: Television Scriptwriter and Producer, Actor **I:** Media & Entertainment **PB:** Brooklyn **SC:** NY/USA **PT:** Morty David; Rose David **ED:** BA in History, University of Maryland, College Park **MIL:** With, US Army Reserve **CW:** Staff writer: Fridays, 1980-82, Saturday Night Live, 1984-85; creator, writer: Norman's Corner, 1989; executive producer, co-creator: (TV series) The Seinfeld Chronicles, 1989, Seinfeld, 1990-98 (Emmy award for Outstanding Comedy Series 1993, Emmy award Outstanding Writing Comedy Series 1993); writer, director Sour Grapes, 1998; executive producer, writer, actor HBO comedy special Larry David: Curb Your Enthusiasm, (TV series) Curb Your Enthusiasm, 2000-11 (AFI award for Best Comedy Series, 2001); executive producer, actor: (films)

Can She Bake a Cherry Pie?, 1983, Radio Days, 1987, New York Stories, 1989, Whatever Works, 2009, The Three Stooges, 2012, (TV appearances) Entourage, 2004, The Paul Reiser Show, 2011; actor, writer, prodr, Clear History, 2013, Triptank, 2014, The League, 2015, SNL, 2015-17, May & Marty, 2016: (TV films) Clear History, 2013; actor, writer: (Broadway play) A Fish In the Dark, 2015

DAVIDSON, WARREN, T: U.S. Representative from Ohio **I:** Government Administration/Government Relations/Government Services **PB:** Troy **SC:** OH/USA **ED:** M.B.A, University of Notre Dame, 2000; B.A., West Point, 1996 **C:** Member, U.S. Representative from Ohio's 8th District, 2016-; Member, Committee on Financial Services

DAVIS, ANTHONY JR., T: Professional Basketball Player **I:** Athletics **DOB:** 03/11/1993 **PB:** Chgo. **SC:** IL/USA **PT:** Son of Anthony and Erainer Davis **ED:** Student, University of Kentucky, Lexington, 2011-12 **C:** Forward, center, New Orleans Pelicans (formerly New Orleans Hornets), 2012-Present **CR:** Member US national team Summer Olympic Games, London, 2012 **AW:** NBA All Star Game MVP Award, 2017, Named a Unanimous 1st Team All-American, Associated Press, US Basketball Writers Association, The Sporting News, National Association Basketball Coaches, 2012; named NCAA Final Four Most Outstanding Player, 2012, College Basketball Player of Year, Associated Press, 2012, The Sporting News, 2012, Defensive Player of Year, National Association Basketball Coaches, 2012, National Freshman of Year, US Basketball Writers Association, 2012, Southeastern Conference Player of Year, 2012, Southeastern Conference Defensive Player of Year, 2012, Southeastern Conference Freshman of Year, 2012; recipient Gold medal, men's basketball, Summer Olympic Games, 2012, Pete Newell Big Man award, National Association Basketball Coaches, 2012, Oscar Robertson trophy, US Basketball Writers Association, 2012, John R. Wooden award, LA Athletic Club, 2012, Adolph F. Rupp trophy, Commonwealth Athletic Club Kentucky, 2012, Naismith trophy, Atlanta Tipoff Club, 2012,NBA All-Star Game MVP, 2017, All-NBA First Team, 2015, 2017, NBA All- Defensive Second Team, 2015, 2017, NBA Blocks Leaderm 2014, 2015, NBA All-Rookie First Team, 2013, NCAA Champion, 2012 **ACH:** Achievements include second freshman in NCAA Division I history named college basketball player of the year by the Associated Press, 2012; member of NCAA Final Four Division I National Championship winning University of Kentucky Wildcats, 2012; first overall pick in the NBA Draft, 2012 **BA:** New Orleans Pelicans, 5800 Airline Drive, Metairie, LA, 70003

DAVIS, DANNY K., T: U.S. Representative from Illinois **I:** Government Administration/Government Relations/Government Services **DOB:** 09/06/1941 **PB:** Parkdale **SC:** AR/USA **MS:** Married **SPN:** Vera Davis **CH:** Jonathon, Stacey **ED:** PhD, Union Institute, 1977; MA, Chicago State University, 1968; BA, Arkansas A. M. & N. College, 1961 **C:** Member, US Congress from 7th Illinois district, 1997-; Member, Committee on Ways and Means; Member committee on education & workforce; US Congress from 7th Illinois district,; Member subcom. of census, US Congress from 7th Illinois district,; Member committee on government reform and oversight, committee on small business, US Congress from 7th Illinois district, **CIV:** Chicago alderman, 1979-90 commissioner Cook. County, 1990-96 candidate Chicago mayor, 1991 founder, president Westside Association for Community Action president National Association Community Health Ctrs. co-chmn. Clinton/Gore/Moseley-Braun Illinois campaigns, 1992 board directors

National Housing Partnership. **AW:** Named to Power 150, Ebony magazine, 2008; recipient Most Influential Black Americans, 2006 **PA:** Democrat **BA:** 2159 Rayburn House Office Building, Washington, DC, 20515

DAVIS, RODNEY LEE, T: U.S. Representative from Illinois **I:** Government Administration/Government Relations/Government Services **DOB:** 01/05/1970 **PB:** Des Moines **SC:** IA/USA **ED:** BA in Political Sci., Millikin University, 1992 **C:** Member, US House Transportation & Infrastructure Committee, 2013-; Member, US House Agricultural Committee, 2013-; Member, US Congress from 13th Illinois District, Washington, 2013-; Staff member to Rep. John Shimkus, US House of Representatives, 1997-2012; Campaign manager, John Shumkus's Congressional Campaign, 1998; Staff member to secretary of state George Ryan, State of Illinois, Springfield, 1992-96 **CIV:** Member board education, St. Mary's Church, **PA:** Republican **BA:** 1740 Longworth House Office Building, Washington, DC, 20515

DAVIS, SUSAN CAROL ALPERT, T: U.S. Representative From California **I:** Government Administration/Government Relations/Government Services **DOB:** 04/13/1944 **PB:** Cambridge **SC:** MA/USA **PT:** George R. Alpert, Dorothy M. (Wexler) Alpert **ED:** MA in Social Work, University of North Carolina, 1968; BA in Sociology, University of California, Berkeley, 1965 **C:** U.S. Congress From 53rd California District, 2003-Present; U.S. Congress From 49th California District, 2001-2003; District 76, California State Assembly, 1994-2000; Executive Director, Aaron Price Fellowship Progressive, San Diego, CA, 1990-1994; Development Associate, KPBS-TV, San Diego, CA, 1979-1983; Development Associate, KPBS-FM, San Diego, CA, 1977 **CR:** Executive Board Member, New Democratic Coalition, National Conference of Christians & Jews, San Diego Consortium & Private Industry Council, Democratic Leadership Council, Vice President, President, San Diego Unified School District Board of Education, 1983-1992 **CIV:** Youth Volunteer, United Way, Volunteer, June Burnett Institute for Children & Families, San Diego, CA **MEM:** President, San Diego League of Women Voters, 1977 **PA:** Democrat **BA:** 1526 Longworth House Office Bldg, Washington, DC, 20515

DAVIS, VIOLA, T: Actress **I:** Media & Entertainment **DOB:** 08/11/1965 **PB:** Saint Matthews **SC:** SC/USA **PT:** Dan Davis; Mary Davis **ED:** Diploma, Juilliard School; Diploma, Rhode Island College **C:** Actress (1992-Present) **CW:** Actress, Films, "The Substance of Fire" (1996); "Out of Sight" (1998); "Traffic" (2000), "The Shrink Is In" (2001), "Kate & Leopold" (2001), "Far from Heaven" (2002), "Antwone Fisher" (2002), "Solaris" (2002), "Get Rich or Die Tryin'" (2005), "Syriana" (2005), "The Architect" (2006), "World Trade Center" (2006), "Disturbia" (2007), "Nights in Rodanthe" (2008), "Doubt" (2008), "Madea Goes to Jail" (2009), "State of Play" (2009), "Knight and Day" (2010), "Eat Pray Love" (2010), "It's Kind of a Funny Story" (2010), "The Help" (2011), "Extremely Loud and Incredibly Close" (2011), "Won't Back Down" (2012), "Beautiful Creatures" (2013), "Prisoners" (2013), "The Disappearance of Eleanor Rigby: Him" (2013), "The Disappearance of Eleanor Rigby: Her" (2013), "Ender's Game" (2013), "The Disappearance of Eleanor Rigby: Them" (2014), "Get On Up" (2014), "Blackhat" (2015), "Suicide Squad" (2016), "Fences" (2016), "Widows" (2018); Actress, TV Films, "The Pentagon Wars" (1998), "Grace & Glorie" (1998), "Amy & Isabelle" (2001), "Father Lefty" (2002), "Stone Cold" (2005), "Jesse Stone: Night Passage" (2006), "Jesse Stone: Death in Paradise" (2006), "Life Is Not a Fairytale: The

Fantasia Barrino Story" (2006), "Fort Pit" (2007), "Jesse Stone: Sea Change" (2007), "The Andromeda Strain" (2008), U.S. of Tara (2009), "Sofia the First" (2013); Actress, TV Series, "City of Angels" (2000), "Law & Order: Special Victims Unit" (2003-2008), "Century City" (2004), "Traveler" (2007), "How to Get Away with Murder" (2014-Present); Actress, Broadway Plays, "Seven Guitars" (1996), "King Hedley II" (2001), "Fences" (2010); Actress, Executive Producer, Films, "Lila & Eve" (2015), "Custody" (2016) **AW:** Named an The 100 Most Influential People in the World, TIME Magazine (2012); Virtuoso Award, Santa Barbara International Film Festival (2009); Academy Award for Best Supporting Actress (2016); Golden Globe for Best Supporting Actress (2016); Time 100 Most Influential (2017); Primetime Emmy for Outstanding Lead Actress in a Drama Series (2015); Tony Award for Best Featured Actress in a Play (2001); Best Actress in a Play (2010); Best Breakthrough Performance - Female, "Doubt," National Board Review (2008); Lead Actress Award, "The Help," African American Film Critics Association (2012); Best Actress, "The Help," Critics' Choice Movie Award (2012); Outstanding Performance by a Female Actor in a Leading Role, "The Help," Screen Actors Guild Awards (2012); Outstanding Actress in a Motion Picture, "Won't Back Down," National Association for the Advancement of Colored People Image Award (2013); Favorite Actress in a New TV Series, "How to Get Away with Murder," People's Choice Award (2015); Outstanding Performance by a Female Actor in a Drama Series, "How to Get Away with Murder," Screen Actors Guild Awards (2015, 2016); Outstanding Actress in a Drama Series, "How to Get Away with Murder," National Association for the Advancement of Colored People Image Awards (2015); Outstanding Lead Actress in a Drama Series, "How to Get Away with Murder," Emmy Award (2015); King Hedley II, 2001 (Best Performance by a Leading Actress in a Play, "King Hedley," Tony Awards (2001); Fences, 2010 (Best Performance by a Leading Actress in a Play, "Fences" Tony Award (2010) **ACH:** Achievements include becoming the first African-American woman to win a Primetime Emmy Award for Outstanding Lead Actress in a Drama Series, 2015, Outstanding Lead Actress, Primetime Emmy's, 2015.

DAVISON, JON, T: Vocalist **I:** Media & Entertainment **PB:** Laguna Beach **SC:** CA/USA **CW:** (Albums)(With Yes) Heaven & Earth, 2014,(With Sky Cries Mary) This Timeless Turning, 1993, Moonbathing on Sleeping Leaves, 1997, Fresh Fruits for the Liberation, 1998, Seeds, 1999, Here and Now, 2005, Small Town, 2007, Space Between the Drops, 2009, Taking the Stage :1997-2005, 2011(With Glass Hammer) If, 2010, Cor Cordium, 2011, The Stories of H.P. Lovecraft, 2012, Perilous, 2012, The Inconsolable Secret, 2013, Ode to Echo, 2014, Untold Tales, 2017

DAWKINS, RICHARD, T: Evolutionary Biologist, Ethologist **I:** Sciences **DOB:** 03/26/1941 **PB:** Nairobi **SC:** Kenya **PT:** Son of Clinton John and Jean Mary Vyvyan (Ladner) Dawkins; **ED:** D Univ. (hon.), Open University, 2003; DSc (hon.), University Hull, 2001; DSc (hon.), University Westminster, 1997; LittD (hon.), Australian National University, Canberra, 1996; LittD (hon.), St. Andrews University, 1995; DSc, Oxford University, 1989; DPhil, Oxford University, 1966; MA, Oxford University, 1966; BA, Oxford University, 1961 **C:** Professorial Fellow, New College, 1995-; Charles Simonyi Professor of the Pub. Understanding of Sci., Oxford University, England, 1995-; Fellow, New College, 1970-90; Ad Hominem Reader, Zoology, Oxford University, 1990-95; Univ. Lecturer, Zoology, Oxford University,

England, 1970-90; Research Student, Oxford University, 1962-66; Assistant Professor Zoology, University California, Berkeley, 1967-69; Research Assistant to Professor N. Tinbergen Federal Reserve System, 1965-67 **CR:** Invited lecturer in field member selection committee for Dawkins Prize Balliol College, Oxford, 2004 patron Sunday Times Oxford Lit. Festival, 2003 member David Attenborough Studi Committee Natural History Museum, London, 2005, pub. engagement committee, 2003 judge, selection committee BAFTA TV Awards, 2003, Grierson Awards Sci. Section, 2003 chairman Michael Faraday award Selection Committee, 2003 consultant Independent Schools Parents' Organization, 1999 member International Centre for Life Scientific Adv. Group, Newcastle upon Tyne, 1997 hon. associate National Secular Society Ltd., London, 1996 hon. chairman, sci. engineering tech. committee Oxford University, 1996 member sci. consultative committee British Broadcasting Corp., 1986-91 council member Association for the Study Animal Behavior, 1972-79 hon. associate New Humanist committee fellow Scientific Investigation of Claims of the Paranormal, Skeptical Inquirer humanist laureate International Academy Humanism **CIV:** Founder, board trustee, Richard Dawkins Foundation for Reason and Sci., 2006- Member, Oxford Trust Centre for Sci. Communications in Oxfordshire, 2002 Member, British Museum Develop. Trust Council, 2001 Advisor, The Vega Sci. Trust, University Sussex, 1999 **CW:** Author: The Selfish Gene, 1976, 1989, The Extended Phenotype, 1982, The Blind Watchmaker, 1986 (Royal Society Lit. award, 1987, LA Times Literary prize, 1987), River Out of Eden: A Darwinian View of Life, 1995 (Number One Bestseller, Sunday Times List), Climbing Mount Improbable, 1996 (Number One Bestseller, Observer List), Unweaving the Rainbow: Science, Delusion and the Appetite for Wonder, 1997, A Devil's Chaplain, 2003, The Ancestor's Tale: A Pilgrimage to the Dawn of Evolution, 2004, The God Delusion, 2006 (Publishers Weekly Bestseller), The Greatest Show on Earth: The Evidence for Evolution, 2009; columnist, senior editor Free Inquiry, Council for Secular Humanism, advisor British Academy TV Awards, edited with M. Dawkins and T.R. Halliday The Tinbergen Legacy, 1991, editorial advisor to several journals, European editor Animal Behavior Monographs, 1972-73, Animal Behaviour, 1974-78, executive editor Oxford Surveys in Evolutionary Biology, 1983-86, founding editor Episteme Journal, 2002; editor: Best American Science and Nature Writing, 2003; board advisor TIME Future of Life Summit, 2003, member adv. board Encyclopedia of Evolution, Oxford University Publishing, Artificial Life, member editorial adv. board Websters Encarta Encyclopedia, Journal of Memetics, member editorial board Biology and Philosophy, member external adv. board Oxford Today, consultant Young Encyclopedia of Science, Oxford University Publishing, televised lecture on the Evolution of Human Purpose, 1982, presenter BBC Horizon Programme: Nice Guys Finish First, 1985, BBC Horizon Programme: The Blind Watchmaker, 1986 (Sci. Tech prize for Best TV Documentary Sci. Programme of the Year, 1987), BBC Discussion Programme: Thinking Aloud, 1986, presenter, author Break the Science Barrier with Richard Dawkins, Channel 4, Equinox, 1996, and other TV interviews, discussions, and presentations, edited in several journals; contributor articles to professional journals; invited forwards in books; writer, presenter: Documentary The Root of All Evil?, 2006,(Book) The Magic of Reality: How We Know What's Really True, 2011, An Appetite for Wonder: The Making of a Scientist, 2013, Brief Candle in the Dark: My Life in Science, 2015, Science in the Soul: Selected Writings of a Passionate Rationalist, 2017(

Documentary) The Enemies of Reason, 2007, The Genius of Charles Darwin, 2008, The Purpose of Purpose, 2009, Faith School Menace, 2010, Beautiful Minds, 2012, Sex, Death and the Meaning of Life, 2012, The Unbelievers, 2013 **AW:** Named Hon. Fellow, Balliol College, Oxford University, 2004, Humanist of Year, 1996; named one of The World's Most Influential People, TIME magazine, 2007, Top 100 Pub. British Intellectuals, Prospect Magazine, 2004; recipient Golden Plate award, Academy Achievement, 2006, Shakespeare prize for contribution to British Culture, Alfred Toepfer Foundation, 2005, Bicentennial Kelvin medal, Royal Philosophical Society Glasgow, 2002, Medal of Presidency of the Italian Republic, Rimini, 2001, Kistler prize, USA, 2001, International Cosmos prize, Osaka, Japan, 1997, Nakayama prize for achievement in human sci., 1994, Michael Faraday award, Royal Society London, 1990, Silver medal, Zoological Society London, 1989, Hon. Fellowship, Regent's College, London, 1988,Daily Telegraphs List of 100 Greatest Living Geniuses, 2007, Richard Dawkins Award, 2003 **MEM:** Fellow: Royal Society, Royal Society Lit.; mem.: British Humanist Association (vice president 1996), British Association Advancement of Sci. (president biological scis. section 1997), Trinity College Univ. Philosophical Society (hon. patron 2004) **H:** Computer programming **BA:** New Coll U Oxford Oxford OX1 3BN England, 11605 Meridian Market VW Ste 124, Falcon, CO, 80831

DAY-LEWIS, DANIEL, T: Actor **I:** Media & Entertainment **DOB:** 04/29/1957 **ED:** Student, Bedales and Bristol Old Vic Theatre School; Honorary LittD, University of Bristol, 2010 **CW:** Actor, (Plays) Class Enemy, Funny Peculiar, Bristol, England, Look Back In Anger, Dracula, Bristol And London, Another Country, London, Futurists, Romeo, Thisbe, R.S.C., Hamlet, 1989, (TV Series) Frost In May, 1982, My Brother Jonathan, 1985, (TV Films) Artemis 81, 1981, The Insurance Man, 1986, (Films) Sunday Bloody Sunday, 1971, Ghandi, 1982, How Many Miles To Babylon?, 1982, The Bounty, 1984, A Room With A View, 1986, My Beautiful Laundrette, 1986, Nanou, 1986, The Unbearable Lightness Of Being, 1988, Stars And Bars, 1988, Eversmile, New Jersey, 1989, My Left Foot, 1989, The Last Of The Mohicans, 1992, The Age Of Innocence, 1993, In The Name Of The Father, 1993, The Crucible, 1996, The Boxer, 1997, Gangs Of New York, 2003, The Ballad Of Jack And Rose, 2005, There Will Be Blood, 2007, Nine, 2009, Lincoln, 2012, Phantom Thread, 2017 **AW:** Knight Commander of the Most Excellent Order of the British Empire (KBE), Her Majesty Queen Elizabeth II, 2014, The 100 Most Influential People in the World, TIME Magazine, 2013, British Academy of Film And TV Arts, Best Performance By An Actor In A Motion Picture-Drama, Golden Globe Award, Hollywood Foreign Press Association, Outstanding Performance By A Male Actor In A Leading Role, Screen Actors Guild, Academy Award For Best Actor, Lincoln, 2013, Best Actor, New York Film Critics Circle, Boston Society of Film Critics, National Society of Film Critics, Critics Choice Awards, Lincoln, 2012, Critics Choice Award, Broadcast Film Critics Association, Best Performance By An Actor In A Motion Picture-Drama, Golden Globe Award, Hollywood Foreign Press Association, Outstanding Performance By A Male Actor In A Leading Role, Screen Actors Guild, Best Leading Actor, British Academy of Film And TV Arts, Academy Award For Best Actor In A Leading Role, There Will Be Blood, 2008, Best Actor, New York Film Critics Circle, There Will Be Blood, 2007, Best Actor In Leading Role, British Academy of Film And TV Arts, Gangs Of New York, 2003, Academy Award For Best Actor, 1989, British Academy of

Film And TV Arts, My Left Foot, 1990 **BA:** Julian Belfrage Associates, 46 Albemarle Street, London, United Kingdom, W1S 4DF

DAYTON, MARK BRANDT, T: U.S. Representative of Minnesota **I:** Government Administration/Government Relations/Government Services **DOB:** 01/26/1947 **PB:** Minneapolis **SC:** MN/USA **ED:** BA cum laude in Psychology, Yale University, 1969 **C:** Governor, State of Minnesota, 2011-; US Senator from Minnesota, 2001-07; State auditor, State of Minnesota, 1991-95; Commissioner energy and economic devel., State of Minnesota, 1983-86; Commissioner economic devel., State of Minnesota, 1978; Staff member for Governor Rudy Perpich, State of Minnesota, 1977; Legis. assistant to Senator Walter Mondale, US Senate,; Counselor, administrator, Social Service agency, Boston, 1972-76; Teacher general sci., New York City Pub. School, 1969-71 **CR:** Member Senator Paul Wellstone's Re-election Campaign, 1995-96 **AW:** Recipient Public Service award, Minnesota State Federation Council for Exceptional Children, 2003, Legis. of Year, Am. Ambulance Association, 2003, Golden Triangle, Minnesota National Farmers Union, 2003, 2002, Distinguished Citizen award, Minnesota Veterans Foreign Wars, 1995, President's award, National Association for the Advancement of Colored People Minnesota chapter, 1995 **PA:** Democrat

DE BLASIO, BILL, T: Mayor of New York City **I:** Government Administration/Government Relations/Government Services **DOB:** 05/08/1961 **PB:** New York City, May 8, 1961 **PT:** Son of Warren and Maria (De Blasio) Wilhelm; **ED:** MA in International & Public Affairs, Columbia University, 1987; BA, New York University, 1984 **C:** Mayor, New York City, 2014-; Public advocate, New York City, 2010-13; City councilman District 39, New York City Council, 2001-09; Regional director, US Department Housing & Urban Devel. (HUD), New York City, 1996-99; Aide to Deputy Mayor Bill Lynch, New York City, **CR:** Chairman General Welfare committee New York City Council **CIV:** Member, Community School Board 15, New York City **PA:** Democrat **BA:** Office of Bill de Blasio, City Hall, New York, NY, 10007

DE GETTE, DIANA LOUISE, T: U.S. Representative from Colorado, lawyer **I:** Government Administration/Government Relations/Government Services **DOB:** 07/29/1957 **PB:** Tachikawa **PT:** Daughter of Richard Louis and Patricia Anne (Rose) De Gette; **ED:** JD, New York University School Law, 1982; BA in Political Sci., magna cum laude, Colorado College, 1979 **CT:** Bar: US Supreme Court 1989, US Court Appeals (10th cir.) 1984, US District Court Colorado 1982, Colorado 1982 **C:** Member, US Congress from 1st Colorado district, 1996-; Member,Committee on Education and the Workforce, Committee on Armed Services; Vice-chair energy & commerce committee;; Chief deputy whip, US Congress from 1st Colorado district,; Assistant minority leader, Colorado House of Reps., 1995-96; Member, Colorado House of Reps., 1992-96; Of counsel, McDermott & Hansen, Denver, 1993-96; Sole practice, Denver, 1986-93; Associate, Coghill & Goodspeed, Professional Corporation, Denver, 1984-86; Deputy state pub. defender, Colorado State Pub. Defender, Denver, 1982-84 **CR:** Lead-whip State Children's Health Insurance Progressive co-chair Congl. Diabetes Caucus, Congl. Bipartisan Pro-Choice Caucus member Mayor's Management Review Commission Social Services, Denver Women's Commission resolutions chair Denver Dem. Party, 1986 **CIV:** Board directors, Planned Parenthood of Rocky Mountains, Board directors,

New York University School Law Root-Tilden Progressive, 1986-92 **CW:** Editor: Trial Talk magazine, 1989-92 **AW:** Named a Root-Tilden scholar, New York University School Law, 1979; recipient Vanderbilt medal, 1982 **MEM:** Mem.: Denver Bar Association, Colorado Women's Bar Association, Colorado Trial Lawyers Association (board directors, executive committee 1986-92), Colorado Bar Association (board governors 1989-91), Pi Gamma Mu, Phi Beta Kappa **H:** Reading, backpacking, gardening **PA:** Democrat **BA:** 2368 Rayburn House Office Bldg, Washington, DC, 20515

DE HAVILLAND, OLIVIA, T: Actress **I:** Media & Entertainment **DOB:** 07/01/1916 **PB:** Tokyo **SC:** Japan **PT:** Daughter of Walter Augustus and Lilian Augusta (Ruse) de H.; **SPN:** Married Marcus Goodrich, August 26, 1946 (div. August 28, 1953); Married Pierre Galante **CH:** 1 child, Benjamin Briggs Goodrich (deceased 1991); **ED:** DHL (hon.), American University, Paris, 1994; LittD (hon.), University Hertfordshire, 1998 **CIV:** Trustee Am. College in Paris, 1970-71, Am. Libr. in Paris, 1974-81. **CW:** Actress: (films) Alibi Ike, 1935, The Irish in Us, 1935, A Midsummer Night's Dream, 1935, Captain Blood, 1935, Anthony Adverse, 1936, The Charge of the Light Brigade, 1936, Call it a Day, 1937, It's Love I'm After, 1937, The Great Garrick, 1937, Gold Is Where You Find It, 1938, The Adventures of Robin Hood, 1938, Four's a Crowd, 1938, Hard to Get, 1938, Wings of the Navy, 1939, Dodge City, 1939, The Private Lives of Elizabeth and Essex, 1939, Gone With the Wind, 1939, Raffles, 1939, My Love Came Back, 1940, Santa Fe Trail, 1940, The Strawberry Blonde, 1941, Hold Back The Dawn, 1941, They Died with Their Boots On, 1941, The Male Animal, 1941, In This Our Life, 1942, Princess O'Rourke, 1943, Government Girl, 1943, To Each His Own, 1946 (Academy award for Best Actress, 1947), Devotion, 1946, The Well-Groomed Bride, 1946, The Dark Mirror, 1946, The Snakepit, 1948 (New York Film Critics Circle award, 1949, Laurel Award for Best Performance 1948-53), The Heiress, 1949 (Golden Globe award for Best Actress, 1950, Academy award for Best Actress, 1950, New York Film Critics Circle award, 1949), My Cousin Rachel 1952, That Lady, 1955, Not As A Stranger, 1955, The Ambassador's Daughter, 1955 (Belgian Critics Prix Femina), The Proud Rebel, 1957, Libel, 1959, Light in the Piazza, 1961, Lady in a Cage, 1963 (British films and filming award), Hush, Hush Sweet Charlotte, 1964, The Adventures, 1970, Pope Joan, 1972, Airport '77, 1976, The Swarm, 1978, The Fifth Musketeer, 1979, I Remember When I Paint, 2009; (TV films) Noon Wine, 1966, The Screaming Woman, 1972, Murder is Easy, 1981, Charles and Diana: A Royal Romance, 1982, Anastasia: The Mystery of Anna, 1986 (Golden Globe award for Actress in a Supporting role, 1987), The Woman He Loved, 1988; (TV mini-series) Roots: The Next Generations, 1979, North and South, II, 1986; (TV appearances) The Big Valley, 1965, ABC Stage 67, 1966, The Danny Thomas Hour, 1968, The Love Boat, 1981; made stage debut as Hermia in: Midsummer Night's Dream (Max Reinhardt production), Hollywood Bowl, 1934; (on Broadway) Romeo and Juliet, 1951, Candida, 1952, A Gift of Time, 1962, (summer stock) What Every Woman Knows, Westport, Connecticut, Easthampton, Long Island, 1946, Candida, same plus 9 other summer theatres, 1951; (legitimate) Transcontinental Tour Candida 1951-52, (245 Performances); lecture tours, US, 1971-80; toured Army and Navy hospitals in US, Alaska, Aleutians, South Pacific, 1943-44, Europe, 1957-61; president jury Cannes Film Festival, 1965; participant: narration of France's Bicentennial gift to US Son et Lumiere, 1976, Bicentennial Service, Am. Cathedral in

Paris, 1976; author: Every Frenchman Has One, 1962 **AW:** Recipient Women's National Press Club award for outstanding accomplishment in theater presented by President Truman, 1950, Am. Legion Humanitarian award, 1967, National Medal of Arts, National Endowment for the Arts, 2008; named chevalier Legion d'honneur, 2010. **MEM:** Member Screen Actors Guild, Academy of Motion Picture Arts & Sciences **PA:** Democrat

DE LA RENTA, OSCAR, T: Fashion Designer **I:** Apparel & Fashion **DOB:** 07/22/1936 **PB:** Santa Domingo **SC:** Dominican Republic **PT:** Oscar de la Renta, Maria Antonia (de Fiallo) de la Renta **ED:** Student, Academy San Fernando, Madrid, Spain; Honorary Doctorate, Hamilton College, Clinton, NY, 2013 **C:** Designer, Oscar De La Renta, Ltd., 1966—Present; Designer, Tortuga Bay Hotel, 2006; Designer, Pierre Balmain, Paris, France, 1993—2002; Chairman, Board of Directors, Chief Designer, Oscar De La Renta, Ltd., 1974—2014; Designer, Oscar De La Renta For Jane Derby, 1965—1966; Designer, Custom Clothing, Elizabeth Arden, New York, NY, 1963—1965; Couture Assistant, Lanvin, Paris, France **CR:** Launched, (Signature Fragrances) Oscar, 1977, Fragrance For Men, Pour Lui, 1980, Oscar For Men, 1995, Intrusion, 2002 **CIV:** Board Of Directors, La Casa Del Nino Orphanage & School, Santo Domingo, Dominican Republic, Metropolitan Opera, New York, NY, New York Opera House, Carnegie Hall, Station-WNET, New Yorkers For Children, America's Society, Queen Sofia Spanish Institute, New York, NY **AW:** Carnegie Hall Medal Of Excellence, 2014, Founder's Award, Council On Fashion Designers Of America, 2013, Super Star Award, Night Of Stars, 2009, Designer Of The Year, Council On Fashion Designers Of America, 2000, 2007, Decorated Gold Medal Of Bellas Artes, King Of Spain, 2000, Order Al Mérito De Juan Pablo Duarte, Order Of Cristóbal Colón Dominican Republic, Grand Marshall Of New York Hispanic Day Parade, 2000, Lifetime Achievement Award, Hispanic Heritage Society, 1996, Living Legend Award, American Society Of Perfumers, 1995, Perennial Success Award, Fragrance Foundation, 1991, Lifetime Achievement Award, Council On Fashion Designers Of America, 1990, American Fashion Critic's Hall Of Fame, 1973, The International Best Dressed List Hall Of Fame, 1973, Neiman-Marcus Award, 1968, Golden Tiberius Award, 1968, Coty Award, 1967-1968 **MEM:** President, Council on Fashion Designers of America, 1973—1976, 1986—1988 **ACH:** Achievements include helping to build two schools incorporating orphanages and day-care centers in La Romana and Punta Cana, Dominican Republic **BA:** Oscar De La Renta NYC Headquarters, 550 Seventh Avenue, New York, NY, 10018

DE LAVALLADE, CARMEN, T: Dancer, Choreographer **I:** Media & Entertainment **DOB:** 03/06/1931 **PB:** Los Angeles **SC:** CA/USA **SPN:** Geoffrey Holder (6/26/1955) **CH:** Leo **ED:** Honorary Doctorate of Fine Arts, Juilliard School (2007) **C:** Choreographer, Performer-in-Residence, Yale School of Drama (1970); Guest Artist, American Ballet Theatre (1965); Principal, John Butler Dance Company (1956); Prima Ballerina, Metropolitan Opera (1956); Lead Dancer, Lester Horton Dance Theater (1950-1954); Dancer, Lester Horton Dance Theater (1949-1950); Member, Yale Repertory Theatre; Professor, Yale School of Drama; Partner, De Lavallade-Ailey Dance Company; Guest Artist, Alvin Ailey Dance Company; Choreographer, Dance Theatre of Harlem **CW:** Actor, "Stone Mansion" (2004); Actor, "The Other Brother" (2002); Actor, "The Hours" (2002); Choreographer, "Sweet Bitter Love," Alvin Ailey American Dance Theater (2000); Actor, "Big Daddy" (1999);

Actor, "Lone Star" (1996); Performer, "Rusalka" (1993); Actor, "Blue Bayou" (1990); Performer, Die Meistersinger (1990); Performer, "Porgy & Bess," Metropolitan Opera (1990); Actor, "The Trial of Standing Bear" (1988); Performer, "The Four Marys," American Ballet Theater (1965); Performer, The Frail Quarry (1965); Performer, "L'Enfance du Christ" (1964); Dancer, "Blues Suite" (1962); Performer, Carmina Burana (1959); Actor, "Odds Against Tomorrow (1959); Dancer, "Roots of the Blues," Alvin Ailey Dance Company (1958); Performer, "Amahl and the Night Visitors" (1957); Dancer, "A Drum is a Woman" (1956); Performer, "Aida," Metropolitan Opera (1956); Performer, "Flight," John Butler Dance Company (1956); Performer, "Samson & Delilah" (1956); Performer, "House of Flowers" (1954); Performer, "The Egyptian" (1954); Performer, "Carmen Jones" (1954); Performer, "Lydia Bailey" (1952); Dancer, "The Face of Violence," Lester Horton Dance Co; Performer, "Othello"; Performer, "Death of a Salesman" **AW:** Kennedy Center Honoree (2017); Dance USA Award (2010); Capezio Dance Award (2007); Dance Magazine Award (1964); Clarence Bayfield Award, Actors Equity; Obie Award; Duke Ellington Fellowship Award **MH:** Albert Nelson Marquis Lifetime Achievement Award (2017) **BA:** 585 W End Ave Ste 14G, New York, NY, 10024 **ADD:** 230 W 97th St Apt 5B, New York, NY, 10025 **URL:** http://www.carmendelavallade.com/

DE NIRO, ROBERT, T: Actor **I:** Media & Entertainment **DOB:** 08/17/1943 **PB:** New York **SC:** NY/USA **ED:** Student, Acting, Stella Adler; Student, Acting, Lee Strasberg **C:** Owner, Locanda Verde, New York, NY, 2009—Present; Owner, Ago, Los Angeles, CA, 2008—Present; Co-Founder, Tribeca Film Festival, 2002; Co-Owner, Rubicon, San Francisco, CA, 1994; Co-Owner, Nobu, New York, NY, 1994; Co-Owner, Tribeca Grill, 1990; Co-Founder, Tribeca Productions, 1988; Owner, Ago, New York, NY **CW:** Actor, (Films) The Wedding Party, 1969, Hi, Mom!, 1970, Bloody Mama, 1970, Jennifer On My Mind, 1971, Born To Win, 1971, The Gang That Couldn't Shoot Straight, 1971, Bang The Drum Slowly, 1973, Mean Streets, 1973, The Godfather, Part II, 1974, The Last Tycoon, 1976, Nineteen Hundred, 1976, Taxi Driver, 1976, New York, New York, 1977, The Deer Hunter, 1978, Raging Bull, 1980, True Confessions, 1981, The King Of Comedy, 1982, Once Upon A Time In America, 1984, Falling In Love, 1984, Brazil, 1984, The Mission, 1985, Angel Heart, 1987, The Untouchables, 1987, Midnight Run, 1988, Jacknife, 1989, Stanley & Iris, 1990, Goodfellas, 1990, Awakenings, 1991, Backdraft, 1991, Cape Fear, 1991, Guilty By Suspicion, 1991, Mistress, 1992, Night And The City, 1992, Mad Dog And Glory, 1993, This Boy's Life, 1993, Mary Shelley's Frankenstein, 1994, Casino, 1995, Heat, 1995, The Fan, 1996, Marvin's Room, 1996, Sleepers, 1996, Copland, 1997, Great Expectations, 1998, 15 Minutes, 1999, Analyze This, 1999, Flawless, 1999, The Score, 2001, Showtime, 2002, Analyze That, 2002, City By The Sea, 2002, Godsend, 2004, (Voice Actor) Shark Tale, 2004, Hide And Seek, 2005, (Voice Actor) Arthur And The Invisibles, 2006, Stardust, 2007, Righteous Kill, 2008, What Just Happened?, 2008, Everybody's Fine, 2009, Machete, 2010, Stone, 2010, Little Fockers, 2010, Killer Elite, 2011, Limitless, 2011, New Year's Eve, 2011, Red Lights, 2012, Being Flynn, 2012, Freelancers, 2012, Silver Linings Playbook, 2012, The Big Wedding, 2013, Killing Season, 2013, The Family, 2013, Last Vegas, 2013, Motel, 2013, Grudge Match, 2013, American Hustle, 2013, The Bag Man, 2014, The Intern, 2015, Heist, 2015, Joy, 2015, Dirty Grandpa, 2016, Hands Of Stone, 2016, The Comedian, 2016, The War With Grandpa, 2018, The Irishman, (Plays) Strange Show, 1982; Actor, Exec-

utive Producer, (Films) We're No Angels, 1989, Meet The Parents, 2000, (TV Films) The Wizard Of Lies, 2016; Actor, Producer, Wag The Dog, 1997, The Adventures Of Rocky And Bullwinkle, 1999, Meet The Fockers, 2004; Actor, Director, A Bronx Tale, 1993, The Good Shepherd, 2006; Appearances, (Documentaries) I Knew It Was You: Rediscovering John Cazale, 2010; Producer, (Films) Entropy, 1999, About A Boy, 2002, Stage Beauty, 2004, Rent, 2005; Co-Producer, Thunderheart, 1992; Executive Producer, (TV Films) Tribeca, 1993, Holiday Heart, 2000, For Justice, 2015 The Wizard Of Lie, 2017, (Films) Faithful, 1996, Navy Driver, 2000, Conjugating Niki, 2000; Actor, Executive Producer, Narrator, (Documentaries) Dear America: Letters Home From Vietnam, 1987, Lenny Bruce: Swear To Tell The Truth, 1998 **AW:** Academy Award For Best Supporting Actor, The Godfather, Part II, 1975, Hasty Pudding Award, Harvard University, 1979, Academy Award For Best Actor, Raging Bull, 1981, D.W. Griffith Award for Best Actor, 1990, Greatest Living Movie Star, Empire Magazine, 2004, Kennedy Center Honors, John F. Kennedy Center for the Performing Arts, 2009, Cecil B. DeMille Award, Hollywood Foreign Press Association, 2011, Presidential Medal of Freedom, The White House, 2016 **BA:** Tribeca Productions, 375 Greenwich Street, New York, NY, 10013

DEAL, NATHAN, T: Governor of Georgia, former U.S. Representative from Georgia, lawyer **I:** Government Administration/Government Relations/Government Services **DOB:** 08/25/1942 **PB:** Millen **SC:** Georgia **ED:** JD, Mercer University, 1966; BA, Mercer University, 1964 **C:** Governor, State of Georgia, 2011-; Member US House Energy & Commerce Committee, US Congress from 10th Georgia District, 2007-10; Member, US Congress from 10th Georgia District, 2003-07; Member, US Congress from 9th Georgia District, 2007-10; Member, US Congress from 9th Georgia District, 1993-2003; President pro tempore, Georgia State Senate, 1991-93; Member District 10, Georgia State Senate, 1981-93; Attorney, Hall County, 1977-79; Judge, juvenile court, Hall County, Georgia, 1971-72; Assistant district attorney Northeast cir., Hall County, Georgia, 1970-71; Private law practice, 1979-82 **CR:** Member Speaker's Immigration Task Force, Rural Health Care Coalition, Congressional Vietnam-Era Veterans Caucus, Congressional Travel and Tourism Caucus, Congressional Caucus on Unfunded Mandates, Congressional Boating Caucus **CIV:** Adv. board member of honors programs, N. Georgia College and University, Board of trustees, Mercer University **MIL:** Captain Judge Advocate General Corps US Army, 1966-68 **PA:** Republican **BA:** Office of Nathan Deal, 206 Washington Street, Atlanta, GA, 30334

DEATON, ANGUS STEWART, T: Economist **I:** Education/Educational Services **CN:** University of Southern California **DOB:** 10/19/1945 **PB:** Edinburgh **SC:** Scotland/UK **ED:** Honorary Degree, University College London; Honorary Degree, University of Rome; LittD, University of St. Andrews; PhD, University of Cambridge, 1975; MA, University of Cambridge, 1971; BA, University of Cambridge, 1967 **C:** President, Professor Of Economics, University Of Southern California, 2017-Present; Visiting Professor, Princeton University, New Jersey, 1979-1980; Professor of Econometrics, Bristol University, England, 1976-1983; Director of Economic Studies, Fitzwilliam College, University of Cambridge, England, 1972-1976; Research Officer, Department of Applied Economics, University of Cambridge, England, 1969-1976; Economist, Bank Of England, 1967-1968; Dwight D. Eisenhower Professor of International Affairs, Professor of Economics And International Affairs,

Woodrow Wilson School, Princeton University; William Church Osborn Professor of Public Affairs, Professor of Economics And International Affairs, Princeton University **CR:** Consultant, World Bank, 1980-Present; Fellow, American Association for the Advancement of Science; Fellow, Econometric Society; Fellow, Royal Society of Edinburgh **CIV:** Frisch medal for Applied Econometrics, Econometric Society **CW:** Co-Author, Models And Projections Of Demand In Post-War England, 1972, (With J. Meullbauer) Economics And Consumer Behaviour, 1980; Author, Understanding Consumption, 1995, The Analysis Of Household Surveys: A Microeconometric Approach To Development Policy, 1997, The Great Escape: Health, Wealth, And The Origins Of Inequality, 2013, Letters From America; Assistant Editor, Review of Economic Studies, 1975-1980; Editor, Essays In The Theory And Measurements Of Consumer Behavior, 1981, The Great Indian Poverty Debate, 2005; Associate Editor to Co-Editor To Editor, Econometrica, 1978-1980, 1980-1984, 1984-1988; Contributor, Articles, Professional Journals **AW:** Sveriges Riksbank Prize in Economic Sciences in Memory of Alfred Nobel, 2015, Bi-Annual Feature In Royal Economic Society Newsletter, The Great Escape: Health, Wealth, And The Origins Of Inequality, 2013, BBVA Foundation Frontiers of Knowledge Award, 2012, Frisch Medal For Applied Econometrics, Econometric Society **MEM:** President, American Economic Association, 2009, Econometric Society, National Academy of Sciences, American Philosophical Society **ACH:** Principal fields of interest development economics, econometric, statistical and math. methods and models, consumer economics. **BA:** Princeton University Woodrow Wilson School, 361 Wallace Hall, Princeton, NJ, 08544-0001

DEBAUN, MORGAN, T: CEO **I:** Business Management/Business Services **CN:** Blavity Inc. **ED:** BA in Political Science and Entrepreneurship, Washington University in St. Louis (2012) **C:** Founder and Chief Executive Officer, Blavity Inc. (2014-Present); Business Development and Strategy, Intuit Inc. (2013-2014); Product Management and Marketing Rotational Development Associate, Intuit Inc. (2012-2014)

DEBERTIN, JAY D., T: CEO **I:** Agriculture **CN:** CHS **ED:** MBA, University of Wisconsin, Madison, WI, 1984; Bachelor in Economics, University of North Dakota, Grand Forks, ND, 1982 **C:** Executive Vice President, COO of Energy & Foods, CHS, Inc. (Merger of Cenex and Harvest States), 2011-Present; Executive Vice President, COO of Processing, CHS, Inc. (Merger of Cenex And Harvest States), Inver Grove Heights, MN, 2005-2010; Senior Vice President, Energy Operations, CHS, Inc. (Merger of Cenex And Harvest States), St. Paul, MN, 2001; Vice President, Crude Oil Supply, CHS, Inc. (Merger of Cenex And Harvest States), Denver, CO, 1998-2001; Petroleum Division, CHS, Inc. (Merger of Cenex And Harvest States), 1984 **CR:** Board of Directors, U.S. BioEnergy, 2006-Present, Ventura Foods, LLC, Horizon Milling, National Cooperative Refinery Association **BA:** CHS Inc., PO Box 64089, Saint Paul, MN, 55164-0089

DEEN, PAULA H., T: Television Personality, Restaurant Owner, Chef **I:** Food & Restaurant Services **DOB:** 01/19/1947 **PB:** Albany **SC:** GA/USA **C:** Owner, The Lady and Sons Restaurant, Savannah, Georgia, 1990-; Owner, Catering Business, The Bag Lady, **CR:** Cross-country tour with 90-minute "Paula Deen Live!", 2014 **CIV:** Provided sponsorships and donations of money, cookbooks and other services to community groups and causes, **CW:** Host (TV series) Paula's Home Cooking, Food

Network, 2002-13, Paula's Party; author: (cookbooks) The Lady and Sons Too!, 2001, 2008, The Lady and Sons Just Desserts, 2002, The Lady and Sons Savannah Country Cookbook, 2005, 2008, Christmas with Paula Deen: Recipes and Stories from My Favorite Holiday, 2007, Paula Deen's My First Cookbook, Paula Deen Cuts the Fat: 250 Recipes Lightened Up, 2015; co-author: (with Martha Nesbit) Paula Deen & Friends: Living It Up, Southern Style, 2005, Paula Deen Celebrates!: Best Dishes and Best Wishes for the Best Times of Your Life, 2006, (with Sherry Sulb Cohen) Paula Deen: It Ain't All About the Cookin', 2007, (with Melissa Clark) Paula Deen's The Deen's Family Cookbook, 2009, Paula Deen's Southern Cooking Bible: The New Classic Guide to Delicious Dishes with More Than 300 Recipes, 2011, (with Brandon Branch) Paula Deen's Savannah Style, 2010; author: (magazine) Cooking with Paula Deen, 2006-; actor: (films) Elizabethtown, 2005 **AW:** Named Small Business Person Year in Georgia, U.S. Small Business Administration, 2003, Most Memorable Meal Year at The Lady and Sons restaurant, USA Today, 1999; named one of The 100 Most Powerful Celebrities, Forbes.com, 2008; recipient Georgia Women Entrepreneurs (GWEN) award, Georgia Small Business Devel. Center, 2003

DEFAZIO, PETER ANTHONY, T: U.S. Representative from Oregon **I:** Government Administration/Government Relations/Government Services **DOB:** 05/27/1947 **PB:** Needham **ED:** MS in Public Administration & Gerontology, University Oregon, Eugene, 1977; BA in Economics & Political Sci., Tufts University, Medford, Massachusetts, 1969 **C:** Ranking Member, Committee on Transportation and Infrastructure,2014-; Ranking member, US House Natural Resources Committee, 2013-; Member, US Representative from Oregon's 4th District, 1987-; Chairman, Lane County Board Commissioners, 1985-86; Commissioner, Lane County Board Commissioners, Eugene, 1983-86; Director constituent services, US House of Representatives, 1980-82; Legis. assistant Washington office, US House of Representatives, 1978-80; Senior issues specialist, district field office congressman Jim Weaver, US House of Representatives, Oregon, 1977-78 **CIV:** Board directors, Eugene-Springfield Metropolitan Partnership, **AW:** Recipient Rail Leadership award, Am. Passenger Rail Coalition, 2006, Human Lifetime Achievement award, Human Society US, 2002, Congressional award, Military Production Network, 1995, DC Distinguished Alumnus award, University Oregon Alumni Association, 1994 **MEM:** Mem.: National Association Counties, Association Oregon Counties **PA:** Democrat

DEGENERES, ELLEN LEE LEE, T: Television Personality **I:** Media & Entertainment **DOB:** 01/26/1958 **PB:** Metairie **SC:** LA/USA **PT:** Elliott DeGeneres, Betty DeGeneres **C:** Special Envoy For Global AIDS Awareness, U.S. Department of State, Washington, DC, 2011-Present; Founder, ElevenEleven Record Label, 2010-Present; Performer, Various Comedy Clubs; Emcee, Local Comedy Club, New Orleans, LA **CR:** Launched, Clothing And Lifestyle Brand E.D., 2014-Present; Face of CoverGirl Cosmetics, 2008; Spokesperson, Vitamin Water Zero, American Express **CW:** Comedian, (TV Specials) Young Comedians Reunion, HBO, Women Of The Night, 1986, Command Performances: One Night Stand, 1989; Author, My Point...And I Do Have One, 1995, The Funny Thing Is..., 2003, Seriously...I'm Kidding, 2011; Actress, (Films) Coneheads, 1993, Mr. Wrong, 1996, Goodbye Lover, 1998, (Voice Actress) Dr. Doolittle, 1998, EDTV, 1999, The Love Letter, 1999, Reaching Normal, 1999, (Voice Actress) Finding Nemo, 2003, (Voice Actress) Finding Dory, 2016, (TV Films) On The Edge, 2001,

(TV Series) Open House, 1989, Laurie Hill, 1992; Writer, Director, Actress, (Films) My Short Film, 2004; Actress, Producer, Writer, (TV Series) These Friends Of Mine (Now Ellen), 1993-1998; Actress, Executive Producer, (TV Films) If These Walls Could Talk 2, 2000, (TV Series) The Ellen Show, 2001-2002; Host, Executive Producer, The Ellen Degeneres Show, 2003-Present; Judge, American Idol, 2009-2010; Star, Executive Producer, (TV Specials) Ellen Degeneres: The Beginning, 2000, Ellen Degeneres: Here And Now, 2003; Co-Host, 46th Annual Primetime Emmy Awards, 1994; Host, 38th Annual Grammy Awards, 1996, 39th Annual Grammy Awards, 1997, VH1 Fashion Awards, 1998, 53rd Annual Primetime Emmy Awards, 2001, 54th Annual Primetime Emmy Awards, 2002, VH1 Divas Las Vegas, 2002, 57th Annual Primetime Emmy Awards, 2005, 79th Annual Academy Awards, 2007, 86th Annual Academy Awards, 2014; Appearance, (Documentaries) Wisecracks, 1991; Performer, (Comedy Album) Ellen Degeneres: Taste This, 1996; Composer, (Albums) The Only Holiday Album You'll Ever Need, 2014, (Film) The Interview, 2014, (Books) My Point...And I Do Have One, 1995, The Funny Thing Is.., 2003, Seriously.... I'm Kidding, 2011, Home, 2015, (Television) The Simpsons, 2010, Christmas In Washington, 2010, The Big Bang Theory, 2016, Ellen's Game Of Games, 2017 **AW:** Presidential Medal of Freedom, The White House, 2016, Favorite Humanitarian, People's Choice Awards, 2016, Favorite Daytime TV Host, People's Choice Awards, The Ellen DeGeneres Show, 2014-2016, Primetime Emmy For Outstanding Interactive Media, The Ellen DeGeneres Show, 2012, 2014, Choice Comedian, Teen Choice Awards, 2012, Mark Twain Prize for American Humor, John F. Kennedy Center for the Performing Arts, 2012, The 100 Most Powerful Women, Forbes Magazine, 2010-2015, The 100 Most Powerful Women in Entertainment, The Hollywood Reporter, 2009, 2012-2015, Favorite Talk Show Host, People's Choice Awards, The Ellen DeGeneres Show, 2009-2010, The 100 Most Powerful Celebrities, 2008, Favorite Talk Show Host & Funny Female Star, 2007-2008, Favorite Daytime Talk Show Host, People's Choice Awards, The Ellen DeGeneres Show, 2006, 2012-2013, Outstanding Talk Show Host, Daytime Emmy Awards, National Academy of TV Arts And Sciences, The Ellen DeGeneres Show, 2006-2007, Funny Female Star, 2006, Best TV Series or Specialty (Variety), The Producers Guild of America, 2006, The 100 Most Influential People in the World, TIME Magazine, 2006, Outstanding Talk Show, Daytime Emmy Award, National Academy of TV Arts And Sciences, The Ellen DeGeneres Show, 2006, Outstanding Talk Show Host, The Ellen DeGeneres Show, 2005-2007, Best Talk Show, Daytime Emmy Awards, National Academy of TV Arts And Sciences, Best Talk Show Host, Daytime Emmy Award, National Academy TV Arts And Sciences, The Ellen DeGeneres Show, 2005, Outstanding Talk Show, The Ellen DeGeneres Show, 2004-2007, Annie Award For Outstanding Voice Acting In Animated Feature Production, Finding Nemo, 2004, American Comedy Award For Funniest Female Performer In TV Special, Ellen Degeneres: The Beginning, 2001, Enduring Spirit Award, Amnesty International, 2000, Lucy Award, 2000, Emmy Award For Outstanding Writing For Comedy Series, Peabody Award, Ellen, 1997, American Comedy Award For Funniest Female Performer In TV Special, 46th Annual Primetime Emmy Awards, 1995, Golden Apple Award for Female Discovery of the Year, Hollywood Women's Press Club, 1994, American Comedy Award for Funniest Female Stand-Up Comic, 1991, Funniest Person in America Award for Videotaped Club Performances in New Orleans, Showtime, 1982 **BA:** ICM Partners, 10250 Constellation Boulevard, Los Angeles, CA, 90067

DEL TORO, GUILLERMO, T: Film Director **I:** Media & Entertainment **PB:** Guadalajara **SC:** Jalisco, Mexico **ED:** Attended, University Guadalajara **C:** Film teacher, Mexico; Founder, The Tequila Gang, Mexico; Founder, Necropia, Mexico; Make-up supervisor **CR:** Judge, mentor NHK Awards, 2000 jury member Ind. Film Project's Spirit Awards, 2000, 1999 **CW:** Executive prodr.: (films) Dona Herlinda and Her Son, 1985; executive prodr.: (films) I Murder Seriously, 2002, Chronicles, 2004, The Orphanage, 2007, Splice, 2009, Kung Fu Panda 2, 2011, Puss in Boots, 2011, Rise of the Guardians, 2012, Mama, 2013; prodr.: Rudo y Cursi, 2008, Rage, 2009, Julia's Eyes, 2010, The Thin Yellow Line, 2015; writer, director (films) Cronos, 1993, Mimic, 1997, Hellboy, 2004, Hellboy II: The Golden Army, 2008, Pacific Rim, 2013, writer, director, executive producer The Devil's Backbone, 2001, writer, director, producer Pan's Labyrinth, 2006 (National Society Film Critics award for Best Picture, 2007, BAFTA award for Best Film not in the England Language, 2007), Crimson Peak, 2015; director The Shape of Water, 2017 (Golden Globe for Best Director, 2018) (Academy Award for Best Director): (films) Blade II, 2002; prodr.: (TV series) Hora Marcada; writer, producer (films) Don't Be Afraid of the Dark, 2010, writer The Hobbit: An Unexpected Journey, 2012, The Hobbit: The Desolation of Smaug, 2013, The Hobbit: The Battle of the Five Armies, 2014; co-author: (with Chuck Hogan) The Night Eternal, 2011 **AW:** Named one of The 50 Smartest People in Hollywood, Entertainment Weekly, 2007

DELANEY, JOHN KEVIN, T: U.S. Representative from Maryland **I:** Government Administration/Government Relations/Government Services **DOB:** 04/16/1963 **PB:** Wood-Ridge **ED:** JD, Georgetown University Law Center, 1988; BA, Columbia University, 1985 **C:** Member, Joint Economic Committee, 2013-; Member, US House Financial Services Committee, 2013-; Member, US Congress from 6th Maryland District, Washington, 2013-; Co-founder, executive chairman, CapitalSource, Chevy Chase, 2000-12; Co-founder, Health Care Financial Partners, Inc., 1993-99; Associate, Shaw Pittman, Potts, & Troubridge, 1988-93 **CR:** Founder Blueprint Maryland, 2011- **CIV:** Board directors, National Symphony Orchestra, Board directors, Georgetown University, **AW:** Recipient Ernst & Young Entrepreneur of the Year award **PA:** Democrat

DELANEY, WILLIAM J. III, T: Sysco CEO **I:** Business Management/Business Services **ED:** MBA, University Pennsylvania, 1982; BBA, University Notre Dame, South Bend, Ind., 1977 **C:** President, CEO, Sysco Corp., Houston, 2010-; CEO, CFO, Sysco Corp., Houston, 2009; Executive vice president, CFO, Sysco Corp., Houston, 2007-09; Senior vice president fin. reporting, Sysco Corp., Houston, 2007; President, CEO, Sysco Food Services LLC, Charlotte, North Carolina, 2004-06; Executive vice president, Sysco Food Services LLC, Syracuse, New York, 2002-04; Senior vice president, Sysco Food Services LLC, Syracuse, New York, 1998-2002; CFO, Sysco Food Services LLC, Syracuse, New York, 1996-98; Vice president, Sysco Corp., 1993-94; Treasurer, Sysco Corp., 1991-93; Assistant treasurer, Sysco Corp., 1987-91

DELAURO, ROSA LUISA, T: U.S. Representative from Connecticut **I:** Government Administration/Government Relations/Government Services **DOB:** 03/02/1943 **PB:** New Haven **PT:** Daughter of Ted and Luisa DeLauro; **ED:** MA in International Politics, Columbia University, 1966; BA in Hist. and Polit Sci., cum laude, Marymount College, 1964; Student, Queen Mary College London School Econs. **C:** Co-chair for steering, US House Democratic Steering & Policy Committee, 2003-; Member, US Congress from 3rd Connecticut District, 1991-; Member, Committee on Appropriations; Executive director, EMILY's List, 1989-90; Executive director, Countdown '87, 1987-88; Chief of staff, to Senator Christopher Dodd, US Senate, Washington, 1981-87; Campaign manager, to Senator Christopher Dodd, US Senate, 1979; Executive assistant, devel. administrator, City of New Haven, Connecticut, 1977-78; Campaign manager, City of New Haven, 1977; Executive assistant to Mayor Frank Logue, City of New Haven, 1976-77; Assistant director, director, National Urban Fellows, 1972-75; Administrative assistant, National Urban Fellows, 1969-72; Training associate, Cmty Progress Inc., New Haven, 1967-69 **CR:** Regional director Dukakis for President Campaign, New York, New Jersey, Connecticut, 1988 state director Mondale-Ferraro Presidential Campaign, New Jersey, 1986 city coordinator Carter-Mondale Presidential Campaign, New Jersey, 1977-79 instructor international relations Albertus Magnus College, New Haven, 1967-68 **CIV:** Founder, Kick Butts Connecticut, Founder, Rosa's Readers, 1999 Member, Anti Crime Youth Council, 1993- Organizer, Connecticut Jobs Fair, **AW:** Named a Bartels Fellow, University New Haven; recipient Corneilius Driscoll award, New Haven St. Patrick's Day Committee **PA:** Democrat

DELBENE, SUZAN KAY, T: U.S. Representative from Washington, former state official **I:** Government Administration/Government Relations/Government Services **DOB:** 02/17/1962 **PB:** Selma **SC:** AL/USA **ED:** MBA, University of Washington, 1990; BS in Biology, Reed College, 1983 **C:** Member, US House Judiciary Committee, 2013-; Member, US House Agricultural Committee, 2013-; Member, US Congress from 1st Washington District, Washington, 2013-; Director revenue, State of Washington, Olympia, 2010-12; Management consultant, strategic adv., Global Partnerships, 2008-09; CEO, Nimble Technology, 2000-03; Vice president, drugstore.com, 1998-2000; Corporate vice president mobile communications business, Microsoft Corp., 2004-07; Director marketing & business devel. Interactive Media Group, Microsoft Corp., Redmond, Washington, 1989-98 **PA:** Democrat

DELILLO, DON, T: Writer **I:** Writing and Editing **DOB:** 11/20/1936 **PB:** New York **SC:** NY/USA **ED:** Student, Fordham University, 1954-58 **C:** Writer, 1971- **CW:** Author: (plays) The Engineer of Moonlight, 1979, The Day Room, 1986, Valparaiso, 1999, The Mystery at the Middle of Ordinary Life, 2000, Love-Lies-Bleeding, 2006, The Word for Snow, 2007; short stories in various collections, periodicals; (novels) Americana, 1971, End Zone, 1972, Great Jones Street, 1973, Ratner's Star, 1976, Players, 1977, Running Dog, 1978, The Names, 1982, White Noise, 1985 (Am. Book award 1985, National Book Critics Circle award nominee 1985), Libra, 1988 (International Fiction prize 1989), Mao II, 1991 (PEN-Faulkner award 1992), Underworld, 1997 (William Dean Howells medal, Am. Academy of Arts & Letter for the most distinguished work of fiction of the past 5 years, named one of Best Fiction of the Past 25 Years, New York Times Book Review, 2006), The Body Artist, 2001, Pafko at the Wall, Cosmopolis, 2003, Falling Man, 2007, Point Omega, 2010, The Angel Esmeralda, 2011,(Book) Zerk K, 2016 **AW:** Guggenheim fellow, 1979, Am. Academy Institute Arts and Letters Literature award, 1984,New York Times 100 Notable Books, 2011, IMPAC Award, 2012, Library of Congress Prize for American Fiction, 2013, Norman Mailer Prize for Lifetime Achievement, 2014, National Book Award Medal for Distinguished Contribution to American Letters,2015

DELL, MICHAEL SAUL, T: CEO **I:** Technology **CN:** Dell **DOB:** 02/23/1965 **PB:** Houston **SC:** TX/USA **PT:** Son of Alexander and Lorraine Dell; **ED:** Doctor in Economic Sci. (hon.), University Limerick, 2002; Attended, University Texas, 1983-84 **C:** Chairman, CEO, Dell, Inc., Round Rock, Texas, 2007-; Chairman, Dell, Inc., Round Rock, Texas, 2004-07; Chairman, CEO, Dell, Inc., Round Rock, Texas, 1984-2004; Founder, Dell Computer Corp. (formerly PC's Ltd.), Austin, 1984 **CR:** Board directors Startup America Partnership, LLC, 2011- investor ValleyCrest, 2006- member governing board Indian School Business, Hyderabad, India, 2003- founder MSD Capital, LP., New York City, 1998- board directors Dell Inc., 1984- **CIV:** Co-founder, Michael & Susan Dell Foundation, Austin, 1999- **CW:** Author: Direct From Dell: Strategies that Revolutionized an Industry, 1999 **AW:** Named Chief Executive of Year, Chief Executive Magazine, 2001, CEO of Year, Financial World Magazine, 1993, Entrepreneur of Year, Inc. Magazine, 1990; named one of The World's Richest People, Forbes Magazine, 2007-, The 50 Who Matter Now, CNNMoney.com Business 2.0, 2006, The Forbes 400: Richest Americans, 2005-, The Top 10 Most Powerful People in Business, Fortune Magazine, 2004, 2003; recipient Bower award for Business Leadership, Franklin Institute, 2013, Customer Satisfaction award, JD Power, 1993, 1991 **MEM:** Fellow: American Association for the Advancement of Science **PA:** Republican

DEMCHAK, WILLIAM STANTON, T: Bank Executive **I:** Financial Services **ED:** MBA in Accounting, University Michigan; BS, Allegheny College, 1984 **C:** President, CEO, PNC Financial Services Group, Inc., Pittsburgh, 2013-; President, PNC Financial Services Group, Inc., Pittsburgh, 2012-13; Senior vice chairman, PNC Financial Services Group, Inc., Pittsburgh, 2009-12; Head corporate & institutional banking, PNC Financial Services Group, Inc., Pittsburgh, 2005-09; Vice chairman, CFO, PNC Financial Services Group, Inc., Pittsburgh, 2002-09; Global head, structured finance & credit portfolio, J.P. Morgan Chase & Co., 1997-2002 **CR:** Board of Directors PNC Financial Services Group, Inc., 2013-, Black Rock, Inc., 2003- **CIV:** Board directors, Blue Mountain Credit Alternatives Ltd, Board directors, YMCA of Pittsburgh, Board member, Extra Mile Education Foundation, Board member, Greater Pittsburgh Council Boy Scouts America, **MEM:** Mem.: Financial Services Roundtable

DEMINGS, VAL, T: U.S. Representative from Florida **I:** Government Administration/Government Relations/Government Services **DOB:** 03/12/1957 **PB:** Jacksonville **SC:** Florida **ED:** B.S., Florida State University, 1979; M.P.A., Webster University, 1996 **C:** Member, U.S. Representative from Florida's 10th Congressional District, 2017-; Member, Committee on Homeland Security; Member, Committee on Oversight and Government Reform; Police Office, Orlando P.D.; Police Chief, 2007-12; Commander of Special Operations, 2003-06 **BA:** 238 Cannon HOB, Washington, DC, 20515

DEMPSEY, MARTIN E., T: Former Chairman of the Joint Chiefs of Staff **I:** Government Administration/Government Relations/Government Services **DOB:** 03/14/1952 **PB:** Goshen **ED:** MS in National Security and Strategic Studies, National Defense University, 1996; MMAS, US Army Command and General Staff College, 1988; MA, Duke University, 1984; BS, U.S. Military Academy **C:** Chairman, Joint Chiefs of Staff, US Department Defense, Washington, 2011-; Chief of staff, US Army, Washington, 2011; Commanding general, US Army Training & Doctrine Command (TRADOC), Fort Monroe, Virginia, 2008-11; Acting Commander, US Central

Command (USCENTCOM), MacDil AFB, Florida, 2008; Deputy Commander, US Central Command (USCENTCOM), MacDil AFB, Florida, 2007-08; Commander, Multinational Security Transition Commissioned, Iraq, 2005-07; Program manager, Saudi Arabian National Guard Modernization Program, 2001-03; Special assistant to chairman of Joint Chiefs of Staff, US Department Defense, Washington, 1999-2001; Assistant deputy director Politico-Military Affairs, Europe & Africa, The Joint Staff (J-5),, US Department Defense, Washington, 1998-99; Commander 3rd Armored Cavalry Regiment, US Army, Fort Carson, Colorado, 1996-98; Chief Armor Branch, Combat Arms Div., Officer Personnel Management Directorate, US Total Army Personnel Command, Alexandria, Virginia, 1993-95; Commander Hdqs. & Hdqs. Troop, US Army, Fort Carson, Colorado, 1981-82; S-3 ops, US Army, Fort Carson, Colorado, 1980-81; Commander A Troop, US Army, Fort Carson, Colorado, 1980; Motor officer 1st Squadron, 10th Cavalry, 4th Infantry Div., US Army, Fort Carson, Colorado, 1979-80; Commanding general 1st Armored Division, US Army Europe & 7th Army (USAREUR), Germany, 2004-05; Commanding general 1st Armored Div., US Army Europe & 7th Army (USAREUR), Operation Iraqi Freedom, 2003-04; Commander 4th Battalion, 67th Armor, 1st Brigade, 1st Armored Div., US Army Europe & 7th Army (USAREUR), Germany, 1991-93; S-3 ops to executive officer, US Army Europe & 7th Army (USAREUR), Operation Desert Shield/Storm, Saudi Arabia, 1989-91; S-3 ops to executive officer, US Army Europe & 7th Army (USAREUR), 1989-91; Executive officer 4th Battalion, 67th Armor, 3d Armored Div., US Army Europe & 7th Army (USAREUR), Germany, 1988-89; S-1, US Army Europe & 7th Army (USAREUR), Germany, 1977-78; Support platoon leader, US Army Europe & 7th Army (USAREUR), Germany, 1976-77; Platoon leader B Troop, 1st Squadron, 2d Armored Cavalry, US Army Europe & 7th Army (USAREUR), Germany, 1975-76; Advanced through grades to general, US Army, 2008 **CR:** Instructor to assistant professor Department English US Military Academy, West Point, New York, 1984-87 **AW:** Decorated Joint Chiefs of Staff Identification Badge, Parachutist Badge, Army Achievement Medal, Joint Service Commendation Medal, Meritorious Service Medal, Bronze Star Medal, Bronze Star Medal with V Device, Legion of Merit, Defense Superior Service Medal, Distinguished Service Medal; recipient Distinguished Service award, United Service Organizations, 2011

DEMPSEY, PATRICK, T: Actor **I:** Media & Entertainment **PB:** Lewiston **PT:** William Dempsey; Amanda (Casson) Dempsey **CR:** Face of Men's fragrance Avon (2008) **CW:** Actor: (films) Heaven Help Us, 1985, Meatballs III: Summer Job, 1986, Can't Buy Me Love, 1987, In the Mood, 1987, In a Shallow Grave, 1988, Some Girls, 1988, Loverboy, 1989, Happy Together, 1987, Coupe de Ville, 1990, Run, 1991, Mobsters, 1991, Face the Music, 1993, Bank Robber, 1993, Ava's Magical Adventure, 1994, With Honors, 1994, Bloodknot, 1995, Outbreak, 1995, Hugo Pool, 1997, Denial, 1998, The Treat, 1998, There's No Fish Food In Heaven, 1998, Me and Will, 1999, Scream 3, 2000, Rebellion, 2002, The Emperor's Club, 2002, Sweet Home Alabama, 2002, Shade, 2006, (voice) Brother Bear, 2006, Freedom Writers, 2007, Enchanted, 2007, Made of Honor, 2008, Valentine's Day, 2010, Flypaper, 2011, Transformers: Dark of the Moon, 2011, Bridget Jones's baby, 2016; (TV films) A Fighting Choice, 1986, Merry Christmas Baby, 1991, For Better and for Worse, 1993, J.F.K.: Reckless Youth, 1993, The Right to Remain Silent, 1996, A Season in Purgatory, 1996, Odd Jobs, 1997, The Player, 1997, The Escape, 1997, 20,000 Leagues Under the

Sea, 1997, Crime and Punishment, 1998, Jeremiah, 1998, Chestnut Hill, 2001, Blonde, 2001, Corsairs, 2002, About a Boy, 2003, Lucky 7, 2003, Iron Jawed Angels, 2004; (TV series) Fast Times, 1986, Grey's Anatomy, 2005-15 (Outstanding Performance by an Ensemble in a Drama Series, Screen Actors Guild, 2007), (guest appearances) Will & Grace, 2000-01, Once and Again, 2000-03,Lucky 7, 2003, Karen Sisco, 2003, Iron Jawed Angels, 2004, The Practice, 2004, Private Practice, 2009, Red Nose Day Actually, 2017; executive prodr.: (documentaries) The Peloton Project, 2014 **AW:** Named Favorite Dramatic TV Actor, People's Choice Awards, 2015, Favorite Male TV Star, 2008, 2007; The 100 Most Powerful Celebrities, Forbes.com, 2008, Barbara Walters-10 Most Fascinating People of 2006

DENCH, JUDI, T: Actress **I:** Media & Entertainment **DOB:** 12/09/1934 **PB:** York **SC:** England **PT:** Reginald Arthur Dench, Eleanora Olave (Jones) Dench **ED:** Honorary LittD, Trinity College, 2003; Honorary LittD, Oxford University, 2000; Honorary LittD, York University, 1983; Honorary LittD, Warwick University, 1978; Student, Central School of Speech Training **CR:** BAFTA Fellow, 2001; Lucy Cavendish College Fellow, Cambridge, England, 2005 **CW:** Theatrical Appearances, (Old Vic) Hamlet, Midsummer Night's Dream, Twelfth Night, 1957-1958, The Importance Of Being Earnest, As You Like It, Romeo And Juliet, 1959-1961, (Venice Festival) Romeo And Juliet (Paladino d'Argentino), 1961, (Royal Shakespeare Co., Stratford) The Cherry Orchard, Measure For Measure, A Midsummer Night's Dream, A Penny For A Song, 1961-1962, (Oxford Playhouse) The Alchemist, The Three Sisters, Romeo And Jeanette, 1964, (Oxford And London) The Promise, 1966-1967, (London) Sally Bowles In Cabaret, 1968, (Royal Shakespeare Co., London) Twelfth Night, A Winter's Tale, London Assurance, 1970, (Royal Shakespeare Co., Stratford) The Merchant Of Venice, The Duchess Of Malfi, 1971, Tour Of Japan With Twelfth Night, 1972, (London) London Assurance, 1973, (Oxford And London) The Wolf, 1974, (London) The Good Companions, 1974-1975, The Gay Lord Quex, 1975, (Royal Shakespeare Co., Stratford) Much Ado About Nothing, The Comedy Of Errors, Macbeth, King Lear, 1976-1977, (Royal Shakespeare Co., London) Pillars Of The Community, The Way Of The World, 1977-1978, Cymbeline, 1979, (Aldwych) Juno And The Paycock, 1981, A Kind Of Alaska, The Importance Of Being Earnest, Pack Of Lies, Mr. And Mrs. Nobody, 1988, Antony And Cleopatra, Gertrude In Hamlet, The Cherry Orchard, 1989-1990, The Blough And The Stars, The Sea, Coriolanus, 1992, The Gift Of The Gorgon, 1992-1993, The Seagull, 1994, Filumena In London, 1998, Amy's View In New York, 1999, The Royal Family, 2001, The Breath Of Life, 2002, All's Well That Ends Well, London And Stratford-Up-on-Avon, 2003-2004, Hay Fever, 2006, The Merry Wives Of Windsor, 2006, Madame De Sade, 2009, A Midsummer Nights Dream, 2010, Peter And Alice, 2013, The Vote, 2015, The Winter's Tale, 2015; Director, (Plays) Much Ado About Nothing, Look Back In Anger, The Boys From Syracuse, Romeo And Juliet; Actress, (TV Appearances) Major Barbara, Talking To A Stranger, 1966, Jackanory, Luther, Neighbours, Marching Song, Days To Come, The Comedy Of Errors, Macbeth, Village Wooing, Love In A Cold Climate, A Fine Romance, The Cherry Orchard, Going Gently, Saigon, Mr. And Mrs. Edgehill, 1988, Ghosts, Make And Break, Behaving Badly, Can You Hear Me Thinking, Torch, Absolute Hell, As Time Goes By, Cranford, 2007, (Films) He Who Rides A Tiger, 1965, A Study In Terror, 1965, Four In The Morning, 1965, A Midsummer Night's Dream, The Third Secret, Dead Cert, Wetherby, 1985, A Room With A View, 84

Charing Cross Road, A Handful Of Dust, 1988, Henry V, 1989, Jack & Sarah, 1994, Golden Eye, 1995, A Little Night Music, 1995, Mrs. Brown, Amy's View, 1997, Tomorrow Never Dies, 1997, Shakespeare In Love, 1998, Tea With Mussolini, 1999, The World Is Not Enough, 1999, The Last Of The Blond Bombshells, 2000, Chocolat, 2000, Iris, 2002, The Shipping News, 2002, The Importance Of Being Ernest, 2002, Die Another Day, 2002, (Voice Actress) Home On The Range, 2004, The Chronicles Of Riddick, 2004, Ladies In Lavender, 2004, Pride & Prejudice, 2005, Mrs. Henderson Presents, 2005, (Voice Actress) Doogal, 2006, Casino Royale, 2006, Notes On A Scandal, 2006, Quantum Of Solace, 2008, Nine, 2009, Pirates Of The Caribbean: On Stranger Tides, 2011, Jane Eyre, 2011, J. Edgar, 2011, My Week With Marilyn, 2011, The Best Exotic Marigold Hotel, 2011, Run For Your Wife, 2012, Stars In Shorts, 2012, Skyfall, 2012, Philomena, 2013, The Second Best Exotic Marigold Hotel, 2015, Miss Peregrine's Home For Peculiar Children, 2016, (Voice Actress) Schadenfreude, 2016, Tulip Fever, 2017, Victoria & Abdul, 2017, Murder On The Orient Express, 2017, (TV Films) National Theatre Live: 50 Years On Stage, 2013, Roald Dahl's Esio Trot, 2015, The Vote, 2015; Author, And Furthermore, 2011 **AW:** Praemium Imperiale (Theatre/Film), 2011, Decorated Order of the British Empire, Dame Commander of the British Empire, Order of the Companion Of Honour, 2005, Olivier Award for Lifetime Achievement, 2004, Evening Standard Theater Award, 2004, BAFTA Award For Best Actress, Iris, 2002, Golden Globe Award For Best Supporting Actress, Chocolat, 2000, Walpole Medal, New York, 2000, Benjamin Franklin Medal, Royal Society of the Arts, London, England, 2000, Tony Award For Best Performance By A Leading Role In A Play, Amy's View In New York, 1999, UK Entertainment Personality Of The Year Variety, 1999, Critics Circle Award For Outstanding Service To The Arts, Academy Award For Best Supporting Actress, Shakespeare In Love, 1999, Critics Circle Drama Award, Amy's View, 1997, British Academy of Film And TV Arts Scotland Award, Critics Circle Film Award, Golden Globe Award For Best Actress, Mrs. Brown, 1997, Rothermore Award For Lifetime Achievement, 1997, Oliver Award For Best Actress, Absolute Hell, 1996, Oliver Award Best Actress In A Musical, A Little Night Music, 1996, Laurence Olivier Theatre Award, Evening Standard Drama Award, Drama Magazine Award, Antony and Cleopatra, 1989-1990, BAFTA Award For Best Actress In A Supporting Role, A Handful Of Dust, 1989, Plays And Players Award, SWET Best Actress Award, Laurence Olivier Theatre Award, Pack Of Lies, 1988, Standard Best Actress Award, Plays And Players Award For Best Actress, The Importance Of Being Earnest, 1988, ACE Award, Mr. And Mrs. Edgehill, 1988, SWET Best Actress Award, Evening Standard Drama Award For Best Actress, Plays And Players Award For Best Actress, Variety Club Award Actress Of The Year, Juno And The Paycock, 1981, SWET Best Actress Award For Lady Macbeth, Macbeth, 1976-1977, BAFTA Award For Best Actress, Talking To A Stranger, 1968, BAFTA Award For Most Promising Newcomer, Four In The Morning, 1965 **MEM:** Honorary Member, American Academy of Arts & Sciences **BA:** c/o Julian Belfrage Associates, Adam House, 14 New Burlington Street, London, United Kingdom, -W1S 3BQ

DENHAM, JEFF, T: U.S. Representative from California **I:** Government Administration/Government Relations/Government Services **DOB:** 07/29/1967 **PB:** Hawthorne **SC:** CA/USA **ED:** BS, California Polytechnic State University, San Luis Obispo, 1992; AA, Victor Valley Junior College, 1989 **C:** Member, U.S. House Agricultural Com-

mittee, 2013-; Member, U.S. House Veterans Affairs Committee, 2011-; Member, U.S. House Transportation & Infrastructure Committee, 2011-; Member, U.S. Congress from 10th California District, Washington, 2013-; Member, U.S. House Natural Resources Committee, 2011-13; Member, U.S. Congress from 19th California District, Washington, 2011-13; Member District 12, California State Senate, 2003-10 **AW:** Named Legislator of Year, California State's Sheriff's Association, 2004; recipient Gold award, California Teachers Association, 2005 **PA:** Republican **BA:** 1222 Longworth House Office Building, Washington, DC, 20515

DENHOLLANDER, RACHAEL, T: Former Olympic Gymnast **I:** Athletics **C:** Olympic Gymnast **AW:** Named One of Time's 100 Most Influential People, TIME Magazine (2018)

DENNEHY, BRIAN, T: information Technology Executive **I:** Information Technology and Services **ED:** PhD, University South Carolina; Master in Diplomatic History, Georgetown University; Bachelor in History & English, University Washington **C:** Vice president, consumer tax group, Intuit, Inc.,; Director, channel marketing, Intuit, Inc.,; Group manager, sales and channel marketing, Intuit, Inc.,; Joined, Intuit, Inc., 2001; Various management positions, Coca-Cola Enterprises, Inc.,; Consultant, Bain & Co., Inc.,

DENNIS, JAMES LEON, T: Federal Judge **I:** Law and Legal Services **DOB:** 01/09/1936 **PB:** Monroe **SC:** LA/USA **PT:** Son of Jenner Leon and Hope (Taylo) Dennis; **ED:** LLM, University Virginia, 1984; JD, Louisiana State University, 1962; BS in Business Adminstrn, Louisiana Tech. University, Ruston, 1959 **CT:** Bar: Louisiana 1962 **C:** Judge, US Court Appeals (5th cir.), New Orleans, 1995-; Visiting professor, Tulane Law School, 2003; Del., chairman judiciary committee, Louisiana Constnl. Convention, 1973; Coordinator, Louisiana Constnl. Revision Commission, 1970-72; Associate justice, Louisiana Supreme Court, 1975-95; Judge, Louisiana 2d Circuit Court Appeals, 1974-75; Judge, 4th District Court Louisiana for Morehouse and Ouachita Parishes, 1972-74; Partner, Hudson, Potts & Bernstein, 1965-72; Associate firm, Hudson, Potts & Bernstein, Monroe, 1962-65 **CIV:** Chairman, Louisiana Commission on Bicentennial U.S. Constitution, Member, Louisiana House of Reps., 1968-72 **MIL:** With, US Army, 1955-57 **MEM:** Mem.: American Bar Association (committee on appellate practice), 4th Judicial Bar Association, Louisiana Bar Association, Rotary **BA:** US Courthouse, 600 Camp St Rm 219, New Orleans, LA, USA, 70130-3425

DENT, CHARLIE, T: U.S. Representative from Pennsylvania **I:** Government Administration/Government Relations/Government Services **DOB:** 05/24/1960 **PB:** Allentown **PT:** Son of Walter and Marjorie (Wieder) Dent; **ED:** MPA, Lehigh University, Bethlehem, Pennsylvania, 1993; BA in Foreign Service and International Politics, Pennsylvania State University, 1982 **C:** Chairman, US House Ethics Committee, 2015-17; Committee on Appropriations; Member, US Congress from 15th Pennsylvania Dist, 2005-; Member District 16, Pennsylvania State Senate, 1999-2004; Member District 132, Pennsylvania House of Representatives, 1991-98; Devel. officer, Lehigh University, 1986-90; Sales rep., P.A. Peters, Inc., Allentown **CIV:** Board directors, Crime Victims Council Lehigh County, Board directors, Pennsylvania Commission Crime & Delinquency, Board directors, Pennsylvania Council Arts, Board directors, Ben Franklin Partnership, **PA:** Republican **BA:** 2082 Rayburn HOB, Washington, DC, 20515

DENTON, NICK, T: Publishing Executive **I:** Publishing **CN:** Gawker.com **DOB:** 08/24/1966 **ED:** Grad. in Econs., Oxford University, England **C:** Managing editor, Gawker.com, 2007—16; Founder, temporary editor, ValleyWag, 2006—2007; Founder, pub., Gawker Media (includes Gawker and Wonkette), New York City, New York; Founder, CEO, Moreover Technologies, London, England, 1998—2001; Founder, First Tuesday; Silicon Valley corr., Fin. Times London, San Francisco, California, 1997; Foreign corr., investment corr., internet media writer, Fin. Times London **CW:** Co-author: All That Glitters: The Fall of Barings, 1996 **AW:** Named one of 50 Who Matter Now, CNNMoney.com Business 2.0, 2006, 50 Most Important People on the Web, PC World, 2007, The 100 Agents of Change, Rolling Stone magazine, 2009 **BA:** Gawker Media, 210 Elizabeth St 4th Fl, New York, NY, 10012

DEPP, JOHNNY, T: Actor **I:** Media & Entertainment **DOB:** 06/09/1963 **PB:** Owensboro **PT:** Son of John and Betty Sue (Palmer) Wells; Married Lori Anne Allison, December 20, 1983 (div. 1985); Married Amber Heard, February 3, 2015 (separated May 2016); children: Lily-Rose Melody, Jack Christo **CIV:** Hon. member, The Comanche Nation, Oklahoma **CW:** Guitarist; ex-member bands the Flame, the Kids, Rock City Angels, 1985; actor: (TV series) 21 Jump Street, 1987-90, Hotel, 1987, The Vicar of Dibley, 1999, The Fast Show, 2000, King of the Hill, 2004, This American Life, 2008, Spongebob Squarepants, 2009, Life's Too Short, 2011; (films) A Nightmare on Elm Street, 1984, Private Resort, 1985, Platoon, 1986, Cry-Baby, 1990, Edward Scissorhands, 1990, Freddy's Dead: The Final Nightmare, 1991, American Dreamers, 1992, Benny & Joon, 1993, What's Eating Gilbert Grape, 1993, Ed Wood, 1994, Arizona Dreamer, Don Juan DeMarco, 1995, Dead Man, 1995, Nick of Time, 1996, Donnie Brasco, 1997, The Astronaut's Wife, 1998, L.A. Without a Map, 1998, Fear and Loathing in Las Vegas, 1998, The Source, 1999, The Ninth Gate, 1999, Just to Be Together, 1999, The Astronaut's Wife, 1999, Sleepy Hollow, 1999, The Source, 1999, The Man Who Cried, 2000, Chocolat, 2000, Blow, 2001, From Hell, 2001, Pirates of the Caribbean: The Curse of the Black Pearl, 2003 (Best Actor, Screen Actors Guild Awards, 2004), Once Upon A Time in Mexico, 2003, Secret Window, 2004, Ils se marièrent et eurent beaucoup d'enfants, 2004, Finding Neverland, 2004, The Libertine, 2004, Charlie and the Chocolate Factory, 2005 (Choice Movie Actor: Comedy, Teen Choice awards, 2006), (voice) Corpse Bride, 2005, (narrator) Deep Sea 3D, 2006, Pirates of the Caribbean: Dead Man's Chest, 2006 (Choice Movie Actor: Drama/Action Adventure, Teen Choice Awards, 2006, Best Performance, MTV Movie Awards, 2007), Pirates of the Caribbean: At World's End, 2007 (Choice Movie Actor: Action Adventure, Teen Choice Awards, 2007, Best Comedic Performance, MTV Movie Awards, 2008, Best Villain, 2008), Sweeney Todd: The Demon Barber of Fleet Street, 2007 (Best Performance by an Actor in a Motion Picture - Musical or Comedy, Golden Globe award, Hollywood Foreign Press Association, 2008, Choice Movie Villain, Teen Choice Awards, 2008), Public Enemies, 2009, Alice in Wonderland, 2010, The Tourist, 2010, (voice) Rango, 2011 (Favorite Animated Voice, People's Choice Awards, 2012), Pirates of the Caribbean: On Stranger Tides, 2011, The Rum Diary, 2011, Transcendence, 2014, Tusk, 2014, Into the Woods, 2014, Black Mass, 2015, London Fields, 2015, Yoga Hosers, 2016, Alice Through the Looking Glass, 2016,Fantastic Beasts and Where to Find Them, 2016, Pirates of the Caribbean Dead Men Tell No Tales, 2017, Murder on the Orient Express, 2017, Sherlock Gnomes, 2018, Fantastic Beasts The Crimes of Grindelwald,

2018, Richard Says Goodbye, 2018, Labyrinth 2018 (documentaries) For No Good Reason, 2012, (TV films) Donald Trump's The Art of the Deal: The Movie, 2016; writer, director, actor: The Brave, 1997; actor, prodr.: Dark Shadows, 2012, Mortdecai, 2015; (TV films) Slow Burn, 1986; actor, executive prodr.: (films) The Lone Ranger, 2013; (TV guest appearances) Lady Blue, 1985, Hotel, 1987, The Vicar of Dibley, 1999, (voice) King of the Hill, 2004; (video-voice) Kingdom Hearts II, 2005 **AW:** Named Favorite Dramatic Movie Actor, People's Choice Awards, 2016, Favorite Movie Actor, 2014, Nickelodeon Kids Choice Awards, 2008, People's Choice Awards, 2012, 2011, 2010, Favorite Male Star, Favorite Male Action Star & On-screen matchup (Keira Knightly), 2007, Favorite Male Movie Star, 2008, 2006; named one of 50 Smartest People in Hollywood, Entertainment Weekly, 2007, Top 25 Entertainers of Year, 2007, The 100 Most Powerful Celebrities, Forbes.com, 2008, 2007, 50 Most Powerful People in Hollywood, Premiere magazine, 2006, 2005, 2004, Time Magazine 100 Most Influential People, 2005; recipient Fashion Icon award, Council Fashion Designers of America, 2012, MTV Generation award, MTV Movie Awards, 2012 **BA:** Spanky Taylor Company, 3727 W Magnolia, Burbank, CA, 91505

DERN, LAURA, T: Actress **I:** Media & Entertainment **PT:** Bruce Dern; Diane Ladd **SPN:** Ben Harper, December 23, 2005 (div. September 2013) **CH:** Ellery Walker; Jaya **ED:** Student, Lee Strasberg Institute; Student, Royal Academy Dramatic Art, London **CW:** Actress: (films) White Lightning, 1973, Alice Doesn't Live Here Anymore, 1974, Foxes, 1980, Ladies and Gentlemen, The Fabulous Stains, 1982, Teachers, 1984, Mask, 1985, Smooth Talk, 1985, Blue Velvet, 1986, Haunted Summer, 1988, Fat Man & Little Boy, 1989, Wild At Heart, 1990, Rambling Rose, 1991, Jurassic Park, 1993, A Perfect World, 1993, Citizen Ruth, 1996, Bastard Out of Carolina, 1996, October Sky, 1999, Daddy and Them, 2001, Jurassic Park III, 2001, Novocaine, 2001, I Am Sam, 2001, We Don't Live Here Anymore, 2004, Happy Endings, 2005, The Prize Winner of Defiance, Ohio, 2005, Lonely Hearts, 2006, Year of the Dog, 2007, Tenderness, 2009, Everything Must Go, 2010, Little Fockers, 2010, The Master, 2012, The Fault in Our Stars, 2014, When the Game Stands Tall, 2014, Wild, 2014, 99 Homes, 2014, Bravetown, 2015, Wilson, 2016, The Founder, 2016, Certain Women, 2016, The Founder, 2016, Wilson, 2017, The Good Time Girls, 2017, Downsizing, 2017, Star Wars: The Last Jedi, 2017, The Tale, 2018, JT LeRoy, 2018; (TV films) Happy Endings, 1983, The Three Wishes of Billy Grier, 1984, Afterburn, 1992 (Golden Globe award for Best Actress in TV Movie or Mini-series), Fallen Angels (Murder, Obliquely), 1993, Ruby Ridge, 1996, The Baby Dance, 1998, Damaged Care, 2002, Recount, 2008 (Best Performance by an Actress in a Supporting Role in a Series, Mini-Series or Motion Picture Made for TV, Golden Globe award, Hollywood Foreign Press Association, 2009); (TV guest appearances) Shannon, 1981, Fallen Angels, 1993, Frasier, 1995, Ellen, 1997, The West Wing, 2002, (voice) King of the Hill, 2003; co-prodr.: (TV films) Damaged Care, 2002; actress, co-prodr.: (films) Inland Empire, 2006; actress, executive producer, writer: (TV series) Enlightened, 2011-13 (Golden Globe award for Best Performance by an Actress in a TV Series-Comedy or Musical, 2012) Call Me Crazy: A Five Film, 2013, Kroll Show, 2014, Drunk History, 2014, The Mindy Project, 2015, F is for Family, 2015, Big Little Lies, 2017,(Golden Globe Best Supporting Actress,2018) The Last Man on Earth, 2017, Unbreakable Kimmy Schmidt, 2017, Twin Peaks, 2017; stage appearances include The Palace of Amateurs (New York),

1988, Brooklyn Laundry (LA).; executive prodr.: (TV films) Down Came a Blackbird, 1995; dir.: (TV films) The Gift, 1994.

DERSHOWITZ, ALAN MORTON, T: Retired Law Educator **I:** Law and Legal Services **DOB:** 09/01/1938 **PB:** Brooklyn **SC:** New York **PT:** Son of Harry and Claire Dershowitz **ED:** BA magna cum laude, Brooklyn College, 1959; LLD (hon.), Brooklyn College, 2001; LLB magna cum laude, Yale University, 1962; MA (hon.), Harvard College, 1967; LLD (hon.), Yeshiva University, 1989; PhD (hon.), Haifa University, 1993; LLD (hon.), Hebrew Union College, 1993; LLD (hon.), Syracuse University, 1997; LLD (hon.), Monmouth College; LLD (hon.), Bar Ilan University, 2004; LLD, City University of New York **CT:** Bar: DC 1963, Massachusetts 1968, US Supreme Court 1968 **C:** CNN and Fox News contributor and political analyst; Felix Frankfurter Professor Law, Harvard Law School, 1993—2013; Professor emeritus, Harvard Law School, 2013—; Professor law, Harvard Law School, 1967—2013; Assistant professor law, Harvard Law School, 1964—1967; Fellow, Center for Advanced Study of Behavioral Sciences, 1971—1972; Law clerk to Justice Arthur J. Goldberg, US Supreme Court, 1963—1964; Law clerk to Hon. David L. Bazelon, US Court Appeals (DC Cir.), 1962—1963 **CR:** Consultant to director, National Institute of Mental Health, 1967—1969, President's Commission on Civil Disorders, 1967, President's Committee on Causes of Violence, 1968, National Association for the Advancement of Colored People Legal Defense Fund, 1967—1968, NIMH's President's Commission on Marijuana & Drug Abuse, 1972—1973, Council on Drug Abuse, 1972—, Ford Foundation Study on Law and Justice, 1973—1976; rapporteur Twentieth Century Fund Study on Sentencing, 1975—1976 **CIV:** Chairman civil rights committee, New England region Anti-Defamation League, B'nai B'rith, 1980—1985; board directors ACLU, 1968—1971, 1972—1975, Assembly Behavioral and Social Scis. at National Academy of Sciences, 1973—1976 **CW:** Co-author: (nonfiction) Psychoanalysis, Psychiatry and the Law, 1967, Criminal Law: Theory and Process, 1974; author: The Best Defense, 1982, Reversal of Fortune: Inside the Von Bulow Case, 1986, Taking Liberties: A Decade of Hard Cases, Bad Laws and Bum Raps, 1988, Chutzpah, 1991, Contrary to Public Opinion, 1992, The Abuse Excuse, 1994, Reasonable Doubts: The O.J. Simpson Case and the Criminal Justice System, 1996, The Vanishing American Jew: In Search of Jewish Identity for the Next Century, 1997, Sexual McCarthyism: Clinton, Starr and the Emerging Constitutional Crisis, 1998, The Genesis of Justice: Ten Stories of Biblical Injustice That Led to the Ten Commandments and Modern Law, 2000, Supreme Injustice: How the High Court Hijacked Election 2000, 2001, Letters to a Young Lawyer, 2001, Why Terrorism Works: Understanding the Threat, Responding to the Challenge, 2002, Shouting Fire: Civil Liberties in a Turbulent Age, 2002, America Declares Independence, 2003, The Case for Israel, 2003, America on Trial, 2004, Rights from Wrongs: The Origins of Human Rights in the Experience of Injustice, 2004, The Case for Peace: How the Arab-Israeli Conflict Can Be Resolved, 2005, Drumption: A Knife That Cuts Both Ways, 2006, Blasphemy: How the Religious Right is Hijacking the Declaration of Independence, 2007, Finding Jefferson: A Lost Letter, a Remarkable Discovery, and the First Amendment in an Age of Terrorism, 2008, The Case Against Israeli Enemies: Exposing Jimmy Carter and Others Who Stand in the Way of Peace, 2008, Is That A Right to Remain Silent, 2008, The Case for Moral Clarity: Israel, Hamas and Gaza, 2009, Taking the Stand: My Life in the Law, 2013, Terror Tunnels: The Case for Israel's Just War Against Hamas, 2014, Abraham:

The World's First (But Certainly Not Last) Jewish Lawyer, 2015; (novels) The Advocate's Devil, 1994, Just Revenge, 1999, The Trials of Zion, 2010; editor-in-chief: Yale Law Journal, 1961—62; contributor articles to professional jounals **AW:** Fellow Guggenheim, 1978—79 **MEM: Mem.:** Order of Coif, Phi Beta Kappa

DESANTIS, RON, T: U.S. Representative from Florida, former federal prosecutor **I:** Government Administration/Government Relations/Government Services **DOB:** 09/14/1978 **PB:** Jacksonville **ED:** Grad., US Naval Justice School, 2005; JD, Harvard Law School, 2005; BA in History, Yale University, 2001 **C:** Member, US House Oversight & Government Reform Committee, 2013-; Member, US House Judiciary Committee, 2013-; Member, US House Foreign Affairs Committee, 2013-; Member, US Congress from 6th Florida District, Washington, 2013-; Prosecutor US Attorney's Office (middle district) Florida, US Department Justice,; Legal adv. to Commander SEAL Team, Special Operations Task Force-West, Fallujah, Iraq,; Military prosecutor, Joint Task Force-Guantanamo Commander (JTF-GTMO), Cuba,; Military prosecutor, Trial Service Office Command South East, Naval Station Mayport, Florida, **CR:** Instructor US military law Florida Coastal School Law **MIL:** Lieutenant, Judge Advocate General Corps. US Naval Reserve, 2010-, served in US Navy, 2004-10 **CW:** Author: Dreams From Our Founding Fathers: First Principles in the Age of Obama, 2011 **AW:** Decorated Iraq Campaign medal, Bronze star **MEM: Mem.:** VFW, American Legion **PA:** Republican

DESAULNIER, MARK, T: U.S. Representative From California **I:** Government Administration/Government Relations/Government Services **PB:** Lowell **SC:** MA/USA **ED:** BA in History, College of the Holy Cross **C:** U.S. Representative From 11th California District, 2015-Present; District 7, California State Senate, 2009-Present; Chair, Growth Management Committee, California State Assembly, 2007-2008; District 11, California State Assembly, 2006-2008; Councilmember, Concord, CA, 1991-1993; Former Mayor, Concord, CA; Chair of Labor and Industrial Relations Committee, Elections, Reapportionment and Constitutional Amendments Committee, Transportation and Housing Committee, Budget and Fiscal Review Committee, California State Senate **MEM:** Metropolitan Transportation Commission, California Air Resources Board, Bay Area Air Quality Management District, Association of the Bay Area Government, Future Fund, Children & Families Commission, Board Supervisor, Contra Costa County, Board Supervisor, AfterSchool4All **PA:** Democrat **BA:** 2265 Rayburn House Office Building, Washington, DC, 20515

DESJARLAIS, SCOTT EUGENE, T: U.S. Representative from Tennessee, Physician **I:** Government Administration/Government Relations/Government Services **DOB:** 02/21/1964 **PB:** Des Moines **SC:** IA/USA **PT:** Joe DesJarlais; Sylvia DesJarlais **ED:** MD, School of Medicine, University of South Dakota, 1991; BS in Chemistry & Psychology, University of South Dakota, 1987 **C:** U.S. House of Oversight & Government Reform Committee, Washington, DC, 2011-Present; U.S. House of Education & the Workforce, Washington, DC, 2011-Present; U.S. House Agricultural Committee, Washington, DC, 2011-Present; U.S. Congress, Fourth Tennessee District, Washington, DC, 2011-Present; Physician, General Practitioner, Grand View Medical Center, Jasper, TN; Committee on Foreign Affairs **PA:** Republican **BA:** U.S. House of Representatives, 413 Cannon House Office Building, Washington, DC, 20515

DESTEFANO, JOHNNY, T: Director, Office of Presidential Personnel **I:** Government Administration/Government Relations/Government Services **ED:** Bachelor, St. Louis University, Missouri, 2001 **C:** director, office of presidential personnel, 2017-; senior advisor, John Boehner, 2011-2013; political director, Congressman John Boehner, 2007-2011; Deputy executive director, National Rep. Congl. Committee, Washington, from 2007; Campaign manager, Deborah Pryce's Congl. Campaign, Ohio, 2006; Coalitions director, US House Rep. Conference, 2001-06 **AW:** Named one of The Fabulous 50, Roll Call, 2009

DEUTCH, TED, T: Ranking Member of the House Ethics Committee **I:** Government Administration/Government Relations/Government Services **DOB:** 05/07/1966 **PB:** Bethlehem **PT:** Son of Bernard and Jean Deutch; **ED:** JD, University Michigan Law School, 1990; BA, University Michigan, 1988 **C:** Ranking Member, House Ethics Commitee, 2017-; Member, US Congress from 21st Florida District, 2013-2017; Member, US Congress from 19th Florida District, Washington, 2010-13; Member District 30, Florida State Senate, Tallahassee, 2006-10; Attorney **MEM:** Member American Bar Association, Florida Bar Association, Century Village Democratic Club, Lake Worth West Democratic Club, Greater Boynton Beach Democratic Club, United South County Dem. Club, Deerfield Democratic Club, League of Women Voters, Women's Foundation Palm Beach County, National Safety Council, University Michigan Alumni Association United Jewish Communities, Jewish Federation South Palm Beach County (James & Marjorie Baer Leadership award), Voter's Coalition, Forum Club, National Conference State Legislatures **PA:** Democrat

DEVITO, DANNY, T: Actor **I:** Media & Entertainment **DOB:** 11/17/1944 **PB:** Asbury Park **SC:** New Jersey **PT:** Son of Daniel and Julia (Moccello) DeVito; **SPN:** Married Rhea Perlman, January 28, 1982; **CH:** children: Lucie Chet, Gracie Fan, Jacob Danie **ED:** Grad., American Academy Dramatic Arts, 1966 **C:** Owner, DeVito South Beach, Miami, Florida, 2007-; Co-founder, Jersey Films, 1992 **CW:** Actor: (theater) The Man With a Flower in His Mouth, Sheridan Sq. Playhouse, 1969, The Shrinking Bride, 1971, One Flew Over the Cuckoo's Nest, 1971, DuBarry Was a Lady, 1972, A Phantasmagoria Historia of D. Johann Fauster Magister, Ph.D, M.D., D.D., D.L., etc., 1973, The Many Wives of Windsor (New York Shakespeare Festival), 1974, Where Do We Go From Here?, 1974; (films) Dreams of Glass, 1970, Lady Liberty, 1971, Hurry Up, or I'll Be 30, 1973, Scalawag, 1972, One Flew Over the Cuckoo's Nest, 1975, The Money, 1976, Hot Dogs for Gaugin, Goin' South, 1978, Swap Meet, 1979, Going Ape!, 1981, Terms of Endearment, 1983, Romancing the Stone, 1984, Johnny Dangerously, 1984, Head Office, 1985, Jewel of the Nile, 1985, Wise Guys, 1986, My Little Pony (voice), 1986, Ruthless People, 1986, Tin Men, 1987, Twins, 1988, Other People's Money, 1991, Batman Returns, 1992, Jack the Bear, 1993, Last Action Hero (voice), 1993, Look Who's Talking Now (voice), 1993, Renaissance Man, 1994, Junior, 1994, Mars Attacks!, 1996, The Rainmaker, 1997, Hercules (voice), 1997, The Virgin Suicides, 1999, The Big Kahuna, 1999, Screwed, 2000, What's the Worst That Could Happen, 2001, Heist, 2001, Austin Powers in Goldmember, 2002, Marx Brothers, 2003, Anything Else, 2003, Big Fish (voice), 2003, Family of the Year, 2004, Catching Kringle (voice), 2004, Christmas in Love, 2004, Marilyn Hotchkiss' Ballroom Dancing Charm School, 2005, The OH in Ohio, 2006, Even Money, 2006, Deck the Halls, 2006, The Good Night, 2007, Nobel Son, 2007, Just

Add Water, 2008, House Broken, 2009, When in Rome, 2010, Girl Walks Into a Bar, 2011, Dr. Suess' The Lorax (voice), 2012, Hotel Noir, 2012, All the Wilderness, 2014, Wiener-Dog, 2016, Curmudgeons, 2016, Animal Crackers, 2017, Jim & Andy: The Great Beyond, 2017, Smallfoot, 2018, Dumbo 2019, (TV series) Taxi, 1978-83 (Golden Globe award for Best TV Actor in a Supporting Role, 1980, Emmy award for Outstanding Supporting Actor in a Comedy or Variety or Music Series, 1981), It's Always Sunny in Philadelphia, 2006-16, Deadbeat, 2015; actor, dir.: (films) Throw Momma From the Train, 1987, The War of the Roses, 1989, Death to Smoochy, 2002, Duplex, 2003; actor, prodr.: (films) Get Shorty, 1995, Living Out Loud, 1998, Man on the Moon, 1999, How High, 2001, Be Cool, 2005, Relative Strangers, 2006; actor, executive prodr.: (films) Drowning Mona, 2000, Reno 911!: Miami, 2007; actor, director, prodr.: (films) Hoffa, 1992, Matilda, 1996; actor, dir.: (TV films) Selling of Vince D'Angelo, 1976, The World's Greatest Lover, 1977, Valentine, 1979, All the Kids Do It, 1984, The Ratings Game, 1984; (guest appearances) Starsky and Hutch, 1977, Police Woman, 1977, Amazing Stories, 1986, The Simpsons (voice), 1989, 1991, 1992, Pearl, 1997, Ed, 2002, Friends, 2004, Father of the Pride (voice), 2004; executive prodr.: (TV series) Kate Brasher, 2001, UC: Undercover, 2001, The American Embassy, 2002, Karen Sisco, 2003-04, Reno 911, 2003-; co-exec. prodr.: (films) Pulp Fiction, 1994; prodr.: (films) Reality Bites, 1994, Sunset Park, 1996, Feeling Minnesota, 1996, Gattaca, 1997, Out of Sight, 1998, Erin Brokovich, 2000, The Caveman's Valentine, 2001, Camp, 2003, Along Came Polly, 2004, Freedom Writers, 2007; co-prodr.: (films) 8 Seconds, 1994; executive prodr.: (films) Garden State, 2004, Bye Bye Benjamin, 2006; producer, dir.: (films) St. Sebastian, 2013. **AW:** Recipient Crystal Globe prize for Contribution to Cinema, Karlovy Vary Film Festival, 2007, Star, Hollywood Walk of Fame, 2011; named to New Jersey Hall of Fame, 2010 **BA:** Creative Artists Agency, 2000 Avenue of the Stars, Los Angeles, CA, 90067

DEVOS, ELISABETH (BETSY), T: Secretary of Education **I:** Government Administration/Government Relations/Government Services **DOB:** 01/08/1958 **PB:** Holland, Michigan **SC:** MI/USA **PT:** Daughter of Edgar Dale and Elsa D. (Zwiep) Prince; Married Richard M. DeVos Junior, 1979; four children **ED:** BSc in Business Administration, Calvin College, 1979 **C:** Secretary, Department of Education, Washington, DC, 2017—; Chairman, Michigan State Rep. Party, 2003-2017; Member, National Rep. Committee, 1996-; Chairman, Michigan State Rep. Party, 1996-2000; Rep. National Committeewoman, State of Michigan, 1992-97; Chairman, Kent County (Michigan) Rep. Finance Committee, 1985-88, 96-; Co-chmn., Kent County (Michigan) Rep. Finance Committee, 1983-84 **CR:** Market Research Analyst, Amway Corp., 1979-81; President, Windquest Group **CIV:** Board of Directors, Blodgett Memorial Medical Center, 1986-, Ada (Michigan) Christian School, 1992-, Member, Rep. Congl. Leadership Council **MEM:** Member Economic Club of Grand Rapids **H:** Travel, Boating, Skiing **BA:** US Department of Education, 400 Maryland Ave, SW, Washington, DC, 20202

DEWITT, WILLIAM O. JR., I: Business Management/Business Services **DOB:** 08/31/1941 **PB:** St. Louis **SC:** MO/USA **PT:** Son of William O. and Margaret H. DeWitt **ED:** MBA, Harvard School of Business, Cambridge, Massachusetts, 1965; BA in Economics, Yale University, New Haven, 1963 **C:** Managing Partner, Chairman, St. Louis Cardinals, 1996-; Co-founder, President, Reynolds, DeWitt

& Co., 1979-; With, Gradison & Co., Cincinnati, 1974-79 **CR:** Member, Foreign Intelligence Advisory Board, Washington, 2001-, Chairman, Board of Directors, Gateway Group Inc., Board of Directors US Playing Card Co., Williams Inc., Sena Weller Rohe, Co-chairman, Restaurant Management Inc. **CIV:** Cabinet Member, Multiple Sclerosis Society, Cabinet Member, United Way Cincinnati, Cabinet Member, Cincinnati Fine Arts Fund, Member, Development Board, Yale University, President Rep. Fin. Committee, Hamilton County, Ohio, President, William O. & Margaret H. DeWitt Foundation, President, Fund for Ind. Schools, Cincinnati, Board of Directors, Salvation Army, Board of Directors, Taft Museum, Board of Directors, Cincinnati Art Museum, Board of Directors, Semple Foundation

DIAMOND, JARED MASON, T: Writer, Ecologist, Biologist **I:** Sciences **DOB:** 09/10/1937 **PB:** Boston **SC:** MA/USA **PT:** Lewis K. Diamond; Flora (Kaplan) Diamond **ED:** Honorary PhD, Westfield State University (2009); Honorary PhD, Katholieke Universiteit Leuven, Belgium; Honorary DLitt, Sejong University, Korea (1995); PhD in Physiology and Biophysics, University of Cambridge, England (1961); BA in Biochemical Sciences, Harvard University (1958) **C:** Professor of Geography, University of California, Los Angeles; Professor of Physiology, UCLA Medical School (1968-Present); Writer (1992-Present); Associate Professor, Physiology, UCLA Medical School (1966-1968); Associate in Biophysics, Harvard Medical School (1965-1966); Junior Fellow, Society Fellows, Harvard University (1962-1965) **CR:** Board of Directors, World Wildlife Fund (1993-Present); Contributing Editor, Discover Magazine (1984-Present); Research Associate, Ornithology, LA County Museum of Natural History (1985-Present); American Museum of Natural History (1973-Present) **CW:** Author, "The Avifauna of the Eastern Highlands of New Guinea" (1972); Author, "The Third Chimpanzee: The Evolution and Future of the Human Animal" (1991); Author, "Why is Sex Fun? The Evolution of Human Sexuality" (1997); Author, "Guns, Germs, and Steel: The Fates of Human Societies" (1997); Author, "Collapse: How Societies Choose to Fail or Succeed" (2005); Author, "The World Until Yesterday: What Can We Learn from Traditional Societies?" (2012); Co-author, "Birds of New Guinea" (1986); Author, "The Birds of Northern Melanesia: Speciation, Ecology, and Biogeography" (2001); Co-editor, "Ecology and Evolution of Communities" (1975); Co-editor, "Community Ecology" (1986); Co-editor, "Natural Experiments of History" (2010); Contributor, Chapters to Books; Member, Editorial Board, "Skeptic" Magazine"; Member, Editorial Board, "The Third Chimpanzee for Young People: The Evolution and Future of the Human Animal" (2015) **AW:** Co-recipient, Wolf Foundation Prize for Agriculture (2013); Dickson Prize in Science (2006); Lewis Thomas Prize for Writing about Science (2002); Tyler Prize for Environmental Achievement (2001); Lannan Literary Award for Nonfiction (1999); National Medal of Science (1999); International Cosmos Prize (1998); Elliott Coues Award, American Ornithologists' Union (1998); Skeptics Society Randi Award (1994); Zoological Society of San Diego Conservation Medal (1993); Archie Carr Medal (1989); Franklin L. Burr Medal, National Geographic Society (1979); Distinguished Achievement Award, American Gastroenterological Association (1975); MacArthur Foundation Fellowship (1985); Humanist of the Year, American Humanist Association (2016); Rhone-Poulenc Prize for Science Books (1992); Los Angeles Times Book Prize; Phi Beta Kappa in Science Book Prize (1997); Pulitzer Prize (1998); Cosmos Prize, Japan (1998); Rhone-Poulenc Science Book Prize (1998); Aventis Prize for Science Books (1998); Nathaniel Bowditch Prize, American Philosophical Society (1976) **MEM:** Fellow, American Academy of Arts and Sciences; National Academy of Sciences; Institute of Medicine; American Philosophical Society

DIAMOND, NEIL, T: Singer **I:** Media & Entertainment **PB:** Brooklyn **SC:** NY/USA **PT:** Akeeba Diamond; Rose (Rapaport) Diamond **ED:** Student, New York University **CW:** Singer: (albums) The Feel of Neil Diamond, 1966, Just for You, 1967, Neil Diamond's Greatest Hits, 1968, Velvet Gloves and Spit, 1968, Touching You, Touching Me, 1969, Brother Love's Travelling Salvation Show, 1969, Gold, 1970, Tap Root Manuscript, 1970, Shilo, 1970, Stones, 1971, Do It!, 1971, Hot August Nights, 1972, Moods, 1972, Rainbow, 1973, Jonathan Livingston Seagull, 1973, Greatest Hits, 1974, Serenade, 1974, Gold 1, 1974, Gold 2, 1974, Diamonds, 1975, Focus On, 1975, Beautiful Noise, 1976, And the Singer Sings His Song, 1976, Live at the Greek, 1977, I'm Glad You're Here With Me Tonight, 1977, You Don't Bring Me Flowers, 1978, 20 Golden Greats, 1978, Neil Diamonds, 1979, September Morn, 1980, Jazz Singer, 1980, Best Of, 1981, Solitary, 1981, Love Songs, 1981, On the Way to the Sky, 1981, Live Diamond, 1982, Heart Light, 1982, Song Sung Blue, 1982, Primitive, 1984, Headed For the Future, 1986, Hot August Night II, 1987, The Best Years of Our Lives, 1989, Lovescape, 1991, Neil Diamond The Greatest Hits, 1966-92, 1992, The Christmas Album, 1992, Neil Diamond Glory Road 1968-72, 1992, Live in America, 1994, His 12 Greatest Hits, 1996, As Time Goes By-Movie Album, 1998, Best of Neil Diamond, 1999, Best of The Movie Album, 1999, Three Cord Opera, 2001, The Essential, 2001, Play Me, 2002, Gold, 2005, 12 Songs, 2005, Home Before Dark, 2008, Hot August Night/NYC, 2009, A Cherry Cherry Christmas, 2009, Dreams, 2010, The Very Best of Neil Diamond, 2011, The Classic Christmas Album, 2013, Melody Road, 2014, Acoustic Christmas, 2016, 50th Anniversary Collection, 2017; (videos) Neil Diamond: Greatest Hits Live, 1988, Neil Diamond: Under a Tennessee Moon, 1996; composer: (film scores) Jonathan Livingston Seagull (Grammy award for Best Score Soundtrack, 1973, Golden Globe award for Best Original Score, 1974), Every Which Way but Loose, 1978, The Jazz Singer (also actor), 1980; guest artist network TV shows; (TV specials) Neil Diamond's Christmas Special, 1993 **AW:** Named MusiCares Person of Year, National Academy Recording Arts and Sciences, 2009; named to Rock and Roll Hall of Fame, 2011; recipient Kennedy Center Honors, John F. Kennedy Center Performing Arts, Washington, 2011, Star, Hollywood Walk of Fame, 2012

DIAMOND, PETER ARTHUR, T: Economics Professor **I:** Education/Educational Services **DOB:** 04/29/1940 **PB:** NYC **PT:** Son of Daniel and Dora (Kolsky) D.; **MS:** Married **SPN:** Priscilla Gibbs Myrick, October 16, 1966 **CH:** Matthew, Andrew **ED:** PhD, Massachusetts Institute of Technology, 1963; BA, Yale University, 1960 **C:** Institute professor, Massachusetts Institute of Technology, 1997-; Paul A. Samuelson professor, Massachusetts Institute of Technology, 1992-97; John & Jennie S. MacDonald professor, Massachusetts Institute of Technology, 1989-91; Professor, Massachusetts Institute of Technology, 1970-88; Associate professor economics, Massachusetts Institute of Technology, Cambridge, 1966-70; Acting associate professor, University Calif.-Berkeley, 1965-66; Assistant professor economics, University Calif.-Berkeley, 1963-65 **AW:** Social Sci. Research Council fellow, 1965; Guggenheim Foundation fellow, 1966, 82; recipient Mahalanobis Memorial award Indian Econometric Society, 1980, Newman's prize, 1994, CES fellow, 2000, Killian award, 2003-04, Samu-elson award, 2003, Jean-Jacques Laffont prize, 2005, Robert M. Ball award, 2008; co-recipient Nobel Prize in Economics, The Nobel Foundation, 2010 **MEM:** Fellow Econometric Society (council 1981-86, 2d vice president 1989, 1st vice president 1990, president 1991); member American Economics Association (vice president 1986, president 2003), National Academy Sci (chairman board 1996-98, board member 1998-2001, president 1994-97). **H:** Baseball **PA:** Democrat

DIAZ, ALBERT, T: Federal Judge **I:** Law and Legal Services **PB:** New York City **SC:** New York **ED:** MS in Business Administration, Boston University, 1993; JD, New York University, 1988; BS in Economics, University Pennsylvania, 1983 **CT:** Bar: North Carolina 1995, DC 1990, New York 1989 **C:** Judge, US Court Appeals (4th Cir.), Richmond, Virginia, 2010-; Judge, North Carolina Business Court, Charlotte, North Carolina, 2005-10; Judge, North Carolina Superior Court, Charlotte, North Carolina, 2001-10; Trial attorney, Hunton & Williams, Charlotte and Raleigh, North Carolina, 1995-2001; Reserve appellate defense counsel, Office of Judge Advocate General, Washington, 1995-2000; Appellate government counsel, Office of Judge Advocate General, Washington, 1991-95; Trial and review attorney, Marine Corps Base, Camp Lejeune, North Carolina, 1988-91 **CR:** Speaker in field adj. faculty Central Piedmont Community College, 2006- presiding judge Charlotte Mecklenburg Schools Truancy Court, 2005-10, National HS Mock Trial Championships, 2005, Mecklenburg County Drug Treatment Court, 2002-10 reserve appellate judge USN-Marine Corps Court Criminal Appeals, Washington Navy Yard, Washington, 2005-06 reserve military judge USN-Marine Corps Trial Judiciary, Piedmont Judicial Cir., Camp Lejeune, North Carolina, 2000-05 **MEM:** Mem.: American Bar Association (member Conference of State Trial Judges 2001-), National Bar Association, Mecklenburg County Bar, North Carolina Bar Association (member Minorities in the Profession Committee & Hispanic-Latino Lawyers Committee 1998-), American College of Business Court Judges, Justice Bobbitt Inn of Court (secretary 2004-), Hispanic National Bar Association **BA:** US Court of Appeals Lewis F Powell Jr US Courthouse, 1100 E Main St, Richmond, VA, 23219

DIAZ-BALART, MARIO, T: Congressman **I:** Government Administration/Government Relations/Government Services **CN:** US Congress from 25th Fla. Dist. **DOB:** 09/25/1961 **PB:** Fort Lauderdale **SC:** Florida **ED:** Student, University South Florida **C:** Member, US Congress from 25th Florida District, 2013-; Member, US Congress from 21st Florida District, 2011-13; Member, US Congress from 25th Florida District, Washington, 2003-11; Member District 37, Florida State Senate, Tallahassee, 1993-2000; Member District 112, Florida House of Reps., Tallahassee, 2001-02; Member District 115, Florida House of Reps., Tallahassee, 1989-92; Administrative assistant to Mayor Xavier Suarez, City of Miami, 1985-88; President, Gordeon Sloan Diaz-Balart, Boca Raton, Miami, **AW:** Named Legis. of Year, Florida Optometrics Association, 2000, Florida Association Realtors, 2000, Conservationist of Year, Biscayne Bay Foundation, 1999, Senator of Year, Florida Association Life Underwriters, 1998; recipient Top Pillar award, Florida International University, 2000, Lifetime Legis. Achievement award, Florida Association CC's, 2000, Legis. Distinction award, MADD, 2000, Golden Shovel award, Miami River Marine Grp., 2000, Claude Pepper Memorial award, United Homecare Services, 2000, Distinguished Leadership award, National Alliance Mentally Ill, 1997, Florida Police Benevolent Association, 1996, Government Recognition award,

American Association Poison Control Centers, 1996, Top Forty award, Florida Chamber of Commerce, 2000, 1996, Legis. Courage award, Labor Council Latin American Advancement, 1996, Furtherance of Justice award, Florida Attorneys Association, 1994, Leadership award, Florida Association State Troopers, 1996, 1993, Public Service award, American League Against Discrimination, 1992 **MEM:** Mem.: Spanish American League Against Discrimination, National Association Latino Elected Officials, Westchester Lions Club **H:** Reading, biking, diving **PA:** Republican

DICAPRIO, LEONARDO, T: Actor, Activist **I:** Media & Entertainment **DOB:** 11/11/1974 **PB:** Hollywood **SC:** CA/USA **PT:** George DiCaprio, Irmelin (Indenbirken) DiCaprio **CIV:** Founder, The Leonardo DiCaprio Charitable Foundation, 1998-Present **CW:** Actor, (Films) Critters III, 1991, This Boy's Life, 1993, What's Eating Gilbert Grape?, 1993, The Quick And The Dead, 1995, The Basketball Diaries, 1995, Total Eclipse, 1995, Romeo + Juliet, 1996, Marvin's Room, 1996, Titanic, 1997, The Man In The Iron Mask, 1998, Celebrity, 1998, The Beach, 2000, Dons Plum, 2001, Gangs Of New York, 2002, Catch Me If You Can, 2002, The Departed, 2006, Blood Diamond, 2006, Body Of Lies, 2008, Revolutionary Road, 2008, Shutter Island, 2010, Inception, 2010, J. Edgar, 2011, Django Unchained, 2012, The Great Gatsby, 2013, The Revenant, 2015, Before The Flood, 2016, Omniverse, 2018, (TV Series) Parenthood, 1990, Santa Barbara, 1990, Growing Pains, 1991-92, Greensburg, 2008, Saturday Night Live, 2014; Actor, Producer, (Films) The Aviator, 2004, The Wolf Of Wall Street, 2013; Producer, (Films) Orphan, 2009, Red Riding Hood, 2011, Out Of The Furnace, 2013, Runner, Runner, 2013, Delirium, 2016; Executive Producer, The Assassination Of Richard Nixon, 2004, (Films) The Ides Of March, 2011, (Documentaries) Cowspiracy: The Sustainability Secret, 2014; Writer, Narrator, (Documentary) The 11th Hour, 2007 **AW:** Golden Globe Award For Best Performance By An Actor In A Motion Picture - Drama, Critics' Choice Award For Best Actor, Screen Actors Guild Award For Outstanding Performance By A Male Actor In A Leading Role, BAFTA Award For Best Actor, Academy Award For Best Actor, The Revenant, 2016, Messenger of Peace, UN, 2014, Favorite Dramatic Movie Actor, People's Choice Awards, 2014, Golden Globe Award For Best Performance By An Actor In A Motion Picture - Comedy Or Musical, Critics' Choice Award For Best Actor In A Comedy, The Wolf of Wall Street, 2014, Spotlight Award (Career Collaboration with Martin Scorsese), National Board Review, 2013, National Board Review Award For Best Supporting Actor, Django Unchained, 2012, Teen Choice Award For Choice Movie Actor: Horror/Thriller, Shutter Island, 2010, International Green Award, Cinema for Peace, 2009, The 100 Most Powerful Celebrities, Forbes.com, 2008, The Most Influential People in the World, TIME Magazine, 2007, Golden Globe Award For Best Performance By An Actor In A Motion Picture - Drama, The Aviator, 2005, Platinum Award, Santa Barbara International Film Festival, 2005, Commander, Order of Arts & Letters, Government of France, 2005, The 50 Most Powerful People in Hollywood, Premiere Magazine, 2003-2006, Green Cross Millennium Award for Entertainment Industry Environmental, Global Green USA, 2003 **BA:** Artists Management Group, 9465 Wilshire Boulevard, Suite 519, Beverly Hills, CA, 90212

DIDION, JOAN, T: Writer **I:** Writing and Editing **DOB:** 12/05/1934 **PB:** Sacramento **SC:** CA/USA **ED:** Honorary LittD, Yale University, 2011; Honorary LittD, Harvard University, 2009; BA in English, University of California, Berkeley, 1956 **C:** Contributor, New York Review Of Books; Former Columnist, Esquire; Former Columnist, Life; Former Columnist, Saturday Evening Post; Associate Feature Editor, Vogue Magazine, 1956-1963 **CR:** Speaker in Field **CW:** Author, (Novels) Run, River, 1963, Play It As It Lays, 1970, A Book Of Common Prayer, 1977, Democracy, 1984, The Last Thing He Wanted, 1996, (Non-Fiction) Slouching Towards Bethlehem, 1968, The White Album, 1979, Salvador, 1983, Miami, 1987, After Henry, 1992, Political Fictions, 2001, Where I Was From, 2003, Fixed Ideas: America Since 9.11, 2003, The Year Of Magical Thinking, 2005, We Tell Ourselves Stories In Order To Live: Collected Nonfiction, 2006, Blue Nights, 2011, (Plays) The Year Of Magical Thinking, 2007; Co-Author, (With John Gregory Dunne) (Screenplays) The Panic In Needle Park, 1971, Play It As It Lays, 1972, A Star Is Born, 1976, True Confessions, 1981, Hills Like White Elephants, 1991, Up Close And Personal, 1996 **AW:** National Humanities Medal, 2013, Medal For Distinguished Contribution To American Letters, National Book Foundation, 2007, Evelyn F. Burkey Award For Contributions Bringing Honor And Dignity To Writers Everywhere, Writers Guild of America, 2007, Academy Of Achievement, 2006, Hubert Howe Bancroft Award, 2006, Golden Plate Award, 2006, National Book Award, The Year Of Magical Thinking, 2005, Gold Medal in Belle Lettres & Criticism, American Academy of Arts and Letters, 2005, George Polk Award, 2001, Columbia Journalism Award, 1999, Edward MacDowell Medal, 1996, Morton Dauwen Zabel Prize, American Academy of Arts and Letters, 1978, First Prize, Vogue's Prix De Paris, 1956 **MEM:** American Academy of Arts and Letters, Council on Foreign Relations, American Academy of Arts & Sciences **BA:** 8955 Beverly Boulevard, West Hollywood, CA, 90048

DIESEL, VIN, T: Actor **I:** Media & Entertainment **PB:** New York **SC:** NY/USA **PT:** Delora Vincent **ED:** Student, Hunter College **CW:** Actor, Director, Producer, Writer, (Films) Multi-Facial, 1994; Strays, 1997; Actor, Executive Producer, XXX, 2002, A Man Apart, 2003; Actor, Producer, The Chronicles Of Riddick, 2004; Actor, Producer, (Films) Fast & Furious 6, 2013, Riddick, 2013, Furious 7, 2015; Actor, (Films) Saving Private Ryan, 1998, The Iron Giant (Voice), 1999, Boiler Room, 2000, Pitch Black, 2000, The Fast And The Furious, 2001, Knockaround Guys, 2001, Be Cool, 2005, The Pacifier, 2005, Find Me Guilty, 2006, The Fast And The Furious: Tokyo Drift, 2006, Babylon A.D., 2008, Fast & Furious, 2009, Fast Five, 2011, Guardians Of The Galaxy (Voice), 2014, The Last Witch Hunter, 2015, Furious 7, Billy Lynn's Long Halftime Walk, 2016, XXX: Return Of Xander Cage, 2017, The Fate Of The Furious, 2017, Guardians Of The Galaxy Vol. 2, 2017, Avengers Infinity War, 2017, (TV Films) Into Pitch Black, 2000; Executive Producer, Hitman, 2007, Life Is A Dream, 2014; Producer, (Documentaries) A War Hero, 2012

DIGGINS, JESSICA, T: Cross Country Skier **I:** Athletics **PB:** Afton **SC:** MN/USA **AW:** One Gold World Championship Medal, Team Sprint, 2013, U23 World Championships, Individual Sprint, 2014, Two Silver World Championship Medals, Sprint, 10 Km Freestyle, 2015, 2017, One Bronze World Championship, Team Sprint, 2017, One Olympic Gold Medal, Team Sprint, 2018

DILLER, ELIZABETH E., T: Architect **I:** Architecture & Construction **SC:** Poland **ED:** BArch, Cooper Union School Architecture (1979) **C:** Partner, Diller & Scofidio (Now Diller Scofidio & Renfro), New York City, NY (1979) **CR:** Associate Professor, Architect Design, Princeton University, NJ (1990-Present) **CW:** Works include Institute of Contemporary Art, Boston, MA, Seagrams, NY, Museum of Art & Technology, NY, Blur Building, Media Pavillion for Swiss EXPO 2002, Designed Viewing Platform for Ground Zero, New York City, NY, Brasserie Restaurant, NY, Slither, Gifu, Japan, Loophole, Museum of Contemporary Art, Chicago, IL (1992), Apparatus Drawing, Museum of Modern Art, NY (1993), Case#00-17164, New Museum (1993), Dysfunction, Center d'Art Contemporian de Castres, France (1993), Desiring Eye, I' dentity and Difference, Triennale, Milan, Italy (1994), Pelts, Thaddeus Ropac Gallery, Paris, France (1997), Non-Place, San Francisco Museum of Modern Art (1997), Slow House, At the End of the Century: One Hundred Years of Architecture, Museum of Contemporary Art, LA (1998), The American Lawn: Surface of Everyday Life, Canadian Centre for Architecture, Montreal, Canada (1998), Public Faces/Private Places, Pusan International Arts Festival, Korea (1998), His/Her Bathroom, Thomas Healy Gallery, NY (1998), Dress Code, Landesmuseum, Linz, Austria (1998); Permanent Collections, Travelogues, International Arrivals Terminal 4, JFK Airport, NY, Installation, The Desiring Eye: Reviewing the Slow House, Gallery MA, Tokyo, Japan (1992), Master/Slave, Fondation Cartier, Paris, France, InterClone Hotel, Ataturk Airport for Istanbul Biennial (1997); Dance Collaborations with the Lyon Ballet Opera of France and Charlerol/Danses of Belgium Touring Exhibition EJM1: Man Walking at Ordinary Speed and EJM2: Inertia (1998); Web Project, Refresh, Dia Art Foundation; Video Installation Pageant, Johannesburg Biennial & Rotterdam Film Festival (1997); Permanent Installation, X,Y, Kobe, Japan (1997); Multi-media Work for Stage in Collaboration with Builders Association, Jet Lag (1998); Public Art Commission, Permanent Video Marques, Jump Cuts, United Artists Cineplex, San Jose, CA; Collaborative Dance Work with Charlerol/Danses, Moving Target; Collaborative Theater Work with Dumb Type and Hotel Pro Forma; Business Class, Copenhagen Cultural Capital; Interactive Video Installation, Indigestion, Barbican Art Gallery, London, England; Walter Phillips Gallery, Banff, Canada; Biennial Nagoya, Japan (1997); Electronic Project, Subtopia, Interstate Commerce Commission Gallery, Tokyo, Japan (1997), Several Others; Installations Commissioned by Museum of Modern Art, Whitney Museum, New Museum of Contemporary Art, Walker Art Center, MN, Cartier Foundation, Palais des Beauz-Arts Brussels, and Gallery Ma Tokyo, Japan; Works in Permanent Collections of Museum of Modern Art, Museum of Modern Art, San Francisco, Fond National d'Art Contemporain, Several FRACs, France, Musee de la Mode, Paris, France; Many Private Collections, Co-published with Ricardo Scofidio "Back to the Front: Tourisms of War," FRAC Basse-Normandie (1994), "Flesh: Architectural Probes," Princeton Architectural Press (1995), "Blur: The Making of Nothing," Abrams (2002) **AW:** Named One of the World's Most Influential People, TIME Magazine (2009); Named One of the 100 Most Influential Women in New York City Business, Crain's New York Business (2007); MacDermott Award for Creative Achievement, Massachusetts Institute of Technology; Brunner Prize in Architect, American Academy of Arts and Letters (2003); MacArthur Foundation Award (1999); Chrysler Award for Innovation in Design (1988-1989); Chicago Institute for Architecture and Urbanism Fellowship; Graham Foundation Fellowship (1998-1999); Named One of TIME's 100 Most Influential People, TIME Magazine (2018); Progressive Architecture Design Award, Blur Building; James Beard Foundation Award for Best New Restaurant Design, Brasserie Restaurant,

NY; Obie Award for Creative Achievement, Multimedia Work for Stage in Collaboration with Builders Association, Jet Lag (1998) **MEM:** Fellow, American Academy of Arts & Sciences **BA:** 601 W 26th St, New York, NY, 10001

DIMAS, PYRROS, I: Athletics **C:** Technical Director for USA Weightlifting, 2017 **AW:** 182 Pound Class Weightlifting Gold Medal, XXV Olympic Games, Barcelona, Spain, 1992

DIMON, JAMIE, T: JP Morgan Chase CEO **I:** Financial Services **DOB:** 03/13/1956 **PB:** NYC **PT:** Son of Theodore and Themis Dimon; **ED:** MBA, Harvard Business School, 1982; BA in Psychology & Economics, Tufts University, 1978 **C:** Chairman emeritus, JP Morgan Chase Bank, N.A., 2013-; Chairman, president, CEO, JPMorgan Chase & Co., New York City, 2006-; Chairman, JP Morgan Chase Bank, N.A., 2006-13; President, CEO, JPMorgan Chase & Co., New York City, 2005-06; President, COO, JPMorgan Chase & Co., New York City, 2004-05; Chairman, CEO, Bank One Corp., Chicago, 2000-04; President, Citigroup, Inc., 1998-2000; Chmn, co-CEO, Salomon Smith Barney Holdings Inc., 1998-2000; President, COO, The Travelers Group Inc, 1993-98; CFO, The Travelers Group Inc, 1988-95; President, Primerica Corp., New York City, 1990-93; Executive vice president, CFO, Primerica Corp., New York City, 1989-90; Senior vice president, CFO, Commercial Credit Co., Baltimore, 1986-88; Vice president, assistant to president, American Express Co., New York City, 1982-85 **CR:** Chairman The Clearing House Payments Co., 2007- board directors The Financial Services Roundtable, Catalyst Inc., The Federal Reserve Bank New York, 2007-, J.P. Morgan Chase & Co., 2000-, Yum! Brands, Inc., 1997-2004 **CIV:** Board directors, United Negro College Fund, Board directors, National Center Addiction & Substance Abuse, Member, Council Foreign Relations, Board directors, Mount Sinai Medical Center & Health Systems, Board directors, Economic Club Chicago, Board directors, Chicago Council on Global Affairs, Board directors, Partnership for New York City, Member trustees committee, Chicago Community Trust, Civic committee, Commercial Club Chicago, Trustee, New York University Medical Center, Trustee, University Chicago, **AW:** Named Executive of Year, University Rochester Simon Graduate School Business, 2012, Banker of Year, American Banker, 2009; named one of The 50 Most Influential People in Global Finance, Bloomberg Markets, 2011-13, The World's Most Powerful People, Forbes magazine, 2009-14, The Top 25 Market Movers, US News & World Report, 2009, The Global Elite, Newsweek magazine, 2008, The 25 Leaders Reshaping New York, Crain's New York magazine, 2008, Business People of Year, Fortune magazine, 2010, The 25 Most Powerful People in Business, 2007, The 100 Most Influential People in the World, TIME magazine, 2011, 2009, 2008, 2006; recipient Golden Plate award, Academy Achievement, 2006 **PA:** Democrat

DINARDO, DANIEL NICHOLAS, T: Cardinal **I:** Religious **DOB:** 05/23/1949 **PB:** Steubenville **SC:** OH/USA **PT:** Nicholas DiNardo, Jane (Green) DiNardo **ED:** BS in Technology, Pontifical Gregorian University, 1975; MPhil, Catholic University of America, 1969; BA, Catholic University of America, 1969; Licentiate in Patristics, Augustinianum; Licentiate of Theology, Pontifical Gregorian University **C:** Cardinal-Priest, Sant' Eusebio (Saint Eusebius), 2008-Present; Archbishop, Galveston-Houston, 2006-Present; Elevated To Cardinal, 2007; Co-Adjutor Archbishop, Galveston-Houston, 2004-2006; Bishop, Sioux City, IA, 1998-2005; Ordained, Sioux City, IA, 1997; Co-Adjutor Bishop,

Sioux City, IA, 1997-1998; Founding Pastor, Saint John And Saint Paul Church, Franklin Park, 1994; Co-Administrator, Madonna Del Castello Church, Swissvale, PA, 1991; Director, Villa Stritch Residence For American Priests Working For The Holy See, Rome, Italy, 1986-1989; Staff Member, Pontifical Congregation Of Bishops, Rome, Italy, 1984-1990; Assistant Chancellor, Pittsburgh, PA, 1981-1993; Part Time Professor, Spiritual Director To The Seminarians, Saint Paul's Seminary, 1981; Ordained Priest, Pittsburgh, PA, 1977; Parochial Vicar, Saint Pius X Church, Pittsburgh, PA; Assistant Secretary Education, Pittsburgh, PA **CR:** Ad Hoc Committee To Oversee The Use Of The Catechism, U.S. Conference Of Catholic Bishops; Advisor, National Association Of Pastoral Musicians; Board Trustee, Catholic University Of America; Board Member, National Catholic Partnership For Persons With Disabilities; Chair, U.S. Bishops' Committee On Pro-Life Activities, 2009-Present; Pontifical Council For Pastoral Care Of Migrants And Itinerant People, Pontifical Council For Culture, 2009-Present; Vice President, U.S. Conference of Catholic Bishops (USCCB), 2013-Present **AW:** Knight Grand Cross of the Order of Merit of the Italian Republic, 2008 **BA:** Archdiocese of Galveston Houston, 1700 San Jacinto Street, PO Box 907, Houston, TX, 77001-0907

DINGELL, DEBORAH, T: U.S. Representative from Michigan, former lobbyist, volunteer **I:** Government Administration/Government Relations/Government Services **ED:** Master in Liberal Studies, Georgetown University, 1998 **C:** Member, U.S. House of Representatives from Michigan's 12th District, 2015-, Member, Committee on Energy and Commerce; Former executive director global community relations and government relations, GM,; Lobbyist, GM, 1977 **CIV:** Co-founder, Children's Inn at National Institutes of Health, Bethesda, Maryland, Vice chairman, GM Foundation, Member executive committee, co-chair Breast Cancer Committee and the Government Relations Committee, Barbara Karmanos Cancer Center, Vice chair, Barbara Karmanos Cancer Center, Member, Dem. National Committee, Founding chair, National Women's Health Resource Center, Washington, **AW:** Named one of The 100 Most Powerful Women in DC, Washingtonian magazine, 2009 **BA:** 116 Cannon House Office Building, Washington, DC, 20515

DINKLAGE, PETER, T: Actor **I:** Media & Entertainment **DOB:** 06/11/1969 **PB:** Morristown **SC:** NJ/USA **PT:** Son of John Dinklage and Diane Dinklange; **ED:** Attended, Welsh School Music & Drama, Cardiff, Wales; Attended, Royal Academy Dramatic Arts, London; BA in Drama, Bennington College, Vermont, 1991 **CW:** Actor: (films) Living in Oblivion, 1995, Bullet, 1996, Safe Men, 1998, Pigeonholed, 1999, Never Again, 2001, Human Nature, 2001, 13 Moons, 2002, Just a Kiss, 2002, The Station Agent, 2003, Tiptoes, 2003, Elf, 2003, 89 Seconds at Alcázar, 2004, Jail Bait, 2004, Surviving Eden, 2004, The Baxter, 2005, Escape Artists, 2005, Lassie, 2005, Fortunes, 2005, The Limbo Room, 2006, Find Me Guilty, 2006, Little Fugitive, 2006, Penelope, 2006, Death at a Funeral, 2007, Ascension Day, 2007, Underdog, 2007, The Chronicles of Narnia: Prince Caspian, 2008, Saint John of Las Vegas, 2009, I Love You Too, 2010, The Last Rites of Ransom Pride, 2010, A Little Bit of Heaven, 2011, Ice Age: Continental Drift (voice), 2012, A Case of You, 2013, Low Down, 2014, X-Men: Days of Future Past, 2014, The Angriest Man in Brooklyn, 2014, Taxi, 2015, Pixels, 2015, The Boss, 2016, Angry Birds (voice), 2016, Rememory, 2017, Three Billboards Outside Ebbing, Missouri, 2017, Three Christs, 2017, I Think We're Alone Now,

2018, Avengers Infinity War, 2018; (TV series) I'm with Her, 2004, Threshold, 2005-06, Nip/Tuck, 2006, Game of Thrones, 2011-, SNL, 2013, Sesame Street, 2013, The David S Pumpkins Animated Halloween Special, 2017, My Dinner with Herve, 2018; (TV films) Testing Bob, 2005, Ultra, 2006; actor, producer (films) Pete Smalls Is Dead, 2010, actor, executive producer Knights of Badassdom, 2013 **AW:** Emmy Award for Outstanding Supporting Actor in a Drama Series, 2011, 2015, 2018; Golden Globe Award for Best Performance by an Actor in a Supporting Role in a Series, Mini-Series or Motion Picture Made for TV, 2012

DION, CELINE, T: Musician, Singer, Songwriter **I:** Media & Entertainment **DOB:** 03/30/1970 **PB:** Charlemagne, Quebec **SC:** Charlemagne Quebec Can. **PT:** Daughter of Adhémar Dion and Thérèse Tanguay; **ED:** Doctorate in Music (hon.), University Laval, Quebec City, 2008 **CIV:** Goodwill Ambassador, UN, 2010- **CW:** Singer: (albums) Unison, 1990 (Album of Year, 1990), Celine Dion, 1992, Colour of My Love, 1993 (Multi-Platinum, 1994), Premieres Anees, 1994, Dion Chante Plamondon, 1994, Des Mots Qui Sonnent, 1995, Live A Paris, 1996, Falling Into You, 1997 (Grammy award for Album of Year, Best Pop Album, 1997), C'est Pour Vivre, 1997, The Collection, 1982-88, 1997, Let's Talk About Love, 1997 (Billboard Music award for Best Album, 1998), S'il suffisait d'aimer, 1998, These are Special Times, 1998, All The Way, 1999, The French Album, 2001, Classique: A Love Collection, 2001, A New Day Has Come, 2002, One Heart, 2003, 1 Fille & 4 Types, 2003, Miracle, 2004, A New Day, 2004, On Ne Change Pas, 2005, Du Soleil au Coeur, 2006, D'Amour Francaise, 2006, D'Elles, 2007, En Amour, 2007, Ihre Schönsten Weihnachstlieder, 2007, Taking Chances, 2007, Sans attendre, 2012, Loved Me Back to Life, 2013, Encore un soir, 2016, (soundtracks) Real Love, 1979, Beauty & the Beast, 1991 (Grammy award for Best Pop Performance by a Duo or Group with Vocal, 1992, Best-selling Single, 1992, Academy award for Best Song, 1992), Sleepless in Seattle, 1993, Through the Fire, 1994, Titanic (single My Heart Will Go On), 1999 (Grammy award for Record of Year, 1999, Grammy award for Best Female Pop Vocal, 1999, Billboard Music award for Best Soundtrack Single, 1998), (shows) The Colosseum, Caesars Palace, Las Vegas, 2003-07, 2015-, Films, Muppet's Most Wanted, 2014; **AW:** Named one of The 100 Most Powerful Celebrities, Forbes Magazine, 2008; Recipient Icon Award, Billboard Music Awards, 2016, Companion of Order of Canada, Governor General of Canada, 2013, Légion d'honneur, France, 2008, Star, Hollywood Walk of Fame, 2004, Canada's Walk of Fame, 1999, Best-Selling Canadian Artist, World Music Awards, 2008, Legend award, 2007, Chopard Diamond award for Best-Selling Female Artist of All Time, 2004 **BA:** Special Artists Agency, 9465 Wilshire Boulevard, Beverly Hills, CA, 90212

DJOKOVIC, NOVAK, T: Professional Tennis Player **I:** Athletics **DOB:** 05/22/1987 **PB:** Belgrade **PT:** Son of Srdjan and Dijana Djokovic; **C:** Professional tennis player, ATP Tennis, 2003 **CW:** Author: Serve to Win: The 14-Day Gluten-Free Plan for Physical and Mental Excellence, 2013 **AW:** Named ATP Player of Year, 2011-12, ATP Most Improved Player, 2006; named one of The 100 Most Influential People in the World, TIME magazine, 2012; recipient Order of Serbian National Defense in America, 2011, Order of St. Sava, Patriarch Irinej of Serbia, 2011, ATP Player of the Year, 2014-15, 2017, ATP Most Improved Player, 2007, Arthur Ashe Humanitarian Award, 2012 **ACH:** Achievements include winning 30 career singles titles, ATP; winner, Amersfoort, 2006, Metz, 2006, Adelaide, 2007, Sony Ericsson Open, 2007, 2011, 2012, Estoril Open, 2007, Rogers Masters, 2007, BA-CA Tennis Trophy, 2007; BNP Paribas Open, Indian Wells, 2008, 2011, Italian Open, 2008, 2011, Masters Cup, 2008, Barclays ATP World Tour Finals London, 2008, Dubai Tennis Championships, 2009, 2010, 2011; Serbia Open, 2009, 2011, Mutua Madrid Open, 2011; winning Grand Slam singles events: Australian Open, 2008, 2011, 2012, 2013, 2015, 2016; Wimbledon, 2011, 2014, 2015, 2018; US Open, 2011, 2015, French Open, 2016;

DOERR, JOHN, T: Venture Capitalist at Kleiner Perkins **I:** Financial Services **DOB:** 06/29/1951 **PB:** St. Louis **SC:** MO/USA **ED:** MBA, Harvard Business School, 1976; MSEE in Electrical Engineering, Rice University, 1974; BS in Electrical Engineering, Rice University, 1973 **C:** Member,USA Economic Recovery Advisory Board,2009-17; Adv. Board Member, Generation Investment Management, Inc., 2007-; Founder, CEO, Silicon Compilers, 1981-; Partner, Kleiner Perkins Caulfield & Byers, Menlo Park, California, 1980-; Salesman, Intel Corp., 1974-80 **CR:** Member President's Economic Recovery Advisory Board, 2009-11 Board of Directors Zynga Inc., 2013-, iControl Networks Inc., 2008-, Amyris Biotechnologies Inc, 2006-, Zazzle.com, Inc., 2005-, Palm, Inc., 2003-05, Google Inc., 1999-, Move, Inc., 1998-2008, Homestore.com, 1998-, Handspring Inc., 1998-2003, Drugstore.com, 1998-2004, Amazon.com, 1996-2010, Netscape Communications Corp., 1994-, Intuit, 1990-2007, Sun Microsystems Inc., 1982-2006 **AW:** Named a Distinguished Alumnus, Rice University, 1997; Named One of America's Best Leaders, US News & World Report, 2009, The 50 Most Important People on the Web, PC World, 2007, The Forbes 400: Richest Americans, 2006-; Named to The California Hall of Fame, 2010, Fellow, American Academy of Arts and Sciences, 2009 **MEM:** Fellow: American Academy Arts & Sciences

DOGGETT, LLOYD, T: U.S. Representative from Texas **I:** Government Administration/Government Relations/Government Services **DOB:** 10/06/1946 **PB:** Austin **SC:** TX/USA **ED:** BBA in Business, University Texas, Austin, 1967; JD with honors, University Texas School Law, 1970 **CT:** Bar: Texas 1971, US District Court (western district) Texas 1972, US Court Appeals (5th cir.) 1972 **C:** Member, US Congress from 35th Texas District, 2013—; Member, US Congress from 25th Texas District, 2005—2013; Member, US Congress from 10th Texas District, 1995—2005; Justice, Texas Supreme Court, Austin, 1989-94; Partner, Doggett & Jacks, Austin, Texas, 1975-88; Member District 14, Texas State Senate, 1973-85 **CR:** Adjunct professor University Texas School Law, 1989—1994; chair Task Force on Judicial Ethics Texas Supreme Court, 1992—1994 **CIV:** Board directors Consumers Union US, 1976—1981, 1986—1989 **AW:** Named Business Advocate of Year, Texas Association Mex.-American Chamber of Commerce, 2006, Best Elected Official, Austin Chronicle, 2010; named an Outstanding State Senator, Common Cause, 1980, Outstanding Jurist in Texas, Mexico American Bar Association, 1993; named one of The Five Outstanding Young Texans, Texas Jaycees, 1977, The Best Legislators, Texas Monthly magazine, 1979, 1981; recipient James Madison award, Freedom of Information Foundation Texas, 1990, First Amendment award, National Society Professional Journalists, 1990, Environmental Champion award, Texas League Conservation Voters, 2006, Legis. Achievement award, American Association Retired Persons, 2008, Arthur B. DeWitty award for outstanding achievement in human rights, Austin chapter National Association for the Advancement of Colored People **MEM:** Mem.: Texas Consumer

Association (president 1973) **BA:** US House of Representatives, 201 Cannon HOB, Washington, DC, 20515

DOLAN, TIMOTHY MICHAEL CARDINAL, T: Cardinal, Archbishop **I:** Religious **DOB:** 02/06/1950 **PB:** Saint Louis **PT:** Son of Robert and Shirley Radcliffe Dolan. **ED:** Doctorate in American Church History, Catholic University America, 1985; BA in Philosophy, Cardinal Glennon College, 1972; STL, Pontifical University of Saint Thomas Aquinas (Angelicum) **C:** Cardinal-priest, of Nostra Signora di Guadalupe a Monte Mario (Our Lady of Guadalupe on Monte Mario), 2012-; Archbishop, of New York, 2009-; Elevated to cardinal, 2012; Apostolic administrator, of Green Bay, Wisconsin, 2007-08; Appointed apostolic administrator, of Green Bay, Wisconsin, 2007; Archbishop, of Milwaukee, 2002-09; Ordained, of Natchesium (Natchez), 2001; Appointed Titular Bishop, of Natchesium (Natchez), 2001; Rector, Pontifical North American College, Rome, 1994-2001; Vice rector, director of spiritual formation and professor of church history, Kenrick-Glennon Seminary, St. Louis, 1992-94; Secretary, Apostolic Nunciature, Washington, 1987-92; Associate pastor, Immacolata Parish, Richmond Heights, Missouri, 1976-79; Auxiliary bishop, of Saint Louis, 2001-02; Liaison for Archbishop John L. May, of Saint Louis, 1983-87; Ordained priest, of Saint Louis, 1976 **CR:** Member XIII Ordinary Council of the Secretariat General of the Synod of Bishops, Pontifical Council for Promoting New Evangelization, Congregation for the Oriental Churches, 2011-, Pontifical Council for Social Communications, 2011- president US Conference Catholic Bishops (USCCB), 2010-13 Apostolic Visitator to seminaries in Ireland, 2010 chairman Catholic Relief Services (CRS), 2007-10 faculty member department ecumenical theology Pontifical University of Saint Thomas Aquinas (Angelicum), 1994-2001 visiting professor church history Pontifical Gregorian University, Rome, 1994-2001 adjunct professor theology Saint Louis University **CW:** Author: Some Seed Fell on Good Ground-The Life of Edwin V. O'Hara, 1992 **AW:** Named one of The 100 Most Influential People in the World, TIME magazine, 2012; recipient Knight Grand Cross of the Order of Saint Maurice and Saint Lazarus, 2011

DOLE, BOB, I: Government Administration/Government Relations/Government Services **DOB:** 07/22/1923 **PB:** Russell **SC:** Kansas **PT:** Son of Doran R. and Bina Dole; **ED:** Doctor (hon.), University Kansas, 2012; LLD (hon.), Washburn University, Topeka, 1969; LLB, Washburn Municipal University, Topeka, 1952; AB, Washburn Municipal University, Topeka, 1952; Student, University Arizona, 1948-49; Student, University Kansas, 1941-43 **CT:** Bar: Kansas 1952 **C:** Special counsel, Alston & Bird LLP, Washington, 2003-; Of counsel, Verner, Liipfert, Bernhard, McPherson & Hand, 1997-2002; Chairman, Republican National Committee, 1971-73; Chairman, US Senate Finance Committee, 1981-85; Minority leader, 1987-95; Majority leader, 1995-96; Majority leader, 1985-87; US Senator from Kansas, 1969-96; Member, US Congress from 1st Kansas District, 1963-69; Member, US Congress from 6th Kansas District, 1961-63; Attorney, Russell County, 1953-61; Sole practice, Russell, Kansas, 1953-61; Member, Kansas House of Reps., 1951-53 **CR:** Republican Presidential candidate, 1996 Republican Vice-Presdl. candidate, 1976 co-chair President Commission on Care for Americans Returning Wounded Warriors, 2007- chairman International Commission on Missing Persons in the Former Yugoslavia, 1997-2001 member Martin Luther King Junior Federal Holiday Commission, 1984, National Commission

on Social Security Reform, 1983, Commission on Security & Cooperation in Europe, 1977, US National Commission for the UN Educational, Scientific, & Cultural Organization, 1973, 1970 advisor General Agreement of Tariff and Trades Ministerial Trade Conference, 1982, US Del. to Study the Arab Refugee Problem, 1967, President's Del. to Study the Food Crisis in India, 1966, US Del. to the UN Food & Agricultural Organization, 1979, 1977, 1975, 1974, 1968, 1965 **CIV:** Chairman, National WWII Memorial, 1997-2004 Chairman, Dole Foundation, **MIL:** With US Army, WW II **CW:** Author: Great Political Wit: Laughing (Almost) All the Way to the White House, 1998, Great Presidential Wits (...I Wish I Was in the Book): A Collection of Humorous Anecdotes and Quotations, 2001, One Soldier's Story: A Memoir, 2005 (New York Times Bestseller list, 2005); co-author (with George McGovern, Donald Messer): Ending Hunger Now: A Challenge to Persons of Faith, 2005; co-author: (with Elizabeth Dole Richard Norton Smith and Kerry Tymchuk) (autobiography) Unlimited Partners: Our American Story, 1996 **AW:** Decorated Bronze Star with oak cluster, Purple Heart (2); named one of The 50 Top Lobbyists, Washingtonian magazine, 2007; recipient Theodore Roosevelt award, NCAA, 1998, Presidential Medal of Freedom, The White House, 1997, Horatio Alger award, Horatio Alger Association Distinguished Ams., 1988 **MEM:** Mem.: DAV, VFW, 4-H Fair Association, Am. Legion, Kiwanis, Elks, Shriners, Masons, Kappa Sigma **PA:** Republican

DOLE, ELIZABETH HANFORD, T: Former U.S. Senator from North Carolina, Former U.S. Cabinet official **I:** Government Administration/Government Relations/Government Services **PB:** , **PT:** Daughter of John Van and Mary Ella (Cathey) Hanford; **MS:** Married **SPN:** Robert Joseph Dole, December 6, 1975; **CH:** Robin **ED:** BA in Political Sci., with honors, Duke University, 1958; Postgrad., Oxford University, England, 1959; MA in Education & Government, Harvard University, 1960; JD, Harvard Law School, 1965 **CT:** Bar: DC 1966 **C:** Chair, National Republican Senatorial Committee (NRSC), 2005—2007; Commissioner, Federal Trade Commission, Washington, DC, 1973-79; Deputy assistant to President, The White House, Washington, DC, 1971-73; Associate director legislative affairs, then executive director, Pres.'s Committee for Consumer Interests, Washington, DC, 1968-71; Private law practice, Washington, DC, 1967-68; Staff assistant to assistant secretary for education, US Department Health Education & Welfare (Department of Health), Washington, DC, 1966-67; US Senator from North Carolina, 2003—2009; President, American Red Cross, 1991-99; Secretary, US Department Labor, 1989-90; With, Robert Dole Presidential Campaign, 1987-88; Secretary, US Department Transportation, 1983-87; Assistant to President for public liaison, The White House, 1981-83; Director, Human Services Group, Office of Executive Branch Management, Office of Pres.-Elect, 1980; Chairman, Voters for Reagan-Bush, 1980 **CR:** Member nominating committee North Carolina Consumer Council, 1972; founder Elizabeth Dole Foundation, 2006 **CIV:** Trustee Duke University, 1974-88; member council Harvard Law School Associates, member visiting committee Harvard School Pub. Health, 1992-95; member board overseers Harvard University, 1989-95; hon. chair, Project RoundHouse, 2001. **CW:** Co-author (with Bob Dole Richard Norton Smith and Kerry Tymchuk): (autobiography) Unlimited Partners: Our American Story, 1996; author: Hearts Touched With Fire: My 500 Most Inspirational Quotes, 2006 **AW:** Recipient Arthur S. Flemming award U.S. Government, 1972, Humanitarian award National Commission Against Drunk Driving, 1988, Distinguished Alumni award Duke University, 1988, North Carolina award, 1991, Lifetime Achievement award (Breaking The Glass Ceiling) Women Executives in State Government, 1993, North Carolinian of the Year award North Carolina Press Association, 1993, Radcliffe medal, 1993, Leadership award League of Women Voters, 1994, Maxwell Finland award National Foundation Infectious Diseases, 1994, Distinguished Service award National Safety Council, 1989, Raoul Wallenberg award for Humanitarian Service, 1995, Christian Woman of Year award, 1996, S. Roger Horchow award for Greatest Public Service by a Private Citizen, 1999; named one of America's 200 Young Leaders, Time magazine, 1974, The World's 10 Most Admired Women, Gallup Poll, 1988, One of 10 Most Fascinating people 1996 Barbara Walter's Special, Most Inspiring Political Figure 1996 MSNBC, 3rd Most Admired Woman in American Good Housekeeping, 1996, 98, The Most Powerful Women in the World, Forbes magazine, 2005; selected for Safety and Health Hall of Fame International, 1993; inducted into National Women's Hall of Fame, 1995. **MEM:** Member Phi Beta Kappa, Pi Lambda Theta, Pi Sigma Alpha. **PA:** Republican

DOMINGO, PLACIDO, T: Opera Singer **I:** Media & Entertainment **DOB:** 01/21/1941 **PB:** Madrid **SC:** Spain **PT:** Placido Francisco Domingo Ferrer; Pepita Embil Echanáz; **ED:** Doctorate (hon.), Harvard University, 2011; Doctorate (hon.), Oxford University, England, 2003; Doctorate (hon.), Chopin Music Academy, Poland, 2003; Doctorate (hon.), Anáhuac University, Mexico, 2001; Doctorate (hon.), Washington College, Chestertown, Maryland, 2000; Doctorate (hon.), Georgetown University, 1992; Doctorate (hon.), New York University, 1990; Doctorate (hon.), Univ. Complutense de Madrid, 1989; Doctorate (hon.), Oklahoma City University, 1984; Doctorate (hon.), Philadelphia College Performing Arts, 1982; Doctorate (hon.), Royal No. College Music, England, 1982; Student, National Conservatory Music, Mexico City **C:** Eli and Edythe Broad general director, LA Opera, 2000-; Member, founder, The Three Tenors, 1990-2003; General director, Washington National Opera, 1994-2011 **CIV:** Founder, Operalia, The World Opera Competition, 1993- **CW:** Singer: (Operas) (star tenor with opera cos. including) La Scala, Covent Garden, Hamburg State Opera, Vienna State Opera, New York City Opera, San Francisco Opera, National Hebrew Opera in Tel-Aviv, (leading roles 185 opera including) Don Rodrigo, Ofello, Walkure, Tosca, Andrea Chenier, Don Carlo, Carmen, La Boheme, Errani, Parsifal, Idomeneo, Simon Boccanegra, Rigoletto, Pablo Neruda, Il Postino, Cyrano de Bergerac, Iphigenie en Tauried, (films) Traviata, 1983, Carmen, 1984, Otello, 1986, (made more than 100 recs. including 93 full-length opera) BMG (formerly RCA), DGG, Sony, Decca/London, Philips, Time Warner, (made more than 100 recs. including 97 full-length opera) EMI (Angel), made more than 50 videos, (performed in concert) PBS TV special (with Jose Carreras & Luciano Pavorotti) The Three Tenors, 1994, PBS TV special (with Kiri Te Kanawa, Carol Neblett, Renata Scotto, Teresa Stratas, and Shirley Verrett) Placido Domingo: My Favorite Roles, 2012, (albums) My Christmas, 2015; conductor numerous performances at major opera houses including: Metropolitan Opera, London's Covent Garden, Vienna State Opera, music dir.: Seville World's Fair; actor(voice): (films) Beverly Hills Chihuahua, 2008, The Book of Life, 2014; author: (books) My First Forty Years, 1983, Placido Domingo - Por Amor, 1999 **AW:** Decorated Real Orden de Isabel la Catolica, Premio Principe de Asturias, Gran Cruz de la Orden del Merito Civil Spain, Orden del Águila Azteca Mexico, Commander de la Legion d'Honneur, Commandeur

Arts et Lettres, and Grande Medaille de la Ville de Paris France, Hon. Knight Commander Order of Brit. Empire; named a Kennedy Center honoree, 2000; recipient Wolf Foundation Prize in the Arts, Israel, 2012, Birgit Nilsson prize, Birgit Nilsson Foundation, 2009, Presidential Medal of Freedom, The White House, 2002, 9 Grammy awards, 3 Latin Grammy awards **MEM:** Mem.: Royal Academy Music (hon.)

DONALD, AARON, T: Professional Football Player **I:** Athletics **DOB:** 05/23/1991 **PB:** Pittsburgh **SC:** PA/USA **ED:** University of Pittsburgh **C:** Los Angeles Rams, 2014- **AW:** Pro Bowl, 2014–2017, First-team All-Pro, 2015–2017, AP NFL Defensive Player of the Year, 2017, NFL Defensive Rookie of the Year, 2014, PFWA All-Rookie Team, 2014, ACC Defensive Player of the Year,2013, Bronko Nagurski Trophy, 2013, Chuck Bednarik Award, 2013, Lombardi Award, 2013, Outland Trophy, 2013, Unanimous All-American, 2013, First-team All-ACC, 2013, First-team All-Big East, 2012, Second-team All-Big East, 2011 **BA:** 29899 Agoura Road, Agoura Hills, CA, 91301

DONALD, BERNICE BOUIE, T: Federal Judge,- Legal Association Administrator **I:** Government Administration/Government Relations/Government Services **DOB:** 09/17/1951 **PB:** Desoto County **SC:** Mississippi **ED:** Student, National Judicial College, 1983-84; JD, University Memphis, 1979; BA in Sociology, University Memphis, 1974 **CT:** Bar: Tennessee 1979, US Federal Court 1979, US Supreme Court 1989 **C:** Judge, US Court Appeals (6th Cir.), Memphis, 2011-; Judge, US District Court (western district) Tennessee, Memphis, 1995-2011; Judge, US Bankruptcy Court (western district) Tennessee, Memphis, 1988-96; Judge, General Sessions Criminal Court of Shelby County, Tennessee, 1982-88; Staff attorney, Shelby County Public Defenders Office, 1980-82; Staff attorney, Memphis Area Legal Services, 1980; Manager, South Central Bell Telephone Co., 1975-80; Clerk, South Central Bell Telephone Co., 1971-75 **CR:** Member adv. committee on bankruptcy rules Judicial Conference, 1996-; faculty member Federal Judicial Center, 1991-; National Judicial College, 1992-; adjunct professor Shelby State Community College, 1980-84; Cecil C. Humphreys School of Law, 1985-88; judge in residence, Washington University, Missouri, 2014, American University School of Law, Washington, DC, 2014; lecturer, presenter in field **CIV:** Board directors Midtown Mental Health, 1990-92, 94-96 Memphis in May, 1994-97, Leadership Memphis, Inc., 1993-96, University Memphis Alumni Board, 1994-, Memphis Race Relations and Diversity Institute, 1994-, Federal Judicial Center, Stax Museum of American Soul, Stax Academy Charter School, former board directors numerous religious and civic organizations including Calvary St. Ministry, Memphis Literacy Council, YWCA; co-founder 4-Life **CW:** Featured in Essence magazine, Ebony magazine, Jet magazine, Memphis magazine, Dollars and Sense magazine, Black Enterprise magazine; board editor American Bar Journal, 2003-11 **AW:** Recipient Community Services award, National Conference Christians and Jews, 1986, Martin Luther King Community Service award, Young Careerist award, State of Tennessee Raleigh Bureau Professional Women, plaques and certs., William Brennan award, University Virginia, 2014; named Citizen of Year Excelsior Chapter of Eastern Star, Woman of Year Pentecostal Church of God in Christ **MEM:** Member American Bar Association (member standing committee on Gavel awards 1989-95, member adv. committee Central and Eastern European Law Initiative 1999-, member house of delegates 1993-95, 99-, chair, commission on racial and ethnic diversity in the profession,

1994-97, board governors 1999-, liason labor and employment law section 1999-, Law Libr. Congress 1999-, Appellate Judges Conference 1999-2000, Africa Legal Tech. Assistance Project 2000-, member legal opportunity scholarship committee 2000-, Mus.'s board directors 2000-, numerous judicial administration division committees, secretary 2008-11, Spirit of Excellence award, 2011 (also founder), American Bar Foundation (president 2012-), National Association Women Judges (treasurer 1986-87, secretary 1987-88, vice president 1988-89, president elect 1989-90, president 1990-91), American Judges Association, National Center State Courts, National Bar Association (co-chair, program committee judicial council 2011-14, William H. Hastie award, 2013), Tennessee Bar Association (board directors 1997-98), Memphis County Bar Association, Shelby County Bar Association, American Trial Lawyers Association, Association of Women Attorneys (president 1991, board directors), National Conference Bankruptcy Judges (board directors 1993-96), National Conference of Women's Bar Association (board member), National Conference of Special Court Judges (secretary), Leadership Memphis (president 1987, board directors), International Women's Forum, Memphis Bar Association (board directors 1993), American Judicature Society (board directors, 2013-), Zeta Phi Beta (Alpha Eta Zeta chapter). **H:** Reading, crossword puzzles, music, bicycling, walking **BA:** 100 East Fifth Street, Cincinnati, OH, 45202

DONNELLY, JOE, T: U.S. Senator from Indiana **I:** Government Administration/Government Relations/Government Services **DOB:** 09/29/1955 **PB:** Massapequa **SC:** NY/USA **ED:** JD, University Notre Dame Law School, 1981; BA in Government, University Notre Dame, 1977 **C:** Member, US Senate Special Committee on Aging, 2013-; Member, US Senate Armed Services Committee, 2013-; Member, US Senate Agricultural, Nutrition & Forestry Committee, 2013-; US Senator from Ind., 2013-; Owner, Marketing Solutions, Mishawaka, Ind., 1996-; Member, US House Veterans' Affairs Committee, 2011-13; Member, US House Agricultural Committee, 2007-09; Member, US House Financial Services Committee, 2007-13; Member, US Congress from 2nd Ind. district, 2007-13; Attorney, Nemeth, Masters & Feeney Law Firm, 1981-96 **CR:** Member Ind. State Election Board, 1988-89 **CIV:** Chairman Bishop's Appeal Campaign, St. Anthony de Padua Parish, 1994-96 Member, St. Anthony de Padua Parish, President, Mishawaka Marian High School Board Education, 2000-01 Member, Mishawaka Marian High School Board Education, 1997-2001 **MEM:** Mem.: American Bar Association, Ind. State Bar Association **PA:** Democrat **BA:** Office of Joe Donnelly, 720 Hart Senate Office Building, Washington, DC, 205010

DONNELLY, SCOTT CHRISTOPHER, T: Manufacturing Executive **I:** Manufacturing **ED:** BEE, University of Colorado, 1984 **C:** Chairman, president, CEO, Textron, Inc., Providence, 2010-; President, CEO, Textron, Inc., Providence, 2009-10; President, COO, Textron, Inc., Providence, 2009; Executive vice president, COO, Textron, Inc., Providence, 2008-09; President, CEO, General Electric Aviation, 2005-08; Senior vice president, director, GE Global Research, Schenectady, New York, 2000-05; Vice president global tech. system, GE Medical Systems, 1997-2000; General manager, GE Industrial Systems Tech., 1995-97; With, GE Aerospace, Syracuse, New York, 1989-95 **CR:** Board directors Textron Inc., 2009- **CIV:** Board director, United Way Greater Cincinnati, Member, NIST Visiting Committee on Advanced Tech., Member engineering adv. committee, Center for Innovation in Minimally

Invasive Therapy, Massachusetts General Hospital, Member engineering adv. committee, Cornell University, Member engineering adv. committee, University of Colorado, Trustee, Siena College

DONOVAN, DANIEL, T: U.S. Representative from New York **I:** Government Administration/Government Relations/Government Services **DOB:** 11/06/1956 **PB:** Staten Island **SC:** NY/USA **PT:** Daniel Michael Donovan; Katherine Bolewicz Donovan **ED:** J.D., Fordham University, 1988,; B.A., St. John's University, 1978 **C:** Member, U.S. Representative from New York's 11th District, 2015-,; Member, Committee on Foreign Affairs,; Member, Committee on Homeland Security,; District Attorney, Richmond County, NY, 2003-2015,; President, Staten Island Deputy Borough, 2002-2003,; Staff, Staten Island Borough President Guy V. Molinari, 1996-2002,; Assistant District Attorney, Manhattan, 1989-1996 **BA:** 1541 Longworth HOB, Washington, DC, 20515

DOOCY, STEVE, T: Author and Television Personality **I:** Writing and Editing **PB:** Algona **SC:** IA/USA **ED:** BJ, University of Kansas **C:** All American New Year, 2004; Fox and Friends, 1998 **CW:** Author, (Books) The Mr. and Mrs. Happy Handbook, 2007, Tales from the Dad Side, 2008

DORSEY, JACK, T: Internet Company Executive, Software Architect **I:** Business Management/Business Services **DOB:** 11/19/1976 **PB:** St. Louis **PT:** Son of Tim and Marcia (Smith) Dorsey. **ED:** Attended, University Calif.-Berkeley; Attended, New York University; Attended, University Mo.-Rolla, 1995-98 **C:** Co-founder, CEO, Square, Inc., San Francisco, 2009-; CEO, Twitter, Inc., San Francisco, 2015-; Executive chairman, Twitter, Inc., San Francisco, 2011-; Non-exec. chairman, Twitter, Inc., San Francisco, 2008-11; CEO, Twitter, Inc., San Francisco, 2007-08; Co-founder, Twitter, Inc., San Francisco, 2007; Creator, Twitter.com, San Francisco, 2006; Co-founder, Obvious Corp. (spun off Twitter, Inc.), 2006; With, Odeo, 2006; Owner of co. to dispatch couriers, taxis and emergency services from the web, California, 2000; Worked with dispatch co., Manhattan, New York, 1999-2000 **CR:** Member advisory board Ustream.tv, 2009- board directors The Walt Disney Co., 2013-, BUILD, 2011-, Square, Inc., 2009-, Twitter, Inc., 2007- **AW:** Named Innovator of Year, American Banker, 2012; named one of The 40 Under 40, Fortune magazine, 2011-14, Technology's Best & Brightest Young Entrepreneurs, BusinessWeek magazine, The 100 Most Influential People in the World, TIME magazine, 2009; named to TR35, an outstanding innovator under the age of 35, Massachusetts Institute of Technology Tech. Rev.; recipient Innovator of the Year award, The Wall St. Journal, 2012

DOUDNA, JENNIFER A., I: Education/Educational Services **ED:** PhD in Biochemistry, Harvard University, 1989; BA in Chemistry, Pomona College, Claremont, California, 1985 **C:** Professor biochemistry and molecular biology, University California, Berkeley, 2003-; Henry Ford II professor molecular biophysics and biochemistry, Yale University, New Haven, 1999-2002; Assistant, then associate professor, Yale University, New Haven, 1994-98; Postdoc. research fellow biomedical sci., University Colorado, 1991-94; Postdoc. research fellow molecular biology, Massachusetts General Hosp./Harvard Medical School, Boston, 1989-91 **CR:** Faculty scientist, physical biosciences division Lawerence Berkeley National Laboratory, 2003- R.B. Woodward visiting professor Harvard University, 2000-01 investigator Howard Hughes Medical Institute, 1997- **CIV:** Board trustees, Pomona College, 2001- **CW:** Contributor articles

to professional journals **AW:** Recipient Eli Lilly award in biological chemistry, American Chemical Society, 2001, Alan T. Waterman award, National Science Foundation, 2000, David & Lucile Packard Foundation Fellow award, 1996, Beckman Young Investigator award, Arnold & Mabel Beckman Foundation, 1996, Johnson Foundation prize for innovative research, 1996, Searle Scholar award, 1996, Lucille P. Markey Scholar award in biomedical sci., 1991, National Research Service award in biomedical sci., 1986 **MEM:** Fellow: Am. Academy Arts & Scis.; mem.: National Academy of Sciences (Award for initiatives in research 1999), Institute Medicine **ACH:** Achievements include research in the molecular structures of RNA molecules as the basis for understanding their biological function; research in understanding how RNA molecules in cells and viruses control gene expression by regulating the synthesis and localization of proteins; first to discover how the structure of a special type of RNA, called a ribozyme, enables it to catalyze chemical reactions inside a cell

DOUGLAS, ALEXANDER, T: CEO **I:** Business Management/Business Services **CN:** Staples **ED:** University of Virginia **C:** CEO, Staples, 2018-; Senior Vice President/Global CCO, Coca Cola, 2013-18 **BA:** 500 Staples Drive, Framingham, MA, 01702

DOUGLAS, MICHAEL, T: Actor **I:** Media & Entertainment **DOB:** 09/25/1944 **PB:** New Brunswick **SC:** NJ/USA **ED:** BA, University of California, Santa Barbara, 1967; Honorary LittD, St. Andrew's University, Scotland, 2006 **CW:** Actor, (Films) Cast A Giant Shadow, 1966, Hail Hero, 1969, Adam At 6 A.M., 1970, Summertree, 1971, Napoleon And Samantha, 1972, Coma, 1978, Running, 1979, It's My Turn, 1981, The Star Chamber, 1983, A Chorus Line, 1985, Fatal Attraction, 1987, Wall Street, 1987, Black Rain, 1989, The War Of The Roses, 1989, Shining Through, 1992, Basic Instinct, 1992, Falling Down, 1993, Disclosure, 1994, The American President, 1995, The Ghost And The Darkness, 1996, A Song For David, 1996, The Game, 1997, A Perfect Murder, 1998, Wonder Boys, 1999, Still Life, 1999, Traffic, 1999, Don't Say A Word, 2001, You, Me And Dupree, 2006, King Of California, 2007, Ghosts Of Girlfriends Past, 2009, Solitary Man, 2009, Beyond A Reasonable Doubt, 2009, Wall Street: Money Never Sleeps, 2010, Haywire, 2011, Last Vegas, 2013, And So It Goes, 2014, Ant-Man, 2015, Unlocked, 2017, Flatliners, 2017, We Have Always Lived In The Castle, 2017, Ant-Man and The Wasp, 2018, (TV Series) Streets Of San Francisco, 1972—1976, (TV Films) Behind The Candelabra, 2013; Actor, Producer, (Films) The China Syndrome, 1979, Romancing The Stone, 1984, Jewel Of The Nile, 1985, The Ghost And The Darkness, 1996, One Night At McCool's, 2001, It Runs In The Family, 2003, The In-Laws, 2003, The Sentinel, 2006, Beyond The Reach, 2014; Producer, (Films) One Flew Over The Cuckoo's Nest, 1975, Flatliners, 1990, Made In America, 1993, The Rainmaker, 1997, Godspeed, Lawrence Mann, 2004 **AW:** Genesis Award, Genesis Prize Foundation, 2015, Golden Globe Award For Best Performance By An Actor In A Mini-Series Or Motion Picture Made For TV, Screen Actors Guild Award For Outstanding Performance By A Male Actor In A TV Movie Or Miniseries, Behind the Candelabra, 2014, Emmy Award For Outstanding Lead Actor In A Miniseries Or Movie, Behind the Candelabra, 2013, New Jersey Hall of Fame, 2012, David O. Selznick Achievement Award, Producers Guild of America, 2009, American Film Institute, 2009, Lifetime Achievement Award, Savannah Film Festival, 2007, Career Achievement Award, National Board Review, 2007, Cecil B. DeMille Award, Hollywood Foreign Press Association, 2004, Academy Award For Best Actor In A Leading

Role, Golden Globe Award For Best Performance By An Actor In A Motion Picture - Drama, 1987, National Board Review Award For Best Actor, Wall Street, 1987, BAFTA Award For Best Film, One Flew Over the Cuckoo's Nest, 1977, Academy Award For Best Picture, Golden Globe Award For Best Motion Picture - Drama, One Flew Over the Cuckoo's Nest, 1975 **BA:** 15030 Ventura Boulevard, #710, Sherman Oaks, CA, 91403

DOWNES, GEOFF, T: Songwriter, Musician **I:** Media & Entertainment **PB:** Stockport **SC:** England **CW:** (Solo Album) The Light Program, 1987, Vox Humana, 1992, Evolution,1996, The World Service, 2000, Shadows & Reflections, 2003, Elecctronica, 2010 (With Asia) Asia, 1982, Alpha, 1983, Astra, 1985, Then and Now, 1990, Aqua, 1992, Aria, 1994, Arena, 1996, Rare, 1999, Aura, 2000, Silent Nation, 2004, Phoenix, 2008, Omega, 2010, XXX, 2012, Gravitas, 2014 (With Yes) Drama, 1980, Fly From Here, 2011, Heaven and Earth, 2014 (With the Buggles) The Age of Plastic ,1980, Adventures in Modern Recording, 1981 **AW:** Rock and Roll Hall of Fame, 2017

DOWNEY, ROBERT JR., T: Actor **I:** Media & Entertainment **DOB:** 04/04/1965 **PB:** NYC **PT:** Son of Robert Downey and Elsie Ford; **C:** Co-founder production co., Team Downey, 2010 **CW:** Actor: (films) Pound, 1970, Greaser's Palace, 1972, Up the Academy, 1980, Baby It's You, 1983, Firstborn, 1984, Deadwait, 1985, To Live and Die in LA, 1985, Tuff Turf, 1985, Weird Science, 1985, America, 1986, Back to School, 1986, Less Than Zero, 1987, The Pick-Up Artist, 1987, Johnny Be Good, 1988, Rented Lips, 1988, Nineteen Sixty-Nine, 1988, True Believer, 1989, Chances Are, 1989, That's Adequate, 1990, Air America, 1990, Too Much Sun, 1991, Soapdish, 1991, Chaplin, 1992, Heart and Souls, 1993, Short Cuts, 1993, Natural Born Killers, 1994, Only You, 1994, Restoration, 1994, Hail Caesar, 1994, Richard III, 1995, Home for the Holidays, 1995, Danger Zone, 1996, One Night Stand, 1997, Hugo Pool, 1997, Two Girls and a Guy, 1997, The Gingerbread Man, 1998, US Marshals, 1998, In Dreams, 1999, Friends & Lovers, 1999, Bowfinger, 1999, Black and White, 1999, Wonder Boys, 2000, Auto Motives, 2000, Lethargy, 2002, The Singing Detective, 2003, Whatever We Do, 2003, Gothika, 2003, Eros, 2004, Game 6, 2005, Kiss, Kiss, Bang, Bang, 2005, Good Night and Good Luck, 2005, The Shaggy Dog, 2006, A Scanner Darkly, 2006, Fur: An Imaginary Portrait of Diane Arbus, 2006, Zodiac, 2007, Lucky You, 2007, Charlie Bartlett, 2007, Iron Man, 2008, Tropic Thunder, 2008, The Soloist, 2009, Sherlock Holmes, 2009 (Best Performance by an Actor in a Motion Picture-Comedy or Musical, Golden Globe award, Hollywood Foreign Press Association, 2010), Iron Man 2, 2010, Due Date, 2010, Sherlock Holmes: A Game of Shadows, 2011, The Avengers, 2012, Iron Man 3, 2013, Chef, 2014, Avengers: Age of Ultron, 2015, Captain America: Civil War, 2016, The Nice Guys, 2016, Spider Man Homecoming, 2017, Avengers Infinity War, 2018, All Star Weekend, 2018, The Voyage of Dr Dolittle, 2019,Infinity War 2 2019; (TV series) Saturday Night Live, 1985-86, Ally McBeal, 2000-01; (TV miniseries) Mussolini: The Untold Story, 1985; Ally McBeal 2000-02, Family Guy, 2005 (TV films) Mr. Willowby's Christmas Tree, 1995; (plays) American Passion, 1983, Alms for the Middle Class, 1983, Fraternity, 1984; actor, writer (documentaries) The Last Party, 1993, actor, co-prodr. (films) A Guide to Recognizing Your Saints, 2006, actor, executive producer The Judge, 2014; singer: (albums) The Futurist, 2004; executive prodr.: (films) Playing It Forward: Imagine Dragons, 2015 **AW:** Named Favorite Dramatic Movie Actor, People's Choice Awards, 2015, Favorite Action Movie

Star, 2014, Favorite Movie Actor, 2015, 2013; named one of Forbes' List of Hollywood's Highest-Paid Actors (#1), 2013, The 10 People Who Mattered, Newsweek, 2008, The 100 Most Influential People in the World, TIME magazine, 2008; recipient Generation award, MTV Movie Awards, 2015, American Cinematheque award, 2011

DOYLE, MICHAEL F., **T:** U.S. Representative from Pennsylvania **I:** Government Administration/ Government Relations/Government Services **DOB:** 08/05/1953 **SC:** Swissvale **PT:** Michael Doyle; Rosemarie (Fusco) Doyle **ED:** BS in Community Development, Pennsylvania State University (1975) **C:** Member, U.S. Congress from the 14th Pennsylvania District (2003-Present); Member, U.S. Congress from the 8th Pennsylvania District (1995-2003); Co-Founder, Agent, Eastgate Insurance Agency, Pittsburgh, PA (1983-1994); Chief of Staff to Senator Frank Pecora, Harrisburg, PA (1979-1994); Executive Director, Turtle Creek Valley Citizens Union, Pennsylvania (1977-1979); Member, Committee on Energy and Commerce **CR:** Member, Swissvale Borough Council (1977-1981) **MEM:** National Democratic Club; Italian Sons and Daughters of America; Ancient Order of Hibernians; Lions **H:** Golf; Italian cooking; Piano **PA:** Democrat

DREYFUSS, RICHARD, **T:** Actor **I:** Media & Entertainment **DOB:** 10/29/1947 **PB:** New York **SC:** NY/ USA **ED:** Coursework, San Fernando Valley State College **CIV:** Alternate Military Duty, Los Angeles County General Hospital (1969-1971); Participant, Civil Rights Marches; Lobbyist for Amnesty Bills **CW:** Actor, "Book Club" (2018); Actor, "The Last Laugh" (2018); Actor, "Shots Fired" (2017); Actor, "Madoff" (2016); Actor, "Madoff" (2016); Actor, "Zipper" (2015); Actor, "Your Family or Mine" (2015); Actor, "Your Family or Mine" (2015); Actor, "Very Good Girls" (2013); Actor, "Paranoia" (2013); Actor, "Squatters" (2013); Actor, "Cas & Dylan" (2013); Actor, "Coma" (2012); Actor, "The Big Valley" (2011); Actor, "Parenthood" (2011); Actor, "Weeds" (2010); Actor, "Piranha 3D" (2010); Actor, "Red" (2010); Actor, "The Lightkeepers" (2009); Actor, "My Life in Ruins" (2008); Actor, "W." (2008); Actor, "Prophesy and Honor" (2007); Actor, "Prophesy and Honor" (2007); Actor, "Poseidon" (2006); Actor, "Coast to Coast" (2004); Actor, "Silver City" (2004); Actor, "Sly Fox" (2004); Actor, "Copshop" (2004); Actor, "The Producers" (2004); Actor, "The Producers" (2004); Actor, Producer, "The Education of Max Bickford" (2001-2002); Actor, "Who Is Cletis Tout?" (2001); Actor, "The Day Reagan Was Shot" (2001); Voice Actor, "Rudolph the Red-Nosed Reindeer and the Island of Misfit Toys" (2001); Actor, "The Crew" (2000); Actor, "Fail Safe" (2000); Actor, "The Old Man Who Read Love Stories" (2000); Actor, "Lansky" (1999); Actor, "Krippendorf's Tribe" (1998); Actor, "A Fine and Private Place" (1998); Actor, "Oliver Twist" (1997); Actor, "Night Falls on Manhattan" (1997); Voice Actor, "The Call of the Wild: Dog of the Yukon" (1997); Voice Actor, "James and the Giant Peach" (1996); Actor, "Mad Dog Time" (1996); Actor, "The American President" (1995); Actor, "Past Perfect" (1995); Co-Author, "The Two Georges" (1995); Actor, "Mr. Holland's Opus" (1995); Actor, "The Last Word" (1995); Actor, "Silent Fall" (1994); Executive Producer, "Quiz Show" (1994); Actor, "Lost in Yonkers" (1993); Actor, "Another Stakeout" (1993); Actor, "Death and the Maiden" (1992); Host, "The Class of the 20th Century" (1991); Actor, Producer, "Prisoner of Honor" (1991); Actor, "What About Bob?" (1991); Actor, Producer, "Once Around" (1991); Actor, "Rosencrantz and Guildenstern Are Dead" (1991); Actor, "Postcards from the Edge" (1990); Actor, "Let It Ride" (1989); Actor, "Always"

(1989); Actor, "Moon Over Parador" (1988); Actor, "Tin Men" (1987); Actor, "Stakeout" (1987); Actor, "Nuts" (1987); Actor, "Stand By Me" (1986); Actor, "Down and Out in Beverly Hills" (1986); Actor, "The Buddy System" (1984); Actor, "Total Abandon" (1983); Actor, "Total Abandon" (1983); Actor, "Whose Life Is It Anyway?" (1981); Actor, "The Competition" (1980); Actor, "Othello" (1979); Actor, "The Big Fix" (1978); Actor, Producer, "The Big Fix" (1978); Actor, "Julius Caesar" (1978); Actor, "The Goodbye Girl" (1977); Actor, "Close Encounters of the Third Kind" (1977); Actor, "Victory at Entebbe" (1976); Actor, "Jaws" (1975); Actor, "Inserts" (1975); Actor, "The Apprenticeship of Duddy Kravitz" (1974); Actor, "The Second Coming of Suzanne" (1974); Actor, "American Graffiti" (1973); Actor, "Dillinger" (1973); Actor, "A Touch of Grace" (1973); Actor, The New Dick Van Dyke Show (1973); Actor, "The Mod Squad" (1973); Actor, "Gunsmoke" (1973); Actor, "Catch-22" (1973); Actor, "Two for the Money" (1972); Actor, "Shadow of a Gunman" (1972); Actor, "Untold Damage" (1971); Actor, "The Young Lawyers" (1971); Actor, "The Bold Ones: The New Doctors" (1970); Actor, "Room 222" (1970); Actor, "Hello Down There" (1969); Actor, "The Ghost & Mrs. Muir" (1969); Actor, "The New People" (1969); Actor, "The Young Runaways" (1968); Actor, "Judd for the Defense" (1968); Actor, "Felony Squad" (1968); Actor, "The Graduate" (1967); Actor, "Hey, Landlord" (1967); Actor, "Occasional Wife" (1967); Actor, "Valley of the Dolls" (1967); Actor, "The Big Valley" (1967); Actor, "Please Don't Eat the Daisies" (1967); Actor, "That Girl" (1967); Actor, "The Second Hundred Years" (1967); Actor, "Bewitched" (1966); Actor, "Gidget" (1966); Actor, "Ben Casey" (1965); Actor, "Karen" (1964); Director, Writer, "Present Tense" **AW:** Recipient, Golden Globe Award for Best Actor in a Motion Picture - Comedy or Musical (1978); Recipient, Academy Award for Best Actor in a Leading Role (1977) **MEM:** American Federation of TV and Radio Artists; American Civil Liberties Union; Equity Association; Screen Actors Guild **BA:** Agency for the Performing Arts N.Y., 135 West 50th Street, 17th Floor, New York, NY, 10020

DRONEY, CHRISTOPHER FITZGERALD, **T:** Federal Judge **I:** Law and Legal Services **DOB:** 06/22/1954 **PB:** Hartford **SC:** Connecticut **PT:** Married Elizabeth Kelly, October 13, 1979. **ED:** JD, University Connecticut School Law, 1979; BA, College Holy Cross, 1976 **C:** Judge, US Court Appeals (2nd Cir.), 2011-; Judge, US District Court Connecticut, Hartford, Connecticut, 1997-2011; Mayor, City of West Hartford, 1985-89; Deputy mayor, City of West Hartford, 1983-85; US attorney District Connecticut, US Department Justice, New Haven, 1993-97; Partner, Reid & Riege PC, Hartford, Connecticut, 1983-93 **CIV:** member US Attorney General's Advisory Committee, 1996-97. **CW:** Notes and comments editor Connecticut Law Rev., 1978-79. **BA:** 40 Foley Square, New York, NY, 10007

DRUDGE, MATT, **I:** Media & Entertainment **DOB:** 10/27/1967 **PT:** Robert Drudge **C:** Host, Radio Show, Premiere Radio Networks, Inc. (2001-Present); Founder, Editor, The Drudge Report Website (1995-Present); Host, Radio Show, ABC Network (1999-2000); Host, TV Show, "Drudge" (1998-1999); Gift Shop Manager, CBS-TV, LA **CW:** Author, "Drudge Manifesto" (2000) **AW:** Named One of the Top 25 Web Celebs, Forbes Magazine (2007, 2006); Named One of the 100 Most Influential People, TIME Magazine (2006) **ACH:** Achievements include Drudge Report listing as #2 on the top 10 web moments that changed the world at the 1998 Webby awards for news break of the Monica Lewinsky scandel

DUCEY, DOUG, **T:** Governor of Arizona **I:** Government Administration/Government Relations/ Government Services **DOB:** 04/09/1964 **PB:** Toledo **ED:** BS in Fin., Arizona State University, 1986 **C:** Governor, State of Arizona, 2015-; State treasurer, State of Arizona, 2011-15; CEO, Cold Stone Creamery,; With, Procter & Gamble,; With, Hensley & Co., **CR:** Past president Greater Phoenix Economic Club, Young Entrepreneur's Organization (Arizona Chapter) member State Land Election Board surveyor general chairman State Loan Commission, State Board Investment, Arizona **AW:** Named Father of Year, Father's Day Council, American Diabetes Association, 2009, Entrepreneurial Fellow, Eller College of Management , University Arizona, 2006; named to W.P. Carey School of Business Hall of Fame, Arizona State University, 2004; recipient Tom and Madena Stewart Lifetime Compassion award, Make-A-Wish Foundation Arizona Chapter, 2012, Golden Chain award, Mult-Unit Foodservice Operators, Spirit of Philanthropy award, Association Fundraising Profls. **PA:** Republican

DUDAMEL, GUSTAVO, **T:** Director of the Los Angeles Philharmonic **I:** Fine Art **DOB:** 01/26/1981 **PB:** Barquisimeto **ED:** Studied conducting with Rodolfo Saglimbeni, José Antonio Abreu; Student, L.American Violin Academy; Student, Jacinto Lara Conservatory **C:** Director of the Los Angeles Philharmonice, 2011-; Principal conductor, Gothenburg Symphony Orchestra, Sweden, 2007-; Music director, LA Philharmonic Orchestra, 2009-; Music director, Simón Bolívar Symphony Orchestra, Venezuela, 1999-; Guest conductor, Chicago Symphony Orchestra, 2007; Music director, Amadeus Chamber Orchestra, Venezuela, 1996-99 **CR:** Guest conductor Vienna Philharmonic Orchestra, San Francisco Symphony, Royal Concertgebouw Orchestra, City of Birmingham Symphony Orchestra, Dresden Staatskapelle, Royal Liverpool Philharmonic signed to Deutsche Grammophon, 2006- **CW:** Recordings include Beethoven: Symphonies Nos. 5 & 7, 2006, Birthday Concert for Pope Benedict XVI, 2007, Brahms Symphony No. 4, 2011 (Best Orchestral Performance, Grammy Awards, 2012) **AW:** Named Gramophone Artist of Year, 2011; named one of The World's Most Influential People, TIME magazine, 2009, 12 People to Watch, Newsweek magazine, 2008; recipient City of Toronto Glenn Gould Protégé prize, 2009, Echo award for New Artist of Year, 2007, Premio de la Latinidad, Union Latina, 2007, Pegasus prize, Spoleto Festival, 2006, Gustav Mahler Conducting prize, Germany, 2004,Leonard Bernstein Lifetime Achievement Award for the Elevation of Music in Society, Longy School, 2014

DUFFIELD, DAVID A., **T:** Co-CEO of Workday Inc **I:** Business Management/Business Services **DOB:** 09/21/1940 **PB:** Shaker Heights, OH **ED:** MBA, Cornell University, 1964; BS in Electrical Engineering, Cornell University, 1962 **C:** Co-founder, Workday, Incline Village, Nevada, 2005-; CEO, PeopleSoft Inc., Pleasanton, California, 2004; CEO, PeopleSoft Inc., Pleasanton, California, 1987-99; President, PeopleSoft Inc., Pleasanton, California, 1987-99; Founder, Chairman, PeopleSoft Inc., Pleasanton, California, 1987-2004; Founder, Chairman, Integral Systems Inc., Walnut Creek, California, 1972-87; Co-founder, Information Associates,; Marketing Rep., System Engineer, IBM, 1964-69 **CR:** Co-founder Maddie's Fund, Alameda, California, 1999- **CIV:** Maddie's Fund, 1994 **AW:** Named one of Forbes 400: Richest Americans, 2006-

DUFFY, SEAN PATRICK, **T:** U.S. Representative From Wisconsin, Prosecutor **I:** Government Administration/Government Relations/Government Services **DOB:** 10/03/1971 **PB:** Hayward

SC: WI/USA PT: Thomas Walter Duffy; Carol Ann (Yackel) Duffy ED: JD, William Mitchell College of Law, St. Paul, MN, 1999; BA in Marketing, St. Mary's University, San Antonio, TX, 1994 C: U.S. Congress from Seventh Wisconsin District, 2011-Present; U.S. House of Financial Services Committee, 2011-Present; District Attorney, Ashland County, Wisconsin, 2002-2010 CW: Cast Member, (MTV Reality Series) The Real World: Boston, 1997, Road Rules: All Stars, 1998, Real World/Road Rules Challenge: Battle of the Seasons, 2002; Color Commentator, ESPN's Great Outdoor Games, 2003 AW: The Politics 40 Under 40, TIME Magazine, 2010 ACH: Achievements include national recognition as a professional lumberjack athlete, holding titles as a two-time world champion in the 90-foot speed climb and three-time champion in the 60-foot climb, as well as an accomplished log-roller PA: Republican

DUJARDIN, JEAN, T: Actor I: Media & Entertainment PB: Paris SC: France PT: Jacques Dujardin CW: Actor: (films) If I Were a Rich Man, 2002, All Girls Are Crazy, 2003, Welcome to the Roses, 2003, Le convoyeur, 2004, Mariages!, 2004, Lucky Luke and the Daltons, 2004, La vie de Michel Muller est plus belle que la võtre, 2005, The Brice Man, 2005, L'amour aux trousses, 2005, Il ne faut jurer...de rien!, 2005, Office of Strategic Services 117: Cairo, Nest of Spies, 2006, Counter Investigation, 2007, Hellphone, 2007, Cherche fiancé tous frais payés, 2007, 99 francs, 2007, Ca$h, 2008, Un homme et son chien, 2008, Office of Strategic Services 117 - Lost in Rio, 2009, Lucky Luke, 2009, The Clink of Ice, 2010, Little White Lies, 2010, A View of Love, 2010, The Artist, 2011 (Golden Globe award for Best Performance by an Actor in a Motion Picture-Comedy or Musical, 2012, Screen Actors Guild award for Outstanding Performance by a Male Actor in a Leading Role, 2012, BAFTA award for Best Leading Actor, 2012, Academy award for Best Performance by an Actor in a Leading Role, 2012), Möbius, 2013, 9 Month Stretch, 2013, The Wolf of Wall Street, 2013, The Monuments Men, 2014, The Connection, 2014, Un Plus Une, 2015, Up for Love, 2016, Brice 3, 2016, Chacun Sa Vie, 2017, Sahara, 2017, I Feel Good, 2018, Le Retour du Heros, 2018; (TV series) Un gars, une fille, 1999-2003; (TV films) Deux sur la balancoire, 2007, Le Débarquement, 2013; dir.: (TV series) Palizzi, 2008; actor, writer, director, producer, SNL, 2012, Le Debarquement,2013, Platane, 2013 (films) The Players, 2012, member humorist band Nous C Nous ACH: Achievements include being the first Frenchman to win the Academy Award for Best Actor

DUKE, ELAINE COSTANZO, T: Former U.S. Secretary of Homeland Security I: Military & Defense Services PB: Ohio PT: Daughter of Frank Costanzo ED: MBA, Chaminade University, Honolulu; BS in Business Management, New Hampshire College C: Acting Secretary, US Department of Homeland Security, Washington, DC, 2017; U.S. Deputy Secretary of Homeland Security, December 2017-; Owner, principal, Elaine Duke & Associates, LLC, Woodbridge, 2010-2017; Under secretary for management, US Department Homeland Security, 2008-10; Deputy under secretary for mgmt, US Department Homeland Security, 2007-08; Deputy chief procurement officer, US Department Homeland Security, 2004-06; Deputy assistant administrator, Transportation Security Administration, 2002-04; Director office contract policy, Department Navy, U.S Department of Defense,; Deputy director hull, mechanical and electrical division in Contracts Directorate Naval Sea Systems Command, Department Navy, US Department of Defense,; Staff assistant secretary

installations and environmental, Department of the Navy, US Department Defense,; Deputy director contracting department Pub. Works. Center, Department Navy, US Department Defense, Pearl Harbor, Hawaii,; Contracting officer, US Air Force,; Director acquisition & grant services, Federal R.R. Administration,; Deputy director contracting & property management, Smithsonian Institution CIV: Board directors, Western Fairfax Christian Ministries, 2010- AW: Recipient Distinguished Pub. Service award, US Coast Guard, Secretary Medal, US Department Homeland Security, Commander Award for Pub. Service, Department Army, Silver Medal for Customer Service, Transportation Security Administration (TSA), Presidential Meritorious Rank award, 2007 BA: Department of Homeland Security, 245 Murray Lane SW, Washington, DC, 20528

DUKUREH, JAHA, T: Activist I: Nonprofit & Philanthropy ED: Bachelors Degree, Business Administration, Georgia Southwestern State University,2013 C: Lead Campaigner,End FGM Guardian Global Media Campaign; Founder, Safe Hands for Girls,2015- AW: Time 100 Most Influential, 2016

DUNAWAY, FAYE, T: Actress I: Media & Entertainment DOB: 12/14/1941 PB: Bascom SC: FL/USA PT: John Dunaway, Grace Dunaway SPN: Terrence O'Neill, 1983, Divorced 3/1987; Peter Wolf, 8/7/1974, Divorced 1979 CH: Liam Walker ED: Degree in Theater, University of Florida, 1962; Student, Boston University CW: Appearances, (As Original Member) Lincoln Center Repertory Co., New York, NY, Off-Broadway, Hogan's Goat; Actress, (Plays) Curse Of The Aching Heart, 1982, (Films) Bonnie And Clyde, 1967, Hurry Sundown, 1967, Puzzle Of A Downfall Child, The Happening, 1967, The Thomas Crown Affair, 1968, A Place For Lovers, 1969, The Arrangement, 1969, The Extraordinary Seaman, 1969, Little Big Man, 1970, The Puzzle Of A Downfall Child, 1970, Doc, 1971, La Maison Sous Les Arbres, 1971, Oklahoma Crude, 1973, The Three Musketeers, 1973, Chinatown, 1974, The Towering Inferno, 1974, The Four Musketeers, 1975, Three Days Of The Condor, 1975, Network, 1976, The Voyage Of The Damned, 1976, The Eyes Of Laura Mars, 1978, The Champ, 1979, The First Deadly Sin, 1980, Mommie Dearest, 1981, The Wicked Lady, 1982, Ordeal By Innocence, 1984, Supergirl, 1984, Barfly, 1987, Burning Secret, 1988, La Partita, 1988, Midnight Crossing, 1988, The Gamble, 1989, On A Moonlit Night, 1989, Wait Until Spring, Bandini, 1989, The Handmaid's Tale, 1990, Three Weeks In Jerusalem, 1990, Scorchers, 1990, Arrowtooth Waltz, 1991, Double Edge, 1992, Arizona Dream, 1993, The Temp, 1993, Even Cowgirls Get The Blues, 1994, Don Juan DeMarco, 1995, En Brazos De La Mujer Madura, 1996, The Chamber, 1996, Albino Alligator, 1996, Dunston Checks In, 1996, Twilight Of The Golds, 1997, Drunks, 1997, Fanny Hill, 1998 Love Lies Bleeding, 1999, The Messenger: The Story Of Joan Of Arc, 1999, The Thomas Crown Affair, 1999, The Yards, 2000, Stanley's Gig, 2000, Changing Hearts, 2002, The Rules Of Attraction, 2002, Mid-Century, 2002, The Calling, 2002, Blind Horizon, 2004, The Last Goodbye, 2004, El Padrino, 2004, Jennifer's Shadow, 2004, Ghosts Never Sleep, 2004, Love Hollywood Style, 2005, Rain, 2006, The Gene Generation, 2007, Cougar Club, 2007, Say It In Russian, 2007, Flick, 2007, Dr. Fugazzi, 2008, La Rabbia, 2008, The Magic Stone, 2009, The Seduction Of Dr. Fugazzi, 2009, The Bait, 2009, 21 And Wake-Up, 2009, Master Class, 2014, The Bye Bye Man, 2017, The Case For Christ, 2017, Inconceivable, 2017, (TV Films) Hogan's Goat, 1971, The Woman I Love, 1972, After The Fall, 1974, The Disappearance Of

Aimee, 1976, Evita Peron, 1981, The Country Girl, 1982, 13 At Dinner, 1985, Beverly Hills Madame, 1986, Raspberry Ripple, 1986, Casanova, 1987, Cold Sassy Tree, 1989, Columbo: It's All In The Game, 1994, Mother Love, 1995, A Family Divided, 1995, The People Next Door, 1996, Rebecca, 1997, Twilight Of The Golds, 1997, Gia, 1998, A Will Of Their Own, 1998, Running Mates, 2000, The Biographer, 2002, Anonymous Rex, 2004, Back When We Were Grownups, 2004, Pandemic, 2007, Midnight Bayou, 2009, A Family Thanksgiving, 2010, Documentary Now!, 2016, Faye Dunaway: Live From The TCM Classic Film Festival, 2017, (TV Appearances) Seaway, 1965, The Trials Of O'Brien, 1966, Road To Avonlea, 1995, Touched By An Angel, 2001, Soul Food, 2002, Alias, 2002-2003, (TV Miniseries) Ellis Island, 1984, Christopher Columbus, 1985, (TV Series) It Had To Be You, 1993, A Will Of Their Own, 1998; Actor, Director, Producer, (Films) The Yellow Bird, 2001; Author, Looking For Gatsby: My Life, 1995; Co-Executive Producer, Actress, (Films) Cold Sassy Tree, 1989, Silhouette, 1990 AW: Special Tribute Award, Almería International Short Film Festival, 2007, Career Achievement Award, Chicago International Film Festival, 2001, Honorary Golden Alexander, Thessaloniki Film Festival, 2001, Lifetime Achievement Award, ShoWest, 1995, Emmy Award For Guest Actress In Drama, Columbo: It's All In The Game, 1994, Academy Award For Best Actress, Network, 1976, Most Promising Newcomer Award, British Film Academy, 1968 BA: Don Buchwald & Associates, Fortitude, 6500 Sunset Boulevard, Suite 2200, Los Angeles, CA, 90069

DUNCAN, ALLYSON K., T: Federal Judge I: Law and Legal Services DOB: 09/05/1951 PB: Durham SC: NC/USA ED: JD, Duke University, 1975; BA, Hampton University, 1972 C: Judge, U.S. Court of Appeals, Fourth Circuit, 2003-Present; Partner, Kilpatrick Stockton LLP, Raleigh, NC, 1998-2003; Commissioner, North Carolina Utilities Commission, 1991-1998; Associate Judge, North Carolina Court of Appeals, 1990; Associate Professor, North Carolina Central University School of Law, 1986-1990; Appellate Attorney, Assistant To Deputy General Counsel, Assistant To Chairman, Equal Employment Opportunity Commission, 1978-1986; Law Clerk To Hon. Julia Cooper Mack, District of Columbia Court Appeals, Washington, DC, 1977-1978; Associate Editor, Lawyers Cooperative Publication Co., 1976-1977 MEM: President, Wake County Bar Association, 2002-2003, President-Elect, North Carolina Bar Association, 2002 BAR: District of Columbia, 1977, North Carolina, 1975 BA: 1100 E Main Street, #501, Richmond, VA, 23219

DUNCAN, JEFF, T: U.S. Representatives from South Carolina I: Government Administration/Government Relations/Government Services DOB: 01/07/1966 PB: Simpsonville SC: SC/USA PT: Son of John T. and Dianne M. Duncan; ED: Grad., South Carolina Bankers School; BA, Clemson University, 1988 CT: Accredited Auctioneer Real Estate designation, Cert. Auctioneers Institute designation C: Member, U.S. House Natural Resources Committee, Washington, 2011-; Member, Republican Study Committee; Member, U.S. House Homeland Security Committee, Washington, 2011-; Member, U.S. House Foreign Affairs Committee, Washington, 2011-; Member, U.S. Congress from 3rd South Carolina District, Washington, 2011-; Chairman, South Carolina House Agricultural, Natural Resources & Environmental Affairs Committee, 2007-11; Member District 15, South Carolina House of Reps., 2002-10; President, corp. auctioneer, J. Duncan Associates, Clinton, South Carolina, CR: Member Clinton Board Zoning Appeals, 1995-99

CIV: Board of Directors, Laurens County C. of C., 2002-07 Board of Directors, Piedmont Wilderness Institute, Clinton, 2001-06 Board of Directors, South Carolina Waterfowl Association, 1997-2002 Board of Directors, Clinton Uptown Devel. Association, 1993-97 AW: Named Legislator of Year, South Carolina Recreation & Parks Association, South Carolina Wildlife Federation, 2007; recipient Guardian of Small Business award, National Federation Ind. Business, 2006, Palmetto Leadership award from, South Carolina Policy Council, 2003 PA: Republican

DUNCAN, JOHN JAMES JR., T: U.S. Representative from Tennessee I: Government Administration/Government Relations/Government Services DOB: 07/21/1947 PB: Lebanon, Tennessee ED: JD, George Washington University National Law Center, 1973; BS in Journalism, University Tennessee, Knoxville, 1969 CT: Bar: Tennessee 1973 C: Member, US Congress from 2nd Tennessee district, 1988-; Member, Committee on Transportation and Infrastructure, Committee on Oversight and Government Reform; State Trial Judge, Knox County, 1981-88; Private Practice Attorney, Knoxville, 1973-81 CIV: Elder, Eastminster Presbyterian Church, MIL: Positions Captain US Army National Guard/USAR, 1970-87 AW: Named one of Top 5 Most Fiscally Conservative Members of the House and Senate, National Taxpayers Union; Recipient Golden Bulldog Award, Watchdogs of Treasury, Super Hero Award, Citizens Against Government Waste, Hartranft Award, Airline Operators & Pilots Association, 1999 MEM: Mem.: Am. Legion, Sertoma Club, Elks, Shriners, Masons PA: Republican BA: 2207 Rayburn HOB, Washington, DC, 20515

DUNCAN, TIM, T: Professional Basketball Player I: Athletics DOB: 04/25/1976 PB: Christiansted, VI, April 25, 1976 PT: Son of William and Ione Duncan; ED: BA in Psych., Wake Forest, 1997 C: Center, forward, San Antonio Spurs, 1997-2016 CR: Member US Olympic Men's Basketball Team, Athens, 2004 CIV: Founder, executive vice president, Tim Duncan Foundation, AW: Named Sportsman of Year, Sports Illus., 2003, NBA Player of Year, The Sporting News, 2003, 2002, MVP, NBA 2003, 2002, Co-MVP, NBA All-Star Game, 2000, MVP, NBA Finals, 2005, 2003, 1999, NBA Rookie of Year, 1998, NCAA Men's Basketball Player of Year, Associated Press, 1997; named to NBA All-Defensive First Team, 2007-08, 2005, 1999-2003, All-NBA First Team, 2013, 2007, 1998-2005, Western Conference All-Star Game, NBA, 2013, 2000-11, 1998; recipient John R. Wooden award, 1997, Naismith Player of Year award, 1997,NBA Shooting Stars Champion,2008 NBA Teammate of the Year, 2015 ACH: Achievements include being a member of the NBA Championship winning San Antonio Spurs, 1999, 2003, 2005, 2014 BA: San Antonio Spurs, One AT&T Center, San Antonio, TX, 78219

DUNGY, TONY, T: NFL Coach I: Athletics DOB: 10/06/1955 PB: Jackson SC: MI/USA PT: Son of Wilbur and Cleomane Dungy ED: BA in Business Administration, University of Minnesota, 1977 C: Analyst, Football Night in America, NBC Sports, 2009-; Head Coach, Indianapolis Colts, 2002-09; Head Coach, Tampa Bay Buccaneers, 1996-2001; Defensive Coordinator, Minnesota Vikings, 1992-95; Defensive Backs Coach, Kansas City Chiefs, 1989-91; Defensive Coordinator, Pittsburgh Steelers, 1984-88; Defensive Back coach, Pittsburgh Steelers, 1982-83; Defensive Assistant, Pittsburgh Steelers, 1981-83; Defensive Backs Coach, University of Minnesota, 1980; Professional Football Player, New York Giants, 1980; Professional Football Player, San Francisco 49ers, 1979;

Professional Football Player, Pittsburgh Steelers, 1977-78 CIV: Active, Am. Diabetes Association, Active, United Way Central Ind., Active, Ind. Black Expo, Active, Black Coaches Association National Convention, Active, Basket of Hope, Active, All Pro Dad, Active, Boys & Girls Clubs, Active, Big Brothers Big Sisters, Active, Athletes in Action, Founder, Mentors for Life, Tampa Bay, Active, Prison Crusade Ministry, Active, Fellowship Christian Athletes CW: Author: Quiet Strength: The Principles, Practices, & Priorities of a Winning Life, 2007 (#1 New York Times bestseller); Co-author: Uncommon, 2009 (Publishers Weekly bestseller), (children's book) You Can Be a Friend, 2011 AW: Named Best Coach-Mgr., ESPY Awards, 2007; Named One of The World's Most Influential People, TIME magazine, 2007; Named to Ind. Hall of Fame, 2008; Recipient, Fatherhood Award, National Fatherhood Initiative, 2002, Amos Alonzo Coaching Award, 2007, Pro Football Hall of Fame, 2016, Indianapolis Colts Ring of Honor, 2010, NFL 2000s All-Decade Team, Super Bowl Champion, XIII, XLI ACH: Achievements include member of Super Bowl XIII Championship winning Pittsburgh Steelers, 1979; head coach of Super Bowl XLI Championship winning Indianapolis Colts, 2007; one of two African-American head coaches to lead a NFL team to the Super Bowl, 2007; first African-American head coach to win a Super Bowl, 2007; one of three individuals to win the Super Bowl as a player and head coach

DUNN, NEAL, T: U.S. Representative from Florida I: Government Administration/Government Relations/Government Services DOB: 02/16/1953 PB: New Haven SC: CT/USA ED: BA, Washington and Lee University; Medical Degree, George Washington University of Medicine & Health Services; Medical Internship, Walter Reed Army Medical Center C: Committee on Agriculture, Committee on Science, Space and Technology, Committee on Veterans' Affairs, Republican Study Committee, U.S. House of Representatives from Florida's Second District, 2017-Present MIL: U.S. Army, 1989-2010 BA: 423 Cannon HOB, Washington, DC, 20515

DUPERREAULT, BRIAN, T: CEO I: Business Management/Business Services CN: Marsh & McLennan Companies, Inc. DOB: 05/08/1947 ED: BS,St. Joseph's University, Philadelphia, 1969 C: Pres, CEO,AIG, 2017-; Pres., CEO & board directors, Marsh & McLennan Companies, Inc., New York City, New York, 2008-; Chairman, ACE Ltd., 1994—2007; CEO, ACE Ltd., 1994—2004; President, ACE Ltd., 1994—1999; Chmn., CEO, Am. International Underwriters, American International Group, Inc. (AIG); Executive vice president, Foreign General Insurance, American International Group, Inc. (AIG) CR: Board directors Bank N.T. Butterfield & Sons Ltd.; chairman board directors ACE Ltd., 1994—2007; board directors Tyco International Ltd., 2004— CIV: Member board trustees St. Joseph's University; board directors Insurance Information Institute, Center on Philanthropy, New York City BA: AIG Headquarters, 80 Pine Street,4th Floor, New York, NY, 10005

DURANT, KEVIN WAYNE, T: Professional Basketball Player I: Athletics DOB: 09/29/1988 PB: Washington SC: DC/USA PT: Son of Wayne and Wanda Pratt ED: Student, The University of Texas at Austin, 2006-07 C: Forward-guard, Golden State Warriors, 2016-; Forward-guard, Oklahoma City Thunder, 2008-16; Forward-guard, Seattle SuperSonics, 2007-08 CR: Member US national team Summer Olympic Games, London, 2012, FIBA World Championships, Turkey, 2010 AW: Named NBA MVP, 2014, NBA All-Star Game MVP, 2012, 1st Team All-NBA, NBA, 2010-13, 1st Team All-Rookie,

2008, NBA Rookie of Year, Associated Press, 2008, National Player of Year, 2007, 1st Team NCAA All-American, 2007, College Basketball Player of Year, The Sporting News, 2007, Division 1 Player of Year, National Association Basketball Coaches, 2007, Jordan All-American Classic Game MVP, 2006, McDonald's All-American Game co-MVP, 2006; named to Western Conference All-Star Team, NBA, 2010-13, McDonald's All-American Team, 2006; recipient Gold medal, men's basketball, Summer Olympic Games, 2012, Gold medal, FIBA World Championship, 2010, John R. Wooden award, 2007, Naismith College Player of Year award, Atlanta Tipoff Club, 2007, Adolph Rupp Trophy, 2007, Oscar Robertson Trophy, US Basketball Writers Association, 2007, NBA Scoring Champion, 2010-12, 2014, All-NBA Second Team, 2016-17, All-NBA Frist Team, 2010-14, NBA All-Star, 2010-2017, NBA Most Valuable Player, 2014, NBA Finals MVP, 2017, NBA Champion, 2017 ACH: Achievements include being the second overall pick in the NBA Draft, 2007; leading the NBA in: scoring, 2010-12; free-throw percentage, 2013; becoming the youngest scoring champion in NBA history (21 years old), 2010

DURBIN, DICK, T: U.S. Senator from Illinois I: Government Administration/Government Relations/Government Services DOB: 11/21/1944 PB: East St. Louis SC: Illinois PT: Son of William and Ann Durbin; ED: JD, Georgetown University, Washington, 1969; BS in Econs., Georgetown University, Washington, 1966 CT: Bar: Illinois 1969 C: Chairman, US Senate Defense Appropriations Subcommittee, 2013-; Assistant Minority Leader (minority whip), 2015-; US Senator from Illinois, 1997-; Assistant Majority Leader (majority whip), 2007-15; Assistant Minority Leader (minority whip), 2005-07; Member, US Congress from 20th Illinois District, 1983-97; Partner, Durbin & Lestikow, Springfield, Illinois, 1979-82; Staff Minority Leader, Illinois State Senate, 1972-77; Parliamentarian, Illinois State Senate, 1969-77; Chief Legal Counsel to Lieutenant Governor Paul Simon, State of Illinois, 1969-72 CR: Co-chmn. Democratic Platform Committee, 2000 Associate Professor Medical Humanities Southern Illinois University, 1978- CIV: Staff, Office Illinois Department Business & Economic Devel., Washington, Connecticut, Adv., American Council Young Political Leaders, 1981 Candidate for Illinois Lieutenant Governor, 1978 Board directors, Springfield Youth Soccer, Board Directors, Old Capitol Art Fair, Board Directors, United Way Springfield, Board Directors, Catholic Charities AW: Recipient Lifetime Achievement award, American Lung Association, Public Service award, American Chemical Society, 2005, Leadership award, National Organization Fetal Alcohol Syndrome, 2005, Ground Water Protector award, National Ground Water Association, 2005, Excellence in Immunization award, National Partnership Immunization, 2001, Friend of Agriculture award, Illinois Farm Bureau, 2000 MEM: Mem.: National Association for the Advancement of Colored People, Trial Lawyers Association, Sangamon County Bar Association, Illinois Bar Association PA: Democrat BA: Office of Dick Durbin, 711 Hart Senate Building, Washington, DC, 20510

DUTKOWSKY, ROBERT M., T: Computer Company Executive I: Technology DOB: 01/02/1955 ED: BS in Industrial Engineering & Labor Relations, Cornell University, 1977 C: CEO, board directors, Tech Data Corp., Clearwater, Florida, 2006-; Chairman, president, CEO, Egenera Inc., Marlboro, Massachusetts, 2004-06; Chairman, president, CEO, J.D. Edwards & Co., Inc., 2002-04; President, assembly test division, Teradyne Inc.,

2001-02; Chairman, president, CEO, GenRad Inc., 2000-02; President, data general, EMC Corp., 1999; Executive vice president, marketing and channels, EMC Corp., 1997-99; Various senior management positions, including vice president, distribution, Asia Pacific, worldwide sales & marketing, RS/6000 business, IBM Corp., 1977-97 **CR:** Board directors McAfee Inc., 2001-07, SEPATON Inc. **AW:** Recipient Ellis Island Medal of Honor, 2000

DUVALL, ROBERT, T: Actor **I:** Media & Entertainment **DOB:** 01/05/1931 **PB:** San Diego **SC:** CA/USA **PT:** Son of William Howard Duvall **MS:** Married **SPN:** Luciana Pedraza, (October); Sharon Brophy, May 1, 1991 (div. 1996); Gail Youngs, August 1982 (div. 1986); Barbara Benjamin, 1964 (div. 1975); **ED:** Grad., Principia College, Illinois; Student, Neighborhood Playhouse, New York City **MIL:** With U.S. Army, 1953—54 **CW:** Actor: (films) To Kill a Mockingbird, 1963, Captain Newman, M.D., 1964, The Chase, 1965, Countdown, 1968, The Detective, 1968, Bullitt, 1968, True Grit, 1969, The Rain People, 1969, M*A*S*H, 1970, The Revolutionary, 1970, THX-1138, 1971, Lawman, 1971, The Godfather, 1972 (New York Film Critics award for Best Supporting Actor, 1972), Tomorrow, 1972, The Great Northfield, Minnesota Raid, 1972, Joe Kidd, 1972, Lady Ice, 1973, Badge 373, 1973, The Outfit, 1974, The Conversation, 1974, The Godfather Part II, 1974, Breakout, 1975, The Killer Elite, 1975, Network, 1976, The Seven Per Cent Solution, 1976, The Eagle Has Landed, 1977, The Greatest, 1977, The Betsy, 1978, Apocalypse Now, 1979 (BAFTA award for Best Supporting Actor, 1980), The Great Santini, 1980, True Confessions, 1981, The Pursuit of D.B. Cooper, 1981, Tender Mercies, 1983 (Academy award for Best Actor, 1984, Golden Globe award for Best Performance by an Actor in a Motion Picture - Drama, 1984), The Stone Boy, 1984, The Natural, 1984, The Lightship, 1986, Let's Get Harry, 1986, Belizaire the Cajun, 1986, Hotel Colonial, 1987, Colors, 1988, Convicts, Roots in a Parched Ground, The Handmaid's Tale, 1990, A Show of Force, 1990, Days of Thunder, 1990, Rambling Rose, 1991, Newsies, 1992, Falling Down, 1993, Geronimo, 1993, Wrestling Ernest Hemingway, 1993, The Paper, 1994, The Stars Fell on Henrietta, 1995, The Scarlet Letter, 1995, Sling Blade, 1996, Phenomenon, 1996, A Family Thing, 1996, Gingerbread Man, 1997, Deep Impact, 1998, A Civil Action, 1999, Gone in Sixty Seconds, 2000, A Shot at Glory, 2000, The Sixth Day, 2000, John Q, 2002, Gods and Generals, 2003, Open Range, 2003, Secondhand Lions, 2003, Kicking & Screaming, 2005, Thank You For Smoking, 2005, Lucky You, 2007, We Own the Night, 2007, Four Christmases, 2008, The Road, 2009, Get Low, 2009, Seven Days in Utopia, 2011, Jayne Mansfield's Car, 2012, One Shot, 2012, Jack Reacher, 2012, The Judge, 2014; director, writer, The Judge, 2014, Wild Horses, 2015, In Dubious Battle, 2016, Widows, 2018; (films) Angelo My Love, 1983; actor, prodr.: (films) Crazy Heart, 2009; actor, director, producer, writer: (films) The Apostle, 1997, Assassination Tango, 2002; actor, producer, writer: (films) A Night in Old Mexico, 2013; actor: (TV films) Fame is the Name of the Game, 1966, Ike: The War Years, 1980, The Terry Fox Story, 1983, Stalin, 1992 (Golden Globe award for Best Performance by an Actor in a Mini-Series or Motion Picture Made for TV, 1993), The Man Who Captured Eichmann, 1996, Hemingway & Gellhorn, 2012; (TV miniseries) Ike, 1979, Lonesome Dove, 1989 (Golden Globe award for Best Performance by an Actor in a Mini-Series or Motion Picture Made for TV, 1990); actor, executive prodr.: (TV miniseries) Broken Trail, 2006 (Primetime Emmy for Outstanding Lead Actor in a Miniseries or a Movie & Outstanding Miniseries, Academy TV Arts and Scis., 2007, Primetime Emmy

for Outstanding Miniseries, 2007), Hemingway & Gellhorn, 2012; (stage appearances) A View From the Bridge, 1965 (Obie award), Wait Until Dark, 1966, American Buffalo, 1977; dir.: (documentaries) We're Not the Jet Set, 1977. **AW:** Recipient National Association Theatre Owners Award, National Medal of Arts National Endowment for the Arts, 2005, Lifetime Achievement Award San Francisco International Film Festival, 2010, Star, Hollywood Walk of Fame, 2003; Decorated National Defense Service Medal **BA:** PO Box 520, The Plains, VA, 20198

DUVERNAY, AVA, T: Film Director, Producer **I:** Media & Entertainment **PB:** Long Beach **SC:** CA/USA **CW:** (Film) Saturday Night Life,2006, Compton in C Minor, 2007, This is the Life, 2008, TV One Night Only: Live From the Essence Music Festival, 2010, My Mic Sounds Nice, 2010, I Will Follow, 2010, Essence Presents: Faith Through the Storm, 2010, Middle of Nowhere, 2012, The Door, 2013, Venus Vs, 2013, Say Yes, 2013, HelloBeautiful Interludes Live: John Legend, 2013, Scandal, 2013, Selma, 2014, For Justice, 2015, Chapter 1, Chapter, 2 Chapter 3, 2015, Queen Sugar, 2016, August 28: A Day in the Life of People, 2016, 13th, 2016, (Primetime Emmy for Outstanding Documentary, 2016, Primetime Emmy for Outstanding Writing for Nonfiction Programming Family Feud, 2017, A Wrinkle in Time, 2018 **AW:** Time 100 Most Influential, 2017

DYLAN, BOB, T: Singer **I:** Media & Entertainment **DOB:** 05/24/1941 **PB:** Duluth **SC:** MN/USA **ED:** Honorary MusD, Princeton University, 1970; Student, University of Minnesota, 1960 **C:** Solo Artist, 1961—Present **CW:** Musician, (Albums) Bob Dylan, 1962, The Freewheelin' Bob Dylan, 1963, The Times They Are A-Changin', 1964, Another Side Of Bob Dylan, 1964, Bringing It All Back Home, 1965, Highway 61 Revisited, 1965, Blonde On Blonde, 1966, John Wesley Harding, 1967, Bob Dylan's Greatest Hits, 1967, Nashville Skyline, 1969, Self Portrait, 1970, New Morning, 1970, Bob Dylan's Greatest Hits, Vol. 2, 1971, Dylan, 1973, Planet Waves, 1974, Blood On The Tracks, 1975, Desire, 1976, Hard Rain, 1976, Street Legal, 1978, Masterpieces, 1978, Slow Train Coming, 1979, Bob Dylan At Budokan, 1979, Saved, 1980, Shot Of Love, 1981, Infidels, 1983, Real Live, 1984, Empire Burlesque, 1985, Biograph, 1985, Knocked Out Loaded, 1986, Down In The Groove, 1988, Oh Mercy, 1989, Under The Red Sky, 1990, The Bootleg Series, Volumes 1-3: (Rare And Unreleased 1961-1991), 1991, Good As I Been To You, 1992, World Gone Wrong, 1993, Bob Dylan's Greatest Hits, Vol. 3, 1994, MTV Unplugged, 1995, Time Out Of Mind, 1997, The Best Of Bob Dylan, 1997, The Bootleg Series, Vol. 4: The Royal Albert Hall Concert, 1998, Essential Bob Dylan, 2000, The Best Of Bob Dylan, Vol. 2, 2000, The Very Best Of Bob Dylan, 2000, Love And Theft, 2001, The Bootleg Series, Vol. 5, Live 1975, The Rolling Thunder Revue, 2002, The Bootleg Series, Vol. 6: Live 1964, 2004, Live At The Gaslight 1962, 2005, Modern Times, 2006, The Bootleg Series, Vol. 8: Tell Tale Signs, 2008, Together Through Life, 2009, Christmas In The Heart, 2009, The Bootleg Series, Vol. 9: The Witmark Demos: 1962-1964, 2010, Bob Dylan In Concert-Brandeis University 1963, 2011, Tempest, 2012, The Bootleg Series, Vol. 10: Another Self Portrait, 1969-1971, 2013, Shadows In The Night, 2015, Fallen Angles, 2016, Triplicate, 2017, (Soundtracks) Pat Garrett And Billy The Kid, 1973, Wonder Boys, 2000, Masked And Anonymous, 2003, The Bootleg Series, Vol. 7: No Direction Home: The Soundtrack, 2005, (With Various Artists) The Concert For Bangladesh, 1971, Bob Dylan 30th Anniversary Concert Celebration, 1993, (With The Band) Before The Flood, 1974, The

Basement Tapes, 1976, The Bootleg Series, Vol. 11: The Basement Tapes Complete, 2014, (Soundtrack With The Band & Others) The Last Waltz, 1978, (With The Grateful Dead) (Albums) Dylan And The Dead, 1988, (With The Traveling Wilburys) Traveling Wilburys Vol. 1, 1988, Traveling Wilburys Vol. 3, 1990; Appearances, (Documentaries) Don't Look Back, 1967; No Direction Home, 2005; The Other Side Of The Mirror: Bob Dylan Live At The Newport Folk Festival 1963-1965, 2007; Performer, (Films) The Last Waltz, 1978; Actor, (Films) Pat Garret And Billy The Kid, 1973, Hearts Of Fire, 1987; Actor, Composer, Director, Editor, Writer, (Films) Renaldo And Clara, 1978; Actor, Composer, Writer, Masked And Anonymous, 2003, (TV Films) The Madhouse On Castle Street, 1963; Director, Editor, (Films) Eat The Document, 1972; Author, Tarantula, 1971, Writings And Drawings By Bob Dylan, 1973, Tarantula: Poems, 1994, Lyrics: 1962-2001, 2004, Lyrics: Since 1962, 2014, (Memoirs) Chronicles, Vol. 1, 2004, (Art Books) Drawn Blank, 1994, The Drawn Blank Series, 2008, The Brazil Series, 2010, The Asia Series, 2011, Revisionist Art: Thirty Works By Bob Dylan, 2013, Bob Dylan: Face Value, 2014 **AW:** Nobel Prize in Literature, 2016, Musicares Person of the Year, 2015, Legion D'Honneur, 2013, Presidential Medal of Freedom, The White House, 2012, National Medal of Arts Award, National Endowment for the Arts, 2009, Special Citation for Profound Impact on Popular Music & American Culture, Pulitzer Prize Board, 2008, Grammy Award For Best Contemporary Folk Album, Best Solo Rock Vocal Performance, Modern Times, 2007, Prince of Asturias, 2007, Prince of Asturias Arts Award, Prince of Asturias Foundation, 2007, Quills Award-Biography/Memoir, Chronicles, Vol. 1, 2005, Grammy Award For Best Contemporary Folk Album, Love And Theft, 2002, The Nashville Songwriters Hall of Fame, 2002, Academy Award For Best Original Song For "Things Have Changed", Wonder Boys, 2001, Grammy Award For Album Of Year, Grammy Award For Best Contemporary Folk Album, Grammy Award For Best Male Rock Vocal Performance For "Cold Irons Bound", Time Out Of Mind, 1998, Kennedy Center Honors, John F. Kennedy Center for the Performing Arts, 1997, Grammy Award For Best Traditional Folk Album, World Gone Wrong, 1994, Lifetime Achievement Award, Grammy Awards, 1991, Grammy Award For Best Rock Performance By A Duo Or Group With Vocal, Traveling Wilburys Vol. 1, 1990, Ordre des Arts et des Lettres, Government of France, 1990, The Rock & Roll Hall of Fame, 1988, The Songwriters Hall of Fame, 1982, Grammy Award For Best Male Rock Vocal Performance For "Gotta Serve Somebody", Slow Train Coming, 1980, Grammy Award For Album Of Year, The Concert For Bangladesh, 1973 **ACH:** Achievements include devising and popularizing folk-rock **BA:** Columbia Records, 550 Madison Avenue, New York, NY, 10022

EARHARDT, AINSLEY HAYDEN, T: News Correspondent **I:** Media & Entertainment **DOB:** 09/20/1977 **ED:** BA in Mass Communications, University South Carolina **C:** Host, Fox and Friends, 2016-; Corr., FOX News Channel, New York City, 2007-; Weekday news anchor, KENS-TV, San Antonio, 2004-07; News corr., WLTX-TV, Columbia, South Carolina, 2000-04 **AW:** Named Outstanding Young Alumna, University of South Carolina School Journalism & Mass Communications, 2007, Best Personality of Year, Columbia Metropolitan Magazine, 2004; named one of Most Beautiful Woman on Planet Earth, MoFoPolitics.com, 2011; recipient Young Alumni award, University of South Carolina, 2007

EASTERBROOK, FRANK HOOVER, T: Federal Judge **I:** Law and Legal Services **DOB:** 09/03/1948 **PB:** Buffalo **SC:** NY/USA **PT:** George Edmund Easterbrook; Vimy (Hoover) Easterbrook **ED:** JD, The University of Chicago (1973); BA, Swarthmore College (1970) **C:** Judge, U.S. Court of Appeals for the Seventh Circuit, Chicago, IL (1985-Present); Senior Lecturer, The University of Chicago (1985-Present); Chief Judge, U.S. Court of Appeals for the Seventh Circuit, Chicago, IL (2006-2013); Principal Employee, Lexecon Inc., Chicago, IL (1980-1985); Lee & Brena Freeman Professor, The University of Chicago (1984-1985); Professor of Law, The University of Chicago (1981-1985); Assistant Professor of Law, The University of Chicago (1978-1981); Deputy Solicitor General, US Department of Justice, Washington, DC (1978-1979); Assistant to Solicitor General, US Department of Justice, Washington, DC (1974-1977); Law Clerk to Honorable Levin H. Campbell, U.S. Court of Appeals for the First Circuit, Boston, MA (1973-1974) **CR:** Member, Advisory Committee on Tender Offers, Securities and Exchange Commission, Washington, DC (1983) **CIV:** Trustee, James Madison Memorial Fellowship Foundation (1988-Present) **CW:** Co-author, "Antitrust" (1981); Co-author, "The Economic Structure of Corporate Law" (1991); Editor, Journal of Law & Economics, Chicago, IL (1982-1991); Contributor, Articles to Professional Journals **AW:** Prize for Distinguished Scholarship, Emory University, Atlanta, GA (1981) **MEM:** American Association for the Advancement of Science; American Law Institute; Mont Pelerin Society; Order of Coif; Phi Beta Kappa **BAR:** The District of Columbia Bar **BA:** US Ct Appeals Everett McKinley Dirksen Fed Bldg, 219 S Dearborn St Ste 2746, Chicago, IL, USA, 60604-1803

EASTERBROOK, STEVE, T: Food Service Executive **I:** Food & Restaurant Services **PB:** Watford **SC:** Hertfordshire Eng. **ED:** Attended, Durham University **C:** President, CEO, McDonald's Corp., 2015-; Chief Brand Officer, McDonald's 2013-2015; CEO, PizzaExpress Ltd. and Wagamama Ltd., 2011-13; Senior executive vice president, chief global office, McDonald's Corp., 2013-15; Corp., executive vice president, chief brand officer then president McDonald's Europe, McDonald's Corp., 2010-11; Senior vice president, division president Northern Europe, McDonald's Corp., 2007-10; President, CEO McDonald's UK division, McDonald's Corp., 2006-07; Deputy managing director McDonald's UK, McDonald's Corp., 2005-06; Regional vice president, UK's southern region, McDonald's Corp., 2001-05; Various positions in fin., operations and supply chain, including financial reporting manager, McDonald's Corp., 1993-2001; Accountant, Price Waterhouse,

EASTON, ELLIOT, T: Musician **I:** Media & Entertainment **PB:** Brooklyn **SC:** NY/USA **MS:** Married **SPN:** Jill Easton **CH:** Sydney **CW:** Solo Album, "Change No Change" (1985); Album with The Cars, "The Cars" (1978), "Candy-O" (1979), "Panorama" (1980), "Shake it Up" (1981), "Heartbeat City" (1984), "Door to Door" (1987), "Move Like This" (2011); Album with Tiki Gods, "Easton Island" (2013) **AW:** Inductee, Rock & Roll Hall of Fame (2018)

EASTWOOD, CLINT, T: Actor, Director **I:** Media & Entertainment **DOB:** 05/31/1930 **PB:** San Francisco **SC:** CA/USA **PT:** Son of Clinton and Margaret Ruth Eastwood **SPN:** Dina Ruiz, March 31, 1996 (div. December 2014); Maggie Johnson, December 19, 1953 (div. May 14, 1984); **CH:** Kyle, Alison, Morgan **ED:** Attended, LA City College; DFA (hon.), Wesleyan University, 2000 **C:** Worked as Lumberjack

in Oregon Before Being Drafted into the U.S. Army **CR:** Owner Malpaso Records Co., Mission Ranch Resort, Carmel, California, Tehama Golf Club, Carmel, Calif; Co-founder, Partner Tehama Inc.; Co-owner Pebble Beach Co. **CIV:** Member National Council Arts, 1972-78; Member Board Monterey Jazz Festival; Chairman Monterey Peninsula Foundation; Hon. Board of Governors Entertainment Industry Foundation; Mayor City of Carmel, California, 1986-88; California State Parks Commissioner for Carmel, 2002-; Vice-chair California State Parks & Recreation Commission; National Spokesman Take Pride in Am., 2005-. **CW:** Actor: (TV series) Rawhide, 1959-1966; (films) Revenge of the Creature, 1955, Francis in the Navy, 1955, Lady Godiva, 1955, Tarantula, 1955, Never Say Goodbye, 1956, The First Travelling Saleslady, 1956, Star in the Dust, 1956, Away All Boats, 1956, Escapade in Japan, 1957, Ambush at the Cimmaron Pass, 1958, Lafayette Escadrille, 1958, Ambush at Cimarron Pass, 1958, A Fistful of Dollars, 1964, For a Few Dollars More, 1965, The Good, the Bad and the Ugly, 1966, The Witches, 1967, Hang 'Em High, 1968, Coogan's Bluff, 1968, Where Eagles Dare, 1968, Paint Your Wagon, 1969, Two Mules for Sister Sara, 1970, Kelly's Heroes, 1970, The Beguiled, 1971, Dirty Harry, 1971, Joe Kidd, 1972, Magnum Force, 1973, Thunderbolt and Lightfoot, 1974, The Enforcer, 1976, Every Which Way But Loose, 1978, Escape from Alcatraz, 1979, Any Which Way You Can, 1980, City Heat, 1984, The Dead Pool, 1988, Pink Cadillac, 1989, In the Line of Fire, 1993; Actor, Dir.: (films) Play Misty For Me, 1971, High Plains Drifter, 1973, The Eiger Sanction, 1975, The Outlaw Josey Wales, 1976, The Gauntlet, 1977, Bronco Billy, 1980, The Rookie, 1990, Gran Torino, 2008 (National Board Review Award for Best Actor, 2008); actor, director, prodr.: (films) Firefox, 1982, Honkeytonk Man, 1982, Sudden Impact, 1983, Pale Rider, 1985, Heartbreak Ridge, 1986, White Hunter Black Heart, 1990, Unforgiven, 1992 (Academy Award for Best Director & Best Picture, 1992, Golden Globe Award for Best Director, 1993), A Perfect World, 1993, The Bridges of Madison County, 1995, Absolute Power, 1997, True Crime, 1999, Space Cowboys, 2000, Blood Work, 2002, Million Dollar Baby, 2004 (Golden Globe Award for Best Director, 2005, Director's Guild Award for Best Feature, 2005, Academy Award for Best Director & Best Picture, 2005); Actor, Prodr.: (films) Tightrope, 1984, The Exchange, 2008 (Special Prize, Festival de Cannes, 2008), Trouble with the Curve, 2012; dir.: (films) Breezy, 1973; (TV episodes) Amazing Stories (Vanessa in the Garden episode), 1985; (TV miniseries) The Blues-(Piano Blues episode), 2003; Director, Prodr.: (films) Bird, 1988, Midnight in the Garden of Good and Evil, 1997, Mystic River, 2003, Flags of Our Fathers, 2006, Letter from Iwo Jima, 2006, Changeling, 2008, Invictus, 2009 (Best Director Award, National Board Review, 2009), Hereafter, 2010, J.Edgar, 2011, Jersey Boys, 2014, American Sniper, 2014 (National Board Review Award for Best Director, 2014), Sully, 2016; Prodr. The 12:17 to Paris, 2018, A Star is Born, 2018: (films) The Stars Fell on Henrietta, 1995; Pxecutive Prodr.: (films) Thelonious Monk-Straight, No Chaser, 1989; Singer: (singles) Unknown Girl, 1981, Rowdy, For You, For Me, For Evermore, Cowboy in a Three Piece Suit, 1981, (albums) Rawhide's Clint Eastwood Sings Cowboy Favorites, 1962. **AW:** Named One of The 100 Most Influential People of 2005, TIME magazine, 2005; Named to The California Hall of Fame, 2006; Recipient Henrietta Award for World Film Favorite, Hollywood Foreign Press. Association, 1971, Cecil B. DeMille Award, 1988, Irving G. Thalberg Memorial Award, Academy Motion Picture Arts & Sciences, 1995, Life Achievement Award, Film Society at Lincoln Center, 1996, Am.

Film Institute, 1996, Kennedy Center Honors, John F. Kennedy Center Performing Arts, 2000, Lifetime Career Achievement Award, New York National Board Review, 2000, Hank Award, Henry Mancini Institute, 2003, Lifetime Achievement Award, Screen Actors Guild, 2003, Milestone Award, Producers Guild America, 2006, Lifetime Achievement Award, Directors Guild America, 2006, Stanley Kubrick Britannia Award for Excellence in Film, British Academy Film & Television Arts/LA, 2006, Golden Boot Award, Motion Picture & Television Fund, 2006, Jack Valenti Humanitarian Award, Motion Picture Association Am., 2007, Legion d'Honneur Order, Government of France, 2007, Career Achievement Award, Palm Springs International Film Society, 2009, Modern Master Award, Santa Barbara Film Festival, 2009, Golden Palm Award, Cannes Film Festival, 2009, Legion d'Honneur Commander, Government of France, 2009, National Medal of Arts Award, National Endowment for the Arts, 2009, James Smithson Bicentennial Medal, Smithsonian Institution, 2012 **MEM:** Fellow: American Academy Arts & Sciences **BA:** Leonard Hirshan, 1680 Clearview Dr, Beverly Hills, CA, 90210

EBERSOLE, CHRISTINE, T: Actress **I:** Media & Entertainment **DOB:** 12/21/1953 **PB:** Chicago **SC:** IL/USA **SPN:** Peter Bergman (div.) **ED:** Student, American Academy Dramatic Arts; Student, McMurray College **C:** Actress, 1975- **CW:** Actress: (stage productions) Angel Street, 1976, Green Pond, 1978, On the Twentieth Century, 1978, Oklahoma!, 1979, Camelot, 1980, The Three Sisters, 1982, Geniuses, 1983, Harrigan 'n Hart, 1985, Getting Away with Murder, 1996, Gore Vidal's The Best Man, 2000, 42nd Street, 2001 (Tony award, best actress in a musical, 2001), Dinner at Eight, 2002, Steel Magnolias, 2005, Grey Gardens, 2005 (Outer Critics' Cir. award outstanding actress in a musical 2006, OBIE award Village Voice 2006, Drama Desk award outstanding actress in a musical 2006, Tony award best performance by a leading actress in a musical, 2007), Blithe Spirit, 2009; (films) Tootsie, 1982, Amadeus, 1984, Thief of Hearts, 1984, Mac and Me, 1988, (TV movies) The Doll Maker, 1984, Acceptable Risks, 1986, (TV series) The Cavanaughs, 1986; cast member Saturday Night Live. (Films) Ghost Dad, 1990, Dead Again, 1991, Folks!, 1992, The Lounge People, 1992, My Girl 2, 1994, Richie Rich, 1994, Black Sheep, 1996, Pie in the Sky, 1996, Til There Was You, 1997, My Favorite Martian, 1999, True Crime , 1999, Confessions of a Shopaholic, 2009, The Big Wedding, 2013, The Wolf of Wall Street, 2013(Television) American Dreamer, 1990, Murphy Brown, 1990, Empty Nest, 1991, Rachel Gunn, RN, 1992, Dying to Love You, 1993, Gypsy, 1993, Hey Arnold, 1996, Ally McBeal, 1998, An Unexpected Family, 1996, Just Shoot Me!, 1998, Double Platinum, 1999, Mary and Rhoda, 2000, Will & Grace, 2001, Crossing Jordan, 2004, Related, 2005, Cashmere, 2008, Lipstick Jungle, 2008, Law & Order:SVU, 2008, Samantha Who?, 2009, Royal Pains, 2009, Ugly Betty, 2010, Retired at 35, 2011, Sullivan & Son, 2012, American Horror Story:Coven, 2013, Unbreakable Kimmy Schmidt, 2015, Madam Secretary, 2015, Crisis in Six Scenes, 2016, Search Party, 2016(Theatre) War Paint, 2016 **AW:** Co-recipient Nightlife award for outstanding cabaret duo in a major engagement, 2007

EDGE, GRAEME, T: Musician, Songwriter, and Poet **I:** Media & Entertainment **PB:** Rocester **SC:** Staffordshire, England **CW:** Albums with Moody Blues, "The Magnificent Moodies" (1965), "Days of Future Passed" (1967), "In Search of the Lost Chord" (1968), "On the Threshold of a Dream" (1969), "To Our Children's Children's Children" (1969), "A Question of Balance" (1970), "Every

Good Boy Deserves Favour" (1971), "Seventh Sojourn" (1972), "Octave" (1978), "Long Distance Voyager" (1981), "The Present" (1983), "The Other Side of Life" (1986), "Sur La Mer" (1988), "Keys of the Kingdom" (1991), "Strange Times" (1999), "December" (2003); Solo Album, "Kick Off Your Muddy Boots" (1975), "Paradise Ballroom" (1977) **AW:** Inductee, Rock & Roll Hall of Fame (2018)

EDWARDS, JOHN BEL, T: U.S. Governor from Louisiana **I:** Government Administration/Government Relations/Government Services **DOB:** 04/18/1979 **PB:** New Orleans **SC:** LA/USA **ED:** JD, Louisiana State University Law School, 1999; BS in Engineering, U.S. Military Academy, 1988 **C:** Governor, State of Louisiana, 2015-; Member District 72, Louisiana House of Reps., 2008-2015; Chair special committee on military and vets. affairs committee, Louisiana House of Reps.; Member civil law and procedure committee, education committee, judiciary committee, house committee on homeland security, joint committee on homeland security, Louisiana House of Reps.; Attorney **PA:** Democrat **BA:** Office of the Governor, P.O. Box 94004, Baton Rouge, LA, 70804

EDWARDS, MARC A., I: Education/Educational Services **PB:** 1964 **ED:** PhD in Environmental Engineering, University of Washington, Seattle, 1991; MS in Environmental Engineering, University of Washington, Seattle, 1988; BS in Biophysics, State University of New York, Buffalo, 1986 **C:** Charles P. Lunsford professor, department of civil and environmental engineering, Virginia Poly. Institute and State University, Blacksburg, 2004-; Faculty member, Virginia Poly. Institute and State University, Blacksburg, 1997-2004; Faculty member, University Colorado, Boulder, **CR:** President Association Environmental Engineering and Sci. Professors **CW:** Contributor articles to sci. journals **AW:** Named a MacArthur Fellow, The John D. and Catherine T. MacArthur Foundation, 2007; recipient Walter L. Huber Civil Engineering Research prize, American Society of Civil Engineers, 2003, Presidential Faculty Fellow CAREER award, National Science Foundation, 1996, H.P. Eddy award, Water Pollution Control Federation, 1990

EFRON, ZAC, T: Actor, Singer **I:** Media & Entertainment **PB:** San Luis Obispo **SC:** CA/USA **PT:** David Efron; Starla Efron **CW:** Actor: (TV films) The Big Wide World of Carl Laemke, 2003, Triple Play, 2004, Miracle Run, 2004, If You Lived Here, You'd Be Home Now, 2006, High School Musical, 2006 (Choice Breakthrough Star award, Choice Chemistry award, Teen Choice Awards, 2006); High School Musical 2, 2007, Robot Chicken DC Comics Special II: Villains in Paradise (voice), 2014; (TV series) Summerland, 2004-05; (films) The Derby Stallion, 2005, Hairspray, 2007 (Breakthrough Performance, MTV Movie Awards, 2008); High School Musical 3: Senior Year, 2008 (Best Male Performance, MTV Movie Awards, 2009, Choice Movie Rockstar Moment, 2009), 17 Again, 2009 (Choice Movie Actor: Drama, Teen Choice Awards, 2012), Charlie St. Cloud, 2010, New Year's Eve, 2011, Liberal Arts, 2012, Dr. Seuss' The Lorax (voice), 2012, The Lucky One, 2012 (Choice Movie Actor: Drama, Choice Movie Actor: Romance, Teen Choice Awards, 2012), The Paperboy, 2012, At Any Price, 2012, Parkland, 2013, Neighbors, 2014, We Are Your Friends, 2015, Dirty Grandpa, 2016, Neighbors 2: Sorority Rising, 2016, Mike and Dave Need Wedding Dates, 2016; The Disaster Artist, 2017, Baywatch, 2017, The Greatest Showman, 2017, The Beach Bum, 2018, Extremely Wicked, Shockingly Evil and Vile, 2018; actor, executive

producer (films) That Awkward Moment, 2014; singer: (albums) High School Musical, 2006, Hairspray, 2007, High School Musical 2, 2007, High School Musical 3: Senior Year, 2008 (Choice Movie Actor: Comedy, Teen Choice Awards, 2009, Choice Actor Music/Dance, Teen Choice Awards, 2009) **AW:** Named Favorite Dramatic Movie Actor, People's Choice Awards, 2013, Favorite Movie Star Under 25, 2011; named one of The World's Most Influential People, TIME magazine, 2009, The 100 Most Powerful Celebrities, Forbes.com, 2008, Top 25 Entertainers of Year, Entertainment Weekly, 2007

EGGERS, DAVID, T: Writer **I:** Writing and Editing **PB:** Boston **SC:** MA/USA **CW:** Author, (Books) (Nonfiction) A Heartbreaking Work Of Staggering Genius, 2000, Teachers Have It Easy: The Big Sacrifices And Small Salaries Of Americas Teachers, 2005, Surviving Justice: Americas Wrongfully Convicted And Exonerated, 2005, Zeitoun, 2009, The Monk Of Mokha, 2018, (Nonfiction) You Shall Know Our Velocity, 2002, Sacrament, 2003, The Unforbidden Is Compulsory; Or, Optimism, 2004, How We Are Hungry, 2004, Short Short Stories, 2005, What Is The What: The Autobiography Of Valentino Achak Deng, 2006, How The Water Feels To The Fishes, 2007, The Wild Things – Novel Inspired By Where The Wild Things Are, 2009, A Hologram For The King, 2012, The Circle, 2013, Your Fathers, Where Are They? And The Prophets, Do They Live Forever?, 2014, Stories Upon Stories, 2016, Heroes Of The Frontier, 2016, Lifters, 2018, (Humor) Giraffes? Giraffes!, 2003, Your Disgusting Head, 2004, Animals Of The Ocean, In Particular The Giant Squid, 2006, Cold Fusion, 2009,(Screenplays) Away We Go, 2009, Where The Wild Things Are, 2009, Promised Land, 2012, The Circle, 2017

EHRENREICH, BARBARA, T: writer **I:** Writing and Editing **DOB:** 08/26/1941 **PB:** Butte **PT:** Daughter of Ben Howes and Isabelle (Oxley) Alexander; Married John H. Ehrenreich, August 6, 1966; children: Rosa, Benjamin; Married Gary Stevenson, December 10, 1983 **ED:** Doctor (hon.), La Trobe University, Melbourne, Australia; Doctor (hon.), UMass-Lowell; Doctor (hon.), John Jay College; Doctor (hon.), College of Wooster, Ohio; Doctor (hon.), State University of New York, Old Westbury; Doctor (hon.), Reed College; PhD in Biology, Rockefeller University, 1968; BA in Chemical Physics, Reed College, 1963 **C:** Columnist, The Guardian, United Kingdom, 1992-; Fellow, Institute Policy Studios, Washington, 1982-; Essayist, Time magazine, 1991-97; Columnist, Mother Jones magazine, 1986-89; Editor, Seven Days magazine, 1974; Fellow, New York Institute Humanities, New York City, 1980; Free-lance writer, lecturer,; Assistant professor, SUNY-Old Westbury, 1971-74; Editor, Health Policy Adv. Center, New York City, 1969-70 **CW:** Author: For Her Own Good: 150 Years of the Experts' Advice to Women, 1978, (with Deirdre English) The American Health Empire, 1970, (with John Ehrenreich) Witches, Midwives and Nurses: A History of Women Healers, 1972, (with D. English) Complaints and Disorders: The Sexual Politics of Sickness, 1973, The Hearts of Men: American Dreams and the Flight from Commitment, (with E. Hess & G. Jacobs) Re-Making Love: The Feminization of Sex, 1986, (with others) The Mean Season: The Attack on the Welfare State, 1987, Fear of Falling: The Inner Life of the Middle Class, 1989, The Worst Years of Our Lives: Irreverent Notes From An Age of Greed, 1990, Kipper's Game, 1993, Blood Rites: Origins and History of the Passions of War, 1997, Nickeled and Dimed: On (Not) Getting by in America, 2001 (Christoper award, 2002, LA Times Book award, 2002, New York Times Bestseller list), Bait and Switch: The (Futile) Pursuit of

the American Dream, 2005, Dancing in the Streets: A History of Collective Joy, 2007, This Land is Their Land: Reports From a Divided Nation, 2008, Bright Sided: How the Relentless Promotion of Positive Thinking Has Undermined America, 2009, Living with a Wild God, 2014; contributing editor: Ms magazine, 1981-, Mother Jones magazine, 1988-, Leavs magazine, 1988-. **AW:** Recipient National Magazine award, 1980, Ford Foundation award for Humanistic Perspectives on Contemporary Issues, 1981; Guggenheim fellow, 1987, Sydney Hillman award for Journalism.National Magazine Award, 2002, Puffin Nation Prize for Creative Citizenship, 2004, Freedom from Want Medal, 2007

EID, ALLISON HARTWELL, T: Federal Judge **I:** Law and Legal Services **PB:** Seattle **SC:** WA/USA **ED:** Temple Bar scholar, London; JD, University Chicago, 1991; BA in Am. Studies with honors, Stanford University, 1987 **CT:** Bar: 1991 **C:** Judge, U.S. Court of Appeals for the Tenth Circuit,2017-; Justice, Colorado Supreme Court, 2006-17; Solicitor general, State of Colorado, 2005-06; Former chief legal officer, Colorado Attorney General,; Associate professor law, University Colorado, 1998-2005; Former attorney, Arnold & Porter, Denver,; Clerk to Justice Clarence Thomas, US Supreme Court, 1993; Clerk to Judge Jerry E. Smith, US Court of Appeals for Fifth Circuit, Houston, 1991; Former special assistant and speechwriter, US Department Education, **CR:** Member Permanent Committee for Oliver Wendell Holmes Devise, 2002- **MEM:** Mem.: Am. Law Institute, Order of the Coif, Phi Beta Kappa **BA:** 1823 Stout St, Denver, CO, 80202

EISGRUBER, CHRISTOPHER LUDWIG, T: President of Princeton University **I:** Education/Educational Services **DOB:** 09/24/1961 **PB:** West Lafayette **SC:** IN/USA **PT:** Son of Ludwig Maria and Eva R. Eisgruber **MS:** Married **SPN:** Lori A. Martin, June 14, 1987; **CH:** Danny **ED:** JD, The University of Chicago, 1988; MLitt in Politics, Oxford University, 1987; AB in Physics, Princeton University, 1983 **C:** President, Princeton University, 2013-; Laurance S. Rockefeller Professor Public Affairs Woodrow Wilson School Public Affairs & the Univ. Center for Human Values, Princeton University, 2004-13; Provost, Princeton University, 2004-13; Director Law & Public Affairs Program, Princeton University, 2001-04; Professor Law, New York University School Law, New York City, 1995-2004; Associate Professor, New York University School Law, New York City, 1993-95; Assistant Professor, New York University School Law, New York City, 1990-93; Law Clerk to Justice John Paul Stevens, Supreme Court of the U.S., Washington, 1989-90; Law Clerk to Hon. Patrick Higginbotham, U.S. Court Appeals (5th Cir.), Dallas, 1988-89 **CW:** Editor in Chief University Chicago Law Rev., 1987-88; Co-convenor Colloquium in Constitutional Theory, 1993-97; Author: Constitutional Self Government, 2001, The Next Justice: Repairing the Supreme Court Appointments Process, 2007; Co-author: (with Lawrence G. Sager) Religious Freedom and the Constitution, 2007; Co-editor: (with Andres Sajo) Global Justice and the Bulwarks of Globalism: Human Rights in Campus, 2005 **AW:** Rhodes Scholar, 1983. **MEM:** Mem.: American Law Institute **BA:** Office of the President Princeton University, 1 Nassau Hall, Princeton, NJ, 08544

EK, DANIEL, T: entrepreneur, technologist **I:** Technology **DOB:** 02/21/1983 **ED:** Attended, Royal Institute Tech., Sweden **C:** Co-founder, CEO, Spotify, London, 2006-; Founder, Advertigo,; CEO, Torrent,; Chief tech. officer, Stardoll,; Chief tech. officer, Jajja Communications, **AW;** Named one of The 100 Most Influential People in the World, TIME magazine, 2012, The 40 Under 40, Fortune magazine, 2011-13,Time 100 Most Influential, 2017

ELBA, IDRIS, I: Media & Entertainment **DOB:** 09/06/1972 **PB:** London **SC:** England **PT:** Winston Elba; Eve Elba **CW:** Actor: (TV series) Ruth Rendell Mysteries, 1996, Insiders, 1997, Ultraviolet, 1998, Dangerfield, 1999, The Wire, 2002-04, The Office, 2009; (films) Sorted, 2000, Buffalo Soldiers, 2001, One Love, 2003, The Gospel, 2005, Daddy's Little Girls, 2007, The Reaping, 2007, 28 Weeks Later, 2007, American Gangster, 2007, This Christmas, 2007, Prom Night, 2008, RocknRolla, 2008, The Human Contract, 2008, The Unborn, 2009, Obsessed, 2009, The Losers, 2010, Takers, 2010, Thor, 2011, Ghost Rider: Spirit of Vengeance, 2011, Prometheus, 2012, They Die by Dawn, 2012, Pacific Rim, 2013, Mandela: Long Walk to Freedom, 2013, Thor: The Dark World, 2013, Second Coming, 2014, The Gunman, 2015, Avengers: Age of Ultron, 2015, Zootopia (voice), 2016, The Jungle Book (voice), 2016, Bastille Day, 2016, Finding Dory (voice), 2016, Star Trek Beyond, 2016; (TV films) Sometimes in April, 2005, World of Trouble, 2005, All in the Game, 2006; actor, executive producer (films) Legacy, 2010, No Good Deed, 2014, actor, producer Beasts of No Nation, 2015 (Screen Actors Guild award for Outstanding Performance by a Male Actor in a Supporting Role, 2016), A Hundred Streets, 2016; executive prodr.: (films) Demons Never Die, 2011; (documentaries) Idris Elba's How Clubbing Changed the World, 2012, Mandela, My Dad and Me, 2015; actor, executive producer (TV series) Luther, 2010-15 (Golden Globe award for Best Performance by an Actor in a Mini-Series or Motion Picture Made for TV, 2012, National Association for the Advancement of Colored People Image award for Outstanding Actor in a TV Movie, Mini-Series or Dramatic Special, 2011, 2014, Critics' Choice award for Best Actor in a Movie Made for TV or Limited Series, 2016, Screen Actors Guild award for Outstanding Performance by a Male Actor in a TV Movie or Mini-Series, 2016), TV appearances Absolutely Fabulous, 1995, The Governor, 1996, Silent Witness, 1997, London's Burning, 2001, CSI: Miami, 2003, The Big C, 2010; singer: (albums) Big Man, 2006, Kings Among Kings, 2009, High Class Problems Vol. 1, 2010 **AW:** Named Best Actor, BET Awards, 2011, 2010

ELLIOTT, MISSY, I: Media & Entertainment **DOB:** 07/01/1971 **PB:** Portsmith **SC:** VA/USA **CW:** Musician: (albums) Supa Dupa Fly, 1997, Da Real World, 1999, Miss E...So Addictive, 2001, Under Construction, 2002, This Is Not A Test!, 2003, The Cookbook, 2005, Block Party, 2009, (songs) The Rain (Supa Dupa Fly), 1997 (Best Video of Year, Rolling Stone, 1997, Best Clip and Best New Artist, Billboard Video Music Awards, 1997), Hot Boyz, 1999 (Top Hot R&B/Hip Hop Single and Top Hot Rap Single, Billboard Year-End Charts, 2000), Get Ur Freak On, 2001 (Soul Train Lady of Soul award for Best R&B/Soul or Rap Music Video, 2001, 2002, Best Single of Year, Rolling Stone, 2001, Grammy award for Best Rap Solo, 2002), One Minute Man, 2001 (Soul Train Lady of Soul award for Best R&B/ Soul or Rap Music Video, 2002), Work It, 2002 (Best Single, Rolling Stone, 2002, Soul Train Music award for Rest R&B/Soul or Rap Music Video, 2003, Best Song and Best Music Video, Soul Train Lady of Soul Awards, 2003, Video of Year and Best Hip Hop Video, MTV Video Music Awards, 2003, Grammy award for Best Female Rap Solo Performance, 2004), Scream aka Itchin, 2002 (Grammy award for Best Female Rap Solo Performance, 2003), Lose Control, 2005 (Best Dance Video and Best Hip Hop Video, MTV Video Music Awards, 2005, Grammy award for Best Short Form Music Video, 2006), We Run This, 2006 (MTV Video Music award for Video Special Effects, 2006)(Film) Pootie Tang, 2001, Ultrasounds: Hip Hop Dollars, 2003, Honey, 2003, Fade to Black, 2004, Shark Tale,

2004, Just for Kicks, 2005 **AW:** Named Best Female Hip-Hop Artist, BET, 2002, Best Female Artist, Best R&B Artist, Rolling Stone, 2002, Top Hot R&B/Hip Hop Singles & Tracks Artists - Female, Billboard Year-End Charts, 2001, Top Hot Rap Artist and Top Hot Female Rap Artist, 2000, Best Rap Artist of Year, Rolling Stone, 1997; named one of 50 Greatest Hip Hop Artists, VH1, 2003; recipient Best Female Hip-Hop Artist award, BET Awards, 2008, 2006, 2004, 2003, Favorite Female Hip-Hop Artist award, Am. Music Awards, 2005, 2003

ELLISON, KEITH MAURICE, T: U.S. Representative from Minnesota, Lawyer **I:** Law and Legal Services **DOB:** 08/04/1963 **PB:** Detroit **SC:** MI/USA **PT:** Leonard Ellison; Clida Ellison **ED:** JD, University of Minnesota School of Law (1990); BA in Economics, Wayne State University, Detroit, MI (1987) **C:** Member, U.S. Congress from the Fifth Minnesota District, Washington, DC (2007-Present); Member, District 58B, Minnesota House of Representatives, Minneapolis, MN (2003-2007); Attorney, Hassan & Reed Ltd. (1998-2007); Executive Director, Legal Rights Center (1993-1998); Associate, Linquist & Vennum (1990-1993); Member, Committee on Financial Services, Committee on Foreign Affairs, Judiciary Committee **AW:** Recipient, Distinguished Service Award, Sierra Club (2011); Recipient, Trailblazer Award, American-Arab Anti-Discrimination Committee (2007) **ACH:** First Muslim elected to US Congress; first African-American elected to Congress from Minnesota **PA:** Democratic–Farmer–Labor Party

ELLISON, LARRY, T: Entrepreneur **I:** Information Technology and Services **CN:** Oracle Corporation **DOB:** 08/17/1944 **PB:** New York **SC:** NY/USA **ED:** Student, University of Chicago, 1965-1966; Student, University of Illinois, Urbana-Champaign, 1963-1965 **C:** Executive Chairman, Chief Technology Officer, Oracle Corporation, Redwood, CA, 2014-Present; Chairman, Oracle Corporation, Redwood, CA, 1995-2004; Chairman, Oracle Corporation, Redwood, CA, 1990-1992; President, Oracle Corporation, Redwood, CA, 1978-1996; CEO, Oracle Corporation, Redwood, CA, 1977-2014; Co-Founder (With Bob Miner & Ed Oates), Oracle Corporation, Redwood, CA, 1977; President, Systems Division, Omex Corp., 1972-1977; Amdahl, Inc., Santa Clara, CA, 1967-1971; Systems Architect, Amdahl, Inc., Santa Clara, CA **CR:** Trustee, U.S. Council International Business; Board of Directors, Apple Computer, Inc., 1997-2002; Oracle Corp., 1977-Present **AW:** The Forbes 400: Richest Americans, 2006-Present, The World's Richest People, Forbes Magazine, 1999-Present, Forbes Fifth Wealthiest In The U.S., Eighth Wealthiest In The World, 2018, World's Most Powerful People, Forbes Magazine, 2013, The Business People of the Year, Fortune Magazine, 2010, The 50 Who Matter Now, CNNmoney.com Business 2.0, 2006, Bio-IT Champion, Bio-Itworld, 2002, Industry Achievement Award, 1997, Distinguished Information Sciences Award, Association of Information Technology Professionals, 1996, Leadership Award For Global Integration, 1994, Entrepreneur of the Year, Harvard Business School, 1990 **H:** Yachting, Tennis, Guitar **BA:** The Ellison Medical Foundation, 104 E Ridgeville Boulevard, Mount Airy, MD, 21771

ELLISON, MARVIN RAY, T: Chairman **I:** Retail/ Sales **CN:** J.C. Penney Company Inc **ED:** MBA, Emory University Goizueta School Business; BBA in Marketing, University of Memphis, 1989 **C:** Chairman, J.C. Penney, 2016-; CEO, J.C. Penney Co Inc., 2015-; President, J.C. Penney Co. Inc., 2014-15; Executive vice president, US Stores, The Home Depot, Inc., 2008-14; President, Northern Division, The Home Depot, Inc., 2006-08; Senior

vice president, global logistics, The Home Depot, Inc., 2005-06; Vice president, global logistics, The Home Depot, Inc., 2004-05; Vice president, loss prevention, The Home Depot, Inc., 2002-04; Various management and executive positions including director, assets protection, Target Corp., 1987-2002 **CR:** Board of Directors J.C. Penney & Co. Inc., 2014-, FedEx Corp., 2014-, US Home Systems Inc., 2012-, H&R Block, Inc., 2011-14

ELROD, JENNIFER WALKER, T: Federal Judge **I:** Law and Legal Services **DOB:** 09/06/1966 **PB:** Port Arthur **SC:** Texas **ED:** JD, Harvard Law School, 1992; BA in Economic, Baylor University, 1988 **CT:** Bar: Texas 1992 **C:** Judge, US Court Appeals (5th Cir.), 2007-; Trial judge, 190th District Court, Harris County, Texas, 2002-07; Associate, Baker Botts L.L.P., Houston, 1994-2002; Law clerk to Hon. Sim Lake, US District Court (so. district) Texas, 1992-94 **CR:** Adj. faculty University Houston Law Center, 1995 **AW:** Recipient President award for Outstanding Service, Houston Bar Association, Thomas Gibbs Gee award for Outstanding Pro Bono Work, Baker Botts L.L.P. **MEM:** Mem.: State Bar Texas (member Texas Center Legal Ethics & Professionalism Board) **BA:** John Minor Wisdom U.S. Court of Appeals Building Fifth Circuit, 600 Camp St, New Orleans, LA, 70130

ELS, ERNIE, T: Professional Golfer **I:** Athletics **DOB:** 10/17/1969 **PB:** Kempton Park **SC:** South Africa **PT:** Son of Cornelius and Hester Els **ED:** Diploma, Jan de Klerk Tech. College **C:** Professional Golfer, PGA Tour, 1994 **CR:** Member, South African National Team Dunhill Cup, 1992, 93, 94, 95, 96, 97, 98, 99, 2000, World Cup, 1992, 93, 96, 97, 2001, Member, International Team, Presidents Cup, 1996, 98, 2000, 03, 07, 09, 2011, Host, Ernie Els Invitational, South Africa, Golf Course Designer, Ernie Els Design, Founder Ernie Els Wines, Ernie Els Wine & Golf Safaris **CIV:** Founder, Ernie Els & Fancourt Foundation **AW:** Recipient, Lifetime Membership, PGA European Tour, 1998; Named PGA Tour Rookie of Year, 1994, European Tour Player of Year, 1994, 2002, 2003, South African Sportsman of Year, 1994, World Golf Hall of Fame, 2011, Payne Stewart Award, 2015, European Tour Order of Merit Winner, 2003, 2004, PGA Tour Rookie of the Year, 1994, European Tour Player of the Year, 1994, 2002, 2003, Sunshine Tour Order of Merit Winner, 1991-92, 1994-95 **MEM:** Member, Ocean Club (Paradise Island, The Bahamas) **ACH:** Achievements include winning PGA Tour Major Championships: US Open, 1994, 97, British Open, 2002, 2012; 58 career international victories; 19 career PGA Tour victories **H:** Squash, Movies, Winemaking

ELWAY, JOHN ALBERT, T: Former NFL Player, Broncos General Manager **I:** Athletics **DOB:** 06/28/1960 **PB:** Port Angeles **SC:** WA/USA **PT:** Son of John Albert and Janet (Jordan) Elway; **ED:** BA in Economics, Stanford University, 1983 **C:** Executive vice president football ops, general manager, Denver Broncos, 2014-; Owner, John Elway's Manhattan Beach Toyota, California, 2007-; Co-owner, John Elway's Crown Toyota, Ontario, California, 2004-; Restaurant co-owner, Elway's, Denver, 2004-; Executive vice president football operations, Denver Broncos, 2011-14; Co-owner, CEO, Colorado Crush, Arena Football League, 2002-09; Co-owner, John Elway AutoNation, 1997-2006; Quarterback, Denver Broncos, 1983-98 **CIV:** Founder, The Elway Foundation, Quarterbacks coach, Cherry Creek HS, Greenwood Village, Colorado, 2007 Chairman, Rocky Mountain Regional National Kidney Foundation, Member mayor's council on physical fitness, City of Denver, **CW:** (TV appearances) Home Improvement, 1994, Las Vegas, 2004, (film appearances) Resurrecting the Champ, 2007 **AW:** Named Executive of Year, Arena Football League, 2007, Super Bowl XXXIII MVP, 1998, Edge NFL Man of Year, 1992, American Football Conference Offensive MVP/Player of Year, 1993, 1987, NFL MVP/Player of Year, Associated Press, 1987, NFL All-Pro, 1997, 1996, 1993, 1987, 1986; named to The NFL Hall of Fame, 2004, The College Football Hall of Fame, 2000, The Colorado Sports Hall of Fame, 1999, The 1990's All-Decade Team, American Football Conference Pro Bowl Team, 1998, 1997, 1996, 1994, 1993, 1991, 1989, 1987, 1986, Sporting News NFL All-Pro Team, 1987, Sporting News College All-American Team, 1982, 1980; recipient Founders award, Arena Football League **ACH:** Achievements include being the first overall selection in the NFL Draft, 1983; leading the NFL in: pass attempts, 1985, 1993; pass completions, passing yards, 1993; member of Super Bowl Championship winning Denver Broncos, 1998, 1999 **H:** Hunting, fishing, golf

EMANUEL, RAHM ISRAEL, T: Mayor, Chicago, Former White House Chief of Staff, Former U.S. Representative from Illinois **I:** Government Administration/Government Relations/Government Services **DOB:** 11/29/1959 **PB:** Chicago **SC:** IL/USA **PT:** Benjamin M. Emanuel, Marsha (Smulevitz) Emanuel **ED:** Honorary Doctor in Public Service, George Washington University, 2009; MA in Speech & Communications, Northwestern University, 1985; BA in Liberal Arts, Sarah Lawrence College, Bronxville, NY, 1981 **C:** Mayor, City of Chicago, 2011-Present; Chief of Staff to President, The White House, Washington, DC, 2009-2010; Chairman, U.S. House Democratic Caucus, 2006-2009; U.S. Congress From Fifth Illinois District, 2003-2009; Managing Director, Dresdner Kleinwort Wasserstein, Chicago, IL, 1999-2002; Director of Special Projects, Senior Advisor for Policy & Strategy, The White House, Washington, DC, 1995-1998; Assistant to President, Director of Political Affairs, Deputy Director of Communications, The White House, Washington, DC, 1993-1995; National Finance Director, Clinton/Gore Campaign, 1991-1992; Senior Advisor, Chief Fundraiser, Mayoral Campaign of Richard M. Daley, 1988-1989; National Campaign Director, Democratic Congressional Campaign Committee (DCCC), 1987-1988; Senior Advisor, Chief Fundraiser, Rep. Paul Simon's Campaign for U.S. Senate, 1984; Illinois Public Action Council, 1981-1983; Finance Director, David L. Robinson Campaign for U.S. Congress, 1980 **CR:** Board of Directors, Freddie Mac (Federal Home Loan Mortgage Corp.), 2000-2001, Vice Chairman, Chicago Illinois Housing Authority, 1998, Co-Director, Presidential Inaugural Committee, 1993 **CW:** Co-Author, (With Bruce Reed) The Plan: Big Ideas for America, 2006 **AW:** The 100 Agents of Change, Rolling Stone Magazine, 2009, The Global Elite, Newsweek Magazine, 2008, The 50 Most Powerful People in DC, GQ Magazine, 2007, 2009, Great Laker Award, Healing Our Waters-Great Lakes Coalition, 2007, Alumni Achievement Citation, Sarah Lawrence College, 2001 **PA:** Democrat

EMMER, TOM, T: U.S. Representative from Minnesota **I:** Government Administration/Government Relations/Government Services **DOB:** 03/03/1961 **PB:** South Bend, Ind., March 3, 1961 **ED:** JD, William Mitchell College Law, 1988; BA in History, University Alaska, Fairbanks, 1984 **C:** Mem., US Congress from 6th Minnesota District, Washington, 2014-; Member, Committee on Financial Services, Republican Study Committee; Managing partner, Emmer Law Firm, 2005-; Member health policy & finance committee, Minnesota House of Reps., 2005-06; Member District 19B, Minnesota House of Reps., 2005-11; Councilman, City of Delano, 2003-04; Councilman, City of Independence, 1995-2002 **PA:** Republican **BA:** 315 Cannon House Office Building, Washington, DC, 20515

ENGEL, ELIOT LANZE, T: U.S. Representative from New York, Ranking Minority Member of the House Foreign Affairs Committee **I:** Government Administration/Government Relations/Government Services **DOB:** 02/18/1947 **PB:** New York **SC:** NY/USA **PT:** Philip Engel, Sylvia (Bleend) Engel **ED:** JD, New York Law School, 1987; MS in Guidance and Counseling, City University of New York Herbert H. Lehman College, 1973; BA in History, Hunter-Lehman College, 1969 **C:** U.S. Congress From 16th New York District, 2013-Present; Ranking Minority Member, House of Foreign Affairs Committee, 2013-Present; U.S. Congress From 17th New York District, 1993-2013; U.S. Congress From 19th New York District, 1989-1993; District 81, New York State Assembly, 1977-1988; Guidance Counselor, New York Public Schools, 1973-1975; Teacher, Department Chairman, New York Board of Education, 1969-1976; Counselor, Advisor, New York Urban Corps, 1968 **CIV:** Vice President, Park-East Independent Democratic Club, New York, 1970-1971, Delegate, Bronx Committee For Democratic Voters, 1971-1976, Delegate, Steering Committee, Youth Caucus, Democratic National Convention, 1972, Committeeman, Bronx County Democratic Committee, New York, 1972, Vice President, Independent Democrats Of Co-Op City, 1972-1973, Executive Council, New York State New Democratic Coalition, 1973-1975, President, Independent Democrats Of Co-Op City, 1974-1975, Founder, New Democratic Club, Co-Op City, 1975, President, New Democratic Club, Co-Op City, 1975-1976, Judicial Delegate, New York Supreme Court Convention, First Judicial District, 1975-1976, Vice President, Bronx Committee For Democratic Voters, 1975-1976, District Leader, New York Supreme Court Convention, First Judicial District, 1976 **CW:** Columnist, Co-op City News, 1972 **AW:** Notable Americans Award, Historic Preservation Of America, Humanitarian Award, United Field Representatives & Staff Union, Distinguished Service Award, Council on Negro Women, Inc., Legislator of the Year, Children Are Precious, 1990, Man of the Year Award, FDR Independent Democrat Club, 1976 **MEM:** Board of Directors, Americans For Democratic Action, 1974, United Fund for Teachers, Zionist Organization of America, Knights Of Pythias **PA:** Democrat **BA:** U.S. House of Representatives, 2161 Rayburn House Office Bldg, Washington, DC, 20515

ENGEL, ZACHARY, T: Chef **I:** Food & Restaurant Services **C:** Chef De Cuisine, Shaya New Orleans; Pastry Assistant, Domenica **AW:** James Beard Award for Rising Star Chef of the Year, 2017

ENGELBERT, CATHY, T: CEO of Deloitte **I:** Business Management/Business Services **DOB:** 01/01/1900 **ED:** B.S., Accounting, Lehigh University, 1986 **C:** CEO, Deloitte,2015-; Chairman/CEO, Deloitte & Touche, 2014-15; Partner, DELOITTE, 1986-

ENGLE, ROBERT FRY III, T: Economist, Finance Educator **I:** Education/Educational Services **DOB:** 11/10/1942 **PB:** Syracuse **SC:** NY/USA **ED:** Doctor (hon.), HEC International Business School, Paris, 2005; Doctor (hon.), University of Southern Switzerland, 2003; PhD in Economics, Cornell University, Ithaca, New York, 1969; MS in Physics, Cornell University, Ithaca, New York, 1966; BS in Physics, with honors, Williams College, Williamstown, Massachusetts, 1964 **C:** Professor Emeritus and Research Professor,USCD, 2003-; Michael Armellino professor management of fin. services, New York University Stern School of Business, 2000-; Emeritus professor and distinguished research professor, University of California, San Diego, 2003-; Chair department economics, University of California, San Diego, 1990-94; Professor economics, University California, San Diego, 1977-2003; Associate professor, University California, San Diego, 1975-77; Associate professor, Massachusetts Institute of Technology, Cambridge, 1974-75; Assistant professor, Massachusetts Institute of Technology, Cambridge, Massachusetts, 1969-74 **CR:** Research associate National Bureau Economic Research, 1987- **CW:** Editor: Cointegration, Casuality, and Forecasting: A Festschrift in Honour of Clive W.J. Granger, 1999; co-editor: Journal Applied Econometrics, 1985-89; associate editor:, 1988-, associate editor: Journal Regional Sci., 1978-, associate editor: Journal Forecasting, 1985-, member editorial bd.: Real Estate Economics, 2004-; contributor articles to professional journals **AW:** Recipient Nobel prize in economics, 2003, Excellence in Teaching award, Massachusetts Institute of Technology Grad. Economic Association, 1974-75 **MEM:** Fellow: Institute Quantitative Research in Fin., Am. Fin. Association, Econometric Society (council member 1994), Am. Statistical Association, Am. Academy Arts & Sciences; mem.: Society Fin. Econometrics (founding member), Am. Economic Association, National Academy of Sciences **BA:** Kaufman Management Center, 44 West Fourth Street, 9-62, New York, NY, 10012

ENZI, MICHAEL BRADLEY, T: U.S. Senator from Wyoming **I:** Government Administration/Government Relations/Government Services **DOB:** 02/01/1944 **PB:** Bremerton **PT:** Son of Elmer Jacob and Dorothy (Bradley) Enzi; **ED:** MBA, Denver University, 1968; BBA, George Washington University, 1966 **C:** Chairmen, Senate Budget Committee, 2015-; US Senator from Wyoming, 1997-; Chairman, US Senate Health, Education, Labor & Pensions Committee, 2005-07; Commissioner We. Interstate Commission Higher Education, Wyoming State Senate, 1995-96; Member, Wyoming State Senate, Cheyenne, 1991-96; Member, Wyoming House of Reps., Cheyenne, 1986-91; Accounting manager, Dunbar Well Service, Inc., Gillette, 1985-97; President, NZ Shoes, Inc., Sheridan, Wyoming, 1983-96; President, NZ Shoes, Inc., Gillette, Wyoming, 1969-95; Mayor, City of Gillette, Wyoming, 1975-82 **CR:** Member Education Commission States, 1989-93 **CIV:** President, Wyoming Association Mcpls., Cheyenne, 1980-82 Board directors, Black Hills Corp., 1992-96 Chairman board directors, First Wyoming Bank, Gillette, 1978-88 **AW:** Named Policy Maker of Year, Association Career & Tech. Education, 2005, Legis. of Year, Biotechnology Industry Organization, 2005, Am. Society Consultant Pharmacists, 2004; recipient TechNet Founders Cir. award, 2005, Leadership award, National Organization Fetal Alcohol Syndrome, 2005, Congl. Leadership award, Food Industry Association, 2005, Small Investor Empowerment award, National Association Real Estate Investment Trusts, 2002, W. Stuart Symington award, Air Force Association, 2001 **MEM:** Mem.: Lions, Wyoming Jaycees (president 1973-74), Shriners, Masons, Wyoming Order of DeMolay (state master councilor 1963-64), Scottish Rite, Sigma Chi **H:** Fishing, bicycling, soccer, hunting **PA:** Republican **BA:** Office of Michael Enzi, 379A Senate Russell Office Building, Washington, DC, 20510

EPSTEIN, THEO NATHAN, T: professional sports team executive **I:** Other **DOB:** 12/29/1973 **PB:** NYC **PT:** Son of Leslie and Ilene Epstein **ED:** JD, University San Diego, 1998; BA in American Studies, Yale University, 1995 **C:** President baseball operations, Chicago Cubs, 2011-; Executive vice president, general manager, Boston Red Sox, 2006-11; General manager, Boston Red Sox, 2002-05; Director baseball operations, San Diego Padres,

2000-02; Baseball operations assistant, San Diego Padres, 1998-2000; Summer intern, media relations, San Diego Padres, 1992-98 **AW:** Named Major League Baseball Executive of Year, Baseball America, 2008; recipient Executive of the Decade, The Sporting News, 2009, Carl Maddox Sport Management award, US Sports Academy, 2007, Time 100 Most Influential, 2017, Sporting News Executive of the Year, 2016, Esurance MLB Award for Best Executive, 2016 **ACH:** Achievements include becoming the youngest general manager in Major League Baseball history, 2002 **BA:** Wrigley Field, 1060 West Addison Street, Chicago, IL, 60613

ERGEN, CHARLES W., T: Chairman **I:** Business Management/Business Services **CN:** Dish Network Corp **DOB:** 03/01/1953 **PB:** Oak Ridge **SC:** TN/USA **ED:** MBA, Wake Forest University, 1976; BS in Business & Accounting, University Tennessee, Knoxville, 1974 **C:** Chairman, EchoStar Corp., Inverness, Colorado, 2009-; Chairman, Dish Network Corp, 2017-; Chairman/CEO, Dish Network Corp. 2015-17; President, CEO, DISH Network Corp. (formerly Echostar Communications Corp.), Englewood, Colorado, 2015-; Chairman, DISH Network Corp. (formerly Echostar Communications Corp.), Englewood, Colorado, 2011-; Chairman, president, CEO, EchoStar Corp., Inverness, Colorado, 2007-09; Founder, chairman, president, CEO, DISH Network Corp. (formerly Echostar Communications Corp.), Englewood, Colorado, 1980-2011; Professional Blackjack Player, Las Vegas, Nevada; Financial Analyst, Frito-Lay, 1976-80 **CR:** Board of Directors, EchoStar Corp., 2007-, DISH Network Corp. (formerly Echostar Communications Corp.), 1980- **AW:** Named CEO of Year, Frost & Sullivan, 2001, Space Industry Business Man of Year, Aviation Week Magazine, 2000, Business Person of Year, Rocky Mountain News, 2001, 1996, Rocky Mountain Region Master Entrepreneur of Year, INC. Magazine, 1991; Named One of Top 10 CEO's, Forbes magazine, 2007, The World's Richest People, 2000-, The Forbes 400: Richest Americans, 1999-; Named to Consumer Electronics Hall of Fame, 2012; Recipient, Star Award, Home Satellite TV Association, 1988 **MEM:** Mem.: Satellite Broadcasting Communications Association (co-founder) **ACH:** Achievements include spearheading the movement for the Satellite Home Viewer Improvement Act in 1999 which gave American consumers the right to watch local TV channels via satellite; testifying before Congress regarding other video competition issues on several occasions **H:** Mountain climbing, Poker, Basketball **BA:** EchoStar Corp, 100 Inverness Terrace E, Englewood, CO, 80112

ERICKSON, RALPH R., T: Federal Judge **I:** Law and Legal Services **DOB:** 04/28/1959 **PB:** Thief River Falls **SC:** MN/USA **ED:** JD, University of North Dakota (1984); BA, Jamestown College (1980) **C:** Judge, U.S. Court of Appeals for the Eighth Circuit (2017-Present); Chief Judge, U.S. District Court for the District of North Dakota (2009-2016); Judge, U.S. District Court for the District of North Dakota, Fargo, ND (2003-2009); District Judge, East Central Judicial District Court, ND (1995-2003); County Judge, Traill, Steele, Nelson & Griggs Counties Court, ND (1994); Magistrate Judge, Cass County Court, ND (1993-1994); Private Practice Attorney, West Fargo, ND (1984-1994) **BA:** Thomas F. Eagleton Courthouse, 111 South 10th Street, St. Louis, MO, 63102

ERNST, JONI KAY, T: U.S. Senator from Iowa **I:** Government Administration/Government Relations/Government Services **DOB:** 07/01/1970 **PB:** Red Oak **PT:** Daughter of Richard and Marilyn Ernst; **ED:** MPA, Columbus College, 1995; BA

in Psychology, Iowa State University, 1992 **C:** Member, Iowa Senate from the 12th District, 2011-2014; Member, US Senate Small Business & Entrepreneurship Committee, 2015-; Member, US Senate Armed Services Committee, 2015-; Member, US Senate Homeland Security & Governmental Affairs Committee, 2015-; Member, US Senate Agricultural Nutrition & Forestry Committee, 2015-; US Senator from Iowa, 2015-; Member District 48, Iowa State Senate, 2011-14; Auditor, Montgomery County, Iowa, 2004-10; Emergency coordinator, Montgomery County, 2001-03; Job Training Partnership Act coordinator, Midlands Technical College, 1997-99; Human resources applicant tester, Blue Cross/Blue Shield, 1996-97; Saleswoman, Parisian Shoes, 1993-95 **CR:** Montgomery County chair Romney for President, 2011-12 co-chair Montgomery County Republican Party, 2006-12 **CIV:** Coordinator, Santa Lucia Festival of Lights Coronation Ceremony, 2011-13 National guard voting assistance officer, 2009-12 Vol. crisis counselor, ACCESS Women's Shelter, 1991-92 Sunday sch.& confirmation teacher, Mamrelund Lutheran Church of Stanton, 2004- **PA:** Republican **BA:** The Office of Joni Ernst, 111 Russell Senate Office Building, Washington, DC, 20510

ERVING, JULIUS, T: Former NBA Player **I:** Athletics **DOB:** 02/22/1950 **PB:** East Meadow **SC:** NY/USA **PT:** Son of Julius Erving and Callie Lindsey; **ED:** Grad., University of Massachusetts, 1986; Doctorate (hon.), U.Mass., 1983; Doctorate (hon.), Temple University, 1983 **C:** President, The Erving Group, 1997—; President, JDREGI; Executive Vice President, Orlando Magic, 1997—2003; Vice President, RDV Sports, Orlando, 1997—2003; In-studio Analyst, NBC Sports, 1993—1997; Co-owner, Coca-Cola Bottling Co., Philadelphia, Pennsylvania, 1987—2007; Forward, Guard, Philadelphia 76ers, 1976-87; Forward, Guard, New York Nets, Am. Basketball Association, 1973-76; Forward, Guard, Virginia Squires, Am. Basketball Association, 1971-73 **CR:** Former Board of Directors Meridian Bancorp, Converse Shoe Co., Darden Restaurants, Inc., The Sports Authority, LCI, Saks Inc. (formerly Proffitt's, Inc.); Board of Directors Fusion Telecommunications, 2003— **CIV:** Trustee NBA International, Basketball Hall of Fame; Board of Directors New York State Sports Commission **CW:** Actor: (films) The Fish That Saved Pittsburgh, 1979 **AW:** Named Rookie of Year Am. Basketball Association (American Bar Association), 1972, 1st Team All-ABA, 1973-76, American Bar Association MVP, 1974-76, American Bar Association Playoffs MVP, 1974, 1976, 1st Team American Bar Association All-Def., 1976, NBA All-Star Game MVP, 1977, 83, 1st Team All-NBA, 1978, 1980-83, NBA MVP, 1981, Man of Year Am. Express, 1985, Sportsman of Year David Zinkoff Memorial Foundation, 1986; Recipient Liberty Bell award Philadelphia Mayor Frank Rizzo, 1978, Cert. Appreciation Easter Seals, 1982, Best Friend Award Police Athletic League Phila, 1982, Walter Kennedy Citizenship Award, 1983, Jackie Robinson Award Ebony Magazine, 1983, Whitney M. Young Award Urban League, 1984, Father Flanagan Award Boys Town Nebraska, 1984, Biddy Basketball Award, 1984, Sports Award Big Brothers Inc., New York City, 1985, Appreciation Award Lupus Foundation Am., 1985; Named to American Bar Association Eastern Conference All-Star Team, 1972-76, NBA Eastern Conference All-Star Team, 1977-87, Univ. Massachusetts Hall of Fame, 1980, NBA 35th Anniversary All-Time Team, 1980, Naismith Memorial Basketball Hall of Fame, 1993, NBA 50th Anniversary All-Time Team, 1996,40 Most Important Athletes of All Time,1994, Nassau County Sports Hall of Fame, 2004 **ACH:** Achievements include leading the American Bar Association in: offensive rebounds, 1972; minutes,

1973; field goal attempts, points per game, 1973, 1974, 1976; field goals made, 1974-76; points, 1974, 1976; member of American Bar Association championship winning New York Nets, 1974, 1976; NBA championship winning Philadelphia 76ers, 1983

ESHOO, ANNA GEORGES, T: U.S. Representative from California **I:** Government Administration/Government Relations/Government Services **DOB:** 12/13/1942 **PB:** New Britain **PT:** Daughter of Fred and Alice Alexandre Georges; **ED:** AA in English, with honors, Canada College, 1975 **C:** Member, US Congress from 18th California District, 2013-; Member, Committee on Agriculture, Committee on Natural Resources; Member, US Congress from 14th California District, Washington, 1993-2013; President, San Mateo County Board Supervisors, 1986; Member, San Mateo County Board Supervisors, 1982-92; Chair, San Mateo Democratic Party, 1978-82; With, Arcata National Corp., 1966-70; With, Alcoa, Inc., 1963-66 **CR:** Member Democratic National Committee, 1981-92, National Committee Presidential Nominations, 1981 chief-of-staff to Speaker Leo McCarthy California State Assembly, 1981 **CIV:** Co-founder, San Mateo Women's Hall of Fame, Chair board directors, San Mateo County General Hospital, 1984-92 **AW:** Named one of The 10 Most Powerful Women of Silicon Vs, San Jose Mercury News, 2011 **MEM:** Mem.: League Women Voters, League Conservation Voters, Democratic Activists for Women Now, Junior League Palo Alto **PA:** Democrat

ESPAILLAT, ADRIANO, T: U.S. Representative From New York **I:** Government Administration/Government Relations/Government Services **DOB:** 09/27/1954 **PB:** Santiago **SC:** Dominican Republic **PT:** Ulises Espaillat, Melba Rodriguez Espaillat **ED:** BS in Political Science, City University of New York, Queens College, 1978 **C:** Committee on Education and the Workforce, Committee on Foreign Affairs, Committee on Small Business, U.S. House of Representatives From New York's 13th District, 2017; District 31, New York State Senate, 2011-2016; District 72, New York State Assembly, 1997-2010; Director, Project Right Start, 1994-1996; Director, Washington Heights Victim Services Community Office, 1992-1994; Manhattan Court Services Coordinator, New York City Criminal Justice Agency, 1980-1988 **CR:** Past President, 34th Precinct Community Council Member; Governor's Dominican American Advisory Board, New York, 1991-1993; Executive Board, Community Planning Board 12, 1986-1991 **CIV:** Mediator, Washington Heights Inwood Conflict Resolutions & Mediation Center, New York, NY, Board of Directors, Dominican American National Roundtable **PA:** Democrat **BA:** 1630 Longworth House Office Building, Washington, DC, 20515

ESPOSITO, PHILIP ANTHONY, T: Retired Professional Hockey Player **I:** Athletics **DOB:** 02/20/1942 **PB:** Sault St. Marie **SC:** Ont./Can. **PT:** Son of Patrick J. and Frances S. (Dipietro) Esposito; **ED:** Student Pub. Schools, Sault Ste. Marie **C:** President, General Manager, Alternate Governor, Tampa Bay Lightning, Tampa, Florida, 1992-97; Head Coach, New York Rangers, New York City, New York, 1986, 87, 1989; Vice President, General Manager, New York Rangers, New York City, New York, 1986-89; TV Commentator, New York Rangers, New York City, 1981-86; Player, New York Rangers, New York City, 1975-81; Player, Boston Bruins, 1967-75; Player, Chicago Black Hawks, 1963-67 **CW:** Author (with Gerald Eskenaz): Hockey is My Life, 1972; Author: (with Tony Esposito) We Can Teach You How to Play Hockey, 1972; Author: (with Dick Dew) Winning Hockey for Beginniners, 1976 **AW:** Named to Hall of Fame; Recipient Player of the

Year, Sporting News E Division, 1972-73, 1971-72, Art Ross Trophy for Leading Scorer, 1971-74, 1969, Hart Memorial Trophy for Most Valuable Player, NHL, 1969 **MEM:** Mem.: Order of Can.

ESSERMAN, LAURA JEAN, **T:** oncologist, educator **I:** Medicine & Health Care **DOB:** 03/24/1957 **PB:** Harvey **ED:** MBA, Stanford Grad. School Business, 1993; MD, Stanford University, 1983; BS, Harvard University **C:** Director, Carol Franc Buck Breast Care Center,; Co-leader, University California Cancer Center Breast Oncology Program, San Francisco,; Affiliate faculty, Institute for Health Policy Studies & Medical Informatics Program,; Professor surgery & radiology, University California, San Francisco,; Staff member, Mount Zion Hospital, San Francisco, 1993; Resident general surgery, Stanford Medical Center, 1990-91; Resident, Stanford Medical Center, 1988-90; Fellow surgery, Stanford Medical Center, 1985-88; Resident medical oncology, Stanford Medical Center, 1983-85; Intern general surgery, Stanford Medical Center, 1983-84

ESTEFAN, GLORIA MARIA, **T:** Singer **I:** Media & Entertainment **DOB:** 09/01/1957 **PB:** Havana **SC:** Cuba **ED:** BA in Psychology, University Miami, Florida, 1978; MusD (hon.), University Miami, Florida, 1993 **C:** Co-owner, Miami Dolphins, 2009—; Co-owner, Bongos Cuban Cafe, Puerto Vallarta, Mexico; Co-owner, Bongos Cuban Cafe, Mexico City, Mexico; Co-owner, Bongos Cuban Cafe, Hollywood, Florida; Co-owner, Costa d'Este, Vero Beach, 2008—; Co-owner, Bongos Cuban Cafe, Miami, 2000—; Co-owner, Bongos Cuban Cafe, Orlando, 1997—; Vice president, Estefan Enterprises, Inc.; Co-owner, The Cardozo, Miami; Co-owner, Cabana Beach Resort (formerly Palm Court Resort Hotel), Vero Beach; Co-owner, Cafe Cardozo; Co-owner, Larios on the Beach **CR:** Board directors Univision Communications Inc. **CW:** Member group Miami Sound Machine, 1975-; singer: (albums) Otra Vez, 1981, Rio, 1982, A Toda Maquina, 1984, Eyes of Innocence, 1984, Primitive Love, 1985, Let It Loose, 1987, Cuts Both Ways, 1989, Into The Light, 1991, Greatest Hits, 1992, Mi Tierra, 1993 (Grammy award for Best Tropical Latin Album, 1994), Christmas Through Your Eyes, 1993, Hold Me, Thrill Me, Kiss Me, 1994, Abriendo Puertas, 1995 (Grammy award for Best Tropical Latin Performance, 1996), Destiny, 1996, Gloria Estefan: The Evolution Tour Live in Miami, 1997, gloria!, 1998, Everlasting Gloria, 1999, Alma Caribena, 2000 (Grammy award for Best Traditional Tropical Latin Album, 2001), No Me Dejes De Querer, 2000, Greatest Hits Volume II, 2001, Que Siga La Tradicion, 2001, Live in Atlantis, 2002, Unwrapped, 2003, Live & Unwrapped, 2004, 90 Millas, 2007 (Billboard Latin Music awards for Female Tropical Album of Year, Tropical Airplay Song of Year, 2008, Latin Grammy awards for Best Traditional Tropical Album and Best Tropical Song, 2008), Miss Little Havana, 2011, The Standards, 2013, Soy Mujer, 2015; actress: (films) Music of the Heart, 1999, (TV films) Club Med, 1986, For Love or Country: The Arturo Sandoval Story, 2000, (TV appearances) Glee, 2012; Broadway musical based on life story: On Your Feet!, 2015; author: (children's books) The Magically Mysterious Adventures of Noelle the Bulldog, 2005, Noelle's Treasure Tale, 2006; collaborator: (cookbook) Estefan Kitchen, 2008. **AW:** Recipient Star, Hollywood Walk of Fame, 1983, Person of Year award, Latin Recording Academy, 2008, Spirit of Hope awards, Latin Billboard Awards, 2011, 26 Grammy awards, The Presidential Medal of Freedom, The White House, 2015, Kennedy Center Honors, 2017 **BA:** Univision Communications Inc, 605 3rd Ave 12Fl, New York, NY, 10158

ESTES, RONALD GENE, **T:** U.S. Representative from Kansas **I:** Government Administration/Government Relations/Government Services **DOB:** 07/19/1956 **PB:** Topeka **SC:** KS/USA **PT:** Son of Billy Dale and Mary Lou (Hendrickson) E. **ED:** MBA, Tennessee Tech. University, 1983; BSCE, Tennessee Tech. University, 1978 **C:** Member, U.S. House of Representatives from Kansas's 4th District, 2017, Member, Commitee on Education and the Workforce, Committee on Homeland Security, Republican Study Committee; State Treasurer, State of Kansas, 2011-2017; Treasurer, Sedgwick County, Kansas, 2004-10; Management Information Consultant, Andersen Consultant, Nashville,; Team Manager, Procter & Gamble Co., Jackson, Tennessee, 1979-81 **AW:** Named One of Outstanding Young Men of Am., 1985. **MEM:** Member Am. Production and Inventory Control Society (Cert.), Tennessee Tech. Alumni Association (Board of Directors 1979-81), Alpha Phi Omega (Chairman Sectional 70 1983-85), Omicron Delta Kappa, Phi Kappa Phi, Beta Gamma Sigma **H:** Athletics **PA:** Republican **BA:** 2452 Rayburn HOB, Washington, DC, 20515

ESTY, ELIZABETH HENDERSON, **T:** U.S. Representative from Connecticut, Former State Legislator **I:** Government Administration/Government Relations/Government Services **DOB:** 08/25/1959 **PB:** Oak Park **SC:** IL/USA **ED:** JD, Yale Law School, 1985; BA, Harvard University, 1981 **C:** Member, U.S. House Space, Sci., & Tech. Committee, 2013-; Member, Committee on Veterans Affairs; Member, U.S. Transportation & Infrastructure Committee, 2013-; Member, U.S. Congress from 5th Connecticut District, 2013-; Member District 103, Connecticut House of Reps., 2008-10; Councilwoman, Town of Cheshire, Connecticut, 2005-08; Senior research scholar, Yale University,; Associate, Sidley Austin LLP,; Law clerk to Hon. Robert Keeton, US District Court Massachusetts, 1985-86 **CR:** Adjunct professor American University **CIV:** Board member, Cheshire Pub. Lib., Vol. legal adv.; Connecticut League Women Voters Consensus Project, Lay member, Committee on Minister for New Haven Association of United Church Christ, **PA:** Democrat **BA:** 221 Cannon House Office Building, Washington, CT, 20515

EVANS, DWIGHT, **T:** U.S. Representative from Pennsylvania **I:** Government Administration/Government Relations/Government Services **DOB:** 05/16/1954 **PB:** Philadelphia **PT:** Son of Henry Evans and Jean E. Odoms **ED:** Grad., La Salle College, 1975; Grad., Community College of Philadelphia, 1973 **C:** Member District 203, Pennsylvania House of Representatives, 1981-16; Member, U.S. House of Representatives from Pennsylvania's 2nd District, 2016-; Chairman, Dem. Appropriations Committee, 1991-; Member, Northwest Polit Coalition & Pennsylvania Council Neighborhoods,; Member, City-Wide Political Alliance,; Vice chairman, Dem. County Executive Committee, Pennsylvania,; Former elementary school teacher,; Former counselor, Urban League Pennsylvania **CR:** Board directors Pennsylvania Black Alliance for Educational Options, National Black Alliance for Educational Options **CIV:** Board directors, Am. Diabetes Association, Board directors, Fox Chase Cancer Center, Board directors, Pub. School Employee's Retirement Systems, Board directors, Pennsylvania Convention Center & Visitor's Bureau, Board directors, Am. Red Cross, Pennsylvania, **AW:** Recipient Service award, Pennsylvania Association Child Care Agencies, Outstanding Achievement award, Pennsylvania Legal Service, 1993, 1979, Distinguished Gentleman award, African Am. Heritage Celebrations, 1993 **MEM:** Mem.: Pub. School Employee Retirement

Syst. Board **H:** Reading, patron of the arts, sports **PA:** Democrat **BA:** 1105 Longworth HOB, Washington, DC, 20515

EVANS, RONALD M., **T:** Professor, Biologist **I:** Education/Educational Services **DOB:** 04/17/1949 **ED:** PhD in Microbiology and Immunology, UCLA, 1974; BA in Bacteriology, UCLA, 1970 **C:** Professor, March of Dimes Chair in Molecular and Developmental Biology, Salk Institute for Biological Studies, San Diego, 1998-; Investigator, Howard Hughes Medical Institute, La Jolla, California, 1985-; Professor Gene Expression lab Salk Institute Biological Studies, Howard Hughes Medical Institute, La Jolla, California, 1986-; Director Gene Expression Laboratory, Salk Institute for Biological Studies, San Diego,; Senior Member molecular biology and virology laboratory Salk Institute Biological Studies, Howard Hughes Medical Institute, La Jolla, California, 1984-86; From Assistant to Associate Professor Tumor Virology Laboratory Salk Institute Biological Studies, Howard Hughes Medical Institute, La Jolla, California, 1978-84; Assistant Research Professor Department of Molecular Cell Biology, Rockefeller University, New York City, 1975-78 **CR:** Lecturer in Field, Speaker Burroughs Wellcome Visiting Professor University of Massachusetts, 1998 Woodward Visiting Professor Memorial Sloan-Kettering, 1996 S. Richard Hill, Junior Visiting Professor University of Alabama, 1995 Member Sci. Adv. Board Osaka Bioscience Institute, 1999-, Dana Farber Cancer Institute, 1996- Member External Sci. Adv. Board Massachusetts General Hospital, 1996- Organizer Numerous Conferences in Field Member Alfred P. Sloan Junior Selection Committee GM Cancer Research Foundation, 1991 Member Program Committee Searle Scholars, 1989-91 Founder and Chair Sci. Adv. Board Ligand Pharmaceutical, 1988- Member National Adv. Committee Pew Scholars Program in Biomedical Scis., 1987-2000 Member Molecular Neurobiology Study Section National Institutes of Health, 1984-85, Member Molecular Biology Study Section, 1983-86 Member External Sci. Adv. Committee City of Hope, 1987 Member Sci. Adv. Board SIBIA, 1983- Chairman Faculty Salk Institute Biological Studies Howard Hughes Medical Institute, La Jolla, 1997-98, La Jolla, 1993-94 Adjunct Professor Department Neurosciences University California, San Diego, 1995-, Adjunct Professor Department of Biomedical Scis. School Medicine, 1989-, Adjunct Professor Department of Biology, San Francisco, 1985- **CIV:** Member Fellowship Screening Committee, Am. Cancer Society, 1987-90 **CW:** Editor: Molecular Endocrinology, 1993-97; Editor: (Associate Editor) Molecular Brain Research, 1985-93, Journal Neuroscience, 1985-90, Neuron, 1987-93; Member Editorial Board Receptors and Channels, 1992-93, Genes and Development, 1992-, Hormones and Signalling, 1996-, Cell Metabolism, -; co-editor: Current Opinion in Cell Biology, 1993; Contributor of Several Articles to Professional Journals **AW:** Named most cited researcher, Institute Scientific Information, 1997, California Scientist of Year, California Museum Sci. and Industry and the California Museum Foundation, 1994; recipient Wolf Foundation Prize in Medicine, 2012, Albany Medical Center prize in Medicine and Biomedical Research, 2007, Gairdner Foundation International award, 2006, Harvey prize in Human Health, 2006, Glenn T. Seaborg medal, 2005, Grande Médaille d'Or, France, 2005, Albert Lasker award for Basic Medical Research, Lasker Foundation, 2004, Alfred P. Sloan Junior Prize, GM Cancer Research Foundation, 2003, Award for Distinguished Achievement in Metabolic Research, Bristol-Myers Squibb, 2000, Fred Conrad Koch Award, Endocrine Society, 1999, Gerald Aurbach

Memorial Award, Association Bone and Mineral Research, 1997, Morton Award, University Liverpool, Biochemical Society, 1996, Dickson Prize in Medicine, University of Pittsburgh, 1994-95, Transatlantic Medal, Society Endocrinology, 1994, Award for Cancer Research, Robert J. and Claire Pasarow Foundation, 1993, Osborne and Mendel Award, Am. Institute Nutrition, 1992, Rita Levi Montalcini Award, Fidia Research Foundation Neuroscience, 1991, Gregory Pincus Memorial Award, Worcester Foundation Experimental Biology, 1991, Van Meter/Rorer Pharmaceutical Prize, Am. Thyroid Association, 1989, Louis S. Goodman and Alfred Gilman Award, Am. Society Pharmacology and Experimental Therapeutics, 1988, Gregory Pincus Medal, Laurentian Society, 1988; Fellow, National Institutes of Health, 1975-78; Research Associate Fellow, Cancer Research Committee California, 1975,The Albany Medical Center Prize, 2012 **MEM:** Fellow: Am. Academy Arts and Sciences; Mem.: National Academy of Sciences, Am. Philosophical Society, Institute of Medicine, Am. Association Cancer Research (Chair Cancer Research Committee 2001, Pezcoller International Award 2001, Eleventh C.P. Rhoads Memorial Award 1990), Harvey Society, Am. Academy Microbiology, Am. Society Microbiology (Fellow), Society Neuroscience, Society Devel. Biology, Endocrine Society (Edwin B. Astwood Lectureship Award 1993)

EVERT, CHRIS, T: Retired Professional Tennis Player **I:** Athletics **DOB:** 12/21/1954 **PB:** Fort Lauderdale **SC:** FL/USA **PT:** Daughter of James and Colette Evert; **MS:** Married **SPN:** Greg; Andy Mill, July 30, 1988 (div. 2006); John Lloyd, April 17, 1979 (div. 1987) **CH:** Alexander James, Nicholas Joseph, Colton Jack **C:** Owner, Evert Enterprises/IMG, Boca Raton, Florida, 1989-; Olympics commentator, CBS Sports, 1992; Professional tennis player, 1972-89 **CR:** Commentator NBC Sports tennis events winner numerous tournaments including U.S. Junior Championship, 1970, 71, U.S. Open, 1975, 76, 77, 78, 80, 82, Wimbledon Singles, 1974, 76, 81, doubles, 1976, Australian Open, 1982, 84, French Open Singles, 1974, 75, 79, 80, 83, 85, 86, Virginia Slims, 1972, 73, 75, 77, 87, European Women's Open, Geneva, 1987, Eckerd Open, 1987 special advisor to U.S. National Tennis Team by U.S. Tennis Association board directors International Tennis Hall of Fame trustee Women's Sports Foundation **CIV:** Founder Chris Evert Charities, Inc., Healthy Start. **CW:** Corp. spokesperson and rep., appearing in TV commls. and print advertisements; host and organizer Chris Evert Pro-Celebrity Tennis Classic, 1989, 90, 92, 93, 94, 95, 96, 97, 98, 99. **AW:** Recipient Lebair Sportsmanship trophy, 1971; named Female Athlete of Year Associated Press, 1974, 75, 77, 80, Athlete of Year Sports Illustrated, 1976, Greatest Woman Athlete of Last 25 Years Women's Sports Foundation, 1985, Flo Hyman award Women's Sports Foundation, 1990, Providencia award Palm Beach County Convention and Visitors Bureau, 1991; named one of Top 10 Romantic People of 1989, Korbel; inducted Madison Sq. Garden Walk of Fame, 1993, inductee, International Tennis Hall of Fame, 1995,Tennis Channel Top 100 of All Time, Special Merit from the International Tennis Hall of Fame, 2013, International Tennis Hall of Fame, 1995 **MEM:** Member U.S. Lawn Tennis Association (Top Women's Singles Player award 1974), National Honor Society, Florida Sports Foundation (board directors), Women's Tennis Association (president 1982-91, executive committee, Sportsmanship award 1979, Player Service awards 1981, 86, 87). **BA:** Chris Evert Charities, 7200 West Camino Real, Suite 310, Boca Raton, FL, 33433

EZEKWESILI, OBIAGELI, T: Accountant **I:** Financial Services **DOB:** 04/28/1963 **ED:** Master's Degree in International Law and Diplomacy, University of Lagos; Master of Public Administration, Kennedy School Harvard University **C:** Co-Founder, Transparency International, 2012-; Vice-President, World Banks Africa Division, 2007-12; Federal Ministers, Solid Minerals of Nigeria, 2005-06; Federal Minister, Education of Nigeria, 2006-07 **AW:** Time 100 Most Influential, 2015

FAIRBANK, RICHARD D., T: Capital One CEO **I:** Financial Services **ED:** MBA, Stanford University, California, 1981; BA in Econs., Stanford University, California, 1972 **C:** Chairman, President, CEO, Capital One Financial Corp., McLean, Virginia, 2005-; Chairman U.S. Region, MasterCard, Inc., 2002-04; Chairman, CEO, Capital One Financial Corp., McLean, Virginia, 1994-2003; Consultant, Strategic Planning Associates, 1981-87 **CR:** Board of Directors MasterCard International Global Board, 2004-, MasterCard U.S. Region, 1995-2004 **AW:** Named Business Leader of Year, Washingtonian Magazine, Best CEO, Institutional Investor Magazine **BA:** Capitol One Headquarters, 1680 Capital One Drive, Mclean, VA, 22102

FALDO, NICK, T: Professional Golfer **I:** Athletics **DOB:** 07/18/1957 **PB:** Hertfordshire **PT:** Married Valerie Faldo; children: Natalie, Matthew, Georgia, Emma. **C:** Professional golfer, PGA, 1976-; Member, Four Tours Championship Team, 1990; Member, Hennessy Cognac Cup Team, 1984; Member, Hennessy Cognac Cup Team, 1982; Member, Hennessy Cognac Cup Team, 1980; Member, Hennessy Cognac Cup Team, 1978; Member, Kirin Cup Team, 1987; Member, Nissan Cup Team, 1986; Member, Dunhill Cup Team, 1985, 86, 87, 88, 91, 93; Member, World Cup Team, 1977, 91, 98; Captain, European Ryder Cup Team, 2008; Member, European Ryder Cup Team, 1977, 79, 81, 83, 85, 87, 89, 91, 93, 95, 97 **AW:** Winner Brit. Open, 1987, 90, 92, Masters Tournament, 1989, 90, 96, Brit. Youths Amateur Championship, 1975, English Amateur Championship, 1975, Skol Laeger Individual, 1977, Brit. PGA Championship, 1978, 80, 81, ICL Tournament, 1979, Haig Whiskey TPC, 1982, Martini International, 1983, Car Care Plan International, 1983, 84, Lawrence Batley International, 1983, Ebel European Masters Swiss Open, 1983, Sza Pines Heritage Classic, 1984, Spanish Open, 1987, Open de France, 1983, 88, 89, Volvo Masters, 1988, Volvo PGA Championship, 1989, Dunhill Brit. Masters, 1989, Suntory World Match Play, 1989, 90, Carroll's Irish Open, 1991, 92, 93, Scandinavian Masters, 1992, GA European Open, 1992, Toyota World Matchplay, 1992, Johnnie Walker Classic, 1990, 93, Alfred Dunhill Open, 1994, Doral/Ryder Open, 1995, Nissan Open, 1997; named European Rookie of Year, 1977, UBS Cup, 2001, 2002, 2003; recipient MBE award, 1987; leading money winner European Tour, 1983, 92, winner Master Tourn., 1996; elected World Golf Hall of Fame, 1997,Payne Stewart, 2014, Knight Bachelor, 2009, Member of the British Empire, 1998, BBC Sports Personality of the Year, 1989, PGA Player of the Year, 1990

FALK, THOMAS J., T: Personal Care Corporation Executive **I:** Consumer Goods and Services **PB:** Waterloo **SC:** IA/USA **ED:** MS in Management, Stanford University, CA (1988); Bachelor in Accounting, University of Wisconsin (1980) **C:** Chairman, Kimberly-Clark Corporation, Texas (2003-Present); Chief Executive Officer, Kimberly-Clark Corporation, Texas (2002-Present); Board of Directors, Kimberly-Clark Corporation, Texas (1999-Present); Chief Operating Officer, Kimberly-Clark Corporation (1999-2002); President, Kimberly-Clark Corporation (1999-2003); Group President, Global Tissue, Pulp and Paper, Kimberly-Clark Corporation (1998-1999); Group President, North America Consumer Products, Kimberly-Clark Corporation (1995); Group President, Infant and Child Care, Kimberly-Clark Corporation (1993); Senior Vice President, Analysis and Administration, Kimberly-Clark Corporation (1991); Vice President, Operations Analysis and Control, Kimberly-Clark Corporation (1990); Operations Manager, Infant Care, Diaper Plant, Kimberly-Clark Corporation, Beech Island, SC (1989); Director, Corporate Strategic Analysis, Kimberly-Clark Corporation (1987); Senior Financial Analyst, Kimberly-Clark Corporation (1986); Senior Auditor, Kimberly-Clark Corporation (1984); With Internal Audit Staff, Kimberly-Clark Corporation, Neenah, WI (1983); With, Alexander Grant & Co. **CR:** Board of Directors, Centex Corporation (2003-Present); Grocery Manufacturers of America, Inc.; Dallas Regional Advisory Board; JP Morgan Chase; Member, Board of Directors, Catalyst, University of Wisconsin Foundation, Centex Corporation **CIV:** Board of Governors, Boys and Girls Clubs of America; Board of Directors, University of Wisconsin Foundation **AW:** Sloan Fellow, Stanford University Graduate School of Business (1988)

FALLIN, MARY COPELAND, T: Governor of Oklahoma **I:** Government Administration/Government Relations/Government Services **DOB:** 12/09/1954 **PB:** Warrensburg **SC:** MO/USA **PT:** Daughter of Joseph Newton and Mary (Duggan) Copeland **MS:** Married **SPN:** Wade Christensen **ED:** Attended, University Central Oklahoma, 1979-81; BS, Oklahoma State University, 1977; Attended, Oklahoma Baptist University, 1973-75 **C:** Governor, State of Oklahoma, Oklahoma City, 2011-; Member, US Congress from 5th Oklahoma district, Washington, 2007-11; Lieutenant governor, State of Oklahoma, Oklahoma City, 1995-2007; Member, Oklahoma House of Reps., Oklahoma City, 1990-94; Real estate associate, Pippin Properties, Inc., Oklahoma City, 1990-94; District manager, Lexington Hotel Suites, Oklahoma City, 1988-90; Director sales, Residence Inn Hotel, Oklahoma City, 1984-87; Marketing director, Brian Head Hotel & Ski Resort, Utah, 1983-84; Sales rep., Associated Petroleum, Oklahoma City, 1982-83; State travel coordinator, Oklahoma Department Tourism, Oklahoma City, 1981-82; Business manager, Oklahoma Department Securities, Oklahoma City, 1979-81 **CR:** Chairman National Governors Association 2013-14 **CIV:** Member, del. Oklahoma Federation Rep. Women member American Legis. Exchange Council, National Conference State Legislatures member adv. board Trail of Tears active Crossings Community Church **AW:** Named Distinguished Former Student, University Central Oklahoma, National Legislator of Year, Oklahoma Ladies in the News, Woman of Year, Girl Scouts Am., 1998, Ladies in Communications, 1998; named to The Oklahoma Aviation Hall of Fame, 1998, The Oklahoma Women's Hall of Fame; recipient Clarence E. Page award, Women in the News award, Women in Communications, Small Business Adv. award, National Federation Ind. Small Business, Guardian of Small Business award, Bi-liner award, 1997 **MEM:** Mem.: Aerospace States Association (chairman 2003-05) **PA:** Republican

FALLON, JIMMY, T: Talk Show Host, Actor **I:** Media & Entertainment **DOB:** 09/19/1974 **PB:** Queens **SC:** NY/USA **PT:** Son of James W. and Gloria (Feeley) Fallon **ED:** BA in Communications, College St. Rose, Albany, New York, 2009 **C:** Television Personality 1998- **CW:** Actor: (TV series) Saturday Night Live, 1998-2004; (TV miniseries)

Band of Brothers, 2001; (films) Almost Famous, 2000, Anything Else, 2003, The Entrepreneurs, 2003, Taxi, 2004, Fever Pitch, 2005, Doogal (voice), 2006, Arthur and the Invisibles (voice), 2006, Factory Girl, 2006, The Year of Getting to Know Us, 2008, Whip It, 2009, Arthur and the Revenge of Maltazard (voice), 2009, Arthur 3: The War of the Two Worlds (voice), 2010, Bucky Larson: Born to Be a Star, 2011, Rise of the Guardians (voice), 2012; executive producer, writer, creator (TV series) Guys With Kids, 2012-13, TV appearances Spin City, 1998, Gossip Girl, 2009, Family Guy, 2009, 30 Rock, 2009-12; co-author (with Gloria Fallon): I Hate This Place: The Pessimist's Guide to Life, 1999; author: Thank You Notes, 2011, Thank You Notes 2, 2012, (children's book) Snowball Fight, 2005, Your Baby's First Word Will Be DADA, 2015; performer: (comedy album) The Bathroom Wall, 2003; co-host (TV specials) MTV Movie Awards, 2001, host MTV Video Music Awards, 2002, MTV Movie Awards, 2005, 62nd Primetime Emmy Awards, 2010, (TV series) Late Night with Jimmy Fallon, 2009-14 (Favorite Late Night Talk Show Host, People's Choice Awards, 2012, 2013, 2015), The Tonight Show Starring Jimmy Fallon, 2014- (Favorite Late Night Talk Show Host, People's Choice Awards, 2016), guest host Saturday Night Live, 2013 (Outstanding Guest Actor in a Comedy Series, Emmy Awards, 2014); singer: (comedy album) Blow Your Pants Off, 2012 (Best Comedy Album, Grammy Awards, 2013), (Film) Get Hard, 2015, Ted 2, 2015, Jurassic World, 2015, Jem and the Holograms, 2015, Popstar: Never Stop Never Stopping, 2016 (Television) Lip Sync Battle, 2015, Louie, 2015, The Spoils Before Dying, 2015, The Jim Gaffigan Show, 2015, Maya & Marty, 2016, 74th Golden Globe Awards, 2017 **AW:** Named Entertainer of Year, Entertainment Weekly, 2014, Webby Person of Year, International Academy Digital Arts & Sciences, 2009; named one of The 100 Most Influential People in the World, TIME magazine, 2013, The 50 Most Beautiful People, People magazine, 2002, People's Choice Award for Favorite Late Night Talk Show Host, 2013-2017, Primetime Emmy for Outstanding Creative Achievement in Interactive Media, 2010,2015, Primetime Emmy for Outstanding Interactive Program, 2014, Grammy for Best Comedy Album, 2013 **BA:** Creative Artists Agency, 2000 Avenue of the Stars, Los Angeles, CA, 90067

FAMA, EUGENE FRANCIS, T: Economics Professor **I:** Education/Educational Services **DOB:** 02/14/1939 **PB:** Boston **ED:** DSc (hon.), Tufts University, 2002; DSc (hon.), Catholic University, Leuven, Belgium, 1995; LLD (hon.), De Paul University, Chicago, 1989; LLD (hon.), University Rochester, New York, 1987; PhD, University Chicago, 1964; MBA, University Chicago, 1963; DSc (hon.), Tufts University, Medford, Massachusetts, 2002; BA in Romance Languages, magna cum laude, Tufts University, Medford, Massachusetts, 1960 **C:** Robert R. McCormick Distinguished service professor finance, University Chicago Grad. Booth School Business, 1993-; Theodore O. Yntema Distinguished service professor finance, University Chicago Grad. Booth School Business, 1984-93; Theodore O. Yntema professor finance, University Chicago Grad. Booth School Business, 1973-84; Professor, University Chicago Grad. Booth School Business, 1968-73; Associate professor, University Chicago Grad. Booth School Business, 1966-68; Assistant professor finance, University Chicago Grad. Booth School Business, 1963-65 **CR:** Board directors, director research, member investment strategy committee Dimensional Fund Advisors, 1982- visiting professor UCLA Anderson Grad. School Management, 1982-95, Catholic University Leuven & European Institute Advanced Studies in Management, Belgium, 1975-76 **CW:** Associate editor Journal Finance, 1971-73, 1977-80, American Economic Rev., 1975-77, Journal Monetary Economics, 1984-96; co-author (with M. Miller): The Theory of Finance, 1972; adv. editor Journal Financial Economics, 1974-; author: Foundations of Finance, 1976; contributor articles to professional journals **AW:** Co-recipient Nobel Memorial Prize in Economic Sciences (Sveriges Riksbank prize), Royal Swedish Academy Sciences, 2013; named to The Malden Catholic HS Athletic Hall of Fame, 1992; recipient Graham & Dodd Best Perspective award, Financial Analysts Journal, 2012, Onassis prize in Finance, 2009, Morgan Stanley American Financial Association award for Excellence in Finance, 2007, Fred Arditti Innovation award, Chicago Mercantile Exchange, 2007, Nicholas Molodovsky award, Chartered Financial Analyst Institute, 2006, Deutsche Bank prize in Financial Economics, 2005, Chaire Francqui, 1982 **MEM:** Fellow: American Finance Association, American Academy Arts & Sciences, Econometric Society; mem.: American Economic Association, Beta Gamma Sigma

FANNING, THOMAS ANDREW, T: Utilities Executive **I:** Business Management/Business Services **DOB:** 03/12/1957 **PB:** Morristown **SC:** NJ/USA **PT:** Son of James E. and Marjorie (Van Morstein) F. **MS:** Married **SPN:** Beverly Booher (3/14/1987) **CH:** Matthew Ryan, Bradley Stephen **ED:** MS in Finance, Georgia Institute Tech., Atlanta, 1980; BS in Industrial Management, Georgia Institute Tech., Atlanta, 1979 **C:** Chairman, President, CEO, Southern Co., 2010-; President, Southern Co., 2010; Executive Vice President, COO, Southern Co., 2008-10; Executive Vice President, CFO, Treasurer, Southern Co., 2003-08; President, CEO Gulf Power, Southern Co., 2002-03; Executive Vice President, CFO, Georgia Power, Southern Co., 1999-2002; Vice President, CFO Mississippi Power, Southern Co.; Senior Vice President, Strategy, Southern Co.; Treasurer, Southern Electrical International, Atlanta, 1986; Director, Corporate Finance, Southern Co. Services, Atlanta, 1988; Supervisor, Southern Co. Services, Atlanta, 1988; With, Southern Co. Services, Atlanta, 1983-86; Financial Analyst, Southern Co., Atlanta, 1980 **CR:** Board of Directors Southern Co., 2010-, Member, Federal Reserve Bank Board of Directors, (Chairman 2015-); Member Vulcan Materials Board of Directors **AW:** Georgia Federal Management Scholar, 1979, National Merit Scholar Advisory Board, Georgia Institute Tech., 2003- **MEM:** Member, Phi Eta Sigma

FARENTHOLD, BLAKE, T: U.S. Representative from Texas **I:** Government Administration/Government Relations/Government Services **DOB:** 12/12/1962 **PB:** Corpus Christi **ED:** JD, St. Mary's University School Law, San Antonio, 1989; BS in Radio, TV and Film, University Texas, Austin, 1985 **C:** Member, Committee on the Judiciary, Washington, 2011-; Member, US House Transportation & Infrastructure Committee, Washington, 2011-; Member, US House Oversight & Government Reform Committee, Washington, 2011-; Member, US Congress from 27th Texas District, Washington, 2011-; Co-host, Lago in the Morning, NewsRadio station 1360 KKTX, Corpus Christi, 1999-2010; Founder, president, Farenthold Consulting LLC, Corpus Christi, 1997-2010; Attorney, Kleberg Law Firm, Corpus Christi, 1989-97; President, Austin Party Line, 1983-85; Disc jockey, KSJL, San Antonio, 1982; Disc jockey, KITY, Llano, 1981; Disc jockey, KITE, Corpus Christi, 1980; Disc jockey, KZFM, Corpus Christi, 1978-80; Disc jockey, KRYS, Corpus Christi, 1977-78; Owner, BFP Mobile Entertainment, 1976-84 **CIV:** Member leadership, Social Media Club Corpus Christi, Board directors, Saint James Episcopal School, Corpus Christi, 1992-2000 Board directors, Texas State Aquarium, **PA:** Republican

FARR, DAVID NELSON, T: Electronics Company Execuitve **I:** Information Technology and Services **ED:** MBA, Vanderbilt University Owen Graduate School Management, 1981; BS in Chemistry, Wake Forest University, 1977 **C:** Chairman, CEO, Emerson Electric Co., 2010-; Chairman, President, CEO, Emerson Electric Co., 2005-10; Chairman, CEO, Emerson Electric Co., 2004-05; CEO, Emerson Electric Co., 2000-04; From Member Staff to CEO, Emerson Electric Co., St. Louis, 1981-2000 **CR:** Board of Directors IBM Corp., 2012-, DPH Holdings Corp., 2002-09 Member The Business Council, Washington, The Delphi Corporation, United Way of Greater St. Louis. **CIV:** Member, Civic Progress, Board of Directors, Greater St. Louis Area Council, Boy Scouts of America, Board of Directors, Municipal Theatre Associate, St. Louis,

FARRELL, THOMAS FRANCIS II, T: CEO **I:** Oil & Energy **CN:** Dominion Energy Inc **PB:** Fort Buckner, Okinawa, **SC:** Japan **ED:** JD, University Virginia, 1979; BA in Econs., University Virginia, 1976 **C:** Chairman, president, CEO, Dominion Resources, Inc., 2007-; CEO, Dominion Energy, 2000-04; President, CEO, Dominion Resources, Inc., 2006-07; President, COO, Dominion Resources, Inc., 2004-06; Executive vice president, Dominion Resources, Inc., 1999-2003; Executive vice president, general counsel, corp. secretary Virginia Power, Dominion Resources, Inc.,; Senior vice president corp. affairs, Dominion Resources, Inc., 1997-99; Vice -president, general counsel, Dominion Resources, Inc., Richmond, Virginia, 1995-97; Partner, McGuire, Woods, Beatle & Booth, 1981-95 **CR:** Board directors Altria Group, Inc., 2008-, Dominion Resources, Inc., 2005- **MEM:** Member Virginia Bar Association (executive committee, chairman young lawyers section), Virginia Law Foundation (member continuing legal education committee).

FARROW, RONAN, T: Television Personality, Former Federal Agency Administrator **I:** Media & Entertainment **DOB:** 12/19/1987 **PB:** NYC **SC:** New York **PT:** Son of Woody Allen and Mia Farrow. **ED:** Doctor (hon.), Dominican University California, 2012; JD, Yale Law School, New Haven, 2009; BA, Bard College, Annandale-on-Hudson, New York, 2004 **C:** Host Ronan Farrow Daily, MSNBC, 2014-; Special advisor to the secretary for global youth issues, US Department State, 2011-12; Special advisor humanitarian and NGO affairs in the office of special rep. for Afghanistan and Pakistan, US Department State, Washington, 2009-11; Spokesperson for youth, UNICEF,; Legal counsel, US House Foreign Affairs Committee, Washington,; Summer associate, Davis Polk & Wardell, New York City, **CR:** Rep. Genocide Intervention Network **CW:** Contributor articles to various publications including the LA Times, International Herald Tribune and Wall St Journal(Books),War on Peace: The End of Diplomacy and the Decline of American Influence,2018 **AW:** Named Up-and-Coming Politician of Year, Harper's Bazaar, 2010, New Activist of Year, New York Magazine, 2009; named one of The 30 Under 30 in Law & Policy, Forbes magazine, 2011; recipient McCall-Pierpaoli Humanitarian award, Refugee's International, 2008; Rhode Scholar, Oxford University, 2012, Time 100 Most Influential, 2018 **PA:** Democrat **BA:** MSNBC, 30 Rockefeller Plz, New York, NY, 10112

FASO, JOHN J., T: U.S. Representative from New York **I:** Government Administration/Government Relations/Government Services **DOB:** 08/25/1952

PB: Massapequa **SC:** NY/USA **MS:** Married **SPN:** Mary Frances Faso **CH:** Nicholas, Margaret **ED:** JD, Georgetown University, 1979; BA, State University of New York, Brockport, 1974 **C:** Partner, Manatt, Phelps & Phillips LLP, Albany, NY, 2003-Present; U.S. House of Representatives From New York's 19th District, 2017; Minority Leader, New York State Assembly, Albany, NY, 1998-2002; New York State Assembly, Albany, NY, 1987-2002; Executive Director, New York State Senate Office, Washington, DC, 1981-1983; Staff House Government Operations Committee, U.S. House of Representatives, Washington, DC, 1979-1981; Counselor, Rapport, Meyers, Griffen & Whitbeck, Hudson, NY; House Budget Committee, House Agriculture Committee **CR:** Board Member, Buffalo Fiscal Stability Authority, 2003-2006 **CIV:** New York State Legislative Bill Drafting Commission; Albany Member, Columbia County Republican Committee; Chairman, Kinderhook Town Republican Committee **AW:** Distinguished Public Service Award, Nelson A. Rockefeller College of Public Affairs & Policy, 1997, Guardian of Small Business Award, National Federation of Independent Businesses, 1996 **MEM:** Knights of Columbus, Lions, Elks **PA:** Republican

FASSBENDER, MICHAEL, T: Actor **I:** Media & Entertainment **PB:** Heidelberg **SC:** Germany **PT:** Josef Fassbender; Adele Fassbender **C:** Owner, Peanut Productions **CW:** Actor: (TV series) Hearts and Bones, 2001, NCS Manhunt, 2002, Holby City, 2002, Hex, 2004-05, William and Mary, 2005, Murphy's Law, 2005, Trial & Retribution, 2006, Agatha Christie's Poirot, 2006; (TV miniseries) Band of Brothers, 2001, The Devil's Whore, 2008; (TV films) Carla, 2003, Gunpowder, Treason & Plot, 2004, A Most Mysterious Murder: The Case of Charles Bravo, 2004, A Bear Named Winnie, 2004, Sherlock Holmes and the Case of the Silk Stocking, 2004, Our Hidden Lives, 2005, Wedding Belles, 2007; (films) 300, 2006, Angel, 2007, Hunger, 2008, Eden Lake, 2008, Blood Creek, 2009, Fish Tank, 2009, Inglourious Basterds, 2009, Centurion, 2010, Jonah Hex, 2010, Jane Eyre, 2011, X-Men: First Class, 2011, A Dangerous Method, 2011, Shame, 2011, Haywire, 2012, Prometheus, 2012, 12 Years a Slave, 2013, The Counselor, 2013, Frank, 2014, X Men: Days of Future Past, 2014, Macbeth, 2015, Steve Jobs, 2015, X-Men: Apocalypse, 2016, Weightless, 2016, Trespass Against Us, 2016, The Light Between Oceans, 2016; Song to Song, 2017, Alien: Covenant, 2017, The Snowman, 2017; actor, executive producer (films) Slow West, 2015, actor, producer Assassin's Creed, 2016; actor: (video game) Fable III (voice), 2010 **AW:** Recipient Spotlight award, National Board Review, 2011

FAUCI, ANTHONY, T: Immunologist **I:** Medicine & Health Care **DOB:** 12/24/1940 **PB:** Brooklyn **SC:** NY/USA **PT:** Son of Stephen A. and Eugenia A. Fauci. **ED:** DSc (hon.), Duke University, 1995; DSc (hon.), University Connecticut Health Ctr, 1994; DSc (hon.), State University of New York, Farmingdale, 1994; DSc (hon.), Bates College, 1993; DSc (hon.), Bard College, 1993; DSc (hon.), Medical College Wisconsin, 1993; DSc (hon.), Long Island University, 1992; DSc (hon.), St. John's University, 1991; DSc (hon.), Universita di Roma, 1990; DSc (hon.), Mount Sinai School Medicine, 1990; DSc (hon.), Hahnemann University, 1990; DSc (hon.), Georgetown University, 1990; DSc (hon.), College Holy Cross, 1987; MD, Cornell University Medical College, New York City, 1966; AB, College of Holy Cross, Worcester, Massachusetts, 1962 **CT:** Diplomate Am. Board Infectious Diseases, Am. Board Allergy & Immunology, Am. Board Internal Medicine **C:** Director, National Institute Allergy & Infectious Diseases (NIAID), 1984-; Chief immunoregulation laboratory, National Institute Allergy & Infectious Diseases (NIAID), 1980-; Associate director to director, National Institutes of Health Office AIDS Research, Bethesda, Maryland, 1988-94; Deputy clinical director, National Institutes of Health, 1977-80; Head clinical physiology section, National Institutes of Health, 1974-80; Senior investigator, National Institutes of Health, 1972-74; Senior staff fellow, National Institutes of Health, 1970-71; Clinical associate, National Institute Allergy & Infectious Diseases (NIAID), Bethesda, Maryland, 1968-70; Chief resident department medicine, New York Hosp.-Cornell Medical Center, 1971-72; Assistant resident department medicine, New York Hosp.-Cornell Medical Center, 1967-68; Intern, New York Hosp.-Cornell Medical Center, 1966-67 **CR:** Lecturer in field consultant Naval Medical Center, Bethesda, 1972- **CIV:** Trustee, Doris Duke Charitable Foundation, **CW:** Editor: Harrison's Principles of Internal Medicine; Contributor, Numerous Articles to Professional Journals **AW:** Named Scientist of Year, R&D Magazine, 2005, America's Best in Sci. & Medicine, CNN/TIME Magazine, 2001, 10th most-cited HIV/AIDS researcher, Institute for Sci. Information, 1996-2006, 9th most cited scientist in immunology, 1993-2003, 13th most cited scientist amongst pub. journal articles, 1983-2002; named one of The 25 Greatest Pub. Servants Over Past 25 Years, Council Excellence in Government, 2008, America's Best Leaders, US News & World Report, 2008, The Top 50 Sci. Leaders, Sci. America, 2003; recipient Presidential Medal of Freedom, The White House, 2008, Mary Woodard Lasker award for pub. service, Albert & Mary Lasker Foundation, 2007, National Sci. Medal, National Science Foundation, 2007, Ellis Island Family Heritage award, Statue of Liberty-Ellis Island Foundation, 2003, Frank Annunzio Humanitarian award, Christopher Columbus Fellowship Foundation, 2001, Frank Brown Berry prize, US Medical & Delta Dental Plan California, 1999, Thomas J. D'Alesandro Junior award, Associate Italian Am. Charities, 1997, Maryland Gov.'s Citation, 1997, Ellen Browning Scripps medal, Scripps Federation Medicine & Research, 1996, David Rumbough Sci. award, Juvenile Diabetes Federation International, 1996, Theobald Smith award, Albany Medical College, 1995, Cartwright prize, Columbia University College Physicians & Surgeons, 1993, Humanitarian award, Tiro a Segno Federation, 1993, Outstanding Achievement award, Howard University, 1992, Dr. Nathan Davis award, American Medical Association, 1992, Thomas H. Ham-Louis R. Wasserman award, Am. Society Hematology, 1992, Pres.'s award, New York Academy Sci., 1990, International Chiron prize, 1990, Lifetime Sci. award, Institute Advanced Studies Immunology & Aging, 1990, Helen Hayes award for medical research, 1989, Lee P. Brown National Pub. Service award, National Academy Pub. Administration./Nat. Society Pub. Administration, 1989, AIDS Research award, National Hemophilia Federation, 1989, Leadership award, Columbus Citizens Foundation, Inc., 1988, Disting Clinical Educator award, National Institutes of Health Clinical Center, 1988, Clemons von Pirquet award, Georgetown University Medical Center, 1986, Arthur S. Fleming award, 1983, Meritorious Service award, US Public Health Service, 1979,Robert Koch Prize, 2013 **MEM:** Master: American Association for the Advancement of Science (Westinghouse award 1988); fellow: American College of Physicians (Richard & Hinda Rosenthal award 1995, John Phillips Memorial award 1997), Am. Academy Microbiology, New York Academy Medicine (hon. Extraordinary Accomplishments award 2004), Am. Academy Arts & Scis., Am. Academy Allergy Asthma & Immunology (hon.), Am. Medical Writers Association (hon. John P. McGovern award 1997); mem.: National Academy of Sciences, Am. Philosophical Society, Royal Academy Medicine (Spain), Royal Danish Academy Sci. & Letters, Institute Medicine (council member), Association Am. Physicians (recorder 1988-93, councillor 1993-), Am. Society Clinical Investigation, Infectious Diseases Society America (Squibb award 1983), International AIDS Society, Am. Federation Clinical Research (president 1980-81), Am. Society Cell Biology, Am. Society Virology, Am. Association Immunologists (progressive chairman 1982-85, Kober lecturer 1988, Lifetime Achievement award 2005) **H:** Running, Tennis **BA:** Nat Inst Allergy & Infectious Diseases, Bldg 31 Claude D Pepper Bldg 7A03 31 Center Dr MS 2520, Bethesda, MD, 20892

FAULKNER, JUDY, T: Founder of Epic Systems **I:** Information Technology and Services **DOB:** 08/01/1943 **ED:** Doctor in Computer Sci., University Wisconsin; MS in Computer Sci., University Wisconsin; BS in Mathematics, Dickinson College, 1965 **C:** Founder, CEO, Epic Systems Corp. (originally known as Human Services Computing, Inc.), Verona, Wisconsin, 1979-; Worked as healthcare software developer,; Taught computer sci., University Wisconsin, Madison, **AW:** Named one of The Forbes 400: Richest Americans, 2012-, The 100 Most Powerful Women, Forbes magazine, 2014, The 100 Most Influential People in Healthcare, Modern Healthcare Magazine, 2011; recipient Alice Paul Merit award, Moorestown Friends School, 2011, Forbes "Most Powerful Woman in Healthcare"

FAUST, DREW GILPIN, T: President of Harvard University **I:** Education/Educational Services **DOB:** 09/18/1947 **PB:** NYC **PT:** Daughter of McGhee Tyson and Catharine (Mellick) Gilpin; **ED:** LLD (hon.), Princeton University, 2010; Doctor (hon.), Peking University, 2008; Doctor (hon.), University Pennsylvania, 2008; Doctor of Humanities (hon.), Yale University, 2008; LHD (hon.), Bowdoin College, 2007; PhD, University Pennsylvania, Philadelphia, 1975; MA, University Pennsylvania, Philadelphia, 1971; BA magna cum laude, Bryn Mawr College, Pennsylvania, 1968 **C:** President, Harvard University, Cambridge, Massachusetts, 2007-; Lincoln professor history, Harvard University, Cambridge, Massachusetts, 2001-; Dean Radcliffe Institute Advanced Study, Harvard University, Cambridge, Massachusetts, 2001-07; Annenberg professor history, University Pennsylvania, Philadelphia, 1989-2000; Stanley I. Sheerr professor hist., University Pennsylvania, Philadelphia, 1988-89; Professor, University Pennsylvania, Philadelphia, 1984-89; Associate professor, University Pennsylvania, Philadelphia, 1980-84; Assistant professor American civilization, University Pennsylvania, Philadelphia, 1976-80 **CR:** Board directors Staples, Inc., 2012- **CIV:** Trustee, Andrew Mellon Foundation, 2002-07 **CW:** Author: A Sacred Circle: The Dilemma of the Intellectual in the Old South, 1977, James Henry Hammond and the Old South: A Design for Mastery, 1982 (Jules F. Landry award, 1982, Charles Sydney award, 1983), The Creation of Confederate Nationalism: Ideology and Identity in the Civil War South, 1988, Southern Stories: Slaveholders in Peace and War, 1992, Mothers of Invention: Women of the Slaveholding South in the American Civil War, 1996 (Avery Craven prize, 1996, Francis Parkman prize, Society American Historians, 1997), This Republic of Suffering: Death and the American Civil War, 2008 (Bancraft prize, Columbia University, 2009); member editorial board Journal Southern Hist., 1981-86, Pennsylvania Magazine Hist. & Biography, 1986-89, Journal American Hist., 1991-; contributor articles to professional journals **AW:** Named an Elizabeth

Hall fellow, Concord Academy, 2003; named one of The 100 Most Powerful Women, Forbes magazine, 2011-14, 2007-09, The 100 Most Influential People in the World, TIME magazine, 2007; recipient Article prize, Berkshire Conference Women's Historians, 1991; fellow Massachusetts Hist. Society, 2002, Guggenheim Foundation, 1987, American Council Learned Societies, 1986, Stanford University Humanities Center, 1983-84 **MEM:** Mem.: American Philosophical Society, American Academy Arts & Sciences, Southern Association Women Historians (president 1998-99, membership committee 1988-), Hist. Society Pennsylvania (board member 1988-91), American Studies Association (council member 1988-90), Organization American Historians (chair progressive committee 1987, council member 1999-2002, chair Avery Craven Prize committee, 1991, 1997), American Hist. Association (vice president professional division 1992-92, council member 1992-), Southern Hist. Association (executive council 1987-90, chair nominating committee 1993, president 1999-2000)

FEDERER, ROGER, **T:** Professional Tennis Player **I:** Athletics **DOB:** 08/08/1981 **PB:** Basel **SC:** Switzerland **PT:** Robert Federer; Lynette Federer **C:** Founder, RF-RogerFederer Fragrance Line (2003-Present); Professional Tennis Player, Association of Tennis Professionals (1998) **CR:** Member, Swiss National Team, Summer Olympic Games, London, England (2012); Member, Swiss National Team, Summer Olympic Games, Beijing, China (2008); Member, Swiss National Team, Summer Olympic Games, Athens, Greece (2004); Member, Swiss National Team, Summer Olympic Games, Sydney, Australia (2000); Davis Cup (1999-Present) **CIV:** Goodwill Ambassador, UNICEF (2006-Present) **AW:** Named Sportsman of the Year, Laureus World Sports Awards (2006); Academy Outstanding Athlete of the Year, U.S. Sports Academy (2005, 2006); BBC Sports Overseas Personality of the Year (2004, 2006); International Tennis Federation World Champion (2004-2007); Ambassador for Tennis, International Tennis Writers Association (2004-2006): Player of the Year (2004-2006); ATPtennis.com Fans' Favorite (2004-2006): ATP Player of the Year (2004, 2006); Swiss of the Year (2003); Named One of the 100 Most Powerful Celebrities, Forbes.com (2008); Named One of the Most Influential People in the World of Sports, Business Week (2007); Named One of the World's Most Influential People, TIME Magazine (2007); Silver Medal, Men's Singles, Summer Olympic Games (2012); Gold Medal, Men's Doubles (2008); Arthur Ashe Humanitarian of the Year Award, ATP (2006); Stefan Edberg Sportsmanship Award (2004, 2006); ATP Player of the Year (2006-2007, 2009); ATP Fan Favorite (2003, 2008-2017); ATP Sportsmanship Award (2004-2009, 2011-2017); Arthur Ashe Humanitarian Award (2013) **ACH:** Achievements include winner, Hamburg Masters, 2002, 2004-05, Wimbledon, 2003-07, 2009, 2012, 2017 Australian Open, 2004, 2006-07, 2010, 2017, 2018, US Open, 2004-08, French Open, 2009, Basel, 2006-08; Qatar Open, 2005, 2006, 2011, Western & Southern Group Fin. Masters, 2005, 2007, 2009, Pacific Life Open, 2006, NASDAQ-100 Open, 2006, Gerry Weber Open, 2006, 2008, Rogers Cup, 2006, Japan Open, 2006; Masters Series, Madrid, 2006, 2009, 2012, Masters Cup, 2006, Tennis Masters Cup Shanghai, 2006, 2007, French Open, 2009; 76 career singles titles, 17 Grand Slam titles, 8 doubles titles; became first player since 1988 to win three legs of the Grand Slam in the same year, 2004; holding record for consecutive wins (42) on grass-court, 2006; tied record of 160 consecutive weeks as the top-ranked player in men's tennis, 2007 **H:** Golf; Soccer; Skiing; Music; Video Games; Playing Cards

FEDEROFF, HOWARD J., **T:** Dean of University of California Medical School **I:** Education/Educational Services **DOB:** 03/24/1953 **PB:** Chicago **PT:** Son of Harry and Esther (Rosen) F.; Married Wendy P. Solovay, October 16, 1983; children: Allison, Monica. **ED:** MD, Albert Einstein College Medicine, 1983; PhD, Albert Einstein College Medicine, 1979; BA, Earlham College, 1974 **CT:** Diplomate in internal medicine and in endocrinology and metabolism Am. Board Internal Medicine. **C:** Dean, University of California, 2015-; Professor, University Rochester School Medicine and Dentistry, New York, 1995-; Associate professor, Albert Einstein College Medicine, Bronx, New York, 1993-95; Assistant professor, Albert Einstein College Medicine, Bronx, New York, 1988-93; Clinical and research fellow, Massachusetts General Hospital, Boston, 1985-88; Intern, resident, Massachusetts General Hospital, Boston, 1983-85 **CR:** Sci. adv. board Alexion Pharms., New Haven, Connecticut, 1994-95 consultant Astra Arcus Pharms., 1995. **CW:** Contributor numerous papers, articles to professional journals **BA:** University of California, School of Medicine, 1001 Health Sciences rd, Irvine, CA, 92617

FEINSTEIN, DIANNE, **T:** U.S. Senator from California **I:** Government Administration/Government Relations/Government Services **DOB:** 06/22/1933 **PB:** San Francisco **SC:** CA/USA **PT:** Leon Goldman; Betty (Rosenburg) Goldman **MS:** Married **SPN:** Richard C. Blum (1/20/1980); Bertram Feinstein (11/11/1962, Deceased) **CH:** Katherine Anne **ED:** BA in History, Stanford University (1955); Honorary LLB, Golden Gate University (1977); Honorary Doctor of Public Administration, University of Manila (1981); Honorary Doctor of Public Service, University of Santa Clara (1981); Honorary JD, Antioch University (1983); Honorary JD, Mills College (1985); Honorary LHD, University of San Francisco, CA (1988) **C:** Ranking Member, Senate Judiciary Committee (2017); Vice Chair, Senate Intelligence Committee (2015-2017); US Senator from California (1992—Present); Member, Mayor's Committee on Crime; Chairman, Advisory Committee, Adult Detention (1967-1969); With, California Women's Board Terms & Parole (1960-1966); Fellow, Coro Foundation, San Francisco, CA (1955-1956); Chair, US Senate Narcotics Caucus (2009—2015); Chair, Joint Committee on Printing (2009—2013); Chair, US Senate Select Committee on Intelligence (2009—2015); Chair, Joint Committee on the Library (2007); Chair, US Senate Rules & Administration Committee (2007—2009); Mayor, City of San Francisco, CA (1978-1988); President, San Francisco Board of Supervisors, San Francisco, CA (1970-1971, 1974-1975, 1978); Member, San Francisco Board of Supervisors, San Francisco, CA (1970-1978) **CR:** Member, Executive Committee, US Conference of Mayors (1983-1988); Democratic Nominee for Governor of California (1990); Member, National Committee on U.S.-China Relations **CIV:** Member, Bay Area Conservation & Development Commission (1973-1978) **AW:** Woman of Achievement Award, Business and Professional Women's Clubs, San Francisco, CA (1970); Distinguished Woman Award, San Francisco Examiner (1970); Coro Foundation Award (1979); Scopus Award, American Friends of the Hebrew University (1981); French Legion of Honor (1984); Brotherhood/Sisterhood Award, National Conference of Christians and Jews (1986); Commander's Award, U.S. Army (1986); Distinguished Civilian Award, U.S. Navy (1987); Coro Leadership Award (1988); President Medal, University of California, San Francisco (1988); Lifetime Achievement Award, National AIDS Foundation (1993); Awareness Achievement Award, Board of Sponsors, Breast Cancer Awareness (1995);

Donald Santarelli Award, National Organization for Victims Assistance (1996); Congressional Excellence Award, MADD (1997); Paul E. Tsongas Award, Lymphoma Research Association of America (1997); Abraham Lincoln Award, Illinois Council Against Handgun Violence (1998); Congressional Award, National Association of Police Organizations (1999); Celebration of Courage Award, Handgun Control, Inc. (1999); Congressional Champion Award, Coalition of Cancer Research (1999); Winning Spirit Award, Women's Information Network Against Breast Cancer, 2000, Recognition award, Susan G. Komen Breast Cancer Foundation (2000); Woodrow Wilson Award, Woodrow Wilson International Center Scholars (2001); Torch of Liberty Award, Anti-Defamation League (2002); Dr. Nathan Davis Award, American Medical Association (2002); Public Service Award, American Society of Hematology (2003); Leadership Award, Alta Med Health Services Corp. (2004); Pat Brown Legacy Award (2004); Lifetime of Idealism Award, City Year (2004); Legislator of the Year Award, California School Resource Officers' Association (2004); National Distinguished Advocacy Award, American Cancer Society (2004); Women of Achievement Award, Century City Chamber of Commerce (2004); Friend of Watershed Award, Ventura County Association of Water Agencies (2004); Outstanding Member of the US Senate Award, National Narcotic Officers Association Coalition (2005); Named Number One Mayor, All-Pro City Management Team City and State Magazine (1987); Person of the Year, National Guard Association of California (1995); Funding Hero, Breast Cancer Research Foundation (2004); Named One of the Congressional Quarterly's Top 50 Members of Congress (2000); Most Powerful Women, Forbes Magazine (2005) **MEM:** Trilateral Commission; President, Japan Society of Northern California (1988-1989); Inter-American Dialogue; National Committee on U.S.-China Relations **PA:** Democrat **BA:** Office of Dianne Feinstein, 331 Hart Senate Office Building, Washington D.C., DC, 20510

FEINZAIG, LESLIE, **T:** CEO of the Females Founders Alliance **I:** Business Management/Business Services **ED:** MBA in Business, Harvard Business School, 2005-07; Bsc in Industrial Relations, 1999-2001 **C:** Founder & CEO, Female Founders Alliance, 2017-; Owner, Venture Kits, 2016-; Mentor, Techstars, 2015-; Judge & Mentor, Social Venture Partners Seattle, 2017-; Organizer, Seattle Startup Week, 2017-

FENTY, ROBYN (RIHANNA), **T:** Singer **I:** Media & Entertainment **DOB:** 02/20/1988 **PB:** St. Michael **PT:** Daughter of Ronald and Monica Fenty **C:** Singer, recording artist, 2005 **CR:** Model, spokesperson Covergirl, 2007- **CW:** Singer: (albums) Music of the Sun, 2005, A Girl Like Me, 2006, Good Girl Gone Bad, 2007, Rated R, 2009, Loud, 2010 (Favorite Soul/R&B Album, American Music Awards, 2011), Talk That Talk, 2011 (Favorite Soul/R&B Album, American Music Awards, 2012), Unapologetic, 2012 (Top R&B Album, Billboard Music Awards, 2013, Best Urban Contemporary Album, Grammy Awards, 2014), ANTI, 2016, (songs) (featuring Jay-Z) Umbrella, 2007 (Monster Single of Year, Video of Year, MTV Video Music Awards, 2007, Best Rap/Sung Collaboration, Grammy Awards, 2008), Shut Up and Drive, 2007 (Favorite R&B Song, People's Choice Awards, 2007), Don't Stop the Music, 2007 (Best R&B/Urban Dance Track, International Dance Music Awards, 2008), (with T.I.) Live Your Life, 2008 (Best Hip-Hop Collaboration, BET Hip-Hop Awards, 2009), (with Jay-Z and Kanye West) Run This Town, 2009 (Favorite Music Collaboration, People's Choice Awards, 2009, Best Rap/Sung Collaboration, Best Rap Song, Grammy

Awards, 2010), Only Girl (in the World), 2010 (Best Dance Recording, Grammy Awards, 2011), (with Eminem) Love the Way You Lie, 2010 (Favorite Song, People's Choice Awards, 2010, Best Hip-Hop Song of Year, Soul Train Music Awards, 2010, Top Rap Song, Billboard Music Awards, 2011), (featuring Calvin Harris) We Found Love, 2011 (Video of Year, MTV Video Music Awards, 2012, Best Short Form Music Video, Grammy Awards, 2013), Diamonds, 2012 (Top R&B Song, Billboard Music Awards, 2013), (with Eminem) Monster, 2013 (Best Rap/Sung Collaboration, Grammy Awards, 2015); actress: (films) Bring It On: All or Nothing, 2006, Battleship, 2012 (Choice Breakout in a Film, Teen Choice Awards, 2012), Annie, 2014, Home (voice), 2015, Valerian and the City of a Thousand Planets,2017, Ocean's 8, 2018 **AW:** Named Sexiest Woman Alive, Esquire, 2011, Favorite R&B Artist, People's Choice Awards, 2013, 2012, Favorite Pop Artist, 2010, Entertainer of Year, World Music Awards, 2007, Best Female Pop Artist, 2007, Best Female R&B Artist, 2007, Favorite Pop/Rock Female Artist, American Music Awards, 2008, Favorite Soul/R&B Female Artist, 2015, 2013, 2010, 2008, 2007, Top R&B Artist, Billboard Music Awards, 2013, Top Radio Songs Artist, 2013, Top Streaming Artist, 2012, Top Female Artist, 2011, Top Dance Club Artist, 2010, Top Digital Song Artist of the Decade, 2009, Female Artist of Year, 2008, 2006; named one of The 100 Most Powerful Women in Entertainment, Hollywood Reporter, 2014, The 100 Most Influential People in the World, TIME magazine, 2012, The Top 25 Entertainers of Year, Entertainment Weekly, 2007; recipient Michael Jackson Video Vanguard award, MTV Video Music Awards, 2016, Fan-Voted Billboard Chart Achievement award, Billboard music Awards, 2016, Icon award, American Music Awards, 2013, 33 Barbados Music Awards, Female R&B artist award, BET Awards, 2011, Viewer's Choice award, 2010, Women of Year award, Glamour Magazine, 2009, Choice R&B Artist award, Teen Choice Awards, 2007, 2006, Female Breakout Artist award, 2006, Viewer's Choice award, BET Awards, 2009

FERGUSON, BOB, T: State Attorney General, Lawyer **I:** Law and Legal Services **PT:** Murray Ferguson; Betty Ferguson **ED:** JD, New York University, 1995; BA in Political Science, University of Washington **C:** Attorney General, State of Washington, 2013-Present; King County Council, 2003-2012; Litigator, Preston, Gates, and Ellis, Seattle, WA; Chief Clerk to Judge Myron Bright, U.S. Court of Appeals, Eighth Circuit; Law Clerk, Chief Judge William Fremming Nielsen, Federal District Court, Eastern District, Washington, Spokane, WA **AW:** Time 100 Most Influential People, 2017 **PA:** Democrat **BA:** Office of the Attorney General, 1125 Washington Street SE, PO Box 40100, Olympia, WA, 98504-0100

FERGUSON, DREW A., T: U.S. Representative from Georgia **I:** Government Administration/Government Relations/Government Services **DOB:** 11/15/1966 **PB:** Langdale **SC:** AL/USA **ED:** University of Georgia,1988; D.M.D,Medical College of Georgia, 1992 **C:** Member, U.S. Representative from Georgia's 3rd Congressional District, 2017-; Member, Committee on Budget; Member, Committee on Education and the Workforce; Member, Committee on Transportation and Infrastructure; Mayor, West Point, Georgia, 2008-16; Member, West Point Board of Alderman, 1997-99; Dentist, Medical College of Georgia, 1998-2016 **BA:** 1032 Longworth HOB, Washington, DC, 20515

FERGUSON, ROGER WALTER JR., T: CEO **I:** Business Management/Business Services **CN:** TIAA **DOB:** 10/28/1951 **PB:** Washington **ED:** PhD (hon.), Webster University; PhD (hon.), Lincoln College; PhD in Economics, Harvard University, 1981; JD cum laude, Harvard University, 1979; BA in Economics, magna cum laude, Harvard University, 1973 **CT:** Bar: New York 1983 **C:** President, CEO, Teachers Insurance & Annuity Foundation College Retirement Equities Fund (TIAA-CREF), New York City, 2008-; Group fin. market strategist, Swiss Reinsurance Co., Zurich, 2006-08; Member executive board, Swiss Reinsurance Co., Zurich, 2006-08; Chairman, Swiss Re Am. Holdings Corp., Armonk, New York, 2006-08; Vice chairman, Federal Reserve Systems, Washington, 1999-2006; Member board governors, Federal Reserve Systems, Washington, 1997-2006; Associate to partner, McKinsey & Co., Inc., New York City, 1984-97; Attorney, Davis Polk & Wardwell, New York City, 1981-84 **CR:** Member President's Economic Recovery Advisory Board, 2009- chairman Fin. Stability Forum, 2003-, Comn. Global Fin. Systems, 2003-, Group Ten Working Party on Financial Sector Consolidation, 1999-2001, Joint Year 2000 Council, 1998-2000 **CIV:** Board overseers, Harvard University, 2003- Past treasurer, Friends of Education, Board trustees, Carnegie Endowment International Peace, Board trustees, Institute Advanced Study, 2004 Trustees' committee, Museum Modern Art, New York City **AW:** Named one of 25 Leaders Reshaping New York, Crain's New York magazine, 2008; recipient Distinguished Service award, Bond Market Association; fellow (hon.), University Cambridge Pembroke College, 2004-, 1973-74 **MEM:** Mem.: Council Foreign Relations **PA:** Democrat

FERNANDES, TONY, T: CEO **I:** Leisure, Travel & Tourism **CN:** AirAsia Berhad **PB:** Kuala Lumpur **SC:** Maylasia **C:** Founder, Tune Hotels Sdn Bhd (2007-Present); Chief Executive Officer, AirAsia Berhad (2003-Present); Founder, Caterham F1 Formula One Team (2010-2014) **AW:** Named One of TIME's 100 Most Influential People, TIME Magazine (2015); American Express CEO of the Year (2003)

FERREIRA, STACEY, T: CEO of Forge **I:** Business Management/Business Services **ED:** BA in Creativity and Innovation, New York University (2011); Coursework, Xavier College Preparatory (2011) **C:** Member, Board of Directors, Watermark (2017-Present); Chief Executive Officer & Co-founder, Forge (2015-Present); Member, Technology Advisory Board, Xavier College Preparatory (2014-Present) **CW:** Author, Book, "2 Billion Under 20" (2015)

FERRELL, WILL, T: Actor **I:** Media & Entertainment **DOB:** 07/16/1967 **PB:** Irvine **PT:** Son of Lee and Kay Ferrell; **ED:** BA in Sports Information, University Southern California, 1989 **C:** Comedian with group, The Groundlings,; Comedian, Actor, 1997- **CW:** Actor: (films) Men Seeking Women, 1997, Austin Powers-International Man of Mystery, 1997, The Thin Pink Line, 1998, The Suburbans, 1999, Austin Powers: The Spy Who Shagged Me, 1999, Dick, 1999, Superstar, 1999, Drowning Mona, 2000, The Ladies Man, 2000, Jay and Silent Bob Strike Back, 2001, Zoolander, 2001, Old School, 2003, Elf, 2003, Melinda and Melinda, 2004, The Wendell Baker Story, 2005, Kicking & Screaming, 2005, Bewitched, 2005, Wedding Crashers, 2005, The Producers, 2005 (Golden Globe award-Best Performance by an Actor in a Supporting Role in a Motion Picture, Hollywood Foreign Press Association, 2006), Winter Passing, 2005, Stranger Than Fiction, 2006, Curious George (voice), 2006, Blades of Glory, 2007, Semi-Pro, 2008, Land of the Lost, 2009, The Other Guys, 2010, Megamind (voice), 2010, Everything Must Go, 2011, The Lego Movie (voice), 2014, Zeroville, 2016, Zoolander 2, 2016, Daddy's Home, 2017, The House, 2017, Zeroville, 2018; (TV films) Bucket of Blood, 1995; (TV series) Saturday Night Live, 1995-2002; (Broadway plays) You're Welcome America: A Final Night With George W. Bush, 2009; (TV miniseries) The Spoils of Babylon, 2014; actor, writer (films) A Night at the Roxbury, 1998, Anchorman: The Legend of Ron Burgundy, 2004, actor, writer, executive producer Step Brothers, 2008, actor, producer, writer Talladega Nights: The Ballad of Ricky Bobby, 2006 (Choice Movie Actor: Comedy, Teen Choice Awards, 2007), Anchorman 2: The Legend Continues, 2013, actor, producer Tim and Eric's Billion Dollar Movie, 2012, Casa de mi Padre, 2012, The Campaign, 2012, Welcome to Me, 2014, Get Hard, 2015, Daddy's Home, 2015, actor, executive producer (TV series) Eastbound & Down, 2009-, (TV films) A Deadly Adoption, 2015; executive prodr.: (films) Hot Rod, 2007; (TV films) Assistance, 2013, Mission Control, 2014; (TV series) Drunk History, 2013-15; No Activity, 2017; prodr.: (films) Bachelorette, 2012, The Boss, 2016; TV appearances include Grace Under Fire, 1995, Living Single, 1995, Cow and Chicken (voice), 1997-2001, King of the Hill (voice), 1999, Strangers with Candy, 2000, Family Guy (voice), 2001, 2005, The Merrick & Rosso Show, 2009, SpongeBob SquarePants (voice), 2009, The Office, 2011, Papanatos, 2011, Funny or Die Presents, 2010-11(Film) Daddy's Home 2, 2017(Television Produced) LA to Vegas, 2018, Succession, 2018 **AW:** Named one of The 100 Agents of Change, Rolling Stone magazine, 2009, The 50 Smartest People in Hollywood, Entertainment Weekly, 2007, The Top 25 Entertainers of Year, 2007, The 50 Most Powerful People in Hollywood, Premiere magazine, 2005-06; recipient Mark Twain Prize for American Humor, John F. Kennedy Center for the Performing Arts, 2011, Best Comedian of 2015 by British GQ Men of the Year Award, **BA:** Werner- Gold-Miller, 4024 Radford ave, Studio City, CA, 91604

FERRIOLA, JOHN J., T: CEO and President at Nucor Corp. **I:** Business Management/Business Services **C:** Chairman, Nucor Corp., Charlotte, North Carolina, 2014-; CEO, Nucor Corp., Charlotte, North Carolina, 2013-; President, Nucor Corp.,2011-; President, COO, Nucor Corp., Charlotte, North Carolina, 2011-13; COO steelmaking operations, Nucor Corp., Charlotte, North Carolina, 2007-11; Executive vice president, Nucor Corp., Charlotte, North Carolina, 2002-07; Vice president, Nucor Corp., Charlotte, North Carolina, 1996-2001; General manager, Vulcraft, Grapeland, Texas, 1995; General manager, Nucor Steel, Crawfordsville, Ind., 1998-2001; General manager, Nucor Steel, Norfolk, Nebraska, 1995-98; Manager maintenance and engineering, Nucor Steel, Jewett, Texas, 1992-95 **CR:** Chairman World Steel Association, 2016-; Chairman, American Iron and Steel Institute. **BA:** Nucor Corp, 1915 Rexford Rd, Charlotte, NC, 28211

FETTER, TREVOR, T: Healthcare Industry Executive **I:** Health, Wellness and Fitness **DOB:** 01/16/1960 **PB:** San Diego **SC:** CA/USA **MS:** Married **CH:** Two Children **ED:** MBA, Harvard University (1986); BS in Economics, Stanford University (1982) **C:** Chairman, Tenet Healthcare Corporation (2015-Present); President, Chief Executive Officer, Tenet Healthcare Corporation, Dallas, Texas (2003-2015); President, Acting Chief Executive Officer, Tenet Healthcare Corporation, Dallas, Texas (2003); President, Tenet Healthcare Corporation, Dallas, Texas (2002-2003); Chairman, Chief Executive Officer, Broad Lane, Inc., San Francisco, CA (2000-2002); Executive Vice President, Chief Financial Officer, Tenet Healthcare Corporation, Dallas, Texas (1996-2000); Executive Vice President, Tenet Healthcare Corporation, Dallas, Texas (1995-1996); Executive Vice President, Chief Financial Officer,

Metro-Goldwyn-Mayer, Inc.; Senior Vice President, MGM/UA Communications Co. (1988); With Investment Banking Division, Merrill Lynch Capital Markets **CR:** Board of Trustees, Healthcare Leadership Council; Member, Board, Hartford Financial Services Group, Inc. **CIV:** Chairman, Board, Santa Catalina Island Conservancy; Trustee, Santa Barbara Zoological Garden

FETTERMAN, LISA, T: CEO **I:** Food & Restaurant Services **CN:** Nomiku **ED:** BA, Journalism, Metropolitan Studies, American Studies, New York University (2006-2010) **C:** Founder and Chief Executive Officer, Nomiku (2012-Present); Chief Executive Officer, Lower East Kitchen (2010-2012); Editor, SMITH Magazine (2008-2011) **AW:** Named to Zagat 30 Under 30, Zagat, The Infatuation Inc.

FEULNER, EDWIN PHD, T: Think-Tank Executive **I:** Research **CN:** The Heritage Foundation **DOB:** 08/12/1941 **PB:** Chicago **SC:** IL/USA **PT:** Edwin John Feulner; Helen J. (Franzen) Feulner **SPN:** Linda C. Leventhal (3/8/1969) **CH:** Edwin John, III; Emily V. **ED:** Honorary LHD, Thomas More College, Manchester, NH (2005); Honorary Doctorate in Public Service, Hillsdale College, Michigan (2004); Honorary LLD, St. Norbert College, De Pere, WI (2002); Honorary LLD, Pepperdine University, Malibu, CA (2000); Honorary DLitt, Grove City College, Pennsylvania (1994); Honorary LLD, Gonzaga University, Spokane, WA (1992); Honorary LLD, Bellevue College, Nebraska (1987); Honorary Doctorate in Social Sciences, Hanyang University, Seoul, Republic of Korea (1982); Honorary Degree, Universidad Francisco Marroquin, Guatemala City, Guatemala (1982); Honorary LHD, Nichols College, Dudley, MA (1981); PhD, University of Edinburgh, Scotland (1981); MBA, University of Pennsylvania, Philadelphia, PA (1964); BS, Regis University, Denver, CO (1963) **C:** President, The Heritage Foundation, Washington, DC (2017-Present); Chairman, Asian Studies Center for Heritage Foundation (2013-Present); Chung Ju-Yung Fellow, Heritage Foundation (2013-Present); Founder, Heritage Foundation (2013-Present); President, American Medical Association (2017-2018); Counselor to Vice Presidential Candidate Jack Kemp (1996); President, The Heritage Foundation, Washington, DC (1977-2013); Chairman, Institute for European Defense & Strategic Studies (1977-1996); Executive Director, U.S. House Republican Study Committee (1974-1977); Campaign Manager, Crane for Congress Committee (1972); Administrative Assistant to Republican Philip M. Crane, U.S. House of Representatives (1970-1974); Confidential Assistant to Secretary Melvin Laird, U.S. Department of Defense (1969-1970); Research Analyst, U.S. House Republican Conference (1968-1969); Public Affairs Fellow, Hoover Institution (1966-1968); Fellow, Center for Strategic & International Studies (1965-1966); Richard Weaver Fellow, London School of Economics (1965) **CR:** Advisory Board, Public Diplomacy Collaborative, John F. Kennedy School of Government, Harvard University (2009-Present); Distinguished Visiting Professor, Hanyang University, Seoul, Republic of Korea (2001-Present); Gingrich/Mitchell Task Force on United Nations Reform (2005-2008); International Financial Institute Advisory Committee (1999-2000); Congressional Policy Advisory Board (1997-2001); National Advisory Board, Center for Education and Research in Free Enterprise, Texas Agricultural and Mechanical University (1995-1996); Vice-Chairman, National Committee on Economic Growth and Tax Reform (1995-1996); Advisory Committee on American Political Channel (1994-1996); U.S. Committee on Improving Effectiveness of the United Nations (1989-1993); White House Consultant on Domestic

Policy (1987); Distinguished Fellow, Mobilization Concepts, Development Center, National Defense University (1983-1989); Carlucci Commission on Foreign Assistance (1983); U.S. Advisory Committee on Public Diplomacy (1982-1994); Chairman, U.S. Information Agency (1982-1991); Public Delegate, United Nations Second Special Session on Disarmament (1982); President's Commission, White House Fellows (1980-1981); Executive Committee, Presidential Transition (1979-1980); U.S. Delegate, IMF/World Bank (1974-1976); **CIV:** Life Trustee, Regis University (2013-Present); Executive Council, America's Future Foundation (1998-Present); Trustee, Sarah Scaife Foundation (1988-Present); Vice Chairman, Board of Directors, Roe Foundation (1983-Present); Vice Chairman of Board, Intercollegiate Studies Institute (1979-Present); Trustee, Regis University (2005-2013); Chairman, Intercollegiate Studies Institute (2003-2006); Multimedia Supercorridor International Advisory Council, Malaysia (2001-2005); Secretary, Korea-U.S. Exchange Council (2001-2004); Trustee, National Chamber Foundation (1998-2011); Board of Visitors, George Mason University (1996-2004); Trustee, Acton Institute (1995-2002); Trustee, International Republican Institute (1995-2001); Executive Committee, Council on National Policy (1993-2001); Trustee, Regis University (1991-2001); Trustee, St. James School (1990-1998); Vice Chairman of Board, Aequus Institute (1989-2015); Chairman, Intercollegiate Studies Institute (1989-1993); Trustee, Sequoia National Bank (1987-1999); Chairman, Citizens for American Education Foundation (1985-1989); Trustee, American Council on Germany, New York (1982-1992); Trustee, Lehrman Institute (1981-1990); Trustee, Institute for Research on Economics Taxation (1980-1987); Vice Chairman, Trustee, Manhattan Institute Policy Studies (1977-1986); Trustee, Foundation Francisco Marroquin; Council of Advisors, Bryce Harlow Foundation **CW:** Author, "The American Spirit" (2012); Author, "Getting America Right" (2006); Author, "Leadership for America" (2000); Author, "Intellectual Pilgrims" (1999); Author, "The March of Freedom" (1998); Author, "Conservatives Stalk the House" (1983); Author, "Looking Back" (1981); Author, "Public Policy Review" (1977-2001); Author, "Congress and the New International Economic Order" (1976); Contributor, Articles to Professional Journals, Newspapers, Chapters to Books **AW:** Presidential Gold Medal, Czech Republic (2014); Ronald Reagan Lifetime Achievement Award, Council of National Policy (2013); Bradley Prize (2012); One of the Most Influential U.S. Conservatives, The Daily Telegraph (2010); Charles Hoeflich Lifetime Achievement Award, Intercollegiate Studies Institute (2009); The Seven Most Powerful Conservatives, Forbes Magazine (2009); The 50 Most Powerful People in Washington, DC, GQ Magazine (2007); Truman-Reagan Medal of Freedom (2006); Walter Judd Freedom Award, Fund for American Studies (2004); Thomas Jefferson Servant Leadership Award, Council of National Policy (1996); Man of the Year, Wharton School (1993); Director's Service Award, U.S. Information Agency (1992); Superior Public Service Award, Department of Navy (1987); Free Enterprise Man of the Year, Texas Agricultural and Mechanical University (1985); Distinguished Alumni Award, Regis University (1985); American Eagle Award, Invest-in-American National Council (1983); Washington Award, Freedom Foundation (1979-1980); Decorated Presidential Recognition Medal; Order of Diplomatic Service; Merit-Gwanghwa Medal, Republic of Korea; Order of Brilliant Star with Grand Cordon, Republic of China **MEM:** President, Philadelphia Society (2013-2014); Treasurer, Mont Pelerin Society (2000-2014); Senior Vice President, Treasurer, Mont Pelerin

Society (1998-2000); President, Treasurer, Mont Pelerin Society (1996-1998); Chairman, International Committee of the G.K. Chesterton Society (1989-1992); President, Philadelphia Society (1982-1983); Treasurer, Mont Pelerin Society (1979-1996); Treasurer, Philadelphia Society (1964-1979); Union League, New York, NY; Metropolitan Club; Reform Club, London, England; Bohemian Club, San Francisco, CA; Knights of Malta; Knights of the Holy Sepulchre; Alpha Kappa Psi; Member, American Economics Association; Institute d'Etudes Politiques **MH:** Albert Nelson Marquis Lifetime Achievement Award (2017) **H:** Model railroading **PA:** Republican **BA:** 214 Massachusetts Avenue NE, The Heritage Foundation, Washington, DC, 20002 **ADD:** 1250 S Washington Street, Unit 721, Alexandria, VA, 22314

FEY, TINA, T: Actress, Comedienne **I:** Media & Entertainment **DOB:** 05/18/1970 **PB:** Upper Darby **PT:** Daughter of Donald and Jeanne (Xenakes) Fey **ED:** BA in Drama, University of Virginia, 1992 **C:** Performer, Second City comedy troupe, Chicago **CW:** Writer (TV series) Saturday Night Live, 1997-2006, The Colin Quinn Show, 2002, (TV special) Saturday Night Live: 25th Anniversary, 1999, NBC 75th Anniversary Special, 2002; actress: (films) Man of the Year, 2006, Beer League, 2006, Aqua Teen Hunger Force Colon Movie (voice), 2007, Baby Mama, 2008, The Invention of Lying, 2009 (Teen Choice award for Choice Movie Actress: Comedy, 2010), Date Night, 2010, Megamind (voice), 2010, Admission, 2013, Anchorman 2: The Legend Continues, 2013, Muppets Most Wanted, 2014, This Is Where I Leave You, 2014, Monkey Kingdom, 2015, Sisters, 2015, Whiskey Tango Foxtrot, 2016; (TV series) Saturday Night Live, 2000-06; actress, writer (films) Mean Girls, 2004, actress, producer Sisters, 2015, Whiskey Tango Foxtrot, 2016, actress, writer, co-prodr. (TV series) 30 Rock, 2006-13 (Emmy award for Outstanding Comedy Series, Academy TV Arts & Scis., 2007, 2008, Golden Globe award for Best Performance by an Actress in a TV Series - Musical or Comedy, Hollywood Foreign Press Association, 2008, 2009, Screen Actors Guild award for Outstanding Performance by a Female Actor in a Comedy Series, 2008, 2010, 2013, Producers Guild of America award for Best Episodic TV-Comedy, 2008, Writers Guild of America award for Best Comedy Series, 2008, 2009, Emmy award for Outstanding Lead Actress in a Comedy Series, Academy TV Arts & Scis., 2008, Golden Globe award for Best TV Series - Musical Or Comedy, Hollywood Foreign Press Association, 2009, Danny Thomas Producer of Year award in Episodic TV - Comedy, Producers Guild America, 2009, Danny Thomas Producer of Year award in Episodic TV-Comedy, Producers Guild America, 2010, Emmy award for Outstanding Writing for a Comedy Series, 2013), narrator (documentaries) Monkey Kingdom, 2015; executive prodr.: (TV films) Cabot College, 2014, Family Fortune, 2015; guest appearances include (TV series) Upright Citizens Brigade, 1999, The Real World/Road Rules Extreme Challenge, 2001, Saturday Night Live: Presidential Bash 2008 (Emmy award for Outstanding Guest Actress in a Comedy Series, Academy TV Arts & Scis., 2009); author: Bossypants, 2011; co-host The 70th Golden Globe Awards, 2013, The 71st Golden Globe Awards, 2014, The 72nd Golden Globe Awards, 2015, Family Fortune, 2015, Unbreakable Kimmy Schmidt, 2015, Inside Amy Schumer, 2015, SNL, 2015, Maya & Marty, 2016, Difficult People, 2016, The Kicker, 2016, Great News, 2017 **AW:** Named a Funny Female Star, People's Choice Awards, 2009; named Entertainer of Year, Associated Press, 2008, Entertainment Weekly, 2001; named one of The 100 Agents of Change, Rolling Stone magazine, 2009,

The 100 Most Powerful Women in Entertainment, The Hollywood Reporter, 2008-14, 10 People Who Mattered, Newsweek, 2008, 25 Leaders Reshaping New York, Crain's New York magazine, 2008, The Ten Most Fascinating People of 2008, Barbara Walters special, The 100 Most Powerful Celebrities, Forbes.com, 2008, The 50 Most Powerful Women in New York City, New York Post, 2008, 2007, The Top 25 Entertainers of Year, Entertainment Weekly, 2007, The 100 Most Influential People in the World, TIME magazine, 2009, 2007; recipient Mark Twain Prize for American Humor, John F. Kennedy Center for the Performing Arts, 2010 **BA:** 3 Arts Entertainment, 9460 Wilshire Blvd. 7th Floor, Beverly Hills, CA, 90212

FIELD, SALLY, T: Actress **I:** Media & Entertainment **PB:** Pasadena **SC:** CA/USA **PT:** Richard Dryden Field; Margaret (Morlan) Field **SPN:** Alan Greisman, December 15, 1984 (div. 1993); Steven Craig, September 16, 1968 (div. 1975) **CH:** Sam; Peter; Eli **ED:** Student, Actor's Studio, 1975 **CIV:** Board of directors, Vital Voices Global Partnership **CW:** Actress: (TV series) Gidget, 1965-66, The Flying Nun, 1967-70, The Girl With Something Extra, 1973-74, Brothers & Sisters, 2006-11 (Emmy award for Outstanding Lead Actress in a Drama Series, 2007, Screen Actors Guild award for Outstanding Performance by a Female Actor in a Drama Series, 2009); (films) The Way West, 1967, Stay Hungry, 1976, Heroes, 1977, Smokey and the Bandit, 1977, Hooper, 1978, The End, 1978, Norma Rae, 1979 (Academy award for Best Actress in a Leading Role, 1980), Beyond the Poseidon Adventure, 1979, Smokey and the Bandit II, 1980, Back Roads, 1981, Absence of Malice, 1981, Kiss Me Goodbye, 1982, Places in the Heart, 1984 (Academy award for Best Actress in a Leading Role, 1984), Murphy's Romance (also executive producer), 1985, Surrender, 1987, Punchline, 1987 (also producer), Steel Magnolias, 1989, Soapdish, 1991, Not Without My Daughter, 1991, Homeward Bound: The Incredible Journey, 1993 (voice), Mrs. Doubtfire, 1993, Forrest Gump, 1994, Homeward Bound II: Lost in San Francisco, 1996 (voice), Eye for an Eye, 1996, Where the Heart Is, 2000, Say It Isn't So, 2001, Legally Blonde 2: Red, White & Blonde, 2003, Two Weeks, 2006, The Amazing Spider-Man, 2012, Lincoln, 2012 (New York Film Critics Cir., Boston Society Film Critics, African American Film Critics Association awards for Best Actress, 2012), The Amazing Spider-Man 2, 2014, Hello, My Name Is Doris, 2015, Little Evil, 2017; (TV films) Maybe I'll Come Home In the Spring, 1971, Marriage: Year One, 1971, Home for the Holidays, 1972, Bridger, 1976, Sybil, 1976 (Emmy award for Outstanding Lead Actress in a Drama or Comedy Special, 1977), All the Way Home, 1981, Merry Christmas George Bailey, 1997, A Cooler Climate, 1999, David Copperfield, 2000; (TV mini-series) David Copperfield, 1986, A Women of Independent Means, 1995; (TV appearances) The Hollywood Squares, 1966, Rowan & Martin's Laugh-In, 1968, Carol Burnett & Co., 1979, Saturday Night Live, 1993, King of Hill (voice), 1997, Murphy Brown, 1998, ER, 2000-06, The Court, 2002, Conviction, 2005, Brothers and Sisters, 2006-11, Spielberg, 2017, Maniac, 2018; director, executive prodr.: (TV films) The Christmas Tree, 1996; dir.: (TV episodes) From the Earth to the Moon, 1998; (films) Beautiful, 2000; prodr.: (films) Dying Young, 1991; executive prodr.: (documentaries) The Lost Children of Berlin, 1997.(Stage) The Goat, or Who is Sylvia?, 2002, The Glass Menagerie, 2017 **AW:** Recipient Golden Plate award, Academy Achievement, 2005

FIELDS, MARK, T: Ford CEO **I:** Automotive **DOB:** 01/24/1961 **PB:** Bklyn. **PT:** Son of Gerald S. and Elinor Fields; **ED:** MBA, Harvard Business School,

1989; BA in Economics, Rutgers University, 1983 **C:** President, CEO, Ford Motor Co., 2014-; COO, Ford Motor Co., 2012-14; Executive vice president, president Americas, Ford Motor Co., 2005-12; Executive vice president, Ford Europe, Ford Motor Co., 2004-05; Group vice president, Premier Automotive Group, Ford Motor Co., 2002-04; Rep. director, president, Mazda Motor Corp., 1999-2002; Senior managing director of marketing, sales & customer service, Mazda Motor Corp., 1998; Senior adviser, Mazda Motor Corp., 1998; Managing director, Ford of Argentina, 1997-98; Served in a variety of sales and marketing positions, Ford Motor Co., Dearborn, Michigan, 1990-96; Joined, Ford Motor Co., Dearborn, Michigan, 1989 **CR:** Board directors Ford Motor Co., 2014- **AW:** Recipient Innovator of the Year, CNBC's Asian Business Leader, 2001, Global Leader of Tomorrow, World Economic Forum, 2000

FIENNES, RALPH, T: Actor **I:** Media & Entertainment **PB:** Ipswitch, Suffolk **SC:** England **PT:** Mark Fiennes; Jini (Jennifer Lash) Fiennes **MS:** Married **SPN:** Alex Kingston, 1993 (div. Oct 28, 1997) **ED:** Student, Royal Academy Dramatic Art; Student, Chelsea College Art and Design **CW:** Actor: (theatre productions) with Royal Shakespeare Co., Broadway debut in Hamlet, 1995 (Tony award for Lead Actor in a Play), Ivanov, 1997, Richard II and Coriolanus, 2000, The Talking Cure, 2002, Brand, 2003, Julius Caesar, 2005, Faith Healer, 2006, First Love, 2007, Oedipus the King, 2008, The Tempest, 2011, Man and Superman, 2015, The Master Builder, 2016, (films) Wuthering Heights, 1992, The Baby of Macon, 1993, Schindler's List, 1993, New York Film Critics Circle award for Best Supporting Actor 1993), Quiz Show, 1994, Strange Days, 1995, The English Patient, 1996, Oscar & Lucinda, 1997, (voice) The Prince of Egypt, 1998 The Avengers, 1998, Taste of Sunshine, 1999, End of the Affair, 1999 Spider, 2002, The Good Thief, 2002, Red Dragon, 2002, Maid in Manhattan, 2002, The Chumscrubber, 2005, The Constant Gardener, 2005, (voice) Wallace & Gromit: The Curse of the Were-Rabbit, 2005, Harry Potter and the Goblet of Fire, 2005, The White Countess, 2005, Harry Potter and the Order of the Phoenix, 2007, Bernard and Doris, 2008, In Bruges, 2008, The Duchess, 2008, The Hurt Locker, 2009, The Reader, 2008, Clash of the Titans, 2010, Nanny McPhee Returns, 2010, Harry Potter and the Deathly Hallows: Part 1, 2010, Harry Potter and the Deathly Hallows: Part 2, 2011, Wrath of the Titans, 2012, Skyfall, 2012, Great Expectations, 2012, The Grand Budapest Hotel, 2014, Two Women, 2014, A Bigger Splash, 2015, Spectre, 2015, Hail, Caesar!, 2016, Kubo and the Two Strings (voice), 2016, The Lego Batman Movie, 2017, Sea Sorrow, 2017, Holmes and Watson, 2018 (TV films) Prime Suspect, 1991, A Dangerous Man: Lawrence After Arabia, 1992, Prime Suspect, 1991 How Proust Can Change Your Life, 2002, Bernard and Doris, 2008, Page Eight, 2011, Rev, 2011-14, Turks & Caicos, 2014, Salting the Battlefield, 2014; actor, prodr.: (films) Onegin, 1999; actor, director, prodr.: (films) Coriolanus, 2011; actor, dir.: (films) The Invisible Woman, 2013; (TV appearances) Masterpiece Contemporary, 2011, Rev, 2011

FIERI, GUY, T: Restaurateur, Television Personality **I:** Media & Entertainment **DOB:** 01/22/1968 **PB:** Colombus **PT:** Son of James and Penelope Ferry; **ED:** BS in Hospitality Management, University Nevada, Las Vegas, 1990 **C:** Founder, manager, Guy's American Kitchen and Bar, New York City, 2012-; Co-founder, Guy's Burger Joint (on Carnival Cruise Lines), 2011-; Co-founder, manager, Tex Wasabi's, Sacramento, 2007-; Co-founder, manager, Tex Wasabi's, Santa Rosa, 2003-; Co-founder, manager, Johnny Garlic's, Roseville, California, 2008-; Co-founder, manager, Johnny Garlic's,

Windsor, California, 1999-; Co-founder, manager, Johnny Garlic's, Santa Rosa, California, 1996-; District manager, Louise's Trattoria,; Manager, Stouffer's Restaurant, Long Beach, California, **CR:** Spokesperson T.G.I. Friday's, 2008-09 **CIV:** Past president, Restaurant Association Redwood Empire, Board directors, California Restaurant Association Educational Foundation, Launched CWK (Cooking With Kids), 2011 **CW:** Contestant, winner The Next Food Network Star, 2006, guest judge, host (TV series) Guy's Big Bite, Food Network, 2006-, Diners, Drive-Ins and Dives, 2007-, Ultimate Recipe Showdown, 2008-10, Tailgate Warriors, 2011, co-host Rachel versus Guy: Celebrity Cook-Off, 2012, host (game show) Minute to Win It, NBC, 2010-11, (road tour) Guy Fieri Road Show, 2009, Guy's Grocery Game, 2013-; author: (cookbooks) Diners, Drive-ins, and Dives: An All-American Road Trip with Recipes!, 2008 (#1 New York Times bestseller), More Diners, Drive-ins and Dives: Another Drop-Top Culinary Cruise Through America's Finest and Funkiest, 2009, Guy Fieri Food, 2011, Guy on Fire: Grilling, Tailgating, Camping, and more!, 2014

FILO, DAVID, T: Co-Founder of Yahoo **I:** Technology **SC:** WI/USA **ED:** BS in Computer Engineering, Tulane; MS, Stanford University **C:** Co-Founder, Yahoo (1994-Present) **CIV:** Yellow Chair Foundation (2000-Present)

FINCH, JENNIE, T: Retired Softball Player **I:** Athletics **DOB:** 09/03/1980 **PB:** La Mirada **PT:** Daughter of Doug and Bev Finch; **ED:** Degree in Communications, University Arizona, 2002 **C:** Conducts softball camps throughout the U.S.; Pitcher, Chicago Bandits (National Pro Fastpitch),; Member, U.S.A. Women's Softball Team, Beijing Olympics, 2008; Member, U.S.A. Women's Softball Team, Athens Olympics, 2004; Color commentator, Women's College World Series, ESPN, 2003 **CW:** Co-host This Week in Baseball, ESPN, co-author, Throw Like a Girl: How to Dream Big and Believe in Yourself, 2011; **AW:** Co-recipient Ruby award for Most Outstanding Female Senior Student Athlete, University Arizona; named First Team All American, National Fastpitch Coach's Association, 2002, 2001, 2000; recipient Honda award for Nation's Best Softball Player, 2002, 2001 **ACH:** Achievements include winning a NCAA-record 60 consecutive games as a pitcher over three seasons; having her number retired at the University of Arizona on May 9, 2003; being a member of the University of Arizona NCAA Championship Team, 2001; being a member of the U.S.A. Women's Softball Gold Medal Team, International Softball Federation World Championships, 2002, Athens Olympic Games, 2004, Silver Medal Team, Beijing Olympics, 2008

FINCHER, DAVID, T: Director **I:** Business Management/Business Services **DOB:** 08/28/1962 **PB:** Denver **SC:** CO/USA **PT:** Howard Kelly Fincher; Claire Mae (Boettcher) Fincher **C:** Co-founder, Propaganda Films, 1987; With, Industrial Light & Magic, 1981-83 **CW:** Dir.: (films) Alien 3, 1992, Seven, 1995, The Game, 1997, The Fight Club, 1999, Panic Room, 2002, Zodiac, 2007, The Curious Case of Benjamin Button, 2008 (National Board Review award for Best Director, 2008, London Film Critics' Cir. award for Director of Year, 2009), The Social Network, 2010 (National Board Review award for Best Film, 2010, New York Film Critics Cir., 2010, Boston Society Film Critics award for Best Director, Best Picture, 2010, Golden Globe award for Best Director - Motion Picture, Hollywood Foreign Press Association, 2011, Critics' Choice Movie award for Best Picture, 2011), The Girl with the Dragon Tattoo, 2011, Gone Girl, 2014;

(music videos) Don Henley, Sting, The Wallflowers, Paula Abdul, Aerosmith, Madonna, Michael Jackson, George Michael, Rolling Stones (Grammy award for Best Music Video Love is Strong, 1995), Steve Winwood, The Motels, Iggy Pop, Billy Idol, A Perfect Circle, Justin Timberlake and Jay Z (Grammy award for Best Music Video, 2014); executive prodr.: (films) Ambush, 2001, Chosen, 2001, The Follow, 2001, Star, 2001, Powder Keg, 2001, The Ticker, 2002, Lords of Dogtown, 2005, Love and Other Disasters, 2006; director, executive prodr: (TV series) House of Cards, 2013- (Emmy award for Outstanding Directing for a Drama Series, 2013), Mindhunter, 2017; dir.: (TV commericals) for Nike, Coca-Cola, Budweiser, Heineken, Pepsi, Levi's, Converse, AT&T, and Chanel.

FINK, LARRY, T: CEO of BlackRock **I:** Real Estate **DOB:** 11/02/1952 **PB:** L.os Angeles **SC:** California **ED:** MBA in Real Estate, UCLA Anderson School Management, 1976; BA in Political Sci., UCLA, 1974 **C:** Co-founder, chairman, CEO, BlackRock, Inc., 1987-; Chairman, Nomura BlackRock Asset Management,; Managing director, member management committee, head mortgage & real estate products group, co-head taxable fixed income div., First Boston Corp., 1976-88 **CIV:** Co-chmn. board trustees, New York University Hospital Center, Co-chmn. board trustees, member executive committee, Mount Sinai New York University Health, Trustee, member executive committee, chairman financial affairs committee, New York University, 2001- **AW:** Named one of The 50 Most Influential People in Global Finance, Bloomberg Markets, 2011-14, The Business People of Year, Fortune magazine, 2010, The World's Most Powerful People, Forbes magazine, 2009-14; recipient Woodrow Wilson award for Corporate Citizenship, Woodrow Wilson International Center for Scholars, 2010, John E. Anderson Distinguished Alumnus award, UCLA, 2007, ABANA Achievement Award, 2016 **H:** Art, fishing, skiing **PA:** Democrat

FIRE, ANDREW ZACHARY, T: Biologist, Pathology Professor **I:** Education/Educational Services **DOB:** 04/27/1959 **PB:** Palo Alto **SC:** CA/USA **ED:** PhD in Biology, Massachusetts Institute of Technology, 1983; BA in Math., University of California, Berkeley, 1978 **C:** Professor department pathology and genetics, Stanford University School of Medicine, California, 2003-; Staff member department embryology, Carnegie Institution of Washington, Baltimore, 1986-2003; Postdoc. fellow, Medical Research Council Laboratory Molecular Biology, Cambridge, England, 1983-86 **CR:** Member board sci. counselors National Center Biotechnology, National Institutes of Health adjunct professor biology Johns Hopkins University, Baltimore, 1989-2003 **CW:** Contributor articles in professional journals **AW:** Recipient Paul Ehrlich & Ludwig Darmstaedter prize, Germany, 2006, Nobel prize in physiology/medicine, 2006, Massry prize, 2005, Lewis S. Rosenstiel award, Brandeis University, 2005, Gairdner Foundation International award, 2005, Dr. H.P. Heinken prize in biochemistry and biophysics, Netherlands Academy Arts & Sci., 2004, Wiley prize, Rockefeller University, 2003, Meyenburg prize, Germany, 2002, Genetics Society of America medal, 2002, Maryland Distinguished Young Scientist award, 1997 **MEM:** Fellow: Am. Academy Arts & Scis.; mem.: National Academy of Sciences (award in Molecular Biology 2003), Institute Medicine **ACH:** Achievements include discovery of process now known as RNAi (with Craig C. Mello), that double-stranded RNA can quash the activity of specific genes

FIRTH, COLIN ANDREW, T: Actor **I:** Media & Entertainment **PB:** Grayshott **SC:** England **PT:** David Norman Lewis; Shirley Jean (Rolles) Firth **ED:** Attended, Barton Peveri College **CW:** Actor: (films) Another Country, 1981, Dutch Girls, 1985, 1919, 1985, A Month in the Country, 1987, Apartment Zero, 1988, Valmont, 1989, Wings of Fame, 1990, Femme Fatale, 1991, The Hour of the Pig, 1993, The Deep Blue Sea, 1994, Playmaker, 1994, Circle of Friends, 1995, The English Patient, 1996, Fever Pitch, 1997, A Thousand Acres, 1997, Shakespeare in Love, 1998, My Life So Far, 1999, The Secret Laughter of Women, 1999, Blackadder Back & Forth, 1999, Relative Values, 2000, Bridget Jones's Diary, 2001, The Importance of Being Earnest, 2002, Hope Springs, 2003, What a Girls Wants, 2003, Girl with the Pearl Earrings, 2003, Love Actually, 2003, Bridget Jones: The Edge of Reason, 2004, Where the Truth Lies, 2005, Nanny McPhee, 2005, The Last Legion, 2007, And When Did You Last See Your Father?, 2007, Then She Found Me, 2007, Mamma Mia!, 2008, Easy Virtue, 2008, A Single Man, 2009 (Best Leading Actor, Brit. Academy Film and TV Arts, 2010), The King's Speech, 2010 (Best Actor, New York Film Critics Cir., 2010, Best Performance by an Actor in a Motion Picture-Drama, Golden Globe Awards, 2011, Outstanding Performance by a Male Actor in a Leading Role, Screen Actors Guild, 2011, Outstanding Performance by a Cast in a Motion Picture, Screen Actors Guild, 2011, Best Actor in a Leading Role, Academy Awards, 2011, Best Actor, Critics' Choice Movie Awards, 2011), Main Street, 2010, Tinker Tailor Soldier Spy, 2011, Arthur Newman, 2012, Gambit, 2012, The Railway Man, 2013, Devil's Knot, 2013, Magic in the Moonlight, 2014, Before I Go to Sleep, 2014, Kingsman: The Secret Service, 2014, Genius, 2016, Deep Water, 2016, Bridget Jones's Baby, 2016, Red Nose Day Actually, 2017, Kingsman The Golden Circle, 2017, The Happy Prince, 2018,The Mercy, 2018, Mamma Mia Here We go Again, 2018, Mary Poppins Returns, 2018; (TV films) Camille, 1984, Tales from the Hollywood Hills: Pat Hobby Teamed with Genius, 1987, The Secret Garden, 1987, Tumbledown, 1989, Out of the Blue, 1991, Hostages, 1993, The Deep Blue Sea, 1994, Master of the Moor, 1994, The Widowing of Mrs. Holroyd, 1995, Conspiracy, 2001; (TV miniseries) Lost Empires, 1986, Pride and Prejudice, 1995, Nostromo, 1997; (plays) Another Country, 1983, The Lonely Road, 1985, Desire Under the Elms, 1987, The Caretaker, 1991, Chatsky, 1993, Three Days of Rain, 1999; executive prodr.: (documentaries) In Prison My Whole Life, 2007, The People Speak UK, 2010; prodr.: Amá, 2015; (films) Eye in the Sky, 2015, Loving, 2016 **AW:** Named one of The 100 Most Influential People in the World, TIME Magazine, 2011; Recipient Best Dressed Actor Award, Elle Magazine, 2010 **MEM:** Mem.: Royal Shakespeare Co.

FISCHER, DEB, T: U.S. Senator from Nebraska **I:** Government Administration/Government Relations/Government Services **DOB:** 03/01/1951 **PB:** Lincoln, Nebraska **PT:** Daughter of Jerry Fischer; **ED:** BS in Education, University Nebraska, Lincoln, 1988 **C:** Member, US Senate Small Business & Entrepreneurship Committee, 2013-; Member, US Senate Indian Affairs Committee, 2013-; Member, US Senate Environment & Public Works Committee, 2013-; Member, US Senate Commerce, Sci. & Transportation Committee, 2013-; Member, US Senate Armed Services Committee, 2013-; US Senator from Nebraska, 2013-; Rancher, Sunny Slope Ranch, 1972-; Member District 43, Nebraska State Legislature, 2005-13 **CR:** Commissioner Nebraska Coordinating Commission for Post-Secondary Education, 2000 **CIV:** Member, Valentine Rural High School Board Education, 1990-2004 **MEM:** Mem.: Philanthropic and Educational Organization for Women, Society for Range Management, Sandhills Cattle Association **PA:** Republican

FISH JR., JAMES C C., T: President of Waste Management **I:** Other **DOB:** 01/01/1900 **ED:** Bachelors in Accounting, Arizona State University; MBA, Finance, University of Chicago **CT:** CPA **C:** President/CEO, Waste Management, 2017-; Exec VP/CFO,Waste Management, 2012-16; Senior VP: Eastern Group, Waste Management, 2011-12; Director Financial Planning & Analysis, Waste Management, 2001-03

FISHBURNE, LAURENCE, T: Actor **I:** Media & Entertainment **PB:** Augusta **SC:** GA/USA **PT:** Laurence John Fishburne Jr.; Hattie Bell Crawford Fishburne **MS:** Married **SPN:** Gina Torres (September 20, 2002); Hajna O. Moss, (July 1, 1985) (div.) **CH:** Delilah; Langston Issa; Montana Isis **ED:** HHD (hon.), Howard University, 2009 **CW:** Stage appearances include Section D, 1975, Eden, 1976, Short Eyes, 1984, Loose Ends, 1988, Urban Blight, 1988, Two Trains Running, 1992 (Tony award for Best Featured Actor, 1992), Fences, 2006, Thurgood, 2008 (Drama Desk award for Outstanding Solo Performance, 2008); actor: (films) Cornbread, Earl and Me, 1975, Apocalypse Now, 1979, Fast Break, 1979, Willie and Phil, 1980, Death Wish II, 1982, Rumble Fish, 1983, The Cotton Club, 1984, The Color Purple, 1985, Band of the Hand, 1986, Quicksilver, 1986, Gardens of Stone, 1987, Cherry 2000, 1987, A Nightmare on Elm Street 3: Dream Warriors, 1987, School Daze, 1988, Red Heat, 1988, King of New York, 1990, Cadence, 1991, Class Action, 1991, Boyz N the Hood, 1991, Deep Cover, 1992, What's Love Got To Do With It, 1993, Searching For Bobby Fischer, 1993, Higher Learning, 1995 (National Association for the Advancement of Colored People Image award for Outstanding Supporting Actor in a Motion Picture, 1996), Bad Company, 1995, Just Cause, 1995, Othello, 1995, Fled, 1996, Event Horizon, 1997, The Matrix, 1999, (voice) Osmosis Jones, 2001, Biker Boyz, 2003, The Matrix Reloaded, 2003, Mystic River, 2003, The Matrix Revolutions, 2003, Assault on Precinct 13, 2005, Mission Impossible III, 2006, Bobby, 2006, (voice) TMNT, 2007, (voice) 4: Rise of the Silver Surfer, 2007, The Death and Life of Bobby Z, 2007, Twenty-One, 2008, Armored, 2009, Predators, 2010, Contagion, 2011, The Colony, 2013, Man of Steel, 2013, Khumba, 2013, Ride Along, 2014, The Signal, 2014, Rudderless, 2014, Standoff, 2015, Batman v Superman: Dawn of Justice, 2016, Passengers, 2016, John Wick: Chapter Two, 2016, Last Flag Flying, 2017, Where'd You Go Bernadette, 2018, Ant Man and the Wasp, 2018 (TV films) If You Give a Dance, You Gotta Pay the Band, 1972, A Rumor of War, 1980, I Take These Men, 1983, For Us the Living: The Medgar Evers Story, 1983, The Father Clements Story, 1987, Decoration Day, 1990, The Tuskegee Airmen, 1995 (National Association for the Advancement of Colored People Image award for Outstanding Actor in a TV Movie or Mini-Series, 1996), Before Your Eyes, 1996, Thurgood, 2011 (National Association for the Advancement of Colored People Image award for Outstanding Actor in a TV Movie, Mini-Series or Dramatic Special, 2015), Have a Little Faith, 2011, (TV series) The Six O'Clock Follies, 1980, CSI: Crime Scene Investigation, 2008-11, Hannibal, 2013-14, (TV Mini-Series) Roots, 2016, Madiba, 2016; (TV appearances) Trapper John, M.D., 1981, Strike Force, 1982, M*A*S*H, 1982, Hill Street Blues, 1981, Miami Vice, 1986, Pee-wee's Playhouse, 1986, 1987, Spenser: For Hire, 1987, The Equalizer, 1989, Tribeca, 1993; actor, director, producer, writer: (films) Once in the Life, 2000; actor, executive prodr.: (films) Hoodlum, 1997, Black

Water Transit, 2009, (TV films) Miss Ever's Boys, 1997 (National Association for the Advancement of Colored People Image award for Outstanding Lead Actor in a TV Movie or Mini-Series, 1998), Always Outnumbered, 1998; actor, prodr.: (films) Akeelah and the Bee, 2006, Five Fingers 2006, (TV series) Black-ish, 2014- (National Association for the Advancement of Colored People Image award for Outstanding Supporting Actor in a Comedy Series, 2015), The Muppets, 2015, Roots,2016, Madiba, 2017 **AW:** Recipient Artist of the Year Award, Harvard University, 2007

FITCH, WILLIAM C., T: Former Professional Basketball Coach **I:** Athletics **DOB:** 05/19/1934 **PB:** Cedar Rapids **ED:** Student, Coe College **C:** Coach, L.A. Clippers, 1994-98; Coach, New Jersey Nets, 1989-92; Coach, Houston Rockets, 1983-88; Coach, Boston Celtics, 1979-83; Coach, Cleveland Cavaliers, 1970-79; Basketball coach, University Minnesota, Minneapolis, 1968-70; Basketball coach, Bowling Green State University, 1967-68; Basketball coach, University North Dakota, Grand Forks, 1962-67; Basketball coach, Coe College, Cedar Rapids, 1958-62 **AW:** Named NBA Coach of Year, 1976, 80; coach NBA championship team, 1981,Chuck Daly Lifetime Achievement Award, 2012-13; Top 10 Coaches in NBA History **ACH:** Coached more games than any other NBA coach.

FITTIPALDI, EMERSON, T: Semi-Retired Racing Driver **I:** Athletics **DOB:** 12/12/1946 **PB:** Sao Paulo **SC:** Brazil **PT:** Son of Wilson and Juze Fittipaldi **MS:** Married **SPN:** Teresa Fittipaldi, 1983 **CH:** Tatiana, Juliana, Jayson **ED:** Student, Jim Russell School Motor Racing **C:** Winner Marlboro Challenge, 1992; Winner Indianapolis 500, 1989; Designer Race Cars, Owner Car Dealership, Brazil, 1982-84; Winner Formula One World title, 1972; Became Formula One racer, Europe, 1970; Founder, Fittipaldi Motoring Accessories, **AW:** Motorsport Hall of Fame, 2001 **ADD:** care Internat Auto Fedn 8 pl de la Concorde, Paris, YT, France, F-75008

FITZPATRICK, BRIAN, T: U.S. Representative from Pennsylvania **I:** Government Administration/ Government Relations/Government Services **DOB:** 12/17/1973 **PB:** Levittown **SC:** PA/USA **ED:** J.D., Penn State, 2001; M.B.A., Penn State, 2001; B.A., La Salle University, 1996 **C:** Member, U.S. House of Representatives fro Pennsylvania's 8th District, 2017-; Member, Committee on Foreign Affairs; Member, Committee on Homeland Security; Member, Committee on Small Business; National Supervisor, Bureau's Public Corruption Unit, 2002-2016; Judicial Clerk, Eastern District of Pennsylvania, 2001-02 **BA:** 514 Cannon HOB, Washington, DC, 20515

FLAKE, JEFF, T: U.S. Senator from Arizona **I:** Government Administration/Government Relations/ Government Services **DOB:** 12/31/1962 **PB:** Snowflake, Arizona **PT:** Son of Dean Maeser and Nerita (Flock) Flake; **ED:** MA in Political Sci., Brigham Young University, 1987; BA in International Relations, Brigham Young University, 1986 **C:** Member, US Senate Special Committee on Aging, 2013-; Member, US Senate Judiciary Committee, 2013-; Member, US Senate Energy & Natural Resources Committee, 2013-; Member, US Senate Foreign Relations Committee, 2013-; US Senator from Arizona, 2013-; Member, US Congress from 6th Arizona District, 2003-13; Member, US Congress from 1st Arizona District, 2001-03; Executive Director, Goldwater Institute, Arizona, 1992-99; Lobbyist, Rossing Uranium, 1990-92; Executive Director, Foundation for Democracy, Namibia, 1989-90 **CW:** Appeared in (documentaries) How Democracy Works Now: Twelve Stories, 2010, (TV Special) Rival Survival,

2014 **AW:** Named one of The 10 Best Members of Congress, Esquire magazine, 2008 **PA:** Republican **BA:** The Office of Jeff Flake, Senate Russell Office Building 413, Washington, DC, 20510

FLAUM, JOEL MARTIN, T: Federal Judge **I:** Law and Legal Services **DOB:** 11/26/1936 **PB:** Hudson **SC:** NY/USA **PT:** Louis Flaum, Sally (Berger) Flaum **ED:** LLD, John Marshall Law School, 2002; LLM, Northwestern University, 1964; JD, Northwestern University, 1963; BA, Union College, Schenectady, NY, 1958 **C:** Judge, U.S. Court of Appeals, Seventh Circuit, 1983-Present; Chief Judge, U.S. Court of Appeals, Seventh Circuit, 2000-2006; Judge, U.S. District Court, Northern District, Illinois, Chicago, IL, 1975-1983; First Assistant, U.S. Attorney, Northern District, U.S. Department of Justice, Chicago, IL, 1972-1975; First Assistant, Attorney General of Illinois, Cook County, Illinois, 1969-1972; Assistant State's Attorney, Cook County, Illinois, 1965-1969 **CR:** Adjunct Professor, Northwestern University, School of Law, 1993-2000; Lecturer, DePaul University College of Law, 1987-1988; Illinois Law Enforcement Commission, 1970-1972; Consultant, U.S. Department of Justice, Law Enforcement Assistance Administration, 1970-1971; Fellow, Ford Foundation, 1963-1964; Fellow, Chicago Bar Foundation; Fellow, American Bar Foundation **CIV:** Visiting Committee, University of Chicago Law School, 1983-1986; Advisory Committee, U.S. Coast Guard Academy, 1990-1993; Law Board, Northwestern University School of Law, 1983-Present **MIL:** Lieutenant Commander, JACG, U.S. Naval Reserve, 1981-1992 **CW:** Northwestern University Law Review, 1962-1963; Contributor, Articles, Legal Journals **MEM:** Licentiate, Chicago Bar Foundation, Licentiate, American Bar Foundation, Federal Bar Association, American Judicature Society, Navy-Marine Corps Retired Judges Advisors Association, Maritime Law Association, Chicago Inn of Court, Seventh Circuit Bar Association, Illinois Bar Association, Naval Reserve Association, Lawyers Club of Chicago **BAR:** State of Illinois, 1963 **BA:** U.S. Court of Appeals, Seventh Circuit, 219 S Dearborn Street, Chicago, IL, USA, 60604-1702

FLAY, BOBBY, T: Executive Chef **I:** Food & Restaurant Services **DOB:** 12/10/1964 **PB:** New York **SC:** NY/USA **PT:** Bill Flay, Dorothy Flay **ED:** Diploma, French Culinary Institute, 1984 **C:** Editor-In-Chief, Bon Appétit Magazine, Condé Nast Publications, 2016-Present; Executive Chef, Owner, Bobby's Burger Palace, Washington, DC, 2011-Present; Executive Chef, Owner, Bobby's Burger Palace, Philadelphia, PA, 2010-Present; Executive Chef, Owner, Bobby's Burger Palace, Uncasville, CT, 2009-Present; Executive Chef, Owner, Bar Americain, Uncasville, CT, 2009-Present; Executive Chef, Owner, Bobby's Burger Palace, Eatontown, NJ, 2008-Present; Executive Chef, Owner, Bobby's Burger Palace, Paramus, NJ, 2008-Present; Executive Chef, Owner, Bobby's Burger Palace, Lake Grove, NY, 2008-Present; Executive Chef, Owner, Mesa Grill, Bahamas, Atlantis Paradise Island, 2007-Present; Executive Chef, Owner, Bobby Flay Steak, Atlantic City, NJ, 2006-Present; Executive Chef, Owner, Bar Americain, New York, NY, 2005-Present; Executive Chef, Owner, Mesa Grill Las Vegas, Caesar's Palace, 2004-Present; Executive Chef, Owner, Mesa Grill, New York, NY, 1991-Present; Partner, Bolo, New York, NY, 1993-2007; Executive Chef, Miracle Grill, New York, NY, 1984-1991; Executive Chef, Owner, Bobby's Burger Palace, College Park, MD; Executive Chef, Owner, Bobby's Burger Palace, East Garden City, NY; Buds And Jams; Joe Allen's **CR:** Cooking Segment Host, CBS the Early Show, Master Instructor, Visiting Chef, French Culinary Institute, Chef's Council on Chefs For Humanity, Celebrity Judge, Wickedly

Perfect, 2005 **CW:** Co-Author, (Cookbooks) (With Joan Schwartz) Bold American Food, 1994, (With Stephanie Banyas and Sally Jackson) Bobby Flay's Grill It!, 2008, Bobby Flay's Burgers, Fries, and Shakes, 2009, (With Stephanie Banyas and Miriam Garron) Bobby Flay's Throwdown!: More Than 100 Recipes From Food Network's Ultimate Cooking Challenge, 2010, (With Stephanie Banyas and Sally Jackson) Bar Americain, 2011, Barbecue Addiction, 2013, Brunch at Bobby's: 140 Recipes for the Best Part of the Weekend, 2015; Author, From My Kitchen to Your Table, 1998, Boy Meets Grill, 1999, Bobby Flay Cooks American, 2001, Boy Gets Grill, 2004, Bobby Flay's Grilling for Life: 75 Healthier Ideas for Big Flavor From the Fire, 2005, Bobby Flay's Mesa Grill Cookbook: Explosive Flavors From Southwestern Kitchen, 2007; Host, (TV Series) Main Ingredients With Bobby Flay, Grillin' & Chillin', 1996, The Main Ingredient, Hot Off the Grill, 1998, Boy Meets Grill, 2003, Grill It! With Bobby Flay, 2008, (Reality Series) America's Next Great Restaurant, 2011, Food Nation, BBQ With Bobby Flay, Throwdown! With Bobby Flay, 2006-Present, (Radio Show) Bobby Flay Radio, SIRIUS XM Radio, 2009-Present, Brunch @ Bobby's, 2010-Present, Three Days to Open With Bobby Flay, 2012-Present, Beat Bobby Flay, 2013-Present; Host, Executive Producer, Bobby Flay's Barbecue Addiction; Co-Host, Worst Cooks in America, 2012; Chef, (TV Series) Iron Chef America; Judge, Food Network Star, 2006-2014; Guest Appearance, (TV Series) The Best Thing I Ever Ate, 2009-2011; Appearance, Entourage, 2011; Executive Producer, (TV Series) Sandwich King, 2011-2012 **AW:** Star, Hollywood Walk of Fame, 2015, Daytime Emmy for Outstanding Culinary Program, Bobby Flay's Barbecue Addiction, 2012, Emmy Award Winner for Best Culinary Program, Grill It! With Bobby Flay, 2009, Who's Who of Food & Beverage in America, 2007, National TV Food Show Award-Bobby Flay Chef Mentor, James Beard Foundation, 2005, Emmy Award Winner for Outstanding Service Show Host, Boy Meets Grill, 2005, IACP Award for Design, International Association of Culinary Professional Award For Design, Bold American Food, 1995, Outstanding Graduate Award, French Culinary Institute, 1993, Rising Star Chef of the Year, James Beard Foundation, 1993

FLEISCHMANN, CHUCK, T: U.S. Representative from Tennessee, Lawyer **I:** Law and Legal Services **DOB:** 10/11/1962 **PB:** New York City **SC:** NY/USA **PT:** Son of Max and Rose Marie Fleischmann **ED:** JD, University Tennessee College Law, Knoxville, 1986; BA in Political Sci., magna cum laude, University Illinois, Urbana-Champaign, 1983 **C:** Member, US House Small Bus. Com., Washington, 2011-; Member, Committee on Appropriations; Member, US House Science Space & Technology, Washington, 2011-; Member, US House Natural Resources Committee, Washington, 2011-; Member, US Congress from 3rd Tennessee District, Washington, 2011-; Founder, partner, Fleischmann & Fleischmann, Chattanooga, 1987 **CR:** Past chairman Chattanooga Lawyers Pro Bono Committee **CIV:** Board directors, National Craniofacial Association, Board directors, Cherokee Area Council Boy Scouts of America, Chattanooga **CW:** Radio talk show host Chuck Fleischmann Show, Chattanooga **MEM:** Mem.: Chattanooga Bar Association (past president) **PA:** Republican

FLEMING, PEGGY GALE, T: Former Olympic Figure Skater **I:** Athletics **DOB:** 07/27/1948 **PB:** San Jose **SC:** CA/USA **PT:** Daughter of Albert Eugene and Doris Elizabeth (Deal) F. **MS:** Married **SPN:** Greg Jenkins, June 13, 1970 **CH:** Andy, Todd **ED:** Student, Colorado College, 1966 **C:** Figure Skater, 1958- **CR:** Skating commentator for ABC Wide

World of Sports appears in commls. for Concord Watch **CIV:** National chairman Easter Seals trustee Women's Sports Foundation **CW:** Performer with Ice Capades, from 1968, Ice Follies; performer 7 TV spls.; guest appearance, Fantasy Island; Ambassador of goodwill, UNICEF; actor: (films) Blades of Glory, 2007. **AW:** Recipient Sports award ABC-TV, 1967; named Woman of Year Reader's Digest, 1969, Female Athlete of Year A.P., 1968; named to Colorado Hall of Fame, 1969,Lombardi Award of Excellence, 2003 **MEM:** Member U.S. Figure Skating Association Clubs: Broadmoor Figure Skating (Colorado Springs, Colorado). **ACH:** Juvenile ice skating champion Southwest Pacific and Pacific Coast, 1960, novice champion, 1961, senior champion, 1963, junior champion Southwest Pacific, 1962; 2d place national novice champion, 1962, 3d national junior champion, 1963; U.S. ladies champion, 1964-68; 2d place North America competition, 1965; 3d place world championship competition, 1965; world champion, 1966, 67, 68; North America ladies champion, 1967; 1st place gold medal for women's figure skating Olympic Games, 1968 **BA:** IMG, 304 Park Avenue South, Penthouse North, New York, NY, 10010

FLETCHER, LOUISE, T: Actress **I:** Media & Entertainment **PB:** Birmingham **SC:** AL/USA **PT:** Robert Capers Fletcher; Estelle (Caldwell) Fletcher **SPN:** Jerry Bick, July 18, 1959 (div. November 1978) **CH:** John Dashiell; Andrew Wilson **ED:** LHD, (hon.), Western Maryland College, 1986; LHD (hon.), Gallaudet University, 1982; Student acting with Jeff Corey; BA, University North Carolina, 1957 **CIV:** Board directors Deafness Research Foundation, 1980- **CW:** Actress: (films) Thieves Like Us, 1973, Russian Roulette, 1974, One Flew Over the Cuckoo's Nest, 1975 (Academy award as Best Actress), Exorcist II: The Heretic,, 1976, The Cheap Detective, 1977, The Magician, 1978, Natural Enemies, 1979, The Lucky Star, 1979, The Lady in Red, 1979, Strange Behavior, 1980, Brainstorm, 1981, Strange Invaders, 1982, Once Upon a Time in America, 1982, Firestarter, 1983, Overnight Sensation, 1983, Invaders from Mars, 1985, The Boy Who Could Fly, 1985, Nobody's Fool, 1986, Flowers in the Attic, 1987, Two Moon Junction, 1987, Blue Steel, 1988, Best of the Best, 1989, Shadowzone, 1989, Blind Vision, 1990, The Player, 1991, Return to Two Moon Junction, 1993, Tollbooth, 1993, Virtuosity, 1995, Mulholland Falls, 1995, 2 Days in the Valley, 1995, Edie & Pen, 1995, High School High, 1995, Girl Gets Moe, 1996, Heartless, 1996, Love Kills, 1998, A Map of the World, 1999, More Dogs than Bones, 1999, Cruel Inventions, 1999, Time Served, 1999, Very Mean Men, 2000, Silver Man, 2000, Seeing in the Dark, 2000, Big Eden, 2000, Touched by a Killer, 2001, After Image, 2001, Manna from Heaven, 2002, Finding Home, 2003, Clipping Adam, 2004, Dancing in Twilight, 2005, Aurora Borealis, 2005, Fat Rose and Squeaky, 2006, The Last Sin Eater, 2007, The Genesis Code, 2010, Cassadaga, 2011, A Perfect Man, 2013; (TV films) Heartless, 1997, The Devil's Arithmetic, 1999, Time Served, 1999, A Time to Remember, 2003, A Dad for Christmas, 2006, Of Two Minds, 2012; (TV appearances) Maverick, Wagon Train, The Law-Man, Playhouse 90, The Millionaire, Alfred Hitchcock, Thou Shalt Not Commit Adultery, 1978, A Summer to Remember, 1984, Island, 1984, Second Serve, 1985, Hoover, 1986, The Karen Carpenter Story, 1988, Nightmare on the 13th Floor, 1988, Twilight Zone, 1988, Final Notice, 1989, The Hitchhiker, 1990, Tales from the Crypt, 1991, In a Child's Name, 1991, Boys of Twilight, 1991, The Fire Next Time, 1992, Civil Wars, 1993, Star Trek: Deep Space Nine, 1993-99, The Haunting of Cliff House, Dream On, 1994, Someone Else's Child, 1994, VR5, 1994, 95, Picket Fences, 1996, Stepford Husbands, 1996,

Twisted Path, 1997, Breastmen, 1997, Married to a Stranger, 1997, Profiler, 1997, The Practice, 1998, Brimstone, 1998, Joan of Arcadia, 2004, 7th Heaven, 2005, Heroes, 2009, Private Practice, 2010-11, Shameless, 2011-12, Girlboss, 2017; **MEM:** Member National Institute Deafness and Other Communicable Disorders (adv. board)

FLETCHER, WILLIAM A., T: Federal Judge **I:** Law and Legal Services **DOB:** 06/06/1945 **PB:** Philadelphia **SC:** PA/USA **PT:** Son of Richard A. and Betty Binns Fletcher. **ED:** JD, Yale University, 1975; BA, Oxford University, 1970; BA, Harvard University, 1968 **C:** Judge, US Court Appeals (9th cir.), San Francisco, 1998-; Professor Law, University California, Berkeley, 1984-98; Acting Professor Law, University California, Berkeley, 1977-84; Law Clerk to Justice William J. Brennan, US Supreme Court, Washington, 1976-77; Law Clerk to Presiding Justice, US District Court California, San Francisco, 1975-76 **CR:** Member Am. Law Institute Professor Salzburg Seminar on Am. Legal Institutions with Office of Emergency Preparedness, Executive Office of the President, 1970-72 **MIL:** Lieutenant U.S. Navy, 1970-72 **MEM:** Mem.: California Bar Association

FLOOD, EMMET, T: White House Attorney **I:** Law and Legal Services **ED:** BA, University of Dallas; JD, Yale University; MA, University of Texas at Austin; PHD, University of Texas at Austin **C:** White House Attorney, Washington D.C. (2018-Present); Partner, Williams & Connolly **PA:** Republican

FLORES, BILL, T: U.S. Representative from Texas **I:** Government Administration/Government Relations/Government Services **DOB:** 02/25/1954 **PB:** Cheyenne **SC:** WY/USA **PT:** Joe P. Flores; Ruth Ann (Kennedy) Flores **ED:** MBA, Houston Baptist University (1985); BBA in Accounting, Texas Agricultural and Mechanical University, Cum Laude (1976) **C:** Chairman, Republican Study Committee (2015-Present); Member, Committee on Energy and Commerce; Member, US House Natural Resources Committee, Washington, DC (2011-Present); Member, US House Budget Committee, Washington, DC (2011-Present); Member, US Congress from the 17th Texas District, Washington, DC (2011-Present); Co-founder, President, Chief Executive Officer, Phoenix Exploration Co., Houston, Texas (2006-2009); Senior Vice President, Chief Financial Officer, Gryphon Exploration Co., Houston, Texas (2001-2005); Senior Vice President, Chief Financial Officer, TransEnergy, Houston, Texas (1999); Corporate Senior Vice President, Chief Financial Officer, Western Atlas Inc., Houston, Texas (1997-1998); Executive Vice President, Director of Marine Drilling, Chief Financial Officer, Marine Drilling Cos., Inc., Sugar Land, Texas (1991-1997); Vice President of Finance, Keyes Offshore Companies, Sugar Land, Texas (1980-1990); Controller, ABC, Houston, Texas (1978-1980); Senior Accountant, Peat, Marwick & Mitchell Co., Houston, Texas (1976-1978); Staff Accountant, Peat, Marwick & Mitchell Co., Amarillo, Texas (1976) **CIV:** Board of Trustees, Houston Baptist University; Commissioner, Texas Real Estate Commission; Board of Directors, Alley Theatre, Houston, Texas; Board of Directors, Past President, Texas Agricultural and Mechanical Association of Former Students **H:** Skiing; Flying **PA:** Republican **BA:** 1030 Longworth House Office Building, Washington, DC, 20515

FLOYD, HENRY FRANKLIN, T: Federal Judge **I:** Law and Legal Services **DOB:** 11/05/1947 **PB:** Brevard **SC:** NC/USA **ED:** JD, University South Carolina, 1973; BA, Wofford College, 1970 **C:** Judge, US Court Appeals (4th Cir.), 2011-; Judge, US Dis-

trict Court South Carolina, Spartanburg, 2003-11; Cir. judge, 13th Judicial Cir. Court South Carolina, 1992-2003; Private law practice, Pickens, South Carolina, 1973-92; Member, South Carolina House of Reps., Columbia, 1972-78 **BA:** US Court Appeals, 1100 E Main St, Richmond, VA, 23219

FLOYD, RAYMOND, T: Professional Golfer **I:** Athletics **CN:** PGA **DOB:** 09/04/1942 **PB:** Fort Bragg **SC:** NC/USA **ED:** Coursework, University of North Carolina (1960) **C:** Professional Golfer, Senior PGA (1992-Present); Professional Golfer, PGA (1961-1992) **CR:** Assistant Captain, U.S. Team, Ryder Cup (2008); U.S. Team, Ryder Cup (1969, 1975, 1977, 1981, 1983, 1985, 1991, 1993); Captain, U.S. Team, Ryder Cup (1989) **AW:** Runner-up, Boeing Championship (2006); Three Top Ten Finishes in Nine Starts (2006); Winner, Wendy's Champion Tour (2006); UBS Cup Member, Winning U.S. Team (2004); Winner, 2000 Ford Senior Players Championship (2000); Winner, Ford Senior Players Championship (2000); Winner, Senior Tour Championship (1994); Winner, Northville Long Island Classic, Senior PGA (1993); Winner, Doral Ryder Open (1992); Winner, GTE North Classic (1992); Elected, World Golf Hall of Fame (1989); Vardon Trophy (1983); Byron Nelson Award (1983); Player of Year, Golf Magazine (1976); Rookie of the Year, Golf Magazine (1963) **ACH:** Winner PGA tournament, 1969, 82 St. Petersburg Open, 1963, St. Paul Open, 1965, Jacksonville Open, 1969, Am. Golf Classic, 1969, Kemper Open, 1975, Masters, 1976, World Open, 1976, Byron Nelson Golf Classic, 1977, Pleasant Valley Golf Classic, 1977, Brazilian Open, 1978, Greater Greensboro Open, 1979, Canadian PGA, 1981, Vardon Trophy, 1983, Ryder Cup, 1969, 75, 77, 81, 83, 85, Doral Eastern Open, 1980, 81, Tournament Players Championship, 1981, Westchester Classic, 1981, Memorial Tournament, 1982, Memphis Classic, 1982, PGA Championship, 1982, $1Million Sun City Challenge, 1982, Houston Open, 1985, Chrysler Team Championship, 1985, U.S. Open, 1986, Walt Disney/Oldsmobile Classic, 1986, Skins Game, 1988, RMCC Invitational, 1990, Doral-Ryder Open, 1992, GTE North Classic, 1992, Ralph's Senior Classic, 1992, Senior Tour Championship, 1992, Thailand Srs., 1992, Northville Long Island Classic, 1993, The Tradition, 1994, Senior Skins Game, 1994, 95, 96, 97, 98, 06, Las Vegas Srs. Classis, 1994, Senior Tour Championship, 1994, PGA Srs. Championship, 1995, Burnet Senior Classic, 1995, Ford Senior Players Championship, 1996; captain Ryder Cup, 1989; inducted in PGA/World Golf Hall of Fame, 1989, winner father-son tourn. w/son Raymond Junior, 1995, 96, 97, w/son Robert, 2000, 01, winner Par 3 Shootout, 2000. **BA:** 505 S Flagler Dr, Palm Beach, FL, 33401

FONDA, JANE, T: Actress **I:** Media & Entertainment **DOB:** 12/21/1937 **PB:** NYC **SC:** NY/USA **PT:** Daughter of Henry and Frances (Seymour) F. **SPN:** Tom Hayden, January 20, 1973 (div. 1990); Roger Vadim August 14, 1965, (div. January 16, 1973); **CH:** Vanessa, Troy Garity **ED:** Student, Vassar College **CW:** Appeared on Broadway stage in There Was a Little Girl, 1960, The Fun Couple, 1962, 33 Variations, 2009; appeared in Actor's Studio production Strange Interlude, 1963; actress: (films) Tall Story, 1960, A Walk on the Wild Side, 1962, The Chapman Resort, 1962, Period of Adjustment, 1962, Sunday in New York, 1963, In the Cool of the Day, 1963, The Love Cage, 1963, La Ronde, 1964, Cat Ballou, 1965, The Chase, 1966, Any Wednesday, 1966, The Game Is Over, 1967, Hurry Sundown, 1967, Barefoot in the Park, 1967, Barbarella, 1968, Spirits of the Dead, 1969, They Shoot Horses, Don't They?, 1969 (New York Film Critics Circle award for Best Actress), Klute, 1970 (New York Film Critics Circle award for Best

Actress, National Society Film Critics award, Golden Globe award for Best Actress, Academy award for Best Actress), All's Well, 1972, Steelyard Blues, 1973, A Doll's House, 1973, The Blue Bird, 1976, Fun with Dick and Jane, 1977, Julia, 1977 (Golden Globe award for Best Actress), California Suite, 1978, Comes a Horseman, 1978, Electric Horseman, 1979, Nine to Five, 1980, On Golden Pond, 1981, Rollover, 1981, Agnes of God, 1985, The Morning After, 1986, Retour, 1987, Leonard Part 6, 1987, Old Gringo, 1988, Stanley and Iris, 1990, Monster-in-Law, 2005, Georgia Rule, 2007, All Together, 2011, Peace, Love & Misunderstanding, 2011, Lee Daniels' The Butler, 2013, Better Living Through Chemistry, 2014, This Is Where I Leave You, 2014, Youth, 2015, Fathers and Daughters, 2015, Our Souls at Night, 2017, Book Club, 2018; actress, prodr.: Coming Home, 1978 (Golden Globe award for Best Actress, Academy award for Best Actress), The China Syndrome, 1979; (TV films) A String of Beads, 1961, Lily: Sold Out, 1981, The Dollmaker (Emmy award for Best Actress), 1984; (TV miniseries) A Century of Women, 1994; (TV series) The Newsroom, 2012-, The Simpsons, 2014, Grace and Frankie, 2015, Elena and the Secret of Avalor, 2016, Elena of Avalor, 2017; appeared in: (exercise videos) Jane Fonda's Workout, 1982, Jane Fonda: Prime Time Walkout, 2010, Jane Fonda: Prime Time Fit & Strong, 2010, Jane Fonda's Prime Time: Trim, Tone & Flex, 2011, Jane Fonda's Prime Time: Firm & Burn, 2011, many others; author: Jane Fonda's Workout Book, 1981, Women Coming of Age, 1984, Jane Fonda's New Workout & Weight-Loss Program, 1986, Jane Fonda's New Pregnancy Workout & Total Birth Program, 1989, (autobiography) My Life So Far, 2005, Prime Time: Love, Health, Sex, Fitness, Friendship, Spirit-Making the Most of Your Life, 2011. **AW:** Recipient Golden Globe award for Most Promising Newcomer, 1962, Golden Apple prize for Female Star of Year Hollywood Women's Press Club, 1977, People's Choice award for Favorite Motion Picture Actress, 1980-83, Career Achievement award National Board Review, 2005, Women in Hollywood Tribute award Elle Magazine, 2008, Lifetime Achievement award New York Women's Agenda, 2009; named to The California Hall of Fame, 2008.

FORD, HARRISON, T: Actor **I:** Media & Entertainment **DOB:** 07/13/1942 **PB:** Chicago **SC:** IL/USA **PT:** Christopher Ford; Dorothy Nidelman Ford;; ;; **MS:** Divorced **SPN:** Melissa Mathison (3/14/1983, Divorced 1/6/2001); Mary Marquardt (6/18/1964, Divorced 10/3/1979) **CH:** Willard; Benjamin **ED:** Coursework, Ripon College **CIV:** Board of Directors, Archaeological Institute of America, Boston, MA (2008-Present); Honorary Board Member, Wings of Hope; Board of Directors, Conservation International **CW:** Actor, "Blade Runner 2049" (2017); Actor, "Toxic Puzzle-Hunt for the Hidden Killer" (2017); Actor, "Star Wars: The Force Awakens" (2015); Actor, "The Age of Adaline" (2015); Actor, "The Expendables 3" (2014); Actor, "Ender's Game" (2013); Actor, "Anchorman 2: The Legend Continues" (2013); Actor, "Paranoia" (2013); Actor, "42" (2013); Actor, "Cowboys & Aliens" (2011); Actor, Executive Producer, "Extraordinary Measures" (2010); Actor, "Morning Glory" (2010); Actor, "Crossing Over" (2009); Actor, "Indiana Jones and the Kingdom of the Crystal Skull" (2008); Actor, "Firewall" (2006); Actor, "Hollywood Homicide" (2003); Actor, Executive Producer, "K-19: The Widowmaker" (2002); Actor, "What Lies Beneath" (2000); Actor, "Random Hearts" (1999); Actor, "Six Days Seven Nights" (1998); Actor, "Air Force One" (1997); Actor, "Devil's Own" (1996); Actor, "Sabrina" (1995); Actor, "A Hundred and One Nights" (1995); Actor, "Clear and Present Danger" (1994); Actor, "The

Young Indiana Jones Chronicles" (1993); Actor, "The Fugitive" (1993); Actor, "Patriot Games" (1992); Actor, "Regarding Henry" (1991); Actor, "Presumed Innocent" (1990); Actor, "Indiana Jones and the Last Crusade" (1989); Actor, "Working Girl" (1988); Actor, "Frantic" (1988); Actor, "Mosquito Coast" (1986); Actor, "Witness" (1985); Actor, "Indiana Jones and the Temple of Doom" (1984); Actor, "Return of the Jedi" (1983); Actor, "Blade Runner" (1982); Actor, "Raiders of the Lost Ark" (1981); Actor, "The Empire Strikes Back" (1980); Actor, "Hanover Street" (1979); Actor, "More American Graffiti" (1979); Actor, "The Frisco Kid" (1979); Actor, "Apocalypse Now" (1979); Actor, "Force 10 From Navarone" (1978); Actor, "Star Wars" (1977); Actor, "Heroes" (1977); Actor, "The Possessed" (1977); Actor, "James A. Michener's Dynasty" (1976); Actor, "Judgement: The Court-Martial of Lieutenant William Calley" (1975); Actor, "The Conversation" (1974); Actor, "Kung-Fu" (1974); Actor, "Petrocelli" (1974); Actor, "American Graffiti" (1973); Actor, "Gunsmoke" (1972-1973); Actor, "Dan August" (1971); Actor, "The Intruders" (1970); Actor, "Getting Straight" (1970); Actor, "Zabriske Point" (1970); Actor, "My Friend Tony" (1969); Actor, "F.B.I." (1969); Actor, "Love, American Style" (1969); Actor, "The Mod Squad" (1968); Actor, "The Long Ride Home" (1967); Actor, "Luv" (1967); Actor, "The Men From Shiloh" (1967); Actor, "Ironside" (1967); Actor, "Dead Heat on a Merry-Go-Round" (1966) **AW:** Recipient, Board of Governors Award, American Society Cinematographers (2012); Recipient, Jules Verne Spirit of Nature Award (2006); Recipient, Lifetime Achievement Award, American Film Institute (2000) **PA:** Democrat

FORD, TOM, T: fashion designer **I:** Textiles **DOB:** 08/27/1962 **PB:** Austin, Texas **PT:** Son of Tom Ford and Shirley Burton; **ED:** BFA in Architectural Design, Parsons School Design, New York City, 1986; Student, New York University **C:** Founder, President, CEO, Tom Ford Co., 2005-; Creative Director Yves Saint Laurent Rive Gauche, YSL Beauté line, Gucci, 2000-04; Creative Director, Gucci, 1994-2004; Design Director, Gucci, 1992-94; Chief Women's Ready-to-wear Designer, Gucci, 1990-92; Design Director, Perry Ellis Women's Am. Division, 1988-90; Senior Designer, Cathy Hardwick, 1986-88; Intern, Chloé, Paris, **CR:** Lines Include Menswear, Beauty, Eyewear, Men's and Women's Accessories Collaborator Fragrance and Beauty Products Line Tom Ford for Estee Lauder, 2005- **CW:** Director, Writer, Producer (films) A Single Man, 2009 (Movie) Nocturnal Animals, 2015 **AW:** Named a Maverick, Details magazine, 2007; Menswear Designer of Year, Council Fashion Designers America, 2015, 2008, Accessory Designer of Year, 2002, Womenswear Designer of Year, 2001, International Designer of Year, 1996, Designer of Year, GQ magazine, 2001, Best Fashion Designer, TIME magazine, 2001, International Man of Year, British GQ, 2000, Best Designer of Year, Fashion Editor's Club Japan, 2001, International Designer of Year, 1996, Designer of Year for Yves Saint Laurent Rive Gauche, VH1/Vogue Fashion Awards, 2002, Womenswear Designer of Year, 1999, 1996, Menswear Designer of Year, 1996, Future's Best New Designer, 1995; named one of The 100 Most Influential People in the World, TIME magazine, 2011; recipient Geoffrey Beene Lifetime Achievement award, Council Fashion Designers of America, 2014, Superstar award, Fashion Group International Night Stars, 2000, Commitment to Life award, AIDS Project, LA, 1999, Style Icon award, Elle Style Awards, 1999, Satellite Auteur Award, 2016

FORLENZA, VINCENT A., T: CEO of Becton Dickinson & Co **I:** Business Management/Business Services **ED:** MBA, Wharton Grad. School, University Penn., 1980; BS in Chemical Engineering, Lehigh University **C:** Chairman, Becton, Dickinson & Co., Franklin Lakes, New Jersey, 2012-; President, CEO, Becton, Dickinson & Co., Franklin Lakes, New Jersey, 2011-17; President, COO, Becton, Dickinson & Co., Franklin Lakes, New Jersey, 2010-11; President, Becton, Dickinson & Co., Franklin Lakes, New Jersey, 2009-10; Executive Vice President, Becton, Dickinson & Co., Franklin Lakes, New Jersey, 2006-08; President BD Biosciences, Becton, Dickinson & Co., San Jose, California, 2003-06; Senior Vice President Strategy and Devel., Becton, Dickinson & Co., Franklin Lakes, New Jersey, 1999-2003; Various Positions Including Product Manager, President Diagnostic Systems, President Microbiology Systems, Becton, Dickinson & Co., Franklin Lakes, New Jersey, 1980-98 **CIV:** Trustee, Valley Hospital, Member, University Maryland Baltimore County Board of Visitors, **BA:** 1 Becton Drive, Franklin Lakes, NJ, 07417-1880

FORTENBERRY, JEFFREY LANE, T: U.S. Representative from Nebraska **I:** Government Administration/Government Relations/Government Services **DOB:** 12/27/1960 **PB:** Baton Rouge **SC:** LA/USA **ED:** MA in Theology, Franciscan University, Steubenville, Ohio, 1996; Master in Pub. Policy, Georgetown University, Washington, 1986; BA Econs., Louisiana State University, 1982 **C:** Member, U.S. Congress from 1st Nebraska district, 2005-; Member, Committee on Agriculture, Committee on Foreign Affairs, Republican Study Committee; At-large member, City Council, Lincoln, Nebraska, 1997-2001; Sales rep., Sandhills Pub., 1998-2005; Pub. rels.-found. activities director, Sandhills Pub., Lincoln, Nebraska, 1995-98; Assistant director, Downtown Devel. District, Baton Rouge, 1989-92; Research associate economist, Gulf South Research Institute, New Iberia, Louisiana, 1987-89; Member economic analysis team, US Senate Subcommittee for Intergovernmental Relations, 1986 **CR:** Member small business committee U.S. Congress, member foreign affairs committee, member agriculture committee **PA:** Republican

FOSS, ERIC J., T: Chairman, President, and CEO of Aramark Corp. **I:** Business Management/Business Services **DOB:** 03/13/1958 **ED:** BS in Marketing, Ball State University, 1980 **C:** President, CEO, ARAMARK, Philadelphia, 2012-; Chairman, Aramark Corp, 2015-; CEO Pepsi Beverages Co., PepsiCo, Inc., Purchase, New York, 2010-11; Chairman, CEO, Pepsi Bottling Group, Inc., Somers, New York, 2008-10; President, CEO, Pepsi Bottling Group, Inc., Somers, New York, 2006-08; COO, Pepsi Bottling Group, Inc., Somers, New York, 2005-06; President North America, Pepsi Bottling Group, Inc., Somers, New York, 2001-05; Executive vice president, general manager No. Am., Pepsi Bottling Group, Inc., Somers, New York, 2000-01; Senior vice president US sales & field marketing, Pepsi Bottling Group, Inc., Somers, New York, 1999-2000; General manager Central Europe, Pepsi Cola Co., 1996-99; General manager North America Great West business unit, Pepsi Cola Co., 1994-96; Vice president retail strategy North America, Pepsi Cola Co., 1990-94; Sales, marketing & management positions, Pepsi Cola Co., 1982-90 **CR:** Member industry affairs council Grocery Manufacturers Am. board directors United Dominion Realty Trust, Pepsi Bottling Group, Inc. **BA:** 1101 Market Street, Philadelphia, PA, 19107

FOSTER, BILL, T: U.S. Representative from Illinois **I:** Government Administration/Government Relations/Government Services **DOB:** 10/07/1955 **PB:**

Madison **SC:** WI/USA **PT:** George William Foster; Jeanette Raymond Foster **MS:** Married **SPN:** Aesook Byon (11/2008); Ann Christine Oswall (3/31/1983, Divorced 10/1996) **CH:** George Billy; Christine **ED:** PhD, Harvard University (1983); BA in Physics, University of Wisconsin (1976) **C:** Member, US House Financial Services Committee (2013-Present); Member, Committee on Science, Space, & Technology; Member, US Congress from the 11th Illinois District (2013-Present); Member, US House Financial Services Committee (2008-2011); Member, US Congress from the 14th Illinois District, Washington, DC (2008-2011); Research Physicist, Fermi National Accelerator Laboratory, Batavia, IL (1984-2006); Founder, Chief Executive Officer, Electronic Theatre Controls, Inc., Middleton, WI (1976-1979) **CR:** Board of Directors, Electronic Theatre Controls, Inc., Middleton, WI **CIV:** Board of Directors, Batavia Foundation for Educational Excellence (1996-2001) **AW:** Rossi Prize for Astrophysics, American Astronomical Society (1989); Federal Energy & Water Management Award, US Department of Energy (1998); Particle Accelerator Science & Technology Award, IEEE (1999); Fermilan Technology Award for Digital Multiplier Integrated Circuit (1999) **MEM:** Fellow, American Physical Society **ACH:** Achievements include particle accelerator designer Fermilab Antiproton Recycler Ring; integrated circuit designer High Speed Phototomultiplier Digitizer. **PA:** Democrat **BA:** 1224 Longworth House Office Building, Washington, DC, 20515

FOSTER, JODIE, T: Actress, Film Director, Producer **I:** Media & Entertainment **DOB:** 11/19/1962 **PB:** LA **PT:** Daughter of Lucius and Evelyn (Almond) F. **MS:** Married **SPN:** Alexandra Hedison, April 2014. **CH:** Charles, Kit **ED:** Degree (hon.), Smith College, 2000; DArts (hon.), University of Penn., 2006; DFA (hon.), Yale University, 1997; BA in Lit. cum laude, Yale University, 1985 **C:** Owner, chair, Egg Pictures Production Co., LA, 1990-2001 **CW:** Actress: (films) Napoleon and Samantha, 1972, Kansas City Bomber, 1972, One Little Indian, 1973, Tom Sawyer, 1973, Alice Doesn't Live Here Anymore, 1974, Taxi Driver, 1976, Echoes of a Summer, 1976, Bugsy Malone, 1976, Freaky Friday, 1976, Moi, Fleur Bleue, 1977, Casotto, 1977, The Little Girl Who Lives Down the Lane, 1977, Candleshoe, 1977, Foxes, 1980, Carny, 1980, O'Hara's Wife, 1982, The Hotel New Hampshire, 1984, The Blood of Others, 1984, Five Corners, 1987, Siesta, 1987, Stealing Home, 1988, The Accused, 1988 (Academy award for Best Actress, 1989, Best Performance by an Actress, Golden Globe award, Hollywood Foreign Press Association, 1989), Backtrack, 1989, The Silence of the Lambs, 1991 (Best Actress in Drama, Golden Globe award, Hollywood Foreign Press Association, 1992, Academy award for Best Actress, 1992, BAFTA award for Best Actress, 1992), Shadows and Fog, 1992, Sommersby, 1993, Maverick, 1994, Contact, 1997, Anna and The King, 1999, Panic Room, 2002, A Very Long Engagement, 2004, Flightplan, 2005, Inside Man, 2006, The Brave One, 2007, Nim's Island, 2008, Carnage, 2011, Elysium, 2013; (TV films) Menace on the Mountain, 1970, My Sister Hank, 1972, Alexander, 1973, Rookie of the Year, 1973, Smile, Jenny, You're Dead, 1974, The Secret Life of T.K. Dearing, 1975, Svengali, 1983; (TV appearances) The Doris Day show, 1969, Julia, 1969, Mayberry, R.F.D, 1969, Gunsmoke, 1969, 1971, 1972, The Courtship of Eddie's Father, 1969, 1970, 1971, Disneyland, 1970, Nanny and the Professor, 1970, Daniel Boone, 1970, Adam-12, 1970, My Three Sons, 1971 The Paul Lunde Show, 1972, Ghost Story, 1972, Ironside, 1972, Bonanza, 1972, The Amazing Chan and the Chan Clan, 1972, The Partridge Family, 1973, Kung Fu, 1973, The Addams

Family, 1973, Bob & Carol & Ted & Alice, 1973, The New Perry Mason, 1973, Love Story, 1973, Paper Moon, 1974, Medical Center, 1975, Frasier, 1996, The X-Files, 1997, Statler and Waldorf: From the Balcony, 2005, The Simpsons, 2009, Makers: Women Who Make America, 2014, Hotel Artemis, 2016; actress, dir.: (films) Little Man Tate, 1991; actress, prodr.: (films) Mesmerized, 1986, Nell, 1994, The Dangerous Lives of Altar Boys, 2002, The Brave One, 2007, The Beaver, 2011; director, prodr.: (films) Home For the Holidays, 1995; dir.: (TV episode) Tales from the Darkside, 1988, (films) Money Monster, 2016; executive prodr.: (TV films) The Baby Dance, 1998; (films) Waking the Dead, 2000. **AW:** Named one of The 50 Smartest People in Hollywood, Entertainment Weekly, 2007; recipient Star, Hollywood Walk of Fame, 2016, Cecil B. DeMille award, Hollywood Foreign Press Association, 2013, Sherry Lansing Leadership award, The Hollywood Reporter, 2007 **BA:** PMK/HBH Public Realtions, 700 San Vicente Ave, West Hollywood, CA, 90069

FOSTER, NORMAN, T: Architect **I:** Architecture & Construction **DOB:** 06/01/1935 **PB:** Reddish **SC:** England **ED:** Honorary DSc, University of Dundee, 2008; Honorary DSc, London Institute, 2001; Honorary DSc, Negev, Israel, 2001; Honorary DSc, London, England, 1996; Honorary DSc, Oxford, England, 1996; Honorary DSc, Eindhoven, Netherlands, 1996; Honorary DSc, Kent Institute of Design, 1994; Honorary DSc, Manchester, England, 1992; Honorary DSc, Humberside, England, 1992; Honorary DSc, Valencia, Spain, 1992; Honorary DSc, Royal College of Art, 1991; Honorary DSc, Bath, England, 1986; Honorary LittD, East Anglia, England, 1980; MArch, Yale University, 1962; Diploma in Architecture, Manchester University, 1961 **C:** President, Norman Foster Foundation, 2017-Present; Principal, Foster Associates (Now Foster And Partners), London, England, 1967-Present; Consultant Architect, University of East Anglia, 1978-1987 **CR:** Collaborator, Buckminster Fuller, 1968-1983; Council, Architectural Association, 1969-1971; External Examiner, Royal Institute of British Architects, 1971-1973; Vice President, Architectural Association, 1974; IBM Fellow, Aspen Design Conference, 1980; Council, R.C.A., 1981; Visiting Professor, Bartlett School of Architecture, 1998-1999, Harvard University Graduate School of Design, 2000; Former Teacher, University of Pennsylvania, Architectural Association, London, London Polytechnic, Bath Academy of Arts; Honorary Fellow, American Institute of Architects; Honorary Fellow, Royal Inc. of Architects, Scotland; Honorary Fellow, Royal Academy of Engineering; Honorary Fellow, Institution of Structural Engineers **CW:** Contributor, Articles, Architectural And Technology Publications, 2005 **AW:** Finance Times Industrial Architecture Award, 1967, 1970-1971, 1974, 1981, 1984, 1993, R.S.A. Business And Industry Awards, International Design Awards, Finniston Award, Structural Steel Award, 1972, 1978, 1980, 1984, 1986, 1992, 1999, R.S. Reynolds International Memorial Award, Head Office, Willis, Faber And Dumas, Ipswich, England, 1976, R.S. Reynolds International Memorial Award, Sainsbury Centre For Visual Arts, Norwich, England, 1979, Ambrose Congreve Award, 1980, Royal Gold Medal For Architecture, 1983, R.S. Reynolds International Memorial Award, Hong Kong And Shanghai Banking Corp. Headquarters, 1986, Interiors USA Award, 1988, 1992-1994, Berlin Art Grand Prize, 1989, Knighthood, 1990, Trustees Medal, Royal Institute of British Architects, 1990, Royal Institute of British Architects Awards, Chicago Arts Award, 1990, Mies Van Der Rohe Pavilion Award, 1991, Gold Medal, French Academy of Architects, 1991, Arnold W. Brunner Memorial

Prize, 1992, Premio Alcantara Award, 1993, Winner, Competition, Reichstag New German Parliament, Berlin, Germany, 1993, Concrete Society Awards, Benedictus Award, 1993, 1999, Gold Medal, Fellow, American Institute of Architects, 1994, Queens Export Achievement Award, 1995, Order Of North Rhine Westphalia, 1995, Man Of The Year, MIPIM, 1996, Silver Medal, Chartered Society Of Designers, 1997, Prince Philip Designers Prize, 1997, Order Of Merit, 1997, Pritzker Architecture Prize, The Hyatt Foundation, 1999, Life Peer, 1999, Visual Arts Award, 2000, Fifth South Bank Show Award, 2001, Auguste Perret Prize 2002, Praemium Imperiale Award For Architecture, 2002, German Order Pour Le Merite For Sciences And Arts, 2002, Prince Of Asturias Award, 2009 **MEM:** Officer, Order of Arts and Letters Ministry of Culture, France, Foreign Honorary Member, American Association for the Advancement of Science, C.S.D., Associate, Royal Academy, Royal Designers for Industry, Association of the Academie Royale de Belgique, Foreign Member, Royal Academy of Fine Arts, Sweden, European Academy of Sciences and Arts, Honorary Member, Und Deutscher Architeken, Royal Designer for Industry, International Academy of Architecture **BA:** Foster & Partners, 22 Riverside, 34 Hester Road, London, United Kingdom, SW11 4AN

FOSTER, SUTTON, T: Actress **I:** Media & Entertainment **DOB:** 03/18/1975 **PB:** Statesboro **SC:** GA/USA **ED:** Postgrad., Hunter College, New York City; Postgrad., Carnegie Mellon University **C:** Actress, 1989- **CW:** Actor: (Broadway plays) Les Misérables, 1987-2003, Grease, 1994-98, Annie, 1997, Scarlet Pimprenel, 1997-2000, Thoroughly Modern Millie, 2002-04 (Tony award for Best Performance by an Actress in a Leading Role in a Musical, 2002), Little Women, 2005, The Drowsy Chaperone, 2006-07 (LA Ovation award lead actress in a musical, 2006), Young Frankenstein, 2007-08, Shrek The Musical, 2008-10, Anything Goes, 2011-12 (Tony award for Best Performance by an Actress in a Leading Role in a Musical, 2011), Violet, 2014-; (TV series) Flight of the Conchords, 2007, Bunheads, 2012-13, Younger, 2014, Psych, 2014; (films) Shrek the Musical, 2013, Gravy, 2014,(Films) The Angriest Man in Brooklyn, 2014, The Nobodies, 2014, Gravy, 2015, Mired, 2016(Television) Say Yes to the Dress, 2014, Younger, 2015, Elementary, 2015, Mad Dogs, 2016, The Good Wife, 2016, Match Game, 2016, Gilmore Girl: A Year in the Life, 2016, Instinct, 2017(Theatre) The Wild Party, 2015, Defying Gravity: The Songs of Stephen Schwartz, 2016, Sweet Charity, 2016

FOX, MICHAEL J., T: Actor **I:** Media & Entertainment **DOB:** 06/09/1961 **ED:** Honorary MD, Karolinska Institute, 2010; GED, 1995 **CR:** Founder, The Michael J. Fox Foundation for Parkinson's Research, 2000-Present; Lottery Hill Entertainment **CW:** Actor, (Films) Midnight Madness, 1980, Class Of '84, 1981, Back To The Future, 1985, Teen Wolf, 1985, Light Of Day, 1986, The Secret Of My Success, 1987, Bright Lights, Big City, 1988, Casualties Of War, 1989, Back To The Future, Part II, 1989, Back To The Future, Part III, 1990, The Hard Way, 1991, Life With Mikey, 1993, For Love Or Money, 1993, Where The Rivers Flow North, 1993, Greedy, 1994, Cold Blooded, 1995, Blue In The Face, 1995, The American President, 1995, Mars Attacks!, 1996, The Frighteners, 1996, Interstate 60, 2002, (Voice Actor) Homeward Bound: The Incredible Journey, 1993, (Voice Actor) Homeward Bound II: Lost In San Francisco, 1996, (Voice Actor) Stuart Little, 1999, (Voice Actor) Atlantis: The Lost Empire, 2001, (Voice Actor) Stuart Little 2, 2002, (Voice Actor) Stuart Little 3: Call Of The Wild, 2006, The Magic 7, 2009, Drew: The Man Behind The Poster,2013, Annie, 2014,

Being Canadian, 2015, Back In Time, 2015, Mr. Calzaghe, 2015, Archie, 2016, (TV Films) Letters From Frank, 1979, Poison Ivy, 1985, High School USA, 1985, I Am Your Child, 1997, (TV Series) Leo And Me, 1976, Palmerstown USA, 1980, Family Ties, 1982-1989, Spin City, 1996-2000; TV Appearances, Lou Grant, 1979, Family, 1980, Trapper John, M.D., 1981, The Love Boat, 1983, Night Court, 1984, Tales From The Crypt, 1991, Scrubs, 2004, Boston Legal, 2006, Rescue Me, 2009, The Good Wife, 2010-13, Curb Your Enthusiasm, 2011; Executive Producer, (TV Series) Anna Says, 1999, Otherwise Engaged, 2002; Actor, Executive Producer, (TV Series) The Michael J. Fox Show, 2013-2014, Jimmy Kimmel Live, 2015, Nightcap, 2016, Oscars, 2017; Author, Lucky Man: A Memoir, 2001, Always Looking Up: The Adventures Of An Incurable Optimist, 2009, A Funny Thing Happened On The Way To The Future, 2010 **AW:** Emmy Award, Outstanding Lead Actor In A Comedy Series, Family Ties, 1986-1988, Golden Globe Award, Best Actor In Comedy Series, Family Ties, 1989, Golden Globe Award, Best Actor In Comedy Series, Spin City, 1998-2000, Emmy Award, Best Actor In Comedy Series, Spin City, 2000, Golden Plate Award, Academy of Achievement, 2005, America's Best Leaders, U.S. News & World Report, 2007, The 100 Most Influential People in the World, TIME Magazine, 2007, Emmy Award, Outstanding Guest Actor In A Drama Series, Rescue Me, 2009, Publishers Weekly Bestseller, Grammy Award, Best Spoken Word Album, Always Looking Up: The Adventures Of An Incurable Optimist, 2010 **BA:** Michael J. Fox Foundation for Parkinson's Research, PO Box 4777, New York, NY, 10163

FOXX, JAMIE, T: Actor, Comedian **I:** Media & Entertainment **DOB:** 12/13/1967 **PB:** Terrell **SC:** TX/USA **PT:** Shaheed Abdulah; Louise Annette D. **CH:** Corinne Bishop; Annalise **ED:** Studied Classical Piano, Juilliard School of Fine Arts; Student, U.S. International University, San Diego, CA (1986-1988) **C:** Host, "The Foxxhole," Sirius Radio **CW:** Actor, TV Series, "In Living Color" (1991-1994); Actor, Director, Producer, Writer, TV Series, "The Jamie Foxx Show" (1996); Comedian, Executive Producer, Writer, TV Special, "Jamie Foxx: I Might Need Security" (2002); Actor, Films, "Toys" (1992), "The Truth About Cats and Dogs" (1996), "The Great White Hype" (1996), "Booty Call" (1997), "The Players Club" (1998), "Held Up" (1999), "Any Given Sunday" (1999), "Bait" (2000), "Date from Hell" (2001), "Ali" (2001), "Shade" (2003), "Breakin' All the Rules" (2004), "Collateral" (2004), "Ray" (2004), "Stealth" (2005), "Jarhead" (2005), "Miami Vice" (2006), "Dreamgirls" (2006), "The Kingdom" (2007), "The Soloist" (2009), "Law Abiding Citizen" (2009), "Valentine's Day" (2010), "Due Date" (2010), Voice Actor, "Rio" (2011), "Horrible Bosses" (2011), "Django Unchained" (2012), "White House Down" (2013), Voice Actor, "Rio 2" (2014), "The Amazing Spider-Man 2" (2014), "Horrible Bosses 2" (2014), "Annie" (2014), "A Million Ways to Die in the West" (2014), "Sleepless" (2017), "Baby Driver" (2017), "Robin Hood" (2018), "All Star Weekend" (2018); Actor, TV Films, "Redemption: The Stan Tookie Williams Story" (2004), "When I was 17" (2011), "Jackie Robinson" (2016); Appearance, "David Blaine, Real or Magic" (2013); Host, "Beat Shazam" (2017); Appearance, "White Famous" (2017); Voice Actor, TV Series, "C-Bear and Jamal" (1996); Director, TV Film, "Night Tales" (2011); Executive Producer, Writer, TV Series, "From G's to Gents" (2008-2009), "In the Flow with Affion Crockett (2011); Singer, Albums, "Peep This" (1994), "Unpredictable" (2005), "Intuition" (2008), "Best Night of My Life" (2010), "Hollywood: A Story of a Dozen Roses" (2015); Singer, Songs, with Kanye West, "Gold Digger" (2005), with T-Pain, "Blame It" (2008) **AW:** Named Favorite Male

Artist, Soul/Rhythm & Blues, American Music Award (2006); Entertainer of the Year, National Association for the Advancement of Colored People Image Award (2013); Outstanding Male Artist, National Association for the Advancement of Colored People Image Awards (2006, 2009); Named One of the 10 Most Fascinating People of 2005, Barbara Walters Special (2005); Named One of the 100 Most Influential People in the World, TIME Magazine (2005); Recipient, Star, Hollywood Walk of Fame (2007); Outstanding Lead Actor in a Comedy Series, "The Jamie Foxx Show," National Association for the Advancement of Colored People Image Award (1997); Outstanding Supporting Actor in a Motion Picture, "Ali," National Association for the Advancement of Colored People Image Award (2002); Best Actor, "Ray," National Board of Review, Motion Pictures (2004); Best Actor, "Ray," Boston Film Critics Award (2004); Best Actor in a Musical or Comedy, "Ray," Golden Globe Award (2005); Outstanding Performance by a Male Actor in Leading Role, "Ray," Screen Actors Guild Award (2005); Best Actor in a Leading Role, "Ray," Academy Award (2005); Best Duet, "Gold Digger," with Kanye West, BET Award (2006); Video of Year, "Gold Digger," BET Awards (2006); Best R&B Performance by a Duo or Group with Vocals, "Blame It," with T-Pain, Grammy Award (2010)

FOXX, VIRGINIA ANN, T: Chairwoman of the House Education Committee **I:** Government Administration/Government Relations/Government Services **DOB:** 06/29/1943 **PB:** New York City **SC:** NY/USA **MS:** Married **SPN:** Thomas A. Foxx **CH:** 1 Child **ED:** EdD in Curriculum and Teaching, Higher Education, University of North Carolina, Greensboro, 1985; MACT, University of North Carolina, Chapel Hill, 1972; AB in English, University of North Carolina, Chapel Hill, 1968 **C:** Chairwoman of the House Education Committee 2017-; Secretary, US House Republican Conference, Washington, 2013-; Member, US Congress from 5th North Carolina District, Washington, 2005-; Member, North Carolina State Senate, Raleigh, 1995-2004; Owner, Operator, Grandfather Nursery, Banner Elk, North Carolina; President, Consultant, Maryland Community College, Spruce Pine, North Carolina, 1987-94; Department of Secretary Management, North Carolina Department Administration; Assistant Dean, General College, Appalachian State University; Professor of Sociology, Appalachian State University, Boone, North Carolina; Professor, Caldwell Community College, Hudson, North Carolina; Secretary, Research Assistant, University of North Carolina, Chapel Hill **CIV:** Member, Watauga County Board Education, 1976-88 **AW:** Recipient, Reagan Award, National Republican Congressional Committee (NRCC), 2010, Contributions to Sociology Award, North Carolina Sociological Association, 2002, Alan Keith-Lucas Friend of Children Award, North Carolina Child Care Association, 2002, Guardian of Small Business Award, National Federation Ind. Business, 2000, North Carolina Carpathian award, 1994, Distinguished Fundraising Award, YMCA, 1993, Order of the Long Leaf Pine, North Carolina Governor Jim Martin, 1992, North Carolina Distinguished Women's Award, 1990, Award for Outstanding Citizenship, Exceptional Pub. Service, Watauga County League Women Voters, 1988, Outstanding Pub. Official Award, North Carolina Christmas Tree Association **MEM:** Member, National Association Women Legislators, American Legis. Exchange Conference, NCCBI, North Carolina Center Pub. Policy Research, North Carolina Women's Forum **PA:** Republican **BA:** Boone District Office of Virginia Foxx, 400 Shadowline Dr Suite 205, Boone, NC, 28607

FOY, CLAIRE, T: Actress **I:** Media & Entertainment **PB:** Stockport **SC:** England **CW:** (Films) Season of the Witch, 2011, Wreckers, 2011, Vampire Academy, 2014, RoseWater, 2014, The Lady in the Vale, 2015, Breathe, 2017, Unsane, 2018, First Man, 2018, The Girl in the Spiders Web, 2018 (Television) Being Human, 2008, Doctors, 2008, Little Dorrit, 2008, 10 Minute Tales, 2009, Terry Pratchetts Going Postal, 2010, Pulse, 2010, Upstairs Downstairs, 2010, The Promise, 2011, The Nights Watch, 2011, Hacks, 2012,White Heat, 2012, Crossbones, 2014, The Great War:The Peoples Story, 2014, Frankenstein and the Vampyre: A Dark and Stormy Night, 2014, Wolf Hall, 2015, The Crown, 2016-17(Screen Actors Guild Award for Outstanding Performance by a Female Actor in a Drama Series 2017-18, Golden Globe for Best Actress in a Television Series, 2017)

FOYT, ANTHONY JOSEPH JR., T: Auto Racing Crew Chief, Former Professional Auto Racer **I:** Athletics **DOB:** 01/16/1935 **PB:** Houston **SC:** TX/USA **MS:** Married **SPN:** Lucy Zarr, 1955; **CH:** A.J. 3rd, Jerry, Terry Lynn. **ED:** Student pub. schools **C:** Owner, Conseco/A.J. Foyt Enterprise Corp.,; Auto racer, 1953-82 **CR:** Professional horse breeder and trainer, Houston; board of directors Riverway Bank, Houston, SCI Corp., Houston. **AW:** Named Racing Driver of Year, Auto Racing Fraternity Greater New York, 1963, Outstanding Am. Driver of Year, 1967, International Motorsports Hall of Fame Inductee, 2000, Nascars 50 Greatest Drivers, 1998, Inducted in the first class National Sprint Car Hall of Fame, 1990, Inducted in the first class into the Motorsports Hall of Fame of America, 1989, Inducted in the National Midget Auto Racing Hall of Fame, 1988 **ACH:** Achievements include winning Indianapolis 500, 1961, 64, 67, 77; winner U.S. Auto Club championship, 1960, 61, 63, 64, 67, 75, 79; winner Twenty Four Hours of Le Mans (France), 1967, Schaefer 500, 1973, Pocono 500, 1975, 79, Daytona 500, 1972, national championship stock car div. U.S. Auto Club, 1968, 78, 79, Twenty Four Hours of Daytona, 1983, 85, Twelve Hours of Sebring, 1985. **BA:** Fort Racing, 19480 Stokes Road, Waller, TX, 77484

FRANCHITTI, DARIO, T: Race Car Driver **I:** Athletics **PB:** Edinburgh **SC:** Scotland **C:** Race car driver NASCAR, Ganassi Racing, 2008-; Race car driver IndyCar Series, Andretti Green, 2003-07 **CR:** 1st pl. Peak Antifreeze Indy 300 Chicagoland Speedway, 2007 2nd pl. Honda 200 Mid-Ohio Sports Car Course, 2007 1st pl. Iowa Corn Indy 250 Iowa Speedway, 2007 1st pl. Indy 500 Indianapolis Motor Speedway, 2012, 2010, 2007 2nd pl. Kansas Lottery Indy 300 Kansas Speedway, 2007 2nd pl. Indy Grand Prix Sonoma Infineon Raceway, 2006 1st pl. Toyota Indy 400 California Speedway, 2005 2nd pl. Firestone Indy 200 Nashville Speedway, 2007, 1st pl. Firestone Indy 200, 2005 1st pl. SunTrust Indy Challenge Richmond International Raceway, 2007, 2nd pl. SunTrust Indy Challenge, 2005 1st pl. Honda Indy 225 Pikes Peak International Raceway, 2004 2nd pl. ABC Supply Co. A.J. Foyt 225 Milwaukee Mile, 2007, 2005, 1st pl. Menards A.J. Foyt 225, 2004 **AW:** Named IndyCar Series Champion, Indy Racing League, 2007; recipient Jerry Titus award, Am. Automobile Racing Writers and Broadcasters Association, 2008 **H:** Reading, video games, skiing

FRANCO, JAMES, T: Actor **I:** Media & Entertainment **DOB:** 06/25/1905 **PB:** Palo Alto, California **SC:** Palo Alto, California **PT:** Son of Doug and Betsy Franco. **ED:** BA in in English Lit., UCLA, 2008 **C:** Teacher film and English departments, New York University,; Teacher film and English departments, CalArts,; Teacher film and English departments, UCLA,; Teacher film and English departments, USC **CR:** Owner Rabbit Bandini Productions **CW:** Actor: (films) Never Been Kissed, 1999, Whatever It Takes, 2000, At Any Cost, 2000, If Tomorrow Comes, 2000, Some Body, 2001, James Dean, 2001, Blind Spot, 2001, Spider-Man, 2002, Deuces Wild, 2002, City by the Sea, 2002, Sonny, 2002, Mean People Suck, 2003, The Car Kid, 2003, Spider-Man 2, 2004, The Great Raid, 2005, Fool's Gold, 2005, Tristan & Isolde, 2006, Annapolis, 2006, The Wicker Man, 2006, Flyboys, 2006, Good Times Max, 2007, An American Crime, 2007, Finishing the Game, 2007, Camille, 2007, Spider-Man 3, 2007, In the Valley of Elah, 2007, Pineapple Express, 2008, Nights in Rodanthe, 2008, Milk, 2008, Date Night, 2010, Eat Pray Love, 2010, 127 Hours, 2010, Your Highness, 2011, Rise of the Planet of the Apes, 2011, The Stare, 2012, About Cherry, 2012, The Iceman, 2012, The Letter, 2012, Maladies, 2012, Tar, 2012, Spring Breakers, 2013, Lovelace, 2013, Oz the Great and Powerful, 2013, This Is the End, 2013, Palo Alto, 2013, Third Person, 2013, Homefront, 2013, Good People, 2014, The Interview, 2014; actor, actor: (films) True Story, 2014, Queen of the Desert, 2015, Every Thing Will Be Fine, 2015, Wild Horses, 2015, The Little Prince (voice), 2015, Richard Peter Johnson, 2015; (director, executive producer, writer): The Ape, 2004; actor, director, writer (films) Good Time Max, 2007, Sal, 2011, actor, director, writer, producer The Broken Tower, 2011, Child of God, 2013, Black Dog, Red Dog, 2016, actor, director, producer Interior. Leather.Bar., 2013, actor, executive producer Don Quixote: The Ingenious Gentleman of La Mancha, 2015, Memoria, 2015, Yosemite, 2015, The Labyrinth (voice), 2016, writer, producer Holy Land, 2014, actor, producer I Am Michael, 2015, The Adderall Diaries, 2015, writer, director Bukowski, 2015, actor, director Zeroville, 2016; actor, The Little Prince, 2015, Memoria, 2015, The Night Before, 2015, The Labyrinth, 2016, Goat, 2016, Sausage Party,2016, Burn Country, 2016, King Cobra, 2016, The Caged Pillows, 2016, In Dubious Battle,2016, Why Him?, 2016, The Institute, 2017, The Disaster Artist, 2017, Alien Covenant, 2017, Don't Come Back From the Moon, 2017,The Vault, 2017, This is Your Death, 2017, The Heyday of the Insensitive Bastards, 2017, Actors Anonymous, 2017, Kill the Czar, 2017, The Long Home, 2018, Artic Justice Thunder Squad, 2018, Kin, 2018, Pretenders, 2018: (TV films) To Serve and Protect, 1999; (TV series) Freaks and Geeks, 1999-2000, General Hospital, 2009-12; TV appearances Pacific Blue, 1997, Profiler, 1999, Hollywood Heights, 2012, The Mindy Project, 2013; author: Palo Alto: Stories, 2010, Strongest of the Litter, 2012, A California Childhood, 2013, Actors Anonymous, 2013, Comedy Central Roast of James Franco, 2013, SNL, 2014, Naked and Afraid, 2014, Deadbeat, 2015, Angie Tribeca, 2016,11.22.63, 2016, Mother May I Sleep with Danger?, 2016, High School Lover, 2017, The Deuce, 2017, The Ballad of Buster Scruggs, 2018 **AW:** Named Man of the Year, Hasty Pudding Theatrical Society, 2009

FRANCONA, TERRY JON, T: Former MLB Manager **I:** Athletics **DOB:** 04/22/1959 **PB:** Aberdeen, South Dakota **PT:** Son of Tito F.; **SPN:** children: Nick, Alyssa, Leah, Jamie **CH:** Married Jacque Lang, January 9, 1982; **ED:** Student, University Arizona **C:** Baseball Analyst Sunday Night Baseball, ESPN, 2011-; Manager, Cleveland Indians, 2012-; Manager, Boston Red Sox, 2004-11; Bench Coach, Oakland A's, 2003; Bench Coach, Texas Rangers, 2002; Special Assistant, Baseball Operations, Cleveland Indians, 2001; Third Base Coach, Detroit Tigers, 1996; Manager, Philadelphia Phillies, 1997-2000; Manager, Dominican Winter League, 1995; Manager, Birmingham AA, 1993-95; Manager, Chicago Single-A South Bend, 1992; Hitting Instructor, Gulf Coast Rookie League, Chicago White Sox Organization, Sarasota, 1991; First Baseman/outfielder, Milwaukee Brewers, 1989-90; First Baseman/outfielder, Cleveland Indians, 1988; First Baseman/outfielder, Cincinnati Reds, 1987; First Baseman/outfielder, Chicago Cubs, 1986; First Baseman/outfielder, Montreal Expos, 1981-85 **CW:** Author: Francona: The Red Sox Years, 2013 **AW:** Named American League Manager of Year, Major League Baseball, 2013, Top Managerial Prospect in Minors, Baseball America, 1994, Minor League Manager of Year, 1993, Southern League Manager of Year, 1993; recipient Golden Spikes award, USA Baseball, 1980, AL Manager of the Year, 2016 **ACH:** Achievements include managing the Boston Red Sox to Two World Series Titles 2004, 2007; manager of American League All-Start Team, 2005 **H:** Golf **BA:** Independent Sports & Entertainment, LLC, 2029 Century Park East Suite 1550, Los Angeles, CA, 90067

FRANK, JOACHIM, T: Structural Biologist, Educator, Biophysicist **I:** Sciences **ED:** PhD in Biophysics, Tech. University, Munich, 1970; Diploma in Physics, University Munich **C:** Professor of Biochemistry and Molecular Biophysics, Columbia University, 2008-; Distinguished scientist structural biology, Wadsworth Center,; Director laboratory computational biology and macromolecular imaging, Wadsworth Center, Albany, New York **CR:** Research professor, cell biology, New York University Medical School; adjunct professor, biochemistry and molecular biophysics, Columbia University, New York City professor biology State University of New York, Albany investigator Howard Hughes Medical Institute, 1998- **CW:** Author: 5 books; contributor 200 articles to sci. journals **AW:** Nobel Prize in Chemistry, 2017, Wiley Prize in Biomedical Sciences, 2017, Benjamin Franklin Medal in Life Science, 2014, National Academy of Sciences, 2006, Fellow of the American Academy of Arts and Sciences, 2006, Humboldt Research Award, 1994 **MEM:** Fellow: Am. Academy Arts Scis., Biophys. Society (Elizabeth Roberts Cole award 1993), American Association for the Advancement of Science; mem.: National Academy of Sciences

FRANKEL, LOIS JANE, T: U.S. Representative from Florida **I:** Government Administration/Government Relations/Government Services **DOB:** 05/16/1948 **PB:** New York City **ED:** JD, Georgetown University Law Center, 1973; BA magna cum laude, Boston University, 1970 **C:** Member, US House Transportation & Infrastructure Committee, 2013-; Member, US House Foreign Affairs Committee, 2013-; Member, US Congress from 22nd Florida District, Washington, 2013-; Mayor, City of West Palm Beach, Florida, 2003-11; Minority leader, Florida House of Reps., 2000-02; Member District 85, Florida House of Reps., 1995-2003; Member District 83, Florida House of Reps., Tallahassee, 1987-93; Partner, Searcy Denney, Scarola, Barnhart & Shipley, 1978-94; Assistant Public Defender, West Palm Beach, Florida, 1974-78; Law Clerk to Hon. David Norman, DC Superior Court, Washington, 1973-74 **CR:** Chair AIDS Task Force, 1986-90 **AW:** Recipient Allen Morris Most Promising Freshman Award, 1988, Up and Comers Government Award S. Florida Business Jour.-Price Waterhouse, 1988, Nelson Poynter Civil Liberties Award, 1988, Florida Brotherhood Award, 1989, Weizmann Institute Sci. Award, 1989, Brotherhood award Association Retarded Citizens/Fla., 1989, Ann. Legis. Award Florida Children's Forum, 1990, First Legis. award Florida Student Nursing Association, 1990, Outstanding Legislator award Florida Federation Business and Professional Women, 1990, Commr.'s award for Prevention of Child Abuse and Neglect U.S. Department Health and Human Services, 1991, Award American Heart Association, 1992, Political Courage award American Lung Association, 1992; named Freshman Friend Education FTP-NEA, 1987, Citizen of Year National Association of Social Workers, 1989, Child Adv. of Year, 1989, Children's Home Society, 1989, Child Care Connection, 1990. **MEM:** Member National Organization of Women, League of Women Voters, Florida Bar Association, Academy Florida Trial Lawyers, Florida Association Women Lawyers (Past President Palm Beach County Chapter), Palm Beach County Bar Association, Jewish Federation Palm Beach County, Executive Women Palm Beaches , Economic Devel. Council Palm Beach County, Gold Coast Business and Professional Women, American Cancer Society, Jewish Family and Children's Services, Domestic Assault Shelter (Founder) **H:** Sports, music **PA:** Democrat

FRANKLIN, ARETHA LOUISE, T: Singer **I:** Media & Entertainment **DOB:** 03/25/1942 **PB:** Memphis **SC:** TN/USA **YOP:** 2018-08-16 **PT:** Daughter of Clarence L. and Barbara (Siggers) Franklin; **ED:** ArtsD (hon.), Harvard University, 2014; MusD (hon.), Yale University, 2010; MusD (hon.), University of Pennsylvania, 2007; MusD (hon.), Berklee College Music, Boston, 2006; MusD (hon.), University of Detroit, 1987 **CW:** Singer: (albums) Aretha, 1961, Electrifying, Tender Moving and Swinging, 1962, Laughing on the Outside, 1963, Unforgettable, Songs of Faith, Running Out of Fools, 1964, Yeah, 1965, Soul Sister, 1966, Queen of Soul, Take It Like You Give It, Lee Cross, Greatest Hits, I Never Loved a Man, Once in a Lifetime, Aretha Arrives, 1967, Lady Soul, Greatest Hits, Vol. 2, Best of Aretha Franklin, Live at Paris Olympia, Aretha Now, 1968, Soul 69, Today I Sing the Blues, Soft and Beautiful, Aretha Gold's, Satisfaction, I Say a Little Prayer, 1969, This Girl's in Love with You, Spirit in the Dark, Don't Play that Song, 1970, Live at the Fillmore West, Young Gifted and Black, Aretha's Greatest Hits, 1971, Amazing Grace, 1972, Hey Hey Now, Firest 12 Sides, 1973, Let Me Into Your Life, 1974, With Every Thing I Feel in Me, You, 1975, Sparkle, Ten Years of Gold, 1976, Sweet Passion, 1977, Almighty Fire, Star Collection, 1978, La Diva, 1979, Aretha, 1980, Who's Zoomin' Who, 1985, One Lord, One Faith, One Baptism, 1987, Aretha Sings the Blues, 1965, 85, Lady Soul, 1988, Through the Storm, 1989, What You See is What You Sweat, 1991, Jazz to Soul, 1992, Aretha After Hours, Chain of Fools, 1993, Unforgettable: A Tribute to Dinah Washington, 1995, Love Songs, 1997, The Delta Meets Detroit, A Rose Is Still A Rose, 1998, Amazing Grace, 1999, The Queen in Waiting: The Columbia Years 1960-1965, 2002, So Damn Happy, 2003, Jazz Moods: 'Round Midnight, 2005, Jewels in the Crown: All Star Duets with the Queen, 2007 (Grammy award for Best Gospel Performance, 2008), This Christmas Aretha, 2008, Sunday Morning Classics, 2009, A Woman Falling Out of Love, 2011, Knew You Were Waiting: The Best of Aretha Franklin 1980-1998, Aretha: A Woman Falling Out of Love, 2011 , Aretha Franklin Sings the Great Diva Classics, 2014 (National Association for the Advancement of Colored People Image award for Outstanding Album, 2015); actress: (films) Blues Brothers, 1980, Shindig! Presents Soul, Shindig! Presents Groovy Gals, 1991, History of Rock 'N' Roll, 1995, Blues Brothers 2000, 1998; (TV films) Bob Hope on Campus, 1975, Aretha Franklin: The Queen of Soul, 1988; (TV miniseries) Motown 40: The Music Is Forever, 1998; appearances in documentaries Immaculate Funk, 2000, Tom Dowd & the Language of Music, 2003, Singing in the Shadow: The Children of Rock Royalty, 2003, From The Heart / The Four Tops 50th Anniversary and Celebration, 2004, Atlantic Records: The House that Ahmet Built, 2007; performer (Showtime production): Aretha, 1986; performer: Presidential Inauguration Jimmy Carter, 1977, Presidential Inauguration Bill Clinton, 1992, Presidential Inauguration Barack Obama, 2009; featured in documentary Muscle Shoals, 2013 **AW:** Named Person of Year, MusiCares Foundation, 2008, Number One Female Singer 16th International, Jazz Critics Poll, 1968, Top Female Vocalist, 1967; named one of Billboard Hot 100 All-Time Top Artists, Billboard magazine, 2008, 100 Greatest Singers of All Time (ranked No. 1), Rolling Stone magazine, 2008, 100 Greatest Artists of All Time, 2004; named to Gospel Music Hall of Fame, 2012, Michigan Rock & Roll Legends Hall of Fame, 2005, UK Music Hall of Fame, 2005, Rock & Roll Hall of Fame, 1987, Hollywood Walk of Fame, 1979; recipient Grammy award for Best Gospel-Soul Vocal Performance by a Duo or Group (with Mary J. Blige), 2008, Key to City of Memphis, 2008, Vanguard award, National Association for the Advancement of Colored People, 2008, Grammy award for Best Traditional R&B Vocal Performance, 2006, 2004, Presidential Medal of Freedom, The White House, 2005, National Medal of Arts, 1999, Kennedy Center Honor, John F. Kennedy Center Performing Arts, Washington, 1994, Grammy Lifetime Achievement award, 1994, Grammy Living Legend award, 1991, Grammy award for Best Soul Gospel Performance, 1989, American Music award, 1984, Grammy award for Best R&B Duo Performance (with George Michael), 1987, Grammy award for Best Soul Gospel Performance, 1973, Grammy award for Best Female R&B Vocal Performance, 1988, 1986, 1982, 1968-75 **MEM:** Mem.: Delta Sigma Theta (hon.) **ACH:** Achievements include recognition as the first female artist to be inducted into the Rock and Roll Hall of Fame; accredited with having the most million-selling singles of any female artist **BA:** William Morris Agency, One William Morris Place, Beverly Hills, CA, 90212

FRAZIER, KENNETH C., **T:** Merck CEO **I:** Business Management/Business Services **DOB:** 12/17/1954 **PB:** Philadelphia, December 17, 1954 **ED:** JD, Harvard University, 1978; BA in Political Sci., Pennsylvania State University, 1975 **CT:** Bar: U.S. Supreme Court 2002, U.S. District Court (eastern district) Pennsylvania 1978, Pennsylvania 1978 **C:** Chairman, President, CEO, Merck & Co., Inc. (formerly Schering-Plough Corp.), Whitehouse Station, New Jersey, 2011-; President, Merck & Co., Inc. (formerly Schering-Plough Corp.), Whitehouse Station, New Jersey, 2010; Executive Vice President, President Global Human Health, Merck & Co., Inc. (formerly Schering-Plough Corp.), Whitehouse Station, New Jersey, 2007-10; Executive Vice President, General Counsel, Merck & Co., Inc. (formerly Schering-Plough Corp.), Whitehouse Station, New Jersey, 2006-07; Senior Vice President, General Counsel, Merck & Co., Inc. (formerly Schering-Plough Corp.), Whitehouse Station, New Jersey, 1999-2006; Vice President, Deputy General Counsel, Merck & Co., Inc. (formerly Schering-Plough Corp.), 1999; Vice President Pub. Affairs, Assistant General Counsel, Merck & Co., Inc. (formerly Schering-Plough Corp.), 1997-98; Vice President Pub. Affairs, Merck & Co., Inc. (formerly Schering-Plough Corp.), 1994-96; Vice President, General Counsel, Secretary, Astra Merck, 1992-94; Partner Department of Litigation, Drinker Biddle & Reath, 1978-92 **CR:** Member CLO Roundtable-U.S., Corp. Executive Bd.'s General Counsel Roundtable Member Adv. Board CorporateProBono.Org, Rand Institute for Civil Justice Member Adv. Board Health Law and Policy Center, Seton Hall University Member Adv. Board Law and Economic Center, Univ. Pennsylvania Chairman Ethics Resource Center Board of

Directors Legal Services New Jersey, Cornerstone Christian Academy, Pennsylvania State Univ., Merck & Co., Inc., 2011-, ExxonMobil Corp., 2009- **AW:** Named to Am. Law Institute Council, 2003 **MEM:** Mem.: American Bar Association, Am. Law Institute, Pennsylvania Bar Association, Council on Foreign Relations

FRECHET, JEAN, **T:** Chemist **I:** Sciences **DOB:** 08/18/1944 **ED:** Doctorate (hon.), University Ottawa, 2004; Doctorate (hon.), University Lyon, 2002; PhD, Syracuse University, 1971; PhD, State University of New York, Syracuse, 1971; MSc, State University of New York, Syracuse, 1969 **C:** Head materials synthesis, Lawrence Berkeley National Laboratory, 1999-; H. Rapoport chair organic chemistry, University California, Berkeley, 2003-; Professor chemistry, University California, Berkeley, 1996-; P.J. Debye chair chemistry, Cornell University, Ithaca, New York, 1996-98; IBM professor chemistry, Cornell University, Ithaca, New York, 1987-95; Professor chemistry, University Ottawa, Canada, 1982-87; Associate professor chemistry, University Ottawa, Canada, 1978-82; Assistant professor chemistry, University Ottawa, Canada, 1973-78 **CR:** Visiting scientist IBM Research Laboratory, San Jose, California, 1979, 83 vice dean grad. studies and research University Ottawa, 1983-87 consultant Kodak, 1997-05, Xenoport, 2000-, Intermolecular, 2005-, Nanomix, 2006-, ICI, 2004- board directors Ontario Center for Materials Research, Toronto, Dendritic Nanotechnologies, Inc, NOVOMER, NTERYX. **CW:** Contributor numerous articles to professional journals; patentee in field. **AW:** Recipient International Union Pure and Applied Chemistry award, 1983, Polymer Society Japan, 1986, A.K. Doolittle award, 1986, Cooperative Research award Am. Chemical Society, 1994, Applied Polymer Chemical award Am. Chemical Society, 1996, 00, Kosar Memorial award Society Imaging Sci. Tech., 1999, Salute to Excellence award Am. Chemical Society, 2001, Esselen award chemistry pub. service, 2005, medal Macro Group UK, 2006, Arthur C. Cope award, Am. Chemical Society, 2007; A.C. Cope scholar Am. Chemical Society, 2001; numerous research grants,Erasmus Medal, 2013, University of California Department of Chemistry Teaching Award, 2010, Herman Mark Award, 2009, Dickson Prize in Science, 2007 **MEM:** Fellow American Association for the Advancement of Science; member National Academy of Sciences, NAE, Am. Academy Arts and Scis. **H:** Oenophile

FREEMAN, MORGAN, **T:** Actor **I:** Media & Entertainment **DOB:** 06/01/1937 **PB:** Memphis **SC:** Tennessee **PT:** Son of Grafton Curtis and Mayme Edna (Revere) F.; **SPN:** Married Jeanette Adair Bradshaw, October 22, 1967 (div. 1979); Married Myrna Colley-Lee, June 16, 1984 (div. September 15, 2010); **CH:** children: Alphonse, **ED:** Student, LA City College **MIL:** With US Air Force, 1955—59, Former Mechanic US Air Force **CW:** Actor, Hello Dolly (Broadway), 1967, Jungle of Cities, 1969, The Recruiting Officer, 1969, Scuba-Duba, 1969, Purlie (American National Theatre and Academy Theatre, New York City), 1970, Black Visions, 1972, Sisyphus and the Blue-Eyed Cyclops, 1975, Cockfight, 1977, Mighty Gents, 1978 (Clarence Derwent Award, Drama Desk award), White Pelicans, 1978, Coriolanus, also Julius (New York Shakespeare Festival), 1979, Mother Courage and Her Children, 1980, Othello & All's Well That Ends Well (both Dallas Shakespeare Festival), 1982, Buck, 1983, Medea and the Doll, 1984, The Gospel at Colonus (Obie awards), 1988, The Country Girl, 2008; (films) Who Says I Can't Ride a Rainbow, 1971, Brubaker, 1980, Eyewitness, 1980, Harry and Son, 1983, Teachers, 1984, Street Smart, 1987,

Clean and Sober, 1988, Lean On Me, 1989, Johnny Handsome, 1989, Driving Miss Daisy, 1989 (Golden Globe award for Best Performance by an Actor in a Motion Picture-Drama, 1990), Glory, 1989, The Bonfire of the Vanities, 1990, Robin Hood: Prince of Thieves, 1991, Unforgiven, 1992, The Shawshank Redemption, 1994, Outbreak, 1995, Seven, 1995, Chain Reaction, 1996, Moll Flanders, 1996, Deep Impact 1997, Kiss The Girls, 1997, The Long Way Home, 1996, Hard Rain, 1998, Water Damage, 1999, Mutiny, 1999, Nurse Betty, 2000, High Crimes, 2002, The Sum of All Fears, 2002, Dreamcatcher, 2003, Bruce Almighty, 2003, The Big Bounce, 2004, Million Dollar Baby, 2004 (Screen Actors Guild award for Outstanding Performance by a Male Actor in Supporting Role, 2005, Academy award for Best Supporting Actor, 2005), Unleashed, 2005, (voice) Batman Begins, 2005, War of the Worlds (Narrator), 2005, March of the Penguins (Narrator), 2005, An Unfinished Life, 2005, Edison, 2005, Lucky Number Slevin, 2006, Gone Baby Gone, 2007, The Bucket List, 2007, Wanted, 2008, The Dark Knight, 2008, Red, 2010, Born to Be Wild (narrator), 2011, Dolphin Tale, 2011, The Magic of Belle Isle, 2012, The Dark Knight Rises, 2012, We the People, 2012, Olympus Has Fallen, 2013, Oblivion, 2013, Now You See Me, 2013, Last Vegas, 2013, (Voice) The Lego Movie, 2014, Transcendence, 2014, Lucy, 2014, Dolphin Tale 2, 2014, We the People (narrator), 2014, Last Knights, 2015, Ted 2, 2015, Momentum, 2015, London Has Fallen, 2016, Going in Style, 2016, Now You See Me 2, 2016, Ben-Hur, 2016,Going in Style, 2017, Just Getting Started, 2017, The Nutcracker and the Four Realms, 2018 (documentaries) JFK: A President Betrayed (Narrator), 2013, Island of Lemurs: Madagascar (Narrator), 2014; actor, executive prodr.: (films) Under Suspicion, 2000, Along Came a Spider, 2001, Levity, 2003, 10 Items or Less, 2006, Invictus, 2009 (National Board Review award for Best Actor, 2009, African-American Film Critics Association award for Best Actor, 2009); actor, prodr.: (films) The Maiden Heist, 2009, Life Itself, 2014, 5 Flights Up, 2014; dir.: (films) Bopha!, 1993; actor: (TV films) Hollow Image, 1979, Attica, 1980, The Marva Collins Story, 1981, The Atlanta Child Murders, 1985, Resting Place, 1986, Flight for Life, 1987, Clinton and Nadine, 1988, Mutiny, 1999; , Smithsonian Channel's Sound Revolution, 2008, Stephen Fry in America, 2008, Saturday Night Live, 2010, Madam Secretary, 2015-2016 (TV Mini Series-voice) Slavery and the Making of America, 2005; Regular Cast Mem.: (TV Series) The Electric Company, 1971-77; Executive Prodr.: (Documentaries) Through the Wormhole, 2010-15, (TV Series) Madam Secretary, 2014-16. **AW:** Named Favorite Movie Icon, People's Choice Awards, 2012; Recipient Spencer Tracy Award, UCLA, 2006, Kennedy Center Honors, John F. Kennedy Center for the Performing Arts, 2008, Career Achievement award, Palm Springs International Film Festival, 2010, Life Achievement award, American Film Institute, 2011, Cecil B. DeMille Award, Hollywood Foreign Press Association, 2012 **BA:** William Morris Agency, 1325 Avenue of the Americas, New York, New York, NY, 10019

FRELINGHUYSEN, RODNEY P., **T:** Chair, Former U.S. Representative from New Jersey **I:** Government Administration/Government Relations/Government Services **CN:** House Appropriations Committee **DOB:** 04/29/1946 **PB:** New York **SC:** NY/USA **PT:** Peter Hood Ballantine Frelinghuysen, Jr. **ED:** Honorary Degree, Drew University, 2004; BA, Hobart College, Geneva, NY, 1969; Graduate Student, Trinity College, Hartford, CT **C:** Chair, House Appropriations Committee, 2017-Present; U.S. Congress From 11th New Jersey District, 1995-

Present; Chairman, Assembly Appropriations Committee, New Jersey General Assembly, 1992-1994; Chairman, Assembly Appropriations Committee, New Jersey General Assembly, 1988-1989; New Jersey General Assembly, 1983-1994; Director, Morris County Board of Chosen Freeholders, 1980; Morris County Board of Chosen Freeholders, 1974-1983; State and Federal Aid Coordinator, Administrative Assistant, Morris County, 1972 **CIV:** Board Member, Morristown Salvation Army; (Board of Directors) United Way, 1979-1982, Peck School, Newark Museum, Morristown Memorial Hospital **MIL:** 93rd Engineer Battalion, U.S. Army, Vietnam, 1969-1971 **AW:** Legislator of the Year, New Jersey Association of Mental Health Agencies, New Jersey Association of Retarded Citizens; Hero of the Taxpayer Award, Americans for Tax Reform; Science Coalition's Champion of Science Award, Rutgers University and Princeton University; Legislator of the Year, VFW **MEM:** VFW, American Legion, New Jersey Historical Society **PA:** Republican **BA:** U.S. House of Representatives, 2306 Rayburn House Office Bldg, Washington, DC, 20515

FRIEDEN, THOMAS R., T: Federal Agency Administrator **I:** Government Administration/Government Relations/Government Services **DOB:** 12/07/1960 **PB:** NYC **ED:** MPH, Columbia University Mailman School Pub. Health, 1986; MD, Columbia University College Physicians & Surgeons, New York City, 1986; BA, Oberlin College, Ohio, 1982 **C:** Administrator Agency Toxic Substances & Disease Registry (ATSDR), US Department Health & Human Services, 2009-; Director Centers Disease Control & Prevention (CDC),, US Department Health & Human Services, 2009-; Medical officer, World Health Organization, New Delhi, 1996-2001; Commissioner, New York City Department Health & Mental Hygiene, 2002-09; Director Bureau Tuberculosis Control, assistant commissioner, New York City Department Health & Mental Hygiene, 1992-96; EIS (epidemiologic intelligence service) officer, New York City Department Health & Mental Hygiene, 1990-92; Fellow in infectious disease, Yale University, New Haven, 1989-90; Medical intern, resident, Columbia Presbyterian Hospital, 1986-89

FRIEDLAND, MICHELLE, T: Federal Judge **I:** Law and Legal Services **CN:** U.S. Court of Appeals for the Ninth Circuit **DOB:** 07/04/1972 **PB:** Berkeley **SC:** CA/USA **MS:** Married **SPN:** Daniel Kelly **ED:** JD, Stanford Law School, Stanford University (2000); Fulbright Scholar, Oxford University (1996); BS in Ecology & Population Biology, Stanford University (1995) **C:** Judge, U.S. Court of Appeals for the Ninth Circuit (2014-Present); Partner, Munger, Tolles & Olson LLP (2010-2014); Associate, Munger, Tolles & Olson LLP, San Francisco, CA (2004-2010); Lecturer in Law, Stanford Law School (2002-2004); Law Clerk to Justice Sandra Day O'Connor, Supreme Court of the U.S. (2001-2002); Law Clerk to Honorary David Tatel, U.S. Court of Appeals for the District of Columbia Circuit (2000-2001) **AW:** Recipient, President's Pro Bono Service Award, State Bar of California (2013); Recipient, LGBT Award, American Civil Liberties Union of Southern California (2009); Recipient, Wiley W. Manuel Award, President's Pro Bono Service Award (2006) **BA:** 95 7th St, San Francisco, CA, 94103

FRIEDMAN, SONIA, T: Theatre Producer **I:** Media & Entertainment **CW:** "Accidental Death of an Anarchist" (1990), "Tartuffe" (1991), "The Queen and I" (1994), "The Libertine" (1995), "Shopping and Fucking" (1996), "Blue Kettle/Heart's Desire"(1997), "The Steward of Christendom" (1997), "Three Sisters" (1997), "Spoonface Steinberg" (1999), "Speed the Plow" (2000), "Noises Off" (2000), "A Day in the Death of Joe Egg" (2001), "Benefactors" (2002), "Up for Grabs (2002), "Afterplay" (2002), "What the Night is For" (2002), "Macbeth" (2002), "Ragtime" (2003), "A Day in the Death of Joe Egg" (2003); Broadway, "Sexual Perversity in Chicago" (2003), "Absolutely! (Perhaps)" (2003), "Hitchcock Blonde" (2003), "See You Next Tuesday" (2003), "Jumpers" (2003), "Calico" (2004), "Endgame" (2004), "Guantánamo" (2004), "The Woman in White" (2004), "By the Bog of Cats" (2005), "Whose Life is it Anyway" (2005), "The Home Place" (2005), "As You Like It" (2005), "Shoot the Crow" (2005), "Celebration" (2005), "Otherwise Engaged" (2005), "The Woman in White" (2005) "Donkeys' Years" (2006-2007), "On the Third Day" (2006), "Eh Joe" (2006), "Bent" (2006), "Faith Healer" (2006), "Love Song" (2006), "Rock 'n' Roll" (2006), "King of Hearts" (2007), "The Dumb Waiter" (2007), "Boeing-Boeing" (2007-2009), "In Celebration" (2007), "Rock 'n' Roll" (2007), "Is He Dead?" (2007), "Hergé's Adventures of Tintin, a Musical Version of Tintin in Tibet" (2007), "Dealer's Choice" (2007), "Boeing-Boeing," Australia (2008); Broadway, "That Face" (2008), "Under the Blue Sky" (2008), "The Seagull" (2008), "No Man's Land" (2008), "La Cage Aux Folles" (2008), "Maria Friedman: Re-Arranged" (2008), UK Tour, "Dancing at Lughnasa" (2009), "A View from the Bridge" (2009), "A Little Night Music" (2009), "The Norman Conquests" (2009), "The Mountaintop" (2009), "Arcadia" (2009), "Othello" (2009), "Prick Up Your Ears" (2009), "After Miss Julie" (2009), "Legally Blonde" (2009), "Jerusalem" (2010-2012), "Private Lives" (2010), "The Prisoner of Second Avenue" (2010), "All My Sons" (2010), "A View from the Bridge" (2010), "Shirley Valentine and Educating Rita" (2010), "La Bete" (2010), "A Flea in Her Ear" (2010), "La Cage Aux Folles" (2010-2012), "The Children's Hour" (2011), "Clybourne Park" (2011), "Arcadia" (2011), "The Book of Mormon" (2011, 2013, 2014, 2015, 2016, 2017, 2018), "Much Ado About Nothing" (2011), "Betrayal" (2011), "Top Girls" (2011), US Tour, "The Mountaintop" (2011), "Master Class" (2012), "Absent Friends" (2012), "Hay Fever" (2012), "Death of a Salesman" (2012), "Nice Work If You Can Get It" (2012-2013), "The Sunshine Boys" (2012), "A Chorus of Disapproval" (2012-2013), "Richard the Third" (2012-2013), "Twelfth Night" (2012-2013), "Old Times" (2013), "Merrily We Roll Along" (2013), "Chimerica" (2013), "The Sunshine Boys" (2013), "Los Angeles, Twelfth Night & Richard III" (2013), "Mojo" (2013), "Ghosts" (2013), "1984" (2013, 2015, 2016), "Shakespeare in Love" (2014), "King Charles III" (2014), "Electra, Frank McGuinness Translation" (2014), "Sunny Afternoon" (2014), "The River" (2014), "The Nether" (2014), "Ghosts," NY (2013), "Bend It Like Beckham" (2015), "Hamlet" (2015), "Farinelli and The King" (2015), "King Charles III" (2015), "A Christmas Carol" (2015), "Funny Girl" (2016), "Harry Potter and the Cursed Child" (2016, 2017, 2018), "Sunny Afternoon," UK Tour (2016), "Nice Fish" (2016), "Dreamgirls" (2016, 2017, 2018), "The Glass Menagerie" (2017), "Travesties" (2017), "Funny Girl," UK Tour (2017), "Who's Afraid of Virginia Woolf?" (2017), "The Ferryman, Royal Court Theatre, (2017), "Our Ladies of Perpetual Succour" (2017), "The Ferryman," Gielgud Theatre (2017, 2018), "Hamlet, Harold Pinter Theatre (2017), "1984," NY (2017), "Ink," Duke of Yorks Theatre (2017/2018), "Farinelli and the King," NY (2017, 2018), "The Birthday Party, Harold Pinter Theatre (2018), "Mean Girls," NY (2018), "Travesties," NY (2018), "Harry Potter and the Cursed Child," NY (2018), "Harry Potter and the Cursed Child, Melbourne, Australia (2019), "The Ferryman," Bernard B. Jacobs Theatre, NY (2018), "The Jungle," Playhouse Theatre (2018), "Consent," Harold Pinter Theatre (2018); **AW:** Named One of TIME's 100 Most Influential People, TIME Magazine (2018); Tony Award Nominee for Best Revival

FRITZ, LANCE M., T: Rail Transportation Company Executive **I:** Other **ED:** MBA, Northwestern University; Bachelor in Mechanical Engineering, Bucknell University **C:** President, CEO, Union Pacific Corp., 2015-; COO, Union Pacific Corp., 2014-15; Executive vice president operations, Union Pacific Corp., 2010-14; Vice president operations, Union Pacific Corp., 2009-10; Vice president, labor relations, Union Pacific Corp., 2008-09; Regional vice president, Southern Region, Union Pacific Corp., 2006-08; Regional vice president, Northern Region, Union Pacific Corp., 2005-06; Vice president, general manager, Energy, Union Pacific Corp., 2000-05; General manager, Fiskars Inc., 1997-2000; Business analyst, Cooper Industries, 1991-94; Worked in marketing and operating positions, Cooper Industries; Worked, operations & manufacturing management, General Electric Co. **CR:** Board directors Union Pacific Corp., 2015-, Member, Board of Directors, Assn. of American Railroads, U.S. Chamber of Commerce. Member, Business Roundtable, STRATCOM Consultation Committee **CIV:** Board directors, Omaha Symphony, Board directors, United Way of the Midlands

FUDGE, MARCIA LOUISE, T: U.S. Representative from Ohio, Former Mayor **I:** Government Administration/Government Relations/Government Services **DOB:** 10/29/1952 **PB:** Cleve. **ED:** JD, Cleveland Marshall College Law, Cleveland State University, 1983; BS in Business Administration, Ohio State University, Columbus, 1975 **C:** Member, US Congress from 11th Ohio District, 2009-; Member, Committee on Agriculture, Committee on Science, Space, and Technology; Mayor, City of Warrensville Heights, Ohio, 2000-08; Chief of staff to Rep. Stephanie Tubbs Jones, US House of Representatives, 1999-2001; Staff personal property tax department, Cuyahoga County Auditor's Office,; Various positions including director budget & finance, Cuyahoga County Prosecutor's Office, Cleveland, **CR:** Chairperson Congressional Black Caucus (Canadian Broadcasting Co.), 2013- **CIV:** Member, AIPAC Mission-Israel, 2008 Visiting referee, acting judge, Bedford Municipal Court, Cuyahoga County, Active, Glenville Church of God, **AW:** Named Municipal Leader of Year, Northeast Ohio Municipal Leader magazine, 2007; recipient American Voice award, 2014, Patricia Roberts Harris Medallion award for excellence in government service, 2007, Russell T. Adrine Citizen of Year award, 2005, Trailblazer of Year award, Norman S. Minor Bar Association, 2005 **MEM:** Mem.: Delta Sigma Theta (president 1996-2000, co-chair national social action commission 2000-04) **PA:** Democrat

FUKUYAMA, FRANCIS, T: Political Scientist, Author **I:** Government Administration/Government Relations/Government Services **DOB:** 10/27/1952 **PB:** Chicago **SC:** IL/USA **ED:** Honorary Doctorate, Doane College, Crete, NE (2001); Honorary Doctorate, Connecticut College, New London, CT (1995); PhD in Soviet Foreign Policy, Harvard University (1981); Intern, U.S. Arms Control and Disarmament Agency (1976); BA in Classics, Cornell University (1974); Honorary Doctorate, Doshisha University, Japan **C:** Olivier Nomellini Senior Fellow at the Freeman Spogli Institute International Studies, Resident of the Center of Democracy, Development, and the Rule of Law, Stanford University, California (2010-Present); Bernard Schwartz Professor of International Political Economy, Director of International

Development Program, Johns Hopkins University, Paul H. Nitze School Advanced International Studies (2001-2010); Omer L. and Nancy Hirst Professor of Public Policy, Director of International Commerce and Policy Program, George Mason University (1996-2001); Senior Social Scientist, The RAND Corp., Santa Monica, CA (1995-1996); Consultant, The RAND Corp., Santa Monica, CA (1990-1994); Deputy Director of Policy Planning Staff, U.S. Department of State, Washington, DC (1989-1990); Senior Staff Member, Political Science Department, The RAND Corp., Santa Monica, CA (1983-1989); Policy Planning Staff, U.S. Department of State, Washington, DC (1981-1982); Associate Social Scientist, The RAND Corp., Santa Monica, CA (1979-1981); Consultant, Pan Heuristics, Inc., Los Angeles, CA (1978-1979) **CR:** Co-Director, Project on the Information and Biological Revolution RAND/George Mason University (1996-1999); Director, New Sciences Project, Johns Hopkins School of Advanced International Studies (1996-1999); Director, SAIS Telecommunications Project (1994-1996); Fellow, Foreign Policy Institute (1994-1996); Visiting Lecturer, Department of Political Science, University of California, Los Angeles (1989, 1986); Member, Advisory Board, FINCA International, Inter-American Dialogue, National Endowment Democracy, National Interest, New American Foundation **CIV:** Member, President's Council on Bioethics (2001-2005); Member, U.S. Delegate, Egyptian-Israeli Talks on Palestinian Autonomy (1981-1982); Board of Trustees, RAND Corp.; Board of Governors, Pardee Rand Graduate School **CW:** Author, "Political Order and Political Decay: From the Industrial Revolution to the Present Day" (2014); Author, "The Origins of Political Order" (2011); Author, "Falling Behind: Explaining the Development Gap between Latin America and the U.S." (2008); Author, "America at the Crossroads: Democracy, Power, and the Neoconservative Legacy" (2006); Author, "State-Building: Governance and World Order in the 21st Century" (2004); Author, "Our Posthuman Future: Consequences of the Biotechnology Revolution" (2002); Co-Editor, with Caroline S. Wagner, "Information and Biological Revolutions: Global Governance Challenges-Summary of a Study Group" (1999); Author, "The Great Disruption: Human Nature and the Reconstitution of Social Order" (1999); Co-Author, with Abram Shulsky, "The Virtual Corporation and Army Organization" (1997); Author, "The End of Order" (1997); Author, "Trust: The Social Virtues and the Creation of Prosperity" (1995); Co-Author, with Kongdan Oh, "The US-Japan Security Relationship After the Cold War" (1993); Author, "The End of History and the Last Man" (1992); Author, "Gorbachev and the New Soviet Agenda in the Third World" (1989); Author, "Soviet Civil-Military Relations and the Power Projection Mission" (1987); Author, "Moscow's Post-Brezhnev Reassessment of the Third World" (1986); Member, Editorial Board, Journal of Democracy; Chairman, Editorial Board, The American Interest; Contributor, Chapters to Books, Articles to Professional Journals **AW:** Graduate Fellow, National Security Program, Center for International Affairs, Harvard University (1979); Fellow, Center for Science and International Affairs, Harvard University (1978-1979) **MEM:** Council on Civil Society; Board of Directors, National Endowment for Democracy; Global Business Network; Founding Member, Pacific Council on International Policy; American Political Science Association; Council on Foreign Relations **BA:** 616 Serra Street, Stanford, CA, 94305

FUTTER, ELLEN VICTORIA, T: President **I:** Business Management/Business Services **CN:** American Museum of Natural History **DOB:** 09/21/1949 **PB:** New York City **SC:** NY/USA **PT:** Daughter of Victor and Joan Babette (Feinberg) Futter **ED:** Degree (hon.), Williams College, 2004; Degree (hon.), Skidmore College, 2003; DHL (hon.), Amherst College; DHL (hon.), Yale University, 2000; DHL (hon.), Long Island City College, 1995; DHL (hon.), City College of New York, 1996; DHL (hon.), Hofstra University, 1994; LLD (hon.), New York Law School; LLD (hon.), Hamilton College, 1985; LLD (hon.), Columbia University, New York City, 1984; JD, Columbia Law School, New York City, 1974; AB, magna cum laude, Barnard College, New York City, 1971; Student, University of Wisconsin, Madison **C:** President, American Museum of Natural History, New York City, 1993-; President, Barnard College, 1981-93; Acting President, Barnard College, 1980-81; Associate, Milbank, Tweed, Hadley & McCloy, New York City, 1974-80 **CR:** Board of Directors Viacom, 2006-07, American International Group (AIG), 1999-2008, Bristol-Myers Squibb Co., 1999-2005, JPMorgan Chase & Co., 1997-2013, Consolidated Edison New York, 1997-, Chair Federal Reserve Bank New York, 1992-93, Board of Directors, 1988-93 **AW:** Named One of The 50 Most Powerful Women in New York, Crain's New York Business, 2011, 2009, The 100 Most Influential Women in New York City Business, 2007; Recipient, Mark Schubart Award in Education, Lincoln Center Institute Arts in Education, 2008, Lawrence A. Wien Prize for Social Responsibility, Columbia Law School, 2008, Woman of Achievement Award, Women in Devel. New York, 2006, Alexander Hamilton Award, Manhattan Institute Policy Research, 2002, Rachel Carson Award, 2014 **MEM:** Fellow: American Academy Arts & Sciences; Mem.: American Bar Association, Council Foreign Relations, National Institute Social Sciences, Association Bar City of New York, New York State Bar Association, Economic Club New York, Century Club, Cosmopolitan Club, Phi Beta Kappa **BAR:** Bar: New York 1975

GABBARD, TULSI, T: U.S. Representative from Hawaii **I:** Government Administration/Government Relations/Government Services **DOB:** 04/12/1981 **PB:** Leloaloa **PT:** Daughter of Gerald Mike and Carol (Porter) Gabbard; **ED:** Grad., Alabama Military Academy Accelerated Officer Candidate School, 2007; BBA in International Business, Hawaii Pacific University, 2009 **C:** Member, US House Homeland Security Committee, 2013-; Member, US House Foreign Affairs Committee, 2013-; Member, US Congress from 2nd Hawaii District, Washington, 2013; City councilwoman District 6, City of Honolulu, 2011-12; Legislative aide to Senator Daniel K. Akaka, US Senate, 2006-09; Member District 42, Hawaii House of Reps., 2002-04 **CR:** Vice chair Dem. National Committee co-founder Stand Up For America (SUFA), 2011, Health Hawaii Coalition (HHC), 2000 **AW:** Decorated German Armed Forces Badge for Military Proficiency in Gold, Combat Medical Badge, Army Good Conduct medal, Army Achievement medal with oak leaf cluster, Army Commendation medal, Meritorious Service medal; named one of The 10 Most Powerful Women in DC, Elle magazine, 2014 **MEM:** Mem.: Military Police Regimental Association (life), National Guard Association US (life) **H:** Surfing **PA:** Democrat

GAETZ, MATT, T: Unites States Representative from Florida **I:** Government Administration/Government Relations/Government Services **PB:** Hollywood **SC:** CA/USA **PT:** Don Gaetz **ED:** JD, College William and Mary, Williamsburg, Virginia, 2007; BS, Florida State University, Tallahassee, 2003 **C:** Member, U.S.house of Representatives Florida's 1st District, 2017-; Member District 4, Florida House of Reps., Tallahassee, 2010-2017; Attorney

CR: Member Niceville Valparaiso C. of C., Navarre C. of C., Fort Walton Beach C. of C., Destin C. of C. **CIV:** Board member, AMIkids, Emerald Coast **MEM:** Mem.: Okaloosa Bar Association **PA:** Republican **RE:** Baptist

GAIMAN, NEIL RICHARD, T: Novelist, Comics Writer, Screenwriter **I:** Writing and Editing **DOB:** 11/10/1960 **PB:** Portchester **SC:** England **PT:** David Bernard Gaiman, Sheila Gaiman **ED:** Student, Whitgift School, London, England **CIV:** Patron, Science Fiction Foundation and Open Rights Group **CW:** Author, Numerous Works of Prose, Graphic Novels, and Comics, (Novels) Angels & Visitations, 1993, Neverwhere, 1996, Smoke & Mirrors, 1998, Stardust, 1999, American Gods, 2001, Coraline, 2002, Adventures in the Dream Trade, 2002, American Gods: The Monarch of the Glen, Legends II, 2004, Anansi Boys, 2005, MirrorMask: A Really Useful Book, 2006, Fragile Things, 2006, M is for Magic, 2007, The Graveyard Book, 2008, The Ocean at the End of the Lane, 2013, Trigger Warning, 2015, (Comic Book Series) The Sandman, 1989-1996, (Children's Books) The Day I Swapped My Dad for Two Goldfish, 1997, The Wolves in the Walls, 2003, Melinda, 2005, MirrorMask, 2005, Odd and the Frost Giants, 2008, The Dangerous Alphabet, 2008, Chu's Day, 2013, Fortunately, the Milk, 2013, (Speech) Make Good Art, 2013; Co-Author, (Novels) (With Terry Pratchett) Good Omens, 1990, (With Stephen Jones) Now We Are Sick, 1991, (With Gene Wolfe and Randy Broecker) A Walking Tour of the Shambles, 2002, (With Michael Reaves) InterWorld, 2007, (With Chris Bachalo and Mark Buckingham) The Absolute Death, 2009; Writer, Producer, (Films) Beowulf, 2007; Writer, (Films) A Short Film About John Bolton, 2003, (Screenplays) Princess Mononoke, 1997, (TV Miniseries) Neverwhere, 1996, (TV Episodes) Day of the Dead, Babylon 5, 1998; Producer, (Films) Stardust, 2007; Co-Editor, (With Ed Kramer) The Sandman: Book of Dreams, 1996, (With Maria Dahvana Headley) Unnatural Creatures, 2013 **AW:** Squiddy Award for Best Writer, 1990-1994, World Fantasy Award, The Sandman, 1991, Favorite Writer, Comics Buyer's Guide, 1991-1993, Defender of Liberty Award, Comic Book Legal Defense Fund, 1993, Haxtur Award, Spain, 1993-1995, Kemi Award for Best International Writer, Finland, 1994, HQ Award for Best Foreign Writer, Comic, Brazil, 1994-1998, Yellow Kid Award, 1995, Lucca Award for Best Writer, Italy, 1997, Sproing Award, Norway, 1998, Nax Und Moritz Award for Best Foreign Writer, 1998, Mythopoeic Fantasy Award for Adult Literature, Stardust, 1999, Bram Stoker Award for Best Illustrated Narrative, The Sandman, 2000, 2004, Bram Stoker Award for Best Work for Young Readers, Coraline, 2001, Bram Stoker Award for Best Novel, American Gods, 2001, Hugo Award for Best Novel, Nebula Award for Best Novel, Locus Award for Best Fantasy Novel, American Gods, 2002, Hugo Award for Best Novella, Nebula Award for Best Novella, Locus Award for Best Young Adult Book, Coraline, 2003, Angoulême International Comics Festival Prize, The Sandman, 2004, Quill Book Award for Graphic Novels, 2005, Mythopoeic Fantasy Award for Adult Literature, Anansi Boys, 2006, Comic-Con Icon Award, 2007, Bob Clampett Humanitarian Award, 2007, John Newbery Medal, American Library Association, The Graveyard Book, 2009, Galaxy Award for Most Popular Foreign Author, China, 2009-2010, Boston Public Library Literary Lights for Children, 2010, Kurt Vonnegut Junior Award for Literature, 2010 **BA:** Casarotto Ramsay & Associates Limited, Waverley House, 7-12 Noel Street, London, United Kingdom, W1F 8GQ

GALLAGHER, MIKE, T: U.S. Representative from Wisconsin **I:** Government Administration/Government Relations/Government Services **DOB:** 03/03/1984 **PB:** Green Bay **SC:** WI/USA **ED:** Phd, Georgetown, 2010-15; M.A., Government, 2011-13; M.A.,Security Studies, 2010-12; MSSI, National Intelligence University, 2009-10; B.A., Woodrow Wilson School of Public and International Affairs at Princeton, 2002-2006 **C:** Member,U.S. House of Representatives from Wisconsin's 8th District, 2017-; Member, Committee on Armed Services; Member, Committee on Homeland Security; Foreign Policy Advisor, Committee on Foreign Relations, 2015- **MIL:** U.S. Marine Corps Reserves, 2006-13 **BA:** 1007 Longworth HOB, Washington, DC, 20515

GALLAGHER, THOMAS C., I: Business Management/Business Services **C:** Chairman, CEO, Genuine Parts Co., 2012-; Chairman, president, CEO, Genuine Parts Co., 2005-12; President, CEO, director, Genuine Parts Co., 2004-05; President, COO, director, Genuine Parts Co., 1990-2004; Executive vice president, Genuine Parts Co., 1989-90; Joined, Genuine Parts Co., 1963; With, SP Richards Co., 1983 **CR:** Board directors STI Classic Funds, Oxford Industries

GALLEGO, RUBEN, T: U.S. Representative from Arizona **I:** Government Administration/Government Relations/Government Services **ED:** Graduate in International Relations, Harvard University **C:** Member US House of Representatives from Arizona 7th District, 2015-; Member, Committee on Armed Services, Committee on Natural Resources; Member District 16, Arizona House Of Representatives, 2011-2015; Vice Chairman, Arizona Dem. Party; Chief of Staff, Councilman Michael Nowakowski **CR:** Board directors Valley Citizens League, Children's Museum **MIL:** Served with US Marine Corps, Iraq **CW:** Contributor, Articles to the Phoenix Business Journal **PA:** Democrat

GARAMENDI, JOHN RAYMOND, T: U.S. Representative from California **I:** Government Administration/Government Relations/Government Services **DOB:** 01/24/1945 **PB:** Mokelumne Hill **SC:** CA/USA **ED:** MBA, Harvard Business School, 1974; BA in Business, University Calif.-Berkeley, 1966 **C:** Member, US Congress from 3rd California District, 2013-; Member, Committee on Agriculture, Committee on Natural Resources, Republican Study Committee; Member, US Congress from 10th California District, Washington, 2009-13; Lieutenant governor, State of California, 2007-09; Partner, Yucaipa Companies, 1998; Deputy secretary, US Department Interior, 1995-98; Insurance commissioner, State of California, 2003-07; Insurance commissioner, State of California, 1991-95; Member District 1, California State Senate, 1977-91; Member District 7, California State Assembly, 1975-77; Rancher near, Sacramento County,; Vol., US Peace Corps, 1966-68 **CIV:** Member, Ocean Protection Council, 2007-09 Member, California Emergency Council, 2007-09 Chair, California State Lands Commission, 2007-09 Chair, California Commission on Economic Growth, 2007-09 Board member, Operation Respect, 1998-2002 Board member, National Heritage Institute, 1998-2002 Board member, International Fund for Animal Welfare, 1998-2009 Trustee, California State University, 2007-09 Regent, University California, 2007-09 Member advisory board, University California Don Bren School Management, 1998-2009 Member, National Park Foundation, 1998-2001 Member, National Association Service & Conservation Corps, 1998-2001 Chairman, University California Merced Foundation, 1999-2009 **AW:** Recipient Glenn Seaborg award, University California, 2009 **PA:** Democrat **BA:** 322 Cannon House Office Building Washington, DC 20515, Washington, DC, USA, 20515

GARCETTI, ERIC MICHAEL, T: Mayor of Los Angeles **I:** Government Administration/Government Relations/Government Services **DOB:** 02/04/1971 **PB:** LA **ED:** Studied, London School Economics; Studied, Oxford University; MA in International Relations, Columbia University, New York City; BA in International Relations, Columbia University, New York City **C:** Mayor, City of LA, 2013-; President, LA City Council, 2006-12; Councilman District 13, LA City Council, 2001-13; Assistant professor diplomacy & world affairs, Occidental College, LA,; Instructor international affairs, University Southern California, **CR:** Board of directors Roth Family Foundation, International Criminal Court Alliance founding board member, Pobladores Fund of Liberty Hill Foundation **CIV:** Board of directors, California Committee Human Rights Watch, Board of directors, Parents International Ethiopia, Board of directors, Dem. Leadership for 21st Century, Board of directors, LA County Young Democrats **AW:** Named LA's Favorite Elected Official, LA Alternative Press, 2003; named one of 25 Angelenos who stand out for potential to shape lives in LA, LA Business Journal, 2004; recipient John F. Kennedy New Frontier award, Green Cross Millennium award, President Mikhail Gorbachev, Tiger award, Valley Industry & Commerce Association, Olson award, Human Rights Watch, 2002; grantee Young Leaders Fellow, French-Am. Foundation, 2006; Asia 21 Fellow, Asia Society, 2006; Next Generation Leadership fellow, Rockefeller Foundation, 1998 **H:** Photography, piano, jazz piano **PA:** Democrat **BA:** City Hall Office, 200 N Spring St Rm 475, Los Angeles, CA, 90012

GARDNER, CORY SCOTT, T: U.S. Senator from Colorado **I:** Government Administration/Government Relations/Government Services **DOB:** 08/22/1974 **PB:** Yuma, Colorado, August 22, 1974 **PT:** Son of John W. Gardner and Cindy L. (Pagel) Gardner; **ED:** JD, University Colorado, 2001; BA in Political Sci., Colorado State University, 1997 **C:** Chairman, National Republican Senatorial Committee, 2017-, Member, Committee on Commerce, Science, and Transportation, Member, Committee on Energy and Natural Resources,; Member, Committee on Foreign Relations,; Member,Committee on Small Business and Entrepreneurship; US Senator from Colorado, Washington, 2015-; Member, US House Energy & Commerce Committee, Washington, 2011-15; Member, US Congress from 4th Colorado District, Washington, 2011-15; Minority whip, Colorado House of Reps., Denver, 2007-11; Member District 63, Colorado House of Reps., Denver, 2007-11; Legislative director, to Senator Wayne Allard, US Senate, Washington, 2002-05; Communications director, to Senator Wayne Allard, US Senate, Washington, 2001-02; Farm equip. dealer, 2005-11; Farm equip. dealer, 1997-98 **PA:** Republican **BA:** Office of Cory Gardner, 354 Russell Senate Office Building, Washington, DC, 20510

GARFIELD, ANDREW RUSSELL, T: Actor **I:** Media & Entertainment **PB:** Los Angeles **SC:** CA/USA **ED:** Grad., Central School Speech and Drama, 2004 **CW:** Actor: (films) Mumbo Jumbo, 2005, Boy A, 2007, Lions for Lambs, 2007, The Other Boleyn Girl, 2008, Red Riding: 1974, 2009, Red Riding: 1983, 2009, Red Riding: 1980, 2009, The Imaginarium of Doctor Parnassus, 2009, Air, 2009, Never Let Me Go, 2010, The Social Network, 2010, The Amazing Spider-Man, 2012, The Amazing Spider-Man 2, 2014, Silence, 2016, Breathe,2017, Under the Silver Lake,2018; (TV series) Sugar Rush, 2005, Doctor Who, 2007, Freezing, 2007, Trial and Retribution,2007, Boy A,2007, Red Riding, 2009, SNL, 2001,2014; (plays) Mercy, 2004, Kes, 2004 (Most Promising Newcomer Theatre award, Manchester Evening News, 2004), The Laramie Project, 2005, Romeo & Juliet, 2005, Beautiful Thing, 2006, Burn/Chatroom/Citizenship, 2006, The Overwhelming, 2006; (Broadway plays) Death of a Salesman, 2012, Angels in America, 2017, The Children's Monologues, 2017, Angels in America,2018(Tony for Best Performance by an Actor in a Leading Role in a Play) actor, producer (films) 99 Homes, 2014 **AW:** Co-recipient Most Promising Newcomer, London Theatre Critics Cir., 2007; recipient Milton Shulman award for Outstanding Newcomer, Evening Standard Theatre Awards, 2006

GARG, OOSHMA, T: CEO **I:** Business Management/Business Services **CN:** Gobble, Inc. **DOB:** 01/01/1900 **ED:** BS in Bio Mechanical Engineering (2009) **C:** Founder & Chief Executive Officer, Gobble, Inc. (2010-Present); Founder & Chief Executive Officer, Anapata (2008-2010); Sales and Trading Summer Associate (2008)

GARLAND, GREGORY CYRIL, T: Chairman, CEO **I:** Business Management/Business Services **CN:** Phillips 66 **ED:** BSChemE, Texas A&M University (1980) **C:** Chairman, Chief Executive Officer, Phillips 66 (2012-Present); Senior Vice President of Exploration & Production for the Americas, ConocoPhillips, Houston, TX (2010-2012); President, Chief Executive Officer, Chevron Phillips Chemical Co., The Woodlands, Texas (2008-2010); Senior Vice President of Planning & Specialty Products, Chevron Phillips Chemical Co. (2001-2008); Senior Vice President of Planning & Strategic Transactions, Chevron Phillips Chemical Co. (2000-2001); General Manager, Qatar/Middle East, Phillips Petroleum Co., Chevron Phillips Chemical Co. (1997-2000); General Manager of Natural Gas Liquids, Chevron Phillips Chemical Co. (1995-1997); Manager of Planning & Development, Planning and Technology, Chevron Phillips Chemical Co. (1994-1995); Manager, K-Resin Business Unit, Chevron Phillips Chemical Co. (1992-1994); Manager of Olefins Business Unit, Chevron Phillips Chemical Co. (1989-1992); Business Development Director, Chevron Phillips Chemical Co. (1988-1989); Business Service Manager of Advanced Materials, Chevron Phillips Chemical Co. (1986-1988); Sales Engineer of Plastics Resins, Chevron Phillips Chemical Co. (1982-1986); Project Engineer of Plastics Technology Center, Chevron Phillips Chemical Co., Bartlesville, OK (1980-1982) **CR:** Board of Directors, Amgen, Inc. (2013-Present); Board of Directors, Phillips 66 (2012-Present) **CIV:** Chemical Engineering Industrial Advisory Board, Texas A&M University; Board of Directors, Executive Committee Member, American Chemistry Council; Board of Directors, Junior Achievement of Southeast Texas **MEM:** Board of Directors, Executive Committee Member, National Petrochemicals & Refining Association **BA:** Phillips 66, 3010 Briarpark Dr, Houston, TX, 77042

GARLAND, MERRICK BRIAN, T: Federal Judge **I:** Law and Legal Services **DOB:** 11/13/1952 **PB:** Chicago **SC:** IL/USA **PT:** Cyril Garland; Shirley Garland **ED:** JD, Harvard Law School, Magna Cum Laude, 1977, AB, Harvard University, Summa Cum Laude, 1974 **C:** Chief Judge, U.S. Court of Appeals, District of Columbia Circuit, Washington, DC, 2013-Present; Judge, U.S. Court of Appeals, District of Columbia Circuit, Washington, DC, 1997-Present; Principal Associate Deputy Attorney

General, U.S. Department of Justice, Washington, DC, 1994-1997; Deputy Assistant Attorney General, Criminal Division, U.S. Department of Justice, Washington, DC, 1993-1994; Partner, Arnold & Porter LLP, Washington, DC, 1992-1993; Assistant U.S. Attorney, District of Columbia, U.S. Department of Justice, Washington, DC, 1989-1992; Associate Independent Counsel, U.S. Department of Justice, Washington, DC, 1987-1988; Partner, Arnold & Porter LLP, Washington, DC, 1985-1989; Associate, Arnold & Porter LLP, Washington, DC, 1981-1985; Special Assistant to Attorney General, U.S. Department of Justice, Washington, DC, 1979-1981; Law Clerk, Justice William J. Brennan, Jr., U.S. Supreme Court, Washington, DC, 1978-1979; Law Clerk, Hon. Henry J. Friendly, Second Circuit, U.S. Court of Appeals, New York, NY, 1977-1978 **CR:** Committee on Judicial Security, U.S. Judicial Conference, 2008-Present; Committee on Judicial Branch, 2001-2005; Lecturer, Harvard University Law School, 1985-1986 **CIV:** President, Harvard University, 2009-2010; Board of Overseers, Harvard University, 2003-2010 **CW:** Author, (Articles) Deregulation and Judicial Review, Harvard Law Review, 1985, Antitrust and State Action, Yale Law Journal, 1987, Antitrust and Federalism, Yale Law Journal, 1987 **MEM:** American Law Institute; Phi Beta Kappa **BAR:** Tenth Circuit, U.S. Court of Appeals, 1996; Fourth Circuit, U.S. Court of Appeals, 1983; U.S. Supreme Court, 1983; District of Columbia and Ninth Circuits, U.S. Court of Appeals, 1980; U.S. District Court, District of Columbia, 1980; District of Columbia, 1979 **BA:** U.S. Court of Appeals, 333 Constitution Avenue NW, Washington, DC, 20001-2866

GARNETT, KEVIN MAURICE, T: Professional Basketball Player **I:** Athletics **DOB:** 05/19/1976 **PB:** Mauldin **SC:** SC/USA **PT:** O'Lewis McCullough; Shirley Irby Garnett **C:** Forward, Brooklyn Nets (2013-Present); Forward, Boston Celtics (2007-2013); Forward, Minnesota Timberwolves (1995-2007) **CR:** Owner, Official Block Family, Inc.; Member, US Olympic Men's Basketball Team, Sydney, Australia (2000) **AW:** Named Defensive Player of the Year, NBA (2008); NBA Player of the Year, The Sporting News (2004); NBA MVP (2004); NBA All-Star Game MVP (2003); Named One of the 100 Most Powerful Celebrities, Forbes.com (2008); Named One of the Most Influential People of the Next Decade, Newsweek (1997); Named to NBA All-Defensive First Team (2000-2005, 2008, 2011); Named to All-NBA First Team (2000, 2003-2004, 2008); Named to Eastern Conference All-Star Team, NBA (2008-2011, 2013); Named to Western Conference All-Star Team (1997, 1998, 2000-2007); J. Walter Kennedy Citizenship Award (2006); Espy Award, Best NBA Player, ESPN (2004); Gold Medal, Sydney Olympic Games (2000) **ACH:** Achievements include leading the NBA in: defensive rebounds, 2003-07; field goals, field goal attempts, 2004; total rebounds, 2004, 2005; rebounds per game, 2004-07; being the first player in NBA history to reach at least 18,000 points, 10,000 rebounds, 4,000 assists, 1,200 steals and 1,500 blocks; member of the NBA Championship winning Boston Celtics, 2008 **H:** Yoga; Music

GARRETT, GEOFFREY PHD, T: Dean **I:** Education/Educational Services **CN:** The Wharton School of Business **ED:** PhD, Duke University, 1990; MA, Duke University, 1984; BA, Australian National University (ANU), 1980 **C:** Dean, Reliance professor management & private enterprise, University Pennsylvania Wharton School Business, Philadelphia, 2014-; Dean, professor business, University New South Wales Australian School Business, Sydney, 2013-14; Dean, University Sydney School Business, 2012-13; Founding CEO,

professor political sci., US Studies Centre, 2008-12; Senior fellow, Pacific Council on International Policy, Sydney, 2008-09; President, Pacific Council on International Policy, Sydney, 2005-08; Professor international relations, business administration, communications & law, University Southern California, 2001-05; Dean, UCLA International Institute, 2001-05; Director Ronald W. Burkle Center on International Relations, UCLA, 2001-05; Vice provost international studies, professor political sci., UCLA, 2001-05; Founding director Leitner Program in International Political Economy, Yale University, 1999-2001; Director Program in Ethics, Politics, & Economics, Yale University, 1999-2001; Founding co-dir. European Studies Council, Yale University, 1998-2000; Professor political sci., Yale University, New Haven, 1997-2001; Associate professor multinational management, University Pennsylvania Wharton School Business, 1995-97; Assistant professor to full professor, Stanford University, 1988-97; Fellow in politics University College, Oxford University, 1986-88 **CR:** Member editorial board Global Policy, 2008, European Political Sci. Review, 2007-, Review of International Organizations, 2004-, World Politics, 2004-10, International Organization, 1997-2003, Comparative Political Studies, 1996-2005, Political Research Quarterly, 1996-2005, Political Behavior, 1989-95 board directors Capital Markets Cooperative Research Centre, 2011-13, CEMS, 2011-13, The Asia Foundation, 2012-, The Asia Foundation Australia, 2010-, US Studies Centre, 2008-13, Pacific Council on International Policy, 2005-08 visiting fellow Juan March Institute, 1998 national fellow Stanford University Hoover Institution, 1993-94 visiting professor Stanford University Graduate School Business, 1993-94 visiting fellow public policy program Australian National University, 1992 fellow Center for Advanced Study in the Behavioral Sciences, 1991-92 visiting fellow Wissenschaftszentrum, Berlin, 1990-93 **CW:** Author: Partisan Politics in the Global Economy, 1998; co-editor (with Frank Dobbin & Beth Simmons): The Global Diffusion of Markets & Democracy, 2008; co-editor: (with James Alt, Simone Chambers, Margaret Levi Paula McClain) The Encyclopedia of Political Sci., 2010 **AW:** Named one of The Top 50 Most Influential People in Education, The Australian, 2012; Fulbright Scholar, 1981-86 **MEM:** Fellow: Australian Academy Social Sciences; mem.: Council on Foreign Relations **BA:** The Wharton School, 1000 Steinberg Hall 3620 Locust Walk, Philadelphia, PA, 19104

GARRETT, THOMAS A., T: U.S. Representative from Virginia **I:** Government Administration/Government Relations/Government Services **DOB:** 03/27/1972 **PB:** Atlanta **ED:** JD, University Richmond; BA, University Richmond **C:** Member, U.S. House of Representatives for Virginia's 5th District, 2017-; Member, Committee on Foreign Affairs; Member, Committee on Homeland Security; Member, Committee on Education and the Workforce; Member, Republican Study Committee; Member District 22, Virginia State Senate, 2012-2017; Member General Laws and Tech. Committee, Courts of Justice Committee, Education and Health Committee & Privileges and Elections Committee, Virginia State Senate,; Commonwealth attorney, Louisa County, Virginia, **PA:** Republican **BA:** 415 Cannon House Office Building, Washington, DC, 20515

GARTEN, INA, I: Media & Entertainment **DOB:** 02/02/1948 **PB:** Brooklyn **SC:** NY/USA **PT:** Charles H. Rosenberg; Florence Rosenberg **ED:** MBA, George Washington University **C:** Specialty food store owner, manager, chef, Barefoot Contessa, East Hampton, New York, 1985-96; Specialty food

store owner, manager, chef, Barefoot Contessa, Southampton, New York, 1978-85; Former budget analyst, Office Management & Budget, The White House **CW:** Author: Barefoot Contessa Cookbook, 1999, Barefoot Contessa Parties!, 2001, Barefoot Contessa Family Style, 2002, Barefoot in Paris, 2004, Barefoot Contessa at Home, 2006, Barefoot Contessa: Back to Basics, 2008, Barefoot Contessa: How Easy Is That?, 2010, Barefoot Contessa Foolproof: Recipes You Can Trust, 2012, Barefoot Contessa: Make It Ahead, 2014; host (cooking show) Barefoot Contessa: Back to Basics, Food Network, 2002- (Daytime Emmy award for Best Culinary Host, 2009), columnist 'Entertaining is Fun!', Martha Stewart Living magazine, 1999-, 'Entertaining', O, The Oprah Magazine, 2003-, 'Ask the Barefoot Contessa', House Beautiful magazine, 2006-10

GATES, BILL, T: Software Company Executive, Philanthropist **I:** Technology **DOB:** 10/28/1955 **PB:** Seattle **SC:** WA/USA **MS:** Married **SPN:** Melinda Gates **ED:** Student, Harvard University; LLD (hon.), Harvard University, 2007 **C:** Technology adv., Microsoft Corp., Redmond, Washington, 2014—; Co-founder, Traf-O-Data Co., Seattle, Washington, 1972—1973; Non-exec. chairman, Microsoft Corp., Redmond, Washington, 2008—2014; Chief software architect, Microsoft Corp., Redmond, Washington, 2000—2006; CEO, Microsoft Corp., Redmond, Washington, 1981—2000; Executive vice president development activities, Microsoft Corp., Redmond, Washington, 1982—1983; Chairman board, Microsoft Corp., Redmond, Washington, 1981—2008; President, Microsoft Corp., Redmond, Washington, 1977—1982; General partner, Microsoft Corp., Redmond, Washington, 1975—1977; Co-founder, Microsoft Corp., Albuquerque, New Mexico, 1975 **CR:** Board directors Microsoft Corp., 1981—, ICOS Corp., 1990—2005, Berkshire Hathaway Inc., 2004—; speaker Consumer Electronics Show, 2006, 2008; chairman, CEO Cascade Investment LLC, Kirkland, Washington; founder Corbis, 1989 **CIV:** Founder, chairman William H. Gates Foundation, 1994—2000; co-founder Gates Learning Foundation (formerly Gates Libr. Foundation), 1997—2000; co-founder, co-chair, trustee Bill & Melinda Gates Foundation, 2000— **CW:** Co-author (with Nathan Myhrvold & Peter Rinearson): The Road Ahead, 1995 (No. 1 New York Times bestseller); author: Business at the Speed of Thought, 1999 (New York Times, USA Today, Wall St. Journal, Amazon.com bestsellers) **AW:** Co-recipient (with Melinda Gates) Lasker-Bloomberg Public Service award, Albert & Mary Lasker Foundation, 2013; named a Knight Commander of British Empire (KBE), Her Majesty Queen Elizabeth II, 2005; named CEO of Year, Chief Executive magazine, 1994, Innovator of Year, Consumer Electronics Association, 2006; named an Honorary Trustee, Peking University, 2007; named one of The Top 50 Cyber Elite, TIME magazine, 1998, The Three Persons of Year, 2005, The 100 Most Influential People in the World, 2004, 2005, 2006, The World's Richest People, Forbes magazine, 1996—, The Top 100 Most Influential People in Media, The Guardian, 2001, The Top 200 Collectors, ARTnews magazine, 2004, The World's Most Powerful People, Forbes magazine, 2009—14, The Forbes 400: Richest Americans, 1986—, The 50 Who Matter Now, CNNMoney.com Business 2.0, 2006, The 25 Most Powerful People in Business, Fortune Magazine, 2007, The Global Elite, Newsweek magazine, 2008, The 100 Agents of Change, Rolling Stone magazine, 2009; recipient Howard Vollum award, Reed College, Portland, Oregon, 1984, National Tech. medal, US Department Commerce, 1992, James C. Morgan Global Humanitarian award, 2006, Einstein award,

Hebrew University, 2008, Indira Gandhi prize for Peace, Disarmament and Develop. for work with Gates Foundation, 2009, Bower award for Business Leadership, Franklin Institute, 2010, Silver Buffalo award, Boy Scouts of America, 2010, Presidential Medal of Freedom, The White House, 2016 **H:** Art, reading, golf, bridge, tennis **BA:** The Bill and Melinda Gates Foundation, PO Box 23350, Seattle, WA, 23350

GATES, MELINDA FRENCH, T: Charitable Foundation Administrator **I:** Nonprofit & Philanthropy **DOB:** 08/15/1964 **PB:** Dallas **SC:** TX/USA **PT:** Daughter of Raymond Joseph and Elaine Agnes (Amerland) French; **ED:** LHD (hon.), Duke University, 2013; Doctor (hon.), University of Cambridge, 2009; MBA, Duke University Fuqua School of Business, 1987; BS in Computer Sci. & Economics, Duke University, 1986 **C:** Co-chair, trustee, Bill & Melinda Gates Foundation, Seattle, 2000-; General manager information products, Microsoft Corp., Redmond, Washington, 1987-96 **CR:** Board of Directors The Washington Post Co., 2004-10, drugstore.com, 1999-2006 **CIV:** Trustee, Duke University, 1996-2003 Co-chair, Washington State Governor's Commission on Early Learning, **AW:** Co-recipient (with Bill Gates) Lasker-Bloomberg Public Service award, Albert & Mary Lasker Foundation, 2013; named one of The Global Elite, Newsweek magazine, 2008, The 50 Women to Watch, The Wall St. Journal, 2008, 2006, The World's 100 Most Influential People, TIME magazine, 2006, The Three Persons of Year, 2005, The 100 Most Powerful Women, Forbes magazine, 2005-14,Time 100 Most Influential, Dame Commander of the Order of the British Empire, 2013, Padma Bhushan, 2015, Presidential Medal of Freedom, 2016, Legion of Honour, 2017, Otto Hahn Peace Medal, 2016 **MEM:** Mem.: Bilderberg Group **H:** Running

GEBBIA, JOE, T: Co-founder **I:** Business Management/Business Services **CN:** Airbnb **PB:** Atlanta **SC:** GA/USA **ED:** BFA, Rhode Island School of Design **C:** Co-founder, Neighborhood (2017-Present); Co-founder/Chief Performance Officer, Airbnb (2008-Present) **AW:** Named to Fortune Magazines 40 Under 40 (2013)

GEHRY, FRANK, T: Architect **I:** Architecture & Construction **DOB:** 02/28/1929 **PB:** Toronto **SC:** Canada **ED:** Doctorate (hon.), Princeton University, 2013; Doctorate (hon.), University Edinburgh, 2000; Doctorate (hon.), Harvard University, 2000; Doctorate (hon.), Yale University, 2000; Doctorate (hon.), University Southern California, 2000; LLD (hon.), University Toronto, 1998; Doctorate (hon.), Southern California Institute Architecture, 1997; Doctorate (hon.), California College Arts and Crafts; Doctorate (hon.), Whittier College, 1995; HHD (hon.), Occidental College, 1993; DEng (hon.), Tech. University Nova Scotia, 1989; Doctorate of Visual Arts (hon.), California Institute Arts, 1987; DFA (hon.), Otis Art Institute at Parsons School Design, 1989; DFA (hon.), Rhode Island School Design, 1987; Postgrad., Harvard University, 1956-57; BArch, University Southern California, 1954 **CT:** Registered professional architect, California **C:** Principal, Gehry Partners, LLP (formerly Frank O. Gehry & Associates and Gehry & Krueger, Inc.), Santa Monica, California, 1962-; Project designer, planner, Pereira & Luckman, LA, 1957-58; Planning, design and project director, Victor Gruen Associates, LA, 1958-61; Designer, Victor Gruen Associates, LA, 1953-54 **CR:** Distinguished professor architecture Columbia University, New York City; visiting professor UCLA, 1998; visiting scholar Federal Institute Tech., Zürich, Switzerland, 1996-97; Eliot Noyes chair Harvard University, 1984; Charlotte Davenport Professorship

in Architecture Yale University, 1999, 1987-89, 1985, 1982, William Bishop chair, 1979 **CIV:** Trustee, Hereditary Disease Foundation, Santa Monica, California, 1970- **CW:** Principal works include Loyola Law School, LA, 1978-92, Temporary Contemporary Museum, 1983, California Aerospace Museum, 1984, Frances Goldwyn Regional Branch Libr., Hollywood, California, 1986, U.C.I. Information and Computer Sci./Engring. Research Laboratory and Engring Center, Irvine, California, 1986-88, Vitra International Manufacturing Facility and Design Museum, Weil am Rhein, Germany, 1989, Chiat/Day Hdqs., Venice, California, 1991, Advanced Tech. Laboratories Building, University Iowa, Iowa City, 1992, University Toledo Center for Visual Arts, Toledo, Ohio, 1992, Olympic Fish, Olympic Village, Barcelona, 1992, Walt Disney Concert Hall, LA, 1993, Frederick R. Weisman Art Museum, Minneapolis, 1993, Vitra International Hdqs., Basel, Switzerland, 1994, Am. Center, Paris, 1994, Team Disneyland Administration Building, Anaheim, California, 1995, Dancing House, Prague, 1995, EMR Communication and Tech. Center, Bad Oeynhausen, Germany, 1995, Nationale-Nederlanden Building, Prague, Czech Republic, 1996, Guggenheim Museum, Bilbao, Spain, 1997, Vontz Center for Molecular Studies, University Cincinnati, Ohio, 1999, Der Neue Zolihof, Dusseldorf, Germany, 1999, DG Bank Hdqrs., Berlin, Germany, 2000, Experience Music Project, Seattle, 2000, Bard College Center for the Performing Arts, Annandale-on-Hudson, New York, 2001, The Walt Disney Concert Hall, LA, 2002, Peter B. Lewis Weatherhead School Management Case Western Reserve University, Cleveland, 2003, Ray and Maria Stata Center, Massachusetts Institute of Technology, Cambridge, Massachusetts, 2003, Pritzker Pavilion, Millennium Park, Chicago, Illinois, 2004, MARTa, Headford, Germany, 2005, IAC/Interactive Corp. West Coast Hdqs., L.A., California, 2005, Marqués de Riscal Winery, Elciego, Spain, 2006, IAC/Interactive Corp. East Coast Hdqs., New York City, 2007, Peter B. Lewis Libr., Princeton, 2008, Lou Ruvo Center for Brain Health, Las Vegas, 2010, New World Center, Miami Beach, 2011, Opus Hong Kong, 2011, Biomuseo, Panama City, 2014, Louis Vuitton Foundation, Paris, 2014, and several others, selected exhibition designs, , ,; work featured in major architectural publications including Newsweek, Time, Forbes, Economist, Vanity Fair, Art in America, Wall Street Journal, New York Times, LA Times, Washington Post, Le Monde, L'Express, El Correo and Frankfurter Allgemeine,(Principal Work)Dr Chau Chak Wing Building, University of Technology Sydney, 2014, Facebook West Park, Menlo Park California, 2015, Pierre Boulez Concert Hall, 2017, Frank Gehry Residence, 2017(In Progress) Guggenheim Abu Dhabi, Abu Dhabi, United Arab Emirates,Philadelphia Museum of Art, Philadelphia, Pennsylvania underground expansion, Began 2010 **AW:** Named Chancellor, City of Bilbao, Spain, 1998, Hon. Consul, 1997; recipient Presidential Medal of Freedom, The White House, 2016, Prince of Asturias award, 2014, Golden Lion for Lifetime Achievement, Foundation La Biennale di Venezia, 2008, Lifetime Achievement award, Am. for the Arts, 2000, Lotus medal of Merit, Lotos Club, 1999, Gold medal, Royal Architectural Institute Canada, 1998, Friedrich Kiesler prize, Friedrich Kiesler Foundation, 1998, National Medal of Arts, National Endowment of the Arts, 1998, Dorothy and Lilian Gish award, 1994, Praemium Imperiale award, Japan Art Association, 1992, Wolf prize in art, Wolf Foundation, 1992, Pritzker Architecture prize, The Hyatt Foundation, 1989,Harvard Arts Medal, 2016, J Paul Getty Medal, 2015 **MEM:** Fellow: Am. Institute Architects (Gold medal 1999), American Association for the Advancement of Science, American Academy of

Arts and Letters (Arnold W. Brunner Memorial prize in architecture 1983); mem.: Royal Academy Arts (hon. academician 1998), National Academy Design (academician 1994), Am. Academy Rome (trustee 1989) **BA:** Gehry Partners LLP, 12541 Beatrice St, Los Angeles, CA, 90066

GELLER, MARGARET JOAN, T: Astrophysicist, Educator **I:** Sciences **DOB:** 12/08/1947 **PB:** Ithaca **SC:** NY/USA **PT:** Daughter of Seymour and Sarah Geller. **ED:** DSc (hon.), University of Rovira i Virgili, Tarragona, Spain, 2009; DSc (hon.), Colby College, 2009; DSc (hon.), University of Massachusetts, Dartmouth, 2000; DSc (hon.), Gustavus Adolphus College, 1997; DSc (hon.), Connecticut College, 1995; PhD, Princeton University, 1975; MA, Princeton University, 1972; AB, University of California, Bekeley, 1970 **C:** Astrophysicist, Smithsonian Astrophys. Observatory, Cambridge, 1983-; IBM lecturer, Colby College, 2010; Lecturer, Ford Motor Co., University Michigan, 2008; Assistant professor, Harvard University, Cambridge, 1980-83; Research associate, Harvard College Observatory, Cambridge, Massachusetts, 1978-80 **CR:** Distinguished fellow University of California, Irvine, California, 2006 distinguished lecturer National Science Foundation, 2004 Hilldale lecturer University Wisconsin, 1999 Bethe lecturer Cornell University, 1996 Hogg lecturer Royal Astro. Society Can., 1993 Brickwedde distinguished lecturer JHU, 1993 Goodspeed-Richardo lecturer University Pennsylvania, 1992 **CW:** Contributor articles to professional journals; member editorial board Sci., 1991-94 **AW:** Named Ford Motor Co. Distinguished Lecturer, University Michigan, 2008, Libr. Lion, New York Pub. Libr., 1997; recipient Magellanic Premium prize, Am. Philosophical Society, 2008, ADION medal, 2003, Klopsteg award, Am. Association Physics Teachers, 1996, Newcomb-Cleve. prize, 1989-90; fellow, MacArthur Foundation, 1990-95,Karl Schwarzschild Medal, 2014, Julias Edgar Lilienfeld Prize, 2013, James Craig Watson Medal, 2010 **MEM:** Fellow: American Association for the Advancement of Science, APS; mem.: National Academy of Sciences (council member 2000-03, James Craig Watson medal 2010), Associate Univs. Research in Astronomy (dir.-at-large), Am. Astron Society (Henry Norris Russell lecturer 2010, councillor 1985-88), Am. Academy Art and Scis. (council member), International Astron Union, Phi Beta Kappa (senator 1998-99)

GENNETTE, JEFFREY, T: Chairman and CEO of Macy's Inc. **I:** Retail/Sales **CN:** Macy's, Inc. (formerly Federated Dept. Stores Inc.) **ED:** BA in English & Art History, Stanford University, California, 1983 **C:** Chairman, Macy's Inc. 2018-; Chief Executive Officer, Macy's Inc. 2017-;; President, Macy's Inc. 2014-2017; Chief merchandising officer Macy's Inc., Macy's, Inc. (formerly Federated Department Stores Inc.), 2009-2014; Regional vice president Broadway stores, Carter Hawley Hale Stores Inc.,; Vice president, manager Emporium/Weinstocks stores, Carter Hawley Hale Stores Inc., 1994; Store manager, Food and Agriculture Organization Schwarz Union Square, San Francisco, 1989-90; Chairman, CEO Macy's West, Macy's, Inc. (formerly Federated Department Stores Inc.), 2008-09; Chairman, Macy's Northwest, Macy's, Inc. (formerly Federated Department Stores Inc.), Seattle, 2005-08; Executive vice president, director stores, Macy's Central, Macy's, Inc. (formerly Federated Department Stores Inc.), Atlanta, 2004-05; Senior vice president, general merchandise manager Macy's West, Macy's, Inc. (formerly Federated Department Stores Inc.), 2001-04; Vice president, store manager, Macy's, Inc. (formerly Federated Department Stores Inc.), Minneapolis, 1993-94; Store manager, Macy's, Inc. (formerly

Federated Department Stores Inc.), Santa Rosa, California, 1990-93; Various positions in stores & merchandise, Macy's, Inc. (formerly Federated Department Stores Inc.), 1983-89; Joined Macy's West division, Macy's, Inc. (formerly Federated Department Stores Inc.), San Francisco, 1983 **CR:** Board directors Macy's Inc., 2006- **BA:** 7 West 7th St, Cincinnati, OH, 45202

GEORGE, PAUL, T: Professional Basketball Player **I:** Athletics **PB:** Palmdale **SC:** CA/USA **ED:** Fresno State, 2008-10 **C:** Oklahoma City Thunder, Small Forward, 2017-; Indiana Pacers, Small Forward, 2010-17 **AW:** NBA All-Star, 2013, 2014, 2016–2018, All-NBA Third Team, 2013, 2014, 2016, NBA All-Defensive First Team, 2014, NBA All-Defensive Second Team 2013, 2016, NBA Most Improved Player 2013, NBA All-Rookie Second Team, 2011

GERARD, RED, T: Olympic Snowboarder **I:** Athletics **PB:** Rocky River **SC:** CO/USA **AW:** Olympic Gold Medal in Slopestyle, 2018

GERE, RICHARD, T: Actor **I:** Media & Entertainment **DOB:** 08/31/1949 **PB:** Philadelphia **SC:** PA/USA **ED:** Attended, University of Massachusetts **CIV:** Co-founder, Tibet House; Creator, The Gere Foundation; Chairman, Board of Directors, International Campaign for Tibet **CW:** Played trumpet, piano, guitar and bass and composed music with various musical groups; Acting appearances with Provincetown Playhouse in Great God Brown, Camino Real, Rosencrantz and Guildenstern are Dead; Off-Broadway productions Killer's Head, Richard Farina: Long Time Coming and Long Time Gone, Back Bog Beast Bait; Broadway productions Taming of the Shrew, Midsummer Night's Dream, Habeas Corpus, Bent, Grease; Appeared in and composed music for Volpone at Seattle Repertory Theatre; Actor: (films) Report to the Commissioner, 1975, Baby Blue Marine, 1976, Looking for Mr. Goodbar, 1977, Days of Heaven, 1978, Blood Brothers, 1978, Yanks, 1979, American Gigolo, 1980, An Officer and a Gentleman, 1982, Breathless, 1983, Beyond the Limit, 1983, The Cotton Club, 1984, King David, 1985, Power, 1986, No Mercy, 1986, Miles from Home, 1988, Internal Affairs, 1990, Pretty Woman, 1990, Rhapsody in August, 1991, Sommersby, 1993, Mr. Jones, 1993, Intersection, 1994, First Knight, 1995, Primal Fear, 1996, Red Corner, 1997, The Jackal, 1997, An Alan Smithee Film: Burn Hollywood Burn, 1998, Runaway Bride, 1999, Autumn in New York, 2000, Dr. T and the Women, 2000, The Mothman Prophecies, 2002, Unfaithful, 2002, Chicago, 2002, (Screen Actors Guild Award for Outstanding Performance by a Cast in a Motion Picture), Shall We Dance?, 2004, Bee Season, 2005, The Hoax, 2007, The Hunting Party, 2007, I'm Not There, 2007, Nights in Rodanthe, 2008, Brooklyn's Finest, 2009, Amelia, 2009, The Double, 2011, Arbitrage, 2012, Movie 43, 2013, Henry & Me (voice), 2013, The Second Best Exotic Marigold Hotel, 2015, The Benefactor, 2015, Norman: The Moderate Rise and Tragic Fall of a New York Fixer, 2016, The Dinner, 2017, Three Christs, 2017; (TV films) Strike Force, 1975, And the Band Played On, 1993; (TV appearances) Kojak, 1973; Actor, Executive Producer: (films) Final Analysis, 1992, Mr. Jones, 1993, Sommersby, 1993; Actor, Producer: (films) Hachiko: A Dog's Story, 2009, Time Out of Mind, 2014; author: Pilgrim Photo Collection, 1998 **AW:** Recipient, Marian Anderson Award, City of Philadelphia, 2007, Joel Siegel Humanitarian Award, Critics Choice Awards, 2009, Medal of Gratitude, Albanian President Bamir Topi, 2012, George Eastman Award for Distinguished Contribution to the Art of Film, George Eastman House International Museum for Photograph and Film, 2012

BA: Gere Foundation Hirsch Wallerstein Hayum Matlof LLP, 10100 Santa Monica Blvd Ste 1700, Los Angeles, CA, 90067

GERKEN, HEATHER K., T: Law Educator **I:** Education/Educational Services **ED:** JD, University of Michigan, Summa Cum Laude, 1994; AB, Princeton University, Summa Cum Laude, 1991 **C:** Co-Founder, Adviser, San Francisco Affirmative Litigation Project, Yale Law School; Dean, Yale University, 2017-Present; J. Skelly Wright Professor of Law, Yale Law School, 2008-Present; Professor, Yale Law School, 2006-2008; Visiting Professor of Law, Yale Law School, New Haven, CT, 2005-2006; Professor, Harvard Law School, 2005-2006; Eugene P. Beard Faculty Fellow, Center for Ethics and the Profession, Harvard University, 2003-2004; Assistant Professor of Law, Harvard Law School, Cambridge, MA, 2000-2005; Associate, Jenner & Block LLP, 1996-2000; Law Clerk, Justice David H. Souter, U.S. Supreme Court, Washington, DC, 1995-1996; Law Clerk, Hon. Stephen Reinhardt, U.S. Court of Appeals, Ninth Circuit, Los Angeles, CA, 1994-1995 **CR:** Senior Adviser, Obama for America, 2008; Academic Steering Committee, Chair, Democratic Governance Working Group, The Tobin Project; Academic Advisor, The Roosevelt Institute; Board of Supervisors, Center on Law and Redistricting **CIV:** (Trustee) Campaign Legal Center, Yale Law Journal **CW:** Author, The Democracy Index: Why Our Election System Is Failing and How to Fix It, 2009; Contributor, Articles, Professional Journals **AW:** Yale Law Women Faculty Teaching Award, Yale Law School, 2009; Sachs-Freund Award for Teaching Excellence, Harvard Law School, 2003 **MEM:** Redistricting Task Force, American Bar Association; American Law Institute **BAR:** District of Columbia, 1998; State of Maryland, 1997

GERMANOTTA, STEFANI (LADY GAGA), T: Singer, Songwriter **I:** Media & Entertainment **DOB:** 03/28/1986 **PB:** Yonkers **SC:** NY/USA **PT:** Daughter of Joseph and Cynthia (Bissett) Germanotta. **ED:** Attended, New York University Tisch School of Arts, New York City **C:** Creative Director, Polaroid, 2010-; Co-founder, Born This Way Foundation, 2012-; Former Songwriter, Interscope Records, **CW:** Singer: (albums) The Fame, 2008 (Best Album of Year, World Music Awards, 2010, Best International Album, Brit Music Awards, 2010, Best Electronic or Dance Album, Grammy Awards, 2010, Top Electronic/Dance Album, Billboard Music Awards, 2011), The Cherrytree Sessions, 2009, The Fame Monster, 2009 (Best Pop Vocal Album, Grammy Awards, 2011), Born This Way, 2011 (Top Dance Album, Billboard Music Awards, 2012), ARTPOP, 2013, (with Tony Bennett) Cheek to Cheek, 2014 (Best Traditional Pop Vocal Album, Grammy Awards, 2015), Joanne, 2016, (songs) Just Dance, 2008 (Best Pop Dance Track, International Dance Music Awards, 2009), Poker Face, 2008 (Best Dance Recording, Grammy Awards, 2010, Best Song of Year, World Music Awards, 2010), Bad Romance, 2009 (Best Female Video, Best Pop Video, Best Dance Music Video, Video of Year, MTV Video Music Awards, 2010, Best Female Pop Vocal Performance, Best Short Form Music Video, Grammy Awards, 2011), (featuring Beyonce) Telephone, 2010 (Best Collaboration, MTV Video Music Awards, 2010, Video of Year, BET Awards, 2010), Alejandro, 2010 (Best Pop Dance Track, International Dance Music Awards, 2011), Born this Way, 2011 (Favorite Album of Year, People's Choice Awards, 2012); appeared in (TV series) Gossip Girl, 2009, (TV specials) Lady Gaga Presents The Monster Ball Tour at Madison Square Garden, 2011, host A Very Gaga Thanksgiving, 2011; actress: (films) Machete Kills, 2013; (TV series) American Horror Story, 2015-16 (Best

Performance by an Actress in a Leading Role in a Series, Limited Series or Motion Picture Made for TV, Golden Globe Awards, 2016), (cameo appearances) Men in Black 3, 2012, Sin City: A Dame to Kill For, 2014 **AW:** Named Top Dance Artist, Billboard Music Awards, 2012, 2011, Top Pop Artist, 2011, Best New Artist, World Music Awards, 2010, Best Pop/Rock Artist, 2010, Crossover Artist of Year, Latin Billboard Music Awards, 2010, Favorite Pop/Rock Female Artist, American Music Awards, 2010, Favorite Pop Artist, People's Choice Awards, 2010, Favorite Breakout Music Artist, 2010, Best New Artist, MTV Video Music Awards, 2009, Breakthrough Solo Artist, International Dance Music Awards, 2009; named one of The 100 Most Powerful Women in Entertainment, Hollywood Reporter, 2013, 2011, The 100 Most Powerful Women, Forbes magazine, 2010-14, The 100 Most Influential People in the World, TIME magazine, 2010, Barbara Walters' 10 Most Fascinating People of Year, 2009; recipient Randy Shilts Visibility award, Servicemembers Legal Defense Network (SLDN), 2011, Best Video with a Message, MTV Video awards, 2011, Best Female Video, 2011, Fashion Icon award, Council Fashion Designers America (CFDA), 2011, Best Dressed of Year award, Vogue Magazine, 2010, GLAAD Media award for Outstanding Music Artist, 2010, Teen Choice award for Choice Music: Female Artist, 2010, International Breakthrough Act award, Brit Music Awards, 2010, International Female Solo Artist award, 2010, Guinness World Record, Most Powerful Popstar, 2015

GERVAIS, RICKY, T: Actor **I:** Media & Entertainment **DOB:** 06/25/1961 **PB:** Reading **PT:** Son of Lawrence Raymond and Eva Sophia Gervais; **ED:** BA in Philosophy, Univ. College, London **C:** Disc jockey, XFM Radio Station, London,; Actor 1999- **CW:** Actor: (films) Dog Eat Dog, 2001, Valiant (voice), 2005, For Your Consideration, 2006, Night at the Museum, 2006, Stardust, 2007, Ghost Town, 2008, Night at the Museum: Battle of the Smithsonian, 2009, Spy Kids: All the Time in the World in 4D (voice), 2011, Escape from Planet Earth (voice), 2013, Muppets Most Wanted, 2014, Night at the Museum: Secret of the Tomb, 2014, The Little Prince (voice), 2015; (actor, director co-writer): The Invention of Lying, 2009; actor: (TV films) Legend of the Lost Tribe (voice), 2002; (TV series) The 11 O'Clock Show, 1998, Meet Ricky Gervais, 2000; actor, writer, director (TV series) Extras, 2005-07 (Primetime Emmy award for Outstanding Lead Actor in a Comedy Series, Academy TV Arts and Scis., 2007, Golden Globe award for Best TV Series - Musical or Comedy, 2008, BAFTA award for Best Comedy Performance, 2007), writer Bruiser, 2000, Meet Ricky Gervais, 2000, The Sketch Show, 2001, Homer Simpson: This Is Your Wife, The Simpsons, 2006, Life's Too Short, 2011-13; writer, prodr.: TV series The Office (US version), 2005-13; writer, executive producer, actor (TV series) The Ricky Gervais Show, 2010-12; writer, executive producer, actor, director (TV series) Derek, 2012-14; director, co-writer: films Cemetery Junction, 2010; executive prodr.: (TV films) The Making of Derek, 2013; actor, writer, director (TV series) The Office (UK version), 2001-03 (Golden Globe award for Best Actor in a TV Series - Musical or Comedy, 2004, BAFTA award for Best Comedy Performance, Situation Comedy award, 2002, 2003, 2004); performer: (TV comedy special) Comic Relief 2003: The Big Hair Do, 2003, Out of England: The Stand-Up Special, 2008, Out of England 2: The Stand-Up Special, 2010; author (illustrated by Rob Steen): (children's books) Flanimals, 2005, More Flanimals, 2006, (Film) Special Correspondents, 2016, David Brent: Life on the Road, 2016, Blazing Samurai, 2017, (Television) Galavant, 2015, BoJack Horseman, 2015, 73rd Golden Globe Awards, 2016

AW: Co-recipient Rave award for podcast, Wired magazine, 2006; named London's Funniest Man, Time Out magazine, No. 3 on the list Brit. Culture's Top 50 Movers and Shakers, BBC 3, 2004; named one of The 100 Most Influential People in the World, TIME magazine, 2010; recipient O.K. Comedy award, 2003

GERWIG, GRETA, T: Actress **I:** Media & Entertainment **DOB:** 08/04/1983 **PB:** Sacremento **SC:** California/USA **ED:** Diploma, Barnard College (2006) **CW:** Actress, "Isle of Dogs" (2018); Actress, "Lady Bird" (2017); Actress, "Saturday Night Light" (2017); Actress, "The Mindy Project" (2016); Actress, "Wiener-Dog" (2016); Actress, "Jackie" (2016); Actress, "20th Century Women" (2016); Actress, "Mistress America" (2015); Actress, "Maggie's Plan" (2015); Actress, "Portlandia" (2015); Actress, "How I Met Your Dad" (2014); Actress, "Eden" (2014); Actress, "The Humbling" (2014); Actress, "To Rome with Love" (2012); Actress, "Lola Versus" (2012); Actress, "Frances Ha" (2012); Actress, "China IL" (2011); Actress, "No Strings Attached" (2011); Actress, "Damsels in Distress" (2011); Actress, "Arthur" (2011); Actress, "Greenberg" (2010); Actress, "Art House" (2010); Actress, "Northern Comfort" (2010); Actress, "The Dish & the Spoon" (2010); Actress, "The House of the Devil" (2009); Actress, "You Wont Miss Me" (2009); Actress, "Baghead" (2008); Actress, "Yeast" (2008); Actress, "Nights and Weekends" (2008); Actress, "Quick Feet, Soft Hands" (2008); Actress, "I Thought You Finally Completely Lost It" (2008); Actress, "Hannah Takes the Stairs" (2007); Actress, "LOL" (2006) **AW:** Listee, Time 100 Most Influential (2018)

GHANI, RULA, T: First Lady of Afghanistan **I:** Government Administration/Government Relations/Government Services **SC:** Lebanon **ED:** Masters Degree in Political Studies, American University of Beirut (1974); Diploma, Sciences Po (1969) **CR:** First Lady of Afghanistan (2014-Present) **AW:** Named One of TIME's 100 Most Influential People, TIME Magazine (2015)

GIANFORTE, GREG R., T: U.S. Representative from Montana, Former Information Technology Executive **I:** Government Administration/Government Relations/Government Services **ED:** PhD in Computer Sci. (hon.), Montana State University, 2007; MS in Computer Sci., Stevens Institute Tech.; BEE, Stevens Institute Tech. **C:** Member, U.S. House of Representatives from Montana's at-large District, 2017-, Member, Committee on Natural Resources, Committee on Oversight and Government Reform; Founder, RightNow Technologies, Inc., 1995-; Chairman, president and CEO, RightNow Technologies, Inc.; Founder, president, Brightwork Devel. Corp. (acquired by McAfee Associates), 1986-94; Vice president, North America Sales, McAfee Associates, Inc. (formerly Network Associates, Inc.); Managing director, Bozeman Tech. Incubator Inc.; With, AT&T Bell Laboratories **CIV:** Founder Bootstrap Montana **CW:** Author: Bootstrapping Your Business: Start and Grow a Successful Company with Almost No Money; pub. Eight to Great: Eight Steps to Delivering an Exceptional Customer Experience, 2008 **AW:** Recipient Entrepreneur of the Year, Ernst & Young, 2003, Stevens Honor award, Stevens Institute Tech., 2003, Hall of Fame, CRM, 2007 **BA:** 1419 Longworth HOB, Washington, DC, 20515

GIBBONS, JULIA SMITH, T: Federal Judge **I:** Law and Legal Services **DOB:** 12/23/1950 **PB:** Pulaski **SC:** Tennessee **PT:** Daughter of John Floyd and Julia Jackson (Abernathy) Smith; **SPN:** Married William Lockhart Gibbons, August 11, 1973; **CH:** children: Rebecca Carey, William Lockhart Junior

ED: JD, University Virginia, 1975; BA, Vanderbilt University, 1972 **CT:** Bar: Tennessee 1975. **C:** Judge, US Court Appeals (6th cir.), Memphis, 2002-; Chief Judge, US District Court (we. district) Tennessee, Memphis, 1994-2000; Judge, US District Court (we. district) Tennessee, Memphis, 1983-2002; Judge, 15th Judicial Cir., Memphis, 1981-83; Legal Advisor, Governor Lamar Alexander, Nashville, 1979-81; Associate, Farris, Hancock, Gilman, Branan, Lanier & Hellen, Memphis, 1976-79; Law Clerk to Judge, US Court Appeals, 1975-76 **AW:** Recipient She Knows Where She's Going Award, Girls, Inc., 1992, Outstanding Judge of Year Award, Memphis Lawyers, 1985 **MEM:** Master: Leo Bearman, Senior Am. Inn of Court; fellow: Memphis and Shelby County Bar Foundation, Tennessee Bar Foundation, Am. Bar Foundation; mem.: Central Gardens Association, Tennessee Women's Forum, Association for Women Attorneys (president 1993, Marion Griffin-Frances Loring award 1992), Federal Judges Association, Memphis Bar Association (Heroine for Women in Law award 2000, Outstanding Judge of Year award 2001), Memphis Rotary Club (Treasurer 1991-92, vice president 1992-93, Paul Harris Fellow, president 1994-95), Phi Beta Kappa, Order of Coif **BA:** 100 East Fifth Street, Cincinnati, OH, USA, 45202

GIBBS, BOB, T: U.S. Representative From Ohio **I:** Government Administration/Government Relations/Government Services **DOB:** 06/14/1954 **PB:** Peru **SC:** IN/USA **ED:** BA, Agriculture Technical Institute, Ohio State University, 1974 **C:** U.S. Congress From Seventh Ohio District, 2013-Present; U.S. House Transportation & Infrastructure Committee, 2011-Present; U.S. House Agricultural Committee, 2011-Present; U.S. Congress From 18th Ohio District, Washington, DC, 2011-2013; U.S. District 22, Ohio State Senate, 2009-2010; U.S. District 97, Ohio House of Representatives, 2003-2008; Owner, Gibbs Enterprises LLC, 2004-2009; Co-Founder, Owner, Hidden Hollow Farms LLC, Holmes County, Ohio, 1978-2004 **AW:** Watchdog Treasury Award, United Conservatives of Ohio, 2004, Guardian of Small Business Award, National Federation of Independent Business, 2004, Legislator of the Year Award, Ohio Restaurant Association, All-America Award, National Pork Producers Council **MEM:** Board of Trustees, Ohio Farm Bureau Federation, 1985-Present, Past President, Ohio Farm Bureau Federation, National Federation of Independent Business, Ashland Area Chamber of Commerce, Wadsworth Chamber of Commerce, Holmes County Chamber of Commerce, Pheasants Forever **PA:** Republican **BA:** U.S. House of Representatives, 329 Cannon House Office Building, Washington, DC, 20515

GIBBS, JOE JACKSON, T: Former NFL Coach **I:** Athletics **DOB:** 11/25/1940 **PB:** Mocksville, North Carolina **ED:** MS, San Diego State University, 1966; BS, San Diego State University, 1964; Attended, Cerritos Junior College **C:** Founder, Owner, Joe Gibbs Racing, 1991-; Special Adv. to Owner, Washington Redskins, 2008-; Head Coach, Team President, Washington Redskins, 2004-07; Head Coach, Washington Redskins, 1981-92; Offensive Coordinator, San Diego Chargers, 1979-80; Offensive Coordinator, Tampa Bay Buccaneers, 1978; Running Backs Coach, St. Louis Cardinals, 1973-77; Running Backs Coach, University Arkansas, 1971-72; Offensive Line Coach, University Southern California, 1969-70; Offensive Line Coach, Florida State University, 1967-68; Offensive Line Coach, San Diego State University, 1964-66 **CR:** Sports Commentator NBC, 1993-98 **CW:** Co-author (with Jerry B. Jenkins): Joe Gibes: Fourth and One, 1992; co-author: (with Ken Abraham) Racing to Win: Establish Your Game Plan For Success, 2003,

(Books)Game Plan For Life, 2009 **AW:** Named NFL Coach of the Year, The Sporting News, 1991, 1983, 1982, Associated Press NFL Coach of the Year, 1983, 1982, United Press International NFL Coach of Year, 1982; named one of Redskins' Ring of Fame, The Most Influential People in the World of Sports, Business Week, 2007; Named to Pro Football Hall of Fame, 1996 **ACH:** Achievements include being a member of Super Bowl Championship winning Washington Redskins, 1983, 1988, 1992; winning four NASCAR Championships, 2000, 2002, 2005,2015,Sporting News Cup, 1982-83, Sporting News COY, 1982-83, 1991, Super Bowl Champion XVII, XXII, XXVI

GIBSON, BOB, T: Former Professional Baseball Player **I:** Athletics **DOB:** 11/09/1935 **PB:** Omaha **SC:** NE/USA **PT:** Son of Pack Gobson and Victoria Gibson; **ED:** Student, Creighton University **C:** Special adv., St. Louis Cardinals,; Special adv. to American League president Gene Budig, Major League Baseball, 1998; Broadcaster, KMOX Sports Div., St. Louis,; Coach, Atlanta Braves, 1982-84; Coach, New York Mets, 1981-82; Pitcher, St. Louis Cardinals, 1959-75 **CW:** Co-author (with Lonnie Wheeler): Stranger to the Game: The Autobiography of Bob Gibson, 1996; (with Reggie Jackson & Lonnie Wheeler) Sixty Feet, Six Inches: A Hall of Fame Pitcher and a Hall of Fame Hitter Talk About How the Game Is Played, 2009 **AW:** Recipient National League Cy Young award, 1968, 1970, Golden Glove award, 1965-73; named National League Most Valuable Player, 1968, World Series Most Valuable Player, 1964, 1967; named to National League All-Star Team, 1962, 65-70, 72, The Baseball Hall of Fame, 1981,Major League Baseball All-Century Team, 1999, World Series Champion, 1964, 1967, NL Wins Leader, 1970, MLB ERA Leader, 1968, NL Strikeout Leader, 1968 **ACH:** Achievements include Pitching a no-hitter against the Pittsburgh Pirates, August 14, 1971

GIBSON, MEL, T: Actor, Film Director and Producer **I:** Media & Entertainment **DOB:** 01/03/1956 **PB:** Peekskill **SC:** NY/USA **PT:** Son of Hutton Peter Gibson & Anne Patricia (Reilly) G.; **MS:** Married **SPN:** Robyn Denise Moore, June 7, 1980 (div. December 23, 2011); **CH:** Hannah, Edward, Christian, William, Louis, Milo, Thomas **ED:** LHD (hon.), Loyola Marymount University, 2003; Grad., National Institute Dramatic Art, Sydney, Australia, 1977 **C:** Founder, Icon Productions, **CW:** Actor: (films) Summer City, 1977, Mad Max, 1979, Tim, 1979, Mad Max II: The Road Warrior, 1981, Gallipoli, 1981, The Year of Living Dangerously, 1982, Attack Force Z, 1982, Mrs. Soffel, 1984, The River, 1984, The Bounty, 1984, Mad Max Beyond Thunderdome, 1985, Lethal Weapon, 1987, Tequila Sunrise, 1988, Lethal Weapon 2, 1989, Hamlet, 1990, Air America, 1990, Bird on a Wire, 1990, Lethal Weapon 3, 1992, Maverick, 1994, Pocahontas (voice), 1995, Ransom, 1996, Conspiracy Theory, 1997, Lethal Weapon 4, 1998, Payback, 1999, What Women Want, 2000, The Patriot, 2000, Chicken Run (voice), 2000, The Million Dollar Hotel, 2000, We Were Soldiers, 2002, Signs, 2002, Edge of Darkness, 2010, The Beaver, 2011, Machete Kills, 2013, The Expendables 3, 2014, Blood Father, 2016, Hacksaw Ridge, 2016, Daddy's Home 2, 2017, The Bombing, 2018; actor, director (films) The Man Without a Face, 1993, actor, producer Forever Young, 1992, The Singing Detective, 2003, actor, director, producer Braveheart, 1995 (Academy award for Best Director, 1995, Academy award for Best Picture, 1995, Golden Globe award for Best Director, 1995, Critics' Choice award for Best Director, 1995, Special Achievement in Filmmaking award, National Board Rev. Motion Pictures, 1995), screenwriter, director, producer The Passion of the

Christ, 2004, Apocalypto, 2006, screenwriter, actor, producer Get the Gringo, 2012, executive producer (TV films) The Three Stooges, 2000, Invincible, 2001,Family Curse, 2003, Complete Savages, 2004, Clubhouse, 2004, Carrier, 2008,; Leonard Cohen: I'm Your Man, 2005; prodr.: (films) Stonehearst Asylum, 2014; appeared in documentary Who Killed the Electric Car?, 2006, appearances in plays (with Nimrod Theatre Co.) Death of a Salesman, Romeo and Juliet, (with South Australian Theatre Co.) Oedipus, Henry IV, Cedoona **AW:** Named Innovator of Year, The Hollywood Reporter, 2004, Man of Year, Hasty Pudding Theatricals, Harvard University, 1997, Favorite Motion Picture Actor, People's Choice Awards, 2004, 2003, 2003, 2001, 1997, 1991; named one of The World's Most Powerful Celebrities, Forbes magazine, 2004, 50 Most Powerful People in Hollywood, Premiere magazine, 2003-06 **BA:** The Spanky Taylor Company, 3727 W Magnolia, Suite 300, Burbank, CA, 91505

GILL, VINCE, T: country musician, singer **I:** Media & Entertainment **DOB:** 04/12/1957 **PB:** Norman **PT:** Son of J. Stanley Gill; Married Janis Oliver, 1980 (div. 1997); 1 child, Jenny; Married Amy Grant, March 2000; 1 child, Corrina. **CW:** With Pure Praire League, 1980, The Time Jumpers, 2010; appeared on Dire Straits album, On Every Street, 1991; performed duets with Reba McEntre, Emmylou Harris, Patty Loveless, Ricky Skaggs; solo albums include: Turn me Loose, 1984, The Things That Matter, 1985, The Way Back Home, 1987, The Best of Vince Gill, 1989, When I Call Your Name, 1989, Pocket Full of Gold, 1991, I Never Knew Lonely, 1992, I Still Believe in You, 1992, Let There Be Peace on Earth, 1993, When Love Finds You, 1994, Vince Gill and Friends, 1994, Souvenirs, 1995, High Lonesome Sound, 1996, The Key, 1998, Let's Make Sure We Kiss Goodbye, 2000, Next Big Thing, 2003, Christmas, 2003, These Days, 2006, Guitar Slinger, 2011, Bakersfield, 2013, Down to My Last Bad Habit, 2016; numerous musical videos. **AW:** Recipient Grammy award for Best Male Country Performance 1990, 1992, 1994-98, 2003, 2007, Best Country Song, 1992, 1995, Best Country Collaboration With Vocals, 1991, 1996, Best Country Instrumental Performance, 1998, 2001, 2009, Best Country Gospel Album, 2005, Best Country Album, 2008; 2 Country Music Association Awards, 1991, Instrumentalist of Year award The Nashville Network/Music City News, 1991, 3 Gold albums, 7 Platinum albums, numerous Country Music Association awards, including Male Vocalist of Year, 1991-95, Song of Year, 1992, 1993, 1996, Entertainer of Year, 1993, 1994, Album of Year, 1993, Vocal Event of Year, 1996, 2007, Country Single of Year award Am. Music Awards, 1994, Academy Country Music Awards, 1984, 1992, 1993, Academy Country Music Home Depot Humanitarian award, 2006, TNN/Music City News awards, 1991-94, 1996, Music City News Songwriters Awards, 1990-94, BMI awards, 1987, 1991-93, 1995, 1996, Nashville Music Awards, 1994-96, Christian Country Music Association Awards, 1996, Minnie Pearl award, 1993, Harmony award, 1993, Tennessean of Year award, 1994, Outstanding Nashvillian of Year award Kiwanis, 1994, Orville H. Gibson Lifetime Achievement award, 1997, BMI Icon award, 2014, Irving Waugh Award of Excellence, Country Music Association Awards, 2014; Vince Gill Tennessee PGA Junior Golf Tournament named in his honor, 1997; named to Nashville Songwriters Hall of Fame, 2005, Country Music Hall of Fame, 2007, Hollywood Walk of Fame, 2012, CMA Humanitarian Award, 2017, 2017 Grammy for Best American Roots Song, 2017

GILLIBRAND, KIRSTEN ELIZABETH RUTNICK, T: U.S. Senator from New York **I:** Government Administration/Government Relations/Government Services **DOB:** 12/09/1966 **PB:** Albany **PT:** Daughter of Douglas P. and Polly (Noonan) Rutnick; **ED:** JD, UCLA School Law, 1991; AB in Asian Studies, magna cum laude, Dartmouth College, Hanover, New Hampshire, 1988 **CT:** Bar: US District Court (southern & eastern district) New York, DC 1993, New York 1992 **C:** US Senator from New York, Washington, 2009-; Member, US Congress from 20th New York District, Washington, 2007-09; Partner commercial litigation practice, Boies, Schiller & Flexner LLP, Albany, New York, 2001-07; Special counsel to secretary, US Department Housing & Urban Devel. (HUD), Washington, 2000-01; Law clerk to Hon. Roger J. Miner, US Court Appeals (2nd cir.), 1992-93; Associate, Davis, Polk & Wardwell LLP, 1993-2000; Associate, Davis, Polk & Wardwell LLP, 1991-92 **CIV:** Member adv. board, Brennan Center Justice, Board member, Commission Greenway Heritage Conservancy Hudson River Valley, Board member, Eleanor Roosevelt Legacy Committee, Chairman, Women's Leadership Forum Network **CW:** Author: Off the Sidelines: Raise Your Voice, Change the World, 2014 **AW:** Named one of The 100 Most Influential People in the World, TIME magazine, 2014, The 50 Most Powerful Women in New York, Crain's New York Business, 2011, 2009; recipient American Jurisprudence Book award **MEM:** Mem.: American Bar Association, Association Bar City of New York (chairman committee on government ethics 1998-99, 2000-), Women's Bar Association, Blue Dog Coalition **PA:** Democrat

GILLON, MICHAEL, T: Astronomer **I:** Sciences **C:** Member, CHEOPS Team, 2013-; Scientist, University of Liege, 2009-; Postdoctoral Stay, University of Geneva, 2006-09 **AW:** Time 100 Most Influential, 2017

GINGRICH (NEWTON LEROY GINGRICH), NEWT, T: Writer, Former U.S. Representative from Georgia **I:** Government Administration/Government Relations/Government Services **DOB:** 06/17/1943 **PB:** Harrisburg **PT:** Son of Robert Bruce and Kathleen (Daugherty) Gingrich; **ED:** PhD in European History, Tulane University, New Orleans, 1971; MA, Tulane University, New Orleans, 1968; BA, Emory University, Atlanta, 1965 **C:** Founder, Center for Health Transformation, 2003-; Panelist Crossfire, CNN, 2013-14; Founder, Committee for New American Leadership, Washington, 2000; Political analyst, Fox News Channel, 1999-2011; Chairman, The Gingrich Group, 1999-2011; Speaker of House, US Congress from 6th Georgia District, Washington, 1995-99; Member, US Congress from 6th Georgia District, Washington, 1979-99; Assistant professor history, West Georgia College, Carrollton, 1970-78 **CR:** Candidate for Republican nomination 2012 US Presidential Election; Distinguished visiting fellow Hoover Institution, Stanford University, 1999-; senior fellow American Enterprise Institute (AEI), 1999-; co-founder Conservative Opportunity Society; speaker, chairman emeritus GOPAC; adjunct professor Reinhardt College, Waleska, Georgia, 1994-95 **CW:** Author: (nonfiction) To Renew America, 1995, Lessons Learned the Hard Way: A Personal Report, 1998, Winning The Future: A 21st Century Contract With America, 2005, Rediscovering God in America: Reflections on the Role of Faith in Our Nation's History and Future, 2006, Drill Here, Drill Now, Pay Less: A Handbook for Slashing Gas Prices and Solving Our Energy Crisis, 2008, To Save America: Stopping Obama's Secular-Socialist Machine, 2010, A Nation Like No Other: Why American Exceptionalism Matters, 2011, $2.50 A

Gallon: Why Obama Is Wrong and Cheap Gas Is Possible, 2012, Breakout: Pioneers of the Future, Prison Guards of the Past and the Epic Battle That Will Decide America's Fate, 2013; co-author (with Marianne Gingrich): Window of Opportunity: A Blueprint for the Future, 1984; co-author: (with Vince Haley & Rick Tyler) Real Change: From the World that Fails to the World that Works, 2008; co-author: (with Callista Gingrich) (nonfitcion) Rediscovering God in America, 2012; co-author: (with William R. Forstchen) (novels) Nineteen Forty-Five, 1995, Gettysburg: A Novel of the Civil War, 2003, Grant Comes East: A Novel of the Civil War, 2003, Never Call Retreat: Lee and Grant: The Final Victory, 2005, Pearl Harbor: A Novel of December 8th, 2007, Days of Infamy, 2008, To Try Men's Souls: A Novel of George Washington and the Fight for American Freedom, 2010, Valley Forge: George Washington and the Crucible of Victory, 2010, The Battle of the Crater: A Novel, 2011, Victory at Yorktown: A Novel, 2012; co-author: (with Pete Earley) Duplicity: A Novel, 2015, Treason: A Novel, 2016; executive prodr.: (documentaries) Rediscovering God in America II: Our Heritage, 2009, America at Risk, 2010, Nine Days that Changed the World, 2010,(Books) Understanding Trump, 2017 **AW:** Named Legis. Conservationist of Year, Georgia Wildlife Foundation, 1998, Georgia Citizen of Year, March of Dimes, 1995, Man of Year, TIME magazine, 1995; named one of The 50 Highest-Earning Political Figures, Newsweek, 2010, The 25 Most Influential Republicans, Newsmax Magazine, 2008; recipient National Minority Health Month Foundation award, 2005, Health Quality award, National Committee Quality Assurance, 2005, Sci. Pioneer award, Sci. Coalition, 2001; Carl E. Sander Political Leadership Scholar, University Georgia School Law, 2009 **MEM:** Mem.: American Association for the Advancement of Science, Georgia Conservancy, Kiwanis **PA:** Republican

GINSBURG, RUTH BADER, T: Associate Justice of the U.S. Supreme Court **I:** Government Administration/Government Relations/Government Services **DOB:** 03/15/1933 **PB:** Brooklyn **PT:** Daughter of Nathan and Celia (Amster) Bader; **ED:** DHL (hon.), Hebrew Union College, 1988; LLD (hon.), Harvard University, 2011; LLD (hon.), Princeton University, 2010; LLD (hon.), Willamette University, 2009; LLD (hon.), University Pennsylvania, 2007; LLD (hon.), George Washington University Law School, 1997; LLD (hon.), Jewish Theological Seminary America, 1997; LLD (hon.), Wheaton College, 1997; LLD (hon.), Brandeis University, 1996; LLD (hon.), University Illinois, 1995; LLD (hon.), Long Island University, 1994; LLD (hon.), Smith College, 1994; LLD (hon.), Columbia University, 1994; LLD (hon.), New York University, 1994; LLD (hon.), Radcliffe College, 1994; LLD (hon.), Lewis & Clark College, 1992; LLD (hon.), Rutgers University, 1991; LLD (hon.), Amherst College, 1991; LLD (hon.), Brooklyn Law School, 1987; LLD (hon.), DePaul University, 1985; LLD (hon.), Georgetown University, 1985; LLD (hon.), Vermont Law School, 1984; LLD (hon.), American University, 1981; LLD (hon.), Lund University, Sweden, 1969; LLB, Columbia Law School, New York City, 1959; AB, Cornell University, Ithaca, New York, 1954 **CT:** Bar: DC 1975, US Supreme Court 1967, New York 1959 **C:** Associate justice, US Supreme Court, Washington, 1993-; Judge, US Court Appeals (DC cir.), Washington, 1980-93; Professor, Rutgers University School Law, Newark, 1969-72; Associate professor, Rutgers University School Law, Newark, 1966-69; Assistant professor, Rutgers University School Law, Newark, 1963-66; Professor, Columbia Law School, 1972-80; Associate director project international procedure, Columbia Law School, 1962-63; Research associate, Columbia

Law School, 1961-62; Law clerk to Hon. Edmund L. Palmieri, US District Court (southern district) New York, 1959-61 **CR:** Visiting faculty Aspen Institute, Colorado, 1990, Salzburg Seminar American Studies, Austria, 1984, University Strasbourg, 1975, University Amsterdam, 1975, Harvard Law School, 1971, New York University School Law, 1978 fellow Center Advanced Study in Behavioral Scis., Stanford, California, 1977-78 board directors ACLU, 1974-80, general counsel, 1973-80 founder, director ACLU Women's Rights Project, 1972 **CW:** Author: (with Anders Bruzelius) Civil Procedure in Sweden, 1965, Swedish Code of Judicial Procedure, 1968, (with H.H. Kay & K. M. Davidson) Text, Cases and Materials on Sex-Based Discrimination, 1974; contributor numerous articles to books, legal texts & professional journals **AW:** Named one of Washington's Most Influential Women Lawyers, The National Law Journal, 2010, The 100 Most Powerful Women in DC, Washingtonian magazine, 2009, The 100 Most Powerful Women, Forbes magazine, 2007-10, 2005, 2004; named to The National Women's Hall of Fame, 2002; recipient Fordham-Stein Ethics prize, Fordham University, 2001 **MEM:** Fellow: Federal Bar Association (hon. life), American Academy Arts & Sciences, American Bar Foundation (board directors 1979-89), American College Trial Lawyers (hon.); mem.: American Bar Association, American Association for the Advancement of Science, Council Foreign Relations, American Law Institute (council member 1978-93) **ACH:** Achievements include recognition as the second woman and the first Jewish woman to serve on the US Supreme Court **H:** Opera, reading mysteries, watching old movies, horseback riding, water-skiing, golf **BA:** US Supreme Court, One First St NE, Washington, DC, USA, 20543-0000

GIULIANI, RUDY, T: Lawyer, Former Mayor of NYC **I:** Government Administration/Government Relations/Government Services **DOB:** 05/28/1944 **PB:** Brooklyn **SC:** NY/USA **PT:** Son of Harold Angelo and Helen (D'Avanzo) Giuliani; **ED:** LLD (hon.), Drexel University Earle Mack School Law, 2008; D in Pub. Administration (hon.), The Citadel, 2007; Degree (hon.), Middlebury College, 2005; Degree (hon.), Loyola College, 2005; JD magna cum laude, New York University, 1968; AB, Manhattan College, 1965 **C:** Attorney to President Donald Trump, 2018-; Informal Cybersecurity Advisor to Donald Trump, 2017; Chair, cybersecurity and crisis-management practice, senior advisor to executive chairman, Greenberg Traurig LLP, 2016-; Chairman, CEO, Giuliani Partners LLC, New York City, 2002-; Partner, Bracewell & Giuliani LLP, New York City, 2005-16; Chairman, CEO Giuliani Capital Advisors LLC, New York City, 2004-07; Mayor, New York City, 1994-2001; Attorney, Anderson Kill Olick & Oshinsky PC, New York City, 1990-93; Attorney, White & Case, New York City, 1989-90; Attorney, Patterson, Belknap, Webb & Tyler, New York City, 1977-81; US attorney (southern district) New York, US Department Justice, New York City, 1983-89; Associate attorney general, US Department Justice, Washington, 1981-83; Associate deputy attorney general, US Department Justice, Washington, 1975-77; Executive assistant US attorney, chief narcotics section, & chief special prosecutions section, US Department Justice, Washington, 1973-75; Assistant US attorney (southern district) New York, US Department Justice, New York City, 1970-73; Law clerk to Hon. Lloyd Francis McMahon, US District Court (southern district) New York, New York City, 1968-70 **CR:** Member Iraq Study Group (ISG), 2006 speaker Republican National Convention, New York City, 2004 Republican candidate for mayor New York City, 1997 Republican candidate for mayor New York City, 1993 Republican candidate for mayor New York City, 1989 **CW:**

Author ((with Ken Kurson)): Leadership, 2002; appeared in (films) Anger Management, 2003 **AW:** Named a Knight Commander of the British Empire (KBE), Her Majesty Queen Elizabeth II, 2002; named Consultant of Year, Consultant magazine, 2002, Person of Year, TIME magazine, 2001; named one of The 50 Highest-Earning Political Figures, Newsweek, 2010; recipient Special Achievement award for Pub. Service, National Italian-American Foundation (NIAF), 2007, Margaret Thatcher Medal of Freedom, Atlantic Bridge, 2007, Golden Plate award, Academy of Achievement, 2003, Ronald Reagan Freedom award, 2002, Fiorella LaGuardia Public Service award for Valor & Leadership in the Time of Global Crisis, Episcopal Diocese of New York, 2002, Order of the Merit of Savoy, 2001, The Hundred Year Association New York Gold Medal award, 1998, Margaret Thatcher Medal of Freedom, 2007 **PA:** Republican

GLASER, DANIEL S., T: CEO of Marsh & McLennon **I:** Business Management/Business Services **C:** CEO/President, Marsh & McLennan Companies, 2013-; Group President, COO, Marsh & McLennan Companies, New York City, 2011-13; Chairman, CEO, Marsh Inc., 2007-11; Regional president Am. International Underwriters (AIU) UK/Ireland division, AIG Europe (UK) Ltd., 2002-07; Managing director, AIG Europe (UK) Ltd., 2002-07; President Global Energy Division, Am. International Group, Inc. (AIG), 2000-02; President, COO, Willis Risk Solutions,; Broker, Marsh Inc., 1982 **BA:** Marsh McLennan Companies, 1166 Avenue Of The Americas, New York, NY, 10036

GLASS, DENNIS ROBERT, T: CEO and President of Lincoln National Group **I:** Business Management/Business Services **DOB:** 10/04/1949 **PB:** Milwaukee **SC:** MN/USA **PT:** Son of Robert Joseph and Carmella (Bellart) Glass; **ED:** MBA, University Wisconsin-Madison, 1973; Bachelors, University Wisconsin-Madison, 1971 **C:** President, CEO, Lincoln Financial Group, Philadelphia, 2007-; President, COO, Lincoln Financial Group, Philadelphia, 2006-07; President, CEO, Jefferson-Pilot Corp., 2004-06; President, COO, Jefferson-Pilot Corp., 2001-04; President fin. operations, CFO, Jefferson-Pilot Corp., 1999-2001; Executive vice president, CFO, Jefferson-Pilot Corp.,; Senior vice president, CFO, Jefferson-Pilot Corp., 1993; Executive vice president, CFO, Protective Life Corp., 1991-93; Senior vice president, chief fin. officer, Portman Cos., Atlanta, 1983-91; Director fin., treasurer, Portman Cos., Atlanta, 1983; Manager treasury operations, Northwestern Mutual Life Insurance Co., Milwaukee, 1983; Vice president, treasurer, Northwestern Mutual Life Insurance Co., Milwaukee, 1977-82; Investment analyst, Northwestern Mutual Life Insurance Co., Milwaukee, 1973-77 **CR:** Member academic staff University Wisconsin, Mliw., 1973-83 member adv. board Wachovia. **CIV:** Member, Greensboro Partnership, Member, Leadership Atlanta, 1985-86 Organizer, United Way, Milwaukee, Board member, Wachovia Bank North Carolina, Greensboro, Board member, Life Office Management Association, Board member, Insurance Marketplace Standards Association, Board member, Am. Council Life Insurers, **BA:** Lincoln Nat, 150 North Radnor Chester Rd, Radnor, PA, 19087

GLASS, PHILIP, T: Composer, Musician **I:** Media & Entertainment **DOB:** 01/31/1937 **PB:** Balt. **PT:** Son of Benjamin C. and Ida (Gouline) Glass; **ED:** Studied flute, Peabody Conservatory; Composition studies with, Darius Milhaud; Composition studies with, Steve Reich; Composition studies with, Nadia Boulanger, Paris, 1964-66; Composition studies with, William Bergsma; Compo-

sition studies with, Vincent Persichetti, 1962; MS in Composition, Julliard School Music, 1964; AB, The University of Chicago, Illinois, 1956 **C:** Founder, director, Philip Glass Ensemble, 1967-; Founder, Chatham Sq. Productions, New York City, 1972; Owner, Dunvagen Music Pubs.,; Worked and studied with Ravi Shankar, 1965-66; Composer in residence, Pittsburgh Pub. School, 1962-64; Began creating music for theatre while studying in Paris, **CW:** (Books)Music by Philip Glass,1987,Words Without Music: A memoir, 2015,Composer of incidental music, film scores, chamber music, choral works and songs; various European concert tours, 1968—, US tours, 1972—; composer: Strung Out, 1967, In Again Out Again, 1967, Pieces in the Shape of a Square, 1968, How Now, 1968, Red Horse Animation, 1968, Two Pages, 1968, Music in Similar Motion, 1969, Music in Contrary Motion, 1969, Music in Eight Parts, 1969, Music in Fifths, 1969, Gradus, 1969, Music with Changing Parts, 1971, Music in Twelve Parts, 1971—74, Music for Voices, 1972, Another Look at Harmony, 1975, The Lost Ones, 1975, The St. and the Football Player, 1975, Einstein On The Beach, 1976, Modern Love Waltz, 1977, Dressed Like an Egg, 1977, Fourth Series Part I, 1978, Music for a Performance/ Reading by C. DeJong: Fourth Series Part II, 1978, Cascando, 1979, Geometry of a Cir., 1979, Mercier and Camier, 1979, Dance No. 2, 1979, Dance No. 4, 1979, Mad Rush: Fourth Series Part III, 1979, Madrigal Opera: The Panther, 1980, Satyagraha, 1980, Facades, 1981, Vessels, 1981, Habeve Song, 1982, The Photographer, 1982, Hymn to the Sun, 1982, The Photographer, 1983, Akhnaten, 1983, The Civil Wars: A Tree is Best Measured When It Is Down, 1983, Pages from Cold Harbor, 1983, Floe, 1983, String Quartet No. 2: Co., 1983, Endgame, 1984, Glassworks, 1984, Dance from Akhnaten, 1984, String Quartet No. 3: Mishima, 1985, The Juniper Tree, 1985, Songs from Liquid Days, 1986, Three Songs, 1986, In the Upper Room, 1986, Dialogue, 1986, A Descent Into the Maelstrom, 1986, The Light for Orchestra, 1987, Itaipu, 1988, The Fall of the House of Usher, 1988, 1000 Airplanes on the Roof, 1988, The Making of the Representative for Planet 8, 1988, The Canyon, 1988, String Quartet No. 4: Boczak, 1989, Hydrogen Jukebox, 1989, The White Raven, 1991, The Voyage, 1992, Orphée, chamber opera after Cocteau, 1993, Low Symphony, 1993, La Belle et la Bête, 1994, Symphony No. 2, 1994, The Marriages Between Zones Three, Four and Five, 1997, Aguas de Amazonia, 1999, Passage, 2001, The Man in the Bath, 2001, Dancissimo, 2001, Notes, 2001, Diaspora, 2001, Voices for Organ, Didgeridoo and Narrator, 2001, Philip on Film, 2001, The Elephant Man, 2002, Symphony No. 6 Plutonian Ode, 2002, Glasswork, 2003, Taoist Sacred Dance, 2003, Orion, 2004, A Musical Portrait of Chuck Close, 2005, Chaotic Harmony, 2006, Life: A Journey Through Time, 2006, Passion of Ramakrishna, 2006, Book of Longing, 2007, Four Moments for Two Pianos, 2008, The Bacchae, 2009, The American Four Seasons, 2009, Black & White Scherzo, 2011, IBM Centennial Film, 2011, Project Rebirth, 2011, The Perfect American, 2013, (films) North Star: Mark Di Suvero, 1977, Koyaanisqatsi, 1983, Mishima, 1984, Dead End Kids, 1986, Hamburger Hill, 1987, Powaqqatsi, 1987, The Thin Blue Line, 1988, Mindwalk, 1990, A Brief History of Time, 1992, Candyman, 1992, Anima Mundi, 1992, Compassion in Exile, 1992, Candyman II: Farewell to the Flesh, 1995, Jenipapo, 1995, The Secret Agent, 1996, Bent, 1997, Kundun, 1997, Dracula, 1999, The Hours, 2002 (The Anthony Asquith Award for Achievement in Film Music, British Academy Film Award (BAFTA), 2003), Nagoygatsi, 2002, The Fog of War, 2003, Secret Window, 2004, Taking Lives, 2004, Undertow, 2004, Declaring Genius, 2004, La Moustache, 2005, Faith's Corner, 2005, Neverwas, 2005, The Giant Buddhas, 2005, Roving Mars, 2006, Nasiona, 2006, Notes on a Scandal, 2006, The Illusionist, 2006 (Best Composer, 2006 Critics Choice award, Broadcast Film Critics Association, 2007), Cassandra's Dream, 2007, No Reservations, 2007, Glass: A Portrait of Philip in 12 Parts, 2007, Animals in Love, 2007, Objects and Memory, 2008, What are you Looking For, 2008, Les regrets, 2009, Transcendent Man, 2009, Mr. Nice, 2010, Astral City: A Spiritual Journey, 2010, Icarus at the Edge of Time, 2010, When the Dragon Swallowed the Sun, 2010, They were There, 2011, Portals, 2011, Rebirth, 2011, Elena, 2011, Londoness, 2011, O Apostolo, 2012, Stoker, 2013; composer, keyboard artist (films) The Truman Show, 1998 (Golden Globe award, American Society of Composers Film & TV award, 1999); composer: (ballets) Witches of Venice, 1995, (dance opera) Les enfants terrible, 1996, (theatre) In the Penal Colony, 2000, (Operas) Monsters of Grace, 1999, Galileo Galilei, 2002, Waiting for the Barbarians, 2005; composer: (with Henry Hwang) The Sound of Voice, 2003; composer: (special events) Ceremonial Music at 1984 Olympics, original music for Atlanta Olympic Games, 1996, (benefit compact disc for Gehlek Rimpoche and Jewel Heart Organization) Dreaming Awake, Concerto for violin and orchestra, 1987, Concerto Fantasy for Two Timpanists and Orchestra, 2000, Tirol Concerto, piano and orchestra, 2000, Concerto for Cello and Orchestra, 2001, Concerto for Harpsichord and Orchestra, 2002, (Pandemic) Facing AIDS (documentary), 2002, (chamber and instrumental music) String Quartet, 1966, (vocal and choral music) Knee Play No. 3, 197 **AW:** Named Musician of Year, Musical Am. magazine, 1985, composition grantee, Menil Foundation, 1974, National Endowment for the Arts, 1974-75, Changes, Inc., 1971-72, Foundation for Contemporary Performance Arts, 1970-71, Fulbright, 1966-67; recipient Praemium Imperiale (music), Japan Art Association, 2012, Frederick Loewe award for Film Composing, Palm Springs International Film Society, Palm Springs International Film Festival, 2007, Contemporary Music award, Classical Brit Awards, 2004, George Peabody medal, Peabody Consultant Music, 2000, Art of Freedom award, Om Sarwasvati Hring Soha Tibet House, 2000, Young Composer's award, Ford Foundation, 1964-66, Benjamin award, 1961-62, Lado prize, 1961-67, Broadcast Music Industry award, 1960, National Medal of Arts, 2015 **MEM:** Mem.: PRS, American Society of Composers **BA:** Dunvagen Music Publishers, 40 Exchange Place, Suite 1906, New York, NY, 10005

GLAUBER, ROY J., T: Theoretical Physicist I: Sciences **DOB:** 09/01/1925 **PB:** NYC **SC:** NY/USA **PT:** Emanuel B. Glauber; Felicia (Fox) Glauber **MS:** Divorced **SPN:** Cynthia Marshall Rich (7/26/1960, Divorced 6/1976) **CH:** Jeffrey M.; Valerie M. **ED:** BS in Physics, Harvard University, Summa Cum Laude (1946); MA, Harvard University (1947); PhD in Physics, Harvard University (1949); Honorary Doctorate, University of Essen, Germany (1997); Honorary Doctorate, Friedrich-Alexander University, Germany (2006); Honorary DSc, University of Arizona, Tucson, AZ (2006) **C:** Mallinckrodt Professor of Physics, Harvard University, Cambridge, MA (1976—Present); Professor, Harvard University, Cambridge, MA (1962-1976); Associate Professor, Harvard University, Cambridge, MA (1956-1962); Assistant Professor, Harvard University, Cambridge, MA (1953-1956); Lecturer, Harvard University, Cambridge, MA (1952-1953); Lecturer, California Institute of Technology, Pasadena, CA (1951-1952); Research Fellow, Swiss Federal Polytechnic Institute, Zürich, Switzerland (1950); Member, Institute for Advanced Study, Princeton, NJ (1949-1951); Staff, Theoretical Physics Division,

Los Alamos Laboratory, NM (1944-1946) **CR:** Visiting Lecturer, Ecole d'Été de Physical, Théorique, Les Houches, France (1954, 1964); Visiting Lecturer, University of California, Berkeley (1955, 1957, 1963); Visiting Lecturer, University of Colorado, Boulder (1958, 1961); Visiting Lecturer, University of Washington, Seattle, WA (1960); Visiting Lecturer, Brandeis University, Waltham, MA (1961); Visiting Lecturer, University of Leningrad, USSR (1964); Visiting Lecturer, City University of New York (1970); Adjunct Professor of Physics, University of Arizona, Tucson, AZ (1988—Present); Director, Enrico Fermi International School of Physics, Varenna, Italy (1967); Guest Professor, European Organization of Nuclear Research, Geneva, Switzerland (1972-1973); Visiting Staff, European Organization of Nuclear Research, Geneva, Switzerland (1983); Visiting Professor, NORDITA, Copenhagen, Denmark (1974); Lorentz Professor, University of Leiden, The Netherlands (1974); Visiting Professor, College of France, Paris, France (1983); Freese Lecturer, Rensselaer Polytechnic Institute (1986); Racah Lecturer, Hebrew University, Jerusalem, Israel (1988); Touschek Lecturer, Frascati Laboratory, Italy (1988); Advisory Board, Program for Science and Technology for International Security, Massachusetts Institute of Technology (1983—Present); Trustee, Ivy Fund (1961-1992, 1995-2004); Director, Mackenzie Funds, Inc. (1993-2004); Consultant, Clinton Anderson Laboratory, Los Alamos National Laboratory, NM; Board of Directors, Center Arms Control and Non Proliferation (2006-Present); Honorable Professor, Zhejiang University, Hangzhou, China (2007); Honorable Professor, Xian Jiaotong University, China (2007); Honorable Professor, Tongji University, Shanghai, China (2007) **CW:** Author, "Quantum Theory of Optical Coherence" (2007); Editor, "Quantum Optics" (1989-1995); Member, Editorial Board, Journal of Mathematical Physics (1961-1963); Member, Editorial Board, Nuclear Physics B. (1972-1993); Contributor, Articles to Professional Journals **AW:** Named Fulbright Lecturer (1954); A.A. Michelson Medal, Franklin Institute (1985); A. von Humbolt Research Award (1989); Dannie Heineman Prize (1996); Willis E. Lamb Prize (2006); Co-recipient, Nobel Prize in Physics (2005); Fellow, National Research Council (1946-1949); Fellow, Atomic Energy Commission (1949-1950); Fellow, Frank B. Jewett Bell Laboratories (1950-1951); Fellow, Guggenheim (1966-1967, 1972-1973); Albert A. Michelson Medal (1985); ForMemRS (1997); Heineman Prize (1996); Dannie N. Heineman Prize in Mathematical Physics (1996); Max Born Award (1985) **MEM:** Fellow, American Academy of Arts and Sciences; American Physical Society; American Optical Society; Honorary Member, Royal Society of New Zealand; National Academy of Sciences; Foreign Member, Royal Society of London; Advisory Board, National Center of Arms Control Non-Proliferation; Phi Beta Kappa; Sigma Xi **BA:** Harvard U Lyman Lab Physics Lyman 331, 331 17 Oxford St, Cambridge, MA, 02138

GLAVINE, TOM, T: Former Professional Baseball Player I: Athletics **DOB:** 05/25/1966 **PB:** Concord **SC:** MA/USA **PT:** Son of Fred and Millie Glavine **ED:** Grad., Billerica Memorial HS, Massachusetts, 1984 **C:** Pitcher, Atlanta Braves, 2008-09; Pitcher, New York Mets, 2002-07; Pitcher, Atlanta Braves, 1987-2002 **CR:** National League Players' Rep., Major League Player's Association, Former Atlanta Braves' Team Rep. **CIV:** Host, Georgia Transplant Foundation Ann. Spring Training, Hon. chairman, Georgia Council on Child Abuse, Vol., National Sports Committee, Leukemia Society Am. **AW:** Named World Series Most Valuable Player, 1995, National League Pitcher of Year, Sporting News, 2000, 1991; Named to National League All-Star

Team, 2006, 2004, 2002, 2000, 1996-98, 1991-93; Recipient, Bart Giamatti Award for Community Service, Baseball Assistance Team, 2006, Good Guy Award, New York Chapter Baseball Writers Association Am., 2007, Joan Payson Award for Humanitarian Service, New York Chapter Baseball Writers of Am., 2004, Good Guy Award, New Jersey Sportswriters, 2004, Babe Ruth Award, 1995, National League Cy Young Award, 1998, 1991, Silver Slugger Award, 1998, 1995-96, 1991, World Series Champion, 1995, Baseball Hall of Fame, 2014, NL wins Leader, 1991-93, 1998, 2000, World Series Champion, 1995 **ACH:** Achievements include leading the National League in: wins, 1991-1993, 1998, 2000; complete games, 1991; shutouts, 1992; starts, 1993, 1996, 1999-2002; member of the World Series championship winning Atlanta Braves, 1995; recording his 300th career win, August 5, 2007 **BA:** National Baseball Hall of Fame, 25 Main Street, Cooperstown, NY, 13326

GLOR, JEFF, T: News Correspondent I: Media & Entertainment **DOB:** 07/12/1975 **PB:** Tonawanda **SC:** NY/USA **ED:** BA in Journalism and Economics, Syracuse University, New York, Magna Cum Laude, 1997 **C:** Anchor, Sunday Edition, CBS Evening News, CBS News, 2012-Present; Special Correspondent, CBS This Morning, CBS News, 2011-Present; News Anchor, The Early Show, CBS News, 2011-2012; Anchor, Saturday Edition, CBS Evening News, National Correspondent, CBS News, 2009-2010; National Correspondent, The Early Show, CBS News, New York, NY, 2007-2010; News Anchor, Weekday Reporter, WHDH-TV, Boston, MA, 2003-2007; Co-Anchor, Reporter Evening News, WSTM-TV, 2000-2003; Morning News Anchor, WSTM-TV, 1997-2000; News Writer, WSTM-TV, Syracuse, NY, 1997 **CW:** Creator, Producer, (Blog) Author Talk **AW:** Best Male News Anchor, Syracuse New Times **BA:** CBS News Headquarters, 51 W 52nd Street, New York, NY, 10103

GLOVER, DANNY, T: Actor I: Media & Entertainment **PT:** James Glover, Carrie (Hunley) Glover **MS:** Married **SPN:** Eliane Cavalleiro, 2009; Asake Bomani, 1975, Divorced 2000 **CH:** Mandisa **ED:** Honorary DFA, San Francisco State University, 1997; Degree in Economics, San Francisco State University **C:** Researcher, Mayor's Office, San Francisco, 1971-1975 **CR:** Appointed Goodwill Ambassador, UN Development Program, 1998; American Conservatory Theatre's Black Actor Workshop **CW:** Actor, (Broadway Debut) Master Harold... And The Boys, Lyceum Theatre, 1982, (Stage Productions) The Blood Knot, 1982, The Island, Sizwe Banzi Is Dead, Macbeth, Suicide In B Flat, Nevis Mountain Dew, Jukebox, (Films) Escape From Alcatraz, 1979, Chu Chu And The Philly Flash, 1981, Out, 1982, The Stand-In, 1984, Iceman, 1984, Places In The Heart, 1984, Birdy, 1984, Silverado, 1985, Witness, 1985, The Color Purple, 1985, Lethal Weapon, 1987, Bat 21, 1988, Lethal Weapon II, 1989, Predator 2, 1990, Flight Of The Intruder, 1991, A Rage In Harlem, 1991, Pure Luck, 1991, Grand Canyon, 1992, Lethal Weapon III, 1992, Bopha!, 1993, Maverick, 1994, Angels In The Outfield, 1994, Operation Dumbo Drop, 1995, The Rainmaker, 1997, Wings Against The Wind, 1998, Beloved, 1998, Lethal Weapon 4, 1998, (Voice Actor) Prince Of Egypt, 1998, (Voice Actor) Antz, 1998, The Monster, 1999, Boesman And Lena, 2000, Wings Against The Wind, 1999, The Royal Tenenbaums, 2001, The Cookout, 2004, Saw, 2004, Manderlay, 2005, Missing In America, 2005, The Shaggy Dog, 2006, (Voice Actor) Barnyard: The Original Party Animals, 2006, Dreamgirls, 2006, Shooter, 2007, Be Kind Rewind, 2008, Blindness, 2008, Death At A Funeral, 2010, (Voice Actor) Alpha And Omega, 2010, I Want To Be A Soldier, 2010, Five Minarets

In New York, 2010, Heart Of Blackness, 2010, Mooz-Lum, 2011, Son Of Morning, 2011, Age Of The Dragons, 2011, Donovan's Echo, 2011, Mysteria, 2011, Supremacy, 2012, LUV, 2012, Sins Expiation, 2012, Chasing Shakespeare, 2012, The Lighthouse, 2012, The Bouquet, 2013, Highland Park, 2013, The Shift, 2013, Space Warriors, 2013, Muhammad Ali's Greatest Fight, 2013, Tula: The Revolt, 2013, Extraction, 2013, Rage, 2014, The Ninja Immovable Heart, 2014, Supremacy, 2014, 2047-Sights Of Death, 2014, Beyond The Lights, 2014, Back In The Day, 2014, (Voice Actor) Yellowbird, 2014, Day Of The Mummy, 2014, Toxin, 2015, About Scout, 2015, Checkmate, 2015, Waffle Street, 2015, Gridlocked, 2015, Diablo, 2015, Consumed, 2015, Andron, 2015, Dirty Grandpa, 2016, Complete Unknown, 2016, Mr. Pig, 2016, Dark Web, 2016, Back In The Day, 2016, Almost Christmas, 2016, Monster Trucks, 2016, Extortion, 2017, The Good Catholic, 2017, Donald Trump, The Kock Brothers And Their War On Climate Science, 2017, Buckout Road, 2017, Proud Mary, 2018, Sorry To Bother You, 2018, Come Sunday, 2018, Death Race: Beyond Anarchy, 2018, Killing Winston Jones, The Old Man And The Gun, 2018, (TV Films) The Face Of Rage, 1983, Mandela, 1987, Dead Man Out, 1989, Freedom Song, 2000, Legend Of Earthsea, 2004, The Exonerated, 2005, Hannah's Law, 2012, Shuffleton's Barbershop, 2013, Americans Dad!, 2013, Muhammad Ali's Greatest Fight, 2013,Criminal Minds, 2016, Mozart In The Jungle, 2016, Tour De Pharmacy, 2017, Cold Case File, 2017, The Christmas Train, 2017, (TV Miniseries) Chiefs, 1983, Lonesome Dove, 1989, Queen, 1993, (TV Episodes) Hill Street Blues, Lou Grant, Many Mansions, Others; Host, Civil War Journal, 1993; Actor, Executive Producer, (Films) To Sleep With Anger, 1990, 3 A.M., 2001, Bamako, 2006, (TV Films) America's Dream, 1996, Buffalo Soldiers, 1997; Actor, Co-Producer, (Films) The Saint Of Fort Washington, 1993; Actor, Producer, (TV Films) Good Fences, 2003; Executive Producer, (Films) The Harimaya Bridge, 2009, Dum Maaro Dum, 2011, Seto Surya, 2016, (TV Films) Deadly Voyage, 1996, (Documentaries) Trouble The Water, 2008, Soundtrack For A Revolution, 2009, The Disappearance Of McKinley Nolan, 2010, Shenandoah, 2012, The House I Live In, 2012, This Changes Everything, 2015, Shadow World, 2016, Angels Are Made Of Light, 2016; Co-Producer, (Films) Salt Of This Sea, 2008, Highway, 2012, Concerning Violence, 2014; Actor, Associate Producer, (Films) Bad Ass 3: Bad Asses On The Bayou, 2015 **AW:** National Association For The Advancement Of Colored People Image Award For Outstanding Actor In A TV Movie, Mini-Series Or Dramatic Special, Freedom Song, 2001, National Association For The Advancement Of Colored People Image Award For Outstanding Lead Actor In A Motion Picture, Beloved, 1999, National Association For The Advancement Of Colored People Image Award For Outstanding Lead Actor In A TV Movie Or Mini-Series, Queen, 1995, National Association For The Advancement Of Colored People Image Award For Outstanding Lead Actor In A Drama Series, Mini-Series Or TV Movie, Mandela, 1990, National Association For The Advancement Of Colored People Image Award For Outstanding Lead Actor In A Motion Picture, Mandela, 1989, Theatre World Award, Master Harold...And The Boys, Lyceum Theatre, 1982 **BA:** Principal Entertainment, 9255 W Sunset Boulevard, Suite 500, West Hollywood, CA, 90069

GLOVER, DONALD, T: Actor, Writer, Director **I:** Media & Entertainment **PB:** Edwards Airforce Base **SC:** CA **CW:** (Studio Albums), Camp, 2011, Because the Internet, 2013, Awaken, My Love, 2016(Grammy for Best Traditional R&B Song) (Film) Mystery Team, 2009, The Muppets, 2011,

The To Do List, 2013, Clapping for the Wrong Reasons, 2013, Alexander and the Terrible, Horrible, No Good, Very Bad Day, 2014, Chicken and Futility, 2014, The Lazarus Effect, 2015, Magic Mike XXL, 2015, The Martian, 2015, Spider-Man: Homecoming, 2017, Solo: A Star Wars Story, 2018, The Lion King, 2019(Television) 30 Rock, 2006, Human Giant, 2007, Community, 2009, Robot Chicken, 2010, Comedy Central Presents Donald Glover, 2010, Regular Show, 2011, Donald Glover Weirdo, 2012, Sesame Street, 2013, Girls, 2013, Adventure Time, 2013, Ultimate Spider-Man, 2015, China, II, 2015, Atlanta, 2016,(Golden Globe Best Actor in a Television Comedy 2016, Primetime Emmy for Outstanding Lead Actor and Directing) Deadpool, 2018

GLUSKI, ANDRÉS R., T: Power Distribution Company Executive **I:** Oil & Energy **ED:** PhD in economic, Univ. of Virginia; MA, Univ. of Virginia; BA, Wake Forest Univ. **C:** Director, president, CEO, AES Corp., Arlington, Virginia, 2011-; Executive vice president, COO, AES Corp., Arlington, Virginia, 2007-11; Executive vice president, regional president Latin Am., AES Corp., Arlington, Virginia, 2006-07; Senior vice president Caribbean & Central Am., AES Corp., Arlington, Virginia, 2003-06; Management positions in Venezuela & Chile, AES Corp., Arlington, Virginia, 1997-2003; Executive vice president corp. banking, Banco de Venezuela,; Executive vice president fin., CANTV, Venezuela, **CR:** Board member, US-Brazil CEO Forum, US-India CEO Forum; Board Member, The AES Corporation, Waste Management and AES Gener; Chairman, Americas Society/Council of the Americas; Director, the Edison Electric Institute. **MEM:** Mem.: Phi Beta Kappa

GODARD, JEAN-LUC, T: Film Director **I:** Fine Art **DOB:** 04/30/1905 **PB:** Paris, **SC:** Paris, **SPN:** Son of Paul and Odile Godard Married Anna Karina, March 2, 1961 (div.); **CH:** Married Anna Karina, March 3, 1961 (div. 1967); Married Anne Wiasemsky, July 22, 1967 (div. 1979). **ED:** Educated, Lyceé Buffon, Paris **C:** Journalist, film critic, Cahiers du Cinema, **CW:** Director, producer, writer: (films and documentaries) Opération Béton, 1954, Une Femme Coquette, 1955, Tous les garçons s'appelent Patrick, 1957, Charlotte et son Jules, 1958, A Bout de Souffle, 1959 (prix Jean Vigo), Le sept peches captiaux, 1961, The Little Soldier, The Carabiniers, 1963, Une Femme est une Femme, 1961, Vivre et sa Vie, 1962, Weekend, 1967, La Chinoise, 1967, Les plus belles escroqueries du Monde, 1963, Une femme mariée, 1964, Band of Outsiders, 1964, Alphaville, 1965, Pierrot le fou, 1965, Sympathy for the Devil, Lion du Vietnam, 1967, Le plus vieux metier du monde, 1967, Vangelo '70, 1967, Un film comme les autres, 1968, British Sounds, 1969, Made in U.S.A., 1966, Masculine-Feminine, 1966, One Plus One, 1968, One American Movie: 1 A.M., 1969, Le Vent d'est, 1969, Lotte in Italia, 1970, Vladmir et Rosa, 1971, Tout va bien, 1972, Numero deux, 1975, Ici et ailleurs, 1976, Bugsy, 1979, Sauve qui peut, 1980, Every Man for Himself, 1980, Passion, 1982, First Name: Carmen, 1984, Hail Mary, 1985, Detective, 1985, King Lear, 1988, Nouvelle Vasue, 1989, Allemagne Neuf Zero, 1991, Contre L'Oubli, 1992, Helas Pour Moi, 1993, Momentous Events: Russia in the 90s, 1993, JLG by JLG, 1995, For Ever Mozart, 1996, The Old Place, 2000, In Praise of Love, 2001, Notre musique, 2004, Vrai faux passeport, 2006, Reportage amateur Maquette expo, 2006, Film socialisme, 2010, Goodbye to Language, 2014, Bridges of Sarajevo, 2014, Image et Parole,2018 numerous others; author: Godard on Godard: Critical Writings by Jean-Luc Godard, 1986. **AW:** Recipient special prize Festival of Venice, 1962, Prix Pasinetti, 1962; ,

hon. award Academy Awards, 2011. **MEM:** Member Superior Council French Language

GOFF, GREGORY J., T: Oil and Gas Company Executive **I:** Oil & Energy **ED:** MBA, University Utah, 1981; BS, University Utah, 1978 **C:** President, CEO, Andeavor (formerly Tesoro Corp.), 2017-; President, CEO, Tesoro Corp., 2010-2017; Senior vice president, commercial, ConocoPhillips, 2008-10; President, strategy, integration and specialty business, refining, marketing and transportation, ConocoPhillips, 2006-08; President, US Lower 48 and Latin America exploration and production business, ConocoPhillips, 2004-06; President, Europe and Asia Pacific downstream activities, ConocoPhillips, 2002-04; Chairman, managing director, Conoco Ltd., England, 2000; Managing director, CEO Conoco JET Nordic, Conoco Inc., 1998-2000; Joined, Conoco Inc., 1981 **CR:** Board directors ChevronPhillips Chemical Co., PolyOne Corporation, American Fuel & Petrochemical Manufacturers; **CIV:** Member downstream committee, Am. Petroleum Institute, National adv. board, University Utah Business School,

GOHMERT, LOUIE, T: U.S. Representative from Texas **I:** Government Administration/Government Relations/Government Services **DOB:** 08/18/1953 **PB:** Pittsburg **SC:** TX/USA **PT:** Son of Louis Buller and E. Sue (Brooks) Gohmert; **ED:** Attended, School International Training, Putney, Vermont; JD, Baylor University School Law, Waco, Texas, 1977; BA, Texas Agricultural and Mechanical University, 1975 **CT:** Bar: US Supreme Court 1986, US Court Appeals (5th cir.) 1986, US District Court (eastern & southern districts) Texas 1978, Texas 1978 **C:** Member, US Congress from 1st Texas District, 2005-; Member, Committee on the Judiciary, Committee on Natural Resources, Republican Study Committee; Judge, 12th Court Appeals Texas, 2002-03; Judge, Smith County District Court, Tyler, 1992-2002; Private practice attorney, Tyler, 1986-92; Partner, Freeman, Smithson & Gohmert, Tyler, 1986; Associate, Potter Guinn Law Firm, Tyler, Texas, 1982-86; Assistant district attorney, 76th Judicial District, Mount Pleasant, Texas, 1978 **CIV:** Deacon, Green Acres Baptist Church, Tyler, **MIL:** Captain Judge Advocate General Corps US Army, 1978-82, Fort Benning, Georgia **MEM:** Mem.: Texas Agricultural and Mechanical Alumni Association (president Smith County chapter 1988), State Bar Texas, Smith County Bar Association (treasurer 1989), Rotary **H:** Sports, creative writing **PA:** Republican

GOLDBERG, SUSAN, T: Magazine Editor **I:** Writing and Editing **PB:** Michigan **ED:** BA in Journalism, Michigan State University, East Lansing **C:** Editor, National Geographic, New York, 2014-; Executive Editor, Bloomberg News, San Francisco, 2010-2014; Editor, The Plain Dealer, Cleveland, 2007-10; Deputy Managing Editor, USA Today, 1989-99; Executive Editor, San Jose Mercury News, 2003-07; Vice President, San Jose Mercury News, 2001-07; Managing Editor, San Jose Mercury News, 1999-2003; Acting City Editor, San Jose Mercury News,; Assistant City Editor, San Jose Mercury News, 1987-89; Assistant City Editor, Detroit Free Press,; Reporter, Seattle Post-Intelligencer, **CR:** Board Directors Accrediting Council on Education in Journalism and Mass Communications Chair Managing Editors Leadership and Management Committee Associated Press **CIV:** Member board visitors, Northwestern University Medill School Journalism, Board directors, The City Club, Board directors, Business Vols. Unlimited, Board member Silicon Valley chapter, American Cancer Society, 2003- **CW:** Talking Toilets with Matt Damon, 2017 **AW:** Washington Magazine Most Powerful Women, 2017

GOLDBERG, WHOOPI, T: Actress, Comedienne **I:** Media & Entertainment **DOB:** 11/13/1955 **PB:** NYC **SC:** NY/USA **PT:** Daughter of Robert and Emma (Harris) Johnson **C:** Member, Blake St. Hawkeyes, Berkeley, California, 1980-84; Member, San Diego Repertory Theatre, 1975-80 **CW:** Actress: (plays) Living on the Edge of Chaos, 1988 (California theatre award for Outstanding Achievement, 1988); (Broadway plays) A Funny Thing Happened on the Way to the Forum, 1996-98, Funny Girl, 2002, Xanadu, 2008; actress, producer (Broadway plays) Ma Rainey's Black Bottom, 2003, actress, writer (one-person show Broadway plays) Whoopi Goldberg on Broadway, 1984-85; actress: (films) Citizen, 1982, The Color Purple, 1985 (Golden Globe for Best Actress Motion Picture Drama, 1986), Jumpin' Jack Flash, 1986, Burglar, 1986, Fatal Beauty, 1987, The Telephone, 1987, Clara's Heart, 1988, Homer and Eddie, 1989, Beverly Hills Brats, 1989, Comicitis, 1989, The Long Walk Home, 1990, Ghost, 1990 (Academy award for Best Supporting Actress, 1991, Golden Globe for Best Supporting Actress Motion Picture, 1991), Soapdish, 1991, Blackbird Fly, 1991, The Player, 1992, Sister Act, 1992, House Party 2, 1992, Sarafina!, 1992, Made in America, 1993, National Lampoon's Loaded Weapon 1, 1993, Sister Act 2: Back in the Habit, 1993, (voice) The Lion King, 1994; actress, actress: (films) Naked in New York, 1993, The Little Rascals, 1994, Corrina, Corrina, 1994, Star Trek: Generations, 1994, (voice) The Pagemaster, 1994, Boys on the Side, 1995, Moonlight and Valentino, 1995, Theodore Rex, 1995, Bogus, 1996, The Ghost of Mississippi, 1996, Eddie, 1996, Tales from the Crypt Presents: Bordello of Blood, 1996, The Associate, 1996, (voice) A Christmas Carol, 1997, How Stella Got Her Groove Back, 1998, (voice) The Rugrats Movie, 1998, Alegria, 1998, Deep End of the Ocean, 1999, Jackie's Back!, 1999, Girl, Interrupted, 1999, (voice) A Second Chance at Life, 2000, More Dogs Than Bones, 2000, Kingdom Come, 2001, Monkeybone, 2001, Rat Race, 2001, (narrator) Golden Dreams, 2001, Star Trek: Nemesis, 2002, Blizzard, 2003, Jiminy Glick in La La Wood, 2004, (voice) Pinocchio 3000, 2004, Racing Stripes, 2005, Doogal, 2006, Everyone's Hero, 2006, If I Had Known I Was Genius, 2007, (voice) Snow Buddies, 2008, Madea Goes to Jail, 2009, For Colored Girls, 2010, Toy Story 3, 2010, A Little Bit of Heaven, 2011, The Little Engine That Could, 2010, Teenage Mutant Ninja Turtles, 2014, Top Five, 2014, Big Stone Gap, 2014, Black Dog, Red Dog, 2015, King of the Dance Hall, 2016, 9/11, 2017, the List, 2018; (voice) Savva. Heart of the Warrior, 2015, : (TV films) My Past Is My Own, 1989, Kiss Shot, 1989, Defenders of Dynatron City, 1992, (voice) Yuletide in the 'hood, 1993, In the Gloaming, 1997, (voice) Mother Goose: A Rappin' and Rhymin' Special, 1997, Cinderella, 1997, A Knight in Camelot, 1998, Jackie's Back!, 1999, The Magical Land of the Leprechauns, 1999, Alice in Wonderland, 1999, (voice) Madeline: My Fair Madeline, 2002, It's a Very Muppet Christmas Movie, 2002, Sensitive Men, 2013; actress, executive producer (TV films) Call Me Claus, 2001, What Makes a Family, 2001, A Day late and a Dollar Short, 2014, actress, producer Good Fences, 2003; actress: (TV films) A Muppets Christmas: Letter to Santa, 2008; (TV series) Star Trek: The Next Generation, 1988-94, (voice): (TV appearances) Captain Planet and the Planeteers, 1990, Baghdad Cafe, 1990, Happily Ever After: Fairy Tales for Every Child, 1997, Foxbusters, 1999, Liberty's Kids, 2002, Littleburg, 2004, Everybody Hates Chris, 2006, Entourage, 2008, Life on Mars,

2008, The Cleaner, 2009, Glee, 2012-14, Once Upon a Time in Wonderland, 2013-14; actress, executive producer (TV series) Whoopi, 2003, (TV films) Delores & Jermaine, 2015; actress: (TV specials) Circus of the Stars #15, 1990, Tales from the Whoop: Hot Rod Brown, Class Clown, 1990; director, writer, performer (TV specials) Comic Relief, 1986; co-prodr.: (films) The Mao Game, 1999; executive prodr.: (TV films) Ruby's Bucket of Blood, 2001, A Day Late and a Dollar Short, 2014; (TV series) Strong Medicine, 2000, Wow, I Never Knew That!, 2011; (documentaries) Moms Mabley: I Got Somethin' to Tell You, 2011; prodr.: (TV series) Hollywood Squares, 1998-2002; (TV mini-series) Oh What A Time It Was, 1999; author: Alice, 1992, Whoopi Goldberg Book, 1997, Whoopi's Big Book of Manners, 2006, Is It Just Me?, Or Is It Nuts Out There?, 2010, Whoopi Goldberg: Inside the Whoopi Cushion, 2012; co-author: (children's book) Sugar Plum Ballerinas # 1: Plum Fantastic, 2008, Sugar Plum Ballerinas # 2: Toeshoe Trouble, 2009, Sugar Plum Ballerinas # 3: Perfectly Prima, 2010, Sugar Plum Ballerinas #4: Terrible Terrel, 2010, Sugar Plum Ballerinas #5: CATastrophe, 2011; host (TV series) The Whoopi Goldberg Show, 1992-93, (radio show) Wake-up with Whoopi, 103.5 KTU, 2006, co-host (TV series) The View, 2007- (Emmy award for Outstanding Talk Show host (with other co-hosts), 2009); prodr.: (Broadway plays) Sister Act, 2011, Thoroughly Modern Millie (Tony award for Best Musical, 2002) **AW:** Named Entertainer of Year, National Association for the Advancement of Colored People, 1990; named one of The World's Most Influential People, TIME magazine, 2009; recipient Mark Twain Prize for American Humor, John F. Kennedy Center for Performing Arts, 2001, Star on Hollywood Walk of Fame, 2001, Humanitarian of Year award, Starlight Foundation, 1989, Hans Christian Andersen award for outstanding achievement by a dyslexic, 1987, Grammy award for Album, Whoopi Goldberg: Direct from Broadway, 1985 **MEM:** Mem.: National Rifle Association

GOLDMAN, LEE, T: Dean, Cardiologist, Educator **I:** Education/Educational Services **DOB:** 01/06/1948 **PB:** Philadelphia **ED:** MPH, Yale University, 1973; MD, Yale University, 1973; BA, Yale University, 1969; **CT:** Diplomate Am. Board Internal Medicine (board directors 1996-), Am. Board Cardiovasc. Disease; **C:** Harold & Margaret Hatch professor, executive vice president health and biomedical scis., dean Faculties of Health Scis. and Medicine, Columbia University College of Physicians and Surgeons, New York City, 2006-; Chief executive, Columbia University Medical Center; Chair Department Medicine, University California, San Francisco, 1995-2006; Professor, associate dean, University California, San Francisco; Professor, Harvard Medical School, 1989-95; Associate professor, Harvard Medical School, 1983-89; Assistant professor medicine, Harvard Medical School, 1978-83; Fellow in cardiology, Yale-New Haven Hospital, 1976-78; Resident in medicine, Massachusetts General Hospital, Boston, 1975-76; Resident in medicine, University California, San Francisco, 1974-75; Intern, University California, San Francisco, 1973-74 **CR:** Member Operating Committee Partners Health Care Inc., 1993-95 Institute Medicine, 1995-, Association Professor Medicine, 1995-2006, President 2002, Board Directors, 1998-2000 Board Directors UCSF Stanford Health Care, 1997-2000; **CIV:** Board Directors Temple Shir Tikva, Wayland, Massachusetts, President, 1986-88; **CW:** Editor-in-chief Am. Journal Medicine, 1997-2005; Associate Editor New England Journal Medicine, 1989-95; Contributor Numerous Articles to Professional Journals; **AW:** Henry J. Kaiser Family Foundation Scholar, 1982-87, Robert Williams

Award 2009; **BA:** Columbia U Coll of Physicians & Surgeons, 630 W 168th St, P&S 2-401, New York, NY, 10032

GOMEZ, JIMMY, T: U.S. Representative from California **I:** Government Administration/Government Relations/Government Services **DOB:** 11/25/1974 **PB:** Fullerton **SC:** California **ED:** B.A., Political Science, University of California; Masters Degree, Public Policy, Harvard University's John F Kennedy's School of Government **C:** Member, U.S. House of Representatives from California's 34th District, 2017; Member, Committee on Oversight and Government Reform; Member, Committee on Natural Resources; Member. California State Assembly from District 51, 2012-2017; Majority Whip, State Assembly, 2013-2014 **BA:** 1226 Longworth HOB, Washington, DC, 201515

GOMEZ, SELENA MARIE MARIE, T: Actress, Singer **I:** Media & Entertainment **PB:** Grand Prairie **SC:** TX/USA **PT:** Ricardo Joel Gomez; Mandy (Cornett) Teefey **C:** Founder, lead singer, Selena Gomez & the Scene, 2008 **CIV:** UNICEF Goodwill Ambassador, 2009- **CW:** Actress: (TV series) Barney & Friends, 2002-03, The Suite Life of Zack & Cody, 2006, Hannah Montana, 2007-08, Wizards of Waverly Place, 2007-12 (Favorite TV Actress, Nickelodeon Kids' Choice Awards, 2009, 2010, 2011), We Day, 2014, The Voice, 2015, Inside Amy Schumer, 2016, SNL , 2016; (films) Spy Kids 3-D: Game Over, 2003, Another Cinderella Story, 2008, Horton Hears a Who! (voice), 2008, Princess Protection Program, 2009, Wizards of Waverly Place: The Movie, 2009, Ramona and Beezus, 2010, Monte Carlo, 2011, Spring Breakers, 2012, Hotel Transylvania (voice), 2012 (Favorite Animated Movie Voice, People's Choice Awards, 2016), Aftershock, 2012, Getaway, 2013, Rudderless, 2014, Behaving Badly, 2014, Hotel Transylvania 2 (voice), 2015, The Big Short, 2015, In Dubious Battle, 2016, The Revised Fundamentals of Caregiving, 2016, Neighbors 2: Sorority Rising, 2016, In Dubious Battle, 2016, Puppy!, 2017, Hotel Transylvania 3, 2018, A Rainy Day in New York, 2018, The Voyage of Doctor Dolittle, 2019; actress, executive producer (TV films) The Wizards Return: Alex versus Alex, 2013; singer: (albums) ((Selena Gomez & the Scene)) Kiss & Tell, 2009, A Year Without Rain, 2010, When The Sun Goes Down, 2011, (solo albums) Stars Dance, 2013, Revival, 2015(Studio Albums)(Selena Gomez and the Scene) Kiss & Tell,2009, A Year Without Rain, 2010, When the Sun Goes Down, 2011(Solo Albums) Stars Dance, 2013, Revival **AW:** Named Choice Music Group (with the Scene), Teen Choice Awards, 2012; Recipient Best Pop Video (for Come and Get It), MTV Video Music Awards, 2013

GONZALEZ, RICHARD A., T: Pharmaceutical Executive **I:** Pharmaceuticals **DOB:** 01/21/1954 **ED:** MS in BioChemistry, University Miami; BS in BioChemistry, University Houston, 1976 **C:** CEO AbbVie (formerly Abbott), 2013-; President Abbot Ventures, Inc., Abbott Labs, Abbott Park, Illinois, 2009-2013; Executive vice president pharmaceutical products group, Abbott Labs, Abbott Park, Illinois, 2010-; President, COO Abbott Labs, Abbott Park, Illinois, 2006-07; President, COO medical products, Abbott Labs, Abbott Park, Illinois, 2001-06; Senior vice president hospital products, Abbott Labs, Abbott Park, Illinois, 1998-2001; Vice president Health Systems division, Abbott Labs, Abbott Park, Illinois, 1995-98; Divisional vice president, general manager, Abbott Labs, Abbott Park, Illinois, 1992-95; Numerous positions in division diagnostics, Abbott Labs, Abbott Park, Illinois, 1977-92; Research biochemist, University Miami School Medicine, **CR:** Board directors Abbott

Labs, 2001-07 **CIV:** Member board directors, Shed Aquarium, Member board directors, Lyric Opera Chicago, **AW:** Named one of 50 Most Important Hispanics in Tech. & Business, Hispanic Engineer & Information Tech. magazine, 2005

GONZALEZ, VINCENTE, T: U.S. Representative from Texas **I:** Government Administration/Government Relations/Government Services **PB:** Corpus Christi **SC:** TX/USA **ED:** J.D., Texas Wesleyan School of Law, 1996; B.A., Embry-Riddle Aeronautical University, 1992 **C:** Member, U.S. Representative from Texas 15th District, 2017-; Member, Committee on Financial Services; Founder/Lawyer, V. Gonzalez & Associates, 1997-

GONZÁLEZ COLÓN, JENNIFER, T: Resident Commission of Puerto Rico **I:** Government Administration/Government Relations/Government Services **DOB:** 08/05/1976 **PB:** San Juan **C:** Minority Leader, Puerto Rico House of Representatives, 2013-2017,; Chair, Puerto Rico Republican Party, 2015-,; Resident Commissioner of Puerto Rico, 2017-Speaker of house, Puerto Rico Legislature, 2009-; At-large rep., Puerto Rico Legislature, 2005-17; Member Budget and Assignments, Ethics, Government, Internal Affairs, San Juan Devel. and Women's Affairs Committees, Puerto Rico Legislature,; Chairwomen Government Affairs Committee, Puerto Rico Legislature,; Rep., District 4, Puerto Rico Legislature, 2002-05; State director, Youth of Progressive New Party, **PA:** New Progressive Party

GOOD, LYNN JONES, T: Electrical Power Company Executive **I:** Oil & Energy **DOB:** 04/18/1959 **ED:** BS in Systems Analysis & Accounting, Miami University, Oxford, Ohio, 1981 **C:** Vice chair, president, CEO, Duke Energy Corp., Charlotte, North Carolina, 2013-; President, CEO, Duke Energy Corp., Charlotte, North Carolina, 2013; Group executive, CFO, Duke Energy Corp., Charlotte, North Carolina, 2009-13; Group executive, president commercial business, Duke Energy Corp., Charlotte, North Carolina, 2007-09; Senior vice president, treasurer, Duke Energy Corp., Charlotte, North Carolina, 2006-07; Executive vice president, CFO, Cinergy, 2005-06; Vice president finance, controller, Cinergy, 2005; Vice president, controller, Cinergy, 2003-05; Vice president finance project strategy, Cinergy, 2003; Partner, Deloitte & Touche LLC, Cincinnati, 2002-03; Partner, Arthur Andersen, 1992-2002; Various positions, Arthur Andersen, 1981-2002 **CR:** Board directors Duke Energy Corp., 2013-, Hubbell Inc., 2009- **CIV:** Board member, Bechtler Museum Modern Art, Charlotte, North Carolina, **AW:** Named one of The 50 Most Powerful Women in Business, Fortune magazine, 2013-15

GOODELL, ROGER STOKOE, T: National Football League commissioner **I:** Business Management/Business Services **DOB:** 02/19/1959 **PB:** Jamestown **PT:** Son of Charles Ellsworth and Jean (Rice) Goodell **ED:** BA in Economics, Washington & Jefferson College, 1981 **C:** Commissioner, NFL, New York City, 2006-; Assistant to president, American Football Conference (AFC), 1987-90; Executive vice president, COO, NFL, New York City, 2001-06; Executive vice president business, properties & club services, NFL, New York City, 2000-01; Executive vice president football devel., NFL, New York City, 1997-2000; Senior vice president league & football devel., NFL, New York City, 1995-97; Vice president international operations, business devel., NFL, New York City, 1992-95; Executive director club relations & international devel., NFL, New York City, 1991-92; Director club administration & international devel., NFL, 1990-91; Public relations assistant, NFL, New York City, 1984-87; Member

public relations, administration, New York Jets, 1983-84; Intern, NFL, New York City, 1982-83 **CIV:** Member board New York City chapter, Big Brothers & Big Sisters, **AW:** Named one of The 50 Most Powerful People in Sports, Sports Illustrated, 2013, The Most Influential People in the World of Sports, Business Week, 2008, 2007, 50 Most Influential People Sports Business, Street & Smith's SportsBus. Journal, 2007-09 **ACH:** Achievements include helping launch NFL Network

GOODING, CUBA, T: Actor **I:** Media & Entertainment **DOB:** 01/02/1968 **PB:** Bronx **SC:** NY/USA **PT:** Cuba Gooding; Shirley Gooding; **CW:** Actor: (films) Coming to America, 1988, Sing, 1989, Boyz N the Hood, 1991, Gladiator, 1992, A Few Good Men, 1992, Hitz, 1992, Judgement Night, 1993, Lightning Jack, 1994, Losing Isaiah, 1995, Outbreak, 1995, Jerry Maguire, 1996 (Academy award for Best Supporting Actor, 1997), The Audition, 1996, As Good As It Gets, 1997, What Dreams May Come, 1998, Instinct, 1999, Men of Honor, 2000, Pearl Harbor, 2001, Rat Race, 2001, In the Shadows, 2001, Boat Trip, 2002, Psychic, 2003, The Fighting Temptations, 2003, Radio, 2003, Home on the Range (voice), 2004, Lightfield's Home Videos, 2005, Shadowboxer, 2005, Dirty, 2005, End Game, 2006, Norbit, 2007, What Love Is, 2007, Daddy Day Camp, 2007, American Gangster, 2007, Hero Wanted, 2008, Linewatch, 2008, The Devil's Tomb, 2009, Lies & Illusions, 2009, Hardwired, 2009, Wrong Turn at Tahoe, 2009, The Hit List, 2011, Sacrifice, 2011, Red Tails, 2012, One in the Chamber, 2012, Deception, 2013, Something Whispered, 2013, Summoned, 2013, The Butler, 2013, Machete Kills, 2013; actress: Selma, 2014; actor: The Book of Negroes, 2015; (TV films) Kill or Be Killed, 1990, Murder with Motive: The Edmund Perry Story, 1992, Daybreak, 1993, The Tuskegee Airmen, 1995, Gifted Hands: The Ben Carson Story, 2009, Firelight, 2012 (National Association for the Advancement of Colored People Image award for Outstanding Actor in a TV Movie, Mini-Series or Dramatic Special, 2013), Guilty, 2013; (TV miniseries) The Book of Negroes, 2015; (TV series) American Crime Story: The People v. O.J. Simpson, 2016, American Horror Story: Roanoke, 2016. Katrina, American Crime Story, 2018; TV appearances Hill Street Blues, 1986-87, MacGyver, 1989-91, Empire, 2015, Forever, 2015, Big Time in Hollywood, FL, 2015, actor, producer (films) A Murder of Crows, 1999, Harold, 2008, actor, executive producer Freedom, 2014; actor: (Broadway plays) The Trip to Bountiful, 2013, Chicago, 2018.

GOODLATTE, ROBERT WILLIAM, T: Chairman of the House Judiciary Committee,U.S. Representative from Virginia, Lawyer **I:** Government Administration/Government Relations/Government Services **DOB:** 09/22/1952 **PB:** Holyoke **SC:** MA/USA **ED:** JD, Washington & Lee University School Law, Lexington, Virginia, 1977; BA in Government, Bates College, Lewiston, Maine, 1974 **CT:** Bar: U.S. Court of Appeals for the Fourth Circuit 1981, Virginia 1978, Massachusetts 1977 **C:** Chairman, U.S. House Judiciary Committee, 2013-; Member, U.S. Congress from 6th Virginia District, 1993-; Vice ranking member, U.S. House Judiciary Committee, 2009-10; Ranking member, U.S. House Agricultural Committee, 2007-08; Chairman, U.S. House Agricultural Committee, 2003-07; Partner, Bird, Kinder & Huffman, Roanoke, 1981-93; Private law practice, Roanoke, Virginia, 1979-81; District manager to Rep. M. Caldwell Butler, U.S. House of Representatives, 1977-79 **CIV:** Member adv. board, United Way Roanoke Valley, 1988-92 Chairman 6th Congressional District, Republican Party Virginia, 1983-88 Chairman, Roanoke City Rep. Committee, 1980-83 **H:** Tennis, swimming, hiking, reading **PA:** Republi-

can **BA:** Office of Robert Goodlatte, 2309 Rayburn HOB, Washington, DC, 20515

GOODMAN, JOHN, T: Actor **I:** Media & Entertainment **PB:** St. Louis **SC:** MO/USA **PT:** Leslie Goodman; Virginia Roos (Loosmoor) Goodman **MS:** Married **SPN:** Annabeth Hartzog (October 27, 1989) **CH:** Molly Evangeline **ED:** BFA in Theater, Southwest Missouri State University, 1975; Student, Meramac Community College **CW:** Performer dinner and children's theater productions, off-Broadway plays; appeared on Broadway in Loose Ends, 1979, Big River, 1985, Cat on a Hot Tin Roof, 2005, Waiting for Godot, 2009; actor: (films) Jailbait Babysitter, 1977, The Survivors, 1983, Eddie Macon's Run, 1983, Revenge of the Nerds, 1984, C.H.U.D., 1984, Maria's Lovers, 1985, Sweet Dreams, 1985, True Stories, 1986, The Big Easy, 1987, Burglar, 1987, Raising Arizona, 1987, The Wrong Guys, 1988, Everybody's All-American, 1988, Punchline, 1988, Sea of Love, 1989, Always, 1989, Stella, 1990, Arachnophobia, 1990, King Ralph, 1990, Barton Fink, 1991, The Babe, 1992, Matinee, 1993, Born Yesterday, 1993, We're Back! A Dinosaur's Story (voice), 1993, The Hudsucker Proxy, 1994, The Flintstones, 1994, Pie in the Sky, 1996, Mother Night, 1996, Fallen, 1997, Combat!, 1997, The Borrowers, 1997, The Big Lebowski, 1998, Blues Brothers 2000, 1998, Dirty Work, 1998, The Real Macaw (voice), 1998, Rudolph the Red Nosed Reindeer: The Movie, (voice) 1998, The Runner, 1999, Bringing Out the Dead, 1999, Coyote Ugly, 2000, O Brother, Where Art Thou?, 2000, What Planet Are You From?, 2000, Hitting the Wall, 2000, The Adventures of Rocky & Bullwinkle, 2000, My First Mister, 2000, One Night at McCool's, 2000, The Emperor's New Groove (voice), 2000, Storytelling, 2001, Happy Birthday, 2001, Monsters, Inc. (voice), 2001, Dirty Deeds, 2002, Masked and Anonymous, 2003, The Jungle Book 2 (voice), 2003, Home of Phobia, 2004, Clifford's Really Big Movie (voice), 2004, Beyond the Sea, 2004, Marilyn Hotchkiss Ballroom Dancing & Charm School, 2005, Cars (voice), 2006, Drunkboat, 2007, Death Sentence, 2007, Evan Almighty, 2007, Bee Movie (voice), 2007, Speed Racer, 2008, Gigantic, 2008, In the Electric Mist, 2008, Confessions of a Shopaholic, 2009, Alabama Moon, 2009, Pope Joan, 2009, The Princess and the Frog (voice), 2009, Drunkboat, 2010, Happy Feet Two (voice), 2011, Red State, 2011, The Artist, 2011, Extremely Loud and Incredibly Close, 2011, Flight, 2012, ParaNorman (voice), 2012, Argo, 2012, Trouble with the Curve, 2012, Flight, 2012, The Hangover Part III, 2013, The Internship, 2013, Monsters University (voice), 2013, Inside Llewyn Davis, 2013, Spring Break '83, 2014, The Monuments Men, 2014, Transformers: Age of Extinction (voice), 2014, The Gambler, 2014, Trumbo, 2015, Love the Coopers, 2015, 10 Cloverfield Lane, 2016, Ratchet and Clank (voice), 2016, Going Under, 2016, The Coldest City, 2016, Patriots Day, 2016, Bunyan and Babe, 2017, Kong Skull Island, 2017, Atomic Blonde, 2017, Once Upon a Time in Venice, 2017, Transformers: The Last Knight,Valerian and the City of a Thousand Planets, Captive State,2018; (TV series) Roseanne, 1988-96, Normal, Ohio, 2000, Center of the Universe, 2004-05, Father of the Pride, 2004-05, Treme, 2010-11, Damages, 2011; (TV films) The Face of Rage, 1983, Heart of Steel, 1983, Murder Ordained, 1987, Frosty Returns (voice), 1992, A Streetcar Named Desire, 1995, The Jack Bull, 1999, On the Edge, 2001, The Year Without a Santa Claus, 2006, You Don't Know Jack, 2010, Downwardly Mobile, 2012, It's a Spongebob Christmas!, 2012, Alpha House, 2013-14; (TV mini-series) Chiefs, 1983; (TV appearances) The Equalizer, 1987, Moonlighting, 1987, Grand, 1990, Grace Under Fire, 1993, Soul Man, 1997-98, The Simpsons, 1999, Futurama,

1999, Now and Again, 1999-2000, Pigs Next Door, 2000, Ed, 2001, Freedom: A History of Us, 2003, The West Wing, 2003-04, The Odd Job Jack, 2006, Studio 60 on the Sunset Strip, 2006, King of the Hill (voice), 2007, The Emperor's New School (voice), 2007, Community, 2011-12, Spongebob Squareparents, 2012, Dancing on the Edge, 2013, Alpha House 2012; actor, producer (TV films) Kingfish: A Story of Huey P. Long, 1995 **AW:** Recipient Spotlight award, National Board Review, 2012, Creative Arts Primetime Emmy for Outstanding Guest Actor in Drama Series, Academy TV Arts and Scis., 2007

GOODMAN, SHIRA D., T: Retail Office and Business Products Executive **I:** Retail/Sales **PB:** Chgo. **SC:** IL/USA **ED:** MS in Strategy and Marketing, Massachusetts Institute of Technology Sloan School Management; JD, Harvard Law School; BA, Princeton University, New Jersey **C:** CEO, Staples, 2016-2018; Executive vice president, human resources, Staples, Inc., Framingham, Massachusetts, 2009-; Executive vice president, marketing, Staples, Inc., Framingham, Massachusetts, 2001-09; Senior vice president, business delivery, Staples, Inc., Framingham, Massachusetts,; Joined as senior vice president, Staples Direct, Staples, Inc., Framingham, Massachusetts, 1992; Various management positions, Bain & Co., Inc., 1986-92 **CR:** Board of Directors CarMax Business Services, LLC, 2007-, The Stride Right Corp., 2002-07

GOODNIGHT, JAMES H., T: CEO of SAS **I:** Information Technology and Services **DOB:** 01/06/1943 **PB:** Wilmington **SC:** NC/USA **ED:** PhD in Statistics, North Carolina State University **C:** President & CEO, SAS Institute Inc., Cary, North Carolina, 1976-; Co-founder, Chairman, SAS Institute Inc.,; Faculty, North Carolina State University, 1972-76 **CR:** Adjunct Professor North Carolina State University, 1976-. **CIV:** Started, SAS inSchool, Founder, Cary Academy, Cary, North Carolina, 1996 **AW:** Named One of Am.'s 25 Most Fascinating Entrepreneurs, Inc. Magazine, 2004, 20th Century's Great Am. Business Leaders, Harvard Business School, 2004, World's Richest People, Forbes Magazine, 2001-, Forbes 400: Richest Americans, 1999- **MEM:** Fellow Am. Statistical Association

GORDER, JOE, T: Valero CEO **I:** Oil & Energy **ED:** MBA, Our Lady of the Lake University, 1992; BBA, University of Missouri, St. Louis, 1979 **C:** President, CEO, Valero Energy Corp., 2014-; President, COO, Valero Energy Corp., 2012-14; Executive vice president marketing & supply, chief commercial officer, Valero Energy Corp., 2011-12; Executive vice president marketing & supply, Valero Energy Corp., 2005-11; Senior vice president corporate devel., Valero Energy Corp., San Antonio, 2003-05; Vice president business devel., Ultramar Diamond Shamrock,; Director comml./ indsl. sales, Diamond Shamrock,; Assistant treasurer, Diamond Shamrock,; Director information systems, Diamond Shamrock

GORDON, JEFF, T: Former Professional Stock Car Racer **I:** Athletics **DOB:** 08/04/1971 **PB:** Vallejo **SC:** CA/USA **PT:** Son of William Grinnell Gordon and Carol Ann (Houston) Bickford; **C:** Announcer, Fox NASCAR, 2015-; Global business advisor, Axalta, 2015-; Retired, 2015; Race car driver NASCAR, Hendrick Motorsports, 1993-2015 **CR:** 1st pl. Ford EcoBoost 400 Homestead-Miami Speedway, 2012 1st pl. Samsung 500 Texas Motor Speedway, 2009 1st pl. Subway Fresh Fit 500 Phoenix International Raceway, 2011, 2007 1st pl. USG Sheetrock 400 Chicagoland Speedway, 2006 1st pl. Protection One 400 Kansas Speedway, 2002, 2001 1st pl. UAW-Daimler Chrysler 400 Las Vegas Motor Speedway, 2001 1st pl. Kmart 400 Michigan International

Speedway, 2001, 1st pl. Pepsi 400, 1998 1st pl. Dodge/Save Mart 350 Infineon Raceway, 2006, 2004, 1st pl. Save Mart/Kragen 350, 2000, 1999, 1998 1st pl. Global Crossing at the Glen Watkins Glen International Raceway, 2001, 1st pl. Frontier at the Glen, 1999, 1st pl. Bud at the Glen, 1998, 1997 1st pl. Auto Club 500 California Speedway, 2004, 1st pl. California 500, 1999, 1997 1st pl. Tyson Holly Farms 400 North Wilkesboro Speedway, 1996 1st pl. Advanced Auto Parts 500 Martinsville Speedway, 2005, 1st pl. Subway 500, 2005, 2003, 1st pl. Virginia 500, 2003, 1st pl. National Association of Performing Artists AutoCare 500, 1999, 1st pl. Goody's Headache Powder 500, 1997, 1st pl. Hanes 500, 1996 1st pl. UAW-Ford 500 Talladega Superspeedway, 2007, 1st pl. Aaron's 499, 2007, 2005, 2004, 1st pl. DieHard 500, 2000, 1996 1st pl. Pennsylvania 400 Pocono Raceway, 2012, 1st pl. Pocono 500, 2011, 2007, 1st pl. Pennsylvania 500, 1998, 1st pl. Pocono 500, 1997, 1st pl. UAW-GM Teamwork 500, 1996 1st pl. Chevrolet Monte Carlo 400 Richmond International Raceway, 2000, 1st pl. Pontiac Excitement 400, 1996 1st pl. MBNA Platinum 400 Dover International Speedway, 2001, 1st pl. Miller 500, 1996, 1st pl. MBNA 500, 1996, 1995 1st pl. Dodge Avenger 500 Darlington Raceway, 2007, 1st pl. Pepsi Southern 500, 1998, 1st pl. TranSouth Fin. 400, 1996, 1st pl. Mountain Dew Southern 500, 2002, 1997, 1996, 1995 1st pl. CMT 300 New Hampshire International Speedway, 1998, 1997, 1st pl. Slick 50 300, 1995 1st pl. Daytona 500 Daytona International Speedway, 2005, 1999, 1997, 1st pl. Pepsi 400, 2004, 1998, 1995 1st pl. Sharpie 500 Bristol Motor Speedway, 2002, 1st pl. Food City 500, 1998, 1997, 1996, 1995 1st pl. Labor Day Classic 500 Atlanta Motor Speedway, 2011, 1st pl. Bass Pro Shops MBNA 500, 2003, 1st pl. Cracker Barrel 500, 1999, 1st pl. National Association of Performing Artists 500, 1998, 1st pl. Purolator 500, 1995 1st pl. Air Corps Delco 400 North Carolina Speedway, 1998, 1st pl. GM Goodwrench Service Plus 400, 1998, 1st pl. Goodwrench Service 400, 1997, 1st pl. Goodwrench 500, 1995 1st pl. Brickyard 400 Indianapolis Motor Speedway, 2004, 2001, 1998, 1994 1st pl. Bank of Am. 500 Lowe's Motor Speedway, 2007, 1st pl. UAW-GM Quality 500, 1999, 1st pl. Coca-Cola 600, 1998, 1997, 1994 **CIV:** Founder, Jeff Gordon Foundation, 1999 **AW:** Named NASCAR Driver of Year, 2001, 1998, 1997, 1995, Winston Cup Series Champion, 2001, 1998, 1997, 1995, Rookie of Year, 1993; named one of The 100 Most Powerful Celebrities, Forbes.com, 2008, The Most Influential People in the World of Sports, Business Week, 2007; named to McDonald's All-Star Team, 1995, 1994; recipient Chevrolet Lifetime Achievement award, 2015, Heisman Humanitarian award, 2012,Bristol Motor Speedway Legends Plaza Inductee, 2016, Order of the Long Leaf Pine, 2016, Denise McCluggage Award, 2016, Nation Motorsports Press Association Spirit Award, 2015, Bill France Award of Excellence, 2015 **ACH:** Achievements include becoming the 2nd youngest Winston Cup Champion ever at age 24; becoming the first NASCAR driver to reach $100 million in career winnings, 2009; all-time winningest Cup Series driver at Indianapolis Motor Speedway, Kansas Speedway, Pocono Raceway, Sonoma Raceway **BA:** Jeff Gordon Inc, 4345 Papa Joe Hendrick Blvd, Charlotte, NC, 28262

GORDON-LEVITT, JOSEPH, T: Actor **I:** Media & Entertainment **PB:** LA **SC:** CA/USA **PT:** Dennis Levitt; Jane Gordon **ED:** Attended, Columbia University **C:** Co-founder, hitRECord, 2005 **CW:** Actor: (TV films) Stranger on My Land, 1988, Settle the Score, 1988, Dark Shadows, 1990, Changes, 1991, Hi Honey - I'm Dead, 1991, Plymouth, 1991, Partners, 1993, Gregory K, 1993, The Great Elephant Escape, 1995; (TV series) Dark Shadows, 1991, The Powers

That Be, 1992-93, Roseanne, 1993-95, 3rd Rock from the Sun, 1996-2001; (films) A River Runs Through It, 1992, Holy Matrimony, 1994, The Road Killers, 1994, Angels in the Outfield, 1994, The Juror, 1996, Sweet Jane, 1998, 10 Things I Hate About You, 1999, Picking Up the Pieces, 2000, Forever Lulu, 2000, Manic 2001, (voice) Treasure Planet, 2002, Latter Days, 2003, Mysterious Skin, 2004, Brick, 2005, Havoc, 2005, Shadowboxer, 2005, The Lookout, 2007, Stop-Loss, 2008, Miracle at St. Anna, 2008, Uncertainty, 2008, Killshot, 2008, Big Breaks, 2009, Women in Trouble, 2009, (500) Days of Summer, 2009, G.I. Joe: The Rise of Cobra, 2009, Inception, 2010, Hesher, 2010, 50/50, 2011, The Dark Knight Rises, 2012, Premium Rush, 2012, Lincoln, 2012, (voice) The Wind Rises, 2013, Sin City: A Dame to Kill For, 2014, The Walk, 2015, The Night Before, 2015, Snowden, 2016; Star Wars: The Last Jedi (voice cameo), 2017; director, producer, writer, composer (films) Sparks, 2009, actor, executive producer Looper, 2012, actor, director, writer Don Jon, 2013

GORDY, BERRY, T: Entrepreneur, Film Producer, Recording Industry Executive **I:** Media & Entertainment **DOB:** 11/28/1929 **PB:** Detroit **SC:** MI/ USA **CH:** Berry IV; Hazel Joy; Terry James; Kerry A.; Sherry R.; Kennedy W.; Stefan K.; Rhonda Ross-Kendrick **ED:** Honorary PhD in Music, Eastern Michigan University (1971) **C:** Chairman, Board of Directors, West Grand Media (1998-Present); Founder, Jobete Music Co., Inc. (1997-Present); Founder, Motown Record Corp. (1961-Present); Executive Producer, Motion Pictures **CW:** Writer, "Motown: The Musical" (2013); Writer, "Lennon" (2005); Author, "To Be Loved: The Music, the Magic, the Memories of Motown" (1994); Executive Producer, "Berry Gordy's the Last Dragon" (1984); Director, "Mahogany" (1975); Executive Producer, "Bingo Long Traveling All-Stars and Motor Kings" (1975); Executive Producer, "Lady Sings the Blues" (1972); Song Writer, "Money-That's What I Want"; Producer, Writer, Composer and Lyricist **AW:** Recipient, Pioneer Award, Songwriters Hall of Fame (2013); Recipient, Candle Award for Lifetime Achievement in Arts and Entertainment, Morehouse College (2005); Recipient, Legend Award, Rainbow/Push Coalition (2001); Recipient, A.G. Gaston Lifetime Achievement Award, Black Entertainment/Bank of America (2001); Recipient, Wall St. Project Millennium Award, Rainbow/Push (2000); Inductee, National Business Hall of Fame, Junior Achievement (1998); Recipient, Legend Award, BESLA (1998); Recipient, AmericanL Legend Award, American Society of Composers Pop Music Awards (1998); Recipient, Lifetime Achievement Award, NABOB (1998); Inductee, Hollywood Walk of Fame (1996); Recipient, 20th Century Award, Black Radio Exclusive (1993); Recipient, Generation Award, Congressional Black Caucus Foundation (1993); Recipient, Lifetime Achievement Award, Black Business Association (1993); Recipient, Abe Olman Publishing Award, Songwriters Hall of Fame (1993); Recipient, Trustees Award, National Academy of Recording Arts and Sciences (1991); Inductee, Rock and Roll Hall of Fame (1988); Recipient, Gordon Grand Fellowship, Yale University (1985); Inductee, Minority Hall of Fame, Atlanta University School of Business Administration (1981); Recipient, Whitney M. Young Junior Award, L.A. Urban League (1980); Named, Leading Entrepreneurs of the Nation, Babson College (1978); Recipient, Annual American Music Award for Iutstanding Contribution to the Music Industry (1975); Recipient, Golden Mike and Martin Luther King, Jr.'s Leadership Award, NATRA (1969); Recipient, Business Achievement Award, Interracial Council for Business Opportunity (1967) **MEM:** NAACP;

Academy of Motion Picture Arts and Sciences; BMI, Directors Guild of America

GORE, AL, **T:** Enviormental Activist, 45th Vice President of the U.S. **I:** Environmental Services **DOB:** 03/31/1948 **PB:** Washington **SC:** DC/USA **PT:** Son of Albert and Pauline (LaFon) Gore; **ED:** LLD, LHD in Ecology and Evolutionary Biology (hon.), University Tennessee, Knoxville, 2010; Attended, Vanderbilt University Law School; Attended, Vanderbilt University Divinity School, Nashville; BA cum laude, Harvard University, 1969 **C:** Partner, head climate change solutions group, Kleiner Perkins Caufield & Byers, Menlo Park, California, 2007-; Co-founder, chairman, Generation Investment Management Inc., London, 2004-; Co-founder, chairman, Current TV, San Francisco, 2005-13; Democratic Candidate for President, 2000; Vice President of the U.S., Washington, DC 1993-2001; US Senator from Tennessee, 1985-93; Member, U.S. Congress from 6th Tennessee District, 1983-85; Member, U.S. Congress from 4th Tennessee District, 1977-83; Homebuilder and land developer, Tanglewood Home Builders Co., 1971-76; Investigative reporter, editorial writer, The Tennessean, 1971-76 **CR:** Visiting professor UCLA, 2001-, Middle Tennessee State University, 2001, Fisk University, 2001, Columbia University School Journalism, 2001 chairman Alliance for Climate Protection, 2006- board of directors World Resources Institute, 2005-, Apple Inc. (formerly Apple Computer Inc), 2003- senior advisor, Google, Inc., 2001- **MIL:** Served with U.S. Army, 1969-71 **CW:** Author: Earth in the Balance: Ecology and the Human Spirit, 1992, Let the Glory Out: My South and It's Politics, 2000, An Inconvenient Truth: The Planetary Emergency of Global Warming and What We Can Do About It, 2006 (Quill Book award for current events, 2006, Grammy award for Best Spoken Word Album for audio book, 2009), The Assault on Reason: How the Politics of Fear, Secrecy, and Blind Faith Subvert Wise Decision Making, Degrade Our Democracy, and Put Our Country and Our World in Peril, 2007 (Quill Book award for current events, 2007), Our Choice: A Plan to Solve the Climate Crisis, 2009, The Future: Six Drivers of Global Change, 2013, (children's books) An Inconvenient Truth: The Crisis of Global Warming, 2007; co-author (with Joseph Kaufman): The World According to Al Gore: An A-To-Z Compilation of His Opinions, Positions, and Public Statements, 2000; co-author: (with Tipper Gore) Joined at the Heart: The Transformation of the American Family, 2002; host, co-prodr. (documentaries) An Inconvenient Truth, 2006 (Special award, Humanitas Prize Board, 2006) **AW:** Named Policy Leader of Year, Scientific American magazine, 2006; named one of The 50 Highest-Earning Political Figures, Newsweek, 2010, The 100 Agents of Change, Rolling Stone magazine, 2009, The World's Most Influential People, TIME magazine, 2007, 2006; recipient James C. Morgan Global Humanitarian award, Tech Museum, 2009, Dan David prize, Dan David Foundation, 2008, Nobel Peace Prize, Norweigan Nobel Committee, 2007, Principe de Asturias prize, Fundación Príncipe de Asturias, 2007, Founders award, International Academy TV Arts & Sciences, 2007, World Tech. award for policy, World Tech. Network, 2006, Webby Lifetime Achievement award, International Academy Digital Arts & Sciences, 2005 **MEM:** Fellow: American Academy Arts & Sciences; mem.: Farm Bureau, Tennessee Jaycees, American Legion, VFW **PA:** Democrat **BA:** Office of the Honorable Al Gore & Tipper Gore, 3810 Bedford Avenue # 250, Nashville, TN, 37215

GORMAN, JAMES P., **T:** Morgan Stanley CEO **I:** Business Management/Business Services **DOB:** 07/14/1958 **PB:** Melbourne **SC:** Australia **ED:** MBA, Columbia University, 1987; Bachelor of Law, University of Melbourne, 1982; Bachelor's Degree, University of Melbourne **C:** Chairman, Morgan Stanley Smith Barney, LLC, 2009-; Chairman, president, CEO, Morgan Stanley, New York City, 2012-; President, CEO, Morgan Stanley, New York City, 2010-11; Co-pres., co-head strategic planning, Morgan Stanley, New York City, 2007-09; President, COO global wealth management group, Morgan Stanley, New York City, 2005-08; Executive vice president acquisitions, strategy and research, Merrill Lynch & Co., Inc., 2005; President global private client, Merrill Lynch & Co., Inc., 2002-05; Head USPC client relationship group, Merrill Lynch & Co., Inc., 2001-02; Executive vice president, chief marketing officer, Merrill Lynch & Co., Inc., 1999-2001; Senior partner, McKinsey & Co., New York, 1997-99; Member partner election committee, McKinsey & Co., 1997-99; Chairman New York personnel operating committee, McKinsey & Co., 1996-99; Co-head personal fin. services practice North America, McKinsey & Co., 1992-96; Partner, McKinsey & Co., 1992-97; Attorney, Phillips Fox & Masel, Melbourne, Australia, 1982-85 **CR:** Board of Directors Morgan Stanley, 2010-, MSCI Inc., 2007-09; Chairman Security Industry & Financial Markets Association, 2006 **CIV:** Trustee, Columbia Business School, Chairman Board of Directors, Graham-Windham, **AW:** Named one of The 50 Most Influential People in Global Finance, Bloomberg Markets, 2014, 2011 **BA:** Morgan Stanley, 1585 Broadway, New York, NY, 10036

GORSKY, ALEX, **T:** Chairman and CEO of Johnson & Johnson **I:** Business Management/Business Services **DOB:** 05/24/1960 **ED:** MBA, University Pennsylvania Wharton School Business, 1996; BS, US Military Academy, West Point, 1982 **C:** Chairman, CEO, Johnson & Johnson, 2012-; CEO, Johnson & Johnson, 2012; Vice chairman executive committee, Johnson & Johnson, 2011-12; Worldwide chairman medical devices & diagnostics group (MD&D), member executive committee, Johnson & Johnson, 2009-11; CEO, head Pharma North America, Novartis Pharmaceuticals Corp., 2005-08; COO, head general medicines, Novartis Pharmaceuticals Corp., 2004-05; Group chairman Europe, the Middle East & Africa, Johnson & Johnson, London, 2003-04; President, Janssen Pharmaceutica Inc., New Jersey, 2001-03; Various positions including sales rep. & in sales & marketing divisions, Janssen Pharmaceutica Inc., New Jersey, 1988-2001 **CR:** Board directors Johnson & Johnson, 2012- **CIV:** Board directors, Doylestown Hospital, **AW:** Named Honorable Mentor, Healthcare Businesswomen's Association, 2009 **MEM:** Mem.: Philadelphia College Pharmacy, National Alliance on Aging, National Alliance for the Mentally Ill **H:** Running **BA:** Johnson & Johnson, 1 Johnson & Johnson Plaza, New Brunswick, NJ, 08933

GORSUCH, NEIL MCGILL, **T:** Associate Justice of the U.S. Supreme Court **I:** Law and Legal Services **DOB:** 08/29/1967 **PB:** Denver, August 29, 1967 **PT:** Son of David Ronald Gorsuch and Anne McGill Burford; **ED:** DPhil, Oxford University, England; JD cum laude, Harvard University, Cambridge, Massachusetts, 1991; BA with honors, Columbia University, New York City, 1988 **CT:** Bar: DC 1997, Colorado 1994, New York 1992 **C:** Associate Justice, Supreme Court of the U.S., Washington D.C., 2017-; Adjunct professor, University Colorado Law School, 2007-2017; Judge, US Court Appeals 10th cir., Denver, 2006-; Principal deputy asso-

ciate attorney general, acting associate attorney general, US Department Justice, DC, 2005-06; Partner, Kellogg, Huber, Hansen, Todd & Evans, 1998-2005; Associate, Kellogg, Huber, Hansen, Todd & Evans, DC, 1995-97; Law clerk to Justice Byron R. White & Justice Anthony M. Kennedy, US Supreme Court, DC, 1993-94; Law clerk to Hon. David B. Sentelle, US Court Appeals DC cir., 1991-92 **CR:** Board directors, executive committee Judicial Conference US Committee Rules Practice & Procedure, 2010-, Federal Judges Association, 2009- **CW:** Contributor articles to professional journals **AW:** Recipient Joseph Stevens Pub. Service award, Harry S. Truman Foundation, 2007, Edmund J. Randolph award for Outstanding Service, US Department Justice, 2006; Harry S. Truman scholar, 1987-90, Marshall scholar, 1992-95 **MEM:** Mem.: Phi Beta Kappa **BA:** US Supreme Court, 1 First St NE, Washington, DC, 20543

GOSAR, PAUL ANTHONY, **T:** U.S. Representative From Arizona, Dentist **I:** Government Administration/Government Relations/Government Services **DOB:** 11/27/1958 **PB:** Rock Springs **ED:** DDS, Creighton Boyle School of Dentistry, 1985; BS, Creighton University, 1981 **C:** U.S. Congress, Fourth Arizona District, 2013-Present; U.S. House of Natural Resources Committee, 2011-Present; U.S. House of Oversight & Government Reform Committee, 2011-Present; U.S. Congress, First Arizona District, Washington, DC, 2011-2013; Private Dental Practice, Flagstaff, AZ **AW:** Dentist of the Year, Hall of Fame, Arizona Dental Association **MEM:** Past Vice Chairman, Council on Government Affairs, American Dental Association; Past President, Arizona Dental Association; Northern Arizona Dental Society **PA:** Republican

GOSLING, RYAN, **T:** Actor **I:** Media & Entertainment **PB:** Cornwall **SC:** ON/Canada **PT:** Thomas Ray Gosling; Donna Gosling **CH:** Esmeralda Amada; Amada Lee **CW:** Actor: (films) Frankenstein and Me, 1996, Remember the Titans, 2000, The Believer, 2001, The Slaughter Rule, 2002, Murder By Numbers, 2002, The U.S. of Leland, 2003, The Notebook, 2004, Stay, 2005, Half Nelson, 2006 (Best Breakthrough Performance - Male National Board Review, 2006), Fracture, 2007, Lars and the Real Girl, 2007, All Good Things, 2010, Crazy, Stupid, Love, 2011, Drive, 2011, The Ides of March, 2011, The Place Beyond the Pines, 2012, Gangster Squad, 2013, The Big Short, 2015, Weightless, 2016, The Nice Guys, 2016, La La Land, 2016, Song to Song, 2017, Blade Runner 2049, 2017, First Man, 2018; (TV films) Nothing Too Good for a Cowboy, 1998, The Unbelievables, 1999; (TV series) The Mickey Mouse Club, 1993-94, Breaker High, 1997-98, Young Hercules, 1998-99, (TV appearances) Are You Afraid of the Dark?, 1995, Ready or Not, 1996, Flash Forward, 1996, The Adventures of Shirley Holmes, 1996, Goosebumps, 1996, Road to Avonlea, 1996, Kung Fu: The Legend Continues, 1996, PSI Factor: Chronicles of the Paranormal, 1996, Hercules: The Legendary Journeys, 1999, I'm Still Here, 2005, SNL, 2015-17; actor, executive producer (films) Blue Valentine, 2010, Only God Forgives, 2013; prodr.: (documentaries) ReGeneration, 2010; producer, director, writer (films) Lost River, 2014; executive prodr.: (films) White Shadow, 2013; musician ((with Dead Man's Bones)): (albums) Self-Titled, 2009

GOSSARD, STONE CARPENTER, **T:** Musician **I:** Media & Entertainment **DOB:** 07/20/1966 **PB:** Seattle **SC:** WA/USA **C:** Guitarist, Member, Pearl Jam, 1991-2001,; Solo Artist, 2001- **CW:** Musician: (albums with Green River) Come On Down, 1985, Dry As a Bone, 1987, Rehab Doll, 1988, (albums with Mother Love Bone) Shine, 1989, Apple, 1990,

Mother Love Bone, 1992, (albums with Temple of the Dog) Temple of the Dog, 1991, (albums with Pearl Jam) Ten, 1991 (Jeremy - Video of Year, Best Group Video, Best Metal/Hard Rock Video, Best Direction, MTV Music Video Awards, 1993), Alive, 1991, Vs., 1993, Vitalogy, 1994 (Spin the Black Circle - Best Hard Rock Performance, Grammy Awards, 1996), No Code, 1996, Yield, 1998, Binaural, 2000, Riot Act, 2002, Pearl Jam, 2006, Backspacer, 2009, Lightning Bolt, 2013; Numerous Collaborations, Sub Pop 200, 1988, This House is Not a Motel, 1989, Sub Pop Rock City, 1989, Another Pyrrhic Victory, 1989, Endangered Species, 1990, Dry As a Bone, 1990, Afternoon Delight, 1992, Hype!, 1996, Wild and Wooly: The Northwest Rock Collection, 2000, Sleepless in Seattle: The Birth of Grunge, 2006 (Albums with Mother Love Bone), Thrash and Burn: The Metal Alternative, 1993, The Best of Grunge Rock, 1993, Alterno-Daze: Natural 90s Selection, 1995, Proud to Be Loud, 1997, Alternative Moments, 2001, The Road Mix: Music from the Television Series One Tree Hill, Volume 3, 2007,(Solo Album) Bayleaf, 2001, Moonlander, 2013 **AW:** Named Favorite Pop/Rock New Artist, Favorite New Heavy Metal/Hard Rock Artist, American Music Awards, 1993, Favorite Alternative Artist, Favorite Heavy Metal/Hard Rock Artist, 1996, Favorite Alternative Artist, 1999, Grammy for Best Recording Package, 2015, Rock and Roll Hall of Fame Inductee, 2017 **BA:** Agricultural and Mechanical Records, 70 Universal City Plz, Universal City, CA, 91608

GOTTHEIMER, JOSH, T: U.S. Representative from New Jersey **I:** Government Administration/Government Relations/Government Services **ED:** J.D., Harvard Law, 2004; B.A., University of Pennsylvania, 1997 **CT:**; **C:** Member, U.S. Representative fro New Jersey's 5th District, 2017-; Member, Committee on Financial Services; General Manager for Advertising and Strategy, Microsoft, 2012-2015; Senior Counselor,Chairman of the Federal Communications Commission,2010-2012; Special Assistant/Speechwriter,, For Hilary Clinton, 1998-2001 **CW:** (Novels)Ripple of Hope: Great American Civil Rights Speeches, 2003, Power in Words: The Stories Behind Barack Obama's Speech's from the State House to the White House, 2011 **BA:** 213 Cannon HOB, Washington, DC, 20515

GOULD, RONALD MURRAY, T: Federal Judge **I:** Law and Legal Services **DOB:** 10/17/1946 **PB:** St. Louis **SC:** MO/USA **PT:** Son of Harry H. and Sylvia C. (Sadofsky) Gould; **ED:** JD, University of Michigan, 1973; BS in Econs., University of Pennsylvania, 1968 **CT:** Bar: U.S. Court Appeals (federal cir.) 1986, U.S. District Court (eastern district) Washington 1982, Supreme Court of the U.S. 1981, U.S. Court Appeals (9th cir.) 1980, U.S. District Court (we. district) Washington 1976, Washington 1975 **C:** Judge, U.S. Court Appeals (9th Cir.), Seattle, 1999-; Partner, Perkins Coie, Seattle, 1981-99; Associate, Perkins Coie, Seattle, 1975-80; Law Clerk to Hon. Justice Potter Stewart, Supreme Court of the U.S., Washington, 1974-75; Law Clerk to Hon. Wade H. McCree Junior, U.S. Court Appeals (6th Cir.), Detroit, 1973-74 **CR:** Adjunct Professor University of Washington Law School, 1986-89 **CIV:** Board of Trustees, Bellevue Community College, 1993-99 Citizens Cabinet Member, Governor Mike Lowry, Seattle, 1993-96 Board of Directors Economic Devel. Council, Seattle and King County, 1991-94 Executive Board Chief, Seattle Council Boy Scouts of Am., 1984- Member Community Relations Council, Jewish Federation of Greater Seattle, 1985-88 **CW:** Editor-in-Chief: Michigan Law Rev., 1972-73; Editor: Washington Civil Procedure Deskbook, 1981 **MEM:** Fellow: American Bar Association (Antitrust Section, Litigation Section);

Mem.: Am. Judicature Society, King County Bar Association (Distinguished Service Award 1987), Washington State Bar Association (Board of Governors 1988-91, President 1994-95), 9th Judicial Cir. Hist. Society (Board of Directors 1994-), Supreme Court Hist. Society **H:** Reading, Chess **BA:** 95 7th St, St. Louis, CA, 94013

GOWDY, TREY, T: Chair of the House Oversight Committee, U.S. Representative from South Carolina **I:** Government Administration/Government Relations/Government Services **DOB:** 08/22/1964 **PB:** Greenville **SC:** SC/USA **PT:** Son of Harold Watson and Novalene (Evans) Gowdy **ED:** JD, University South Carolina School Law, 1989; BA in History, Baylor University, Waco, Texas, 1986 **C:** Chair, House Oversight Committee, 2017-; Member, US House Ethics Committee, 2013-; Member, US House Oversight & Government Reform Committee, Washington, 2011-; Member, US House Education & the Workforce Committee, Washington, 2011-; Member, US House Judiciary Committee, Washington, 2011-; Member, US Congress from 4th South Carolina District, Washington, 2011-; Solicitor, Seventh Judicial Cir. Court, Spartanburg, South Carolina, 2001-10; Federal prosecutor Office US Attorney, US Department Justice, Greenville, 1994-2000; Attorney, Nelson Mullins Riley & Scarborough LLP, Greenville, 1991-93; Law clerk to Hon. G. Ross Anderson, Junior, US District Court (District South Carolina), Anderson, 1990-91; Law clerk to Hon. John P. Gardner, South Carolina Court Appeals, 1989-90 **CR:** Chairman US House Select Committee on the Events Surrounding the 2012 Terrorist Attack in Benghazi, 2014- **PA:** Republican

GRABER, SUSAN P., T: Federal Judge **I:** Law and Legal Services **DOB:** 07/05/1949 **PB:** Oklahoma City **SC:** OK/USA **PT:** Julius A. Graber; Bertha (Fenyves) Graber **ED:** JD, Yale University (1972); BA, Wellesley College (1969) **C:** Judge, United Court of Appeals for the Ninth Circuit, Portland, OR (1998-Present); Associate Justice, Oregon Supreme Court, Salem, OR (1990-1998); From Judge to Presiding Judge, Oregon Court of Appeals, Salem, OR (1988-1990); Mediator, U.S. District Court for the District of Oregon (1986-1988); Arbitrator, Oregon Circuit Court for the Fourth Judicial District (1985-1988); Judge Pro Tempore, Multonomah County District Court (1983-1988); From Associate to Partner, Stoel Rives Boley Jones & Grey, Portland, OR (1978-1988); Associate, Taft Stettinius & Hollister, Cincinnati, OH (1975-1978); Associate, Jones Gallegos Snead & Wertheim, Santa Fe, NM (1974-1975); Assistant Atorney General, Bureau of Revenue, Santa Fe, NM (1972-1974) **CIV:** Board of Directors, U.S. District Court of Oregon Historical Society (1985-Present); Board of Directors, Oregon Law Foundation (1990-1991); Board of Visitors, School of Law, University of Oregon (1986-1993); Member, Governor's Advisory Council on Legal Services (1979-1988) **MEM:** Chair, Oregon Appellate Judges Association (1992-1993); Vice Chair, Oregon Appellate Judges Association (1991-1992); Secretary-Treasurer, Oregon Appellate Judges Association (1990-1991); Program Chair, Oregon Judicial Conference (1990); Education Committee, Oregon Judicial Conference (1988-1991); Pro Bono Committee, Oregon State Bar (1988-1990); Chair Executive of Committee, Ninth Circuit Judicial Conference (1987-1988); Judicial Administration Committee, Oregon State Bar (1985-1987); Phi Beta Kappa; American Law Institute; ABA; Master, American Inns of Court **BAR:** Oregon (1978); Ohio (1977); New Mexico (1972) **BA:** 95 7th St, San Francisco, CA, 94013

GRAF, STEFFI, T: Former Professional Tennis Player **I:** Athletics **DOB:** 06/14/1969 **PB:** Bruhl **SC:** Germany **PT:** Daughter of Peter and Heidi Graf; **C:** Designer, Steffi Graf Handbags, 2002-; Founder, Steffi Graf Marketing, 1996; WTA 1982- **CIV:** Founder, Children of Tomorrow, 1998- Ambassador, World Wildlife Fund (WWF), **AW:** Winner numerous professional women's tennis tournaments including The Golden Grand Slam (Australian Open, French Open, Wimbledon, US Open, Olympics), 1988, Berlin Open, 1988, Wimbledon, 1989, 1991, 1992, 1993, 1995, 1996, US Open, 1989, 1993, 1995, 1996, Australian Open, 1989, 1990, 1994, French Open, 1993, 1995, 1996, 1999, Olympic Gold Medal, 1988; retired from competition, 1999; named WTA Player of Year, 1987-90, 1993-96; recipient Olympic Medal of Honor, IOC, 1999, Female Sports Award of the Last Decade, Espy, 1999; named to Tennis Hall of Fame, 2004,ITF World Champion, 1987-90, 1993, 1995-96, German Sportsperson of the Year, 1986-89, International Tennis Hall of Fame, 2004, German Sports Hall of Fame, 2008 **ACH:** Achievements include 107 Career Titles; finished WTA season ranked no. 1, 1987-90, 1993-96; ranked no. 1 in world for more consecutive weeks than any other player in tennis history; ranks 1st all-time in career prize money ($21 million); only person to win a Grand Slam on four different surfaces; only person to win a Calendar Year Golden Slam, 1988 **ADD:** Steffi Graf Sport GmBH, Mallaustrasse 75, Mannheim, YT, Germany, 68219

GRAHAM, ASHLEY, T: Model **I:** Apparel & Fashion **PB:** Lincoln **SC:** NE/USA **C:** Judge, Americas Next Top Model, 2016; Backstage Host, Miss Universe and Miss USA, 2016-17; Designer, Lingerie for Addition Elle, 2013; Model,Ford Models, 2003-; Model,Wilhelmina Models, 2001-03 **CW:** (Book) A New Model: What Confidence, Beauty, and Power Really Look Like, 2017 **AW:** Time 100 Most Influential, 2017

GRAHAM, AUBREY (DRAKE), T: Singer, Rapper, Actor **I:** Media & Entertainment **PB:** Toronto **SC:** ON/Canada **PT:** Dennis Graham; Sandi Graham **CW:** Actor: (TV series) Degrassi: The Nest Generation, 2001-09; singer: (mixtape) Room for Improvement, 2006, Comeback Season, 2007, (albums) So Far Gone, 2009 (Rap Recording of Year, Juno Awards, 2010), Thank Me Later, 2010, Take Care, 2011 (Best Rap Album, Grammy Awards, 2013), Nothing Was the Same, 2013, If You're Reading This It's Too Late, 2015, If You're Reading This It's Too Late, 2015, Views, 2016, More Life, 2017, Scary Hours, 2018 (songs) Best I Ever Had, 2009 (Top Rap Song, Billboard Music Awards, 2009), (featuring Lil Wayne) HYFR, 2011 (Best Hip-Hop Video, MTV Video Music Awards, 2012), Hold On, We're Going Home, 2013 (Best Hip-Hop Video, MTV Video Music Awards, 2014) **AW:** Named Best Male Hip Hop Artist, Black Entertainment (BET) Awards, 2012, Top Rap Artist, Billboard Music Awards, 2016, Top New Hip Hop Artist/R&B Artist, 2009; recipient Hal David Starlight award, Songwriters Hall of Fame, 2011, Grammy for Best Rap Song, 2017, Grammy for Best Sung Performance, 2017

GRAHAM, FRANKLIN, T: Evangelist, Missionary **I:** Religious **DOB:** 07/14/1952 **PB:** Asheville **PT:** Son of Billy and Ruth Bell Graham; **ED:** Doctorate (hon.), Liberty University; Doctorate (hon.), National University; Doctorate (hon.), Lees McRae College; Doctorate (hon.), LeTourneau University; Doctorate (hon.), Toccoa Falls College; Doctorate (hon.), Whitworth College; BA, Appalachian State University, Boone, North Carolina, 1978 **C:** President, Billy Graham Evangelistic Association (BGEA), 2001-; CEO, Billy Graham Evangelistic Association (BGEA), 2000-; First vice chairman,

Billy Graham Evangelistic Association (BGEA), 1995-; Evangelist, Billy Graham Evangelistic Association (BGEA), 1989-; President, CEO, Samaritan's Purse, 1979-; Board member, Samaritan's Purse, 1978 **CR:** Board of Directors Harvest Christian Fellowship **CW:** Author: Bob Pierce: This One Thing I Do, 1983, Rebel with a Cause, 1995, Miracle in a Shoebox, 1995, Living Beyond the Limits, 1998, The Name, 2002, It's Who You Know: The One Relationship that Makes All the Difference, 2002, Kids Praying for Kids, 2003, A Wing and a Prayer, 2005; co-author (with R. Rhoads): All For Jesus: A Devotional, 2003 **AW:** Named Daniel of Year, World magazine, 2002, Tar Heel of Year, The News & Observer, Charlotte, North Carolina, 1992; recipient William Booth award, Salvation Army **BA:** Billy Graham Evangelistic Association, 1 Billy Graham Parkway, Charlotte, NC, 28201

GRAHAM, LINDSEY OLIN, T: U.S. Senator from South Carolina **I:** Government Administration/Government Relations/Government Services **DOB:** 07/09/1955 **PB:** Seneca **PT:** Son of Florence James and Millie Graham. **ED:** Doctor in Public Administration (hon.), The Citadel, Charleston; Doctor in Public Service (hon.), Presbyterian College, Clinton, South Carolina; HD (hon.), Francis Marion University, Florence, South Carolina; LHD (hon.), Allen University, Columbia, South Carolina; LHD (hon.), College Charleston, South Carolina; LHD (hon.), Winthrop University, Rock Hill, South Carolina; LLD (hon.), Coker College, Hartsville, South Carolina; LLD (hon.), Erskine College, Due West, South Carolina; LLD (hon.), South Carolina State University, Orangeburg; LLD (hon.), Southern Wesleyan University, Central, South Carolina; LLD (hon.), University South Carolina; JD, University South Carolina, 1981; MPA, University South Carolina, 1978; BS in Psychology, University South Carolina, 1977 **C:** Member, US Senate Homeland Security & Governmental Affairs Committee, 2009-; Member, US Senate Select Committee on Aging, 2007-; Member, US Senate Veterans Affairs Committee, 2007-; Member, US Senate Budget Committee, 2004-; Member, US Senate Armed Services Committee, 2002-; Member, US Senate Judiciary Committee, 2002-; US Senator from South Carolina, 2002-; Member, US Senate Select Committee on Intelligence, 2007-09; Member, US Senate Agricultural, Nutrition & Forestry Committee, 2007-09; Member, US Senate Health, Labor, Education & Pensions Committee, 2002-04; Member, US House Armed Services Committee, 1999-2002; Member, US House Judiciary Committee, 1997-2002; Member, US House International Relations Committee, 1995-98; Member, US House Education & Workforce Committee, 1995-2002; Member, US Congress from 3d South Carolina District, 1995-2001; Member, South Carolina House of Reps., 1992-95; City attorney, Central, South Carolina, 1990-94; Private practice, 1988-94; Assistant county attorney, County of Oconee, South Carolina, 1988-92; Cir. trial counsel, US Air Force Europe, 1984-88; Area defense counsel, Shaw AFB, 1982-84 **CR:** Candidate for the 2016 Republican Party presidential nomination **CIV:** Member, Anderson Chamber of Commerce, Board directors, Rosa Clark Free Medical Clinic, Seneca, South Carolina, Member, Corinth Baptist Church, **AW:** Decorated Meritorious Service medal; recipient Minuteman of Year award, Reserve Officers Association, 2004 **MEM:** Mem.: Retired Officers Association, American Cancer Society (Oconee County Chapter fundraising chairman), Seneca Sertoma, American Legion Post 120, Walhalla Rotary **PA:** Republican

GRAMMER, KELSEY, T: Actor **I:** Media & Entertainment **PB:** St. Thomas **SC:** VI/USA **PT:** Sally Grammer; Allen Grammer **ED:** Studied, Juilliard School, New York City **CW:** Actor: (TV series) Cheers, 1984-93, Frasier, 1993-2004 (People's Choice award for Favorite Male in New TV Series, Emmy award for Best Lead Actor in a Comedy Series, 1994, 1995, 1998, Golden Globe award for Best Actor in TV Series, 1996, 2000, Emmy award for Outstanding Lead Actor in a Comedy Series, 2004), Back to You, 2007-08, Hank, 2009-10, Boss, 2011-12 (Golden Globe award for Best Performance by an Actor in a TV Series-Drama, 2012), Partners, 2014, (films) Toy Story 2 (voice), 1999, 15 Minutes, 1999, New Jersey Turnpikes, 1999, Standing on Fishes, 1999, The Real Howard Spitz, 1998, Down Periscope, 1996, Anastasia (voice), 1997, X-Men: The Last Stand, 2006, 15 Minutes, 2001, Even Money, 2006, Back to You, 2007, Swing Vote, 2008, Fame, 2009, Middle Men, 2010, Crazy on the Outside, 2010, I Don't Know How She Does It, 2011, Legends of Oz: Dorothy's Return (voice), 2013, Think Like a Man Too, 2014, Reach Me, 2014, Transformers: Age of Extinction, 2014, The Expendables 3, 2014, Breaking the Bank, 2014, Baby, Baby, Baby, 2015, Neighbors 2: Sorority Rising, 2016, Storks (voice), 2016, Bunyan and Babe (voice), 2017, Nest, 2016, (TV mini-series) Kennedy, 1983, George Washington, 1984, Crossings, 1986, (TV films) Dance 'til Dawn, 1988, Beyond Suspicion, 1993, The Innocent, 1994, London Suite, 1996, The Pentagon Wars, 1998, The Sports Pages, 2001, Killing Jesus, 2015, (TV appearances) Kate and Allie, Wings, Tracy Ullman Show, The Simpsons, 1990-2010, The Troop, 2010, 30 Rock, 2010, Boss, 2011, Partners, 2014, Who Do You Think You Are?, 2014, Killing Jesus, 2015, The Last Tycoon, 2016, Trollhunters, 2016, Modern Family, 2017(Off-Broadway) Plenty, A Month in the Country, Sunday in the Park with George, Quartermaine's Terms, (Broadway) Macbeth, Othello, La Cage aux Folles, 2010, Finding Neverland, 2015-16; executive prodr.: (TV series) Fired Up, 1997, In-Laws, 2002, Gary the Rate, 2003, Medium, 2005-11, Kelsey Grammer Presents: The Sketch Show, 2005, The Game, 2006-13; voice (video) Bartok the Magnificent, 1999, (TV films) Animal Farm, 1999, The Hand Behind the Mouse: The Ub Iwerks Story, 1999; featured in documentary: Best of Enemies, 2015; author: (autobiography) So Far, 1995

GRANDE, ARIANA, T: Singer, Actress **I:** Media & Entertainment **PB:** Boca Raton **SC:** FL/USA **PT:** Edward Butera; Joan Grande **CIV:** Co-founder, Kids Who Care **CW:** Actress: (Broadway plays) 13, 2008; (plays) Cuba Libre, 2012, A Snow White Christmas, 2012; (TV films) 7 Secrets with Victoria Justice, 2010, Swindle, 2013; (films) Snowflake, the White Gorilla (voice), 2011, Zoolander 2, 2016; (TV series) Victorious, 2010-13, Sam & Cat, 2013-14; singer: (albums) Yours Truly, 2013, My Everything, 2014, Dangerous Woman, 2016, Sweetener, 2018 **AW:** Named Favorite Breakout Artist, People's Choice Awards, 2014, Favorite Female Pop/Rock Artist, American Music Awards, 2015, New Artist of Year, 2013

GRANGER, KAY, T: U.S. Representative from Texas **I:** Government Administration/Government Relations/Government Services **DOB:** 01/18/1943 **PB:** Greenville **SC:** TX/USA **ED:** Doctor in Pub. Service (hon.), Tennessee Wesleyan College; DHL (hon.), Texas Wesleyan University; BS magna cum laude, Texas Wesleyan University, 1965 **C:** Member, US Congress from 12th Texas district, 1997-; Member, Committee on Appropriations; Vice chair House Rep. Conference, US Congress from 12th Texas district, 2007-09; Mayor, City of Fort Worth, 1991-95; City councilwoman, City of Fort Worth, 1989-91; Member private industry council, City of Fort Worth, 1988-89; Member zoning committee,

City of Fort Worth, 1981-89; Principal, owner, Kay Granger & Associates,; Principal, owner, G&R Insurance Agency, Fort Worth, **CIV:** Board visitors, US Air Force Academy, Board trustees, Southwestern University, Georgetown, Texas, **CW:** Author: What's Right About America?, 2006 **AW:** Named to Fort Worth Business Hall of Fame, Texas Women's Hall of Fame, 1999; recipient Brotherhood/Sisterhood citation, National Conference Community & Justice Fort Worth/Tarrant County Region, 2006, National Association Manufacturers award, 2006, Community Health Defender award, National Association Community Health Centers, 2006 **MEM:** Meadowbrook Business & Professional Womens Association, East Fort Worth Business & Professional Association (board directors), International Sister Cities Association, Am. Planning Association, East Fort Worth C. of C. **PA:** Republican **BA:** 1026 Longworth House Office Building, Washington, DC, 20515

GRANT, BUD, T: Former NFL Coach **I:** Athletics **DOB:** 05/20/1927 **PB:** Superior, Wisconsin **ED:** Student, University Minnesota **C:** Head Coach, Minnesota Vikings, NFL, 1967-84, 85; Head Coach, Winnipeg Blue Bombers, Canadian Football League, 1957-66; Football Player, Winnipeg Blue Bombers, Canadian Football League, 1953-56; Football Player, Philadelphia Eagles, NFL, 1951-52; Basketball Player, Minneapolis Lakers, NBA, 1949-51 **AW:** Coach Can. Football League championships, 1958-59, 61-62. Coached in Super Bowls IV, VIII, IX, XI, NFL; NFL Coach of the Year, The Sporting News, 1969; NFL Hall of Fame, 1994, Grey Cup Champion, 1958-59, 1961-62, , NFL Champion, 1969, CFL Coach of the Year, 1965, NFL Coach of the Year, 1976 **ACH:** Achievements include earning nine varsity letters in football, basketball and baseball at University Minnesota after having overcome polio at the age of ten.

GRANT, HUGH, T: Actor **I:** Media & Entertainment **DOB:** 09/09/1960 **PB:** London **SC:** England **PT:** James Grant; Finvola Susan (MacLean) Grant **CH:** Tabitha; Felix Chang **ED:** BA in English Lit. with honors, Oxford University, England, 1982 **C:** Formed, Simian Films **CW:** Debuted on stage at Nottingham Playhouse; formed revue group The Jockeys of Norfolk, 1985; actor: (films) Privileged, 1982, Maurice, 1987, White Mischief, 1988, The Lair of White Worm, 1988, The Dawning, 1988, Remando al Viento, 1988, La Nuit Bengali, 1988, Impromptu, 1991, Crossing the Line, 1991, Bitter Moon, 1992, The Remains of the Day, 1993, Four Weddings and a Funeral, 1994 (Golden Globe award for Best Actor, 1994, BAFTA award for Best Actor, 1994), Sirens, 1994, Restoration, 1994, The Englishman Who Went Up a Hill But Came Down a Mountain, 1995, Nine Months, 1995, An Awfully Big Adventure, 1995, Sense and Sensibility, 1995, Extreme Measures, 1996, Notting Hill, 1999, Mickey Blue Eyes, 1999, Small Time Crooks, 2000, Bridget Jones's Diary, 2001, About a Boy, 2002, Two Weeks Notice, 2002, Love Actually, 2003, Bridget Jones: The Edge of Reason, 2004, Travaux on sait quand ça commence, 2005, American Dreamz, 2006, Music and Lyrics, 2007, Did You Hear About the Morgans?, 2009, The Pirates! Band of Misfits (voice), 2012, Cloud Atlas, 2012, The Rewrite, 2014, The Man from U.N.C.L.E., 2015, Florence Foster Jenkins, 2016, Paddington 2; (guest appearances) A Very Peculiar Practice, 1986 **AW:** Stanley Kubrick Britannia award for Excellence in Film, BAFTA, 2003

GRANT, HUGH, T: CEO of Monsanto **I:** Agriculture **DOB:** 03/23/1958 **PB:** Larkhall **SC:** Scotland **ED:** MBA, International Management Center, Buckingham, England; MS, Edinburgh University,

Scotland; BS in Molecular Biology and Agricultural Zoology with honors, Glasgow University, Scotland **C:** Chairman/CEO, Monsanto, 2012-; Chairman, President, CEO, Monsanto Co., 2003-12; Executive Vice President, COO, Monsanto Co., 2000-03; Vice President, COO, Monsanto Co., 2000; Co-Pres. Agricultural Sector, Pharmacia Corp., 1998 **CR:** Member International Adv. Board Scottish Enterprise Member Executive Committee Microedit Summit Campaign **CIV:** Board of Governors, United Way St. Louis, Board of Trustee, Donald Danforth Plant Sci. Center, Member, Civic Progress, **MEM:** Mem.: Biotechnology Industry Organization, International Policy Council on Agriculture, Food and Trade, CropLife International **BA:** 800 North Lindbergh Blvd, Saint Louis, MI, 63167

GRASSLEY, CHUCK, T: U.S. Senator from Iowa **I:** Government Administration/Government Relations/Government Services **DOB:** 09/17/1933 **PB:** New Hartford **SC:** IA/USA **PT:** Son of Louis Arthur and Ruth (Corwin) Grassley; **ED:** Postgrad., University of Iowa, 1957-58; MA in Political Sci., University of No. Iowa, 1956; BA, University of No. Iowa, 1955 **C:** Chairman, U.S. Senate Narcotics Caucus, 2015-; Chairman, U.S. Senate Judiciary Committee, 2015-; US Senator from Iowa, 1981-; Chairman, Congressional Joint Committee on Taxation, 2005-06; Chairman, U.S. Senate Finance Committee, 2003-07; Chairman, U.S. Senate Special Committee on Aging, 2001; Chairman, U.S. Senate Special Committee on Aging, 1997-2001; Member, U.S. Congress from 3rd Iowa District, Washington, DC 1975-81; Instructor political sci., Charles City Community College, 1967-68; Instructor political sci., Drake University, 1962; Assembly line worker, 1961-71; Member, Iowa House of Reps., 1959-75; Sheet metal shearer, 1959-61; Farmer, **AW:** Recipient Health Policy Hero award, National Research Center for Women & Families, 2009, National Energy Leadership award, National Bio-Diesel Board, 2003, Legis. of Year, Biotechnology Industry Organization, 2003, National Leadership award, National Citizens' Coalition Nursing Home Reform, 2002, Patients' Champions award, American Chiropractic Association, 2001, Excellence in Public Service award, American Academy Pediatrics, 2001, Bipartisan Hero award, National Association Pediatric Nurse Associate & Practitioners, 2001, American Financial Leadership award, Financial Services Roundtable, 2001, Ester Peterson Senior Advocate award, United Seniors Health Cooperative, 2000, Excellence in Health Service award, National Association Community Health Centers, 1998, Congressional award, Cmty Anti-Drug Coalitions of America, 1997 **MEM:** Member American Farm Bureau, Iowa Hist. Society, Black Hawk County Hist. Society, Masons, Pi Gamma Mu, Kappa Delta Pi. **PA:** Republican **BA:** Federal Bldg Rm 120, 210 Walnut St, Des Moines, IA, 50309

GRASZ, L(EONARD) STEVEN, T: Federal Judge **I:** Law and Legal Services **DOB:** 11/14/1961 **PB:** Chappell **SC:** Nebraska **PT:** Son of Jesse Howard and Jane (Jankovsky) G.; Married Verlyne Rene Dannehl, August 31, 1985; 1 child, Caylen. **ED:** JD, University Nebraska, 1989; BS, University Nebraska, 1984 **CT:** Bar: Nebraska 1989, U.S. District Court Nebraska 1989, U.S. Court Appeals (8th cir.) 1991, (D.C. cir.) 1992. **C:** Judge,U.S. Court of Appeals for the Eighth Circuit,2018-; Chief deputy attorney general, State of Nebraska, Lincoln, 1991-2002; Associate, Kutak Rock and Campbell, Omaha, 1989-91; Legis. assistant, U.S. Congresswoman Virginia Smith, Washington, 1984-85 **CIV:** Adviser Farm House Fraternity, Lincoln, 1992- member Douglas County GOP Cen. Committee, Omaha, 1992-. **CW:** Executive editor Nebraska Law

Rev., 1988-89. **MEM:** Member Nebraska Bar Association, Order of Coif. **H:** Basketball **PA:** Republican **BA:** Thomas F. Eagleton Courthouse, 111 South 10th Street, St. Louis, MO, 63102

GRAVES, GARRET, T: U.S. Representative from Louisiana **I:** Government Administration/ Government Relations/Government Services **DOB:** 01/31/1972 **PB:** Baton Rouge **SC:** LA/USA **ED:** American University, Washington, DC,1996; Louisiana Tech University,1993-95; University of Alabama, Tuscaloo, 1990-1991; Graduated from Catholic High School, Baton Rouge,1990 **C:** Member, House of Representative from Louisiana's 6th District, 2015-; Member, Committee on Natural Resources; Member, Committee on Transportation; Member, Republican Study Committee; Manager, Louisiana Coastal Protection and Restoration Authority, 2008-2014; Aide, U.S. Senator Committee on Commerce, Science and Transportation, 2005-08 **BA:** 430 Cannon HOB, Washington, DC, 20515

GRAVES, JAMES EARL, T: Federal Judge **I:** Law and Legal Services **DOB:** 11/19/1953 **PB:** Clinton **SC:** MS/USA **ED:** LLD (hon.), Millsaps College; MPA, Syracuse University Maxwell School Citizenship & Public Affairs, 1981; JD, Syracuse University, 1980; BA in Sociology, Millsaps College, 1975 **C:** Judge, U.S. Court of Appeals for the Fifth Circuit, Jackson, 2011-; Presiding justice, Mississippi Supreme Court, 2009-11; Justice, Mississippi Supreme Court, 2001-11; Cir. court judge, 7th Cir. District, 1991-2001; Director child support enforcement div. Department Human Services, State of Mississippi, Jackson, 1990-91; Special assistant attorney general, State of Mississippi, 1986-90; Legal counsel, Human Services Div., Mississippi Attorney General Office, 1989-90; Legal counsel, Health Law Div., Mississippi Attorney General Office, 1986-89; Associate attorney, Walker & Walker, 1984-86; Partner, Murrain & Graves, 1983-84; Staff attorney, Central Mississippi Legal Services, Jackson, Mississippi, 1980-83; Clerk, Department of Community Devel., Syracuse, New York, 1978-79 **CR:** Instructor trial advocacy Harvard Law School, 1998-2000 adjunct professor media and civil rights law Jackson State University, 1980-97 **CIV:** Coach, student mock trial teams, Active pub. school activities, **AW:** Named Parent of Year, 2000-01; recipient Humanized Educated award, Mississippi Association of Educators, 2002, Special Achievement award, Jackson Federal Executive Association, 2002, Commissioner's award, U.S. Department Health & Human Services, 2001, Thurgood Marshall award, Jackson's Martin Luther King Celebration, 2002, 1994, Judge of Year award, National Conference Black Lawyers, 1992 **MEM:** Mem.: Mississippi Bar Foundation (Law-Related Public Educated award 2002), Magnolia Bar Association (Government Service award 1993, R. Jess Brown award 1994, Government Service award 1998), Hinds County Bar Association (Innovation award 2000), National Bar Association (Distinguished Jurist award 1996) **BA:** John Minor Wisdom U.S. Court of Appeals Building Fifth Circuit, 600 Camp St, New Orleans, LA, 70130

GRAVES, SAM, T: U.S. Representative from Missouri **I:** Government Administration/Government Relations/Government Services **DOB:** 11/07/1963 **PB:** Fairfax **SC:** MO/USA **PT:** Samuel Bruce Graves, Janice A. (Hord) Graves **ED:** BS in Agronomy, University of Missouri, Columbia, MO, 1986 **C:** U.S. Congress from Sixth Missouri District, 2001-Present; Chairman, U.S. House Small Business Committee, 2011-2015; District 12, Missouri State Senate, 1995-2000; District 4, Missouri House of Representatives, 1993-1995 **AW:** Voice of Missouri

Business Award, Associated Industries, 1999, Missouri Physical Therapy Association Award, 1997, Outstanding Young Farmer in U.S., Missouri Junior Chamber of Commerce, 1996, Tarkio, Missouri Community Betterment Award, 1995, Outstanding Young Farmer in U.S., Farm Bureau, 1991, Outstanding Young Farmer in Missouri, Missouri Farm Bureau, 1990 **MEM:** Farm Bureau, Rotary **PA:** Republican

GRAVES, TOM, T: U.S. Representative from Georgia **I:** Government Administration/Government Relations/Government Services **DOB:** 02/03/1970 **PB:** St. Petersburg, Florida, February 3, 1970 **ED:** Grad., Coverdale Leadership Institute; BBA in Finance, University Georgia **C:** Member, Committee on Agriculture, Committee on Education and the Workforce; Member, US Congress from 14th Georgia District, 2013-; Member, US Congress from 9th Georgia District, Washington, 2010-13; Member District 12, Georgia House of Reps., 2005-10; Member District 10, Georgia House of Reps., 2003-05 **AW:** Named Legislator of the Year, Georgia Retail Association, 9th District Republican Party, 2009, American Legislative Exchange Council, 2009; recipient Legislative Entrepreneur of the Year award, Freedom Works Foundation, Guardian of Small Business award, National Federation of Ind. Business **MEM:** Mem.: American Legislative Exchange Council **PA:** Republican

GRAY, GLENDA, T: Physician and Scientist **I:** Medicine & Health Care **ED:** University of Witwatersrand, 1980 **C:** Member, Academy of Science of South Africa; Executive Director, Pediatric HIV Research Unit, Chris Hani Baragwanath Hospital **AW:** Time 100 Most Influential, 2017-, A Rated National Research Foundation Scientist **MEM:** American Academy of Microbiology

GREEN, ALEXANDER N., T: U.S. Representative from Texas **I:** Government Administration/Government Relations/Government Services **DOB:** 09/01/1947 **PB:** New Orleans **SC:** LA/USA **ED:** JD, Texas Southern University Thurgood Marshall School of Law, 1974; Attended, Tuskegee Institute Tech., Alabama; Attended, Florida Agricultural and Mechanical University **C:** Member, U.S. Congress from 9th Texas district, 2005-; Member, Committee on Financial Services; Justice of peace, Harris County, Texas, 1977-2004; Founder, managing partner, Green, Wilson, Dewberry & Fitch, Houston, 1974 **CIV:** Past President Houston branch, NAACP **AW:** Named one of 100 Most Influential Black Americans, Ebony magazine, 2006; named to Power 150, 2008; recipient Mickey Leland Humanitarian award, National Association for the Advancement of Colored People, 2006, Citation for Service, Am. Federation Teachers, 1983, Outstanding Leadership award, Black Heritage Society, 1981, Distinguished Service award, Houston Citizens C. of C., 1978 **PA:** Democrat **BA:** 2347 Rayburn House Office Building, Washington, DC, 20515

GREEN, CEELO, T: Singer, Songwriter, Record Producer **I:** Media & Entertainment **PB:** Atlanta **SC:** GA/USA **C:** Member, Gnarls Barkley, 2006-; Member, Goodie Mob, 1991 **CW:** Singer: (albums) Cee-Lo Green & His Perfect Imperfections, 2002, Cee-Lo Green...Is the Soul Machine, 2004, Art of Noise: The Best of Cee-Lo, 2006, Closet Freak: The Best of Cee-Lo Green the Soul Machine, 2006, The Lady Killer, 2011, Cee-Lo's Magic Moment, 2012, Cee-Lo Green...Is Everybody's Brother, 2012, (with Goodie Mob), Heart Blanche, 2015, Soul Food, 1995, Still Standing, 1998, World Party, 1999, (with Gnarls Barkley) St. Elsewhere, 2006 (Best Alternative Music Album, Grammy Awards, 2007), The Odd

Couple, 2008, (songs) Crazy, 2006 (Best Urban/Alternative Performance, Grammy Awards, 2007, ranked #1 on Rolling Stone mag.'s Top 50 Songs of the Decade 2000-2009), Smiley Faces, 2006 (Best Editing, MTV Video Music Awards, 2007), Run, 2008 (Best Art Direction, Best Choreography, MTV Video Music Awards, 2008), (solo recording) Forget You!, 2010 (Best Urban/Alternative Performance, Grammy Awards, 2011), (with Melanie Fiona) Fool For You, 2011 (Best R&B Song, Best Traditional R&B Vocal Performance, Grammy Awards, 2012); vocal coach, judge (TV series) The Voice, 2011-13; actor: (films) Hotel Transylvania (voice), 2012; reality TV personality CeeLo Green's The Good Life, 2014 **AW:** Named Best International Male, Brit. Phonographic Industry (BRIT) Awards, 2011; recipient Best Group award (with Gnarls Barkley), Black Entertainment TV (BET) Awards, 2007

GREEN, GENE, **T:** U.S. Representative from Texas **I:** Government Administration/Government Relations/Government Services **DOB:** 10/17/1947 **PB:** Houston, October **PT:** Son of Garland B. and Evelyn (Clark) Green; **ED:** JD, University Houston Bates College Law, 1977; BBA, University Houston, 1971 **CT:** Bar: Texas 1977 **C:** Chair, US House Ethics Committee, 2008-09; Member, US Congress from 29th Texas District, 1993-; Member, Committee on Energy and Commerce; Chair, US House Standards of Official Conduct Committee, 2008-09; Member District 6, Texas State Senate, 1987-93; Member District 140, Tex House of Reps., 1981-85; Member District 95, Tex House of Reps., 1973-81 **AW:** Named Legislator of Year, National Council Community Behavioral Healthcare, 2008; Recipient Honor Award, Houston Bureau Tuberculosis Control, 2008, Champion of Women's Health Award, Susan G. Komen for the Cure Advocacy Alliance, 2008, Safety Net Champion Award, National Association Hospitals, 2007, Alfred K. Whitehead Legis. Award, International Association Fire Fighters, 2004, Distinguished Community Health Award, National Association Health Centers, 2008, 2003, Medal of Honor for Directing Funding for Cancer Research, US Oncology, Inc., 2003, Legis. Open Door Award, National Association Credit Management, 2003 **MEM:** Mem.: Coastal Conservation Association, Texas Hist. Society, League United Latin Am. Citizens (hon.) **PA:** Democrat

GREEN, JOHN, **T:** Radio Broadcast Editor and Author **I:** Writing and Editing **C:** Writer 2005-; Prod. editor, NPR,; Former contributor, NPR's All Things Considered; Former contributor, WBEZ Pub. Radio **CW:** Author: (novels) Looking for Alaska, 2005 (Named Top Ten Best Books for Teens, 2005, Michael L. Printz award, American Library Association, 2006), An Abundance of Katherines, 2006,(Books) Let it Snow: Three Holiday Romances, 2008, Will Grayson, Will Grayson, 2010, The Fault in Our Stars, 2012, Turtles All the Way Down, 2017(Short Stories) The Approximate Cost of Loving Caroline, 2006, The Great American Morp, 2007, Freek the Geak, 2009, Reasons, 2011, Double on Call and Other Short Stories, 2012 **AW:** Los Angeles Times Book Prize, Innovator Award, 2013

GREEN, KIRSTEN, **T:** Venture Capitalist **I:** Financial Services **PB:** San Francisco **SC:** CA/USA **ED:** B.A., University of California, 1989-93 **C:** General Partner/Founder, Forerunner Ventures, 2010-; Advisor, TSG Consumer Partners, 2009-10; Equity Research Analyst,Bank of America, 1998-2002 **AW:** Time 100, 2017 **ACH:** CPA, CFA

GREENAWAY, JOSEPH ANTHONY JR., **T:** Federal Judge **I:** Law and Legal Services **DOB:** 11/16/1957 **PB:** London **SC:** United Kingdom **PT:** Son of Joseph

Anthony Senior and Brucel May (Lynch) G. **ED:** JD, Harvard University, 1981; BA in History, Columbia University, 1978 **C:** Judge, US Court Appeals (3rd Cir.), 2010-; Judge, US District Court New Jersey, Newark, 1996-2010; In-house Counsel, Johnson & Johnson, New Brunswick, New Jersey, 1990-96; Assistant US Attorney, Chief Narcotics Division, US Department Justice, Newark, 1985-90; Lawyer, Kramer, Levin, Nessen, Kamin & Frankel, New York City, 1981-82, 83-85; Law Clerk to Hon. Vincent L. Broderick, US District Court (so. district) New York, 1982-83 **CR:** Weintraub Lecturer, Rutgers University Law School, 1998; Adjunct Professor, Rutgers University Law School, 2002-06; Cardozo School Law, 2006-, Columbia College, 2007- **CIV:** Past Secretary Columbia University Alumni Association, Board Directors, New York City, Board Directors Columbia University National Council, Chair Emeritus, Columbia College Black Alumni Council, Board Visitors, Columbia College **CW:** Presenter in field **AW:** Recipient Proclamation Newark City Council, 1990, Medal of Excellence, Columbia University, 1997; Distinguished Service Award, American Corp. Counsel Association, 1997, Distinguished Jurist award, Garden State Bar Association, 1999, John Jay Award, Columbia University, 2003, Excellence Award, Thurgood Marshall College Fund, 2007, Roger M. Yancey Award, Garden State Bar Association, 2007, Scales Justice Award of Excellence, Caribbean Bar Association, 2008, YMWCA Greater Newark Leaders and Legends Award, 2008, Trailblazer Award, New Jersey Women Lawyers Association, 2011; Named Minority Achiever of Year, East Orange YMCA, 1997, Earl Warren Legal Scholar **MEM:** Member American Bar Association, Garden State Bar Association, Federal Judges Association, American Corp. Counsel Association, Garden State Bar Association, Columbia College Alumni Association **H:** Golf **BA:** 601 Market St, Philadelphia, PA, 19106

GREENGARD, PAUL, **T:** neuroscientist, educator **I:** Medicine & Health Care **DOB:** 12/11/1925 **PB:** NYC **ED:** PhD in Biophysics, Johns Hopkins University, Baltimore, 1953; AB in Math. & Physics, Hamilton College, Clinton, New York, 1948 **C:** Director Fisher Center for Alzheimer's Disease Research, Rockefeller University, New York City, 1995-; Vincent Astor professor, head. Laboratory Molecular & Cellular Neurosci., Rockefeller University, New York City, 1983-; Professor pharmacology & psychiatry, Yale University School Medicine, New Haven, 1968-83; Director department biochemistry, Geigy Research Laboratories, Ardsley, New York, 1959-67; Visiting scientist National Heart Institute, National Institutes of Health, 1958-59; Fellow National Institute Neurological Diseases & Blindness,, National Institutes of Health, Bethesda, Maryland, 1956-58; Paraplegia Foundation fellow, National Institute Medical Research, England, 1955-56; National Foundation Infantile Paralysis fellow, Molteno Institute, Cambridge University, England, 1954-55; National Science Foundation fellow in neurochemistry, Institute Psychiatry, University London, 1953-54 **CR:** Member board sci. governors Scripps Research Institute, La Jolla, California; Andrew D. White prof.-at-large Cornell University, Ithaca, New York, 1981-81; visiting professor Vanderbilt University, Nashville, 1967-68; visiting associate professor, professor pharmacology Albert Einstein College Medicine, New York City, 1961-70 **CIV:** Co-founder, Pearl Meister Greengard Prize annual award for women scientists, Board directors, Michael Stern Parkinson's Research Foundation **AW:** Recipient Nobel Prize in Physiology/Medicine, The Nobel Foundation, 2000, Senior Scholar award, Ellison Medical Foundation, 1999, Award for Medical Research, Metropolitan Life Foundation, 1998, Mayor's award for

Excellence in Sci. & Tech., New York City, 1998, Award for Pioneering Achievements in Health, Charles A. Dana Foundation, 1997, Biochem. Society Thudichum medal, 1996, Karl Spencer Lashley prize, American Philosophical Society, 1993, Goodman & Gilman award in receptor pharmacology, 1992, Bristol-Myers award for Distinguished Achievement in Neuroscience Research, 1989, 3M Life Scis. award, Federation Am. Societies Experimental Biology, 1987, Award in Biology & Medical Sciences, New York Academy Sciences, 1980, Ciba-Geigy Drew award, 1979, Dickson Prize & Medal in Medicine, University Pittsburgh, 1977 **MEM:** Mem.: National Academy of Sciences, National Alliance Research Schizophrenia & Depression (Lieber prize 1996), Society Neurosci. (Gerard prize 1994), American Association for the Advancement of Science, American Neurological Association (hon.)

GREGORY, ROGER LEE, **T:** Federal Judge **I:** Law and Legal Services **DOB:** 07/17/1953 **PB:** Philadelphia **SC:** Pennsylvania **PT:** Son of George Lee and Fannie Mae (Washington) G.; Married Carla Eugenia Lewis, September 6, 1980; children: Adriene Leigh, Rachel Leigh. **ED:** JD, University Michigan, 1978; BA, Virginia State University, 1975 **CT:** Bar: Michigan 1978, Virginia 1980, US Court Appeals (6th cir.) 1978, US Court Appeals (4th cir.) 1980. **C:** Chief Judge, US Court of Appeal 4th Circuit, 2016-; Judge, US Court of Appeals (4th cir.), Richmond, 2001-; Managing partner, chairman litigation secretary, Wilder & Gregory, Richmond, 1982-2001; Associate attorney, Hunton & Williams, Richmond, Virginia, 1980-82; Associate attorney, Butzel, Long, Gust, Klein & Van Zile, Detroit, 1978-80 **CR:** Board visitors Virginia Commonwealth University, Richmond, 1985-adjunct professor Virginia State University, 1981-1985. **CIV:** Board directors Industrial Devel. Authority, Richmond, 1984-, Richmond chapter YMCA, 1989-. **MEM:** Me. Cen. Virginia Legal Aid Society (executive committee), Old Dominion Bar Association (president), Richmond Bar Association (board directors), Metro C. of C. (board directors 1989-), Alpha Kappa Mu, Alpha Mu Gamma. **BA:** US Ct Appeals 4th Cir, 1000 E Main St Rm 212, Richmond, VA, 23219

GREIDER, CAROLYN WIDNEY, **T:** Molecular biologist, educator **I:** Sciences **DOB:** 04/15/1961 **PB:** San Diego **ED:** PhD in Molecular Biology, University California, Berkeley, 1987; BA in Biology, University California, Santa Barbara, 1983 **C:** Daniel Nathans professor & director department molecular biology and genetics, Johns Hopkins University School Medicine, Baltimore, 2003-; Professor oncology, Johns Hopkins University School Medicine, Baltimore, 2001-; Interim director department molecular biology and genetics, Johns Hopkins University School Medicine, Baltimore, 2002-03; Professor, Johns Hopkins University School Medicine, Baltimore, 1999-2003; Associate professor department molecular biology and genetics, Johns Hopkins University School Medicine, Baltimore, 1997-99; Investigator, Cold Spring Harbor Laboratory, New York, 1994-97; Associate staff investigator, Cold Spring Harbor Laboratory, New York, 1992-94; Assistant investigator, Cold Spring Harbor Laboratory, New York, 1990-92; Fellow, Cold Spring Harbor Laboratory, New York, 1988-90 **CR:** Consultant Amgen, Inc., 1998-2002 organizer Gordon Research Conference Nucleic Acids, Providence, 1998 member National Bioethics Adv. Commission, 1996-2001 member sci. adv. board Geron Corp., 1992-96 visiting lecturer State University of New York, Stony Brook, 1991-97 **CW:** Member editorial board Cancer Cell, 2001-, Molecular Cancer Research, 2003-; contributor numerous articles and revs. to professional journals, chapters to books **AW:** Recipient Nobel prize in physiology/medicine, 2009, Louisa Gross Horwitz prize, Columbia University, 2007, Albert Lasker award for Basic Medical Research, 2006, Wiley prize in biomed scis., 2006, Lila Gruber Cancer Research award, 2006, Lewis S. Rosenstiel award, Brandeis University, 1999, Passano Foundation award, 1999, Gairdner Foundation International award, 1998, Senior Scholar award, Ellison Medical Foundation, 1998; Pew Biomed. Scis. scholar, 1990-94, Regents scholar, University California, 1981 **MEM:** Fellow: American Association for the Advancement of Science, American Academy Microbiology, American Academy Arts & Scis.; mem.: National Academy of Sciences (Richard Lounsbery award 2003), Institute Medicine, American Society Biochemistry & Molecular Biology (Schering-Plough Sci. Achievement award 1997), American Society Microbiology, American Association Cancer Research (Gertrude Elion Cancer Research award 1994, Cornelius Rhoads award 1996), American Society Cell Biology (council member 1998-2001, Glenn Foundation award 1995), Phi Beta Kappa **ACH:** Achievements include along with Elizabeth Blackburn, discovery of telomerase, a key enzyme in cancer and anemia research

GREITENS, ERIC ROBERT, **T:** Former Governor of Missouri **I:** Government Administration/Government Relations/Government Services **DOB:** 04/10/1974 **PB:** St. Louis **PT:** Son of Robert and Becky Greitens; **ED:** LHD (hon.), Tufts University, 2012; PhD in Politics, Oxford University, 2000; MA in Development Studies, Oxford University, 1998 **C:** Governor, State of Missouri, 2017-2018; CEO, The Mission Continues, St. Louis, 2007-; White House fellow, US Department Housing & Urban Devel. (HUD), 2005-06 **CR:** Senior fellow Washington University Olin School Business, University Missouri Harry S. Truman School Public Affairs **CW:** Author: Strength and Compassion: Photographs and Essays, 2008 (Grand Prize winner New York Book Festival, 2009), The Heart & the Fist: The Education of a Humanitarian, the Making of a Navy SEAL, 2011 **AW:** Decorated Military Outstanding Volunteer Service medal, Joint Service Achievement medal, Navy Commendation medal, Joint Service Commendation medal, Purple Heart, Bronze Star; named HOOAH award, Major George A. Smith Memorial Fund, 2009, Navy Reserve Junior Line Officer of the Year, Association US Navy, 2011; named one of The 100 Most Influential People in the World, TIME magazine, 2013; recipient Charles Bronfman prize, 2012, President's Volunteer Service award, The White House, 2008 **H:** Running, Tae Kwon Do

GRETZKY, WAYNE DOUGLAS, **T:** Retired Professional Hockey Player, Former Professional Hockey Coach **I:** Athletics **DOB:** 01/26/1961 **PB:** Brantford **SC:** Ont. Canada **PT:** Son of Walter and Phyllis Gretzky **C:** Executive director, Team Canada, World Cup of Hockey, 2004; Special advisor, Team Canada, Olympic Games, Vancouver,; Executive director, Team Canada, Olympic Games, Torino, Italy, 2006; Executive director, Team Canada, Olympic Games, Salt Lake City, 2002; Head coach, Phoenix Coyotes, 2005-09; Director hockey operations, alternate governor, Phoenix Coyotes, 2001-09; Managing partner, Phoenix Coyotes, 2000-09; Investor, Los Arcos Sports LLC / Phoenix Coyotes, 1999-2009; Center, New York Rangers, 1996-99; Center, St. Louis Blues, 1996; Center, LA Kings, 1988-96; Center, Edmonton Oilers, 1979-88; Center, Indianapolis Racers (World Hockey Association), 1978; Center, Sault Ste. Marie Greyhounds, 1977-78; Center, Peterborough Petes (Junior Ontario Hockey Association), 1977-78 **AW:** Named All-Star Game MVP, 1999, 1989, 1983,

Dodge Performer of Year, 1986-87, 1984-85, Can. Athlete of Year, 1985, NHL Player of Year, Sporting News, 1981-87, Man of Year, 1981, Sportsman of Year, Sports Illustrated, 1982, Rookie of Year, World Hockey Association, 1978-79; named one of Most Influential People in the World of Sports, Business Week, 2008; named to NHL All-Star Team, 1997-99, 1980-94; recipient Lester Patrick Trophy, 1993-94, Conn Smythe Trophy, 1988, 1985, Emery Edge award, 1986-87, 1984-85, 1983-84, Lester B. Pearson award, 1986-87, 1984-85, 1982, Art Ross Memorial Trophy, NHL, 1993-94, 1990-91, 1989-90, 1981-87, Lady Byng Memorial Trophy, 1993-94, 1991-92, 1990-91, 1979-80, Lemms Family award, 1977-78, William Hanley Trophy, 1977-78, Hart Memorial Trophy, 1974-80, Hockey Hall of Fame, 1999, International Ice Hockey Federation Centennial All-Star Team, Ontario Sports Hall of Fame, 2004, World Cup of Hockey Champion, 2004, The Hockey News Book Top 60, 2007 World Hockey Association Hall of Fame Legend of the Game, 2010, **ACH:** Achievements include being the record holder for points, goals, assists, overtime assists and others; being a member of the Stanley Cup Champion Edmonton Oilers, 1984, 1985, 1987, 1988; having his number, 99, retired by Edmonton Oilers, 1999 and Los Angeles Kings, 2002; being inducted into the Hockey Hall of Fame, 1999

GREUENEBERG, SARAH, **T:** Chef **I:** Food & Restaurant Services **PB:** Houston **SC:** TX/USA **ED:** Associate's Degree, Art Institute of Houston, 2001 **C:** Owner/Head Chef, Monteverde Restaurant & Pastificio, 2016-Present; Executive Chef, Spiaggia, 2010; Chef De Cuisine, Spiaggia, 2008; Purchasing Sous Chef, Spiaggia, 2007; Spiaggia, 2005; Sous Chef, Brennan's of Houston, 2003 **AW:** James Beard Award for Best Chef, 2017

GRIFFIN, BLAKE AUSTIN, **T:** Professional Basketball Player **I:** Athletics **DOB:** 03/16/1989 **PB:** Oklahoma City **SC:** OK/USA **PT:** Son of Tommy and Gail Griffin. **ED:** Student in pre-health and exercise sci., University of Oklahoma, Norman, 2007-09 **C:** Forward, Detroit Pistons, 2018-; Forward, LA Clippers, 2009-2018; **CR:** Production intern Funny or Die, LA, 2011 **AW:** Named Rookie of Year, NBA, 2011, College Basketball Player of Year, The Sporting News, 2009, 1st Team All-American, Associated Press, 2009, Player of Year, 2009, Big 12 Conference, 2009, 1st Team All-Conference, 2008, Associated Press, 2008, 1st Team All-District, National Association Basketball Coaches, 2008, US Basketball Writers Association, 2008; named to Western Conference All-Star Team, NBA, 2011-13, All-Rookie Team, Big 12 Conference, 2008,All-NBA Third Team, 2015, All-NBA Second Team, 2012-14, NBA All-Star, 2011-2015 **ACH:** Achievements include being the first overall pick in the NBA Draft, 2009; winning the NBA All-Star Slam Dunk Contest, 2011 **BA:** Detroit Pistons Little Caesars Arena 2645 Woodward Avenue, Little Caesars Arena 2645 Woodward Avenue, Detroit, MI, 48201-3028

GRIFFIN, RICHARD ALLEN, **T:** Federal Judge **I:** Law and Legal Services **DOB:** 04/15/1952 **PB:** Traverse City **SC:** Michigan **ED:** JD, University Michigan, 1977; BA magna cum laude, We. Michigan University, 1973 **CT:** Bar: Michigan 1977 **C:** Judge, US Court Appeals (6th cir.), 2005-; Judge, Michigan Court Appeals, 1989-2005; Founder, partner, Read & Griffin, Traverse City, Michigan, 1985-88; Partner, Coulter, Cunningham, Davison & Read, 1981-85; Associate, Williams, Coulter, Cunningham, Davison & Read, 1977-81; Law clerk to Hon. Ross W. Campbell, Michigan Court Appeals (23rd cir.), 1975-77 **CR:** Chairman Long Lake Township Building Authority, 1987-88 **BA:** US Ct Appeals 540 Potter Stewart Courthouse, 100 E Fifth St, Cincinnati, OH, 45202

GRIFFITH, HOWARD MORGAN, **T:** U.S. Representative from Virginia **I:** Government Administration/Government Relations/Government Services **DOB:** 03/15/1958 **PB:** Philadelphia **SC:** PA/USA **PT:** A. Hundley Griffith; Charlotte Virginia (Burford) Griffith **ED:** JD, Washington Lee University, Lexington, VA (1983); BA, Emory & Henry College, with Honors, VA (1980) **C:** Member, US House Energy & Commerce Committee, Washington, DC (2011-Present); Member, US Congress from the Ninth Virginia District, Washington, DC (2011-Present); Partner, Head, Roanoke/Salem Office, Albo & Oblon LLP (2007-Present); Majority Leader, Virginia House of Delegates (2000-2010); Member, District 8, Virginia House of Delegates (1994-2010); Partner, Griffith & Varney, Salem, MA (1987-1989); Private Practice, Salem, MA (1989-2007); Private Practice, Salem, VA (1984-1987); Associate, Lutins & Shapiro, Roanoke, VA (1983-1984) **CIV:** Board of Visitors, Emory & Henry College; Chairman, Catawba District, Boy Scouts of America (1984-1986); Member, Blue Ridge Mountains Council, Boy Scouts of America; District Chairman, Boy Scouts of America (1988-1991); Advisor, Sponsor, Legal Explorers Post, Boy Scouts of America, Salem, MA (1988-1989); Chairman, Salem Republican Party (1991-1994); Chairman, Salem Republican Party (1986-1988); Member, State Central Committee, Republican Party, VA; Member, St. Paul's Episcopalian Church, Salem, MA; Board of Trustees, Jamestown-Yorktown Foundation; Former Member, Board of Directors, Easter Seals, VA; Board of Directors, Stonegate Swim Club, Salem, MA (1991-Present); Board of Directors, Legal Aid Society, Roanoke Valley, VA (1991-1992) **AW:** Silver Beaver Award, Boy Scouts of America (1994) **MEM:** President, Salem/Roanoke County Bar Association (1995-1996); The Virginia Bar Association; Board of Directors, Lions (1988-1990) **BAR:** U.S. District Court for the District of Virginia (1985); Virginia State Bar (1983) **H:** Swimming; Ornithology: Ichthyology **PA:** Republican

GRIFFITH, THOMAS BEALL, **T:** Federal Judge **I:** Law and Legal Services **DOB:** 07/05/1954 **PB:** Yokohama **SC:** Japan **PT:** Son of Robert Elmon and Jane (Beall) Griffith; **ED:** JD, Thw University of Virginia, 1985; BA, Brigham Young University, 1978 **CT:** Bar: DC 1991, North Carolina 1985 **C:** Judge, U.S. Court Appeals (DC cir.), Washington, 2005-; Assistant to the president, general counsel, Brigham Young University, Provo, Utah, 2000-05; Legal counsel, U.S. Senate, Washington, 1995-99; Partner, Wiley, Rein & Fielding LLP, Washington, 1999-2000; Partner, Wiley, Rein & Fielding LLP, Washington, 1993-95; Associate, Wiley, Rein & Fielding LLP, Washington, 1989-93; Associate, Robinson, Bradshaw & Hinson P.A., Charlotte, North Carolina, 1985-89 **CR:** Member Secretary Edn.'s Commission on Opportunity in Athletics (Title IX Commission), 2002-03 general counsel Adv. Commission on Electronic Commerce, 1999-2000 ex officio council member, Administrative Law & Regulatory Practice American Bar Association, 1996-99, member executive committee Central European and Eurasian Law Initiative, 1995- **BA:** US Court of Appeals, 333 Constitution Ave NW, Washington, DC, 20001

GRIFFITH, TRICIA, **T:** CEO **I:** Insurance **CN:** Progressive **ED:** B.S., Illinois State University **C:** CEO, Progressive, 2015-; Personal Lines COO, Progressive, 2014-16; Claim Group President, Progressive, 2008-14; Chief Human Resources Officer, Progressive, 2002-08 **AW:** Fortune 100 Most Powerful Women, 2016

GRIFFITH-JOYNER, FLORENCE, T: Former Professional Track and Field Athlete **I:** Athletics **DOB:** 12/21/1959 **PB:** Los Angeles **SC:** CA/USA **ED:** Student, California State University, Northridge; Student, University of California, Los Angeles; Honorary PhD, American University, Washington, DC, 1994 **C:** Co-Owner, NUCO Nails, Camarillo, CA, 1994—Present **CIV:** Co-Chairperson, President, Council on Physical Fitness and Sports, 1993—Present; Founder, The Florence Griffith Joyner Youth Foundation **CW:** Designer, Line Of Sportswear, Uniforms For NBA Independent Pacers; Actor, (Film) The Chaser, (TV Drama) Santa Barbara; Guest, 227 TV Sitcoms, Numerous Talk Shows; Host, Commentator, Various Sports Events **AW:** Collegiate Champion, 400 Meters, NCAA, 1981, Collegiate Champion, 200 Meters, 1983, Silver Medal, 200 Meters, Olympic Games, Los Angeles, CA, 1984, Sports Woman Of The Year, U.S. Olympic Committee, 1988, Jesse Owens Outstanding Track And Field Athlete, TAC, 1988, Sports Personality Of The Year, Tass News Agency, 1988, Athlete Of The Year, Track And Field, 1988, Gold Medal, 4 X 100 Meter Relay, Silver Medal, 200 Meters, World Championships, Gold Medal, 100 Meters, Olympic Games, Silver Medal, 4 X 400 Meter Relay, Three Gold Medals, Summer Olympic Games, Seoul, South Korea, 1988, Silver Medal, Summer Olympic Games, Seoul, South Korea, 1988, International Jesse Owens Award, Most Outstanding Amateur Athlete, 1988, Most Outstanding Physique of the 1980's, International Federation of Bodybuilders, 1988, Award For Outstanding Contribution To The Field Of Athletics, Harvard Foundation, 1989, Sports Award, Extraordinary Accomplishments in Athletics, Essence Magazine, 1989, Golden Camera Award, German Advertising Industry, 1989, James E. Sullivan Memorial Award, Most Outstanding Athlete In America, 1989 **ACH:** Achievements include Am. record holder World Cup 4x100 meter relay, 1981; NCAA 200 meters record holder, 1983; World track records at 100 and 200 meters, 1988; 1st Am. woman to win 4 medals in single Olympic Games; World record Olympic Quarterfinals 200 meters

GRIJALVA, RAÚL M., T: U.S. Representative From Arizona **I:** Government Administration/Government Relations/Government Services **DOB:** 02/19/1948 **PB:** Tucson **SC:** AZ/USA **ED:** BA in Sociology, University of Arizona, 1988 **C:** Ranking Member, House Committee On Natural Resources, 2007-Present; U.S. Congress From 3rd Arizona District, 2013-Present; Ranking Member, Committee On Natural Resources, 2013-Present; U.S. Congress From Seventh Arizona District, 2003-2013; Chairman, Pima County Board of Supervisors, 2000-2002; Pima County Board of Supervisors, 1989-2003; Director, El Pueblo Neighborhood Center, 1975-1986; Board Member, Tucson Unified School District, 1974-1986; Assistant Dean, Hispanic Student Affairs, University of Arizona **PA:** Democrat **BA:** Office of Raul Grijalva, 1511 Longworth HOB, Washington, DC, 20515

GRISHAM, JOHN RAY, T: Writer **I:** Writing and Editing **PB:** Jonesboro **ED:** JD, University Mississippi School Law, 1981; BS in Accounting, Mississippi State University, 1977 **C:** Member District 7, Mississippi House of Reps., Jackson, 1984-90; Private law practice, Southaven, Mississippi, 1981-91; Writer 1989- **CW:** Author: (novels) A Time to Kill, 1989, The Firm, 1991, The Pelican Brief, 1992, The Client, 1993, The Chamber, 1994, The Rainmaker, 1995, The Runaway Jury, 1996, The Partner, 1997, The Street Lawyer, 1998, The Testament, 1999, The Brethren, 2000, A Painted House, 2001, Skipping Christmas, 2002, The Summons, 2002, The King of Torts, 2003, Bleachers, 2003, The Last Juror, 2004, The Broker, 2005, Playing for Pizza, 2007, The Appeal, 2008 (#1 Publishers Weekly bestseller), The Associate, 2009 (#1 Publishers Weekly bestseller), Ford County, 2009 (#1 Publishers Weekly bestseller), The Confession, 2010 (#1 Publishers Weekly, New York Times bestsellers, Harper Lee prize for Legal Fiction, 2011), The Litigators, 2011, Calico Joe, 2012, The Racketeer, 2012, Sycamore Row, 2013, Gray Mountain, 2014, Rogue Lawyer, 2015, (non-fiction) The Innocent Man: Murder and Injustice in a Small Town, 2006, (children's books) Theodore Boone: Kid Lawyer, 2010, Theodore Boone: The Abduction, 2011, Theodore Boone: The Accused, 2012, Theodore Boone: The Activist, 2013, (screenplays) The Gingerbread Man, 1998, (A Non-Legal Thriller) The Tumor, 2016; producer (films) A Time to Kill, 1996; executive prodr.: (TV films) The Street Lawyer, 2003; actor, director, producer (films) Mickey, 2006,(Books) Theodore Boone: The Scandal, 2016, The Whistler, 2016, Camino Island, 2017, The Rooster Bar, 2017(Short Story) Partners, 2016, Witness to a Trial, 2016 **BAR:** Bar: Mississippi 1981 **PA:** Democrat **RE:** Baptist

GRISHAM, MICHELLE LUJAN, T: U.S. Representative from New Mexico, Former State Agency Administrator **I:** Government Administration/ Government Relations/Government Services **DOB:** 10/24/1959 **PB:** Los Alamos **PT:** Daughter of Buddy and Sonja Lujan **ED:** JD, University of New Mexico School of Law, 1987; BA, University of New Mexico, 1981 **C:** Member, US House Oversight & Government Committee, 2013-; Member, US House Budget Committee, 2013-; Member, US House Agricultural Committee, 2013-; Member, US Congress from 1st New Mexico District, Washington, 2013-; Co-owner, Delta Consulting Group, 2008-; Commissioner, Bernalillo County, New Mexico, 2011-12; Secretary, New Mexico Department Health, Santa Fe, 2004-07; Director, N.Mex Agency on Aging, 1992-2004; Director, lawyer referral for the elderly progressive, N.Mex State Bar **PA:** Democrat **BA:** 214 Cannon House Office Building, Washington, DC, 20515

GROSS, DAVID JONATHAN, T: Physicist **I:** Sciences **DOB:** 02/19/1941 **PB:** Washington **SC:** DC/USA **PT:** Son of Bertram M. and Nora (Faine) G. **MS:** Married **SPN:** Jacquelyn Savani, August 12, 2001; Shulamith Toaff, March 30, 1962; **CH:** Ariela, Elisheva; Miranda Savani (stepdaughter) **ED:** Doctor (hon.), University Libre de Bruxelles, 2010; Doctor (hon.), University of Cambodia, 2010; Doctor (hon.), Hong Kong University of Sci. and Tech., 2008; Doctor (hon.), University of Cambridge, England, 2008; Doctor (hon.), De La Salle University, Manila, Philippines, 2008; Doctor (hon.), The Ohio State University, 2007; Doctor (hon.), Sao Paulo University, Brazil, 2006; Doctor (hon.), Hebrew University, 2001; Doctor (hon.), University of Montpellier, 2000; PhD, University of California, Berkeley, 1966; BSc, Hebrew University, Jerusalem, 1962 **C:** Institute for Quantum Studies, 2017-; Professor physics, University of California, Santa Barbara, 1997-; Jones professor physics emeritus, Princeton University, 1997-; Gluck professor theoretical physics, University of California, 2001-02; Frederick W. Gluck chair theoretical physics, director Kavli Institute Theoretical Physics, University of California, 1997-2012; Jones professor physics, Princeton University, 1995-97; Eugene Higgens professor physics, Princeton University, 1986-95; Professor, Princeton University, 1973-86; Associate professor, Princeton University, 1971-73; Assistant professor physics, Princeton University, New Jersey, 1969-71; Harvard Society of Fellows junior fellow, Harvard University, 1966-69 **CR:** Chair XXV Solvay Conference Physics, 2011, XXIII Solvay Conference Physics, 2005, Franqui Prize Committee, 2012, Solvay Sci. Committee Physics, 2006-, International Adv. Committee Indian Center Theoretical Studies, Bangalore, India Solvay Centenary chair Solvay Institute, Brussels, 2011 Solvay professor University Brussels, 2008 Rothschild professor Cambridge University, 2007 chair, evaluation committee Scuola Internazionale Superiore di Studi Avanzati, Italy, 1994 invited lecturer for several universities visiting professor Lawrence Radiation Laboratory, Berkeley, California, 1992, Hebrew University, Jerusalem, 1984, Ecole Normale Superioure, Paris, 1988-89, Paris, 1983, European Organization of Nuclear Research, Geneva, 1993, Geneva, 1968-69 **CIV:** Director, Jerusalem Winter School, 1999- **CW:** Associate editor Nuclear Physics, 1972- **AW:** Recipient Alfred P. Sloan fellow, 1970-74, MacArthur Prize fellow, 1987, Dirac medal, 1988, Harvey prize, Technion-Israel Institute Tech., 2000, Oscar Klein medal, Stockholm University, 2000, grande médaille, French Academy Sciences, 2004, Golden Plate award, Academy Achievement, 2005; co-recipient High Energy and Particle Physics prize, European Physical Society, 2003, Nobel prize in physics, 2004. **MEM:** Fellow American Association for the Advancement of Science, Am. Physical Society (J. J. Sakurai prize 1986), Am. Academy Arts and Scis.; member National Academy Scis., European Academy Scis. (elected member, 2004), Tata Institute Fundamental Research, The Academy Scis. Developing World (elected member, 2007); member International Adv. Committee International Institute Physics (chair, 2009-), Am. Philosophical Society (elected member, 2007), Academy International Philosophie des Scis. (elected member, 2009), Chinese Academy Scis. (foreign member, elected member, 2011). **ACH:** Research, numerous publications in field; discovered asymptotic freedom, 1973; proposal of non-Abelian gauge theories of the strong interactions, 1973, heterotic string theory, 1984; discovery of (with H. David Politzer and Frank Wilczek) asymptotic freedom in the theory of the strong interaction. **BA:** Univ Calif Kohn Hall 1219, Santa Barbara, CA, 93106

GROSS, MARK, T: Food Retailing Company Executive **I:** Food & Restaurant Services **PB:** 1963 **ED:** JD, University of Pennsylvania, 1990; BA, Dartmouth College, 1985 **C:** CEO, Supervalu, 2016-; Founder, president, Surry Investment Advisors LLC, 2006-2016; President, GU Markets, 2003; Executive vice president, GU Markets, 2001-03; Board directors, C & S Wholesale Grocers, Inc., Keene, New Hampshire, 1997; Corp. executive vice president, C & S Wholesale Grocers, Inc., Keene, New Hampshire, 2002; CFO, C & S Wholesale Grocers, Inc., Keene, New Hampshire, 2001; General counsel, C & S Wholesale Grocers, Inc., Keene, New Hampshire, 1997; Senior vice president, C & S Wholesale Grocers, Inc., Keene, New Hampshire, 1997-2002; Mergers and acquisitions partner, Skadden, Arps, Slater, Meagher & Flom, New York City, **CR:** Board of Directors Food Industry Alliance, New York, Monadnock Waldorf School **BA:** Supervalu, 7075 Flying Cloud Dr, Eden Prairie, MN, 55344

GROSSMAN, ROBERT IVIN, T: Dean of NYU Medical School **I:** Education/Educational Services **DOB:** 09/28/1947 **PB:** New York **SC:** NY/USA **ED:** MD, University Pennsylvania, 1973; BS, Tulane University, 1969 **CT:** Cert. Neuroradiology, Radiology **C:** CEO, New York University Langone Medical Center, 2007-; Saul J. Farber dean, New York University School Medicine, 2007-; Louis Marx professor radiology, chairman Department Radiology, professor neurosurgery, neurology, physiology and neuroscience,

New York University School Medicine, 2001-; Chairman Diagnostics Radiology Study Section, University Pennsylvania Medical Center, 1997-2000; Chief neuroradiology, University Pennsylvania Medical Center, 1987; Professor radiology, neurosurgery and neurology, University Pennsylvania Medical School, Philadelphia, 1987; Associate professor, University Pennsylvania Medical School, Philadelphia, 1984-87; Assistant professor radiology, University Pennsylvania Medical School, Philadelphia, 1981-84; Fellow in neuroradiology, Massachusetts General Hospital, Boston, 1979-81; Resident in radiology, University Pennsylvania Medical School, Philadelphia, 1976-79; Resident in neurosurgery, University Pennsylvania Medical School, Philadelphia, 1974-76; Intern, Beth Israel Hospital, Boston, 1973-74 **CR:** Member National Adv. Council Biomedical Imaging and Bioengineering National Institutes of Health, 2003-07, chairman, 1997-2000, member Diagnostic Radiology Study Section, 1995-2000 **CW:** Author: Neuroradiology: The Requisites, 1994, Magnetic Resonance Techniques in Clinical Trials in Multiple Sclerosis, 1999; associate editor Magnetic Resonance Medicine, 1991-; contributor articles to medical journals **AW:** Recipient Outstanding Contributions in Research Award, Am. Society Neuroradiology Education and Research Foundation, 2004, Javits Neuroscience Investigator Award, National Institutes of Health, 1999 **MEM:** Fellow: International Society Magnetic Resonance in Medicine, Am. College Radiology; mem.: Am. Society Neuroradiology (pres.-elect 2005-06, former vice president), Alpha Omega Alpha **BA:** NYU Medical School, 550 1st Ave, New York, NY, 10016

GROTHMAN, GLENN, T: U.S. Representative from Wisconsin **I:** Government Administration/Government Relations/Government Services **DOB:** 06/03/1955 **PB:** Milw. **ED:** JD, University Wisconsin, Madison; BBA, University Wisconsin, Madison **C:** Member, U.S. House of Representatives from Wisconsin's 6th District, 2015-; Member, Committee on the Budget; Member, Committee on Education and the Workforce; Member, Committee on Oversight Government Reform; Member, Joint Economic Committee; Member, Republican Study Committee; Member District 20, Wisconsin State Senate, 2005-; Vice chair majority caucus, Wisconsin State Assembly, 1999-2004; Member District 59, Wisconsin State Assembly, 1993-2004 **CIV:** Board directors, Kettle Moraine Symphony Orchestra, **AW:** Named Legislator of Year, Wisconsin Guild Midwives, 2006, Ind. Business Association, 2000, Pro-Life Wisconsin, 1995; recipient Milk Bottle award, Wisconsin Dairy Business Association, 2006, 2004, Guardian of Small Business award, National Federation Ind. Businesses, 2000, Outstanding Legislator award, Wisconsin Counties Association, 1998, Sanctity of Life award, Wisconsin Right to Life, 2004, Pro-Life Hero award, 1996 **MEM:** Mem.: Washington County Bar Association, University Wisconsin Madison Alumni Association, Kiwanis West Bend Early Risers, Loyal Order Moose West Bend **PA:** Republican

GRUBBS, ROBERT HOWARD, T: Chemistry Professor **I:** Education/Educational Services **DOB:** 02/27/1942 **PB:** Calvert City **SC:** KY/USA **PT:** Son of Henry Howard and Faye (Atwood) Grubbs; **ED:** PhD in Chemistry, Columbia University, New York City, 1968; MS in Chemistry, University Florida, Gainesville, 1965; BS in Chemistry, University Florida, Gainesville, 1963 **C:** Co-Founder, Materia, 1998; Victor & Elizabeth Atkins professor chemistry, California Institute Tech., Pasadena, 1990-; Professor chemistry, California Institute Tech., Pasadena, 1978-90; Associate professor, Michigan State University, East Lansing, 1973-78; Assistant professor, Michigan State University, East Lansing,

1969-73; National Institutes of Health postdoc. fellow, Stanford University, California, 1968-69 **CR:** Hon. professor Shanghai Institute Organic Chemistry, Chinese Academy Scis., 2001 **CW:** Contributor, articles to professional journals **AW:** Recipient Ulysses Medal, Univ. College Dublin, 2007, Golden Plate award, Academy Achievement, 2006, Havinga Medal, Leiden University, The Netherlands, 2006, Nobel prize in chemistry, 2005, Bristol-Myers Squibb Distinguished Achievement award, 2004, Tetrahedron prize, 2003, Benjamin Franklin Medal in Chemistry, Franklin Institute, Philadelphia, 2000, Fluka prize, 1998, Nagoya Medal of Organic Chemistry, 1997, Tchr.-Scholar award, Camille and Henry Dreyfus Foundation, 1975-78, Senior Scientist award, Alexander von Humboldt Foundation, 1975; Alfred P. Sloan Fellow, 1974-76,Fellow of the Royal Society, 2017, AIC Gold Medal, 2010 **MEM:** Fellow: Am. Academy Arts & Scis., Royal Society Chemistry (hon.); mem.: National Academy of Sciences, Am. Chemical Society (National award in Organometallic Chemistry 1988, Arthur C. Cope award 1990, Award in Polymer Chemistry 1995, Herman F. Mark Polymer Chemistry award 2000, Herbert C. Brown award 2001, Arthur C. Cope award 2002, Richard C. Tolman Medal 2003, Pauling Medal 2003, Kirkwood Medal 2005, award for creative invention 2009), Royal Irish Academy (hon.) **ACH:** Achievements include research in homogeneous or heterogeneous catalysis **PA:** Democrat

GRUENDER, RAYMOND W., T: Federal Judge **I:** Law and Legal Services **DOB:** 07/05/1963 **PB:** St. Louis **SC:** MO/USA **ED:** JD, Washington University, 1987; MBA, Washington University, 1987; BA, Washington University, 1984 **C:** Judge, U.S. Court of Appeals for the Eighth Circuit, 2004-; U.S. attorney Eastern District of Missouri, US Department State, 2001-04; Assistant U.S. attorney, Eastern District of Missouri, U.S. Department State, St. Louis, 2000-01; Assistant U.S. attorney, Eastern District of Missouri, U.S. Department State, St. Louis, 1990-94; Partner, Thompson Coburn LLP, 1994-2000; Associate, Lewis, Rice and Fingersh, 1987-90 **BA:** US Courthouse, 111 S Tenth St, Saint Louis, MO, 63102

GUÐMUNDSDÓTTIR, BJÖRK, I: Media & Entertainment **DOB:** 11/21/1965 **PB:** Reykjavik **SC:** Iceland **PT:** Gudmundur and Hildur Runa **SPN:** Matthew Barney, 2000 (div. 2012); Thor Eldon, 1986 (div. 1988) **CH:** Sindri Eldon; Isadora **CW:** Recording artist solo album at age 11; performer with several bands; formed theatrical/rock ensemble KUKL, 1980s; recording artist with The Sugarcubes: (albums) Life's Too Good, 1986, Here Today, Tomorrow, Next Week, 1989; solo artist: (albums) Debut, 1993, Post, 1995, Telegram, 1997, Homogenic, 1997, Vespertine, 2001, Family Tree, 2002, Greatest Hits, 2002, Medulla, 2004, Volta, 2007, Biophilia, 2011, Vulnicura, 2015; (soundtracks) Selmasongs: Dancer in the Dark, 2000, Drawing Restraint 9, 2005; actor: (films) Juniper Tree, 1990,Pret-a-Porter , 1994, Dancer in the Dark, 2000 (Best Actress, Cannes Film Festival), Drawing Restraint 9, 2005, (voice only) Anna and the Moods, 2007 (retrospective exhibition) Museum Modern Art, New York 2015. **AW:** Named Webby awards Artist of the Year, 2012; recipient Polar Music Prize, Royal Swedish Academy Arts, 2010, Q Inspiration award, 2005, Brit Award for International Female, 1994

GUTH, ALAN HARVEY, T: Physicist, Researcher **I:** Sciences **DOB:** 02/27/1947 **PB:** New Brunswick **PT:** Son of Hyman and Elaine (Cheiten) G. **MS:** Married **SPN:** Susan Tisch, March 28, 1971 **CH:** Lawrence David, Jennifer Lynn **ED:** PhD in Physics, Massachusetts Institute of Technology, 1972; SB and

SM, Massachusetts Institute of Technology, 1969 **C:** Victor F. Weisskopf professor physics, Massachusetts Institute of Technology, Cambridge, 1992-; Jerrold Zacharias professor physics, Massachusetts Institute of Technology, Cambridge, 1989-91; Professor, Massachusetts Institute of Technology, Cambridge, 1986-89; Associate professor Physics, Massachusetts Institute of Technology, Cambridge, 1980-86; Research associate, Stanford Linear Accelerator Center, California, 1979-80; Research associate, Cornell University, Ithaca, New York, 1977-79; Research associate, Columbia University, New York City, 1974-77; Instructor, Princeton University, 1971-74 **CR:** Physicist Harvard-Smithsonian Center for Astrophysics, 1984-89, visiting scientist, 1990-91. **AW:** Alfred P. Sloan fellow, 1981, Margaret MacVicar Faculty Fellow, Massachusetts Institute of Technology; named to Sci. Digest's list of America's 100 Brightest Scientists Under 40, 1984, Esquire Mag.'s list of Men and Women Under 40 Who Are Changing the Nation, 1985, Newsweek's list of 25 Top American Innovators, 1989; recipient Lilienfeld Prize 1992, Benjamin Franklin medal for Physics, Frankling Institute, 2001, Dirac prize, International Center for Theoretical Physics in Trieste, 2002, Gruber Prize in Cosmology; co-recipient Kavli Prize in Astrophysics, 2014,Fundamental Physics Prize, 2012, Gruber Prize in Cosmology, 2004 **MEM:** Fellow American Association for the Advancement of Science, American Physical Society (member executive committee astrophysics div. 1986-88, vice chairman astrophysics div. 1988-89, chairman div. 1989-90), American Academy Arts and Sciences; member National Academy of Sciences, American Astronomical Society **ACH:** Achievements include being originator of inflationary model of early universe.

GUTHRIE, BRETT, T: U.S. Representative from Kentucky **I:** Government Administration/Government Relations/Government Services **DOB:** 05/18/1964 **PB:** Florence, Alabama **PT:** Son of Lowell M. and Carolyn P. (Holt) Guthrie **ED:** MA in Public & Private Management, Yale University, 1997; BS in Mathematical Economics, US Military Academy, 1987 **C:** Member, US Congress from 2nd Kentucky District, Washington, 2009-; Member, Committee on Energy and Commerce, Committee on Education and the Workforce, Republican Study Committee; Member District 32, Kentucky State Senate, Frankfort, 1998-2009; Director operations, Trace Die Casting, **CIV:** Board directors, United Way, Vol., Potter Children's Home, Member, Warren County Rep. Executive Committee, **MEM:** Mem.: American Society Quality, National Association Manufacturing **PA:** Republican

GUTHRIE, SAVANNAH, T: Broadcast Journalist **I:** Media & Entertainment **DOB:** 12/28/1971 **PB:** Melbourne **ED:** JD magna cum laude, Georgetown University Law Center, 2002; BA in Journalism, cum laude, University Arizona, 1993 **C:** Co-anchor The Today Show, NBC News, 2012-; Co-anchor The Daily Rundown,, MSNBC, 2010-11; Co-anchor third hour segment The Today Show, NBC News, 2011-12; Chief legal analyst, NBC News, 2011-12; White House corr., NBC News, 2008-11; Legal analyst corr., NBC News, 2007-08; Legal affairs corr., Court TV, Washington, 2006-07; National trial corr., Court TV, 2004-06; Litig. associate, Akin Gump Strauss Hauer & Feld LLP, Washington, 2002-03; Freelance reporter, WRC-TV, Washington, 2000-02; Anchor, reporter, KVOA-TV, Tucson, 1995-99; Anchor, reporter, KMIZ-TV, Columbia, Missouri, 1993-95 **MEM:** Mem.: Order of the Coif, Pi Beta Phi

GUTIERREZ, MAURICIO, T: CEO **I:** Oil & Energy **CN:** NRG Energy **ED:** Master in Mineral and Petroleum Economics, French Petroleum Institute; Master in Mineral and Petroleum Economics, Colorado School Mines; BS in Industrial Engineering, Universidad Panamericana **C:** CEO, NRG Energy, 2015-; Executive vice president, COO, NRG Energy, Inc., 2010-15; Senior vice president commercial operations, NRG Energy, Inc., 2008-09; Executive vice president commercial operations, NRG Energy, Inc., 2007-10; Vice president commercial operations trading, NRG Energy, Inc., 2006-07; Portfolio director, NRG Energy, Inc., 2004-05; Managing director, Dynegy, Inc., 2004; Senior power trader, asset manager, Dynegy, Inc., 2000-04; Senior consultant, project manager, Dynegy, Inc., 1994-98 **MEM:** Mem.: US Association for Energy Economics, Colorado School of Mines Alumni Association

GUTIÉRREZ, LUIS VICENTE, T: U.S. Representative from Illinois **I:** Government Administration/Government Relations/Government Services **DOB:** 12/10/1953 **PB:** Chgo. **ED:** BA magna cum laude in English, Northeastern Illinois University, 1975 **C:** Member, US House Judiciary Committee, 2013-; Member, US Senate Permanent Select Committee on Intelligence, 2011-; Member, US House Financial Services Committee, 1993-; Member, US Congress from 4th Illinois District, 1993-; President pro tempore, Chicago City Council, 1992; Alderman 26th Ward, Chicago City Council, 1986-93; Administrative assistant Mayor's Subcommittee on Infrastructure, City of Chicago, 1984-85; Social worker, Illinois Department Children & Family Services, 1979-83 **CR:** Chairman Housing, Land Acquisition & Disposition Committee, 1989-93 **CW:** Author: Still Dreaming: My Journey From the Barrio to Capitol Hill, 2013 **PA:** Democrat

GUTMANN, AMY PH.D, T: President **I:** Education/Educational Services **CN:** Pennsylvania State University **DOB:** 11/19/1949 **PB:** Brooklyn **SC:** NY/USA **PT:** Michael Doyle (1976) **CH:** Abigail **ED:** PhD in Political Sci., Harvard University, 1976; MSc in Political Sci., London School Economics, 1972; BA magna cum laude, Harvard-Radcliffe College, 1971 **C:** President, University Pennsylvania, Philadelphia, 2004-; Provost, Princeton University, New Jersey, 2001-04; Laurance S. Rockefeller University Professor of Politics and the University Center for Human Values, Princeton University, New Jersey, 1990-2004; Academic advisor to president, Princeton University, New Jersey, 1997-98; Dean faculty, Princeton University, New Jersey, 1995-97; Founding director University Center for Human Values, Princeton University, New Jersey, 1998-2001; Founding director University Center for Human Values, Princeton University, New Jersey, 1990-95; Director ethics and pub. affairs program, Princeton University, New Jersey, 1997-2000; Director ethics and pub. affairs program, Princeton University, New Jersey, 1990-95; Director political philosophy program, Princeton University, New Jersey, 1987-89; Director grad. studies department politics, Princeton University, New Jersey, 1986-88; Andrew W. Mellon Professor, Princeton University, New Jersey, 1987-90; Professor politics, Princeton University, New Jersey, 1987-2004; Associate professor politics, Princeton University, New Jersey, 1981-86; Assistant professor politics, Princeton University, New Jersey, 1976-81 **CR:** Visitor Institute for Advanced Study, Princeton University, 1981-82 visiting Rockefeller Faculty Fellow, Center for Philosophy and Pub. Policy, University Maryland, 1984-85 visiting professor, Kennedy School Government, Harvard University, 1988-89, adv. council, 1996-2001 Tanner lecturer, Stanford University, 1994-95 academic adv. board

Institute Human Sciences, Vienna, 2001- member board directors, executive committee, Centers for Advanced Study in Behavioral Sciences, Stanford University, 1998-, Princeton University Press, 1996- secondary faculty appointment Annenberg School for Communications, 2004-, chair, Presdl Commission for the Study of Bioethical Issues, 2009- board dirs, The Vanguard Group, 2006- **CIV:** Trustee, Carnegie Corp., 2005- **CW:** Author: Liberal Equality, 1980, Democratic Education, 1987, 2nd edition, 1999; co-author: (with Dennis Thompson) Democracy & Disagreement, 1996, (with Anthony Appiah) Color Conscious, 1996 (award North America Society Social Philosophy), Identity in Democracy, 2003, (with Dennis Thompson) Why Deliberative Democracy? 2004; editor: Democracy and the Welfare State, 1988, Multiculturalism, 1992, Freedom of Association, 1998, University Center for Human Values Series, Princeton University Press, 1992-; co-editor: (with Dennis Thompson) Ethics and Politics, 3d edition, 1997; member editl board Teachers' College Record, 1990-95, Cambridge Studies in Philosophy and Pub. Policy, 1991-, Raritan, 1995-, Journal Political Philosophy, 1995-, Handbook of Political Theory, 1999-, Annual Reviews, 2001-05; international adv. board Ethicities, 2000-. **AW:** Fellowship, National Endowment of the Humanities, 1977, Am. Council Learned Societies, 1978-79, University Hong Kong, 1998-99; Grant, Spencer Foundation, 1995-98, Senior Scholar Award, 1999-2003; recipient Gustavus Myers Center for Study of Human Rights in North America Award, 1997, North America Society for Social Philosophy Book Award, 1996-97, Ralph J. Bunche Award, Am. Political Sci. Association, 1997, Bertram Mott Award, Am. Association Univ. Professors, Rider College, 1998, President's Distinguished Teaching Award, 2000, Centennial Medal, Harvard University, 2003, others. **MEM:** Member Association Practical and Professional Ethics (executive committee, 1990-), Am. Society Political and Legal Philosophy (president 2001-04); fellow Am. Academy of Arts and Sciences, National Academy of Education, Am. Academy Political and Social Sci. **BA:** Office of the President, 201 Old Main, University Park, PA, 16802

GUY, BUDDY, T: Blues Guitarist **I:** Media & Entertainment **DOB:** 07/30/1936 **PB:** Lettsworth **SC:** LA/USA **C:** Began to play guitar professionally in Chicago, 1957-; Owner, Buddy Guy Legends, Chicago,; Toured widely, performing in international blues and folk festivals, concert halls, clubs, **CW:** Recordings include Hoodoo Man Blues, 1965, Stone Crazy, 1965, With the Blues, 1965, Hoodoo Man Blues, 1966, Its My Life, Baby!, 1966, I Left My Blues in San Francisco, 1967, Coming at You, 1968, A Man and His Blues, 1968, I Left My Blues in San Francisco, 1968, This is Buddy Guy, Blues Today, 1968, Hot and Cool, 1969, First Time I Met Blues-Python, 1969, Buddy and the Juniors, 1970, South Side Blues Jam, 1970, In the Beginning, 1971, Play the Blues, 1972, Hold That Plane!, 1972, Buddy Guy & Junior Wells Play the Blues, 1972, Hot & Cool, 1969, I Was Walking Through the Woods, 1974, Got to Use Your Head, 1979, Dollar Done Fell, 1980, Drinkin' TNT 'n' Smokin' Dynamite, 1982, DJ Play My Blues, 1982, Buddy Guy, 1983, Ten Blue Fingers, 1985, Atlantic Blues: Chicago, 1986, Chess Masters, 1987, Breaking Out, 1988, I Ain't Got No Money, 1989, Damn Right, I've Got the Blues, 1991 (Grammy award for Best Contemporary Blues Recording 1991), Alone and Acoustec, 1991, Feels Like Rain, 1993 (Grammy award for Best Contemporary Blues Album 1994), Live in Montreux, 1992, My Time After Awhile, 1992, Slippin' In, 1994 (Grammy award for Best Contemporary Blues Recording 1995), Buddy Guy Live: The Real Deal, 1996, Buddy's Blues, 1997, As

Good As It Gets, 1998, Blues Master, 1998, Heavy Love, 1998, Buddy's Baddest: The Best of Buddy Guy, 1999, Every Day I Have the Blues, 2000, Sweet Tea, 2001, Double Dynamite, 2001, Blues Singer, 2003 (Grammy award for Best Traditional Blues Album 2003), Jammin' Blues Electric & Acoustic, 2003, Live At the Mystery Club, 2003, A Night of the Blues, 2005, Bring 'Em In, 2005, Live: The Real Deal, 2006, Goin' Home: A Tribute to Fats Domino, 2007, Skin Deep, 2008, The Definitive Buddy Guy, 2009, Living Proof, 2010 (Grammy award for Best Contemporary Blues Album 2010), Icon, 2011, Live At Legends, 2012, Rhythm & Blues, 2013, Born To Play Guitar, 2015 (Grammy award for Best Blues Album, 2016); author: (autobiography) When I Left Home: My Story, 2012. **AW:** Recipient Century award Billboard Magazine, 1993, Grammy award for Best Contemporary Blues Recording "Stevie Ray Vaughan Shuffle", 1997 (with B.B. King, Bonnie Raitt, Dr. John and others), 23 W.C. Handy Blues Awards, Billboard Magazine Century award, Presidential National Medal of Arts, Kennedy Center Honors, John F. Kennedy Center Performing Arts, Washington, 2012, Induction into Musician Hall of Fame and Museum, 2014, Lifetime Achievement award, Grammy Awards, 2015; named to Louisiana Music Hall of Fame, 2008, Rock and Roll Hall of Fame, 2005, Grammy for Best Blues Album, 2016

GWYNN, REGINA, T: Co-founder & CEO **I:** Business Management/Business Services **CN:** TresseNoire **ED:** MBA in Marketing and Entrepreneurship, Northwestern University (2009); BS in Marketing, Rutgers, The State University of New Jersey (2001); Coursework, Fashion Buying & Merchandising, Fashion Institute of Technology (1997) **C:** Co-founder, Black Women Talk Tech (2017-Present); Co-founder & Chief Executive Officer, TresseNoire (2014-Present); Senior Advisor, Culture Shift Labs (2013-2017); Marketing, The Apparel Group, Ltd. (2011-2015)

GYLLENHAAL, JAKE, T: Actor **I:** Medicine & Health Care **DOB:** 07/05/1905 **PB:** LA, **SC:** LA, **PT:** Son of Stephen Gyllenhaal and Naomi Foner. **ED:** Attended, Columbia University **CW:** Actor: (films) City Slickers, 1991, A Dangerous Woman, 1993, Josh and S.A.M., 1993, Homegrown, 1998, October Sky, 1999, Donnie Darko, 2001, Bubble Boy, 2001, Lovely and Amazing, 2001, The Good Girl, 2002, Moonlight Mile, 2002, Highway, 2002, The Day After Tomorrow, 2004, Proof, 2005, Jarhead, 2005, Brokeback Mountain, 2005 (National Board Review award for Best Supporting Actor, 2005, British Academy Film and TV Arts award for Actor in a Supporting Role, 2006, MTV Movie award for Best Performance, 2006), Zodiac, 2007, Rendition, 2007, Brothers, 2009, Prince of Persia: The Sands of Time, 2010, Love and Other Drugs, 2010, Source Code, 2011, Prisoners, 2013, Enemy, 2013, Nailed, 2014, Accidental Love, 2015, Southpaw, 2015, Everest, 2015, Demolition, 2015, Nocturnal Animals, 2016, Lief, 2017, Okja, 2017, Stronger, 2017, Wild Life, 2018, The Sisters Brothers, 2018; (plays) This is Our Youth (London Evening Standard Theatre award for Outstanding Newcomer, 2002), If There Is, I Haven't Found It Yet, 2012, Constellations, 2014-2015, Little Shop of Horrors, 2015, Sunday in the Park with George, 2016-2017; actor, executive producer (films) End of Watch, 2012, actor, producer Nightcrawler, 2014 **AW:** Named one of The 50 Most Powerful People in Hollywood, Premiere magazine, 2006; recipient Best Supporting Actor award, National Board Rev., 2005

HABERMAN, MAGGIE, T: White House Correspondent **I:** Writing and Editing **DOB:** 07/07/1905 **PB:** New York City, New York **SC:** New York City, New York **C:** Political Correspondent, New York Times, 2017; Political Analyst, CNN, 2014; Senior Reporter, Politico, 2010; New York Post, 1996

HACKETT, JAMES PATRICK, T: President of Ford Motor Company **I:** Automotive **DOB:** 04/22/1955 **PB:** Columbus, Ohio **ED:** Bachelor in General Studies, University Michigan, 1977 **C:** President/CEO, Ford Motor Co, 2017-; Chairman, Ford Smart Mobility, 2016-17; CEO, Steelcase, Inc,., Grand Rapids, 2013-14; President, CEO, Steelcase, Inc., Grand Rapids, Michigan, 1994-2013; Executive vice president, COO, North America, Steelcase, Inc., Grand Rapids, Michigan, 1994; Executive vice president, Steelcase Ventures subsidiary, Steelcase, Inc., Grand Rapids, Michigan, 1994; President, Turnstone subsidiary, Steelcase, Inc., Grand Rapids, Michigan, 1993-94; Senior vice president, sales & marketing, Steelcase, Inc., Grand Rapids, Michigan, 1990-93; Director, national accounts, Steelcase, Inc., Grand Rapids, Michigan, 1986-90; Regional manager, Steelcase, Inc., Houston, 1984-86; Management positions, Steelcase, Inc., Grand Rapids, Michigan, 1981-84; Various sales & management positions, The Proctor & Gamble Co., 1977-81 **CR:** Trustee University Michigan, board directors Ford Motor Co., 2013-, Fifth Third Bancorp, 2001-, Northwestern Mutual Life, 2000- **BA:** 1 American Road, Dearborn, MI, 48126

HACKMAN, GENE, T: Actor **I:** Media & Entertainment **DOB:** 05/16/1905 **PB:** San Bernardino, **SC:** San Bernardino, **PT:** Son of Eugene Ezra Hackman; **MIL:** US Marine Corps, 1946-49 **CW:** Actor: (films) Mad Dog Coll, 1961, Lilith, 1964, Hawaii, 1966, First to Fight, 1967, A Covenant With Death, 1967, Bonnie and Clyde, 1967, First to Fight, 1967, The Split, 1968, Riot, 1969, The Gypsy Moths, 1969, Downhill Racer, 1969, I Never Sang for My Father, 1969, Marooned, 1970, Doctor's Wives, 1971, The Hunting Party, 1971, The French Connection, 1971 (Academy award for Best Actor, 1971, Golden Globe award, Brit. Academy award, New York Film Critics award), Cisco Pike, 1971, Prime Cut, 1972, The Poseidon Adventure (Brit. Academy award), 1972, Scarecrow, 1973 (Cannes Film Festival award), The Conversation, 1974, Zandy's Bride, 1974, Young Frankenstein, 1974, The French Connection II, 1975, Bite the Bullet, 1975, Night Moves, 1975, Lucky Lady, 1975, A Bridge Too Far, 1977, The Domino Principle, 1977, March or Die, 1977, Superman, 1978, Superman II, 1980, All Night Long, 1981, Reds, 1981, Two of a Kind (voice only), 1983, Under Fire, 1983, Uncommon Valor, 1983, Misunderstood, 1984, Eureka, 1984, Target, 1985, Twice in a Lifetime, 1985, Power, 1986, Superman IV: The Quest for Peace, 1987, No Way Out, 1987, Another Woman, 1988, Bat*21, 1988, Split Decisions, 1988, Mississippi Burning, 1988 (Best Actor award National Society Film Critics), Full Moon in Blue Water, 1988, The Package, 1989, Postcards From The Edge, 1989, Class Action, 1989, Loose Cannons, 1990, Narrow Margin, 1990, Company Business, 1991, Unforgiven, 1992 (Academy award for Best Supporting Actor, Golden Globes, New York, LA, Boston Film Critics, National Soc.Film Critics awards), The Firm, 1993, Geronimo: An American Legend, 1993, Wyatt Earp, 1994, The Quick and the Dead, 1995, Crimson Tide, 1995, Get Shorty, 1995, Extreme Measures, 1996, The Chamber, 1996, The Birdcage, 1996, The Magic Hour, 1997, Absolute Power, 1997, Enemy of the State, 1998, Antz (voice only), 1998, Twilight, 1998, The Replacements, 2000, The Mexican, 2001, Heartbreakers, 2001, Heist, 2001, The Royal Tenenbaums, 2001 (Golden Globe for Best Actor in a Comedy 2001, Chicago Film Critics award for Best Actor 2002, National Society Film Critics award 2002, AFI award 2002), Behind Enemy Lines, 2001, Runaway Jury, 2003, Welcome to Mooseport, 2004, The Unknown Flag Raiser of Iwo Jima, 2016; actor, executive prodr.: (films) Under Suspicion, 1999; actor: (TV films) Ride with Terror, 1963, Shadow

on the Land, 1968, My Father and My Mother, 1968; (TV appearances) The U.S. Steel Hour, 1959, 60, 62, The Defenders, 1961, 63, Look up and Live, 1963, Naked City, 1963, The DuPont Show of the Week, 1963, East Side/West Side, 1963, The Trials of O'Brien, 1966, The F.B.I., 1967, The Invaders, 1967, The Iron Horse, 1967, I Spy, 1968; co-author: (novels) (with Daniel F. Lenihan) Wake of the Perdido Star: A Novel, 2000, Justice for None: A Novel, 2004, Escape from Andersonville: A Novel of the Civil War, 2008; author: (novels) Payback at Morning Peak, 2011, Pursuit, 2014 **AW:** Named Star of Year, National Association Theatre Owners, 1974; recipient Cecil B. DeMille award, 2003

HADDISH, TIFFANY, T: Actress **I:** Media & Entertainment **DOB:** 06/18/1905 **PB:** Los Angeles, California **SC:** Los Angeles, California **CW:** (Films) The Urban Demographic, 2005, Meet the Spartans, 2008, Janky Promoters, 2009, Wax On, F*ck Off, 2010, Driving by Braille, 2011, What My Husband Doesn't Know, 2012, Christmas Wedding, 2013, 4Play, 2014, patterns of Attraction, 2014, Wishes, 2014, School Dance, 2014, All Between Us, 2015, Kean, 2016, Mad Families, 2017, Girls Trip, 2017, Boosters, 2017, Uncle Drew, 2018, Night School,2018, The List, 2018, The Lego Movie Sequel, 2019, The Secret Life of Pets 2,2019(Television) That's So Raven, 2005, Bill Bellamy's Who's Got Jokes?, 2006, My Name is Earl, 2006, It's Always Sunny in Philadelphia, 2006, The Underground, 2006, Nick Cannon Presents: Short Circuitz, 2007, Just Jordan, 2007, Racing for Time, 2008, In the Motherhood, 2009, Secret Girlfriend, 2009, Real Husbands of Hollywood, 2013-14, If Loving You is Wrong, 2015, New Girl, 2014, Trip Tank, 2014, The Carmichael Show, 2015, Legends of Chamberlain Heights, 2016,Tiffany Haddish: She Ready! From the Hood to Hollywood, 2017, SNL, 2017, Drunk History, 2018, The Last O.G., 2018 (Books)The Last Black Unicorn, 2017 **AW:** Time 2018 Most Influential

HAGER, DAVID A., T: CEO of Devon Energy Corp **I:** Oil & Energy **DOB:** 10/14/1956 **PB:** Indianapolis **SC:** IN/USA **MS:** Married **SPN:** Alice Hager **CH:** 3 children **ED:** MBA, Southern Methodist University; Bachelor in Geophysics, Purdue University; Completed Executive Management Program, Harvard University; Completed Executive Management Programs, Duke University **C:** President/CEO, Devon Energy Corp, 2015-; COO, Devon Energy Corp, 2013-15; Executive vice president, Exploration & Production, Devon Energy Corp., 2009-13; Vice president, U.S. Offshore operations, Oryx Energy Co., 1997-; Board directors, Devon Energy Corp., 2007-09; Senior vice president, COO, Kerr-McGee Corp.(merged with Anadarko Petroleum Corp.), 2005-06; Senior vice president, oil and gas exploration & production, Kerr-McGee Corp., 2003-05; Vice president, Exploration & Production, Kerr-McGee Corp.(merged with Anadarko Petroleum Corp.), 2002-03; Vice president, Gulf of Mexico & Worldwide Deepwater Exploration & Production, Kerr-McGee Corp.(merged with Anadarko Petroleum Corp.), 2001-02; Vice president, Worldwide Deepwater Exploration & Production, Kerr-McGee Corp.(merged with Anadarko Petroleum Corp.), 2000-01; Vice president, international operations, Kerr-McGee Corp., 2000; Vice president, Gulf of Mexico Operations, Kerr-McGee Corp., 1999-2000; Project director, New Areas Exploration & Production, director, operations Planning Drilling & Facilities Engineering, Oryx Energy Co., 1995-97; Joined, Sun Oil Co., 1981; Exploration geophysicist, Mobil Oil Corp., 1979 **CR:** Board of directors Pride International, Inc., 2008

HALEY, NIKKI RANDHAWA, T: Former Ambassador to the UN, Former Governor of South Carolina, Former State Legislator **I:** Government Administration/Government Relations/Government Services **DOB:** 01/20/1972 **PB:** Bamberg **ED:** BS in Accounting, Clemson University, 1994 **C:** Ambassador to the UN, Washington D.C.2017-; Governor, State of South Carolina, Columbia, South Carolina, 2011-2017; Majority whip, South Carolina House of Reps., Columbia, South Carolina, 2006-10; Member District 87, South Carolina House of Reps., Columbia, 2004-10; CFO, Exotica International, 1996-2004; Accounting supervisor, FCR, Inc., 1994-96 **CR:** Board directors Lexington Sheriff's Foundation, 2004-06, Lexington Medical Foundation, 2004 **CIV:** Board member, Mount Horeb United Methodist Church **CW:** Author: (memoir) Can't Is Not An Option: My American Story, 2012 **AW:** Named one of The Politics 40 Under 40, TIME Magazine, 2010, The 50 Politicos to Watch, Politico, 2010 **MEM:** Mem.: National Rifle Association, West Metro Rep. Women, Lexington Rotary Club **PA:** Republican **BA:** U.S. Department of State, 2201 C Street NW, Washington, DC, 20037

HALL, JEFFREY CONNOR, T: Biology Educator Emeritus, Behavioral Genetics Researcher **I:** Education/Educational Services **DOB:** 05/03/1945 **PB:** Brooklyn **SC:** NY/USA **ED:** PhD in Genetics, University Washington, 1971; MS, University Washington, 1969; AB, Amherst College, 1967 **C:** Visiting professor, University of Maine, Orono, 2007-; Professor emeritus biology, Brandeis University, Waltham, Massachusetts, 2007-; Professor biology, Brandeis University, Waltham, Massachusetts, 1986-2007; Associate professor biology, Brandeis University, Waltham, Massachusetts, 1979-86; Assistant professor biology, Brandeis University, Waltham, Massachusetts, 1974-79; Fellow behavioral genetics, California Institute Tech., 1971-73 **AW:** Nobel Prize in Physiology or Medicine 2017,Co-recipient The Shaw Prize in Life Science and Medicine, 2013, Canada Gairdner International award, 2012, Louisa Gross Horwitz prize, Columbia University, 2011, Peter and Patricia Gruber Foundation Neuroscience prize, 2009, Genetics Society of America medal, 2003,Wiley Prize, 2013, Shaw Prize, 2013 **MEM:** Mem.: American Academy of Arts & Sciences, National Academy of Sciences

HALL, JOHN LEWIS, T: Physicist, Researcher **I:** Sciences **PB:** , **PT:** Son Of John Ernest And Elizabeth Rae (Long) H **SPN:** Married Marilyn Charlene Robinson, March 1, 1958 **CH:** Thomas Charles, Carolyn Gay, Jonathan Lawrence **ED:** PhD (hon.), University of Paris, 1989; DS (hon.), The Ohio State University,2008; DS (hon.),University of Moscow, 2007; DSc (hon.), Carnegie Mellon University, Pittsburgh, 2006; DS(hon.), The republic legions,2004; PhD in Physics, Carnegie Mellon University, Pittsburgh, 1961; MS in Physics, Carnegie Mellon University, Pittsburgh, 1958; BS in Physics, Carnegie Mellon University, Pittsburgh, 1956 **C:** Adjunct Professor, Na. Institute Standards & Tech. (formerly National Bureau Standards), Boulder, Colorado, 2005-; Senior Fellow Emeritus, Na. Institute Standards & Tech. (formerly National Bureau Standards), Boulder, Colorado, 2005-; Senior Scientist, Na. Institute Standards & Tech. (formerly National Bureau Standards), Boulder, Colorado, 1975-2004; Physicist, Na. Institute Standards & Tech. (formerly National Bureau Standards), Boulder, Colorado, 1962-75; Postdoc. Research Associate, National Bureau Standards, Washington, 1961-62 **CR:** Lecturer University Colorado, Boulder, 1977-Consultant Los Alamos Sci. Laboratories, 1963-65 Consultant Numerous Firms in Laser Industry, 1974-. **CW:** Contributor Articles to Professional

Journals; Patentee in Laser Tech.; Editor: Laser Spectroscopy 3, 1977 **AW:** Recipient IR-100 Award IR Magazine, 1975, 77, National Bureau Standards Stratton Award, 1971, E.U. Condon Award, 1979, Gold Medal Department Commerce, 1969, 74, 2002, Presidential Meritorious Executive Award, 1980, 2002, Meritorious Alumnus Award Carnegie Mellon University, 1985, Humboldt Senior Scientist Award Munich, 1989, A.V. Astin Award NIST, 2000, Rabi Award IEEE, 2004, Golden Plate Award, Academy Achievement, 2006; Co-Recipient Nobel Prize For Physics, 2005; Named Knight French Legion Honor, 2004; Sherman Fairchild Distinguished Scholar California Tech., 1992. **MEM:** Fellow Optical Society Am. (Board of Directors 1980-82, Charles H. Townes Award 1984, Frederic Ives Medal 1991, Max Born Award 2002), Am. Physical Society (Davisson-Germer Award 1988, Arthur L. Schawlow Prize 1993); Member National Academy of Sciences **H:** Photography, Travel, Invention **ADD:** 14074 Blue River Trl, Broomfield, CO, 80023 **URL:** nobelprize.org (search physics 2005)

HALL, KEITH D., T: Director of the Congressional Budget Office **I:** Government Administration/ Government Relations/Government Services **ED:** PhD in Economics, Purdue University; MA in Economics, Purdue University; BA in Economics, University Virginia **C:** Director of the Congressional Budget Office, 2015-; Commissioner Bureau Labor Statistics, U.S. Department Labor, 2008-12; Chief economist Council Economic Advisors, Executive Office of President,; Chief economist econs./ statistics administration, U.S. Department Commerce,; Senior international economist research division, U.S. International Trade Commission,; Chief division applied econs., U.S. International Trade Commission, **BA:** Fort House Office Building, Second and D Streets, SW, Washington, DC, 20515

HALL, PETER W., T: Federal Judge **I:** Law and Legal Services **DOB:** 11/09/1948 **PB:** Hartford **SC:** CT/USA **ED:** JD, Cornell University, 1977; MA, University of North Carolina, 1974; BA, University of North Carolina, 1971 **C:** Judge, U.S. Court Appeals (2nd cir.), 2004-; U.S. attorney eastern district, U.S. Department Justice, Vermont, 2001-04; Partner, Reiber, Kenlan, Schwiebert, Hall and Facey, Rutland, Vermont, 1986-2001; 1st assistant US attorney, District VT, U.S. Department Justice, 1982-86; Assistant U.S. atty, District Vermont, U.S. Department Justice, 1978-82; Law clerk to Hon. Albert W. Coffrin, 1977-78 **BA:** US Court of Appeals, 40 Foley Sq, New York, NY, 10007

HAMILTON, DAVID FRANK, T: Federal Judge **I:** Law and Legal Services **DOB:** 07/02/1957 **PB:** Bloomington **SC:** Indiana **PT:** Son of Richard Hamilton. **ED:** JD, Yale University, 1983; BA Magna Cum Laude, Haverford College, 1979 **CT:** Bar: US Supreme Court 1992, US Court Appeals (7th cir.) 1985, US District Court (so. district) Ind. 1984, Ind. 1984 **C:** Judge, US Court Appeals (7th cir.), Indianapolis, 2009-; Chief judge, US District Court (so. district) Ind., Indianapolis, 2008-09; Judge, US District Court (so. district) Ind., Indianapolis, 1994-2009; Counsel to Governor, State of Ind., Indianapolis, 1989-91; Partner, Barnes & Thornburg, Indianapolis, 1991-94; Associate, Barnes & Thornburg, Indianapolis, 1984-88; Law Clerk to Hon. Richard D. Cudahy, US Court Appeals (7th cir.), 1983-84 **CR:** Chair Ind. State Ethics Commission, 1991-94. **CIV:** Board Directors Ind. Civil Liberties Union, 1987-88 Board Visitors Ind. University School Law, 2000-07 **AW:** Fulbright Scholar, 1979-80; Recipient Sagamore of the Wabash, Governor Evan Bayh, 1991. **MEM:** Mem.: Am. Inns of Court (president chapter 2001-03), Phi Beta Kappa **BA:** 219 S. Dearborn Street Room 2722, Chicago, IL, 60604

HAMILTON, LEWIS, I: Athletics **DOB:** 01/07/1985 **PB:** Stevenage **SC:** England **PT:** Anthony Hamilton; Carmen Hamilton **C:** Race car driver Formula One, Mercedes AMG Petronas, 2013-; Race car driver Formula One, McLaren, 2007-12 **CR:** 1st place, Italian Grand Prix, 2012, Abu Dhabi Grand Prix, 2011, Belgian Grand Prix, 2010, Singapore Grand Prix, 2009, Chinese Grand Prix, 2011, 2008, German Grand Prix, 2011, 2008, Brit. Grand Prix, 2008, Monaco Grand Prix, 2008, Australian Grand Prix, 2008, Japanese Grand Prix, 2007, Hungarian Grand Prix, 2012, 2009, 2007, Can. Grand Prix, 2012, 2010, 2007, US Grand Prix, 2012, 2007 **AW:** Named Member Order of the Brit. Empire (MBE), 2008; Named one of The 100 Most Influential People in the World, TIME Magazine, 2016 **ACH:** Achievements include being the first backed Formula One race car driver; winning the FIA Formula One World Championship, 2008 **H:** Guitar, music

HAMM, JON, T: Actor **I:** Media & Entertainment **DOB:** 03/10/1971 **PB:** St. Louis **SC:** MO/USA **PT:** Daniel Hamm; Deborah Hamm **ED:** BA in English, University Missouri, St. Louis, 1993 **CW:** Actor: (films) Space Cowboys, 2000, Early Bird Special, 2001, Kissing Jessica Stein, 2001, We Were Soldiers, 2002, Ira and Abby, 2006, The Ten, 2007, The Day the Earth Stood Still, 2008, Shrek Forever After (voice), 2010, The Town, 2010, Bridesmaids, 2011, The Congress (voice), 2013, Million Dollar Arm, 2014, Minions (voice), 2015, Absolutely Fabulous: The Movie, 2016, Marjorie Prime, 2016, Aardvark, 2016, Keeping Up with the Joneses, 2016, Majorie Prime, 2017, Baby Driver, 2017, Aardvark, 2017, Beirut, 2018, Nostalgia, 2018, Tag, 2018; (TV series) Providence, 2000-01, The Division, 2002-04, What About Brian, 2006-07, The Unit, 2006-07, The Increasingly Poor Decisions of Todd Margaret, 2012, Wet Hot American Summer: First Day of Camp, 2015-, TripTank , Toast of London, 2015, Wander Over Yonder, 2016, Angie Tribeca, 2016, All or Nothing, 2016, The Last Man on Earth, 2016, Spongebob Squarepants, 2017, Tour De Pharmacy, 2017, Big Mouth, 2017, Travel Man, 2017, Good Omens, 2018(voice), 2015-16; (TV films) Clear History, 2013; actor, producer (TV series) Mad Men, 2007-15 (Golden Globe award for Best Performance by an Actor in a TV Series - Drama, 2008, 2016, Emmy award for Outstanding Leading Actor in a Drama Series, 2015), (films) Friends With Kids, 2012, actor, executive producer (TV series) A Young Doctor's Notebook, 2012-13

HAMMERGREN, JOHN HARVEY, T: CEO **I:** Business Management/Business Services **CN:** McKesson Corp. **DOB:** 02/20/1959 **PB:** St. Paul **SC:** MN/USA **ED:** MBA, Xavier University, 1987; BBA, University Minnesota, 1981 **C:** Chairman,CEO, McKesson Corp. (formerly McKesson HBOC, Inc.), 2002-; President, McKesson Corp. (formerly McKesson HBOC, Inc.), 2001-18; Co-pres, co- CEO, McKesson Corp. (formerly McKesson HBOC, Inc.), 1999-2001; CEO supply chain management, McKesson Corp. (formerly McKesson HBOC, Inc.), 1997-99; Group president, McKesson Health Systems, 1997-99; Executive vice president, president, CEO supply management business, McKesson HBOC, Inc., 1996-99; President med./ surgical division, Kendall Healthcare Products Co., Mansfield, Massachusetts, 1991-96; With, Baxter Healthcare Corp./American Hospital Corp. & Lyphomed Inc., 1981-91 **CR:** Chairman Healthcare Leadership Council, 2008-09 member, The Business Roundtable, The Business Council board directors Hewlett Packard Co., 2005-13, McKesson Corp., 1999- **CW:** Co-author (with Phil Harkins): Skin in the Game: how Putting Yourself First Today Will Revolutionize Healthcare Tomorrow, 2008 **AW:** Recipient Warren Bennis award for Leadership,

2004, Cap Gemini Ernst & Young Leadership award for Global Integration, 2004 **BA:** McKesson Corp, One Post St, San Francisco, CA, USA, 94104

HANABUSA, COLLEEN WAKAKO, T: U.S. Representative from Hawaii **I:** Government Administration/Government Relations/Government Services **DOB:** 05/04/1951 **PB:** Honolulu **SC:** HI/USA **PT:** June Hanabusa, Isao Hanabusa **ED:** JD, University of Hawaii William S. Richardson School of Law, 1977; MA in Sociology, University of Hawaii, 1975; BA in Economics and Sociology, University of Hawaii, 1973 **C:** U.S. House of Natural Resources Committee, Washington, DC, 2011-Present; U.S. House of Armed Services Committee, Washington, DC, 2011-Present; U.S. Congress From First Hawaii District, Washington, DC, 2011-Present; Private Practice Attorney, 1998-Present; President, Hawaii State Senate, 2007-2010; Majority Leader, Hawaii State Senate, 2003-2007; Vice President, Hawaii State Senate, 2001-2002; District 21, Hawaii State Senate, Honolulu, HI, 1999-2010; Attorney, Sakurai & Sing, AAL, ALC, 1990-1998; Partner, Koshiba & Young, 1980-1990; Private Practice Attorney, 1978-1980; Legal Researcher, Madison, WI, 1978; Committee On Science, Space, And Technology **CR:** Delegate, Hawaii State Judicial Conference, 1991-1993 **CIV:** Trustee, St. Andrew's Primary School, 1984-1987 **MEM:** American Bar Association, Hawaii State Bar Association, Ikenobo Ikebana Society of America **H:** Reading **PA:** Democrat **BA:** 422 Cannon House Office Building, Washington, DC, 20515

HANCOCK, HERBERT JEFFREY, T: Composer, Pianist, Publisher **I:** Fine Art **DOB:** 04/12/1940 **PB:** Chgo. **PT:** Son of Wayman Edward and Winnie (Griffin) Hancock **ED:** Student, New School Social Research, 1967; Student, Manhattan School Music, 1962; Student, Roosevelt University, Chicago, 1960; Student, Grinnell College, Iowa, 1956-60 **CR:** President Harlem Jazz Music Center, Inc. founder Hancock and Joe Productions, 1989- owner-pub. Hancock Music Co., 1962- **CW:** Performer: Chicago Symphony Orchestra, 1982, Coleman Hawkins, 1960, Donald Byrd, 1960-63, Miles Davis Quintet, 1963-68; recorded with Chick Corea, scored (films) Blow Up, 1966, The Spook Who Sat By the Door, 1973, Death Wish, 1974, A Soldier's Story, 1984, Jo Jo Dancer, Your Life is Calling, 1986, Action Jackson, Colors, 1988, Harlem Nights, 1989, Livin' Large, 1991, scored and appeared 'Round Midnight, 1986 (Academy award for Best Original Score, 1986), albums Takin' Off, 1963, Succotash, Speak Like a Child, 1968, Fat Albert Rotunda, 1969, Mwandishi, 1971, Crossings, Sextant, 1972, Headhunters, 1973, Thrust, The Best of Herbie Hancock, 1974, Man-Child, 1975, The Quintet, V.S.O.P., 1977, Sunlight, 1978, An Evening with Herbie Hancock and Chick Corea in Concert, Feets Don't Fail Me Now, 1979, Monster, Greatest Hits, 1980, Lite Me Up, 1982, Future Shock, 1983, (with Foday Musa Suso albums) Village Life, 1985, (with Dexter Gordon albums) The Other Side of 'Round Midnight, 1987, Perfect Machine, 1988, Jamming, 1992, Cantaloupe Island, Tribute to Miles, 1994, Dis Is Da Drum, 1995, The New Standard, 1996, 1 + 1, 1997, Gershwin's World, 1998 (Grammy award for Best Instrumental Jazz Performance, and Best Instrumental Arrangement for St. Louis Blues, 1999), albums Night Walker, 2000, Jammin' with Herbie Hancock, 2000, Mr. Funk, 2001, Future 2 Future, 2001, Day Dreams, 2002, Directions in Music: Live at Massey Hall, 2002 (Grammy award for Best Jazz Instrumental Album, and Best Jazz Instrumental Solo for My Ship, 2003), Live: Detroit/ Chicago, 2005, Possibilities, 2005, Baraka, 2006, Piano Fiesta, 2006, Joni Mitchell Project, 2007, River: The Joni Letters, 2007 (Grammy award for Album of Year, Best Contemporary Jazz Album,

2008), Crossings, 2007, Then and Now: The Definitive Herbie Hancock, 2008, The Imagine Project, 2010; performer: (songs) A Change Is Gonna Come, 2010 (Grammy award for Best Improvised Jazz Solo, 2011), Imagine, 2010 (Grammy award for Best Pop Collaboration with Vocals, 2011); featured in documentaries Keep on Keepin' On, 2014(Television) Girl Meets World, 2014; (Films) Miles Ahead, 2015, River of Gold, 2016, Valerian and the City of a Thousand Planets, 2017 **AW:** Named Top Jazz Artist, Black Music magazine, 1974, Jazzman of Year, Down Beat magazine, 1974; named one of America's Best Leaders, US News & World Report, 2008, The 100 Most Influential People in the World, TIME magazine, 2008; named to Critic's Poll for talent deserving wider recognition, Down Beat magazine, 1967; recipient Kennedy Center Honors, John F. Kennedy Center Performing Arts, Washington, 2013, Image award, Outstanding Jazz Artist, National Association for the Advancement of Colored People, 2008, Star, Hollywood Walk of Fame, 1994, All-Star Band New Artist award, Record World, 1968, Citation of Achievement, Broadcast Music, Inc., 1963, Kennedy Center Honors, 2013 **MEM:** Mem.: National Academy TV Arts and Scis., National Academy Recording Arts and Scis., Broadcast Music, Jazz Musicians Association, Pioneer (Grinnell College).

HANDEL, KAREN C., T: U.S. Representative from Georgia **I:** Government Administration/Government Relations/Government Services **DOB:** 04/30/1962 **PB:** Nashville **C:** Member, U.S. House of Representatives from Georgia's 6th District, 2017-; Member, Committee on Education and the Workforce, Committee on the Judiciary, Republican Study Committee; Senior vice president pub. policy, Susan G. Komen for the Cure, Washington, 2011-12; Chairman, Fulton County Board Commissioners, Georgia, 2003-06; Secretary state, State of Georgia, Atlanta, 2007-10; Deputy chief of staff to Governor Sonny Perdue, State of Georgia, Atlanta, 2002-03; President, CEO, North Fulton Chamber of Commerce, 2000-02; Manager government and community relations, KPMG,; Manager international communications, CIBA Vision,; Deputy chief of staff to Vice President Dan Quayle & Marilyn Quayle, The White House, Washington,; Executive assistant to vice president government affairs, Hallmark Co., Washington,; Clerk typist, American Association Retired Persons, **AW:** Named a Georgia Diva, B2B Magazine; named one of The Most Influential Atlantans, Atlanta Business Chronicle, Georgia's Most Influential Political Leaders, James magazine, The 100 Most Influential Political Leaders in Georgia, Georgia Trend **PA:** Republican **BA:** 1211 Longworth HOB, Washington, DC, 20515

HANKS, TOM, T: Actor **I:** Media & Entertainment **DOB:** 07/09/1956 **PB:** Concord **SC:** CA/USA **ED:** Student, California State University, Sacramento, CA **CW:** Actor, (Films) He Knows You're Alone, 1980, Splash, 1984, Bachelor Party, 1984, The Man With One Red Shoe, 1985, Volunteers, 1985, The Money Pit, 1986, Nothing In Common, 1986, Every Time We Say Goodbye, 1986, Dragnet, 1987, Big, 1988, Punchline, 1988, Turner And Hooch, 1989, The 'Burbs, 1989, Joe Versus The Volcano, 1990, The Bonfire Of The Vanities, 1990, A League Of Their Own, 1992, Radio Flyer, 1992, Sleepless In Seattle, 1993, Philadelphia, 1993, Forrest Gump, 1994, Apollo 13, 1995, (Voice Actor) Toy Story, 1995, Saving Private Ryan, 1998, You've Got Mail, 1998, (Voice Actor) Toy Story 2, 1999, The Green Mile, 1999, Cast Away, 2000, Road To Perdition, 2002, Catch Me If You Can, 2002, The Terminal, 2004, The Ladykillers, 2004, (Cameo Appearance) Elvis Has Left The Building, 2004, The Polar Express, 2004, The Da Vinci Code, 2006, (Voice Actor) Cars, 2006, The Simpsons Movie,

2007, Charlie Wilson's War, 2007, The Great Buck Howard, 2008, Angels & Demons, 2009, (Voice Actor) Toy Story 3, 2010, Extremely Loud And Incredibly Close, 2011, Cloud Atlas, 2012, Captain Phillips, 2013, Saving Mr. Banks, 2013, Bridge Of Spies, 2015, Inferno, 2016, The Circle, 2017, Mark Felt: The Man Who Brought Down The Whitehouse, 2017, The Post, 2017, Toy Story 4, (TV Films) Mazes And Monsters, 1982, I Am Your Child, 1997, Killing Lincoln, 2013, (TV Series) Bosom Buddies, 1980—1982, (Broadway Plays) Lucky Guy, 2013; Actor, Writer, Director, That Thing You Do!, 1996; Actor, Producer, Director, (Films) Larry Crowne, 2011; Actor, Executive Producer, Ithaca, 2015; Actor, Producer, A Hologram For The King, 2016, Sully, 2016; Producer, (Films) My Big Fat Greek Wedding, 2002, Connie And Carla, 2004, Neil Young: Heart Of Gold, 2006, The Ant Bully, 2006, Parkland, 2013, My Big Fat Greek Wedding 2, 2016, (Documentaries) Beyond All Boundaries, 2009; Executive Producer, (TV Films) We Stand Alone Together, 2001, Game Change, 2012, (TV Series) Big Love, 2006—2011, The 3 Minute Talk Show, 2011, (TV Miniseries) John Adams, 2008, The Pacific, 2010, 30 Rock, 2011, Killing Lincoln, 2013, Toy Story Of Terror, 2013, The Assassination Of President Kennedy, 2013, Last Week Tonight With John Oliver, 2014, The Sixties, 2014, Olive Kitteridge, 2014, The Greatest Event In Television History, 2014, Toy Story That Time Forgot, 2014, The Seventies, 2015, The Eighties, 2016, Maya And Marty, 2016, The Nineties, 2017, The David S. Pumpkins Animated Halloween Special, 2017, (Films) My Life In Ruins, 2009, Where The Wild Things Are, 2009, (Documentaries) He Has Seen War, 2011, The Sixties, 2014, The Seventies, 2015, The Eighties, 2016; Producer, Director, Writer, (TV Miniseries) From The Earth To The Moon, 1998, Band Of Brothers, 2001 **AW:** Presidential Medal Of Freedom, The White House, 2016, Kennedy Center Honors, John F. Kennedy Center for the Performing Arts, Washington, DC, 2014, David L. Wolper Award For Outstanding Producer Of Long-Form TV, Producers Guild Of America, Game Change, 2013, Norman Lear Achievement Award In Television, Producers Guild Of America, 2011, Emmy Award For Outstanding Miniseries, The Pacific, 2010, The World's Most Influential People, TIME Magazine, 2009, Honoree, Film Society of Lincoln Center, 2009, David L. Wolper Producer Of Year Award In Long-Form TV, Producers Guild of America, 2009, Emmy Award For Outstanding Miniseries, John Adams, 2008, 100 Most Powerful Celebrities, Forbes.com, 2007, Honorary Member, U.S. Army Ranger Hall Of Fame, 2006, The 50 Most Powerful People In Hollywood, Premiere Magazine, 2004—2006, Britannia Award For Excellence In Film, British Academy of Film & TV, Los Angeles, CA, 2004, Emmy Awards For Best Directing, Best Miniseries, Band Of Brothers, 2002, AFI Life Achievement Award, American Film Institute, 2002, Actor Of The Year, Hollywood Film Festival, 2002, Golden Globe Award For Best Actor, Cast Away, 2001, New York Film Critics Circle Award For Best Actor, Cast Away, 2000, Distinguished Public Service Award, U.S. Navy, 1999, Emmy Award For Best Miniseries, From The Earth To The Moon, 1998, Academy Award For Best Actor, Golden Globe Award For Best Actor, American Comedy Award For Funniest Actor In A Motion Picture, Screen Actors Guild Award For Outstanding Performance By A Male Actor In A Leading Role, Man Of The Year, Hasty Pudding Theatrical Society, National Board Review Award For Best Actor, Forrest Gump, 1995, Academy Award For Best Actor, Golden Globe Award For Best Actor, Philadelphia, 1994, Louella O. Parsons Award, Hollywood Women's Press Club, 1994, American Comedy Award For Funniest Actor In A Motion Picture, A League

Of Their Own, 1993, Star, Hollywood Walk Of Fame, 1992, Golden Globe Award For Best Actor, American Comedy Award For Funniest Actor In A Motion Picture, Big, 1989, Golden Apple Award, Hollywood Women's Press Club, 1988 **MEM:** First Vice President, American Academy of Motion Picture Arts & Sciences, 2009—Present, Vice President, American Academy of Motion Picture Arts & Sciences, 2007—2009, American Federation of TV and Radio Artists, Screen Actors Guild, International Thespian Society, Actors' Equity Association **BA:** Playtone Productions, P.O Box 7340, Santa Monica, CA, 90406

HANNA-ATTISHA, MONA, T: Public Health Advocate **I:** Medicine & Health Care **PB:** Sheffield, England **SC:** Sheffield, England **ED:** B.S., M.P.H,University of Michigan; M.D.,Michigan State University **C:** Co-Chair, March of Science, 2017- **AW:** Times Most Influential People in 2016,

HANNITY, SEAN PATRICK PATRICK, T: Political Commentator, Writer **I:** Media & Entertainment **DOB:** 12/30/1961 **PB:** NYC **PT:** Son of Hugh and Lillian (Flynn) Hannity; **ED:** PhD (hon.), Southeastern University, 2006 **C:** Host Hannity, FOX News Channel, 2009-; Host Hannity's America, FOX News Channel, 2007-; Host The Sean Hannity Show, ABC Radio Network, New York City, 2001-; Co-host Hannity & Colmes, FOX News Channel, New York City, 1996-2009; Afternoon drive host, Station 77WABC, New York City, 1998-2001; Late night host, Station 77WABC, New York City, 1997-98; Substitute host, Station 77WABC, New York City, 1996; With, Station WGST, Atlanta, 1992-96; With, Station WVNN, Huntsville, Alabama, 1990-92 **CW:** Author: Let Freedom Ring: Winning the War of Liberty Over Liberalism, 2002 (New York Times bestseller), Deliver Us From Evil: Defeating Terrorism, Despotism, and Liberalism, 2004 (New York Times bestseller), Conservative Victoy: Defeating Obama's Radical Agenda, 2010 (#1 New York Times bestseller) **AW:** Named one of The 50 Highest-Earning Political Figures, Newsweek, 2010, Top 100 Talk Hosts in America, Talkers Magazine, 2003; recipient National Talk Show Host of Year award, Radio & Records magazine, 2004, 2003, Marconi award for Network Syndicated Personality of Year, National Association Broadcasting, 2007, Marconi award for Talk Show Host of Year, 2003, Freedom of Speech award, Talkers Magazine, 2003,Talkers Magazine, 100 Most Important Talk Show Hosts,2009 **PA:** Republican

HANSEN, LARS PETER, T: Economics Professor **I:** Education/Educational Services **DOB:** 10/26/1952 **PB:** Urbana **SC:** IL/USA **PT:** Son of Roger Gaurth and Anna Lou (Rees) H. **MS:** Married **SPN:** Grace Renjuei Tsiang, August 25, 1984 **ED:** PhD in Economics, University of Minnesota, 1978; BS in Mathematics & Political Sci., Utah State University, 1974 **C:** Founding Director Becker Friedman Institute for Research in Economics, The University of Chicago, 2009-; David Rockefeller Distinguished Service Professor in Economics, Statistics & the College, The University of Chicago, 2010-; Homer J. Livingston Professor Economics, The University of Chicago, 1990-2010; Chairman Department Economics, The University of Chicago, 1998-2002; Director Graduate Studies, The University of Chicago, 1988-94; Professor, The University of Chicago, 1984-90; Associate Professor, The University of Chicago, 1982-84; Associate Professor, Carnegie-Mellon University, Pittsburgh, 1980-81; Assistant Professor Economics, Carnegie-Mellon University, Pittsburgh, 1978-80 **CR:** Visiting Associate Professor Economics, The University of Chicago, 1981-82, Massachusetts Institute of Technology, Boston, 1983, Harvard University, Cambridge, Massachusetts, 1986 Visiting Research Professor Stanford University Grad. School Business, 1989-90, The University of Chicago Graduate School Business, 2003-05, Nemmers Visiting Professor Department Economics Northwestern University, 2007, Visiting Professor Keio University School Business & Commerce, 2009 Board of Governors The Stevanovich Center for Financial Mathematics **CW:** Co-editor Econometrica, 1986-. **AW:** Sloan Fellow, 1982; Recipient Erwin Plein Nemmers Prize in Economics, 2006; Co-recipient Frisch Medal, 1984, CME Group-MSRI in Quantitative Applications, 2008, BBVA Foundation Frontiers of Knowledge Award in Economics, Finance & Management, 2011, Nobel Memorial Prize in Economic Sciences (Sveriges Riksbank Prize), Royal Swedish Academy Sciences, 2013,Frisch Medal, 1984, **MEM:** Fellow Econometric Society (President, 2007), American Finance Association, National Academy of Sciences; Member American Association for the Advancement of Science **H:** Skiing **BA:** University of Chicago, 5801 S Ellis Ave,, Chicago, IL, 60637

HARBAUGH, EDITH, T: CEO **I:** Technology **CN:** LaunchDarkly **ED:** BS in Engineering, Harvey Mudd College; Coursework, Economics, Pomona College **C:** Mentor, HMC INQ, Harvey Mudd College Entrepreneurial Network (HMCEN) (2017-Present); Contributing Writer (2015-Present); Co-host, "To Be Continuous" (2015-Present); Startup Mentor, Alchemist Accelerator (2015-Present); Chief Executive Officer/Co-founder, LaunchDarkly, Catamorphic Co. (2014-Present)

HARBAUGH, JIM, T: Head Coach of the University of Michigan **I:** Athletics **DOB:** 12/23/1963 **PB:** Toledo **SC:** OH/USA **PT:** Son of Jack Avon and Jacqueline M. (Cipiti) Harbaugh; **ED:** BA in Communications, University of Michigan, 1987 **C:** Head Football Coach, University Michigan Wolverines, Ann Arbor, 2014-; Head Football Coach, San Francisco 49ers, 2011-14; Head Football Coach, Bradford M. Freeman director football, Stanford University Cardinals, 2006-11; Head Football Coach, University San Diego Toreros, 2004-06; Offensive Assistant, Oakland Raiders, 2002-03; Volunteer Assistant Coach, Western Kentucky University Athletics, Bowling Green, Kentucky, 1994-2001; Quarterback, Carolina Panthers, 2001; Quarterback, San Diego Chargers, 1999-2000; Quarterback, Baltimore Ravens, 1998-99; Quarterback, Indianapolis Colts, 1994-98; Quarterback, Chicago Bears, 1987-93 **CR:** Co-owner, Founding Partner, Panther Racing, 1997- **CW:** Appeared in (TV series) Saved By the Bell: The New Class, 1996, Arli$$, 1997 **AW:** Named to The American Football Conference Pro Bowl Team, 1995, Indianapolis Colts Ring of Honor, 2005; Named NFL Co-Comeback Player of Year, Associated Press, 1995, AFC Player of Year, United Press International, 1995, NFL All-Pro, 1995, NFL Coach of Year Associated Press, 2011; Recipient Woody Hayes Coach of Year award, 2010,Big 10 MVP,1986, Pioneer League Champion, 2005, 2006, NFL Coach of the Year, NFC Champions, 2012 **BA:** Athletic Department of University of Michigan, 1000 South State Streen, Ann Arbor, MI, 48109

HARDEN, JAMES E. JR., T: Professional Basketball Player **I:** Athletics **DOB:** 08/26/1989 **PB:** LA **PT:** James Harden; Monja Willis **ED:** Coursework, Arizona State University, Tempe, AZ (2007-2009) **C:** Guard, Houston Rockets (2012-Present); Guard, Oklahoma City Thunder (2009-2012) **CR:** Member, U.S. National Team, Summer Olympic Games, London, England (2012) **AW:** Named NBA Most Valuable Player (2018); NBA Assists Leader (2017); All-NBA First Team (2014-2015, 2017); NBA All-Star (2013-2017); All NBA Third Team (2013);

Named to Western Conference All-Star Team, NBA (2013); Named NBA Sixth Man of the Year (2012); Pacific 10 Conference Player of the Year (2009); First Team All-Pacific 10 Conference (2009); First Team All-American, Associated Press, National Association of Basketball Coaches, U.S. Basketball Writers Association, The Sporting News, Basketball Times (2009)

HARDIMAN, THOMAS MICHAEL, T: Federal Judge **I:** Law and Legal Services **DOB:** 07/08/1965 **PB:** Winchester **SC:** MA/USA **PT:** Son of Robert and Judith Hardiman **ED:** JD, Georgetown University Law Center, 1990; BA, University Notre Dame, 1987 **C:** Judge, US Court Appeals (3rd cir.), Philadelphia, 2007-; Judge, US District Court (we. district) Pennsylvania, Pittsburgh, 2003-07; Partner, Reed Smith LLP, 1999-2003; Partner, Titus & McConomy LLP (formerly Cindrich & Titus), Pittsburgh, 1996-99; Associate, Titus & McConomy LLP (formerly Cindrich & Titus), Pittsburgh, 1992-96; Associate, Skadden, Arps, Slate, Meagher & Flom LLP, Washington, 1990-92 **CR:** Alternate hearing member Disciplinary Board, Pennsylvania Supreme Court, 1999-2003, hearing officer, 1995-99 **CIV:** President, Big Brothers Big Sisters of Greater Pittsburgh, Inc., 1999-2000 Director, Big Brothers Big Sisters of Greater Pittsburgh, Inc., 1995- **AW:** Recipient Nancy B. Zappala Service award, Big Brothers Big Sisters of Greater Pittsburgh, Inc., 2002 **MEM:** Mem.: American Bar Association (member House Delegates 1996-98), Pennsylvania Bar Association (member professionalism committee 1999-2003), Allegheny County Bar Association, DC Bar Association, Massachusetts Bar Association **BA:** US Court of Appeals, 601 Market St, Philadelphia, PA, 19106

HARDY, TOM, T: Actor **I:** Media & Entertainment **DOB:** 06/25/1905 **PB:** Hammersmith, United Kingdom **SC:** Hammersmith, United Kingdom **CW:** (Film) Black Hawk Down, 2001, Deserter, 2002, Star Trek: Nemesis, 2002, The Reckoning, 2003, Dot the i, 2003, LD 50 Lethal Dose, 2003, EMR, 2004, Layer Cake, 2004, Marie Antoinette, 2006, Minotaur, 2006, Scenes of a Sexual Nature, 2006, Flood, 2007, WAZ, 2007, The Inheritance, 2007, Sucker Punch, 2008, RocknRolla, 2008, Bronson, 2008, Thick as Thieves, 2009, Perfect, 2009, Inception, 2010, Sergeant Slaughter, My Big Brother, 2011, Tinker Tailor Soldier Spy, 2011, Warrior, 2011, This Means War, 2012, The Dark Night Rises, 2012, Lawless, 2012, Locke, 2013, The Drop, 2014, Child 44, 2015, Mad Max:Fury Road, 2015, London Road, 2015, Legend, 2015, The Revenant, 2015, Dunkirk, 2017, Venom, 2018(Television) Band of Brother, 2001, Colditz, 2005, The Virgin Queen, 2005, Gideons Daughter, 2005, A for Andromeda, 2006, Sweeney Todd, 2006, Cape Wrath, 2007, Oliver Twist, 2007, Stuart: A Life Backwards, 2007, Wuthering Heights, 2008, The Take, 2009, Driven to Extremes, 2013, Poaching Wars, 2013, Peaky Blinders, 2014, CBeebies Bedtime Stories, 2017, Taboo, 2017

HARMENING, JEFFREY L., T: Chairman and CEO of General Mills Inc. **I:** Business Management/Business Services **ED:** MBA, Harvard University, 1994; Bachelor's, DePauw University, Greencastle, Ind., 1989 **C:** CEO General Mills 2017-;; Chairman, Board of Directors 2018-.; President, COO, General Mills Inc, 2016-17; executive v.p., Chief Operating Officer U.S. Retail Segment 2014-2016,; CEO General Mills Cereal Partners Worldwide 2012-2014; senior v.p. General Mills 2011-2012;; President Big G division, General Mills, Inc., 2007-2011; Vice president General Mills, General Mills, Inc., 2004-; Vice president marketing Cereal Partners Worldwide (joint venture General Mills/Nestlé), General Mills, Inc., Lausanne, Switzerland, 2003-07; marketing

director Big G new enterprises & foodservice new business, General Mills, Inc., 2000-03; Various marketing positions in Betty Crocker, Yoplait USA & Big G cereals divisions, General Mills, Inc.,; Joined, General Mills, Inc., 1994 **BA:** General Mills Inc, 1 General Mills Blvd, Minneapolis, MN, 55426

HARMON, MARK, T: Actor **I:** Media & Entertainment **DOB:** 09/02/1951 **PB:** Burbank **SC:** CA/USA **PT:** Tom Harmon; Elyse Knox **MS:** Married **SPN:** Pam Dawber (March 21, 1987) **CH:** Sean; Ty Christian **ED:** Degree in communications cum laude, UCLA, 1974 **CW:** Actor: (films) Comes a Horseman, 1978, Beyond the Poseidon Adventure, 1979, Let's Get Harry, 1987, Summer School, 1987, The Presidio, 1988, Stealing Home, 1988, Worth Winning, 1989, Till There Was You, 1991, Cold Heaven, 1992, Wyatt Earp, 1994, Magic in the Water, 1995, The Last Supper, 1995, Casualties, 1997, The First to Go, 1997, Fear and Loathing in Las Vegas, 1998, The Amati Girls, 2000, I'll Remember April, 2000, Local Boys, 2002, Freaky Friday, 2003, Chasing Liberty, 2004, Weather Girl, 2009, Justice League Crisis on Two Earths, 2010, Certain Prey, 2011 (TV films) Eleanor and Franklin: The White House Years, 1977, Getting Married, 1978, Little Mo, 1978, Getting Married, 1978, The Dream Merchants, 1980, Goliath Awaits, 1981, Intimate Agony, 1983, Prince of Bel Air, 1986, Deliberate Stranger, 1986, After the Promise, 1987, Sweet Bird of Youth, 1989, Dillinger, 1991, Long Road Home, 1991, Fourth Story, 1991, Shadow of a Doubt, 1991, Original Sins, 1995, For All Time, 2000, Crossfire Trail, 2001, And Never Let Her Go, 2001, Certain Prey, 2011, (TV series) Sam, CBS, 1978, Centennial, 1978-79, 240-Robert, 1979-80, Flamingo Road, 1981-82, St. Elsewhere, 1983-86, Reasonable Doubts, 1991-93, Charlie Grace, 1995-96, Chicago Hope, 1996-2000, NCIS, 2003-12, (guest appearances) Adam-12, 1975, Strangers, 1996, The Legend of Tarzan, 2001, The West Wing, 2002, Judge Advocate General, 2003, JAG, 2003, NCIS, 2003, Retrosexual, 2004, Certain Prey, 2011, Family Guy, 2012, NCIS New Orleans, 2014 **AW:** Named Sexiest Man Alive, People magazine, 1986

HARPER, BRYCE, T: Professional Baseball Player **I:** Athletics **DOB:** 10/16/1992 **PB:** Las Vegas **SC:** NV/USA **PT:** Son of Ron and Sheri Harper. **ED:** Student, College Southern Nevada, North Las Vegas, 2009-10 **C:** Outfielder, Washington Nationals, 2010-; Catcher, College Southern Nevada Coyotes, 2009-10 **AW:** Named National League Rookie of Year, Baseball Writers Association America, 2012; named to National League All-Star Team, Major League Baseball, 2013, 2012; recipient Golden Spikes award, USA Baseball, 2010,All Star, 2015-17,National League MVP, 2015, NL Hank Aaron Awar, 2015, NL Home Run Leader, 2015, Golden Spikes Award, 2010 **ACH:** Achievements include being the first overall pick in Major League Baseball's Amatuer Draft, 2010; becoming the first teenaged positon player in Major League Baseball history selected to the All-Star Game, 2012

HARPER, GREGG, T: Chairman of the House Administration Committee,U.S. Representative from Mississippi, lawyer **I:** Government Administration/Government Relations/Government Services **DOB:** 06/01/1956 **PB:** Jackson **PT:** Son of C. Douglas and Lois (Livingston) H.; Married Sidney Hancock, August 11, 1979. **ED:** JD, University Mississippi, 1981; BS in Chemistry, Mississippi College, 1978 **CT:** Bar: Mississippi 1981, U.S. District Court (no. and so. dists.) Mississippi 1981, U.S. Court Appeals (5th cir.) 1981. **C:** Chairman, House Administration Committee, 2017-; Member, US House Ethics Committee (formerly House Standards of Official Conduct Committee), 2009-;

Member, US Congress from 3rd Mississippi District, 2009-; City prosecutor, City of Richland, Mississippi, 2006-09; City prosecutor, City of Brandon, Mississippi, 2003-09; Attorney, Sanford and Harper, 1995-2009 **CR:** Legal vol. for Senator Jim Talent, 2006 legal vol. 2000 Presidential Recount, Ohio, 2004, Florida, 2000 **CIV:** Board attorney, Mississippi Baptist Children's Village, 2004- Chair, Rankin County Rep. Executive Committee, 2000-08 Del., Rep. National Convention, New York, 2004 Del., Rep. National Convention, Philadelphia, 2000 **AW:** Named one of The 50 Politicos to Watch, Politico, 2010 **MEM:** Member Association Trial Lawyers Am., Mississippi Bar Association, Mississippi Trial Lawyers Association (board governors 1986-). **PA:** Republican

HARRELSON, WOODY, T: Actor **I:** Media & Entertainment **PB:** Midland **PT:** Charles Voyde Harrelson; Diane Lou Oswald **MS:** Married **SPN:** Laura Louie (December 28, 2008); Nancy Simon, June 29, 1985 (div. January 20, 1986) **CH:** Deni Montana; Zoe Giordano; Makani Ra **ED:** BA in Theater Arts and English, Hanover College, Ind. **CW:** Actor: (TV series) Cheers, 1985-93 (Emmy award for Outstanding Supporting Actor in a Comedy Series, 1989), True Detective, 2014,SNL, 2014 (TV films) Bay Coven, 1987, Killer Instinct, 1988, Mother Goose Rock 'n' Rhyme, 1990, Game Change, 2012, (films) Wildcats, 1986, Eye of the Demon, 1987, Cool Blue, 1990, Doc Hollywood, 1991, Ted and Venus, 1991, L.A. Story, 1991, White Men Can't Jump, 1992, Indecent Proposal, 1993, The Cowboy Way, 1994, I'll Do Anything, 1994, Natural Born Killers, 1994, The Sunchaser, 1996, The People versus Larry Flynt, 1996, Kingpin, 1996, Wag the Dog, 1997, The Thin Red Line, 1998, The Hi-Lo Country, 1998, Edtv, 1999, Austin Powers: The Spy Who Shagged Me, 1999, Grass (voice), 1999, Play It to the Bone, 1999, American Saint, 2000, Scorched, 2002, Anger Management, 2003, She Hate Me, 2004, After the Sunset, 2004, North Country, 2005, The Prize Winner of Defiance, Ohio, 2005, A Prairie Home Companion, 2006, (voice) Free Jimmy, 2006, A Scanner Darkly, 2006, The Walker, 2007, No Country for Old Men, 2007 (Screen Actors Guild award for Outstanding Performance by a Cast in a Motion Picture, 2008), The Grand, 2007, Battle in Seattle, 2007, Semi-Pro, 2008, Sleepwalking, 2008, Transsiberian, 2008, Seven Pounds, 2008, Management, 2008, Zombieland, 2009, 2012, 2009, The Messenger, 2009 (National Board Review award for Best Supporting Actor, 2009), Defendor, 2010, Friends with Benefits, 2011, Rampart, 2011 (African American Film Critics Association award for Best Lead Actor, 2011), The Hunger Games, 2012, Seven Psychopaths, 2012, Now You See Me, 2013, Free Birds (voice), 2013, Out of the Furnace, 2013, The Hunger Games: Catching Fire, 2013, The Hunger Games: Mockingjay - Part 1, 2014, Triple Nine, 2015, The Hunger Games: Mockingjay - Part 2, 2015, By Way of Helena, 2015, Wilson, 2016, Triple 9, 2016, Now You See Me 2, 2016,The Duel, 2016, LBJ, 2016, The Edge of Seventeen, 2016, Lost in London, 2017, The Glass Castle, 2017, Three Billboards Outside Ebbing Missouri, 2017, Shock and Awe, Solo A Star Wars Story, 2018, Venom, 2018 (TV appearances) Will & Grace, 2001; executive prodr.: (TV series) 2014-15; (TV host) Comedy Club All-Star IV, 1990; understudy Broadway prodn.: Biloxi Blues; starred in Off-Broadway prodns.: The Boys Next Door, 1987, The Zoo Story; actor, playwright: Two on Two, Furthest From the Sun, 1993

HARRINGTON, PADRAIG, T: Professional Golfer **I:** Athletics **PB:** Dublin **SC:** Ireland **C:** Professional Golfer (1995) **CR:** Member, Great Britain and Ireland Team, Seve Trophy (2005, 2003, 2002, 2000); Member, Team Europe, Ryder Cup (2010, 2008, 2006, 2004, 2002, 1999); Member, Irish Team, World Cup (2005, 2004, 2003, 2002, 2001, 2000, 1999, 1998, 1997, 1996); Dunhill Cup (2000, 1999, 1998, 1997, 1996) **AW:** Named PGA Tour Player of Year (2008); Order of Merit, PGA European Tour (2006); Winner, PGA European Tour Events including BMW Asian Open (2003), Dunhill Links Championship (2002), Volvo Masters Andalucia (2001), BBVA Open Turespaña Masters Comunidad de Madrid (2000); Winner, Portugal Masters (2016), Irish Open (2007), Linde German Masters (2004), Omega Hong Kong Open (2004), Deutsche Bank-SAP Open TPC of Europe (2003), Brazil Sao Paulo 500 Years Open (2000), Peugeot Spanish Open (1996); Winner, PGA Tour events including the PGA Championship (2008), British Open (2007, 2008), Dunlop Phoenix (2006), Barclays Classic (2005), Honda Classic (2005); Winner, Other Events including Honda Classic (2015), Grand Slam of Golf (2012), Member of Ryder Cup Winning Team Europe (2002, 2004, 2006, 2010), Irish PGA Championship (1998, 2004, 2005), Target World Challenge Presented by Williams (2002);; ; **ACH:** Achievements include winning PGA European Tour events including Peugeot Spanish Open, 1996, Brazil Sao Paulo 500 Years Open, 2000, BBVA Open TurespaÄ±a Masters Comunidad de Madrid, 2000, Volvo Masters Andalucia, 2001, Dunhill Links Championship, 2002, BMW Asian Open, 2003; winner, Deutsche Bank-SAP Open TPC of Europe, 2003, Omega Hong Kong Open, 2004, Linde German Masters, 2004, Irish Open, 2007; winner, PGA Tour events including the Honda Classic, 2005, Barclays Classic, 2005, Dunlop Phoenix, 2006, British Open, 2007, 2008, PGA Championship, 2008, Portugal Masters, 2016; winner, other events including the Irish PGA Championship, 1998, 2004, 05, Target World Challenge presented by Williams, 2002; Grand Slam of Golf, 2012; member of Ryder Cup winning Team Europe, 2002, 2004, 2006, 2010, Winner of the Honda Classic, 2015

HARRIS, ANDY, T: U.S. Representative from Maryland **I:** Government Administration/Government Relations/Government Services **DOB:** 01/25/1957 **PB:** Brooklyn **SC:** NY/USA **PT:** Son of Zoltán and Irene Harris; **ED:** MHS in Health Policy & Management, Johns Hopkins University, 1995; MD, Johns Hopkins University, 1980; BS in Human Biology, Johns Hopkins University, 1977 **C:** Member, US House Transportation & Infrastructure Committee, 2011-; Member, Republican Study Committee; Member, US House Space, Science & Tech. Committee, 2011-; Member, US House Natural Resources Committee, 2011-; Member, US Congress from 1st Maryland District, Washington, 2011-; Minority whip, Maryland State Senate, 2003-10; Member District 7, Maryland State Senate, 2002-10; Member District 9, Maryland State Senate, 1998-2003; Commanding, Johns Hopkins Naval Reserve Medical Unit, 1989-92; Associate professor department anesthesiology & critical care medicine, Johns Hopkins University School Medicine,; Chief obstetric anesthesiology, Johns Hopkins Hospital,; Intern & resident, Johns Hopkins Hospital, 1980-84 **CR:** Member Education, Health & Environmental Affairs committee **CIV:** Vice president, St. Joseph's School Home-Sch. Association, 1992-94 Member board directors, Maryland Leadership Council, 1995- Member board directors, Sherwood Community Association, 1987-93 President, Thornleigh Improvement Association, 1984-86 **MIL:** Commander US Naval Reserve, 1988-2010, Iraq **MEM:** Mem.: American Society Obstetric Anesthesia & Perinatology (board directors 1996-), Md.-DC Society Anesthesiologists (executive committee 1996-, president 2005-) **PA:** Republican

HARRIS, ED, T: Actor **I:** Media & Entertainment **PB:** Englewood **SC:** NJ/USA **PT:** Bob L. Harris and Margaret (Sholl) Harris **MS:** Married **SPN:** Amy Madigan (November 21, 1983) **CH:** Lily Dolores **ED:** BFA, California Institute of Arts, Valencia, 1975; Student, University Oklahoma, Norman, 1972-73; Student, Columbia University, 1969-71 **CIV:** Trustee California Institute of Arts, Valencia, 1985-. **CW:** Actor: (plays) A Streetcar Named Desire, Sweet Bird of Youth, Julius Caesar, Hamlet, Camelot, Are You Lookin?, Time of Your Life, Learned Ladies, Kingdom of Earth, Grapes of Wrath, Present Laughter, Balaam, Killers' Head, Fool for Love (Obie award 1983), Prairie Avenue (LA Drama Critics Circle award 1981), Scar, 1985 (San Francisco Critics award), Precious Sons, 1986 (Theater World award), Simpatico, 1994, 95, Taking Sides, 1996, Wrecks, 2006, (repertory plays) Servant of Two Masters, Ohio, Claptrap, Cambridge, Massachusetts, 1985, Pirates of Penzance at New York Shakespeare Festival, Glass Menagerie, Long Wharf, New Haven, 1986, Bobby Gould in Hell, 1989, (films) Coma, 1978, Borderline, 1978, Knightriders, 1980, Dream On, 1980, Creepshow, 1981, The Right Stuff, 1982, Swing Shift, 1982, Under Fire, 1982, Places in the Heart, 1983, A Flash of Green, 1984, Alamo Bay, 1984, Sweet Dreams, 1985, Code Name: Emerald, 1985, Walker, 1987, To Kill a Priest, 1988, Jacknife, 1989, The Abyss, 1989, State of Grace, 1990, Glengarry Glen Ross, 1992, Needful Things, 1993, The Firm, 1993, China Moon, 1994, Milk Money, 1994, Apollo 13, 1995 (Screen Actors Guild award for Outstanding Performance by a Cast, 1996), Just Cause, 1995, Eye for an Eye, 1995, Nixon, 1995, The Rock, 1996, Absolute Power, 1997, Stepmom, 1998, The Truman Show, 1998 (Golden Globe award for Best Performance by an Actor in a Supporting Role in a Motion Picture, 1999), The Third Miracle, 1999, Waking the Dead, 2000, The Prime Gig, 2000, Enemy at the Gates, 2001, Buffalo Soldiers, 2001, A Beautiful Mind, 2001, Just a Dream, 2002, The Hours, 2002, Masked and Anonymous, 2003, The Human Stain, 2003, Radio, 2003, A History of Violence, 2005 (National Society Film Critics award for Best Supporting Actor, 2006), Winter Passing, 2005, Cleaner, 2007, Gone Baby Gone, 2007, National Treasure: Book of Secrets, 2007, Touching Home, 2008, The Way Back, 2010, Once Fallen, 2010, Virginia, 2010, Salvation Boulevard, 2011, That's What I Am, 2011, Man on a Ledge, 2012, Sweetwater, 2013, Phantom, 2013, Snowpiercer, 2013, Pain & Gain, 2013, Gravity (voice), 2013, The Face of Love, 2013, Planes: Fire & Rescue (voice), 2014, Frontera, 2014, Cymbeline, 2014, Run All Night, 2014, The Adderall Diaries, 2015, In Dubious Battle,2016, Rules Don't Apply,2016, A Crooked Somebody,2017, Mother!, 2017, Kodachrome,2017, Geostorm, 2017 (TV films) The Amazing Howard Hughes, 1977, The Seekers, 1979, The Aliens Are Coming, 1980, The Last Innocent Man, 1987, Paris Trout, 1991, Running Mates, 1992, The Stand, 1994, Riders of the Purple Sage (also executive producer), 1997, Game Change, 2012 (Golden Globe award for Best Performance by an Actor in a Supporting Role in a Series, Mini-series or Motion Picture Made for TV, 2013), (TV mini-series) Empire Falls, 2005, (TV appearances) The Rockford Files, 1978, Lou Grant, 1979, 80, 81, Barnaby Jones, 1979, CHiPs, 1981, Hart to Hart, 1981, Cassie and Co., 1982, Frasier, 1995, Riders of the Purple Sage, 1996, Empire Falls,2005, The Armenian Genocide, 2006, Game Change, 2012, Westworld,2016; actor, director, prodr.: (films) Pollock, 2000; actor, director, producer, writer: (films) Appaloosa, 2008. **MEM:** Member Screen Actors Guild, Equity.

HARRIS, EMMYLOU, T: Singer **I:** Media & Entertainment **DOB:** 04/02/1947 **PB:** Birmingham **SC:** AL/USA **PT:** Walter Harris; Eugenia Harris **MS:** Divorced **SPN:** Tom Slocum (1969, Divorced 1970) **CH:** Hallie; Meghann **ED:** Honorary PhD, Berklee College of Music (2009); Coursework, University of North Carolina at Greensboro **CIV:** President, Country Music Foundation (1983) **CW:** Musician, "Old Yellow Moon" (2013); Musician, "Hard Bargain" (2011); Musician, "All I Intended to Be" (2008); Musician, "The Very Best of Emmylou Harris: Heartaches & Highways" (2005); Musician, "Stumble Into Grace" (2003); Musician, "Nobody's Darling But Mine" (2002); Musician, "O Brother, Where Art Thou?" (2001); Musician, "Red Dirt Girl" (2000); Musician, "Spyboy" (1998); Musician, "A Tribute to Tradition" (1998); Musician, "The Horse Whisperer" (1998); Musician, "Wrecking Ball" (1995); Musician, "Songs of the West" (1994); Musician, "Cowgirl's Prayer" (1993); Musician, "At the Ryman" (1992); Musician, "Duets" (1990); Musician, "Bluebird" (1988); Musician, "Angel Band" (1987); Contributing Musician, with Dolly Parton and Linda Ronstadt, "Trio" (1987); Musician, "Thirteen" (1986); Musician, "The Ballad of Sally Rose" (1985); Co-Writer, Co-Producer, "The Ballad of Sally Rose" (1985); Musician, "White Shoes" (1983); Musician, "Last Date" (1982); Musician, "Evangeline" (1981); Musician, "Roadie" (1980); Musician, Blue Kentucky Girl (1979); Musician, "Light of the Stable" (1979); Musician, "Quarter Moon In A Ten Cent Town" (1978); Musician, "Profile: Best of Emmylou Harris" (1978); Featured, "The Last Waltz" (1978); Musician, "Luxury Liner" (1977); Musician, "Pieces of the Sky" (1975); Musician, "Elite Hotel" (1975); Musician, "The Gliding Bird" (1969); Singer, Fallen Angels Band, Europe, U.S. of America **AW:** Recipient, Grammy Award for Best Americana Album (2014); Named, Country Music Hall of Fame (2008); Recipient, Grammy Award for Best Female Country Vocal Performance (2006); Recipient, Golden Plate Award, Academy Achievement (2004); Named, Alabama Music Hall of Fame (2003); Named, Lifetime Achievement Performer (2002); Recipient, Grammy Award for Best Contemporary Folk Album (2001); Recipient, Grammy Award for Best Country Collaboration with Vocals (1999); Recipient, Orville H. Gibson Lifetime Achievement Award (1996); Recipient, Grammy Award for Best Contemporary Folk Album (1996); Recipient, Grammy Award for Best Country Performance (1993); Recipient, Grammy Award for Best Country Performance (1988); Recipient, Academy Country Music Award for Album of the Year (1987); Recipient, Grammy Award for Best Female Country Vocal Performance (1984); Recipient, Grammy Award for Best Country Performance (1981); Named, Female Vocalist of the Year, Country Music Association (1980); Recipient, Grammy award for Best Female Country Vocal Performance (1979); Recipient, Grammy Award for Best Female Country Vocal Performance (1976); Recipient, Patrick J. Leahy Humanitarian Award, Americana Music Awards; Recipient, Grammy Award for Album of Year **MEM:** Fellow, American Academy of Arts and Sciences

HARRIS, NEIL PATRICK PATRICK, T: Actor **I:** Media & Entertainment **DOB:** 06/15/1973 **PB:** Albuquerque **SC:** NM/USA **PT:** Ron Harris; Sheila H. Harris **CW:** Actor: (TV series) Doogie Howser, 1989-92 (People's Choice award for Favorite Male Performer in a New TV Series, 1990, Young Artists award for Best Young Actor in Series, 1989, 1990, 1991, 1992), Captain Planet and the Planeteers (voice), 1990, Spider-Man (voice), 2003, How I Met Your Mother, 2005-14; (TV films) Too Good to be True, 1988, Home Fires Burning, 1989, Cold Sassy Tree, 1989, A Stranger in the Family, 1991, Sudden Fury: A Family Torn Apart, 1993, Snowbound: The Jim and Jennifer Stolpa Story, 1994, The Man in the Attic, 1994, Not Our Son, 1995, Legacy of Sin: The William Coit Story, 1995, My Antonia, 1995, The Christmas Wish, 1998, Joan of Arc, 1999, The Wedding Dress, 2001, Sweeney Todd: The Demon Barber of Fleet Street in Concert, 2001, The Christmas Blessing, 2005, Yes, Virginia (voice), 2009; (films) Clara's Heart, 1988, The Purple People Eater, 1988, Animal Room, 1995, Starship Troopers, 1997, The Proposition, 1998, The Next Best Thing, 2000, The Mesmerist, 2001, Undercover Brother, 2002, Mesmirist, 2002, Harold and Kumar Go to White Castle, 2004, The Golden Blaze (voice), 2005, Justice League: The New Frontier (voice), 2008, Harold & Kumar Escape from Guantanamo Bay, 2008, Cloudy with a Chance of Meatballs (voice), 2009, The Best and the Brightest, 2010, Beastly, 2011, Company, 2011, The Smurfs, 2011, A Very Harold & Kumar 3D Christmas, 2011, The Muppets, 2011, American Reunion, 2012, The Smurfs 2 (voice), 2013, Cloudy with a Chance of Meatballs 2 (voice), 2013, A Million Ways to Die in the West, 2014, Gone Girl, 2014, Downsizing, 2017; (films, internet) Dr. Horrible's Sing-Along Blog, 2008,Prop 8: The Musical, 2008, Neil's Puppet Dreams, 2012, (TV appearances) B.L. Stryker, 1989, Blossom, 1991, Roseanne, 1992, Capitol Critters (voice), 1992, Quantum Leap, 1993, Murder, She Wrote, 1993, The Outer Limits, 1996, Homicide: Life on the Streets, 1997, Stark Raving Mad, 1999, Will & Grace, 2000, Static Shock (voice), 2001, Son of the Beach, 2001, Ed, 2001, Spider-Man: The Animated Series (voice), 2002, Justice League (voice), 2002, Touched By An Angel, 2002, Boomtown, 2003, Law & Order: Criminal Intent, 2004, Numb3rs, 2005, Jack & Bobby, 2005, Me, Eloise, 2006, Family Guy (voice), 2007-09, Sesame Street, 2008, Robot Chicken (voice), 2009, The Penguins of Madagascar (voice), 2009-10, Glee, 2009 (Emmy award for Outstanding Guest Actor in a Comedy Series, 2010), American Horror Story, 2015, Ant and Dec's Saturday Night Takeaway, 2015,A Series of Unfortunate Events, Mystery Science 3000, 2017 (musicals) Fiddler on the Roof, 1991, Rent, 1997-98, Cabaret, 1998, Sweeney Todd: The Demon Barber of Fleet Street, 1999; (plays) Romeo and Juliet, 1998, Proof, 2002, Assassins, 2004, All My Sons, 2006, Hedwig and the Angry Itch, 2014 (Drama Desk award for Outstanding Actor in a Musical, 2014, Tony award, Best Leading Actor in a Musical, 2014); host 61st Primetime Emmy Awards, 2009, 65th Primetime Emmy Awards, 2013, 67th Annual Tony Awards, 2013, (TV series) Best Time Ever with Neil Patrick Harris, 2015-; dir.: (off-Broadway) Nothing to Hide, 2013; author: Neil Patrick Harris: Choose Your Own Autobiography, 2014 **AW:** Named Favorite TV Comedy Actor, People's Choice Awards, 2012, 2011; named one of The 10 Most Fascinating People of 2014, Barbara Walters Special, The 100 Most Influential People in the World, TIME magazine, 2010

HART, KEVIN, T: Actor, Comedian **I:** Media & Entertainment **PB:** Philadelphia **SC:** PA/USA **PT:** Henry Hart; Nancy Hart **CW:** Actor: (TV films) North Hollywood, 2001, Class of '06, 2002, Dante, 2005, The Weekend, 2007, Little in Common, 2011; actor, writer, executive producer (TV films) Keep It Together, 2014; actor: (films) Paper Soldiers, 2002, Death of a Dynasty, 2003, Scary Movie 3, 2003, Along Came Polly, 2004, Soul Plane, 2004, The 40-Year-Old Virgin, 2005, In the Mix, 2005, Scary Movie 4, 2006, The Last Stand, 2006, Fool's Gold, 2008, Drillbit Taylor, 2008, Superhero Movie, 2008, Meet Dave, 2008, Extreme Movie, 2008, Not Easily Broken, 2009, Something Like a Business, 2010, Death at a Funeral, 2010, Little Fockers, 2010, Let Go, 2011, 35 and Ticking, 2011, Exit Strategy, 2012, Think Like a Man, 2012 (BET award for Best Actor, 2012), The Five-Year Engagement, 2012, This Is the End, 2013, Grudge Match, 2013, Ride Along, 2014, About Last Night, 2014, Think Like a Man Too, 2014, Top Five, 2014, The Wedding Ringer, 2015, Get Hard, 2015, Ride Along 2, 2016, Central Intelligence, 2016, The Secret Life of Pets (voice), 2016; TV appearances The Big House, 2004, Barbershop, 2005, Love, Inc., 2006, Party Down, 2009, Modern Family, 2011-12, actor, executive producer (TV series) Real Husbands of Hollywood, 2013-15 (National Association for the Advancement of Colored People Image award for Outstanding Actor in a Comedy Series, 2014), stand-up comedy tour I'm a Grown Little Man, 2009, Seriously Funny, 2010, Laugh At My Pain, 2011, Let Me Explain, 2013, Kevin Hart: What Now?, 2016, host MTV Video Music Awards, 2012 **AW:** Named Favorite Comedic TV Actor, People's Choice Awards, 2016, Entertainer of Year, National Association for the Advancement of Colored People Image Awards, 2014; recipient Comedic Genius award, MTV Movie Awards, 2015

HART, OLIVER D'ARCY, T: Economist **I:** Financial Services **DOB:** 10/09/1948 **PB:** London **SC:** England **PT:** Philip D'Arcy Hart; Ruth D'Arcy (Meyer) Hart **MS:** Married **SPN:** Rita B. Goldberg (6/09/1974) **CH:** Daniel S.; Benjamin P. **ED:** Honorary PhD, Warwick University (2012); Honorary PhD, London Business School (2011); Honorary PhD, University of Paris-Dauphine (2009); Honorary PhD, Copenhagen Business School (2009); Honorary PhD, University of Basel, Switzerland (1994); Honorary PhD, Free University of Brussels (1992); PhD, Princeton University (1974); MA, Warwick University, England (1972); BA, Cambridge University (1969) **C:** Andrew E. Furer Professor of Economics, Harvard University, Cambridge, MA (1997-Present); Professor of Economics, Harvard University, Cambridge, MA (1993-Present); Professor of Economics, Massachusetts Institute of Technology, Cambridge, MA (1984-1993); Professor of Economics, London School of Economics (1981-1985); Lecturer of Economics, Cambridge University, England (1975-1981); Lecturer of Economics, University of Essex, England (1974-1975) **CR:** Centennial Visiting Professor, London School of Economics (1997-Present); Marvin Bower Fellow, Harvard University Business School, Boston, MA (1988-1989) **CW:** Author, "Firms, Contracts, and Financial Structures" (1995); Editor, "Review of Economic Studies" (1979-1983); Contributor, Articles to Professional Journals **AW:** Recipient, Nobel Prize in Economics (2016); Fellow, John Simon Guggenheim Foundation (1987-1988) **MEM:** Council, Econometric Society (1983-Present); President, American Law and Economic Association (2006-2007); Vice President, American Economic Association (2006); Fisher-Schultze Lecturer, Econometric Society (1988); Correspondent, British Academy; American Academy of Arts and Sciences; Fellow, Econometric Society **H:** Listening to music **BA:** Harvard University, Dept of Economics, Cambridge, MA, 02138-0000

HARTWELL, LELAND HARRISON, T: Geneticist, Educator **I:** Education/Educational Services **DOB:** 10/30/1939 **PB:** LA **SC:** CA/USA **PT:** Son of Marjorie (Taylor) Hartwell; **ED:** PhD in Biology, Massachusetts Institute of Technology, 1964; BS, California Institute Tech., Pasadena, 1961 **C:** Co-dir., chief scientist Biodesign Institute Center Sustainable Health, Arizona State University, Tempe, 2010-; Faculty, Virginia G. Piper chair personalized medicine, Arizona State University, Tempe, 2010-; President, director, Fred Hutchison Cancer Research Center, Seattle, 1997-2010; Faculty, Fred Hutchison

Cancer Research Center, Seattle, 1996-97; Adjunct professor medicine, University Washington School Medicine, Seattle, 2003-10; Am. Cancer Society research professor genetics, University Washington School Medicine, Seattle, 1990-2010; Professor genome scis., University Washington School Medicine, Seattle, 1973-2010; Associate professor, University Washington School Medicine, Seattle, 1968-73; Associate professor, University California, Irvine, 1967-68; Assistant professor, University California, Irvine, 1965-67; Postdoc. fellow, Salk Institute Biological Studies, La Jolla, California, 1964-65 **CR:** Chairman sci. adv. board Canary Foundation **CW:** Member editorial board Journal Cell Biology, 1988-91, Molecular Biology of the Cell, 1991-93, Molecular & Cellular Biology; contributor articles to professional journals **AW:** Recipient Washington State Medal of Merit, 2003, Massry prize, Meira & Shaul G. Massry Foundation, Nobel prize in physiology/medicine, 2001, Léopold Giffuel prize, Association Research Cancer, France, 2000, Am. Cancer Society medal of honor, 1999, Distinguished Alumni award, California Institute Tech., 1999, Komen Brinker award for sci. distinction, Susan G. Komen Breast Cancer Foundation, 1998, Albert Lasker award for basic medical research, 1998, Louisa Gross Horwitz prize, Columbia University, 1995, Carnegie Mellon Dickson award, 1996, Warren Triennial prize, Massachusetts General Hospital, 1995, Katherine Berkan Judd award, Memorial Sloan Kettering Cancer Center, 1994, Rosenstiel award, Brandeis University, 1993, Simon Shubitz award, University Chicago, 1992, Gairdner Foundation International award, 1992, Hoffman LaRoche Mattia award, 1991, Alfred P. Sloan award, GM Cancer Research Foundation, 1991, National Institutes of Health Merit award, 1990, Eli Lilly award in microbiology and immunology, 1973; fellow John Simon Guggenheim Memorial Foundation, 1983-84; scholar Am. Cancer Society; 1996 Laureate, Passano Foundation, Inc. **MEM:** Mem.: National Academy of Sciences, Am. Association Cancer Research, Am. Academy Microbiology, Genetics Society America (president 1990), Am. Society Cell Biology (Keith Porter award 1995), Am. Society Microbiology, Am. Academy Arts & Scis. **ACH:** Achievements include patents in field **BA:** Ariz State U Biodesign Inst, 1001 S McAllister Ave, Tempe, AR, 85287

HARTZ, HARRIS L., T: U.S. Circuit Judge **I:** Law and Legal Services **CN:** U.S. Court of Appeals for the Tenth Circuit **DOB:** 01/20/1947 **PB:** Baltimore **SC:** MD/USA **PT:** Alvin Sidney Hartz; Muriel (Abrams) Hartz **CH:** Jacob Cameron; Andrew Samuel **ED:** JD, Harvard Law School, Magna Cum Laude (1972); Coursework in Physics, The Graduate School, Princeton University (1967-1968); AB, Harvard University, Summa Cum Laude (1967); Diploma, Farmington High School, NM (1963) **C:** Judge, U.S. Court of Appeals for the Tenth Circuit, Albuquerque, NM (2001-Present); Special Counsel, Stier, Anderson & Malone, LLC (1999-2001); Chief Judge, New Mexico Court of Appeals (1997-1999); Judge, New Mexico Court of Appeals (1988-1999); Partner, Miller, Stratvert, Torgerson & Brandt (Now Miller Stratvert P.A.) (1983-1988); Director, Miller, Stratvert, Torgerson & Brandt (Now Miller Stratvert P.A.) (1983-1988); Associate, Miller, Stratvert, Torgerson & Brandt (Now Miller Stratvert P.A.) (1982-1983); Associate, Poole, Tinnin & Martin, P.A. (1979-1982); Attorney, Executive Director, Governor's Organized Crime Prevention Commission, Albuquerque, NM (1976-1979); Assistant Professor, College of Law, University of Illinois, Champaign-Urbana (1976); Assistant U.S. Attorney, U.S. Department Justice, Albuquerque, NM (1972-1975) **CR:** Member, Advisory Board, George Mason Judicial Education Program (2018-Present); Member, Committee on Federal-State Jurisdiction U.S. Judicial Conference (2013-Present); Advisor, Principles of Government Ethics Project, The American Law Institute (2011-Present); Member, Board of Overseers, Searle Civil Justice Institute (2008-Present); The American Law Institute (1993-Present); President, H. Vearle Payne American Inn of Court (2015-2017); Member, Dean's Advisory Committee, University of California, Irvine School of Law (2012-2017); Chair, Appellate Judges Education Institute (2005-2006); Chairman, Appellate Judges Conference, ABA (2004-2005); Board of Directors, Appellate Judges Education Institute (2003-2006); Member, Standing Committee on Rules of Practice and Procedure (2002-2010); Board of Directors, Appellate Judges Education Institute (2002-2006); Chair, Appellate Practice Insurance, The American Law Institute (2001-2002); Member, Executive Committee, Council of Chief Judges, ABA (1997-1999); Member, Chief Judges Education Committee, Appellate Judges Conference, ABA (1997-1998); Advisor, Restatement of the Law Third Agency, The American Law Institute (1996-2004); Member, Advisory Committee, ABA (1995-1997); Standing Committee on the Law, ABA (1995-1997); National Security, ABA (1995-1997); Member, Dean's Advisory Committee, University of California, Irvine School of Law (1982-1983) **CIV:** Chair, Rhodes Scholarship Selection Committee, NM (1999-2002); Chair, Selection Committee, New Mexico Ethics in Business Awards, Central New Mexico Community College (1999-2001); Republican Nominee, New Mexico Supreme Court (1996); Republican Nominee, New Mexico Supreme Court (1992); Co-chairman, Quality Assurance Committee, National Association of State Racing Commissioners (1988); Chairman, New Mexico Racing Commission (1987-1988); Republican Nominee, New Mexico Supreme Court (1986); Member, Executive Committee, Bernalillo County Republic Party, Albuquerque, NM (1982-1983) **CW:** Author, "Evaluating Judges," Duke Law Journal Legal Workshop (2018); Co-author, "The Law of Judicial Precedent" (2016); Author, "How Do Judges Think?," Denver Law Review (2014); Co-author, "Symposium: The Restyled Federal Rules of Evidence," William & Mary Law Review (2012); Author, "Evaluating Judges," Duke Law Journal Legal Workshop (2010); Board of Editors, Litigation Journal (1983-1986); Case and Developments Editor, Harvard Law Review (1971-1972); Editor, Harvard Law Review **AW:** Judge of the Year, Albuquerque Bar Association (2007); Founders' Award, National Kidney Foundation, Inc., NM (1997); Nominee, Joan Pew Award, National Association of State Racing Commissioners (1988) **MEM:** President, Albuquerque Rotary (1996-1997); Chairman, Albuquerque Committee on Foreign Relations (1981-1982); President, Albuquerque Committee on Foreign Relations (1980); The Phi Beta Kappa Society (1966) **BAR:** U.S. Court of Appeals for the Tenth Circuit (1973); U.S. District Court for the District of New Mexico (1972); State Bar of New Mexico (1972) **BA:** 201 3rd St NW Ste 1870, U.S. Circuit Judge, U.S. Court of Appeals, Albuquerque, NM, 87102

HARTZLER, VICKY J., T: U.S. Representative from Missouri **I:** Government Administration/Government Relations/Government Services **DOB:** 10/13/1960 **PB:** Archy **SC:** MO/USA **ED:** MEd, Central Missouri State University, 1992; EdB, University of Missouri, Columbia, MO, 1983 **C:** U.S. House Armed Services Committee, Washington, DC, 2011-Present; U.S. House Agricultural Committee, Washington, DC, 2011-Present; U.S. Congress From Fourth Missouri District, Washington, DC, 2011-Present; Chairperson, Missouri Women's Council, 2005-2007; Missouri House Of Representatives, Jefferson City, MO, 1995-2001 **CR:** Co-Owner, Hartzler Equipment Co. **CIV:** Former President, Cass County Farm Bureau **CW:** Author, Running God's Way: Step by Step to a Successful Political Campaign, 2008 **PA:** Republican **BA:** 2235 Rayburn HOB, Washington, DC, 20515

HASLAM, BILL, T: U.S. Governor from Tennessee **I:** Government Administration/Government Relations/Government Services **DOB:** 08/23/1958 **PB:** Knoxville **SC:** TN/USA **PT:** Jim Haslam; Natalie L. Haslam **ED:** BA in History, Emory University **C:** Governor, State of Tennessee (2011-Present); Mayor, City of Knoxville, TN (2003-2011); Owner, Tennessee Smokies; President, Pilot Corporation (1985-2003); Manager, Pilot Travel Centers (1983-1985) **CR:** Board Member, Tennessee Technology Development Corporation (2008-Present); Advisory Council on Historical Preservation (2008-Present) **CIV:** Former Board Member, Diversity Task Force of Nine Counties, One Vision; Former Board Member, Emerald Avenue Youth Foundation; Former Board Member, Cornerstone Foundation and World Vision; Vice Chairman, Knoxville Museum Art; Campaign Chairman, Foothills Land Conservancy; Executive Committee Chairman, Young Life of Knoxville; Chairman & President, Project GRAD; Chairman, East Tennessee Center for Non-Profit Management; Elder, Cedar Springs Presbyterian Church **MEM:** Chairman, Salvation Army; United Way of Greater Knoxville **H:** Bicycling; Running **PA:** Republican

HASPEL, GINA, T: Director of the CIA **I:** Government Administration/Government Relations/Government Services **C:** Director, CIA, 2018-; Deputy Director, CIA, 2017-2018; Director, National Clandestine Services, 2013 **AW:** Donovan Award, Presidential Rank Award, Intelligence Medal of Merit

HASSAN, MUSTAFA, T: Child-Protection Manager **I:** Social Work **C:** Child Protection Manager, International Rescue Committee **AW:** Named One of TIME's 100 Most Influential People, TIME Magazine (2015)

HASTINGS, ALCEE LAMAR, T: U.S. Representative from Florida **I:** Government Administration/Government Relations/Government Services **DOB:** 09/05/1936 **PB:** Altomonte Springs **SC:** FL/USA **PT:** Julius C. Hastings, Mildred L. Hastings **ED:** JD, Florida A&M University, 1963; BS in Zoology & Botany, Fisk University, Nashville, TN, 1958; Student, Howard University School of Law **C:** Committee On Rule, Commission On Security And Cooperation In Europe, U.S. Congress From 20th Florida District, 2013-Present; U.S. Congress From 23d Florida District, Washington, 1993-2013; Private Practice Attorney, 1989-1992; Judge, U.S. District Court, Southern District, Florida, 1979-1989; Judge, Circuit Court of Broward County, Florida, 1977-1979; Private Practice Attorney, Fort Lauderdale, FL, 1966-1977; Associate, Allen & Hastings, Fort Lauderdale, FL, 1963-1966 **CR:** Lecturer, Consultant, Peace Corps Volunteers, Avon Park, FL, 1966 **CIV:** Trustee, Bethune Cookman College, Trustee, Broward Community College, Board of Directors, Broward County Council on Human Relations, Board of Directors, Florida Voters League, Board of Directors, Broward County Sickle Cell Anemia Foundation, Board of Directors, Child Advocacy, Inc., Board of Directors, Urban League of Broward County **CW:** Host, (TV Series) Pride, Station WPLG; Columnist, West Side Gazette **AW:** Citizen of the Year, Zeta Phi Beta, 1978, Sam Delevoe Human Rights Award, Community Relations Board of Broward County, 1978, Humanitarian Award, Broward County Young

Democrats, 1978, Man of the Year, Committee of Italian American Affairs, 1979, Chairman's Award, National Bar Association, 1981, Glades Festival of Afro Arts Award, Zeta Phi Beta, 1981, The 100 Most Influential Black Americans, Ebony Magazine, 2006, The Power 150, 2008 **MEM:** National Organization of Women, National Association for the Advancement of Colored People, Miami-Dade Chamber of Commerce, American Civil Liberties Union, Family Christian Association **BAR:** State of Florida, 1963 **PA:** Democrat **BA:** 2353 Rayburn House Office Building, Washington, DC, 20515

HASTINGS, REED, T: CEO **I:** Other **CN:** Netflix **DOB:** 10/08/1960 **PB:** Boston **SC:** MA/USA **ED:** MS in Computer Science, Stanford University, CA (1988); BA, Bowdoin College, Brunswick, Maine (1983) **C:** Co-founder, Chairman, President, Chief Executive Officer, Netflix, Inc., Los Gatos, CA (1998-Present); Chief Executive Officer, Technology Network (1998-1999); Founder, Chief Executive Officer, Pure Atria Software (1991-1997); High School Math Teacher, U.S. Peace Corps, Swaziland (1983-1986) **CR:** Board of Directors, Facebook, Inc. (2011-Present); Board of Directors, Microsoft Corporation (2007-Present); Board of Directors, Netflix, Inc. (1997-Present) **CIV:** Founding Member, EdVoice.net; Founding Member, Pacific Collegiate School; Founding Member, Aspire Public Schools; Founding Member, NewSchools.org; President, California State Board of Education (2000-2004) **AW:** Named a Maverick, Details Magazine (2007); Named Business Person of the Year, Fortune Magazine (2010); Named One of the 30 Most Respected CEOs, Barron's (2010); Named One of the 100 Agents of Change, Rolling Stone Magazine (2009); Named One of the 100 Most Influential People in the World, TIME Magazine (2005, 2011); Named to the Video Business Hall of Fame (2007)

HATCH, ORRIN GRANT, T: U.S. Senator from Utah **I:** Government Administration/Government Relations/Government Services **DOB:** 03/22/1934 **PB:** Homestead Park **SC:** Pennsylvania **PT:** Son of Jesse and Helen (Kamm) H.; Married Elaine Hansen, August 28, 1957; children: Brent, Marcia, Scott, Kimberly, Alysa, Jess. **ED:** LLD (hon.), Southern Utah University, 1990; LLD (hon.), Pepperdine University, 1990; MS (hon.), Defense Intelligence College, 1982; LLD (hon.), University Maryland, 1981; LLD (hon.), University Pittsburgh, 1999; JD, University Pittsburgh, 1962; BS in History, Brigham Young University, 1959 **CT:** Bar: Pennsylvania 1962, Utah 1962 **C:** Chairman, US Senate Finance Committee, 2015-; Member, US Senate Judiciary Committee, 1977-; President pro tempore, 2015-; US Senator from Utah, 1977-; Chairman, US Senate Labor & Human Resources Committee, 1981-87; Chairman, US Senate Judiciary Committee, 2003-05; Chairman, US Senate Judiciary Committee, 2001; Chairman, US Senate Judiciary Committee, 1995-2001; Partner, Hatch & Plumb, Salt Lake City, 1976; Partner, Thomson, Rhodes & Grigsby, Pittsburgh, 1962-69 **CR:** Board of directors, US Holocaust Memorial Museum **CW:** Author: The Equal Rights Amendment: Myths and Realities, 1983, Understanding the Doctrines of Christ, 1995, Square Peg: Confessions of a Citizen Senator, 2003; contributor articles to newspapers and professional journals **AW:** Recipient Excellence in Public Service award American Academy Pediatrics, 1988, Senator of Year award National Multiple Sclerosis Society, 1996, Lifetime Achievement award Asian Association Utah, 1998, Small Investor Empowerment award National Association Real Estate Investment Trusts, 2001, Campbell award, American Society Law Enforcement Training, 2002, Elmer P. Martin Public Service award Great Blacks in Wax Museum, 2003, Legis. of Year award Biotechnology Industry Organization, 2003, National Leadership award, Coalition for Juvenile Justice, 2004, Edmund J. Randolph award US Department Justice, 2004, Lifetime Achievement award Operation Kids, 2004, C. W. Bill Young Congl. award National Marrow Donor Program, 2006, Executive Dir.'s award US Office Rehabilitation, 2009; named Champion of MedTech. Innovation, Advanced Medical Techs. Association, 2007; named one of America's Best Leaders US News & World Report, 2009 **MEM:** Member American Bar Association., National Bar Association, Utah Bar Association, Pennsylvania Bar Association, American Judicature Society **H:** Golf, poetry, piano playing, composer lyrics **PA:** Republican **BA:** Office of Orrin Hatch, 125 S State St Federal Bldg Rm 8402, Salt Lake City, TX, 84138-1191

HATHAWAY, ANNE, T: Actress **I:** Media & Entertainment **PB:** Brooklyn **SC:** NY/USA **PT:** Gerard Hathaway; Kate McCauley **C:** Spokeswoman, Lancôme, 2008 **CW:** Actress: (TV series) Get Real, 1999-2000, Elmos Christmas Countdown, 2007, SNL, 2008, The Simpsons, 2009-2010, Family Guy, 2010, 83rd Academy Awards, 2011, Hit Record on TV, 2015, Lip Sync Battle, 2015, Documentary Now!, 2016; (films) The Princess Diaries, 2001, The Other Side of Heaven, 2001, (voice) The Cat Returns, 2002, Nicholas Nickleby, 2002, Ella Enchanted, 2004, The Princess Diaries 2: Royal Engagement, 2004, (voice) Hoodwinked, 2005, Havoc, 2005, Brokeback Mountain, 2005, The Devil Wears Prada, 2006, Becoming Jane, 2007, Get Smart, 2008, Rachel Getting Married, 2008 (Best Actress, National Board Review, 2008, Best Actress, Critics Choice Awards, 2009), Passengers, 2008, Bride Wars, 2009 (Choice Movie Actress: Comedy, Teen Choice Awards, 2009), Valentine's Day, 2010, Alice in Wonderland, 2010, (voice) Rio, 2011, One Day, 2011, The Dark Knight Rises, 2012, Les Misérables, 2012 (Best Supporting Actress, Critics Choice Awards, 2013, Best Performance by an Actress in a Supporting Role in a Motion Picture, Golden Globe award, Hollywood Foreign Press Association, 2013, Outstanding Performance by a Female Actor in a Supporting Role, Screen Actors Guild, 2013, Best Supporting Actress, British Academy Film and TV Arts, 2013, Best Supporting Actress, Academy Awards, 2013), Don Jon's Addiction, 2013, (voice) Rio 2, 2014, Don Peyote, 2014, Interstellar, 2014, The Intern, 2015, Alice Through the Looking Glass, 2016, Colossal, 2016, Ocean's 8, 2018, Serenity, 2018, Nasty Women, 2018; (plays) Twelfth Night, 2009; actress, producer (films) Song One, 2014, Grounded, 2015, The Children's Monologues, 2017 **AW:** Named Woman of Year, Hasty Pudding Theatrical Society, 2010; Recipient Women in Hollywood Tribute Award, Elle Magazine, 2008

HAWKE, ETHAN, T: Actor **I:** Media & Entertainment **DOB:** 11/06/1970 **PB:** Austin **SC:** TX/USA **PT:** James Hawke; Leslie (Green) Hawke **ED:** Attended, Carnegie Mellon University, 1988-89 **C:** Co-founder, artistic director, Malaparte Theatre Co., New York City, 1992-2000 **CIV:** Co-founder, Lions Fiction award, 2001 **CW:** Actor: (plays) Casanova, 1991, A Joke, The Seagull, 1992, Sophistry, Henry IV, 2003-04, Hurlyburly, 2005, The Coast of Utopia (Part 1: Voyage), 2006, The Coast of Utopia (Part 2: Shipwreck), 2006, The Coast of Utopia (Part 3-Salvage), 2007, The Cherry Orchard, 2009, The Winter's Tale, 2009, Blood from a Stone, 2010-11, Ivanov, 2012, Macbeth, 2013; (films) Explorers, 1985, Lion's Den, 1988, Dead Poet's Society, 1989, Dad, 1989, White Fang, 1991, Mystery Date, 1991, A Midnight Clear, 1992, Waterland, 1992, Alive, 1993, Rich in Love, 1993, Floundering, 1994, Reality Bites, 1994, White Fang II, 1994, Quiz Show, 1994, Before Sunrise, 1995, Search & Destroy, 1995, Gattaca, 1997, Great Expectations, 1998, The Newton Boys, 1998, The Velocity of Gary, 1998, Joe the King, 1999, Snow Falling on Cedars, 1999, Tell Me, 2000, Hamlet, 2000, (voice) Waking Life, 2001, Tape, 2001, Training Day, 2001, The Jimmy Show, 2001, Taking Lives, 2004, Assault on Precinct 13, 2005, Before the Devil Knows You're Dead, 2007, What Doesn't Kill You, 2008, Daybreakers, 2009, Brooklyn's Finest, 2009, Life in New York, 2009, The Woman in the Fifth, 2011, Sinister, 2012, Vigilandia, 2013, The Purge, 2013; actor, (films) Getaway, 2013, Boyhood, 2014, Predestination, 2014, Cymbeline, 2014, Good Kill, 2014, 10,000 Saints, 2015, Sinister 2, 2015, The Phenom, 2015, Maggie's Plan, 2015, Born to Be Blue, 2015, Regression, 2015, Maudie, 2016, In a Valley of Violence, 2016, The Magnificent Seven, 2016, Valerian and the City of a Thousand Planets, 2017, First Reformed, 2017, 24 Hours to Live, 2017, Juliet, Naked, 2018, Blaze, 2018 (writer, director); (TV appearances) Alias, 2003; dir.: (films) Chelsea Walls, 2001; actor, producer (TV films) Exit Strategy, 2012; dir.: (films) Straight to One, 1994; (plays) Things We Want, 2007; director, writer, actor (films) The Hottest State, 2007, actor, writer Before Sunset, 2004, Before Midnight, 2013, director, featured in documentary Seymour: An Introduction, 2014; dir.: (plays) A Lie of the Mind, 2010; (actor, director): Clive, 2013; author: (novels) The Hottest State, 1996, Ash Wednesday, 2002 **AW:** Co-recipient Louis XIII Genius award, Critics' Choice Awards, 2014; named to The Texas Film Hall of Fame, 2004

HAWKES, GREG, T: Musician **I:** Media & Entertainment **DOB:** 06/08/1905 **PB:** Fulton, Maryland **SC:** Fulton, Maryland **ED:** Berklee College of Music **CW:** (Solo Albums) Niagara Falls, 1983, The Beatles Uke, 2008, (Albums with the Cars) The Cars,1978, Candy-O,1979, Panorama, 1980, Shake It Up, 1981, Heartbeat City, 1984, Door to Door, 1987, Move Like This, 2011 **AW:** Rock and Roll Hall of Fame, 2018

HAWKINS, PAULA, T: Writer **I:** Writing and Editing **PB:** Salisbury **SC:** Rhodesia **CW:** (Books)Guerrilla Learning: How to Give Your Kids a Real Education With or Without School,2001,Confessions of a Reluctant Recessionista,2009,All I Want for Christmas 2010,One Minute to Midnight,2011, The Reunion, 2013, The Girl on the Train, 2015, Into the Water, 2017

HAYDEN, CARLA DIANE, T: 14th Librarian of Congress **I:** Library Management/Library Services **DOB:** 08/10/1952 **PT:** Daughter of Bruce Kenard and Colleen (Dowling) Hayden. **ED:** LHD (hon.), Morgan State University, 2001; LHD (hon.), University Baltimore, 2000; PhD, University Chicago, 1987; MA in Libr. and Information Sci., University Chicago, 1977; BA, Roosevelt University, 1973 **C:** 14th Librarian of Congress, 2016-; President of the American Library Association, 2003-2004; Executive director, CEO, Enoch Pratt Free Libr., Baltimore, 1993-; 1st deputy commissioner, chief libr., Chicago Pub. Libr., 1991-93; Member faculty, School Libr. and Information Sci., Pittsburgh, 1987-91; Libr. services coordinator, Museum Sci. and Industry, Chicago, 1982-87; Assistant professor School Libr. and Information Sci., University Pittsburgh,; Children's and young adult libr., Chicago Pub. Libr., 1973-81 **CR:** Adjunct professor University Maryland, College Park, 1995-faculty member Long Island University, New York, 1994, Columbia University, New York City, 1990, 91 board directors Baltimore Gas & Electric Co., 2008- **CIV:** Board directors Maryland African Am. Museum Corp., Baltimore City Hist. Society, Baltimore Reads, Greater Baltimore Cultural Alliance,

Franklin and Eleanor Roosevelt Institute and Libr., New York City, Baltimore, Goucher College, PALINET, University Pittsburgh School Information Scis. **CW:** Contributor numerous articles to professional journals **AW:** Named Libr. of Year Libr. Journal, 1995, One of Md.'s Top 100 Women Warfield Business Record 1996, Daily Record, 2003, Woman of Year Ms. magazine, 2003; recipient Legacy of Literacy award DuBois Cir., 1996, Torch Bearer award Coalition of 100 Black Women, 1996, Andrew White medal Loyola College, 1997, Pres.'s medal Johns Hopkins University, 1998, Pro Urbe award College Notre Dame Maryland, 2004, Whitney M. Young Junior award Greater Baltimore Urban League, 2004, Leader award YWCA, Balt, 2004, Medal of Distinction Barnard College, 2005. **MEM:** Mem.: Maryland Libr. Association, Pub. Libr. Association, American Library Association (pres.-elect 2002-03, president 2003-04, immediate past president 2004-05, chairman committee on accreditation and spectrum initiative) **BA:** Library of Congress, 101 Independence Ave SE, Washington, DC, 20540

HAYES, GREGORY JAMES, **T:** CEO and President of United Technologies **I:** Business Management/Business Services **DOB:** 11/19/1960 **ED:** BS in Economics, Purdue University, 1982 **CT:** CPA **C:** Chairman, United Technologies Corp, 2016-; President, CEO, United Technologies Corp., Hartford, Connecticut, 2014-; Senior vice president, CFO, United Technologies Corp., Hartford, Connecticut, 2008-14; Vice president accounting & investor relations, United Technologies Corp., Hartford, Connecticut, 2006-08; Vice president accounting & controls, United Technologies Corp., Hartford, Connecticut, 2004-06; Vice president, controller, United Technologies Corp., Hartford, Connecticut, 2003-04; Financial management positions through vice president finance & information system aerospace, Sundstrand Corp., 1989-99; Accountant, Arthur Andersen, **CR:** Board directors Nucor Corp., 2014-, United Technologies Corp., 2014- **BA:** United Technologies Corp, 10 Farm Springs Rd., Farmington, CT, 06032

HAYES, SEAN, **T:** Actor, Comedian **I:** Media & Entertainment **DOB:** 06/26/1905 **PB:** Chgo., **SC:** Chgo., **PT:** Son of Ron and Mary Hayes. **ED:** PhD (hon.), Illinois State University, 2013; Attended, Illinois State University **CR:** Co-founder production company Hazy Mills **CW:** Music director Pheasant Run Theatre, Chicago, comedian Second City Improvisational Comedy Group, stand-up comedian in clubs in LA and Chicago; actor: (TV films) A & P, 1996, How Murray Saved Christmas, 2014; (films) Billy's Hollywood Kiss, 1998, Sin City Spectacular (Episode: Penn & Teller's Sin City Spectacular), 1999, Martin and Lewis, 2002, Pieces of April, 2003, Win a Date with Tad Hamilton!, 2004, The Bucket List, 2007, Igor (voice), 2008, Soul Men, 2008, Cats & Dogs: The Revenge of Kitty Galore (voice), 2010, The Three Stooges, 2012, Hit and Run, 2012, Monsters University, 2013, How Murray Saved Christmas, 2014, The Emoji Movie, 2017; (TV series) Will & Grace, 1998-2006 (Emmy award for Outstanding Supporting Actor in a Comedy, 2000, Outstanding Performance by an Ensemble in a Comedy Series, Screen Actors Guild award, 2001, Outstanding Performance by a Male Actor in a Comedy Series, Screen Actors Guild award, 2002, 2003, 2006), The Millers, 2014, The Comeback, 2014, Crowded, 2016, Maya & Marty, 2016, Hairspray Live, 2016, Tangled:The Series, 2017; actor, executive producer (TV series) Sean Saves the World, 2013-, TV appearances Silk Stalkings, 1996, Scrubs, 2001, 30 Rock, 2007, Portlandia, 2012, Up All Night, 2012, Smash, 2013; actor: (Broadway plays) Promises, Promises,

2010; voice Buzz Lightyear of Star Command: The Adventure Begins, 2000, Cats & Dogs, 2001, The Cat in the Hat, 2003, Monsters University, 2013; executive prodr.: (TV series) Situation: Comedy, 2005; executive prodr.: (TV films) Stephen's Life, 2005; executive prodr.: (TV films) What News?, 2007, (TV series) Hot in Cleveland, 2010-, Grimm, 2011-; executive prodr.: (TV series) The Soul Man, 2012-; prodr.: (TV films) Man Stroke Woman, 2008

HAYNES, CATHARINA D., **T:** Federal Judge, Lawyer **I:** Law and Legal Services **DOB:** 11/09/1963 **PB:** Melbourne **SC:** FL/USA **ED:** JD, Emory University, 1986; BS in Psychology, Florida Institute of Technology, 1983 **CT:** Consumer and Commercial Law, U.S. Supreme Court, 1997 **C:** Judge, U.S. Court of Appeals, Fifth Circuit, Dallas, TX, 2008-Present; Partner, Baker & Botts LLP, Dallas, TX, 2007-2008; Presiding Judge, Dallas Civil District Court, Dallas, TX, 2005; Judge, 191st District Court of Texas, Dallas, TX, 1999-2006; Partner, Baker & Botts LLP, Dallas, TX, 1995-1998; Associate, Baker & Botts LLP, Dallas, TX, 1988-1994; Associate, Thompson & Knight LLP, Dallas, TX, 1986-1988 **CR:** Founding Fellow, Dallas Association of Young Lawyers Foundation, 2002-Present; Fellow, Dallas Bar Foundation, 2002-Present; Fellow, College of the State Bar of Texas, 2001-Present; Chair, Texas Court Reporters Certification Board, Austin, TX, 2003-2006; Volunteer Judge, Pro Bono Clinic, Legal Aid of Northwest Texas, 2003-2006 **CIV:** Attorneys Serving the Community, 2006-Present, Board Member, Vickery Meadow Learning Center, 2005-Present, Volunteer, Instructor, Vickery Meadow Learning Center, 2003-Present, Dallas Inn Court, 1990-1991 **AW:** Texas Super Lawyer, Texas Monthly & Law & Politics, 2007, Outstanding Achievement Award, Florida Tech Alumni Association, 2006, Presidential Commendation, State Bar of Texas, 2006, Award of Excellence, Dallas Association of Young Lawyers Foundation, 2005, Louise B. Raggio Award, Dallas Women Lawyers Association, 2004, Outstanding Board Member Award, 2003, Jo Anna Moreland Outstanding Committee Chair Award, Dallas Bar Association, 1996, 2002 **MEM:** Insurance Law Section Council, State Bar of Texas, 2002-Present, College of the State Bar of Texas, 1991-Present, Professional Ethics Committee, State Bar of Texas, 2006-2007, Co-Chair, Courthouse Committee, Dallas Bar Association, 2005, Advisory Committee, Dallas Association of Women Lawyers, 2003-2007, Co-Chair, Bench/Bar Conference Committee, Dallas Bar Association, 2002, ADR Section Council, Dallas Bar Association, 2001-2003, At-Large Director, Dallas Bar Association, 2001, Supreme Court of Texas Jury Task Force, State Bar of Texas, 1996-1997, Co-Chair, Judiciary Committee, Dallas Bar Association, 1996 **BAR:** U.S. District Court, Northern, Southern, Eastern, and Western Districts, Texas; U.S. Court of Appeals, Fifth and Tenth Circuits; State of Texas, 1986 **BA:** John Minor Wisdom U.S. Court of Appeals Building, Fifth Circuit, 600 Camp Street, New Orleans, LA, 70130

HAYWARD, JUSTIN, **T:** Singer and Guitarist **I:** Media & Entertainment **PB:** Swindon **SC:** Wiltshire, England **CW:** Solo Albums, "Blue Jays" (1975), "Songwriter" (1977), "Night Flight" (1980), "Moving Mountains" (1985), "Classic Blue" (1989), "Justin Hayward and Friends Sing the Moody Blues Classic Hits" (1994), "The View from the Hill" (1996), "Live in San Juan Capistrano" (1998), "Spirits of the Western Sky" (2013), "Spirits...Live" (2014), "All the Way" (2016); Albums with Moody Blues, "The Magnificent Moodies" (1965), "Days of Future Passed" (1967), "In Search of the Lost Chord" (1968), "On the Threshold of a Dream" (1969), "To Our Children's Children's Children"

(1969), "A Question of Balance" (1970), "Every Good Boy Deserves Favour" (1971), "Seventh Sojourn" (1972), "Octave" (1978), "Long Distance Voyager" (1981), "The Present" (1983), "The Other Side of Life" (1986), "Sur La Mer" (1988), "Keys of the Kingdom" (1991), "Strange Times" (1999), "December" (2003) **AW:** Inductee, Rock & Roll Hall of Fame (2018)

HECK, DENNY, **T:** U.S. Representative from Washington **I:** Government Administration/Government Relations/Government Services **DOB:** 07/19/1952 **PB:** Vancouver **SC:** Canada **ED:** Coursework, Portland State University (1974-1975); BA, Evergreen State College (1973) **C:** Member, U.S. House of Financial Services Committee (2013-Present); Member, 10th Washington District, U.S. Congress, Washington (2013-Present); Chief Executive Officer, TVW Television Network (1993-2003); Chief of Staff to Governor Booth Gardner, State of Washington, Olympia, WA (1990-1993); Minority Leader, Washington House of Representatives (1977-1985); Member, District 17, Washington House of Representatives (1976-1986); Co-Founder, Director, Intrepid Learning Solutions; Member, House Permanent Select Committee on Intelligence **CIV:** Board Member, Washington State History Museum,; Trustee, Evergreen State College **CW:** Author, "Our Times" (2008); Author, "The Enemy You Know" (2002); Author, "Challenges and Opportunities: The Transformation of Washington's Schools" (1987) **PA:** Democrat **BA:** # 203, 1423 E 29th St, Tacoma, WA, 98404-4008

HECKMAN, JAMES JOSEPH, **T:** Economist, Educator **I:** Education/Educational Services **DOB:** 04/19/1944 **PB:** Chgo. **SC:** IL/USA **PT:** Son of John Jacob and Bernice Irene (Medley) Heckman; **ED:** LLD (hon.), Colorado College, 2001; LHD (hon.), Bard College, 2004; Doctor (hon.), Pontifical University, Chile, 2009; Doctor (hon.), University of Montreal, 2004; Doctor (hon.), Mexico State Autonomous University, 2003; Doctor (hon.), University of Chile, 2002; PhD in Economics, Princeton University, New Jersey, 1971; MA in Economics, Princeton University, New Jersey, 1968; BA in Math., summa cum laude, Colorado College, 1965 **C:** Director Economics Research Center, University of Chicago, 1997-; Henry Schultz distinguished service professor economics, The University of Chicago, 1995-; Director Center Program Evaluation, Harris School Pub. Policy, The University of Chicago, 1991-; Henry Schultz professor economics, The University of Chicago, 1985-95; Professor economics, The University of Chicago, 1976-85; Associate professor economics, The University of Chicago, 1973-76; Lecturer, then associate professor, Columbia University, 1970-74; Aerospace systems engineer, Martin Marietta Corp., 1968 **CR:** Professor sci. and society Univ. College Dublin, 2006- distinguished chair microeconometrics Univ. College London, 2004-08 senior research fellow Am. Bar Foundation, 1991- Alfred Cowles distinguished visiting professor Yale University, 2008-, A. Whitney Griswold professor economics, 1988-90, Irving Fisher professor economics, 1984 senior research associate National Bureau Econs. Research, 1987-, 1977-85, research associate, 1970-77 **CW:** Author, editor Longitudinal Analysis of Labor Market Data, 1985, Inequality in America: What Role for Human Capital Policy?, 2003, Law and Employment: Lessons From Latin America and the Caribbean, 2004, Global Perspectives on the Rule of Law, 2010; co-author (author, editor): Handbook of Econometrics (numerous editions); member editorial board Journal Applied Econometrics, 2007-; contributor articles to professional journals **AW:** Recipient Distinguished Contribution to Pub. Policy for

Children award, Society Research in Child Devel., 2009, Theodore W. Schultz award, Am. Agricultural Economics Association Foundation, 2007, Sun Yefang Economic Sci. award, 2007, Ulysses medal, Univ. College Dublin, 2006, Dennis J. Aigner award for applied econometrics, Journal Econometrics, 2007, 2005, Medal of Excellence, Center Excellence for Children's Well-Being, Montreal University, 2004, Nobel Prize in economics, 2000, Louis T. Benezet Distinguished Alumnus award, Colorado College, 1985,Frisch Medal, Econometric Society, 2014, Spirit of Erikson Award, 2014 **MEM:** Fellow: American Association for the Advancement of Science, Econometric Society, Am. Academy Arts. & Scis., Society Labor Economics (Jacob Mincer award for Lifetime Achievement 2005), Am. Statistical Association (Chicago chapter Statistician of Year 2002), International Statistical Institute; mem.: National Academy of Sciences, Am. Economic Association (John Bates Clark medal 1983), Am. Philosophical Society, National Academy Education, Irish Economic Association (life), Phi Beta Kappa

HEEGER, ALAN JAY, T: Physicist, Educator **I:** Education/Educational Services **DOB:** 01/22/1936 **PB:** Sioux City **SC:** IA/USA **PT:** Son of Peter J. and Alice (Minkin) Heeger; **ED:** PhD (hon.), Abo Akademie University, Finland, 1998; DTech (hon.), Linköping University, Sweden, 1996; DSc (hon.), University Alicante, Spain, 2006; DSc (hon.), Trinity College, University of Dublin, 2005; DSc (hon.), Bar Ilan University, Israel; DSc (hon.), Japan Adv. Institute Sci. & Tech.; DSc (hon.), Southern China University Tech.; DSc (hon.), University of Nebraska, 1999; DSc (hon.), University Mons, Belgium, 1993; PhD in Physics, University of California, Berkeley, 1961; BA with high distinction, University of Nebraska, 1957 **C:** Professor physics, University of California, Santa Barbara, 1982-; Director Institute Polymers & Organic Solids, University of California, Santa Barbara, 1983-2000; Acting vice provost research, University of Pennsylvania, 1981-82; Director Research Laboratory Structure of Matter, University of Pennsylvania, 1974-81; Professor physics, University of Pennsylvania, 1966-82; Associate professor, University of Pennsylvania, 1964-66; Assistant professor, University of Pennsylvania, Philadelphia, 1962-64 **CR:** Co-founder, vice-chmn. CytomX, Inc., 2006- co-founder, chairman CBritu, Inc., Santa Barbara, 2005- co-founder, chief scientist Konarka Technologies, Inc., Lowell, Massachusetts, 2001- founder, president UNIAX Corp., Santa Barbara, 1990-94 Morris Loeb lecturer Harvard University, 1973 **CW:** Editor-in-chief Synthetic Metals journal, 1983-2000, contributor sci. articles to professional journals **AW:** Recipient Italgas prize, Eni Inc., Italy, 2007, Nobel prize in chemistry, 2000, President medal, University Pennsylvania, 2000, Balzan prize, Balzan Foundation, Italy/Switzerland, 1995, John Scott medal, City of Philadelphia, 1989; Alfred P. Sloan Fellow **MEM:** Fellow: Am. Physics Society (Buckley prize for solid state physics 1983); mem.: NAE, National Academy of Sciences, Korean Academy Scis. (foreign) **ACH:** Achievements include patents in field **H:** Skiing

HEES, BERNARDO VIEIRA, T: Food Products Executive **I:** Government Administration/Government Relations/Government Services **ED:** MBA, University Warwick, England; BA in Economics, Pontificia Universidade Católica, Rio de Janeiro **C:** CEO, The Kraft Heinz Co. (formally known as H.J. Heinz Co.), Pittsburgh, 2013-; Partner, 3G Capital Partners Ltd., 2010-; CEO, Burger King Holdings, Inc., Miami, 2010-13; CEO, America Latina Logistica, 2005-10; Director superintendent, America Latina Logistica, 2004; Operational planning manager, CFO, comml officer,

America Latina Logistica, 2004; COO, America Latina Logistica, 2003; Vice president, marketing, America Latina Logistica, 2002-03; Logistics analyst, America Latina Logistica, 1998-2000; With, Banco Marka, 1995-96; With, Shell Brazil,; With, Banco Marka Nacional de Desenvolvimento Econômico e Social, **CR:** Board directors Burger King Holdings, Inc., 2010-13, America Latina Logistica, 2005-10

HEIDEN, ERIC, T: Former Olympic Speed Skater **I:** Athletics **PB:** 1959 **C:** Skater, Olympic Winter Games, Lake Placid, 1980; Skater, Olympic Winter Games, 1976 **AW:** Recipient 5 Olympic Gold medals, 1980; Olympic record breaker 500, 1,000, 1,500, and 5,000 meter races; world record breaker 10,000 meter race; 1st person in Olympic history to win 5 individual Gold medals at one Games,Oscar Mathisen, 1977-1980, James E Sullivan, 1980, Olympic Hall of Fame, 1983, Wisconsin Athletic Hall of Fame, 1990, United Press international Athlete of the Year, 1980, 50 Greatest Athletes of the 20th Century, 1999 **BA:** Heiden Orthopedics, 2200 Park Ave, Park City, UT, 84060

HEINRICH, MARTIN TREVOR, T: U.S. Senator from New Mexico **I:** Government Administration/Government Relations/Government Services **DOB:** 10/17/1971 **PB:** Fallon **PT:** Son of Peter C. and Shirley A. (Bybee) Heinrich; **ED:** Postgraduate studies in Community & Regional Planning Program, University New Mexico; BSc in Engineering, University Missouri, 1995 **C:** Member, US Joint Economic Committee, 2013-; Member, US Senate Select Committee on Intelligence, 2013-; Member, US Senate Energy & Natural Resources Committee, 2013-; US Senator from New Mexico, 2013-; Member, US House Natural Resources Committee, 2009-13; Member, US House Armed Services Committee, 2009-13; Member, US Congress from 1st New Mexico District, 2009-13; President, Albuquerque City Council, 2006; Member, Albuquerque City Council, 2003-07; Natural resources trustee, State of New Mexico,; Executive director, Cottonwood Gulch Foundation, 1996-2001 **CIV:** Board member, Southeast Heights Neighborhood Association, Board member, New Mexico Wilderness Alliance, Board member, Albuquerque Open Space Adv. Board, **CW:** Appeared in (TV special) Rival Survival., 2014 **PA:** Democrat **BA:** Office of Martin Heinrich, 303 Hart Senate Office Building, Washington, DC, 20510

HEINSOHN, THOMAS WILLIAM, T: Professional Basketball Broadcaster **I:** Athletics **DOB:** 08/26/1934 **PB:** Jersey City **PT:** Son of William B. and Bessie (Paul) H.; Married Diane Regenhard, September 2, 1956; children: Donna Marie, Paul T., David **ED:** BSBA, Holy Cross College, 1956 **CT:** Chartered Life Underwriter **C:** Commentator, CBS Sports, New York City, 1980-; Coach, Boston Celtics, 1969-78; Basketball player, Boston Celtics, 1956-65; Life insurance underwriter, Boston, 1956 **AW:** NBA Champion, 1957, 1959-1965, NBA All-Star, 1957, 1961-1965, All-NBA Second Team, 1963-1964, NBA Rookie of the Year, 1957, NBA Coach of the Year, 1973, NBA All-Star Game Head Coach, 1972-1974, 1976 **BA:** TD Garden, 100 Legends Way, Boston, MA, 02114

HEITKAMP, HEIDI, T: U.S. Senator **I:** Government Administration/Government Relations/Government Services **DOB:** 10/30/1955 **PB:** Breckenridge **SC:** MN/USA **PT:** Daughter of Raymond Bernard and Doreen LaVonne (Berg) H. **MS:** Married **SPN:** Darwin K. Lange, June 9, 1984; **CH:** Alethea Ruth, Nathan Dennis **ED:** JD, Lewis & Clark Law School, 1980; BA, University of North Dakota, 1977 **CT:** Bar: North Dakota, US District Court North Dakota **C:**

Member, US Senate Small Business & Entrepreneurship Committee, 2013-; Member, US Senate Indian Affairs Committee, 2013-; Member, US Senate Homeland Security & Governmental Affairs Committee, 2013-; Member, US Senate Banking, Housing & Urban Affairs Committee, 2013-; Member, US Senate Agricultural, Nutrition & Forestry Committee, 2013-; US Senator from North Dakota, 2013-; Attorney General, State of North Dakota, Bismarck, 1993-2001; Tax Commissioner, State of North Dakota, Bismarck, 1986-92; Administrative Counsel, Office North Dakota State Tax Commission, Bismarck, North Dakota, 1985-86; Assistant Attorney General, Office North Dakota State Tax Commissioner, Bismarck, North Dakota, 1981-85; Attorney Enforcement Division, EPA, Washington, 1980-81; Research Assistant, Natural Resources Law Institute, Portland, Oregon, 1979; Executive Director, Northwest Environmental Defense Center, Portland, Oregon, 1978-79; Legislative Intern, North Dakota Legislative Council, Bismarck, 1977; Intern Assistant, Environmental Study Conference, Washington, 1976 **CR:** Vice-chmn. Multistate Tax Commission, 1987-88, Chairman 1988-89 Board of Directors Dakota Gasification Co., 2001-12 **CIV:** Crusade Chairperson American Cancer Society, North Dakota, 1988-89 **AW:** Toll Fellow Council State Governments, 1986; Recipient Young Achiever Award National Council Women, 1987; Named One of The 20 Young Lawyers Making a Difference, American Bar Association Barrister Magazine, 1990 **MEM:** Member Federation Tax Administrators, Midwestern States Association Tax Administrators, North Dakota Bar Association, National Association Attorney Generals **H:** Triathlon competitions, Racquetball, Biking, Softball, Running **PA:** Democrat **BA:** Office of Heidi Heitkamp, SH-516 Hart Senate Office Building, Washington, DC, 20510

HELLER, DEAN ARTHUR, T: U.S. Senator from Nevada **I:** Government Administration/Government Relations/Government Services **DOB:** 05/10/1960 **PB:** Castro Valley **PT:** Married Lynne Brombach, children: Hilary, Harrison, Andrew, Emmy. **ED:** BS with honors, University Southern California, 1985 **C:** Member, US Senate Commerce, Sci. & Transportation Committee, Washington, 2011-; Member, US Senate Special Committee on Aging, Washington, 2011-; Member, US Senate Energy & Natural Resources Committee, Washington, 2011-; US Senator from Nevada, Washington, 2011-; Member, US Congress from 2nd Nevada District, Washington, 2007-11; Member, Nevada State Assembly, Carson City, 1990-94; Secretary state, State of Nevada, Carson City, 1994-2006; Chief deputy state treasurer, State of Nevada, Carson City,; Stockbroker, broker, trader, Pacific Stock Exchange, **CIV:** Board directors, Western Nevada Community College Foundation, **MEM:** Mem.: Western Nevada Chamber of Commerce Foundation, Boys & Girls Club Western Nevada, North American Securities Administrators Association **ACH:** Achievements include being the first secretary of state in the nation to demand a voter-verifiable paper audit trail printer on touch-screen voting machines **H:** Stockcar racing **PA:** Republican **BA:** Office of Dean Heller, 324 Hart Senate Office Building, Washington, DC, 20510

HEMINGER, GARY R., T: CEO and Chairman at Marathon Petroleum Corp. **I:** Business Management/Business Services **ED:** MBA, Univ. of Dayton, 1982; Bachelor accounting, Tiffin Univ., 1976 **C:** Chairman,CEO, Marathon Petroleum Corp, 2017-; Chairman,CEO, Mplx LP, 2012-; President,Chairman, CEO, Marathon Petroleum Corp., 2011-17; Executive vice president downstream, Marathon Oil Corp., 2005-11; Executive vice president, Marathon Oil Corp., 2001-05; Executive vice president supply trans. & marketing, Marathon Ashland Petroleum LLC, 2001; Senior vice president business develop., Marathon Ashland Petroleum LLC, 1999-2001; Vice president business develop., Marathon Ashland Petroleum LLC, 1998-99; Manager business develop & joint interest, Marathon Oil Corp., 1996-98; Vice president we. div. Speedway SuperAm., Marathon Oil Corp., 1991-95; Management positions, Marathon Oil Corp., Houston, 1976-91 **CR:** Chairman downstream committee Am. Petroleum Institute member Oxford Institute Energy Studies board directors Fifth Third Bancorp. **CIV:** Chairman board trustees, Tiffin Univ. **BA:** Marathon Petroleum, 539 South Main Street, Findlay, OH, 45840

HEMSLEY, STEPHEN J., T: CEO **I:** Health, Wellness and Fitness **CN:** United Healthcare **PB:** 1952 **ED:** BS, Fordham University, 1974 **C:** CEO, UnitedHealth Group, Inc., Detroit, 2006-; Board directors, UnitedHealth Group, Inc., Detroit, 2000-; President, UnitedHealth Group, Inc., Detroit, 1999-; COO, UnitedHealth Group, Inc., Detroit, 1998-2006; Senior executive vice president, UnitedHealth Group, Inc., Detroit, 1997-98; CFO Arthur Anderson Worldwide, Arthur Anderson and Co..; Managing partner strategy and planning, Arthur Andersen and Co..; General manager tech. activities and knowledge initiatives, Arthur Andersen and Co., **CR:** Board trustee Minnesota Pub. Radio, Univ. of St. Thomas, Minnesota board directors Provell, Inc., 1997-2001 **CIV:** Trustee, Minnesota Pub. Radio, 2002-

HEMSWORTH, CHRIS, I: Media & Entertainment **DOB:** 08/11/1983 **PB:** Melbourne **SC:** VIC/Australia **PT:** Craig Hemsworth; Leonie Hemsworth **CW:** Actor: (TV series) Home and Away, 2004-07; (films) Star Trek, 2009, Ca$h, 2010, Thor, 2011, The Cabin in the Woods, 2011, The Avengers, 2012, Snow White and the Huntsman, 2012 (Choice Summer Male Movie Star, Teen Choice Awards, 2012), Red Dawn, 2012, Star Trek Into Darkness, 2013, Rush, 2013, Thor: The Dark World, 2013, Blackhat, 2015, Avengers: Age of Ultron, 2015, Vacation, 2015, In the Heart of the Sea, 2015, The Huntsman: Winter's War, 2016, Ghostbusters, 2016 **AW:** Named Sexiest Man Alive, People magazine, 2014, Favorite Action Movie Actor, People's Choice Awards, 2016, Favorite Action Movie Star, 2013

HENDERSON, KAREN LECRAFT, T: Federal Judge **I:** Law and Legal Services **DOB:** 07/11/1944 **PB:** Oberlin **SC:** OH/USA **ED:** JD, University of North Carolina, 1969; BA, Duke University, 1966 **C:** Judge, U.S. Court of Appeals, District of Columbia Circuit, Washington, DC, 1990-Present; Judge, U.S. District Court, South Carolina, Columbia, SC, 1986-1990; Partner, Sinkler, Gibbs & Simons, P.A., Columbia, SC, 1983-1986; Deputy Attorney General, Director Of Criminal Division, 1982; Senior Assistant Attorney General, Director Of Special Litigation Section, 1978-1982; Assistant Attorney General, Columbia, SC, 1973-1978; Partner, Wright & Henderson, Chapel Hill, NC, 1969-1970 **CIV:** Appointed, District Court Advisory Committee **MEM:** Litigation Section And Urban, State And Local Government Law Section, American Bar Association, American Law Institute, Supreme Court Historical Society, Federal Judges Association, Federal American Inn Of Court, American Judicature Society, Government Law Section, Trial And Appellate Practice Section, Federal Judges Association, South Carolina Bar Association, North Carolina Bar Association **BA:** U.S. Court of Appeals, 333 Constitution Avenue NW, Washington, DC, 20001-2802

HENDERSON, RICKEY HENLEY, T: Former MLB Player **I:** Athletics **DOB:** 12/25/1958 **PB:** Chicago **SC:** IL/USA **C:** Special Instructor, New York Mets (2006-2007); First Base Coach, New York Mets (2007-2010); Special Instructor, Athletics (2010); Retired (2007); Outfielder, San Diego Surf Dawgs (2005); Outfielder, LA Dodgers (2003); Outfielder, Newark Bears (2003); Outfielder, Boston Red Sox (2002); Outfielder, Seattle Mariners (2000); First Base Coach, New York Mets (2007); Special Instructor, New York Mets (2007); Outfielder, New York Mets (1998-2000); Outfielder, Anaheim Angels (1997); Outfielder, San Diego Padres (2001); Outfielder, San Diego Padres (1995-1997); Outfielder, Toronto Blue Jays (1993); Outfielder, New York Yankees (1984-1989); Outfielder, Oakland Athletics (1998); Outfielder, Oakland Athletics (1993-1995); Outfielder, Oakland Athletics (1989-1993); Outfielder, Oakland Athletics (1979-1984); Draft Pick, Oakland Athletics (1976) **AW:** Named American League MVP (1990); American League Championship Series MVP (1989); Named to National Baseball Hall of Fame, Baseball Writers' Association America (2009); Named to American League Silver Slugger Team, Sporting News (1981, 1985, 1990); Named to American League All-Star Team (1980, 1982-1988, 1990, 1990-1991); Golden Shoe Award, Sporting News (1983); Silver Shoe Award (1982); Golden Glove Award, American League (1981) **ACH:** Achievements include leading the American League in: stolen bases, 1980-86, 88-91, 98; runs 1981, 85, 86, 89, 90; hits (135), 1981; on-base percentage (.439), 1990; member of the World Series Championship winning Oakland Athletics, 1989; Toronto Blue Jays, 1993; holding Major League Baseball records for: stolen bases in one season (130), 1982, career stolen bases (1,406), runs scored (2,295), lead-off home runs (81)

HENSARLING, JEB, I: Government Administration/Government Relations/Government Services **DOB:** 05/29/1957 **PB:** Stephenville, Texas **PT:** Son of Charles and Ann (Brock) Hensarling; **ED:** JD, University Texas, Austin, 1982; BA in Economics, Magna Cum Laude, Texas Agricultural and Mechanical University, 1979 **C:** Chairman, US House Financial Services Committee, Washington, 2013-; Member, US Congress from 5th Texas District, Washington, 2003-; Co-chair, Joint Select Committee on Deficit Reduction, Washington, 2011; Chairman, US House Republican Conference, Washington, 2011-13; CEO, Family Support Assurance Corp., Dallas, 2001-02; Vice president, Green Mountain Energy, Austin, 1999-2001; Owner, San Jacinto Ventures, 1996-99; Vice President, Maverick Capital, Dallas, 1993-96; Owner, Principal, F-H & Associates, Dallas,.; Attorney, Oppenheimer, Harrison, Blend & Tate, San Antonio,; State Director to Rep. Phil Gramm, US House of Representatives, 1985-89 **CR:** Chairman Republican Study Committee, 2007-09 Executive Director National Republican Senatorial Committee (NRSC), 1991-93 **CIV:** Member Adv. Board, Children's Education Fund, Board of Directors, Texas Pub. Policy Foundation, Board of Directors, American Cancer Soc.-Dallas Metro Area **AW:** Recipient Fighter for Free Enterprise Award, Hero of the Taxpayer Award, Small Business Adv. Award, Spirit of Enterprise Award, True Blue Award, Family Research Council **PA:** Republican **BA:** Office of Jeb Hensarling, 228 Rayburn HOB, Washington, DC, 20515

HENSON, TARAJI PENDA, T: Actress **I:** Media & Entertainment **PB:** Washington **SC:** DC/USA **PT:** Boris Henson; Bernice Henson **ED:** Graduate, Howard University, Washington, DC, 1995 **CW:** Actress: (films) Streetwise, 1998, The Adventures of Rocky & Bullwinkle, 2000, All or Nothing, 2001, Baby Boy, 2001, Hair Show, 2004, Hustle & Flow, 2005, Four Brothers, 2005, Something New, 2006, Smokin' Aces, 2006, Talk to Me, 2007, The Family That Preys, 2008, The Curious Case of Benjamin Button, 2008 (National Association for the Advancement of Colored People Image award for Outstanding Supporting Actress in a Motion Picture, 2009), Not Easily Broken, 2009, I Can Do Bad All by Myself, 2009, Hurricane Season, 2009, Date Night, 2010, Once Fallen, 2010, The Karate Kid, 2010, Peep World, 2010, The Good Doctor, 2011, Larry Crowne, 2011, Think Like a Man, 2012, From the Rough, 2013, Think Like a Man Too, 2014, Term Life, 2016, Hidden Figures, 2016, Proud Mary, 2018, Arimony, 2018, The Best of Enemies, 2018, Wreck it Ralph 2, 2018, What Men Want, 2019; (TV series) The Division, 2003-04, Boston Legal, 2007-08, Person of Interest, 2011-15 (National Association for the Advancement of Colored People Image award for Outstanding Supporting Actress in a Drama Series, 2014), Empire, 2015- (Golden Globe award for Best Performance by an Actress in a TV Series - Drama, 2016, National Association for the Advancement of Colored People Image award for Outstanding Actress in a Drama Series, 2016); (TV films) Satan's School for Girls, 2000, Murder, She Wrote: The Last Free Man, 2001, Taken from Me: The Tiffany Rubin Story, 2011; TV appearances Sister, Sister, 1997, ER, 1998, Saved by the Bell: The New Class, 1998, Smart Guy, 1997-98, Felicity, 1998-99, Pacific Blue, 1999, Strong Medicine, 2000, Holla, 2002, All of Us, 2004, Half & Half, 2005, House M.D., 2005, CSI: Crime Scene Investigation, 2006, Eli Stone, 2008, The Cleveland Show, 2010, Person of Interest, 2011, Season of Love, 2014, Empire, 2015, FIFA Women's World Cup, 2015, SNL, 2015, Ice Age The Great Eggscapade, 2016, The Simpsons, 2017; actress, executive producer (films) No Good Deed, 2014 (National Association for the Advancement of Colored People Image award for Outstanding Actress in a Motion Picture, 2015), Seasons of Love, 2015

HERBERT, GARY RICHARD, T: Governor of Utah **I:** Government Administration/Government Relations/Government Services **DOB:** 05/07/1947 **PB:** American Fork **PT:** Son of Duane and Carol Herbert; **ED:** Attended, Brigham Young University, Provo, Utah **CT:** Lic. real estate broker 1969 **C:** Chair, National Governors Association, 2015-16; Governor, State of UT, 2009-; Lieutenant governor, State of UT, 2005-09; Commissioner, Utah County Commission, Salt Lake City, 1990-2004; President, Herbert & Associates Inc., Orem, Utah, **CR:** Chairman Utah Adv. Council Intergovernmental Rel., Utah County Council Governments, Mountainland Association Governments president Utah State Association County Commissioners & Councils, 2000 **CIV:** Board directors, Provo/Orem C. of C., **MEM:** Mem.: Utah Association Counties (vice president 2002, president 2003), Utah Association Counties Insurance Mutual (past president), Utah Association Realtors, National Association Realtors (chairman Local Fiscal Affairs Committee 1999) **H:** Golf, tennis **PA:** Republican

HERD, WHITNEY WOLFE, T: CEO **I:** Business Management/Business Services **CN:** Bumble **DOB:** 07/01/1989 **PB:** Salt Lake City **SC:** UT/USA **ED:** BA, Southern Methodist University **C:** Founder, Bumble (2014-Present); Vice President of Marketing, Tinder Inc. (2012-2014) **AW:** Listee, Time 100 Most Influential (2018)

HERNANDEZ, ENRIQUE JR., T: Security System Company Executive **I:** Technology **DOB:** 11/02/1955 **PB:** Los Angeles **SC:** CA/USA **ED:** JD, Harvard University, 1980; AB, Harvard University, Cum Laude, 1977 **C:** Chairman, CEO, Inter-Con Security Systems, Inc., 1984-Present; Co-Founder, Principal Partner,

Interspan Communications; Litigation Attorney, Brobeck, Phleger & Harrison, Los Angeles, CA CR: U.S. National Infrastructure Advisory Committee, 2002-Present; (Board of Directors) Wells Fargo & Co., 2003-Present, Tribune Co. 2001-Present, Nordstrom Inc., 1997-Present, McDonald's Corporation, 1996-Present; Non-Executive Chairman, Nordstrom Inc., 2006-Present CIV: (Committee Member) Harvard University Resources Committee, Harvard College Visiting Committee; Board of Trustees, Los Angeles County Museum of Art; Board of Trustees, University of Notre Dame; Vice Chairman, Board Director, Children's Hospital, Los Angeles, CA; Chairman, Board of Regents, Loyola High School, Los Angeles, CA; President, Board, Los Angeles Police Commission, 1993-1995

HERRERA, CAROLINA, T: Fashion Designer **I:** Textiles **DOB:** 01/08/1939 **PB:** Caracas **PT:** Daughter of Guillermo and Maria Cristina Pacanins; **C:** Founder, head designer, Carolina Herrera Ltd., New York City, 1981-; CH Carolina Herrera lifestyle brand, Carolina Herrera Ltd., 2008; Herrera for Men, Herrera Studio and W by Carolina Herrera lines, Carolina Herrera Ltd., 1992; Jewelry collections, Carolina Herrera Ltd., 1990; Carolina Herrera Collection II sportswear line, Carolina Herrera Ltd., 1989; Fragrance line (currently has 10 fragrances), Carolina Herrera Ltd., 1988; Couture bridal collection, Carolina Herrera Ltd., 1987; Publicist for fashion house of Emilio Pucci, Caracas **CR:** Board directors Mimi So, 2004-, Council Fashion Designers of America, 1999- **AW:** Named to International Best-Dressed List, Vanity Fair magazine, 1971-80; recipient Couture Council award for Artistry of Fashion, 2014, Golden Plate award, Academy Achievement, 2005, Geoffrey Beene Lifetime Achievement award, Council Fashion Designers of America, 2008, Womenswear Designer of Year award, 2004, Spain's Gold Medal for Merit in Fine Arts, King Juan Carlos II, 2002, Special Distinction to Career in World of Design, International Fashion Center New York, 1995, Mary Ann Magnin award, 1994, Presidential medal, Pratt Institute, 1990, Latin America Designer Fashion award, 1987, Style Awards Designer of the Year, 2012

HERRERA BEUTLER, JAIME LYNN, T: U.S. Representative from Washington, Former State Legislator **I:** Government Administration/Government Relations/Government Services **DOB:** 11/03/1978 **PB:** Glendale **ED:** BA in Communications, University Washington, Seattle, 2004; AA, Bellevue Community College, 2003 **C:** Member, US House Transportation & Infrastructure, Washington, 2011-; Member, Committee on Appropriations; Member, Republican Study Committee; Member, US House Small Business Committee, Washington, 2011-; Member, US Congress from 3rd Washington District, Washington, 2011-; Assistant minority fl. leader, Washington House of Reps.,; Member District 18, Washington House of Reps., 2007-10; Senior legis. aide to Rep. Cathy McMorris Rodgers, US House of Representatives, Washington, 2005-07; Intern, Office Political Affairs, The White House, **CIV:** Vol., Ground Zero, 9/11, New York City, 2001 **AW:** Named one of The Politics 40 Under 40, TIME Magazine, 2010 **PA:** Republican

HERRMAN, ERNIE, T: President and CEO of Tjx Companies Inc. **I:** Retail/Sales **C:** CEO, Tjx Companies Inc, 2016-; President, TJX Companies, Inc., 2011-; Group president, TJX Companies, Inc., 2008-11; President Marmaxx Group, TJX Companies, Inc., 2007-08; Senior executive vice president, TJX Companies, Inc., 2007-11; Executive vice president, president, Marmaxx Group, TJX Companies, Inc., 2005-07; Executive vice pres-

ident, COO, Marmaxx Group, TJX Companies, Inc., 2004-05; Executive vice president, merchandising, Marmaxx Group, TJX Companies, Inc., 2001-04; Senior vice president, merchandising, TJX Companies, Inc., 1998-2001; Vice president, general merchandise manager, TJX Companies, Inc., 1996-98; Vice president, senior merchandise manager, TJX Companies, Inc., 1995-96; Buyer, TJX Companies, Inc., Framingham, Massachusetts, 1989 **BA:** TJX Headquarters, 770 Cochituate Road, Framingham, MA, 01701

HERZOG, WERNER, T: Screenwriter, Director **I:** Media & Entertainment **PB:** Munich **SC:** Germany **PT:** Dietrich Herzog; Elizabeth Stipetic **ED:** Grad., Duquesne University, Pittsburgh; Student, University of Munich **CW:** Producer, writer, director (films) Signs of Life, 1968, Even Dwarfs Started Small, 1970, Fata Morgana, 1971, Aguirre, the Wrath of God, 1972, The Enigma of Kaspar Hauser, 1974, Heart of Glass, 1976, Stroszek, 1977, Nosferatu the Vampyre, 1979, Woyzeck, 1979, Fitzcarraldo, 1982, Where the Green Ants Dream, 1984, Cobra Verde, 1987, Scream of Stone, 1991, Lessons of Darkness, 1992, Invincible, 2001, The Wild Blue Yonder, 2005, Rescue Dawn, 2007, producer, writer, director, actor Salt and Fire, 2016; dir.: (films) Bad Lieutenant: Port of Call New Orleans, 2009, My Son My Son What Have Ye Done, 2009, Queen of the Desert, 2015, Salt and Fire, 2016; (documentaries) Into the Inferno, 2016; director, writer (films) My Son, My Son, What Have Ye Done, 2009, Queen of the Desert, 2015, producer, writer, director (documentaries) Land of Silence and Darkness, 1971, The Great Ecstasy of Woodcarver Steiner, 1974, Echoes From a Somber Empir, 1990, Bells from the Deep, 1993, Little Dieter Needs to Fly, 1997, My Best Fiend, 1999, Pilgrimage, 2001, Wheel of Time, 2003, The White Diamond, 2004, Grizzly Man, 2005 (New York Film Critics Cir. award for Best Non-Fiction Film, 2005, Directors' Guild of America award for Outstanding Directorial Achievement in Documentary, 2006), Encounters at the End of the World, 2007, Cave of Forgotten Dreams, 2010 (National Society Film Critics award for Best Non-fiction Film, 2011), Into the Abyss, 2011, (TV films) The Flying Doctors of East Africa, 1969, Handicapped Future, 1971, How Much Wood Would a Woodchuck Chuck, 1976, God's Angry Man, 1980, Huie's Sermon, 1980, The Dark Glow of the Mountains, 1984, Ballad of the Little Soldier, 1984, Wodaabe - Herdsmen of the Sun, 1989, Jag Mandir, 1991, The Transformation of the World Into Music, 1994, Gesualdo: Death for Five Voices, 1995, Wings of Hope, 2000, (exhibitions) Whitney Biennial, Whitney Museum Am. Art, 2012, executive producer, writer, co-dir. (documentaries) Happy People: A Year in the Taiga, 2011; executive prodr.: (documentaries) The Act of Killing, 2012, The Look of Silence, 2014; dir.: Into the Abyss, 2011; director, writer (documentaries) On Death Row, 2012-13, director, producer Lo and Behold, Reveries of the Connected World, 2016, film appearances include Man of Flowers, 1983, Bride of the Orient, 1989, Hard to Be a God, 1990, Tales from the Opera, 1994, What Dreams May Come, 1998, Julien Donkey-Boy, 1999, Incident at Loch Ness, 2004, Mister Lonely, 2007, The Grand, 2007, Jack Reacher, 2012, The Wind Rises (voice), 2013, Home from Home: Chronicle of a Vision, 2013, Penguins of Madagascar (voice), 2014; author: (books) Of Walking In Ice, 1981, Fitzcarraldo: The Original Story, 1983 **AW:** Named one of The 100 Most Influential People in the World, TIME magazine, 2009; recipient Film Society Directing award, San Francisco International Film Festival, 2006

HERZOG, WHITEY, T: Professional Baseball Player (Retired), Coach, Executive **I:** Athletics **DOB:** 11/09/1931 **PB:** New Athens **SC:** IL/USA **C:** Retired, Major League Baseball, 1994; Senior vice president, director player personnel, California Angels, 1991-94; Vice president, St. Louis Cardinals, 1990; Manager, St. Louis Cardinals, 1980-90; Manager, Kansas City Royals, 1975-79; Interim manager, California Angels, 1974; Coach, California Angels, 1974-75; Manager, Texas Rangers, 1973; Director player devel., New York Mets, 1967-72; Coach, New York Mets, 1966; Coach, Kansas City Athletics, 1965; Scout, Kansas City Athletics, 1964; Infielder, outfielder, Detroit Tigers, 1963; Infielder, outfielder, Baltimore Orioles, 1961-62; Infielder, outfielder, Kansas City Athletics, 1958-60; Infielder, outfielder, Washington Senators, 1956-58 **AW:** Named Sporting News Man of Year, 1982, National League Manager of Year, 1982, 85, 87, Am. League Manager of Year, 1976, United Press International Executive of Year, 1981-82; named to National Baseball Hall of Fame, 2009, Kansas City Royals Hall of Fame, St Louis Cardinals Hall of Fame, 2014 **ACH:** Achievements include manager of World Series championship winning St. Louis Cardinals, 1982

HEWSON, MARILLYN ADAMS, T: Lockheed Martin CEO **I:** Aviation **DOB:** 12/27/1953 **PB:** Junction City **ED:** MS in Economics, University Alabama; BBA, University Alabama **C:** President, CEO, Chairman, Lockheed Martin Corp., Bethesda, Maryland, 2013-; President, COO, Lockheed Martin Corp., Bethesda, Maryland, 2012; Executive vice president electronic systems business, Lockheed Martin Corp., Bethesda, Maryland, 2010-12; President Lockheed Martin Systems Integration, Lockheed Martin Corp., Owego, New York, 2008-10; Executive vice president global sustainment, Lockheed Martin Aeronautics Co., Lockheed Martin Corp., Fort Worth, 2007-08; President, general manager Kelly Aviation Center (affiliate), Lockheed Martin Corp., San Antonio, 2006; General manager logistics services, Lockheed Martin Corp., 2006; Senior vice president corporate shared services, Lockheed Martin Corp., 2001-06; Vice president global supply chain management, Lockheed Martin Corp., 2000-01; Corporate vice president internal audit, Lockheed Martin Corp., Bethesda, Maryland, 1998-2000; Director consolidated material systems & business management, Aeronautics Material Management Center, Lockheed Martin Corp., Fort Worth, 1995-98; Director commercial practices, Lockheed Martin Corp., 1995; Various positions, then director operations control, Lockheed Martin Corp., 1993-95; Senior industrial engineer Aeronautical Systems Co.,, Lockheed Martin Corp., Marietta, Georgia, 1983; Economist Bureau Labor Statistics, US Department Labor **CR:** Chair board directors Sandia Corp., 2010-13; board directors Lockheed Martin Corp., 2012-; E.I. DuPont de Nemours & Co., 2007-; Carpenter Technology Corp., 2002-06 **CIV:** Board visitors, University Alabama Culverhouse College Commerce & Business Administration; Board trustees, Association US Army Council Trustees **AW:** Named one of The 100 Most Powerful Women, Forbes magazine, 2013-14; The 50 Most Powerful Women in Business, Fortune magazine, 2010-15; recipient Woman of the Year award, United Service Organizations, 2012 **MEM:** Mem.: Economic Club Washington DC

HEWSON, PAUL (BONO), T: Musician **I:** Media & Entertainment **DOB:** 05/10/1960 **PB:** Dublin **PT:** Son of Brendan Robert and Iris (Rankin) Hewson; **ED:** LLD (hon.), University Penn., 2004; LLD (hon.), University Dublin, Trinity College, 2003 **C:** Co-owner, Clarence Hotel, Dublin, 1992-; Singer, songwriter, U2, 1978 **CR:** Managing director, co-founder Elevation Partners, Menlo Park, California, 2004- **CIV:** Launched, "Red" Campaign, 2006 Founder, spokesman, board director, Debt, Aids, Trade in Africa (DATA)-organization officially opened its offices in 2002, 1999- **CW:** Albums with U2 include Boy, 1980, October, 1981, War, 1983, Under a Blood Red Sky, 1983, The Unforgettable Fire, 1984, Wide Awake in America, 1985, The Joshua Tree, 1987 (Grammy awards for Best Album, Best Performance by a Group), Rattle and Hum, 1988, Achtung Baby, 1991 (Grammy award for Best Rock Group Vocal, 1993), Zooropa, 1993, Pop, 1997, The Best of 1980-1990, 1998, Million Dollar Hotel, 2000, All That You Can't Leave Behind, 2000 (Grammy awards for Album of Year, Best Pop Performance, Best Rock Performance, Best Rock Album, 2001), Hasta la Vista Babe!: Live From Mexico City, 2000, The Best of 1990-2000, 2002, How to Dismantle an Atomic Bomb, 2004 (Grammy awards for Best Rock Album, Album of Year, Best Rock Group Performance, Song of Year for 'Sometimes You Can't Make It on Your Own', Best Rock Song for 'City of Blinding Lights', 2006), No Line on the Horizon, 2009, Songs of Innocence, 2014, Songs of Experience, 2017 films/videos Under a Blood Red Sky: U2 Live at Red Rocks, 1984, U2: Rattle and Hum, 1988, film appearances include In Darkest Hollywood: Cinema & Apartheid, 1993, Entropy, 1999, Across the Universe, 2007, TV appearances Entourage, 2005, Rewind, 2007, Across the Universe, 2007, American Idol, 2007, U2 3D, 2008, Bruno, 2009, From the Sky Down, 2011, Anton Corbijn Inside Out, 2011, B.B. King- The Life of Riley, 2012, The Resurrection of Victor Jara, 2012, Arcade Fire in Here Comes the Night Time, 2013, Muscle Shoals, 2013, 2009; composer: (film scores) They Call it an Accident, 1982, In the Name of The Father, 1993, Golden Eye, 1995, Gangs of New York, 2002 (World Soundtrack award for Best Original Song Written for a Film, 2003), (song for film Mandela: Long Walk to Freedom) Ordinary Love (with U2), 2013 (Golden Globe award for Best Original Song - Motion Picture, 2014), (Broadway plays) Spider-Man: Turn Off the Dark, 2011; writer, producer, actor (films) The Million Dollar Hotel, 2000, featured in documentary Muscle Shoals, 2013; co-author (with U2 & Neil McCormick): U2 by U2, 2006, **AW:** Named Top Touring Artist (with U2), Billboard Music Awards, 2012, MusiCares Person of Year, 2003, Most Powerful Artist in Music, Q magazine, 2002; named an Honorary Knight Commander of the Most Excellent Order of the British Empire, Queen Elizabeth II, 2007; named one of The 100 Agents of Change, Rolling Stone magazine, 2009, 100 Most Influential People, Time Magazine, 2006, Three Persons of Year, 2005, VH1: 100 Sexiest Artists, 2002; named to Rock and Roll Hall of Fame (with U2), 2005, Music Hall of Fame, UK, 2004; recipient Man of Peace prize, Paris, 2008, Philadelphia Liberty medal, 2007, Liberty medal for humanitarian work in Africa, 2007, Board Directors Special Tribute award, Council Fashion Designers Am., 2007, Liberty medal, National Constitution Center, 2007, Chairman's award, National Association for the Advancement of Colored People Image Awards, 2007, Neruda award, Chile, 2006, World's Best-Selling Rock Act, World Music Awards, 2006, Portuguese Order of Liberty, 2005, Ambassador of Conscience award, Amnesty International, 2005, Grammy Award for Best Rock Performance by a Duo or Group (Vertigo), 2005, Grammy Award for Best Long Form Music Video (U2: Zoo TV Live from Sydney), 1995, TED prize, Tech., Entertainment , Design Conference, 2004, Freedom award, National Civil Rights Museum, 2004, Best-Selling Irish Artist (with U2), World Music Awards, 2007, 1998, 1993

HICE, JODY, T: U.S. Representative from Georgia **I:** Government Administration/Government Relations/Government Services **DOB:** 04/22/1960 **PB:** Atlanta **SC:** GA/USA **ED:** Doctor of Ministry, Luther Rice Seminary, Atlanta, GA; MDiv, Southwestern Baptist Theological Seminary, Fort Worth, TX; BA, Asbury College, Wilmore, KY **C:** U.S. Congresswoman, 10th Georgia District (2014-Present); Senior Pastor, The Summit Church, Loganville, GA (2011-2013); Senior Pastor, Bethlehem First Baptist Church, GA (2005-2010); First Vice President, Georgia Baptist Convention (2004-2005); Committee on Armed Services, U.S. Congress; Committee on Natural Resources, U.S. Congress; Committee on Oversight and Government Reform, U.S. Congress; Republican Study Committee, U.S. Congress; Professor of Preaching, Luther Rice Seminary **CR:** Host, "The Jody Hice Show" (Formerly "Let Freedom Ring") **MEM:** National Rifle Association; Georgia Carry; Georgia Gun Owners; Georgia Sports Shooting Association; Gun Owners of America **PA:** Republican

HICKENLOOPER, JOHN WRIGHT, T: Governor of Colorado **I:** Government Administration/Government Relations/Government Services **DOB:** 02/07/1952 **PB:** Narberth, Pennsylvania, February 7, 1952 **ED:** MS in Geology, Wesleyan University, 1980; BA in English, Wesleyan University, 1974 **C:** Governor, State of Colorado, 2011-; Mayor, City and County of Denver, 2003-11; Founder, The Wynkoop Brewing Co., 1988-98; Exploration geologist, Buckhorn Petroleum, Denver, 1981-86 **CIV:** Co-founder, Chinook Fund, Co-founder, CultureHaus, Board directors, Volunteers for Outdoor Colorado, Board directors, Denver Civic Ventures, Board directors, Denver Art Museum, Board directors, Denver Metro Convention and Visitors Bureau, Board directors, Colorado Business Committee for the Arts **AW:** Named one of The Top Pub. Officials of Year, Governing Magazine, 2005, The Top Five Big City Mayors of America, TIME Magazine, 2005 **PA:** Democrat

HICKS, HOPE, T: Former White House Director of Communications **I:** Government Administration/Government Relations/Government Services **PT:** Caye Ann Hicks; Paul Burton Hicks **ED:** B.A., Southern Methodist University **C:** White House Director of Communications, 2017-2018; Press Secretary, Trump Campaign, 2015-2016; Trump Organization, 2014; Public Relations, Hiltzik Strategies, 2012

HIGDON, JENNIFER, T: Composer **I:** Fine Art **CW:** (Opera) Cold Mountain, 2015 **AW:** Grammy for Best Contemporary Classical Composition, 2010, 2018, Pulitzer Prize for Music, 2009

HIGGINS, BRIAN, T: U.S. Representative from New York **I:** Government Administration/Government Relations/Government Services **DOB:** 10/06/1959 **PB:** Buffalo **SC:** NY/USA **PT:** Dan Higgins; Mary Higgins **ED:** MA in Public Policy and Administration, Harvard University John F. Kennedy School of Government (1996); MA in History, Buffalo State College (1985); BS in Political Science, Buffalo State College (1984) **C:** Member, US Congress from the 26th New York District (2013-Present); Member, Committee on Foreign Affairs, Committee on Homeland Security; Member, US Congress from the 27th New York District (2005-2013); Member, District 145, New York State Assembly (1998-2004); Lecturer, History & Economics, Buffalo State College; Member, Buffalo Common Council (1987-1993) **AW:** Forty Under Forty Award, Business First Newspaper; Scholar, Judge John D. Hillary Scholarship Award; Inaugural Western New York Harvard Graduate Fellowship (1995) **PA:** Democrat

HIGGINS, CLAY, T: U.S. Representative from Louisiana **I:** Government Administration/Government Relations/Government Services **DOB:** 08/24/1961 **PB:** New Orleans **SC:** LA/USA **MS:** Married **SPN:** Becca Higgins **ED:** Louisiana State University, 1979-1983, 1989-1990 **C:** Member, U.S. House of Representatives from Louisiana's 3rd District, 2017-; Member, Committee on Homeland Security; Member, Committee on Science, Space, and Technology; Member, Committee on Veteran's Affairs; Sheriff, St. Landry Parish,2008-2016; Reserve Officer, Opelousas Louisiana, 2004-08 **BA:** 1711 Longworth HOB, Washington, DC, 20515

HIGGINSON, STEPHEN ANDREW, T: Federal Judge, Former Federal Prosecutor **I:** Law and Legal Services **DOB:** 04/12/1961 **PB:** Boston **SC:** MA/USA **ED:** JD, Yale University, 1987; Master in Philosophy, Cambridge University, 1984; AB summa cum laude, Harvard University, 1983 **C:** Judge, US Court Appeals (5th Cir.), New Orleans, 2011-; Associate professor law, Loyola University New Orleans College Law, 2004-11; Chief of appeals, US Department Justice, 1995; Assistant US attorney (eastern district) Louisiana, US Department Justice, 1993-2011; Assistant US attorney District Massachusetts, Criminal Division, US Department Justice, Boston, 1989-93; Law clerk to Justice Byron R. White, US Supreme Court, 1988-89; Law clerk to Hon. Patricia M. Wald, US Court Appeals (DC Cir.), 1987-88 **CR:** Deputy director special projects Presidential Rule of Law Initiative US Department State, 1997-98 **AW:** Harvard Scholar, Cambridge University **BA:** John Minor Wisdom U.S. Court of Appeals Building Fifth Circuit, 600 Camp St, New Orleans, LA, 70130

HIGGS, PETER WARE, T: Theoretical Physicist **I:** Sciences **DOB:** 05/29/1929 **PB:** Newcastle **PT:** Son of Thomas Ware and Gertrude Maud Higgs; **ED:** DSc (hon.), University Durham, 2013; DSc (hon.), Heriot-Watt University, 2012; DSc (hon.), University Cambridge, 2012; DSc (hon.), University College London, 2010; DSc (hon.), King's College London, 2009; DSc (hon.), University Swansea, 2008; DSc (hon.), University Glasgow, 2002; DSc (hon.), University Edinburgh, 1998; DSc (hon.), University Bristol, 1997; PhD, Kings College, London, 1954; MSc, Kings College, London, 1951; BSc in Physics, Kings College, London, 1950 **C:** Professor emeritus, University Edinburgh, 1996-; Professor theoretical physics, University Edinburgh, 1980-96; Reader math & physics, University Edinburgh, 1970-80; Lecturer mathematical physics, University Edinburgh, 1960-70; Temporary lecturer mathematics, Univ. College, 1959-60; ICI research fellow, Imperial College, 1957-58; ICI research fellow, University College, 1956-57 **AW:** Co-recipient Nobel Prize in Physics, Royal Swedish Academy Sciences, 2013, Prince of Asturias award for Technical & Scientific Research, 2013, J.J. Sakurai prize for Theoretical Particle Physics, American Physical Society, 2010, Wolf prize in Physics, Wolf Foundation, Israel, 2004, High Energy and Particle Physics Prize, European Physical Society, 1997; named to The Order of the Companions of Honor, 2013; recipient Edinburgh medal, Edinburgh International Sci. Festival, 2013, Nonino prize Man of Our Time prize, 2013, Freedom of the City of Bristol, 2013, Higgs medal, Royal Society of Edinburgh, 2012, Edinburgh award, 2011, Oskar Klein Memorial Lecture & Medal, Stockholm Academy Sciences, 2009, Royal Medal, Royal Society Edinburgh, 2000, Paul Dirac medal, Institute of Physics, 1997, James Scott prize, 1993, Scottish Sci. award, 1990, Rutherford Medal, 1984, Hughes Medal, Royal Society, 1981; fellow, Swansea University, 2008, Royal Society, 1983, Royal Society Edinburgh, 1974 **MEM:** Fellow: Institute of Physics (hon.), Royal Scottish

Society of Arts (hon.); mem.: Saltire Society (hon.) **ACH:** Achievements include discovery of the mechanism that gives masses to all elementary particles in particle physics; first to conduct pioneering work that has led to the insight of mass generation, whenever a local gauge symmetry is realized asymmetrically in the world of sub-atomic particles **H:** Walking, music, swimming **BA:** University of Edinburgh, JCMB Building, Room 4417, Old College, South Bridge,, Edinburgh, EH8 9YL

HILL, FAITH, T: Singer **I:** Media & Entertainment **DOB:** 09/21/1967 **PB:** Jackson **PT:** Daughter of Ted and Edna Perry; **C:** With, Warner Brothers Records, 1993-; Launched fragrance, True, 2010; Launched fragrance, Faith Hill Parfums, 2009 **CIV:** Co-organizer, Nashville Rising benefit concert, 2010 Founder, Faith Hill Family Literacy Project, 1996 **CW:** Singer: (albums) Take Me As I Am, 1993, It Matters To Me, 1995, Faith, 1998, Breathe, 1999 (Billboard Hot 100 Airplay Track of Year, 2000, Am. Music Awards Favorite Country Album, 2001, Top Selling Album, Can. Country Music Association, 2001, Grammy award for Best Country Album, 2001), Cry, 2002 (Best Female Country Vocal Performance Grammy, 2003, Hottest Female Video of Year, Country Music TV Flameworthy Video Music Awards, 2003), Fireflies, 2005, Sunshine & Summertime, 2005, Joy to the World, 2008, Illusion, 2013, The Rest of Our Life, 2017(Compilation Albums) Piece of my Heart, 1996, There You'll Be, 2001, The Hits, 2007, Deep Tracks, 2016 (songs) It's Your Love, 1997 (4 Academy Country Music awards for Song of Year, Single of Year, Video of Year, Vocal Event of Year, 1998), This Kiss, 1998 (Video of Year award, Country Music Association, 1998, Academy Country Music, TNN/Music City News, 1999, Single of Year, Academy Country Music, 1999), Just to Hear You Say You Love Me, 1998 (Vocal Event of Year, Academy Country Music, Music City News, 1999, Music City News Song of Year award, 1999), Breathe, 1998 (Grammy award for Best Country Vocal Performance, 2001), (with Tim McGraw) Let's Make Love, 1998 (Grammy award for Best Country Collaboration with Vocals, 2001), Like We Never Loved at All, 2005 (Grammy award for Best Country Collaboration with Vocals, 2006); performer: (film soundtracks) Practical Magic, 1998, How the Grinch Stole Christmas, 2000, Pearl Harbor, 2001, (TV soundtracks) King of the Hill; actor: (films) The Stepford Wives, 2004(Television) Touched by an Angel, 1997, CMT Crossroads,2011, Dixieland, 2015, The Voice Season 11, 2016, Pickler & Ben,2017 **AW:** Named one of 30 Most Powerful Women in America, Ladies Home Journal, 2001; recipient Best Country Collaboration With Vocals (with Tim McGraw), Grammy awards, 2006, Best CountryVocal Performance, Best Country Album, & Best Country Collaboration with Vocals, 2001, 5 Platinum awards, Can. Recording Industry Association, 2001, Favorite Pop-Rock Female Artist, Am. Music Awards, 2001, Favorite Female Country Artist, 2006, 2001-03, Favorite Female Performer, People's Choice Awards, 2001-03, Female Country Artist of Year, Country Weekly, 2000, Female Vocalist of Year, TNN/CTM Country Weekly Music Awards, 2001, TNN/Music City News, 2000, Female Star of Tomorrow, 1995, #1 Adult Contemporary Artist of Decade, Billboard, 2009, Hot 100 Singles Female Artist of Year, 2000, Top Country Female Artist, 1994, Female Vocalist of Year, Academy Country Music, 2001, 1999, New Female Vocalist of Year, 1993

HILL, FRENCH, T: U.S. Representative from Arkansas **I:** Government Administration/Government Relations/Government Services **DOB:** 12/05/1956 **PB:** Little Rock **SC:** AR/USA **ED:** BS in Economics, Vanderbilt University, 1979 **C:** Member, US House

Financial Services Committee, Washington, 2015-; Member, Republican Study Committee; Mem., US Congress from 2nd Arkansas District, Washington, 2015-; Founder, chairman, CEO, Delta Trust & Banking Corp., Little Rock, 1999-; Executive officer, First Commercial Corp., Little Rock, 1993-98; Special assistant to President, executive secretary Economic Policy Council, The White House, 1991-93; Deputy assistant secretary for corporate finance, US Department Treasury, Washington, 1989-93; Senior economic policy official, US Department Treasury, 1989-93; Director, Mason Best Co., 1984-89; Assistant to Senator John Tower, US Senate Banking, Housing & Urban Affairs Committee, 1982-84 **CR:** Chairman board Access Plans, Inc., 2009- board directors HillAlliance HealthCard, Inc., 2009-, Access Plans USA Inc., 2003-09, Syair Designs LLC, 2000-, Research Solutions LLC, 1999-, Delta Trust & Banking Corp., 1999- **AW:** Named Arkansas Museum Trustee of the Year, 1999; named an Outstanding Young Arkansan, Arkansas Jaycees, 1993; named one of The Most Powerful Men in Business, AY magazine, 2010, The 40 Under 40, Arkansas Business, 1996; recipient The Henry award, State of Arkansas, 2007, Edwin Hanlon award for Contributions to the City's Arts & Humanities, 2002, Distinguished Service award, US Department Treasury, 1993 **PA:** Republican

HIMES, JIM, T: U.S. Representative from Connecticut, former nonprofit organization executive **I:** Government Administration/Government Relations/Government Services **DOB:** 07/05/1966 **PB:** Lima **ED:** LHD (hon.), University Bridgeport, 2012; Master in Philosophy, Oxford University, England, 1990; BA, Harvard College, 1988 **C:** National finance chairman, Democratic Congressional Campaign Committee (DCCC), 2013-; Member, US Congress from 4th Connecticut District, 2009-; Member, Committee on Financial Services, Committee on Intelligence; Vice president, Enterprise Community Partners, Inc. (formerly Enterprise Foundation), 2007-09; Head Northeast operations, Enterprise Community Partners, Inc. (formerly Enterprise Foundation), 2004-07; Joined, Enterprise Community Partners, Inc. (formerly Enterprise Foundation), 2003; Entry level to vice president, Goldman Sachs & Co., Latin America, New York, 1990-2002 **CR:** Chairman Greenwich Democratic Town Committee member Greenwich Board Estimate & Taxation commissioner Greenwich Housing Authority, 2002 **CIV:** Elder, First Presbyterian Church, Greenwich, Board directors, Fairfield County Community Foundation, Adv. board member, Family Assets, Inc., Bridgeport, Former chairman board directors, Aspira of Connecticut, Bridgeport **PA:** Democrat

HIRONO, MAZIE KEIKO, T: U.S. Senator from Hawaii **I:** Government Administration/Government Relations/Government Services **DOB:** 11/03/1947 **PB:** Fukushima **ED:** JD, Georgetown University Law Center, 1978; BA, University Hawaii, 1970 **C:** Member, US Senate Veterans' Affairs Committee, 2013-; Member, US Senate Judiciary Committee, 2013-; Member, US Senate Armed Services Committee, 2013-; US Senator from Hawaii, 2013-; Member, US House Ethics Committee, 2011-13; Member, US Congress from 2nd Hawaiian District, 2007-13; Lieutenant governor, State of Hawaii, 1994-2002; Member District 22, Hawaii House of Reps., 1993-94; Member District 32, Hawaii House of Reps., 1985-93; Member District 20, Hawaii House of Reps., 1983-85; Member District 12, Hawaii House of Reps., Honolulu, 1981-83; Member, Shim, Tam, Kirimitsu & Naito, 1984-88; Deputy attorney general, State of Hawaii, Honolulu, 1978-80 **CR:** Board directors National Asian Pacific American Bar Association chair Hawaii Policy Group,

National Commission on Teaching & America's Future, Governors Task Force on Sci. and Tech. **CIV:** Deputy chair, Dem. National Committee, 1997, Board directors, Blood Bank of Hawaii, Board directors, Moiliili Community Center, Honolulu, 1984-, Board directors, Nuuanu YMCA, Honolulu, 1982-2004 **MEM:** Member U.S. Supreme Court Bar, Hawaii Bar Association, Phi Beta Kappa. **PA:** Democrat

HIRSCH, JUDD, T: Actor **I:** Media & Entertainment **PB:** New York **SC:** NY/USA **PT:** Joseph Sidney Hirsch; Sally (Kitzis) Hirsch **SPN:** Bonni Chalkin, December 24, 1992 (div. 2005); Elisa Sadaune, 1956 (div. 1958) **CH:** Montana; London; Alexander **ED:** BS in Physics, City College of New York, 1960 **C:** Actor 1971- **CW:** Broadway appearances in Barefoot in the Park, 1966, Knock Knock, 1976 (Drama Desk award for Best Featured Actor), Chapter Two, 1977-78, Talley's Folly, 1980, I'm Not Rappaport, 1985-86, (Tony award for Best Actor in a Play, 1986, Outer Critics Circle award, 1986), Conversations with My Father, 1992 (Tony award for Best Actor in a Play, 1992, Outer Critics Circle award, 1992), A Thousand Clowns, 1996, Art, 1998, I'm Not Rappaport, 2002, Sixteen Wounded, 2004; off-Broadway appearances in On the Necessity of Being Polygamous, 1963, Scuba Duba, 1967-69, King of the U.S., 1972, Mystery Play, 1972, Hot L Baltimore, 1973, Prodigal, 1973, Knock Knock, 1975, Talley's Folly, 1979 (Obie award), The Seagull, 1983, I'm Not Rappaport, 1985, Below the Belt, 1996; regional appearances include Theater for Living Arts, Philadelphia, Line of Least Existence, Harry Noon and Night, The Recruiting Officer, 1969-70, Annenberg Center, Philadelphia, Hough in Blazes, 1971, Seattle Repertory, Conversations with My Father, 1991, Scarborough, England, 1994, London, 1995, Chapel Hill, North Carolina, Death of a Salesman, 1994, Long Wharf Theater Robbers, 1995, Manitoba Theatre Center, Winnipeg and Royal Alexandra Theatre, Toronto, Death of A Salesman, 1997, Art, London, 1999, 2001; stock and tours A Thousand Clowns, Threepenny Opera, Fantastiks, Woodstock, New York, 1964, Peterpat, Houston and Fort Worth, 1970, Harvey, Chicago, 1971, And Miss Reardon Drinks a Little, Palm Beach, Florida, 1972, I'm Not Rappaport, national tour, 1986-87, Conversations With My Father, Doolittle Theatre, LA, 1993, Art, national tour, 1999-2000; (TV series) Delvecchio, 1976-77, Rhoda, 1977, Taxi, 1978-83 (Emmy award for Best Actor in a Comedy Series, 1981, 1983), Dear John (Golden Globe award for Best Performance by an Actor in a Television Series - Comedy or Musical, 1989), 1988-92, George and Leo, 1997, Regular Joe, 2003, Numb3rs, 2005-2010, (voice) American Dad!, 2009, Damages, 2011-12, Forever, 2014-15; (TV films) The Law, 1974, Fear on Trial, 1975, The Legend of Valentino, 1975, The Halloween That Almost Wasn't, 1979, Sooner or Later, 1979, Marriage Is Alive and Well, 1980, First Steps, 1985, Brotherly Love, 1985, The Great Escape-Untold Story, 1988, She Said No, 1990, Betrayal of Trust, 1993, Color of Justice, 1997, Rocky Marciano, 1999, Who Killed the Federal Theatre, 2003, Silent Witness, 2011; (films) King of the Gypsies, 1978, Ordinary People, 1980, Without a Trace, 1983, Teachers, 1984, The Goodbye People, 1984, Running on Empty, 1988, Independence Day, 1996, Man On the Moon, 1999, A Beautiful Mind, 2001, Zeyda and the Hitman, 2004, Polish Bar, 2010, Tower Heist, 2011, The Muppets, 2011, Altered Minds, 2013, Independence Day: Resurgence, 2016, Wild Oats, 2016; director Squaring the Circle, 1962, Not Enough Rope, 1973, Talley's Folly, 1981, Art, 2000-01.(Film) The Meyerowtiz Stories, 2017 (Television) The Goldbergs, 2015, The Big Bang Theory, 2016, Family Guy, 2016, Superior Donuts, 2017 **MEM:** Member Academy Motion Picture

Arts and Scis., Academy TV Arts and Scis., Actors Equity Association, Screen Actors Guild, American Federation of TV and Radio Artists, SSDC

HITCHCOCK, KEN, T: Head Coach **I:** Athletics **CN:** Dallas Stars **DOB:** 12/17/1951 **PB:** Edmonton **SC:** AB/Canada **ED:** Student, University of Alberta, Edmonton, AB, Canada **C:** Head Coach, Dallas Stars, 2017-Present; Head Coach, St. Louis Blues, 2011-2017; Head Coach, Columbus Blue Jackets, 2006-2010; Pro Scout, Philadelphia Flyers, 2006; Head Coach, Philadelphia Flyers, 2002-2006; Head Coach, Dallas Stars, 1996-2002; Coach All-Star Games, IHL, 1993-1995; Head Coach, Kalamazoo Wings, 1993-1994; Assistant Coach, Philadelphia Flyers, 1990-1993; Head Coach, Kamloops Blazers, 1984-1990 **CR:** Assistant Coach, Team Canada, Olympic Games, Sochi, Russia, 2014, Assistant Coach, Team Canada, Olympic Games, Vancouver, BC, Canada, 2010, Head Coach, Team Canada, IIHF World Championships, 2008 **AW:** Jack Adams Award, 2012 **ACH:** Achievements include being the head coach of Stanley Cup Champion Dallas Stars, 1999 **BA:** Hockey Canada Father David Bauer Arena, 2424 University Drive NW, Calgary, AB, Canada, -T2N 3Y9

HO, JAMES C., T: Federal Judge **I:** Law and Legal Services **DOB:** 02/27/1973 **PB:** Taipei **SC:** Taiwan **ED:** JD with high honors, University Chicago, 1999; BA in Pub. Policy with honors, Stanford University, California, 1995 **CT:** Bar: DC, Texas, Virginia **C:** Judge,U.S. Court of Appeals for the Fifth Circuit,2018-; Partner, Gibson Dunn and Crutcher, Dallas, 2010-; Solicitor general, State of Texas, 2008-10; Of counsel, Gibson Dunn and Crutcher, Dallas,; Attorney, office legal counsel, The White House, Washington,; Attorney, civil rights division, US Department Justice, Washington,; Chief counsel to John Cornyn, US Senate, Washington,; Law clerk to the Honorable Clarence Thomas, US Supreme Court, Washington,; Law clerk to the Honorable Jerry E. Smith, US Court Appeals 5th Cir.,; Legis. aide to Quentin Kopp, California State Senate, **CR:** Adjunct professor law University Texas Law School **CIV:** Board governors, Dallas Symphony Orchestra, Board directors, Asian Pacific American Bar Association Educational Fund, Board directors, The Tony Patiño Fellowship, Inc., Board directors, Human Rights Initiative North Texas, Inc., Board directors, Dallas Holocaust Museum, **CW:** Contributor articles to professional journals **AW:** Named a Rising Star, Law360, 2011, Texas Super Lawyers, 2008; named one of Minority 40 Under 40, The National Law Journal, 2011, 25 Extraordinary Minorities in Texas Law, Texas Lawyer, 2009, 35 Under 35, The Hill, 2005 **MEM:** Fellow: Dallas Bar Foundation, Texas Bar Foundation, American Bar Foundation; mem.: American Bar Association, Dallas Asian American Bar Association (secretary), National Asian Pacific American Bar Association (co-chmn. judiciary committee, Best Lawyers Under 40 2006, Presidential award 2009), State Bar Texas, American Law Institute, The Federalist Society Law and Pub. Policy Studies **BA:** John Minor Wisdom U.S. Court of Appeals Building Fifth Circuit, 600 Camp St, New Orleans, LA, 70130

HOBSON, MELLODY, T: Investment Company Executive **I:** Financial Services **DOB:** 04/03/1969 **PB:** Chgo. **PT:** Daughter of Dorothy Ashley; **ED:** BA, Princeton University Woodrow Wilson School International Relations, 1991 **C:** President, Ariel Capital Management, Inc., 2000-; Chair, board trustees, Ariel Investment Trust,; Senior vice president, director marketing, Ariel Capital Management, Inc., 1994-2000; Vice president marketing, Ariel Capital Management, Inc., Chicago,

1991-94 **CR:** Spokesperson Ariel/Schwab Black Investor Survey columnist Black Enterprise financial corr. ABC's Good Morning America board directors Groupon, 2011-, Starbucks Corp., 2005-, Dreamworks Animation SKG, Inc., 2004-, The Estée Lauder Companies Inc., 2003- **CIV:** Chair, After School Matters, 2012- Board trustees, Princeton University, Board directors, Field Museum, Board directors, Chicago Pub. Libr., Board directors, Chicago Pub. Education Fund, Board directors, The Sundance Institute, **AW:** Named a Woman to Watch, Fortune magazine, 2008, Global Leader of Tomorrow, World Economic Forum, Switzerland, 2001; named one of The Top 25 Nonbank Women in Fin., US Banker, 2009, 50 Women to Watch, The Wall St. Journal, 2008, The 30 Leaders of the Future, Ebony magazine, The 40 under 40, Crain's Chicago Business, 1999; named to The Power 150, Ebony magazine, 2008; recipient Luminary award, Girl Scouts of Greater Chicago & Northwest Ind., 2010 **MEM:** Mem.: Council Foreign Relations

HOEVEN, JOHN HENRY III, T: U.S. Senator from North Dakota **I:** Government Administration/Government Relations/Government Services **DOB:** 03/13/1957 **PB:** Bismarck, North Dakota, March 13, 1957 **ED:** MBA, Northwestern University Kellogg School Management, 1981; BA in Hist. & Economics, Dartmouth College, Hanover, New Hampshire, 1979 **C:** Chairman, Senate Indian Affairs Committee, 2017-; Member, US Senate Indian Affairs Committee, Washington, 2011-17; Member, US Senate Agricultural, Nutrition & Forestry Committee, Washington, 2011-; Member, US Senate Energy & Natural Resources Committee, Washington, 2011-; Member, US Senate Appropriations Committee, Washington, 2011-; US Senator from North Dakota, Washington, 2011-; Governor, State of North Dakota, Bismarck, 2000-10; President, CEO, Bank of North Dakota (BND), 1993-2000; Executive vice president, First Western Bank, Minot, North Dakota, 1986-93 **CR:** Chair health & human services committee, natural resources committee National Governors Association chair Midwestern Governors Association, Governors' Ethanol Coalition, Interstate Oil & Gas Compact Commission **CIV:** Trustee, Bismarck State College, Chair, Minot Area Devel. Corp., Board directors, Harold Schafer Leadership Center, Board directors, Bismarck YMCA, Board directors, North Dakota Economic Devel. Association, Board directors, North Dakota Small Business Investment Co., Board directors, North Dakota Bankers Association, Board directors, First Western Bank & Trust, **PA:** Republican **BA:** The Office of John Hoeven, 338 Russell Senate Office Building, Washington, DC, 20510

HOFFMAN, DUSTIN, T: Actor **I:** Media & Entertainment **DOB:** 08/08/1937 **PB:** LA **SC:** CA/USA **PT:** Son of Harry and Lillian Hoffman; **ED:** Studied with, Barney Brown, Lonny Chapman & Lee Strasberg.; Student, Pasadena Playhouse; Student, Santa Monica City College **CW:** Stage debut: Sarah Lawrence College production of Yes Is for a Very Young Man; Broadway debut: A Cook for Mr. General, 1961; appeared in Endgame, The Quare Fellow, In The Jungle of Cities, A Country Scandal, The Dumbwaiter, The Room, Waiting for Godot, Picnic on the Battlefield, Dirty Hands, The Cocktail Party, All Theatre Company of Boston, Three Men on a Horse, 1964, Harry, Noon and Night, 1965, The Journey of the Fifth Horse (Obie award 1966), 1966, Fragments, 1966, Eh? (Drama Desk award 1967, Verna Rice award 1967, Theatre World award 1967), 1966, Jimmy Shine, 1968, Death of a Salesman, 1984, The Merchant of Venice, 1989; recorded: Death of a Salesman on Caedmon Records (Drama Desk award 1984); actor: (films) The Tiger Makes Out, 1967, The Graduate, 1967

(BAFTA award for Best Actor 1969, Golden Globe award for Most Promising Newcomer 1968), Madigan's Millions, 1969, Sunday Father, 1969, Midnight Cowboy, 1969 (BAFTA award for Best Actor 1970), John and Mary, 1969 (BAFTA award for Best Actor 1970), Little Big Man, 1970, Who Is Harry Kellerman and Why Is He Saying Those Terrible Things About Me?, 1971, Straw Dogs, 1971, Alfredo, Alfredo, 1972, Papillon, 1973, Lenny, 1974, All the President's Men, 1976, Marathon Man, 1976, Straight Time, 1978, Agatha, 1979, Kramer versus Kramer, 1979 (Academy award for Best Actor, 1979, Golden Globe award for Best Actor 1980), Tootsie, 1982 (Golden Globe award for Best Actor 1983, BAFTA award for Best Actor 1984), Ishtar, 1987, Rain Man, 1988 (Academy award for Best Actor 1989, Golden Globe award for Best Actor 1989), Family Business, 1989, Dick Tracy, 1990, Billy Bathgate, 1991, Hook, 1991, Hero, 1992, Outbreak, 1995, American Buffalo, 1996, Sleepers, 1996, Mad City, 1997, Wag the Dog, 1997, Sphere, 1998, Messenger: The Story of Joan of Arc, 1999, (voice) Tuesday, 2001, Moonlight Mile, 2002, Confidence, 2003, Runaway Jury, 2003, I Heart Huckabees, 2004, Finding Neverland, 2004, Meet the Fockers, 2004, Lemony Snicket's A Series of Unfortunate Events, 2004, (voice) Racing Stripes, 2005, The Lost City, 2005, Perfume: The Story of a Murderer, 2006, Stranger Than Fiction, 2006, Mr. Magorium's Wonder Emporium, 2007, (voice) Kung Fu Panda, 2008, (voice) The Tale of Despereaux, 2008, Last Chance Harvey, 2008, Little Fockers, 2010, (voice) Kung Fu Panda 2, 2011, Chef, 2014, The Boychoir, 2014, The Cobbler, 2014, The Program, 2015, (voice) Kung Fu Panda 3, 2016, The Meyerowitz Stories, 2017(TV films) Roald Dahl's Esio Trot, 2015, (TV mini-series) Medici: Masters of Florence, 2016; actor, executive prodr.: Straight Time, 1978; actor: (TV films) Journey of the Fifth Horse, 1966, The Star Wagon, 1967, (voice) The Point, 1971, Death of a Salesman, 1985 (Emmy award for Best Actor 1986, Golden Globe award for Best Actor, 1986), A Wish for Wings That Work, 1991; TV series: (voice) Liberty's Kids, 2002, Luck, 2011-12; producer, Roald Dahls Esio Trot, 2015, Medici Masters of Florence, 2016 (films) A Walk on the Moon, 1999, The Furies, 1999; executive prodr.: (TV films) The Devil's Arithmetic, 1999; dir.: (films) Quartet, 2012. **AW:** Decorated Officer National Order Arts & Letters, France, 1995, Hon. Commander, 2009; recipient Lifetime Achievement award, Golden Globes, Hollywood Foreign Press, 1997, AFI Lifetime Achievement award, 1999, Chmn.'s award Palm Springs International Film Society, 2009, Kennedy Center Honors, John F. Kennedy Center Performing Arts, Washington, 2012. **MEM:** Fellow: Am. Academy Arts and Sciences

HOFFMAN, REID, T: Social Networking Company Executive, Venture Capitalist **I:** Business Management/Business Services **DOB:** 08/05/1967 **PB:** Stanford **SC:** CT/USA **ED:** Master in Phil., Oxford Univ., London, 1993; BS with Distinction in Symbolic Systems, Stanford Univ., 1990 **C:** Partner, Greylock Partners, Menlo Park, California, 2009-; Co-founder, executive chairman, LinkedIn Corp., Mountain View, California, 2009-; Angel investor, Aufklarung, LLC, 2001-; CEO, LinkedIn Corp., Mountain View, California, 2008-09; Chairman, president products, LinkedIn Corp., Mountain View, California, 2007-08; Founding CEO, LinkedIn Corp., Mountain View, California, 2003-07; Executive vice president, PayPal Inc., 2001-02; Founder, SocialNet,; With division human interface design, Apple Computers, Inc.,; Angel investor, Friendster, Inc.,; Principal investor, Nanosolar, Inc., **CR:** Member advisory board Center for Citizen Media, 2006-, Lulan LLC, 2003-, WeAttract.com, EZCab board directors Startup America Partnership, 2011-,

Grassroots Enterprises, 2007-, Zynga, Inc., 2008-14, Kiva.org, 2006-, Tagged, 2005-, Mozilla Corp., 2005-, Vendio, 2003-, Six Apart, 2003-, Jumpstart Tech., LLC **CIV:** Chair advisory council, Westcoast, 2008- Member provost council, College Eight, University California, San Francisco, 2006- **CW:** Co-author (with Ben Casnocha): The Start-Up of You: Adapt to the Future, Invest in Yourself, and Transform Your Career, 2012; co-author: (with Ben Casnocha & Chris Yeh) The Alliance: Managing Talent in the Networked Age, 2014 **AW:** Named one of The World's Most Powerful People, Forbes magazine, 2013, The Business People of Year, Fortune magazine, 2010, The 50 Who Matter Now, CNNMoney.com Business 2.0, 2006,Honorary Commander of the order of the British Empire, 2017, Academy of Achievement, 2014, Presidential Ambassador for Global Entrepreneurship, 2014 **BA:** Linkedin Corporation, 599 N Mathilda Ave, Sunnyvale, CA, 94085

HOFSTADTER, DOUGLAS RICHARD, T: Professor **I:** Education/Educational Services **CN:** Indiana University **DOB:** 02/15/1945 **PB:** New York **SC:** NY/USA **PT:** Robert Hofstadter, Nancy (Givan) Hofstadter **MS:** Married **SPN:** Carol Ann Brush, 1985 **CH:** Daniel Frederic, Monica Marie **ED:** PhD in Physics, University of Oregon, 1975; MS, University of Oregon, 1972; BS in Mathematics, Stanford University, With Distinction, 1965 **C:** Professor of Cognitive Science, Computer Science, Indiana University, Bloomington, IN, 1988-Present; Walgreen Professor of Cognitive Science, University of Michigan, Ann Arbor, MI, 1984-1988; Associate Professor, Indiana University, 1980-1984; Assistant Professor of Computer Science, Indiana University, Bloomington, IN, 1977-1980 **CR:** Guggenheim Fellow, 1980-1981, Adjunct Professor of Psychology, Philosophy, History, And Philosophy Of Science, Comparative Literature, Director, Center For Research On Concepts And Cognition, Indiana University **CW:** Author, Godel, Escher, Bach: An Eternal Golden Braid, 1979, Metamagical Themas, 1985, Ambigrammi, 1987, Fluid Concepts And Creative Analogies, 1995, Rhapsody On A Theme By Clement Marot, 1996, Le Ton Beau De Marot, 1997; Editor, (With Daniel C. Dennett) The Mind's I, 1981; Columnist, Metamagical Themas In Science in America, 1981-1983, (Books) Eugene Onegin: A Novel Versification, 1991, I Am A Strange Loop, 2007, The Discovery Of Dawn, 2007, That Mad Ache, 2009, Surfaces And Essences: Analogy As The Fuel And Fire Of Thinking, 2013 **AW:** Pulitzer Prize For General Nonfiction, 1980, American Book Award, 1980 **MEM:** Cognitive Science Society, American Association of Artificial Intelligence, American Literature Translators Association **BA:** Center for Research Concepts & Cognition, 510 N Fess Street, Bloomington, IN, USA, 47408-3822

HOGAN, LARRY, T: Governor of Maryland **I:** Government Administration/Government Relations/ Government Services **PB:** Washington, DC **SC:** DC/ USA **PT:** Lawrence Joseph Hogan, Ilona (Modly) Hogan **ED:** BA in Government & Political Science, Florida State University (1978) **C:** Governor, State of Maryland (2015-Present); Founder, President, Chief Executive Officer, The Hogan Companies, MD (1985-Present); Governor-elect, State of Maryland (2014-2015); Cabinet Secretary to Governor Bob Ehrlich, State of Maryland, Annapolis, MD (2003-2007) **CR:** Founder, Chairman, Change Maryland (2011-Present); Delegate to Republican National Convention (1976, 1980, 1984, 1988) **PA:** Republican

HOGAN, TIMOTHY, T: Photographer **I:** Media & Entertainment **PB:** Santa Monica, California **SC:** Santa Monica, California **ED:** Graduate, Syracuse University; **C:** Founder, director of theFINproject.

com, 2012-; Founded Timothy Hogan Photography Inc. 1999; Opened first studio, 2000 **AW:** Awarded in Communication Arts Photography Annual for his Graphics Photo Annual

HOLCOMB, ERIC JOSEPH, T: Governor of Indiana **I:** Government Administration/Government Relations/Government Services **ED:** Grad., Hanover College, 1990 **C:** Governor, State of Indiana, 2017-; Chief of staff to Senator Dan Coats, US Senate, Washington, 2013-; Chairman, Ind. Republican Party, Indianapolis, 2011-13; Deputy chief staff for Governor Mitch Daniels, State of Ind., Indianapolis **CR:** Campaign manager for Governor Mitch Daniels, Ind., 2008, Congressman John N. Hostettler, Mayor Terry Mooney, City of Vincennes, Ind. **MIL:** Served in US Navy **PA:** Republican

HOLDING, GEORGE E.B., T: U.S. Representative from North Carolina **I:** Government Administration/Government Relations/Government Services **DOB:** 04/17/1968 **PB:** Raleigh, North Carolina, April 17, 1968 **ED:** JD, Wake Forest University School Law, 1996; BA in Classical Studies with honors, Wake Forest University, 1991 **C:** Member, US Congress from 2nd North Carolina District, Washington, 2017-; Member, Committee on Ways and Means, Republican Study Committee; Member, US House Judiciary Committee, 2013-; Member, US House Foreign Affairs Committee, 2013-; Member, US Congress from 13th North Carolina District, Washington, 2013-17; US attorney, US Department Justice, 2006-11; First assistant US attorney (eastern district) North Carolina, US Department Justice, 2002-06; Attorney, Maupin Taylor, Raleigh, 2001-02; Legislative counsel to Senator Jesse Helms, US Senate, 1999-2001; Associate, Kilpatrick Stockton LLP, Raleigh, North Carolina, 1997-98; Law clerk to Hon. Terrence Boyle, US District Court (eastern district) North Carolina, 1996-97 **PA:** Republican **BA:** 1110 Longworth House Office Building, Washington, DC, 20515

HOLLAND, CINDY, T: VP of Content Acquisition at Netflix **I:** Business Management/Business Services **ED:** Stanford University **C:** VP, Content Acquisition/Original Series, Netflix, 2002-; VP, Business Development, Kozmo, 1999-2001; Head of Acquisitions, Mutual Film Company, 1998-99; VP, Development, Baltimore/Spring Creek Productions, 1994-98 **AW:** Time 100 Most Influential, 2018

HOLLINGSWORTH, TREY, T: U.S. Representative from Indiana **I:** Government Administration/Government Relations/Government Services **PB:** Clinton **SC:** TN/USA **ED:** Master's in Public Policy, Georgetown University, 2014; BS in Engineering, University of Pennsylvania **C:** U.S. House of Representatives from Indiana's 9th District, 2017-Present; Committee on Financial Services

HOLM, GEORGE L., I: Food & Restaurant Services **ED:** BS, Grand Canyon Univ. **C:** President, CEO, Performance Food Group, Richmond, Virginia, 2008-; President, CEO, Vistar Corp., Centennial, Colorado, 2002-08; CEO, Roma Food Enterprises; Senior management positions, Alliant Foodservice Inc., US Foodservice Inc., Sysco Corp.

HOLMES, JEROME A., T: Federal Judge **I:** Law and Legal Services **DOB:** 11/18/1961 **PB:** Washington **SC:** D.C. **ED:** MPA, John F. Kennedy School Government, Harvard University, 2000; JD, Georgetown University, 1988; BA cum laude, Wake Forest University, 1983 **CT:** Bar: US District Ct (eastern district) Oklahoma 2005, US District Ct (no. district) Oklahoma, US District Ct (we. district) Oklahoma 1999, US Supreme Court 1998, Pennsylvania 1988,

Oklahoma 1997, Washington, DC 1991 **C:** Judge, US Court Appeals (10th cir.), 2006-; Director, Crowe & Dunlevy, PC, Oklahoma City, 2005-06; Assistant US attorney (we. district) Oklahoma, US Department Justice, 1994-2005; Associate, Steptoe & Johnson LLP, 1991-94; Law clerk to Hon. William J. Holloway, US Court Appeals (10th Cir.), 1990-91; Law clerk to Hon. Wayne E. Alley, US District Court (we. district) Oklahoma, 1988-90 **AW:** Recipient Am. Jur award in Consumer Protection, 1988, John McTigue Essay award, 1988 **MEM:** Mem.: Oklahoma Bar Association Board Governors (vice president) **BA:** 1823 Stout St, Denver, CO, 80202

HOLT, LESTER STEVEN, T: News Correspondent **I:** Media & Entertainment **DOB:** 03/08/1959 **PB:** Marin County **SC:** California **ED:** Doctorate (hon.), Pepperdine University, 2012; Degree in government, California State University, Sacramento **C:** Anchor, NBC Nightly News, NBC News, 2015-; Anchor Dateline NBC, NBC News, 2011-; Contributor, weekend anchor NBC Nightly News, NBC News, 2007-; Co-anchor weekend edition Today, NBC News, 2003-; Reporter, corr., NBC News, 2000-; Interim anchor, NBC Nightly News, NBC News, 2015; Anchor evening news, WBBM-TV, Chicago, 1986-2000; Reporter, weekend anchor, KCBS-TV, LA, 1982-83; Reporter, weekend anchor, WCBS-TV, New York City, 1983-86; Reporter, WCBS-TV, New York City, 1981-82 **CR:** Host Dateline on ID, Investigation Discovery Network announcer Westminster Kennel Club Dog Show, USA Network, 2008, 2007, 2006 **CW:** Multiple film and TV series appearances **AW:** Named one of The 100 Most Influential People in the World, TIME Magazine, 2016; recipient Robert F. Kennedy Journalism award, 1990,California Hall of Fame,2015, NABJ Journalist of the Year, 2016

HOOD, LEROY EDWARD, T: Systems Biologist, Genomics, Proteomics Educator **I:** Sciences **DOB:** 10/10/1938 **PB:** Missoula **PT:** Son of Thomas Edward and Myrtle Evylan (Wadsworth) Hood; **ED:** DSc (hon.), Mount Sinai School of Medicine, 2011; DSc (hon.), University Warwick, England, 2009; DSc (hon.), University Edinburgh, Scotland, 2008; DSc (hon.), College of Wooster, Ohio, 2007; PhD (hon.), Ben-Gurion University of the Negev, Israel, 2005; DSc (hon.), Medical College of Wisconsin, Milwaukee, 2005; LHD (hon.), Loyola University, 2005; DSc (hon.), Pennsylvania State University, 2001; DSc (hon.), Bates College, Maine, 1999; DSc (hon.), Whitman College, Walla Walla, 1995; DSc (hon.), Wesleyan University, 1992; LHD (hon.), John Hopkins University, 1990; DSc (hon.), University Southern California, LA, 1989; DSc (hon.), University British Columbia, 1988; DSc (hon.), Mount Sinai School of Medicine, City University of New York, 1987; DSc (hon.), Montana State University, 1986; PhD in Biochemistry, California Institute Tech., 1968; MD, Johns Hopkins University, Baltimore, 1964; BS in Biology, California Institute Tech., 1960 **C:** Affiliate professor, departments of microbiology and immunology, University of British Columbia, 2002-; Co-founder, president, Institute of Systems Biology, Seattle, 1999-; Professor at large, Keck Graduate Institute of Applied Life Sciences, 1999-; Full faculty member, molecular and cellular biology program, University of Washington, 2004-; Affiliate professor, departments of bioengineering, computer science and immunology, University of Washington, 2000-; William Gates III professor biomedical sci., founder & chairman department molecular biotechnology, University of Washington School Medicine, Seattle, 1992-99; Professor, departments of bioengineering and immunology, adjunct professor, departments of medicine and computer science, University of Washington, Seattle, 1992-99; Director, National Science Foundation,

Science and Technology Center for Molecular Biotechnology, University of Washington, Seattle, 1992-2000; Director, National Science Foundation Science and Technology Center for Molecular Biotechnology, California Institute Tech., 1989-92; Director, Cancer Center, California Institute Tech., 1981-90; Chairman division of biology, California Institute Tech., Pasadena, 1980-89; Bowles professor of biology, California Institute Tech., Pasadena, 1977-92; Professor of biology, California Institute Tech., Pasadena, 1975-77; Associate professor biology, California Institute Tech., Pasadena, 1973-75; Assistant professor of biology, California Institute Tech., Pasadena, 1970-73; National Institutes of Health postdoctoral fellow, California Institute of Tech., 1964-67; National Institutes of Health predoctoral fellow, California Institute of Tech., 1963-64; Senior investigator, immunology branch, GL&C, National Cancer Institute, National Institutes of Health, 1967-70; Staff scientist, US Public Health Service, Bethesda, Maryland, 1967-70; Medical officer, US Public Health Service, 1967-70 **CR:** Member College of Fellows American Institute for Medical and Biological Engineering member of several board of directors and scientific adv. boards invited lecturer in field **CW:** Author (with others): Biochemistry, a Problems Approach, 1974, Molecular Biology of Eukaryotic Cells, 1975, Immunology, 1978, Essential Concepts of Immunology, 1978, The Code of Codes: Scientific and Social Issues in the Human Genome Project, 1992; co-editor: Advances in Immunology, 1987, Genetics: From Genes to Genomics, 1999; contributor numerous articles to professional journals; member of several editorial boards **AW:** Named Scientist of Year, R&D Magazine, 1993, California Scientist of the Year, 1985; named one of The 100 Agents of Change, Rolling Stone magazine, 2009, Forbes Magazine's Top 25 Most Influential Biotech Leader, 1999, Science Digest's 100 Top Innovators: Development of Highly Sophisticated Instruments for the Synthesis and Analysis of Genes and Proteins, 1985; named to National Inventors Hall of Fame, 2007; recipient National Medal of Science, 2012, Kistler prize, Foundation for the Future, 2010, Wharton Infosys Business Transformation award, University Pennsylvania, 2006, Heinz award for tech., economy & employment, 2006, Biotechnology Heritage award, Chemical Heritage Foundation and Biotechnology and Industry Organization, 2004, Award for excellence in molecular diagnostics, Association Molecular Pathology, 2003, Lemelson-MIT prize for invention & innovation, 2003, Kyoto prize, Inamori Foundation, Japan, 2002, Innovation in Bioscience award, The Economist, 2002, Association Biomolecular Resource Facilities award, 2000, Steven C. Beering award, Ind. University School of Medicine, 1989, Cetus award for Biotechnology, 1989, Rabbi Shai Shacknai Memorial prize in immunology and cancer research, Hebrew University, 1988, Isco award for significant contributions to the field of biochemical instrumentation, University of Nebraska-Lincoln, 1987, Louis Pasteur award for Medical Innovation, 1987, Dickson prize in medicine for contributions to immunology and molecular biology, 1987, Albert Lasker Basic Medical Research award, 1987, Analytical prize, German Society for Clinical Chemistry award: The Development of Microchemical Facilities for High-Sensitivity Protein Sequencing, 1986, Ellis Island Medal of Honor, 2016, NAS Award for Chemistry in to Society, 2017 **MEM:** Fellow: American Association for the Advancement of Science, American Academy of Microbiology, World Technology Network, American Academy of Microbiology (American Society for Microbiology); mem.: American Medical Association, NAE (Fritz J. and Dolores H. Russ prize 2011), National Academy of Sciences, Association for Laboratory Automation, Association of American Physicians, American Society for Biochemistry and Molecular Biology, American Chemical Society, American Association of Immunologists, Society of Toxocology (hon.), American Association for Clinical Chemistry (hon.), European Molecular Biology Organization, International Society of Molecular Evolution National., Society for Integrative and Comparative Biology, Institute Medicine, American Philosophical Society, American Academy Arts & Sciences, Sigma Xi **ACH:** Achievements include development of the automated DNA sequencer in 1986, the key technology enabling the Human Genome Project; invention of the protein synthesizer, an instrument that assembles long peptides from amino acid subunits; invention of the DNA synthesizer for synthesizing DNA fragments, a key development for gene mapping and the polymerase chain reaction **H:** Photography, running, reading

HOPKINS, ANTHONY, T: Actor **I:** Media & Entertainment **DOB:** 12/31/1937 **PB:** Port Talbot **SC:** South Wales/United Kingdom **PT:** Son of Richard Arthur and Muriel Annie (Yeates) H. Abigail; **SPN:** Jennifer Ann Lynton, January 13, 1973 (div. April 30, 2002); Petronella Barker, September 1967 (div. 1972); **CH:** Abigail **ED:** Fellow (hon.), St. David's College, Lampeter, Wales, 1992; DLitt (hon.), University of Wales, 1988; Student, Royal Academy Dramatic Art, London, 1961-63; Student, Welsh College Music and Drama, Cardiff, Wales, 1954-56 **CIV:** Member, Greenpeace, Patron, Rehabilitation for Addicted Prisoners Trust, **CW:** Actor: (London stage debut) Julius Caesar, 1964; member National Theatre Co., 1966-73; Juno and the Paycock, 1966, A Flea in Her Ear, 1966, Three Sisters, 1967, The Dance of Death, 1967, As You Like It, 1967, The Architect and the Emperor of Assyria, 1971, A Woman Killed with Kindness, 1971, Coriolanus, 1971, The Taming of the Shrew, 1972, Macbeth, 1972, Equus (Best Actor award New York Drama Desk, Best Actor award Outer Critics Circle, Best Actor award), New York City, 1974-75, (LA Drama Critics award), LA, 1977, The Tempest, LA, 1979, Old Times, New York City, 1983, The Lonely Road, London, 1985, Pravda, National Theatre, London, 1985-86 (Olivier award 1985), King Lear, National Theatre, London, 1986-87, Antony & Cleopatra, National Theatre, London, 1987, M Butterfly, Shaftesbury Theatre, London, 1989, (also director) August, 1994, (films) Red, White and Zero, 1967, The Lion in Winter, 1968, Hamlet, 1969, The Looking Glass War, 1969, When Eight Bells Toll, 1971, Young Winston, 1972, A Doll's House, 1973, The Girl from Petrovka, 1974, Juggernaut, 1974, A Bridge Too Far, 1977, Audrey Rose, 1977, International Velvet, 1978, Magic, 1978, The Elephant Man, 1980, A Change of Seasons, 1980, The Bounty, 1984, The Good Father, 1985, 84 Charing Cross Road, 1986, The Dawning, 1988, A Chorus of Disapporoval, 1989, Silence of the Lambs, 1991 (Academy award for Best Actor 1992, Best Actor award Boston Film Critics 1992, Best Actor award New York Film Critics 1992, Best Film Actor award BAFTA 1992), Freejack, 1992, Spotswood/The Efficiency Expert, 1992, Howard's End, 1992, Bram Stoker's Dracula, 1992, Chaplin, 1992, Remains of the Day, 1993 (Best Actor award National Society Film Critics, 1993), Shadowlands, 1993 (Best Actor award National Board Rev. 1993, National Society Film Critics, 1993), The Trial, 1993, The Road to Welville, 1994, Legends of the Fall, 1994, The Innocent, 1993, Nixon, 1995, August, 1996, Surviving Picasso, 1996, The Edge, 1997, Amistad, 1997, The Mask of Zorro, 1998, Meet Joe Black, 1998, Instinct, 1999, Titus, 1999, Mission Impossible II, 2000, How the Grinch Stole Christmas (voice), Hannibal, 2001, Hearts in Atlantis, 2001, The Devil and Daniel Webster, 2001, Bad Company, 2002, Red Dragon, 2002, The Human Stain, 2003, Alexander, 2004, Proof, 2005, The World's Fastest Indian, 2005, All the King's Men, 2006, Fracture, 2007, Beowulf (voice), 2007, The City of Your Final Destination, 2007, The Wolfman, 2010, You Will Meet a Tall Dark Stranger, 2010, The Rite, 2011, Thor, 2011, 360, 2011, Hitchcock, 2012, Red 2, 2013, Thor: The Dark World, 2013, Noah, 2014, Solace, 2014, Kidnapping Freddy Heineken, 2015, Blackway, 2015, Misconduct, 2016, Collide, 2016, Transformers The Last Knight, Thor:Ragnarock, 2017; (TV films) A Heritage and Its History, 1968, Vanya, Hearts and Flowers, Three Sisters, The Peasant's Revolt, Dickens, Danton, The Poet Game, Decision to Burn, War and Peace, Cuculus Canorus, Lloyd George, Q.B. VII, 1971, Find Me, A Childhood Friend, Possessions, All Creatures Great and Small, 1975, The Lindbergh Kidnapping Case, 1976 (Emmy award for Outstanding Lead Actor in a Drama or Comedy Special), Victory at Entebbe, 1976, Dark Victory, Mayflower: The Pilgrim's Adventure, 1979, The Bunker, 1980 (Emmy award for Outstanding Lead Actor in a Limited Series or a Special), Peter and Paul, 1980, Othello, 1981, Little Eyolf, 1981, The Hunchback of Notre Dame, 1982, A Married Man, 1984, The Arch of Triumph, 1984, Hollywood Wives, 1984, Guilty Conscience, 1984, Mussolini and I, 1985, Blunt, 1985, The Tenth Man, 1988, Across the Lake, 1988, Heartland, 1989, Great Expectations, 1989, To Be The Best, 1990, One Man's War, 1991, To be the Best, 1992, Selected Exits, 1993, American Masters, 2007, The Dresser, 2015, Westworld, 2016, King Lear, 2018 (TV Mini-series) War and Peace (Best TV Actor award Society Film and TV Arts), 1972, (TV documentaries) Freedom: A History of Us, 2003, (TV appearances) Department S, 1970, The Man Outside, 1972, Childhood, 1974, Strangers and Brothers, 1984, (TV series) Hannibal, 2012; actor, executive prodr.: (films) Bobby, 2006; actor, director, writer: (films) Slipstream, 2007; composer: (albums) Composer, 2012. **AW:** Decorated Commander of Order of Brit. Empire, 1987, Knights Bachelor, 1993, Commander of Order of Arts & Letters, France, 1996; named one of Top 100 Movie Stars of All Time, Empire (U.K.) Magazine, 1997; recipent Star on Hollywood Walk of Fame, 2003, Cecil B. DeMille award, Hollywood Foreign Press. Association, 2006. **BA:** Creative Artists Agency, 2000 Avenue of the Stars, Los Angeles, CA, 90067

HORNE, MARILYN BERNEICE, T: Mezzo-soprano **I:** Media & Entertainment **DOB:** 01/16/1934 **PB:** Bradford **SC:** PA/USA **PT:** Daughter of Bentz and Berneice Horne; **ED:** LHD (hon.), Kean College, 1977; DLitt (hon.), St. Peter's College; MusD (hon.), Juillard School Music, 1994; MusD (hon.), Brown University, 1984; MusD (hon.), Jersey City State College, 1973; MusD (hon.), Rutgers, The State University of New Jersey 1970; Student, University of Southern California **CR:** Vocal program director Music Academy of the West, Santa Barbara, California, 1995- **CIV:** Founder, Marilyn Horne Foundation, **CW:** Singer: (Operas) (debut) as Hata in The Bartered Bride, 1954, (La Scala debut) Oepidus Rex, 1969, (Metropolitan Opera debut) as Adalgisa in Norma, 1970, (other roles) Rosina in Barber of Seville, Cleonte in The Siege of Corinth, Isabella in L'Italiana in Algieri, Carmen at Metropolitan Opera, 1972-73, Laura in Harvest, Chicago Lyric Opera, Marie in Wozzeck, San Francisco Opera, (appeared in) Phigenie en Tauride, Semiramide, Samson et Dalila at Metropolitan Opera, 1987, The Ghost of Versailles, 1991, Pelléas et Mélisande, 1995, Venice Festival by invitation of Igor Stravinsky, Am. Opera Society, New York City, for several seasons, Vancouver Opera, Philharmonic Hall, New York City, Paris, Dallas, Houston, Covent Garden, London, roles at La Scala, Italy, Rossini Opera Festival, Pesaro, Italy, Metropolitan Opera, 1987, (recital debuts) Madrid, Dresden, East Berlin, 1987; performer: (at inauguration) of U.S. President Clinton, 1993, annual recital at Carnegie Hall, European tour with husband for Department State, 1963; recording artist London, Columbia, Deutsche Grammaphon and RCA records, recs. include soundtrack Carmen Jones(Live Recorded)Corigliano: The Ghosts of Versailles,1992,Rossini: L'italiana in Algeri,1986,Rossini: Semiramide,1990,Verdi: Falstaff,1992,Vivaldi: Orlando furioso,1989(Novels)Marilyn Horne: The Song Continues,2004 Marilyn Horne:My Life,1983 **AW:** Named Musician of Year, Musical Am., 1995; named to Hollywood Bowl Hall of Fame, 2001, Am. Classical Music Hall of Fame, 1999; recipient Opera honor, National Endowment for the Arts, 2009, Opera News award, 2008, Pres.'s Merit award, National Academy of Recording Arts and Sciences, 2001, Commander, French Order Arts and Letters, Kennedy Center honor, 1995, National Arts medal, 1992, Distinguished Daughter of Pennsylvania Silver medal, San Francisco Opera, 1990, Silver medal, Covent Garden Royal Opera House, 1989, George Peabody award, 1989, Fidelio Gold medal, 1988, Gold Merit medal National Society Arts and Letters, 1987, Commendatore al merito della Repubblica Italiana, 1983, Premio d'Oro, Italy, 1982, Handel medallion, 1980, Grammy awards, 1994, 1983, 1981, 1964 **MEM:** Fellow: Am. Academy Arts and Sciences **ACH:** Achievements include having the leading exponent florid vocal style, music of Rossini, Handel, Vivaldi

HORVITZ, HOWARD, T: Biologist, Educator **I:** Education/Educational Services **DOB:** 05/08/1947 **PB:** Chicago **SC:** IL/USA **PT:** Oscar Horvitz, Mary Horvitz **ED:** BS in Mathematics and Economics, Massachusetts Institute of Technology, 1968; MA in Biology, Harvard University, 1972; PhD in Biology, Harvard University, 1974; Honorary MD, University of Rome, 2004 **C:** Founding Member, McGovern Institute for Brain Research, Massachusetts Institute Of Technology, Cambridge, MA, 2001—Present; David H. Koch Professor of Biology, Massachusetts Institute Of Technology, Cambridge, MA, 2000—Present; Professor, Massachusetts Institute Of Technology, Cambridge, MA, 1986—Present; Whitehead Professor of Biology, Massachusetts Institute Of Technology, Cambridge, MA, 1999-2000; Career Development Associate, Professor of Biology, Whitehead Institute, Massachusetts Institute Of Technology, Cambridge, MA, 1982-1985; Associate Professor, Massachusetts Institute Of Technology, Cambridge, MA, 1981—1986; Assistant Professor, Massachusetts Institute Of Technology, Cambridge, MA, 1978—1981; Postdoctorate Fellow, MRC Laboratory Molecular Biology, Cambridge, England; Howard Hughes Medical Institute Investigator **CR:** Medical Advisory Board, Gairdner Foundation, 2007—Present; Consultant, Scientific Advisory Board, Novartis Institute for Biomedical Research, 2003—Present; Consultant, Scientific Advisory Board, Genpath Pharmacies, 2003—Present; Consultant, Scientific Advisory Board, Idun Pharmaceuticals, Inc., 1993—Present; Neurobiologist, Geneticist, Massachusetts General Hospital, Boston, MA, 1989—Present; Investigator, Howard Hughes Medical Institute, 1988—Present; Fellow, Royal Society, 2009; Consultant, Scientific Advisory Board, Axys Pharmacies, Inc., 1998—2002; Chair, Development Biology Review Committee, Swedish Foundation for Strategic Research, 1996; Advisory Board, Umea Center for Molecular Pathogenesis, Sweden, 1993—1996; Scientific Review Committee, Amyotrophic Lateral

Sclerosis (ALS) Association, 1990—1995; Scientific Advisory Board, Jane Coffin Childs Memorial Fund For Medical Research, 1989—1997; Science Advisory Board, Hereditary Disease Foundation, 1987—1993; Co-Organizer, Gordon Conference on Development Biology, 1985; Advisor, Department of Biochemistry And Molecular Biology, Harvard University, 1984—1990; Woodrow Wilson Fellow, 1968; Advisory Board, World Health Organization Special Programme for Research & Training In Tropical Diseases; Advisory Council, National Center for Human Genome Research, National Institutes Of Health; Fellow, American Association for the Advancement of Science; Fellow, American Academy of Microbiology; Fellow, American Academy of Arts & Sciences **CW:** Author, (With Others) The Role Of Intercellular Signals: Navigation, Encounter, Outcome, 1979, Genetic Maps, 1980, Nematodes As Biological Models, 1980, Development Of The Nervous Systems, 1981, Repair And Regeneration Of The Nervous Systems, 1982, The Nematode Caenorhabditis Elegans, 1988; Editorial Board, Journal of Neurogenetics, 1982—1988, Journal of Neuroscience, 1984—1989, Developmental Biology, 1985—1995, Development, 1986—1993, Genes And Development, 1986—1998, Neuron, 1987—1990, Cell, 1987—1999, The New Biologist, 1989—1992, Genetic Analysis: Techniques And Applications, 1990—1995, Current Biological, 1992—1995, Annual Review of Genetics, 1993—1997, Neurobiology Of Disease, 1994—2000, Cancer Research, 1995—2000, Journal of Cell Biology, 1997—2000, Proceedings Of The National Academy Of Sciences, 1997—2001, Trends In Genetics, 1987—Present, Current Opinion In Neurobiology, 1990—Present, Cell Death & Differentiation, 1994—Present, Invertebrate Neuroscience, 1994—Present, Genome Biology, 1999—Present, Journal of Experimental Therapeutics And Oncology, 1995—Present; Contributor, Articles, Professional Journals **AW:** Research Career Development Award, National Institutes Of Health, 1981—1986, Spencer Award In Neurobiology, Columbia University, 1986, Warren Triennial Prize, Massachusetts General Hospital, 1986, U.S. Steel Foundation Award In Molecular Biology, 1988, Method To Extend Research In Time Award, National Institutes Of Health, 1991, V.D. Mattia Award, Roche Institute Molecular Biology, 1993, Hans Sigrist Award, 1994, Charles A. Dana Award For Pioneering Achievements In Health And Education, Institute of Medicine, National Academy Of Sciences, 1995, Ciba-Drew Award For Biomedical Science, 1996, Rosenstiel Award, Brandeis University, 1998, Passano Award For The Advancement of Medical Science, 1998, Alfred P. Sloan Jr. Prize, GM Cancer Research Foundation, 1998, Gairdner Foundation International Award, 1999, Paul Ehrlich & Ludwig Darmstaedter Prize, Germany, 2000, Segerfalk Award, 2000, March Of Dimes Prize In Developmental Biology, 2000, Louisa Gross Horwitz Prize, 2000, Charles-Leopold Mayer Prize, French Academy of Sciences, 2000, Bristol-Myers Squibb Award For Distinguished Achievement In Neuroscience, 2001, Genetics Prize, Peter Gruber Foundation, 2002, American Cancer Society Medal Of Honor, 2002, Wiley Prize In Biomedical Sciences, 2002, Nobel Prize In Physiology/Medicine, 2002, Alfred G. Knudson Award, National Cancer Institute, 2005, Centennial Medal, Harvard University, 2005, Killian Faculty Achievement Award, Massachusetts Institute Of Technology, 2006 **MEM:** National Academy of Sciences, American Philosophical Society, Physiological Society of London, Helminthological Society of Washington, Executive Committee, American Society of Cell Biology, Society of Neuroscience, Society of Nematologists, Society of Developmental Biology, American Association

for Cancer Research, Institute of Medicine, Membership Committee, Genetics Society of America, 1984—1986, Board of Directors, Genetics Society of America, 1990—1996, Vice President, Genetics Society of America, 1994, President, Genetics Society of America, 1995 **ACH:** Achievements include patents in field **BA:** Massachusetts Institute of Technology, Department of Biology, Room 68, 425 77 Massachusetts Avenue, Cambridge, MA, 02139

HOSSEINI, KHALED, T: Writer **I:** Writing and Editing **DOB:** 03/04/1965 **PB:** Kabul **SC:** Afghanistan **ED:** MD, University of California, San Diego, 1993; BS in Biology, Santa Clara University, California, 1988 **C:** Internist, Kaiser Medical Offices, Mountain View, California,; Internist, Cedars-Sinai Hospital, 1996-2004; Residency, Cedars-Sinai Hospital, LA,; Writer, 2003- **CIV:** Goodwill envoy, UN High Commissioner for Refugees, 2006 Provide humanitarian assistance in Afghanistan, The Khaled Hosseini Foundation, **CW:** Author: (novels) The Kite Runner, 2003 (Publishers Weekly bestseller, #1 New York Times bestseller), A Thousand Splendid Suns, 2007 (Publishers Weekly bestseller), And the Mountains Echoed, 2013 **AW:** Named one of the 100 Most Influential People in the World, TIME magazine, 2008; recipient Humanitarian award, UN Refugee Agency,Goodreads Choice Award, 2013, Book Sense Book of the Year, 2008 **BA:** The Khaled Hosseini Foundation, 4848 San Felipe Road, #150-221, San Jose, CA, 95135

HOUSTON, DANIEL J., T: CEO of Principal Financial Group **I:** Financial Services **ED:** Bachelor, Iowa State University,1984 **C:** Chairman, Principal Financial Group inc, 2016-; President/CEO, Principal Life Insurance, 2014-; President of Retirement & Insurance, Principal Financial Group Inc, 2009-14; President, retirement, investor services division, Principal Financial Group, Inc., 2008-; Executive vice president, Principal Fin. Group Inc., 2006-08; Senior vice president, Principal Fin. Group Inc., 2000-06; Vice president, Principal Fin. Group Inc., 1997-2000; Regional vice president, Principal Fin. Group Inc., 1993-97; Regional director, group, pension sales, Principal Fin. Group Inc., 1990-93; Group, pension consultant, Principal Fin. Group Inc., 1988-90; Senior group, pension rep., Principal Fin. Group Inc., 1986-88; Group rep., Dallas group, pension office, Principal Fin. Group Inc., 1984-86 **CR:** Board of Directors Catalyst Health Solutions, 2005- **MEM:** Mem.: Employee Benefits Research Institute **BA:** Principal Financial Group Inc, 711 High St, Des Moines, IA, 50392

HOWARD, JEFFREY R., T: Federal Judge **I:** Law and Legal Services **DOB:** 11/04/1955 **PB:** Claremont **SC:** NH/USA **ED:** JD, Law Center, Georgetown University, 1981; BA, Plymouth State College-University of New Hampshire, 1978 **C:** Chief Judge, U.S. Court Of Appeals For The First Circuit, 2015-Present; Judge, U.S. Court of Appeals, First Circuit, 2002-Present; Private Practice, Jeffrey R. Howard, Esq., 2001-2002; Partner, Choate Hall & Stewart, 1997-2001; Attorney General, State Of New Hampshire, 1993-1997; U.S. Attorney, District Of New Hampshire, Concord, NH, 1989-1992; Deputy Attorney General, State Of New Hampshire, 1988-1989; Office Of New Hampshire Attorney General, 1981-1988 **CR:** Attorney General Advisory Committee, Attorney Generals Thornburg & Barr **AW:** Citizen of the Year, Salisbury, NH, 2000 **BA:** 1 Courthouse Way, Boston, MA, 02210

HOWARD, TERRENCE DASHON DASHON, T: Actor **I:** Media & Entertainment **PB:** Chicago **SC:** IL/USA **PT:** Tyrone Howard Williams; Anita (Hawkins) Williams **ED:** LHD, South Carolina State University, 2012; Attended, Pratt Institute **CW:** Actor: (TV films) The Jacksons: An American Dream, 1992, The O.J. Simpson Story, 1995, Shadow-Ops, 1995, Mama Flora's Family, 1998, King of the World, 2000, Boycott, 2001, Lackawanna Blues, 2005 (National Association for the Advancement of Colored People Image award for Outstanding Actor in a TV Movie, Mini-series or Dramatic Special, 2006), Their Eyes Were Watching God, 2005, Wifey, 2007; (TV series) Tall Hopes, 1993, Sparks, 1996-98, Street Time, 2003, Law & Order: LA, 2010-11, Hawaii Five-0, 2012 (National Association for the Advancement of Colored People Image award for Outstanding Actor in a Drama Series, 2016), Hada Madrina, 2015-, Wayward Pines, 2015-, Empire, 2015, Wayward Pines, 2016, Philip K Dicks Electric Dreams, 2017; (films) Who's the Man?, 1993, Mr. Holland's Opus, 1995, Lotto Land, 1995, Dead Presidents, 1995, Sunset Park, 1996, Johns, 1996, Double Tap, 1997, Butter, 1998, Spark, 1998, The Players Club, 1998, Valerie Flake, 1999, Best Laid Plans, 1999, The Best Man, 1999 (National Association for the Advancement of Colored People Image award for Best Actor, 2000), Big Momma's House, 2000, Investigating Sex, 2001, Angel Eyes, 2001, Glitter, 2001, Hart's War, 2002, Biker Boyz, 2003, Love Chronicles, 2003, Crash, 2004 (Screen Actors Guild award for Outstanding Performance by a Cast in a Motion Picture, 2006, Outstanding Supporting Actor in a Motion Picture, National Association for the Advancement of Colored People Image Awards, 2006), Ray, 2004, Hustle & Flow, 2005, The Salon, 2005, Four Brothers, 2005, Animal, 2005, Get Rich or Die Tryin', 2005 (National Board Review award for Breakthrough Performance Actor, 2005), Idlewild, 2006, The Brave One, 2007, August Rush, 2007, The Hunting Party, 2007, Awake, 2007, Iron Man, 2008, Fighting, 2009, The Princess and the Frog (voice), 2009, Little Murder, 2011, Winnie, 2011, Red Tails, 2012, On the Road, 2012, The Company You Keep, 2012, Movie 43, 2013, Dead Man Down, 2013, House of Bodies, 2013, The Butler, 2013, Prisoners, 2013, The Best Man Holiday, 2013; actor: (films) Lullaby, 2013, Sabotage, 2014, Lullaby, 2013, St. Vincent, 2014, Cardboard Boxer, 2016, Term Life, 2016; actor, executive producer (films) Love Beat the Hell Outta Me, 2000; (actor, executive producer): (films) Pride, 2007; actor, co-exec. producer (films) The Ledge, 2011; actor: (Broadway plays) Cat on a Hot Tin Roof, 2008; (host): (TV series) Independent Lens, 2003-07; singer: (albums) Shine Through It, 2008 **MEM:** Mem.: Phi Beta Sigma (hon.)

HOWE, STEVE, T: Musician, Songwriter **I:** Media & Entertainment **PB:** London **SC:** England **CW:** (Albums) Beginnings, 1975, The Steve Howe Album, 1979, Turbulence, 1991, The Gran Scheme of Things, 1993, Mothballs, 1994, Homebrew, 1996, Masterpiece Guitars with Martin Taylor, 1996, Quantum Guitar, 1998, Portraits of Bob Dylan, 1999, Homebrew 2, 2000, Natural Timbre, 2001, Skyline, 2002, Elements, 2003, Spectrum, 2005, Homebrew 3, 2005, Motif, 2008, Homebrew 4, 2010, Time, 2011, Homebrew 5, Homebrew 6 (Books) The Steve Howe Guitar Collection, Steve Howe with Tony Bacon,1994,Steve Howe Guitar Pieces, Steve Howe tablatures, 1980

HOYER, STENY HAMILTON, T: Chair of the House Agriculture Committee **I:** Government Administration/Government Relations/Government Services **DOB:** 06/14/1939 **PB:** New York City **PT:** Son of Steen T. and Jean Baldwin (Slade) H.; **SPN:** Married Judith Elaine Pickett, June 17, 1961 (deceased February 1997); **CH:** children: Susan, Stefany, Anne. **ED:** LLB, Georgetown University,

1966; BS in Political Sci., University Maryland, 1963 **CT:** Bar: Maryland 1966 **C:** Assistant Minority Leader (minority whip), US Congress from 5th Maryland District, 2011-; Member, US Congress from 5th Maryland District, 1981-; Chairman, US House Democratic Caucus, 1989-95; Majority Leader, US Congress from 5th Maryland District, 2007-11; Assistant Minority Leader (minority whip), US Congress from 5th Maryland District, 2003-07; Deputy Majority Leader (deputy majority whip), US Congress from 5th Maryland District, 1987-89; Private Law Practice, 1981-89; Associate, Hoyer & Fannon, District Heights, Maryland, 1969-81; President, Maryland State Senate, 1975-79; Member, Maryland State Senate, 1966-79; Associate, Haislip & Yewell, Marlow Heights, Maryland, 1966-69; Executive Assistant to Senator Daniel B. Brewster, US Senate, 1962-66 **CIV:** Member Maryland Board Higher Education, 1979-81 Member Baltimore Council Foreign Relations Board Visitors University Maryland School Pub. Affairs **AW:** Named Champion of Pediatric Research, Children's National Medical Center, 1995, Washingtonian of Year, Washington magazine, 1988, State Official of Year, Maryland Municipal League, 1971; named an Outstanding Young man, Maryland Jaycees, 1975; recipient Leadership award, National Org. on Fetal Alcohol Syndrome, 2005, Nathan Davis award for Outstanding Government Service, American Medical Association, 2008, Freedom award, National Association Secretaries of State, 2003, Excellence in Immunization award, National Partnership for Immunization, 2001, Jack Niles Medal of Honor, Pub. Employees Roundtable, 1999, Pub. Service award, Am. Association Pub. Health Dentistry, 1997, Excellence in Pub. Service award, Am. Academy Pediatrics, 1991 **MEM:** Member University Maryland Alumni Association (trustee), Phi Sigma Alpha, Omicron Delta Kappa, Delta Theta Phi, Sigma Chi. **PA:** Democrat **BA:** Office of Steny Hoyer, 1705 Longworth House Office Building, Washington, DC, 20515

HUDSON, JENNIFER, T: singer, actress **I:** Media & Entertainment **DOB:** 09/12/1981 **PB:** Chicago **SC:** IL/USA **PT:** Daughter of Samuel Simpson and Darnell Donnerson; **CR:** Spokesperson Weight Watchers, 2010- **CW:** (appeared as contestant): American Idol, 2004; actress: (films) Dreamgirls, 2006 (National Board Review award for Best Female Breakthrough Performance, 2006, New York Film Critics Cir., African American Film Critics Association awards for Best Supporting Actress, 2006, BAFTA award for Best Actress in a Supporting Role, 2007, Golden Globe award for Best Performance by an Actress in a Supporting Role in a Motion Picture, 2007, Critics' Choice award for Best Supporting Actress, Broadcast Film Critics Association, 2007, Screen Actors Guild award for Outstanding Performance by a Female Actor in a Supporting Role, 2007, Academy award for Best Supporting Actress, 2007, National Association for the Advancement of Colored People Image award for Outstanding Supporting Actress in a Motion Picture, 2007, BET award for Best Actress, 2007), Sex and the City: The Movie, 2008, The Secret Life of Bees, 2008, Fragments, 2009, The Three Stooges, 2012, The Inevitable Defeat of Mister and Pete, 2013, Black Nativity, 2013, Lullaby, 2014, Chi-Raq, 2015, Sing, 2016, Sandy Wexler, 2017; (TV series) Smash, 2013; (TV films) Call Me Crazy: A Five Film, 2013, Confirmation, 2016,Inside Amy Schumer, 2016, Hairspray, 2016, Ant and Decs Saturday Night Takeaway, 2017, The Voice, 2017; (Broadway plays) The Color Purple, 2015; singer: (albums) Jennifer Hudson, 2008 (National Association for the Advancement of Colored People Image award for Outstanding Album, 2009, Grammy award for Best R&B Album, 2009), I Remember Me, 2011,

JHUD, 2014, (songs) (with Fantasia Barrino) I'm His Only Woman, 2008 (National Association for the Advancement of Colored People Image award for Outstanding Collaboration, 2009); performed Star-Spangled Banner Super Bowl XLIII, 2009; author: (memoir) I Got This: How I Changed My Ways and Lost What Weighed Me Down, 2012 **AW:** Named Outstanding New Artist, National Association for the Advancement of Colored People Image Awards, 2009, Best New Artist, Black Entertainment TV (BET) Awards, 2007; named one of The 10 Actors to Watch, Variety, 2006; recipient Humanitarian award, People's Choice Awards, 2014, Sammy Davis Junior award for Entertainer of Year, Soul Train Awards, 2007, ShoWest Female Star of Tomorrow award, National Association Theatre Owners, 2006 **BA:** Creative Artists Agency, 2000 Avenue of the Stars, Los Angeles, CA, 90067

HUDSON, RICHARD LANE JR., T: U.S. Representative from North Carolina, former legislative staff member **I:** Government Administration/Government Relations/Government Services **DOB:** 11/04/1971 **PB:** Franklin **ED:** BA, University North Carolina, Charlotte, 1996 **C:** Member, US House Homeland Security Committee, 2013-; Member, Republican Study Committee; Member, US House Education & the Workforce Committee, 2013-; Member, US House Agricultural Committee, 2013-; Member, US Congress from 8th North Carolina District, Washington, 2013-; Founder, Cabarrus Marketing Group, Concord, 2011-12; Campaign manager, Pat McCrory for Governor, North Carolina, 2008; Chief of staff to Rep. Mike Conaway, US House of Representatives, Washington, 2009-11; Chief of staff to Rep. John R. Carter, US House of Representatives, Washington, 2006-08; Chief of staff to Rep. Virginia Foxx, US House of Representatives, Washington, 2005-06; District director to Rep. Robin Hayes, US House of Representatives, Washington, 2000-05; Communications director, North Carolina Republican Party, 1997-99; Customer service, Carolina Power & Light Co., 1997; Deputy campaign manager, Steve Arnold for Lieutenant Governor, North Carolina, 1996; Field director, Richard A. Vinroot for Governor, North Carolina, 1996 **CIV:** Chapt. secretary, Jaycees, 2000-04 Bd trustees, Rowan-Cabarrus Community College, 2001-05 Member, Order of Omega, Member, Omicron Delta Kappa, Member, Phi Eta Sigma, Board governors, University North Carolina Charlotte Alumni Association, 1999-2002 **AW:** Named Man of Year, North Carolina Federation of Young Reps., 1999 **MEM:** Mem.: F.A.A.M., Magnolia Lodge No. 53, North Carolina State Society Washington, Texas State Society Washington, RAMS, House Chief of Staff Associate, Republican Club Capitol Hill, Kappa Alpha Order (president University North Carolina Charlotte Alumni chapt. 1998-) **H:** Hunting **PA:** Republican

HUFFMAN, JARED WILLIAM, T: U.S. Representative from California **I:** Government Administration/Government Relations/Government Services **DOB:** 02/18/1964 **PB:** Independence, Missouri **PT:** Son of William Ward and Phyllis Jean Huffman; **SPN:** Married Susan E. Musgrove, May 13, 1995; **CH:** 2 children **ED:** JD Cum Laude, Boston College, 1990; BA in Political Sci. magna cum laude, University California, Santa Barbara, 1986 **CT:** Bar: California 1990, US District Court (Northern District) California 1990 **C:** Member, US House Natural Resources Committee, 2013-; Member, US House Budget Committee, 2013-; Member, US Congress from 2nd California District, Washington, 2013-; Member District 6, California State Assembly, 2006-12; Senior Attorney, Natural Resources Defense Council,; Partner, The Legal Solutions Group LLP, San Rafael, California,; Partner, Boyd

Huffman Williams & Urla, San Francisco, 1992-96; Associate, McCatchen Doyle Brown & Enersen, San Francisco, 1990-92 **CR:** Commissioner Marin County Adult Criminal Justice Commission, San Rafael, 1996- Board of Directors Marin Municipal Water District, Corte Madera, California **CW:** Contributing Editor Legal Practice Guide, 1995-96 **AW:** Recipient Millenium Leadership Award, Marin Ind. Journal and Marin Community Foundation, 2000 **MEM:** Member Rotary Club San Rafael **H:** Volleyball, golf, basketball, fishing, tennis, winemaking **PA:** Democrat **BA:** 1406 Longworth House Office Building, Washington, DC, 20515

HUFFMAN, STEVE, T: CEO **I:** Technology **CN:** Reddit **C:** CEO, Reddit, 2015-; Owner/Founder, Reddit,2005-06

HUIZENGA, BILL, T: U.S. Representative from Michigan **I:** Government Administration/Government Relations/Government Services **DOB:** 01/31/1969 **PB:** Zeeland, Michigan **ED:** BA, Calvin College, 1991 **C:** Member, US House Financial Services Committee, Washington, 2011-; Member, Republican Study Committee; Member, US Congress from 2nd Michigan District, Washington, 2011-; Co-owner, Huizenga Gravel Co., Jenison, Michigan,; Member District 90, Michigan House of Reps., Michigan, 2003-09; Co-chmn., Ottawa County Republican Party, 2001; Director pub policy to US Representative Pete Hoekstra, US House of Representatives, 1996-2002; Board director, Vanderbilt Pub. School Academy, 1998-2001; Board director, Holland Board Realtors, 1995-96 **AW:** Named Advisor of Year, W. Michigan chapter Alzheimers Association, 2000 **MEM:** Mem.: National Federation Independent Business **PA:** Republican

HULL, BOBBY, T: Professional Hockey Player (Retired) **I:** Athletics **DOB:** 01/03/1939 **PB:** Point Anne **SC:** Ont./Canada **PT:** Son of Robert Edward and Lena (Cook) Hull; **C:** Ambassador, Chicago Blackhawks, 2007-; Left wing, Hartford Whalers, 1979-80; Left wing, Winnipeg Jets, 1972-79; Left wing, Chicago Blackhawks, 1957-72 **CR:** Lecturer throughout U.S. and Canada commissioner World Hockey Association, 2003-04 commentator, Hockey Night in Canada president Bobby Hull Enterprises member, Team Canada, Canada Cup, 1976 **CW:** Author: Hockey is My Game, 1967 **AW:** Named Officer of the Order of Canada, 1978, Most Valuable Player, World Hockey Association, 1973; named to NHL Second All-Star Team, 1971, 1963, NHL First All-Star Team, 1972, 1964-70, 1962, 1960, Can. Sports Hall of Fame; recipient City of Hope Award, 1965, Lester Patrick Trophy, NHL, 1969, Lady Byng Memorial Trophy, 1965, Hart Memorial Trophy, 1966, 1965, Art Ross Trophy, 1966, 1962, 1960,Hockey Hall of Fame, 1983, Hockey News List of 100 Greatest Hockey Players, 1998, Honoured Member of the Manitoba Hockey Hall of Fame, Member of the Manitoba Sports Hall of Fame, Inaugural member of the World Hockey Association Hall of Fame, Honored Member of the Ontario Sports Hall of Fame **ACH:** Achievements include being a member of Stanely Cup Champion Chicago Blackhawks, 1961; being inducted into the Hockey Hall of Fame, 1983; having his number, 9, retired by Chicago Blackhawks and Winnipeg Jets

HULTGREN, RANDY, T: U.S. Representative from Illinois **I:** Government Administration/Government Relations/Government Services **DOB:** 03/01/1966 **PB:** Park Ridge, Illinois **ED:** JD, Chicago Kent College Law, 1993; Grad., Bethel College, 1988 **C:** Member, US House Transportation & Infrastructure Committee, 2011-; Member, Committee on Science, Space and Technology; Member, US House Agricultural Committee, 2011-; Member, US

Congress from 14th Illinois District, Washington, 2011-; Member District 48, Illinois State Senate, 2007-10; Member District 95, Illinois House of Reps., 2003-07; Member District 40, Illinois House of Reps., 1999-2002; Board member, DuPage County, 1995-99 **PA:** Republican

HUNT, HELEN, T: Actress **I:** Media & Entertainment **DOB:** 06/15/1963 **PB:** LA **SC:** CA/USA **PT:** Gordon Hunt; Jane Hunt **MS:** Divorced **SPN:** Matthew Carnahan (Partner); Hank Azaria (7/17/1999, Divorced 12/18/2000) **CH:** Makena' Lei Gordon Carnahan **ED:** Coursework, University of California, Los Angeles **C:** Co-owner Production Company, Hunt/Tavel Productions **CW:** TV Appearances, "Amy Prentiss" (1974), "The Swiss Family Robinson" (1975-1976), "The Fitzpatricks" (1977), "The Bionic Women" (1978), "Weekend, Mary Tyler Moore Show" (1977), "Family" (1976, 1980), "Facts of Life" (1980), "Knots Landing" (1980, 1981), "Darkroom" (1981), "Gimmie a Break!" (1982), "It Takes Two" (1982), "Highway to Heaven" (1985), "St. Elsewhere" (1984-1986), "The Hitchiker" (1987), "China Beach" (1990), "The Trials of Rosie O'Neill" (1990), "My Life and Times" (1991), "Friends" (1995); TV Films, "Pioneer Woman" (1973), "All Together Now" (1975), "Death Scream" (1975, "Having Babies" (1976), "The Spell" (1977), "Transplant" (1979), "Angel Dusted" (1981), "I Think I'm Having a Baby" (1981), "The Best Little Girl in the World" (1981), "The Miracle of Cathy Miller" (1981), "Child Bride of Short Creek" (1981), "Desperate Lives" (1982), "Quarterback Princess" (1983), "Bill: On His Own" (1983), "Choices of the Heart" (1983), "Sweet Revenge" (1984), "Shooter" (1988), "American Playhouse: Land of Little Rain" (1989), "Incident at Dark River" (1989), "Into the Badlands" (1991), "Murder in New Hampshire: The Pamela Wojas Smart Story" (1991), "In the Company of Darkness" (1993), "Twelfth Night, or What You Will" (1998), "Empire Falls" (2005), "Shots Fired" (2017); TV Series, "Mad About You" (1992-1999), Producer, Three Episodes, "Mad About You"; Director, Five Episodes, "Mad About You"; "Rollercoaster" (1977), "Girls Just Want To Have Fun" (1985), "Waiting to Act" (1985), "Trancers" (1985); "Empire" (1985); "Peggy Sue Got Married" (1986), "Project X" (1987), "Stealing Home" (1988), "Miles From Home" (1988), "The Frog Prince" (1988), "Next of Kin" (1989), "Trancers II" (1991); "The Waterdance" (1992), "Only You" (1992), "Bob Roberts" (1992), "Mr. Saturday Night" (1992), "Trancers III (1992), "Sexual Healing" (1993), "Kiss of Death" (1995), "Twister" (1996), "As Good As It Gets" (1997), "Ride It Out" "Dr. T and the Women" (2000), Pay It Forward" (2000), Cast Away (2000), "What Women Want" (20007), "Curse of the Jade Scorpion" (2001), "A Good Women" (2004), "Bobby" (2006), "Soul Surfer" (2011), Voice Actor, "Jock the Hero Dog" (2011), "The Sessions" (2012), "The Surrogate" (2012), "Decoding Annie Parker" (2013); Actress, Director, Producer, Writer, Films, "Then She Found Me" (2007), "Ride" (2014), "I Love You, Daddy" (2017), "The Miracle Season" (2018); Plays, "Life (X)3" (2003); Voice Actor, "Galtar and the Golden Lance" (1985); Voice Actor, "The Nativity" (1986); Voice Actor, "The Easter Story" (1989), Voice Actor, "Captain Planet and the Planeteers" (1990), Voice Actor, "The Simpsons" (1998) **AW:** Named One of 50 Most Beautiful People, People Magazine (1998); Best Actress, Musical or Comedy, "Mad About You," Golden Globe Awards (1994, 1995); Best Leading Actress in a Comedy Series, "Mad About You," Emmy Award (1996) **BA:** Creative Artists Agency, 2000 Avenue of the Stars, Los Angeles, CA, 90067

HUNTER, DUNCAN DUANE, T: U.S. Representative from California, military officer **I:** Gov-

ernment Administration/Government Relations/Government Services **DOB:** 12/07/1976 **PB:** San Diego **PT:** Son of Duncan Lee and Lynne (Layh) Hunter; **ED:** Grad., US Marine Corps Officer Candidate School, 2002; BBA, San Diego State University, 2001 **C:** Member, US Congress from 50th California District, 2013-; Member, Committee on Foreign Affairs, Committee on Science, Space and Technology; Member, US Congress from 52nd California District, Washington, 2009-13; Active duty, US Marine Corps Reserve, Afghanistan, 2007; Promoted to captain, US Marine Corps Reserve, 2006; Lieutenant Battery A, 1st Battalion, 11th Marines, US Marine Corps Reserve, Fallujah, Iraq, 2004; Lieutenant 1st Marine Division, US Marine Corps Reserve, Iraq, 2003; Lieutenant, US Marine Corps Reserve, 2002; Former business analyst, San Diego, **PA:** Republican

HUNTER, HOLLY, T: Actress **I:** Media & Entertainment **DOB:** 03/20/1958 **PB:** Conyers **SC:** GA/USA **ED:** BFA, Carnegie-Mellon University (1980) **CIV:** Board of Directors, California Abortion Rights Action League **CW:** Actress, Films, "The Burning" (1981), "Swing Shift" (1984), "Broadcast News" (1987), "Raising Arizona" (1987), "End of the Line" (1988), "Always" (1989), "Miss Firecracker" (1989), "Animal Behavior" (1989), "Once Around" (1991), "The Piano" (1993), "The Firm" (1993), "Home for the Holidays" (1995), "Copycat" (1995), "Crash" (1996), "A Life Less Ordinary" (1997), "Living Out Loud" (1998), "Jesus' Son" (1999), "Things You Can Tell Just By Looking at Her" (2000), "Woman Wanted" (2000), "Timecode" (2000), "O Brother, Where Art Thou" (2000), "Moonlight Mile" (2002), "Levity" (2003), "Little Black Book" (2004), Voice Actor, "The Incredibles" (2004), "Nine Lives" (2005), "The Big White" (2005), "Jackie" (2012), "Portraits in Dramatic Time" (2011), "Won't Back Down" (2012), "Paradise" (2013), "Manglehorn" (2014), "Batman v Superman: Dawn of Justice" (2016), "Weightless" (2016), "Strange Weather" (2016), "Breakable You" (2016), "The Big Sick" (2017), "Song to Song" (2017), Voice Actor, "Incredibles 2" (2018); Actor, TV Films, "Svengali" (1983), "An Uncommon Love" (1983), "With Intent to Kill" (1984), "A Gathering of Old Men" (1987), "Roe versus Wade" (1989), "Crazy in Love" (1992), "The Positively True Adventures of the Alleged Texas Cheerleader-Murdering Mom" (1993), "Harlan County War" (2000), "When Billie Beat Bobby" (2001); Actor, TV Mini-series, "Top of the Lake" (2015), "Bonnie and Clyde" (2013), "Here and Now" (2018); Actor, Broadway Stage Productions, "Crimes of the Heart" (1982), "The Wake of Jamey Foster" (1982), "Impossible Marriage" (1998); Actor, Regional Stage Productions, "Buried Child," "A Doll's House," "Artichoke"; Actor, Other Stage Productions, "A Lie of the Mind," "LA," "Battery, New York City," "Miss Firecracker Contest" (1984), "The Person I Once Was," New York City, NY; Actress, Executive Producer, Films, "Thirteen" (2003); Actor, TV Series, "Saving Grace" (2007-2010) **AW:** Named One of the Top 25 Entertainers of the Year, Entertainment Weekly (2007); Star, Hollywood Walk of Fame (2008); Lucy Award, Women in Film (2009); Golden Globe Award for Best Actress (1994); Academy Award for Best Actress (1994); Emmy Award for Best Actress in a Miniseries or Special (1989); Emmy Award for Best Actress in a Miniseries or Special (1993); CableACE Award for Best Actress in a Movie or Miniseries (1994) **BA:** Eric Kranzler Management, 360 9111 Wilshire Blvd, Beverly Hills, CA, 90210

HUPPERT, ISABELLE ANN, T: Actress **I:** Media & Entertainment **DOB:** 03/16/1953 **PB:** Paris **SC:** France **PT:** Raymond Huppert; Annick Beau **MS:** Married **SPN:** Ronald Chammah (1982)

CH: Lolita; Lorenzo; Angelo ED: Educated, Lycee de Saint-Cloud, Ecole national des langues orientales vivantes CW: Actress: (films) Faustine et le bel Été, 1972, The Bar at the Crossing, 1972, César and Rosalie, 1972, Successive Slidings of Pleasure, 1974, Going Places, 1974, Serious as Pleasure, 1975, The Common Man, 1975, Rosebud, 1975, The Big Delirium, 1975, The Judge and the Assassin, 1976, The Lacemaker, 1977, Return to the Beloved, 1979, Loulou, 1980, Coup de torchon, 1981, Godard's Passion, 1982, Entre Nous, 1983, My Best Friend's Girl, 1983, Story of Women, 1988, Seobe, 1989, Malina, 1991, Amateur, 1994, La séparation, 1994, The Swindle, 1997, The School of Flesh, 1998, Keep It Quiet, 1999, La fausse suivante, 2000, 8 Women, 2002, Ghost River, 2002, Me and My Sister, 2004, Gabrielee, 2005, Private Property, 2006, Hidden Love, 2007, Home, 2008, The Sea Wall, 2008, Villa Amalia, 2009, Copacabana, 2010, My Little Princess, 2011, My Worst Nightmare, 2011, Captive, 2012, Amour, 2012, In Another Country, 2012, Lines of Wellington, 2012, Dormant Beauty, 2012, Dead Man Down, 2013, The Nun, 2013, Michael H- Profession: Director 2013, Tip Top, 2013, Abuse of Weakness, 2013, The Disappearance of Elanor Rigby, 2013, Paris Follies, 2014, Dior and I, 2014, Louder Than Bombs, 2015, Valley of Love, 2015, Macadam Stories, 2015, Things to Come, 2016, Elle, 2016,(Golden Globe for Best Picture 2017) Tout de Suite Maintenant, 2016, Closes Encounters with Vilmos Zsigmond, 2016, Souvenir, 2016, Souvenir, 2016, What Tears Us Apart, 2016, Barrage, 2017, Happy End, 2017, Claire's Camera, Madame, Hyde, 2017, Reinventing Marvin, 2017, Eva, 2018, The Widow, 2018, Une Jeunesse Doree, 2018, many others; (TV films) Le prussien, 1971, Le drakkar, 1973, Madame Baptiste, 1974, No Trifling with Love, 1977, Gulliver's Travels (voice), 1996, Medee, 2001, Isabelle Huppert, Une Vie Pour Jouer, 2001, Law & Order: Special Victims Unit, 2010, False Confessions, 2016, I Love Isabelle Huppert, 2017, The Romanoffs, 2018 AW: Recipient Prix Susanne Blachetti, 1976, Prix Bistingo, 1976, Prix César, 1978, Gold Palm, Cannes, 1978, Prix d'interpretation, Cannes, 1978, chevalier Légion d'honneur, 1999, officier, 2009.

HURD, MARK VINCENT, T: CEO **I:** Technology **CN:** Oracle **DOB:** 01/01/1957 **PB:** New York City **SC:** NY/USA **ED:** BBA, Baylor University, Waco, Texas (1979) **C:** Co-Chief Executive Officer, Oracle Corp., Redwood City, CA (2014-Present); President, Oracle Corp., Redwood City, CA (2010-2014); Chairman, President, Chief Executive Officer, Hewlett-Packard Co., Palo Alto, CA (2006-2010); President, Chief Executive Officer, Hewlett-Packard Co., Palo Alto, CA (2005-2006); President, Chief Executive Officer, NCR Corp., Dayton, Ohio (2003-2005); President, Chief Operating Officer, NCR Corp., Dayton, Ohio (2002-2003); Co-president, NCR Corp., Dayton, Ohio (2001-2002); Executive Vice President, NCR Corp. (2000-2001); Chief Operating Officer, Teradata, Division of NCR Corp. (2000-2002); Senior Vice President, Teradata Solutions Group, Division of NCR Corp. (1998-2000); With, NCR Corp. (1980-2005) **CR:** Board of Directors, Oracle Corp. (2010-Present); Board of Directors, News Corp. (2008-2010); Board of Directors, Hewlett-Packard Co. (2005-2010) **CIV:** Board of Trustees, Dayton Area Chapter, American Red Cross; Board of Visitors, Fuqua School Business Duke University **CW:** Co-author, "The Value Factor: How Global Leaders Use Information" (2004) **AW:** Named One of the 25 Most Powerful People in Business, Fortune Magazine (2007); Named One of the 50 Who Matter Now, CNNMoney.com Business 2.0 (2006, 2007) **H:** Tennis **BA:** Oracle Corporation, 500 Oracle Parkway, Redwood Shores, CA, 94065

HURD, WILL, T: U.S. Representative from Texas **I:** Government Administration/Government Relations/Government Services **DOB:** 08/19/1977 **PB:** San Antonio **SC:** TX/USA **PT:** Son of Mary Alice and Robert Hurd. **ED:** BS in Computer Sci., Texas Agricultural and Mechanical University, 2000 **C:** Member, US Congress from 23rd Texas District, Washington, DC 2015-; Member, Committee of Homeland Security, House Permanent Select Committee on Intelligence; Senior adv., FusionX, LLC, San Antonio, 2009-14; Partner, Crumpton Group, 2009-13; Case officer, CIA, 2000-09 **CR:** Board member World Affairs Council San Antonio, 2014- **PA:** Republican

HURDLE, CLINT, T: Professional Baseball Manager **I:** Athletics **DOB:** 07/30/1957 **PB:** Big Rapids, Michigan, July 30, 1957 **C:** Manager, Pittsburgh Pirates, 2010-; Batting coach, Texas Rangers, 2009-10; Guest analyst, MLB Network, 2009; Manager, Colorado Rockies, 2002-09; Batting coach, Colorado Rockies, 1997-2002; Minor league coach and instructor, Colorado Rockies, 1994-96; Manager, New York Mets Minor League Systems, 1988-93; Outfielder, St. Louis Cardinals, 1986; Outfielder, New York Mets, 1987; Outfielder, New York Mets, 1985; Outfielder, New York Mets, 1983; Outfielder, Cincinnati Reds, 1982; Outfielder, Kansas City Royals, 1977-81 **CR:** Coach National League All-Star Team, 2004 **CIV:** National spokesman, Prader-Willi Syndrome Association **AW:** Named National League Manager of Year, Major League Baseball, 2013, Sporting News Manager of the Year Award, 2013 **BA:** PNC Park, 115 Federal Street, Pittsburgh, PA, 15212

HURT, WILLIAM, T: Actor **I:** Media & Entertainment **DOB:** 03/20/1950 **PB:** Washington **SC:** DC **ED:** BA in Drama, Tufts University, 1972; DFA (hon.), Tufts University, 2005; Student, Juilliard School **C:** Joined, Circle Repertory Theatre, New York City, New York, 1977; Performed Regularly With, Ashland Shakespeare Festival, Oregon; Joined, Oregon Shakespeare Festival, 1975 **CW:** Actor: (theatre) Henry V, 1977, My Life, 1977, Ulysses in Traction, Lulu, 1978, Fifth of July, 1978, Hamlet, 1979, Mary Stuart, 1979, Childe Byron, 1981, The Diviners, 1981, The Great Grandson of Jedediah kohler, 1982, Richard II, 1982, A Midsummer Night's Dream, 1982, Hurlyburly, 1984, Joan of Arc at the Stake, 1985, Love Letters, 1989, Beside Herself, 1989, Ivanov, 1991, (films) Altered States, 1980, Eyewitness, 1981, Body Heat, 1981, The Big Chill, 1983, Gorky Park, 1983, Kiss of the Spider Woman, 1985 (Academy award for Best Actor, 1986), Children of a Lesser God, 1986, Broadcast News, 1987, A Time of Destiny, 1988, The Accidental Tourist, 1988, I Love You To Death, 1990, Marilyn Hotchkiss' Ballroom Dancing and Charm School (voice), 1990, Alice, 1990, The Doctor, 1991, Until the End of the World, 1991, The Plague, 1992, Mr. Wonderful, 1993, Trial by Jury, 1994, Second Best, 1994, Secrets Shared with a Stranger, 1994, Smoke, 1995, Michael, 1996, Jane Eyre, 1996, A Couch in New York, 1996, Loved, 1997, Dark City, 1998, Lost in Space, 1998, One True Thing, 1998, The Big Brass Ring, 1999, Sunshine, 1999, Do Not Disturb, 1999, The 4th Floor, 1999, The Simian Line, 2000, Artificial Intelligence: AI, 2001, The Contaminated Man, 2001, Rare Birds, 2001, Changing Lanes, 2002, Nearest to Heaven, 2002, Tuck Everlasting, 2002, The Tulse Luper Suitcases: The Moab Story, 2003, The Blue Butterfly, 2004, The Village, 2004, A History of Violence, 2005 (New York Film Critics Circle award for Best Supporting Actor, 2005), Neverwas, 2005, Syriana, 2005, Beautiful Ohio, 2006, The Good Shepherd, 2006, Mr. Brooks, 2007, Into the Wild, 2007, Noise, 2007, Yellow Handkerchief, 2008, Vantage Point, 2008, The Incredible Hulk,

2008, Endgame, 2009, The River Why, 2010, Robin Hood, 2010, Shadows, 2011, Late Bloomers, 2011, Hellgate, 2011, Maddened by His Absence, 2012, The Host, 2013, The Disappearance of Eleanor Rigby: Him, 2013, The Disappearance of Eleanor Rigby: her, 2013, Winter's Tale, 2014, Days and Nights, 2014, The Disappearance of Eleanor Rigby: Them, 2014, Race, 2016, The Moon and the Sun, 2016, Captain America: Civil War, 2016, The King's Daughter, 2017 (TV films) Verna: United Service Organizations Girl, 1978, All the Way Home, 1981, The Miracle Maker (voice), 2000, The Flamingo Rising, 2001, Master Spy: The Robert Hanssen Story, 2002, Frankenstein, 2004, Hunt for Justice, 2005, Too Big to Fail, 2011, The Challenger Disaster, 2013, (TV miniseries) The Best of Families, 1977, Dune 2000, Bonnie and Clyde, 2013, Beowulf: Return to the Shieldlands, 2016, (TV series) Riviere-des-Jeremie, 2001, Damages, 2009, Humans, 2015, Trial, 2016-, Beowolf, 2016, Goliath, 2016; actor, co-prodr.: (films) The Legend of the Sasquatch (voice), 2006. **AW:** Recipient 1st Spencer Tracy award for Outstanding Screen Performances and Professional Achievement, UCLA, 1988. **BA:** Creative Artists Agency, 2000 Avenue of the Stars, Los Angeles, CA, 90067

HURWITZ, ANDREW DAVID, T: Federal Judge **I:** Law and Legal Services **DOB:** 10/01/1947 **PB:** New York **SC:** NY/USA **SPN:** Dr. Sally Hurwitz **ED:** JD, Yale Law School, 1972; AB in Public & International Affairs, Princeton University, 1968 **C:** Judge, U.S. Court of Appeals, Ninth Circuit, Phoenix, AZ, 2012-Present; Vice Chief Justice, Arizona State Supreme Court, 2009-2012; Associate Justice, Arizona State Supreme Court, Phoenix, AZ, 2003-2009; Partner, Martori Meyer Hendricks & Victor (Now Osborn Maledon), 1995-2003; Partner, Martori Meyer Hendricks & Victor (Now Osborn Maledon), 1983-1995; Associate, Martori Meyer Hendricks & Victor (Now Osborn Maledon), 1974-1980; Law Clerk To Justice Potter Stewart, U.S. Supreme Court, Washington, DC, 1973-1974; Law Clerk To Hon. J. Joseph Smith, U.S. Court of Appeals, Second Circuit, 1972-1973; Law Clerk To Hon. Jon O. Newman, U.S. District Court, Connecticut, 1972 **CR:** Co-Chair, Transition Team, Governor Janet Napolitano, State Of Arizona, 2002, Distinguished Visiting From Practice, 2001, Visiting Professor of Law, Civil Procedure, 1994-1995, Visiting Professor of Law, Arizona State University, Sandra Day O'Connor College of Law, 1994-1995, President, Arizona Board Of Regents, 1992-1993, Arizona Board Of Regents, 1988-1996, Chief Of Staff To Governor Rose Mofford, State Of Arizona, 1988, Chief Of Staff To Governor Bruce Babbitt, 1980-1983, Adjunct Professor of Law, Ethics, Supreme Court Litigation, Legislative Process, and Civil Procedure, 1977-1980, 1988, 2004-Present **CIV:** Secretary, Children's Action Alliance, 2002-2003, Board of Directors, Children's Action Alliance, 1999-2003, Chair, City Of Phoenix Street Environment Committee, 1989-1990, Board of Directors, Arizona Center For Law In Public Interest, 1986-1988, Chair, City Of Phoenix Neighborhood Improvement Committee, 1986-1988 **MIL:** U.S. Army National Guard/U.S. Army Reserve, 1969-1975 **MEM:** Committee on Rules of Professional Conduct, State Bar of Arizona, 1985-1990, Examination & Bar Review Committee, State Bar of Arizona, 1986-1987, Phi Beta Kappa **BAR:** U.S. Court of Appeals, Seventh Circuit, 1987, U.S. Tax Court, 1987, U.S. Court of Appeals, Second Circuit, 1977, U.S. District Court, Connecticut, 1977, U.S. Supreme Court, 1976, U.S. Court of Appeals, Ninth Circuit, 1975, U.S. District Court, Arizona, 1975, Arizona, 1974, Connecticut, 1973 **PA:** Democrat **BA:** 95 7th Street, San Francisco, CA, 94013

HUTCHINSON, ASA, T: Governor of Arkansas **I:** Government Administration/Government Relations/Government Services **DOB:** 12/03/1950 **PB:** Bentonville **SC:** AR/USA **PT:** John M. Hutchinson; Coral (Mount) Hutchinson **MS:** Married **SPN:** Susan Burrell **CH:** Asa III; Sarah; John; Seth **ED:** JD, University of Arkansas School of Law (1975); BS in Accounting, Bob Jones University (1972) **C:** Governor, State of Arkansas (2015-Present); Senior Partner, The Asa Hutchinson Law Group, PLC, Rogers, AR (2008-Present); Founding Partner, Chief Executive Officer, Hutchinson Group, LLC, Washington, DC (2005-Present); Partner, Venable LLP, Washington, DC (2007); Partner, Venable LLP, Washington, DC (2005-2006); Under Secretary for Border & Transportation Security, US Department of Homeland Security, Washington, DC (2003-2005); Member, US Congress from the Third Arkansas District (1996-2001); Partner, Karr & Hutchinson, Fort Smith, AR (1986-1996); Administrator Drug Enforcement Administration (DEA), US Department of Justice, Washington, DC (2001-2003); US Attorney, Western District of Arkansas, US Department of Justice (1982-1985); City Attorney, City of Bentonville, AR (1977-1978) **CR:** Chairman, Arkansas State Republican Committee (1990-1995); Conductor, Democracy Workshops in Russia (1994); Delegate, White House Conference on Aging (1995); Board of Directors, The Constitution Project, SAFLINK Corporation (2005-Present); Board of Directors, Fortress International Group; Board of Directors, Pinkerton Government Services; Board of Directors, Intergraph Government Solutions **AW:** Named One of Ten Outstanding Young Leaders in Arkansas, Arkansas Jaycees (1986); Civic Star, Director General, Colombian National Police; Order Al Merito Civil Libertador Simon Bolivar by President of Bolivia **MEM:** ABA; National Association of Former US Attorneys; Benton County Bar Association; Arkansas Bar Association **BAR:** U.S. Court of Appeals for the Fifth Circuit; U.S. Court of Appeals for the Eighth Circuit; Supreme Court of the U.S.; Arkansas Bar Association **PA:** Republican **BA:** Office of the Governor, 500 Woodlane St, Little Rock, AR, 72201

HWANG, SHELLEY, T: Surgeon **I:** Medicine & Health Care **ED:** M.P.H., University of California at Berkeley, 2006; M.D., University of California at Los Angeles, 1991 **C:** Surgeon-in-Chief, Ucsf Helen Diller Family Cancer Center, University of California, San Francisco, School of Medicine, 2009 - 2011; Professor in Residence, Surgery, University of California, San Francisco, School of Medicine, 2009 - 2011; Chief, Division Of Breast Surgery Oncology, University of California, San Francisco, School of Medicine, 2008 - 2011; Associate Professor in Residence, Surgery, University of California, San Francisco, School of Medicine, 2004 - 2009; Assistant Professor in Residence, Surgery, University of California, San Francisco, School of Medicine, 1998 - 2004; Senior Reigstrar, General Surgical Oncology, Singapore General Hospital, 1998 - 1999; Fellow, Breast Surgical Oncology, Memorial Sloan Kettering Cancer Center, 1996 - 1997; Resident, General Surgery, Cornell University, 1992 - 1996; Intern, General Surgery, Kaiser Foundation Hospital, 1991 - 1992 **AW:** Time 100 Most Influential, 2016 **BA:** Duke University, Durham, NC, 27708

HYDE-SMITH, CINDY, T: U.S. Senator from Mississippi **I:** Government Administration/Government Relations/Government Services **DOB:** 05/10/1959 **PB:** Brookhaven **SC:** MI/USA **ED:** Bachelor, University of Southern Mississippi; AA, Copiah-Lincoln Community College **C:** U.S. Senator from Mississippi (2018-Present); Commissioner, Mississippi Department of Agriculture and Commerce (2012-2018); Member, District 39, Mississippi State Senate (2000-2012); Congressional Affairs Consultant; Farmer **MEM:** Mississippi Cattleman's Association; Mississippi Wildlife Federation; American Cancer Society **PA:** Republican

HYMAN, JENNIFER, T: Rental Company Executive **I:** Business Management/Business Services **ED:** MBA, Harvard University, Cambridge, MA 2009; BA in Social Studies, Harvard University, Cambridge, MA 2002 **C:** Co-founder, CEO, Rent the Runway, New York City, 2008-; Director business devel., IMG, 2006-07; Senior manager sales, Wedding Channel, 2005-06; Senior manager leisure program devel., Starwood Hotels & Resorts Worldwide, Inc., 2002-05 **AW:** Named one of The 40 Under 40, Fortune magazine, 2012, Crain's New York Business, 2012, The Top 100 More Influential Women in Tech. (with partner Jennifer Fleiss), Fast Co., 2011, The Recode 100,2017

IACOCCA, LEE, T: Former Automobile Executive **I:** Automotive **DOB:** 10/15/1924 **PB:** Allentown, Pennsylvania **PT:** Son of Nicola and Antoinette (Perrotto) I.; Married Mary McCleary, September 29, 1956 (deceased May 16, 1983), children: Kathryn Lisa Hentz, Lia Antoinette Nagy; Married Peggy Johnson, April 17, 1986 **ED:** ME, Princeton University, 1946; BS, Lehigh University, 1945 **C:** Founder, Olivio Premium Products, 2000-; Founder, EV Global Motors, 1999-; Principal, Iacocca Partners, 1994-; President, Lee Iacocca & Associates, Inc.,; Chairman, CEO, Chrysler Corp., Highland Park, Michigan, 1979-93; President, COO, Chrysler Corp., Highland Park, Michigan, 1978-79; President, Ford Motor Co., 1970-78; Executive vice president, Ford Motor Co., 1967-69; Vice president car & truck group, Ford Motor Co., 1965-69; General manager, Ford Motor Co., 1960-65; Vice president, Ford Motor Co.,; Vehicle market manager, Ford Motor Co., 1960; Car marketing manager, Ford Motor Co., 1957-60; Truck marketing manager div. office, Ford Motor Co., 1956-57; District sales manager, Ford Motor Co., Washington, 1946-56; Successively member field sales staff, various merchandising and training activities, assistant directors sales manager, Ford Motor Co., Philadelphia,; With, Ford Motor Co., Dearborn, Michigan, 1946-78 **CIV:** chairman The Statue of Liberty-Ellis Island Foundation, 1982 founder, The Iacocca Foundation, 1984- **CW:** Co-author: (with William Novak) Iacocca: An Autobiography, 1984, (with Sonny Kleinfeld) Talking Straight, 1988, (with Catherine Whitney) Where Have All the Leaders Gone?, 2007; actor (TV appearances) Miami Vice, 1986 **AW:** Wallace Memorial fellow Princeton University, S Roger Horchow Award, 1985, Portfolio 18th Greatest CEO of All Time **MEM:** Member NAE, Tau Beta Pi. Clubs: Detroit Athletic.

ICAHN, CARL CELIAN, I: Business Management/Business Services **DOB:** 02/16/1936 **PB:** Queens **SC:** NY/USA **ED:** Student, New York University School Medicine; BA in Philosophy, Princeton University, New Jersey, 1957 **C:** Chairman, CVR Energy Inc., 2012-; Chairman, Tropicana Entertainment Inc., 2010-; Chairman board, XO Holdings, Inc. (formerly XO Communications), 2003-; Board chairman, American Railcar Industries, Inc., 1994-; Board chairman, American Property Investors, Inc., 1990-; Founder, Icahn Capital, Inc., 1987-; Chairman, ACF Industries, Inc., St. Charles, Missouri, 1984-; Board chairman, Starfire Holding Corp. (formerly Icahn Holding), 1984-; Chairman board, ImClone Systems Inc., 2006-08; Chairman board, GB Holdings, 2000-07; President, Stratosphere Corp., 1998-2004; Board chairman, Maupintour Holdings, LLC, 1998-2002; Chairman, president, CEO, Trans World Airlines Inc., New York City, 1985-93; Chairman, president, Icahn & Co., New York City, 1968-2005; Options manager, Gruntal & Co., 1964-68; Options manager, Tessel, Patrick & Co., New York City, 1963-64; Apprentice broker, Dreyfus Corp., New York City, 1960-63 **CR:** Non-exec. chairman Federal-Mogul Corp., 2008-, board directors, 2007-, Yahoo! Inc., 2008-09, WCI Communities, Inc., 2007-, ImClone Systems Inc., 2006-08, WestPoint International, Inc., 2005-, American Railcar Industries Inc., 1994-, Cadus Pharmaceutical Corp., 1993-2010, Starfire Holding Corp., 1984- **CIV:** Founder, Carl C. Icahn Charter School, New York City, Founder, Icahn House, New York City, **MIL:** Served in US Army, 1960-61 **AW:** Named one of The 100 Most Influential People in the World, TIME magazine, 2014, The 50 Most Influential People in Global Finance, Bloomberg Markets, 2013-14, The World's Richest People, Forbes Magazine, 2007-, The Forbes 400: Richest Americans, 2006-, The Top 200 Collectors, ARTnews magazine, 2004 **H:** Collector Old Masters and Impressionist art

IGE, DAVID Y., T: Governor of Hawaii **I:** Government Administration/Government Relations/Government Services **DOB:** 01/15/1957 **PB:** Honolulu **SC:** HI/USA **ED:** MBA, University of Hawaii, Manoa, Hawaii (1985); BS in Electrical Engineering, University of Hawaii, Manoa, Hawaii (1979) **C:** Governor, State of Hawaii (2014-Present); Project Manager, R.A. Ige & Associates Inc. (2003-Present); Member, District 16, Hawaii State Senate (2003-2014); Member, District 17, Hawaii State Senate (1995-2002); Member, District 43, Hawaii House of Representatives (1986-1993); Vice President of Engineering, Net Enterprise Inc. (2001-2002); Project Manager, Pihana Pacific LLC (1999-2001); Senior Administrator, Gte-Hawaiian Telephone Co. (1981-1999); Electronics Engineer & Analyst, Pacific Analysis Corp.; Board Director, Pacific Space Center; Vice Chairman, Media, Arts, Science & Technological Committee; Chairman, Intergovernment Affairs Committee; Member, Commission to Commemorate the 90th Anniversary of Okinawan Immigration; Member, Task Force on Hawaiian Service; Member, Honolulu Financial Center Task Force; Former Chairman, Education Committee **MEM:** IEEE; Newtown Estates County Association; Pearl City Community Association **PA:** Democrat

IGER, BOB, T: Disney CEO **I:** Business Management/Business Services **DOB:** 02/10/1951 **PB:** NYC **SC:** NY/USA **PT:** Son of Arthur and Mimi Iger; **ED:** BA magna cum laude, Ithaca College, 1973 **C:** President, CEO, Walt Disney Co., Burbank, California, 2005-; President, COO, Walt Disney Co., Burbank, California, 2000-05; President, Walt Disney International, 1999-2000; Chairman, ABC Grp., 1999-2000; President, ABC, Inc., New York City, 1996-99; President, COO, Capital Cities/ABC Inc., New York City, 1994-96; Executive Vice President, Capital Cities/ABC Inc., New York City, 1993-94; President, ABC Entertainment, 1989-92; President, ABC TV Network Grp., 1992-94; Executive Vice President, ABC TV Network Grp., 1988-89; Vice President progressive planning & acquisition, ABC Sports, 1987-88; Vice president progressive planning, devel., ABC Sports, 1985-87; Various positions, ABC-TV Sports, 1976-85; Studio supervisor, ABC-TV, 1974-76 **CR:** Board directors Lincoln Center Performing Arts Board of Trustees, Ithaca College, Museum TV & Radio, American Film Institute (AFI) board member US-China Business Council, 2011- member President's Export Council, 2011- Board of Directors Apple Inc., 2011-, Hulu, 2009-, The Walt Disney Co., 2000- **CIV:** Trustee, Ithaca College, **AW:** Named CEO of

Year, Chief Executive magazine, 2014, Market-Watch, 2006; named one of The Best CEO's, Institutional Investor magazine, 2008-11, The 25 Most Powerful People in Business, Fortune magazine, 2006-07, The 50 Who Matter Now, CNNMoney.com Business 2.0, 2006; recipient Milestone award, Producers Guild of America, 2014, Ambassador for Humanity award, USC Shoah Foundation Institute for Visual History and Education, 2012, Trustee award, National Academy TV Arts & Scis., 2005

IKUTA, SANDRA SEGAL, T: Federal Judge **I:** Law and Legal Services **DOB:** 06/24/1954 **PB:** Los Angeles **SC:** California **ED:** JD, UCLA, 1988; MS, Columbia University, 1978; AB, University California Berkeley, 1976; Student, Stanford University, 1972-74 **C:** Judge, US Court Appeals (9th cir.), 2006-; Deputy secretary, general counsel, California Resources Agency, 2004-06; Partner, O'Melveny & Myers LLP, 1997-2004; Associate, O'Melveny & Myers LLP, 1990-97; Law clerk to Justice Sandra Day O'Connor, US Supreme Court, Washington, 1989-90; Law clerk to Hon. Alex Kozinski, US Court Appeals (9th Cir.), 1988-89 **BA:** US Ct Appeals, 95 Seventh St, San Francisco, CA, 94103

ILLSLEY, JOHN, T: Musician **I:** Media & Entertainment **PB:** Leicester **SC:** England **CW:** Solo Album, "Never Told a Soul" (1984), "Glass" (1988), "Live in Les Baux De Provence" (2007), "Beautiful You" (2008), "Streets of Heaven" (2010), "Testing the Water" (2014), "Live in London" (2014), "Long Shadows" (2016); Albums with Dire Straits, "Dire Straits" (1978), "Communique" (1979), "Making Movies" (1980), "Money for Nothing" (1988), "Live at the BBC" (1995), "Sultans of Swing: The Very Best of Dire Straits" (1998), "Private Investigations: The Best of Dire Straits" (2005) **AW:** Inductee, Rock & Roll Hall of Fame (2018)

IMMELT, JEFFREY ROBERT, T: CEO **I:** Oil & Energy **CN:** General Electric **DOB:** 02/19/1956 **PB:** Cincinnati **SC:** OH/USA **PT:** Joseph Francis Immelt, Donna Rosemary (Wallace) Immelt **ED:** Honorary Doctorate in Public Service, University of Maryland, 2011; Honorary Doctorate, Michigan State University, 2010; Honorary Doctorate, Worcester Polytechnic Institute, 2008; Honorary DEng, University of Notre Dame, 2007; Honorary Doctorate, Georgia Institute of Technology, 2007; Honorary Doctorate in Business, Northeastern University, 2006; Honorary LLD, Pepperdine University, 2004; Honorary LLD, Dartmouth College, 2004; MBA, Harvard Business School, 1982; BA in Applied Mathematics, Dartmouth College, 1978 **C:** Chairman, CEO, General Electric Co., 2001-Present; Chairman, NBC Universal, Inc., 2007-2011; President, CEO, GE Medical Systems, 1997-2000; Vice President, General Manager, GE Plastics America, 1992-1996; Vice President, Consumer Service, GE Appliances, 1989-1991; Various Positions, GE Plastics, 1982-1989; Corporate Marketing Department, General Electric Co., 1982; Vice President, Worldwide Marketing And Product Management, GE Appliances **CR:** Fellow, American Academy of Arts & Sciences, The Business Council, 2006-2007, Board of Directors, Federal Reserve Bank of New York, 2006-2011, President's Economic Recovery, 2009-2011, President's Economic Recovery Advisory Board, 2011, Chairman, President's Council On Jobs & Competitiveness, 2011-2013, General Electric Co., 2000-Present **CIV:** Board of Directors, Catalyst, Robin Hood, New York, NY **AW:** The 50 Most Influential People In Global Finance, Bloomberg Markets, 2011, 2014, The World's Most Powerful People, Forbes Magazine, 2009-2014, The 100 Most Influential People In The World, TIME Magazine, 2008, National Equal Justice Award, National Association For The

Advancement Of Colored People Legal Defense & Educational Fund, Inc., 2008, The 25 Most Powerful People In Business, Fortune Magazine, 2007, CEO Coach of the Year, American Football Coaches Foundation, 2006, Man of the Year, Financial Times, 2003 **PA:** Republican **BA:** General Electric Co., 3135 Easton Turnpike, Fairfield, CT, 06431-0002

IÑÁRRITU, ALEJANDRO GONZÁLEZ, T: Film Director, Producer **I:** Media & Entertainment **DOB:** 08/15/1963 **PB:** Mexico City **SC:** Mexico **C:** Founder, Zeta Films, 1991; Director, Televisa, Mexico **CW:** Director, (Films) Timbre, El, 1996, Powder Keg, 2001; Director, Producer, (Films) Amores Perros, 2000, September 11, 2002, 21 Grams, 2003, Babel, 2006; Executive Producer, (Films) Nine Lives, 2005, Toro Negro, 2005, Mother and Child, 2009, En La Estancia, 2014; Director, Producer, Writer, (Films) Biutiful, 2010, Birdman or (The Unexpected Virtue of Ignorance), 2014, The Revenant, 2015; Associate Producer, The Last Elvis, 2012 **AW:** Golden Globe Award, Best Motion Picture - Drama, Babel, 2007; Golden Globe Award, Best Screenplay, Birdman or (The Unexpected Virtue of Ignorance), 2015; The Darryl F. Zanuck Award, Outstanding Producer of Theatrical Motion Pictures, Birdman or (The Unexpected Virtue of Ignorance), 2015; Academy Awards, Best Director, Best Original Screenplay, Best Picture, Birdman or (The Unexpected Virtue of Ignorance), 2015; Producers Guild of America Award, Birdman or (The Unexpected Virtue of Ignorance); Golden Globe Awards, Best Director, Best Picture - Drama, The Revenant, 2016; BAFTA Award, David Lean Award for Direction, The Revenant, 2016; Academy Award, Best Director, The Revenant, 2016

INFANTINO, GIANNI, T: Sports Association Executive **I:** Business Management/Business Services **DOB:** 03/23/1970 **C:** President, Federation International Football Association (FIFA), 2016-; General secretary, Union European Football Associations (UEFA), 2009-16; Deputy general secretary and director governance & legal affairs division, Union European Football Associations (UEFA), 2007-09; Interim CEO, Union European Football Associations (UEFA), 2007; Director legal affairs and club licensing, Union European Football Associations (UEFA), 2004-07; Joined, Union European Football Associations (UEFA), Nyon, Switzerland, 2000; Secretary general, University Neuchâtel International Center for Sports Studies, Switzerland,; Advisor to the Italian, Spanish and Swiss football leagues

INHOFE, JIM, T: U.S. Senator from Oklahoma **I:** Government Administration/Government Relations/Government Services **DOB:** 11/17/1934 **PB:** Des Moines **PT:** Son of Perry and Blanche Mountain Inhofe; **ED:** BA, University Tulsa, 1973 **C:** Chairman, Senate Environment Committee, 2015-2017; Ranking minority member, US Senate Environment & Public Works Committee, 2007-; US Senator from Oklahoma, 1994-; Chairman, US Senate Environment & Public Works Committee, 2003-07; Member, US Congress from 1st Oklahoma District, 1987-94; Mayor, City of Tulsa, 1978-84; Member, Oklahoma State Senate, 1969-77; Member, Oklahoma House Reps., 1967-69; President, Quaker Life Insurance Co. **CIV:** Member, Tulsa Area Safety Council, Member, Tulsa Airport Authority **CW:** Author: The Greatest Hoax: How the Global Warming Conspiracy Threatens Your Future, 2012 **AW:** Recipient National Guardian award, Lincoln House Heritage Institute, 2002, William S. Lee award leadership, Nuclear Energy Institute, 2001, Democracy award, International Foundation Election Systems, 1996 **MEM:** Mem.: Friends of American Diabetes Association **PA:** Republican

INSLEE, JAY ROBERT, T: Governor of Washington, former U.S. Representative from Washington **I:** Government Administration/Government Relations/Government Services **DOB:** 02/09/1951 **PB:** Seattle **PT:** Son of Frank E. and Adele A. (Brown) Inslee; **ED:** JD magna cum laude, Willamette University School Law, Salem, Oregon, 1976; BA in Economics, University Washington, Seattle, 1973; Attended, Stanford University, 1969-70 **C:** Governor, State of Washington, Olympia, 2013-; Member, US Congress from 1st Washington District, Washington, 1999-2012; Member, US Congress from 4th Washington District, Washington, 1993-95; Member District 14, Washington State House of Reps., 1988-92; Regional director, US Department Health & Human Services (Department of Health and Human Services), Seattle, 1997-98; Attorney, Gordon, Thomas, Honeywell, Malanca, Peterson & Daheim, Seattle, 1995-96; Attorney, Peters, Fowler & Inslee, Selah, Washington, 1976-92 **CIV:** Board directors, Selah, Washington School Bond Committee, 1980 Board directors, New Valley Osteopathic Hospital, Yakima, Washington, 1984-88 Charter member, Hoopaholics, Seattle, 1988- **CW:** Co-author (with Bracken Hendricks): Apollo's Fire: Igniting America's Clean Energy Economy, 2007 **PA:** Democrat

IRONS, JEREMY, T: Actor **I:** Media & Entertainment **PB:** Cowes **SC:** England **PT:** Paul Dugan Irons; Barbara Anne (Sharpe) Irons **CIV:** Goodwill ambassador, Food and Agriculture Organization of UN, 2011- **CW:** Actor: (plays) John the Baptist in Godspell, 1973, Mick in The Caretaker, 1974, Petruchio in The Taming of the Shrew, 1975, James Jameson in Rear Column, 1978, The Real Thing, 1984 (Tony award for Best Actor in a Play, 1984); actor, actor: (plays) Harry Thunder in Wild Oats, 1976, Richard II, 1986, Leontes in Winter's Tale, 1986, The Rover, 1986, Henrik in Embers, 2006, Impressionism, 2009; (films) Nijinsky, 1979, The French Lieutenant's Woman, 1981, Betrayal, 1982, Moonlighting, 1982, The Wild Duck, 1983, Swann in Love, 1983, The Mission, 1985, Chorus of Disapproval, 1988, Australia, 1988, Dead Ringers, 1988 (New York Film Critics' Circle award for Best Actor, 1988), Danny, the Champion of the World, 1989, Reversal of Fortune, 1990 (Academy award for Best Actor, 1991, Golden Globe award for Best Actor, 1991), Kafka, 1991, Waterland, 1992, Damage, 1992, M. Butterfly, 1993, The House of the Spirits, 1994, (voice) The Lion King, 1994, Die Hard with a Vengeance, 1995, Stealing Beauty, 1996, Lolita, 1997, The Chinese Box, 1997, Man in the Iron Mask, 1998, Dungeons and Dragons, 2000, Fourth Angel, 2000, And Now Ladies and Gentlemen, 2001, Callas Forever, 2001, Mathilde, 2003, Being Julia, 2003, Merchant of Venice, 2004, Kingdom of Heaven, 2004, Casanova, 2004, Inland Empire, 2006, Eragon, 2006, Appaloosa, 2008, The Pink Panther 2, 2009, Margin Call, 2011, The Words, 2012, Night Train to Lisbon, 2013, Beautiful Creatures, 2013, High-Rise, 2015, The Man Who Knew Infinity, 2015, La corrispondenza, 2016, Race, 2016, Batman v Superman: Dawn of Justice, 2016, Assassin's Creed, 2016; (TV films) Charles Ryder in Brideshead Revisited, 1980-81, Alex Hepburn in The Captain's Doll, 1982, Tales from Hollywood, 1992, Longitude, 1999, Last Call, 2001, Elizabeth I, 2005 (Emmy award for Outstanding Supporting Actor in a miniseries or movie, 2006, Golden Globe award for Best Performance by an Actor in a Supporting Role in a Series, Mini-Series or Motion Picture Made for TV, 2007, Screen Actors Guild award for Outstanding Performance by a Male Actor in a TV Movie or Mini-series, 2007), The Colour of Magic, 2008, (voice) The Magic 7, 2008, Georgia O'Keefe, 2009, Henry IV, Part 1, 2012, Henry IV, Part 2, 2012; (documentaries) The Wind Gods, 2013, (narrator) Ash

Runners, 2010, Another Way Home, 2012, Game of Lions, 2013 (Emmy award for Outstanding Narrator, 2014), : (TV series) The Borgias, 2011-13; dir.: (TV films) Mirad, 1997; prodr.: (documentary) Trashed, 2012 **AW:** Decorated officier des Artes et Lettres (France)

IRVING, JOHN WINSLOW, T: Writer **I:** Writing and Editing **DOB:** 03/02/1942 **PB:** Exeter **PT:** Son of Colin F.N. and Frances Winslow Irving; **ED:** MFA, University Iowa, 1967; BA, University New Hampshire, 1965; Student, University Vienna; Student, University Pittsburgh **C:** Head wrestling coach, Vermont Academy, 1987-89; Assistant wrestling coach, Fessenden School, 1984-86; Assistant wrestling coach, Northfield Mount Hermon School, 1981-83; Faculty, Brandeis University, Massachusetts, 1978-79; With, Bread Loaf Writer's Conference, 1976; Assistant professor English, Mount Holyoke College, South Hadley, Massachusetts, 1975-78; Writer-in-residence, University Iowa, 1972-75; Assistant professor English, Windham College, Putney, Vermont, 1967-69, 70-72; Writer,1968-; Assistant wrestling coach, Phillips Exeter Academy, New Hampshire, 1964-65 **CW:** Author: (novels) Setting Free the Bears, 1968, The Water-Method Man, 1972, The 158-Pound Marriage, 1974, The World According to Garp, 1978 (National Book award (paperback), 1980), The Hotel New Hampshire, 1981, The Cider House Rules, 1985, A Prayer for Owen Meany, 1989, Trying to Save Piggy Sneed, 1993, A Son of the Circus, 1994, A Widow for One Year, 1998, The Fourth Hand, 2001, A Sound Like Someone Trying Not to Make a Sound, 2004, Until I Find You, 2005, Last Night in Twisted River, 2009, In One Person, 2012, Avenue of Mysteries, 2015, (nonfiction) The Imaginary Girlfriend, 1996, My Movie Business, 1999, (screenplays) The Cider House Rules, 1999 (Academy award for Best Adapted Screenplay, 1999),(Book) Darkness As a Bride, 2018 **AW:** Named to The National Wrestling Hall of Fame, 1992; recipient Golden Plate award, Academy Achievement, 2005; fellow John Simon Guggenheim Memorial Foundation, 1976-77, National Endowment Arts, 1974-75; grantee Rockefeller Foundation, 1971-72

IRWIN, HALE S., T: Former Professional Golfer **I:** Athletics **CN:** Sr. PGA **DOB:** 06/03/1945 **PB:** , **PT:** Son of Hale S. and Mabel M. (Philipps) I. **MS:** Married **SPN:** Sally Jean Stahlhuth, September 14, 1968; **CH:** Becky, Steven **ED:** BS in Marketing, University Colorado, 1968 **C:** Joined, Senior PGA, 1995-; Professional golfer, 1968-; Vice president, PGA Am., 1979; Tour director, PGA Am., 1978-79 **CIV:** State chairman Missouri Easter Seal campaign, 1977. **AW:** World Golf Hall of Fame, 1992, Champions Tour Leading Money Winner, 1997, 1998, 2002, Champions Tour Player of the Year, 1997, 1998, 2002, Champions Tour Rookie of the Year, 1995, Byron Nelson Award, 1996-98, 2002, Charles Schwab Cup, 2002, 2004 **MEM:** Member Phi Gamma Delta. **ACH:** Achievements include tour victories Heritage Classic, 1971, 73, 94, U.S. Open, 1974, 79, Western Open, 1975, Atlanta Golf Classic, 1975, 77, Glen Campbell-Los Angeles, 1976, Florida Citrus, 1976, Hall of Fame Classic, 1977, Hawaiian Open, 1981, Buick Open, 1981, Inverrary Classic, 1982, Bing Crosby Pro-Am, 1984, Memorial Tournament, 1983, 85, Bahamas Classic, 1986. **PA:** Republican **BA:** Irwin Golf Managment, 1962 Blake Street, Suite 250, Denver, CO, 80202

ISAACSON, WALTER, T: Think-Tank Executive **I:** Business Management/Business Services **CN:** The Aspen Inst. **DOB:** 05/20/1952 **PB:** New Orleans **SC:** Lousiana **ED:** BA, Harvard University, Cambridge, Massachusetts, 1974; MA, Oxford University, England, 1976 **C:** Pres., CEO, The Aspen Institute, Washington, DC, 2003—; Political corr., TIME magazine, Washington, DC, 1979-81; Staff writer, TIME magazine, New York City, New York, 1978-79; Reporter, columnist, States-Item, New Orleans, Louisiana, 1977-78; Reporter, Sunday Times London, London, England, 1976-77; Chairman, Broadcasting Board Governors, 2010—2012; Chmn., CEO, CNN News Group, 2001—2003; Editorial director, Time Inc., New York City, New York, 2000—2001; Editor, New Media Time Inc., New York City, New York, 1993—1995; Managing editor, TIME magazine, New York City, New York, 1995—2000; Assistant managing editor, TIME magazine, New York City, New York, 1991-93; Senior editor, TIME magazine, New York City, New York, 1985-91; Associate editor, TIME magazine, New York City, New York, 1981-84 **CR:** Board directors United Continental Holdings, Inc. (formerly United Airlines Corp.), 2006, Tulane University, National Constitution Center, Shakespeare Theatre of Washington; board overseers Harvard University; vice-chairperson Louisiana Recovery Authority, 2005—2007; chairman board Teach for America **CW:** Author: Pro and Con, 1983, Kissinger: A Biography, 1992, Benjamin Franklin: An American Life, 2003, Einstein: His Life and Universe, 2007 (Quill Book award for biography, 2007, Communication Award (Book)-Best Book award, National Academy of Sciences, 2008), American Sketches: Great Leaders, Creative Thinkers, and Heroes of a Hurricane, 2009, Steve Jobs: A Biography, 2011, The Innovators: How a Group of Hackers, Geniuses, and Geeks Created the Digital Revolution, 2014; co-author: (with Evan Thomas) The Wise Men: Six Friends and the World They Made, 1986 (Harry Truman Book prize 1987); editor: Profiles in Leadership: Historians on the Elusive Quality of Greatness, 2010,(Books) Leonardo Da Vinci, 2017 **AW:** Rhodes scholar, 1974; recipient Overseas Press Club award, New York City, 1981, 84, 87; named one The 100 Most Influential People in the World, TIME magazine, 2012,Nichols Chancellor's Medal at Vanderbilt University **MEM:** Member Council Foreign Relations, Century Association, Metropolitan Club of Washington. **BA:** Aspen Inst, One Dupont Cir Northwest Ste 700, Washington, DC, 20036

ISAKSON, JOHNNY, T: U.S. Senator from Georgia **I:** Government Administration/Government Relations/Government Services **DOB:** 12/28/1944 **PB:** Atlanta **SC:** GA/USA **MS:** Married **SPN:** Dianne (Davison) Isakson **CH:** John; Kevin; Julie **ED:** BBA, University of Georgia, 1966 **C:** Chairman, Senate Veterans Affairs Committee, 2015-;; Chairmen of the Senate Ethics Committee, 2015-; Vice Chairman, US Senate Select Committee on Ethics, 2009-; US Senator from Georgia, 2005-; Member, US Congress from 6th Georgia District, 1999-2005; Member, Georgia State Senate, 1994-96; Republican Leader, Georgia House of Reps., 1983-90; Member, Georgia House of Reps., 1976-90; CEO, Fairgreen Capital LP, Atlanta, 1996-99; President, Northside Realty, Atlanta, 1979-98 **CR:** Chairman Georgia State Board Education, 1996-99 **CIV:** Sunday School teacher Mount Zion Methodist Church, 1978-, Advisory Board, Federal National Mortgage Association, Board of Trustees Kennesaw State University, Georgia Board of Directors Georgia Club, Metro Atlanta C. of C., Georgia C. of C., Riverside Bank **MIL:** Served as SSG with Georgia National Guard, 1967-72, served with US Air Force, 1966-67 **AW:** Recipient Blue Key Award, University of Georgia, 1998, Tax fighter Award, National Tax Limitation Committee, Hero of Taxpayers Award, Americans for Tax Reform, Guardian Small Business Award, National Federation Independent Business, Distinguished Service Award, Georgia Municipal Association, Best Legis. in America Award, Rep. National Committee, 1989 **MEM:** Mem.: Realty Alliance (president), National Association Realtors (executive committee) **PA:** Republican

ISHIGURO, KAZUO, T: Author **I:** Writing and Editing **DOB:** 11/08/1954 **PB:** Nagasaki **SC:** Japan **PT:** Son of Shizuo and Shizuko (Michida) Ishiguro; **ED:** MA in Creative Writing, University East Anglia, Norwich, England, 1980; BA in Lit. and Philosophy, University Kent, Canterbury, England, 1978 **C:** Resettlement worker, W. London Cyrenians Ltd., 1981-83; Residential social worker, W. London Cyrenians Ltd., England, 1979-80; Writer, 1982-; Community worker, Renfrew Social Works Department, Scotland, 1976 **CW:** Author: (novels) A Pale View of Hills, 1982, An Artist of the Floating World, 1985 (Whitbread Book award, 1986, Scanno prize, Italy, 1995), The Remains of the Day, 1989 (Man Booker prize for fiction, 1989), The Unconsoled, 1995 (Cheltenham prize, 1995), When We Were Orphans, 2000, Never Let Me Go, 2005 (Alex award, American Library Association, 2006, one of 100 best English-lang. novels from 1923 to 2005, TIME magazine), The Buried Giant, 2015, (short fiction) Nocturnes: Five Stories of Music and Nightfall, 2009, (screenplays) A Profile of Arthur J. Mason, 1984, The Gourmet, 1986, The Saddest Music in the World, 2003, The White Countess, 2005 **AW:** Decorated Knight, Order of Arts & Letters, France, 1998, Officer, Order of Brit. Empire, 1995; named one of The 50 Greatest Brit. Writers since 1945, The Times, UK, 2008, Nobel Prize in Literature,2017,Time 100 Greatest English Language Novels, Novel 1923 **MEM:** Fellow: Royal Society Lit. (Winifred Holtby award 1983) **H:** Music, guitar, piano, cinema **BA:** Rogers Coleridge White, 20 Powis Mews, London, United Kingdom, W11 1JN

ISSA, DARRELL EDWARD, T: U.S. Representative from California **I:** Government Administration/Government Relations/Government Services **DOB:** 11/01/1953 **PB:** Cleveland, November 1, 1953 **ED:** BA in Business, Siena Heights University, Adrian, Michigan, 1976; AA, Kent State University, Ohio, 1976 **C:** Member, US Congress from 49th California District, 2003-; Member, Committee on Transportation and Infrastructure; Chairman, US House Oversight & Government Reform Committee, 2011-15; Member, US Congress from 48th California District, Washington, 2001-03; Founder, CEO, Directed Electronics, Vista, California, 1982-99 **CR:** Former director Bus.-Industry Political Action Committee co-chair US-Philippines Caucus, California Civic Rights Initiative, 1996 **CIV:** Board trustees, Siena Heights University, **MIL:** Served with US Army, 1970-80 **AW:** Named Angel of Year, North County Solutions for Change, 2004, Entrepreneur of Year, Inc. magazine, 1994; recipient Ellis Island Medal of Honor **MEM:** Mem.: Consumer Electronics Association (past chair), Electronics Industries Association (past board gov.'s), San Diego County C. of C., San Diego Economic Devel. Association **PA:** Republican **BA:** 2347 Rayburn House Office Bldg, Washington, DC, 20515

ISSAC, OSCAR, T: Actor **I:** Media & Entertainment **SC:** Guatemala **CW:** Actor, (Films) Illtown, 1998, All About The Benjamins, 2002, Lenny The Wonder Dog, 2004, PU-239, 2006, The Nativity Story, 2006, The Life Before Her Eyes, 2007, Che: Part One, 2008, Body Of Lies, 2008, Agora, 2009, Balibo, 2009, Robin Hood, 2010, Sucker Punch,2010, W.E., 2011, 10 Years, 2011, Drive, 2011, For Greater Glory, 2012, Revenge For Jolly!, 2012, The Bourne Legacy, 2012, Won't Back Down, 2012, Inside Llewyn Davis, 2013, In Secret, 2013, The Two Faces Of January, 2014, Ticky Tacky, 2014, A Most Violent, 2014, Ex Machina, 2015, Mojave, 2015, Star Wars: The Force

Awakens, 2015, X-Men: Apocalypse, 2016, The Promise, 2016, Lightningface, 2017, Suburbicon, 2017, Star Wars: The Last Jedi, 2017, Annihilation, 2018, Operation Finale, 2018, Life Itself, 2018, At Eternity's Gate,2018, Law And Order Criminal Intent, 2006, Show Me A Hero, 2015, Star Wars Rebels, 2018, (Theatre) The Two Gentleman Of Verona, 2005, Beauty Of The Father, 2006, Romeo And Juliet, 2007, Grace, 2008, We Live Here, 2011, Hamlet, 2017 **AW:** TIME Most Influential, 2016

IVEY, KAY ELLEN, T: Governor of Alabama **I:** Government Administration/Government Relations/Government Services **DOB:** 10/15/1944 **PB:** Repton, Alabama, October 15, 1944 **PT:** Daughter of Boardman Nettles and Barbara Elizabeth Ivey. **ED:** Cert. in Strategic Leadership for State Executives, Duke University, 1989; Cert. in Banking, University South Alabama; Cert. in Marketing, University Colorado, 1975; BS, Auburn University, 1967 **C:** Governor, State of Alabama, 2017-.; Lieutenant governor, State of Alabama, 2011-2017; Treasurer, State of Alabama, 2003-11; Director government affairs, Alabama Commission Higher Education, 1985-98; Executive vice president, St. Margaret's Hospital Foundation, 1982-85; Reading clerk, Alabama House of Reps., 1981-82; Cabinet officer, Office of the Governor, State of Alabama, Montgomery, 1979-81; Assistant vice president, Merchants National Bank, Mobile, Alabama, 1970-79; Teacher, coach forensics, Rio Linda HS, California, 1968-69 **CR:** Owner, consultant Ivey Enterprises, Montgomery, 1982- speaker in field. **CIV:** Member adv. board School Business Auburn University, 1980-83 candidate Alabama State Auditor, 1982 secretary Alabama div. Am. Cancer Society, 1985- board directors Alabama Girl's State School, 1983-85, Stetson Hoedown Rodeo Queen's Pageant, Montgomery, Montgomery YMCA board trustees Sheriff's Boys and Girls Ranches. charter trustee, Alabama Banking School **CW:** Editor (audio-visual presentation) What Price Freedom (award of Excellence), 1976, St. Margaret's Hospital Heart tabloid, 1983. **MEM:** Member Industrial Developers Alabama, Young Men's Business Organization, Pub. Relations Council Alabama (board directors 1976-82), Daughters of the American Revolution (state chairman 1985-86), Alabama Young Bankers (past president), Alabama Bankers Association (chairman education committee, consultant), Alabama Forestry Association, Alpha Gamma Delta (distinguished citizen award 1986), Montgomery Rotary Club (director, Paul Harris award), Homemakers Am. (hon.), Future Farmers Am. **H:** Horseback riding, public speaking **PA:** Republican **BA:** Office of the Governor, 600 Dexter Ave., Montgomery, AL, 61030

IZZO, THOMAS, T: College Basketball Coach **I:** Athletics **CN:** Michigan State University Spartans **DOB:** 01/30/1955 **PB:** Iron Mountain **SC:** MI/USA **ED:** Honorary Degree, Michigan State University; Honorary Degree, Northern Michigan University; Graduate, Northern Michigan University, 1977 **C:** Head Basketball Coach, Michigan State University Spartans, 1995-Present; Assistant Coach, Recruiting Coordinator, University of Tulsa Golden Hurricane, 1986; Assistant Coach, Michigan State University Spartans, 1986-1995; Assistant Coach, Michigan State University Spartans, East Lansing, MI, 1983-1986; Assistant Coach, Northern Michigan University Wildcats, 1979-1983; Head Coach, Ishpeming High School, Michigan, 1977-1979 **CR:** Head Coach, USA Pan American Games, 2003, Assistant Coach, Goodwill Games, 2001 **CIV:** Active, Coaches Vs. Cancer, Catholic Social Services/St. Vincent Home for Children, Lansing, MI, Sparrow Hospital **AW:** District V Coach of the Year, U.S. Basketball Coaches Association, 2012,

Big 10 Conference Coach of the Year, 2009, 2012, Clair Bee Award, 2005, Division I Coach of the Year, National Association Basketball Coaches, 2001, 2012, District XI Coach of the Year, 1999, 2001, National Coach of the Year, Basketball News, U.S. Basketball Writers Association, 1998, Associated Press, 1998, Upper Peninsula Hall Of Fame, 1998, Henry Iba Award, 1998, Big Ten Coach of the Year, 1998, Northern Michigan University Hall Of Fame, 1990 **ACH:** Achievements include head coach of the NCAA Men's Basketball National Championship winning Michigan State University Spartans, 2000 **BA:** Michigan State University Athletic Department, 222 Breslin Center, Jensen Fieldhouse, East Lansing, MI, 48824-0000

JACKMAN, HUGH, T: Actor **I:** Media & Entertainment **DOB:** 10/12/1968 **PB:** Sydney **SC:** NSW/Australia **PT:** Son of Chris Jackman **ED:** Grad., Western Australian Academy Performing Arts, Perth, 1994; Student, Actor's Center, Sydney; BA in Journalism, University of Technology, Sydney, 1991 **C:** Owner, The Laughing Man Marketplace, New York City, 2011-; Co-founder, Seed Productions, Australia; Co-founder, Seed Productions, LA; Actor, 1994- **CW:** Actor: (TV series) Correlli, 1995, Snowy River: The McGregor Saga, 1993, Halifax f.p: Afraid of the Dark, 1998, Oklahoma!, 1999; (films) Hey Mr. Producer, 1998, Paperback Hero, 1999, Erskineville Kings, 1999, X-Men, 2000, Someone Like You, 2001, Swordfish, 2001, Kate & Leopold, 2001, Standing Room Only, 2002, X2, 2003, Van Helsing, 2004, The Fountain, 2006, X-Men: The Last Stand, 2006, Scoop, 2006, The Prestige, 2006, (voice) Flushed Away, 2006, Happy Feet, 2006, Uncle Jonny, 2008, Australia, 2008, Snow Flower and the Secret Fan, 2011, Butter, 2011, Real Steel, 2011, (voice) Rise of the Guardians, 2012, Les Misérables, 2012 (Golden Globe award for Best Performance by an Actor in a Motion Picture-Comedy or Musical, 2013), Movie 43, 2013, Prisoners, 2013, X-Men: Days of Future Past, 2014, Chappie, 2015, Pan, 2015, Eddie the Eagle, 2016, Broadway 4D, 2016; actor, producer (films) Deception, 2008, X-Men Origins: Wolverine, 2009 (Teen Choice award for Choice Movie Actor: Action Adventure, 2009), The Wolverine, 2013; actor: (other stage appearances) Beauty and the Beast, Oklahoma!, Carousel, 2002; (Broadway plays) The Boy from Oz, 2003 (Tony Award for Best Actor in a Musical, 2004, Drama Desk Award for Best Actor in a Musical, 2004), A Steady Rain, 2009, Hugh Jackman, Back on Broadway, 2011-12, The River, 2014-15; host Tony Awards, 2003, 2004, 2005 (Emmy Award for Outstanding Individual Performance in a Variety or Musical Program, 2005), 2014, The Oscars, 2009; (Television) Viva Laughlin, 2007, Sesame Street, 2010, WWE Raw, 2011, SNL, 2011, Top Gear, 2013, Christmas in Washington, 2013, WWE Raw, 2014; (Movies) X-Men: Apocalypse, 2016, Logan, 2017, The Greatest Showman, 2017, The Front Runner, 2018; (Theatre) The River, 2014, An Evening with Hugh Jackman, 2015, Broadway to Oz, 2015 **AW:** Named Favorite Action Star, People's Choice Awards, 2012, 2010, Sexiest Man Alive, People magazine, 2008; recipient Star, Hollywood Walk of Fame, 2012, Special Tony Award Actors' Equity Association, 2012 **BA:** The Spanky Taylor Company, 3727 W Magnolia, Suite 300, Burbank, CA, 91505

JACKSON, ALAN, T: Musician **I:** Media & Entertainment **PB:** Newnan **SC:** GA/USA **PT:** Son of Eugene and Ruth Jackson; **ED:** Student, W. Georgia College **CW:** Musician: (albums) Here in the Real World, 1990, Don't Rock the Jukebox, 1991 (Album of Year, Academy Country Music, 1991), A Lot About Livin' (and a Little 'Bout Love), 1992, Honky Tonk Christmas, 1993, Who I Am, 1994, The Greatest Hits Collection, 1995, Everything I Love,

1996, High Mileage, 1998, Under the Influence, 1999, When Somebody Loves You, 2000, Drive, 2002 (Album of Year, Academy Country Music Awards, 2002), What I Do, 2004, Like Red on a Rose, 2006, Live at Texas Stadium, 2007, Good Time, 2008, Freight Train, 2010, Thirty Miles West, 2012, Precious Memories, 2012, Precious Memories Volume II, 2013 (Top Christian Album, Billboard Music Awards, 2014), The Bluegrass Album, 2013, Angels and Alcohol, 2015, (songs) Don't Rock the Jukebox, 1991 (Single Record of Year, Academy Country Music, 1991, American Society of Composers Country Song of year, 1992, Single of Year, Music Record of Year, Country Music Association Awards, 1993), Chattahoochee, 1993 (Single Record of Year, Academy Country Music Awards, 1993, Single of Year, Academy Country Music Awards, 1993), Where Were You (When the World Stopped Turning), 2002 (Best Country Song, Grammy Awards, 2002), It's Five O'Clock Somewhere (with Jimmy Buffett, 2003 (Single of Year, Vocal Event of Year, Academy Country Music Awards, 2003), As She's Walking Away, 2010 (Vocal Event of Year award, Academy Country Music, 2011, Single of Year, Song of Year, Country Music Association Awards, 2002) **AW:** Named Male Vocalist of Year, Country Music Association Awards, 2002, Entertainer of Year, Academy Country Music Awards, 2002, 1995, Male Vocalist of Year, 1995, 1994, Country Songwriter of Year, American Society of Composers, 1992; recipient Impact award, CMT Music Awards, 2014, Star, Hollywood Walk of Fame, 2010, Triple Play award, Country Music Association Awards, 1992, 1991, 1990, Grammy Award for Best Country Collaboration with Vocals, 2011, Billboard Music Awards, 2014 Top Christian Album **BA:** Alan Jackson Fan Club, PO Box 121945, Nashville, TN, 37212

JACKSON, CURTIS (FIFTY CENT), T: Rap Artist, Actor **I:** Media & Entertainment **DOB:** 07/06/1976 **PB:** Queens **PT:** Son of Sabrina **CW:** Performer: (soundtracks) Power of the Dollar, 2000, (albums) Guess Who's Back?, 2002, Get Rich or Die Tryin', 2003, 24 Shots, 2003, The Massacre, 2005 (Favorite Rap Album, American Music Awards, 2005, Album of Year, Billboard Music Awards, 2005, Top 200 Album of Year, Billboard Music Awards, 2005), Curtis, 2007, Before I Self-Destruct, 2009, Street King Immortal, 2015; performer: (with G-Unit) (albums with G-Unit) Beg for Mercy, 2003; performer: (songs) How to Rob, 1999, Wanksta, 2002, In Da Club, 2003 (Top R&B/Hip-Hop Song, American Society of Composers, 2004, Top Rap Song, American Society of Composers, 2004, Pop Songwriter of Year, American Society of Composers, 2004); actor: (films) Get Rich or Die Tryin', 2005, Righteous Kill, 2008, Twelve, 2010, Morning Glory, 2010, Escape Plan, 2013, Vengeance, 2013, Southpaw, 2015, Popstar: Never Stop Never Stopping, 2016, The Pursuit, 2017, Den of Thieves, 2018, Escape Plan,2018; actor, producer, writer (films) All Things Fall Apart, 2011, actor, executive producer Caught in the Crossfire, 2010, actor, producer Setup, 2011, Freelancers, 2012, The Frozen Ground, 2013; executive prodr.: (TV series) Power, 2014-; author: (autobiography) From Pieces to Weight: Once Upon a Time in Southside Queens, 2005, The 50th Law, 2009 **AW:** Named Best Rap Performance by a Duo or Group (with Eminem & Dr. Dre, Grammy Awards, 2010, Best Rap/Hip-Hop Artist, World Music Awards, 2007, Best Male Pop Artist, 2005, Artist of Year, Hip-Hop Artist of Year, Rap Artist of Year, Hot 100 Artist of Year, Billboard Music Awards, 2005; named one of The 100 Most Powerful Celebrities, Forbes.com, 2008 **BA:** APA Agency, 135 W 50th St, New York, NY, 10020

JACKSON, GLENDA, **T:** British Legislator, Actress **I:** Government Administration/Government Relations/Government Services **DOB:** 05/09/1936 **PB:** Birkenhead **SC:** Cheshire/England **PT:** Daughter of Harry and Joan J. **SPN:** Roy Hodges, 1958 (div. 1976); **CH:** Daniel **ED:** LLM (hon.), University of Nottingham, 1992; DLitt (hon.), University of Liverpool, 1978 **C:** Member of Parliament for Labor Party representing Hampstead and Highgate,, Parliament, London, England 1992-; Under secretary of state Department Environment and Transport, Parliament, London, England 1997-99 **CW:** Made stage debut as student in Separate Tables, Worthing, England, 1957; first appeared London (England) stage as Ruby in All Kinds of Men, Arts Theatre, 1957; appeared in Hammersmith, 1962, The Idiot, 1963, Alfie, 1963, Stratford Season, 1965; Love's Labour's Lost, Hamlet, The Investigation, 1965, Marat-Sade, 1965, Puntila, 1965, Three Sisters, 1967, Fortune, 1967, Collaborators, 1973, as Solange in The Maids, 1974, Rose, New York City, London, 1980-81, Phaedra, New York City, 1984-85, Strange Interlude, 1985, Macbeth, 1988 The White Devil, 1976, Scenes from an Execution, 1990, Mother Courage, 1990, Edward Albee's Three Tall Women, 2017, (Tony Award for Best Performance by an Actress in a Leading Role in a Play); actress: (films) The Extra Day, 1956, This Sporting Life, 1963, Marat-Sade, 1967, Tell Me Lies, 1968, Negatives, 1968, Women in Love, 1969 (Academy award for Best Actress 1970), The Music Lovers, 1970, Sunday, Bloody Sunday, 1971, The Boy Friend, 1971, Mary Queen of Scots, 1971, Triple Echo, 1972, The Nelson Affair, 1973, A Touch of Class (Academy award for Best Actress 1974), 1973, The Devil Is a Woman, 1974, Hedda, 1975, The Maids, 1975, The Romantic Englishwoman, 1975, The Incredible Sarah, 1976, Nasty Habits, 1977, The Class of Miss MacMichael, 1978, House Calls, 1978, Steve, 1978, Lost and Found, 1979, HealtH, 1980, Hopscotch, 1980, The Return of the Soldier, 1982, Giro City, 1982, Turtle Diary, 1985, Business as Usual, 1987, Beyond Therapy, 1987, Salome's Last Dance, 1988, Doombeach, 1989, The Rainbow, 1989, (voice) The Real Story of Humpty Dumpty, 1990 King of the Wind, 1990; (TV films) The Patricia Neal Story, 1981, Sakharov, 1984, Strange Interlude, 1988, A Murder of Quality, 1991, The House of Bernarda Alba, 1991, The Secret Life of Arnold Bax, 1992, (voice) A Wave of Passion: The Life of Alexandra Kollontai, 1994; (TV appearances) ITV Play of the Week, 1957-61, Z Cars, 1963, Half-Hour Story, 1967, The Wednesday Play, 1965-68, American Theatre, 1968, ITV Saturday Night Theatre, 1969, BBC Play of the Month, 1970, Elizabeth R, 1971, The Morecambe & Wise Show, 1980. **AW:** Named a Commander of the Order of the British Empire, Queen Elizabeth II, 1978 **PA:** British Labour Party **BA:** House of Commons, London, SW1A 0AA

JACKSON, JESSE LOUIS, **T:** Civil Rights Activist, Clergyman **I:** Religious **DOB:** 10/08/1941 **PB:** Greenville **SC:** South Carolina **PT:** Son of Noah Robinson, Charles Henry (Stepfather) and Helen Burns Jackson; **ED:** Degree (hon.), Georgetown University; Degree (hon.), Howard University; Degree (hon.), University Rhode Island; Degree (hon.), Oral Roberts University; Degree (hon.), Oberlin University; Degree (hon.), Pepperdine University; Degree (hon.), North Carolina AT State University; MDiv, Chicago Theological Seminary, 2000; Student, Chicago Theological Seminary, 1964-66; BA in Sociology and Economics, North Carolina AT State University, 1964; Student, University Illinois, 1959-60 **C:** Founder, The Wall St. Project, 1997-; Founder, national president, Rainbow/Push Coalition, Inc., Chicago, 1996-; Founder, Citizenship Education Fund, 1984; Special envoy of the President & Secretary State for the Promotion of Democracy in Africa, US Department State, Washington, 1997-2000; Shadow senator from DC, US Senate, Washington, 1991-96; Founder, national president, National Rainbow Coalition Inc., Chicago, 1984-96; Founder, PUSH-Excel and PUSH for Economic Justice, 1977-96; Founder, executive director, Operation PUSH (People United to Serve Humanity), Chicago, 1971-96; National director, Operation Breadbasket project, Southern Christian Leadership Conference, 1967-71; Chicago director, Operation Breadbasket project, Southern Christian Leadership Conference, Chicago, 1966-67; Ordained to ministry, Baptist Church, 1968 **CR:** Lecturer for high schools, colleges, professor audiences in Am., Europe candidate for Dem. nomination US Presidential Election, 1987-88, 1983-84 **CIV:** Active Black Coalition for United Community Action, 1969. **CW:** Host, Both Sides with Jesse Jackson, CNN, 1992-2000; Author: Straight From the Heart, 1987, Keep Hope Alive, 1989; co-author: (with Jesse L. Jackson, Junior) Legal Lynching: Racism, Injustice, and the Death Penalty, 1996, It's About the Money: How You Can Get Out of Debt, Build Wealth, and Achieve Your Financial Dreams!, 1999; appeared in: (documentaries) The Nine Lives of Marion Barry, 2009 **AW:** Recipient Presidential Award National Medical Association, 1969, Humanitarian Father of Year Award National Father's Day Committee, 1971, Presidential Medal of Freedom, 2000; named Third Most Admired Man in Am. Gallup Poll, 1985, one of six new leaders on the rise US News World Report, 100 Most Influential Black Americans Ebony magazine, 2006; named to Power 150 Ebony magazine, 2008. **BA:** 930 East 50th Street, Chicago, IL, 60615

JACKSON, MICHAEL J., **T:** Automotive Retailer Company Executive **I:** Automotive **CN:** AutoNation, Inc. **C:** Chairman, CEO, AutoNation, Inc., Fort Lauderdale, FL, 1999-Present; President, CEO, Mercedes-Benz USA, Inc., 1999; Senior Marketing Executive, Mercedes-Benz USA, Inc.; District Manager, Mercedes-Benz North America; Managing Partner, Euro Motorcars, Bethesda, MD; Technician, Mercedes-Benz Dealership, Cherry Hill, NJ **CR:** Chairman, Board of Directors, Atlanta Federal Reserve Bank; Director, Fort Lauderdale Museum of Art **AW:** Two-Time Automotive Executives Dream Team, Automotive News, Four-Time Marketing 100, Advertising Age, All-Star Dealer Award, Sports Illustrated, 1990, Automobile Hall Of Fame, 2003, Automotive Industry Leader Of the Year, 2003, South Florida's CEO Magazine CEO Of The Year, 2006, Wayne Huizenga School Of Business Entrepreneur Hall Of Fame, 2006, 50 Visionary Dealers Of All Time, Automotive News, 2009 **BA:** AutoNation Inc., 110 SE 6th Street, Fort Lauderdale, FL, 33301-5000

JACKSON, O'SHEA (ICE CUBE), **T:** Rap Artist, Actor **I:** Media & Entertainment **PB:** Los Angeles **SC:** CA/USA **PT:** Hosea Jackson; Doris Jackson **MS:** Married **SPN:** Kim Woodruff (April 26, 1992) **CH:** O'Shea Junior; Darryl; Kereema; Shareef **ED:** Attended, Phoenix Institute Tech. **C:** Founder, Lynch Mob Records, LA **CR:** Founder Cubevision Production Co. **CW:** Albums: (with N.W.A.) Straight Outta Compton, 1989, (with Westside Connection) Bow Down, 1996, Terrorist Threats, 2003, (solo) Amerikkka's Most Wanted, 1990, Kill At Will, Death Certificate, 1991, The Predator, 1992, Lethal Injection, 1993, War & Peace, Vol. 1, 1998, War & Peace, Vol. 2, 2000, Laugh Now, Cry Later, 2006, Raw Footage, 2008, I Am the West, 2010, Everythang's Corrupt, 2014; actor: (films) Boyz n the Hood, 1991, Trespass, 1992, Higher Learning, 1995, Anaconda, 1997, I Got the Hook Up, 1998, Three Kings, 1999, Ghosts of Mars, 2001, Barbershop, 2002, Torque, 2004, xXx: State of the Union, 2005, First Sunday, 2008, Rampart, 2011, 21 Jump Street, 2012, 22 Jump Street, 2014, The Book of Life, 2014, Straight Outta Compton, 2015, Ride Along 2, 2016, Barbershop: The Next Cut, 2016, xXx: Return of Xander Cage, 2017, Fist Fight, 2017, Last Friday, 2018 actor, writer: (films) The Glass Shield, 1995; actor, prodr.: (films) All About the Benjamins, 2002, Friday After Next, 2002, Barbershop 2: Back in Business, 2004, Are We There Yet?, 2005, Are We Done Yet?, 2007, The Longshots, 2008, The Janky Promoters, 2009, Ride Along, 2014, Ride Along 2, 2016, Barbershop: The Next Cut, 2016; actor, executive prodr.: (films) Friday, 1995, Dangerous Ground, 1997, The Players Club, 1998, Next Friday, 2000, Barbershop 2: Back in Business, 2005, Lottery Ticket, 2010; executive prodr.: (films) Beauty Shop, 2005; executive prodr.: (TV series) Barbershop, 2005, Black.White., 2006, Are We There Yet?, 2010-12, The Rebels, 2014 **AW:** Named to Rock and Roll Hall of Fame (as member of N.W.A), 2016

JACKSON, PHIL, **T:** Former Professional Basketball Coach **I:** Athletics **DOB:** 09/17/1945 **PB:** Deer Lodge **SC:** MO/USA **PT:** Son of Charles and Elisabeth (Funk) Jackson; **ED:** LHD (hon.), University North Dakota; BA in Religion, Psychology & Philosophy, University North Dakota, 1967 **C:** President, New York Knicks, 2014-17; Head coach, LA Lakers, 2005-11; Head coach, LA Lakers, 1999-2004; Head coach, Chicago Bulls, 1989-98; Assistant coach, Chicago Bulls, 1987-89; Head coach, Albany Patroons, Continental Basketball Association, 1982-87; Assistant coach, New Jersey Nets, 1980-82; Forward, New Jersey Nets, 1978-80; Forward, New York Knicks, 1967-78 **CW:** Co-author (with George Kalinsky): Take It All, 1970; co-author: (with Charley Rosen) Maverick, 1975, More Than A Game, 2002; co-author: (with Hugh Delehanty) Sacred Hoops: Spiritual Lessons of a Hardwood Warrior, 1996, Eleven Rings: The Soul of Success, 2013; author: The Last Season: A Team in Search of Its Soul, 2004, Journey to the Ring: Behind the Scenes with the 2010 NBA Champion Lakers, 2010 **AW:** Named NBA Coach of Year, 1996; named one of NBA Ten Greatest Coaches, 1997; named to Naismith Memorial Basketball Hall of Fame, 2007; recipient Theodore Roosevelt Rough Rider award, 1992,NBA All-Star Game Head Coach, 1992, 1996, 2000, 2009, Basketball Hall of Fame, 2007 **ACH:** Achievements include member of NBA Championship winning New York Knicks, 1970, 73; head coach of NBA Championship winning Chicago Bulls, 1991, 92, 93, 96, 97, 98; Los Angeles Lakers, 2000, 01, 02, 09, 10; holding the record for NBA Championship wins as both a player and coach (13)

JACKSON, SAMUEL L., **I:** Media & Entertainment **DOB:** 12/21/1948 **PB:** Washington **SC:** DC/USA **PT:** Elizabeth (Montgomery) Jackson **MS:** Married **SPN:** LaTanya Richardson (January 14, 1980) **CH:** Zoe **CW:** Actor: (TV series) Happily Ever After: Fairy Tales for Every Child, 1995-99, (voice) The Boondocks, 2005-10; (TV films) The Trial of the Moke, 1978, Uncle Tom's Cabin, 1987, Common Ground, 1990, Dead and Alive: The Race for Gus Farace, 1991, Simple Justice, 1993, Assault at West Point, 1994, Against the Wall, 1994, Honor Deferred, 2006, The Sunset Limited, 2011, Prohibition, 2011, Curiosity, 2011, 2012 Spike Video Game Awards, 2012, The Colbert Report, 2012, Generations, 2013, Agents of Shield, 2013-2014,Black Dynamite, 2014; (films) Together for Days, 1972, Ragtime, 1981, Eddie Murphy Raw, 1987, Coming to America, 1988, School Daze, 1988, Mystery Train (voice), 1989, Do The Right Thing, 1989, Sea of Love, 1989, A Shock to the System,

1990, Def by Temptation, 1990, Betsy's Wedding, 1990, Mo' Better Blues, 1990, The Exorcist III, 1990, Goodfellas, 1990, Return of Superfly, 1990, Jungle Fever, 1991, Strictly Business, 1991, Juice, 1992, White Sands, 1992, Patriot Games, 1992, Johnny Suede, 1992, Jumpin' at the Boneyard, 1992, Fathers and Sons, 1992, National Lampoon's Loaded Weapon 1, 1993, Amos & Andrew, 1993, Menace II Society, 1993, Jurassic Park, 1993, True Romance, 1993, Hail Caesar, 1994, Fresh, 1994, Hail Caesar, 1994, The New Age, 1994, Pulp Fiction, 1994, Losing Isiah, 1995, Kiss of Death, 1995, Fluke, 1995, Die Hard With a Vengeance, 1995, The Great White Hype, 1996, Trees Lounge, 1996, The Search for One Eye Jimmy, 1996, A Time to Kill, 1996, The Long Kiss Goodnight, 1996, 187, 1997, Jackie Brown, 1997, Hard Eight, 1997, Sphere, 1998, Out of Sight, 1998, The Negotiator, 1998, Rules of Engagement, 1999, Mefisto in Onyx, 1999, Star Wars Episode I: The Phantom Menace, 1999, Deep Blue Sea, 1999, Shaft, 2000, Unbreakable, 2000, Changing Lanes, 2002, Star Wars: Episode II - Attack of the Clones, 2002, XXX, 2002, Basic, 2003, S.W.A.T., 2003, In My Country, 2004, Twisted, 2004, Kill Bill: Vol. 2, 2004, (voice) The Incredibles, 2004, Coach Carter, 2005 (Outstanding Actor in a Motion Picture, National Association for the Advancement of Colored People Image Awards, 2006), xXx: State of the Union, 2005, Star Wars: Episode III Revenge of the Sith, 2005, The Man, 2005, Freedomland, 2006, Snakes on a Plane, 2006, Black Snake Moan, 2006, Home of the Brave, 2006, Resurrecting the Champ, 2007, 1408, 2007, Jumper, 2008, Star Wars: The Clone Wars, 2008, Lakeview Terrance, 2008, Soul Men, 2008, The Spirit, 2008, (voice) Astro Boy, 2009, Mother and Child, 2009, Unthinkable, 2010, Iron Man 2, 2010 The Other Guys, 2010, Captain America: The First Avenger, 2011, Thor, 2011, Meeting Evil, 2012, The Avengers, 2012, (voice) Zambezia, 2012, Django Unchained, 2012 (Outstanding Supporting Actor in a Motion Picture, National Association for the Advancement of Colored People Image Awards, 2013), Turbo (voice), 2013, Oldboy, 2013, Reasonable Doubt, 2014, RoboCop, 2014, Captain America: The Winter Soldier, 2014, Kite, 2014, Big Game, 2014, Kingsman: The Secret Service, 2015, Barely Lethal, 2015, Avengers: Age of Ultron, 2015, Chi-Raq, 2015, The Hateful Eight, 2015, Cell, 2016, The Legend of Tarzan, 2016, Miss Peregrine's Home for Peculiar Children, 2016, Eating You Alive, 2016, xXx:Return of Xander Cage, 2017, Kong:Skull Island, 2017, The Hitman's Bodyguard, 2017, Unicorn Store, 2017, Incredibles 2, 2018, Blazing Samurai, 2018, Life Itself, 2018, The Last Full Measure, 2018, Glass, 2019, Son of Shaft, 2019; (plays) The Mountaintop, 2011; actor, prodr.: (films) Eve's Bayou, 1997, Cleaner, 2007; actor, executive prodr.: (films) The Caveman's Valentine, 2001, Formula 51, 2001, The Samaritan, 2012, (TV films) Afro Samurai: Resurrection (voice), 2009. **AW:** Recipient American Cinematheque award, 2008, Star, Hollywood Walk of Fame, 2006, Dream Keeper award, I Have A Dream Foundation, 2005

JACKSON LEE, SHEILA, T: U.S. Representative from Texas **I:** Government Administration/Government Relations/Government Services **DOB:** 01/12/1950 **PB:** Queens, New York **PT:** Daughter of Erica Shelwyn and Jason Cornelius Bennett; **ED:** JD, University Virginia School Law, Charlottesville, 1975; BA in Political Sci., with honors, Yale University, New Haven, 1972 **CT:** Bar: Texas **C:** Member, US Congress from 18th Texas District, 1995-; Member, Committee on Homeland Security, Committee on the Judiciary; Founder Congl. Children's Caucus, US Congress from 18th Texas District,; Councilwoman, Houston City Council, 1990-94; Associate Judge, City of Houston

Municipal Court, 1987-89; Senior Attorney, United Energy Resources, Inc., 1980; Trial Attorney, Fulbright & Jaworski, 1978-80; Senior Counsel Select Committee on Assassinations, US Congress, 1977-78 **AW:** Named one of 100 Most Influential Black Americans, Ebony Magazine, 2006; Named to Power 150, 2008; recipient Phillip Burton Immigration & Civil Rights policy Award, Immigrant Legal Resource Center, 2006, Top Women in Sci. Award, National Tech. Association Scientists & Engineers, 1998 **MEM:** Mem.: Texas Municipal Judges Association, State Bar Association Justice Committee **PA:** Democrat **BA:** 2187 Rayburn House Office Building, Washington, DC, 20515

JACOBS, BRADLEY S., T: Transportation and Logistics Services Company Exec **I:** Logistics and Supply Chain **C:** Chairman, CEO XPO Logistics, Greenwich, Connecticut, 2011-; Co-founder, chairman, CEO, United Rentals, Greenwich, 1997-2007; Founder, chairman, CEO, United Waste Systems, Inc., 1989-97; Chairman, COO, Hamilton Resources Ltd., 1984-89; CEO, Amerex Oil Associates, Inc., 1979-83

JACOBS, DENNIS G., T: Federal Judge **I:** Law and Legal Services **DOB:** 02/28/1944 **PB:** New York **SC:** NY/USA **PT:** Son of Harry N. and Rose J.; Married Judith Weissman. **ED:** LLD (hon.), St. John's University, 2009; JD, New York University School Law, 1973; MA, New York University, 1965; BA, Queens College, 1964 **C:** Judge, US Court Appeals (2d Cir.), New York City, 1992-; Chief judge, US Court Appeals (2d Cir.), New York City, 2006-13; Partner, Simpson Thacher & Bartlett, New York City, 1980-92; Associate, Simpson Thacher & Bartlett, New York City, 1973-80 **CR:** Chairman Committee on Judicial Resources, Judicial Conference of US, 1999-2004, member, 1997- lecturer Queens College, 1967-69 **AW:** Recipient James Madison award, Federalist Society, 2009, Outstanding Public Service award, New York Intellectual Property Law Association, 2009, Eugene J. Keogh award for Distinguished Public Service, New York University, 2004, Learned Hand award for Excellence in Jurisprudence, Federal Bar Council, 2003 **BA:** 40 Foley Square, New York, NY, USA, 10007

JACOBS, MARC, T: Fashion Designer **I:** Apparel & Fashion **DOB:** 04/09/1963 **PB:** New York **SC:** NY/USA **ED:** Student, Parsons School of Design, The New School, New York, NY **C:** Designer, Mark Jacobs, New York, NY, 1988-Present; Developer, Marc By Marc Jacobs Line, Marc Jacobs, 2001; Creative Director, Louis Vuitton, Paris, France, 1997-2013; Head Designer, Perry Ellis, New York, NY, 1989-1992; Marc Jacobs Label Debut, 1986; Jacobs Duffy Designs Inc.; Designer, Ruben Thomas Inc. (Under Sketchbook Label), New York, NY; Stock Boy, Charivari, New York, NY **CR:** Creative Director, Diet Coke, 2013; Co-Host, Metropolitan Museum of Art Costume Institute Gala, New York, NY, 2009 **CW:** Subject of Documentary, Marc Jacobs and Louis Vuitton, 2007, The Red Carpet Issue, 2010, L'effet Mad men, 2010, In Vogue: The Editor's Eye, 2012, Scatter My Ashes at Bergdorf's, 2013; Actor, (Films) Disconnect, 2012 **AW:** Council of Fashion Designers of America, Womenswear Designer of the Year, 2016, Geoffrey Beene Lifetime Achievement Award, Council of Fashion Designers of America, 2011, Council of Fashion Designers Of America Lifetime Achievement Award, 2011, The 100 Most Influential People in the World, TIME Magazine, 2010, The 100 Agents of Change, Rolling Stone Magazine, 2009, Fragrance Foundation's Hall of Fame, 2009, Designer of the Year Award, Accessories Council of Excellence, 2007, Women's Designer of the Year Award, 1992, 2010, Perry Ellis Award for New Fashion Talent, 1987,

Design Student of the Year Award, Parsons School of Design, 1984, Chester Weinberg Gold Thimble Award, 1984, Perry Ellis Gold Thimble Award, 1984 **PA:** Democrat **BA:** Marc Jacobs Headquarters, 72 Spring Street, Second Floor, New York, NY, 10012

JAGGER, MICK, T: Singer **I:** Media & Entertainment **DOB:** 07/26/1943 **PB:** Dartford **SC:** Kent Eng. **PT:** Son of Joe and Eva Jagger; 1 child (with Marsha Hunt) Karis; Married Bianca Perez Morena de Macias, May 12, 1971 (div. November 1979); children: Jade, Karis; Married Jerry Hall, November 21, 1990 **ED:** Student, London School Econs., 1962-64 **C:** Lead singer, The Rolling Stones, 1962-; Lead singer, SuperHeavy, 2011 **CW:** Singer: (albums with The Rolling Stones) England's Newest Hitmakers: The Rolling Stones, 1964, 12 X 5, 1964, The Rolling Stones, Now!, 1965, Out of Our Heads, 1965, December's Children (And Everybody's), 1965, Big Hits, High Tide, & Green Grass, 1966, Aftermath, 1966, Got Live if You Want It!, 1966, Between the Buttons, 1967, Flowers, 1967, Their Satanic Majesties Request, 1967, Beggars Banquet, 1968, Through the Past, Darkly (Big Hits Vol. 2), 1969, Let It Bleed, 1969, Get Yer Ya-Yas Out!: The Rolling Stones in Concert, 1970, Hot Rocks, 1964-1971, 1971, Sticky Fingers, 1971, More Hot Rocks: Big Hits and Fazed Cookies, 1972, Exile on Main Street, 1972, Goats Head Soup, 1973, It's Only Rock and Roll, 1974, Metamorphosis, 1975, Made in the Shade, 1975, Rolled Gold+: The Very Best of the Rolling Stones, 1975, Black and Blue, 1976, Love You Live, 1977, Some Girls, 1978, Emotional Rescue, 1980, Sucking in the Seventies, 1981, Tattoo You, 1981, "Still Life" (American Concert, 1981), 1982, Undercover, 1983, Rewind (1971-1984), 1984, Dirty Work, 1986, Singles Collection: The London Years, 1989, Steel Wheels, 1989, Flashpoint, 1990, Jump Back: The Best of the Rolling Stones, 1993, Voodoo Lounge, 1994 (Grammy Award for Best Rock Album, 1994), Stripped, 1995, Bridges to Babylon, 1997, No Security, 1999, Forty Licks, 2002, Singles: 1965-1967, 2004, Live Licks, 2004, A Bigger Bang, 2005, Rarities 1971-2003, 2005, GRRR!, 2012, (soundtracks) Shine a Light, 2008, (albums with The Rolling Stones & other artists) Jamming With Edward, 1972, The Rolling Stones Rock 'N' Roll Circus, 1996, (albums with SuperHeavy) SuperHeavy, 2011, (solo albums) She's The Boss, 1985, Primitive Cool, 1987, Wandering Spirit, 1993, Goddess In the Doorway, 2001, The Very Best of Mick Jagger, 2007, (soundtracks) Alfie, 2004 ((with David A. Stewart) Golden Globe award for best original song "Old Habits Die Hard", 2005), Superheavy, 2011; Singles: Miracles Worker, With Superheavy, 2011, T.H.E., with Will.i.am and Jennifer Lopez, 2011, Gotta get a Grip/ England Lost, 2017 performer: (films) Gimme Shelter, 1970, Sympathy for the Devil, 1970, Ladies and Gentlemen: The Rolling Stones, 1974, Let's Spend the Night Together, 1983, Rolling Stones: Live At the Max, 1991, Voodoo Lounge, 1995, The Rolling Stones Rock 'N' Roll Circus, 1996, The Rolling Stones Bridges to Babylon Tour '97-98, 1997, Four Flicks, 2003, The Biggest Bang, 2007, Shine a Light, 2008, Some Girls Live in Texas '78, 2011; appeared in (documentaries) 25 X 5: The Continuing Adventures of the Rolling Stones, 1989, Being Mick, 2001, Stones in Exile, 2010, Crossfire Hurricane, 2012, The Rolling Stones: Charlie Is My Darling, 2012, Muscle Shoals, 2013; actor: (films) Performance, 1969, Ned Kelly, 1970, Freejack, 1992, Bent, 1997, The Man From Elysian Fields, 2001, Being Mick, 2001, Mayer of the Sunset Strip, 2003, Shine a Light, 2008, The Bank Job, 2008, Stones in Exile, 2010, Ladies and Gentleman: The Rolling Stones, 2010, Some Girls: Live in Texas '78, 2011, (TV appearances) The Knights of Prosperity, 2007; prodr.: (films) Enigma, 2001, The Women,

2008; prodr.: (films) Get on Up, 2014 **AW:** Named Greatest Touring Band of All Time, World Music Awards, 2006; named an Honorary Knight Commander of the Most Excellent Order of the British Empire, Her Majesty Queen Elizabeth II, 2003; named to The Rock and Roll Hall of Fame (as member of The Rolling Stones), 1989 **BA:** Special Artists Agency, 9465 Wilshire Boulevard, Beverly Hills, CA, 90212

JAGR, JAROMIR, T: Professional Hockey Player **I:** Athletics **CN:** Florida Panthers **DOB:** 02/15/1972 **PB:** Kladno **SC:** Czech Republic **C:** Calgary Flame, 2017-Present; Right Wing, Florida Panthers, 2015-Present; Right Wing, New Jersey Devils, 2013-2015; Right Wing, Boston Bruins, 2013; Right Wing, Dallas Stars, 2012-2013; Right Wing, Philadelphia Flyers, 2011-2012; Right Wing, Avangard Omsk (Continental Hockey League), Russia, 2008-2011; Captain, New York Rangers, 2006-2008; Right Wing, New York Rangers, 2004-2008; Right Wing, Washington Capitals, 2001-2004; Right Wing, Pittsburgh Penguins, 1990-2001; Right Wing, Poldi Kladno, 1988-1990 **CR:** Co-Owner, HC Kladno; Owner, Jagr Bar; Prague Member, Team Czech Republic, Olympic Games, Vancouver, BC, Canada, 2010; Prague Member, Team Czech Republic, Olympic Games, Torino, Italy, 2006; Prague Member, Team Czech Republic, Olympic Games, Salt Lake City, UT, 2002; Prague Member, Team Czech Republic, Olympic Games, Nagano, Japan, 1998 **AW:** 100 Greatest NHL Players, 2017, Bill Masterton Memorial Trophy, NHL, 2016, NHL Eastern Conference Champion, 2013, Medal Of Merit, 2010, NHL Player of the Year, Sporting News, 1999-2000, 2006, Lester B. Pearson Award, 1999-2000, 2006, Hart Memorial Trophy, 1999, Golden Stick Trophy For Czech Republic Player of the Year, 1995-1996, 1999-2000, 2002, 2005-2008, Best NHL Player, ESPY Awards, 2006, NHL All-Star Game, 1992-1993, 1996, 1998-2004, 2016, Czechoslovakian League All-Star Team, 1989-1990, Second All-Star Team, NHL, 1997, First All-Star Team, 1995-1996, 1998-2001, 2006, Art Ross Trophy, 1995, 1998-2001, All-Rookie Team, 1991 **ACH:** Achievements include being a member of Stanley Cup Champion Pittsburgh Penguins, 1991, 1992; being a member of gold medal winning Czech Republic Hockey Team, Nagano Olympics, 1998, bronze medal team, Torino Olympics, Italy, 2006; setting the New York Rangers franchise record for goals in a season with 54 goals, 2006; setting the NHL record for most regular-season overtime goals, 2012 **BA:** Florida Panthers, BankAtlantic Center, One Panther Parkway, Sunrise, FL, 33323

JAHREN, (A.) HOPE, T: Geochemist, Educator **I:** Sciences **ED:** PhD, University California, Berkeley, 1996; BA, University Minnesota, Minneapolis, 1991 **C:** Professor, Johns Hopkins University, 2006-; Associate professor, Johns Hopkins University, 2003-06; Assistant professor geobiology, Johns Hopkins University, Baltimore, 1999-2003; Assistant professor geochemistry, Georgia Institute Tech., 1996-99; Postdoctoral researcher ecosystem sci. division, University California, Berkeley, 1996 **CW:** Contributor articles to sci. journals **AW:** Named one of Brilliant 10, Popular Sci. magazine, 2005; recipient Macelwane medal, Am. Geophysical Union, 2005 **MEM:** Fellow: Geological Society Am. (Donath award 2001)

JAMES, E.L., T: Writer, Former Broadcast Executive **I:** Writing and Editing **DOB:** 03/07/1963 **PB:** London **ED:** Attended, University of Kent **C:** Writer 2011- **CW:** Author: Fifty Shades of Grey, 2011 (named to New York Times Best Seller List,

nominee for Best Romance, Goodreads Choice award, 2011), Fifty Shades Darker, 2012, Fifty Shades Freed, 2012, Grey: Fifty Shades of Grey, 2015, (Books) Grey: Fifty Shades of Grey As Told by Christian, 2015, Darker: Fifty Shades Darker as Told by Christian, (Film Produced) Fifty Shades of Grey, 2015, Fifty Shades Darker, 2017, Fifty Shades Freed, 2018 **AW:** Named Person of the Year, Publisher's Weekly, 2012; named one of The 100 Most Powerful Women in Entertainment, Hollywood Reporter, 2012-13, The 10 Most Fascinating People of 2012, Barbara Walters Special, The 100 Most Influential People in the World, TIME magazine, 2012, Time 100 Most Influential People in the World, 2012, Publishers Weekly Person of the Year, 2012 **BA:** Vintage Books & Anchor Books, 1745 Broadway, 12-1,, New York, NY, 10019

JAMES, LEBRON RAYMONE, T: Professional Basketball Player **I:** Athletics **DOB:** 12/30/1984 **PB:** Akron **PT:** Son of Gloria James and McClelland Anthony **C:** Forward, Los Angeles Lakers, 2018-; Forward, Cleveland Cavaliers, 2014-2018; Co-founder, partner, LRMR Innovative Marketing & Branding, Cleveland; Forward, Miami Heat, 2010-14; Forward, Cleveland Cavaliers, 2003-10 **CR:** Vice president NBA Players Association, 2015-; member US national team Summer Olympic Games, London, 2012, Beijing, 2008, Athens, Greece, 2004 **CIV:** Founder, board directors, LeBron James Family Foundation, 2004- **CW:** (cohost): ESPY Awards show, 2007; (guest host):(TV series) Saturday Night Live, 2007; featured on cover Vogue, 2008, appeared in (documentaries) More Than A Game, 2008, (TV series) Entourage, 2009; co-author (with Buzz Bissinger): Shooting Stars, 2009; (films) Trainwreck, 2015 **AW:** Named Male Athlete of Year, Associated Press, 2013, Sportsman of Year, Sports Illus., 2012, NBA Finals MVP, 2016, 2013, 2012, NBA MVP, 2013, 2012, 2010, 2009, NBA Player of Year, The Sporting News, 2009, 2006, NBA All-Star Game MVP, 2008, 2006, NBA Rookie of Year, 2004, National HS Player of Year, USA Today, 2003; named one of The 10 Most Fascinating People of 2010, Barbara Walters Special, The 40 Under 40, Fortune magazine, 2010, The 100 Agents of Change, Rolling Stone magazine, 2009, The Most Influential People in the World of Sports, Business Week, 2008, 2007, The 100 Most Powerful Celebrities, Forbes.com, 2008, The 100 Most Influential People in the World, TIME magazine, 2013, 2005; named to The NBA All-Defensive 1st Team, 2009-13, The Power 150, Ebony magazine, 2008, The All-NBA 1st Team, NBA, 2008-14, 2006, The Eastern Conference All-Star Team, 2005-16, NBA All-Rookie First Team, 2004; recipient Best Male Athlete award, Black Entertainment TV (BET), 2006-07, Gold medal, men's basketball, Summer Olympic Games, 2012, 2008, Bronze medal, men's basketball, 2004,Time 100 Most Influential, 2017, NBA All-Star, 2017, All-NBA First Team, 2017, J Walter Kennedy Citizenship Award **ACH:** Achievements include being the first overall pick in the NBA Draft, 2003; leading the NBA in: minutes, 2005, 2007; field goals, 2005, 2008; free throws, 2009; points per game, 2008; being a member of NBA Finals championship winning Miami Heat, 2012, 2013, Cleveland Cavaliers, 2016; the youngest player in NBA history to score 20,000 points, 2013 **BA:** Los Angeles Lakers, El Segundo, CA, 90245

JANNEY, ALLISON, T: Actress **I:** Media & Entertainment **DOB:** 11/19/1960 **PB:** Dayton **SC:** OH/USA **PT:** Jervis Spencer Janney Jr.; Macy (Putnam) Brooks **ED:** Private studies in acting, Neighborhood Playhouse, New York City; BA, Kenyon College **CW:** Actress: (films) Big Night, 1996, Private Parts, 1997, Primary Colors, 1998, Six Days, Seven Nights, 1998, The Ice Storm, 1997, Celebrity,

1998, 10 Things I Hate About You, 1999, Drop Dead Gorgeous, 1999, Nurse Betty, 2000, American Beauty, 1999, Leaving Drew, 2000, Finding Nemo (voice), 2003, How to Deal, 2003, Over the Hedge (voice), 2006, Hairspray, 2007, Juno, 2007, Pretty Ugly People, 2008, Prop 8: The Musical, 2008, Away We Go, 2009, Life During Wartime, 2009, The Help, 2011, The Oranges, 2011, Margaret, 2011, Liberal Arts, 2012, A Thousand Words, 2012, Struck by Lightning, 2012, Touchy Feely, 2013, The Way, Way Back, 2013, Trust Me, 2013, Bad Words, 2013, Brightest Star, 2013, Mr. Peabody & Sherman (voice), 2014, Days and Nights, 2014, The Rewrite, 2014, Tammy, 2014, Get on Up, 2014, The DUFF, 2015, Spy, 2015, Minions (voice), 2015, The Night Is Young, 2015, Tallulah, 2016, Finding Dory (voice), 2016, Miss Peregrine's Home for Peculiar Children, 2016, The Girl on the Train, 2016, A Happening of Monumental Proportions, Sun Dogs, 2017, I, Tonya, 2017(Golden Globe for Best Supporting Actress), (Academy Award for Best Supporting Actress) (Broadway), (Screen Actors Guild Award for Best Supporting Actress), Present Laughter, 1996, A View From The Bridge, 1997 (Outer Critics Circle award, Drama Desk award), 9 to 5, 2008 (Drama Desk award for Outstanding Actress in a Musical, 2009), (TV series) The West Wing, 1999-2006, (Emmy award for Outstanding Supporting Actress in a Drama Series, 1999, 2000, 2001, Emmy award for Outstanding Lead Actress in a Drama Series, 2002, 2004), Mom, 2013- (Emmy award for Outstanding Supporting Actress in a Comedy Series, 2014, 2015), (TV films) Friday Night Dinner, 2012, (TV appearances) Family Guy, 2010, In Plain Sight, 2010, Lost, 2010, Phineas and Ferb, 2008-12, Glenn Martin DDS, 2011, Mr. Sunshine, 2011, The Big C, 2012, Veep, 2013, Masters of Sex, 2013-15, (Emmy award for Outstanding Guest Actress in a Drama Series, 2014), Web Therapy, 2014, The Simpsons, 2016, Comedy Bang! Bang!, 2016, F is for Family, 2017, Nobodies, 2017, American Dad!, 2017, DuckTales, 2018 (TV miniseries) A Girl Thing, 2000

JARVIK, ROBERT KOFFLER, T: Biomedical Research Scientist **I:** Sciences **DOB:** 05/11/1946 **PB:** Midland **SC:** Michigan **PT:** Son of Norman Eugene and Edythe (Koffler) Jarvik **SPN:** Marilyn vos Savant **CH:** Tyler; Kate **ED:** DSc (hon.), Hahnemann University, 1985; DSc (hon.), Syracuse University, 1983; MD, University Utah, 1976; Ms in Medical Engineering, New York University, 1971; BA, Syracuse University, New York, 1968 **C:** Founder, President, Chief Executive Officer, Jarvik Research Inc., New York, NY (Now Jarvik Heart, Inc.) (1988-Present); President, Symbion, Inc., Salt Lake City (1978-1987); Assistant Research Professor of Surgery, The University of Utah, Salt Lake City, UT (1979-1987); Assistant Director of Experimental Laboratories, The University of Utah, Salt Lake City, UT (1976-1982); Research Assistant, Division of Artificial Organs, The University of Utah, Salt Lake City, UT (1971-1976) **CW:** Section Editor, "International Journal of Artificial Organs" (1979-1988) **AW:** Named Inventor of Year, Intellectual Property Owners Association, 1983; recipient Golden Plate award, American Academy Achievement, 1983, Gold Heart award, Utah Heart Association, 1983, John W. Hyatt award, Society Plastics Engineers, 1983 **ACH:** Achievements include invention of the first permanently-implantable artificial heart, the Jarvik-7; Development of a highly reliable innovative left ventricular assist system, the Jarvik 2000 Flow-Maker, a thumb-sized battery operated pump that fits directly into the left ventricle and pushes oxygenated blood throughout the body

JAYAPAL, PRAMILA, T: U.S. Representative from Washington **I:** Government Administration/Government Relations/Government Services **DOB:** 06/19/1905 **PB:** Chennai, Tamil Nadu, India **SC:** Chennai, Tamil Nadu, India **ED:** M.B., Northwestern University, 1990; A.B., Georgetown University, 1986 **C:** Member, U.S. House of Representatives from Washingtons 7th District, 2017-; Member, Committee on Budget; Member, Committee on Judiciary; Member, Washington Senate from the 37th District, 2015-16; Founder, Hate Free Zone, 2001-12

JEFFERTS SCHORI, KATHARINE, T: Bishop **I:** Religious **DOB:** 03/26/1954 **PB:** Pensacola **SC:** FL/USA **ED:** MDiv, Church Div. School of the Pacific, Berkeley, California, 1994; PhD in Oceanography, Oregon State University, Corvallis, 1983; MS in Oceanography, Oregon State University, Corvallis, 1977; BS in Marine Biology, Stanford University, 1974 **C:** Chief pastor, presiding bishop, Episcopal Church USA, New York City, 2006-; Bishop, Episcopal Diocese of Nevada, Las Vegas, 2001-06; Consecrated, bishop, 2001; Assistant rector, Episcopal Church of the Good Samaritan, Corvallis, Oregon, 1994-2001; Ordained, priest, 1994; Ordained, deacon, 1994; Worked in oceanography, including at the National Marine Fisheries Service in Seattle, **CW:** Author: A Wing and a Prayer: A Message of Faith and Hope, 2007 **ACH:** Achievements include becoming the first woman to lead a church in the worldwide Anglican Communion, 2006

JEFFRIES, HAKEEM SEKOU, T: U.S. Representative from New York, State Legislator (Retired), Lawyer **I:** Government Administration/Government Relations/Government Services **DOB:** 08/04/1970 **PB:** Brooklyn **SC:** NY/USA **ED:** JD, New York University, Magna Cum Laude (1997); MS in Public Policy, Georgetown University (1994); BA in Political Science, State University of New York at Binghamton (1992) **C:** Chair, Democratic Policy and Communications Committee (2017-Present); Member, U.S. House Judiciary Committee (2013-Present); Member, U.S. House Budget Committee (2013-Present); Member, U.S. Congress from the Eighth New York District, Washington, DC (2013-Present); Member District 57, New York State Assembly, Albany, NY (2007-2013); Litigation Counsel, CBS Corp. (2003-2006); Associate, Paul, Weiss, Rifkind, Wharton & Garrison (1999-2003); Law Clerk for Honorable Harold Baer, Junior, U.S. District Court for the Southern District of New York, New York (1998); Staff Member, Office of Mayor Sharon Pratt Kelly; Member, Committee on Education **CR:** Civil Rights and Civil Liberties Instructor, Crown Heights Youth Collective **CIV:** Member, Freedom Democrats, Brooklyn, NY; Member, 77th Precinct Community Council, New York **AW:** Named, One of the 40 Under 40, Crain's New York Business (2006) **MEM:** President, Black Attorneys for Progress **PA:** Democrat

JELINEK, CRAIG, T: Costco CEO **I:** Business Management/Business Services **DOB:** 08/08/1952 **ED:** BA, San Diego State University, 1975 **C:** President, CEO, Costco Wholesale Corp., Issaquah, Washington, 2011-; President, COO, Costco Wholesale Corp., Issaquah, Washington, 2010-11; Executive vice president, COO merchandising, Costco Wholesale Corp., Issaquah, Washington, 2004-10; Executive vice president, COO northern division, Costco Wholesale Corp., Issaquah, Washington, 1995-2004; Senior vice president operations northeastern region, Costco Wholesale Corp., Issaquah, Washington, 1992-95; Vice president, regional operations manager LA region, Costco Wholesale Corp., Issaquah, Washington, 1986-92; Joined, Costco Wholesale Corp., Issaquah, Washington, 1984; Operations manager L.A. division, Fed-Mart; Various positions, Gemco **CR:** Board of directors, Costco Wholesale Corp., 2010-

JENKINS, BARRY, T: Film Director, Producer **I:** Media & Entertainment **PB:** Miami **SC:** FL/USA **CW:** (Film) Medicine for Melancholy, 2008, Moonlight, 2016,(Golden Globe for Best Picture, 2017, Academy Award for Best Picture, 2017) Dear White People, 2017, If Beale Street Could Talk, 2018 **AW:** Time 100 Most Influential, 2017

JENKINS, EVAN H., T: U.S. Representative from West Virginia **I:** Government Administration/Government Relations/Government Services **DOB:** 09/12/1960 **PB:** Huntington **SC:** WV/USA **PT:** Son of John E. and Dorothy C. Jenkins **C:** Member, U.S. House of Representatives from West Virginia's 3rd District, 2015-; Member, Committee on Appropriations; Member District 5, W. Virginia State Senate, 2002-; Executive director, W. Virginia Medical Association, 1999-; Member, W. Virginia House of Dels., 1994-98; With, W. Virginia State C. of C., 1992-99; Attorney, Jenkins Fenstermaker PLLC, 1987-92 **CR:** Member U.S. Delegation to Taiwan, Am. Council Young Political Leaders Former Business Law Instructor, Marshall University **CIV:** Member community adv. committee, YMCA Activate America, Organizer, W. Virginia Health Initiative Inc. and W. Virginia Center for Patent Safety, Past. member, board directors, Western W. Virginia Chapter Am. Red Cross, President board director, Operation Business and Education Succeeding Together, President board director, Leadership W. Virginia, Board director, W. Virginia EPSCORE, Board director, W. Va.Coun. on Economics in Education, Board director, Riverview Manor, Board director, Huntington Main St., Board director, Cabell County Community Services Organization, Past president, Big Brothers/Big Sisters of the Tri-State, **AW:** Recipient Medical Executive Meritorious Achievement Award, American Medical Association, 2006 **MEM:** Mem.: W. Virginia Bar Association, Cabell County Bar Association, American Bar Association, Dem. Leadership Council (adv. board) **PA:** Democrat

JENKINS, JO ANN, T: CEO **I:** Nonprofit & Philanthropy **CN:** AARP **PB:** Mon Louis Island **SC:** AL/USA **ED:** Political Science, Spring Hill College; Stanford Executive Program, Stanford University's Graduate School of Business **C:** CEO, AARP, 2014-; COO, AARP, 2013-14

JENKINS, LYNN M., T: U.S. Representative from Kansas **I:** Government Administration/Government Relations/Government Services **DOB:** 06/10/1963 **PB:** Topeka **SC:** KS/USA **MS:** Single **SPN:** Scott M. Jenkins, 1983, Divorced 2009 **CH:** Hayley, Hayden **ED:** BS, Weber State College, 1985; AA, Kansas State University, 1984 **CT:** CPA **C:** Vice Chair, U.S. House Republican Conference, 2013-Present; U.S. Congress From 2nd Kansas District, 2009-Present; Treasurer, State Of Kansas, 2002-2009; District 20, Kansas State Senate, 2000-2003; District 52, Kansas House Of Representatives, 1998-2000; Committee On Financial Services, Ways And Means Committee, Republican Study Committee **CR:** College Savings Plan Network, Pooled Money Investment Board **MEM:** Kansas Society of CPAs, National Association of Unclaimed Property Administrator, Senior Vice President, National Association of State Treasurers **PA:** Republican **BA:** 1526 Longworth HOB, Washington, DC, 20515

JENNER, CAITLYN, T: Television Personality, Motivational Speaker, Former Olympic Athlete **I:** Media & Entertainment **DOB:** 10/28/1949 **PB:** Mt. Kisco **SC:** NY/USA **PT:** William Hugh Jenner, Ester R. (McGuire) Jenner **MS:** Single **SPN:** Kris Kardashian, 4/21/1991, Divorced 3/23/2015; Linda Thompson, 1/5/1981, Divorced 2/10/1986; Chrystie Crownover, 12/15/1972, Divorced 1/1981

CH: Burton "Burt", Cassandra "Casey", Brandon, Sam "Brody", Kendall, Kylie, Kourtney Kardashian (Stepdaughter), Kim Kardashian (Stepdaughter), Khloé Kardashian (Stepdaughter), Robert "Rob" Kardashian (Stepson) **ED:** Graduate, Graceland College, Lamoni, IA, 1973 **C:** Founder, President, 8634 Inc., 1976-Present; U.S. Olympic Team, Montreal, QC, Canada, 1976; U.S. Olympic Team, Munich, Germany, 1972; Owner, Founder, Bruce Jenner Aviation **CR:** National Spokesperson, General Aviation Task Force, 1991, Neo-Life Health Care Products, Kodak, IBM, General Mills, Cisco Systems, Deloitte Services; President, Fitness Council, FXTV; Lecturer, Colleges and Universities, Business and Industrial Conventions; Motivational Speaker; Sports Commentator; Entrepreneur; Commercial Spokesperson **CIV:** Active, Special Olympics; Governor Council, Physical Fitness Advisory Boards, Angel Planes; National Advisory Committees, Children's Miracle Flights, California Special Olympics, Family Sports Day on Council of Champions, Children's Hope Foundation, Global Mind Network, Icons of the 20th Century, International Student Travel & Youth, Make-A-Wish Foundation - KJ; Honorary Committee, Martin Luther King National Holiday Celebration, National Dyslexia Research Foundation, President's Council on American Intercultural Student Exchange (AISE), David Rickey & Co., National Council on Recording for the Blind, World T.E.A.M., San Jose City College Trust, Motorsports Hall of Fame **CW:** Author, (With Philip Finch) Decathlon Challenge: Bruce Jenner's Story, 1977, Bruce Jenner's Guide to Family Fitness, 1978, Bruce Jenner's Guide to the Olympics, 1980, 1984, Bruce Jenner's the Athletic Body: A Complete Fitness Guide for Teenagers - Sports, Strength, Health, Agility, 1984, Finding the Champion Within: A Step-by-Step Plan for Reaching Your Full Potential, 1999; Co-Creator, (With Kris Jenner) Women's Defense and Fitness Program; Actor, (Films) Can't Stop the Music, 1980, Jack and Jill, 2011, The Hungover Games, 2014; Producer, Actor, (TV Films) Grambling's White Tiger, 1981, The Steeler and the Pittsburgh Kid; Reality TV Personality, Keeping Up With the Kardashians, 2007-2015, I Am Cait, 2015-2016; Guest Appearances, (TV Series) CHiPS, 1981, The Fall Guy, 1984, Murder She Wrote, 1985, (Voice Actor) King of the Hill, 2002; Host, Star Games; Guest Host, ABC's Good Morning America, 1988, ABC's Home Show; Sports Commentator, ABC Sports, NBC Sports; TV Infomercials, Superstep, StairClimber Plus, Super Fit, The Best Health and Fitness with Kris and Bruce Jenner, (With Gary Player) Rhythm Golf, Minimax; TV Infomercial Appearances, Wheaties, Minolta, London Fog **AW:** Olympic Gold Medal in Decathlon, 1976, James E. Sullivan Trophy, Outstanding Amateur Athlete of the Year, 1976, Track and Field Performer of the Year Award, Sport Magazine, 1976, Male Athlete of the Year, Associated Press Poll, 1976, Outstanding International Spokesperson of the Year, 1978, Olympic Hall of Fame, 1986, Celebrity Outreach Award, 1993, Bay Area Hall of Fame, San Jose, CA, 1993, The Most Fascinating Person, Barbara Walters Special, 2015, Arthur Ashe Courage Award, ESPY Awards, 2015, TIME 100 Most Influential People, 2016, Ten Outstanding Young Men in America, U.S. Jaycees **ACH:** Established Bruce Jenner Classic Track Meet; featured as subject in numerous magazines and newspapers including Sports Illus., GQ, People.; In April 2015, identified as a women, becoming the most high-profile American to come out as transgender during a 20/20 interview with Diane Sawyer; Caitlyn Jenner, formerly Bruce, introduced on the cover of Vanity Fair on June 1, 2015; broke Twitter history twice in 2015, first time with interview with Diane Sawyer and second time with Vanity Fair cover announcement regarding transgender transition.

JIANLIN, WANG, T: Founder **I:** Real Estate **CN:** Dalian Wanda Group **PB:** Cangxi County **SC:** Sichuan Province, China **C:** Chairman/President/Founder, Dalian Wanda Group Co. Ltd, 1989-Present

JIMENEZ, CHRISTINA, T: Activist **I:** Nonprofit & Philanthropy **CN:** United We Dream **PB:** Ecuador **SC:** Ecuador **C:** Founder, United We Dream (2008-Present) **AW:** Named to TIME's 100 Most Influential, TIME Magazine (2018)

JING, CHAI, T: Journalist **I:** Media & Entertainment **DOB:** 06/02/1905 **PB:** Linfen, China **SC:** Linfen, China **ED:** Changsha Railway Institute, 1995; Master of Fine Arts, Peking University **C:** Reporter,China Central Television, 2001-13 **CW:** (Books) Use my Lifetime to Forgot, 2001 Insight,2012(Documentary)Under the Dome,2014 **AW:** Time 100 Most Influential, 2015

JOBS, LAURENE POWELL, T: Educational Association Administrator **I:** Education/Educational Services **DOB:** 11/06/1963 **PB:** Palo Alto **SC:** CA/USA **ED:** MBA, Stanford University, 1991; BA, BSE, University Pennsylvania, 1985 **C:** Member, White House Council for Community Solutions, 2010-; Co-founder, board chair, College Track, 1997-; Founder, chair, Emerson Collective,; Co-founder, Terravera,; Fixed-income trading strategist, Goldman Sachs,; Fixed-income trading strategist, Merrill Lynch Asset Management, **CR:** Chair, Board of Directors, XQ; Member, chairman's advisory board of the Council on Foreign Relations, Member, Board directors Conservation International, Stand for Children, NewSchools Venture Fund, Stanford Schools Corp., New American Foundation, EdVoice, Global Fund for Women, Teach for America, Achieva, Udacity; **CIV:** Adv. board, Stanford Grad. School Business, **AW:** Named one of The 100 Most Powerful Women, Forbes magazine, 2012-14 **BA:** College Track, 117 Broadway Ave, Oakland, CA, 94607

JOEL, BILLY, T: Musician **I:** Media & Entertainment **DOB:** 05/09/1949 **PB:** Bronx **SC:** NY/USA **PT:** Son of Howard and Rosalind (Nyman) Joel **SPN:** Christie Brinkley, March 23, 1985 (div. August 25, 1994); Elizabeth Webber, September 5, 1973 (div. August 25, 1982); **CH:** Alexa Ray **ED:** D in Musical Arts (hon.), Manhattan School Music, 2008; DFA (hon.), Syracuse University, 2006; MusD (hon.), Stony Brook University, 2015; MusD (hon.), Southampton College, 2000; LHD (hon.), Hofstra University, 1997; HMD (hon.), Berklee College Music, 1993; LHD (hon.), Fairfield University, 1991 **C:** Solo recording artist, 1972-; Co-founder, Long Island Boat Co., 1996; Performed in piano bars under name Bill Martin, LA, 1973; Joined band, Attila, 1970; Joined band, The Hassles, Long Island, 1968 **CIV:** Established The Rosalind Joel Scholarship, City College of New York, 1996 **CW:** Albums: (with The Hassles) The Hassles, 1967, Hour of the Wolf, 1968; (with Attila) Attila, 1970; (solo albums) Cold Spring Harbor, 1971, Piano Man, 1973, Streetlife Serenade, 1974, Turnstiles, 1975, The Stranger, 1977, 52nd Street, 1978 (Grammy award for Album of Year, 1979, Grammy award for Best Male Pop Vocal Performance, 1979), Glass Houses, 1980 (Grammy award for Best Male Rock Vocal Performance, 1980), Songs in the Attic, 1981, The Nylon Curtain, 1982, An Innocent Man, 1983, Billy Joe's Greatest Hits, Vols. I and II, 1985, The Bridge, 1986, Kohuept: Live from the Soviet Union, 1987, Storm Front, 1989, River of Dreams, 1993, Billy Joe's Greatest Hits, Vol. III, 1997, 2000 Years: Millenium Concert, 2000, Essential Billy Joel, 2001, Fantasies & Delusions: Music For Solo Piano, 2001, My Lives, 2005, 12 Gardens Live, 2006; numerous

appearances in TV series, documentaries, and TV films; author: Goodnight My Angel: A Lullabye, 2005, New York State of Mind, 2005, Billy Joel: The Definitive Biography, 2014. **AW:** Recipient Grammy Legend award, 1990, Humanitarian award, Cathedral of St. John the Divine, 1990, Billboard Century Music award, 1994, American Society of Composers Founder's award, 1997, Am. Music Awards award of Merit, 1999, James Smithson Bicentennial Medal of Honor, 2000, Johnny Mercer award, The Songwriter's Hall of Fame, 2001, Star, Hollywood Walk of Fame, 2005, Kennedy Center Honors, John F. Kennedy Center Performing Arts, Washington, 2013; named Music Cares Person of Year, 2002; named to The Songwriter's Hall of Fame, 1992, The Rock and Roll Hall of Fame, 1999, The Long Island Music Hall of Fame, 2006, The Hit Parade Hall of Fame, 2009, Gershwin Prize for Popular Song, 2014. **ACH:** Achievements include premiering first production tour of the USSR by an American popular artist, 1987; inspiring Broadway musical Movin' Out, 2002; making history for the most performances at Madison Square Garden, 65th show on July 1, 2015.

JOHN, ELTON HERCULES, T: Musician **I:** Media & Entertainment **DOB:** 03/25/1947 **PB:** Pinner **SC:** Middlesex/England **PT:** Son of Stanley and Sheila Eileen (Farebrother) Dwight; **ED:** PhD with honors, Royal Academy Music, 2002; Attended, Royal Academy Music, London, 1959-64 **C:** Solo performer and with, Elton John Band, 1969-; Member of the group, Bluesology, 1965-67; Begin playing piano, 1951 **CIV:** Established, Elton John Aids Foundation, 1992- President, Watford Football Club, 1990- Chairman, Watford Football Club, 1976-90 Patron, Amnesty International, Scholarship Fund-Royal Academy of Music, Patron, The Globe Theatre, Patron, Terrence Higgins Trust, Patron, International AIDS Vaccine Initiative, Patron, Gus Dudgeon Foundation, **CW:** Composer: (albums) Empty Sky, 1969, Elton John, 1970, Tumbleweed Connection, 1970, 11.17.70, 1971, Madman Across the Water, 1971, Honky Chateau, 1972, Don't Shoot Me I'm Only The Piano Player, 1973, Goodbye Yellow Brick Road, 1973, Caribou, 1974, Greatest Hits, 1974, Captain Fantastic and the Brown Dirt Cowboy, 1975, Rock of the Westies, 1976, Here and There, 1976, Blue Moves, 1976, Greatest Hits Vol. II, 1977, A Single Man, 1978, Victim of Love, 1979, 21 at 33, 1980, The Fox, 1981, Jump Up!, 1982, Too Low for Zero, 1983, Breaking Hearts, 1984, Ice on Fire, 1985, Leather Jackets, 1986, Elton John Live in Australia with the Melbourne Symphony Orchestra, 1987, Reg Strikes Back, 1988, Sleeping with the Past, 1989, To Be Continued, 1990, The One, 1992, Greatest Hits 1976-1986, 1992, Duets, 1993, Made in England, 1995, Love Songs, 1996, The Big Picture, 1997, Elton John and Tim Rice's Aida, The Muse, 1999, Elton John One Night Only-The Greatest Hits, 2000, Songs From the West Coast, 2001, Greatest Hits 1970-2002, 2002, Peachtree Road, 2004, The Captain & The Kid, 2006, Rocket Man – Number Ones, 2007, The Diving Board, 2013, Wonderful Crazy Night, 2016, (album with Leon Russell) The Union, 2010, (album with Pnau) Good Morning to the Night, 2012, (soundtracks) Friends, 1971, The Lion King, 1994 (Best Original Song Academy award for Can You Feel the Love Tonight?), The Muse, 1999, The Road to El Dorado, 2000, Gnomeo & Juliet, 2011, (Broadway musicals) The Lion King, 1998 (6 Tony awards), Aida, 2000 (Tony award for Best Original Score, Grammy award for Best Musical Show Album, 2001), Lestat, 2006, Billy Elliot the Musical, 2005 (New York Drama Critics' Cir. award for Best Musical, 2009, Drama Desk awards for Outstanding Musical, Outstanding Music, 2009, Tony award for Best Musical, 2009); actor: (films) Tommy, 1975;

as himself Spice World, 1997, The Country Bears, 2002, Elton John: Me, Myself & I (autobiography), 2007; actor(voice only)Nashville, 2016, Kingsman: The Golden Circle, 20127: (films) The Lion King, 1994, The Road to El Dorado, 2000; performed at Live Aid, 1985, Freddie Mercury Tribute Concert, 1992, Live 8, 2005, Funeral of Princess Diana at Westminster Abbey, 1997, Concert for Diana at Wembley Stadium in London, in honor of Diana Princess of Wales 46th Birthday, 2007, 52nd Grammy awards, piano duet with Lady Gaga, 2010, Queen's Diamond Jubilee Concert outside Buckingham Palace, 2012, appeared in (documentaries) Being Mick, 2001, performance shows The Red Piano Tour, The Colosseum at Caesars Palace, Las Vegas, 2003-09, The Million Dollar Piano, The Colosseum at Caesars Palace, Las Vegas, 2011- **AW:** Decorated Knighted Queen Elizabeth II, Commander of the Order of the British Empire (CBE); named one of The 100 Most Influential People in the World, TIME magazine, 2010, The Billboard Hot 100 Top All-Time Artists, Billboard Magazine, 2008; named to The Rock & Roll Hall of Fame, 1994, Songwriters Hall of Fame, 1992; recipient PRS for Music Heritage award, 2010, Maori award, 2007, Disney Legends award, 2006, Kennedy Center Honors, John F. Kennedy Center Performing Arts, 2004, Grammy Legend award, 2001, Grammy award for Best Male Pop Vocal Performance for the song Candle in the Wind, 1997, Grammy award for Best Male Pop Vocal Performance for song Can You Feel The Love Tonight, 1994, Grammy award for Best Instrumental Composition for Basque, 1991, Best British Male Artist Brit award, 1991, Grammy award for Best Pop Performance by a Duo or Group for the song-That's What Friends Are For, performed with Dionne Warwick & Friends, 1987, Star on the Hollywood Walk of Fame, 1975, 11 Ivor Novello awards, 1973-2000, Best Pop Collaboration with Vocals,Grammy, 2011, Best Play(As Producer), Tony Award, 2010 **MEM:** Fellow: British Academy Songwriters and Composers **ACH:** Achievements include first popular Western singer to perform in USSR, 1979; released biggest selling single of all time, Candle in the Wind, 1997 with over 33,000,000 copies sold **BA:** Universal Music Group, 2220 Colorado Ave, Santa Monica, CA, 90404

JOHNS, JASPER, T: Artist **I:** Fine Art **DOB:** 05/15/1930 **PB:** Augusta **PT:** Son of Jasper and Jean (Riley) J. **ED:** Student, University South Carolina, 1947-48 **CW:** Exhibitions include, Leo Castelli Gallery, New York City, 1958, 60, 61, 63, 66, 68, 76, 81, 84, Minami Gallery, Tokyo, 1965, 75, Galerie Rive Droite, Paris, 1959, 61, Galleria D'Arte Del Naviglio, Milan, 1959, Ileana Sonnabend, Paris, 1963, Columbia Museum Art (South Carolina), 1960, Jewish Museum, New York City, 1964, White-chapel Gallery, London, 1964, Pasadena Museum (California), 1965, Smithsonian Institution National Collection Fine Arts, 1966, Arts Council Great Britain, 1974-75, Whitney Museum Am. Art, 1977, Kunsthalle, Cologne, 1978, Centre Pompidou, Paris, 1978, Hayward Gallery, London, 1978, Seibu Museum, Tokyo, 1978, San Francisco Museum Modern Art, 1978, Kunstmuseum, Basel, 1979, Des Moines Art Center, 1983, St. Louis Art Museum, 1985, Museum Modern Art, 1986, Kunsthalle, 1986, Wight Art Gallery UCLA, 1987, Galerie Daniel Templon, Paris, 1987, Museum Contemporary Art, L.A., 1987, Venice Biennale, 1958, 64, 78, Philadelphia Museum Art, 1988, Walker Art Center, Minneapolis, 1990, Museum Fine Arts, Houston, 1990, Fine Arts Museum San Francisco, 1990, Montreal Museum Fine Arts, 1990, National Gallery Art, Washington, 1990, Kunstmus. Basel, 1990, Hayward Gallery, London, 1990, St. Louis Art Museum, 1991, Center for Fine Arts, Miami, 1991,

Denver Art Museum, 1991, Brooke Alexander Editions, New York City, 1991, Whitney Museum Am. Art, New York City, 1991, Harvard University Art Museum, 1992, San Diego Museum Art, 1992, Cana Art Gallery, Seoul, 1991, Gagosian Gallery, New York, 1992, Palaus de Luppe, La Fondation Vincent Van Gogh, Arles, France, 1992, Milwaukee Art Museum, 1992, Galeria Weber Alexander Cobo, Madrid, 1992, National Academy Design, New York City, 1996, Philadelphia Museum of Art, 1999, Art Institute Chicago, 1999, Kunst Museum, Basel, 2007; represented in permanent collections Museum Modern Art, Albright-Knox Art Gallery, Buffalo, Tate Gallery, London, Moderna Museet, Stockholm, Stedelijik Museum, Amsterdam, The Netherlands, Whitney Museum, New York City, Kunstmuseum, Basel, Centre Pompidou, Art Institute Chicago, Baltimore Museum Art, Cleveland Museum Art, Kunsthaus Zurich, Minneapolis Institute Art, National Gallery Art, San Francisco Museum Modern Art, Virginia Museum Fine Arts, Richmond, Walker Art Center, others; illustrator (book) In Memory of My Feelings, 1967,(Exhibitions) National Gallery, 2007 **AW:** Recipient 1st prize Print Biennale Ljubljana, Yugoslavia, prize IX Sao Paulo (Brazil) Biennale, Skowhegan medal for painting Skowhegan School of Painting and Sculpture, Skowhegan medal for Graphics, Mayors award of Honor for Arts and Culture City of New York, Wolf prize for Painting, Wolf Foundation, 1986, International prize Venice Biennale, 1988, National Medal of Arts, The White House, 1990, Presidential Medal of Freedom, 2010; named to The South Carolina Hall of Fame, 1989 **MEM:** Member Am. Academy Arts and Letters (Gold medal for graphic art), Royal Academy of Arts, National Institute of Arts and Letters, Am. Academy of Arts and Scis

JOHNSON, BILL, T: U.S. Representative from Ohio **I:** Government Administration/Government Relations/Government Services **DOB:** 11/10/1954 **PB:** Roseboro **SC:** NC/USA **ED:** MA, Georgia Institute Tech (1984); BA, Troy University, Summa Cum Laude, AL (1979) **C:** Member, US House Natural Resources Committee, Washington, DC (2011-Present); Member, US House Veterans affairs Committee, Washington, DC (2011-Present); Member, US House Foreign Affairs Committee, Washington, DC (2011-Present); Member, US Congress from the Sixth Ohio District, Washington, DC (2011-Present); Chief Information Officer, Stoneridge Inc., Warren, Ohio (2006-2010); Co-founder, J2 Business Solutions, Inc. (2003-2006); Co-founder, Johnson-Schley Management Group, Inc. (1990-2003); Member, Committee on Energy and Commerce, Committee on Science, Space and Technology **MIL:** Retired, Lieutenant Colonel, U.S. Air Force (1999); Career Military Officer, Director, Chief Information Officer, Staff, U.S. Special Operations Command, U.S. Air Force (1973-1999) **AW:** Decorated National Defense Service Medal; Air Force Commendation Medal; Air Force Meritorious Service Medal **PA:** Republican

JOHNSON, DWAYNE (THE ROCK) DOUGLAS, T: Actor **I:** Media & Entertainment **DOB:** 05/02/1972 **PB:** Hayward **SC:** CA/USA **PT:** Rocky Johnson; Ata (Maivia) Johnson **ED:** BA in Criminology and Physiology, University of Miami (1995) **C:** Professional Wrestler (1997-2013) **CW:** Actor, Films, "Beyond the Mat" (1999), "Longshot" (2000), "The Mummy Returns" (2001), "The Scorpion King" (2002), "The Rundown" (2003), "Walking Tall" (2004), "Be Cool" (2005), "Doom" (2005), "Southland Tales" (2006), "Gridiron Gang" (2006), "The Game Plan" (2007), "Get Smart" (2008), "Race to Witch Mountain" (2009), Voice, "Planet 51" (2009), "Tooth Fairy" (2010), "The Other Guys" (2010), "Journey 2: The Mysterious Island" (2012), "G.I. Joe: Retal-

iation" (2013), "Empire State" (2013), "Pain & Gain" (2013), "Fast & Furious 6" (2013), "Hercules" (2014), "Furious 7" (2015), "San Andreas" (2015), "Central Intelligence" (2016), Voice, "Moana" (2016), "The Fate of the Furious" (2017), "Baywatch" (2017), "Jumanji, Welcome to the Jungle" (2017), "Rampage" (2018), "Skyscraper" (2018), "Fighting with My Family" (2018); Wrestler, TV Series, "WWF Superstars of Wrestling" (1996), "WWF Monday Night Raw" (1997-2015), "Sunday Night Heat" (1998-2004), "WWE Smackdown!" (1999-2013); TV Appearances include "That 70s Show" (1999), "The Net" (1999) "SNL" (2000), "Star Trek: Voyager" (2000), "Cory in the House" (2007), "Hannah Montana" (2007), "Wizards of Waverly Place" (2009), "Transformers Prime" (2010), "Family Guy" (2010), "The Hero" (2013), "Wake Up Call" (2014), "Lifeline" (2017); Actor, Producer, Films, "Snitch" (2013); Executive Producer, TV Series, "The Hero" (2013); Actor, Executive Producer, TV Series, "Ballers" (2015-Present) **AW:** People's Choice Award for Favorite Premium Cable TV Actor (2016) **ACH:** Achievements include being the 7 time World Wrestling Federation champion

JOHNSON, EARVIN "MAGIC" JR., T: Development Company Executive, Retired Professional Basketball Player **I:** Athletics **DOB:** 08/14/1959 **PB:** Lansing **SC:** MI/USA **PT:** Earvin Johnson; Christine Johnson **MS:** Married **SPN:** Cookie Johnson (1991) **CH:** EJ Johnson; Elisa Johnson; Andre Johnson **ED:** Student, Michigan State University (1979) **C:** Studio Analyst, NBA Countdown (2008-Present); Owner, LA Sparks (2014); President, LA Lakers (2017-Present); Co-owner, LA Dodgers (2012—Present); Guard, LA Lakers (1996); Guard, LA Lakers (1979—1991); Studio Analyst, ESPN, ABC Sports (2008—Present); Co-chairman, Executive Steering Committee for Diversity, NASCAR (2004—Present); Chairman, Magic Johnson Entertainment, Magic Johnson Productions & Magic Johnson Enterprises (1997—Present); Chairman, Chief Executive Officer, Johnson Development Corporation (1993—Present); Studio Analyst, Turner Sports (2001—2008); Sportscaster, NBC-TV (1993-1994); Vice President, Co-owner, LA Lakers (1994—2010); Head Coach, LA Lakers (1994) **CIV:** Founder, Magic Johnson Foundation (1991—Present) **CW:** Author, Autobiography, "Magic" (1983); Author, "What You Can Do to Avoid AIDS" (1992); Author, "32 Ways to Be a Champion in Business" (2008); Co-author, "Magic's Touch" (1989); Co-author, "My Life" (1992); Co-author, "When the Game Was Ours" (2009) **AW:** Named to First Team NCAA All-American, Associated Press (1979); Named One of NCAA Final Four Most Outstanding Player (1979); Named First Team All-Rookie (1980); NBA Finals MVP (1980, 1982, 1987); Named to First Team All-NBA (1983—1991); NBA MVP (1987, 1989, 1990); NBA All-Star Game MVP (1990, 1992); Player of the Year, Sporting News (1987); Named one of the 50 Greatest Players in NBA History (1996); Named One of the Most Influential Black Americans, Ebony Magazine (2006); Named, One of the Power 150 (2008); Named One of the Most Influential People in the World of Sports, Business Week (2007, 2008); Named to Western Conference All-Star Team, NBA (1980, 1982—1992); Inductee, Michigan State University Athletics Hall of Fame (1992); Inductee, Naismith Memorial Basketball Hall of Fame (2002); Inductee, National Collegiate Basketball Hall of Fame (2009); All-Around Contributions to Team Success Award, IBM (1984); Schick Pivotal Player Award (1984); J. Walter Kennedy Citizenship Award, NBA (1992); Gold Medal, Men's Basketball, Summer Olympic Games, Barcelona, Spain (1992); AdColor Award (2008) **ACH:** Achievements include member of NCAA National Championship winning Michigan State University

Spartans, 1979; being the first overall pick in the NBA Draft, 1979; member of NBA Championship winning Los Angeles Lakers, 1980, 1982, 1985, 1987, 1988; leading the NBA in: steals per game, 1981, 1982; assists, 1983, 1986, 1987; assists per game, 1983, 1984, 1986, 1987; free throw percentage, 1989; being the all-time NBA career leader in assists per game (11.2) **BA:** Johnson Devel Corp & Magic Johnson Found, 9100 Wilshire Blvd, Beverly Hills, CA, 90212

JOHNSON, EDDIE BERNICE, T: U.S. Representative from Texas, Ranking Member of the House Committee on Science, Space and Technology **I:** Government Administration/Government Relations/Government Services **DOB:** 12/03/1935 **PB:** Waco **SC:** Texas **PT:** Daughter of Lee Edward and Lillie Mae (White) Johnson; **ED:** LLD (hon.), Paul Quinn College, 1993; LLD (hon.), Houston-Tillotson College, 1993; LLD (hon.), Texas College, 1989; LLD (hon.), Jarvis College, 1979; LLD (hon.), Bishop College, 1979; MPA, Southern Methodist University, Dallas, 1976; BSN, Texas Christian University, 1967; Diploma in Nursing, St. Mary's College, University Notre Dame, South Bend, Ind., 1955 **C:** Ranking Member, House Committee on Science, Space and Technology, 2010-; Member, US Congress from 30th Texas district, 1993-; Member District 23, Texas State Senate, 1987-93; Vice president, Visiting Nurse Association Texas, Dallas, 1981-87; Executive assistant to administrator for primary health care policy, Department Health, Education and Welfare, Washington, 1979-81; Dallas regional director, Department Health, Education and Welfare, 1977-79; Member District 33, Texas House of Reps., 1973-77; Chief psychiatric nurse, Vets. Administration Hospital, Dallas, 1956-72 **CR:** President Eddie Bernice Johnson & Associates, Inc. consultant division urban affairs Zales Corpn., Dallas, 1976-77 executive assistant personnel division Neiman-Marcus, Dallas, 1972-75 **AW:** Named one of The Most Influential Black Americans, Ebony magazine, 2006; named to Power 150, 2008; recipient 25th Anniversary Outstanding Achievement award, National Black Caucus State Legislators, Woman of Year award, 100 Black Men of America, Inc., 2001, Visionary award, National Organization Black Elected Legis. Women, 2001, Pres.'s award, National Conference Black Mayors, 2001, Heroes award, Texas National Association for the Advancement of Colored People, 2000, Citizenship award, National Conference Christians & Jews, 1985 **MEM:** Mem.: Alpha Kappa Alpha **PA:** Democrat

JOHNSON, HENRY C. JR., T: U.S. Representative from Georgia **I:** Government Administration/Government Relations/Government Services **DOB:** 10/02/1954 **PB:** Washington, DC, October 2, 1954 **ED:** JD, Texas Southern University, 1979; BA, Clark University, 1976 **C:** Member, US Congress from 4th Georgia District, 2007-; Member, Committee on Armed Services, Committee on the Judiciary; Partner, Johnson & Johnson Law Group LLC, Decatur, Georgia,; Judge, State Court of Georgia,; Judge, Magistrate Ct,, DeKalb County, Georgia, **CR:** Chairman Budget Committee DeKalb County Board Commissioners, member **AW:** Named to Power 150, Ebony magazine, 2008 **MEM:** Mem.: State Bar Georgia, Georgia Lawyers Foundation, Georgia Association Criminal Defense Attorneys, DeKalb County Law Libr. **PA:** Democrat **BA:** 2240 Rayburn HOB, Washington, DC, 20515

JOHNSON, JIMMIE KENNETH, T: Professional Stock Car Racer **I:** Athletics **DOB:** 09/17/1975 **PB:** El Cajon, California **PT:** Son of Gary and Cathy Johnson; **C:** Co-founder, The Jimmie Johnson Foundation, 2006-; Racecar Driver NASCAR, Hendrick

Motorsports, 2002-; Driver, Truck Series, Randy Moss Motorsports, 2008 **CR:** 1st pl. Aaron's 499 Talladega Superspeedway, 2011 1st pl. Toyota/Save Mart 350 Infineon Raceway, Sonoma, California, 2010 1st pl. Food City 500 Bristol Motor Speedway, 2010 1st pl. Hollywood Casino 400 Kansas Speedway, 2011, 1st pl. Camping World RV 400, 2008 1st pl. Subway Fresh Fit 500 Phoenix International Raceway, 2008, 1st pl. Checker O'Reilly Auto Parts 500, 2009, 2008, 2007 1st pl. AAA Texas 500 Texas Motor Speedway, 2012, 1st pl. Dickies 500, 2007 1st pl. Chevy Rock-n-Roll 400 Richmond International Raceway, 2008, 2007, 1st pl. Crown Royal 400, 2007 1st pl. Crown Royal Curtiss Shaver 400 Indianapolis Motor Speedway, 2012, 1st pl. Allstate 400 at The Brickyard, 2009, 2008, 2006 1st pl. Daytona 500 Daytona International Speedway, 2013, 2006 1st pl. Shelby Am. Las Vegas Motor Speedway, 2010, 1st pl. UAW-DaimlerChrysler 400, 2007, 1st pl. UAW-DaimlerChrysler 400, 2006, 1st pl. United Auto Workers DiamlerChrysler 400, 2005 1st pl. Pep Boys Auto 500 Atlanta Motor Speedway, 2007, 1st pl. Kobalt Tools 500, 2007, 1st pl. Bass Pro Shops/MBNA 500, 2004 1st pl. Tums Fast Relief 500 Martinsville Speedway, 2012, 1st pl. Goody's Fast Pain Relief 500, 2009, 1st pl. TUMS QuikPak 500, 2008, 1st pl. Goody's Cool Orange 500, 2007, 1st pl. Subway 500, 2007, 2006, 2004 1st pl. Pennsylvania 500 Pocono Raceway, 2004, 1st pl. Pocono 500, 2004 1st pl. Bojangles' Southern 500 Darlington Raceway, 2012, 1st pl. Mountain Dew Southern 500, 2004, 1st pl. Carolina Dodge Dealers 400, 2004 1st pl. Lenox Industrial Tools 301 New Hampshire International Speedway, 2010, 1st pl. Sylvania 300, 2003, 1st pl. New England 300, 2003 1st pl. Bank of America 500 Lowes Motor Speedway, 2009, 1st pl. United Auto Workers GM-Quality 500, 2005, 1st pl. UAW-GM Quality 500, 2004, 1st pl. Coca-Cola 600, 2005, 2004, 2003 1st pl. FedEx 400 Dover International Speedway, 2012, 1st pl. AAA 400, 2010, 1st pl. Dover 400, 2009, 2009, 1st pl. MBNA RacePoints 400, 2005, 1st pl. MBNA All-Am. Heroes 400, 2002, 1st pl. MBNA Platinum 400, 2002 1st pl. Auto Club 500 California Speedway, 2010, 1st pl. Pepsi 500, 2009, 2008, 1st pl. Sharp AQUOS 500, 2007, 1st pl. National Association of Performing Artists Auto Parts 500, 2002 **CIV:** Co-founder, Jimmie Johnson Foundation, 2006- **CW:** Commentator ESPN, spokesperson Chevrolet division GM; (host): (weekly radio show) Not What You Expected; appeared in (documentaries) 24/7 Jimmie Johnson: Race to Daytona, 2010 **AW:** Named Male Athlete of Year, Associated Press, 2009, NASCAR Nextel Cup Champion, 2013, 2010, 2009, 2008, 2007, 2006, NASCAR Athlete of Decade, 2000's, The Sporting News, 2009, NASCAR Driver of Year, 2009-10, 2006-08, 2013 Pat Schauer Memorial Rookie of Year, American Speed Association, 1998; recipient ESPY award, Best Driver, ESPN, 2008, Forbes Most Influential Athletes, 2011-12 **ACH:** Achievements include being the first driver in history to win four consecutive NASCAR Cup Series championships, 2006-09

JOHNSON, JIMMY, T: Sports Commentator, Former Football Coach **I:** Athletics **DOB:** 07/16/1943 **PB:** Port Arthur **SC:** TX/USA **ED:** BA, University Arkansas, 1965 **C:** Co-host, NFL Sunday, Fox, 2002-; Head coach, general manager, Miami Dolphins, 1996-99; Sports commentator, football analyst, Fox Network, 1994-95; Head coach, Dallas Cowboys, Dallas, TX, 1989-94; Head coach, University Miami, Miami, FL, 1983-88; Head coach, Oklahoma State University, OK, 1979-83; Assistant coach, University Pittsburg, 1977-78; Assistant coach, University Arkansas, AR, 1973-76; Assistant coach, University Oklahoma, Norman, OK, 1970-72; Assistant coach, Iowa State University, IA, 1968-68; Assistant coach, Wichita State University,

KS, 1967; Assistant coach, Louisiana Tech. University, LA, 1965 **AW:** Coach NCAA Division I championship team, 1987, Super Bowl (XXVII, XXVIII) championship team, 1992-93; named Coach of Year Walter Camp Foundation, 1986-87, NFL Coach of Year College & Pro Football Newsweekly, 1990, United Press International, 1990, Associated Press, 1990, Football Digest, 1991; recipient Seattle Gold Helmet award, 1986.

JOHNSON, KEVIN, T: CEO **I:** Food & Restaurant Services **CN:** Starbucks **PB:** Bellevue **SC:** WA/USA **ED:** B.A., Business Administration, New Mexico State University **C:** President/CEO, Starbucks 2017-; President/COO, Starbucks, 2015-17; CEO, Juniper Networks, 2008-13; President of Platform & Services, 2007-08; Co-President of Platform and Services, 2005-07

JOHNSON, MICHAEL, T: Retired Professional Sprinter **I:** Athletics **DOB:** 09/13/1967 **PB:** Dallas **SC:** TX/USA **ED:** Coursework, Baylor University (1990) **C:** Retired (1991) **CR:** BBC Sports Commentator **AW:** Gold Medal, 200 Meters, Goodwill Games (1990, 1994); Gold Medal, 4 x 100 Relay, Olympics, Barcelona, Spain (1992); Gold Medal, 200 Meters and 400 Meters, Summer Olympics, Atlanta, GA (1996); Winner, 200 Meters, World Athletic Championships (1991); Winner, 400 Meters, World Athletic Championships (1993); U.S. National Champion, 200 Meters (1990-1992, 1995); Named Athlete of the Year, USA Track & Field (1993-1994); Male Athlete of the Year, Associated Press (1996); Gold Medal, 400 Meters, World Championship (1997); Gold Medalist, 400m & 4 x 400m, Olympics, Sydney, Australia (2000); Three Time Recipient, Jesse Owens Award; Track and Field Hall of Fame (2004)

JOHNSON, MIKE, T: U.S. Representative from Louisiana **I:** Government Administration/Government Relations/Government Services **DOB:** 01/30/1972 **PB:** Shreveport **SC:** LA/USA **ED:** JD, Louisiana State University, 1998; BS, Louisiana State University, 1995 **C:** Committee on the Judiciary, Committee on Natural Resources, Louisiana House of Representatives from Louisiana's District 4, 2017-Present; Louisiana House of Representatives from Louisiana's District 8, 2015-2017; Trustee, Ethics and Religious Liberty Commission, 2004-2012 **BA:** 327 Cannon HOB, Washington, DC, 20515

JOHNSON, R. MILTON, T: CEO **I:** Business Management/Business Services **CN:** HCA **DOB:** 12/15/1956 **ED:** BBA, Belmont University **CT:** CPA, 1981 **C:** President, HCA, Inc., 2011-; Board of Directors, HCA, Inc., 2009-; CFO, HCA, Inc., 2004-; Executive Vice President, HCA, Inc., 2004-11; Senior Vice President, Controller, HCA, Inc., 1998-2004; Vice President, Tax, HCA, Inc., 1995-98; Director, Tax, HealthTrust (merged with HCA, Inc.), 1987-95; Tax Manager, Research & Planning Area, HCA, Inc., 1982-87; Accountant, Ernst & Young LLP **CIV:** Member, Conference Board, Council of Financial Executives, Board of Directors, Sarah Cannon Research Institute, Board of Directors, Siloam Family Health Center, Board of Directors, McNeilly Center for Children, Board Director, HCA Foundation, Board of Trustees, Board of Regents, Belmont University

JOHNSON, RANDY, T: Retired Professional Baseball Player **I:** Athletics **DOB:** 09/10/1963 **PB:** Walnut Creek **PT:** Son of Bud and Carol Johnson; **ED:** Attended, University Southern California **C:** Retired, Major League Baseball, 2010; Pitcher, San Francisco Giants, 2008-09; Pitcher, New York Yankees, 2005-06; Pitcher, Arizona Diamond-

backs, 2007-08; Pitcher, Arizona Diamondbacks, Phoenix, 1999-2004; Pitcher, Houston Astros, 1998; Pitcher, Seattle Mariners, 1990-98; Pitcher, Montreal Expos, 1988-89 **AW:** Named Sportsman of Year, Sports Illus., 2001, World Series Co-MVP, Major League Baseball, 2001, National League Outstanding Pitcher, Major League Baseball Players Association, 2000, Am. League Outstanding Pitcher, 1995, Pitcher of Year, Sporting News, 1995; named to Hall of Fame, Major League Baseball, 2015, National League All-Star Team, 2004, 1999-2002, Am. League All-Star Team, 1997, 1993-95, 1990; recipient National League Babe Ruth award, 2001, Warren Spahn award, Oklahoma Sports Museum, 1999-2002, National League Cy Young award, 1999-2002, Am. League Cy Young award, 1995 **ACH:** Achievements include pitched a no-hitter versus Detroit Tigers, 1990; becoming the first pitcher since Nolan Ryan to lead the National League in ERA and strikeouts in the same year, 1999; becoming the first pitcher since Mickey Lolich to win three games in the same World Series, 2001; being a member of the World Series Champion Arizona Diamondbacks, 2001; pitching a perfect game versus Atlanta Braves, 2004; holding the Major League Baseball record for career strikeouts by a left-handed pitcher; being ranked 2nd for career strikeouts; recording his 300th career win against the Washington Nationals, June 4, 2009

JOHNSON, RON, T: U.S. Senator from Wisconsin **I:** Government Administration/Government Relations/Government Services **DOB:** 04/08/1955 **PB:** Mankato **PT:** Daughter of Dale Robert and Jeanette Elizabeth (Thisius) Johnson; **ED:** BA in Accounting, University Minnesota, 1977 **C:** Chairman, Senate Homeland Security Committee, 2015; Member, US Senate Homeland Security & Governmental Reform Committee, Washington, 2011-; Member, US Senate Special Committee on Aging, Washington, 2011-; Member, US Senate Appropriations Committee, Washington, 2011-; Member, US Senate Budget Committee, Washington, 2011-; US Senator from Wisconsin, Washington, 2011-; Owner, president, PACUR, LLC, 1997-; From machine operator and accountant to general manager, PACUR, LLC, Oshkosh, Wisconsin, 1979-97; Accountant, Jostens Inc., Minneapolis, 1977-79 **CIV:** Active, Unified Catholic School Systems, Oshkosh, Active, Oshkosh C. of C. Partners in Education Council, **AW:** Recipient Stephen Mosling Commitment to Education award, Oshkosh C. of C., 2009 **PA:** Republican **BA:** Office of Ron Johnson, 328 Hart Senate Office Building, Washington, DC, 20510

JOHNSON, SAMUEL ROBERT, T: U.S. Representative from Texas **I:** Government Administration/Government Relations/Government Services **DOB:** 10/11/1930 **PB:** San Antonio **ED:** Grad., National War College; Grad., Armed Forces Staff College; MA in International Affairs, George Washington University; BBA, Southern Methodist University, Dallas, 1951 **C:** Member, US Congress from 3rd Texas District, 1991-; Member, Committee on Ways and Means, Joint Committee on Taxation; Member, Texas House of Reps., 1984-91; Air Division Commdr., US Air Force,; Wing Commdr., US Air Force,; Member Thunderbirds, US Air Force,; Director Air Force Fighter Weapons School, US Air Force,; Prisoner of War, US Air Force, 1966-73; Fighter Pilot, US Air Force,; Career Military Officer, US Air Force, 1950-79 **AW:** Decorated Bronze Star with Valor, 2 Legions of Merit, 2 Purple Hearts, 4 Air medals, 2 Silver Stars **PA:** Republican **BA:** 2304 Rayburn House Office Building, Washington, DC, 20515

JOLIE, ANGELINA, T: Actress **I:** Media & Entertainment **DOB:** 06/04/1975 **PB:** Los Angeles **SC:** CA/USA **PT:** Daughter of Jon Voight and Marcheline Bertrand **SPN:** Brad Pitt (8/2014); Billy Bob Thornton (3/5/2000, Divorced 5/27/2003); Jonny Lee Miller (3/3/1996, Divorced 2/3/1999) **ED:** Student, New York University; Student, Strasberg Theatre Institute, New York City **CR:** Co-founder, Maddox Jolie-Pitt Foundation (MJP), 2006-, Goodwill Ambassador, UN High Commissioner for Refugees, Geneva, 2001-, Former Professional Model, LA, New York City, London **CW:** Actress: (films) Lookin' to Get Out, 1982, Cyborg 2, 1993, Angela & Viril, 1993, Hackers, 1995, Without Evidence, 1995, Foxfire, 1996, Mojave Moon, 1996, Love Is All There Is, 1996, True Women, 1997, Playing God, 1997, Hell's Kitchen, 1998, Playing by Heart, 1998 (National Board Rev. Award for Best Breakthrough Performance), Pushing Tin, 1999, The Bone Collector, 1999, Girl, Interrupted, 1999 (Academy Award for Best Supporting Actress, Golden Globe award for Best Supporting Actress, Screen Actors Guild award for Best Supporting Actress, Broadcast Film Critics award for Best Supporting Actress), Dancing in the Dark, 2000, Gone in Sixty Seconds, 2000, Original Sin, 2001, Life or Something Like It, 2002, Lara Croft Tomb Raider: The Cradle of Life, 2003, Beyond Borders, 2003, Taking Lives, 2004, Shark Tale (voice), 2004, Sky Captain and the World of Tomorrow, 2004, Alexander, 2004, Mr. and Mrs. Smith, 2005, The Good Shepherd, 2006, Beowulf (voice), 2007, A Mighty Heart, 2007, Kung Fu Panda (voice), 2008, Wanted, 2008, Changeling, 2008 (African American Film Critics Association award for Best Actress), Salt, 2010, The Tourist, 2010, Kung Fu Panda 2 (voice), 2011, Kung Fu Panda 3 (voice), 2016, First they Killed My Father, 2017, The Breadwinner, 2017; (TV films) George Wallace, 1997 (Golden Globe award for Best Supporting Actress), Gia, 1998 (Screen Actors Guild award for Best Actress, Golden Globe award for Best Actress), Kung Fu Panda Holiday, 2010; dir.: (films) In the Land of Blood and Honey, 2011; actress, executive producer (films) Maleficent, 2014, producer, director Unbroken, 2014, actress, producer, director, writer By the Sea, 2015, appearances in music videos for recording artists Meat Loaf, Lenny Kravits, Antonello Venditti, The Lemonheads **AW:** Named Favorite Female Action Star, People's Choice Awards, 2009; Named an Honorary Dame Commander of the Most Excellent Order of the British Empire, Her Majesty Queen Elizabeth II, 2014; Named one of Forbes' List of Hollywood's Highest-Paid Actresses (#1), 2013, The 100 Most Powerful Women in Entertainment, The Hollywood Reporter, 2014, 2008, The 50 Smartest People in Hollywood, Entertainment Weekly, 2007, The Top 25 Entertainers of Year, 2007, The 100 Most Powerful Women, Forbes magazine, 2010-14, The 100 Most Powerful Celebrities, 2007-12, Barbara Walters 10 Most Fascinating People of Year, 2006, The 100 Most Influential People in the World, TIME magazine, 2008, 2006, The 50 Most Powerful People in Hollywood, Premiere magazine, 2006; Recipient, Jean Hersholt Humanitarian award, Academy Motion Picture Arts & Sciences, 2014, Nansen Refugee Award, UN, 2011, Heart of Sarajevo Award, 2011, Global Humanitarian Award, UN Association USA, 2005, Cambodian Citizenship for Conservation Work, King Norodom Sihamoni, 2005

JOLY, HUBERT BERNARD, T: CEO **I:** Business Management/Business Services **CN:** Best Buy Co./Best Buy Inc. **DOB:** 08/11/1959 **PB:** Laxou **SC:** France **ED:** MPA, Institute d'Etudes Politiques, Paris, France (1983); MBA, Ecole des Hautes Etudes Commercial, Jouy-en-Josas, France (1981) **C:** Chief Executive Officer, Best Buy Co., Richfield, MN (2012-Present); President, Chief Executive Officer, Carlson Companies, Inc., Minnetonka, MN (2008-2012); Executive Vice President, Monitoring U.S. Assets, Deputy Chief Financial Officer, Vivendi Universal (2002-2004); Executive Vice President, Corporate Chief Information Officer, Vivendi Universal (2002); Senior Vice President, North American Integration, Vivendi Universal (2001-2002); Chief Executive Officer, Havas Interactive Inc. (1999-2000); Vice President, EDS Europe (1998-1999); Chairman, EDS Progical (1996-1999); President, EDS France, Paris, France (1996-1999); Co-Leader, European Electronics Practice, McKinsey & Co., Paris, France (1994-1996); Principal, McKinsey & Co., Paris, France (1993-1996); Principal, McKinsey & Co., New York, NY (1992-1993); Principal, McKinsey & Co., Paris, France (1990-1991); Manager, McKinsey & Co., Paris, France (1985-1989); Associate, McKinsey & Co., San Francisco, CA (1984-1985); Associate, McKinsey & Co., Paris, France (1983-1984); Consultant, Partner, McKinsey & Co. (1982-1996); Assistant Chairman, Chief Executive Officer, Sacilor, Paris, France (1981-1982); Chief Executive Officer, Video Games Division, Vivendi Universal, Los Angeles, CA **CR:** Best Buy Inc. (2012-Present); Polo Ralph Lauren (2009-Present); Board of Directors, The Rezidor Hotel Group (2008-2012); Member, World European Forum, Global Leaders for Tomorrow (1996) **CIV:** U.S. Department of Commerce Travel & Tourism Advisory Board (2010-Present); World Travel and Tourism Council (2008-Present); Member, Executive Committee, Minnesota Business Partnership (2008-Present); Chairman, CWT Board of Directors (2008-Present); Board Member, Minneapolis Institute of Arts (2008-Present); Board Member, American Chamber of Commerce in France (1998-Present) **CW:** Author, "Wake Up Europe!" (1999); Author, "Excellence in Electronics" (1993); Contributor, Articles to Professional Journals **MEM:** Center d'Etude Prospective es Stratègique **BA:** Best Buy Inc, 7601 Penn Ave South, Richfield, MN, 55423

JONES, CHARLES E., T: CEO of FirstEnergy **I:** Oil & Energy **CN:** FirstEnergy **ED:** Bachelors of Science,University of Akron; MIT Reactor Technology Program **C:** CEO, President, Director, FirstEnergy, 2015-; Executive VP, First Energy, 2014-15; President of Utilities, FirstEnergy, 2010-2013

JONES, CHERRY, T: Actress **I:** Media & Entertainment **DOB:** 11/21/1956 **PB:** Paris **SC:** France **C:** Founder, American Repertory Theatre, Cambridge, MA (1980-Present); Guest Artist, Arena Stage, Washington, DC (1983-1984) **CW:** Actress, "Awake" (2012); Actress, "The Beaver" (2011); Actress, "New Years Eve" (2011); Actress, Broadway, "Mrs. Warren's Profession" (2010); Actress, "24" (2009-2010); Actress, "Mother and Child" (2009); Actress, Broadway, "Faith Healer" (2006); Actress, "Swimmers" (2005); Actress, Broadway, "Doubt" (2005); Actress, "The Village" (2004); Actress, "Ocean's Twelve" (2004); Actress, "Signs" (2002); Actress, "Divine Secrets of the Ya-Ya Sisterhood" (2002); Actress, "What Makes a Family" (2001); Actress, "The Perfect Storm" (2000); Actress, "Erin Brockovich" (2000); Actress, "Cradle Will Rock" (1999); Actress, "Murder in a Small Town" (1999); Actress, "The Lady in Question" (1999); Actress, "The Horse Whisperer" (1998); Voice Actress, "Out of the Past" (1998); Actress, "The Tears of Julian Po" (1997); Actress, "The Tears of Julian Po" (1997); Actress, "The Tears of Julian Po" (1997); Actress, "Housesitter" (1992); Actress, "The Big Town" (1987); Actress, "Light of Day" (1987); Actress, "Alex: The Life of a Child" (1986); Actress, American Repertory Theatre, "King Lear," "Twelfth Night," "Major Barbara," "Caucasian Chalk Circle," "The Serpent Woman," "Platonov," Life is a Dream," "The School for Scandal," "The Thress Sister," "As You Like It," "Baby with the Bathwater," "A Midsummer Night's Dream," "Journey of the Fifth Horse," "The Glass Menagerie"; Actress, Off Broadway, "Desdemona," "Goodnight Desdemona," "Baltimore Waltz," "And Baby Makes Seven," "Light Shining in Buckinghamshire," "Big Time," "Ballad of Soapy Smith," "I Am a Camera," "The Philanthropist," "The Importance of Being Earnest"; Actress, Broadway, "Angels in America," "Our Country's Good," "Macbeth," "Stepping Out," "The Heiress" **AW:** Recipient, Primetime Emmy for Outstanding Supporting Actress in a Drama Series, Academy TV Arts & Sciences (2009); Recipient, Obie Award, The Village Voice (2005); Recipient, Outstanding Actress in a Play (2005); Named, Outstanding Lead Actress (2005); Recipient, Tony Award for Best Performance by a Leading Actress in a Play (2005); Recipient, Drama Desk Award for Outstanding Actress in a Play (2005); Recipient, Tony Award for Best Actress (1995); Recipient, Outer Critics Circle Award; Recipient, Lucille Lortel Award **BA:** William Morris Endeavor Entertainment, 9601 Wilshire Blvd. 3rd Floor, Beverly Hills, CA, 90210

JONES, DOUG, T: U.S. Senator from Alabama **I:** Government Administration/Government Relations/Government Services **DOB:** 05/04/1954 **PB:** Fairfield **SC:** AL/USA **SPN:** Louise New Jones **ED:** Law, Samford University; B.A., University of Alabama **C:** Member, U.S. Senate from Alabama, 2018-; Member, Committee on Banking, Housing, and Urban Affairs; Member, Committee on Health, Education, Labor and Pensions; Member, Committee on Homeland Security and Governmental Affairs; Member, Special Committee on Aging; Attorney, Northern District of Alabama,1997-2001; Lawyer, Private Practice, 2001-2013; General Special Master, Environmental Clean-Up Case, 2004; Founder, Jones & Hawley, 2013- **BA:** 326 Russell Senate Office Building, Washington, DC, 20510

JONES, EDITH HOLLAN, T: Federal Judge **I:** Law and Legal Services **DOB:** 04/07/1949 **PB:** Philadelphia **SC:** PA/USA **ED:** JD with honors, University Texas, 1974; BA Cornell University, 1971 **CT:** Bar: US District . (southern & northern districts) Texas, US Court Appeals (5th & 11th circuits), US Supreme Court 1979, Texas 1974 **C:** Chief Judge,U.S. Court of Appeals for the Fifth Circuit,2006-12; Judge, US Court Appeals (5th Cir.), Houston, 1985-; Chief judge, US Court Appeals (5th Cir.), Houston, 2006-12; Partner, Andrews & Kurth, Houston, 1982-85; Associate, Andrews & Kurth, Houston, 1974-82 **CR:** General counsel Republican Party of Texas, 1981-83 **CIV:** Member board director, Boy Scouts of America **MEM:** Master: American Bar Association; mem.: Garland Walker American Inns of Court, Houston Bar Association, State Bar Texas **PA:** Republican **BA:** Fifth Circuit US Ct Appeals, 600 Camp St, New Orleans, LA, USA, 70130

JONES, JAMES EARL, T: Actor **I:** Media & Entertainment **DOB:** 01/17/1931 **PB:** Arkabutla **SC:** MS/USA **PT:** Son of Robert Earl and Ruth (Williams) J. **MS:** Married **SPN:** Cecilia Hart, March 15, 1982; **CH:** Flynn Earl **ED:** ArtsD (hon.), New York University, 1994; LHD (hon.), Columbia College, 1982; DFA (hon.), Yale University, 1982; DFA (hon.), Princeton University, 1980; Studied with Lee Strasburg, Ted Danielewsky; Diploma, Am. Theatre Wing, 1957; LHD (hon.), University of Michigan, 1970; BA, University of Michigan, 1953 CW: Films: Dr.Strangelove, 1964, The Comedians, 1967, The Comedians in Africa, 1967, The End of the Road, 1970, The Great White Hope, 1970, King A filmed Record, 1970, Malcolm X, 1972, The Man, 1972, Claudine, 1974, The River Niger,1976, The Bingo Long Traveling All-Stars & Motor Kings 1976, Swashbuckler, 1976, Deadly Hero,1976, The Greatest, 1977, Star Wars, 1977, Exorcist II: The Hereic, 1977, The Last Remake of Beau Geste, 1977, The Empire Strikes Back, 1980, Bushido Blade, 1981, The FLights of Dragons, 1982, Blood Tide, 1982, Return of the Jedi, 1983, City Limits, 1985, Soul Man, 1986,Gardens of Stone, 1987, My Little Girl, 1987, Pinocchio and the Emperor of the Night,1987, Matewan, 1987,Coming to America, 1988, Three Fugitives, 1989, Field of Dreams, 1989, Best of the Best, 1989, Convicts, 1990,The Ambulance, 1990, Grim Prairie Tales, 1990, Scorchers, 1991, Patriot Games, 1992, Freddie as FRO7, 1992, Dreamrider, 1993, Sneakersm 1992, Dream Rider, 1993, Sommersby, 1993, The Sandlot,1993, The Excessive Force, 1993, The Meteor Man, 1993,Naked Gun 33 1/3 The Final Insult, 1994, Clean Slate, 1994, The Lion King, 1994, Clear and Present Danger, 1994, Jefferson in Paris, 1995, Judge Dredd, 1995, A Family Thing, 1996, Good Luck, 1996, Casper A Spirited Beginning, 1997, Gang Related, 1997, Primary Colors, 1998, The Lion King II, 1998, Our Friend Martin,1999, On the QT, 1999, Undercover Angel, 1999, The Annihilation of Fish, 1999, Fantasia 2000, 1999, Finders Fee, 2001, Robots, 2005, The Sandlot 2, 2005, The Benchwarmers, 2005, Click, 2006, Scary Movie 4, 2006, Welcome Home Roscoe Jenkins, 2008, Quantum Quest A Cassini Space Odyssey, 2009, Jack and the Beanstalk, 2010, Star Tours- The Adventure Continue, 2011, Gimme Shelter, 2013, The Angriest Man in Brooklyn, 2014, Driving Miss Daisy, 2014, Rogue One: A Star Wars Story, 2016, Warning Shot, 2017, The Lion King, Mufasa, 2019 AW: Named Distinguished Artist, LA Music Center Club, 1994; recipient The Village Voice Off-Broadway award, 1962, Theatre World award, 1962, Hon. Doctoral Degree, Black Am. Culture Festival, 1969, Grammy award, 1976, medal for spoken language, American Academy of Arts and Letters, 1981, Office of Black Ministries Toussaint medallion, 1982, Theater Hall of Fame award, 1985, Emmy award for performance in children's programming, Soldier Boys, CBS Schoolbreak Special, 1987-88, LA Film Teachers Association Jean Renoir award, 1990, Commonwealth award Distinguished Service in the Dramatic Arts, Bank of Del., 1991, National Medal of Arts for outstanding contribution to cultural life of country, 1992, Hall of Fame Image award for great contribution to arts, National Association for the Advancement of Colored People, 1992, UCLA medal, 1993, John Houseman award, The Acting Co., 1995, Special award for contbns. to theater, Drama Desk, 2008, Lifetime Achievement award, Screen Actors Guild, 2009, Honorary award Academy Motion Picture Arts & Sciences, 2011; numerous other acting awards, nominations-Obie, Drama Desk, Tony, Golden Globe, Outer Critics Cir., ACE, others. MEM: Fellow Am. Academy Arts and Sciences; member National Council of Arts (Presidential appt. to adv. board 1962, presidential appointee 1970-76), Actors' Equity Association, Screen Actors Guild, Am. Federation TV and Radio Artists, Theatre Communications Group (board directors 1962). ACH: Can commonly be seen on TV commericals for Verizon (formerly Bell Atlantic). BA: Horatio Productions, P.O. Box 610, Pawling, NY, 12564

JONES, JERRY, T: Professional Sports Team Owner I: Media & Entertainment DOB: 10/13/1942 PB: LA ED: MBA, University Arkansas, 1970; Grad., University Arkansas, 1965 C: Owner, president, general manager, Dallas Cowboys, 1989-; Founder, Jones Oil and Land Lease, Oklahoma,; Executive vice president, Modern Security Life, Springfield, Missouri, 1965-69 CR: Member LA stadium working group National Football League, member business ventures committee, member special committee on league econs., member broadcast committee, member management council executive committee CIV: Co-founder, Gene and Jerry Jones Family Center for Children, 1998 Co-founder, Gene and Jerry Jones Family Charities, Active, The Rise School of Dallas, Active, The Family Pl., Active, Kent Waldrep Paralysis Foundation, Active, Happy Hill Farm Acad./Home, Active, Children's Medical Center of Dallas, Member national adv. board, Salvation Army, 1998- Member national board, Boys and Girls Club of Am., CW: Appeared in (TV series) Entourage, 2010 AW: Elected, Pro Football Hall of Fame, 2018; Co-recipient Hope award, National Multiple Sclerosis Society, 2005, Annette G. Strauss Humanitarian award, Family Gateway Organization, 2003, Children's Champion award for philanthropy, Dallas for Children Organization, 2002, Chmn.'s award, Boys and Girls Club of Am., 2001, Evangeline Booth award, Salvation Army, 1999; named Partner of Year, 1999; named one of The Most Influential People in the World of Sports, Business Week, 2008, 2007, 50 Most Influential People in Sports Business, Street & Smith's SportsBus. Journal, 2007-09, Forbes 400: Richest Americans, 2006- MEM: Mem.: Salvation Army William Booth Society H: Hunting, fishing, tennis, water-skiing, skiing

JONES, JOHN PAUL, T: Musician I: Media & Entertainment DOB: 05/05/1905 PB: London SC: London C: Musician, recording artist, member, Led Zeppelin, 1968-80 CW: Musician: (albums with Led Zeppelin) Led Zeppelin, 1968, Led Zeppelin II, 1969, Led Zeppelin III, 1970, Led Zeppelin IV, 1971, Houses of the Holy, 1973, Physical Graffiti, 1975, The Song Remains the Same, 1976, Presence, 1976, In Through the Out Door, 1979, Coda, 1982, Remasters, 1990, BBC Sessions, 1997, Early Days: The Best of Led Zeppelin Volume One, 2000, Latter Days: The Best of Led Zeppelin Volume Two, 2002, How the West Was Won, 2003, Mothership, 2007, Definitive Collection, 2008, Celebration Day, 2012 (Grammy award for Best Rock Album, 2014), (solo albums) Zooma, 1999, The Thunderthief, 2001, (with Them Crooked Vultures) Them Crooked Vultures, 2009, (with Seasick Steve) You Can't Teach an Old Dog New Tricks, 2011, Hubcap Music, 2013; also performed with Rolling Stones, Paul McCartney, Jimmy Page, others(Film) Ms Brown, You've Got a Lovely Daughter The Song Remains the Same, 1976, Give my Regards to Broad Street, 1984, Scream for Help, 1984, The Secret Adventures of Tom Thumb 1993, Risk, 1994, Celebration Day, 2012 AW: Named to Rock and Roll Hall of Fame (as member of Led Zeppelin), 1995, Polar Music prize Royal Swedish Academy Music, 2006, Kennedy Center Honors, John F. Kennedy Center Performing Arts, Washington, 2012.

JONES, JULIO, T: Professional Football Player I: Athletics DOB: 02/08/1989 PB: Foley SC: AL/USA ED: University of Alabama C: Atlanta Falcons, Wide Receiver, 2011- AW: Pro Bowl, 2012, 2014–2017, First-team All-Pro, 2015–2017, NFL receiving yards leader, 2015, NFL receptions co-leader, 2015, BCS national champion, 2009, SEC champion, 2009, SEC Freshman of the Year, 2008, First-team All-SEC, 2010, Second-team All-SEC, 2008, USA Today High School All-American, 2007 BA: 4400 Falcon Parkway, Flowery Branch, FL, 30542

JONES, K. C., T: Professional Basketball Coach I: Athletics DOB: 05/25/1932 PB: Taylor ED: Educated, University San Francisco C: New England Blizzard, 1997-98; Head coach, New England Blizzard, ABL, Hartford, Connecticut, 1997-; Assistant coach, Boston Celtics, 1995-07; Head coach, Seattle SuperSonics, NBA, 1990-92; Assistant coach, consultant player personnel director, Seattle SuperSonics, NBA, 1989-90; Vice president basketball operations, Boston Celtics, NBA, 1988-89; Coach, Boston Celtics, NBA, 1983-88; Assistant coach, Boston Celtics, NBA, 1977-83; Coach, Capital Bullets (later Washington), 1973-76; Coach, San Diego Conquistadores, Am. Basketball Association, 1972-73; Assistant coach, Los Angeles Lakers, NBA, 1971-72; Coach, Brandeis University, Waltham, Massachusetts, 1967-71; Player, Boston Celtics, NBA, 1958-67 CR: Member gold medal U.S. Olympic Basketball Team, 1956 member NCAA Championship Team, 1955, NBA Championship Team, 1959-66 coach NBA All-Star Game, 1975, 84, 86 CIV: Served with U.S. Army, 1956-58. AW: Coach NBA Championships, 1984, 86; named to San Francisco Bay Area Sports Hall of Fame, 1989, Naismith Memorial Basketball Hall of Fame, 1989,NBA Champion, 1959-1966, NCAA Champion, 1955, 1956, NBA Champion as Coach, 1984,1986, NBA All-Star Game Head Coach, 1975, 1984-1987

JONES, KIMBERLY (LIL KIM), T: Rap Artist, Actress I: Media & Entertainment PB: Brooklyn SC: NY/USA PT: Linwood Jones; Ruby Mae Jones CW: Singer, Albums, "Hard Core" (1996), "Notorious K.I.M." (2000), "La Bella Mafia" (2003), "The Naked Truth" (2005), "The Meaning of Family" (2005); Films, "Money Talks" (1997), "Moulin Rouge!" (2001); Composer, "High School High" (1996), "Booty Call" (1997), "Nothing to Lose" (1997), "Dr. Doolittle 2" (2001); Actress, Films, "She's All That" (1999), "Longshot" (2000), "Juwanna Mann" (2002), "Gang of Roses" (2003), "Nora's Hair Salon" (2004), "You Got Served" (2004), "Lil Pimp" (2005), "There's a God on the Mic" (2005), "Life After Death: The Movie - Ten Years Later" (2007), "Superhero Movie" (2008), "Can't Stop Won't Stop: A Bad Boy Story" (2017); Guest Appearances, TV Series, "V.I.P." (1999), "DAG" (2001), "Moesha" (2001), "American Dreams" (2003); Performer, "Dancing with the Stars" (2009)

JONES, KIRA ORANGE, T: Teacher I: Education/Educational Services ED: B.A., Wesleyan University; M.Ed., Harvard University C: SVP, Regional Operations for Teach for America,2016-; Regional Director,Teach for America New Orleans- Louisiana Delta,2007-2016 AW: Time 100 Most Influential, 2015, Peter Jennings Award

JONES, LESLIE, T: Comedian I: Media & Entertainment PB: Memphis SC: TN/USA CW: (Film) For Love of the Game, 1999, National Security, 2003, Repos, 2006, Gangsta Rap: The Glockumentary, 2007, Internet Dating, 2008, Something Like a Business, 2010, Lottery Ticket, 2010, The Company We Keep, 2010, House Arrest, 2012, Christmas in Compton, 2012, Top 5, 2104, Kony Montana, 2014, We Are Family,2015, Trainwreck, 2015, Ghostbusters,2016, Sing (Television) In the House, 1996, Coach, 1997, The Way We Do it, 2001, Girlfriends, 2004, Mind of Mencia, 2007, American Body Shop, 2007, Chelsea Lately, 2010, Problem Child: Leslie Jones, 2010, Daddy Knows Best, 2012, Sullivan and Son, 2013, See Dad Run, 2013, The League, 2013, SNL, 2014-, Workaholics, 2014, The Awesomes, 2015, The Blacklist, 2016, Kevin (Probably) Save the World, 2018 AW: Time 100 Most Influential, 2017

JONES, RACHEL BAY BAY, **T:** Actress and Singer **I:** Media & Entertainment **PB:** New York City **SC:** NY/USA **CW:** Actress, Theatre, "Meet Me in St Louis" (1989), "Grand Hotel" (1990), "Fiddler on the Roof" (2000), "Hair" (2009), "Woman on the Verge of a Nervous Breakdown" (2010), "A Christmas Story: The Musical" (2011), "Pippin" (2012-2013), "Dear Evan Hansen" (2015-2016) **AW:** Tony Award for Best Featured Actress in a Musical (2017); Grammy Award for Best Musical Theater Album (2018)

JONES, TODD, **T:** Publix CEO **I:** Business Management/Business Services **C:** President, Publix Super Markets, Inc., 2007-; Senior vice president product business devel., Publix Super Markets, Inc., Lakeland, Florida, 2005-07; Vice president Jacksonville division, Publix Super Markets, Inc., 2003-05; Regional director, Publix Super Markets, Inc., 1999-2003; District manager, Publix Super Markets, Inc., 1997-99; Store manager, Publix Super Markets, Inc., Jacksonville, Florida, 1988-97; Front service clerk to various store level positions, Publix Super Markets, Inc., New Smyrna Beach, Florida, 1980-88

JONES, VAN, **T:** Advocate, Former Federal Official **I:** Government Administration/Government Relations/Government Services **DOB:** 09/20/1968 **PB:** Jackson **ED:** JD, Yale Law School, New Haven, 1993; BS in Communications & Political Sci., University Tennessee, Martin, 1990 **C:** Panelist, Crossfire, CNN, 2013-; President, co-founder, Rebuild the Dream, 2011-; Senior fellow, Center for American Progress, Washington, 2010-; Senior policy adv., Green For All, Oakland, 2010-; Professor, environmental policy & politics, Princeton University, 2010-11; Special advisor for green jobs, enterprise & innovation, The White House Council on Environmental Quality (CEQ), Washington, 2009; Founding president, Green For All, Oakland, 2008-09; Co-founder, Color Of Change, 2005; Co-founder, Ella Baker Center for Human Rights, 1996; Founder, Bay Area PoliceWatch, 1993; Intern, Lawyers Committee for Civil Rights, San Francisco, **CIV:** Trustee, Robert F. Kennedy Center for Justice & Human Rights, Trustee, National Resources December Council (NRDC) **CW:** Co-author (with Ariane Conrad): The Green Collar Economy: How One Solution Can Fix Our Two Biggest Problems, 2008, Rebuild the Dream, 2012, Beyond the Messy Truth: How We Come Apart, How We Come Together, 2017 **AW:** Named a Young Global Leader, World Economic Forum, 2005; named an Environmental Hero, TIME magazine, 2008; named one of The 100 Most Influential People in the World, 2009, The 100 Agents of Change, Rolling Stone magazine, 2009, The Daring Dozen, George Lucas Foundation, 2008, The 25 Most Influential/Inspiring African Americans, Essence Magazine, 2008, The 12 Most Creative Minds, Fast Company, 2008; named to The Power 150, Ebony magazine, 2010; recipient Inforum's 21st Century Leadership award, Commonwealth Club of California, 2010, President's award, National Association for the Advancement of Colored People, 2010, Individual Thought Leadership, Energy & Environment award, Aspen Institute, 2009, President's award, National Association for the Advancement of Colored People, 2010, Eco-Entrepreneur award, Howard University Institute Entrepreneurship, Leadership & Innovation, 2009, Hubert H. Humphrey Civil Rights award, 2009, Puffin/Nation prize for creative citizenship, 2008, Community Leadership award, San Francisco Foundation, 2008, Community Environmental Leadership Award, Global Green USA, 2008, Paul Wellstone award, Campaign America's Future, 2008, Hunt Prime Mover award, 2008, Green award, Elle magazine,

2008, Reebok International Human Rights award, 1998; International Ashoka Fellowship, 2000, Next Generation Leadership Fellowship, Rockefeller Foundation, 1997-98 **PA:** Democrat

JONES, WALTER BEAMAN JR., **T:** U.S. Representative from North Carolina **I:** Government Administration/Government Relations/Government Services **DOB:** 02/10/1943 **PB:** Pitt County, North Carolina **PT:** Son of Walter Beaman Jones; **ED:** BA in Hist., Atlantic Christian College, Wilson, North Carolina, 1967 **C:** Member, US House Armed Services Committee, 1995-; Member, Committee on Homeland Security, Committee on Oversight and Government Reform, Committee on House Administration; Member, US Congress from 3rd North Carolina District, 1995-; Member, US House Financial Services Committee, 1995-2012; Member, North Carolina House of Reps., 1983-92; President, Judson Co., 1990-94; President, Benefit Reserves, Inc., 1989-94; Salesman, Dunn Associate, 1973-82; Manager, Walter B. Jones Office Supply Co., 1967-73 **CIV:** With, North Carolina National Guard, 1967-71 Member adv. board, Disabled Children's Relief Fund, **AW:** Named a Friend of the Farmer, Am. Farm Bureau Federation, Friend of the Family, Christian Coalition; named Guardian of Small Business, National Federation Ind. Business, Taxpayer Hero, Council Citizens against Government Waste; recipient Spirit of Enterprise award, US C. of C., Pro-Nat. Security award, Center Security Policy, Golden Bulldog award, Watchdogs of the Treasury, Inc., George L. Murphy award, United Seniors Association, George (Buck) Gillispie Congl. award, Meritorious Service, Blinded Am. Vets. Foundation, 2004 **PA:** Republican **BA:** 2333 Rayburn House Office Building, Washington, DC, 20515

JORDAN, ADALBERTO JOSE, **T:** Federal Judge **I:** Law and Legal Services **DOB:** 12/07/1961 **PB:** Havana **SC:** Cuba **ED:** JD, University of Miami (1987); BA, University of Miami (1984) **C:** Judge, U.S. Court of Appeals for the Eleventh Circuit, Miami, FL (2012-Present); Judge, U.S. District Court for the Southern District of Florida, Miami, FL (1999-2012); Chief, Appellate Division, U.S. Department of Justice, Miami, FL (1998-1999); Deputy Chief, Appellate Division, U.S. Department Justice, Miami, FL (1996-1998); Assistant U.S. Attorney for the Southern District of Florida, U.S. Department of Justice, Miami, FL (1994-1999); Partner, Steel, Hector & Davis, Miami, FL (1994); Associate, Steel, Hector & Davis, Miami, FL (1989-1994); Law Clerk to Justice Sandra Day O'Connor, Supreme Court of the U.S., Washington, DC (1988-1989); Law Clerk to Honorable Thomas Alonzo Clark, U.S. Court of Appeals for the Eleventh Circuit (1987-1988) **CR:** Adjunct Professor, University of Miami School of Law (1990-Present) **BA:** 56 Forsyth St NW, Atlanta, GA, 30303

JORDAN, JIM, **T:** U.S. Representative from Ohio **I:** Government Administration/Government Relations/Government Services **DOB:** 02/17/1964 **PB:** Urbana **SC:** OH/USA **ED:** JD, Capital University, Columbus, 2001; MA in Education, Ohio State University, Columbus, 1991; BS in Economics, University of Wisconsin, Madison, 1986 **C:** Member, US House Select Committee on the Events Surrounding the 2012 Terrorist Attack in Benghazi, 2014-;; Member, Committee on the Judiciary, Committee on Oversight and Government Reform; Member, US Congress from 4th Ohio District, 2007-; Chairman, Republican Study Committee, 2011-13; Member, District 12, Ohio State Senate, 2001-07; Member, District 85, Ohio House of Reps., Columbus, 1995-2000; Assistant Wrestling Coach, Ohio State University Buckeyes, Columbus, **AW:** Named Pro-life Legis. of Year, United Conserva-

tives of Ohio, 1998; Recipient, Defender of Life Award, Ohio Right to Life Society, Leadership in Government Award, Ohio Roudtable/Freedom Forum, 2001; Big Ten/NCAA Wrestling Champion, 1986, 1985 **MEM:** Mem.: Citizens Against Government Waste, Mad River Valley Young Rep. Club **PA:** Republican

JORDAN, KENT A., **T:** Federal Judge **I:** Law and Legal Services **DOB:** 10/24/1957 **PB:** West Point **SC:** NY/USA **PT:** Amos Azariah Jordan; MarDeane (Carver) Jordan **MS:** Married **SPN:** Michelle Weaver (4/25/1981) **ED:** JD, Georgetown University, Cum Laude (1984); BA in Economics, Brigham Young University, with High Honors (1981) **C:** Judge, U.S. Court of Appeals for the Third Circuit (2006-Present); Judge, U.S. District Court for the District of Delaware (2002-2006); Vice President, General Counsel, Corporate Service Co., Wilmington, DE (1997-2002); Partner, Morris, James, Hitchens & Williams, Wilmington, DE (1993-1997); Associate, Morris, James, Hitchens & Williams, Wilmington, DE (1992-1993); Chief, Civil Division, U.S. Department of Justice, Wilmington, DE (1991-1992); Assistant U.S. Attorney Delegate, U.S. Department of Justice, Wilmington, DE (1987-1992); Associate, Potter Anderson & Corroon, Wilmington, DE (1985-1987); Law Clerk to the Honorable James L. Latchum, U.S. District Court, Wilmington, DE (1984-1985) **CR:** Adjunct Professor, University of Pennsylvania (2005-Present); Adjunct Professor, Vanderbilt University (2003-Present); Member, Delaware Supreme Court, Wilmington, DE (2000-2002); Delaware Supreme Court, Wilmington, DE (1997); Ombudsman (1995-2002); Member, Advisory Committee, U.S. District Court for the District of Delaware (1995-1998); Adjunct Professor, Widener University Law School, Wilmington, DE (1995-1996); Secretary, Board of Bar Examiners **CIV:** Past President, Board of Directors, Community Legal Aid Society, Wilmington, DE (1994-1997); Member, Greater Hockessin Area Development Association (1991-2001) **CW:** Contributor, Articles to Professional Journals **MEM:** President, Richard S. Rodney American Inn of Court (2005-2007); Council Member, Intellectual Property Section, Delaware State Bar Association (1996-1998); Counselor, Richard S. Rodney American Inn of Court (1996-1998); Secretary-Treasurer, Richard S. Rodney American Inn of Court (1994-1996); Delaware Chapter, Federal Bar Association; American Intellectual Property Law Association **BAR:** District of Columbia Court of Appeals (1996); U.S. Court of Appeals for the Federal Circuit (1995); Supreme Court of the U.S. (1994); U.S. Court of Appeals for the Third Circuit (1988); U.S. District Court for the District of Delaware (1985); Delaware (1984) **BA:** 601 Market St, Philadelphia, PA, 19106 **ADD:** US Ct Appeals, 844 King St Lock Box 10, Wilmington, NC, 19801

JORDAN, MICHAEL JEFFREY, **T:** Professional Sports Team Executive, Retired Professional Basketball Player **I:** Business Management/Business Services **DOB:** 02/17/1963 **PB:** Bklyn. **SC:** NY/USA **PT:** Son of James and Deloris Jordan; **ED:** Student, University of North Carolina at Chapel Hill 1981-84 **C:** Majority owner, chairman, Charlotte Hornets (formerly Charlotte Bobcats), 2014-; Majority owner, chairman, Charlotte Bobcats, 2010-14; Minority owner, managing member basketball operations, Charlotte Bobcats, 2006-10; Retired player, NBA, 2003; Guard, Washington Wizards, 2001-03; President basketball operations, Washington Wizards, 1999-2000; Minor league baseball player, Chicago White Sox AA Team, 1994-95; Guard, Chicago Bulls, 1995-98; Guard, Chicago Bulls, 1984-93 **CR:** Founder MJ Basketball Holdings, LLC, Jordan Brand Clothing, 1997-; owner Michael

Jordan's: The Restaurant, 1993- **CW:** Author: RareAir: Michael on Michael, 1993; co-author (with Tinker Hatfield): Driven From Within, 2005; actor: (films) Space Jam, 1996, He Got Game, 1998 **AW:** Named NBA Finals MVP, 1996-98, 1991-93, Male Athlete of Year, Associated Press, 1993, 1992, 1991, NBA MVP, 1998, 1996, 1992, 1991, 1988, NBA Defense Player of Year, 1988, NBA All-Star Game MVP, 1998, 1996, 1988, Slam-Dunk Championship winner, 1988, 1987, Seagram's NBA Player of Year, 1987, NBA Rookie of Year, 1985, First Team All-Am., Sporting News, 1983-84; named one of The 100 Most Powerful Celebrities, Forbes.com, 2008, Most Influential People in the World of Sports, Business Week, 2008, 2007; named to Naismith Memorial Basketball Hall of Fame, 2009, NBA All-Def. Team, 1996-98, 1988-93, All-NBA First Team, 1996-98, 1987-93, Eastern Conference All-Star Team, NBA, 2002-03, 1996-98, 1985-93; recipient Presidential Medal of Freedom, The White House, 2016, Wooden award, 1984, Naismith award, 1984 **ACH:** Achievements include member of the NCAA Division I Men's Basketball Championship winning University of North Carolina Tar Heels, 1982; member of the Gold Medal winning US Olympic basketball team, 1984, 92; leading the NBA in: points, 1985, 1987-93, 1996-98; scoring average, 1987-93, 1996-98; minutes, 1987-89; steals, 1988, 1990, 1993; holding the record for most points in an NBA playoff game (63), 1986; member of the NBA Championship winning Chicago Bulls, 1991, 92, 93, 96, 97, 98 **H:** Golf **BA:** Jump Inc, 676 North Michigan Avenue, Suite 293, Chicago, IL, 60611

JORDAN, MICHAEL B. B., T: Actor **I:** Media & Entertainment **PB:** Santa Ana **SC:** CA/USA **CW:** (Film) Black and White, 1999, Hardball, 2001, Blackout, 2007, Pastor Brown, 2009, Red Tails, 2012, Chronicle, 2012, Fruitvale Station, 2013, Justice League:The Flashpoint Paradox, 2013, That Awkward Moment, 2014, Fantastic Four, 2015, Creed, 2015, Black Panther, 2018(Television) The Sopranos, 1999, Cosby, 1999, The Wire, 2002, All My Children, 2003, CSI: Crime Scene Investigation, 2006, Without a Trace, 2006, Cold Case, 2007, Burn Notice, 2009, Bones, 2009, The Assistants, 2009, Friday Night Lights, 2009, Law and Order:Criminal Intent, 2010, Lie to Me, 2010, Parenthood, 2010, House, 2012, County, Ridiculousness, 2014, Boondocks, 2014, Running Wild with Bear Grylls, 2015, Fahrenheit 451, Raising Dion, 2019

JOYCE, DAVID, T: U.S. Representative from Ohio **I:** Government Administration/Government Relations/Government Services **PB:** Cleveland **SC:** OH/USA **ED:** J.D., University of Dayton, 180-82; B.S., University of Dayton, 1975-79 **C:** Member, U.S. Representative from Ohio's 14 District, 2013-; Member, Committee on Appropriations; Prosecutor, Geauga County, 1988-; Public Defender, Geauga County, Ohio, 1985-88; Public Defender, Cuyahoga Country, Ohio, 1983-84

JOYCE, THOMAS P., T: Consumer Products Company Executive **I:** Manufacturing **C:** President, CEO, member Board of Directors, Danaher Corporation, 2014-; Executive vice president, Danaher Corp., 2006-2014; President, Hach Co. (subsidiary Danaher Corp.), 2001-02; Vice president, group executive, Danaher Corp., 2002-06; Various general management positions, Danaher Corp.; Joined, Danaher Corp., 1990

JOYNER KERSEE, JACKIE, T: Retired Track and Field Athlete **I:** Athletics **DOB:** 03/03/1962 **PB:** East St. Louis **SC:** Illinois **PT:** Daughter of Alfred and Mary Joyner; Married Bob Kersee, January 11, 1986. **ED:** DHL (hon.), George Washington University, St. Louis, 1999; DHL (hon.), Howard University, 1999; DHL (hon.), Spelman College, 1998; DHL (hon.), Fontbonne College, St. Louis, 1998; DHL (hon.), Harris-Stowe State College, 1993; LLD (hon.), Iona College, 1994; LLD (hon.), Washington University, St. Louis, 1992; BA in History, UCLA, 1985 **C:** Retired, 2001; Member USA Track & Field Olympic Team, 1996; Member USA Track & Field Olympic Team, 1992; Member USA Track & Field Olympic Team, 1988; Member USA Track & Field Olympic Team, 1984; Basketball Player, Richmond Rage, ABL, 1996 **CR:** President, Founder JJK & Associates., Inc. **CIV:** Founder JJK Community Foundation, 1989 (now JJK Youth Center Foundation, 1997-), Jackie Joyner Kersee Boys & Girls Club chairman St. Louis Sports Commission, 1996-2000, chairman emeritus, 2001-. **CW:** Author: (autobiography) A Kind of Grace: The Autobiography of the World's Greatest Female Athlete, 1997; Co-author: A Woman's Place Is Everywhere, 1994. **AW:** Recipient Broderick Cup, 1985, James E. Sullivan Award, 1986, Jesse Owens Award, 1986, 87, Am. Black Achievement Award, Ebony magazine, 1987, 1st Female Athlete of Year Award, Sporting News, 1988, Jim Thorpe Award, 1993, Jackie Robinson "Robie" Award, 1994, Parenting Leader Award, Parenting Magazine, Jesse Owens Humanitarian Award, 1999, Humanitarian Award, Women Sports and Fitness, Pres.'s Award, National Conference Black Mayors; named Athlete of Year, Track & Field News, 1986, Female Athlete of Year, Associated Press, 1987, Female of Year, International Association Athletics Federations, 1994, St. Louis Ambassadors Sportswoman of Year, Hon. Harlem Globetrotter, Woman Athlete of Century, Sports Illustrated, 1999; inductee National Boys and Girls Club Hall of Fame, Dick Enberg Award, 2011, NCAA Silver Anniversary Awards Honoree, 2010, Order of Licoln, 2005, St Louis Walk of Fame, 2000, Jack Kelly Fair Play Award, 1997 **ACH:** Achievements include winner of 4 consecutive National Junior Pentathlon Championships; winner long jump, World Championships, Rome, 1987; winner Mobil Indoor Grand Prix, 1987; winner long jump, Pan Am. Games, 1987; winner heptathlon, World Championships, Stuttgart, Germany, 1993; winner hepthathlon, Goodwill Games, New York City, 1998; winner silver medal for heptathlon, LA Olympic Games, 1984; winner gold medal for heptathlon, Seoul Olympic Games, 1988; winner gold medal for long jump, Seoul Olympic Games, 1988; winner gold medal for heptathlon, Barcelona Olympic Games, 1992; winner bronze medal for long jump, Barcelona Olympic Games, 1992; winner bronze medal for long jump, Atlanta Olympic Games, 1996; set and still holds World Record for heptathlon, Seoul Olympic Games, 9/23/1988 **BA:** Jackie Joyner-Kersee Foundation, 101 Jackie Joyner-Kersee Circle, East St Louis, IL, 62204

JUN, LEI, T: Founder of Xiaomi Inc **I:** Technology **DOB:** 06/21/1905 **PB:** Xiantao, China **SC:** Xiantao, China **ED:** Bachelors Degree in Computer Science, Wuhan University **C:** Advisor, Cheetah Mobile Inc, 2018-; Co-Founder, YY Inc, 2016-; Chairman/CEO/Co-Founder, Xiaomi Corp, 2010-; Co-Founder, Joyo.Com Ltd, 2005-

JUNE, CARL HOWARD, T: Immunologist **I:** Medicine & Health Care **DOB:** 07/13/1953 **ED:** MD, Baylor College of Medicine, Houston, TX, 1979; BS in Biology, Naval Academy, Annapolis, MD, 1971 **CT:** Certificate in Medical Oncology; Diplomate, American Board of Internal Medicine **C:** Director, Translational Research Programs, Abramson Cancer Center, University of Pennsylvania, 1999-Present; Professor, Pathology & Laboratory Medicine, University of Pennsylvania, Philadelphia, PA, 1999-Present; Professor, Department of Medicine, Department of Cell & Molecular Biology, Uniformed Services, University of Health Sciences, Bethesda, MD, 1995-1999; Fellow, American College Of Physicians, 1991; Head, Department of Immunology, Founder, Immune Cell Biology Program, Naval Medical Research Institute, Maryland, 1990-1995; Postdoctorate Training In Transplantation Biology, Fred Hutchinson Cancer Research Center, Seattle, WA, 1983-1986; Graduate Training In Immunology & Malaria, World Health Organization, Geneva, Switzerland, 1978-1979 **CR:** Investigator, Abramson Family Cancer Research Institute, 1999-Present **CW:** Contributor, Articles, Professional Journals **AW:** Alpha Omega Alpha Medical Society, 1978, Frank Brown Berry Prize In Federal Medicine, 1997, Lifetime Achievement Award, Leukemia And Lymphoma Society Of America, 2002, William Osler Award, University Of Pennsylvania School Of Medicine, 2002, Federal Laboratory Award For Excellence In Technology Transfer, 2005, Bristol-Myers Squibb Freedom To Discover Award, 2005–2009, Elected, Institute Of Medicine, 2012, Elected, American Academy Of Arts And Sciences, 2014, Hamdan Award For Medical Research Excellence, 2014, Taubman Prize For Excellence In Translational Medical Science, 2014, Karl Landsteiner Memorial Award, AABB, 2014, Paul Ehrlich And Ludwig Darmstaedter Prize, 2015, Most Influential, TIME, 2018 **MEM:** American Association of Clinical Oncology **ACH:** Achievements include research in various mechanisms of lymphocyte activation that relate to immune tolerance and adoptive immunotherapy **BA:** June Lab, Room 554 BRB II/III, 421 Curie Boulevard, Philadelphia, PA, 19104-6160

JUSTICE, JAMES "JIM" CONLEY JR., T: Governor of West Virginia **I:** Government Administration/Government Relations/Government Services **DOB:** 04/27/1951 **PB:** Charleston **SC:** WV/USA **PT:** James Conley Justice, Sr., Edna Ruth (Perry) Justice **MS:** Married **SPN:** Cathy (Comer) Justice, 1975 **CH:** Jay; Jill **ED:** BA, MBA, Marshall University; Student, University of Tennessee **C:** Governor, West Virginia, 2017-Present; Owner, Mechel, 2015-Present; Owner, Bluestone Industries and Bluestone Coal Corporation, 1993-Present; Businessman, 1977-2017; Founder, Bluestone Farms, 1977; Owner or CEO of Over 50 Businesses Including Greenbrier, Sulphur Springs, West Virginia **CR:** Developer, Stoney Brook Plantation, Monroe County, West Virginia; Endorsed, United Mine Workers; Host, Greenbrier Classic **CIV:** Girls Basketball Coach, Greenbrier East High School, 2003-Present; President, Beckley Little League, 1992-Present; Head Coach, Boys Basketball Teams, Greenbrier East High School, 2011-2017; Thundering Herd Golf Team, Marshall University; James C. Justice National Scout Camp, Summit Bechtel Family National Scout Reserve; Marshall University; Cleveland Clinic; Dream Tree for Kids **AW:** Winner, State Championship, Girls Basketball, Greenbrier East High School, 2012 **MEM:** Director, Mountain State Coal Classic, 1995-Present **ACH:** seven time national corn growing champion; **PA:** Republican

KAEPERNICK, COLIN RAND, T: Former Professional Football Player/Civil Rights Activist **I:** Athletics **DOB:** 11/03/1987 **PB:** Milwaukee **SC:** WI/USA **PT:** Rick Kaepernick; Teresa Kaepernick **ED:** Bachelor in Business Management, University of Nevada, Reno (2011) **C:** Free Agent (2016-Present); Quarterback, San Francisco 49ers (2011) **AW:** Time 100 Most Influential (2017); Offensive Player of Year, Western Athletic Conference (Women's Army Corps) (2008, 2010); Named Most Valuable Player, Humanitarian Bowl (2008); Freshman of the Year (2007) **ACH:** Achievements include holding the NFL record for most rushing yards (182) in a game by a quarterback, 2012

KAGAN, ELENA, T: Associate Justice of the U.S. Supreme Court **I:** Government Administration/Government Relations/Government Services **DOB:** 04/28/1960 **PB:** New York City **SC:** NY/USA **PT:** Daughter of Robert and Gloria (Gittelman) Kagan **ED:** JD magna cum laude, Harvard Law School, 1986; MPhil, Worchester College, Oxford, England, 1983; BA in History, summa cum laude, Princeton University, New Jersey, 1981 **C:** Associate Justice, US Supreme Court, 2010-; Solicitor General, US Department Justice, Washington, 2009-10; Charles Hamilton Houston Professor of Law, Dean, Harvard Law School, Cambridge, Massachusetts, 2003-09; Professor, Harvard Law School, Cambridge, Massachusetts, 2001-03; Visiting Professor of Law, Harvard Law School, Cambridge, Massachusetts, 1999-2001; Deputy Assistant to President for Domestic Policy, Deputy Director, Domestic Policy Council, The White House, Washington, 1997-99; Associate Counsel to President, The White House, Washington, 1995-96; Professor, University of Chicago Law School, 1995; Assistant Professor, University of Chicago Law School, 1991-95; Associate, Williams & Connolly LLP, Washington, 1989-91; Law Clerk to Justice Thurgood Marshall, US Supreme Court, 1987-88; Law Clerk to Hon. Abner Mikva, US Court Appeals (DC cir.), 1986-87 **CW:** Contributor, Articles to Professional Journals **AW:** Named one of The 100 Most Influential People in the World, TIME magazine, 2013, The 100 Most Powerful Women, Forbes magazine, 2010, The 10 Most Powerful Women in Washington, Fortune magazine, 2010, The 100 Most Powerful Women in DC, Washingtonian magazine, 2009, Washington's Most Influential Women Lawyers, The National Law Journal, 2010, The 50 Most Influential Women Lawyers in America, 2007; Recipient, Teaching Excellence Award, University Chicago Law School, 1993 **ACH:** Achievements include recognition as the first woman to serve as Solicitor General of the U.S. **PA:** Democrat **BA:** US Supreme Court, One First St NE, Washington, DC, 20543

KAHNEMAN, DANIEL, T: Psychologist **I:** Health, Wellness and Fitness **DOB:** 03/05/1934 **PB:** Tel Aviv **ED:** Doctor (hon.), Erasmus University, 2009; Doctor (hon.), University of Rome, 2007; Doctor (hon.), U. Alberta, 2006; Doctor (hon.), University of Paris, 2006; Doctor (hon.), University of Milan, 2005; Doctor (hon.), University of Wurzburg, 2004; Doctor (hon.), University of East Anglia, 2004; Doctor (hon.), Harvard University, 2004; Doctor (hon.), University of British Columbia, 2004; Doctor (hon.), The New School, New York City, 2003; Doctor (hon.), Ben-Gurion University, 2003; Doctor (hon.), University of Trento, 2002; DSc (hon.), University of Pennsylvania, 2001; PhD in Psychology, University of California, Berkeley, 1961; BA in Psychology & Math., Hebrew University, Jerusalem, 1954 **C:** Professor of Public Affairs Emeritus, Senior Scholar, Woodrow Wilson School, Princeton University, 2007-; Eugene Higgins Professor of Psychology Emeritus, Princeton University, 2007-; Fellow, Center for Rationality, Hebrew University, 2000-; Eugene Higgins Professor of Psychology, Professor of Public Affairs, Princeton University, 1993-2007; Professor of Psychology, University of California, Berkeley, 1986-94; Professor of Psychology, University of British Columbia, Canada, 1978-86; Professor, Hebrew University, 1973-78; Associate Professor, Hebrew University, 1970-73; Senior Lecturer, Hebrew University, 1966-70; Lecturer of Psychology, Hebrew University, 1961-66 **CR:** Visiting Scholar, Russell Sage Foundation, 1991-92; Associate Fellow, Canadian Institute for Advanced Research, 1984-86; Fellow, Center

Advanced Studies in Behavioral Scis., Stanford, California, 1977-78; Visiting Scientist, Applied Psychological Research Unit, University of Cambridge, England, 1968-69; Lecturer of Psychology, Fellow, Center for Cognitive Studies, Harvard University, 1966-67; Visiting Scientist, Department of Psychology University of Michigan, 1965-66 **MIL:** Second Lieutenant to Lieutenant, Israel Defence Forces, 1954 **CW:** Member, Editorial Board Thinking and Reasoning, Environmental and Resource Economics; Contributor, Articles to Professional Journals; Author: Thinking, Fast and Slow, 2011 (Communication award, National Academy of Sciences, 2011) **AW:** Named one of The 50 Most Influential People in Global Finance, Bloomberg Markets, 2011-12; Recipient, The Economist's 7th Most Influential Economist in the World, 2015, Presidential Medal of Freedom, The White House, 2013, Talcott Parsons Prize, American Academy Arts & Sciences, 2011, Award for Outstanding Life Contributions to Psychology, American Psychological Association, 2007, Frank P. Ramsey Medal, Decision Analysis Society, 2006, Thomas Schelling Prize, 2006, Career Achievement Award, Society Medical Decision Making, 2002, Grawemeyer Prize in Psychology, University of Louisville, 2002, Nobel Prize in Economics, Royal Swedish Academy Sci., 2002, Hilgard Award for Lifetime Contribution to General Psychology, 1995, Warren Medal, Society of Experimental Psychologists, 1995, Distinguished Scientific Contribution Award, Society for Consumer Psychology, 1992, Distinguished Scientific Contribution Award, American Psychological Society, 1982, William James Fellow, American Psychological Society **MEM:** Fellow: Econometric Society, Can. Psychological Association, American Psychological Association, American Psychological Society, American Academy Arts & Sciences; mem.: National Academy of Sciences, Society Judgment & Decision Making (president 1992-93), Society Economic Sci., Psychonomic Society, Brit. Academy (corr.), Society Experimental Psychologists 1992-93

KAINE, TIM, T: U.S. Senator from Virginia **I:** Government Administration/Government Relations/Government Services **DOB:** 02/26/1958 **PB:** St. Paul **SC:** MN/USA **PT:** Albert A. Kaine, Mary Kathleen (Burns) Kaine **MS:** Married **SPN:** Anne Bright Holton, 11/24/1984 **CH:** Annella, Woody, National **ED:** JD, Harvard Law School, Cum Laude, 1983; AB, University of Missouri, Summa Cum Laude, 1979 **C:** U.S. Senate Armed Services Committee, 2013-Present; U.S. Senate Foreign Relations Committee, 2013-Present; U.S. Senate Budget Committee, 2013-Present; U.S. Senator From Virginia, 2013-2016; Chairman, Democratic National Committee, Washington, DC, 2009-2011; Governor, State Of Virginia, 2006-2010; Lieutenant Governor, State Of Virginia, 2002-2006; Mayor, City Of Richmond, 1998-2001; City Council, City Of Richmond, 1994-1998; Private Law Practice, Richmond, VA, 1984-2001; Law Clerk To Hon. R. Lanier Anderson, III, U.S. Court of Appeals, 11th Circuit, 1983-1984 **CR:** Professor of Law, University of Richmond Law School; Chairman, Southern Governors Association, 2008-2009; Democratic Party Nominee For Vice President Of The U.S., 2016 **CIV:** Board of Directors, Historic Jackson Ward Foundation **CW:** Contributor, Articles, Professional Journals **AW:** Pro Bono Public Award, Richmond Bar Association, 1995 **MEM:** American Bar Association, Virginia Bar Association, Richmond Bar Association **PA:** Democrat **BA:** Democratic National Committee, 430 S Capitol Street, Washington, DC, 20003

KALANICK, TRAVIS CORDELL, T: Former CEO **I:** Business Management/Business Services **CN:** Uber **PB:** Los Angeles **SC:** CA/USA **PT:** Donald Kalanick; Bonnie Kalanick **ED:** UCLA (1994-1998) **C:** Founder, CEO, Uber, San Francisco, 2009-17; Head P2P Initiatives, Akami Technologies, 2007-08; Founder, CEO, Red Swoosh, 2001-07; Co-founder, Scour.net, 1998-2000 **AW:** Named one of The 100 Most Influential People in the World, TIME magazine, 2014, The 40 Under 40, Fortune magazine, 2013-14

KALING, MINDY, T: Actress, Scriptwriter, Television Producer **I:** Media & Entertainment **DOB:** 06/24/1979 **PB:** Cambridge **SC:** MA/USA **PT:** Avu Kaling; Swati Kaling **ED:** BA in Playwriting, Dartmouth College, Hanover, NH (2001) **CW:** Actress, Executive Producer, Writer, "The Mindy Project" (2012-Present); Actress, "Ocean's 8" (2018); Actress, "A Wrinkle in Time" (2018); Actress, "Champions" (2018); Actress, "Animals" (2017); Actress, "The Muppets" (2015); Author, "Why Not Me?" (2015); Actress, "The Night Before" (2015); Voice Actress, "Inside Out" (2015); Actress, "Sesame Street" (2014); Actress, "This Is the End" (2013); Actress, "The Five-Year Engagement" (2012); Voice Actress, "Wreck-It Ralph" (2012); Actress, "No Strings Attached" (2011); Author, "Is Everyone Hanging Out Without Me? (And Other Concerns)" (2011); Voice Actress, "Despicable Me" (2010); Actress, "Unaccompanied Minors" (2006); Actress, Co-Producer, "The Office" (2005-2012); Actress, "Curb Your Enthusiasm" (2005); Actress, "The 40 Year Old Virgin" (2005); Co-Writer, Actress, "Matt & Ben" (2003) **AW:** Named, One of the 100 Most Influential People in the World, Time Magazine (2013); Named, Outstanding Performance by an Ensemble in a Comedy Series, Screen Actors Guild (2007-2008); Recipient, Best Play Prize, New York International Fringe Festival (2003); Featured, U.S. Comedy Arts Festival, Aspen, CO (2003); Named, "One of the Top Ten Theatrical Events of 2003," Time Magazine (2003)

KALUUYA, DANIEL, T: Actor **I:** Media & Entertainment **PB:** London **SC:** England **CW:** (Film) Shoot the Messenger, 2006, Much Ado About a Minor Ting, 2007, Cass, 2008, Chatroom,2010, Baby, 2010, Johnny English Reborn, 2011, Beginning, 2012, Welcome to the Punch, 2013, Jonah, 2013, Kick-Ass 2, 2013, Sicario, 2015, Get Out, 2017, Black Panther, 2018, Widows,2018(Television) The Whistleblowers, 2007, Comedy: Shuffle, 2007, Skins, 2007, Delta Forever, 2008, Silent Witness, 2008, That Mitchell and Webb Look, 2008, Doctor Who, 2009, Lewis, 2009, FM, 2009, The Philanthropist, 2009, 10 Minute Tales, 2009, Psychoville,2009,Comedy Lab, 2010, Harry and Paul,2010, Coming Up, 2011, The Fades, 2011, Black Mirror,2011, Random,2011, Babylon, 2014, Watership down, 2018

KANDARIAN, STEVEN A., T: Metlife CEO **I:** Insurance **ED:** MBA, Harvard Business School, 1980; JD, Georgetown University Law Center, 1978; BA in Economics, Clark University, 1974 **C:** Chairman, president, CEO, MetLife, Inc., 2012-; President, CEO, MetLife, Inc., 2011; Executive vice president, chief investment officer, MetLife, Inc., 2005-11; Executive director, Pension Benefit Guaranty Corp. (PBGC), 2001-04; Founder, managing partner, Orion Partners, LP,; President, founder, Eagle Capital Holdings, 1990-93; Managing director, Lee Capital Holdings, Boston, 1984-90; With, State St. Bank,; With, LCB Holdings, Inc.,; Investment banker, Rotan Mosle, Inc., Houston, **CR:** Board directors MetLife, Inc., 2011- board trustees MassMutual Premier Funds, MassMutual Participation Investors, MassMutual Corp. Investors

KANDEL, ERIC RICHARD, T: Neuroscientist, Educator **I:** Medicine & Health Care **DOB:** 11/07/1929 **PB:** Vienna **PT:** Son of Herman and Charlotte (Zimels) Kandel **ED:** MD, New York University School Medicine, 1956; BA, Harvard College, 1952 **C:** Professor department biochemistry and molecular biophysics, Columbia University College Physicians & Surgeons, 1992-; Univ. professor, Columbia University College Physicians & Surgeons, 1983-; Professor department physiology and psychiatry, Columbia University College Physicians & Surgeons, New York City, 1974-; Founding director Center Neurobiology & Behavior, Columbia University College Physicians & Surgeons, New York City, 1974-83; Associate professor department physiology and psychiatry, New York University School Medicine, 1965-74; Staff psychiatrist, Harvard Medical School, Boston, 1964-65; Resident in psychiatry, Harvard Medical School, Boston, 1960-64; Research associate neurophysiology laboratory, National Institutes of Health, Bethesda, 1957-60; Intern, Montefiore Hospital, New York City, 1956-57 **CR:** Senior investigator Howard Hughes Medical Institute, Chevy Chase, Maryland, 1984- **CW:** Author: Cellular Basis of Behavior: An Introduction to Behavioral Neurobiology, 1976, Cellular Biology of Neurons, 1977, A Cell Biological Approach to Learning, 1978, Behavioral Biology of Aplysia: A Contribution to the Comparative Study of Opisthobranch Molluscs, 1979, Essentials of Neural Science Value Pack, 1995, Psychiatry, Psychoanalysis, and the New Biology of Mind, 2005, (autobiography) In Search of Memory: The Emergence of a New Science of Mind, 2006 (LA Times Book award for sci. & tech., 2006); co-author (with James H. Schwartz & Thomas M. Jessell): Essentials of Neural Science and Behavior, 1995; editor: Molecular Neurobiology in Neurology and Psychiatry, 1987; co-editor: Molecular Aspects of Neurobiology, 1986, Principles of Neural Science, 2000; contributor articles to professional journals, (Film) In Search of Memory, 2008 **AW:** Recipient Viktor Frankl award, Vienna, 2008, Nobel Prize in Physiology/Medicine, The Nobel Foundation, 2000, Heineken prize, 2000, Wolf Foundation Prize in Medicine, Israel, 1999, Charles A. Dana award for pioneering achievement in health, 1997, New York City Mayor's award for excellence in sci. and tech., 1994, FO Schmitt medal in neurosci., 1993, Harvey prize, Technion-Israel Institute Tech., 1993, Jean-Louis Signoret's prize, 1992, Warren Triennial prize, 1992, Bristol-Myers Squibb award for distinguished achievement in neurosci. research, 1991, Robert J. & Claire Pasarow Foundation award in neurosci., 1989, Distinguished Service award, American Psychiatric Association, 1989, National Medal Sci., The White House, 1988, Gairdner Foundation International award, 1987, Howard Crosby Warren medal, Society Experimental Psychologists, 1984, Albert Lasker award for Basic Medical Research, 1983, Dickson prize in biology & medicine, 1982, Karl Spencer Lashley prize in neurobiology, 1981, Solomon A. Berson Medical Alumni Achievement award, 1979, Lucy G. Moses prize for research in basic neurology, 1977, Lester N. Hofheimer prize for research, 1977, Henry L. Moses award, Montefiore Hospital, 1959, Grand Decoration of Honour in Silver with Star for Services to the Republic of Austria, 2012, Benjamin Franklin Medal for Distinguished Achievement in the Sciences, 2006 **MEM:** Fellow: American Association for the Advancement of Science; mem.: National Academy of Sciences, Academy Scis. France, Am. Philosophical Society, New York Academy Scis., International Brain Research Organization, Society Neuroscis. (president 1980-81) **ACH:** Achievements include patents in field

KANNE, MICHAEL STEPHEN, T: Federal Judge **I:** Law and Legal Services **DOB:** 12/21/1938 **PB:** Rensselaer **SC:** Indiana **ED:** Postgrad., University Birmingham, England, 1975; Postgrad., Boston University, 1963; JD, Ind. University, 1968; BS, Ind. University, 1962; Student, St. Joseph's College, Rensselaer, 1957-58 **CT:** Bar: Ind. 1968 **C:** Chair, Committee Judicial Security, 2009-; Judge, US Judicial Conference Committee Space & Facilities, 1998-; Judge, US Court Appeals (7th cir.), Chicago, 1987-; Member, Committee Judicial Security, 2005-09; Member, Committee Defender Services, 1997-2003; Chairman, US Courts Design Guide, 1988-95; Judge, US District Court (no. district) Ind., Hammond, 1982-87; Judge, 30th Judicial Cir. of Ind., 1972-82; Attorney, City of Rensselaer, 1972; Sole Practice, Rensselaer, 1971-72; Associate, Nesbitt and Fisher, Rensselaer, 1968-71 **CR:** Faculty National Institute for Trial Advocacy, South Bend, Ind., 1978-88 Lecturer law St. Frances College, 1990-91, St. Joseph's College, 1976-89 **CIV:** Trustee, St. Joseph's College, 1984-2000 Board Visitors, Ind. University School Law, 1987- **MIL:** 1st Lieutenant US Air Force, 1962-65 **AW:** Named Outstanding Alumnus, Today's Catholic Teacher, 1991; Recipient Distinguished Grad. Award, National Catholic Educational Association, Distinguished Service Award, St. Joseph's College, 1973 **MEM:** Mem.: Federal Bar Association, Jasper County Bar Association (president 1972-76), Ind. State Bar Association (board directors 1977-79, Presidential citation 1979), Law Alumni Association Ind. University (president 1980) **H:** Weightlifting **BA:** US Ct Appeals, 219 S Dearborn St, Chicago, IL, USA, 60604

KANTOR, JODI M., T: Editor **I:** Writing and Editing **DOB:** 04/21/1975 **PB:** New York City **SC:** NY/USA **SPN:** Ron Lieber **ED:** Attended, Harvard Law School, 1998; Grad., Columbia University, 1996 **C:** Editor, Arts & Leisure, New York Times, 2003-; Washington Correspondent, New York Times,; New York Editor, Slate online magazine, 1998-2003; Urban Fellow, Mayor's Office Operations, New York City, **CW:** Author: The Obamas, 2012; guest appearances The Today Show and Charlie Rose **AW:** Named to, Crain's New York Business "40 under 40", 2004; recipient Columbia Young Alumni Achievement award; Dorot Fellowship, Israel, 1996-97, Pulitzer Prize, 2018, Time 100 Most Influential, 2018 **BA:** New York Times, 242 W 41st, New York, NY, 10036

KAO, CHARLES KUEN, T: Electrical Engineer, Educator **I:** Engineering **DOB:** 11/04/1933 **PB:** Shanghai **PT:** Son of Chun-Hsien and Tisung Fong K.; **SPN:** Married May Wan Wong, September 19, 1959; **CH:** children: Simon M.T., Amanda Medical Corps **ED:** PhD in Electrical Engineering, University London, 1965; BSc in Electrical Engineering, University London, 1957 **C:** Founder, Chairman, CEO, ITX Services Ltd., Hong Kong, 2003-09; Chairman, CEO, Transtech Standard Ltd.,; Executive Scientist, Director Research, ITT Advanced Tech. Center, Shelton, Connecticut, 1983-87; Vice President, Director Engineering, Electro Optical Products div./ITT, Roanoke, Virginia, 1981-83; Chief Scientist, Electro Optical Products div./ITT, Roanoke, Virginia, 1974-81; Professor Electronics, Chairman Department, Vice Chancellor, Chinese University Hong Kong, 1987-96; Professor Electronics, Chairman Department, Univ. President, Chinese University Hong Kong, 1970-74; Principal Research Engineer, Standard Telecomm. Laboratory Ltd., Harlow, England, 1960-70; Devel. Engineer, Standard Telephones & Cables Ltd., London, 1957-60 **CW:** Author: Optical Fiber Technology II, 1981, Optical Fibers Systems: Technology, Design and Applications, 1982, Optical Fibre, 1988, A Choice Fulfilled–The Business of High Technology, 1991; Contributor Articles to Professional Journals; Patentee in Field. **AW:** Decorated Commander Brit. Empire, 1993; Recipient Morey Award Am. Ceramic Society, 1976, Stewart Ballantine Medal Franklin Institute, 1977, Rank prize Rank Trust Funds, 1978, LM Ericsson International Prize, 1979, Gold Medal Armed Forces Communications and Electronics Association, 1980, International C & C Prize Foundation for C & C Promotion, Japan, 1987, New Materials Prize Am. Physical Society, 1989, Gold Medal International Society for Optical Engineering, 1992, Japan Prize The Sci. and Tech. Foundation Japan, 1996, Morris Liebmann Memorial Award, 1978, Faraday Medal, 1989; Marconi International Fellow, 1985; Co-recipient Nobel Prize in Physics, 2009. **MEM:** Fellow: IEEE (Alexander Graham Bell medal 1985), Royal Academy Engineering (U.K.) (Prince Philip medal 1996), Royal Society (U.K.), Chinese Academy Sciences; mem.: NAE (Charles Stark Draper prize 1999), European Academy Sciences and Arts, Academia Sinica (Taiwan), Royal Swedish Academy Engineering Sciences **ACH:** Achievements include first to use fiber optics in telecommunications; patents in field **ADD:** Unit 1708 Office Tower, 1 Harbor Rd, Hong Kong, YT, Hong Kong, Wan Chai

KAO, MINN H., T: Co-Founder of Garmin **I:** Business Management/Business Services **PB:** Zhushan **SC:** Taiwan **ED:** PhD in Electrical Engineering, University of Tennessee; MS in Electrical Engineering, University of Tennessee; BS, National Taiwan University **C:** Director, Garmin International, Inc.,; Chairman, CEO, Garmin Corp.,; Co-founder, Garmin Corp., 1989; Systems analyst, Teledyne Systems,; With, Magnavox Advanced Products, **AW:** Named one of 50 Who Matter Now, Business 2.0, 2007, Forbes 400: Richest Americans, 2006- **MEM:** Mem.: NAE

KAPTUR, MARCIA CAROLYN, T: U.S. Representative from Ohio **I:** Government Administration/ Government Relations/Government Services **DOB:** 06/17/1946 **PB:** Toledo **SC:** KS/USA **ED:** Honorary LLD, University of Toledo (1993); Attended, Massachusetts Institute of Technology; Attended, University of Manchester, England; MA in Urban Planning, University of Michigan, Ann Arbor, MI (1974); BA in History, University of Wisconsin, Madison, WI (1968) **C:** Member, Committee on Appropriations; Member, US Representative from the Ninth Ohio District (1983-Present); Assistant Director, Urban Affairs and Domestic, Executive Office of the President, The White House (1977-1979); Director, Planning, National Center of Urban Ethnic Affairs, Washington, DC (1975-1977); Urban Planner, Toledo-Lucas County Plan Commissions (1969-1975) **AW:** Legislator of the Year Award, National Mental Health Association; Director's Award, Georgetown University, Edmund A. Walsh School Foreign Service; Ellis Island Medal of Honor (2002); Americanism Award, VFW (1999) **MEM:** University of Michigan Urban Planning Alumni Association; American Institute of Certified Planners; American Planning Association; Polish American Historical Association; Democratic Women's Campaign Association; Urban League; Fulton County Democratic Women's Club; Lucas County Democratic Business & Professional Women's Club **PA:** Democrat

KARDASHIAN, KIM, T: Businesswoman, Model **I:** Media & Entertainment **DOB:** 10/21/1980 **PB:** Los Angeles **SC:** CA/USA **PT:** Daughter of Robert Kardashian and Kris Jenner, Bruce Jenner (Stepfather, now known as Caitlyn Jenner); Married Damon Thomas, January 22, 2000 (div. 2004); Married Kris Humphries, August 20, 2011 (div.) **C:** Co-creator, retail store, Kardashian Khaos, Las Vegas, 2011-; Clothing designer (with Kourtney and Khloé), Kardashian Kollection, 2011-; Clothing designer (with Kourtney and Khloé), K-Dash, 2010-; Contributing beauty editor, OK! magazine, 2009-; Co-owner, D-A-S-H clothing store, Calabasas, Miami, New York City, 2006-; Launched multiple fragrances; Co-designer, jewelry line for Virgins, Saints, and Angels, 2010; Owner, Kimsaprincess Productions LLC,; Fashion stylist to the stars; Closet designer CR: Creator, designer mobile game Kim Kardashian: Hollywood, 2014- spokesmodel, PerfectSkin co-creator, Kardashian Glamour Tan, 2010 CW: Appears in reality TV series Keeping Up with the Kardashians, 2007-, Kourtney & Kim Take New York, 2011-12, Kourtney & Kim Take Miami, 2013, Kourtney & Khloe Take The Hamptons, 2014-15; actress: (films) Disaster Movie, 2008, Tyler Perry's Temptation, 2013; featured in (video) Workout with Kim Kardashian, 2008, Fit In Your Jeans By Friday, 2009, (music video) Fall Out Boy, co-founder, chief fashion stylist ShoeDazzle, 2009-; executive prodr.: (TV series) SPINdustry, 2010; co-author (with Kourtney & Khloé Kardashian): (nonfiction) Kardashian Konfidential, 2010, (novels) Dollhouse, 2011; spokesperson Skechers Shape-Ups, guest appearance (TV series) Beyond the Break, 2006, How I Met Your Mother, 2009, CSI:NY, 2009, 90210, 2010, 30 Rock, 2012, Drop Dead Diva, 2012, American Dad! (voice), 2013, (Television) Celebrities Undercover, 2014, I Am Cait, 2015, Dash Dolls, 2015, (Movies) Oceans 8, 2018 AW: Named Favorite TV Celebrity Reality Star, People's Choice Awards, 2012; named one of The 10 Most Fascinating People of 2013, Barbara Walters Special, The 10 Most Fascinating People of 2011

KARLIN, BEN, T: Producer and Writer **I:** Media & Entertainment **PB:** Needham **SC:** MA/USA **CW:** Writer, (Television) The Daily Show, 2000-2006, The Colbert Report, 2005-2008, Modern Family, 2011-2014, Future Man, 2017, (Television Movie) Three Strikes, 2006, The King of 7B, 2015, (Film) 50/50, 2011, A.C.O.D., 2013 **AW:** Primetime Emmy for Outstanding Variety, Music or Comedy Program, The Daily Show, 2002-2007, Primetime Emmy for Outstanding Writing for a Variety, Music, or Comedy Program, The Daily Show, 2003-2006, Primetime Emmy for Outstanding Comedy Series, Modern Family, 2013-2014

KARP, DAVID, T: Internet Company Executive, Web Developer **I:** Information Technology and Services **DOB:** 07/06/1986 **PB:** New York City **SC:** NY/USA **PT:** Son of Michael D. and Barbara (Ackerman) Karp. **C:** Founder, CEO, Tumblr Inc., New York City, 2007-; Chief tech. officer, UrbanBaby, Tokyo, 2002-06 **CR:** Adjunct professor New York University **AW:** Named The Best Young Tech Entrepreneur, Business Week, 2009; named one of The 40 Under 40, Crain's New York Business, 2011, The Top 35 Innovators in the World Under the Age of 35, Massachusetts Institute of Technology Technology Review, 2010

KARPEL, CRAIG S., I: Writing and Editing **PB:** Midland **SC:** TX/USA **MS:** Married **ED:** AB, Columbia University, 1965 **C:** Contributing editor, Harper's magazine, New York City, 1985-92 **CW:** Author: The Rite of Exorcism, 1974, The Retirement Myth, 1995, The 12-Step Guide for the Recovering Obama Voter, 2012; contributor numerous articles to magazines and newspapers, U.S., South America, Europe, Africa, Asia

KARPLUS, MARTIN, T: Theoretical Chemist **I:** Sciences **DOB:** 03/15/1930 **PB:** Vienna **SC:** Austria **ED:** BA, Harvard University, 1950; PhD, California Institute Tech., 1953; DSc (hon.), University of Sher-

brooke, Quebec, Can., 1998; MA (hon.), Oxford University, 1999; PhD (hon.), Bar-Ilan University, 2014 **C:** Theodore William Richards Professor Emeritus, Harvard University, Cambridge, Massachusetts, 1999—; Theodore William Richards Professor of Chemistry, Harvard University, Cambridge, Massachusetts, 1979-99; Professor, Harvard University, Cambridge, Massachusetts, 1966—1999; Professor, Columbia University, New York City, New York, 1960-66; Associate Professor, University Illinois, 1960; Assistant Professor chemistry, University Illinois, 1957-60; National Science Foundation Fellow, Oxford University, England, 1953-55 **CR:** Professor, University Paris VII, 1974-75, College de France, Paris, 1980; Professor Associè University Paris-Sud, 1980-81, University of Strasbourg, France, spring 1992, 94-95, professor conventionné, 1995—; Eastman professor Oxford University, 1999-2000. **CW:** Author: (with R.N. Porter) Atoms and Molecules: An Introduction for Students of Physical Chemistry, 1970, (with C.L. Brooks III and B.M. Pettitt) Proteins: A Theoretical Perspective of Dynamics, Structure and Thermodynamics, 1988; Author, Numerous Articles **AW:** Recipient Fresenius Award Phi Lambda Epsilon, 1965, Harrison Howe Award American Chemical Society, 1967, Outstanding Contribution Award International Society Quantum Biology, 1979, Distinguished Alumni Award California Institute Tech., 1986, Irving Langmuir Award American Physical Society, 1987, Theoretical Chemistry Award American Chemical Society, 1993, Pauling Award Northwest Section, 2004, Joseph O. Hirschfelder Prize in Theoretical Chemistry University Wisconsin Theoretical Chemistry Institute, 1995, Computers in Chemical & Pharmaceutical Research Award American Chemical Society, 2001, Anfinsen Award Protein Society, 2001, Lifetime Achievement Award Theoretical Biophysics, 2008, G.N. Ramchandran Award Indian Biophys. Society, 2009; Co-recipient Nobel Prize in Chemistry, Royal Swedish Academy Sciences, 2013; Named Westinghouse Scholar, 1947, Christian B Anfinsen Award, 2001, Fellow of the Royal Society, 2000 **MEM:** Member National Academy of Sciences, American Academy Arts & Sciences, International Academy Quantum Molecular Sci., Netherlands Academy Art & Sciences (foreign), Royal Society U.K. (foreign) **BA:** Massachusetts Hall, Cambridge, MA, 02138

KASBAR, MICHAEL J., T: Energy Executive **I:** Oil & Energy **C:** President, CEO, World Fuel Services, Inc. (subsidiary World Fuel Services Corp.), Miami, Florida, 2012-; Board directors, World Fuel Services, Inc. (subsidiary World Fuel Services Corp.), Miami, Florida, 1995-; President, COO, World Fuel Services, Inc. (subsidiary World Fuel Services Corp.), Miami, Florida, 2002-12; CEO marine fuel service, World Fuel Services, Inc. (subsidiary World Fuel Services Corp.), Miami, Florida, 1995-2002; Co-founder, officer, director, TransTec New York, 1985-94

KASICH, JOHN RICHARD, T: Governor of Ohio **I:** Government Administration/Government Relations/Government Services **DOB:** 05/13/1952 **PB:** McKees Rocks **SC:** PA/USA **ED:** BA, Ohio State University, 1974 **C:** Governor, State of Ohio, Columbus, 2011-; Instructor business classes, Ohio State University,; Chairman, New Century Project, Columbus, Ohio, 2001-10; Managing director, investment banking division, Lehman Brothers, Columbus, Ohio, 2001-08; Chairman, US House Budget Committee, Washington, 1995-2001; Member, US Congress from 12th Ohio District, Washington, 1983-2001; Member District 15, Ohio State Senate, 1979-82; Administrative assistant to Rep. Buz Lukens, Ohio State Senate, 1975-77 **CR:**

Candidate for the 2016 Republican Party presidential nomination honorary chairman Recharge Ohio, 2008- **CW:** Author: Courage is Contagious: Ordinary People Doing Extraordinary Things to Change the Face of America, 1998, Stand for Something: The Battle for America's Soul, 2006, Every Other Monday: Twenty Years of Life, Lunch, Faith and Friendship, 2010; host (TV series) Heartland with John Kasich, guest host The O'Reilly Factor **PA:** Republican **BA:** Office of John Kasich, Riffe Center, 30th Floor, 77 South High Street, Columbus, OH, 43215

KATKO, JOHN MICHAEL, T: U.S. Representative from New York **I:** Government Administration/Government Relations/Government Services **DOB:** 11/09/1962 **PB:** Syracuse **PT:** Son of Andrew and Mary Lou (O'Connor) Katko; **ED:** JD cum laude, Syracuse University, 1988; BA in Political Sci. cum laude, Niagara University, 1985 **C:** Member, US Congress from 24th New York District, Washington, 2015-; Positions included, supervisor narcotics section, narcotics chief, organized crime drug enforcement task force coordinator, Binghamton office supervisor, team leader, Grand Jury coordinator; From special assistant U.S. atty (eastern district) Virginia to criminal division, narcotic & dangerous drug section, US Department Justice, 1994-2014 **CIV:** Hockey coach, Camillus Youth Hockey Association, New York, **PA:** Republican

KATSAS, GREGORY GEORGE, T: Federal Judge **I:** Law and Legal Services **DOB:** 08/06/1964 **PB:** Boston **SC:** Massachusetts **ED:** JD, Harvard Law School, Cambridge, Massachusetts, 1989; BA, Princeton University, New Jersey, 1986 **C:** Judge of the U.S. Court of Appeals, District of Columbia Circuit,2017-; Deputy White House Council, U.S., 2017; Partner, Jones Day LLP, 2009-; Assistant attorney general civil division, US Department Justice, 2008-09; Acting associate attorney general, US Department Justice, 2007-08; Principal deputy associate attorney general, US Department Justice, 2006-08; Deputy assistant attorney general civil division, US Department Justice, 2001-06; Attorney, Jones Day LLP, Washington, 1992-2001; Law clerk to Justice Clarence Thomas, US Supreme Court, 1990-91; Law clerk to Hon. Edward Becker, US Court Appeals (3d Cir.), 1989-90 **AW:** Recipient Secretary of Defense medal for Exceptional Pub. Service, US Department Defense, 2009, Edmund Randolph award for Outstanding Service, US Department Justice, 2009, Attorney General's Distinguished Service award, 2006 **MEM:** Mem.: American Bar Association **BA:** 333 Constitution Ave NW, Washington, DC, 20001

KATZMANN, ROBERT ALLEN, T: Federal Judge **I:** Law and Legal Services **DOB:** 04/22/1953 **PB:** New York **SC:** NY/USA **ED:** JD, Yale University, 1980; PhD in Government, Harvard University, 1978; MA in Government, Harvard University, 1975; AB summa cum laude, Columbia University, 1973 **CT:** Bar: Massachusetts 1982, New York, US Court Appeals (1st cir.) 1983, DC 1984, US District Court Massachusetts 1984 **C:** Adjunct professor law, New York University, New York City, 2001-; Chief judge, US Court Appeals (2nd cir.), 2013-; Judge, US Court Appeals (2nd cir.), 1999-; President, Governance Institute, Washington, 1986-99; William J. Walsh professor government, professor law, Georgetown University, 1992-99; Adjunct professor law, public policy, Georgetown University, Washington, 1984-92; Acting director government studies, Brookings Institution, Washington, 1998; Fellow, Brookings Institution, Washington, 1985-99; Research associate, Brookings Institution, Washington, 1981-85; Law clerk to Hon. Hugh H. Bownes, US Court Appeals (1st cir.), Concord, New Hampshire, 1980-81 **CR:** Visiting professor political sci. UCLA, Washington program, 1990-92 visiting chair, Wayne Morse professor law and politics University Oregon, 1992 consultant Federal Courts Study Committee, 1990 adjunct professor law New York University, 2001- **CW:** Author: Regulatory Bureaucracy: The Federal Trade Commission and Antitrust Policy, 1980, Institutional Disability: The Saga of Transportation Policy for the Disabled, 1986, Courts and Congress, 1997; co-editor: Managing Appeals in Federal Courts, 1988; editor: Judges and Legislators, 1988, The Law Firm and the Public Good, 1995; editor, co-author, Daniel Patrick Moynihan: The Intellectual in Public Life, 1998, 2d edit, 2004; article and book editor Yale University Law Journal, 1979-80,The Marden Lecture: The Legal Profession and the Unmet Needs of the Immigrant Poor, 21 Geo. J. of Legal Ethics 3,2008,Madison Lecture: Statutes, 2012,; When Legal Representation is Deficient: The Challenge of Immigration Cases for the Courts, 143 Daedalus,2014,Judging Statutes, 2014 **AW:** Recipient Chas. E. Merriam award, Am. Political Sci. Association, 2001 **MEM:** Fellow: American Academy Arts & Sciences; mem.: American Bar Association (vice chair committee on government operations and separation of powers 1991-94, pub. member administration conference 1992-95, administrative law section), American Association Law Schools (chairman legis. section 1999-2000), American Political Sci. Association (Charles E. Merriam award 2001), American Judicature Society (board directors 1992-98), Phi Beta Kappa **BA:** US Court of Appeals 2d Cir, 40 Foley Sq, New York, NY, USA, 10007-1502

KAUR, RUPI, **T:** Writer **I:** Writing and Editing **PB:** Punjab **SC:** India **CW:** Author, (Books) Milk and Honey, 2015, The Sun and Her Flowers, 2017

KAVANAUGH, BRETT MICHAEL, **T:** Federal Judge **I:** Law and Legal Services **DOB:** 02/12/1965 **PB:** Washington **SC:** DC/USA **PT:** Son of Edward and Martha Kavanaugh; **ED:** JD (hon.), Yale Law School, 1990; BA cum laude, Yale College, 1987 **CT:** Bar: DC 1992, Maryland 1990 **C:** Nominee, Associate Justice, Supreme Court of the U.S., 2018; Judge, U.S. Court Appeals (DC cir.), 2006-; Assistant to President, staff secretary, The White House, Washington, DC 2003-06; Senior Associate Counsel to President, The White House, Washington, DC 2003; Associate counsel to President, The White House, Washington, 2001-03; Partner, Kirkland & Ellis LLP, 1999-2001; Partner, Kirkland & Ellis LLP, 1997-98; Associate counsel, Office Ind. Counsel Kenneth W. Starr, US Department Justice, 1994-98; Law clerk to Justice Anthony M. Kennedy, Supreme Court of the U.S., Washington, DC 1993-94; Attorney, Office Solicitor General, US Department Justice, Washington, 1992-93; Law clerk to Hon. Alex Kozinski, US Court Appeals (9th cir.), 1991-92; Law clerk to Hon. Walter K. Stapleton, US Court Appeals (3rd cir.), 1990-91 **BA:** US Court of Appeals, 333 Constitution Ave NW Rm 3004, Washington, DC, 20001

KAYATTA, WILLIAM JOSEPH JR., **T:** Federal Judge, Lawyer **I:** Law and Legal Services **DOB:** 10/27/1953 **PB:** Pawtucket **SC:** RI/USA **ED:** JD, Harvard Law School, Magna Cum Laude (1979); BA, Amherst College, Magna Cum Laude (1976) **C:** Judge, U.S. Court of Appeals for the First Circuit, Portland, ME (2013-Present); Partner, Pierce Atwood LLP, Portland, ME (1986-2013); Associate, Pierce Atwood LLP, Portland, ME (1980-1986); Law Clerk to Chief Judge Frank M. Coffin, U.S. Court of Appeals for the First Circuit (1979-1980) **CR:** Member, Maine Board of Bar Examiners (1986-1990); Chairman, Maine Board of Bar Examiners (1988-1989); Member, Maine Professional Ethics

Commission (1995-Present) **CW:** Contributor, Articles to Professional Journals **AW:** Named Best Lawyers in America, Chambers USA (2007); Howard H. Dana Award, Maine State Bar Association (2010) **MEM:** Standing Committee for the Federal Judiciary, ABA; Maine State Bar Association; Cumberland County Bar Association; American Law Institute; President, Maine State Bar Foundation (2004-Present); Fellow, American College of Trial Lawyers **BAR:** Maine State Bar Association (1980); U.S. District Court of the District of Maine; U.S. Court of Appeals for the First Circuit; U.S. District Court of the District of Maine; U.S. Court of Appeals for the Ninth Circuit; Supreme Court of the U.S. **ACH:** Editor & officer Harvard Law Review, 1977-79. **BA:** 1 Courthouse Way,, Boston, MA, 02210

KEAN, STEVEN J., **T:** CEO **I:** Oil & Energy **CN:** Kinder Morgan **ED:** JD, University of Iowa, Iowa City, Iowa; BA, Iowa State University, Ames, Iowa **C:** Chair/Chief Executive Officer, Kinder Morgan, Canada (2017-Present); President/Chief Executive Officer, Kinder Morgan Inc. (2015-Present); President/Chief Operating Officer, Kinder Morgan (2013-Present); Executive Vice President, Chief Operating Officer, Kinder Morgan, Inc., Houston, Texas (2006-Present); Executive Vice President of Operations, Kinder Morgan, Inc. (2005-2006); President, Intrastate Pipeline Group, Kinder Morgan Energy Partners, L.P., Kinder Morgan, Inc. (2002-2005); Vice President, Strategic Planning, Natural Gas Pipeline Group, Kinder Morgan, Inc. (2002); With, Enron; With, Utilicorp; With, El Paso Natural Gas

KEANE, MARGARET, **I:** Financial Services **ED:** MBA, St. John's University, Queens, NY (1986); BA in Government & Politics, St. John's University, Queens, NY (1981) **C:** President, Chief Executive Officer, U.S. Consumer Retail Finance, General Electric Capital (Now Synchrony Financial), Stamford, CT (2011-Present); President, Chief Executive Officer, Retail Consumer Financial Unit, General Electric Capital (2004-2011); Senior Vice President, Operations for Consumer Finance of the Americas, General Electric Capital (2002-2004); Chief Quality Officer, General Electric Capital, Stamford, CT (2000-2002); Retail Bank Operations Director, Citibank, New York City, NY **AW:** Named One of the 50 Most Powerful Women, Fortune Magazine (2015); Named One of the 25 Most Powerful Women in Finance, American Banker (2011); Named One of the 25 Most Powerful Women in Finance, U.S. Banker (2007-2010)

KEATING, WILLIAM RICHARD, **T:** U.S. Representative from Massachusetts **I:** Government Administration/Government Relations/Government Services **DOB:** 09/06/1952 **PB:** Norwood **SC:** MA/USA **ED:** JD, Suffolk University (1985); MA, Boston College (1982); BA, Boston College, Magna Cum Laude (1974) **C:** Member, U.S. House Homeland Security Committee (2013-Present); Member, U.S. House Foreign Affairs Committee (2013-Present); Member, U.S. Congress from Ninth Massachusetts District (2013-Present); Member, U.S. House Small Business Committee (2011-2013); Member, U.S. Congress from 10th Massachusetts District, Washington, DC (2011-2013); District Attorney, Norfolk County, Canton, MA (1999-2010); Member Norfolk, Bristol & Plymouth District, Massachusetts State Senate, Boston, MA (1985-1998); Member, Eighth Norfolk District, Massachusetts House of Representative (1979-1985); Member, 19th Norfolk District, Massachusetts House of Representatives, Boston, MA (1977-1979) **CR:** Former Chairman of Steering, Policy, and Public Safety Committees, Massachusetts State Senate **AW:** Named, Legis-

lator of the Year, Massachusetts Bar Association (1992); Named, Legislator of the Year, Massachusetts Victim Witness Board (1989); Named, Legislator of the Year, Massachusetts Police Association (1988); Named, Legislator of the Year, Massachusetts Municipal Association (1980) **MEM:** LMV; Massachusetts Legislators Association; Massachusetts Bar Association; Knights of Columbus; Sons of Italy; Jaycees **PA:** Democrat **BA:** 315 Cannon House Office Bldg, Washington, DC, 20515

KEATON, DIANE, **T:** Actress **I:** Medicine & Health Care **DOB:** 05/07/1905 **PB:** Santa Ana, **SC:** Santa Ana, **PT:** Daughter of Jack and Dorothy (Keaton) Hall; **ED:** Student, Neighborhood Playhouse, New York City, 1968 **CW:** Appeared on New York stage in Hair, 1968, Play It Again Sam, 1969, The Primary English Class, 1976; actress: (films) Lovers and Other Strangers, 1970, Play It Again Sam, 1972, The Godfather, 1972, Sleeper, 1973, The Godfather Part II, 1974, Love and Death, 1975, I Will, I Will... For Now, 1975, Harry and Walter Go To New York, 1976, Annie Hall, 1977 (New York Film Critics Circle award for Best Actress, 1977, National Society Film Critics award for Best Actress, 1977, Academy award for Best Actress, 1978, BAFTA award for Best Actress, 1978, Golden Globe award for Best Motion Picture Address - Musical/Comedy, 1978), Looking for Mr. Goodbar, 1977, Interiors, 1978, Manhattan, 1979, Reds, 1981, Shoot the Moon, 1982, Little Drummer Girl, 1984, Mrs. Soffel, 1984, Crimes of the Heart, 1986, Radio Days, 1987, Baby Boom, 1987, The Good Mother, 1988, The Lemon Sisters, 1990, The Godfather Part III, 1990, Father of the Bride, 1991, Manhattan Murder Mystery, 1993, (voice) Look Who's Talking Now, 1993, Father of the Bride 2, 1995, Marvin's Room, 1996, First Wives Club, 1996, The Only Thrill, 1997, The Other Sister, 1999, Hanging Up, 2000, Town and Country, 2001, Plan B, 2001, Something's Gotta Give, 2003 (National Board Review award for Best Actress, 2003, Golden Globe award for Best Actress in a Musical or Comedy, 2004), The Family Stone, 2005, Smother, 2007, Mama's Boy, 2007, Because I Said So, 2007, Mad Money, 2008, Morning Glory, 2010, Darling Companion, 2012, The Big Wedding, 2013, And So It Goes, 2014, 5 Flights Up, 2014, Finding Dory (voice), 2016, Hampstead, 2017, Book Club, 2018; (TV films) Running Mates, 1992, Amelia Earhart, 1994, Sister Mary Explains It All, 2001, Tilda, 2011; director, writer: (documentaries) Heaven, 1987; actress, prodr.: (films) The Lemon Sisters, 1990; (TV films) Crossed Over, 2002, On Thin Ice, 2003, Surrender, Dorothy, 2005, Tilda, 2011, The Young Pope, 2016; dir.: (films) Wildflower, 1991, Unstrung Heroes, 1995; executive prodr.: (TV films) Northern Lights, 1997, (TV series) Pasadena, 2001; actress, executive prodr.: (films) Love the Coopers, 2015; author: (photography) Reservations, 1980; editor: (with Marvin Heiferman) Still Life, 1983, Mr. Salesman, 1994; author: (memoir) Then Again, 2011, Let's Just Say It Wasn't Pretty, 2014 **AW:** Recipient Trustees award, International Center Photography, 2008.

KEENAN, BARBARA MILANO, **T:** Federal Judge **I:** Law and Legal Services **DOB:** 03/01/1950 **PB:** Vienna **SC:** Austria **ED:** LLM, University Virginia, 1992; JD, George Washington University, 1974; BA, Cornell University, 1971 **C:** Judge, US Court Appeals (4th Cir.), 2010-; Associate justice, Virginia Supreme Court, Richmond, 1991-2010; Judge, Virginia Court Appeals, 1985-91; Judge, Fairfax County Cir. Court, 1982-85; Judge, Fairfax County General District Court, 1980-82; Private law practice, 1976-80; Assistant commonwealth attorney, Fairfax County, Virginia, 1974-76 **AW:** Recipient American Jurisprudence award, Fairfax Bar Association, 1995 **BA:** US Court Appeals, 1100 E Main St, Richmond, VA, 23219

KEITH, TOBY, T: Musician, Producer **I:** Media & Entertainment **DOB:** 07/08/1961 **PB:** Clinton **SC:** NY/USA **PT:** Son of H.K. and Joan Covel; **ED:** Degree (hon.), Villanova University, Pennsylvania **C:** Founder, Show Dog Nashville Records, 2005-; Signed with, DreamWorks, Nashville, 1999; Signed with, Mercury Records, Nashville, 1984-99; Defensive end, Oklahoma Outlaws, US Football League (USFL) team,; Defensive end, Oklahoma City Drillers, minor league, semi-pro football team,; Member, The Easy Money Band,; Worked in oil industry, **CW:** Singer: (albums) Toby Keith, 1993, Christmas to Christmas, 1995, Boomtown, 1995, Blue Moon, 1996, Dream Walkin', 1997, Greatest Hits, Vol. 1, 1998, How Do You Like Me Now?, 1999 (Album of Year, Academy Country Music Awards, 2000), Pull My Chain, 2001, Unleashed, 2002 (Favorite Country Album, American Music Awards, 2003), 20th Century Masters- The Millennium, 2003, Shock 'n Y'all, 2003 (Album of Year, Academy Country Music Awards, 2003, Best Country Album, Am. Music Awards, 2004), Greatest Hits 2, 2004, Honkytonk University, 2005, White Trash with Money, 2006, Big Dog Daddy, 2007, A Classic Christmas, 2007, Love Me If You Can, 2007, That Don't Make Me a Bad Guy, 2008, American Ride, 2009, Bullets in the Gun, 2010, Clancy's Tavern, 2011, Hope On the Rocks, 2012, Drinks After Work, 2013, 35 MPH Town, 2015, (songs) Should've Been A Cowboy, 1993 (Most Played Song of Decade in the 90's, Billboard), How Do You Like Me Now?, 2000 (Named Most Played Song of 2000, Billboard), Whiskey Girl, 2003 (Hottest Video of Year, Country Music TV Music Awards, 2005), As Good As I Once Was, 2005 (Music Video of Year, Country Music Association Awards, 2005), Red Solo Cup, 2011 (Music Video of Year, Country Music Association Awards, 2012, Video of Year, Academy Country Music Awards, 2012); actor: (films) Broken Bridges, 2006; (writer, producer, actor): Beer for My Horses, 2008 (Tex Ritter award, Academy Country Music, 2009) **AW:** Named Country Artist of Year, Billboard Music Awards, 2005, Favorite Male Country Artist, Am. Music Awards, 2006, 2004, Top Male Vocalist, Academy Country Music Awards, 2003, 2000, Entertainer of Year, 2003, 2002; recipient Country Album Artist of Year, Country Music Association, 2005 **ACH:** Achievements include invited by George W. Bush to addresss at MacDill Air Force Base in Tampa, Florida, site of US Cent. Command and headquarters of General Tommy Franks; a super-patriotic response to September 11th that became one of country's most highly charged political statements; songwriting, 12 of his 16 #1 hits have been self-penned; radio airplay, 8 Billboard country #1's and eight R&R country #1's from his DreamWorks Records alone; sales of more than $13.5 million **BA:** TKO Artist Management, 3100 West End Ave, Nashville, TN, 37203

KELLEY, DAVID E., T: Executive Producer, Writer **I:** Writing and Editing **DOB:** 04/04/1956 **PB:** Waterville **SC:** ME/USA **PT:** Jack Kelley **ED:** JD, Boston University, 1983; BA, Princeton University, 1979 **C:** CEO, David E. Kelley Productions, Inc., L.A. **CW:** Writer, story editor, executive story editor, supervising producer, executive prodr.: (TV series) L.A. Law (Emmy award for Outstanding Drama Series 1989, 1990, Emmy award for Outstanding Writing in a Drama Series 1990); writer, executive prodr.: (TV series) Picket Fences (Emmy award for Outstanding Drama Series 1993, 1994), Chicago Hope, 1994-2000, The Practice, 1997-2004 (Golden Globe award for Best TV Drama 1998, Emmy award for Outstanding Drama Series, 1998, 1999), Ally McBeal, 1997-2002 (Golden Globe winner, Emmy award for Best TV Series-Musical or Comedy 1997, 1998, Emmy award for Outstanding Comedy

Series 1999), Snoops, 1999-2000, Boston Public, 2000-04, Girl's Club, 2002, The Brotherhood of Poland, New Hampshire, 2003, Boston Legal, 2004-08, The Law Firm, 2005, The Wedding Bells, 2007, Legally Mad, 2009, Harry's Law, 2011-12, Monday Mornings, 2013, The Crazy Ones, 2013, Goliath, 2016, Big Little Lies, 2016, Mr Mercedes, 2017 (TV films) Life on Mars, 2008, Legally Mad, 2010, Wonder Woman, 2011

KELLY, ALFRED F. JR., T: CEO of Visa **I:** Business Management/Business Services **ED:** MBA, Iona College, 1981; BA in Liberal Arts, Iona Coll, 1980 **C:** CEO, Visa, 2016-; President, head global consumer group, American Express Co., 2007-10; Group president U.S. consumer & small business service, American Express Co., 2000-07; President consumer card services group TRS, American Express Co., 1998-2000; Executive vice president, general manager consumer marketing TRS, American Express Co., 1997-98; Executive vice president general manager U.S. consumer card marketing, American Express Co.,; Joined, American Express Co., 1987; Head Info systems, The White House, Washington, 1985-87; With, PepsiCo, Inc., 1981-85; Adj. assistant professor, Iona College, New Rochelle, New York, 1980-85 **CR:** Board of Directors MetLife, Inc., 2009-, Hershey Co., 2005-07 **CIV:** Trustee, Iona College, New Rochelle, New York, Vice chairman, Wall St. Charity Golf Classic, Board of Directors, Carvel Children's Rehabilitation Center, Board of Directors, Concern Worldwide USA, Board of Directors, Iona Prepatory School, Trustee, New York Presbyterian Hospital, Trustee, St. Joseph's Seminary & college, **AW:** Recipient The Journal News Westchester Business Leader of the Year award, 2009 **MEM:** Mem.: Council Foreign Relations **BA:** Visa, One Market Plaza, San Francisco, CA, 94105

KELLY, GARY CLAYTON, T: Chairman and CEO at Southwest Airlines Co. **I:** Aviation **DOB:** 03/12/1955 **PB:** San Antonio **SC:** Texas **PT:** Son of Clayton Kelly; **SPN:** Married Carol G. Kelly; **CH:** Caroline, Elizabeth **ED:** BBA in Accounting, University Texas, 1977 **CT:** CPA, Texas **C:** Chairman, CEO, Southwest Airlines Co., Dallas, 2008-; President, Southwest Airlines Co.,2008-17; Chairman, CEO, Southwest Airlines Co., Dallas, 2008; Vice Chairman, CEO, Southwest Airlines Co., Dallas, 2004-08; Executive Vice President, CFO, Southwest Airlines Co., Dallas, 2001-04; Vice President Finance, CFO, Southwest Airlines Co., Dallas, 1989-2001; Controller, Southwest Airlines Co., Dallas, 1986-89; Controller, Systems Center Inc., Irving, Texas,; Audit Manager, Arthur Young & Co., Dallas, **CR:** Board Directors Jefferson-Pilot Corp., Air Transport Association America, Southwest Airlines Co., 2004- **CIV:** Member Advisory Council, McCombs School Business, Univ. Texas, Austin, **AW:** Named CEO of Year, Dallas Business Journal, 2011; Named One of The 25 Most Influential Executives, Business Travel News, 2004; Named to The McCombs School Business Hall of Fame, 2013; Recipient McLane Leadership in Business award, Texas A & M University, 2013, Distinguished Alumnus Award, University Texas Austin, 2010, Recipient 2016 Tony Jannus Award for Distinguished Achievement in Commercial Air Transportation; **H:** Guitar **BA:** Southwest Airlines Co, 2702 Love Field Dr, Dallas, TX, 75235

KELLY, JANE LOUISE, T: Federal Judge **I:** Law and Legal Services **DOB:** 10/28/1964 **PB:** Greencastle **SC:** IN/USA **ED:** JD, Harvard Law School, 1991; BA, Duke University, 1987 **C:** Judge, US Court Appeals (8th Cir.), Cedar Rapids, 2013-; Supervising attorney, Office Federal Public Defender, Cedar

Rapids, Iowa, 1999-2013; Assistant federal public defender (northern district) Iowa, Office Federal Public Defender, 1994-2013; Visiting instructor, University Illinois College Law, 1993-94; Law clerk to Hon. David R. Hansen, US Court Appeals (8th Cir.), 1992-93; Law clerk to Hon. Donald J. Porter, US District Court South Dakota, 1991-92 **BA:** Thomas F. Eagleton Courthouse, 111 South 10th Street, Saint Louis, MO, 63102

KELLY, JOHN FRANCIS, T: White House Chief of Staff **I:** Government Administration/Government Relations/Government Services **PB:** Boston **SC:** MA/USA **ED:** Graduate, National War College, 1995; Graduate, U.S. Army Infantry Advanced Courses, Fort Benning, GA, 1980; BS, University of Massachusetts, 1976; Graduate, School for Advanced Warfare; Graduate, Marine Corps Command & Staff College **C:** Secretary, Homeland Security, 2017-Present; Chief of Staff, Office of the President, Washington, DC, 2017—Present **MIL:** Commander, U.S. Southern Command, Doral, FL, 2012-2017; Advanced Through Ranks to General, U.S. Marine Corps, 2012; Senior Military Assistant to Secretary, U.S. Department of Defense, Washington, DC, 2011-2012; Commander, Marine Forces Reserve & Marine Forces North, 2009-2011; Commanding General, Multi-Nation Force-West, Baghdad, Iraq, 2008-2009; Commanding General, I Marine Expeditionary Force, Forward, 2007-2008; Legislative Assistant to Commandant, U.S. Marine Corps, 2004-2007; Assistant Division Commander, First Marine Division, 2002-2004; Assistant Chief of Staff, G-3, Second Marine Division, 2001-2002; Special Assistant, Supreme Allied Commander Europe, Saceur, NATO, Mons, Belgium, 1999-2001; Commandant's Liaison Officer, U.S. House of Representatives, U.S. Marine Corps, 1995-1998; Commanding Officer, First Light Armored Reconnaissance Battalion, First Marine Division, 1992-1994; Head of Offensive Tactics Section to Director of Infantry Officer Course, Basic School, Quantico, VA, 1987-1990; Assignment Monitor, U.S. Marine Corps Headquarters, 1981-1984; Battalion Operations Officer, Second Marine Division, 1987; Rifle & Weapons Platoon Commander, Second Marine Division, 1984-1987; Rifle & Weapons Platoon Comdr, Second Marine Division, 1976-1980; Second Lieutenant, U.S. Marine Corps, 1976; U.S. Marine Corps, 1970-1972 **AW:** Decorated Kuwait Liberation Medal; Global War on Terrorism Service Medal; Global War on Terrorism Expeditionary Medal; Marine Corps Expeditionary Medal; Joint Meritorious Unit Award; Navy & Marine Corps Achievement Medal; Navy & Marine Corps Commendation Medal; Meritorious Service Medal; Two Legion of Merits With Valor V; Defense Superior Service Medal; Defense Distinguished Service Medal **BA:** The White House, 1600 Pennsylvania Avenue NW, Washington, DC, 20500

KELLY, MEGYN MARIE, T: News Anchor, Reporter **I:** Media & Entertainment **DOB:** 11/18/1970 **PB:** Syracuse **SC:** NY/USA **PT:** Daughter of Linda Kelly; **ED:** JD, Albany Law School, 1995; BA in Political Sci., Syracuse University, New York, 1992 **C:** Host, Sunday Night with Megyn Kelly, 2017-; Host, The Kelly File, Fox News Channel, 2013-17; Regular contributor The O'Reilly Factor, Fox News Channel,; Host America Live, Fox News Channel, 2010-13; Host America's Newsroom, Fox News Channel, 2007-09; General assignment reporter, Fox News Channel, Washington, DC 2004-07; General assignment reporter, WJLA-TV, Washington, 2004; Corporate litigator, Jones Day, New York City, Chicago, Washington, 1995-2004 **CW:** Author, (Book) Settle, 2016 **AW:** Named one of The 100 Most Influential People in the World, TIME magazine, 2014

KELLY, MIKE, T: U.S. Representative from Pennsylvania **I:** Government Administration/Government Relations/Government Services **DOB:** 05/10/1948 **PB:** Pittsburgh **SC:** PA/USA **ED:** BA, University of Notre Dame (1970) **C:** Member, US House Oversight & Government Reform Committee, Washington, DC (2011-Present); Member, US House Foreign Affairs Committee, Washington, DC (2011-Present); Member, US House Education & the Workforce Committee, Washington, DC (2011-Present); Owner, Kelly Chevrolet-Cadillac, Inc. (1995-Present); Member, US Congress from the Third Pennsylvania District, Washington, DC (2011); Employee, Kelly Chevrolet-Cadillac, Inc., Butler, PA (1970-95); Member, US Committee on Ways and Means **CR:** Former Member, Butler School Board of Education, Butler City Council **AW:** Named to Butler Area Sports Hall of Fame (1999) **PA:** Republican

KELLY, PAUL JOSEPH JR., T: Federal Judge **I:** Law and Legal Services **DOB:** 12/06/1940 **PB:** Freeport **SC:** NY/USA **PT:** Paul J. Kelly; Jacqueline M. (Nolan) Kelly **ED:** JD, Fordham University (1967); BBA, University of Notre Dame (1963) **C:** Senior Judge, U.S. Court of Appeals for the Tenth Circuit (2018-Present); Judge, US Court of Appeals for the Tenth Circuit, Santa Fe, NM (1992-2018); Partner, Hinkle, Cox, Eaton, Coffield & Hensley, Roswell, NM (1971-1992); Associate Firm, Hinkle, Cox, Eaton, Coffield & Hensley, Roswell, NM (1967-1971); Law Clerk, Cravath, Swaine & Moore, New York City, NY (1964-1967) **CR:** Chair, Tenth Circuit, Uniform Criminal Jury Instruction Committee; Tenth Circuit Rules Committee Member; Committee on Codes of Conduct (2010-Present); US Judicial Conference, Civil Rules Advisory Committee (2002-2007); US Judicial Conference, Committee on the Judicial Branch (1994-1999); New Mexico Public Defender; Board Member, Judiciary Committee, New Mexico House of Representatives; Chairman, Consumer and Public Affairs Committee (1976-1981); New Mexico Board of Bar Examiners (1982-1985) **CIV:** Member, Eastern New Mexico State Fair Board (1978-1983); Member, Appellate Judges Nominating Commission (1989-1992); President, Roswell Drug Abuse Committee (1970-1971); President, Oliver Seth Inn of Court (1993-Present); Board of Visitors, Fordham University School of Law (1992-2006); Treasurer, New Mexico Young Republicans (1968-1969); Vice Chairman, New Mexico Young Republicans (1969-1971); President, Chaves County Young Republicans (1971-1972); President, Parish Council, Roman Catholic Church (1971-1976); President, Roswell Symphony Orchestra Society (1973-1975); Treasurer, Roswell Symphony Orchestra Society (1970-1973); Board of Directors, Roswell Symphony Orchestra Society (1969-1982); Board of Directors, Santa Fe Orchestra (1992-1993); Board of Directors, Chaves County Mental Health Association (1974-1977); Board of Directors, Roswell Girls Club; Board of Directors, Zia Council Girl Scouts of America **MEM:** Vice President, Young Lawyers Section, State Bar of New Mexico (1969); Continuing Legal Education Committee (1970-1973); Co-chairman, Insurance Sub-committee (1972-1973); Bench-Bar Committee (1994-Present); Federal Bar Association **BAR:** State Bar of New Mexico (1967) **BA:** 1823 Stout St, Denver, CO, USA, 80202

KELLY, ROBIN LYNNE, T: U.S. Representative from Illinois **I:** Government Administration/Government Relations/Government Services **DOB:** 04/30/1956 **PB:** New York City **SC:** NY/USA **ED:** PhD, Northern Illinois University, 2004; MA in Counseling, Bradley University, 1982; BA in Psychology, Bradley University, 1977 **C:** Member, Committee on Foreign Affairs; Member, U.S. House Space, Sci. & Technology Committee, 2013-; Member, U.S. House Oversight & Government Reform Committee, 2013-; Member, U.S.Congress from 2nd Illinois District, Washington, 2013-; Chief Administrative Officer, Cook County, Illinois, 2011-13; Chief of Staff to Treasurer, State of Illinois, Springfield, 2007-11; Member District 38, Illinois House of Reps., 2002-06; Director Community Affairs, Village of Matteson, 1992-2006; Minority Student Services Director, Bradley University, 1990-92; Associate Director, The Youth Shelter, 1987-90; Director Crisis Nursery, Crittenton Care & Counseling Center, 1984-87 **CR:** Board Member Hate Crimes Commission, 2005- Commissioner, Cook County Human Rights Commission, 1998- **CIV:** Trustee, Bradley University, 2003- Board Member, Bradley Univ. Council, 1998- Board Member, Rich Township Food Pantry Board, 1995- Board Member, Illinois Theatre Center, 1993- **AW:** Named to The Centurion Society, Bradley University, 2009 **PA:** Democrat **BA:** District, "3649 West 183rd St Hazel Crest", 60429, IL, Zimbabwe, USA

KELLY, SCOTT J., I: Aviation **DOB:** 02/21/1964 **PB:** Orange **SC:** NJ/USA **PT:** Richard Kelly; Patricia Kelly **ED:** MS in Aviation Systems, The University Tennessee, Knoxville (1996); BSEE, State University of New York Maritime College (1987) **C:** Astronaut, NASA Johnson Space Center, Houston, TX (1996-Present); Test Pilot, US Navy, Patuxent River, Maryland (1994-1996); Test Pilot Student, US Navy Test Pilot School (1993-1994); Pilot, US Navy, Fighter Squadron 143, US Ship Dwight D. Eisenhower (1990-1993); Naval Pilot, US Navy Fighter Squadron 101, Oceana, VA (1989-1990); Student Pilot, US Navy, Naval Air Station Beeville, Texas (1987-1989); Commissioned Ensign, State University of New York Maritime College (1987); Lieutenant Commander, US Navy **CR:** Commander, International Space Station-Expedition 45 (2015); One-Year Crew Member, Soyuz TMA-16M (2015); Commander, International Space Station-Expedition 26 (2011); Flight Engineer, International Space Station-Expedition 25 (2010); Commander, STS-118 Mission (Endeavour) to International Space Station (2007); Pilot, STS 103 Mission (1999); Astronaut, Office Space Station Branch Chief, NASA Back-Up Crew Member, ISS Expedition; Director of Operations, NASA, Star City, Russia **AW:** Recipient, Korolev Diploma, Fédération Aéronautique Internationale (1999); Decorated, Sea Service Deployment Ribbon; Decorated, Kuwait Liberation Medal; Decorated, Southwest Asia Service Medal; Decorated, Navy Unit Commendations; Decorated, National Defense Service Medal; Decorated, Navy Achievement Medal; Decorated, Navy Commendation Medal; Decorated, Defense Superior Service Medal; Recipient, NASA Exceptional Service Medal; Recipient, NASA Space Flight Medal **MEM:** Fellow, Associate, Society of Experimental Test Pilots; Association of Space Explorers **ACH:** Achievements include being the first flight pilot to fly an F-14 with an experiment digital flight control system installed and performed subsequent high angle of attack and departure testing; Logged over 3,700 flight hours in more than 30 different aircraft and has over 250 carrier landings; will set the record for the longest space mission for an American and NASA astronaut at the International Space Station, March 27, 2015 until March 1, 2016 (1 year in space) **H:** Running; Weightlifting

KELLY, TRENT, T: U.S. Representative from Mississippi **I:** Government Administration/Government Relations/Government Services **DOB:** 03/01/1966 **PB:** Union **SC:** MS/USA **ED:** MD, U.S. Army War College, 2010; Law Degree, University OF Mississippi, 1994; BBA, University of Mississippi; Associate's Degree, East Central Community College **C:** Committee on Agriculture, Committee on Small Business, Committee on House Armed Services Committee, Republican Study Committee, U.S. House of Representative's from Mississippi's First District, 2015-Present; District Attorney, Mississippi's First Judicial District, 2012-2015 **BA:** 1721 Longworth House Office Building, Washington, DC, 20515

KENNEDY, ANTHONY MCLEOD, T: Associate Justice of the U.S. Supreme Court **I:** Government Administration/Government Relations/Government Services **DOB:** 07/23/1936 **PB:** Sacramento **SC:** CA/USA **PT:** Son of Arthur J. and Gladys McLeod Kennedy; **ED:** JD (hon.), University Santa Clara, 1988; JD (hon.), University Pacific, 1988; LLB, Harvard University, 1961; Student, London School Economics, 1957-58; AB, Stanford University 1958 **CT:** Bar: California 1962, US Tax Court 1971. **C:** Associate justice, US Supreme Court, Washington, 1988-2018; Judge, US Court Appeals (9th Cir.), Sacramento, 1975-88; Adjunct professor constitutional law, McGeorge School Law, University Pacific, 1965-88; Partner, Evans, Jackson & Kennedy, 1967-75; Private practice, Sacramento, 1963-67; Associate, Thelen, Martin, Johnson, & Bridges, San Francisco, 1961-63 **CR:** Member board student advisors Harvard Faculty, 1960-61, Advisory Committee on Codes of Conduct, 1979-87, Committee on Pacific Territories, 1979-88 (chairman, 1982-88), Federal Judicial Center, 1987-88. **MIL:** Served in California Army National Guard, 1961-62 **AW:** Named one of The 100 Most Influential People in the World, TIME magazine, 2012, The 50 Most Powerful People in DC, GQ magazine, 2007; recipient Golden Plate award, Academy Achievement, 2005 **MEM:** Fellow American Bar Foundation (honorary), American College Trial Lawyers (honorary); member American Bar Association, Sacramento County Bar Association, State Bar California, Phi Beta Kappa. **BA:** US Supreme Court, 1 First St NE, Washington, DC, USA, 20543-0001

KENNEDY, JOE III, T: U.S. Representative from Massachusetts **I:** Government Administration/Government Relations/Government Services **DOB:** 10/04/1980 **PB:** Boston **SC:** MA/USA **PT:** Son of Joseph Patrick and Sheila Brewster (Rauch) Kennedy; **ED:** JD, Harvard Law School, 2009; BS in Industrial Engineering, Stanford University, 2003 **C:** Member, US House Sci., Space & Tech. Committee, 2013-; Member, Committee on Energy and Commerce; Member, US House Foreign Affairs Committee, 2013-; Member, US Congress from 4th Massachusetts District, Washington, 2013-; Assistant district attorney, Middlesex County, Massachusetts, 2011-12; Prosecutor, Cape Cod & Islands, Massachusetts, 2009-11; Vol., Peace Corps, Dominican Republic, 2004-06 **PA:** Democrat

KENNEDY, KATHLEEN, T: Film Producer **I:** Media & Entertainment **DOB:** 01/01/1954 **PB:** Berkeley **SC:** CA/USA **ED:** BA in Telecommunications and Film, San Diego State University, 1975 **C:** President, Lucasfilm Ltd., Walt Disney, 2012-; Co-founder (with Frank Marshall), president, producer, Kennedy-Marshall Co., 1994-2012; Co-founder (with Steven Spielberg & Frank Marshall) and president, Amblin Entertainment, Universal City, California, 1984-92; Various posts including camera operator, video editor, floor director and news production coordinator, KCST, San Diego, **CR:** President Producers Guild of Am., 2001-06 **CIV:** Board Director, Michael J. Fox Foundation for Parkinson's Research, **CW:** Associate prodr.: (films) Poltergeist, 1982, Twilight Zone-The Movie, 1983, Indiana Jones and the Temple of Doom, 1984, Reform School Girls, 1986; prodr.: (films) E.T. The Extra-Terrestrial, 1982; (with Quincy Jones, Frank Marshall, and Spielberg) The Color Purple, 1985, (with Marshall and Art Levinson) The Money Pit, 1986; (with Marshall and Spielberg) Empire of the Sun, 1987, Always, 1989; (with Richard Vane) Arachnophobia, 1990; (with Marshall and Gerald R. Molen) Hook, 1991; (with Robert Watts) Alive, 1993; (with Molen) Jurassic Park, 1993, (with Marshall) Milk Money, 1994; (with Clint Eastwood) The Bridges of Madison County, 1995, Twister, 1996; (with Steven Spielberg), The Six Sense, 1999, Snow Falling on Cedars, 1999, A Map of the World, 1999, Artifical Intelligence: AI, 2001, Jurassic Park III, 2001, Seabiscuit, 2003, The Young Black Stallion, 2003, War of the Worlds, 2005, (with Spielberg) Munich, 2005, The Diving Bell and the Butterfly, 2007, The Curious Case of Benjamin Button, 2008, Hereafter, 2010, (with Spielberg) The Adventures of Tintin, 2011, (with Spielberg) War Horse, 2011, Lincoln, 2012, Star Wars: Episode VII - The Force Awakens, 2015; executive prodr.: (films) Roller Coaster Rabbit, 1990, A Dangerous Woman, 1993, (with Spielberg) Schindler's List, 1993 (Academy award for Best Picture 1993), Trail Mix-Up, 1993, A Far Off Place, 1993, Balto, 1995, Congo, 1995, The Indian in the Cupboard, 1995, Indiana Jones and the Kingdom of the Crystal Skull, 2008; (with Marshall and Spielberg) Gremlins, 1984, The Goonies, 1985, Back to the Future, 1985, Young Sherlock Holmes, 1985, *batteries not included, 1987, Jurassic Park: The Lost World, 1997, Dad, 1989, Back to the Future Part II, 1990, Gremlins 2: The New Batch, 1990, Back to the Future Part III, 1990, Joe Versus the Volcano, 1990, Cape Fear, 1991, We're Back! A Dinosaur's Story, 1993, (with Marshall) Fandango, 1985; (with Marshall, Spielberg, and David Kirschner) An American Tail, 1986; (with Marshall, Spielberg, Peter Guber, and Jon Peters) Innerspace, 1987; (with Spielberg) Who Framed Roger Rabbit, 1988; (with Marshall, Spielberg, and George Lucas) The Land Before Time, 1988; (with Marshall and Lucas) Indiana Jones and the Last Crusade, 1989; (with Marshall and Kirschner) An American Tail: Fievel Goes West, 1991; (with Peter Bogdanovich) Noises Off, 1992; (with Marshall and Molen); (with Molen, Kirschner, William Hanna, and Joseph Barbera) The Flintstones, 1994, Olympic Glory, 1999, Signs, 2002, The Last Airbender, 2010, The Secret World of Arrietty, 2010; executive producer TV Tummy Trouble, 1989, The Sports Pages, 2001; (TV films) Movies Rock, 2007, The Special Relationship, 2010. **AW:** Named one of the 50 Most Powerful Women in Busines, Fortune Magazine, 2015, The 100 Most Powerful Women in Entertainment, The Hollywood Reporter, 2006-14, 50 Smartest People in Hollywood, Entertainment Weekly, 2007; recipient David O. Selznick Achievement award in Theatrical Motion Pictures, Producers Guild Am., 2008

KENNEDY, THOMAS A., T: CEO **I:** Military & Defense Services **CN:** Raytheon **ED:** Doctorate Degree, Engineering, UCLA; M.S., Air Force Institute; B.S., Rutgers **C:** Chairman, Forcepoint, 2015-; CEO/Chairman, Raytheon, 2014-; VP, Raytheon,2010-2013; COO, Raytheon,2013-2014

KENNEY, JAMES F., T: Mayor of Philadelphia **I:** Government Administration/Government Relations/Government Services **DOB:** 08/08/1958 **PB:** Phila. **ED:** BA in Political Sci., La Salle University, Philadelphia, 1980 **C:** Mayor, Philadelphia, 2016-; Councilman-at-large, Philadelphia City Council, 1992-2015; Chief of staff to Senator Vincent J. Fumo, Pennsylvania State Senate, 1984-92; Administrative assistant, Senator Vincent J. Fumo, Pennsylvania State Senate, Harrisburg, 1980-84 **CR:** Vice chairman laws & government committee, pub. property & pub. works committee, rules committee Philadelphia City Council, chairman environmental committee, legis. oversight committee

CIV: Founding member, Gallagher's St Patrick's Day Observance, Del., Dem. National Convention, 1980-92 Member, Pennsylvania Dem. State Committee **MEM:** Mem.: Columbus Civic Association, Philadelphia Irish Society, Jokers New Year's Association **PA:** Democrat

KERRY, JOHN FORBES, I: Government Administration/Government Relations/Government Services **DOB:** 12/11/1943 **PB:** Denver **PT:** Son of Richard John and Rosemary (Forbes) K. **MS:** Married **SPN:** Teresa Heinz (5/26/1995); Julia Stimson Thorne, (5/23/1970, Divorced 7/25/1988) **CH:** Alexandra, Vanessa, Henry John IV (Stepchild), André (Stepchild), Christopher (Stepchild) **ED:** PhD (hon.), University Massachusetts, 1988; JD, Boston College Law School, 1976; BA in Political Science, Yale University, 1966 **C:** Secretary, US Department State, Washington, 2013-; Democratic Nominee for President, US Presidential Election, 2004; Member, Joint Select Committee on Deficit Reduction, 2011; Chairman, US Senate Foreign Relations Committee, 2009-13; Chairman, US Senate Small Business & Entrepreneurship Committee, 2007-09; Chairman, US Senate Small Business & Entrepreneurship Committee, 2001-03; Chairman, US Senate Small Business & Entrepreneurship Committee, 2001; Chairman, Democratic Senatorial Campaign Committee (DSCC), 1987-89; US Senator from Massachusetts, 1985-2013; Lieutenant Governor, State of Massachusetts, Boston, 1983-85; Partner, Kerry & Sragow, Boston, 1979-82; Assistant District Attorney, Middlesex County, 1976-79; National Coordinator, Vietnam Vets. Against The War, 1969-71 **CIV:** Democratic Candidate for Congress from 5th Massachusetts District, 1972, Board of Visitors, Walsh School Foreign Service, Georgetown University **MIL:** Served to Lieutenant (junior grade), U.S. Naval Reserve, 1966-69 **CW:** Author: The New Soldier, 1971, The New War: The Web of Crime That Threatens America's Security, 1997, A Call to Service: My Vision for a Better America, 2003; Co-author (with Teresa Heinz Kerry) This Moment on Earth: Today's New Environmentalists and Their Vision for the Future, 2007 **AW:** Decorated Purple Hearts (2), Bronze Star with Oak Leaf Cluster, Silver Star; Named one of The 100 Most Influential People in the World, TIME magazine, 2014 **MEM:** Member: Vietnam Vets. America (founder) **BAR:** Bar: Massachusetts 1976 **PA:** Democrat

KERSHAW, CLAYTON EDWARD, T: Professional Baseball Player **I:** Athletics **DOB:** 03/19/1988 **PB:** Dallas **C:** Pitcher, L.A. Dodgers, 2008 **CIV:** Vol., Arise Africa, Zambia, 2011 Founder, Kershaw's Challenge, **CW:** Co-author (with E. Kershaw): Arise: Live Out Your Faith and Dreams on Whatever Field You Find Yourself, 2012 **AW:** Named National League Most Valuable Player, Major League Baseball, 2014, National League Outstanding Pitcher, Major League Baseball Players Association, 2011; named to National League All-Star Team, Major League Baseball, 2011-14; recipient Branch Rickey award, Rotary Club Denver, 2013, Warren Spahn award, Oklahoma Sports Museum, 2013, 2011, Roberto Clemente award, Major League Baseball, 2012, National League Gold Glove award, 2011, National League Cy Young award, Baseball Writers' Association America, 2014, 2013, 2011,All Star, 2015-17, NL Wins Leader, 2011, 2014, 2017, NL ERA Leader, 2011-14, 2017,NL Strikeout Leader, 2011,2013, 2015, Roberto Clemente Award, 2012, Marvin Miller Man of the Year Award, 2014, Marvin Miller Man of the Year Award, 2014, Warren Spahn Award, 2011, 2013, 2014, 2017 **ACH:** Achievements include leading the National League in: wins, 2011; earned run average, strikeouts, 2011, 2013; pitched his first career no hitter, June 18, 2014

KETHLEDGE, RAYMOND MICHAEL, T: Federal Judge **I:** Law and Legal Services **DOB:** 12/11/1966 **PB:** Summit **ED:** JD magna cum laude, University Michigan, 1993; BA in History, University Michigan, 1989 **CT:** Bar: Michigan 1990 **C:** Judge, US Court Appeals (6th cir.), Detroit, 2008-; Partner, Bush Seyferth Kethledge and Paige PLLC, Troy, Michigan, 2003-08; Partner, Feeney Kellett Weinner & Bush, 2002-03; Counsel, Ford Motor Co., 2001-02; Partner litigation department, Honigman Miller Schwartz and Cohn, 2001; Associate, Honigman Miller Schwartz and Cohn, Detroit, 1998-2001; Law clerk to Justice Anthony Kennedy, US Supreme Court, 1997-98; Judiciary counsel to Senator Spencer Abraham, US Senate, 1995-97; Associate, Sidley & Austin LLP, 1994; Law clerk to Hon. Ralph B. Guy, Junior, US Court Appeals (6th cir.), 1993-94 **CR:** Vol. New Leaders New Schools, Community Legal Services **CW:** Lead Yourself First: Inspiring Leadership Through Solitude,2017 **MEM:** Mem.: Order of Coif **BA:** US Ct Appeals 540 Potter Stewart US Courthouse, 100 E Fifth St, Cincinnati, OH, 45202

KEYS, ALICIA, T: Singer, Musician **I:** Media & Entertainment **DOB:** 01/25/1981 **PB:** New York City **SC:** NY/USA **PT:** Daughter of Craig Cook and Terri Augello; **ED:** Attended, Columbia University, New York City **C:** Global Creative Director, BlackBerry, 2013; Singer, Songwriter, 2001- **CIV:** Co-founder, Global Ambassador, Keep a Child Alive, **CW:** Singer: (albums) Songs in A Minor, 2001 (Favorite Soul/R&B Album, American Music Awards, 2002, Top R&B/Hip-Hop Album, Billboard R&B/Hip-Hop Awards, 2002, Best R&B Album, Grammy Awards, 2002, Outstanding Album, National Association for the Advancement of Colored People Image Awards, 2002, R&B/Soul Solo Artist Album of Year, Soul Train Lady of Soul Awards, 2002), The Diary of Alicia Keys, 2003 (Best R&B Album, Grammy Awards, 2005), Unplugged, 2005, As I Am, 2007 (Best Soul/R&B Album, American Music Awards, 2008, Outstanding Album, National Association for the Advancement of Colored People Image Awards, 2008), The Element of Freedom, 2009, Girl on Fire, 2012 (Best R&B Album, Grammy Awards, 2014), (songs) Fallin', 2001 (Best R&B Song, Best Female R&B Vocal Performance, Song of Year, Grammy Awards, 2002), You Don't Know My Name, 2003 (Best R&B Song, Grammy Awards, 2005), If I Ain't Got You, 2004 (R&B/Hip-Hop Single of Year, Billboard Music Awards, 2004, Best R&B Video, MTV Video Music Awards, 2004, Best Female R&B Vocal Performance, Grammy Awards, 2005, Outstanding Music Video, Outstanding Song, National Association for the Advancement of Colored People Image Awards, 2005), Karma, 2004 (Best R&B Video, MTV Video Music Awards, 2005), (featuring Tony! Toni! Toné!) Diary, 2004, (with Usher) My Boo, 2004 (Best R&B Performance by a Duo or Group with Vocals, Grammy Awards, 2005), Unbreakable, 2005 (Outstanding Music Video, Outstanding Song, National Association for the Advancement of Colored People Image Awards, 2006), No One, 2007 (Best Female R&B Vocal Performance, Best R&B Song, Grammy Awards, 2008, Favorite R&B Song, People's Choice Awards, 2009), Superwoman, 2008 (Best Female R&B Vocal Performance, Grammy Awards, 2009), (with Jay Z) Empire State of Mind, 2009 (Best Collaboration, BET Awards, 2010, Best Rap/Sung Collaboration, Best Rap Song, Grammy Awards, 2011), Un-Thinkable (I'm Ready), 2010 (Outstanding Music Video, National Association for the Advancement of Colored People Image Awards, 2011), Empire State of Mind (Part II) Broken Down, 2010, Girl On Fire, 2012 (Outstanding Music Video, National Association for the Advancement of Colored People Image Awards, 2013), We Are Here,

2014 (Outstanding Song, National Association for the Advancement of Colored People Image Awards, 2015); actress: (films) Smokin' Aces, 2007, The Nanny Diaries, 2007, The Secret Life of Bees, 2008, The Ninth Wave, 2014, (TV guest appearances) The Cosby Show, 1985, Saturday Night Live, 2001, Charmed, 2001, American Dreams, 2003; executive prodr.: (TV films) Firelight, 2012; executive producer, composer (films) The Inevitable Defeat of Mister and Pete, 2013; author: Tears for Water: Songbook of Poems and Lyrics, 2004, (children's book) Blue Moon: From the Journals of MaMa Mae and LeeLee, 2014; judge (reality singing competition) The Voice, 2016-, (Music) Here, 2016 (Film) The Gospel, 2016, Here in Times Square, 2016, CMT Crossroads, 2016, Landmarks Live: Great Performances, 2017, The Soundtrack of My Life, 2017, Marriage Boot Camp, 2018 **AW:** Named Favorite Female Singer, People's Choice Awards, 2005, Best Selling R&B Artist, World Music Awards, 2008, 2004, 2002, Outstanding Female Artist, National Association for the Advancement of Colored People Image Awards, 2013, 2008, 2005, 2002, Outstanding New Artist, 2002, Best R&B Female Artist, BET Awards (Black Entertainment TV), 2010, 2008, 2005, Best New Artist, 2002, Favorite Female Soul/R&B Artist, American Music Awards, 2004, Favorite New Soul/R&B Artist, 2002, Best New Artist, Grammy Awards, 2002, Female Artist of Year, Billboard Music Awards, 2002, Female R&B/Hip-Hop Artist of Year, 2004, Female Artist of Year, 2001; named one of The 100 Greatest Artists of All Time, VH1, 2010, The 100 Most Powerful Celebrities, Forbes.com, 2008, The 100 Most Influential People in the World, TIME magazine, 2005, The 50 Most Influential African-Americans, Ebony Magazine, 2004; recipient Humanitarian award, Black Entertainment TV, 2009, Time 100 Most Influential, 2017, Grammy for Best Rap Sung Collabortation, 2011, Grammy for Best Rap Song, 2011, Grammy for Best R&B Album, 2014, Peoples Choice Awards for Favorite R&B Song, 2009 **BA:** 42 West, 220 W 42nd St 12th Fl, New York, NY, 10036

KHAN, SHAHID, T: Manufacturing Executive, Professional Sports Team Executive **I:** Business Management/Business Services **ED:** BS in Mechanical Engineering, University Illinois, Urbana-Champaign, 1971 **C:** Owner, Fulham FC, Barclays Premier League, 2013-; Owner, Jacksonville Jaguars, NFL, Florida, 2012-; Owner, CEO and president, Flex-N-Gate Corp., 1980-; Chairman, Bio-Alternative, LLC, Illinois,; Chairman, Smart Structures, LLC, Illinois,; Founder, auto parts designer & manufacturer, Bumper Works, 1978-80; Product and tooling design engineer, Flex-N-Gate Corp., Illinois, 1970-78 **CR:** Member Daimler-Chrysler Minority Supplier Council **CIV:** Member business adv. council, University of Illinois College of Business, Member board of visitors, University of Illinois College of Engineering **AW:** Recipient Minority Business Leadership award, National Minority Supplier Devel. Council, 2007, Distinguished Alumnus award, Univ. Illinois Department Mechanical and Industrial Engineering, 1999 **MEM:** Mem.: World Presidents Organization

KHANNA, ROHIT, T: U.S. Representative from California **I:** Government Administration/Government Relations/Government Services **DOB:** 09/13/1976 **PB:** Philadelphia **SC:** PA/USA **PT:** Grandmother, Amarnath Vidyalankar **ED:** BA, Economics, University of Chicago, 1998; Yale Law School, 2001 **C:** Member, U.S. House of Representatives from California's 17th District, 2017-,; Member, Committee on Armed Services,; Member, Committee on the Budget,; Lawyer, Wilson, Sonsini, Goodrich and Rosati, 2011-,; Deputy Assistant Secretary, U.S. Department of Commerce, 2009-2012 **CW:** Author

(Novel) Entrepreneurial Nation: Why Manufacturing is Key to America's Future, 2012 **BA:** 513 Cannon HOB, Washington, DC, 20515

KIDMAN, NICOLE, T: Actress **I:** Media & Entertainment **DOB:** 06/20/1967 **PB:** Honolulu **PT:** Daughter of Anthony David and Janelle Ann (Glenny) Kidman; **CIV:** Goodwill ambassador, UN Devel. Fund for Women, UNIFEM, 2006- **CW:** Actress (films) BMX Bandits, 1983, Bush Christmas, 1983, Wills & Burke, 1985, Archer's Adventure, 1985, Windrider, 1986, Watch the Shadows Dance (Nightmaster), 1986, Bit Part, 1987, Emerald City, 1989, Dead Calm, 1989, Days of Thunder, 1990, Flirting, 1991, Billy Bathgate, 1991, Far and Away, 1992, Malice, 1993, My Life, 1993, Batman Forever, 1995, To Die For, 1995 (Golden Globe award for Best Actress, Boston Society Film Critics award for Best Actress), Portrait of a Lady, 1996, The Peacemaker, 1997, Practical Magic, 1998, Eyes Wide Shut, 1999, The Others, 2001, Birthday Girl, 2001, Moulin Rouge, 2001 (Golden Globe award for Best Actress), The Hours, 2002 (Academy award for Best Actress, Golden Globe award for Best Actress, BAFTA award for Best Actress in a Leading Role), Dogville, 2003, The Human Stain, 2003, Cold Mountain, 2003, The Stepford Wives, 2004, Birth, 2004, The Interpreter, 2005, Bewitched, 2005, Fur: An Imaginary Portrait of Diane Arbus, 2006, Happy Feet (voice), 2006, The Invasion, 2007, Margot at the Wedding, 2007, The Golden Compass, 2007, Australia, 2008, Nine, 2009, Just Go With It, 2011, Trespass, 2011, Stoker, 2012, The Paperboy, 2012, Stoker, 2013, The Railway Man, 2013, Grace of Monaco, 2014, Before I Go to Sleep, 2014, Paddington, 2015, Strangerland, 2015, Queen of the Desert, 2015, Secret in Their Eyes, 2015, The Guardian Brothers (voice), 2016, Genius, 2016, How to Talk to Girls at Parties, 2016, Lion, 2016, The Killing of a Sacred Deer, 2017, The Beguiled, 2017, The Upside, 2017, Boy Erased, 2018, Aquaman, 2018, Sex and the City 3, Det Erin Bell, 2018 (TV films) Hemingway & Gellhorn, 2012; prodr.: (films) In the Cut, 2003, Monte Carlo, 2011; actress, producer (films) Rabbit Hole, 2010, The Family Fang, 2015, (TV appearances) Five Mile Creek, 1983, Chase Through the Night, 1983, Matthew and Son, 1984, Vietnam, 1985, Bangkok Hilton, 1989, actress (plays) The Blue Room, London, 1997-98, Broadway, 1998-99, Photograph 51, London, 2015, Hello Ladies the Movie, 2014, Big Little Lies, 2017, Top of the Lake, 2017 **AW:** Named Companion of the Order of Australia, 2006, Australian of Year, New South Wales, 2004; named one of The 100 Most Powerful Celebrities, Forbes.com, 2008, 2007, 50 Most Powerful People in Hollywood, Premiere magazine, 2003-06; recipient Women in Hollywood Tribute award, ELLE magazine, 2008, Citizen award, UN, 2004, star on Hollywood Walk of Fame, 2003, ShoWest Distinguished Decade Achievement award, 2002

KIHUEN, RUBEN, T: U.S. Representative from Nevada **I:** Government Administration/Government Relations/Government Services **DOB:** 04/25/1980 **PB:** Guadalajara, Jalisco, Mexico, April 25, 1980 **SC:** Guadalajara Jalisco Mexico **ED:** Student in pub. administration, University Oklahoma, Norman; BS in Education, University Nevada, Reno; Attended, Community College Southern Nevada, North Las Vegas **C:** Member, U.S. House of Representatives from Nevada's 4th District, 2017-. Member, Committee on Financial Services; Member Clark 10 District, Nevada State Senate, 2010-2017; Regional rep. Senator Harry Reid, US Senate, 2005-06; Member District 11, Nevada State Assembly, 2007-10; Personal assistant to Rep. Richard Perkins, Nevada State

Assembly, 2002; Academic advisor, Community College Southern Nevada,; Student recruiter, Community College Southern Nevada, 1999-2005; Base vote director, Nevada State Dem. Party, 2004-05; Former deputy field director 3d district Congl. campaign, Nevada State Dem. Party **CIV:** Vol., Profls. and Youth Building a Commitment, Vol., St. Vincent's Shelter, Board directors, Vol. Center Southern Nevada, **MEM:** Mem.: National Council Hispanic State Legislators, Latin C. of C., National Association Latino Elected and Appointed Officials **PA:** Democrat **BA:** Nev State Assembly, 401 S Carson St Rm 3159, Carson City, NV, 89701-4747

KILDEE, DAN, T: U.S. Representative from Michigan **I:** Government Administration/Government Relations/Government Services **DOB:** 08/11/1958 **PB:** Flint **ED:** BS in Community Development Administration, Central Michigan University, 2008 **C:** Member, US House Financial Services Committee, 2013-; Member, Budget Committee; Assistant minority whip, US Congress from 5th Michigan District, 2013-; Member, US Congress from 5th Michigan District, Washington, 2013-; Founder, CEO, Genesee County Land Bank, 2002-09; Treasurer, Genesee County, Michigan, 1997-2009; Commissioner, Genesee County, Michigan, 1985-97; Member, Flint Board Education, Michigan, 1977-85; Youth specialist, Whaley Children's Center, 1976-85 **CR:** Co-founder, president The Center for Community Progress, 2009-12 **PA:** Democrat

KILMEADE, BRIAN, T: Television Personality **I:** Media & Entertainment **PB:** New York **SC:** NY/USA **C:** Co-Host,Fox and Friends, 2008-; Guest Co-Host, The Five, 2012-17 **CW:** (Books) The Games do Count: Americas Best and Brightest on the Power of Sports, 2004, Its How You Play the Game: The Powerful Sports Moments that Taught Lasting Values to Americas Finest, 2007, George Washington's Secret Six: The Spy Ring that Saved the American Revolution,2013, Thomas Jefferson and the Tripoli Pirates: The Forgotten War that Changed American History,2015,Andrew Jackson and the Miracle of New Orleans: The Battle That Shaped Americas Destiny, 2017

KILMER, DEREK, T: U.S. Representative from Washington, Former State Legislator **I:** Government Administration/Government Relations/Government Services **DOB:** 01/01/1974 **PB:** Port Angeles, Clallam County **ED:** DPhil, University Oxford, 2003; BA in Public Affairs, Princeton University Woodrow Wilson School Public & International affairs, 1996 **C:** Member, US House Sci., Space & Technology Committee, 2013-; Member, US House Armed Services Committee, 2013-; Member, US Congress from 6th Wash District, Washington, 2013-; Member, Committee on Appropriations; Member District 26, Washington State Senate, 2007-12; Member District 26, Washington House of Reps., 2005-07; Management consultant, McKinsey & Co.,; Vice president economic development board, Tacoma-Pierce Co., **AW:** Named Honorary Fire Chief, Washington Fire Chiefs, Legislator of the Year, Washington Council Police & Sheriffs; recipient Legislative Business Star award, Enterprise Washington's Business Institute, LEADER award (3), Washington Economic Development Association **MEM:** Mem.: Tacoma Community College (board trustees) **PA:** Democrat

KIM, CHLOE, T: Olympic Snowboarder **I:** Athletics **DOB:** 07/21/1905 **PB:** Long Beach, California **SC:** Long Beach, California **AW:** One Olympic Gold Medal, Halfpipe, 2018, 4 Winter X Games Superpipe Gold Medals,2015,2016,2018, One Winter X Games Superpipe Silver Medal, 2014, One

Winter X Games Superpipe Bronze Medal,2017, 2 Gold Winter Youth Medals, 2016

KIMMEL, JIMMY, T: Television Personality **I:** Media & Entertainment **DOB:** 11/13/1967 **PB:** Brooklyn **SC:** NY/USA **PT:** James Kimmel, Joan (Iacono) Kimmel **ED:** Student, Arizona State University; Student, University of Nevada, Las Vegas **C:** Television Personality, 1997-Present **CW:** Host, Writer, (TV Series) The Man Show, 1999-2003; Host, Writer, Executive Producer, (Voice Actor) Crank Yankers, 2002-2007, Jimmy Kimmel Live, 2003-Present; Writer, Executive Producer, The Andy Milonakis Show, 2005-2007; Executive Producer, (TV Films) Big Night of Stars, 2008, Alligator Boots, 2009, Ace in the Hole, 2009, (TV Series) The Adam Carolla Project, 2005; Host, White House Correspondents' Dinner; Co-Host, Win Ben Stein's Money, 2001-2002; Actor, (Films) Down to You, 2000, (Voice Actor) Road Trip, 2000, (Voice Actor) Garfield, 2004, (Voice Actor) The Smurfs 2, 2013, (TV Films) Channel 101, 2006; Guest Appearances, (Films) Pitch Perfect 2, 2015, Ted 2, 2015, Miss Famous, 2015, The Boss Baby, 2017, Sandy Wexler, 2017, Brad's Status, 2017, The Heyday Of The Insensitive Bastards, 2017, (TV Series) Charmed, 1999, Entourage, 2004, Drawn Together, 2006, Robot Chicken (Voice), 2006, Hot in Cleveland, 2011, Brody Stevens: Enjoy It!, 2013, The Middle, 2014, Shark Tank, 2014, Tim & Eric's Bedtime Stories, 2014, The Bachelor, 2015, The Grinder, 2016, The Real O'Neals, 2016, Trailer Park Boys, 2016, Pitch, 2016, Curb Your Enthusiasm, 2017, (TV Programs) 64th Primetime Emmys, 2012, 68th Primetime Emmy Awards, 2016, 89th Academy Awards, 2017, 90th Academy Awards, 2018 **AW:** Daytime Emmy For Outstanding Game Show Host, Win Ben Stein's Money, 1999, Writers Guild Award for Best Comedy/Variety Series, 2012, The 100 Most Influential People in the World, TIME Magazine, 2013, Hollywood Walk of Fame, 2013, Variety's Power of Comedy Award, 2013, Writers Guild of America Award for Comedy, 2016 **BA:** c/o Jimmy Kimmel Live, 6834 Hollywood Boulevard, Los Angeles, CA, 90028

KIND, RONALD JAMES, T: U.S. Representative from Wisconsin **I:** Government Administration/ Government Relations/Government Services **DOB:** 03/16/1963 **PB:** La Crosse **SC:** WI/USA **PT:** Son of Elroy and Greta Kind; **ED:** JD, University Minnesota, 1990; MA, London School Economics, 1986; BA with honors, Harvard University, 1985 **C:** Member, US Congress from 3rd Wisconsin District, 1997-; Member, Committee on Ways and Means; Prosecutor, La Crosse County, Wisconsin, 1992-96; Associate, Quarles & Brady, Milwaukee, 1990-92 **CR:** Chairman New Democrat Coalition, 2013- **MEM:** Mem.: New Dem. Network, La Crosse Optimists Club **PA:** Democrat

KING, ANGUS STANLEY JR., T: U.S. Senator from Maine **I:** Government Administration/Government Relations/Government Services **DOB:** 03/31/1944 **PB:** Alexandria **SC:** VA/USA **MS:** Married **SPN:** Mary J. Herman, 1984 **CH:** Angus III, Duncan, James, Benjamin, Molly **ED:** LLD (hon.), Bowdoin College, 2007; JD, University of Pennsylvania, 1969; BA, Dartmouth College, 1966 **CT:** Bar: Maine 1969. **C:** Member, U.S. Senate Select Committee on Intelligence, 2013-; Member, U.S. Senate Rules & Administration Committee, 2013-; Member, U.S. Senate Budget Committee, 2013-; Member, U.S. Senate Armed Services Committee, 2013-; U.S. Senator from Maine, 2013-; Distinguished Lecturer, Bowdoin College, Brunswick, Maine, 2004-; Governor, State of Maine, Augusta, Maine, 1995-2003; Partner, Smith, Lloyd & King, Brunswick, Maine, 1975-83; Chief Counsel to Senator William D.

Hathaway, US Senate Subcommittee on Alcoholism and Narcotics, Washington, 1972-75; Staff Attorney, Pine Tree Legal Assistance, Showhegan, Maine, 1969-72 **CR:** TV host, Co-prodr. Maine Watch, Maine Pub. Broadcasting Network, 1975-93 Vice President, General Counsel Swift River/Hafslund Co., 1983 Founder, President Northeast Energy Management Inc., Brunswick, Maine, 1989-94 **PA:** Independent **BA:** Office of Angus King, 133 Hart Building, Washington, DC, 20510

KING, BILLIE JEAN MOFFITT, T: Retired Professional Tennis Player **I:** Other **DOB:** 11/22/1943 **PB:** Long Beach **PT:** Daughter of Willard J. and Betty Moffitt; Married Larry King (div. 1987), September 17, 1965 **ED:** PhD (hon.), University Massachusetts, 2000; PhD (hon.), University Pa, 1999; Degree (hon.), Trinity College, 1998; PhD (hon.), California State University, 1997; Student, California State University at Los Angeles, 1961-64 **C:** Director, official spokesperson, World Team Tennis, Chicago, 1985-; Commentator, analyst Wimbeldon and other tennis events, HBO, New York City,; Member, Tennis Challenge Series, 1977, 78; Professional, 1968-84; Amateur tennis player, 1958-67 **CR:** Winner, Singles champion tournaments include: Wimbledon, 1966-68, 72, 73,75, U.S. Open, 1967, 71, 72, 74, Australian Open, 1968, French Open, 1972 Doubles champion Wimbledon, 1961, 62, 65, 67, 68, 70-73, 79 U.S. Open, 1965, 67, 74, 80, French Open, 1972 mixed doubles champion Wimbledon, 1967, 71, 73, 74, U.S. Open, 1967, 71, 73, French, 1967, 70, Australian, 1968 winner 29 Virginia Slims singles titles, 1970-77, 4 Colgate titles, 1977, Federation Cup, 1963-67, 76-79, Wightman Cup, 1961-67, 70, 77, 78 World Tennis Team All-Star, 3 times host Colgate women's sports TV special The Lady is a Champ, 1975 sports commentator ABC-TV, 1975-78founder Women's Tennis Association, 1973, president, 1973-75, 80-81 founder, Women's Sports Found, 1974, Professional World TeamTennis, 1974, World TeamTennis Professional League, 1981, World TeamTennis Recreational League, 1985, World TeamTennis Charities, 1987 co-founder, pub. WomenSports magazine, 1974, Kingdom, Inc., San Mateo, California founding member, Women's Sports Legends first woman commissioner (Team Tennis League) professional sports history, 1984 TV commentator HBO-Sports Wimbeldon coverage captain Federal Cup for USA, 1995 consultant Virginia Slims World Championship Seriesmember, Planned Parenthood, US Professional Tennis Association, US Professional Tennis Registry, Chicago Area Women's Sports Association, advisory bd,, Areta Sports award nomination committee, Jim Thorpe Pro sports nomination committee award, sports advisory board for the Vic Braden Neurology Research Institute, US Tennis Association Player Devel. Committee board directors Challenger Center, Elton John AIDS Foundation, S.A.F.E., National AIDS Fund, Altria Group, Inc., Women's Sports Foundation ambassador Adventures in Movement Charity coach Federal Cup Women's Tennis Team, 1995-96, 98-2003, USA Olympic Women's Tennis Team, 1996, 2000 national spokesperson Literary Vols. Am. tennis teacher to profls **CW:** Author: Tennis to Win, 1970, (with Kim Chapin) Billie Jean, 1974, (with Greg Hoffman) Tennis Love: A Parent's Guide to the Sport, 1978, (with Frank Deford) The Autobiography of Billie Jean King, 1982 (with Cynthia Starr) We Have Come a Long Way, The Story of Women's Tennis, 1988. **AW:** Named Sportsperson of Year, 1972, Top 40 Athletes, 1994, Sports Illustrated; Woman Athlete of Year, A.P., 1967, 73, Top Woman Athlete of Year, 1972; Woman of Year, Time magazine, 1976, One of 10 Most Powerful Women in Am., Harper's Bazaar, 1977, One of 25 Most Influential Women in Am., World

Almanac, 1977, One of 100 Most Important Ams. of 20th Century, Life magazine, 1990, woman of the Year, Women in Sports & Events, 2002; named to International Tennis Hall of Fame, 1987, National Women's Hall of Fame, 1990, Chicago Gay and Lesbian Hall of Fame, 1999, Court of Champions, US Tennis Association National Tennis Center, 2003, The California Hall of Fame, 2006; WTA Hon. Membership award, 1986, Female Teaching Pro of the Decade, 1994, Lifetime Achievement award, March of Dimes, 1994, Flo Hymnal award, Women's Sports Found, 1997, "Player Who Makes a Difference award", 1997, US Olympic Committee National Tennis Coach of the Year award, 1997, National Women's Law Center honoree, 1997, Elizabeth Blackwill award for Courage, William & Hobart Smith Colleges, 1998, Arthur Ashe award for Courage, ESPN, 1999, Community Role Model award, LA Gay & Lesbian Center, 1999, NFL Players Association Lifetime Achievement award, 1999, Sports Illustrated "Athletes Who Changed the Game award, 1999, Capitol award, GLAAD, 2000, Radcliffe medal, Radcliffe College, 2002, Internat Olympic Committee Women & Sport World Trophy, 2002, National Association Collegiate Women Athletic Administrators award of Honor, 2002, Pillipe Chatrier award, International Tennis Federation, 2003, Presidential Medal of Freedom, The White House, 2009,Souther California Tennis Hall of Fame, 2011, ESPNW'S Impact 25, 2014, Sunday Times Sports Women of the Year Lifetime Achievement Award, 2007 **ACH:** Won 71 singles titles, including 12 Grand Slam singles titles; won 20 Wimbledon titles; First woman to win more than $100,000 in a single season in any sport; Highest singles ranking 1(5 times between 1966-72); defeated Bobby Riggs in "The Battle of the Sexes" tennis match, September 20, 1973, Houston, Texas

KING, CAROLE, T: Singer **I:** Media & Entertainment **DOB:** 05/08/1905 **PB:** Bklyn., **SC:** Bklyn., **SPN:** Married Gerry Goffin, 1959 (div. 1968); Married Charles Larkey; Married Rick Evers, 1977 (deceased, 1978); Married Rick Sorensen; 1982; **CH:** children: Louise, Sherry, Molly, Levi. **ED:** Student, Queens College **CW:** Co-writer (with Gerry Goffin): Will You Love Me Tomorrow?, Go Away, Little Girl, Up on the Roof, (with Jerry Wexler) Natural Woman, The Locomotion, Take Good Care of My Baby, (with Toni Stern) It's Too Late, 1971; albums include: Music, 1971, Tapestry, 1971 (Grammy awards for Album of Year, Record of Year for It's Too Late, Song of Year for You've Got a Friend, Best Female Pop Vocal Performance for Tapestry, 1972), Simple Things, Pearls: Songs of Goffin and King, Rhymes & Reasons, 1972, Fantasy, 1973, Wrap Around Joy, 1974, Really Rosie, 1975, Thoroughbred, 1975, Her Greatest Hits: Songs of Long Ago, 1978, One To One, 1982, Speeding Time, 1983, City Streets, 1989, Colour of Your Dreams, 1993, In Concert, 1994, A Natural Woman, 1994, The Carnegie Hall Concert, 1996, Pearls/Time Gone By, 1998, Super Hits, 2000, Love Makes the World, 2001, The Living Room Tour, 2005, Love Makes the World-Deluxe Edition, 2007, Welcome To My Living Room (DVD), 2007, Live at the Troubadour, 2010, A Holiday Carole, 2011; (film composer) Head, 1968, Murphy's Romance, 1985, The Care Bears Movie, 1985; (off-Broadway theater appearances) A Minor Incident, 1989; (Broadway appearances) Blood Brothers, 1994; (film appearances) Murphy's Romance, 1985, Russkies, 1987, (TV films) Hider in the House, 1989; (TV series) The Tracy Ullman Show, 1989, The Trials of Rosie O'Neill, 1991, Gilmore Girls, 2002, 2005,Gilmore Girls: A Year in the Life, 2016; A Natural Woman: A Memoir, 2012. **AW:** Recipient Lifetime Achievement award, Grammy Awards, 2013, Gershwin prize for Popular Song, Library of Congress, 2013, Kennedy Center

Honors, John F. Kennedy Center Performing Arts, Washington, 2015; named to Rock & Roll Hall of Fame, 1990; named MusiCares Person of Year, Grammy Awards, 2014.

KING, KELLY S., **T:** CEO of BB&T Corp **I:** Financial Services **DOB:** 09/12/1948 **PB:** Raleigh **SC:** NC/USA **MS:** Married **CH:** 2 children **ED:** Grad., Rutgers University, 1981; MBA, East Carolina University, 1971; BSBA, East Carolina University, 1970 **C:** Chairman, CEO, BB&T Corp. (Branch Banking and Trust Co.), Winston-Salem, North Carolina, 2009-; President, CEO, BB&T Corp. (Branch Banking and Trust Co.), Winston-Salem, North Carolina, 2009; COO, BB&T Corp. (Branch Banking and Trust Co.), Winston-Salem, North Carolina, 2004-08; Management Positions inc. Manager Ctrl & Metropolitan Regions, City Executive, Business Services Manager, Consumer Loan Manager, Marketing Officer, & Branch Network Manager, BB&T Corp. (Branch Banking and Trust Co.), Winston-Salem, North Carolina, 1988-2004; Joined, BB&T Corp. (Branch Banking and Trust Co.), Winston-Salem, North Carolina, 1972; Marketing Professor, East Carolina University, Greenville, North Carolina, 1971-72 **CR:** Past Board Member Am. Bankers Association Past Vice-chmn. Am. Bankers Council **CIV:** Chair, Piedmont Triad Leadership Group, United Way Tocqueville Leadership Campaign & United Way Tocqueville Leadership Society Member, Financial Services Roundtable & Triangle Community Foundation Leadership Council Board Member, North Carolina Chamber of Commerce Board of Trustees, St. Augustine?s College, Mission Emanuel, North Carolina Center for Non-Profits, North Carolina Economic Devel. Commission, North Carolina Child Advocacy Institute, North Carolina Community College Foundation & Winston-Salem Downtown Church Center, North Carolina Bankers Association **MEM:** Member Raleigh C. of C. (Economic Devel. Adv. Council). Clubs: Capital City (Raleigh) (Board of Governors). **BA:** 200 West Second Street, Winston-Salem, NC, 27101

KING, PETER THOMAS, **T:** U.S. Representative from New York, lawyer **I:** Government Administration/Government Relations/Government Services **DOB:** 04/05/1944 **PB:** NYC **PT:** Son of Peter E. King; Married Rosemary Wiedel; children: Sean, Erin. **ED:** JD, University Notre Dame Law School, 1968; BA in Hist., St. Francis College, Brooklyn, 1965 **CT:** Bar: New York 1968 **C:** Member, US Congress from 2nd New York District, 2013-; Member, Permanent Select Committee on Intelligence, Committee on Financial Services; Chairman, US House Homeland Security Committee, 2011-13; Chairman, US House Homeland Security Committee, 2005-07; Member, US Congress from 3rd New York District, 1993-2013; Comptroller, Nassau County, New York, 1981-93; Member, Town Council, Hempstead, New York, 1977-81; General counsel, New York Off-Track Betting Corp., 1977; Executive assistant to county executive, Nassau County, New York, 1974-76; Deputy attorney, Nassau County, New York, 1972-74; Private law practice, 1968-72 **CW:** Author: Terrible Beauty, 1999, Deliver Us From Evil, 2002, Vale of Tears, 2003 **AW:** Named Man of Year, FBI Emerald Society, Patriot of Year, Reserve Officers Association; recipient Friend of Labor award, Civil Service Employees Association, Guardian of Small Business award, National Federation Ind. Business, Spirit of Enterprise award, US C. of C., Interfaith Understanding award, Jewish Chatauqua Society of the Wantagh Suburban Temple, Distinguished Service award, Institute Pub. Affairs of the Orthodox Jewish Congregations of Am., Frederick Olmstead award, Labor Enforcement Alliance, 2003, Huey award, Vets. of Vietnam War, Cert. of Honor, Long Island Committee Soviet

Jewry, Cert. of Achievement, Excellence in Fin. Reporting, Governor Fin. Officers Association, 1985-91 **MEM:** Mem.: Nassau County Fire Fighters Emerald Society (hon.), Catholic War Vets. (Cert. of Achievement), Sons of Italy, Vets. Corps of 69th Infantry, AMVETS (life), American Legion, Ancient Order of Hibernians, Knights of Columbus (Citizen of Year) **PA:** Republican

KING, REGINA, **T:** Actress **I:** Media & Entertainment **PB:** Los Angeles **SC:** CA/USA **PT:** Thomas King; Gloria King **CW:** Actress: (TV series) 227, 1985-90, Leap of Faith, 2002, The Boondocks, 2005-14, 24, 2007, Southland (also director 1 episode, Off Duty), 2009-13 (National Association for the Advancement of Colored People Image award for Outstanding Directing in a Dramatic Series, 2013), The Leftovers, 2015-2017, American Crime, 2015-2017,(Emmy award for Outstanding Supporting Actress in a Limited Series or a Movie, 2015, 2016, National Association for the Advancement of Colored People Image award for Outstanding Supporting Actress in a Drama Series, 2016), Seven Seconds, 2018; (TV films) Where the Truth Lies, 1999, If These Walls Could Talk 2, 2000, Damaged Care, 2002, Living Proof, 2008, Divorce: A Love Story, 2013, The Gabby Douglas Story, 2014, Pariah, 2015, The Adventures of Hooligan Squad in World War II, 2016; (films) Boyz n the Hood, 1991, Poetic Justice, 1993, Higher Learning, 1995, Friday, 1995, A Thin Line Between Love and Hate, 1996, Jerry Maguire, 1996, Rituals, 1998, How Stella Got Her Groove Back, 1998, Enemy of the State, 1998, Mighty Joe Young, 1998, Down to Earth, 2001, Daddy Day Care, 2003, Legally Blonde 2: Red, White & Blonde, 2003, A Cinderella Story, 2004, Ray, 2004, Miss Congeniality 2: Armed and Fabulous, 2005, (voice) The Ant Bully, 2006, This Christmas, 2007, Our Family Wedding, 2010, (voice) Planes: Fire & Rescue, 2014, If Beale Street Could Talk, 2018; actress, prodr.: (films) Final Breakdown, 2002; dir.: (TV films) Let the Church Say Amen, 2013; director, executive producer (documentaries) Story of a Village, 2014

KING, ROBERT BRUCE, **T:** Federal Judge **I:** Government Administration/Government Relations/Government Services **DOB:** 01/29/1940 **PB:** White Sulphur Springs **SC:** West Virginia **ED:** JD, West Virginia College of Law, 1968; BA, West Virginia University, 1961 **CT:** Bar: US Tax Court 1991, US Claims Court 1985, US District Court (eastern district) Kentucky 1975, US Supreme Court 1974, US District Court (no. district) West Virginia 1972, US Court Appeals (4th cir.) 1970, US Court Appeals West Virginia 1968, US District Court (so. district) West Virginia 1968, West Virginia 1968 **C:** Judge, US Court Appeals (4th cir.), Richmond, Virginia, 1998-; Partner, King Allen Guthrie & McHugh, 1981-98; US Attorney, Southern District of West Virginia, Charleston, 1977-81; Partner, Spilman, Thomas, Battle and Klostermeyer, 1981; Partner, Spilman, Thomas, Battle and Klostermeyer, Charleston, 1976-77; Associate, Spilman, Thomas, Battle and Klostermeyer, Charleston, 1975; Assistant US attorney, Southern District of West Virginia, Charleston, 1970-74; Associate, Haynes and Ford, Lewisburg, West Virginia, 1969-70; Law clerk Chief Judge John A. Field, Junior, US District Court (so. district) West Virginia, Charleston, 1968-69; Research Assistant, State and Community Planning Office, Office of R&D, West Virginia University, Morgantown, West Virginia, 1966-68; Assistant Manager, Sam Snead All-Am. Golf Course, Sharpes, Florida, 1965 **CR:** Member 4th Cir. Judicial Council Visiting Committee College of Law of West Virginia University, 1997- Member Judicial Investigation Commission of West Virginia, 1990-94 **MIL:** Member US Air Force, 1961-64,

Member, West Virginia National Guard, 1957-59 **AW:** Scholar Patrick Duffy Koontz **MEM:** Fellow: Am. Bar Foundation, Am. College Trial Lawyers; mem.: American Bar Association, Am. Board Trial Advocates (West Virginia chapter president 1986-90), Judicial Conference of 4th Cir. Court Appeals, West Virginia Law School Association, West Virginia University Alumni Association, Greenbrier County Bar Association, Kanawha County Bar Association, West Virginia Bar Association, West Virginia Golf Association, US Golf Association, Order of the Coif, Phi Alpha Delta, Pi Sigma Alpha **BA:** 1100 E Main St #501, Richmond, VA, 23219

KING, STEPHEN EDWIN, **T:** Writer **I:** Writing and Editing **DOB:** 09/21/1947 **PB:** Portland **SC:** ME/USA **PT:** Donald King, Nellie Ruth (Pillsbury) King **ED:** BS, University of Maine, Orono, ME, 1970 **C:** Columnist, Entertainment Weekly, 2003-2010; Writer-in-Residence, University of Maine, 1978-1979; Teacher of English, Hampden Academy, Maine, 1971-1973 **CW:** Author: (Novels) Carrie, 1974, Salem's Lot, 1975, The Shining, 1977, The Stand, 1978, The Dead Zone, 1979, Firestarter, 1980, Cujo, 1981, The Dark Tower I: The Gunslinger, 1982, Christine, 1983, Pet Sematary, 1983, Cycle of the Werewolf, 1985, It, 1986, The Eyes of the Dragon, 1987, Misery, 1987, The Dark Tower II: The Drawing of the Three, 1987, The Tommyknockers, 1988, The Dark Half, 1989, The Stand, the Complete and Uncut Edition, 1990, Needful Things, 1990, The Dark Tower III: The Waste Lands, 1991, Gerald's Game, 1992, Dolores Claiborne, 1993, Insomnia, 1994, Rose Madder, 1995, Desperation, 1996, The Green Mile, 1996, The Dark Tower IV: Wizard & Glass, 1997, Bag of Bones, 1998, The Girl Who Loved Tom Gordon, 1999, Dreamcatcher, 2001, From a Buick 8, 2002, The Dark Tower V: Wolves of the Calla, 2003, The Dark Tower VI: Song of Susannah, 2004, The Dark Tower VII: The Dark Tower, 2004, The Colorado Kid, 2005, Cell, 2006, Lisey's Story, 2006, Duma Key, 2008, Under the Dome, 2009, Blockade Billy, 2010, 11/22/63, 2011, The Dark Tower: The Wind Through the Keyhole, 2012, Joyland, 2013, Doctor Sleep, 2013, Mr. Mercedes, 2014, Revival, 2014, Finders Keepers, 2015, The Bazaar of Bad Dreams, 2015, (As Richard Bachman) Rage, 1977, The Long Walk, 1979, Roadwork, 1981, The Running Man, 1982, Thinner, 1984, The Regulators, 1996, Blaze: A Posthumous Novel, 2007 (Non-Fiction Books) Danse Macabre, 1981, On Writing: A Memoir of the Craft, 2000, Guns, 2013, (Fiction/Non-Fiction Books) Secret Windows: Essays and Fiction on the Craft of Writing, 2000, (Short Story Collections) Night Shift, 1978, Different Seasons, 1982, Skeleton Crew, 1985, Four Past Midnight, 1990, Nightmares & Dreamscapes, 1993, Everything's Eventual: 14 Dark Tales, 2002, Just After Sunset, 2008, Full Dark, No Stars, 2010, (Original Screenplays) Creepshow, 1982, Cat's Eye, 1984, Silver Bullet, 1985, Maximum Overdrive, 1986, Golden Years, 1991, Sleepwalkers, 1992; Co-Author, (With Peter Straub) The Talisman, 1984, Black House, 2001, (With Stewart O'Nan) Faithful: Two Diehard Boston Red Sox Fans Chronicle the Historic 2004 Season, 2005; Creator, Writer, Executive Producer, (Films) Riding the Bullet, 2004, (TV Films) Desperation, 2006, (TV series) Golden Years, 1991, Kingdom Hospital, 2004, (TV Miniseries) The Stand, 1994, The Shining, 1997, Storm of the Century, 1999; Executive Producer, (TV Films) The Diary of Ellen Rimbauer, 2003; Actor, (Films) Knightriders, 1981, Creepshow, 1982, Maximum Overdrive, 1986, Creepshow II, 1988, Pet Sematary, 1989, Sleepwalkers, 1992, Thinner, 1996, Gotham Cafe, 2005, (TV Films) The Langoliers, 1995, Rose Red, 2002, (TV Appearances) Frasier, 2000, (Voice Actor) Diary of the Dead, 2008, (Books) Finders

Keepers, 2015, End of Watch, 2016, Sleeping Beauties, 2017, The Outsider, 2018 **AW:** The 100 Most Powerful Celebrities, Forbes.com, 2008, Lifetime Achievement Award, Canadian Literature Guild, 2007, Quill Award for Best Sports Book, Season, 2005, Horror Writers' Association, 2003, Distinguished Contribution to American Letters Medal, National Book Foundation, 2003, O. Henry Award, 1996, Golden Pen Award, Spokane Public Library, Washington, DC, 1986, Best Fiction Writer of the Year, Us Magazine, 1982, Hugo Award, World Science Fiction Convention, 1982, British Fantasy Award, 1982, Career Alumni Award, University of Maine, 1981, Six Bram Stoker Awards, Six Horror Guild Awards, Five Locus Awards, Three World Fantasy Awards **MEM:** Writer's Guild, Screen Writers of America, Screen Artists Guild, Author's Guild of America **PA:** Democrat **ADD:** c/o Arthur Greene, 101 Park Avenue, New York, NY, 10178

KING, STEVE, T: U.S. Representative from Iowa **I:** Government Administration/Government Relations/Government Services **DOB:** 05/28/1949 **PB:** Storm Lake **SC:** IA/USA **PT:** Marilyn Kelly, 1972 **MS:** Married **ED:** Student, Northwest Missouri State University, 1967-70 **C:** Member, US Congress from 4th Iowa District, 2013-; Member, Committee on Agriculture, Committee on the Judiciary, Committee on Small Business; Member, US Congress from 5th Iowa District, Washington, 2003-13; Member District 6, Iowa State Senate, Des Moines, 1997-2003 **CIV:** Member St. Martin's Catholic Church board directors Odebolt Community Housing. **MEM:** Member Iowa Cattleman's Association, Land Improvement Contractors America, US Chamber of Commerce, Odebolt Chamber of Commerce, SAC County Farm Bureau **PA:** Republican

KINGSLEY, BEN, T: Actor **I:** Media & Entertainment **DOB:** 12/31/1943 **PB:** Scarborough **PT:** Son of Rahimtulla Harji and Anna Lyna (Goodman) Bhanji; Married Angela Morrant, 1966 (div. 1972), children: Thomas, Jasmine,; Married Alison Sutcliffe, July 1, 1978 (div. February 1992), children, Edmund, Ferdinand,; Married Alexandra Christmann (div. 2005); Married Daniela Lavender, 2007 **ED:** MA (hon.), Salford University **C:** Associate artist, Royal Shakespeare Co., England, 1968 **CW:** Appeared in plays including Hamlet, 1975-76, Othello, 1985-86, Edmund Kean, 1981-83; actor: (films) Fear Is the Key, 1972, Gandhi, 1981 (Academy award for Best Actor, 1982), Betrayal, 1982, Turtle Diary, 1984, Sleeps Six, 1984, Harem, 1985, Maurice, 1987, Testimony, 1987, Pascali's Island, 1988, Without a Clue, 1988, Slipstream, 1989, (voice) Romeo-Juliet, 1990, The Children, 1990, O, Quinto Macacao, 1990, Una Vita Scellerata, 1991, L'Amore Necessario, 1991, Bugsy, 1991, (voice) Freddie as F.R.O.7, 1992, Sneakers, 1992, Dave, 1993, Innocent Moves, 1993, Searching for Bobby Fisher, 1993, Schindler's List, 1993, Death and the Maiden, 1994, Species, 1994, Twelfth Night: Or What You Will, 1996, The Assignment, 1997, Photographing Fairies, 1997, Parking Shots, 1998, Rules of Engagement, 1999, (voice) A Force More Powerful, 1999, The Confession, 1999, Sexy Beast, 2000, Spooky House, 2000, What Planet Are You From, 2000, (voice) Artificial Intelligence: A.I., 2001, The Triumph of Love, 2001, Tuck Everlasting, 2002, House of Sand and Fog, 2003, Thunderbirds, 2004, Suspect Zero, 2004, A Sound of Thunder, 2005, Mrs. Harris, 2005, Oliver Twist, 2005, BloodRayne, 2005, The Inquiry, 2006, Lucky Number Slevin, 2006, You Kill Me, 2007, The Last Legion, 2007, Transsiberian, 2008, War, Inc., 2008, The Love Guru, 2008, The Wackness, 2008, Elegy, 2008, Fifty Dead Men Walking, 2008, Shutter Island, 2010, Prince of Persia: The Sands of Time, 2010, Hugo, 2011,

(voice) Noah's Ark: The New Beginning, 2012, The Dictator, 2012, A Common Man, 2012, Iron Man 3, 2013, A Birder's Guide to Everything, 2013, Walking with the Enemy, 2013, Ender's Game, 2013, The Physician, 2013, Eliza Graves, 2014, (voice) The Boxtrolls, 2014, Learning to Drive, 2014, Robot Overlords, 2014, Exodus: Gods and Kings, 2014, Night at the Museum: Secret of the Tomb, 2014, Knight of Cups (voice), 2015, Life, 2015, Self/less, 2015, The Walk, 2015, The Jungle Book (voice), 2016, Collide, 2016, The Ottoman Lieutenant, 2017, War Machine, 2017, An Ordinary Man, 2017, Backstabbing for Beginners, 2017, Security, 2017, Nomis, 2018 (TV films) A Misfortune, 1973, Barbara of the House of Grebe, 1973, Antony and Cleopatra, 1974, The Brotherhood, 1975, An Impeccable Elopement, 1975, Remember Me, 1975, Beata Beatrix, 1975, The Artisan, 1975, Thank You Comrades, 1978, Kean, 1982, The Merry Wives of Windsor, 1982, Camille, 1984, Stanley's Visoipn, 1986, Murderers Among Us: The Simon Weisenthal Story, 1988 (Distinguished Service award 1989), Leini: The Train, 1990, The War That Never Ends, 1991, Joseph, 1995, Moses, 1996, Weapons of Mass Distraction, 1997, Crime and Punishment, 1998, The Tale of Sweeny Todd, 1998, Alice in Wonderland, 1999, Mrs. Harris, 2005, (TV series) Coronation Street, 1966-67, Oxbridge Blues, 1986, Crime and Punishment, 1998, (TV miniseries) Dickens of London, 1976, The Secret of the Sahara, 1987, Anne Frank: The Whole Story, 2001, Tut, 2015, (TV appearances) Orlamdo, 1966, Skin Deep, 1966, The Rhyme, But No Reason, 1966, The Adventurer, 1973, Wessex Tales, 1973, Play for Today, 1973, Silas Marner, 1987, The Sopranos, 2006, Garfunkel and Oates, 2014, Tut, 2015(Outstanding Performance by a Male Actor in a Miniseries or TV Movie), Watership, 2017. **AW:** Recipient Padma Shri award Government of India, 1984, Grammy award for Best Spoken Word or Nonmusical Recording for "The Words of Ghandi; " named Best Actor and Best Newcomer Brit. Academy Film and TV Arts, 1982, Best Actor Standard Film Awards, London, 1983; knighted by Queen Elizabeth II, 2001. **MEM:** Mem.: Academy Motion Picture Arts & Scis.(Evening Standard Film award/Best Actor for Schindler's List 1995, Golden Camera Berlin award), Brit. Academy Film & TV Arts

KINNEY, JEFFREY PATRICK, T: Writer, Game Designer, Cartoonist **I:** Writing and Editing **ED:** Attended, University of Maryland, College Park **C:** Writer 2007-; Creator, Poptropica.com,; Designer/developer, online games, Boston **CW:** Author: (children's book series) Diary of a Wimpy Kid, 2007 (#1 New York Times bestseller); Diary of a Wimpy Kid: Rodrick Rules, 2008, Diary of a Wimpy Kid Do-It-Yourself Book, 2008, Diary of a Wimpy Kid: The Last Straw, 2009, Diary of a Wimpy Kid: Dog Days, 2009, The Wimpy Kid Movie Diary, 2010, Diary of a Wimpy Kid: The Ugly Truth, 2010, Diary of a Wimpy Kid: Cabin Fever, 2011, Diary of a Wimpy Kid: The Third Wheel, 2012, Diary of a Wimpy Kid: Hard Luck, 2013, Diary of a Wimpy Kid: The Long Haul, 2014, Diary of a Wimpy Kid: Old School, 2015, (Books) Diary of a Wimpy Kid: Double Down, 2016, Diary of a Wimpy Kid: The Getaway, 2017 **AW:** Named one of The World's Most Influential People, TIME magazine, 2009

KINZINGER, ADAM, T: U.S. Representative from Illinois **I:** Government Administration/Government Relations/Government Services **DOB:** 02/27/1978 **PB:** Kankakee **SC:** IL/USA **ED:** BA, Illinois State University, Normal, 2000 **C:** Member, U.S. House Energy & Commerce Committee, Washington, 2011-; Member, Committee on Foreign Affairs;

Member, U.S. Congress from 16th Illinois District, 2013-; Captain, pilot, U.S. Air Force, 2005-; Member, U.S. Congress from 11th Illinois District, Washington, 2011-13; Served with Air Force Special Operations, Air combat Command, Air Mobility Command, Air National Guard, U.S. Air Force,; 2d lieutenant, U.S. Air Force, 2003 **CR:** Board member McLean County, Illinois **AW:** Decorated Valley Forge Cross, Airman's medal; named Hero of Year, Southeast Wisconsin American Red Cross; named one of The Politics 40 Under 40, TIME Magazine, 2010 **MEM:** Mem.: National Rifle Association, Illinois Rifles Association **PA:** Republican

KIRK, JIM, T: Newspaper Editor **I:** Writing and Editing **ED:** Bachelor in Mass Communications, Illinois State University, Normal, IL **C:** Editor, Los Angeles Times, 2017-Present; Senior Vice President, Editor-In-Chief, Chicago Sun-Times Media, 2012—2017; Chief, Editorial Operations, Crain's Chicago Business, 2011—2012; Managing Editor, Chicago News Cooperative, 2010—2011; U.S. Government Team Leader, Bloomberg News, Washington, DC, 2009—2010; Associate Managing Editor, Business News, Chicago Tribune, 2005—2009; Marketing & Advertising Reporter, Columnist, Business Editor, Chicago Tribune, 1997—2005; Midwest Managing Editor, Adweek; Business Reporter, Columnist, Chicago Sun-Times **BA:** 202 W 1st Street, Los Angeles, CA, 90012

KIRK, MARK STEVEN, T: U.S. Senator from Illinois **I:** Government Administration/Government Relations/Government Services **DOB:** 09/15/1959 **PB:** Champaign **PT:** Son of Francis Gabriel and Judith Ann (Brady) Kirk; **ED:** JD, Georgetown University, 1992; MS, London School of Economics, 1982; BA in History, Cornell University, 1981 **CT:** Bar: Illinois 1992, D.C. 1993. **C:** US Senator from Illinois, Washington, 2010-2017; Member, US Senate Special Committee on Aging, Washington, 2010-; Member, US Senate Banking, Housing & Urban Affairs, Washington, 2010-; Member, US Senate Veterans Affairs Committee, Washington, 2010-; Member, US Senate Appropriations Committee, Washington, 2010-; Member, US Senate Armed Services Committee, Washington, 2010-; US Senator from Illinois, Washington, 2010-; Member, US Congress from 10th Illinois District, Washington, 2001-10; Counsel, US House International Relations Committee, Washington, 1995-99; Attorney, Baker & McKenzie LLP, Washington, 1993-95; Special assistant to assistant secretary for Inter-American affairs, US Department State, Washington, 1991-93; Officer, The World Bank, Washington, 1990; Chief of staff to Rep. John Porter, US House of Representatives, Washington, 1984-90; Parliamentary aide, Julian Critchley, London, 1982-83 **CR:** Board directors Population Resource Center, Princeton, New Jersey. **CIV:** Organizer Bush/Quayle Campaign, Northern Illinois, 1988, Dole for President, 1988, various states campaigner Porter for Congress, Northern Illinois, 1984-90. Lieutenant US Naval Reserve, 1989-. **CW:** Contributor articles to various newspapers. **AW:** Kellogg Fellow, Chicago, 1980, Radm James Fellow, Washington, 1984; recipient Council of Jewish Federation award Washington, 1988, Commander's Cross of the Order of Merit of the Republic of Poland, 2012 **MEM:** Member Navy League, Naval Reserve Association, New Trier Rep. Organization **H:** Backpacking, skydiving **PA:** Republican **BA:** Office of Mark Kirk, 387 RUSSELL SENATE OFFICE BUILDING, Washington, DC, 20510

KISSINGER, HENRY ALFRED, T: International Consulting Company Executive, Former U.S. Secretary of State **I:** Government Administration/Government Relations/Government Services **DOB:** 05/27/1923 **PB:** Fuerth **SC:** Germany **PT:** Son of

Louis and Paula (Stern) Kissinger; **ED:** PhD, Harvard University, 1954; MA, Harvard University, 1952; AB in Political Sci. summa cum laude, Harvard University, 1950 **C:** Founder, chairman, Kissinger Associates, Inc., New York City, 1982-; Chancellor, College William & Mary, 2001-05; Secretary, US Department State, Washington, 1973-77; Assistant to President for national security affairs, National Security Council, Washington, 1968-75; Associate director Center International Affairs, Harvard University, 1957-60; Director defense studies program, Harvard University, 1958-69; Faculty member Department Government & Center International Affairs, Harvard University, 1954-69; Executive director, Harvard International Seminar, 1951-69 **CR:** Hon. counselor Asia Society Policy Institute (ASPI), 2014- board directors Freeport-McMoRan Copper & Gold Inc., 1995-2001, American Express Co., 1986-96 member Commission on the Integrated Long-Term Strategy of the National Security Council & Defense Department, 1986-88, President's Foreign Intelligence Advisory Board, 1984-90 chairman National Bipartisan Commission on Central America, 1983-84 director special studies project Rockefeller Brothers Fund, 1956-58 study director nuclear weapons & foreign policy Council Foreign Relations, 1955-56 director Psychological Strategy Board, 1952 consultant US Department State, 1965-68, Rand Corp., 1961-68, US Arms Control & Disarmament Agency, 1961-68, National Security Council, 1961-62, Weapons Systems Evaluation Group, US Department Defense, 1959-60, Operations Coordinating Board, 1955, Operations Research Office, 1950-51 **CIV:** Board trustees, Institute International Education, 1999- **MIL:** Captain Military Intelligence Reserve, 1946-49, served with Counter Intelligence Corps US Army, 1943-46 **CW:** Author: A World Restored: Metternich, Castlereagh and the Problems of Peace, 1812-22, 1957, Nuclear Weapons and Foreign Policy, 1957, The Necessity for Choice: Prospects of American Foreign Policy, 1961, The Troubled Partnership: A Re-Appraisal of the Atlantic Alliance, 1965, American Foreign Policy: Three Essays, 1969, White House Years, 1979, For the Record: Selected Statements, 1981, Years of Upheaval, 1982, Observations: Selected Speeches and Essays 1982-1984, 1985, Diplomacy, 1994, Years of Renewal, 1999, Does America Need a Foreign Policy?: Toward a Diplomacy for the 21st Century, 2001, Vietnam: A Personal History of America's Involvement in and Extrication from the Vietnam War, 2002, Crisis: The Anatomy of Two Major Foreign Policy Crises: Based on the Record of Henry Kissinger's Hitherto Secret Telephone Conversations, 2003, On China, 2011, World Order, 2014; co-author: Kissinger Transcripts: The Top Secret Talks With Beijing and Moscow, 1999; editor: Problems of National Strategy: A Book of Readings, 1965; contributor articles to professional journals **AW:** Decorated Bronze star; co-recipient Nobel Peace prize, Norwegian Nobel Committee, 1973; recipient Henry A. Grunwald award for Public Service, Lighthouse International, 2013, Israel's President's medal, 2012, Hopkins-Nanjing award, 2007, Woodrow Wilson award for Public Service, Smithsonian Institution, 2006, Medal of Liberty, 1986, Presidential Medal of Freedom, The White House, 1977, Hope award for International Understanding, 1973, Dwight D. Eisenhower Distinguished Service medal, VFW, 1973, Theodore Roosevelt award, International Platform Association, 1973, Distinguished Public Service award, American Institute Public Service, 1973, Woodrow Wilson prize for Best Book in Fields of Government, Politics & International Affairs, 1958 **MEM:** Mem.: American Academy Arts & Sciences, Council Foreign Relations, American Political Sci. Association, Century Club, New York City Book Club, Metropolitan Club (Washington), Phi Beta Kappa **PA:** Republican

KLEIN, CALVIN RICHARD, T: Fashion Designer **I:** Apparel & Fashion **DOB:** 11/19/1942 **PB:** Bronx **SC:** NY/USA **PT:** Leo Klein, Flore (Stern) Klein **ED:** Honorary Doctorate, Fashion Institute of Technology, New York, NY, 2003; Student, Fashion Institute of Technology, New York, NY **C:** Designer, Calvin Klein (a Phillips-Van Heusen Company), New York, NY, 2003-Present; Founder, President, Designer, Calvin Klein Ltd., New York, NY, 1968-2003 **CR:** Designer, Calvin Klein Watches and Jewelry, CK One Lifestyle, Calvin Klein Underwear, Calvin Klein Golf, The Khaki Collection, Calvin Klein Home, Calvin Klein Jeans, Calvin Klein Sport, CK Calvin Klein, Calvin Klein Collection **AW:** Lifetime Achievement Award, Council on Fashion Designers of America, 2001, Womenswear/Menswear Designer of the Year, Council on Fashion Designers of America, 1993, Woolmark Award for Career Achievement, 1987, Outstanding American Talent in Women's Fashion Design, 1986, 1982-1983, Hall of Fame Award, Coty American Fashion Critics', 1975, America's 25 Most Influential People, TIME Magazine **MEM:** Council on Fashion Designers of America **BA:** Calvin Klein Europe, Via Montenapoleone 29, Milan, Zimbabwe, 20121

KLEIN, NAOMI, T: Journalist **I:** Media & Entertainment **PB:** Montreal **SC:** QC, Canada **PT:** Michael Klein; Bonnie Sherr Klein **ED:** Attended, University Toronto **C:** International syndicated columnist; Editor, This Magazine; Intern, Toronto Globe & Mail **CW:** Author: (books) No Logo: Taking Aim at the Brand Bullies, 2000 (Can. National Business Book award, 2001, Prix Médiations, 2001), Fences & Windows: Dispatches from the Front Lines of the Globalization Debate, 2002, The Shock Doctrine: The Rise of Disaster Capitalism, 2007 (New York Times bestseller, Warwick prize for Writing, England, 2009); syndicated columnist Toronto Star, The Nation, New York Times, In These Times, Globe & Mail, This Magazine, The Guardian; co-dir.(with Avi Lewis): (documentaries) The Take, 2004,(Book) This Changes Everything: Capitalism vs. The Climate, 2014, No is Not Enough: Resisting Trump's Shock Politics and Winning the World We Need, 2017 (Documentary) The Shock Doctrine, 2009, This Changes, Catastroika, 2012, Everything, 2015 **AW:** Named one of The 100 Agents of Change, Rolling Stone Magazine, 2009; Freda Kirchway Fellow, Nation Institute, 2005, Miliband Fellow, London School Economics, 2002

KLINE, KEVIN DELANEY, T: Actor **I:** Media & Entertainment **DOB:** 10/24/1947 **PB:** St. Louis **SC:** MO/USA **PT:** Son of Robert Joseph and Peggy (Kirk) K.; **MS:** Married **SPN:** Phoebe Cates, March 5, 1989; **CH:** Owen, Greta **ED:** Adv. program diploma, Juilliard School Drama Division, New York City, 1972; BA in Speech and Theatre, Ind. University **C:** Founding member, The Acting Co., New York City, 1972-76 **CR:** Appointed artistic associate New York Shakespeare Festival, 1993. **CW:** Actor: (Broadway) On the Twentieth Century, 1978 (Tony award for Best Performance by a Featured Actor in a Musical, 1978), Loose Ends, 1979, Pirates of Penzance, 1980 (Tony award for Best Leading Actor in a Musical, Obie award), Arms and the Man, 1985, The Play What I Wrote, 2003, Cyrano de Bergerac, 2007; (off-Broadway) Richard III, 1983, Henry V, 1984, Hamlet, 1986 (Obie award), Much Ado About Nothing, 1988, Measure for Measure, 1993, The Seagull, 2001, Mother Courage, 2006, King Lear, 2007; actor, dir.: (off-Broadway) Hamlet, 1990; actor: (Broadway) Ivanov, 1997, Henry IV, Parts I & II, 2003 (Drama Desk award for Best Actor, 2004); (films) Sophie's Choice, 1982, Pirates of Penzance, 1983, The Big

Chill, 1983, Silverado, 1985, Violets are Blue, 1985, Cry Freedom, 1987, A Fish Called Wanda, 1988 (Academy award for Best Supporting Actor, 1989), The January Man, 1989, I Love You To Death, 1989, Soapdish, 1991, Grand Canyon, 1991, Consenting Adults, 1991, Chaplin, 1992, Dave, 1993, George Balanchine's The Nutcracker (voice), 1993, Princess Caraboo, 1994, French Kiss, 1995, The Hunchback of Notre Dame (voice), 1996, Fierce Creatures, 1997, In & Out, 1997, The Ice Storm, 1997, A Midsummer Night's Dream, 1999, Wild Wild West, 1999, The Road to El Dorado (voice), 2000, The Anniversary Party, 2001, Life as a House, 2001, The Emperor's Club, 2002, De-lovely, 2004, The Pink Panther, 2006, A Prairie Home Companion, 2006, Trade, 2007, Definitely, Maybe, 2008, The Tale of Despereaux (voice), 2008, The Conspirator, 2010, No Strings Attached, 2011, Darling Companion, 2012, The Last of Robin Hood, 2013, Last Vegas, 2013, My Old Lady, 2014, Ricki and the Flash, 2015, Dean, 2016, Beauty and the Beast, 2017; (TV films) As You Like It, 2006 (Outstanding Performance by a Male Actor in a TV Movie or Miniseries, Screen Actors Guild, 2008); (TV series) Bob's Burgers (voice), 2011-14; dir.: (TV film) Hamlet, 1990. **AW:** Kevin Kline awards to recognize outstanding achievement in professional theatre in greater St. Louis, Missouri area, named in his honor, 2006; recipient Lifetime Achievement award Lucille Lortel Awards, 2007.

KLOBUCHAR, AMY JEAN, T: U.S. Senator from Minnesota **I:** Government Administration/Government Relations/Government Services **DOB:** 05/25/1960 **PB:** Plymouth **PT:** Daughter of Jim and Rose Katherine (Heuberger) Klobuchar; **ED:** JD, University Chicago Law School, 1985; BA, Yale University, 1982 **C:** Ranking Member, Senate Rules Committee, 2017,; US Senator from Minnesota, 2007-; Attorney, Hennepin County, 1999-2007; Member, Minnesota Supreme Court Jury Task Force,; Partner, Gray Plant Mooty LLP, 1993-98; Associate partner, Dorsey & Whitney LLP, 1985-93 **AW:** Named Super Lawyer, Minnesota Law & Politics; named one of 10 Attorneys of Year, Minnesota Lawyer, 2001; recipient Achievement and Leadership award, Ann Bancroft, 2004, Leadership award, MADD, 2001, Alumni of Year award, Wayzata High School, 1999, 40 Under 40 award, CityBus., 1996 **MEM:** Mem.: Minnesota County Attorneys Association (president 2002-03) **H:** Cross-country bicycling **PA:** Democrat **BA:** Office of Amy Klobuchar, 302 Hart Senate Office Building, Washington, DC, 20510

KLOSS, KARLIE, T: Model **I:** Media & Entertainment **PB:** Chicago **SC:** IL/USA **C:** IMG Models, IMG Worldwide Inc. (2012-Present); Victoria Secret Angel (2011-2014); NEXT Model Management (2008-2012) **AW:** Named One of TIME's 100 Most Influential People, TIME Magazine (2016)

KLOTMAN, MARY E., T: Dean of the Duke School of Medicine **I:** Education/Educational Services **ED:** Fellow in Infectious Diseases, Medicine, Duke University, 1983 - 1985; Resident, Medicine, Duke University, 1980 - 1983; M.D., Duke University, 1980 **C:** Dean , Duke School of Medicine, 2017- **AW:** Duke University School of Medicine Distinguished Alumni Award, 2015 **MEM:** Academy of Medicine, 2014

KLUBER, COREY, T: Professional Baseball Player **I:** Athletics **PB:** Birmingham **SC:** AL/USA **C:** Pitcher, Cleveland Indians, 2011-Present **AW:** AL Cy Young Award, 2014, 2017, AL Wins Leader, 2014, 2017, All-Star, 2016-2017, AL ERA leader, 2017

KNIGHT, STEVE, T: U.S. Representative from California **I:** Government Administration/Government Relations/Government Services **PB:** Majove **ED:** High School, Palmdale High School **C:** Member, US Congress from California's 25th District.; Member District 36, California State Assembly, 2008-2015; Member, Palmdale City Council, California, 2005-; Member judiciary committee, natural resources committee, housing and community devel. committee, select committee on aerospace, select committee on alcohol and drug abuse, California State Assembly,; Vice chair local government committee, California State Assembly,; Officer, LAPD, California, **BA:** Longworth House Office Building, 41319 12th St W Ste 105, Washington, DC, 20515

KNOLL, ANDREW HERBERT, T: Professor of Earth and Planetary Sciences **I:** Education/Educational Services **DOB:** 04/23/1951 **PB:** West Reading **SC:** PA/USA **PT:** Son of Robert Samuel and Anna Augusta (Meyer) K. **MS:** Married **SPN:** Marsha Craig, June 22, 1974; **CH:** Kirsten C., Robert A. **ED:** DSc (hon.), University of Southern Denmark, 2014; DSc (hon.), The University of Chicago, 2014; DSc (hon.), Lehigh University, 1998; PhD (hon.), Uppsala University, Sweden, 1996; PhD, Harvard University, 1977; MA, Harvard University, 1974; BA with highest honors, Lehigh University, 1973 **C:** Fisher Professor Natural History Department of Organismic and Evolutionary Biology, Harvard University, Cambridge, Massachusetts, 2000-; Professor Earth and Planetary Sci., Harvard University, Cambridge, Massachusetts, 1985-; Curator Botanical Museum, Harvard University, Cambridge, Massachusetts, 1985-; Associate Dean Faculty Arts and Scis., Harvard University, Cambridge, Massachusetts, 2000-03; Chairman Department of Organismic and Evolutionary Biology, Harvard University, Cambridge, Massachusetts, 2004-05; Chairman Department Organismic and Evolutionary Biology, Harvard University, Cambridge, Massachusetts, 1992-98; Professor Biology, Harvard University, Cambridge, Massachusetts, 1985-2000; Associate Professor, Harvard University, Cambridge, Massachusetts, 1982-85; Assistant Professor Geology, Oberlin College, Ohio, 1977-82 **CR:** Member Committee on Planetary Biology U.S. Space Sci. Board, 1982-88, National Research Council Board on Earth Scis., 1987-88, 92-95, Space Studies Board, 1989-90, 97-2000 Crosby Visiting Lecturer Massachusetts Institute of Technology, 1999 Member Sci. Team NASA MER 2003 Mars Mission **CIV:** Board of Directors U.S. National Museum National Hist., 1993-97. **CW:** Associate Editor: Paleobiology, 1980-92, Precambrian Research, 1985?2012, Trends in Ecology and Evolution, 1987-92, Rev. of Palaeobotany and Palynology, 1987-2012, Am. Journal Sci., 1990-2004, Geology, 1992-98, Palaios, 1996-2002, Palaeography Palacoclimatology Palaeocology, 1997-2012, International Journal Plant Scis., 1998?; Mitteilungen aus dem Museum fer Naturkunde Geowissenschaftliche Reihe (Humboldt Museum), Berlin, 1999-, Proceedings of the National Academy Scis., 2010-2013, Acta Geologica Sinica 2013-; Author, Co-author: (book) Life on a Young Planet, 2003, Evolution of Primary Producers in the Sea, 2007, Fundamentals of Geobiology, 2012, Biology: How Life Works, 2013; Contributor More Than 350 Articles to Professional Publications **AW:** Named one of Time/CNN America's Best Scientists, 2002; Recipient Mary Clark Thompson Medal, National Academy Scis., 2012, Palaeontology International Award, Dinopolis Foundation, Spain, 2009, Wollaston Medal, Geological Society London, 2007, Medal, Paleontological Society, 2005, Bownocker Medal, The Ohio State University, 2005, Moore Medal, Society Sedimentary Geology, 2005, Chang Prize in Paleon-

tology, Am. Museum Natural History, 2001, Walcott Medal, National Academy Scis., 1987; Fellow, Guggenheim, 1987, Geological Society Am., Linnean Society, London, Am. Academy Arts and Scis., 1987; Foreign Fellow, National Academy Scis., India, 2013, Visiting fellow, Gonville and Caius College, Cambridge, England, 1991-92, Oparin Medal, 2014, Foreign Member, Royal Society, 2015 **MEM:** Fellow: American Association for the Advancement of Science, European Union Geoscis. (hon.), Am. Academy Microbiology; member NAS(Walcott Medal, 1987, Mary Clark Thompson Medal, 2012), Botanical Society Am., Am. Philosophical Society, Paleontol. Society (Schuchert Award 1987, Medal, 2005), Am. Academy Microbiology, US National Academy Scis., Am. Philosophical Society, Phi Beta Kappa (Sci. Book Award, 2003), Royal Society London (Foreign Member, 2015). **H:** Travel, Reading, Cooking, Choral Music

KNOPFLER, DAVID, T: Singer-Songwriter and Guitarist **I:** Media & Entertainment **PB:** Glasgow **SC:** Scotland **MS:** Married **SPN:** Leslie Stroz **CW:** Album with Dire Straits, "Dire Straits" (1978), "Communique" (1979), "Making Movies" (1980), "Money for Nothing" (1988), "Live at the BBC" (1995), "Sultans of Swing: The Very Best of Dire Straits" (1998), "Private Investigations: The Best of Dire Straits" (2005); Solo Albums, "Release" (1983), "Behind the Lines" (1985), "Cut the Wire" (1986), "Lips Against the Steel" (1988), "Lifelines" (1991), "The Giver" (1993), "Small Mercies" (1995), "Wishbones" (2001), "Ship of Dreams" (2004), "Songs for the Siren" (2006), "Anthology: 1983-2008" (2009), "Acoustic" (2011), "Made in Germany" (2013), "Grace" (2015), "Anthology Vol. 2 & 3" (2016) **AW:** Inductee, Rock & Roll Hall of Fame (2018)

KNOPFLER, MARK, T: Singer-Songwriter and Guitarist **I:** Media & Entertainment **DOB:** 08/12/1949 **PB:** Glasgow **SC:** Scotland **ED:** Diploma in English Lit., University of Leeds, England, 1973 **C:** Founder, Lead Guitarist, Vocalist, Composer Rock Group, Dire Straits, 1977-96; Lecturer, Loughton College, England, 1973-77; Rock Music Critic, Reporter, Yorkshire (England) Evening Post, 1968-70 **CW:** Albums: (with Dire Straits) Dire Straits, 1978, Communiqu?, 1979, Making Movies, 1980, Love Over Gold, 1982, Twisting By the Pool, 1983, Alchemy, 1984, Brothers in Arms, 1986 (Best Group Vocal Rock Performance, Grammy Awards, 1986, Best Short Form Music Video, 1987), Money for Nothing, 1988, On Every Street, 1991, On the Night, 1993, Live at the BBC, 1995, Sultans of Swing: The Very Best of Dire Straits, 1998, Brothers in Arms 20th Ann. Educated (Grammy award for Best Surround Sound Album, 2005), Private Investigations, 2005, (with Bob Dylan) Slow Train Coming, Infidels, 1983, Down in the Groove, 1988 (with Steely Dan) Gaucho, 1980, Citizen Steely Dan, 1993, Showbiz Kids, 2000, (with Van Morrison) Beautiful Vision, 1982, (with Chet Adkins) Stay Tuned, 1985 (Best Country Instrumental Performance, Grammy Awards, 1986), Sails, 1987, C.G.P., 1988, Neck and Neck, 1990 (Best Country Vocal Collaboration & Best Country Instrumental Performance, Grammy Awards, 1991), Pickin' the Hits, 1997, Chet Picks on the Grammys, 2002, Essential Chet Atkins, 2004, 2007, (solo albums) Screenplaying, 1993, Golden Heart, 1996, Night in London, 1996, Metroland, 1999, Sailing to Philadelphia, 2000, Ragpicker's Dream, 2002, Shot at Glory, 2002, Why Aye Man, 2002, Shangri-La, 2004, One Take Radio Sessions, 2005, All the Roadrunning, 2006, Real Live Roadrunning, 2006, Kill to Get Crimson, 2007, Get Lucky,2009, Privateering,2012, Tracker, 2015; composer (films) Local Hero, 1983, Cal, 1984, Comfort and Joy, 1985, The Princess Bride, 1987, Last Exit to Brooklyn, 1989, Wag the Dog, 1997, Hooves of

Fire, 1999, A Shot at Glory, 2000; producer (film soundtracks) Officer and a Gentleman, 1982, Color of Money, 1986, Twister, 1996, Sult, 1997, 200 Cigarettes, 1999, America's Sweethearts, 2001, Bandits, 2001, North Country, 2005. **AW:** Named One of 100 Greatest Guitarists of All Time, Rolling Stone; Recipient 6 Grammy Awards, Order of the Brit. Empire, 1999, Rock and Roll Hall of Fame, 2018

KNOWLES, BEYONCÉ GISELLE, T: Singer, Actress **I:** Media & Entertainment **DOB:** 09/04/1981 **PB:** Houston **SC:** TX/USA **PT:** Mathew Knowles, Celestine "Tina" (Beyincé) Knowles **MS:** Married **SPN:** Shawn Corey Carter, 4/4/2008 **CH:** Blue Ivy, Rumi, Sir **ED:** Student, Alief Elsik High School, Houston, TX; Student, High School for the Performing and Visual Arts, Houston, TX **C:** Solo Artist, 2003-Present; Singer, Destiny's Child, 1997-2005 **CR:** Co-Owner, Tidal, 2015-Present; Co-Launched, (With Tina Knowles) Deréon By Beyoncé, C&A Clothing Stores, 2010, Sasha Fierce for Deréon, 2009, House of Dereon Fashion Line, 2005; Launched, (Fragrances) Beyoncé Heat, 2010, Emporio Armani Diamonds, 2007, True Star Gold, 2005, Tommy Hilfiger's True Star Fragrance, 2004; Spokesperson, L'Oreal, Pepsi, Nintendo, Vizio **CW:** Singer, (With Destiny's Child) (Albums) Destiny's Child, 1998, The Writing's on the Wall, 1999, Survivor, 2001, Eight Days of Christmas, 2001, Destiny Fulfilled, 2004, #1's, 2005, (Songs) Say My Name, 2000, (Solo) Dangerously in Love, 2003, Live at Wembley, 2004, B'Day, 2006, I Am... Sasha Fierce, 2008, 4, 2011, Beyoncé, 2013, Lemonade, 2016, (Songs) Dangerously in Love 2, 2003, (Featuring Jay-Z) Crazy in Love, 2003, (With Luther Vandross) The Closer I Get to You, 2004, (With Stevie Wonder) So Amazing, 2005, Irreplaceable, 2006, Single Ladies (Put a Ring on It), 2008, Halo, 2009, (With Lady Gaga) Telephone, 2010, Love on Top, 2011, (Featuring Jay-Z) Drunk in Love, 2013, 7/11, 2014, Formation, 2016, Hold Up, 2016, Lemonade, 2016; Actress, (Films) Austin Powers in Goldmember, 2002, The Fighting Temptations, 2003, The Pink Panther, 2006, Dreamgirls, 2006, Cadillac Records, 2008, Obsessed, 2009, (Voice Actress) Epic, 2013, The Lion King; Executive Producer, Director, (Documentaries) Life is But a Dream, 2013; Appearance, Cover Model, Sports Illustrated Swimsuit Issue, 2007 **AW:** Video of the Year, Best Direction, Best Cinematography, Best Editing, MTV Video Music Awards, Formation, 2016, Best Female Video, MTV Video Music Awards, Hold Up, 2016, Breakthrough Long Form Video, MTV Video Music Awards, Lemonade, 2016, Fashion Icon Award, Council on Fashion Designers of America, 2016, Best R&B Performance, Best R&B Song, Grammy Awards, Drunk in Love, 2015, Best Editing, MTV Video Music Awards, 7/11, 2015, Michael Jackson Video Vanguard Award, MTV Video Music Awards, 2014, Outstanding Female Artist, National Association for the Advancement of Colored People Image Awards, Favorite Soul/R&B Album, American Music Awards, Beyoncé, 2014, The 100 Most Influential People in the World, TIME Magazine, 2013-2014, The 100 Most Powerful Women in Entertainment, Hollywood Reporter, 2013, Best Traditional R&B Performance, Grammy Awards, Love on Top, 2013, World's Most Beautiful Woman!, People Magazine, 2012, Video Director of the Year, (With Alan Ferguson) Black Entertainment TV (BET) Awards, 2012, BBC Radio 4's Woman's Hour Power List, 2016, Issue of Essence Magazine, 2012, Top R&B Album, Billboard Music Awards, 4, 2012, New York Association of Black Journalists Writing Award for a Story Titled Eat, Play, Love, 2011, Millennium Award, Billboard Music Awards, 2011, The 100 Most Powerful Women, Forbes Magazine, 2010-2014, Choice Music: R&B Artist, Teen Choice Awards, 2010, Best Female R&B Vocal Performance, Best R&B Song, Song of the Year, Grammy Awards, Single Ladies (Put a Ring on It), 2010, Best Female Pop Vocal Performance, Grammy Awards, Halo, 2010, Best Collaboration, MTV Video Music Awards, Telephone, 2010, Best Contemporary R&B Album, Grammy Awards, I Am... Sasha Fierce, 2010, Outstanding Female Artist, National Association for the Advancement of Colored People Image Awards, 2009, 2015, Favorite Female Soul/R&B Artist, American Music Awards, 2009, 2011-2012, 2014, Nominee, Choice Female Hottie, Teen Choice Awards, 2009, Album of the Year, Soul Train Music Awards, I Am... Sasha Fierce, 2009, Best Female R&B/Soul Artist, Soul Train Music Awards, 2009, Song of the Year, Soul Train Music Awards, Best R&B Song, Teen Choice Awards, Best Choreography, Video of the Year, MTV Video Music Awards, Video of the Year, BET Awards, Single Ladies (Put A Ring On It), 2009, The 100 Most Powerful Celebrities, 2008-2012, Award for Outstanding Contribution to the Arts, World Music Awards, 2008, The 50 Most Powerful Women in New York City, New York Post, 2007-2008, International Artist Award, American Music Awards, 2007, Video of the Year, BET Awards, Best Female R&B/Soul Single, Soul Train Music Awards, Irreplaceable, 2007, Best Contemporary R&B Album, Grammy Awards, B'Day, 2007, Best Female R&B Artist, 2006-2008, 2012, Female R&B/Hip-Hop Artist of the Year, Billboard Music Awards, 2006, Best R&B Performance By a Duo or Group With Vocals, Grammy Awards, So Amazing, 2006, Favorite Female Performer, People Choice Awards, 2004, 2008, Sammy Davis Junior Award for Entertainer of the Year, Soul Train Music Awards, 2004, Best International Female Solo Artist, British Phonographic Industry (BRIT) Awards, 2004, Entertainer of the Year, 2004, Best Collaboration, BET Awards, Best R&B Song, Best Rap/Sung Collaboration, Grammy Awards, Crazy in Love, 2004, Best R&B Performance By a Duo or Group With Vocals, Grammy Awards, The Closer I Get to You, 2004, The 50 Most Influential African-Americans, Ebony Magazine, 2004, Best Female R&B Vocal Performance, Grammy Awards, Dangerously in Love 2, 2004, Best Contemporary R&B Album, Grammy Awards, Best Female R&B/Soul Album, Soul Train Music Awards, Dangerously in Love, 2004, Best Female Video, Best R&B Video, MTV Video Music Awards, Crazy in Love, 2003, Best R&B Performance By a Duo or Group With Vocals (For Title Track), Grammy Awards, Survivor, 2002, Best R&B Song, Best R&B Performance By a Duo or Group With Vocals, Grammy Awards, Say My Name, 2001 **BA:** Floor 24, 1412 Broadway, New York, NY, 10018-9235

KNOX, CHUCK, T: Former Professional Football Coach **I:** Other **DOB:** 04/27/1932 **PB:** Sewickley **PT:** Son of Charles McMeehan and Helen (Keith) K.; Married Shirley Ann Rhine, August 2, 1952; children: Christeen, Kathy, Colleen, Chuck **ED:** Postgrad., Pennsylvania State University, 1955; BA, Juniata College, 1954 **C:** Head football coach, Los Angeles Rams, 1992-94; Head football coach, Seattle Seahawks, 1983-91; Head football coach, vice president football operations, Buffalo Bills, 1978-82; Head football coach, Los Angeles Rams, 1973-78; Assistant football coach, Detroit Lions, 1967-72; Assistant football coach, New York Jets, 1963-66; Assistant football coach, University Kentucky, 1961-62; Assistant football coach, Wake Forest College, 1959-60 **AW:** Named NFL Coach of Year, Sporting News, 1973, 80, NFL Coach of Year, Seattle Gold Helmet Committee, 1983, 84, AP NFL Coach of the Year, 1973, 1980, 1984 **MEM:** Big Canyon Country

KNUTH, DONALD ERVIN, T: Computer Sciences Educator **I:** Education/Educational Services **CN:** Stanford University **DOB:** 01/10/1938 **PB:** Milwaukee **SC:** WI/USA **PT:** Ervin Henry Knuth; Louise Marie (Bohning) Knuth **SPN:** Nancy Jill Carter (6/24/1961) **CH:** John Martin; Jennifer Sierra **ED:** DSc, University of Bordeaux (2007); Honorary DSc, National Academy of Sciences of the Republic of Armenia (2005-2006); Honorary DLitt, Concordia University, Wisconsin (2006); Honorary DSc, Eidgenössische Technische Hochschule Zürich (2005); Honorary DSc, Université de Montréal (2004); Honorary DSc, UAntwerpen (2003); Honorary DSc, Aristotle University of Thessaloniki (2003); Honorary DSc, Harvard University (2003); Honorary DSc, University of Oslo (2002); Honorary DSc, Athens University of Economics and Business (2001); Honorary DSc, University of Tübingen (2001); Honorary DSc, Williams College (2000); Honorary DLitt, University of Waterloo (2000); Honorary DSc, University of St Andrews (1998); Honorary DSc, Duke University (1998); Honorary DSc, Masarykova Univerzita (1996); Honorary DSc, Adelphi University (1993); Pochetnogo Doktora, St. Petersburg University (1992); Doctor Technology, KTH Royal Institute of Technology (1991); Honorary DSc, Concordia University (1991); Honorary DSc, Dartmouth College (1990); Honorary DSc, Grinnell College (1989); Honorary DSc, Valparaiso University (1988); Honorary DSc, Brown University (1988); Honorary DSc, University of Oxford (1988); Honorary DSc, Stony Brook University (1987); Honorary DSc, Université Paris-Sud (1986); Honorary DSc, University of Rochester (1986); Honorary DSc, University of Pennsylvania (1986); Honorary DSc, Muhlenberg College (1986); Honorary DSc, Lawrence University (1985); Honorary DSc, Luther College, Decorah, IA (1985); Honorary DSc, Case Western Reserve University (1980); PhD in Mathematics, California Institute of Technology (1963); MS, Case Institute of Technology (Now Case Western Reserve University) (1960); BS, Case Institute of Technology (Now Case Western Reserve University), Summa Cum Laude (1960) **C:** Professor Emeritus, The Art of Computer Programming, Stanford University (1993-Present); Professor, Electrical Engineering, Stanford University (1977-Present); Professor, The Art of Computer Programming, Stanford University (1990-1992); Fletcher Jones Professor, Computer Science, Stanford University (1977-1989); Professor, Computer Science, Stanford University (1968-1977); Associate Professor, Mathematics, California Institute of Technology (1966-1968); Assistant Professor, Mathematics, California Institute of Technology (1963-1966) **CR:** Visiting Professor, Computer Science, University of Oxford (2002-2017); Guest Professor, Mathematics, University of Oslo (1972-1973); Staff Mathematician, Institute for Defense, Analysis-Communication Research Division (1968-1969); Consultant, Burroughs Corporation (Now Unisys), Pasadena, CA (1960-1968); Invited Lecturer in Field, University of Oxford **CW:** Member, Editorial Board, Transactions on Algorithms, Association for Computing Machinery (2004-Present); Member, Editorial Board, Theory of Computing (2004-Present); Member, Editorial Board, Japan Journal of Industrial and Applied Mathematics (1997-Present); Member, Editorial Board, Journal of Graph Algorithms and Applications (1996-Present); Member, Editorial Board, Journal of Experimental Algorithmics (1996-Present); Member, Editorial Board, Electronic Journal of Combinators (1994-Present); Member, Editorial Board, The Mathematica Journal (1990-Present); Member, Editorial Board, Random Structures & Algorithms (1990-Present); Member, Editorial Board, Journal of Computer Science and Technology (1989-Present); Member, Editorial Board, Applied Mathematics Letters (1987-2000); Member, Editorial Board, Discrete and Computational Geometry (1986-2012); Member, Editorial Board, Combinatorica (1985-1998); Member, Editorial Board, Software-Practice and Experience (1979-Present); Member, Editorial Board, Journal of Computer and System Sciences (1969-Present); Member, Editorial Board, Journal of Algorithms (1979-2004); Author, "Computers and Typesetting " (1986); Author, "The Art of Computer Programming" (1968); Author, "3:16 Bible Texts Illuminated" **AW:** 2018 began for me with an absolutely incredible 80th birthday celebration called Knuth80, held in the delightful city of Piteå in northern Sweden. It's impossible for me to thank adequately all of the wonderful people who contributed their time to making this event such a stunning success, certainly one of the greatest highlights of my life. Many of the happenings were also captured digitally in state-of-the-art audio and video, so that others will be able to share some of this joy. I'll link to that data when it becomes available.; Honorary Fellow, Magdalen College, Oxford (2005-Present); Recipient, Kyoto Prize, Inamori Foundation (1996); Recipient, Harvey Prize, Israel Institute of Technology (1995); Recipient, W. Wallace McDowell Award, IEEE (1995); Recipient, Adelskold Medal, Swedish Academy of Science (1994); Recipient, Lester R. Ford Award, Mathematics Association of America (1993); Recipient, Gold Medal Award, Case Alumni Association (1990); Recipient, J.D. Warnier Prize (1989); Recipient, Franklin Medal (1988); Recipient, Steele Prize for Expository Writing, American Mathematics Society (1987); Recipient, Steele Prize for Expository Writing, American Mathematics Society (1986); Recipient, Computer Science Education Award, Association for Computing Machinery (1986); Recipient, Software Systems Award, Association for Computing Machinery (1986); Recipient, Golden Plate Award, American Academy of Achievement (1985); Recipient, W. Wallace McDowell Award, IEEE (1982); Distinguished Fellow, British Computer Society (1980); Recipient, Priestley Award, Dickinson College (1981); Recipient, W. Wallace McDowell Award, IEEE (1980); Recipient, National Medal of Science, President James Carter (1979); Recipient, Distinguished Alumni Award, California Institute of Technology (1978); Recipient, Lester R. Ford Award, Mathematics Association of America (1975); Recipient, Alan M. Turing Award, Association for Computing Machinery (1974); Fellow, John Simon Guggenheim Memorial Foundation (1972-1973); Recipient, Grace Murray Hopper Award, Association for Computing Machinery (1971); Fellow, National Science Foundation (1960); Fellow, Woodrow Wilson National Fellowship Foundation (1960); Recipient, Computer Pioneer Award, IEEE; Recipient, John von Neumann Medal, IEEE,BBVA Foundation Frontiers of Knowledge Award, 2010, Faraday Medal, 2011, Fellowship of the Royal Society, 2003 **MEM:** Foreign Member, Royal Society London (2003); Committee on Composition Technology, American Mathematics Society (1978-1981); Member, General Technology Achievement Awards Subcommittee, Association for Computing Machinery (1975-1979); National Lecturer, Association for Computing Machinery (1966-1967); Visiting Scientist, Association for Computing Machinery (1966-1967); Chairman, Subcommittee on ALGOL, Association for Computing Machinery (1963-1964); American Academy of Arts and Sciences; The Computer Museum; National Academy of Sciences; Honorary Member, Editorial Board, IEEE; Society Industrial and Applied Mathematics; Mathematics Association of America; Foreign Associate, Academy of Science, Paris; Foreign Associate, Academy of Science, Oslo; Foreign Associate, Academy of Science, Munich; Foreign Associate, Academy of Science, St. Petersburg; NAE; American Guild of Organists; American Philosophical Society **MH:** Albert Nelson Marquis Lifetime Achievement Award (2017) **ACH:** Patents in field **H:** Playing pipe organ; Reading; Writing **BA:** Stanford University, 450 Serra Mall, Stanford, CA, 94305 **ADD:** 1063 Vernier Pl, Stanford, CA, 94305 **URL:** http://www-cs-faculty.stanford.edu/knuth

KOBILKA, BRIAN KENT, T: Molecular Biologist **I:** Sciences **PB:** Little Falls **PT:** Son of Franklyn A. and Betty L. (Faust) Kobilka; **ED:** MD cum laude, Yale University School Medicine, 1981; BS in Biology & Chemistry, University Minnesota, 1977 **C:** Co-founder, ConfometRX, Santa Clara, California, 2009-; Professor molecular & cellular physiology, Stanford Univ., 1989-; Investigator, Howard Hughes Medical Institute (HHMI), Chevy Chase, Maryland, 1987-2003; Assistant professor medical, Duke Univ.,; Research fellow, Duke Univ.,; Internal medical res., Barnes Hospital, St. Louis, **AW:** Co-recipient Nobel Prize in Chemistry, Royal Swedish Academy Sciences, 2012; recipient Javits Neuroscience Investigator, National Institute Neurological Disorders & Stroke, 2004, John J. Abel award in Pharmacology, American Society for Pharmacology & Experimental Therapeutics, 1994,National Academy of Sciences, 2011 **MEM:** Mem.: National Academy of Sciences

KOCH, CHARLES, T: Chemicals Executive **I:** Business Management/Business Services **CN:** Koch Industries, Inc. **DOB:** 11/01/1935 **PB:** Wichita **SC:** KS/USA **ED:** BS in General Engineering, Massachusetts Institute of Technology (1957); MS in Mechanical Nuclear Engineering, Massachusetts Institute of Technology (1958); MS in Chemical Engineering, Massachusetts Institute of Technology (1959); Doctor of Science (Hon.), George Mason University; JD (Hon.), Babson College; PhD in Commerce (Hon.), Washburn University **C:** Chmn., CEO, Koch Industries, Inc., Wichita, 1967—; President, Koch Industries, Inc., Wichita, 1966-74; Chairman, Koch Engineering Co., Inc., Wichita, 1967-78; President, Koch Engineering Co., Inc., Wichita, 63-71; Vice president, Koch Engineering Co., Inc., Wichita, 1961-63; Engineer, Arthur D. Little, Inc., Cambridge, Massachusetts, 1959-61 **CR:** Board of Directors, Intrust Bank, N.A., Mercatus Center **CIV:** Chairman Institute Humane Studies, Claude R. Lambe Charitable Foundation, Charles G. Koch Charitable Foundation **CW:** "The Science of Success : How Market-Based Management Built the World's Largest Private Company"; "Market-Based Management"; "Good Profit" **AW:** Named one of The World's Richest People, Forbes magazine, 1999—, The Forbes 400: Richest Americans, 2006—, The World's Most Powerful People, 2010—14, The 100 Most Influential People in the World, TIME magazine, 2011, 2014, The 50 Most Influential People in Global Finance, Bloomberg Markets, 2012; recipient Leadership award, National Foundation Teaching Entrepreneurship, Adam Smith award, American Legis. Exchange Council, Brotherhood/Sisterhood award, National Conference Christians & Jews, Distinguished Citizen award, Boy Scouts of America, Free Enterprise award, Council National Policy, Spirit of Justice award, Heritage Foundation, Director's award for Global Vision in Energy, New York Mercantile Exchange, 1999, National Distinguished Service award, Tax Foundation, 2000, Spirit Excellence award, Urban League Wichita **MEM:** Member, Flint Hills National; Member, Mount Pelerin Society; Member, The Vintage Club **PA:** Republican

KOCH, DAVID HAMILTON, T: Businessman, Philanthropist **I:** Business Management/Business Services **DOB:** 05/03/1940 **PB:** Wichita **SC:** KS/USA **PT:** Son of Frederick and Mary (Robinson) Koch **ED:** MSChemE, Massachusetts Institute of Technology, 1963; BSChemE, Massachusetts Institute of Technology, 1962 **C:** Executive Vice President, Koch Industries, Inc., Wichita, Kansas, 1981-2018; With, Koch Industries, Inc., Wichita, Kansas, 1970-; Chairman, Board of Directors, CEO, Chemical Tech. Grp., LLC (subsidiary Koch Industries, Inc.); Board of Directors, Koch Industries, Inc., Wichita, Kansas; Research Engineer and Process Design Engineer, Sci. Design Comp. (affiliate of Halcon International, Inc.), New York City; Research Engineer and Process Design Engineer, Halcon International, Inc., New York City, 1967-70; Research Engineer and Process Design Engineer, Arthur D. Little, Inc., Cambridge, Massachusetts, 1964-67; Research Engineer and Process Design Engineer, Amicon Corp., Cambridge, 1963-64 **CR:** Board of Directors, Hospital for Special Surgery, New York City **CIV:** Active, Libr. Congress James Madison Council, Washington, Active, National Cancer Adv. Board, National dinner chairman, Rep. Gov.'s Association, 1999 Member Libertarian Party Candidate for V.P. US, 1980 Board of Directors, corp. life member, Massachusetts Institute of Technology, Vice-chmn., Board of Directors, Am. Ballet Theatremem, Chmn.'s council, Metropolitan Museum Art, New York City, Board of Advisors, John Hopkins Medical Center, Board associate, Whitehead Institute, Cambridge, Massachusetts, Board Visiting, M.D. Anderson Cancer Adv. Board, Houston, Board of Overseers, TV Station WGBH, Boston, Board of Directors, CATO Institute, Washington, Board of Directors, Reason Foundation, Santa Monica, California, Board of Directors, Institute Human Origins, Phoenix, Board of Directors, Aspen Institute, Colorado, Board of Directors, TV Station WNET, New York City, Board of Directors, Rockefeller University, New York City, Board directors, Am. Museum Natural Hist., New York City, Board of Governors, Deerfield Academy, Massachusetts, Board of Governors, New York Presbyterian Hospital, New York City, Board of Trustees, Johns Hopkins University, Board of Trustees, Prostate Cancer Foundation, LA, Board of Trustees, House Ear Institute, LA, Member Board of Overseers and Managers, Board of Trustees, Memorial Sloan Kettering Cancer Center, New York City **AW:** Named 10th Ann. Gala Honoree, New York Academy Medicine, 2004, Businessman of Year, Manhattan Rep. Party, 2002; Named One of The 10 Most Fascinating People of 2014, Barbara Walters Special, The 50 Most Influential People in Global Finance, Bloomberg Markets, 2012, The 100 Most Influential People in the World, TIME magazine, 2014, 2011, The World's Most Powerful People, Forbes magazine, 2010-14, The Forbes 400: Richest Americans, 2006-, The World's Richest People, 2001-; Recipient, Leadership Award, National Foundation Teaching Entrepreneurship, Corporate Leadership Excellence Award, Society Memorial Sloan-Kettering, 2005, Corporate Citizenship Award, Woodrow Wilson International Center Scholars, 2004 **MEM:** Mem.: New York Explorers Club, New York Racquet & Tennis Club, New York River Club **ACH:** holder, 4 U.S. patents; **H:** Skiing, Tennis, Golf **PA:** Republican **BA:** Koch Industries Inc, 4111 E 37th St N, Wichita, KS, 67220

KOCHHAR, CHANDA, T: Bank Executive **I:** Financial Services **DOB:** 11/19/1961 **PB:** Jodhpur **SC:** India **ED:** Master in Management Studies, Jamnalal Bajaj Institute Management Studies; MBA, Jaihind College; BA, Jaihind College, 1982 **C:** Managing director, CEO, ICICI Bank, 2009-; Board directors, ICICI Bank, 2001-; Joint managing director, CFO, ICICI Bank, 2007-09; Deputy managing director, ICICI Bank, 2006-07; Executive director retail business, ICICI Bank, 2001-06; Head retail fin. division, ICICI Bank, 2000-01; General manager, head major clients group, ICICI Bank, 1998; Head infrastructure industry group, ICICI Bank, 1996; Joined as management trainee, ICICI Bank, India, 1984 **CR:** Director ICICI Prudential Life Insurance Co. Ltd., ICICI International Ltd. vice-chairperson ICICI Bank Canada, ICICI Bank UK Plc chairperson ICICI Investment Management Co. Ltd., ICICI Bank Eurasia LLC **AW:** Named Businesswoman of Year, The Economic Times, India, 2005, Retail Banker of Year, The Asian Banker, 2004; named one of The 50 Most Influential People in Global Finance, Bloomberg Markets, 2011, The 100 Most Powerful Women, Forbes magazine, 2009-14, The 50 Most Powerful People in Asian Business, Fortune magazine, 2011, The International Power 50, 2008-13, 2005; recipient Rising Star award, Retail International Banker, 2006 **ADD:** ICICI Bank Ltd PO Box 20, Banjara Hills PO, Hyderabad, YT, India, -500 034

KOENIG, SARAH, T: Journalist **I:** Writing and Editing **PB:** New York City **SC:** NY/USA **ED:** Coursework, University of Chicago (1990) **C:** Producer, "Serial" (2013-Present); Producer, "This American Life" (2004-Present) **AW:** Named One of TIME's 100 Most Influential People, TIME Magazine (2015); Peabody Award (2006)

KONDO, MARIE, T: Organizing Consultant **I:** Writing and Editing **SC:** Japan **CW:** Author, "The Life-Changing Manga of Tidying Up: A Magical Story" (2017); Author, "The Illustrated Guide to the Life-Changing Magic of Tidying Up" (2015); Author, "The Life-Changing Magic of Tidying Up: The Japanese Art of Decluttering and Organizing" (2011) **AW:** Named One of TIME's 100 Most Influential People, TIME Magazine (2015)

KOOLHAAS, REMMENT, T: Architect **I:** Architecture & Construction **DOB:** 11/17/1944 **PB:** Rotterdam, Netherlands **ED:** Degree, Architectural Association School, London, 1972 **C:** Founder, Volume Magazine, 2005-; Professor grad. school design, Harvard University, 1995-; Founder, director, Office Metropolitan Architecture, Rotterdam, Netherlands, 1978-; Director, Office Metropolitan Architecture, New York City,; Founder, Office Metropolitan Architecture, London, 1975-78; Former journalist, writer film screenplays **CR:** Co-founder Volume Magazine, 2005; director Project on the City, Harvard University; professor practice of architecture and urban design, Grad. School Design, 1995-; adjunct professor architecture, 1990-95; professor architecture, Rice University, Houston, 1991-92, Technical University, Delft, Netherlands, 1988-89; architectural associate, London, 1976 **CW:** Principal works include Netherlands Dance Theater, The Hague, 1987, Nexus Housing, Fukuoka, Japan, 1991 (Best Building in Japan, The Architectural Institute of Japan, 1992), Kunsthal, Rotterdam, 1992, Lille Grand Palais, France, 1994, Educatorium Utrecht (Netherlands) University, 1997, Maison at Bordeaux, France, 1998, Netherlands Embassy, Berlin, Villa Dall'Ava, Paris (Prix d'Architecture, Le Moniteur, Paris, 1991), China Central TV Hdqs., 2008; author: Delirious New York: A Retroactive Manifesto for Manhattan, 1995; Rem Koolhaas Conversations with Students, 1996; author:(with Bruce Mau)) S,M,L,XL, 1998; author:(with Jacques Lucan)) OMA Rem Koolhaas Living, Vivre, Leben, 1999; author: (with Bernard Colenbrander, Michelle Provoost) Dutchtown: A City Center Design by OMA, 2000; exhibitions include Guggenheim Museum, New York City, 1978, Max Protech Gallery, 1988, Museum Modern Art, 1988, 1994, 1995, Architectur Museum, Basel, Switzerland, 1988, Boymans Museum, Rotterdam, 1989, Institute Francais d'Architecture, Paris, 1989, Stedeliijk Museum, Amsterdam, The Netherlands, 1990, Colegio de Arquitectos, Barcelona, Spain, 1990, Musee de Beaux Arts, Lille, 1990; guest editor Wired magazine; co-founder with Mark Wigley and Ole Bourman, Volume Magazine, 2005; (Principal Works) Riga Port City, 2009, 23 East 22nd Street, New York City, 2010, Bryghusprojektet, Danish Architecture Centre, Copenhagen, 2008–, New Court, St. Swithin's Lane,London, 2010, De Rotterdam, Rotterdam, 2013 Garage Museum of Contemporary Art, Moscow, 2014; Taipei Performing Arts Centre, Taipei, 2012–, Marina Abramovic Community Centre Obod Cetinje – MACCOC, Cetinje, 2012-, The Factory, Manchester 2019; (Books) Content, 2004, Serpentine Gallery, 2007, Project Japan: Metabolism Talks, 2011 **AW:** Named one of The 100 Most Influential People in the World, TIME magazine, 2008; recipient Johannes Vermeer award, 2013, Jencks award, Royal Institute British Architects, 2012, Golden Lion of the Venice Biennale of Archit. for Lifetime Achievement, 2010, Wired Rave award in Architecture, 2005, Legion d'Honneur, 2001, Pritzker Architecture prize, The Hyatt Foundation, 2000, Progressive Architecture award, 1974, Time 100 Most Influential People, 20008 **MEM:** Mem.: Am. Academy Arts & Scis.(hon. foreign)

KOONTZ, DEAN, T: Writer **I:** Writing and Editing **DOB:** 07/09/1945 **PB:** Everett **SC:** PA/USA **ED:** LittD (hon.), Shippensburg University, Pennsylvania, 1989; BS, Shippensburg University, Pennsylvania, 1966 **C:** Freelance writer, Orange, California, 1969-; Teacher, Mechanicsburg HS, Pennsylvania, 1967-69; Teacher, Appalachian Poverty Progressive, Saxton, Pennsylvania, 1966-67 **CW:** Author: (novels) Star Quest, 1968, Fear That Man, 1969, The Fall of the Dream Machine, 1969, The Dark Symphony, 1969, Hell's Gate, 1970, Dark of the Woods, 1970, Beastchild, 1970, Anti-Man, 1970, The Crimson Witch, 1971, Warlock!, 1972, Time Thieves, 1972, Starblood, 1972, The Flesh in the Furnace, 1972, A Darkness in My Soul, 1972, The Haunted Earth, 1973, Demon Seed, 1973, A Werewolf Among Us, 1973, Hanging On, 1973, After the Last Race, 1974, Nightmare Journey, 1975, Night Chills, 1976, The Vision, 1977, Whispers, 1980, Phantoms, 1983, Darkfall, 1984, Twilight Eyes, 1985, Strangers, 1986, Twilight Eyes (Expanded Version), 1987, Watchers, 1987, Lightning, 1988, Midnight, 1989, The Bad Place, 1990, Cold Fire, 1991, Hideaway, 1992, Dragon Tears, 1993, Mr. Murder, 1993, Winter Moon, 1994, Dark Rivers of the Heart, 1994, Intensity, 1996, Tick Tock, 1996, Santa's Twin, 1996, Demon Seed (Revised Version), 1997, Sole Survivor, 1997, Fear Nothing, 1998, False Memory, 1999, Seize the Night, 1999, From the Corner of His Eye, 2000, One Door Away from Heaven, 2001, By the Light of the Moon, 2002, The Face, 2003, Odd Thomas, 2003, The Taking, 2004, Life Expectancy, 2004, Velocity, 2005, Frankenstein Book 1: Prodigal Son, 2005, Frankenstein Book 2: City of Night, 2005, Forever Odd, 2005, The Husband, 2006, Brother Odd, 2006, The Good Guy, 2007, The Darkest Evening of the Year, 2007, Odd Hours, 2008, In Odd We Trust, 2008, Bliss to You, 2008, Your Heart Belongs to Me, 2008, I Trixie, Who Is Dog, 2009, Relentless, 2009, Frankenstein Book 3: Dead and Alive, 2009, Frankenstein: Prodigal Son (Graphic Novel), 2009, Breathless, 2009, A Big Little Life, 2009, Frankenstein: Lost Souls, 2010, Odd is On Our Side (Graphic Novel), 2010, Trixie & Jinx, 2010, Darkness Under the Sun (Novella), 2010, What the Night Knows, 2010, Fear Nothing, Vol.

1 (Graphic Novel), 2010, Frankenstein: The Dead Town, 2011, The Moonlit Mind (Novella), 2011, 77 Shadow Street, 2011, Nevermore, 2011, Odd Interlude #3, 2012, Odd Interlude #2, 2012, House of Odd (Graphic Novel), 2012, Odd Interlude #1, 2012, Odd Apocalypse, 2012, Deeply Odd, 2013, The City, 2014, Innocence, 2013, Saint Odd, 2014, Ashley Bell, 2015, (novels) (as David Axton) Prison of Ice (later Icebound), 1975, Icebound, 1995, (novels) (as Leonard Chris) Hung, 1970, (as Deanna Dwyer) Demon Child, 1971, Legacy of Terror, 1971, Children of the Storm, 1972, Dance with the Devil, 1972, The Dark of Summer, 1972, (as Brian Coffey) Blood Risk, 1973, Surrounded, 1974, The Wall of Masks, 1975, The Face of Fear, 1977, The Voice of the Night, 1980, (as Anthony North) Strike Deep, 1974, (as Aaron Wolfe) Invasion (inspiration for Winter Moon 1994), 1975, (as John Hill) The Long Sleep, 1975, (as K. R. Dwyer) Shattered, 1973, Chase, 1972, Dragonfly, 1975, Chase (Revised Version), 1995, (as Leigh Nichols) The Key to Midnight (Revised), 1979, The Eyes of Darkness, 1981, The House of Thunder, 1982, Twilight (Later: The Servants of Twilight), 1984, The Servants of Twilight, 1990, Shadow Fires, 1990, The Eyes of Darkness, 1996, (as Owen West) The Funhouse, 1980, The Mask, 1981, (as Richard Paige) The Door to December, 1985, (non-fiction) The Underground Lifestyles Handbook, 1970, The Pig Society, 1970, Writing Popular Fiction, 1972, How To Write Best-Selling Fiction, 1981, Life is Good! Lessons in Joyful Living, 2004, Christmas Is Good!: Trixie Treats And Holiday Wisdom, 2005, Bliss to You: Trixie's Guide to a Happy Life, 2008, A Big Little Life: A Memoir of a Joyful Dog, 2009, (short story collections) Soft Come the Dragons, 1970, Strange Highways, 1995, (children's books) Oddkins: A Fable for All Ages, 1988, Santa's Twin, 1996, The Paper Doorway: Funny Verse and Nothing Worse, 2001, Every Day's a Holiday: Amusing Rhymes for Happy Times, 2003, Robot Santa: The Further Adventures of Santa's Twin, 2004, (comic book) Dean Koontz's Nevermore, 2011,(Books) Odd Thomas: You Are Destined to be Together Forever, 2014, Last Light, 2015, Ashley Bell, 2015, The Silent Corner, 2017, The Whispering Room, 2017, The Crooked Staircase, 2018 **ACH:** Achievements include having ten hardcovers and thirteen paperbacks reach #1 on the New York Times Bestseller list

KORDESTANI, OMID R., T: Information Technology Executive **I:** Information Technology and Services **PB:** Tehran **SC:** Iran **ED:** MBA, Stanford University Graduate School of Business, 1991; BSEE, San Jose State University, California, 1984 **C:** Executive Chairman, Twitter, 2015-; President, global sales operations & business devel., Google, Inc., 2014-; Senior adv., Google, Inc., 2009-14; Senior vice president global sales & business development, Google, Inc., 2006-09; Senior vice president, worldwide sales & field operations, Google, Inc., Mountain View, California, 1999-2006; Vice president, business devel. & sales, Netscape, 1995-99; Various marketing, product management & business devel. positions, Go Corp.,; Various marketing, product management & business devel. positions, 3DO Co.,; Product marketing manager, Hewlett-Packard Co., **CR:** Board directors Vodafone Group Public Ltd. Co., 2013- **AW:** Named one of The Forbes 400: Richest Americans, 2006-, The 100 Most Influential People in the World, TIME magazine, 2006

KORNBERG, ROGER, T: Biochemist **I:** Sciences **CN:** Stanford University **PB:** St. Louis **SC:** MO/USA **PT:** Arthur Kornberg; Sylvy Ruth (Levy) Kornberg **ED:** PhD in Chemistry, Stanford University, CA (1972); BS in Chemistry, Harvard University, Cambridge, MA (1967) **C:** Professor, Structural Biology,

Stanford University School of Medicine (1978-Present); Winzer Professor, Structural Biology, Stanford University School of Medicine; Chairman, Department, Stanford University School of Medicine (1984-1992); Assistant Professor, Biological Chemistry, Harvard Medical School (1976-1977); Member, Science Staff, MRC Laboratory of Molecular Biology (1974-1975); Junior Fellow, MRC Laboratory of Molecular Biology (1973-1974); Postdoctoral Fellow, MRC Laboratory of Molecular Biology, Cambridge, England (1972-1973) **CR:** Co-chairman, Skolkovo Science and Technical Council (2010-Present) **CW:** Contributor, Articles to Professional Journals **AW:** Louisa Gross Horwitz Prize, Columbia University (2006); Nobel Prize in Chemistry (2006); Dickson Prize, University of Pittsburgh (2006); GM Cancer Research Award (2005); Massry Prize (2003); Pasarow Award in Cancer Research (2003); Merck Award, American Society of Biochemistry & Molecular Biology (2002); Welch Foundation Award in Chemistry (2001); Hoppe-Seyler Award, Society of Biochemistry & Molecular Biology, Germany (2001); Gairdner Foundation International Award (2000); Harvey Prize, Technion-Israel Institute Technician (1997); Ciba-Drew Award (1990); Passano Award (1982); Eli Lilly Award (1981) **MEM:** National Academy of Sciences; Foreign Associate, European Molecular Biology Organization; American Academy of Arts & Sciences; Honorary Member, Japanese Biochemistry Society

KOTB, HODA, T: News Correspondent **I:** Media & Entertainment **DOB:** 08/09/1964 **PB:** Norman **ED:** BA in Broadcast Journalism, Virginia Tech., 1986 **C:** Co-host fourth hour segment Today Show, Kathie Lee and Hoda, NBC, 2007-; Corr., Dateline NBC, New York City, 1998-; Host Your Total Health (syndicated), NBC, 2004-08; Anchor, reporter, WWL-TV, New Orleans, 1992-98; Weekend anchor, reporter, WINK-TV, Fort Myers, Florida, 1989-91; Morning anchor, general assignment reporter, WQAD-TV, Moline, Illinois,; Anchor, WXVT-TV, Greenville, Mississippi,; News assistant, CBS News, Cairo, 1986 **CIV:** Board directors, Virginia Tech Alumni Association, 2010- **CW:** Author: Hoda: How I Survived War Zones, Bad Hair, Cancer and Kathie Lee, 2010, Ten Years Later: Six People Who Faced Adversity and Transformed Their Lives, 2013, Where We Belong: Journeys That Show Us The Way, 2016,(Book) Hoda: How I Survived War Zones, Bad Hair, Cancer and Kathie Lee, 2010, Ten Years Later: Six People Who Faced Adversity and Transformed Their Lives, 2013, Where They Belong: The Best Decisions People Almost Never Made, 2016 **AW:** Recipient Alfred I. duPont-Columbia University award, 2008, George Foster Peabody award, 2006, Gracie award, Alliance Women in Media, 2003, Headliner award, 2002, Edward R. Murrow award, Radio-TV News Directors Association, 2002 **MEM:** Mem.: Delta Delta Delta

KOUFAX, SANDY, T: Retired MLB Player **I:** Athletics **DOB:** 12/30/1935 **PB:** Brooklyn **C:** Special Advisor, LA Dodgers, 2013-; Broadcaster, NBC Sports, 1966-73; Minor League Pitching Instructor, LA Dodgers, 1979-90; Pitcher, LA Dodgers, 1958-66; Pitcher, Brooklyn Dodgers, 1955-57 **AW:** Recipient Babe Ruth award Major League Baseball, 1963, 1965 Cy Young Award, 1963, 1965, 1966, Hutch Award, 1966; Named National League Pitcher of Year The Sporting News, 1963-66, World Series MVP, 1963, 1965, Major League Player of Year, 1963, 1965, National League MVP, 1963; Named to National League All-Star Team, 1961-66, Baseball Hall of Fame, 1972, Four Best Living Players Voted by Fans, 2015, Sporting News Baseballs 100 Greatest Players, 1999 **ACH:** Achievements include member of World Series championship winning

Los Angeles Dodgers, 1959, 1963, 1965; leading the National League in: strikeouts, 1961, 1963, 1965, 1966; earned run average, 1962-66; wins, 1963, 1965, 1966; shutouts, 1963, 1964, 1966; innings, complete games, 1965, 1966, starts, 1966; pitching a no-hitter against the: New York Mets, June, 30, 1962; San Francisco Giants, May 11, 1963; Philadelphia Phillies, June, 4, 1964; winner of the National League Triple Crown for pitchers (league leader in wins, strikeouts and earned run average), 1963, 1965, 1966; pitching a perfect game against the Chicago Cubs, September 9, 1965 **BA:** Sports Placement Service, Inc., 330 West 11th Street Suite 105, Los Angeles, CA, 90015

KOUM, JAN BORIS, **T:** Entrepreneur, Computer Engineer **I:** Technology **CN:** WhatsApp **PB:** Kiev **SC:** Soviet Union **ED:** Student, San Jose University (1994-1997) **C:** Co-Founder, CEO, WhatsApp, Inc. (Acquired by Facebook, Inc., 2014), Santa Clara, CA, 2009-Present; Infrastructure engineer, Yahoo! Inc., Sunnyvale, CA, 1997-2007; Security tester, Ernst & Young **CR:** Board of Directors, Facebook, Inc., 2014-Present **AW:** The Forbes 400: Richest Americans, 2014-Present, The 40 Under 40, Fortune Magazine, 2014 **RE:** Jewish

KRAFT, ROBERT K., **I:** Athletics **DOB:** 07/05/1941 **PB:** Brookline **SC:** MA/USA **SPN:** Myra (Hiatt) K. (6/1963, Deceased 7/20/2011) **CH:** Jonathan, Daniel, Joshua, David **ED:** MBA, Harvard University; Grad., Columbia University, New York City **C:** Principal Owner, Chairman, CEO, New England Patriots, 1994-; Chairman, Carmel Container Systems, Ltd., Israel; President, International Forest Products Group Cos.; With, Rand-Whitney Group, Inc., Worcester, Massachusetts; President, New England TV Corp., 1986-91; Founder, International Forest Products, 1972; Chairman, Chestnut Hill Management; Owner, Foxboro Stadium, Massachusetts **CR:** Board of Directors, Viacom Inc., 2006-, Federal Reserve Bank Boston Chairman Fin. Committee NFL, 1998- **CIV:** Board of Overseers, Boston Symphony Orchestra, Boston Museum of Science, Board of Trustees, Boston College, Trustee Emeritus, Columbia University, Member Executive Committee, Dana-Farber Cancer Institute **AW:** Named One of The Most Influential People in the World of Sports, Business Week, 2008, 2007, The 50 Most Influential People in Sports Business, Street & Smith's Sports-Business Journal, 2007-09, The Forbes 400: Richest Americans, 2006-; Recipient, Theodore Roosevelt Award, National Association for the Advancement of Colored People, 2006 **H:** Golf, Tennis

KRAMER, RICHARD J., **T:** Manufacturing Executive **I:** Manufacturing **DOB:** 10/30/1963 **PB:** Cleve. **ED:** BS in Business Administration, John Carroll University, 1986 **CT:** CPA **C:** Chairman, president, CEO, Goodyear Tire & Rubber Co., 2010-; President, CEO, Goodyear Tire & Rubber Co., 2010; COO, Goodyear Tire & Rubber Co., 2009-10; President North American Tire, Goodyear Tire & Rubber Co., 2007-09; Executive vice president, CFO, Goodyear Tire & Rubber Co., 2004-07; Senior vice president strategic planning & restructuring, Goodyear Tire & Rubber Co., 2003-04; Vice president fin. North American Tire, Goodyear Tire & Rubber Co., 2002-03; Vice president corp. fin., Goodyear Tire & Rubber Co., 2000-03; Partner, PricewaterhouseCoopers,; With, PricewaterhouseCoopers, 1987-2000 **CR:** Board directors Sherwin-Williams Co., 2012-, Goodyear Tire & Rubber Co., 2010

KRASINSKI, JOHN, **T:** Actor **I:** Media & Entertainment **PB:** Boston **SC:** MA/USA **PT:** Ronald Krasinski; Mary Clare Krasinski **ED:** Grad., National Theater Institute; BA in English Literature, Brown University, Providence, Rhode Island, 2001 **C:** Script intern, Late Night with Conan O'Brien **CW:** Actor: (TV series) The Office, 2005-13 (Outstanding Performance by an Ensemble in a Comedy Series, Screen Actors Guild, 2007, 2008); TV appearances Ed, 2003, Law & Order: Criminal Intent, 2004, CSI: Crime Scene Investigation, 2005, Without a Trace, 2005, Arrested Development, 2013, BoJack Horseman, 2014-15, Lip Sync Battle, 2015, Robot Chicken, 2016, Tom Clancy's Jack Ryan, 2018; actor: (films) Doogal, 2004, Kinsey, 2004, Taxi, 2004, Duane Hopwood, 2004, Jarhead, 2005, For Your Consideration, 2006, Dreamgirls, 2006, The Holiday, 2006, License to Wed, 2007, Shrek the Third (voice), 2007, Leatherheads, 2008, Monsters versus Aliens (voice), 2009, Away We Go, 2009, It's Complicated, 2009, Something Borrowed, 2011, The Muppets, 2011, Nobody Walks, 2012, Big Miracle, 2012, Monsters University (voice), 2013, The Wind Rises, 2013, Kahlil Gilbran's The Prophet (voice), 2014, Aloha, 2015, 13 Hours: The Secret Soldiers of Benghazi, 2016, Manchester by the Sea, 2016, The Hollars, 2016, Past Forward, 2016, Born in China, 2017, Animal Crackers, 2017, Detroit, 2017, A Quiet Place, 2018 (off-Broadway) Dry Powder, 2016; actor, director, writer (films) Brief Interviews with Hideous Men, 2009, actor, producer, writer Promised Land, 2012, actor, producer, director The Hollars, 2016; executive prodr.: (TV series) Lip Sync Battle, 2015

KRAUSE, CHERYL, **T:** Federal Judge **I:** Law and Legal Services **CN:** (3rd Cir.) US Court Appeals **DOB:** 01/01/1968 **PB:** St Louis **SC:** MO/USA **ED:** JD, Stanford Law School, 1993; BA, University Pennsylvania, 1989 **C:** Judge, US Court Appeals (3rd Cir.), 2014-; Partner, Dechert LLP, Philadelphia, 2006-14; Shareholder, Hangley Aronchick Segal & Pudlin, 2003-06; Assistant US attorney (southern district) New York, US Department Justice, New York City, 1997-2002; Associate, David Polk & Wardwell, New York City, 1996-97; Law clerk, Heller Ehran White & McAuliffe LLP, San Francisco, 1995-96; Lecturer, visiting scholar, Stanford Law School, 1995-96; Law clerk to Justice Anthony Kennedy, US Supreme Court, 1994-95; Law clerk to Hon. Alex Kozinski, US Court Appeals (9th Cir.), 1993-94 **CR:** Founder Philadelphia Project, 2011- board directors Committee on Seventy, 2007- outside counsel Philadelphia Board Ethics, 2007- vol. attorney The Veterans Consortium Pro Bono Program, 2005- lecturer evidence & cybercrime University Pennsylvania Law School, 2003-06 lectr trial practice Columbia Law School, 2002 barrister American Inns of Court University Pennsylvania Law School chapter, 2003-05 regional rep. Stanford Law School Alumni Association, 2003 founder, president Stanford Law School Alumni Association New York, 1996-98 **AW:** Recipient, Steve M. Block Civil Liberties award **MEM:** Mem.: Federal Bar Association (member executive committee 2003-), Professional Women's Roundtable of Philadelphia (member advisory committee 2005-), Association Bar City of New York (committee on professional & judicial ethics 2001-03), American Bar Association (member steering committee young lawyers' division white collar crime section 2004-06), Pennsylvania Bar Association, Philadelphia Bar Association **BA:** 601 Market St, Philadelphia, PA, 19106

KRAVITZ, LENNY, **T:** Singer, Guitarist, Actor **I:** Media & Entertainment **PB:** New York **SC:** NY/USA **PT:** Sy Kravitz; Roxy Roker **C:** Founder, Kravitz Design Inc., New York City, 2003 **CW:** Singer: (albums) Let Love Rule, 1989, Mama Said, 1991,

Are You Gonna Go My Way, 1993, Circus, 1995, 5, 1998 (Grammy award for Best Male Rock Vocal Performance for song Fly Away, 1998, Grammy award for Best Male Rock Vocal Performance for song American Woman, 1999), Greatest Hits, 2000 (Grammy award for Best Male Rock Vocal Performance for song Again, 2000), Lenny, 2001 (Grammy award for Best Male Rock Vocal Performance for song Dig In, 2001), Baptism, 2004, It is Time for a Love Revolution, 2008, Black and White America, 2011, Strut, 2014, Raise Vibration,; actor: (films) The Rugrats Movie (voice), 1998, Precious, 2009, The Hunger Games, 2012, The Butler, 2013, The Hunger Games: Catching Fire, 2013 **AW:** Recipient Officer of Arts and Literature award, France, 2011

KRIMBILL, H. MICHAEL, **T:** CEO **I:** Oil & Energy **CN:** NGL Energy Partners LP **C:** Chief Executive Officer, NGL Energy Partners LP (2010-Present); Chief Financial Officer/Principal Executive, NGL Energy Partners LP (2012-2013); President/Chief Financial Officer, Energy Transfer Partners, L.P. (2004-2007); President/Chief Executive Officer, Heritage Propane Partners (2000-2005); Vice President/Chief Financial Officer, Heritage Propane Partners (1990-1999)

KRISHNAMOORTHI, RAJA, **T:** U.S. Representative from Illinois **I:** Government Administration/ Government Relations/Government Services **DOB:** 07/19/1973 **PB:** New Delhi **SC:** India **ED:** B.A., Princeton, 1995; J.D., Harvard Law, 2000 **C:** Member, U.S. House of Representative's from Illinois' 8th District, 2017-; Member, Committee on Education and the Workforce; Member, Committee on Oversight and Government Reform; Deputy State Treasurer, Illinois, 2008-09; Illinois Special Assistant Attorney General, 2006-07; Staff, Illinois Housing Development Authority, 2005-07; Campaign Staff, Barack Obama, 2004, 2008; Clerk, U.S. District Court for Northern District of Illinois, 2000-2002 **BA:** 515 Cannon HOB, Washington, DC, 20515

KROEMER, HERBERT, **T:** Professor of Electrical and Computer Engineering **I:** Education/Educational Services **DOB:** 08/25/1928 **PB:** Weimar **SC:** Germany **ED:** Doctor (hon.), University Colorado, 2001; Doctor (hon.), University Lund, Sweden, 1998; Doctor (hon.), Tech. University Aachen, Germany, 1985; PhD in Theoretical Physics, University Gottingen, Germany, 1952 **C:** Professor Department Electrical and Computer Engineering, University California, Santa Barbara, 1976-; Donald W. Whittier Chair Electrical Engineering, University California, Santa Barbara,; Faculty Research Lecturer, University California, Santa Barbara, 1985-96; Teacher Electrical Engineering, University Colorado, Boulder, 1968-76; Research Physicist, Varian, Inc., 1959-66; Research Physicist, RCA Corp., 1954-59; Semiconductor Researcher, German Postal Service, 1952-54 **CW:** Author: Thermal Physics, 1990, Quantum Mechanics for Engineering, Materials Science, and Applied Physics, 1994; Contributor Articles to Professional Journals **AW:** Decorated Grand Cross, Order of Merit Federal Republic of Germany; Recipient Nobel prize in physics, 2000, Alexander von Humboldt Medal, European Geoscis. Union, 1994, Heinrich Welker Medal, International Symposium GaAs & Related Compounds, 1982, IEEE Medal of Honor, 2002 **MEM:** Mem.: IEEE (Jack Morton Award 1986, Medal of Honor 2002), National Academy of Sciences (Foreign Associate), Am. Physical Society (Foreign), Electron Devices Society (J.J. Ebers Award 1973), National Academy Engineering (Foreign Associate)

KROENKE, STANLEY, I: Athletics **DOB:** 07/29/1947 **PB:** Cole Camp, Missouri **SPN:** Married Ann Walton, 1974; **CH:** children: Whitney, Josh. **ED:** MBA, University of Missouri, 1973; BS in Business, University of Missouri, 1969 **C:** Majority Shareholder, Arsenal Football Club, London, 2007-; Owner, Colorado Rapids, 2003-; Owner, Colorado Mammoth, 2002-; Owner, Colorado Avalanche, 2000-; Owner, Denver Nuggets, 2000-; Owner, Pepsi Center, Denver, 2000-; Vice chairman, co-owner, St. Louis Rams, 1995-; Co-owner, Dick's Sporting Goods, Colorado,; Owner, Colorado Crush, 2002-09; Owner, Kroenke Sports Enterprises,; Chairman, THF Realty,; Chairman, owner, The Kroenke Group., Columbia, Missouri, **CR:** Board Directors Community Investment Partnership Funds I and II, St. Louis, Boone County National Bank, Columbia, Central Bancompany, Jefferson City Co-owner Screaming Eagle Vineyard, Napa Valley, California, 2006-. **CIV:** Trustee College of the Ozarks Member Board Greater St. Louis Area Council Boy Scouts of Am., St. Louis Art Museum **AW:** Named One of Most Influential People in the World of Sports, Business Week, 2008, Forbes 400: Richest Americans, 2006

KRUGMAN, PAUL, T: Economics Professor **I:** Education/Educational Services **DOB:** 02/28/1953 **PB:** Albany **SC:** NY/USA **PT:** Son of David Krugman and Anita Alman; **ED:** BA, Yale University, New Haven, 1974; PhD, Massachusetts Institute of Technology, 1977; LLD (hon.), University of Toronto, 2013 **C:** Distinguished Scholar Luxembourg Income Study Center, The Graduate Center, City University of New York, New York City, New York, 2014—; Professor Economics & International Affairs, Princeton University, New Jersey, 2000—; Professor Economics, Stanford University, California, 1994—1996; Professor Economics, Massachusetts Institute of Technology, Cambridge, 1983—1994; Associate Professor, Massachusetts Institute of Technology, Cambridge, 1979—1983; Assistant Professor, Yale University, New Haven, Connecticut, 1977—1979 **CR:** Research Associate National Bureau Economic Research, 1979—; International Policy Economist Council Economic Advisers, Washington, 1982—1983; Member Board of Advisors Institute International Economics, Washington, 1986—; Columnist Slate Magazine, 1996—1999, Fortune, 1997—1999, New York Times, 2000—; **CW:** Author (academic books): Adjustment in the World Economy, 1987, Exchange-Rate Instability (Lionel Robbins Lectures), 1988, Rethinking International Trade, 1990, Has the Adjustment Process Worked?, 1991, Geography and Trade (Gaston Eyskens Lecture Series), 1991, Currencies and Crises, 1992, What Do We Need to Know About the International Monetary System?, 1993, World Savings Shortage, 1994, Development, Geography, and Economic Theory (Ohlin Lectures), 1995, The Self Organizing Economy, 1996; Co-author: Market Structure and Foreign Trade: Increasing Returns, Imperfect Competition, and the International Economy, 1985, Trade Policy and Market Structure, 1989, The Risks Facing the World Economy, 1991, Foreign Direct Investment in the U.S., 1995, EMU and the Regions, 1995, The Spatial Economy - Cities, Regions and International Trade, 1999, numerous Econs. textbooks; editor/co-editor Strategic Trade Policy and the New International Economics, 1986, Exchange Rate Targets and Currency Bands, 1991, Empirical Studies of Strategic Trade Policy, 1994, Trade with Japan : Has the Door Opened Wider?, 1995, Currency Crises, 2000; author (general audience): The Age of Diminished Expectations: US Economic Policy in the 1990s, 1990, Peddling Prosperity: Economic Sense and Nonsense in an Age of Diminished Expectations, 1995, Pop Inter-

nationalism, 1996, The Accidental Theorist and Other Dispatches from the Dismal Science, 1998, The Return of Depression Economics, 1999, Fuzzy Math: The Essential Guide to the Bush Tax Plan, 2001, The Great Unraveling: Losing Our Way in the New Century, 2003, The Conscience of a Liberal, 2007, The Return of Depression Economics and the Crisis of 2008, 2008, End This Depression Now!, 2012; appeared in (films) Get Him to the Greek, 2010 **AW:** Co-recipient Nikkei Prize, 2001; Named One of The Top 25 Market Movers, US News & World Report, 2009, The World's Most Influential People, TIME magazine, 2009, The 100 Agents of Change, Rolling Stone magazine, 2009, The 50 Highest-Earning Political Figures, Newsweek, 2010, The 50 Most Influential People in Global Finance, Bloomberg Markets, 2011—13, The Top Global Thinkers, Foreign Policy, 2012; Recipient John Bates Clark Medal, American Economic Association, 1991, Eccles Prize for Excellence in Economic Writing, 1991, Alonso Prize, Regional Sci. Association, 2002, Nobel Prize in Economics, Royal Swedish Academy Sciences, 2008, National Journalism Award for Commentary, Scripps Howard Foundation, 2008, James Joyce Award, Literary & Historical Society, 2013,Princess of Asturias Award, 2004 **MEM:** Fellow: American Academy Arts & Sciences, Econometric Society; Mem.: Group of Thirty **BA:** The Graduate Center, CUNY, 365 Fifth Avenue, New York, NY, 10016

KRZANICH, BRIAN M., T: CEO of Intel **I:** Information Technology and Services **DOB:** 05/09/1960 **PB:** Santa Clara **SC:** CA/USA **ED:** BS in Chemistry, San Jose State University, 1982 **C:** CEO, Intel Corp., 2013-2018; Executive vice president, COO, head worldwide manufacturer, Intel Corp., 2012-13; Senior vice president, general manager, manufacturing & supply chain, Intel Corp., 2010-12; Vice president, general manager, manufacturing & supply chain, Intel Corp., 2007-10; Vice president, Intel Corp., Santa Clara, California, 2005-07; General manager, assembly test, Intel Corp., 2005-07; Various positions, assembly test, Intel Corp., 2003-05; Plant manager, Fab 17, Intel Corp., 1997-2001; Plant manager, Fab 6, Intel Corp., Arizona, 1996-97; Manufacturing manager, Fab 12, Intel Corp., Arizona, 1994-96; Process engineer, various locations, Intel Corp.,; Joined, Intel Corp., 1982 **CR:** Board directors Semiconductor Industry Association, Lilliputian Corp. **AW:** Recipient Achievement award, Intel Corp., 1999. **BA:** Intel Corp, 2200 Mission College Blvd, Santa Clara, CA, 95054-1549

KRZYZEWSKI, MIKE, T: College Basketball Coach **I:** Athletics **DOB:** 02/13/1947 **PB:** Chicago **SC:** IL/USA **PT:** Son of William and Emily M. (Pituch) Krzyzewski; **ED:** BS, US Military Academy, 1969 **C:** Head basketball coach, Duke University Blue Devils, Durham, North Carolina, 1980—; Head basketball coach, US Military Academy, West Point, New York, 1975-80; Assistant coach, Ind. University, 1974—1975; Head basketball coach, US Military Academy Prep School, Fort Belvoir, Virginia, 1972—1974 **CR:** Assistant coach US Men's National Basketball Team, 1979, 1984, 1992, head coach, 2006—, 2008, 2012, 2016 **CIV:** Chairman Children's Miracle Network Telethon; board directors V Foundation; with Comprehensive Cancer Center, NABC Coaches versus Cancer; board directors K Lab Human Performance; fundraising leader Emily Krzyzewski Center Immaculate Conception Catholic Church, Durham, North Carolina **MIL:** Served US Army, 1967—69, officer US Army, 1969—74, retired captain US Army, 1974 **CW:** Co-author (with Bill Brill): A Season Is a Lifetime: The Inside Story of the Duke Blue Devils and Their Championships Seasons, 1993; (with

Donald T. Phillips) Leading with the Heart: Coach K's Successful Strategies for Basketball, Business and Life, 2000, 5 Point Play: Duke's Journey to the 2001 National Championship, 2001, (with Jamie Krzyzewski Spatola) Beyond Basketball: Coach K's Keywords for Success, 2006, The Gold Standard: Building a World-Class Team, 2009 **AW:** Named Metropolitan New York Basketball Writer's Coach of Year, 1977, Coach of Year, Atlantic Coast Conference (ACC), 1984, 1986, 1997, 1999, 2000, National Coach of Year, Basketball Times, 1997, CBS/Chevrolet, 1986, 2000, Sporting News, 1992, United Press International, 1986, Victor awards, 2001, Sportsman of Year, Sporting News, 1992, Sports Illus., 2011, Coach of Decade, NABC, 1990, America's Best Coach, Time/CNN, 2001, 3d Best Coach All Time, CBS show; named to Naismith Memorial Basketball Hall of Fame, 2001; recipient Naismith College Coach of Year Award, 1989, 1992, 1999, Wooden award, Legends of Coaching, 2000, GTE (now Verizon) Reads with the NABC Lit. Champion award, 2000, Gold medal, Summer Olympic Games, Beijing, 2008, Summer Olympic Games, London, 2012, Summer Olympic Games, Rio de Janeiro, 2016,The Lincoln Academy of Illinois, 2014, Chicago History Museum Making History Award, 2013, Sports Illustrated Sportsman of the Year, 2011, Time Americas Best Coach Award, 2001 **MEM:** Mem.: NCAA (basketball issues committee), National Association Basketball Coaches (president 1998—99, District Coach of Year 1977, 1984, 1992, 1994, 1999, 2000, National Coach of Year 1991, 1999) **ACH:** Achievements include coaching the Duke University Blue Devils to the NCAA Final Four, 1986, 88, 89, 90, 91, 92, 94, 99, 2001, 2004, 2010, 2015; head coach of the NCAA Division I National Championship winning Duke University Blue Devils, 1991, 92, 2001, 2010, 2015; one of five coaches in NCAA history to earn 3 or more national championships along with John Wooden, Adolph Rupp, Bob Knight and Jim Calhoun; second head coach in Division I NCAA men's basketball history to reach 900 career wins, 2011; becoming NCAA Division I men's basketball all-time winningest head coach (903 victories), November 15, 2011; became the first NCAA Division I men's basketball coach to reach 1,000 career wins on January 25, 2015 **BA:** Cameron Indoor Stadium, 115 Whitford Dr, Durham, NC, 27705

KUCIJ, TIMOTHY MICHAEL, T: Composer, Arranger, Pianist **I:** Fine Art **CN:** Self-Employed **DOB:** 09/02/1954 **PB:** Whittier **SC:** CA/USA **PT:** Theodore G. Kucij; June Krebs Kucij **SPN:** Paulina V. Jimenez (1979) **ED:** ThM, Christian Bible College, Cum Laude (1983); BA in Music, California State Polytechnic University, Pomona (1978); Studied with Frank Sanucci, Edward D. Berryman, Thurla Wallis, Kathreen Prout, Eddy L. Manson, Henry Charles Smith, Joseph P. Free, Ronald Gearman (1965-1978); Coursework, Sherwood Music Conservatory, Chicago, IL (1965-1968); Graduate Coursework, Central Baptist Theological Seminary; Graduate Coursework, Maranatha Baptist Bible College (Now Maranatha Baptist University) **CT:** Licensed Minister, Baptist Church (1982) **C:** Freelance Composer, Arranger & Pianist (2014-Present); Quality Engineering Manager, UTC Aerospace Systems, Pomona, CA (2008-2014); Senior Quality Engineer, UTC Aerospace Systems, Pomona, CA (2008-2011); Senior Quality System Manager, TRW Automotive (Now ZF Friedrichshafen AG), Carson, CA (1998-2004); Senior Quality Engineer, Hi-Shear Corporation (Now Lisi Aerospace), Torrance, CA (1996-1998); Division Quality Assurance Engineer, Rexroth Corporation Piston Pump Division (Now Bosch Rexroth USA), Fountain Inn, SC (1992-1994); Quality Assurance Staff Specialist, Swedlow, Inc., Garden Grove, CA

(1990-1992); Manager of Quality Assurance, Composites Division, Swedlow, Inc., Garden Grove, CA (1988-1990); Senior Engineer of Quality and Reliability, Swedlow, Inc., Garden Grove, CA (1986-1988); Reliability Engineer, Advanced Systems Division, Northrop Corporation (Now Northrop Grumman Corporation), Pico Rivera, CA (1984-1986); Technical Writer, Honeywell Inc. (Now Honeywell International Inc.), West Covina, CA, Minneapolis, MN (1977-1984) **CR:** Music Teacher, Piano, Organ and Composition, CA (1971-1981); Active Pulpit Supply, Local Baptist Churches; Lecturer, Technology and Engineering **CIV:** Assistant Pastor, Calvary Baptist Tabernacle, Gardena, CA (2000-2004); Associate Pastor, Bethel Baptist Church, Torrance, CA (1996-2000); Pastor, First Missionary Baptist Church, Gardena, CA (1994-1996); Member, School Board, Church Council, Calvary Baptist Church, La Verne, CA (1989-1992); Board of Directors, Garden Grove Symphony Orchestra (Now The Orange County Symphony) (1989-1990); Music Director, Calvary Baptist Church, La Verne, CA (1988-1992); Bible Teacher, Calvary Baptist Church, La Verne, CA (1988-1992); Music Director, Covina Baptist Temple (1985-1987); Youth Director, Covina Baptist Temple (1985-1987); Pastor, Victory Baptist Church, Pine City, MN (1982-1983); Assistant to Local Pastors of Baptist Churches, Texas, Georgia, Wisconsin, Minnesota and California (1978-1982) **CW:** Musician, Recordings, KRC Records (1993-Present); Musician, "A Place Somewhere" (2003); Musician, "LifeSongs" (2003); Editor, "The Golden State Baptist" (1995-1996); Performer, Busch-Reisinger Museum, Harvard University (1972-1974); Performer, Pipe Organ, Wiltern Theater (1966-1968); Debut, Los Angeles, CA (1966); Performer, Organ and Piano; Composer, Score for Piano, "Persistence"; Composer, Score for Piano, "The Storm"; Composer, Score for Piano, "Purity"; Composer, Score for Piano, "Remembrance"; Composer, Score for Piano, "Your Song"; Composer, Score for Piano, "Yearning"; Composer, Score for Piano, "Compassion"; Composer, Score for Piano, "A Little Jingle"; Composer, Score for Piano, "A Familiar Song"; Composer, Score for Piano, "Images"; Composer, Score for Piano, "Paulina"; Composer, Score for Piano, "Afterthought"; Composer, Score for Piano, "Blue Fragrance"; Composer, Score for Piano, "Sunset"; Composer, Score for Piano, "Then"; Composer, Score for Piano, "Piano Lesson # 1"; Composer, Score for Piano, "Chase"; Composer, Score for Piano, "Unrest"; Composer, Score for Piano, "Nebulae"; Composer, Score for Piano, "Distress"; Composer, Score for Piano, "Retrograde"; Composer, Score for Piano, "Frolic"; Composer, Score for Piano, "The Happy Whistler"; Composer, Score for Piano, "The Little Toy March"; Composer, Score for Piano, "Hope"; Composer, Score for Piano, "Teardrops"; Composer, Score for Piano, "Reminisce"; Composer, Score for Piano, "Wind Chimes"; Composer, Score for Piano, "A Place Somewhere"; Composer, Score for Piano, "Rainbows"; Composer, Score for Piano, "The Bicentennial Rag"; Composer, Score for Piano, "The Pulsar Rag"; Composer, Score for Piano, "Dazzling Fingers"; Composer, Score for Piano, "The Butterfly Rag"; Composer, Score for Piano, "Serenity"; Composer, First 25 Original Pieces Written in Honor of American Bicentennial; CDs, Music Housed in LA County Library (Now County of Los Angeles Public Library); CDs, Music Housed in Dallas Public Library; CDs, Music Housed in Houston Public Library; Scorebook, Music Housed in Los Angeles Public Library; Scorebook, Music Housed in St. Louis Public Library; CDs & Scorebook, Music Housed in Atlanta-Fulton County Library (Now Atlanta-Fulton Public Library System); CDs & Scorebook, Music Housed in Master's College Library (Now The

Master's University Library); CDs & Scorebook, Music Housed in California State Polytechnic University Library; Scorebook, Music Housed in University of South Carolina Library (Now Thomas Cooper Library); CDs, Music Housed in Chicago Public Library; Music Housed in Juilliard School of Music Library (Now The Lila Acheson Wallace Library); CDs, Music Housed in California Baptist University Library (Now Ann Gabriel Library); CDs & Scorebook, Music Housed in Biola University Library; CDs & Scorebook, Music Housed in The New York Public Library; CDs & Scorebook, Music Housed in Cleveland Public Library; Scorebook, Music Housed in Boston Public Library; CDs & Scorebook, Music Housed in Harvard University Library (Now Harvard Library); CDs, Music Housed in University of Kansas Gorton Music Library (Now Thomas Gorton Music and Dance Library); CDs & Scorebook, Music Housed in Greenville County Library; CDs, Music Housed in Central Baptist Theology Seminary Library; CDs, Music Housed in Torrance Public Library; CDs, Music Housed in Whittier Public Library; Music Housed in Others; Scored Comprehensive Piano Arrangement, "Jesus Loves Me"; Scored Comprehensive Piano Arrangement, "Over the Rainbow"; Songwriter, "Jesus is the Answer"; Songwriter, "O Jesus"; Contributor, Articles to Various Periodicals; Composer, Scores of Original Piano Pieces; Performed Nationally, Piano & Pipe Organ; Composer, Scores of Comprehensive Piano Arrangements **AW:** Albert Nelson Marquis Lifetime Achievement Award (2017); Distinguished Alumnus Award, California State Polytechnic University (1989); Named One of Outstanding Young Men in America, US Jaycees (Now JCI Inc.) (1980); Performer's Certificate (1967); First Prize, Southern California Organ Competition (1966) **MEM:** The Gospel Coalition, Inc.; Founders Ministries (Now Founders Ministries, Inc.); Creation Research Society; Broadcast Music, Inc.; American Composers Forum; Christian Fellowship of Art Music Composers; American Society for Quality **MH:** Albert Nelson Marquis Lifetime Achievement Award (2017) **PA:** Republican **ADD:** 2711 Westfield Pl, Claremont, CA, 91711 **URL:** http://www.timkucij.com

KUDLOW, LAWRENCE ALAN, T: Director, National Economic Council, Former Financial News Correspondent, Economist **I:** Financial Services **DOB:** 08/20/1947 **PB:** NYC **PT:** Son of Irving H. and Ruth (Grodnick) K.; **MS:** Married **SPN:** Judy Pond, July 11, 1987. **ED:** LLD (hon.), Monmouth University, 2009; Postgrad., Woodrow Wilson School, Princeton University, 1971-73; BA in History, University Rochester, 1969 **C:** Director of the National Economic Council, Office of the White House, 2018-; Host The Kudlow Report, CNBC, 2009-2018; Economics editor, National Review Online (NRO), 2001-; Founder, CEO, Kudlow & Co., LLC,; Co-host The Call, CNBC,; Host The Larry Kudlow Show, WABC Radio,; Host, Kudlow & Company, CNBC, 2005-08; Co-host Kudlow & Cramer, CNBC, 2002-05; Co-host America Now, CNBC, 2001-02; Economic counsel, A.B. Laffer & Associates, San Diego,; Chief economist, senior managing director, chairman investment policy committee, Bear Stearns & Co., Inc., New York City, 1986-94; President, CEO, Lawrence Kudlow & Associates, Washington, 1983-86; Associate director economics & planning, Office Management & Budget, Executive Office of President, Washington, 1982-83; Assistant director economic policy, Office Management & Budget, Executive Office of President, Washington, 1981-82; Chief economist, Bear Stearns & Co., New York City, 1979-81; Corp. vice president, chief economist, Paine Webber, Jackson & Curtis, New York City, 1975-79; Staff economist, Federal Reserve Bank New York, New York City, 1973-75 **CR:** Frequent commentator PBS's MacNeil-Lehrer

Report, Nightly Business Report, CNN's Crossfire, ABC's Business World other network appearances include This Week with David Brinkley, Nightline, 60 Minutes and Larry King Live regular panelist CNBC's Strictly Business Disting Scholar, Mercatus Center, George Mason University **CIV:** Board directors Am. Council on Germany, Institute Educational Affairs, Change New York, Empire Foundation, Madison Center for Educational Affairs, Emergency Shelter, Inc. former member board governors Smith Richardson Foundation **CW:** Contributor op-ed. articles to Wall Street Journal, New York Times, Washington Times and other journals; author: American Abundance: The New Economic and Moral Prosperity, 1998, Tide: Why Tax Cuts Are the Key to Prosperity and Freedom, 2005 **AW:** Named one of The Top 25 Market Movers, US News & World Report, 2009 **MEM:** Member fiscal policy studies adv. council Am. Enterprise Institute, New York State Legis. Committee on Private-Public Co-operation, U.S. C of C., Hudson Institute Center, Heritage Foun., Cato Inst, Union League Club, Capitol Hill Club, Princeton Club, National Women's Rep. Club. **H:** Tennis, golf **PA:** Republican **BA:** National Economic Council Office of the White House, 1600 Pennsylvania Avenue NW, Washington, DC, 20500

KUNDERA, MILAN, T: Writer **I:** Writing and Editing **DOB:** 04/01/1929 **PB:** Prague **SC:** Czechoslovakia **PT:** Son of Lidvik and Milada (Janosikova) K.; **MS:** Married **SPN:** Vera Hrabankova, 1967 **ED:** D.h.c., University Michigan, 1983; Student Film Faculty, Academy Music & Dramatic Arts, Prague **C:** Professor, Ecole des Hautes Études en Scis. Sociales, Paris, 1980-94; Professor, University Rennes, France, 1975-80; Assistant professor film Film Faculty, Academy Music and Dramatic Arts, 1958-69; Writer, 1967- **CW:** Author: Směšné lásky (pub. as Laughable Loves, 1974; Czech Writers' Pub. House prize 1969, Zert, 1967 (pub. as The Joke, 1969; Czech Writers' Union prize 1968), La Vie est ailleurs, 1973 (pub. as Life Is Elsewhere, 1974, Prix Medicis 1973), La Valse aux adieux, 1976 (pub. as The Farewell Waltz, 1973; Premio Letterario Mondello 1978), Le Livre du rire et de l'oubli, 1979 (pub. as The Book of Laughter and Forgetting, 1980), Jakub a pan, 1971 (pub. as Jacques le Fataliste et son maître, hommage Denis Diderot, Jacques and His Master), L'Insoutenable Légèreté de l'être, 1984 (pub. as The Unbearable Lightness of Being, 1984; L.A. Times book prize for fiction 1984), L'Art du roman, 1986 (pub. as The Art of the Novel, 1987), L'Immortalità, 1990 (pub. as Immortality, 1991), Les Testaments Trahis (Testaments Betrayed 1996), 1993, La Lenteur (The Slowness 1996), 1995, Identity. A Novel, 1998, L'Ignorance, 2000,(Book) The Festival of Insignificance, 2014 **AW:** Recipient Commonwealth award distinguished service in lit., 1981, Prix Europa for lit., 1982, Jerusalem prize, 1985, Acadmie Française Critics prize, 1987, Nell Sachs prize, 1987, Osterichisheve state prize, 1987, Ind. award for foreign fiction, 1991, Prix Mondial Cino Del Duca, 2009, Ovid Prize, 2011 **ADD:** c/o Gallinard, 5 Rue Sebastien-Bottin, Paris, YT, France, 75007

KUSAMA, YAYOI, T: Sculptor, Painter **I:** Fine Art **DOB:** 03/22/1929 **PB:** Matsumoto-shi **SC:** Nagano/ Japan **ED:** Student, Kyoto Arts and Crafts School, Japan, 1948-1949 **C:** President, Japan Education Co., 1977 **CW:** Author, (Books) Manhattan Suicide Addict, 1978, Christopher Homosexual Brothel, 1983, The Hustler's Grotto of Christopher Street, 1983, Lost in Swapland, 1992, Others; Contributor, Articles, Magazines and Newspapers; Producer, Star, Kusama's Self-Obliteration; Organizer, Presenter, Worldwide Events **AW:** Fourth International Experimental Film Competition Prize, Ann Arbor

Film Festival Prize, Second Maryland Film Festival Prize, Kusama's Self-Obliteration, 1968, Tenth Literature New Writers Award, The Hustler's Grotto of Christopher Street, 1983, Best Gallery Show Prize, International Association of Art Critics, 1995-1997, Education Minister's Art Encouragement Prize, Foreign Minister's Commendations, 2000, Asahi Prize, 2001, Dark Navy Blue Ribbon Medal, 2002, Nagano Governor Prize Contribution in Encouragement of Art and Culture, 2003, Praemium Imperiaie (Painting), Japan Art Association, 2006, Decorated Officer **ACH:** Invented infinity mirror room. **ADD:** Kusama Building, 109 Bentencho, Tokyo, Japan, -1013

KUSHNER, JARED COREY, T: Senior Advisor to the President **I:** Government Administration/Government Relations/Government Services **DOB:** 01/10/1981 **PB:** Livingston **SC:** NJ/USA **PT:** Charles B. Kushner, Seryl Kushner **ED:** Student, New York University Stern School of Business; Student, New York University Law School; BA, Harvard University, 2003 **C:** Senior Advisor to the President, 2017-Present; Director of the Office of American Innovation, 2017-Present; Owner, Politicsnj.com, 2007-Present; Owner, Public, New York Observer, 2006-Present; Principal, Kushner Companies; Intern, Square Mile Capital **CW:** Appearance, (TV Series) Gossip Girl, 2010 **AW:** Time 100 Most Influential People, 2017-Present **ACH:** Achievements include being involved in purchase or sale of more than 35 buildings since age 19; purchase of 666 Fifth Avenue, the largest single building transaction in the country **BA:** New York Observer, 9th Floor, 915 Broadway, New York, NY, 10010

KUSHNER, TONY, T: Playwright, Scriptwriter **I:** Writing and Editing **DOB:** 07/16/1956 **PB:** NYC **SC:** New York **PT:** Son of William Kushner and Sylvia Deutscher; **ED:** Student, New York University; Student, Columbia University **CR:** Playwright-in-residence Juilliard School of Drama, 1990-92 director literary services Theatre Communications Group, New York City, 1990-91 guest artist, grad. theater program Yale University, New York University & Princeton University, 1989-associate artistic director New York Theatre Workshop, 1987 **CW:** Author: (plays) A Bright Room Called Day, 1990, Angels in America: A Gay Fantasia on National Themes Part I "Millenium Approaches", 1992 (Pulitzer Prize for Drama, 1993, Tony award for Best Play, 1993), Part II "Perestroika", 1993 (Tony award for Best Play, 1994), Slavs!, 1994, Thinking about the Longstanding Problems of Virtue and Happiness, 1995 (Lambda Literary award, 1996), Dybbuk and Other Tales of the Supernatural, 1997, Death and Taxes, 2000, Homebody/Kabul, 2001, Caroline, or Change, 2003 (Obie award, 2004), Only We Who Guard the Mystery Shall Be Unhappy, 2004; adaptor (plays) The Illusion (Pierre Corneille), 1988, A Dybbuk (S.Y. Ansky), 1995, Good Person of Setzuan (Bertolt Brecht), 1999, Mother Courage and Her Children (Bertolt Brecht), 2006,The Intelligent Homosexual's Guide to Capitalism and Socialism with a Key to the Scriptures, 2009, Tiny Kushner, 2009, (Operas) Brundibar, 2003, director, author Yes Yes No No: The Solice of Solstice, Apogee/ Perigee, Bestial/Celestial Holiday Show, 1985, In Great Eliza's Golden Time, 1986, writer (TV miniseries) Angels in America, 2003 (Emmy award, Outstanding Writing for a Miniseries, Movie or a Dramatic Series, 2004), (films) Munich, 2005, Lincoln, 2012 (Best Screenplay, New York Film Critics Cir., Boston Society Film Critics, 2012, Best Adapted Screenplay, Critics Choice Awards, 2013, Best Screenplay, National Society Film Critics, 2013) **AW:** Recipient National Medal of Arts, National Endowment for the Arts, 2012, Puffin/

Nation Prize, 2011, Steinberg Distinguished Playwright award, 2008, American Academy of Arts and Letters award, 1994, London Evening Standard award, 1992, Will Glickman playwriting prize, 1992, Kesserling award, National Arts Club, 1992, John Whiting award, Arts Council of Great Britain, 1990, Princess Grace award, 1986; grantee National Education Association, 1993, 1987, 1985 **MEM:** Mem.: American Academy of Arts and Letters **BA:** 114 Fifth Ave, New York, NY, 10011

KUSTER, ANN MCLANE, T: U.S. Representative from New Hampshire, lobbyist **I:** Government Administration/Government Relations/Government Services **DOB:** 09/05/1956 **PB:** Concord **PT:** Daughter of Malcolm and Susan (Neidlinger) McLane; **ED:** JD, Georgetown University Law Center, 1984; BS in Environmental Policy, Dartmouth College, 1978 **C:** Member, US House Veterans' Committee, 2013-; Member, US House Small Business Committee, 2013-; Member, US House Agricultural Committee, 2013-; Member, US Congress from 2nd New Hampshire District, Washington, 2013-; Owner, consultant, Newfound Strategies, LLC, 2001-; Of counsel, Rath, Young & Pignatelli,; Staff member to Rep. Pete McCloskey, US House of Representatives, Washington, 1978-81 **CR:** Del. Democratic National Convention, 2008, 2004, New Hampshire Delegation, Boston, 2004 co-chair New Hampshire Women for Obama member New Hampshire steering committee Barack Obama's Presidential Campaign, 2007-08, John Kerry's Presidential Campaign, 2003-04 founder Women's Fund of New Hampshire **CW:** Co-author (with Susan McLane): The Last Dance: Facing Alzheimer's with Love and Laughter, 2006 **AW:** Recipient Rainbow award, Riverbend Community Mental Health Center, 2008, Marilla M. Ricker Achievement award, New Hampshire Women's Bar Assn, 2004 **MEM:** Mem.: American Academy Adoption Attorneys **PA:** Democrat

KUSTOFF, DAVID F., T: U.S. Representative from Tennessee, Lawyer, Former Prosecutor **I:** Government Administration/Government Relations/Government Services **DOB:** 10/08/1966 **PB:** Memphis **ED:** JD, University of Memphis, 1992; BBA, University of Memphis, 1989 **C:** Member, U.S. House of Representatives from Tennessee's 8th District, 2017-, Member, Republican Study Committee; US attorney (we. district) Tennessee, US Department of Justice, Memphis, 2006-08; Partner, Kustoff & Strickland PLLC, Memphis, **CIV:** Head, Bush-Cheney election effort, 2004 Head, Bush-Cheney election effort, Tennessee, 2000 Chairman, Shelby County Rep. Party, Tennessee, **BAR:** Tennessee Bar: 1992 **BA:** 508 Cannon House Office Building, Washington, DC, 20515

KWAN, KEVIN, T: Novelist **I:** Writing and Editing **CW:** (Novels) Crazy Rich Asians, 2013, China Rich Girlfriend,2015, Rich People Problems, 2016 **AW:** Time 100 Most Influential, 2018

LA MALFA, DOUG, T: U.S. Congressman from California **I:** Government Administration/Government Relations/Government Services **DOB:** 07/02/1960 **PB:** Oroville, California, July 2, 1960 **ED:** BS, California Poly. State University, San Luis Obispo, 1982; AA, Butte College, 1980 **C:** Member, US House Foreign Affairs Committee, 2013-; Member, US House Financial Services Committee, 2013-; Member, US Congress from 1st California District, Washington, 2013-; Owner, manager, Dsl Lamalfa Family Partnership, 1990-; Member District 4, California State Senate, 2010-12; Member District 2, California State Assembly, 2002-08; Vice chairman, Butte County Rep. Central Committee, 1992-2002 **CR:** Founding director California Rice Commission **CIV:** Past chairman, Richvale Foundation Boosters **PA:** Republican

LA RUSSA, TONY JR., T: President of Baseball Operations **I:** Athletics **CN:** Boston Red Sox **DOB:** 10/04/1944 **PB:** Tampa **SC:** FL/USA **MS:** Married **SPN:** Elaine Coker, 12/31/1973; Luzette Sarcone, Divorced 1973 **CH:** Andrea, Averie, Bianca, Devon **ED:** JD, Florida State University College of Law, 1978; BA, University of South Florida, 1969; Student, University of Tampa **C:** Manager, St. Louis Cardinals, 1996-2011; Manager, Oakland Athletics, 1986-1995; Manager, Chicago White Sox, 1979-1986; Manager, Iowa Oaks, American Association, 1979; Coach, Chicago White Sox, 1978; Minor League Minor League Manager, Knoxville Sox, Southern League, 1978; Coach, St. Louis Cardinals, 1977; Infielder, Chicago Cubs, 1973; Infielder, Atlanta Braves, 1971; Infielder, Oakland Athletics, 1968-1971; Infielder, Kansas City Athletics, 1963 **CR:** Manager, American League All-Star Team, 1988, National League All-Star Team, 2005 **CIV:** Co-Founder, Tony LaRussa's Animal Rescue Foundation, 1991-Present **CW:** Author, One Last Strike: Fifty Years in Baseball, Ten and a Half Games Back, and One Final Championship Season, 2012 **AW:** American League Manager of the Year, Major League Baseball, 1983, 1988, 1992, Named To The National Italian American Sports Hall Of Fame, 1998, National League Manager of the Year, 2002, C.I. Taylor Award, Negro League Hall Of Fame, 2004, The Missouri Sports Hall Of Fame, 2006, The Hispanic Heritage Baseball Museum Hall Of Fame, 2010, Ellis Island Family Heritage Award (Sports), 2012, Baseball Hall Of Fame, 2013, St. Louis Cardinals Hall Of Fame, 2014 **BAR:** State of Florida, 1979 **ACH:** Achievements include manager of the World Series Championship winning Oakland Athletics, 1989; St. Louis Cardinals, 2006, 2011; becoming the second manager in Major League Baseball history to win the World Series in both leagues; winning his 2,500th career game as a manager, 2009 **BA:** St. Louis Cardinals Busch Stadium, 250 Stadium Plaza, Saint Louis, MO, USA, 63102-1722

LABRADOR, RAUL RAFAEL, T: U.S. Representative from Idaho **I:** Government Administration/ Government Relations/Government Services **DOB:** 12/08/1967 **PB:** Carolina, Puerto Rico, December 8, 1967 **ED:** JD, University Washington, 1995; BA in Spanish, Brigham Young University, 1992 **C:** Member, Judiciary Committee; Member, US House Natural Resources Committee, Washington, 2011-; Member, US House Ethics Committee, Washington, 2011-; Member, US Congress from 1st Idaho District, Washington, 2011-; Member District 14B, Idaho House of Reps., 2007-10; Managing partner, Labrador Law Offices,; Attorney, Belnap & Curtis, 1998; Associate, Herrington Law Offices,; Associate, Cusack & Knowles, 1998-2000; Law clerk, US District Court, Idaho, 1996-98 **PA:** Republican

LAFLEUR, GUY, T: Retired Professional Hockey Player **I:** Athletics **DOB:** 09/20/1951 **PB:** Thurso **SC:** Que. Can. **PT:** Son of Rejean and Pierrette Lafleur; **ED:** Student pub. schools **C:** Director of corporate affairs, Quebec Nordiques, 1992-93; Right wing, Quebec Nordiques, 1989-91; Right wing, New York Rangers, 1988-89; Right wing, Montreal Canadiens, 1971-85; Right wing, Quebec Remparts, 1969-71 **CR:** Owner Bleu Blanc Rouge, Rosemere, Quebec, 2008- Guy LaFleur Mike's Signature, Berthierville, Quebec, 2002- vice president public relations Titrex, 1993 **AW:** Named Knight of the National Order of Quebec, 2005, NHL Player of Year, Sporting News, 1978, 1977; named to Can. Sports Hall of Fame, 1996, Order of Canada, 1980; recipient Lou Marsh Trophy, 1977, Hart Memorial Trophy, 1978, 1977, Conn Smythe Trophy, 1977, Lester B. Pearson Award, 1978, 1977, 1976, Art Ross Trophy, 1978, 1977, 1976, 1976,100 Greatest

NHL Players in History, 2017 **ACH:** Achievements include being a member of Stanely Cup Champion Montreal Canadiens, 1973, 1976, 1977, 1978, 1979

LAGASSE, EMERIL, T: Chef **I:** Food & Restaurant Services **DOB:** 10/15/1959 **PB:** Fall River **SC:** MA/USA **PT:** John Lagasse, Hilda Lagasse **ED:** Student, Culinary Arts, France; Honorary Doctorate, Johnson & Wales University, Providence, RI; BS in Culinary Arts, Johnson & Wales University, Providence, RI **C:** Owner, Chef, Emeril's Italian Table, Sands Casino Resort, Bethlehem, PA, 2011-Present; Owner, Chef, E2 Emeril's Eatery, Charlotte, NC, 2011-Present; Owner, Chef, Burgers And More By Emeril, Sands Casino Resort, Bethlehem, PA, 2009-Present; Owner, Chef, Lagasse's Stadium, Las Vegas, NV, 2009-Present; Owner, Chef, Emeril's Chop House, Sands Casino Resort, Bethlehem, PA, 2009-Present; Host, Cooking Show, Essence of Emeril (The Fine Living Network), 2008-Present; Owner, Chef, Table 10, Las Vegas, NV, 2008-Present; Owner, Chef, Emeril's Gulf Coast Fish House, Gulfport, MS, 2007-Present; Owner, Chef, Emeril's Atlanta, GA, 2003-Present; Owner, Chef, Tchoup Chop Restaurant, Orlando, FL, 2003-Present; Owner, Chef, Delmonico Steakhouse Restaurant, Las Vegas, NV, 1999-Present; Owner, Chef, Emeril's Orlando, Orlando, FL, 1999-Present; Owner, Chef, Delmonico Restaurant And Bar, New Orleans, LA, 1998-Present; Food Correspondent, Good Morning America, ABC, 1998-Present; Owner, Chef, Emeril's New Orleans Fish House Restaurant, Las Vegas, NV, 1995-Present; Host, Cooking Show, Essence of Emeril (The Food Network), 1994-Present; Owner, Chef, Nola Restaurant, New Orleans, LA, 1992-Present; Owner, Chef, Emeril's Restaurant, New Orleans, LA, 1990-Present; Owner, Chef, Emeril's Miami Beach, FL, 2003-2011; Host, Cooking Show, Emeril Live (The Food Network), 1997-2007; Executive Chef, Commander's Palace, New Orleans, LA, 1983-1990 **CR:** Partner, T-Fal to Develop Emerilware Fryer, Grill/Panini Maker and Steamer, 2006-Present, Emeril Professional Stoneware, 2005-Present, Partner, All-Clad Metalcrafters For Emerilware, 1999-Present, Emerilware Cookware and Gourmet Kitchen Tools Brought The HSN, 2007, Launches Emeril's Gourmet Produce With Pride of San Juan, 2004, Launches Emerilware Electric Appliance Collection And Emerilware Cast Iron Cookware, 2004, Launches Emeril's Gourmet Meats With Sara Lee Foods, 2004, Introduces Clog Line Called Emeril By Sanita, 2003, Launches A California Wines Line Called Emeril's Classics With Fetzer Vineyards, 2002, Launches Emerilware Knives With Wusthof-Trident, 2002, Launches Emeril's Original, Gourmet Food Line of Seasonings, Salad Dressing, Pasta Sauces and More, 2000 **CIV:** Established, Emeril Lagasse Foundation, 2002, Dedication, Emeril Lagasse Foundation Culinary Arts Studio, 2011 **CW:** Author, (Cookbooks) Emeril's New New Orleans Cooking, 1993, Louisiana Real And Rustic, 1996, Emeril's Creole Christmas, 1997, Emeril's TV Dinners, 1998, Every Day's A Party, 1999, Prime Time Emeril: More TV Dinners From America's Favorite Chef, 2001, There's A Chef In My Soup, 2002, From Emeril's Kitchens: Favorite Recipes From Emeril's Restaurants, 2003, There's A Chef In My Family, 2004, Emeril's Potluck: Comfort Food With A Kicked-Up Attitude, 2004, Emeril's Delmonico: A New Orleans Restaurant With A Past, 2005, There's A Chef In My World, 2006, Emeril 20-40-60: Fresh Food Fast, 2009, Emeril At The Grill: A Cookbook For All Seasons, 2009, Farm To Fork: Cooking Local, Cooking Fresh, 2010, Sizzling Skillets And Other One-Pot Wonders, 2011, Emeril's Kicked-Up Sandwiches: Stacked With Flavor, 2012, Emeril's Cooking With Power: 100 Delicious Recipes Starring Your Slow Cooker, Multi Cooker, Pressure Cooker, And Deep Fryer, 2013,

Essential Emeril: Favorite Recipes And Hard-Won Wisdom From My Life In The Kitchen, 2015; Judge, (TV Series) Top Chef, 2011; Host, The Originals With Emeril, Cooking Channel, 2011-Present, Emeril's Table, Hallmark Channel, 2011-Present, Emeril Live, Cooking Channel, Fresh Food Fast, Cooking Channel, 2010-Present, Live, Call-In Radio Program Cooking With Emeril, Martha Stewart Living Radio On SIRIUS XM, 2009-Present, Planet Green: Emeril Green, 2008-Present, The Emeril Lagasse Show, Ion TV, 2010; Co-Writer, (Column) Everyday Food Magazine; Guest Appearances, Jon & Kate Plus 8, 2009, Voice, The Princess And The Frog, 2009; Competitor, Super Chef Battle, Iron Chef America, 2010, Stars In Comedy Series Emeril, 2001; Mentor, On The Menu, 2014 **AW:** Honor By The James Beard Foundation For Dedicated Efforts To Further The Culinary Arts In America, The Emeril Lagasse Foundation, 2011, Lifetime Achievement Award, Food Network's South Beach Wine & Food Festival, 2009, Gaming Hall of Fame, 2008, Restaurateur of the Year, New Orleans City-business, 2007, Menumasters Hall of Fame, 2006, Distinguished Service Award, Wine Spectator Magazine, 2005, Executive of the Year, Restaurants & Institutions Magazine, 2004, Grand Award, Wine Spectator Magazine, 1999, Salute To Excellence Award, National Restaurant Association, 1998, Chef of the Year, GQ Magazine, 1998, Most Intriguing People of the Year, People Magazine, 1998, Cable ACE Award For Best Informational Series-Emeril Live, 1997, Ivy Award For Restaurants And Institutions, 1994, American Express For Fine Dining Hall Of Fame, 1994, Best Esquire Award For Restaurant of the Year, 1993, Best Chef Southeast, James Beard Foundation, 1991, Food And Wine Award For One Of America's Top 25 New Chefs, 1991, Esquire Award For Restaurant of the Year, 1991, America's Top Twenty-Five New Chefs, Food & Wine, 1991 **ACH:** Achievements include being first celebrity chef to have meals and recipes developed for NASA and served in Space, 2006; restaurants have received several awards and acknowledgements; The Emeril Lagasse Foundation raises millions of dollars each year with the culinary event Carnivale du Vin

LAHOOD, DARIN M., T: U.S. Representative from Illinois **I:** Government Administration/Government Relations/Government Services **ED:** JD, John Marshall Law School, 1997; Bachelor in Political Sci., Loras College, Dubuque, Iowa **CT:** Bar: Illinois 1997 **C:** Member, U.S. House of Representatives from Illinois's 18th District, 2015-, Member Committee on Natural Resources, Committee on Science, Space, and Technology; Member District 37, Illinois State Senate, Springfield, 2011-2015; Attorney, Miller, Hall & Triggs, Peoria, Illinois, 2006-; Lead terrorism prosecutor for district Nevada, Office of U.S. Attorney, 2005-06; Federal prosecutor, Office of US Attorney, Las Vegas, Nevada, 2001-05; Assistant state's attorney, Cook County, Tazewell County, Illinois, 1997-2001; Legis assistant, appropriations committee assistant, U.S. House of Representatives, Washington, DC 1990-94 **CR:** Adjunct professor criminal law University of Nevada Las Vegas, 2003-05 **CIV:** Member, St. Vincent de Paul Parish, Illinois, Board directors, The Center Prevention of Abuse, 2006-10 Former board member, Salvation Army, Former board member, Big Brothers/Big Sisters, **PA:** Republican **BA:** 1424 Longworth HOB, Washington, DC, 20515

LAI, JIMMY, I: Publishing **DOB:** 12/08/1948 **PB:** Guangzhou **SC:** Guangdong, China **C:** President, founder, Apple Daily, Taiwan, 2003-; President, founder, Apple Daily, Hong Kong, 1995-; President, founder, Next Magazine, Taiwan, 2001-; President, founder, Next Magazine, Hong Kong,

1989-; Founder, AdMart, 1999; President, founder, Giordano, Hong Kong, 1981-96 **CR:** Chairman Next Media Ltd., 1999- **RE:** Catholic

LAMAR, KENDRICK, T: Rapper **I:** Media & Entertainment **PB:** Compton **SC:** CA/USA **CW:** Rapper (albums) Section.80, 2011, Good Kid, M.A.A.D City, 2012, To Pimp a Butterfly, 2015 (Grammy award for Best Rap Album, 2016), Damn, 2017 (songs) Bad Blood (with Taylor Swift), 2014 (Grammy award for Best Music Video, 2016), i, 2014 (Grammy awards for Best Rap Song, Best Rap Performance, 2015), Alright, 2015 (MTV Video Music award for Best Direction, 2015, Grammy award for Best Rap Performance, Best Rap Song, 2016), These Walls (featuring Bilal, Anna Wise & Thundercat), 2015 (Grammy award for Best Rap/Sung Collaboration, 2016) **AW:** Named Best Male Hip-Hop Artist, BET Awards, 2015, 2013, Best New Artist, 2013, American Music Awards, Favorite Rap Album, 2017,BET Best Male Hi-Hop Artist, 2017, Grammy for Best Rap Song and Performance, 2015, Best Rap Song, 2016, Best Rap Collaboration, 2016,Best Rap Album 2016

LAMBERT, MIRANDA LEIGH, T: Musician **I:** Media & Entertainment **DOB:** 11/10/1983 **PB:** Longview **SC:** TX/USA **PT:** Richard Lee Lambert, Beverly June (Hughes) Lambert **C:** Country Girl Group, Pistol Annies, 2011-Present; Solo Musician, 2001-Present **CIV:** Founder, Owner, Redemption Ranch, Tishomingo, OK, 2014-Present **CW:** Contestant, (Reality TV Series) Nashville Star, 2003; Musician, (Albums) Miranda Lambert, 2001, Kerosene, 2005, Crazy Ex-Girlfriend, 2007, Revolution, 2009, Four the Record, 2011, Platinum, 2014, The Weight of These Wings, 2016, (With Pistol Annies) Hell on Heels, 2011, Hush Hush, 2013, (Songs) White Liar, 2009, The House That Built Me, 2010, Over You, 2011, Mama's Broken Heart, 2011, Automatic, 2014, (With Keith Urban) We Were Us, 2013, (With Carrie Underwood) Somethin' Bad, 2014, (With Little Big Town) Smokin' And Drinkin', 2014, (Television Performances) CMT Cross Country, 2007, The Voice, 2011, Law & Order: SVU, 2012 **AW:** Vocal Event of the Year, Academy Country Music Awards, Smokin' and Drinkin', 2016, Best Country Album, Grammy Awards, Album of the Year, Academy Country Music Awards, Platinum, 2015, Collaborative Video of the Year, CMT Music Awards, Somethin' Bad, 2015, Song of the Year, Academy Country Music Awards, Automatic, 2015, Milestone Award, 2015, Album of the Year, Country Music Association Awards, Platinum, 2014, Female Video of the Year, CMT Music Awards, Single of the Year, Country Music Association Awards, Automatic, 2014, Vocal Event of the Year, ACAD Country Music Awards, Musical Event of the Year, Country Music Association Awards, We Were Us, 2014, Single Record of the Year, Academy Country Music Awards, Mama's Broken Heart, 2014, Song of the Year, Single Record of the Year, Academy Country Music Awards, Performance of the Year, CMT Music Awards, Over You, 2013, Female Video of the Year, CMT Music Awards, Mama's Broken Heart, 2013, Female Video of the Year, CMT Music Awards, Song of the Year, Country Music Association Awards, Over You, 2012, Album of the Year, Academy Country Music Awards, Four the Record, 2012, Best Female Country Vocal Performance, Grammy Awards, Single Record of the Year, Video of the Year, Song of the Year, Academy Country Music Awards, Female Video of the Year, CMT Music Awards, The House That Built Me, 2011, Academy Country Music Awards, 2010-2016, Female Vocalist of the Year, Country Music Association Awards, 2010-2015, Video of the Year, Academy Country Music Awards, Female Video of the Year, CMT Music Awards, White Liar,

2010, Album of the Year, Academy Country Music Awards, Album of the Year, Country Music Association Awards, Revolution, 2010, Music Video of the Year, Song of the Year, Country Music Association Awards, The House That Built Me, 2010, Album of the Year, Academy Country Music Awards, Crazy Ex-Girlfriend, 2008, Top New Female Vocalist, 2007, Cover Girl Fresh Face of Country Music Award, 2005, Third-Place Winner, Nashville Star, 2003 **BA:** Frontpage Publicity, 1188 Ben Collier Road, Charlotte, NC, 37036-5900

LAMBORN, DOUGLAS L., T: U.S. Representative from Colorado **I:** Government Administration/Government Relations/Government Services **DOB:** 05/24/1954 **ED:** JD, University Kansas, 1985; Bachelor in Journalism, University Kansas, 1978 **C:** Member, US Congress from 5th Colorado district, 2006-;; Member, Committee on Education and the Workforce, Committee on Natural Resources, Committee on Rules; Private General Practice Attorney, Colorado Springs, 1987-; Member Natural Resources Committee Vets. Affairs Committee, Armed Services Committee, US Congress from 5th Colorado District; President Pro-tem, Chairman State, Vets. & Military Affairs Committee, Colorado State Senate,; Member District 9, Colorado State Senate, Denver, 1997-2006; Rep. Whip, Colorado House of Reps., 1997; Member, Colorado House of Reps., 1995-97 **CR:** Member We. States Reps. Leadership Conference, 1993, 1989 **CIV:** Former member citizen's adv. committee, Pikes Peak Area Council Govt.'s, Member prin.'s adv. council, Antelope Trails Elementary School, Colorado Springs, **PA:** Republican

LAMPERT, EDDIE, T: CEO **I:** Consumer Goods and Services **CN:** Sears Holdings **PB:** Roslyn **SC:** NY/US **ED:** B.S.,Economics, Yale University **C:** CEO, Sears Holdings Corp, 2013-; Founder, ESL Partners LP, 1989-; Chairman/CEO/Founder, ESL Investments Inc, 1988-

LANCE, LEONARD, T: U.S. Representative from New Jersey, former state legislator **I:** Government Administration/Government Relations/Government Services **DOB:** 06/25/1952 **PB:** Easton **PT:** Son of Wesley L. and Anne (Anderson) L.; Married Heidi A. Rohrbach. **ED:** MPA, Princeton University, 1982; JD, Vanderbilt University, 1977; BA, Lehigh University, 1974 **C:** Member, US Congress from 7th New Jersey District, 2009-; Member, Committee on Energy and Commerce; Minority leader, New Jersey State Senate from District 23, 2004-07; Member, New Jersey State Senate from District 23, 2002-09; Member, New Jersey General Assembly from District 23, Trenton, 1991-2002; Assistant counsel to Gov, State of New Jersey, Trenton, New Jersey, 1983-90; Law clerk to judges, Warren County Court, Belvidere, New Jersey, 1977-78 **CIV:** Member Grandin Libr. Board, Clinton, New Jersey, 1990-2000, New Jersey Council for Humanities, Trenton, 1994- trustee Newark Museum, 1995-, Centenary College, Hackettstown, New Jersey, 1998-, McCarter Theatre, 1998-2007. **MEM:** Member Princeton Club New York, Phi Beta Kappa. **PA:** Republican **BA:** 2352 Rayburn HOB, Washington, DC, 20515

LANCE, RYAN MICHAEL, T: Oil Industry Executive **I:** Oil & Energy **PB:** Blythville **SC:** AR/USA **ED:** BS in Petroleum Engineering, Montana Tech of the University of Montana, Butte, MT, 1984 **C:** Chairman, CEO, Conocophillips, Houston, TX, 2012-Present; Senior Vice President, Exploration & Production-International, Conocophillips, Houston, TX, 2009-2012; President, Exploration & Production, Europe, Asia, Africa, Middle East, Conocophillips, 2007-2009; Senior Vice President of Technology, Conocophillips, 2007; Senior Vice President of Technology & Major Projects, Conocophillips, 2006-2007; President, Strategy, Integration, and Specialty Business, Conocophillips, 2005-2006; President, Exploration & Production Asia Pacific, Conocophillips, 2003-2005; Vice President, Lower 48, Conocophillips, Houston, TX, 2002-2003; General Manager, Lower 48 & Canada, Phillips Petroleum, Houston, TX, 2001-2003; Vice President, Western North Slope, ARCO, Alaska, 1998-2001; Planning Manager, Vaster Resources, Houston, TX, 1996-1998; Exploration Engineering Manager, ARCO, Alaska, 1994-1996; Supervisor, Coalbed Methane Operations, ARCO, Midland, TX, 1992-1994; Operations, ARCO, Bakersfield, CA, 1989-1992; Engineer, ARCO, Alaska, 1984-1989 **CR:** President, Board of Trustees, Spindletop International; Board of Directors, Conocophillips, 2012-Present **CIV:** Advisory Board Member, Montana Tech Foundation; Board Member, Independent Petroleum Association of America and American Petroleum Institute **MEM:** Society of Petroleum Engineers **BA:** ConocoPhillips, PO Box 2197, Houston, TX, 77252

LANDMAN, JONATHAN, T: Deputy Managing Editor at the New York Ttimes **I:** Writing and Editing **PB:** NYC **SC:** NY/USA **ED:** MS in Journalism, Columbia University, 1978; BA in History, Amherst College, 1974 **C:** Culture editor, The New York Times Co. 2009-; Deputy managing editor, digital journalism, The New York Times Co., 2005-09; Enterprise editor, The New York Times Co., 2003-05; Metropolitan editor, The New York Times Co., 1999-2003; Week in Review editor, The New York Times Co., 1994-99; Deputy editor, The New York Times Co., 1992-94; Assistant editor, The New York Times Co., 1991-92; Assistant metropolitan editor, The New York Times Co., 1990-91; Assistant national editor, The New York Times Co., 1989-90; Deputy city editor, New York Daily News, 1985-87; Reporter, Newsday, 1984-85; Reporter, assistant city editor, Chicago Sun-Times, 1979-84 **AW:** Recipient Alfred I. duPont-Columbia University award, 2007 **MEM:** Mem.: Board of Trustees, Amherst College

LANE, NATHAN, T: Actor **I:** Media & Entertainment **DOB:** 02/03/1956 **PB:** Jersey City **PT:** Son of Daniel and Nora Lane; **C:** Actor, 1978- **CW:** Appeared in plays: (off-Broadway) A Midsummer Night's Dream, Dedication or the Stuff of Dreams, 2005, The Iceman Cometh, 2015; (Broadway) Present Laughter, 1982-83, Merlin, 1983, Raving, New York City 1984, She Stoops to Conquer, New York City, 1984, The Common Pursuit, 1984-85, A Backer's Audition, New York City, 1985, The Wind in the Willows, 1985, Measure for Measure, 1985 (St. Clair Bayfield award for Shakespearean Performance, 1986), The Common Pursuit, 1986-87, Claptrap, New York City, 1987, Uncounted Blessings, 1988, The Film Society, 1988, The Lisbon Traviata, 1989 (Drama Desk award for Best Actor in a Play, 1990, Lucille Lortel award), A Pig's Valise, 1989, Some Americans Abroad, 1990, Bad Habits, 1990, Lips Together, Teeth Apart, 1991, On Borrowed Time, 1991-92, Guys and Dolls, 1992-95 (Drama Desk award for Outstanding Actor in a Musical, 1992, Obie award for Sustained Excellence of Performance, 1992, Outer Critics Cir. awards), Laughter on the 23rd Floor, 1993-94 Love!, Valour!, Compassion!, 1995 (Drama Desk award for Outstanding Featured Actor in a Play, 1995, Obie award for Ensemble Acting, 1995, Outer Critics Cir. awards), A Funny Thing Happened on the Way to the Forum, 1996-98 (Tony award for Best Actor in a Musical, 1996, Drama Desk award for Outstanding Actor in a Musical, 1996, Outer Critics Cir. awards), The Man Who Came to Dinner, 2000, The Producers, 2001-02, 2003 (Drama Desk award for Outstanding Actor in a Musical, 2001, Tony award for Best Actor in a Musical, 2001, Olivier award for Best Actor in a Musical, 2005), Trumbo Red White and Blacklisted, 2003, The Frogs, 2004, The Odd Couple, 2005-06, Butley, 2006-07, November, 2008, Waiting for Godot, 2009, The Addams Family, 2010, The Nance, 2013, It's Only a Play, 2014-15; (TV films) Valley of the Dolls, 1981, The Last Mile, 1992, The Wizard of Oz in Concert: Dreams Come True, 1995, The Boys Next Door, 1996, Merry Christmas, George Bailey, 1997, The Man Who Came to Dinner, 2000, Laughter on the 23rd Floor, 2001, A Muppets Christmas: Letters to Santa, 2008, The Money, 2014; (TV series) One of the Boys, 1982, One Saturday Morning, 1997, Encore!Encore!, 1998-99, George and Martha, 1999, Teacher's Pet, 2000-02 (Daytime Emmy award for Outstanding Performer in an Animated Program, 2001), The Good Wife, 2012-14, American Crime Story: The People v. O.J. Simpson, 2016; actor, executive prodr.: (TV series) Charlie Lawrence, 2003, Local Talent, 2012; actor: (films) Walls of Glass, 1985, Ironweed, 1987, The Lemon Sisters, 1990, Joe Versus the Volcano, 1990, He Said, She Said, 1991, Frankie and Johnny, 1991, Life With Mikey, 1993, Addams Family Values, 1993, (voice) The Lion King, 1994, The Birdcage, 1996 (Screen Actors Guild award for Outstanding Performance by a Cast, Am. Comedy award for Best Performance by an Actor in a Motion Picture-Musical or Comedy, 1996), Mousehunt, 1997, (voice) The Lion King II: Simba's Pride, 1998, The Best Man, 1999, At First Sight, 1999, (voice) Stuart Little, 1999, Isn't She Great?, 2000, Trixie, 2000, Love's Labour's Lost, 2000, (voice) Titan A.E., 2000, Nicholas Nickelby, 2002 (National Board Review award for Best Ensemble Performance, 2002), (voice) Stuart Little 2, 2002, Austin Powers in Goldmember, 2002, (voice) Teacher's Pet, 2004, Win a Date with Tad Hamilton!, 2004, (voice) The Lion King 1 1/2, 2004, The Producers, 2005, (voice) Stuart Little 3: Call of the Wild, 2006, Swing Vote, 2008, (voice) Astro Boy, 2009, The Nutcracker in 3D, 2010, Mirror Mirror, 2012, The English Teacher, 2013; (TV guest appearances) Miami Vice, 1985, The Days and Nights of Molly Dodd, 1989, 1990, 1991, (voice) The American Experience, 1991, (voice) Timon and Pumbaa, 1995 (Daytime Emmy award for Outstanding Performer in an Animated Program, 1996), Frasier, 1995, Mad About You, 1997, Sex and the City, 2002, Absolutely Fabulous, 2004, 30 Rock, 2007, Modern Family, 2010-15.(Theatre) The Iceman Cometh, 2015, White Rabbit, Red Rabbit, 2016, The Front Page, 2016, Angels in America, 2017, (Tony Award,Best Performance by an Actor in a Featured Role in a Play); (Films) No Pay, Nudity, 2016, Carrie Pilby, 2016, Sidney Hall, 2017; (Television) The Good Wife, 2012, The Money, 2014, The People v OJ Simpson: American Crime Story, 2016, Difficult People, 2016, Maya & Marty, 2016, The Blacklist, 2018 **AW:** Named to Am. Theatre Hall of Fame, 2008, Hollywood Walk of Fame, 2006; recipient Distinguished Achievement in Musical Theatre award, The Drama League, 2010, Human Rights Campaign Equality award, 2007, Trevor Project Hero award, 2007, Am. Theatre Wing Honor, 2006, Vito Russo award, GLAAD, 2002, People's Choice award for Favorite Male Performer in a New TV Series, 1999 **BA:** Anonymous Content, 3532 Hayden Avenue, Culver City, CA, 90232

LANG, DAVID, T: Composer **I:** Media & Entertainment **DOB:** 01/08/1957 **PB:** Los Angeles **SC:** CA/USA **ED:** DMA, Yale School Music, 1989; MMA, Yale School Music, 1983; MMus, University of Iowa, 1980; AB with honors, Stanford University,

1978 C: Co-founder, Co-artistic Director, Bang on a Can music festival, Brooklyn, 1987-; Co-founder, Red Poppy Music, New York City, CW: Composer: Writing on Water, The Most Dangerous Room in the House, 1997 (Bessie award, 1999), Loud Love Songs, 2004, The Little Match Girl Passion, 2007 (Pulitzer Prize in Music, 2008), (Operas) The Carbon Copy Building, 1999 (OBIE award for Best New Am. Work, Village Voice, 2000), The Difficulty of Crossing a Field, 1999, (albums) Are You Experienced?, 1991, The Passing Measures, 2001, Child, 2003, Elevated, 2005,(Works) The Difficulty of Crossing a Field, 1999, Battle Hymns, 2009, The Little Match Girl Passion, 2007, Death Speaks, 2012,The Whisper Opera, Crowd Out, 2014, The National Anthems, 2014,Anatomy Theater, 2016, The Loser,2016, Symphony for a Broken Orchestra,(Film Soundtracks) Requiem for a Dream,2000, Amelia, 2002, Untitled, 2009, The Woodmans, 2012, La Grande Bellezza,2014,Youth,2015, Wildlife,2017 AW: Recipient Pulitzer Prize in Music, 2008, Kennedy Ctr./Friedheim award, 1992, BMW Music-Theater prize, 1990, Rome prize, Am. Academy in Rome, 1990; fellow Guggenheim Foundation, 1986; grantee New York Foundation Arts, National Endowment Arts, Foundation Contemporary Arts, 2002; Revson fellowship, New York Philharmonic, 1985 MEM: Mem.: American Academy of Arts and Letters (Academy award in Music 2009)

LANGE, JESSICA PHYLLIS, T: Actress I: Media & Entertainment PB: Cloquet PT: Al Lange and Dorothy Florence (Sahlman) Lange SPN: Francisco Paco Grande, July 29, 1971 (div. 1981) CH: Alexandra; Hannah Jane ED: Student Mime, with Etienne DeCroux, Paris; Student, University Minnesota C: Model, Wilhelmina Agency, New York City; Dancer, Opera Comique, Paris CR: Model Marc Jacobs Beauty, 2014 CIV: Goodwill ambassador, UNICEF, Ambassador, Save the Children, 2008- CW: Actress: (films) King Kong, 1976, All That Jazz, 1979, How to Beat the High Cost of Living, 1980, The Postman Always Rings Twice, 1981, Frances, 1982, Tootsie, 1982 (Academy award for Best Supporting Actress, 1983), Sweet Dreams, 1985, Crimes of the Heart, 1986, Everybody's All American, 1988, Far North, 1988, Music Box, 1989, Men Don't Leave, 1990, Cape Fear, 1991, Night and the City, 1992, Blue Sky, 1994 (Golden Globe award for Best Actress in a Drama, 1995, Academy award for Best Actress, 1995), Losing Isaiah, 1995, Rob Roy, 1995, A Thousand Acres, 1997, Hush, 1998, Cousin Bette, 1998, Titus, 1999, Prozac Nation, 2001, Masked and Anonymous, 2003, Big Fish, 2003, Broken Flowers, 2005, Don't Come Knocking, 2005, Neverwas, 2005, Bonneville, 2006, The Vow, 2012, In Secret, 2013, The Gambler, 2014, Wild Oats, 2016, (TV films) Cat on a Hot Tin Roof, 1984, O'Pioneers!, 1992, A Streetcar Named Desire, 1995 (Golden Globe award for Best Performance by an Actress in a Mini-series or Motion Picture Made for TV, 1996), Normal, 2003, Sybil, 2007, Grey Gardens, 2009 (Emmy award for Outstanding Actress, Mini-series or Movie, 2009), (TV series) American Horror Story, 2011-15 (Golden Globe award for Best Performance by an Actress in a Supporting Role in a Series, Mini-Series or Motion Picture Made for TV, 2012, Screen Actors Guild award for Outstanding Performance by a Female Actor in a Drama Series, 2012, Emmy award for Outstanding Supporting Actress in a Mini-series or Movie, 2012, 2014); (TV miniseries) Horace and Pete, 2016, (plays) Angel on My Shoulder, North Carolina, 1980, (Broadway) A Streetcar Named Desire, 1992, The Glass Menagerie, 2005, in London, 2007, Long Day's Journey into Night, 2016 (Tony award for Best Leading Actress in a Play, 2016); actress, prodr.: (films) Country, 1984; author, photographer: 50 Photographs, 2008; author: (children's picture book) It's About a Little Bird, 2013.

LANGELLA, FRANK, T: Actor I: Media & Entertainment DOB: 01/01/1940 PB: Bayonne SC: NJ/USA PT: Frank A. Langella, Angelina Langella MS: Single SPN: Ruth Weil, 6/14/1977, Divorced 1996 CH: Two Children ED: Student, Seymour Falk; BA in Drama, Syracuse University, 1959 C: Actor, 1963-Present CIV: Board of Directors, Berkshire Festival CW: Actor, (Broadway Shows) Yerma, 1966, A Cry of Players, 1968, Seascape, 1974-1975, Dracula, 1977-1980, Passion, 1983, Design for Living, 1984, Hurlyburly, 1985, Sherlock's Last Case, 1987, The Father, 1996, Present Laughter, 1996-1997, Fortune's Fool, 2002, Match, 2004, Frost/Nixon, 2007, A Man for All Seasons, 2008, Man and Boy, 2011, The Father, 2016, (Other Stage Appearances) The Immoralist, 1963, Benito Cereno, 1964, The Old Glory, 1964-1965, Good Day, 1965-1966, The White Devil, 1965-1966, Long Day's Journey Into Night, 1966, The Skin of Our Teeth, 1966, The Cretan Woman, 1966, The Devils, 1967, Iphigenia at Aulis, 1967, The Prince of Hamburg, Cleveland Playhouse Co., 1967-1968, The Prince of Hamburg, Long Island Festival Repertory, 1968, Cyrano de Bergerac, 1971, A Midsummer Night's Dream, 1972, The Relapse, The Tooth of Crime, 1972, The Taming of the Shrew, 1973, The Seagull, 1974, Ring Round the Moon, 1975, After the Fall, 1984, Booth, 1994, Les Liaisons Dangereuses, 2006, Frost/Nixon, 2006, (Films) Diary of a Mad Housewife, 1970, The Twelve Chairs, 1970, The Deadly Trap, 1972, The Wrath of God, 1972, Dracula, 1979, Those Lips Those Eyes, 1980, Sphinx, 1981, The Men's Club, 1986, Masters of the Universe, 1987, And God Created Woman, 1988, True Identity, 1991, 1492: Conquest of Paradise, 1992, Dave, 1993, Body of Evidence, 1993, Brainscan, 1994, Junior, 1994, Bad Company, 1995, Cutthroat Island, 1995, Eddie, 1996, Lolita, 1997, I'm Losing You, 1998, Alegría, 1998, Small Soldiers, 1998, The Ninth Gate, 1999, Stardom, 2000, Sweet November, 2001, House of D, 2004, The Novice, 2004, Breaking the Fifth, 2004, How You Look to Me, 2005, Return to Rajapur, 2005, Good Night, and Good Luck, 2005, Superman Returns, 2006, Starting Out in the Evening, 2007, The Caller, 2008, Frost/Nixon, 2008, (Voice Actor) The Tale of Despereaux, 2008, The Box, 2009, Wall Street: Money Never Sleeps, 2010, All Good Things, 2010, Unknown, 2011, Robot & Frank, The Time Being, 2012, Muhammad Ali's Greatest Flight, 2013, (Voice Actor) Noah, 2014, Muppets Most Wanted, 2014, Draft Day, 2014, 5 to 7, 2014, Parts Per Billion, 2014, Grace of Monaco, 2014, (Voice Actor) Kahlil Gilbran's The Prophet, 2014, The Driftless Area, 2015, Captain Fantastic, 2016, Youth in Oregon, 2016, (TV Films) Benito Cereno, 1965, Good Day, 1967, The Mark of Zorro, 1974, The Ambassador, 1974, The Seagull, 1975, The American Woman: Portraits of Courage, 1976, Eccentricities of a Nightingale, 1976, Sherlock Holmes, 1981, I, Leonardo: A Journey of the Mind, 1983, Liberty, 1986, The Doomsday Gun, 1994, Moses, 1996, Kilroy, 1999, Jason and the Argonauts, 2000, Cry Baby Lane, 2000, 111 Gramercy Park, 2003, Now You See It..., 2005, The Water is Wide, 2006, 10.5: Apocalypse, 2006, All the Way, 2016, (TV Series) The Americans, 2015-Present; Original Member, Lincoln Center Repertory Training Co., 1963;; Stage Directing Debut, John and Abigail, 1969; Appearance, Erie (Pennsylvania) Playhouse, 1960; Apprentice, Pocono Playhouse, Mountain Home, PA; Author, (Memoir) Dropped Names: Famous Men and Women As I Knew Them, 2012 AW: Tony Award for Best Leading Actor in a Play, The Father, 2016, The Ten Most Fascinating People, Barbara Walters, 2008, African American Film Critics Association Award for Best Actor, Frost/Nixon, 2008, Tony for Best Leading Actor in a Play, Drama Desk Award for Outstanding Actor in a Play, Outer Critics Circle Award for Outstanding Actor in a Play, Tony

Award for Best Performance by a Leading Actor in a Play, Frost/Nixon, 2007, Boston Society of Film Critics Award for Best Actor, Starting Out in the Evening, 2007, Tony for Best Supporting Actor, Fortune's Fool, 2002, Drama League Award, Dracula, 1978, Tony Award for Best Featured Actor, Drama Desk Award, Seascape, 1975, National Board Review Award for Best Supporting Actor, Diary of a Mad Housewife, 1971, Drama Desk Award, A Cry of Players, 1968, Obie Award, Good Day, 1966, Obie Award, The White Devil, 1966, Obie Award, The Old Glory, 1965 MEM: Actors' Equity Association, Screen Actors Guild BA: Circle of Confusion, 8931 Ellis Avenue, Los Angeles, CA, 90034

LANGEVIN, JAMES R., T: U.S. Representative from Rhode Island I: Government Administration/Government Relations/Government Services DOB: 04/22/1964 PB: Providence SC: RI/USA PT: Son of Richard Raymond and June Katherine (Barrett) Langevin. ED: MPA, Harvard University John F. Kennedy School Government, 1994; BA, Rhode Island College, 1990 C: Member, US Congress from 2nd Rhode Island District, Washington, 2001-; Member, Committee on Armed Services,; Committee on Homeland Security; Secretary of state, Rhode Island, Providence, 1995-2001; Member District 29, Rhode Island House of Reps., Providence, 1988-94 CIV: Board directors, Rhode Island Shelter, Board directors, Big Brothers Rhode Island, Board directors, Pari Ind. Living Center, Pawtucket, Rhode Island, Board directors, Hope Alzheimer's Center, Cranston, Rhode Island, H: Reading, public speaking, community involvement PA: Democrat

LANKFORD, JAMES, T: U.S. Senator from Oklahoma I: Government Administration/Government Relations/Government Services DOB: 03/04/1968 PB: Dallas SC: TX/USA ED: MDiv, Southwestern Baptist Theological Seminary, Fort Worth, 1994; BS in Secondary Education, University Texas, 1990 C: US Senator from Oklahoma, 2015-; Chairman, US House Republican Policy Committee, Washington, 2013-15; Chairman, US House Energy, Policy, Health Care, & Entitlements Subcommittee, Washington, 2013-15; Member, US House Transportation & Infrastructure Committee, Washington, 2011-13; Member, US House Oversight & Government Reform Committee, Washington, 2011-15; Member, US House Budget Committee, Washington, 2011-15; Member, US Congress from 5th Oklahoma District, Washington, 2011-15; Director, Falls Creek Summer Youth Camp, Davis, Oklahoma, 1996-2009; Staff member, Baptist General Convention Oklahoma, 1996-2009 MEM: Mem.: National Rifle Association, Heritage Foundation, Edmond Chamber of Commerce, Deer Creek Chamber of Commerce PA: Republican

LANSBURY, ANGELA BRIGID, T: Actress I: Media & Entertainment DOB: 10/16/1925 PB: London PT: Daughter of Edgar and Moyna (Macgill) L.; Married Richard Cromwell, September 27, 1945 (div. August 1946); Married Peter Shaw, August 12, 1949 (deceased January 29, 2003); children: Anthony Peter, Dei ED: LHD (hon.), Boston University, 1990; Student, Feagin School Drama, New York City, 1940-42; Student, Webber-Douglas School Drama, London, 1939-40 C: Actress, 1944- CR: Host Tony Awards, 1968, 1971, 1987, 1988, and 1989, 45th Ann. Emmy Awards spokesperson ALS Association, 2008-. CW: Actress: Gaslight, 1944, National Velvet, 1944, The Picture of Dorian Gray, 1944 (Golden Globe award for Best Performance by an Actress in a Supporting Role in a Motion Picture, 1945), The Harvey Girls, 1946, The Hoodlum Saint, 1946, Till the Clouds Roll By, 1946, The Private Affairs of Bel Ami, 1947, If Winter Comes, 1948, Tenth Avenue

Angel, 1948, State of the Union, 1948, The Three Musketeers, 1948, The Red Danube, 1949, Samson and Delilah, 1949, Kind Lady, 1951, Mutiny, 1952, Remains to be Seen, 1953, A Life at Stake, 1955, The Purple Mask, 1956, A Lawless Street, 1956, Please Murder Me, 1956, The Court Jester, 1956, The Long Hot Summer, 1958, Reluctant Debutante, 1958, A Breath of Scandal, 1960, Dark at the Top of the Stairs, 1960, Season of Passion, 1961, Blue Hawaii, 1961, All Fall Down, 1962, Manchurian Candidate, 1962 (Golden Globe award for Best Performance by an Actress in a Supporting Role in a Motion Picture, 1962), In the Cool of the Day, 1963, Dear Heart, 1964, The World of Henry Orient, 1964, The Greatest Story Ever Told, 1965, Harlow, 1965, The Amorous Adventures of Moll Flanders, 1965, Mister Buddwing, 1966, Something for Everyone, 1970, Bedknobs and Broomsticks, 1971, Death on the Nile, 1978, The Lady Vanishes, 1980, The Mirror Crack'd, 1980, The Pirates of Penzance, 1982, The Company of Wolves, 1983, Beauty and the Beast, 1991, Your Studio and You, 1995, Beauty & the Beast: Enchanted Christmas (voice), 1997, Anastasia (voice), 1997, Nanny McPhee, 2005, Mr. Popper's Penguins, 2011; (TV series) Murder, She Wrote, 1984-96 (Golden Globe awards for Best Performance by an Actress is a TV Series 1984, 1986, 1991, 1992), Murder, She Wrote: A Story to Die For, 2000, Murder, She Wrote: The Last Free Man, 2001, Murder, She Wrote: The Celtic Riddle, 2003; appeared in TV mini-series Little Gloria, Happy at Last, 1982, Lace, 1984, Rage of Angels, part II, 1986; (TV films) The First Olympics-Athens 1896, A Talent for Murder, Gift of Love, 1982, Shootdown, 1988, The Shell Seekers, 1989, The Love She Sought, 1990, Mrs. 'Arris Goes to Paris, 1992, (musical) Mrs. Santa Claus, 1996; appeared in plays Hotel Paradiso, 1957, A Taste of Honey, 1960, Anyone Can Whistle, 1964, Mame (on Broadway), 1966, 83 (Tony award for Best Museum Actress 1966), Dear World, 1968 (Tony award for Best Museum Actress 1969), All Over (London Royal Shakespeare Co.), 1971, Prettybelle, 1971, Gypsy, 1974 (Tony award for Best Museum Actress 1975, Sarah Siddons award), The King and I, 1978, Sweeney Todd, 1979 (Tony award for Best Museum Actress 1979, Sarah Siddons award), Hamlet, National Theatre, London, 1976, A Little Family Business, 1983, Deuce, 2007, Blithe Spirit, 2009 (Drama Desk award for Oustanding Featured Actress, 2009, Tony award for Best Performance by a Featured Actress in a Play, 2009), A Little Night Music, 2009-2011, Gore Vidal's The Best Man, 2012, Driving Miss Daisy, 2013, Blithe Spirit, 2014; TV appearances Law & Order: SVU, 2005; author: Angela Lansbury's Positive Moves - My Personal Plan for Fitness and Well-Being, 1990,(Films) Ultraman Zero: The Revenge of Belial, Driving Miss Daisy, 2014, Mary Poppins Returns, 2018, (Television) Murder, She Wrote: South by Southwest, 1997, The Unexpected Mrs. Pollifax, 1999, Murder, She Wrote A Story to Die For, 2001, Touched by an Angel, 2002, Murder She Wrote: The Celtic Riddle, 2003, The Blackwater Lightship, 2004, Law & Order: Trial by Jury, 2005, Great Performances, 2015, Little Women, 2017 AW: Named Woman of Year, Harvard Hasty Pudding Theatricals, 1968, Commander of British Empire by Queen Elizabeth II, 1994; named to Theatre Hall of Fame, 1982, TV Hall of Fame, 1996; recipient British Academy award, 1991, Silver Mask Lifetime Ach. Award, British Academy Film & TV Arts, 1992, Lifetime Achievement award, Screen Actors' Guild, Hollywood, 1997,Nat. Medal of the Arts, The White House, 1997, Special Citation for Contribution to American theater, New York Drama Critics' Cir., 2009, 16 Emmy Award Nominations, 8 Golden Globe Nominations, 6 Golden Globe Awards, British Columbia Forbes Peopling of America award-Ellis Island Family Her-

itage Awards, 2012, Honorary Academy award for Lifetime Achievement, Academy Motion Picture Arts & Sciences, 2014. **BA:** 635 N Bonhill Rd, Los Angeles, CA, 90049

LAPIERRE, WAYNE R. JR., T: NRA CEO **I:** Business Management/Business Services **DOB:** 11/08/1949 **PB:** Schenectady **SC:** NY/USA **ED:** MA in Government, Boston College; BA in Education, Siena College, Loudonville, New York, 1971 **C:** CEO, executive vice president, chief national spokesperson, National Rifle Association, Fairfax, Virginia, 1991-; Director federal affairs, National Rifle Association, Fairfax, Virginia, 1981-86; Director state and local affairs, National Rifle Association, Fairfax, Virginia, 1979-80; Executive director, NRA-Inst. Legis. Action, Fairfax, Virginia, 1986-91; State liaison, NRA-Inst. Legis. Action, Fairfax, Virginia, 1978-79 **CR:** Board of Trustees National Rifle Association Foundation president National Firearms Museum Fund **CIV:** Board directors, National Fish & Wildlife Foundation, Board directors, American Association Political Consultants, Board directors, American Conservative Union, **CW:** Author: Guns, Crime, and Freedom, 1994, Guns, Freedom, and Terrorism, 2003, Corporate Fascism: How America's Companies Are Butting into the Private Lives of Their Employees, 2005, The Global War on Your Guns: Inside the UN Plan To Destroy the Bill of Rights, 2006, The Essential Second Amendment Guide, 2007, America Disarmed: Inside the U.N. and Obama's Scheme to Destroy the Second Amendment, 2011; co-author (with James Jay Baker): Shooting Straight: Telling the Truth About Guns in America, 2002; host (syndicated TV series) Crime Strike **AW:** Named one of The 100 Most Influential People in the World, TIME magazine, 2013, The 25 Most Influential Republicans, Newsmax magazine, 2008, The 50 Most Powerful People in DC, GQ magazine, 2007

LARSEN, JOAN L., T: Federal Judge **I:** Law and Legal Services **PB:** Waterloo **SC:** IA/USA **ED:** BA, University of Northern Iowa; JD, Northwestern University **C:** Judge, U.S. Court of Appeals for the Sixth Circuit (2017-Present); Associate Justice, Michigan Supreme Court (2015-2017)

LARSEN, RICHARD RAY, T: U.S. Representative from Washington **I:** Government Administration/ Government Relations/Government Services **DOB:** 06/15/1965 **PB:** Arlington, Washington, June 15, 1965 **ED:** MPA, University Minnesota; BA, Pacific Lutheran University, Tacoma **C:** Member, US Congress from 2nd Washington district, 2001-; Member, Committee on Armed Services; Member, Committee on Transportation and Infrastructure; Co-chair Congl. Methamphetamine Caucus, US Congress from 2nd Washington district,; Chair, Snohomish County Council, Washington, 1999; Councilman, Snohomish County Council, Washington,; Economic devel. official, Port of Everett, Washington,; Director pub. affairs, Washington State Dental Association, **AW:** Named Friend of the National Pks., National Pks. Conservation Association **PA:** Democrat

LARSON, BRIE, T: Actress **I:** Media & Entertainment **PB:** Sacramento **SC:** CA/USA **CW:** Actress: (films) Special Delivery, 1999, 13 Going on 30, 2004, Sleepover, 2004, Madison, 2005, Just Peck, 2009, Tanner Hall, 2009, House Broken, 2009, Greenberg, 2010, Scott Pilgrim versus the World, 2010, The Trouble with Bliss, 2011, Rampart, 2011, Treatment, 2011, 21 Jump Street, 2012, The Spectacular Now, 2013, Don Jon, 2013, Short Term 12, 2013; (plays) The Gambler, 2014; (films) Digging for Fire, 2015, Trainwreck, 2015, Room, 2015 (Golden Globe award for Best Performance by an

Actress in a Motion Picture - Drama, 2016, Critics' Choice award for Best Actress, 2016, Screen Actors Guild award for Outstanding Performance by a Female Actor in a Leading Role, 2016, BAFTA award for Best Actress, 2016, Academy award for Best Actress, 2016), Free Fire, 2016, Basmati Blues, 2016, Kong: Skull Island, 2017, The Glass Castle, 2017, Unicorn Store, 2017, Basmati Blues, 2017; (TV films) Schimmel, 2000, Right on Track, 2003, Entry Level, 2012; (TV series) Raising Dad, 2001-02, U.S. of Tara, 2009-11; TV appearances Hope & Faith, 2003, Ghost Whisperer, 2008, The League, 2011, Community, 2013-14, Comedy Bang! Bang!, 2015, SNL, 2016; singer: (albums) Finally Out of P.E., 2005

LARSON, JOHN BARRY, T: U.S. Representative from Connecticut **I:** Government Administration/ Government Relations/Government Services **DOB:** 07/22/1948 **PB:** Hartford **SC:** CT/USA **PT:** Son of Raymond and Pauline (Nolan) Larson; **ED:** BS in Education, Cen. Connecticut State University, 1971 **C:** Member, US House Ways & Means Committee, 2005-; Member, US Congress from 1st Connecticut district, 1999-; Member, US House Select Committee on Energy Independence & Global Warming,; President pro tempore, Connecticut State Senate, 1987-95; Member, Connecticut State Senate, 1983-94; Partner, Larson & Lysik Insurance, 1977-90; HS teacher, 1972-77 **CR:** Chairman US House Democratic Caucus, 2009-13, vice chairman, 2007-09 founder, chair ConneCT96 Project, 1996 member East Hartford Board Education, 1978-79, East Hartford Town Council, 1979-83 **AW:** Named Man of Year, United Irish Societies, 1990, Legislator of Year, Catholic Charities/Cath. Family Services, 1989, Connecticut Valley Girl Scouts, 1989, Junior League Connecticut, 1988; recipient Child Advocacy Legis. Leadership award, Connecticut Coalition Children, 1991, Connecticut AIDS Consortium/United Way Connecticut Appreciation award, 1991, Alzheimer's Association Recognition award, 1991, Distinguished Alumni award, Cen. Connecticut State University, 1987, Legis. Leadership award, Connecticut Association Human Services, 1987, Outstanding Alumni award, East Hartford HS National Honor Society, 1985; fellow Yale Bush Center Child Devel. **MEM:** Mem.: Hartford Club **PA:** Democrat

LASORDA, TOMMY, T: Retired Professional Baseball Team Manager **I:** Athletics **DOB:** 09/22/1927 **PB:** Norristown **PT:** Son of Sam and Carmella (Covatto) Lasorda; **ED:** Student pub. schools, Norristown **C:** Senior adv. to chairman, L.A. Dodgers, 2004-; With, L.A. Dodgers, 1956-; Senior vice president, L.A. Dodgers, 1998-2004; Interim general manager, L.A. Dodgers, 1998; Vice president fin., L.A. Dodgers, 1996-98; Manager, L.A. Dodgers, 1976-96; Coach, L.A. Dodgers, 1973-76; Manager minor league clubs, L.A. Dodgers, Pocatello, Idaho, Ogden, Utah, Spokane, Albuquerque, 1965-73; Pitcher, Kansas City Athletics, 1956; Pitcher, Brooklyn Dodgers, 1954-55 **CW:** Co-author (with David Fisher): (autobiography) The Artful Dodger, 1985; co-author: (with Bill Plaschke) I Live for This!: Baseball's Last True Believer, 2007 **AW:** Named coach, National League All-Star team, 1993, 1986, 1983-84, 1977, National League Manager Year, Baseball Writers Association Am., 1988, 1983, Sporting News, 1988, Baseball Writers' Association Am., 1988, Associated Press, 1977, United Press International, 1977, 2d National League manager to win pennant first two years as manager, L.A. Dodgers winner, National League pennant, 1988, 1981, 1978, 1977, Pitcher of Year, International League, 1958; named to Baseball Hall of Fame, 1997; recipient Milton Richman Memorial award, Association Professional Baseball Players Am., World Championship, 1988, 1981,Baseball America Manager of the Year, 1988, Sporting News Co-Manager, 1988, Amos Alonzo Slagg Coaching Award, 2000, **MEM:** Mem.: Professional Baseball Players Am., Variety Club of California (vice president)

LATIFAH, QUEEN, T: Rapper, Songwriter, Singer, Actress, and Producer **I:** Media & Entertainment **DOB:** 03/18/1970 **PB:** Newark **PT:** Daughter of Lance and Rita (Bray) Owens. **ED:** Student, Borough of Manhattan C.C. **C:** Co-founder, CEO, Flavor Unit Entertainment, 1993-; Launched perfume line, Queen,; Spokeswoman, CoverGirl,; Spokeswoman, Revlon, **CW:** Actress: (films) House Party 2, 1991, Jungle Fever, 1991, Juice, 1992, Who's the Man, 1993, My Life, 1993, Set It Off, 1996, (Named Best Actress, American Black Film Festival, NAACP Image Award) Hoodlum, 1997, The Wizard of Oz, 1998, Living Out Loud, 1998, Sphere, 1998, The Bone Collector, 1999, (voice) Bringing Out the Dead, 1999, The Country Bears, 2002, Brown Sugar, 2002, (voice) Pinocchio, 2002, Chicago, 2002, (Screen Actors Guild Award: Outstanding Performance by a Cast) Scary Movie 3, Barbershop 2: Back in Business, 2004, Taxi, 2004, Last Holiday, 2006, (voice) Ice Age: The Meltdown, 2006, Stranger Than Fiction, 2006, (voice) Arctic Tale, 2007, Hairspray, 2007, (voice) Ice Age: Dawn of the Dinosaurs, 2009, Valentine's Day, 2010, Just Wright, 2010, The Dilemma, 2011, Joyful Noise, 2012, (voice) Ice Age: Continental Drift, 2012, House of Bodies, 2013, Miracles from Heaven, 2016, (voice) Ice Age: Collision Course, 2016; Girls Trip, 2017; actress, executive prodr.: (films) Bringing Down the House, 2003 National Association for the Advancement of Colored People Image award for Outstanding Actress in a Motion Picture, 2004), (TV films) Steel Magnolias, 2012, Bessie, 2015 (Screen Actors Guild award for Outstanding Performance by a Female Actor in a TV Movie or Mini-series, 2016, (Emmy Award for Outstanding Television Movie-as a producer); actress, prodr.: (films) The Cookout, 2004, Beauty Shop, 2005, The Perfect Holiday, 2007, Mad Money, 2008, The Secret Life of Bees, 2008; executive prodr.: (films) Who's Your Caddy?, 2007, Percentage, 2013, November Rule, 2015, Brotherly Love, 2015, The Secrets of Emily Blair, 2016, The Perfect Match, 2016, (TV films) Wifey, 2007, (TV series) Let's Stay Together, 2011-14, The Queen Latifah Show, 2013-2015, Ice Age, The Great Egg-Scapade, 2016, Star, 2016-,Scream (executive producer); (documentaries) The Art of Organized Noize, 2016; actress: (TV films) Sister in the Name of Rap, 1992, Mama Flora's Family, 1998, Living with the Dead, 2002, (voice) Crash Nebula, 2004, The Muppets' Wonderful Wizard of Oz, 2005, Life Support, 2007 (Golden Globe award for Best Performance by an Actress in a Mini-Series or Motion Picture Made for TV, 2008, National Association for the Advancement of Colored People Image award for Outstanding Performance by a Female Actor in a TV Movie or Miniseries, 2008), The Wiz Live!, 2015, Flint, 2017; host, executive prodr.: The Queen Latifah Show, 1999-2001; (TV appearances) In Living Color, 1991, Fresh Prince of Bel Air, 1991, Living Single, 1993, Mad TV, 1997, Living Single, 1996, 1997, Spin City, 2001, Kung Faux, 2003, The Fairly OddParents, 2004, Eve, 2004, Entourage, 2010, Hot in Cleveland, 2014; composer: (films) New Jack City, 1991, White Man Can't Jump, 1992, Girls Town, 1996; singer: (albums) All Hail the Queen, 1990, The Nature of Sista, 1991, X-tra Naked, 1992, Black Reign, 1994, Order In The Court, 1998, She's the Queen: A Collection of Hits, 2002, The Dana Owens Album, 2004, Trav'lin' Light, 2007, Persona, 2009; talk-show host, executive prodr.: The Queen Latifah Show, 2013-14 (People's

Choice award for Favorite New Talk-Show Host, 2014); author: Ladies First: Revelations of a Strong Woman, 1999, Queen of the Scene, 2006. **AW:** Soul Train Music award, 1995, Sammy Davis Junior award, 1995, Entertainer of Year award, 1995, Grammy award for best rap solo performance, 1995, Artist of the Year award, Harvard Foundation, 2003, Lifetime Achievement award, BET Awards, 2010; named Best New Artist, New Music Seminar, 1990, Best Female Rapper, Rolling Stone Readers' Poll, 1990, Woman of the Year Glamour magazine, 2006; named one of 50 Most Influential African-Americans, Ebony magazine 2004, named to Hollywood Walk of Fame, 2005, Power 150, Ebony magazine 2008; New Jersey Hall of Fame, 2011. **ACH:** Achievements include becoming first hip-hop artist honored with star on the Hollywood Walk of Fame

LATTA, ROBERT EDWARD, T: U.S. Representative from Ohio **I:** Government Administration/ Government Relations/Government Services **DOB:** 04/18/1956 **PB:** Bluffton **SC:** OH/USA **PT:** Delbert Leroy Latta, Rose Mary (Kiene) Latta **ED:** JD, University of Toledo, 1981; BA, Bowling Green State University, 1978 **C:** U.S. Congress from Fifth Ohio District, 2007-Present; District 6, Ohio House of Representatives, 2001-2007; District 2, Ohio State Senate, Columbus, OH, 1997-2000; Wood County Commissioner, Bowling Green, OH, 1991-1996; Associate Counsel, TrusCorp International Co. Ltd., 1983-1989; Attorney, Cheetwood & Davies, Bowling Green, OH, 1982-1983; Attorney, Marshall & Melhorn, LLC, Toledo, OH, 1981-1982; Committee on Energy and Commerce, Republican Study Committee; Chair, Criminal Justice Committee, Ohio House of Representatives **CIV:** Wood County Historical Society **AW:** Legislator Appreciation Award, Ohio Association of Alcohol, Drug Addiction, & Mental Health Services, Distinguished Legislator Award, Ohio Economic Development Association, 2007, Patriot Award, U.S. Sportsmen's Alliance, 2002, Legislator of the Year, League of Ohio Sportsmen, 2000, Ohio Farmers Union, 2000, Major General Charles Dick Award for Legislative Excellence, Ohio National Guard Association, 1999, Watchdog of Treasury Award, United Conservatives of Ohio, 1998, 2000, 2005 **MEM:** Vice President, Kiwanis, 1990-1991, President, Kiwanis, 1991-1992, Trustee, Wood County Bar Association, 1991-1995, National Rifle Association, National Federation of Independent Business, Ohio Rifle & Pistol Association, Wood County Historical Society, Omicron Delta Kappa **BAR:** Ohio, 1981 **PA:** Republican **BA:** 2448 Rayburn House Office Bldg, Washington, DC, 20515

LAUDER, WILLIAM P., T: Chairman **I:** Business Management/Business Services **CN:** Estée Lauder **DOB:** 04/11/1960 **PT:** Son of Leonard A. and Evelyn Hausner Lauder **ED:** Student, University of Grenoble, France; BS in Economic, University of Pennsylvania, 1983 **C:** Executive chairman, Estée Lauder Companies, Inc., New York City, 2009-; Vice president, general manager to president, Origins Natural Resources Inc., 1990-98; CEO, Estée Lauder Companies, Inc., New York City, 2008-09; President, CEO, COO, Estée Lauder Companies, Inc., New York City, 2004-08; COO, Estée Lauder Companies, Inc., 2003-04; From regional marketing director Clinique USA to group president, Estée Lauder Companies, Inc., New York City, 1986-2003; Associate merchandising manager New York Divsn./Dallas Store, Macy's, 1985-86 **CR:** Director, member nominating committee Jarden Corp., 2011- director, member audit committee GLG Partners, Inc., 2006- director NYC2012, Inc., True Temper Sports Inc., 2006- member board directors The Fresh Air Fund, 92nd Street Y **AW:** Named one

of 25 Leaders Reshaping New York, Crain's New York magazine, 2008 **MEM:** Trustee for University of Pennsylvania, Chairman of the Fresh Air Fund

LAUPER, CYNDI, T: Singer, Actress **I:** Media & Entertainment **DOB:** 06/20/1953 **PB:** Queens **SC:** NY/USA **PT:** Fred Lauper, Catrine Lauper **ED:** Student, Katie Agresta, New York, NY, 1974 **C:** Musical Group, Blue Angel, New York, NY, 1980; Tour Guest, Doc West's Disco Band Flyer **CIV:** Board of Directors, Co-Founder, True Colors Fund, 2008-Present, Honorary Chair, Co-Founder, True Colors Residence **CW:** Featured, German TV Music Program; Singer, (Albums) She's So Unusual, 1983, A Night To Remember, 1989, Hat Full Of Stars, 1993, Twelve Deadly Cyns...And Then Some, 1995, Sisters Of Avalon, 1997, Merry Christmas...Have A Nice Life, 1998, Feels Like Christmas, 2001, Shine, 2002, The Essential Cyndi Lauper, 2003, At Last, 2003, The Body Acoustic, 2006, Bring Ya To The Brink, 2008, Memphis Blues, 2010, Detour, 2016; Co-Writer, (Songs) Girls Just Want To Have Fun, She Bop, Money Changes Everything, Time After Time, Goonies R Good Enough, 1985, True Colors, 1986, A Night To Remember, 1989; Contributor, A Very Special Christmas, 1992, A Very Special Christmas, Vol. 2, 1993; Star, (Videos) Girls Just Want To Have Fun, Time After Time, Others; Actress, (Films) Vibes, 1988, Off And Running, 1991, Life With Mikey, 1993, The Opportunists, 2000, Here And There, 2009, Dirty Movie, 2011, (Voice Actress) Henry & Me, 2014, (TV Films) Mother Goose Rock N' Rhyme, 1990, The Happy Prince, 1999, Christmas Dream, 2000, (TV Appearances) Mad About You, Bones, 2009-2015, Happily Divorced, 2012, Bob's Burgers, 2012, Front And Center, 2014, (Broadway) The Three Penny Opera, 2006; Host, (Docu-Series) Cyndi Lauper: Still So Unusual, WE Television, 2013; Performer, Concert Tours, Japan, Australia, Hawaii And England; Co-Creator, Music And Lyrics, (Broadway) Kinky Boots, 2013; Author, Cyndi Lauper: A Memoir, 2012 **AW:** Grammy Award For Best Musical Theater Album, Kinky Boots, 2014, Tony Award For Best Original Score Music And/Or Lyrics Written For The Theatre, Kinky Boots, 2013, Emmy Award For Outstanding Guest Actress In A Comedy Series, Mad About You, 1995, Grammy Award For Best Album Package, She's So Unusual, 1985, Best New Artist, Grammy Awards, 1985 **ACH:** Achievements include first woman to win the composing Tony award category solo **BA:** So What Arts Management and Media Inc., 890 West End Avenue, Suite 1A, New York, NY, 10025

LAUREN, RALPH, T: Apparel Designer **I:** Apparel & Fashion **CN:** Polo Ralph Lauren Corp. (formerly Polo Fashions, Inc.) **DOB:** 10/14/1939 **PB:** , **PT:** Son of Frank and Fraydl (Kotlar) Lifshitz **ED:** HDL (hon.), Brandeis University, 1996; DFA (hon.), Pratt University, 1988; Student, Baruch College, City College of New York **C:** Executive chairman, chief creative officer, Polo Ralph Lauren Corp. (formerly Polo Fashions, Inc.), 2015-; Ralph Lauren Home Collection, Polo Ralph Lauren Corp. (formerly Polo Fashions, Inc.), 1983; Polo/Ralph Lauren Luggage, Polo Ralph Lauren Corp. (formerly Polo Fashions, Inc.), 1982; Fragrances Polo for Men, Lauren for Women (others to follow), Polo Ralph Lauren Corp. (formerly Polo Fashions, Inc.), 1979; Polo Leathergoods, Polo/Ralph Lauren for Boys, Polo Ralph Lauren Corp. (formerly Polo Fashions, Inc.), 1978; Ralph Lauren Womenswear, Polo Ralph Lauren Corp. (formerly Polo Fashions, Inc.), New York City, 1971; Established various lines including Polo Men's Wear Co., Polo Ralph Lauren Corp. (formerly Polo Fashions, Inc.), New York City, 1968; Founder, CEO, chairman, Polo Ralph Lauren Corp. (formerly Polo Fashions, Inc.), New York

City, 1967-2015; Neckwear designer, Polo division Beau Brummel, New York City, 1967-69; Rep., Rivetz Necktie Manufacturers, New York City,; Assistant buyer, Allied Stores, New York City,; Salesperson, Brooks Brothers, New York City, **CR:** Designer sportswear Team USA, opening and closing ceremonies 2014 Winter Olympics, Sochi, Russia, 2012 Summer Olympics, London; opened RL Restaurant, Chicago, 1999; chairman Polo Ralph Lauren Corp. (flagship store New York City, 65 other stores in US and 140 stores worldwide) **AW:** Knight Commander of the Order of the British Empire, 2017 **ACH:** Achievements include establishing the Pink Poney Campaign to address the significant lack of access to cancer screening, education, outreach and quality cancer care, 2000; opening the Ralph Lauren Center for Cancer Care and Prevention to provide individuals, many of who are medically underserved, with access to the highest quality cancer screening and treatment services; establishing the American Heroes Fund following September 11, 2001 **BA:** Ralph Lauren, 652 Madison Ave, New York, NY, 10022

LAURIE, HUGH, T: Actor **I:** Media & Entertainment **PB:** Oxford **SC:** England **PT:** George Ranald Mundell; Patricia (Laidlaw) Mundell **ED:** Attended, Cambridge University **CW:** (actor, writer): (TV series) Alfresco, 1983-84; A Bit of Fry and Laurie, 1986-95; (actor, director) Fortysomething, 2003; actor: Blackadder the Third, 1987, Les Girls, 1988, Blackadder Goes Forth, 1989, (voice) Treasure Island, 1993, Tracey Takes On..., 1996, (voice) Preson Pig, 2000, Little Grey Rabbit, 2000, Stuart Little, 2003, House, M.D., 2004-12, SNL, 2006, Later with Jools Holland, 2011, Veep, 2015, The Night Manager, 2016, Chance, 2016 (For House M.D.-Best Performance by an Actor in a TV Series-Drama, Hollywood Foreign Press Association Golden Globe award, 2006, Best Performance by an Actor in a TV Series-Drama, Golden Globe award, Hollywood Foreign Press Association, 2007, Outstanding Performance by a Male Actor in a Drama Series, Screen Actors Guild, 2007, Choice TV Actor: Drama, Teen Choice Awards, 2007, Outstanding Performance by a Male Actor in a Drama Series, Screen Actors Guild, 2009); (TV films) Cambridge Footlights Revue, 1982, The Crystal Cube, 1983, Mrs. Capper's Birthday, 1985, The Laughing Prisoner, 1987, Hysteria 2!, 1989, All or Nothing at All, 1993, The Adventures of Mole, 1995, The Place of Lions, 1997, The Nearly Complete Utter History of Everything, 1999, Life with Judy Garland: Me and My Shadows, 2001, The Young Visitors, 2003; (films) Plenty, 1985, Peter's Friends, 1992, A Pin for the Butterfly, 1994, Sense and Sensibility, 1995, 101 Dalmatians, 1996, The Borrowers, 1997, The Man in the Iron Mask, 1998, Cousin Bette, 1998, Stuart Little, 1999, Blackadder Back and Forth, 1999, Carnivale, 2000, The Piano Tuner, 2001, Stuart Little 2, 2002, Flight of the Phoenix, 2004, The Big Empty, 2005, Valiant, 2005, Street Kings, 2008, (voice) Monsters versus Aliens, 2009, Hop, 2011, Arthur Christmas, 2011, The Oranges, 2011, Mr. Pip, 2012, Tomorrowland, 2015, The Canterville Ghost, 2017; author: (novels) The Gun Seller, 1998; singer: (albums) Let Them Talk, 2011, Didn't It Rain, 2013 **AW:** Named Favorite TV Doctor, People's Choice Awards, 2011, Favorite TV Drama Actor, 2011, 2010, Favorite Male TV Star, 2009; named an Honorary Knight Commander of the Most Excellent Order of the British Empire, Queen Elizabeth II, 2007; recipient Musician of Year award, GQ, 2011

LAVER, RODNEY GEORGE, T: Former Professional Tennis Player **I:** Athletics **DOB:** 08/09/1938 **PB:** Rockhampton **SC:** QLD, Australia **ED:** Educated, Pub. Schools **C:** 1st player, Grand Slam Twice, 1969; 1st player, Grand Slam Twice, 1962; French champion, 1969; French champion, 1962; USA champion, 1969; USA champion, 1962; Wimbledon champion, 1968-69; Wimbledon champion, 1961-62; Australian champion, 1969; Australian champion, 1962; Australian champion, 1960; Player, San Diego Friars, 1976-78; Player, World Championship Tennis, 1970; Player, Australian Davis Cup Team, 1973; Player, Australian Davis Cup Team, 1958-63 **CW:** Author: How To Play Winning Tennis, 1964, Education of a Tennis Player, 1971 **AW:** Decorated Order Brit. Empire,Australian Sports Medal, 2000 **BA:** 3009 Via Conquistador, Carlsbad, CA, 92009

LAWRENCE, BRENDA LEE, T: U.S. Representative from Michigan, Mayor **I:** Government Administration/Government Relations/Government Services **DOB:** 10/18/1954 **PB:** Detroit **SC:** MI/USA **ED:** BS in Public Administration, Central Michigan University, 2005 **C:** Mem., US Congress from 14th Michigan District, Washington, 2014-; Mayor, City of Southfield, Southfield, 2001-; President, City of Southfield, 1999-2001; Councilman, City of Southfield, Southfield, Michigan, 1997-99; From letter carrier to human resources management, US Postal Service (USPS), 1978-2008 **CR:** Member school board City of Southfield, 1992-96 **AW:** Recipient Woman of Year award, ABWA Millenium Chapter, Brotherhood award, Jewish War Veterans, Michigan, Black Woman Achiever award, Distinguished Leadership & Future Leaders award for Exemplary Leadership, Leadership Oakland, 2004 **PA:** Democrat

LAWRENCE, JENNIFER, T: Actress **I:** Media & Entertainment **DOB:** 08/15/1990 **PB:** Louisville **SC:** KY/USA **PT:** Daughter of Gary and Karen Lawrence **CW:** Actress: (films) Garden Party, 2008, The Poker House, 2008, The Burning Plain, 2008, Winter's Bone, 2010, Like Crazy, 2011, The Beaver, 2011, X-Men: First Class, 2011, Devil You Know, 2012, The Hunger Games, 2012 (MTV Movie award for Best Female Performance, 2012, Teen Choice award for Choice Movie Actress: Sci-Fi/Fantasy, 2012, Critics Choice award for Best Actress in an Action Movie, 2013), House at the End of the Street, 2012, Silver Linings Playbook, 2012 (Critics Choice award for Best Actress in a Comedy, 2013, Golden Globe award for Best Performance by an Actress in a Motion Picture-Comedy or Musical, 2013, Screen Actors Guild award for Outstanding Performance by a Female Actor in a Leading Role, 2013, Academy award for Best Performance by an Actress in a Leading Role, 2013), The Hunger Games: Catching Fire, 2013 (Teen Choice award for Choice Movie Actress: Sci-Fi/Fantasy, 2014), American Hustle, 2013 (Golden Globe award for Best Performance by an Actress in a Supporting Role in a Motion Picture, 2014, Brit. Academy Film and TV Arts award for Best Supporting Actress, 2014), X-Men: Days of Future Past, 2014 (Teen Choice award for Choice Movie Actress: Sci-Fi/ Fantasy, 2014), Serena, 2014, The Hunger Games: Mockingjay - Part 1, 2014 (Teen Choice award for Choice Movie Actress: Sci-Fi/Fantasy, 2015), The Hunger Games: Mockingjay - Part 2, 2015, Joy, 2015 (Golden Globe award for Best Performance by an Actress in a Motion Picture - Musical or Comedy, 2016), X-Men: Apocalypse, 2016, Passengers, 2016, Mother!, Red Sparrow, 2018, X-Men: Dark Phoenix,2018; (TV films) Company Town, 2006, Not Another High School Show, 2007; (TV series) The Bill Engvall Show, 2007-09; narrator (documentaries) A Beautiful Planet, 2016 **AW:** Named Favorite Action Movie Actress, People's Choice Awards, 2015, Favorite Movie Actress, 2015, 2013; named one of The 10 Most Fascinating People of 2013, Barbara Walters Special, The 100 Most Influential People in the World, TIME magazine, 2013, The 100 Most Powerful Women in Entertainment, The Hollywood Reporter, 2012-14, Top Ten Actors to Watch, Variety magazine, 2010

LAWSON, ALFRED J. JR., T: U.S. Representative from Florida **I:** Government Administration/Government Relations/Government Services **DOB:** 09/21/1948 **PB:** Tallahassee, September 21, 1948 **ED:** MSPA, Florida State University, 1973; BS, Florida Agricultural & Mechanical University, 1970 **C:** Member of the U.S. House of Representatives from Florida's 5th District, 2017-,; Member, Committee on Agriculture, Committee on Small Business; President, Lawson and Associates Inc., 1984-; Insurance agent, Northwestern Mutual Life Insurance Co., 1976-; Member banking and insurance committee, governmental oversight and accountability committee, health regulation committee, reapportionment committee, rules committee, Florida State Senate,; Vice chair general government appropriations committee, select committee on Fla's inland waters, Florida State Senate,; Minority leader, Florida State Senate, 2008-10; Member District 6, Florida State Senate, Tallahassee, 2000-10; Member District 8, Florida House of Reps., Tallahassee, 1982-2001 **AW:** Named to Million Dollar Round Table, 1975-93, Florida Agricultural and Mechanical University Sports Hall of Fame, 1989; recipient National Sales Achievement award, 1977-93, National Alumni Outstanding Service award, Florida Agricultural and Mechanical University Alumni, 1985, Outstanding Community Leadership award Tallahassee Urban League, 1985, Distinguished Alumni award Florida State University, 1989, Leadership award, 1996. Meritorious award Florida Agricultural and Mechanical University, 1989, Legislature Service award Organized Fisherman Florida, 1989-90, Outstanding Legislature Service award Sierra Club, 1990, Environmental Leadership award Nature Conservancy, 1990, Rosewood award, 1996; named Florida Insurance Agent of Year, 1979, Legislator of Year, Florida Student Association, 1985. **MEM:** Member National Association for the Advancement of Colored People, Association Life Underwriters, Florida Agricultural and Mechanical University Boster Club & National Alumni Association, Tallahassee C. of C. (board member), Florida State University Alumni Club (adv. committee), Tallahassee Urban League (board member), Boy Scouts America. **PA:** Democrat **BA:** 1337 Longworth House Office Building, Washington, DC, 20515

LE CARRE, JOHN, T: Writer **I:** Writing and Editing **DOB:** 10/19/1931 **PB:** Poole, Dorset **SC:** England **PT:** Son of Ronald Thomas Archibald and Olive (Glassy) Cornwell; **ED:** Doctorate (hon.), University Bath; Doctorate (hon.), University Southampton; Doctorate (hon.), St. Andrews University; Doctorate (hon.), University Exeter; BA in Modern Languages, Bern University, Switzerland, 1956 **C:** Consul, Brit. Foreign Service, Hamburg, Germany, 1963-64; 2d secretary embassy, Brit. Foreign Service, Bonn, Germany, 1961-63; Writer, 1961-; Member, Brit. Foreign Service, 1959-64; Tutor, Eton College, Berkshire, England, 1956-58 **CW:** Author: (novels) Call for the Dead, 1961, A Murder of Quality, 1962, The Spy Who Came in from the Cold, 1963 (Brit. Crime Novel of Year, 1963, Somerset Maugham award, 1963, Edgar Allen Poe award for Best Novel, 1963), The Looking-Glass War, 1965, A Small Town in Germany, 1968, The Naïve and Sentimental Lover, 1971, Tinker, Tailor, Soldier, Spy, 1974, The Honourable Schoolboy, 1977 (James Tait Black Memorial prize, 1978), Smiley's People, 1979, The Little Drummer Girl, 1983, A Perfect Spy, 1986, The Russia House, 1989 (Nikos Kasanzakis prize, 1991), The Secret Pilgrim, 1990, The Night Manager, 1993, Our Game, 1995, The Tailor of Panama, 1996, Single & Single, 1999, The Constant Gardener, 2001, Absolute Friends, 2003, The Mission Song, 2006, A Most Wanted Man, 2008, Our Kind of Traitor, 2010, A Delicate Truth, 2013, (nonfiction) The Unbearable Peace, 1991, (screenplays) End of the Line, 1970, A Murder of Quality, 1991, The Tailor of Panama (also executive producer), 2001; actor: (films) The Little Drummer Girl, 1984,(Book) A Legacy of Spies, 2017 (Nonfiction) Not One More Death, 2006, Afterword, 2014, The Pigeon Tunnel: Stories from My Life, 2016 **AW:** Named one of The 50 Greatest Brit. Writers Since 1945, The Times, UK; recipient Malaparte prize, 1987, Grand Master award, Mystery Writers of America, 1986, Diamond Dagger award, Crime Writers Association, 1988, Gold Dagger award, 1978,Goethe Medal, 2011

LE GUIN, URSULA KROEBER, T: Writer **I:** Writing and Editing **DOB:** 10/21/1929 **PB:** Berkeley **YOP:** 2018-01-22 **PT:** Daughter of Alfred Louis and Theodora (Kracaw) Kroeber **ED:** MA, Columbia University, New York City, 1952; BA, Radcliffe College, Cambridge, Massachusetts, 1951 **CIV:** Active, Planned Parenthood Federation America, Active, Environmental Defense Fund, Active, Oregon Nature Conservancy **CW:** Author: Planet of Exile, 1966, Rocannon's World, 1966, City of Illusion, 1967, A Wizard of Earthsea, 1968, The Left Hand of Darkness, 1969, The Tombs of Atuan, 1970, The Lathe of Heaven, 1971, The Farthest Shore, 1972, The Dispossessed, 1974, The Wind's Twelve Quarters, 1975, Very Far Away from Anywhere Else, 1976, Orsinian Tales, 1976, The Word for World is Forest, 1976, The Language of the Night, 1979, rev. edition, 1992, Leese Webster, 1979, Malafrena, 1979, The Beginning Place, 1980, Hard Words, 1981, The Compass Rose, 1982, The Eye of the Heron, 1983, Cobbler's Rune, 1983, King Dog, 1985, Always Coming Home, 1985, Buffalo Gals, 1987, Wild Oats and Fireweed, 1988, A Visit from Dr. Katz, 1988, Catwings, 1988, Solomon Leviathan, 1988, Fire and Stone, 1989, Catwings Return, 1989, Dancing at the Edge of the World, 1989, Tehanu, 1990, Searoad, 1991, Fish Soup, 1992, A Ride on the Red Mare's Back, 1992, Blue Moon Over Thurman Street, 1993, Wonderful Alexander and the Catwings, 1994, Going Out With Peacocks, 1994, A Fisherman of the Inland Sea, 1994, Four Ways to Forgiveness, 1995, Unlocking the Air, 1996; author: ((with Diana Bellessi)) The Twins, The Dream, 1997; translation Lao Tzu: Tao Te Ching: A Book About the Way and the Power of the Way, 1997; author: Steering the Craft, 1998, Jane on Her Own, 1999, Sixty Odd, 1999, The Telling, 2000, The Other Wind, 2001, Tales From Earthsea, 2001, The Birthday of the World, 2002, Tom Mouse, 2002, Changing Planes, 2003, The Wave in the Mind, 2004, Gifts, 2004, Incredible Good Fortune, 2006, Voices, 2006, Powers, 2007, Lavinia, 2008, short stories, numerous poems, screenplays; translator: Kalpa Imperial by Angelica Gorodischer, 2003, Selected Poems of Gabriela Mistral, 2003; contributor articles to professional journals **AW:** Recipient Locus Readers award novel, 1973, collection, 1984, 96, story, 1995, 2002, 2003, story and novel, 2001, Jupiter award 1975-76, Lewis Caroll Shelf award 1979, International Fantasy award 1988, Howard D. Vursell award Am. Academy Arts and Letters, 1991, Pushcart prize, 1991, Boston Globe-Hornbook award for excellence in juvenile fiction, 1968, Newbery Honor medal, 1972, Nebula award (novel) 1969, 75, 90, (story) 1975, 1996, Hugo award (novel) 1969, 75, (story) 1974, 88, Gandalf award, 1979, Kafka award, 1986, National Book award, 1972, H.L. Davis award Oregon Institute Literary Arts, 1992, Hubbub annual poetry award, 1995,

Asimov's Reader's award, 1995, 03, James Tiptree Junior award, 1995, 97, Retrospective award, 1996, Theodore Sturgeon award (story), 1995, Prix Lectures-Jeunesse award, 1987, Bumbershoot Arts award, Seattle, 1998, Lifetime Achievement award Robert Kirsch/L.A. Times, 2000, Lifetime Achievement award Pacific Northwest Booksellers Association, 2001, Endeavor award, 2001, 03, Willamette Writers Lifetime Achievement award, 2002, PEN/Malamud award for short fiction, 2002, World Fantasy award, 2002, Grand Master award SFW, 2003, Margaret A. Edwards award, 2004, Literary award PEN Center USA, 2005, Maxine Cushing Gray award for literary achievement, 2006, CES Wood Distinguished Writers award, 2006, Gallun award for outstanding contribution to the genre of sci. fiction, 2007; Arbuthnot lecturer American Library Association, 2004,Medal for Distinguished Contribution to American Letters, 2014, **MEM:** Mem.: PEN (PEN/USA award 2005), Sci. Fiction Writers Association (Damon Knight Memorial Grand Master award 2003), Sci. Fiction Research Association, Amnesty International, Phi Beta Kappa **BA:** Curtis Brown Ltd, 10 Astor Place, New York, NY, 10003

LE PEN, MARINE, T: French Government Official **I:** Government Administration/Government Relations/Government Services **DOB:** 08/05/1968 **PB:** Neuilly sur Seine **PT:** Daughter of Jean-Marie Le Pen and Pierrette Lalanne; **ED:** Master in Criminal Law, University Paris II-Assas, 1991; Master in Law, University Paris II-Assas, 1990 **CT:** Cert.: (in legal profession) 1992 **C:** MEP, North-West France constituency, European Parliament, 2009-; Councillor, Nord-Pas-de-Calais Regional Council, 2010-; President, National Front Party, 2011-; Municipal councillor, Hénin Beaumont, France, 2008-11; MEP, Île-de-France constituency, European Parliament, 2004-09; Councillor, Île-de-France Regional Council, 2004-09; Councillor, Nord-Pas-de-Calais Regional Council, France, 1998-2004; Executive vice president, National Front Party, 2007-10; Vice president, National Front Party, 2004-07; Director legal services, National Front Party, France, 1998-2004; Lawyer, Paris Bar, 1992-98 **CR:** Member central committee National Front, member political bureau, member executive committee **AW:** Named one of The 100 Most Influential People in the World, TIME magazine, 2011 **PA:** National Front **ADD:** Front National, 76-78 rue des Suisses, Nanterre, YT, France, 92000

LEAHY, PATRICK JOSEPH, T: U.S. Senator from Vermont **I:** Government Administration/Government Relations/Government Services **DOB:** 03/31/1940 **PB:** Montpelier **SC:** Vermont **PT:** Son of Howard and Alba (Zambon) L.; Married Marcelle Pomerleau, August 25, 1962; children: Kevin, Alicia, Mark. **ED:** JD, Georgetown University Law Center, 1964; BA in Political Sci., St. Michael's College, Vermont, 1961 **CT:** Bar: Vermont 1964, DC 1979, US Court Appeals (2d cir.) 1966, Vermont Federal District Court 1965, US Supreme Court 1968. **C:** President pro tempore emeritus, 2015-; US Senator from Vermont, 1975-; Chairman, US Senate Judiciary Committee, 2007-15; Chairman, US Senate Judiciary Committee, 2001-03; Chairman, US Senate Judiciary Committee, 2001; Chairman, US Senate Agricultural Nutrition & Forestry Committee, 1987-95; President pro tempore, 2012-15; State's attorney, Chittenden County, Vermont, 1966-75 **CR:** US rep. to UN General Assembly, 2004 **CIV:** Board visiting, National District Attorney Association, 1971-74 Board visiting, National College Deaf, DC, Board visiting, Gallaudet University, DC, Board visiting, US Military Academy, West Point, New York, Board regents, Smithsonian Institute, Washington, **AW:** recipient Award Distin-

guished Public Service, Medical Library Association, 2003, Champion for Real and Lasting Change award, Save the Children, 2005, Robert Vaughh FOIA Legend award, American University Washington College Law, 2009, John Heinz award for Greatest Public Service by Elected or Appointed Official, 2013. named one of The 50 Most Powerful People in DC, GQ magazine, 2007 **MEM:** Member National District Attorneys Association (vice president 1971-74) **PA:** Democrat

LEAR, NORMAN MILTON, T: Producer, Writer, Director **I:** Media & Entertainment **DOB:** 07/27/1922 **PB:** New Haven **PT:** Son of Herman and Jeanette (Seicol) Lear; **ED:** HHD, Emerson College, 1968; Student, Emerson College, 1940-42 **C:** Founder, Act III Comms., 1987-; Engaged in pub. relations, 1945-49 **CIV:** Founder, Business Enterprise Trust , Trustee, Museum Broadcasting, President, Am. Civil Liberties Foundation Southern, California, 1973- Board dirs, People for the American Way, **CW:** Comedy writer, 1950-54; dir.(writer): (TV and films), 1954-59; prodr.: (films) Never Too Late, 1965, Start the Revolution Without Me, 1970; (TV series) Hot L Baltimore, 1975, All That Glitters, A Year at the Top, 1977, The Baxters, 1979, Sunday Dinner, 1991; executive producer, creator (TV series) Sanford and Son, 1972-77, Maude, 1972-78, Good Times, 1974-79, One Day at a Time, 1975-84, 704 Hauser, 1994; executive prodr.: (films) Fried Green Tomatoes, 1991, Way Past Cool, 2000, Stand By Me, 1986, Princess Bride, 1987, Way Past Cool,2003, Pete Seeger: The Power of Song, 2007; (TV series) The Andy Williams Show, 1962, The Nancy Walker Show, 1976, Heartsounds, 1984, a.k.a. Pablo, 1984, Channel Umptee-3, 1997; prodr.(director, creator): All in the Family, 1971 (4 Emmy awards 1970-73, Peabody award, 1977), The Powers That Be, 1992; producer, writer, American Masters, 2008, American Divided, 2016 (films) Come Blow Your Horn, 1963, Divorce American Style, 1967, The Night They Raided Minsky's, 1968, producer, director, writer Cold Turkey, 1971, writer Scared Stiff, 1953, creator (TV series) The Jeffersons, 1975-85, Fernwood 2-Night, 1977, writer (TV films) The Little Rascals, 1977, director, executive producer Maggie Bloom, 2000, subject of documentary Norman Lear: Just Another Version of You, 2016; author: Even This I Get to Experience, 2014 **AW:** Decorated Air medal with 4 oak leaf clusters; named Man of Year Hollywood chapter, National Academy Television Arts and Scis., 1973, Broadcaster of Year, International Radio and TV Society, 1973, Association Business Managers, 1972, Showman of Year, Publicists Guild, 1971-77, One of Top Ten Motion Picture Producers, Motion Picture Exhibitors, 1968, 1967, 1963; named to TV Academy Hall of Fame, 1984; recipient Achievement award in TV, Producers Guild Am., 2006, National Arts Medal, 1992, International award of Year, National Association TV Program Executives, 1987, Mass Media award, Am. Jewish Committee Institute of Human Relations, 1986, Distinguished Am. award, 1984, Gold medal International Radio and TV Society, 1981, 1st Amendment Lecturer Ford Hall Forum, 1981, William O. Douglas award Pub. Counsel, 1981, Mark Twain award, International Platform Association, 1977, Humanitarian award, National Conference of Christians and Jews, 1976 **MEM:** Mem.: American Federation of TV and Radio Artists, Writers, and Directors, Caucus Producers, Directors Guild Am., Writers Guild Am. (Valentine Davies award 1977) **BA:** Act III Communications, 100 N Crescent Dr Suite 250, Beverly Hills, CA, 90210

LEDECKY, KATIE, T: Swimmer **I:** Athletics **DOB:** 03/17/1997 **PB:** Washington **SC:** Dc?USA **AW:** 1 Gold Medal in the 2012 Olympics,4 Gold Medals in the 2013 World Championships, 5 Pan Pacific Championships Gold Medal, 5 World Championships Gold Medals, 4 Gold Medals and 1 Silver in the 2016 Olympics, 5 Gold Medals and 1 Silver in the 2017 World Championships,Time 100 Most Influential 2016, Sportswoman of the Year by the Woman's Sports Foundation,2017 **BA:** U.S. Olympic Committee Headquarters, 92 S Tejon St, Colorado Springs, CO, 80903

LEE, BARBARA JEAN, T: U.S. Representative from California **I:** Government Administration/ Government Relations/Government Services **DOB:** 07/16/1946 **PB:** El Paso **SC:** TX/USA **ED:** MSW, University California, Berkeley, 1975; BA, Mills College, California, 1973 **C:** Member, US Congress from 13th California District, 2013-; Member, US House Budget Committee,; Member, US House Appropriations Committee,; Member, US Congress from 9th California District, Washington, 1998-2013; Member, California State Senate, 1996-98; Member District 16, California State Assembly, 1992-96; Member District 13, California State Assembly, 1990-92; Chief of staff to Rep. Ron Dellums, US House of Representatives, 1976-86; Northern California Presidential campaign coordinator, 1972 **CR:** Member California Defense Conversion Council, California Commission Status Women, California Coastal Conservancy/ Dist. Export Council co-chair Congressional Progressive Caucus founder California Commission Status African American Males chair California Rainbow Coalition, Congressional Black Caucus, 2009-11 **CIV:** Board directors, Bay Area Black United Fund, Member adv. board, Alameda Boys Club, **AW:** Named one of The Most Influential Black Americans, Ebony magazine, 2006; named to The Power 150, 2008 **MEM:** Mem.: League of Women Voters, Black Women Organized Political Action, Ronald V. Dellums Democratic Club (founder), John George Democratic Club **PA:** Democrat

LEE, MIKE, T: U.S. Senator From Utah **I:** Government Administration/Government Relations/ Government Services **DOB:** 06/04/1971 **PB:** Mesa **SC:** AZ/USA **PT:** Rex E. Lee; Janet (Griffin) Lee **ED:** JD, Brigham Young University, Provo, UT, Magna Cum Laude, 1997; BA in Political Science, Brigham Young University, Provo, UT, Cum Laude, 1994 **C:** Chairman, U.S. Senate Republican Steering Committee, 2015-Present; Committee on Armed Services, 2011-Present; Joint Economic Committee, 2011-Present; U.S. Senate Foreign Relations Committee, Washington, DC, 2011-Present; U.S. Senate Energy & Natural Resources Committee, Washington, DC, 2011-Present; U.S. Senate Judiciary Committee, Washington, DC, 2011-Present; U.S. Senator From Utah, Washington, DC, 2011-Present; U.S. Congressional Joint Economic Committee, Washington, DC, 2011; Partner, Howrey LLP, Salt Lake City, UT, 2007-2010; Law Clerk, Hon. Samuel A. Alito, U.S. Supreme Court, Washington, DC, 2006-2007; General Counsel, Gov. Jon Huntsman, State of Utah, Salt Lake City, UT, 2005-2006; Assistant U.S. Attorney, District of Utah, U.S. Department of Justice, Salt Lake City, UT, 2002-2005; Partner, Sidley & Austin LLP, Washington, DC, 2000-2002; Law Clerk, Hon. Samuel A. Alito, U.S. Court of Appeals, Third Circuit, Newark, 1998-1999; Law Clerk, Hon. Dee V. Benson, U.S. District Court of Utah, 1997-1998 **CW:** Author, (Books) The Freedom Agenda: Why a Balanced Budget Amendment is Necessary to Restore Constitutional Government, 2011, Our Lost Constitution: The Willful Subversion of America's Founding Document, 2015 **AW:** The Politics 40 Under 40, TIME Magazine, 2010 **MEM:** Federalist Society of Law & Public Policy Studies **BAR:** District of Columbia, 1999; State of Utah, 1998 **PA:** Republican **BA:** Howrey LLP, 170 S Main Street, Suite 400, Salt Lake City, UT, 84101-3636

LEE, SPIKE, T: Film Producer, Director, Screenwriter **I:** Media & Entertainment **DOB:** 03/20/1957 **PB:** Atlanta **SC:** Georgia **PT:** Son of William James Edwards and Jacqueline (Shelton) L.; **SPN:** Married Tonya Lewis, October 2, 1993; **CH:** children: Satchel, Jackson **ED:** MFA, New York University, 1982; BA, Morehouse College, 1979 **CR:** Owner, 40 Acres & a Mule Filmworks, 1986-, 40 Acres & a Mule Musicworks, 1987-94, Spike's Joint, 1994-, Chairman, Spike/DDB, 1996- Moderator, Moorehouse College Black Athletes Forum, 2007 **CIV:** Trustee Morehouse College, 1992- **CW:** Actor, Director, Producer, Writer: (films) She's Gotta Have It, 1986, School Daze, 1988, Do the Right Thing, 1989, Mo' Better Blues, 1990, Jungle Fever, 1991, Malcolm X, 1992, Crooklyn, 1994, Clockers, 1995, Summer of Sam, 1999, Red Hook Summer, 2012; actor, director, prodr.: (films) Girl 6, 1996, The Original Kings of Comedy, 2000; director, producer, writer: (films) Joe's Bed-Stuy Barbershop: We Cut Heads, 1983 (Student Director award Academy Motion Pictures Arts & Sciences), He Got Game, 1998, Bamboozled, 2000, She Hate Me, 2004, Da Blood of Jesus, 2014, Chi-Raq, 2015; director, prodr.: (films) Original Kings of Comedy, 2001, 25th Hour, 2002, Miracle at St. Anna, 2008; actor, producer (films) 3 A.M., 2001; dir.: (films) Last Hustle in Brooklyn, 1977, The Answer, 1980, Sarah, 1981, Inside Man, 2006 (Director of Motion Picture, TV Movie, National Association for the Advancement of Colored People Image Awards, 2007); Lovers & Haters, 2007, Oldboy, 2013, (documentaries) Michael jackson's Journey from Motown to Off the Wall, 2016, 2 Fists Up, 2016, Rodney King, 2017, Brave Visions for Moncler, 2017, Black Klansman, 2018; prodr.: (films) The Best Man, 1999, Love and Basketball, 2000, Mania Days, 2014; executive prodr.: (films) Drop Squad, 1994, New Jersey Drive, 1995, Tales from the Hood, 1995, Home Invaders, 2001; director, prodr.: (documentaries) Get on the Bus, 1996, 4 Little Girls, 1997, A Huey P. Newton Story, 2001, Jim Brown: All American, 2002, When the Levees Broke: A Requiem in Four Acts, 2006 (2006 George Polk award for Documentary TV, Creative Arts Primetime Emmy award for Outstanding Writing for Nonfiction Programming, Academy TV Arts and Scis., 2007), Kobe Doin' Work, 2009, If God Is Willing and Da Creek Don't Rise, 2010; (short films) Jesus Children of America, 2005, All the Invisible Children, 2005; (TV films) Sucker Free City, 2004; dir.: (TV films) Freak, 1998, M.O.N.Y., 2008; director, executive producer (TV films) Da Brick, 2011, Mike Tyson: Undisputed Truth, 2013, Katt Williams Priceless Afterlife, 2014, Jerrod Carmichael Love at the Store, 2014, She's Gotta Have It, 2017; (TV appearances) Into the Comics: Part 1, 1992; Dir.: (TV series) Shark (pilot), 2006; Author: Spike Lee's Gotta Have It: Inside Guerilla Filmmaking, 1987, Uplift the Race: The Construction of School Daze, 1988, Do the Right Thing: A Spike Lee Joint, 1989, Mo' Better Blues, 1990, By Any Means Necessary: The Trials and Tribulations of the Making of "Malcolm X", 1992; Co-author: (with Ralph Wiley) Best Seat in the House, 1997, (with Tonya Lewis Lee) Please, Baby Please, 2002, (with Kaleem Aftab) Thats My Story and I'm Sticking to It, 2005 **AW:** Named to The Power 150, Ebony magazine, 2008; recipient Academy Honorary award, Governors Awards, 2015, National Association for the Advancement of Colored People President's award, National Association for the Advancement of Colored People Image Awards, 2015, Dorothy & Lillian Gish prize, 2013, Wexner prize, Wexner

Center Foundation, 2008, Special Achievement award, African-American Film Critics Association, 2006, Ossie Davis Humanitarian award, Black Movie Awards, 2006, Filmmaker Trumpet award, 2003, French Academy Cinema award, 2002 **MEM:** Fellow Am. Academy Arts & Scis. **BA:** 40 Acres & a Mule, 124 Dekalb Ave Ste 2, Brooklyn, NY, 11217

LEE JONES, TOMMY LEE, T: Actor **I:** Media & Entertainment **PB:** San Saba **SC:** TX/USA **PT:** Clyde L. and Lucille Marie (Scott) Jones; **ED:** BA in English, cum laude, Harvard University, 1969 **CW:** Actor: (Broadway plays) A Patriot for Me, 1969, Fortune and Men's Eye's, 1969, Four on a Garden, 1971, Blue Boys, 1972, Ulysses in Nighttown, 1974, True West, 1981; (films) Love Story, 1970, Eliza's Horoscope, 1972, Life Study, 1972, Jackson County Jail, 1976, Rolling Thunder, 1977, The Betsy, 1978, Eyes of Laura Mars, 1978, Coal Miner's Daughter, 1980, Back Roads, 1981, Nate and Hayes, 1983, The River Rat, 1984, Black Moon Rising, 1986, The Big Town, 1987, Stormy Monday, 1988, The Package, 1989, Fire Birds, 1990, JFK, 1991, Under Siege, 1992, The Fugitive, 1993 (Academy award for Best Actor in a Supporting Role, 1994, Golden Globe award for Best Performance by an Actor in a Supporting Role in a Motion Picture, 1994), House of Cards, 1993, Heaven and Earth, 1993, Blown Away, 1994, The Client, 1994, Natural Born Killers, 1994, Blue Sky, 1994, Cobb, 1994, Batman Forever, 1995, Men in Black, 1997, Volcano, 1997, U.S. Marshals, 1997, Small Soldiers (voice only), 1998, Double Jeopardy, 1999, Rules of Engagement, 2000, Space Cowboys, 2000, Men in Black II, 2002, The Hunted, 2003, The Missing, 2003, Man of the House, 2005, A Prairie Home Companion, 2006, In the Valley of Elah, 2007, No Country for Old Men, 2007 (Screen Actors Guild award for Outstanding Performance by a Cast in a Motion Picture, 2008), In the Electric Mist, 2009, The Company Men, 2010, Captain America: The First Avenger, 2011, Men in Black III, 2012, Hope Springs, 2012, Lincoln, 2012 (Screen Actors Guild award for Outstanding Performance by a Male Actor in a Supporting Role, 2013), The Family, 2013, Criminal, 2016, Jason Bourne, 2016, Mechanic: Resurrection, 2016, Shock and Awe, 2017, Just Getting Started, 2017, Ad Astra, 2019; (TV films) Smash-Up on Interstate 5, 1976, Charlie's Angels, 1976, The Amazing Howard Hughes, 1977, The Rainmaker, 1982, The Executioner's Song, 1982 (Emmy award for Outstanding Lead Actor in a Limited Series or Special, 1983), The Park is Mine, 1985, Yuri Nosenko, KGB, 1986, Broken Vows, 1987, Stranger on My Land, 1988, April Morning, 1988, Gotham, 1988; (TV miniseries) Lonesome Dove, 1989, The Good Old Boys, 1995, The Sunset Limited, 2011; actor, director, producer (films) The Three Burials of Melquiades Estrada, 2005, actor, director, executive producer, writer The Homesman, 2014, actor, director, writer (TV films) The Good Old Boys, 1995, actor, director, executive producer The Sunset Limited, 2011 **AW:** Named one of The Top 25 Entertainers of Year, Entertainment Weekly, 2007; named to The Texas Cowboy Hall of Fame, 2009

LEFKOWITZ, ROBERT, T: Physician **I:** Medicine & Health Care **DOB:** 04/15/1943 **PB:** New York City **SC:** New York **PT:** Son of Max and Rose (Levine) Lefkowitz; **ED:** BA, Columbia College, New York City, 1962; MD, Columbia University College Physicians and Surgeons, New York City, 1966 **CT:** Diplomate Am. Board Internal Medicine **C:** Professor Biochemistry, Duke University Medical Center, Durham, North Carolina, 1985—; James B. Duke Professor Medicine, Duke University Medical Center, Durham, North Carolina, 1982—; Professor Medicine, Duke University Medical Center, Durham, North Carolina, 1977—; Associate Professor Medicine, Duke University Medical Center, Durham, North Carolina, 1973—1977 **CR:** Established Investigator American Heart Association, 1973—1976; Investigator Howard Hughes Medical Institute (HHMI), Durham, 1976—; Visiting Professor New York University, 1996 **CW:** Author: Receptor Binding Studies in Adrenergic Pharmacology, 1978, Receptor Regulation, 1981, Principles of Biochemistry, 1983 **AW:** Co-recipient Nobel Prize in Chemistry, Royal Swedish Academy Sciences, 2012; recipient Young Scientist award, Passano Foundation, 1978, George Thorn award, Howard Hughes Medical Institute, 1979, Oppenheimer award, 1982, Gordon Wilson medal, American Clinical & Climatol. Association, 1982, Lita Annenberg Hazen award, 1983, Outstanding Research award, International Society Health Research, 1985, H.B. Van Dyke award, College Physicians & Surgeons Columbia University, 1986, Steven C. Beering award, Ind. University School Medicine, 1986, North Carolina award in Sci., 1987, International award, Gairdner Foundation, 1988, Novo Nordsk Biotechnology award, 1990, Basic Research prize, 1990, Biomedical Research award, Association American Medical Colleges, 1990, City of Medecin award, North Carolina, 1991, The Giovani Lorenzini prize for basic biomedical research, 1992, Alumnus award for Distinguished Achievement in Cardiovasc. Research, Columbia University College Physicians & Surgeons, 1992, Joseph Mather Smith prize, 1993, The Endocrine Society Gerald D. Aurbach Lecturer award, Institute of Medicine National Academy of Sciences, 1995, J. David Gladstone Institutions Distinguished Lecture award, 1996, Ciba award, Hypertension Research award, 1996, Glorney-Raisbeck award in cardiology, New York Academy Medicine, 1997, Novartis/Drew award in Biomedical Research, 2000, F.E. Shideman-Sterling award, University Minnesota, 2001, Louis & Artur Lucian award for Research in Circulatory Disease, 2001, Peter Harris Distinguished Scientist award, International Society for Heart Research, 2001, 15th Ann. Pasarow Cardiovasc. Research award, The Robert J. & Claire Pasarow Foundation, 2002, Bio/Tech. Winter Symposia Feodor Lynen award, Medal of Merit, International Academy Cardiovasc. Sciences, 2003, IPSEN Endocrinology prize, Foundation IPSEN, Paris, 2003, Foundation Lefoulon-Delalande Grand Prize for Sci. award, Institute France, 2003, Founding Distinguished Scientist award, American Heart Association, 2003, Herbert Tabor Lecture award, American Society Biological Chemistry & Molecular Biology, 2004, Shaw prize, Life Sci. & Medicine, Shaw Prize Foundation, 2007, National Medal Sci., The White House, 2007, BBVA Frontiers of Knowledge award, 2009, Research Achievement award, American Heart Association, 2009, Distinguished Lecture award, Basic Sci., Heart Failure Society America, 2007, National Sci. medal, 2007, Research Achievement award, AHA, 2009, Steven's Triennial prize, Columbia University College Physicians & Surgeons, 2009, Foundation Frontiers of Knowledge award, 2010, Achievement award, SBS Society Biomol. Scis., 2011, Norman Weiner award, Am. Society Pharmacology & Experimental Therapeutics, 2011, Kober medal, Association Am. Physicians, 2012; International Academy Cardiovasc. Scis., 2002 **MEM:** Mem.: National Academy of Sciences (Jessie Stevenson Kovalenko medal 2001), Institute Medicine, American Heart Association Basic Research Society, American Academy Arts & Sciences, American Federation Clinical Research (member national council 1978—83, sec.-treas. 1980—83), Endocrine Society (Fred Conrad Koch award 2001), American Society Pharmacology & Experimental Therapeutics (John J. Abel award 1978, Goodman and Gilman award 1986), Association American Physicians

(treasurer 1989—94, Francis Gilman Blake award 2001), American Society Clinical Investigation (counselor 1982—85, pres.-elect 1986—87, president 1987—88), American Society Biological Chemists, Japanese Biochemical Society (hon.) **BA:** Duke U Med Ctr, Ctr 467 Carl Bldg PO Box 3821, Durham, NC, 22710

LEGEND, JOHN, T: Musician **I:** Media & Entertainment **DOB:** 12/28/1978 **PB:** Springfield **PT:** Son of Ronald and Phyllis Stephens; **ED:** BA in English, University Pennsylvania, 1999 **C:** Signed to KonMan Entertainment prod. co. (name changed to G.O.O.D. Music), 2003; Music director, producer, Counterparts a cappella group, University Penn., Philadelphia, 1998-99; President music department, choir director, Bethel African Methodist Episcopal Church, Scranton, Pennsylvania, 1995-2004 **CW:** Musician: (albums) John Stephens, 2000, Solo Sessions Vol. 1: Live at the Knitting Factory, 2003, Live at SOB's, 2003, Get Lifted, 2004 (Grammy award for Best R&B Album, 2006), Once Again, 2006, Different Strokes by Different Folks, 2005, Evolver, 2008, Love in the Future, 2013, (with The Roots) Wake Up, 2010 (Grammy award for Best R&B Album, 2011, National Association for the Advancement of Colored People Image award for Outstanding Album, 2011), (songs) Ordinary People, 2004 (Grammy award for Best Male R&B Vocal Performance, 2006), Family Affair, 2005 (Grammy award for Best Group Vocal R&B Performance, 2007), Heaven, 2006 (Grammy award for Best Male R&B Vocal Performance, 2007), Save Room, 2006, (with Al Green) Stay With Me (By the Sea), 2008 (Grammy award for Best Duo R&B Vocal Performance, 2009), Hang On In Their, 2010 (Grammy awards for Best R7B Album, Best Traditional R&B Vocal Performance, 2011), Shine, 2010 (Grammy award for Best R&B Song, 2011), All of Me, 2013 (National Association for the Advancement of Colored People Image award for Outstanding Song, 2014, Top Radio Song, Top Streaming Song-Audio, Billboard Music Awards, 2015), You & I (Nobody in the World), 2013 (National Association for the Advancement of Colored People Image award for Outstanding Music Video, 2015), One Man Can Change the World (with Big Sean and Kanye West), 2015 (MTV Video Music award for Video with a Social Message, 2015); musician, composer (songs) Glory (with Common), 2014 (Golden Globe award for Best Original Song, 2015, Critics' Choice award for Best Song, 2015, Academy award for Best Original Song, 2015, Grammy award for Best Song Written for Visual Media, 2016), contributor pianist, vocalist songs and albums by Kanye West, Lauryn Hill, Jay-Z, Black Eyed Peas, Alicia Keys, Janet Jackson, Twista, Slum Village; actor: (films) Loverboy, 2004, Soul Men, 2008; mentor (reality TV competition) Duets, 2012 **AW:** Named Favorite Male Artist, American Music Awards, 2014, Outstanding Male Artist, National Association for the Advancement of Colored People Image Awards, 2014, Best R&B Act, Music of Black Origins Awards, 2005, Best New Artist, BET Awards, 2005; named one of The World's Most Influential People, TIME magazine, 2009; recipient President's award, National Association for the Advancement of Colored People Image Awards, 2016, Humanitarian award, BET Awards, 2010, Most Influential Songwriter award, MTV Japan, 2006 **BA:** William Morris Endeavor Entertainment, 9601 Wilshire Blvd 3rd Fl, Beverly Hills, CA, 90210

LEGGETT, ANTHONY JAMES, T: Physics Professor **I:** Sciences **PB:** London **ED:** PhD in Theoretical Physics, Merton College, Oxford; Degree in physics, Merton College, Oxford; Student, Balliol College, Oxford, England **C:** John D. and Catherine T. Macarthur Professor, University Illinois,

Urbana-Champaign, 1983-; Professor, University Sussex (UK), 1978-83; Reader, University Sussex (UK), 1971-78; Member Faculty, University Sussex (UK), 1967-71 **CR:** Researcher Urbana, Illinois, Kyoto, Japan Lecturer in Field **CW:** Author: The Problems of Physics, 1987, Quantum Tunnelling in Condensed Media, 1992; Contributor Articles to Professional Journals **AW:** Recipient Nobel Prize in Physics, 2003, Wolf Prize in Physics, Wolf Foundation, Israel, 2003, John Bardeen Prize, 1994, Paul Dirac Medal and Prize, Institute of Physics, UK, 1992, Fritz London Memorial Award, 1981, Simon Memorial Prize, Institute of Physics, UK, 1981, Maxwell Medal and Prize, 1975, KBE, 2004, Honorary Dlitt, 2005 **MEM:** Fellow: American Physical Society, Institute Physics, UK (hon.), Royal Society, UK; Mem.: Russian Academy of Sciences, National Academy of Sciences (associate), Am. Academy Arts & Sciences, Am. Philological Society **ACH:** Achievements include research in condensed matter physics, high-temperature superconductivity, foundations of quantum mechanics.

LEIBOVITZ, ANNIE, T: Photographer **I:** Media & Entertainment **DOB:** 10/02/1949 **PB:** Waterbury **SC:** CT/USA **ED:** BFA, San Francisco Art Institute, 1971 **C:** Photographer, Conde Nast, Vogue, 1998-; Photographer, Conde Nast, Vanity Fair, 1980-; Proprietor, Annie Leibovitz Studio, New York City,; Chief Photographer, Rolling Stone, 1973-83; Photographer, Rolling Stone, 1970-83 **CW:** Works exhibited in various galleries and museums, including the National Portrait Gallery, Washington DC, 1991, The Corcoran Gallery, 1999; Author, Photographs: Annie Leibovitz 1970-1990, 1992, Olympic Portraits: Annie Leibovitz, 1996, Annie Leibovitz: Women,(with essay by Susan Sontag) 1999, American Music, 2003, A Photographer's Life: 1990-2005, 2006, Annie Leibovitz at Work, 2008, Pilgrimage, 2012; Creator, Official Portfolio for 26th Olympic Games, Atlanta, 1995, (Books) Annie Leibovitz Potraits, 2005-2016 **AW:** Recipient, Photographer of Year Award, Am. Society Magazine Photographers, 1984, Innovation in Photography Award Am. Society Magazine Photographers, 1987, Clio Award, 1987, Campaign of Decade Award Advertising Age magazine, 1987, Infinity Award for Applied Photography, International Center for Photography, 1990, Medal of Distinction, Barnard Coll, 2000, Wexner Prize, Wexner Center Arts, 2012; Named One of Top 10 Living Artists, ARTnews magazine, 1999, The 50 Most Powerful Women in New York City, New York Post, 2008; Named to Art Dirs Club Hall of Fame, 1999, Named Living Legend, Libr Congress, 2000, Commandeur French Govt's Ordre des Arts et des Lettres, 2006 **ACH:** Was asked by Queen Elizabeth II to take her portrait for a state visit to Virginia, 2007. **BA:** Contact Press Images, 341 West 38th Street, New York, NY, 10018

LEMANN, JORGE PAULO, T: Investor **I:** Financial Services **ED:** MBA, Harvard Business School, 1961; BA/BS, Harvard University **C:** Co-founder, 3G Capital Inc.,; Member adv. board, DaimlerChrysler,; Board member, Swiss Re,; Board member, Gillette Co.,; Board member, Lojas Americanas S.A.,; Founder, board member, Fundacao Estudar,; Chairman, Latin Am. Adv. Committee of the New York Stock Exchange,; Partner, GP Investimentos Ltda,; Majority shareholder, InBev, Belgium,; Member board of directors, Brahma, 1990-99; Sold to Credit Suisse First Boston, Banco Garantia, 1998; Founded, Banco Garantia, 1971 **CIV:** Founder, Lemann Scholars program, 1998 **AW:** Named one of 50 Most Influential People in Global Fin., Bloomberg Markets, 2013, World's Richest People, Forbes magazine, 2004- **ACH:** Achievements include winning the Swiss tennis nationals and going on to play at Wimbledon **ADD:** 3G Capital, Rua Humaita 275 9 andar, Rio de Janeiro, YT, Brazil, 22261-001

LEMIEUX, MARIO, T: Retired Professional Hockey Player **I:** Athletics **DOB:** 10/05/1965 **PB:** Montreal **SC:** QC/Canada **C:** Co-owner, chairman, Pittsburgh Penguins, 1998-; CEO, Pittsburgh Penguins, 1998-2006; Player, Pittsburgh Penguins, Pittsburgh, 2000-06; Player, Pittsburgh Penguins, 1984-97 **CR:** Member Team Can., World Cup of Hockey, 2004, Team Can., Olympic Games, Salt Lake City, 2002 **CIV:** Founder, Mario Lemieux Foundation **AW:** Named NHL Player of Year, Sporting News, 1996, 1993, 1989, 1988, NHL Rookie of Year, 1985, MVP, NHL All-Star game, 1990, 1988, 1985, Player of the Year, Can. Hockey League, 1983-84; named to Order of Canada, 2010, National Order of Quebec, 2009, International Ice Hockey Federation Hall of Fame, 2008, NHL All-Star game, 2001, 1996-97, 1992-93, 1990, 1986-89; recipient Bill Masterson Memorial Trophy, 1993, Guy LaFleur Trophy, 1983-84, Michael Bossy Trophy, 1983-84, Jean Beliveau Trophy, 1983-84, Michel Briere Trophy, 1983-84, Art Ross Memorial Trophy, 1996-97, 1992-93, 1988-89, Conn Smythe Trophy, 1991-92, Hart Memorial Trophy, 1996, 1993, 1988, Calder Memorial Trophy, 1985,Recipient of the Order of Hockey in Canada, 2016, 100 Greatest NHL Players, 2017 **ACH:** Achievements include being the only player in NHL history to score a goal 5 different ways in a single game, 1988; being a member of the Stanley Cup Champion Pittsburgh Penguins, 1991, 1992; being inducted to Hockey Hall of Fame without mandatory 3 year waiting period, 1997; being a member of the gold medal Canadian Hockey Team, Salt Lake City Olympic games, 2002; being a member of the World Cup Champion Team Canada, 2004; being the owner of the Stanley Cup Champion Pittsburgh Penguins, 2009, 2016; having #66 retired by the Pittsburgh Penguins, Team Canada, and Laval Titan **BA:** Mario Lemieux Foundation, Two Chatham Center, Suite 1661, Pittsburgh, PA, 15219

LENDL, IVAN, T: Retired Professional Tennis Player **I:** Athletics **DOB:** 03/07/1960 **PB:** Ostrava **SC:** Czechoslovakia **AW:** Winner, Italian Junior Singles, 1978, French Junior Singles, 1978, Wimbledon Junior Singles, 1978, Spanish Open Singles, 1980, 81, South America Open Singles, 1981, Can. Open Singles, 1980, 81, World Championship Tennis Tournament of Champions Singles, 1982, World Championship Tennis Masters Singles, 1982, World Championship Tennis Finals Singles, 1982, Volvo Masters, 1983, Can. Open, 1983, 89, French Open, 1984, 86, 87, Monte Carlo Open, 1985, 88, Suntory Cup, 1985, Tournament of Champs, 1985, 89, U.S. Clay, 1985, U.S. Open, 1985, 86, 87, Mercedes Cup, 1985, Australian Indoor, 1985, 89, European Champion, 1985, AT&T Challenge, 1986, 88, Nabisco Masters, 1986, U.S. Pro Indoor, 1986, 91, Lipton International Players Championship, 1986, 88, 89, Italian Open 1986, 88, Volvo International, 1986, Australian Open, 1989, 90, Chicago Volvo, 1989, Eagle Classic, 1989, EC Champ, 1989, German Open, 1989, Hamlet Challenge Cup, 1989, Nabisco Grand Prix Bonus, 1989, Passing Slot Tournament, 1989, Stella Artois, 1989, 90, Stockholm Open, 1989, Sky Dome World Tennis, 1990, Memphis Volvo Indoor, 1991, Beckenham Tournament, 1991, Marlboro Championship, 1991,ITF World Champion, 1985-87, ATP Player of the Year, 1985, 1986, 1987 **H:** Golf, Hockey **BA:** 400 5 1/2 Mile Road, Goshen, CT, 06756

LENK, KATRINA, T: Actress, Singer **I:** Media & Entertainment **ED:** Northwestern University **CW:** (Theatre) Hedwig and the Angry Inch, 2001, The

Caucasian Chalk Circle, 2005, IWitness,2007, Lovelace: A Rock Musical, 2008, The Miracle Worker, 2010, Spider-Man: Turn Off the Dark, 2012-13, Once,2013-15, Indecent, 2015-16, The Band's Visit, 2016-17, Indecent,2017, The Band' Visit, 2017 (Tony for Best Actress in a Musical, 2018)

LENO, JAY, T: Comedian **I:** Media & Entertainment **DOB:** 05/28/1950 **PB:** New Rochelle **SC:** NY/USA **PT:** Son of Angelo and Cathryn (Muir) Leno; **ED:** BA in Speech Therapy, Emerson College, Boston, 1972 **C:** Worked as Rolls-Royce auto mechanic and deliveryman,; Television Personality, Actor, 1976- **CW:** Stand-up comedian playing Carnegie Hall, Caesar's Palace, others, numerous appearances on Late Night with David Letterman, writer (TV series) Good Times, 1974-79, exclusive guest host The Tonight Show, 1987-92, host, producer, writer, 1992-2009, 2010-14 (Emmy award for Outstanding Variety, Music or Comedy Series, 1995, People's Choice award for Favorite Late Night Talk Show Host, 2006), The Jay Leno Show, 2009-10, producer, host (Showtime special) Jay Leno and the American Dream, 1986, Saturday Night Live, 1986, Jay Leno's Family Comedy Hour, 1987, executive producer, host (documentaries) Jay Leno's Garage: The Ultimate Car Week, 2014, film appearances include Fun with Dick and Jane, 1977, American Hot Wax, 1978, Americathon, 1979, Collision Course, 1989, Dave, 1993, Wayne's World 2, 1993, Major League 2, 1994, The Flintstones, 1994, The Birdcage, 1996, Space Cowboys, 2000, John Q, 2002, Stuck on You, 2003, Mr 3000, 2004, The Astronaut Farmer, 2006, The Great Buck Howard, 2008, (voice only) What's up Hideous Sun Demon?, We're Back! A Dinosaur's Story, 1993, Robots, 2005, Ice Age: The Meltdown, 2006, Cars, 2006, Igor, 2008, TV appearances include The Bernie Mac Show, 2003, Joey, 2005, Entourage, 2009, Louie, 2012, numerous others; author: Leading with my Chin, 1996, If Roast Beef Could Fly, 2004, How to be the Funniest Kid in the Whole Wide World (or Just in your Class), 2005,(Film) Unstable Fables: Tortoise vs Hare, 2008, I'm Still Here, 2010, Delivery Man, 2013, Elf: Buddy's Musical Christmas, 2014, Ted 2, 2015 (Television) Real Husbands of Hollywood, 2013, Episodes, 2014, Phineas and Ferb, 2014, The 7D, 2014, The Muppets, 2015, Last Man Standing, 2015, Mickey and the Roadster Racers, 2017 **AW:** Named one of The World's Most Influential People, TIME magazine, 2009, The 100 Most Powerful Celebrities, Forbes.com, 2008, 2007; named to TV Hall of Fame, 2014; recipient Mark Twain Prize for American Humor, John F. Kennedy Center for the Performing Arts, 2014; Mark Twain Prize for American Humor, 2014, Primetime Emmy for Outstanding Short Format Non-Fiction Program, 2011, People's Choice Award for Favorite Late Night Talk Show Host, 2006, Hollywood Walk of Fame, 2000 **BA:** c/o Big Dog Productions Inc, PO Box 7855, Burbank, CA, 91510

LEO, LEONARD A., T: Legal Association Administrator, Lawyer **I:** Law and Legal Services **ED:** JD, Cornell University, 1989; AB, Cornell University, 1987 **C:** Executive vice president, The Federalist Society for Law & Pub. Policy Studies, Washington; Law clerk to Hon. Raymond Randolph, US Court Appeals (DC Cir.); Law clerk to Hon. Randall Rader, US Court Federal Claims **CR:** Chairman US Commission for International Religious Freedom (USCIRF), 2009-, commissioner, 2007- Catholic strategist Bush-Cheney campaign, 2004 **CIV:** Board directors, Catholic Action Network, Board directors, Men's Leadership Foundation, Board directors, Youth Leadership Foundation, Board directors, National Catholic Prayer Breakfast **CW:** Contributor articles to professional journals;

co-editor: Presidential Leadership: Rating the Best and Worst in the White House, 2004 **MEM:** Mem.: Sovereign Order of Malta **BAR:** Bar: US Court Appeals (DC Cir.), US Court Appeals (Federal Cir.), US Supreme Court, Washington DC, New Jersey **BA:** The Federalist Society, 1015 18th St Northwest Ste 425, Washington, DC, 20036

LEONARD, KAWHI, T: Professional Basketball Player **I:** Athletics **DOB:** 06/29/1991 **PB:** Los Angeles **SC:** CA/USA **ED:** San Diego State, 2009-11 **C:** San Antonio Spurs, Small Forward, 2011- **AW:** NBA champion,2014, NBA Finals MVP, 2014, NBA All-Star, 2016, 2017, All-NBA First Team, 2016, 2017, NBA Defensive Player of the Year, 2015, 2016, NBA All-Defensive First Team, 2015–2017, NBA All-Defensive Second Team, 2014, NBA All-Rookie First Team, 2012, NBA steals leader, 2015, Consensus second-team All-American, 2011, First-team All-MWC, 2010, 2011, California Mr. Basketball, 2009 **BA:** Impact Sports Management, 2401 NW 2nd Avenue, Suite 200, Boca Raton, FL, 33431

LEONE, DOUGLAS, T: Global Managing Partner **I:** Business Management/Business Services **CN:** Sequoia Capital **PB:** Genoa **SC:** Italy **ED:** MS in Management, Massachusetts Institute of Technology Sloan School of Management (1988); MS in Industrial Engineering, Columbia University (1986); BS in Mechanical Engineering, Cornell University (1979) **C:** Global Managing Partner, Sequoia Capital (2012-Present); Managing Partner, Sequoia Capital (1996-2012); Sequoia Capital (1988) **AW:** Named One of Forbes Top 10 Investors (2017)

LEPAGE, PAUL RICHARD, T: Former Governor **I:** Government Administration/Government Relations/Government Services **DOB:** 10/09/1948 **PB:** Lewiston, Maine **PT:** Son of Gerard A. and Theresa B. (Gagnon) LePage **ED:** MBA, University Maine, 1975; BBA, Husson College, Bangor, Maine, 1971 **C:** Governor, State of Maine, Augusta, 2011-; Head, LePage and Kasevich,; General Manager, Marden's Surplus and Salvage,; President, Paul LePage Associates, Inc., Waterville, Maine, 1985-2011; CFO, Forster Manufacturing Co., Inc., Wilton, Maine, 1984-85; Director Finance & Administration, Interstate Food Processing Corp., Fort Fairfield, Maine, 1983-84; Controller, Scott Paper Co., Winslow, Maine, 1979-83; Director of Finance, Maine State Housing Authority, Augusta, Maine, 1977-79; Treasurer, General Manager, Arthurette Lumber Co., Canada, 1971-77 **CR:** Mayor Waterville teacher Kennebec Vallery Vocational Institute, Waterville, 1986- **CIV:** Vice President, Mid-Maine United Way Program, Waterville, 1985-86 Task Force Leader, Town of Perth-Andover, Canada, 1976-77 **MEM:** Maine Forest Products Council, American Association Council, National Association Accountants, Mid-Maine Chamber of Commerce, Maine Chamber of Commerce & Industry, Toastmasters, Rotary, Elks **H:** Furniture making, softball, racquetball, ice hockey **PA:** Republican

LESTER, GILLIAN, T: Dean **I:** Education/Educational Services **CN:** Columbia Law School **ED:** JSD, Standford Law School, 1998; LLB, University Toronto Faculty of Law, 1990; BSc, University British Columbia, 1986 **C:** Dean, Columbia Law School, 2015-; Werner and Mimi Wolfen Research Professor, University California Berkeley School of Law; Alexander F. & May T. Morrison professor law, University California Berkeley School of Law, 2006-15; Acting dean, University California Berkeley School of Law, 2013-14; Acting dean, University California Berkeley School of Law, 2012-13; Associate dean for JD Program and Curricular Planning, University California Berkeley School of Law, 2010-13; Co-dir., Berkeley Center for Health,

Economic and Family Security, 2010-12; Prof.-in-residence, University Chicago Law School, 2011; Professor law, UCLA School of Law, 1999-2006; Acting professor, UCLA School of Law, 1994-99; Teaching fellow, Stanford Law School, 1992-93; Consultant on health legislation, World Health Organization, Geneva, 1993-94; Intern, Health Legislation Unit, World Health Organization, Geneva, 1991; Judicial clerkship to Chief Justice of Ontario Charles Dubin, Supreme Court of Ontario, Court of Appeal, 1990-91; Summer associate, banking group, Goodman & Goodman, Toronto, 1989; Summer associate, labour group, Campney & Murphy, Vancouver, 1988; Lab technician, department psychology, University British Columbia, 1986-87; Teaching assistant, department psychology, University British Columbia, 1984-87 **CR:** Visiting professor Radzyner School of Law, Interdisciplinary Center, Herzliya, Israel, 2013 Sidney Austin visiting professor law Harvard Law School, 2008-09 distinguished visiting professor University Southern California Gould School of Law, 2008 visiting professor law and Sloan fellow Georgetown University Law Center, 2000 **CW:** Contributor chapters to books, articles; co-author: Jumping the Queue: An Inquiry Into the Legal Treatment of Students with Learning disabilities, 2002, Employment Law Stories, 2006, Employment Law, 2008, Employment Law Cases and Materials, 5th educated, 2012; author: Family Security Insurance: A New Foundation for Economic Security, 2010 **BA:** Columbia Law School, 435 W 116 St, New York, NY, 10025

LETTERMAN, DAVID, T: Talk Show Host, Producer, Comedian, Writer **I:** Media & Entertainment **DOB:** 04/12/1947 **PB:** Indianapolis **SC:** IN/USA **PT:** Joseph Letterman, Dorothy (Hofert) Letterman **MS:** Married **SPN:** Regina Lasko, 3/19/2009, Michelle Cook, 7/2/1968, Divorced 10/1978 **CH:** Harry Joseph **ED:** Graduate, Ball State University, 1969 **C:** Radio Talk Show Host, 1974-1975; Weatherman and TV Announcer, 1970-1974 **CR:** Co-owner, Rahal Letterman Racing **CIV:** Founder, The Letterman Foundation for Courtesy and Grooming **CW:** Performer, The Comedy Store, Los Angeles, CA, 1975; Actor, (TV Appearances) Mary, 1978, Mork & Mindy, 1978, Murphy Brown, 1993, The Nanny, 1995, Seinfeld, 1996, Cosby, 1998, Others, (Films) Cabin Boy, 1994, Eddie, 1996, Private Parts, 1997, Man on the Moon, 1999, I'm Still Here, 2010; Host, Writer, Executive Producer, The Late Show with David Letterman, CBS, 1993-2015; Host, The David Letterman Show, 1980, Late Night with David Letterman, NBC, 1982-1993; Executive Producer (Worldwide Pants, Inc.), (TV Series) The Bonnie Hunt Show, 1995-1996, The Late Late Show With Tom Snyder, 1995-1999, The High Life, 1996, Everybody Loves Raymond, 1996-2005, Late Late Show with Craig Kilburn, 1999-2005, Welcome to New York, 2000-2001, Ed, 2000-2004, Late Late Show with Craig Ferguson, 2005, Knights of Prosperity, 2007, (Documentary) The Youngest Candidate, 2008, (TV Films) Coming Home: Military Families Cope with Change, 2009, Families Stand Together: Feeling Secure in Tough Times, 2009; Co-Author, Late Night with David Letterman: The Book, The Late Night with David Letterman Book of Top Ten Lists, 1990, An Altogether New Book of Top Ten Lists, 1991, Late Night Fun Facts, 2008, This Land Was Made for You and Me (But Mostly Me), 2013 **AW:** Emmy Award for Outstanding Host or Hostess in a Variety Series, The David Letterman Show, 1981, Emmy Award for Outstanding Writing in a Variety or Music Program, Late Night with David Letterman, 1984-1987, Emmy Award for Outstanding Variety, Music or Comedy Program, The Late Show With David Letterman, 1994, 1998-2002, People's Choice Award for Favorite Late Night Talk Show Host, The Late Show With David Letterman, 2005, The 100 Most Powerful Celebrities, Forbes.com, 2007-2008, Johnny Carson Award for Comedic Excellence, The Comedy Awards, 2011, Kennedy Center Honors, John F. Kennedy Center for the Performing Arts, Washington, DC, 2012 **MEM:** Sigma Chi **BA:** Creative Artists Agency, 9830 Wilshire Boulevard, Beverly Hills, CA, 90212

LEVIN, SANDER MARTIN, T: U.S. Representative from Michigan **I:** Government Administration/Government Relations/Government Services **DOB:** 09/06/1931 **PB:** Detroit **SC:** MI/USA **PT:** Son of Saul R. and Bess (Levinson) L. **MS:** Single **SPN:** Married Victoria Schlafer, 1957 (deceased September 4, 2008); **CH:** Jennifer, Andrew, Madeleine, Matthew **ED:** LLB, Harvard University, 1957; MA in International Relations, Columbia University, 1954; BA, University Chicago, 1952 **C:** Member, US Congress from 9th Mich District, 2013-; Acting chairman, US House Ways & Means Committee, 2010-11; Member, US Congress from 12th Mich District, Washington, 1983-2013; Assistant administrator, US Agency for International Develop. (USAID), Washington, 1977-81; Fellow, John F. Kennedy School Government, Institute Politics, Harvard University, Cambridge, Massachusetts, 1975; Member, Michigan State Senate, 1965-70; Supervisor, Oakland County Board Supervisors, Michigan, 1961-64; Private law practice, 1971-77; Private law practice, 1957-64 **CR:** Adjunct professor law Wayne State University, Detroit, 1971-74 **CIV:** Chairman Michigan Democratic Committee, 1968-69 Democratic Candidate for Governor, 1970, 74. **AW:** Recipient Public Policy award, American Society Training & Devel. award, 1997 **PA:** Democrat

LEVINE, ADAM NOAH, T: Singer **I:** Media & Entertainment **DOB:** 03/18/1979 **PB:** Los Angeles **SC:** CA/USA **PT:** Son of Fred and Patsy (Noah) Levine **ED:** Attended, Five Towns College, Dix Hills, New York **C:** Signed to, Octone Records, 2001-; Singer, Maroon 5, 2002-; Signed to, Reprise Records, 1997-99; Singer, Kara's Flowers, 1994-2002 **CW:** Singer: (albums) (with Kara's Flowers) The Fourth World, 1997, (with Maroon 5) Songs About Jane, 2002, It Won't Be Soon Before Long, 2007, Hands All Over, 2010, Overexposed, 2012, V, 2014, Red Pill Blues, 2017 (songs) This Love, 2004 (Best Pop Performance by a Duo or Group With Vocals, Grammy Awards, 2006), Makes Me Wonder, 2007 (Best Pop Performance by a Duo or Group With Vocals, Grammy Awards, 2008); vocal coach, judge (TV series) The Voice, 2011-; actor: (films) Begin Again, 2013, Pitch Perfect 2, 2015, Unity, 2015, Klown Forever, 2015, Popstar: Never Stop Never Stopping, 2016, Fun Mom Dinner, 2017, The Clapper, 2017 **AW:** Named Sexiest Man Alive, People magazine, 2013, Top Hot 100 Artist, Billboard Music Awards, 2013, Favorite Group, People's Choice Awards, 2015, Favorite Band, 2013, 2012, Favorite Adult Contemporary Artist, American Music Awards, 2013, Favorite Pop/Rock Band, Duo or Group, 2012, 2011, Best New Artist, Grammy Awards, 2005, MTV Video Music Awards, 2004, Best New Group, World Music Awards, 2004 **BA:** Press Here Publicity, 138 West 25th Street, 9th Floor, New York, NY, 10001

LEVITT, MICHAEL, T: Chemistry Professor **I:** Education/Educational Services **DOB:** 05/09/1947 **PB:** Pretoria **SC:** South Africa **ED:** PhD in Computational Biology, Gonville & Gaius College, Cambridge, 1971; BSc in Physics, King's College, London, 1967 **C:** Professor structural biology, Stanford University, California, 1987-; Blaise Pascal Research professor, Foundation de l'Ecole Normale Superieure, Paris, 2003-04; Associate chairman Department Structural Biology, Stanford University, 2005-10; Chairman Department Structural Biology, Stanford University, 1993-2004; Chairman Department Chemical Physics, The Weizmann Institute of Sci., Rehovot, 1980-83; Professor chemical physics, The Weizmann Institute of Sci., Rehovot, Israel, 1980-87; Associate professor physics, The Weizmann Institute of Sci., Rehovot, 1979; Professor, Medical Research Council Laboratory of Molecular Biology, Cambridge, Massachusetts, 1986-87; Staff scientist, Medical Research Council Laboratory of Molecular Biology, Cambridge, England, 1971-79 **CR:** Member editorial board Proceedings National Academy Sci., 2002-reviwer Swedish National Research Foundation, 1992 reviewer Brit. Medical Research Council, 1992 ad hoc reviewer US Department Energy, 1989-96, National Science Foundation, 1989-96, National Institutes of Health, 1989-96 **CW:** Author: A Simplified Representation of Protein Conformations for Rapid Simulation of Protein Folding, 1976; co-author: Conformations Using a Macromolecular Energy Minimization Procedure, 1969, Computer Simulation of Protein Folding, 1975, Structural Patterns in Globular Proteins, 1976, Automatic Identification of Secondary Structure in Globular Proteins, 1977, Refinement of Large Structures by Simultaneous Minimization of Energy and R Factor, 1978, various publications; editorial board Structure, 1986, Current Opinion in Structural Biology, 1986; editor: Journal of Molecular Biology, 2001- **AW:** Co-recipient Nobel Prize in Chemistry, Royal Swedish Academy Sciences, 2013; recipient Anniversary prize, Federation European Biochemical Societies, 1986, Delano Award, 2014, ISCB Fellow, 2015, Academy of Sciences, 2002 **MEM:** Fellow: American Academy of Arts & Sciences, Royal Society; mem.: National Academy of Sciences

LEVY, MARV, T: Former NFL Coach **I:** Athletics **DOB:** 08/03/1925 **PB:** Chicago **SC:** IL/USA **ED:** MA, Harvard University, 1951; BA, Coe College, Cedar Rapids, Iowa, 1950 **C:** Buffalo Bills Administrator, 2006-2007; General Manager, Vice President Football Operations, Buffalo Bills, 2006-07; Vice President, Buffalo Bills, 1995-97; Head Coach, Buffalo Bills, 1986-97; Head Coach, Chicago Blitz, US Football League, 1984; Head Coach, Kansas City Chiefs, 1978-82; Head Coach, Montreal Alouetts, Can. Football League, 1973-77; Special Teams Coach, Washington Redskins, 1971-72; Special Teams Coach, LA Rams, 1970; Kicking Teams Coach, Philadelphia Eagles, 1969; Head Coach, College William & Mary, Williamsburg, Virginia, 1964-68; Head Coach, University of California Golden Bears, Berkeley, 1960-63; Head Coach, University of New Mexico, 1958-59; Assistant Coach, University of New Mexico, 1956-58; Assistant Coach, Coe College, Cedar Rapids, Iowa, 1953-55; High School Coach, St. Louis, 1951-52 **MIL:** Served U.S. Army Air Corps., 1943-46 **CW:** Author: Marv Levy: Where Else Would You Rather Be?, 2004 **AW:** Named NFL Coach of the Year, United Press International, 1995, 1988, AFC Coach of the Year, 1995, 1993, 1988; Named to The Pro Football Hall of Fame, 2001; Recipient Annis Stukus trophy (Coach of the Year), Can. Football League, 1974 **ACH:** Achievements include leading the Buffalo Bills to four consecutive Super Bowl appearances, 1990-94

LEWIS, CARL, T: Retired Professional Track and Field Athlete **I:** Athletics **DOB:** 07/01/1961 **PB:** Birmingham **SC:** AL/USA **PT:** William McKinley Lewis, Jr.; Evelyn (Lawler) Lewis **ED:** Student, University of Houston **C:** Member, U.S. Olympic Team (1980, 1984, 1988, 1992, 1996) **CIV:** Founder, Carl Lewis Foundation **CW:** Musician, Album, "Break it Up" (1986) **AW:** Named US Athlete of the Year (1981—1984, 1987, 1988, 1991); Athlete of the Year, Track & Field News (1982—1984); Male Athlete of the Year,

Associated Press (1983, 1984); Athlete of the Year, United Press International (1983, 1984); 1980's World Athlete of the Decade, Track & Field News; Olympic Athlete of the Century (2000); Named to US Olympic Hall of Fame (1985); Named to New Jersey Hall of Fame (2010); James E. Sullivan Award, Best Amateur Athlete (1981); Jesse Owens Award (1982); Gold Medal, 100m, Long Jump, 4X100m Relay, World Championships, Helsinki, Finland (1983); Gold Medal, 100m, 200m, Long Jump, 4X100m Relay, Summer Olympic Games, Los Angeles, CA (1984); Gold Medal, Long Jump, Pan America Games, Indianapolis, IN (1987); Gold Medal, 100m, Long Jump, 4X100m Relay, World Championships, Rome, Italy (1987); Gold Medal, 100m, Long Jump, Summer Olympic Games, Seoul, Korea (1988); Silver Medal, 200m (1988); Gold Medal, 100m, 4X100m Relay, World Championships, Tokyo, Japan (1991); Silver Medal, Long Jump (1991); Gold Medal, Long Jump, 4X100m Relay, Summer Olympic Games, Barcelona, Spain (1992); Bronze Medal, 200m, World Championships, Stuttgart, Germany (1993); Gold Medal, Long Jump, Summer Olympic Games, Atlanta, GA (1996); Inductee, New Jersey Hall of Fame (2010); Inductee, Texas Track and Field Coaches Association Hall of Fame (2016); Sports Illustrated Olympian of the Century (2000) **BA:** Cleve Lewis Management, 12460 Crabaple Rd, Alpharetta, GA, 30004

LEWIS, JASON, T: U.S. Representative from Minnesota **I:** Government Administration/Government Relations/Government Services **DOB:** 09/23/1955 **PB:** Waterloo **SC:** IA/USA **ED:** M.A. University of Colorado, 1992; B.A., University of Iowa, 1979 **C:** Member, U.S. House of Representatives from Minnesota's 2nd District, 2017-; Member, Committee on Budget; Member, Committee on Education and the Workforce; Member, Committee on Transportation and Infrastructure; Host, The Jason Lewis Show, 2011-2014 **BA:** 418 Cannon HOB, Washington, DC, 20515

LEWIS, JOHN ROBERT, T: U.S. Representative from Georgia **I:** Government Administration/Government Relations/Government Services **DOB:** 02/21/1940 **PB:** Troy **PT:** Married Lillian Miles, 1968 (deceased December 31, 2012); 1 child, John-Miles **ED:** BA in Religion & Philosophy, Fisk University, 1963; BA in Theology, American Baptist Theological Seminary, Nashville, 1961 **C:** Member, US Congress from 5th Georgia District, Washington, 1987-; Member, Congressional Black Caucus; Member, US House Ways & Means Committee; Community affairs director, National Consumer Cooperative Bank, 1980-82; City councilman, City of Atlanta, Atlanta, 1983-86 **CR:** Board directors Robert F. Kennedy Memorial, National Democratic Institute for International Affairs, Martin Luther King Junior Center for Social Change, Friends of Volunteers in Service to America, African Am. Institute; associate director ACTION, 1977-80; director Voter Education Project, 1970-77; associate director Field Foundation, 1966-67; founder, chair Student Non-Violent Coordination Committee, 1963-66 **CIV:** member Martin Luther King Center for Social Change, African American Institute, Robert F. Kennedy Memorial **CW:** Co-author (with Michael D'Orso): Walking With the Wind: A Memoir of the Movement, 1998 (Robert F. Kennedy Book award, 1999); co-author: (with Brenda Jones) Across That Bridge: Life Lessons and a Vision for Change, 2012; co-author: (with Andrew Aydin & Nate Powell) March: Book One, 2013 **AW:** Named one of The Most Influential Black Americans, Ebony magazine, 2006-08; recipient Presidential Medal of Freedom, The White House, 2010, Wiley A. Branton award, Washington Lawyers' Committee, 2009, Dole Leadership award, Robert J.

Dole Institute Politics, University Kansas, 2007, Golden Plate award, Academy Achievement, 2004, Allies for Justice award, National Lesbian and Gay Law Association, 2004, Edwin T. Dahlberg award, American Baptist Churches USA, 2003, William Mott Junior Parks Leadership award, National Parks Conservation Association, 2002, Springarn award, National Association for the Advancement of Colored People, 2002, John F. Kennedy Profile in Courage Award, 2001, We the People award, National Constitution Ctr, 2001, Helen Keller Achievement award for Advocacy, American Foundation for the Blind, 2001, Raoul Wallenberg medal, University Michigan, 2000, Martin Luther King Junior Non-Violent Peace Prize, 1999, Pinnacle award for Lifetime Achievement, ACDelco, 1999, Eleanor Roosevelt award for Human Rights, 1998, Time 100 Most Influential, 2017 **MEM:** Mem.: Faith & Politics Institute, Americans for Democratic Action (president 1993-95) **PA:** Democrat

LEWIS, RAMSEY EMANUEL JR., T: Pianist, Composer **I:** Media & Entertainment **DOB:** 05/27/1935 **PB:** Chgo. **PT:** Son of Ramsey Emanuel and Pauline (Richards) L.; Married Geraldine Taylor, April 7, 1954 (div. March 1989); children– Vita Denise, Ramsey Emanuel III, Marcus Kevin, Dawn, Kendall, Frayne, Robert; **Marr ED:** Doctorate (hon.), University South Carolina, 2000; ArtsD (hon.), University Illinois, 1995; DHL (hon.), DePaul University, Chicago, 1993; DHL (hon.), University Illinois, Chicago, 1995; DHL (hon.), De Paul University, 1993; Student, De Paul University, 1954-55; Student, University Illinois, 1953-54; Student, Chicago Music College, 1947-54 **C:** Manager record department, Hudson-Ross, Inc., Chicago, 1954-56 **CR:** Art Tatum professor in jazz studies Roosevelt University, Chicago, 1999-. **CW:** Organizer Ramsey Lewis Trio, 1956; he plays with various formats from solo, duo (with Dr. Billy Taylor), trio, quartet, quintet, sextet, septet and on up to symphony orchestras, 1st professional appearance, Chicago 1957, appeared New York City, 1958-, San Francisco, 1962, played Randall's Island Jazz Festival, New York City, 1959, Saugatuck (Michigan) Jazz Festival, 1960, Newport (Rhode Island) Jazz Festival, 1961, 63, numerous jazz concerts at various festivals and univs. since 1961; toured with New Sounds of 1963; appeared in film Save the Children, 1973; recipient Grammy awards for The In Crowd 1965, Hold It Right There 1966, Hang on Sloopy 1973); albums include Another Voyage, 1970, The Piano Player, 1970, Them Changes, 1970, Back To The Roots, 1971, Upendo Ni Pamoja, 1972, Funky Serenity, 1973, Legacy, 1978, Best of Ramsey Lewis, 1981, Salongo, 1976, Sun Goddess, 1974, Tequila Mockingbird, 1977, Ramsey, 1979, Routes, 1980, (with Nancy Wilson) The Two of Us, 1984, Fantasy, 1985, Keys to the City, 1987, A Classic Encounter (with London Philharmonic Orchestra), 1988, Urban Renewal, 1989, We Meet Again (with Billy Taylor), 1989, The Electric Collection, 1991, Ivory Pyramid, 1992, Sky Island, 1993, Maiden Voyage, 1994, Urban Knights, 1995, Between The Keys, 1996, Urban Knights II, 1997, Dance of the Soul, 1998, Appasionate, 1999, Urban Knights III, 2001, Urban Knights IV, 2001, Meant to Be, 2002, Urban Knights V, 2003, Simple Pleasures, 2003, Time Flies, 2004, Urban Knights VI, 2005, With One Voice, 2005, Song from the Heart: Ramsey, 2009, Taking Another Look, 2011; composer: Sound of Spring, Fantasia for Drums, Look-a-Here, Sound of Christmas; organizer, Rams' L Productions, Inc., Chicago, 1966, Ramsel Pub. Co., Chicago, 1966, Ivory Pyramid Productions, Inc., 1995-2000, The Pathlink Company, 2001; host weekly jazz TV show, Station B.E.T. (cable TV) Ramsey Lewis on Jazz Central, 1990-99; host radio show The Ramsey Lewis Morning Show, 1997-,

Station WNUA, Chicago, Legends of Jazz with Ramsey Lewis, 1990-; artistic director Jazz series at Ravinia Festival Chicago, 1993-; numerous TV appearances; lecturer various univs.; performance at White House, 1995. **AW:** Recipient Records and Radio Industry Achievement award as Personality of Year, 1999, 2000, National Academy of Recording Arts and Sciences Gov.'s award, 2000; named Person of Week ABC Nightly News, 1995; elected laureate Lincoln Academy, Springfield, iilinois, 1997, Golden Globe for Best Jazz Performance, 1965, Golden Globe for Best Rhythm and Blues Group, 1966, Golden Globe Best Rhythm and Blue Instrumental, 1973 **BA:** Universal Attractions Agency, 15 West 36th Street, 8th Floor, New York, NY, 10018

LIDSTROM, NICKLAS, T: Retired Professional Hockey Player **I:** Athletics **DOB:** 04/28/1970 **PB:** Vasteras **SC:** Sweden **C:** Scout, Detroit Red Wings, 2012-; Captain, Detroit Red Wings, 2006-12; Defenseman, Detroit Red Wings, 1991-2012 **CR:** Member Team Sweden, World Cup of Hockey, 2004, Team Sweden, Olympic Games, Vancouver, 2010, Torino, Italy, 2010, Salt Lake City, 2002, Nagano, Japan, 1998 **AW:** Named NHL Player of the Decade, Sporting News, 2009; named to Second All-Star Team, NHL, 2010, 2009, First All-Star Team, 2011, 2008, 2007, 2006, 1998-2003, NHL All-Star Game, 2011, 2009, 2008, 2007, 1998-2004, 1996, All-Rookie Team, NHL, 1992; Recipient Conn Smythe Trophy, 2002, James Norris Memorial Trophy, 2011, 2008, 2007, 2006, 2003, 2002, 2001, 100 Greatest NHL Players of All Time, 2017, Michigan Sports Hall of Fame, 2014, IIHF Hall of Fame, 2014, Hockey Hall of Fame, 2015 **ACH:** Achievements include being a member of Stanley Cup Champion Detroit Red Wings, 1997, 1998, 2002, 2008; being the first European captain to win the Stanley Cup, 2008; being a member of gold medal winning Swedish Hockey Team, Torino Olympics, Italy, 2006; setting NHL record of most games played (1,564) with a single team; having his number 5 retired by the Detroit Red Wings, 2014; being inducted into the Michigan Sports Hall of Fame, 2014; being inducted into the Hockey Hall of Fame, 2015

LIEU, TED W., T: U.S. Representative from California **I:** Government Administration/Government Relations/Government Services **ED:** JD, Georgetown University, 1994; BA in Political Sci., Stanford University, 1991; BS in Computer Sci., Stanford University, 1991 **C:** Member US House of Representative's from California's 33rd District, 2015-; Member, Committee on Appropriations; Member District 28, California State Senate, 2010-2015; Member District 53, California State Assembly, 2005-10; Attorney, US Air Force,; Attorney, Judge Adv. General Corps.,; Member, Torrance Environmental Quality & Energy Conservation Commission,; Member, Torrance City Council, **MIL:** Major US Air Force Reserve **PA:** Democrat **BA:** 1223 Longworth HouseOffice Building, Washington, DC, 20515

LIGHTFOOT, ROBERT M. JR., T: NASA Administrator **I:** Sciences **PB:** Montevallo **SC:** Alabama **ED:** Bachelor in Mechanical Engineering, University Alabama, 1986 **C:** Nasa Administrator, 2017-; Associate administrator, NASA, 2012-; Assistant associate administrator space shuttle program, office space operations, NASA, Washington, 2003-05; Director propulsion test directorate, Stennis Space Center, NASA, 2002; Deputy director propulsion test directorate, Stennis Space Center, NASA, 2001-02; Chief propulsion test operations, Stennis Space Center, NASA, 1999-2001; Director, Marshall Space Flight Center, NASA, 2009-12; Deputy director, Marshall Space Flight

Center, NASA, 2007-09; Manager space shuttle propulsion office, Marshall Space Flight Center, NASA, 2005-07; Test engineer, program manager, Marshall Space Flight Center, NASA, 1989 **CR:** Member adv. board college mechanical engineering University Alabama, fellow college engineering, 2009, distinguished department fellow, department mechanical engineering, 2007 **AW:** Recipient Presidential Rank award for Distinguished Executives, 2010, Outstanding Leadership medal, NASA, 2007, Presidential Rank award for Meritorious Executives, 2006, Spaceflight Leadership Recognition award, 2000, Silver Snoopy award, 1999, NASA Exceptional Achievement medal, 1996

LIGHTHIZER, ROBERT E., T: U.S. Trade Representative **I:** Government Administration/Government Relations/Government Services **CN:** Office of the U.S. Trade Representative **PB:** Ashtabula **SC:** OH/USA **ED:** JD, Georgetown University, 1973; BA, Georgetown University, 1969 **C:** U.S. Trade Representative, Washington, DC, 2017-Present; Practice Leader, Legislative/Lobbying, Skadden, Arps, Slate, Meagher & Flom, Washington, DC; Partner, Practice Leader, International Trade And Transactions, Skadden, Arps, Slate, Meagher & Flom, Washington, DC **CR:** Chief Of Staff, U.S. Senate Committee of Finance, 1981-1983; Deputy U.S. Trade Representative, Rank Of Ambassador, Treasurer, Republican Presidential Campaign, 1996; Speaker On Trade And Tax Issues, Politics, And Other Developments, Washington, DC; Board Director For Several Charitable And Political Groups **CW:** Contributor, Articles, Professional Publications and Journals **MEM:** International Bar Association **BAR:** District of Columbia, 1973 **BA:** Office of the U.S. Trade Representative, 600 17th Street NW, Washington, DC, 20005

LIMBAUGH, RUSH HUDSON III, T: RadioTalk Show Host **I:** Media & Entertainment **DOB:** 01/12/1951 **PB:** Cape Girardeau **PT:** Son of Rush Hudson Junior and Mildred Carolyn (Armstrong) Limbaugh; **ED:** Grad., Elkins Institute Radio & Tech.; Student Southeast Missouri State University **C:** Radio talk show host, The Rush Limbaugh Show, New York City, 1988-; Radio talk show host, KFBK-AM radio, Sacramento, 1984-88; Political commentator, KMBZ radio, Kansas City, 1983-84; Director sales & special events, Kansas City Royals,; Director group sales, Kansas City Royals, 1979-83; Disc jockey, WHB radio, Kansas City, 1975-78; Disc jockey, KQV radio, Pittsburgh, 1971 **CR:** Pub. The Limbaugh Letter, 1995- **CW:** Author: The Way Things Ought To Be, 1992 (#1 New York Times bestseller), See, I Told You So, 1993 (#1 New York Times bestseller), Rush Revere and the Brave Pilgrims: Time Travel Adventures with Exceptional Americans, 2013, Rush Revere and the First Patriots: Time-Travel Adventures with Exceptional Americans, 2014, Rush Revere and the Star-Spangled Banner: Time-Travel Adventures with Exceptional Americans, 2015, Rush Revere and the Presidency, 2016; TV/film appearances include Hearts Afire, 1994, Forget Paris, 1995, The Drew Carey Show, 1998, weekly analyst ESPN's Sunday NFL Countdown, 2003 **AW:** Named Man of Year, Human Events magazine, 2007, Greatest Radio Talk Show Host of All Time, Talkers magazine, 2002; named one of The 50 Highest-Earning Political Figures, Newsweek, 2010, The World's Most Influential People, TIME magazine, 2009, The Ten Most Fascinating People of 2008, Barbara Walters, The 100 Most Powerful Celebrities, Forbes.com, 2008; named to, National Association Broadcasters Hall of Fame, 1998, Radio Hall of Fame, 1993; recipient William F. Buckley, Junior award for Media Excellence, Media Research Center, 2007, Marconi Radio award for Syndicated Radio Personality of

Year, National Association Broadcasters, 2005, 2000, 1995, 1992 **ACH:** Achievements include having the most-listened-to radio show in the US since 1991 **PA:** Republican

LINCECUM, TIM, T: Professional Baseball Player **I:** Athletics **DOB:** 06/15/1984 **PB:** Bellevue **SC:** WA/USA **PT:** Son of Chris and Rebecca Lincecum. **ED:** Attended, University of Washington, Seattle, 2003-06 **C:** Pitcher, San Francisco Giants, 2007-2015; Pitcher, Texas Rangers 2016 **CR:** Coach Giants Challenger Clinic, 2007 **AW:** Named National League Pitcher of Year, The Sporting News, 2009, National League Outstanding Pitcher, Major League Baseball Players Association, 2008, 1st team All-American, Collegiate Baseball, 2006, National Freshman of Year, 2004, Freshman of Year, PAC-10 Conference, 2004, Pitcher of Year, 2004; named to National League All-Star Team, Major League Baseball, 2009-11; recipient Babe Ruth award, 2010, National League Cy Young award, Baseball Writers' Association America, 2009, 2008, Harry S. Jordan award, San Francisco Giants, 2007, Golden Spikes award, USA Baseball, 2006,World Series Champion, 1966, 1970, 1983, AL Wins Leader, 1975, 1977, AL ERA Leader, 1973, 1975, Gold Glove Award, 1976-1979 **ACH:** Achievements include leading the National League in: strikeouts, 2008-10; complete games (4), 2009; member of World Series Championship winning San Francisco Giants, 2010, 2012, 2014; pitched a no-hitter against the San Diego Padres on July 13, 2013, pitched his second no-hitter against the San Diego Padres on June 25, 2014

LINCOLN, ANDREW, T: Actor **I:** Media & Entertainment **PB:** London **SC:** England **CW:** (Film) Boston Kickout, 1995, Understanding Jane, 1998, A Mans Best Friend, 1999, Human Traffic, 1999, Gangster No. 1, 2000, Offending Angels, 2000, Love Actually, 2003, Enduring Love, 2004, These Foolish Things, 2006, Hey Good Looking!, 2006, Scenes of a Sexual Nature, 2006, Heartbreaker, 2010, Made in Dagenham, 2010, (Television) Drop the Dead Donkey, 1994, N7, 1995, Over Here, 1996, Bramwell, 1996, This Life, 1996, The Woman in White, 1997, Bomber, 2000, Shipwrecked, 2000, A Likeness in Stone, 2000, Teachers, 2001, Trevor's World of Sport, 2003, State of mind, 2003, The Canterbury Tales, 2003, Holby City, 2004, Lie With Me, 2004, Whose Baby?, 2004, Afterlife, 2005, This Life +10, Wuthering Heights, 2009, The Things I Haven't Told You, 2009, Monnshot, 2009, Strike Back, The Walking Dead, 2010, Red Nose Day Actually, 2017, Robot Chicken, 2017

LINEBARGER, TOM, T: CEO **I:** Manufacturing **CN:** Cummins **PB:** Indianapolis **SC:** IN/USA **SPN:** Michele Linebarger **ED:** Master's Degree, Stanford School of Engineering; MBA, Stanford Graduate School of Business, 1993 **C:** Chairman/CEO, Cummins Inc, 2012-; President/COO, Cummins Inc, 2008-2011; Exec VP/Pres Power Generation, Cummins Inc, 2005-2008

LINKLATER, RICHARD, I: Media & Entertainment **DOB:** 07/30/1960 **PB:** Houston **SC:** TX/USA **PT:** Charles W. Linklater III; Diane Margaret (Krieger) **ED:** Student, University Texas; Student, Sam Houston State University **C:** Founder, Detour Filmprodn., Austin, Texas **CIV:** Founder, artistic director Austin Film Society **CW:** Director, producer, writer, cinematographer, editor: (films) It's Impossible to Learn to Plow by Reading Books, 1988; director, producer, writer, actor: (films) Slacker, 1991; director, producer, writer: (films) Dazed and Confused, 1993, Before Sunset, 2004, Before Midnight, 2013, Boyhood, 2014 (New York Film Critics Cir. award for Best Director,

2014, Boston Society Film Critics awards for Best Director, Best Screenplay, 2014, Golden Globe award for Best Director, 2015, Critics' Choice award for Best Director, 2015, BAFTA awards for Best Film, Best Director, 2015), Everybody Wants Some!!, 2016; director, prodr.: (films) Bad News Bears, 2005, Me and Orson Welles, 2008; writer, dir.: (films) Before Sunrise, 1995, The Newton Boys, 1998, Fast Food Nation, 2006, A Scanner Darkly, 2006, Fast Food Nation, 2006, Bernie, 2011; dir.: (films) Suburbia, 1997, School of Rock, 2003; dir.: (documentary) Inning by Inning: A Portrait of a Coach, 2008; actor: (films) Underneath, 1995, Scotch and Milk, 1998, Spy Kids, 2001, The Hottest State, 2006, RSO (Registered Sex Offender), 2008; director, producer, actor: (animated film) Waking Life, 2001; executive prodr.: (films) I Dream Too Much, 2014. **AW:** Co-recipient Louis XIII Genius award, Critics' Choice Awards, 2014; named to Texas Film Hall of Fame, 2007

LINNEY, LAURA, T: Actress **I:** Media & Entertainment **DOB:** 05/26/1905 **PB:** New York City **SC:** New York City **PT:** Daughter of Romulus Linney and Ann Leggett Perse; **ED:** Grad., Juilliard School, 1989; BFA, Brown University, 1986 **CW:** Actress: (films) Lorenzo's Oil, 1992, Searching for Bobby Fischer, 1993, Blind Spot, 1993, Dave, 1993, A Simple Twist of Fate, 1994, Congo, 1995, Primal Fear, 1996, The Truman Show, 1998, Absolute Power, 1998, Lush, 1999, You Can Count on Me, 2000, The House of Mirth, 2000, Running Mates, 2000, Maze, 2000, The Laramie Project, 2002, The Mothman Prophecies, 2002, The Life of David Gale, 2003, Mystic River, 2003, Love Actually, 2003, P.S., 2004, Kinsey, 2004, The Squid and the Whale, 2005, The Exorcism of Emily Rose, 2005, Driving Lessons, 2006, Jindabyne, 2006, The Hottest State, 2006, Man of the Year, 2006, Breach, 2007, The Nanny Diaries, 2007, The Savages, 2007, The Other Man, 2008, The City of Your Final Destination, 2009, Sympathy for Delicious, 2010, Morning, 2010, The Details, 2011, (voice) Arthur Christmas, 2011, Hyde Park on Hudson, 2012, The Fifth Estate, 2013, Mr. Holmes, 2015, Genius, 2016, Teenage Mutant Ninja Turtles: Out of the Shadows, 2016, Sully, 2016, Nocturnal Animals, 2016, The Dinner, 2017 (TV films) Tales of the City, 1993, More Tales of the City, 1998, Love Letters, 1999, Wild Iris, 2001,King of the Hill, 2002, Frasier 2003-4, American Dad, 2006 (TV miniseries) John Adams, 2008 (Outstanding Lead Actress in a Miniseries or a Movie, Emmy Awards, 2008, Best Performance by an Actress in A Miniseries or Motion Picture Made for TV, Golden Globe Awards, 2009, Outstanding Performance by a Female Actor in a TV Movie or Miniseries, Screen Actors Guild, 2009); actress, prodr.: (TV series) The Big C, 2010-13 (Best Performance by an Actress in a TV Series-Comedy or Musical, Golden Globe Awards, 2011, Outstanding Lead Actress in a Miniseries or Movie, Emmy Awards, 2013), Inside Amy Schumer, 2016, Red Nose Day Actually, 2017, Last Week Tonight with John Oliver, 2017, Ozark, 2017, Sink Sank Sunk, 2017 (Broadway plays) Six Degrees of Separation,1990, Sight Unseen, 1992, The Seagull, 1992, Hedda Gabler, 1994, Holiday, 1995, Honour, 1998, Uncle Vanya, 2000, The Crucible, 2002, Sight Unseen, 2004, Les Liaisons Dangereuses, 2008, Time Stands Still, 2010, The Little Foxes, 2017.

LIPINSKI, DANIEL, T: U.S. Representative from Illinois **I:** Government Administration/Government Relations/Government Services **DOB:** 07/15/1966 **PB:** Chgo. **PT:** Son of William and Marie Lipinski; **ED:** PhD in political sci., Duke Univ., 1998; MA, Stanford Univ., 1989; BS, Northwestern Univ., 1988 **C:** Member, U.S. Congress from 3rd Dist Illinois, 2005-; Member transportation committee, U.S. House of Representatives,; Member sci., space and technology committee, U.S. House of Representatives.; Associate professor, Univ. Tennessee, 2001-04; Associate professor, Notre Dame Univ., 2000-01 **PA:** Democrat

LIPINSKI, TARA KRISTEN, T: Professional Figure Skater **I:** Athletics **DOB:** 06/10/1982 **PB:** Philadelphia **SC:** PA/USA **C:** Professor figure skater, Stars On Ice, 1998 **CR:** National spokesperson Campaign for Tobacco-Free Kids **CW:** Actor (TV appearance): 7th Heaven, 2003, The Wayne Brady Show, 2003,(Television) Generation Jets, 2003, The Metro Chase, 2004, Still Standing, 2005, What's New, Scooby-Doo?, 2005, Malcolm in the Middle, 2006, Superstore, 2016 **AW:** Recipient Gold Medal, Winter Olympic Games, 1998, 1st Place, Rattle and Roll, 1998, 2nd Place, National Championship, 1998, 1st National Senior, 1997, 1st Place, Champion Series Final, 1998, 1997, World Championships, 1997, Hershey's Kisses Challenge, 1997, 3rd Place, Trophy Lalique, 1996, 2nd Place, Nations Cup, 1996, 1st (team), Postal Service Challenge, 1996, 2nd Place, Skate Can., 1996, Mary Lou Retton award, U.S. Olympic Festival, 1994,Olympic Committee Female Athlete of the Year, 1997, U.S. Figure Skating Hall of Fame, 2006 **ACH:** Achievements include youngest Olympic Festival gold medalist at age 12 **H:** Reading, cooking, tennis

LITHGOW, JOHN ARTHUR, T: Actor **I:** Media & Entertainment **PB:** Rochester **SC:** NY/USA **PT:** Arthur Lithgow; Sarah Jane (Price) Lithgow **MS:** Married **SPN:** Mary Yeager (1981); Jean Taynton, September 10, 1966 (div. 1980) **CH:** Ian; Phoebe; Nathan **ED:** ArtsD (hon.), Harvard University, 2005; Postgrad., London Academy Music and Dramatic Art, 1967-69; Grad. magna cum laude, Harvard University, 1967 **C:** Printmaker, founder, Lithgow Graphics **CW:** Actor: (films) Obsession, 1976, The Big Fix, 1978, Rich Kids, 1979, All That Jazz, 1979, Blow Out, 1981, I'm Dancing as Fast as I Can, 1982, The World According to Garp, 1982, Twilight Zone: The Movie, 1983, Terms of Endearment, 1983, 2010: The Year We Make Contact, 1984, Footloose, 1984, Adventures of Buckaroo Banzai Across the 8th Dimension, 1984, The Glitter Dome, 1984, Santa Claus: The Movie, 1985, Mesmerized, 1986, The Manhattan Project, 1986, Harry and the Hendersons, 1987, Distant Thunder, 1988, Out Cold, 1989, Memphis Belle, 1990, At Play in the Fields of the Lord, 1991, Richochet, 1991, Raising Cain, 1992, Cliffhanger, 1993, The Pelican Brief, 1993, Good Man in Africa, 1994, Silent Fall, 1994, Princess Caraboo, 1994, Hollow Point, 1995, (voice) Special Effects: Anything Can Happen, 1996, Officer Buckle and Gloria, 1998, Johhny Skidmarks, 1998, Homegrown, 1998, A Civil Action, 1998, Portofino, 1999, (voice) Rugrats in Paris: The Movie-Rugrats II, 2000, C-Scam, 2000, (voice) Shrek, 2001, Orange County, 2002, The Life and Death of Peter Sellers, 2004, Kinsey, 2004, Dreamgirls, 2006, Confessions of a Shopaholic, 2009, The Macabre World of Lavender Williams, 2009, Leap Year, 2010, Rise of the Planet of the Apes, 2011, The Campaign, 2012, This is 40, 2012, Love Is Strange, 2014, The Homesman, 2014, Interstellar, 2014; (TV films) Mom, the Wolfman and Me, 1983, Not in Front of the Children, 1982, The Day After, 1983, Resting Place, 1986, Baby Girl Scott, 1987, Traveling Man, 1989, Ivory Hunters, 1990, The Boys, 1991, The Wrong Man, 1993, Love, Cheat and Steal, 1993, Then There Were Giants, 1994, American Cinema, 1994, World War II: When Lions Roared, 1994, The Tuskegee Airmen, 1995, My Brother's Keeper, 1995, Redwood Curtain, 1995, Christmas in Washington, 1996, E=mc², 2005, Classical Baby (Im Grown Up Now): The Poetry Show, 2008, Timms Valley, 2013; (TV series) 3rd Rock from the Sun, 1996-2001 (Emmy award for Outstanding Lead Actor in a Comedy Series 1996,

1997, 1999, Golden Globe award for Best Actor in a TV Series Musical and Comedy 1996), Twenty Good Years, 2006-08, Once Upon a Time in Wonderland, 2013-14; (mini-series) Don Quixote, 1999; (TV appearances) Amazing Stories, 1985 (Emmy for Outstanding Guest Performer in a Drama Series 1986), Tales from the Crypt, 1989, Cosby, 1996, Paloozaville, 2008, Dexter, 2009 (Golden Globe award for Best Performance by a Supporting Actor in a Series, Mini-Series, or Motion Picture Made for TV, 2010, Emmy award for Outstanding Guest Actor in a Drama Series, 2010); (Broadway plays) Sweet Smell of Success, 2000-03 (Tony for Best Male Actor 2002), The Retreat from Moscow, 2004, Dirty Rotten Scoundrels, 2005, All My Sons, 2008, Mr & Mrs. Fitch, 2009, The Columnist, 2011; (plays) The Magistrate, 2013; (one man shows) John Lithgow: Stories by Heart, 2008; singer: (albums) Singing in the Bathtub, 1999; author: (children's books) The Remarkable Farkle McBride, 2000, Marsupial Sue, 2001, I'm a Manatee, 2003, Carnival of the Animals, 2004, (memoir) Drama: An Actor's Education, 2011. **AW:** Named to Theater Hall of Fame, 2005

LITTON, ANDREW, T: Director of the New York City Ballet **I:** Fine Art **DOB:** 05/16/1959 **PB:** New York City **SC:** NY/USA **ED:** Doctorate (hon.), University of Bournemouth; MBA, Juilliard School of Music, New York City; BS, Juilliard School of Music, New York City **C:** Director, New York City Ballet,2014; Music Director, Principal Conductor, Bergen Philharmonic Orchestra, Norway, 2003-; Music Director Emeritus, Dallas Symphony Orchestra, 2007-; Conductor Laureate, Bournemouth Symphony Orchestra, 1994-; Music Director, Dallas Symphony Orchestra, 1994-2006; Conductor, Bournemouth Symphony Orchestra, 1988-94 **CR:** Guest Conductor LA Opera House, Israel Orchestra, Moscow Orchestra, Welsh National Opera, England National Opera, Dallas Symphony Orchestra, Philadelphia Orchestra, Bergen Philharmonic, Scottish Chamber Orchestra, NHK Orchestra, Dresden Philharmonic, St. Louis Symphony Orchestra Artistic Director Sommerfest Concerts Minnesota Orchestra, 2003- **AW:** Recipient Elgar Society Medal, Sanford Medal for Musical Achievement, Yale University, 2003; Winner BBC International Conductors Competition **BA:** David H. Koch Theater, 20 Lincoln Center Plaza, New York, NY, 10023

LIU, JOANNE, T: Medical Association Administrator **I:** Medicine & Health Care **PB:** Quebec City **SC:** Canada **ED:** Master in Management, McGill University, Canada (2014); MD, McGill University, Canada (1991) **C:** International President, Médecins Sans Frontières, Geneva, Switzerland (2013-Present); Board of Directors, Médecins Sans Frontières, Geneva, Switzerland (2010-Present); Paediatric Emergency Physician, CHU Sainte-Justine Hōspital for Children, Montreal, Canada (2000-Present); President, Board of Directors, Médecins Sans Frontières, Canada (2004-2009); Program Manager, Desk Operations, Médecins Sans Frontières (1999-2002); Joined, Médecins Sans Frontières (1996); Fellowship in Paediatric Emergency Medicine, New York University School of Medicine, New York City, NY (1994-1996); Residency in Paediatrics, Université de Montréal, Canada (1991-1995); Head of Mission, Médecins Sans Frontières, Central African Republic; Head of Mission & Pediatric Consultant, Médecins Sans Frontières, Republic of the Congo; Medical Consultant, Médecins Sans Frontières, Honduras; Field Doctor, Médecins Sans Frontières, Kenya; Head of Mission, Médecins Sans Frontières, Ethiopia; Medical Coordinator, Médecins Sans Frontières, Indonesia; Medical Coordinator, Medical Consultant & Field Doctor, Médecins Sans Frontières, Haiti; Medical Coordinator, Head of

Mission, Médecins Sans Frontières, Nigeria; Head of Mission, Médecins Sans Frontières, Palestine; Medical Coordinator, Médecins Sans Frontières, Uganda; Medical Coordinator, Médecins Sans Frontières, Sudan; Medical Coordinator, Médecins Sans Frontières, Bulgaria; Medical Coordinator, Médecins Sans Frontières, Lebanon; Head, Paediatric Department, Médecins Sans Frontières, Sri Lanka; Refugee Camp Physician, Médecins Sans Frontières, Mauritania **CR:** Invited Professor in Paediatric Emergency, Fudan University, Shanghai, China (2010); Associate Professor, Université de Montréal **MEM:** Fellow, Royal College of Physicians and Surgeons of Canada **ADD:** Médecins Sans Frontières 78 rue de Lausanne, Case Postale 116, Geneva, YT, Switzerland, 1211

LIVERIS, ANDREW N., T: Dow Chemical CEO **I:** Engineering **DOB:** 05/05/1954 **PB:** Darwin **SC:** Australia **ED:** Ph.D (hon.), University of Queensland; BS in Chemical Engineering, University of Queensland, 1976 **C:** Chairman, president, CEO, Dow Chemical Co., Midland, Michigan, 2006-; President, CEO, Dow Chemical Co., Midland, Michigan, 2004-06; President, COO, Dow Chemical Co., Midland, Michigan, 2003-04; Business group president, Dow Chemical Co., 2000-04; Vice president specialty chems., Dow Chemical Co., Midland, 1998-2000; President, Dow chemical pacific, Dow Chemical Co., Hong Kong, 1995-98; Vice president, Dow Chemical Co., 1994-95; General manager, Dow Chemical Co., 1993-94; Group business director, Dow Chemical Co., Midland, Michigan, 1992-93; General manager all operations, Dow Chemical Co., Thailand, 1989-92; Joined, Dow Chemical Co., 1976 **CR:** Member National Petroleum Council, US-India CEO Forum member executive committee Business Council board member, Peterson Institute for International Economic vice chairman, Business Roundtable chairman, US-China Business Council board directors, IBM Corp., 2010-, Citigroup Inc., 2005-, Dow Chemical Co., 2004- **CIV:** Board member, Lake Huron Area Council, Boy Scouts Am., Board of Trustees, Herbert H. and Grace A. Dow Foundation, Trustee, Tufts Univ., **AW:** Recipient Premier of Queensland's Expatriate Achievement award, 2007, Alumnus of Year, University Queensland, 2005 **MEM:** Fellow: Institute Chemical Engineers (UK); mem.: Am. Chemistry Council, Soap and Detergent Association, U.S. Climate Action Partnership

LIVINGSTON, DEBRA ANN, T: federal judge, educator **I:** Law and Legal Services **DOB:** 04/15/1959 **PB:** Waycross **SC:** Georgia **PT:** Daughter of Robert Livingston; **ED:** JD magna cum laude, Harvard University, 1984; BA magna cum laude, Princeton University, 1980 **C:** Judge, US Court Appeals (2nd. Cir.), 2007-; Vice dean, Columbia Law School, New York City, 2005-06; Paul J. Kellner professor law, Columbia Law School, New York City, 2004-07; Professor law, Columbia Law School, New York City, 2000-07; Associate professor law, Columbia Law School, New York City, 1994-2000; Assistant professor law, University Michigan Law School, 1992-94; Deputy chief of appeals, US Department Justice, 1990-91; Assistant US attorney (so. district) New York, US Department Justice, 1986-91; Associate, Paul, Weiss, Rifkind, Wharton & Garrison, 1991-92; Associate, Paul, Weiss, Rifkind, Wharton & Garrison, 1985-86; Law clerk to Hon. J. Edward Lumbard, US Court Appeals (2nd Cir.), 1984-85 **CR:** Commissioner New York City Civilian Complaint Review Board, 1994-2003 legal consultant UN High Commissioner for Refugees, Bangkok, 1982-83 **CW:** Co-author: Comprehensive Criminal Procedure, 2001 **BA:** 40 Foley Square, New York, NY, 10007

LOBIONDO, FRANK A., T: U.S. Representative from New Jersey **I:** Government Administration/ Government Relations/Government Services **DOB:** 05/12/1946 **PB:** Bridgeton **ED:** BA in Business Administration, St. Joseph's University, Pennsylvania, 1968 **C:** Member, US Congress from 2nd New Jersey district, 1995-; Member transportation and infrastructure committee, armed services committee, US Congress from 2nd New Jersey district,; Member, New Jersey General Assembly from District 1, 1988-94; Member, Cumberland County Board Freeholders, New Jersey, 1985-88; Operations manager, LoBiondo Brothers Motor Express, Inc., Rosenhayn, New Jersey, 1968-94 **CIV:** Hon. chairman annual fund raising drive, Cumberland County Hospice, 1992 Chairman, Cumberland County chapter Am. Heart Association, 1989-90 Founder, Cumberland County Environmental Health Task Force, 1987 Liaison, Cumberland County Health and Welfare Department, 1985-88 Member, Cumberland County Economic Devel. Board, 1985-88 President, Cumberland County Guidance Center, 1982-84 Board directors, Literacy Vols. Am., Cape May County chapter, 1991- Trustee, YMCA, 1990-94 Trustee, YMCA, 1981-84 Board directors, YMCA, Vineland, 1978-94 **AW:** Recipient South Jersey Breast Cancer Coalition award, 2005, Friend of National Pks. award, National Pks. Conservation Association, 2005, Guardian of Small Business award, National Federation Independent Business **MEM:** Mem.: Vineland, New Jersey Rotary **PA:** Republican

LOBO, KEVIN A., T: CEO **I:** Business Management/ Business Services **CN:** Stryker Corporation **ED:** Bachelors, McGill University; Masters Degree, University of Toronto **C:** Chairman, Stryker Corporation (2014-Present); President/Chief Executive Officer, Stryker Corporation (2012-2014); President of Orthopedics, Stryker Corporation (2011-2012); President of Neurotechnology & Spine, Stryker Corporation (2011); President of Medical Products Canada, Johnson & Johnson Services, Inc. (2005-2006)

LODGE, JOHN, T: Musician **I:** Media & Entertainment **PB:** Erdington **SC:** Birmingham, England **ED:** Birmingham College of Advanced Technology for Engineering **CW:** (Solo Albums) Blue Jays,1975, Natural Avenue, 1977, 10,000 Light Years Ago, 2015(Albums with the Moody Blues) Days of Future Passed, 1967, In Search of the Lost Chord, 1968, On the Threshold of a Dream, 1969, To our Children's Children's Children, 1969, A Question of Balance, 1970, Every Good Boy Deserves Favour, 1971, Seventh Sojourn, 1972, Octave, 1978, Long Distance Voyager, 1981, The Present, 1983, The Other Side of Life, 1986, Sur La Mer, 1988, Keys of the Kingdom,1991, Strange Times, 1999, December, 2003 **AW:** Rock and Roll Hall of Fame (2018)

LOEBSACK, DAVE, T: U.S. Representative from Iowa, Former Political Science Professor **I:** Government Administration/Government Relations/ Government Services **DOB:** 12/23/1952 **PB:** Mount Vernon **ED:** PhD in Political Sci., University California Davis, 1985; MA in Political Sci., Iowa State University, 1976; BS in Political Sci., Iowa State University, 1974 **C:** Member, US Congress from 2nd Iowa district, 2007-; Member armed services committee, education & labor committee, US Congress from 2nd Iowa district,; Professor political sci., Cornell College, 1982-2006 **CR:** Board member UN Am. former president Iowa Conference Political Scientists former chair Cornell College Politics Department **CIV:** Chair, Linn Phoenix Club, 2002-05 Local leader, Bill Bradley Presidential Campaign, 2000 Linn County coordinator, Howard Dean for President, 2000 **MEM:** Mem.: Humanities Iowa Speakers Bureau **PA:** Democrat

LOFGREN, ZOE, T: U.S. Representative from California **I:** Government Administration/Government Relations/Government Services **DOB:** 12/21/1947 **PB:** Palo Alto **SC:** CA/USA **PT:** Milton R. Lofgren; Mary Violet Lofgren **ED:** JD, Santa Clara Law, University of Santa Clara, Cum Laude (1975); BA in Political Science, Stanford University (1970) **C:** Member, U.S. Congress from 19th California District (2013—Present); Chair, U.S. House of Representatives, Committee on Standards of Official Conduct (Now House Committee on Ethics) (2009—2011); Member, U.S. Congress from 16th California District (1995—2013); Member, Santa Clara County Board of Supervisors (1981-1994); Partner, Webber & Lofgren (1978—1980); Administrative Assistant to Representative Don Edwards, U.S. House of Representatives, San Jose, CA (1970—1978) **CR:** Adjunct Professor, Immigration Law (1981—1994); Founding Executive Director, Community Housing Developers, Santa Clara County (1978—1981); Law Teacher, Santa Clara Law, University of Santa Clara (1976—1978) **CIV:** Board of Trustees, San Jose-Evergreen Community College District (1979—1981); Active People Acting in Community Together **AW:** Bancroft-Whitney Award for Excellence in Criminal Procedure (1973) **MEM:** President, Santa Clara Law School Alumni Association (1978); Vice President, Santa Clara Law School Alumni Association (1977); DC Bar Association (Now BADC); Santa Clara County Bar Association **BAR:** The State Bar of California; The District of Columbia Bar **PA:** Democrat **BA:** US House of Representatives, 1401 Longworth House Office Bldg, Washington, DC, 20515-0516

LOHIER, RAYMOND JOSEPH JR., T: Federal Judge **I:** Law and Legal Services **DOB:** 12/01/1965 **PB:** Montreal **SC:** Canada **PT:** Son of Raymond and Flocie Lohier **MS:** Married **SPN:** Donna Hae Kyun Lee **ED:** JD, New York University, 1991; AB cum laude, Harvard University, 1988 **C:** Judge, US Court Appeals (2nd Cir.), New York City, 2010-; Senior counsel, US Attorney; Chief, US Department Justice, New York City, 2007-10; Deputy chief Securities and Commodities Fraud Task Force, US Department Justice, New York City; Deputy chief then chief Narcotics Unit, US Department Justice, New York City; Assistant US attorney (southern district) New York, US Department Justice, New York City, 2000-10; Senior trial lawyer, US Department Justice, Washington, 1998-2000; Trial attorney Civil Rights division, US Department Justice, Washington, 1997-98; Associate, Cleary, Gottlieb Steen & Hamilton, New York City, 1993-97; Law clerk to Hon. Robert P. Patterson, Junior, US District Court (southern district) New York, New York City, 1992-93 **AW:** Recipient Vanderbilt Medal **BA:** US Court of Appeals Thurgood Marshall US Courthouse, 40 Foley Sq, New York, NY, 10007

LOKEN, JAMES BURTON, T: Federal Judge **I:** Law and Legal Services **DOB:** 05/21/1940 **PB:** Madison **SC:** Wisconsin **PT:** Son of Burton Dwight and Anita (Nelson) Loken; **ED:** LLB magna cum laude, Harvard University, 1965; BS, University Wisconsin, 1962 **C:** Chief judge, US Court Appeals (8th cir.), St. Paul, 2003-10; Judge, US Court Appeals (8th cir.), St. Paul, 1990-2003; Staff assistant, Office of President of U.S., Washington, 1970-72; General counsel, Pres.'s Committee on Consumer Interests, Office of President of U.S., Washington, 1970; Partner, Faegre & Benson, Minneapolis, 1973-90; Associate attorney, Faegre & Benson, Minneapolis, 1967-70; Law clerk to associate justice Byron White, US Supreme Court, Washington, 1966-67; Law clerk to Hon. J. Edward Lumbard, US Court Appeals (2d Cir.), New York City, 1965-66 **CW:** Editor: Harvard Law Rev., 1964-65 **MEM:** Mem.: Am. Law Institute, Phi Beta Kappa, Phi Kappa Phi **H:** Golf, running **BA:** Thomas F. Eagleton Courthouse, 111 South 10th Street, Saint Louis, MO, 63102

LONG, BILLY, T: U.S. Representative from Missouri **I:** Government Administration/Government Relations/Government Services **DOB:** 08/11/1955 **PB:** Springfield **ED:** Grad., Missouri Auction School, Kansas City **C:** Member, US House Transportation & Infrastructure Committee, Washington, 2011-; Member, Committee on Energy and Commerce; Member, US House Homeland Security Committee, Washington, 2011-; Member, US Congress from 7th Missouri District, Washington, 2011-; Owner, Billy Long Auctions, LLC, **CR:** Former talk radio show host KWTO AM 560, Springfield, Missouri **MEM:** Mem.: National Rifle Association, Greater Springfield Board Realtors, Missouri Professional Auctioneers Hall of Fame, Missouri Professional Auctioneers Association (former president), National Auctioneers Association (member national board directors), National Association Realtors, Springfield Area C. of C., Southeast Rotary Club **PA:** Republican

LONG, DAVID H., T: CEO **I:** Business Management/Business Services **CN:** Liberty Mutual **C:** Chairman, Liberty Mutual Group, Inc., Boston, MA (2013-Present); President, Chief Executive Officer, Liberty Mutual Group, Inc., Boston, MA (2011-Present); President, International, Liberty Mutual Group, Inc., Boston, MA (2009-Present); President, Liberty Mutual Group, Inc., Boston, MA (2010-2011); From Executive Vice President of National Market to President of Commercial Business Insurance Unit, Liberty Mutual Group, Inc., Boston, MA (1985-2008) **BA:** Liberty Mutual Group, 175 Berkeley St, Boston, MA, 02116-9500

LONG, MICHAEL J., T: Electronics Executive **I:** Business Management/Business Services **ED:** Student, Milwaukee School Engineering; BBA, University Wisconsin **C:** Chairman, president, CEO, Arrow Electronics, Inc., 2009-; President, CEO, Arrow Electronics, Inc., 2009; President, COO, Arrow Electronics, Inc., 2008-09; Senior vice president, president Global Components, Arrow Electronics, Inc., 2006-08; President North America and Asia/Pacific components, Arrow Electronics, Inc., 2006; President, COO Arrow North Am. Computer Products (now Arrow Enterprise Computing Solutions), Arrow Electronics, Inc., 1998-2005; President Gates/Arrow Distributing, Arrow Electronics, Inc., 1995-99; President Capstone Electronics, Arrow Electronics, Inc., 1994; Joined, Arrow Electronics, Inc., 1991; Various leadership positions, Schweber Electronics, 1983-90 **CR:** Board of directors, AmerisourceBergen **CIV:** Board of directors, Denver Zoo **AW:** Named one of Top 25 Executives, Computer Reseller News, 2004, 2002

LONG, WILLIAM B., T: Administrator of the Federal Emergency Management Agency **I:** Government Administration/Government Relations/ Government Services **DOB:** 04/06/1975 **PB:** Newton **SC:** North Carolina **ED:** B.S., M.P.A., Appalachian State University; Naval Postgraduate School's Executive Leadership Program **C:** Statewide Planner/ School Safety Coordinator, Georgia Emergency Management Agency, 1999-2001; Federal Emergency Management Agency, Hurricane Program Manager, 2001-06; Southeast Regional Director for Beck Disaster Recovery, 2007-08; Head, Alabama Emergency Management Agency, 2008-11; Executive V.P., Hagerty Consulting, 2011-17; Administrator, Federal Emergency

Manager Agency, 2017- **BA:** 500 C Street, SW, Washington, DC, 20472

LOPEZ, JENNIFER, T: Actress, Singer, Dancer **I:** Media & Entertainment **DOB:** 07/24/1969 **PB:** Bronx **SC:** NY/USA **PT:** David Lopez, Guadalupe Lopez **CR:** (Launched) J-Lo By Jennifer Lopez, 2001, Lingerie Line, 2004, (Signature Fragrances) Glow, 2002, Still, 2004, Miami Glow, 2005, Live Jennifer Lopez, 2005, Love At First Glow, 2006, Live Luxe, 2006, Glow After Dark, 2007, Deseo, 2008, Sunkissed Glow, 2009, My Glow, 2009; Owner, Madre's Restaurant, Pasadena, CA, 2002—2008 **CW:** Dancer, (TV Series) In Living Color, 1991—1993; Backup Dancer, (Music Video For Janet Jackson) That's The Way Love Goes, 1993; Actress, (TV Series) Second Chances, 1993—1994, South Central, 1994, Hotel Malibu, 1994, (Films) My Family, 1995, Money Train, 1995, Jack, 1996, Blood And Wine, 1996, Anaconda, 1997, Selena, 1997, U-Turn, 1997, (Voice Actress) Antz, 1998, Out Of Sight, 1998, The Cell, 2000, The Wedding Planner, 2001, Angel Eyes, 2001, Enough, 2002, Maid In Manhattan, 2002, Gigli, 2003, Jersey Girl, 2004, Shall We Dance?, 2004, Monster-In-Law, 2005, An Unfinished Life, 2005, Bordertown, 2007, The Back-Up Plan, 2010, What To Expect When You're Expecting, 2012, (Voice Actress) Ice Age: Continental Drift, 2012, Parker, 2013, Lila & Eve, 2015, (Voice Actress) Home, 2015, (Voice Actress) Ice Age: Collision Course, 2016, (Live Television) Bye Bye Birdie Live, 2018; Actress, Producer, El Cantante, 2007, The Boy Next Door, 2015; Producer, (Films) Feel The Noise, 2007; Executive Producer, (TV Series) South Beach Tow, 2011—2013, The Fosters, 2013—2015; Actress, Executive Producer, (TV Series) Shades Of Blue, 2015—Present; TV Appearances, How I Met Your Mother, 2010; Singer, (Albums) On The 6, 1999, J.Lo, 2001, J To Tha L-O!: The Remixes, 2002, This Is Me...Then, 2002, Rebirth, 2005, Como Ama Una Mujer, 2007, Brave, 2007, Love?, 2011, Dance Again: The Hits, 2012, A.K.A., J To Tha L-O! The Remixes, 2012, 2014, Por Primera Vez; Judge, (TV Series) American Idol, 2010—2012, 2014—2016, Shades Of Blue, 2016, World Of Dance, 2017-Present; Co-Creator, (Reality TV Series) Q'Viva!: The Chosen, 2012; Author, True Love, 2014 **AW:** The 50 Most Beautiful People in the World, People Magazine, 1997, ALMA Award For Outstanding Actress, Selena, 1998, Most Fashionable Female Artist, VH1/Vogue Fashion Awards, 1999, ALMA Award For Outstanding Actress, Out Of Sight, 1999, Female Entertainer of the Year, American Latino Media Arts Awards (ALMA), 2000, #1 Spot in FHM Magazine's 100 Sexiest Women List, 2000-2001, Most Influential Artist, 2002, Female Star of the Year, ShoWest Awards/National Association of Theatre Owners, 2002, Best-Selling Latin Female Artist, World Music Awards, 2002, Favorite Hip-Hop/R&B Female Artist, American Music Awards, 2003, Children's Humanitarian Award, Children's Hospital of Los Angeles, 2004, The 25 Most Influential Hispanics, TIME Magazine, 2005, Crystal Award, Women in Film, Los Angeles, CA, 2006, The 50 Most Beautiful, People en Español, 2006, The 100 Most Influential Hispanics, 2007, Artists For Amnesty Award, Berlin International Film Festival/Amnesty International, Bordertown, 2007, Favorite Latin Artist, 2007, 2011, The 100 Most Powerful Celebrities, Forbes.com, 2008, Latin Pop Album Of Year, Billboard Latin Music Awards, Como Ama Una Mujer, 2008, Barbara Walters Ten Most Fascinating People, 2010, Glamour Women of the Year, 2011, World's Most Beautiful Woman!, People Magazine, 2011, Ally for Equality Award, Human Rights Campaign, 2013, Star, Hollywood Walk of Fame, 2013, Icon Award, Billboard Music Awards, 2014, People's Choice Awards for Favorite TV Crime Drama Actress, Shades of Blue, 2017 **BA:** Simon

Fields Nuyorican Productions, 1100 Glendon Avenue, Suite 920, Los Angeles, CA, 90024

LOREE, JAMES M., T: CEO of Stanley Black & Decker **I:** Business Management/Business Services **ED:** BA in Economics, Union College, Schenectady, New York **C:** CEO, Stanley Black & Decker, 2016-; President, Stanley Black & Decker, Inc, 2013-16; Executive vice president, COO, Stanley Black & Decker, Inc. (formerly Stanley Works), 2009-2016; Executive vice president fin., CFO, Stanley Black & Decker, Inc. (formerly Stanley Works), New Britain, Connecticut, 1999-2009; Vice president fin. & strategic planning, auto fin. services unit GE Capital, General Electric Co., 1995-99; Head GE Capital Corp. Sourcing, General Electric Co., 1993-95; Member capital services staff, General Electric Co., 1990-93; General manager motors business, General Electric Co., 1988-90; Member corp. audit staff, corp. business devel., General Electric Co., 1983-88; Member fin. management staff, General Electric Co., Utica, New York, 1980-83

LOREN, SOPHIA, T: Actress **I:** Media & Entertainment **DOB:** 09/20/1934 **PB:** Rome **SC:** Italy **PT:** Daughter of Riccardo Scicolone and Romilda Villani **SPN:** Carlo Ponti, April 12, 1967 (deceased January 9, 2007); **CH:** Carlo Junior, Edoardo **ED:** Student, Scuole Magistrali Superiori **CW:** Actress: (films) E Arrivato l'Accordatore, 1951, Africa sotto i Mari, La Favorita, La Tratta Delle Bianche, 1952, Aida, Tempi Nostri, Ci Troviamo in Gellera, La Domenica Della Buona Genti, Il Paese dei Campanelli, Un Giorno in Pretura, Due Notti con Cleopatra, Pelegrini d'Amore, Attila, Carosello Napoletano, 1953, Miseria e Nobilta, Gold of Naples, Woman of the River, Too Bad She's Bad (Best Actress award Buenos Aires Festival), 1954, Lucky To Be A Woman, Sign of Venus, The Millers Wife, Scandal in Sorrento, 1955, Pride and Passion, Boy on a Dolphin, Legend of The Lost, 1957, Desire Under the Elms, Houseboat, The Key (Best Actress award Japan), 1958, That Kind of Woman, Black Orchid, 1959 (Best Actress Venice Festival, David Di Donatello award Italy, Victoire Popularity award France), Heller in Pink Tights (Best Actress Rapallo Festival Italy), It Started in Naples, A Breath of Scandal, The Millionaires, 1960, Two Women, (11 Best Actress awards including Oscar, Hollywood, Di Donatello award, Cannes Film Festival, New York Critics, Golden Globe, Brit. Film Academy, others from Ireland, Japan, Belgium, Spain, France, W. Ger., also other awards), El Cid, Madame, Bocaccio 70, 1961, The Condemned of Altona, Five Miles to Midnight, 1962, Yesterday, Today and Tomorrow, (Best Actress Di Donatello award, Golden Globe award), 1963, The Fall of the Roman Empire, Marriage Italian Style, 1964 (Best Actress Di Donatello award, Golden Globe award, Alexander Korda award Brit. Film Institute, others), Operation Crossbow, Lady L, Judith, 1965, Arabesque, A Countess From Hong Kong, 1966, Happily Ever After, Ghosts, Italian Style (Best Foreign Actress Diploma USSR), 1967, More Than A Miracle, (Ramo d'Oro award Italy, other awards), 1968, Sunflower (Best Actress Di Donatello award), 1969, The Priest's Wife, 1970, Lady Liberty, White Sister, 1971, Man of La Mancha, 1972, The Voyage (Di Donatello award), 1973, Brief Encounter, The Verdict, 1974, The Cassandra Crossing, A Special Day, 1977, Firepower, 1978, Brass Target, 1979, Blood Feud, 1981, Ready to Wear (Prêt-à-Porter), 1994, Grumpier Old Men, 1995, Messages, 1996, Soleil, 1997, Destinazione Verna, 1999, Between Strangers, 2002, Too Much Romance.It's Time for Stuffed Peppers, 2004, Nine, 2009, My House is Full of Mirrors, 2010, Cars 2, 2011, La Voce Umana, 2013, Sophia Loren: Live from the TCM Classic Film Festival, 2016; (TV films) Sophia Loren: Her

Own Story, 1980, Angela, 1982, Aurora, 1985, Mother Courage, 1986, The Fortunate Pilgrim (Best Actress of Year for TV mini-series), 1987, La Ciociara, 1989, Running Away, 1989, Francesca and Nunziata, 2001, Lives of the Saints, 2004, My House is Full of Mirrors, 2010. **AW:** Recipient numerous awards including Nastro d'Argento, Italy, 14 Bambi and Bravo Popularity awards, Federal Republic Germany, 3 Prix Uilenspigoel Fiamingo award, Belgium, Popularity awards Am. Legion, Texas Cinema Exhibitors, 4 Snosiki Popularity awards, Finland, 2 Best Actress awards Bengal Film Journalists Association, India, Box-Office Favourite Medal, Italy, Helene Curtis award, U.S.A., Simpatia Popularity award, Italy, Rudolph Valentino Screen Services award, Italy, Best Actress award Moscow Film Festival, Hon. Academy award, 1990; Star, Hollywood Walk of Fame, 1994; named Most Popular Actress in Italy. **BA:** Case Postale 430, 1211 Geneve 12, Geneve, Switzerland, 1200

LOUDERMILK, BARRY DEAN, T: U.S. Representative from Georgia, former state legislator **I:** Government Administration/Government Relations/Government Services **DOB:** 12/22/1963 **PB:** Riverdale **ED:** BA in Occupational Education and Information Systems Tech., Wayland Baptist University, Plainview, Texas **C:** Member, Committee on Financial Services, Committee on Science, Space and Technology, Committee on House Administration; Mem.US Congress from 11th Georgia District, Washington, 2014-; Co-owner, president, Innovative Network Systems, Inc., Cartersville, Georgia, 1995-; Member District 14, Georgia State Senate, 2013; Member District 52, Georgia State Senate, 2011-13; Member District 14, Georgia House of Reps., 2005-11 **CR:** Chairman Bartow County Rep. Party, 2000-04 **AW:** Named Pub. Servant of Year, Advocates for Children, 2006, National Legis. of Year, Civil Air Patrol, 2006, State of Georgia Legis. of Year, 2006; named one of 50 Most Influential Georgians, James Magazine, 2008 **PA:** Republican **BA:** 329 Cannon House Office Building, Washington, DC, 20515

LOUGANIS, GREG E(FTHIMIOS), T: Retired Professional Diver **I:** Athletics **DOB:** 01/29/1960 **PB:** San Diego **SC:** CA/USA **PT:** Son of Peter E. and Frances I. (Scott) Louganis **ED:** BA in Drama, University California, 1983; Student, University Miami, 1978-80 **C:** Retired, 1989; Former member, US National Diving Team, **CR:** Motivational speaker dog agility expert judge Red Bull Cliff Diving Tour mentor US Olympic Diving Team coach Hill-Nickleodeon Sport Theater, 1997 color commentary US Diving Nats., 1990, Circus of the Stars, 1986, US Diving Championships, 1985, US Olympic Festival, 1985 **CW:** Author: Breaking the Surface, 1995, For the Life of Your Dog, 1999; prodr.: (video diary) Breaking the Surface; actor: (plays) Working, 1978; (plays, Camelot), 1978; (plays) Carousel, 1978, Equus, 1980, Dance Kaleidoscope, 1987, Cinderella, 1989, The Boyfriend, 1990, Jeffrey, 1994, The Only Thing Worse You Could Have Told Me..., 1995, Just Say No, 1999, Nunsense A-Men, 1999; actor: (TV series) Battle of the Sexes, 1979, The Brain, 1985, NBC Superstars, 1985, Battle of the Network Stars, 1985, Circus of the Stars, 1986; host (TV series) Where Are They Now?, 1997; actor: (TV series) Hollywood Sqs., 1986; actor: (films) 16 Days of Glory, 1985, Dirty Laundry, 1985, Object of Desire, 1990, Mighty Ducks II, 1992, It's My Party, 1995, Touch Me, 1997; actor, trainer (competition show) Splash, 2013, Celebrity Splash, 2013, subject of (feature-length documentary) Back on Board, 2014,(Film) Sabre Dance, 2015, Entourage, 2015 **AW:** Named Five-time US Olympic Festival Titles, Four-time FINA World Cup Gold Medalist, Three-time NCAA champion, winner

5 World Diving Championships (platform and springboard), 1986, winner 47 U.S. National Diving Titles; named to International Swimming Hall of Fame, 1993, Olympic Hall of Fame, 1985; recipient US Olympic Committee's Robert J. Kane award, 1994, Jesse Owens award, 1987, James E. Sullivan award, Amateur Athletic Union, 1984, Gold medal (platform and springboard), Seoul Olympic Games, 1988, Gold medal, Pan Am. Games, 1987, 1983, 1979, Maxwell House/US Olympic Committee Spirit award, Olympic Games, 1988, 2 Gold medals, 1988, 1984, Silver medal on 10 m platform, 1976,California Sports Hall of Fame, 2013

LOUIS-DREYFUS, JULIA, T: Actress **I:** Media & Entertainment **DOB:** 01/13/1961 **PB:** NYC **PT:** Daughter of Gérard and Judith (LeFever) Louis-Dreyfus; **ED:** Doctor in Arts (hon.), Northwestern University, 2007; Attended, Northwestern University, 1980-82 **C:** Member, Second City and the Practical Theatre Co., Chicago, **CW:** Actress: (TV series) Saturday Night Live, 1982-85, Day by Day, 1986-89, The Art of Being Nick, 1986, Seinfeld, 1989-98 (Emmy award for Best Supporting Actress in a Comedy Series, 1996, Am. Comedy award for Best Supporting Actress, 1993, 1994, 1995, 1997, 1998, Golden Globe award for Best Supporting Actress, 1994, Screen Actors Guild award for Outstanding Performance by a Female Actor in a Comedy Series, 1997, 1998), The New Adventures of Old Christine, 2006-10 (Emmy award for Outstanding Lead Actress in a Comedy Series, 2006); actress, prodr.: (TV series) Watching Ellie, 2002-03; actress, producer and executive prodr.: (TV series) Veep, 2012- (Emmy award for Outstanding Lead Actress in a Comedy Series, 2012, 2013, 2014, 2015, 2016, Screen Actors Guild award for Outstanding Performance by a Female Actor in a Comedy Series, 2014), Web Therapy, 2012, Inside Amy Schumer, 2015; (TV appearances) Family Ties, 1988, Dinosaurs, 1991, The Single Guy, 1995, Hey Arnold, 1997, Curb Your Enthusiasm, 2000, 2001, 2009, (voice) The Simpsons, 2001, Arrested Development, 2002, 2004, 2005, 30 Rock, 2010, Web Therapy, 2010; (films) Soul Man, 1986, Troll, 1986, Hannah and Her Sisters, 1986, National Lampoon's Christmas Vacation, 1989, Jack the Bear, 1993, North, 1994, Father's Day, 1997, Deconstructing Harry, 1997, (voice) A Bug's Life, 1998, Gilligan's Island, 1999, Speak Truth to Power, 2000, (voice) Planes, 2013, Enough Said, 2013; (TV films) London Suite, 1996, (voice) Animal Farm, 1999, Gepetto, 2000; prodr.: (documentaries) Generosity of Eye, 2015 **AW:** Named one of 100 Most Influential People in the World, TIME magazine, 2016, The 100 Most Powerful Women in Entertainment, The Hollywood Reporter, 2014; named to TV Academy Hall of Fame, 2014; recipient Star, Hollywood Walk of Fame, 2010, Prime Time Emmy for Comedy Series, 2015-17, Prime Time Emmy Outstanding Lead Actress in a Comedy Series, 2012-17

LOVATO, DEMI, T: Actress, Singer **I:** Media & Entertainment **PB:** Albuquerque **SC:** NM/USA **PT:** Patrick Lovato; Diana (Hart) Lovato **C:** Actress, 2002-; Singer, 2008- **CIV:** Spokesperson, Join the Surge Campaign!, DoSomething.org, Spokesperson, PACER **CW:** Actress: (TV series) Barney & Friends, 2002-03, As the Bell Rings, 2007-08, Sonny With A Chance, 2009-11 (Choice TV Breakout Star: Female, Teen Choice Awards, 2009); (TV films) Camp Rock, 2008, Princess Protection Program, 2009, Camp Rock 2: The Final Jam, 2010, (TV appearances) Prison Break, 2006, Just Jordan, 2007, Grey's Anatomy, 2010 (Favorite TV Guest Star, People's Choice Awards, 2011), Extreme Makeover: Home Edition, 2010, Glee, 2013-14; singer: (albums) Don't Forget, 2008, Here We Go Again, 2009, Unbroken, 2011, Demi, 2013; judge The

X Factor, 2012-14 (Favorite Celebrity Judge, People's Choice Awards, 2013); author: Staying Strong: 365 Days a Year, 2013, (Music) Confident, 2015, Tell Me You Love Me, 2017,(Film) Jonas Brothers: The 3D Concert Experience, 2009, Demi Lovato: Stay Strong, 2012, Smurfs: The Lost Village, 2017, Demi Lovato: Simply Complicated, 2017, Charming, 2018(Television) Matador, 2014, RuPaul's Drag Race, 2015, From Dusk Till Dawn: The Series, 2015, We Day, 2015, Victoria's Secret Swim Special, 2016, Project Runway, 2017, The Voice of Germany, 2017 **AW:** Named Choice Summer Female Music Star, Teen Choice Awards, 2012, Favorite Female Artist, People's Choice Awards, 2014, Favorite Pop Artist, 2012, Time 100 Most Influential, 2017

LOVE, MIA, T: U.S. Representative from Utah **I:** Government Administration/Government Relations/Government Services **DOB:** 12/06/1975 **PB:** Brooklyn **SC:** NY/USA **PT:** Daughter of Jean Mexine and Mary Bourdeau; **ED:** BA, University Hartford, Connecticut, 1998 **C:** Member, US House Financial Services Committee, 2015-; Mem.-elect, US Congress from 4th Utah District, 2014-; Mayor, City of Saratoga Springs, 2010-13; Councilwoman, City of Saratoga Springs, Utah, 2003-10 **CR:** Former flight attendant Continental Airlines **CIV:** Member national advisory council on African-American outreach, Republican National Committee, 2014- **PA:** Republican

LOVELL, JAMES ARTHUR JR., T: Astronaut (Retired) **I:** Sciences **DOB:** 03/25/1928 **PB:** Cleveland **SC:** IL/USA **PT:** James A. Lovell; Blanch Lovell **SPN:** Marilyn Gerlach (6/6/1952) **CH:** Barbara Lynn; James Arthur; Susan Kay; Jeffrey C. **ED:** Graduate, Advanced Management Program, Harvard Business School (1971); Graduate, Aviation Safety School, University of Southern California (1961); BS, US Naval Academy (1952); Coursework, University of Wisconsin (1946-1948) **C:** Senior Vice President of Administration, Executive Vice President, Centel Corp., Chicago, IL (1980-1991); President, Fisk Telephone Systems (1977-1981); Chief Executive Officer, Bay-Houston Towing Co. (1975); With, Bay-Houston Towing Co. (1973); Retired (1973); Deputy Director, Science and Applications, Directorate Manned Spacecraft Center, NASA (1971-1973); Spacecraft Commander, Apollo 13 (1970); Backup Commander, Apollo 11 (1969); Command Module Pilot, Apollo 8 (1968); Commander, Gemini XII (1966); Pilot, Gemini VI (1965); Advanced through Grades to Captain, US Navy (1965); Backup Pilot, Gemini IV; Astronaut, Manned Spacecraft Center, NASA (1962); Flight Instructor, Safety Officer, Fighter Squadron 101, Naval Air Station, Oceana, VA; Test Pilot, Navy Air Test Center (now US Naval Test Pilot School), Patuxent River, MD (1958-1961); Enlisted, US Navy (1952); Served in, Korean War **CW:** TV Appearance, "The Colbert Report" (2007); Cameo, TV Series, "Situation Critical" (2007); Cameo, Film, "In the Shadow of the Moon" (2007); Speaker, TV Series, "Pritzker Military Library Presents" (2006); Cameo, Film, "The American Experience" (2005); Cameo, Film, "Conquering Space: The Moon and Beyond" (2005); Speaker, "Failure is Not an Option" (2003); Speaker, "AFI Life Achievement Award: A Tribute to Tom Hanks" (2002); Cameo, TV Series, "Modern Marvels" (2001); Cameo, TV Series, "Lateline" (199) Cameo, Film, "Apollo 13: For the Record" (1995); Technical Consultant, Cameo, Film, "Apollo 13" (1995); Co-author, "Lost Moon: The Perilous Voyage of Apollo 13," with Jeffrey Kluger (1994); Cameo, "Apollo 13: To the Edge and Back" (1994); Cameo, TV Series, "Spaceflight" (1985); Cameo, TV Series, "VIP Schaukel" (1977); Cameo, Film, "The Man Who Fell to Earth" (1976); TV Appearance, "The Tonight Show Starring Johnny Carson" (1970) **AW:** Silver Buffalo, Boy Scouts of America (1992); Distinguished Eagle Scout Award (1976); Grand Medallion

Award, Aero Club France (1972); Congressional Space Medal of Honor (1970); Robert H. Goddard Memorial Trophy (1969); H.H. Arnold Trophy (1969); General Thomas D. White US Air Force Space Trophy (1969); Robert J. Collier Trophy (1968); Named Man of the Year, Time Magazine (1968); Harmon International Trophy (1966-1967); Decorated Naval Aviator Badge, NASA (1965); Naval Astronaut Wings, NASA (1965); National Defense Service Medal, NASA (1965); Navy Commendation Medal, NASA (1965); Air Medal, NASA (1965); Distinguished Flying Cross with Gold Service Star, NASA (1965); Exceptional Service Medal, NASA (1965); Distinguished Service Medal, NASA (1965); Presidential Medal of Freedom; Hubbard Medal, National Geographic Society; FAI De Laval Medal; Gold Space Medals; Légion d'honneur **MEM:** Fellow, American Astronautical Society; Fellow, Society of Experimental Test Pilots; Past President, National Eagle Scout Association; Board of Governors, National Space Society; Board of Directors, Lindbergh Foundation; Association of Space Explorers; Golden Eagles; Toastmasters; Alpha Phi Omega **ACH:** First man to journey twice to the moon, during which an explosion from an oxygen tank damaged the service module and the crew converted the lunar module into a "lifeboat" that kept them alive in space until they used the ship's remaining power to land safely on Earth; Command module pilot of Apollo 8, the first manned voyage to the moon; Among the first humans to leave Earth's gravity; Among the first humans to see the far side of the moon; Made 10 lunar orbits; Commander of Gemini XII, the final Gemini mission, which proved the feasibility of astronauts working outside of the ship; Experimented with photography in space; Pilot of Gemini VII, the first time 14 days were spent in space; The crew of Gemini VII flew 20 experiments, the most of any Gemini mission, investigated the effects of extended periods in space on human body, and had the first rendezvous (with Gemini VI) of 2 manned maneuverable spacecrafts

LOWENTHAL, ALAN STUART, T: U.S. Representative from California **I:** Government Administration/Government Relations/Government Services **DOB:** 03/08/1941 **PB:** New York City **SC:** NY/USA **ED:** PhD, Ohio State University (1967); MA, Ohio State University (1965); BA, Hobart College (1962) **C:** Member, U.S. House Natural Resources Committee (2013-Present); Member, U.S. House Foreign Affairs Committee (2013-Present); Member, U.S. Congress from 47th California District, Washington, DC (2013-Present); Member, Committee on Transportation and Infrastructure, Republican Study Committee; Member, District 27, California State Senate (2004-2012); Member, District 54, California State Assembly (1998-2004); City Councilman, City of Long Beach, CA (1992-1998); Member, Human Relations Commission (1990-1992); Professor, Community Psychology, California State University, Long Beach, CA (1969-2008) **CIV:** Member, Advisory Board, St. Mary's Medical Center (1992-1998) **AW:** Named Legislator of the Year, California State Firefighters Association (2002); League of California Cities (2001) **PA:** Democrat **BA:** 515 Cannon House Office Bldg, Washington, DC, 20515

LOWEY, NITA MELNIKOFF, T: U.S. Representative from New York **I:** Government Administration/Government Relations/Government Services **DOB:** 07/05/1937 **PB:** New York City **PT:** Married Stephen Lowey, 1961; children: Dona, Jacqueline, Douglas **ED:** BA in Marketing, Mount Holyoke College, Massachusetts, 1959 **C:** Chair of the House Appropriations Committee, 2017-; Member, US Congress from 17th New York District, 2013-2017; Member, US Congress from 18th New York District, 1993-2013; Member, US Congress from 20th New York

District, 1989-92; Assistant secretary of state, State of New York, 1985-87; Assistant to secretary of state for economic devel. & neighborhood preservation, director division economic opportunity, State of New York, Albany, 1975-85; Community activist **CIV:** Board directors, Windward School, Board directors, Effective Parenting Information for Children, Board directors, Close-Up Foundation **AW:** Named Legislator of Year, MADD; named one of The Most Powerful Women in New York City, New York Post, 2007, The 10 Women's Health Heroes, Reader's Digest, 1999; recipient Responsible Choices award, Planned Parenthood Federation America, Congressional Leadership award, Coalition to Stop Gun Violence, 2001, Excellence in National Pub. Leadership award, National Assembly Health & Human Service Organizations, 1999, Herbert Tenzer award for Public Service, Five Towns Jewish Council, 1999 **MEM:** Mem.: Women's Network of YWCA **PA:** Democrat **BA:** Office of Nita Lowey, 2365 Rayburn HOB, Washington, DC, 20515

LOWRY, GLENN DAVID, T: Director of the Museum of Modern Art **I:** Museums & Institutions **DOB:** 09/28/1954 **PB:** NYC **PT:** Son of Warren and Laure (Lynn) L.; Married Susan Chambers, August 24, 1974; children: Nicholas, Alexis, William. **ED:** PhD (hon.), Penn. Academy Fine Arts, 2000; PhD, Harvard University, 1982; MA, Harvard University, 1978; BA, Williams College, 1976 **C:** Director, Museum Modern Art (MoMA), New York City, 1995-; Director, Art Gallery Ontario, Toronto, Canada, 1990-95; Curatorial coordinator, Arthur M. Sackler and the Freer Gallery Art, Smithsonian Institution, Washington, 1987-89; Curator Near Eastern art, Arthur M. Sackler and the Freer Gallery Art, Smithsonian Institution, Washington, 1984-90; Director, Joseph and Margaret Muscarelle Museum Art, Williamsburg, Virginia, 1982-84; Curator Oriental art, Museum Art, Rhode Island School Design, Providence, 1981-82; Research assistant, Archeological Survey of Mediterranean Town of Amalfi, Italy, 1980; Assistant curator, Fogg Art Museum, Harvard University, Cambridge, Massachusetts, 1978-80 **CR:** Member adv. council department art history and archaeology Columbia University, Smithsonian Council steering committee Aga Kahn Architect award. **CIV:** Trustee Metro Toronto Convention and Visitors Association **CW:** Co-author: Fatehpur-Sikri: A Source Book, 1985, From Concept to Context: Approaches to Asian and Islamic Calligraphy, 1986, An Annotated Checklist of the Vever Collection, 1988, A Jeweler's Eye: Art of the Book from the Vever Collection, 1988, Timur and the Princely Vision: Persian Art and Culture in the Fifteenth Century, 1989, Europe and the Arts of Islam: The Politics of Taste, 1991 **AW:** Recipient Institute Turkish Studies Travel award Smithsonian Institution, 1980, Special Exhibitions award, 1987, Scholarly Studies award, 1990., Officer of Order Arts & Letters award, 2004, Government France **MEM:** Member Association Am. Art Museum Directors, College Art Association, Am. Academy Arts & Scis **BA:** Museum of Modern Art, 11 W 53rd St, New York, NY, 10019

LUCAS, FRANK DEAN, T: U.S. Representative from Oklahoma **I:** Government Administration/ Government Relations/Government Services **DOB:** 01/06/1960 **PB:** Cheyenne **PT:** Married Lynda L. Bradshaw, 1988; 3 children. **ED:** BS in Agricultural Economics, Oklahoma State University, 1982 **C:** Vice Chairman, House Science Committee, 2015,; Member, Committee on Financial Services,; Committee on Science, Space, and Technology; Member, US Congress from 3rd Oklahoma District, Washington, 2003-; Chairman, US House Agrl Committee, Washington, 2011-15; Member, US Congress from 6th Oklahoma District, Washington, 1994-2003; Member, Oklahoma House of Reps., 1989-94 **AW:** Named a Property Rights Champion, League of Property Voters, 2002, Congl. Conservation Champion, 2001; recipient Champion of Small Business award, Small Business Survival Committee, Guardian of Small Business award, National Federation Ind. Business, Staff of Life award, Oklahoma Wheat Commission, Friend of the Farm Bureau award, Am. Farm Bureau Federation, Wheat Champion award, National Association Wheat Growers **MEM:** Mem.: Oklahoma Cattlemen's Association, Oklahoma Farmer's Union, Oklahoma Farm Bureau **PA:** Republican **BA:** 2405 Rayburn HOB, Washington, DC, 20515

LUCAS, GEORGE WALTON JR., T: Filmmaker **I:** Media & Entertainment **DOB:** 05/14/1944 **PB:** Modesto **SC:** CA/USA **PT:** Son of George Walton Lucas, Senior, and Dorothy Ellinore (Bomberger) Lucas **ED:** BFA, University of Southern California, 1966; Student, Modesto Junior College **C:** Founder, chairman, CEO, Lucasfilm Ltd., San Rafael, California, 1971-2012; Co-founder, American Zoetrope, 1969 **CR:** Chairman, Film Foundation, Joseph Campbell Foundation, Artists Rights Foundation, George Lucas Educational Foundation, Member TV Board Councilors University of Southern California **CIV:** Member, Advisory Board, Science Fiction Museum and Hall of Fame **CW:** Assistant to Francis Ford Coppola (films) The Rain People, 1969, Creator, Short Film, Director, Co-writer THX-1138:4EB, 1970, THX-1138, 1971, Director, Co-writer, American Graffiti, 1973, Director, Author, Screenplay, Star Wars, 1977; Executive Producer: (films) More American Graffiti, 1979, The Empire Strikes Back, 1980, Raiders of the Lost Ark, 1981, Indiana Jones and the Temple of Doom, 1984, Labyrinth, 1986, Howard the Duck, 1986, Willow, 1988, Tucker, 1988, Radioland Murders, 1994, (co-author screenplay) Return of the Jedi, 1983; Co-executive Producer (films) Mishima, 1985; Co-author (Co-executive Producer): (films) Indiana Jones and the Last Crusade, 1989; Director, Executive Producer (films) Star Wars: Episode I The Phantom Menace, 1999, Star Wars: Episode II Attack of the Clones, 2002, Star Wars: Episode III Revenge of the Sith, 2005 (Favorite Movie and Favorite Movie Drama, People's Choice Award, 2006), Writer, Executive Producer Indiana Jones and the Kingdom of the Crystal Skull, 2008, Red Tails, 2012, Strange Magic, 2015, (TV series) Star Wars: The Clone Wars, 2008-13; Executive Producer (TV series): The Young Indiana Jones Chronicles, 1992-93, Star Wars The Clone Wars, 2008, Double Victory: The Tuskegee Airmen at War, 2012: (documentaries) Manifest Destiny, 2011 **AW:** Named One of The Forbes 400: Richest Americans, 2009-12, The 100 Most Powerful Celebrities, Forbes.com, 2008; Named to The California Hall of Fame, 2009, The Science Fiction Hall of Fame, 2009; Recipient, Kennedy Center Honors, John F. Kennedy Center Performing Arts, Washington, 2015, National Medal of Arts, National Endowment for the Arts, 2012, Cinema Vanguard Award, African American Film Critics Association, 2011, Golden Lion for Lifetime Achievement, Venice Film Festival, 2009, Lifetime Achievement Award, American Film Institute, 2005, Irving G. Thalberg Memorial Award, Academy of Motion Picture Arts & Sciences, 1991

LUCAS, ROBERT EMERSON JR., T: Economist, Educator **I:** Education/Educational Services **DOB:** 09/15/1937 **PB:** Yakima **SC:** Washington **ED:** DSc (hon.), Technion-Israel Institute Tech., 1996; PhD (hon.), University Montréal, 1998; PhD (hon.), Athens University Economics & Business, 1994; PhD (hon.), University Paris-Dauphine, 1992; PhD in Economics, University Chicago, 1964; BA in History, University Chicago, 1959 **C:** John Dewey distinguished service professor economics, University Chicago, 1980-; Chairman department economics, University Chicago, 1986-88; Vice chairman department economics, University Chicago, 1975-83; Professor economics, University Chicago, 1975-80; Ford Foundation visiting research professor economics, University Chicago, 1974-75; Professor, Carnegie Mellon University, 1970-74; Associate professor, Carnegie Mellon University, 1967-70; Assistant professor economics, Carnegie Mellon University, Pittsburgh, 1963-67 **CR:** Visiting professor economics Northwestern University, 1981-82 **CW:** Author: Studies in Business-Cycle Theory, 1981, Models of Business Cycles, 1985, Recursive Methods in Economic Dynamics, 1989, Lectures on Economic Growth, 2001; co-editor: Rational Expectations and Econometric Practice, 1981; associate editor Journal Economic Theory, 1972-78, Journal Monetary Economics, 1977-, editor Journal Political Economy, 1988-; contributor articles to professional journals **AW:** Recipient Nobel prize in economics, 1995; fellow John Simon Guggenheim Memorial Foundation, 1981-82, Brookings Institution, 1961-62; grantee Woodrow Wilson Fellowship, 1959-60 **MEM:** Fellow: Am. Academy Arts & Scis. (council member 1991-95), Econometric Society (president 1997); mem.: National Academy of Sciences, Am. Economic Association (vice president 1987, member executive committee 1980-82), Am. Philosophical Society, European Academy Arts, Scis. & Humanities, Phi Beta Kappa **ACH:** Achievements include developing and applying the hypothesis of rational expectations, and thereby having transformed macroeconomic analysis and deepened out understanding of economic policy **BA:** University of Chicago, 1126 East 59th Street, Chicago, IL, 60637

LUCERO, CARLOS, T: Federal Judge **I:** Law and Legal Services **CN:** US Ct. Appeals (10th cir.) **DOB:** 11/23/1940 **PB:** Antonito **SC:** CO/USA **ED:** JD, George Washington University, 1964; BA, Adams State College **C:** Judge, US Court Appeals (10th cir.), 1995-; Senior partner, Lucero, Lester & Sigmund, Alamosa, Colorado,; Private practice, Alamosa, Colorado, 1966-95; Law clerk to Judge William E. Doyle, US District Court, Colorado, 1964-65 **CR:** Member President Carter's Presidential Panel on Western State Water Policy **CIV:** Board directors, Sante Fe Opera Association of New Mexico,; Board directors, Colorado Hist. Society, **AW:** Recipient Distinguished Alumnus award, George Washington University, Outstanding Young Man of Colorado award, Colorado Jaycees; fellow Paul Harris, Rotary Foundation **MEM:** Fellow: International Society Barristers, International Academy Trial Lawyers, Colorado Bar Foundation (president), Am. College Trial Lawyers, Am. Bar Foundation; mem.: American Bar Association (member action committee to reduce court cost and delay, member adv. board American Bar Association journal, member committee on the availability of legal services), Colorado Rural Legal Services (board directors), Colorado Hispanic Bar Association (Professional Service award), National Hispanic Bar Association, San Luis Valley Bar Association (president), Colorado Bar Association 1977-78, (member ethics committee), Order of the Coif **BA:** 1823 Stout St, Denver, CO, 80202

LUCIANO, JUAN RICARDO, T: Archer Daniels CEO **I:** Engineering **PB:** San Nicolas **ED:** MS in Industrial Engineering, Buenos Aires Institute of Tech., 1985; BS in Industrial Engineering, Buenos Aires Institute of Tech., 1983 **C:** President, CEO, Archer Daniels Midland Co., 2015-; President,

COO, Archer Daniels Midland Co., 2014; Executive vice president, COO, Archer Daniels Midland Co., Decatur, Illinois, 2011-14; Executive vice president, president performance division, The Dow Chemical Co., 2010-11; Senior vice president, hydrocarbons & energy, basic plastics, & joint ventures, The Dow Chemical Co., 2008-10; Business group president, hydrocarbons & energy, The Dow Chemical Co., 2007-08; Global business vice president, olefins & aromatics, The Dow Chemical Co., 2006-07; Business vice president, engineering polymers, The Dow Chemical Co., 2004-06; Global business director, polypropylene, The Dow Chemical Co., 2001-04; Global business director, LDPE/PRIMACOR/SARAN/Slurry PE, The Dow Chemical Co., 2000-01; Business director, chelants, specialty chemicals, The Dow Chemical Co., 1999-2000; Senior marketing manager, Americas polyglycols, specialty chemicals, The Dow Chemical Co., 1996-99; Sales, marketing manager, specialty chemicals, The Dow Chemical Co., 1994-96; Joined, The Dow Chemical Co., 1985 **CR:** Board directors Archer Daniels Midland Co., 2014-, Wilmar International Ltd., 2012- **CIV:** Governor, Boys & Girls Clubs America

LUCKEY, PALMER, T: Entrepreneur **I:** Business Management/Business Services **PB:** Long Beach **SC:** CA/USA **ED:** Coursework, California State University **C:** Facebook (2014-2017); Founder, Oculus, Facebook Technologies, LLC (2012-2014) **AW:** Named One of TIME's 100 Most Influential People, TIME Magazine (2016); Named Forbes Richest Entrepreneurs Under 40 (2016)

LUETKEMEYER, BLAINE, T: U.S. Representative from Missouri **I:** Government Administration/Government Relations/Government Services **DOB:** 05/07/1952 **PB:** Jefferson City **ED:** BA, Lincoln University, 1974 **C:** Member, US Congress from 3rd Missouri District, 2013-; Member, Financial Services Committee, Republican Study Committee; Member, US Congress from 9th Missouri District, 2009-13; Member District 115, Missouri House of Reps., 1999-2004; Insurance agent, owner, Luetkemeyer Insurance Agency, 1988-2009; Vice president, loan officer, Bank of St. Elizabeth, 1976-2009; Bank examiner, State of Missouri, 1974-76; Farmer, 1968-88 **CR:** Board governors Capital Region Medical Center, 2002-, 1990-93 **CIV:** Member board trustees, Village of St. Elizabeth, 1978-87 **MEM:** Mem.: American Family Insurance Agents' Association **PA:** Republican

LUJAN, BEN RAY SR., T: U.S. Representative from New Mexico **I:** Government Administration/Government Relations/Government Services **PB:** Nambe, 1935 **ED:** Attended, College Santa Fe **C:** Member, U.S. House of Representative from New Mexico's 3rd District, 2009-; Member, Committee on Energy and Commerce; Speaker of the house, New Mexico House of Reps., 2001-09; Majority leader, New Mexico House of Reps., 1999-2001; Democratic whip, New Mexico House of Reps., 1983-99; Member District 46, New Mexico House of Reps., 1975-2012; Member, Santa Fe County Commission, 1970-74; Iron worker, Zia Co., Los Alamos, New Mexico, **PA:** Democrat

LUPONE, PATTI, T: Actress, Singer **I:** Media & Entertainment **DOB:** 04/21/1949 **PB:** Northport **SC:** NY/USA **PT:** Orlando Joseph LuPone; Angela Louise (Patti) LuPone **MS:** Married **SPN:** Matthew Johnston (12/12/1988) **CH:** Joshua Luke **ED:** BFA, The Juilliard School (1972) **C:** Actress (1972-Present) **CIV:** Volunteer, Craft and Folk Art Museum (1999-2000) **CW:** Off-Broadway Productions Include "The Woods," "School for Scandal,"

"The Lower Depths," "Stage Directions"; Regional Productions Include "The Lady with the Torch" (2004), "The Little Foxes" (2005), "Anyone Can Whistle" (2005), "Rise and Fall of the City of Mahogany" (2007); Broadway Productions Include "The Three Sisters" (1973, 1975), "The Beggar's Opera" (1973), "Measure for Measure" (1973), "Scapin" (1973), "Next Time I'll Sing to You" (1974), "The Robber Bridegroom" (1975), "Edward II" (1975), "The Time of Your Life" (1975), "The Water Engine" (1978), "Working" (1978), "Evita" (1979), "Oliver!" (1984), "Accidental Death of an Anarchist" (1984), "Anything Goes" (1987), "Company" (1993), "Master Class" (1995), "The Old Neighborhood" (1997), "Noises Off" (2001), "Anything Goes" (2002), "Children & Art" (2005), "Sweeney Todd" (2005), "Gypsy" (2008), "An Evening with Patti LuPone & Mandy Patinskin" (2011), "The Anarchist" (2012), "Shows for Days" (2015); London Productions, "Les Miserables" (1985), "Sunset Boulevard" (1993); Actress, Films, "King of the Gypsies" (1978, 1979), "Fighting Back" (1982), "Witness" (1985), "Wise Guys" (1986), "Driving Miss Daisy" (1989), "Family Prayers" (1993), "State and Maine" (1999), "Just Looking" (1999), "Bad Faith" (1999), "The 24 Hour Woman" (1999), "Summer of Sam" (1999), "Bad Faith" (2000), "State and Main" (2000), "The Victim" (2001), "Heist" (2001), "City by the Sea" (2002), "Cold Blooded" (2003), "Company" (2011), "Union Square" (2011), "Parker" (2013); TV Films, "The Time of your Life" (1976), "LBJ: The Early Years" (1987), "The Water Engine" (1992), "Family Prayers" (1993), "The Song Spinner" (1995), "Her Last Chance" (1996), "Family Brood" (1998), "Bonanno: A Godfather's Story" (1999), "Sweeney Todd: The Demon Barber of Fleet Street in Concert" (2001), "Life at Five Feet" (2002), "Monday Night Mayhem" (2002), "Strip Search" (2004), "Open Books" (2010), "The Miraculous Year" (2011), "People in New Jersey" (2013); TV Series, "Life Goes On" (1989-1993), "Falcone" (2000); TV Appearances, "Law & Order" (1990), "Frasier" (1993), "Remember WENN" (1996), "Saturday Night Live" (1998), "Touched by an Angel" (2001), "Oz" (2003), "Will & Grace" (2005), "Ugly Betty" (2007), "30 Rock" (2009-2010), "Army Wives" (2012), "American Horror Story" (2013-2014), "Girls" (2014); Singer, Albums, "Patti LuPone Live," "Matters of the Heart," "The Lady With the Torch," "The Lady With the Torch... Still Burning"; Author, "Patti Lupone: A Memoir" (2010); Theatre, "War Paint" (2017), "Company" (2018); Film, "The Comedian" (2016); Television, "Law and Order: SVU" (2014), "Penny Dreadful" (2015), "Dinner with Family with Brett Gelman and Brett Gelman's Family" (2015), "Steven Universe" (2016), "Crazy Ex-Girlfriend" (2017), "BoJack Horseman" (2017) **AW:** Named One of the 50 Most Powerful Women in New York City, New York Post (2008); Named to Theatre Hall of Fame (2007); John Houseman Award (2006); Grammy Awards for Best Classical Album, Best Opera Recording, "Rise and Fall of the City of Mahogany" (2009); Tony Award for Best Actress in a Musical, "Evita" (1980); Drama Desk Award for Outstanding Actress in a Musical, (Evita) (1980); Drama Desk Award, Outstanding Actress in a Musical, "Anything Goes" (1987); Drama Desk Award for Outstanding Actress in a Musical, "Gypsy" (2008); Tony Award for Best Performance by a Leading Actress, "Gypsy" (2008) **ACH:** First American actress to win an Olivier award in England, 1985.

LYNCH, BARBARA, T: Musician **I:** Media & Entertainment **PB:** 1964 **C:** Writer 2009-; Owner, B&G Oysters, Ltd., Boston, 2003-; Chef, owner, No. 9 Park, Boston, 1998-; Executive chef, Galleria Italiana, Boston, 1995-98; Chef, Rocco's, Boston, 1993-95; Chef, Figs, Boston,; Chef, Olives,; Chef,

Michaela's,; Head chef, dinner cruise ship, Martha's Vineyard, **CW:** (subject): (documentaries) Amuse Bouche - A Chef's Tale; Boston 24/7,(Book) Stir: Mixing It Up in The Italian Tradition, 2009, Out of Line, A life playing with Fire, 2017 **AW:** Named Best Chef, Northeast, James Beard Foundation, 2003; named one of America's Best New Chefs, Food & Wine magazine, 1996,James Beard Award for Who's Who in Food & Beverage, 2013, James Beard for outstanding Wine Program, 2012, Amelia Earhart Award, 2009, Time Top 100 Most Influential, 2017

LYNCH, DAVID K., T: Film Producer, Director, Screenwriter **I:** Media & Entertainment **DOB:** 01/20/1946 **PB:** Missoula **SC:** MT/USA **PT:** Donald Lynch; Sunny Lynch **MS:** Married **SPN:** Emily Stofle (2009); Mary Sweeney (2006, Divorced 2006); Mary Fisk (6/21/1977, Divorced 1987); Peggy Reavey (1967, Divorced 1974) **CH:** Jennifer; Austin; Riley; Lula **ED:** Student, Pennsylvania Academy of Fine Arts, Philadelphia, PA **CW:** Co-screenwriter, Director, Films, "Eraserhead" (1978), "The Elephant Man" (1980), "Dune" (1984); Screenwriter, Director, Films, "Blue Velvet" (1986), "Wild at Heart" (1990), "Twin Peaks: Fire Walk With Me" (1992), "Lost Highway" (1997), "Driven to It" (1999), "The Straight Story" (1999), "Mulholland Drive" (2001), "Dumbland" (2002), "Rabbits" (2002), "Darkened Room" (2002), "Inland Empire" (2006), "Duran Duran Unstaged" (2014); Co-director, "Lumiere et Compagnie" (1995); Creator, TV Series, "American Chronicles" (1990), "On the Air" (1992), "Hotel Room" (1993), Performance Piece, "Industrial Symphony #1" (1989); Actor, Creator, TV Series, "Twin Peaks" (1990-1991); Actor, TV Series, "The Cleveland Show" (2010-2011); Guest Appearances, Voice Actor, "Family Guy" (2010); Singer, Album, "Crazy Clown Time" (2011) **AW:** Grantee, American Film Institute; Academy Award, "The Elephant Man"; Palme d'Or, Cannes International Film Festival **MEM:** Directors Guild of America

LYNCH, SANDRA LEA, T: Federal Judge **I:** Law and Legal Services **DOB:** 07/31/1946 **PB:** Oak Park **SC:** IL **PT:** Daughter of Bernard Francis and Eugenia Tyus Lynch; **ED:** JD Cum Laude, Boston University, 1971; AB in Philosophy, Wellesley College, 1968 **CT:** Bar: Supreme Court of the U.S. 1974, Massachusetts 1971 **C:** Chief Judge, U.S. Court Appeals (1st Cir.), Boston, 2008-15; Judge, U.S. Court Appeals (1st Cir.), Boston, 1995-; Partner, Foley, Hoag & Eliot, Boston, 1978-95; General Counsel, Massachusetts Department Education, Boston, 1974-78; Assistant Attorney General, Commonwealth of Massachusetts, Boston, 1974; Law Clerk to Hon. Raymond J. Pettine, US District Court, Providence, **CR:** Instructor Boston Univ. Law School, 1973-74 **CIV:** Past Co-chair Leading Industries Committee, Greater Boston C. of C., **CW:** Contributor Articles to Professional Journals **AW:** Recipient Distinguished Service Award, Planned Parenthood, 1991, Distinguished Alumnae Award, Wellesley College, 1997, Boston University Law School, 1993 **MEM:** Mem.: American Bar Association, Boston Bar Association (President 1992-93, Judicial Excellence Award 2001), Massachusetts Bar Association, National Association Women Judges, Women's Forum **BA:** US Ct Appeals, One Courthouse Way Ste 8710, Boston, MA, 02210-3010

LYNCH, STEPHEN, T: Editor of the New York Times **I:** Media & Entertainment **C:** Editor in Chief, New York Post, 2016-

LYNCH, STEPHEN F., T: U.S. Representative from Massachusetts **I:** Government Administration/ Government Relations/Government Services **DOB:** 03/31/1955 **PB:** Boston **SC:** MA/USA **PT:** Son of Frances and Anne (Havlin) Lynch; **ED:** MPA, Harvard University, 1999; JD, Boston College, 1991; BS, Wentworth Institute of Tech., 1988 **C:** Member, US Congress from 8th Massachusetts District, 2013–; Member, Financial Services Committee, Oversight and Government Reform Committee; Member, US Congress from 9th Massachusetts District, 2001-13; Member 1st Suffolk District, Massachusetts State Senate, Boston, 1996-2001; Member 4th Suffolk District, Massachusetts House of Reps., Boston, 1994-96; Private Law Practice,; Ironworker, General Dynamics Shipyard, 1973-91; Ironworker, General Motors,; Ironworker, US Steel Plant, **CR:** Co-founder Congressional Labor and Working Families Caucus **MEM:** Mem.: Boston Ironworkers Union (President Local 7) **PA:** Democrat

LYNN, LORETTA WEBB, T: Singer **I:** Media & Entertainment **DOB:** 04/14/1935 **PB:** Butcher Hollow **PT:** Daughter of Ted and Clara (Butcher) Webb; Married Oliver V. Lynn, Junior, January 10, 1948 (deceased 1996); children: Betty Sue Lynn Markworth (deceased), Jack Benny (deceased), Clara Lynn Lyell, Erne **ED:** Student pub. schools **CR:** Sec.-treas. Loretta Lynn Enterprises vice president United Talent, Inc. hon. chairman board Loretta Lynn Western Stores. **CIV:** Hon. rep. United Giver's Fund, 1971 **CW:** Country vocalist with MCA records, 1961– (numerous gold albums); albums: Loretta Lynn Sings, 1963, Before I'm Over You, 1964, Songs from My Heart, 1965, Hymns, 1965, Blue Kentucky Girl, 1965, (with Ernest Tubb) Mr. & Mrs. Used to Be, 1965, I Like Em' Country, 1966, You Aint Woman Enough, 1966, Don't Come Home a Drinkin', 1967, Ernest Tubb & Loretta Lynn Singin' Again, 1967, Singin' With Feelin', 1967, Fist City, 1968, Who Says God id Dead!, 1968, Your Squaw is on the Warpath, 1969, (with Ernest Tubb) If We Put Our Heads Together, 1969, Woman of the World / To Make a Man, 1969, Wings Upon Your Horns, 1970, Loretta Lynn Writes 'em & Sings 'em, 1970, Coal Miner's Daughter, 1970, I Wanna Be Free, 1971, (with Conway Twitty) We Only Make Believe, 1971, You're Lookin' At Country, 1971, (with Conway Twitty) Lead Me On, 1972, One's on the Way, 1972, Here I Am Again, 1972, Entertainer of the Year - Loretta, 1973, (with Conway Twitty) Louisiana Woman, Mississippi Man, 1973, Love is the Foundation, 1973, They Don't Make 'em Like My Daddy, 1974, (with Conway Twitty) Country Partners, 1974, Back to the Country, 1975, (with Conway Twitty) Feelin's, 1975, Home, 1975, When the Tingle Becomes a Chill, 1976, (with Conway Twitty) United Talent, 1976, Somebody, Somewhere, 1976, I Remember Patsy, 1977, (with Conway Twitty) Dynamic Duo, 1977, Out of My Head and Back in Bed, 1978, (with Conway Twitty) Honky Tonk Heroes, 1978, We've Come a Long Way Baby, 1979, (with Conway Twitty) Diamond Duet, 1979, Loretta, 1980, Lookin' Good, 1980, (with Conway Twitty) Two's a Party, 1981, I Lie, 1981, Making Love from Memory, 1982, Lyin', Cheatin', Woman Chasin', Honky Tonkin', Whiskey Drinkin' You, 1983, Just a Woman, 1985, Who Was That Stranger, 1988, (with Conway Twitty) Making Believe, 1989, The Country Music Hall of Fame, 1991, Greatest Hits Live, 1992, Country's Favorite Daughter (reissue), 1993, (with Dolly Parton and Tammy Wynette) Honky Tonk Angels, 1993, Making More Memories, 1994, All Time Gospel Favorites, 1997, Still Country, 2000, Van Lear Rose, 2004, Full Circle, 2016, Wouldn't It Be Great, 2018; author: Coal Miner's Daughter, 1976, Still Woman Enough, 2002, You're Cookin' It Country, 2004, Honky Tonk Girl: My Life in Lyrics, 2012; appearance (TV film)

Loretta Lynn: The Seasons of My Life, 1992, Big Dreams and Broken Hearts: The Dottie West Story, 1995; discs include (boxed set) Honky Tonk Girl: The Loretta Lynn Collection, 1994, (MCA special products) Hymns, 1995, Christmas Without Daddy, 1995, On Tour #1, 1996, On Tour #2, 1996, 20th Century Masters: The Millenium Collection, 1999, Still Woman Enough, 2000 **AW:** Named Country Music Association Female Vocalist of Year 1967, 1972, 1973, Entertainer of Year, 1972, Top Duet of 1972, 1973, 1974, 1975, Entertainer of Decade, Academy Country Music 1980; recipient Grammy award 1971, American Music award 1978, Johnny Cash Visionary award, Country Music Television Music award, 2005, Pioneer award, Academy County Music, 1995, Kennedy Center Honors. John F. Kennedy Center for the Performing Arts, 2003, Grammy Lifetime Achievement, 2010, Presidential Medal of Freedom, The White House, 2013; inducted into Country Music Hall of Fame, 1988, Songwriter's Hall of Fame, 2008; first country female vocalist to record certified Gold album, Grammy for Recording Academy Honor Award, 2007, Grammy for Presidents Merit Award, 2010,Grammy for Lifetime Achievement, 2010, Grammy for Best Country Album, 2017, Presidential Medal of Freedom, 2013, Academy of Country Music Awards, 2014, Crystal Milestone, Americana Music Association Awards, 2014, Nashville Music City Walk of Fame, 2015 **BA:** c/o Loretta Lynn Ranch, 44 Hurricane Mills Rd, Hurricane, TN, 37078

LYNN JR (COMMON), LONNIE, T: Rap Artist, Actor **I:** Media & Entertainment **PB:** Chicago **SC:** IL/USA **CW:** Singer: (albums) Can I Borrow a Dollar?, 1992, Resurrection, 1994, One Day It'll All Make Sense, 1997, Like Water for Chocolate, 2000, Electric Circus, 2002, Be, 2005, Finding Forever, 2007, Time Travelin', 2008, Universal Mind Control, 2008, The Dreamer, The Believer, 2011, Nobody's Smiling, 2014, (songs) Love of My Life (An Ode to Hip Hop), 2002 (Grammy award for Best R&B Song, 2003), Southside, 2007 (Grammy award for Best Duo Rap Performance, 2007); singer, composer (songs) Glory (with John Legend), 2014 (Golden Globe award for Best Original Song, 2015, Critics' Choice award for Best Song, 2015, Academy award for Best Original Song, 2015, Grammy award for Best Song Written for Visual Media, 2016); actor: (films) Smokin' Aces, 2006, Wanted, 2008, Terminator Salvation, 2009, Just Wright, 2010, (voice) Happy Feet Two, 2011, New Year's Eve, 2011, The Odd Life of Timothy Green, 2012, Pawn, 2013, Now You See Me, 2013, X/Y, 2014, Every Secret Thing, 2014, Selma, 2014 (National Association for the Advancement of Colored People Image award for Outstanding Supporting Actor in a Motion Picture, 2015), Run All Night, 2015, Being Charlie, 2015, Coco, 2016, Barbershop: The Next Cut, 2016, Suicide Squad, 2016, John Wick Chapter 2,2017, A Happening of Monumental Proportions, 2017, Love Beats Rhymes, 2017, Megan Leavey, 2017, Girls Trip, 2017, The Tale, 2018, All About Nina, 2018, Three Seconds, 2018, Smallfoot, 2018, Hunter Killer, 2018, The Hate U Give, 2018; (TV series) Hell on Wheels, 2011-14; (TV films) Ali 70 from Las Vegas, 2012, The Wiz Live!, 2015; actor, producer (films) LUV, 2012; prodr.: (documentaries) Magic Men, 2013 **AW:** Recipient Centric award, Black Entertainment TV (BET) Awards, 2012

LYNNE, JEFF, T: Rock Musician, Composer **I:** Media & Entertainment **PB:** Birmingham **SC:** AL/ USA **CW:** Musician with The Nightriders, England, The Move, also The Electric Light Orchestra; albums include No Answer, 1971, ELO, II, 1973, On the Third Day, 1973, Eldorado, 1974, Face the Music, 1975, Ole ELO, 1976, A New World Record,

1976, The Light Shines On, 1977, 3 Light Years, 1978, ELO, 1978, Out of the Blue, 1978, Discovery, 1979, The Light Shines On, Vol. 2, 1979, Greatest Hits, 1979, Xanadu, 1980, Box of Their Best, 1980, Secret Messages, 1984, Balance of Power, 1986, Afterglow, 1990, ELO Part II, 1991, (with Traveling Wilburys) Traveling Wilburys, 1988, Traveling Wilburys Vol. 3, 1990, Zoom, 2001, Alone in the Universe, 2015, (solo) Armchair Theatre, 1990, Beatles Anthology, 1995; producer various artists including Dave Edmunds, George Harrison, Daryl Hall **AW:** Recipient Grammy award (with Traveling Wilburys), 1990., Rock and Roll Hall of Fame Inductee, 2017, Songwriters Hall of Fame Nominee, 2014, 2016-17

MA, SHAN-LYN, T: CEO **I:** Business Management/ Business Services **CN:** Zola **ED:** MBA, General Management, Stanford University Graduate School, 2006; Bachelor of Commerce, University of New South Wales, **C:** CEO and Founder, Zola, 2013–; CPO, Chlo + Isabel,2012-13; GM and Founder, Gilt Groupe, 2010-12; Senior Director of Product Management, Gilt Groupe, 2008-10

MA, YO-YO, T: Cellist **I:** Media & Entertainment **DOB:** 10/07/1955 **PB:** Paris **PT:** Son of Hiao-Tsiun Ma and Marina Lu; **ED:** MusD (hon.), Harvard University, 1991; AB, Harvard University, 1976; Studied with Leonard Rose, Juilliard School Music, New York City, 1962; Studied with Janos Scholz **C:** Founder & artistic director, Silk Road Project Inc., Providence, 1998–; Recording artist, Sony Classical,; Appeared with Pablo Casals, Isaac Stern, Leonard Bernstein, Emanuel Ax, Jaime Laredo, performs throughout world with major orchestras,; Debut at age 9, Carnegie Hall, New York City, **CR:** Guest star Arthur, Mister Rogers' Neighborhood, Sesame Street member President Barack Obama's Committee on Arts and Humanities, 2009 messenger of peace UN, 2006- **CIV:** Head, Children's Orchestra Society, Manhasset, New York, **CW:** Musician: (albums) Portrait of Yo-Yo Ma, Anything Goes (with Stephanie Grapelli), Yo-Yo Ma at Tanglewood, Cello Suites Inspired By Bach, Portrait of Cello Works, Premieres, Great Cello Concertos, 1989, Japanese Melodies, 1990, Hush, 1992, Made in America, 1993, The New York Album, 1994, Appalachia Waltz, 1996, Bach: Unaccompanied Cello Suites, 1997, The Protecting Veil/Wake Up... And Die, 1998, Plays Piazzolla, 1998, Soul of the Tango, 1998, Simply Baroque, 1999, Lulie the Iceberg, 1999, Solo, 1999, Appalachian Journey, 2000, Phantasmagoria, 2000, Yo-Yo Ma Plays the Music of John Williams, 2002, Silk Road Journeys: When Strangers Meet, 2002, Obrigado Brazil, 2003, Belle Epoque, 2003, Plays Ennio Morricone, 2004, Silke Road Journeys: Beyond the Horizon, 2004, The Dvorak Album, 2004, Vivaldi's Cello, 2004, Silk Road Journeys: Beyond the Horizon, 2005, Memoirs of a Geisha, 2005, The Essential Yo-Yo-Ma, 2005, Appassionato, 2006, New Impossibilities, 2007, Songs of Joy & Peace, 2008, The Goat Rodeo Sessions (with Stuart Duncan, Edgar Meyer and Chris Thile), 2011 (Grammy awards for Best Folk Album, Best Engineered Album, 2013), Songs from the Arc of Life (with Kathryn Stott), 2015. **AW:** Named one of America's Best Leaders US News & World Report, 2007, Musician of the Year, Musical America, 2008; recipient Avery Fisher prize, 1978, Glen Gould prize, 1999, National Medal of the Arts, 2001, Dan David prize, 2006, Sonning Music prize, 2006, Presidential Medal of Freedom, The White House, 2010, Kennedy Center Honors, John F. Kennedy Center Performing Arts, Washington, 2011, Polar Music prize, 2012, Golden Baton award, Midwest Young Artists, 2014, Fred Rogers Legacy award, Fred Rogers Center Early Learning and Children's Media, Saint Vincent College, 2014,

Commander of the Order of Arts and Letters, 2016 **MEM:** Mem.: American Academy of Arts and Letters (hon.) **BA:** Sound Postings, 11 Water Street Suite 2b, Arlington, MA, 02476

MACARTHUR, TOM, T: U.S. Representative from New Jersey **I:** Government Administration/ Government Relations/Government Services **DOB:** 10/16/1960 **PB:** Hebron **SC:** Palestine **ED:** BA, Hofstra University, 1982 **C:** Member, US Congress from 3rd New Jersey Dist, Washington, 2015-; Member, Committee on Financial Services; Mayor, City of Randolph, 2013-14; Deputy mayor, City of Randolph, 2012-13; Councilman, Randolph Township, New Jersey, 2010-13; Chairman, CEO, York Risk Services Group, Inc., New Jersey, 1999-2010; Insurance adjuster, New York City, **CIV:** Co-founder, St. Peter's Sandy Relief Fund, **PA:** Republican

MACDIARMID, ALAN GRAHAM, I: Education/ Educational Services **DOB:** 04/14/1927 **PB:** Masterton **SC:** New Zealand **ED:** PhD in Chemistry, University of Cambridge (1955); PhD in Chemistry, University of Wisconsin (1953); MS, University of Wisconsin (1952); MSc, University of New Zealand (1950); BSc, University of New Zealand (1948) **C:** Blanchard Professor, Chemistry, University of Pennsylvania, Philadelphia, PA (1998-2007); Professor, Chemistry, University of Pennsylvania, Philadelphia, PA (1964-2007); Sloan Fellowship, University of Pennsylvania, Philadelphia, PA (1959-1963); From Instructor to Associate Professor, University of Pennsylvania, Philadelphia, PA (1955-1964); Assistant Lecturer in Chemistry, St. Andrews University (1955) **CR:** Visiting Professor, Kyoto University, Japan **AW:** Nobel Prize in Chemistry (2000); Francis J. Clamer Medal, Franklin Institute (1993); Royal Society of Chemical Centenary Medal; Chemical Pioneer Award (1984); Doolittle Award (1982); Marshall Award (1982); Frederic Stanley Kipping Award (1970) **MEM:** Royal Society of Chemistry; American Chemical Society **ACH:** Achievements include preparation and characterization of organosilicon compounds; preparation and charachterization of derivatives of sulfur nitrides and quasi one-dimensional semiconducting and metallic covalent polymers such as polyacetylene and its derivatives

MACFARLAND, SEAN, T: Retired Three Star General **I:** Military & Defense Services **PB:** New York City **SC:** NY/USA **C:** Deputy Commanding General, U.S. Army Training and Doctrine Command (2017-2018); Commander, Coalition Against ISIS (2015-2016) **MIL:** U.S. Army (1981-2018) **AW:** Named One of TIME's 100 Most Influential People, TIME Magazine (2016); Legion of Merit; Bronze Star Medal

MACFARLANE-BARROW, MAGNUS, T: Founder **I:** Nonprofit & Philanthropy **CN:** Mary's Meals **SC:** Scotland **C:** Founder, Mary's Meals (2002-Present) **AW:** Named One of TIME's 100 Most Influential, TIME Magazine (2015)

MACK, KHALIL, T: Professional Football Player **I:** Athletics **PB:** Fort Pierce **SC:** FL/USA **ED:** Student, University of Buffalo **C:** Defensive End, Oakland Raiders, 2014-Present **AW:** NFL Defensive Player of the Year, 2016, Butkus Award (Pro), 2016, Pro Bowl, 2015–2017, First-team All-Pro, 2015-2016, PFWA All-Rookie Team, 2014, MAC Defensive Player of the Year, 2013, First-team All-American, 2013, First-team All-MAC, 2011–2013;

MACKEY, JOHN P., T: Food Products Company Executive **I:** Business Management/Business Services **PT:** Son of Bill and Margaret Mackey; **ED:** Student, University of Texas, Austin; Student, Trinity College, San Antonio, Texas **C:** CEO, Whole Foods, 2017-.; Co-CEO, Whole Foods Market, Inc., Austin, 2010-2016; CEO, Whole Foods Market, Inc., Austin, 1980-2010; President, Whole Foods Market, Inc., Austin, 2001-04; Co-founder, chairman, Whole Foods Market, Inc., Austin, 1978-2009; Owner, Safer Way Natural Foods, Austin, 1978-80 **AW:** Named Overall National Entrepreneur of Year, Ernst & Young, 2003 **ACH:** Achievements include hiking entire Applachian Trail (2168 miles), 2002 **H:** Yoga, meditation, scuba diving

MACKINNON, RODERICK, T: Neuroscientist, Educator **I:** Education/Educational Services **DOB:** 02/19/1956 **PB:** Burlington **SC:** MA/USA **ED:** PhD (hon.), Tufts University, Medford, Massachusetts, 2002; MD, Tufts University, Medford, Massachusetts, 1982; BA, Brandeis University, Waltham, Massachusetts, 1978 **C:** John D. Rockefeller Junior professor, Rockefeller University, New York City, 1996-; Assistant professor to professor department neurobiology, Harvard Medical School, 1989-96; Postdoc. fellow, Brandeis University, 1986-89; Postdoc. fellow, Beth Israel Hospital, Harvard University, Boston, 1985-86 **CR:** Investigator Howard Hughes Medical Institute, Chevy Chase, Maryland, 1997- **AW:** Recipient Louisa Gross Horwitz prize, Columbia University, 2003, Nobel prize for chemistry, 2003, Gairdner Foundation International award, 2001, Lewis S. Rosentiel award for distinguished work in basic medical sci., 2000, Albert Lasker award for basic medical research, 1999, Newcomb Cleveland prize, American Association for the Advancement of Science, 1998, Young Investigator award, Biophysical Society, 1995, Bijvoet Medal, 2004 **MEM:** Mem.: National Academy of Sciences, Alpha Omega Medical Honor Society **H:** Kayaking **BA:** Rockefeller U Lab Molecular Neurobiology & Biophysics, 1230 York Ave, New York, NY, 10065

MACLAINE, SHIRLEY, T: Actress **I:** Media & Entertainment **DOB:** 05/17/1905 **PB:** Richmond, **SC:** Richmond, **PT:** Daughter of Ira O. and Kathlyn (MacLean) Beatty; **SPN:** Married Steve Parker, September 17, 1954 (div. 1982); **CH:** 1 child, Stephanie Sachiko. **CW:** Actress: (Broadway) Me and Juliet, 1953, Pajama Game, 1954, (films) The Trouble With Harry, 1954, Artists and Models, 1954, Around the World in 80 Days, 1955-56, Hot Spell, 1957, The Matchmaker, 1957, The Sheepman, 1957, Some Came Running, 1958, Ask Any Girl, 1959, Career, 1959, Can-Can, 1959, The Apartment, 1959, Children's Hour, 1960, The Apartment, 1960, Two for the Seesaw, 1962, Irma La Douce, 1963, What A Way to Go, The Yellow Rolls Royce, 1964, John Goldfarb Please Come Home, 1965, Gambit and Woman Times Seven, 1967, The Bliss of Mrs. Blossom, Sweet Charity, 1969, Two Mules for Sister Sara, 1969, Desperate Characters, 1971, The Possession of Joel Delaney, 1972, The Other Half of the Sky: A China Memoir, 1975, The Turning Point, 1977, Being There, 1979, A Change of Seasons, 1980, Loving Couples, 1980, Terms of Endearment, 1983 (Academy award for Best Actress, 1984, Golden Globe award for Best Actress, 1984), Cannonball Run II, 1984, Madame Sousatzka, 1988 (Golden Globe award for Best Actress, 1989), Steel Magnolias, 1989, Waiting For the Light, 1990, Postcards From the Edge, 1990, Defending Your Life, 1991, Used People, 1992, Wrestling Ernest Hemingway, 1993, Guarding Tess, 1994, Evening Star, 1995, Mrs. Winterbourne, 1996, Carolina, 2003, Bewitched, 2005, In Her Shoes, 2005, Rumor Has It..., 2005, Closing the Ring, 2007, Valentine's Day, 2010, Bernie, 2011, The Secret Life of Walter Mitty, 2013, Elsa & Fred, 2014, Wild Oats, 2016, The Last Word, 2016, The Little Mermaid, 2017, Nicole, 2019 (TV appearances) Shirley's World, 1971-72, Shirley

MacLaine: If They Could See Me Now, 1974-75, Gypsy in My Soul, 1975-76 (Emmy award for Outstanding Special: Comedy-Variety or Music, 1976), Where Do We Go From Here?, 1976-77, Shirley MacLaine at the Lido, 1979, Shirley MacLaine... Every Little Movement, 1980, Downton Abbey, 2012-13, Glee, 2014, A Heavenly Christmas, 2016 (TV films) Out On A Limb, 1987, The West Side Waltz, 1995, Joan of Arc, 1999, These Old Broads, 2001, Hell on Heels: The Battle of Mary Kay, 2002, Anne of Green Gables: A New Beginning, 2008, Coco Chanel, 2008, (TV mini-series) Salem Witch Trials, 2002; (directorial debut) Bruno, 2000; co-dir.: documentary: China The Other Half of the Sky; star US tour stage musical Out There Tonight, 1990; author: Don't Fall Off the Mountain, 1970, The New Celebrity Cookbook, 1973, You Can Get There From Here, 1975, Out on a Limb, 1983, Dancing in the Light, 1985, It's All in the Playing, 1987, Going Within: A Guide for Inner Transformation, 1989, Dance While You Can, 1991, My Lucky Stars: A Hollywood Memoir, 1995, The Camino: A Journey of the Spirit, 2000, Out On A Leash: Exploring The Nature of Reality and Love, 2003, Sage-ing While Age-ing, 2007, I'm All Over That: and Other Confessions, 2011, What if...a lifetime of questions, speculations, reasonable guesses, and a few things I know for sure, 2013, Above the Line: My Wild Oats, 2016; editor: McGovern: The Man and His Beliefs, 1972. **AW:** Recipient Kennedy Center Honors, John F. Kennedy Center Performing Arts, Washington, 2013, Lifetime Achievement award, American Film Institute, 2012

MACY, WILLIAM H., T: Actor **I:** Medicine & Health Care **DOB:** 03/13/1950 **PB:** Miami **SC:** FL/USA **PT:** William Hall Macy; Lois (Overstreet) Macy **ED:** Attended, Bethany College **CR:** Founding member Atlantic Theatre Co., New York City, St. Nicholas Theater, Chicago **CIV:** Spokesperson, United Cerebral Palsy **CW:** Actor: (TV miniseries) The Awakening Land, 1978; (TV series) ER, 1994-98, Above Suspicion, 1995, Shameless, 2011- (Screen Actors Guild Award for Outstanding Performance by a Male Actor in a Comedy Series, 2015); (TV films) The Cradle Will Fall, 1983, The Boy Who Loved Trolls, 1984, The Dining Room, 1984, The Murder of Mary Phagan, 1988, In the Line of Duty: Siege at Marion, 1992, A Private Matter, 1992, The Water Engine, 1992, The Heart of Justice, 1993, Texan, 1994, The Writing on the Wall, 1994, In the Shadow of Evil, 1995, Andersonville, 1996, The Night of the Headless Horseman, 1999, It's a Very Merry Muppet Christmas Movie, 2002, Reversible Errors, 2004; (actor, writer): The Con, 1998; A Slight Case of Murder, 1999; Door to Door, 2002 (Screen Actors Guild award for Outstanding Performance by a Male Actor in a TV Movie or Miniseries, 2003, Emmy award for Best Actor in a TV Movie, 2003, Emmy award for Best Writing for a TV Movie, 2003); The Wool Cap, 2004; (actor, director) Lip Service, 1988; actor, executive producer, writer (TV films) Family Man, 2008; actor: (TV appearances) Kate & Allie, 1984, Spenser: For Hire, 1985-88, The Equalizer, 1985, L.A. Law, 1986, Law & Order, 1990, Civil Wars, 1991, Bakersfield P.D., 1993, Frasier, 1993, Superman, 1996, King of the Hill, 1997, The Lionhearts, 1998, Hercules, 1998, Sports Night, 1998, Batman Beyond, 1999, Out of Order, 2003, The Unit, 2007, ER, 2009, Shameless, 2011-; (films) Foolin' Around, 1980, Somewhere in Time, 1980, Without a Trace, 1983, The Last Dragon, 1985, Radio Days, 1987, House of Games, 1987, Things Change, 1988, Homicide, 1991, Shadows and Fog, 1992, Benny & Joon, 1993, Searching for Bobby Fischer, 1993, Twenty Bucks, 1993, Being Human, 1993, The Client, 1994, Oleanna, 1994, Murder in the First, 1995, Roommates, 1995, Tall Tale, 1995, Evolver, 1995,

Mr. Holland's Opus, 1995, Down Periscope, 1996, Fargo, 1996, Hit Me, 1996, Ghosts of Mississippi, 1996, Colin Fitz, 1996, Air Force One, 1997, Boogie Nights, 1997, Wag the Dog, 1997, Jerry and Tom, 1998, Pleasantville, 1998, Psycho, 1998, (voice) The Secret of National Institute of Mental Health 2: Timmy to the Rescue, 1998, A Civil Action, 1998, Happy, Texas, 1999, Mystery Men, 1999, Magnolia, 1999, Panic, 2000, State and Main, 2000, Jurassic Park III, 2001, Focus, 2001, Welcome to Collinwood, 2002, The Cooler, 2003, Seabiscuit, 2003, Cellular, 2004, Sahara, 2005, Edmond, 2005, Thank You for Smoking, 2006, (voice) Doogal, 2006, Bobby, 2006, Inland Empire, 2006, (voice) Everyone's Hero, 2006, He Was a Quiet Man, 2007, Wild Hogs, 2007, Bart Got a Room, 2008, The Deal, 2008, (voice) The Tale of Despereaux, 2008, Shorts, 2009, Marmaduke, 2010, Dirty Girl, 2010, The Lincoln Lawyer, 2011, The Surrogate, 2012, The Sessions, 2012, A Single Shot, 2013, Trust Me, 2013, Two-Bit Waltz, 2014, Cake, 2014, Walter, 2015, Blood Father, 2015, Room, 2015, Stealing Cars, 2015, Dial a Prayer, 2015, Blood Father, 2016, The Layover, 2017, Krystal, 2017; (plays) American Buffalo, 1975, Speed-the-Plow, 2009; (writer) (TV series) thirtysomething, 1987; writer: TV films Every Woman's Dream, 1996, writer: TV films Just a Walk in the Park, 2002; executive prodr.: (films) Transamerica, 2005; actor, director, executive producer, writer (films) Rudderless, 2014 **AW:** Recipient Star, Hollywood Walk of Fame, 2012

MADDEN, JOHN, T: Retired Sportscaster, Retired Professional Football Coach **I:** Media & Entertainment **DOB:** 04/10/1936 **PB:** Austin **PT:** Son of Earl and Mary O'Flaherty M.; Married Virginia Madden; children: Mike, Joe. **ED:** MA, California Poly. University, 1961; BS, California Poly. University, 1959 **C:** Special adv. to commissioner, NFL, 2009-; Sports commentator, football analyst, NBC Sunday Night Football, 2006-09; Sports commentator, football analyst, Monday Night Football (ABC), 2002-06; Sports commentator, football analyst, Fox Sports, 1994-2002; Sports commentator, football analyst, CBS Sports, 1979-93; Head football coach, Oakland Raiders, Am. Football League (now Am. Football Conference, National Football League), 1969-79; Linebackers coach, Oakland Raiders, Am. Football League (now Am. Football Conference, National Football League), 1967-69; Defensive coordinator, California State University, San Diego, 1964-66; Head football coach, Hancock Junior College, 1962-64; Assistant coach, Hancock Junior College, Santa Maria, California, 1960-62; Professional football player, Philadelphia Eagles, 1959 **CR:** Head coach Am. Football Conference Pro Bowl Team, 1971-75 **CW:** Author: Hey, Wait a Minute, I Wrote a Book!, 1984; One Knee Equals Two Feet (and Everything Else You Wanted To Know About Football), 1987, One Size Doesn't Fit All, 1993; co-author (with Dave Anderson) All Madden: Hey, I'm Talking Pro Football, 1996, (with Peter Kaminsky) John Madden's Ultimate Tailgating, 1998, (with Bill Gutman) John Madden's Heroes of Football, 2006; developer (software) John Madden Football, 1988, John Madden Football II, 1993. **AW:** Recipient Emmy awards for sports broadcasting, 1982, 83, 85, 86, 87, 88, Pete Rozelle Radio-TV award, 2002; named NFL Coach of Year Am. Football League, Pro Football Weekly 1969, Sports Personality of Year Am. Sportscasters Association, 1985, 1992; named one of The Most Influential People in the World of Sports, BusinessWeek, 2007, '08, Top 50 Sportscasters Am. Sportscasters Association, 2009; named to The Pro Football Hall of Fame, 2006,NSSA Hall of Fame Inductee, 1984 **ACH:** Achievements include coaching the Oakland Raiders to seven American Football Conference Western Division

titles, 1969, 1970, 1972-76; head coach of Super Bowl XI championship winning Oakland Raiders, 1977 **BA:** Madden Charities Inc, 5955 Coronado Lane, Pleasanton, CA, 94588

MADDON, JOE, T: Professional Baseball Manager **I:** Athletics **DOB:** 09/19/1954 **PB:** Hazleton **ED:** LittD (hon.), Lafayette College, 2010; BS in Economics, Lafayette College, Easton, Pennsylvania, 1976 **C:** Manager, Chicago Cubs, 2015-; Manager, Tampa Bay Devil Rays, 2005-14; Bench coach, California Angels, 2000-05; Interim manager, California Angels, 1999; Interim manager, California Angels, 1996; Bench coach, California Angels, 1996; First base coach, California Angels, 1995; Bullpen coach, California Angels, 1994; Director player develop., California Angels, 1994; Roving hitting instructor, California Angels, 1987-93; Coordinator, California Angels Arizona Instructional League, 1984-93; Manager, Midland Minor League Baseball, 1985-86; Manager, Peoria Minor League Baseball,; Manager, Salem Minor League Baseball,; Manager, Idaho Falls Minor League Baseball, 1981 **AW:** Named American League Manager of Year, Baseball Writers' Association America, 2011, 2008, The Sporting News, 2008,Manager of the Year, 2015, World Series Champion, 2002, 2016

MADDOW, RACHEL ANNE, T: Television and Radio Personality, Political Commentator **I:** Media & Entertainment **DOB:** 04/01/1973 **PB:** Castro Valley **PT:** Daughter of Bob and Elaine Maddow **ED:** LLD (hon.), Smith College, Northampton, Massachusetts, 2010; DPhil in Political Sci., Lincoln College, Oxford University, England, 2001; BA in Pub. Policy, Stanford University, California, 1994 **C:** Host, The Rachel Maddow Show,, MSNBC, 2008-; Political analyst, MSNBC, 2008-; Host, The Rachel Maddow Show, Air America Radio, New York City, 2005-10; Co-host, (with Chuck D. & Liz Winstead) Unfiltered, Air America Radio, New York City; Host, Big Breakfast, WRSI, Northhampton, Massachusetts, 2002-04; Co-host, Dave in the Morning Show, Station WRNX-100.9 FM; Host, Station WRNX-100.9 FM, Holyoke, Massachusetts **CR:** Regular contributor, former guest host Countdown with Keith Olbermann regular panelist Race for the White House with David Gregory, 2008-09, Tucker, MSNBC, 2005-08 **CW:** Author: Drift: The Unmooring of American Military Power, 2012, Monthly Opinion Column, Washington Post, 2013 **AW:** Named Outstanding Host, Gracie Allen award, 2012, Lesbian/Bi Woman of Year, AfterEllen.com's Visibility Awards, 2008; named one of The 100 Most Powerful Women, Forbes magazine, 2010, The 50 Highest-Earning Political Figures, Newsweek, 2010, The 100 Agents of Change, Rolling Stone magazine, 2009, 40 Under 40, The Advocate magazine, 2009, Crain's New York Business, 2009, Top 100 Gay Men & Women Who Moved Culture, Out magazine, 2008; recipient John Steinbeck award, Martha Heasley Cox Center for Steinbeck Studies, San Jose State University, 2012, Walter Cronkite Faith & Freedom award, Interfaith Alliance, 2010, Maggie award, Planned Parenthood Federation America, 2010, GLAAD Media award, Gay & Lesbian Alliance Against Defamation, 2010, Proclamation of Honor, California State Senate, 2009, Gracie award, Alliance Women in Media, 2009; fellow AIDS Legal Referral Panel, San Francisco; grantee Ludlam Health Policy Fellowship, John Gardner Pub. Service Fellowship, 1994; Rhodes Scholar, 1995, Emmy for Outstanding Live Interview, 2017, Emmy for Outstanding News Discussion and Analysis, 2011, 2017

MADDUX, GREG, T: Former Professional Baseball Player **I:** Athletics **DOB:** 04/14/1966 **PB:** San Angelo, Texas **ED:** Grad., High School, Las Vegas

C: Special assistant to the general manager, Texas Rangers, 2012-; Retired, Major League Baseball, 2008; Pitcher, San Diego Padres, 2007-08; Pitcher, LA Dodgers, 2008; Pitcher, LA Dodgers, 2006; Pitcher, Atlanta Braves, 1993-2003; Assistant to the general manager, Chicago Cubs, 2010-11; Pitcher, Chicago Cubs, 2004-06; Pitcher, Chicago Cubs, 1986-92 **CIV:** Co-founder, Maddux Foundation, 1993- **AW:** Named National League Outstanding Pitcher, Major League Baseball Players Association, 1998, 1995, 1994, National League Pitcher of Year, The Sporting News, 1992-95; named to All-Time Rawlings Gold Glove Team, 2007, National League All-Star Team, Major League Baseball, 2000, 1994-98, 1992, 1988; recipient William J. Slocum award, Baseball Writers' Association America, New York Chapter, 2009, Cy Young award, Baseball Writers' Association America, 1992-95, Gold Glove award, 2004-08, 1990-2002, Baseball Hall of Fame, 2014, World Series Champion, 1995, MLB Wins Leader, 1992,1994, 1995, MLB ERA Leader, 1993-1995, 1998 **ACH:** Achievements include leading the National League in: starts, 1990-93, 2000, 03, 05; innings, 1991-95; wins, 1992, 94, 95; ERA, 1993-95, 98; complete games, 1993-95; shutouts, 1994, 95, 98, 2000, 01; being the first pitcher in Major League Baseball history to win the Cy Young award for four consecutive years, 1992-95; being a member of the World Series Championship winning Atlanta Braves, 1995; becoming 13th pitcher in MLB history to throw 3,000 strikeouts, 2005; holding the all-time record for Gold Glove awards with 18

MAGILL, M. ELIZABETH, T: Dean, Law Educator **I:** Education/Educational Services **PB:** Fargo **SC:** ND/USA **PT:** Daughter of Frank John and Mary Louise (Timlin) Magill; **ED:** JD, University of Virginia School of Law, Charlottesville, 1995; BA in History, Yale University, New Haven, 1988 **CT:** Bar: Maryland 1997 **C:** Richard E. Lang professor law, dean, Stanford Law School, California, 2012-; Elizabeth D. and Richard A. Merrill professor, University of Virginia School of Law, 2011-12; Vice dean, University of Virginia School of Law, 2009-12; Horace W. Goldsmith research professor, University of Virginia School of Law, 2007-10; Joseph Weintraub-Bank of America distinguished professor law, University Virginia School of Law, 2006-12; John V. Ray research professor, University Virginia School of Law 2003-06; Professor, University Virginia School of Law 2002-12; Associate professor law, University Virginia School of Law Charlottesville, 1997-2002; Law clerk to Hon. Ruth Bader Ginsburg, Supreme Court of the U.S., Washington, DC 1996-97; Law clerk to Hon. J. Harvie Wilkinson III, U.S. Court Appeals (4th Cir.), 1995-96; Summer associate, Covington & Burling LLP, Washington, DC 1994; Senior legis. assistant for energy and natural resources to Senator Kent Conrad, U.S. Senate, Washington, DC 1988-92 **MEM:** Mem.: American Bar Association (vice-chair judicial rev. subcom., associate reporter Administrative Procedure Act Project) **BA:** Stanford Law School, Room N305, Neukom Building, 450 Serra Mall, Stanford, CA, 94305

MAGUIRE, TOBEY, T: Actor **I:** Media & Entertainment **DOB:** 06/27/1975 **PB:** Santa Monica **SC:** CA/USA **PT:** Vincent Maguire; Wendy Maguire **CW:** Actor: (films) The Wizard, 1989, This Boy's Life, 1993, Healer, 1994, SFW, 1994, Revenge of the Red Baron, 1994, Joyride, 1996, The Ice Storm, 1997, Deconstructing Harry, 1997, Pleasantville, 1998, Fear and Loathing in Las Vegas, 1998, Ride with the Devil, 1999, The Cider House Rules, 1999, Wonder Boys, 2000, Don's Plum, 2001, Spider-Man, 2002, Spider-Man 2, 2004, The Good German, 2006, Spider-Man 3, 2007, Brothers, 2009, The Details, 2011, Life of Pi, 2012, The Great Gatsby, 2013, Labor Day,

2014, Pawn Sacrifice, 2014; voice (films) Cats & Dogs, 2001, The Boss Baby, 2017; Producer (films) Good People, 2014, Z for Zachariah, 2015, The 5th Wave, 2016; actor: (TV films) Tales from the Whoop: Hot Rod Brown Class Clown, 1990, Spoils of War, 1994, A Child's Cry for Help, 1994, Seduced by Madness: The Diane Borchardt Story, 1996; (TV series) Great Scott!, 1992; (TV miniseries) The Spoils of Babylon, 2014; actor, executive producer (films) Seabiscuit, 2003, actor, producer Pawn Sacrifice, 2014; executive prodr.: (TV films) Rock of Ages, 2003; prodr.: (films) 25th Hour, 2002, Whatever We Do, 2003, Country Strong, 2010, Seeking Justice, 2011, Rock of Ages, 2012, Z for Zachariah, 2015, The 5th Wave, 2016; guest appearances on: Blossom, 1991, Roseanne, 1991, Eerie, Indiana, 1991, Wild & Crazy Kids, 1992, Walker, Texas Ranger, 1994, Tracey Takes On, 1996

MAHER, BILL, T: Political Commentator **I:** Media & Entertainment **DOB:** 01/20/1956 **PB:** New York **SC:** NY/USA **PT:** Son of Bill and Julie (Berman) Maher. **ED:** BA in English & Hist., Cornell University, New York City, 1978 **C:** Minority owner, New York Mets, 2012-; Host, Real Time With Bill Maher, HBO, 2003-; Creator, host Politically Incorrect, ABC, 1996-2002; Creator, host Politically Incorrect, Comedy Central, New York City, 1993-96; Host, Catch a Rising Star Comedy Club, New York City, 1979 **CIV:** Board directors, PETA, Adv. board member, The Reason Project, **CW:** Stand-up performances include The Bob Monkhouse Show, Late Night with David Letterman, The Tonight Show, (HBO specials) One Night Stand, 1989, 1992, Stuff that Struck Me Funny, 1995, The Golden Goose Special, 1997, Be More Cynical, 2000, Victory Begins at Home, 2003, I'm Swiss, 2005, The Decider, 2007, "...But I'm Not Wrong", 2010; actor: (films) DC Cab, 1993, Ratboy, 1986, House II: The Second Story, 1987, Cannibal Women in the Avocado Jungle of Death, 1989, Pizza Man, 1991, Say What?, 1992, Don't Quit Your Day Job, 1996, Bimbo Movie Bash, 1997, EDtv, 1998, Tomcats, 2001, The Aristocrats, 2005, Swing Vote, 2008; (TV series) Sara, 1985; (TV films) Club Med, 1986, Out of Time, 1988, The Weinerville Election Special: From Washington British Columbia, 1996, (TV appearances) Alice, 1985, Hard Knocks, 1987, Rags to Riches, 1987, Max Headroom, 1987, Newhart, 1988, Murder, She Wrote (2 episodes), 1989-90, The Midnight Hour, 1990, Charlie Hoover (4 episodes), 1991, (TV appearances:) Married With Children, 1993, (TV appearances) Roseanne, 1993, The Jackie Thomas Show, 1993; appeared in, producer (documentaries) Religulous, 2008; author: True Story : A Novel, 1994, Does Anybody Have a Problem With That? Politically Incorrect's Greatest Hits, 1996, Does Anybody Have a Problem with That? The Best of Politically Incorrect, 1997, When You Ride Alone You Ride With Bin Laden: What the Government Should Be Telling Us to Help Fight the War on Terrorism, 2003, Keep the Statue of Liberty Closed: The New Rules, 2004, New Rules: Polite Musings from a Timid Observer, 2005, The New New Rules: A Funny Look at How Everybody But Me Has Their Head Up Their Ass, 2011 **AW:** Named one of The 50 Highest-Earning Political Figures, Newsweek, 2010, Comedy Central's 100 Greatest Stand-Ups of All Time; recipient Johnny Carson Producer of Year award, Producers Guild of America, 2007, Pres.'s award for Championing Free Speech, LA Times Press Club, 2002, CableACE award for best talk show host, National Academy Cable Programming, 1995, CableACE award for best talk show series, 1995, CableACE award, 1990 **PA:** Democrat **BA:** Brillstein-Grey Entertainment, 9150 Wilshire Boulevard, Beverly Hills, CA, 90212

MAHONY, ROGER MICHAEL, T: Cardinal, Archbishop Emeritus **I:** Religious **DOB:** 02/27/1936 **PB:** Hollywood **SC:** CA/USA **PT:** Son of Victor James and Loretta Marie (Baron) Mahony **ED:** AA, Our Lady Queen of Angels Seminary, 1956; BA, Saint John's Seminary College, 1958; BST, Saint John's Seminary College, 1962; MSW, Catholic University America, 1964 **C:** Cardinal-priest, of Santi Quattro Coronati (Four Crowned Saints), 1991—; Pastor, Saint Genevieve's Parish, Fresno, California, 1967—1968; Administrator, Saint Genevieve's Parish, Fresno, California, 1964—1967; Executive Director, Infant of Prague Adoption Service, Catholic Welfare Bureau, Fresno, California, 1964—1970; Diocesan Director, Catholic Charities and Social Services, Fresno, California, 1964—1970; Assistant Pastor, Saint John's Cathedral, Fresno, California, 1962—1964; Auxiliary Bishop and Vicar General, Fresno, California, 1975—1980; Chancellor, Fresno, California, 1970—1977; Ordained Priest, of Fresno, California, 1962; Archbishop Emeritus of Los Angeles, 2011—; Elevated to Cardinal, 1991; Archbishop, of Los Angeles, California, 1985—2011; Bishop of Stockton, California, 1980—1985; Ordained, of Tamascani, 1975; Appointed Titular Bishop, of Tamascani, 1975; Rector, Saint John's Cathedral, Fresno, California, 1973—1980; Assistant Pastor, Saint John's Cathedral, Fresno, California, 1968—1973 **CR:** Faculty Extension Division, Fresno State University, 1965—1967; Secretary, U.S. Catholic Bishops Ad Hoc Committee on Farm Labor, National Conference Bishops, 1970—1975; Chairman, Committee on Public Welfare and Income Maintenance, National Conference Catholic Charities, 1969—1970; Administrative Committee, National Conference Catholic Bishops, 1976—1979, 1982—1985, 1987—1990, 1992—1995, 1998—2001, Committee, Migration and Refugees, 1976—1995, Chairman, Committee on Farm Labor, 1981—1992, Committee, Moral Evaluation of Deterrence, 1986—1988, Consultant Committee, Chairman for Prolife Activities, 1990—1995; Committee, Social Development and World Peace U.S. Catholic Conference, 1985—1993, Chairman, International Policy Section, 1987—1993; Committee, Justice and Peace, Pontifical Councils, 1984—1998, Pastoral Care of Migrants and Itinerant People, 1986—1991, Chairman, Committee Domestic Policy, 1998—2001; President-delegate Special Assembly for America of the Synod of Bishops, 1997; Member Congregation for the Oriental Churches, Prefecture for the Economic Affairs of the Holy See, Canon Law Society **CIV:** Active Mexican-American Council for Better Housing, 1968—1972, Federal Commission Agricultural Workers, 1987—1993, Urban Coalition of Fresno, California, 1968—1972, Fresno County Economic Opportunities Commission, 1964—1966, Fresno County Alcoholic Rehabilitation Committee, 1966—1967, Fresno City Charter Review Committee, 1968—1970, Fresno Redevelopment Agency, 1970—1975, Los Angeles 2000 Committee, 1985—1988, Blue Ribbon Committee Affordable Housing City of Los Angeles, 1988; Member, Commission to Draft an Ethics Code, Los Angeles City Government, 1989—1990; Trustee Saint Agnes Hospital, Fresno, 1969—1973, Catholic University America, 1984—1988, 1998—; Named chaplain to Pope Paul VI, 1967; Chaplain Saint Vincent de Paul Society, 1964—1970; Board of Directors West Coast Regional Office Bishops Committee for Spanish-Speaking, 1967—1970; Chairman, California Association Catholic Charities Directors, 1965—1969; Trustee Saint Patrick's Seminary, Archdiocese of San Francisco, 1974—1975; Board of Directors Fresno Community Workshop, 1965—1967, Rebuild Los Angeles, 1992—1995 **AW:** Named Young Man of Year, Fresno Junior Chamber of Commerce, 1967 **BA:** Archdiocese Los Angeles 3424 Wilshire Blvd, Los Angeles, CA, 90010

MAIDA, ADAM JOSEPH CARDINAL, T: Cardinal, Archbishop Emeritus **I:** Religious **DOB:** 03/18/1930 **PB:** East Vandergrift **SC:** Pennsylvania **PT:** Son of Adam and Sophie (Cieslak) Maida. **ED:** JD, Duquesne University, 1964; JCL, Pontifical Lateran University, Rome, 1960; STL, Saint Mary's University, Baltimore, 1956; BA, Saint Vincent College, Latrobe, Pennsylvania, 1952 **CT:** Bar: US Supreme Court, US District Court (western district) Pennsylvania, Pennsylvania **C:** Cardinal-priest, of Santi Vitale, Valeria, Gervasio e Protasio (Saints Vitalis, Valeris, Gervase, and Protase), 1994-; Archbishop Emeritus, of Detroit, 2009-; Superior, Cayman Islands, Antilles, 2000-09; Elevated to Cardinal, 1994; Archbishop, of Detroit, 1990-2009; Ordained, of Green Bay, Wisconsin, 1984; Bishop, of Green Bay, Wisconsin, 1984-89; Associate Pastor, Vice-chancellor, General Counsellor, of Pittsburgh, 1965-83; Ordained Priest, of Pittsburgh, 1956 **CR:** Past assistant professor theology, LaRoche College adjunct professor, Duquesne University School Law, 1971-83 chairman National Conference of Catholic Bishops (NCCB), Canonical Affairs Committee, 1992, member NCCB Bishops' and President's Committee, Economic Concerns of the Holy See, Migration and Refugee Services, Nominations of Conference Officers, Pro-Life Committee, Committee of the Polish Apostolate Member U.S. Catholic Conferences Ex Corder Ecclesiae Committee, Congregation for Catholic Education, Congregation for the Clergy, Pontifical Council for Interpretation of Legislative Texts, Pontifical Council for Pastoral Care of Migrants and Itinerant Peoples, Cardinal Commission for the Supervision of the Institute for Works of Religion, Roman Curia **CIV:** Trustee, Basilica of the National Shrine of the Immaculate Conception, Catholic University America, Michigan Catholic Conference, Papal Foundation Philadelphia Chairman Board Trustees, Sacred Heart Major Seminary, Saints Cyril and Methodius Seminary Member Board Governor Ave Maria School Law Board Director National Catholic Bioethics Center Board Directors Pope John XXIII Medical-Moral Research and Education Centre, Braintree, Massachusetts Chairman Board Trustees Michigan Catholic Conference Member Pope John Paul II Cultural Foundation, Rome Episcopal Moderator, President Pope John Paul II Cultural Foundation **CW:** Author Ownership Control and Sponsorship of Catholic Institutions, 1975, Church Property, Church Finances and Church-Related Corporations, A Canon Law Handbook, 1983; educated, The Tribunal Reporter-A Casebook and Commentary on the Ground for Annulment in the Catholic Church, 1970, Issues in the Labor-Management Dialogue: Church Perspectives, 1982. **BA:** Cathedral of the Most Blessed Sacrament, 9844 Woodward Ave, Detroit, MI, 48202

MALAIHOLLO, NATASIA, T: CEO **I:** Technology **CN:** Wyzerr, Inc. **ED:** BA in Legal Studies, University of California, Berkeley (2005-2008) **C:** Board Member, Cincinnati Reds (2017-Present); Chief Executive Officer, Wyzerr, Inc. (2014-Present); Events Associate, Vator (2014-2015); Chief Executive Officer, Sooligan (2011-2014); Patent Specialist, Sughrue Mion PLLC (2011-2012)

MALKOVICH, JOHN GAVIN, T: Actor **I:** Media & Entertainment **DOB:** 12/09/1953 **PB:** Christopher **SC:** IL/USA **MS:** Married **SPN:** Nicoletta Peyran, 9/20/1989; Glenne Headly, 8/2/1982, Divorced 1/1988 **CH:** Amandine, Loewy **ED:** Student, Eastern Illinois University; Degree in Theater, Illinois State University **CR:** Co-Founder, Steppenwolf Theatre, Chicago, IL, 1976 **CW:** Actor, (Theatrical Debut) In True West, 1982, (Theatrical Appearances) Death Of A Salesman, 1984, Burn This, 1987, States Of

Shock, (Films) Places In The Heart, 1984, The Killing Fields, 1984, Eleni, 1985, Making Mr. Right, 1987, The Glass Menagerie, 1987, Empire Of The Sun, 1987, Miles From Home, 1988, Dangerous Liaisons, 1988, The Sheltering Sky, 1990, Queen's Logic, 1991, The Object Of Beauty, 1991, Shadows And Fog, 1992, Jennifer 8, 1992, Of Mice And Men, 1992, In The Line Of Fire, 1993, Alive, 1993, Touchstone, 1994, Para De La Nuages, 1994, Mary Reilly, 1994, Mulholland Falls, 1996, Der Unhold, 1996, The Portrait Of A Lady, 1996, Primary Colors, 1997, Con Air, 1997, The Man In The Iron Mask, 1998, Rounders, 1998, Le Temps Retrouvé, 1999, The Libertine, 1999, Ladies Room, 1999, Joan Of Arc, 1999, Being John Malkovich, 1999, Shadow Of The Vampire, 2000, Les Ames Forte, 2001, Knockaround Guys, 2001, Je Rentre A La Maison, 2001, Ripley's Game, 2002, Hotel, 2001, The Dancer Upstairs, 2002, Johnny English, 2003, The Hitchhiker's Guide To The Galaxy, 2005, Colour Me Kubrick, 2005, Klimt, 2006, The Call, 2006, Eragon, 2006, Drunkboat, 2007, Gardens Of The Night, 2007, In Tranzit, 2007, (Voice Actor) Beowulf, 2007, Burn After Reading, 2008, Changeling, 2008, Jonah Hex, 2010, Secretariat, 2010, Red, 2010, Drunkboat, 2011, Transformers: Dark Of The Moon, 2011, Lines Of Wellington, 2012, Warm Bodies, 2013, Educazione Siberiana, 2013, Red 2, 2013, Cut Bank, 2014, The Casanova Variations, 2014, (Voice Actor) Penguins Of Madagascar, 2014, Zoolander 2, 2016, Dominion, 2016, Deepwater Horizon, 2016, Psychogenic Fugue, 2016, Unlocked, 2016, The Wilde Wedding, 2017, I Love You, Daddy, 2017, About Love: Only For Adults, 2017, Bullet Heads, 2017, Valley Of The Gods, 2018, (TV Films) Word Of Honor, 1981, American Dream, 1981, Death Of A Salesman, 1985, Rocket To The Moon, 1986, Santabears High Flying Adventure, 1987, Old Times, 1991, Heart Of Darkness, 1994, RKO 281, 1999, Les Miserables, 2000, Napoleon, 2002, (TV Series) Crossbones, 2014; Executive Producer, (Films) The Accidental Tourist, 1988, Somewhere Else, 2000, Abel, 2010, Young Adult, 2011; Producer, (Films) Ghost World, 2000, The Loner, 2001, Found In The Street, 2001, The Dancer Upstairs, 2002, Ripley's Game, 2002, Johnny English, 2003, A Talking Picture, 2003, The Libertine, 2004, Kill The Poor, 2006, Art School Confidential, 2006, Juno, 2007, The Perks Of Being A Wallflower, 2012, Chavez, 2014; Co-Executive Producer, (Films) The Dancer Upstairs, 2002; Actor, Executive Producer, (Films) Cesar Chavez, 2014; Director, Balm In Gilead, 1984-1985, Arms And The Man, 1985, The Caretaker, 1986, Coyote Ugly, 1985, Libra, 1994, Steppenwolf, 1994, The Infernal Comedy: Confessions Of A Serial Killer, 2011 **AW:** American Comedy Award, Being John Malkovich, 2000, Emmy Award For Outstanding Supporting Actor In A Mini-Series Or A Special, Death Of A Salesman, 1986, Obie Award, Clarence Derwent Award, In True West, 1982 **BA:** Principato Young Management, 9465 Wilshire Boulevard, Suite 900, Beverly Hills, CA, 90212

MALLORY, TAMIKA, T: Activist **I:** Other **PB:** New York **SC:** NY/USA **C:** Owner/Creator, Mallory Consulting; Transition Committee, For Bill De Blasio, 2014 **AW:** Time Most Influential, 2017 **MEM:** Board of Directors for Gathering for Justice

MALLOY, DAN, T: Governor of Connecticut **I:** Government Administration/Government Relations/Government Services **DOB:** 07/21/1955 **PB:** Stamford **SC:** CT/USA **PT:** Son of William F. and Agnes Egan Malloy; **ED:** JD, Boston College, 1980; BA Magna Cum Laude, Boston College, 1977 **CT:** Bar: U.S. District Court (eastern & southern districts) New York, U.S. District Court Connecticut, New York, Massachusetts, Connecticut **C:** Governor, State of Connecticut, 2011-; Mayor, City of Stamford, Connecticut, 1995-2011; Partner, Abate & Fox, Stamford, Connecticut, 1985-95; Assistant District Attorney, Kings County, Brooklyn, 1980-84 **CR:** Lecturer Family Law Training Seminar Special Master, Connecticut Superior Court Member Board Fin. Stamford Board Education, 1994-95, City of Stamford, 1983-94 **CIV:** Member Adv. Board, U.S. Conference Mayors, Member Task Force on Youth and End., National League of Cities, Member Fair Policy Steering Committee, National League of Cities, 1997-98 Vice Chair Mayors and Pub. Schools Task Force, U.S. Conference Mayors, Vice President, Connecticut Conference Municipalities, Treasurer, Connecticut Conference Municipalities, 1997-98 Past Board of Directors, CTE, Past Board of Directors, Liberation Programs, Inc., Past Board of Directors, Teen Life Center, Member Executive Committee, Democratic National Committee, Member, Democratic National Committee, Chairman, Democratic Municipal Officials Organization **AW:** Recipient John F. Kennedy Profile in Courage Award, 2016 **MEM:** Mem.: Association of Trial Lawyers of America, American Bar Association, Connecticut Trial Lawyers Association, Connecticut Bar Association, National Trial Lawyers Association **PA:** Democrat

MALONE, KARL, T: Former NBA Player **I:** Athletics **DOB:** 07/24/1963 **PB:** Summerfield, Louisiana **ED:** Attended, Louisiana Tech University, Ruston, 1981-85 **C:** Assistant Coach, Utah Jazz, 2013-; Director Basketball Promotions, Assistant Strength and Dieting Coach, Louisiana Tech University Bulldogs, 2007; Power Forward, LA Lakers, 2004-05; Power Forward, Utah Jazz, Salt Lake City, 1985-2003 **CR:** Member US National Team Summer Olympic Games, Atlanta, 1996, Barcelona, 1992 **CIV:** Works with, Utah Special Olympics, Founder, Karl Malone Foundation for Kid's, **AW:** Named NBA Most Valuable Player, 1999, 1997, 1st Team All-Defense, NBA, 1997-99, Most Valuable Player, NBA All-Star Game, 1993, 1989, 1st Team All-NBA, NBA, 1989-99, 1st Team All-Rookie, 1986; named one of 50 Greatest Players in NBA History, 1996; named to Naismith Memorial Basketball Hall of Fame, 2010, Western Conference All-Star Team, NBA, 2000-02, 1988-98; recipient Gold medal, men's basketball, Atlanta Olympic Games, 1996, Barcelona Olympic Games, 1992 **ACH:** Achievements include leading the NBA in: free throw attempts, 1989-93, 1997, 1998; free throws made, 1989-1993, 1997-99; defensive rebounds, 1991, 1995 **BA:** Karl Malone Used Car Outlet, 10736 South State St, Sandy, UT, 84070

MALONEY, CAROLYN BOSHER, T: U.S. Representative from New York **I:** Government Administration/Government Relations/Government Services **DOB:** 02/19/1948 **PB:** Greensboro **PT:** Daughter of R.G. and Christine (Clegg) Bosher; Married Clifton H.W. Maloney, 1976 (deceased September 25, 2009); children: Christina, Virginia. **ED:** BA, Greensboro College, 1968 **C:** Chair, US House Democratic Caucus Task Force on Homeland Security, 2003-; Chair, US Congressional Joint Economic Committee (JEC), 2007-; Member, US Congress from 12th New York District, 2013-; Member, US House Oversight & Government Reform Committee,; Member, US House Financial Services Committee,; Ranking member, Joint Economic Committee, 2005-07; Member, US Congress from 14th New York District, 1993-2013; City councilwoman District 8, New York City, 1983-93; Director special projects, Office of New York State Senate Minority Leader Manfred Ohrenstein, 1980-82; Executive director adv. council, Office of New York State Senate Minority Leader Manfred Ohrenstein, 1979-82; Senior progressive analyst cities committee, New York State Assembly, 1977-79; Legislative aide housing committee, New York State Assembly, 1977; Special assistant center career & occupational education, New York City Board Education, 1975-76; Community affairs coordinator welfare education progressive, New York City Board Education, New York City, 1972-75 **CR:** Member US del. International Conference on Population and Devel., The Hague, Netherlands, Fourth World Conference on Women, Beijing **CIV:** active Association for a Better New York, Manhattan Women's Political Caucus. **CW:** Author: Rumors of Our Progress Have Been Greatly Exaggerated: Why Women's Lives Aren't Getting Any Easier – and How We Can Make Real Progress for Ourselves and Our Daughters, 2008 **AW:** Decorated Military Order of the Purple Heart; recipient Queens Women of Distinction award, Queen's Women's Political Caucus, Global Peace award, Peace Action, Ellis Island Medal of Honor, Distinguished Pub. Service award, National Family Planning and Reproductive Health Association, Women's Leadership award, UN Family Planning, 2002, Special Impact award, Healthy Mothers, Healthy Babies, 2000 **MEM:** Mem.: Hadassah (Myrtle Wreath award), National Organization of Women, National Association for the Advancement of Colored People **PA:** Democrat **BA:** 2308 Rayburn House Office Building, Washington, DC, 20515

MALONEY, SEAN PATRICK, T: U.S. Representative from New York **I:** Government Administration/Government Relations/Government Services **DOB:** 07/30/1966 **PB:** Sherbrook **SC:** Canada **PT:** James Francis Maloney; Joan Caroline (Daley) Maloney **ED:** JD, University of Virginia (1992); BA, University of Virginia (1988); Coursework, Georgetown School of Foreign Service, Washington, DC (1984-1986) **CT:** Washington, DC (1994); New York (1993) **C:** Member, U.S. House Transportation & Infrastructure Committee (2013-Present); Member, U.S. House Agricultural Committee (2013-Present); Member, U.S. Congress from the 18th New York District, Washington, DC (2013-Present); Partner, Orrick, Herrington & Sutcliffe LLP (2011-2012); First Deputy Secretary to Governor, State of New York, Albany, NY (2007-2009); Associate, Willkie Farr & Gallagher LLP, New York, NY (2003-2007); Chief Operating Officer, Kiodex, Inc., New York, NY (2000-2003); Vice President, General Counsel, Kiodex, Inc., New York, NY (2000); Assistant to President, Staff Secretary, The White House, Washington, DC (1997-2000); Associate, Willkie Farr & Gallagher LLP, New York, NY (1992-1997) **AW:** Grantee, Next Generation Leadership Fellowship, Rockefeller Foundation (2002-2003) **H:** Soccer; Running **PA:** Democrat **BA:** 1027 Longworth House Office Building, Washington, DC, 20515

MANCHIN, JOSEPH III, T: U.S. Senator from West Virginia **I:** Government Administration/Government Relations/Government Services **DOB:** 08/24/1947 **PB:** Farmington **SC:** WV/USA **PT:** Son of John and Mary Manchin; **ED:** BS in Business & Economics, West Virginia University, 1970 **CT:** Cert. pilot **C:** Chairman, National Governors Association, 2010; Co-host "No Labels Radio: A Town Hall with America", Sirius XM Radio, 2013-; Member, U.S. Senate Select Committee on Aging, Washington, 2010-; Member, U.S. Senate Energy & Natural Resources Committee, Washington, 2010-; Member, U.S. Senate Armed Services Committee, Washington, 2010-; US Senator from West Virginia, Washington, 2010-; Governor, State of West Virginia, 2005-10; Secretary of state, State of West Virginia, Charleston, 2001-05; Member, West Virginia State Senate, 1986-92; Member, West Virginia House of Delegates, 1982-86; Operator, Manchin's Carpet Center, Marion County, West Virginia, 1970 **MEM:** Mem.: National Rifle Association **PA:** Democrat **BA:** Office of Joseph Manchin, 306 Hart Senate Office Building, Washington, DC, 20510

MANFRED, ROB, T: MLB Commissioner **I:** Athletics **PB:** Rome **PT:** Son of Robert Dean and Phyllis (Aquino) M.; **SPN:** Married Colleen Feely, June 5, 1982 **CH:** children: Megan, Francis Michael, Jane, Mary Clare **ED:** JD Magna Cum Laude, Harvard Law School, Massachusetts, 1983; BS, Cornell University, Ithaca, New York, 1980 **CT:** Bar: Massachusetts 1983, D.C. 1984. **C:** Commissioner, Major League Baseball, 2015-; COO, Major League Baseball, 2013-; Commr.-elect, Major League Baseball, 2014-15; Executive Vice President Labor Relations & Human Resources, Major League Baseball, New York City, 1998-2013; Partner, Morgan, Lewis & Bockius, LLP, 1991-98; Associate, Morgan, Lewis & Bockius, LLP, 1984-91; Law Clerk to Hon. Joseph L. Tauro, US District Court Mass, 1983-84 **MEM:** Mem.: American Bar Association (Member Labor Section), DC Bar Association, Massachusetts Bar Association **BA:** The Office of the Commissioner of Baseball Robert D. Manfred Jr., Commissioner 245 Park Avenue, 31st Floor, New York, NY, 10167

MANNING, ANNA, T: CEO **I:** Insurance **CN:** Reinsurance Group of America **ED:** Bachelor's Degree, University of Toronto **C:** Chief Executive Officer, Reinsurance Group of America Inc. (2017-Present); President, Reinsurance Group of America Inc. (2015-2017); Senior Executive Vice President, Global Structured, Reinsurance Group of America Inc. (2015); Executive Vice President/Head, U.S., Reinsurance Group of America (2011-2015); Executive Vice President & Chief Operating Officer, International Business, Reinsurance Group of America, International Corporation (2008-2011) **BA:** 16600 Swingley Ridge Road, Chesterfield, MO, 63017-1706

MANNING, JOHN F., T: Dean of Harvard Law School **I:** Law and Legal Services **DOB:** 04/11/1961 **PB:** LA **ED:** JD magna cum laude, Harvard University, 1985; AB in History summa cum laude, Harvard University, 1982 **CT:** Bar: California 1990, Pennsylvania 1986 **C:** Dean, Harvard Law School, 2013-; Professor, Harvard Law School, Cambridge, Massachusetts, 2004-; Professor, Columbia Law School, New York City, 1994-2004; Asst to, US Solicitor General, 1991-94; Associate, Gibson, Dunn & Crutcher, Washington, 1989-91; Law clerk to Justice Antonin Scalia, US Supreme Court, 1988; Atty.-advisor Office Legal Counsel, US Department Justice, 1986-88; Law clerk to Judge Robert H. Bork, US Court Appeals DC Cir., 1985

MANNING, PEYTON WILLIAMS, T: Former NFL Player **I:** Athletics **DOB:** 03/24/1976 **PB:** New Orleans **SC:** LA/USA **PT:** Son of Archie and Olivia (Williams) Manning; **ED:** BA in Speech Communications, University Tennessee, 1998 **C:** Retired,; Quarterback, Denver Broncos, 2012-16; Quarterback, Indianapolis Colts, 1998-2012 **CR:** Founder The Peyback Foundation, 1999- **CW:** Co-author (with Archie Manning): A Father, His Sons and a Football Legacy, 2000; co-author: (with Archie & Eli Manning) Family Huddle, 2009 **AW:** Named Sportsman of Year, Sports Illus., 2013, NFL Comeback Player of Year, Associated Press, 2012, Super Bowl XLI MVP, NFL, 2007, Pro Bowl MVP, 2005, NFL Athlete of Decade, 2000's, The Sporting News, 2009, NFL Player of Year, 2008, 2004, 2003, NFL Offensive Player of Year, Associated Press, 2013, 2004, 1st Team All-Pro, 2013, 2012, 2009, 2008, 2005, 2004, 2003, NFL MVP, 2013, 2009, 2008, 2004, 2003; named one of The Most Influential People in the World of Sports, Business Week, 2008, 2007; named to The American Football Conference Pro-Bowl Team, NFL, 2013-14, 2012, 2010, 2009, 2008, 2007, 2006, 2005, 2004, 2003, 2002, 2000, 1999; recipient Walter Payton Man of Year

award, 2005, Byron "Whizzer" White Humanitarian award, 2005, ESPY award, Best Championship Performance, ESPN, 2007, ESPY award, Best NFL Player, 2004, John Wooden Trophy, Athletes for a Better World, 2004, Bert Bell award, Maxwell Club, 2004, 2003, Henry P. Iba Citizen Athlete award, 2002, American Dream award, Hudson Institute, 2001, Johnny Unitas award, 1997, Davey O'Brien award, Davey O'Brien Foundation, 1997, Maxwell award, Maxwell Football Club, 1997,Super Bowl Champion XLI, 50, Pro Bowl, 2014, Sports Illustrated Sportsman of the Year, 2013, NFL Passing Yard Leader of the Year, 2004, 2013, Bert Bell Award, 2013 **ACH:** Achievements include leading the NFL in: interceptions, 1998, pass attempts, 1998, completions, 2000, 2003, passing yards, 2000, 2003, touchdown passes, 2000, 2004, 2006; member of Super Bowl XLI winning Indianapolis Colts, 2007; setting the all-time NFL postseason record for 300-yard passing games (7), 2010; setting the all-time NFL record for touchdown passes (509), 2014; member of Super Bowl 50 winning Denver Broncos, 2016 **BA:** PeyBack Foundation, PO Box 3367, Englewood, CO, 80155

MANSELL, KEVIN B., T: CEO **I:** Retail/Sales **CN:** Kohl's Corporation **PB:** St. Louis **SC:** MO/USA **ED:** Coursework, University of Missouri **C:** Chairman, President, CEO, Kohl's Corporation, Menomonee Falls, WI (2009-Present); President, Chief Executive Officer, Kohl's Corporation, Menomonee Falls, WI (2008-2009); President, Kohl's Corporation, Menomonee Falls, WI (1999-2008); Senior Executive Vice President, Merchandising and Marketing, Kohl's Corporation, Menomonee Falls, WI (1998-1999); General Merchandise Manager, Kohl's Corporation, Menomonee Falls, WI (1987); Divisional Merchandise Manager, Kohl's Corporation, Menomonee Falls, WI (1982-1987); Positions in Merchandising and Buying, May Department Stores; With Venture Store Division, May Department Stores (1975) **CR:** Board of Directors, Kohl's Corporation (1999-Present)

MARCHANT, KENNY EWELL, T: U.S. Representative from Texas **I:** Government Administration/Government Relations/Government Services **DOB:** 02/23/1951 **PB:** Bonham **ED:** Attended, Nazarene Theological Seminary, Kansas City, Missouri; DHL (hon.), Southern Nazarene University, Bethany, Oklahoma, 1999; BA, Southern Nazarene University, Bethany, Oklahoma, 1974 **C:** Member, US Congress from 24th Texas district, 2005-; Member, Committee on Ways and Means, Committee on Ethics, Republican Study Committee; Chair House Rep. Caucus, Texas House of Reps., 1999-2003; Member, Texas House of Reps., Austin, 1987-2004; Mayor, City of Carrollton, Carrollton City Council, 1984-87; Councilman, Carrollton City Council, Texas, 1980-84 **AW:** Named a Top Ten Legislator, Texas Monthly magazine; named Top Pro-Family Legislator of Year, Am. Family Association, Legislator of Year, Texas Municipal League, Citizen of Year, Metrocrest C. of C. **PA:** Republican **BA:** 2369 Rayburn House Office Building Washington, DC 20515, Washington, DC, 20515

MARCUS, STANLEY, T: Federal Judge **I:** Law and Legal Services **DOB:** 03/27/1946 **PB:** New York **SC:** NY/USA **ED:** JD, Harvard University, 1971; BA, City University of New York, 1967 **C:** Judge, US Court Appeals (11th cir.), 1997-; Judge, US District Court (so. district) Florida, Miami, 1985-97; US attorney, Southern District of Florida, Miami, 1982-85; Chief U.S. organized crime section, Detroit Strike Force, 1980-82; Special attorney, deputy chief U.S. organized crime section, Detroit Strike Force, 1978-79; Assistant attorney, US District Court (eastern district)NY, 1975-78; Associate, Botein, Hays, Sklar &

Herzberg, New York City, 1974-75; Law clerk, Hon. John Bartels, US District Court (eastern district), New York, **CR:** Member Federal Bar Association, Florida Bar Assn, New York Bar Association **MIL:** Member US Army, 1968-74 **BA:** 56 Forsyth St NW, Atlanta, GA, USA, 30303

MARGULIES, JULIANNA, I: Media & Entertainment **DOB:** 06/04/1905 **PB:** Spring Valley, New York **SC:** Spring Valley, New York **PT:** Daughter of Paul and Francesca (Gardner) Margulies; **ED:** BA, Sarah Lawrence College, 1989 **CW:** Actress: (films) Out for Justice, 1991, Traveller, 1997, Paradise Road, 1997, A Price Above Rubies, 1997, The Newton Boys, 1998, The Big Day, 1999, What's Cooking, 2000, (voice) Dinosaur, 2000, Ten Unknowns, 2001, The Man From Elysian Fields, 2001, (voice) Love Gets You Twisted, 2002, Ghost Ship, 2002, Evelyn, 2002, Slingshot, 2005, The Darwin Awards, 2006, Snakes on a Plane, 2006, Beautiful Ohio, 2006, City Island, 2009, Stand Up Guys, 2012; (TV series) Philly Heat, 1994, ER, 1994-2000 (Emmy award for Best Supporting Actress-Drama, 1995, Screen Actors Guild award for Outstanding Performance by an Ensemble in a Drama Series, 1997, 1998, 1999), Canterbury's Law, 2008, The Good Wife, 2009-16 (Best Performance by an Actress in a TV Series-Drama, Golden Globe award, Hollywood Foreign Press Association, 2010, Outstanding Performance by a Female Actor in a Drama Series, Screen Actors Guild, 2010, 2011, Emmy award for Outstanding Lead Actress in a Drama Series, 2011, 2014); (TV mini-series) The Grid, 2004; (TV films) The Mists of Avalon, 2001, Jenifer, 2001, Hitler: The Rise of Evil, 2003; (TV appearances) Law & Order, 1993, Murder, She Wrote, 1993, Homicide: Life on the Street, 1994, Scrubs, 2004, The Sopranos, 2006, 2007, 2009; (theater appearances) The Substance of Fire, At Home, Fefu and Her Friends, The Substance of Fire, Living Expenses, Dan Drift, Book of Names, Balm in Gilead, In the Boom Boom Room, The Vagina Monologues, 2000, Festen, 2006; author: (children's book) Three Magic Balloons, 2015 **AW:** Named one of The 100 Most Powerful Women in Entertainment, The Hollywood Reporter, 2014

MARINO, THOMAS ANTHONY, T: U.S. Representative from Pennsylvania **I:** Government Administration/Government Relations/Government Services **DOB:** 08/13/1952 **PB:** Lycoming County **SC:** PA/USA **ED:** JD, Dickinson School of Law, Carlisle, PA (1988); BA in Political Science & Education, Lycoming College, Magna Cum Laude, Williamsport, PA (1985); AA, Williamsport Area Community College (1983) **C:** Member, US House Judiciary Committee, Washington, DC (2011-Present); Member, US House Homeland Security Committee, Washington, DC (2011-Present); Member, US House Foreign Affairs Committee, Washington, DC (2011-Present); Member, US Congress from 10th Pennsylvania District, Washington, DC (2011-Present); Business Law Attorney, DeNaples Management (2007-2009); US Attorney, Middle District of Pennsylvania, US Department of Justice, Philadelphia, PA (2002-2007); District Attorney, Lycoming County, PA (1996-2002); Associate, McNerney, Page, Vanderlin & Hall, Williamsport, PA (1988-1996) **PA:** Republican

MARIOTA, MARCUS ARDEL TAULAUNIU, T: NFL Quarterback **I:** Athletics **DOB:** 10/30/1993 **PB:** Honolulu **SC:** HI/USA **PT:** Son of Toa and Alana (Deppe) Mariota. **ED:** Attending, University Oregon, 2011- **C:** Quarterback, Tennessee Titans, 2015- Quarterback, University of Oregon Ducks, Eugene, 2011 **AW:** Named 1st Team All-American, Associated Press, 2014, Pac-12 Offensive Player of the Year, 2014, Pac-12 Championship Game

MVP, 2014, Alamo Bowl MVP, 2013, Fiesta Bowl MVP, 2013, Pac-12 Offensive Freshman of the Year, 2012; recipient Johnny Unitas Golden Arm award, The Golden Arm award, 2014, Walter Camp award, Walter Camp Football Foundation, 2014, Davey O'Brien award, Davey O'Brien Foundation, 2014, Heisman Memorial Trophy, Heisman Trust, 2014,Maxwell Award, 2014, Manning Award, 2014 **BA:** Tennessee Titans Headquarters, Saint Thomas Sports Park 460 Great Circle Rd., Nashville, TN, 37228

MARKEY, ED, T: U.S. Senator from Massachusetts **I:** Government Administration/Government Relations/Government Services **DOB:** 07/11/1946 **PB:** Malden **SC:** Massachusetts **PT:** Son of John E. and Christine M. Markey; **ED:** JD, Boston College, 1972; BA, Boston College, 1968 **CT:** Bar: Massachusetts **C:** Member, US Senate Environment & Public Works Committee, 2014-; Member, US Senate Small Business & Entrepreneurship, 2013-; Member, US Senate Foreign Relations Committee, 2013-; Member, US Senate Commerce, Sci. & Transportation Committee, 2013-; US Senator from Massachusetts, 2013-; Chairman, US House Energy Independence & Global Warming Committee, 2007-11; Member, US Congress from 5th Massachusetts District, 2013; Member, US Congress from 7th Massachusetts District, 1976-2013; Member District 16, Massachusetts House of Reps., 1973-76 **CIV:** Served with US Army Reserve, 1968-73 **CW:** Member editorial staff: Boston College Law Rev. **MEM:** Member Massachusetts Bar Association (Massachusetts Legislator of Year 1975) Clubs: K.C. **PA:** Democrat **BA:** Office of Ed Markey, 225 Dirksen Senate Office Building, Washington, DC, 20510

MARKS, ROBERT JACKSON, T: Electrical Engineer **I:** Engineering **DOB:** 08/25/1950 **PB:** Sutton **SC:** WV/USA **PT:** Son of Robert Jackson and Lenore Ethyl (Hersman) M. **MS:** Married **SPN:** Connie Lynn Jewett, July 28, 1974 **CH:** Jeremiah Jackson Jewett, Joshua Jackson Jewett, Marilee Melodie **ED:** PhD in Electrical Engineering, Texas Tech University, 1977; MSEE, Rose-Hulman Institute Tech., 1973; BSEE, Rose-Hulman Institute Tech., 1972 **C:** Professor, University Washington, Seattle, 1987-; Associate professor, University Washington, Seattle, 1982-87; Assistant professor electrical engineering, University Washington, Seattle, 1978-82; Research assistant, Texas Tech University, Lubbock, 1974-77; Reliability engineer, Naval Weapons Center, Crane, Ind., 1973-74 **CR:** Consultant Applied Physics Laboratory, Seattle, 1978-79, Appa Systems Inc., Bellevue, Washington, 1981-82, Tech. Arts Corp., Seattle, 1983-84, Flow Ind., 1987-89. **CW:** Contributor articles to professional journals,(Books) Computational Intelligence: A Dynamic System Perspective, 1999, Neural Smithing: Supervised Learning in Feedforward Artificial Neural Networks, 1999, Handbook of Fourier Analysis and Its Applications, 2009, New Perspectives, World Scientific, Singapore, 2013, Introduction to Evolutionary Informatics, 2017 **MEM:** Member IEEE (senior member; chairman pro tempore neural networks com 1988-, Centennial medal and cert. 1984, Outstanding Branch Councilor-Advisor award 1982), Optical Society Am. (hon. member Puget Sound section), Society Photo-optical Instrumentation Engineers, Sigma Xi, Eta Kappa Nu. **PA:** Republican **BA:** U Wash, Dept Elec Engring, Seattle, WA, 98195

MARLEY, ZIGGY, T: Singer **I:** Media & Entertainment **DOB:** 10/17/1968 **PB:** Kingston, Jamaica **PT:** Son of Bob and Rita Marley; **SPN:** Married Orly Agai; **CH:** children: Judah Victoria, Gideon Robert Nesta, Abraham Selassie Robert Nesta,

Isaiah Sion Robert Nesta; from a previous relationship: Daniel, Ju **C:** Co-founder, Band Member (with siblings Stephen, Sharon & Cedella Marley), Ziggy Marley and the Melody Makers, 1970-2000 **CIV:** Founder, URGE (Unlimited Resources Giving Enlightenment), Founder, Ghetto Youths International, 1992 **CW:** Musician: (albums with The Melody Makers) Play The Game Right, 1985, Hey World!, 1986, Conscious Party, 1988 (Best Reggae Album, Grammy Awards, 1989), One Bright Day, 1989 (Best Reggae Album, Grammy Awards, 1990), Jahmekya, 1991, Joy and Blues, 1993, Free Like We Want 2 B, 1995, Fallen is Babylon, 1997 (Best Reggae Album, Grammy Awards, 1998), Spirit of Music, 1999, Ziggy Marley & the Melody Makers Live, Vol. 1, 2000, (solo albums) Dragonfly, 2003, Love is My Religion, 2006 (Best Reggae Album, Grammy Awards, 2007), Family Time, 2009 (Best Musical Album for Children, Grammy Awards, 2010), Wild and Free, 2011, In Concert, 2012 (Best Reggae Album, Grammy Awards, 2014), Fly Rasta, 2014 (Best Reggae Album, Grammy Awards, 2015), Ziggy Marley, 2016(Live Albums) Love is My Religion Live, 2008, Ziggy Live From Soho, 2009, Ziggy Marley in Concert, 2013, We Are the People Tour, 2017 **BA:** Bob Marley Music Inc, 76 9th Ave Ste 1110, New York, NY, 10011

MARROW, TRACY (ICE-T), T: Rap Artist, Actor **I:** Media & Entertainment **PB:** Newark **SC:** NJ/USA **PT:** Solomon Morrow; Alice Morrow **MS:** Married **SPN:** Nicole Austin (December 31, 2005) **CH:** Chanel Nicole; Tracy Junior; Letesha **MIL:** Served in US Army Rangers, 1979-81 **CW:** (solo albums) Rhyme Pays, 1987, Power, 1988, The Iceberg/Freedom of Speech...Just Watch What You Say, 1989, O.G. Original Gangster, 1991, Home Invasion, 1993, Ice-T VI: Return of the Real, 1996, The Seventh Deadly Sin, 1999, Greatest Hits: The Evidence, 2001, Gang Culture, 2004, Gangsta Rap, 2006 (with King Tee), Criminal Vortex,2018, Havin' a T Party, 1991, (with Body Count) Body Count, 1992, Born Dead, 1994, Violent Demise: The Last Days, 1997, Murder 4 Hire, 2006, Manslaughter, 2014, Bloodlust, 2017, (collaboration albums) Breaking and Entering, 1983, Rhyme Syndicate Comin' Through, 1988, Murder Squad Nationwide, 1995, $port Ya Vest in the West, 1997, Pimp to Eat, 2000, WWW Aggression, 2000, Repossession, 2004, Urban Legends, 2008; Actor: (films) Breakin', 1984, Breakin' 2, 1984, New Jack City, 1991, Ricochet, 1991, Trespass, 1992, Why Colors?, 1992, Surviving the Game, 1994, Tank Girl, 1995, Johnny Mnemonic, 1995, Mean Guns, 1997, The Deli, 1997, Beyond Utopia, 1997, Crazy Six, 1998, Final Voyage, 1999, Corrupt, 1999, The Wrecking Crew, 1999, Sonic Impact, 1999, The Heist, 1999, Frezno Smooth, 1999, Urban Menace, 1999, Stealth Fighter, 1999, Corrupt, 1999, Guardian, 2000, Gangland, 2000, Luck of the Draw, 2000, The Alternates, 2000, Stranded, 2001, Kept, 2001, Crime Partners, 2001, 3000 Miles to Graceland, 2001, Point Doom, 2001, Deadly Rhapsody, 2001, 'R Xmas, 2001, Ticker, 2001, Out Kold, 2001, Ablaze, 2001, On the Edge, 2002, Tracks, 2002, Good Hair, 2009, The Passions of Jesus Christ, 2012, Santorini Blue, 2013, Once Upon a Time in Brooklyn, 2013, Crossed the Line, 2014, What Now, 2015, The Ghetto, 2015, How We Met,2016, Bloodrunners,2017; (TV films) Exiled, 1998, The Disciples, 2000; (TV series) Players, 1997-98, Law and Order: Special Victims Unit, 2000-, 30 Rock, 2011-13, Chicago P.D., 2014-15; (reality TV personality) Ice Loves Coco, 2011-13; co-host with wife (talk show) Ice and Coco, 2015-; executive prodr.: (documentaries) 25 to Life: Ice T Presents, 2008, Planet Rock: The Story of Hip-Hop and the Crack Generation, 2011, Something from Nothing: The Art of Rap, 2012, Iceberg Slim: Portrait of a Pimp, 2012; author: The Iceberg/Freedom

of Speech, Just Watch What You Say, 1989, The Ice Opinion, 1994, Ice: A Memoir of Gangster Life and Redemption from South Central to Hollywood, 2011; co-author: Mirror Image, 2013.

MARS, BRUNO, T: Singer, Songwriter, Music Producer **I:** Media & Entertainment **DOB:** 10/08/1985 **PB:** Honolulu **SC:** HI/USA **PT:** Pete Hernandez; Bernadette Hernandez **C:** Production Team, The Smeezingtons **CW:** Singer, (Albums) Doo-Wops & Hooligans, 2010, (Compilation Album) The Twilight Saga: Breaking Dawn - Part 1: Original Motion Picture Soundtrack, 2011, Unorthodox Jukebox, 2012, 24K Magic, 2016, (Songs) Just the Way You Are, 2010, Grenade, 2010, The Lazy Song, 2011, Let It Rain, 2011, Locked Out of Heaven, 2013, Treasure, 2013, (With Mark Ronson) Uptown Funk, 2014; Co-Writer, Guest Vocalist, (Song by B.o.B) Nothin' on You, 2010, (Song by Travie McCoy) Billionaire, 2010; Performer, Super Bowl XLVIII Half-Time Show, 2014; Actor, (Films) Honeymoon in Vegas, 1992, Rio 2, 2014 **AW:** Artist of the Year, Favorite Pop/Rock, Favorite Soul/RnB, American Music Awards; Favorite Pop/Rock Song, Favorite Soul/Rock, 24K Magic, American Music Awards; Song of Year, Nothin' on You, Soul Train Music Awards, 2010; Favorite Pop/Rock Male Artist, American Music Awards, 2011; Best Male Pop Vocal Performance, Grammy Awards, 2011; Top Radio Song, Just the Way You Are, Billboard Music Awards, 2011; The 100 Most Influential People in the World, TIME Magazine, 2011; 14 ASCAP Pop Music Awards, 2011-2017; Favorite Male Artist, People's Choice Awards, 2012; Best Male Video, Locked Out of Heaven, MTV Video Music Awards, 2013; Best Choreography, Treasure, MTV Video Music Awards, 2013; Best Pop Vocal Album, Unorthodox Jukebox, Grammy Awards, 2014; Best Male Video, MTV Video Music Awards, 2015; (With Mark Ronson) Record of the Year, Best Pop Duo/Group Performance, Best Remixed Recording, Non-Classical, Uptown Funk, Grammy Awards, 2016; Favorite Soul/RnB, Video of the Year, That's What I Like, American Music Association, 2017; Best Male R&B/Pop Artist, BET Awards, 2017; 24K Magic, Video of the Year, 2017 **BA:** Lower 2C01, 1633 Broadway, New York, NY, 10019-6708 **ADD:** c/o Atlantic Records, 1290 Avenue of the Americas, New York, NY, 10104

MARSHALL, KERRY JAMES, T: Artist **I:** Fine Art **DOB:** 10/17/1955 **PB:** Birmingham **SC:** AL/USA **ED:** BFA, Otis College of Art and Design, Los Angeles, CA, 1978 **C:** Associate Professor, University of Illinois, Chicago, IL; Production Designer, Praise House & Sankofa, 1991 **CR:** Art Instructor, Los Angeles City College, 1980-1983; Art Faculty, Los Angeles Southwest College, 1981-1985; Fellow, National Endowment for the Arts and Visual Art, 1991; Adjunct Assistant Professor, School of Art And Design, University of Illinois, Chicago, IL, 1993-1994 **CW:** Contributor, Articles, Professional Journals; Appearance, (Television) Art:21, 2001 **AW:** Visual Arts Grantee, Illinois Arts Council, 1992, Grantee, Tiffany Foundation, 1993, Herb Alpert Award, California Institute of the Arts, 1997, John D. And Catherine T. MacArthur Foundation, 1997, Distinguished Artist Fellowship And Stillwater Foundation Grant, College of Fine Arts, University of Texas, Austin, TX, 2004, Time 100 Most Influential, 2017, Fifth Star Award, City Of Chicago, 2017 **MEM:** Illinois Arts Council

MARSHALL, ROGER, T: U.S. Representative from Kansas **I:** Government Administration/Government Relations/Government Services **DOB:** 08/09/1960 **PB:** El Dorado **SC:** KS/USA **ED:** M.D., University of Kansas, 1987; B.S., Kansas State University; A.S.,Butler Community College, 1980 **C:**

Member, U.S. Representative from Kansas 1st District, 2017-; Member, Committee on Agriculture; Member, Committee on Science, Space and Technology; Member, Committee on Small Business; U.S. Army Reserve, 1984-1991 **BA:** 312 Cannon HOB, Washington, DC, 20515

MARTIN, BEVERLY BALDWIN, T: Federal Judge **I:** Government Administration/Government Relations/Government Services **DOB:** 08/07/1955 **PB:** Macon **SC:** Georgia **ED:** JD, University Georgia, 1981; BA, Stetson University, Deland, Florida, 1976 **CT:** Bar: Georgia 1981. **C:** Judge, US Court Appeals (11th Cir.), 2010-; Judge, US District Court (No. District) Georgia, Atlanta, 2000-10; US Attorney, US Department Justice, Macon, 1998-2000; Assistant U.S. Attorney (Middle District Georgia), US Department Justice, Macon, 1994-98; Trial and Appellate Court Litigator, Senior Assistant Attorney General and Director Business and Professional Regulation Division, Office of Attorney General State of Georgia, Macon, 1984-94; Associate, Martin, Snow, Grant & Napier, Macon, Georgia, 1981-84 **MEM:** Member Georgia Bar Association, Macon Bar Association, Am. Judicature Society, Georgia Association Women Lawyers, Lawyers Club of Atlanta **BA:** 56 Forsyth St NW, Atlanta, GA, 30303

MARTIN, GEORGE RAYMOND RICHARD, T: Writer **I:** Writing and Editing **DOB:** 09/20/1948 **PB:** Bayonne **PT:** Son of Raymond Collins and Margaret (Brady) Martin **ED:** MS in Journalism, cum laude, Northwestern University, Evanston, Illinois, 1971; BS in Journalism, summa cum laude, Northwestern University, Evanston, Illinois, 1970 **C:** Writer-in-residence, Clarke College, 1978-79; Instructor journalism, Clarke College, Dubuque, Iowa, 1976-78; Founder, chairman, Windy City Sci. Fiction Writers' Workshop, Chicago, 1972-76; Communications & education coordinator, Cook County Legal Assistance Foundation, Chicago, 1972-74; Sportswriter, public relations officer, New Jersey Department Parks, Bayonne, 1971; Journalism intern, Medill News Service, Washington, 1971 **CW:** Author: (novels) Dying of the Light, 1977, Windhaven, 1981, Fevre Dream, 1982, The Armageddon Rag, 1983; co-author: Dead Man's Hand, 1990, Shadow Twin, 2005, Hunter's Run, 2008; author: (children's book) The Ice Dragon, 2006, (novels) (A Song of Ice and Fire series) A Game of Thrones, 1996 (Locus Fantasy award, 1997), A Clash of Kings, 1998 (Locus Fantasy award, 1999), A Storm of Swords, 2000 (Locus Fantasy award, 2001), A Feast for Crows, 2005 (#1 New York Times bestseller, #1 Wall St. Journal bestseller), A Dance with Dragons, 2011, Feast Crows, 2014, The World of Ice & Fire: The Untold History of Westeros and the Game of Thrones, 2014, A Knight of the Seven Kingdoms, 2015, (short story collections) A Song for Lya, 1976, Songs of Stars and Shadows, 1977, Sandkings, 1981, Songs the Dead Men Sing, 1983, Nightflyers, 1985, Tuf Voyaging, 1987, Portraits of His Children, 1987, Quartet, 2001, GRRM: A RRetrospective, 2003, Dreamsongs: A RRetrospective, 2007, Starlady/Fast-Friend, 2008; editor, contributor numerous volumes (science fiction and superhero anthology series) Wild Cards, 1987-, contributor numerous works of short fiction and essays to anthologies and sci. fiction & fantasy publications, writer, story editor (TV series) The Twilight Zone, 1986, writer, producer Beauty and the Beast, 1987-90, writer, producer, co-creator Game of Thrones, 2011- (Primetime Emmy for Outstanding Drama Series, 2015-16, 2018); co-editor (with Gardener Dozois): Rogues, 2014, (Books) The Sons of the Dragon, 2017 **AW:** Named one of The 10 Most Fascinating People of 2014, Barbara Walters Special; Recipient The 100 Most Influential

People in the World, TIME magazine, 2011 **MEM:** Mem.: Writers' Guild America West, Sci. Fiction & Fantasy Writers America (South-Ctrl. regional director 1977-79, vice president 1996-98) **BA:** Fevre River Packet Co., Inc., 102 San Salvador Ln, Santa Fe, NM, 87501

MARTIN, STEVE, T: Actor, Comedian **I:** Media & Entertainment **DOB:** 08/14/1945 **PB:** Waco **PT:** Son of Glenn and Mary Lee Martin; Married Victoria Tennant, November 20, 1986 (div. 1994); Married Anne Stringfield, July 28, 2007, 1 child. **ED:** Student, UCLA; Student, Long Beach State College **C:** Executive producer TV show, Domestic Life, 1984; Actor 1967- **CIV:** Trustee, L.A. Museum Art, **CW:** TV writer for Smothers Brothers (co-winner Emmy award 1969), Sonny and Cher, Pat Paulsen, Ray Stevens, Dick Van Dyke, John Denver, Glen Campbell; nightclub comedian; performer: (TV specials) Steve Martin: A Wild and Crazy Guy, 1978, Comedy is Not Pretty, 1980, Steve Martin's Best Show Ever, 1981; (comedy albums) Let's Get Small, 1977 (Grammy award 1977), A Wild and Crazy Guy, 1978 (Grammy award 1978), Comedy is Not Pretty, 1979, The Steve Martin Brothers, 1982; actor, screenwriter: (films) The Absent Minded Waiter, 1977, The Jerk, 1979, Pennies From Heaven, 1981, Dead Men Don't Wear Plaid, 1982, The Man With Two Brains, 1983, All of Me, 1984 (National Society Film Critics award for Best Actor 1984, New York Film Critics' Circle award for Best Actor 1984), L.A. Story, 1991; actor, writer, executive prodr.: (films) Three Amigos, 1986, Roxanne, 1987 (National Society Film Critics award Best Actor 1988); actor: (films) Sergeant Pepper's Lonely Hearts Club Band, 1978, The Muppet Movie, 1979, The Kids Are Alright, 1979, The Lonely Guy, 1984, Little Shop of Horrors, 1986, Planes, Trains and Automobiles, 1987, Dirty Rotten Scoundrels, 1988, Parenthood, 1989, My Blue Heaven, 1990, Father of the Bride, 1991, Grand Canyon, 1991, Housesitter, 1992, Leap of Faith, 1993, Mixed Nuts, 1994, A Simple Twist of Fate, 1994, Sergeant Bilko, 1995, The Spanish Prisoner, 1998, Bowfinger, 1999, Joe Gould's Secret, 2000, Novocaine, 2001, Bringing Down the House, 2003, Looney Tunes: Back in Action, 2003, Cheaper by the Dozen, 2003, Jiminy Glick in La La Wood, 2004, Shopgirl, 2005 (also writer, producer), Cheaper by the Dozen 2, 2005, Baby Mama, 2008, It's Complicated, 2009, The Big Year, 2010, Home (voice), 2015; (theatre) Waiting For Godot, 1988; actor, writer: (films) The Pink Panther, 2006, The Pink Panther 2, 2009; (TV films) And the Band Played On, 1993, Rutles 2: Can't Buy Me Lunch, 2002; (TV appearances) 30 Rock, 2008; screenwriter: (films) Easy Money, 1983, Bowfinger, 1999, Traitor, 2008; author: (nonfiction) Cruel Shoes, 1977, Pure Drivel, 1998; (novels) Shopgirl, 2000, The Pleasure of My Company, 2003, An Object of Beauty, 2010; (children's books) The Alphabet From A To Y With Bonus Letter Z!, 2007, Late for School, 2010; (autobiography) Born Standing Up: A Comic's Life, 2007; (plays) Picasso at the Lapin Agile and Other Plays, 1993; musician: (albums) The Crow: New Songs for the Five-Sting Banjo, 2009 (Grammy award for Best Bluegrass Album, 2010), Rare Bird Alert, 2011, Love Has Come for You (with Edie Brickell), 2013(Grammy for Best American Roots Song 2013),(Film) Love the Coopers, 2015, Billy Lynns's Long Halftime Walk, 2016(Television)SNL, 2009, 2012, 2015, Maya & Marty, 2016, Oh, Hello On Broadway, 2017 **AW:** Named one of The 50 Most Powerful People in Hollywood, Premiere magazine, 2006; recipient American Film Institute Life Achievement award, 2015, Honorary Academy award for Lifetime Achievement, Academy Motion Picture Arts & Sciences, 2014, Entertainer of the Year award, International Bluegrass Music Awards, 2011,

Kennedy Center Honors, John F. Kennedy Center for Performing Arts, 2007, Mark Twain prize for American Humor, 2005, Georgie award, American Guild Variety Artists, 1978, 1977

MARTINEZ, PEDRO JAIME, T: Former Major League Baseball Player **I:** Athletics **DOB:** 07/25/1971 **PB:** Manoquayabo **SC:** Dominican Republic **PT:** Son of Paolino and Leopoldino Martinez **ED:** Student, Ohio Dominican College **C:** Studio Analyst, MLB Network, 2015-; Special Assistant to General Manager, Boston Red Sox, 2013-; Pitcher, Philadelphia Phillies, 2009; Pitcher, New York Mets, 2005-08; Pitcher, Boston Red Sox, 1998-2004; Pitcher, Montreal Expos, 1994-97; Pitcher, LA Dodgers, 1992-93 **CW:** Author (with Michael Silverman): Pedro, 2015 **AW:** Named All-Star Game MVP, Major League Baseball, 1999, Pitcher of Year, The Sporting News, 2000, 1999, 1997, Minor League Player of Year, 1991; Named to Hall of Fame, Major League Baseball, 2015, American League All-Star Team, 2002, 1998-2000, National League All-Star Team, 2006, 2005, 1997, 1996; Recipient, American League Cy Young Award, 2000, 1999, National League Cy Young Award, 1997, National Baseball Hall of Fame, 2015 **ACH:** Achievements include leading the National League in: earned run average, complete games, 1997; leading the American League in: wins, 1999; earned run average, 1999-2003; strikeouts, 1999, 2000, 2002; shutouts, 2000; capturing Major League Baseball's Triple Crown for a pitcher (leading a league in wins, earned run average and strikeouts), 1999; member of World Series Championship winning Boston Red Sox, 2004 **BA:** Pedro Martinez Charity, PO BOX 990045, Boston, MA, 02199

MARTINEZ, SUSANA, T: Governor of New Mexico, Former Prosecutor **I:** Government Administration/Government Relations/Government Services **DOB:** 07/14/1959 **PB:** Rio Grande Valley **SC:** TX/USA **PT:** Jake Martinez; Paula Martinez **ED:** JD, University of Oklahoma, 1986; BA in Criminal Justice, University of Texas, El Paso, TX, 1981 **C:** Governor, State of New Mexico, Santa Fe, NM, 2011-Present; District Attorney, Doña Ana County District Attorney's Office, Las Cruces, NM, 1996-2010; Assistant District Attorney, Doña Ana County District Attorney's Office, Las Cruces, NM, 1986-1992 **AW:** Woman of the Year, Heart Magazine, 2008; New Mexico Prosecutor of the Year, State Bar of New Mexico, 2010; The 100 Most Influential People in the World, TIME Magazine, 2013 **PA:** Republican

MASSIE, THOMAS HAROLD, T: U.S. Representative from Kentucky, Farmer **I:** Government Administration/Government Relations/Government Services **DOB:** 01/13/1971 **PB:** Huntington **ED:** MS in Electrical Engineering, Massachusetts Institute of Technology; BS in Electrical Engineering, Massachusetts Institute of Technology **C:** Member, US House Transportation & Infrastructure Committee, 2013-; Member, US House Sci., Space & Technology Committee, 2013-; Member, US House Oversight & Government Reform Committee, 2013-; Member, US Congress from 4th Kentucky District, Washington, 2013-; Judge-exec., Lewis County, Kentucky, 2011-12; Co-founder, chairman, chief technology officer, SensAble Technologies, Inc. (formerly SensAble Devices Inc.), 1993-2003 **AW:** Lemelson-MIT Student Prize, 1995 **PA:** Republican

MAST, BRIAN, T: U.S. Representative from Florida **I:** Government Administration/Government Relations/Government Services **PB:** Grand Rapids **SC:** MI/USA **ED:** American Military University, 2008-10; A.L.B, Harvard University Extension School, 2016 **CR:** Member, U.S. Representative from Florida's 18th District, 2017-; Member, Committee on

Foreign Affairs; Member, Committee on Transportation and Infrastructure; U.S. Army, 2000-2012; Explosive Specialist, Department of Homeland Security 2012-15; Analyst, National Nuclear Security Administration, 2011-12 **AW:** During Military Service, Bronze Medal Star, Purple Heart, Defense Meritorious Service Medal, Army Commendation Medal with "V"

MATHAS, THEODORE A., T: New York Life CEO **I:** insurance **DOB:** 04/04/1967 **ED:** JD, University Virginia, 1992; AB, Stanford University, 1989 **C:** Chairman, president, CEO, New York Life Insurance Co., New York City, 2009-; President, CEO, New York Life Insurance Co., New York City, 2008-09; President, COO, New York Life Insurance Co., New York City, 2007-08; Vice-chmn., COO, member executive management committee, New York Life Insurance Co., New York City, 2006-07; Executive vice president, co-head life & annuity, New York Life Insurance Co., New York City, 2004-06; COO life & annuity, New York Life Insurance Co., New York City, 2001-04; COO agency department, New York Life Insurance Co., New York City, 1999-2001; Senior vice president, New York Life Insurance Co., New York City, 1998-2004; President NYLIFE Securities, New York Life Insurance Co., New York City, 1997-99; President Eagle Strategies Corp. subsidiary, New York Life Insurance Co., New York City, 1996-99; Corp. vice president, New York Life Insurance Co., New York City, 1995-98; Attorney, Debevoise & Plimpton, **CR:** Chairman Am. Council Life Insurers, 2012-, board directors, 2007-, New York Life Insurance Co., 2006-, Haier New York Life Insurance Ltd. **CW:** Member Univ. Virginia Law Review **MEM:** Mem.: Order of the Coif

MATHER, JOHN C., T: Astrophysicist **I:** Medicine & Health Care **DOB:** 08/07/1946 **PB:** Roanoke **SC:** Virginia **ED:** BA in Physics, Swarthmore College, Pennsylvania, 1968; PhD in Physics, University California, Berkeley, 1974; DSc in Physics (hon.), Swarthmore College, 1994; DSc in Physics (hon.), University Notre Dame, South Bend, 2011; DSc in Physics (hon.), University Maryland, College Park, 2008 **C:** Senior Scientist, NASA/Goddard Space Flight Center, 1993—; Head Infrared Astrophysics Branch, NASA/Goddard Space Flight Center, Greenbelt, Maryland, 1988—1989; Study Scientist Cosmic Background Explorer Satellite, NASA/Goddard Space Flight Center, Greenbelt, Maryland, 1976—1982; Lecturer Astronomy, Columbia University, New York City, New York, 1975—1976; NAS/NRC Research Associate, NASA/Goddard Institute Space Studies, New York City, New York, 1974—1976; Project Scientist COBE, NASA/Goddard Space Flight Center, Greenbelt, Maryland, 1982—; Principal Investigator FIRAS on COBE, NASA/Goddard Space Flight Center, Greenbelt, Maryland, 1976—; Astrophysicist, NASA/Goddard Space Flight Center, Greenbelt, Maryland, 1976—; Senior Project Researcher, James Webb Space Telescope, 2002; Researcher, Next Generation Space Telescope, 1995—2002; Head Office of Chief Scientist, NASA, Washington, DC, 2007—2008; Senior Scientist, NASA/Goddard Space Flight Center, Greenbelt, Maryland, 1989—1990; Head Infrared Astrophysics Branch, NASA/Goddard Space Flight Center, 1990—1993 **CR:** Chairman External Adv. Board University Chicago Center Astrophys. Research in the Antarctic, 1992—1995; Member Lunar Astrophysics Management Operations Working Group NASA, Washington, 1992; Member National Research Council Board Physics and Astronomy, 1998—2001; Member Astrophysics Subcommittee NASA Adv. Council, 2006—2007 **CIV:** President John and Jane Mather Foundation for Science and the Arts, 2007— **CW:** Co-author (with John Boslough): The Very First Light: The True Inside Story of the Scientific Journey Back to the Dawn of the Universe, 1996; Contributor Articles to Professional Journals **AW:** Co-recipient Nobel Prize in Physics, 2006; Finalist Discover Magazine Tech. Award, 1993; Named a Goddard Fellow, 1994; Named one of The World's Most Influential People, TIME Magazine, 2007; Named to Aviation Week & Space Tech. Hall of Fame, 1997, Newton HS Hall of Fame, New Jersey, 2003; Recipient National Science Foundation Fellowship, Hon. Woodrow Wilson Fellowship, 1968—70, Hertz Foundation Fellowship, 1970—74, National Space Achievement Award, Rotary Club, 1991, National Air & Space Museum Trophy, 1991, Aviation Week & Space Tech. Laurels award for space/missles, 1992, John Scott Award, City of Philadelphia, 1995, Marc Aaronson Memorial Prize, 1998, Benjamin Franklin Medal in Physics, Franklin Institute, 1999, Presidential Rank Award, NASA, 2003, 2008, Cosmology Prize, Peter Gruber Foundation, 2006, Antoinette de Vaucouleurs Medal, University Texas, 2007, Robinson prize, Newcastle University, 2008, Gold Medal, Prime Minister of India, 2009, Award, New Jersey Educational Association, 2010, **MEM:** Fellow: Am. Physical Society; mem.: American Institute of Aeronautics and Astronautics (Astronautics Space Sci. award 1993), National Academy of Sciences, Am. Academy Arts & Scis. (Rumford prize 1996), Society Photo-Optical Instrumentation Engineers (George W. Goddard award 2005), International Astronomical Union, Am. Astronomical Society (councilor 1998—2001, Dannie Heineman prize astrophysics 1994), Phi Beta Kappa, Sigma Xi **ACH:** Achievements include proposing Cosmic Background Explorer Satellite, led team to successful launch in 1989; measured spectrum of cosmic microwave background radiation to unprecedented accuracy **PA:** Democrat **BA:** Office of Chief Scientist, t NASA 300 E St Northwest, Washington D.C., DC, 20546

MATHERS, MARSHALL (EMINEM), T: Rap Artist, Producer **I:** Media & Entertainment **DOB:** 10/17/1973 **PB:** St. Joseph **SC:** MO/USA **PT:** Marshall Bruce Mathers, Jr.; Deborah R. (Nelson) Mathers-Briggs **MS:** Divorced **SPN:** Kimberley Anne Scott (Remarried 1/14/2006, Divorced 12/19/2006); Kimberley Anne Scott (6/14/1999, Divorced 10/11/2001) **C:** Founder, Producer, Shady Records, New York City, NY (1999-Present); Performer, D12 (1996-Present); Solo Artist (1992) **CIV:** Founder, The Marshall Mathers Foundation **CW:** Performer, Albums, "Infinite" (1997), "The Slim Shady LP" (1999), "The Marshall Mathers LP" (2000), "Devil's Night" (2001), "The Eminem Show" (2002), "Encore" (2004), "Curtain Call" (2005), "The Re-Up" (2006), "Relapse" (2009), "Recovery" (2010), "The Marshall Mathers LP 2" (2013), "Revival" (2017); Performer, Songs, "The Real Slim Shady" (2000), "Lose Yourself" (2002), Featuring Dr. Dre & 50 Cent, "Crack a Bottle" (2009), "Not Afraid" (2009), Featuring Rihanna, "Love the Way You Lie" (2010), "Monster" (2013); Performer, Producer, Albums with D12, "Devil's Night" (2001), "D12 World" (2004); Producer, Albums by Obie Trice, "Cheers" (2003), "Second Round's on Me" (2006); Albums by 50 Cent, "Get Rich or Die Tryin'" (2003), "The Massacre" (2005); Actor, Films, "8 Mile" (2002); Appearances Include TV Series, "Saturday Night Live" (1999, 2000, 2002, 2004, 2010), "Entourage" (2005, 2010), "Detroit Rubber" (2013); Appearances, Films, "Funny People" (2009); Author, "The Interview" (2014), "Bodied" (2017), Autobiography, "The Way I Am" (2008); Documentaries, "50 Cent: The New Breed" (2003), "Something from Nothing: The Art of Rap" (2012), "How to Make Money Selling Drugs" (2012), "Not Afraid: The Shady Records Story" (2015), "Stretch and Bobbito: Radio that Changed Lives" (2015), "The Defiant Ones" (2017) **AW:** Named Top Artist, Billboard Music Award (2011); Top Male Artist, Billboard Music Award (2011); Top Rap Artist, Billboard Music Awards (2011, 2014); Artist of the Decade, Billboard Music Award (2009); Favorite Male Artist, People's Choice Award (2011); Favorite Hip-Hop Artist, People's Choice Awards (2012, 2011, 2010); Favorite Male Musical Performer, People's Choice Awards (2003, 2005); Best Selling Rap/Hip-Hop Artist, World Music Award (2005); Best Selling Pop/Rock Artist, World Music Awards (2003, 2005); Best American Male Artist, World Music Award (2003); Favorite Hip-Hop/R&B Male Artist, American Music Awards (2003, 2005, 2006, 2010); Favorite Pop/Rock Male Artist, American Music Award (2003); Named One of the 100 Greatest Artists of All-Time, Rolling Stone Magazine, VH1; Five Source Hip Hop Music Awards; Seven Teen Choice awards, 12 MTV Video Music Awards, 12 Detroit Music Awards; Best Rap Album, "The Slim Shady LP," Grammy Award (2000); Best Rap Album, "The Marshall Mathers LP," Grammy Award (2001); Album of Year, "The Eminem Show," Billboard Music Award (2002); Best R&B/Hip Hop Album of Year, "The Eminem Show," Billboard Music Award (2002); Favorite Pop/Rock Album, "The Eminem Show," American Music Award (2003); Favorite Hip-Hop/R&B Album, "The Eminem Show," American Music Award (2003); Best Rap Album, "The Eminem Show," Grammy Award (2003); Favorite Rap/Hip-Hop Album, "The Encore," American Music Award (2005); (Favorite Rap/Hip-Hop Album, "Relapse," American Music Awards (2009); Best Rap Album, "Relapse," Grammy Award (2010); Favorite Rap-Hip Hop Album, "Recovery," American Music Award (2010); Best Rap Album, "Recovery," Grammy Award (2011); Top Rap Album, "Recovery," Billboard Music Award (2011); Top Rap Album, "The Marshall Mathers LP 2," Billboard Music Award (2014); Best Rap Album, "The Marshall Mathers LP 2," Grammy Award (2015); Best Rap Solo Performance, "The Real Slim Shady," Grammy Award (2001); Academy Award for Best Original Song, "Lose Yourself," Academy Motion Picture of Arts & Sciences (2002); Best Rap Solo Performance, "Lose Yourself," Grammy Award (2004); Best Rap Song, "Lose Yourself," Grammy Award (2004); Best Rap Performance by a Duo or Group, "Crack a Bottle," Grammy Award (2010); Best Rap Solo Performance, "Not Afraid," Grammy Award (2011); Hip-Hop Song of Year, "Love the Way You Lie," Soul Train Music Award (2010); Top Rap Song, "Love the Way You Lie," Billboard Music Award (2011); Favorite Song, "Love the Way You Lie," People's Choice Award (2011); Favorite Music Video, "Love the Way You Lie," National Association for the Advancement of Colored People Image Award (2011); Best Rap/Song Collaboration, "Monster," Grammy Award (2015); Academy Award for Best Original Song (2002); Golden Globe for Best Original Song (2002) **BA:** William Morris, 1325 Avenue of the Americas, New York, NY, 10019

MATHESON, SCOTT MILNE JR., T: Federal Judge **I:** Law and Legal Services **DOB:** 07/18/1953 **PB:** Salt Lake City **SC:** Utah **PT:** Son of Scott Milne and Norma (Warenski) M. **MS:** Married **SPN:** Robyn Kuida, August 12, 1978; **CH:** Heather Blair, Briggs James. **ED:** JD, Yale University, 1980; MA, Oxford University, England; AB, Stanford University, 1975 **CT:** Bar: D.C., 1981, Utah 1986. **C:** Judge, US Court Appeals (10th Cir.), 2010-; Pub. Policy Scholar, Woodrow Wilson International Center for Scholars, 2006-07; US Attorney District Utah, US Department Justice, Salt Lake City, 1993-97; Deputy Attorney, Salt Lake County Attorney's Office, 1988-89; Hugh B. Brown Endowed Chair,

University Utah S.J. Quinney College Law, Salt Lake City, 2009-10; Dean, University Utah S.J. Quinney College Law, Salt Lake City, 1998-2006; Professor Law, University Utah S.J. Quinney College Law, Salt Lake City, 1991-2010; Associate Dean, University Utah S.J. Quinney College Law, Salt Lake City, 1990-93; Associate Professor Law, University Utah S.J. Quinney College Law, Salt Lake City, 1985-91; Associate, Williams & Connolly LLP, Washington, 1981-85 **CR:** Visiting Associate Professor JFK School Government Harvard University, Cambridge, Massachusetts, 1989-90 Adv. Committee on Rules of Evidence Utah Supreme Court, 1987-93, Utah Constitutional Revision Commission, 1987-93, Adv. Committee on the Local Rules of Practice, US District Court Utah, 1993-97 Gubernatorial Candidate, State of Utah, 2004, Chair Utah Mine Safety Commission, 2007-08. **CIV:** Chairman U.N. Day for State of Utah, 1991 Member Univ. Committee on Tanner Lectures on Human Values University Utah, 1993-2000, Honors Program Adv. Committee University Utah, 1986-88, Adv. Board Hinckley Institute Politics University Utah, 1990-93, Governor Board, 1998-2006 Trustee Legal Aid Society of Salt Lake, 1986-93, President, 1987 Trustee TreeUtah, 1992-93 campaign manager Matheson for Governor, 1976, 1980 Vol. State Director Clinton/Gore '92. **CW:** Contributor Articles to Professional Journals **AW:** Recipient Up'n Comers award Zions Bank, 1991, Faculty Achievement Award Burlington Resources Foundation, 1993, Distinguished Service to Federal Bar Award Federal Bar Association, Utah Chapter, 1998, Special Recognition Award Utah Minority Bar Association, 1999, College Law Faculty Service Award 2009; Named One of Outstanding Young Men of Am., 1987, 1988; Rhodes Scholar. **MEM:** Member American Bar Association, Association Am. Law Schools (Chair Section on Mass Committee Law 1993), Utah State Bar, Salt Lake County Bar Association (Executive Committee 1986-92), Golden Key National Honor Society (Hon. 1990), Phi Beta Kappa **BA:** 1823 Stout St, Denver, CO, 80202

MATLIN, MARLEE, I: Media & Entertainment **PB:** Morton Grove **SC:** IL/USA **PT:** Don Matlin; Libby Matlin **MS:** Married **SPN:** Kevin Grandalski (August 29, 1993) **CH:** Brandon Joseph; Tyler Daniel; Sara Rose; Isabelle Jane **ED:** Attended William Rainey Harper College; LHD (hon.), Gallaudet University, 1987 **CR:** Spokeswomen, National Captioning Institute **CIV:** Board directors Very Special Arts, Starlight Foundation **CW:** Actress: (films) Children of a Lesser God, 1986 (Academy award for Best Actress in a Leading Role, 1987, Golden Globe award for Best Performance by an Actress in a Motion Picture - Drama, 1987), Walker, 1987, Linguini Incident, 1991, The Player, 1992, Hear No Evil, 1993, Snitch, 1996, It's My Party, 1996, In Her Defense, 1998, When Justice Fails, 1998, Freak City, 1999, Two Shades of Blue, 2000, Askari, 2001, Excision, 2012, The One I Love, 2014, How to Make Love Like an Englishman, 2014, Silent Knights, 2015 (TV films) Bridge to Silence, 1989, Against Her Will: The Carrie Buck Story, 1994, When Justice Fails, 1997, Dead Silence, 1997, Kiss My Act, 2001, Sweet Nothing in My Ear, 2008, (TV series) Reasonable Doubts, 1991-93, The L Word, 2007-09, Switched at Birth, 2011-14, (TV appearances) Picket Fences, 1993-96, Seinfeld, 1993, The Larry Sanders Show, 1992, Spin City, 1996, ER, 1999, Judging Amy, 1999, The West Wing, 2000?06, The Practice, 2000, Gideon's Crossing, 2001, Extreme Makeover: Home Edition, 2003, The Division, 2003, Law & Order: Special Victims Unit, 2004-05, Desperate Housewives, 2005, My Name is Earl, 2006-07, CSI: New York, 2006, Nip/Tuck, 2008, Family Guy (voice), 2012-14; performer Dancing with the Stars, 2008, Nip/Tuck, 2008, Sweet Nothing in my Ear, 2008, Seth & Alex's Comedy Show, 2009, The Celebrity Apprentice, 2011, Comedy Central Roast of Donald Trump, 2011, CSI; Crime Scene Investigation, Switched at Birth, 2011, Family Guy, 2012, Glee, 2014, Cosmos: A Spacetime Odyssey, 2014, The Magicians, 2017, Quantico, 2018; actress, executive prodr.: (TV films) Where the Truth Lies, 1999; executive prodr.: (TV films) Eddie's Million Dollar Cook-Off, 2003; author: Deaf Child Crossing, 2002, I'll Scream Later, 2009. **AW:** Recipient Star, Hollywood Walk of Fame, 2009

MATSUI, DORIS OKADA, T: U.S. Representative from California **I:** Government Administration/ Government Relations/Government Services **DOB:** 09/25/1944 **PB:** Dinuba, California **ED:** BA in Psychology, University California, Berkeley, 1966 **C:** Member, US Congress from 6th California District, 2013-; Member, Committee on Budget, Committee on Natural Resources; Member, US Congress from 5th California District, 2005-13; Government Relations Adv., Collier, Shannon & Scott PLLC, Washington, 1999-2005; Senior Adv. to President, The White House, Washington, 1993-99 **CR:** Member Clinton-Gore Transition Team, 1992-93 **CIV:** Board Regents, Smithsonian Institute, Past Board Trustees, Sacramento Children's Home, Past Board Trustees, Arena Stage, Past Board Trustees, Crocker Art Museum, Board Trustees, Meridian International Center, Board Trustees, Woodrow Wilson Center, **AW:** Recipient Rosalie Stern Award, University California Alumni Association, Newmyer Award, Sidwell Friends School, Mentor Award, University Southern California Sacramento School Pub. Administration, Advocates Award, National Association Mental Health, Action for Breast Cancer Awareness Award **MEM:** Mem.: Junior League Sacramento, Women's Club Sacramento **PA:** Democrat **BA:** 2312 Rayburn House Office Building, Washington, DC, 20515

MATTHEWS, CHRIS, T: Political Commentator, writer **I:** Media & Entertainment **DOB:** 12/17/1945 **PB:** Phila. **PT:** Son of Herbert Charles and Mary Teresa (Shields) Matthews; **ED:** LittD (hon.), University Rochester, 2014; Doctor (hon.), Chestnut Hill College; Doctor (hon.), Anna Maria College; Doctor (hon.), New England School Law; Doctor (hon.), Beaver College; Doctor (hon.), Fontbonne College; Doctor (hon.), Niagara University; Doctor (hon.), Loyola College, Maryland; Doctor (hon.), St. Leo University; LLD (hon.), College Holy Cross, Worcester, Massachusetts, 2003; BA in Economics, College Holy Cross, Worcester, Massachusetts, 1967 **C:** Host Hardball with Chris Matthews, MSNBC, 1999-; Host, syndicated program, The Chris Matthews Show, 2002-13; Host Hardball with Chris Matthews, CNBC, 1997-2002; Former national syndicated columnist, San Francisco Chronicle,; Bureau chief, columnist, San Francisco Examiner, Washington, 1987-2000; Political analyst, CBS This Morning, Washington, 1987; Aide to Speaker Tip O'Neill, US House of Representatives, Washington, 1981-87; Speechwriter to President Jimmy Carter, The White House, Washington, 1977-79; Staff assistant, US Senate Budget Committee, Washington, 1974-77; Staff member to Senator Edward Muskie, US Senate, Washington, 1973-74; Legis. assistant to Senator Frank Moss, US Senate, Washington, 1971-73 **CIV:** Trade devel. advisor, US Peace Corps, Swaziland, 1968-70 **CW:** Author: Kennedy & Nixon: The Rivalry That Shaped Postwar America, 1996, Hardball: How Politics is Really Played- Told By One Who Knows the Game, 1999, Now, Let Me Tell You What I Really Think, 2001, American: Beyond Our Grandest Notions, 2002, Life's a Campaign : What Politics Has Taught me About Friendship, Rivalry, Reputation and Success, 2007, Jack Kennedy: Elusive Hero, 2011, Tip and the Gipper:When Politics Worked, 2013; contributor articles to The New Republic, US News & World Report, New York Times, Christian Sci. Monitor, American Politics; actor: (films) Man of the Year, 2006(Books) Bobby Kennedy: A Raging Spirit, 2017 **AW:** Named one of The 50 Highest-Earning Political Figures, Newsweek, 2010; recipient Lincoln Award, Union League Philadelphia **PA:** Democrat

MATTIS, JAMES, T: U.S. Secretary of Defense **I:** Government Administration/Government Relations/Government Services **DOB:** 09/08/1950 **PB:** Seattle **SC:** WA/USA **ED:** Graduate, Amphibious Warfare School; Graduate, Command and Staff College; Graduate, National War College **C:** Secretary, U.S. Department of Defense, Washington, DC, 2017—Present; Executive Secretary, U.S. Department of Defense, Washington, DC, 1996-1998 **MIL:** Commander, U.S. Central Command (USCENTCOM), Tampa, FL, 2010—2013; Commander, U.S. Joint Forces Command (USJFCOM), Norfolk, VA, 2007—2010; Supreme Allied Commander For Transformation (SACT), NATO, Brussels, Belgium, 2007—2009; Advanced Through Grades To General, U.S. Marine Corps, 2007; Commanding General, U.S. Marine Corps I Marine Expeditionary Force, Commander, U.S. Marine Corps Forces Central Command, U.S. Marine Corps, Camp Pendleton, CA, 2006—2007; Commander, U.S. Marine Corps Combat Development Command, Deputy Commandant For Combat Development, U.S. Marine Corps, 2004—2006; Commander, First Marine Division, U.S. Marine Corps, 2003—2004; Commander, Seventh Marines Regiment, U.S. Marine Corps, 1994-1996; Commissioned Second Lieutenant, U.S. Marine Corps, 1972; Director, Manpower Plans & Policy Division, U.S. Marine Corps, Washington, DC; Senior Military Assistant To Deputy Secretary, U.S. Department of Defense; Commander, First Battalion, Seventh Marines Regiment, U.S. Marine Corps, Saudi Arabia; Assistant Division Operations Officer, Executive Officer, Seventh Marines Regiment, U.S. Marine Corps; Battalion Landing Team Assistant Operations Officer, First Marine Brigade, U.S. Marine Corps; Rifle & Weapons Platoon Commander, Third Marine Division, U.S. Marine Corps; Commander, Task Force 58, U.S. Marine Corps, Afghanistan; Commander, First Marine Expeditionary Brigade, U.S. Marine Corps, Afghanistan **AW:** Decorated Defense Distinguished Service Award With Oak Leaf Cluster, Navy Distinguished Service Medal, Defense Superior Service Medal, Legion Of Merit, Bronze Star With Combat V, Meritorious Service Medal With Two Gold Award Stars, Navy & Marine Corps Achievement Medal, Combat Action Ribbon, Presidential Unit Citation, Joint Meritorious Unit Award, Navy Unit Commendation, Navy & Marine Corps Meritorious Unit Commendation, Marine Corps Expeditionary Medal, National Defense Service Medal With Two Bronze Service Stars, Southwest Asia Service Medal With Two Bronze Service Stars, Afghanistan Campaign Medal, Iraq Campaign Medal, Global War On Terror Expeditionary Medal, Global War On Terrorism Service Medal, Humanitarian Service Medal, Sea Service Deployment Ribbon With Bronze Service Star, Marine Corps Recruiting Service Ribbon With Bronze Service Star, Kuwait Liberation Medal, Saudi Arabia, Kuwait Liberation Medal, Kuwait **ACH:** Achievements include serving in Operation Desert Storm, Operation Enduring Freedom and Operation Iraqi Freedom **BA:** Department of Defense, 2 N Rotary Road, Arlington, VA, 20301

MAYNE, THOM, T: Architect **I:** Architecture & Construction **DOB:** 01/19/1944 **PB:** Waterbury **SC:** Connecticut **PT:** Son of Walter and Bernice (Gornall) M.; Married Blythe Alison Mayne, August 8, 1981; **SPN:** Married Susan Burnham, September 10, 1964 (div. 1970); **CH:** 1 child, Richard; children: Sam, Cooper **ED:** MArch, Harvard University, 1978; BArch, University Southern California, 1968 **C:** Board directors, Southern California Institute Architecture, Santa Monica, California, 1983-; Member faculty, UCLA School Art and Architecture, Santa Monica, California, 1972-; Architect, Morphosis, Santa Monica, California, **CR:** Adjunct professor UCLA, 1993 member visiting faculty California State College, Pomona, 1971, Miami University, Ohio, 1982, Washington University, St. Louis, 1984, University Texas, Austin, 1984, University Pennsylvania, 1985, Columbia University, New York City, 1986, Harvard University, 1988, Clemson University, 1991, Yale University, 1991, UCLA, 1986, 92, University Illinois, Urbana-Champaign, 1992-93, Tech. University, Vienna, Austria, 1993, Berlage Institute, Amsterdam, 1993, Hochschule für Andgewandt Kunst, Vienna, 1991, 93 lecturer in field adjudicator numerous awards member President Barack Obama's Committee on Arts and Humanities, 2009 **CW:** Architectural one-man exhibitions include 2 AES Gallery, San Francisco, 1988, Cheney Cowles Museum, Spokane, Washington, 1989, Walker Arts Center, Minneapolis, 1989, Gallery of Architecture, LA, 1989, Contemporary Arts Center, Cincinnati, 1989, San Francisco Museum Modern Art, 1990, Graham Foundation, Chicago, 1990, Aedes Galerie and Architecture Forum, Berlin, 1990, Fenster Architekturgalerie, Frankfurt, Germany, 1990, Gallery MA, Toyko, 1990, Laguna (California) Art Museum, 1991, G201 Gallery, Ohio, 1991, 1-Space Gallery, Chicago, 1992, Sadock & Uzzan Galerie, Paris, 1992, Diane Farris Gallery, 1993; group exhibitions include Umwelt Galerie, Stuttgart, Germany, 1978, The Architectural Gallery, Venice, California, 1979, La Jolla (California) Museum of Contemporary Art, 1982, Institute Contemporary Arts, London, 1983, Architectural Association, London, 1983, National Academy of Design, New York City, 1983, 88, Museum Modern Art, San Francisco, 1983, California Museum Sci. and Industry, 1984, G.A. Gallery, Tokyo, 1985, 87, 90, Max Protech Gallery, New York City, 1985, 86, I.D.C., New York City, 1986, Axis Gallery, Tokyo, Milan, Paris, 1988, Pacific Design Center, LA, 1988, Australia Center for Contemporary Arts, Victoria, 1988, Cooper-Hewitt Museum, New York City, 1988, Aedes Galerie für Architektur und Raum, Berlin, 1988, Kirsten Kiser Gallery, 1988, 89, Visual Arts Ontario, Toronto, 1988, Gallery Functional Art, Santa Monica, California, 1989, Deutsches Architektur Museum, Frankfurt, 1989, US Information Agency, Moscow, 1989-90, Lameier Sculpture Park, St. Louis, 1989, Gwenda Jay Gallery, Chicago, 1990, Sadock & Uzzan Galerie, 1991, Bannatyne Gallery, Santa Monica, 1991, ROM Galleri for Arkitektur, Oslo, 1992, 65 Thompson Street Gallery, New York City, 1992; architectural projects include Sequoyah Education and Research Center, Santa Monica, 1977 (Progressive Architecture award 1974), Flores Residence, 1979 (Progressive Architecture award 1980), Sedlak Residence, 1980 (American Institute of Architects award 1981), Western Melrose Office Bldg, 1981 (Progresstive Architecture award 1982), Hermosa Beach Central Business District (Progressive Architecture award 1984), 72 Market Street Restaurant, 1983 (American Institute of Architects award 1985, CCAIA award 1986), Bergren Residence, 1984 (American Institute of Architects award 1985, CCAIA award 1986, National American Institute of Architects award 1986), Cedar Sinai Comprehensive Cancer

Center, L.A., 1988 (Progressive Architecture award 1987, American Institute of Architects award 1988, CCAIA award 1989), Arts Park Performing Pavilion, 1988, (Progressive Architecture award 1989), Leon Max Showroom, LA, 1988 (CCAIA award 1990, Architectural Record Interior award 1990), Club Post Nulear, Laguna Beach, California, 1988, Berlin Wall Competition, 1988, Expo '90 Folly, Osaka, Japan, 1989, The Emery Center Performing Arts, 1989, Temple University Commodity Credit Corp., Philadelphia, 1989, Politix, 1990 (American Institute of Architects award 1990), Salick Health Care Corp. Hdqs., 1990 (American Institute of Architects award 1992, CCAIA award 1993), Visual Performing Arts School at Thomas More College, Crestview, New York, 1990, MTV Studios, LA, 1990, Higashi Azabu Tower, Tokyo, 1991, Yuzen Vintage Car Museum, LA, 1991 (American Institute of Architects award 1993), Disney Institute and Town Center Competition, Orlando, Florida, 1991, Cranbrook Academy Gatehouse Competition (Pilkington Planar prize 1993), Spreebogen Master Plan, Berlin, 1993, Check Point Charlie Office Building, Berlin, 1993; contributor articles to professional journals, University of Toronto Graduate House, Toronto, Ontario, Canada, 2000, Hypo Alpe-Adria Center, Klagenfurt, Austria, 2002, Caltrans District 7 Headquarters, Los Angeles, California, 2004, Science Center School, Los Angeles, California, 2004, University of Cincinnati Student Recreation Center, Cincinnati, Ohio, 2006, Public housing in Madrid, Spain, 2006, Wayne L. Morse U.S. Courthouse, Eugene, Oregon, 2006, San Francisco Federal Building, San Francisco, California, 2006, Cahill Center for Astronomy and Astrophysics at the California Institute of Technology, Pasadena, California, 2009 National Oceanic Atmospheric Administration (NOAA) Satellite Operation Facility, Suitland, Maryland, 2007, New Academic Building at 41 Cooper Square, The Cooper Union for the Advancement of Science and Art, New York, New York, 2009, Perot Museum of Nature & Science, Victory Park, Dallas, Texas, 2012 Bill and Melinda Gates Hall, Cornell University, Ithaca, New York, 2013, Emerson College Los Angeles Center, Los Angeles, California, 2014 **AW:** Rome Prize fellow Am. Academy Rome, 1987; recipient Architecture award Am. Academy Arts and Letters, 1992, Pritzker Architecture prize Hyatt Foundation, 2005. **MEM:** Fellow Am. Academy Arts and Sciences; member American Institute of Architects (Gold medal, 2013), Am. Academy Design. **H:** Skiing, Traveling **PA:** Democrat **BA:** Morphosis Architecture, 3440 Wesley St, Culver City, CA, 90232

MAYOPOULOS, TIMOTHY J., T: Fannie Mae CEO **I:** Real Estate **DOB:** 03/07/1959 **PB:** Reading **PT:** Son of Harry B. and Eleanor Ida (Raifsnider) M.; Married Amy F. Lefkof, April 28, 1990; 1 child, Philip Alexander. **ED:** JD cum laude, New York University, 1984; AB with distinction, Cornell University, 1980 **CT:** Bar: New York 1985, US District Court (southern & eastern districts New York) 1987, US Court Appeals (2nd cir.) 1993, Supreme Court, 1993, US District Court (eastern & western districts Arkansas) 1994, US Court Appeals (8th cir.), 1995. **C:** President, CEO, Fannie Mae (Federal National Mortgage Association), Washington, 2012-; Executive vice president, general counsel, corp. secretary, chief administrative officer, Fannie Mae (Federal National Mortgage Association), Washington, 2009-12; Executive vice president, general counsel, Bank of America Corp., Charlotte, North Carolina, 2004-08; Managing director, general counsel, corp. investment bank, Americas, Deutsche Bank AG, 2002-04; Managing director, senior deputy general counsel, Americas, Credit Suisse First Boston,; Associate general counsel,

Donaldson, Lufkin & Jenrette, 1996; Associate ind. counsel, Office Ind. Counsel Kenneth Starr, 1994-96; Associate, Davis, Polk & Wardwell, New York City, 1986-94; Law clerk to Hon. William C. Conner, US District Court (southern district New York), New York City, 1984-86 **MEM:** Member Federal Bar Council, Association of Bar of City of New York, New York State Bar Association, Securities Industry Association, Order of the Coif. **BA:** Office of Fannie Mae, 3900 Wisconsin Ave, Washington, DC, 201510

MAYS, WILLIE HOWARD JR., T: Retired Professional Baseball Player **I:** Athletics **DOB:** 05/06/1931 **PB:** Westfield **SC:** Alabama **PT:** Son of William Howard and Ann M.; Married Margherite Wendell Chapman, 1956 (div. 1961), 1 adopted son, Michael; Married Mae Louise Allen, November 27, 1971 **ED:** LHD (hon.), Yale University, 2004 **C:** Special Assistant to the President, Ballys Casino Atlantic City,1979-1985; Special assistant to the president, team emissary, San Francisco Giants, 1986-; Retired, Major League Baseball, 1973; Outfielder, New York Mets, 1972-73; Outfielder, San Francisco Giants, 1958-72; Outfielder, New York Giants, 1951-57; Outfielder, Minneapolis Millers, Am. Association, 1951; Outfielder, Trenton Inter-State League, 1950-51; Outfielder, Birmingham Black Barons, 1948-50 **CIV:** Served with Army of the U.S., 1952-54. **CW:** Author: Willie Mays: My Life In and Out of Baseball, 1966, Say Hey: The Autobiography of Willie Mays, 1988,(Book) Willie Mays: The Life, The Legend, 2010 **AW:** Named MVP National League, 1954, 65, Player of Year Sporting News, 1954, Baseball Player of Decade, 1970, Male Athlete of Year Associated Press, 1954, National League Rookie of Year, 1951, Sportsman of Decade, Congress Racial Equality, 1991; named to National League All-Star Team, 1954-73, Rawlings All-Time Gold Glove Team, 2007; recipient Hickok Belt, 1954, Gold Glove award, 1957-68, 1st Commissioner's award, 1970, Roberto Clemente award, 1971, Golden Plate awarded to America's Captains of Achievement by Am. Academy Achievement, 1976, Spirit of Life award City of Hope, 1988, Legendary Star award HBO Video, Golden Bat award to commemorate 600 home runs, Presidential Medal of Freedom, The White House, 2015; inducted into Alabama Sports Hall of Fame, Black Hall of Fame, 1973, Baseball Hall of Fame, 1979, California Hall of Fame, 2007,Beacon of Life Award, 2010 **ACH:** Achievements include member of World Series championship winning New York Giants, 1954; leading the Nationl League in: batting average, 1954; triples, 1954, 1955, 1957; home runs, 1955, 1962, 1964, 1965; stolen bases, 1956-59; runs, 1958, 1961; hits, 1960; holding Major League Baseball's record for putouts by an outfielder (7095)

MCADAM, LOWELL CLAYTON, T: CEO **I:** Telecommunications **CN:** Verizon **DOB:** 05/28/1954 **ED:** MBA, University of San Diego, 1983; BS in Engineering, Cornell University, 1976 **CT:** EIT **C:** Chairman, President, CEO, Verizon Communications, Inc., 2012-Present; Chairman, Verizon Wireless, Inc., 2010-Present; President, CEO, Verizon Communications, Inc., 2011; President, COO, Verizon Communications, Inc., 2010-2011; President, CEO, Verizon Wireless, Inc., 2007-2010; Executive Vice President, COO, Verizon Wireless, Inc., 2000-2007; Executive Director, International Applications and Operations, Airtouch Communications, 1993; Pacific Bell, 1983-1993; Vice President, Bay Area Marketing, Pacific Bell; President, CEO, Primeco Personal Commission; COO, Primeco Personal Commission; Vice President, International Operations, Airtouch Communications; General Manager, South Bay Customer Services, Pacific Bell **CR:** (Board of Directors) Verizon

Communications, Inc., 2011-Present, Verizon Wireless, Inc., 2003-Present, Cellular Telecommunications & Internet Association (CTIA)

MCAVOY, JOHN JOSEPH, T: CEO **I:** Oil & Energy **CN:** Con Edison **DOB:** 08/22/1960 **PB:** Bronx **SC:** NY/USA **PT:** Son of Bernard C. and Mary B. McA. **MS:** Married **SPN:** Kathleen F., May 30, 1981 **CH:** Kelly Frances, Maureen Nicole, Siobhan Mary, Jacqueline Marie **ED:** MBA, New York University, 1987; BS in Engineering, Manhattan College, Bronx, 1980 **CT:** Lic. senior reactor operator U.S. Nuclear Regulatory Commission, 1984-95; system operator North American Electric Reliability Corp., 2005-10 **C:** President, CEO, Consolidated Edison, Inc., New York City, 2014-; President, CEO, Orange & Rockland Utilities, Inc. (O&R), New York, 2012-13; Senior vice president central operations, Consolidated Edison of New York, 2009-12; Vice president system & transmission operations, Consolidated Edison of New York, 2006-09; Operations evaluator, Institute Nuclear Power Operations, Atlanta, 1988-90; Plant manager, Indian Point 2 Nuclear Power Plant, Con Edison Co., Buchanan, New York, 1995-97; Operations manager, Indian Point 2 Nuclear Power Plant, Con Edison Co., Buchanan, New York, 1992-95; Director quality assurance, Indian Point 2 Nuclear Power Plant, Con Edison Co., Buchanan, New York, 1990-92; Shift supervisor, Indian Point 2 Nuclear Power Plant, Con Edison Co., Buchanan, New York, 1985-88 **CR:** Board directors Consolidated Edison, Inc., 2013- system operator North American Electric Reliability Corp., 2005-10 senior reactor operations US Nuclear Regulatory Commission, 1984-95 **CIV:** Youth coach Mahopac (New York) Sports Association, 1994- trustee Intrepid Air, Sea & Space Museum, 2010- **BA:** 4 Irving Place, New York, NY, 10003

MCBRIDE, DANNY, T: Actor **I:** Media & Entertainment **DOB:** 12/29/1976 **PB:** Statesboro **SC:** GA/USA **ED:** Attended, North Carolina School of Arts **C:** Night manager, Holiday Inn, Burbank, California **CW:** Actor: (films) All the Real Girls, 2003, Hot Rod, 2007, The Heartbreak Kid, 2007, Drillbit Taylor, 2008, Pineapple Express, 2008, Tropic Thunder, 2008, Land of the Lost, 2009, Despicable Me (voice), 2010, Due Date, 2010, Kung Fu Panda (voice), 2011, 30 Minutes or Less, 2011, As I Lay Dying, 2013, This Is the End, 2013, The Sound and the Fury, 2014, Don Verdean, 2015, Aloha, 2015, Hell and Back (voice), 2015, Rock the Kasbah, 2015, Sausage Party (voice), 2016, Zeroville, 2016, The Angry Birds Movie (voice), 2016, In Dubious Battle, 2016, The Disaster Artist, 2017, Alien: Covenant -Prologue: Last Supper, 2017, Alien: Covenant, 2017, Arizona, 2018; (TV films) Clear History, 2013; actor, writer (films) The Foot Fist Way, 2006, actor, executive producer Your Highness, 2011, actor, executive producer, writer (TV series) Eastbound & Down, 2009-2013, Vice Principals, 2016-2017; executive prodr.: (films) The Comedy, 2012, Prince Avalanche, 2013, Joe, 2013, Manglehorn, 2014, Masterminds, 2016; (documentaries) Hot Sugar's Cold World, 2015

MCBRIDE, MARTINA, T: Country Music Singer **I:** Media & Entertainment **DOB:** 07/29/1966 **PB:** Medicine Lodge **SC:** KS/USA **PT:** Daughter of Daryl and Jeanne (Clark) Schiff; **C:** Backup singer, Garth Brooks, 1992-93; Vocalist, assorted bands, Wichita, Kansas,; Vocalist, Schiffters, 1975-86 **CW:** Singer: (albums) The Time Has Come, 1992, The Way That I Am, 1993, Wild Angels, 1995, Evolution, 1997, Martina McBride Christmas, 1998, Emotion, 1999, White Christmas, 1999, Greatest Hits, 2001, Martina, 2003, Timeless, 2005, Waking Up Laughing, 2007, Martina McBride: Live In

Concert, 2008, Shine, 2009, Eleven, 2011, The Classic Christmas Album, 2013, Everlasting, 2014, Reckless, 2016, (albums with various artists) Girls Night Out, 1999; author: (cookbook) Around the Table: Recipes and Inspiration for Gatherings Throughout the Year, 2015 **AW:** Nominee Female Vocalist Year, Am. Music Awards, 2003, Country Music Association, 2001, 1999, 1998, 1996, Horizon award, 1994, Top Female Vocalist, Academy Country Music, 2001, 2000, 1998, 1993, Video Year for "Concrete Angel", Country Music Association, 2003, Best Female Country Vocal Performance for "Blessed", Grammy, 2002, Single Year for "Blessed", Country Music Association, 2002, Best Country Female Vocal Performance for "I Love You", Grammy, 1999, Video Year for "A Broken Wing", Academy Country Music, 1999, Song Year for "A Broken Wing", 1999, Single Year for "A Broken Wing", 1999, Country Music Association, 1998, Video Year for "A Broken Wing", 1998, Best Country Collaboration with Vocals for "Still Holding You" with Clint Black, Grammy, 1997, Vocal Event Year for "Still Holding On" with Clint Black, Country Music Association, 1997, Best Country Female Vocal Performance for "Safe In The Arms of Love", Grammy, 1995, Album Year for "Wild Angels", Country Music Association, 1996, Vocal Event Year for "On My Own" with Reba McEntire, Linda Davis, and Trisha Yearwood., 1996, Best Country Collaboration with Vocals for "Own My Own" with Reba McEntire, Linda Davis, and Trisha Yearwood, Grammy, 1995, Video Year for "Independence Day", Academy Country Music, 1994, Best Country Song for "Independence Day", Grammy, 1994; recipient Favorite Female Artist, Country Weekly, 2003, Favorite Female Artist, Country, Am. Music Awards, 2003, Best Female Artist, Country Radio Music Awards, 1996, Country Female Artist Year, Billboard Music Award, 2002, Female Vocalist Year award, Country Music Association, 2004, 2003, Female Vocalist Year, Country Music Association Award, 2002, Top Female Vocalist, Academy Country Music award, 2004, 2003, Academy Country Music, 2002, Female Video Year for "Concrete Angel", CMT Flameworthy Award, 2003, Female Video Year for "Blessed", CMT Flameworthy Awards, 2002, Video Year for "Safe In The Arms of Love", Nashville Music Awards, 1996, Country Album Year for "Wild Angels", 1996, Best Southern Gospel, Country Gospel or Bluegrass Gospel for "Amazing Grace - A Country Salute To Gospel", Grammy Awards, 1995, Gold Clio for Country Music Video Year for "Independence Day", Clio Awards, 1995, Video Year for "Independence Day", TNN Music City News Award, 1995, Nashville Music Awards, 1995, Best Video Year for "Independence Day", Great Brit. Music Awards, 1994, Music Video Year for "Independence Day", Country Music Association Awards, 1994, Breakthrough Artist Video for "My Baby Loves Me", Music Row Ind. Summit Award, 1994 **BA:** Big Machine Records, 1219 16th Ave S, Nashville, TN, 37212

MCCAIN, JOHN, T: Former U.S. Senator from Arizona **I:** Government Administration/Government Relations/Government Services **DOB:** 08/29/1936 **PB:** Canal Zone **SC:** Panama **YOP:** 2018-08-25 **PT:** Son of John Sidney and Roberta (Wright) McCain; **ED:** Grad. U.S. Naval Academy, 1958; Grad., National War College, 1974; Degree (hon.), Johns Hopkins University, 1999; Degree (hon.), Colgate University, 2000; Degree (hon.), University of Penn., 2001; Degree (hon.), Wake Forest University, 2002; Degree (hon.), University of Southern California, 2004 **C:** Chairman, Senate Armed Services Committee, 2015-; Member, U.S. Senate Homeland Security & Governmental Affairs Committee, 2009—; Chairman, U.S. Senate Indian Affairs Com-

mittee, 1995—1997; Ranking Member, U.S. Senate Armed Services Committee, 2009—2015; Member, U.S. Congress from 1st Arizona District, 1983—1986; Director, Navy Senate Liaison Office, Washington, DC, 1977-81; Member, U.S. Senate Energy & National Resources Committee, 2009—; Chairman, U.S. Senate Armed Services Committee, 2015—; Member, U.S. Senate Armed Services Committee, 1987—; U.S. Senator from Arizona, 1987—; Republican Nominee for President, US Presidential Election, 2008; Chairman, U.S. Senate Commerce Sci. & Transportation Committee, 2003—2005; Chairman, U.S. Senate Commerce Sci. & Transportation Committee, 1997—2001; Chairman, U.S. Senate Indian Affairs Committee, 2005—2007 **CR:** Board of Directors Nixon Center for Peace & Freedom, Community Assistance League, Phoenix, 1981—; Chairman International Republican Institute, 1993—; Candidate for Republican Presidential Nomination, 2000; Member Commission on Intelligence Capabilities of U.S. Regarding Weapons of Mass Destruction, 2004; Speaker Republican National Convention, New York City, 2004 **MIL:** Served in U.S. Navy, 1958—81, Prisoner of War, 1967—73, Vietnam, Became Captain U.S. Navy, 1977 **CW:** Co-author (with Mark Salter): Faith of My Fathers, 1999, Worth the Fighting For: What I Learned from Mavericks, Heroes, and Politics, 2002, Why Courage Matters: The Way to a Braver Life, 2004, Character Is Destiny: Inspiring Stories Every Young Person Should Know and Every Adult Should Remember, 2005, Hard Call: Great Decisions and the Extraordinary People Who Made Them, 2007; Appeared in By the People: The Election of Barack Obama, 2009 **AW:** Decorated Legion of Merit, Silver Star, Bronze Star, Purple Heart, Distinguished Flying Cross, Vietnamese Legion of Honor; Named Cancer Survivor of Year, Cancer Rsch./Treatment Fund, 2004; Named One of The 25 Most Influential People in America, TIME magazine, 1997, The 100 Most Influential People in the World, 2006, 2008, The 10 People Who Mattered, Newsweek, 2008; Recipient Excellence in Public Service Award, American Academy Pediatrics, 1999, Friendship Award, League Latin American Citizens, 1999, Freedom Award, Intrepid Museum Foundation, 1999, John F. Kennedy Profile in Courage Award, John F. Kennedy Library Foundation, 1999, Paul H. Douglas Ethics in Government Award, University of Illinois Institute Government & Pub. Affairs, 2000, William Penn Mott Junior Park Leadership Award, National Parks Conservation Association, 2001, Citizen Patriot Award, Citizen Patriot Organization, 2003, Arthur T. Marix Congressional Leadership Award, Military Officers Association of America, 2004, Economic Patriot Award, Concord Coalition, 2004, Evelyn F. Burkey Award, Writers Guild of America East, 2004, Distinguished Leadership Award, American Ireland Fund, 2005 **MEM:** Mem.: VFW, Society of the Cincinnati, Am. Legion **PA:** Republican **BA:** The Office of John Mccain, 218 Russell Senate Office Building, Washington, DC, 20510

MCCARRICK, THEODORE EDGAR CARDINAL, T: Cardinal, Archbishop Emeritus **I:** Religious **DOB:** 07/07/1930 **PB:** NYC **PT:** Son of Theodore Egan and Margaret T. (McLaughlin) McCarrick. **ED:** PhD in Sociology, Catholic University, 1963; MA in Social Sciences, Catholic University, 1960; AM in History, Saint Joseph's Seminary, 1958; AB in Philosophy, Saint Joseph's Seminary, 1954 **C:** Cardinal-priest, of Santi Nereo e Archilleo (Saints Nereus and Achilleus), 2001-; Archbishop emeritus, of Washington, 2006-; Elevated to cardinal, 2001; Archbishop, of Washington, 2001-06; Appointed archbishop, of Washington, DC, 2000; Superior, of Turks and Caicos, Antilles, 1998; Archbishop, of Newark, 1986-2000; First bishop, of Metuchen, New Jersey, 1982-86; Appointed first bishop, of Metuchen, 1981; Ordained, of Rusibisir (Rusibisir), 1977; Appointed Titular Bishop, of Rusibisir (Rusibisir), 1977; President, Catholic University Puerto Rico, 1965-69; Domestic prelate, 1965; Instructor department sociology, Catholic University America, 1961-65; Assistant to rector, director development, Catholic University America, 1963-65; Dean students, Catholic University America, 1961-63; Assistant chaplain, Catholic University America, Washington DC, 1959-61; Auxiliary bishop, of New York, 1977-81; Secretary to Terrence Cardinal Cooke, of New York, 1971-77; Associate secretary for education, of New York, 1969-71; Ordained priest, of New York, 1958 **CR:** Chairman domestic policy committee U.S. Conference of Catholic Bishops, 2002-05, chairman international policy committee, 1996-99, chairman Committee Aid to Churches in Central and Eastern Europe, 1992-96 Episcopal promoter Apostleship of the Sea, 1989-92 member U.S. Committee on International Religious Freedom, 1999-2001, U.S. Secretary of State's Advisory Committee on Religious Freedom Abroad, 1996-99, Federal Commission for Study of Migration and Economic Development, 1989 chairman Puerto Rico Advisory Council on Technical and Vocational Education, 1968-69, Governor's Commission for Higher Education in Puerto Rico, 1968, U.S. Bishops Committee on Migration, 1992-95, 1986-89 chaplain Knights of Malta, 1978-82 member policy board Pontifical Commission for Migrants and Refugees, 1987, Washington Consortium, Peace Corps, 1962-63 **CIV:** President, Papal Foundation, 1997- Secretary-treasurer, Papal Foundation, 1988-96 **AW:** Decorated Officer of the Order of Cedars of Lebanon President of Lebanon; recipient Global Citizen award, Whitehead School Diplomacy & International Relations, Seton Hall University, 2007, Eleanor Roosevelt award for Human Rights, 2000

MCCARTHY, CORMAC, T: Writer **I:** Writing and Editing **DOB:** 07/20/1933 **PB:** Providence **PT:** Son of Charles Joseph and Gladys (McGrail) McCarthy **MIL:** Served in US Air Force, 1953-57 **CW:** Author: (novels) The Orchard Keeper, 1965 (William Faulkner Foundation award, 1965), Outer Dark, 1968, Child of God, 1974, Suttree, 1979, Blood Meridian, or The Evening Redness in the West, 1985, All the Pretty Horses, 1992 (National Book award for fiction, 1992, National Book Critics Circle award for fiction, 1993), The Crossing, 1994, Cities of the Plain, 1998, No Country for Old Men, 2005, The Road, 2006 (James Tait Black Memorial Prize for fiction, 2006, Pulitzer Prize for fiction, 2007, Quill Book award for general fiction, 2007), (screenplays) The Gardener's Son, 1976, (plays) The Stonemason, 1995, The Sunset Limited, 2006 **AW:** Named a MacArthur Fellow, John D. & Catherine T. MacArthur Foundation, 1981; recipient PEN/Saul Bellow award for Achievement in Am. Fiction, 2008, Jean Stein award, American Academy of Arts and Letters, 1991; grantee creative writing fellowship, John Simon Guggenheim Memorial Foundation, 1969, Traveling fellowship, American Academy of Arts and Letters, 1965-66, Ingram-Merrill Foundation, 1959-60, Pulitzer Prize for Fiction, 2007, IMPAC Award, 2007-08, Maltese Falcon Award, 2008, Premio Ignotus, 2008, Best of the James Tait Black, 2012 **BA:** ICM Partners, 10250 Constellation Blvd., Los Angeles, CA, 90067

MCCARTHY, KEVIN OWEN, T: House Majority Leader **I:** Government Administration/Government Relations/Government Services **DOB:** 01/26/1965 **PB:** Bakersfield **SC:** CA/USA **ED:** MBA, California State University, Bakersfield, 1994; BBA, California State University, Bakersfield, 1989; Student, Bakersfield College **C:** Majority Leader, 2014-Present; U.S. Congress From 23rd California District, 2013-Present; Assistant Majority Leader (Majority Whip), 2011-2014; Chief Deputy Whip, 2009-2011; Assistant Whip, 2006-2009; U.S. Congress From 22nd California District, 2007-2013; Minority Leader, California State Assembly, 2004-2006; District 32, California State Assembly, 2002-2007; District Director To Rep. Bill Thomas, U.S. House Of Representatives; Owner, Kevin O's Deli; Owner, Bakersfield Batting Range **CR:** Chairman, Young Republican National Federation, 1999-2001 **CIV:** Trustee, District Board, Kern Community College, 2000-2002; Kern County Republican Central Committee, 1992-Present; Coach, YMCA, 1999-Present; Executive Director, McCarthy Foundation, 2000-Present; Board of Directors, Head Start, Board of Directors, First Book, 2001-Present **CW:** Co-Author, (With Eric Cantor & Paul Ryan) Young Guns: A New Generation of Conservative Leaders, 2010 **AW:** The Ten Members to Watch in the 112th Congress, Roll Call, 2011, The 50 Politicos to Watch, Politico, 2010 **MEM:** Rotary **PA:** Republican **BA:** Office of Kevin McCarthy, 2421 Rayburn House Office Building, Washington, DC, 20515

MCCARTHY, MELISSA ANN, T: Actress **I:** Media & Entertainment **DOB:** 08/26/1970 **PB:** Plainfield **SC:** NJ/USA **PT:** Michael McCarthy; Sandra McCarthy **CW:** Actress, Executive Producer, Writer, "The Boss" (2016); Actress, "Ghostbusters" (2016); Actress, "Spy" (2015); Actress, Producer, Writer, "Tammy" (2014); Actress, "St. Vincent" (2014); Actress, "Identity Thief" (2013); Actress, "The Hangover Part III" (2013); Actress, "The Heat" (2013); Actress, "This Is 40" (2012); Actress, "Bridesmaids" (2011); Actress, "Mike & Molly" (2010-2016); TV Appearance, "Private Practice" (2010); Actress, "Life as We Know It" (2010); Actress, "The Back-up Plan" (2010); TV Appearance, "Rita Rocks" (2009); Actress, "Just Add Water" (2008); Actress, "Pretty Ugly People" (2008); Actress, "Samantha Who?" (2007-2009); Actress, "The Captain" (2007); Actress, "The Nines" (2007); Actress, "Cook-Off!" (2006); TV Appearance, "Curb Your Enthusiasm" (2004); Actress, "The Life of David Gale" (2003); TV Appearance, "Kim Possible" (2002-2005); Actress, "Pumpkin" (2002); Actress, "The Third Wheel" (2002); Actress, "White Oleander" (2002); TV Appearance, "The Lost World" (2001); Actress, "Gilmore Girls" (2000-2007); TV Appearance, "D.C." (2000); Actress, "Drowning Mona" (2000); Actress, "Charlie's Angels" (2000); Actress, "Go" (1999) **AW:** Named, Favorite Comedic TV Actress, People's Choice Awards (2016); Named, Favorite Comedic Movie Actress (2015-2016); Named, One of the 100 Most Powerful Women in Entertainment, Hollywood Reporter (2013); Recipient, Best Supporting Actress Award, Boston Society of Film Critics (2011); Named, One of the 100 Most Powerful Women in Entertainment, Hollywood Reporter (2011)

MCCARTNEY, PAUL, T: Musician **I:** Media & Entertainment **DOB:** 06/18/1942 **PB:** Liverpool **PT:** Son of James and Mary Patricia (Mohin) McCartney; **ED:** MusD (hon.), Yale University, 2008 **C:** Solo artist, 1970-; Singer, guitarist, Wings, 1971-81; Singer, guitarist, The Beatles, 1962-70; Singer, guitarist, other various groups, 1956-62; Singer, guitarist, Silver Beatles,; Singer, guitarist, Johnny and the Moondogs,; Singer, guitarist, Quarrymen, **CW:** Musician: (albums with The Beatles) Please Please Me, 1963, Introducing... The Beatles, 1964, Meet The Beatles!, 1964, The Beatles' Second Album, 1964, A Hard Day's Night, 1964, Help!, 1965, Rubber Soul, 1965, Revolver, 1966, Sergeant Pepper's Lonely Hearts Club Band, 1967 (Best Pop Vocal Album, Best Album of Year, Grammy Awards, 1968), Magical Mystery Tour, 1967, The Beatles (commonly known as The White Album), 1968, Yellow Submarine, 1969, Abbey Road, 1969, Let It Be, 1970 (Best Score Soundtrack Album for a Motion Picture, Grammy Awards, 1971), (songs) Love Me Do, 1962, Please Please Me, 1963, She Loves You, 1963, I Want to Hold Your Hand, 1963, All My Loning, 1964, Can't Buy Me Love, 1964, A Hard Day's Night, 1964 (Best Performance by a Vocal Group, Grammy Awards, 1965), Eight Days a Week, 1965, Yesterday, 1965, Michelle, 1965 (Best Song of Year, Grammy Awards, 1965), We Can Work It Out, 1965, Eleanor Rigby, 1966 (Best Contemporary Solo Vocal Performance, Grammy Awards, 1965), Penny Lane, 1967, All You Need Is Love, 1967, Hey Jude, 1968, Let It Be, 1970, (albums with Wings) Wild Life, 1971, Red Rose Speedway, 1973, Band on the Run, 1973 (Best Historical Album, Grammy Awards, 2012), Venus and Mars, 1975, Wings at the Speed of Sound, 1976, London Town, 1978, Back to the Egg, 1979, (songs) Live and Let Die, 1973 (Best Instrumental Arrangement Accompanying Vocalist(s), Grammy Awards, 1974), Jet, 1973, Band on the Run, 1974 (Best Pop Performance by a Duo or Group with Vocal, Grammy Awards, 1975), (solo albums) McCartney, 1970, Ram, 1971, McCartney II, 1980, Tug of War, 1982, Pipes of Peace, 1983, Give My Regards to Broad Street, 1984, Press to Play, 1986, Flowers in the Dirt, 1989, Off the Ground, 1993, Flaming Pie, 1997, Run Devil Run, 1999, Driving Rain, 2001, Chaos and Creation in the Backyard, 2005, Memory Almost Full, 2007, Kisses on the Bottom, 2012 (Best Traditional Pop Vocal Album, Grammy Awards, 2013), New, 2013, (songs) Maybe I'm Amazed, 1970, Cut Me Some Slack (with Dave Grohl, Krist Novoselic and Pat Smear), 2013 (Best Rock Song, Grammy Awards, 2014); appeared in (films) A Hard Day's Night, 1964, Help!, 1965, (TV films) Magical Mystery Tour, 1967, (animated feature film) Yellow Submarine, 1968, (documentaries) Let It Be, 1970, Good Ol' Freda, 2013, actor, writer (films) Give My Regards to Broad Street, 1984, writer, producer (animated films films) Rupert and the Frog Song, 1984, Eat the Rich, 1987, Tuesday, 2001, Al's Brain in 3-D, 2009, Pirates of the Caribbean: Dead Men Tell No Tales, 2017, Tropical Island Hum, 2004; author: Blackbird Singing: Poems and Lyrics, 1965-2001, 2002, Wingspan: Paul McCartney's Band on the Run, 2002; co-author: Each One Believing: Paul McCartney On Stage, Off Stage, and Backstage, 2004, (children's book) High in the Clouds: An Urban Furry Tail, 2005, (Television) The Simpsons, 1995, SNL, 2005, 30 Rock, 2012, Bojack Horseman, 2015 **AW:** Decorated Knight Commander (KBE), 1997, Order of Brit. Empire (OBE), 1965; named Songwriter of Year, American Society Composers, Authors & Publishers, 2009; recipient Best Music Film award for Live Kisses, Grammy Awards, 2014, Lifetime Achievement award (as member of The Beatles), 2014, French Legion of Honour, Government of France, 2012, Kennedy Center Honors, John F. Kennedy Center Performing Arts, Washington, 2010, Gershwin prize, Libr. Congress, 2010, BRIT award for Outstanding Contribution to Music, Brit. Phonographic Industry, 2008, Lifetime Achievement award, People for Ethical Treatment of Animals (PETA), 1996, Award of Merit, American Music Awards, 1993, Grammy Lifetime Achievement award, National Academy Recording Arts & Scis., 1990, Ivor Novello award, Brit. Academy Songwriters, Composers & Authors, 1989; fellow Brit. Academy Songwriters, Composers & Authors, 2000, inducted, Rock & Roll Hall of Fame (as solo artist), 1999, Rock & Roll Hall of Fame (as member of The Beatles), 1988, Musicares Person of the Year, 2012 **MEM:** Fellow:

American Academy Arts & Sciences, Royal College Music; mem.: Royal Academy Music (hon.) **BA:** Paul Freundlich Associates Media, 451 Greenwich Street, New York, NY, 10013

MCCASKILL, CLAIRE CONNER, T: U.S. Senator from Missouri **I:** Government Administration/Government Relations/Government Services **DOB:** 07/25/1953 **PB:** Rolla, Missouri, July 25, 1953 **PT:** Daughter of William Young and Betty Anne (Ward) McCaskill **ED:** JD, University Missouri, Columbia, 1978; BS in Political Sci., University Missouri, Columbia, 1975 **C:** Ranking Member, Senate Homeland Security Committtee, 2017-; US Senator from Missouri, 2007-; Auditor, State of Missouri, Jefferson City, 1999-2007; Member, Missouri House of Reps., 1982-88; County prosecutor, County of Jackson, Missouri, 1993-99; Assistant prosecutor, County of Jackson, Missouri; Private law practice, 1989-91; Law clerk, Missouri Court Appeals (western district), Kansas City, 1978-79 **PA:** Democrat

MCCAUL, MICHAEL THOMAS, T: Chair of the House Homeland Security Committee,U.S. Representative from Texas **I:** Government Administration/Government Relations/Government Services **DOB:** 01/14/1962 **PB:** Dallas **ED:** Attended, Harvard University John F. Kennedy School Government; JD, St. Mary's University, San Antonio, 1987; BS, Trinity University, San Antonio, 1984 **C:** Chairman, US House Homeland Security Committee, 2013-; Member, US Congress from 10th Texas District, 2005-; Member, US House Ethics Committee (formerly House Standards of Official Conduct Committee),; Federal prosecutor, pub. integrity section, US Department Justice, Washington, 1990-99; Chief Terrorism & National Security section, State of Texas, 2002; Deputy attorney general, State of Texas, 2000-02; Special assistant attorney general, State of Texas, 1999-2000; Deputy attorney general, State of Texas, Austin, Texas, 1987-90 **CR:** Vice chairman US-Mex. Inter-Parliamentary Group, 2005 **PA:** Republican **BA:** Office of Michael Mccaul, 2001 Rayburn House Office Building, Washington, DC, 20515

MCCLINTOCK, TOM, T: U.S. Representative from California **I:** Government Administration/Government Relations/Government Services **DOB:** 07/10/1956 **PB:** Bronxville, New York **PT:** Son of Thomas Miller and Marianne (Christy) McClintock; **ED:** BA, UCLA, 1978 **C:** Member, US Congress from 4th California District, Washington, 2009-; Member, Committee on Transportation and Infrastructure; Member District 19, California State Senate, 2000-08; Republican whip, California House of Reps., 1984-89; Member District 38, California House of Reps., 1996-2000; Member District 28, California House of Reps., 1982-92; Chief of staff to Senator Ed Davis, California State Senate, 1980-82 **CR:** Director economic & regulatory affairs National Tax Limitations Foundation, 1995-96 director Center California Taxpayer, 1992-94 chairman Ventura County Republican Party, 1979-81 political columnist Thousand Oaks News Chronicle, 1976-80 local government consultant Conejo Valley Board Realtors, 1975-76 resolution chairman California State Republican Central Committee, 1985-92, member, 1973-2001 charter state president California State Republican Org., 1973-74 **AW:** Recipient Medal of Merit, Ventura County Peace Officers Association, Benjamin Franklin award, California Printing Industry **PA:** Republican **BA:** 1406 Longworth House Office Building, Washington, DC, 20515

MCCOLLUM, BETTY, T: U.S. Representative from Minnesota **I:** Government Administration/Government Relations/Government Services **DOB:** 07/12/1954 **PB:** Mpls. **ED:** BS in Education, College St. Catherine, 1987 **C:** Member, U.S. Congress from Minnesota 4th District, Washington, 2001-; Member, Committee on International Relations; Member education and workforce committee, resources committee; Member, Appropriations Committee; Member rules and administrative legis. committee, Minnesota House Reps.; Chair legis. commission on economic status of women, Minnesota House Reps.; Assistant majority leader, Minnesota House Reps.; Member transportation and transit committee, Minnesota House Reps.; Member general legis. committee, vet. affairs and elections committee, Minnesota House Reps.; Member education committee, environmental and natural resources committee, Minnesota House Reps.; Member, Minnesota House Reps., 1992-2000; Retail store manager, Minnesota **CIV:** Member, St. Croix Valley Council Girl Scouts **MEM:** Mem.: Am. Legion Auxiliary, VFW Auxiliary **PA:** Dfl

MCCONAUGHEY, MATTHEW, I: Media & Entertainment **DOB:** 11/04/1969 **PB:** Uvalde **SC:** TX/USA **PT:** Jim McConaughey; Kay McConaughey **MS:** Married **SPN:** Camila Alves (June 9, 2012) **CH:** Levi, Vida, Livingston **ED:** BA in Film Production, University Texas, Austin, 1993 **CW:** Actor: (films) My Boyfriend's Back, 1993, Dazed and Confused, 1993, The Return of The Texas Chainsaw Massacre, 1994, Angels in the Outfield, 1994, Submission, 1995, Judgement, 1995, Boys on the Side, 1995, Lone Star, 1996, A Time to Kill, 1996, Larger than Life, 1996, Glory Daze, 1996, Scorpion Spring, 1997, Amistad, 1997, Contact, 1997, The Rebel, 1998, The Newton Boys, 1998, Making Sandwiches, 1998, South Beach, 1999, Last Flight of the Raven, 1999, Edtv, 1999, U-571, 2000, The Wedding Planner, 2001, Thirteen Conversations About One Thing, 2001, Frailty, 2001, Reign of Fire, 2002, How To Lose a Guy in 10 Days, 2003, Tiptoes, 2003, Two for the Money, 2005, Failure to Launch, 2006, We Are Marshall, 2006, Fool's Gold, 2008, Ghosts of Girlfriends Past, 2009, The Lincoln Lawyer, 2011, Bernie, 2011 (New York Film Critics Cir. award for Best Supporting Actor, 2012, National Society Film Critics award for Best Supporting Actor, 2013), Killer Joe, 2011, Mud, 2012, Magic Mike, 2012 (New York Film Critics Cir. award for Best Supporting Actor, 2012, National Society Film Critics award for Best Supporting Actor, 2013), The Paperboy, 2012, Dallas Buyers Club, 2013 (Golden Globe award for Best Performance by an Actor in a Motion Picture - Drama, 2014, Critics' Choice award for Best Actor, 2014, Screen Actors Guild award for Outstanding Performance by a Male Actor in a Leading Role, 2014, Academy award for Best Actor in a Leading Role, 2014), The Wolf of Wall Street, 2013, Interstellar, 2014, The Sea of Trees, 2015, Free State of Jones, 2016, Gold, 2016, Kubo and the Two Strings (voice), 2016, Sing, Gold, 2016, The Dark Tower, 2017, White Boy Rick, 2018, Serenity, 2018, The Beach Bum, 2018 (voice), 2016; actor, executive prodr.: (films) Sahara, 2005, (TV series) True Detective, 2014-15; actor, prodr.: (films) Surfer, Dude, 2008; actor: (TV films) Absolute Evel: The Evel Knievel Story, 2005; (TV appearances) Unsolved Mysteries, 1992, (voice) King of the Hill, 1999, Sex and the City, 2000, Eastbound & Down, 2010-12; (TV documentary) Freedom: A History of Us, 2003. **AW:** Named Sexiest Man Alive, People magazine, 2005; named one of The 100 Most Influential People in the World, TIME magazine, 2014; recipient Star, Hollywood Walk of Fame, 2014, Favorite Male Action Star, People's Choice Award, 2006

MCCONNELL, MITCH, T: U.S. Senator from Kentucky **I:** Government Administration/Government Relations/Government Services **DOB:** 02/20/1942 **PB:** Tuscumbia **SC:** AL/USA **PT:** Addison Mitchell McConnell, Julia (Shockley) McConnell **MS:** Married **SPN:** Elaine Lan Chao, 2/6/1993 **CH:** Eleanor Hayes, Claire Redmon, Marion Porter **ED:** JD, University of Kentucky, 1967; BA, University of Louisville, With Honors, 1964 **C:** Majority Leader, 2015-Present; U.S. Senator From Kentucky, 1985-Present; Minority Leader, 2007-2015; Assistant Majority Leader (Majority Whip), 2002-2007; Judge, Jefferson County, Louisville, KY, 1978-1985; Deputy Assistant Attorney General, U.S. Department of Justice, Washington, DC, 1974-1975; Private Law Practice, Louisville, KY, 1970-1974; Chief Legislative Assistant To Sen. Marlow Cook, U.S. Senate, Washington, DC, 1968-1970 **CIV:** Chairman, Jefferson County Republican Committee, 1973-1974, Co-Chairman, National Child Tragedies Coalition, 1981, Chairman, Founder, Kentucky Task Force On Exploited And Missing Children, 1982, President's Partnership On Child Safety **AW:** Commendation, National Trust On Historical Preservation In the U.S., 1982, Conservationist of the Year Award, League of Kentucky Sportsmen, 1983, Certificate Of Appreciation, American Correctional Association, 1985, Golden Plow Award, American Farm Bureau Federation, 1996, Freedom Award, National Council on Union Burma, 1999, Sam Rainsy Party Freedom Award, 2002, Kentucky Warbler Migratory Songbird Conservation Award, U.S. Fish & Wildlife Service, Kentucky Department of Fish And Wildlife Resources, 2002, Defender Of Freedom Award, James Madison Center for Freedom of Speech, 2002, Distinguished Service Award, American Farm Bureau, 2002, The 50 Most Powerful People In District of Columbia, GQ Magazine, 2007 **MEM:** President, Kentucky Association of County Judge Executives, 1982, Advisory Board, National Institute of Justice, 1982-1984 **BAR:** State of Kentucky, 1967 **H:** Fly-fishing, Cooking **PA:** Republican **BA:** Gene Snyder U.S. Courthouse, Room 630, 601 West Broadway, Louisville, KY, USA, 40202-2228

MCCORMACK, ERIC, T: Actor **I:** Media & Entertainment **PB:** Toronto **SC:** ON/Canada **PT:** James Keith; Doris McCormack **ED:** Grad., Ryerson University School Theatre, Toronto **C:** Founder, Big Cattle Productions; Member, Stratford Shakespearean Festival, Canada, 1985-89 **CW:** Actor: (plays) A Midsummer Night's Dream, Henry V, The Three Sisters, Some Girl(s), 2006; (TV films) The Boys From Syracuse, 1986, Much Ado About Nothing, 1987, Relentless: Mind of a Killer, 1993, Family of Strangers, 1993, Miracle on Interstate 880, 1993, Call of the Wild, 1993, Double, Double, Toil and Trouble, 1993, Island City, 1994, The Man Who Wouldn't Die, 1994, Townies, 1996, Night Visitors, 1996, Borrowed Hearts, 1997, The Audrey Hepburn Story, 2000, In From the Night, 2005, Best Thing Ever, 2009, Stuck, 2009, Who is Clark Rockefeller?, 2010, Romeo Killer: The Chris Porco Story, 2013; (TV series) Street Justice, 1992-93, Lonesome Dove: The Series, 1994, Lonesome Dove: The Outlaw Years, 1995, Will & Grace, 1998-2006 (Emmy award for Outstanding Lead Actor in a Comedy, 2001), Dead Like Me, 2004, Trust Me, 2009, Pound Puppies (voice), 2010-12, Perception, 2012, American Dad!, 2012, Robot Chicken, 2013, The Mysteries of Laura, 2015, Full Circle, 2015, A Heavenly Christmas, 2016, Travelers, 2016; (TV miniseries) A Will of Their Own, 1998; (films) The Lost World, 1992, Return to the Lost World, 1992, Giant Steps, 1992, Exception to the Rule, 1997, Free Enterprise, 1998, Holy Man, 1998, Here's to Life, 2000, Break a Leg, 2005, The Sisters, 2005, My One and Only, 2009, Textuality, 2011, Knife

Fight, 2012, Barricade, 2012, Knife Fight, 2012, Romali Series,2013, Considering Love and Other Magic, 2016; (Broadway plays) The Music Man, 2001; TV appearances The New Adventures of Old Christine, 2009-10; executive prodr.: (TV series) Lovespring International, 2006; actor, prodr.: (TV series) Perception, 2012

MCCREADY, MIKE, T: Musician **I:** Media & Entertainment **DOB:** 04/05/1966 **PB:** Pensacola **SC:** FL/USA **C:** Solo Artist (2009-Present); Lead Guitarist, Vocalist, Pearl Jam (1991-2009); Member Band, Shadow **CW:** Musician, "Live at Third Man Records" (2016); Musician, "Live at the Moore 1995" (2015); Musician, "Seattle Symphony- Sonic Evolution" (2015); Musician, "Lightning Bolt," Pearl Jam (2013); Musician, "Backspacer," Pearl Jam (2009); Musician, "Pearl Jam," Pearl Jam (2006); Musician, "Waiting..." (2004); Musician, "Live Seattle, WA 12/13/03" (2003); Musician, "Riot Act," Pearl Jam (2002); Musician, "The Rockfords," The Rockfords (2000); Musician, "Binaural," Pearl Jam (2000); Musician, "Yield," Pearl Jam (1998); Musician, "No Code," Pearl Jam (1996); Musician, "Vitalogy," Peal Jam (1994); Musician, "Vs.," Pearl Jam (1993); Musician, "Mother Love Bone," Mother Love Bone (1992); Musician, "Temple of the Dog," Temple of the Dog (1991); Musician, "Ten," Pearl Jam (1991); Musician, "Alive," Peal Jam (1991); Musician, "Apple," Mother Love Bone (1990); Musician, "Shine," Mother Love Bone (1989) **AW:** Inductee, Rock and Roll Hall of Fame (2017); Named, Favorite Alternative Artist, American Music Awards (1999); Named, Favorite Alternative Artist, Favorite Heavy Metal/Hard Rock Artist, American Music Awards (1996); Named, Best Hard Rock Performance, Grammy Awards (1996); Named, Favorite Pop/Rock New Artist, Favorite New Heavy Metal/Hard Rock Artist, American Music Awards (1993): Named, Video of the Year, Best Group Video, Best Metal/Hard Rock Video, Best Direction, MTV Music Video Awards (1993)

MCCURRY, STEVE, T: Photographer **I:** Other **DOB:** 04/23/1950 **PB:** Darby **SC:** PA/USA **ED:** Graduate, Penn State University, 1974; **CW:** Publications include From These Hands: A Journey Along the Coffee Trail, 2015, Untold: The Stories Behind the Photographs, 2013, The Iconic Photographs, 2011, The Unguarded Moment, 2009, In the Shadow of Mountains, 2007, Looking East, 2006, Steve McCurry, Phaidon 55 series, 2005, The Path to Buddha: A Tibetan Pilgrimage, 2003; 2012, Sanctuary: The Temples of Angkor, 2002, South Southeast, 2000, Portraits, 1999; 2012, Monsoon.1988; 1995; **AW:** Awards include Leica Hall of Fame Award, St. Moritz, Switzerland, 2011, Lowell Thomas GOLD, 2006, National Press Photographers Association, 2005, The Lucie Award for Photojournalism, International Photography Awards, 2003, Co-recipient of the New York Film Festival Gold for documentary, Afghan Girl: Found, New York Film Festival, 2003, Award of Excellence for "Women of Afghanistan," French Art Directors Association, 2002, Special Recognition Award, United Nations, International Photographic Council, 2002, Photographer of the Year, American Photo Magazine, 2002, Book of the Year: "South SouthEast", Pictures of the Year International, 2000, Oliver Rebbot Memorial Award: Best Photographic Reporting from Abroad on Gulf War Coverage, Overseas Press Club, 1992, First Place, Gulf War News Story: Kuwait: After the Storm, Picture of the Year Competition, 1992, Our World Photo Winner, "Red Boy", Life Magazine: 'The Eisenstaedt Awards, 1988, Medal of Honor for coverage of the 1986 Philippine Revolution, Philippines, 1987, Magazine Photographer of the Year National Press Photographers Association, 1984, Robert Capa

Gold Medal for coverage of the war in Afghanistan for Time, 1980; **ACH:** McCurry's portrait, "Afghan Girl, 1984, was named as the most recognized photograph in the history of the National Geographic magazine;

MCDANIEL, RONNA, T: Chair **I:** Government Administration/Government Relations/Government Services **CN:** Republican National Committee **PB:** Austin **SC:** TX/USA **ED:** B.A., Brigham Young University **C:** Chair, Republican National Committee, 2017-; Michigan Representative to the RNC, 2014; Michigan Board of Marriage and Family Therapy, 2013

MCDONALD, AUDRA ANN, T: Actress, Singer **I:** Media & Entertainment **DOB:** 07/03/1970 **PB:** Berlin **SC:** Germany **PT:** Stanley McDonald; Kathryn McDonald **ED:** Attended, School Arts., California; BFA in Voice, Juilliard School, 1993 **CW:** Stage appearances include (operas) La Voix Humaine/Send, 2006, Rise and Fall of the City of Mahogany, 2007 (Grammy awards for best classical album and best opera recording, 2009); (regional plays) Man of La Mancha, Evita, The Wiz, A Chorus Line, Grease, Anything Goes, The Real Inspector Hound, Anyone Can Whistle, 2005; (concerts) Carnegie Hall, 2011; (Broadway plays) The Secret Garden, Man of La Mancha, 1989, Carousel, 1994 (Tony award best featured actress in a musical, 1994, Outer Critics Circle award outstanding actress in a musical, 1994), Master Class, 1995-97 (Tony award best featured actress in a musical, 1996, LA Ovation award best featured actress in a musical, 1996), Ragtime, 1998-99 (Tony award for best featured actress in a musical, 1998), Sweeney Todd, 2000, A Raisin in the Sun, 2004 (Tony award best featured actress in a play, 2004, Drama Desk award best featured actress in a play, 2004), See What I Wanna See (formerly titled R Shomon), 2005, 110 in the Shade, 2007 (Drama Desk award outstanding actress in a musical 2007), The Gershwins Porgy and Bess, 2012 (Drama Desk award outstanding actress in a musical, 2012, Tony award best performance by an actress in a leading role in a musical, 2012), Lady Day at Emerson's Bar & Grill, 2014 (Drama Desk award outstanding actress in a play, 2014, Tony award, Best Leading Actress in a Play, 2014); (TV series) Bill Cosby pilot, 1996, Mister Sterling, 2003, The Bedford Diaries, 2006, Kidnapped, 2006-07, Private Practice, 2007-; (TV Movies) Having Our Say: The Delaney Sisters' First 100 Years, 1999, Annie, 1999, The Last Debate, 2000, Wit, 2001 (Emmy award nom. best supporting actress, 2001), A Raisin in the Sun, 2008; (films) Seven Servants, 1996, The Object of My Affection, 1998, Cradle Will Rock, 1999, It Runs in the Family, 2003, The Best Thief in the World, 2004; concert performances include S'Wonderful, Some Enchanted Evening, Christa Ludwig and James Levine Recital, Revelation in Courthouse Park, Requiem Canticles, Carnegie Hall; singer: (albums) Leonard Bernstien's New York, 1996, Sings Rodgers & Hart, 1996, George & Ira Gershwin: Standards & Gems, 1998, George Gershwin: 100th Birthday Celebration, 1998, Broadway in Love, 2000, Marie Christine: A New Musical, 2000, Broadway Cares: Home for the Holidays, 2001, Dreamgirls in Concert, 2002, (solo albums) Way Back to Paradise, 1998, How Glory Goes, 2000, Happy Songs, 2002, Build a Bridge, 2006, Go Back Home, 2013. **AW:** Recipient Theatre World award, 1994, Drama League award for distinguished achievement in musical theatre, 2000

MCDORMAND, FRANCES, T: Actress **I:** Media & Entertainment **PB:** Chicago **SC:** IL/USA **PT:** Vernon W. McDormand; Noreen E. (Nickleson) McDormand **ED:** BA, Bethany College, 1979;

MFA, Yale University School Drama, 1982 **CW:** Stage appearances include: Awake and Sing!, New York City, 1984, Painting Churches, New York City, 1984, The Three Sisters, Minneapolis, 1985, New Jersey, 1991, All My Sons, New Haven, 1986, A Streetcar Named Desire, New York City, 1988, Moon for the Misbegotten, 1992, Sisters Rosensweig, New York City, 1993, The Swan, New York City, 1993, To You, the Birdie!, 2002, Far Away, 2002, The Country Girl, New York City, 2008, Good People, 2011 (Tony award for Best Performance by an Actress in a Leading Role in a Play, 2011); (films) Blood Simple, 1984, Crime Wave, 1986, Raising Arizona, 1987, Mississippi Burning, 1988 (National Board Review award for Best Supporting Actress, 1988), Chattahoochee, 1990, Darkman, 1990, Miller's Crossing, 1990, Hidden Agenda, 1990, The Butcher's Wife, 1991, Passed Away, 1992, Short Cuts, 1993 (Golden Globe award for Best Ensemble Cast, 1994), Beyond Rangoon, 1995, Plain Pleasures, 1996, Fargo, 1996 (National Board Review award for Best Actress, 1996, Academy award for Best Actress in a Leading Role, 1997, Am. Comedy award for Funniest Actress in Motion Picture, 1997, Broadcast Film Critics Association award for Best Actress, 1997, Screen Actors Guild award for Outstanding Performance by Female Actor in Leading Role, 1997), Lone Star, 1996, Primal Fear, 1996, Palookaville, 1996, Paradise Road, 1997, Johnny Skidmarks, 1998, Madeline, 1998, Talk of Angels, 1998, Wonder Boys, 1999, Almost Famous (Boston Society Film Critics award for Best Supporting Actress, 2000, Broadcast Film Critics Association award for Best Supporting Actress, 2001), Man Who Wasn't There, 2001, City by the Sea, 2002, Laurel Canyon, 2002, Something's Gotta Give, 2003, Last Night, 2004, North Country, 2005, Aeon Flux, 2005, Friends With Money, 2006, Miss Pettigrew Lives for a Day, 2008, Burn After Reading, 2008, This Must be the Place, 2011, Transformers: Dark of the Moon, 2011, Moonrise Kingdom, 2012, Madagascar 3: Europe's Most Wanted (voice), 2012, Promised Land, 2012, The Good Dinosaur (voice), 2015, Hail, Caesar!, 2016, Three Billboards Outside, Ebbing, Missouri, 2017, (Recipient Academy Award for Best Actress, Recipient Golden Globe Award for Best Actress, Recipient Screen Actors Guild Award for Best Actress); Isle of Dogs, 2018; (TV films) Scandal Sheet, 1985, Vengeance: The Story of Tony Cimo, 1986, Crazy In Love, 1992, Good Old Boys, 1995, Hidden in America, 1996, (narrator) Precinct Hollywood, 2005; (TV appearances) The Twilight Zone, 1986, The Equalizer, Spencer: For Hire, Hill Street Blues, 1985, Hunter, 1985, Legwork, 1986-87, State of Grace, 2001, The Simpsons, 2006, Olive Kitteridge, 2014; actress, executive prodr.: (TV Mini-series) Olive Kitteridge, 2014 (Screen Actors Guild award for Outstanding Performance by a Female Actor in a TV Movie or Mini-series, 2015, Emmy award for Outstanding Lead Actress in a Mini-series or Movie, 2015).

MCEACHIN, DONALD A., T: U.S. Representative from Virginia **I:** Government Administration/Government Relations/Government Services **DOB:** 10/10/1961 **PB:** Nuremberg **SC:** West Germany **SPN:** Colette McEachin **ED:** M.Div., Samuel Dewittt Proctor School of Theology at Virginia Union University, 2008; J.D., University of Virginia, 1986, B.S., American University, 1982 **C:** Member, U.S. House of Representatives from Virginia's 4th District, 2017-; Member, Committee on Armed Services; Member, Committee on Natural Resources; Member, Virginia Senates 9th District, 2008-17; Member, Virginia House of Delegates 74th District, 1996-2002, 2006-2008 **BA:** 314 Cannon HOB, Washington, DC, 20515

MCENROE, JOHN PATRICK JR., **T:** Professional Tennis Player (Retired), Host **I:** Media & Entertainment **DOB:** 02/16/1959 **PB:** Wiesbaden **SC:** Germany **PT:** Son of John Patrick and Kathy McEnroe; **ED:** Student, Stanford University; Grad., Trinity School, New York City, 1977 **C:** Host, McEnroe, 2004; Host, The Chair, 2002; Tennis sportscaster, USA Network, 1993; Winner (with Jonas Bjorkman), Doubles Title SAP Open, 2006; Winner, Wimbledon Doubles, 1992; Winner, Tournament of Champions, 1981, 83; Winner, Wimbledon Singles, 1981, 83, 84; Winner, World Championship Tennis Championship, 1979, 83; Winner, U.S. Open Men's Singles Championship, 1979, 80, 81, 84; Winner, Grand Prix Masters Tournament, New York City, 1979; Played on, victorious U.S. Davis Cup Team, 1978, 79, 81, 82, 92; Professional tennis player, 1978-93; Winner, National College Athletic Association Intercollegiate U.S. Men's Singles title, 1978; Winner junior titles, French Junior Singles, 1977; Winner junior titles, French Mixed Doubles, 1977; Winner numerous U.S. junior singles and doubles titles, **CR:** Owner John McEnroe Gallery. **CW:** Co-author (with James Kaplan): (autobiography) You Cannot Be Serious, 2000; author: Serious, 2003 **AW:** Inducted, Tennis Hall of Fame, 1999,ITF World Champion, 1981,1983, 1984, ATP Player of the Year, 1981, 1983, 1984, ATP Most Improved Player, 1978, World Number 1 Male Player, Davis Cup Commitment Award **MEM:** Mem: Men's Seniors' Tour Circuit, 1994. **ACH:** Achievements include winner 21 Singles Titles, Senior Champions Tour, 1998-2005

MCENTIRE, REBA, **T:** Musician, Actress **I:** Media & Entertainment **DOB:** 03/28/1955 **PB:** McAlester **SC:** Oklahoma **PT:** Daughter of Clark Vincent and Jacqueline (Smith) McE.; **SPN:** Married Charlie Battles, June 21, 1976 (div. 1987); Married Narvel Blackstock, June 3, 1989 (div. October 2015); **CH:** 1 Child, Shelby Steven McEntire **ED:** Student Elementary Education, Music, Southeastern State University, Durant, Oklahoma, 1976 **C:** Recording Artist, Valory Music Co., 2008—; Recording Artist, MCA Records, 1984—2008; Recording Artist, Mercury Records, 1978-83 **CIV:** Spokesperson Middle Tennessee United Way, 1988, National and State 4-H Alumni, Bob Hope's Hope for a Drug Free Am.; National spokesperson Am. Lung Association, 1990-91. **CW:** Albums: Reba McEntire, 1977, Out of a Dream, 1979, Feel the Fire, 1980, Heart to Heart, 1981, Unlimited, 1982, Behind the Scene, 1983, Just a Little Love, 1984, My Kind of Country, 1984, Have I Got a Deal for You, 1985, The Best of Reba McEntire, 1985, Reba Nell McEntire, 1986, Whoever's in New England, 1986, What Am I Gonna Do About You, 1987, Greatest Hits, 1987, Merry Christmas To You, 1987, The Last One To Know, 1988, Reba, 1988, Sweet 16, 1989, Rumor Has It, 1990, Reba Live, 1989, For My Broken Heart, 1991, Forever in Your Eyes, 1992, It's Your Call, 1992, Greatest Hits Vol. 2, 1993, Read My Mind, 1994, Oklahoma Girl, 1994, Starting Over, 1995, What If It's You, 1996, If You See Him, 1998, Forever Reba, 1998, Moments and Memories: The Best of Reba, 1998, Star Profile, 1999, So Good Together, 1999, The Secret of Giving: A Christmas Collection, 1999, I'll Be, 2000, Greatest Hits Vol. III: I'm a Survivor, 2001, Room to Breathe, 2003, The Christmas Collection: The Best of Reba, 2003, Reba #1's, 2005, The Best of Reba McEntire, 2007, Reba Duets, 2007, 50 Greatest Hits, 2008, Love Revival, 2008, Keep On Loving You, 2009, All the Women I Am, 2010, Love Somebody, 2015, My Kind of Christmas, 2016, Sing it Now: Songs of Faith and Hope, 2017, Icon, 2014, Love Somebody, 2015; actress: (stage) Annie Get Your Gun, 2001 South Pacific, 2006, (films) Tremors, 1990, The Little Rascals, 1994, North, 1994, One Night at McCool's, 2001, (voice)

The Fox & the Hound 2, 2006, (voice) Charlotte's Web, 2006, Romances of the Republics, 2015, The Land Before Time: Journey of the Brave (TV films) The Gambler Returns: The Luck of the Draw, 1991, The Man From Left Field, 1993, Buffalo Girls, 1995, (TV series) Malibu Country, 2012-13, (TV appearances) Country Gold, 1982, Bob Hope Winterfest Christmas Show, 1987, (video) Wrestlemania VIII, 1992, Evening Shade, 1993, Frasier, 1994, The Roseanne Show, 1998, (voice) Hercules, 1998, One Life to Live, Working Class, 2011; actress, co-exec. prodr.: (TV series) Reba, 2001-07 (Favorite Female Performer in a New TV Series, People's Choice Awards, 2002); actress, executive prodr.: (TV films) Is There Life Out There?, 1994, Forever Love, 1998, Secret of Giving, 1999, (TV series) Malibu Country, 2012-13, Kelly Clarksons Cautionary Christmas Music Tale, 2013, Baby Daddy, 2015, Best Time Ever with Neil Patrick Harris, 2015, Disney Parks Christmas Day Parade,2015, The Voice, 2015, Last Man Standing, 2016, Americas Got Talent, 2016; (host) Academy Country Music awards, 2004-12; Author: (with Tom Carter) Reba: My Story, 1995, Comfort from a Country Quilt, 2000. **AW:** Recipient numerous awards in Country music including Distinguished Alumni award Southeastern State University, Female Vocalist award Country Music Association, 1984, 85, 86, 87, Grammy award for Best Country Vocal Performance, 1987, Grammy award, Best Country Vocal Collaboration for "Does He Love You" with Linda Davis, 1994, Entertainer of Year award Country Music Radio Awards, 1994, Female Vocalist award, 1994; named Entertainer of Year, Country Music Association, 1986, Female Vocalist of Year Academy Country Music, 1984, 1985, 1986, 1987, 1992, Top Female Vocalist, 1984, 1985, 1986, 1987, 1991, 1994, Milestone award, 2015, International Artist Achievement award, 2004, Am. Music award Favorite Female Country Artist, 1988, 1990, 1991, 1992, 1993, 1994, 1998, 2004, Am. Music award, 1989, 1990, 1991, 1992, Favorite Country Album, 1991, 1993, 1995, Favorite Female Musical Performer, People's Choice Awards, 1992, 1993, Favorite Female Country Performer, 1992, 1994, 1995, TNN Viewer's Choice Awards, 1993, Favorite Female Country Artist, Billboard, 1994, Favorite Country Album award Am. Music Awards, 1995, Favorite Female Country Vocalist, 1995, Favorite Female Artist-Country, 2004, Favorite Female Vocalist award People's Choice Awards, 1995, Top Female Vocalist of Year award Academy Country Music, 1995, Entertainer of Year award, 1995, Home Depot Humanitarian award, 2002, Leading Lady award, 2003, Special award for Most Female Vocalist Wins, 2005, Favorite Female Vocalist award TNN Viewer's Choice Awards, 1995, Star on the Walk of Fame, 1999; named to Country Music Hall of Fame, 2011 **MEM:** Member Country Music Association, Academy County Music, National Academy Recording Arts and Scis., Grand Ol' Opry, American Federation of TV and Radio Artists, Nashville Songwriters Association Inc. **ACH:** Record for most CMA Award Nominations **BA:** c/o Starstruck Entertainment, 40 Music Square West, Nashville, TN, 37203

MCEWAN, IAN RUSSELL, **T:** Writer **I:** Writing and Editing **DOB:** 06/21/1948 **PB:** Aldershot **SC:** Hampshire, England **PT:** Son of David and Rose Lilian Violet (Moore) McEwan **ED:** DLitt (hon.), Univ. College, London, 2008; MA in Lit., University East Anglia, Norwich, England, 1971 **CW:** Author: (novels) The Cement Garden, 1978, The Comfort of Strangers, 1981, The Child in Time, 1987 (Whitbread award, 1987, Prix Fémina Etranger, France, 1993), The Innocent, 1990, Black Dogs, 1992, Enduring Love, 1997, Amsterdam, 1998 (Booker Prize for fiction, 1998), Atonement, 2001 (National Book Critics Cir. award for fiction, 2002, TIME mag-

azine Best Novel of 2002, W.H. Smith Lit. award, 2002, LA Times prize for fiction, 2003, Santiago prize for European Novel, 2004), Saturday, 2005 (New York Times bestseller, James Tait Black Memorial prize, 2005), On Chesil Beach, 2007 (Galaxy Book of Year, Brit. Book Awards, 2008), Solar, 2010, Sweet Tooth, 2012, The Children Act, 2014, (short story collections) First Love, Last Rites, 1975 (Somerset Maugham award, Society Authors, 1976), In Between the Sheets, 1978, ((children's book)) Rose Blanche, 1985, The Daydreamer, 1994, (screenplays) The Ploughman's Lunch, 1985, Sour Sweet, 1989, The Good Son, 1993, (plays) The Imitation Game, 1981, (Book) Nutshell, 2016,(Screenplay) On Chesil Beach, 2017, The Children Act, 2017 **AW:** Named Reader's Digest Author of Year, 2008, Commander Order of Brit. Empire (CBE), 2000; recipient Herold & Ethel L. Stellfox Visiting Scholar & Writers Program award, Dickinson College, Carlisle, Pennsylvania, 2005, Shakespeare Prize, Alfred Toepfer Foundation, Germany, 1999 **MEM:** Fellow: Am. Academy Arts & Scis., Royal Society Arts, Royal Society Lit.

MCFADDEN, DANIEL LITTLE, **T:** Economics Professor **I:** Education/Educational Services **DOB:** 07/29/1937 **PB:** Raleigh **PT:** Son of Robert S. and Alice (Little) McFadden; **ED:** PhD (hon.), North Carolina St. University, 2006; Doctor (hon.), Univ. College London, 2003; LLD, University Chicago, 1992; PhD in Economics, University Minnesota, 1962; BS in Physics, University Minnesota, 1957 **C:** Presidential professor health economics, University Southern California, 2011-; Professor emeritus, University California, Berkeley, California, 2006-; Director Statistics Research Center, Massachusetts Institute of Technology, Massachusetts, 1986-88; James R. Killian chair, Massachusetts Institute of Technology, Cambridge, Massachusetts, 1984-91; Professor economics, Massachusetts Institute of Technology, Cambridge, Massachusetts, 1979-91; Chairman department economics, University California, Berkeley, 1995-96; Director Econometrics Laboratory, University California, Berkeley, 1996-2006; Director Econometrics Laboratory, University California, Berkeley, 1991-95; E. Morris Cox professor & chair economics, University California, Berkeley, 1990-2006; Professor economics, University California, Berkeley, 1968-79; Associate professor, University California, Berkeley, California, 1966-68; Assistant professor economics, University California, Berkeley, 1963-66; Assistant professor economics, University Pittsburgh, 1962-63 **CR:** Sherman Fairchild distinguished scholar California Institute Tech., 1990 Irving Fisher research professor Yale University, New Haven, 1977-78 board directors National Bureau Economic Research, 1980-83, 1976-77 member executive com Transportation Research Board, 1975-78 member economics advisory panel National Science Foundation, 1969-71 visiting associate professor University Chicago, 1966-67 **CIV:** Member adv. committee, City of Berkeley Coordinated Transit Project, 1975-76 **CW:** Co-author: Urban Travel Demand: A Behavioral Analysis, 1975, Microeconomic Modeling and Policy Analysis, 1984; co-editor: Essays on Economic Behavior Under Uncertainty, 1974, Production Economics, Vols. I and II, 1978, Structural Analysis of Discrete Data with Econometric Applications, 1981, Preferences, Uncertainty, and Optimality, 1990, Handbook of Econometrics Vol. IV, 1994; editor: Journal Statistical Physics, 1968-70; associate editor: Journal Econometrics, 1977-78; member editorial board American Economic Rev., 1971-74, Journal Math. Economics, 1973-77, Transportation Research, 1978-80, member adv. committee Journal Applied Economics, 1996-; contributor articles to professional journals **AW:** Co-recipient Nobel Prize in Economics, The Nobel Foundation, 2000; recipient Richard Stone Prize in Applied Economics, Journal Applied Econometrics, 2000-01, Nemmers Prize in Economics, Northwestern University, 2000, Outstanding Teacher award, Massachusetts Institute of Technology, 1981; Ford Faculty Research Fellow, 1966-67, Earhart Fellow, 1960-61, Ford Foundation Behavioral Sci. Fellow, 1958-62, Frisch Medal, 1986 **MEM:** Fellow: Econometrics Society (Fisher-Schultz lecturer 1979, vice president 1984, president 1985, fellow 1969, Frisch Medal 1986); mem.: National Academy of Sciences, American Philosophical Society, Math. Association America, American Statistical Association, American Economic Association (member executive committee 1985-87, vice president 1994, pres.-elect 2004, John Bates Clark Medal 1975), American Academy Arts & Sciences **H:** Bicycling, tennis, squash, sailing, skiing **PA:** Democrat **BA:** University of California, Berkeley Department of Economics, 508-1 Evans Hall #3880, Berkeley, CA, 94720

MCGARRY, MICHAEL, T: Chairman **I:** Manufacturing **CN:** PPG Industries **ED:** B.A., University of Texas at Arlington **C:** Chairman, Ppg Industries Inc, 2016-; CEO, Ppg Industries Inc, 2015-2016; President/COO, Ppg Industries Inc, 2015-2015 **MEM:** Board Member, Pittsburgh Glass Works LLC

MCGOVERN, JIM, T: U.S. Representative from Massachusetts **I:** Government Administration/Government Relations/Government Services **DOB:** 11/20/1959 **PB:** Worcester **SC:** MA/USA **PT:** Son of Walter and Mindy McGovern; **ED:** MA in Pub. Administration, American University, 1984; BA, American University, 1981 **C:** Member, US Congress from 2nd Mass District, 2013-; Member, House Rules Committee; Member, US Congress from 3rd Mass District, Washington, 1997-2013; Staff positions including spokesman, legis. director, senior aide to Rep. Joe Moakley, US House of Representatives, 1981-96; Aide to Senator George McGovern, US Senate, 1977-80 **CR:** Manager George McGovern for President, 1984 delivered McGovern presidential nomination speech Dem. National Convention, San Francisco, 1984 leader Congressional Investigation on El Salvador, 1989 **CIV:** Candidate for U.S. Congress, 1996 vol. Mount Carmel House board directors Jesuit International Vols. **PA:** Democrat **BA:** 438 Cannon House Office Building Washington, DC 20515, Washington, DC, 20515

MCGRAW, TIM, T: Singer, Musician **I:** Media & Entertainment **DOB:** 05/01/1967 **PB:** Delhi, Louisiana, May 1, 1967 **PT:** Son of Tug McGraw; **CW:** Musician: (albums) Tim McGraw, 1993, Not a Moment Too Soon, 1994 (triple-platinum, Album of Year, Academy County Music Awards, 1994), All I Want, 1995, Everywhere, 1997 (Album of Year, Country Music Association Awards, 1998), A Place in the Sun, 1999 (Album of Year, Country Music Association Awards, 1999), Tim McGraw Greatest Hits, 2000, Set the Circus Down, 2001 (Best Country Album, Am. Music Awards, 2002), Tim McGraw and the Dancehall Doctors, 2002, Live Like You Were Dying, 2004 (Most Inspiring Video of Year, Country Music Television Music award, 2005, Single Record of Year, Academy Country Music Awards, 2005, Favorite Country Album, Am. Music Awards, 2005), Tim McGraw Reflected Greatest Hits Vol. 2, 2006 (Favorite Country Album, Am. Music Awards, 2006), Let it Go, 2007, Greatest Hits: Limited Edition, 2008, Collector's Edition, 2008, Greatest Hits Vol. 3, 2008, Limited Edition: Greatest

Hits: Volumes 1, 2 & 3, 2008, Southern Voice, 2009, Number One Hits, 2010, Emotional Traffic, 2012, Two Lanes of Freedom, 2013, Sundown Heaven Town, 2014, Damn Country Music, 2015,The Rest of Our Life,2017 (songs) It's Your Love, 1997 (Single of Year, Song of Year, Academy Country Music Awards, 1998), Grown Men, 2001 (Single of Year, Radio Music Association, 2001), (with Faith Hill) Let's Make Love, 2001 (Grammy award for Vocal Collaboration, 2001); singer Live Like You Were Dying, 2004 (Single of Year, Song of Year, Country Music Association Awards, 2004, Song of Year, Academy Country Music Awards, 2005); musician (with Tracy Lawrence and Kenny Chesney) Find Out Who Your Friends Are, 2007 (Musical Event of Year, Country Music Association Awards, 2007, Vocal Event of Year, Academy Country Music Awards, 2008), (with Kenny Chesney) Feel Like a Rock Star, 2012 (Musical Event of Year, Country Music Association Awards, 2012), (with Taylor Swift and Keith Urban) Highway Don't Care, 2013 (Musical Event of Year, Music Video of Year, Country Music Association Awards, 2013, Video of Year, Academy Country Music Awards, 2014), Humble and Kind, 2015 (Video of Year, CMT Music Awards, 2016); actor: (films) Black Cloud, 2004, Friday Night Lights, 2004, Flicka, 2006, Four Christmases, 2008, The Blind Side, 2009, Dirty Girl, 2010, Country Strong, 2010, Tomorrowland, 2015, The Shack,2016 (TV appearances) The Jeff Foxworthy Show, 1997, Sesame Street, 2000, SNL, 2008, Who Do You Think You Are, 2011, Cake Boss, 2013, Repeat After Me, 2015, The Voice, 2016 **AW:** Named Favorite Country Music Icom, People's Choice Awards, 2014; recipient Best Country Collaboration With Vocals (with Faith Hill), 2006, Favorite Male Performer, People's Choice Awards, 2006, Favorite Male Musical Performer, 2004, Country Male Artist, Radio Music Awards, 2003, Favorite Male Artist, Blockbuster Award, 2001, Male Artist of Year, TNN/Music City News, 1999, Entertainer of Year, Country Music Association, 2001, Male Vocalist of Year, 2000, 1999, Vocal Event of Year, 1997, Academy Country Music, 1998, 1997, Top Male Vocalist, 1998, 1999, 1994, Favorite Male Country Artist, Am. Music Awards, 2007, 2005, 2003, 2001, 2002, Favorite New Artist, 1995, Grammy for Best Country Collaboration, 2006, Grammy for Best Male Country Vocals, 2005 **BA:** McGrawFan, P.O. Box 128138, Nashville, TN, 37212

MCGREGOR, CONOR ANTHONY, T: Professional Boxer and Mixed Martial Artist **I:** Athletics **DOB:** 07/19/1988 **PB:** Crumlin **SC:** Ireland **PT:** Tony McGregor, Margaret McGregor **SPN:** Dee Devlin **CH:** Conor Jack, Jr. **C:** Launched, (With David August) Men's Formal Wear Line, August McGregor, 2017 **CR:** Sponsored, Beats by Dre, Monster Energy, Reebok, Bud Light, Burger King **CW:** Appearance, (Film) Conor McGregor: Notorious, 2017, (Television) The Ultimate Fighter 22, 2015, The Notorious, 2015, The 13th Jockey, 2017, All Access: Mayweather vs. McGregor, (Video Game) Call of Duty: Infinite Warfare, 2016 **AW:** Top 100 Most Influential People, TIME Magazine, 2017, Best Box Office Draw, Wrestling Observer Newsletter, 2016-2017, Fight of the Year, Bleacher Report, Fox Sports, Best Fighter and Nominee for Best Breakthrough Athlete, ESPYs, RTÉ Sports Person of the Year, RTÉ Sport, Mixed Martial Arts Most Valuable, Most Charismatic, Wrestling Observer Newsletter, 2016, Best on Interviews, Wrestling Observer Newsletter, 2015-2017, Fighter of the Year, Sherdog, Feud of the Year, Most Outstanding Fighter of the Year, Wrestling Observer Newsletter, 2015-2016, Fighter of the Year, Bleacher Report, ESPN, Fox Sports, Severe MMA, MMA Mania, MMA Junkie, MMA Fighting, World MMA Awards, December Knockout of the Month, MMA

Junkie, Event of the Year, MMA Fighting, MMA Mania, Sherdog, 25 Hottest Sex Symbols, Rolling Stone, Knockout of the Year, Sherdog, Male Fighter of the Year, The MMA Community, Ireland's Most Stylish Man, VIP Style Awards, 2015, Irish Pro Fighter of the Year, Severe MMA, International Fighter of the Year, World MMA Awards, 2014-2015, Breakthrough Fighter of the Year, Sherdog, 2014, Best UFC Newcomer, MMA Insider, 2013 **ACH:** CWFC Featherweight Champion; CWFC Lightweight Champion; UFC Featherweight Champion; UFC Interim Featherweight Champion; UFC Lightweight Champion

MCGREGOR, EWAN GORDON, T: Actor **I:** Media & Entertainment **DOB:** 03/31/1971 **PB:** Crieff **SC:** Perthshire/Scotland **PT:** Son of James and Carol McGregor **ED:** LLD, University of Ulster, 2001 **C:** Co-founder (with John Lee Miller, Sean Pertwee, Jude Law, Sadie Frost), Natural Nylon (production co.) **CW:** Actor: (films) Being Human, 1993, Shallow Grave, 1994, The Pillow Book, 1994, Blue Juice, 1995, Emma, 1996, Trainspotting, 1996, Brassed Off, 1996, A Life Less Ordinary, 1997, Velvet Goldmine, 1998, Little Voice, 1998, Eye of the Beholder, 1999, Star Wars: Episode I-The Phantom Menace, 1999, Moulin Rouge, 2001, Black Hawk Down, 2001, Star Wars: Episode II-Attack of the Clones, 2002, Down With Love, 2003, Young Adam, 2003, Big Fish, 2003, Star Wars: Episode III-Revenge of the Sith, 2005, The Island, 2005, (voice) Robots, 2005, Valiant, 2005, Stay, 2005, Cassandra's Dream, 2007, Incendiary, 2008, Deception, 2008, Angels & Demons, 2009, Amelia, 2009, The Men Who Stare at Goats, 2009, I Love You Phillip Morris, 2010, The Ghost Writer, 2010, Nanny McPhee Returns, 2010, Beginners, 2010, Haywire, 2012; actor: (films) Perfect Sense, 2011, Salmon Fishing in the Yemen, 2012, The Impossible, 2012, Jack the Giant Slayer, 2013, August: Osage County, 2013, Son of a Gun, 2014, Mortdecai, 2015, Last Days in the Desert, 2015, Miles Ahead, 2015, Jane Got a Gun, 2015, Our Kind of Traitor, 2016, American Pastoral, 2016, T2 Trainspotting, 2017, Beauty and the Beast, 2017, Zoe, 2018, Christopher Robin, 2018; (TV films) Lipstick on Your Collar, 1993, Doggin' Around, 1994, Motor Bike: Round the World Trip, 2004, The Corrections, 2012; TV guest appearances include Tales from the Crypt, 1989, ER, 1994, Kavanagh QC, 1994, Karaoke, 1996, The Polar Bears of Churchill with Ewan McGregor, 2002, Long Way Round, 2004, Long Way Down, 2007, The Battle of Britain, 2010, Ewan McGregor: Cold Chain Mission, 2012, Bomber Boys, 2012, The Corrections, 2013, Hebrides: Islands on the Edge, 2013, Doll & Em, 2015, Highlands: Scotland's Wild Heart, 2016, Fargo, 2017 (Golden Globe for Best Actor in a Miniseries Television Film, 2017); actor (plays) Guys and Dolls, 2005; (Broadway plays) The Real Thing, 2014; executive producer, writer (documentaries) Long Way Round, 2004, Long Way Down, 2007, actor, co-producer (films) Nora, 2000, co-executive producer (documentaries) Marley Africa Roadtrip, 2011 **AW:** Named Officer of the Order of the British Empire, 2013; Named One of British Culture's Top 50 Movers and Shakers, BBC 3, 2004, The 100 Top Movie Stars of All Time, Empire magazine, 1997; Recipient, ALFS Award, 1997

MCHENRY, PATRICK TIMOTHY, T: U.S. Representative from North Carolina **I:** Government Administration/Government Relations/Government Services **DOB:** 10/22/1975 **PB:** Mecklenburg **ED:** BA in Hist., Belmont Abbey College, 1999; Attended, North Carolina State University **C:** Chief deputy whip, US Congress from 10th North Carolina District, 2014-; Member, Committee on Financial Services, Government Reform, Republican Study Committee; Member, US Congress from 10th North Carolina District, 2005-; Member, North Carolina State House Reps., 2003-05; Special assistant to Secretary Elaine L. Chao, US Department Labor, Washington, 2000; Owner & broker, McHenry Real Estate, Gastonia, North Carolina,; Executive, DCI/New Media, Inc., Washington, **CIV:** Board directors, United Success by Six Youth Progressive, **AW:** Named a Protector of Property Rights, Property Rights Alliance, Hero of the Taxpayer, Ams. for Tax Reform, Small Business Champion, Small Business and Entrepreneurship Council; named one of The Politics 40 Under 40, TIME Magazine, 2010; recipient Spirit of Enterprise award, US C. of C. **MEM:** Mem.: Gaston C. of C., National Rifle Association, Gastonia Rotary Club **PA:** Republican **BA:** 2334 Rayburn House Office Building, Washington, DC, 20515

MCHUGH, CAROLYN BALDWIN, T: Federal Judge **I:** Law and Legal Services **DOB:** 07/12/1957 **PB:** Abington **SC:** PA/USA **ED:** JD, The University of Utah S.J. Quinney College of Law (1982); BA, The University of Utah (1978) **C:** Judge, U.S. Court of Appeals for the Tenth Circuit, Salt Lake City, Utah (2014-Present); Presiding Judge, Utah Court of Appeals, Salt Lake City, Utah (2012-2014); Associate Presiding Judge, Utah Court of Appeals, Salt Lake City, Utah (2010-2011); Judge, Utah Court of Appeals, Salt Lake City, Utah (2005-2014); Shareholder, Parr Brown Gee & Loveless (1987-2005); Associate, Parr Brown Gee & Loveless (1983-1987); Law Clerk to Honorary Bruce S. Jenkins, U.S. District Court of Utah, Salt Lake City, Utah (1982-1983) **CR:** Adjunct Professor of Law, The University of Utah S.J. Quinney College of Law (1991-1992, 2011-Present); Member, Utah Judicial Conduct Commission (2010-Present) **CIV:** Trustee, Legal Aid Society of Salt Lake (2004-2005); President, Catholic Community Services (2002); Trustee, Catholic Community Services (1996-2003) **AW:** Dorothy Merrill Brothers Award for the Advancement of Women in the Legal Profession (2009); Named Christine M. Durham Utah Woman Lawyer of Year (2001); The University of Utah College of Law Young Alumna of Year (1997) **MEM:** Board Member, Appellate Section, Utah State Bar (2010-Present); President, Women Lawyers of Utah (1996-1997); Chairperson, Distinguished Committee, Utah State Bar (1996) **BA:** 1823 Stout St, Denver, CO, 80212

MCILROY, RORY, T: Professional Golfer **I:** Athletics **DOB:** 05/04/1989 **PB:** Holywood **SC:** Northern Ireland/UK **PT:** Gerry McIlroy, Rosie McIlroy **MS:** Married **SPN:** Erica Stoll, 4/2017 **C:** Professional Golfer, 2007-Present **CR:** European Team, Ryder Cup, 2010, 2012, Great Britain and Ireland Team, Vivendi Trophy With Severiano Ballesteros, 2009 **CIV:** Ambassador, UNICEF, Ireland **AW:** PGA Tour Player of the Year, 2012, 2014, Vardon Trophy, PGA of America, 2012, Golf Magazine Player of the Year, 2012, PGA of America Player of the Year, 2012, Irish Independent Young Sports Star of the Year, 2006, Belfast Telegraph Young Sports Star of the Year, 2006, Irish Examiner Young Sports Star of the Year, 2005-2006, Willie Gill Award, Best Senior Player in Ireland, 2005-2006, Junior Sports Personality of the Year in Ireland, 2004, Tom Montgomery Award, Best Under 18 Player in Ireland, 2004 **ACH:** Achievements include winning amateur events: Irish Boys Championship, 2004, Irish Youth Championship, 2004, Warrenpoint Scratch Cup, 2004, Irish Close Championship, 2005, 2006, West of Ireland Championship, 2005, 2006; Ballyliffin Scratch Cup, 2005, Rosapenna Scratch, 2005, English Under 21 Stroke Play Championship, 2006, Mullingar Scratch Cup, 2006, European Amateur Championship, 2006, Sherry Cup, 2007; winning European Tour events: Dubai Desert Classic, 2009, UBS Hong Kong Open,

2011, Dubai World Championship, 2012, Emirates Australian Open, 2013; winning PGA Tour events: Quail Hollow Championship, 2010, Honda Classic, Deutsche Bank Championship, BMW Championship, 2012, WGC-Bridgestone Invitational, 2014; member of Ryder Cup winning Team Europe, 2010, 2012; winning PGA Tour major titles: US Open, 2011, PGA Championship, 2012, 2014, British Open, 2014; setting the US Open record for most strokes under par (16 under), 2011; becoming the number 1 player in the world, 2014,Tour Championship Winner, 2016,WGV-Cadillac Match Play, 2015, Wells Fargo Championship, 2015 Deutsche Bank Championship, 2016,Winner of the Arnold Palmer Invitational, 2018 **RE:** Roman Catholic **BA:** International Sports Management Ltd., Cherry Tree Farm, Cherry Tree Lane, Rostherne, Cheshire, United Kingdom, -HA14 3RZ

MCKEE, ANN, T: Neuropathologist **I:** Medicine & Health Care **PB:** Appleton **SC:** WI/USA **ED:** Student, University of Wisconsin–Madison; Student, Case Western Reserve University School of Medicine **C:** Chief Neuropathologist, New England Veterans Administration; Medical Centers Director, Boston University CTE Center and Neuropathology Core for the Boston University Alzheimer's Disease Center; Associate Director, Boston University ADC **AW:** TIME 100 Most Influential, 2018 **BA:** 940 Belmont Street, Brockton, MA, 02301

MCKEE, THEODORE A., T: Federal Judge **I:** Law and Legal Services **DOB:** 06/05/1947 **PB:** Rochester **SC:** NY/USA **ED:** JD magna cum laude, Syracuse University College of Law, 1975; BA, State University of New York, Cortland, 1969 **C:** Chief judge, US Court Appeals (3d cir.), 2010-16; Judge, US Court Appeals (3d cir.), Philadelphia, 1994-; Judge orphans' court division, Court of Common Pleas, 1st Judicial Dist, 1992; Judge major felony program, Court of Common Pleas, 1st Judicial Dist, 1986; Judge, Court of Common Pleas, 1st Judicial Dist, Pennsylvania, 1984-94; General counsel, Philadelphia Parking Auth., 1983; Deputy city solicitor, Law Department, Philadelphia, 1980-83; Lecturer, Rutgers University College of Law, 1980-91; Assistant US attorney, Eastern District General Crimes Unit, Narcotics and Firearms Unit, then Political Corruption Unit,; Assistant US attorney, Eastern District, Pennsylvania, 1977-80; Attorney, Wolf, Block, Schorr & Solis-Cohen, Philadelphia, 1975-77; Director of minority recruitment & admissions, State University of New York, Binghamton, 1969-72 **CR:** Board directors Diagnostic and Rehabilitation Center of Philadelphia **CIV:** Member adv. board, City Year for Philadelphia, Trustee, Edna McConnell Clark Foundation, **MEM:** Mem.: American Bar Association, Pennsylvania Bar Associate, Philadelphia Bar Associate, Temple Inn of Court, Barristers' Association Philadelphia, Am. Law Institute, National Bar Association, Crime Prevention Association (board directors) **BA:** 601 Market St, Philadelphia, PA, 19106

MCKENZIE, KEVIN PATRICK, T: Director **I:** Media & Entertainment **CN:** American Ballet School **DOB:** 04/29/1954 **PB:** Burlington **PT:** Son of Raymond James and Ruth (Davison) McKenzie **ED:** Attended, Washington School Ballet **C:** Artistic director, Am. Ballet Theatre, New York City, 1992-; Associate artistic director and choreographer, New Amsterdam Ballet; Artistic associate, Washington Ballet, 1991-92; Permanent guest artist, Washington Ballet, 1989; Principal dancer, Am. Ballet Theatre, New York City, 1979-91; Principal dancer, Joffrey Ballet, New York City, 1974-78; Member corps de ballet, National Ballet of Washington, 1972-74 **CR:** Founding board member Kaatsbaan International Dance Center, 1991-; pres-

ident board directors Am. Ballet Theatre Dancers Fund, Inc., 1982-89 **CW:** Performer: (films) Unicorn, 1971; dancer Houston Ballet, 1978, Spoleto Festival, 1980, 1984, Theatre des Champs Elysees, Paris, 1981, Sadler's Wells Theatre, London, 1981, Asami Maki Ballet Co., Tokyo, 1983, Aspen Festival, 1982, La Bayadere, Carmen, Cinderella, Coppelia, Dim Lustre, Don Quixote, Giselle, The Garden of Villandry, Jardin aux lilas, The Leaves Are Fading, Pillar of Fire, Raymonda, Requiem, Rodeo, Romeo and Juliet, The Sleeping Beauty, Swan Lake, La Sylphide, Paquita, Sylvia Pas de Deux, Theme and Variations; producer, director The Party of the Year, 1982; choreographer Groupo Zambaria Ballet, 1984, Liszt Etudes, 1991, Lucy and the Count, 1992, The Nutcracker, 1993, Don Quixote, 1995, (Swan Lake ballets) Am. Ballet Theatre, 2000, Metropolitan Opera House, 2001; created roles Adrienne Dellos' The Blind Man's Daughter, Seoul, Korea, 1986, Amnon V''Tamar, S.P.E.B.S.Q.S.A., appeared with Martine Van Hamel Swan Lake, National Ballet of Cuba, Havana, 1986, appeared with Merrill Ashley Tchaikowsky Pas de Deux, Bolshoi Theatre, Moscow, 1986 **AW:** Recipient naming of Kevin McKenzie Day, City of Burlington, 1985, Performing Arts award, Am. Ireland Fund, 1994, Artistic Achievement medal, Mayor Burlington, Vermont, 1984, Department State, U.S. Government, 1972, Silver medal, Varna International Ballet Competition, Bulgaria, 1972, Dance Magazine Award, 1999

MCKEOWN, M. MARGARET, T: Federal Judge **I:** Law and Legal Services **DOB:** 05/11/1951 **PB:** Casper **SC:** WY/USA **PT:** Robert Mark McKeown; Evelyn Margaret (Lipsack) McKeown **ED:** JD, Georgetown University (1975); BA in International Affairs and Spanish, University of Wyoming (1972) **C:** Judge, U.S. Court of Appeals for the Ninth Circuit, San Diego, CA (1998-Present); Managing Director, Strategic Planning and Client Relations, Perkins Coie, Seattle, WA (1990-1995); Partner, Member Executive Committee, Perkins Coie, Seattle, WA (1981-1998); Special Assistant, The White House, Washington, DC (1980-1981); Special Assistant, U.S. Department of the Interior, Washington, DC (1980-1981); Associate, Perkins Coie, Washington, DC (1979-1980); Associate, Perkins Coie, Seattle, WA (1975-1979) **CR:** Board of Directors, RAND Institute for Civil Justice (2003-Present); Adjunct Professor, University of San Diego (2003-Present); Lecturer, University of Washington Law School (2000-2001); Executive Committee, Ninth Circuit (2001-2004); Chair, Committee on Codes of Conduct (2009-Present); Judicial Conference (2001-Present); Member, Gender Bias Task Force (1992-1993); Representative, Ninth Circuit Judicial Conference, San Francisco, CA (1985-1989); Trustee, The Public Defender, Seattle, WA (1982-1985) **CIV:** National Board of Directors, Girl Scouts of the U.S., New York City, NY (1976-1987); Board of Directors, YMCA of Greater Seattle; Member, Executive Committee, Washington Council of International Trade; Board General Counsel, Downtown Seattle Association (1986-1989); Member, Executive Committee, Corporate Council for the Arts, Seattle, WA (1988-1998); Board of Directors, Family Services, Seattle, WA (1982-1984) **CW:** Author, "Girl Scout's Guide to New York" (1990); Contributor, Chapter to Book, Articles to Professional Journals **AW:** Named One of the Top 50 Women Lawyers, National Law Journal (1998); Washington's Winningest Trial Lawyers, Washington Journal (1992); Named One of the 100 Young Women of Promise, Good Housekeeping (1985); Rising Stars of the 80's Award, Legal Times Washington (1983); Fellow, Japan Leadership (1992-1993); Outstanding Lawyer Award, Seattle-King County Bar Association (1992) **MEM:** Fellow, ABA; House of Delegates, ABA (1990-1996); Judicial Advisory Committee to Standing Committee on Ethics, ABA (2001-2005); Joint Commission to Evaluate Code of Judicial Conduct, ABA (2003-2007); Chair, ABA (2004-2005); Standing Committee, Federal Judicial Improvements, ABA; Chair, ABA (2006-Present); Justice Center Coordinator Council, ABA (2006-Present); Committee Member, World Justice Project, ABA (2007-Present); Advisory Panel, Professor Responsibility, ABA (2007-Present); Louis M. Welsh Chapter, American inns of Court; Board of Directors, American Judicature Society (2001-Present); Association of Business Trial Lawyers (2002-Present); Executive Committee Member, Association of Business Trial Lawyers (2007-Present); American Intellectual Property Law Associate; American Law Institute; Board of Directors, National Association Iolta Programs (1989-1991); President, Board of Directors, Washington Women Lawyers (1978-1979); President, Trustee, Legal Foundation Washington (1989-1990); Trustee, Secretary, Seattle-King County Bar Association (1984-1985); Chairman, Judicial Recommendations, Washington Bar Association (1989-1990); Trustee, Federal Bar Association, Western District, Washington, DC (1980-1990); Board of Directors, White House Fellows Foundation (1998-Present); President, White House Fellows Foundation (2000-2001) **BAR:** The District of Columbia Bar (1982); Washington State Bar Association (1975) **H:** Travel; Classical Piano; Hiking; Gourmet Cooking; Tennis **BA:** 95 7th St, San Francisco, CA, 94013

MCKINLEY, DAVID B., **T:** U.S. Representative from West Virginia **I:** Government Administration/Government Relations/Government Services **DOB:** 05/28/1947 **PB:** Wheeling **ED:** BS in Engineering, Purdue University, West Lafayette, Ind., 1969 **C:** Member, US House Energy & Commerce Committee, 2011-; Member, US Congress from 1st West Virginia District, 2011-; Member, Republican Study Committee; Founder, principal, McKinley & Associates, Wheeling, 1981-; Member District 3, West Virginia House of Delegates, 1981-94 **CIV:** Chairman, West Virginia Rep. Party, 1992-96 **AW:** Named one of The 50 Most Influential People in West Virginia, West Virginia Executive Magazine **MEM:** Mem.: National Society Professional Engineers **PA:** Republican

MCMAHON, LINDA EDWARDS, **T:** Administrator **I:** Business Management/Business Services **CN:** Small Business Administration **DOB:** 10/04/1948 **PB:** New Bern **SC:** NC/USA **PT:** Henry Edwards; Evelyn Edwards **ED:** BA in French, East Carolina University (1969) **C:** Administrator, Small Business Administration, Washington, DC (2017-Present); Chief Executive Officer, World Wrestling Entertainment, Inc. (1997-2009); President, World Wrestling Entertainment, Inc. (1993-2000); Co-Founder, Board of Directors, World Wrestling Entertainment, Inc., Stamford, CT (1980-2017); Paralegal, Covington & Burling LLP **CR:** Member, International Advisory Council, APCO Worldwide (2013-Present) **CIV:** Member, Connecticut Board of Education (2009-Present); Board of Trustees, Sacred Heart University (2004-Present) **CW:** Producer, "WWE: Smackdown!" (1999-Present); Producer, "WWE: Sunday Night Heat" (1998-Present); Producer, "WWE: Raw is War" (1997-Present); Executive Producer, "WWE Experience" (2004) **PA:** Republican **BA:** Small Business Association, 409 Third Street SW, Washington, DC, 20024

MCMASTER, H.R., **T:** Former U.S. National Security Advisor **I:** Government Administration/Government Relations/Government Services **DOB:** 07/24/1962 **ED:** BS, U.S. Military Academy; PhD, University of North Carolina Chapel Hill **C:** National Security Advisor, 2017-2018,; Director of the U.S. Army Training and Doctrine Command's Army Capabilities Integration Center, 2014-,; Commanding General, Maneuver Center of Excellence at Fort Benning, 2012-14,; Director, Concept Development and Learning at the U.S. Army Training and Doctrine Command, Fort Monroe, 2008-10,; Special Assistant to the Commander, Multinational Force, Iraq, 2007-08,; Director, Commander's Advisory Group at US Central Command, 2003-04,; Assistant Professor of History, US Military Academy. 1994-96,; National Security Affairs Fellow, Hoover Institution, 2002-03 **MIL:** U.S. Army, 1984- **CW:** Author: (Books) Dereliction of Duty, 1997 **BA:** 1600 Pennsylvania Ave N.W., Washington, DC, 20502

MCMASTER, HENRY DARGAN, **T:** Governor of South Carolina **I:** Government Administration/Government Relations/Government Services **DOB:** 05/27/1947 **PB:** Columbia **SC:** SC/USA **PT:** John Gregg McMaster, Ida Bacot (Dargan) McMaster **ED:** JD, University of South Carolina School of Law, 1973; BA in History, University of South Carolina, 1969 **C:** Governor, State Of South Carolina, 2017-Present; Lieutenant Governor, State Of South Carolina, 2015-Present; Attorney General, State Of South Carolina, 2003-2011; Partner, Tompkins & McMaster, Columbia, SC, 1985-2003; Head, Law Enforcement Coordinating Committee, District of South Carolina, 1981-1985; U.S. Attorney, District of South Carolina, Columbia, SC, 1981-1985; Partner, Tompkins & McMaster, Columbia, SC, 1974-1981; Attorney, Legislative Assistant To Rep. Strom Thurmond, U.S. Senate, Washington, DC, 1973-1974 **CR:** Chairman, South Carolina Republican Party, 1994-2002; Board of Directors, South Carolina Policy Council, 1991-2003; South Carolina Commission on Higher Education, 1991-1994 **CW:** Contributor, Articles, Legal Publications **MEM:** Province Commander, Kappa Alpha, 1975-1991, Deputy Province Commander, Kappa Alpha, 1974-1975, American Bar Association, South Carolina Bar Association, Richland County Bar Association, Centurian Society, Caroliniana Ball Club, Phi Delta Phi, St. Andrew's Society **BAR:** U.S. Supreme Court, 1978, U.S. Court of Appeals, Fourth Circuit, 1976, U.S. Court of Claims, 1974, U.S. District Court, South Carolina, 1973, South Carolina, 1973 **PA:** Republican

MCMILLON, DOUG, **T:** Retail Executive **I:** Retail/Sales **DOB:** 10/12/1966 **PB:** Memphis **SC:** TN/USA **PT:** Son of Morris and Laura McMillon; **ED:** MBA in Finance, University of Tulsa, 1991; BA in Business Administration, University of Arkansas, 1989 **C:** President, CEO, Wal-Mart Inc., 2018-; President, CEO, Wal-Mart Stores, Inc., 2014-2018; President, CEO, Sam's Club Division, 2005-09; Executive Vice President Merchandising & Replenishment, Sam's Club Division, 2002-05; President, CEO, Wal-Mart International, 2009-14; Executive Vice President, Wal-Mart Stores, Inc., 2005-09; Senior Vice President, General Merchandise Manager, Wal-Mart Stores, Inc., 1999-2002; Rejoined Company, Wal-Mart Stores, Inc., 1991; Buyer Trainee in Sporting Goods, Wal-Mart Stores, Inc., 1984 **CR:** Board of Directors Wal-Mart Stores, Inc., 2013- **CIV:** Director Emeritus, The Sunshine School, Bentonville, Arkansas, Member Executive Board, Center Retailing Excellence, University Arkansas, Board of Advisors, National Council La Raza, **AW:** Named One of The World's Most Powerful People, Forbes Magazine, 2014

MCMORRIS-RODGERS, CATHY, **T:** U.S. Representative from Washington **I:** Government Administration/Government Relations/Government Services **DOB:** 05/22/1969 **PB:** Salem **SC:** MA/USA **ED:** MBA, University of Washington, 2002; BA, Pensacola Christian College, Florida, 1990 **C:** Chair, U.S. House Republican Conference, 2013-; Member, U.S. Congress from 5th Washington District, 2005-; Member, Committee on Energy and Commerce; Vice chair, U.S. House Republican Conference, 2009-12; Minority leader, Washington State House of Reps., 2002-03; Member District 7, Washington State House of Reps., 1995-2005 **AW:** Named one of The 100 Most Powerful Women in DC, Washingtonian magazine, 2009; recipient Gold Medal, Ind. Business Association, 1996, Guardian of Small Business award, National Federation Ind. Business, 1996, Sentinal award, Washington State Law Enforcement Association, 1996, Cornerstone award, Association Washington Business, 1995-96 **MEM:** Mem.: Washington Women for Survival of Agriculture, Washington Rural Health Association, Washington State Farm Bureau (Legislator of Year 1997), Washington State Cattlemen's Association **PA:** Republican

MCMULLEN, RODNEY, **T:** CEO **I:** Retail/Sales **CN:** The Kroger Co. **PB:** Willamstown **SC:** KY/USA **ED:** BS in Accounting, University Kentucky, 1981; BBA in Finance, University Kentucky, 1981; MS in Accounting, University Kentucky, 1982 **CT:** CPA **C:** Chmn., CEO, The Kroger Co., Cincinnati, Ohio, 2015—; Assistant treasurer, The Kroger Co., Cincinnati, Ohio, 1988-90; Financial analyst, The Kroger Co., Cincinnati, Ohio, 1985-88; CEO, The Kroger Co., Cincinnati, Ohio, 2014; Pres., COO, The Kroger Co., Cincinnati, Ohio, 2009—2013; Vice chairman, The Kroger Co., Cincinnati, Ohio, 2003—2009; Executive vice president strategy, planning & finance, The Kroger Co., Cincinnati, Ohio, 2000—2003; Senior vice president, CFO, The Kroger Co., Cincinnati, Ohio, 1997-2000; Group vice president, CFO, The Kroger Co., Cincinnati, Ohio, 1995-97; Vice president financial services & control, The Kroger Co., Cincinnati, Ohio, 1993-95; Vice president planning & capital management, The Kroger Co., Cincinnati, Ohio, 1990-93 **CR:** Board directors Cincinnati Financial Co., 2001—, The Kroger Co., 2003— **CIV:** Trustee Xavier University, Business Partnership Foundation, Gatton College Business and Economics, University Kentucky **BA:** Kroger Headquarters, The Kroger Co 1014 Vine St, Cincinnati, OH, 45202

MCNAIR, ROBERT C., **I:** Business Management/Business Services **PB:** Tampa **SC:** FL/USA **ED:** LHD (hon.), University of South Carolina, Columbia, 1999; BS, University of South Carolina, Columbia, 1958 **C:** Chairman, CEO, Houston Texans, 1999-; Founder, Houston NFL Holdings, 1998; Chairman, CEO, RCM Fin. Services LP; Chairman, CEO, Palmetto Partners, Ltd.; Chairman, The McNair Group; Founder, CEO, Cogen Techs. Energy Group, Houston; Chairman, US Telesys, Inc.; Chairman, Cypress Telecommunications Corp. **CR:** Speaker in field member audit, fin., stadium and expansion committees NFL, chairman investment committee chairman emeritus The Texas Bowl board directors Mosher, Inc., Federal Reserve Bank, Dallas, Houston owner, thoroughbred horse farm Stonerside Stable, Kentucky **CIV:** Chairman, Board of Trustees McNair Foundation, Free Enterprise Institute, President, Houston Grand Opera Association, Board of Trustees, Baylor College Medicine, Houston, Sigma Chi Foundation, Museum Fine Arts, Greater Houston Partnership, Greater Houston Convention Center and Visitors Bureau, Board of Governors, Rice University, Founder, Cotswold Project, Houston Elder Memorial Dr. Presbyterian

Church, Houston **AW:** Named Entrepreneur of Decade, Houston Tech. Center, 2009; Named One of Forbes 400: Richest Americans, 2006-; Named to Texas Business Hall of Fame; Recipient, President & Mrs. George H.W. Bush Community Impact Award, Fellowship Christian Athletes, National Patriotism, Responsible Citizenship and Community Involvement Award, Freedoms Foundation at Valley Forge, Denton A. Cooley Leadership Award, Texas Heart Institute, Trailblazer Award, Houston Advertising Federation, City Builder Award, South Main Center Association, Distinguished Citizen Award, Sam Houston Area Council of Boy Scouts America, Rotary Club Houston, Distinguished Am. Award, National Football Foundation Houston Chapter, Herman W. Lay Memorial Award, Association Private Enterprise Education, Outstanding Business Leader Award, Northwood University, Torch of Liberty Award, ADL

MCNERNEY, JERRY, T: U.S. Representative from California, Engineer **I:** Government Administration/Government Relations/Government Services **DOB:** 06/18/1951 **PB:** Alburquerque **SC:** NM/USA **ED:** PhD in Engineering & Math., University New Mexico, 1981; MS, University New Mexico, 1975; BS, University New Mexico, 1973; Attended, US Military Academy, West Point, New York **C:** Member, US Congress from 9th California District, 2013-; Member, US Congress from 11th California District, Washington, 2007-13; CEO, Hawt Power Inc., 2003-04; Senior engineer, field manager, Wind Turbine Co., 1999-2003; Energy consultant various cos., PG&E, FloWind, Electric Power Rsch Institute, 1994-98; Senior engineer, US Wind Power/Kenetech Inc., 1985-94; Contractor, Sandia National Laboratories, Kirkland Air Force Base, **MEM:** Mem.: American Math. Society, American Society Mechanical Engineers **H:** Reading, hunting, running, hiking **PA:** Democrat **BA:** 1431 Longworth House Office Building, Washington, DC, 20515

MCREYNOLDS, JOHN W., I: Oil & Energy **C:** President, CFO and Board Cirectors, Energy Transfer Equity, LP, 2005-; Partner, Hunton & Williams LLP, 1979-2005; Attorney, Hunton & Williams LLP, 1978 **CR:** Board directors Energy Transfer Partners, LP, 2004-, LE GP LLC, 2004

MCSALLY, MARTHA ELIZABETH, T: U.S. Representative from Arizona, Retired Military Officer **I:** Government Administration/Government Relations/Government Services **DOB:** 03/22/1966 **PB:** Warwick **SC:** NY/USA **PT:** Daughter of Bernard and Eleanor McSally; **ED:** LLD in Civil Law (hon.), Rhode Island College; MS in Strategic Studies, Air War College; MPP, Harvard University John F. Kennedy School Government; BS, US Air Force, 1988 **C:** Member, US Congress from 2nd Arizona District, Washington, 2014-; Member, Committee on Armed Services, Committee on Homeland Security; Adv. on national security issues to Senator Jon. Kyl, US Senate; Commander, 354th Fighter Squadron, Davis-Monthan AFB, 2004-06; Flight Commander then director operations 612 Combat Operations Squadron, 12th Air Force Headquarters, Davis-Monthan AFB,; Retired, US Air Force, 2010; Advanced through ranks to colonel, US Air Force, 1988 **CR:** Professor George Marshall European Center for Security Studies, Garmisch-Partenkirchen, Germany, 2011- **AW:** Named a Woman Who Leads, University Arizona Women's Studies Advisory Council, 2005; recipient Lifetime Achievement award, National Center for Women in Policing, Woman on the Move award, Tucson YWCA, David C. Shilling award, Air Force Association, 2005, Al Neuharth Free Spirit award, 2002 **ACH:** Achievements include becoming the first woman in US history to fly a combat airctaft into enemy territory, 1995; the first woman to command a U.S. Air Force fighter squadron **PA:** Republican

MCWHORTER, DIANE, T: Journalist, Author **I:** Writing and Editing **DOB:** 11/01/1952 **PB:** Tupelo **SC:** MI/USA **ED:** BA in Comparative Lit., Wellesley College **C:** Writer, New York City **CW:** Author: Carry Me Home: Birmingham, Alabama,The Climactic Battle of the Civil Rights Revolution, 2001 (Pulitzer prize for general nonfiction, 2002, named New York Times Notable Book, winner, Southern Book Critics Circle award, 2001, J. Anthony Lukas Book prize, 2002, English Speaking Union Ambassador award, 2002, Sidney Hillman Foundation award, 2002), A Dream of Freedom: The Civil Rights Movement from 1954 to 1968, 2004 (New York Times Notable Children's Book, 2004, USA Today Best Children's History, 2004, on American Library Association Best New Book for Young Adults list, 2004); contributor articles to newspapers, chapters to books **AW:** Recipient Clarence Cason award, 2003; Guggenheim fellowship, Am. Academy in Berlin, 2009, Holtzbrinck fellowship, 2007, Pulitzer Prize, 2002, J. Anthony Lukas Book Prize, 2002, National Endowment for the Humanities, 2015

MEAD, MATTHEW HANSEN, T: Governor from Wyoming **I:** Government Administration/Government Relations/Government Services **DOB:** 03/11/1962 **PB:** Jackson, Wyoming, March 11, 1962 **PT:** Son of Peter Bradford and Mary (Hansen) Mead; **ED:** JD, University Wyoming School Law, 1987; BA, Trinity University, San Antonio, Texas, 1984 **C:** Governor, State of Wyoming, 2011-; Co-owner, Mead Land & Livestock, LLC,; US attorney Wyoming, US Department Justice, 2001-07; Partner, Mead & Phillips, 1997-2001; Private law practice, Cheyenne, 1995-97; Assistant US attorney, US Department Justice, 1991-95; Deputy county attorney, Cambell Co. Atty Office, Wyoming, 1987-90 **CR:** Board directors Wyoming Bank & Trust **PA:** Republican **BA:** Idelman Mansion, 2323 Carey Ave., Cheyenne, WY, 82002

MEADOWS, MARK RANDALL, T: U.S. Representative from North Carolina **I:** Government Administration/Government Relations/Government Services **DOB:** 07/28/1959 **PB:** Verdun **ED:** BS in Business Management, University South Florida, 1981 **C:** Member, US House Transportation & Infrastructure Committee, 2013-; Member, US House Oversight & Government Committee, 2013-; Member, US House Foreign Affairs Committee, 2013-; Member, US Congress from 11th North Carolina District, 2013-; owner, Highland Properties, 1990-; Chairman, Macon County Republican Party, 2002; Owner sandwich shop, 1986-90; Director customer relations & public safety, Tampa Electric, 1983-86 **PA:** Republican

MEARS, RICK RAVON, T: Professional Race Car Driver **I:** Athletics **DOB:** 12/03/1951 **PB:** Wichita **PT:** Son of Bill Ravon and Mae Louise (Simpson) M. **MS:** Married **SPN:** Christyn Bowen, November 28, 1986; **CH:** Clint Ravon, Cole Ray **ED:** Student public schools **C:** Consultant, Penske Racing Team, 1993-; Retired, 1992; Member, Penske Racing Team, 1978-92; Professional race car driver, 1973-92 **AW:** Winner 3d annual Firecracker 250, Japan Grand Prix Off-Road Race, 1973, 74, Nor-Cal 100 1974, several regional and national Formula Vee and Super Vee Races, 1974, 3d Place Sprint Buggy Open-Wheel Pikes Peak Hill Climb, 1976, Indianapolis 500, 1979, 84, 88, 91, Trenton Race, 1979, Atlanta Race, 1979, National Championship, 1979, Mexico City Race, 1980, 81, 2 Atlanta Races, 1981, Riverside Race, 1981, Michigan Race, 1981, Watkins Glen Race, 1981, National Championship Auto Racing Team, 1979, 81, 82, 4 Indy Car Races, 1982, Michigan 200 Indy Car Race, 1983, Triple Crown Championship, 1983, 84, 2nd Indy 500, 1984, Pocono 500, 1985, 87, Milwaukee Indy Car Race, 1988, 89, Laguna Seca Race, 1989, Phoenix Race, 1989, 90, Michigan 500, 1991, total 29 national championship races in 203 career starts; named co-Rookie of the Year Indianapolis 500, 1978, Rookie of Year Championship Division U.S. Auto Club, 1976, Am. Auto Racing Writers and Broadcasters Association Auto Racing All American, 1979, Driver of Decade, Associated Press, 1989, One of 10 Champions for Life, Driver of Year Awards, 1992; recipient U.S. Driver of Year Jerry Titus Memorial trophy, 1981,International Motorsports Hall of Fame, 1997, Motorsports Hall of Fame of America, 1998, Penske Hall of Fame, 2017 **ACH:** Qualified on front row Indianapolis 500, 1978; set closed course Indianapolis car speed record Michigan International Speedway, 1986; scored 4 pole positions Michigan International Speedway, 1986, 4th Indianapolis 500 pole, 1988, 3 pole positions Phoenix International Raceway, 1990, 6th pole at Indianapolis 500, 1991; first driver in Indianapolis car history to win poles at Indianapolis, Michigan and Pocono Races, 1988.

MEDINA, GABRIEL, T: Professional Surfer **I:** Athletics **PB:** Sao Paulo **SC:** Brazil **C:** Surfer (2003-Present) **AW:** Champion, Vans Triple Crown of Surfing (2015); World Champion (2014); World Junior Champion, World Surf League (WSL) (2013); Nine Time World Surf League (WSL) Event Winner **ACH:** 2013 WSL World Junior Champion; 2014 World Champion; 2015 Vans Triple Crown of Surfing Champion; 9 Time World Surf League Event Winner

MEEHAN, PATRICK LEO, T: U.S. Representative from Pennsylvania **I:** Government Administration/Government Relations/Government Services **DOB:** 10/20/1955 **PB:** Cheltenham, Pennsylvania **ED:** JD, Temple University School Law, Philadelphia, 1986; BA, Bowdoin College, Brunswick, Maine, 1978 **CT:** Bar: US Court Appeals (3rd cir.), US District Court (eastern district) Pennsylvania, Pennsylvania **C:** Member, US House Ethics Committee, 2013-; Member, US House Transportation & Infrastructure Committee, Washington, 2011-; Member, US House Oversight & Government Reform Committee, Washington, 2011-; Member, US House Homeland Security Committee, Washington, 2011-; Member, US Congress from 7th Pennsylvania District, Washington, 2011-; Partner, Conrad O'Brien PC, Philadelphia, 2008-10; US Attorney (Eastern District) Pennsylvania, US Department Justice, Philadelphia, 2001-08; District Attorney, Delaware County, Pennsylvania, 1996-2001; Senior Counsel, Executive Director to Senator Arlen Specter, US Senate, 1992-94; Associate, Dilworth, Paxon, Kalish & Kauffman, Philadelphia,; Former Official, NHL, **MEM:** Del. County Bar Association **PA:** Republican

MEEKS, GREGORY WELDON, T: U.S. Representative from New York **I:** Government Administration/Government Relations/Government Services **DOB:** 09/25/1953 **PB:** NYC **PT:** Son of James Weldon and Mary (McNeal) Meeks; Married Simone-Marie Meeks; children: Ebony Renee, Aja J., Nia-Aiyana. **ED:** JD, Howard University School Law, Washington, 1978; BA in Hist., Adelphi University, Garden City, New York, 1975 **C:** Member, US Congress from 5th New York District, 2013-; Member, Committee on Financial Services, Committee on Foreign Affairs; Member, US Congress from 6th New York District, 1998-2013; Member, New York State Assembly, 1993-98; Supervising judge, New York State Workers' Compensation Board, 1987-93; Judge, New York State Workers' Compensation

Board, 1985-87; Hearing officer, New York Family Court, 1984-85; Assistant counsel, State Investigations Commission, 1983-84; Assistant special narcotics prosecutor, Office of Special Narcotics Prosecutor, New York City, 1981-83; Assistant district attorney, Queens District Atty.'s Office, 1978-81 **CIV:** Board directors Rockaway Peninsula Civic Association, 1983-1991, Peninsula General Hospital, 1989- chairman board Joseph P. Addabbo Family Health Care Center, 1990-92 **AW:** Recipient National Association for the Advancement of Colored People Political Leadership award, 1989, Outstanding Vol. Mentor award, New York Mentoring, 1990, Community Leader award Boy Scouts America, 1992, William Garvin Pub. Service award, 2004, Congressional Leadership award, National Urban League, 2006; named one of The Most Influential Black Americans Ebony magazine, 2006; named to The Power 150 Ebony magazine, 2008. **MEM:** Member American Bar Association, Macon B. Allen Black Bar Association (vice president), Queens County Bar Association, Far Rockaway National Association for the Advancement of Colored People (Political Leadership award 1989), Alpha Phi Alpha **PA:** Democrat

MEHROTRA, SANJAY, T: CEO **I:** Engineering **CN:** Micron Technology, Inc. **ED:** MS in Electrical Engineering & Computer Science, University of California, Berkeley; BS in Electrical Engineering & Computer Science, University of California, Berkeley **C:** President, Chief Executive Officer, Micron Technology, Inc. (2017-Present); President, Chief Executive Officer, SanDisk Corp. (2011-2016); President, SanDisk Corp. (2006-2011); Chief Operating Officer, SanDisk Corp. (2001-2011); Various Positions Including Director Memory Design and product engineering, vice president engineering, product Development, Senior Vice President of Engineering, Executive Vice President, SanDisk Corp.; Co-founder, SanDisk Corp. (1988); Senior Engineering and Engineering Management Positions, Integrated Device Technologies, Inc.; Senior Engineering and Engineering Management Positions, Atmel Corp.; Senior Engineering and Engineering Management Positions, SEEQ Technologies, Inc.; Senior Engineering and Engineering Management Positions, Intel Corp. **CR:** Board of Directors, SanDisk Corp. (2010-Present); Cavium Networks, Inc. (2009-Present); Divio Board of Advisors, University of California, Berkeley **CIV:** Member, Engineering Advisory Board, University of California, Berkeley **BA:** Micron Technology, 8000 South Federal Way PO Box 6, Boise, ID, 83716-0006

MEIER, RICHARD, T: Architect **I:** Architecture & Construction **DOB:** 10/12/1934 **PB:** Newark **SC:** New Jersey **PT:** Son of Jerome and Carolyn (Kaltenbacher) M.; Married Katherine Gormley, January 21, 1978 (div.); children: Joseph Max, Ana Moss **ED:** PhD (hon.), Mercy College, 2004; PhD (hon.), North Carolina State University, 2004; PhD (hon.), University Bucharest, 2001; PhD (hon.), Pratt School Fine Arts, 1999; PhD (hon.), Wheaton College, 1998; PhD (hon.), Parsons School Design, 1998; PhD (hon.), University Naples, Italy, 1991; BArch, Cornell University, Ithaca, New York, 1957 **CT:** Registered professional architect, New York, New Jersey, Connecticut, Michigan, Virginia, Florida, Ind., Georgia, California, Illinois, Iowa, Texas, Oregon **C:** Architect, principal, Richard Meier & Partners, 1980-; Principal architect, Richard Meier & Associates, New York City, 1963-80; Architect, Marcel Breuer & Associates, 1960-63; Architect, Skidmore, Owings & Merrill, 1959-60; Architect, Davis, Brody & Wisniewski, New York City, 1959; Architect, Frank Grad & Sons, New Jersey, 1957 **CR:** Resident architect Am. Academy

Rome, 1973-74; visiting critic Pratt Institute, 1960-62, 65, Princeton, 1963, Syracuse University, 1964; William Henry Bishop visiting professor architecture Yale University, 1975, 77; visiting critic, 1967, 72, 73, 77, Davenport professor, 2008; visiting professor Harvard University, 1977, UCLA, 1988; Eliot Noyes visiting critic in architecture, 1980-81 Harvey S. Perloff visiting professor architecture UCLA, 1987, 88, 90, 2000; adjunct professor architecture Cooper Union, New York City, 1963-73; member adv. council Cornell University College Art, Architecture and Planning; member Jerusalem Committee Exhibitions, XV Triennale, Milan, 1973, Museum Modern Art, New York City, 1975, 81, Princeton University, Biennale, Venice, Italy, 1976, Cooper-Hewitt Museum, New York City, 1976-77, Leo Castelli Gallery, New York City, 1977, 94, Rosa Esman Gallery, New York City, 1978, 80, New Jersey State Museum, 1978, Modernism Gallery, San Francisco, Wadsworth Atheneum, Hartford, Connecticut, High Museum Art, Atlanta Harvard University, Max Protech Gallery, 1980, Syracuse University, Whitney Museum Art, New York City, 1982, Knoll International, Tokyo, Japan, 1988, October Gallery, London, 1990, Royal Palace, Naples, Italy, 1991, Palazzo delle Esposizione, Rome, 1993, Aichi Prefectural Museum Art, Nagoya, Japan, 1996, LTB Foundation, London, 2008 professor Cooper Union, 1963-66, 66-69, 69-73 **CW:** Principal works include Westbeth Artists Housing, New York City, Bronx Devel. Center, New York, Smith House, Darien, Connecticut, Douglas House, Harbor Springs, Michigan, Shamberg House, Mount Kisco, New York, Hoffman and Saltzman Houses, East Hampton, New York; houses in Old Westbury, New York, Pound Ridge, New York, Palm Beach, Florida, Pittsburgh; Twin Parks NE Housing, New York City, Atheneum, New Harmony, Ind., New York, Hartford Seminary, Connecticut, Museum für Kunsthandwerk, Frankfurt, Germany, Des Moines Art Center, High Museum Art, Atlanta, Bridgeport Center, New York, Daimler-Benz Office and Laboratory Complex, Ulm, Germany, Weishaupt Forum, Schwendi, Germany, City Hall and Cen. Libr., The Hague, The Netherlands, Corp. Hdqs., Royal Dutch Paper Mills, Hilversum, The Netherlands, Cornell University Alumni and Admissions Center, Ithaca, New York, Canal Hdqs., Paris, Espace Pitot, Montpellier, France, Maybury Office Park, Edinburgh, Hypolux Bank Building, Luxembourg, Museum Contemporary Art, Barcelona, Spain, Arp Museum, Rolandseck, Germany, Swiss Volksbank, Basel Office Building, Singapore, The Getty Center, LA, SwissAir Hdqs., Melville, New York, Federal Courthouse, Islip, New York, Phoenix, Museum TV & Radio, LA, Gagosian Gallery, LA, Rachofsky House, Dallas, Church of Year 2000, 173 & 176 Perry St., New York City, 2002 (Royal Institute Brit. Architects award 2006), Frieder Burda Collection Museum, Baden-Badem, Germany, 2004 (Royal Institute Brit. Architects award 2006), Rome, Ara Pacis, Rome, 2006, 165 Charles St., New York City, 2006, One Grand Army Plz., Brooklyn, 2008, Rothschild Tower, Tel Aviv, 2008-, others; author: Richard Meier Architect, vol. 1, 1964-68, vol. 2, 1985-91, vol. 3, 1992-99, vol. 4, 2000-04, On Architecture, 1982, Richard Meier Collages, 1990, The Getty Center Design Process, J. Paul Getty Trust, 1991, Richard Meier Sculpture, 1994; contributor articles to professional journals,(Principal Works) International Coffee Plaza, Hamburg, Germany, 2010, Bodrum Houses, Bodrum, Turkey, 2010, Vinci Partners Corporate Headquarters, Rio de Janeiro, Brazil, 2012,Vitrum Apartments, Bogotá, Colombia, 2013, Teachers Village, Newark, New Jersey, 2013,Engel & Völkers, HafenCity, Hamburg, Germany, 2015 **AW:** Decorated officer de l'Ordre des Arts et des Lettres (France), 1984; recipient Arnold Brunner Memorial prize, American

Academy of Arts and Letters, 1972, Albert S. Bard Civic award, City Club New York, 1973, 1st honor award for excellence in architecture and urban design, 1977, R.S. Reynolds Memorial award, 1977, Architectural Record award of excellence for design, 1964, 68, 69, 70, 77, Am. Institute Steel Construction award, 1978, 79, design award 1st prize Kunsthandwerk Competition, Frankfurt am Main, Federal Republic Germany, 1980, Pritzker Prize for Architecture, 1984, Praemium Imperiale, Japan, 1997, Am. Institute Architects, LA Chapter Gold Medal, 1998, El Gobierno del Distrito Federal "Huesped Distinguido de la Ciudad de Mexico," 2000, American Institute of Architects 25-Yr. award for Smith House, 2000, New York Magazine award for Architect, 2003, Frate Sole International award for Sacred Architecture, 2004, Dedalo Minosse International Prize for Commissioning a Building - Quinquennial Hon. award, Associazione Liberi Architetti, 2004, Pratt Legend award, 2004, Sidney L. Strauss award, New York Society Architects, 2004, Gold medal for Architecture, Am. Academy Arts and Letters, 2008, The Pres.'s medal Architectural League New York, 2009, Ellis Island Family Heritage award (Arts/Architecture), 2012,A+ Life Achievemant Award, 2010 **MEM:** Fellow American Institute of Architects (medal of honor New York chapter 1980, national design committee 1972-74, 30 American Institute of Architects national awards 1968-2006, 50 chapter awards New York 1965-2006, Chicago Architect award, 1995, 5 Progressive Architecture awards 1979, 89, 90, 91, 95, Gold medal 1997), Am. Academy Arts & Sci., 1995; member National Academy of Design (academician), International Institute Architects, Royal Institute Brit. Architects (Royal Gold medal 1989), Belgian Royal Academy Art (Lifetime Achievement award Guild Hall 1991, commdr. de l'Ordre des Arts et Lettres, France, 1992). **BA:** Richard Meier & Ptnrs, 475 10th Ave Fl 6, New York, NY, 10018

MELLO, CRAIG CAMERON, T: Biologist, Educator **I:** Education/Educational Services **DOB:** 10/18/1960 **PB:** New Haven **ED:** PhD in Biology, Harvard University, 1990; BS in Biochemistry, Brown University, Providence, 1982 **C:** Howard Hughes Medical Institute Investigator, 2000-; Blais Univ. chair in molecular medicine, University Massachusetts Medical School, 2003-; Professor program in molecular medicine, University Massachusetts Medical School, Worcester, 1994-; Postdoc. research fellow, Fred Hutchinson Cancer Research Center, Seattle, 1990-94 **CR:** Investigator Howard Hughes Medical Institute, 2000- **CW:** Contributor articles to professional journals **AW:** Co-recipient Nobel prize in physiology/medicine, 2006; recipient Paul Ehrlich & Ludwig Darmstaedter prize, Germany, 2006, Dr. Paul Janssen award for biomed. research, Johnson & Johnson, 2006, Gairdner Foundation International award, 2005, Lewis S. Rosenstiel award, Brandeis University, 2005, Massry prize, 2005, Wiley prize in biomed. scis., Rockefeller University, 2003; Pew scholar, University California, San Francisco, 1995 **MEM:** Fellow: Am. Academy Arts & Sciences; mem.: National Academy of Sciences (Award in molecular biology 2003) **ACH:** Achievements include discovery of the process now known as RNAi (with Andrew Z. Fire), that double-stranded RNA can quash the activity of specific genes

MENDES, SHAWN, T: Singer **I:** Media & Entertainment **DOB:** 07/08/1905 **PB:** Toronto, Ontario **SC:** Toronto, Ontario **CW:** (Film) Handwritten, 2015, Illuminate, 2016, Shawn Mendes, 2018 **AW:** Time 100 Most Influential, 2018

MENDEZ, LINDSAY, T: Actress and Singer **I:** Media & Entertainment **PB:** Norwalk **SC:** CA/USA **CW:** Actress, Theatre, "Grease" (2007-2008), "Everyday Rapture" (2010), "Godspell" (2011-2012), "Wicked" (2013-2014), "Significant Other" (2017), "Carousel" (2018); Singer, "Grease Revival" (2008), "New York City Christmas" (2009), "Everyday Rapture" (2010), "Godspell" (2011), "35MM: A Musical Exhibition" (2012), "This Time" (2013), "Kerrigan-Lowdermilk Live" (2013), "Dogfight" (2013), "21 Chump Street" (2014) **AW:** Tony Award for Best Actress in a Musical (2018)

MENEAR, CRAIG ALBERT, T: CEO **I:** Business Management/Business Services **CN:** The Home Depot, Inc. **PB:** Flint **SC:** Michigan **ED:** BA in Business, Michigan State University Eli Broad College Business, 1979 **C:** President, CEO, The Home Depot, Inc., 2014-; President US retail, The Home Depot, Inc., Atlanta, 2014; Executive vice president merchandising, The Home Depot, Inc., Atlanta, 2007-14; Senior vice president merchandising, The Home Depot, Inc., Atlanta, 2003-07; Merchandising vice president hardware, The Home Depot, Inc., Atlanta,; Merchandising vice president Southwest division, The Home Depot, Inc., Atlanta; Division merchandise manager, The Home Depot, Inc., Atlanta; Joined, The Home Depot, Inc., 1997; With, Montgomery Ward; With, Grace Home Ctrs.; With, Builders Emporium; With, IKEA Wholesale, Inc. **CR:** Board directors The Home Depot, Inc., 2014- chairman The Home Depot Foundation **BA:** The Home Depot Inc, 2455 Paces Ferry Rd NW, Atlanta, GA, 30339-4024

MENENDEZ, ROBERT, T: U.S. Senator from New Jersey **I:** Government Administration/Government Relations/Government Services **DOB:** 01/01/1954 **PB:** New York City **SC:** NY/USA **PT:** Son of Mario and Evangelina (Lopez) M. **SPN:** Jane Jacobsen, June 5, 1976 (div. 2005); **CH:** Alicia, Robert **ED:** JD, Rutgers University, 1979; BA in Political Sci. and Urban Studies, St. Peter's College, 1976 **CT:** Bar: New Jersey 1980 **C:** U.S. Senator from New Jersey, 2006-; Chairman, U.S. Senate Foreign Relations Committee, 2013-15; Chairman, Democratic Senatorial Campaign Committee (DSCC), 2009-11; Chairman, U.S. House Democratic Caucus, 2003-06; Member, U.S. Congress from 13th New Jersey District, 1993-2006; Member District 33, New Jersey State Senate, 1992-93; Member District 33, New Jersey General Assembly, 1987-91; Mayor, City of Union City, 1986-92; Attorney, Diaz & Menendez, Union City, New Jersey, 1980-92 **CR:** Co-chair Hillary Rodham Clinton Presidential Campaign, 2007-08 **CIV:** CFO Union City Board Education, 1978-82, Trustee, 1974-78 Member Alliance Civic Association, 1982-92, President 1981 Member Gov.'s Hispanic Adv. Committee, Trenton, New Jersey, 1984- Member Gov.'s Ethnic Adv. Committee, Washington, 1985 **AW:** Recipient Community Service award Gran Logia del Norte, 1981, Outstanding Service award Hispanic Law Enforcement, 1981, Outstanding Community Service Revista Actualidades, 1982, U.S. Conference Mayors Award, 1987, 1988, 1991, Distinguished Citizen Award University Medicine and Dentistry New Jersey, 1994, Man of Year Award Kiwanis, 1994, Justice of Cyprus Award, Cyprus Federation Am., 1995, Am. Hellenic Institute Public Service Achievement Award, 1997, Lifetime Achievement Award Hispanic Business Roundtable, 2000, Excellence in Education Award, Ana G. Mendez University System, 2003, Capital Award National Council of La Raza, 2003, Paraskevaides Award, 16th Annual Cyprus Conference, 2005; Named Man of the Year, Armenian National Committee New Jersey, 2007 **MEM:** Member American Bar Association, Federal Bar Association New

Jersey Bar Association, Hispanic Bar Association, Hudson County Bar Association, New Jersey Employment & Training Commission, New Jersey Mayors Coalition, New Jersey Hispanic Leadership Opportunities Program (Chairman), Hispanic Elected and Apptd Ofcls. Organization (Chairman); Hoboken Elks Club, North Hudson Lawyers Club (Chairman) **H:** Chess, Racquetball **PA:** Democrat **BA:** Office of Bob Menendez, 528 Hart Senate Office Building, Washington, DC, 20510

MENG, GRACE, T: U.S. Representative from New York, former state legislator **I:** Government Administration/Government Relations/Government Services **DOB:** 10/01/1975 **PB:** Queens **PT:** Daughter of Jimmy K. Meng **ED:** JD, Yeshiva University, Benjamin N. Cardozo School Law, 2002; BA, University Michigan, 1997 **C:** Vice Chair, Democratic National Committee, 2017-; Member, US House Small Business Committee, 2013-; Member, US House Foreign Affairs Committee, 2013-; Member, US Congress from 6th New York District, Washington, 2013-; Member District 22, New York State Assembly, Flushing, 2009-13; Partner, Yoon & Kim, LLP,; Campaign worker, Barack Obama's Presidential Campaign, 2008; Campaign worker for, Hillary Rodham Clinton Senatorial Campaign, 2006; Campaign worker for, Lieutenant Governor David Paterson, 2006; Campaign worker for, New York State Governor Eliot Spitzer, 2006; Campaign worker for, Fernando Ferrer, 2005; Campaign manager, to Assemblyman Jimmy K. Meng, New York State Assembly,; District office administrator, counsel, to Assemblyman Jimmy K. Meng, New York State Assembly, **CIV:** Pro bono attorney, Sanctuary for Families, New York City, **AW:** Named one of The 40 Under 40, Crain's New York Business, 2013 **PA:** Democrat **BA:** 1317 Longworth HOB, Washington, DC, 20515

MERCER, REBEKAH, T: Foundation Director **I:** Nonprofit & Philanthropy **PB:** Yorktown Heights **SC:** NY/USA **ED:** M.A. Management Science and Engineering, Stanford University **C:** Director, Mercer Foundation,; Trader, Renaissance Technologies; Owner, Ruby et Violette **CW:** (Books)Clinton Cash, 2015

MERKLEY, JEFF, T: U.S. Senator from Oregon **I:** Government Administration/Government Relations/Government Services **DOB:** 10/24/1956 **PB:** Eugene **SC:** OR/USA **PT:** Son of Darrell and Betty Merkley; **ED:** MA in Public Policy, Princeton University, 1982; BA in International Relations, Stanford University, 1979 **C:** Member, US Senate Health, Education Labor & Pensions Committee, Washington, 2009-; Member, US Senate Environment & Pub. Works Committee, Washington, 2009-; Member, US Senate Banking, Housing & Urban Affairs Committee, Washington, 2009-; Member, US Senate Budget Committee, Washington, 2009-; US Senator from Oregon, Washington, 2009-; Speaker, Oregon House of Reps., Salem, 2007-09; Minority Leader, Oregon House of Reps., Salem, 2003-07; Member District 46, Oregon House of Reps., Salem, 1999-2009; Executive Director, World Affairs Council Oregon, 1996-2003; Director Housing Devel., Human Solutions, 1995-96; Executive Director, Portland Habitat for Humanity, 1991-94; Managing Partner, Computer Medics, 1989-91; Analyst, Congressional Budget Office, 1985-89; Presidential Intern, 1982-85 **PA:** Democrat **BA:** Office of Jeff Merkley, 313 Hart Senate Office Building, Washington, DC, 20510

MERLO, LARRY J., T: CVS Health CEO **I:** Business Management/Business Services **ED:** Grad., University of Pittsburgh, School of Pharmacy **C:**

President, CEO, CVS Health Corp. (formerly CVS Caremark Corp.), Woonsocket, Rhode Island, 2011-; President, COO, CVS Caremark Corp., Woonsocket, Rhode Island, 2010-11; Executive vice president, CVS Caremark Corp., Woonsocket, Rhode Island, 2007-10; Executive vice president stores, CVS Corp., Woonsocket, 2000-07; President, CVS Pharmacy Inc., Woonsocket, Rhode Island, 2007-11; Executive vice president stores, CVS Pharmacy, Inc., Woonsocket, Rhode Island, 1998-2000; Senior vice president stores, CVS Pharmacy, Inc., Woonsocket, Rhode Island, 1994-98 **CR:** Member Business Roundtable member board executive committee National Association Chain Drug Stores (NACDS), former chairman, vice chairman, 2009-10 board directors CVS Caremark Corp., 2010- **CIV:** Board Trustee, University of Pittsburgh

MERTON, ROBERT COX, T: Economist, Educator **I:** Education/Educational Services **DOB:** 07/31/1944 **PB:** New York City **SC:** NY/USA **PT:** Son of Robert K. and Suzanne (Carhart) Merton. **ED:** PhD in Business Administrn. (hon.), University Macau, 2014; DSc (hon.), Chinese University Hong Kong, 2014; PhD (hon.), University of Catolica de Chile, 2014; PhD (hon.), University of National Mayor San Marcos, Peru, 2004; PhD (hon.), University of Nacional Federico Villarreal, Lima, Peru, 2004; Doctor (hon.), University of Paris Dauphine, 1997; DSc (hon.), Claremont Grad. University, 2008; DSc (hon.), Athens University Economics and Business, 2003; DSc (hon.), National Sun Yat-Sen University, Taiwan, 1998; DSc (hon.), University of Lausanne, Switzerland, 1996; LLD (hon.), The University of Chicago, 1991; MA (hon.), Harvard University, 1989; PhD in Economics, Massachusetts Institute of Technology, 1970; MS in Applied Math., California Institute Tech., 1967; BS in Engineering Math., Columbia University, New York City, 1966 **C:** Resident scientist, Dimenional Holdings, 2009-; Professor fin., School Management, 2010-; Univ. professor emeritus, Harvard University, 2010-; Distinguished professor fin., Alfred P. Sloan School Management, Massachusetts Institute of Technology, 2010-; Hon. professor, Saint-Petersburg University Management and Economics, Russia, 2011; Hon. professor, HEC, Paris, 1995; Hon. professor, St. Petersburg University Management and Economics., 2011; John & Natty McArthur Univ. professor, Harvard University, Boston, 1998-2010; George Fisher Baker professor business administration, Harvard University, Boston, 1988-98; Visiting professor fin., Harvard University, Boston, 1987-88; J.C. Penney professor management, Alfred P. Sloan School Management, Massachusetts Institute of Technology, 1980-88; Professor, Alfred P. Sloan School Management, Massachusetts Institute of Technology, 1974-80; Associate professor, Alfred P. Sloan School Management, Massachusetts Institute of Technology, 1973-74; Assistant professor fin., Alfred P. Sloan School Management, Massachusetts Institute of Technology, 1970-73; Research assistant, economics instructor, Massachusetts Institute of Technology, Cambridge, Massachusetts, 1968-70 **CR:** Member competitive markets adv. council Chicago Mercantile Exchange, 2004- co-founder, chief sci. officer, board of directors, Integrated Fin. Ltd., 2002-07 member adv. board, nuServe, 2001-04, eCredit.com, 2000-02 co-founder, member, management committee Long-Term Capital Management, L.P., Greenwich, Connecticut, 1993-99 chairman board of directors, Daedalus Software, Inc., 2008- board of directors, Dimensional SmartNest LLC, 2010-14, Trinsum Group, 2007-08, Dimensional Funds, 2003-09, Peninsula Banking Group, 2003-10, Community First Fin. Group, 2003-10, Vical Inc., 2002-, MF Risk, Inc., 2001-09,

Travelers Investment Management Co., 1987-91, Nova Fund, 1980-88 senior advisor Platinum Grove Asset Mgnt., 2008, J.P. Morgan & Co., Inc., 1999-2000, Salomon Inc., 1988-92 research associate, National Bureau Economic Research, 1979- **CIV:** Member international adv. board, Middle East Sci. Fund, 2008- Board trustees, College Retirement Equities Fund, 1988-96 Board advisors, Santa Clara University Center Innovation in Fin. & Investment, 2008- Hon. member board directors, Angelo Roncalli International Committee, 2003- Hon. member board directors, International Raoul Wallenberg Foundation, 2003- **CW:** Author: Continuous-Time Finance, 1990; co-author: Cases in Financial Engineering: Applied Studies of Financial Innovation, 1995, The Global Financial System: A Functional Perspective, 1995, Teacher's Manual for Cases in Financial Engineering: Applied Studies of Financial Innovation, 1996; editor: The Collected Scientific Papers of Paul A. Samuelson, 1972; co-editor: Ann. Rev. Fin. Economics, 2007-; associate editor International Economic Rev., 1972-77, Journal Fin., 1973-77, Journal Money, Credit and Banking, 1974-79, Journal Banking and Fin., 1977-79, 1992-2003, Journal Fin. Economics, 1977-83, Geneva Papers Risk and Insurance, 1989-96, Journal Fixed Income, 1991-2012, adv. editor Rev. Devel. Fin., 2009-; contributor numerous articles to professional journals **AW:** Named one of 40 People of Power & Influence in Fin., Institutional Investor magazine, 2007; named to Risk Hall of Fame, Risk Magazine, 2002, Derivatives Hall of Fame, Derivatives Strategy Magazine, 1998; recipient Lifetime Achievement award, Fin. Intermediation Research Society, 2014, Excellence award, World Federation Exchanges, 2013, Group Melamed-Arditti Innovation award, CME, 2011, Hamilton medal, Royal Irish Academy, 2010, Robert A. Muh. award, Massachusetts Institute of Technology, 2009, Excellance award, Hastings on Hudson HS, 2009, Kolmogorov medal, University London, 2010, Tjailing C. Koopmans Asset award, Tilburg University, 2009, Distinguished Fin. Educator award, Fin. Education Association, 2008, PRIMIA Higher Standard award, Professional Risk Managers' International Association, 2006, Nicholas Molodovsky award, Association Investment Management & Research, 2003, Lifetime Achievement award, Risk Magazine, 2003, Boston University, 1999, Distinguished Alumni award, California Institute Tech., 1999, Michael I. Pupin medal, Columbia University, 1998, Nobel prize in economics, 1997, FORCE award for financial innovation, Duke University Fuqua School Business, 1993, Distinguished Scholar award, Eastern Fin. Association, 1989 Roger Murray prize, Institute Quantitative Research in Fin., 1986, 1985, Leo Melamed prize, University Chicago, 1983, Salgo-Noren award for excellence in thcg., Massachusetts Institute of Technology, 1971-72 **MEM:** Fellow: Econometric Society, Am. Academy Arts & Scis., Fin. Management Association, Am. Fin. Association (board directors 1982-84, 1987-88, president 1986), International Association Fin. Engineers (senior Fin. Engineer of Year award 1993); mem.: National Academy of Sciences, Society Fin. Studies (vice president 1993), Bachelier Fin. Society (hon.), Tau Beta Pi, Sigma Xi **BA:** MIT, 77 Massachusetts Ave, Office of E62-634, Cambridge, MA, 02139

MESSER, LUKE, T: U.S. Representative From Indiana **I:** Government Administration/Government Relations/Government Services **DOB:** 02/27/1969 **PB:** Evansville **SC:** IN/USA **ED:** JD, School of Law, Vanderbilt University, 1994; BA, Wabash College, 1991 **C:** Chairman, Republican Policy Committee; Committee on Financial Services; U.S. House Foreign Affairs Committee, 2013-Present; U.S. House Education & The Workforce Committee, 2013-Present; U.S. House Budget Committee, 2013-Present; U.S. Congress, Sixth Indiana District, Washington, DC, 2013-Present; President, CEO, Hoosiers for Economic Growth (HEG), 2010-2012; President, CEO, School Choice Indiana, 2010-2012; Partner, Ice Miller LLP, 2006-2010; Assistant Floor Majority Leader, Indiana House of Representatives, Indianapolis, IN, 2005-2006; District 57, Indiana House of Representatives, Indianapolis, IN, 2003-2007; Executive Director, Indiana Republican Party, Indianapolis, IN, 2001-2005; Associate, Barnes & Thornburg Law Firm, Indianapolis, IN, 2000-2001; Legal Counsel, Rep. Jim Duncan, U.S. House of Representatives, Washington, DC, 1999; Legal Counsel, U.S. House Subcommittee for Government Reform, 1998-1999; Press Secretary, Rep. Ed Bryant, U.S. House of Representatives, 1997; Associate Counsel, Koch Industries, 1995-1996 **CR:** Co-Chair, John McCain's Presidential Campaign, Indiana, 2008; Campaign Manager, Virginia Blankenbaker's Congressional Campaign, 1998 **CW:** Author, (Children's Books) Hoosier Heart, 2006 **PA:** Republican **ADD:** U.S. House of Representatives, 508 Cannon House Office Building, Washington, DC, 20515

MESSIER, MARK DOUGLAS, T: Retired Professional Hockey Player **I:** Athletics **DOB:** 01/18/1961 **PB:** Edmonton **SC:** AB/Canada **C:** Special Assistant to President, New York Rangers, 2009-13; Hockey Analyst, NHL on Versus; Center, Captain, Vancouver Canucks, 1997-2000; Center, Captain, New York Rangers, 2000-05; Center, Captain, New York Rangers, 1991-97; Captain, Edmonton Oilers, 1988-91; Center, Edmonton Oilers, 1979-91; Center, Cincinnati Stingers, 1979; Center, Indianapolis Racers, 1978 **AW:** Named NHL Player of Year, Sporting News, 1992, 1990; Named to Order of Hockey in Canada, 2013, NHL All-Star Game, 2004, 2000, 1996-98, 1994, 1988-92, 1986, 1982-84, Sporting News All-Star Team, 1991-92, 1989-90, 1982-83, 1981-82; Recipient Lester Patrick Trophy, 2009, Hart Memorial Trophy, 1992, 1990, Lester B. Pearson Award, 1991-92, 1989-90, Conn Smythe Trophy, 1984, Hockey Hall of Fame, 2007, 100 Greatest NHL Players in History, 2017, Officer of the Order of Canada, 2017 **ACH:** Achievements include being a member of Stanley Cup Champion Edmonton Oilers, 1984, 1985, 1987, 1988, 1990, New York Rangers, 1994; having his number, 11, retired by New York Rangers, 2006, Edmonton Oilers, 2007; being inducted into the Hockey Hall of Fame, 2007

MESSING, DEBRA, T: Actress **I:** Media & Entertainment **DOB:** 08/15/1968 **PB:** Brooklyn **SC:** NY/USA **PT:** Brian Messing; Sandra (Simons) Messing **ED:** MA in Fine Arts, New York University; BA in Theater summa cum laude, Brandeis University, 1990 **CW:** Actress: (films) Walk in the Clouds, 1995, McHale's Navy, 1997, Prey, 1997, Celebrity, 1998, The Mothman Prophecies, 2002, Hollywood Ending, 2002, Along Came Polly, 2004, (voice) Garfield, 2004, The Wedding Date, 2005, (voice) Open Season, 2006, Purple Violets, 2007, Lucky You, 2007, The Women, 2008, Nothing Like the Holidays, 2008, Like Sunday, Like Rain, 2014,Search, 2018; (TV series) Ned and Stacey, 1995, Prey, 1998, Will & Grace, 1998-2006 (Emmy award for Outstanding Lead Actress in a Comedy Series, 2003), Smash, 2012-13, The Starter Wife, 2008, The Mysteries of Laura, 2014-; (TV miniseries) It Could Be Worse, 2013; (Broadway plays) Outside Mullingar, 2014; TV appearances include NYPD Blue, 1994-95, Partners, 1995, Seinfeld, 1996-97, (voice) King of the Hill, 2002, Law & Order: Special Victims Unit, 2011, actress, executive producer, Smash, 2012, Project Runaway, 2012, The Mysteries of Laura, 2014, Jeopardy, 2015, Match Game, 2016, Nightcap, 2016, Dirty Dancing, 2017 (TV films) Wright versus Wrong, 2010, actress, co-exec. producer Mother's Day, 2013

METCALF, LAURIE, T: Actress **I:** Media & Entertainment **DOB:** 05/31/1905 **PB:** Edwardsville, **SC:** Edwardsville, **PT:** Daughter of James and Libby M.; **SPN:** Married Jeff Perry, 1983 (div. 1992); Married Matt Roth, 1993 (div., 2014); **CH:** children: Mae Akins, Donovan (adopted), Zoe; **ED:** BA in Theatre, Illinois State University, 1976 **C:** Founding ensemble member, Steppenwolf Theatre, Chicago,; Actress, 1978- **CW:** Actress: (Off-Broadway appearances) Balm in Gilead (debut, Theatre World award), 1984; (Stage appearances) Who's Afraid of Virginia Woolf?, 1982, Coyote Ugly, 1985, Bodies Rest, and Motion, 1986, Educating Rita, 1987 (Joseph Jefferson award for Best Performance by a Principal Actress in a Play), Little Egypt, 1987, Killers, 1988, All My Sons, 2006 (LA Ovation award for Best Lead Actress in a Play, 2006), A Long Day's Journey into Night, 2012, Domesticated, 2013; (Broadway plays) My Thing of Love, 1995, November, 2008, Brighton Beach Memoirs, 2009, The Other Place, 2013, Misery, 2015-16; (films) Desperately Seeking Susan, 1985, Making Mr. Right, 1987, Stars and Bars, 1988, The Appointments of Dennis Jennings, 1988, Candy Mountain, 1988, Miles from Home, 1988, Uncle Buck, 1989, Internal Affairs, 1989, Pacific Heights, 1990, Frankie and Johnny, 1991, JFK, 1991, Mistress, 1992, A Dangerous Woman, 1993, Blink, 1994, The Secret Life of Houses, 1994, Leaving Las Vegas, 1995, Dear God, 1996, (voice) Toy Story, 1995, Hellcab, 1997, U-Turn, 1997, Scream 2, 1997, Bulworth, 1998, (voice) Toy Story 2, 1999, Treasure Planet, 2002, Steel City, 2006, Beer League, 2006, (voice) Meet the Robinsons, 2007, Georgia Rule, 2007, Stop-Loss, 2008, (voice) Toy Story 3, 2010; (TV films) Execution of Raymond Graham, 1985, Always Outnumbered, 1998, The Long Island Incident, 1998, Ballon Farm, 1999, Two Families, 2002, Phil at the Gate, 2003, The Farm, 2009, Strange Brew, 2010; (TV series) Saturday Night Live, 1981, Roseanne, 1988-97 (Emmy award for Outstanding Supporting Actress in a Comedy Series, 1993, 1994), The Norm Show, 1999, (voice) God, The Devil and Bob, 2000, Charlie Lawrence, 2003, Easy Money, 2008, The Big Bang Theory, 2007-15; (TV appearances) The Equalizer, 1986, The Dharma & Greg, 1997, King of the Hill, 1997, 3rd Rock from the Sun, 1998, The Norm Show, 2001, Malcolm in the Middle, 2004, Frasier, 2004, Without a Trace, 2005, Monk, 2006, Grey's Anatomy, 2006, Desperate Housewives, 2006, My Boys, 2006, The Virgin of Akron, Ohio, 2007, Raines, 2007, The Goodwin Games, 2013, Getting On, 2013-15, The McCarthys, 2014-15. (Television) Horace and Pete, 2016, Portlandia, 2017, Playing House, 2017,(Film) Lady Bird, 2017, Toy Story 4, 2019(Theatre) Misery, 2015, A Doll's House Part 2, 2017,(Tony Award for Best Actress in a Play 2017) "A Doll's House, Part 2", Three Tall Women, 2018 (Tony Award for Best Performance by an Actress in a Featured Role in a Play)

MEYER, DANNY, I: Food & Restaurant Services **DOB:** 03/14/1958 **PB:** St. Louis **SC:** MO/USA **ED:** BA in Political Sci., Trinity College **C:** Founder, Marta, 2014-; Founder, The Modern, 2013-; Founder, North End Grill, 2012-; Founder, Untitled, 2011-; Founder, Maialino, 2010-; Founder, Hospitality Quotient, 2010-; Founder, Union Square Events, 2005-; Founder, Shake Shack, 2004-; Founder, Blue Smoke and Jazz Standard, 2002-; CEO, Union Square Hospitality Group, 1998-; Founder, Grammercy Tavern, 1994-; Founder, Union Square Cafe, 1985-; Founder, Cafe 2 & Terrace 5 at The Museum of Modern Art; Founder, Tabla, 1998-2010; Founder, Eleven Madison Park, 1998-2011; Assistant manager, Pesca, New York City, 1984-85; Cook County field director, Rep. John Anderson's Presidential Campaign, Chicago, 1980 **CIV:** Co-chair, Union Square Partnership, Member executive committee, Madison Square Park Conservancy, Member executive committee, New York City & Co., Member board directors, City Strength, Member board directors, Share Our Strength **CW:** Co-author (with Michael Romano): Union Square Cafe Cookbook, 1994 (Julia Child award International Association Culinary Profls.); co-author: Second Helpings from Union Square Cafe, 2001; author: Setting the Table: The Transforming Power of Hospitality in Business, 2006 **AW:** Named One of The 25 Leaders Reshaping New York, Crain's New York magazine, 2008; Recipient Outstanding Restaurant Award (Gramercy Tavern), James Beard Foundation, 2008

MEYER, URBAN, T: College Football Coach **I:** Professional Training & Coaching **DOB:** 07/10/1964 **PB:** Ashtabula **PT:** Son of Urban (Bud) Frank and Gisela Meyer **ED:** MA in Sports Administration, Ohio State University; BS in Psychology, University Cincinnati, 1986 **C:** Head football coach, Ohio State University Buckeyes, 2011-; College football analyst, ESPN, 2011; Head football coach, University Florida Gators, Gainesville, 2005-10; Head football coach, University Utah Utes, 2003-04; Head football coach, Bowling Green University Falcons, 2001-02; Wide receivers coach, University Notre Dame Fighting Irish, 1996-2000; Wide receivers coach, Colorado State University Rams, 1990-95; Quarterbacks/wide receivers coach, Illinois State University Redbirds, 1989; Linebackers coach, Illinois State University Redbirds, 1988; Receivers coach, Ohio State University Buckeyes, 1987; Tight ends coach, Ohio State University Buckeyes, 1986; Defensive backs coach, St. Xavier High School, Cincinnati, 1985 **AW:** Named Eddie Robinson Coach of Year, Football Writers Association America, 2004, National Coach of Year, Home Depot, 2004, Mountain West Conference Coach of Year, 2004, 2003, National Coach of Year, The Sporting News, 2003, Mid. American Conference Coach of Year, 2001; recipient Victor award, 2004, Woody Hayes Trophy award,2012 Columbus Touchdown Club, 2004, George Munger award for Collegiate Coach of Year, Maxwell Club, 2004, National Coach of Year, Pro Football Weekly, 2004, Sports Illustrated Coach of the Decade, 2009,Victor Award, 2004, Sporting News National Coach of the Year, 2003 **ACH:** Achievements include coaching the University of Florida Gators to Two Bowl Championship Series (BCS) National Championships, 2006, 2008; coaching the Ohio State Buckeyes to the College Football Playoff Championship (Certified Financial Planner), 2014 **BA:** Woody Hayes Athletic Center, 2491 Olentangy River Road, Columbus, OH, 43210

MEYERS, SETH, T: Actor, Writer, Television Producer, Comedian **I:** Media & Entertainment **DOB:** 12/28/1973 **PB:** Evanston **PT:** Son of Hilary Claire and Laurence Meyers **ED:** Grad., Northwestern University, Evanston, Illinois **C:** Host, Late Night with Seth Meyers, 2014-; Weekend Update co-anchor with Cecily Strong, Saturday Night Live, 2013-14; Solo anchor, Saturday Night Live, 2008-13; Weekend Update co-anchor with Amy Poehler, Saturday Night Live, 2006-08; Head writer, Saturday Night Live, 2006-14; Co-head writer with Tina Fey & Andrew Steele, Saturday Night Live, 2006-07; Writing supervisor, Saturday Night Live, 2005-06; Cast member, Saturday Night Live, 2001 **CR:** Keynote speaker White House Correspondents' Association Dinner, 2011 host The 66th Primetime Emmy Awards, 2014, ESPY awards, 2011, 2010, Microsoft Co. Meeting, Seattle, 2009, Webby awards, 2009, 2008 **CW:** Actor: (films) See this Movie, 2004, Perception, 2005, American Dreamz, 2006, Journey to the Center of the Earth, 2008, Nick and Norah's Infinite Playlist, 2008, Spring Breakdown,

2009, I Don't Know How She Does It, 2011, New Year's Eve, 2011, (TV guest appearances) Spin City, 2001, The Mindy Project, 2012, The Office, 2013; co-prodr.: (films) Hot Rod, 2007; prodr.: Mac-Gruber, 2010; (creator, voice artist, writer, executive producer): The Awesomes, 2013-15,(Film) The Interview, 2014,(Television) The Awesomes, 2013, Portlandia, 2015, Difficult People, 2015, Lady Dynamite, 2016, This is Us, 2016 **AW:** Named one of The 100 Most Influential People in the World, TIME magazine, 2014,Primetime Emmy for Outstanding Original Music and Lyrics, 2011 **ACH:** Achievements include winner of third season of Bravo's Celebrity Poker Showdown

MICHAELS, LORNE, T: Television Producer **I:** Media & Entertainment **DOB:** 11/17/1944 **PB:** Toronto **SC:** Ont./Canada **ED:** Doctorate (hon.), Ryerson University; Grad., University of Toronto, 1966 **C:** Chairman board, founder, Broadway Video, New York City,; Writer, Rowan and Martin's Laugh-In, NBC, LA, 1968-75; Former producer, Canadian Broadcasting Co., Toronto, **CW:** Writer, producer (TV series) The Hart & Lorne Terrific Hour, 1970, writer, executive producer Saturday Night Live, 1975-80 (Best Comedy/ Variety - Series, Writers Guild America, 2009), 1985-; prodr.: (TV series) The New Show, 1984; executive prodr.: Sunday Night, 1988, The Kids in the Hall, 1989-94, Late Night with Conan O'Brien, 1993-2009, The Vacant Lot, 1994, 30 Rock, 2006-13 (Primetime Emmy for Outstanding Comedy Series, Academy TV Arts and Scis., 2007, 2008, Danny Thomas Producer of Year Award in Episodic TV - Comedy, Producers Guild America, 2009, Danny Thomas Producer of Year award in Episodic TV - Comedy, Producers Guild America, 2010), Late Night with Jimmy Fallon, 2009-14, Up All Night, 2011-13, Portlandia, 2011-14, Late Night with Seth Meyers, 2014-, The Tonight Show Starring Jimmy Fallon, 2014-, (TV special), Late Night with Seth Meyers, 2014, Mulaney, 2014, The Maya Rudolph Show, 2014, Man Seeking Man, 2015, Documentary Now, 2015, Maya & Marty, 2016, Late Night with Conan O'Brian: 10 Anniversary Special, 2003, Night of Too Many Stars, 2003, Saturday Night Live: 25th Anniversary; co-exec. producer (TV special) Rolling Stone Presents Twenty Years of Rock & Roll, 1987, writer, producer Lily Tomlin, 1975, The Paul Simon Special, 1977, Steve Martin's Best Show Ever, 1981; prodr.: (TV films) Things We Did Last Summer, 1977; executive prodr.: The Rutles: All You Need Is Cash, 1978, Mr. Mike's Mondo Video, 1979, Simon and Garfunkel: The Concert in Central Park, 1982, The Rutles 2: Can't Buy Me Lunch, 2002, Michael Che Matters, 2016; co-writer (TV films) Gilda Live, 1980, writer, producer (films) Three Amigos, 1986, Nothing Lasts Forever, 1984, Wayne's World, 1992; producer, prodr.: (films) Coneheads, 1983, Wayne's World II, 1993, Tommy Boy, 1995, Stuart Saves His Family, 1995, Black Sheep, 1996, Kids in the Hall: Brain Candy, 1996, A Night at the Roxbury, 1998, Superstar, 1999, The Ladies Man, 2000, Enigma, 2001, Mean Girls, 2004, Hot Rod, 2007, Baby Mama, 2008, Mac-Gruber, 2010, The Guilt Trip, 2012, Brother Nature, 2015, Whiskey Tango Foxtrot, 2016, Masterminds, 2016 **AW:** Named Broadcaster of Year, International Radio and TV Society, 1992; named one of The 100 Most Influential People in the World, TIME magazine, 2008; named to Order of Canada, 2002, TV Academy Hall of Fame, 1999; recipient Presidential Medal of Freedom, The White House, 2016, Webby Film & Video Lifetime Achievement, International Academy Digital Arts and Scis., 2008, Star on Hollywood Walk of Fame, 11 Emmy awards, Herb Sargent award for Comedy Excellence, Writers Guild of America, 2007, Mark Twain Prize, John F. Kennedy Center Performing Arts, 2004, George Foster Peabody award for Saturday Night Live, 1990

MICHALSKI, PATTY, T: Executive Editor **I:** Writing and Editing **CN:** USA Today **C:** Executive Editor, USA Today, 2017-Present; Interim Editor in Chief, USA Today, 2016-2017; Managing Editor, USA Today, 2013-2017; Editorial Mobile Manager, USA Today, 2010-2013; News Director, USA Today, 2003-2010

MICKELSON, PHIL, T: Professional Golfer **I:** Athletics **DOB:** 06/16/1970 **PB:** San Diego **SC:** CA/USA **PT:** Son of Philip and Mary Mickelson; **ED:** BS in Psychology, Arizona State University, Tempe, 1992 **C:** Professional golfer, PGA, 1992 **CR:** Member US team Ryder Cup, 2012, 2010, 2008, 2006, 2004, 2002, 1999, 1997, 1995, Presidents Cup, 2011, 2009, 2007, 2005, 2003, 2000, 1998, 1996, 1994 **CIV:** Founder, The Phil and Amy Mickelson Charitable Fund **CW:** Co-author (with Donald T. Phillips): One Magical Sunday (But Winning Isn't Everything), 2005; appeared in (TV series) Entourage, 2008 **AW:** Recipient Fred Haskins award, 1990, 1991, 1992, Jack Nicklaus award, 1990, 1991, 1992; won NCAA Championships, 1989, 1990, 1992; 1st team All-American with Sun Devils; Espy Award for Best Male Golfer, Best Championship Performance, ESPN, 2004; named one of The 100 Most Powerful Celebrities, Forbes.com, 2008, The 100 Most Influential People in the World, TIME magazine, 2010; named to World Golf Hall of Fame, 2012; named Player of Year Golf magazine, 2013,Haskins Award, 1990, 1991, 1992 **ACH:** Achievements include 1st left-hander to win US Amateur, 1990; 1st player in PGA history to win same tournament as amateur and profesional (No. Telecom Open); winner PGA Tour events: Northern Telecom Open, 1991, 1995; Buick Invitational, 1991, 2000, 2001; The International, 1993; Mercedes Championship, 1994, 1998; Nortel Open, Phoenix Open, GTE Byron Nelson Golf Championship, NEC World Series of Golf, 1996; Bay Hill Invitational, Sprint International, 1997; AT&T Pebble Beach National Pro-Am, 1998, 2005, 2007, 2012; Bell South Classic, 2000, 2005, 2006; MasterCard Colonial, 2000; THE TOUR Championship, 2000, 2009; Canon Greater, 2001; Canon Greater Hartford Open, 2002; Bob Hope Chrysler Classic, 2002, 2004; FBR Open, 2005; THE PLAYERS Championship, Deutsche Bank Championship, 2007; Northern Trust Open, 2008, 2009; Crowne Plaza Invitational, 2008; Shell Houston Open, 2011; winner Major Championships: The Masters, 2004, 2006, 2010; PGA Championship, 2005; Open Championship (British Open), 2013; member of the President's Cup winning US national team: 1994, 1996, 2000, 2005, 2007, 2009; member of the Ryder Cup winning US national team: 1999, 2008; winner World Golf Championship events: CA Championship, HSBC Champions, 2009 **H:** Flying

MIDLER, BETTE, T: Singer, Actress **I:** Media & Entertainment **DOB:** 12/01/1945 **PB:** Honolulu **SC:** HI/USA **PT:** Fred Midler; Ruth (Schindel) Midler **ED:** Coursework, University of Hawaii **C:** Actress (1966-Present); Singer (1972) **CIV:** Founder, New York Restoration Project (1995-Present) **CW:** Co-Producer, "Priscilla: Queen of the Desert" (2011-Present); Actress, "Freak Show" (2017); Performer, "Hello Dolly" (2017); Actress, "The Voice" (2016); Singer, "It's the Girls!" (2014); Actress, "Bette Midler: One Night Only" (2014); Performer, "I'll Eat You Last: A Chat with Sue Mengers" (2013); Actress, "Parental Guidance" (2012); Actress, "The Showgirl Must Go On" (2010); Voice Actress, "Cats & Dogs: The Revenge of Kitty Galore" (2010); Actress, "Paul O'Grady's Christmas" (2010); TV Appearance, "Kathy Griffin: My Life on the D-List" (2009); Performer, "Bette Midler: The Showgirl Must Go On" (2008-2010); Actress, "The Woman" (2008); Actress, "The Women" (2008); Actress, "Then She Found Me" (2007); Actress, "Then She Found Me" (2007); Singer, "Cool Yule" (2006); Singer, "Bette

Midler Sings the Peggy Lee Songbook" (2005); Actress, "The Stepford Wives" (2004); Actress, "The Stepford Wives" (2004); Singer, "Bette Midler Sings The Rosemary Clooney Songbook" (2003); Executive Producer, "Divine Secret of the Ya-Ya Sisterhood" (2002); Executive Producer, "Some of My Best Friends" (2001); Actress, "Drowning Mona" (2000); Singer, "Bette" (2000); Executive Producer, Composer, "Bette" (2000); Actress, "Isn't She Great" (1999); Actress, "Get Bruce" (1999); Singer, "Bathhouse Betty" (1998); Actress, "That Old Feeling" (1997); Actress, "The First Wives Club" (1996); Singer, "Bette of Roses" (1995); Actress, "Get Shorty" (1995); Actress, "Hocus Pocus" (1993); TV Appearance, "Gypsy" (1993); Actress, "Scenes From a Mall" (1991); Actress, "For the Boys" (1991); Singer, "Some People's Lives" (1990); Actress, "Stella" (1990); Singer, "Beaches" (1989); Actress, "Beaches" (1988); Voice Actress, "Oliver and Company" (1988); Actress, "Big Business" (1988); TV Appearance, "Bette Midler's Mondo Beyondo" (1988); Performer, "Outrageous Fortune" (1987); Performer, "Down and Out in Beverly Hills" (1986); Performer, "Ruthless People" (1986); Singer, "Mud Will Be Flung Tonight" (1985); Author, "The Saga of Baby Divine" (1984); Singer, "No Frills" (1984); Performer, "Jinxed" (1982); Author, "A View from a Broad" (1981); Singer, "Divine Madness" (1980); Performer, "Divine Madness" (1980); Performer, "Bette! Divine Madness" (1979-1980); Singer, "Songs for the New Depression" (1979); Singer, "The Rose" (1979); Performer, "The Rose" (1979); Singer, "Thighs and Whispers" (1979); Singer, "Live at Last" (1977); Singer, "Broken Blossom" (1977); Performer, "Bette Midler's Clams on the Half Shell Revue" (1975); Singer, "Bette Midler" (1973); Performer, "Bette Midler: Special Concert" (1973); Singer, "The Divine Miss M" (1972); Actress, "Tommy," Seattle Opera Co. (1971); Actress, "Salvation" (1970); Performer, "Hawaii" (1966); Actress, "Fiddler on the Roof" (1964-1972) **AW:** Recipient, Sammy Cahn Lifetime Achievement Award, Songwriters Hall of Fame (2012); Recipient, Golden Globe Award for Best Actress in a Mini-Series or Movie Made for Television (1994); Recipient, Emmy Award (1992); Recipient, Golden Globe Award (1991); Recipient, Grammy Award for Record of the Year (1990); Inductee, Hollywood Walk of Fame (1986); Recipient, Grammy Award for Best Female Pop Performance (1981); Two-Time Recipient, Golden Globe Award (1979); Recipient, Emmy Award (1978); Recipient, Grammy Award for Best New Artist (1974); Recipient, Special Tony Award (1973); Recipient, After Dark Ruby Award (1973); Recipient, Tony Award for Best Actress

MIKITA, STAN, T: Professional Hockey Player **I:** Athletics **PB:** Sokolce **SC:** Slovak Republic **C:** Centre, Chicago Blackhawks, 1960-1980 **AW:** NHL's First All-Star Team, 1962-1964, 1966-1968, Art Ross Trophy, 1964-1965, 1967-1968, Lady Byng Memorial Trophy, 1967-1968, Hart Memorial Trophy, 1967-1968, Lester Patrick Trophy, 1976, Hockey Hall of Fame, 1983

MILES, THOMAS JOHN, I: Law and Legal Services **DOB:** 06/14/1905 **PT:** Son of William F. and Joan M. Miles. **ED:** JD, Harvard Law School, Cambridge, Massachusetts, 2003; PhD, University Chicago, 2000; BA, Tufts University, Medford, Massachusetts, 1990 **C:** Assistant professor law, University Chicago Law School, 2004-; Doctoral fellow, Am. Bar Foundation, 1998-2000

MILLER, JEFF, T: CEO of Halliburton **I:** Oil & Energy **CN:** Halliburton **ED:** B.A., Mcneese State University; M.B.A., Texas A&M University **CT:** CPA **C:** President/CEO, Halliburton Co, 2017-; President, Halliburton Co, 2014-2017; Exec VP/COO, Halliburton Co, 2012-

2014; Senior VP Global Bus Dev & Mktg, Halliburton Co, 2011-2012 **MEM:** Board Member, Halliburton, 2014-; Board Member, Atwood Oceanics, 2013

MILLER, JOHN LAURENCE, T: Professional Golfer **I:** Athletics **PB:** San Francisco **SC:** CA/USA **PT:** Laurence O. Miller; Ida (Meldrum) Miller **MS:** Married **SPN:** Linda Strouse (September 17, 1969) **CH:** John Strouse; Kelly; Casi; Scott; Brent; Todd **ED:** Student, Brigham Young University, 1965-69 **C:** Professional golfer, 1969 **CR:** President Johnny Miller Enterprises, Inc. golf commentator, NBC **CW:** Author: Pure Golf, 1976, Johnny Miller's Golf for Juniors, 1987 **AW:** Named PGA Player of Year, 1974; elected to Golf Hall of Fame, 1999, World Golf Hall of Fame, 1998, PGA Tour Leading Money Winner, 1974 **ACH:** Achievements include major tournaments won in the Southern Open, 1971, Heritage Classic, 1972, 74, Ortago Golf Classic, New Zealand, 1972, U.S. Open at Oakmont County Club, 1973, Lancome Trophy Tournament, Paris 1973, 74, Bing Crosby Pro Am, 1974, Phoenix Open, 1974, 75, Dean Martin-Tucson Open, 1974, 75, Tournament of Champions, 1974, Westchester Classic, 1974, World Open, 1974, Dunlop Phoenix, Japan, 1974, Kaiser International, 1974, 75, Bob Hope Desert Classic, 1975, 76, British Open Crown, 1976, NBC Tucson Open, 1976, Jackie Gleason Inverarry Classic, 1980, Sun City, 1981, Joe Garagiola Tucson Open, 1981, Glen Campbell L.A. Open, 1981, Wickes Andy Williams San Diego Open, 1982, Honda Inverrary Classic, 1983, AT&T Pebble Beach National Pro-Am, 1987, 94, World Cup individual titles, 1973, 75, Ryder Cup, 1975, 81.

MILLER, ROBERT G., T: Albertsons CEO **I:** Business Management/Business Services **PB:** Louisville **ED:** Attended executive management program, Stanford University, California; Attended, Orange Coast College, Costa Mesa, California **C:** Chairman, SuperValu, Inc., Eden Prairie, Minnesota, 2013-; President & CEO, AB Acquisition, LLC, 2013-; CEO, Albertsons LLC, 2006-; Chairman, Wild Oats Markets, Boulder, Colorado, 2004-06; Chairman, Rite Aid Corp., Camp Hill, Pennsylvania, 1999-2007; CEO, Rite Aid Corp., Camp Hill, Pennsylvania, 1999-2003; Vice chairman, COO, Kroger Co., Cincinnati, 1999; Vice chairman board, CEO, Fred Meyer Inc., 1998-99; Chairman board, president, CEO, Fred Meyer Inc., Portland, Oregon, 1991-98; CEO, Albertson's Inc., 2006-13; Executive vice president retail operations, Albertson's Inc., 1989-91; With, Albertson's Inc., 1961-89 **CR:** Chairman Distribution Trucking Co. Inc. director Food Marketing Institute, 2008-, Nordstrom Inc., 2005- director, non-exec. chairman Wild Oats Markets Inc., 2004-06 director Rite Aid Corp., 1999-2011, Harrah's Entertainment Inc., 1999- **BA:** Albertsons Headquarters, 250 Parkcenter Blvd, Boise, ID, 83706

MILLER, STEPHEN, T: Senior Advisor to the President **I:** Government Administration/Government Relations/Government Services **C:** Senior Advisor to the President,Washington D.C., 2017- Press secretary to Rep. John Shadegg, US House of Representatives, Washington, 2009-10 **PA:** Republican

MILLER, VON, T: Professional Football Player **I:** Athletics **DOB:** 03/29/1989 **PB:** DeSoto **SC:** TX/USA **ED:** Bachelor in Univ. Studies, Texas A&M University, College Station, 2011 **C:** Linebacker, Denver Broncos, 2011-Present **AW:** Super Bowl MVP,Named NFL Defensive Rookie of Year, Associated Press, 2011, AFC Defensive Player of the Month, November, 2012 and October, 2014, AFC Defensive Player of the Week, Week 11, 2011 and Week 12, 2012; recipient Butkus award, Butkus Foundation, 2012, 2010,Super Bowl 50 Champion,

Super Bowl 50 MVP, Pro Bowl, 2014-2017, First Team All-Pro,2012,2015, 2016, Second-Team All-Pro, 2011, 2014, 2017, NFL Defensive Rookie of the Year, 2011, Butkus Award Pro, 2012, Butkus Award, 2010, First- Team All- American, 2009-10, First Team All- Big 12, 2009-10 **ACH:** Super Bowl 50 Champion,Achievements include member of College-Level First-team All-Big 1, 2009 and 2010, Freshman All-Big 12, 2007; member of NFL First-team All-American 2009, 2010, Second-team All-Pro, 2011, 2014, First-team All-Pro, 2012, 2015, Pro Bowl 2011, 2012, 2014, 2015-2017; member of Super Bowl 50 winning Denver Broncos, 2016; being named Most Valuable Player for Super Bowl 50 in 2016

MILLETT, PATRICIA ANN, T: Federal Judge, Lawyer **I:** Law and Legal Services **DOB:** 09/01/1963 **PB:** Dexter **SC:** ME/USA **SPN:** Robert King **ED:** JD magna cum laude, Harvard Law School, 1988; BA in Political Sci., summa cum laude, University Ill, Urbana-Champaign, 1985 **CT:** Bar: U.S. Supreme Court, U.S. Court Appeals (2d, 3rd, 4th, 5th, 6th, 7th, 8th, 9th, 10th, DC & Federal Cir.), DC, Massachusetts **C:** Judge, U.S. Court Appeals (DC Cir.), Washington, 2013-; Partner, co-chair Supreme Court practice group, Akin Gump Strauss Hauer & Feld LLP, Washington, 2007-13; Assistant to solicitor general, U.S. Department Justice, 1996-2007; Appellate staff, civil division, U.S. Department Justice, 1992-96; Law clerk to Hon. Thomas Tang, U.S. Court Appeals (9th cir.), 1990-92; Staff litigation department, Miller & Chevalier, Washington, 1988-90 **CW:** Contributor articles to professional journals **AW:** Named one of Washington's Most Influential Women Lawyers, The National Law Journal, 2010; recipient Attorney General's Distinguished Service award, U.S. Department Justice, 2004 **MEM:** Mem.: American Bar Association, DC Bar **BA:** US Court Appeals, 333 Constitution Ave NW, Washington, DC, 20001

MILLIGAN, JOHN F., T: Former President and CEO at Gilead Sciences **I:** Sciences **ED:** PhD in Biochemistry, University of Illinois; Bachelor's, Chemistry, Ohio Wesleyan University **C:** CEO, Gilead Sciences inc, 2016-18; President, Gilead Sciences, Inc., 2008-18; COO, Gilead Sciences, Inc., 2007-16; CFO, Gilead Sciences, 2002-08; Executive vice president, Gilead Sciences, Inc., 2003-08; Principal accounting officer, CFO, Gilead Sciences, Inc., 2002-08; Senior vice president, Gilead Sciences, Inc., 2002-03; Vice president corp. devel., Gilead Sciences, Inc., 2000-02; Corp. devel., Gilead Sciences, Inc., 1998-2000; Director project management, project team leader, Gilead Hoffmann-La Roche Tamiflu collaboration, Gilead Sciences, Inc., 1996-98; Research scientist, Gilead Sciences, Inc., 1990-96 **AW:** Named Top Biotech. Industry CFO in the US, Institutional Investor magazine, 2006-08, Bay Area CFO of Year, 2006; Am. Cancer Society postdoctoral fellow, University California San Francisco

MILLIGAN, STEPHEN D., T: CEO **I:** Business Management/Business Services **CN:** Western Digital Corporation **DOB:** 01/01/1900 **ED:** Bachelors Degree in Accounting, The Ohio State University **C:** Chief Executive Officer, Western Digital Corporation (2013-Present); President, Western Digital Corporation (2012-2013); President/Chief Executive Officer, Hitachi Global Storage Tech (HGST, Inc.) (2009-2012); Chief Financial Officer, Hitachi Global Storage Tech (HGST, Inc.) (2007-2009); Senior Vice President/Chief Financial Officer, Western Digital Corporation (2004-2007); Vice President of Finance, Western Digital Corporation (2002-2004)

MINAJ, NICKI, T: Rap Artist **I:** Media & Entertainment **DOB:** 12/08/1984 **PB:** St. James **SC:** Port of Spain Trinidad and Tobago **PT:** Daughter of Robert and Carol Maraj **C:** Signed with, Young Money Entertainment, 2009 **CW:** Singer: (albums) Pink Friday, 2010 (Favorite Rap/Hip-Hop Album, American Music Awards, 2011), Pink Friday: Roman Reloaded, 2012 (Favorite Rap/Hip-Hop Album, American Music Awards, 2012, Top Rap Album, Billboard Music Awards, 2013), The Pink Print, 2014 (Favorite Rap/Hip-Hop Album, American Music Awards, 2015), (songs) Super Bass, 2011 (Top Streaming Song-Video, Billboard Music Awards, 2012), Starships, 2012 (Best Female Video, MTV Video Music Awards, 2012), Anaconda, 2014 (Best Hip-Hop Video, MTV Video Music Awards, 2015); judge American Idol, 2013; actress: (films) Ice Age: Continental Drift (voice), 2012, The Other Woman, 2014, Barbershop: The Next Cut, 2016 **AW:** Named Top Streaming Artist, Billboard Music Awards, 2013, Top Rap Artist, 2013, Favorite Hip-Hop Artist, People's Choice Awards, 2016, 2013, Favorite Rap/Hip-Hop Artist, American Music Awards, 2015, 2012, 2011, Best Female Hip-Hop Artist, Black Entertainment TV (BET) Awards, 2015, 2014, 2013, 2012, 2011, 2010, Best New Artist, 2010; named one of The 100 Most Influential People in the World, TIME Magazine, 2016, American Music Award, Favorite Rap/ Hip Hop Artist, 2015

MINNELLI, LIZA, T: Singer, Actress **I:** Media & Entertainment **PB:** Los Angeles **SC:** CA/USA **PT:** Vincente Minnelli; Judy (Garland) Minnelli **SPN:** Mark Gero (December 4, 1979) (div.); Jack Haley Junior (September 15, 1974) (div. 1979); Peter Allen (March 3, 1967) (div. June 24, 1972) **CW:** Actress: (theater) Wish You Were Here, 1961, Take Me Along, 1961, Best Foot Forward, 1963, Flower Drum Song, 1961, The Diary of Anne Frank, 1961-62, Carnival!, 1964, Time Out for Ginger, 1964, The Fantasticks, 1964, Flora, the Red Menace, 1965 (Tony award), The Pajama Game, 1966, Liza, 1974, Chicago, 1975, The Act, 1977-78 (Tony award), The Owl and the Pussycat, 1978-79, The Rink, 1984, Love Letters, 1994, Victor Victoria, 1997; (films) Charlie Bubbles, 1967, The Sterile Cuckoo, 1969, Tell Me That You Love Me, Junie Moon, 1970, Cabaret, 1972 (Golden Globe award for Best Actress, Academy award for Best Actress, BAFTA award for Best Actress in a Leading Role), That's Entertainment, 1974, Lucky Lady, 1975, A Matter of Time, 1976, Silent Movie, 1976, New York, New York, 1977, Arthur, 1981, Rent A Cop, Arthur on the Rocks, 1988, Stepping Out, 1991, The OH in Ohio, 2006; singer: (albums) Liza! Liza!, 1964, It Amazes Me, 1965, There Is a Time, 1966, Liza Minnelli, 1966, Come Saturday Morning, 1969, New Feelin', 1970, The Singer, 1973, Tropical Nights, 1977, Liza Minnelli at Carnegie Hall, 1987, Results, 1989, Maybe This Time, 1996, Gently, 1996, Minnelli on Minnelli, 2000, (with Herbie Hancock, Johnny Mathis, Donna Summer), Liza's Back!, 2003, Liza's at the Palace, 2008, Confessions, 2010; (TV films) Parallel Lives, 1994, The West Side Waltz, 1995, Jackie's Back!, 1999; appeared on TV in own special Liza With a Z, 1972 (Emmy award for Outstanding Single Program); (TV appearances) Goldie and Liza Together, 1980, Baryshnikov on Broadway, 1980, The Princess and the Pea, Showtime, 1983, A Time to Live, 1985, Sam Found Out, 1988, Liza Minnelli Live from Radio City Music Hall, The Wonderful World of Oz: 50 Years of Magic, 1990, A Century of Cinema, 1994, My Favorite Broadway: The Leading Ladies, 1999, (TV series) Arrested Development, 2003-05 2013, Law & Order: Criminal Intent, 2006, Drop Dead Diva, 2009, The Oh in Ohio, 2006; international tour with Frank Sinatra, Sammy Davis Junior, 1988. **AW:** Recipient, Italy's

David di Donatello award (twice), the Valentino award, Drama Desk award, 2009, Tony award for Best Special Theatrical Event, 2009

MINOR, LLOYD B., T: Medical School Dean **I:** Education/Educational Services **DOB:** 05/25/1957 **PB:** Little Rock **SC:** AR/USA **ED:** M.D, Brown University, 1982, SC.B, Brown University, 1979; **C:** Dean, Stanford University's School of Medicine, 2012-; Provost, Johns Hopkins University, 2009-2012; Andelot Professor and Director (chair) of the Department of Otolaryngology–Head and Neck Surgery and otolaryngologist-in-chief at Johns Hopkins Hospital, 2003-2009; professor, Johns Hopkins University, 2001-2003; associate professor, 1997-2001, assistant professor, 1993-1997, completed clinical fellowship, Nashville, Tennessee,1992-1993; resident, 1988-1992, University of Chicago Medical Center, completed research fellowship, University of Chicago, from 1984 until 1988,; residency training, Duke University Medical Center, 1982-1984; **AW:** Recipient, the Prosper Ménière Society's Gold Medal, 2010; winner, Joseph Toynbee Memorial Medal, Royal Society of Medicine and Royal College of Surgeons, 2015; **MEM:** Fellow, American College of Surgeons, American Academy of Otolaryngology – Head and Neck Surgery; Member, National Academy of Medicine; **ACH:** Discovered superior canal dehiscence syndrome

MINSHEW, KATHRYN, T: Founder, CEO **I:** Human Resources **CN:** The Muse **SC:** NJ/USA **ED:** BA in Political Science, French, Duke University **C:** CEO/Founder, The Muse, 2011-Present; Business Analyst, McKinsey & Company, 2008-2010

MIRANDA, LIN-MANUEL, T: Composer **I:** Media & Entertainment **DOB:** 01/16/1980 **PB:** New York City **SC:** NY/USA **ED:** LHD (hon.), Yeshiva University, 2009; BA, Wesleyan University, 2002 **CR:** Member New York City Theater Subdistrict Council, 2015 board member Young Playwrights, Inc. **CW:** Composer, lyricist, performer (Broadway plays) In the Heights, 2008-11 (Theatre World award, 2007, Drama Desk award for Outstanding Ensemble Performance, 2007, Outer Critics Cir. award for Outstanding Musical, 2007, Lucille Lortel award for Outstanding Musical, 2007, Obie award for Music & Lyrics, 2007, Best Musical, Best Orchestrations, and Best Choreography, Tony Awards, 2008, Best Score, Tony Awards, 2008, Grammy award for Best Musical Show Album, 2009, Oliver award for Outstanding Achievement in Music for original London production, 2016), translations West Side Story, 2009, co-composer, lyricist Bring it On: The Musical, 2012 (Emmy award with Tom Kitt for the song, Bigger, 2014), composer, lyricist, performer, Hamilton, 2015-16 (New York Drama Critics' Cir. award for Best Musical, 2015, Drama Desk award for Outstanding Music, 2015, Drama Desk award for Outstanding Lyrics, 2015, Drama Desk award for Outstanding Book of a Musical, 2015, Pulitzer Prize in Drama, 2016, Grammy award for Best Musical Theatre album, 2016, 10 Lortel awards, 3 Outer Critic Circle awards, 8 Drama Desk awards, New York Drama Critics Circle award for Best New Musical, OBIE for Best New American Play, Edward M. Kennedy Prize for Drama Inspired by American History, 2015, Tony awards for Best Musical, Best Original Score, Best Book of a Musical, 2016), The Hamilton Mixtape, 2016, The Hamilton Instrumentals, 2017 appeared in Merrily We Roll Along, City Center Encores!, 2012, Tick, Tick...Boom!, 2014, voice to audiobook recordings The Brief Wondrous Life of Oscar Wao, Dante Discover the Secrets of the Universe; actor: (films) The Odd Life of Timothy Green, 2012, Looking for Maria Sanchez, 2013, Speech & Debate, 2016, Hamilton's

America, 2016, Moana, 2016, Speech and Debate, 2017, Mary Poppins Returns, 2018; (TV films) Freestyle Love Supreme, 2012; TV credits include The Electric Company, Sesame Street, The Sopranos, House, Modern Family, Do No Harm, How I Met Your Mother (Television) Last Week Tonight with John Oliver, 2016, Drunk History, 2016, Saturday Night Live, 2016, My Brother, My Brother and Me, 2017, Bojack Horseman, 2017, The Magic School Bus Rides Again, 2017, Curb Your Enthusiasm, 2017, Duck Tales, 2017 **AW:** Named one of The 100 Most Influential People in the World, TIME Magazine, 2016, 40 Under 40, Crain's New York Business, 2009; recipient MacArthur Foundation award, 2015, National Arts Club Medal of Honor, American Society of Composers Foundation Richard Rodgers New Horizons award, Clarence Derwent award for Most Promising Male Performance, In the Heights, Actor's Equity Foundation, 2007, Theater World award for Outstanding Debut Performance, 2007, Primetime Emmy for Outstanding Original Music, 2014, Tony Award, Hamilton, Best Book of a Musical, Best Original Score **MEM:** Mem.: Dramatists Guild (council member)

MIRREN, HELEN, T: Actress **I:** Media & Entertainment **DOB:** 07/26/1945 **PB:** London **SC:** England **PT:** Daughter of Basil and Katherine Mirren; **C:** With, Peter Brook's Center International de Recheres Theatrales, Africa, 1972-73; Joined, Royal Shakespeare Co., 1967 **CW:** Actress: (theatre) National Youth Theatre, Antony and Cleopatra, 1965, Royal Shakespeare Co., 1967, The Revenger's Tragedy, All's Well That Ends Well, Much Ado About Nothing, 1968, Batholomew Fair, 1969, Richard III, Hamlet, The Two Gentlemen of Verona, 1970, Enemies, 1971, Lady McBeth, 1974-75, Teeth 'n' Smiles, 1975, The Bed Before Yesterday, 1975, The Roaring Girl, Henry VI, 1977-78, Measure for Measure, 1979, The Duchess of Malfi, 1980-81, Faith Healer, 1981, Barbican, 1983, Extremities, 1984, Madame Bovary, 1987, Two Way Mirror, 1988, Sex Please We're Italian, 1991, A Month in the Country, 1994, The Audience, 2013 (Drama desk award outstanding actress in a play, 2015, Tony award Best Performance by an Actress in a Leading Role in a Play, 2015); (films) Herostratus, 1967, A Midsummer Night's Dream, 1968, Red Hot Shot, 1969, Age of Consent, 1969, Miss Julie, 1972, Savage Messiah, 1972, O Lucky Man!, 1973, Hamlet, 1976, The Quiz Kid, 1979, Caligula, 1979, The Hussy, 1980, The Fiendish Plot of Dr. Fu Manchu, 1980, The Long Good Friday, 1980, Excalibur, 1981, Cal, 1984, 2010, 1984, White Nights, 1984, Coming Through, 1985, Heavenly Pursuits, 1985, The Mosquito Coast, 1986, Pascali's Island, 1987, When the Whales Came, 1988, The Cook, the Thief, His Wife, and Her Lover, 1989, Bethune, The Making of a Hero, 1990, The Comfort of Strangers, 1990, Where Angels Fear to Tread, 1991, The Gift, 1991, The Hawk, 1991, The Prince of Jutland, 1991, The Madness of King George, 1994, The Snow Queen, 1995, Some Mother's Son, 1996, Ciritical Care, 1997, Teaching Mrs. Tingle, 1998, Greenfingers, 2000, The Pledge, 2001, No Such Thing, 2001, Last Orders, 2001, Gosford Park, 2001 (National Society Film Critics award for Best Supporting Actress, 2002, New York Film Critics Circle award for Best Supporting Actress, 2001), Calendar Girls, 2003, The Clearing, 2004, Raising Helen, 2004, Shadowboxer, 2005, The Queen, 2006 (New York Film Critics Circle award for Best Actress, 2006, National Board Rev. award for Best Actress, 2006, National Society Film Critics award for Best Actress, 2007, Critics Choice award for Best Actress, 2007, Golden Globe award for Best Performance by an Actress in a Motion Picture - Drama, 2007, Academy award for Best Actress in a Leading Role, 2007, BAFTA award for Best Actress in a Leading Role, 2007, Screen Actors Guild award for Outstanding Performance by a Female Actor in a Leading Role, 2007), National Treasure: Book of Secrets, 2007, Inkheart, 2008, The Last Station, 2009, State of Play, 2009, Love Ranch, 2010, Red, 2010, The Tempest, 2010, Brighton Rock, 2010, The Debt, 2010, Arthur, 2011, The Door, 2012, Hitchcock, 2012, Red 2, 2013, The Hundred-Foot Journey, 2014, Woman in Gold, 2015, Eye in the Sky, 2015, Trumbo, 2015; actress, director (films) Happy Birthday, 2001; actress: (TV films) Bellamira, 1974, Caesar and Claretta, 1974, The Philanthropist, 1975, The Collection, 1976, As You Like It, 1978, S.O.S. Titanic, 1979, Mrs. Reinhardt, 1981, A Midsummer Night's Dream, 1981, Cymbeline, 1982, Soft Targets, 1982, Faerie Tale Theatre, 1987, Red Kind White Knight, 1988, Prime Suspect, 1991 (BAFTA award for Best Actress, 1992), Prime Suspect 2, 1992 (BAFTA award for Best Actress, 1993), Prime Suspect 3, 1993 (BAFTA award for Best Actress, 1994), Prime Suspect 4: The Lost Child, 1995, Prime Suspect 4: Inner Circles, 1995, Prime Suspect 4: Scent of Darkness, 1995 (Emmy award for Outstanding Lead Actress in a Miniseries or Movie, 1996), Losing Chase, 1995, Prime Suspect 5: Errors of Judgement, 1996, The Passion of Avn Road, 1999 (Emmy award for Outstanding Lead Actress in a Miniseries or Movie, 1999), On the Edge, 2001, Georgetown, 2002, Door to Door, 2002, The Roman Spring of Mrs. Stone, 2003, Prime Suspect 6: The Last Witness, 2003, Elizabeth I, 2005 (Emmy award for Outstanding Lead Actress in a Miniseries or Movie, 2006, Golden Globe award for Best Performance by an Actress in a Miniseries or Motion Picture Made for TV, 2007 **AW:** Named Dame Commander of the Most Excellent Order of the British Empire, Her Majesty Queen Elizabeth II, 2003; recipient Fellowship award, Brit. Academy Film and TV Arts, 2014, Sherry Lansing Leadership award, The Hollywood Reporter, 2010, Distinction in Theatre award, Geffen Playhouse, 2007 **MEM:** Mem.: PTO **BA:** Creative Artists Agency, 2000 Avenue of the Stars, Los Angeles, CA, 90067

MITCHELL, PAUL, T: U.S. Representative from Michigan **I:** Government Administration/Government Relations/Government Services **DOB:** 11/14/1946 **ED:** BA, Michigan State University, 1978 **C:** Committee on Education and the Workforce, Committee on Oversight and Government Reform, Committee on Transportation, House of Representatives from Louisiana's Tenth District, 2017-Present; Chairman, Faith and Freedom Coalition of Michigan, 2013-Present; Owner, Ross Medical Education Center, 2004-Present **BA:** 211 Cannon HOB, Washington, DC, 20515

MNUCHIN, STEVEN, T: U.S. Secretary of the Treasury, Investment Company Executive (Retired) **I:** Business Management/Business Services **CN:** Dune Capital Management, LP **DOB:** 12/21/1962 **PB:** New York **SC:** NY/USA **ED:** BA, Yale University **C:** Secretary, U.S. Department of Treasury, Washington, DC (2017-Present); Chairman, Chief Executive Officer, Dune Capital Management, LP (2004-Present); Chairman, Chief Executive Officer, One West Bank Group, LLC (2009-2017); Chief Executive Officer, SFM Capital Management LP (2003-2004); Vice Chairman, English as Second Language Investments Inc. (2003); Executive Vice President, Chief Information Officer, Goldman Sachs Group, Inc. (Formerly Goldman, Sachs & Co.) (2001-2002); Various Management Positions, Goldman Sachs Group, Inc. (Formerly Goldman, Sachs & Co.) (1985-2001) **CR:** Board of Trustees, New York Presbyterian Medical Center (2004-Present); Board of Directors, Kmart Holding Corp. (Merged Sears Holding Corp.) (2003-Present); Yale Development Board; Trustee, Whitney Museum of American Art;

Hirshhorn Museum & Sculpture Garden, Riverdale Country School **PA:** Republican **BA:** US Treasury Department, 1500 Pennsylvania Ave, Washington, DC, 20220

MOCK, JANET, T: Activist **I:** Nonprofit & Philanthropy **PB:** Honolulu **SC:** HI/USA **ED:** BA, University of Hawaii at Manoa; MA, New York University **CW:** Author, "Surpassing Certainty: What My Twenties Taught Me" (2017); Author, "Redefining Realness: My Path To Womanhood, Identity, Love & So Much More" (2014) **AW:** Named to TIME's 100 Most Influential, TIME Magazine (2018)

MODRICH, PAUL LAWRENCE, T: Biochemistry Professor **I:** Education/Educational Services **DOB:** 06/13/1946 **PB:** Raton **ED:** Postgrad., Harvard University, 1973-74; PhD in Biochemistry, Stanford University, 1973; BS in Biology, Massachusetts Institute of Technology, 1968 **C:** Investigator Howard Hughes Medical Institute, Duke University, 1994-; James B. Duke professor biochemistry, Duke University,; Director program in genetics, Duke University, 1989-92; Professor biochemistry, Duke University, 1984; Associate professor biochemistry, Duke University, 1980; Assistant professor biochemistry, Duke University, 1976; Assistant professor chemistry, University California, Berkeley, 1974 **CW:** Contributor articles to professional journals; associate editor: Biochemistry, 1992-94, member editorial adv. board, 1986-91, 95-; member editorial board Nucleic Acids Research, 1980-82, Journal Biological Chemistry, 1982-83. **AW:** Recipient award in enzyme chemistry Pfizer, 1983, National Academy of Sciences, 1993, Mott prize in cancer research GM, 1996, Medal of Honor for basic research, American Cancer Society, 2005, Pasarow Foundation award in cancer research; co-recipient Nobel Prize in Chemistry, 2015 **MEM:** Fellow: American Academy Arts & Sciences; Member National Institutes of Health (member biochemistry study section 1980-84, National Institutes of Health NIGMS merit award 1986), American Society Biochemistry and Molecular Biology (councillor 1989-92, 97-, member publications committee 1995-97), Institute Medicine; foreign associate National Academy of Sciences **BA:** Department of Biochemistry Duke University, 156A Nanline H Duke Bldg, Durham, NC, 27710

MOERNER, WILLIAM, T: Chemist, Physicist **I:** Sciences **CN:** Stanford University **DOB:** 06/24/1953 **PB:** Pleasanton **SC:** CA/USA **PT:** William Alfred Moerner, Bertha Frances Moerner **MS:** Married **SPN:** Sharon Judith Stein, 6/19/1983 **CH:** Daniel Everett **ED:** PhD in Physics, Cornell University, 1982; MS in Physics, Cornell University, 1978; BEE in Physics and Electrical Engineering, Washington University, St. Louis, MO, 1975; AB in Mathematics, Washington University, St. Louis, MO. 1975 **C:** Chemistry Chairman, Stanford University, 2011—Present; Professor of Chemistry, Stanford University, California, 1998—Present; Professor of Applied Physics, Stanford University, California, 2005; Harry S. Mosher Professor of Chemistry, Stanford University, California, 2002; Professor And Distinguished Chair, Physical Chemistry And Biochemistry, University of California, San Diego, California, 1995-1998; Research Staff Member And Photorefractive Polymer Project Leader, IBM Almaden Research Center, San Jose, CA, 1989-1995; Manager, Laser-Materials Interactions, IBM Almaden Research Center, San Jose, CA, 1988-1989; Research Staff, IBM Almaden Research Center, San Jose, CA, 1981-1988; Research Assistant, Cornell University, 1978-1981; National Science Foundation Graduate Fellow, Cornell University, Ithaca, NY, 1975-1978; Langsdorf Engineering Fellow, Washington University, St. Louis, MO, 1971-1975

CR: General Chair, Topical Meeting On Persistent Spectral Hole-Burning, 1991; Samuel L. McElvain Lecturer, Department of Chemistry, University of Wisconsin, 1993; Visiting Guest Professor, Laboratory For Physical Chemistry, Swiss Institute of Technology, Switzerland, 1993-1994; Ehrenfest Colloquium Lecturer, University of Leiden, The Netherlands, 1994; A.D. Little Lecturer, Department of Chemistry, Massachusetts Institute Of Technology, 1995; Robert Burns Woodward Visiting Professor, Harvard University, 1997-1998 **CIV:** Tenor, San Jose Symphonic Choir, 1983-1991; Official Observer, American Radio Relay League, Santa Clara Valley, CA, 1987-1988; Assistant Technology Coordinator, American Radio Relay League, Santa Clara Valley, CA, 1990-1995; Assistant Emergency Coordinator, American Radio Relay League, Santa Clara Valley, CA, 2000—2008; Tenor, Stanford Symphonic Chorus, 2000—Present **CW:** Single Molecule Optical Detection, Imaging, And Spectroscopy, 1997, Guest Editor, Special Issue, Accounts Of Chemical Research On Single Molecules And Atoms, 1996, Author, Editor, Persistent Spectral Hole-Burning: Science And Applications, 1988, Advising Editor, Chemical Physics Letters, Chemical Physical Chemical, Contributor, Articles, Technical Publications **AW:** Wilkinson Outstanding Young Electrical Engineer Award, National Winner, Eta Kappa Nu, 1984, IBM Outstanding Technical Achievement Awards For Photon-Gated Persistent Spectral Hole-Burning, 1988, Single-Molecule Detection And Spectroscopy, 1992, Earle K. Plyler Prize For Molecular Spectroscopy, 2001, Co-Recipient, Wolf Foundation Prize In Chemistry, Israel, 2008, Irving Langmuir Prize, 2009, Pittsburg Spectroscopy Award, 2012, Peter DeBye Award In Physical Chemistry, American Chemical Society, 2013, Engineering Alumni Achievement Award, Washington University, 2013, Co-Recipient, Nobel Prize In Chemistry, Royal Swedish Academy of Sciences, 2014 **MEM:** Chair, GRC Single-Molecule Approaches To Biology, Society of Photo-Optical Instrumentation Engineers, 2010, Organizer, Symposium On Chemistry Of Single Molecules, American Chemical Society, 1997, Program Committee, Society of Photo-Optical Instrumentation Engineers, 1996-1998, March Meeting, American Physical Society, 1993, Chair, Fundamental And Applied Spectroscopy Technical Group, Optical Society of America, 1992-1994, Symposium Organizer, Laser Science Topical Group, American Physical Society, 1992, General Chair And Founder, Advising Chair, Topical Conference On Persistent Spectral Hole-Burning Science And Applications, Optical Society of America, 1991, 1993-1994, Symposium Organizer, Materials Research Society, 1991, Symposium Organizer, Annual Meeting, IEEE, 1989, Senior Member, Assistant Treasurer, Lasers And Electro-Optics Society Annual Meeting, IEEE, 1988-1989, Biophysics Society, President, IBM Amateur Radio Club, 1987-1988, Co-Editor, Optical Society of America, American Academy of Arts And Sciences, American Association For The Advancement Of Science, National Academy Of Sciences **ACH:** Achievements include single molecule detection and spectroscopy being a patentee in strain-sensitive spectral features detection method, device, photorefractive polymers, photoswitchable fluorescent protein, single photon source **H:** Fellow, American Physical Society; Geoffrey Frew Fellow, Australian Academy of Sciences **BA:** Department of Chemistry, M/C 5080 Stanford University, 375 N-S Mall, Stanford, CA, 94305

MOLINARI, SUSAN, T: Lobbyist, Former U.S. Representative from New York **I:** Government Administration/Government Relations/Government Services **DOB:** 03/27/1958 **PB:** Staten Island **SC:**

NY/USA **PT:** Daughter of Guy Victor and Marguerite (Wing) Molinari; **ED:** MA, State University of New York, Albany, 1982; BA, State University of New York, Albany, 1980 **C:** Vice president public policy & government relations Americas, Google Inc., Washington, 2012-; Chairman, The Century Council, 2001-; Founder, chair, Susan Molinari Strategies LLC, 2010-12; Senior principal government relations & strategy section, Bracewell & Giuliani LLP, Washington, 2008-10; President, Ketchum Pub. Affairs, 2004-08; Chairman, CEO, The Washington Group, 2001-08; Anchor, CBS News Saturday Morning, New York City, 1997-98; Vice chairman, US House Republican Conference, 1995-97; Member, US Congress from 13th New York District, 1993-97; Member, US Congress from 14th New York District, 1990-93; Minority leader, New York City Council, 1986-90; Member District 1, New York City Council, 1986-90; Ethnic community liaison, Republican National Committee, 1983-84; Financial assistant, National Republican Governors Association,; Research analyst, New York State Senate FinanceCom.,; Intern to Senator Christopher Mega, New York State Senate, **CR:** Visiting fellow John F. Kennedy School Government, Harvard University, 1998 **CIV:** Board member, Children's Health Foundation, Member, Commission on Federal Election Reform, Member, March of Dimes Advisory Board, Member, Toyota North American Diversity Advisory Board, **CW:** Author: (with Elinor Burkett) Representative Mom: Balancing Budgets, Bill and Baby in the U.S. Congress, 1998. **AW:** Named a Top Lobbyist, The Hill, 2009; named Housing Person of the Year, National Housing Conference, 2003, Woman of the Year, Glamour magazine, 1996; named one of The 50 Top Lobbyists, Washingtonian magazine, 2007 **PA:** Republican

MOLLENKOPF, STEVEN, T: CEO **I:** Technology **CN:** Qualcomm **ED:** M.S., University of Michigan; B.S., Virginia Polytechnic Institute **C:** CEO, Qualcomm, 2014-; COO and President, Qualcomm, 2011-14; Executive Vice President and President of QCT, Qualcomm, 2008-11; Executive Vice President, Qualcomm, 2008

MONDALE, WALTER FREDERICK, T: Lawyer, Former Vice President of U.S. **I:** Law and Legal Services **DOB:** 01/05/1928 **PB:** Ceylon **PT:** Son of Theodore Sigvaard and Claribel Hope (Cowan) M. **SPN:** Joan Adams, December 27, 1955 (deceased February 3, 2014); **CH:** Theodore, Eleanor Jane (deceased September 17, 2011), William **ED:** LLB cum laude, University of Minnesota, 1956; BA cum laude, University of Minnesota, 1951 **CT:** Bar: Minnesota 1956. **C:** Senior counsel, Dorsey & Whitney LLP, Minneapolis, 1997-; Partner, Dorsey & Whitney LLP, Minneapolis, 1987-93; Presidential envoy to Indonesia, US Department State, 1998; US ambassador to Japan, U.S. Department State, Tokyo, 1993-96; Democratic nominee for President U.S., 1984; Partner, Winston & Strawn LLP, 1981-87; Member, National Security Council, 1977-81; Vice President of the U.S., 1977-81; US Senator from Minnesota, 1964-77; Attorney general, State of Minnesota, 1960-64; Private practice law, Minneapolis, 1956-60; Law clerk to Justice Thomas F. Gallagher, Minnesota Supreme Court, Minneapolis, 1956 **CR:** Chairman National Democratic Institute for International Affairs, 1986-93 **CW:** Author: The Accountability of Power Toward a Responsible Presidency, 1975, The Good Fight: A Life in Liberal Politics, 2010; co-author: (with William Regis Farrell) Crisis and Opportunity in a Changing Japan, 1999, (with Terry Gydesen) Twelve Years and Thirteen Days: Remembering Paula and Sheila Wellstone, 2003 **AW:** Named Distinguished Univ. Fellow in Law & Public Affairs, University Minnesota Hubert H. Humphrey Institute Public Affairs; recipient Lifetime Achievement award, The American Lawyer magazine, 2011 **PA:** Democrat

MONDELLO, MARK T., T: Electronics Executive **I:** Business Management/Business Services **ED:** BSME, University South Florida **C:** CEO, Jabil Circuit, Inc. 2013-; COO, Jabil Circuit, Inc., 2002-2013; Senior vice president business devel., Jabil Circuit, Inc., 1999-2002; Vice president business devel., Jabil Circuit, Inc., 1997-99; Project manager, Jabil Circuit, Inc., 1993-97; Production line supervisor, Jabil Circuit, Inc., St. Petersburg, Florida, 1992-93; Former project manager on commercial and def.-related aerospace programs, Moog, Inc., **CIV:** Board directors, All Children's Hospital,

MONEO, RAFAEL, T: Architect **I:** Architecture & Construction **DOB:** 05/09/1937 **PB:** Tudela, Navarra **SC:** Spain **PT:** Son of Rafael and Maria Teresa (Vallés) **MS:** Married **SPN:** Belén Feduchi **CH:** Belén, Teresa, Clara Matilde **ED:** DArch, Madrid, 1963; Degree in architecture, Madrid, 1961 **C:** Josep Lluís Sert professor architect, Grad. School Design, Harvard University, Cambridge, Massachusetts, 1991-; Professor architect, Grad. School Design, Harvard University, Cambridge, Massachusetts, 1985-; Chairman Department Architect, Grad. School Design, Harvard University, Cambridge, Massachusetts, 1985-90; Professor architect, Madrid, 1981-85; Professor architect, Barcelona, 1970-80; Fellow, Spanish Academy, Rome, 1963-65 **CW:** Principal works include Bankinter, Madrid, Logroño Hall, Mérida Roman Art Museum, Atocha Station, Madrid, Seville (Spain) Airport, Auditorium of Barcelona, Kursaal Auditorium and Congress Center, Thyssen-Bornemesza Museum, Madrid, Davis Museum Wellesley College, Miro Foundation Museum, Mallorca, Diagonal Building, Barcelona, Museums of Modern Art and Architecture, Stockholm, 1994-98, City Hall Extension, Urcia, 1998, Barcelona Concert Hall & Cultural Center, 1999, Kursaal Concert Hall & Cultural Center, San Sebastian, 1999, Audrey Jone Beck Building, Museum Fine Arts, Houston, 2000. **AW:** Recipient Arnold W. Brunner Member prize in Architecture, Am. Academy Arts and Letters, 1993, Pritzker Architect prize, 1996, Gold medal International Union of Architects, 1996, Antonio Feltrinelli prize, 1998. **BA:** Harvard Graduate School of Design, Gund Hall 207 48 Quincy St, Cambridge, MA, 02138

MONTANA, JOE JR., T: Retired Professional Football Player **I:** Athletics **DOB:** 06/11/1956 **PB:** New Eagle **PT:** Son of Joseph C. Montana, Senior and Theresa M. Montana **ED:** BBA in Marketing, University Notre Dame, 1978 **C:** Member new business devel. department, Viking Components Inc., Rancho Santa Margarita, California, 1999-2000; Retired, NFL, 1995; Quarterback, Kansas City Chiefs, 1993-95; Quarterback, San Francisco 49ers, 1979-93 **CW:** Author (with Alan Steinberg): Cool Under Fire, 1989 **AW:** Named Male Athlete of Year, Associated Press, 1990, 1989, Man of Year, The Sporting News, 1989, Player of Year, 1989, Offensive Player of Year, Associated Press, 1989, NFL MVP, 1989, 1st Team All-Pro, 1990, 1989, 1987, NFL Comeback Player of Year, Associated Press, 1986, Super Bowl MVP, NFL, 1990, 1985, 1982; named to NFL 75th Anniversary All-Time Team, Super Bowl Silver Anniversary Team, NFL All-Decade Team, 1980s, Pro Football Hall of Fame, 2000, National Football Conference Pro Bowl Team, NFL, 1994, 1991, 1990, 1988, 1984-86, 1982, Greatest Athlete of the 20th Century, 1999, Sports Illustrated, Number One Clutch Quarterback of All Time, 2006, AP Athlete of the Year, 1989, 1990 **ACH:** Achievements include leading the NFL in: pass completion percentage, 1980, 1981, 1985, 1987, 1989, attempts, 1982; passing touchdowns, 1982, 1987; passer rating, 1987, 1989; member of Super Bowl Championship winning San Fransisco 49ers, 1982, 1985, 1989, 1990 **H:** Winemaking **BA:** Ballantine Book Publicity, 1745 Broadway, New York, NY, 10019

MONTOYA, JUAN PABLO, T: Professional Racing Driver **I:** Athletics **DOB:** 09/20/1975 **PB:** Bogota, Colombia **C:** Racecar Driver NASCAR, Team Penske, 2014-; Racecar Driver NASCAR, Chip Ganassi Racing, 2007-14; Racecar Driver Formula One, McLaren, 2005-06; Racecar Driver Formula One, Williams, 2001-04 **CR:** 1st pl. IZOD series IndyCar 500, 2015, 1st pl., 2000 1st pl. Heluva Good! Sour Cream Dips at the Glen Watkins Glen International, 2010 1st pl. Toyota/Save Mart 350 Infineon Raceway, 2007 3rd pl. Turkish Grand Prix, 2005 1st pl. Brazilian Grand Prix, 2005, 2004 3rd pl. San Marino Grand Prix, 2006, 2004, Hungarian Grand Prix, 2003 2nd pl. French Grand Prix, 2003 3rd pl. Can. Grand Prix, 2003 2nd pl. Monaco Grand Prix, 2006, 1st pl., 2003 3rd pl. Belgian Grand Prix, 2002 1st pl. German Grand Prix, 2003, 2nd pl., 2005, 2002 1st pl. Brit. Grand Prix, 2005, 2nd pl., 2003, 3rd pl., 2002, Austrian Grand Prix, 2002 2nd pl. Malaysian Grand Prix, 2004, 2002, Australian Grand Prix, 2003, 2002, Japanese Grand Prix, 2001, Italian Grand Prix, 2003, 1st pl., 2005, 2001 2nd pl. European Grand Prix, 2003, 2001, Spanish Grand Prix, 2002, 2001 **CIV:** Goodwill ambassador, UN, Founder, Formula Smiles Foundation, **AW:** Named NASCAR Nextel Cup Rookie of Year, 2007, Autosport International Driver of the Year, 2003, Newcomer of Year, Laureus World Sports Awards, 2002, Autosport Rookie of the Year, 2001; recipient Lorenzo Bandini trophy, 2002, Indianapolis 500 Rookie of the Year, 2000, 1999 CART Rookie of the Year, 1999 **ACH:** Achievements include being the only driver to win a CART series title, the Indianapolis 500 and the 24 Hours of Daytona, all in the first attempt **H:** Video games, snowboarding, golf

MOOLENAAR, JOHN, T: U.S. Representative from Michigan **I:** Government Administration/Government Relations/Government Services **DOB:** 05/08/1961 **PB:** Midland **SC:** MI/USA **ED:** MPA, Harvard University, MA **C:** Member, U.S. House of Representatives from Michigan's 4th District (2015-Present); Member, Committee on Appropriations, Republican Study Committee; Member, District 36, Michigan State Senate (2010-2015); Member, District 98, Michigan House of Representatives (2002-2008); Councilman, Midland City Council, MI; Director, Business Development, MITECH+; Lecturer, Saginaw Valley State University; Former Administrator, Midland Academy of Advanced and Creative Studies; Director, Small Business Center, Midland Michigan Development Corporation; Product Market Developer, Dow Chemical **PA:** Republican **BA:** 117 Cannon House Office Building, Washington, DC, 20515

MOONEY, ALEXANDER XAVIER, T: U.S. Representative from West Virginia **I:** Government Administration/Government Relations/Government Services **DOB:** 06/07/1971 **PB:** Washington **ED:** BA in Philosophy, Dartmouth College, 1993 **C:** Member, U.S. House of Representatives from West Virginia's 2nd District, 2015-; Member,House Financial Services Committee; Member, Republican Study Committee; Chairman, Republican Party of Maryland, 2011-13; Member District 3, Maryland State Senate, 1999-2011; Vice president legislative analysis, CNP Action, Inc., 1995-98; Legislative analyst, US House Republican Conference, 1995; Staff assistant to Rep. Roscoe G. Bartlett, US House of Representatives, 1993-95 **MEM:** Mem.: Knights of Columbus **PA:** Republican

MOONVES, LESLIE, T: CEO I: Media & Entertainment **CN:** CBS **DOB:** 10/06/1949 **PB:** New York **SC:** NY/USA **PT:** Herman Moonves, Josephine (Schleifer) Moonves **ED:** Graduate, New York Neighborhood Playhouse School Theatre, New York, NY, 1973; BA in Spanish, Bucknell University, Lewisburg, PA, 1971 **C:** Chairman, Viacom, Inc. (Now CBS Corp.), New York, NY, 2016-Present; President, CEO, Viacom, Inc. (Now CBS Corp.), New York, NY, 2006-Present; Co-President, Co-COO, Viacom, Inc. (Now CBS Corp.), New York, NY, 2004-2005; Chairman, CEO, CBS TV, 2003-2004; President, CEO, CBS TV, 1998-2003; Executive Vice President, CBS/Broadcast Group, 1995-1997; President, CBS Entertainment, Los Angeles, CA, 1995-1997; President, Warner Brothers TV, Burbank, CA, 1993-1995; President, Lorimar Television, Burbank, CA, 1989-1993; Executive Vice President, Creative Affairs, Lorimar Television, Culver City, CA, 1988-1990; Vice President, Movies & Mini-Series, Lorimar Television, Culver City, CA, 1985-1988; Vice President, Movies & Mini-Series, 20th Century Fox Television, Los Angeles, CA, 1982-1985; Vice President of Development, Saul Ilson Productions, Columbia Pictures TV, Burbank, CA, 1981-1982; Development Executive, Catalina Productions, Burbank, CA, 1980-1981 **CR:** Board of Directors, CBS Corp., 2005-Present; KB Home, 2004-Present; Westwood One, Inc., 2004-2006 **CIV:** Trustee, American Film Institute, National Council for Families & TV, Entertainment Industries Council; Co-Chair, Los Angeles Board of Governors, Museum of TV & Radio (Now Paley Center for Media); Board of Directors, Los Angeles Free Clinic; Leadership Advisory Board, NCAA **CW:** Actor, (TV Appearances) Cannon, 1976, Gemini Man, 1976, The Six Million Dollar Man, 1977, Midnight Caller, 1986, (TV Films) The Enola Gay: The Men, the Mission, the Atomic Bomb, 1980 **AW:** Sherrill Corwin Award, American Jewish Committee, 1998, The Most Powerful Man in Hollywood, Entertainment Weekly Magazine, 2000, Showman of the Year, Variety Magazine, 2000, Career Achievement Award, Casting Society of America, 2000, Alumni Association Award for Achievement in a Chosen Profession, Bucknell University, 2002, Gold Medal Award, International Radio & TV Society, 2003, Champion for Children Award, UNICEF, 2005, Milestone Award, Producers Guild of America, 2012, Television Hall of Fame, 2013 **MEM:** Executive Committee, National Academy of Television Arts and Sciences; Board of Directors, Hollywood Radio & TV Society, 1988-1991; President, Hollywood Radio & TV Society, 1991 **PA:** Democrat **BA:** Viacom Inc., 1515 Broadway, New York, NY, 10036

MOORE, ALECIA "PINK" B., T: Singer **I:** Media & Entertainment **DOB:** 09/08/1979 **PB:** Doylestown **SC:** PA/USA **C:** Model, Spokesperson, CoverGirl, 2012—Present **CW:** Singer, (Albums) Can't Take Me Home, 2000, M!ssundaztood, 2001, Try This, 2003, I'm Not Dead, 2006, Funhouse, 2008, Greatest Hits...So Far!!!, 2010, The Truth About Love, 2012, Beautiful Trauma, 2017, (Songs) There U Go, 2000, Most Girls, 2000, You Make Me Sick, 2001, Get The Party Started, 2001, (With Mya, Lil' Kim, & Christina Aguilera) Lady Marmalade, 2001, Don't Let Me Get Me, 2002, Just Like A Pill, 2002, Family Portrait, 2002, Trouble, 2003, God Is A DJ, 2003, Stupid Girls, 2006, Who Knew, 2006, Ur + Ur Hand, 2006, Sober, 2008, So What, 2008, Please Don't Leave Me, 2009, Raise Your Glass, 2010, F**Kin' Perfect, 2010; Film Appearances Ski To The Max, 2000, Rollerball, 2002, Charlie's Angels: Full Throttle, 2003, Catacombs, 2007, Get Him To The Greek, 2010; Actress, (Films) (Voice Actress) Happy Feet II, 2011, Thanks For Sharing, 2012, Billy On The Street, 2015, Janis: Little Girl Blue, 2015,

Popstar: Never Stop Never Stopping, 2016 **AW:** Best Collaboration (With Nate Ruess), Just Give Me a Reason, MTV Video Music Awards, 2013, The World's Most Powerful Celebrities, Forbes Magazine, 2010, BMI Pop Award, Broadcast Music, Inc., U + Ur Hand, 2008, BMI Pop Award, Broadcast Music, Inc., Who Knew, 2008, Best Pop Video, MTV Video Music Awards, Stupid Girls, 2006, Best Female Rock Vocal Performance, Grammy Awards, Trouble, 2004, Best International Female Solo Artist, Brit Awards, 2003, Best Selling American Pop Female Artist, World Music Awards, 2003, Best Pop Collaboration With Vocals, Grammy Awards, Lady Marmalade, 2002, Best Female Video, Best Dance Video, MTV Video Music Awards, Favorite Song, Nickelodeon Kids' Choice Awards, Get the Party Started, 2002, Favorite Female Artist, Nickelodeon Kids' Choice Awards, 2002, The 100 Sexiest Artists, VH1, 2002, Favorite Female - New Artist, Blockbuster Entertainment Awards, 2001, Video of the Year, Best Video From A Film, MTV Video Music Awards, Lady Marmalade, 2001, Best Pop New Artist, Billboard Music Awards, 2000, Top Accomplished Women Entertainers, CEOWORLD Magazine **BA:** La Face Records, 1 Capital City Plaza, 3350 Peachtree Road, Suite 1500, Atlanta, GA, 30326

MOORE, GORDON EARLE, T: Electronics Executive (Retired) **I:** Business Management/Business Services **DOB:** 01/03/1929 **PB:** San Francisco **SC:** CA/USA **PT:** Son of Walter Harold and Florence Almira (Williamson) Moore; **ED:** PhD in Chemistry and Physics, California Institute Tech., Pasadena, 1954; BS in Chemistry, University California, Berkeley, 1950; Attended, San Jose State University **C:** Chairman emeritus, Intel Corp., 1997-2006; Chairman, Intel Corp., 1979-97; CEO, Intel Corp., 1979-87; President, CEO, Intel Corp., Santa Clara, California, 1975-79; Co-founder, executive vice president, Intel Corp., Santa Clara, California, 1968-75; Director R&D, Fairchild Semiconductor Corp., 1959-68; Co-founder, manager engineering department, Fairchild Semiconductor Corp., Mountain View, California, 1957-59; Member tech. staff, Shockley Semiconductor Laboratory, Palo Alto, California, 1956-57 **CR:** Board directors Transamerica Corp., Varian Associates Inc., Gilead Scis., Inc., 1996-, member business adv. board, 1991-96 **CIV:** Co-founder, chairman, Gordon & Betty Moore Foundation, 2000- Senior trustee, California Institute Tech., 2001- Chairman, California Institute Tech., 1995-2001 **AW:** Named one of World's Richest People, Forbes magazine, 2001, Forbes Richest Americans, 1999-; named to National Inventors Hall of Fame, 2009; recipient Distinguished Alumnus award, California Institute Tech., Advancement of Research medal, Am. Society Metals, Perkin medal, Society Chemical Industry, 2004, Bower award for business leadership, Franklin Institute, Philadelphia, 2002, Fellow award, Computer History Museum, 1998, John Fritz medal, Am. Association Engineering Societies, 1993, Presidential Medal of Freedom, The White House, 2002, National Medal Tech., 1990, Nierenberg Prize, 2006, IEEE Medal of Honor, 2008 **MEM:** Fellow: American Association for the Advancement of Science, IEEE (Founders medal 1977, Medal of Honor 2008, Computer Pioneer medal), Royal Society Engineering; mem.: NAE, Am. Physical Society **ACH:** Achievements include recognition as the prognosticator of 'Moore's Law', his prediction that the number of transistors and other components that could be economically placed on a chip would double every year (later revised to every 18 months) **H:** Fishing, golf

MOORE, GWENDOLYNNE SOPHIA, T: U.S. Representative from Wisconsin **I:** Government Administration/Government Relations/Government Services **DOB:** 04/18/1951 **PB:** Racine, Wisconsin **ED:** BA in

Political Sci., Marquette University, Milwaukee, 1978 **C:** Vice Chair Congl. Womens Caucus, US Congress from 4th Wisconsin district, 2009-; Member, US Congress from 4th Wisconsin district, 2005-; Member, Committee on the Budget; Member, Committee on Financial Services; Member District 4, Wisconsin State Senate, 1993-2004; Member, Wisconsin State Assembly, 1989-92 **AW:** Named one of Most Influential Black Americans, Ebony Magazine, 2006; Named to Power 150, 2008 **PA:** Democrat

MOORE, JULIANNE, T: Actress **I:** Media & Entertainment **PB:** Fayetteville **SC:** NC/USA **PT:** Peter Moore; Anne Love Smith **ED:** BFA, Boston University **C:** With, The Guthrie Theater (1988-1989) **CW:** Actress: (theatre) Serious Money, 1987, Bone-the-Fish, 1988, Ice Cream with Hot Fudge, 1990, Uncle Vanya; (Broadway) The Vertical Hour, 2006; (TV soap operas) As the World Turns (Emmy award for Outstanding Ingenue in Daytime Drama Series, 1988), The Edge of Night; (TV films) Money, Power, Murder, 1989, Lovecraft, 1991, The Last to Go, 1991, Cast a Deadly Spell, 1991, (voice) A Child's Garden of Poetry, 2011, Game Change, 2012 (Emmy award for Outstanding Lead Actress in a Mini-series or Movie, 2012, Golden Globe award for Best Performance by an Actress in a Mini-series or Motion Picture Made for TV, 2013, Screen Actors Guild award for Outstanding Performance by a Female Actor in a TV Movie or Mini-series, 2013); (films) The Hand That Rocks the Cradle, 1992, The Gun in Betty Lou's Handbag, 1992, Body of Evidence, 1993, Benny & Joon, 1993, The Fugitive, 1993, Short Cuts, 1993, Vanya on 42nd Street, 1994, Roommates, 1995, Nine Months, 1995, Safe, 1995, Assassins, 1995, Surviving Picasso, 1996, The Myth of Fingerprints, 1997, The Lost World: Jurassic Park, 1997, Hellcab, 1997, Boogie Nights, 1997, Chicago Cab, 1998, The Big Lebowski, 1998, Psycho, 1998, Map of the World, 1999, Magnolia, 1999, Cookie's Fortune, 1999, An Ideal Husband, 1999, The End of the Affair, 1999, Hannibal, 2001, Evolution, 2001, The Shipping News, 2001, Far From Heaven, 2002, The Hours, 2002, Laws of Attraction, 2004, The Forgotten, 2004, The Prize Winner of Defiance, Ohio, 2005, Freedomland, 2006, Children of Men, 2006, Next, 2007, I'm Not There, 2007, Savage Grace, 2007, Blindness, 2008, A Single Man, 2009, Chloe, 2009, The Kids Are All Right, 2010, 6 Souls, 2010, Crazy, Stupid, Love., 2011, Being Flynn, 2012, The English Teacher, 2012, What Maisie Knew, 2012, Don Jon, 2013, Carrie, 2013, Non-Stop, 2014, Maps to the Stars, 2014, Still Alice, 2014 (National Board Review award for Best Actress, 2014, Golden Globe award for Best Actress in a Motion Picture - Drama, 2015, Critics' Choice award for Best Actress, 2015, Screen Actors Guild award for Outstanding Performance by a Female Actor in a Leading Role, 2015, BAFTA award for Best Leading Actress, 2015, Academy award for Best Actress, 2015), The Hunger Games: Mockingjay - Part 1, 2014, Seventh Son, 2014, Freeheld, 2015, The Hunger Games: Mockingjay - Part 2, 2015, Wonderstruck, 2017, Suburbicon, 2017, Kingsman: The Golden Circle, 2017; actress, executive prodr.: (films) Marie and Bruce, 2004; (TV appearances) 30 Rock, 2009-13, Game Change, 2012, Inside Amy Schumer, 2016, Difficult People, 2016; author: (children's books) Freckleface Strawberry, 2007, Freckleface Strawberry and the Dodgeball Bully, 2009, Freckleface Strawberry: Best Friends Forever, 2011, My Mom is a Foreigner, But Not to Me, 2013. **AW:** Recipient Star, Hollywood Walk of Fame, 2013

MOORE, KAREN NELSON, T: Federal Judge **I:** Government Administration/Government Relations/Government Services **DOB:** 11/19/1948 **PB:** Washington **SC:** D.C. **ED:** JD magna cum laude, Harvard University, 1973; AB magna cum laude, Radcliffe

College, 1970 **CT:** Bar: US Court Appeals (6th cir.) 1984, US Supreme Court 1980, US Court Appeals (DC cir.) 1974, Ohio 1976, DC 1973 **C:** Judge, US Court Appeals (6th cir.), Cleveland, 1995-; Professor, Case Western Reserve Law School, Cleveland, 1982-95; Associate professor, Case Western Reserve Law School, Cleveland, 1980-82; Assistant professor, Case Western Reserve Law School, Cleveland, 1977-80; Associate, Jones, Day, Reavis & Pogue, Cleveland, 1975-77; Law clerk to Hon. Harry A. Blackmun, US Supreme Court, Washington, 1974-75; Law clerk to Hon. Malcolm R. Wilkey, US Court Appeals (DC Cir.), Washington, 1973-74 **CR:** Visiting professor Harvard Law School, 1990-91 **CIV:** Trustee, Radcliffe College, Cambridge, 1980-84 Trustee, Lakewood Hospital, Ohio, 1978-85 **CW:** Member Harvard Law Rev., 1971-73; contributor articles to professional journals **MEM:** Fellow: Am. Bar Foundation; mem.: Harvard University Alumni Association (board directors 1984-87), Am. Law Institute, Phi Beta Kappa **BA:** 100 East Fifth Street, Cincinnati, OH, USA, 45202

MORAN, JERRY, T: U.S. Senator from Kansas **I:** Government Administration/Government Relations/Government Services **DOB:** 05/29/1954 **PB:** Great Bend **SC:** KS/USA **PT:** Son of Raymond Edwin and Madeline Eleanor (Fletcher) Moran; **ED:** JD, The University of Kansas School of Law, 1981; BS in Economics, The University of Kansas 1976 **C:** Chairmen, National Republican Senatorial Committee, 2013-2015; Member, U.S. Senate Veterans Affairs Committee, 2011-; Member, U.S. Senate Appropriations Committee, 2011-; Member, U.S. Senate Banking, Housing, & Urban Affairs Committee, 2011-; U.S. Senator from Kansas, 2011-; Member, U.S. Senate Special Committee on Aging, 2011-13; Member, U.S. Senate Small Business & Entrepreneurship Committee, 2011-13; Member, U.S. Senate Homeland Security & Governmental Affairs Committee, 2011-13; Member, U.S. Congress from 1st Kansas District, 1997-2011; Majority leader, Kansas State Senate, 1995-96; Member District 37, Kansas State Senate, 1989-96; Deputy attorney, Rooks County, Kansas, 1987-95; Partner, Jeter & Moran, 1983-87; Special assistant attorney general, State of Kansas, Topeka, 1982-85 **CR:** Chairman National Republican Senatorial Committee (NRSC), 2013-15 **CIV:** President, The University of Kansas School of Law, 1994-95 Vice president, The University of Kansas School of Law, 1993-94 Board of Governors, The University of Kansas School of Law, Board of Directors, Kansas Chamber of Commerce & Industry, 1996-97 **AW:** Named a Guardian of Small Business, National Federation Independent Business, 2010, 2008; named Home Care Hero of Year, Kans, Home Care Association, 1998; recipient Distinguished Leadership award, American Association for Marriage & Family Therapy, 2007, Wheat Leader of the Year award, National Association Wheat Growers & US Wheat Associates, 2004, Small Business Advocate award, Small Business Survival Committee, 2004, Intergovernmental Leadership award, League of Kansas Municipalities, 2003, Jim Edwards Alumnus of the Year award, Leadership Kansas, 2003, Legislative award, National Rural Health Association, 1999 **PA:** Republican

MORENO, RITA, T: Actress **I:** Media & Entertainment **DOB:** 12/11/1931 **PB:** Humacao **SC:** Puerto Rico **CW:** Spanish dancer since childhood, night club entertainer; actress: (Broadway) The Sign in Sidney Brustein's Window, 1964-65, Gantry, 1969-70, The Last of the Red Hot Lovers, 1970-71, The National Health, 1974, The Ritz, 1975, Wally's Cafe, 1981, The Odd Couple, 1985; (off-Broadway) After Play, 1995, (London production) Sunset

Blvd., 1996; (films) Singin' in the Rain, 1952, The King and I, 1956, West Side Story, 1961 (Academy award for Best Actress in a Supporting Role, 1962, Golden Globe award for Best Supporting Actress, 1962), Night of the Following Day, 1968, Carnal Knowledge, 1971, The Four Seasons, 1981, I Like It Like That, 1994, Angus, 1995, The Wharf Rat, 1995, Slums of Beverly Hills, 1998, Carlo's Wake, 1999, Blue Moon, 2000, Pinero, 2001, King of the Corner, 2004, Lolo's Cafe, 2006, Play It By Ear, 2006, Rio 2 (voice), 2014, Six Dance Lessons in Six Weeks, 2014, Remember Me, 2016; (TV films) Dominic's Dream, 1974, Out to Lunch, 1974, Anatomy of a Seduction, 1979, Evita Peron, 1981, Portrait of a Showgirl, 1982, Best Defense, 1995, The Spree, 1998, The Rockford Files: If It Bleeds...It Leads, 1999, Open House, 2003, Copshop, 2004, Nicky Deuce, 2013, Old Soul, 2014, A Gift of Miracles, 2015; (TV series) The Electric Company, 1971-77, Where on Earth Is Carmen Sandiego? (voice), 1994-99, Oz, 1997-2003, Law & Order: Criminal Intent 2006-07, Cane, 2007, In Plain Sight, 2010, Happily Divorced 2011-13; (TV appearances) The Rockford Files, 1974 (Emmy award for Outstanding Lead Actress for a Single Appearance in a Drama or Comedy Series, 1978), The Muppet Show, 1976 (Emmy award for Outstanding Continuing or Single Performance by a Supporting Actress in Variety or Music, 1977), The Love Boat, 1983, Miami Vice, 1989, B.L. Stryker, 1989-90, Top of the Heap, 1991, Strong Medicine, 2003, The Guardian, 2003, Copshop, 2004, Law and Order, 2005, American Family, 2002, In Plain Sight, 2010, One Day at a time, 2017-, many others; author: Rita Moreno, 2013. **AW:** Recipient Grammy award for Best Recording, 1973, Antoinette Perry award for Best Supporting Actress Broadway Play, 1975, Star, Hollywood Walk of Fame, 1995, National Osteoporosis Foundation award, 2000, Presidential Freedom medal, 2005, National Medal of Arts award, National Endowment for the Arts, 2010, Lifetime Achievement award, Screen Actors Guild, 2014, Kennedy Center Honors, John F. kennedy Center Performing Arts, Washington, 2015; named to The California Hall of Fame, 2007. **ACH:** Achievements include being in the Guinness Book of World Records as the one of two female performers to win Academy, Grammy, Tony and Emmy awards.

MORIKIS, JOHN G., T: CEO, Chairman, and President of Sherwin-Williams Co. **I:** Business Management/Business Services **ED:** Masters in Business, National Louis University; BBA, St. Joseph's College **C:** Chairman, Sherwin-Williams Co, 2017-; CEO, Sherwin-Williams Co. 2016-; President, Sherwin-Williams Co., 2016-; President, COO, Sherwin-Williams Co., 2006-16; President Paint Stores Group, Sherwin-Williams Co., 1999-2006; President, general manager Eastern Division Paint Stores Group, Sherwin-Williams Co., 1998-99; Senior vice president, director marketing Paint Stores Group, Sherwin-Williams Co., 1997-98; Management trainee, Sherwin-Williams Co., Cleveland, 1984 **CIV:** Board directors, American Red Cross Greater Cleveland chapter, **BA:** 101 West Prospect Avenue, Cleveland, OH, 44115-1075

MORITZ, MICHAEL J., T: Venture Capitalist **I:** Financial Services **PB:** Cardiff **SC:** United Kingdom **ED:** MBA, University Pennsylvania Wharton School Business, 1978; MA in Hist., University Oxford, 1976 **C:** Chairman, Sequoia Capital, 2012-; General partner, managing director, Sequoia Capital, 1986-2012; Founder, Technologic Partners,; With, Time Warner,; Corr., TIME magazine, 1979 **CR:** Board directors LinkedIn Corp., 2011-, Klarna AB, 2010-, Sugar Inc., 2007, kayak.com, 2007-, Green Dot Corp., 2003, 24/7 Customer, 2003-, Google, Inc., 1999-2007, PayPal, Inc., 1999-2002, Yahoo! Inc., 1995-2003, Flextronics International Ltd., 1993-2005

CW: Author: The Little Kingdom: The Private Story of Apple Computer, 1986,Co Author: Going for Broke: The Chrysler Story,1986 **AW:** Named one of Forbes 400: Richest Americans, 2009, The Richest People in Britain, London's Sunday Times, 50 Who Matter Now, Business 2.0, 2007, The Most Influential People in the World, TIME magazine, 2007, Knight Commander of the Order of the British,2013

MORITZ, NANCY LOUISE, T: Federal Judge, Former State Supreme Court Justice **I:** Law and Legal Services **DOB:** 03/03/1960 **PB:** Beloit **SC:** KS/USA **ED:** JD, Washburn University, 1985; BBA, Washburn University, 1982 **C:** Judge, U.S. Court Appeals (10th Cir.), Lawrence, Kansas, 2014-; Associate justice, Kansas Supreme Court, 2011-14; Judge, Kans Court Appeals, 2004-11; Appellate coordinator, US Department Justice, 1999-2004; Assistant US atty District Kansas, U.S. Department Justice, Kansas City, 1995-2004; Associate, Spencer Fane Britt & Browne, Overland Park, Kansas, 1989-95; Law clerk to Hon. Patrick F. Kelly, U.S. District Court Kansas, 1987-89; Research attorney to Justice Harold Herd, Kansas Supreme Court, 1985-87 **CIV:** Board governors, Washburn Law School, Member, Kansas Continuing Legal Education Commission, Chair, Kansas Bar Journal, Board editors, Kansas Bar Journal, **MEM:** Mem.: Kansas Bar Association **BA:** 1823 Stout St, Denver, CO, 80202

MORRIS, DESMOND (JOHN), T: Zoologist, Writer, Artist **I:** Sciences **PT:** Son of Harry Howe Morris and Dorothy Marjorie (Hunt) Fuller **MS:** Married **SPN:** Ramona Joy Baulch, July 30, 1952 **CH:** Jason **ED:** DSc (hon.), Reading University, England, 1998; DPhil, Oxford University, England, 1954; BSc, Birmingham University, England, 1951 **C:** Research fellow, Wolfson College, Oxford, 1973-81; Director, Institute Contemporary Arts, London, 1967-68; Curator mammals, Zoological Society London, 1959-67; Head Granada T.V. and Film Unit,, Zoological Society of London, 1956-59; Research worker zoology, University of Oxford, England, 1954-56 **CW:** Author: Biology of Art, 1962, Apes and Monkeys, 1965, Big Cats, 1965, Mammals: A Guide to the Living Species, 1966, The Naked Ape, 1968, The Human Zoo, 1969, Intimate Behavior, 1971, Manwatching: A Field Guide to Human Behavior, 1977, The Soccer Tribe, 1981, The Book of Ages, 1983, The Art of Ancient Cyprus, 1985, Bodywatching: A Field Guide to the Human Species, 1985, The Illustrated Naked Ape, 1986, Catwatching, 1986, Dogwatching, 1986, The Secret Surrealist, 1987, Catlore, 1987, The Animals Roadshow, 1988, The Human Nestbuilders, 1988, Horsewatching, 1988, The Animal Contract, 1990, Animalwatching, 1990, Babywatching, 1991, Christmas Watching, 1992, The World of Animals, 1993, The Human Animal, 1994, Body Talk, A World Guide to Gestures, 1994, The Naked Ape Trilogy, 1994, Illustrated Cat Watching, 1994, Illustrated Babywatching, 1995, Illustrated Dogwatching, 1996, Catworld: A Feline Encyclopedia, 1996, The Human Sexes, 1997, Illustrated Horsewatching, 1998, Cool Cats: The 100 Cat Breeds of the World, 1999, Body Guards, 1999, Dogs: A Dictionary of Dog Breeds, 2001, Peoplewatching, 2002, The Nature of Happiness, 2004, The Naked Woman, 2004, Watching: Encounters With Humans and Other Animals, 2006, Fantastic Cats, 2006, The Naked Man, 2008, Baby: The Amazing Story of the First Two Years of Life, 2008, Planet Ape, 2009, Owl, 2009, Child, 2010, Monkey, 2013, The Artistic APE: Three Million Years Art, 2013, others; co-author: (with Ramona Morris) Men and Snakes, 1965, Men and Apes, 1966, Men and Pandas, 1966, The Giant Panda, 1981, Gestures: Their Origins and Distribution, 1979; autobiography Animal Days, 1979, The Naked Eye, 2000; editor: Primate Ethology,

1969, (fiction) Inrock, 1983; contributor numerous articles to zoological journals; one-man shows include Mayor Gallery, London, 1997, Pub. Art Gallery, Buxton, 1997, Keitelman Gallery, Brussels, 1998, Rossaert Gallery, Antwerp, 1998, Witteveen Gallery, Amsterdam, 1999, Museum Modern Art, Ostend, 2002, others,(Book) Leopard, 2014, Bison, 2015(Film) Zootime, 1956, Life, 1965, The Human Race, 1982, The Animals Roadshow, 1987, The Animal Contact, 1989, Animal Country, 1992, The Human Animal, 1994, The Human Sexes, 1997

MORRIS, MAREN LARAE, T: Country Music Singer **I:** Media & Entertainment **DOB:** 04/10/1990 **PB:** Arlington **SC:** TX/USA **PT:** Greg Morris, Kellie Morris **MS:** Married **SPN:** Ryan Hurd, 3/24/2018 **CW:** Singer, (Albums) Walk On, 2005, All That It Takes, 2007, Live Wire, 2011, Hero, 2016, (Extended Plays) Maren Morris, 2015, (Songs) My Church, 80s Mercedes, (With Dierks Bentley) I'll Be the Moon, 2016, I Could Use a Love Song, (With Thomas Rhett) Craving You, (With Vince Gill) Dear Hate, Once, 2017, (With Zedd and Grey) The Middle, Rich, (With Niall Horan) Seeing Blind, 2018; Songwriter, (Songs) (Songs By Tim McGraw) Last Turn Home, 2014, (Songs By Aubrey Peeples) Blind, 2014, (Songs By Kelly Clarkson) Second Wind, 2015, (Songs By Jessie James Decker) Clint Eastwood, 2015, (Songs By Connie Britton and Lennon & Maisy) This is Real Life, 2015, (Songs By Caitlyn Shadbolt) Shoot Out the Lights, 2015, (Songs By Clare Bowen and Sam Palladio) Wake Up When It's Over, 2015, (Songs By Aubrey Peeples) Mess Worth Making, 2015, (Songs By Brothers Osborne) Greener Pastures, 2016, (Songs By Aubrey Peeples) The Book, Caged Bird, 2016, (Songs By Hayden Panettiere and Will Chase) Boomtown, 2016, (Songs By The Henningsens) Jesus or a Bullet, 2016, (Songs By Kree Harrison) Your Whiskey, 2016, (Songs By Bridgit Mendler) Out for Love, 2017, (Songs By Jessie James Decker) Shoot Out the Lights, Too Young to Know, Open All Night, Hold a Candle, 2017; Appearances, (TV Shows) Saturday Night Live, CMT Crossroads, 2016, NCIS: New Orleans, 2017 **AW:** Honoree, Artists of the Year Awards, CMT, 2018, Top Country Female Artist, Billboard Music Awards, 2018, Best New Country Artist, Radio Disney Music Awards, 2017, New Female Vocalist of the Year, ACM Awards, 2017, Best Country Solo Performance, My Church, Grammy Awards, 2017, New Artist of the Year, CMA Awards, 2016 **ACH:** Grammy for Best Country Solo Performance, 2017, CMA New Artist of the Year, 2016 **BA:** Red Light Management, 8439 Sunset Boulevard, 2nd Floor, Los Angeles, CA, 90069

MORRISON, TONI, T: Writer, Educator, Retired Literature and Language Professor **I:** Writing and Editing **DOB:** 02/18/1931 **PB:** Lorain **SC:** OH/USA **PT:** George Wofford; Ella Ramah (Willis) Wofford **ED:** Honorary LittD, University of Geneva (2011); Honorary LittD, Rutgers, The State University of New Jersey (2011); Honorary LittD, University of Oxford (2005); Honorary Degree, Princeton University (2013); Honorary Degree, University of Paris; Honorary Degree, Oberlin College; Honorary Degree, Sarah Lawrence College; Honorary Degree, Dartmouth College; Honorary Degree, University of Michigan; Honorary Degree, Brown University; Honorary Degree, Georgetown University; Honorary Degree, Yale University; Honorary Degree, Columbia University; Honorary Degree, University of Pennsylvania; Honorary Degree, Harvard University; MA in American Literature, Cornell University, New York City, NY (1955); BA in English, Howard University, Washington, DC (1953) **C:** Retired (2006); Director, Princeton Atelier, Princeton University (1994-2006); Robert

F. Goheen Professor of Humanities, Princeton University, Princeton, NJ (1989-2006); Albert Schweitzer Professor of Humanities, State University of New York, Albany, NY (1984-1989); Associate Professor of English, State University of New York, Purchase, NY (1971-1972); Senior Editor, Random House, New York City, NY (1967-1983); Associate Editor, Random House, Syracuse, NY (1965-1967); Instructor English, Howard University (1957-1964); Instructor of English, Texas Southern University, Houston, Texas (1955-1957) **CR:** international Cordorcet Chair, Ecole Normale Superieure & College, France (1994); Presenter of Massey Lecturers, Harvard University (1990); Clark Lecturers, Trinity College (1990); Jeannette K. Watson Distinguished Professor, Syracuse University, NY (1988); Obert C. Tanner Lecturer, University of Michigan, Ann Arbor, MI (1988); Visiting Lecturer, Bard College, NY (1986-1988); Yale University, New Haven, CT (1976-1977) **CW:** Author, Novels, "The Bluest Eye" (1970), "Sula" (1974), "Song of Solomon" (1977), "Tar Baby" (1981), "Beloved" (1987), "Jazz" (1992), "Paradise" (1999), "Love" (2003), "A Mercy" (2008), "Home" (2012), "God Help the Child" (2015), Nonfiction, "The Black Book" (1974), "Playing in the Dark: Whiteness and the Literary Imagination" (1992), "The Dancing Mind" (1996), "Remember: The Journey to School Integration" (2004), "What Moves at the Margins: Selected Essays, Reviews and Speeches" (2008), Plays, "Dreaming Emmett" (1986); Co-author with Slade Morrison, Children's Literature, "The Big Box" (2002), "The Book of Mean People" (2002), "The Lion or the Mouse?" (2003), "The Ant or the Grasshopper?" (2003), "The Poppy or the Snake?" (2003); Editor, "Race-ing Justice, En-Gendering Power: Essays on Anita Hill, Clarence Thomas, and the Construction of Social Reality" (1992); "To Die for the People: The Writings of Huey P. Newton" (1995); Co-editor, "Birth of a Nation'hood: Gaze, Script, Spectacle in the O.J. Simpson Case" (1997) **AW:** Named One of the 30 Most Powerful Women in America, Ladies' Home Journal (2001); Named to the New Jersey Hall of Fame (2008); Presidential Medal of Freedom, The White House (2012); Norman Mailer Prize for Lifetime Achievement (2009); Golden Plate Award, Academy of Achievement (2005); Elizabeth Cady Stanton Award, National Organization of Women; Living Legends Award, Library of Congress (2000); National Humanities Medal (2000); Medal for Distinguished Contribution to American Letters, National Book Foundation (1996); Nobel Prize for Literature, Swedish Academy (1993); New York State Governor's Art Award (1986); Medal of Distinction, Barnard College (1979); Ohioana Book Award, "Sula" (1975); National Book Critics Circle Award, "Song of Solomon" (1977); Robert F. Kennedy Memorial Book Award, "Beloved" (1988); Anisfield-Wolf Book Award, "Beloved" (1988); Unitarian Universalist Association's Frederic G. Melcher Book Award, "Beloved" (1988); Pulitzer Prize for Fiction, "Beloved" (1988); Named Best American Novel Published in Previous 25-Years, New York Times Book Review, "Beloved" (2006); ALA's Coretta Scott King Award, "Remember: The Journey to School Integration" (2005) **MEM:** American Academy of Arts and Letters; National Council of the Arts; Author's Guild **ACH:** Achievements include becoming first African American woman to win the Nobel Prize in Literature **BA:** The Random House Publishing Group, 1745 Broadway 18th Floor, New York, NY, 10019

MOSCHINI, SILVINA, T: President of Transparent Business **I:** Business Management/Business Services **ED:** Latino Growth Leadership Program, Stanford University, 2016-20; Endeavor Strategic Growth Program, Stanford University, 2016 **C:** Co-Founder/President, Transparent Business,

2009-; CEO, She Works! , 2016-; Founder, Yandiki , 2014-; Internet & Technology Contributing Expert, CNN, 2012

MOSKOVITZ, DUSTIN AARON, T: CEO **I:** Information Technology and Services **CN:** Asana **PB:** Gainesville **SC:** FL/USA **PT:** Richard A. Moskovitz; Nancy Siegel **ED:** Student Majored in Economics, Harvard University, 2002-04 **C:** Co-Founder, Good Ventures, 2011-; Co-founder, Asana, 2008-; Vice president engineering, Facebook, Inc., Palo Alto, California, 2004-08; Co-founder, Facebook, Inc., Palo Alto, California, 2004 **AW:** Named one of The Forbes 400: Richest Americans, Forbes magazine, 2011-

MOSS, ELISABETH, T: Actress **I:** Media & Entertainment **DOB:** 07/07/1905 **PB:** LA **SC:** LA **PT:** Daughter of Ron Moss; **CW:** Actress (TV films) Bar Girls, 1990, It's Spring Training, Charlie Brown!, 1992, Midnight's Child, 1992, Frosty Returns, 1992, Gypsy, 1993, Escape to Witch Mountain, 1995, Naomi & Wynonna: Love Can Build a Bridge, 1995, Earthly Possessions, 1999, Spirit, 2001, (TV series) Lucky Chances, 1990, Picket Fences, 1992-95, The West Wing, 1999-2006, Invasion, 2005-06, Mad Men, 2007-15, (TV miniseries) Top of the Lake, 2013 (Golden Globe award for Best Performance by an Actress in a Mini-Series or Motion Picture Made for TV, 2014) The Simpsons, 2013, The Handmaid's Tale, 2017-, (films) Suburban Commando, 1991, Once Upon a Forest, 1993, Imaginary Crimes, 1994, Separate Lives, 1995, The Last Supper, 1995, A Thousand Acres, 1997, Angelmaker, 1998, The Joyriders, 1999, Mumford, 1999, Anywhere But Here, 1999, Girl, Interrupted, 1999, West of Here, 2002, Heart of America, 2003, Temptation, 2003, Virgin, 2003, The Missing, 2003, Bittersweet Place, 2005, They Never Found Her, 2007, Day Zero, 2007, Honored, 2007, The Attic, 2008, New Orleans, Mon Amour, 2008, El Camino, 2008, The Pack, 2008, Did You Hear About the Morgans?, 2009, A Buddy Story, 2010, The Pack, 2010, Get Him to the Greek, 2010, Smoking/Non-Smoking, 2012, Darling Companion, 2012, On the Road, 2012, Listen Up Philip, 2014, The One I Love, 2014, Meadowland, 2015, Truth, 2015, High-Rise, 2015, The Free World, 2016, The Bleeder, 2016, The Seagull, 2016, Mad to Be Normal, 2016, The Square, 2017, The Seagull, 2018, The Old Man and the Gun, 2018 (ballets) Sleeping Beauty, New York City Ballet, The Nutcracker, Joffrey Ballet, (plays) Sound of Music, Christmas Dragon, Big Tush/Little Tush, Franny's Way, (Broadway plays) Speed-the-Plow, 2008, actress, producer (films) Queen of Earth, 2015 **AW:** Primetime Emmy, Outstanding Lead Actress in a Drama Series, 2017, The Handmaids Tale, Outstanding Drama Series, 2017, Golden Globe for Best Actress, 2014, Top of the Lake

MOTTA, DICK, T: Former Professional Basketball Coach **I:** Athletics **C:** Weber State,1962-1968; Chicago Bulls, 1968-1976,; Washington Bullets, 1976-1980,; Dallas Mavericks, 1980-1987,; Sacramento Kings, 1990-1991,; Dallas Mavericks, 1994-1996,; Denver Nuggets, 1996-1997 **AW:** NBA Coach of the Year, 1971, NBA All-Star Game Head Coach, 1979, Big Sky Coach of the Year, 1965, Big Sky Champion, 1965, 1966, 1968

MOTZ, DIANA GRIBBON, T: Federal Judge **I:** Law and Legal Services **DOB:** 07/15/1943 **PB:** Washington **SC:** D.C./USA **PT:** Daughter of Daniel McNamara and Jane (Retzler) Gribbon; **ED:** LLB, University of Virginia, 1968; BA, Vassar College, 1965 **CT:** Bar: Supreme Court of the U.S. 1980, U.S. Court Appeals (4th cir.) 1969, U.S. District Court Maryland 1969 **C:** Judge, U.S. Court Appeals (4th cir.), 1994-; Judge, Maryland Court of Special Appeals, 1991-94; Partner, Frank, Bernstein, Conaway & Goldman, Baltimore, 1986-91; Chief of Litigation, State of Maryland, Baltimore, 1981-86; Assistant Attorney General, State of Maryland, Baltimore, 1972-81; Associate, Piper & Marbury, Baltimore, 1968-71 MEM: Mem.: American Bar Association, Federal Courts Study Committee, Lawyers Round Table, Maryland Bar Foundation, Am. Bar Foundation, Am. Law Institute, Baltimore City Bar Association (Executive Committee 1988), Maryland Bar Association, Wranglers Law Club BA: 1100 E Main St #501, Richmond, VA, 23219

MOULTON, SETH WILBUR, T: U.S. Representative from Massachusetts I: Government Administration/Government Relations/Government Services DOB: 10/24/1978 PB: Salem SC: MA/USA PT: Son of Wilbur Thomas and Lynn Alice (Meader) Moulton. ED: MBA, PPA, Harvard University, 2011; BS in Physics, Harvard University, Connecticut, 2001 C: Mem., US Congress from 6th Massachusetts District, Washington, 2014-; Member, Budget Committee, Armed Services Committee, Small Business Committee; Managing director, Texas Central Railway, 2011-12 CR: Managing director Texas Central Railway, 2011 CW: Appeared in (documentaries) No End in Sight, 2007 AW: Decorated Commendation medal, Bronze star PA: Democrat

MOYNIHAN, BRIAN THOMAS, T: CEO of Bank of America I: Financial Services DOB: 10/09/1959 PB: Marietta ED: JD, University Notre Dame Law School, 1984; BA, Brown University, 1981 C: Chairman, president, CEO, Bank of America Corp., 2014-; CEO Merrill Lynch, Bank of America Corp., 2009; President, CEO, Bank of America Corp., 2010-14; Head consumer banking, Bank of America Corp., 2009-10; President global banking, global wealth & investment management, Bank of America Corp., 2009; President global corporate & investment banking, Bank of America Corp., 2007-09; Executive vice president, general counsel, Bank of America Corp., 2008-09; President global wealth & investment management, Bank of America Corp., Charlotte, North Carolina, 2004-07; Executive vice president brokerage & wealth management, FleetBoston Financial Corp., 2000-04; Executive vice president, FleetBoston Financial Corp., 1999-2000; Senior vice president, Fleet-Boston Financial Corp., 1998-99; Managing director corporate strategy & devel., FleetBoston Financial Corp., 1994-2000; Deputy general counsel, Fleet-Boston Financial Corp., 1993-94; Partner, Edwards & Angell LLP, 1991-93; Associate, Edwards & Angell LLP, 1984-91 CR: Board directors Bank of America Corp., 2010- CIV: Past chairman, Providence Haitian Project, Inc., Past chairman, Travelers Aid Society, Rhode Island, Board directors, Boys & Girls Clubs of Boston, Board directors, YouthBuild Boston, BA: Bank of America Corp, 100 N Tryon St, Charlotte, NC, 28255

MUELLER, ROBERT SWAN III, T: Special Prosecutor of the U.S. I: Law and Legal Services DOB: 08/07/1944 PB: New York City SC: NY/USA PT: Son of Robert Swan Junior and Alice C. (Truesdale) Mueller MS: Married SPN: Ann Standish, September 3, 1966; CH: Cynthia, Melissa ED: JD, University of Virginia School of Law, 1973; MA in International Relations, New York University, 1967; BA, Princeton University, 1966 CT: Bar: Massachusetts, US District Court Massachusetts, US Court Appeals (1st cir.), California, US District Court (northern district) California, US Ct Appeals (9th cir.). C: Special Prosecutor, 2017-; Partner, WilmerHale LLP, 2014-; Director FBI, US Department Justice, 2001-13; Acting Deputy Attorney General, US Department Justice, 2001; US Attorney

(Northern Dist) California, US Department Justice, 1998-2001; Senior Litigator, Homicide Section, DC US Attorney's Office, US Department Justice, Washington, 1995-98; Partner, Hale & Dorr LLP, Washington, 1993-95; Assistant Attorney General Criminal Division, US Department Justice, Washington, 1990-93; Assistant to Attorney General for Criminal Matters, US Department Justice, Washington, 1989-90; Partner, Hill & Barlow, Boston, 1988-89; Deputy US Attorney, US Department Justice, Boston, 1987-88; US Attorney, US Department Justice, Boston, 1986-87; 1st Assistant US Attorney, US Department Justice, Boston, 1985; Chief Criminal Division Massachusetts District, US Department Justice, Boston, 1982-85; Chief Criminal Division, US Department Justice, San Francisco, 1981-82; Chief Unit Special Prosecutions, US Department Justice, San Francisco, 1980-81; Assistant US Attorney (Northern District) California, US Department Justice, San Francisco, 1976-80; Associate, Pillsbury, Madison & Sutro, San Francisco, 1973-76 CR: Lead Investigator Ind. Investigation into National Football League's Handling of Ray Rice Domestic Violence Incident, 2014 CIV: Captain U.S. Marine Corps, 1967-70 Vietnam. AW: Decorated Bronze Star, Purple Heart, Vietnamese Cross of Gallantry; Recipient Thomas Jefferson Foundation Medal in Law University Virginia, 2013; Named One of The 50 Most Powerful People in DC, GQ Magazine, 2009. MEM: Mem.: American College Trial Lawyers, California Bar Association, Massachusetts Bar Association BA: Department of Justice, 950 Pennsylvania Ave, NW, Washington, DC, 20530

MUHAMMAD, IBTIHAJ, T: Olympic Fencer I: Athletics PB: Maplewood SC: NJ/USA ED: International Relations and African American Studies double major, Duke University, 2007 C: Founder, Louella, 2014- AW: Olympic Bronze medal in Fencing, 2016 Summer Olympics;

MUHLY, NICO, T: Composer I: Fine Art SC: VT/USA ED: Wheeler School; English Degree, Columbia University; Masters in Music, Juilliard CW: (Album) Speaks Volumes,2007 Joshua, 2008, Mothertongue, 2008, The Reader, 2009, I Drink the Air Before Me, 2010, A Good Understanding by Los Angeles Master Chorale, 2010, Seeing is Believing by the Aurora Orchestra, 2011, Drones with Bruce Brubaker, 2012, Cycles with James McVinnie, 2013, Two Boys from the Metropolitan Opera production, 2014, Keep In Touch by Nico Muhly & Nadia Sirota, 2016, Confessions by Nico Muhly & Teitur, 2016,Planetarium with Bryce Dessner, James McAlister, and Sufjan Stevens, 2017

MUILENBURG, DENNIS A., T: CEO, Chairman, and President at Boeing Co. I: Aviation ED: MS in Aeronautics & Astronautics, University of Washington, Seattle; BS in Aerospace Engineering, Iowa State University, 1986 C: Chairman, president, CEO, The Boeing Co., 2016-; Various engineering and program management positions, The Boeing Co., 1985-; President, CEO, Boeing Defense, Space & Security, 2009-13; President, CEO, The Boeing Co., 2015-16; Vice chairman, president, COO, The Boeing Co., 2013-15; Executive vice president, The Boeing Co., 2009-13; President global services & support, The Boeing Co., 2008-09; General manager combat systems division & progressive manager Future Combat Systems, The Boeing Co., 2003-08; Then vice president programs & engineering Boeing Air Traffic Management, The Boeing Co., 2001-03; Including director weapon systems Joint Strike Fighter progressive, The Boeing Co., CR: Executive committee member Business Roundtable board directors Caterpillar Inc., 2011- CIV: Board of Directors, St. Louis Sports

Commission, Board Trustee, Washington University, St. Louis, Board Trustee, National World War II Museum, Board of Trustees, St. Louis Sci. Center MEM: Fellow: American Institute of Aeronautics and Astronautics (associate), Royal Aeronautical Society; mem.: Aerospace Industries Association (chairman board governors, member executive committee), Association US Army (vice president community relations Gateway chapter) BA: The Boeing Company, 100 N Riverside Plz, Chicago, IL, 60606

MUIR, DAVID, T: News Correspondent I: Media & Entertainment DOB: 11/08/1973 PB: Syracuse ED: Doctor of Media (hon.), Northeastern University, 2015; LittD (hon.), Ithaca College, 2015; Attended, University Salamanca, Spain; Attended, Institute Political Journalism, Georgetown University; BA magna cum laude, Ithaca College, New York, 1995 C: Co-anchor, 20/20, 2013-; Anchor World News, ABC News, 2014-; Weekend anchor World News, ABC News, 2007-; Reporter, anchor, ABC News, New York City, 2003-; Anchor World News with David Muir, ABC News, 2011-13; Co-anchor Primetime, ABC News, 2004-11; Anchor World News Now, ABC News, 2003-04; Reporter, anchor, WCVB-TV, Boston,; Reporter, anchor, WTVH-TV, Syracuse, New York, AW: Named one of Syracuse's Best News Anchors, Syracuse News Times; recipient Jessica Savitch award of Distinction for Excellence in Journalism, Ithaca College, 2015, Edward R. Murrow award for investigative reporting, 2013, Associated Press Best Enterprise Reporting award, National Headliner award,TV Week, 12 to Watch in TV News, 2013

MUKHERJEE, SIDDHARTHA, T: Oncologist, Educator I: Education/Educational Services DOB: 07/21/1970 PB: New Delhi ED: MD, Harvard Med School, 2000; PhD in Immunology, Magdalen College, Oxford University; Grad., Stanford University, California CT: Cert. in medical oncology, diplomate American Board Internal Medicine C: Assistant professor medicine, Columbia University, New York City, 2009-; Former faculty, Harvard Medical School, Boston,; Internist, oncology fellow, Massachusetts General Hospital, CR: Staff cancer physician Columbia University Medical Center, 2009- CW: Author: The Emperor of All Maladies: A Biography of Cancer, 2010 (one of Top 10 Books of 2010, New York Times, O-The Oprah magazine, Pulitzer prize for general nonfiction, 2011); contributor articles to professional journals,(Book) The Laws of Medicine: Field Notes from an Uncertain Science, 2015, The Gene: An Intimate History, 2016 AW: Rhodes Scholar, 1993-95,Gabrielle Angel's Leukemia Foundation Award, 2010, New York Times Magazine 100 Notable Books of 2010, 2010, LA Times Book Award,2011, Pulitzer Prize, 2011, PEN-E O Wilson Literary Science Writing Award, 2011, Cancer Leadership Award, 2011, Time 100 Best Non-Fiction Books of All Time, 2011, Time 100 Most Influential People, 2011, Padma Shri, 2014, Washington Post 10 Best Books of 2016

MULLALLY, MEGAN, T: Actress I: Media & Entertainment DOB: 11/12/1958 PB: Los Angeles SC: CA/USA PT: Carter Mullally; Martha Mullally ED: Student, Northwestern University CW: Actress: (TV films) Rainbow Drive, 1990, Winchell, 1998, Everything Put Together, 2000, The Pact, 2002, Bad Mother's Handbook, 2008; (TV series) My Life and Times, 1991, Fish Police, 1992, Rachel Gunn, RN, 1992, Will and Grace, 1998-2006 (Emmy award for Supporting Actress in a Comedy Series, 2000, 2006, Outstanding Comedy Series award, 2000, Am. Comedy award, 2001, Outstanding Female Actor award, 2001, Screen Actors Guild award for

Outstanding Actress in a Comedy Series, 2001, 2002, 2003), Children's Hospital, 2008-13, In the Motherhood, 2009, Party Down, 2010, Breaking In, 2012, Out There, 2013, Axe Cop (voice), 2012-13; (Broadway plays) Grease, 1994, How to Succeed in Business Without Really Trying, 1995-96, Young Frankenstein, 2008, It's Only a Play, 2014, (off-Broadway) Annapurna, 2015; host (talk show) Megan Mullally Show, 2006-07; actress: (films) Once Bitten, 1985, Last Resort, 1986, About Last Night, 1986, Anywhere But Here, 1999, Best Man in Grass Creek, 1999, Everything Put Together, 2000, Monkey Bone, 2001, Speaking of Sex, 2001, Stealing Harvard, 2002, (voice) Teacher's Pet, 2004, Rebound, 2005, (voice) Bee Movie, 2007, Fame, 2009, Smash, 2012, Somebody Up There Likes Me, 2012, The Kings of Summer, 2013, G.B.F., 2013, Date and Switch, 2014, Apartment Troubles, 2014, Alexander and the Terrible, Horrible, No Good, Very Bad Day, 2014,Hotel Transylvania 2, 2015, Why Him, 2016, Lemon, 2017, Infinity Baby, 2017, The Disaster Artist, 2017 (voice) Hotel Transylvania 2, 2015, (guest appearance): (TV series) Murder, She Wrote, 1988, China Beach, 1989, Wings, 1990, Herman's Head, 1991, Seinfeld, 1993, Frasier, 1997, Mad About You, 1997, Caroline in the City, 1997, Just Shoot Me!, 1998, 3rd Rock from the Sun, 2000, King of the Hill, 2002, 30 Rock, 2008, Parks and Recreation, 2009-15, Happy Endings, 2011-13, Bob's Burgers (voice), 2011-15, Up All Night, 2012, Randy Cunningham: 9th Grade Ninja (voice), 2012-15, Web Therapy, 2013, Axe Cop, 2013, Sofia the First, 2013, Trophy Wife, 2014, You, Me and the Apocalypse, 2015, Life in Pieces, 2016; member band Nancy and Beth, 2012-, Supreme Music Program; musician: (albums) (with Supreme Music Program) The Sweetheart Break-In, Big as a Berry, Free Again!

MULLIGAN, DEANNA MARIE, T: CEO **I:** Insurance **CN:** Guardian Life **DOB:** 07/24/1963 **PB:** West Point **SC:** Nebraska **PT:** Daughter of Paul Arthur and Judith Maureen (Bottger) Predoehl; **MS:** Married **SPN:** Stephen Edward Mulligan, December 26, 1985 **ED:** MBA, Stanford University Graduate School Business, 1989; BS in Business, University Nebraska, 1985 **C:** President, CEO, Guardian Life Insurance Co. of America, New York City, 2011-; President, COO, Guardian Life Insurance Co. of America, New York City, 2010-11; Executive vice president, individual life & disability business, Guardian Life Insurance Co. of America, New York City, 2008-10; Senior vice president, AXA Financial Services, Inc., New York City, 2000-06; Principal, McKinsey & Co., Inc., New York City, 1992-97,98-2000; Senior vice president life & annuity, New York Life Insurance Co., New York City,; Assistant vice president, New York Life Insurance Co., New York City, 1990-92; Director, corporate planning, New York Life Insurance Co., New York City, 1989-90; Intern, Hewlett-Packard Co., 1988; Consultant, Woodmen Accident & Life, Hayward, California, 1985-87 **CR:** Board directors The Guardian Life Insurance Co. of America, 2011- **CIV:** Vol. Friendly Visitor Program, Napa, California, 1987 member planning forum, New York City director Project Renewal, New York City, trustee Red Cross of Greater New York, 2000-. **AW:** National Merit scholar, 1981.; named one of The 50 Most Powerful Women in Business, Fortune magazine, 2011, 2013, The 50 Most Powerful Women in New York, Crain's New York Business, 2011 **BA:** Guardian Life, 7 Hanover Square, New York, NY, 10004

MULLIN, MARKWAYNE, T: U.S. Representative From Oklahoma, Plumber, Rancher **I:** Government Administration/Government Relations/Government Services **DOB:** 07/26/1977 **PB:** Tulsa **SC:** OK/USA **ED:** AAS in Construction Technology,

Institute of Technology, Oklahoma State University, 2010; Student, Missouri Valley College, 1996 **C:** Republican Study Committee; Radio Host, "House Talk"; U.S. House Natural Resources Committee, 2013-Present; U.S. House Transportation & Infrastructure Committee, 2013-Present; U.S. Congress, Second Oklahoma District, 2013-Present; Owner, Mullin Plumbing, Mullin Farms, Mullin Properties, Mullin Services, 1997-Present **MEM:** Cherokee Nation **PA:** Republican

MULLIS, KARY BANKS, T: Biochemist **I:** Sciences **DOB:** 12/28/1944 **PB:** Lenoir, North Carolina **PT:** Son of Cecil Banks Mullis and Bernice Alberta (Barker) Fredericks; **ED:** DSc (hon.), University South Carolina, 1994; PhD in Biochemistry, University California, Berkeley, 1973; BS in Chemistry, Georgia Institute Tech, 1966 **C:** Founder, Chief Scientific Officer, Altermune LLC, Newport Beach, California, 2003-; Distinguished Researcher, Children's Hospital, Oakland Research Institute, California, 2003-; Vice President Molecular Biology, Burstein Technologies, Irvine, California, 1999-2003; Vice President Molecular Biology, Vyrex Inc., La Jolla, 1997-98; Vice President Research, Atomic Tags, Inc., La Jolla, California, 1992-93; Private Consultant Nucleic Acid Chemistry, California, 1987-2002; Director Molecular Biology, Xytronyx, Inc., San Diego, 1986-88; Scientist, Cetus Corp., Emeryville, California, 1979-86; Postdoc. Fellow, University California, San Francisco, 1977-79; Postdoc. Fellow, University Kansas Medical School, Kansas City, 1973-76; Lecturer Biochemistry, University California, Berkeley, 1962 **CR:** Distinguished Visiting Professor University South Carolina College Sci. & Math., 1994- **CIV:** Board of Directors, National Organization Reform Marijuana Laws, 2000- **CW:** Author: (autobiography) Dancing Naked in the Mind Field, 1998; Contributor Articles to Professional Journals,(Books) The Polymerase Chain Reaction, 1994, The Unusual Origin of the Polymerase Chain Reaction, 1990 **AW:** Named California Scientist of Year, 1992, Scientist of Year, R&D Magazine, 1991; Named to National Inventors Hall of Fame, 1998; Recipient Nobel prize in Chemistry, 1993, Japan Prize, Japan Sci. & Tech. Foundation, 1993, Chiron Corp. Biotechnology Research Award, Am. Society Microbiology, 1992, Robert Koch Award, 1992, National Biotech. Award, 1991, Gairdner Foundation International Award, 1991, Allan Award, German Society Clinical Chemistry, 1990, Preis Biochemische Analytik Award, 1990, National Inventors Hall of Fame, 1998 **MEM:** Mem.: Am. Academy Achievement,, Am. Chemical Society **ACH:** Achievements include patents in field **H:** Astrology, surfing **BA:** 19010 Gschwend Rd, Philo, CA, 95466

MULVANEY, MICK, T: Director of the Office of Management and Budget **I:** Government Administration/Government Relations/Government Services **CN:** Consumer Financial Protection Bureau **DOB:** 07/21/1967 **PB:** Alexandria **SC:** VA/USA **PT:** Michael Mulvaney, Kathleen Mulvaney **ED:** Graduate, Owner's and President's Management Program, Harvard Business School, 2006; JD, University of North Carolina, Chapel Hill, 1992; BS, Georgetown University School of Foreign Service, With Honors, 1989 **C:** Director, Consumer Financial Protection Bureau, 2017-Present; Director, Office of Management and Budget, Washington, DC, 2017-Present; U.S. House Budget Committee, Washington, DC, 2011-Present; U.S. Congress From Fifth South Carolina District, Washington, DC, 2011-Present; U.S. House of Representatives, South Carolina's Fifth District, 2011-2017; U.S. House Small Business Committee, Washington, DC, 2011-2017; District 16, South Carolina State Senate, Columbia, SC, 2009-2011; District 45, South

Carolina House of Representatives, Columbia, SC, 2007-2009; Attorney, Mulvaney & Fisher PA, Charlotte, NC, 1997-2000; Attorney, James, McElroy & Diehl, Charlotte, NC, 1992-1997 **CR:** Franchise Owner-Operator, Salsarita's Fresh Cantina, 2009-Present **CIV:** Board of Visitors, University of South Carolina, Lancaster, SC, Youth Baseball Coach, Lancaster County Parks & Recreation **MEM:** Founding Member, Indian Land Rotary **PA:** Republican **BA:** Office of Management and Budget, 1650 Pennsylvania Avenue NW, Washington, DC, 20502

MUNDELL, ROBERT, T: Economist **I:** Education/Educational Services **CN:** Columbia University **PB:** Kingston **SC:** ON/Canada **PT:** William C. Mundell, Lila (Knifton) Mundell **ED:** Honorary PhD, University of Paris, 1992; Honorary PhD, Renmin University, China, 1985; PhD, Massachusetts Institute of Technology, 1956; MA, University of Washington, Seattle, WA, 1954; BA, University of British Columbia, Vancouver, BC, Canada, 1953; Student, London School of Economics **C:** University Professor, Columbia University, 2001-Present; Professor of Economics, Columbia University, New York, NY, 1974-2001; Professor of Economics, Chairman of the Department, University of Waterloo, 1972-1974; Professor, University of Chicago, 1966-1971; Ford Foundation Visiting Research Professor of Economics, University of Chicago, 1965-1966; Rockefeller Visiting Research Professor of International Economics, Brookings Institution, Washington, DC, 1964-1965; Visiting Professor of Economics, McGill University, Montreal, QC, Canada, 1963-1964; Senior Economist, International Monetary Fund, Washington, DC, 1961-1963; Visiting Professor of Economics, School of Advanced International Studies, Bologna Center, Johns Hopkins University, Bologna, Italy, 1959-1961; Acting Assistant Professor of Economics, Stanford University, California, 1958-1959; Economics Instructor, University of British Columbia, 1957-1958; Postdoctorate Fellow in Political Economy, University of Chicago, 1956-1957 **CR:** Fellow, John Simon Guggenheim Memorial Foundation, 1970-1971; Fellow, American Academy of Arts & Sciences **CW:** Author, The International Monetary System: Conflict And Reform, 1965, Man And Economics, 1968, International Economics, 1968, Monetary Theory: Interest, Inflation And Growth In The World Economy, 1971; Co-Editor, Monetary Problems Of The International Economy, 1969, Trade Balance Of Payments And Growth, 1971, Policy Formation In An Open Economy, 1974, The International Monetary System, 1978, A Monetary Agenda For The World Economy, 1984, Global Disequilibrium, 1992, Debt, Deficit And Economic Importance, 1992, Building The New Europe, 1993, Inflation And Growth In China, 1996; Contributor, Articles, Professional Journals **AW:** Companion Of The Order Of Canada, 2003, Nobel Prize In Economics, Royal Swedish Academy of Sciences, 1999, Distinguished Fellow Award, American Economic Association, 1997, Jacques Rueff Medal, France, 1983, Grantee, National Science Foundation, 1967-1970 **MEM:** American Economic Association **BA:** 35 Claremont Avenue, New York, NY, 10027

MUNOZ, OSCAR, T: United Continental CEO **I:** Business Management/Business Services **ED:** MBA, Pepperdine University, 1986; BS, University Southern California, 1982 **C:** President, CEO, United Continental Holdings, Inc., 2016-; President, CEO, United Continental Holdings, Inc., Chicago, 2015-; Medical leave, United Continental Holdings, Inc., 2015-16; Executive vice president, CFO, CSX Corp., Jacksonville, Florida, 2003-15; CFO, vice president AT&T Consumer Services, AT&T Corp., Basking Ridge, New Jersey, 2001-03; Senior vice president fin. And administration,

Qwest Comms. International Inc., Denver, 2000; CFO, vice president, U.S. West Retail Markets, Denver, 1999-2000; Vice president fin., controller, USWEST Comms. Inc., Denver, 1997-99; Executive director, Coca-Cola Co., Atlanta, 1996-97; CFO, region vice president, Coca-Cola Enterprises, Inc., Hollywood, California, 1991-96; Division controller, director fin. operations, assistant corp. controller, Coca-Cola Enterprises, Inc., L.A. and Atlanta, 1986-91; Fin. analyst, accounting manager, manager fin. control, Pepsico Inc., L.A. and Purchase, New York, 1983-86 **MEM:** Mem.: Fin. Executives Institute

MURAI, KEVIN M., I: Business Management/ Business Services **PB:** 1964 **ED:** BSEE, University of Waterloo, Ontario **C:** President, CEO and director, SYNNEX Corp., Fremont, California, 2008-; Co-CEO, Synnex Corp., Fremont, California, 2008; President, COO, Ingram Micro, Inc., 2005-07; President, COO, Ingram Micro N. Am., 2002-05; COO, Ingram Micro US, 2000-02; President, Ingram Micro US, 2000-01; Executive Vice President, Ingram Micro, Inc., Santa Ana, California, 2000-05; Senior Vice President, Ingram Micro, Inc., 1997-2002; President, Ingram Micro Can., 1997-2000; Vice President, Operations, Ingram Micro Can., Canada, 1993-97; Joined, Ingram Micro, Inc., 1988; Manager, Management Information Services, Verifact, Inc., Ontario, Canada

MURAKAMI, HARUKI, T: Writer **I:** Writing and Editing **DOB:** 01/12/1949 **PB:** Kyoto **ED:** Student in Theater Arts, Waseda Univ. **C:** Associate professor, William Howard Taft Univ., Santa Ana, California, 1993-2001; Associate professor, Princeton Univ., 1992-93; Associate researcher, Princeton Univ., 1991-92; Writer 1979-; Owner, Peter Cat Jazz Bar, Tokyo, 1974-81 **CW:** Author: Hear the Wind Sing, 1979 (Gunzo New Writer award), Pinball, 1980, A Wild Sheep Chase, 1982 (Noma Lit. award for new writers), Hard boiled Wonderland and End of the World, 1985 (Junichi Tanizaki award), Norwegian Wood, 1987, The Elephant Vanishes, 1993, Dance Dance Dance, 1994, Wind-up Bird Chronicle, 1996 (Yomiuri Lit. award), Underground, 1997, South of the Border, West of the Sun, 2000, Sputnik Sweetheart, 2002, After the Quake, 2003, Kafka on the Shore, 2005, Blind Willow, Sleeping Woman, 2006, IQ84, 2011, Colorless Tsukuru Tazaki and His Years of Pilgrimage, 2014,(Book) Killing Commendatore, 2017 **AW:** Hans Christian Anderson Literature Award, 2016, Frank O'Connor Short Story Away, 2006, World Fantasy Award, 2006 **BA:** Knopf Doubleday Group, 1745 Broadway, New York, NY, 10019

MURDOCH, JAMES, T: Broadcast Executive **I:** Media & Entertainment **CN:** 21st Century Fox Inc. **DOB:** 12/13/1972 **PB:** , **PT:** Son of Rupert and Anna Maria (Torv) Murdoch; **ED:** Attended, Harvard University, 1991-95 **C:** Chairman Sky, 2016-; Chairman 21st Century Fox, 2016-; Chairman supervisory board, Sky Deutschland AG, Frankfort, Germany, 2013-; Co-COO, 21st Century Fox Inc., 2014-; Executive chairman, News Corp. International, London, 2011-12; Chairman, CEO, News Corp. International, New York City, 2011; Deputy COO, 21st Century Fox Inc., 2013-14; Deputy COO, News Corp., New York City, 2011-13; Chairman, CEO Europe & Asia, News Corp., London, 2007-11; Chairman, Brit. Sky Broadcasting Group Plc, 2007-12; CEO, Brit. Sky Broadcasting Group PLC (BSkyB), Middlesex, England, 2003-07; Chairman, CEO, STAR TV, Hong Kong, 2000-03; Executive vice president, News Corp., New York City, 1996-2000; Chairman, Festival Records,; Founder, Rawlus Entertainment LLC, 1995 **CR:** Board advertising True[X] Media, 2014-; Member, board directors Tesla, 2017-. Sky

Deutschland AG, 2013-, Sotheby's Holding, Inc., 2010-12, GlaxoSmithKline plc, 2009-12, Brit. Sky Broadcasting Group PLC (BSkyB), 2003-, News Corp., 2007-, 2000-03

MURDOCH, RUPERT, T: Broadcast Executive **I:** Media & Entertainment **CN:** 21st Century Fox News Corp **DOB:** 03/11/1931 **PB:** Melbourne **SC:** Australia **ED:** BA, BS, Oxford University; MA, Worcester College, Oxford, England, 1953 **C:** Chmn., CEO, 21st Century Fox, 2013—2015,; Executive Co-Chairman of 21st of 21st Century Fox, 2015-; Chmn., CEO, Fox News, 2016—; Chmn., CEO, 21st Century Fox, 2013—; Executive chairman, News Corp., Ltd., New York City, New York, 2013—; Chairman, DirecTV Group, 2003—2007; Chairman, Brit. Sky Broadcasting Group PLC (BSkyB), 1999—2007; Chmn., CEO, News Corp., Ltd., New York City, New York, 1991—2013; CEO, News Corp., Ltd., 1979—1991; Publisher, New York Post, 2005; Publisher, New York Post, 1976—1986 **CR:** Chairman STAR Group Ltd., 1993—1998; board directors Philip Morris Cos. Inc., 1989—2002, China Netcom Group Corp. Ltd., 2001—2005, Brit. Sky Broadcasting Group PLC (BSkyB), 1990—2007; owner, pub. numerous newspapers, magazines, TV operations in USA, Australia, UK, Asia **AW:** Named Companion of the Order of Australia, 1984, Knight Order of St. Gregory the Great, 1998; named one of The Forbes 400: Richest Americans, 1999—, The 100 Most Influential People in the World, TIME magazine, 2004, 2005, 2008, The 50 Who Matter Now, CNNMoney.com Business 2.0, 2006, 2007, The 25 Most Powerful People in Business, Fortune magazine, 2007, The Most Influential People in the World of Sports, Business Week, 2007, 2008, The Global Elite, Newsweek magazine, 2008, The Top 25 Market Movers, US News & World Report, 2009, The World's Most Powerful People, Forbes magazine, 2009—14 **H:** Sailing **BA:** 1211 Ave of Americas, rmurdoch@21cf.com, New York, NY, 10036

MURGUIA, MARY HELEN, T: Federal Judge **I:** Law and Legal Services **DOB:** 09/06/1960 **PB:** Kansas City **SC:** KS/USA **PT:** Alfred Murguia; Amalia Murguia **ED:** JD, University of Kansas, 1985; BS, BA, University of Kansas, 1982 **C:** Judge, U.S. Court of Appeals, Ninth Circuit, Phoenix, AZ, 2010-Present; Judge, U.S. District Court, Arizona, Phoenix, AZ, 2000-2010; Director, Executive Office of U.S. Attorneys, U.S. Department of Justice, Washington, DC, 1999-2000; Principal Deputy Director, Executive Office of U.S. Attorneys, U.S. Department of Justice, Washington, DC, 1999; Counsel to Director's Staff, Executive Office of U.S. Attorneys, U.S. Department of Justice, Washington, DC, 1998-1999; Assistant U.S. Attorney, District of Arizona, U.S. Department of Justice, Phoenix, AZ, 1990-2000; Assistant District Attorney, Wyandotte County District Attorney's Office, 1985-1990 **CR:** Director, Executive Office of U.S. Attorneys, 1999-2000; Principal Deputy Director, Executive Office of U.S. Attorneys, 1999; Counsel to Director's Staff, Executive Office of U.S. Attorneys, 1998-1999 **BA:** 95 7th Street, Los Angeles, CA, 94103

MURKOWSKI, LISA ANN, T: U.S. Senator for Alaska **I:** Government Administration/Government Relations/Government Services **DOB:** 05/22/1957 **PB:** Ketchikan **SC:** AK/USA **PT:** Frank Hughes Murkowski, Nancy (Gore) Murkowski **MS:** Married **SPN:** Verne Martell, 8/22/1987 **CH:** Nicholas, Matthew **ED:** JD, Willamette College, 1985; BA in Economics, Georgetown University, 1980 **C:** Chairman, Senate Energy Committee, 2015-Present; U.S. Senate Appropriations Committee, 2009-Present; U.S. Senator From Alaska, 2002-Present; Vice Chairman, U.S. Senate Republican Conference, 2009-

2010; Majority Leader, Alaska House Of Representatives, Anchorage, AK, 2002; District 18, Alaska House Of Representatives, 2000-2002; District 14, Alaska House Of Representatives, Anchorage, AK, 1998-2000; Private Law Practice, 1989-1996; Attorney, Hoge & Lekisch, 1989-1996; Attorney, Anchorage District Court, Anchorage, AK, 1987-1989 **CR:** Director, First Bank, Mayor's Task Force on the Homeless, 1990-1991, State Central Committee, District 14 Republican Chair, 1993-1998, Commissioner, Anchorage Equal Rights Commission, 1997-2002, Citizens Advisory Board, Joint Committee Military Bases In Alaska, 1998-Present **CIV:** Trustee, Catholic Services, President, Government Hill Elementary PTA, Director, Alaskan Drug Free Youth, YWCA, Arctic Power **AW:** Food Safety Award, National Food Processors Association, 2003, Outstanding Volunteer Award, Alaska School District, 1998, 2000, Community Leadership Award, FBI Director, 1993 **MEM:** Alaska Bar Association, Anchorage Bar Association, Board of Directors, Alaska Federation of Republic Women, Anchorage Republican Women's Club, Midnight Sun Republican Women **PA:** Republican **BA:** Office of Lisa Murkowski, 522 Hart Senate Office Building, Washington, DC, 20510

MURPHY, BOBBY, T: Co-Founder of Snapchat **I:** Technology **DOB:** 07/08/1905 **PB:** Berkeley, California **SC:** Berkeley, California **ED:** B.S.,Stanford **C:** Co-Founder/CTO, Snapchat, 2011- **CIV:** Snap Foundation, 2017 **AW:** Time 100 Most Influential, 2014

MURPHY, CHRISTOPHER SCOTT, T: U.S. Senator from Connecticut **I:** Government Administration/Government Relations/Government Services **DOB:** 08/03/1973 **PB:** White Plains **SC:** NY/USA **PT:** Scott Murphy; Catherine Murphy **ED:** JD, University of Connecticut School of Law (2002); BA in History & Political Science, Williams College, with Honors, Massachusetts (1996); Coursework, Exeter College, Oxford University, England **C:** Member, U.S. Congressional Joint Economic Committee (2013-Present); Member, U.S. Senate Foreign Relations Committee (2013-Present); Member, U.S. Senate on Health, Education, Labor & Pensions Committee (2013-Present); U.S. Senator from Connecticut (2013-Present); Member, U.S. Congress from the Fifth Connecticut District (2007-2013); Member, District 16, Connecticut State Senate (2003-2006); Attorney, Ruben, Johnson, & Morgan, PC, Hartford, CT (2002-2006); Member, District 81, Connecticut House of Representatives (1998-2002) **CR:** Member, Southington Planning & Zoning Commission (1997-1999); Staff Member, Connecticut State Senate Majority Caucus (1996-1998) **PA:** Democrat **BA:** U.S. House of Representatives, 412 Cannon House Office Bldg, Washington, DC, 20515 **ADD:** Office of Chris Murphy, 136 Hart Senate Office Bldg., Washington, DC, 20510

MURPHY, DONNA, T: Actress **I:** Media & Entertainment **DOB:** 03/07/1959 **PB:** Corona **SC:** NY/USA **ED:** Student, New York University School of the Arts **CW:** Actor: (Broadway plays) They're Playing Our Song, The Human Comedy, The Mystery of Edwin Drood; actor, (Broadway plays) Passion, 1994 (Tony award best actress in a musical, 1994, Drama Desk award, Drama League award), The King and I, 1996 (Tony award best actress in a musical, 1996, Drama League award), Wonderful Town, 2003-04 (Tony nom. best actress in a musical, 2004, Drama Desk award best actress in a musical, 2004, Drama League award, 2004), Children & Art, 2005, Love-Musik, 2007 (Outer Critics Cir. award outstanding actress in a musical, 2007, Drama Desk award outstanding actress in a musical, 2007); (plays) Song of Singapore, Privates on Parade, Showing Off,

Birds of Paradise, Little Shop of Horrors, A...My Name Is Alice, Twelve Dreams, 1995, Hello Again, 1994, Follies, 2007, Anyone Can Whistle, 2010; (TV series) Murder One, 1995-96; actor: (TV series) Law & Order, 1993 (Tony award best actress in a musical, 1994, Drama Desk award, Drama League award), The Practice, 1998, Ally McBeal, 1998, What About Joan, 2001, Hack, 2002-03, Trust Me, 2009; (TV miniseries) LIBERTY! The American Revolution, 1997; (TV films) Tales from the Hollywood Hills: A Table at Ciro's, 1987, Power, Passion and Murder, 1987, Passion, 1996, Someone Had to Be Benny, 1996 (Cable ACE award, 1996, Daytime Emmy, 1996), The Day Lincoln Was Shot, 1998, The Last Debate, 2000; (films) Jade, 1995, October 22, 1998, Star Trek: Insurrection, 1998, The Astronaut's Wife, 1999, Center Stage, 2001, The Door in the Floor, 2004, Spiderman 2, 2004, Ira and Abby, 2006, World Trade Center, 2006, The Fountain, 2006, The Nanny Diaries, 2007, Higher Ground, 2010; actor(voice): (films) Tangled, 2010 (Tony award best actress in a musical, 1994, Drama Desk award, Drama League award)

MURPHY, EDDIE, T: Actor, Comedian **I:** Media & Entertainment **DOB:** 04/03/1961 **PB:** Bklyn. **PT:** Son of Charles Edward and Lillian Murphy, Vernon Lynch (stepfather); **SPN:** Married Nicole Mitchell, March 18, 1993 (div. April 17, 2006); **CH:** Bria, Myles Mitchell, Shayne Audra, Zola Ivy, Bella Zehra; **ED:** Student pub. schools, Brooklyn **C:** Host, 35th Ann. Emmy Awards, 1983; With, Saturday Night Live, New York City, 1980-84; Performed at various New York City clubs, including, The Comic Strip,; Began performing, Richard M. Dixon's White House, Long Island, New York, **CW:** Actor: (films) 48 Hrs., 1982, Trading Places, 1983, Best Defense, 1984, Beverly Hills Cop, 1984, The Distinguished Gentleman, 1992, Beverly Hills Cop III, 1994, The Nutty Professor, 1996, Metro, 1997, Mulan (voice), 1998, Dr. Dolittle, 1998, Holy Man, 1998, Bowfinger, 1999, Shrek (voice), 2001, Dr. Dolittle 2, 2001, Showtime, 2002, The Adventures of Pluto Nash, 2002, I Spy, 2002, Daddy Day Care, 2003, The Haunted Mansion, 2003, Shrek 2 (voice), 2004, Dreamgirls, 2006 (African-American Film Critics Association award for Best Supporting Actor, 2006, Critics Choice award for Best Supporting Actor, 2007, Golden Globe award for Best Performance by an Actor in a Supporting Role in a Motion Picture, 2007, Screen Actors Guild award for Outstanding Performance by a Male Actor in a Supporting Role, 2007, Broadcast Film Critics Association award for Best Supporting Actor, 2007), Shrek the Third (voice), 2007, Meet Dave, 2008, Imagine That, 2009, (voice) Shrek Forever After, 2010, A Thousand Words, 2012, Mr. Church, 2016; (actor, executive producer): The Golden Child, 1986; The Nutty Professor II: The Klumps, 2000; Harlem Nights, 1989; actor, executive producer (TV films) Beverly Hills Cop, 2015; (actor, producer): (films) Vampire in Brooklyn, 1995; Life, 1999; Tower Heist, 2011; (actor, writer, producer) Norbit, 2007; (actor, writer) Beverly Hills Cop II, 1987; Coming to America, 1988; Another 48 Hrs., 1990; actor, writer: films Boomerang, 1992; actor: (TV films) Eddie Murphy Delirious, 1983, Eddie Murphy Raw, 1987; actor (voice only), executive producer (TV series) The PJ's, 1999-2001 **AW:** Recipient Mark Twain Prize for American Humor, John F. Kennedy Center for the Performing Arts, 2015, Star, Hollywood Walk of Fame, 1996

MURPHY, PHILIP D., T: Governor of New Jersey, Former Ambassador, Investment Company Executive, Professional Sports Team Executive **I:** Government Administration/Government Relations/Government Services **DOB:** 08/16/1957 **PB:** Needham **SC:** Massachusetts **ED:** MBA, University Pennsylvania Wharton School Business, Philadelphia, 1983; AB in Economics, Harvard University, Cambridge, Massachusetts, 1979 **C:** Governor, State of New Jersey, Trenton, NJ, 2018-; Principal owner, Sky Blue Soccer, Somerset, New Jersey, 2009-; US ambassador to Germany, US Department State, Berlin, 2009-13; Principal, Murphy Endeavors, LLC, Red Bank, New Jersey,; National finance chair, Democratic National Committee, Washington, 2006-09; Senior director, Goldman Sachs Group, Inc., 2003-06; Co-head, investment management division, Goldman Sachs Group, Inc., 1999-2003; President, Goldman Sachs Asia, Goldman Sachs Group, Inc., 1997-99; Head, German region, Goldman Sachs Group, Inc., Frankfurt, Germany, 1993-97; Summer associate to numerous positions of increasing responsibility in the US, Europe and Asia, Goldman Sachs Group, Inc., 1982-2006 **CR:** Member management committee Goldman Sachs, sponsor, women's network **CIV:** Member bid. committee, USA Soccer, Huntsman program adv. board, University Pennsylvania, Board directors, US Soccer Foundation, Board president, 180 Turning Lives Around, Board trustees, Center Am. Progress, Chairman, executive committee, Local Initiatives Support Corp., Board trustees, special contribution fund, National Association for the Advancement of Colored People, Pres./CEO search committee, National Association for the Advancement of Colored People, Former co-chair, Renewing Our Schools, Securing Our Future: A Task Force on Public Education for the 21st Century, Former chair, benefits rev. task force, State of New Jersey, Former trustee, The Goldman Sachs Foundation, Former trustee, Prosperity New Jersey, Former member grad. executive board, Asian adv. board, Wharton School Business, **AW:** Named Business Leader of Year, Am. Woman's Economic Devel. Corp., 2003 **PA:** Democrat **BA:** New Jersey State House, 125 West State Street, Trenton, NJ, 08608

MURPHY, STEPHANIE, T: U.S. Representative from Florida **I:** Government Administration/Government Relations/Government Services **DOB:** 09/16/1978 **PB:** Ho Chi Minh City **SC:** Vietnam **ED:** B.A., Economics, College of William and Mary,2000; Masters of Science Degree, Georgetown University,2004 **C:** Member, U.S. Representative from Florida's 7th District, 2017-; Member, Committee on Armed Services; Member, Committee on Small Business; Faculty, Rollings College, 2014-16; Foreign Affairs Specialist, U.S. Department of Defense, 2004-08 **BA:** 1237 Longworth HOB, Washington, DC, 20515

MURRAY, ANDY, T: Professional Tennis Player **I:** Athletics **DOB:** 05/15/1987 **PB:** Dunblane **PT:** Son of William and Judith (Erskine) Murray; **C:** Professional tennis player, ATP, 2005 **CR:** Member British national team Summer Olympic Games, Rio de Janeiro, 2016, London, 2012 **AW:** Named LTA Young Player of Year, 2004, BBC Young Sports Personality of Year, 2004; recipient Arthur Ashe Humanitarian of Year award, 2014, Gold medal, men's singles, Summer Olympic Games, 2016, Gold medal, men's singles; Silver medal, mixed doubles, 2012,ATP Player of the Year,2016, Arthur Ashe Humanitarian of the Year Award, 2016, Knight Bachelor, 2017, ITF Player of the Year, 2016, Freeman of Merton, 2014, Freeman of Stirling, 2014, BBC Sports Personality of the Year, 2013, 2015, 2016 **ACH:** Achievements include 35 career titles and ATP world ranking: 2; winner Grand Slam men's singles final: US Open, 2012; Wimbledon Championships, 2013, 2016;

MURRAY, BILL, T: Actor, Writer **I:** Media & Entertainment **DOB:** 06/04/1905 **PB:** Wilmette, **SC:** Wilmette, **PT:** Edward Murray; Lucille Murray **SPN:** Jennifer Butler, July 4, 1997 (div. June 2008); Margaret Kelly, January 25, 1981 (div. January 1994) **CH:** Homer; Luke; Jackson; Caleb **ED:** Student, Second City Workshop, Chicago; Student, Regis College, Denver **CR:** Team psychologist St. Paul Saints baseball club co-owner Caddyshack Restaurant, Jacksonville, Florida part owner minor league baseball teams Charleston RiverDogs, St. Paul Saints, Hudson Valley Renegades, Brockton Rox **CW:** Performer, Second City Comedy Troupe, 1973-75; voice, National Lampoon Radio Hour, 1975; actor, writer: Saturday Night Live, 1977-80 (Emmy award for Outstanding Writing in a Comedy-Variety or Music Series, 1977); actor: (films) Next Stop, Greenwich Village, 1976, Meatballs, 1979, Mr. Mike's Mondo Video, 1979, Where the Buffalo Roam, 1980, Caddyshack, 1980, Loose Shoes, 1980, Stripes, 1981, Tootsie, 1982, Ghostbusters, 1984, The Razor's Edge, 1984, Nothing Lasts Forever, 1984, Little Shop of Horrors, 1986, Scrooged, 1988, Ghostbusters II, 1989, What About Bob?, 1991, Groundhog Day, 1993, Mad Dog and Glory, 1993, Ed Wood, 1994, Kingpin, 1996, Larger Than Life, 1996, Space Jam, 1996, The Man Who Knew Too Little, 1997, With Friends Like These, 1998, Veeck As In Wreck, 1998, Rushmore, 1998, Wild Things, 1998, The Cradle Will Rock, 1999, Scout's Honor, 1999, Hamlet, 1999, Company Man, 1999, Charlie's Angels, 2000, Speaking of Sex, 2001, The Royal Tenenbaums, 2001, Osmosis Jones, 2001, Coffee and Cigarettes, 2003, Lost in Translation, 2003 (Golden Globe award for Best Actor in a Musical or Comedy, 2004), Garfield: The Movie (voice), 2004, The Life Aquatic with Steve Zissou, 2004, Broken Flowers, 2005, The Lost City, 2005, Garfield: A Tail of Two Kitties (voice), 2006, The Darjeeling Limited, 2007, Get Smart, 2008, City of Ember, 2008, The Limits of Control, 2009, Get Low, 2009, Zombieland, 2009, Fantastic Mr. Fox (voice), 2009, Passion Play, 2010, Moonrise Kingdom, 2012, Hyde Park on Hudson, 2012, A Glimpse Inside the Mind of Charles Swan III, 2012, The Monuments Men, 2014, The Grand Budapest Hotel, 2014, St. Vincent, 2014, Dumb and Dumber To, 2014, Aloha, 2015, Rock the Kasbah, 2015, The Jungle Book (voice), 2016, Ghostbusters, 2016, Isle of Dogs, 2018; (TV Mini-series) Olive Kitteridge, 2014 (Emmy award for Outstanding Supporting Actor in a Mini-series or Movie, 2015); SNL, 2015, Parks and Recreation, 2015, A Very Murray Christmas, 2015, Angela Tribeca, 2016, Vice Principals, 2016, Bill Murray and Brian Doyle- Murray's Extra Innings, 2017; actor, director, prodr.: (films) Quick Change, 1990, (TV films) The Rutles: All you Need Is Cash, 1978, (TV series) Stories from My Childhood (voice), 1998, The Sweet Spot, 2002; executive producer, writer, actor: (films) A Very Murray Christmas, 2015; author: Cinderella Story: My Life in Golf, 1999.

MURRAY, PATTY, T: U.S. Senator from Washington **I:** Government Administration/Government Relations/Government Services **DOB:** 10/11/1950 **PB:** Seattle **SC:** WA/USA **PT:** Daughter of David L. and Beverly A. (McLaughlin) Johns **MS:** Married **SPN:** Robert R. Murray, June 2, 1972; **CH:** Randy P., Sara A. **ED:** BA, Washington State University, 1972 **C:** Senate Assistant Democratic Leader, 2017-,; Senate Health Committee, 2015-,; Ranking Member Senate Health Committee, 2015,; Secretary of the Senate Democratic Conference, 2007-2017,; Chairwoman,U.S. Senate Budget Committee, 2013-2015; Chairwoman, U.S. Senate Budget Committee, 2013-; Member, U.S. Senate Rules & Administration Committee, 2007-; US Senator from Washington, 1993-; Co-chair, Joint Select Committee on Deficit Reduction, 2011; Chairwoman, U.S. Senate Veterans' Affairs Committee, 2011-13; Member, Washington State Senate, Seattle, 1989-92; Instructor,

Shoreline Community College, Seattle, 1984-88; Legislative lobbyist, Organization for Parent Education, Seattle, 1977-84; Citizen lobbyist, various educational groups, Seattle, 1983-88; Secretary, various companies, Seattle, 1972-76 **CR:** Secretary U.S. Senate Democratic Conference, 2007- chairwoman Democratic Senatorial Campaign Committee (DSCC), 2011-13, 2001-03 **CIV:** Member board Shoreline School, Seattle, 1985-89 member steering committee Demonstration for Education, Seattle, 1987 founder, chairman Organization for Parent Education, Washington, 1981-85 1st Congressional Rep. Washington Women United, 1983-85. **CW:** Co-author (with Catherine Whitney): Nine and Counting: The Women of the Senate, 2000 **AW:** Recipient Outstanding award Washing. Women United, 1986, Recognition of Service to Children award Shoreline PTA Council, 1986, Golden Acorn Service award, 1989; Outstanding Service award Washington Women United, 1986, Outstanding Service to Pub. Education award Citizens Educational Center Northwest, Seattle, 1987, Washington State Legis. of Year, 1990, George Falcon Spike award National Association Railroad Passengers, 2003, Person of Year award Washington State VFW, 2004; named one of The 10 Members to Watch in the 112th Congress, Roll Call, 2011 **PA:** Democrat **BA:** Office of Patty Murray, 154 Russell Senate Office Building, Washington, DC, 20510

MUSGRAVES, KACEY LEE, T: Musician **I:** Media & Entertainment **PB:** Mineola **SC:** TX/USA **CW:** Musician, (Albums) Movin' On, 2002, Wanted: One Good Cowboy, 2003, Kacey Musgraves, 2007, Same Trailer Different Park, 2013, Pageant Material, 2015, A Very Kacey Christmas, 2016, Golden Hour, 2018, (Songs) Merry Go Round, 2013, Follow Your Arrow, 2013, (Television) Nashville Star, 2007, CMT Crossroads, 2014, Hollywood Medium With Tyler Henry, 2017, Nashville, 2017 **AW:** Country Music Association Award For Song Of Year, Follow Your Arrow, 2014, Grammy Award For Best Country Song, Merry Go Round, 2014, Grammy Award For Best Country Album, Academy Country Music Award For Album Of Year, Same Trailer Different Park, 2014, New Artist of the Year, Country Music Association Awards, 2013

MUSK, ELON, T: CEO of Spacex **I:** Business Management/Business Services **DOB:** 06/28/1971 **PB:** Pretoria **ED:** Attended, Stanford University, 1995; BA in Physics, BS in Economics, University Pennsylvania, 1994; Attended, Queen's University, Kingston, Ontario, Can. **C:** Founder/CEO, The Boring Company, 2016-; CEO/Co-Founder, Neuralink, 2016-; Co-Founder, OpenAI, 2015-; Chairman, product architect, CEO, Tesla Motors, Inc., 2008-; Co-founder, Tesla Motors, Inc., Palo Alto, California, 2003-; Founder, CEO, chief tech. officer, SpaceX (Space Explorations Technologies Corp.), Hawthorne, California, 2002-; Chairman, Tesla Motors, Inc., 2003-08; Co-founder, chairman, CEO, PayPal (merger of X.com and Confinity Inc.), acquired by eBay Inc.), 2001-02; Co-founder, chairman, CEO, X.com, 1999-2001; Co-founder, chief tech. officer, chairman, CEO,, Zip2 (acquired by Compaq Computer Corp.), 1995-99; Software devel., Microsoft Corp., Redmond, Washington,; Software devel., Rocket Sci.,; With, Pinnacle Research, **CR:** Past member National Academy of Sciences Aeronautics and Space Engineering Board chairman board directors SolarCity, Foster City, California, 2006- board directors Planetary Society, Pasadena, California, 2003- **CIV:** Member engring adv. board, Stanford University, Chairman board directors, Musk Foundation, Board trustee, X-Prize Foundation, **AW:** Named a Living Legend in Aviation, Kitty Hawk Foundation, 2010; named

Businessperson of Year, Fortune magazine, 2013, Aviation Week 2008 Laureate; named one of The 10 Most Fascinating People of 2014, Barbara Walters Special, The CNN 10: Thinkers, 2013, The 50 Most Influential People in Global Finance, Bloomberg Markets, 2013-14, The World's Most Powerful People, Forbes magazine, 2012-14, America's 20 Most Powerful CEOs 40 and Under, 2012, The 40 Under 40, Fortune magazine, 2010, The 100 Most Influential People in the World, TIME magazine, 2013, 2010, The 100 Agents of Change, Rolling Stone magazine, 2009, The 75 Most Influential People of the 21st Century, Esquire magazine, 2008, The 50 Who Matter Now, Business 2.0, 2007; recipient Von Braun Trophy, National Space Society, 2009, National Conservation Achievement award, National Wildlife Federation, 2008, George Low award, American Institute Aeronautics & Astronautics, 2007/2008, INDEX Design award, 2007, Innovator of Year award, R&D Magazine, 2007, Entrepreneur of Year award, Inc Magazine, 2007, Product Design award, Global Green USA, 2006 **MEM:** Fellow: World Tech. Network **ACH:** An unmanned capsule that was built by Space Exploration Technolgies Corporation (SpaceX) was the first non-governmental spacecraft to launch to the space station on May 22, 2012, leading to a new era of partnership between the public and private spaceflight programs. **BA:** 3500 Deer Creek Road, Palo Alto, CA, 94304

MUTI, RICCARDO, T: Director of the Chicago Symphony Orchestra **I:** Media & Entertainment **DOB:** 07/28/1941 **PB:** Naples **ED:** Doctor (hon.), Westminster Choir College, Princeton, New Jersey; LLD (hon.), Warwick University, England; MusD (hon.), Mount Holyoke College; MusD (hon.), Curtis Institute Music, University Bologna; MusD (hon.), University Pennsylvania; Diploma in Composition and Conducting, Milan Conservatory; Studied piano, Conservatory San Pietro a Majella, Naples **C:** Music director, Chicago Symphony Orchestra, 2010-; Founder, conductor, Luigi Cherubini Youth Orchestra, Italy, 2004-; Music director designate, Chicago Symphony Orchestra, 2009-10; Music director, Teatro alla Scala, Milan, 1986-2005; Music director, Philadelphia Orchestra, 1980-92; Principal conductor, Philharmonia Orchestra, London, 1972-82; Principal conductor, music director, Maggio Musicale Fiorentino, Florence, Italy, 1968-80 **CR:** Guest conductor Berlin Philharmonic, Bayerischer Rundfunk, New York Philharmonic, Orchestre National de France, Vienna Philharmonic artistic director Pentecost Festival, Salzburg, 2007- conductor Salzburg Festival, Austria, 1971- **AW:** Decorated Order of Friendship, Russia, Knight of Brit. Empire, Queen Elizabeth II, Order of Merit, Federal Republic of Germany, Cavaliere di Gran Croce, Italy; recipient Wolf prize in arts (music), Wolf Foundation, Israel, 2000,2nd Class, Gold and Silver Star, Order of the Rising Sun, 2016, Knight Commander, Order of the British Empire, 2000 **MEM:** Mem.: Am. Academy Arts & Scis. (foreign), Royal Academy Music (hon.)

MYERS, ROLLAND, T: Investment Counselor **I:** Financial Services **ED:** Diploma, St. Louis Country Day School, 1963; AB cum laude in History and Lit., Harvard University, 1966; Postgrad. Faculties of Social Scis. and Law, University Edinburgh, Scotland, 1966-1967; Postgrad. Foundation Nationale des Sciences Politiques and Faculte de Lettres et des Sciences Humaines, University Paris, 1967-1968 **C:** Trainee global credit department, The Chase Manhattan Bank, N.A. (now JPMorgan Chase Bank, N.A.), New York City, New York, 1968-69, Member 32nd special development program, 1969; Strategic planner (for the Caribbean) international department,

1969-70; Securities analyst, marketing rep., fiduciary investment department, 1970; Associate, Smith, Barney & Co., Inc. (now Morgan Stanley Smith Barney LLC and Citi Institutional Clients Group), New York City, New York, 1971; Account executive New York sales department, 1971-72; Institutional account executive (for Japan, Hong Kong, Singapore, Australia, and Canada) New York international sales department, 1972-74; 2nd vice president, stockholder, 1975-76; V.P., stockholder, Smith Barney, Harris Upham & Co., Inc. (subsidiary SBHU Holdings, Inc.), 1976-78; President and principal, W.H. Graham & Sons, family investment office, 1977-present; Investment counsel, 1982-2011; **CR:** Ltd. partner Croke-Patterson-Campbell Mansion, Ltd., Denver, 1975-87; president, chairman executive committee, board directors Fifty-Five Residents Corp., New York City, 1980-84; board directors Fifty-Six Danbury Rd. Association, Inc., New Milford, Connecticut, 1984-; **CIV:** Trustee, member corp. Bishop Rhinelander Foundation (Episcopal Chaplaincy at Harvard and Radcliffe Colleges), Cambridge, 1973-75; vice president, treasurer, board directors The Whitehill Graham Foundation, St. Louis, 1976—; board directors, fin. committee, bylaws committee, member corp. Eliot Pratt Education Center, Inc. (The Pratt Ctr.: Your Connection with the Natural World), New Milford, 1987-94; bylaws/governance committee, member corp. Kent (Connecticut) Land Trust, Inc., 1989—, treasurer, 1989-93, board directors, 1989-2003, adv. board, 2003-; board directors, fin. committee, member corp. Kent Art Association, 2010-; trustee, Kent Art Association Charitable Trust, 2011-, board directors, finance committee Hunt Hill Farm Trust, Inc. (The Silo), an affiliate of the Smithsonian Institution, New Milford, 2015-; project financier Restoration of 1851 Samuel Curtiss Hosford House, National Register Historic District, Falls Village, Connecticut, 1984-86; commissioner Housatonic River Commission, Warren, Connecticut, 1985-93, vice chairman, 1986-87, chairman, 1988-92; commissioner Conservation, Inland Wetlands and Watercourses Commission, Kent, 1988-93, vice chairman, 1988-92; member schools and scholarships committee, Office of Admissions and Fin. Aid, Harvard and Radcliffe Colleges, 1991-99. **MEM:** Member Cum Laude Society, Mary Institute and St. Louis Country Day School Alumni Association, Harvard Alumni Association, Capitol Hill Club (Washington), Harvard Club (New York City), Hasty Pudding-Inst. of 1770 (Cambridge), Wyoming Business Alliance, Wyoming Heritage Foundation, St. Andrew's Society, New England Society in City New York, St. George's Society New York **H:** Skiing, snowboarding, weight training, tennis, distance walking, history, genealogy, fine arts, writing, architecture and design, political science; **PA:** Republican **BA:** W H Graham & Sons Investment Counsel 1818 Evans Ave Ste 207, 1818 Evans Ave Ste 207, Cheyenne, WY, 82001-4664

NADAL, RAFAEL, T: Professional Tennis Player **I:** Athletics **DOB:** 06/03/1986 **PB:** Manacor **SC:** Mallorca Spain **PT:** Son of Sebastian and Ana Maria. **C:** Professional tennis player, ATP Tour, 2001 **CR:** Member Spanish national team Summer Olympic Games, Beijing, 2008, Athens, Greece, 2004, Davis Cup, 2011, 2009, 2008, 2004 **CIV:** Founder, Fundacion Rafa Nadal, 2007- **CW:** Co-author (with John Carlin): Rafa, 2011 **AW:** Named ATP Newcomer of Year, 2003; named one of The World's Most Influential People, TIME magazine, 2009; recipient Gold medal, men's singles tennis, Summer Olympic Games, Beijing, 2008, Newcomer of Year, Laureus World Sports Awards, 2006,ATP Player of the Year, 2008,2010,2013,2017, Most Improved Player, 2005, ATP Star of Tomorrow, 2003, Comeback of the Year,

2013, Stefan Edberg Sportsmanship Award, 2010, Arthur Ashe Humanitarian of the Year,2011 **ACH:** Achievements include winner 60 career singles titles, 8 career doubles titles; member of Davis Cup winning Spanish Tennis Team, 2004; winner Grand Slam titles: French Open, 2005-08, 2010-14, 2017, 2018, Wimbledon, 2008, 2010, Australian Open, 2009, US Open, 2010, 2013, 2017; **ADD:** c/o Carlos Costa IMG Tennis, Planta Via Augusta 4, Barcelona, YT, Spain, 8006

NADELLA, SATYA, T: CEO **I:** Business Management/Business Services **CN:** Microsoft **DOB:** 06/06/1967 **PB:** Hyderabad **PT:** Son of Bukkapuram Nadella Yugandhar and Prabhavati Yugandhar **ED:** MBA, University Chicago Booth School Business; MS in Computer Sci., University Wisconsin, 1990; BS in Electronics & Telecommunication, Manipal Institute Technology, 1987 **C:** CEO, Microsoft, 2014-; Executive vice president cloud & enterprise, Microsoft, 2013-14; President server & tools business (STB), Microsoft Corp., Redmond, Washington, 2011-13; Senior vice president research & devel., Online Services division, Microsoft, 2009-11; Senior vice president search, portal & advertising platform group, Microsoft, 2008-09; Corporate vice president Microsoft business solutions, Microsoft, 2002-08; General manager commerce platforms group, Microsoft; Leader Central marketing & business devel., Microsoft, 1999-2002; Founder Central small business online service, Microsoft, Redmond, Washington; Program manager Windows developer relations group, Microsoft; Joined, Microsoft, 1992; Software devel. engineer, Sun Microsystems Inc. **CR:** Board directors Microsoft, 2014-, Riverbed Technology, Inc., 2013-14 **AW:** Named one of The World's Most Powerful People, Forbes magazine, 2014

NADER, RALPH, T: Advocate, Lawyer, Writer **I:** Law and Legal Services **DOB:** 02/27/1934 **PB:** Winsted **PT:** Son of Nadra and Rose (Bouziane) Nader. **ED:** LLB with distinction, Harvard University, 1958; AB magna cum laude, Princeton University, 1955 **CT:** Bar: US Supreme Ct 1959, Massachusetts 1959, Connecticut 1958 **C:** Founder of, numerous non-profit orgn.'s, 1969-; Others, numerous non-profit orgn.'s,; Center Justice & Democracy, numerous non-profit orgn.'s, 1998; Center Insurance Research, numerous non-profit orgn.'s, 1995; Center Women's Policy Studies, numerous non-profit orgn.'s, 1972; Including Center for Study of Responsive Law, numerous non-profit orgn.'s, 1969; Founder, director, Pub. Citizen, Washington, 1971-80; Staff member to assistant secretary, US Department Labor, Washington, 1964; Professor hist. & government, University Hartford, 1961-63; Private law practice, Hartford, Connecticut, 1959-61 **CIV:** US presidential candidate, Ind. Party, 2008 US presidential candidate, Ind. Party, 2004 US presidential candidate, Green Party, 2000 US presidential candidate, Green Party, 1996 **CW:** Author: Unsafe at Any Speed, 1965, Working on the System: A Manual for Citizen's Access to Federal Agencies, 1972, Action for a Change, 1972, You and Your Pension, 1973, Taming the Giant Corporation, 1976, The Lemon Book, 1980, The Big Boys, 1986, Winning The Insurance Game, 1990, No Contest: Corporate Lawyers and the Perversion of Justice in America, 1996, The Ralph Nader Reader, 2000, Crashing the Party: Taking on the Corporate Government in an Age of Surrender, 2002, In Pursuit of Justice: Collected Writing, 2004, The Good Fight: Declare Your Independence and Close the Democracy Gap, 2004, Civic Arousal, 2004, The Seventeen Traditions: Lessons From an American Childhood, 2007, Only the Super Rich Can Save Us!, 2009, Getting Steamed to Overcome Corporatism: Build It Together to Win, 2011, The

Seventeen Solutions: New Ideas for Our American Future, 2012, Unstoppable: The Emerging Left-Right Alliance to Dismantle the Corporate State, 2014; co-author (with John Abbots): Menace of Atomic Energy, 1979; co-author: (with Wesley J. Smith) Collision Course: The Truth About Airline Safety, 1993; editor: Whistle Blowing: The Report on the Conference on Professional Responsibility, 1972, The Consumer and Corporate Accountability, 1973; co-editor: Corporate Power in America, 1973, Verdicts on Lawyers, 1976, Who's Poisoning America, 1981; actor: (documentaries) The Greatest Movie Ever Sold, 2011,(Book) Return to Sender: Unanswered Letters to the President, 2015, Breaking Through Power: It's Easier Than We Think,2016 **AW:** Named one of The 10 Outstanding Young Men of Year, US Junior Chamber of Commerce, 1967; recipient Nieman Fellows award, 1965-66 **MEM:** Mem.: American Association for the Advancement of Science, American Bar Association, Phi Beta Kappa **PA:** Independent

NADLER, JERRY, T: U.S. Representative from New York, lawyer **I:** Government Administration/Government Relations/Government Services **DOB:** 06/13/1947 **PB:** Bklyn. **PT:** Married Joyce L. Miller, 1976; 1 child, Michael. **ED:** JD, Fordham University School Law, 1978; AB in Government, Columbia University, 1969 **C:** Member, US Congress from 10th New York District, 2013-; Member, Committee on the Judiciary, Committee on Transportation and Infrastructure; Ranking minority member, US House Subcommittee on Comml./Adminstrv. Law, 1997-2000; Member, US House Subcommittee on Construction, 1997-2006; Member, US House Subcommittees on Surface Transportation, Water Resources, & Environment, 1993-94; Member, US Congress from 8th New York District, 1993-2013; Member District 67, New York State Assembly, 1983-92; Member District 69, New York State Assembly, 1977-82; Law clerk, Morgan, Finnegan, Pine, Foley and Lee, 1976; Democratic district leader, 69th Assembly District Part A, 1973-77; Executive director, Community Free Dem., 1972; Democratic leader, 67th Assembly District Part C, 1969-71; Member, Community Planning Board Number 7, Manhattan, 1967-71 **CR:** Chairman Assembly Committee on Corps, Authorities and Commission, 1991-92, Assembly Consumer Affairs & Protection Committee, 1987-90, Assembly Committee on Ethics & Guidance, 1985-86, Assembly Subcom. on Mass Transit and Rail Freight, 1979-86 **CIV:** Founder, chairman West Side Peace Committee, 1969-71 **AW:** recipient Recognition award New York State Nurses Association, 1982, Distinguished Service award Coalition on Domestic Violence, 1989, Legislator of Year award International Association Firefighters, 2003; Pulitzer scholar Columbia University **MEM:** Member National Organization of Women (Assembly Member of Year from New York chpt, 1980), National Association for the Advancement of Colored People, New York Bar Association, New York Civil Liberties Union (honor roll), Citizens Union, League Conservation Voters, New Democratic Coalition, Americans for Democratic Action (board directors, national vice president). **PA:** Democrat **BA:** 2109 Rayburn Hall Office Building, Washington, DC, 20515

NAKAMURA, SHUJI, T: Engineering Educator **I:** Engineering **DOB:** 05/22/1954 **PB:** Seto, Japan, May 22, 1954 **ED:** DEng (hon.), Hong Kong University Sci. & Technology, 2008; DEng, University Tokushima, 1994; MEE, University Tokushima, 1979; BEE, University Tokushima, Japan, 1977 **C:** Professor of Materials at UCSB, 2008-; Professor materials, electrical and computer engineering department, University California, Santa Barbara, 1999-; Director, Solid State Lighting

& Display Center, University California, Santa Barbara,; Senior researcher department R&D, Nichia Chemical Industry, Ltd., 1993-99; Group head R&D 2nd section, Nichia Chemical Industry, Ltd., 1989-93; Group head R&D 1st section, Nichia Chemical Industry, Ltd., 1985-88; R&D staff, Nichia Chemical Industry, Ltd., 1979-84 **CR:** Visiting research associate electronic engineering University Florida, 1988-89 **CW:** Member editorial bd.: Applied Physics Society, 1998-2000; published several papers **AW:** Co-recipient Nobel Prize in Physics, Royal Swedish Academy Sciences, 2014; named Silicon Valley Intellectual Property Law Association Inventor of Year, 2012, Cree Professor in Solid State Light and Display Endowed chair, 2001; recipient Technological & Engineering Emmy award, National Academy Television, Arts & Sciences (National Academy of Television Arts and Sciences), 2012, Harvey prize, Technion Israeli Institute Technology, 2009, Prince of Asturias prize for Technical & Scientific Research, 2008, Czochralski award, 2007, Millennium Tech. prize for his inventions in light and laser tech., Millennium Prize Foundation, 2006, Benjamin Franklin medal in engineering, Franklin Institute, 2002, LEOS Distinguished Lecturer award, 2001, OSA Nick Holonyak award, 2001, Asahi award, 2001, Crystal Growth and Crystal Tech. award, 2000, Honda award, 2000, Carl Zeiss Research award, 2000, Takayanagi award, 2000, Julius-Springer prize for applied physics, 1999, British Rank prize, 1998, Jack A. Morton award, IEEE, 1998, C&C award, Innovation in Real Materials award, 1998, Society Medal award, Materials Research Society, 1997, Okochi Memorial award, 1997, Special Recognition award, Society for Information Display, 1996, IEEE Lasers and Electro-Optics Society Engineering Achievement award, 1996, Nishina Memorial award, 1996, Sakurai award, 1995, Best Paper award, Japanese Applied Physics Society, 1997, 1994, Nikkei Business Publications Engineering award, 1996, 1994, National Inventors Hall of Fame, 2015, Mountbatten Medal, 2017, Zayed Future Energy Prize, 2018 **MEM:** Mem.: NAE (Draper prize 2015) **ACH:** Achievements include development of first group-III nitride-based blue/ green LEDs; design of first group-III nitride-based violet laser diodes; patents in field

NAPOLITANO, GRACE, T: U.S. Representative From California **I:** Government Administration/ Government Relations/Government Services **DOB:** 12/04/1936 **PB:** Brownsville **SC:** TX/USA **PT:** Miguel Flores, Maria Alicia (Ledezma) Flores **ED:** Student, Texas Southmost College; Student, Los Angeles Trade-Technical College; Student, Cerritos College **C:** Committee on Financial Services, Committee on Foreign Affairs, U.S. Congress from 32nd California District, 2013-Present; U.S. Congress from 38th California District, 2003-2013; U.S. Congress from 34th California District, Washington, DC, 1999-2003; California State Assembly, 1993-1998; Mayor, City of Norwalk, 1989-1990; City Councilwoman, City of Norwalk, California, 1986-1992 **CIV:** Active, Cerritos College Foundation **MEM:** US/Mexico Sister Cities Association, Veterans of Foreign Wars, Lions Club **PA:** Democrat **BA:** 4401 Santa Anita Avenue, Suite 201, El Monte, CA, 91731

NASH, STEVE, T: Professional Basketball Player **I:** Athletics **DOB:** 02/07/1974 **PB:** Johannesburg **ED:** Bachelor, Santa Clara University, California, 1996 **C:** Point guard, LA Lakers, 2012-2015; Co-Owner, Vancouver Whitecaps, 2011-; Manager, Canada Men's National Basketball Team,2012-; Part Time Consultant, Golden State Warriors, 2015-; Point guard, LA Lakers, 2012-; Point guard, Dallas Mavericks, 1998-2004; Point guard, Phoenix Suns, 2004-12; Point guard, Phoenix Suns, 1996-98 **CR:**

General manager senior men's national team Canada Basketball, 2012- **CIV:** Founder, Steve Nash Foundation, 2001- **AW:** Elected Naismith Memorial Basketball Hall Of Fame, 2018; Named NBA Player of Year, The Sporting News, 2006, Man of Year, GQ magazine, 2005, MVP, NBA, 2005-06, Best NBA Player, ESPY awards, 2005; named one of 100 Most Influential People, Time Magazine, 2006; named to All-NBA First Team, 2005-07, All-NBA Third Team, 2003, 2002, Western Conference All-Star Team, NBA, 2012, 2010, 2008, 2007, 2005, 2003, 2002; recipient J. Walter Kennedy Citizenship award, 2007, Lou Marsh trophy, 2005, Lionel Conacher award, 2006, 2005, 2002,Phoenix Suns Ring of Honor, All-NBA Second Team, 2008,2010 **ACH:** Achievements include winner of the NBA All-Star Weekend Skills Challenge, 2005, 2010; leading the NBA in: assists, 2005-07, 2010, 2011; free throw percentage, 2006, 2010 **BA:** c/o Phoenix Suns, 201 E Jefferson St, Phoenix, AR, 85004

NASH, WILLIAM D., T: retail executive **I:** Retail/Sales **ED:** Bachelor in Business Accounting, James Madison University **C:** President, CEO, CarMax, 2016-; executive v.p. CarMax 2012-2016; Senior vice president, Merchandising, CarMax, Inc., 2010-2011; Vice president, Merchandising, CarMax, Inc., 2007-10; Auction manager, CarMax, Inc., 1997; Auction director, assistant vice president, auction services and vice president, auction services, CarMax, Inc.,; Various positions, pub. accounting, Circuit City

NASHAN, KEVIN, T: Chef **I:** Food & Restaurant Services **PB:** Chicago **SC:** IL/USA **C:** Owner/Chef, The Peacemaker, 2014-Present; Owner/Chef, Sidney Street Cafe, 2003-Present **AW:** Restaurant of the Year, St. Louis Magazine, 2013, James Beard Award for Best New Chef, 2017

NATALICIO, DIANA SIEDHOFF, T: Academic Administrator **I:** Education/Educational Services **DOB:** 08/25/1939 **PB:** St. Louis **SC:** MO/USA **PT:** Daughter of William and Eleanor J. (Biermann) Siedhoff. **ED:** PhD (hon.), Universidad Autonoma de Nuevo Leon; PhD (hon.), Smith College; PhD in Linguistics, University of Texas, 1969; MA in Portuguese language, University of Texas, 1964; BS in Spanish summa cum laude, Saint Louis University, 1961 **C:** President, University of Texas, El Paso, 1988-; Vice president academy affairs, University of Texas, El Paso, 1984-88; Dean College Liberal Arts, University of Texas, El Paso, 1980-84; Acting dean liberal arts, University of Texas, El Paso, 1979-80; Associate dean liberal arts, University of Texas, El Paso, 1977-79; Chairman department modern languages, University of Texas, El Paso, 1973-77 **CR:** Board directors El Paso branch Federal Reserve Board Dallas, chairman, 1989 member Presidential Adv. Commission on Educational Excellence for Hispanic Ams., 1991 board directors Sandia Corp., Trinity Industries board directors National Action Council for Minorities in Engineering, 1993- member National Sci. Board 1994-2006 member NASA Adv. Council, 1994-96 board member Fund for Improvement of Post-Secondary Education, 1993-97 board directors Fogarty International Center of National Institutes of Health, 1993-96 board chair Am. Association Higher Education, 1995-96 board directors U.S.-Mexico Commission for Educational and Cultural Exchange, 1994-. **CIV:** Board directors United Way El Paso, 1990-93, chairman needs survey committee, 1990-91, chairman education division, 1989 chairman Quality Education for Minorities Network in Math. Sci. and Engineering, 1991-92 chairperson Leadership El Paso, Class 12, 1989-90, member adv. council, 1987-90, participant, 1980-81 member Historically Black Colleges

and Univs./Minority Institutions Consortium on Environmental Tech. chairperson, 1991-93 trustee Rockefeller Foundation **CW:** Co-author: Sounds of Children, 1977; contributor articles to professional journals **AW:** Recipient Harold W. McGraw. Junior prize in education, 1997, Torch of Liberty award Anti-Defamation League B'nai B'rith, 1991, Conquistador award City of El Paso, 1990, Humanitarian award El Paso chapter National Conference of Christians and Jews, 1990, Distinguished Alumnus Award, University Texas Austin, 2006; named to El Paso Women's Hall of Fame, 1990, Texas Women's Hall of Fame, 1998. **MEM:** Member Philosophical Society Texas **H:** Hiking, bicycling, skiing, skating

NAUGHTON, JAMES, T: Actor **I:** Media & Entertainment **DOB:** 05/18/1905 **PB:** Middletown **SC:** Middletown **PT:** Son of James Joseph and Rosemary (Walsh) N.; **SPN:** children: Gregory J., Keira P. **CH:** Married Pamela Parsons, October 1968; **ED:** MFA, Yale University, 1970; BA, Brown University, 1967 **C:** Actor 1971- **CW:** Broadway appearances include Edmund in Long Day's Journey Into Night, 1971 (Theatre World award, New York Drama Critics award, Vernon Rice award 1971), Stone in City of Angels (Tony award 1990, Drama Desk award), I Love My Wife, 1977, Whose Life Is It Anyway, 1980, Chicago, 1996 (Tony award, 1997); films include Paper Chase, 1972, Second Wind, 1975, A Stranger is Watching, 1981, Cat's Eye, 1982, The Glass Menagerie, 1987, The Good Mother, 1988, First Kid, 1996, The First Wives Club, 1996, The Proprietor, 1996, Oxygen, 1999, Labor Pains, 2000, Fascination, 2004, The Devil Wears Prada, 2006; TV appearances include: (series) Faraday and Company, 1973-74, Planet of the Apes, 1974, Making the Grade, 1982, Trauma Center, 1983, The Cosby Mysteries, 1994; (movies) F. Scott Fitzgerald and The Last of the Belles, 1974, The Last 36 Hours of Dr. Durant, 1975, The Bunker, 1981, My Body, My Child, 1982, Parole, 1982, The Last of the Great Survivors, 1984, Between Darkness and the Dawn, 1985, Sin of Innocence, 1986, Necessity, 1988, Blown Away, 1990, The Birds II: Land's End, 1994, Couples, 1994, Cagney & Lacey: The Return, 1994, Cagney & Lacey: Together Again, 1995, Mixed Blessings, 1995, The Truth About Jane, 2000; director (plays) Surface to Air, 2007.(Theatre) The Price, 1999, Our Town, 2003, Prymate, 2004, Democracy, 2004(Film) Factory Girl, 2006, Suburban Girl, 2007, Gossip Girl, 2009, Warehouse 13, 2009, Hostages, 2013, Turks & Caicos, 2014, The Blacklist, 2015 **AW:** Recipient Tony award Leading Actor in a Musical, 1997.

NAVRATILOVA, MARTINA, T: Former Professional Tennis Player **I:** Athletics **DOB:** 10/18/1956 **PB:** Prague **PT:** Daughter of Miroslav Navratil and Jana Navratilova **ED:** Hon. doctorate, George Washington University, 1996; Student, schools in Czechoslovakia **C:** Professional tennis player, 2003-06; Professional tennis player, 1973-94; Tennis commentator/broadcaster, HBO Sports, 1995-99 **CR:** Member World Team Tennis, 1990- player U.S. Fed Cup Team, 2003, 1995, 1989, 1986, 1982, Czech Federal Cup Team, 1975 **CIV:** Co-founder Rainbow Card **CW:** Author: (with George Vecsey) Martina, 1985; (with Liz Nickles) The Total Zone, 1995, Breaking Point, 1996, Killer Instinct, 1997, Shape Your Self: My 6-Step Diet and Fitness Plan to Achieve the Best Shape of Your Life, 2006; columnist; performer Dancing With the Stars, 2012 **AW:** Winner Czechoslovak National singles, 1972-74, U.S. Open singles, 1983, 84, 86, 87, U.S. Open doubles, 1977, 78, 80, 83, 84, 87, 90, U.S. Open mixed doubles, 1987, 2006, Virginia Slims Championsips, 1978, 83, 84, 85, 86, Virginia Slims Championships, 1991, Wimbledon singles, 1978,

79, 82, 83, 84, 85, 86, 87, 90, Wimbledon women's doubles, 1976, 79, 81, 82, 83, 84, 86, Wimbledon mixed doubles, 1985, 93, 95, 2003, French Open singles, 1982, 84, Australian Open singles, 1981, 83, 85, Australian Doubles (with Betsy Nagelsen) 1980, (with Pam Shriver), 1982, 84, 85, 87, 88, 89, Australian Mixed Doubles, 2003, Roland Garros (with Pam Shriver), 1985, 87, 89, Italian Open doubles (with Gabriela Sabatini), 1987, (with Pam Shriver) COREL WTA Tour doubles team of year, 1981-89, triple Crown at U.S. Open, 1987; recipient Women's Sports Foundation Flo Hyman award, 1987, BBC Lifetime Achievement Award, 2003, Eugene L. Scott award, International Tennis Hall of Fame, 2010; named Female Athlete of the Decade (1980s) The National Sports Review, United Press International, and Associated Press, WTA Player of Year, 1978-79, 82-86, Women's Sports Foundation Sportswoman of Year, 1982-84, Hon. Citizen of Dallas, Associated Press Female Athlete of Year, 1983; named to International Tennis Hall of Fame, 2000; Martina Navratilova Day proclaimed in Chicago, 1992,ITF World Champion, 1979, 1982-86, BBC Sports Personality of the Year Lifetime Achievement Award, 2003, Czech Sport Legend Award, 2006 **MEM:** Member Women's Tennis Association (director, executive committee, president), Women's Tennis Association Tour Player's Association (president 1979-80, 83-84, 94-95) **ACH:** Achievements include being the holder of 167 singles titles and 173 doubles titles; holder of record of singles-match wins (1,309), 1991; holds record for 109 consecutive doubles matches won (with Pam Shriver) **BA:** Little Brown And Company, 1290 Avenue of the Americas, New York, NY, 10104

NAYEF, MOHAMMED BIN BIN, T: Crown Prince of Saudia Arabia **I:** Government Administration/Government Relations/Government Services **DOB:** 06/21/1905 **PB:** Jeddeh, Saudi Arabia **SC:** Jeddeh, Saudi Arabia **C:** Crown Prince of Saudi Arabia,- First Deputy Prime Minister,2015-17; Minister of the Interior, Saudi Arabia,2012-17; Deputy Crown Prince of Saudi Arabia,Second Deputy Prime Minister,2015 **AW:** Time 100,2016, French Legion of Honor,2016

NEAL, RICHARD EDMUND, T: U.S. Representatives from Massachusetts **I:** Government Administration/Government Relations/Government Services **DOB:** 02/14/1949 **PB:** Worcester **SC:** MA/USA **PT:** Edmund J. Neal; Mary H. (Garvey) Neal **MS:** Married **SPN:** Maureen Conway (12/20/1975) **CH:** Rory; Brendan; Maura; Sean **ED:** Postgraduate Coursework, University of Massachusetts, Amherst (1982); MPA, University of Hartford, CT (1976); BS, American International College, Springfield, MA (1972) **C:** Member, House Ways and Means Committee (2013-Present); Member, US Congress from the First Massachusetts District (2013-Present); Member, US Congress from the Second Massachusetts District (1989-2013); Mayor, City of Springfield, MA (1984-1988); City Councilman, City of Springfield, MA (1978-1983); Administrative Aide to Mayor, City of Springfield, MA (1973-1978) **CR:** Lecturer, History & Politics, Springfield Technical Community College, MA (1973-1983); Lecturer, Business & Government, Western New England College, Springfield, MA (1979-1982); Project Director, Springfield Technical Community College (1979-1982) **CIV:** Trustee, American Red Cross; Trustee, YMCA, Springfield, MA **AW:** Named to Outstanding Young Men in America, US Junior Chamber of Commerce, Springfield, MA; John F. Kennedy Award & Ambassador's Award, Holyoke, MA; St. Patrick's Day Committee; International Leadership Award, American Ireland Fund (2002); Alumni Achievement Award, American International College Alumni Association (1985) **MEM:**

President, American International College Alumni Association (1980); Trustee, Springfield Library and Museum Association; Valley Press Club; John Boyle O'Reilly Club, Springfield, MA **PA:** Democrat

NEESON, LIAM, T: Actor **I:** Media & Entertainment **PB:** Ballymena **SC:** Ireland **PT:** Barney Neeson and Kitty Neeson **SPN:** Natasha Richardson (July 3, 1994) (Deceased March 18, 2009) **CH:** Michael Richard Antonio; Daniel Jack **ED:** PhD (hon.), Queen's University, Belfast, 2009 **CW:** Theatrical appearances include (Broadway) The Judas Kiss, 1998, Anna Christie, 1993 (Theatre World award, 1993); actor: (films) Excalibur, 1981, Krull, 1983, The Bounty, 1984, The Innocent, 1984, Lamb, 1986, Duet for One, 1986, The Mission, 1986, A Prayer for the Dying, 1987, Suspect, 1987, Satisfaction, 1988, The Good Mother, 1988, Next of Kin, 1989, Darkman, 1990, Crossing the Line, 1990, Ruby Cairo, 1991, Shining Through, 1992, Under Suspicion, 1992, Husbands and Wives, 1992, Leap of Faith, 1992, Ethan Fromme, 1992, Schindler's List, 1993, Nell, 1994, Rob Roy, 1995, Before and After, 1996, Michael Collins, 1996, Les Miserables, 1998, Star Wars: Episode I-The Phantom Menace, 1999, The Haunting, 1999, Gun Shy, 2000, K-19: The Widowmaker, 2002, Gangs of New York, 2002, Love Actually, 2003, Kinsey, 2004, Kingdom of Heaven, 2005, Batman Begins, 2005, Breakfast on Pluto, 2005, (voice) The Chronicles of Narnia: The Lion, the Witch, and the Wardrobe, 2005, (voice) The Chronicles of Narnia: Prince Caspian, (voice) Ponyo on the Cliff, 2008, The Other Man, 2008, Taken, 2008, Five Minutes of Heaven, 2009, Chloe, 2009, Clash of the Titans, 2010, The A-Team, 2010, Unknown, 2011, The Grey, 2012, Wrath of the Titans, 2012, Battleship, 2012, The Dark Knight Rises, 2012, Taken 2, 2012, The Gentleman Prize-fighter, 2012, (voice) Khumba, 2013, Third Person, 2013, Anchorman 2: The Legend Continues, 2013, (voice) The Nut Job, 2014, (voice) The Lego Movie, 2014, Non-Stop, 2014, (voice) Kahlil Gibran's The Prophet, 2014, A Million Ways to Die in the West, 2014, A Walk Among the Tombstones, 2014, Taken 3, 2015, Run All Night, 2015, Ted 2, 2015, A Christmas Star, 2015, Operation Chromite, 2016, A Monster Calls, 2016, Silence, 2016, Mark Felt: The Man Who Brought Down the White House, 2017, The Commuter, 2018, Widows, 2018, Hard Powder, 2018; (TV appearances) Play for Today, 1978, BBC2 Playhouse, 1980, A Woman of Substance, 1985, Arthur the King, 1985, Miami Vice, 1986, Hold the Dream, 1986, Screen Two, 1988, The Great War of the Shaping of the 20th Century, 1996, Empires: The Greeks, 2000, Evolution, 2001, Liberty's Kids, 2002, Patrick, 2004, The Simpsons, 2005, The Big C, 2010, Life's Too Short, 2011, (voice) Star Wars: The Clone Wars,2011-14 Family Guy, 2014, Rev, 2014, Key & Peele, 2014, Wild Japan, 2014, Inside Amy Schumer, 2016, Dream Corp, 2016, Red Nose Day Actually, 2017, The Orville, 2017 Breadwinners, 2014; prodr: (plays) James-X, 2011 **AW:** Named an Officer of the Order of the British Empire (OBE), Her Majesty Queen Elizabeth II 1999

NEIDORFF, MICHAEL F., T: CEO **I:** Health, Wellness and Fitness **CN:** Centene Corporation **DOB:** 11/19/1942 **PB:** Philadelphia **SC:** PA/USA **PT:** A. Harvey Neidorff; Shirley R. (Rubin) Neidorff **MS:** Married **SPN:** Noemi Karpati **ED:** MA, St. Francis College (1966); BS, Trinity University (1965) **C:** Chairman, President, Chief Executive Officer, Centene Corporation, St. Louis, MO (2004-Present); President, Chief Executive Officer, Centene Corporation, St. Louis, MO (1996-2004); Treasurer, Centene Corporation, St. Louis, MO (1996-2001); President, Chief Executive Officer, Group Health Plan, Inc., St. Louis, MO (1995-1996); President, Chief Executive Officer, Physician Health Plan

(1985-1995); Manager, Miles Laboratories, Ltd. (1969-1975) **CR:** Board of Directors, Mark Twain Bank, St. Louis, MO; Board of Directors, Miles Laboratories, Ltd. (1967-1985); Board of Directors, Brown Shoe Co. Inc. **CIV:** Board of Trustees, St. Louis Symphony Orchestra, St. Louis, MO; Board of Directors, St. Louis Area Council, Boy Scouts of America, Grand Center, St. Louis, MO **MEM:** Missouri Managed Healthcare Association

NELSON, BILL, T: U.S. Senator From Florida **I:** Government Administration/Government Relations/Government Services **DOB:** 09/29/1942 **PB:** Miami **SC:** FL/USA **PT:** C.W. Nelson, Nannie (Merle) Nelson **MS:** Married **SPN:** Grace H. Cavert, 2/19/1972 **CH:** C. William, Nan Ellen **ED:** JD, University of Virginia, 1968; BA, Yale University, 1965 **C:** Ranking Member, Senate Commerce Committee, 2015-Present; Chairman, U.S. Senate Space, Aeronautics & Related Sciences Subcommittee, 2007-Present; U.S. Senator from Florida, 2001-Present; Chairman, U.S. Senate Special Committee on Aging, 2013-2015; Treasurer, Insurance Commissioner, State of Florida, Tallahassee, FL, 1995-2000; Attorney, Maguire, Vorrhis & Wells, Pennsylvania, 1991-1994; Payload Specialist 1, Space Shuttle Columbia Seventh Orbital Mission, 1986; U.S. Congress from 11th District of Florida, Washington, DC, 1983-1991; U.S. Congress from Ninth District of Florida, Washington, DC, 1979-1983; Florida House of Representatives, Tallahassee, FL, 1972-1978; Attorney, Nelson, Normile & Dettmer, Melbourne, FL, 1970-1979 **CIV:** Board of Directors, American Astronautical Society; Florida Space Business Roundtable **MIL:** U.S. Army, 1968-1970; Served to Captain, U.S. Army Reserve, 1965-1975 **CW:** Author, Mission: An American Congressman's Voyage to Space, 1988 **AW:** President's Award, Florida State Conference, National Association for the Advancement of Colored People, 2001, Debus Award, National Space Club, Florida Committee, 1993, Public Service Award, National Crystallography Association, 1988 **MEM:** Florida Bar Association, Brevard County Bar Association, Association of Space Explorers **BAR:** State of Florida, 1968 **PA:** Democrat **BA:** Office of Bill Nelson, 716 Senate Hart Office Building, Washington, DC, 20510

NELSON, LARRY GENE, T: Professional Golfer **I:** Athletics **PB:** Ft. Payne **SC:** AL/USA **MS:** Married **SPN:** Gayle **ED:** Student, Kennesaw Junior College **C:** Professional golfer, 1971 **AW:** Named to World Golf Hall of Fame, PGA Tour, 2006 **ACH:** Winter Jackie Gleason-Inverrary Classic, 1979, Western Open, 1979, Ryder Cup, 1979, 81, Atlanta Classic, 1980, U.S. PGA Championship, 1981, 87, Greensboro Open, 1981, U.S. Open, 1983; Senior Tour wins include FleetBoston Classic, 2000, 2001, Foremost Insurance Championship, 2000, Bank One Senior Championship, Vantage Championship, MasterCard Championship, 2001, Royal Caribbean Championship, Farmers Charity Classic, SBC Championship, Constellation Energy Classic, 2003, Greater Hickory Classic, FedEx Kinko's Classic, 2004, Administaff Small Business Classic,2004, Winner of the Bass Pro Shops Legends of Gold, 2015-16

NELSON, WILLIE HUGH, T: Musician **I:** Media & Entertainment **DOB:** 04/30/1933 **PB:** Abbott **SC:** TX/USA **ED:** Mus D (hon.), Berklee College of Music, 2013; Student, Baylor University **C:** Personal appearances, throughout the U.S., 1964-; Personal appearances, Grand Ole Opry, Nashville, 1964-; Owner, Pedernales Golf Club/Willie Nelson's Cut-N-Putt,; Founder, Pedernales Records, Austin, Texas, 2007; Founder, Pedernales Studios, Spicewood, Texas,; Recording artist, RCA records,; Recording artist, Columbia,;

Recording artist, Atlantic,; Formed own band,; Bass player, Ray Price's band,; Announcer, host country music shows, local Texas stas.,; Salesman, **CR:** Co-founder Willie Nelson's Biodiesel **CW:** Musician: (albums) Love & Pain, 1961, And Then I Wrote, 1962, Here's Willie Nelson, 1963, Country Willie: His Own Songs, 1965, Country Favorites: Willie Nelson Style, 1966, Live Country Music Concert, 1966, Make Way for Willie Nelson, 1967, Texas in My Soul, 1968, Good Times, 1968, My Own Peculiar Way, 1969, Both Sides Now, 1970, Laying My Burdens Down, Yesterday's Wine, 1971, Willie Nelson & Family, 1971, The Willie Way, 1972, The Words Don't Fit the Picture, 1972, Shotgun Willie, 1973, Phases and Stages, 1974, Red Headed Stranger, 1975 (Grammy award Best Country Vocal Performance for song "Blue Eyes Crying In The Rain", 1975), Willie Nelson Live, 1976, The Sound in Your Mind, 1976, The Troublemaker, 1976, To Lefty from Willie, 1977, Stardust, 1978 (Grammy award Best Country Vocal Performance for song "Georgia on My Mind", 1978), Waylon & Willie, 1978 (Grammy award Best Country Vocal Performance By A Duo Or Group for song "Mammas Don't Let Your Babies Grow Up to Be Cowboys", 1978), Willie and Family Live, 1978, The Electric Horseman, 1979, Sings Kris Kristofferson, 1979, One for the Road, 1979, Pretty Paper, 1979, San Antonio Rose, 1980, Honeysuckle Rose, 1980 (Grammy award Best Country Song for "On The Road Again", 1980), Blue Skies, 1981, Somewhere over the Rainbow, 1981, Pancho & Lefty, 1983 (Vocal Duo Year (with Merle Haggard) Country Music Association Awards, 1983), Old Friends, 1982, Always on My Mind, 1982 (Grammy award Best Country Vocal Performance for song "Always On My Mind", 1982, Country Music Association awards: Album Year, 1982, Single Year for "Always On My Mind", 1982), Tougher Than Leather, 1983, Without a Song, 1983, Take It to the Limit, 1983, Music from Songwriter, 1984, Portrait in Music, 1984, Angel Eyes, 1984, City of New Orleans, 1984, Me and Paul, 1985, Half Nelson, 1985 (Vocal Duo Year (with Julio Iglesias) Country Music Association Awards, 1984), Brand on My Heart, 1985, Funny How Time Slips Away, 1985, Partners, 1986, The Promiseland, 1986, Island in the Sea, 1987, Seashores of Old Mexico, 1987, What a Wonderful World, 1988, Horse Called Music, 1989, Born for Trouble, 1990, The IRS Tapes: Who'll Buy My Memories?, Willie Nelson, 1993, Across the Borderline, 1993, Moonlight Becomes You, 1994, Healing Hands of Time, 1994, Pancho, Lefty and Rudolph, 1995, Six Hours at Pedernales, 1995, Just One Love, 1996, Spirit, 1996, How Great Thou Art, 1996, Christmas with Willie Nelson, 1997, Hill Country Christmas, 1997, Teatro, 1998, Life's Railway to Heaven, 1998, Back to Back: Willie Nelson and Patsy Cline, 1998, Night and Day, 1999, Clean Shirt, 2000, Outlaws, 2000, Memories of Hank Williams, Senior, 2000, Me and the Drummer, 2000, Milk Cow Blues, 2000, Good Ol' Country Singin', 2000, Rainbow Connection, 2001, Tales Out of Luck, 2001, The Great Divide, 2002, Home is Where You're Happy, 2002, All of Me Live...in Concert, 2002, Stars & Guitars, 2002 (Grammy award (with Lee Ann Womack) Best Country Collaboration With Vocals for song "Mendocino County Line", 2002), Night Life, 2002, Country Willie, 2002, Is There Something on Your Mind, 2002, On the Road Again, 2002, Honky Tonk Heroes, 2003, Broken Promises, 2003, Reunion - Can't Get the Hell Out of Texas, 2003, Willie Nelson and Friends: Live and Kickin', 2003, Standard Time, 2003, Keepsake, 2003, Run That By Me One More Time, 2003, I Just Don't Understand, 2003, Live in Amsterdam, 2004, Music Legends: The Best of Willie Live, 2004, Live at Billy Bob's Texas, 2004, It Always Will Be, 2004, Songs for Tsunami Relief, 2005, Countryman, 2005, You Don't Know Me,

2006, Just a Couple of Outlaws, 2006, All American Country, 2006, Last of the Breed, 2007 (Grammy award Best Country Vocal Collaboration, 2008), Willie Nelson Christmas, 2007, Gravedigger, 2007, Moment of Forever, 2008, Naked Willie, 2009, Country Music, 2010, I Let My Mind Wander: The Best of Willie Nelson, 2010, (with Wynton Marsalis) Here We Go Again: Celebrating the Genius of Ray Charles, 2011, Heroes, 2012, Let's Face the Music and Dance, 2013, Band of Brothers, 2014, Summertime: Willie Nelson Sings Gershwin, 2016, (with Merle Haggard) Django & Jimmie, 2015; appeared on (album by Waylon Jennings) Good Hearted Woman, 1972 (Single Year (with Waylon Jennings) Country Music Association Awards, 1976), appeared with various artists (albums) Wanted: The Outlaws, 1976 (Vocal Duo Year (with Waylon Jennings) Country Music Association (Certified Medical Assistant) Awards, 1976, Album Year (with Waylon Jennings, Tompall Glaser, Jessi Colter) Country Music Association Awards, 1976); actor: (films) The Electric Horseman, 1979, Honeysuckle Rose, 1980, Thief, 1981, Barbarosa, 1982, Songwriter, 1984, Red-Headed Stranger, 1986, Starlight, 1996, Gone Fishin', 1997, Wag the Dog, 1997, Stardust, 2000, The Journeyman, 2001, The Big Bounce, 2004, The Dukes of Hazzard, 2005, Half Baked, Beerfest; appearances include (films) Anthem, 1997, Dill Scallion, 1999, Austin Powers: The Spy Who Shagged Me, 1999 AW: Named Entertainer Year, Country Music Association (Certified Medical Assistant), 1979; named to, Country Music Hall of Fame, 1993, Nashville Songwriters Association International Hall of Fame, 1973; recipient Kris Kristofferson award-first recipient of this lifetime achievement award, Nashville Songwriters Association International, 2013, Grammy Lifetime Achievement award, 1989, Special Humanitarian award, National Farmers Organization, 1986, citation for Top Album Artist, Billboard magazine, 1976 ACH: Swing Vote, 2008; actor, co-writer musical score : (TV films) Stagecoach, 1986; performer: (theme song for film) Welcome Home, 1989, (songs) Cowboys Are Frequently, Secretly (Fond of Each Other), 2006, (movie soundtrack, Brokeback Mountain) He Was a Friend of Mine, 2005; (TV films appearances include) Where the Hell's That Gold, 1988, Once Upon a Texas Train, 1989, A Pair of Aces, 1990, Born for Trouble, 1990, Another Pair of Aces: Three of a Kind, 1991, Big Country, 1994, Big Dreams and Broken Hearts: The Dottie West Story, 1995, The Beach Boys: Nashville Sounds, 1996, Starlight, 1996, Farm Aid '96, 1996, Outlaw Justice, 1998; author: (autobiography) I Didn't Come Here (and I Ain't Leavin'), 1988, The Facts of Life: and Other Dirty Jokes, 2003, A Tale Out of Luck, 2008, (memoir) Roll Me Up and Smoke Me When I Die: Musings from the Road, 2012; co-author (with Turk Pipkin): The Tao of Willie: A Guide to the Happiness in Your Heart, 2006; co-author: (with David Ritz) It's a Long Story: My Life, 2015(Album) For the Good Times: A Tribute to Ray Price, 2016, Gods Problem Child, 2017, Last Man Standing,2018; Achievements include performing Cowboys Are Frequently, Secretly (Fond of Each Other), which may be the first gay cowboy song by a major recording artist BA: 12400 Street Hwy 71 W, Suite 350, Austin, TX, 78738

NELSONS, ANDRIS, T: Conductor **I:** Media & Entertainment **DOB:** 11/18/1978 **PB:** Riga **SC:** Latvia **C:** Music Director, Boston Symphony Orchestra, 2014-; Music Director, Leipzig Gewandhaus Orchestra, 2018-; Principal conductor, Birmingham (England) Symphony Orchestra, 2008-2015;; Chief conductor of the Nordwestdeutsche Philharmonie of Herford, Germany, 2006-2009; Principal conductor of the Latvian National Opera, 2003-2007; **AW:** Recipient Grammy Award in 2015 (with the Boston Symphony Orchestra) for best Orchestral Performance (Under Stalin's Shadow);

NEWELL, GABE, T: Computer Game Development Company Executive **I:** Business Management/ Business Services **CN:** Valve **PB:** Seattle **SC:** WA/ USA **ED:** Student, Harvard University **C:** President,-co-founder, managing director, Valve Software, Bellevue, Washington, 1996-; Positions in the systems, applications, and advanced technology divisions, Microsoft Corp., 1983-96 **CR:** Speaker in field **CW:** Credited to the following games Half-Life, 1998, Half-Life: Opposing Force, 1999, Half-Life (Game of Year Edition), 1999, Half-Life: Counter Strike, 2000, Gunman Chronicles, 2000, Deus Ex, 2000, Half-Life: Blue Shift, 2001, Deus Ex (Game of Year Edition), 2001, Homeworld 2, 2003, Vampire: The Masquerade-Bloodlines, 2004, Half-Life 2, 2004, Counter-Strike: Condition Zero, 2004 **AW:** Nominee Rave award-Games, WIRED Magazine, 2005

NEWHOUSE, DANIEL, T: U.S. Representative from Washington **I:** Government Administration/Government Relations/Government Services **PB:** Sunnyside **SC:** WA/USA **C:** Member, U.S. House of Representatives from Washington's 4th District, 2015-; Member, Republican Study Committee; State rep. District 15, Washington, 2003-; Farmer, Sunnyside Area,; Member, Fin. Insights & Insurance & Judiciary Committees,; Member, Capital Budget, **MEM:** Mem.: Hop Growers America, Hop Growers Washington, Washington State Farm Bureau **PA:** Republican

NEWSOM, KEVIN, T: Federal Judge **I:** Law and Legal Services **DOB:** 09/22/1972 **PB:** Birmingham **SC:** AL/USA **SPN:** Deborah E. Wilgus **ED:** Diploma, Harvard Law School (1997); Diploma, Samford University **C:** Judge, U.S. Court of Appeals for the Eleventh Circuit (2017-Present); Partner, Chair, Appellate Litigation Group, Bradley Arant Boult Cummings LLP, Birmingham, AL (2007-Present); Solicitor General, State of Alabama (2003-2007); Associate, Covington & Burling, Washington, DC (2001-2003); Law Clerk to Honorable David H. Souter, Supreme Court of the U.S., Washington, DC (2000-2001); Law Clerk to Honorable Diarmund F. O'Scannlain, U.S. Court of Appeals for the Ninth Circuit (1997-1998) **AW:** Named One of the Best Lawyers in America, Appellate Law (2009-2011); Litigation's Rising Stars, The American Lawyer (2007); Distinguished Alumni Award, Federalist Society, Harvard Law School Chapter (2005); Best Brief Award, National Association of Attorneys (2004, 2005, 2007) **MEM:** American Law Institute **BAR:** Supreme Court of the U.S.; U.S. Court of Appeals for the First Circuit; U.S. Court of Appeals for the Second Circuit; U.S. Court of Appeals for the Third Circuit; U.S. Court of Appeals for the Fourth Circuit; U.S. Court of Appeals for the Fifth Circuit; U.S. Court of Appeals for the Sixth Circuit; U.S. Court of Appeals for the Seventh Circuit; U.S. Court of Appeals for the Eighth Circuit; U.S. Court of Appeals for the Ninth Circuit; U.S. Court of Appeals for the Tenth Circuit; U.S. Court of Appeals for the Eleventh Circuit; U.S. District Court for the Northern District of Alabama; U.S. District Court for the Middle District of Alabama; U.S. District Court for the Southern District of Alabama; Alabama State Bar Association; The District of Columbia Bar; State Bar of Georgia **BA:** 56 Forsyth St NW, Atlanta, GA, 30303

NEWTON, CAM, T: professional football player **I:** Athletics **DOB:** 05/11/1989 **PB:** College Park **PT:** Son of Cecil and Jackie Newton; **ED:** Degree in sociology, Auburn University, Alabama, 2015; Attended, Blinn College, Brenham, Texas, 2009; Attended, University Florida, Gainesville, 2007-08 **C:** Quarterback, Carolina Panthers, 2011-; Quarterback, Auburn University Tigers, 2010-11; Quarterback, Blinn College Buccaneers, 2009; Quarterback, University Florida Gators, 2007-08 **CR:** Launched clothing line MADE by Cam Newton **AW:** Named NFL Offensive Rookie of Year, Associated Press, 2011, College Football Player of Year, 2010, 1st Team All-American, 2010, Staten Island. com, 2010, Offensive Player of Year, Southeastern Conference, 2010; named to National Football Conference Pro Bowl Team, NFL, 2013, 2011; recipient Manning award, Sugar Bowl Committee, 2010, Heisman Memorial Trophy, Heisman Trophy Trust, 2010, Walter Camp Player of Year award, Walter Camp Football Foundation, 2010, Maxwell award, Maxwell Football Club, 2010, Davey O'Brien National Quarterback award, Davey O'Brien Foundation, 2010,NFL Offensive Rookie of the Year, 2011, Bert Bell Award, 2015, NFL Offensive Player of the Year, 2015, NFL Most Valuable Player, 2015, First-team All-Pro, 2015, Pro Bowl, 2011, 2013;2015 **ACH:** Achievements include member of National Junior College Athletic Association national championship winning Blinn College Buccaneers, 2009; one of only three players in NCAA Football Bowl Subdivision history with at least 20 touchdowns both rushing and passing in a season, 2010; member of the BCS National Championship winning Auburn University Tigers, 2010; being the first overall pick in the NFL Draft, 2011; setting the NFL record for: passing yards by a rookie in his regular season opener (422 yards), 2011; rushing touchdowns by a quarterback in a single-season, 2011; being the first player in NFL history to pass for more than 4,000 yards and rush for more than 500 yards, 2011; having the most combined yards in Carolina Panthers history; having the the most consecutive seasons with 3,000 yards passing, 2011-14; numerous other NFL and Carolina Panthers records and achievements

NEWTON, WAYNE, T: Entertainer, Actor, Recording Industry Executive **I:** Media & Entertainment **DOB:** 04/03/1942 **PB:** Norfolk **PT:** Son of Patrick and Evelyn (Smith) N.; Married Elaine Okamura, June 1, 1968 (div. 1985); 1 adopted child, Erin; Married Kathleen McCrone, April 9, 1994; 1 child, Lauren Ashley. **ED:** Doctorate (hon.), William Woods University; LHD (hon.), University Nev.-Las Vegas, 1981 **C:** Owner, Tamiment International Resort **CIV:** Supporter St. John's Indian Mission, Levene, Arizona chairman United Service Organizations Celebrity Cir. member Patawomeck Indian Tribe, Virginia **CW:** Appearances include Sands, Caesar's Palace, Desert Inn, Flamingo and Frontier hotels, Las Vegas, Harrah's Club, Reno and Lake Tahoe, I Love New York Concert, Americana Hotel, New York City, Talk of the Town, London, London Palladium, Grand Ole Oprey House, Nashville, 4th of July, Washington, Astrodome, Houston, Hollywood (California) Bowl, Melodyland, Anaheim, California, Circle Star, San Francisco, Sea World, Orlando, Florida, Sherman House, Chicago, Wisconsin State, Iowa State fairs, Valley Forge Music, Westbury Music fairs, Deauville and Eden Roc hotels, Miami Beach, Carlton Club, Bloomington, Minnesota, hotels in Atlantic City, New Jersey, before US troops, Vietnam, Beirut, & Persian Gulf; (TV miniseries) North and South: Book II, 1986; (TV spls.) Opryland, 1973, Joys, 1976, Happy Birthday, Las Vegas, 1977, The Wayne Newton Special, 1982, The Real Las Vegas, 1996, Las Vegas on Ice, 1997, Feed the Children, 1997, Elvis Meets Nixon, 1997, VH1 Divas Las Vegas, 2002; (film appearances) 80 Steps to Jonah, 1969 (also composer), Licence to Kill, 1989, The Adventures of Ford Fairlane, 1990, The Dark Backward, 1991, Best of the Best II, 1993, Night of the Running Man, 1994, Vegas Vacation, 1997, Ocean's Eleven, 2003,

Smokin' Aces, 2006, (voice) Hoodwinked Too! Hood VS. Evil, 2011, 40 West, 2011, Getting Back to Zero, 2013, Sharknado: The 4th Awakens, 2016; video appearances in Who's Your Daddy?, 2003, (voice) Fallout: New Vegas, 2010; host, prodr.: The Entertainer, 2005; (guest appearances) Bonanza, 1966, Here's Lucy, 1968, 1970, Switch, 1976, Vega$, 1979, 1981, The Highwayman, 1988, Full House, 1990, L.A. Law, 1991, Roseanne, 1991, Perfect Strangers, 1992, Renegade, 1994, 1995, Tales from the Crypt, 1994, The Fresh Prince of Bel-Air, 1995, Ellen, 1997, Ally McBeal, 1998, The Pretender, 2000, Las Vegas, 2003-06, My Wife and Kids, 2004, 7th Heaven, 2004, and others; albums include Danke Schoen, 1963, In Person!, 1964, Wayne Newton in Person!, 1964, Summer Wind, 1965, Red Roses for a Blue Lady, 1965, Now!, 1966, It's Only the Good Times, 1967, Old Rugged Cross, 1966, One More Time, 1968, Walking on New Grass, 1968, Can't You Hear the Song?, 1972, Change of Heart, 1978, Daddy Don't You Walk So Fast, 1972, Coming Home, 1989, God Is Alive, 1991, Showstoppers, 1992, Rock of Ages, 1992, A Merry Little Christmas, 1992, Moods & Moments, 1992, Christmas Song, 1995, Branson City Limits, 1998, Real Thing, 2004, Song of the Year: Wayne Newton Style, Tomorrow; author (with Dick Maurice): Once Before I Go, 1989; performer Dancing With the Stars, 2007. **AW:** Recipient citation as distinguished recording artist and humanitarian, 1971; Freedom Lantern award Commonwealth of Massachusetts, 1979, Entertainer of Year award Variety Clubs Southern Nevada, 1973, Gov.'s award Commonwealth of Massachusetts, 1976, cert. of appreciation Governor of Nevada, 1978, Founders award St. Judes Children's Hospital, Humanitarian award Am. Cancer Society Cancer Research Center, Lifetime Achievement award, First Am. in the Arts, 2000, Congl. medal, Honor Society Citizenship award, medal of honor, Department Defense, US Legion of Valor's Citizen award, Jimmie E. Howard Memorial award, Medal of Honor, City Las Vegas, Ellis Island Medal of Honor, 1999, American Legend award, Washington, DC, 1999, VFW Hall of Fame award, Am. Legion Exceptional Citizen award, star on the Hollywood Walk of Fame, award for Daddy Don't Walk So Fast American Society of Composers, platinum record for Danke Schoen, also gold album and gold records; named one of 10 Outstanding Young Men of Am. National Jaycees, 1976; named Most Distinguished Citizen of Year National Conference of Christians and Jews, Outstanding Indian Entertainer of Year Navajo Nation, 1980, Entertainer of Year, Nevada Magazine, Casino Player Magazine, 1999, Top Three Entertainers of the Century in Nevada and Around the World, Reno Gazette Journal, Ambassador Goodwill, State of Nev, Veteran Foreign Wars of US, Hon. Vietnam Veteran, Hon. Green Beret, 1999; knighted; 1998; renamed in his honor Las Vegas' McCarran International Airport main thouroghfare Wayne Newton Blvd.; inducted Gaming Hall of Fame, Am. Gaming Association

NÉZET-SÉGUIN, YANNICK, T: Director of the Philadelphia Orchestra **I:** Media & Entertainment **C:** Music Director Designate, Metropolitan Opera, 2017-; Music director, The Philadelphia Orchestra, 2012-; Music director, Rotterdam Philharmonic Orchestra, 2008-; Principal guest conductor, London Philharmonic Orchestra, 2008-; Artistic director, principal conductor, Orchestre Métropolitain du Grand Montréal, 2000-; Music director designate, The Philadelphia Orchestra, 2010-12 **CW:** Conductor Nino Roto, 2003, Mahler 4, 2004, Flemish Connexion Vol. 5, 2004, Camille Saint-Saens, Symphony No. 3, 2006, Weill Rota, 2006, Bruckner 7, 2007, La Mer Debussy Britten Mercure, 2007, Pierre LaPointe en Concert Dans La Foret

des Mal-Aimés Avec L'Orchestre Métropolitain de Grand Montréal Dirige par Yanick-Nézet-Séguin, 2007, Beethoven Symphony No. 3 'Eroica - Strauss Death and Configuration, 2008, Bruckner 9, 2008, Charles Gounod Roméo et Juliette, 2009, Beethoven, Korngold Violin Concertos, 2009, Bruckner 8, 2009, Ravel, 2009, Fantasy - A Night at the Opera, 2010, Tenor Arias, 2010, Brahms - A German Requiem, 2010, pianist Conversations, 2003, Arianna a Naxos, 2004, Kurt Weill, 2005 **AW:** Recipient National Arts Center award, Governor General for Performing Arts Awards, 2010, Royal Philharmonic Society award, 2009, Virginia-Parker award, Can. Council, 2000, Prix Opus, Conseil québécois de la musique,Companion of the Order of Canada, 2012,Doctorate honoris causa in music, McGill University, 2017

NGUYEN, JACQUELINE HONG-NGOC, T: Federal Judge **I:** Law and Legal Services **DOB:** 05/25/1965 **PB:** Dalat **SC:** South Vietnam **ED:** JD, UCLA School Law, 1991; AB in English, Occidental College, LA, 1987 **C:** Judge, US Court Appeals (9th Cir.), 2012-; Judge, US District Court (central district) California, L.A., 2009-12; Judge, L.A. County Superior Court, Alhambra, 2002-09; Deputy chief general crimes division, US Department Justice, 2000-02; Assistant US attorney (central district) California, US Department Justice, 1995-2000; Litig. associate, Musick, Peeler & Garrett LLP, L.A., 1991-94 **ACH:** Achievements include recognition as the first Vietnamese-American woman ever appointed to the state of California and the first Vietnarnese American article III judge in the U.S. **BA:** 95 7th St, San Francisco, CA, 94103

NIAKAN, KATHY, T: Developmental Biologist **I:** Sciences **ED:** BSc, Cell and Molecular Biology, University of Washington; PhD, University of California **C:** Group Leader, Francis Crick Institute, 2015-; Group Leader, MRC NIMR, 2013-15 **AW:** Time 100 Most Influential, 2016

NIBLOCK, ROBERT A., T: CEO **I:** Consumer Goods and Services **CN:** Lowe's **SC:** FL/USA **ED:** BA in Accounting, University of North Carolina **C:** Chairman, President, CEO, Lowe's Companies, Inc., Mooresville, NC, 2011-Present; Chairman, CEO, Lowe's Companies, Inc., Mooresville, NC, 2005-2011; President, Lowe's Companies, Inc., Mooresville, NC, 2003-2006; Executive Vice President, CFO, Lowe's Companies, Inc., Mooresville, NC, 2001-2003; Senior Vice President, CFO, Lowe's Companies, Inc., Mooresville, NC, 2000-2001; Senior Vice President of Finance, Lowe's Companies, Inc., Mooresville, NC, 1999-2000; Vice President, Treasurer, Lowe's Companies, Inc., Mooresville, NC, 1997-1999; Accountant, Ernst & Young LLP, 1986-1993; Senior Director of Tax, Lowe's Companies, Inc., Mooresville, NC; Director of Tax, Lowe's Companies, Inc., Mooresville, NC **CR:** Board of Directors, ConocoPhillips, 2010-Present, Board of Directors, Lowe's Companies Inc., 2004-Present, Chairman, Retail Industry Leaders Association, 2008-2009, Vice Chairman, Retail Industry Leaders Association, 2006-2007 **BA:** Lowe's Headquarters, 1000 Lowe's Boulevard, Mooresville, NC, 28117

NICHOLAS, HENRY THOMPSON III, T: Philanthropist **I:** Nonprofit & Philanthropy **PB:** Cincinnati **SC:** OH/USA **ED:** PhD in EE, UCLA; MSEE, UCLA; BSEE, UCLA **C:** Co-founder, president, CEO, Broadcom Corp., Irvine, California, 1991-2003; Director microelectronics, PairGain Techs.,; With, TRW, **AW:** Named one of Forbes 400: Richest Americans, 2006-, World's Top Cyber Elite, 1997 Time Digital Magazine, 1997, Top 20 Entrepreneurs, 1997 Red Herring, 1997; recipient Entrepreneur of the Year award, Ernst & Young, 1996,UCLA

School of Engineering Alumni Award, **BA:** Henry T Nicholas Foundation, Orange County, CA, 0

NICHOLSON, JACK, T: Actor **I:** Media & Entertainment **DOB:** 04/22/1937 **PB:** Neptune City **SC:** NJ/USA **PT:** John Nicholson, Ethel May Nicholson-TB **SPN:** Sandra Knight, 6/17/1962, Divorced 8/8/1968 **CH:** Jennifer, Lorraine Broussard **CW:** Actor, (Hollywood Stage Production) Tea and Sympathy; Actor, (Films) Cry-Baby Killer, 1958, Studs Lonigen, 1960, The Little Shop of Horrors, 1960, Ensign Pulver, 1964, The Trip, 1967, Easy Rider, 1969, Five Easy Pieces, 1970, Carnal Knowledge, 1971, A Safe Place, 1971, The Last Detail, 1974, Chinatown, 1974, Tommy, The Passenger, 1975, The Fortune, 1975, One Flew Over the Cuckoo's Nest, 1975, The Missouri Breaks, 1976, The Last Tycoon, 1976, The Shining, 1980, The Postman Always Rings Twice, 1981, Reds, 1981, The Border, 1982, Terms of Endearment, 1983, Prizzi's Honor, 1985, Heartburn, 1986, The Witches of Eastwick, 1987, Broadcast News, 1987, Ironweed, 1987, Batman, 1989, Man Trouble, 1991, A Few Good Men, 1992, Hoffa, 1992, Wolf, 1994, The Crossing Guard, 1995, Mars Attacks!, 1996, The Evening Star, 1996, Blood and Wine, 1996, As Good As It Gets, 1997, The Pledge, 2001, About Schmidt, 2002, Anger Management, 2003, Something's Gotta Give, 2003, The Departed, 2006, The Bucket List, 2007, How Do You Know, 2010; Producer, (Films) Ride the Whirlwind, 1965, The Shooting, 1966, Head, 1968; Director, Drive, He Said, 1971; Actor, Director, (films) Goin' South, 1978, The Two Jakes, 1990 **AW:** New Jersey Hall of Fame, 2010, California Hall of Fame, 2008, MTV Movie Award for Best Villain, The Departed, 2007, Golden Globe Award for Best Actor, About Schmidt, 2003, Cecil B. DeMille Award, American Film Institute, 1999, Academy Award for Best Actor, Golden Globe Award for Best Actor, Screen Actors Guild Award for Best Actor, As Good As It Gets, 1998, Life Achievement Award, 1994, Co-Recipient, (With Bobby McFerrin) Grammy Award for Best Recording for Children, 1987, Academy Award for Best Supporting Actor, Golden Globe Award for Best Actor, Terms of Endearment, 1984, BAFTA Award for Best Supporting Actor, Reds, 1983, BAFTA Award for Best Actor, One Flew Over the Cuckoo's Nest, 1977, Golden Globe Award for Best Actor, One Flew Over the Cuckoo's Nest, 1976, Academy Award for Best Actor, New York Film Critics Circle Award for Best Actor, One Flew Over the Cuckoo's Nest, 1975, BAFTA Award for Best Actor, The Last Detail, 1975, BAFTA Award for Best Actor, Golden Globe Award for Best Actor, New York Film Critics Circle Award for Best Actor, Chinatown, 1974 **BA:** c/o Bresler Kelly & Associates, 11500 W Olympic Boulevard, Suite 510, Los Angeles, CA, 90064-1578

NICKLAUS, JACK WILLIAM, T: Sports Apparel Executive, Professional Golfer (Retired) **I:** Retail/Sales **DOB:** 01/21/1940 **PB:** Columbus **SC:** OH/USA **PT:** Son of Louis Charles, Junior and Helen (Schoener) N. **MS:** Married **SPN:** Barbara Bash, July 23, 1960; **CH:** Jack William II, Steven Charles, Nancy Jean, Gary Thomas, Michael Scott **ED:** LLD (hon.), University of St. Andrews, 1984; Doctor of Athletic arts (hon.), The Ohio State University, 1972; Student, The Ohio State University, 1957-62 **C:** Owner, Nicklaus Golf Equipment Co.,; Partner, Nicklaus Design,; Chairman, CEO, Golden Bear International, Inc., **CR:** Player U.S. Ryder Cup Team, 1987, 1983, 1981, 1977, 1975, 1973, 1971, 1969 **CIV:** Chairman Ohio division Am. Cancer Society, 1967 chairman sports division National Easter Seal Society, 1967. **CW:** Author: My 55 Ways to Lower Your Golf Score, 1964, Take a Tip From Me, 1968, The Greatest Game of All, 1969, Jack Nicklaus' Lesson Tee, 1972, Golf My Way, 1974,

Jack Nicklaus' Playing Lessons, 1976, On and Off the Fairway, 1978, Play Better Golf, Vols. 1-3, 1980, 81, 83, The Full Swing, 1982, My Most Memorable Shots in the Majors, 1988. **AW:** Recipient Byron Nelson award, 1964, 65, 72, 73, Bob Jones award, 1975, Presidential Medal of Freedom, The White House, 2005, Congressional Gold Medal, 2012; named PGA Player of Year, 1967, 72, 73, 75, 76, Dunlop Professional Athlete of Year, 1972, Golfer of Year Professional Golfers Association, 1973, Sportsman of Year, Sports Illus. magazine, 1978, Athlete of the Decade for 1970-79, 1979, Golfer of the '70s, 1979, Golfer of the Century, 1988; named to World Golf Hall of Fame, 1974; named one of Most Influential People in the World of Sports, 2008,Payne Stewart Award, 2000, PGA Tour Lifetime Achievement Award, 2008, Congressional Gold Medal, 2015, **MEM:** Member President's Club Ohio State University, Phi Gamma Delta. **ACH:** Achievements include playing on over 105 golf courses on 5 continents, 12 ranked in US Top 100; hosted 185 professional tournaments 1973-; won 73 official tournaments; major tournaments won include Tournament of Champions, 1963, 64, 71, 73, 77, US Amateur, 1959, 61, US Open, 1962, 67, 72, 80, US Masters, 1963, 65, 66, 72, 75, 86, Brit. Open, 1966, 70, 78, PGA Championship, 1963, 71, 73, 75, 80, International Pro-Amateur, 1973, Tournament Players Championship, 1974, 76, 78, Australian Open, 1964, 68, 71, 75, 76, 78, World Series of Golf, 1962, 63, 67, 70, 76, PGA Seniors Championship, 1991, US Senior Open, 1991, 93.

NIELSEN, KIRSTJEN M., **T:** U.S. Secretary of Homeland Security **I:** Government Administration/ Government Relations/Government Services **PB:** Clearwater **SC:** FL/USA **ED:** B.A., Georgetown School of Foreign Service; J.D. University of Virginia School of Law, 1999 **C:** Secretary, Homeland Security, 2017-; Principal Deputy Chief of Staff, White House, 2017; Chief of Staff, To the Secretary of Homeland Security, 2017

NIEMEYER, PAUL VICTOR, **T:** Federal Judge **I:** Law and Legal Services **DOB:** 04/05/1941 **PB:** Princeton **SC:** NJ/USA **PT:** Son of Gerhart and Lucie (Lenzer) Niemeyer **ED:** JD, University Notre Dame, 1966; Student, University Munich, Federal Republic of Germany, 1962-63; AB, Kenyon College, 1962 **C:** Cir. Judge, US Court Appeals (4th cir.), Baltimore, 1990-; US District Judge, US District Court Maryland, Baltimore, 1988-90; Partner, Piper & Marbury, 1974-88; Associate, Piper & Marbury, Baltimore, 1966-74 **CR:** Chairman, 1996-2000, adv. committee on Federal Rules of Civil Procedure, 1993-2000, select com.-profl. conduct, 1983-85, attorney grievance com.-hearing panel, 1978-81, member standing committee on rules of practice and procedure courts appeals, 1973-88, senior lecturing fellow in appellate advocacy Duke University School of Law, 1994-, lecturer Maryland Court Clerks Association, Maryland Judicial Conference lecturer advanced business law Johns Hopkins University, Baltimore, 1971-75 **CW:** Author: (book) A Path Remembered, 2006; Co-author: Maryland Rules Commentary, 1984, 3d. edition, 2003, Maryland Rules Commentary supplement, 1988; Contributor, Articles to Professional Journals **AW:** Recipient Special Merit Citation, Am. Judicature Society, 1987 **MEM:** Fellow: Am. Law Institute, Maryland Bar Association (Distinguished Service Award Litigation Section 1981), Maryland Bar Foundation, Am. Bar Foundation, Am. College Trial Lawyers; Mem.: Lawyers' Round Table, Wednesday Law Club **BAR:** Bar: US Court Appeals (3d cir.) 1980, US Court Appeals (5th cir.) 1978, US District Court (so. district) Texas 1977, US Supreme Court 1970, US Court Appeals (4th cir.) 1968, US District Court Maryland 1967, Maryland

1966 **PA:** Republican **BA:** 1100 E Main St #501, Richmond, VA, 23219

NIMBLEY, THOMAS, **T:** CEO **I:** Oil & Energy **CN:** PBF Energy **ED:** Student, Manhattan College **C:** Chairman/CEO, PBF Logistics LP, 2016-Present; Chief Executive Officer, PBF Logistics GP LLC, 2013-Present; Chief Executive Officer, PBF Energy Inc., 2010-Present; Chief Executive Officer, PBF Energy Co. LLC, 2010-Present; Chief Executive Officer, PBF Holding Co. LLC, 2010-Present; Chief Executive Officer, PBF Logistics LP, 2013-2016; Executive Vice President/COOPBF Energy Co LLC, 2010; Principal, Nimbley Consultants LLC, 2005-2010

NIXON, CYNTHIA, **T:** Actress **I:** Media & Entertainment **DOB:** 04/09/1966 **PB:** New York **SC:** NY/USA **PT:** Walter Nixon, Anne Nixon **SPN:** Christine Marinoni, 5/27/2012; Danny Mozes **CH:** Samantha, Charles Ezekiel, Max Ellington Nixon-Marinoni **ED:** BA in English, Barnard College, 1988 **C:** Founding Member, The Drama Department, 1996; Actress, 1980-Present **CR:** Gubernatorial Candidate, Governor of New York, 2018 **CW:** Actress, (Plays) The Philadelphia Story, 1980, The Real Thing, 1984, Hurly Burly, 1984, Indiscretions, 1996, Rabbit Hole, 2006, The Prime Of Miss Jean Brodie, 2006, Wit, 2011, The Little Foxes, 2017, (Films) Little Darlings, 1980, Prince Of The City, 1981, Tattoo, 1981, I Am The Cheese, 1983, Amadeus, 1984, The Manhattan Project, 1986, O.C. And Stiggs, 1987, Let It Ride, 1989, Through An Open Window, 1992, The Pelican Brief, 1993, Addams Family Values, 1993, Baby's Day Out, 1994, The Cottonwood, 1996, 'M' Word, 1996, Marvin's Room, 1996, Advice From A Caterpillar, 1999, The Out-Of-Towners, 1999, Igby Goes Down, 2002, The Paper Mache Chase, 2003, Sex And The City: The Movie, 2008, Lymelife, 2008, An Englishman In New York, 2009, Sex And The City 2, 2010, Rampart, 2011, 5 Flights Up, 2014, Stockholm, Pennsylvania, 2015, James White, 2015, The Adderall Diaries, 2015, A Quiet Passion, 2016, The Only Living Boy In New York, 2017, (TV Series) Sex And The City, 1998-2004, The Big C, 2010-2011, Law And Order: Criminal Intent, 2011, World Without End, 2012, 30 Rock, 2012, Alpha House, 2013, Alpha House, 2013-2014, Hannibal, 2014, The Affair, 2015, Broad City, 2016, Killing Reagan, 2016, (TV Miniseries) Tanner '88, 1988, (TV Films) The Seven Wishes Of A Rich Kid, 1979, The Private History Of A Campaign That Failed, 1981, Rascals And Robbers: The Secret Adventures Of Tom Sawyer And Huck Finn, 1982, My Body, My Child, 1982, Fifth Of July, 1982, The Murder Of Mary Phagan, 1988, Women & Wallace, 1990, Love She Sought, The, 1990, Face Of A Stranger, 1991, Love, Lies And Murder, 1991, Kiss-Kiss, Dahlings!, 1992, Sex And The Matrix, 2000, Papa's Angels, 2000, Stage On Screen: The Women, 2002, Tanner On Tanner, 2004, Warm Springs, 2005, Too Big To Fail, 2011 **AW:** Theatre World Award, The Philadelphia Story, 1981, Emmy Award For Outstanding Supporting Actress In A Comedy Series, Sex And The City, 2004, Tony Award For Best Performance By A Leading Actress In A Play, Indiscretions, 2006, Tony for Best Spoken Word Album, An Inconvenient Truth, 2009, Tony Award For Featured Actress In A Play, The Little Foxes, 2017 **BA:** c/o William Morris Agency, One William Morris Place, Beverly Hills, CA, 90212

NOAH, TREVOR, **T:** Television Personality, Comedian **I:** Media & Entertainment **PB:** Johannesburg **SC:** South Africa **PT:** Robert Noah; Patricia Nombuyiselo Noah **C:** Host, The Daily Show with Trevor Noah, 2015-; Contributor, The

Daily Show with Jon Stewart, 2014-15 **CW:** Writer, executive producer, personality (documentaries) Trevor Noah: The Daywalker, 2009, Trevor Noah: Crazy Normal, 2011, (TV specials) Trevor Noah: African American, 2013, Trevor Noah: It's My Culture, 2013, Trevor Noah: Nationwild Comedy Tour, 2015, The Daily Show with Trevor Noah, 2015, Trevor Noah: Lost in Translation, 2015, Trevor Noah: Afraid of the Dark, 2017, Nashville, 2017, The Opposition with Jordan Klepper, 2017; actor: (films) Taka Takata, 2011, Mad Buddies, 2012 **ACH:** Achievements include becoming the first South African stand-up comedian to appear on The Tonight Show, 2013; becoming the first South African comedian to appear on Late Show with David Letterman, 2013

NOEM, KRISTI LYNN, **T:** U.S. Representative from South Dakota **I:** Government Administration/Government Relations/Government Services **DOB:** 11/30/1971 **PB:** Hamlin County, South Dakota, November 30, 1971 **PT:** Daughter of Ron and Corinne (Bergan) Arnold; **ED:** BA in Political Sci., South Dakota State University, 2012; Attended, Mount Marty College, Watertown, South Dakota; Attended, Northern State University, Aberdeen, South Dakota, 1990-92 **C:** Member, US House Armed Services Committee, 2013-; Member, Committee on Ways and Means; Member, US House Agricultural Committee, 2011-; Member at-large, US Congress from South Dakota, Washington, 2011-; Member, US House Natural Resources Committee, Washington, 2011-12; Member, US House Education & the Workforce, Washington, 2011-12; Assistant majority leader, South Dakota House of Representatives, 2009-10; Member District 6, South Dakota House of Representatives, 2006-10; Partial owner, Racota Valley Ranch, Hazel, South Dakota, **AW:** Named an South Dakota Outstanding Young Farmer, 2007; named one of Heroes on the Hill, Indian Country Today Media Network, 2011, The Politics 40 Under 40, TIME Magazine, 2010, The 50 Politicos to Watch, Politico, 2010 **PA:** Republican

NOHRIA, NITIN, **T:** Dean **I:** Education/Educational Services **CN:** Harvard Business School **ED:** PhD in Management, Massachusetts Institute of Technology, 1988; BSChemE, Indian Institute of Technology, Bombay, India, 1984 **C:** Dean, Harvard Business School, 2010-Present; Co-Chair, Leadership Initiative, Harvard Business School, 2009-Present; Richard P. Chapman Professor of Business Administration, Harvard Business School, 1999-Present; Senior Associate Dean, Faculty Development, Harvard Business School, 2006-2009; Director, Research Division, Harvard Business School, 2003-2004; Chair, Organizational Behavior Unit, Harvard Business School, 1998-2002; Associate Professor, Harvard Business School, 1993-1999; Assistant Professor, Harvard Business School, Boston, MA, 1988-1993 **CR:** Co-Founder, The Smart Manager, 2002; Visiting Faculty, London Business School, 1996 **CW:** Co-Author, (Books) Beyond the Hype: Rediscovering the Essence of Management, 1992, Building the Information-Age Organization: Structure, Control, and Information Technologies, 1994, The Best Ideas on Managing Business Change, 1996, The Differentiated Network: Organizations Knowledge Flows in Multinational Corporations, 1997, The Arc of Ambition: Defining the Leadership Journey, 2000, Driven: How Human Nature Shapes Our Choices, 2001, Master Passions: The Interplay of Anxiety, Ambition, and Envy, 2002, Changing Fortunes: The Rise and Fall of the Industrial Corporation, 2002, What Really Works: The 4+2 Formula for Sustained Business Success, 2003, In Their Time: The Greatest Business Leaders of the 20th Century,

2005, Paths to Power: How Insiders and Outsiders Shaped American Business Leadership, 2006, Entrepreneurs, Managers, and Leaders: What the Airline Industry Can Teach Us About Leadership, 2009; Co-Editor, (Books) Networks and Organizations: Structure, Form, and Action, 1992, Breaking the Code of Change, 2000, Handbook of Leadership and Theory Practice, 2010; Author, The Portable MBA Desk Reference, 1998; Contributor, Articles, Professional Journals **AW:** Distinguished Alumnus Medai, indian institute of Technology, 2007 **BA:** Harvard Business School, Morgan Hall, Room 339, 15 Harvard Way, Boston, MA, 2163

NOLAN, CHRISTOPHER, T: Film Director, Producer, Writer **I:** Media & Entertainment **PB:** London **SC:** England **PT:** Brendan Nolan; Christina (Jensen) Nolan **ED:** Attended, University College London **C:** Co-founder, Syncopy Films **CW:** (Director, writer): (films) Doodlebug, 1997; Memento, 2000; Batman Begins, 2005; (director, writer, cinematographer, editor, producer) Following, 1998; dir.: Insomnia, 2002; director, writer, producer (films) The Prestige, 2006, The Dark Knight, 2008, Inception, 2010 (Best Original Screenplay, Writers Guild Awards, 2011), The Dark Knight Rises, 2012, Interstellar, 2014, Quay, 2015, Dunkirk, 2017, writer, producer Man of Steel, 2013; prodr.: (films) Transcendence, 2014

NOLAN, RICK, T: U.S. Representative from Minnesota **I:** Government Administration/Government Relations/Government Services **DOB:** 12/17/1943 **PB:** Brainerd **ED:** Postgraduate studies, St. Cloud State College; BA, University Minnesota, 1966; Attended, St. John's University, 1962 **C:** Member, US House Transportation & Infrastructure Committee, 2013-; Member, US House Agricultural Committee, 2013-; Member, US Congress from 8th Minnesota District, Washington, 2013-; President, Minnesota World Trade Center, Minnesota, 1986-94; President, US Export Corp., 1981-86; Chairman, DRAFT Kennedy President Committee, 1979-80; Member, Presidential Commission on World Hunger, 1978-80; Member, US Congress from 6th Minnesota District, Washington, 1975-81; Member District 53A, Minnesota House of Reps., 1969-73; Social studies teacher, Royalton, Minnesota, 1968-72; Staff assistant to Senator Walter Mondale, US Senate,; Sawmill operator, Emily, Minnesota, **PA:** Dfl **BA:** 2366 Rayburn House Office Building, Washington, DC, 20515

NOOYI, INDRA KRISHNAMURTHY, T: CEO **I:** Business Management/Business Services **CN:** Pepsi **DOB:** 10/28/1955 **PB:** Chennai **SC:** India **ED:** MA in Public & Private Management, Yale University, New Haven, 1980; MBA, Indian Institute Management, Calcutta, 1978; BS in Commerce, Madras Christian College, India, 1976 **C:** Chairwoman, Board of Directors, 2007-2019; CEO, PepsiCo, Inc., Purchase, New York, 2007-2018; CEO, PepsiCo, Inc., Purchase, New York, 2006-07;; President, CFO, PepsiCo, Inc., Purchase, New York, 2001-06;; Senior Vice President, CFO, PepsiCo, Inc., Purchase, New York, 2000-01; Senior Vice President, Strategic Planning, PepsiCo, Inc., Purchase, New York, 1994-2000; Senior Vice President, Strategic Planning and Strategic Marketing, Asea Brown Boveri, 1990-94; Vice president, Director, Corporate Strategy & Planning, Motorola, Inc., 1986-90; Director, International Corp. Strategy Projects, Boston Consultant Group, 1980-86;; Product manager, Mettur Beardsell, Ltd., India;; Product manager, Johnson & Johnson, India **CR:** Appointed Member US-India CEO Forum, 2009-, Successor Fellow, Yale Corp., 2002-, Board of Directors, Grocery Manufacturers Association, Consumer Goods Forum, US-India Business

Council, US-China Business Council, Catalyst Inc., Motorola Solutions, Inc., 2002-07, PepsiCo, Inc., 2001- **CIV:** Board of Directors, US Soccer Federation, Board of Directors, Peterson Institute International Economics, Washington, Board of Directors, Lincoln Center Performing Arts, New York City **AW:** Named a Power Player, Advertising Age, 2009; Named CEO of Year, Global Supply Chain Leaders Group, 2009; Named an Outstanding American of Choice, US Department State, 2007; Named one of The 50 Most Powerful Women in New York, Crain's New York Business, 2011, Crain's New York Business, 2009, America's Best Leaders, US News & World Report, 2008, The 50 Who Matter Now, Business 2.0, 2007, The 100 Most Influential People in the World, TIME magazine, 2007, The 50 Most Powerful Women in Business, Fortune magazine, 2006-15, The 100 Most Powerful Women, Forbes magazine, 2005-14, The 50 Women to Watch, The Wall St. Journal, 2008, 2006, 2005; Recipient, Padma Bhushan award, Government of India, 2007 **MEM:** Fellow: American Academy Arts & Sciences **H:** Guitar

NORCROSS, DONALD, T: United State Representative from New Jersey **I:** Government Administration/Government Relations/Government Services **ED:** AS in Criminal Justice, Camden County College, New Jersey **C:** Member, U.S. House of Representatives from New Jersey's 1st District, 2015-; Vice chair transportation committee, New Jersey State Senate, 2010-2015; Vice chair law and pub. safety committee, New Jersey State Senate, 2010-; Member District 5, New Jersey State Senate, 2010-; Member District 5, New Jersey General Assembly, 2010; President, South Jersey AFL-CIO Central Labor Council,; Assistant business manager, IBEW Local 351, **CIV:** Member executive board, United Way, **PA:** Democrat

NORMAN, GREGORY JOHN, T: Professional Golfer **I:** Athletics **DOB:** 02/10/1955 **PB:** Mount Isa **SC:** Australia **C:** Professional Golfer, PGA Tour, 1983-; Professional Golfer, 1976-; Chairman, CEO, Great White Shark Enterprises Inc., Hobe Sound, Florida, **CR:** Captain International Team Presidents Cup, 2009, Member International Team, 2000, 1998, 1996 Member National Team Four Tours, 1989, Kirin Cup, 1987, Dunhill Cup, 1994-96, 1992, 1985-90, Nissan Cup, 1985-86, Hennessy Cognac Cup, 1982, World Cup, 1978, 1976 **AW:** Winner Brit. Open Championship, 1986, 93, 20 PGA Tour Titles, 68 Additional International Titles; Winner Vardon Trophy, 1989, 90, 94; Recipient Arnold Palmer Award for Leading Money Winner, 1995, Byron Nelson Trophy for the Lowest Scoring Average, 1995; Ranked #1 in World Golf Ranking for 331 Weeks; Named PGA Player of Year, 1995, PGA Tour Player of Year, 1995; Named to World Golf Hall of Fame, 2001, Winner of the 2001 Skins Game, **ACH:** Achievements include being the leading Money Winner PGA Tour 1986, 90. **BA:** Great White Shark Enterprises Inc, 2041 Vista Pkwy Ste Level, West Palm Beach, FL, 33411-6758

NORMAN, RALPH W., T: U.S. Representative from South Carolina **I:** Government Administration/Government Relations/Government Services **DOB:** 06/20/1953 **PB:** Rock Hill **ED:** BS, Presbyterian College, 1973 **C:** Member, U.S. House of Representatives from South Carolina's 5th District, 2017-,; Member, Committee on Science, Space and Technology, Committee on Small Business; Member District 48, South Carolina House of Reps., 2009-17; Member, South Carolina House of Reps., 2004-06 **CIV:** Board visitors, Medical Univ. of South Carolina, **MEM:** Mem.: Young Men's Christian Association (board directors) **BA:** 2350 Rayburn HOB, Washington, DC, 20515

NORQUIST, GROVER GLENN, T: Founder and President of Americans for Tax Reform **I:** Financial Services **DOB:** 10/19/1956 **PB:** Sharon **SC:** PA/USA **PT:** Son of Warren Elliott and Carol (Lutz) Norquist; **ED:** MBA, Harvard University, 1981; BA, Harvard University, 1978 **C:** Founder, president, Americans for Tax Reform, Washington, 1985-; Field director, Citizens for America, Washington, 1985; Chief speechwriter, U.S. C. of C., Washington, 1983-85; Executive director, Americans for Reagan Agenda, Washington, 1982-83; Executive director, College Rep. National Committee, Washington, 1981-82; Executive director, National Taxpayers Union, Washington, 1978-79 **CR:** Chairman emeritus Islamic Free Market Institute member Small Business Survival Committee, 1994 speech writer presidential campaigns, 1988, 1987 economic adv. UNITA, Angola, 1985-88 **CW:** Author: Rock the House, 1995, Leave Us Alone: Getting the Government's Hands Off Our Money, Our Guns, Our Lives, 2008, Debacle: Obama's War on Jobs and Growth and What Can We Do Right Now to Regain our Future, 2012; political columnist Am. Spectator magazine, 1992- **AW:** Named one of The 25 Most Influential Republicans, Newsmax Magazine, 2008, The 50 Most Powerful People in DC, GQ magazine, 2007 **MEM:** Mem.: National Rifle Association (board directors), Am. Society Competitiveness (president), Am. Conservative Union (board directors) **PA:** Republican **BA:** 722 12th ST NW, Suite 400, Washington, DC, 20005

NORTHAM, RALPH SHEARER, T: Governor of Virginia, former Lieutenant Governor of Virginia, former state legislator **I:** Government Administration/Government Relations/Government Services **DOB:** 09/13/1959 **PB:** Nassawadox **PT:** Son of Wescott B. and Nancy B. (Shearer) Northam; **ED:** MD, Eastern Virginia Medical School, 1984; BS, Virginia Military Institute, 1981 **C:** Governor, Commonwealth of Virginia, Richmond, 2018-; Lieutenant governor, Commonwealth of Virginia, Richmond, 2014-2018; Pediatric neurologist, Children's Hospital of the King's Daughters, 1992-; Member District 6, Virginia State Senate, 2008-14; Resident, Brooke Army Medical Center,; Assistant professor neurology, Eastern Virginia Medical School,; Major, US Army, **PA:** Democrat

NORTON, EDWARD, T: Actor **I:** Media & Entertainment **DOB:** 08/18/1969 **PB:** Boston **SC:** MA/USA **PT:** Edward Norton, Robin Norton **ED:** BA in History, Yale University, 1991 **CR:** President Barack Obama's Committee on Arts and Humanities, 2009 **CIV:** UN Goodwill Ambassador for Biodiversity, 2010-Present, President, American Branch, Maasai Wilderness Conservation Trust, Board of Trustees, Enterprise Community Partners **CW:** Actor, (Films) Everyone Says I Love You, 1996, Primal Fear, 1996, The People Versus Larry Flynt, 1996, Rounders, 1998, American History X, 1998, Fight Club, 1999, The Score, 2001, Death To Smoochy, 2002, Red Dragon, 2002, Frida, 2002, The Italian Job, 2003, Kingdom Of Heaven, 2005, Pride And Glory, 2008, Leaves Of Grass, 2009, Stone, 2010, Moonrise Kingdom, 2012, The Bourne Legacy, 2012, The Grand Budapest Hotel, 2014, Birdman Or (The Unexpected Virtue Of Ignorance), 2014, Little Door Gods, 2016, Sausage Party, 2016, Collateral Beauty, 2016, Isle Of Dogs, 2018; Actor, Co-Producer, 25th Hour, 2002; Director, Producer, (Films) Keeping The Faith, 2000; Executive Producer, (Films) Dirty Work, 2004; Actor, Writer, (Films) The Incredible Hulk, 2008; Actor, Producer, Leaves Of Grass, 2009; Executive Producer, (Films) Thanks For Sharing, 2012, (Documentary) My Own Man, 2014; Featured, (Documentary) Salinger, 2013, (Television) The Simpsons, 2000-2013, Modern Family, 2009, SNL, 2013, Stella, 2015, Last Week

Tonight With John Oliver, 2015 **AW:** National Board Review Award For Best Supporting Actor, Birdman Or (The Unexpected Virtue Of Ignorance), 2014, Golden Globe Award For Best Performance By An Actor In A Supporting Role In A Motion Picture, National Board Review Award For Best Supporting Actor, Primal Fear, 1996 **BA:** c/o Brian Swardstrom Endeavor Talent Agency, 9601 Wilshire Boulevard, Floor 3, Beverly Hills, CA, 90210

NORTON, ELEANOR HOLMES, T: Delegate to the U.S. House of Representatives **I:** Government Administration/Government Relations/Government Services **DOB:** 06/13/1937 **PB:** Washington, DC **SC:** DC/USA **PT:** Coleman Holmes; Vela (Lynch) Holmes **ED:** LLB, Yale University (1964); MA in American Studies, Yale University (1963); BA, Antioch College, Ohio (1960) **C:** Delegate at Large, US Congress from Washington, DC (1990-Present); Professor of Law, Georgetown University, Washington, DC (1982-Present); Member, Committees on Government Reform and Transparencies/Infrastructure, US Congress from Washington, DC; Senior Fellow, Urban Institute, Washington, DC (1981-1982); Chairman, Equal Employment Opportunity Commission, Washington, DC (1977-1981); Chairman, New York City Commission on Human Rights (1970-1977); Executive Assistant to Mayor, City of New York, NY (1971-1974); Assistant Legal Director, ACLU (1965-1970); Law Clerk to Judge A. Leon Higgonbotham, Federal District Court (1964-1965) **AW:** Named One of the 100 Most Powerful Women in D.C., Washingtonian Magazine (2009); Named One of the 100 Most Influential Black Americans, Ebony Magazine (2006); Named to Power 150, Ebony Magazine (2008) **BAR:** Supreme Court of the U.S. (1968); Pennsylvania Bar Association (1965) **PA:** Democrat **BA:** 2136 Rayburn HOB, Washington, DC, 20515

NOVAKOVIC, PHEBE N., T: General Dynamics CEO **I:** Business Management/Business Services **ED:** MBA in Strategic Planning & Finance, Wharton School, University of Pennsylvania, 1988; BS, Smith College, Northampton, Massachusetts, 1979 **C:** Chairman, CEO, General Dynamics Corp., 2013-; President, COO, General Dynamics Corp., 2012; Executive vice president marine systems, General Dynamics Corp., 2010-12; Senior vice president, planning & devel., General Dynamics Corp., 2005-10; Vice president strategic planning, General Dynamics Corp., 2002-05; Director strategic planning & devel., General Dynamics Corp., Falls Church, Virginia, 2001-02; Special assistant to secretary & deputy secretary, U.S. Department Defense, Washington, DC 1997-2001; Deputy associate director, Office Management & Budget, Executive Office of the President, Washington, DC 1992-97 **CR:** Board of directors General Dynamics Corp., 2013-, Abbott Laboratories, 2010- **AW:** Named one of The 100 Most Powerful Women, Forbes magazine, 2013-14, The 50 Most Powerful Women in Business, Fortune magazine, 2010-15

NOWITZKI, DIRK WERNER, T: Professional Basketball Player **I:** Athletics **DOB:** 06/19/1978 **PB:** Würzburg **SC:** West Germany **PT:** Son of Joerg and Helen Nowitzki **C:** Forward, Dallas Mavericks, 1998 **MIL:** Served in German Army, 1997-98 **CW:** Featured in Documentary Nowitzki: The Perfect Shot, 2014 **AW:** Named German Sports Personality of Year, 2011, NBA Finals MVP, 2011, NBA Player of Year, The Sporting News, 2007, NBA MVP, 2007; Named to Western Conference All-Star Team, NBA, 2002-12, All-NBA First Team, 2009, 2005-07, All-NBA Second Team, 2008, 2003, 2002; Recipient, Magic Johnson Award, 2014, NBA Teammate of the Year, 2017, NBA Shooting Stars Champion, 2010, NBA Three-Point Shootout Champion, 2006, 50-40-90

Club, 2007, All-NBA Third Team, 2001, 2004, 2012, All-NBA Second Team, 2002, 2003, 2008, 2010, 2011, All-NBA First Team, 2005-07, 2009, NBA All-Star, 2002-2012, 2014-15, NBA Champion, 2011 **ACH:** Achievements include winner of the NBA All-Star Weekend Three-Point Shootout, 2006; member of the NBA Finals Championship winning Dallas Mavericks, 2011; being the first non-American player to receive the Naismith Legacy award, 2012

NUNES, DEVIN GERALD, T: U.S. Congressman from California **I:** Government Administration/Government Relations/Government Services **DOB:** 10/01/1973 **PB:** Tulare, California **ED:** MS in Agricultural, California Poly. State University, 1996; BS in Agricultural Business, California Poly. State University, 1995 **CT:** Cert. California Agricultural Leadership Fellowship Progressive, 2000 **C:** Chairman, US House Permanent Select Committee on Intelligence, 2015-; Member, US Congress from 22nd California District, 2013-; Member, US Congress from 21st California District, Washington, 2003-13; California State Director, US Department of Agriculture, 2001; Farmer, Manager, Nunes Dairy, 1998-2000 **CIV:** Member Board of Trustees, College Sequoias, 1996-2002 **CW:** Author: Restoring the Republic: A Clear, Concise and Colorful Blueprint for America's Future, 2010 **AW:** Named to The Politics 40 Under 40, TIME Magazine, 2010 **PA:** Republican **BA:** 1013 Longworth House Office Bldg Washington DC 201515, Washington, DC, 20515

OATES, JOYCE CAROL, T: Writer, Retired Educator **I:** Writing and Editing **DOB:** 06/16/1938 **PB:** Lockport **PT:** Daughter of Frederic James and Caroline (Bush) Oates **ED:** MA, University of Wisconsin, Madison, 1961; BA, Syracuse University, New York, 1960 **C:** Roger S. Berlind '52 professor humanities/prof. creative writing, Princeton University, 2008-14; Professor, Princeton University, 1987-2008; Writer-in-residence, Princeton University, New Jersey, 1978-81; Professor English, University of Windsor, Canada, 1967-87; Assistant professor, University of Detroit, 1965-67; Writer, 1963-; Instructor English, University of Detroit, 1961-65 **CW:** Author: (novels) With Shuddering Fall, 1964, A Garden of Earthly Delights, 1967 (M.L. Rosenthal award, National Institute Arts & Letters, 1968), Expensive People, 1968, Them, 1969 (National Book award, 1970), Wonderland, 1971, Do with Me What You Will, 1973, The Assassins: A Book of Hours, 1975, Childwold, 1976, Son of the Morning, 1978, Cybele, 1979, Unholy Loves, 1979, Bellefleur, 1980, Angel of Light, 1981, A Bloodsmoor Romance, 1982, Mysteries of Winterthurn, 1984, Solstice, 1985, Marya: A Life, 1986, You Must Remember This, 1987, American Appetites, 1989, Because It Is Bitter, and Because It Is My Heart, 1990, Foxfire: Confessions of a Girl Gang, 1993, What I Lived For, 1994, Zombie, 1995 (Bram Stoker award, 1996, Fisk Fiction prize, Boston Book Review, 1996), We Were the Mulvaneys, 1996, Man Crazy, 1997, My Heart Laid Bare, 1998, Broke Heart Blues, 1999, Blonde, 2000, Middle Age: A Romance, 2001, I'll Take You There, 2002, The Tattooed Girl, 2003, The Falls, 2004 (Prix Femina Etranger, France, 2005), Missing Mom, 2005, Black Girl / White Girl, 2006, The Gravedigger's Daughter, 2007, My Sister, My Love, 2008, Blonde, 2009, Mudwomen, 2012, Daddy Love, 2013, The Accursed, 2013, Carthage, 2014, The Sacrifice, 2015, Jack of Spades, 2015, The Lost Landscape, 2015, (under pseudonym Rosamond Smith) Lives of the Twins, 1987, Soul/Mate, 1989, Nemesis, 1990, Snake Eyes, 1992, You Can't Catch Me, 1995, Double Delight, 1997, Starr Bright Will Be With you Soon, 1999, The Barrens, 2001, (under pseudonym Lauren Kelly) Take Me, Take Me With You, 2003, The Stolen Heart, 2005, Blood Mask, 2006, (novellas) The Triumph of the

Spider Monkey, 1976, I Lock My Door Upon Myself, 1990, The Rise of Life on Earth, 1991, Black Water, 1992, First Love: A Gothic Tale, 1996, Beasts, 2002, Rape: A Love Story, 2003, The Corn Maiden : A Love Story, 2005, (short story collections) By the North Gate, 1963, Upon the Sweeping Flood And Other Stories, 1966, The Wheel of Love And Other Stories, 1970, Marriages and Infidelities, 1972, The Goddess and Other Women, 1974, The Poisoned Kiss And Other Stories from the Portuguese, 1975, The Seduction & Other Stories, 1975, Crossing the Border: Fifteen Tales, 1976, Night-Side, 1977, All the Good People I've Left Behind, 1979, A Sentimental Education: Stories, 1980, Last Days: Stories, 1984, Wild Saturday, 1984, Raven's Wing: Stories, 1986, The Assignation: Stories, 1989, Oates In Exile, 1990, Heat And Other Stories, 1991, Where Is Here?, 1992, Where Are You Going, Where Have You Been?: Selected Early Stories, 1993, Haunted: Tales of the Grotesque, 1994, Demon and Other Tales, 1996, Will You Always Love Me? And Other Stories, 1996, The Collector of Hearts: New Tales of the Grotesque, 1998, Faithless: Tales of Transgression, 2001, I Am No One You Know: Stories, 2004, The Female of the Species: Tales of Mystery and Suspense, 2006, High Lonesome: New & Selected Stories, 2006, The Museum of Dr. Moses: Tales of Mystery and Suspense, 2007, Wild Nights!, 2008, Black Dahlia & White Rose, 2012, (young adult fiction) Big Mouth & Ugly Girl, 2002, Small Avalanches and Other Stories, 2003, Freaky Green Eyes, 2003, Sexy, 2005, After the Wreck, I Picked Myself Up, Spread My Wings, and Flew Away, 2006, Two or Three Things I Forgot to Tell You, 2012, (children's fiction) Come Meet Muffin!, 1998, Where Is Little Reynard?, 2003, (poetry) Women In Love and Other Poems, 1968, Anonymous Sins & Other Poems, 1969, Love and Its Derangements, 1970, Angel Fire, 1973, The Fabulous Beasts, 1975, Women Whose Lives Are Food, Men Whose Lives Are Money, 1978, Invisible Woman: New and Selected Poems, 1982, The Time Traveler, 1989, Tenderness, 1996, (plays) Miracle Play, 1974, Three Plays, 1980, In Darkest America, 1991, I Stand Before You Naked, 1991, Twelve Plays, 1991, The Perfectionist and Other Plays, 1996, New Plays, 1998, Dr. Magic: Six One Act Plays, 2004, A Widow's Story: A Memoir, 2011; contributor numerous essays, short stories and works of criticism to various ,(Books) The Man Without a Shadow, 2016, A Book of American Martyrs, 2017,(As Lauren Kelly) Blood Mask, 2006(Short Fiction) Evil Eye: Four Novellas of Love Gone Wrong, 2013, High Crime Area: Tales of Darkness and Dread,2014, Lovely, Dark, Deep, 2014, The Doll Master and Other Tales, 2016, **AW:** Named Humanist of Year, Am. Humanist Association, 2007; named to New Jersey Hall of Fame, 2012; recipient Ivan Sandorf Lifetime Achievement award, National Book Critics Cir., 2010, Chicago Tribune Lit. prize, 2006, PEN/Malamud award for Excellence in Art of Short Story, 1996, Rea award for Short Story, 1990, Heidemann award, 1990, O. Henry award, 1973, 1967; grantee National Education Association, 1968, 1966

OBAMA, BARACK HUSSEIN JR., T: 44th President of the U.S. **I:** Government Administration/Government Relations/Government Services **DOB:** 08/04/1961 **PB:** Honolulu **SC:** HI/USA **PT:** Barack Obama, Sr., Shirley Ann (Dunham) Obama **MS:** Married **SPN:** Michelle (Robinson) Obama, 10/3/1992 **CH:** Sasha, Malia **ED:** Honorary LLD, Hampton University, 2010; Honorary LLD, University of Michigan, Ann Arbor, MI, 2010; Honorary LLD, University of Notre Dame, 2009; Honorary LLD, Wesleyan University, 2008; Honorary LLD, Harvard University, 2007; Honorary LLD, Southern New Hampshire University, 2007; Honorary LLD,

Xavier University, 2006; Honorary LLD, University of Massachusetts, 2006; Honorary LLD, Northwestern University, 2005; Honorary LLD, Knox College, 2005; JD, Harvard Law School, Magna Cum Laude, 1991; BA in Political Science, Columbia University, 1983; Student, Occidental College, Los Angeles, CA, 1979-1981 **C:** President of the U.S., Washington, DC, 2009-2017; U.S. Senate of Homeland Security & Governmental Affairs Committee, 2007-2009; U.S. Senate of Health, Education, Labor & Pensions Committee, 2007-2009; U.S. Senate Environment & Public Works Committee, 2006-2007; U.S. Senate Veterans' Affairs Committee, 2005-2006; U.S. Senate Foreign Relations Committee, 2005-2006; U.S. Senator From Illinois, 2005-2008; District 13, Illinois State Senate, Springfield, IL, 1997-2005; Of Counsel, Davis, Miner, Barnhill & Galland, Professional Corporation, 1996-2004; Associate, Davis, Miner, Barnhill & Galland, Professional Corporation, 1993-1996; Executive Director, PROJECT VOTE!, Chicago, IL, 1992; Editor-in-Chief, Harvard Law Review, 1990-1991; Director, Developing Communities Project, 1985-1988; Writer, Financial Analyst, Business International Corp., 1984-1985 **CR:** Keynote Speaker, Democratic National Convention, Boston, MA, 2004; Senior Lecturer, University of Chicago Law School, 1996-2004; Lecturer, Constitutional Law, 1992-1996 **CIV:** Founding President, Chairman, Chicago Annenberg Challenge, 1995-1999, Board of Directors, Chicago Annenberg Challenge, 1995-1999, Board of Directors, Chairman, Chicago Lawyers Committee of Civil Rights Under the Law, 1995, Board pf Directors, Joyce Foundation, 1994-2002, Co-Founder, Lugenia Burns Hope Center, 1994, Board of Directors, Woods Fund of Chicago, 1993-2001 **CW:** Author, (Books) Dreams From My Father: A Story of Race and Inheritance, 1995, Audacity of Hope: Thoughts on Reclaiming the American Dream, 2006, Change We Can Believe In: Barack Obama's Plan to Renew America's Promise, 2008, Of Thee I Sing: A Letter to My Daughters, 2010; Appearances, (Documentaries) By the People: The Election of Barack Obama, 2009, (TV Series) Mythbusters, 2010 **AW:** The 40 Under 40, Crains Chicago Business, 1993, Monarch Award for Outstanding Public Service, 1994, "Legal Eagle" Award for Litigation, IVI-IPO, 1995, Freshman Legislator Award, Independent Voters of Illinois, Independent Precinct of Organizations, 1997, Outstanding Legislator Award, Campaign for Better Health Care-Illinois Primary Health Care Association, 1998, Legislative Award, Associated Firefighters of Illinois, 2004, Howard Blake Walker Award, Christopher House, 2005, Chairman's Award, National Association for the Advancement of Colored People, 2005, Harvard Law School Association Award, 2005, Lifetime Achievement Award, Detroit Chapter, National Association for the Advancement of Colored People, 2005, The 100 Most Influential People in the World, TIME Magazine, 2005, 2007-2014, Publishers Weekly Bestseller, Grammy Award for Best Spoken Word or Non-Musical Album, Recording Academy, Dreams From My Father: A Story of Race and Inheritance, 2006, Congressional Leadership Award, National Urban League, 2006, The Most Influential Black Americans, Ebony Magazine, 2006, Best Literary Work in Nonfiction, National Association for the Advancement of Colored People Image Awards, 2007, The 50 Most Powerful People in DC, GQ Magazine, 2007, Grammy Award for Best Spoken Word Album, Recording Academy, Publishers Weekly Bestseller, Audacity of Hope: Thoughts on Reclaiming the American Dream, 2008, The Most Fascinating Person, Barbara Walters, 2008, The Global Elite, Newsweek Magazine, 2008, Person of the Year, TIME Magazine, 2008, 2012, The 100 Agents of Change, Rolling Stone Magazine, 2009, Nobel Peace Prize, Norwegian Nobel Committee,

2009, The Top 25 Market Movers, U.S. News & World Report, 2009, The World's Most Powerful People, Forbes Magazine, 2009-2014, The 50 Highest-Earning Political Figures, Newsweek, 2010, Presidential Medal of Distinction, Government of Israel, 2013 **MEM:** Illinois Bar Association, Cook County Bar Association **ACH:** Achievements include becoming the first African-American to be elected President of the U.S., November 4, 2008; first US sitting President to visit Cuba in 88 years, March 20, 2016; first US sitting President to visit Hiroshima in May, 2016 **H:** Golf **PA:** Democrat **BA:** Office of Barack and Michelle Obama, P.O. Box 91000, Washington, DC, 20066

OBAMA, MICHELLE LAVAUGHN ROBINSON, **T:** Former First Lady **I:** Government Administration/Government Relations/Government Services **DOB:** 01/17/1964 **PB:** Chicago, January 17, 1964 **PT:** Daughter of Fraser C. and Marian Lois (Shields) Robinson; **ED:** JD, Harvard Law School, 1988; BA cum laude in Sociology, Princeton University, 1985 **C:** First Lady of the US, 2009-2017; Vice president community & external affairs, manager business diversity program, University Chicago Medical Center, 2005-08; Executive director community & external affairs, University Chicago Medical Center, 2002-05; Associate dean of students, director community service, University Chicago, 1997-2005; Founding executive director, Public Allies - Chicago, 1993-96; Assistant to Mayor Richard M. Daley, assistant commissioner planning & devel., City of Chicago, 1991-93; Associate marketing & intellectual property, Sidley & Austin LLP, Chicago, 1988-91 **CR:** Hon. chairwoman President Barack Obama's Committee on Arts and Humanities, 2009- board directors Chicago Council on Global Affairs, TreeHouse Foods, Inc., 2005-07 **CIV:** Hon. board chair, Girls Inc., 2010- Board member, Muntu Dance Co., Board member, Facing History and Ourselves, Board member, Otho S.A. Sprague Memorial Institute, **CW:** Appeared in (documentaries) By the People: The Election of Barack Obama, 2009; author: American Grown: How the White House Kitchen Garden Inspires Families, Schools and Communities, 2012 **AW:** Named a Woman to Watch, Crain's Chicago Business, 2009, 2008; named one of The 100 Most Powerful Women in DC, Washingtonian magazine, 2009, The 100 Most Powerful Women, Forbes magazine, 2009-14, The 100 Most Influential People in the World, TIME magazine, 2013, 2011, 2009, The World's 25 Most Inspiring Women, Essence magazine, 2006; recipient Women of Year award, Glamour Magazine, 2009 **MEM:** Mem.: Alpha Kappa Alpha (hon.) **PA:** Democrat **BA:** Office of Barack and Michelle Obama, PO Box 91000, Washington, DC, 20066

O'BRIEN, CONAN, **T:** Talk Show Host, Writer **I:** Media & Entertainment **PB:** Brookline **SC:** MA/USA **PT:** Thomas O'Brien; Ruth (Reardon) O'Brien **ED:** BA in American Hist. & Lit., Harvard University, 1985 **CR:** Staff member The Harvard Lampoon, 1981-85 (president 1983, 84); Television Personality 1983- **CW:** Stage appearances with: The Groundlings (L.A.) 1985-87; writer, performer The Happy Happy Good Show (LA, Chicago) 1988; writer (TV series) Not Necessarily the News (HBO) 1985-87, Saturday Night Live, 1988-91 (NBC, Emmy Outstanding Writing in Comedy series 1989), Lookwell (NBC) 1991; writer, producer The Simpsons (Fox) 1991-93, The Wilton North Report (syndicated) 1987; writer, producer, host Late Night with Conan O'Brien (NBC) 1993-2009 (Best Writing in Comedy/Variety Show Writer's Guild award 1997, TV award Writers Guild America 2000, 2002, 2003, 2005, 2006, Primetime Emmy for Outstanding Writing for a Variety, Music or Comedy Progressive, Academy TV Arts & Sciences, 2007); host Tonight Show

with Conan O'Brien (NBC), 2009-10, Conan (TBS), 2010-; film appearances include Tomorrow Night, 1998, Barenaked in America, 1999, Vanilla Sky, 2001, Bewitched, 2005, The Great Buck Howard, 2008; TV appearances include (voice only) The Simpsons, 1994, The Single Guy, 1996, Arli$$, 1996, (voice only) Dr. Katz, Professional Therapist, 1997, Veronica's Closet, 1998, Spin City, 1998, LateLine, 1999, Space Ghost Coast to Coast, 1999, (voice) Futurama, 1999, Tomorrow Night, 1998, (voice) Robot Chicken, 2005.(Television) Web Therapy, 2011, Christmas in Washington, 2011, Eagleheart, 2012, How I Met Your Mother, 2012, The Penguins of Madagascar, 2012, Cleary History, 2013, White house Correspondents Dinner, 2013, Arrested Development, 2013, Nashville, 2013, It's Always Sunny in Philadelphia, 2013, Real Husbands of Hollywood, 2013, Brody Stevens: Enjoy it, 2013, Family Guy, 2013, 2014 MTV Movie Awards, 2014, The Comeback, 2014, Sharktopus vs Pteracude, 2014, Ground Floor, 2015, Stranger's Soul, 2015, Clipped, 2015, Armcomedy, 2015, One More Happy Ending, 2016, Gute Zeiten Schlechte Zeiten, 2016, Mi Adorable Maldicion, 2017,(Film) Tomorrow Night, 1998, Pootie Tang, 2001, Vanilla Sky, 2001, Storytelling, 2001, End of the Century: The Story of the Ramones, 2003, Bewitched, 2005, Queer Duck: The Movie, 2006, Pittsburgh, 2006, The Great Buck Howard, 2008, Conan O'Brien Can't Stop,2011, Batman: The Dark Knight Returns Part 2, 2013, Now You See Me, 2013, The Secret Life of Walter Mitty, 2013, The Lego Batman Movie, 2017, Sandy Wexler, 2017 **AW:** Named Favorite Talk Show Host, People's Choice Awards, 2011; named one of The 100 Most Influential People in the World, TIME magazine, 2010,Primetime Emmy for Outstanding Writing, 2007, Primetime Emmy for Outstanding Creative Achievement, 2012 **PA:** Democrat **RE:** Irish Catholic

OCASEK, RIC, **T:** Rock Vocalist, Songwriter, Guitar Player, Producer **I:** Media & Entertainment **PB:** Baltimore **SC:** MD/USA **MS:** Married **SPN:** Paulina Porizkova **ED:** Student, Bowling Green State University; Student, Antioch College **C:** Founder, The Cars, 1978 **CW:** Albums with The Cars include Shake It Up, Candy-O, Panorama, 1980, Heartbeat City, 1984, Door to Door,1987, Move Like This, 2011; solo albums include Beatitude,1982 This Side of Paradise, 1987, Fireball Zone, 1991, Troublizing, 1997, Nexterday, 2005; producer groups Weezer, Hole, Bad Religion, Nada Surf, Cakelike, Black 47, Mercury Rev; appeared in films Made In Heaven, 1987, Hairspray, 1988. **AW:** Rock and Roll Hall of Fame, 2018

O'CONNOR, SANDRA DAY, **T:** Former Chancellor of the College of William and Mary, Retired U.S. Supreme Court Justice **I:** Law and Legal Services **DOB:** 03/26/1930 **PB:** El Paso **SC:** TX/USA **PT:** Harry A. Day; Ada Mae (Wilkey) Day **ED:** LLB, Stanford University (1952); BA, Stanford University, with Great Distinction (1950) **C:** Chancellor, College of William & Mary, Williamsburg, VA (2005-2012); Associate Justice, Supreme Court of the U.S., Washington, DC (1981-2006); Judge, Arizona Court of Appeals (1979-1981); Judge, Maricopa County Superior Court, Phoenix, AZ (1975-1979); Chairman, Committee on State, County & Municipal Affairs, Arizona State Senate (1972-1973); Majority Leader, Arizona State Senate (1972-1975); Member, Arizona State Senate (1969-1975); Assistant Attorney General, State of Arizona (1965-1969); Private Law Practice, Maryvale, AZ (1958-1960); Civilian Attorney, Q.M. Market Center, Frankfurt am Main, Germany (1954-1957); Deputy County Attorney, San Mateo, CA (1952-1953) **CR:** Harry Rathbun Visiting Fellow, Office of Religious Life, Stanford University (2008);

Member, Iraq Study Group (2006); Vice Chairman, Arizona Select Law Enforcement Review Commission (1979-1980); Chairman, Maricopa County Superior Court, Judges Training and Education Committee (1977-1979); Arizona Supreme Court Committee to Reorganize Lower Courts (1974-1975); Chairman, Visiting Board, Maricopa County Juvenile Detention Home (1963-1964); Member, National Defense Advisory Committee on Women in Services (1974-1976); Arizona Criminal Code Commission (1974-1976); Maricopa County Board of Adjustments and Appeals (1963-1964) **CIV:** Trustee, Rockefeller Foundation; Member, Cathedral Chapter, Washington National Cathedral (1991-1999); Co-chair, National Advisory Council, Campaign for Civic Mission of Schools (2005-Present); Member, Selection Committee, Oklahoma City National Memorial and Museum (2005-Present); Member, Advisory Board, Smithsonian National Museum of Natural History (2006-Present); Trustee, National Constitution Center **CW:** Author, "The Majesty of the Law: Reflections of a Supreme Court Justice" (2005), "Out of Order: Stories from the History of the Supreme Court" (2013), Children's Books, "Chico: A True Story from the Childhood of the First Woman Supreme Court Justice" (2005), "Finding Susie" (2009); Co-author with H. Alan Day, Memoir, "Lazy B: Growing Up on a Cattle Ranch in the American Southwest" (2002); Developer, Video Game, "Our Courts" (2008) **AW:** Named Woman of the Year, Phoenix Advertising Club (1972); Named One of the World's Most Powerful Women, Forbes Magazine (2005); Named to the National Women's Hall of Fame (1995); Margaret Chase Smith American Democracy Award, National Association of Secretaries of State (2009); Presidential Medal of Freedom, The White House (2009); Harry F. Byrd Junior '35 Public Service Award, Virginia Military Institute (2008); William Green Award for Professional Excellence, University of Richmond (1990); American Association of University Women Achievement Award (1988); Thomas Jefferson Award of Law, University of Virginia (1987); American Bar Association Medal (1997); Sara Lee Frontrunner Award (1997); Fordham-Stein Ethics Prize, Fordham University (1992); Ohio State Law Award, The Ohio State University (1992); Award of Merit, Stanford Law School (1990); Elizabeth Blackwell Award, Hobart & William Smith College (1985); Gimble National Award, Gimble Philadelphia Awards Committee (1982); Distinguished Achievement award, Arizona State University (1980); Annual Award, National Conference of Christians and Jews (1975) **MEM:** Fellow, American Academy of Arts & Sciences; Anglo-American Exchange; Arizona State Personnel Commission; Advisory Board, Stanford Center Ethics (2005-Present); Advisory Committee, American Society of International Law (2001-Present); Arizona Women Lawyer's Association; National Association of Women Judges; Honorary Member, Advisory Committee for Judiciary Leadership Development Council; Arizona Judges' Association; California Bar Association; Chairman, Lawyer Referral Service, Maricopa County Bar Association (1960-1962); Former Member Committee, Legal Aid, Arizona Bar Association; Former Member, Committee of Public Relations, Arizona Bar Association; Former Member, Committee of Lower Court Reorganization, Arizona Bar Association; Former Member, Committee of Continuing Legal Education, Arizona Bar Association; Executive Board, Central European and Euroasian Law Institute, American Bar Association (1990-Present); Executive Committee of Museum Law, Arizona Bar Association (2000-Present); Advisory Commission, Standing Committee on Law Library of Congress, Arizona Bar Association (2002-Present); Commission on Civic Education and Sep-

aration of Powers, Arizona Bar Association (2005-Present) **BAR:** State Bar of Arizona; The State Bar of California

O'CONNOR, SEAN M., I: Business Management/Business Services **C:** CEO, INTL FCStone Inc., 2009-; CEO, International Assets Holding Corp. (merged with FC Stone, Inc.), 2002-2009; Executive director, Standard Bank London Ltd., 1999-2002; CEO, Standard New York Securities, 1994-2002

O'DONNELL, LAWRENCE FRANCIS JR., T: Political Commentator **I:** Media & Entertainment **DOB:** 11/07/1951 **PB:** Boston **SC:** MA/USA **PT:** Son of Lawrence Frances and Frances Marie (Buckley) O'Donnell **MS:** Married **SPN:** Kathryn Hunter Harrold, 1994 **CH:** Elizabeth Buckley Harrold **ED:** AB, Harvard University, 1976 **C:** Host, The Last Word with Lawrence O'Donnell, MSNBC, 2010-; Political analyst, MSNBC, 1996-; Staff director, U.S. Senate Finance Committee, Washington, DC 1993-95; Staff director, U.S. Senate Environment & Pub. Works Committee, Washington, DC 1992-93; Senior advisor to Senator Daniel Patrick Moynihan, U.S. Senate, Washington, DC 1988-92; Self-employed writer, Boston and New York City, 1976-84, 84-87 **CW:** Author: Deadly Force, 1983; associate producer: (films) A Case of Deadly Force, 1986; writer: (TV series) The West Wing (16 episodes), 1999-2006, executive story editor (12 episodes), 1999-2000, co-prodr. (5 episodes, 2000, producer (17 episodes), 2000-01, consulting producer (44 episodes), 2003-05, executive producer (22 episodes), 2005-06; supervisory producer (TV series) First Monday, 2002; creator, executive producer, writer: (TV series) Mister Sperling, 2003; actor: (TV appearances) The West Wing, 2001, The Lyon's Den, 2003, The Practice, 2003, Monk (2 episodes), 2006-08, Big Love (10 episodes), 2006-10; (TV movies) Mrs. Harris, 2005 **MEM:** Member Writers Guild of America **PA:** Democrat **BA:** MSNBC, 30 Rockefeller Plaza, New York, NY, 10112

O'DONNELL, ROSIE, T: Television Personality **I:** Media & Entertainment **DOB:** 03/21/1962 **PB:** Commack **SC:** NY/USA **PT:** Daughter of Edward Joseph and Roseann Teresa (Murtha) O'Donnell; **ED:** Student, Boston University; Student, Dickinson College **C:** Co-host, The View, 2014-15; Co-host, The View, 2006-07; Editor, Rosie magazine, 2000-02; Host, The Rosie Show, 2011-12; Host, Rosie Radio, 2009-11; Host, The Rosie O'Donnell Show, 1995-2002 **CW:** Actress: (films) A League of Their Own, 1992, Sleepless in Seattle, 1993, Another Stakeout, 1993, Car 54, Where Are You?, 1994, I'll Do Anything, 1994, The Flintstones, 1994, Exit to Eden, 1994, Now and Then, 1995, Beautiful Girls, 1996, Harriet the Spy, 1996, A Very Brady Sequel, 1996, Wide Awake, 1996, Get Bruce, 1999, Jackie's Back, 1999, (voice) Tarzan, 1999, Flintstones in Viva Rock Vegas, 2000; (TV films) The Twilight of the Golds, 1997; (TV series) Gimme A Break, 1986-87, Stand By Your Man, 1992, Curb Your Enthusiasm, 2005-11; (Broadway plays) Grease, 1994, Seussical the Musical, 2001, Fiddler on the Roof, 2005; host, comedienne (TV series) Stand-up Spotlight, VH-1, 1993, actress, executive producer (TV films) Riding the Bus with My Sister, 2005; executive prodr.: (TV films) Kids are Punny, 1998; (films) Mina & the Family Treasure, 2004; (Broadway plays) Taboo, 2003-04; (documentaries) The (Dead Mothers) Club, 2014; TV Appearances include Ally McBeal, 1999, Third Watch, 2000, The Practice, 2000, Will & Grace, 2002, Judging Amy, 2003, Queer as Folk, 2005, Nip Tuck, 2006-08, Little Britain USA, 2009, Drop Dead Diva, 2009-10, Web Therapy, 2011-12, Happily Divorced, 2012, The Fosters, 2014-, Mom, 2016, The 100,000 Pyramid, 2016, Match Game,

2016, Hairspray Live, 2016, When We Rise, 2017, American Dad!, 2017, Difficult People, 2017, SMILF, 2017; Author: Find Me, 2002, Celebrity Detox: (The Fame Game), 2007, Rosie O'Donnell's Crafty U: 100 Easy Projects the Whole Family Can Enjoy All Year Long, 2008; Comedienne (TV special) Rosie O'Donnell: A Heartfelt Standup, 2015 **AW:** Named one of The World's Most Influential People, TIME Magazine, 2007; Recipient Tony Award, Isabelle Stevenson Award, 2014, Daytime Emmy Awards for The Rosie O'Donnell Show, 1997-2001, Time 100 Most Influential, 2018 **BA:** 8942 Wilshire Blvd, Beverly Hills, CA, 90210

OERTER, AL, T: Former Professional Athlete in the Discus Throw **I:** Athletics **DOB:** 09/19/1936 **PB:** New York City **PT:** Son of Alfred Adolph and Mary (Strup) O. **SPN:** Married Corinne Benedetto, October, 1958 (div. May 1975); Married Cathy Jo Carroll, July 23, 1983; **CH:** children: Crystiana, Gabrielle **ED:** Student, Kansas University, 1954-59 **C:** Motivational speaker, 1984-2007; Computer Manager, Grumman Data Systems, Bethpage, New York, 1959-84 **CW:** (Art) Art of the Olympian, 2006 **AW:** Four-time Olympic Gold Medalist, 1956, 1960, 1964, 1968; Member Olympic Hall of Fame, Track Hall of Fame; Recipient Olympic Order **BA:** Al Oerter Recreation Center, 134-40 Folwler Ave, Flushing, NY, 11355

OFILI, CHRIS, T: Painter **I:** Fine Art **DOB:** 10/10/1968 **PB:** Manchester **SC:** England/UK **PT:** Michael Ofili, May Ofili **MS:** Married **SPN:** Roba Ofili, 2002 **ED:** Student, Royal College of Art, London, England, 1991-1993; Student, Chelsea School of Art, London, England, 1988-1991; Foundation Course, Tameside College, Ashton-under-Lyne, Manchester, England; Student, Xaverian College, Victoria Park, Manchester, England **C:** Painter, 1992-Present **CR:** Visiting Artist, Painting Workshop, Port of Spain, Trinidad, 2000; Owner, Studio, Lady Chancellor Road, Port of Spain, Trinidad **CIV:** Founder, Prime Mover, Freeness Project **AW:** Commander of the Order of the British Empire, New Year Honours, 2017, TIME 100 Most Influential, 2015, Turner Prize, 1998, Scholarship, Zimbabwe, 1992, One-Year Exchange Scholarship, Universität der Künste Berlin, 1992

O'HALLERAN, TOM C., T: U.S. Representative from Arizona **I:** Government Administration/Government Relations/Government Services **DOB:** 01/24/1946 **C:** Member, U.S. House of Representatives from Arizona's First District (2017-Present); State Senate, AZ (2007-2017); Vice Chairman, Agricultural Committee; Vice Chairman, Environmental Committee; Member, Environmental Committee; Member, Co. & Municipal Committee; State Representative, District One, AZ (2002-2007); State Representative, District 2, AZ (2001-2002); State Senator, District 1, AZ; House of Representatives, AZ **AW:** Recognition Award, Arizona Department of Veterans Service (2006); Leadership Award, Arizona Commission of Indian Affairs (2005); Children & Youth Champion Award, Arizona School Age Coalition (2004); Outstanding Leadership Award (2003-2005); Public Policy Award, Mental Health Association of Arizona (2003) **PA:** Republican **BA:** 126 Cannon House Office Building, Washington, DC, 20515

OHNO, APOLO ANTON, T: Former Olympic Speed Skater **I:** Athletics **DOB:** 05/22/1982 **PB:** Seattle **SC:** WA/USA **C:** Member, U.S. Elite Short Track Speedskating Team, **CW:** Performer: Dancing with the Stars, 2007 (Named Champion, 2007) **AW:** Named 1500 Meter Champion, 2001, 1000 Meter Champion, 2001, 500 Meter Champion, 2001, World Cup Overall Champion, 2001, World

Junior Short Track Champion, 1999, US Champion, 1997; Named to Asian-Am. Hall of Fame, 2007; Recipient Silver Medal, Men's 1500m Short Track, Bronze Medal, Men's 1000m Short Track, Men's 5000m Relay, Winter Olympic Games, 2010, Gold Medal, 500 Meter, 2006, Bronze Medal, Men's Short Track Relay, 2006, Bronze Medal, 1000 Meter, 2006, Silver Medal, Men's 1000 Meter, 2002, Gold Medal, Men's 1500 Meter, 2002, US Champion, 2002, 2001, 1999,Speedskatings Athlete of the Year, 2003 **H:** Music, Badminton, Basketball, Break Dancing **BA:** Brillstein Entertainment Partners, 9150 Wilshire Blvd, Suite 350, Beverly Hills, CA, 90212

OLAJUWON, HAKEEM ABDUL, T: Former NBA Player **I:** Athletics **DOB:** 01/21/1963 **PB:** Lagos, Nigeria **PT:** Son of Salaam and Abike Olajuwon. **ED:** Student, University Houston, 1980-84 **C:** Co-founder, Islamic Da'wah Center, Houston, 2002-; Retired, NBA, 2002; Center, Toronto Raptors, 2001-02; Center, Houston Rockets, 1984-2001 **AW:** Named NBA Finals MVP, 1995, 1994, NBA Defensive Player of Year, 1994, 1993, NBA MVP, 1994, 1st Team All-Def., NBA, 1993-94, 1990, 1987-88, 1st Team All-NBA, 1993-94, 1987-89; Named to Naismith Memorial Basketball Hall of Fame, 2008, We. Conference All-Star Team, NBA, 1992-97, 1985-90, NBA All-Rookie Team, 1985, 1st Team All-American, Sporting News, 1984, FIBA Hall of Fame, 2016 **ACH:** Achievements include member of NBA Finals championship winning Houston Rockets, 1994, 1995 **BA:** DR34M, LLC, 3300 E. Nasa Parkway, The West Mansion, Houston, TX, 77058

OLDMAN, GARY, T: Actor **I:** Media & Entertainment **PB:** London **SC:** England **PT:** Leonard Bertram Oldman; Kathleen (Cheriton) Oldman **ED:** BA, Rose Buford College Speech and Drama, 1979 **CW:** Actor: (theatre) Massacre at Paris, 1980, Chinchilla, 1980, Desperado Corner, 1980, A Waste of Time, 1980, Summit Conference, 1982, Rat in the Skull, 1984, The Pope's Wedding, 1984 (Drama Magazine Best Actor award 1985, Fringe Best Newcomer award 1985-86), The War Plays, 1985, The Desert Air, 1985, Women Beware Women, 1986, Real Dreams, 1986, Serious Money, 1987; (TV films) Meantime, 1984, Honest, Decent and True, 1985, Fallen Angels: Dead End for Delia, 1993, The Firm, 1988, Heading Home, 1991, Jesus, 1999, Friends, 2001, Greg the Bunny, 2002; (TV miniseries) Who Was Lee Harvey Oswald, 1992; (films) Remembrance, 1982, Sid and Nancy, 1986, Prick Up Your Ears, 1987, Track 29, 1988, We Think the World of You, 1988, Criminal Law, 1988, Paris by Night, 1989, Chattahoochee, 1989, Henry & June, 1990, State of Grace, 1990, Rosencrantz and Guildenstern Are Dead, 1990, JFK, 1991, Bram Stoker's Dracula, 1992, True Romance, 1993, Romeo is Bleeding, 1993, The Professional, 1994, Immortal Beloved, 1994, Murder in the First, 1995, The Scarlet Letter, 1995, Basquiat, 1996, The Fifth Element, 1997, Air Force One, 1997, Lost in Space, 1998, Quest for Camelot (aka Magic Sword), 1998, Nobody's Baby, 2001, Hannibal, 2001, Interstate 60, 2002, The Hire: Beat the Devil, 2002, Sin, 2003, Harry Potter and the Prisoner of Azkaban, 2004, Who's Kyle, 2004, Batman Begins, 2005, Harry Potter and the Goblet of Fire, 2005, The Dark Knight, 2008, (voice), Planet 51, 2009, The Book of Eli, 2010, Red Riding Hood, 2011, (voice) Kung Fu Panda, 2011, Harry Potter and the Deathly Hallows: Part 2, 2011, Tinker Tailor Soldier Spy, 2011, Lawless, 2012, The Dark Knight Rises, 2012, Paranoia, 2013, RoboCop, 2014, Dawn of the Planet of the Apes, 2014, Child 44, 2015, Man Down, 2015, Criminal, 2016, The Space Between Us, 2016,The Hitman's Bodyguard, Darkest Hour, 2017, (Recipient Academy Award for Best Actor, Recipient Golden Globe for Best Actor, Recipient Screen Actors Guild Award for

Best Actor) Hunter Killer, 2018; actor, executive prod.: The Contender, 2000; director, writer, prod.: Nil By Mouth, 1997 (BAFTA award for Best Original Screenplay, Best British Film, 1998).

OLIVER, JOHN W., T: Comedian **I:** Media & Entertainment **PB:** Erdington **SC:** United Kingdom **CW:** (Film) The Love Guru, 2008, Moves: The Rise and Rise of the New Pornographers,2011, The Smurfs, 2011, The Smurfs 2, 2013, The Smurfs: The Legend of Smurfy Hollow, 2013, Amusement Park, 2019, The Lion King, 2019(Television)Bleak House, 1985, People Like Us, 2001, My Hero, 2001,Gash, 2003, Green Wing, 2004, The Comic Side of 7 Days, 2005, Mock the Week, 2005, The Daily Show, 2006,(Primetime Emmy for Outstanding Writing for a Variety, Music or Comedy Series,2009-11, Primetime Emmy for Outstanding Variety, Music, or Comedy Series, 2011) John Oliver: Terrifying Times, 2008, Important Things with Demetri Martin, 2009, Community, 2009-14, John Oliver's New York Stand-Up Show, 2010-13,Gravity Falls, 2012, Randy Cunningham:9th Grade Ninja, 2012, Rick and Morty, 2013, Last Week Tonight with John Oliver, 2014,(Primetime Emmy Award for Outstanding Variety Talk Series 2016-17, Primetime Emmy Award for Outstanding Writing for a Variety Series,2016-17,Primetime Emmy Award for Outstanding Interactive Program 2015,2017) The Simpsons, 2014, Robot Chicken, 2014, Danger Mouse, 2016, Bobs Burgers, 2017, The Detour, 2017

OLSON, PETER GRAHAM, T: U.S. Representative from Texas **I:** Government Administration/ Government Relations/Government Services **DOB:** 12/09/1962 **PB:** Ft. Lewis **ED:** JD, University Texas School Law, Austin, 1988; BA in Computer Sci., Rice University, Houston, 1985 **C:** Member, US House Energy & Commerce Committee, Washington, 2011-; Member, US House Transportation & Infrastructure Committee, Washington, 2009-; Member, US House Science & Tech. Committee, Washington, 2009-; Member, US House Homeland Security Committee, Washington, 2009-; Member, US Congress from 22nd Texas District, Washington, 2009-; Chief of staff to Senator John Cornyn, US Senate, Washington, 2002-07; Legis. aide to Senator Phil Gramm, US Senate, Washington, 1998-2002; Naval liaison officer, US Senate, 1995-98 **AW:** Decorated Joint Service Commendation medal, Joint Service Achievement medal, Navy & Marine Corps Achievement medal, Armed Forces Expeditionary medal, Southwest Asia Service medal, Joint Chiefs of Staff Badge **MEM:** Mem.: National Rifle Association, Texas State Society, Rice University R Association, Texas Lyceum (director), Littlefield Society **PA:** Republican

O'MALLEY, SEAN PATRICK CARDINAL, T: Cardinal **I:** Religious **DOB:** 06/29/1944 **PB:** Lakewood **SC:** OH/USA **PT:** Theodore O'Malley; Mary Louise (Reidy) O'Malley **ED:** PhD in Spanish and Portuguese, Catholic University of America (1979); MA in Spanish, Capuchin College, Washington, DC (1972); MA in Religious Education, Capuchin College, Washington, DC (1971); BA in Theology, Capuchin College, Washington, DC (1971); Diploma, Saint Fidelis Seminary, Herman, PA (1967) **C:** Cardinal-Priest of Santa Maria della Vittoria (Saint Mary della Vittoria) (2006-Present); Archbishop, Boston, MA (2003-Present); Cardinal (2006); Bishop, Palm Beach, FL (2002-2003); Bishop, Fall River, MA (1992-2002); Bishop, Saint Thomas (1985-1992); Coadjutor Bishop of Saint Thomas (1984-1985); Ordained, Saint Thomas (1984); Episcopal Vicar of Priests Serving Portuguese, Haitian and Hispanic Communities of Washington, DC (1978-1984); Executive Director, Centro Catolico Hispano of Washington, DC

(1973-1978); Ordained Priest, Order of Friars Minor Capuchin (1970); Ordained Priest, Roman Catholic Church (1970); Professor, Catholic University of America, Washington, DC (1969-1973); **CR:** Member, Presidential Council of the Pontifical Council for the Family (2009-Present); Congregation for the Clergy (2006-Present); Congregation for Institutes of Consecrated Life and Societies of Apostolic Life in the Roman Curia (2006-Present); Chairman Committee on Consecrated Life, U.S. Conference of Catholic Bishops **AW:** Named, Honorary Chaplain, Sovereign Military Order of Malta (1991); Named, Knight Commander of the Order of Infante D. Henrique, Government of Portugal (1985)

OMIDYAR, PIERRE M., T: Founder of Ebay **I:** Internet **DOB:** 06/21/1967 **PB:** Paris **SC:** France **ED:** Honorary Doctor of Public Service, Tufts University (2011); BS in Computer Science, Tufts University (1988) **C:** Launched, First Look Media (2013-Present); Founder, Chairman, eBay, Inc. (1998-Present); Co-founder, Ink Development Corporation (1991); Software Developer, Claris, (Subsidiary of Apple Computer) (1988-1991); With Developer Relations, General Magic, Inc. **CR:** Trustee, Santa Fe Institute; Member, Administration and Finance Committee, Santa Fe Institute; Member, Committee on Trusteeship, Tufts University; Trustee, Tufts University **CIV:** Co-founder, Chief Executive Officer, Omidyar Network; Co-founder, Chair, Board of Directors, Omidyar Foundation (1998-Present); Board Director, Meetup.com **CW:** Producer, Film, "Merchants of Doubt" (2014); Producer, Film, "Spotlight" (2015) **AW:** EY Entrepreneur of the Year National Winner (1999); Named One of Forbes 400 Richest Americans (2006-Present); Named One of the 50 Most Generous Philanthropists, Fortune Magazine (2005); Named One of World's Richest People, Forbes (1999-2007); Light on the Hill Award (with Pam Omidyar), Tufts University

O'NEAL, SHAQUILLE RASHAUN, T: Sportscaster, Retired Professional Basketball Player **I:** Athletics **DOB:** 03/06/1972 **PB:** Newark **PT:** Son of Philip A. Harrison and Lucille O'Neal; **ED:** EdD, Barry University, 2012; Student in broadcasting, Sportscaster University at Syracuse University Staten Island Newhouse School Pub. Communications, New York, 2009; MBA, University Phoenix, 2005; BS, Louisiana State University, Baton Rouge, 2000 **C:** Minority Owner, Sacramento Kings, 2013-; Inside the NBA, 2011-; NBA analyst, Turner Sports, 2011-; Retired, NBA, 2011; Center, Boston Celtics, 2010-11; Center, Cleveland Cavaliers, 2009-10; Center, Phoenix Suns, 2008-09; Center, Miami Heat, Florida, 2004-08; Center, LA Lakers, 1996-2004; Center, Orlando Magic, Florida, 1992-96 **CR:** Owner, clothing line and record label TWIsM member US men's basketball team Olympic Games, Atlanta, 1996, World Championships, Toronto, Canada, 1994 **CIV:** Special deputy, colonel, Maricopa County Sheriff's Department, Arizona, 2006-08 Reserve deputy officer, Bedford County Sheriff's Department, Virginia, 2004-07 Vol., Tempe Police Department, Arizona, Reserve officer, Miami Beach Police Department, Florida, **CW:** Actor: (films) Blue Chips, 1994, Kazaam, 1996, Steel, 1997, The Wash, 2001, After the Sunset, 2004, The Year of the Yao, 2004, Scary Movie 4, 2006; performer: (albums) Shaq Diesel, 1993, Shaq Fu: Da Return, 1994, You Can't Stop the Reign, 1995, The Best of Shaquille O'Neal, 1996, Shaquille O'Neal Presents his Superfriends, Vol. 1, 2002; co-author (with Jackie MacMullan): Shaq Uncut: My Story, 2011 **AW:** Named NBA Finals MVP, 2002, 2001, NBA Player of Year, The Sporting News, 2005, 2000, NBA MVP, 2000, NBA

All-Star Game co-MVP, 2009, NBA All-Star Game MVP, 2004, 2000, NBA Rookie of Year, 1993, 1st Team All-Am., Sporting News, 1992, 1991; named one of 100 Most Powerful Celebrities, Forbes.com, 2008, The Most Influential People in the World of Sports, Business Week, 2007, 50 Greatest Players in NBA History, 1996; named to New Jersey Hall of Fame, 2009, All-NBA 1st Team, 2000-06, 1998, All-NBA 2nd Team, 1999, 1995, Western Conference All-Star Team, NBA, 2009, 2000-04, 1998, 1997, Eastern Conference All-Star Team, 2005-07, 1993-96; recipient Gold medal, men's basketball, Atlanta Olympic Games, 1996, World Championships, 1994,Naismith Basketball Hall of Fame, 2016, FIBA Hall of Fame, 2017 **ACH:** Achievements include being first overall pick in the NBA Draft, 1992; member of NBA Championship winning: Los Angeles Lakers, 2000-2002; Miami Heat, 2006; leading the NBA in: field goals, 1994, 1995, 1999-2001; field goal attempts, 1995; field goal percentage, 1994, 1998-2002, 2004-06; free throw attempts, 1995, 1999-2002, 2004; points, 1995, 1999, 2000; points per game, 1995, 2000 **BA:** Mine O' Mine Inc, P.O. Box 951840, Lake Mary, FL, 32795

O'NEILL, EDWARD, T: Actor **I:** Media & Entertainment **SC:** Youngstown **PT:** Edward Phillip O'Neill; Ruth Ann (Quinlan) O'Neill **MS:** Married **SPN:** Cathy Rusoff (February, 1986) **CH:** Claire; Sophia **ED:** Student, Youngstown State University; Student, Ohio State University **CW:** Actor: (theatre) Knockout (Broadway debut), 1979, Androcles and the Lion, 1986, Lakeboat, 1983, Elm Circle, 1984, Of Mice and Men, 1984; (films) Deliverance, 1972, Cruising, 1980, Dogs of War, 1980, Disorganized Crime, 1989, K-9, 1989, Sibling Rivalry, 1990, The Adventures of Ford Fairlane, 1990, Dutch, 1991, Wayne's World, 1992, Blue Chips, 1993, Little Giants, 1994, Prefontaine, 1997, The Spanish Prisoner, 1997, The Bone Collector, 1999, Lucky Numbers, 2000, Nobody's Baby, 2001, Spartan, 2004, Redbelt, 2008, Wreck-It Ralph (voice), 2012, Finding Dory (voice), 2016, Sun Dogs, 2017; (TV series) Married...with Children, 1987-97, Big Apple, 2001, L.A. Dragnet, 2003-04, John from Cincinnati, 2007, Modern Family, 2009- (Best Actor in a Comedy Series, Emmy Awards, 2010, Outstanding Performance by an Ensemble in a Comedy Series, Screen Actors Guild Awards, 2011); (TV films) The Day the Women Got Even, 1980, Farrell for the People, 1982, When your Lover Leaves, 1983, Popeye Doyle, 1986, A Winner never Quits, 1986, Right to Die, 1987, The Whereabouts of Jenny, 1991, W.E.I.R.D. World, 1995, In the Game, 2004, Inseparable, 2006; (TV miniseries) The 10th Kingdom, 2000; (guest appearances) Another World, 1981, Miami Vice, 1984, Hunter, 1985, The Equalizer, 1985, Spenser: For Hire, 1986, Midnight Caller, 1988, Top of the Heap, 1991, In Living Color, 1994, 8 Simple Rules, 2005, The West Wing, 2004-05, Twenty Good Years, 2006, The Unit, 2006,John from Cincinnati, 2007, WordGirl, 2009, Handy Manny, 2011, Kick Buttowski: Suburban Daredevil, 2011, The Penguins of Madagascar, 2012, Real Husbands of Hollywood, 2013, Family Guy, 2015 **AW:** Recipient, Star, Hollywood Walk of Fame, 2011

ORMAN, SUZE, T: Financial Consultant, Writer, Columnist **I:** Consulting **DOB:** 06/05/1951 **PB:** Chgo. **PT:** Daughter of Morry and Ann Orman; **ED:** Honorary Doctorate in Commercial Science, Bentley University, 2010; LHD (hon.), University Illinois, 2009; BA in Social Work, University Illinois, 1976 **CT:** Cert. fin. planner **C:** Director, Suze Orman Financial Group, 1987-97; Vice president invest-

ments, Prudential Bache Securities, 1983-87; Account executive, Merrill Lynch, 1980-83 **CR:** Motivational speaker **CW:** Author: The 9 Steps to Financial Freedom: Practical & Spiritual Steps so You Can Stop Worrying, 1997 (New York Times bestsellers), The Courage to Be Rich: Creating a Life of Material and Spiritual Abundance, 1999 (New York Times bestsellers, Motivational book award Books for a Better Life, 1999), The Road to Wealth: Suze Orman's Complete Guide to Your Money, 2001 (New York Times bestsellers), The Laws of Money, the Lessons of Life: Keep What You Have and Create What You Deserve, 2003, The Money Book for the Young, Fabulous & Broke, 2005 (Publishers Weekly Bestseller), Women and Money: Owning the Power to Control Your Destiny, 2007, Suze Orman's 2009 Action Plan, 2009 (Publishers Weekly bestseller), Suze Orman's 2010 Action Plan, 2010, The Money Class: Learn to Create Your New American Dream, 2011; co-author (with Linda Mead): You've Earned It, Don't Lose It : Mistakes You Can't Afford to Make When You Retire, 1995; co-prodr., host (PBS special) The Courage to Be Rich, 1999, The Road to Wealth, 2001, The 9 Steps to Financial Freedom, 2004, Suze Orman's Money Class, 2011, host (national syndicated radio talk show) The Suze Orman Show, 2001-15 (CableFAX program award for best show or series in the Talk Show/Commentary, 2008, Gracie Allen award-Nat./Network/Syndication Talk Show category, American Women in Radio and Television, 2003, Gracie Allen award-Individual Achievement-Program Host Category, American Women in Radio and Television, 2005, 2006, Gracie Allen award-Outstanding Talk Show, American Women in Radio and Television, 2007, 2008, 2009, 2013), QVC Network, Financial Essentials Hour; contributing editor: O: The Oprah Magazine; columnist Yahoo! Finance 'Money Matters', Costco Connection magazine, guest appearances Oprah's All Stars Program on OWN TV, regular guest on The View, Today Show and the Oprah Winfrey Show **AW:** Named Outstanding Service Show Host for Suze Orman: For the Young, Fabulous & Broke, National Academy TV Arts & Sciences, 2006; named one of The World's Most Influential People, TIME magazine, 2009, 2008, Top 30 Power Brokers Who Most Influenced Mutual Fund Industry and Affected Money, Smart Money magazine, 1999, The 100 Most Powerful Women, Forbes magazine, 2010; named to Books for a Better Life award Hall of Fame, 2003, the 18th spot on list of Most Influential Women In Media, Forbes magazine, 2009, the top 10 spot on a list of the most influential celebrities of 2013, 100th issue as those "who have revolutionized the way America thinks about money", Worth magazine, 2001; recipient Gracie Allen Tribute award, American Women in Radio and Television, 2010, Touchstone award, Women in Cable Telecommunications, 2010, Visionary award, Council for Economic Education, 2009, Amelia Earhart award, 2008, National Equality award, Human Rights Campaign, 2008, Daytime Emmy award in the category of Outstanding Service Show Host for a PBS Special, The Money Show for the Young Fabulous & Broke, 2006, Daytime Emmy award in the category of Outstanding Service Show Host for a PBS Special, The Laws of Money the Lesson's of Life, 2004, Multiple Sclerosis Society Spirit Award, 2006, Crossing Borders award, Feminist Press, 2003, TJFR Group News Luminaries award, 2002 **ACH:** Achievements include named top 10 motivational speakers in the world, only woman named to this list, so also named top female motivational speaker in the world in 2007 by Business Week; is one of the most recognized and celebrated writers in today's personal finance arena **PA:** Democrat

O'ROURKE, BETO, T: U.S. Representative from Texas, Former City Councilman **I:** Government Administration/Government Relations/Government Services **DOB:** 09/26/1972 **PB:** El Paso **PT:** Son of Pat and Melissa O'Rourke; **ED:** BA in English Lit., Columbia University, 1995 **C:** Member, US House Veterans' Affairs Committee, 2013-; Member, Committee on Armed Services; Member, US House Homeland Security Committee, 2013-; Member, US Congress from 16th Texas District, Washington, 2013-; Co-founder, Stanton Street Technology Group, El Paso, 1999-; City councilman Dist 8, City of El Paso, Texas, 2005-11; Singer, guitarist, Los Dregtones,; Singer, guitarist, Foss, **CW:** Singer, guitarist (albums with Foss) The El Paso Pussycats, 1993, Fewel St., 1994 **PA:** Democrat

ORR, BOBBY, T: Sports Agent, Retired Professional Hockey Player **I:** Athletics **DOB:** 03/20/1948 **PB:** Parry Sound **SC:** Ont. Can. **PT:** Son of Doug and Arva (Steele); **C:** Agent, president, ORR Hockey Group, 2002-; Host Hockey Legends, Canadian Broadcasting Co.,; Assistant to the president, Pandick New England,; Spokesman, Bay Banks, Inc., Boston,; Spokesman, Nabisco Brands, Inc., New York City,; Consultant, NHL,; Consultant, Hartford Whalers,; Assistant coach, Chicago Blackhawks, 1976-77; Defenseman, Chicago Blackhawks, 1978; Defenseman, Chicago Blackhawks, 1976-77; Defenseman, Boston Bruins, 1966-76 **CW:** Author: Orr: My Story, 2013 **AW:** Named Top Defenseman of All Time, The Hockey News, 2010, Officer of Order of Can., 1979, MVP, Canada Cup, 1976, Athlete of Year, Sports Illustrated, Sport Magazine, Male Athlete of Year, Can. CP Poll, 1970; named to World Sports Hall of Fame, 2008; recipient Queen Elizabeth II Diamond Jubilee medal, 2012, Lester Patrick Trophy, 1979, Lester B. Pearson Award, 1975, Loy Marsh Trophy, 1970, Conn Smythe Trophy, 1972, 1970, Hart Memorial Trophy, 1970-72, Art Ross Trophy, 1975, 1970, James Norris Memorial Trophy, 1968-75, Calder Memorial Trophy, 1967,Ranked 31 in ESPN SportsCentury: 50 Greatest Athletes of the 20th Century, 1999, **ACH:** Achievements include being a member of Stanely Cup Champion Boston Bruins, 1970, 1972; being inducted into the Hockey Hall of Fame, 1979; having his number, 4, retired by Boston Bruins, 1979 **BA:** Great North Road America, 11443 S.E. Plandome Drive, Hobe Sound, FL, 33455

OSTEEN, JOEL, T: Minister **I:** Religious **PB:** Houston **SC:** TX/USA **PT:** John Osteen; Dodie Osteen **ED:** Student, Oral Roberts University, 1981-82 **CT:** Ordained 1992 **C:** Senior pastor, Lakewood Church, Houston, 1999-; President, co-owner, Station KTBU Channel 55, Houston, 1998-; Producer, creator, John Osteen TV Program, 1982-99 **CW:** Author: Your Best Life Now: 7 Steps to Living at Your Full Potential, 2004, Living the Joy Filled Life (Six Easy Steps to Living a Life of Victory Abundance and Blessing, 2005, Scriptures and Meditations for Your Best Life Now, 2006, Become a Better You: 7 Keys to Improving Your Life Every Day, 2007 (Publishers Weekly bestseller), Your Best Life Begins Each Morning: Devotions to Start Every New Day of the Year, 2008, It's Your Time: Activate Your Faith, Achieve Your Dreams and Increase in God's Favor, 2009 (Publishers Weekly bestseller), Every Day a Friday: How to Be Happier 7 Days a Week, 2011, I Declare: 31 Promises to Speak Over Your Life, 2012, Break Out!: 5 Keys to Go Beyond Your Barriers and Live an Extraordinary Life, 2013, You Can You Will: 8 Undeniable Qualities of a Winner, 2014, The Power of I Am: Two Words That Will Change Your Life Today, 2015, Fresh Start: The New You Begins Today, 2015; co-author (with Dodie Osteen): Choosing

Life: One Day at a Time, 2006; several compact discs titles and journals/devotional books **AW:** Named Most Influential Christian, Church Report Magazine, 2006; named one of Barbara Walters 10 Most Fascinating People, 2006 **ACH:** Achievements include minister to the one of the largest and most diverse congregations in America; weekly television program appears on six cable networks and internationally in over 100 nations

OSTRIKER, JEREMIAH PAUL, T: Astrophysicist, Educator **I:** Sciences **DOB:** 04/13/1937 **PB:** NYC **PT:** Son of Martin and Jeanne (Sumpf) Ostriker **ED:** MA, University of Cambridge, England, 2002; H.D., DSc., University of Chicago, 1992; PhD in Astrophysics, University of Chicago, 1964; AB in Physics and Chemistry, Harvard University, 1959 **C:** Professor, Columbia University, 2012-; Charles A. Young professor emeritus of astronomy, Princeton University, 2012-; Director Institute Computational Sci. & Engineering, Princeton University, 2005-09; Distinguished visiting professor, Institute Advanced Study, Princeton University, 2004-05; Provost, Princeton University, 1995-2001; Charles A. Young professor of astronomy, Princeton University, 1982-2002; Chairman department astrophysical scis., director Princeton University Observatory, Princeton University, 1979-95; Professor, Princeton University, 1971-2012; Associate professor, Princeton University, 1968-71; Assistant professor, Princeton University, 1966-68; Research associate, lecturer astrophysics, Princeton University, 1965-66; Plumian professor astronomy & experimental philosophy, University Cambridge, 2001-04; Postdoc. fellow, University of Cambridge, England, 1964-65 **CR:** Visiting Miller professor University California, Berkeley, 1990 visiting professor Harvard University, 1987 **CIV:** Hon. trustee, Am. Museum of Natural History, 2007-Trustee, Am. Museum of Natural History, 1997-2006 **CW:** Author: Development of Large-Scale Structure in the Universe, 1991; member editorial board Princeton University Press, 1982-84, 1986, Heart of Darkness: Unravelling the mysteries of the Invisible Universe, 2013; contributor articles to professional journals **AW:** Named Champions of Charge, The White House, 2013; recipient Gruber Cosmology prize, 2015, James Craig Watson medal, 2012, Catherine Wolfe Bruce Gold medal, 2011, Golden Plate award, Am. Academy Achievement, 2001, National Medal Sci., 2000, Karl Schwarzschild medal, German Astronomical Society, 1999, Vainu Bappu Memorial award, Indian National Sci. Academy, 1993; fellow, National Science Foundation, 1960-65, Alfred P. Sloan Foundation, 1970-72; Regents fellow, Smithsonian Institute, 1984-85, Sherman Fairchild fellowship, California Institute Tech., 1977,Fellow of the Royal Society, 2007 **MEM:** Fellow: American Association for the Advancement of Science; mem.: National Academy of Sciences (councilor 1992-95, board governers 1993-95, treasurer 2008-, board governors 2008-), Am. Academy Arts & Scis., Am. Philosophical Society, International Astronomical Union, Am. Astronomical Society (councilor 1978-80, Helen B. Warner prize 1972, Henry Norris Russell prize 1980), Royal Society (foreign), Royal Netherlands Academy Arts & Scis. (foreign), Royal Astronomical Society (associate Gold medal 2004)

OTTER, BUTCH, T: Governor of Idaho **I:** Government Administration/Government Relations/Government Services **DOB:** 05/03/1942 **PB:** Caldwell **SC:** ID/USA **PT:** Son of Joseph Bernard and Regina Mary (Buser) Otter **ED:** PhD (hon.), Mindanao State University, 1980; BA in Political Science, College of Idaho, 1967 **C:** Governor,

State of Idaho, 2007-; Member, US Congress from 1st Idaho District, Washington, 2001-07; Lieutenant Governor, State of Idaho, Boise, 1987-2001; Member, Idaho House of Reps., Boise, 1973-77; International President, J.R. Simplot Co., Caldwell, Idaho, 1982-93; Vice President, Administration, J.R. Simplot Co., Caldwell, Idaho, 1978-82; Assistant Vice President, Administration, J.R. Simplot Co., Caldwell, Idaho, 1976-78; Manager, J.R. Simplot Co., Caldwell, Idaho, 1971-76 **CR:** Member, Idaho International Trade Council, Idaho Agricultural Leadership Council **CIV:** Member, US C. of C., Washington, 1983-84, Member, Presidential Task Force-AID, Washington, 1982-84, Member, Executive Council, Bretton Woods Committee, Committee Member Invest Tech. Devel., State Adv. Council, Washington, 1983-84 **MIL:** Served with Idaho Army National Guard 116th Armored Cavalry, 1968-73 **MEM:** Mem.: Pacific Northwest Waterways Association, Idaho Association Commerce & Industry, Young Presidents Organization, Ducks Unltd., Safari Club International (life), Elks, Moose **H:** Jogging, Music, Fishing **PA:** Republican **BA:** Office of the Governor, State Capitol, PO Box 83720, Boise, ID, 83720

OUBOU, IMAN, T: CEO **I:** Media & Entertainment **CN:** SWAYY Media **ED:** Masters of Science in Biomedical Engineering, University of Colorado, 2011-13; Bachelors of Science in Biochemistry/Molecular Biology, Colorado State University, 2007-11 **C:** Founder/CEO, SWAAY Media, 2016-; Regional Director, Gen Next, 2015-16; Account Executive, The Ruth Group, 2014-15; Research Scientist, Siva Therapeutics Inc, 2013-14

OVECHKIN, ALEXANDER, T: Professional Hockey Player **I:** Athletics **DOB:** 09/17/1985 **PB:** Moscow **PT:** Son of Mikhail and Tatiana Ovechkin. **C:** Captain, Washington Capitals, 2010-; Left wing, Washington Capitals, 2005-; Left wing, Dynamo Moscow (Russian Super League), 2001-05 **CR:** Member Team Russia, Olympic Games, Vancouver, 2010, Torino, Italy, 2006, Team Russia, World Cup of Hockey, 2004, Team Russia, World Championships, 2005, 2004, Team Russia, World Junior Championships, 2003-05 **AW:** Named NHL Player of Year, Sporting News, 2009, 2008, NHL Rookie of Year, 2006; named one of 50 Most Powerful People in DC, GQ magazine, 2009; named to Second All-Star Team, NHL, 2011, All-NHL Team, Sporting News, 2010, 2009, NHL All-Star Game, 2016, 2015, 2011, 2009, 2008, 2007, First All-Star Team, NHL, 2006-10; recipient Wayne Gretzky award, The Hockey News, 2013, Hart Memorial Trophy, 2013, 2009, 2008, Ted Lindsay Award (formerly Lester B. Pearson Award), 2010, Lester B. Pearson Award, 2009, 2008, Maurice Richard Trophy, 2015, 2014, 2013, 2009, 2008, Art Ross Trophy, 2008, Calder Memorial Trophy, 2006,100 Greatest NHL Players, 2017, NHL First All-Star Team, 2013, 2015, NHL Second All-Star Team, 2013, 2014, 2016, NHL All-Star Game, 2017, NHL All-Star Game Superskills Competition, 2008-09, 2011, Lester B. Pearson Award, 2010, Maurice Richard Trophy, 2015, Kharlamov Trophy, 2006-10, 2014, 2015 **ACH:** Achievements include being a member of gold medal Team Russia, World Junior Championships, 2003; being the first overall draft pick in NHL entry draft, 2004

OWEN, PRISCILLA RICHMAN, T: Federal Judge, Former State Supreme Court Justice **I:** Law and Legal Services **DOB:** 10/04/1954 **PB:** Palacios **SC:** TX/USA **ED:** JD, Baylor University School of Law, 1977; BA, Baylor University, 1975 **C:** Judge, U.S. Court of Appeals, Fifth Circuit, New Orleans, LA, 2005-Present; Justice, Supreme Court of Texas, Austin, TX, 1995-2005; Partner, Andrews, Kurth,

Campbell & Jones, 1985-1994; Associate, Andrews, Kurth, Campbell & Jones, 1978-1985; Law Clerk, Sheehy, Lovelace & Mayfield, 1976-1977 **CR:** Liaison to Texas Legal Services for Poor Supreme Court; Advisory Committee on Court-Annexed Mediations, Special Supreme Court of Texas **CIV:** Advisory Board, Houston & Austin Chapter, Federalist Society; Board Member, A.A. White Dispute Resolution Institute, Texas Hearing & Service Dogs **AW:** Outstanding Young Alumna, Baylor University; Young Lawyer of the Year **MEM:** American Bar Association, American Judicature Society, American Law Institute **BAR:** U.S. Court of Appeals, Fourth, Fifth, Eighth, and 11th Circuits, Texas, 1978 **BA:** John Minor Wisdom U.S. Court of Appeals Building, Fifth Circuit, 600 Camp Street, New Orleans, LA, 70130

OWENS, JOHN BYRON, T: Federal Judge **I:** Law and Legal Services **CN:** U.S. Court of Appeals for the Ninth Circuit **PB:** Washington **SC:** DC/USA **MS:** Married **SPN:** Marjorie Purcell-Jones **ED:** JD, Stanford Law School, 1996; BA, University of California, Berkeley, 1993 **C:** Judge, U.S. Court of Appeals, Ninth Circuit, Pasadena, CA, 2014-Present; Partner, Munger, Tolles & Olson LLP, Los Angeles, CA, 2012-2014; Chief, Criminal Division, U.S. Department of Justice, 2010-2011; Deputy Chief, Frauds Section, U.S. Department of Justice, 2008-2010; Assistant U.S. Attorney, Southern District, California, U.S. Department of Justice, 2004-2012; Assistant U.S. Attorney, Central District, U.S. Department of Justice, 2001-2004; Associate, O'Melveny & Myers LLP, Washington, DC, 2000-2001; Trial Attorney, Office of Consumer Litigation, U.S. Department of Justice, 1998-1999; Law Clerk To Justice Ruth Bader Ginsburg, U.S. Supreme Court, Washington, DC, 1997-1998; Law Clerk To Hon. J. Clifford Wallace, U.S. Court of Appeals, Ninth Circuit, 1996-1997 **BA:** 95 7th Street, San Francisco, CA, 94013

PACINO, AL, T: Actor **I:** Media & Entertainment **DOB:** 04/25/1940 **PB:** NYC **SC:** NY/USA **PT:** Son of Salvatore and Rose Pacino **CH:** Julie Marie; Anton, Olivia **ED:** Student, Actors Studio; Student, HS of Performing Arts **C:** Co-artistic director, The Actors Studio, Inc., New York City, 1982-84; Formerly messenger, movie theatre usher, building superintendent,; Formerly mail deliverer editorial offices, Commentary Magazine, **CW:** Actor: (films) Me, Natalie, 1969, The Panic in Needle Park, 1971, The Godfather, 1972 (Best Actor award National Society Film Critics, Academy award nominee), Scarecrow, 1973, Serpico, 1973 (Golden Globe for best actor), The Godfather, Part II, 1974 (BAFTA award for Best Actor), Dog Day Afternoon (BAFTA award for Best Actor), 1975, Bobby Deerfield, 1977, And Justice for All..., 1979, Cruising, 1980, Author! Author!, 1982, Scarface, 1983, Revolution, 1985, Sea of Love, 1989, Dick Tracy, 1990, The Godfather Part III, 1990, Frankie and Johnny, 1991, Glengarry Glen Ross, 1992, Scent of a Woman, 1992 (Academy award for Best Actor, 1992, Golden Globe award for Best Actor), Carlito's Way, 1993, Two Bits, 1995, Heat, 1995, City Hall, 1996, Donnie Brasco, 1997, Devil's Advocate, 1997, The Insider, 1999, Any Given Sunday, 1999, People I Know, 2002, Simone, 2002, Insomnia, 2002, The Recruit, 2003, Gigli, 2003, The Merchant of Venice, 2004, Two for the Money, 2005, 88 Minutes, 2007, Ocean's Thirteen, 2007, Righteous Kill, 2008, The Son of No One, 2011, Jack and Jill, 2011, Stand Up Guys, 2013, (voice) Despicable Me 2, 2013, Manglehorn, 2014, Danny Collins, 2015, Misconduct, 2016, The Pirates of Somalia, 2017, Hangman, 2017, The Irishman, 2019; appeared in a one-act play Off Broadway The Indian Wants the Bronx, opened Astor Pl. Theater on January 17, 1968 (Obie award for

Best Actor in Off-Broadway production 1967-68); (Broadway Plays) Does A Tiger Wear A Necktie?, 1969 (Tony award for Best Featured Actor in a Play, 1969), Camino Real, 1970, The Basic Training of Pavlo Hummel (Tony award for Best Actor in a Play, 1977), 1977, King Richard III, 1979, American Buffalo, 1983, Chinese Coffee, 1992, Salomé, 1992, Hughie, 1996, The Merchant of Venice, 2011, Glengarry Glen Ross, 2012; actor, dir.: (films) Chinese Coffee, 2000, Salomé, 2013; actor: (TV miniseries) Angels in America, 2003 (Golden Globe for Best Actor, Screen Actors Guild Award for Best Actor, 2004, Emmy award Outstanding Lead Actor in a Miniseries or a Movie, 2004); (TV films) You Don't Know Jack, 2010 (Emmy award for Outstanding Lead Actor in a Miniseries or a Movie, 2010, Best Performance by an Actor in a Mini-series in a Motion Picture Made for TV, Golden Globe award, Hollywood Foreign Press Association, 2011, Outstanding Performance by a Male Actor in a Television Movie or Miniseries, Screen Actors Guild, 2011); dir.: (short films) The Local Stigmatic, 1990; (documentaries) Looking for Richard, 1996 (Director Guild of America award for Best Director of Documentary); appeared in: (documentaries) I Knew It Was You: Rediscovering John Cazale, 2010; writer, dir.: (films) Wilde Salome, 2011; actor, executive prodr.: (TV films) Phil Spector, 2013, Untitled Joe Paterno Film, 2018; actor, prodr.: (films) The Humbling, 2014. **AW:** Recipient Lifetime Achievement award Ind. Feature Project Gotham awards, 1996, Cecil B. DeMille Award Hollywood Foreign Press. Association, 2001, Am. Cinematheque Lifetime Achievement award, 2006, Lifetime Achievement award, Am. Film Institute, 2007, Marcus Aurelius Lifetime Achievement award, Rome Film Festival, 2008, Internat award, Variety Club, 2008

PAEZ, RICHARD A., T: Federal Judge **I:** Law and Legal Services **DOB:** 05/05/1947 **PB:** Salt Lake City **SC:** Utah **SPN:** Diane Erickson **ED:** JD, University California, Berkeley, 1972; BA, Brigham Young University, 1969 **C:** Judge, US District Court (9th Cir.), Pasadena, California, 2000-; Judge, US District Court (Central District) California, LA, 1994-2000; Judge, superior ct, Los Angeles, 1993-94; Judge, LA Municipal Court, 1981-94; Act. Executive Director, Legal Aid Foundation of LA, 1980-81; Director Litigation, Legal Aid Foundation of LA, 1978-79; Senior Counsel, Legal Aid Foundation of LA, 1976-78; Staff Attorney, Western Center on Law and Poverty, 1974-76; Staff Attorney, California Rural Legal Assistance, Delano, California, 1972-74 **CIV:** Active, Hollywood-Los Feliz Jewish Community Center, **MEM:** Mem.: California Judicial Council, Mex.-Am. Bar Association LA County, LA County Bar Association, California State Bar Association **BA:** 95 7th St, St. Louis, CA, 94103

PAGE, JIMMY, T: Guitarist **I:** Media & Entertainment **DOB:** 01/09/1944 **PB:** Heston, England **PT:** Son of James Patrick Page & Patricia Elizabeth Gaffikin P **SPN:** Married Jimena; Married Patricia Ecker, 1986 (div. 1995); **CH:** James Patrick III; Scarlet Lilith Eleida **ED:** Doctor (hon.), Berklee College Music, 2014 **C:** Guitarist, The Firm, 1984-86; Guitarist, Led Zeppelin, 1968-80; Guitarist, The Yardbirds, 1966-68; Guitarist, Carter-Lewis & The Southerners, 1964; Guitarist, Neil Christian & the Crusaders, 1961-62 **CIV:** Active in, Action for Brazil's Children Trust, 1998- **CW:** Guitarist (albums with The Yardbirds) Little Games, 1967, (albums with Led Zeppelin) Led Zeppelin, 1968, Led Zeppelin II, 1969, Led Zeppelin III, 1970, Led Zeppelin IV, 1971, Houses of the Holy, 1973, Physical Graffiti, 1975, The Song Remains the Same, 1976, Presence, 1976, In Through the Out Door, 1979, Coda, 1982, Remasters, 1990, BBC Sessions, 1997,

Early Days: The Best of Led Zeppelin Volume One, 2000, Latter Days: The Best of Led Zeppelin Volume Two, 2002, How the West Was Won, 2003, Mothership, 2007, Definitive Collection, 2008, Celebration Day, 2012 (Best Rock Album, Grammy Awards, 2014), (albums with The Honeydrippers) The Honeydrippers: Volume One, 1984, (albums with Roy Harper) Whatever Happened to Jugula?, 1985, (albums with The Firm) Firm, 1985, Mean Business, 1986, (albums with David Coverdale) Coverdale/Page, 1993, (albums with Robert Plant) No Quarter: Jimmy Page and Robert Plant Unledded, 1994, Walking into Clarksdale, 1998, (albums with The Black Crowes) Live at the Greek, 2000, (solo albums) Outrider, 1988; composer: (soundtracks) Death Wish II, 1982; performer: (concert films) The Song Remains the Same, 1976, Unledded, 1994; appeared in (documentaries) It Might Get Loud, 2009 **AW:** Co-recipient Lifetime Achievement award, Grammy Awards, 2005, Grammy Award for Best Hard Rock Performance, 1999; named London's Greatest Guitarist, Total Guitar magazine, 2001; named an Officer of the Most Excellent Order of the British Empire (OBE), Her Majesty Queen Elizabeth II, 2005; named one of The 100 Greatest Guitarists of All Time, Rolling Stone magazine, 2003; named to United Kingdom Music Hall of Fame (as member of Led Zeppelin), 2006, The Rock & Roll Hall of Fame (as member of The Yardbirds, 1992, as member of Led Zeppelin, 1995); recipient Kennedy Center Honors, John F. Kennedy Center Performing Arts, Washington, 2012, Polar Music prize, Royal Swedish Academy Music, 2006 **ACH:** Was highly sought after as a studio sessions guitarist during the early part of his career; his guitar playing appears in recordings by such acts as Sonny Boy Williamson, John Mayall's Bluesbreakes, The Who, The Rolling Stones The Kinks, The Jeff Beck Group, Joe Cocker & Al Stewart **BA:** Genesis Publications, 2 Jenner Road, Guildford, GA, United Kingdom, GU1 3PL

PAGE, LARRY, T: Alphabet CEO **I:** Internet **DOB:** 03/26/1973 **PB:** Ann Arbor **SC:** MI/USA **PT:** Son of Carl Victor and Gloria Page; **ED:** MBA (hon.), IE Business School, Madrid, 2003; MS in Computer Sci., Stanford University, California; BS in Computer Engineering, University Michigan, 1995 **C:** CEO, Google, Inc., Mountain View, California, 2011-; President products, Google, Inc., Mountain View, California, 2001-11; Co-pres., Google, Inc., Mountain View, California, 1998-2001; Co-founder, Google, Inc., Mountain View, California, 1998 **CR:** Speaker Wall St. Journal Tech. Summit, Tech., Entertainment & Design Conference, World Economic Forum board directors Google, Inc., 1998- **CIV:** Member national adv. committee, University Michigan College Engineering, Board trustee, X Prize, 2005- **AW:** Co-recipient (with Sergey Brin) Marconi prize, 2004; named a Young Innovator Who Will Create the Future, Massachusetts Institute of Technology Tech. Rev. Magazine, Power Player, Advertising Age, 2009, Global Leader for Tomorrow, World Economic Forum, 2002; named Businessperson of the Year, Fortune magazine, 2014, Business Leader of Year, Sci. American magazine, 2005, Innovator of Year, R&D Magazine, 2002; named one of The 100 Agents of Change, Rolling Stone magazine, 2009, The 40 Under 40, Fortune magazine, 2009-12, The 25 Most Powerful People in Business, Fortune Magazine, 2007, The 50 Most Important People on the Web, PC World, 2007, America's 20 Most Powerful CEOs 40 and Under, Forbes magazine, 2012, The World's Most Powerful People, 2009-14, The World's Richest People, 2006-, The Forbes 400: Richest Americans, 2006-, The 50 Who Matter Now, CNNMoney.com Business 2.0, 2007, 2006, The 100 Most Influential People in the World, TIME magazine, 2011, 2005,

2004, Persons of Week (with Sergey Brin), ABC World News Tonight, 2004; recipient Golden Plate award, Academy Achievement, 2004, Engineering Graduate award, University Michigan Alumni Society **MEM:** Fellow: American Academy Arts & Scis.; mem.: NAE, Eta Kappa Nu

PAGELS, ELAINE HIESEY, T: Theology Studies Educator, Writer **I:** Writing and Editing **PB:** Palo Alto **PT:** Daughter of William McKinley and Louise Sophia (van Druten) Hiesey **ED:** PhD, Harvard University, 1970; MA, Stanford University, 1965; BA, Stanford University, 1964 **C:** Harrington Spear Paine professor religion, Princeton University, 1982-; From associate professor to professor, chair department religion, Barnard College, Columbia, 1974-82; Assistant professor history religion, Barnard College, Columbia, 1970-74; Writer, 1973- **CW:** Author: The Johannine Gospel in Gnostic Exegesis, 1973, The Gnostic Paul, 1975, The Gnostic Gospels, 1979 (National Book award and National Book Critics Cir. award), Adam, Eve and The Serpent, 1988, Beyond Belief: The Secret Gospel of Thomas, 2003, Reading Judas: The Gospel of Judas and the Shaping of Christianity, 2007 (Book) The Origin of Satan: How Christians Demonized Jews, Pagans, and Heretics, 1995, Revelations: Visions, Prophecy, and Politics in the Book of Revelation, 2012 **AW:** Grantee, National Endowment of the Humanities, 1973; MacArthur prize fellow, 1981-87, Guggenheim fellow, 1979-80, Rockefeller fellow, 1978-79, Hazen fellow, 1975, Mellon fellow, Aspen Institute Humanistic Studies, 1974 **MEM:** Mem.: Am. Academy Religion., Society Biblical Lit., Biblical Theologians Club **BA:** 12 Newlin Rd, Princeton, NJ, 08540

PAI, AJIT VARADARAJ, T: Chairman, Federal Communications Commission **I:** Business Management/Business Services **ED:** JD, University of Chicago Law School (1997); BA, Harvard University, with Honors, Cambridge, MA (1994) **C:** Chairman, Federal Communications Commission (2017-Present); Commissioner, Federal Communications Commission (2012-2017); Partner, Jenner & Block LLP, Washington, DC (2011-2012); Special Advisor to the General Counsel, Federal Communications Commission (2010-2011); Deputy General Counsel, Federal Communications Commission (2007-2010); Associate General Counsel, Federal Communications Commission, Washington, DC (2007); Chief Counsel, U.S. Senate Judiciary Subcommittee on the Constitution, Civil Rights & Property Rights (2005-2007); Senior Counsel on Office Legal Policy, U.S. Department of Justice (2004-2005); Deputy Chief Counsel, U.S. Senate Committee on Administrative Oversight & the Courts, Washington, DC (2003-2004); Associate General Counsel, Verizon Communications Inc. (2001-2003); Law Clerk to the Honorable Martin L.C. Feldman, U.S. District Court for the Eastern District of Louisiana (1997-1998); Honors Program Trial Attorney, Antitrust Division Telecommunication Task Force, U.S. Department of Justice, Washington, DC **CW:** Contributor, Articles to Professional Journals **MEM:** Board Member, District of Columbia Chapter, South Asian Bar Association (2002-2003); District of Columbia Bar Association; Federal Communications Bar Association; Network of Indian Professionals; Federalist Society **BAR:** Kansas; Washington, DC **PA:** Republican **BA:** Federal Communications Commission, 445 12th St SW, Washington, DC, 20554

PAISLEY, BRAD, T: Musician **I:** Media & Entertainment **PB:** Glen Dale **SC:** WV/USA **ED:** Grad., Belmont University, 1995 **CIV:** Founder, The Brad Paisley Foundation, 2001- **CW:** Musician: (albums) Who Needs Pictures, 1999, Part II, 2001, Mud On

The Tires, 2003, Time Well Wasted, 2005 (Album of Year, Academy Country Music Awards, Country Music Association Awards, 2006), A Brad Paisley Christmas, 2006, 5th Gear, 2007, Play, 2008, American Saturday Night, 2009, Hits Alive, 2010, This is Country Music, 2011, Wheelhouse, 2013, Moonshine in the Trunk, 2014, Love and War,2017 (songs) He Didn't Have to Be, 1999 (Song of Year, Single of Year & Video of Year, Country Music Association, 2000), I'm Gonna Miss Her, 2001 (Song of Year, Single of Year & Video of Year, Country Music Association, 2002, Grammy award for Best Male Country Vocal Performance, 2003), Celebrity, 2003 (Song of Year, Single of Year, Video of Year, Country Music Association, 2003), Online, 2007 (Music Video of Year, Country Music Association, 2007, Comedy Video of Year, Country Music TV, 2008, Video of Year, Academy Country Music, 2008), Throttleneck, 2007 (Grammy award for Best Country Instrumental Performance, 2008), Letter to Me, 2007 (Grammy award for Best Male Country Vocal Performance, 2009), Cluster Pluck, 2009 (Grammy award for Best Country Instrumental Performance, 2009), (with Chely Wright) Hard to be a Husband, Hard to be a Wife, 2001 (Vocal Event of Year, Country Music Association, 2001), (with Alison Krauss) Whiskey Lullaby, 2003 (Video of Year, Event of Year, Country Music Association, 2004, Video of Year, Event of Year, Academy Country Music, 2005, Collaborative Video of Year, Country Music TV, 2005), (with Dolly Parton) When I Get Where I'm Going, 2005 (Inspiring Video of Year, Country Music TV, Video of Year & Vocal Event of Year, Academy Country Music, Musical Event of Year, Country Music Association, 2006), (with Andy Griffith) Waitin' on a Woman, 2007 (Music Video of Year, Country Music Association, 2008, Video of Year, Academy Country Music, 2009), (with Keith Urban) Start a Band, 2008 (Vocal Event of Year, Academy Country Music, 2009), (with Carrie Underwood) Remind Me, 2011 (Collaborative Video of Year, CMT Music Awards, 2012); author: Diary of a Player, 2011; judge (reality TV competition) Rising Star, 2014, Repeat After Me, 2015, The Voice, 2015 **AW:** Recipient Favorite Male Country Artist award, American Music Awards, 2010, 2008, Top Male Vocalist award, Academy Country Music, 2007-11, Entertainer of Year award, Country Music Association, 2010, Male Vocalist of Year award, 2007-09, 2000-03

PALAZZO, STEVEN MCCARTY, T: U.S. Representative from Mississippi **I:** Government Administration/Government Relations/Government Services **DOB:** 02/21/1970 **PB:** Gulfport, Mississippi, February 21, 1970 **ED:** MPA, University Southern Mississippi, 1996; BA in Accounting, University Southern Mississippi, 1994 **C:** Member, US House Armed Services Committee, 2011-; Member, US House Sci., Space & Tech. Committee, 2011-; Member, US Congress from 4th Mississippi District, 2011-; Member District 116, Mississippi House of Reps., 2007-11 **MEM:** Mem.: National Rifle Association, American Institute of Certified Public Accountants, Mississippi Society CPA, Marine Corps Association, Rotary Club **PA:** Republican

PALLONE, FRANK JR., T: Ranking Member of Committee on Energy and Commerce, U.S. Representative from New Jersey, Lawyer **I:** Government Administration/Government Relations/Government Services **DOB:** 10/30/1951 **PB:** Long Branch **ED:** JD, Rutgers University School Law, New Jersey, 1978; MA in International Relations, Tufts University School Law & Diplomacy, Massachusetts, 1974; BA cum laude in History & French, Middlebury College, Vermont, 1973 **C:** Ranking member, US House Energy & Commerce Com-

mittee, 2015-; Member, US Congress from 6th New Jersey District, 1993-; Member, US Congress from 3rd New Jersey District, 1988-93; Member District 11, New Jersey State Senate, 1984-88; Councilman, Town of Long Branch, New Jersey, 1982-88; Maritime attorney, New York City, 1982-84; Instructor, Monmouth County Community College; Counsel, Monmouth County Protective Services for the Elderly, New Jersey; Assistant professor sea grant extension progressive, Cook Coll.-Rutgers University, New Jersey, 1980-81; Coastal law specialist, New Jersey Marine Adv. Service, 1980-81 **AW:** Named Outstanding Legislator of Year, VFW, 1999, Legislator of Year, New Jersey Academy Ophthalmology, 1998, Consumer Hero, Consumer Federation America, 1997; recipient International Year of Ocean award, Clean Ocean Action, 1998, Cancer Advocacy award, Cancer Institute New Jersey, 1998 **BAR:** Bar: Pennsylvania, New York, New Jersey, Florida **PA:** Democrat **BA:** U.S. Department of Energy, 100 Independence Ave. S.W., Washington, DC, 20585

PALMER, CARSON HILTON, T: Professional Football Player **I:** Athletics **DOB:** 12/27/1979 **PB:** Fresno **PT:** Son of Bill and Danna Palmer; **ED:** BA in Pub. Policy, University Southern California, 2002 **C:** Quarterback, Arizona Cardinals, 2013-2017; Quarterback, Arizona Cardinals, 2013-; Quarterback, Oakland Raiders, 2011-12; Quarterback, Cincinnati Bengals, 2003-11 **CIV:** Co-founder, Carson Palmer Foundation, 2004- **AW:** Named Pro Bowl MVP, NFL, 2007, College Football Player of Year, The Sporting News, 2002; named to The American Football Conference Pro Bowl Team, 2005-06; recipient Ed Block Courage award, 2006, Heisman Memorial Trophy award, Heisman Trophy Trust, 2002, Pro Bowl, 2015 **ACH:** Achievements include being the first overall selection in the 2003 NFL Draft; leading the NFL in touchdown passes (32), 2005

PALMER, GARY JAMES, T: U.S. Representative from Alabama **I:** Government Administration/Government Relations/Government Services **DOB:** 05/14/1954 **PB:** Haleyville **SC:** AL/USA **PT:** J.C. Palmer, Mae (Lacy) Palmer **MS:** Married **SPN:** Marjorie Ann Cushing, 11/19/1983 **CH:** Claire Elaine, Kathleen Corrie, Robert William **ED:** BS in Operations Management/Management Science, University of Alabama, 1977 **C:** Committee On Ways And Means, Committee On Intelligence, U.S. Representative From Sixth District Alabama, 2015-Present; President, Alabama Policy Institute, 1993-2015; Executive Director, Alabama Policy Institute, 1990-1993; Co-Founder, State Coordinator, Alabama Policy Institute, Birmingham, AL, 1989-1990; Cost Engineer, Project Control Engineer, Rust International, Birmingham, AL, 1981-1989; Cost Engineer, Combustion Engineering, Birmingham, AL, 1980-1981; Business Manager, Bradford And Co., Birmingham, AL, 1979-1980; General Manager, Palmer Truss Co., Hodges, AL, 1977-1978 **CR:** Speaker and Writer in Field **CIV:** Board of Directors, State Policy Network, 1992-1998, President, State Policy Network, 1996-1998 **CW:** Contributor, Articles, Professional Journals **AW:** Outstanding Young Men Of America, 1989, Roe Award, 2002, State Policy Network **MEM:** Rotary **H:** Hunting, Fishing, Golf, History, Skiing

PALMER, JAMES ALVIN, T: Baseball Commentator **I:** Media & Entertainment **DOB:** 10/15/1945 **PB:** NYC **SC:** NY/USA **ED:** Student, Towson State College, Maryland; Student, Arizona State University **C:** Commentator, ABC Sports, 1984-; Commentator, Baltimore Orioles baseball,; Former commentator, Home Team Sports, Bethesda, Maryland,; Pitcher, Baltimore Orioles, 1966-84 **CW:** Performer: TV and print advertisements;

author (with Jack Clary): Jim Palmer's Way to Fitness, 1985; author: (with Jim Dale) Together We Were Eleven Foot Nine: The Twenty-Four Year Friendship of Hall of Fame Pitcher Jim Palmer and Orioles Manager Earl Weaver, 1996 **AW:** Named Am. League Pitcher of Year, The Sporting News, 1976, 1975, 1973; named to All Star Game, 1978, 1977, 1972, 1971, 1970, Baseball Hall of Fame, 1990; recipient Cy Young Memorial award, Am. League, 1976, 1975, 1973,World Series Champion, 1966, 1970, 1983, Gold Glove Award, 1976-1979, AL wins Leader, 1975-1977, AL ERA leader, 1973, 1975,

PALTROW, GWYNETH, T: Actress **I:** Media & Entertainment **DOB:** 09/28/1972 **PB:** Los Angeles **SC:** CA/USA **PT:** Bruce Paltrow; Blythe Danner **ED:** Student, University California Santa Barbara **CR:** Designer ZOEtee's Loves Gwyneth, 2009- launched weekly lifestyle newsletter Goop, 2008- spokesmodel Coach, Estee Lauder, 2005- **CIV:** Board member, Robin Hood Foundation **CW:** Actress (films) Hook, 1991, Shout, 1991, Malice, 1993, Flesh and Bone, 1993, Mrs. Parker and the Vicious Circle, 1994, Jefferson in Paris, 1995, Se7en, 1995, Moonlight and Valentino, 1995, Hard Eight, 1996, The Pallbearer, 1996, Emma, 1996, Out of the Past (voice), 1998, Great Expectations, 1998, Sliding Doors, 1998, Hush, 1998, A Perfect Murder, 1998, Shakespeare in Love, 1998 (Academy award for Best Actress, 1998, Golden Globe award for Best Actress, 1998), The Talented Mr. Ripley, 1999, The Intern, 2000, Duets, 2000, Bounce, 2000, The Anniversary Party, 2001, The Royal Tenenbaums, 2001, Shallow Hal, 2001, Possession, 2002, View From the Top, 2003, Sylvia, 2003, Sky Captain and the World of Tomorrow, 2004, Proof, 2005, Infamous, 2006, Love and Other Disasters, 2006, Running with Scissors, 2006, The Good Night, 2007, Iron Man, 2008, Two Lovers, 2008, Iron Man 2, 2010, Country Strong, 2010, Glee: The 3D Concert Movie, 2011, Contagion, 2011, The Avengers, 2012, Thanks for Sharing, 2012, Iron Man 3, 2013, Mortdecai, 2015, Justin Timberlake The Tennessee Kids, 2016, Spider Man Homecoming, 2017, Man in Red Bandana, 2017, (TV films) Cruel Doubt, 1992, Deadly Relations, 1993, (TV appearances) Glee, 2010-14, Who Do you Think you Are?, 2011, The New Normal, 2012, Web Therapy, 2014, Nightcap, 2016, Planet of the Apps, 2017 (plays) Picnic, The Adventures of Huck Finn, Sweet Bye and Bye, The Seagull, Proof, host (TV series) Spain...On the Road Again, 2008; executive prodr.: (TV special) Stand Up to Cancer, 2012; co-author (with Mario Batali): Spain...A Culinary Road Trip, 2008; author: (cookbook) My Father's Daughter: Delicious, Easy Recipes Celebrating Family and Togetherness, 2011, It's All Good: Delicious, Easy Recipes That Will Make You Look Good and Feel Good, 2013, It's All Easy: Delicious Weekday Recipes for the Super-Busy Home Cook, 2016 **AW:** Named World's Most Beautiful Woman, People magazine, 2013, World's Best Dressed Woman, 2012; named one of The 100 Most Powerful Celebrities, Forbes.com, 2008; recipient Star, Hollywood Walk of Fame, 2010 **MEM:** Mem.: Screen Actors Guild

PANETTA, JIMMY, T: U.S. Representative from California **I:** Government Administration/Government Relations/Government Services **DOB:** 10/01/1969 **PB:** Washington **SC:** DC/USA **MS:** Married **SPN:** Carrie Panetta **ED:** Student, Monterey Peninsula College; BA, International Relations, University of California, Davis; Law Degree, Santa Clara University School of Law **C:** Committee on Agriculture, Committee on Armed Services, U.S. House of Representatives from California's 20th District, 2017-Present; Intelligence Office, Joint Operations Special Operations Command, 2007 **BA:** 228 Cannon HOB, Washington, DC, 20515

PANJABI, RAJ, T: Physician **I:** Medicine & Health Care **PB:** Monrovia **SC:** Liberia **ED:** Bachelor and Medical Degree, University of North Carolina School at Chapel Hill; Masters of Public Health, Johns Hopkins Bloomberg School of Public Health **C:** Founder,Community Health Academy,2017-; CEO,Last Mile Health, 2007- **AW:** Worlds 50 Greatest Leaders by Fortune 500, 2015, 2017, 100 Most Influential by Time in 2016, Ted Prize, 2017

PARCELLS, BILL, T: Sportscaster, Retired Professional Football Coach **I:** Media & Entertainment **DOB:** 08/22/1941 **PB:** Englewood **PT:** Son of Charles and Ida (Naclerio) Parcells; **ED:** BA, Wichita State University, 1964 **C:** Cleveland Browns, Courtesy Consultant, 2014-; Studio analyst, Sunday NFL Countdown, ESPN, 2011-; Team consultant, Miami Dolphins, 2010; Executive vice president football operations, Miami Dolphins, 2007-10; Radio co-host, ESPN Radio, 2007; Studio analyst, Monday Night Countdown, ESPN, 2007; Studio analyst, NFL Pregame Show, ESPN, 2002; Studio analyst, NBC Sports, 1991-92; Head coach, Dallas Cowboys, 2003-07; Chief football operations, New York Jets, 2000-01; Head coach, New York Jets, 1997-2000; Head coach, New England Patriots, 1993-97; Head coach, New York Giants, 1983-91; Defensive coordinator, linebackers coach, New York Giants, 1981-82; Defensive coordinator, New York Giants, 1979-80; Linebackers coach, New England Patriots, 1980-81; Head coach, US Air Force Academy Falcons, Colorado Springs, Colorado, 1978-79; Linebackers coach, Texas Tech University Red Raiders, Lubbock, 1975-77; Linebackers coach, Vanderbilt University Commodores, Nashville, 1973-74; Linebackers coach, Florida State University Seminoles, Tallahassee, 1970-72; Defensive coordinator, US Military Academy Black Knights, 1968-69; Linebackers coach, US Military Academy Black Knights, West Point, New York, 1966-67; Linebackers coach, Wichita State University Shockers, Kansas, 1965; Linebackers coach, Hastings College Broncos, Nebraska, 1964 **CW:** Co-author (with Jeff Coplon): Finding a Way to Win: The Principles of Leadership, Teamwork and Motivation, 1995; co-author: (with Will McDonough) The Final Season: My Last Year as Head Coach in the NFL, 2000; co-author: (with Nunyo Demasio) Parcells: A Football Life, 2014 **AW:** Named NFL Coach of Year, Pro Football Weekly, 1996, 1994, Maxwell Football Club, 1994, Associated Press, 1994, 1986, United Press International, 1994, 1986, Sporting News, 1986; named to The Pro Football Hall of Fame, 2013, NFL 1990s All-Decade Team **ACH:** Achievements include coaching the New York Giants to two Super Bowl Championships, 1986, 1990

PARKER, DOUG, T: American Airlines CEO **I:** Aviation **PB:** NYC **ED:** MBA, Vanderbilt University, Nashville, 1986; BA in Economics, Albion College, Michigan, 1984 **C:** CEO, American Airlines, Inc., Fort Worth, 2013-; CEO, American Airlines Group, Inc., Fort Worth, 2013-; Chairman, CEO, US Airways Group, Inc., Tempe, Arizona, 2005-13; President, US Airways/US Airways Group Inc., Tempe, Arizona, 2005-06; Chairman, president, CEO, America West Airlines, 2001-05; President, COO, America West Airlines, 2000-01; Executive vice president, America West Airlines, 1999-2000; Senior vice president, CFO, America West Airlines, 1995-99; Vice president financial planning & analysis, assistant treasurer, Northwest Airlines,; Various financial management positions, American Airlines, Inc., 1986-91 **CR:** Board directors American Airlines Group, Inc., 2013-, Pinnacle West Capital Corp., 2007-12, Clear Channel Outdoor Holdings Inc., 2005-08 **AW:** Recipient Distinguished Alumnus award, Vanderbilt University Owen Grad. School

Management, 2004 **PA:** Republican **BA:** American Airlines Headquarters, 4333 Amon Carter Boulevard, Fort Worth, TX, 76155

PARKER, MARK G., T: Nike CEO **I:** Business Management/Business Services **PB:** Poughkeepsie **ED:** BS in Political Sci., Pennsylvania State University, 1977 **C:** President, CEO, Nike, Inc. (formerly Blue Ribbon Sports, Inc.), 2006-; President Nike Brand, Nike, Inc. (formerly Blue Ribbon Sports, Inc.), 2001-06; Vice president, general manager global footwear, Nike, Inc. (formerly Blue Ribbon Sports, Inc.), 1998-2001; Vice president consumer product marketing, Nike, Inc. (formerly Blue Ribbon Sports, Inc.), 1993-98; Corp. vice president research design & devel., Nike, Inc. (formerly Blue Ribbon Sports, Inc.), 1988-93; Division vice president footwear research, design and devel., Nike, Inc. (formerly Blue Ribbon Sports, Inc.), 1987-88; Head, special design project teams, Nike, Inc. (formerly Blue Ribbon Sports, Inc.), 1985-87; Manager footwear marketing, Nike, Inc. (formerly Blue Ribbon Sports, Inc.), 1983-85; Director footwear design, Nike, Inc. (formerly Blue Ribbon Sports, Inc.), 1982-83; Director design concepts & engineering, Nike, Inc. (formerly Blue Ribbon Sports, Inc.), Beaverton, Oregon, 1981-82; Manager advanced product design, Nike, Inc. (formerly Blue Ribbon Sports, Inc.), 1980-81; Designer, devel. manager, Nike, Inc. (formerly Blue Ribbon Sports, Inc.), Exeter, New Hampshire, 1979-80; Joined, Nike, Inc. (formerly Blue Ribbon Sports, Inc.), 1979 **AW:** Named a Power Player, Advertising Age, 2009; named one of 50 Most Influential People in Sports Business, Street & Smith's SportsBus. Journal, 2009, The Most Influential People in the World of Sports, Business Week, 2008, 2007 **H:** Running, rock climbing, bicycling, sailing, kayaking, art

PARKER, SARAH JESSICA JESSICA, T: Actress **I:** Media & Entertainment **DOB:** 03/25/1965 **PB:** Nelsonville **SC:** OH/USA **PT:** Stephen Parker; Barbara Parker **CR:** Member President Barack Obama's Committee on Arts and Humanities, 2009 designer clothing line sold exclusively at Steve & Barry's, Bitten, 2007-08 launched fragrance line Dawn, Endless and Twilight, 2009, Covet, 2007, Lovely, 2005 spokesmodel The Gap, 2004-05, Garnier Nutrisse products for L'Oréal, 2003- **CIV:** National ambassador, US Fund for UNICEF **CW:** Actress (theatre) The Innocents, 1976, The Sound of Music, 1977, The War Brides, 1981, The Death of a Miner, 1982, To Gillian on Her 37th Birthday, 1983-84, Terry Neal's Future, 1986, The Heidi Chronicles, 1989, How to Succeed in Business Without Really Trying, 1996, Once Upon a Mattress, 1996, The Commons of Pensacola, 2013, (films) Rich Kids, 1979, Somewhere Tomorrow, 1983, Firstborn, 1984, Footloose, 1984, Girls Just Want to Have Fun, 1985, Flight of the Navigator, 1986, L.A. Story, 1991, Honeymoon in Vegas, 1992, Hocus Pocus, 1993, Striking Distance, 1993, Ed Wood, 1994, Miami Rhapsody, 1995, If Lucy Fell, 1996, Mars Attacks!, 1996, The First Wives Club, 1996, Extreme Measures, 1996, The Substance of Fire, 1996, 'Til There Was You, 1997, A Life Apart: Hasidism in America (voice), 1997, Isn't She Great, 1999, Dudley Do-Right, 1999, State and Main, 2000, Life Without Dick, 2001, Strangers with Candy, 2005, The Family Stone, 2005, Failure to Launch, 2006, Spinning Into Butter, 2007, Smart People, 2008, Did You Hear About the Morgans?, 2009, I Don't Know How She Does It, 2011, New Year's Eve, 2011, Escape from Planet Earth (voice), 2013,Lovelace,2013, All Roads lead to Rome,2016, Best Day of My Life,2017 (TV series) Sex and the City (also co-exec. producer), 1998-2004 (Golden Globe award for Best Supporting Actress, 2000,

2001, 2002, 2004, Emmy award for Outstanding Lead Actress in a Comedy Series, 2004, Screen Actors Guild award for Outstanding Performance by a Female Actor in a Comedy Series, 2001), (TV films) My Body, My Child, 1982, Going for the Gold: The Bill Johnson Story, 1985, A Year in the Life, 1986, The Room Upstairs, 1987, Dadah Is Death, 1988, The Ryan White Story, 1989, Twist of Fate, 1989, In the Best Interest of the Children, 1992, The Sunshine Boys, 1995, Sex and the Matrix, 2000, (TV series) Square Pegs, 1982-83, A Year in the Life, 1987-88, Equal Justice, 1990-91, (TV pilots) The Alan King Show, 1986, host MTV Movie Awards, 2000, actress, producer (films) Sex and the City: The Movie, 2008, Sex and the City 2, 2010, guest appearances include Project Runway, 2007, Glee, 2012,Divorce, 2016, Nightcap,2016 (video) Sesame Beginnings: Moving Together, 2007; prodr.: (documentaries) Pretty Old, 2013 **AW:** Named one of The 100 Most Powerful Women, Forbes magazine, 2010, The 100 Most Powerful Celebrities, 2008, The 50 Most Powerful Women in New York City, New York Post, 2008; recipient Vanguard award, ShoWest, 2008, Am. Civil Liberties Union award, 1995

PARKER, SEAN, T: Venture Capitalist, Entrepreneur **I:** Business Management/Business Services **DOB:** 12/03/1979 **PB:** Herndon **SC:** VA/USA **PT:** Bruce Parker; Diane Parker **C:** Co-Founder, Airtime (2010-Present); Co-Founder, Chairman, Causes, San Francisco, CA (2007-Present); Managing Partner, Founders Fund, San Francisco, CA (2006-Present); Founding President, Facebook, Inc., Palo Alto, CA (2004-2005); Advisor, Facebook, Inc., Palo Alto, CA (2004); Co-Founder, President, Plaxo (2001-2004); Co-Founder, Napster, Inc. (1999-2001) **CR:** Board Member, Votizen, Spotify, Yammer (2009-Present); Co-Founder, Chairman, Causes (2007-Present); Co-Founder, Gowalla **AW:** Named, One of the World's Richest People, Forbes Magazine (2011-Present); Named, The Forbes 400: Richest Americans (2011-Present) **BA:** Founders Fund One Letternam Dr Bldg C Ste 420, Presidio of San Francisco, San Francisco, CA, 94129

PARKER, STUART BLAIN, T: Insurance Company Executive **I:** Insurance **CN:** USAA **ED:** MBA, St. Mary's University, San Antonio, TX; MA in Political Science, Midwestern University; BBA in Management, Valdosta State University, Georgia **CT:** Chartered Life Underwriter; Chartered Financial Consultant **C:** CEO, USAA (United Services Automobile Association) 2015-Present; COO, USAA (United Services Automobile Association) 2014; CFO, USAA (United Services Automobile Association) 2012-2014; President, Financial Planning Services, USAA (United Services Automobile Association), 2004; Certified Financial Planner Practitioner, USAA (United Services Automobile Association), San Antonio, TX, 1998; President, Property & Casualty Insurance Group, Vice President, Financial Planning Services, USAA (United Services Automobile Association) **MIL:** Pilot, U.S. Air Force **MEM:** Financial Planning Association **BA:** USAA, 9800 Fredericksburg Road, San Antonio, TX, 78288

PARSONS, JIM, T: Actor **I:** Media & Entertainment **PB:** Houston **SC:** TX/USA **PT:** Milton Parsons; Judy Parsons **ED:** MA in Dramatic Arts, University San Diego, 2001; BA in Theater, University Houston, 1996 **C:** Founding member, Infernal Bridegroom Productions, Houston **CW:** Actor: (films) Nowhere to Go But Up, 2003, Garden State, 2004, The King's Inn, 2005, The Great New Wonderful, 2005, Heights, 2005, 10 Items or Less, 2006, School for Scoundrels, 2006, On the Road with Judas, 2007, Gardener of Eden, 2007, The Big Year, 2011, The

Muppets, 2011, Sunset Stories, 2012, Wish I Was Here, 2014, Home (voice), 2015, Visions, 2015, Hidden Figures, 2016, A Kid Like Jake,2018; (Broadway plays) The Normal Heart, 2011, Harvey, 2012, An Act of God, 2015, The Boys in the Band, 2018; (TV series) Judging Amy, 2004-05, The Big Bang Theory, 2007-15 (TV Critics Association award for Individual Achievement in Comedy, 2009, TV Chairman's award, National Association Broadcasters, 2010, Emmy award for Outstanding Lead Actor in a Comedy Series, 2010, 2011, 2013, 2014, People's Choice award for Favorite Comedic TV Actor, 2016, Golden Globe award for Best Performance by an Actor in a TV Series-Comedy or Musical, 2011), (voice) Family Guy, 2009-12, Glenn Martin, DDS, 2010, : (TV films) The Normal Heart, 2014, Elf: Buddy's Musical Christmas, 2014, Supermansion, 2016, Michael Jackson's Halloween, 2017, Young Sheldon appeared in TV commercials for Quiznos, Stride Gum, FedEx, others **AW:** Recipient Star, Hollywood Walk of Fame, 2015

PARTON, DOLLY, T: Singer, Composer, Actress **I:** Media & Entertainment **DOB:** 01/19/1946 **PB:** Sevier County **PT:** Daughter of Robert Lee and Avie Lee (Owens) P.; Married Carl Dean, May 30, 1966. **ED:** Doctor in Humane & Musical Letters (hon.), University Tennessee, Knoxville, 2009 **C:** Country music singer, recording artist, composer, actress, radio and TV personality, **CR:** Entrepreneur, owner entertainment park Dollywood, established 1985 founder Dixie Stampede, 1988 built Dollywood Splash Country, Tennessee's largest water park, 2001 **CIV:** Began Dollywood Foundation, 1988 **CW:** Established Velvet Apple Music (BMI); owner of record company Blue Eye Records; radio appearances include: Grand Ole Opry, WSM Radio, Nashville, Cass Walker program, Knoxville; TV appearances include: Porter Wagoner Show, from 1967, Cass Walker program, Bill Anderson Show, Wilburn Brothers Show, Barbara Mandrell Show; recording artist, Mercury, Monument, RCA , CBS record cos.; (albums) Here You Come Again (Grammy award for Best Country Vocal Performance, Female, 1979), Real Love, 1985, Just the Way I Am, 1986, Portrait, 1986, Think About Love, 1986, Trio (with Emmylou Harris, Linda Ronstadt), 1987, (Grammy award for Best Country Vocal Performance by a Duo or Group, 1988), Heartbreaker, Great Balls of Fire, Rainbow, 1988, White Limozeen, 1989, Home for Christmas, 1990, Eagle When She Flies, 1991, Slow Dancing with the Moon, 1993, (with Tammy Wynette and Loretta Lynn) Honky Tonk Angels, 1994, The Essential Dolly Parton, 1995, Just the Way I Am, 1996, Super Hits, 1996, (with others) I Will Always Love You & Other Greatest Hits, 1996, Hungry Again, 1998, Trio II, 1998, Grass is Blue, 1999 (Grammy award for Best Bluegrass Album), Best of the Best-Porter & Doll, 1999, Halos and Horns, 2002, For God and Country, 2003, Makin' Believe, 2003, Live and Well, 2004, Those Were the Days, 2005, Backwoods Barbie, 2008, Better Day, 2011, Blue Smoke, 2014, Pure & Simple, 2016; appears on song "Creepin' In" with Norah Jones, 2004; composer numerous songs including 9 to 5 (Grammy awards for Best Country Vocal Performance, Female, Best Country Song, 1982); actress: (films) Nine to Five, 1980, The Best Little Whorehouse in Texas, 1982, Rhinestone, 1984, Steel Magnolias, 1989, Straight Talk, 1991, Frank McKlusky, C.I., 2002, (voice) Gnomeo & Juliet, 2011, Joyful Noise, 2012; (TV films) A Smoky Mountain Christmas, 1986, Wild Texas Wind, 1991, Unlikely Angel, 1996, Blue Valley Songbird, 1999, A Country Christmas Story, 2013, Dolly Parton's Coat of Many Colors, 2015, Dolly Parton's Christmas of Many Colors: Circle of Love,2016; (TV series) Heavens to Betsy, 1994, Mindin My Own Business, 1996, Reba, 2005, Hannah Montana, 2006-10; author:

Dolly, 1994; music and lyrics (Broadway plays) 9 to 5, 2009; (autobiography) My Life and Other Unfinished Business, 1994, Dream More: Celebrate the Dreamer in You, 2012, (cookbook) Dolly's Dixie Fixin's: Love, Laughter and Lots of Good Food, 2006 **AW:** Recipient (with Porter Wagoner) Vocal Group of Year award, 1968, Vocal Duo of Year award All Country Music Association, 1970, 1971, Nashville Metronome award, 1979, Am. Music award for Best Duo Performance (with Kenny Rogers), 1984, Grammy awards for Best Female Country Vocalist, 1978, 1981, for Best Country Song, 1981, for Best Country Vocal Performance with Group, 1987, People's Choice award, 1980, 1988, Icon award, Broadcast Music, Inc., 2003, US Libr. of Congress Living Legend award, 2004, National Medal of Arts National Endowment for the Arts, 2005, Kennedy Center Honor, John F. Kennedy Center for Performing Arts, 2006, Johnny Mercer award, Songwriter's Hall of Fame, 2007, Grammy Lifetime Achievement award, 2011, Tex Ritter award for "Coat of many Colors," 2016; co-recipient (with Emmylou Harris and Linda Ronstadt) Academy Country Music award for Album of Year, 1987, (with Brad Paisley) Most Inspiring Video of Year for When I Get Where I'm Going, CMT Awards (Country Music TV), 2006, Video of Year and Vocal Event of Year, Academy Country Music award, 2006; Cliffie Stone Pioneer award, Academy Country Music, 2008, Jim Reeves International award, 2009; named Female Vocalist of Year, 1975, 76, Country Star of Year, Sullivan Productions, 1977, Entertainer of Year, Country Music Association, 1978, Female Vocalist of Year, Academy Country Music, 1980; Dolly Parton Day proclaimed, Sevier County, Tennessee, designated October 7, 1967, Los Angeles, September 20, 1979; named to Small Town of Am. Hall of Fame, 1988, East Tennessee Hall of Fame, 1988, Country Music Hall of Fame, 1999, National Academy of Popular Music Songwriters Hall of Fame, 2001, Gospel Music Hall of Fame, 2009, Music City Walk of Fame, 2009, Country Gospel Music Hall of Fame, 2010, National Hall of Fame for Mountain Artisans, 2014; Star on Hollywood Walk of Fame, 1984; bronze statue, Courthouse lawn, Sevierville, Tennessee

PASCRELL, BILL JR., T: U.S. Representative from New Jersey **I:** Government Administration/Government Relations/Government Services **DOB:** 01/25/1937 **PB:** Paterson **SC:** NJ/USA **PT:** Son of William James and Roffie (Loffredo) Pascrell; **MS:** Married **SPN:** Elsie Marie Botto **CH:** William III, David, Glenn **ED:** Postgraduate student, Fairleigh Dickinson University; MA in Philosophical, Fordham University, New York, 1961; BA in Journalism, Fordham University, New York, 1959 **C:** Member, US Congress from 9th New Jersey District, 2013-; Member, Committee on the Budget, Committee on Ways and Means; Member, US Congress from 8th New Jersey District, 1997-2013; Member District 35, New Jersey General Assembly, 1987-90; Member, Paterson Planning Board, New Jersey, 1975-77; Mayor, City of Paterson, New Jersey, 1990-96; President board education, City of Paterson, New Jersey, 1979-82; Director policy, planning & devel., City of Paterson, Paterson, New Jersey, 1979-87; Director public works, City of Paterson, Paterson, New Jersey, 1974-77; Adult school teacher, Dwight Morrow HS, Englewood, New Jersey, 1969-70; Ophthalmic technician, Seymour Pollack Opticians, 1968-74; Adjunct professor, Fairleigh Dickinson University, Madison, New Jersey, 1964-69; Teacher, Paramus HS, New Jersey, 1962-74; Teacher, Junior HS, Clifton, New Jersey, 1962 **CR:** Member ways and means and homeland security committee US Congress, co-chair Congl. Brain Injury Task Force **CIV:** Board directors Passaic County Community College, 1973-79, Boys

Club, 1975- campaign coordinator Robert A. Roe for Governor, New Jersey, 1977 regional coordinator James Florio for Governor, Hudson County, New Jersey, 1981 active County Chairmen for Sen. Frank Lautenberg, New Jersey, 1982 chairman Passaic County Democrats, New Jersey, 1982-1990. **MIL:** Sergeant US Army Reserve, 1962-67, enlisted US Army, 1961-62 **AW:** Named Man of Year, Passaic County Young Democrats, 1983, American Legion John Raad Post, 1983, Unico Passaic County, 1982, Federation italian Societies, 1981, Mother Cabrini Society, 1979; recipient Congl. Recognition award, International Association Fire Fighters, 2001 **MEM:** Mem.: Pat Mone Association, Charles Alfano Association, Riverside Vets., Knights of Columbus, Fordham University Alumni Association, American Cancer Society, Italian-American Federation, Paterson Taxpayers Association, Elks **PA:** Democrat **BA:** 2370 Rayburn House Office Building, Washington, DC, 20515

PATEL, VIKRAM HARSHAD, T: Joint Director **I:** Nonprofit & Philanthropy **CN:** Public Health Foundation of India **DOB:** 05/05/1964 **PB:** Bombay **SC:** India **PT:** Harshad Bhagvat Patel, Bharati Harshad Patel **MS:** Married **SPN:** Gauri Anil Divan, 2/18/1989 **ED:** PhD, London University, 1997; MSc, Oxford University, England, 1989; MB, BChir, Bombay University, 1987 **C:** Joint Director, Centre For Chronic Conditions And Injuries, Public Health Foundation Of India, 2014-Present; Professor Of International Mental Health, Wellcome Trust Senior Research Fellow, London School Of Hygiene & Tropical Medicine, 2005-Present; Lecturer, Research Coordinator, Institute of Psychiatry, UK, 1996-Present; Lecturer, Research Coordinator, Institute of Psychiatry, Goa, 1996-1997; Lecturer, Institute of Psychiatry, UK And University of Zimbabwe, 1993-1995; Senior Registrar, Westmead Hospital, Sydney, NSW, Australia, 1992; Registrar, Maudsley Hospital, London, England, 1989-1992; Rhodes Scholar, Oxford University, 1987-1989; Intern, Goa Medical College, 1986; Founding And Joint Director, Centre For Global Mental Health **CR:** Mental Health Policy Group, India, 2011-Present; National Rural Health Mission ASHA Mentoring Group, India, 2011-Present; Co-Founder, Sangath Society For Child Development And Family Guidance, Goa, 1996-Present; MacArthur Fellow For Population Innovations, 1998; Beit Medical Fellow, Beit Trust, London, England, 1992; Honorary Senior Lecturer, Institute of Psychiatry, London, England; Co-Chair, Grand Challenges In Global Mental Health **CW:** Author, Culture and Common Mental Disorders in Sub-Saharan Africa, 1997, Where There is No Psychiatrist; Editor, Essentials of Clinical Psychiatry in Africa, 1997, Several Lancet Series, 2007, 2011, (Textbooks) Global Mental Health: Principles and Practice, Global Mental Trials; Contributor, Articles, Professional Journals **AW:** Rhodes Scholar Rhodes Trust, Oxford, England, 1987, Wellcome Health Services Research Grantee, Wellcome Trust, London, England, 1995, TIME 100: Most Influential People, 2015 **MEM:** Royal College of Psychiatrists, Indian Psychiatric Society **H:** Trekking, Swimming, Music, Cooking

PATTERSON, JAMES BRENDAN, I: Writing and Editing **DOB:** 05/27/1905 **PB:** Newburgh, New York **SC:** Newburgh, New York **PT:** Son of Charles H. and Isabelle (Morris) Patterson **ED:** MA, Vanderbilt University, Nashville, 1970; BA, Manhattan College, 1969 **C:** Chairman, J. Walter Thompson U.S., 1990-96; With, J. Walter Thompson Co., New York City, 1971-96 **CW:** Author: (novels) The Thomas Berryman Number, 1976 (Edgar Allen Poe award, Mystery Writers America), Season of the Machete, 1977, Virgin, 1980, The Midnight Club, 1988, Hide & Seek, 1996, Miracle on the 17th green, 1996, See How They Run, 1997, When the Wind Blows, 1998, Black Friday, 2000, Cradle & All, 2000, Suzanne's Diary for Nicholas, 2001, The Beach House, 2002, The Jester, 2003, The Lake House, 2003, Sam's Letters To Jennifer, 2004, Honeymoon, 2005, Lifeguard, 2005, Beach Road, 2006, Judge & Jury, 2006, The Quickie, 2007, You've Been Warned, 2007, Sundays at Tiffany's, 2008, Sail, 2008, Swimsuit, 2009 (#1 New York Times bestseller), Private, 2010, The Postcard Killers, 2010, Don't Blink, 2010, Toys, 2011, Now You See Her, 2011, (Alex Cross series) Along Came a Spider, 1992, Kiss the Girls, 1995, Jack & Jill, 1996, Cat and Mouse, 1997, Pop! Goes the Weasel, 1999, Roses are Red, 2000, Violets are Blue, 2001, Four Blind Mice, 2002, The Big Bad Wolf, 2003, London Bridges, 2004, Mary, Mary, 2005, Cross, 2006, Double Cross, 2007 (#1 Publishers Weekly bestseller), Cross Country, 2008 (#1 Publishers Weekly bestseller), Alex Cross's Trial, 2009 (#1 Publishers Weekly bestseller), I, Alex Cross, 2009 (#1 Publishers Weekly bestseller), Cross Fire, 2010 (#1 Publishers Weekly bestseller, #1 New York Times bestseller), Kill Alex Cross, 2011, Merry Christmas Alex Cross, 2012, Run, 2013, Cross My Heart, 2013, Hope To Die, 2014, Cross Justice, 2015, (novels) (Women's Murder Club series) 1st to Die, 2001, 2nd Chance, 2002, 3rd Degree, 2004, 4th of July, 2005, The 5th Horsemen, 2006, The 6th Target, 2007, 7th Heaven, 2008, 8th Confession, 2009, The 9th Judgment, 2010 (#1 Publishers Weekly bestseller), 10th Anniversary, 2011, 11th Hour, 2012, 12th of Never, 2013, Unlucky 13, 2014, 14th Deadly Sin, 2015, 15th Affair, 2016, (novels) (Michael Bennett series) Step on a Crack, 2007, Run for Your Life, 2009, Worst Case, 2010 (#1 Publishers Weekly bestseller), Tick Tock, 2011 (#1 New York Times bestseller), (Daniel X series) The Dangerous Days of Daniel X, 2008, Watch the Skies, 2009, Demons & Druids, 2010, Lights Out, 2015, (children's books) SantaKid, 2004, Maximum Ride:The Angel Experiment, 2005, Maximum Ride: School's Out-Forever, 2006, Maximum Ride: Saving the World and other Extreme Sports, 2007, Maximum Ride:The Final Warning, 2008, MAX: A Maximum Ride Novel, 2009, Fang: A Maximum Ride Novel, 2010, Angel: A Maximum Ride Novel, 2011, Nevermore: The Final Maximum Ride Adventure, 2012, Maximum Ride Forever, 2015, Middle School-The Worst Years of My Life, 2011, Middle School- Get Me Out of Here, 2012; co-author (with Chris Grabenstein): Middle School: I Funny, 2012, Middle School: I Even Funnier, 2013, Middle School: I Totally Funniest, 2015, I Funny TV:A Middle School Story, 2016; co-author: (with Chris Tebbetts) Middle School: Save Rafe!, 2014, Middle School: Just My Rotten Luck, 2015, Public School Superhero, 2015; co-author: (and Gabrielle Charbonnet) (Witch & Wizard Series) Witch & Wizard, 2009; co-author: (and Ned Ruse) Witch & Wizard: The Gift, 2010; co-author: (and Jill Dembowski) Witch & Wizard: The Fire, 2011, Witch & Wizard: The Kiss, 2013; co-author: (and Emily Raymond) Witch & Wizard: The Lost, 2014; co-author: (non-fiction) Against Medical Advice: One Family's Struggle with an Agonizing Medical Mystery, 2008 (#1 Publishers Weekly bestseller), The Murder of King Tut, 2009, Now You See Her, 2011, Kill Me If You Can, 2011; co-author: (with Richard DiLallo) The Christmas Wedding, 2011; co-author: (and Maxine Paetro) Private #1 Suspect, 2012, Confessions: The Private School Murders, 2013, Confessions: The Paris Mysteries, 2014, Confessions of a Murder Suspect, 2014, Confessions: The Murder of an Angel, 2015, Private Vegas, 2015; co-author: (with Mark Sullivan) Private Games, 2012, Private LA, 2014; co-author: (with David Ellis) Guilty Wives, 2012, Mistress,

2013, Invisible, 2014, The Murder House, 2015; co-author: (with Michael Ledwidge) I. Michael Bennett, 2012, Zoo, 2012, Gone, 2013, Burn, 2014, Alert, 2015; co-author: (with Marshall Karp) NYPD Red, 2012; co-author: (with Marshall karp) NYPD Red 2, 2014, NYPD Red 3, 2015, NYPD Red 4, 2016; co-author: (with Mark Pearson) Private London, 2012; co-author: (with Michael Sullivan) Private Berlin, 2013, Private Paris, 2016, Private Rio, 2016; co-author: (with Howard Roughan) Second Honeymoon, 2013, Truth or Die, 2015; co-author: (with Emily Raymond) First Love, 2014; co-author: (with Lisa Papademetrious) Homeroom Diaries, 2014; co-author: (with Chris Grabstein) Treasure Hunters: Danger Down the Nile, 2014, Jacky Ha Ha, 2016; co-author: (with Michael White) Private Down Under, 2014; co-author: (with Chris Grabstein) House of Robots, 2014; co-author: (with Peter de Jonge) Miracle at Augusta, 2015 **AW:** Named one of The 100 Most Powerful Celebrities, Forbes.com, 2008; recipient Effie award, 1983, 6 Clio awards, 1983 **MEM:** Mem.: Phi Beta Kappa

PAUL, CHRIS, T: Professional Basketball Player **I:** Athletics **DOB:** 05/06/1985 **PB:** Winston-Salem **ED:** Attended, Wake Forrest Univ., North Carolina, 2002-05 **C:** Guard, Houston Rockets, 2017-; President, NBA Players Association, 2013-; Guard, LA Clippers, 2011-2017; Guard, New Orleans Hornets, 2005-11 **CR:** Member US national team Summer Olympic Games, London, 2012, Beijing, 2008 **AW:** Named All-Star Game MVP, NBA, 2013, Rookie of Year, 2006, Player of Year, Atlantic Coast Conference, 2004-05, Rookie of Year, 2003-04; named to All-NBA First Team, NBA, 2013, 2012, 2008, All-Defensive First Team, 2013, 2012, 2009, Western Conference All-Star Team, 2008-13, All-Rookie First Team, 2006; recipient Gold medal, men's basketball, Summer Olympic Games, 2012, 2008,NBA All Star, 2008-16, All-NBA First Team, 2014, All-NBA Second Team, 1008, 2015, 2016 **ACH:** Achievements include setting the NBA record for consecutive regular-season games with a steal, (106), 2006-08; leading the NBA in: assists, 2008, 2009; steals, 2009, 2011-13

PAUL, RAND, T: U.S. Senator from Kentucky **I:** Business Management/Business Services **DOB:** 01/07/1963 **PB:** Pittsburgh **SC:** PA/USA **PT:** Ronald Ernest Paul; Carol Wells Paul **ED:** Resident in Ophthalmology, Duke University Medical Center (1990-1993); Intern in Surgery, Georgia Baptist Medical Center (1989); MD, Duke University (1988); BS, Baylor University **C:** Member, U.S. Senate Committee on Foreign Relations, Washington, DC (2013-Present); Member, U.S. Senate on Health, Education, Labor, & Pensions Committee, Washington, DC (2011-Present); Member, U.S. Senate Small Business & Entrepreneurship Committee, Washington, DC (2011-Present); Member, U.S. Senate Homeland Security & Governmental Affairs, Washington, DC (2011-Present); U.S. Senator from Kentucky, Washington, DC (2011-Present); Private Practice, Bowling Green, KY (1993-Present); Member, U.S. Senate Energy & Natural Resources Committee, Washington, DC (2011-2013); Ophthalmologist, Graves-Gilbert Clinic; Staff Member, TJ Samson Community Hospital, Glasgow, KY; Staff Member, Logan County Memorial Hospital, Russellville, KY; Staff Member, Bowling Green Medical Center; Staff Member, Greenview Regional Hospital, Bowling Green, KY **CR:** Presidential Nomination Founder, Chairman, Kentucky Taxpayers United (1994-Present); Candidate, Republican Party (2016) **CIV:** Founder, Southern Kentucky Lions Eye Clinic (1995); Eye Surgeon, Children of the Americas Program **CW:** Author, "The Tea Party Goes to Washington" (2011) **AW:** Named, One of the 100 Most Influential People in the World, Time

Magazine (2013-2014); Recipient, Outstanding Service and Commitment to Seniors, Twilight Wish Foundation (2002); Recipient, Melvin Jones Fellow Award for Dedicated Humanitarian Services; Recipient, Lion of the Year Award, Bowling Green Lions; Recipient, Fines E. Davis Fellow Award for Dedicated Humanitarian Service; Recipient, Governor's Appreciation Award for Sight Conservation **MEM:** Former President, Lions Clubs International **PA:** Republican **BA:** Office of Rand Paul, 167 Russell Senate Office Building, Washington, DC, 20510

PAUL, RON, T: Former U.S. Representative **I:** Government Administration/Government Relations/Government Services **DOB:** 08/20/1935 **PB:** Pittsburgh **PT:** Son of Howard Caspar and Margaret Dumont Paul; **ED:** MD, Duke University Medical Center, Durham, North Carolina, 1961; BA in Biology, Gettysburg College, Pennsylvania, 1957 **C:** Member, US Congress from 14th Texas District, 1997-2013; Member, US Congress from 14th Texas District, 1979-85; Member, US Congress from 14th Texas District, 1976-77; Private Medical Practice, Brazoria County, Texas, 1968; Obstetrics-gynecology Training, University of Pittsburgh, 1965-68; Intern, Resident, Henry Ford Hospital, Detroit, 1961-62 **CR:** Candidate for Republican Nomination 2012 US Presidential Election, 2008 US Presidential Election Libertarian Candidate for President 1988 US Presidential Election **MIL:** Flight Surgeon US Air NG, 1965-68, Flight Surgeon US Air Force, 1963-65 **CW:** Author: Gold, Peace, and Prosperity: The Birth of a New Currency, 1981, The Case for Gold: A Minority Report of the U.S. Gold Commission, 1982, Texas: Foundation for Rational Economics and Education, 1983, Ten Myths About Paper Money: And One Myth About Paper Gold, 1983, Mises and Austrian Economics: A Personal View, 1984, Freedom Under Siege: The U.S. Constitution After 200 Years, 1987, Challenge to Liberty: Coming to Grips with the Abortion Issue, 1990, The Ron Paul Money Book, 1991, A Republic, If You Can Keep It, 2000, The Case for Defending America., 2002, A Foreign Policy of Freedom: Peace, Commerce, and Honest Friendship, 2007, Pillars of Prosperity, 2008, The Revolution: A Manifesto, 2008, End the Fed, 2009, Liberty Defined: 50 Essential Issues That Affect Our Freedom, 2011, The School Revolution: A New Answer for our Broken Education System **AW:** Named one of The 100 Most Influential People in the World, TIME magazine, 2012; Recipient Taxpayer's Best Friend Award, National Taxpayers Union, Torch Freedom Award, Young Conservatives Texas, Leadership Award, Coalition for Peace Through Strength **PA:** Republican

PAULEY, JANE, T: Newscaster, Journalist **I:** Media & Entertainment **DOB:** 10/31/1950 **PB:** Indpls. **SC:** IN/USA **ED:** Doctor of Journalism (hon.), DePauw University, 1978; BA in Political Sci, Ind. University, 1971 **C:** Host, CBS Sunday Morning, 2016-; From co-anchor to corr., NBC News, New York City, 1976-; Host, monthly segment, Your Life Calling, The Today Show, NBC, New York City, 2014-; Host, The Jane Pauley Show, 2004-05; Anchor, Time & Again MSNBC, 1999-2003; Principal anchor, Dateline NBC, New York City, 1999-2003; Co-anchor, Dateline NBC, New York City, 1992-99; Principal corr., Real Life With Jane Pauley, NBC, 1991; Co-anchor, Early Today, NBC, 1982-83; Substitute anchor, NBC Nightly News, 1990-2003; Principal writer, reporter, NBC Nightly News, 1980-82; Co-anchor, The Today Show, NBC, New York City, 1976-90; Co-anchor, WMAQ-TV News, Chicago, 1975-76; Reporter, Station WISH-TV, Indianapolis, 1972-75 **CIV:** Chair adv. board, member board directors, Childrens Health Fund, New York City, Board directors, The Mind Trust, Indianapolis,

2009- Board directors, Pub. Education Needs Civic Involvement in Learning, Member adv. board, International Council Freedom From Hunger, AARP's Ambassador of "Your Life Calling", **CW:** Author: Skywriting: A Life Out of the Blue, 2004 (Publishers Weekly Bestseller), Your Life Calling: Reimagining the Rest of Your Life, 2014 **AW:** Named Best in Business, Washington Journalism Rev., 1990, Broadcaster of Year, International Radio and TV Society, 1986; named to Broadcasting and Cable Hall of Fame; recipient Paul White award, NTNDA, Leonard Zeidenberg First Amendment award, Radio TV News Directors Foundation, Salute to Excellence award, National Association Black Journalists, Wilbur award, Religious Public Relations Council, Clarion award, Association for Women in Communications, Gracie Allen award, Commendation award, Am. Women in Radio and TV, Humanitas award, Maggie award, Nancy Susan Reynolds award, Gabriel award, Edward R. Murrow award, Emmy award,Broadcast and Cable Hall of Fame, 1998, Matrix Award from Association for Women in Communications, Walter Cronkite Award for Excellence in Journalism **MEM:** Fellow: Society for Professional Journalists (hon. chair Jane Pauley task force on mass communications education)

PAULSEN, ERIK, T: U.S. Representative from Minnesota, Former State Legislator **I:** Government Administration/Government Relations/Government Services **DOB:** 05/14/1965 **PB:** Bakersfield **SC:** CA/USA **PT:** Son of Gerald and Janet (Lindfors) Paulsen; **ED:** BA in Math., St. Olaf College, Northfield, Minnesota, 1987 **C:** Chair, Joint Economic Committee, 2018, Member, Bicameral Joint Economic Committee, Committee on Ways and Means, Committee on Health; Member, US Congress from 3rd Minnesota District, 2009-; Business analyst, Target Corp., Minnesota,; Majority leader, Minnesota House Reps. from District 42B, 2003-06; Member district, Minnesota House Reps. from District 42B, 1995-2009; State director 3rd. district, US Congressman Jim Ramstad, Minnesota, 1994; Legis. assistant to, US Congressman Jim Ramstad, Washington, 1991-93; Staff member, field director, US senator Rudy Baschwitz, Minnesota, 1989-90; Marketing manager, CVN Co., 1987-89 **CIV:** Trustee, Minneapolis Institute of Arts, Board directors, Southdale YMCA, Board directors, A Better Chance Foundation, Eden Prairie, Minnesota, **MEM:** Mem.: Eden Prairie C. of C. **PA:** Republican

PAULSON, SARAH CATHARINE CATHARINE, T: Actress **I:** Media & Entertainment **PB:** Tampa **SC:** FL/USA **PT:** Douglas Lyle Paulson II; Catharine Gordon (Dolcater) Paulson **C:** Actress, 1994- **CW:** Actress: (TV guest appearances) Law & Order, 1994, Cracker: Mind Over Murder, 1997, Real Life, 1998, Touched by an Angel, 2001, The D.A., 2004, Desperate Housewives, 2007, Puppy Love, 2008, Law & Order: Special Victims Unit, 2010, Grey's Anatomy, 2010, Blue, 2012; (TV series) American Gothic, 1995-96, Jack & Jill, 1999-2001, Leap of Faith, 2002, Deadwood, 2005, Studio 60 on the Sunset Strip, 2006-07, Cupid, 2009, American Horror Story, 2011-, American Crime Story: The People v. O.J. Simpson, 2016 (Emmy award for Outstanding Lead Actress in a Limited Series or a Movie, 2016, Primetime Emmy for Outstanding Lead Actress in a Miniseries, 2016, Critics Choice for Best Actress in a miniseries, 2016); (TV films) Friends at Last, 1995, Shaughnessy, 1996, The Long Way Home, 1998, Metropolis, 2000, Path to War, 2002, A Christmas Wedding, 2006, Pretty/Handsome, 2008, November Christmas, 2010, Untitled Kari Lizer Project, 2011, Game Change, 2012; (films) Levitation, 1997, The Other Sister, 1999, Held Up, 1999, What Women Want, 2000,

Bug, 2002, Down with Love, 2003, Swimmers, 2005, Piccadilly Jim, 2005, Serenity, 2005, The Notorious Bettie Page, 2005, Diggers, 2006, Griffin & Phoenix, 2006, The Spirit, 2008, Martha Marcy May Marlene, 2011, New Year's Eve, 2011, Mud, 2012, Fairhaven, 2012, The Time Being, 2012, Stars in Shorts, 2012, Twelve Years a Slave, 2013, Carol, 2015, The Runner, 2015, Blue Jay, 2016; (Broadway plays) The Glass Menagerie, 2005, Collected Stories, 2010, (off Broadway) Talley's Folly, 2013,(Film) Rebel in the Rye, 2017, The Post, 2017, Ocean's 8, 2018, Glass, 2019 (Television) American Horror Story: Roanoke, 2016, Feud: Bette and Joan, 2017, American Horror Story:Cult, 2017 Katrina: American Crime Story, 2019 **AW:** Time 100 Most Influential

PAYNE, DONALD MILFORD, T: U.S. Representative from New Jersey **I:** Government Administration/Government Relations/Government Services **DOB:** 07/16/1934 **PB:** Newark, July 16, 1934 **PT:** Son of William Evander and Norma (Garrett) Payne; **ED:** Doctor (hon.), William Paterson University; Doctor (hon.), Essex County College; Doctor (hon.), Drew University; Doctor (hon.), Chicago State University; Grad. student, Springfield College, Massachusetts; BA in Social Studies, Seton Hall University, New Jersey, 1957 **C:** Member, US Congress from 10th New Jersey District,2012-; Member, Committee on Homeland Security, Committee on Transportation and Infrastructure; Member, Newark Municipal Council, 1982-88; Member, Essex County Board Chosen Freeholders, 1972-78; Vice president, Urban Data Systems, Inc., 1969; Executive, Prudential Insurance Co., 1964-69; Teacher, Pulaski Elementary School, Passaic, New Jersey, 1959-64; Teacher, Robert Treat Junior High School, Newark, 1957-59; Teacher, South Side High School, Newark, 1957 **CR:** Chairman Essex County Democratic Committee, 2003-04, Congressional Black Caucus, 1995-97 **CIV:** National president, YMCA, 1970-73 Board directors, Enterprise Works, Board directors, Congl. Award Foundation, Board directors, Discovery Channel Global Education Fund, Board directors, TransAfrica, Board directors, National Endowment Democracy, Chairman, World YMCA Refugee & Rehabilitation Committee, 1973-81 Board directors, Newark YMCA, Board directors, Fighting Back Initiative, Board directors, Newark Day Center, Board directors, Boys and Girls Club Newark, Member congl. del., UN, 2005 Member congl. del., UN, 2003 Member, US Committee for UNICEF, **AW:** Named one of The People to Watch, Sunday Star Ledger, 2007, The Most Influential Black Americans, Ebony magazine, 2006; named to The Power 150, 2008; recipient Africa Grand Leadership Prize award, Celebrate Africa Foundation, 2007, Bishop John T. Walker Distinguished Humanitarian Service award, Africare, 2004, Humanitarian Service award, Isaac Hayes Foundation, 2004, Visionaries for Africa award, Africa Society, 2004, Leadership award, Hudson County Urban League, New Jersey, 2003 **MEM:** Mem.: National Association for the Advancement of Colored People (life), Council Foreign Relations, National Council Negro Women **PA:** Democrat **BA:** 2370 Rayburn House Office Building, Washington, DC, 20515

PEARCE, STEVE, T: U.S. Representative from New Mexico **I:** Government Administration/Government Relations/Government Services **DOB:** 08/24/1947 **PB:** Lamesa **SC:** TX/USA **ED:** MBA, Eastern New Mexico University, Portales, 1991; BBA in Economics, New Mexico State University, Las Cruces, 1970 **C:** Member, US House Financial Services Committee, Washington, 2011-; Member, US Congress from 2nd New Mexico District, Washington, 2011-; Member, Appropriations Committee;

Member, US Congress from 2nd New Mexico District, Washington, 2003-09; Member, New Mexico House of Reps., 1997-2000; Co-owner, operator, Lea Fishing Tools, Inc., 1989-2002; Chief pilot, RUNCO, Inc.,; Chief pilot, check pilot, Marshall Aviation, 1978-81; Owner-operator, crop dusting flying service, Blytheville, Arkansas, 1975-78 **MIL:** Pilot US Air Force, 1970-76, Philippines **AW:** Decorated Air medal, Distinguished Flying Cross; co-recipient VIVA award, Association Commerce and Industry, 2001; named an Outstanding Legislator, New Mexico Tech. Showcase **PA:** Republican

PECK, ART, T: CEO **I:** Retail/Sales **CN:** Gap, Inc. **ED:** MBA, Harvard Business School; BA in Economics, Occidental College, LA, 1977 **C:** CEO, Gap, Inc., 2015-; President growth, innovation & digital (GID) division, Gap, Inc., 2012-15; President Gap North America, Gap, Inc., 2011-12; President Gap Outlet, Gap, Inc., San Francisco, 2008-11; Executive vice president strategy & operations, Gap, Inc., San Francisco, 2005-11; Director, Boston Consulting Group, Inc., 1988-2005; Senior vice president, Boston Consulting Group, Inc., 1982-2005; Financial & marketing positions, Avery Denison, Pasadena, California, **CR:** Board directors Gap, Inc., 2015- Trustee, The Gap Foundation, 2008- **AW:** Named one of The 100 Most Creative People in Business, Fast Company, 2013

PEDROIA, DUSTIN LUIS, T: Professional Baseball Player **I:** Athletics **DOB:** 08/17/1983 **PB:** Woodland **SC:** CA/USA **ED:** Attended, Arizona State University **C:** Second Baseman, Boston Red Sox (2006) **CR:** Member, U.S. National Team World Baseball Classic (2009) **AW:** Named American League MVP, Major League Baseball (2008); American League Rookie of Year (2007); Red Sox Minor League Offensive Player of Year (2005); Named to American League All-Star Team, Major League Baseball (2008-2010, 2013); American League Silver Slugger Award (2008); American League Gold Glove Award (2008, 2011, 2013); World Series Champion (2007, 2013); Heart and Hustle Award (2012) **ACH:** Achievements include member of the World Series Championship winning Boston Red Sox, 2007, 2013; leading the American League in: hits, doubles, 2008; runs, 2008, 2009 **H:** Movies, video games, sports **BA:** Aces Inc, 188 Montague Avenue, 6th Floor, Brooklyn, NY, 11201

PEELE, JORDAN, T: Actor, Director **I:** Media & Entertainment **DOB:** 02/21/1979 **PB:** New York **SC:** NY **C:** (Film) Boner Boyz!, 2008, Little Fockers,2010, 3B, 2010, Wanderlust, 2012, The Sidekick, 2013, Keanu, 2016, Storks, 2016, Get Out,(Director) 2017, Captain Underpants: The First Epic Movie, 2017, Abruptio, 2018,(Television) Mad TV, 2003, Chocolate News, 2008, Reno 911, 2009, The Station, 2009, Supernews!, 2009,Children's Hospital, 2010, Love Bites, 2011, Key and Peel, 2012, The Mindy Project, 2013, Workaholics, 2013, Comedy Bang! Bang!, 2013, Axe Cop, 2013, Modern Family, 2013, Kroll Show, 2013, Bob's Burgers, 2014, Fargo, 2014, Drunk History, 2014, Robot Chicken, 2014, Life in Pieces, 2015, Rick and Morty, 2015, Wet Hot American Summer: First Day of Camp, 2015, Trip Tank, 2015, Supermansion, 2015, The Muppets, 2016, American Dad!, 2016, The Daily show, 2017, Big Mouth, 2017, The Last O.G., 2018 **AW:** Time 100 Most Influential, 2017, Peabody, 2013 **BA:** Principato Young Entertainment, 9465 Wilshire Blvd, Suite 900, Beverly Hills, CA, 90212

PEGULA, TERRY, I: Business Management/Business Services **DOB:** 03/27/1951 **PB:** Carbondale **SC:** PA/USA **ED:** BS in Petroleum and Natural Gas Engineering, Pennsylvania State University, 1973 **C:** Owner, Buffalo Bills, 2014-; Owner,

Buffalo Sabres, 2011-; Founder, president, CEO, East Resources Inc., 1983-2010; With, Felmont Oil; With, Getty Oil **CR:** Operator First Niagara Center, Buffalo associated with Impact Sports Performance co-owner Black River Music, Nashville **PA:** Republican

PEI, I.M., T: Architect **I:** Architecture & Construction **DOB:** 04/26/1917 **PB:** Canton **PT:** Son of Tsu Yee Pei and Lien Kwun Chwong; **ED:** LHD (hon.), American University, Paris, 1990; LHD (hon.), University of Hong Kong, 1990; LHD (hon.), University of Rochester, 1982; LHD (hon.), University of Colorado, 1982; LHD (hon.), Columbia University, New York City, 1980; LLD (hon.), Pace University; LLD (hon.), Chinese University, Hong Kong, 1970; DFA (hon.), University of Rochester; DFA (hon.), Harvard University; DFA (hon.), Northeastern University; DFA (hon.), Dartmouth College, 1991; DFA (hon.), New York University, 1980; DFA (hon.), Brown University, 1980; DFA (hon.), University Massachusetts, 1980; DFA (hon.), Carnegie Mellon University, 1980; DFA (hon.), Rensselaer Poly. Institute, 1978; DFA (hon.), University of Pennsylvania, 1970; MArch, Harvard University, 1946; BArch, Massachusetts Institute of Technology, Cambridge, 1940 **C:** Ind. architect, New York City, 1990-; Founding partner, Pei Cobb Freed & Partners (formerly I.M. Pei & Partners, I.M. Pei & Associates), New York City, 1955-90; Director architectural division, Webb & Knapp, Inc., 1948-55; Assistant professor, Harvard Grad. School Design, 1945-48; With, National Defense Research Committee, 1943-45; Architect, New York City, 1939-42 **CIV:** Member, National Council on Arts, 1981-84 Member, National Council Humanities, 1966-70 **CW:** Principal works include Mile High Center, Denver, National Center Atmospheric Research, Boulder, Colorado, Dallas City Hall, John Fitzgerald Kennedy Libr., Boston, Can. Imperial Bank Commerce Complex, Toronto, Overseas Chinese Banking Corp. Center, Singapore, Dreyfus Chemistry Building, Massachusetts Institute of Technology, East-West Center University Hawaii, Honolulu, Mellon Art Center and Choate Rosemary Hall Sci. Center, Wallingford, Connecticut, Univ. Plz., New York University, Johnson Museum Art Cornell University, Ithaca, New York, Washington Sq. East, Philadelphia, Everson Museum Art, Syracuse, New York, National Gallery Art, East Building, Washington, Wilmington Tower, Raffles City, Singapore, West Wing Museum Fine Arts, Boston, expansion and modernization of Louvre Museum, Paris, Morton H. Meyerson Symphony Center, Dallas, Massachusetts Institute of Technology Arts and Media Center, Jacob K. Javits Convention Center, New York City, Fragrant Hill Hotel, Beijing, Texas Commerce Tower, Houston, Bank of China, Hong Kong, Creative Artists Agency, Beverly Hills, California, Guggenheim Pavilion, Mount Sinai Medical Center, New York City, Rock n' Roll Hall of Fame and Museum, Cleveland, Museum Modern Art, Athens, Greece, Miho Museum of Art, Shiga, Japan, Bilbao Estuary Project, Spain, Four Seasons Hotel, New York City, planning projects include,(Principal Works) Louvre Pyramid, 1993, Rock and Roll Hall of Fame, 1995, Buck Institute on Aging, 1996, Miho Museum, 1997, Bank of China Head Office Building, 1999, Republic of Korea Permenant Mission to the United Nations, 2000, Essensa Condiminum, 2000,Zeughaus Wing at Deutsches Historisches Museum, 2003,MUDAM-Musée d'Art Moderne Grand-Duc Jean, 2006, Suzhou Museum, 2006, Embassy of the People's Republic of China to the U.S. of America, 2006, Museum of Islamic Art, 2008, Macao Science Center, 2009 **AW:** Recipient Oreint und Okzident Preis, Erwin Wickert Foundation, 2006, Legion of Honor, France, 2006, Thomas Jefferson medal

for Distinguished Achievement in the Arts, Humanities or Social Scis., Am. Philosophical Society, 2001, Freedom medal, 1993, Excellence 2000 award, 1991, Colbert Foundation first award for excellence, 1991, UCLA Gold medal, 1990, Praemium Imperiale, Japan Art Association, 1989, National Medal of Art, 1988, Medal of French Legion of Honor, 1988, Medal of Liberty, 1986, Pritzker Architecture prize, 1983, La Grande Medaille D'or L'Académie d'Architecture, 1981, Mayor's award of Honor for Art and Culture, New York City, 1981, National Arts Club Gold medal of honor, 1981, gold medal for architecture, American Academy of Arts and Letters, 1979, Thomas Jefferson Memorial medal for Architecture, 1976; fellow Wheelwright, Harvard University, 1951, Massachusetts Institute of Technology traveling, 1940, Presidental Medal of Freedom, 1992 **MEM:** Fellow: American Institute of Architects (Medal of Honor New York chapter 1963, Gold Medal 1979), ASID (hon.); mem.: National Academy of Design, Urban Design Council, Royal Institute Brit. Architects, Am. Academy and Institute Arts and Letters (chancellor 1978-80), Am. Academy Arts and Scis., National Institute Arts and Letters (Arnold Brunner award 1961) **BA:** Pei Cobb Freed & Partners, 88 Pine Street, New York, NY, 10005

PELLI, CESAR, T: Architect **I:** Architecture & Construction **DOB:** 10/12/1926 **PB:** Tucuman **PT:** Son of Victor V. and Teresa S. Pelli; **ED:** MS in Architecture, University Illinois, 1954; BArch cum laude, University Tucuman, 1949 **C:** Associate, Pelli Clarke Pelli Architect (formerly Cesar Pelli & Associates), New Haven, 1977-; Dean, Yale University School Architecture, New Haven, 1977-84; Associate, Gruen Associates Inc., LA, 1968-77; Associate, Daniel, Mann, Johnson & Mendenhall, 1964-68; Associate, Eero Saarinen & Associates, 1954-64 **CW:** Works include Pacific Design Center and Expansion, LA (Honor award Southern California chapter American Institute of Architects 1976), US Embassy, Tokyo, Museum Modern Art Expansion, New York City, World Fin. Center and Winter Garden, New York City (Bard award 1992), Cleveland Clinic (Honor award American Institute of Architects 1986), Herring Hall, Rice University, Houston (Honor award American Institute of Architects 1986), Carnegie Hall Tower, New York City (Honor award American Institute of Architects 1994, Design award AIA/Conn. 1991), Boyer Center Molecular Medicine Yale University (Design award AIA/Conn. 1991), Bank of Am. Corp. Center, Charlotte, One Can. Sq., London, NTT Corp. Hdqrs., Tokyo (Design award AIA/Conn. 1997), Terminal B/C Reagan Washington National Airport (Design award AIA/Conn. 1998, NE Design award 1999, Design for Transportation award 2000), Aronoff Center for the Arts, Cincinnati (USITT Honor award 1996, Design award AIA/CIN 1996, Design award AIA/Conn. 1997), Petronas Towers, Kuala Lumpur, Malaysia (Design award AIA/Conn. 1999, NE Design award 2000, Honor award American Institute of Architects 2000), Frances Lehman Loeb Art Center Vassar College, Poughkeepsie, New York (Design award AIA/Conn. 1996), International Fin. Center, Hong Kong, National Museum of Art, Osaka, Japan (Design award AIA/Conn. 2005), Overture Center, Madison, Cira Center, Phila. (Am. Architecture award 2006), The Solaire, New York (LEED Gold), Carnival Center Performing Arts, Florida, Minneapolis Central Libr. (AIA/ Conn. award, 2006), Bloomberg Tower, New York City (Urban Land Institute award for excellence, 2005), Orange County Performing Arts Center, Costa Mesa, California (AIA/Conn. award, 2007), Bank of Oklahoma Center, Tulsa, Connecticut Sci. Center, Hartford, Torre de Cristal, Madrid, Torre Libertad, Mexico City, South Station Air Rights

Devel., Boston, Torre Iberdrola, Bilbao, Paradise St. Devel. & One Park West, Liverpool, England, Gran Torre Costanera, Santiago, Chile, Project CityCtr. Hotel and Casino, Las Vegas, Torre Puerto Triana, Seville, Spain, Winnipeg Airport Terminal, National Children's Museum, Washington, DC, Repsol YPF Hdqrs., Buenos Aires, Transby Terminal & Tower, San Francisco; editor Yale Seminars on Architecture, 1981-82; author Observations for Young Architects, 1999,(Principal Works)Iberdrola Tower, office building, Bilbao, Spain,2011,St. Katharine Drexel Chapel, Xavier University of Louisiana, New Orleans, 2012, Unicredit Tower, master plan and mixed-use development, Milan, Italy, 2012, The Landmark, Abu Dhabi, United Arab Emirates, 2013: DePaul University, The Theatre School, Chicago, 2013, Cameron and Edward Lanphier Center, Choate Rosemary Hall, Wallingford, Connecticut, 2015 McKinney & Olive, Mixed-Use Development Dallas, 2016, Hancher Auditorium, University of Iowa Iowa City, Iowa, 2016, The Cabin Stack Prefabricated House, 2016, Eccles Theater, performing arts center, Salt Lake City, 2016, Indiana University School of Informatics, Luddy Hall, Indiana University Bloomington, Indiana, 2017 (In Progress) Cira Center South, Philadelphia, 2012, Sidra Medical Center, Qatar, 2012, Cajasol Tower, office building, Seville, Spain, 2012, Banco Macro Tower, Buenos Aires, Argentina, 2013, Torre Sofia, San Pedro Garza García, Mexico, 2013, Maral Explanada, Mar del Plata, Argentina, 2012, Torre Mitikah, Mexico City, 2014, Transbay Transit Center, San Francisco, 2017, Louis Armstrong International Airport, New Terminal, New Orleans, 2018 **AW:** Recipient Aga Khan award, Aga Khan Trust for Culture, 2004, AIA Gold Medal, 1995, Lyn S. Beedle Lifetime Achievement Award, 2008 **MEM:** Fellow American Institute of Architects (Firm award 1989, named to top ten list of living Am. architects 1991, Gold medal 1995); member National Academy of Design (Arnold M. Brunner Memorial prize 1978), Am. Academy Arts and Letters (academician), International Academy Architecture (academician)

PELOSI, NANCY PATRICIA, T: U.S. Representative From California **I:** Government Administration/Government Relations/Government Services **DOB:** 03/26/1940 **PB:** Baltimore **SC:** MD/ USA **PT:** Thomas J. D'Alesandro, Jr.; Annunciata M. Lombardi **ED:** Honorary LLD, Mills College, 2010; AB in Political Science, Trinity College, 1962 **C:** U.S. Congress, 12th California District, 2013-Present; Minority Leader, 2011-Present; Chair, U.S. House Democratic Steering & Policy Committee, 2003-Present; Speaker of the House, 2007-2011; Minority Leader, 2003-2007; Assistant Minority Leader, Minority Whip, 2002-2003; U.S. Congress, Eighth California District, 1993-2013; U.S. Congress, Fifth California District, 1987-1993; Finance Chairman, Democratic Senatorial Campaign Committee, 1987; Committeewoman, Democratic National Committee, 1984; Chairman, California State Democratic Committee, 1981-1983; Committeewoman, Democratic National Committee, 1980; Chair, Northern California Democratic Party, 1977-1981; Committeewoman, Democratic National Committee, 1976 **CW:** Co-Author, (With Amy Hill Hearth) Know Your Power: A Message to America's Daughters, 2008 **AW:** The Ten Most Powerful Women in Washington, Fortune Magazine, 2009-2010; The 100 Most Powerful Women in DC, Washingtonian Magazine, 2009; The Global Elite, Newsweek Magazine, 2008; The 100 Most Influential People in the World, TIME Magazine, 2007, 2010; The 50 Most Powerful People in DC, GQ Magazine, 2007, 2009; America's Best Leaders, US News & World Report, 2007; Barbara Walters Most Fascinating Persons, 2006; Golden Plate Award,

Academy of Achievement, 2006; The 100 Most Powerful Women, Forbes Magazine, 2005-2014; National Legislation Award, League of United Latin American Citizens, 2004; Legacy Award, Cesar E. Chavez Foundation, 2003; Alan Cranston Peace Award, Global Security Institute, 2003; Congressional Service Award, American Council for Voluntary International Action, 1999; Public Service Award, Federation of American Societies for Experimental Biology, 1997 **ACH:** Achievements include being the first woman in US history to be elected Speaker of the House, 2006 **PA:** Democrat **BA:** Office of Nancy Pelosi, 233 Canon H.O.B., Washington, DC, 20515-0508

PENCE, KAREN, T: Second Lady of the U.S. **I:** Government Administration/Government Relations/Government Services **ED:** B.S.,M.S., Elementary Education, Butler University **C:** Second Lady of the U.S., 2017-; First Lady of Indiana, 2013-2017

PENCE (MICHAEL RICHARD PENCE), MIKE, T: Vice President of the U.S. **I:** Government Administration/Government Relations/Government Services **DOB:** 06/07/1959 **PB:** Columbus **SC:** IN/USA **MS:** Married **SPN:** Karen Pence (June 8, 1985) **CH:** Michael, Charlotte, Audrey **ED:** JD, Ind. University Robert H. McKinney School Law, 1986; BA in History, Hanover College, 1981 **C:** Vice President of the U.S., 2017-; Governor, State of Ind., Indianapolis, 2013-16; Chairman, US House Republican Conference, 2009-11; Chairman, US House Republican Study Committee, 2005-07; Member, US House Foreign Affairs Committee,; Member, US Congress from 6th Ind. District, 2003-13; Member, US Congress from 2nd Ind. District, 2001-03; President, Ind. Policy Rev. Foundation, 1991; Attorney, 1986-91 **CR:** Republican Party nominee for V.P. of the US, 2016 **CW:** Host (radio shows) The Mike Pence Show, 1992-99 **PA:** Republican **BA:** Office of the Vice President, 1600 Pennsylvania Avenue NW, Washington, DC, 20500

PENN, SEAN, T: Actor **I:** Media & Entertainment **DOB:** 08/17/1960 **PB:** Burbank **SC:** CA/USA **C:** Founder, J/P Haitian Relief Organization, 2010 **CW:** Actor, (Films) Taps, 1981, Fast Times At Ridgemont High, 1982, Summerspell, 1983, Bad Boys, 1983, Crackers, 1984, Racing With The Moon, 1984, The Falcon And The Snowman, 1985, At Close Range, 1986, Shanghai Surprise, 1986, Cool Blue, 1988, Colors, 1988, Judgment In Berlin, 1988, Casualties Of War, 1989, We're No Angels, 1989, State Of Grace, 1990, Carlito's Way, 1993, Dead Man Walking, 1995, Loved, 1997, She's So Lovely, 1997, U Turn, 1997, The Game, 1997, Hugo Pool, 1997, Hurlyburly, 1998, The Thin Red Line, 1998, Being John Malkovich, 1999, Sweet And Lowdown, 1999, Up At The Villa, 2000, Before Night Falls, 2000, The Weight Of Water, 2000, The Beaver Trilogy, 2001, I Am Sam, 2001, It's All About Love, 2003, Mystic River, 2003, 21 Grams, 2003, The Assassination Of Richard Nixon, 2004, The Interpreter, 2005, All The King's Men, 2006, Milk, 2008, Fair Game, 2010, The Tree Of Life, 2011, This Must Be The Place, 2011, Gangster Squad, 2013, The Secret Life Of Walter Mitty, 2013, (Voice Actor) The Angry Birds Movie, 2016, The Last Face, 2016, Sound Of Sun, 2016, The Professor And The Madman, 2018, (Documentaries) The Last Party, 1991, A Constant Forge, 2000, Scene Smoking: Cigarettes, Cinema & The Myth Of Cool, 2001, See How They Run, 2001, (TV Films) Hellinger's Law, 1981, The Killing Of Randy Webster, 1981, (Music Videos) Highway Patrolman, 1982, North Dakota, 1992, Dance With The One That Brought You, 1993, (TV Appearances) Ellen, 1997, Friends, 2001, The Barry Williams Show, 2002, Two And A Half Men, 2004, Viva La Bam, 2004,

Family Guy, 2016, The First, 2018, (Broadway Plays) Heartland, 1981, Slab Boys, 1983; Writer, Director, (Films) The Indian Runner, 1991, 11'09"01 - September 11, 2002; Writer, Producer, Director, The Crossing Guard, 1995; Producer, Director, The Pledge, 2001, Into The Wild, 2007; Actor, Writer, Producer, The Gunman, 2015; Narrator, (Documentaries) Dear America: Letters Home From Vietnam, 1987, Dogtown And Z-Boys, 2001; Narrator, Executive Producer, Witch Hunt, 2008 **AW:** Ambassador-at-Large to Haiti, Haiti's Ministry Foreign & Religious Affairs, 2012, International Humanitarian Service Award, American Red Cross, 2012, Peace Summit Award, World Summit of Nobel Peace Laureates, 2012, Stanley Kramer Award, Producers Guild of America, 2011, Desert Palm Achievement Award, Palm Springs International Film Society, 2009, The 100 Agents of Change, Rolling Stone Magazine, 2009, Critics' Choice Award For Best Actor, Broadcast Film Critics Association, 2009, Screen Actors Guild Award For Outstanding Performance By A Male Actor In A Leading Role, Milk, 2009, Academy Award For Best Actor, Academy of Motion Picture Arts & Sciences, Milk, 2008, John Steinbeck Award, San Francisco Chronicle, 2004, Academy Award For Best Actor, Academy of Motion Picture Arts & Sciences, Critics' Choice Award For Best Actor, Broadcast Film Critics Association, Golden Globe Award For Best Actor In Motion Picture/Drama, Hollywood Foreign Press Association, Mystic River, 2003 **BA:** CAA, 2000 Avenue of the Stars, Los Angeles, CA, 90067

PENSKE, ROGER S. JR., T: Retail Executive **I:** Retail/Sales **ED:** Graduate, Lehigh University **C:** Chairman, CEO, Penske Automotive Group, Inc., 1999-Present; Chairman, President, Pennsylvania International Raceway, Inc., 1986-Present; Chairman, Penske Truck Leasing Co., 1982-Present; Chairman, CEO, Penske Corp., 1969-Present; Chairman, United Auto Group Inc., 1999; Chairman, Penske Motorsports (Acquired by Penske Automotive Group, Inc.), 1996-1999; Board of Directors, Penske Motorsports (Acquired by Penske Automotive Group, Inc.), 1995; Chairman, California Speedway Corp., 1994; Chairman, Detroit Diesel Corp., 1987; Chairman, Michigan International Speedway, Inc., 1973; Managing Director, Transportation Resource Partners, LP; Chairman, Detroit Investment Fund; Senior Advisor to Board of Directors, Delphi Corp.; Former Board of Directors, Delphi Corp.; Founder, Penske Racing South Inc.; Founder, Penske Racing Inc.; Founder, Penske Logistics **CR:** (Board of Directors) General Electric Co., 1994-Present, Home Depot, Inc., 2000, Gulfstream Aerospace Corp., 1993, Detroit Renaissance; (Vice Chairman) CarsDirect.com, Inc., 2000-Present, International Speedway Corp., 1999-Present, Delphi Automotive Systems Corp.; Former Board of Directors, Internet Brands, Inc. **CIV:** Board of Directors, Business Leaders for Michigan, Universal Tech. Institute, 2002-Present; The Business Council; Chairman, Downtown Detroit Partnership

PERA, ROBERT J., T: Communications Company Executive, Professional Sports Team Owner **I:** Business Management/Business Services **DOB:** 03/10/1978 **SC:** U.S. **ED:** MS in Electrical Engineering, University California, San Diego; BS in Electrical Engineering, University California, San Diego; BA in Japanese Language, University California, San Diego **C:** Owner, Memphis Grizzlies, 2012-; Founder, CEO, Ubiquiti Networks, Inc., 2005-; Hardware engineer, Apple, Inc., 2003-05 **AW:** Named one of America's 20 Most Powerful CEOs 40 and Under, Forbes magazine, 2012

PERDUE, DAVID ALFRED JR., T: U.S. Senator for Georgia **I:** Government Administration/ Government Relations/Government Services **DOB:** 12/10/1949 **PB:** Macon **SC:** GA/USA **PT:** Son of David A. and Gervaise (Wynn) P. **MS:** Married **SPN:** Bonnie Dunn Perdue (8/26/1972) **CH:** Blake R., David Alfred III **ED:** MS in Operations Research, Georgia Institute Tech., 1975; BS in Industrial Engineering, Georgia Institute Tech., 1972 **CT:** Registered securities principal; cert. financial planner; cert. management consultant **C:** Member, US Senate Special Committee on Aging, 2015-; Member, US Senate Judiciary Committee, 2015-; Member, US Senate Foreign Relations Committee, 2015-; Member, US Senate Budget Committee, 2015-; Member, US Senate Agricultural Nutrition & Forestry Committee, 2015-; US Senator from Georgia, 2015-; Partner, Perdue Partners, Atlanta, 2011-15; Senior Consultant, Gujarat Heavy Chemicals Ltd, New Delhi, 2007-11; Chairman, CEO, Dollar General Corp., Nashville, 2003-07; Chairman, CEO, Pillowtex Corp., Kannapolis, North Carolina, 2002-03; President, CEO, Reebok Brand, Reebok International Ltd., 2001-02; Executive Vice President, Global Supply Chain, Reebok International Ltd., 2001-02; Executive Vice President, Global Operations Units, Reebok International Ltd., 1999-2001; Senior Vice President, Global Supply Chain, Reebok International Ltd., 1998-99; Senior Vice President, Haggar Inc., 1994-98; Senior Vice President, Operations, Sara Lee Corp., Hong Kong, China, 1992-94; President, Westar Holding Co., 1987-92; Vice President, Paul R. Ray & Co., 1986-87; Vice President, Professional Planning Associates, 1983-86; Partner, Kurt Salmon Associates, 1976-83; Staff Consultant, Kurt Salmon Associates, 1972-75 **CR:** Board of Directors, Alliant Energy Corp., 2001-, Dollar General Corp., 2003-07, Jo-Ann Stores, Inc., 2008-11, Liquidity Services, Inc., 2009-14, Cardlytics, Inc., 2010-14, BRG Sports Inc., 2011-14 **CIV:** Member, Georgia Council on Youth, Atlanta, 1972, Atlanta Care Advisory Board, 1983-85 **MEM:** Member, Mortgage Banking Association, Institute Cert. Financial Planners, Institute Management Consultant, Atlanta Athletic Club **H:** Tennis, Golf, Sailing, Reading **PA:** Republican **BA:** Office of David Perdue, 455 Russell Office Building, Washington, DC, 20510

PERDUE, SONNY, T: U.S. Secretary of Agriculture **I:** Government Administration/Government Relations/Government Services **DOB:** 12/20/1946 **PB:** Perry **SC:** GA/USA **PT:** Ervin Perdue; Ophie Perdue **ED:** DVM, University of Georgia College of Veterinary Medicine (1971) **C:** Secretary, Department of Agriculture, Washington, DC (2017-Present); Governor, State of Georgia, Atlanta, GA (2003-2011); President, Pro Tempore, Georgia General Assembly (1997); Member, District 18, Georgia General Assembly, Atlanta, GA (1990-2002); Member, Houston County Planning & Zoning Board; Co-Chair, Joint Commission, Legislative Information Management, Georgia General Assembly; Chairman, Higher Education Committee, Defense Conversion Committee, Georgia General Assembly; Veterinarian (Retired); Majority Leader, Georgia General Assembly **MIL:** Captain, US Air Force, Vietnam (1971-1974) **PA:** Republican **BA:** US Department of Agriculture, 1400 Independence Ave S.W., Washington, DC, 20520

PEREZ, CARMEN, T: Activist **I:** Other **C:** Executive Director, The Gathering for Justice, 2017- **AW:** Time Most Influential, 2017 **MEM:** Co-Chair, Women's March, 2017

PEREZ, THOMAS EDWARD, T: Chairman of the Democratic National Committee **I:** Government Administration/Government Relations/Government Services **DOB:** 10/07/1961 **PB:** Buffalo **PT:** Married Ann Marie Staudenmaier; children: Amalia, Susana, Rafael **ED:** Master in Public Policy, John F. Kennedy School Government, Harvard University, 1987; JD cum laude, Harvard Law School, 1987; AB in International Rels.-Polit. Sci., Brown University, 1983 **CT:** Bar: DC 1998, New York 1988 **C:** Chair, Democratic National Committee, 2017-; Secretary, US Department Labor, Washington, 2013-17; Assistant attorney general Civil Rights Division, US Department Justice, Washington, 2009-13; Secretary Department Labor, Licensing & Regulation (DLLR), State of Maryland, Annapolis, 2007-09; Assistant professor, director clinical law office, University Maryland School Law, Baltimore, 2001-07; Director Office Civil Rights (OCR), US Department Health & Human Services (Department of Health and Human Services), 1999-2002; Special counsel to Senator Edward M. Kennedy, US Senate, 1995-98; Deputy assistant attorney for civil rights, US Department Justice, 1998-99; Deputy chief criminal section, civil rights division, US Department Justice, 1994-97; Trial lawyer, criminal section, civil rights division, US Department Justice, 1989-94; Law clerk to Hon. Zita L. Weinshienk, US District Court Colorado, 1987-89 **CR:** Consultant Vera Institute Justice, New York City, 1997-99; teacher Stanford University, Washington, 1994-96; part time faculty member, George Washington School Public Health **CIV:** Member, Montgomery County Council, 2002-06, council president, 2005 **MEM:** Member Hispanic Bar Association (board directors) **PA:** Democrat **BA:** Democratic National Committee, 430 South Capitol Street Southeast, Washington, DC, 20003

PERKINS, THOMAS B., T: CEO **I:** Retail/Sales **CN:** Core-Mark Holding **ED:** BS, Northern Arizona University **C:** Senior Vice President, Resources, Core-Mark Holding Co., Inc., 2007-2018; Vice President, U.S. Division, Core Mark Holding Co., Inc., 2003-2007; President, Arizona Distribution Center, Core Mark Holding Co., Inc., 2001-2003; President, Spokane Distribution Center, Core Mark Holding Co., Inc., 1996-2000; Controller, Los Angeles Distribution Center, Core Mark Holding Co., Inc., 1993-1996; Controller, Pepsi-Cola Co. **BA:** Core Mark Holding Co. Inc., Suite 415, 395 Oyster Point Boulevard, South San Francisco, CA, 94080

PERLMAN, ITZHAK, T: Violinist **I:** Media & Entertainment **DOB:** 08/31/1945 **PB:** Tel Aviv **SC:** Israel **PT:** Son of Chaim and Shoshana P. **MS:** Married **SPN:** Toby Lynn Friedlander, 1967 **CH:** Noah, Navah, Miriam, Leora, Ariella **ED:** Degree (hon.), Hebrew University; Degree (hon.), Yeshiva University; Degree (hon.), Roosevelt University; Degree (hon.), Brandeis University; Degree (hon.), Yale University; Degree (hon.), Harvard University; Degree (hon.), Tufts University, 1986; Student, Meadowmount School of Music.; Studied with Ivan Galamian & Dorothy DeLay, Juilliard School; Student, Tel Aviv Academy of Music **CR:** Appeared with numerous orchestras including New York Philharmonic, Cleveland Orchestra, Philadelphia Orchestra, National Symphony Orchestra, Berlin Philharmonic, English Chamber Orchestra, London Symphony, London Philharmonic, Royal Philharmonic, BBC Orchestra, Vienna Philharmonic, Israel Philharmonic founder Perlman Music Program, New York, 1998- principal guest conductor Detroit Symphony, 2001-05 music advisor St. Louis Symphony, 2002-04 participant numerous music festivals including Ravinia Festival, Tanglewood Music Festival, Aspen Music Festival, Israel Fes-

tival, Wolf Trap Summer Festival recital tours US, Can., South America, Europe, Israel, Australia, Far East recorded for Angel, London, RCA Victor, DG, Telarc, Teldec, Sony **CIV:** Founder, Perlman Music Program, 1995 **CW:** Albums include Vivaldi: The Four Seasons, 1977 (Grammy award best classical performance 1977), Beethoven: Sonatas For Violin And Piano, 1978 (Gramy award best chamber music performance 1978), Brahms: Concerto For Violin In D, 1978 (Grammy award best classical album 1978), The Spanish Album, 1980 (Grammy award best classical performance 1980), Brahms: Violin And Cello Concerto In A Minor, 1980 (Grammy award best classical performance 1980), Berg: Violin Concerto/Stravinsky: Violin Concerto In D, 1980 (Grammy award best classical performance 1980), Music For Two Violins, 1980 (Grammy award best chamber music performance 1980), Isaac Stern: 60th Anniversary Celebration, 1981 (Grammy award best engineered recording 1981, Grammy award best classical performance 1981), Tchaikovsky: Piano Trio In A Minor, 1981 (Grammy award best chamber music performance 1981), Elgar: Violin Concerto In B Minor, 1982 (Emmy award best classical performance 1982), Chausson: Violin Concerto, 1984, An Isaac Stern Vivaldi Gala, 1985, Beethoven: The Complete Piano Trios, 1987 (Grammy award best chamber music performance 1987), Tradition,1987, Duos, 1987, Bach: Double Concerto, 1987, Mozart Violin Concertos Nos.1 & 2, 1987 (Grammy award best classical performance 1987), Paganini & Giuliani: Duos for Violin and Guitar, 1987, The Italian Album, 1989, Brahms: The 3 Violin Sonatas, 1990 (Grammy award best small ensemble performance 1990) Vivaldi:The Four Seasons,1992, Dvorák In Prague: A Celebration, 1994, Bach: Violin Concertos, 1995, The American Album: Works Of Bernstein, Barber, Foss, 1995 (Grammy award best instrumental soloist performance with orchestra 1995),In the Fiddlers House, 1995, Cinema Serenade, 1997, Holiday Tradition, 1998, Concertos from my Childhood, 1999, John Williams Greatest Hits 1969-1999 Cinema Serenade 2, 1999, Classic Yo-Yo, 2001, Classic Perlman: Rhapsody, 2002, The Essential Itzhak Perlman, 2009, Eternal Echoes, 2012, Violin Sonatas,2015, The Perlman Sound, 2015; appeared in PBS documentary Fiddling for the Future, 1998 (Emmy award outstanding cultural music-dance program 1999); TV specials Perlman in Russia, 1992 (Emmy award outstanding classical program 1992), Itzhak Perlman: In the Fiddler's House, 1996 (Emmy award outstanding cultural music-dance program 1996). **AW:** Recipient Leventritt prize, 1964, Medal of Liberty, 1986, National Medal of Arts, 2000, Kennedy Center Honor, 2003, Golden Plate award, Academy Achievement, 2005, Presidential Medal of Freedom, The White House, 2015; named Musician of Year, Musical Am., 1981; inductee Am. Classical Music Hall of Fame, 2001, Grammy Lifetime Achievement Award, 2008, National Medal of Arts, 2000, Emmy Award for Outstanding Individual Achievement, 1994

PERLMUTTER, DAVID H., T: Physician, Educator **I:** Medicine & Health Care **DOB:** 05/11/1952 **PB:** Brooklyn, New York **ED:** BA, University Rochester, 1974; MD, St. Louis University, 1978 **CT:** Cert. Pediatrics, 1983, Pediatric Gastroenterology and Nutrition, 1990; **C:** Executive Vice Chancellor for Medical Affairs and Dean of the School of Medicine, Washington University, 2015-; Physician in Chief, Sci. Director, Children's Hospital Pittsburgh, 2001—2015; Intern then Resident in Pediatrics, University Pennsylvania School Medicine, Philadelphia, Pennsylvania, 1978-81; Professor Cell Biology and Physiology, University Pittsburgh School Medicine, 2001—; Vira I. Heinz Professor and Chair Pediatrics, University Pittsburgh School

Medicine, 2001—; Director Gastroenterology and Nutrition Division, St. Louis Children's Hospital, 1992—2001; Professor Cell Biology, Physiology, Washington University School Medicine, St. Louis, Missouri, 1989—2001; Donald Strominger Professor of Pediatrics, Washington University School Medicine, St. Louis, Missouri, 1986-89; Assistant Professor Pediatrics, Harvard University School Medicine, Boston, Massachusetts, 1985-86; Instructor Pediatrics, Harvard University School Medicine, Boston, Massachusetts, 1983-85; Fellow in Pediatric Gastroenterology, Harvard University School Medicine, Boston, Massachusetts, 1981-84 **CW:** Editorial Bd.: Hepatology, Am. Journal Physiology; Consultant Editor: Pediatric Research; Contributor Articles to Professional Journals **AW:** Recipient Established Investigator Award Am. Heart Association, 1987, Research Scholar Award Am. Gastroent. Association, 1985, RJR Nabisco Co., 1986, E. Mead Johnson award for Research in Pediatrics, 1994 **MEM:** Member Institute Medicine, Am. Pediatric Society, Association Am. Physicians, Am. Association for the Study of Liver Disease, Society Pediatric Research (council rep. 1990—, former president), Am. Society Cell Biology, Am. Society Clinical Investigation. **BA:** Washington University School of Medicine, 660 S. Euclid Ave, St. Louis, MO, 63110

PERLMUTTER, ED, T: U.S. Representative from Colorado **I:** Government Administration/Government Relations/Government Services **DOB:** 05/01/1953 **PB:** Denver **ED:** JD, University Colorado School Law, 1978; BA, University Colorado, Boulder, 1975 **C:** Member, US Congress from 7th Colorado District, 2006-; Member, Committee on Financial Services, Committee on Science, Space, and Technology; Attorney, Berenbaum, Weinshienk & Eason, Professional Corporation, Denver, 1978-; Member Fin. Services Committee, Homeland Security Committee, US Congress from 7th Colorado District,; Member Pub. Policy & Planning Committee, Joint Legal Services Committee, Colorado State Senate,; President Pro Tempore, Colorado State Senate, Denver, 2001-03; Member District 20, Colorado State Senate, Denver, 1994-2002 **CR:** Fin. Chair Jefferson County Dems. Chair First Judicial & Judicial Performance Commission, 1991-93, Board Trustees, 1989-91 **CIV:** Active, Am. Heart Association, Active, Girl Scouts of America, Active, Jefferson Foundation, Trustee, Midwest Research Institute, PTA member, Maple Grove Elementary School, Golden, Colorado, member, Applewood Community Church, Past Board Directors, National Jewish Medical & Research Center **MEM:** Mem.: American Bar Association, Commercial Law League America, University Colorado Alumni Association, Colorado Trial Lawyers Association, Colorado Oil & Gas Association, Associated General Contractors Colorado, Applewood Business Association, Am. Judicature Society, Am. Bankruptcy Institute, Golden C. of C., West C. of C., Northwest Metro C. of C., Denver Bar Association, Colorado Bar. Association (board governors), Arvada Soccer Association, Table Mountain Soccer Association, Wheat Ridge Soccer Association **PA:** Democrat

PERLMUTTER, SAUL, T: Astrophysicist, Educator **I:** Education/Educational Services **PB:** Champaign-Urbana **SC:** IL/USA **ED:** PhD in Physics, University of California Berkeley, 1986; AB in Physics (magna cum laude), Harvard University, 1981 **C:** Professor, physics department, University of California Berkeley, 2004-; Senior staff scientist, astrophysicist, Lawrence Berkeley National Laboratory,; Postdoctoral researcher, Space Sci. Laboratory, Lawrence Berkeley National Laboratory, 1987-88 **CR:** Leader, International Supernova Cosmology

Project, 1998- **CW:** Contributor articles to professional journals, to Sky and Telescope magazine; guest appearances Pub. Broadcasting Systems, BBC documentaries on astronomy and cosmology **AW:** Co-recipient Nobel Prize in Physics, 2011, Gruber Cosmology prize, 2007, Shaw prize in Astronomy, Shaw Foundation, Hong Kong, 2006; named Scientist of Year, California, 2003; recipient Feltrinelli International prize, Physical & Math. Sciences, Lincei Academy, Rome, 2006, Padua prize, 2005, John Scott award, 2005, E.O. Lawrence award in Physics, Department Energy, 2002, Breakthrough of Year award, Science Magazine, 1998, Henri Chretien award, American Astronomical Society, 1996,Breakthrough Prize in Fundamental Physics, 2015 **MEM:** Fellow: Am. Academy Arts & Scis. **ACH:** Achievements include discovery of the universe's accelerating expansion using supernovae as "standard candles" to measure the cosmic expansion rate

PEROT, ROSS, T: Real Estate Company, Investment Company, Data Processing Executive **I:** Business Management/Business Services **DOB:** 06/27/1930 **PB:** Texarkana **SC:** TX/USA **PT:** Son of Gabriel Ross and Lulu May Perot; **ED:** Educated, US Naval Academy, 1949-53 **C:** Chairman emeritus, Perot Systems Corp., Plano, 2004-; Board member, Perot Systems Corp., Plano, 1997-; Founder, Perot Systems Corp., Washington, 1988-; Founder, The Perot Group, Dallas, 1986-; Chairman, Perot Systems Corp., Plano, 2000-04; Chairman, Perot Systems Corp., Dallas, 1988-92; Board member, Perot Systems Corp., Dallas, 1988-94; Chairman, CEO, also director, Electronic Data Systems Corp., Dallas, to 1986; Sold to GM, Electronic Data Systems Corp., Dallas, 1984; Founder, Electronic Data Systems Corp., Dallas, 1962-84; Data processing salesman, IBM Corp., 1957-62 **CR:** Reform Party candidate US Presidential Election, 1996, ind. candidate, 1992 **CIV:** Served with US Navy, 1953-57. **CW:** Author (books) United We Stand: How We Can Take Back Our Country, 1992, Not for Sale at Any Price: How We Can Save America for Our Children, 1993, Intensive Care: We Must Save Medicare and Medicaid Now, 1995, Preparing Our Country for the 21st Century, 1995, Ross Perot: My Life & the Principles for Success, 1996; co-author (with Pat Choate) Save Your Job, Save Our Country: Why NAFTA Must Be Stopped-Now!, 1993, (with Senator Paul Simon) The Dollar Crisis: A Blueprint to Help Rebuild the American Dream, 1996. **AW:** Recipient Winston Churchill Award, 1986, International Distinguished Entrepreneur Award, University Manitoba, 1988, Raoul Wallenberg Award, Jefferson Award, Patrick Henry Award, Nat, Business Hall of Fame Award, Sarnoff Award, Eisenhower Award, Smithsonian Computerworld Award, Horatio Alger Award.; named one of Forbes 400: Richest Americans, 1999-, World's Richest People, Forbes magazine, 1999-. **BA:** Perot Family Trust, PO Box 269014, Plano, TX, USA, 75026-9014

PERRY, GAYLORD JACKSON, T: Former Professional Baseball Player **I:** Athletics **DOB:** 09/15/1938 **PB:** Williamston **ED:** Student, Campbell College **C:** Pitcher, Kansas City Royals, 1983; Pitcher, Seattle Mariners, 1982-83; Pitcher, Atlanta Braves, 1981; Pitcher, New York Yankees, 1980; Pitcher, San Diego Padres, 1978-79; Pitcher, Texas Rangers, 1975-77, 80; Pitcher, Cleveland Indians, 1972-75; Pitcher, San Francisco Giants, 1962-71; Began professional career with, St. Cloud team, No. League, **CW:** Co-author: Me and the Spitter: An Autobiographical Confession, 1974. **AW:** Recipient Cy Young Member award Am. League, 1972, Cy Young award National League, 1978; member National League All-Star team, 1966, 70, 79, Am. League All-Star team, 1972, 74; inducted into Baseball Hall of Fame, Cooperstown, New York, 1991.,Wins Leader, 1970, 1972, 1978 **BA:** Gaylord Perry Enterprises, 1096 Dale Rd, Spruce Pine, NC, 28777

PERRY, KATY, T: Singer **I:** Media & Entertainment **DOB:** 10/25/1984 **PB:** Santa Barbara **SC:** CA/USA **PT:** Keith Hudson; Mary (Perry) Hudson **C:** Spokesmodel, CoverGirl (2013) **CIV:** Goodwill Ambassador, UNICEF (2013-Present) **CW:** Singer, Albums, "Katy Hudson" (2001), "One of the Boys" (2008), "MTV Unplugged" (2009), "Teenage Dream" (2010), "Teenage Dream: The Complete Confection" (2012), "Prism" (2013), "Witness" (2017); Singer, Songs, "I Kissed a Girl" (2008), Featuring Snoop Dogg, "California Gurls" (2010), Featuring Kanye West, "E.T." (2011); "Last Friday Night (T.G.I.F.)" (2011), "Part of Me" (2012), "Roar" (2013), Featuring Juicy J, "Dark Horse" (2013), Actress, Films, Voice Actor, "The Smurfs" (2011), "The Katy Perry: Part of Me" (2012), Voice Actor, "Smurfs 2" (2013), "Brand: A Second Coming" (2015), "Katy Perry A Prismatic World Tour" (2015), "Katy Perry: Making of the Pepsi Super Bowl Half Time Show" (2015), "Jeremy Scott: The People's Designer" (2015), "Zoolander 2" (2016); Narrator, Documentary, "Katy Perry: Part of Me" (2012); TV appearances, "How I Met Your Mother" (2011), "Raising Hope" (2012) **AW:** Named Top Digital Songs Artist, Billboard Music Award (2014); Top Female Artist, Billboard Music Award (2014); Woman of the Year, Billboard Magazine (2012); Favorite Adult Contemporary Artist, American Music Award (2014); Favorite Pop/Rock Female Artist, American Music Award (2012, 2014): Favorite Female Singer, Nickelodeon's Kids' Choice Award (2011); Sexiest Woman in the World, FHM Magazine (2011); Favorite Tour Headliner, People's Choice Award (2012); Favorite Online Sensation, People's Choice Award (2011); Favorite Pop Artist, People's Choice Award (2013); Favorite Female Artist, People's Choice Award (2013, 2012, 2011); Named One of the 100 Most Powerful Women in Entertainment, Hollywood Reporter (2013); Named, One of the 10 Most Fascinating People of 2011, Barbara Walters Special (2011); Video of the Year, MTV Video Music Award (2011); Cosmopolitan Ultimate Women of the Year Award (2010); Best Track, "I Kissed a Girl," Virgin Media Music Award (2008); Favorite Pop Song, "I Kissed a Girl," People's Choice Award (2009); Choice Music Single, "California Gurls," Teen Choice Award (2010); Choice Summer Song, "California Gurls," Teen Choice Award (2010); Best Collaboration with Kanye West Video, "E.T.," MTV Video Award (2011); Favorite Song of the Year, "E.T.," People's Choice Award (2012); Favorite Music Video, "Last Friday Night (T.G.I.F.)," People's Choice Award (2012); Favorite Music Video, "Part of Me," People's Choice Award (2013); Favorite Song, "Roar," People's Choice Award (2014); Favorite Music Video, "Roar," People's Choice Award (2014); Best Female Video, "Dark Horse," MTV Video Music Award (2014); Single of Year, "Dark Horse," American Music Award (2014); Favorite TV Guest Star, "How I Met Your Mother," People's Choice Award (2012)

PERRY, RICK, T: U.S. Secretary of Energy **I:** Government Administration/Government Relations/ Government Services **DOB:** 03/04/1950 **PB:** Paint Creek **SC:** Texas **PT:** Son of Joseph Ray and Amelia June (Holt) Perry; **ED:** BS in Animal Sci., Texas Agricultural and Mechanical University, 1972 **C:** Secretary of Energy, Washington, DC, 2017—; Governor, State of Texas, Austin, 2000-15; Lieutenant governor, State of Texas, Austin, 1999-2000; Commissioner agricultural, State of Texas, Austin, 1991-99; Member District 64, Texas House of Reps., Austin, 1985-91; Farmer/rancher, **CR:** Candidate for Republican Party nomination 2016 US Presidential Election, 2012 US Presidential Election finance chairman Republican Governors Association, 2008-09, chairman, 2010-11, 2007-08 **MIL:** Captain US Air Force, 1972-77 **CW:** Author: On My Honor: Why the American Values of the Boy Scouts Are Worth Fighting For, 2008, Fed Up!: Our Fight to Save America from Washington, 2010 **AW:** Named Man of Year in Texas Agricultural, Texas County Agricultural Agents Association, 1990; named an Outstanding Tex Leader, John Ben Shepperd Pub. Leadership Institute, 1996; named one of The Most Effective Legislators, Dallas Morning News, 1989; recipient Gerald W Thomas Agriculturist award, Distinguished Eagle Scout award, Boy Scouts America, 1992 **MEM:** Mem.: Texas & Southwestern Cattle Raisers Association, Texas Firemen & Fire Marshals Association (life), National Future Farmers of America Alumni Association, American Legion Post #75 (life), Eagle Scouts **PA:** Republican **BA:** US Department of Energy, 1000 Independence Ave SW, Washington, DC, 20585

PERRY, SCOTT GORDON, T: U.S. Representative from Pennsylvania **I:** Government Administration/ Government Relations/Government Services **DOB:** 05/27/1962 **PB:** San Diego **SC:** CA/USA **ED:** MA in Strategic War Planning, U.S. Army War College, 2012; BBA, Pennsylvania State University, 1991 **C:** U.S. House of Transportation & Infrastructure Committee, 2013-Present; U.S. House of Homeland Security Committee, 2013-Present; U.S. House of Foreign Affairs Committee, 2013-Present; U.S. Congress from Fourth Pennsylvania District, Washington, DC, 2013-Present; Founder, Hydrotech Mechanical Services, Inc,, Dillsburg, PA, 1993-Present; District 92, Pennsylvania House of Representatives, 2007-2012 **MIL:** Colonel, Pennsylvania Army National Guard, 1980-Present **MEM:** Dillsburg VFW Post #6671, Northern York County Representative Club, Republican Club of New York, Dillsburg Legion Post #26 **PA:** Republican **BA:** 54B East Wing, PO Box 202092, Harrisburg, PA, 17120-2092

PERRY, TYLER A., T: Playwright, Actor, Film Director, Producer **I:** Media & Entertainment **DOB:** 09/14/1969 **PB:** New Orleans **SC:** LA/USA **PT:** Emmett R. Perry, Willie Maxine Perry **CW:** Actor, Director, Executive Producer, Writer, Why Did I Get Married Too?, 2010, Madea's Neighbors From Hell, 2014; Actor, Director, Producer, Writer, (Films) Diary of a Mad Black Woman, 2005, Why Did I Get Married?, 2007, Meet the Browns, 2008, The Family That Preys, 2008, Madea Goes to Jail, 2009, I Can Do Bad All By Myself, 2009, Madea's Big Happy Family, 2011, Good Deeds, 2012, Madea's Witness Protection, 2012, A Madea Christmas, 2013, The Single Mom's Club, 2014, (Voice Actor) Boo! A Madea Halloween, 2016, Boo! 2, A Madea Halloween, 2018, Acrimony, 2018, A Madea Family Funeral, 2018; Actor, Director, Executive Producer, Madea's Family Reunion, 2006; Actor, Director, Writer, (Plays) Madea's Family Reunion, 2002, Madea's Class Reunion-The Class That Had No Class, 2003, Madea Goes to Jail, 2005; Actor, Producer, Writer, (Films) Madea's Tough Love, 2015; Actor, (Films) Alex Cross, 2012, Gone Girl, 2014, Teenage Mutant Ninja Turtles: Out of the Shadows, 2016, Brain on Fire, 2016, (TV Films) The Passion, 2016, The Star, 2017, Backseat, 2018; Director, Executive Producer, Writer, If Loving You is Wrong, 2014-Present; Director, Producer, Writer, Daddy's Little Girls, 2007, For Colored Girls, 2010, The Marriage Counselor, 2012-2013, Temptation: Confessions of a Marriage Counselor, 2013, The Haves and the Have Nots, 2013-Present, For Better or Worse, 2013-Present; Director, Producer, (Plays) Woman, Thou Art Loosed, 1999, Behind Closed Doors, 2001; Director, Writer,

What's Done in the Dark, 2006, Aunt Bam's Place, 2012, (TV Series) House of Payne, 2007-Present; Producer, (Film) Peeples, 2013; Writer, (Plays) I Know I've Been Changed, 1999, I Can Do Bad All By Myself, 2000, Meet the Browns, 2004, Diary of a Mad Black Woman, 2005, Why Did I Get Married?, 2007; Author, (Book) Don't Make a Black Woman Take Off Her Earrings: Madea's Uninhibited Commentaries on Love and Life, 2006 **AW:** Barbara Walters' 10 Most Fascinating People, 2009, The 100 Most Powerful Celebrities, Forbes.com, 2008, The 100 Most Influential People in the World, TIME Magazine, 2008, Outstanding Supporting Actor in a Motion Picture, National Association for the Advancement of Colored People, Why Did I Get Married?, 2008, Named to Power 150, 2008, 50 Smartest People in Hollywood, Entertainment Weekly, 2007, Top 25 Entertainers of the Year, 2007, Most Influential Black Americans, Ebony Magazine, 2006, Black Movie Award for Outstanding Achievement in Writing, Diary of a Mad Black Woman, 2006, Quills Award, Humor the Quills Literacy Foundation, Don't Make a Black Woman Take Off Her Earrings: Madea's Uninhibited Commentaries on Love and Life, 2006, BET Comedy Award for Outstanding Lead Actor in a Theatrical Film, BET Comedy Award for Outstanding Writing for a Theatrical Film, Diary of a Mad Black Woman, 2005 **BA:** c/o William Morris Endeavor Entertainment, 9601 Wilshire Boulevard, Third Floor, Beverly Hills, CA, 90210

PESCI, JOE, T: Actor **I:** Media & Entertainment **PB:** Newark **SC:** NJ/USA **PT:** Angelo Pesci; Mary Pesci **CW:** Actor: (films) The Death Collector, 1976, Raging Bull, 1980 (National Board Rev. award for Best Supporting Actor, National Society Film Critics award for Best Supporting Actor, New York Film Critics Cir. award for Best Supporting Actor, BAFTA Award for Best Newcomer), Dear Mr. Wonderful, 1982, I'm Dancing as Fast as I Can, 1982, Easy Money, 1983, Once Upon A Time In America, 1984, Eureka, 1984, Tutti Dentro, 1984, Man on Fire, 1987, Moonwalker, 1988, The Legendary Life of Ernest Hemingway, 1988, Lethal Weapon 2, 1989, Betsy's Wedding, 1990, Goodfellas, 1990 (Academy award for Best Supporting Actor), Home Alone, 1990, The Super, 1991, JFK, 1991, My Cousin Vinny, 1992 (Am. Comedy award for Funniest Actor in a Motion Picture), Lethal Weapon 3, 1992, The Public Eye, 1992, Home Alone 2: Lost In New York, 1992, A Bronx Tale, 1993, Jimmy Hollywood, 1994, With Honors, 1994, Casino, 1995, Gone Fishin', 1997, 8 Heads in a Duffel Bag, 1997, Lethal Weapon 4, 1998, The Good Shepherd, 2006, Love Ranch, 2010, A Warriors Tail, 2015, The Irishman, 2019; (TV series) Half Nelson, 1985, Tales from the Crypt, 1992, SNL, 1992 **AW:** Named Best Supporting Actor (for Goodfellas), Boston Society Film Critics, Chicago Film Critics Association, Kansas City Film Critics Cir., LA Film Critics Association, National Board Rev.

PESSINA, STEFANO, T: CEO Walgreens Boot Alliance **I:** Business Management/Business Services **DOB:** 06/04/1941 **PB:** Pescara **ED:** DBA, Nottingham Business Institute, 2012; DSc (hon.), University Wales Cardiff, 2009; Bachelor, Polytechnic University Milan **C:** CEO, Walgreens Boots Alliance, Inc., 2015-; Acting CEO, The Walgreen Co., Chicago, 2014-15; Executive chairman, Alliance Boots Holdings Ltd., London, 2007-14; Executive deputy chairman, Alliance UniChem, 2004-07; Chief executive, Alliance UniChem, 2001-04; Founder, Alliance Santé, Italy, 1977; With, A.C. Nielson,; Ind. business consultant, **CR:** Board directors The Walgreen Co., 2012-, Alliance Boots Holdings Ltd., 2006-, Galencis, Ltd., 2000- **AW:** Named one of The World's Richest People, Forbes magazine, 2006-; recipient Alkemeon International

prize, National Centre for Research & European Brain Research Institute, 2012, Keynes-Sraffa award, 2009, William L. Ford International award, International Federation Pharmaceutical Wholesalers (IFPW), 2006

PETERS, BERNADETTE, T: Actress **I:** Media & Entertainment **DOB:** 02/28/1948 **PB:** Queens **PT:** Daughter of Peter and Marguerite (Maltese) **SPN:** Lazar; Married Michael Wittenberg, July 20, 1996 (deceased September 26, 2005) **ED:** PhD (Hon.), Hofstra University, Hempstead, New York, 2002; Student, Quintano School for Young Profls., New York City **C:** Actress 1958- **CIV:** Founder, Ann. Broadway Barks fundraiser **CW:** Appeared on TV series All's Fair, 1976-77; (films) The Longest Yard, 1974, Silent Movie, 1976, Vigilant Force, 1976, W.C. Fields and Me, 1976, Silent Movie, 1976, The Jerk, 1979, Heartbeeps, 1981, Tulips, 1981, Pennies from Heaven, 1981 (Golden Globe award for Best Actress), Annie, 1982, Slaves of New York, 1989, Pink Cadillac, 1989, Impromptu, 1991, Alice, 1990, Anastasia (voice), 1997, Cinderella, 1997, Snow Days, 1999, Prince Charming, 2001, Bobbie's Girl, 2002, A Few Good Years, 2002, It Runs in the Family, 2003, Wine and Kisses, 2007, Coming Up Roses, 2011, Legends of Oz: Drothy's Return (voice), 2013, (TV films) Cinderella, 1997, Holiday in Your Heart, 1997, Prince Charming, 2001, Bobbie's Girl, 2002, Adopted, 2005, Living Proof, 2008, (TV appearances) Frasier, 2001, Ally McBeal, 2001, Will & Grace, 2006, Grey's Anatomy, 2008, Ugly Betty, 2009, Smash, 2012-13, Mozart in the Jungle, 2014-, many others, (stage appearances) This is Google, 1957, The Most Happy Fella, 1959, Gypsy, 1961, Curly McDimple, 1967, Johnny No-Trump, 1967, George M!, 1968 (Theatre World award, 1968), Dames at Sea, 1968 (Drama Desk award, 1968), La Strada, 1969, On the Town, 1971, Tartuffe, 1972, Mack and Mabel, 1974, Sally and Marsha, 1982, Sunday in the Park with George, 1983-85, Song and Dance, 1985-86 (Drama League award for Best Actress, 1985, Tony award for Best Actress, 1986, Drama Desk award for Best Actress, 1986), Into the Woods, 1987, The Goodbye Girl, 1992-93, Annie Get Your Gun 1998-99 (Tony award for Best Actress, 1999, Outer Critics Circle award for Best Actress, 1999, Drama Desk award for Best Actress, 1999), Gypsy, 2003, A Little Night Music, 2009, Follies, 2011, (TV mini-series) The Odyssey, 1997; recording artist: (MCA Records) Bernadette Peters, 1980, Now Playing, 1981; albums: I'll Be Your Baby Tonight, 1996, Sondheim Etc: Bernadette Peters Live at Carnegie Hall, 1997, Bernadette Peters Loves Rodgers and Hammerstein, 2002, Sondheim Etc., Etc. Live at Carnegie Hall, 2005; solo concert Radio City Music Hall, 2002; author: Broadway Barks, 2008, Stella is a Star, 2010,(Film) 10 Little Rubber Ducks, 2016, (Television) Girlfriends Guide to Divorce, 2014, The Good Fight, 2017 **AW:** Recipient Hasty Pudding Theatrical award, 1987 Woman of Year award, Sara Siddons Actress of Year award, 1993-94, Actors Fund medal for artistic achievement, 1999, New York City Parks Citizen award, 2006, Sondheim award, 2011, Tony award Isabelle Stevenson award, 2012; named Woman of Year, Police Athletic League, 1999; named to Theatre Hall of Fame **BA:** Katz Public Relations, 1745 Broadway, 17th Floor, New York, NY, 10106

PETERS, GARY CHARLES, T: U.S. Senator from Michigan **I:** Government Administration/Government Relations/Government Services **DOB:** 12/01/1958 **PB:** Pontiac **SC:** Colleen Ochoa **PT:** Herbert Garrett Peters; Madeleine (Vignier) Peters **MS:** Married **CH:** Gary Jr.; Madeleine; Alana **ED:** MA in Philosophy, Michigan State University, East Lansing, MI; JD, Wayne State University

(1989); MBA, University of Detroit (1984); BA, Alma College (1980) **C:** US Senator from Michigan (2015-Present); Member, US Congress from the 14th Michigan District (2013-2015); Member, US Congress from the Ninth Michigan District, Washington, DC (2009-2013); Commissioner, Michigan State Lottery (2003-2008); Member, District 14, Michigan State Senate, Lansing, MI (1994-2002); Vice President, Branch Manager, Paine Webber, Inc., Rochester, MI; Financial Consultant, Resident Manager, Assistant Vice President, Merrill Lynch; Pierce, Fenner & Smith, Inc., Rochester, MI (1980-1989) **CR:** Securities Arbitrator, Mediator, National Association of Securities Dealers; New York Stock Exchange; American Arbitration Association; Adjunct Professor, Oakland University, Rochester, NY (1991-1993); Instructor, Wayne State University (1992-1994) **CIV:** Councilman, City of Rochester Hills, NY (1992-1994), Member, Zoning Board Appeals and Paint Creek Trailways Commission (1992-1994); Officer-at-large, Michigan Democratic Party (1996) **MIL:** Officer, U.S. Navy Reserve (1993-2000, 2001-2005) **AW:** Decorated Military, Outstanding Volunteer Service Medal; Navy and Marine Corps Achievement Medal **MEM:** Michigan State Bar Association; Sierra Club; Phi Beta Kappa **BAR:** State Bar of Michigan (1990) **H:** Hiking; Motorcycling; World Travel; Soaring; Scuba Diving **PA:** Democrat

PETERS, SCOTT H., T: U.S. Representative from California, former city councilman **I:** Government Administration/Government Relations/Government Services **DOB:** 06/17/1958 **PB:** Springfield **ED:** JD, New York University; BA in Economics & Political Sci. magna cum laude, Duke University **C:** Member, US House Sci., Space & Technology Committee, 2013-; Member, US House Armed Services Committee, 2013-; Member, US Congress from 52nd California District, Washington, 2013-; Member, Committee on Education and the Workforce, Committee on Transportation and Infrastructure; Chairman, San Diego Unified Port Commission, 2011; Commissioner, San Diego Unified Port Commission, 2009-12; President, San Diego City Council, 2006-07; Councilman, District 1, San Diego City Council, 2000-08; Deputy company counsel, San Diego, 1991-96; Partner, Peters & Varco LLP, 1996-2000; Attorney, Baker & McKenzie, San Diego,; Attorney, Dorsey & Whitney, Minneapolis,; Economist, EPA, Washington, 1980-81 **PA:** Democrat

PETERSON, ADRIAN, T: Professional Football Player **I:** Athletics **DOB:** 03/21/1985 **PB:** Palestine **SC:** TX/USA **ED:** Student, University of Oklahoma, Norman, OK, 2004—2006 **C:** Running Back, Arizona Cardinals, 2017-Present; Running Back, Minnesota Vikings, 2007—Present; Running Back, New Orleans Saints, 2017 **AW:** Hall of Fame Trophy, 2003, First Team All-Freshman, Associated Press, 2004, First Team All-American, 2004, NFL Offensive Rookie of the Year, 2007, National Football Conference Pro Bowl Team, NFL, 2007—2010, 2012, FedEx Ground Player of the Year, 2008, 2012, NFL Pro Bowl MVP, 2008, ESPY Award, Best Breakthrough Athlete, ESPN, 2008, Bert Bell Award, Maxwell Football Club, 2008, 2012, First Team All-Pro, 2008-2009, 2012, NFL MVP, Associated Press, 2012, NFL Offensive Player of the Year, 2012, NFL MVP, Pro Football Writers America (PFWA), 2012, NFL Most Valuable Player, 2012, NFL Offensive Player Of The Year, 2012, Bert Bell Award, 2012, First Team All-Pro, 2012, 2015, Pro Bowl, 2012-2013, 2015, Second Team All Pro, 2013 **ACH:** Achievements include setting the NFL single-game rushing record (296 yards), 2007; leading the NFL in: rushing yards, 2008, 2012; rushing touchdowns, 2009; one of only seven players in NFL history to rush for 2,000 yards in a single season, 2012 **BA:** Minnesota Vikings, 9520 Viking Drive, Eden Prairie, MN, 55344

PETERSON, COLLIN CLARK, T: Chair of the House Agriculture Committee **I:** Government Administration/Government Relations/Government Services **DOB:** 06/29/1944 **PB:** Fargo **SC:** ND/USA **CH:** Sean, Jason, Elliott **ED:** BA in Business Administration and Accounting, Moorhead State University, 1966 **CT:** CPA Minnesota **C:** Member, US Congress from 7th Minnesota district, 1991-; Chairman, US House Agricultural Committee, 2007-11; Member District 10, Minnesota State Senate, 1976-86 **CIV:** With U.S. Army National Guard, 1963-69. **MEM:** Member Am. Legion, Ducks Unltd., Elks, Sportsmen's Club, Rural Caucus, Mainstream Forum, Cormorant Lakes Sportsmen Club, Congl. Sportsmen's Caucus, Mainstream Forum, Congl. Rural Caucus. **PA:** Democrat **BA:** Office of Collin Peterson, 2204 Rayburn HOB, Washington, DC, 20515

PETITTI, TONY, T: Chief Operating Officer of Major League Baseball **I:** Athletics **ED:** JD, Harvard Law School, Massachusetts, 1986; BA in Econs., Haverford College, Pennsylvania, 1983 **C:** Chief Operating Officer, Major League Baseball, 2015-; President, CEO, MLB Network, 2008-2015; Vice president, general manager, Station WCBS-TV, New York City, 1999-2002; Executive vice president, CBS Sports, 2005-08; Executive producer, CBS Sports, 2002-08; Special adv. to president, CBS Sports; Senior vice president business affairs and programming, CBS Sports, New York City, 1997-99; Senior vice president negotiations, NBC Sports, New York City, 1996-97; Vice president programming, ABC Sports, 1994-96; Director programming, ABC Sports; General attorney, ABC Sports, New York City, Attorney, Cadwalader, Wickersham and Taft, 1986-88 **AW:** Named one of The Most Influential People in the World of Sports, Business Week, 2007, 40 Under 40 Top Executives in the Industry, Sports Business Journal, 2000; recipient Lawrence Forman award, Haverford College, 2006, Five Emmy awards

PETTY, RICHARD, T: Retired Professional Racing Driving **I:** Media & Entertainment **DOB:** 07/02/1937 **PB:** Level Cross **PT:** Son of Lee and Elizabeth T. P.; Married Lynda Owens, 1958 **CH:** children: Kyle, Sharon, Lisa, Rebecca **C:** Co-owner, Car #43, Richard Petty Motorsports, 2009-; Co-owner, Car #43, Petty Enterprises Inc.,; Retired, 1992; Professional race car driver, 35 years **CIV:** Member Pres.'s Council Fitness and Sport **CW:** Actor(voice): (films) Cars, 2006, Swing Vote, 2008 **AW:** Recipient Myers Brothers award National Motorsports Press Association, 1961, 67, 71, Excellence award NASCAR, 1987; named Grand National Rookie of Year, 1959; Most Popular Driver in Grand National, 1962, 64, 68, 70, 74, 75, 76, 77, 78; Martini & Rossi Am. Driver of Year, 1971; Driver of Year National Motorsport Press Association, 1974-75; Driver of Quarter Century, 1991; named one of Most Influential People in the World of Sports, Business Week, 2008; inducted into North Carolina Athletic Hall of Fame, 1973, NASCAR Hall of Fame, 2010,Diecast Hall of Fame, 2011, NASCAR's 50 Greatest Drivers, 1998, Presidential Medal of Freedom, 1992 **MEM:** Member National Association Stock Car Auto Racing (7 time champion; Winston Cup grand national champion 1964, 67, 71, 72, 74, 75, 79) **ACH:** Achievements include entered 1015 Grand National Races, winner 200, 1958-86, with 55 Superspeedway wins; winner Daytona 500, 1964, 66, 71, 73, 74, 79, 81; 1000th career Winston Cup start June 15, 1986 at Michigan International Speedway; 500th consecutive start on August 21, 1988 in Champion Spark Plug 500. **BA:** Richard Petty Museum, 311 Branson Mill Rd, Randleman, NC, 27317

PHELPS, EDMUND STROTHER JR., T: Economics Professor **I:** Education/Educational Services **DOB:** 07/26/1933 **PB:** Evanston **PT:** Son of Edmund Strother and Florence Esther (Stone) Phelps **ED:** DLitt (hon.), Amherst College, 1985; PhD, Yale University, New Haven, 1959; MA, Yale University, New Haven, 1956; BA, Amherst College, Massachusetts 1955 **C:** Director Center Capitalism & Society, Columbia University, 2001-; McVickar professor political economy, Columbia University, 1982-; Professor economics, New York University, 1978-79; Professor economics, Columbia University, 1978-82; Professor economics, Columbia University, New York City, 1971-77; Professor economics, University Pennsylvania, Philadelphia, 1966-71; Associate professor, Yale University, 1963-66; Assistant professor economics, Yale University, 1960-62; Economist, RAND Corp., Santa Monica, California, 1959-60 **CR:** Member adv board New York Forum, 2010; visiting research fellow French Observatory Economic Business Cycles, Paris, 2001-; visiting scholar Russell Sage Foundation, 1993-94; consultant European Bank Reconstruction & Devel., London, 1992-93; visiting associate professor economics Massachusetts Institute of Technology, 1962-63; member Cowles Foundation Research in Economics, Yale University, 1960-66 **CW:** Author: Golden Rules of Economic Growth, 1966, Microeconomic Foundations of Employment and Inflation Theory, 1970, Economic Justice, 1973, Studies in Macroeconomic Theory, 1979, Political Economy, 1986, The Slump in Europe, 1989, Structural Slumps, 1994, Designing Social Inclusion: Tools to Raise Low-End Pay and Employment in Private Enterprise, 2003, others; contributor articles to professional journals **AW:** Recipient Kiel Global Economy prize, 2008, Nobel prize in economics, 2006, Kenan Enterprise award, William R. Kenan Charitable Trust, 1996; fellow John Simon Guggenheim Memorial Foundation, 1978, Social Sci. Research Council, 1966,Chevalier de la Legion d'Honneur, 2008,Piceo Della Mirandola Prize, 2008, Global Economy Prize, 2008, Friendship Award, 2014 **MEM:** Fellow: National Academy of Sciences, American Association for the Advancement of Science, New York Academy Scis., Econometric Society, Am. Economic Association (distinguished executive committee 1976-78, vice president 1983); mem.: Council Foreign Relations, European Academy Scis & Arts (hon.), Economic Club New York, Phi Beta Kappa **BA:** Columbia University, International Affairs, Suite1126, New York, NY, 10027

PHELPS, MICHAEL, T: Professional Swimmer **I:** Athletics **DOB:** 06/30/1985 **PB:** Balt. **PT:** Son of Michael Fred and Deborah Sue Phelps; **ED:** Student, University Michigan **C:** Member, Team Speedo, 2001-; Member, US Men's Olympic Swim Team, Rio de Janeiro, 2016; Member, US Men's Olympic Swim Team, London, 2012; Member, US Men's Olympic Swim Team, Beijing, 2008; Member, US Men's Olympic Swim Team, Athens, 2004; Member, US Men's Olympic Swim Team, Sydney, 2000 **CIV:** Founder, Michael Phelps Foundation, Spokesperson, Boys & Girls Clubs of America, Hon. board member, Pathfinders for Autism, Hon. board member, Boys & Girls Club, Harford County, Maryland, **CW:** Author: Beneath the Surface, 2004, No Limits: The Will to Succeed, 2008 **AW:** Named Male Athlete of Year, Associated Press, 2012, 2008, Sportsman of Year, Sports Illus., 2008, US Olympic Committee, 2008, 2004, Athlete of Year, USA Swimming, 2007, World Swimmer of Year, Swimming World Magazine, 2006-09, 2004, 2003, American Swimmer of Year, 2006-09, 2001-04; named one of The 10 People Who Mattered, Newsweek, 2008, The Ten Most Fascinating People of 2008, Barbara Walters, The Most Influ-

ential People in the World of Sports, Business Week, 2008; recipient Gold medal, 100m, 200m butterfly, 200m individual butterfly, 200m individual medley, US National Championships, 2015, Gold medal, 4x100m freestyle relay, 200m butterfly, 4x200 freestyle relay, 200m individual medley, 4x100m medley relay; Silver medal, 100m butterfly, Summer Olympic Games, 2016, Gold medal, 100m butterfly, 200m individual medley, 4x200m freestyle relay, 4x100m medley relay; Silver medal, 200m butterfly, 4x100m freestyle relay, 2012, Gold medal, 100m butterfly, 100m, 200m freestyle, 200m, 400m individual medley, 4x100, 4x200 freestyle relay, 4x100m medley relay, 2008, Bronze medal, 200m freestyle, 4x100 freestyle relay, 2004, Gold medal, 100m, 200m freestyle, 200m, 400m individual medley, 4x100m medley relay, 4x200m freestyle relay, 2004, Gold medal, 100m butterfly, 200m freestyle, 100m medley relay, Pan Pacific Championships, 2014, Gold medal, 100m, 200m butterfly, 400m, 800m freestyle relay, 400m medley relay, 2010, Gold medal, 400m, 800m freestyle relay, 2006, Gold medal, 200m, 400m individual medley, 400m medley relay; Silver medal, 200m butterfly, 800m freestyle relay, 2002, Gold medal, 100m, 200m butterfly, 800m freestyle, 400m medley; Silver medal, 200m freestyle, individual medley; Bronze medal, 400m team freestyle, World Championships, 2011, Gold medal, 100m, 200m butterfly, 400m, 800m freestyle relay, 400m medley relay; Silver medal, 200m freestyle, 2009, Gold medal, 100m, 200m freestyle, 100m, 200m butterfly, 200m, 400m individual medley, 400m, 800m freestyle relay, 2007, Gold medal, 200m freestyle, 200m individual medley, 400m medley relay, 400m, 800m freestyle relay; Silver medal, 100m butterfly, 2005, Gold medal, 200m butterfly, 200m, 400m individual medley, 400m medley relay; Silver medal, 100m butterfly, 800m freestyle relay, 2003, Gold medal, 200m butterfly, 2001, James Sullivan award, Amateur Athletic Union, 2003, Marca Leyenda, 2008, Laureus Comeback of the Year Award, 2017,Golden Goggle Relay Performance of the Year, 2006, 2007, 2008, 2009, 2016,Golden Goggle Relay Performance of the Year 2006, 2007, 2008, 2009, 2016 **ACH:** Achievements include individual world records in: 400m individual medley, 2008, 200m butterfly, 2009, 100m butterfly, 2009; team world records in: 400m freestyle relay, 2008, 800m freestyle relay, 2008, 400m medley relay, 400m freestyle relay, 2009; breaking the world record for Gold medals in a single Olympic games (8), Beijing, 2008; breaking the all-time record for most career Olympic Gold medals (22), 2016; becoming the most decorated Olympic athlete of all time with 26 medals **BA:** Octagon Olympics & Action Sports, 7 Ocean Street, South Portland, ME, 04106

PHILBIN, GARY M., T: Retail Executive **I:** Retail/Sales **C:** CEO, Dollar Tree Stores, Inc., 2017-; COO, Dollar Tree Stores, Inc., 2007-2017; Senior vice president, stores, Dollar Tree Stores, Inc., 2001-07; Various positions, including president, CEO, chief merchandising officer, board directors, Grand Union (sale to C&S Wholesale Grocers), New Jersey, 1997; Executive vice president, operations and merchandising, Cub Foods, SuperValu, 1996-97; Senior vice president, merchandising, Walbaum, A&P, 1993-96; Various positions, store operations and merchandising, Kroger Co., 1973

PHILLIPS, GREGORY ALAN, T: Federal Judge, Former State Attorney General, Former Federal Prosecutor **I:** Law and Legal Services **DOB:** 08/17/1960 **PB:** Littleton **SC:** CO/USA **ED:** JD, University of Wyoming College Law, 1987; BA in Economics, University of Wyoming, 1983 **CT:** Bar: U.S. Supreme Court, U.S. Court Appeals

(10th cir.), U.S. District Court, Wyoming, Wyoming Supreme Court, Wyoming **C:** Judge, U.S. Court Appeals (10th Cir.), 2013-; Attorney general, State of Wyoming, Cheyenne, Wyoming, 2011-13; Assistant U.S. attorney Dist Court, US Department Justice, Cheyenne, Wyoming, 2003-11; Member, Wyoming State Senate, Cheyenne, Wyoming, 1993-98; Private practice, Cheyenne, Wyoming, 1998-2001; Private practice, Evanston, Wyoming, 1989-98; Law clerk to Hon. Alan Bond Johnson, US District Court, Wyoming, Cheyenne, Wyoming, 1987-89 **MEM:** Mem.: Order of the Coif **PA:** Democrat **BA:** 1823 Stout St, Denver, CO, 80202

PHOENIX, JOAQUIN RAPHAEL, T: Actor **I:** Media & Entertainment **DOB:** 10/28/1974 **PB:** San Juan **SC:** Puerto Rico **PT:** John Bottom; Arlyn Dunetz **CIV:** Board of Directors, The Lunchbox Fund **CW:** Actor, TV Films, "Backwards: The Riddle of Dyslexia" (1984), "Kids Don't Tell" (1985), "Secret Witness" (1988); TV Series, "Morningstar/Eveningstar" (1986); Films, "SpaceCamp" (1986), "Russkies" (1987), "Parenthood" (1989), "Walking the Dog" (1991), "To Die For" (1995), "Inventing the Abbotts" (1997), "U Turn" (1997), "Return to Paradise" (1998), "Clay Pigeons" (1998), "8MM" (1999), "The Yards" (2000), "Gladiator" (2000), "Quills" (2000), "Buffalo Soldiers" (2001), "Signs" (2002), "It's All About Love" (2003), Voice, "Brother Bear" (2003), "The Village" (2004), "Ladder 49" (2004), "Hotel Rwanda" (2004), "Walk the Line" (2005), "Reservation Road" (2007), "Two Lovers" (2008), "The Master" (2012), "The Immigrant" (2013), "Her" (2013), "Inherent Vice" (2014), "Irrational Man" (2015), "Unity" (2015), "You Were Never Really Here" (2017), "Don't Worry, He Won't Get Far on Foot" (2018), "Mary Magdalene" (2018), "The Sisters Brothers" (2018); Actor, Producer, Films, "We Own the Night" (2007); Actor, Producer, Writer, "I'm Still Here" (2010); Television, "Seven Brides for Seven Brothers" (1982), "The Fall Guy" (1984), ABC Afterschool Specials (1984), "Hill Street Blues" (1984), "Murder She Wrote" (1984), "Alfred Hitchcock Presents" (1986), "The New Leave it to Beaver" (1989), "Superboy" (1989) **AW:** Named Favorite Leading Man, People's Choice Awards (2008); Best Performance by an Actor in a Motion Picture-Musical or Comedy, Golden Globe Awards (2006)

PICHAI, SUNDAR, T: Internet Company Executive **I:** Internet **PB:** Chennai **ED:** MS, Stanford University; MBA, University of Pennsylvania Wharton School of Business; Bachelor in Tech., Indian Institute Tech., 1993 **C:** CEO-elect, Google, Inc., Mountain View, California, 2015-; Vice president product management, Google, Inc., Mountain View, California, 2014-; Senior vice president Android, Chrome & Apps, Google, Inc., Mountain View, California, 2013-14; Senior vice president Google Chrome & Apps, Google, Inc., Mountain View, California, 2011-13; Vice president, product management, Google, Inc., Mountain View, California, 2004-11; Management consultant, McKinsey & Co.,; Various engineering & product management positions, Applied Materials, Inc., **CR:** Board of directors Jive Software, Inc., 2011-13 **AW:** Named Palmer Scholar, Siebel Scholar, University of Pennsylvania; recipient Institute Silver Medal, Indian Institute Tech.

PIERCE, DAVID HYDE HYDE, T: Actor **I:** Media & Entertainment **DOB:** 04/03/1959 **PB:** Albany **SC:** NY/USA **ED:** BA in Theatre & English, Yale University, 1981 **C:** Actor, 1988- **CW:** Appeared in plays Beyond Therapy, 1982, Holiday, 1982, Summer, 1983, That's It, Folks! 1983, Candida, 1984, The Seagull, 1984, The Grand Hysteric, 1984, The Three

Zeks, 1984, Tartuffe, 1984, Donuts, 1985, Hamlet, 1986, The Author's Voice, 1987, The Maderati, 1987, Camille, 1987, The Cherry Orchard, 1988, Zero Positive, 1988, Much Ado About Nothing, 1988, The Heidi Chronicles, 1989, Elliot Loves, 1990, It's Only a Play, 1991, Monty Python's Spamalot, 2005, Curtains, 2006 (Tony award best performance by a leading actor in a musical, 2007), Accent on Youth, 2009, La Bête, 2010-2011, Vanya and Sonia and Masha and Spike, 2013, It Shoulda Been You, 2015, Ripcord, 2015, A Life, 2016, Hello Dolly, 2017; films include Bright Lights, Big City, 1988, Crossing Delancey, 1988, Rocket Gibraltar, 1988, The Fisher King, 1991, Little Man Tate, 1991, Sleepless in Seattle, 1993, Addams Family Values, 1993, Wolf, 1994, Nixon, 1995, Hercules, 1998, A Bug's Life, 1998, Jackie's Back!, 1999, Mating Habits of the Earthbound Human, 1999, Isn't She Great, 2000, Chain of Fools, 2000, Wet, Hot, American Summer, 2001, Osmosis Jones, 2001, Full Frontal, 2002, Treasure Planet (voice), 2002, Down with Love, 2003, Forever Plaid, 2008, (voice) Stingray Sam, 2009, The Perfect Host, 2011; TV series include The Powers That Be, 1993, Frasier, 1993-2004 (seven American Comedy awards), SNL, 1995, Caroline in the City, 1995, The Outer Limits, Mighty Ducks, 1996, Happily Every After, 1997, The Simpsons, 1997(2014) Jackie's Back, 1999, Titus, 2001, On the Edge, 2001, Gary the Rat, 2003, The Amazing Screw-On Head, 2006, The Good Wife, 2014, Wet Hot American Summer: First Day of Camp, 2015, When We Rise, 2017, Julie's Greenroom, 2017, Wet Hot American Summer: Ten Year Later, 2017; TV appearances, Sesame Street (voice), 2012,(**AW:** Recipient Q Award 1994, 95, 96, 98, Emmy award, 1995, 98, 99, 2004, Am. Comedy award 1995-2000, Screen Actors Guild Award, 1996, 2000, TV Critics Association award 1997, 1998, TV Guide award, 2000, Isabelle Stevenson Award, Tony Awards, 2010

PIKETTY, THOMAS, T: Economist **I:** Education/ Educational Services **DOB:** 06/07/1905 **PB:** Clichy, Hauts-de-Seine, France **SC:** Clichy, Hauts-de-Seine, France **ED:** École Normale Supérieure; London School of Economics **C:** Professor, EHESS, 2000-; Researcher,French National Centre for Scientific Research, 1995-2000; Assistant Professor, MIT, 1993-95 **CW:** (Novel) Capital in the Twenty-First Century, 2013,About Capital in the Twenty-First Century, 2015,Carbon and Inequality: from Kyoto to Paris,2015,Chronicles: On Our Troubled Times,2016,Why Save the Bankers? And Other Essays on Our Economic and Political Crisis, 2016 **AW:** Time 100 Most Influential, 2015

PILLARD, NINA, T: Federal Judge, Law Educator **I:** Law and Legal Services **DOB:** 03/04/1961 **PB:** Cambridge **SC:** MA/USA **PT:** Richard Pillard; Cornelia Cromwell (Tierney) Pillard **SPN:** David D. Cole **ED:** JD, Harvard Law School, 1987; BA in History, Yale College, 1983 **C:** Judge, U.S. Court of Appeals, District of Columbia Circuit, Washington, DC, 2013-Present; Professor of Law, Georgetown University Law Center, 2005-Present; Associate Professor, Georgetown University Law Center, 2000-2005; Deputy Assistant Attorney General, Office of Legal Counsel, U.S. Department of Justice, 1998-2000; Associate Professor of Law, Georgetown University Law Center, 1997-1998; Assistant, Solicitor General, U.S. Department of Justice, 1994-1997; Assistant Counsel, National Association for the Advancement of Colored People Legal Defense & Educational Fund, Washington, DC, 1992-1994; Assistant Counsel, National Association for the Advancement of Colored People Legal Defense & Educational Fund, New York, NY, 1989-1992; Marvin N. Karpatkin Fellow, American Civil Liberties Union, New York, NY, 1988-1989; Law Clerk,

Hon. Louis H. Pollak, U.S. District Court, Eastern District, Pennsylvania, 1987-1988 **CR:** Professor, Academy Co-Director, Center for Transnational Legal Studies, London, England, 2008-2009; Visiting Fellow, Institute for Advanced Legal Studies, London, England, 2006 **BA:** Georgetown University Law Center, 600 New Jersey Avenue NW, Washington, DC, 20001

PINDER, MIKE, T: Musician and Keyboardist **I:** Media & Entertainment **DOB:** 06/04/1905 **PB:** Erdington, Birmingham, England **SC:** Erdington, Birmingham, England **CW:** (Solo Albums) The Promise,1976, Among the Stars, 1994(Album with The Moody Blues) The Magnificent Moodies, 1965, Days of Future Passed, 1967, In Search of the Lost Chord, 1968, On the Threshold of a Dream, 1969, A Question of Balance, 1970, Every Good Boy Deserves Favour, 1971, Seventh Sojourn, 1972, Octave, 1978 **AW:** Rock and Roll Hall of Fame, 2018

PINE, CHRIS WHITELAW WHITELAW, T: Actor **I:** Media & Entertainment **DOB:** 07/11/1905 **PB:** LA, **SC:** LA, **PT:** Son of Robert Pine and Gwynne Gilford. **ED:** Attended, American Conservatory Theater, San Francisco; BA in English, University California, Berkeley, 2002 **CW:** Actor: (films) Why Germany?, 2004, The Princess Diaries 2: Royal Engagement, 2004, Confession, 2005, The Bulls, 2005, Just My Luck, 2006, Blind Dating, 2006, Smokin' Aces, 2006, Bottle Shock, 2008, Star Trek, 2009, Carriers, 2009, Small Town Saturday Night, 2010, Unstoppable, 2010, (voice) Quantum Quest: A Cassini Space Odyssey, 2010, Celeste & Jesse Forever, 2012, This Means War, 2012, People Like Us, 2012, (voice) Rise of the Guardians, 2012, Star Trek Into Darkness, 2013, Jack Ryan: Shadow Recruit, 2014, Stretch, 2014, Horrible Bosses 2, 2014, Into the Woods, 2014, Z for Zachariah, 2015, The Finest Hours, 2016, Hell or High Water, 2016, Star Trek Beyond, 2016, Wonder Woman, 2017, A Wrinkle in Time, 2018, Outlaw King, 2018; (TV films) Surrender Dorothy, 2006; (TV series) Wet Hot American Summer, 2015, (TV appearances) ER, 2003, CSI: Miami, 2003, Six Feet Under, 2005

PINEDA, ARNEL, T: Singer **I:** Media & Entertainment **PB:** Tonda **SC:** Philippines **CW:** (Solo Album) Arnel Pineda, 1999, AP, 2016, (With the Zoo) Zoology, 2007, (With Journey) Revelation, 2008, Journey: Live in Manila, 2009, Eclipse, 2011 **AW:** Rock and Roll Hall of Fame, 2017

PINGREE, CHELLIE M., T: U.S. Representative from Maine **I:** Government Administration/Government Relations/Government Services **DOB:** 04/02/1955 **PB:** Mpls. **SC:** ME/USA **ED:** Attended Summer Fellows Program, Kennedy School Government, 1996; BA, College of Atlantic, 1976; Attended, Outward Bound, 1970; Attended, University of Southern Maine **C:** Member, U.S. Congress from 1st Maine District, 2009-; Member, Committee on Appropriations; Founder, managing partner, Nebo Lodge, 2006-09; President, CEO, Common Cause, 2003-07; Majority leader, Maine State Senate from District 12, 1996-2000; Member, Maine State Senate from District 12, 1992-2000; Owner, founder, North Island Designs, 1981-93; Farmer, North Island Farm, 1977-80 **CR:** Board directors Wal-Mart Watch, 2005-; member adv. board Main Businesses for Social Responsibility, 2000-; founder, president, North Haven Arts and Enrichment Fund, 1999-2000; member North Haven Grange, 1981- **CIV:** Co-chair, Maine Economic Growth Council, 1995-98; Member, Adv. Committee on Mental Retardation, 1995-96; Member, Commission to Study Poverty Among the Working Poor, 1995-96; Member, Special Committee to Study Nursing Home Rates, 1995-96;

Senator, Maine State Senate, 1992-2000; Member, North Haven Planning Board, 1989-94 Chair, North Haven Tax Assesors, 1980-94; Former chair, SAD 7 School Board, **CW:** Author; photography, design, and production coordinator Maine Island Classics: Sweaters and Stories From Offshore, 1988, Sweaters from the Maine Islands, 1990, North Island Designs, 1992, Maine Island Classics, 1992, North Island Designs 5: A Scrapbook of Sweaters from a Maine Island, 1993 **PA:** Democrat

PINKETT-SMITH, JADA, T: Actress **I:** Media & Entertainment **DOB:** 09/18/1971 **PB:** Baltimore **SC:** MD/USA **PT:** Robson Pinkett; Adrienne (Banfield) Pinkett **MS:** Married **SPN:** Will Smith (December 31, 1997) **CH:** Jaden Christopher Syre, Willow Camille Reign; Trey (Stepchild) **ED:** Attended, North Carolina School Arts **CW:** Actress: (films) Menace II Society, 1993, The Inkwell, 1994, Jason's Lyric, 1994, A Low Down Dirty Shame, 1994, Demon Knight, 1995, The Nutty Professor, 1996, Set It Off, 1996, Blossoms and Veils, 1997, Scream 2, 1997, Woo, 1998, Return to Paradise, 1998, Bamboozled, 2000, Kingdom Come, 2001, Ali, 2001, The Matrix Reloaded, 2003, The Matrix Revolutions, 2003, Collateral, 2004, (voice) Madagascar, 2005, Reign Over Me, 2007, The Women, 2008, (voice) Madagascar: Escape 2 Africa, 2008, (voice) Madagascar 3: Europe's Most Wanted, 2012, Magic Mike XXL, 2015, Bad Moms, 2016, Girls Trip, 2017; (TV films) If These Walls Could Talk, 1996, Maniac Magee, 2003; (TV series) A Different World, 1991-93, Gotham, 2014-16; actress, executive prodr.: (TV series) Hawthorne, 2009-11; executive prodr.: (TV series) All of Us, 2003-07, Gotham, 2014-2017, (films) The Seat Filler, 2004, The Secret Life of Bees, 2008, (documentaries) Free Angela and All Political Prisoners, 2012, Rape For Profit, 2012; prodr.: (films) The Karate Kid, 2010, After Earth, 2013, Annie, 2014; actress, dir.: (films) The Human Contract, 2008; author (children's book): Girls Hold Up This World, 2004 (National Association for the Advancement of Colored People Image award for Outstanding Lit. Work-Children's 2006).

PINSKY, ROBERT NEAL, T: Poet, Educator **I:** Writing and Editing **DOB:** 10/20/1940 **PB:** Long Branch **PT:** Son of Milford Simon and Sylvia (Eisenberg) P.; Married EllenJane Bailey, December 30, 1961; children: Nicole, Caroline, Elizabeth. **ED:** PhD, Stanford University, 1966; BA, Rutgers University, 1962 **C:** Poet Laureate, 1997-2000; Professor creative writing, Boston University, 1989-; Professor, Boston University, 1980-89; Professor English, University California, Berkeley, 1980-89; Member English faculty, Wellesley College, 1968-80; Member English faculty, University Chicago, 1967-68 **CR:** Poetry editor New Republic magazine, 1978 visiting lecturer Harvard University Hurst professor Washington University, St. Louis **CW:** Author: Landor's Poetry, 1968, Sadness and Happiness, 1975, The Situation of Poetry, 1977, An Explanation of America, 1980, History of My Heart, 1984, Poetry and the World, 1988, The Want Bone, 1990, The Inferno of Dante, 1994, The Figured Wheel: New and Collected Poems 1966-1996, 1996, The Sounds of Poetry, 1998, The Handbook of Heartbreak, 1998, Americans' Favorite Poems, 2000, Jersey Rain, 2000, Gulf Music, 2007; editor: (poetry) Slate magazine, 1994-2000 **AW:** Recipient Artists award Am. Academy Arts and Letters, 1979; Saxifrage prize, 1980; William Carlos Williams prize, 1984; Shelley Memorial award, 1996, Harold Washington Lit. award, 1999; Guggenheim fellow, 1980; appointed U.S. poet laureate, 1997,PEN/ Voelcker Award for Poetry, 2004, Manhae Foundation Prize, 2006, Premio Capri, 2009 **MEM:** Member American Academy of Arts and Letters, American Association for the Advancement of Science, PEN

PITINO, RICK, T: College Basketball Coach **I:** Athletics **DOB:** 09/18/1952 **PB:** New York City **ED:** Grad., University Massachusetts, 1974 **C:** Head Coach, University Louisville, 2001-2017; Head Coach, president, Boston Celtics, 1997-2001; Head Coach, University Kentucky, Lexington, 1989-97; Head Coach, Providence University, 1985-87; Head Coach, New York Knicks, 1987-89; Assistant Coach, New York Knicks, 1983-85; Head Coach, Boston University, 1978-83; Assistant Coach, Syracuse University, 1976-78; Assistant Coach, University Hawaii, 1975-76; Grad. Assistant, University Hawaii, 1974 **CW:** Author: (with Bill Reynolds) Born to Coach: A Season with the New York Knicks, 1988, (with Dick Weiss) Full Court Pressure: A Year in Kentucky Basketball, 1992; Success Is a Choice: Ten Steps to Overachieving in Business and Life, 1997, Lead to Succeed, 2000, (with Pat Forde) Rebound Rules: The Art of Success 2.0, 2008, (with Eric Crawford) The One-Day Contract: How to Add Value to Every Minute of Your Life, 2013 **AW:** Named Conference USA Coach of Year, 2005, Southeastern Conference Coach of Year, 1997, 1991, 1990, John Wooden National Coach of Year, 1987, National Association Basketball Coaches National Coach of Year, 1987, New England Coach of Year, 1983, 1979; named to Naismith Memorial Basketball Hall of Fame, 2013, New York City Hall of Fame, 2006, Naismith Memorial Basketball Hall of Fame, 2013 **ACH:** Achievements include head coach of the NCAA Final Four National Championship winning University of Kentucky Wildcats, 1996; University of Louisville Cardinals, 2013

PITT, BRAD, T: Actor, Film Producer **I:** Media & Entertainment **DOB:** 12/18/1963 **PB:** Shawnee **SC:** MO/USA **PT:** Son of Bill and Jane Pitt **SPN:** Angelina Jolie, (August 23, 2014, separated September 2016); Jennifer Aniston, July 29, 2000 (div. October 2, 2005); **CH:** Shiloh Nouvel, Knox Leon, Vivien **C:** Founder, Make It Right Foundation New Orleans, 2007-; Co-founder, Maddox Jolie-Pitt Foundation (MJP), 2006-; Co-founder, Plan B Entertainment, 2002 **CW:** Actor: (films) No Man's Land, 1987, Less Than Zero, 1987, Cutting Glass, 1989, Happy Together, 1990, Across the Tracks, 1991, Thelma and Louise, 1991, Johnny Suede, 1991, Contact, 1992, Cool World, 1992, A River Runs Through It, 1992, Kalifornia, 1993, True Romance, 1993, The Favor, 1994, Interview with the Vampire, 1994 (MTV Movie awards for Best Male Performance, Most Desirable Male, 1995), Legends of the Fall, 1994, Se7en, 1995, 12 Monkeys, 1995 (Golden Globe award for Best Supporting Actor, 1996), Sleepers, 1996, Seven Years in Tibet, 1997, The Devil's Own, 1997, Dark Side of the Sun, 1997, Meet Joe Black, 1998, Fight Club, 1999, Snatch, 2000, The Mexican, 2001, Spy Game, 2001, Ocean's Eleven, 2001, Full Frontal, 2002, Confessions of a Dangerous Mind, 2002, Sinbad: Legend of the Seven Seas (voice only), 2003, Troy, 2004 (Teen Choice award for Choice Movie Actor in Drama/Action Adventure, 2004), Ocean's Twelve, 2004, Mr. & Mrs. Smith, 2005, Babel, 2006, Ocean's Thirteen, 2007, The Assassination of Jesse James by the Coward Robert Ford, 2007, Burn After Reading, 2008, The Curious Case of Benjamin Button, 2008, Inglourious Basterds, 2009, Megamind (voice), 2010, Moneyball, 2011 (New York Film Critics Cir. award for Best Actor, 2011, Boston Society Film Critics award for Best Actor, 2011, National Society Film Critics award for Best Actor, 2011), Happy Feet Two (voice), 2011, The Counselor, 2013, Allied, 2016); actor, producer (films) The Assassination of Jesse James by the Coward Robert Ford, 2007, The Tree of Life, 2011 (National Society Film Critics award for Best Actor, 2012), Killing Them Softly, 2012, Voyage of Time, 2013, World War Z, 2013, 12 Years a Slave, 2013

(The Darryl F. Zanuck award for Outstanding Producer of Theatrical Motion Pictures, Producers Guild of America, 2014, Brit. Academy Film and TV Arts award for Best Film, 2014), Voyage of Time (voice), 2014, By the Sea, 2015, The Big Short, 2015 (The Darryl F. Zanuck award for Outstanding Producer of Theatrical Motion Pictures, Producers Guild of America, 2016), War Machine, 2017, Brad's Status, 2017, Beautiful Boy, 2018, Backseat, 2018, Ad Astra, 2019actor, executive producer Fury, 2014; actor: (TV films) A Stoning in Fulham County, 1988, Too Young to Die, 1990; (TV series) Another World, 1987, Glory Days, 1990, (TV appearances) Growing Pains, 1987-89, Dallas, 1987-88, 21 Jump Street, 1988, Head of the Class, 1989, Freddy's Nightmares, 1989, thirtysomething, 1989, Tales from the Crypt, 1992, Friends, 2001, King of the Hill (voice), 2003, Getaway, 2005; prodr.: (films) The Departed, 2006, Running with Scissors, 2006, Kick-Ass 2, 2013, True Story, 2015, The Lost City of Z, 2016; (TV films) The Normal Heart, 2014 (Stanley Kramer award, Producers Guild of America, 2015, Nightingale, 2014, The OA, 2016, Feud, 2017, The Jim Jefferies Show, 2017); (documentaries) Voyage of Time, 2016; executive prodr.: (films) God Grew Tired of Us: The Story of Lost Boys of Sudan, 2004, Year of the Dog, 2007; executive prodr.: (films) Eat Pray Love, 2010; (documentaries) The House I Live In, 2012, Big Men, 2013; co-prodr.: (films) A Mighty Heart, 2007 (Theatre) 8, 2012; **AW:** Named Favorite Leading Man, People's Choice Awards, 2009, Favorite On Screen Match-Up (with George Clooney), 2008, Favorite Leading Man, 2006, Male Star of Tomorrow, ShoWest Convention, 1993; named one of The 100 Most Powerful Celebrities, Forbes.com, 2008, 2007, The 100 Most Influential People in the World, TIME magazine, 2009, 2008, 2007, Barbara Walters 10 Most Fascinating People of 2006, The 50 Most Powerful People in Hollywood, Premiere magazine, 2004-06; recipient Visionary award (with Plan B Entertainment), Producers Guild of America, 2015

PITTENGER, ROBERT, T: U.S. Representative from North Carolina **I:** Government Administration/Government Relations/Government Services **DOB:** 08/15/1948 **PB:** Dallas **SC:** TX/USA **ED:** BA, University of Texas, 1970 **C:** Member, U.S. House Financial Services Committee, 2013-; Member, Republican Study Committee; Member, U.S. Congress from 9th North Carolina District, Washington, until 2013; Member Dist 39, North Carolina State Senate, 2004-08; Member District 40, North Carolina State Senate, 2003-04; Owner, Robert Pittenger Co., 1989; Assistant to president, Campus Crusade for Christ, 1970-85 **CR:** Chairman Congressional Task Force on Terrorism & Unconventional Warfare, 2014- **PA:** Republican

PIZARRO, PEDRO, T: CEO of Edison Intl **I:** Sciences **ED:** PhD in Chemical Physics, California Institute Tech.; BS in Chemistry, magna cum laude, Harvard Univ. **C:** President/CEO, Edison Intl, 2016-; President Southern California Edison Co, Edison Intl, 2014-16; CEO, Southern California Edison Co, 2011-14; President, Edison Mission Energy, 2011-14; Exec Vp:Power Operations, Southern California Edison Co, 2008-10; Senior vice president, Southern California Edison, Rosemead, California, 2005-; And general manager, Edison Carrier Solutions, Southern California Edison, Rosemead, California,; Vice president, power procurement, Southern California Edison, Rosemead, California, 2000-05; Joined, Southern California Edison, Rosemead, California, 1999; Senior engagement manager, McKinsey & Co., LA, **CIV:** Director, Colburn School Performing Arts, Trustee, House Ear Institute **AW:** Named one of 50 Most Important Hispanics in Tech., Business, Hispanic Engineer and Information Tech. magazine, 2005

PLANT, ROBERT ANTHONY, T: Musician **I:** Media & Entertainment **DOB:** 08/20/1948 **PB:** Bromwich **SC:** Staffordshire Eng. **PT:** Son of Robert C. and Annie C. (Cain) P.; Married Maureen Wilson, November 9, 1969 (div. August 1983); children: Carmen Jayne, Karac Pendragon (deceased July 26, 1977), Logan Romero, Jesse Lee **C:** Lead singer, Led Zeppelin, 1968-80; Lead singer, Band of Joy, 1966-68; Lead singer, Crawling King Snakes, **CW:** Singer: (albums with Led Zeppelin) Led Zeppelin, 1968, Led Zeppelin II, 1969, Led Zeppelin III, 1970, Led Zeppelin IV, 1971, Houses of the Holy, 1973, Physical Graffiti, 1975, The Song Remains the Same, Presence, 1976, In Through the Out Door, 1979, Coda, 1982, Remasters, 1990, BBC Sessions, 1997, Early Days: The Best of Led Zeppelin Volume One, 2000, Latter Days: The Best of Led Zeppelin Volume Two, 2002, How the West Was Won, 2003, Definitive Collection, 2008, Mothership, 2007, Celebration Day, 2012 (Best Rock Album, Grammy Awards, 2014), (solo albums) Pictures at Eleven, 1982, The Principle of Moments, 1983, Shaken 'n' Stirred, 1985, Now and Zen, 1988, Manic Nirvana, 1990, Fate of Nations, 1993, Sixty Six to Timbuktu, 2003, Mighty Rearranger, 2005, Nine Lives, 2006, Lullaby and... The Ceaseless Roar, 2014, Carry Fire, 2017, (albums with The Honeydrippers) The Honeydrippers: Volume One, 1985, (albums with Jimmy Page) No Quarter: Jimmy Page and Robert Plant Unledded, 1994, (albums with Strange Sensation) Dreamland, 2002, Enchanter, 2005, (albums with Alison Krauss) Raising Sand, 2007 (Wide Open Country Video of Year, Country Music TV, Musical Event of Year, Country Music Association, 2008, Record of Year, Album of Year, Best Pop Collaboration with Vocals, Best Country Collaboration with Vocals, Best Contemporary Folk Album, Grammy Awards, 2009), (albums with Band of Joy) Band of Joy, 2010, (album with Alison Krauss) Raising Sand, 2007; performer: (concert films) The Song Remains the Same, 1976, Unledded, 1994 **AW:** Co-recipient Lifetime Achievement award, Grammy awards, 2005; named a Commander of the Most Excellent Order of the British Empire (CBE), Prince Charles of Wales, 2009; named to The Rock and Roll Hall of Fame (as member of Led Zeppelin), 1995; recipient Kennedy Center Honors, John F. Kennedy Center Performing Arts, Washington, 2012, Grammy award for Best Pop Collaboration with Vocals, 2008, Polar Music prize, Royal Swedish Academy Music, 2006, Grammy award for Best Hard Rock Performance, 1999

PLATT, BEN, T: Actor **I:** Media & Entertainment **PB:** Los Angeles **SC:** CA/USA **CW:** (Film) Pitch Perfect, 2012, Pitch Perfect 2, 2015, Ricki and the Flash, 2015, Billy Lynn's Long Halftime Walk, 2016, The Female Brain, 2017, Drunk Parents, 2018, (Television) Will & Grace, 2017(Theatre) The Music Man, 2002, Caroline, or Change, 2004, Dead End, 2005, The Power of Duff, 2012, The Black Suits, 2012, The Book of Morman, 2012-2015, Dear Evan Hansen, 2015, The Secret Garden, 2016, Dear Evan Hansen, 2016(Tony Award for Best Actor in a Musical, 2016 Grammy Award for Best Musical Theatre Album, 2018) **AW:** Time 100 Most Influential, 2017

PLAYER, GARY JIM, T: Professional Golfer, Businessman, Golf Course Designer **I:** Athletics **DOB:** 11/01/1935 **PB:** Johannesburg **PT:** Son of Francis Harry Audley and Muriel (Ferguson) P; Married Vivienne Verwey, January 19, 1957; children: Jennifer, Marc, Wayne, Michele, Theresa, Amanda. **ED:** LLD (hon.), St. Andrews University, Scotland, 1995; Student, King Edward School, Johannesburg **C:** Professional golfer, Senior PGA, 1985-; Professional golfer, 1953-; With, PGA, 1957-85 **CR:** Chair Gary Player Group. **AW:** 3rd man in history to win Grand Slam of Golf; winner over 150 international golf tournaments, 22 Senior Tour tournaments; named Christian Athlete of Year Southern Baptist Convention, 1967, Sportsman of the Year in South Africa, 1955, 56, 59, 61, 63, 65, 72, 74, 78, South African Sportsman of the Century, 1990; Richardson award Golf Writers Association Am., 1975; named to World Golf Hall of Fame, 1974; hon. member R&A, 1994, Skills Challenge, 1994. Won East Rand Open, South Africa, 1955-56, Egyptian Mathchplay, 1955, South African Open, 1956, 60, 65-69, 72, 75-77, 79, 81, Dunlop Tournament, England, 1956, Ampol Tournament, Australia, 1956, 58, 61, Australian PGA, 1957, Coughs Harbour Tournament, Australia, 1957-58, Natal Open, South Africa, 1958-60, 62, 66, 68, Australian Open, 1958, 62-63, 65, 69-70, 74, Transvaal Open, South Africa, 1959, 60, 62, 63, 66, South African PGA, 1959-60, 69, 79, 82, Western Province Open, South Africa, 1959-60, 68, 71-72, Dunlop Masters, South Africa, 1959-60, 63-64, 67, 71-74, 76-77, Brit. Open, 1959, 68, 74, Victoria Open, 1959, Yomiuri Open, Japan, 1961, Masters Tournament, 1961, 74, 78, Sponsored 5000, South Africa, 1963, Liquid Air Tournament, South Africa, 1963, Richelieu Grand Prix, Capetown, 1963, Johannesburg, 1963, NTL Challenge Cup, 1965, World Cup International, 1965, World Series of Golf, 1965, 68, 72, Picadilly World Match Play, England, 1965, 66, 68, 71, 73, Australian Wills Masters, 1968, 69, Dunlop International, Australia, 1970, General Motors Open, South Africa, 1971, 73, 74, 75, 76, Japan Airlines Open, 1972, Brazilian Open, 1972, 74, Rand International Open, South Africa, 1974, General Motors International Classic, South Africa, 1974, Ibergolf Tournament, Spain, 1974, La Manga Tournament, Spain, 1974, General Motors Classic, 1975, ICL Transvaal, South Africa, 1977, World Cup Individual, The Philippines, 1977, Knonenbrau Masters, South Africa, 1979, Sun City, South Am., 1979, Chilean Open, 1980, Trophee Boigny, Ivory Coast, 1980, Australian Tooth Gold Coast Classic, 1981, Johnnie Walker Trophy, Spain, 1981; recipient PGA tour victories (21) Kentucky Derby Open, 1961, Lucky International Open, 1961, Sunshine Open 1961, PGA Championship, 1962, 72, San Diego Open, 1963, Pensacola Open, 1964, 500 Festival Open, 1964, U.S. Open, 1965, Tournament of Champions, 1969, 78, Greater Greensboro Open, 1970, Jacksonville Open, 1971, National Airlines Open, 1971, New Orleans Open, 1972, Southern Open, 1973, Danny Thomas Memphis Classic, 1974, Houston Open, 1978, (Senior PGA tours) (19) Quadel Senior Classic, 1985, General Foods PGA Srs. Championship, 1986, 88, 90, United Hospitals Senior Golf Championship, Denver Post Champions of Golf, Mazda Senior Tournament Players Champion, 1987, Northville Srs., 1987, U.S. Senior Open, 87, 88, PaineWebber World Srs. Invitational, Aetna Challenge, 1988, Southwestern Bell Classic, 1988, USGA Srs., 1988, Senior Brit. Open, 1988, 90, 97, GTE North Classic, The RJR Championship, Royal Caribbean Classic, 1991, Bank One Classic, 1993, 95, Northville Long Island Classic, 1998,PGA Tour Lifetime Achievement, 2012, Payne Stewart Award, 2006 **H:** Thoroughbred horse breeding, farming, exercise, health, diet

PLUMMER, CHRISTOPHER, T: Actor **I:** Media & Entertainment **DOB:** 12/13/1929 **PB:** Toronto **SC:** Ont. Can. **PT:** Son of John and Isabella Mary (Abbott) P. **SPN:** Married Elaine Taylor, 1970; Married Patricia Audrey Lewis, May 4, 1962 (div. 1967); Tammy Grimes, August 19, 1956 (div. 1960); **CH:** Amanda; **ED:** PhD (hon.), University Toronto, Ryerson and Western Ontario; DFA (hon.), New York Julliard School; LLD (hon.), University We. Ontario, 2004; Pupil, C. Herbertcasari; Pupil, Iris Warren; Student pub. and private schools, Can. **CW:** Stage debut in The Rivals with Can. Repertory Theatre, 1950; Broadway debut in Starcross Story, 1954, J.B.; London debut in Becket, 1961; leading actor Cymbeline, Am. Shakespeare Theatre, Stratford, Connecticut, 1955, Royal Shakespeare Co., London and Stratford, Avon, England, 1961-62, Stratford (Ontario) Shakespeare Festival, 1956, 57, 58, 60, 62, 67, National Theatre Co., London; radio roles include Shakespeare, Canada; plays include Home is the Hero, 1954, Twelfth Night, 1954, 70-71, Dark is Light Enough, The Lark, Julius Caesar, The Tempest, 1955, (rearranger with Sir Neville Mariner) Henry VI, 1956, Hamlet, 1957, Winter's Tale, 1958, Much Ado About Nothing, 1958, J.B., 1958, King John, 1960, Romeo and Juliet, 1960, Richard III, 1961, Arturo Ui, 1963, The Royal Hunt of the Sun, 1965, Antony and Cleopatra, 1967, Danton's Death, 1971, Alnsmphitryon 38, 1971, The Constant Wife, The Dark is Light Enough (Theatre World award), Medea, The Lark; (musicals) Cyrano, 1973 (Tony award for Best Actor in a Musical, 1974), The Good Doctor, 1973, Love and Master Will, 1975; performer (with Sir Neville Mariner and rearranged by Michael Lankester) A Midsummer's Night's Dream; Othello, 1982, Macbeth, 1988, No Man's Land, 1993, Barrymore, 1996 (Tony award for Best Actor in a Play, 1997, Drama Desk, Outer Critics Cir. award, Edwin Booth award, Boston Critics' award, Chgo.'s Jefferson award, LA Ovation award Best Actor 1997-98), King Lear, 2004, Inherit the Wind, 2007, A Word or Two, 2012, Hirsch, 2012; made TV debut 1953; TV productions include Little Moon of Alban, Johnny Belinda, 1958, Cyrano de Bergerac, 1962, Oedipus Rex, After the Fall, 1974, The Doll's House, The Prince and the Pauper, Prisoner of Zenda, Hamlet at Elsinore, BBC, 1964, Time Remembered, Captain Brassbound's Conversion, The Shadow Box, 1981, The Thornbirds, 1983, Little Gloria-Happy at Last, A Hazard of Hearts, 1987, Crossings, 1986, Danielle Steele's Secrets, 1992, Liar's Edge, 1992, On Golden Pond, 2001, Night Flight, 2002, Agent of Influence, 2002, Odd Job Jack, 2003, Our Fathers, 2005, Miracle Planet, 2005, American Experience, 2006, The Summit, 2008, Muhammad Ali's Greatest Fight, 2013; star TV series The Moneychangers, 1977, Harrison Bergeron, 1995, We the Jury, 1996, The Conspiracy of Fear, 1996; actor: (films) Stage Struck, 1957, Wind Across the Everglades, 1958, The Fall of the Roman Empire, 1963, Inside Daisy Clover, 1965, Sound of Music, 1965, Triple Cross, 1967, Nobody Runs Forever, 1969, The Battle of Britain, 1969, The Royal Hunt of the Sun, 1969, Lock up your Daughters, 1969, The Phyx, 1970, Waterloo, 1971, The Man Who Would Be King, 1975, The Return of the Pink Panther, 1975, Conduct Unbecoming, 1975, International Velvet, 1978, Murder By Decree, 1979, Starcrash, 1979, The Silent Partner, 1979, Hanover Street, 1979, Somewhere in Time, 1980, Eyewitness, 1981, The Disappearance, 1981, The Amateur, 1982, Dreamscape, 1984, Ordeal by Innocence, 1984, Lily in Love, 1985, The Boss' Wife, 1986, The Boy In Blue, 1986, An American Tail, 1986 (voice), Souvenir, 1987, Dragnet, 1987, Light Years (voice), 1988, Where the Heart Is, 1989, Fire Head, 1991, Star Trek: VI: The Undiscovered Country, 1991, Rock a Doodle, 1992 (voice), Malcolm X, 1992, Wolf, 1994, Dolores Claiborne, 1994, Twelve Monkeys, 1995, Skeletons, 1996, The Arrow, 1997, Hidden Agenda, 1998, The Clown at Midnight, 1998, Blackheart, The Insider, 1999, All the Fine Lines, 1999, The Dinosaur Hunter, 2000, Dracula 2000, A Beautiful Mind, 2001, Nicholas Nickleby, 2002, Ararat, 2002, Blizzard, 2003, Cold Creek Manor, 2003, National Treasure, 2004, Alexander, 2004, Tma, 2005, Must Love Dogs, 2005, Syriana, 2005, The New World, 2005, Inside Man, 2006, Man in the Chair, 2007, The Lake House, 2006, (voice) Up, 2009, (voice) 9, 2009,

Beginners, 2010 (National Board Review award for Best Supporting Actor, 2011, Critics' Choice Movie award for Best Supporting Actor, 2012, Golden Globe award for Best Performance by an Actor in a Supporting Role in a Motion Picture, 2012, Screen Actors Guild award for Outstanding Performance by a Male Actor in a Supporting Role, 2012, BAFTA award for Best Supporting Actor, 2012, Academy award for Best Supporting Actor, 2012), Priest, 2011, The Girl with the Dragon Tattoo, 2011, The Legend of Sarila (voice), 2013, Muhammad Ali's Greatest Fight, 2013, Elsa & Fred, 2014, Hector and the Search for Happiness, 2014, The Forger, 2014, Danny Collins, 2015, Pixies (voice), 2015, Remember, 2015, The Exception, 2016, Howard Lovecraft and the Frozen Kingdon, 2016, The Star, 2017, The Man Who Invented Christmas, 2017, All the Money in the World, 2017, Cliffs of Freedom, 2018, The Last Full Measure, 2018, Boundaries, 2018; (TV films) Winchell, 1998, Four Minute Mile, 2005, Our Fathers, 2005; (TV mini-series) Celebrate the Century, 1999,Nuremberg, 2000, American Tragedy, 2000; actor, executive prodr.: (films) Barrymore, 2011; author: In Spite of Myself: A Memoir, 2008. **AW:** Decorated companion Order of Can., 1968; recipient Theatre World award, 1955, Evening Standard Theatre award, 1961, Delia Austrian medal, 1973, 2 Drama Desk awards, 1973, 82, Antoinette Perry award, 1974, Emmy award National Academy TV Arts and Scis., 1977, Genie award, Can., 1980, Golden Badge of Honor, Austria, 1982, Maple Leaf award National Academy Arts and Letters, many honors England, Austria, Can., Two Tony awards (seven nominations), Two Emmy awards (six nominations), Great Britain's Evening Standard award, Can.'s Genie award, Governor Gen's Lifetime Achievement award, 2001, William Shakespeare award (Will award) classical theatre, National Board Rev. Career Achievement award, New York., Jason Robard's award excellence in memory great friend, 2002; inducted in Am.'s Theatre's Hall of Fame, 1986, Can.'s Walk of Fame, 1997. **BA:** 49 Wampum Hill Road, Weston, CT, 06883

POCAN, MARK, T: U.S. Representative from Wisconsin, former state legislator **I:** Government Administration/Government Relations/Government Services **DOB:** 08/14/1964 **PB:** Kenosha **ED:** BA in Journalism, University Wisconsin, Madison, 1986 **C:** Member, US House Oversight Reform Committee, 2013-; Member, US House Budget Committee, 2013-; Member, Committee on Urban and Local Affairs; Member, Committee on Colleges and Universities; Member, US Congress from 2nd District Wisconsin, Washington, 2013-; Member District 78, Wisconsin State Assembly, 1999-2013; Member, Dane County Board Supervisors, 1991-96 **AW:** Named Legislator of Year, Professional Fire Fighters Wisconsin, 2008, Conservative Champion, Wisconsin League of Conservation Voters, 2006, Council Rep. of the Year, Wisconsin Federation Teachers State Employees, 2002; named to The Wisconsin League of Conservation Voters Honor Roll, 2008; recipient Council Rep. of the Year, Wisconsin Federation Teachers State Employees, 2003, Special Recognition award, ACLU, 2001, Outstanding Young Legislator award, Wisconsin Counties Association, 2008, 2006, Planned Parenthood Rebecca Young Leadership award, 2009, Fair Wisconsin Statewide Leader award, 2009, Voices of Courage Pub. Policy award, Wisconsin Coalition Against Sexual Assault, 2008, Public Policy award, Wisconsin Libr. Association, 2008, Wisconsin AIDS Fund award, 2007, Clean Wisconsin Clean 16 award, 2004, 2002, 2000 **MEM:** Mem.: American Civil Liberties Union **PA:** Democrat

PODESTA, TONY, I: Consulting **DOB:** 10/24/1943 **PB:** Chicago **SC:** IL/USA **PT:** John David; Mary (Kokoris) Podesta **ED:** BA, University of Illinois **C:** Co-founder, president, The Podesta Group, Washington, 1988 **CR:** Visiting professor Georgetown University Law Center **AW:** Named Power Collector, The Washington Post; named one of 50 Most Powerful People in DC, GQ magazine, 2009, 50 Top Lobbyists, Washingtonian magazine, 2007 **H:** Art collecting **PA:** Democrat

POE, TED, T: U.S. Representative from Texas, Former Judge **I:** Law and Legal Services **DOB:** 10/13/1948 **PB:** Temple **ED:** JD, University Houston Law Center, 1973; BA in Political Sci., Abilene Christian University, 1970 **C:** Member, US Congress from 2nd Texas district, 2005-;; Member, Committee on Foreign Affairs, Committee on the Judiciary; Criminal court judge, Harris County, Texas, 1981-2003; Assistant district attorney, Harris County, Texas, 1973-81 **CR:** Instructor University Houston, US Military Academy, West Point, FBI National Academy, Quantico, Virginia **CIV:** Board directors, National Children's Alliance, Past board directors, Abilene Christian University, Past board directors, Roseate Women's Center Abused Women, Past board directors, DARE, Past board directors, MADD, Past board directors, Parents of Murdered Children, Past board directors, Child Abuse Prevention Council, Past board directors, CASA Child Advocates, Past board directors, Children's Assessment Center Houston, **AW:** Named Outstanding Young Lawyer, Houston Bar Association, Outstanding District Judge, Houston Police Officers Assn./Harris County Deputy Sheriffs Association, Best Judge, Kansas Peace Officers Association, Outstanding Instructor, Texas District Attorney Association, Outstanding Judge, Foundation Improvement of Justice; recipient Morton Bard award, National Organization Victims Assistance, Social Change award, Texas Association Against Sexual Assault, Spirit of Enterprise award, US C. of C., Congl. Partnership award, Southeast Texas Regional Planning Commission, 2006 **PA:** Republican

POEHLER, AMY, T: Comedienne, Actress **I:** Media & Entertainment **DOB:** 09/16/1971 **PB:** Newton **SC:** MA/USA **ED:** Grad., Boston College **C:** Performer, Improv Olympic, LA,; Performer, Second City comedy troupe, Chicago, 1993-96 **CW:** Actress: (films) Saving Manhattan, 1998, Tomorrow Night, 1998, Deuce Bigalow: Male Gigolo, 1999, The Devil and Daniel Webster, 2001, Wet Hot American Summer, 2001, Martin & Orloff, 2002, Mean Girls, 2004, Envy, 2004, Southland Tales, 2006, Man of the Year, 2006, Blades of Glory, 2007, Horton Hears a Who! (voice), 2008, Baby Mama, 2008, Hamlet 2, 2008, Monsters versus Aliens (voice), 2009, Alvin and the Chipmunks: The Squeakquel (voice), 2009, Hoodwinked Too! Hood VS. Evil (voice), 2011, Alvin and the Chipmunks: Chip-Wrecked (voice), 2011, The Secret World of Arrietty (voice), 2012, A.C.O.D., 2013, You Are Here, 2013, Free Birds (voice), 2013, Anchorman 2: The Legend Continues, 2013, They Came Together, 2014, Inside Out (voice), 2015, Rileys First Date,2015, A Very Murray Christmas, 2015, Sisters, 2015, The House, 2017; actress, writer, producer (films) Wild Girls Gone, 2005, actress, executive producer Sisters, 2015, actress, writer (TV series) Upright Citizens Brigade, 1998-2000; actress: (TV series) Saturday Night Live, 2001-08, Wet Hot American Summer: First Day of Camp, 2015-; actress, executive producer, writer (TV series) The Mighty B!, 2008-11; executive prodr.: (TV series) Broad City, 2014-15; actress, producer (TV series) Parks and Recreation, 2009- (Golden Globe award for Best Performance by an Actress in a TV Series - Musical

or Comedy, 2014), actress, executive producer Welcome to Sweden, 2014-15, appearances include Apartment 2F, 1997, Spin City, 1998, Undeclared, 2002, Arrested Development, 2004, 30 Rock, 2012, Comedy Bang Bang, 2012 The Awesomes, 2014, host, Broad City, 2014, Welcome to Sweden, 2015, Kroll Show, 2014, Wet Hot American Summer, 2017, Difficult, 2017, Making it, 2017 (online series) Smart Girls at the Party, 2008, co-host The 70th Golden Globe Awards, 2013, The 71st Golden Globe Awards, 2014, The 72nd Golden Globe Awards, 2015; author: Yes Please, 2014 **AW:** Named a Maverick, Details magazine, 2008; named Best Actress-Webby award, International Academy of Digital Arts and Sciences, 2010, Best Actress, 2010; named one of The 100 Most Powerful Women in Entertainment, The Hollywood Reporter, 2013-14, The 100 Most Influential People in the World, TIME magazine, 2011, The 50 Most Powerful Women in New York City, New York Post, 2008; recipient Star, Hollywood Walk of Fame, 2015, Women of Year award, Glamour Magazine, 2009

POITIER, SIDNEY, T: Actor **I:** Media & Entertainment **DOB:** 02/20/1927 **PB:** Miami **SC:** FL/USA **PT:** Son of Reginald and Evelyn (Outten) Poitier **ED:** Student, The Bahamas **CR:** Ambassador to Japan from the Bahamas, 1997; Board of Directors, Walt Disney Co., 1994—2003 **MIL:** Served 1267th Medical Detachment US Army, 1944—45, veteran's hospital, Long Island, NY **CW:** Performer: (Broadway plays) Lysistrata, 1946; Anna Lucasta, 1974; A Raisin in the Sun, 1959—60; director: Carry Me Back to Morningside Heights, 1968; actor: (films) No Way Out, 1950, Cry, the Beloved Country, 1951, Red Ball Express, 1952, Go, Man, Go!, 1954, Blackboard Jungle, 1955, Good-bye, My Lady, 1956, Edge of the City, 1957, Something of Value, 1957, Band of Angels, 1957, The Mark of the Hawk, 1958, The Defiant Ones, 1958, Virgin Island, 1958, Porgy and Bess, 1959, All the Young Men, 1960, A Raisin in the Sun, 1961, Paris Blues, 1961, Pressure Point, 1962, Lilies of the Field, 1963 (Academy Award for Best Actor in a Leading Role, 1963, Golden Globe Award for Best Motion Picture Actor - Drama, 1964), The Long Ships, 1963, The Bedford Incident, 1965, The Greatest Story Ever Told, 1965, A Patch of Blue, 1965, The Slender Thread, 1965, Duel at Diablo, 1966, To Sir, with Love, 1967, In the Heat of the Night, 1967, Guess Who's Coming to Dinner, 1967, The Lost Man, 1969, The Call Me Mister Tibbs!, 1970, Brother John, 1971, The Organization, 1971, The Wilby Conspiracy, 1975, Shoot to Kill, 1988, Little Nikita, 1988, Sneakers, 1992, The Jackal, 1997, Ralph Bunche An American Odyssey, 2001, Tell Them Who You Are, 2004, Mr Warmth The Don Rickles Project, 2008; (TV films) Separate but Equal, 1991, Children of the Dust, 1995, To Sir, with Love II, 1996, Mandela and de Klerk, 1997, David and Lisa, 1998, The Simple Life of Noah Dearborn, 1999, Free of Eden, 1999, The Last Brickmaker in America, 2001; actor, producer (TV films) East of Eden, 1999; actor, director (films) Buck and the Preacher, 1972, A Warm December, 1973, Uptown Saturday Night, 1974, Let's Do It Again, 1975, A Piece of the Action, 1977, actor, writer (story) For Love of Ivy, 1968; director: (films) Stir Crazy, 1980, Hanky Panky, 1982, Fast Forward, 1985, Ghost Dad, 1990; author: (autobiography) This Life, 1980, The Measure of a Man: A Spiritual Autobiography, 2000, Life Beyond Measure, Letters to My Great-Granddaughter, 2008, Montaro Caine, 2013 **AW:** Decorated Hon. Knight Commander of the Most Excellent Order of the British Empire, Her Majesty Queen Elizabeth II; Recipient, Golden Globe Award for World Film Favorite - Male, 1969, Cecil B. DeMille Award, Golden Globe Awards, 1982, Lifetime Achievement Award, Am. Film Institute, 1992, Kennedy Center Honors, 1995,

Lifetime Achievement Award, Screen Actors Guild, 2000, Hall of Fame Award, National Association for the Advancement of Colored People, 2001, Hon. Academy Award, Academy Motion Pictures Arts & Sciences, 2002, Presidential Medal of Freedom, The White House, 2009, Film Society of Lincoln Center Gala Tribute, 2011, Star on Hollywood Walk of Fame, 1994, Spingarn Medal, National Association for the Advancement of Colored People, 2015, BAFTA Fellowship, 2016 **ACH:** Achievements include being first African America to win an Academy Award for a leading role, 1964 **BA:** Creative Artists Agency, 2000 Avenue of the Stars, Los Angeles, CA, 90067

POLICINSKI, CHRIS, T: CEO **I:** Consumer Goods and Services **CN:** Land O'Lakes, Inc. **ED:** MBA, New York University; Honorary BA, University of Notre Dame (1980) **C:** President, Chief Executive Officer, Land O'Lakes, Inc., Arden Hills, MN (2005-Present); Executive Vice President, Chief Operating Officer, Dairy Foods, Land O'Lakes, Inc., Arden Hills, MN (2002-2005); Executive Vice President, Chief Operating Officer, Dairy Foods Value Added Group, Land O'Lakes, Inc., Arden Hills, MN (1999-2002); Vice President Strategy, Business & International Development, Land O'Lakes, Inc., Arden Hills, MN (1997-1999); Management Positions with Pillsbury Co., Kraft General Foods **CR:** Board of Directors, National Council of Farmer Cooperatives; Board of Directors, National Milk Production Federation; Board of Directors, Grocery Manufacturers of America **CIV:** Trustee, Graduate Institute of Cooperative Leadership; Board of Directors, Minnesota Business Partnership; Board of Directors, Greater Twin Cities United Way **MEM:** Board Member, National Council of Farmer Cooperatives; Board Member, Catholic Relief Services **BA:** Land O'Lakes, 4001 Lexington Ave N, Arden Hills, MN, 55126

POLIQUIN, BRUCE LEE, T: U.S. Representative from Maine **I:** Government Administration/Government Relations/Government Services **DOB:** 11/01/1953 **PB:** Waterville **SC:** ME/USA **PT:** Son of Lionel Joseph and Esther Louise (Cyr) P. **ED:** BS in Economics, Harvard University, 1976 **C:** Member, US House Financial Services Committee, Washington, 2015-; Member, Republican Study Committee; Member, US Congress from 2nd Maine District, Washington, 2014-; State treasurer, State of Maine, Augusta, 2011-13; Vice president, director marketing & principal, Avatar Associates, New York City, 1981-96; Director marketing, Evaluation Associates Inc., Norwalk, Connecticut, 1978-80; Marketing rep., Harris Trust & Savings Bank, Chicago, 1976-77 **CIV:** Recruiter Phillips Academy, Andover, Massachusetts **CW:** Contributor articles to professional journals **MEM:** Member Association Investment Management Sales Executives, Political Club for Econs. Growth. **H:** Triathlons, marathons, flying **PA:** Republican **BA:** 1208 Longworth House Office Building, Washington, DC, 20515

POLIS, JARED SCHUTZ, T: U.S. Representative from Colorado, entrepreneur, philanthropist **I:** Government Administration/Government Relations/Government Services **DOB:** 05/12/1975 **PB:** Boulder **PT:** Son of Stephen and Susan (Polis) Schutz; **ED:** BA in Political Sci, Princeton University, New Jersey, 1996 **C:** Member, US Congress from 2nd Colorado District, Washington, 2009-; Member, Committee on Rules, the Committee on Education and the Workforce, the Committee on Ethics, and the House Democratic Steering and Policy Committee; Founder, TechStars, 2006; Founder, Sonora Entertainment Grp., 2001; Founder, Proflowers.com/Proflowers Inc., San Diego, 1998;

Executive director internet startups, Dan's Chocolates,; Executive director internet startups, FrogMagic,; Executive director internet startups, Bluemountain.com,; Sales manager, Blue Mountain Arts, **CR:** Board member Colorado Conservation Voters, Colorado Consumer Health Initiative, Colorado Anti-Defamation League, Latin American Research & Service Agency chair fin. literacy study grp. National Association Sate Boards Education co-chair Colorado Commission HS Improvement chairman Colorado State Board Education, 2004-05, member, 2001-06 member executive committee Boulder County Democrats, 2000-07, Colorado Democratic Party, 2000-07 founder Jared Polis Foundation, 2000- **CIV:** Co-founder, Academy Urban Learning, Denver, 2005 Founder, superintendent, New America School, Thornton, Colorado, 2004 Founder, Community Computer Connection, Aurora, Colorado, Founder, Jared Polis Foundation, 2000 Board directors, Watershed School, Boulder, **AW:** Named an Outstanding Young Coloradoan, Colorado Jaycees, Outstanding Philanthropist, State of Colorado, 2006, Ernst & Young Entrepreneur of Year, 2000; named one of The Politics 40 Under 40, TIME Magazine, 2010, The 50 Politicos to Watch, Politico, 2010, Forty Under 40, Denver Business Journal, 2000; recipient Martin Luther King, Junior Humanitarian award, Community award, Kauffman Foundation, Community Builder award, Anti-Defamation League, Ohtli award, Denver consul general of Mexico, Pacesetter award in education, Boulder Daily Camera, 2007 **PA:** Democrat

POLISI, JOSEPH WILLIAM, T: President of The Juilliard School **I:** Education/Educational Services **DOB:** 12/30/1947 **PB:** NYC **MS:** Married **SPN:** Elizabeth Polisi **ED:** DFA (hon.), Fordham University, Bronx, New York, 2006; DHL (hon.), Juilliard School, 2005; DMA, New England Conservatory Music, 2001; MusD (hon.), Curtis Institute Music, 1990; DHL (hon.), Ursinus College, Collegetown, Pennsylvania, 1986; DMA, Yale University, 1980; Master of Museum Arts, Tufts University, 1975; MusM, Tufts University, 1973; MA in International Relations, Tufts University, 1970; BA in Political Sci., University Connecticut, 1969 **C:** President, The Juilliard School, New York City, 1984-; Dean, College Conservatory of Music University Cincinnati, 1983-84; Dean of faculty, Manhattan School of Music, New York City, 1980-83; Executive officer, Yale School of Music, New Haven, 1976-80 **CR:** Speaker in field **CIV:** Director, Samuels Foundation, Director, Irene Diamond Fund, Director, Edward John Noble Foundation, **CW:** Performances as bassoonist throughout the U.S.; contributor articles to various publications in U.S. and France; author: The Artist as Citizen, 2005, American Muse: The Life & Times of William Schuman, 2008 **AW:** Named Educator of Year, Musical Am. International Director Performing Arts, 2005 **MEM:** Fellow: Am. Academy Arts and Sciences; mem.: Royal Academy Music London (hon.)

POLITZER, HUGH DAVID, T: Physicist, Educator **I:** Education/Educational Services **DOB:** 08/31/1949 **PB:** NYC **PT:** Son of Alan A. and Valerie T. (Diamant) P. **ED:** PhD, Harvard University, 1974; BS, University Michigan, 1969 **C:** Professor theoretical physics, California Institute Tech., 1979-; Member faculty, California Institute Tech., 1975-; Executive officer for physics, California Institute Tech., 1986-88; Junior fellow, Harvard University Society Fellows, 1974-77 **CW:** Author: Asymptotic Freedom: An Approach to String Interactions, 1974; appeared in Fat Man and Little Boy, 1989 **AW:** Recipient J.J. Sakurai prize, 1986; fellow National Science Foundation, 1969-74, Sloan Foundation, 1977-81, Woodrow Wilson grad. fellow,

1969-74, Guggenheim fellow, 1997-98; co-recipient High Energy and Particle Physics prize European Physical Society, 2003, Nobel prize for physics, 2004. **MEM:** Member Am. Physical Society, Harvard Society Fellows, Phi Beta Kappa. **ACH:** Achievements include discovery of asymptotic freedom in the theory of the strong interaction **BA:** Calif Inst Tech High Energy Physics, 1201 E California Blvd Mail Code 452-48, Pasadena, CA, 91106

POLK, MICHAEL B., T: CEO **I:** Business Management/Business Services **CN:** Newell Brands **ED:** MBA in Marketing & General Management, Harvard Business School, 1987; BS in Operations Research & Industrial Engineering, Cornell University, 1982 **C:** CEO, Newell Brands Inc, 2016-; President, CEO, Newell Rubbermaid, 2011-16; President, Unilever Americas, 2007-11; President, Unilever USA, 2005-07; Senior vice president marketing, president Unilever Best Foods North America, Unilever, 2003-05; Group vice president, Kraft Foods International, 2000-01; Group vice president, Kraft Foods North America, 2001-03; Executive vice president, general manager Post cereal division, Kraft Foods North America, 1998-99; President biscuits, snacks, & confections segment, Kraft Foods, Inc., 2001-03; President Asia Pacific Region, Kraft Foods, Inc., 1999-2001; Vice president category sales management & strategy, Kraft Foods, Inc., 1997-98; Various position brand management & sales, Kraft Foods, Inc., 1987-97; Joined, Kraft Foods, Inc., 1987; Manufacturing, research & devel., The Procter & Gamble Co., 1982-85 **CR:** Board directors Yellowstone National Park, GS1, Grocery Manufacturers America & Food Products Association, Retail Industry Leadership Association, The Yankee Candle Co., Inc., 2003- **BA:** 221 River Street, Hoboken, NJ, 07030

POLLAN, MICHAEL, T: Author, Journalist, Professor **I:** Writing and Editing **DOB:** 02/06/1955 **PB:** Long Island **PT:** Son of Stephen and Corky Pollan; **ED:** MA in English, Columbia University, New York City, 1981; BA, Bennington College, Vermont, 1977; Student, Mansfield College, Oxford University, England, 1975 **C:** John S. and James L. Knight professor journalism, University California, Berkeley, 2003-; Series editor, Modern Library Garden Series, 2001-; Contributing writer, New York Times Magazine, 1995-; Director Knight Progressive Sci. & Environmental Journalism, University California, Berkeley,; Contributing editor and writer, New York Times Magazine, 1998-99; Contributing editor, Harper's Magazine, 1995-2003; Executive editor, Harper's Magazine, 1985-94; Senior editor, Harper's Magazine, 1983-85; Senior editor, Channels Magazine, 1981-83; Associate producer, Straight Talk, WOR-TV, 1980; Associate producer, A House Divided, Gateway Productions, 1978; Assistant editor, Politicks & Other Human Interests, 1977-78; Assistant editor, Village Voice, New York City, 1974-76; Reporter, Vineyard Gazette, Massachusetts, 1973 **CR:** Lectures on food, agriculture, health and the environment **CIV:** Advisor, Edible Schoolyard, Advisor, Massachusetts Institute of Technology Collaborative Initiative on Foodsheds, Adv. committee member, The Food Project's Real Food Challenge, Member Stegner Cir. advisors, Trust for Public Land, San Francisco, Board advisors, Alameda County Meals on Wheels, Board advisors, Center Urban Education about Sustainable Agriculture (CUESA), San Francisco, **CW:** Author: Second Nature: A Gardener's Education, 1991 (QPB new Vision award, 1991, named one of the 75 best gardening books of the century, American Horticultural Society, book is taught in many environmental studies and history courses), Place of My Own: The Education of an Amateur Builder, 1997 (John Burroughs

Natural History award, 1997, New York Times Book Review notable book of 1997), The Botany of Desire: A Plant's-Eye View of the World, 2001 (Best Book of the Year by American Booksellers Association and Amazon.com, New York Times Bestseller list, finalist for the Book Sense best book of the year award, 2001, Borders Original Voices award for the Best Non-Fiction Work, 2001, Best Nonfiction Book of Year, Connecticut Center of Book, 2002), The Omnivore's Dilemma: A Natural History of Four Meals, 2006 (one of 10 Best Books of Year, New York Times Book Rev., Amazon.com, Washington Post, and the Boston Globe, 2006, finalist National Book Critics Circle award, 2006, Northern California Book award, 2006, California Book award, 2006, James Beard award for best food writing, 2007), In Defense of Food: An Eater's Manifesto, 2008 (Publishers Weekly and New York Times bestseller), Food Rules: An Eaters Manual, 2010 (New York Times Bestseller List), Cooked-A Natural History of Transformation, 2013, (illustrated version) Food Rules: An Eaters Manual, 2011, (young reader's edition) The Omnivore's Dilemma: The Secrets Behind What You Eat, 2009 (New York Times Bestseller, named one of Booklist's Top Environmental Titles for Youth); numerous essays appeared in many anthologies including Best American Essays (1990, 2003), Best American Science Writing (2004), Norton Book of Nature Writing, and The New Kings of Non-Fiction, articles to professional journals including New York Times Magazine, Harper's Magazine, National Geographic, Mother Jones, The Nation, The New York Review of Books, Vogue, Travel + Leisure, Gourmet, House & Garden and Garden Illustrated, among others; contributor chapters to books; speaker in field, guest appearances The Botany of Desire, 2009, special consultant, co-narrator (documentaries) Food, Inc., 2009, editorial adv. board Orion Magazine, Harvard Design Magazine,(Book) Pollan Family Table, 2014 AW: Finalist National Magazine award for best essay-Out of the Kitchen, Onto the Couch, 2010; named Bon Appétit Magazine's Food Writer of the Year, 2008; named one of The 100 Most Influential People in the World, TIME magazine, 2010, Top 10 New Thought Leaders, Newsweek, 2009, The 100 Agents of Change, Rolling Stone magazine, 2009, Men's Health Magazine's Heroes of Health and Fitness, 2008, The Plenty 20-annual list of dynamic individuals, companies and ideas that are changing the world, Plenty Magazine, 2008; recipient Pioneer in Integrative Medicine award, California Pacific Medical Center, 2011, Lennon Ono Grant for Peace, 2010, George Orwell award, National Council of Teachers of English, 2010, Social Justice Champion award, California Center for Pub. Health, 2010, President's Citation award, American Institute of Biological Sciences, 2009, Voices of Nature award, Natural Resources Defense Council, 2009, President's Citation award, American Institute of Biological Sciences, 2009, Humanities prize, Washington University Center for Humanities, 2008, Truth in Journalism award, American Corn Growers Association, 2008, Pioneer of Precaution award, Center for Health, Environment & Justice, Environmental Research Foundation and the Science and Environmental Health Network, 2006, James Beard award for best magazine feature article for Sustaining Vision in Gourmet Magazine, 2003, Genesis award for Power Steer and An Animal's Place, Humane Society US, 2003, Reuters World Conservation Union Global award for excellence in environmental journalism, 2000, Golden Trowel award, Horticultural Society America, 1999; Fellowship, The National Humanities Center, Research Triangle Park, North Carolina, 2006, Avenali fellowship, Townsend Center for the Humanities, University of California, Berkeley, 2002-03 MEM: Fellow: New York Institute Humanities; mem.: PEN American Center

POMPEO, MIKE, T: U.S. Secretary of State **I:** Government Administration/Government Relations/Government Services **DOB:** 12/30/1968 **PB:** Orange **ED:** JD, Harvard Law School, 1994; BS in Engineering Management, US Military Academy at West Point, 1986 **C:** U.S. Secretary of State, 2018-; Director, Central Intelligence Agency, Washington,D.C., 2017-2018; Member, US House Select Committee on the Events Surrounding the 2012 Terrorist Attack in Benghazi, 2014-2017; Member, US House Energy & Commerce Committee, Washington, 2011-; Member, US Congress from 4th Kansas District, Washington, 2011-17; President, Sentry International, Wichita, Kansas, 2006-; Founder, CEO, Thayer Aerospace, Wichita, Kansas, 1996-2006 **CIV:** Board member, YMCA, Board member, Wichita Metro C. of C., National committeeman, Republican National Convention, 2008- **PA:** Republican **BA:** U.S. Department of State, 2201 C St NW, Washington, DC, 20520

POOLER, ROSEMARY S., T: Federal Judge **I:** Law and Legal Services **DOB:** 06/21/1938 **PB:** New York City **SC:** NY/USA **ED:** Honorary Degree, State University of New York, Albany, NY (1986); Certificate in Senior Management in Government, Harvard University (1978); JD, University of Michigan Law School (1965); MA, University of Connecticut (1961); BA, Brooklyn College (1959) **C:** Judge, U.S. Court of Appeals for the Second Circuit (1998-Present); Judge, U.S. District Court for the Northern District of New York, Syracuse, NY (1994-1998); Judge, Supreme Court, 5th Judicial District (1991-1994); Staff Director, New York State Assembly, Committee on Corporations, Authorities and Communications (1987-1994); Commissioner, New York State Public Services Commission (1981-1986); Chairman, Executive Director, Consumer Protection Board (1975-1980); Common Counsel, City of Syracuse Public Interest Research Group (1974-1975); Assistant Corporation Counsel, Director of Consumer Affairs Unit, Syracuse, NY (1972-1973); With, Michaels and Michaels, Syracuse, NY (1969-1972); With, Crystal, Manes & Rifken, Syracuse, NY (1966-1969) **CR:** Vice President, Legal Affairs, Atlantic States Legal Foundation (1989-1990); Visiting Professor, Syracuse University College of Law (1987-1988) **MEM:** Secretary, Association of Supreme Court Justices of the State of New York (1993-1994); Women's Bar Association of the State of New York; New York State Bar Association; Onondaga County Bar Association

POPOVICH, GREGG CHARLES, T: Professional Basketball Coach **I:** Athletics **DOB:** 01/28/1949 **PB:** Chicago **SC:** IL/USA **MS:** Married **SPN:** Erin Popovich **CH:** Micky; Jill **ED:** BA in Soviet Studies, U.S. Air Force Academy (1970); MA in Physical Education & Sports Sciences, University of Denver **C:** President, Spurs Basketball, San Antonio Spurs (2008-Present); Head Coach, San Antonio Spurs (1996-Present); Executive Vice President of Basketball Operations, San Antonio Spurs (1994-2008); General Manager, San Antonio Spurs (1994-2002); Assistant Coach, Golden State Warriors (1992-1994); Assistant Coach, San Antonio Spurs (1988-1992); Head Coach, Pomona-Pitzer College, Claremont, CA (1979-1987); Assistant Coach, U.S. Air Force Academy (1973-1979) **CR:** Assistant, USA Men's Senior National Team (2002-2004) **MIL:** Second Lieutenant, US Air Force (1970-1975) **AW:** Named, NBA Coach of the Year (2014); Named, NBA All-Star Game Head Coach (2016, 2013); Named, NBA Coach of the Year (2012); Named, NBA All-Star Game Head Coach (2011); Recipient, Distinguished Graduate Award, Air Force Academy (2008); Named, NBA All-Star Game Head Coach (2005); Named, NBA Coach of the Year (2003);

Recipient, Daily Point of Light Award, President George H.W. Bush (1992) **ACH:** Achievements include winning NBA Championships as head coach of the San Antonio Spurs, 1999, 2003, 2005, 2007, 2014; one of five NBA coaches with four or more championship titles **BA:** San Antonio Spurs, One AT&T Ctr, San Antonio, TX, 78219

PORTMAN, NATALIE, T: Actress **I:** Media & Entertainment **DOB:** 06/20/1905 **PB:** Jerusalem **SC:** Jerusalem **PT:** Daughter of Avner and Shelley Hershlag; **ED:** BS in Psychology, Harvard University, 2003 **C:** Founder, HandsomeCharlie Films, 2008 **CR:** Designer Té Casan Vegan Shoe collection, 2008 **CW:** Actress: (films) The Professional, 1994, Developing, 1995, Heat, 1995, Beautiful Girls, 1996, Everyone Says I Love You, 1996, Mars Attacks!, 1996, Star Wars: Episode I-The Phantom Menace, 1999, Anywhere But Here, 1999, Where the Heart Is, 2000, Zoolander, 2001, Star Wars Episode II-Attack of the Clones, 2002, Cold Mountain, 2003, Garden State, 2004, True, 2004, Closer, 2004 (Golden Globe award for Best Supporting Actress, 2005), Domino One, 2005, Star Wars: Episode III-Revenge of the Sith, 2005, Free Zone, 2005, V for Vendetta, 2006, Paris, je t'aime, 2006, Goya's Ghosts, 2006, My Blueberry Nights, 2007, The Darjeeling Limited, 2007, Mr. Magorium's Wonder Emporium, 2007, The Other Boleyn Girl, 2008, Brothers, 2009, Black Swan, 2010 (Best Performance by an Actress in a Motion Picture-Drama, Golden Globe Awards, 2011, Outstanding Performance by a Female Actor in a Leading Role, Screen Actors Guild, 2011, Best Actress in a Leading Role, Academy Awards, 2011, Best Actress award, Boston Society Film Critics, 2011, Best Actress, Critics' Choice Movie Awards, 2011), Your Highness, 2011, Thor, 2011, Thor: The Dark World, 2013, Knight of Cups, 2015, The Heyday of the Insensitive Bastards, 2016, Jackie, 2016, Planetarium, 2016, Song to Song, 2017, Annihilation, 2018, The Death and Life of John F Donovan, 2018; actress, executive prodr.: (films) The Other Woman, 2009, No Strings Attached, 2011; actress, prodr.: (films) Hesher, 2009, Jane Got a Gun, 2016; executive prodr.: (TV films) Scruples, 2012, (documentaries) The Seventh Fire, 2015; actress, producer, director, writer: (films) A Tale of Love and Darkness, 2015; prodr.: (documentaries) Eating Animals, 2016, (films) Pride and Prejudice and Zombies, 2016, Angie Tribeca, 2017; appeared in stage productions including Diary of Anne Frank, 1997, The Seagull, 2001. **AW:** Named one of The 50 Most Powerful Women in New York City, New York Post, 2008; recipient Movie for Humanity award, Venice Film Festival, 2008

PORTMAN, ROB, T: U.S. Senator from Ohio **I:** Government Administration/Government Relations/Government Services **DOB:** 12/19/1955 **PB:** Cin. **PT:** Son of William C. & Joan (Jones) P.; **SPN:** Married Jane Dudley, 1986; **CH:** children: Jed, Will, Sally **ED:** JD, University Michigan Law School, 1984; BA, Dartmouth College, 1979 **C:** Vice chairman finance, National Republican Senatorial Committee (NRSC), 2013-; Member, US Senate Finance Committee, 2013-; Member, US Senate Homeland Security & Governmental Reform Committee, 2011-; Member, US Senate Energy & Natural Resources Committee, 2011-; Member, US Senate Budget Committee, 2011-; US Senator from Ohio, 2011-; Member, Joint Select Committee on Deficit Reduction, Washington, 2011; Member, US Senate Armed Services Committee, Washington, 2011-12; Of counsel, Squires Sanders & Dempsey LLP, Cincinnati & Washington DC, 2007-09; Director Office Management & Budget, Executive Office of the President, Washington, 2006-07; US Trade Rep., Office US Trade Rep., Executive Office of the President, Washington, 2005-06; Member,

US Congress from 2nd Ohio District, 1993-2005; Member, US Del. to UN Subcom. on Human Rights, 1992; Deputy assistant to President for legislative affairs, The White House, Washington, 1989-91; Associate counsel to President, The White House, Washington, 1989-91; Partner, Graydon Head & Ritchey LLP, Cincinnati, 1991-93; Partner, Graydon Head & Ritchey LLP, Cincinnati, 1986-89; Associate, Patton Boggs LLP, Washington, 1984-86 **CIV:** Board trustees Springer School, The United Way, Hyde Park Community United Methodist Church founding trustee Cin.-China Sister City Committee member advisory board, John Glenn School Public Affairs, The Ohio State University, 2008- vice chairman Hamilton County George Bush for President Campaign, 1988, 92 chairman Republican Early Bird Campaign committee, 1992 del. Republican National Convention, 1988, 92 active Hamilton County Republican Party Executive committee, Hamilton County Republican Party Finance Committee **CW:** Co-author (with Cheryl Bauer): Wisdom's Paradise: The Forgotten Shakers of Union Village, 2004 **AW:** Named one of The 10 Members to Watch in the 112th Congress, Roll Call, 2011; recipient Albert Gallatin award, Swiss-American Chamber of Commerce, Leadership on Alcohol & Other Drug Services award, Hamilton County Mental Health & Recovery Services Board, National Leadership award, Community Anti-Drug Coalition of America, 2008, PLANSPONSOR magazine Legend award, Nelson A. Rockefeller Distinguished Public Service award, Nelson A. Rockefeller Center, Dartmouth College, Excellence in Public Service award, John Glenn School Public Affairs, The Ohio State University, 2008 **MEM:** Member Cincinnati World Trade Association **PA:** Republican **BA:** Office of Rob Portman, 448 Russell Senate Office Building, Washington, DC, 20510

POSEN, ZAC, T: Apparel Designer **I:** Textiles **DOB:** 10/24/1980 **PB:** NYC **PT:** Son of Stephen and Susan (Orzack) Posen **ED:** Grad., Central St. Martins College Art and Design, London, 1999-2001; Grad., Parsons School Design, 1999 **C:** Launched bridal gowns, Truly Zac Posen, 2014-; Creative director women's collection and accessories, Brooks Brothers, 2014-; Founder, designer, Outspoke LLC, New York City, 2001-; Launched, Zac Posen for Target, 2008; Intern, Tocca,; Intern, Nicole Miller,; Intern, New York Costume Institute, Metropolitan Museum Art, **CR:** Judge Project Runway, 2013- **CW:** (Television) Project Runway, 2012 **AW:** Named one of 40 Under 40, Crain's New York Business, 2004; recipient Swarovski Perry Ellis award for Womenswear, Council Fashion Designers of America, 2004,Swarovski's Perry Ellis Award for Womensware, 2004

POSEY, BILL, T: U.S. Representative from Florida **I:** Government Administration/Government Relations/Government Services **DOB:** 12/18/1947 **PB:** Washington **SC:** DC/USA **PT:** Walter J. Posey, Beatrice (Tohl) Posey **MS:** Married **SPN:** Mary Ingram, 11/23/1987 **CH:** Pamela J., Catherine L. **ED:** Student, Stetson University, 1978; AA, Brevard Community College, 1969 **C:** Committee On Financial Services, Committee On Science, Space, And Technology, U.S. Congress From Eighth Florida District, 2013-Present; President, CEO, Posey & Co., Rockledge, FL, 1978-Present; U.S. Congress From 15th Florida District, Washington, DC, 2009-2013; District 24, Florida State Senate, Tallahassee, FL, 2003-2009; District 15, Florida State Senate, Tallahassee, FL, 2001-2003; District 32, Florida House Of Representatives, Tallahassee, FL, 1992-2000; Broker, Sherwood Realty Inc., Cocoa, FL, 1974-1978; Manager, Gay & Taylor Inc., St. Petersburg, FL, 1971-1974; President, CEO, Mid Florida Racing Inc., Melbourne, FL, 1969-1971; Quality Assurance

Representative, McDonnell-Douglas, Cape Kennedy, FL, 1966-1969 **CR:** Board of Directors, Rockledge Land Co., Indian Oaks Corp., Rockledge, FL, Rockledge Realty Corp., National Racetrack Clearing House, Rockledge, FL, Founder, Florida Motorsports Hall of Fame, 1986 **CIV:** Rockledge Economic Development Commission, 1985-Present, Business And Industrial Task Force, 1985-Present, Rockledge City Council, 1976-1986, Rockledge Planning Commission, 1974-1976 **CW:** Author, Race Track Promoters Handbook, 1971 **MEM:** President, Cape Kennedy Area Board of Realtors, 1987-Present,Board of Directors, Florida Association Realtors, 1986-Present, Committee 100, Cocoa Beach Chamber Of Commerce, 1974-Present, Brevard County Kiwanis, Masons **PA:** Republican **BA:** 2150 Rayburn HOB, Washington, DC, 20515

POST, GLENN F. III, T: CEO **I:** Telecommunications **CN:** Centurylink **ED:** MBA, Louisiana Technology University, 1976; B.A., Louisiana Technology University, Accounting **C:** Chief Executive Officer Centurylink Inc, 2017-2019; President/CEO, Centurylink Inc, 2010-2017; President/CEO, Centurytel Inc, 2009-6/2010

POTVIN, DENIS CHARLES, T: Professional Hockey Player **I:** Athletics **DOB:** 10/29/1953 **PB:** Hull **SC:** Quebec/Canada **PT:** Son of Armand Jean and Lucille (St. Louis) P. **ED:** Student pub. schools, Hull. **C:** Player, New York Islanders, NHL, 1973-; Captain Stanley Cup championship team, defeating Minnesota North Stars in 5 games, New York Islanders, NHL, 1981; Captain Stanley Cup championship team, defeating Philadelphia Flyers in 6 games, New York Islanders, NHL, 1980; Player, Ottawa 67's, Junior Hockey League, 1967-73 **CW:** Author: Power on Ice, 1977. **AW:** Recipient Calder trophy as Rookie of Year, 1973-74, Norris trophy as best defenseman, 1975-76; member All Star Team, 6 times in 8 years,100 Greatest NHL Players, 2017, Hockey Hall of Fame, 1991, Ottawa Sports Hall of Fame, 1991, Nassau County Sports Hall of Fame,2002,100 Greatest NHL Players,100 Ranger Greats, 2009, Sault Ste Marie Walk of Fame, 2007, Ontario Sports Hall of Fame, 2004

POWELL, COLIN LUTHER, T: Former U.S. Secretary of State, Former Chairman of the Joint Chiefs of Staff **I:** Government Administration/Government Relations/Government Services **DOB:** 04/05/1937 **PB:** New York City **SC:** NY/USA **PT:** Son of Luther and Maud Ariel (McKoy) P.; Married Alma Vivian Johnson, August 25, 1962; children: Michael, Linda, Annemarie **ED:** Grad., National War College, 1976; MBA, George Washington University, 1971; BS in Geology, City University of New York, 1958 **C:** Strategic adv., Kleiner Perkins Caufield & Byers, Menlo Park, California, 2005-; Secretary, US Department State, Washington, 2001-05; Chairman Joint Chiefs of Staff, US Department Defense, Washington, 1989-93; Comdr.-in-chief, US Army Forces Command (FORSCOM), Fort McPherson, Georgia, 1989; Assistant to President for national security affairs, National Security Council, Washington, 1987-89; Deputy assistant to the President for national security affairs, National Security Council, Washington, 1987; Assigned to U.S. V Corps, Europe, 1986-87; Military assistant to secretary defense, US Department Defense, Washington, 1983-86; Assistant div. Commander 4th Infantry Div., US Department Defense, Fort Carson, Colorado, 1981-83; Senior military assistant to deputy secretary, US Department Defense, Washington, 1979-81; Executive assistant to secretary, US Department Energy, Washington, 1979; Commander, 2d Brigade, 101st Airborne Div., Fort

Campbell, Kentucky, 1976-77; Battalion Commander, Republic of Korea, 1973-74; Assistant to deputy director, Office Management & Budget, Washington, 1972-73; Retired, 1993; Advanced through grades to general, 1989; Commissioned 2d lieutenant, U.S. Army, 1958 **CR:** Founding chair America's Promise Alliance, 1997- pub. speaker addressing audiences across the country and abroad **CW:** Author: (with Joseph E. Persico) My American Journey (autobiography), 1995, It Worked For Me: In Life and Leadership, 2012 **AW:** Decorated Purple Heart, Air medal, Bronze Star, Legion of Merit (2); named Hon. Knight Commander Most Honorable Order of Bath, Queen Elizabeth II, 1993; named one of The 50 Highest-Earning Political Figures, Newsweek, 2010; several schools and other institutions have been named in his honor; recipient Legion of Honor, France, 2006, Ellis Island Family Heritage award in Government Service, Statue of Liberty-Ellis Island Foundation, Inc, 2005, Secretary of Energy Distinguished Service Medal, Secretary of State Distinguished Service Medal, Congressional Gold Medal, President's Citizens Medal, Ronald Reagan Freedom award, 1993, Presidential Medal of Freedom (2); White House fellow, 1972-73,Nation Board of Advisors for High Point University, 2014 **MEM:** Member Association U.S. Army, American Academy Arts & Sciences **PA:** Republican **BA:** 1317 Ballantrae Farm Drive, McLean, VA, 22101

POWELL, DINA HABIB, T: Former National Security Advisor for Strategy **I:** Government Administration/Government Relations/Government Services **DOB:** 06/18/1973 **PB:** Cairo **SC:** Egypt **PT:** Daughter of Onsi Habib and Hoda Soliman; **ED:** BA in Humanities, University of Texas, 1995 **C:** Deputy National Security Advisor for Strategy, 2017-2018; Senior Counselor to the President Economic Initiatives, 2017-2018; President, Goldman Sachs Foundation, 2010-; Partner, Goldman Sachs Group, Inc., 2010-; Director global corporate engagement, Goldman Sachs Group, Inc., New York City, 2007-; Managing director, Goldman Sachs Group, Inc., 2007-10; Assistant secretary for educational & cultural affairs, US Department State, Washington, DC 2005-07; Assistant to President for presidential personnel, The White House, Washington, DC 2003-05; Special assistant to President for presidential personnel, The White House, Washington, DC 2001-03; Director congressional affairs, senior adv. through chairman, Republican National Committee, Washington, 1999-2001; Member relations coordinator to Rep. Dick Army, US House of Representatives, Washington, DC **CIV:** Board directors, Vital Voices Global Partnership, Trustee, American University, Cairo, Egypt Member, J. William Fulbright Scholarship Board, **AW:** Recipient Outstanding American by Choice, US Citizenship & Immigration Services, 2007, Outstanding Young Texas Executive award, University of Texas, 2006 **MEM:** Mem.: Council Foreign Relations **PA:** Republican

POWELL, JEROME H., T: Federal Official, Political Scientist **I:** Government Administration/Government Relations/Government Services **DOB:** 02/04/1953 **PB:** Washington **SC:** DC/USA **ED:** JD, Georgetown University, 1979; AB, Princeton University, 1975 **C:** Member board governors, Federal Reserve Systems, Washington, DC 2012-2018, Chairman, 2018-; Partner, The Carlyle Group, 1997-2005; Under secretary for finance, U.S. Department Treasury, 1992; Assistant secretary for domestic finance, U.S. Department Treasury, 1990-92; Consultant, U.S. Department Treasury, Washington, 1990; Senior vice president, Dillon Reed & Co., Inc., 1984-90; Associate, Werbel,

McMillin & Carnelutti, 1982-84; Associate, Davis Polk & Wardwell, New York City, 1981-82; Law clerk to Hon. E.A. Van Graafeiland, U.S. Court Appeals (2nd Cir.), 1979-80; Legis. assistant to Senator Richard S. Schweiker, U.S. Senate, Washington, DC 1976 **CR:** Visiting scholar Bipartisan Policy Center, Washington, DC 2010-12 senior adv. Global Environment Fund, 2008-12 **CIV:** Founding chair, Center City Consortium, Washington, DC Board directors, Nature Conservancy of Washington, DC and Maryland, Board directors, Bendheim Center Finance, Princeton University, Board directors, D.C. Prep, Washington, **PA:** Republican **BA:** Federal Reserve Board, 20th Street and Constitution Avenue N.W, Washington, DC, 20551

POWER, SAMANTHA J., I: Government Administration/Government Relations/Government Services **DOB:** 09/21/1970 **PB:** Dungarvan, Ireland **ED:** JD, Harvard Law School, Cambridge, Massachusetts, 1999; BA, Yale University, New Haven, 1993 **C:** Permanent US rep. to UN, US Department State, New York City, 2013-; Anna Lindh professor practice of global leadership & public policy, Harvard University John F. Kennedy School Government, 2000-; Director for multilateral affairs, National Security Council, 2009-13; Foreign policy adviser, Obama-Biden Presidential Transition Team, 2008; Senior foreign policy adviser, Barack Obama Presidential Campaign, 2008; Foreign policy fellow to Senator Barack Obama, US Senate, 2005-06; Founding executive director Carr Center for Human Rights Policy,, Harvard University John F. Kennedy School Government, 1998-2002; Political analyst, International Crisis Group,; Reporter covering the Yugoslav wars,, US News & World Report, Boston Globe, The Economist and New Republic, 1993-96 **CR:** Columnist TIME magazine, 2007- **CW:** Author: A Problem from Hell: America and the Age of Genocide, 2003 (Pulitzer prize for General Nonfiction, 2003, National Book Critics Cir. award for General Nonfiction, 2003, Artur Ross prize for Best Book in US Foreign Policy, 2003, J. Anthony Lukas Book prize, 2003), Chasing the Flame: Sergio Vieira de Mello and the Fight to Save the World, 2008; co-editor (with Graham Allison): Realizing Human Rights: Moving from Inspiration to Impact, 2000; co-editor: (with Derek Chollet) The Unquiet American: Richard Holbrooke in the World, 2011; featured in documentary Watchers of the Sky, 2014 **AW:** Named one of The 100 Most Powerful Women, Forbes magazine, 2014, The 100 Agents of Change, Rolling Stone magazine, 2009, The 100 Top Scientists & Thinkers of Year, TIME magazine, 2004; recipient National Magazine award for Reporting, 2005 **PA:** Democrat

PRADO, EDWARD CHARLES, T: Federal Judge **I:** Law and Legal Services **DOB:** 06/07/1947 **PB:** San Antonio **SC:** TX/USA **PT:** Edward L. Prado; Bertha (Cadena) Prado **MS:** Married **SPN:** Anita Jung (11/10/1973) **CH:** Maria; Edward C. **ED:** JD, The University Texas at Austin (1972); BA, The University Texas at Austin (1969); AA, San Antonio College (1967) **C:** Judge, U.S. Court of Appeals for the Fifth Circuit, San Antonio, TX (2003-2018); Judge, U.S. District Court for the Western District of Texas, San Antonio, TX (1984-2003); U.S. Attorney, U.S. Department of Justice, San Antonio, TX (1981-1984); Judge, U.S. District Court of Texas, San Antonio, TX (1980); Assistant Public Defender, U.S. Public Defender's Office, San Antonio, TX (1976-1980); Assistant District Attorney, Bexar County District Attorney's Office, San Antonio, TX (1972-1976) **CIV:** Captain, US Army **AW:** Named, Outstanding Young Lawyer of Bexar County (1980) **MEM:** ABA; Texas Bar Association; San Antonio Bar Association; San Antonio Young Lawyers Association; Federal Bar Association **BAR:** Texas

(1972) **PA:** Republican **BA:** John Minor Wisdom U.S. Court of Appeals Building Fifth Circuit, 600 Camp St, New Orleans, LA, 70130

PRATT, CHRIS, I: Media & Entertainment **DOB:** 06/21/1979 **PB:** Virginia **SC:** MN/USA **PT:** Daniel C. Pratt; Kathleen (Indahl) Pratt **CW:** Actor: (films) The Extreme Team, 2003, Strangers with Candy, 2005, Walk the Talk, 2007, Wieners, 2008, Wanted, 2008, Bride Wars, 2009, Deep in the Valley, 2009, Jennifer's Body, 2009, Take Me Home Tonight, 2011, Moneyball, 2011, 10 Years, 2011, What's Your Number?, 2011, The Five-Year Engagement, 2012, Zero Dark Thirty, 2012, Her, 2013, Delivery Man, 2103, The Lego Movie (voice), 2014, Guardians of the Galaxy, 2014, Jurassic World, 2015, Jem and the Holograms, 2015, The Magnificent Seven, 2016, Passengers, 2016; (TV films) Path of Destruction, 2005, Kinect Star Wars: Duel, 2012, Timms Valley, 2013; (TV series) Everwood, 2002-06, The O.C., 2006-07, Parks and Recreation, 2009-

PRESCOTT, EDWARD CHRISTIAN, T: Economist **I:** Education/Educational Services **DOB:** 12/26/1940 **PB:** Glens Falls **SC:** NY/USA **ED:** PhD in Economics, Carnegie Mellon University, Pittsburgh, PA, 1967; MS in Operations Research, Case Western Reserve University, Cleveland, OH, 1963; BA in Mathematics, Swarthmore College, Pennsylvania, 1962 **C:** Adjunct Distinguished Economics Professor, Australia National University, 2014-Present; W.P. Carey Professor and Chair, Department of Economics, Arizona State University, 2003-Present; Professor, Department of Economics, University pf Minnesota, 1999-2003; Professor of Economics, University of Chicago, 1998-1999; Professor, Department of Economics, University of Minnesota, 1980-1998; Professor, Graduate School of Industrial Administration, Carnegie Mellon University, 1975-1980; Associate Professor, Graduate School of Industrial Administration, Carnegie Mellon University, 1972-1975; Assistant Professor Economics, Graduate School of Industrial Administration, Carnegie Mellon University, 1971-1972; Assistant Professor, University of Pennsylvania, 1967-1971; Lecturer, Department of Economics, University of Pennsylvania, 1966-1967 **CR:** Shinsei Bank Visiting Professor, Political Economy, Stern School of Business, New York University, 2005-Present; Senior Monetary Advisor, Federal Reserve Bank of Minneapolis, 2003-Present; Research Associate, National Bureau of Economic Research, 1988-Present; Fellow, U.S. National Academy of Sciences, 2008; Maxwell Pellish Distinguished Visiting Professor of Economics, University of California, Santa Barbara, 2004; Senior Advisor, Research Department, University of California, Santa Barbara, 1980-2003; Visiting Professor of Finance, Kellogg Graduate School of Management, Northwestern University, 1980-1982; Visiting Professor of Economics, 1979-1980; Norwegian School of Business & Economics, 1974-1975; Fellow, John Simon Guggenheim Memorial Foundation, 1974-1975; Economic Policy Fellow, Brookings Institution, Washington, DC, 1969-1970; Fellow, American Academy of Arts & Sciences, Econometric Society **CW:** Co-Author, Recursive Methods in Economic Dynamics, 1989, Barriers to Riches, 2000; Co-Editor, Economic Theory, 1991; Associate Editor, Journal of Econometrics, 1976-1982, International Economic Review, 1980-1990, Journal of Economic Theory, 1990-1992; Contributor, Articles, Professional Journals **AW:** Nobel Prize in Economics, 2004, Erwin Plein Nemmers Prize in Economics, Northwestern University, 2002 **MEM:** President, Society of Advancement Economic Theory, 1992-1994, Society of Economic Dynamics & Control, 1992-1995 **BA:** Arizona State

University, CPCOM 435C Department of Economics, PO Box 879801, Scottsdale, AR, 065257

PRICE, DAVID EUGENE, T: U.S. Representative from North Carolina, education educator **I:** Government Administration/Government Relations/Government Services **DOB:** 08/17/1940 **PB:** Johnson City **PT:** Son of Albert Lee and Elna (Harrell) Price **MS:** Married **SPN:** Lisa Beth Kanwit, July 27, 1968; **CH:** Karen Elizabeth, Michael Edmond. **ED:** PhD in Political Sci., Yale University, 1969; BD in Theology, Yale University, 1964; BA in Am. Hist. and Math., University North Carolina, 1961; Student, Mars Hill College, North Carolina, 1957-59 **C:** Member, US Congress from 4th North Carolina district, 1997-; Co-chair Dem. budget grp., US Congress from 4th North Carolina district,; Member democracy assistance commission, US Congress from 4th North Carolina district,; Chairman homeland security subcommittee, US Congress from 4th North Carolina district,; Member appropriations committee, US Congress from 4th North Carolina district,; Member, US Congress from 4th North Carolina district, 1987-95; Professor political sci. and pub. policy, Duke University, Durham, North Carolina, 1973-86; Legis. aide, Staff of US Senator Edward Lewis Bartlett of Alaska, 1963-67 **CR:** Executive director North Carolina Dem. Party, Raleigh, 1979-80, chairman, 1983-84, member 1983- staff director national committee on presidential nomination Dem. Party, 1981-82 **CW:** Author: Who Makes the Laws, 1972, Bringing Back the Parties, 1984, Policymaking in Congl. Committees, 1979, The Congressional Experience: A View From the Hill, 2000. **AW:** Named a Champion of Sci., Sci. Coalition, 2004, 2002; recipient Hubert H. Humphrey Pub. Service award, Am. Political Sci. Association, Charles Dick Medal of Merit, North Carolina Nat Guard, Engineering Deans Council award, Am. Society Engineering Education, 2003 **MEM:** Member Am. Political Sci. Association, Society Values in Higher Education, Phi Beta Kappa, Kiwanis. **H:** Jogging, music **PA:** Democrat

PRICE, NICK, T: Professional Golfer **I:** Athletics **DOB:** 12/28/1957 **PB:** Durban **SC:** South Africa **MS:** Married **SPN:** Sue Price **CH:** Gregory, Robyn Frances, Kimberly **C:** Professional golfer, PGA, 1977— **AW:** Winner Asseng Invitational, 1979, Canon European Masters, 1980, Italian Open, 1981, South African Masters, Vaals Reef Open, 1982, World Series of Golf, 1983, Trophee Lancome, 1985, ICL International Open, West End South Australian Open, 1989, GTE Byron Nelson Golf Classic, 1991, Canadian Open, Air New Zealand/Shell Open, 1992, PGA Championship, 1992, 1994, H.E.B. Texas Open, The Players Championship, 1993, Canon Greater Hartford Open, Sprint Western Open, Federal Express St. Jude Classic, HondaClassic, 1994, Southwestern Bell Colonial, Motorola Western Open, Bell Canadian Open, Alfred Dunhill Challenge Hassan II Golf Trophy, Zimbabwe Open, British Open, 1994, MCI Classic, 1997, Dimension Data Pro-Am, 1997, 97, Suntory Open, 1999; 3rd PGA Tour Money Leader, 1992, PGA Tour Money Leader, 1993, 10 USPGA Tour Victories, 26 World Wide Victories; recipient Vardon Trophy, 1993; named Player of Year, 1993; recipient, Payne Stewart award, 2002; ASAP/Jim Murray award, 2002; named to World Golf Hall of Fame, 2003,Old Tom Morris Award, 2011, Bob Jones Award, 2005, PGA Tour player of the Year, 1993, Sunshine Tour Order of Merit Winner **ACH:** Achievements include holding PGA Tournament record for lowest score (269), 1994. **BA:** 900 S US Highway 1, Suite 204, Jupiter, FL, 33477

PRIEBUS, REINCE R., T: Political Organization Administrator, Lawyer **I:** Law and Legal Services **PB:** Kenosha **ED:** JD cum laude, University Miami School Law, Coral Gables, Florida, 1998; BS cum laude, University Wisconsin, Whitewater, 1994 **CT:** Bar: US District Court (eastern district) Wisconsin, US District Court (western district) Wisconsin, Wisconsin 1998 **C:** Chairman, Republican National Committee (RNC), Washington, 2011-; General counsel, Republican National Committee (RNC), Washington, 2009-10; Partner litigation practice group, Michael Best & Griedrich LLP, Milwaukee, 1998-2011; Law clerk, National Association for the Advancement of Colored People Legal Defense Fund, L.A.,; Law clerk, US District Court (southern district) Florida; Law clerk, Wisconsin Supreme Court; Law clerk, Wisconsin Court of Appeals **CIV:** Adv. board member, past president, Kenosha Symphony Orchestra, Adv. board member, CareNet Crisis Pregnancy Center, Kenosha, Chair, Southeastern Wisconsin American Heart Association Heart Ball, 2008 Co-chair, Southeastern Wisconsin Am. Heart Association Heart Ball, 2007 Chairman, Republican Party of Wisconsin, 2007-11 Vice chairman, Republican Party of Wisconsin, 2006-07 Treasurer, Republican Party of Wisconsin, Chairman 1st district, Republican Party of Wisconsin, Vice chairman 1st district, Rep. Party of Wisconsin **AW:** Named one of Milwaukee's 40 Under 40, Milwaukee Business Journal, 2008, Time 100 Most Influential, 2017 **MEM:** Mem.: American Bar Association, Kenosha Bar Association, Racine Bar Association, Wisconsin Bar Association, Milwaukee Bar Association **PA:** Republican

PRISING, JONUS, T: CEO **I:** Business Management/Business Services **CN:** Manpowergroup **ED:** MBA, Stockholm School Econs. **C:** Chairman, CEO, Manpowergroup, 2015-; Executive vice president, president North America, Manpower, Inc., Milwaukee, Wisconsin, 2006—; Managing director Italy, Manpower, Inc., Milan, Italy, 2002—2005; Director global accounts Europe, Mid. East and Africa, Manpower, Inc., London, England, 1999—2002; Managing director commercial cleaning equipment division, head global sales and marketing for division, AB Electrolux, London, England, 1995—1999; Managing director commercial cleaning equipment division, AB Electrolux, Paris, France, 1993—1995; Asia-Pacific regional manager, AB Electrolux, Singapore, 1989—1993 **BA:** 100 Manpower Place, Milwaukee, WI, 53212

PRUITT, SCOTT, T: Former Administrator of the Environmental Protection Agency **I:** Government Administration/Government Relations/Government Services **DOB:** 05/09/1968 **PB:** Danville, Kentucky **ED:** JD, University Tulsa, 1993; BA, Georgetown College, 1990 **CT:** Bar: Oklahoma 1993 **C:** Administrator, Environmental Protection Agency, Washington, DC, 2017-2018; Attorney General, State of Oklahoma, 2011-2017; Attorney, Latham Stall Wagner Steele & Lehman PC, Tulsa, Oklahoma,; Co-owner, Managing General Partner, Triple A Oklahoma City Redhawks, 2002-10; Assistant Republican Floor Leader, Oklahoma State Senate, 2002-06; Republican Whip, Oklahoma State Senate, 2000-02; Member Dist 54, District 36, Oklahoma State Senate, Oklahoma City, 1998-2006; Attorney **CIV:** Vice Chairman, Common Ground Committee Broken Arrow Public Schools, Oklahoma deacon First Baptist. Church, Broken Arrow Consultant North American Mission Board of Southern Baptist Convention **MEM:** Mem.: Oklahoma Bar Association, Tulsa County Bar Association **H:** Baseball, tennis, collector of historical documents, family activities **PA:** Republican **BA:** Environmental Protection Agency, 1200 Pennsylvania Avenue, Washington, DC, 20460

PRUSINER, STANLEY, T: Neurologist **I:** Medicine & Health Care **DOB:** 05/28/1942 **PB:** Des Moines **SC:** IA/USA **PT:** Lawrence Albert Prusiner, Miriam (Spigel) Prusiner **ED:** Honorary PhD, Claremont Graduate University, California, 2007; Honorary DSc, Pennsylvania State University, 2001; Honorary DSc, University of Liege, Belgium, 2000; Honorary MD, University of Bologna, Italy, 2000; Honorary DSc, Dartmouth College, Hanover, NH, 1999; Honorary DSc, University of Pennsylvania, Philadelphia, PA, 1998; Honorary PhD, René Descartes University, Paris, France, 1996; Honorary PhD, Hebrew University, Jerusalem, Israel, 1995; MD, University of Pennsylvania, Philadelphia, 1968; AB, University of Pennsylvania, Philadelphia, PA, Cum Laude, 1964; PhD, Rosalind Franklin University, Chicago, IL **CT:** Diplomate, American Board of Neurology **C:** Director, Institute for Neurodegenerative Diseases, University of California, San Francisco, 1999-Present; Professor, University of California, San Francisco, 1984-Present; Professor of Biochemistry, University of California, San Francisco, 1988-2008; Associate Professor, University of California, San Francisco, 1980-1984; Assistant Professor of Neurology, University of California, San Francisco, 1974-1980; Resident in Neurology, University of California, San Francisco, 1972-1974; Intern in Medicine, University of California, San Francisco, 1968-1969 **CR:** Board of Governors, Foundation for Biomedical Research, Washington, DC, 2002-Present; Honorary Member, Board of Directors, American Health Assistance Foundation, Rockville, MD, 2001-Present; Chairman, Scientific Advisory Board, French Foundation, Los Angeles, CA, 1996-Present; Scientific Advisory Board, French Foundation, Los Angeles, CA, 1985-Present; Director, Institute for Neurodegenerative Diseases, Imperial College, London, England, 2007-2008; Board of Directors, International Longevity Center, New York, NY, 2003-2011; Fromm Institute for Lifelong Learning, San Francisco, CA, 2002-2008; Chairman, Board of Directors, Inpro Biotechnology Inc., San Francisco, CA, 2001-2008; Spongiform Encephalopathy Advisory Committee, Food And Drug Administration, 1997-2001; Chairman, Scientific Advisory Board, American Health Assistance Foundation, Rockville, MD, 1986-2000; Advisory Board, Alzheimer's Disease And Related Disorders Foundation, San Francisco, CA, 1985-1991; Scientific Review Committee, Alzheimer's Disease Diagnostic Center & Research Grant Program, California, 1985-1989; Neurology Review Committee, National Institute for Neurodegenerative Diseases (NIND), National Institutes Of Health, Bethesda, MD, 1982-1986, 1990-1992; Alfred P. Sloan Research Fellow, University of California, 1976-1978; Fellow, American Association For The Advancement Of Science, Fellow, Royal College of Physicians, Fellow, American Academy of Arts & Sciences, Fellow, American Society of Microbiology **CIV:** Overseer, Weill Cornell Medical College, New York, NY, 2014-Present; Trustee, University of Pennsylvania, 2000-2005; Trustee, Congregation of Sherith Israel, San Francisco, CA, 1999-2002 **MIL:** Lieutenant Commander, U.S. Public Health Service, 1969-1972 **CW:** Editor, The Enzymes Of Glutamine Metabolism, 1973, Slow Transmissible Diseases Of The Nervous System, Two Volumes, 1979, Prions-Novel Infectious Pathogens Causing Scrapie And CJD, 1987, Prion Diseases Of Humans And Animals, 1992, Prions Prions Prions, 1996, Molecular And Genetic Basis Of Neurologic Disease, Third Edition, 2003, Prion Biology And Diseases, Second Edition, 2004; Author, Madness And Memory: The Discovery Of Prions-A New Biological Principle Of Disease, 2014; Contributor, Articles, Professional Journals **AW:** National Medal for Science, The White House, 2010, George Eastman Medal, 2009, William Beaumont Medal,

2005, Commonwealth Award, 2004, Distinguished Alumni Award, University of Pennsylvania College of Arts & Sciences, 2003, Ellen Browning Scripps Medal, 2000, Sir Hans Krebs Medal, Federation of European Biochemical Societies, 1999, Jubilee Medal, Swedish Medical Society, 1998, Distinguished Achievement Award, American Academy of Neurology, 1998, Benjamin Franklin Medal, Franklin Institute, 1998, K.J. Zulch Prize, Gertrud Reemtsma Foundation, 1997, Nobel Prize In Physiology/Medicine, 1997, Louisa Gross Horwitz Prize, Columbia University, 1997, Amgen Award, Protein Society, 1997, Baxter Award, American Association of Medical Colleges, 1996, Keio International Prize, 1996, Charles Leopold Mayer Prize, French Academy of Sciences, 1996, Pasarow Foundation Prize, 1996, Victor & Clara Soriano Award, World Federation of Neurology, 1996, ICN Virology Prize, 1996, Wolf Foundation Prize In Medicine, Israel, 1996, Paul Hoch Award, American Psychopathology Association, 1995, Paul Ehrlich & Ludwig Darmstaedter Award, Germany, 1995, Caledonian Research Foundation Prize, Royal Society of Edinburgh, 1995, Albert Lasker Award For Basic Medical Research, 1994, Gairdner Foundation International Award, 1993, Richard Lounsbery Award for Extraordinary Achievements in Biology And Medicine, Institute of Medicine, National Academy Of Sciences, 1993, Presidential Award, American Academy of Neurology, 1993, Max Planck Research Award, Alexander Von Humboldt Foundation/Max Planck Society, 1992, Dickson Prize, University of Pittsburgh, 1992, Charles A. Dana Award, 1992, Christopher Columbus Discovery Award, NIH/Medical Society of Genoa, Italy, 1992, Medical Research Award, Metropolitan Life Foundation, 1992, Distinguished Medical Graduate Award, University of Pennsylvania School of Medicine, 1991, Potamkin Prize For Alzheimer's Disease Research, National Institutes Of Health, 1991, George Cotzias Award for Outstanding Research, American Academy of Neurology, 1987, Grantee, Howard Hughes Medical Institute, 1976-1981 **MEM:** President-Elect, American Neurological Association, 2013-Present, Governing Board Member, National Research Council, 2008-2012, Council Member, National Academy Of Sciences, 2007-2010, Board of Directors, Concordia Argonaut Club, 1997-2005, World Jewish Academy of Sciences, Serbian Academy of Sciences, Protein Society, Royal Society of London, American Philosophical Society, American Society of Molecular Biology & Biochemistry, American Society of Cellular Biology, American Society of Cell Biology, Genetics Society of America, American Society of Human Genetics, Society of Neuroscience, American Chemical Society, American Society of Biochemistry & Molecular Biology, American Society of Clinical Investigation, American Society of Virology, American Society of Neurochemistry, American Association of Physicians, American Academy of Neurology, Bohemian Club **BA:** University of California Institute for Neurodegenerative Diseases, 675 Nelson Rising Lane, San Francisco, CA, 94158

PRYOR, JILL ANNE, T: Federal Judge **I:** Law and Legal Services **DOB:** 03/24/1963 **PB:** Harrisburg **SC:** Pennsylvania **PT:** Daughter of Gerald Osmond and Virginia Mary (Tartaglin) P.; **MS:** Married **SPN:** Harry Antrim Austin III, (June 18, 1988) **ED:** JD, Yale Law School, 1988; BA, College of William & Mary, 1985 **CT:** Bar: Georgia 1989, U.S. District Court Northern District of Georgia 1989, Supreme Court of the U.S., U.S. Court of Appeals for the Eleventh Circuit **C:** Judge, U.S. Court of Appeals for the Eleventh Circuit 2014-; Partner, Bondurant, Mixson & Elmore LLP, Atlanta, 1997-2014; Associate, Bondurant, Mixson & Elmore LLP, Atlanta,

1989-97; Law clerk to Hon. J. L. Edmondson, U.S. Court of Appeals for the Eleventh Circuit, Atlanta, 1988-89 **CR:** Member lawyers committee U.S. Court of Appeals for the Eleventh Circuit 1996-2009 **CW:** Contributor articles to professional journals **AW:** Recipient Georgias Top 50 Female Superlawyers, by Law & Politics Media and Atlanta magazine, Georgia's Legal Elite, by Georgia Trend magazine, 2005, 2004 **MEM:** Member American Bar Association, State Bar Georgia, Atlanta Bar Association, Georgia Association Women Lawyers (president 2000-2001; pres.-elect 1999-2000; v.p.- cmty. 1997-99; scholarship com.1995-96), Mortar Board, Phi Beta Kappa, Delta Sigma Rho-Tau Kappa Alpha, Omicron Delta Kappa, Association Trial Lawyers America, Georgia Trial Lawyers Association (editorial committee, verdict, 1996-2000); lawyers club Atlanta, American Inns Court (Barrister, Lumpkin Inn, 1992-94). **ACH:** Senior editor Yale Law jour, 1987-88, editor Yale Law & Policy Review, 1987-88. **BA:** 56 Forsyth St NW, Atlanta, GA, 30303

PRYOR, WILLIAM HOLCOMBE JR., T: Federal Judge, Former State Attorney General, Educator **I:** Law and Legal Services **DOB:** 04/26/1962 **PB:** Mobile **SC:** Alabama **PT:** Son of William Holcombe Senior and Laura Louise (Bowles) Pryor; **ED:** JD with honors, Tulane University, 1987; BA in Legal Studies with honors, Northeast Louisiana University, 1984 **C:** Commissioner, US Sentencing Commission, Washington, 2013-; Judge, US Court Appeals (11th Cir.), Birmingham, 2004-; Attorney general, State of Alabama, Montgomery, 1997-2004; Deputy attorney general, State of Alabama, Montgomery, 1995-97; Associate, Walston, Stabler, Wells, Anderson & Bains, Birmingham, 1991-95; Associate, Cabaniss, Johnston, Gardner, Dumas & O'Neil, Birmingham, Alabama, 1988-91; Law clerk to Hon. John Minor Wisdom, US Court Appeals (5th Cir.), New Orleans, 1987-88 **CR:** Adjunct professor University Alabama School Law, 2006-, Samford University Cumberland School Law, Birmingham, 1989-94 **CIV:** Member national committee, Young Republican National Federation, 1984-86 Member, Alabama Republican Executive Committee, 1994-95 **CW:** Board student editors: Tulane Law Rev., 1985-86, editor-in-chief:, 1986-87, board adv. editors:, 1995- **MEM:** Mem.: Federalist Society (associate), American Law Institute (associate), Order of Coif, Omicron Delta Kappa, Phi Kappa Phi **PA:** Republican **BA:** 56 Forsyth St NW, Atlanta, GA, 30303

PUCK, WOLFGANG, I: Food & Restaurant Services **DOB:** 07/08/1949 **PB:** St. Veit, Austria **ED:** Doctor of Culinary Arts (hon.), Johnson & Wales University, Providence, Rhode Island, 1998 **C:** Partner, Wolfgang Puck Worldwide, Inc., 2000-; Owner, Chef, Wolfgang Puck Catering, 1998-; Owner, Wolfgang Puck Cafes, 1993-; Owner, Wolfgang Puck Express, 1991-; Executive Chef, Partner, CUT, Beverly Hills, California, 2006-; Executive Chef, Partner, 20 21, Minneapolis, 2005-; Executive Chef, Partner, Wolfgang Puck Bar & Grill, Las Vegas, 2004-; Executive Chef, Partner, Postrio Las Vegas, 1998-; Executive Chef, Partner, Chinois Las Vegas, 1998-; Executive Chef, Partner, Spago Las Vegas, 1992-; Executive Chef, Partner, Granita, Malibu, California, 1991-; Executive Chef, Partner, Trattoria del Lupo, Las Vegas, 1989-; Executive Chef, Partner, Postrio, San Francisco, 1989-; Executive Chef, Partner, Chinois on Main, Santa Monica, 1983-; Executive Chef, Partner, Spago, 1982-; Chef, Part Owner, Ma Maison, LA, 1975-; Owner, Wolfgang Puck Fine Dining Group,; Executive Chef, Partner, Vert, Hollywood, California,; Chef, La Tour, Indianapolis, 1973-75; Former Chef, L'Oustau de Baumanière,

Provence,; Former Chef, Maxim's, Paris,; Former Chef, Hotel de Paris, Monaco **CR:** Fund raising Meals on Wheels, A. Cancer Society LA executive chef Governor's Ball, The Oscars, 1995-, Grammy awards celebrations, ESPY awards, American Music Awards, and presidential galas and fundraisers partner with Humane Society US, factory farming animal welfare progressive, 2007- launched line of cookware, food products and small kitchen appliances and gadgets/tools. **CIV:** Founder, Puck-Lazaroff Charitable Foundation, 1982- **CW:** Author: (cookbooks) Modern French Cooking for the American Kitchen, 1982, The Wolfgang Puck Cookbook: Recipes from Spago and Chinois, 1986, Adventures in the Kitchen with Wolfgang Puck, 1991, Pizza, Pasta and More!, 2000, Live, Love, Eat! The Best of Wolfgang Puck, 2002, Wolfgang Puck Makes It Easy, 2004, Wolfgang Puck Makes It Healthy: Light Delicious Recipes and Easy Exercises for a Better Life, 2014, (newspaper columns) Wolfgang Puck's Kitchen, 2003-; regular guest Good Morning America, 1986-; producer (instructional cooking video) Spago Cooking with Wolfgang Puck; appeared in TV series Wolfgang Puck, 2000-2005 (Daytime Emmy for Outstanding Service Show, 2004), Wolfgang Puck's Cooking Class, 2003; actor: (guest appearances) (films) The Weather Man, 2005, (TV series) Who's the Boss?, 1987, Blossom, 1991, Tales from the Crypt, 1992, Ellen, 1996, Frasier, 2000, 2002, Late Night with David Letterman, Tonight Show with Jay Leno, Entertainment Tonight, Hollywood Squares, Wheel of Fortune, ABC News, CBS News, Politically Incorrect with Bill Maher, Las Vegas, 2006, (voice) The Simpsons, 2002, The Late Late Show with Craig Ferguson, E! Entertainment TV, The History Channel, Shark, What's My Line. **AW:** Named Outstanding Chef of the Year, James Beard Foundation, 1998, 1991; named one of The 100 Most Powerful Celebrities, Forbes. com, 2008; recipient Lifetime Achievement award, James Beard Foundation, 2012, Smithfield Foods Outstanding Service award, 2005, Business Statesman of Year award, Harvard Business School of Southern California, 2001, Restaurant of the Year, James Beard Foundation, 1994, Humanitarian of Year award, 1994

PUJJI, PAYAL, T: Executive Chairman **I:** Business Management/Business Services **CN:** Classpass **ED:** B.S., Management Science, MIT, 2001-05 **C:** CEO & Co-Founder, Classpass, 2011-; Founder & Artistic Director, The Sa Dance Company, 2009-; Associate Director, Warner Music Group, 2008-11

PUJOLS, ALBERT, T: Professional Baseball Player **I:** Athletics **DOB:** 01/16/1980 **PB:** Santo Domingo **ED:** Attended, Maple Woods Community College, Kansas City, Missouri, 1999 **C:** First baseman, LA Angels of Anaheim, 2012-; First baseman, St. Louis Cardinals, 2001-11 **CR:** Co-founder Pujols Family Foundation, 2005- co-owner Patrick's Restaurant, Maryland Heights, Missouri first baseman, Dominican Republic national team World Baseball Classic, 2006 **CIV:** Founder, Pujols Family Foundation, 2005 **AW:** Named Best International Player, ESPY awards, 2006, Best Major League Baseball Player, 2006, 2005, National League MVP, Baseball Writers Association America, 2009, 2008, 2005, National League Championship Series MVP, Major League Baseball, 2004, MLB Athlete of Decade, 2000's, The Sporting News, 2009, MLB Player of Year, 2009, 2008, 2003, Marvin Miller Man of Year, Major League Baseball Players Association, 2006, Player of Year, 2009, 2008, 2003, National League Outstanding Player, 2008, 2003, National League Outstanding Rookie, 2001, National League

Rookie of Year, Major League Baseball, 2001; named to National League All-Star Team, 2003-10, 2001; recipient Roberto Clemente award, 2008, National League Gold Glove award, 2010, 2006, Hank Aaron award, 2009, 2003, National League Silver Slugger award, 2008-10, 2004, 2003, 2001,World Series Champion, 2006, 2011, NL Home Run Leader, 2010 **ACH:** Achievements include leading the National League in: hits, doubles, 2003; batting average, 2003; runs, 2003, 2004, 2005, 2009, 2010; home runs, 2009, 2010; RBI, 2010; member of the World Series Champion St. Louis Cardinals, 2006, 2011; becoming the first player in Major League Baseball history to hit 30 or more home runs in first nine seasons, 2009; hit his 500th home run, April 22, 2014 **BA:** National Headquarters of the Pujols Family, 111 Westport Plaza, Suite 255, St Louis, MO, 63146

PYNCHON, THOMAS RUGGLES JR., T: Writer **I:** Writing and Editing **PB:** Glen Cove **SC:** NY/USA **PT:** Thomas Ruggles Pynchon; Katherine Frances Bennett **ED:** BA in English, Cornell University, New York City, 1958 **C:** Former editorial writer, Boeing Aircraft Co., Seattle **MIL:** Served with US Navy, 1955-57 **CW:** Author: (novels) V., 1963 (Best first Novel of Year, William Faulkner Foundation, 1963), The Crying of Lot 49, 1966 (Rosenthal award, American Academy of Arts and Letters, 1967, named one of 100 Best English-lang. Novels from 1923 to 2005, TIME magazine), Gravity's Rainbow, 1973 (National Book award, 1979), Slow Learner, 1984, Vineland, 1990, Deadly Sins, 1994, Mason & Dixon, 1997, Against the Day, 2006, Inherent Vice, 2009 (Publishers Weekly bestseller), Bleeding Edge, 2013; contributor non-fiction works New York Times Book Review and New York Review of Books; contributor numerous short stories to various publications **AW:** Recipient William Dean Howells medal, American Academy of Arts and Letters, 1975; MacArthur Fellow, 1988

QUAYLE, DAN, T: Former Vice President of the U.S. **I:** Government Administration/Government Relations/Government Services **DOB:** 02/04/1947 **PB:** Indpls. **PT:** Son of James Cline and Corinne (Pulliam) Q.; Married Marilyn Tucker, November 18, 1972; children: Tucker Danforth, Benjamin Eugene, Mary Corinne Berger. **ED:** JD, Ind. University Robert H. McKinney School Law, 1974; BS in Political Sci., DePauw University, Greencastle, Ind., 1969 **CT:** Bar: Ind. 1974. **C:** Chairman global investments, Cerberus Capital Management, LP, 2000-; President, Quayle & Associates, Phoenix,; Founder, BTC, 1994; Vice President of the US, Washington, 1989-93; US Senator from Ind., Washington, 1981-89; Member, US Congress from 4th Ind. District, Washington, 1977-81; Teacher business law, Huntington College, 1975; Director, Ind. Inheritance Tax Div., 1973-74; Administrative assistant to Governor, State of Ind., 1971-73; With consumer protection division Office Attorney General, State of Ind., 1970-71; Associate pub., general manager, Huntington Herald-Press, Ind., 1974-76; Court reporter, pressman, Huntington Herald-Press, Ind., 1965-69 **CR:** Distinguished visiting professor American Grad. School International Management, 1997-99 board directors IAP Worldwide Services, Inc., Aozora Bank Ltd., 2000–, K-2, Inc., 2001-07, Bell Automotive, Heckmann Corp., 2007- consultant in field. **CIV:** Chairman Campaign America, 1995-99 hon. trustee emeriti Hudson Institute With Ind. Army National Guard, 1970-76. **CW:** Author: Standing Firm: A Vice-Presidential Memoir, 1994, Worth Fighting For, 1999; co-author (with Diane Medved) The American Family: Discovering the Values That Make Us Strong, 1996 **PA:** Republican **BA:** The Quayle Vice Presidential Learning Center, 815 Warren Street, Hungington, IN, 46750

QUENNEVILLE, JOEL, T: Head Coach **I:** Athletics **CN:** Chicago Blackhawks **DOB:** 09/15/1958 **PB:** Windsor **SC:** ON/Canada **C:** Head Coach, Chicago Blackhawks, 2008-; Scout, Chicago Blackhawks, 2008; Head Coach, St. Louis Blues, 1997-2004; Head Coach, Colorado Avalanche, 2004-08; Assistant Coach, Colorado Avalanche, 1995-96; Head Coach, Springfield Indians (AHL), 1993-94; Assistant Coach, St. John's Maple Leafs (AHL), 1992-93; Defenseman, Player Assistant, St. John's Maple Leafs (AHL), 1991-92; Defenseman, Washington Capitals, 1990-91; Defenseman, Baltimore Skipjacks (AHL), 1990-91; Defenseman, Hartford Whalers, 1983-90; Defenseman, New Jersey Devils, 1982-83; Defenseman, Colorado Rockies, 1980-82; Defenseman, Toronto Maple Leafs, 1979-80 **AW:** Recipient, Jack Adams Award, NHL, 2000 **ACH:** Achievements include being the head coach of Stanley Cup Champion Chicago Blackhawks, 2010, 2013, 2015 **BA:** United Center, 1901 W Madison St, Chicago, IL, 60612

QUIGLEY, MIKE, T: U.S. Representative from Illinois, Former County Commissioner **I:** Government Administration/Government Relations/ Government Services **DOB:** 10/17/1958 **PB:** Carol Stream **ED:** JD, Loyola University School Law, Chicago, 1989; MA in Pub. Policy, University Chicago, 1985; BA in Political Sci., Roosevelt University, Chicago, 1981 **C:** Member, Intelligence Committee; Member, US Congress from 5th Illinois District, 2009-; Rep. from District 10, Cook County Board Commissioners, Chicago, 1998-2009; Attorney, Law Offices of Michael B. Quigley, 1990-2009; Aide to alderman Bernie Hansen, Chicago City Council, 1983-89 **CR:** Instructor political sci. Loyola University, Chicago **AW:** Recipient Human Rights award, Evangelical Catholic Church, Chicago Recycling Coalition award, Distinguished Service award, Illinois Committee for Honest Government, Audobon Leadership award, Human Rights Campaign Equality award, Leon Despres award, Ind. Voters of Illinois, Community Advocate award, Chicago Battered Women's Network, Legislator award, Respiratory Health Association, Pub. Service Award, Chicago House, 2008, Chicago Recycling Coalition award, Community Advocate award, Chicago Battered Women's Network, Leon Despres award, Ind. Voters of Ill./Ind. Precinct Organization, Distinguished Service award, Illinois Committee for Honest Government **MEM:** Mem.: Lakeview C. of C. (Outstanding Pub. Servant award) **PA:** Democrat

QUINCEY, JAMES ROBERT, T: Coca-Cola CEO **I:** Business Management/Business Services **DOB:** 01/08/1965 **ED:** Bachelor in Electronic Engineering, University Liverpool **C:** President,CEO, The Coca-Cola Co., 2016-; President, COO, The Coca-Cola Co., 2015-; President, Europe Group, The Coca-Cola Co., 2013-15; President, Northwest Europe and Nordics Business Unit, The Coca-Cola Co., 2008-12; President, Mexican Division, The Coca-Cola Co., Mexico, 2005-08; President, South Latin Division, The Coca-Cola Co., 2003-05; General manager, South Latin Division, The Coca-Cola Co., 2003; Region manager, The Coca-Cola Co., Uruguay, 2000-03; Region manager, The Coca-Cola Co., Argentina, 2000-03; Deputy to division president, The Coca-Cola Co., Mexico, 1999-2000; Director, learning strategy, L. Am. Group, The Coca-Cola Co., 1996-99; Ptrn., strategy, consulting, The Kalchas Group, **CR:** Board directors Embotelladora Andina S.A., 2006-, Coca-Cola Embonor S.A.

RADER, JAN, T: Fire Chief **I:** Civil Service **C:** Fire Chief, Huntington, WV **AW:** Named One of TIME's 100 Most Influential People, TIME Magazine (2018)

RAE, ISSA, T: Actress, Writer, Director **I:** Fine Art **DOB:** 06/22/1905 **PB:** Los Angeles, California **SC:** Los Angeles, California **CW:** (Online Show) Awkward Black Girl, 2011, (Television) Insecure,2013(Novel) The Misadventures of Awkward Black Girl, 2015(Producer)M.O. Diaries, 2012, How Men Became Dogs, 2013,Little Horribles, 2013, The Choir,2013, Inside Web Series, 2013, Black Actress, 2013, Roomieloverfriends,2013, Hard Times, 2013, So Jaded, 2013, Words with Girls, 2013, Bleach, 2014, Head Cases,2014,Protect and Serve,2014, A Bitter Lime, 2014, First, 2014, Killing Lazarus, 2015, Get Your life, 2015, Insecure, 2016, The Hate U Give, 2018

RAGGI, REENA, T: Federal Judge **I:** Law and Legal Services **DOB:** 05/11/1951 **PB:** Jersey City **SC:** NJ/USA **ED:** JD, Harvard University, Cum Laude, 1976; BA, Wellesley College, 1973 **C:** Judge, U.S. Court of Appeals, Second Circuit, New York, NY, 2002-Present; Judge, U.S. District Court, Eastern District, New York, 1987-2002; Partner, Windels, Marx, Davies & Ives, New York, NY, 1986-1987; Assistant U.S. Attorney, Department of Justice, Brooklyn, NY, 1979-1986; Associate, Cahill, Gordon & Reindel, New York, NY, 1977-1979; Law Clerk, U.S. Court Of Appeals, Seventh Circuit, 1976-1977 **BAR:** State of New York, 1977, U.S. District Court, Eastern District, New York, 1987, U.S. Court of Appeals, Second Circuit, 2002 **BA:** 40 Foley Street, New York, NY, 10007

RAIMONDO, GINA MARIE, T: Governor of Rhode Island, Former State Treasurer **I:** Government Administration/Government Relations/Government Services **DOB:** 05/17/1971 **PB:** Smithfield **SC:** RI/USA **PT:** Daughter of Joseph and Josephine (Piro) Raimondo; **ED:** JD, Yale University Law School, New Haven, 1998; Rhodes Scholar, Oxford University, 1997; BS magna cum laude in Economics, Harvard University, Cambridge, Massachusetts, 1993 **C:** Governor, State of Rhode Island, Providence, 2015-; Gov.-elect, State of Rhode Island, Providence, 2014-15; General treasurer, State of Rhode Island, Providence, 2011-14; Co-founder, general partner, Point Judith Capital, Rhode Island, 2001-10; Senior vice president for fund devel., Village Ventures, 1999-2001; Law clerk to Hon. Kimba Wood, U.S. District Court (southern district) New York, New York City, 1998-99 **CIV:** Trustee, chair quality committee, Women and Infants Hospital, Vice chair board directors, Crossroads Rhode Island, **AW:** Rhodes scholar, Oxford University, England **ACH:** Achievements include being the first woman to serve as the governor of Rhode Island **PA:** Democrat

RAJAN, MADHAV V., T: Professor, academic administrator **I:** Education/Educational Services **ED:** Graduate University of Madras, 1984, master of science in Accounting, Carnegie Mellon University, 1987, Master of science in Industrial Administration, Carnegie Mellon University, 1989, PhD in Accounting in 1990, Carnegie Mellon University; **C:** Dean, Booth School of Business, University of Chicago, 2017-, Senior associate dean for academic affairs, Stanford Graduate School of Business, 2010-2016, professor, Stanford Graduate School of Business 2001-2016, associate professor, University of Pennsylvania, 1996-2000, assistant professor, University of Pennsylvania, 1990-1996 **CR:** Member, board of directors of Cavium, iShares and the Investment Advisory Board of CM Capital. **CW:** Coauthor of Managerial Accounting, 2013. Contributor articles to professional journals. **AW:** Winner, Lifetime of achievement and service to the Stanford Graduate School of Business, 2017, winner David W. Hauck Award, University of Pennsylvania, 2000

RAJAN, RAGHURAM G., T: Bank Executive, Economics Professor **I:** Financial Services **DOB:** 02/03/1963 **PB:** Hamidia **PT:** Son of R and M Govindarajan; **ED:** PhD, Massachusetts Institute of Technology, 1991; MBA, Indian Institute Management, Ahmedabad, 1987; BTech, Indian Institute Tech., New Delhi, 1985 **C:** Governor, Reserve Bank of India, 2013-; On leave, Booth School of Business, University Chicago, 2013-; Economic counselor, director research, International Monetary Fund, Washington, 2003-06; Eric J. Gleacher Distinguished service professor finance, Booth School of Business, University Chicago, 2006-13; Joseph L. Gidwitz professor finance, Booth School of Business, University Chicago, 1997-2003; Professor, Booth School of Business, University Chicago, 1995-96; Assistant professor finance, Booth School of Business, University Chicago, 1991-95 **CR:** Chief economic advisor Government of India, 2012, hon. economic advisor to prime minister, 2008-12, chairman High Level Committee on Fin. Sector Reforms, 2007-08 Fisher Black visiting professor Massachusetts Institute of Technology Sloan School Management, 2000-01 program director corp. fin. National Bureau Economic Research, 1998-2010 visiting professor fin. Kellogg School, Northwestern University, 1996-97 Bertil Danielsson visiting professor banking Stockholm School Economics, 1996-97 **CIV:** Board, Chicago Council Global Affairs, 2008 **CW:** Co-author (with Luigi Zingales): Caving Capitalism from the Capitalists, 2003; author: Fault Lines: How Hidden Fractures Still Threaten the World Economy, 2010 (Fin. Times / Goldman Sachs Business Book of Year Award, 2010); contributor articles to professional journals **AW:** Named one of The 50 Most Influential People in Global Finance, Bloomberg Markets, 2013-14; recipient Global Indian of Year Award, NASSCOM, 2011, Bernhard Harms Prize, Kiel Institute International Economics, 2010, Fischer Black Prize, American Financial Association, 2003, Treffstz Prize, Western Finance Association, 1991; grantee National Science Foundation, 2010-, 2002-07, 1999-2002, 1995-98 **MEM:** Fellow: American Academy Arts and Sciences; mem.: Group of Thirty, Academic Council of Indian School of Business, American Fin. Association (director 2001-04, president 2011) **ACH:** Achievements include research in corporate finance; research in theory of organizations; research in financial intermediation and regulation **H:** Squash, tennis, skiing

RAMAKRISHNAN, VENKATRAMAN, T: Structural Biologist **I:** Sciences **PB:** Chidambaram, Tamil Nadu **SC:** India **ED:** PhD in Physics, Ohio University (1976); BS in Physics, Maharaja Sayajirao University Baroda, India (1971) **C:** Senior Scientist, Group Leader Structural Studies Division, MCR Laboratory of Molecular Biology, Cambridge, England (1999-Present); Professor, Department of Biochemistry, University of Utah (1995-1999; Staff Scientist, Brookhaven National Laboratory, Upton, NY (1983-1995); Postdoctorate Fellow, Department of Chemistry, Yale University, New Haven, CT (1978-1982) **CW:** Contributor, Articles to Professional Journals **AW:** Nobel Prize in Chemistry (2009); Heatley Medal, British Biochemistry Society (2008); Louis Jeantet Prize for Medicine (2007); Fellow, John Simon Guggenheim Memorial Foundation (1991-1992); Knight Bachelor (2012); Padma Vibhushan (2010) **MEM:** Fellow, Royal Society; National Academy of Sciences; Foreign Member, Indian National Science Academy; European Molecular Biology Organization

RAMOS, JORGE, T: Newscaster **I:** Media & Entertainment **DOB:** 03/16/1958 **PB:** Mex. City **ED:** Master in International Studies, University Miami; Grad. in Communications,

Ibero-American University, Mexico City **C:** Anchorman, Noticiero Univision, 1986-; Host, Mundo Latino, Univision TV progressive, 1986; News reporter, Univision, LA, 1984-86 **CR:** Founder Wake Up Reading book club, 2002- **CW:** Author: (autobiography) No Borders: a Journalist's Search for Home, Behind the Mask, The Other Face of America, What I Saw, Hunting the Lion, The Latino Wave, Dying to Cross; contributor weekly column, New York Times Syndicate **AW:** Named one of The 50 Highest-Earning Political Figures, Newsweek, 2010, 25 Most Influential Hispanics, Time Magazine, 2005, Ten Most Admired Latinos, Latino Leaders magazine, 2004; recipient 8 Emmy awards, National Academy Television Arts & Sci., David Brinkley award for Journalistic Excellence, Barry Univ., 2003, Ron Brown award, National Child Labor Committee, 2002, Ruben Salazar award, National Council La Raza, 2002, Maria Moors Cabot award, Columbia Univ., 2001

RANDALL, KIKKAN, T: Cross-Country Skier **I:** Athletics **DOB:** 07/19/1905 **PB:** Salt Lake City, Utah **SC:** Salt Lake City, Utah **AW:** One Olympic Gold Medal, Team Spring, 2018, One Gold World Championship Medal, Team Sprint, 2013, One Silver World Championship, Sprint,2009, One Bronze Championship Medal, Spring, 2017, Alaska Sports Hall of Fame, 2011

RASKIN, JAMIN B., T: U.S. Representative from Maryland **I:** Government Administration/Government Relations/Government Services **DOB:** 12/13/1962 **PB:** Washington **PT:** Son of Marcus Goodman and Barbara Judith (Bellman) R.; Married Sarah Bloom, August 11, 1990; children: Hannah Grace, Thomas Bloom, Tabitha Claire **ED:** JD, Harvard Law School, 1987; BA in Government, Harvard College, 1983 **C:** Member, U.S. House of Representatives from Maryland's 8th District, 2017-; Member, Committee on House Administration, Committee on the Judiciary, Committee on Oversight and Government Reform; Member, District 20, Maryland State Senate, 2007-2017; Professor law, Am. University Washington College Law, 1990-; Associate dean faculty & academy affairs, Am. University Washington College Law, 1994-96; Assistant attorney general, Massachusetts, 1987-89 **CR:** Visiting professor Sciences Po, Paris, 2003-04; chair Maryland State Higher Education Labor Relations board **CIV:** Member 1992 Clinton-Gore Transition Team Justice Department Civil Rights Cluster, Washington, 1992 board directors Washington area National Rainbow Coalition, 1992- **CW:** Author: The Supreme Court versus the American People 2003, We the Students, The Wealth Primary, Contributor articles to professional journals; featured guest on national & local TV & radio shows including Crossfire, C-Span, Diane Rehm Show, NPR, others **AW:** Named Scholar-Tchr. of the Year, Am. University, 2000-2001 **MEM:** Member American Bar Association (co-chair section on administrative law, committee on election law 1998-), Clinton-Gore transition team **BAR:** Bar: Massachusetts 1987 **PA:** Democrat **BA:** 431 Cannon House Office Building, Washington, DC, 20515

RASMUSSEN, STEPHEN SCOTT, T: Nationwide CEO **I:** Insurance **ED:** BS in Business Administration, University of Iowa **C:** President, CEO, Nationwide Mutual Insurance Co., Columbus, Ohio, 2009-; President, COO property & casualty operations, Nationwide Mutual Insurance Co., Columbus, Ohio, 2003-09; President, COO, CalFarm Insurance, 2001-03; Executive vice president, product management, Allied Insurance, 1998-2001; Vice president, underwriting, Allied Insurance,

1986-98; Regional vice president, pacific coast regional office, Allied Insurance, 1982-86; Underwriting & marketing, Allied Insurance, 1974-82 **CIV:** 2002 Walk corp. chair, central Iowa chapter, Juvenile Diabetes Research Foundation, Trustee, Grand View College, Board member, Columbus Metropolitan Library, Board member, Franklin County Convention Facilities Authority, Board member, Insurance Institute for Highway Safety, Board member, National Urban League,

RATCLIFFE, JOHN LEE, T: U.S. Representative from Texas **I:** Government Administration/Government Relations/Government Services **DOB:** 10/20/1965 **ED:** JD, Southern Methodist University, 1989; BA in Government & International Studies, University Notre Dame, 1987 **C:** Member US Congress from 4th Texas District, Washington, 2015-; Member, Judiciary Committee, Committee on Homeland Security, Republican Study Committee; Partner, Ashcroft Sutton Ratcliffe LLC, 2009-14; Partner, The Ashcroft Law Firm LLC, 2009-14; Mayor, City of Heath, Texas, 2004-12; Chief anti-terrorism & national security, US Department Justice, 2004-07; US attorney (eastern district) Texas, US Department Justice, 2007-08 **CR:** Adjunct professor law Texas Wesleyan University, Southern Methodist University **PA:** Republican

RAUNER, BRUCE VINCENT, T: Governor of Illinois, Investment Company Executive (Retired) **I:** Government Administration/Government Relations/Government Services **DOB:** 02/18/1957 **PB:** Chicago **SC:** IL/USA **PT:** Vincent Joseph Rauner; Ann E. (Erickson) Rauner **ED:** MBA, Harvard Business School, Harvard University (1981); BS in Economics, Dartmouth College (1978) **C:** Governor, State of Illinois, Springfield, MA (2015-Present); Chairman, R8 Capital Partners (2012-2014); Chairman, GTCR (Formerly Golder, Thoma, Cressey) (1981-2012) **CR:** Board of Directors, Coinmach Service Corp. (2004-2007) **CIV:** Chairman, Choose Chicago **AW:** Recipient, Community Service Award, Golden Apple Foundation (2011); Recipient, Daley Medal, Illinois Venture Capital Association (2003); Recipient, Lifetime Achievement Award, Association for Corporate Growth **PA:** Republican **BA:** Office of Governor, 207 State House, Springfield, IL, 62706

RAWLINSON, JOHNNIE BLAKENEY, T: Federal Judge **I:** Government Administration/Government Relations/Government Services **DOB:** 12/16/1952 **PB:** Concord **SC:** NC **ED:** JD, University of the Pacific (1979); BS in Psychology, North Carolina A&T State University, Summa Cum Laude (1974) **C:** Judge, U.S. Court of Appeals for the Ninth Circuit (2000-Present); Judge, U.S. District Court for the District of Nevada (1998-2000); From Deputy District Attorney to Assistant District Attorney, Clark County District Attorney's Office (1980-1998); Staff Attorney, Nevada Legal Services (1980); Private Practice, Las Vegas, NV (1979-1980) **BA:** 95 7th St, San Francisco, CA, 94013

RAY, RACHAEL DOMENICA, T: Cookbook Author, television personality **I:** Media & Entertainment **DOB:** 08/25/1968 **PB:** Glens Falls **SC:** New York **C:** Founder, editorial director, Everyday with Rachael Ray magazine, 2005-; Food buyer, Cowan & Lobel, Albany, New York,; Manager Mister Brown's Pub,, Sagamore Resort, Lake George, New York,; Store manager, buyer, Agata & Valentina, New York City,; Manager fresh foods department, Macy's Marketplace, New York City, **CR:** Has own line of cookware and kitchenware founder Nutrish pet food, Rachael's Rescue, Yum-O! Organization, 2007 spokesperson Dunkin Donuts, 2007-, Nabisco, 2006- **CW:** Author: (cookbooks) 30-Minute Meals,

1999, Rachael Ray's Open House Cookbook, 2000, Veggie Meals, 2001, Comfort Foods, 2001, 30-Minute Meals 2, 2003, Get Togethers: Rachael Ray 30 Minute Meals, 2003, $40 a Day: Best Eats in Town, 2004, Cooking 'Round the Clock: Rachael Ray's 30-Minute Meals, 2004, Cooking Rocks!: Rachael Ray's 30-Minute Meals for Kids, 2004, 30-Minute Get Real Meals: Eat Healthy Without Going to Extremes, 2005 (Quills award, 2005), Rachael Ray's 365: No Repeats: Rachael Ray's Open House Cookbook, 2005 (Quills award, 2006), Rachael Ray's Top 30-30 Minute Meals-Comfort Food, 2005, Rachael Ray's 30 Minute Meals-Guy Food, 2005, Rachael Ray's 30 Minute Meals-Kid Food, 2005, Rachael Ray's Express Lane Meals, 2006, Rachael Ray 2, 4, 6, 8: Great Meals for Couples or Crowds, 2006, Classic 30 Minute Meals: The All-Occasion Cookbook, 2006, Rachael Ray's Open House, Revised, 2006, Rachael Ray: Just in Time, 2007, Yum-O! The Family Cookbook, 2008, Rachael Ray's Big Orange Book, 2008, Rachael Ray's Book of 10: More Than 300 Recipes To Cook Every Day, 2009, Rachael Ray's Look + Cook, 2010, The Book of Burgers, 2012, My Year in Meals, 2012, Week In a Day-Five Dishes One Day, 2013, Everyone is Italian on Sunday, 2015; host (TV series) 30 Minute Meals, Food Network, 2001- (Daytime Emmy award for Outstanding Service Show, 2006), $40 A Day, 2002-03, Inside Dish, 2004-05, Rachael Ray's Tasty Travels, 2005-07, Rachael's Vacation, 2008-, co-host Rachael versus Guy: Celebrity Cook-Off, 2012-, host Rachael Ray's Week In a Day, Cooking Channel, 2010-, (syndicated daytime TV talk show) The Rachel Ray Show, 2006- (Daytime Emmy award for Outstanding Talk Show/Entertainment, 2008, 2009); prodr.: (TV series) Viva Daisy!, 2008-09; guest appearances include The Tony Danza Show, Live With Regis and Kelly, Today Show, The View, Tonight Show with Jay Leno, Late Show with David Letterman, Oprah Winfrey Show, Late Night with Conan O'Brien, Larry King Live **AW:** Named Favorite TV Chef, People's Choice Awards, 2011; named an 100 Sexiest Women, FHM-US Magazine, 2006; named one of The 100 Most Powerful Women in Entertainment, Hollywood Reporter, 2008, The 100 Most Powerful Women, Forbes magazine, 2010, The 100 Most Powerful Celebrities, 2008, The 50 Most Powerful Women in New York City, New York Post, 2008, 2007, The 100 Most Influential Women in New York City Business, Crain's New York Business, 2007, 100 Most Influential People, TIME magazine, 2006, 100 Sexiest Women, FHM-US Magazine, 2004

READ, IAN C., T: CEO and Chairman at Pfizer Inc. **I:** Pharmaceuticals **ED:** BSChemE, London University Imperial College, 1974 **CT:** Cert. Institute Chartered Accountants England & Wales, 1978 **C:** Chairman, CEO, Pfizer, Inc., New York City, 2011-; President, CEO, Pfizer, Inc., New York City, 2010-11; Senior vice president, president worldwide pharmaceutical operations, Pfizer, Inc., New York City, 2006-10; Executive vice president Latin America, Pfizer, Inc., 2006; Executive vice president Africa/Middle East, Pfizer, Inc., 2004; Vice president, Pfizer, Inc., 2001-06; Executive vice president Europe/Can., Pfizer, Inc., 2000; President International Pharmaceuticals Group Latin America/Canada, Pfizer, Inc., 1996; Country manager, Pfizer, Inc., Brazil,; CFO, Pfizer, Inc., Mexico,; Operational auditor, Pfizer, Inc., 1978 **CR:** Board member European Federation Pharmaceutical Industries & Associations, US Council for International Business board directors Pfizer Inc., 2010-, Kimberly-Clark Corp., 2007- **AW:** Named a Power Player, Advertising Age, 2008 **BA:** Pfizer Inc, 235 E 42nd St, New York, NY, 10017

REDFORD (CHARLES ROBERT REDFORD), ROBERT, T: Actor, Film Director and Producer **I:** Media & Entertainment **DOB:** 08/18/1937 **PB:** Santa Monica **PT:** Son of Charles Robert and Martha Redford **ED:** DFA (hon.), Brown University, 2008; LHD (hon.), Bard College, 1995; Doctor (hon.), University Massachusetts, 1990; LHD (hon.), University Colorado, 1987; Student, American Academy Dramatic Arts; Student, Pratt Institute Design; Student, University Colorado **C:** Owner ski resort, Sundance, Provo, Utah **CIV:** Founder, president, The Sundance Institute, 1981- **CW:** Stage appearances include: Tall Story, The Highest Tree, Sunday in New York, Barefoot in the Park; actor: (films) War Hunt, 1961, Situation Hopeless But Not Serious, 1965, Inside Daisy Clover, 1965, The Chase, 1966, This Property Is Condemned, 1966, Barefoot in the Park, 1967, Butch Cassidy and the Sundance Kid, 1969, Tell Them Willie Boy is Here, 1969, Little Fauss and Big Halsey, 1970, The Hot Rock, 1972, Jeremiah Johnson, 1972, The Way We Were, 1973, The Sting, 1973, The Great Gatsby, 1974, The Great Waldo Pepper, 1975, Three Days of the Condor, 1975, A Bridge Too Far, 1977, The Electric Horseman, 1979, Brubaker, 1980, The Natural, 1984, Out of Africa, 1985, Legal Eagles, 1986, Havana, 1990, Sneakers, 1992, Indecent Proposal, 1993, Up Close and Personal, 1996, Anthem, 1997, Enredando sombras, 1998, Forever Hollywood, 1999, Spy Game, 2001, The Last Castle, 2001, The Clearing, 2004, An Unfinished Life, 2005, (voice) Charlotte's Web, 2006, All Is Lost, 2013, Captain America: The Winter Soldier, 2014, Truth, 2015, Pete's Dragon, 2016; The Discovery, 2017, Our Souls at Night, 2017, The Old Man and the Gun 2018 (TV appearances) Maverick, 1960, Rescue 8, 1960, Tall Story, 1960, The Deputy, 1960, Hallmark Hall of Fame, 1960, Playhouse 90, 1960, Moment of Fear, 1960, Tate, 1960, Perry Mason, 1960, Play of the Week, 1960-61, Naked City, 1961, The Americans, 1961, Whispering Smith, 1961, Route 66, 1961, Bus Stop, 1961, The New Breed, 1961, Alfred Hitchcock Presents, 1961, The Twilight Zone, 1962, Dr. Kildare, 1962, Alcoa Premiere, 1962, The Alfred Hitchcock Hour, 1963-63, The Untouchables, 1963, The Virginian, 1963 The Dick Powell Show, 1963, Breaking Point, 1963, The Virginian, 1963, The Defenders, 1964; (TV films) The Iceman Cometh, 1960; actor, director, prodr.: (films) Lions for Lambs, 2007, The Company You Keep, 2012; actor, executive prodr.: (films) Downhill Racer, 1969, The Candidate, 1972, All The President's Men, 1976; dir.: (films) Ordinary People, 1980 (Academy award for Best Director, Golden Globe award for Best Director, 1980), Quiz Show, 1994; director, prodr.: (films) The Milagro Beanfield War, 1988, A River Runs Through It, 1993; prodr.: (films) A Civil Action, 1998, The Legend of Bagger Vance, 2000; executive prodr.: (films) Promised Land, 1988, Some Girls, 1988, She's the One, 1996, The Dark Wind, 1991, Slums of Beverly Hills, 1998, How to Kill Your Neighbor's Dog, 2000, Drunktown's Finest, 2014, The Adderall Diaries, 2015, (documentaries) The Unforseen, 2007, Iconoclasts, 2005-12, Watershed: Exploring a New Water Ethic for the New West, 2012, All the President's Men Revisited, 2013, The March, 2014, Death Row Stories, 2014-15, Be Natural: The Untold Story of Alice Guy-Blaché, 2016, American Epic, 2015, The Seer: A Conversation with Wendell Berry, 2015, (TV series) The American West, 2016; actor, prodr.: (films) A Walk in the Woods, 2015, Truth, 2015, Pete's Dragon, 2016, The Discovery, 2017, Our Souls at Night, 2017, The Old Man and the Gun, 2018; executive producer, narrator: Yosemite: The Fate of Heaven, 1989, Incident at Oglala, 1992 **AW:** Named Officer of French Ordre des Arts et des Lettres; named one of The 100 Most Influential People in the World, TIME magazine, 2014, The 100 Sexiest Stars in film history, Esquire magazine, 1994; recipient Presidential Medal of Freedom, The White House, 2016, Legion d'Honneur order, Government of France, 2010, Peter J. Owens award, San Francisco International Film Festival, 2009, Dorothy & Lillian Gish prize, 2008, Kennedy Center Honors, John F. Kennedy Center for the Performing Arts, 2005, Lifetime Achievement award/Honorary Oscar, Academy Motion Picture Arts & Sciences, 2002, Screen Actors Guild Award for Life Achievement, 1996, National Medal of Arts, National Endowment of the Arts, 1996, Cecil B. Demille Golden Globe Award for Lifetime Achievement, 1994, Dartmouth Film Society award, 1990, Audubon medal, 1989 **MEM:** Fellow: American Academy Arts & Sciences; mem.: Land Trust of Napa County (member adv. committee) **BA:** Creative Artists Agency, 2000 Avenue of the Stars, Los Angeles, CA, 90067

REDMAYNE, EDDIE, T: Actor, Model **I:** Media & Entertainment **PB:** London **SC:** England **ED:** Grad, Trinity College, Cambridge, 2003 **CW:** Actor: (TV series) Animal Ark, 1998, Doctors, 2003; (TV miniseries) Elizabeth I, 2005, Tess of the d'Urbervilles, 2008, The Pillars of the Earth, 2010, Birdsong, 2012, War Art with Eddie Redmayne, 2015, CBBC Visits the Wizarding World of Harry Potter and Fantastic, 2017; (plays) Twelfth Night, 2002, The Goat, or Who is Sylvia?, 2004 (50th Evening Standard Theatre awards for Outstanding Newcomer, 2004, Critics' Circle Theatre award for Best Newcomer, 2005), Now or Later, 2008, Red, 2009 (Olivier award for Best Actor in a Supporting Role, 2010, Tony award for Best Performance by a Featured Actor in a Play, 2010, Am. Theatre Wing award for Best Actor, 2010); (films) Like Minds, 2006, The Good Shepherd, 2006, Savage Grace, 2007, The Yellow Handkerchief, 2008, The Other Boleyn Girl, 2008, Powder Blue, 2009, Glorious 39, 2009, Black Death, 2010, Hick, 2011, My Week with Marilyn, 2011, Les Misérables, 2012, The Theory of Everything, 2014 (Golden Globe award for Best Actor in a Motion Picture - Drama, 2015, Screen Actors Guild award for Outstanding Performance by a Male Actor in a Leading Role, 2015, BAFTA award for Best Leading Actor, 2015, Academy award for Best Actor, 2015), Jupiter Ascending, 2015, Thomas & Friends: Sodor's Legend of the Lost Treasure (voice), 2015, The Danish Girl, 2015, Fantastic Beasts and Where to Find Them, 2016, Early Man, 2018, Fantastic Beasts:The Crimes of Grindelwald, 2018; (TV films) The Miraculous Year, 2011

REDSTONE, SUMNER MURRAY, T: Retired Founder of Viacom **I:** Medicine & Health Care **DOB:** 05/27/1923 **PB:** Boston **PT:** Son of Michael and Belle (Ostrovsky) R.; married; children: Brent Dale, Shari Ellin. **ED:** LHD (hon.), New York Institute Tech., 1996; LLD (hon.), Boston University, 1994; LLB, Harvard University, 1947; BA, Harvard University, 1944 **CT:** Bar: Massachusetts 1947, US Court Appeals (1st cir.) 1948, US Court Appeals (8th cir.) 1950, US Court Appeals (9th cir.) 1948, DC 1951, US Supreme Court 1952. **C:** Chairman emeritus, CBS Corp., 2016-; Executive chairman emeritus, Viacom, Inc., New York City, 2016-; Chairman board, National Amusements, Inc., Dedham, Massachusetts, 1986-; CEO, National Amusements, Inc., Dedham, Massachusetts, 1967-; Chairman, CBS Corp., 2006-16; Executive chairman, Viacom, Inc., New York City, 2006-16; CEO, Viacom, Inc., New York City, 1996-2006; Chairman board, Viacom, Inc., New York City, 1987-2006; President, National Amusements, Inc., Dedham, Massachusetts, 1967-99; Partner, Ford, Bergson, Adams, Borkland & Redstone, Washington, 1951-54; Special assistant to attorney general, US Department Justice, Washington, 1948-51; Instructor law and labor management, University San Francisco, 1947; Law secretary, US Court Appeals (9th cir.), San Francisco, 1947-48 **CR:** Professor Boston University Law School, 1982, 85-86 board directors, adv. council TV Academy Arts and Scis. Foundation visiting professor Brandeis University, Waltham, Massachusetts lecturer Harvard Law School, Cambridge, Massachusetts Judge on Kennedy Libr. Foundation, (sel. communications John F. Kennedy Profile in Courage award) board trustee Museum TV and Radio past president Theatre Owners Am. **CIV:** chairman metropolitan division NE Combined Jewish Philanthropies, Boston, 1963 member executive board Combined Jewish Philanthropies of Greater Boston, chairman metropolitan division member corp. New England Medical Center, 1967-, Massachusetts General Hospital Corp. trustee Children's Cancer Research Foundation founding trustee Am. Cancer Society chairman Am. Cancer Crusade, State of Massachusetts, 1984-86 Art Lending Libr. sponsor Boston Museum Sci. chairman Jimmy Fund Foundation, 1960 vice president, member executive committee Will Rogers Memorial Fund hon. chairman Will Rodgers Motion Picture Pioneers Foundation board directors Boston Arts Festival board overseers Dana Farber Cancer Center, Boston Museum Fine Arts member presidential adv. committee on arts John F. Kennedy Libr. Foundation, also judge annual John F. Kennedy Profile in Courage Award committee chairman Corp. Commission on Education Tech., 1996-, presidential appointed chairman, 1996, 1st lieutenant Army of the U.S., 1943-45 **AW:** Decorated Army Commendation medal; named 1 of 10 Outstanding Young Men in New England, Boston Junior C. of C., 1958; recipient William J. German Human Relations award Am. Jewish Committee Entertainment/ Comm. Division, 1977, Silver Shingle award Boston University Law School, 1985, Variety New England Humanitarian award, 1989, Golden Plate award Am. Academy Achievement, 1993, 32d Ann. Salute to Excellence Program, 1993, Business Excellence award University Southern California School Business Administration, 1994, The Stephen S. Wise award The Am. Jewish Congress, 1994, Man of Year award MIPCOM, the International Film and Programme Market for TV, Video, Cable and Satellite, 1994, The Legends in Leadership award Emory University, 1995, Allan K. Jonas Lifetime Achievement award Am. Cancer Society, 1995, Humanitarian award Variety Club International, 1995, Expeditioner's award New York City Outward Bound Center, 1996, Patron Arts award Songwriter's Hall Fame, 1996, Vision 21 award New York Institute Tech., 1996, Trustees award National Academy of Television Arts and Sciences, 1997, Ripple of Hope award Robert F. Kennedy Memorial, 1998, Humanitarian award National Conference Christians and Jews, 1998; named Communicator of Year, B'nai B'rith Comm./ Cinema Lodge, 1980, Man of Year, Entertainment Industries Division of UJA Federation, 1988, Pioneer of Year, Motion Picture Pioneers, 1991, Grad. of Year, Boston Latin School, 1989, Honoree 7th annual fundraiser Montefiore Medical Center, 1995, Hall of Fame award Broadcasting and Cable magazine, 1995; named one of World's Richest People, Forbes Magazine, 1999-2007, Forbes 400: Richest Americans, 2009 **MEM:** Member American Bar Association, National Association Theatre Owners (chairman board directors 1965-66, executive communications 1995-), Theatre Owners Am. (assistant president 1960-63, president 1964-65), Motion Picture Pioneers (board directors), Boston Bar Association, Massachusetts Bar Association, Harvard Law School Association, Am. Judicature Society, Masons, Univ. Club, Harvard Club

REED, JACK, T: U.S. Senator from Rhode Island **I:** Government Administration/Government Relations/Government Services **DOB:** 11/12/1949 **PB:** Providence **PT:** Son of Joseph Anthony and Mary Louise (Monahan) R.; **SPN:** Married Julia Hart, April 16, 2005; **CH:** 1 child, Emily **ED:** JD cum laude, Harvard Law School, 1982; MA in Pub. Policy, Harvard University, 1973; BS in Engineering, US Military Academy, 1971 **CT:** Bar: DC 1982, Rhode Island 1983. **C:** Ranking Member, Senate Armed Services Committee, 2015-; US Senator from Rhode Island, 1997-; Member, US Congress from 2nd Rhode Island District, 1991-97; Member, Rhode Island State Senate, 1984-90; Associate, Edwards & Angell, Providence, 1983-89; Associate, Sutherland, Asbill & Brennan, Washington, 1982-83; Assistant Professor, US Military Academy, West Point, New York, 1977-79 **MIL:** 82nd Airborne Division, 1973-77, Served in US Army, 1967-79 **CW:** Author: (with others) American National Security, 1981. **AW:** Recipient Distinguished Legis. award United Way Southeastern New England, 1988, Distinguished Service award AARP, 1989, John Fogarty award, 1990, Crystal Apple award American Association School Librarians, 1994, Excellence in Public Service award American Academy Pediatrics, 1998, Excellence in Immunization award National Partnership for Immunization, 2001, Congl. Leadership award Coalition to Stop Gun Violence & Education Fund to Stop Gun Violence, 2002, National Excellence in Public Health award Association State & Territorial Health Officials, 2002, Joan Gallagher Legis. award Massachusetts School Libr. Media Association, 2003. **MEM:** Member American Bar Association, Rhode Island Bar Association, DC Bar Association, Environmental and Energy Study Institute, Phi Kappa Phi. **H:** Reading, hiking **PA:** Democrat **BA:** Office of Jack Reed, 728 Hart Senate Office Building, Washington, DC, 20510

REED, TOM, T: U.S. Representative from New York, Lawyer **I:** Government Administration/Government Relations/Government Services **DOB:** 11/18/1971 **PB:** Joliet **PT:** Son of Tom and Betty (Barr) Reed **ED:** JD, Ohio Northern University, 1996; BA in Political Sci., Alfred University, 1993 **C:** Member, US House Ways & Means Committee, 2011-; Member, US Congress from 23rd New York District, 2013-; Private practice, Corning, New York, 1999-; Member, US House Rules Committee, 2011; Member, US House Transportation & Infrastructure Committee, 2010-11; Member, US House Judiciary Committee, 2010-11; Member, US Congress from 29th New York District, Washington, 2010-13; Mayor, City of Corning, New York, 2008-09; Attorney litigation department, Gallo & Iacovangelo, LLP, Rochester, New York, 1997-99 **BAR:** Bar: New York 1997 **PA:** Republican

REEVES, KEANU, T: Actor **I:** Media & Entertainment **DOB:** 05/30/1905 **PB:** Beirut, **SC:** Beirut, **PT:** Son of Samuel Nowlin Reeves and Patricia (Bond) Taylor. **CW:** Actor: (stage) Wolf Boy (debut), For Adults Only, Romeo and Juliet, (films) Flying, 1986, Youngblood, 1986, River's Edge, 1987, Permanent Record, 1988, The Night Before, 1988, The Prince of Pennsylvania, 1988, Dangerous Liaisons, 1988, Bill and Ted's Excellent Adventure, 1989, Parenthood, 1989, I Love You to Death, 1990, Tune in Tomorrow, 1990, Bill and Ted's Bogus Journey, 1991, Point Break, 1991, My Own Private Idaho, 1991, Bram Stoker's Dracula, 1992, Much Ado About Nothing, 1993, Little Buddha, 1994, Even Cowgirls Get the Blues, 1994, Speed, 1994, Johnny Mnemonic, 1995, A Walk in the Clouds, 1995, Feeling Minnesota, 1996, Chain Reaction, 1996, Devil's Advocate, 1997, The Last Time I Committed Suicide, 1997, The Matrix, 1999, The Replacements, 2000, The Watcher, 2000, The Gift, 2000, Hard Ball, 2001, Sweet November, 2001, The Matrix Reloaded, 2003, The Matrix Revolutions, 2003, Something's Gotta Give, 2003, Thumbsucker, 2005, Constantine, 2005, A Scanner Darkly, 2006, The Lake House, 2006, Street Kings, 2008, The Day the Earth Stood Still, 2008, The Private Lives of Pippa Lee, 2009, Henry's Crime, 2010, Generation Um..., 2012, 47 Ronin, 2013, The Whole Truth, 2016, The Neon Demon, 2016, The Bad Batch, 2016, To the Bone, 2017, John Wick: Chapter 2, SPF-18, 2017, Replicas, 2018, Siberia, 2018 (TV films) Letting Go, 1985, Act of Vengeance, 1986, Young Again, 1986, Babes in Toyland, 1986, Under the Influence, 1986, Brotherhood of Justice, 1986, Life Under Water, 1989, Children Remember the Holocaust, 1995, (narrator) The Great Warning, 2003; actor, dir.: (films) Man of Tai Chi, 2013, actor, executive prodr.: (films) John Wick, 2014, Knock Knock, 2015; actor, prodr.: (films) Exposed, 2016; prodr.: (documentaries) Side by Side, 2012, Side by Side Extra: Volumes One-Five, 2014 **AW:** Named one of 50 Most Powerful People in Hollywood, Premiere magazine, 2004-06; recipient Star, Hollywood Walk of Fame, 2005

REICH, STEVE, T: Composer **I:** Fine Art **DOB:** 10/03/1936 **PB:** NYC **SPN:** Married Beryl Korot; **CH:** children: Ezra, Michael **ED:** Doctor (hon.), California Institute Arts, 2000; Student, Cantillation of Hebrew Scriptures, New York City and Jerusalem, 1976-77; Student, Am. Society for Eastern Arts, Seattle and Berkeley, 1973-74; Studies in drumming, Institute for African Studies, University Ghana, 1970; MA in Music, Mills College, 1963; Studies with Bergsma and Persichetti, Julliard School Music, 1958-61; Studies in composition with Hall Overton, 1957-58; BA in Philosophy with honors, Cornell University, 1957; Studies in percussion with Roland Kohloff, 1950-53 **C:** Performed throughout the World, 1971-; Recs. with Various Cos. including, Columbia Records, Deutsche Grammophon, Nonesuch, Disques Shandar, Hungaraton, Angel, ECM, Phillips, Virgin Classics, Argo,; Organized Ensemble, Steve Reich and Musicians, 1966 **CR:** Regents Lecturer University California, Berkeley, 2000. **CW:** Composer, performer: (albums) Come Out, 1967, It's Gonna Rain, 1969, Violin Phase, 1969, Four Organs, 1970, Phase Patterns, 1970, Drumming, 1971, Four Organs, 1973, Six Pianos, 1973, Music for Mallet Instruments, Voices, and Organ, 1973, Music for Eighteen Musicians, 1978 (Grammy award 1999), Octet, 1980, Music for a Large Ensemble, 1980,Tehillim, 1982, The Desert Music, 1984, Sextet, 1986, Six Marimbas, 1986, Electric Counterpoint, 1987, Different Trains, 1988 (Grammy award 1989), The Four Sections, 1987, The Cave, 1994, City Life, 1995, Proverb, 1996, Triple Quartet, 1999, Three Tales, 2002, Dance Patterns, 2002, Cello Counterpoint, 2003, You Are, 2004,Variations for Vibes, Pianos and Strings, 2005, Daniel Variations, 2006, Double Sextet, 2007, 2x5, 2008, Mallet Quartet, 2009, WTC 9/11, 2010, Finishing the Hat, 2011, Radio Rewrite, 2012, Quartet, 2013, Pulse, 2015, Runner, 2016 others; recordings include (10 CD boxed set) Steve Reich Works: 1965-1995; composer: Vermont Counterpoint, Variations for Winds, Strings and Keyboards, Eight Lines for Chamber Orchestra, Piano Phase, Clapping Music, Pendulum Music, Music for Pieces of Wood, Nagoya Marimbas, other works performed by major orchestras and ensembles; commissioned to compose for Holland Festival, 1978, Radio Frankfurt, 1979, San Francisco Symphony, 1980, Rothko Chapel, 1981, West German Radio, Cologne, 1984, Fromm Music Foundation, 1985, Richard Stoltzman, 1985, Brooklyn Academy Music, 1987, Kronos Quartet, 1988, St. Louis Symphony, 1987, (with Beryl Korot) The Cave video opera commissioned by Vienna Festival, Holland Festival, Festival d'Automne à Paris, Theatre de la Monnaie, Brussels, Hebbel Theatre, Berlin, South Bank Centre/Serious Speakout, London and the Brooklyn Academy Music, Next Wave Festival, 1993; 4-concert retrospective Lincoln Center Festival, New York City, 1999, video opera (with Beryl Korot) Three Tales, commissioned by Vienna Festival, Barbican Center, London, SPoleto Festival, Brooklyn Academy Music, Music Strassbourg, Hebbel Theater, Berlin(Books) Writings About Music, 1974, Writings on Music, 2002 **AW:** Recipient Koussevitzky Foundation award, 1981, 2002, Schuman prize Columbia University, 2000, Praemium Imperiale award (Music), Japan Art Association, 2006, Polar Music prize, 2007; named Composer of Year, Musical Am., 2000; Rockefeller Foundation grantee 1975, 78, 81, 90, National Endowment for the Arts grantee, 1974, 76, 91, New York State Council Arts grantee, 1974; Guggenheim fellow, 1978, Montgomery fellow Dartmouth College, 2000; elected to Am. Academy Arts and Letters, 1994, Bayerische Akademie der Schönen Künst, 1995; named Commissioner dans l'Ordre des Arts et des Lettres, 1999 **MEM:** Fellow Am. Academy Arts & Scis.

REICHERT, DAVID GEORGE, T: U.S. Representative from Washington **I:** Government Administration/Government Relations/Government Services **DOB:** 08/29/1950 **PB:** Detroit Lakes **SC:** MN/USA **ED:** AA, Concordia Lutheran College, Portland, Oregon, 1970 **C:** Member, U.S. Congress from 8th Washington district, 2005-; Member, Committee on Ways and Mean; Sheriff, King County Sheriff's Department, Washington, 1997-2004; Police officer, King County Sheriff's Department, Washington, 1972-97 **CIV:** Member adv. board, King County Domestic Violence Council, Member adv. board, King County Criminal Justice Council, Co-chmn., Washington State Partners in Crisis, **CW:** Author: Chasing the Devil: My Twenty Year Quest to Capture the Green River Killer, 2004 **AW:** Named Sheriff of Year, National Sheriffs Association, 2004; recipient 2 Medal of Valor awards, King County Sheriff's Office, Champion of Freedom award, Washington Policy Center **MEM:** Mem.: Washington Association Sheriffs & Police Chiefs (member executive board), Washington State Sheriffs Association (past president) **PA:** Republican

REID, HARRY MASON, T: Former U.S. Representative from Nevada **I:** Government Administration/ Government Relations/Government Services **DOB:** 12/02/1939 **PB:** Searchlight, Nevada, December 2, 1939 **SC:** NV/USA **PT:** Son of Harry and Inez Jaynes Reid; **ED:** LLD (hon.), University Southern Utah, 1984; JD, George Washington University, 1964; BS in History & Political Sci., Utah State University, 1961; AS, Southern Utah State University, 1959 **CT:** Bar: Nevada Bar 1963 **C:** Senate Minority Leader, 2015-2017,; US Senator from Nevada, Washington, 1987-2017; Minority leader, 2015-; US Senator from Nevada, Washington, 1987-; Chairman, US Senate Committee on Environment & Public Works, 2001; Chairman, US Senate Select Committee on Ethics, 2001-03; Majority leader, 2007-15; Minority leader, 2004-07; Assistant majority leader (majority whip), 2001-03; Assistant minority leader (minority whip), 2003-05; Assistant minority leader (minority whip), 2001; Assistant minority leader (minority whip), 1999-2001; Member, US Congress from 1st. Nevada District, Washington, 1983-87; Chairman, Nevada Gaming Commission, 1977-81; Lieutenant governor, State of Nevada, 1971-75; Member, Nevada State Assembly, 1969-70; City attorney, City of Henderson, Henderson, Nevada, 1964-66; Police officer, US Capitol, Washington, 1961-64 **CR:**

Chairman US Senate Democratic Conference, 2005- **CIV:** Board trustees, Southern Nevada Memorial Hospital, 1967-69 **CW:** Author: Searchlight: The Camp that Didn't Fail, 1998 **AW:** Named one of The 50 Most Powerful People in DC, GQ magazine, 2009, 2007; recipient TechNet Founders Cir. award, 2005, Pick and Gravel award, Association American State Geologists, 2004, National Landscape Conservation Systems Champion award, NLCS Coalition, 2004, Inspirational Leadership award, Military Order of Purple Heart, 2003, Distinguished Service award, American Public Works Association, 2003, Arthur T. Marix award, Military Officers Association America, 2003, Award of Merit, The Military Coalition, 2002, Modern Language Association award for Distinguished Public Service, 2002, Friend of Zion award, The Jerusalem Fund, 2000, Public Service award, American Foundation Suicide Prevention, 1999, Humanitarian award, National Asthma Center and National Jewish Hospital, 1984 **MEM:** Mem.: Nevada Athletic Commission, National Conference Lieutenant Governors, American Board Trial Advocates, Clark County Bar Association, Nevada Bar Association, American Bar Association **PA:** Democrat **BA:** Office of Harry Reid, 522 Senate Hart Building, Washington, DC, USA, 20510

REIF, L. RAFAEL, **T:** President **I:** Education/Educational Services **CN:** Massachusetts Institute of Technology **DOB:** 08/21/1950 **PB:** Maracaibo **SC:** Venezuela **ED:** PhD, Stanford University, 1979; MS, Stanford University, 1975; BS, Universidad de Carabobo, Venezuela, 1973 **C:** President, Massachusetts Institute of Technology, Cambridge, 2012-; Provost, Massachusetts Institute of Technology, Cambridge, 2005-12; Head Department Electrical Engineering & Computer Sci., Massachusetts Institute of Technology, Cambridge, 2004-05; Associate head electrical engineering, Massachusetts Institute of Technology, Cambridge, 1999-2004; Director Microsystems Tech. Laboratories, Massachusetts Institute of Technology, Cambridge, 1990-99; Professor, Massachusetts Institute of Technology, 1988; Associate professor, Massachusetts Institute of Technology, Cambridge, 1983-88; Assistant professor electrical engineering, Massachusetts Institute of Technology, Cambridge, 1980-83; Assistant professor, Universidad Simon Bolivar, Caracas, Venezuela, 1973-74 **AW:** Recipient Tribeca Disruptive Innovation award, 2012, Aristotle Award, Semiconductor Research Corp., 2000, U.S. Presidential Young Investigator Award, 1984 **MEM:** Fellow, IEEE; mem.: American Physical Society, Electrochemical Society, Tau Beta Pi

REINHARDT, STEPHEN D., **T:** Federal Judge **I:** Law and Legal Services **PB:** New York **SC:** NY/USA **ED:** BA, Pomona College; LLB, Yale College **C:** Judge, U.S. Court of Appeals for the Ninth Circuit, 1980-2018

RENACCI, JIM, **T:** U.S. Representative from Ohio **I:** Government Administration/Government Relations/Government Services **DOB:** 12/03/1958 **PB:** Monongahela **ED:** BS in Business Administration, Ind. University of Pennsylvania, 1980 **CT:** CPA **C:** Member, US House Ways & Means Committee, Washington, 2013-; Member, US Congress from 16th Ohio District, Washington, 2011-; Member, US House Budget Committee, Washington, 2013; Member, US House Financial Services Committee, Washington, 2011-13; CEO, LTC Companies Group, Wadsworth, Ohio, 2003-10; Founder, president, LTC Management Services, Inc., Wadsworth, Ohio, 1985-2003 **CR:** Partial owner minor league baseball team Lancaster JetHawks, California former owner, general manager Arena Football League team Columbus Destroyers, Ohio mayor

City of Wadsworth, 2004-08 president Wadsworth City Council, 1999-2002 appointed Wadsworth Planning Commission, 1999 **CIV:** Member, Wadsworth Board Zoning Appeals, 1993-94 Vol., Wadsworth Vol. Fire Department, 1984-88 **PA:** Republican **BA:** 328 Cannon HOB, Washington, DC, 20515

RENDLE, STEVEN E., **T:** CEO **I:** Apparel & Fashion **CN:** VF Corp **ED:** Bachelor's Degree, Washington University **C:** Chairman, VF Corp. (2017-Present); Chief Executive Officer, VF Corp. (2017-Present); President, Chief Operating Officer (2015-2017); Senior Vice President of the Americas, VF Corp (2014-2015); Vice President, President:Outdoor, VP Corp (2011-2014); President, Outdoor America, VF Corp (2009-2011); President, North Face (2004-2009); VP:Sales, North Face Inc. (1999-2004)

RENTLER, BARBARA J., **T:** CEO of Ross Stores **I:** Business Management/Business Services **C:** President, CEO, Ross Stores, Inc., 2014-; President, chief merchandising officer, Ross Dress for Less, 2009-14; Senior vice president, Ross Dress for Less, 2001-05; General merchandising manager, Ross Dress for Less, 2001-04; Executive vice president, merchandising, Ross Stores, Inc., 2006-09; Executive vice president, Ross Stores, Inc., 2005-06; Chief merchandising officer, dd's Discounts, Ross Stores, Inc., 2004-06; Group divisional merchandise manager, Ross Stores, Inc., 1999-2001; Vice president, divisional merchandise manager, Ross Stores, Inc., 1996-99; Counselor, Ross Stores, Inc., 1993-96; Various merchandising positions, Ross Stores, Inc., 1986-93 **CR:** Board directors Ross Stores, Inc., 2014- **AW:** Named one of The 50 Most Powerful Women in Business, Fortune magazine, 2014-15 **MEM:** Board Membership of Ross Stores, 2014- **BA:** Ross Stores Inc, 5130 Hacienda Dr, Dublin, BC, 94568-7579

RESTREPO, LUIS FELIPE, **T:** Federal Judge **I:** Law and Legal Services **PB:** Medellin **SC:** Colombia **ED:** JD, Tulane University School of Law (1986); BA, University of Pennsylvania (1981); Coursework, George Mason University **C:** Judge, U.S. Court of Appeals for the Third Circuit (2016-Present); Judge, U.S. District Court for the Eastern District of Pennsylvania (2013-2016); Magistrate Judge, U.S. District Court for the Eastern District of Pennsylvania (2006-2013); Partner, Krasner & Restrepo (1993-2006); Assistant Federal Defender, Office of Federal Public Defenders for the Eastern District of Pennsylvania (1990-1993); Assistant Defender, Defender Association of Philadelphia (1987-1990); Law Clerk, National Prison Project (1986-1987) **BA:** 601 Market St, Philadelphia, PA, 19106

REYNOLDS, KIM, **T:** Governor of Iowa **I:** Government Administration/Government Relations/Government Services **DOB:** 08/04/1959 **PB:** Truro **SC:** MA/USA **ED:** Attended Business Administration & Marketing, Northwest Missouri State University, Maryville; Attended, Southwestern Community College **C:** Governor, State of Iowa, 2017-; Lieutenant governor, State of Iowa, Des Moines, 2011-2017; Member District 48, Iowa State Senate, 2008-10; President, Iowa State County Treasurer's Association, 2000; Treasurer, Clarke County, 1994-2008; Member, Iowa Public Employees Retirement System Board, 1996-2001; Formerly with, Clarke County Treasurer's Office,; Pharmacist assistant, **PA:** Republican

REYNOLDS, RYAN, **T:** Actor **I:** Media & Entertainment **PB:** Vancouver **SC:** BC/Canada **PT:** Jim Reynolds; Tammy Reynolds **C:** Actor, 1991- **CW:** Actor: (TV series) Hillside, 1990, The Odyssey, 1993-94, The Outer Limits, 1995-98, Two Guys, a Girl and a Pizza Place, 1998-2001; (films) Ordinary

Magic, 1993, Life During Wartime, 1997, Coming Soon, 1999, Dick, 1999, Big Monster on Campus, 2000, We All Fall Down, 2000, Finder's Fee, 2001, Van Wilder, 2002, Buying the Cow, 2002, The In-Laws, 2003, Foolproof, 2003, Harold & Kumar Go to White Castle, 2004, Blade: Trinity, 2004, The Amityville Horror, 2005, Waiting, 2005, Smokin' Aces, 2006, The Nines, 2007, Chaos Theory, 2007, Definitely, Maybe, 2008, X-Men Origins: Wolverine, 2009, The Proposal, 2009, Buried, 2010, Green Lantern, 2011 (Favorite Movie Superhero, People's Choice Awards, 2012), The Change Up, 2011; actor: (films) Fireflies in the Garden, 2008, Safe House, 2012, The Croods (voice), 2013, Turbo (voice), 2013, R.I.P.D., 2013, The Voices (voice), 2014, The Captive, 2014, Mississippi Grind, 2015, Woman in Gold, 2015, Self/less, 2015, Criminal, 2016; actor, producer (films) Deadpool, 2016; executive prodr.: (documentaries) The Whale, 2011; (TV films) Murder in Manhattan, 2013,(Film) No Good Deed, 2017, Life, 2017, The Hitman's Bodyguard, 2017, Deadpool 2, 2018, Detective Pikachu, 2019 (Television) Scrubs, 2003, Zeroman, 2004, School of Life, 2005, My Boys, 2007, SNL, 2009, Family Guy, 2011, Top Gear, 2012 **AW:** Named Sexiest Man Alive, People Magazine, 2010, Time 100 Most Influential People, 2017, Critics Choice Awards, 2016, Hollywood Walk of Fame, 2017, People's Choice Awards for Favorite Movie Actor, 2017

RHAMES, VING, **T:** Actor **I:** Media & Entertainment **DOB:** 05/12/1961 **PB:** New York City **SC:** NY/USA **ED:** Graduate, Juilliard School of Drama **CW:** Actor, Broadway Plays, "The Winter Boys" (1984); Films, "Native Son" (1986), "Patty Hearst" (1988), "Casualties of War" (1989), "The Long Walk Home" (1990), "Jacob's Ladder" (1990), "Flight of the Intruder" (1991), "Homicide" (1991), "Stop! Or My Mom Will Shoot" (1992), "The People Under the Stairs" (1992), "Dave" (1993), "The Saint of Fort Washington" (1993), "Bound By Honor Blood In Blood Out" (1993), "Pulp Fiction" (1994), "Drop Squad" (1994), "Kiss of Death" (1995), "Ed McBain's 87th Precinct" (1995), "Mission: Impossible" (1996), "Striptease" (1996), "Con Air" (1997), "Rosewood" (1997), "Dangerous Ground" (1997), "The Split" (1998), "Out of Sight" (1998), "Body Count" (1998), "Entrapment" (1999), "Bringing Out the Dead" (1999), "Mission Impossible II" (2000), Voice, "Final Fantasy: The Spirits Within" (2001), "Baby Boy" (2001), Voice, "Lilo & Stitch" (2002), "Dark Blue" (2002), "Undisputed" (2002), Voice, "Stitch! The Movie" (2003), "Back in the Day" (2004), "Dawn of the Dead" (2004), "Mission: Impossible III" (2006), "Idlewild" (2006), "Animal 2" (2007), "I Now Pronounce You Chuck and Larry" (2007), "The Goods: Live Hard, Sell Hard" (2009), "The Bridge to Nowhere" (2009), "Surrogates" (2009), "Piranha 3D" (2010), "Caged Animal" (2010), "Submission" (2010), "Minkow" (2011), "The River Murders" (2011), "Julia X 3D" (2011), "Seven Below" (2012), "Piranha 3DD" (2012), "Soldiers of Fortune" (2012), "Won't Back Down" (2012), "Mafia" (2012), "Armed Response" (2013), "Force of Execution" (2013), "Percentage" (2014), "Jamesy Boy" (2014), "Minkow" (2015), "Operator" (2015), "Mission: Impossible-Rogue Nation" (2015), "A Sunday Horse" (2015), "Father Figures" (2017), "Mission Impossible-Fallout" (2018); TV Films, "Go Tell It On the Mountain (1985), "Rising Son" (1990), "When You Remember Me" (1990), "Amerique en Otage L" (1991), "Terror on Track 9" (1992), "Deadly Whispers" (1995), "Don King: Only in America" (1997), "American Tragedy" (2000), "Holiday Heart" (2000), "Little John" (2002), "RFK" (2002), "Sins of the Father" (2002), "Aquaman" (2007), "Football Wives" (2007), "Zombie Apocalypse" (2011), "Black Jack" (2011), "A Day Late and a Dollar Short" (2014); TV Series, "Another World"

(1986), "Men" (1989), "UC: Undercover" (2001), "The District" (2002-2003), "The System" (2003), "Gravity" (2010); TV Appearances, "Miami Vice" (1985, 1987), "Crime Story" (1986), "Tour of Duty" (1987), "Spenser: For Hire" (1988), "The Equalizer" (1989), "ER" (1994, 1995, 1996), "New York Undercover" (1995), "The District" (2002, 2003), "The Adventures of Jimmy Neutron: Boy Genius" (2003); Actor, Executive Producer, Film, "King of the Avenue" (2010) **AW:** Golden Globe Award for Best Performance by an Actor in a Mini-Series or Motion Picture Made for TV (1998)

RHIMES, SHONDA, T: Television Producer, Director, Writer **I:** Media & Entertainment **DOB:** 01/13/1970 **PB:** Chgo. **ED:** MFA, University Southern California, 1994; BA in English, Dartmouth College, Hanover, New Hampshire, 1991 **CIV:** Trustee, John F. Kennedy Center for the Performing Arts, 2013- Work with, Writers Guild Foundation, Work with, Planned Parenthood, **CW:** (director, writer): (films) Blossoms and Veils, 1998; (writer) Crossroads, 2002; The Princess Diaries 2: Royal Engagement, 2004; (executive producer, writer): (TV series) Grey's Anatomy, 2005-13 (Norman Felton award for Outstanding Producer of Episodic TV - Drama, Producers Guild of America, 2007, National Association for the Advancement of Colored People Image award for Outstanding Writing in Drama Series, 2007, 2008, 2009, Golden Globe award for Best Drama TV Series, 2007); executive producer, writer (TV series) Private Practice, 2007-13 (National Association for the Advancement of Colored People Image award for Outstanding Writing in Drama Series, 2010, 2011), Scandal, 2012-15; executive prodr.: (TV series) How to Get Away with Murder, 2014-, The Catch, 2016, Still Star Crossed, 2017, For the People, 2017; author: (memoir) Year of Yes: How to Dance It Out, Stand In the Sun and Be Your Own Person, 2015 **AW:** Named one of The 100 Most Powerful Women in Entertainment, The Hollywood Reporter, 2009-15, The 50 Most Powerful Women in Business, Fortune magazine, 2013, The 40 Under 40, Advertising Age, 2007, The 100 Most Influential People in the World, TIME magazine, 2013, 2007; named to The Power 150, Ebony magazine, 2008; recipient Norman Lear Achievement award in TV, Producers Guild of America, 2016

RICE, ANNE, T: Writer **I:** Writing and Editing **DOB:** 10/14/1941 **PB:** New Orleans **SC:** LA/USA **PT:** Howard O'Brien; Katherine (Allen) O'Brien **ED:** MA, San Francisco State College, 1971; BA, San Francisco State College, 1964; Student, Texas Woman's University **C:** Writer, 1965- **CW:** Author: (novels) The Feast of All Saints, 1979, Cry to Heaven, 1982, The Mummy, 1989, Servant of the Bones, 1996, Violin, 1997, Christ the Lord: Out of Egypt, 2005, Christ the Lord: The Road to Cana, 2008, Angel Time, 2009, The Wolf Gift, 2012, The Wolves of Midwinter, 2013, (Vampire Chronicles) Interview with the Vampire, 1976, The Vampire Lestat, 1985, The Queen of the Damned, 1988, The Tale of the Body Thief, 1992, Memnoch the Devil, 1995, The Vampire Armand, 1998, Pandora, 1998, Vittorio the Vampire, 1999, Merrick, 2000, Blood and Gold, 2001, Blackwood Farm, 2002, Blood Canticle, 2003, Interview with the Vampire Claudia's Story, 2012, Prince Lestat, 2014, (novels) (Lives of the Mayfair Witches) The Witching Hour, 1990, Lasher, 1993, Taltos, 1994, (under pseudonym Anne Rampling) Exit to Eden, 1985, Belinda, 1986, (under pseudonym A.N. Roquelaure) The Claiming of Sleeping Beauty, 1983, Beauty's Punishment, 1984, Beauty's Release, 1985, (short fiction) October 4, 1948, 1965, (nonfiction) Called Out of Darkness: A Spiritual Confession, 2008,(Books) Prince Lestat and the Realms of Atlantis, 2016,

Beauty's Kingdom, 2015(Short Fiction) Nicholas and Jean, 1966, The Master of Rampling Gate, 1984

RICE, CONDOLEEZZA, T: Political Science Professor, Former U.S. Secretary of State **I:** Education/Educational Services **DOB:** 11/14/1954 **PB:** Birmingham **SC:** AL/USA **PT:** Daughter of John Wesley and Angelena Ray Rice. **ED:** LLD (hon.), Southern Methodist University, 2012; LHD (hon.), Air University, 2008; PhD (hon.), Boston College, 2006; PhD (hon.), Michigan St. University, 2004; PhD (hon.), University of Louisville, 2004; PhD (hon.), Mississippi College School of Law, 2003; PhD (hon.), National Defense University, 2002; PhD (hon.), University of Notre Dame, 1995; PhD (hon.), The University of Alabama, 1994; PhD (hon.), Morehouse College, 1991; MA in Political Sci., University of Notre Dame, 1975; PhD in Political Sci., University of Denver Josef Korbel School International Studies, 1981; BA cum laude in Political Sci., University of Denver, 1974 **C:** College Playoff Football Selection Committee, 2013-; Founding partner, RiceHadleyGates, Washington, DC 2012-; Denning professor global business & economy, Stanford University Graduate School Business, 2010-; Thomas & Barbara Stephenson senior fellow on pub. policy, The Hoover Institution, Stanford, California, 2009-; Professor, Stanford University, 2009-; Principal, The RiceHadley Group, LLC, San Francisco, 2009-12; Senior adv., Regions Financial Corp., Birmingham, Alabama, 2009; Secretary, U.S. Department State, Washington, 2005-09; Assistant to the President for national security affairs, National Security Council, Washington, DC 2001-05; National security consultant, George W. Bush Presidential Campaign, Washington, DC 2000; Senior fellow, The Hoover Institution, Stanford, California, 1999-2001; Senior fellow, The Hoover Institution, Stanford, California, 1991-93; Director to senior director Soviet & East European Affairs, National Security Council, 1989-91; Special assistant to the President for national security affairs, National Security Council, 1989-91; Special assistant to director of the Joint Chiefs of Staff, U.S. Department Defense, Washington, DC 1986; Provost, Stanford University, 1993-99; Professor, Stanford University, 1993-99; Associate professor, Stanford University, 1987-93; Assistant professor political sci., Stanford University, 1981-87; Assistant director Center for International Security & Arms Control, Stanford University, 1981-86; Political sci. consultant, Stanford University, 1980-81; Intern, The Rand Corp., Santa Monica, California, 1978; Intern, Bureau Educational & Cultural Affairs, U.S. Department State, Washington, DC 1977 **CR:** Board of Directors KiOR, inc., 2011-, Charles Schwab Corp., 1999-2001, Transamerica Corp., 1991-2001, Chevron Corp., 1991-2001 **CIV:** Member, College Football Playoff Selection Committee, 2013- Trustee, John F. Kennedy Center for the Performing Arts, 2009-12 **CW:** Author: Uncertain Allegiance: The Soviet Union and the Czechoslovak Army, 1984, Extraordinary, Ordinary People: A Memoir of Family, 2010, No Higher Honor: A Memoir of My Years in Washington, 2011; co-author (with Alexander Dallin): The Gorbachev Era, 1986; co-author: (with Philip Zelikow) Germany Unified and Europe Transformed, 1995 **AW:** Named one of The 50 Highest-Earning Political Figures, Newsweek, 2010, Glamour's Women of the Year, 2008, The 50 Most Powerful People in DC, GQ Magazine, 2007, The Most Influential Black Americans, Ebony magazine, 2006-08, The 10 Most Fascinating People of 2005, Barbara Walters Special, The 100 Most Powerful Women, Forbes magazine, 2005-08, The 100 Most Influential People in the World, TIME magazine, 2007, 2006, 2005, 2004; recipient President award, National Association for the Advancement of Colored People Image Awards, 2002, Walter J.

Gores award for Excellence in Teaching, Stanford University, 1984, Dean's award for Distinguished Teaching, Stanford University School Humanities and Scis., 1993 **MEM:** Fellow: American Association for the Advancement of Science; mem.: Council Foreign Relations, Augusta National Golf Club (One of Two First Female Members Admitted 2012) **PA:** Republican

RICE, JERRY LEE, T: Former NFL Player **I:** Athletics **DOB:** 10/13/1962 **PB:** Starkville **SC:** MI/USA **PT:** Son of Joe Nathan and Eddie Rice; **ED:** Student, Mississippi Valley State University, 1981-84 **C:** NFL analyst, ESPN, 2011-; Co-host Sports Sunday, Station KNTV NBC-TV, San Francisco, 2006-; Retired, NFL, 2006; Wide receiver, Seattle Seahawks, 2004-05; Wide receiver, Oakland Raiders, 2001-04; Wide receiver, San Francisco 49ers, 1985-2000 **CW:** Co-author (with M. Silver): Rice, 1996; co-author: (with Brian Curtis) Go Long!: My Journey Beyond Fame and the Game, 2007; celebrity dancer Dancing With the Stars, 2006; actor: Without a Paddle: Nature's Calling, 2009 **AW:** Named Pro Bowl MVP, NFL, 1995, Super Bowl XXIII MVP, 1989, NFL MVP, Pro Football Writers Association, 1987, Offensive Player of Year, Associated Press, 1993, 1987, First Team All-Pro, 1992-96, 1986-90; named to Pro Football Hall of Fame, 2010, Am. Football Conference Pro Bowl Team, NFL, 2002, National Football Conference Pro Bowl Team, 1998, 1986-96; recipient Bert Bell award, 1987,College Football Hall of Fame, 2006, Top 100 NFL Player, 1999, First Team All-Pro, 1986-90, 1992-1996 **ACH:** Achievements include member of Super Bowl XIX, XXIII, XXIV, XXIX championship winning San Francisco 49ers, 1985, 1989, 1990, 1995; leading the NFL in: receiving yards, 1986, 1989, 1990, 1993-95; recieving touchdowns, 1986, 1987, 1989-1991, 1993; touchdowns, 1987, 1993; receptions, 1990, 1996; holds NFL career records for: receptions, receiving yards, touchdowns, touchdown receptions, yards from scrimmage, all-purpose yards

RICE, KATHLEEN MAURA, T: U.S. Representative from New York, Former Prosecutor **I:** Government Administration/Government Relations/Government Services **DOB:** 02/15/1965 **PB:** Manhattan **SC:** NY/USA **PT:** Daughter of Laurence and Christine Rice. **ED:** JD, Touro Law Center, 1991; BA, Catholic University, 1987 **C:** Mem.-elect, US Congress from 4th New York District, Washington, 2015-; Member, Committee on Homeland Security, Committee on Veterans' Affairs; District attorney, Nassau County, 2013; District attorney, Nassau County, 2009; District attorney, Nassau County, 2005; Assistant US attorney (eastern district) Pennsylvania, US Department Justice, Philadelphia, 1999-2005; Assistant district attorney, Kings County, New York, 1992-99 **CR:** Co-chair Moreland Commission to Investigate Public Corruption, 2013-14 **MEM:** Mem.: DAASNY (president 2013-) **PA:** Democrat **BA:** 1508 Longworth H.O.B. Washington, DC 20515, Washington, DC, 20515

RICE, TOM, T: U.S. Representative from North Carolina **I:** Government Administration/Government Relations/Government Services **DOB:** 08/04/1957 **PB:** Charleston **SC:** SC/USA **PT:** Son of Hugh Thompson and Katherine Louise (Miller) R. **MS:** Married **SPN:** Wrenzie Lee Calhoun, August 7, 1982 **CH:** Hugh Thompson III, Jacob Calhoun, James Lucas **ED:** JD, University South Carolina, 1982; MS, University South Carolina, 1982; BS in Accounting, University South Carolina, 1979 **CT:** Bar: South Carolina 1982; CPA, South Carolina; cert. tax specialist. **C:** Member, US House Transportation & Infrastructure Committee, 2013-; Member, Committee on Ways and Means; Member, US House

Small Business Committee, 2013-; Member, US House Budget Committee, 2013-; Member, US Congress from 7th South Carolina District, Washington, 2013-; Chairman, Horry County Council, 2010-12; Founding partner, Rice & MacDonald Law Firm, 1997-2012; Partner, Van Osdell, Lester, Howe & Rice, P.A., Myrtle Beach, South Carolina, 1984-97; Senior tax consultant, Deloitte Haskins & Sells, Charlotte, North Carolina, 1982-84 **CR:** Adjunct professor accounting University South Carolina, Myrtle Beach, 1985-86. **CIV:** Vol. Brothers and Sisters Community Action, Columbia, South Carolina, 1978-82 member Probate Adv. Board Horry County, 1989- member vestry Episcopalian Church, 1989-92, treasurer capital building fund, 1989-92, finance chairman, 1990-92 board directors YMCA, Myrtle Beach Haven, 1989-, president 1994-. **AW:** Recipient Outstanding Service award Brothers & Sisters Community Action, 1980, 81. **MEM:** Member South Carolina Bar Association (cert. specialist in taxation and estate planning), South Carolina Association CPAs, Sertoma (Gem award 1987, Centurion award 1988, secretary 1988-89, president 1989-90, chairman board directors 1990-91). **PA:** Republican **BA:** 223 Cannon HOB, Washington, DC, 20515

RICHARDS, KEITH, T: Guitarist **I:** Media & Entertainment **DOB:** 12/18/1943 **PB:** Dartford **SC:** Kent, England **PT:** Bert Richards; Doris (Dupree) Richards **MS:** Married **SPN:** Patti Hanson (12/18/1983); Anita Pallenberg **CH:** Marlon; Angela (Dandelion); Tara (Deceased 6/4/1976); Hansen; Theodora; Alexan **ED:** Coursework, Sidcup Art School **C:** Guitarist, The Rolling Stones (1962) **CW:** Guitarist, Albums with The Rolling Stones, "England's Newest Hitmakers: The Rolling Stones" (1964), "12 X 5" (1964), "The Rolling Stones, Now!" (1964), "Out of Our Heads" (1965), "December's Children (And Everybody's)" (1965), "Big Hits, High Tide, & Green Grass" (1966), "Aftermath" (1966), "Got Live If You Want It!" (1966), "Between the Buttons" (1967), "Flowers" (1967), "Their Satanic Majesties Request" (1967), "Beggars Banquet" (1968), "Through the Past, Darkly (Big Hits Vol. II)" (1969), "Let It Bleed" (1969), "Get Yer Ya-Yas Out!: The Rolling Stones in Concert" (1970), "Hot Rocks 1964-1971" (1971), "Sticky Fingers" (1971), "More Hot Rocks: Big Hits and Fazed Cookies" (1972), "Exile on Main Street" (1972), "Goats Head Soup" (1973), "It's Only Rock and Roll" (1974), "Metamorphosis" (1975), "Made in the Shade" (1975), "Rolled Gold+: The Very Best of the Rolling Stones" (1975), "Black and Blue" (1976), "Love You Live" (1977), "Some Girls" (1978), "Emotional Rescue" (1980), "Sucking in the Seventies" (1981), "Tattoo You" (1981), "Still Life, American Concert, 1981" (1982), "Undercover" (1983), "Rewind (1971-1984)" (1984), "Dirty Work" (1986), "Singles Collection: The London Years" (1989), "Steel Wheels" (1989), "Flashpoint" (1991), "Jump Back: The Best of The Rolling Stones" (1993), "Voodoo Lounge" (1994), "Stripped" (1995), "Bridges to Babylon" (1997), "No Security" (1999), "Forty Licks" (2002), "Singles: 1965-1967" (2004), "Live Licks" (2004), "A Bigger Bang" (2005), "Rarities 1971-2003" (2005), "GRRR!" (2012); Soundtracks, "Shine a Light" (2008); Albums with The Rolling Stones & Other Artists, "The Rolling Stones Rock 'N' Roll Circus" (1996); Singer, Guitarist, Solo Albums, "Talk Is Cheap" (1988), "Keith Richards & The X-Pensive Winos Live at the Hollywood Palladium" (1991), "Main Offender" (1992), "Vintage Vinos" (2010), "Crosseyed Heart" (2015); Performer, Films, "Gimme Shelter" (1970), "Sympathy for the Devil" (1970), "Ladies and Gentlemen: The Rolling Stones" (1974), "Let's Spend the Night Together" (1983), "Rolling Stones: Live at the Max" (1991), "Voodoo Lounge" (1994), "The Rolling Stones Rock 'N' Roll Circus" (1996), "The Rolling Stones Bridges to Babylon Tour '97-98" (1997), "Four Flicks" (2003), "The Biggest Bang" (2007), "Shine a Light" (2008), "Some Girls Live in Texas '78" (2011); Performer, Musical Director, Films, "Hail! Hail! Rock & Roll" (1987); Appeared in Documentaries, "25 X 5: The Continuing Adventures of the Rolling Stones" (1989), "Being Mick" (2001), "Stones in Exile" (2010), "Crossfire Hurricane" (2012), "The Rolling Stones: Charlie is My Darling" (2012), "Muscle Shoals" (2013); Actor, Films, "Pirates of the Caribbean: At World's End (2007), "Pirates of the Caribbean: On Stranger Tides" (2011), "Toots and the Maytals: Reggae Got Soul" (2011), "Rolling Stones: One More Shot" (2012), "Keith Richards: Under the Influence" (2015), "Pirates of the Caribbean: Dead Men Tell No Tales" (2017); Co-author, with James Fox, "Life" (2010); Author, with Art by Theodora Richards, "Gus & Me: The Story of My Granddad and My First Guitar" (2014) **AW:** Named to The Rock and Roll Hall of Fame as Member of The Rolling Stones (1989); Greatest Touring Band of All Time, World Music Awards (2006); Ivor Novello Award for Outstanding Contribution to British Music (1991); Grammy Award for Lifetime Achievement (1986); Nordoff Robbins Silver Clef Award (1982); Living Legend Award, International Rock; Grammy Award for Best Rock Album, "Voodoo Lounge" (1994); Spike TV's Best Cameo Award, Pirates of the Caribbean: At World's End (2008); Number One New York Times Bestseller, "Life"; Mailer Prize for Distinguished Biography, "Life" (2011) **BA:** Universal Music Group, 2220 Colorado Ave, Santa Monica, CA, 90404

RICHARDS, THOMAS EDWARD, T: Information Technology Executive, Former Telecommunications Industry Executive **I:** Information Technology and Services **ED:** MS in Management, Massachusetts Institute of Technology, Cambridge; BA in Economics, University Pittsburgh **C:** President, CEO, CDW Corp., 2011-; President, COO, CDW Corp., Vernon Hills, Illinois, 2009-2011; COO, Qwest Communications International, Inc., Denver, 2008-09; Executive vice president, Business Markets Group, Qwest Communications International, Inc., Denver, 2005-08; Chairman, president and CEO, Clear Communications Corp., 1999-2003; Executive vice president, communications & information products, Ameritech, 1995-99; Various management positions, Bell Atlantic, 1983-95; Various management positions, Bell of Pennsylvania, 1976-83 **CR:** Board directors Tele Danmark (TDK), National Alliance Business **CIV:** Member Pittsburgh council, Boy Scouts America, Board directors, Pittsburgh C. of C., Board directors, Pennsylvania Southwest Economic Devel. Association, Board directors, Pennsylvania Economic League, **AW:** Alfred P. Sloan Fellow

RICHIE, LIONEL B. JR., T: Singer, Lyricist, Theater Producer **I:** Media & Entertainment **DOB:** 06/20/1949 **PB:** Tuskegee **SC:** AL/USA **PT:** Lionel Richie; Alberta Richie **ED:** Honorary MusD, Boston College (1986); Honorary MusD, Tuskegee University (1985); BS in Economics, Tuskegee University (1971) **C:** President, Brockman Music, LA **CW:** Member, Group The Mystics (Name Changed to The Commodores) (1969-1981); Writer, Producer, Songs for Commodores Including "Easy," "Three Times a Lady," "Still," "Sail On, Lady"; Songwriter, Producer, Album for Kenny Rogers; Albums with The Commodores Include "Midnight Magic," "Machine Gun," "Movin' On," "Commodores," "Caught in the Act," "Hot on the Tracks," "Natural High," "Heroes"; Solo Albums, "Lionel Richie" (1982), "Can't Slow Down" (1983), "Dancing on the Ceiling" (1986), "Back to Front" (1992), "Louder Than Words" (1996), "Truly-The Love Songs" (1997), "Time" (1998), "Renaissance" (2001), "Just for You" (2004), "Encore" (2004), "Coming Home" (2006), "Sound of the Season" (2006), "Live" (2007), "Live in Paris" (2007), "Icons: Lionel Richie and the Commodores" (2009), "Just Go" (2009), "20th Century Masters - The Millennium Collection" (2011), "Tuskegee" (2012); Producer, Composer, Songs, "Truly," "All Night Long," "Hello," "Say You, Say Me," "Dancing on the Ceiling," Duet with Diana Ross, "Endless Love," Sung by Kenny Rogers, "Lady," With Michael Jackson, "We Are The World" (1985); Performer, "Oh No/All Night Long," with Luke Bryan (2014); Actor, Films, "Scott Joplin" (1977), "Thank God It's Friday" (1978), "Running with the Night" (1990), "The Preacher's Wife" (1996), "Pariah" (1998), Documentary, "Truth or Dare" (1991), TV Appearance, "Who Do You Think You Are?" (2011), "Lionel Richie: Dancing on the Ceiling" (2011), "Oprah Winfrey's Master Class" (2014) **AW:** Best Young Artist in Film Award (1980); Two National Association for the Advancement of Colored People Image Awards (1983); Favorite Male Vocalist Pop/Rock Award, American Music Academy (1987); Favorite Male Vocalist Soul/R&B Award, American Music Academy (1987); Lifetime Achievement Award, San Remo Festival, Italy (1996); Lifetime Achievement Award, World Music Awards; Golden Note Award, American Society of Composers (2008); Star, Hollywood Walk of Fame (2003); Lifetime Achievement Award, BET (2014); Named to Alabama Music Hall of Fame (1997); Named Man of the Year, Children's Diabetes Foundation (1984); Alumnus of the Year, United Negro College Fund (1984); Favorite Male Singer People Magazine Readers Poll (1985); Entertainer of the Year, National Association for the Advancement of Colored People (1987); MusiCares Person of Year, Grammy Awards (2016); Kennedy Center Honours (2017); American Music Award, "Three Times a Lady" (1979); People's Choice Award for Best Song, "Three Times a Lady" (1979); People's Choice Award for Best Song, "Still" (1980); National Music Publishers Award, "Sail On, Lady" (1980, 1981); People's Choice Award for Best Composer, "Sail On, Lady" (1981); Grammy Award for Album of Year, Can't Slow Down" (1985); Grammy Award, "Truly" (1982); Two American Music Awards, "Truly" (1983); People's Choice Award for Best Song, "Truly" (1983); National Music Publishers Award, "All Night Long" (1984); Three Black Gold Awards, "All Night Long" (1984); American Music Award, "All Night Long" (1984); Two American Music Awards, "Hello" (1985); American Society of Composers Pop Award, "Say You, Say Me" (1987); American Music Award, "Say You, Say Me" (1987); Academy Award for Best Song, "Say You, Say Me" (1986); Golden Globe Award for Best Song, "Say You, Say Me" (1986); Three American Music Awards, "Dancing on the Ceiling" (1987); Grammy Award, "Endless Love" (1982); Two American Music Awards, "Endless Love" (1982); American Movie Award, "Endless Love" (1982); Rojo Award, "Endless Love"; Gold Status in Hong Kong, "Endless Love" (1982); People's Choice Award for Best Song, "Endless Love" (1982); Grammy Awards for Best Song, Record of Year, "We Are the World" (1986); People's Choice Award for Best Song, "We Are the World" (1986); Performance of the Year, CMT Music Awards, "Oh No/All Night Long" (2014); Writer of Year, American Society of Composers (1984, 1985, 1986); Publisher of Year, American Society of Composers (1985) **MEM:** American Society of Composers

RICHMOND, CEDRIC, T: Congressman **I:** Government Administration/Government Relations/ Government Services **CN:** U.S. Representative from Louisiana **DOB:** 09/13/1973 **PB:** New Orleans

SC: Louisiana/USA **ED:** BA, Morehouse College, 1995; JD, Tulane University, 1998; Grad. Executive Program, John F. Kennedy School Government Harvard University **C:** Member, US House Small Business Committee, 2011—; Member, US Congress from 2nd Louisiana District, 2011—; Member District 101, Louisiana House of Reps., 2000—2010 **AW:** Named one of The Politics 40 Under 40, TIME Magazine, 2010 **MEM:** Member, Louisiana Bar Association **PA:** Democrat **BA:** US House of Representatives, 240 Cannon House Office Bldg, Washington, DC, 20515

RICKETTS, PETER, T: Governor of Nebraska **I:** Government Administration/Government Relations/Government Services **DOB:** 08/19/1964 **ED:** MBA in Marketing & Finance, University of Chicago; Bachelor in Biology, University of Chicago **C:** Governor, State of Nebraska, 2015-Present; Senior Vice President, Strategy, Business Development, Senior Vice President, Product Development, Senior Vice President, Marketing, TD Ameritrade Holding Corp., 1993-2005; COO, Executive Vice President, Corporate Secretary, President, Private Client Division, TD Ameritrade Holding Corp., 1993-2005; Union Pacific Railroad; Founder, Drakon, LLC **CR:** TD Ameritrade Holding Corp. 2007-Present, Board Chairman, Platte Institute for Economic Research, 2007, Vice Chairman, TD Ameritrade Holding Corp., 1999-2006, Board of Directors, Chicago Cubs Baseball Team, ZNRG, Inc. **CIV:** Board of Directors, Knights of Columbus; Fund for Omaha Committee, Community Health Charities of Nebraska; Gambling with the Good Life member, Trustee, American Enterprise Institute; Board Advisor, Alumni Capital Network; Representative Forum, Nebraska Coalition for Ethical Research; University of Chicago School of Business; Chairman, Children's Scholarship Fund; Omaha President, Board of Directors, Platte Institute for Economic Research, Inc. **PA:** Republican **BA:** Office of the Governor, PO Box 94848, Lincoln, NE, 68509-4848 **ADD:** TD Ameritrade Holding Corporation, 4211 S 102nd Street, Omaha, NE, 68127

RICKS, DAVID A., T: Pharmaceutical Executive **I:** Pharmaceuticals **ED:** MBA, Ind. University, 1996; BA in Business Management, Purdue University, 1990 **C:** Chairman, CEO, Eli Lilly, 2017-; Senior vice president, president Lilly Bio-Medicines, Eli Lilly & Co., 2012-2016; President, Eli Lilly USA, 2009-11; President, general manager, Eli Lilly China, 2008-09; General manager, Eli Lilly Canada, 2005-08; Vice president sales, Eli Lilly Canada, 2004-05; Marketing director, Eli Lilly Canada, 2002-04; District manager, Eli Lilly & Co., 2001-02; Marketing studies manager, Eli Lilly & Co., 1998-2001; Business devel. associate, Eli Lilly & Co., 1996-98; Account rep., IBM Corp., 1991-94; With, Hewlett-Packard Corp., **CR:** Member, Pharmaceutical Research and Manufactures of America, Central Indiana Corporate Partnership. Chairman Riley Children's Foundation Board of Governors. **H:** Jogging, backpacking

RIDENHOUR, CARLTON, T: Rap Musician **I:** Media & Entertainment **CW:** Performer (as member rap group Public Enemy) Yo Bum Rush the Show, 1987, It Takes a Nation of Millions to Hold Us Back, 1988, Fear, 1990, Apocalypse '91...The Enemy Strikes Back, 1991, producer Promised Land; co-author (song) Fight The Power, 1989 (Grammy nomination); Welcome to the Terrordome, 1989; contributor vocals Janet (Janet Jackson), 1993, Branded (Isaac Hayes), 1995; solo album Autobiography of Mistachuck, 1996, Yo! Bum Rush the Show, 1987, It Takes a Nation of Millions to Hold Us Back, 1988, Fear of a Black Planet, 1990, Apocalypse 91... The Enemy Strikes Black, 1991,

Muse Sick-n-Hour Mess Age, 1994, He Got Game, 1998, There's a Poison Goin' On, 1999, Revolverlution, 2002, New Whirl Odor, 2005, How You Sell Soul to a Soulless People Who Sold Their Soul?, 2007, Most of My Heroes Still Don't Appear on No Stamp, 2012, The Evil Empire of Everything, 2012, Man Plans God Laughs, 2015, If I Can't Change the People Around Me I Change the People Around Me, 2016

RIESS, ADAM GUY, T: Astronomer, Educator **I:** Sciences **DOB:** 12/16/1969 **PB:** Washington **ED:** PhD in Astrophysics, Harvard University, 1996; AM in Astrophysics, Harvard University, 1994; BS in Physics, minor in history, Massachusetts Institute of Technology, 1992 **C:** Professor, physics and astronomy, John Hopkins University, 2006-; Full astronomer, Space Telescope Sci. Institute, Baltimore, 2004-; Associate adjunct professor, John Hopkins University, 2002-06; Associate astronomer, Space Telescope Sci. Institute, Baltimore, 2001-04; Assistant astronomer, Space Telescope Sci. Institute, Baltimore, 1999-2001; Miller Fellow, University California, Berkeley, 1996-99; Doctoral student, Harvard University, 1992-96; Research associate, Lawrence Livermore National Laboratory, 1992; Senior thesis student, Massachusetts Institute of Technology, 1991-92; Undergraduate research assistant, Massachusetts Institute of Technology, 1990-92 **CR:** Invited speaker in field co-taught, Hot Topics in Astrophysics, astronomy and physics department John Hopkins University, 2003 teaching fellow, astronomy Harvard University, 1994, 1993 teaching fellow, physics department, The Physics of Sports Massachusetts Institute of Technology, 1992 **CW:** Contributor articles to professional journals; guest appearance Quirks and Quarks, CPR, 1998, News, BBC, 1998, Science Friday, NPR, 1998, 2001, Headline News, CNN, 1998, Jim Lehrer News Hour, PBS, 1998, Sound Prints, NPR, 2000, NOVA, PBS, 2000, 60 Minutes, CBS, 2003, Scientific American Frontiers, PBS, 2004 **AW:** Co-recipient Nobel Prize in Physics, 2011, Shaw prize in Astronomy, Shaw Foundation, Hong Kong, 2006; finalist Innovator award, Discover Magazine, 2003; named one of Twenty under 40, 2008; recipient Einstein medal, 2011, Thomson Reuters Citation Laureate, 2010, Gruber prize in Cosmology, 2007, Townes prize in Cosmology, University California Berkeley, 2005, Raymond and Beverly Sackler prize, Tel-Aviv University, 2004, International Academy of Astronautics, Laurels for Achievement award, 2004, Best and Brightest award, Esquire Magazine, 2003, Helen B. Warner prize, Am. Astronomical Society, 2003, Bok prize, Harvard University, 2001, Innovator award, Time Magazine, 2000, AURA Sci. award, 2000, STSci Sci. Merit award, 2001, 2000, Trumpler award, Astronomical Society of the Pacific, 1999, National Merit Scholar, 1988; Gilman Scholar, John Hopkins University, 2011; MacArthur Fellow, The John D. and Catherine T. MacArthur Foundation, 2008, Kavli Frontier of Sci. fellow, 2007, Harvard GSAS Merit fellow, 1995, Margaret Weyerhaeuser Jewett Memorial fellowship, 1993 **MEM:** Fellow: Am. Academy Arts and Sciences; mem.: National Academy of Sciences, Phi Beta Kappa **ACH:** Achievements include design of Space Shuttle, Leap Frog Toys, children's educational astronomy toy, 1997-98; published the first evidence that the expansion of the Universe was accelerating % filled with Dark Energy, as a result, Science Magazine called this the Breakthrough Discovery of the Year in 1998 **H:** Bicycling, coin collecting/numismatics, home improvement

RIGALI, JUSTIN FRANCIS, T: Cardinal **I:** Religious **CN:** Roman Catholic Church **DOB:** 04/19/1935 **PB:** Los Angeles **SC:** CA/USA **PT:** Son of Henry

Alphonsus and Frances Irene (White) Rigali. **ED:** LHD (hon.), Saint Louis University, 1995; JCL, Pontifical Gregorian University, 1964; JCL, Pontifical Gregorian University, 1963; Bachelor in Sacred Theology, Catholic University America, 1961 **C:** Cardinal-priest, of Santa Prisca, 2003-; Archbishop emeritus, of Philadelphia, 2011-; Elevated to cardinal, 2003; Archbishop, of Philadelphia, Pennsylvania, 2003-11; Archbishop, of Saint Louis, 1994-2003; Secretary, College of Cardinals, 1990-94; Secretary, Congregation of Bishops, 1989-94; Various Vatican posts, 1985-90; Ordained, of Volsinium (Bolsena), 1985; Appointed Titular Archbishop, of Volsinium (Bolsena), 1985; Professor, Pontifical Ecclesiastical Academy, Rome,; President, Pontifical Ecclesiastical Academy, Rome, 1985-89; Magistral chaplain, Order of the Knights of Malta, 1984; Prelate of honor of His Holiness, 1980; Named Papal Chamberlain to Pope Paul VI, 1967; Served as Apostolic Nunciature to, Madagascar, 1966-70; Associate pastor, Pamona, California, 1964; Worked as English translator for Pope Paul VI,; Director English-language department, Secretariat of State, 1970; Entered the English-language department, Secretariat of State, Vatican City, 1964-70; Assistant, Second Vatican Council, 1963-64; Ordained priest, of Los Angeles, 1961 **CR:** Member Administration of the Patrimony of the Apostolic See, Committee Vox Clara, Congregation for Divine Worship and the Discipline of the Sacraments, Congregation for Bishops, 2007- served on various committees for the U.S. Bishops' Conference apostolic administrator of Scranton, 2009-10 **BA:** Archdiocese of Philadelphia, 222 N 17th St, Philadelphia, PA, 19103

RILEY, PATRICK JAMES, T: Professional Sports Team Executive **I:** Business Management/Business Services **DOB:** 03/20/1945 **PB:** Rome **PT:** Son of Leon R.; Married Chris Riley **CH:** James Patrick, Elisabeth Marie. **ED:** Grad., University Kentucky, 1967 **C:** President basketball operations, Miami Heat, 2003-; Head coach, Miami Heat, 2005-08; Head coach, Miami Heat, 1995-2003; Head coach, New York Knicks, 1991-95; Head coach, LA Lakers, 1981-90; Assistant coach, LA Lakers, 1979-81; Guard, LA Lakers, 1970-75; Guard, Phoenix Suns, 1975-76; Guard, San Diego Rockets, 1967-70 **CR:** Broadcaster NBC Sports, 1990-91 broadcaster LA Lakers games Station KLAC and Station KHJ-TV, 1977-79 **CW:** Author: Show Time: Inside the Laker's Breakthrough Season, 1988, The Winner Within: A Life Plan for Team Players, 1993. **AW:** Co-recipient NBA Executive of Year award, NBA, 2011; recipient Chuck Daly Lifetime Achievement award National Basketball Coaches Association, 2012; named NBA Coach of Year, 1990, 93, 97, NBA Executive of Year The Sporting News, 2011; named to Naismith Memorial Basketball Hall of Fame, 2008,Top 10 Coaches in NBA History, NBA All-Star Game Head Coach, 1982, 1983, 1985-1990, 1993, NBA Coach of the Year, 1990,1993, 1997, NBA Champion as Head Coach, 1982, 1985, 1987-88, 2006. NBA Champion, 1980, NBA Champion, 1972 **ACH:** Achievements include head coach of the NBA Finals Championship winning: Los Angeles Lakers, 1982, 85, 87, 88; Miami Heat, 2006

RIORDAN, RICK, T: Writer **I:** Writing and Editing **PB:** San Antonio **SC:** TX/USA **ED:** Graduate, Univ. Texas, Austin **C:** Former English, history teacher, California and Texas, **CW:** Author: (novels) Big Red Tequila, 1997 (Anthony award for best original paperback novel, 1997, Shamus award for best first private eye novel, 1997), Widower's Two-Step, 1998 (Edgar Allen Poe award for best original paperback novel, 1998), Last King of Texas, 2000, Devil Went Down to Austin, 2001, Cold Springs, 2003 (One of top 10 Crime novels, Am.Libr. Association, 2003), South Town, 2004 (Edgar award, 2004, Publishers Weekly Editor's Pick, 2004), Mission Road, 2005, Rebel Island, 2007, (children's books) Percy Jackson & the Olympians: The Lightning Thief, 2005 (New York Times Bestseller, Selected for Al Roker's Book Club for Kids, The Today Show, Best Book of 2005, School Library Journal, New York Times Notable Book of 2005, Best Book of 2005, Child Magazine, Askews Torchlight award (UK), 2006, Chicago Pub. Library Best of the Best Book List, 2005, VoYA Top Shelf Fiction List for 2005, American Library Association Notable Book of 2005, YALSA Best Book for Young Adults, 2005, Red House Children's Book award (UK), 2006, Cooperative Children's Book Center choice award, 2006, National Council for Teachers of English, Notable Children's Book, 2006, Publishers Weekly National Children's Bestseller, Warwickshire Book award (UK), 2007, recipient of several State Library Association Readers' Choice awards, Mark Twain award, 2008, Rebecca Caudill award, 2009), Percy Jackson & the Olympians: The Sea of Monsters, 2006 (New York Times Bestseller, BookSense National Children's Series Bestseller, BookSense Top Ten Summer Pick for 2006, YALSA Best Book for Young Adults, 2007, Best Book of 2006, Child Magazine, Best Fantasy Sequel of 2006, Kirkus Reviews, Barnes & Noble Best Children's Book of 2006, VOYA Top Shelf Fiction Pick for Middle School Readers, 2006, Cooperative Children's Book Center choice award, 2007, Mark Twain award, 2009), Percy Jackson & the Olympians: The Titan's Curse, 2007 (#1 New York Times Children's Series Bestseller, USA Today Bestseller, BookSense Top Ten Summer Pick for 2007, #1 Publishers Weekly Bestseller, Amazon Best Book of 2007), Percy Jackson & the Olympians: The Battle of the Labyrinth, 2008, Percy Jackson & the Olympians: The Last Olympian, 2009 (#1 USA Today Bestseller, #1 Wall Street Journal Bestseller, #1 Los Angeles Times Bestseller, Wyoming Soaring Eagle Book award, 2011), Percy Jackson & the Olympians: The Demigod Files, 2009, Percy Jackson & the Olympians: The Ultimate Guide, 2010, Percy Jackson's Book of Greek Gods, 2014, Kane's Chronicles: The Red Pyramid, 2010 (#1 New York Times Bestseller, School Library Journal Best Book of 2010, Children's Choice Book award: Best Book Grades 5-6 Book of the Year, 2011, Indian Paintbrush award, 2012), Kane's Chronicles: The Throne of Fire, 2011 (#1 New York Times Bestseller, #1 Wall Street Journal Bestseller), Kane's Chronicles: The Serpent's Shadow, 2012, Kane's Chronicles: Survival Guide, 2012, Heroes of Olympus: The Lost Hero, 2010 (#1 on New York Times, USA Today, Wall Street Journal, Indiebound, and UK Bestsellers lists), Heroes of Olympus: The Son of Neptune, 2011 (#1 on New York Times, USA Today and Wall Street Journal Bestsellers lists), Heroes of Olympus: The Mark of Athena, 2012 (Best Fiction Book for Children in Bulgaria, 2013), Heroes of Olympus: The House of Hades, 2013, Heroes of Olympus: The Blood Olympus, 2014, (Magnus Chase and the Gods of Asgard Series) The Swords of Summer, 2015, (short stories) The Demigold Diaries, 2012, (other children's books) 39 Clues: The Maze of Bones,(Books) The Hammer of Thor, 2016, The Ship of the Dead, 2017, Hotel Valhalla: Guide to the Norse Worlds, 2016, The Hidden Oracle, 2016, The Dark Prophecy, 2017, Camp Half-Blood Confidential,2017, The Burning Maze, 2018 **AW:** Named to Texas Institute Letters, 2003; recipient Children's Choice Book awards, Author of the Year, 2011, Milner award, 2011, Indian Paintbrush Award, 2012, Stonewall Book Award for Children's Literature, 2017 **H:** Reading, swimming, guitar, travel

RIPOLL, SHAKIRA, T: Singer **I:** Media & Entertainment **DOB:** 02/02/1977 **PB:** Barranquilla **PT:** Daughter of William Mebarak Chadid and Nidia Ripoll; **CIV:** Member, President's Advisory Commission on Educational Excellence for Hispanics, 2011 Hon. chairman, Global Campaign for Education, Founder, 3 elementary schools, Colombia, Founder, Barefoot Foundation, Founder, Pies Descalzos, 1996 Global Goodwill Ambassador, UNICEF, 2003- **CW:** Singer: (albums) Magia, 1991, Peligro, 1994, Pies descalzos, 1995, The Remixes, 1995, Dónde Están Los Ladrones?, 1998, MTV Unplugged, 2000, Laundry Service, 2001, Grandes éxitos, 2002, Live & Off the Record, 2004, Fijación Oral Vol. 1, 2005 (Latin Pop Album of Year, Billboard Music Awards, 2005, Grammy Award for Best Lation Rock/Alternative Album, 2006, Spanish Album of Year, National Council La Raza ALMA award (American Latin Media Arts), 2006, Latin Pop Album of Year, Billboard Latin Music Awards, 2006, Latin Grammy award for Album of Year, 2006, Latin Grammy award Best Female Pop Vocal Album, 2006), Oral Fixation Vol. 2, 2005, She-Wolf, 2009, Sale el Sol, 2010, Shakira, 2014, EL Dorado, 2017 (songs) La Tortura, 2005 (Latin Song of Year, Billboard Music Awards, 2005, 4 Billboard Latin Music awards: Hot Latin Song, Hot Latin Vocal Duet, Latin Pop Airplay Song for Duo, Latin Ringtone, 2006, Latin Grammy award for Record of Year, 2006, Latin Grammy award for Song of Year, 2006), Hips Don't Lie, 2006 (MTV Video Music award for Best Choreography, 2006, Billboard Latin Music award for Hot Latin Duet of Year, 2007, Favorite Pop Song, People's Choice Awards, 2007), (with Beyonce) Beautiful Liar, 2006 (Best Collaboration, MTV Video Music Awards, 2007); actress: (TV series) El Oasis, 1996; (films) Zootopia (voice), 2016; vocal coach, judge (TV series) The Voice, 2013, Dreamland, 2014, (Film) Zootopia, 2016 **AW:** Chevalier De L'ordre Des Arts et des Lettres, 2012,Hollywood Walk of Fame, 2011, Named Top Latin Artist, Billboard Music Awards, 2012, Favorite Latin Artist, American Music Awards, 2012, Latin Recording Academy Person of Year, Latin Grammy Awards, 2011, Favorite Latin Artist, American Music Awards, 2010, Outstanding Female Musical Performer, National Council La Raza ALMA award (American Latin Media Arts), 2006, Favorite Latin Artist, American Music Awards, 2006, Best Latin Entertainer, International Reggae & World Music Awards, 2006, Latin Pop Album Artist of Year, Billboard Music Awards, 2005, Favorite Latin Music Artist, American Music Awards, 2005, Best Latin Female Artist, World Music Awards, 2003, Best Female Pop Artist, Billboard Latin Music Awards, 1999, Best Latin Artist, World Music Awards, 1998; named one of The 100 Most Powerful Women, Forbes magazine, 2012-14; recipient 'Chevalier De L'Ordre des Arts et des Lettres medal, 2012, Star, Hollywood Walk of Fame, 2011, Humanitarian award, ALMA Awards, 2008, Spirit of Hope award, Billboard Latin Music Awards, 2006, Best Female award, MTV Europe Awards, 2005, Luna award for Best Latin Pop Artist, 2003, Echo award for Best Female Pop Artist, 2003, Nickelodeon Kids Choice award, 2000, Gardel award, 2000, Casandra award for Best Latin Female Singer, 1997, Eres award for Pop Singer of Year, 1997

RISCH, JIM, T: U.S. Senator from Idaho **I:** Government Administration/Government Relations/Government Services **DOB:** 05/03/1943 **PB:** Milwaukee **SC:** WI/USA **PT:** Son of Elroy A. and Helen B. (Levi) R.; Married Vicki L. Choborda, June 8, 1968; children: James E., Jason S., Jordan D. **ED:** JD, University Idaho, 1968; BS in Forestry, University Idaho, 1965 **C:** Chairmen, Senate Small Business Committee, 2017; Member, US Senate Joint Economic Committee, 2009-; Member, US Senate Select Committee on Intelligence, 2009-; Member, US Senate Select Committee on Ethics, 2009-; Member, US Senate Energy & National Resources Committee, 2009-; Member, US Senate Foreign Relations Committee, 2009-; US Senator from Idaho, 2009-; Partner, Risch Goss & Insinger, Boise, 1975-; Governor, State of Idaho, Boise, 2006-07; Lieutenant governor, State of Idaho, Boise, 2007-09; Lieutenant governor, State of Idaho, Boise, 2003-06; Ind. counsel to Governor, State of Idaho, Boise, 1996; President pro tempore, Idaho State Senate, Boise, 1983-88; Majority leader, Idaho State Senate, Boise, 1997-2002; Majority leader, Idaho State Senate, Boise, 1977-82; Member District 18, Idaho State Senate, Boise, 1995-2002; Member District 18, Idaho State Senate, Boise, 1974-88; Prosecuting attorney, Ada County, Idaho, 1971-75; Chief deputy prosecuting attorney, Ada County, Idaho, 1969-70; Deputy prosecuting attorney, Ada County, Idaho, 1968-69 **CR:** Professor law Boise State University, 1972-75. **CIV:** Board directors National District Attorneys Association, 1973,, Idaho Co., 1992-94, State Legis. Leaders Foundation, 2002 chairman board directors American Trailer Manufacturing Co., 1995- president Idaho Pros. Attorneys, 1970-74 chairman George Bush Presidential Campaign, Idaho, 1988 general counsel Idaho Republican Party, 1991-2002. **MEM:** Member American Bar Association, Idaho Bar Association, Boise Bar Association, Ducks Unlimited, National Rifle Association, National Cattlemans Association, Idaho Cattlemans Association, American Angus Association, Idaho Angus Association, American Legislative Exchange Council, Boise Valley Angus Association, Phi Delta Theta, Xi Sigma Pi **H:** Hunting, fishing, skiing **PA:** Republican **BA:** Office of James Risch, U.S. Senate R SR-483, Washington, DC, 20510

RITCHIE, ROBERT (KID ROCK), T: Singer **I:** Media & Entertainment **DOB:** 06/13/1905 **PB:** Romeo, **SC:** Romeo, **PT:** Son of William and Susan Ritchie; **CW:** Singer: (albums) Grits Sandwiches for Breakfast, 1990, The Polyfuze Method, 1993, Early Mornin' Stoned Pimp, 1996, Devil Without a Cause, 1998, The History of Rock, 2000, Cocky, 2001, Kid Rock, 2003, Live Trucker, 2006, Rock N Roll Jesus, 2007, Born Free, 2010, Rebel Soul, 2012, First Kiss, 2015, Sweet Southern Sugar, 2017, (songs) All Summer Long, 2007 (People's Choice award for Best Rock Song, 2009, CMT Music award for Wide Open Country Video of Year, 2009); actor: (films) Joe Dirt, 2001, (voice) Osmosis Jones, 2001, Biker Boyz, 2003, (voice): (TV series) Stripperella, 2003, (guest appearance) Stacked, 2005, CSI: New York, 2006 **AW:** Recipient World's Best Pop/Rock Male Artist award, World Music Awards, 2008, World's Best Pop Male Artist award, 2008

RIVERA, CHITA, T: Actress, Singer, Dancer **I:** Media & Entertainment **PB:** Washington **SC:** DC/USA **PT:** Pedro Julio Figuerva del Rivero **SPN:** Anthony Mordente (div.) **ED:** Attended, School America Ballet, New York City **C:** Actress 1952- **CW:** Broadway debut: Call Me Madam, 1952; appeared on stage in: Guys and Dolls, Can-Can, Seventh Heaven, Mister Wonderful, West Side Story, Father's Day, Bye Bye Birdie, Three Penny Opera, Flower Drum Song, Zorba, Sweet Charity, Born Yesterday, Jacques Brel is Alive and Well and Living in Paris, Sondheim-A Musical Tribute, Kiss Me Kate, Ivanhoe, Chicago, Bring Back Birdie, Merlin, Jerry's Girls, 1985, The Rink, 1984 (Tony award best actress in a musical, Drama Desk award for outstanding actress in a musical), Can-Can, 1988, Kiss of the Spider Woman (Tony award best actress in a musical, Drama Desk award outstanding actress in a musical), 1993, Nine, 2003, The Dancer's Life, 2005, The Mystery of Edwin Drood, 2012, Ring Them Bell!, 2013, Chita: A Legendary Celebration,2013; performs in cabarets and nightclubs around world; starred in: film Sweet Charity, 1969; cameo appearance in the movie version of Chicago, 2002; numerous TV appearances include Kojak and the Marcus Nelson Murders, 1973, The New Dick Van Dyke Show, 1973-74, Kennedy Center Tonight-Broadway to Washington!, Pippin, 1982, The Mayflower Madam, 1987, Sammy Davis Jr.'s 60th Birthday Celebration, 1990, Ira Gershwin at 100: A Celebration at Carnegie Hall, 1997, Venecia, 2001, Anything Goes, 2000, The Visit, 2001, Will & Grace, 2005, Submissions Only, 2011. **AW:** Recipient Presidential Medal of Freedom, The White House, 2009, Rolex Dance award, Career Transition for Dancers, 2006, Kennedy Center Honor, 2002, Ellis Island Medal of Honor, 2000 **MEM:** Member American Federation of TV and Radio Artists, Screen Actors Guild, Actors Equity Association **ACH:** Achievements include first Hispanic woman to recieve a Kennedy Center Honors award

RIVERA, GERALDO, T: Attorney, Reporter, Author **I:** Media & Entertainment **DOB:** 07/04/1943 **PB:** Brooklyn **SC:** NY/USA **PT:** Son of Cruz and Lillian (Friedman) Rivera; **ED:** JD, Brooklyn Law School, 1969; BS, University Arizona, 1965 **C:** Host radio talk show Geraldo Show, WABC (AM), New York City, 2012-; Host Geraldo at Large, Fox News Channel, 2005-; Special corr., Fox News Channel, 2001-; Host Upfront Tonight, CNBC, New Jersey, 1998-2000; Host Rivera Live,, CNBC, 1994-2001; Reporter, NBC, 1997-2001; Host syndicated talk show, The Geraldo Rivera show, 1987-98; Corr., senior producer 20/20, ABC-TV, 1978-85; Corr., host Good Night America, ABC-TV, 1975-77; Reporter Good Morning America, ABC-TV, 1973-76; Reporter Eyewitness News,, WABC-TV, New York City, 1970-75; Member anti-poverty neighborhood law firms, Harlem Assertion Rights & Community Action Legal Services, New York City, 1968-70 **CW:** Author: (nonfiction) Willowbrook, 1972, Miguel Robles - So Far, 1973, A Special Kind of Courage: Profiles of Young Americans, 1977, Exposing Myself, 1992, HisPanic: Why Americans Fear Hispanics in the US, 2008, The Great Progression: How Hispanics Will Lead America to a New Era of Prosperity, 2009; contestant Celebrity Apprentice, 2015 **AW:** Recipient George Foster Peabody award, 7 Emmy awards, 2 Scripps Howard Journalism awards, Robert F. Kennedy journalism award, 2000, 1975, 1973 **MEM:** Mem.: Tau Delta Phi

RIVERS, DOC, T: Professional Basketball Coach **I:** Athletics **CN:** Los Angeles Clippers **DOB:** 10/13/1961 **PB:** Maywood **SC:** IL/USA **PT:** Grady Alexander Rivers, Betty Rivers **ED:** BA in Pre-Law & Political Science, Marquette University, 1985; Student, Marquette University, 1980-1983 **C:** Head Coach, President, Basketball Operations, Los Angeles Clippers, 2014-Present; Head Coach, Senior Vice President, Basketball Operations, Los Angeles Clippers, 2013-2014; Head Coach, Boston Celtics, 2004-2013; Sports Analyst, ABC Sports, 2003-2004; Head Coach, Orlando Magic, 1999-2003; Sports Analyst, Turner Sports, 1996-1999; Player, San Antonio Spurs, 1994-1996; Player, New York Knicks, 1992-1994; Player, Los Angeles Clippers, 1991-1992; Player, Atlanta Hawks, 1983-1991 **CR:** Assistant Coach, U.S.A. Men's Basketball Team, Goodwill Games, Brisbane, Australia, 2001 **AW:** NBA All-Star Game Head Coach, 2011, Male Coach of the Year, Rainbow Sports Awards, 2000, Head Coach, Eastern Conference, All-Star Team, NBA, 2008, Coach of the Year, 2000, J. Walter Kennedy Basketball Citizenship Award, Pro Basketball Writers, 1990, NBA All-Star Team, 1988, USA Basketball Male Athlete of the Year, 1982 **ACH:** Achievements include coaching the NBA Champion Boston Celtics, 2008 **BA:** Staples Center, 1111 S Figueroa Street, Los Angeles, CA, 90015

ROBBIE, MARGOT, T: Actress **I:** Media & Entertainment **PB:** Dalby **SC:** QLD/Australia **PT:** Sarie Kessler **ED:** Degree, Somerset College, Mudgeeraba, Gold Coast, Australia **C:** Actress, 2008- **CW:** Actress: (films) Vigilante, 2008, About Time, 2013, The Wolf of Wall Street, 2013, Suite Française, 2014, Z for Zachariah, 2015, Focus, 2015, Whiskey Tango Foxtrot, 2016, The Legend of Tarzan, 2016, Suicide Squad, 2016(People's Choice Awards Favorite Action Movie Actress, 2017, Critics Choice Award, Best Actress in an Action Movie, 2017)(; (TV series) Neighbours, 2008-11, Pan Am, 2011-12; actress, associate producer (films) I.C.U., 2009, actress, producer Terminal, 2016, (Film) I, Tonya, 2017, Goodbye Christopher Robin, 2017, Peter Rabbit, 2018, Mary Queen of Scots, 2018, Terminal, 2018, Dreamland, 2018 (Television) Top Gear, 2015, Neighbors 30th: The Stars Reunite, 2015, SNL, 2016 **AW:** Time 100 Most Influential, 2017

ROBBINS, CHUCK, T: Cisco CEO **I:** Business Management/Business Services **ED:** BS in Mathematical Sciences, University North Carolina, Chapel Hill, 1987 **C:** CEO, Cisco Systems, Inc., 2015-; Senior vice president, Worldwide Field Operations, Cisco Systems, Inc., 2012-15; Senior vice president, Americas, Cisco Systems, Inc., 2011-12; Senior vice president, US Enterprise, Commercial & Canada, Cisco Systems, Inc., 2009-11; Senior vice president, US Commercial, Cisco Systems, Inc., 2007-09; Segment vice president, US Channel Sales, Cisco Systems, Inc., 2005-07; Vice president, US Channel Sales, Cisco Systems, Inc., 2002-05; Operations director, US Channels Sales, Cisco Systems, Inc., 1999-2002; Regional manager, Cisco Systems, Inc., 1998-99; Accountant manager, Cisco Systems, Inc., 1997-98; Sales, Ascend Communications, 1996-97; Sales, Wellfleet Communications, 1992-96; Applications developer, NCNB, North Carolina, 1987-92 **CR:** Board directors Cisco Systems, Inc., 2016- **CIV:** Member Georgia Tech. Adv. Board for the President of Georgia Tech, Board member, MS Society of Northern California,

ROBBINS, TIM, T: Actor, Film Director, Scriptwriter **I:** Media & Entertainment **PB:** West Covina **SC:** CA/USA **PT:** Gil Robbins; Mary Robbins **CH:** Miles Guthrie; John Henry; Eva Maria (Stepchild) **ED:** BA with honors, UCLA, 1981 **C:** Founder, artistic director, The Actor's Gang, 1981 **CW:** Actor: (films) No Small Affair, 1984, Toy Soldiers, 1984, Fraternity Vacation, 1985, The Sure Thing, 1985, Howard the Duck, 1986, Top Gun, 1986, Five Corners, 1987, Bill Durham, 1988, Tapeheads, 1989, Eric The Viking, 1989, Miss Firecracker, 1989, Cadillac Man, 1990, Twister, 1990, Jacob's Ladder, 1990, Jungle Fever, 1991, The Player, 1992, Short Cuts, 1993, The Hudsucker Proxy, 1994, The Shawshank Redemption, 1994, Ready to Wear (Prêt-à-Porter), 1994, I.Q., 1994, Nothing to Lose, 1997, Arlington Road, 1999, Austin Powers: The Spy Who Shagged Me, 1999, Mission to Mars, 2000, High Fidelity, 2000, Antitrust, 2001, Human Nature, 2001, The Truth About Charlie, 2002, The Day My God Died (voice), 2003, Mystic River, 2003 (Golden Globe award for Best Supporting Actor in a Drama, 2004, Screen Actors Guild award for Best Supporting Actor, 2004, Academy Award for Best Supporting Actor in a Drama, 2004), Code 46, 2004, Anchorman: The Legend of Ron Burgundy, 2004, War of the Worlds, 2005, The Secret Life of Words, 2005, Zathura: A Space Adventure, 2005, Catch a Fire, 2006, Tenacious D: The Pick of Destiny, 2006, The Lucky Ones, 2008, City of Ember, 2008, Green Lantern, 2011, Thanks for Sharing, 2012, Back to 1942, 2012, Life of Crime, 2013, Welcome to Me, 2014, A Perfect Day, 2015, Majoriee Prime, 2017; (TV films) Quarterback Princess, 1983, Malice in Won-

derland, 1985, Cinema Verite, 2011; (TV series) The Brink, 2015-; (TV Mini-Series) The Spoils of Babylon, 2014; (TV appearances) St. Elsewhere, 1982, Legmen, 1984, Hardcastle and McCormick, 1984, Hill Street Blues, 1984, Moonlighting, 1985, Amazing Stories, 1986, (voice) The Simpsons, 1999, Jack & Bobby, 2005, Portlandia, 2012, The Spoils Before Dying,2015, The Brink, 2015, Here and Now, 2018; actor, director, writer, composer: (films) Bob Roberts, 1992; director, writer, prodr.: (films) Dead Man Walking, 1995, The Cradle Will Rock, 1999; executive prodr.: (films) The Typewriter, the Rifle, and the Movie Camera, 1994, The Spectre of Hope, 2000; dir.: (plays) Ubu Roi, A Midsummer's Night Dream, Methusalem, the Eternal Bourgeois, The Good Woman of Setzuan and others, (TV series) Queen's Supreme, 2003; co-writer: (plays) Alagazam...After the Dog Wars, Violence: The Misadventures of Spike Spangle, Farmer, Carnage, a Comedy, Embedded, and others; musician: (albums) Tim Robbins & The Rogues Gallery Band, 2010 **AW:** Recipient Star on Hollywood Walk of Fame, 2008, Tribute to Ind. Vision Award, Sundance Film Festival, 1997

ROBERTS, BRIAN, T: CEO **I:** Technology **CN:** Comcast Corp. **DOB:** 05/28/1959 **PB:** Philadelphia **SC:** PA/USA **ED:** BS, University of Pennsylvania (1981) **C:** Chairman, President, Chief Executive, Officer, Comcast Corp. (2004—Present); President, Chief Executive Officer, Comcast Corp. (1997—2004); President, Comcast Corp. (1992—1997); Executive Vice President, Comcast Corp. (1986-1992); Vice President of Operations, Comcast Cable Communications, Inc., Philadelphia, PA (1985-1986) **CR:** Board of Directors, The Bank of New York; Board of Trustees, Simon Wiesenthal Center; Founding Co-chair, Philadelphia (2000); Director, Executive Committee CableLabs (1999); Chairman, Board Director, CableLabs **CIV:** Vice Chairman, The Walter Katz Foundation **AW:** Named One of America's Top CEOs, Institute Investor Magazine (2004—2007); Named One of the Most Influential People in the World of Sports, Business Week (2007); Named One of 50 Most Influential People in Sports Business, Street & Smith's SportsBusiness Journal (2009); Named to Cable TV Hall of Fame (2006); Steven J. Ross Humanitarian Award, UJA Federation of New York (2003); Humanitarian Award, Simon Wiesenthal Center (2004); Business People of the Year, Fortune Magazine (2010); All-American Squash Athlete, Silver Medal with U.S. Team (1981, 1985, 1997) **MEM:** Chairman, National Cable & Telecommunications Association (1995—1996, 2005—Present) **H:** Squash **BA:** Comcast Corp, Fl 35 East Twr 1500 Market St Fl 33, Philadelphia, PA, 19102

ROBERTS, JOHN GLOVER JR., T: Associate Justice of the U.S. Supreme Court **I:** Law and Legal Services **DOB:** 01/27/1955 **PB:** Buffalo **SC:** NY/USA **PT:** Son of John Glover and Rosemary (Podrasky) Roberts; **ED:** JD magna cum laude, Harvard Law School, 1979; AB in History summa cum laude, Harvard University, 1976 **CT:** Bar: US Court Appeals (3rd, 7th , and 10th circuits) 1996, US Court Appeals (DC, 5th and 9th circuits) 1988, US Supreme Court 1987, US Court Appeals (federal circuit) 1982, US Court Claims 1982, DC 1981 **C:** Chief justice, US Supreme Court, Washington, 2005-; Judge, US Court Appeals (DC Cir.), Washington, 2003-05; Principal deputy solicitor general, US Department Justice, Washington, 1989-93; Partner, Hogan & Hartson, LLP, Washington, 1993-2003; Partner, Hogan & Hartson, LLP, Washington, 1988-89; Associate, Hogan & Hartson, LLP, Washington, 1986-87; Associate counsel to President Ronald Reagan, The White House, Washington, 1982-86; Special assistant to US Attorney General William French Smith, US Department Justice, Washington, 1981-82; Law clerk to Associate Justice William H. Rehnquist, US Supreme Court, Washington, 1980-81; Law clerk to Honorable Henry Friendly, US Court Appeals (2nd cir.), New York City, 1979-80 **AW:** Named one of The World's Most Powerful People, Forbes magazine, 2012-14, 2009, The 50 Most Powerful People in DC, GQ magazine, 2009, The 100 Most Influential People in the World, TIME magazine, 2007, 2006; recipient Bowdoin Prize for Best Dissertation in the English Language, Harvard University, 1976 **MEM:** Fellow: American Academy Arts & Sciences; mem.: Supreme Court Historical Society, Edward Coke Appellate Inn of Court, American Academy Appellate Lawyers, American Law Institute, Robert Trent Jones Golf Club, Metropolitan Club, Lawyers Club, Phi Beta Kappa **PA:** Republican **BA:** Supreme Court of the U.S., 1 First St NE, Washington, DC, 20453

ROBERTS, JULIA, T: Actress **I:** Media & Entertainment **DOB:** 10/28/1967 **PB:** Smyrna **SC:** GA/ USA **CR:** Global Ambassador, Lancôme, 2010 **CIV:** UNICEF **CW:** Actress, (Films) Blood Red, 1986, Satisfaction, 1987, Mystic Pizza, 1988, Steel Magnolias, 1989, Pretty Woman, 1990, Flatliners, 1990, Sleeping With The Enemy, 1991, Hook, 1991, Dying Young, 1991, The Player, 1992, The Pelican Brief, 1993, I Love Trouble, 1994, Ready To Wear (Prêt-À-Porter), 1994, Something To Talk About, 1995, Mary Reilly, 1996, Everybody Says I Love You, 1996, Michael Collins, 1996, My Best Friend's Wedding, 1997, Conspiracy Theory, 1997, Stepmom, 1998, Notting Hill, 1999, Runaway Bride, 1999, Erin Brockovich, 2000, The Mexican, 2001, America's Sweethearts, 2001, Ocean's Eleven, 2001, Full Frontal, 2002, Confessions Of A Dangerous Mind, 2002, Mona Lisa Smile, 2003, Closer, 2004, Ocean's Twelve, 2004, (Voice Actress) The Ant Bully, 2006, (Voice Actress) Charlotte's Web, 2006, Charlie Wilson's War, 2007, Fireflies In The Garden, 2008, Duplicity, 2009, Valentine's Day, 2010, Eat Pray Love, 2010, Larry Crowne, 2011, (Voice Actress) Love, Wedding, Marriage, 2011, Mirror Mirror, 2012, August: Osage County, 2013, Secret In Their Eyes, 2015, Mother's Day, 2016, Money Monster, 2016, Smurfs: The Lost Village, 2017, Wonder, 2017, (Broadway Plays) Three Days Of Rain, 2006, (TV Films) Baja Oklahoma, 1988, The Normal Heart, 2014; Executive Producer, (TV Films) An American Girl Holiday, 2004, An American Girl Adventure, 2005, (Films) Kit Kittredge: An American Girl, 2008, Jesus Henry Christ, 2012, (Documentaries) Extraordinary Moms, 2011; Narrator, (TV Special) Before Your Eyes: Angelie's Secret, 1995, TV Appearances, Crime Story, 1987, Miami Vice, 1988, Friends, 1996, Murphy Brown, 1998, Sesame Street, 1998, AFI's 100 Years...100 Movies, 1998, In The Wild, 1998, Law & Order, 1999, Silent Angels: The Rett Syndrome Story, 2000, Queens Supreme, 2003, Freedom: A History Of U.S., 2003, Beslan: Three Days In September, 2006, Molly: An American Girl On The Home Front, 2007, Extraordinary Moms, 2011, Makers: Woman Who Make America, 2014, The Normal Heart, 2014, Running Wild With Bear Grylls, 2017 **AW:** American Cinematheque Award, 2007, 100 Most Powerful Celebrities, Forbes.com, 2007, 50 Most Powerful People In Hollywood, Premiere Magazine, 2002—2006, 25 Most Intriguing People, 2001, Academy Award For Best Actress, Golden Globe Award For Best Actress, Screen Actors Guild Award For Outstanding Performance By A Female Actor In A Leading Role, BAFTA Award For Best Performance By An Actress In A Leading Role, Erin Brockovich, 2001, 50 Most Beautiful People (USA), 2000, 2002, National Board Review Arad For Best Actress, Erin

Brockovich, 2000, Special International Star of the Year Award, Showest Convention, 1998, Woman of the Year Award, Hasty Pudding Theatricals, 1997, Favorite Dramatic Motion Picture Actress, 1994, Favorite Comedy/Dramatic Motion Picture Actress, 1992, Favorite Motion Picture Actress, People's Choice Awards, 1991, 1998, Female Star of the Year, National Association of Theatre Owners, 1991, Golden Globe Award For Best Actress, Pretty Woman, 1991, 50 Most Beautiful People In The World, People Magazine, 1990-1991, Golden Globe Award For Best Supporting Actress, Steel Magnolias, 1990 **BA:** Hirsch Wallerstein Matlof and Fishman LLP, 10100 Santa Monica Boulevard, Los Angeles, CA, 90067

ROBERTS, MICHELE A., T: Lawyer, Union Leader **I:** Law and Legal Services **DOB:** 09/14/1956 **PB:** NYC **ED:** JD, Boalt Hall School Law, University California, Berkeley, 1980; BA, Wesleyan University, 1977 **CT:** Bar: Washington DC 1980 **C:** executive director, National Basketball Players Association, 2014-; Partner litigation group, Skadden, Arps, Slate, Meagher & Flom LLP, Washington, 2011-2014; Partner civil/white collar litigation, Akin Gump Strauss Hauer & Feld LLP, Washington, 2004-11; Partner, Shea & Gardner, 2001-04; Partner, Rochon & Roberts, 1992-2001; Attorney, Pub. Defender Service, Washington, 1986-92 **CR:** Member DC Adv. Commission Sentencing past instructor National Institute Trial Advocacy former adj. faculty George Washington University School Law adj. faculty Harvard Law School **AW:** Named one of Top Litig. Trial Lawyers, Chambers Global, 2011, Chambers USA, 2010, Washington's 10 Leading Criminal Defense Lawyers, Legal Times, 2006, America's Top Black Lawyers, Black Enterprise Magazine, 2003, The 100 Most Powerful Women in DC, Washingtonian magazine, 2009, Washingtonian's Big Guns: Top 30 Lawyers in DC, 2007, Washington's Top 75 Lawyers, 2004, 2002 **MEM:** Fellow: American College Trial Lawyers; mem.: American Bar Association, National Association Criminal Defense Lawyers, National Bar Association, DC Bar **BA:** NBA Player's Association, 1133 6th Ave, New York, NY, 10036

ROBERTS, NORA, T: Writer **I:** Media & Entertainment **DOB:** 10/10/1950 **PB:** Silver Spring **SC:** Maryland **C:** Writer 1981- **CW:** Author: (novels) Blithe Images, 1982, Song of the West, 1982, Search for Love, 1982, Island of Flowers, 1982, The Heart's Victory, 1982, From This Day, 1983, Her Mother's Keeper, 1983, Once More with Feeling, 1983, Tonight and Always, 1983, Untamed, 1983, This Magic Moment, 1983, Endings & Beginnings, 1984, Storm Warning, 1984, Promise Me Tomorrow, 1984, Sullivan's Woman, 1984, First Impression, 1984, A Matter of Choice, 1984, Less of a Stranger, 1984, The Law is a Lady, 1984, Rules of the Game, 1984, Opposites Attract, 1984, The Right Path, 1985, Partners, 1985, Night Moves, 1985, Boundary Lines, 1985, Dual Image, 1985, The Art of Deception, 1986, Treasures Lost, Treasures Found, 1986, Risky Business, 1986, A Will and a Way, 1986, Home for Christmas, 1986, Mind Over Matter, 1987, Hot Ice, 1987, Temptation, 1987, Local Hero, 1988, The Name of the Game, 1988, Sweet Revenge, 1988, Impulse, 1989, Gabriel's Angel, 1989, The Welcoming, 1989, Public Secrets, 1990, Genuine Lies, 1991, Carnal Innocence, 1991, Unfinished Business, 1992, Honest Illusions, 1992, Divine Evil, 1992, Private Scandals, 1993, The Best Mistake, 1994, Hidden Riches, 1994, All I Want for Christmas, 1994, True Betrayals, 1995, Montana Sky, 1996, Sanctuary, 1997, Homeport, 1998, The Reef, 1998, River's End, 1999, Carolina Moon, 2000, The Villa, 2001, Midnight Bayou, 2001, Three Fates, 2002, Birthright, 2003, Northern Lights, 2004, Blue

Smoke, 2005 (Quill award for romance, 2007), Angels Fall, 2006 (Quill award for romance, 2006, Quill award for Book of Year, 2006), High Noon, 2007, Tribute, 2008 (Quill award for romance), Black Hills, 2009, The Search, 2010, Chasing Fire, 2011, The Witness, 2012, Whiskey Beach, 2013, The Collector, 2014, The Liar, 2015, Stars of Fortune, 2015, (under pseudonym J.D. Robb) Naked in Death, 1995, Glory in Death, 1995, Immortal in Death, 1996, Rapture in Death, 1996, Ceremony in Death, 1997, Vengeance in Death, 1997, Holiday in Death, 1998, Conspiracy in Death, 1999, Loyalty in Death, 1999, Witness in Death, 2000, Judgment in Death, 2000, Betrayal in Death, 2001, Seduction in Death, 2001, Reunion in Death, 2002, Purity in Death, 2002, Portrait in Death, 2003, Imitation in Death, 2003, Divided in Death, 2004, Visions in Death, 2004, Survivor in Death, 2005, Origin in Death, 2005, Memory in Death, 2006, Born in Death, 2006, Innocent in Death, 2007, Creation in Death, 2007, Strangers in Death, 2008, Salvation in Death, 2008, Promises in Death, 2009, Kindred in Death, 2009, Fantasy in Death, 2010, Indulgence in Death, 2010, Treachery in Death, 2011, New York to Dallas, 2011, Celebrity in Death, 2012, Delusion in Death, 2012, Calculated in Death, 2013, Thankless in Death, 2013, Concealed in Death, 2014, Festive In Death, 2014, Obsession in Death, 2015, Devoted In Death, 2015, Silent Night, "Midnight in Death", 1998, Out of This World, "Interlude in Death", 2001, Bump in the Night, "Haunted in Death", 2006, Dead of Night, "Eternity in Death", 2007, Suite 606, "Ritual in Death", 2008, The Lost, "Missing in Death", 2009, The Other Side, "Possession in DeaTh", 2010; : The Unquiet, "Chaos in Death", 2011, Mirror, Mirror, "Taken in Death", 2013, Down the Rabbit Hole," Wonderment in Death", 2015, Apprentice in Death, 2016, Echos in Death, 2017, Secrets in Death, 2017, Dark in Death, 2018 Leverage in Death,2018(Best Laid Plans, Lawless) Loving Jack, 1989, (Loving Jack, Lawless) Best Laid Plans, 1989, (Loving Jack/ Best Laid Plans) Lawless, 1989, (Times Change) Time Was, 1989, (Time Was) Times Change, 1990, (Born in Trilogy Series) Born in Fire, 1994, Born in Ice, 1995, Born in Shame, 1996, (Dream Trilogy Series) Reflections, 1983, Daring to Dream, 1996, Holding the Dream, 1997, Finding the Dream, 1997, (Key Trilogy Series) Key of Light, 2003, Key of Knowledge, 2003, Key of Valor, 2004, (The Guardian Trilogy) Stars of Fortune, 2015, Bay of Sighs, 2016, Island of Glass, 2016 (In the Garden Trilogy Series) Blue Dahlia, 2004, Black Rose, 2005, Red Lily, 2005, (The Circle Trilogy Series) Morrigan's Cross, 2006, Dance of the Gods, 2006, Valley of Silence, 2006, (Chronicles of the One) Year One, 2017, Of Blood and Bone, 2018(The Sign of Seven Trilogy Series) Blood Brothers, 2007, The Hollow, 2008, The Pagan Stone, 2008, (Inn BoonsBoro Trilogy Series) The Next Always, 2011, The Last Boyfriend, 2012, The Perfect Hope, 2012, (The MacGregors) Playing the Odds, 1985, Tempting Fate, 1985, All the Possibilities, 1985, One Man's Art, 1985, For Now, Forever, 1987, Rebellion, 1988, In From the Cold, 1990, The MacGregor Brides, 1997, The Winning Hand, 1998, The MacGregor Grooms, 1998, The Perfect Neighbor, 1999, (The O'Hurleys) The Last Honest Woman, 1988, Dance the Piper, 1988, Skin Deep, 1988, Without a Trace, 1990, (The Stanislaskis) Taming Natasha, 1990, Luring a Lady, 1991, Falling for Rachel, 1993, (songs) Convincing Alex, 1994, Waiting for Nick, 1997, Considering Kate, 2001, (The Calhoun Women) Courting Catherine, 1991, A Man for Amanda **AW:** Named one of The World's Most Influential People, TIME magazine, 2007; recipient Lifetime Achievement award, Waldenbooks, 1991 **MEM:** Mem.: Novelists, Inc., Crime League America, Sisters in Crime, Mystery Writers America, Romance Writers America (charter member Washington chapter, 7 Golden Medallion awards 1983—89, 14 RITA awards 1992—2006, Lifetime Achievement award 1997, Centennial award, Hall of Fame inductee) **ACH:** Achievements include having 124 out of over 150 novels ranked on the New York Times bestseller list, including 29 that debuted in the number-one spot for a combined 90 weeks; over 280 million copies of her books are in print, having been published in 35 countries **BA:** GP Putnams Sons, 375 Hudson St, New York, NY, 10014

ROBERTS, PAT, T: U.S. Senator from Kansas **I:** Government Administration/Government Relations/Government Services **DOB:** 04/20/1936 **PB:** Topeka **SC:** KS/USA **MS:** Married **SPN:** Frankie Fann (1969) **CH:** David; Ashleigh; Anne-Wesley **ED:** BA in Journalism, Kansas State University (1958) **C:** Chairman, Senate Agricultural Committee (2015-Present); US Senator from Kansas, Washington, DC (1997-Present); Chairman, US Senate Select Committee on Intelligence, Washington, DC (2003-2007); Chairman, US Senate Select Committee on Ethics, Washington, DC (2001); Chairman, US Senate Select Committee on Ethics, Washington, DC (1999-2001); Chairman, US House Agricultural Committee, Washington, DC (1995-1997); Member, US Congress from the First Kansas District, Washington, DC (1981-1997); Administrative Assistant to Representative Keith Sebelius, US House of Representatives, Washington, DC (1968-1980); Administrative Assistant to Senator Frank Carlson, US Senate, Washington, DC (1967-1968); Public, Litchfield Park, AZ (1962-1967) **MIL:** Served, U.S. Marine Corps (1958-1962) **AW:** John H. Chafee Award for Public Service, Republican Main Street Partnership (2003); Public Service Award, American Chemical Society (2001); Wheat Man of the Year, Association of Wheat Growers (1993); Distinguished Service Award, Kansas Farm Bureau; Distinguished Leadership Award, Production Credit Association; American Farmer Award, Future Farmers of America (1986) **PA:** Republican

ROBERTS, ROBIN RENÉ, I: Media & Entertainment **DOB:** 11/23/1960 **PB:** Pass Christian **SC:** MS/USA **PT:** Daughter of Lawrence and Lucimarian Roberts **ED:** BA in Communications, cum laude, Southeastern Louisiana University, 1983 **C:** Co-anchor, Good Morning America, ABC News, 2005-; Host Wide World of Sports, ABC News, 1996-98; Featured Reporter, News Anchor, Good Morning America, ABC News, New York City, 1995-2005; Reporter, Interviewer, Anchor, SportsCenter, ESPN, Bristol, Connecticut, 1990-2005; Sports Anchor, Reporter, WAGA-TV, Atlanta, 1988-90; Sports Anchor, Reporter, WSMV-TV, Nashville, 1986-88; Sports Anchor, Reporter, WLOX-TV, Biloxi, Mississippi, 1984-86; Sports Anchor, Reporter, WDAM-TV, Hattiesburg, Mississippi, 1983-84; Sports Director, WHMD/WFPR Radio, Hammond, Louisiana, 1980-83 **CR:** Host, Academy Awards Pre-show, ABC, 2011, 2009, Appointed FIFA Women's World Cup Adv. Board, 1999 **CW:** Author: From the Heart: Seven Rules to Live By, 2007; Co-author (with Lucimarian Roberts): My Story, My Song, 2012; Co-author: (with Veronica Chambers) Everybody's Got Something, 2014 **AW:** Named a Louisiana Legend, Louisiana Pub. Broadcasting, 2001; Named Journalist of Year, Ebony magazine, 2002; Named one of The 10 Most Fascinating People of 2013, Barbara Walters Special, The 50 Most Powerful Women in New York City, New York Post, 2008, Most Intriguing People in College Basketball, Basketball Times, 1997; Named to Women's Institute Sport & Education Foundation Hall of Fame, 1994; Recipient Walter Cronkite Award for Excellence in Journalism, 2014, 3 Emmy Awards for Sportscasting, Mel Greenberg Media

Award, Women's Basketball Coaches Association, 2001, Excellence in Sports Journalism Award, Center Study of Sport in Society, Northeastern University, 1993, TV Award of Merit, Daughters of the American Revolution, 1990

ROBERTSON, OSCAR, T: Former NBA Player **I:** Athletics **DOB:** 11/24/1938 **PB:** Charlotte **SC:** Tennessee **ED:** BS in Business, University Cincinnati, 1960; LHD (hon.), University Cincinnati, 2007; LHD (hon.), Ind. University, Kokomo, 1994 **C:** Founder, President, CEO, Oscar Robertson Document Management Solutions, LLC, Cincinnati, Ohio, 1997—; Founder, President, CEO, Orflex Ltd., Cincinnati, Ohio, 1995—; Founder, President, CEO, Orpack-Stone Corp., Herrin, Illinois, 1990—; Founder, President, CEO, Orchem, Inc., Fairfield, Ohio, 1981—; General Partner, Oscar Robertson Media Ventures, El Cerrito, California; Guard, Forward, Milwaukee Bucks, 1970-74; Guard, Forward, Cincinnati Royals, 1960-70 **CR:** Member US Men's Basketball Team Summer Olympic Games, Rome, 1960; President NBA Players Association, 1965—1974; Interim Head Basketball Coach University Cincinnati Bearcats, 2004 **AW:** Recipient Gold Medal, men's basketball Summer Olympic Games, 1960, Sports Legacy Award National Civil Rights Museum, William Howard Taft medal Univ. Cincinnati, Lifetime Achievement Award for Entrepreneurship, University Cincinnati College Business Entrepreneurship Center, National Pathfinder Award, Ind. Sports Corp., Ohio Governor's award, Northrop award Boys Club New York, Cincinnati Red, White & Blue award, Greater Cincinnati YMCA Character award, Asian Basketball Confedn. award, Lifetime Achievement award Applause Magazine, Tree of Life award Jewish National Federation; named Sporting News College Player of Year, 1958-60, 1st Team NCAA All-Am. Associated Press, 1958-60, NBA Rookie of Year, 1961, 1st Team All-NBA, 1961-69, NBA All-Star Game MVP, 1961, 64, 69, NBA MVP, 1964, Player of Century National Association Basketball Coaches, 2000; named to Eastern Conference All-Star Team NBA, 1961-72, NBA 35th Anniversary All-Star Team, 1980, Naismith Memorial Basketball Hall of Fame, 1979, NBA 50th Anniversary All-Star Team, 1996, National Collegiate Basketball Hall of Fame, 2006, International Basketball Federation Hall of Fame, 2009., Ind. & Ohio Basketball Halls of Fame, Wisconsin Sports Hall of Fame, National HS Sports Hall of Fame, Naismith Basketball Hall of Fame, 2010 **MEM:** Mem.: National Basketball Retired Players Association (co-founder 1992, president 1992—98) **ACH:** Achievements include leading the NBA in: assists, 1961, 1962, 1964-66, 1969; assists per game, 1961, 1962, 1964-66, 1968, 1969; free throws made, 1964, 1965, 1968, 1969; free throw percentage, 1964, 1968; points per game, 1968; member of NBA championship winning Milwaukee Bucks, 1971

ROBINSON, DAVID, T: Drummer **I:** Media & Entertainment **PB:** Malden **SC:** MA/USA **CW:** Album with The Cars, "The Cars" (1978), "Candy-O" (1979), "Panorama" (1980), "Shake it Up" (1981), "Heartbeat City" (1984), "Door to Door" (1987), "Move Like This" (2011) **AW:** Inductee, Rock & Roll Hall of Fame (2018)

ROBINSON, DAVID MAURICE, T: Former NBA Player **I:** Athletics **DOB:** 08/06/1965 **PB:** Key West **SC:** FL/USA **ED:** BS in Mathematics, US Naval Academy, Annapolis, Maryland, 1987 **C:** Retired, NBA, 2003; Center, San Antonio Spurs, 1989-2003; Commissioned Ensign, U.S. Navy, 1987-89 **CR:** Member, US Olympic Basketball Team, 1996, 1992, 1988 **CIV:** Founder, Patron, The Carver Academy, San Antonio, 1997-, Founder, David Robinson

Foundation, San Antonio, 1992- **AW:** Named NBA Most Valuable Player, 1995, NBA Defensive Player of Year, 1992, 1st Team All-NBA, 1996, 1995, 1992, 1991, NBA Rookie of Year, 1990, College Player of Year, Sporting News, 1987, 1st Team All-Am., 1987, 1986; Named One of America's Best Leaders, US News & World Report, 2009; Named to Naismith Memorial Basketball Hall of Fame, 2009, Western Conference All-Star Team, NBA, 2001, 2000, 1998, 1990-96; Recipient, Gold Medal, Men's Basketball, Atlanta Olympic Games, 1996, Barcelona Olympic Games, 1992, Bronze Medal, Men's Basketball, Seoul Olympic Games, 1988, Wooden Award, 1987, Naismith Award, 1987, Children's Champion Award, 2011, William E Simon Prize for Philanthropic Leadership, 2003, Founder, Carvery Academy, 2001, 2012 NCAA Silver Anniversary Award, Sports Illustrated Sportsman of the Year, 2003, NBA Sportsmanship Award, 2001 **ACH:** Achievements include leading the NBA in: rebounds, 1991, 1996; blocks, 1991, 1992; free throws, 1994-96; scoring, 1994; member of the NBA Championship winning San Antonio Spurs, 1999, 2003 **BA:** Admiral Capital Group, 1150 N Loop 1604 West, Suite 108-505, San Antonio, TX, 78248

ROBINSON, FRANK, T: Major League Baseball Executive, Former Professional Baseball Manager, Retired Professional Baseball **I:** Athletics **DOB:** 08/31/1935 **PB:** Beaumont **PT:** Son of Frank and Ruth (Shaw) R.; Married Barbara Ann Cole, October 28, 1961; children: Frank Kevin, Nichelle **ED:** Student, Xavier University, Cincinnati **C:** Analyst, ESPN, 2007; Special Advisor for Baseball Operations, 2007-2009; Special Assistant to Bud Selig, 2009-2010; Executive Vice President of Baseball Development/ Honorary American League President, 2015-; Senior adv. to commissioner, Major League Baseball, 2011-; Senior vice president major league operations, Major League Baseball, 2010-11; Special assistant to executive vice president baseball operations, special assistant to the commissioner, Major League Baseball, 2006-10; Manager, Washington Nationals (formerly Montreal Expos), 2002-06; Vice president on-field operations, Major League Baseball, 1999-2002; Director baseball operations Arizona Fall League, Major League Baseball, 1997-99; Batting coach, Milwaukee Brewers, 1984; Manager, San Francisco Giants, 1981-84; Manager, Cleveland Indians, 1975-77; Assistant to general manager, Baltimore Orioles, 1991-95; Manager, Baltimore Orioles, 1988-91; Coach, Baltimore Orioles, 1978-80, 85-87; Coach, California Angels, 1977; Outfielder, Cleveland Indians, 1974-76; Outfielder, California Angels, 1973-74; Outfielder, L.A. Dodgers, 1972; Outfielder, Baltimore Orioles, 1966-71; Outfielder, Cincinnati Reds, 1956-65 **CW:** Author: (with Al Silverman) My Life is Baseball, 1967, (with Barry Steinbach) Extra Innings, 1989, Frank the First Year, 1976 **AW:** Named National League Rookie of Year, 1956, National League MVP, 1961, American League MVP, 1966, Major League Player of Year The Sporting News, 1966, World Series MVP, 1966, American League Manager of Year, 1982, 89; named to The National League All-Star Team, 1956-57, 1959, 1961, 1962, 1965, American League All-Star Team, 1966, 1967, 1969-71, 1974, The Baseball Hall of Fame, 1982; recipient Babe Ruth award, 1966, Presidential Medal of Freedom, The White House, 2005, Beacon of Life award Major League Baseball, 2008 **ACH:** Achievements include leading the National League in: runs, 1956, 1962, slugging percentage, 1960-62; on-base percentage, doubles, 1962; leading the American League in: batting average, on-base percentage, slugging percentage, runs, home runs, runs batted in, 1966; member of World Series championship winning Baltimore Orioles, 1966, 1970; winning the

American League Triple Crown in batting (league leader in batting average, home runs and runs batted in), 1966; the only player in Major League Baseball history named Most Valuable Player in both the National and American Leagues, 1961 and 1966 **BA:** Major League Baseball, 245 Park Avenue, New York, NY, 10167

ROBINSON, LORI, T: Commander of USNORTH-COM and NORAD **I:** Military & Defense Services **PB:** Big Spring **SC:** Texas **ED:** Bachelor of Arts in English, University of New Hampshire, 1981; Master of Arts in Education Leadership and Management, Troy State University, 1992; Master's Degree in National Security and Strategic Studies, College of Naval Command and Staff, Naval War College, 1995 **C:** Commander, USNORTHCOM and NORAD, 2016- **MIL:** Second Lieutenant May 24, 1981; First Lieutenant September 11, 1983; Captain September 11, 1985; Major January 1, 1994; Lieutenant Colonel July 1, 1998; Colonel August 1, 2002; Brigadier General July 22, 2008; Major General May, 2011; Lieutenant General May 20, 2013; General October 16, 2014 **AW:** Time 100 Most Influential, 2016 **BA:** Peterson Air Force Base, NORAD, Colorado Springs, CO, 0

ROBINSON, MARILYNNE, I: Writing and Editing **DOB:** 11/26/1943 **PB:** Sandpoint **SC:** ID/USA **PT:** John J. Summers; Ellen (Harris) Summers **ED:** PhD in English Lit., University Washington, 1977; BA, Brown University, 1966 **C:** Member faculty Writer's Workshop, University Iowa, 1991 **CR:** Speaker in field visiting professor University Massachusetts MFA Progressive Poets & Writers, University Kent, England, Amherst College, Massachusetts **CW:** Author: (novels) Housekeeping, 1981 (Hemingway Found./PEN award, 1981), Gilead, 2004 (National Book Critics Cir. prize for fiction, 2004, Pulitzer Prize for fiction, 2005, Ambassador Book award, 2005, Publishers Weekly bestseller, Home, 2008 (LA Times Book prize, 2008, one of the New York Times 100 Notable Books of 2008, Orange prize for fiction, 2009), Lila, 2014, (non-fiction) Mother Country: Britain, the Welfare State and Nuclear Pollution, 1989, The Death of Adam: Essays on Modern Thought, 1998, Absence of Mind: The Dispelling of Inwardness from the Modern Myth of the Self, 2010, When I Was a Child I Read Books, 2012 **AW:** Recipient, National Humanities Medal, National Endowment for the Arts, 2012, Richard & Hinda Rosenthal award, American Academy of Arts and Letters, Mildred & Howard Strauss Living award, 1998

ROBO, JAMES L., T: Chairman, President, and CEO of Nextera Energy Inc. **I:** Business Management/Business Services **ED:** MBA, Harvard Business School; BA summa cum laude, Harvard College **C:** Chairman, CEO, President, Nextera Energy Inc, 2013-; Chairman, CEO, Florida Power and Light Company, 2012-; President, CEO, NextEra Energy, 2012-13.; President, COO, NextEra Energy, Inc. (formerly FPL Group, Inc.), Juno Beach, Florida, 2010-2012; President, COO, FPL Group, Inc., Juno Beach, Florida, 2006-08; Vice president corp. devel. and strategy, FPL Group, Inc., Juno Beach, Florida, 2002-06; President, FPL Energy, LLC, 2002-06; President, CEO Capital TIP/Modular Space, General Electric Co.,; Various positions including general manager distribution operations GE Lighting, general manager Six Sigma GE Lighting, president and CEO GE Mexico, General Electric Co.,; Vice president, Strategic Planning Associates **CR:** Board directors J.B. Hunt Transport Services, Inc., Lowell, Arkansas, 2003- **MEM:** Mem.: Phi Beta Kappa **BA:** NextEra Energy Inc, 700 Universe Blvd, Juno Beach, FL, 33408-0420

ROBY, MARTHA DUBINA, T: U.S. Representative from Alabama **I:** Government Administration/Government Relations/Government Services **DOB:** 07/26/1976 **PB:** Montgomery **ED:** JD, Samford University, Birmingham, Alabama, 2001; BA in Music, New York University, New York City, 1988 **C:** Member, U.S. House Select Committee on the Events Surrounding the 2012 Terrorist Attack in Benghazi, 2014-; Member, U.S. House Armed Services Committee, 2011-; Member, U.S. House Education & Workforce Committee, 2011-; Member, U.S. House Agricultural Committee, 2011-; Member, U.S. Congress from 2nd Alabama District, 2011-; Member, District 7, Montgomery City Council, 2003-10; Attorney, Copeland, Franco, Screws & Gill, **CIV:** Board director, Sav-A-Life Montgomery, Member executive board, Montgomery Weed & Seed, Member, Montgomery Area Business Committee for the Arts, **MEM:** Mem.: Alabama Bar Association, Mississippi Bar Association, Cleveland Ave. YMCA, Britton YMCA **PA:** Republican

ROCK, CHRIS, T: Comedian **I:** Media & Entertainment **DOB:** 02/07/1965 **PB:** Brooklyn **SC:** NY/USA **PT:** Julius Rock; Rosalie (Tingman) Rock **C:** Actor (1985-Present) **CW:** Actor, Films, "Beverly Hills Cop II" (1987), "I'm Gonna Git You Sucka" (1988), "New Jack City" (1991), "Boomerang" (1992), "Panther" (1995), "The Immortals" (1995), "Sergeant Bilko" (1996), "Beverly Hills Ninja" (1997), Voice Actor, "Doctor Dolittle" (1998), "Lethal Weapon 4" (1998), "Dogma" (1999), "Torrance Rises" (1999), "Spin Doctor" (1999), "Nurse Betty" (2000), Voice Actor, "Artificial Intelligence" (2001), "Pootie Tang" (2001), Voice Actor, "Osmosis Jones" (2001), "Jay and Silent Bob Strike Back" (2001), "Bad Company" (2002), "Paparazzi" (2004), Voice Actor, "Madagascar" (2005), "The Longest Yard" (2005), Voice Actor, "Bee Movie" (2007), "You Don't Mess with the Zohan" (2008), Voice Actor, "Madagascar: Escape 2 Africa" (2008), "Good Hair" (2009), "Death at a Funeral" (2010), "Grown Ups" (2010), "2 Days in New York" (2011), "What to Expect When You're Expecting" (2012), Voice Actor, "Madagascar 3: Europe's Most Wanted" (2012), "Grown Ups 2" (2013); Actor, Writer, Director, Films, "I Think I Love My Wife" (2007), "Top Five" (2014); Actor, Writer, Executive Producer, Film, "Down to Earth" (2001); Actor, Director, Producer, Films, "Head of State" (2003); Actor, Writer, Producer, with Nelson George, "CB4" (1993); Actor, TV Series, "Saturday Night Live" (1990-1993), "Def Comedy Jam" (1992), "In Living Color" (1993-1994); TV Appearances, "Miami Vice" (1987), "The Fresh Prince of Bel-Air" (1995), "Martin" (1996), "Homicide: Life on the Street" (1996), Voice Actor, "King of the Hill" (1998), "Chappelle's Show" (2003); Actor, Writer, Executive Producer, TV Series, "The Chris Rock Show" (1997-2000), "Everybody Hates Chris" (2005-2009); Executive Producer, TV Series, "The Hughleys" (1998), "Totally Biased with W. Kamau Bell" (2012-2013); Writer, Executive Producer, Comedy Specials, "Chris Rock: Big Ass Jokes" (1993), "Chris Rock: Bring the Pain" (1996), "Chris Rock: Bigger and Blacker" (1999), "Chris Rock: Never Scared" (2004), "Chris Rock: Kill the Messenger" (2008), Writer, Producer, "Best of Chris Rock" (1999); Narrator, "Whatever Happened to Michael Ray?" (2000); Performer, Comedy Albums, "Born Suspect" (1991), "Roll with the New" (1997), "Bigger & Blacker" (1999), "Never Scared" (2004); Author, "Rock This!" (1998); Film, "A Very Murray Christmas" (2015), "Sandy Wexler" (2017), "The Week of" (2018), Television, "Louie" (2011), "Tosh.0" (2012), "A.N.T. Farm" (2013), "Real Husbands of Hollywood" (2013), "SNL" (2014), "Broad City" (2015), "Empire" (2015), "The Jim Gaffigan Show" (2015), Host, 88th Academy Awards (2016) **AW:** Named One of the 100 Most Influential People in the World, TIME Magazine (2008); Star, Hollywood Walk of Fame (2003); Spotlight Award, National Board Review (2014); Emmy for Outstanding Writing for a Variety or Music Program (1998); Emmy Award for Outstanding Variety, Music or Comedy Special; American Comedy Award for Funniest Male Performer in a TV Special (2000); Grammy Award for Best Comedy Album (2006); Grammy Award for Best Spoken Comedy Album (1997); Grammy Award for Best Spoken Comedy Album (1999)

ROCKWELL, SAM, T: Actor **I:** Media & Entertainment **PB:** Daly City **SC:** CA/USA **PT:** Pete Rockwell; Penny Hess **CW:** Actor: (films) Clownhouse, 1989, Last Exit to Brooklyn, 1989, Teenage Mutant Ninja Turtles, 1990, Strictly Business, 1991, Jack and His Friends, 1992, In the Soup, 1992, Light Sleeper, 1992, Happy Hell Night, 1992, Somebody to Love, 1994, The Search for One-eye Jimmy, 1994, Drunks, 1995, Glory Daze, 1995, Mercy, 1995, Bad Liver & a Broken Heart, 1996, Basquiat, 1996, Box of Moon Light, 1996, Arresting Gena, 1997, Lawn Dogs, 1997, The Call Back, 1998, Jerry and Tom, 1998, Louis & Frank, 1998, Safe Men, 1998, Celebrity, 1998, A Midsummer Night's Dream, 1999, The Green Mile, 1999, Galaxy Quest, 1999, Charlie's Angels, 2000, D.C. Smalls, 2001, Pretzel, 2001, Big Love, 2001, Made, 2001, Heist, 2001, 13 Moons, 2002, Running Time, 2002, Welcome to Collinwood, 2002, Confessions of a Dangerous Mind, 2002, Matchstick Men, 2003, Piccadilly Jim, 2004, The Hitchhiker's Guide to the Galaxy, 2005, The F Word, 2005, Robin's Big Date, 2005, Joshua, 2007, Snow Angels, 2007, The Assassination of Jesse James by the Coward Robert Ford, 2007, Woman in Burka, 2008, Choke, 2008, Frost/Nixon, 2008, Moon, 2009, (voice) G-Force, 2009, Gentlemen Broncos, 2009, Everybody's Fine, 2009, Iron Man 2, 2010, Conviction, 2010, Cowboys & Aliens, 2011, The Sitter, 2011, Seven Psychopaths, 2012, The Way, Way Back, 2013, Trust Me, 2013, A Case of You, 2013, Laggies, 2014, Better Living Through Chemistry, 2014, Poltergeist, 2015, Mr. Right, 2015, The Dark of Night, 2017, Three Billboards Outside Ebbing, Missouri, 2017,(Golden Globe Award for Best Supporting Actor, 2017)(Screen Actors Guild Award for Best Supporting Actor), (Academy Award for Best Supporting Actor), Woman Walks Ahead, 2017, Blaze, 2018, Mute, 2018, Blue Iguana, 2018, The Best of Enemies, 2018, Backseat, 2018; (TV series) Law & Order, 1992-93, Prince Street, 1997-2000, F is for Family, 2015, Inside Amy Schumer, 2016, Saturday Night Live, 2018; (TV films) Subway Stories: Tales from the Underground, 1997; actor, executive producer (films) The Winning Season, 2009, A Single Shot, 2013, Loitering with Intent, 2014, Don Verdean, 2015; executive prodr.: (films) Life at These Speeds, 2016

RODGERS, AARON CHARLES, T: Professional Football Player **I:** Athletics **DOB:** 12/02/1983 **PB:** Chico **PT:** Son of Edward Wesley and Darla Leigh (Pittman) Rodgers **ED:** Student in American studies, University California, Berkeley, 2003-05; Attended, Butte College, Oroville, California, 2002-03 **C:** Quarterback, Green Bay Packers, 2005 **AW:** Named Male Athlete of Year, Associated Press, 2011, FedEx Air & Ground Players of the Year, 2015, FedEx Air NFL Player of Year, 2010, 1st Team NFL All-Pro, 2014, 2011, NFL MVP, Associated Press, 2015, 2011, Super Bowl XLV MVP, NFL, 2010, Holiday Bowl MVP, 2002; named to The National Football Conference Pro Bowl Team, NFL, 2014, 2011-12, 2009; recipient Bart Starr Man of Year award, 2014, Good Guy award, Pro Football Writers of America, 2011,Pro Bowl, 2009, 2011,

2012, 2014-16, Super Bowl Champion XLV, NFL Passing Touchdown Leader, 2016,NFL MVP, 2011, 2014, First Team All-Pro, 2011, 2014, Second Team All-Pro, 2012, Bert Bell Award, 2011 **ACH:** Achievements include member of Super Bowl XLV championship winning Green Bay Packers, 2010

RODRIGUEZ, ALEX, T: Former MLB Player **I:** Athletics **DOB:** 07/27/1975 **PB:** New York City **SC:** NY/USA **PT:** Son of Victor Rodriguez and Lourdes Navarro; **C:** Special Adviser, New York Yankees, 2016-; Third Baseman, New York Yankees, 2004-16; Shortstop, Texas Rangers, 2001-03; Shortstop, Seattle Mariners, 1994-2000 **CR:** Guest Analyst, ALCS and World Series Fox Sports, 2015 Member Dominican Republic National Team World Baseball Classic, 2009, Member U.S. National Team, 2006 **CIV:** Founder, Alex Rodriguez Foundation, 1998- Founder, Grand Slam for Kids, 1996- **CW:** Author: (children's book) Out of the Ballpark, 2007; Co-author (with Greg Brown): Hit a Grand Slam, 1998 **AW:** Named Am. League MVP, 2007, 2005, 2003, Player of Year, Major League Baseball Players Association, 2007, 2002, Am. League Outstanding Player, 2007, 2001-03, 1998, 1996, Major League Baseball Player of Year, The Sporting News, 2007, 2002, 1996; Named One of The 100 Most Powerful Celebrities, Forbes.com, 2008, The Most Influential People in the World of Sports, Business Week, 2008, 2007; Named to Am. League All-Star Team, Major League Baseball, 2011, 2010, 2000-08, 1996-98; recipient Babe Ruth award, Baseball Writers Association America, New York Chapter, 2009, ESPY award, Best Baseball Player, ESPN, 2008, Oscar Charleston Legacy award, Negro Leagues Baseball Museum, 2008, Hitter of Year award, MLB.com, 2007, Gold Glove award, Major League Baseball, 2003, 2002, Hank Aaron award, 2007, 2001-03, Silver Slugger award, 2008, 2007, 2005, 1998-2003, 1996,AL Home Run Leader, 2001-03, 2005, 2007, MLB RBI Leader, 2002, 2007 **ACH:** Achievements include leading the Am. League in: batting average: 1996; runs scored, 1996, 2001, 2003, 2005, 2007; doubles, 1996; hits, 1998; home runs, 2001-03, 2005, 2007; runs batted in (RBI), 2002, 2007; becoming the first player in MLB history to hit at least 35 home runs 11 consecutive seasons, 1998-2008; youngest player in MLB history to hit 500 home runs, August 4, 2007 and 600 home runs, August 4, 2010; recording his 2,500th career hit, September 2, 2009; setting the American League record for RBIs in one inning (7), 2009; member of World Series championship winning New York Yankees, 2009; twenty-ninth player in Major League Baseball history to record 3000 hits by hitting solo home run in the first inning on June 19, 2015 against the Detroit Tigers

RODRIGUEZ, CARLOS A., T: CEO of ADP **I:** Business Management/Business Services **ED:** MBA, Harvard University; BA in Government, Harvard College **C:** President, CEO, Automatic Data Processing, Inc., Roseland, New Jersey, 2011-; President, COO, Automatic Data Processing, Inc., Roseland, New Jersey, 2011; Division president, small business services & professional employer organization to president national accounts services, Automatic Data Processing, Inc., Roseland, New Jersey, 2007-11; Vice president, Automatic Data Processing, Inc.,; President, totalsource & employer services, Automatic Data Processing, Inc., 2000-07; Joined, Automatic Data Processing, Inc., 1999 **CR:** Board directors Hubbell Inc., 2009- **BA:** Automatic Data Processing Inc, 1 ADP Blvd,Mail Stop C421, Roseland, NJ, 07068

RODRIGUEZ, GINA, T: Actress **I:** Media & Entertainment **DOB:** 07/15/1905 **PB:** Chicago, Illinois **SC:** Chicago, Illinois **CW:** (Films) Calling it Quits, 2008, Ten:Thirty One, 2008, Osvaldos, 2009, Our Family Wedding, 2010, Little Spoon, 2010, Go For It!, 2011, Filly Brown,2012, California Winter,2012, Interstate,2013, Enter the Dangerous Mind, 2013, The Price We Pay, 2013, Sleeping with the Fishes,2013, Una Y Otra Y Otra Ve, 2013, Since I Laid Eyes, 2013, Cest Jane, 2014, Sticky Notes, 2016, Deepwater Horizon, 2016, Sharon 1.2.3., 2017, The Star, 2017, Ferdinand, 2017, Annihilation, 2018, Smallfoot, 2018, Miss Bala, 2019(Television) Law & Order, 2004, Jonny Zero, 2005, Law & Order, 2008, Eleventh Hour, 2009 , 10 Things I Hate About You, 2010, Army Wives, 2010, My Super Psycho Sweet 16: Part 2, 2010, Happy Ending, 2011, The Mentalist, 2011, The Bold and the Beautiful, 2011, No Names, 2012, Longmire, 2013, Rizzoli & Isles, 2013, Wild Blue, 2014, Jane the Virgin, 2014,(Golden Globe for Best Actress in a Television Series, 2015) Lip Sync Battle, 2016, Carmen Sandiego, 2019

ROE, PHIL, T: U.S. Representative from Tennessee **I:** Government Administration/Government Relations/Government Services **DOB:** 07/21/1945 **PB:** Clarksville **SC:** TN/USA **ED:** MD, University of Tennessee College of Medicine, Memphis, 1970; BS in Biology, Austin Peay State University, Clarksville, 1967 **C:** Chairmen, House Committee on Veterans Affairs, 2017-; Member, U.S. Congress from 1st Tennessee district, 2009-; Mayor, Johnson City, 2007-09; Vice-mayor, Johnson City, 2003-07; Commissioner, Johnson City Board Commissioners, 2003-08; Private practice obstetrics-gynecology, Johnson City, Tennessee, 1974-2005 **CR:** Del. Tennessee Medical Association; past president Tri-County Medical Society **CIV:** Member, Munsey United Methodist Church, Board of directors, East Tennessee University Foundation, 2006- **MIL:** Major, U.S. Army Medical Corps, 1973-74 **AW:** Recipient Excellence in Philanthropy award, Tennessee Board of Regents **PA:** Republican

ROGERS, HAROLD DALLAS, T: U.S. Representative from Kentucky **I:** Government Administration/Government Relations/Government Services **DOB:** 12/31/1937 **PB:** Barrier **SC:** Kentucky **ED:** LLB, University Kentucky, 1964; BA, University Kentucky, 1962 **CT:** Bar: Louisiana 1964 **C:** Chairman, US House Appropriations Committee, Washington, 2011-; Member, US Congress from 5th Kentucky District, Washington, 1981-; Commonwealth attorney, Pulaski and Rockcastle counties, Kentucky, 1969-80; Private law practice, Somerset, Kentucky, 1967-69; Associate, Smith & Blackburn, 1964-67 **CR:** Member Tennessee Valley Authority Caucus, Congressional Horse Caucus **CIV:** Founder, Southern. Kentucky Economic Council, **MIL:** With KY and North Carolina National Guard, 1957-64 **MEM:** Mem.: Kentucky Commonwealth Attorney Association (past president) **PA:** Republican

ROGERS, JOHN MARSHALL MARSHALL, T: Federal Judge **I:** Law and Legal Services **DOB:** 06/26/1948 **PB:** Rochester **SC:** NY/USA **PT:** Son of Harry Lovejoy III and Virginia Kathryn (Meyers) R.; Married Ying Juan Xiong, 1990. **ED:** JD, University Michigan, 1974; BA, Stanford University, 1970 **CT:** Bar: DC 1975, Kentucky 1980, US Court Appeals, US Supreme Court **C:** Cir. judge, US Court Appeals (6th cir.), 2002-; Professor emeritus, University Kentucky, Lexington, 2002-; Professor, University Kentucky, Lexington, 1986-2002; Associate professor, University Kentucky, Lexington, 1981-86; Assistant professor, University Kentucky, Lexington, 1978-81; Appellate attorney civil div., US Department Justice, Washington, 1974-78; Com-

missioned, US Army Reserve, 1970 **CR:** visiting professor Civil Division US Department Justice, Washington, 1983-85; Fulbright lecturer Foreign Affairs College, Beijing, 1987-88, Zhongshan University, Guangzhou, People's Republic of China, 1994-95; special counsel impeachment committee Kentucky House of Reps., 1991. **CW:** Author: International Law and U.S. Law, 1999; contributor articles to professional journals **MEM:** Member Council on Foreign Relations, Am. Law Institute, Order of Coif, Phi Beta Kappa. **BA:** 100 East Fifth Street, Cincinnati, OH, 45202

ROGERS, JUDITH ANN WILSON, T: Federal Judge **I:** Law and Legal Services **DOB:** 07/27/1939 **PB:** New York **SC:** NY/USA **ED:** Honorary LLD, District of Columbia School Law, 1992; LLM, University of Virginia, 1988; LLB, Harvard University, 1964; AB, Radcliffe College, Cum Laude, 1961 **C:** Judge, U.S. Court of Appeals, District of Columbia Circuit, 1994-Present; Chief Judge, U.S. Court of Appeals, District of Columbia Circuit, 1988-1994; Associate Judge, U.S. Court of Appeals, District of Columbia Circuit, 1983-1988; Corporate Counsel, District of Columbia, 1979-1983; Special Assistant To Mayor For Legislator, District of Columbia, 1974-1979; Coordinator, Legislative Program Office Of the Deputy Mayor, District of Columbia, 1972-1974; General Counsel, Congressional Commission On Organization Of District of Columbia Government, 1971-1972; Attorney, Criminal Division, U.S. Department of Justice, 1969-1971; Attorney, Associate Attorney General's Office, U.S. Department of Justice, 1969-1971; Trial Attorney, San Francisco Neighborhood Legal Assistance Foundation, 1968-1969; Assistant U.S. Attorney, District of Columbia, 1965-1968; Law Clerk, Juvenile Court of the District of Columbia, 1964-1965 **CR:** District of Columbia Law Revision Commission, 1979-1983, Grievance Committee, U.S. District Court of the District of Columbia, 1982-1983, Executive Committee, Conference of Chief Justices, 1993-1994, Fellow, American Bar Association **CIV:** Board of Directors, Wider Opportunities For Women, 1972-1974, Visiting Committee, Harvard University School of Law, 1984-1990, Trustee, Radcliffe College, 1982-1988 **AW:** Citation For Work On District of Columbia Self-Government Act, 1973, Distinguished Public Service Award, District of Columbia Government, 1983, Award, National Bar Association, 1989, Woman Lawyer of the Year, Women's Bar Association of the District of Columbia, 1990 **MEM:** Board of Directors, Conference of Chief Justices, 1988-1994, District of Columbia Bar, National Association of Women Judges, American Law Institute, Phi Beta Kappa **BAR:** District of Columbia, 1965 **BA:** 333 Constitution Avenue NW, Washington, DC, 20001

ROGERS, KENNY, T: Entertainer, Recording Artist **I:** Media & Entertainment **DOB:** 08/21/1938 **PB:** Houston **PT:** Son of Edward Floyd and Lucille (Hester) R.; Married Janice Gordon, May 15, 1958 (div. April 1960), 1 child: Carol; Married Jean Rogers, October 1960 (div. 1963); Married Margo Anderson, October 1964 **ED:** Student, University Houston **C:** Founder, Kenny Roger's Roasters, **CR:** Recording artist, Liberty Records, 1976-82, RCA Records, 1983-88, Warner Records, 1988-93, Atlantic Records, 1993-94, Magnatone Records, 1996-97, co-founder and rec. artist, Dreamcatcher Entertainment, 1998-2000. **CIV:** Hon. captain 1988 US Gymnastics Team. **CW:** Appeared on American Bandstand, 1958; member Bobby Doyle Trio, 1959-66, Christy Minstrels, 1966-67, The First Edition, 1967-69, Kenny Rogers and The First Edition, 1969-75, solo career, 1975-; hosted TV spls. Kenny Rogers Classic Weekend, 1988-90, Kenny, Dolly & Willie, 1989, Kenny Rogers in Concert,

1989, Goodwill Games, 1990; starred in TV series Rollin' with The First Edition, 1972; appeared in movies Six Pack, 1982; actor: (TV appearances) The Muppet Show, 1979, Evening Shade, 1991, A&E The Real West, 1993, MacShayne, 1994, Touched by an Angel, 2000, Reno 911, 2004,How I Met Your Mother, 2009 (TV films) Saga of Sonora, 1973, Kenny Rogers as the Gambler, 1980, Coward of the County, 1981, Gambler, Part II, 1983, Wild Horses, 1985, Gambler III: The Adventure Continues, 1987, Christmas in America, 1989, The Gambler Returns, Gambler IV: The Luck of the Draw, 1991, Rio Diablo, 1993, Gambler V: Playing for Keeps, 1994, MacShayne: Winner Takes All,1994, MacShayne: The Final Roll of Dice, 1994 Big Dreams & Broken Hearts: The Dottie West Story, 1995; recordings include: That Crazy Feeling (Gold single), I Don't Need You (Brit. Country Music Association award, Academy Country Music award), Love is What We Make It, 1985, The Heart of the Matter, 1985, They Don't Make Them Like They Used To, What About Me, I Prefer the Moonlight, 1987, When You Put Your Heart in It, 1988 (official theme song US Gymnastics Federation), Christmas in America, 1989, Love Is Strange, 1990, Greatest Country Hits, 1990, If Only My Heart Had a Voice, 1993, Greatest Hits, 1994; (albums): Kenny Rogers-Lucille, 1976, Love or Something Like It, 1978, The Gambler, 1978, Kenny, 1979, Gideon, 1980, Share Your Love, 1981, Eyes That See in the Dark, 1983, Something Inside So Strong, 1989, Timepiece, 1994, The Gift, 1996, Across My Heart, 1997, Christmas From the Heart, 1998, She Rides Wild Horses, 1999, Christmas Greetings, 2000, There You Go Again, 2000, The Way It Used to Be, 2001, Calico Silver, 2002, Heart of the Matter, 2003, Back to the Well, 2003, Christmas with Kenny, 2004, Water & Bridges, 2006, After Dark, 2006, 50 Years, 2008, The Love of God, 2011, Amazing Grace, 2012, You Can't Make Old Friends, 2013; author: Kenny Roger's America, 1986, Your Friends and Mine, 1987, Christmas in Canaan, 2002, Luck or Something Like It: A Memoir, 2012. **AW:** Named Cross-Over Artist of Year Billboard magazine, 1977, named Top Male vocalist People magazine, 1979, 80; recipient Country Music Association award, 1978, 79, Star, Hollywood Walk of Fame, 1979, Am. Music award, Best Male Vocalist, Best Album, 1984, Am. Music award, Best Male Country Vocalist, Best Album, 1985, Country Music Foundation Roy Acuff award, 1985, UN Peace award, 1984, Recording Industry Association Am. Most Awarded Artist award, 1984 (11 platinum, 18 gold albums), Grammy award for Best Male Country Vocal, 1977, 79, co-recipient (with Ronnie Milsap) for Best Country Vocal Duet, 1987, 1st Harry Chapin award for Humanitarianism American Society of Composers, 1988, Horatio Alger award, 1990, Awd. for sales in excess of ten million copies for "Greatest Hits", Lifetime Achievement Awd., Songwriters Hall of Fame, N.A.R.M. Chmns. Awd. for Sustained Achievement, 1999, American Eagle award, National Music Council, 2010; numerous other music awards, Texas Country Music Hall of Fame, 2017, Willie Nelson Lifetime Achievement Award, 2013, Country Music Hall of Fame,2013 **BA:** 103 Paradise Dr, Hendersonville, TN, 37075

ROGERS, MIKE D., T: U.S. Representative from Alabama **I:** Government Administration/Government Relations/Government Services **DOB:** 07/16/1958 **PB:** Hammond **SC:** IN/USA **ED:** JD, University of Birmingham, 1991; MPA, Jacksonville State University, 1985; BA in Political Sci., Jacksonville State University, 1981 **C:** Member, US Congress from 3rd Alabama District, 2003-; Member, Alabama House of Representatives, 1994-2002; Associate then Partner, Rogers, Young, Wollstein and Hughes; Attorney, Bolt, Isom, Jackson and

Bailey; Community Rep., Psychiatric Counselor, Northeast Alabama Regional Medical Center; Director, Dislocated Worker's Project, United Way of Etowah County **CR:** Member, Committee on Appropriations **CIV:** Active, State Rep. Executive Committee, 1990-; Member, Calhoun County Commission, 1987-91 **PA:** Republican

ROHRABACHER, DANA TYRONE, T: U.S. Representative from California **I:** Government Administration/Government Relations/Government Services **DOB:** 06/21/1947 **PB:** Coronado **SC:** CA/USA **PT:** Son of Donald and Doris Rohrabacher **ED:** MA in American Studies, University of Southern California, 1976; BA in History, Long Beach State College, 1969; Student, LA Harbor College **C:** Member, US Congress from 48th California District, 2013-;; Member, Committee on Homeland Security, Committee on Veterans' Affairs; Member, US Congress from 46th California District, 2003-13; Member, US Congress from 45th California District, 1993-2003; Member, US Congress from 42nd California District, Washington, 1989-93; Speechwriter, Special Assistant to President Ronald Reagan, The White House, Washington, 1981-88; Assistant Press Secretary, Reagan/Bush Committee, 1980; Editorial Writer, Orange County Register, 1979-80; Reporter, City News Svc./Radio News West, LA **CR:** Distinguished Lecturer, International Terrorism Conference, Paris, 1985 **AW:** Recipient, Distinguished Alumnus Award, LA Harbor College, 1987 **H:** Surfing, Whitewater rafting **PA:** Republican

ROKITA, TODD, T: U.S. Representative from Indiana **I:** Government Administration/Government Relations/Government Services **DOB:** 02/09/1970 **PB:** Munster, Ind **ED:** JD, Ind. University School of Law, Indianapolis, 1995; BA in Political Sci., Wabash College, Crawfordsville, Ind., 1992 **C:** Member, US House Administration Committee, Washington, 2011-; Member, Committee on Transportation and Infrastructure, Republican Study Committee; Member, US House Education & the Workforce Committee, Washington, 2011-; Member, US House Budget Committee, Washington, 2011-; Member, US Congress from 4th Ind. District, Washington, 2011-; Secretary of State, State of Ind., Indianapolis, 2003-11; Deputy Secretary of State, State of Ind., Indianapolis, 1997-2003; General Counsel to Secretary of State, State of Ind., Indianapolis, 1997 **CR:** Board of Directors Election Assistance Commission Member Dir.'s Cir. Ind. Council Economic Education **CIV:** Member, St. Thomas More Parish, Board of Directors, St. Joseph's College Ind., Board of Directors, St. Vincent Foundation **AW:** Named Small Business Statesman of Year, National Federation Ind. Businesses; Recipient Indianapolis Choice Award, Indianapolis Chapter National Association Women Business Owners, Merit Award, International Association Commercial Administrators; Grantee Toll Fellowship, Council State Governments, Rodel Fellowship in Pub. Leadership, Aspen Institute, Colorado **MEM:** Mem.: National Rifle Association, Ind. State Bar Association (Past Chair, Member Aviation Law Committee), Employers Support of Guard & Reserve, Knights of Columbus **PA:** Republican **BA:** 2439 Rayburn House Office Building, Washington, DC, 20515

ROLLINS, SONNY, T: Composer, Musician **I:** Fine Art **DOB:** 09/07/1930 **PB:** NYC **PT:** Son of Walter and Valborg (Solomon) R. **SPN:** Married Dawn Finney, 1956 (div.); Married Lucille Pearson, September 7, 1959 (deceased November 2004) **ED:** PhD (hon.), Rutgers University, 2009; PhD (hon.), Colby College, 2007; MusD (hon.), Berklee College Music, 2003; Doctor of Music, New England Conservatory of Music, 2002; ArtsD, Duke University,

1999; ArtsD, Wesleyan University, 1998; ArtsD, Long Island University, 1998; ArtsD, Bard College, 1992 **C:** Co-founder, Doxy Records, New York City, 2005-; Tenor saxophonist, 1971-; Leader, Max Roach-Clifford Brown Quintet, 1956-57; Member, Max Roach-Clifford Brown Quintet, 1955-57; Tenor saxophonist, 1961-68; Tenor saxophonist, 1946-59 **CW:** Ann.concert tours in Europe and Asia; composer (songs) Airegin, Alfie's Theme, Blessing in Disguise, Blue 7, Doxy, East Broadway Run Down, He's Younger Than You Are, Movin' Out, Oleo, On Impulse, Pent-Up House, Sonnymoon for Two, St. Thomas, Tenor Madness, The Bridge, Freedom Suite, Way Out West; performer (albums) Sonny Rollins Quartet, 1951, Sonny & the Stars, 1951, Mambo Jazz, 1951, Movin' Out, 1954, Sonny Rollins Quintet, 1954, Taking Care of Business, 1955, Work Time, 1955, Saxophone Colossus, 1956, Sonny Rollins Plus Four, 1956, Three Giants, 1956, Tenor Madness, 1956, Sonny Boy, 1956, Tour de Force, 1956, Way Out West, 1957, Sounds of Sonny, 1957, Newk's Time, 1957, A Night at the Village Vanguard, 1957, Freedom Suite, 1958, Shadow Waltz, 1958, The Bridge, 1962, What's New?, 1962, Our Man in Jazz, 1962, Sonny Meets Hawk!, 1963, All the Things You Are, 1963, Now's the Time, 1964, There Will Never Be Another You, 1965, Alfie, 1966, East Broadway Run Down, 1966, Next Album, 1972, Horn Culture, 1973, Cutting Edge, 1974, Nucleus, 1975, The Way I Feel, 1976, Easy Living, 1977, Don't Stop the Carnival, 1978, Green Dolphin Street, 1978, Don't Ask, 1979, Love at First Sight, 1980, No Problem, 1981, Reel Life, 1982, Sunny Days, Stary Nights, 1984, Solo Album, 1985, G-Man, 1986, Dancing in the Dark, 1987, Falling in Love with Jazz, 1989, Here's to the People, 1991, Old Flames, 1993, The Meeting, 1994, Without a Song, 1995, Sonny Rollins Plus Three, 1996, Global Warming, 1998, Dearly Beloved, 1998, This is What I Do, 2000 (Grammy award for Best Instrumental Jazz Performance, 2001), Scoops, 2002, Solid, 2002, Without a Song: The 9/11 Concert, 2005 (Grammy award for Best Jazz Instrumental Solo: Why Was I Born?, 2006), Sonny Please, 2006, Soneymoon, 2007, Then and Now, 2008, Sonny, Please, Road Shows, vol. 1, 2008, Road Shows, vol. 2, 2011, Road Shows, Vol 3, 2014, Road Shows, Vol 4 Holding the Stage, 2016 **AW:** Named to Big Band & Jazz Hall of Fame, 1999; recipient Kennedy Center Honors, John F. Kennedy Center Performing Arts, 2011, National Medal of Arts, National Endowment for the Arts, 2010, Edward MacDowell Medalist, 2010, Polar Music prize, Sweden, 2007, Golden Plate award, Academy Achievement, 2006, Lifetime Achievement award, National Academy Recording Arts and Scis., 2004; Guggenheim fellow, 1972

ROMETTY, GINNI, T: CEO **I:** Business Management/Business Services **CN:** IBM Corp. **DOB:** 07/29/1957 **PB:** Chgo. **ED:** BS in Computer Sci. & Electrical Engineering with high honors, Northwestern University, Evanston, Illinois, 1979 **C:** Chairman, president, CEO, IBM Corp., 2012-; President, CEO, IBM Corp., 2012; Senior vice president, group executive IBM sales, marketing & strategy, IBM Corp., 2010-11; Senior vice president, global sales & distribution, IBM Corp., 2005-10; Senior vice president global business services, IBM Corp., 2002-05; General manager global services Americas, IBM Corp.,; General manager strategy, marketing & sales operations, global services worldwide, IBM Corp.; Various positions including general manager global insurance & financial services sector, IBM Corp.; Business & information tech. consultant, IBM Corp., 1985-91; Systems engineer, IBM Corp., Detroit, 1981-85; Applications & system devel. staff, General Motors Co., 1979-81 **CR:** Board directors IBM Corp., 2012-, American International Group (AIG), 2006-09 **CIV:**

Board trustees, Northwestern University, Board overseers, board managers, Memorial Sloan Kettering Cancer Center **AW:** Named a Global Business Influential, TIME magazine, 2002; named one of The 50 Most Influential People in Global Finance, Bloomberg Markets, 2012, The 100 Most Influential People in the World, TIME magazine, 2012, The 50 Most Powerful Women in New York, Crain's New York Business, 2011, 2009, The World's Most Powerful People, Forbes magazine, 2013-14, The 100 Most Powerful Women, 2011-14, 2008-09, The Next 20 Female CEOs, Pink Magazine & Forté Foundation, 2006, The 50 Most Powerful Women in Business, Fortune magazine, 2006-15; recipient Alumni Merit award, Northwestern Alumni Association, 2010, Carl Sloane award, Association Management Consultant Firms, 2006 **MEM:** Mem.: Council on Foreign Relations

ROMNEY, MITT, T: investment company executive, former Governor of Massachusetts **I:** Government Administration/Government Relations/Government Services **DOB:** 03/12/1947 **PB:** Detroit **PT:** Son of George Wilcken and Lenore (Lafount) Romney; **ED:** Doctor (hon.), Liberty University, 2012; MBA, Harvard Business School, 1975; JD, Harvard Law School, 1975; BA, Brigham Young University, Provo, Utah, 1971 **C:** Chairman executive committee, Solamere Capital, LLC, Boston, 2013-; Republican Candidate for President, US Presidential Election, 2012; Governor, Commonwealth of Massachusetts, 2003-07; President, CEO, Salt Lake Organizing Committee (Winter Olympics), Utah, 1999-2002; Managing partner, CEO, Bain Capital, LLC, Boston, 1984-2001; Chairman, CEO, Bain & Co., Inc., Boston, 1991-2001; Vice president, Bain & Co., Inc., Boston, 1978-84; Consultant, Bain & Co., Inc., Boston, 1977-78; Consultant, Boston Consulting Group, 1975-77 **CR:** Candidate for the 2012 Republican Party presidential nomination candidate for the 2008 Republican Party presidential nomination board directors Marriott International, Inc., 2012-, 2009-11, Bethesda, Maryland, 1992-2002, Staples Inc., Framingham, Massachusetts, 1986-2001 **CIV:** Member national executive board, Boy Scouts of America, Member visiting committee, Harvard Business School, Member adv. board, Brigham Young University School Business, President, Boston Stake Latter Day Saints Church, 1986-94 **CW:** Author: Turnaround: Crisis, Leadership, and the Olympic Games, 2004, No Apology: The Case for American Greatness, 2010 (#1 Publishers Weekly bestseller) **AW:** Named one of The 100 Most Influential People in the World, TIME magazine, 2012; Baker scholar, Harvard Business School, 1975 **MEM:** Mem.: Belmont Hill Club **PA:** Republican

RONAN, SAOIRSE, T: Actress **I:** Media & Entertainment **PB:** Bronx **SC:** NY/USA **PT:** Monica (née Brennan) and Paul Ronan **CW:** (Film) I Could Never Be Your Woman, 2007, The Christmas Miracle of Jonathan Toomey, 2007, Atonement, 2007, Death Defying Acts, 2007, City of Ember, 2008, The Lovely Bones, 2009, Arrietty, 2010, The Way Back, 2010, Hanna, 2011, Violet and Daisy, 2011, Byzantium, 2012, The Host, 2013, How I Live Now, 2013, Justin and the Knights of Valour, 2013, The Grand Budapest Hotel, 2014, Muppets Most Wanted, 2014, Lost River, 2014, Stockholm, Pennsylvania, 2015, Brooklyn, 2015, Loving Vincent, 2017, Lady Bird, 2017 (Golden Globe Best Actress in a Motion Picture 2018) On Chesil Beach, 2017, The Seagull, 2018, Mary Queen of Scots, 2018 (Television) The Clinic, 2003, Proof, 2005, Robot Chicken, 2014, SNL, 2017

RONSTADT, LINDA MARIE MARIE, T: Singer **I:** Media & Entertainment **DOB:** 05/23/1905 **PB:** Tucson **SC:** AZ/USA **PT:** Gilbert Ronstadt; Ruthmary (Copeman) Ronstadt **CH:** Mary Clementine; Carlos **ED:** Doctorate (hon.), Berklee College Music, 2009 **CW:** Recording artist numerous albums including Evergreen 1967, Evergreen Vol. 2, 1967, Linda Ronstadt, The Stone Poneys and Friends, Vol. 3, 1968, Hand Sown, Home Grown, 1969, Silk Purse, 1970, Linda Ronstadt, 1972, Don't Cry Now, 1973, Heart Like a Wheel, 1974 (Grammy award for Best Country Vocal Performance, Female, I Can't Help It (If I'm Still In Love With You), 1975), Different Drum, 1974, Prisoner In Disguise, 1975, Hasten Down the Wind, 1976 (Grammy award for Best Pop Vocal Performance, 1976), Greatest Hits, 1976, Simple Dreams, Blue Bayou, 1977, Living in the U.S.A., 1978, Mad Love, Greatest Hits Vol. II, 1980, Get Closer, 1982, What's New, 1983, Lush Life, 1984, For Sentimental Reasons, 1986, Trio (with Dolly Parton, Emmylou Harris), 1986 (Academy Country Music award for Best Album, 1987, Grammy award for Best Country Performance by a Duo or Group with Vocals, 1987), 'Round Midnight, 1987, Canciones de Mi Padre, 1987 (Grammy award for Best Mexican-American Performance, 1988, Emmy award for Outstanding Individual Performance in a Variety or Music Program, 1989), Cry Like a Rainstorm-Howl Like the Wind, 1989 (Grammy awards for Best Pop Vocal Performance by a Duo or Group with Vocal, Don't Know Much, 1989, Best Pop Vocal Performance by a Duo or Group with Vocal, All My Life, 1990), Mas Canciones, 1991 (Grammy award for Best Mexican-American Album, 1993), Frenesi, 1992 (Grammy award for Best Tropical Latin Album, 1992), Winter Light, 1993, Feels Like Home, 1995, Dedicated to the One I Love, 1996 (Grammy award for Best Musical Album for Children, 1996), We Ran, 1998, Trio 2, (with Emmylou Harris & Dolly Parton), 1999 (Grammy award for Best Country Collaboration with Vocals, After the Gold Rush, 1999), Western Wall: The Tucson Sessions (with Emmylou Harris), 1999, A Merry Little Christmas, 2000, Hummin' to Myself, 2004, Adieu False Heart, 2006, Standards with Nelson Riddle Orchestra,2008, Duets, 2014; actress: (Broadway) Pirates of Penzance, 1981 (Tony award for Best Performance by a Leading Actress in a Musical, 1981), (films) The Pirates of Penzance, 1983, (off Broadway) La Boheme, 1984, (TV films) Corridos: Tales of Passion & Revolution, 1987, The Young Indiana Jones Chronicles, 1993; author: Simple Dreams: A Musical Memoir, 2013, Simple Dreams: A Musical Memoir, 2013 **AW:** named Best New Female Artist, Academy Country Music Awards, 1974; named one 100 Greatest Women of Rock 'n' Roll, VH1, 1999; named to Arizona Music and Entertainment Hall of Fame, 2007, Rock and Roll Hall of Fame, 2014; recipient National Medal of Arts, National Education Association, 2014

ROONEY, FRANCIS, T: U.S. Representative from Florida **I:** Government Administration/Government Relations/Government Services **DOB:** 12/04/1953 **ED:** PhD (hon.), University of Notre Dame, 2006; JD, Georgetown University, 1978; AB, Georgetown University, 1975 **CT:** 100-Ton Master's License, U.S. Coast Guard **C:** Member, U.S. House of Representatives from Florida's 19th District 2017-;; Member, Committee on Education and the Workforce, Committee on Foreign Affairs, Economic Committee; Chairman, President, CEO, Rooney Holdings, Inc., Naples, Florida, 1984; US Ambassador to The Holy See, US Department State, 2005-08 **CR:** Board of Directors Laredo Petroleum, Inc., 2010-, Vetra Energy Group, LLC, 2009-, Helmerich and Payne, Inc., 2008-, Florida Corp., 2008-09, Cimarex Energy Co., 2002-05, BOK Fin. Corp., 1995-2005, BOL Fin. Corp., Oklahoma Capital Investment

Board, New York Stock Exchange, NASDAQ Vice Chairman Oklahoma Turnpike Authority Transition Team for Governor-Elect Brad Henry State of Oklahoma, Director, 20/20 Committee, Washington Adv. Council Center for Strategic and International Studies **CIV:** Member, School of Architecture Council, University of Notre Dame, Board Advisor, Panama Canal Authority, Trustee, Center for the Study of the Presidency and Congress, Member, Sovereign Military Order of Malta (Federal Association), Washington **MEM:** Mem.: Young President's Org. (director 1992-98, international president 1997-98) **BAR:** Bar: Texas, DC; **PA:** Republican **BA:** 120 Cannon HOB, Washington, DC, 20515

ROONEY, TOM, T: U.S. Representative from Florida, Lawyer **I:** Government Administration/ Government Relations/Government Services **DOB:** 11/21/1970 **PB:** Phila. **SC:** PA/USA **PT:** Son of Patrick J. Rooney; **ED:** JD, University of Miami School Law; MA in Political Sci., University of Florida; BS in English Lit., Washington and Jefferson College, Pittsburgh; Student, Syracuse University, New York **CT:** Bar: Florida 1999 **C:** Member, U.S. Congress from 17th Florida District, 2013-; Member, Committee on Agriculture, Committee on Armed Services, Committee on Armed Services; Member, U.S. Congress from 16th Florida District, Washington, 2009-13; Attorney, Kramer, Sopko & Levenstein, P.A., Stuart, Florida, 2008-09; Board directors, Children's Services Council Palm Beach County, 2006-08; Assistant attorney general, State of Florida, 2004-06; Commissioned officer Judge Advocate General Corps, special assistant U.S. attorney, U.S. Army, Fort Hood, Texas, 1999-2004 **CIV:** Board of directors, Children's Place at Home Safe, South Lake Worth, Florida, **PA:** Republican

ROSBASH, MICHAEL, T: Biology Professor, Researcher **I:** Education/Educational Services **PB:** Kansas City **ED:** PhD in Biophysics, Massachusetts Institute of Technology (1970) **C:** Peter Gruber Endowed Chair in Neuroscience, Brandeis University (2012-Present); Professor, Department of Biology, Brandeis University (1986-Present); Associate Professor, Department of Biology, Brandeis University (1980-1986); Assistant Professor, Department of Biology, Brandeis University (1973-1980); Postdoctoral Position, University of Edinburgh (1972-1974); Investigator, Howard Hughes Medical Institute; Director, National Center for Behavioral Genomics, Brandeis University **AW:** Nobel Prize in Physiology or Medicine (2017); Co-recipient, The Shaw Prize in Life Science and Medicine (2013); Wiley Prize (2013); Canada Gairdner International Award (2012); Massry Prize (2012); Horwitz Prize, Columbia University (2011); Peter and Patricia Gruber Foundation Neuroscience Prize (2009); Fulbright Fellowship, Institut de Biologie Physico-Chimique, Paris, France **MEM:** American Academy of Arts & Sciences, National Academy of Sciences **BA:** MS008 Brandeis University Shapiro Science Center, 2-24B PO Box 549110, Waltham, MA, 02454

ROSE, IRWIN ALLEN, T: Biochemist, Educator **I:** Sciences **DOB:** 07/16/1926 **PB:** Brooklyn **SC:** NY/USA **PT:** Harry; Ella Greenwald Royze **ED:** PhD in Biochemistry, The University of Chicago (1952); BS, The University of Chicago (1948) **C:** Distinguished Professor-in-Residence, Department of Physiology and Biophysics, University of California, Irvine, School Medicine (1997-2015); Retired, Fox Chase Cancer Center (1995); Researcher, Fox Chase Cancer Center, Philadelphia, PA (1963-1995); Faculty, Department of Biochemistry, Yale University, New Haven, CT (1954-1963) **CW:** Contributor, Articles to Professional Journal **AW:** Nobel Prize in Chemistry

(2004) **MEM:** National Academy of Sciences **ACH:** Achievements include discovery of ubiquitin-mediated protein degradation

ROSE, PETER EDWARD, T: Retired Professional Baseball Player, Retired Professional Baseball Coach **I:** Athletics **DOB:** 04/14/1941 **PB:** Cin. **PT:** Son of Harry Rose; Married Karolyn Ann Englehardt (div.); children: Fawn, Peter; Married Carol Woliung, April 1984; children: Cara, Tyler **C:** Color Analyst, Fox, 2015-2017; Now host syndicated show Talk Sports with Pete Rose, Station WGTO-AM, Orlando, Florida,; Host weekly radio show Pete Rose on Baseball, Station WCKY, Cincinnati, 1992; Player, Montreal Expos, 1984; Player, Philadelphia Phillies, 1979-83; Manager, Cincinnati Reds, 1987-89; Player manager, Cincinnati Reds, 1984-87; Player, Cincinnati Reds, 1963-78 **CW:** Author: (with Bob Hertzel) Charlie Hustle, 1975, Winning Baseball, 1976, (with Peter Golenback) Pete Rose on Hitting, 1985, (with Roger Kahn) Pete Rose: My Story, 1989, Pete Rose: My Prison Without Bars, 2004; TV appearances include Babe Ruth, 1991, Arli$$, 1996, Savage Skies, 1996, Veronica's Closet, 1997, Wrestlemania XIV, 1998, Wrestlemania XV, 1999, Wrestlemania XVI, 2000. **AW:** Named National League Rookie of Year, 1963, Most Valuable Player, 1973, Most Valuable Player World Series, 1975, National League Player of Year The Sporting News, 1968, Ball Player of Decade, 1979; named to National League All-Star Team, 1965, 67-71, 73-79, 80-81, member of MLB All-Century Team, 1999,Mariners Hall of Fame, 2012,Baseball Hall of Fame, 2015 **ACH:** Achievements include being second player in baseball history to exceed 4000 hits, all time leader in hits.

ROSEN, JACKY, T: U.S. Representative from Nevada **I:** Government Administration/Government Relations/Government Services **PB:** Chicago **SC:** IL/USA **ED:** B.A., University of Minnesota, Minneapolis **C:** Member, U.S. House of Representatives from Nevada's 3rd District, 2017-; Member, Committee on Armed Services; Member, Committee on Science, Space, and Technology

ROSENBAUM, ROBIN STACIE, T: Federal Judge **I:** Law and Legal Services **DOB:** 07/11/1966 **PB:** Chapel Hill **SC:** NC/USA **ED:** JD, University of Miami School of Law, 1991; BA, Cornell University, 1988 **C:** Judge, U.S. Court of Appeals, 11th Circuit, 2014-Present; Judge, U.S. District Court, Southern District, Florida, 2012-2014; Magistrate Judge, U.S. District Court, Southern District, Florida, 2007-2012; Chief, Economics Crime Section, U.S. Department of Justice, 2002; Assistant U.S. Attorney, Southern District, U.S. Department of Justice, 1998-2007; Law Clerk, Hon. Stanley Marcus, U.S. Court of Appeals, 11th Circuit, 1998; Associate, Holland & Knight LLP, 1996-1997; Staff Counsel, Office of Independent Counsel Dan Pearson, 1995-1996; Trial Attorney, Federal Programs Bench, U.S. Department of Justice, 1991-1995 **CR:** Adjunct Professor, University of Miami School of Law, 2009-Present **BA:** 56 Forsyth Street NW, Atlanta, GA, 30303

ROSENSTEIN, ROD J., T: U.S. Deputy Attorney General **I:** Government Administration/Government Relations/Government Services **DOB:** 01/13/1965 **PB:** Philadelphia **SC:** PA/USA **PT:** Robert Jacob Rosenstein, Gerry M. (Stoloff) Rosenstein **ED:** JD, Harvard University, 1989; BS in Economics, University of Pennsylvania, Philadelphia, PA, 1986 **CT:** Certificate, U.S. Court of Appeals, District of Columbia, 1990 **C:** 37th Deputy Attorney General, Washington, DC, 2017-Present; U.S. Attorney District Maryland, U.S. Department of Justice, Baltimore, MD, 2005-2017; Associate

Counsel, Office of Independent Counsel, Washington, DC, 1995-1997; Principal Deputy Assistant Attorney General, Tax Division, U.S. Department of Justice, Washington, DC, 2002-2005; Deputy Assistant Attorney General, Criminal Matters, U.S. Department of Justice, Washington, DC, 2001-2002; Assistant U.S. Attorney, District of Maryland, U.S. Department of Justice, Washington, DC, 1997-2001; Special Assistant Criminal Division, U.S. Department of Justice, Washington, DC, 1994-1995; Counsel To Deputy Attorney General, U.S. Department of Justice, Washington, DC, 1993-1994; Trial Attorney, Public Integrity Section, Washington, DC, 1990-1993; Law Clerk To Hon. Douglas H. Ginsburg, U.S. Court of Appeals, District of Columbia Circuit, Washington, DC, 1989-1990 **BAR:** U.S. Court of Appeals, First, Second, Tenth And 11th Circuits, 2004, U.S. Tax Court, 2003, U.S. Court of Appeals, Eighth Circuit, 2003, Maryland, 2002, U.S. Supreme Court, 2002, U.S. Court of Appeals, Fourth Circuit, 1998, U.S. Court of Appeals, Ninth Circuit, 1992, District of Columbia, 1992, U.S. Court of Appeals, Fifth Circuit, 1991, Pennsylvania 1989 **BA:** U.S. Attorneys Office, 36 S Charles Street, 4th Floor, Baltimore, MD, 21201

ROSKAM, PETER JAMES, T: U.S. Representative from Illinois, Former State Legislator, Lawyer **I:** Government Administration/Government Relations/Government Services **DOB:** 09/13/1961 **PB:** Hinsdale **PT:** Son of Verlyn Ronald and Martha (Jacobsen) Roskam; **ED:** JD, Illinois Institute Tech., 1989; BA, University Illinois, 1983 **CT:** Bar: Illinois 1989 **C:** Member, US House Select Committee on the Events Surrounding the 2012 Terrorist Attack in Benghazi, 2014-; Member, Committee on Ways and Means; Member, US Congress from 6th Illinois district, 2007-; Member District 20, Illinois State Senate f, 2000-06; Member District 40, Illinois General Assembly, Springfield, 1993-99; Partner, Salvi & Roskam, Wheaton, Illinois, 1994-2006; Executive director, Educational Assistance Ltd., Glen Ellyn, Illinois, 1987-93; Legal assistant to Rep. Henry Hyde, US Congress, Washington, 1986-87; Legis. assistant to Rep. Tom Delay, US Congress, Washington, 1985-86; Teacher, All Saints HS, St. Thomas, 1984-85 **AW:** Named a Hero of Taxpayer, Americans for Tax Reform, 2005 **PA:** Republican

ROS-LEHTINEN, ILEANA CARMEN, T: U.S. Representative from Florida **I:** Government Administration/Government Relations/Government Services **DOB:** 07/15/1952 **PB:** Havana **SC:** Cuba **PT:** Enrique Emilio Ros; Amanda (Adato) Ros **ED:** PhD in Higher Education, University of Miami (2004); MS in Educational Leadership, Florida International University, Miami, FL (1986); BA in Education, Florida International University, Miami, FL (1975); AA, Miami-Dade Community College, FL (1972) **C:** Member, US Congress from the 27th Florida District, Washington, DC (2013-Present); Founder, Chief Administrator, Eastern Academy, Miami-Dade County, FL (1978-Present); Chairwoman, US House Foreign Affairs Committee, Washington, DC (2011-2013); Member, US Congress from the 18th Florida District, Washington, DC (1989-2013); Member, District 34, Florida State Senate, Tallahassee, FL (1987-1989); Member, District 110, Florida House of Representatives, Tallahassee, FL (1983-1986) **CR:** Co-chair, Congressional Vision Caucus (2008-Present); National Marine Sanctuary Caucus (2008-Present) **AW:** Education Award, Hispanic Heritage Foundation (2007); Named Official of the Year, Youth Crime Watch America (2001); National Legislation Award, LULACH (1999) **MEM:** Bi-lingual Private School Association **PA:** Republican

ROSS, DENNIS ALAN, T: U.S. Representative from Florida **I:** Government Administration/Government Relations/Government Services **DOB:** 10/18/1959 **PB:** Lakeland, Florida **PT:** Son of William A. and Loyola Ross; Married Cindy Hartley, August 6, 1983; children: Shane, Travis **ED:** JD, Samford University, 1987; BS in Business, Auburn University, 1981 **CT:** Bar: Florida 1987, US District Court (middle district) Florida 1987 **C:** Member, US House Financial Services Committee, 2013-; Member, US Congress from 15th Florida District, 2013-; Partner, Ross Vecchio P.A. (formerly Ross Williams & Deal PA), Lakeland, 1989-; Member, US House Judiciary Committee, 2011-13; Member, US House Ethics Committee, 2011-13; Member, US House Education & Workforce Committee, 2011-13; Member, US Congress from 12th Florida District, Washington, 2011-13; Member District 63, Florida House of Reps., Tallahassee, 2000-08; Staff counsel, Walt Disney World Co., Lake Buena Vista, Florida, 1989; Associate, Holland & Knight, Lakeland, 1987-89 **CIV:** Chairman Polk County Republican Party, Lakeland, 1992-95. **AW:** Recipient Legis. Leadership award The Trust for Public Lands, 2001, Florida Workers Adv. Outstanding Freshman award, 2001, AIF Champion Business award, 2006; named Legis. of Year Florida Building Material Association, 2001, Florida Automobile Dealers, 2003, Trucking Association, 2005, Florida League Cities, 2006, Florida Association Insurance Agents, 2006. **MEM:** Member Lakeland Bar Association (past president), Lakeland Kiwanis Club (board member 1987). **PA:** Republican **BA:** 436 Cannon HOB, Washington, DC, 20515

ROSS, DIANA, T: Singer, Actress, Entertainer, Fashion Designer **I:** Media & Entertainment **DOB:** 03/26/1944 **PB:** Detroit **SC:** MI/USA **PT:** Daughter of Fred and Ernestine R.; Married Robert Ellis Silberstein, January 1971 (div. 1976); children: Rhonda, Tracee, Chudney; Married Arne Naess, October 23, 1985 (div. 2000, deceased 2004); child **C:** President, music pub.; President, Rossville; President, Rosstown; President, Chondee Inc.; President, RTC Management Corp.; President, Anaid Film Productions, Inc.; President, Diana Ross Enterprises, Inc. **CR:** Began mini-residency, Wynn Las Vegas hotel & Casino 2018 **CW:** Started in Detroit as member the Primettes; lead singer until 1969, Diana Ross and the Supremes; solo artist, 1969-; albums include Diana Ross, 1970, 76, Everything Is Everything, 1971, I'm Still Waiting, 1971, Lady Sings The Blues, 1972, Touch Me In The Morning, 1973, Original Soundtrack of Mahogany, 1975, Baby It's Me, 1977, The Wiz, 1978, Ross, 1978, 83, The Boss, 1979, Diana, 1981, To Love Again, 1981, Why Do Fools Fall In Love?, 1981, Silk Electric, 1982, Endless Love, 1982, Swept Away, 1984, Eaten Alive, 1985, Chain Reaction, 1986, Diana's Duets, 1987, Workin' Overtime, 1989, Red Hot Rhythm and Blues, 1987, Surrender, 1989, Ain't No Mountain High Enough, 1989, The Force Behind the Power, 1991, Stolen Moment: The Lady Sings... Jazz & Blues, 1993, Musical Memories Forever, 1993, The Remixes, 1994, A Very Special Season, 1994, Making Spirits Bright, 1994, Take Me Higher, 1995, Voice of Love, 1996, Gift of Love, 1996, The Greatest, 1998, The Real Thing, 1998, Every Day is a New Day, 1999, Love From...Diana Ross, 2001, The #1's, 2004, Complete Symphony, 2004, The Blue Album, 2006, I Love You, 2007; films include Lady Sings the Blues, 1972, Mahogany, 1975, The Wiz, 1978; NBC-TV special, An Evening With Diana Ross, 1977, Diana, 1981, numerous others; TV movie Out of Darkness, 1994; author: Secrets of a Sparrow, 1993, Diana Ross: Going Back, 2002, Upside Down: Wrong Turns, Right Turns and the Road Ahead **AW:** Recipient citation V.P. Humphrey for efforts on behalf President Johnson's Youth

Opportunity Program, citation Mrs. Martin Luther King and Rev. Abernathy for contribution to Southern Christian Leadership Conference cause, awards Billboard, Cash Box and Record World as worlds outstanding singer, Grammy award, 1970, Female Entertainer Year National Association for the Advancement of Colored People, 1970, Cue award as Entertainer Year, 1972, Golden Apple award, 1972, Gold medal award Photoplay, 1972, Antoinette Perry award, 1977, Golden Globe award, 1972, BET (Black Entertainment Television) Walk Fame award, 1999, Heroes award, National Academy of Recording Arts and Sciences, New York Chapter, 2000, Kennedy Center Honors, John F. Kennedy Center for Performing Arts, 2007, Presidential Medal of Freedom, The White House, 2016, recipient American Music Lifetime Achievement Award, 2017; named to The Rock & Roll Hall Fame, 1988

ROSS, STEPHEN MICHAEL, T: Real Estate Company Executive, Professional Sports Team Owner **I:** Real Estate **DOB:** 05/10/1940 **PB:** Detroit **SC:** MI/USA **ED:** LLM in Taxation, New York University, 1966; JD, Wayne State University, 1965; BS, University of Michigan, 1962 **C:** Majority Owner, Miami Dolphins, 2009-Present; Founder, Chairman, CEO, The Related Companies L.P., New York, NY, 1972-Present; Co-Owner, Miami Dolphins, 2008-2009; Founder, Director, Charter Municipal Mortgage Acceptance Co.; Director, Insignia Fin. Group, Inc.; Tax Attorney, Coopers & Lybrand, Detroit, MI **CR:** Chairman, Real Estate Board of New York, Equinox Fitness Clubs **CIV:** Trustee, Juvenile Diabetes Research Foundation, Jewish Association for Services for the Aged, Jackie Robinson Foundation, Solomon R. Guggenheim Museum, National Building Museum, Levin Institute, Urban Land Institute, New York Presbyterian Hospital, and Lincoln Center, Chairman, Board of Trustees, Centerline Holding Co. **AW:** Forbes 400: Richest Americans, 2006-Present, The Harry B. Helmsley Distinguished New Yorker Award, The Real Estate Board of New York, 2005, Jack D. Weiler Award, United Jewish Appeal, 2003, Leadership in Tourism Award, New York City & Co., 2002, The 100 Most Influential Leaders in Business, Crain's New York Business, 2002; Henry Pearce Award, Jewish Association for Services for the Aged, 2001, Owner & Developer of the Year, New York Construction News, 2000, "What New York Needs" Award, The Dow Fund, 1999, Tree of Life Award, 1998, Housing Person of the Year, National Housing Conference **MEM:** Director, Real Estate Board of New York

ROSS, WILBUR, T: Secretary, U.S. Department of Commerce **I:** Government Administration/Government Relations/Government Services **CN:** W.L. Ross & Co., LLC **DOB:** 11/28/1937 **PB:** Weehawken **SC:** NJ **PT:** Son of Wilbur Louis and Agnes (O'Neill) R. **MS:** Married **SPN:** Hilary Geary; Betsy McCaughey, December 7, 1995 (div. 2000); Judith Nodine, May 26, 1961 (div. 1995); **CH:** Jessica, Amanda **ED:** AB in English Lit., Yale University, 1959; MBA with distinction, Harvard Business School, 1961 **C:** Secretary, U.S. Department of Commerce, Washington, DC, 2017-; Chmn., CEO, W.L. Ross & Co., LLC, New York City, New York, 2000—2017; Chmn., chief investment officer, Rothschild Recovery Fund, New York City, New York, 1997-2000; CEO, News Communications Inc., New York City, New York, 1996-98; Senior managing director, Rothschild, Inc., New York City, New York, 1976-2000; President, Faulkner, Dawkins and Sullivan Securities Corp., New York City, New York, 1964-76; Associate, Wood, Struthers and Winthrop, New York City, New York, 1963-64 **CR:** Board directors Casella Waste Systems Inc., 1999-2003, International Steel Group, Inc., Cleveland,

2002-04, Ohizumi Manufacturing Co., Japan, 2003-, Burlington Industries, 2003-, Marquis Who's Who LLC, 2003-06, Marquis Who's Who Inc., 2004-06, Japan, Mittal Steel Co., 2004-06, International Coal Group, 2005-11, International Textile Group, 2005—, Arcelor Mittal Steel Co., 2005-, Montpelier Re Holdings, Ltd., 2006-10, Wagon, PLC, 2006-08, BankUnited Inc., 2009-, The Greenbrier Companies Inc., 2009-13, Sun Bancorp Inc., 2010-, Talmer Bancorp, Inc., 2010-, Air Lease Corp., 2010-13; director Ocluen Fin. Corp., 2013-. **CIV:** Treasurer New York State Democratic Committee, 1980-83, American Federation Arts, 1993—95, The New Museum, 1993—95; vice chairman Brooklyn Museum, 1981—95; chairman univ. council committee on art Yale University, 1983-88; chairman National Academy of Design, New York City, 1985—89, American Art Forum, Smithsonian Institution, 1987—; trustee, vice chairman National Museum American Art, Washington, DC 1986-91, chairman, 1991—94; trustee, Museum American Financial History, chairman, Japan Society, 2010-, Brookings Institution, Economic Studies Council, 2011-, Yale University School Management, board advisor, 2009-, Harvard Business School, board deans advisors, Gustave Hyde Center National Museum American Indian, 2001—11, National Museum American Financial History, Whitney Museum American Art, Preservation Foundation of Palm Beach; trustee Sarah Lawrence College, 1986—91, chairman art gallery, 1984—91; president Parrish Art Museum, 1991-95; chairman New York Hist. Society, 1993-94; board directors Smithsonian Institute National Board, 1994—, chairman board 1995; national chairman Smithsonian Bicentennial Celebration, 1996; board directors Turnaround Management Association, 2001—; chairman Absolute Recovery Hedge Fund, Ltd., Hamilton, Bermuda, Taiyo Fund, 2003-13, Japan Real Estate Recovery Fund, 2003-08; director Palm Beach Civic Association, 2005-, Yale University School Management; member committee on univ. relations, committee on capital markets regulation Harvard University **MIL:** With US Army, 1961-63 **AW:** Named one of The Forbes 400: Richest Americans, 2006—, 50 Most Influential People in Global Fin., Bloomberg Markets, 2011; recipient Legend in Leadership award, Yale School Management, 2005, Order if the Rising Sun, Gold, and Silver Star, Ambassador Sumio Kusaka, 2015 **MEM:** Fellow Jonathan Edward College of Yale University; member Financial Analysts Federation (chartered), Sterling Fellow Yale University, The Business Round Table, Bath and Tennis Club, Everglades Club, Harvard Business School Club New York (board directors), Beach Club. **H:** Collecting art **BA:** U.S. Department of Commerce, 1401 Constitution Ave NW,, Washington, DC, 20230

ROTH, ALVIN ELIOT, T: Economics Professor **I:** Education/Educational Services **DOB:** 12/18/1951 **PB:** NYC **PT:** Son of Ernest and Lillian (Caesar) R.; Married Emilie Matarasso, May 22, 1977; children: Aaron Leon, Benjamin Nathaniel. **ED:** Doctor of Economics and Management Honoris Causa, Lund University, 2014; DHL (hon.), University Pittsburgh, 2014; Doctor Honoris Causa, University Amsterdam, 2014; Doctor Honoris Causa, Technion-Israel Institute of Technology, 2013; PhD, Stanford University, 1974; MS, Stanford University, 1973; BS, Columbia University, 1971 **C:** President, American Economics Association, 2017-; Craig and Susan McCaw Professor of Economics, Department of Economics, Stanford University, 2013-; George Gund Professor Economics and Business Administration emeritus, Harvard University, Boston, 2012-; McCaw Senior Visiting Professor of Economics, Department of Economics, Stanford University, 2012; George Gund Professor

Economics and Business Administration, Harvard University, Boston, 1998-2012; Professor business administration, University Pittsburgh, 1985; A.W. Mellon professor economics, University Pittsburgh, 1982-98; Professor department of business administration and Department Economics, University Illinois, Urbana, 1979-82; Associate professor, University Illinois, Urbana, 1977-79; Assistant professor department business administration and department econs., University Illinois, Urbana, 1974-77 **CR:** Senior fellow Stanford Institute for Economic Policy Research, 2013- research associate National Bureau of Economic Research, 1998- visiting professor, department economics University Tel Aviv, Israel, 1995 Bogen Visiting Professor, Department Economics Hebrew University of Jerusalem, Israel, 1995 Mendes-France visiting professor economics The Technion, Haifa, Israel, 1986 Beckman Associate Center for Advanced Study, University Illinois, 1981 institute associate Institute for Mathematical Studies in Social Sciences, Stanford University, 1978 **CW:** Author: Axiomatic Models of Bargaining, 1979, Game-Theoretic Models of Bargaining, 1985, Laboratory Experimentation in Economics, 1987, The Shapley Value, 1988, (with M. Sotomayor) Two-Sided Matching: A Study in Game Theoretic Modeling and Analysis, 1990, (with J. Kagel) Handbook of Experimental Economics, 1995, (with B. Holmstrom and P. Milgron) Game Theory in the Tradition of Bob Wilson, 2002, Who Gets What and Why, 2015; published several articles in peer-reviewed journals **AW:** Recipient Founders' prize Texas Instruments Foundation, 1980, Lanchester prize, Operations Research Society of America, 1990, T.W. Schultz prize, Department Economics, University Chicago, 2006; co-recipient NKR Terasaki Medical Innovation award, American Transplant Congress, 2012, Nobel Memorial Prize in Economic Sciences (Sveriges Riksbank Prize), Royal Swedish Academy Sciences, 2012, Golden Goose award, 2013; Guggenheim fellow, 1983-84; Fellow Center for Philosophy of Sci., University Pittsburgh, 1983; A.P. Sloan research fellow, 1984-86; Economic Theory Fellow, Society for the Advancement of Economic Theory, 2013; named one of 10 Outstanding Young Americans award, US Jaycees, 1984. **MEM:** Fellow Econometric Society, American Academy Arts & Sciences, American Association for the Advancement of Science; charter fellow Society for Economic Measurement; member American Economic Association, National Bureau of Economic Research, National Academy of Sciences

ROTH, PHILIP, T: Writer **I:** Writing and Editing **DOB:** 03/19/1933 **PB:** Newark **SC:** NJ/USA **YOP:** 2018-05-22 **ED:** Student, Rutgers University, New Jersey; AB in English, Bucknell University, Lewisburg,, Pennsylvania, 1954; MA in English Lit., University Chicago, 1955; LittD (hon.), Harvard University, 2003 **C:** Retired, University of Pennsylvania, 1991; Adjunct Professor Comparative Lit., University of Pennsylvania, 1967—1991; Writer in Residence, Princeton University, 1962-64; Faculty, Iowa Writers Workshop, 1960-62; English Teacher, University Chicago, 1956-58 **CR:** Distinguished Professor City University of New York Hunter College, 1989—1992 **CW:** Author: (novels) Goodbye, Columbus, 1959 (Daroff Award, Jewish Book Council of America, 1960, National Book Award, 1960), Letting Go, 1962, When She Was Good, 1967, Portnoy's Complaint, 1969, Our Gang, 1971, The Great American Novel, 1973, My Life As a Man, 1974, Deception: A Novel, 1990, Operation Shylock: A Confession, 1993 (PEN/Faulkner Award for Fiction, 1994), Sabbath's Theater, 1995 (National Book Award, 1995), The Plot Against America, 2004 (Sidewise Award for Alternate Hist.,

2005), Everyman, 2006 (PEN/Faulkner Award for Fiction, 2007), Indignation, 2008, The Humbling, 2009, Nemesis, 2010, (Zuckerman novels) The Ghost Writer, 1979, Zuckerman Unbound, 1981, The Anatomy Lesson, 1983, The Prague Orgy, 1985, The Counterlife, 1986 (National Book Critics Circle award, 1986), American Pastoral, 1997 (Prix du Meilleur Livre Étranger, France, 2000, Pulitzer Prize for Fiction, 1997), I Married a Communist, 1998, The Human Stain, 2000 (PEN/Faulkner Award for Fiction, 2001, WH Smith Lit. Award, 2001, Prix Médicis Étranger, France, 2002), Exit Ghost, 2007, (Kepesh novels) The Breast, 1972, The Professor of Desire, 1977, The Dying Animal, 2001, (story collections) Reading Myself and Others, 1976, A Philip Roth Reader, 1980, Shop Talk, 2001, (memoirs) The Facts: A Novelist's Autobiography, 1988, Patrimony: A True Story, 1991 (National Book Critics Circle award, 1991), Numerous Short Stories, Essays and Narratives **AW:** Named to New Jersey Hall of Fame, 2010; Recipient Lit. Medal of Honor, National Arts Club, 1991, Karel Capek Prize, Czech Republic, 1994, National Medal of Arts, The White House, 1998, Gold Medal in Fiction, American Academy of Arts and Letters, 2001, Award for Distinguished Contribution to Am. Letters, National Book Foundation, 2002, PEN/Nabokov Award for Lifetime Achievement, 2006, PEN/Saul Bellow Award for Achievement in American Fiction, 2007, Man Booker International Prize, 2011; Grantee Guggenheim Foundation, 1959—60, Rockefeller Foundation, 1966, Commander of the Legion, Republic of France, 2013, Lifetime Achievement Award from PEN/ALLEN Foundation, Prince of Asturias Award for Literature, 2012, Library of Congress Creative Achievement Award, 2012,

ROTH, VERONICA, T: Writer **I:** Writing and Editing **PB:** New York **SC:** NY/USA **ED:** Creative Writing, Northwestern University **CW:** (Books) Divergent, 2011, Insurgent, 2012, Allegiant, 2013, The World of Divergent: The Path to Allegiant,2013, Four: A Divergent Collection, 2014, We Can Be Mended, 2017, Carve the Mark, 2017, The Fates Divide, 2018(Short Story) Hearken, 2013

ROTHFUS, KEITH JAMES, T: U.S. Representative from Pennsylvania, Lawyer **I:** Law and Legal Services **DOB:** 04/25/1962 **PB:** Endicott **ED:** JD, University Notre Dame Law School, 1994; BS in Information Systems, State University of New York, Buffalo, 1984 **C:** Member, US House Judiciary Committee, 2013-; Member, Committee on Financial Services,; Republican Study Committee; Member, US House Homeland Security Committee, 2013-; Member, US Congress from 12th Pennsylvania District, Washington, 2013-; Director Faith Based & Community Initiatives, US Department Homeland Security, Washington, 2006-07 **CIV:** Board directors, Veterans Leadership Program of Western Pennsylvania (VLP), **PA:** Republican

ROTHMAN, PAUL B., T: dean, medical educator **I:** Education/Educational Services **ED:** MD, Yale University, 1984 **C:** CEO, Johns Hopkins Medicine, 2012-; Dean, Johns Hopkins University, 2012-; Dean, Roy J. and Lucille A. Carver College Medicine, University Iowa, 2008-12; Head, professor internal medicine, Roy J. and Lucille A. Carver College Medicine, University Iowa, 2004-08; Richard J. Stock professor immunology and microbiology, chief pulmonary allergy and critical care medicine division, Columbia University College Physicians and Surgeons, New York City, 1997; Resident, Columbia-Presbyn. Medical Center, New York City, **CR:** Member Am. Thoracic Society Asthma Immunology and Inflammation Program Committee, Am. Academy Allergy, Asthma and Immunology Grant Review Committee, Israel Cancer Research Fund International Sci. Adv. Board, Immunologic

Scis. Study Section, National Institutes of Health **CW:** Contributor articles to professional journals **AW:** Recipient Pharmacia Allergy Research Foundation International Award, Leukemia Society of America Scholar Award, Pew Scholars Award, Pfizer Scholars Award, James S. McDonnell Foundation Career Devel. Award **MEM:** Fellow: Am. College Physicians; mem.: Association Am. Physicians, Collegium Internationale Allergologicum, Am. Society for Clinical Investigation, Council of Association of Am. Physicians, Association Professors of Medicine

ROTHSCHILD, JEFF, T: Vice President of Infrastructure Software at Facebook **I:** Internet **DOB:** 06/08/1905 **PB:** , U.S. **SC:** , U.S. **ED:** BS, MS,Vanderbilt University,1977,1979 **C:** Vice President of Infrastructure Software, Facebook, 2005-; Co-Founder, Mendocino Software, 2003-2008; Co-Founder,Veritas Software, 1988-; Co-Founder,Mpath Interactive, 1999-; Advisor, Venture Partner,Accel Partners, 1999-

ROUNDS, MIKE, T: U.S. Senator, South Dakota **I:** Government Administration/Government Relations/Government Services **DOB:** 10/24/1954 **PB:** Huron **SC:** SD/USA **ED:** BS in Political Science, South Dakota State University, Brookings, SD (1977) **C:** U.S. Senator from South Dakota (2015-Present); Governor, State of South Dakota, Pierre, SD (2003-2011); Majority Leader, South Dakota State Senate (1995-2002); Minority Whip, South Dakota State Senate (1993-1994); Member, District 24, South Dakota State Senate, SD (1991-2002); Partner, Fischer, Rounds & Associates, Inc. **CIV:** President, Pierre-Ft. Pierre Exchange Club; Vice President, St. Joseph School Home & School Association; Board president, Oahe YMCA **MEM:** Chairman, Midwestern Governors Association; Elks; Ducks Unlimited; Knights of Columbus, Pierre Elks Lodge **H:** Racquetball; Hunting; Boating; Camping **PA:** Republican

ROUSEY, RONDA JEAN, T: Mixed Martial Artist **I:** Athletics **DOB:** 02/01/1987 **PB:** Riverside County **SC:** CA/USA **PT:** Daughter of Ron and AnnMaria DeMars (Waddell) Rousey. **C:** Professional mixed martial artist, UFC, 2011-; Women's Bantamweight Champion, UFC, 2012-15 **CW:** Actress: (films) The Expendables 3, 2014, Furious 7, 2015; guest appearance (films) Entourage, 2015; author: My Fight/Your Fight, 2015 **AW:** Named Female Fighter of Year, World Mixed Martial Artist awards, 2012-13, Best Fighter, ESPY Awards, 2015, Female Athlete of Year, 2015, 2014; named one of The 100 Most Influential People in the World, TIME Magazine, 2016, The 10 Most Fascinating People of 2015, Barbara Walters Special; recipient Bronze medal in Judo, Olympic Games, 2008, Gold medal, Pan American Games, 2007

ROUZER, DAVID, T: U.S. Representative From North Carolina **I:** Government Administration/Government Relations/Government Services **DOB:** 02/16/1972 **PB:** Landstuhl **SC:** Germany **ED:** BA in Agricultural Business Management & Chemical, North Carolina State University, 1994 **C:** Transportation and Infrastructure Committee, Agriculture Committee, U.S. House of Representatives From North Carolina's Seventh District, 2015-Present; District 12, North Carolina State Senate, 2009-2013; Associate Administrator, U.S. Department of Agriculture, 2005-2006; Assistant to Dean, North Carolina State College Agricultural & Life Sciences, 2001-2002; Legislative Aide, Senior Policy Advisor to Senator Jesse Helms, U.S. Senate, 1996-2001; Owner, Rouzer Co. **PA:** Republican **BA:** 424 Cannon House Office Building, Washington, DC, 20515

ROVNER, ILANA D., T: Federal Judge **I:** Law and Legal Services **DOB:** 08/21/1938 **PB:** Riga **SC:** Latvia **ED:** Honorary DHL, Spertus College of Judaica, 1992; Honorary LittD, Mundelein College, 1989; Honorary LittD, Rosary College, 1989; JD, Illinois Institute of Technology, 1966; Postgraduate, Georgetown University, 1961-1963; Postgraduate, University London King's College, 1961; AB, Bryn Mawr College, 1960 **C:** Circuit Judge, U.S. Court of Appeals, Seventh Circuit, Chicago, IL, 1992-Present; District Judge, U.S. District Court, Northern District, State of Illinois, Chicago, IL, 1984-1992; Deputy Governor, Legal Counsel, Gov. James R. Thompson, Chicago, IL, 1977-1984; Chief of Public Protection, U.S. Attorney's Office, Chicago, IL, 1976-1977; Deputy Chief Of Public Protection, U.S. Attorney's Office, Chicago, IL, 1975-1976; Assistant U.S. Attorney, U.S. Attorney's Office, Chicago, IL, 1973-1977; Judicial Clerk, U.S. District Court, Northern District, State of Illinois, Chicago, IL, 1972-1973 **CR:** Fairness Committee, U.S. Court of Appeals, Seventh Circuit, 1996-Present; Race And Gender Fairness Committee, U.S. Court of Appeals, Seventh Circuit, 1993-Present; Judicial Conference, U.S. Committee of Court Administration Case Management, 2000-2006; Gender Study Task Force, U.S. Court of Appeals, Seventh Circuit, 1995-1996; Civil Justice Reform Act Advisory Committee, U.S. Court of Appeals, Seventh Circuit, 1991-1995; Gannon-Proctor Commission On The Status Of Women In Illinois, 1982-1984 **CIV:** Board of Directors, Rehabilitation Institute of Chicago, 1998-Present, Central And East European Law Initiative Volunteer, American Bar Association, 1997-Present, Trustee, Illinois Institute of Technology, 1989-Present, Board of Overseers, Illinois Institute of Technology/Kent College of Law, 1983-Present, Visiting Committee, University of Chicago Law School, 2000-2003, Chair, Illinois State Selection Committee, Rhodes Scholarship Trust, 1998-2000, Visiting Committee, Northwestern University School of Law, 1993-1998, Visiting Committee, University of Chicago Law School, 1993-1996, Board of Visitors, Northern Illinois University College of Law, 1992-1994, Advisory Council, Rush Center For Sports Medicine, Chicago, IL, 1991-1996, Trustee, Bryn Mawr College, Pennsylvania, 1983-1989 **AW:** Women Of Valor Award, B'nai B'rith International, 2008, Chicago Legal Legends Award, American Constitution Society, 2008, Professionalism Award, American Inns Court of the Seventh Circuit, 2008, Lifetime Achievement Award, Northwestern University Jewish Law Students Association, 2008, Inaugural Speaker, Distinguished Judge Series, Continuing Legal Education Program, Illinois Attorney General Office, 2007, Inaugural Judge Abraham Lincoln Marovitz Mentoring Award, Chicago Bar Association And Foundation Lend-A-Hand Program, 2005, Hero Of Liberty Award, National Liberty Museum, 2005, Thurgood Marshall Career Achievement Award, Association of Corporate Counsel Chicago Chapter, 2005, Justice John Paul Stevens Award, Chicago Bar Association, 2005, Lifetime Achievement Award, Jewish Judges Association of Illinois, 2004, Vanguard Award, Chicago Bar Association And Lesbian And Gay Bar Association of Chicago, 2004, Decalogue Society of Lawyers, 2004, Chicago Historical Society Trailblazers Award, 2003, Today's Chicago Women Hall Of Fame, 2002, First Woman Award, Georgetown University Law Center, 2001, Chicago Bar Association Alliance For Women And Women's Bar Association of Illinois, 2000, First Woman Award (In Conjunction With Chicago Bar Association Alliance For Women), Women's Bar Association of Illinois, 2000, Award, Chicago Attorneys Council Of Hadassah, 1999, 15 Chicago Women Of The Century, Chicago Sun Times, 1999, Arabella Babb Mansfield Award, National Association of Women Lawyers, 1998, Merit Award, Decalogue Society Of Lawyers, 1997, Hebrew Immigrant Aid Society of Chicago 85th Anniversary Honoree, 1996, First Myra Bradwell Woman Of Achievement Award, Women's Bar Association of Illinois, 1994, First Woman Award, Valparaiso University School of Law, 1993, Louis Dembitz Brandeis Medal For Distinguished Legal Service, Brandeis University, 1993, Citation Of Honor, Decalogue Society Of Lawyers, 1991, Annual Award, Chicago Foundation For Women, 1990, Annual Award, Women's Bar Association of Illinois, 1989, ORT Women's American Community Service Award, 1987-1988, Service Award, Spertus College Of Judaica, 1987, Commendation Defense Of Prisoners Committee, Chicago Bar Association, 1987, Professional Achievement Award, Illinois Institute of Technology, 1986, Woman Of Achievement, Chicago Women's Club, 1986, Today's Chicago Woman Of The Year, 1985, Annual Guardian Police Award, 1977, Special Achievement Award, U.S. Department of Justice, 1976, Annual National Law And Social Justice Leadership Award, League To Improve The Community, 1975, Special Commendation Award, 1975 **MEM:** Chicago Bar Association, Jewish Judges Association of Illinois, Decalogue Society Of Lawyers, Chicago Council on Lawyers, Women's Bar Association of Illinois, Federal Judges Association, Kappa Beta Pi, Honorary Member, Phi Alpha Delta, Selection Committee, Chicago Chapter, Federal Bar Association, 1977-1980, Treasurer, Chicago Chapter, Federal Bar Association, 1978-1979, Secretary, Chicago Chapter, Federal Bar Association, 1979-1980, Second Vice President, Chicago Chapter, Federal Bar Association, 1980-1981, First Vice President, Chicago Chapter, Federal Bar Association, 1981-1982, President, Chicago Chapter, Federal Bar Association, 1982-1983, Second Vice President, Seventh Circuit, Chicago Chapter, Federal Bar Association, 1983-1984, Vice President, Seventh Circuit, Chicago Chapter, Federal Bar Association, 1984-1985 **BAR:** Federal Trial Bar, Northern District, State of Illinois, 1982, U.S. Supreme Court, 1981, U.S. Court of Appeals, Seventh Circuit, 1977, U.S. District Court, Northern District, State of Illinois, 1972, State of Illinois, 1972 **BA:** 219 S Dearborn Street, Room 2722, Chicago, IL, 60604

ROWLING, J.K., T: Writer **I:** Writing and Editing **DOB:** 07/31/1965 **PB:** Gloucestershire **SC:** England **PT:** Daughter of Peter and Anne Rowling **ED:** LLD (hon.), Aberdeen University, 2006; Degree (hon.), University of Edinburgh, 2004; Degree (hon.), University of St. Andrews, 2000; LittD (hon.), Harvard University, 2008; LittD (hon.), University of Exeter, 2000; LittD (hon.), Dartmouth College, 2000; LittD (hon.), Napier University, 2000; BA in French and Classics, University of Exeter, England, 1986 **C:** Teacher, Scotland, 1990-94; Former researcher, Amnesty International; Writer 1997- **CIV:** First ambassador to president, One Parent Families/Gingerbread, London, 2000- Numerous philanthropic donations and vol. work for various charities including Comic Relief, Multiple Sclerosis Society Great Britain, others **CW:** Author: (Harry Potter series) Harry Potter and the Philosopher's Stone (published in US as Harry Potter and the Sorcerer's Stone), 1997 (Smarties Book Prize Gold winner, 1997, British Book awards Children's Book of Year, 1998, Premio Cento per la Letteratura Infantile, 1998, Anne Spencer Lindbergh Prize for children's lit., 1998, American Booksellers Association ABBY award, 1999, Sorcieres Prix, 1999, Birmingham Cable Children's Book award, Young Telegraph Paperback of Year, Sheffield Children's Book award), Harry Potter and the Chamber of Secrets, 1998 (Smarties Book Prize Gold winner, 1998), Harry Potter and the

Prisoner of Azkaban, 1999, Harry Potter and the Goblet of Fire, 2000, Harry Potter and the Order of the Phoenix, 2003, Harry Potter and the Half-Blood Prince, 2005 (Quill award for Book of Year, 2005, Brit. Book of Year, 2006), Harry Potter and the Deathly Hallows, 2007, (supplement to Potter series) Quidditch Through the Ages, 2001, Fantastic Beasts & Where to Find Them, 2001, (children's stories) The Tales of Beedle the Bard, 2008, (novels) The Casual Vacancy, 2012, Very Good Lives: The Fringe Benefits of Failure and the Importance of Imagination, 2015, History of Magic in North America, 2016, Fourteenth Century-Seventeenth Century, 2016, Seventeenth Century and Beyond, 2016, Rappaport's Law, 2016; author: (under pseudonym Robert Galbraith) The Cuckoo's Calling, 2013, The Silkworm, 2014, Career of Evil, 2015, (Books) Short Stories from Hogwarts of Power, Politics, and Pesky Poltergeists, 2016, Short Stories from Hogwarts of Heroism, Hardship and Dangerous, 2016, Hogwarts: An Incomplete and Unreliable Guide, 2016 **AW:** Named Entertainer of Year, Entertainment Weekly, 2007, No. 1 on Top 10 authors list, Amazon.com, 1995-2005; named an Hon. Knight Légion d'honneur, France, 2009, Officer of the Most Excellent Order of the British Empire (OBE), Prince of Wales, 2001; named one of The 100 Most Powerful Women in Entertainment, Hollywood Reporter, 2013, Brit. Top 50 Movers and Shakers, BBC 3, The 100 Most Powerful Celebrities, Forbes magazine, 2008, The 100 Most Powerful Women, 2011-13, 2005; recipient Beacon award for Targeted Philanthropy, 2013, City of Edinburgh award, 2008, Rave award for Business, WIRED Magazine, 2007 **BA:** C/O Bloomsbury Publishing PLC, 50 Bedford Square, London, WC1B 3DP

ROY, PATRICK, T: Professional Hockey Player (Retired) **I:** Athletics **DOB:** 10/05/1965 **PB:** Quebec City **SC:** Canada **PT:** Michel Roy; Barbara (Miller) Roy **C:** Head Coach, Vice President of Hockey Operations, Colorado Avalanche (2013-2016); Head Coach, Quebec Remparts, QMJHL (2005-2013); Vice President of Hockey Operations, Quebec Remparts, QMJHL (2003-2013); Goaltender, Colorado Avalanche (1995-2003); Goaltender, Montreal Canadiens (1984-1995); Owner, General Manager, Quebec Remparts, QMJHL **CR:** Talk-Show Hockey Analyst, L'Antichambre (2012-Present) **AW:** Recipient, Jack Adams Award (2014); Recipient, Jack Adams Award (2014); Named, Colorado Sports Hall of Fame (2004); Recipient, William M. Jennings Trophy (2002); Recipient, Conn Smythe Trophy as Playoff MVP (2001); Recipient, Vezina Trophy (1992); Recipient, William M. Jennings Trophy (1992); Named, Sporting News All-Star Team (1992); Named, First All-Star Team, NHL (1992); Named, Second All-Star Team (1991); Named, First All-Star Team, NHL (1990); Named, Sporting News All-Star Team (1989-1990); Recipient, Vezina Trophy (1989-1990); Recipient, Trico Goaltender Award (1989-1990); Named, First All-Star Team, NHL (1989); Named, Second All-Star Team (1988); Recipient, William M. Jennings Trophy (1987-1989); Named, All-Rookie Team (1986); Recipient, Conn Smythe Trophy as Playoff MVP (1986) **ACH:** Achievements include being a member of Stanley Cup Champion Montreal Canadiens, 1986, 1993, Colorado Avalanche, 1996, 2001; being the first goaltender to record 500 NHL victories, 2001; holding the record for most NHL wins by a goaltender with 551, 2003-2009; setting the record for most NHL playoff wins by a goaltender with 151; having his number, 33, retired by Colorado Avalanche, 2003 and Montreal Canadiens, 2008; being inducted into the Hockey Hall of Fame, 2006 **BA:** Les Remparts De Quebec, Colisee Pepsi, 250 Boulevard Wilfrid-Hamel, Quebec, QC, Canada, G1L 5A7

ROYBAL-ALLARD, LUCILLE, T: U.S. Representative from California **I:** Government Administration/Government Relations/Government Services **DOB:** 06/12/1941 **PB:** Boyle Heights **SC:** CA/USA **PT:** Daughter of Edward Ross and Lucille (Beserra) Roybal; **ED:** BA in Speech, California State University, LA, 1965 **C:** Member, U.S. Congress from 40th California District, 2013-; Member, House Appropriations Committee; Member, U.S. Congress from 34th California District, 2003-13; Member, U.S. Congress from 33th California District, Washington, 1993-2003; Member District 56, California State Assembly, 1986-92; Assistant director, Alcoholism Council East LA,; Employee, United Way, **CR:** Chair Congl. Hispanic Caucus, 1999-2000 member Congl. Children's Working Grp., Homeland Security Task Force, Livable Communities Task Force **AW:** Recipient Madre y Mujer award, Kimberly-Clark, 2006 **PA:** Democrat

ROYCE, ED, T: Chairman of the House Foreign Affairs Committee **I:** Government Administration/Government Relations/Government Services **DOB:** 10/12/1951 **PB:** Los Angeles **SC:** CA/USA **ED:** BA in Business Administration, California State University, Fullerton, CA (1977) **C:** Chairman, US House Foreign Relations Committee (2013-Present); Member, US Congress from the 39th California District (2013-Present); Member, US Congress from the 40th California District (2003-2013); Member, US Congress from the 39th California District, Washington, DC (1993-2003); Member, District 32, California State Senate (1983-1992; Tax Manager, Southwestern Portland Cement Company **AW:** Named Child Advocate of the Year, California Association Service for Children (1987); Legislator of the Year, Orange County Republican Committee (1986); Visionaries for Africa Award, Africa Society, National Summit on Africa (2004): Taxpayers Hero Award, Citizens Against Government Waste (1994); Taxpayers Friend Award, National Taxpayers Union (1994); Medal of Commendation, Veterans of Foreign Wars (1985) **MEM:** Anaheim Chamber of Commerce; Fullerton Chamber of Commerce; Literacy Volunteers of America **ACH:** Achievements include writing nation's 1st felony stalking law; writing bill for Foster Family Home Insurance Fund, creating foster parent recruitment and training programs **PA:** Republican **BA:** Office of Ed Royce, 2310 Rayburn House Office Building, Washington, DC, 20515

RUBIO, MARCO ANTONIO, T: U.S. Senator from Florida **I:** Government Administration/Government Relations/Government Services **DOB:** 05/28/1971 **PB:** Miami **PT:** Son of Mario and Oria (Garcia) Rubio; **ED:** JD, University Miami School Law, 1996; BS in Political Science, University Florida, 1993; Student, Tarkio College, 1989-90 **C:** Member, US Senate Foreign Relations Committee, Washington, 2011-; Member, US Senate Small Business & Entrepreneurship, Washington, 2011-; Member, US Senate Select Committee on Intelligence, Washington, 2011-; Member, US Senate Commerce, Sci. & Transportation Committee, Washington, 2011-; US Senator from Florida, Washington, 2011-; Visiting professor, Florida International University Metropolitan Center, 2008; Speaker, Florida House of Reps., 2006-08; Majority leader, Florida House of Reps., 2003-06; Member District 111, Florida House of Reps., 2000-08; City commissioner, West Miami, Florida, 1998-2000 **CR:** Candidate for the 2016 Republican Party Presidential nomination political analyst Univision, 2008 **CW:** Author: 100 Innovative Ideas for Florida's Future: A Plan of Action, 2006, An American Son: A Memoir, 2012, American Dreams: Restoring Economic Opportunity for Everyone, 2015 **AW:**

Named one of The 100 Most Influential People in the World, TIME magazine, 2012; recipient Freshman Legislator of Year, Florida Petroleum Marketers Association **PA:** Republican **BA:** Office of Marco Rubio, 284 Russell Senate Office Building, Washington, DC, 20510

RUDDY, CHRISTOPHER, T: News Media Executive **I:** Media & Entertainment **DOB:** 01/28/1965 **PB:** Mineola **SC:** NY/USA **PT:** Son of Francis and Marie (Lynch) R. **ED:** MS in Econs., London School Econs., 1988; BA in History, St. John's University, Jamaica, New York, 1987 **C:** Started Newsmax Media, 1998; Reporter, Pittsburgh Tribune Rev., Greensburg, Pennsylvania, 1994-1998; Reporter, New York Post, New York City, 1993-94; Editor, New York Guardian, New York City, 1990-93; High School Teacheer, Bronx, New York; **CR:** Member, Media Fellow, Hoover Institution on War, Revolution and Peace, Member, Board of directors, Financial Publishers Association, Member, International Council; **CW:** Catastrophe: Clinton's Role in America's Worst Disaster, 2002, Bitter Legacy: NewsMax Reveals the Untold Story of the Clinton-Gore Years, 2002, The Strange Death of Vincent Foster: An Investigation, 1997, Vincent Foster: The Ruddy Investigation, 1996;; ;; **AW:** Recipient Courage in Journalism award Western Journalism Center, 1994; Media fellow Stanford University, 1996. **MEM:** Member New York Press Club. **BA:** NewsMax Media, 560 VILLAGE BOULEVARD SUITE 270, West Palm Beach, FL, 33409

RUDOLPH, JEFFREY N., T: President of the Calinfornia Science Center **I:** Museums & Institutions **ED:** MBA, Yale University, New Haven; BA, University of California, Berkeley **C:** President, California Sci. Center Foundation,; President, CEO, California Sci. Center,; Executive Director, California Sci. Center,; Deputy Director, California Sci. Center, LA,; Executive Director, State of California Intergovernmental Personnel Act Adv. Board,; Program Analyst to the Legis. Budget Committee, California State Legislature, **CR:** Board of Directors EXPO Center, Museum Trustees Association Adv. Council of Directors, Sci. Museums Exhibits Collaborative, National Health Sci. Consortium Member California Council on Sci. and Tech. **MEM:** Mem.: Association Sci.-Tech. Centers (Past President), American Association Museums (Chairman 2004-06)

RUIZ, RAUL, T: U.S. Representative from California, Physician **I:** Government Administration/Government Relations/Government Services **DOB:** 08/25/1972 **PB:** Coachella **SC:** CA/USA **ED:** MS in Public Health, Harvard T.H. Chan School of Public Health (2007); MPP, John F. Kennedy School of Government, Harvard University (2001); MD, Harvard Medical School, Harvard University (2001); BS, University of California, Los Angeles (1994) **C:** Member, U.S. House Veterans' Affairs Committee (2013-Present); Member, U.S. House of Natural Resources Committee (2013-Present); Member, U.S. Congress, 36th California District, Washington, DC (2013-Present); Senior Associate Dean, University of California, Riverside, School of Medicine (2011-2012); Emergency Physician, Eisenhower Medical Center; Consultant, El Salvadoran Ministry Health; Consultant, Serbian Ministry Health **CR:** Medical Director, J/P Haitian Relief Organization (2010); Founder, Coachella Healthcare Initiative (2010) **AW:** Recipient, Commander's Award for Public Service, 82nd Airborne Division, U.S. Army (2011) **PA:** Democrat **BA:** Ste F, 43875 Washington St, Palm Desert, CA, 92211-8249

RUMSFELD, DONALD HENRY, T: Former U.S. Secretary of Defense **I:** Government Administration/Government Relations/Government Services **DOB:** 07/09/1932 **PB:** Chgo. **ED:** PhD (hon.), Hampden-Sydney College; PhD (hon.), RAND Grad. School, 1993; PhD (hon.), Illinois Wesleyan University; PhD (hon.), Claremont Grad. School, California; PhD (hon.), Bryant College; PhD (hon.), National College Education; PhD (hon.), Tuskegee Institute; PhD (hon.), Park College; LLD (hon.), Lake Forest College, 1975; PhD (hon.), Illinois College; PhD (hon.), De Paul University College Commerce; AB, Princeton University, 1954 **C:** Distinguished visiting fellow Hoover Institution, Stanford University, 2007-; Chairman, Gilead Sciences, Inc., Foster City, California, 1997-2001; Chairman, CEO, General Instrument Corp., Chicago, 1990-93; Senior adv., William Blair & Co., Chicago, 1985-90; Special presidential ambassador to Mid. East, The White House, 1983-84; Chairman CEO, G.D. Searle & Co., Skokie, Illinois, 1985; President, CEO, G.D. Searle & Co., Skokie, Illinois, 1977-85; Secretary, US Department Defense, Washington, 2001-06; Secretary, US Department Defense, Washington, 1975-77; Chief of staff to President, The White House, Washington, 1974-75; Chair transition to the presidency of Gerald R. Ford, The White House, Washington, 1974; US ambassador & permanent rep. to NATO, US Department State, Brussels, 1973-74; Director Cost of Living Council, The White House, Washington, 1971-73; Counsellor to the President, The White House, Washington, 1970-73; Director Office of Economic Opportunity & assistant to the President, The White House, Washington, 1969-70; Member, US Congress from 13th Illinois District, Washington, 1963-69; Investment broker, A.G. Becker & Co., Chicago, 1960-62; Member staff to Rep. Robert Griffin, US House of Representatives, 1959; Administrative assistant to Rep. David Dennison, US House of Representatives, 1957-59 **CR:** Member General Advisory Committee on Arms Control & advisor to the government on national security affairs, 1983-84, US Joint Advisory Commission on US/Japan Relations, 1983-84, National Commission on Pub. Service, 1987-90, National Economic Commission, 1988-89, Commission on US/Japan Relations, 1989-91 special presidential envoy on the Law of the Sea Treaty, 1982-83, senior advisor to the President panel on Strategic Systems, 1983-84, chairman US Commission to Assess the Ballistic Missile Threat to the U.S., 1998 commissioner US Federal Trade Deficit Rev. Commission, 1999-2000 U.S. Commission to Assess National Security Space Management & Organization, 2000 board visitors, National Defense University, 1988-92. **CW:** Author:Strategic imperatives in East Asia,1998, Known and Unknown: A Memoir, 2011 (#1 New York Times bestseller), Rumsfeld's Rules: Leadership Lessons in Business, Politics, War, and Life, 2013; appeared in (documentaries) The World According to Dick Cheney, 2013, The Unknown Known, 2014 **AW:** Recipient Distinguished Eagle Scout award, 1975, Presidential Medal of Freedom, The White House, 1977, Outstanding Chief Executive Officer in the Pharmaceutical Industry award, 1980, George Catlett Marshall award, 1984, Woodrow Wilson award, 1985, Dwight David Eisenhower medal, 1993, James H. Doolittle award, 2003, Ronald Reagan Freedom award, 2003, Gerald R. Ford medal, 2004, Defender of the Constitution award, Conservative Political Action Conference, 2011 **PA:** Republican

RUPPERSBERGER, DUTCH, T: U.S. Representative from Maryland **I:** Government Administration/Government Relations/Government Services **DOB:** 01/31/1946 **PB:** Baltimore **SC:** Maryland **PT:** Son of Charles Albert and Margaret (Wilson) Ruppersberger; **ED:** BA, University Maryland, 1967; JD, University Baltimore, 1970 **CT:** Bar: Maryland 1972, US Supreme Court 1977; **C:** Member, US Congress from 2nd Maryland District, 2003—; Ranking member, US House Permanent Select Committee on Intelligence, 2011—2015; Member, US House Permanent Select Committee on Intelligence, 2003—2015; Partner, Ruppersberger, Winter, Clark & Mister, Timonium, Maryland, 1980—1994; Assistant state's attorney, Baltimore County State's Attorney, Towson, 1972-80; Law clerk to presiding justice, Baltimore County Cir. Court, Towson, 1970-72; Claims adjuster, US Fidelity & Guaranty Co., Baltimore, Maryland, 1969-70; Social worker, Baltimore City Schools, 1967-69 **CR:** Chief investigation div. State's Atty.'s Office, Towson, 1972—1980; liaison Baltimore County Police Dept./Md. State Police, 1973—1980; **CIV:** Legal council Baltimore County Athletic League; president Topfield Condominium Association, Cockeysville, Maryland, 1975—1978; campaign manager Senator Francis X. Kelly, Annapolis, 1980—1985; councilman Baltimore County Council, 1985—1994; coach, v.p Cockeysville Recreation Council, 1978—; president Greater Timonium Community Council, Maryland, 1980—; board directors Timonium Methodist Church, 1984—; **AW:** Named one of Outstanding Young Marylanders, Jaycees, 1979; recipient Appreciation award, Baltimore County Order Fraternal Police, 1977, 1979; **MEM:** Mem.: University Maryland Alumni Association (vice president), National College District Attorneys (adv. 1974—80), Baltimore County Bar Association (chairman bench-bar committee), Maryland Bar Association (grievance committee), Masons;

RUSCHA, EDWARD JOSEPH IV, T: Artist **I:** Fine Art **DOB:** 12/16/1937 **PB:** Omaha **SC:** NE/USA **MS:** Married **SPN:** Danna Knego (1967) **CH:** Edward Joseph **ED:** Coursework, Chouinard Art Institute, Los Angeles, CA (1956-1960) **CR:** Numerous Visiting Artist Positions Including University of California, Los Angeles (1969-1970), U.S. Representative, Venice Biennale (2005) **CIV:** Trustee, Museum of Contemporary Art, Los Angeles, CA **CW:** Author, "Twentysix Gasoline Stations" (1962), "Various Small Fires" (1964), "Some Los Angeles Apartments" (1965), "The Sunset Strip" (1966), "Thirtyfour Parking Lots" (1967), "Royal Road Test" (1967), "Business Cards" (1968), "Nine Swimming Pools" (1968), "Crackers" (1969), "Real Estate Opportunities" (1970), "Records" (1971), "A Few Palm Trees" (1971), "Colored People" (1972), "Hard Light" (1978), "Country Cityscapes" (2001), "ME and THE" (2002), "Ed Rusha and Photography" (2004), "OH/NO" (2008), "Dirty Baby" (2010); Noted for Numerous Graphite, Gunpowder and Pastel Drawings, Over 200 Limited-edition Prints; Producer, Director, Films "Premium" (1970), "Miracle" (1974); Began Showing Works, Ferus Gallery, LA (1963); First International Show, Galerie Rudolf Zwirner, Cologne, Germany (1968); Works Include Paintings, "Standard Station," Amarillo, Texas (1963), "Annie" (1963), "Smash" (1963), "Electric" (1964), Mural, Miami-Dade Public Library, FL (1985); One-man Exhibitions Include Minnesota Institute of the Arts (1972), Nigel Greenwood Ltd., London, England (1970, 1973, 1980), Leo Castelli Gallery, New York City, NY (10 Shows) (1973-Present), Albright-Knox Art Gallery, Buffalo, NY (1976), Stedelijk Museum, Amsterdam, The Netherlands (1976), Fort Worth Art Museum (1977), San Francisco Museum Modern Art (1982), Whitney Museum of American Art (1982), Vancouver Art Gallery (1982), Contemporary Arts Museum, Houston, Texas (1983), Los Angeles County Museum of Art (1983), James Corcoran Gallery, Los Angeles, CA (1985), Gagosian Galleries, Chelsea, NY (2002, 2013), Beverly Hills, CA (2003),

Other Museums; Exhibited in Group Shows at 64th Whitney Biennial (1987), Centre Pompidou, Paris, France (1989), Museum Boymans-van Beuningen, Rotterdam, The Netherlands (1990), Ghislaine Hussenot, Paris, France (1990), Fundacio Caixa, Barcelona, Spain (1990), Serpentine Gallery, London, England (1990), Museum of Contemporary Art, Los Angeles, CA (1990-1991), Robert Miller Gallery, New York City, NY (1992), Thaddaeus Ropac, Salzburg, Austria (1992); Represented in Permanent Collections Including Museum of Modern Art, Los Angeles County Museum Art, Whitney Museum, Hirshhorn, Washington, DC, Miami-Dade Public Library, Denver Public Library, J. Paul Getty Museum, Los Angeles, CA, Harry Ransom Center, University of Texas, Austin, and Others; Retrospective of Works on Paper, J. Paul Getty Museum, Los Angeles, CA (1998); Paintings Exhibited, Gagosian Gallery, Beverly Hills, CA (1999), Metro Plots, NY (1999); Retrospective of Career Hirshhorn Museum (2000), Sculpture Garden, Washington, DC (2000), Museum of Contemporary Art, Chicago, IL, Miami Art Museum, Modern Art Museum, Fort Worth, Texas, Hayward Gallery (2009), Modern Art Museum of Fort Worth (2011), Denver Art Museum (2011), Museum of Contemporary Art, FL (2012), Exhibitions, Kunsthistorisches Museum (2012) **AW:** Named One of the 100 Most Influential People in the World, TIME Magazine (2013); Fellow, Guggenheim Fellow (1971) **MEM:** Fellow, American Academy of Arts & Sciences; Art Department, American Academy of Arts & Letters

RUSH, BOBBY L., T: U.S. Representative from Illinois **I:** Government Administration/Government Relations/Government Services **DOB:** 11/23/1946 **PB:** Albany **ED:** MA in Theology, McCormick Theological Seminary, 1998; MA in Political Sci., University Illinois, 1992; BA in Political Sci., Roosevelt University, Chicago, 1974 **C:** Member, US Congress from 1st Illinois District, 1993-; Member, energy and commerce committees; Chairman, capitol devel. committee, hist. landmark preservation committee,; Chairman, budget/govt. operations committee,; Chairman, environmental protection, energy and pub. utilities committee,; Deputy chairman, Illinois Dem. Party, 1990; Dem. committeeman, Central Illinois, 1990; Dem. committeeman, Chicago 2nd ward, 1984, 88; City alderman, Chicago, 1984-93; Insurance agent, Prudential Insurance Co.,; Associate dean, Daniel Hale Williams University,; Fin. planner, Sanmar Fin. Planning Corp.,; **CIV:** Founder, Illinois Black Panther Party, Past coordinator, Free Medical Clinic, Past coordinator, Free Breakfast for Children, **AW:** Named one of Power 150, Ebony magazine, 2008, Most Influential Black Americans, 2006; recipient Distinguished Political Leadership award, Chicago Black United Communities, Outstanding Business and Professional Achievement award, South End Jaycees, Outstanding Community Service award, Henry Booth House, Outstanding Young Man award, Operation PUSH, Enterprise Zone award, Illinois Department Commerce and Community **PA:** Democrat

RUSH, GEOFFREY, T: Actor **I:** Media & Entertainment **DOB:** 07/06/1951 **PB:** Toowomba **SC:** QLD/Australia **PT:** Roy Baden; Merle Rush **ED:** LittD (hon.), University Queensland; Diploma, University Queensland **CW:** Actor: (plays) Wrong Side of the Moon, 1971, Lock Up Your Daughters, 1972, Assault With a Deadly Weapon, 1972; actor, (plays) Twelfth Night, 1972, Ruling Class, 1972, You're a Good Man Charlie Brown, 1972, Puss in Boots, 1972, Juno and the Paycock, 1973, Expresso Bongo, 1973, National Health, 1973, The Imaginary Invalid, 1973, Suddenly at Home, 1973, Aladdin, 1973, Hamlet on Ice, 1973, Godspell, 1974, The Rivals, 1974, The Philanthropist, 1974, Present Laughter, 1974, Jack and the Beanstalk, 1975-77; actor, (plays) King Lear, 1978, Point of Departure, 1978, Waiting for Godot, 1979, On Our Selection, 1979, Teeth and Smiles, 1980, Revenger's Tragedy, 1981, No End of Blame, 1982, You Can't Take It With You, 1981, A Midsummer Night's Dream, 1978, Mother Courage, 1982, Silver Lining, 1982, The Prince of Homburg, 1982, Royal Show, 1983, Blood Wedding, 1983, Netherwood, 1983, The Marriage of Figaro, 1983, Pal Joey, 1983, The Blind Giant is Dancing, 1983, Sunrise, 1983, Benefactors, 1986, On Parliament Hill, 1987, Shepherd on the Rocks, 1987, The Winter's Tale, 1987, Tristram Shandy-Gent, 1988, Les Enfants du Paradis, 1984; actor, (plays) The Importance of Being Earnest, 1988, Troilus & Cressida, 1989, Marat/Sade, 1990, The Comedy of Errors, 1990, The Government Inspector, 1991, Uncle Vanya, 1992, The Dutch Courtesan, 1993, Oleanna, 1993, The Drowsy Chaperone, 2010; (Broadway plays) Exit the King, 2009 (Drama Desk award for Outstanding Actor, 2009, Tony award for Best Performance by a Leading Actor in a Play, 2009); (films) Hoodwink, 1980, Starstruck, 1981, Twelfth Night, 1985, On Our Selection, 1994, Five Easy Pizzas, 1994, Children of the Revolution, 1996, Shine, 1996 (BAFTA award Best Actor, 1997, Golden Globe award for Best Performance in Motion Picture, 1997, Screen Actors Guild award for Outstanding Performance, 1997, Academy award for Best Actor, 1997), Oscar & Lucinda, 1997, Les Misérables, 1998, Shakespeare in Love, 1998 (BAFTA award Best Supporting Actor, 1999), Elizabeth, 1998, Mystery Men, 1999, House on Haunted Hill, 1999, Quills, 2000 (New York Film Critics Online award for best actor, 2000), The Tailor of Panama, 2001, Lantana, 2001, Frida, 2002, The Banger Sisters, 2002, Swimming Upstream, 2003, Ned Kelly, 2003, Finding Nemo (voice), 2003, Pirates of the Caribbean: The Curse of the Black Pearl, 2003, Intolerable Cruelty, 2003, The Life and Death of Peter Sellers, 2004 (Golden Globe award for Best Actor Miniseries or TV Movie, 2005, Screen Actors Guild Award for Best Actor in a TV Movie or Miniseries, 2005, Emmy award for Outstanding Lead Actor in a Miniseries or a Movie, 2005), Munich, 2005, Candy, 2006, Pirates of the Caribbean: Dead Man's Chest, 2006, Pirates of the Caribbean: At World's End, 2007, Elizabeth: The Golden Age, 2007, The Warrior's Way, 2010, Pirates of the Caribbean: On Stranger Tides, 2011, (voice) Green Lantern, 2011, The Eye of the Storm, 2011, The Best Offer, 2013, The Book Thief, 2013, The Daughter, 2015, Minions (voice), 2015, Holding the Man, 2015, Gods of Egypt, 2016, Final Portrait, 2017, Genius, 2017, Pirates of the Caribbean Dead Men Tell No Tales,2017, Land Down Under, 2019; (TV series) Consumer Capers, 1979-81, Menotti, 1980-81, The Burning Piano, 1992, Mercury, 1996, Lowdown, 2010-12, Being Brendo, 2012, Animal Acts, 1984-86, Teen Ages, 1984-86, Carols-By-Lazerlight, 1984-86, The 1985 Scandals, 1986, Pearls Before Swine, 1986, The Merry Wives of Windsor, 1987, The Wolf's Banquet, 1989, Popular Mechanicals 2, 1992, Aristophane's Frogs, 1992; co-translator The Government Inspector, 1991, writer (with George Whaley) ((TV film)) Clowning Around, 1992, (with John Clarke) (plays) Aristophane's Frogs, 1992, Call Me Sal, 1996, Children of the Revolution, 1997, actor, executive producer (films) The King's Speech, 2010 **AW:** Recipient Raymond Langford award, Australian Film Institute, 2009

RUSHDIE, SALMAN, T: Writer **I:** Writing and Editing **DOB:** 06/19/1947 **PB:** Mumbai **SC:** India **PT:** Anis Ahmed Rushdie; Negin (Butt) Rushdie **ED:** Honorary PhD, Chapman University, Orange, CA; MA in History, King's College, with Honors, University of Cambridge, England (1968) **C:** Distinguished Writer in Residence, English Department, Emory University, Atlanta, GA (2007-Present); Freelance Advertising Copywriter, Ayer Barker; Freelance Advertising Copywriter, Ogilvy & Mather **CR:** Honorary Professor, Massachusetts Institute of Technology; President, Massachusetts Institute of Technology; PEN American Center (2004-2006) **CW:** Author, "Grimus" (1975) "Midnight's Children" (1981), "Shame" (1983), "The Jaguar Smile: A Nicaraguan Journey" (1987), "The Satanic Verses" (1988), "Haroun and the Sea of Stories" (1990), "Imaginary Homelands: Essays and Criticism 1981-1991" (1992); Co-author, with R. Jhabvala and V. S. Naipaul, "Homeless by Choice" (1992); Author, "East, West" (1994), "The Moor's Last Sigh" (1995), "The Ground Beneath Her Feet" (1999), "Fury" (2001), "Step Across This Line: Collected Nonfiction 1992-2002" (2002), "Shalimar the Clown" (2005), "The Enchantress of Florence" (2008), "Luka and the Fire of Life" (2010), "Joseph Anton-A Memoir" (2012), "Two Years Eight Months and Twenty-Eights Nights: A Novel" (2015); Editor, "Best American Short Stories" (2008), "The Golden Rush" (2017) **AW:** Named, Honorary Knight Commander, Most Excellent Order of the British Empire, Her Majesty Queen Elizabeth II (2008); Best of Booker Award (2008); Commandeur de l'Ordre des Arts et des Lettres (1999); Budapest Grand Prize for Literature (1998); Mantova Literature Prize (1997); Aristeion Literature Prize, European Union (1996); State Prize for European Literature, Austria (1994); Prix Colette, Switzerland (1993); Kurt Tucholsky Prize, Sweden (1992); Outstanding Lifetime Achievement in Cultural Humanism, Harvard University; India Abroad Lifetime Achievement Award; Hutch Crossword Fiction Prize, India; Booker Prize (1981, 1988); Whitbread Novel Award (2007); Knighthood (2007); Hans Christian Andersen Literature Award (2014); Booker Prize for Fiction (1981); English Speaking Union Literature Award (1981); James Tait Black Memorial Prize (1982); Booker of Bookers Prize (1993); Best of Booker Prize (2008); Prix de Meilleur Livre Etranger (1984); Whitbread Novel Award (1988); German Author of the Year Award (1988); Writer's Guild Prize for Children's Fiction (1991); Whitbread Novel Award (1995); British Book Awards, Author of the Year (1995) **MEM:** Fellow, Royal Society of Literature; Honorary Member, American Academy of Arts and Letters **BA:** The Random House Publishing Group, 1745 Broadway 18th Floor, New York, NY, 10019

RUSSELL, BILL, T: Professional Basketball Player **I:** Athletics **DOB:** 02/12/1934 **PB:** Monroe **SC:** LA/USA **PT:** Charles Russell, Katie Russell **ED:** Honorary LHD, Dartmouth College, Hanover, NH, 2009; Honorary LHD, Suffolk University, Boston, MA, 2007; BA, University of San Francisco, 1956 **C:** Vice President of Basketball Operations to Executive Vice President, Sacramento Kings, 1988-1989; Head Coach, Sacramento Kings, 1987-1988; Head Coach, Seattle Supersonics, 1973-1977; Sportscaster, CBS-TV, 1980-1983; Sportscaster, ABC-TV, 1969-1980; Head Coach, Boston Celtics, 1966-1969; Center, Boston Celtics, 1956-1969 **CW:** Appearances, (TV Series) Cowboy in Africa; Co-Host, The Superstars, ABC-TV, 1978-1979; Co-Author, (With Taylor Branch) Second Wind: Memoirs of an Opinionated Man, 1979, (With David Faulkner) Russell Rules: 11 Lessons on Leadership From the Twentieth Century's Greatest Winner, 2001, (With Alan Steinberg) Red and Me: My Coach, My Lifelong Friend, 2009 **AW:** Presidential Medal of Freedom, The White House, 2010-2011, We Are Boston Leadership Award, Mayor's Office of New Bostonians, 2008, The FIBA Hall of Fame, 2007, FIBA Hall of Fame, 2007, The National Collegiate Basketball Hall of Fame, 2006, The 50 Greatest Athletes of the 20th Century, ESPN, 1999; The NBA 50th Anniversary

Team, 1996, The Greatest Player in the History of NBA, Professional Basketball Writers Association of America, 1980, The NBA 35th Anniversary Team, 1980, The Bay Area Sports Hall of Fame, 1980, The Naismith Pro Basketball Hall of Fame, 1974, The NBA 25th Anniversary Team, 1971, Athlete of the Decade of the 1960s, The Sporting News, 1970, The NBA All-Defensive Team, 1969, Sportsman of the Year, Sports Illustrated, 1968, NBA All-Star Game MVP, 1963, First Team All-NBA, 1959, 1963, 1965, The University of San Francisco Athletic Hall of Fame, 1959, The NBA All-Star Team, 1958-1969; Second Team All-NBA, 1958, 1960-1962, 1964, 1966-1968, NBA MVP, 1958, 1961-1963, 1965, Gold Medal in Men's Basketball, Summer Olympics Games, Melbourne, VIC, Australia, 1956 **ACH:** Achievements include member of NCAA National Championship winning University of San Francisco Dons, 1955, 1956; member of NBA Championship winning Boston Celtics, 1957, 1959-66, 1968, 1969; becoming the first African American head coach in NBA history, 1966 **BA:** The Literary Group International, 1357 Broadway, Suite 316, New York, NY, 10018

RUSSELL, STEVE, T: State Legislator **I:** Government Administration/Government Relations/Government Services **ED:** BS, Ouachita Baptist University, 1985 **C:** U.S. House of Representatives from Oklahoma's 5th District, 2015,; Member, Committee on Armed Services,; Committee on Oversight and Government Reform,; House Republican Steering Committee; Member District 45, Oklahoma State Senate, 2008-13; **CR:** Featured speaker Premiere Speaker's Bureau **MIL:** Served 21 years through Lieutenant Colonel, with Airborne & Ranger qualification, serving in Kosovo, Kuwait, Afghanistan & in Operation Iraqi Freedom, U.S. Army **CW:** Author: We Got Him! A Memoir of the Hunt and Capture of Saddam Hussein **AW:** Decorated Valorous Unit award, Combat Infantryman Badge U.S. Army, Bronze Star with Valor Device & Oak Leaf Cluster, Legion of Merit **PA:** Republican **BA:** 128 Cannon HOB, Washington, DC, 20515

RUTHERFORD, JOHN, T: U.S. Representative from Florida **I:** Government Administration/Government Relations/Government Services **DOB:** 09/02/1952 **ED:** Grad., National Executive Institute; Grad., Florida National Academy; Grad., Florida State University **C:** Member, U.S. House of Representatives from Florida's 4th District 2017-; Member, Committee on Homeland Security, Committee on Veterans' Affairs; Sheriff, City of Jacksonville, 2003-2015; Director corrections, City of Jacksonville, 1995-2003; Chief patrol, City of Jacksonville,; Chief traffic and special operations, City of Jacksonville,; Chief services, City of Jacksonville,; Captain, City of Jacksonville,; Director region five criminal justice training center, City of Jacksonville,; Lieutenant patrol and detective division, City of Jacksonville,; Sergeant, City of Jacksonville,; Uniformed patrolman, City of Jacksonville, Florida **ACH:** Achievements include created several programs within Jacksonville including Justice and the Revolving Door, Operation Showdown, and Anti-Litter **BA:** 230 Cannon House Office Building, Washington, DC, 20515

RUTLEDGE, THOMAS M., T: Charter Communications CEO **I:** Telecommunications **ED:** Grad. advanced management progressive, Harvard University, 1995; BA in Econs., California University, Pennsylvania, 1977 **C:** Director, president, CEO, Charter Communications, Inc., 2012-; COO, Cablevision Systems Corp., 2004-11; President cable & communications, Rainbow Media Holdings LLC, 2002-04; President, Time Warner Cable, 2001; Senior executive vice president, Time Warner Cable, 1991-2001; Division president, Am. TV &

Communications, Portland, Maine,; Division president, Am. TV & Communications, Austin, Texas,; Manager trainee, Am. TV & Communications, 1977 **CR:** Chairman, member executive committee National Cable & Telecomm. Association board directors Cable TV Laboratories, Inc., National Cable Satellite Corp. **CIV:** Board directors, CTAM Educational Foundation, **BA:** Charter Communications, 400 Atlantic St, Stamford, CT, 06901

RYAN, MATT, T: Professional Football Player **I:** Athletics **DOB:** 05/17/1985 **PB:** Exton **SC:** PA/USA **PT:** Son of Michael and Bernice Ryan. **ED:** BS in Management, Boston College, 2007 **C:** Quaterback, Atlanta Falcons, 2008-Present **AW:** Named NFL Offensive Rookie of Year, Associated Press, 2008, Player of Year, Atlantic Coast Conference, 2007, MVP, MPC Computers Bowl, 2005; named to National Football Conference Pro Bowl Team, NFL, 2012, 2010; recipient Manning award, Sugar Bowl Committee, 2007, Johnny Unitas Golden Arm award, 2007,Pro Bowl, 2014, 2016, First-Team All-Pro, 2016, NFL Most Valuable Player, 2016, NFL Offensive Player of the Year, 2016, Bert Bell Award, 2016, NFL Passer Rating Leader, 2016 **ACH:** Achievements include being the third overall pick by the Atlanta Falcons in the NFL Draft, 2008

RYAN, NOLAN, T: Professional Baseball Team Executive, Former Professional Baseball Player **I:** Business Management/Business Services **DOB:** 01/31/1947 **PB:** Refugio **SC:** CA/USA **PT:** Son of Lynn Nolan and Martha (Hancock) Ryan; **ED:** Student, Alvin Junior College, Texas, 1966-69 **C:** CEO, Texas Rangers, 2010-13,; Special Assistant, Houston Astros, 2014-; President, Texas Rangers, 2008-; Pitcher, Texas Rangers, 1989-93; Pitcher, Houston Astros, 1980-88; Pitcher, California Angels, 1972-79; Pitcher, New York Mets, 1968-71; Pitcher, New York Mets, New York City, 1966 **CR:** Investor, partner Express Bank Texas, 2003- owner, Corpus Christi Hooks (Houston Astros AA team), 2004-, Round Rock Express (Pacific Coast League AAA team), Texas, Waterfront Steakhouse and Grill, Bass Inn cattle rancher, China Grove, Ray and Gonzalvez, Texas **CIV:** Vice chairman, Texas Pks. and Wildlife Commission, 1995-97 Commissioner, Texas Pks. and Wildlife Commission, 1995-2001 Founder, board directors, Nolan Ryan Foundation, Board directors, Natural Resources Foundation, Texas, Board directors, Texas Water Foundation, Board directors, Justin Cowboy Crisis Fund, **CW:** Co-author (with Steve Jacobson): Nolan Ryan: Strike-Out King, 1975; co-author: (with Bill Libby) Nolan Ryan: The Other Game, 1977; co-author: (with Joe Torre) Pitching and Hitting, 1977; co-author: (with Harvey Frommer) Throwing Heat: The Autobiography of Nolan Ryan, 1988; co-author: (with Tom House) Nolan Ryan's Pitcher's Bible, 1991; co-author: (with Jerry Jenkins) Miracle Man: Nolan Ryan, The Autobiography, 1992; co-author: (with others) Kings of Hill, 1992 **AW:** Named Am. League Pitcher of Year, Sporting News, 1977; named to Baseball Hall of Fame, 1999, National League All-Star Team, 1989, 1985, 1981, Am. League All-Star Team, 1979, 1977, 1975, 1972-73 **ACH:** Achievements include holding over 53 Major League records including most seasons pitched (27), most strikeouts (5,714) and most no-hit games (7); being the only Major League Baseball player to have his uniform retired by three different teams, the Angels, Astros and Rangers; holding Guinness Book of World Records for throwing the fastest baseball pitched (100.9 miles per hour)

RYAN, PAUL DAVIS JR., T: Speaker of the House **I:** Government Administration/Government Relations/Government Services **DOB:** 01/29/1970 **PB:**

Janesville **SC:** WI/USA **PT:** Paul Murray Ryan, Sr., Elizabeth A. (Hutter) Ryan **ED:** Honorary Doctorate, Miami University, Ohio, 2009; BS in Economics & Political Science, Miami University, Ohio, 1992 **C:** Speaker, U.S. House Of Representatives, 2015-Present; U.S. Congress From First Wisconsin District, Washington, DC, 1999-Present; Chairman, U.S. House Ways & Means Committee, 2015-2017; Chairman, U.S. House Budget Committee, 2011-2015; Marketing Consultant, Ryan Inc. Central, Janesville, WI, 1997-1998; Legislative Director To Representative Sam Brownback, U.S. House Of Representatives, Washington, DC, 1995-1997; Economic Advisor, Speechwriter To Bill Bennett & Jack Kemp, Empower America, Washington, DC, 1993-1995; Aide To Senator Bob Kasten, U.S. Senate, Washington, DC, 1992 **CR:** Republican Party Candidate For Vice President, 2012 **CW:** Co-Author, (With Eric Cantor & Kevin McCarthy) Young Guns: A New Generation Of Conservative Leaders, 2010; Author, The Way Forward: Renewing The American Idea, 2014 **AW:** The 50 Most Influential People In Global Finance, Bloomberg Markets, 2012, The 100 Most Influential People In The World, TIME Magazine, 2011, 2016, Freedom & Prosperity Award, Mason Contractors Association of America, 2011, Leadership Award, Jack Kemp Foundation, 2011, The 50 Politicos To Watch, Politico, 2010, Guardian Of Small Business Award, National Federation of Independent Business, 2010, Award For Manufacturing Legislative Excellence, National Association of Manufacturers, 2009 **MEM:** Janesville YMCA, Janesville Bowmen Inc. **PA:** Republican

RYAN, TIM, T: U.S. Representative from Ohio **I:** Government Administration/Government Relations/Government Services **DOB:** 07/16/1973 **PB:** Niles **SC:** OH/USA **PT:** Rochelle Ryan **ED:** JD, Franklin Pierce Law Center, Concord, NH, 2000; BA in Political Science, Bowling Green State University, 1995; Student, Youngstown State University **C:** U.S. Congress From 13th Ohio District, 2013-Present; U.S. Congress From 17th Ohio District, Washington, 2003-2013; District 32, Ohio State Senate, Columbus, 2001-2002; Congressional Aide To Rep. James A. Traficant, U.S. House Of Representatives, 1995-1997; Committee On Appropriations, Committee On The Budget; Intern, Trumbull County Prosecutor's Office **AW:** Friend Of National Parks Award, National Parks Conservation Association, 2005, Legislative Leadership Award For Domestic Manufacturing, U.S. Business And Industry Council, 2004 **MEM:** International Narcotic Enforcement Officers Association, Ancient Order of Hibernians, Sons of Italy, Elks **PA:** Democrat **BA:** 1126 Longworth HOB, Washington, DC, 20515

RYLANCE, MARK, T: Actor, Playwright **I:** Media & Entertainment **DOB:** 01/18/1960 **PB:** Ashford, Kent **SC:** England **PT:** David Waters; Anne (Skinner) Waters **ED:** Student, Royal Academy of Dramatic Arts, London, England (1978-1980) **C:** Artistic Director, Shakespeare's Globe Theatre, London, England (1995-2005); Associate Member, Royal Shakespeare Co. **CW:** Artistic Director, Actor, Plays, "The Two Gentlemen of Verona" (1996), "A Chaste Maid in Cheapside" (1997), "Henry V" (1997), "The Merchant of Venice" (1998), "The Honest Whore" (1998), "Antony and Cleopatra" (1999), "Hamlet" (2000), "Cymbeline" (2001), "The Golden Ass" (2002), "Twelfth Night" (2002), "Richard II" (2003), "Measure for Measure" (2004), "The Tempest" (2005), "The Storm" (2005), "Nice Fish" (2013, 2016); Actor, Plays, "Desperado Corner" (1981), "Hamlet" (1988), "Much Ado About Nothing" (1993), "Henry V" (1993), "As You Like It" (1994), "True West" (1994), "Macbeth"

(1995), "Life x 3" (2000), "Boeing Boeing" (2007), "I Am Shakespeare" (2007), "Peer Gynt" (2008), "Endgame" (2009-Present), "La Bete" (2010-2011), "Jerusalem" (2009), "Richard III" (2013), "Twelfth Night" (2013), "Farinelli and the King" (2015); Actor, TV Films, "Wallenberg: A Hero's Story" (1985), "Incident in Judea" (1991), "Love Lies Bleeding" (1993), "Loving" (1995), "Leonardo" (2003), "Richard II" (2003), "The Government Inspector" (2005); Actor, films, "The McGuffin" (1986), "Hearts of Fire" (1987), "The Grass Arena" (1991), "Prospero's Books" (1991), "Institute Benjamenta" (1995), "Angels and Insects" (1995), "Intimacy" (2001), "The Other Boleyn Girl" (2008), "Blitz" (2011), "Anonymous" (2011), "Days and Nights" (2014), "The Gunman" (2015), "Bridge of Spies" (2015), "The BFG" (2016), "Dunkirk" (2017), "Ready Player One" (2018); Actor, TV Series, "Wallenberg: A Hero's Story" (1985), "Love Lies Bleeding" (1993), "Loving" (1995), "Hamlet" (1995), "Henry V" (1997), "Changing Stages" (2001), "Leonardo" (2003), "Richard II" (2003), "The Government Inspector" (2005), "Bing" (2014-2015); Actor, TV Miniseries, Wolf Hall (2015) **AW:** Olivier Award for Best Actor, "Much Ado About Nothing" (1994); Best Performance by a Leading Actor in a Play, "Boeing Boeing," Tony Award (2008); Best Featured Actor in a Play, "Twelfth Night," Tony Award (2014); Best Actor, "The Government Inspector," BAFTA Award (2006); Best Newcomer, "The Grass Arena," BBC Radio Times Award (1991); Outstanding Actor in a Play, "The Other Boleyn Girl," Drama Desk Award (2008); Best Supporting Actor, "Bridge of Spies," BAFTA Award (2016); Best Supporting Actor, "Bridge of Spies," Academy Award (2016)

SABAN, NICK, T: College Football Coach, Former Professional Football Coach **I:** Athletics **DOB:** 10/31/1951 **PB:** Fairmont **PT:** Son of Nicholas Lou and Mary Saban; **ED:** MA in Sports Administration, Kent State University, 1975; BS in Business, Kent State University, 1973 **C:** Head coach, University Alabama Crimson Tide, Tuscaloosa, 2007-; Head coach, Miami Dolphins, 2005-07; Head coach, Louisiana State University Fighting Tigers, Baton Rouge, 2000-05; Defensive coordinator, Cleveland Browns, 1991-94; Head coach, Toledo University Rockets, 1990; Secondary coach, Houston Oilers, 1988-89; Head coach, Michigan State University Spartans, 1995-2000; Secondary coach & defensive coordinator, Michigan State University Spartans, East Lansing, 1983-87; Secondary coach, US Naval Academy Midshipmen, Annapolis, 1981; Secondary coach, Ohio State University Buckeyes, Columbus, 1980-81; Secondary coach, W. Virginia University Mountaineers, Morgantown, 1978-79; Outside linebackers coach, Syracuse University Orangemen, 1977; Linebackers coach, Kent State University Golden Flashes, 1975-76; Grad. assistant, Kent State University Golden Flashes, 1973-74 **CIV:** Active, Children's Miracle Network, Founder, Nick's Kids, **CW:** Co-author (with Sam King): Tiger Turnaround: LSU's Return to Football Glory, 2001; co-author: How Good Do You Want to Be, 2005 **AW:** Named Coach of Year, Southeastern Conference,2003, 2009,2016 National Coach of Year, The Sporting News, 2008, Securities and Exchange Commission Coach of Year, 2008, Associated Press, 2008, 2003, National Coach of Year, 2008, 2003; named to The Alabama Sports Hall of Fame, 2013; recipient Bobby Bowden National Collegiate Coach of Year award, Over the Mountain Touchdown Club, 2011-13; Amos Alonzo Stagg Coaching, 2010, Home Depot Coach of Year award, ESPN, ABC Sports, 2008, Walter Camp Coach of Year award, Walter Camp Football Foundation, 2008, Coach of Year award, Liberty

Mutual, 2008, Eddie Robinson Coach of Year award, Football Writers Association America, 2008, Eddie Robinson Coach of Year award, 2003, Paul "Bear" Bryant award, National Sportscasters & Sportswriters Association, 2003, George Munger Award, 2016, , Alabama Sports Hall of Fame, 2013 **ACH:** Achievements include head coach of the BCS National Championship winning Louisiana State University Fighting Tigers, 2003; University of Alabama Crimson Tide, 2009, 2011, 2012 **H:** Golf **BA:** The University of Alabama Department of Intercollegiate Athletics, Box 870323, Tuscaloosa, AL, 35487

SABETI, PARDIS CHRISTINE, T: Researcher **I:** Research **DOB:** 12/25/1975 **PB:** Tehran **ED:** MD summa cum laude, Harvard Medical School, Boston, 2006; DPhil, University Oxford, 2002; MS, University Oxford, 1998; BS, Massachusetts Institute of Technology, Cambridge, 1997 **C:** Post-doctoral fellow genomics and infectious disease, Broad Institute of Massachusetts Institute of Technology and Harvard, Cambridge, Massachusetts, 2003-; Grad. research fellow, University Oxford, 1997-2000 **CR:** Corp. member, board trustees Massachusetts Institute of Technology Corp., Cambridge, Massachusetts, 1999-2004 **CW:** Musician (writer, singer): (five-song CD) Headlight Waves (Billboard Songwriting Contest Hon. Mention, 2006) **AW:** Named Trailblazer, Sci. Spectrum Magazine, 2006; recipient award in biomed. sci., Burroughs Wellcome Career, 2006; fellow, Damon Runyon Cancer Research Foundation, 2004-, L'Oreal For Women in Sci., L'Oreal U.S.A., 2004, Paul and Daisy Soros Fellowships, 2001-03; Scholarship, Rhodes Trust, 1997-2000 **MEM:** Mem.: American Society of Composers (associate)

SABRINA, DANIELLE, T: CEO of What Vibes Your Tribe **I:** Business Management/Business Services **DOB:** 01/01/1900 **ED:** Business, Southern New Hampshire University, 2003; Business Marketing,-Southern NH University, 2001 **C:** Business Development, Media, Brand Strategy,Creative Direction, What Vibes Your Tribe, 2008-; Contributor, The Huffington Post, 2015-18; Director, Financial Planning for the NPA, 2003-08

SALL, JOHN, T: Co-Founder of the SAS Institute **I:** Information Technology and Services **PB:** Rockford **SC:** IL/USA **ED:** MS, No. Illinois University; BS, Beloit College **C:** Leader, JMP Business Division; Co-founder, executive vice president, SAS Institute, Cary, North Carolina,1976- **AW:** Named one of Forbes 400: Richest Americans, 2006-

SALOVEY, PETER, T: Academic Administrator, psychology professor **I:** Education/Educational Services **DOB:** 02/21/1958 **PB:** Cambridge **SC:** Massachusetts **PT:** Son of Ronald and Elaine Y. (Gross) S.; Married Marta Elisa Moret, June 15, 1986. **ED:** Doctor of Laws (hon.), Harvard University, Cambridge, Massachusetts, 2014; PhD (hon.), Shanghai, Jiao Tong University, Shanghai, China, 2014; DHL (hon.), National Tsing Hua University, Hsinchu City, Taiwan, 2014; DEd (hon.), University Pretoria, South Africa, 2009; MPhil in Psychology, Yale University, New Haven, Connecticut, 1984; MS in Psychology, Yale University, New Haven, Connecticut, 1983; PhD in Psychology, Yale University, New Haven, Connecticut, 1986; MA in Sociology, Stanford University, California, 1980; BA in Psychology, Stanford University, California, 1980 **CT:** Lic. psychologist, Connecticut **C:** President, Yale University, 2013-; Provost, Yale University, New Haven, 2008-13; Dean, Yale College, 2004-08; Dean Grad. School Arts and Scis., Yale University, 2003-04; Chris Argyris professor psychology, professor management and epidemiology and pub. health, Yale University,

2001-13; Chairman department psychology, Yale University, 2000-03; Professor psychology, epidemiology and pub. health, Yale University, 1995-2001; Associate professor, Yale University, 1990-95; Assistant professor, Yale University, New Haven, 1986-90 **CR:** Consultant psychologist West Haven (Connecticut) VA Medical Center, 1986- deputy director Center for Interdisciplinary Research on AIDS, 1997-2006 member National Science Foundation Social Psychology Adv. Committee, 1994-97 member National Institute of Mental Health National Adv. Mental Health Council, 2003-07, National Institute of Mental Health Behavioral Sci. Task Force, 2000, **CW:** Author: Peer Counseling, 1983, The Remembered Self, 1993, Psychology, 1993, The Emotionally Intelligent Manager, 2004; editor: Reasoning Inference & Judgement in Clinical Psychology, 1988, The Psychology of Jealousy and Envy, 1991, Emotional Development and Emotional Intelligence, 1997, At Play in the Fields of Consciousness, 1999, The Wisdom in Feeling: Psychological Processes in Emotional Intelligence, 2002, Social Psychology of Health, 2003, Key Readings in Emotional Intelligence, 2004; editor: Rev. of General Psychology, 1996-2002; associate editor Psychological Bulletin, 1991-96, Emotion, 2000-2002; contributor articles to professional journals **AW:** Named Presidential Young Investigator, National Science Foundation, Washington, 1990, Mensa Education & Research Foundation award 2001, National Cancer Society CIS Partner research award, 2001, SAMHSA Excellence award, 2005, Exceptional Lifetime Achievement Award, International Conference on Advances in Management, 2009. American Academy of Arts and Sciences, 2013, National Academy of Medicine, 2013, Lifetime Achievement Award, Connecticut Psychological Association, 2015, Outstanding Contribution to Health Psychology, American Psychological Association, 2015, Ellis Island Medal of Honor, 2016 **MEM:** Fellow American Psychological Association, American Association for the Advancement of Science, Associate Psychological Sci., International Society for Research on Emotion (treasurer 1992-96), Society for General Psychology (president 2004), Phi Beta Kappa, Sigma Xi, Court Academy Sci. & Engineering, 2009. **ACH:** Achievements include research on psychological consequences of the arousal of mood and emotion, emotional intelligence, and motivators of health-protective behaviors, especially those relevant to the prevention of cancer and HIV/AIDS. **H:** Bluegrass Music **PA:** Democrat

SAMPRAS, PETE, T: Professional Tennis Player (Retired) **I:** Athletics **DOB:** 08/12/1971 **PB:** Washington **SC:** DC/USA **PT:** Son of Sam and Georgia Sampras **MS:** Married **SPN:** Bridgette Wilson, September 30, 2000, **CH:** Christian Charles, Ryan Nikolaos **C:** ATP, 1988- **CR:** Member U.S. Davis Cup team., named to Olympic Team Atlanta, 1996 **CIV:** chairman ATP Tour Charities program, 1992. **CW:** Co-author (with Pete Bodo): A Champion's Mind: Lessons from a Life in Tennis, 2008 **AW:** Winner tournaments including Philadelphia, 1990, Manchester, 1990, US Open, 1990, 1993, Grand Slam Cup, 1990, L.A., 1991, Indianapolis, 1991, Lyon, 1991, IBM/ATP Tour World Championship-Frankfurt, 1991, 94, US Pro Indoor, 1992, Lipton International, 1993, Wimbledon, 1993, 94, 95, 97, 98, 99, 2000; Australian Open, 1994, 97, Italian Open, 1994, US Open, 1990, 93, 95, 96, 2002, San Jose Open, 1996, Memphis Open, 1996, ATP Tour World Championship/Hannover, Germany, 1996, Australian Open Wimbledon, 1997, Advanta Championships, 1998, Champions Cup, 2007; ranked # 1 during 1993, 94 season, finalist Australian Open, 1995; retired, 2003; named to International Tennis Hall of Fame, 2007 **ACH:** Achievements include 1st male to win the US Open, Wimbledon, and Australian Open in succession, member US Davis Cup Team, 1991, became only the fourth player to finish as No. 1 three (or more) consecutive years, 1st player to surpass $5 million in a season, all-time leader in career earnings, named ATP Tour Player of the Year, 1993-94, Jim Thorpe Tennis Player, 1993.

SAMUELI, HENRY, T: Chief Technology Officer **I:** Technology **CN:** Broadcom Inc. **DOB:** 09/20/1954 **PB:** Buffalo **SC:** NY/USA **PT:** Son of Aron and Sala (Traubman) S.; **MS:** Married **SPN:** Susan Faye Eisenberg, August 22, 1982; **CH:** Leslie Pamela, Jillian Meryl, Erin Sydney **ED:** PhD in Electrical Engineering, UCLA, 1980; MSEE, UCLA, 1976; BSEE, UCLA, 1975 **C:** Chief Technical Officer, Broadcom Inc, 2018-; Chief Technical Officer, Broadcom Ltd, 2016-; Chief Technical Officer, Co-Founder, Broadcom Corp, 2009-16; Technology Advisor, Co-Founder, Broadcom Corp, 2008-09; Chairman,CTO,Co-Founder,Broadcom Corp, 2003-2008; Distinguished adjunct professor, electrical engineering and computer sci., UCLA, 2003-; Chairman, Broadcom Corp., Irvine, California, 2012-; Co-founder, chief tech. officer, Broadcom Corp., Irvine, California, 1991-; Professor, UCLA, 1994-95; Associate professor, UCLA, 1990-94; Assistant professor, UCLA, 1985-90; Chairman, Broadcom Corp., Irvine, California, 2003-08; Vice president research & devel. & co-chmn., Broadcom Corp., Irvine, California, 1991-2003; Co-founder, chief scientist, PairGain Techs., Inc., Tustin, California, 1988-94; Consultant, TRW Inc., Redondo Beach, California, 1985-89; Section manager, TRW Inc., Redondo Beach, California, 1983-85; Staff engineer, TRW Inc., Redondo Beach, California, 1980-83 **CR:** Co-owner Anaheim Ducks (formerly Mighty Ducks of Anaheim), 2005- **AW:** Named one of Top 20 Entrepreneurs of 1997, The Red Herring Magazine, 1997, one of Top 50 Cyber Elite, Time Digital Magazine, 1997; Schools Engineering at both University California Irvine and UCLA named in honor of; recipient Presidential award, University California, 2000, Irvine medal, 2000, Alumnus of Year award, UCLA School of Engineering and Applied Sci., 2000, Golden Plate award, Academy Achievement, 2006, Marconi Prize, 2012 **MEM:** Fellow: IEEE (Circuits and Systems Society Industrial Pioneer award 2000), Am. Academy Arts & Sci.; mem.: NAE **ACH:** Holder of 22 US patents. **PA:** Republican **BA:** 1320 Ridder Park Drive, San Jose, CA, USA, 95131

SANCAR, AZIZ, T: Biochemist, Molecular Biologist **I:** Sciences **DOB:** 09/08/1946 **PB:** Savur-Mardin **SC:** Turkey **ED:** PhD in Molecular Biology, University of Texas, Dallas, Texas (1977); MD, Istanbul Medical School (1969) **C:** Sarah Graham Kenan Professor, Biochemistry and Biophysics, University of North Carolina School of Medicine, Chapel Hill, NC (1997-Present); Associate Professor, Biochemistry, University of North Carolina School of Medicine, Chapel Hill, NC (1982-1997) **CR:** Co-founder, Carolina Turk Evi, Aziz and Gwen Sancar Foundation **CW:** Contributor, Chapters to Books, Several Articles to Professional Publications **AW:** Co-recipient, Nobel Prize in Chemistry (2015); North Carolina Distinguished Chemist Award; Merit Award, National Institutes of Health (1966); Scientific Achievement Award, Turkish Scientific and Technical Council (1995); American Society for Photobiology Award (1990); Presidential Young Investigator Award, National Science Foundation (1984-1989); Vehbi Koc Award (2007) **MEM:** Fellow, American Academy of Arts & Sciences; Fellow, Third World Academy of Sciences; American Academy of Microbiology; Honorary Member, Turkish Academy of Sciences; National Academy of Sciences

SANCHEZ, NICOLE, T: CEO of Credit Hero **I:** Business Management/Business Services **DOB:** 01/01/1900 **ED:** M.B.A, Harvard Business School, 2010; B.A., Harvard University, 2006 **C:** Investment Partner, XFactor Ventures, 2017-; Founder and CEO, Credit Hero, 2016-; Founder and CEO, VIXXEN, 2014-15; Case Team Leader, Bain & Company, 2010-13

SÁNCHEZ, LINDA TERESA, T: U.S. Representative From California **I:** Government Administration/Government Relations/Government Services **DOB:** 01/28/1969 **PB:** Orange **SC:** CA/USA **PT:** Ignacio Sánchez, Maria (Macias) Sánchez **ED:** JD, University of California, Los Angeles, 1995; BA in Spanish Literature, University of California, Berkeley, 1991 **C:** Chair, Congressional Hispanic Caucus, 2015-Present; U.S. House Select Committee On The Events Surrounding The 2012 Terrorist Attack In Benghazi, 2014-Present; U.S. Congress From 38th California District, 2013-Present; Ranking Member, U.S. House of Ethics Committee, 2011-Present; U.S. Congress From 39th California District, 2003-2013; Compliance Officer, International Brotherhood of Electrical Workers, National Electrical Contractors Association, 1998-2002; Law Clerk To Chief Justice Terry Hatter, Jr., U.S. District Court, Central District, California **CR:** Lecturer, National Association of Elected & Appointed Officials, 1998-Present; Campaign Aide, Loretta Sanchez For U.S. Congress, 1996, 1998 **CW:** Co-Author, (With Loretta Sanchez) Dream In Color: How The Sanchez Sisters Are Making History In Congress, 2008 **MEM:** International Brotherhood of Electrical Workers (Local 441) **BAR:** State of California, 1995 **PA:** Democrat **BA:** Suite 140, 12440 Imperial Highway, Norwalk, CA, 90650-8307

SANDERS, BERNIE, T: U.S. Senator From Vermont **I:** Government Administration/Government Relations/Government Services **DOB:** 09/08/1941 **PB:** Brooklyn **SC:** NY/USA **PT:** Eli Sanders; Dorothy (Glassberg) Sanders **MS:** Married **SPN:** Jane O'Meara, 1988 **CH:** Levi, Heather, Carina, David **ED:** BA, University of Chicago, 1964; Student, Brooklyn College **C:** Ranking Member, Senate Budget Committee, 2015-Present; U.S. Senator From Vermont, 2007-Present; Chairman, U.S. Senate Veterans' Affairs Committee, 2013-2015; Member-at-Large, U.S. Congress From Vermont, 1991-2007; Faculty Member, Hamilton College, Clinton, NY, 1990; Faculty Member, Harvard University, Cambridge, MA, 1989; Mayor, Burlington, VT, 1981-1989; Director, American People's Historical Society, Burlington, VT, 1976-1981; Freelance Writer, Carpenter, Youth Counselor, 1964-1976 **CR:** Candidate, Democratic Party Presidential Nomination, 2016 **CIV:** Chairman, Vermont Liberty Union Party, 1975-1976; (Candidate) Vermont Governor, 1972, 1976, 1986, U.S. Senate, 1971, 1974 **CW:** Author, (Books) Outsider in the House, 1997, The Speech: A Historic Filibuster on Corporate Greed and the Decline of Our Middle Class, 2011 **AW:** The Ten Most Fascinating People, Barbara Walters Special, 2015 **PA:** Independent

SANDERS, SARAH HUCKABEE, T: White House Press Secretary **I:** Government Administration/Government Relations/Government Services **PT:** Mike Huckabee; Janet Huckabee **C:** White House Press Secretary, 2017-; White House Principal Deputy Press Secretary, 2017; Campaign manager, John Boozman for Senate, 2010; With, Educational Department, Washington, 2004; Executive director, Huck PAC **AW:** Named one of The Politics 40 Under 40, TIME Magazine, 2010 **PA:** Republican

SANDOVAL, BRIAN EDWARD, T: Governor of Las Vegas **I:** Government Administration/Government Relations/Government Services **DOB:** 08/05/1963 **PB:** Redding **SC:** CA/USA **PT:** Ronald L. Sandoval; Gloria Sandoval **ED:** JD, The Ohio State University (1989); Bachelor's Degree in English & Economics, University of Nevada (1986) **CT:** Washington, DC; California; Nevada **C:** Governor, State of Nevada (2011-Present); Judge, U.S. District Court for the District of Nevada, Reno, NV (2005-2009); Attorney General, State of Nevada, Carson City, NV (2003-2005); Attorney, Sandoval Law Office, Reno, NV (1999-2003); Attorney, Gamboa, Sandoval & Stovall, Reno, NV (1995-1999); Member, Nevada State Assembly (1995-1997); Attorney, Robinson, Belaustegui, Robb & Sharp, Reno, NV (1991-1995); Attorney, McDonald, Carano, Wilson, McCune Bergin, Frankovich & Hicks, Reno, NV (1989-1991) **CR:** Chairman, Nevada Gaming Commission (1999-2001); Member, Nevada Gaming Commission (1998-2001); Member, State and Local Officials' Advisory Committee, U.S. Department of Homeland Security **CIV:** Board of Trustees, Washoe County Law Library, Nevada,; Board of Trustees, St. Jude's Ranch for Children; Board of Trustees, Children's Cabinet, Reno, NV **AW:** Named, Public Lawyer of the Year, Nevada St. Bar Associate (2004); Recipient, Torch of Liberty, Anti-Defamation League (2003) **PA:** Republican **BA:** Grant Sawyer State Office Building, 555 East Washington Ave, Suite 5100, Las Vegas, NV, 89101

SANFORD, MARK, T: U.S. Representative from South Carolina **I:** Government Administration/Government Relations/Government Services **DOB:** 05/28/1960 **PB:** Fort Lauderdale **SC:** FL/USA **PT:** Son of Marshall Clement and Peggy (Pitts) Sanford; **ED:** MBA, University Virginia Darden Grad. School Business Administration, 1988; BBA, Furman University, Greenville, South Carolina, 1983 **C:** Member, US House Transportation Committee, 2013-; Member, Committee on International Relations,; Committee on Government Reform,; Committee on Science, Joint Economic Committee; Member, US Congress from 1st South Carolina District, 2013-; Governor, State of South Carolina, Columbia, 2003-11; Member, US Congress from 1st South Carolina District, Washington, 1995-2001; Principal, Norton & Sanford Real Estate Investment, 2001-02; Principal, Norton & Sanford Real Estate Investment, 1993-95; Real estate broker, Brumley Co., Charleston, South Carolina, 1990-91; Principal, Southeastern Partners, 1989-93; Financial analyst, Chemical Realty Corp., 1988-90; Training positions, Goldman Sachs,; Project supervisor, Beachside Real Estate, Isle of Palms, Charleston County, 1984-86; Associate, Coldwell Banker, 1983 **CR:** Chairman Republican Governors Association, 2008-09 **MIL:** Member US Air Force **CW:** Author: The Trust Committed to Me, 2000 **MEM:** Mem.: Preservation Society Charleston **H:** Windsurfing, running **PA:** Republican **BA:** 2211 Rayburn HOB, Washington, DC, 20515

SANTI, ERNEST SCOTT, T: CEO **I:** Business Management/Business Services **CN:** Illinois Tool Works Inc. **ED:** Masters Degree, Kellogg School of Management Northwestern University (1992); Bachelors in Accounting, University of Illinois (1983) **C:** Chairman/Chief Executive Officer, Illinois Tool Works Inc. (2015-Present); President/Chief Executive Officer, Illinois Tool Works Inc. (2012-2015); Vice Chairman, Illinois Tool Works Inc. (2008-2012); Executive Vice President, Illinois Tool Works Inc. (2004-2008)

SARANDON, SUSAN, T: Actress **I:** Media & Entertainment **DOB:** 10/04/1946 **PB:** NYC **SC:** NY/USA **PT:** Phillip Leslie Tomalin; Lenora Marie (Criscione)

Tomalin **MS:** Divorced **SPN:** Chris Sarandon (12/16/1967, Divorced 1979) **CH:** Eva Maria Livia Amurri; Jack Henry Robbins; Miles Guthrie Robbins **ED:** BA in Drama and English, Catholic University of America (1968) **CW:** Actress, Plays, "An Evening with Richard Nixon" (1972), "A Coupla White Chicks Sittin' Around Talkin'" (1980-1981), "A Stroll in the Air," "Albert's Bridge," "Private Ear, Public Eye," "Extremities" (1982), "Exit the King" (2009); Actress, Films, "Joe" (1970), "Lady Liberty" (1972), "The Rocky Horror Picture Show" (1975), "Lovin' Molly" (1974), "The Front Page" (1974), "The Great Waldo Pepper" (1975), "Dragon Fly" (1976), "Crash" (1976), "The Other Side of Midnight" (1977), "The Last of the Cowboys" (1978), "Checkered Flag or Crash" (1978), "Pretty Baby" (1978), "King of the Gypsies" (1978), "Something Short of Paradise" (1979), "Loving Couples" (1980), "Atlantic City" (1980), "Tempest" (1982), "The Hunger" (1983), "The Buddy System" (1984), "Compromising Positions" (1985), "The Witches of Eastwick" (1987), "Bull Durham" (1988), "Sweet Hearts Dance" (1988), "A Dry White Season" (1989), "The January Man" (1989), "White Palace" (1990), "Thelma and Louise" (1991), "The Player" (1992), "Light Sleeper" (1992), "Bob Roberts" (1992), "Lorenzo's Oil" (1992), "The Client" (1994), "Little Women" (1994), "Safe Passage" (1994), "Dead Man Walking" (1995), Voice Actor, James and the Giant Peach" (1996), Voice Actor, "187" (1997), "Illuminata" (1998), "Twilight" (1998), "Joe Gould's Secret" (1999), "Baby's in Black" (1999), "Cradle Will Rock" (1999), "Anywhere But Here" (1999), Voice Actor, "Rugrats in Paris: The Movie - Rugrats II" (2000), "The Banger Sisters" (2002), "Igby Goes Down" (2002), "Noel" (2004), "Shall We Dance?" (2004), "Alfie" (2004), "Jiminy Glick in La La Wood" (2004), "Elizabethtown" (2005), "In the Valley of Elah" (2007), "Mr. Woodcock" (2007), "Emotional Arithmetic" (2007), "Enchanted" (2007), "Bernard and Doris" (2008), "Speed Racer" (2008), "The Lovely Bones" (2009), "Leaves of Grass" (2009), "Wall Street: Money Never Sleeps" (2010), "Jeff, Who Lives at Home" (2012), "Robot and Frank" (2012), "Arbitrage" (2012), "Irwin & Fran" (2012), "That's My Boy" (2012), "The Wedding" (2012), "Cloud Atlas" (2012), "The Company You Keep" (2012), "Snitch" (2013), "Irwin & Fran" (2013), "The Big Wedding" (2013), "Ping Pong Summer" (2013), "Tammy" (2014), "The Calling" (2014), "About Ray" (2015), Voice Actor, "Hell and Back" (2015), "Kid Witness" (2016), "Mothers and Daughters" (2016), "Spark" (2016), "Ace the Case" (2016), "My Entire High School Sinking into the Sea" (2016), "A Bad Moms Christmas" (2017), "Going Places" (2018), "The Death and Life of John F. Donovan" (2018); Actress, TV Films, "The Haunting of Rosalind" (1973), "F. Scott Fitzgerald and The Last of the Belles" (1974), "Who Am I This Time" (1982), "A.D." (1985), "Mussolini: The Decline and Fall of Il Duce" (1985), "Earthly Possessions" (1999), "Ice Bound" (2003), "The Exonerated" (2005), "You Don't Know Jack" (2010), "The Miraculous Year" (2011), Voice Actor, "Cassius and Clay" (2016); Actress, TV Series, "A World Apart" (1970-1971), "Search for Tomorrow" (1972-1973), "Rescue Me" (2006-2007), "The Big C" (2012), "Louie" (2012), "Mike and Molly" (2013), "Doll & Em" (2014), "The Secret Life of Marilyn Monroe" (2015), "Moonbeam City" (2015), "Cassius and Clay" (2016), "Skylanders Academy" (2016), "American Dad" (2016), "Feud: Bette and Joan" (2017), "Ray Donovan" (2017), "Rick and Morty" (2017), "Neo Yokio" (2017); TV Appearances, "Friends" (2001), "Malcolm in the Middle" (2002), "30 Rock" (2011, 2012); Actress, TV Miniseries, "Children of Dune" (2003); Narrator, Films, "The Shape of Water" (2008); Actress, Executive Producer, Films, "Stepmom" (1998), "Moonlight Mile" (2002), "The Meddler" (2015);

Executive Producer, Documentaries, "Waiting for Mamu" (2013), "Storied Streets" (2014), "Silenced" (2014), "Radical Grace" (2014), "Deep Run" (2015) **AW:** Named to New Jersey Hall of Fame (2010); Bette Davis Lifetime Achievement Award, Boston University (2008); Prix Genie Best Foreign Actress Award, "Atlantic City" (1981); Best Actress Award, "Tempest," Venice Film Festival (1982); Academy Award for Best Actress, "Dead Man Walking" (1996) **MEM:** American Federation of TV and Radio Artists; Screen Actors Guild; Actors Equity; Academy Motion Picture of Arts and Sciences; National Organization of Women; MADRE; Amnesty International; ACLU **BA:** International Creative Management, 40 West 57th Street, New York, NY, 10019

SARBANES, JOHN PETER SPYROS, T: U.S. Representative from Maryland, Lawyer **I:** Government Administration/Government Relations/ Government Services **DOB:** 05/22/1962 **PB:** Baltimore **SC:** MD/USA **PT:** Son of Paul S. and Christine (Dunbar) Sarbanes; **ED:** JD, Harvard University, 1988; AB cum laude, Woodrow Wilson School Public & International Affairs, Princeton University, 1984 **CT:** Bar: DC, Maryland 1988 **C:** Member, US Congress from 3nd Maryland district, 2007-; Member, Committee on Energy and Commerce; Member education & workforce committee, resources committee, government oversight committee, US Congress from 3nd Maryland district,; Chairman health care practice, Venable LLP, 2000-06; Member hiring committee, Venable LLP, 1992-96; Associate through partner, Venable LLP, Baltimore, 1989-2006; Law clerk to Hon. J. Frederick Motz,, US District Court Maryland, 1988-89 **CR:** Special assistant to superintendent schools State of Maryland president Pub. Justice Center, Baltimore, 1994-97 **CIV:** Special assistant, State Superintendent Schools, Maryland, Board member, Institute for Christian & Jewish Studies, **AW:** Fulbright Scholar, 1985 **MEM:** Mem.: American Bar Association, Maryland Bar Association, DC Bar **PA:** Democrat

SARGENT, THOMAS JOHN, T: Economics Professor **I:** Education/Educational Services **DOB:** 07/19/1943 **PB:** Pasadena **PT:** Son of Charles Robert and Helen Alma (Drucker) S.; **MS:** Married **SPN:** Judith Leslie Tam, September 3, 1964 (div. April 1982) **CH:** Robert John, Judy Tam, Anne Catherine **ED:** PhD in Economics (hon.), European University Institute, 2008; PhD in Economics (hon.), Stockholm School Economics, 2003; PhD, Harvard University, 1968; BA, University Calif.-Berkeley, 1964 **C:** Berkeley professor economics & business, New York University, New York City, 2002-; Distinguished fellow Becker Friedman Institute for Research in Economics, University Chicago, 2011-; Donald Lucas professor economics emeritus, Stanford University, 2002-; Senior fellow Hoover Institution, Stanford University, California, 1987-; David Rockefeller professor economics, University Chicago, 1991-98; Donald Lucas professor economics, Stanford University, 1998-2002; Professor economics, University Minnesota, 1975-87; Associate professor economics, University Minnesota, Minneapolis, 1971-75; Associate professor economics, University Pennsylvania, Philadelphia, 1970-71; Research associate, Carnegie Institute Tech., Pittsburgh, 1967-68 **CR:** Visiting scholar Stanford University Hoover Institution, 1985-87 visiting professor economics Harvard University, Cambridge, Massachusetts, 1981-82 Ford Foundation visiting research professor economics University Chicago, 1976-77 member Brookings Panel on Economic Activity, 1973 advisor Federal Reserve Bank, Minneapolis, 1971-87 researcher National Bureau Economic Research, 1979-,

1969-73 **CW:** Author: Macroeconomic Theory, 1979, Dynamic Macroeconomic Theory, 1987, Bounded Rationality in Macroeconomics, 1993, The Conquest of American Inflation, 1999; co-editor: (with R. Lucas) Rational Expectations and Econometric Practice, 1981; editor: Energy, Foresight and Strategy, 1985; co-author: (with R. Manuelli) Exercises in Dynamic Macroeconmic Theory, 1987, (with L. Hansen) Rational Expectations Econometrics, 1991, Robustness, 2008, (with F. Velde) The Big Problem of Small Change, 2002, (with L. Ljungqvist) Recursive Macroeconomic Theory, 2d edition, 2004; contributor articles to professional journals **AW:** Recipient Univ. medal University Calif.-Berkeley, 1964, Mary Elizabeth Morgan prize University Chicago Department Econs., 1979, Erwin Plein Nemmers prize Northwestern University, 1996-97, CME Group MSRI prize in Innovative Quantitative Applications, 2011; co-recipient Nobel Prize in Economics, Swedish Royal Academy Sciences, 2011; named Marshall Lecturer, Cambridge, England, Moore Distinguished scholar California Institute Tech., 2000-01; Woodrow Wilson Harvard Grad. Prize fellowships National Science Foundation,NAS Award for Scientific Reviewing, 2011 **MEM:** Fellow Econometric Society (council member 1987-1992, 1995-99, 2d vice president 2003, 1st vice president 2004, president 2005), National Academy of Sciences (National Academy of Sciences award for Scientific Reviewing, 2011), American Academy Arts & Sciences; member American Economic Association (member executive committee 1986-88, vice president 2000-01, pres.-elect 2004, president 2007), Society Economic Dynamics and Control (president 1989-92), Phi Beta Kappa. **BA:** Department of Economics, New York University 19 W. 4th Street, 6th Floor, New York, NY, 10012

SARKESSIAN, ANITA, T: Founder **I:** Nonprofit & Philanthropy **CN:** Feminist Frequency **SC:** Canada **ED:** Bachelor's Degree in Communication Studies, California State University; Master's Degree in Social and Political Thought, York University **C:** Executive Director, Feminist Frequency (2009-Present) **AW:** Named One of TIME's 100 Most Influential People, TIME Magazine (2015)

SARKISIAN, CHERILYN "CHER", T: Singer **I:** Media & Entertainment **DOB:** 05/20/1946 **PB:** El Centro **SC:** CA/USA **PT:** Gilbert LaPiere, Georgia LaPiere **MS:** Single **SPN:** Gregg Allman, 6/30/1975, Divorced 1/16/1979; Sonny Bono, 10/27/1964, Divorced 6/26/1975 **ED:** Student, Jeff Corey **CW:** Singer, (With Sonny Bono) Sonny And Cher, 1964-1974; Host, (TV Series) Cher, 1975-1976, The Sonny And Cher Show, 1976-1977; Film Appearances, (With Sonny Bono) Good Times, 1966, Chastity, 1969; Actress, (Films) Come Back To The Five And Dime, Jimmy Dean, Jimmy Dean, 1982, Silkwood, 1983, Mask, 1985, The Witches Of Eastwick, 1987, Suspect, 1987, Moonstruck, 1987, Mermaids, 1990, The Player, 1992, Pret-A-Porter, 1994, Faithful, 1996, Tea With Mussolini, 1999, Stuck On You, 2003, Burlesque, 2010, (Voice Actress) Zookeeper, 2011, Mamma Mia! Here We Go Again, 2018, (TV Films) Club Rhino, 1990, If These Walls Could Talk, 1996, Happy Birthday Elizabeth: A Celebration Of Life, 1997; Executive Producer, (TV Films) Sonny & Me: Cher Remembers, 1998; Singer, (Albums) Black Rose, 1980, Cher, 1988, Heart Of Stone, 1989, Love Hurts, 1991, It's A Man's World, 1996, The Casablanca Years, 1996, Believe, 1998, Not Commercial, 2000, Living Proof, 2002, Closer To The Truth, 2013; Special TV Appearances, Cher: Live At The MGM Grand In Las Vegas, 1999, Will & Grace, 2000, 2002, Cher: The Farewell Tour, 2003; Performer, (Special TV Presentation) VH1 Divas Live 2, 1999, VH1 Divas Las Vegas, 2002 **AW:** Glamour Magazine

Women of the Year Lifetime Achievement Award, 2010, TV Land Award, 2007, Emmy Award For Outstanding Variety, Music Or Comedy Special, Cher: The Farewell Tour, 2003, Lifelong Contribution to Music Industry Award, World Music Award, 2000, Lucy Award for Women in Film, 2000, Grammy Award For Best Dance Recording, Believe, 1999, Star on Hollywood Walk of Fame, 1998, Vanguard Award, GLAAD, 1998, Double Platinum, Heart of Stone, 1989, People's Choice Award for Favorite All-Around Female Star, 1989, Golden Globe Award, 1988, Academy Award For Best Actress, Moonstruck, 1988 **BA:** c/o Warner Brothers Records, 3300 Warner Boulevard, Burbank, CA, USA, 91505

SASOUR, LINDA, **T:** Executive Director of the Arab American Association of New York **I:** Nonprofit & Philanthropy **PB:** Brooklyn **SC:** NY/USA **C:** Co-Chair, Women's March, 2017-; Executive Director, Arab American Association of New York, 2005- **AW:** Time 100 Most Influential, 2017

SASSE, BEN, **T:** U.S. Senator from Nebraska **I:** Government Administration/Government Relations/Government Services **DOB:** 02/22/1972 **PB:** Plainview **SC:** NY/USA **PT:** Son of Gary Lynn and Linda K. (Dunklau) Sasse; **ED:** PhD in American History, Yale University, New Haven; MA in Liberal Arts, St. John's College, 1998; AB, Harvard University, Cambridge, Massachusetts, 1994; Attended, Oxford University, 1992 **C:** U.S. Senator from Nebraska, 2015-; Member, Committee on Armed Services, Member Committee on Banking, Housing, and Urban Affairs, Member Joint Economic Committee, Member Committee of the Judiciary; President, Professor history, Midland University, Freemont, Nebraska, 2010-; Assistant Professor public affairs, University of Texas Lyndon B. Johnson School of Public Affairs, Austin, 2009-10; Assistant secretary for planning & evaluation, U.S. Department Health & Human Services, 2007-09; Counselor to secretary, U.S. Department Health & Human Services 2006-07; Chief staff to Rep. Jeff Fortenberry, U.S. House of Reps., Washington, 2005; Chief of staff Office Legal Policy, U.S. Department Justice, 2003-05; Associate consultant, Boston Consulting Group, 1994-95 **CW:** Co-editor: Here We Stand!: A Call From Confessing Evangelicals For A Modern Reformation, 1996 **AW:** Recipient George Washington Egleston Prize, Theron Rockwell Field Prize **PA:** Republican **BA:** Office of Ben Sasse, 136 Russell Senate Office Building, Washington, DC, 20510

SATHER, GLEN CAMERON, **T:** President of New York Rangers **I:** Business Management/Business Services **CN:** New York Rangers **DOB:** 09/02/1943 **PB:** High River **SC:** Alta. Canada **C:** President, New York Rangers, 2000-; Head coach, New York Rangers, 2003-04; General manager, New York Rangers, 2000-15; Alternate governor, Edmonton Oilers, 1990-2000; President, Edmonton Oilers, 1982-2000; General manager, Edmonton Oilers, 1981-2000; Head coach, Edmonton Oilers, 1977-89; Left wing, Minnesota North Stars, 1975-76; Left wing, Montreal Canadiens, 1974-75; Left wing, St. Louis Blues, 1973-74; Left wing, New York Rangers, 1971-73; Left wing, Pittsburgh Penguins, 1969-71; Left wing, Boston Bruins, 1967-69 **CR:** General manager, head coach Team Canada, World Cup of Hockey, 1996 **AW:** Named to World Hockey Association Hall of Fame, 2010, Hockey Hall of Fame, 1997; recipient Jack Adams Award, NHL, 1986, Alberta Sports Hall of Fame and Museum, 1996 **ACH:** Achievements include being the head coach of Stanley Cup Champion Edmonton Oilers, 1984, 1985, 1987, 1988; being the president and general manager of Stanley Cup Champion Edmonton Oilers, 1990

SATRIANO, PIETRO, **T:** CEO of U.S. Foods **I:** Food & Restaurant Services **CN:** US Foods **ED:** M.B.A, Harvard Business School, 1990-92; B.A., Economics, Harvard, 1982-85 **C:** CEO, US Foods, 2015-; CMO, US Foods, 2011-2015; President, Loyalty One Canada, 2009-11; Executive VP Food Segment, Loblaw Companies, 2007-08; Executive VP Loblaw Brands, Loblaw Companies, 2002-06

SCALISE, STEVE, **T:** Dean of Louisiana Congressional Delegation **I:** Government Administration/Government Relations/Government Services **DOB:** 10/06/1965 **PB:** New Orleans **SC:** LA/USA **ED:** BS in Computer Programming, Louisiana State University, 1989 **C:** Dean, Louisiana Congressional Delegation, 2017-; Assistant majority leader (majority whip), 2014-; Member, U.S. Congress from 1st Louisiana District, 2008-; Chairman, Republican Study Committee, 2013-14; Member District 9, Louisiana State Senate, 2008; Member District 82, Louisiana House of Reps., 1996-2007; Software engineer, computer programmer, Louisiana, **CIV:** Board member, Jefferson Senior Center, Board member, American Italian Renaissance Foundation, Board member, Teach For America, New Orleans, **AW:** Named a Man of Year, Central Metairie Chap. AARP, 1998; named, Associated Builders & Contractors, 2001, Legislator of Year, New Orleans Regional Chamber of Commerce, 2001, Citizens Against Lawsuit Abuse, 1999, Alliance for Good Government Jefferson/New Orleans chap.; named one of The 50 Politicos to Watch, Politico, 2010; recipient Outstanding Legislator award, Victims & Citizens Against Crime, Business Champion award, New Orleans Regional Chamber of Commerce, Patrick F. Taylor Rep. Leadership award, Distinguished Service award, Louisiana Restaurant Association, Letter of Commendation, US Naval Reserve **MEM:** Mem.: Young Leadership Council New Orleans, Louisiana Young Rep. **PA:** Republican **BA:** Office of Steve Scalise, 2338 Rayburn HOB, Washington, DC, 20515

SCARAMUCCI, ANTHONY, **T:** Hedge Fund Manager **I:** Financial Services **ED:** JD, Harvard Law School, 1989; BA in Economics, summa cum laude, Tufts University, Medford, Massachusetts, 1986 **C:** Director of Communication, White House,2017.; Co-founder, managing partner, SkyBridge Capital, LLC, 2005-; Managing director, investment management division, Neuberger Berman, LLC, 2003-05; Managing director, private asset management group, Neuberger Berman, LLC, 2001-03; Co-founder, senior partner, Oscar Capital Management LLC, 1996-2001; Vice president private wealth management, Goldman Sachs & Co., 1993-96; Various positions, Goldman Sachs & Co., 1989-93 **CR:** Member adv. committee New York City Fin. Services **CIV:** Member board overseers, School Arts & Scis., Tufts University, Board directors, Brain Tumor Foundation, Board directors, Lymphoma Foundation, **CW:** Author: Goodbye Gordon Gekko: How to Find Your Fortune Without Losing Your Soul, 2010 **MEM:** Mem.: Phi Beta Kappa

SCARBOROUGH, JOE, **T:** Talk Show Host **I:** Media & Entertainment **DOB:** 04/09/1963 **PB:** Atlanta **SC:** GA/USA **PT:** Son of George Francis and Mary Joanna (Clark) Scarborough; **ED:** JD, University Florida College Law, 1990; BA, University Alabama, 1985 **CT:** Bar: Florida 1991 **C:** Co-host, Morning Joe, MSNBC, 2007-; Host Scarborough Country, MSNBC, 2003-07; Partner, Beggs & Lane, Florida,; Member government reform committee, judiciary committee, armed service committee, US Congress from 1st Florida District,; Member, US Congress from 1st Florida District, Washington, 1995-2001; Attorney, Pennsylvania, 1990 **CR:** Board

directors Emerald Coast Pediatrics Primary Care, Inc. co-chmn. New Federalists **CW:** Author: Rome Wasn't Burnt in a Day: The Real Deal on How Politicians, Bureaucrats, and Other Washington Barbarians are Bankrupting America, 2004, The Last Best Hope: Restoring Conservatism and America's Promise, 2009 (Publishers Weekly bestseller), The Right Path: From Ike to Reagan, How Republicans Once Mastered Politics--and Can Again, 2013,(Music) Mystified, 2017 **AW:** Named one of The 100 Most Influential People in the World, TIME magazine, 2011, The 50 Highest-Earning Political Figures, Newsweek, 2010; recipient Guardian of Senior Rights, 60 Plus Association, Taxpayer's Hero award, Council for Citizens Against Government Waste, Spirit of Enterprise award, US C. of C., Guardian of Small Business award, National Federation Ind. Business, Friend of Taxpayer award, Americans for Tax Reform **PA:** Republican

SCHAEFER III, HENRY F., **T:** Computational and Theoretical Chemist **I:** Education/Educational Services **CN:** University of Georgia **DOB:** 06/08/1944 **PB:** Grand Rapids **SC:** MI/USA **PT:** Son of Henry Frederick Junior and Janice Christine (Trost) S. **MS:** Married **SPN:** Karen Regine Rasmussen, September 2, 1966; **CH:** Charlotte, Pierre, Theodore, Rebecca, Caleb **ED:** Doctor (hon.), Babes-Bolyai University, Cluj-Napoca, Romania, 2009; Doctor (hon.), NorthEastern Hill University, Shillong, India, 2008; Doctor (hon.), Huntington University, 2002; Doctor (hon.), Beijing Institute Tech., 1999; Doctor (hon.), University Sofia, 1999; Doctor (hon.), University Plovdiv, 1998; PhD in Chemical Physics, Stanford University, 1969; BS in Chemical Physics, Massachusetts Institute of Technology, 1966 **C:** Graham Perdue professor, director Center for Computational Quantum Chemistry, University Georgia, Athens, 1987-; From assistant professor to professor chemistry, University California, Berkeley, 1969-87 **CR:** Appointed Professeur d'Echange University Paris, 1977, Gastprofessor Eidgenössische Technische Hochschule, Zürich, 1994, 95, 97, 2000, 02, 04, 06, 08, 10 professor, Ludwig Maximilian University, Munich, 2012, 2013, 2014, 2015 Wilfred T. Doherty professor, director Institute Theoretical Chemistry, University Texas, Austin, 1979-80, chemistry professor emeritus University California, Berkeley, 2004- lecturer in field. **CW:** Author: Science and Christianity: Conflict or Coherence? 2010; contributor articles to professional journals including Electronic Structure of Atoms and Molecules: A Survey of Rigorous Quantum Mechanical Results, 1972, Modern Theoretical Chemistry, 1977, Quantum Chemistry, 1983, A New Dimension to Quantum Chemistry, 1994; editor Molecular Physics, 1991-94, editor in chief, 1995-2005 **AW:** Recipient Pure Chemistry award Am. Chemical Society, 1979, Leo Hendrik Baekeland award, 1983, Schrödinger Medal, 1990, Centenary medal Royal Society Chemistry, London, 1992, Gold medal Comenius University, Bratislava, Slovakia, 2000, Biennial Gold medal University Sofia, 2009; Sloan fellow, 1972, Guggenheim fellow, 1976-77; named one of 100 Outstanding Young Scientists in Am., Sci. Digest, 1984, named 3d Most Highly cited chemist in world Science Watch, 1992,ACS Peter Debye Award, 2014, Joseph O. Hirschfelder prize, 2005, ACS Award in Theoretical Chemistry, 2003 **MEM:** Fellow Japan Society Promotion Sci., American Association for the Advancement of Science, IUPAC, Am. Physical Society, Am. Sci. Affiliation, Am. Academy Arts and Scis., Royal Society Chemistry (London), Am. Chemical Society (Peter Debye award, 2014), Chemical Research Society India, 2015; member International Academy Quantum Molecular Sci., Am. Chemical Society (chairman division physical chemistry 1992, award in theoretical chemistry 2003, Ira M. Remsen award

2003, Ide P. Trotter prize Texas Agricultural and Mechanical University, 2011), World Association Theoretical and Computational Chemists (president 1996-2005, Joseph O. Hirschfelder prize, 2005, Biennial Grand award, Sofia University 2008, Alexander von Humboldt award 2012, SURA Distinguished Scientist award 2012), Am. Institute Chemists (Chemical Pioneer award, 2013), H Index of 108. **BA:** U Georgia, Ctr Computational Quantum Chemistry, Athens, GA, 30602

SCHAKOWSKY, JANICE, T: U.S. Representative from Illinois **I:** Government Administration/Government Relations/Government Services **DOB:** 05/26/1944 **PB:** Chicago **PT:** Daughter of Irwin and (Cosnow) Danoff; **ED:** BS, University Illinois, 1965 **CT:** Cert. Elementary Teacher Illinois **C:** Member, US Congress from 9th Illinois District, 1999-; Member, Committee on Energy and Commerce, Permanent Select Committee on Intelligence; Member, US House Government Reform Committee, 1999-2000; Member, US House Banking & Financial Services Committee, 1999-2000; Member, Illinois House of Reps., 1990-98; Executive director, Illinois State Council Senior Citizens, Chicago, 1985-90; Organizer, Illinois Pub. Action Council, Chicago, 1976-85; Teacher, Chicago Board Education, 1965-67 **CIV:** Del., National Dem. Convention, 1988 Member Governing Council, American Jewish Congress, 1990- Member Steering Committee, Cook County Dem. Women, 1986-90 Board Directors, 4 C's Day Care Council, Evanston, Board Directors, Illinois Pub. Action, **AW:** Named Legislator of Year, Illinois Association Community Mental Health Agencies, 1994, Coalition Citizens with Disabilities/Ill. Council Senior Citizens, 1993, Illinois Nurses Association, 1992, Champaign County Health Care Association, 1992, Community Action Association, 1991, Rookie of Year, Illinois Environmental Council, 1991; named an Outstanding Legislator, Interfaith Council for Homeless, 1993 **MEM:** Mem.: National Organization of Women, ACLU, Rogers Park Hist. Society, Evanston Friends of Libr., Evanston Hist. Society, Evanston Mental Health Association, Illinois Pro-Choice Alliance, National Council Jewish Women **H:** Travel, horsebackriding, reading **PA:** Democrat **BA:** 2367 Rayburn House Office Building, Washington, DC, 20515

SCHARF, CHARLES W., T: Banking Executive **I:** Financial Services **PB:** 1965 **ED:** MBA, New York University; BA, Johns Hopkins University, 1987 **C:** CEO, Director Bank of New York, Mellon 2017-. Chairman Board of Directors, 2018-; CEO, Visa Inc., Foster City, 2012-2017;; Managing director, partner, One Equity Partners LLC, New York City, 2011-12; CEO retail financial services, JPMorgan Chase & Co., New York City, 2004-11; Head retail banking, Bank One Corp., Chicago, 2002-04; Executive vice president, CFO, Bank One Corp., Chicago, 2000-02; CFO global corporate & investment bank, Citigroup, Inc., 1999-2000; Various senior positions to CFO, Salomon Smith Barney, 1995-98; With, Commercial Credit Corp., 1987-95 **CR:** Board directors Microsoft, Inc., 2014-, Visa U.S.A., Inc., 2012-, Visa Inc., 2012-, 2007-11, Travelers Property Casualty Corp., 2002-05 **CIV:** Board trustees, Johns Hopkins University **BA:** Bank of New York-Mellon, 225 Liberty Street New York, NY 10286, New York, NY, 10284

SCHATZ, BRIAN EMANUEL, T: U.S. Senator from Hawaii **I:** Government Administration/Government Relations/Government Services **DOB:** 10/20/1972 **PB:** Ann Arbor **SC:** MI/USA **PT:** Son of Irwin Schatz; **ED:** BA in Philosophy, Pomona College, Claremont, California, 1994 **C:** Member, U.S. Senate Commerce, Sci. & Transportation Committee, 2013-;

Member, U.S. Senate Indian Affairs Committee, 2013-; Member, U.S. Senate Energy & Natural Resources Committee, 2013-; U.S. Senator from Hawaii, 2012-; Lieutenant governor, State of Hawaii, Honolulu, 2010-12; Chairman, Democratic Party of Hawaii, 2008-10; CEO, Helping Hands Hawaii, 2002-10; Member District 25, Hawaii House of Reps., 2002-06; Member District 24, Hawaii House of Reps., 1998-2002; Teacher, Punahou School, **CR:** Member Democratic Party State Central Committee, 1997-98 **CIV:** Candidate, Lieutenant Governor Hawaii, 2010 **AW:** Named Community Leader of Year, Bank of Hawaii, 2004; recipient Environmental Hero Award, National Oceanic & Atmospheric Administration (National Oceanographic and Atmospheric Administration), Pres.'s Award, Hawaii Audubon Society **PA:** Democrat **BA:** Office of Brian Schatz, 722 HART SENATE OFFICE BUILDING, Washington, DC, 20510

SCHEKMAN, RANDY WAYNE, T: Molecular Biology Administrator, Biochemist **I:** Sciences **CN:** University of California, Berkeley **DOB:** 12/30/1948 **PB:** St. Paul **SC:** MN/USA **MS:** Married **CH:** One Child **ED:** Honorary PhD, University of Geneva, 1997; PhD in Biochemistry, Stanford University, 1975; BA, University of California, Los Angeles, 1970 **C:** Editor, eLife, 2011-Present; Co-Chair, Department of Molecular And Cellular Biology, University of California, Berkeley, 1997-Present; Professor, University of California, Berkeley, 1983-Present; Head, Division of Biochemistry And Molecular Biology, University of California, Berkeley, 1990-1997; From Assistant To Associate Professor, University of California, Berkeley, 1976-1983; Fellow, University of California, San Diego, 1974-1976 **CR:** Fellow, Woodrow Wilson Foundation, 1970; Fellow, Cystic Fibrosis Foundation, 1974; Fellow, John S. Guggenheim Foundation, 1982-1983; Proceeding of the National Academy Sciences (PNAS), 2006-2011; Fellow, Royal Society, 2013 **AW:** Research Award In Microbiology & Immunology, Eli Lilly, 1987, Lewis S. Rosenstiel Award In Basic Biomedical Science, 1994, Gairdner Foundation International Award, 1996, Amgen Award Lecturer, Protein Society, 1999, Berkeley Faculty Research Lecturer, University of California, 1999, Albert Lasker Award For Basic Medical Research, Albert & Mary Lasker Foundation, 2002, Louisa Gross Horwitz Prize, Columbia University, 2002, Massry Prize, University of Southern California Keck School of Medicine, 2010, E.B. Wilson Medal, 2010, Co-Recipient, Nobel Prize In Physiology Or Medicine, Karolinska Institute, 2013 **MEM:** American Society of Microbiology, American Society of Biochemists & Molecular Biologists, Honorary Member, Japanese Biochemical Society, Foreign Associate, EMBO., Foreign Member, Royal Society, 2013, American Academy of Arts & Sciences, 2000, President, American Society of Cell Biology, 1999, National Academy of Sciences, 1992 **ACH:** Achievements include research on molecular mechanism of secretion and membrane assembly in eucaryotic cells. **BA:** University of California, Department of Molecular Cell Biology, 401 Barker Hall, Spc 3202, Berkeley, CA, 94720-3202

SCHELLING, THOMAS, T: Economist **I:** Education/Educational Services **CN:** University of Maryland **DOB:** 04/14/1921 **PB:** Oakland **SC:** CA/USA **ED:** AB in Economics, University of California, Berkeley, 1944; PhD in Economics, Harvard University, 1951; Honorary Doctorate, Yale University, 2009 **C:** Distinguished Professor of Economics Emeritus, University of Maryland, 2003—Present; Professor of Economics And Public Affairs, University of Maryland, College Park, MD, 1990—2003; Lucius N. Littauer Professor of Political Economy, Harvard University, 1969—1990; Professor of

Economics, Harvard University, Cambridge, MA, 1958-1990; Associate Professor to Professor of Economics, Yale University, New Haven, CT, 1953-1958; Economist, Executive Office Of the President, The White House, Washington, DC, 1951—1953; Economist, The Marshall Plan, Paris, Copenhagen, Denmark, 1948—1950; Economist, U.S. Bureau Of Budget, Washington, DC, 1945—1946 **CR:** Senior Staff Member, Rand Corp., Santa Monica, CA, 1958—1959; Chairman, Research Advisory Board, Committee on Economic Development, Washington, DC, 1978—1981, 1984—1985; Military Economic Advisory Panel, CIA, 1980—1985; Director, Institute of the Study Of Smoking Behavior & Policy, Harvard University, 1984—1990; Co-Faculty Member, New England Complex Systems Institute; Fellow, American Association For The Advancement Of Science; Fellow, Association For Public Policy Analysis And Management; Fellow, American Economic Association **CW:** Author, National Income Behavior, 1951, International Economics, 1958, The Strategy of Conflict, 1960, Arms and Influence, 1966, Micromotives and Macrobehavior, 1978, Thinking Through the Energy Problem, 1979, Choice and Consequence, 1984, Strategies of Commitment, 2006; Co-Author, (with Morton H. Halperin) Strategy and Arms Control, 1961 **AW:** Nobel Prize in Economic Science, 2005, Award, Behavioral Research Relevant To The Prevention Of Nuclear War, National Academy Of Sciences, 1993, Frank E. Seidman Distinguished Award in Political Economy, 1977, Distinguished Fellow Award, American Economic Association **MEM:** President, American Economic Association, National Academy Of Sciences, Institute of Medicine, President, Eastern Economic Association, 1996 **BA:** University of Maryland, 3114 Tydings Hall, 7343 Preinkert Drive, College Park, MD, 20742

SCHERZER, MAX, T: Professional Baseball Player **I:** Athletics **DOB:** 07/27/1984 **PB:** St. Louis **SC:** MO/USA **PT:** Brad Scherzer; Jan Scherzer **ED:** Student in Business, University of Missouri, Columbia, MO **C:** Pitcher, Washington Nationals, 2015-Present; Pitcher, Detroit Tigers, 2010-2015; Pitcher, Arizona Diamondbacks, 2008-2009 **AW:** University of Missouri Intercollegiate Athletics Hall of Fame, 2011; American League All-Star Team, Major League Baseball, 2013; American League Cy Young Award, Baseball Writers Association of America, 2013, 2016-2017; Wins Leader, 2013-2014, 2016; NL Strikeout Leader, 2016-2017 **ACH:** Achievements include leading the American League in: wins, 2013 **BA:** Detroit Tigers, 2100 Woodward Avenue, Detroit, MI, 48201-3470

SCHIFF, ADAM BENNETT, T: U.S. Representative from California, lawyer **I:** Government Administration/Government Relations/Government Services **DOB:** 06/22/1960 **PB:** Framingham **PT:** Son of Edward Maurice and Sherrill Ann (Glovsky) Schiff; **ED:** JD cum laude, Harvard University, 1985; BA, Stanford University, 1982 **CT:** Bar: California 1986 **C:** Member, US House Select Committee on the Events Surrounding the 2012 Terrorist Attack in Benghazi, 2014-; Ranking member, US House Permanent Select Committee on Intelligence, 2015-; Member, US House Appropriations Committee, 2013-; Member, Committee on Transportation and Infrastructure and Committee on Veterans' Affairs; Member, US Congress from 28th California District, 2013-; Member, US House Permanent Select Committee on Intelligence, 2013-15; Member, US Congress from 29th California District, 2003-13; Member, US Congress from 27th California District, Washington, 2001-03; Member, California State Senate, 1996-2000; Prosecutor US Attorney's Office (central district) California, US Department

Justice, 1987-93; Associate, Gibson, Dunn & Crutcher LLP, LA, 1986 **CR:** Special assignment to Czechoslovakia US Department Justice, Bratislava, Slovakia, 1992 **CIV:** Mock trial coach, Burbank HS, National board member, Big Brothers Big Sisters of America, **MEM:** Mem.: Glendale Chamber of Commerce, Burbank Chamber of Commerce **H:** Creative writing **PA:** Democrat **BA:** 1019 Longworth House Office Building, Washington, DC, 20515

SCHLIFSKE, JOHN E., T: Northwestern Mutual CEO **I:** Insurance **PB:** Milw. **ED:** Master in Fin. & Accounting, Northwestern University, Evanston, Illinois, 1983; BA in economics, Carleton College, Northfield, Minnesota, 1981 **C:** Chairman, CEO, Northwestern Mutual Life Insurance Co., 2010-; President, The Northwestern Mutual Life Insurance Co., 2009-10; President, CEO Russell Investment subsidiary, The Northwestern Mutual Life Insurance Co., 2008-09; Executive vice president, investment products, services & affiliates, The Northwestern Mutual Life Insurance Co., 2004-08; Various investment & real estate management positions, The Northwestern Mutual Life Insurance Co., 1987-2004 **CR:** Board directors Russell Investment Co., Kohl's Corp., 2011- member board trustees The Northwestern Mutual Life Insurance Co. **CIV:** Member, Greater Milwaukee Committee, Board member, Metropolitan Milwaukee Association Commerce, Board member, Froedert Health, Board member, Children's Hospital Wisconsin

SCHLOSSER, ERIC, T: Writer **I:** Writing and Editing **PB:** New York **SC:** NY/USA **PT:** Herbert Schlosser; Judith (Gassner) **ED:** Graduate Degree in British Imperial History, Oxford University; Studied American History, Princeton University **C:** Writer, contributor, Atlantic Monthly Magazine, Boston,; Writer, 1994- **CW:** Playwriter Americans, Arcola Theatre, 2003, We The People, Shakespeare's Globe Theatre, 2007, co-producer, co-narrator Food, Inc., 2008; executive prodr.: There Will Be Blood, 2008; author: Fast Food Nation, 2000, Reefer Madness, 2003, Command and Control: Nuclear Weapons, the Damascus Accident and the Illusion of Safety, 2013; co-author (with Charles Wilson): Chew On This, 2006; television appearances 60 Minutes, CNN, NBC Nightly News, Fox News, works published in Rolling Stone, Vanity Fair, The New Yorker, The New York Times, and The Nation,(Books) Chew on This, 2006, Gods of Metal, 2015 **AW:** Recipient Sidney Hillman Foundation Award, 1995, National Magazine Award for Reporting, 1994 **ACH:** Achievements include several months on New York Times best-seller list, 2004-2005; co-screenwriter, executive producer for the film based on first book produced, Fast Food Nation in 2006

SCHMIDT, BRIAN, T: Astronomer **I:** Sciences **CN:** ANU Research School of Astronomy & Astrophysics **DOB:** 02/24/1967 **PB:** Missoula **SC:** Montana **ED:** PhD in Astronomy, Harvard University (1993); AM in Astronomy, Harvard University (1992); BS in Physics, BS in Astronomy, University of Arizona (1989) **C:** Vice-Chancellor, Australian National University (2015-Present); Laureate Fellow, Australian Research Council, Australian National University (2010—Present); Distinguished Professor, Australian National University, Research School of Astronomy & Astrophysics (2010—Present); Federation Fellow, Australian Research Council, Australian National University (2005—2009); Professional Fellow, Australian Research Council, Australian National University (2003—2005); Research Fellow, Australian National University, Mount Stromlo & Siding Spring Observatories (Now Research School of

Astronomy & Astrophysics) (1997—1999); Post-doctoral Fellow, Australian National University, Mount Stromlo & Siding Spring Observatories (Now Research School of Astronomy & Astrophysics), Canberra, Australia (1995—1996); CfA Postdoctoral Fellow, Harvard-Smithsonian Center for Astrophysics, Cambridge, MA (1993-1994); Fellow, Australian National University, Research School Astronomy & Astrophysics (1992—2002); Astronomer, Australian National University, Research School of Astronomy & Astrophysics **CR:** Australia Telescope Steering Committee (2010—Present); Australian Astronomical Observatory Advisory Committee (2010—Present); National Committee Member, Astronomy of Australian Academy (2010—Present); AURA Gemini Oversight Council (2008—Present); Non-executive Director, Astronomy Australia Ltd. (2007—Present); Member, Steering Committee, Australian Square Kilometre Array (2001—Present); Lecturer, A3002, Observational Cosmology, Australian National University (2004—2005); Board Member, Anglo Australian Telescope Board (2004—2008); Chair, Australian Decade Plan Working Group on International Facilities (2004—2005); Chair, Working Group, Australian National Academy LOFAR (2003—2004); Australia Telescope National Facility Time Allocation Committee (2002—2004); Chair, Australian Time Allocation Committee (2002—2003); Member, ESSENCE-Project to Measure the Equation of State of Dark Energy, REACT-Gamma Ray Burst Follow-up Program, Australia Major National Research Facility Selection Panel (2001); Co-convenor, Astronomy Graduate Program, Australian National University (1999—2001); Coordinator, Extension Course, Astronomy by Astronomers, Australian National University (1999—2001); Lecturer, P2023, Observational Astronomy, Australian National University (1999); Lecturer, A06, Introductory Astrophysics, Australian National University (1996—1998); Teaching Fellow, Astronomy 45 (Introductory Astrophysics), Harvard University (1992); Teaching Fellow, A-35, Harvard University (1991); Teaching Fellow, A-17, Harvard University (1990—1991); Teaching Fellow, Astronomy 14, Harvard University (1989—1990); Teaching Assistant, Astronomy 101, University of Arizona (1988); Scientific Leader, Skymapper Telescope and Southern Sky Survey **CW:** Contributor, Articles to Professional Journals Including The Astrophysics Journal, Nature, and The Astrophysics Journal Letters **AW:** Order of Australia (2013); Dirac Medal (2012); Fellow of the Royal Society (2012); Nobel Prize in Physics (2011); Gruber Cosmology Prize (2007); Co-recipient Shaw Prize in Astronomy, Shaw Foundation, Hong Kong (2006); Padova Citta' dele Stelle Prize (2005); Marc Aaronson Memorial Lecturer (2005); Scientist of the Year, Bulletin Magazine (2004); Dean's Lecture, University of Western Australia (2004); Australian Academy of Science 50th Anniversary Lecture (2004); Vainu Bappu Medal, Astronomical Society of India (2002); Harley Wood Lecture, The Astronomical Society of Australia Inc. (2001); Burbridge Lecture, Auckland Astronomical Society (2001); Oliphant Lecture (Inaugural), Australian Academy of Sciences (2001); Pawsey Medal, Australian Academy of Science (2001); Bok Prize for Outstanding Astronomical Thesis, Harvard University (2000); Australian Government Malcolm McIntosh Prize in Physical Sciences (Inaugural) (2000); Finalist, University of New South Wales Eureka Prize for Scientific Research (1999); Research Breakthrough of the Year, Science Magazine (1998); Named ISI Most Cited Australian in Space Sciences (1997—2007); NASA Graduate Student, Researchers Program Fellowship (1992—1993) **MEM:** Council Member, The Astronomical Society of Australia, Inc. (2001-2003); Fellow, Jap-

anese Society for Promotion of Science; Australian Academy of Sciences; National Academy of Sciences; American Astronomical Society; The Phi Beta Kappa Society **H:** Food; Wine; Running

SCHMIDT, ERIC EMERSON, T: Information Technology Executive **I:** Information Technology and Services **DOB:** 04/27/1955 **PB:** Falls Church **SC:** VA/USA **ED:** PhD in Computer Sci., University of California, Berkeley, 1982; MS in Computer Sci., University of California, Berkeley, 1979; BSEE, Princeton University, New Jersey, 1976 **C:** Chairman, Alphabet Inc, 2015-17; Executive chairman, Google, Inc., Mountain View, California, 2011-2017; Chairman, CEO, Google, Inc., Mountain View, 2001-11; Chairman, CEO, Novell, Inc., Provo, Utah, 1997-2001; President, Sun Tech. Enterprises, Inc., Mountain View, California, 1991-94; Chief technology officer, Sun Microsystems, Mountain View, California, 1994-97; Vice president general systems group, Sun Microsystems, Mountain View, California, 1988-91; Vice president, general manager software products division, Sun Microsystems, Mountain View, California, 1985-88; Software director, Sun Microsystems, Mountain View, California, 1984-85; Software manager, Sun Microsystems, Mountain View, California, 1983-84; Member research staff, Xerox PARC, Palo Alto, California, 1980-83; Research intern, Xerox PARC, Palo Alto, California, 1979-80; Formerly with, Zilog,; Formerly with, Bell Laboratories, **CR:** Member President's Council of Advisors on Sci. & Tech. (PCAST), 2009- chairman New America Foundation, 2008- board directors Apple Inc., 2006-09, Google, Inc., 2001- **CIV:** Trustee, Princeton University, **CW:** Co-author (with Jonathan Rosenberg): How Google Works, 2014 **AW:** Named one of The Business People of Year, Fortune Magazine, 2010, The Top 25 Market Movers, US News & World Report, 2009, The 50 Most Influential People in Sports Business, Street & Smith's SportsBus. Journal, 2008, The Global Elite, Newsweek magazine, 2008, The Top 200 Art Collectors, ARTnews, 2007-, The 25 Most Powerful People in Business, Fortune Magazine, 2007, The 50 Most Important People on the Web, PC World, 2007, The 50 Who Matter Now, Business 2.0, 2007, The World's Richest People, Forbes Magazine, 2006-, The Forbes 400: Richest Americans, 2004- **MEM:** Fellow: American Academy Arts & Sciences; mem.: IEEE, Association Computing Machinery, Sigma Xi **ACH:** Achievements include patents in field **BA:** 1600 Amphitheatre Parkway, Mountain View, CA, 94043

SCHMIDT, MIKE, T: Professional Baseball Player (Retired) **I:** Health, Wellness and Fitness **DOB:** 09/27/1949 **PB:** Dayton **SC:** OH/USA **PT:** Donna Wightman (1973) **MS:** Married **CH:** Jessica Roe; Jonathan Michael **ED:** BBA, Ohio University, Athens, OH **C:** Hitting Coach, Phillies (2002-Present); Third Base Coach, Team USA (2009); Auxiliary Coach, U.S. National Team, World Baseball Classic (2009); Manager, Clearwater Threshers (2003-2004); Player, Philadelphia Phillies (1972-1989); Co-Owner, Mike Schmidt's Philadelphia Hoagies **CR:** Spokesperson, Participate in the Lives of American Youth, Nike **CIV:** Founder, Charity Fishing Tournament, Mike Schmidt Winner's Circle Invitational (1999-Present) **CW:** Co-Author, with Glen Waggoner, "Clearing the Bases: Juiced Players, Shrinking Ballparks, Sham Records, and a Hall of Famer's Search for the Soul of Baseball" (2006); Author, "The Mike Schmidt Study: Building a Hitting Foundation" (1994); Co-Author, with Rob Ellis, "The Mike Schmidt Study: Hitting Theory, Skills, and Technique" (1994); Co-Author, with Barbara Walder, "Always on the Offense" (1982) **AW:** Inductee, Baseball Hall of Fame (1995); Named, National League All-Star Team (1989); Named, National League All-Star Team (1986-1987); Recipient, Silver Slugger Award (1986); Recipient, Golden Glove Award (1986); Named, National League Most Valuable Player (1986); Recipient, Lou Gehrig Memorial Award (1983); Recipient, Silver Slugger Award (1980-1984); Named, National League Most Valuable Player (1980-1981); Named, World Series Most Valuable Player (1980); Named, National League All-Star Team (1979-1984); Recipient, Golden Glove Award (1976-1984); Named, National League All-Star Team (1976-1977); Named, National League All-Star Team (1974) **ACH:** Achievements include hitting his 500th career home run, 1987; having his uniform #20 retired by the Philadelphia Phillies, 1990 **BA:** National Baseball Hall of Fame, 25 Main Street, Cooperstown, NY, 13326

SCHMITTLEIN, DAVID C., **T:** Dean of the MIT Business School **I:** Education/Educational Services **ED:** PhD, Columbia University; M.Phil in Business, Columbia University; BA magna cum laude in Math., Brown University **C:** John C. Head III dean, Massachusetts Institute of Technology Sloan School Management, 2007-; Interim dean, Wharton School, University Pennsylvania, 2007; Deputy dean, Wharton School, University Pennsylvania, 2000-07; Ira A. Lipman professor, professor marketing, Wharton School, University Pennsylvania,; Faculty member, Wharton School, University Pennsylvania, 1980-2007 **CR:** Member Global Agenda Council for Marketing and Branding, World Economic Forum distinguished scholar in residence   John M. Olin School Business, Washington University visiting professor Faculty of Econs. Tokyo University adv. board School Econs. and Management, Tsinghua University international adv. council Guanghua School Management, Peking University academic adv. board China Europe International Business School (CEIBS) international adv. board Groupe HEC **CW:** Contributor articles to professional journals **MEM:** Mem.: Institute for Operations Research and Management Scis. (INFORMS), Am. Statistical Association, Am. Marketing Association

SCHNEIDER, BRAD, **T:** U.S. Representative from Illinois **I:** Government Administration/Government Relations/Government Services **DOB:** 08/20/1961 **PB:** Denver **SC:** CO/USA **ED:** MBA, Kellogg Graduate School of Management, Northwestern University, 1988; BS in Industrial Engineering, Northwestern University, 1983 **C:** U.S. House Small Business Committee, 2013-Present; U.S. House Foreign Affairs Committee, 2013-Present; U.S. Congress, Tenth Illinois District, Washington, DC, 2013-Present; Founder, Cadence Consulting Group, LLC, 2008-Present; Director, Strategic Services Group, Blackman Kallick, 2003-2008; Managing Principal, David Dann Adler Schneider, LLC, 1997-2003; Founder, Managing Principal, Schneider Consulting Group, 1994-1997; Head of Strategy, Mergers & Acquisitions, Commerce Clearing House, 1993-1994; Senior Consultant, Price Waterhouse, 1983 **PA:** Democrat

SCHNITZER, ALAN D., **T:** CEO **I:** Insurance **CN:** Travelers Companies **DOB:** 12/06/1965 **PB:** Dallas **SC:** TX/USA **ED:** JD, Columbia University, 1991; BSE, Wharton School, University of Pennsylvania, Magna Cum Laude, 1988 **C:** CEO, Travelers Companies, 2015-Present; Vice-Chairman, Chief Legal Officer, Travelers Companies, Inc., Saint Paul, MN, 2007-Present; Partner, Corporate Law Practice, Simpson Thacher & Bartlett, LLP, New York, NY, 1999-Present; Associate, Simpson Thacher & Bartlett, LLP, New York, NY, 1991-1999 **CIV:** Board

Director, Audit Committee, Legal Aid Society **CW:** Columbia Law Review **AW:** Harlan Fiske Stone Scholar **MEM:** American Bar Association, New York State Bar Association, Association of the Bar of the City of New York **BAR:** State of New York, 1992 **BA:** 485 Lexington Avenue, New York, NY, 10017

SCHOLES, MYRON SAMUEL, **T:** Economics Professor **I:** Education/Educational Services **DOB:** 07/01/1941 **PB:** Timmins **SC:** ON/Canada **ED:** Doctor (hon.), University Leuven, 1998; Doctor (hon.), McMaster University, 1990; Doctor (hon.), University Paris-Dauphine, 1989; PhD in Fin., University Chicago, 1969; MBA, McMaster University, Hamilton, Ontario, 1964; BA in Economics, McMaster University, Hamilton, Ontario, 1962 **C:** Frank E. Buck professor fin. emeritus, Stanford University, California, 1996-; Co-founder, managing partner, chairman, Platinum Grove Asset Management LP (formerly Oak Hill Platinum Partners), Rye Brook, New York, 1999-2005; Co-founder, principal, Long-Term Capital Management, Greenwich, Connecticut, 1994-98; Senior research fellow Hoover Institution, Stanford University, California, 1988-96; Professor law, Frank E. Buck professor fin., Stanford University, California, 1983-96; Associate professor, Massachusetts Institute of Technology, 1972-73; Assistant professor fin., Massachusetts Institute of Technology, Cambridge, Massachusetts, 1968-72; Edward Eagle Brown professor fin., University Chicago, 1979-82; Director Center Research in Security Prices, University Chicago, 1975-81; Professor, University Chicago, 1975-79; Associate professor, University Chicago, 1973-74; Fin. instructor, University Chicago, 1967-68; Research associate Center Math. Studies in Business & Economics,, University Chicago, 1966-67 **CR:** Board directors Dimensional Fund Advisors, Am. Century Companies Inc., Chicago Mercantile Exchange, 2000- managing director, senior advisor Salomon Brothers, 1990-93 **CIV:** Board trustees, Math. Scis. Research Institute, Berkeley, California, **CW:** Co-author: Taxes and Business Strategies: A Planning Approach, 1991; contributor articles to professional journals **AW:** Recipient Nobel prize in economics, 1997 **MEM:** Mem.: Am. Fin. Association (vice president 1989, president 1990), Econometrics Society **BA:** Stanford Business School, 655 Knight Way, Stanford, CA, 94305

SCHON, NEAL, **T:** Guitarist **I:** Media & Entertainment **PB:** Tinker Air Force Base **SC:** OK/USA **CW:** (Solo) Late Nite,1989,Beyond the Thunder,1995,Electric World, 1997, Piranha Blues, 1999, Voice, 2001, I on U ,2005, The Calling, 2012, So U, 2014 Vortex, 2015,(with Santana), Santana III, 1971, Caravanserai, 1972, Santana IV, 2016 (with Azteca) Azteca, 1972, Pyramid of the moon, 1973, (with Journey) Journey, 1975, Look into the Future, 1976, Next, 1977, Infinity, 1978, Evolution, 1979, Departure, 1980,Escape, 1981, Frontiers, 1983, Raised on Radio, 1986, Trial by Fire, 1996, Arrival, 2001, Generations,2005, Revelation,2008, Eclipse, 2011,(Jan Hammer) Untold Passion, 1981, Here to Stay, 1982,(with HSAS) Through the Fire, 1984, (with Bad English) Bad English, 1989, Backlash 1991,(with Hardline) Hot Cherie EP, 1992, Double Eclipse, 1992, Cant Find My Way EP, 1992, II ,200, (with Paul Rodgers) Muddy Water Blues: A Tribute to Muddy Waters, 1993, The Hendrix Set, 1993, Now, 1997, Paul Rodgers & Friends Live at Montreux 1994, 2011, (with Just If I) All One People,1993, (with Abraxas Pool) Abraxas Pool,1997,(with Soul SirkUS), World Play, 2006 **AW:** Rock and Roll Hall of Fame, 2017

SCHRADER, KURT, **I:** Government Administration/Government Relations/Government Services **DOB:** 10/19/1951 **PB:** Bridgeport, Connecticut, October 19, 1951 **ED:** DVM, University of Illinois, 1977; BS, University of Illinois, 1975; BA in Government, Cornell University, Ithaca, New York, 1973 **C:** Member, US Congress from 5th Oregon district, 2009-; Member, Committee on Energy and Commerce; Member District 20, Oregon State Senate, 2003-08; Member District 23, Oregon House of Reps., 1997-2003; Veterinarian, Owner, Manager, Clackamas County Vet. Clinic, Oregon City, **CR:** Member Canby Planning Commission, 1981-96 **AW:** Recipient Distinguished Leadership by Community Planner Award, Am. Planning Association **MEM:** Mem.: Am. Association Equine Practitioners, Oregon Vet. Association, Am. Vet. Medical Association, Canby C. of C., Oregon City C. of C., Oregon Farm Bureau, National Federation Ind. Business **PA:** Democrat

SCHRIOCK, STEPHANIE, **T:** Political Advocacy Association Administrator **I:** Government Administration/Government Relations/Government Services **ED:** MA in Political Management, George Washington University, 1997; BS in Pub. Administration, Mankato State University, 1995 **C:** President, EMILY's List, 2010-; Campaign manager, Al Franken for Senate, Minnesota, 2008; Chief of staff for Senator Jon Tester, US Senate, Washington, DC 2006-10; National fin. director, Howard Dean's Presidential Campaign, 2003-04; Campaign manager, David Walters for Senate, Oklahoma City,; Campaign manager, Bill Luther for Congress, Minnesota, 1998; Fin. director, South Carolina Dem. Party,; Fin. director, Mary Rieder for Congress, 1996

SCHROCK, RICHARD ROYCE, **T:** Chemist **I:** Sciences **DOB:** 01/04/1945 **PB:** Berne, Ind. **PT:** Son of Noah J. and Martha A. Habegger S.; **ED:** PhD, Harvard University, 1971; AB, University California, Riverside, 1967 **C:** Frederick G. Keyes Professor Chemistry, Massachusetts Institute of Technology, 1989-; Professor, Massachusetts Institute of Technology, 1980-89; Associate Professor, Massachusetts Institute of Technology, 1978-80; Assistant Professor, Massachusetts Institute of Technology, 1975-78; Research Chemist, Central Research & Devel. Department, E.I. du Pont de Nemours & Co., Wilmington, Del., 1972-75 **CW:** Associate Editor: Organometallics; Contributor Articles to Professional Journals **AW:** Recipient Chancellors Award, University Calif, 2006, Distinguished Alumnus Award, University California, 2006, Nobel Prize in Chemistry, 2005, August Wilhelm von Hofmann Medal, German Chemical Society, 2005, Sir Edward Frankland Prize, Royal Society Chemistry, 2004, Sir Geoffrey Wilkinson Medal, 2002, Bailar Medal, University Illinois, 1998; National Science Foundation Postdoc. Fellow, Cambridge University, 1971-72,Basolo Medal, 2007, Member of the Royal Society, 2008, Basolo Medal, 2007, Member of the Royal Society, 2008, **MEM:** Mem.: National Academy of Sciences, American Association for the Advancement of Science, Am. Chemical Society (Organometallic Chemistry award 1985, Harrison Howe award 1990, Humboldt award 1994, Inorganic Chemistry award 1996, Arthur C. Cope award 2001, F. Albert Cotton award 2006, Theodore W. Richards medal 2006, Basolo medal 2007), Am. Academy Arts & Scis.

SCHUMER, AMY, **T:** Comedienne, Actress **I:** Media & Entertainment **PB:** New York **SC:** NY/USA **PT:** Gordon Schumer; Sandra (Jones) Schumer **MS:** Married **SPN:** Chris Fischer (2018) **ED:** Post graduate studies, William Esper Studio, 2003-05; BA in Theatre, Towson University, 2003 **C:** Actress,

Comedian, 2003- **CW:** Actress: (plays) Keeping Abreast; (films) Sleepwalk with Me, 2012, Price Check, 2012, Seeking a Friend for the End of the World, 2012, Thank You for Your Service, 2016; actress, writer (films) Trainwreck, 2015 (Critics' Choice award for Best Actress in a Comedy, 2016), appeared in (TV series) Realty Bites Back, 2008, A Different Spin with Mark Hoppus, 2010, Delocated, 2012, (TV specials) Last Comic Standing, 2007, host, executive producer (TV series) Inside Amy Schumer, 2013- (Emmy award for Outstanding Variety Sketch Series, 2015), performer, executive producer (TV specials) Amy Schumer: Mostly Sex Stuff, 2012, Amy Schumer Live at the Apollo, 2015, appeared in, executive producer Women Who Kill, 2013; performer: (comedy albums) Cutting, 2011; actress: (TV appearances) 30 Rock, 2009, Cupid, 2009, Curb Your Enthusiasm, 2011, Louie, 2012, Girls, 2013-14, BoJack Horseman (voice), 2015, TripTank (voice), 2015; author: The Girl With the Lower Back Tattoo, 2016,(Film) I Feel Pretty, 2018(Television) , The Simpsons, 2016, Family Guy, 2016, Bob's Burgers, 2016, Amy Schumer: The Leather Special, 2017, Family Feud, 2017 **AW:** Named one of The 10 Most Fascinating People of 2015, Barbara Walters Special **RE:** Jewish

SCHUMER, CHUCK, T: U.S. Senator from New York **I:** Government Administration/Government Relations/Government Services **DOB:** 11/23/1950 **PB:** Brooklyn **SC:** NY/USA **PT:** Son of Abraham and Selma (Rosen) S.; Married Iris Weinshall, September 21, 1980; children: Jessica Emily, Alison **ED:** JD with honors, Harvard University, 1974; BA magna cum laude, Harvard University, 1971 **C:** Senate Minority Leader, 2017-; Chairman, US Senate Democratic Policy & Communications Center (DPCC), 2011-2017; Vice chairman, US Senate Democratic Conference, 2007-2017; Chairman, US Senate Rules & Administration Committee, 2009-2015; Chairman, US Senate Democratic Policy & Communications Center (DPCC), 2011-; Chairman, US Senate Rules & Administration Committee, 2009-; Vice chairman, Congressional Joint Economic Committee (JEC), 2009-; Vice chairman, US Senate Democratic Conference, 2007-; US Senator from New York, 1998-; Chairman, Joint Economic Committee (JEC), 2007-09; Chairman, Democratic Senatorial Campaign Committee (DSCC), 2005-09; Member, US Congress from 9th New York District, 1993-99; Member, US Congress from 10th New York District, 1983-93; Member, US Congress from 16th New York District, 1981-83; Chairman committee on oversight & investigation, New York State Assembly, 1979; Chairman subcom. on city management and governance, New York State Assembly, 1977; Member, New York State Assembly, 1975-80; Associate, Paul, Weiss, Rifking, Wharton and Garrison, 1974; Staff member to Senator Claiborne Pell, US Senate, 1973 **CIV:** Board directors, New York Philharmonic **CW:** Co-author (with Daniel Squadron): Positively American: Winning Back the Middle-Class Majority One Family at a Time, 2007 **AW:** Herbert Tenzer award for Pub. Service, Five Towns Jewish council, 1995, Criminal Justice Legis. award, New York State Bar Associate, 1999, Leadership in Government award, Columbia University Business School, 1999, Travers J. Bell Mem award of Distinction, New York District Economic Education Found, Securities Industry, Associate, 1999, Pub. Policy Achievement award, Amer. Cancer Society, 2000, Sound Guardian award, New York Audobon and Consultant Industry Council of Westchester, 2002 **MEM:** Member Jewish War Veterans, B'nai Brith, Phi Beta Kappa **BAR:** Bar: New York 1975 **PA:** Democrat **BA:** Office of Chuck Schumer, 322 Hart Senate Office Building, Washington, DC, 20510

SCHWEIKERT, DAVID, T: U.S. Representative from Arizona, Real Estate Agent, Former State Legislator **I:** Government Administration/Government Relations/Government Services **DOB:** 03/03/1962 **PB:** L.A. **SC:** CA/USA **ED:** MBA, Arizona State University, 2005; BA in Finance & Real Estate, Arizona State University, 1985 **C:** Member, Congress Joint Economic Committee; Member, U.S. House Space, Sci. & Technology Committee, 2013-; Member, U.S. House Small Business Committee, 2013-; Member, U.S. Congress from 6th Arizona District, 2013-; Member, U.S. House Financial Services Committee, 2011-12; Member, U.S. Congress from 5th Arizona District, Washington, 2011-13; Real estate agent, Fountain Hills, Arizona,; Treasurer, Maricopa County, Arizona, 2004-07; Chief deputy treasurer, Maricopa County, 2004; Majority whip, Arizona House of Representatives, 1993-94; Member District 28, Arizona House of Representatives, 1991-95 **CR:** Chair Arizona State Board of Equalization, 1995-2004 **PA:** Republican

SCORSESE, MARTIN, T: Film Director, Film Producer **I:** Media & Entertainment **CN:** World Cinema Foundation **DOB:** 11/17/1942 **PB:** Flushing **SC:** NY/USA **PT:** Charles Scorsese; Catherine (Cappa) Scorsese **SPN:** Helen Morris (1999); Barbara De Fina (1985, Divorced 1991); Isabella Rossellini (1979, Divorced 1982); Julia Cameron (12/30/1975, Divorced 1/19/1977); Laraine Marie Brennan (5/15/1965, Divorced 1971) **CH:** Catherine Terese Glinora Sophia; Domenica Elizabeth **ED:** MA in Film Communications, New York University (1966); BS in Film Communications, New York University (1964); Honorary Doctorate, Royal College Art; Honorary Doctorate, Yale University; Honorary Doctorate, Williams College Yale University; Honorary Doctorate, Bard College; Honorary Doctorate, Wesleyan University; Honorary Doctorate, Princeton University; Honorary Doctorate, New York University **C:** Founder, World Cinema Foundation (2007-Present); Faculty Assistant, Instructor of Film, New York University, New York City, NY (1963-1970) **CW:** Director, Executive Producer, "Boardwalk Empire" (2010-Present); Director "The Irishman" (2019); Director "Silence" (2016); Director, "Vinyl" (2016); Director, "The Audition" (2015); Executive Producer, "The Third Side of the River" (2014); Director, Producer, "The 50 Year Argument" (2014); Executive Producer, "The Wannabe" (2014); Executive Producer, "Glickman" (2013); Executive Producer, "The Family" (2013); Director, "The Wolf of Wall Street" (2013); Executive Producer, "Surviving Progress" (2011); Director, Executive Producer, "George Harrison: Living in the Material World" (2011); Director, "Hugo" (2011); Director, "A Letter to Elia" (2010); Director, "Public Speaking" (2010); Director, "Shutter Island" (2010); Appearance, "30 Rock" (2009); Producer, "The Young Victoria" (2009); Appearance, "Entourage" (2008); Executive Producer, "Lymelife" (2008); Director, "Shine a Light" (2008); Director, Producer, "The Departed" (2006); Director, Producer, "No Direction Home: Bob Dylan" (2005); Director, Executive Producer, "The Aviator" (2004); Director, "The Gangs of New York" (2002); Appearance, "Curb Your Enthusiasm" (2002); Director, "Bringing Out the Dead" (1999); Producer, "The Hi-Lo Country" (1998); Executive Producer, "Kicked in the Head" (1997); Director, "Kundun" (1997); Executive Producer, "Grace of My Heart" (1996); Producer, "Clockers" (1995); Director, "Casino" (1995); Executive Producer, "Quiz Show" (1994); Executive Producer, Naked in New York (1994); Producer, "Mad Dog and Glory" (1993); Director, "The Age of Innocence" (1993); Executive Producer, "Guilty by Suspicion" (1991); Director, "Cape Fear" (1991); Executive Producer, "Akira Kurosawa's Dreams"

(1990); Producer, "The Grifters" (1990); Director, "Goodfellas" (1990); Director, "New York Stories" (1989); Director, "The Last Temptation of Christ" (1988); Executive Producer, "Round Midnight" (1986); Director, "The Color of Money" (1986); Director, "After Hours" (1985); Director, "The King of Comedy" (1983); Director, "Raging Bull" (1980); Director, "The Last Waltz" (1978); Director, "New York, New York" (1977); Director, "Taxi Driver" (1976); Director, "Alice Doesn't Live Here Anymore" (1975); Director, "Italianamerican" (1974); Director, "Street Scenes" (1970); Director, "Mean Streets" (1973); Director, "Boxcar Bertha" (1972); Director, "Who's That Knocking at My Door?" (1968) **AW:** Recipient Spotlight Award for Career Collaboration with Leonardo DiCaprio, National Board Review (2013); Golden Globe Award for Best Director, Motion Picture (2012); Fellow, British Academy of Film and Television Arts (2012); National Board Review Award for Best Director (2011); National Board Review Award for Best Film (2011); Boston Society Film Critics Award for Best Director (2011); Emmy Award for Outstanding Directing for a Drama Series (2011); Cecil B. DeMille Award, Hollywood Foreign Press Association (2010); Columbia-DuPont Journalism Award (2007); Golden Globe Award for Best Director (2007); Named, One of the World's Most Influential People, TIME Magazine (2007); Directors Guild of America Award for Outstanding Directorial Achievement in Feature Film (2007); Academy Award for Best Director (2007); Kennedy Center Honors, John F. Kennedy Center Performing Arts (2007); New York Film Critics Circle Award for Best Director (2006); National Board Review Award for Best Director (2006); Grammy Award for Best Long Form Music Video (2006); Ellis Island Family Heritage Award (2004); Evelyn F. Burkey Award, Writers Guild of America East (2003); Lifetime Achievement Award, Directors Guild of America (2003); Ray of Light Award, Dalai Lama (1998); Lifetime Career Award, Lincoln Center Film Society (1998); Life Achievement Award, American Film Institute (1997); Wexner Prize, Wexner Center for Arts, Columbus, Ohio (1996); Golden Lion Award, Venice Film Festival (1995); Britannia Award, Britain Academy of Film & TV Arts (1993); American Cinematheque Award (1991); Screen Producers Guild Prize (1965); Edward L. Kingsley Foundation Award (1964); Peabody Award; Decorated Commandeur, De La Legion D'Honneur France **MEM:** Fellow, American Academy of Arts and Sciences; Jefferson Humanities Lecturer, National Endowment of the Humanities; Honorary Member, American Academy of Arts and Letters **MH:** Albert Nelson Marquis Lifetime Achievement Award (2017) **BA:** 110 W 57th St Fl 5, Sikelia Productions, New York, NY, 10019

SCOTT, AUSTIN, T: U.S. Representative from Georgia **I:** Government Administration/Government Relations/Government Services **DOB:** 12/10/1969 **PB:** Augusta **SC:** GA/USA **PT:** Jim Scott; Becky Scott **ED:** BBA, University of Georgia, Athens, Greece (1993) **CT:** RHU, The American College (2000); CHFC, The American College (1995); Chartered Life Underwriter, The American College (1995) **C:** Member, U.S. House Armed Services Committee, Washington, DC (2011-Present); Member, U.S. House Agricultural Committee, Washington, DC (2011-Present); Member, U.S. Congress from the Eighth Georgia District, Washington, DC (2011-President); Owner, Insurance Agent & Investment Salesman, The Southern Group, LLC (1998-Present); Member, District 153, Georgia State House of Representatives (2004-2010); Member, District 138, Georgia State House of Representatives (2003-2004); Member, District 165, Georgia State House of Representatives, GA

(1997-2003); Senior Agent, The Principal Financial Group (1993-1998); Agent, Life of South Agency (1992-1993) **CR:** Member, American Legislative Exchange Council (2004) **MEM:** Life Member, National Rifle Association; National Association of Insurance Financial Advisers **PA:** Republican

SCOTT, BOBBY, T: Ranking Member of the Committee on Education,U.S. Representative from Virginia, lawyer **I:** Government Administration/Government Relations/Government Services **DOB:** 04/30/1947 **PB:** Washington **PT:** Son of Charles Waldo and Mae (Hamlin) Scott. **ED:** LLD (hon.), Commonwealth College, Hampton, Virginia, 1988; JD, Boston College School Law, 1973; BA, Harvard University, Cambridge, Massachusetts, 1969 **C:** Chairman, Committee on Education and the Workforce, 1993-; Member, US Congress from 3rd Virginia district, 1993-; Member, Virginia State Senate, 1983-93; Member, Virginia House of Delegates, 1978-83; Lawyer, private practice, Newport News, Virginia, 1973-91 **CIV:** Member adv. committee, Peninsula Boy Scouts America, Board president, National Association for the Advancement of Colored People, Newport News, Chairman 1st district, Virginia Dem. Party, Virginia, 1980-85 Board directors, Hampton Roads March of Dimes, President board directors, Peninsula Legal Aid Center, Hampton, Virginia, 1977-81 **AW:** Named an Outstanding Legislator, Southern Health Association, 1989; named one of 100 Most Influential Black Americans, Ebony magazine, 2006; recipient Distinguished Service award, Virginia State Fraternal Order Police, 1987, Child Advocate award, Virginia Academy Pediatrics, 1987, Brotherhood Citation award, National Conference Christians & Jews, 1985 **MEM:** Mem.: Peninsula C. of C., Sigma Pi Phi, Alpha Phi Alpha **PA:** Democrat

SCOTT, DAVID ALBERT, T: U.S. Representative from Georgia **I:** Government Administration/Government Relations/Government Services **DOB:** 06/27/1945 **PB:** Aynor **SC:** SC/USA **PT:** Albert Scott, Mamie (Polite) Scott **ED:** MBA, University of Pennsylvania, 1969; BA, Florida A&M University, 1967 **C:** U.S. Congress From 13th Georgia District, 2003-Present; Chairman, Rules Committee, Georgia Senate, Atlanta, GA, 1994-2002; Chairman, Education Committee, Georgia Senate, Atlanta, GA, 1993; Georgia Senate, Atlanta, GA, 1983-2002; Georgia House Of Representatives, Atlanta, GA, 1975-1982; Agriculture Committee, Financial Services Committee; President, Owner, Dayn-Mark Advertising, Atlanta, GA **CR:** Chairman, Atlanta Fulton Senate Delegation, 1992-1994 **CIV:** Executive Board of Directors, University of Pennsylvania Wharton School of Business **CW:** Creator, Producer, Director, (Films) Langston!, (National Radio Programs) Inside Black America **AW:** Power 150, 2008, Most Influential Black Americans, Ebony Magazine, 2006, Telly Award, 1994, Silver Microphone Award, 1986, 1992-1994, Four Emmy Awards, Best Cultural Affairs Program Award, National Academy Of Television Arts And Sciences, Special Recognition, Congressional Black Caucus, Bronze Jubilee Award, Langston!, Special Community Service Award, Mayor Of Chicago, James Weldon Johnson Journalism Award, National Association For The Advancement Of Colored People, Special Citation, City Of Highland Park, Michigan, Special Broadcasting Community Service Award, Detroit City Council, Special Tribute, Michigan House Of Representatives, Inside Black America **MEM:** National Association For The Advancement Of Colored People, Black Caucus, National Association of Black Elected Officials, Board of Directors, Georgia Chamber of Commerce, Georgia Business Council, Alpha Phi Alpha **H:** Reading, Writing, Movies, Theater **PA:** Democrat

SCOTT, PHIL, T: Governor of Vermont **I:** Government Administration/Government Relations/Government Services **DOB:** 09/04/1958 **PB:** Barre **SC:** VT/USA **ED:** BS, University of Vermont (1980) **C:** Governor, State of Vermont (2017-Present); Lieutenant Governor, State of Vermont (2011-2017); Co-owner, Debois Construction, Middlesex, VT (1986-Present); Member, Washington District, Vermont State Senate, VT (2001-2011); Co-owner, Shoneys Restaurant, Berlin, VT **CIV:** President, Associated General Contractors (1998); President, Associated General Contractors (1997); Founder, Wheels for Warmth (2004-Present) **MEM:** President, Associated General Contractors (1997-1998) **PA:** Republican **BA:** Office of the Governor, 109 State Street Pavilion, Montpelier, VT, 05609

SCOTT, RICK, T: Governor of Florida, Investment Company Executive **I:** Government Administration/Government Relations/Government Services **DOB:** 12/01/1952 **PB:** Bloomington **PT:** Son of Orba and Esther Scott; **ED:** JD, Southern Methodist University, 1978; BSBA, University Missouri, 1975 **CT:** Bar: Texas **C:** Governor, State of Florida, 2011-; Founder, Conservatives For Patients' Rights (CPR), 2009-19; Co-founder, chairman, Solantic Corp., Jacksonville, Florida, 2001-11; President, CEO, Richard L. Scott Investments, LLC, Naples, Florida, 1997-2001; Chairman, CEO, Columbia/ HCA Healthcare Corp., Nashville, 1987-97 **CR:** Board directors Secure Computing Corp., 2006-08, Solantic Corp., 2001-11, CyberGuard, 2001-03 **CIV:** Member national board, The United Way, 1997-2003 **AW:** Named CEO of the Year, Financial World magazine, 1995; named one of America's 25 Most Influential People, TIME magazine, 1996, The Top 25 Performers, US News & World Report, 1995; recipient Entrepreneurship award, George Washington University, 2007, Second Century award for Excellence in Health Care, Columbia University School Nursing, 1995 **MEM:** Mem.: Business Council, Business Roundtable, Healthcare Leadership Council **PA:** Republican **BA:** Office of Rick Scott, 400 S. Monroe St., Tallahassee, FL, 32399

SCOTT, TIM, T: U.S. Senator from South Carolina **I:** Government Administration/Government Relations/Government Services **DOB:** 09/19/1965 **PB:** Charleston **PT:** Son of Ben Scott Senior and Frances Scott **ED:** BS in Political Sci., Charleston Southern University, 1988 **C:** Member, US Senate Special Committee on Aging, 2013-; Member, US Senate Small Business & Entrepreneurship Committee, 2013-; Member, US Senate Health, Education, Labor & Pensions Committee, 2013-; Member, US Senate Energy & Natural Resources Committee, 2013-; Member, US Senate Commerce, Sci. & Transportation Committee, 2013-; US Senator from South Carolina, 2013-; Member, US House Rules Committee, Washington, 2011-13; Member, US Congress from 1st South Carolina District, Washington, 2011-13; Member District 117, South Carolina House of Reps., 2008-11; Chairman, Charleston County Council, 2007-08; Councilman, Charleston County Council, 1995-2008; Partner, Pathway Real Estate Group, LLC, Charleston; Owner, Tim Scott Allstate, Charleston **CR:** Co-chmn. financial services committee Allstate National Advisory Board, 2004-08 **AW:** Named an The 50 Politicos to Watch, Politico, 2010; recipient South Carolina Agency Owner of Year award **PA:** Republican **BA:** The Office of Tim Scott, 717 Hart Senate Office Building, Washington, DC, 20510

SCULLY, VINCENT EDWARD EDWARD, T: Sports Broadcaster **I:** Media & Entertainment **DOB:** 11/29/1927 **PB:** Bronx **PT:** Son of Vincent Aloysius and Bridget (Freehill) S.; Married Sandra Hunt, November 11, 1973; children: Michael, Kevin,

Todd, Erin, Kelly, Catherine Anne. **ED:** LLD (hon.), Pepperdine University, Malibu, California, 2008; BA, Fordham University, Bronx, New York, 1949 **C:** Sports announcer, LA Dodgers, 1957-; Sports announcer, NBC-TV, 1982-89; Sports announcer, CBS-TV, 1975-82; Sports announcer, Brooklyn Dodgers, 1950-57; Broadcaster, 1950-2016 **CIV:** Served with US Naval Reserve, 1944-45 **AW:** Recipient TV award Look magazine, 1959, Ford C. Frick award, 1982; named Sportscaster of Year in California, 1959, 60, 63, 69, 71, 73-75; National Sportscaster of Year, 1966, 78, 82; named to Fordham University Hall of Fame, 1976, National Baseball Hall of Fame, 1982, California Sports Hall of Fame, 2008; named one of Top 50 Sportscasters Am. Sportscasters Association, 2009,Commissioners Historic Achievement Award, 2014, Presidential Medal of Freedom, 2016 **MEM:** Member American Federation of TV and Radio Artists, Screen Actors Guild, Catholic Actors, TV Academy Arts and Scis. Clubs: Lambs (New York City); Bel Air Country, Beach

SEATON, DAVID T., T: CEO **I:** Architecture & Construction **CN:** Fluor **ED:** B.S. Degree, University of South Carolina; Post Grad Certificate, Thunderbird School of Global Management **C:** Chairman/CEO, Fluor Corp,2/2012-; Chief Executive Officer, Fluor Corp, 2011-2012; Chief Operating Officer, Fluor Corp, 2009-2011; Senior Pres:Energy,Fluor Corp, 2009-2009; Pres:Energy & Chemicals,Fluor Corp, 2007-2009; Senior VP:Corp Sales Board,Fluor Corp, 2005-2007; Senior VP:Chemical Business, Fluor Corp, 2004-2005; Senior VP:Oil & Gas Sales, Fluor Corp, 2002-2004 **BA:** 6700 Las Colinas Blvd, Irving, TX, 75039

SEAVER, TOM, T: Former Professional Baseball Player **I:** Athletics **DOB:** 11/17/1944 **PB:** Fresno **PT:** Son of Charles H. and Betty Lee (Cline) S.; Married Nancy Lynn McIntyre, June 9, 1966; children: Sarah, Anne Elizabeth **ED:** Student, University of Southern California, 1965-68; Student, Fresno City College, 1964 **C:** Analyst, New York Yankees, 1989-1993,; Analyst, New York Mets, 1995-2005; Pitcher, Boston Red Sox, 1986; Pitcher, Chicago White Sox, 1984-86; Pitcher, Cincinnati Reds, 1977-82; Member, World Series Championship team, New York Mets, 1969; Pitcher, New York Mets, 1967-77, 83-84, 87; Pitcher, Jacksonville (Florida) Suns, 1966 **CR:** Announcer New York Yankees WPIX-TV, New York City, New York Mets, 1999- **CIV:** Served with US Marine Corps Reserve, 1963 **CW:** Author: (with Lee Lowenfish) The Art of Pitching, 1984, (with Alice Seigel) Tom Seaver's Baseball Card Book, 1985, (with Herb Resnicow) novel Beanball, 1989 **AW:** Recipient Cy Young award National League, 1969, 73, 75; named Rookie of Year Baseball Writers Association Am., 1967, National League Pitcher of Year Sporting News, 1969, 73, 75, Sportsman of Year Sports Illustrated, 1969; named to National League All-Star team, 1969-73, 75-78, to Baseball Hall of Fame Baseball Writers Association Am., 1992 **ACH:** Achievements include being credited with more than 300 career victories; pitched over 3,000 career strikeouts.

SEBERT, KESHA, T: Singer **I:** Media & Entertainment **DOB:** 03/01/1987 **PB:** Los Angeles **SC:** CA/USA **PT:** Pebe Sebert **CW:** Singer: (albums) Animal, 2010, Cannibal, 2010, I Am the Dance Commander + I Command You to Dance: The Remix Album, 2011, Warrior, 2012, (with the Flaming Lips) Lipsha, 2013, Rainbow, 2017 (songs) Tik Tok, 2009, (featuring 3OH!3) Blah Blah Blah, 2010, Your Love Is My Drug, 2010, We R Who We R, 2010, Blow, 2011; author: (autobiography) Kesha: My Crazy Beautiful Life, 2012; reality TV personality Kesha: My Crazy Beautiful Life, 2013, judge (reality

TV competition) Rising Star, 2014 **AW:** Named Best New Act, MTV Europe Music Awards, 2010, Time 100 Most Influential, 2018

SEGER, BOB, T: Musician **I:** Media & Entertainment **PB:** Ann Arbor **SC:** MI/USA **PT:** Stewart Seger; Charlotte Seger **CW:** Recorded for Capitol Records then recorded (with duo Teegarden and Van Winkle) Smokin O.P.'s, 1972, Back in 72, 1973, Seven, 1974, for Warner Bros Ramblin Gamblin Man, 1969, Mongrel, 1970, currently recording for Capitol Records and touring with own back-up group, The Silver Bullet Band, albums include Beautiful Loser, 1975, Live Bullet, Night Move, 1976, Stranger in Town, 1978, Against The Wind, 1980, Nine Tonight, 1981, The Distance, 1982, Like a Rock, 1986, The Fire Inside, 1991, It's A Mystery, 1995, Face the Promise, 2006, Ride Out, 2014, I Knew You When, 2017, songs include Turn The Page (with Jason Aldean for CMT Crossroads: Bob Seger and Jason Aldean), 2014 (Performance of Year, CMT Music Awards, 2015) **AW:** Named to Songwriters Hall of Fame, 2012, Rock & Roll Hall of Fame, 2004

SEINFELD, JERRY, T: Comedian, Actor, Television Producer, Scriptwriter **I:** Media & Entertainment **PB:** Brooklyn **SC:** NY/USA **PT:** Kalman Seinfeld, Betty S. Seinfeld **ED:** Degree In Theatre Communications, Queens College, New York, 1976 **C:** Stand-up Comedian, 1976 **CW:** Joke-Writer, Actor, (TV Series) Benson, 1980-1981; Actor, Co-Writer, Producer, Seinfeld, 1990-1998; Actor, (TV Films) The Ratings Game, 1984, (TV Specials) The Tommy Chong Roast, 1986, The Seinfeld Chronicles, 1989, (Films) The Thing About My Folks, 2005, Top Five, 2014; Executive Producer, Comedian, 2002; Writer, Actor, A Uniform Used To Mean Something..., 2004, Hindsight Is 20/20..., 2004; Writer, Producer, Actor, (Voice) (Films) Bee Movie, 2007; Writer, Jerry Seinfeld-Stand-Up Confidential, 1987; Guest Appearances, The Larry Sanders Show, 1992, News Radio, 1995, Curb Your Enthusiasm, 2004-2009, Louie, 2012-2014, The Jim Gaffigan, 2016, Mystery Science Theater 3000, 2017; Creator, Producer, The Marriage Ref, 2010-2011; Creator, Host, Comedians In Cars Getting Coffee, 2012-Present; Director, (Broadway Plays) Long Story Short, 2010-2011; Performer, (TV Special) Talking Funny, 2011; Author, Seinlanguage, 1993, (Children's Book) Halloween, 2002, Top Five, 2014, Jerry Before Seinfeld, 2017 **AW:** American Comedy Award For Funniest Male Performer In A TV Series, Seinfeld, 1992-1993, Emmy Award For Outstanding Comedy Series, Seinfeld, 1993, Golden Globe Award For Outstanding Performance By An Ensemble In A Comedy Series, Seinfeld, 1995, 1997-1998, People's Choice Award For Favorite TV Comedy Series, Seinfeld, 1998, The 100 Most Powerful Celebrities, Forbes.com, 2008,; Producers Guild Of America Award For Outstanding Digital Series, Comedians In Cars Getting Coffee, 2015-2016 **RE:** Jewish

SELES, MONICA, T: Professional Tennis Player (Retired) **I:** Athletics **DOB:** 12/02/1973 **PB:** Novi Sad **SC:** Serbia **PT:** Daughter of Karolj and Esther Seles. **C:** Professional tennis player, 1989-2008 **CR:** Member WTA Tour Players' Council, 1998-99, U.S. Fed Cup Team, 2000, 1999, 1996 **CIV:** Active, Special Olympics, **CW:** Co-author (with Nancy Ann Richardson): Monica: From Fear to Victory, 1996; author: Getting a Grip, 2009; performer: (TV series) Dancing with the Stars, 2008 **AW:** Named Player Who Makes a Difference, Family Circle Cup, 1999, Female Pro Athlete of Year, Florida Sports Hall of Fame, 1998, Comeback Player of Year, TENNIS Magazine, 1995, Female Athlete of Year, Associated Press, 1992, 1991, Player of Year, WTA Tour, 1991, Most Improved Player, 1990, Female

Rookie of Year, TENNIS Mag./Rolex Watch, 1989, Sportswoman of Year, Yugoslavia, 1985; recipient Sanex Hero of Year Award, WTA Tour, 2002, Flo Hyman Memorial Award, Women's Sports Foundation, 2000, Commitment to Community Award, Florida Times-Union, 1999, Comeback Player of Year Award, WTA Tour, 1998, 1995, Rado Topspin Award, 1990, Ted Tinling Diamond Award, 1990,30 Legends of Women's Tennis: Past, Present and Future, Time Magazine, International Tennis Hall of Fame, 2009 **ACH:** Achievements include 3rd player in the Open-era to capture the Australian and Roland Garros in same calendar year; World #1 ranked player, 1991, 92, 95; youngest #1 ranked player in tennis history for women and men at 17 years, 3 months, 9 days; Winner Grand Slam titles: Roland Garros, 1990, 91, 92, French Open, 1990, 91, 92, U.S. Open, 1991, 92, Australian Open, 1991, 92, 93, 96; Winner 53 Career Singles Titles and 6 Career Doubles Titles, WTA Tour.

SELF, BILL, T: College Basketball Coach **I:** Athletics **DOB:** 12/27/1962 **PB:** Okmulgee **SC:** OK/USA **PT:** Married Cindy Self **CH:** Lauren, Tyler **ED:** Master in Athletic Administration, Oklahoma State University, 1989; BSBA, Oklahoma State University, 1985 **C:** Head coach, University Kansas, 2003-; Head coach, University Illinois Champaign-Urbana, 2000-03; Head coach, University Tulsa, 1997-2000; Head coach, Oral Roberts University, 1993-97; Assistant coach, Oklahoma State University, 1986-93; Assistant coach, University Kansas, 1985-86 **CR:** Board member National Association Basketball Coaches member competition committee USA Men's Basketball, 2005- **AW:** Finalist Naismith College Coach of Year award 2000-03, 2009; named Don Haskins Coach of Year, Western Athletic Conference, 2009; John and Nellie Wooden Coach of Year, Utah Tipoff Club, 2000, National Coach of Year, The Sporting News, 2000, 2009, 2012, Associated Press, 2009, Big 12 Coach of Year, 2006, 2009, 2011, 2012, District VI Coach of Year US Basketball Writers Association, 2011, Naismith College Coach of Year, 2012, Adolph F. Rupp cup Commonwealth Athletic Club Kentucky, 2012; recipient Henry Iba award US Basketball Writers Association, 2009, Guardians of Game Pillar award Service National Association Basketball Coaches, 2011,Basketball Hall of Fame, 2017, NABC Coach of the Year, 2016, AP College Coach of the Year, 2016, AP Big 12 Coach of the Year, 2016, Bleacher Report National Coach of the Year, 2016, USA Today National Coach of the Year, 2016, John R. Wooden Award Legends of Coaching Award, 2013, Oklahoma Sports Hall of Fame, 2013 **ACH:** Achievements include coaching the Univeristy of Tulsa to Western Athletic Conference regular season championship, 1999, 2000; coaching the University of Illinois to Big Ten regular season championship, 2001, 2002; coaching the University of Kansas to Big 12 regular season championship, 2005-09; head coach of the NCAA Men's Basketball National Championship winning University of Kansas Jayhawks, 2008 **BA:** Allen Fieldhouse, 1651 Naismith Dr, Lawrence, KS, 66044

SELLECK, TOM, T: Actor **I:** Media & Entertainment **PB:** Detroit **SC:** MI/USA **PT:** Robert D. Selleck; Martha Selleck **MS:** Married **SPN:** Jillie Joan Mack, (August 7, 1987); Jacquelyn Ray (May 15, 1971) (div. August 10, 1982) **CH:** Kevin (Stepchild); Hannah Margaret **ED:** Ph.D (hon.), Pepperdine University **CIV:** Board member, Michael Josephson Institute Ethics **CW:** Actor: (films) Myra Breckinridge, 1970, The Seven Minutes, 1971, Daughters of Satan, 1972, Shadow of Fear, 1973, Terminal Island, 1973, Midway, 1976, The Washington Affair, 1977, The Gypsy Warriors, 1978, Coma, 1978, High Road to China, 1983, Lassiter, 1984, Runaway, 1985,

Three Men and a Baby, 1987, Her Alibi, 1989, An Innocent Man, 1989, Quigley Down Under, 1990, Three Men and a Little Lady, 1990, Folks!, 1992, Christopher Columbus: The Discovery, 1992, Mr. Baseball, 1992, Open Season, 1995, In and Out, 1997, The Love Letter, 1999, Angus Magillicutty, 2003, (voice) Meet the Robinsons, 2007, Killer, 2010; (TV films) The Movie Murderer, 1970, A Case of Rape, 1974, Returning Home, 1975, Bunco, 1977, Superdome, 1978, The Chinese Typewriter, 1979, The Sacketts, 1979, Divorce Wars: A Love Story, 1982, Louis L'Amour's The Shadow Riders, 1982, Broken Trust, 1995, Running Mates, 2000, Touch 'Em All McCall, 2003, Twelve Mile Road, 2003, Reversible Errors, 2004, Ike: Countdown to D-Day, 2004; actor, executive prodr.: (TV films) Ruby Jean and Joe, 1996, Last Stand at Saber River, 1998, Louis l'Amour's Crossfire Trail, 2000, Monte Walsh, 2003, Jesse Stone: Stone Cold, 2005, Jesse Stone: Night Passage, 2006, Jesse Stone: Death in Paradise, 2006, Jesse Stone: Sea Change, 2007, Jesse Stone: Thin Ice, 2009, Jesses Stone: No Remorse, 2010, Jesse Stone: Innocents Lost, 2011, Jesse Stone: Benefit of the Doubt, 2012, Jesse Stone: Lost in Paradise; (TV series) The Young and the Restless, 1973-74, Magnum P.I. 1980-88, The Closer, 1998, Las Vegas, 2007-08, Blue Bloods, 2010-; (TV appearances) Lancer, 1969, Bracken's World, 1969, Sarge, 1971, Wide World Mystery, 1973, The F.B.I., 1973, Owen Marshall: Counselor at Law, 1973, Lucas Tanner, 1975, Marcus Welby, M.D., 1974-75, Lucas Tanner, 1975, Mannix, 1975, The Streets of San Francisco, 1975, Doctor's Hospital, 1976, Most Wanted, 1976, Charlie's Angels, 1976, Taxi, 1978, The Rockford Files, 1978-79, Stockard Channing in Just Friends, 1979, Concrete Cowboys, 1979, Simon & Simon, 1982, Murder, She Wrote, 1986, Friends, 1996, 2000, Boston Legal, 2006; prodr., Las Vegas, 2007, Blue Bloods, 2010, North America, 2013, Arnie, 2014: (TV series) Magnum P.I., 1985-87, B.L. Stryker, 1989, The Closer, 1998; executive prodr.: (TV films) Revealing Evidence: Stalking the Honolulu Strangler, 1990, Silver Fox, 1991 **AW:** Recipient Horizon award, US Congress, 1997 **MEM:** National Rifle Association

SENSENBRENNER, JIM, T: U.S. Representative from Wisconsin **I:** Government Administration/ Government Relations/Government Services **DOB:** 06/14/1943 **PB:** Chicago **SC:** IL/USA **PT:** Son of James and Margaret Sensenbrenner; **ED:** JD, University Wisconsin, Madison, 1968; AB in Political Sci., Stanford University, California, 1965 **CT:** Bar: US Supreme Court 1972, Wisconsin 1968 **C:** Member, U.S. House of Representatives from Wisconsin's 5th District, 2003-; Member, Committee on the Judiciary; Member, Committee on Foreign Affairs; Member, US Congress from 9th Wisconsin district, 1979-2003; Chairman judiciary committee, US Congress from 5th Wisconsin district, 2001-07; Chairman sci. committee, US Congress from 5th Wisconsin district, 1997-2001; Assistant minority leader, Wisconsin State Senate, 1977-79; Member, Wisconsin State Senate, 1975-79; Member, Wisconsin State Assembly, 1969-75 **MEM:** Mem.: Am. Philatelic Society, Chenequa Country Club, Capitol Hill Club **PA:** Republican

SERRANO, JOSÉ ENRIQUE, T: U.S. Representative from New York **I:** Government Administration/Government Relations/Government Services **DOB:** 10/24/1943 **PB:** Mayagüez **SC:** Puerto Rico **PT:** José E. Serrano; Hipolita (Soto) Serrano **ED:** Coursework, Lehman College, City University of New York (1961) **C:** Member, U.S. Congress from 15th New York District (2013-Present); Member, U.S. House Appropriations Committee (1996-Present); Member, U.S. Congress from 16th New York District (1993-2013); Member, U.S.

House Appropriations Committee (1993-1995); Member, U.S. Congress from 18th New York District (1990-1993); Member District 73, New York State Assembly (1983-1990); Member District 75, New York State Assembly (1975-1983); Member, New York City Board of Education, New York, NY (1969-1974); With, Manufacturers Hanover Trust Co. (1961-1969) **MIL:** With, 172nd Support Battalion Medical Corps, US Army (1964-1966) **AW:** Recipient, Friend of the National Parks Award, National Parks Conservation Association (2005); Recipient, Distinguished Public and Community Service, Hunter College Center or Puerto Rican Studies (2003); Named, Man of the Year Award, Bronx Puerto Rican Day Parade (2003); Recipient, Congressional Recognition Award, National Council La Raza (1993); Recipient, Evelina Lopez Antonetty Award **PA:** Democrat **BA:** 2354 Rayburn House Office Building, Washington, DC, 20515

SESSIONS, JEFF, T: U.S. Attorney General **I:** Government Administration/Government Relations/ Government Services **DOB:** 12/24/1946 **PB:** Hybart, Alabama, December 24, 1946 **PT:** Son of Jefferson Beauregard and Abbie (Powe) S.; Married Mary Montgomery Blackshear, August 9, 1969; children: Mary Abigail, Ruth Blackshear, Samuel Turner **ED:** JD, University Alabama, 1973; BA, Huntingdon College, Montgomery, Alabama, 1969 **CT:** Bar: Alabama 1973. **C:** U.S. Attorney General, Washington, DC, 2017—; Ranking member, US Senate Judiciary Committee, 2009-2017; US Senator from Alabama, 1997-2017; Attorney general, State of Alabama, Montgomery, 1995-97; Partner, Stockman, Bedsole & Sessions, Mobile, 1993-94; Associate then partner, Stockman & Bedsole Attorneys, Mobile, Alabama, 1977-81; US attorney, US Department Justice, Mobile, Alabama, 1981-93; Assistant US attorney (southern district) Alabama, US Department Justice, Mobile, Alabama, 1975-77; Associate, Guin, Bouldin & Porch, Russellville, Alabama, 1973-75 **CR:** Member U.S. Attorney Gen's. adv. committee, 1987-89, vice-chmn. 1989 **CIV:** Presidential elector State of Alabama, 1972 trustee, member executive committee Mobile Bay Area Partnership for Youth, 1981-95 chairman administrative board Ashland Pl. United Methodist Church, Mobile, 1982 1st vice president Mobile Lions Club, 1993-94. Captain US Army Reserve, 1975-85 **AW:** Recipient U.S. Attorney Gen's. award for significant achievements in the war against drug trafficking, US Department Justice, 1992, George (Buck) Gillespie Congl. award, Blinded Americans Veterans Foundation, 2000, National Leadership award, Civil War Preservation Trust, 2004, Distinguished Eagle Scout award, Guardian of Small Business award, Minuteman of the Year award, Reserve Officers Association, Service to Agricultural award, AL Farmers Federation, Teddy Roosevelt Environmental award, Watchdog of the Treasury award, Legislative Achievement award, US Chamber of Commerce, 2009 **MEM:** Member American Bar Association, Alabama Bar Association, Mobile Bar Association **PA:** Republican **BA:** US Department of Justice, 950 Pennsylvania Ave NW, Washington, DC, 20530

SESSIONS, PETER ANDERSON, T: Chairman of the US House Rules Committee **I:** Government Administration/Government Relations/Government Services **DOB:** 03/22/1955 **PB:** Waco **SC:** TX/USA **PT:** William Steele Sessions; Alice June (Lewis) Sessions **ED:** BS in Political Science, Southwestern University, Georgetown, Texas (1978) **C:** Chairman, US House Rules Committee (2013-Present); Member, US Congress from 32nd Texas District (2003-Present); Chairman, National Republican Congressional Committee (NRCC) (2009-2013); Member, US Congress from

5th Texas District (1997-2003); Vice President, Public Policy, National Center of Policy Analysis, Dallas, Texas (1994-1995); Various Positions Including District Manager Marketing, Southwestern Bell Telephone Co., Dallas, Texas (1978-1994) **CIV:** Member, National Committee, National Eagle Scout Association; Member, Advisory Board, HomeAid Dallas; Advisor to President, Special Olympics Texas; Member, Executive Board, Circuit Ten Council, Boy Scouts of America; Board of Trustees, Southwestern University (2007-Present); Team Leader, Adopt–A–Shoreline, White Rock Lake, Dallas, Texas (1996-Present); Active, United Methodist Church **AW:** Taxpayer Hero Award, Citizens Against Government Waste (2009); Guardian of Small Business Award, National Federation of Independent Business (2009); National Leadership Award, National Down Syndrome Society (2008); Distinguished Legislator Award, City of Dallas, Texas (2008); Visionary Award, American Academy of Ophthalmology (2007); Ben Franklin Public Policy Award, National Association of Mutual Insurance Companies (2007); Public Service Award, Association of Air Medical Services (2007); National Distinguished Eagle Scout Award (1999) **MEM:** Rotary Club **H:** Hiking; Mountain Climbing; Running **PA:** Republican **BA:** Office of Peter Sessions, 2233 Rayburn House Office Building, Washington, DC, 20515

SEWELL, TERRI ANDREA, T: U.S. Representative from Alabama, Lawyer **I:** Government Administration/Government Relations/Government Services **DOB:** 01/01/1965 **PB:** Selma **SC:** AL/USA **PT:** Andrew A. Sewell; Nancy (Gardner) Sewell **ED:** JD, Harvard University (1992); MA, University of Oxford, with Honours; BA, Princeton University (1986) **C:** Member, US House of Space, Science & Technology Committee (2011-Present); Member, US House of Agricultural Committee (2011-Present); Member, US Congress from 7th Alabama District, Washington, DC (2011-Present); Partner, Maynard, Cooper & Gale PC, Birmingham, AL (2004-2010); Chair, House of Transportation Committee (2001-2007); Associate, Davis, Polk & Wardwell (1994-2004); Member, Committee on Natural Resources; Committee on Transportation and Infrastructure; Staff Member to Senator Howell Heflin, Alabama State Senate; Law Clerk to Chief Judge U.W. Clemon, U.S. District Court for the Northern District of Alabama; Staff Member to Representative Richard Shelby, US House of Representatives, Washington, DC **CIV:** Member, Community Advisory Board, Birmingham Minority Health & Research Center, University of Alabama; Board Treasurer & Chair, Finance Committee, St. Vincent's Foundation; Board Member, Girl Scouts of Cahaba Council; Member, Corporate Partners Council, Birmingham Art Museum; Member, Governor Board, Alabama Council on Economic Education **PA:** Democrat

SHAH, RISHI U., T: Owner **I:** Business Management/Business Services **CN:** Outcome Health **SC:** IL/USA **ED:** Student, Northwestern University; Student, Harvard University **C:** Founder, CEO, Board directors, ContextMedia, (Now Outcome Health) Inc., Chicago, 2006- **CIV:** Past chairman, Institute Student Business Education, Evanston, Illinois **CW:** Board advisors Northwestern Business Rev. **AW:** Named one of 40 Under 40, Crain's Chicago Business, 2009

SHAHEEN, JEANNE, T: U.S. Senator from New Hampshire **I:** Government Administration/Government Relations/Government Services **DOB:** 01/28/1947 **PB:** St. Charles, Missouri **PT:** Daughter of Ivan E. and Belle E. Bowers; **ED:** Master of Social Sci. in Political Sci., University Mississippi, 1973;

BA, Shippensburg University, 1969 **C:** Ranking Member, Senate Small Business Committee, 2015-; US Senator from New Hampshire, 2009-; Chair, US Senate Foreign Relations Subcommittee on European Affairs, 2009-13; Director Institute Politics, Harvard University, Cambridge, Massachusetts, 2005-07; National Chair, John Kerry's Presidential Campaign, 2004; Vice Chair, Democratic National Convention Committee, 2004; Gov, State of New Hampshire, Concord, 1997-2003; Member District 21, New Hampshire State Senate, 1991-96; Campaign Manager, Governor Paul McEachon, 1988; Campaign Manager, Governor Paul McEachon, 1986; Campaign Manager, Gary Hart's Presidential Campaign, 1984; Campaign Manager, President Jimmy Carter's Presidential Campaign, New Hampshire, 1980 **CR:** Chair Education Commission States, 2000-01 **PA:** Democrat **BA:** Office of Jeanne Shaheen, 506 Hart Senate Office Building, Washington, DC, 20510

SHALHOUB, TONY, T: Actor, Television Producer **I:** Media & Entertainment **PB:** Green Bay **SC:** WI/USA **PT:** Joe Shalhoub; Helen Shalhoub **ED:** Attended, Yale University; BA in Drama, University Southern Maine, 1977 **CW:** Actor: (Broadway plays) The Odd Couple, 1985, The Heidi Chronicles; (plays) Waiting for Godot, For Dear Life, Zero Positive, Rameau's Nephew, 1988, Conversations with My Father, 1992, The Scene, 2007, Lend Me a Tenor, 2010, Golden Boy, 2012, Act One,2014, The Mystery of Love and Sex, 2015, Happy Days,2015, The Band's Visit, 2017 (Tony for Best Performance by a Leading Actor in a Musical, 2018), The Price, 2017; (films) Longtime Companion, 1990, Quick Change, 1990, Barton Fink, 1991, Honeymoon in Vegas, 1992, Searching for Bobby Fischer, 1993, Addams Family Values, 1993, I.Q., 1994, Big Night, 1996 (National Society Film Critics award for Best Supporting Actor, 1996), Men in Black, 1997, Gattaca, 1997, A Life Less Ordinary, 1997, Primary Colors, 1998, Paulie, 1998, The Siege, 1998, The Impostors, 1998, A Civil Action, 1998, The Tic Code, 1998, The Man Who Wasn't There, 2001, Spy Kids, 2001, Thir13en Ghosts, 2001, Men in Black II, 2002, Life or Something Like It, 2002, Impostor, 2002, Something More, 2003, Against the Ropes, 2003, Spy Kids 3-D: Game Over, 2003, T for Terrorist, 2003, The Great New Wonderful, 2005, (voice) Cars, 2006, Maybe It's in the Water, 2006, Careless, 2007, 1408, 2007, How Do You Know, 2010, (voice) Cars 2, 2011, Pain & Gain, 2013, The Adventures of Beatle, 2014, Teenage Mutant Ninja Turtles (voice), 2014, Guns for Hire, 2015, Custody, 2016, (voice) Teenage Mutant Ninja Turtles: Out of the Shadows, 2016, Breakable You, 2016, Final Portrait, 2017, Cars 3,2017; (TV films) Alone in the Neon Jungle, 1988, Money, Power, Murder, 1989, Day One, 1989, Gypsy, 1993, Radiant City, 1996, That Championship Season, 1999, The Heart Department, 2001, Too Big to Fail, 2011, Five, 2011, Friday Night Dinner, 2012, Hemingway & Gellhorn, 2012, (video game) Fallout: A Post-Nuclear Role-Playing Game, 1997; (TV series) Wings, 1991-97, Stark Raving Mad, 1999-2000, Monk, 2002-09 (Golden Globe award, 2002, Emmy award for Best Actor in a Comedy, 2003, Screen Actors Guild Award for Best Actor in a Comedy Series, 2004, Screen Actors Guild award for Outstanding Performance by a Male Actor in a Comedy Series, 2005, Emmy award for Outstanding Lead Actor in a Comedy Series, 2005, 2006), We Are Men, 2013, Nurse Jackie, 2015, The Blacklist, 2016, Braindead, 2016, The Marvelous Mrs Maisel, 2017; actor, director (films) Made Up, 2002, actor, executive producer AmericanEast, 2008, Feed the Fish, 2009

SHANAHAN, PATRICK M., T: Deputy Secretary of Defense **I:** Government Administration/Government Relations/Government Services **CH:** 3 children **ED:** MS in Mechanical Engineering & Management, Massachusetts Institute of Technology; BS in Mechanical Engineering, University of Washington **C:** Deputy Secretary of Defense, Washington, 2017-; Senior vice president, supply chain and operations worldwide, Boeing Co., 2016-2017; Vice president, general manager, airplane programs, Boeing commercial airplanes, Boeing Co., 2008-16; Vice president, general manager, 787 dreamline program, Boeing Co., 2004; Vice president, general manager, Boeing missile defense system, Boeing Co., Washington, 2004; Vice president, general manager, rotorcraft system, Boeing Co., Philadelphia; Vice president, general manager, Boeing commercial airplanes, Boeing Co.; Director, 767 manufacturing business unit, director, tooling business unit, fabrications division, Boeing Co.; Program manager, Boeing 767-400ER, Boeing Co.; Joined, Boeing Co., 1986 **CIV:** Secretary, treasurer Am. Helicopter Society board directors Am. Parkinson Disease Association, 2004 fellow Society Manufacturing Engineers, The Royal Aeronautical Society **MEM:** Mem.: American Helicopter Society(treasurer; secretary)

SHAPIRO, ROBERT, T: Partner **I:** Law and Legal Services **CN:** Glaser Weil Fink Jacobs Howard Avchen & Shapiro LL **DOB:** 09/02/1942 **PB:** Plainfield **SC:** NJ/USA **ED:** JD, Loyola University, LA, 1968; BS in Fin., UCLA, 1965 **CT:** Bar: California 1969, U.S. Court Appeals (9th cir.) 1972, U.S. District Court (Central, No. and So. Dists.) California 1982. **C:** Partner, Christensen, Glaser, Fink, Jacobs, Weil & Shapiro (now Glaser, Weil, Fink, Jacobs, Howard & Shapiro, LLP), LA, 1995-; Of counsel, Christensen, Glaser, Fink, Jacobs, Weil & Shapiro (now Glaser, Weil, Fink, Jacobs, Howard & Shapiro, LLP), LA, 1988-95; Of Counsel, Bushkin, Gaims, Gaines, Jonas, LA, 1987-88; Sole Practice, LA, 1972-87; Deputy District Attorney, Office of District Attorney, LA, 1969-72 **CR:** Lecturer in Field; Co-founder Legalzoom.com, Inc., 1999- **CIV:** Board of Directors, Brent Shapiro Foundation for Drug Awareness, **CW:** Author: When The Press Calls: A Lawyer's View, 1991, The Search For Justice: A Defense Attorney's Brief on the O.J. Simpson Case, 1996; co-author: (with Walt W. Becker) Misconception, 2001; Frequent Guest on Network and Cable TV Shows; Called Upon for Legal Expertise. **AW:** Recipient American Jurisprudence Award Bancroft Whitney, 1969; Named Pro-bono Lawyer the Year, State of Nevada; Named One of The 100 Super Lawyers, LA Daily Journal, The 100 Most Influential Lawyers in America, The National Law Journal, 2013 **MEM:** Member National Association Criminal Defense Lawyers, California Attorneys for Criminal Justice, Trial Lawyers for Pub. Justice (Founder 1982), Century City Bar Association (Best Criminal Defense Attorney 1993). **H:** Avid sport fan to basketball and boxing. **BA:** Office of Robert Shapiro, 10250 Constellation Blvd, 19th Floor, Los Angeles, CA, 90067

SHARPLESS, KARL, T: Chemist, Educator **I:** Sciences **DOB:** 04/28/1941 **PB:** Philadelphia **SC:** Pennsylvania **ED:** BA, Dartmouth College, Hanover, New Hampshire, 1963; PhD, Stanford University, California, 1968; Doctor (hon.), Dartmouth College, 1995; Doctor (hon.), Royal Institute Tech., Stockholm, 1995; Doctor (hon.), Tech. University Munich, 1995; Doctor (hon.), Catholic University Louvain, Belgium, 1996; Doctor (hon.), Wesleyan University, 1999 **C:** Professor Skaggs Institute Chemical Biology, Scripps Research Institute, 1996—,; W. M. Keck professor chemistry, Scripps Research Institute, La Jolla, California, 1990—,;

Faculty, Department of Chemistry, Stanford University, 1977-80,; Arthur C. Cope Professor, Massachusetts Institute of Technology, Cambridge, Massachusetts, 1987—1990,; Faculty, Massachusetts Institute of Technology, Cambridge, Massachusetts, 1970-77, 1980-90,; Postdoctoral Associate, Harvard University, Cambridge, Massachusetts, 1969—1970,; Postdoctoral Associate, Stanford University, 1968—1969 **CR:** Honorary Distinguished Professor Hong Kong Poly. University, 2002; visiting Professor Kitasato University, Japan, 2002—; **AW:** Recipient Allan Day Award, Philadelphia Organic Chemists Club, 1985, Pual Janssen Award for Biomedical Research, Belgium, 1988, Prelog Medal, Swiss Federal Institute Tech., Zurich, 1988, Chemical Pioneer Award, Am. Institute Chemists, 1988, Scheele Medal, Swedish Academy Pharmaceutical Scis., 1991, Cliff Hamilton Award, University of Nebraska, 1995, King Faisal International Prize for Sci., Saudi Arabia, 1995, Microbial medal, Kitasato Institute, Tokyo, 1997, Harvey Sci. & Tech. prize, Technion-Israel Institute Tech., 1998, Rylander Award, Organic Reactions Catalysis Society, 2000, Chiralty Medal, Italian Chemical Society, 2000, John Scott Medal, City of Phila, 2001, Benjamin Franklin Medal, Franklin Institute, Philadelphia, 2001, Wolf Prize in chemistry, Wolf Foundation, Israel, 2001, Nobel Prize in Chemistry, 2001, Rylander Award, 2000, Chemical Sciences Award, 2000, Harvey Prize, 1998, Microbial Chemistry Medal, 1997, Tetrahedron Prize, 1993 **MEM:** Fellow: American Association for the Advancement of Science, Am. Academy Arts & Scis., Royal Society Chemistry (hon.); mem.: National Academy of Sciences (Award in Chemical Scis. 2000), Am. Chemical Society (Creative Work in Synthetic Organic Chemistry Award 1983, Harrison Howe award 1987, Remsen award 1989, Arthur C. Cope award 1992, Roger Adams Award 1997, Richards Medal 1998, Top 75 Contributors to Chemical Enterprise 1998) **BA:** Scripps Rsch Inst, 10550 N Torrey Pines Rd, La Jolla, CA, 92037-1000

SHATNER, WILLIAM, T: Actor **I:** Media & Entertainment **DOB:** 03/22/1931 **PB:** Montreal **SC:** Que. Can. **PT:** Son of Joseph and Anne S.; Married Gloria Rosenberg, August 12, 1956 (div. March 1969); three children; Married Marcy Lafferty, October 20, 1973 (div. 1996); Married Nerine Kidd, November 15, 1997 (deceased 1999); Married Elizabeth Martin, 2001 **ED:** BA, McGill University, 1952 **CW:** Stage debut, 1952; appeared Montreal Playhouse, summers 1952, 53; played juvenile roles Canadian Repertory Theatre, Ottawa, 1952-53, 53-54; appeared Stratford Shakespeare Festival, Ontario, 1954-56; Broadway appearances include Tamburlaine the Great, 1956, The World of Suzie Wong, 1958, A Shot in the Dark, 1961; films include The Brothers Karamazov, 1958, The Explosive Generation, 1961, Judgement at Nuremburg, 1961, The Intruder, 1962, The Outrage, 1964, Dead of Night, 1974, The Devil's Rain, 1975, Star Trek: The Motion Picture, 1979, The Kidnapping of the President, 1979, Star Trek: The Wrath of Khan, 1982, Airplane II: The Sequel, 1982, Star Trek III: The Search for Spock, 1984, Star Trek IV: The Voyage Home, 1986, (director) Star Trek V: The Final Frontier, 1989, Star Trek VI: The Undiscovered Country, 1991, National Lampoon's Loaded Weapon, 1992, Star Trek: Generations, 1994, Trekkies, 1997, Free Enterprise, 1998, Shoot or be Shot, 2000, Groom Lake, 2000, Miss Congeniality, 2000, American Psycho II, 2001, Osmosis Jones, 2001, Dodgeball: A True Underdog Story, 2004, Miss Congeniality 2: Armed and Fabulous, 2005, The Wild (voice), 2006, Over the Hedge (voice), 2006, Gonzo Ballet, 2007, Live Life, 2007, Quantum Quest: A Cassini Space Odyssey (voice), 2010, Horrorween, 2010, Escape from Planet Earth, 2013, A Christmas Horror Story,

2015, When Elephents Were Young, 2015, Range 15, 2016, Creators The Past, 2016, Malevolent, 2016, Batman vs Two-Face, 2017; also TV movies and appearances on The Andersonville Trial, The Bastard, 1978, Disaster on the Coastliner, 1979, Secrets of a Married Man, 1984, North Beach and Rawhide, 1985, Columbo, 1993, The Kid (voice), 2001, A Carol Christmas, 2003, Gotta Catch Santa Claus, 2008; TV series Star Trek, 1966-69, animated series, 1973-75, Barbary Coast, 1975-76, The Babysitter, 1979, T.J. Hooker, 1982-86; host (TV series) Rescue 911, CBS, 1989-96, Third Rock From the Sun, 1996, The Practice, 2004 (Emmy award for Outstanding Guest Actor in a Drama Series 2004), Boston Legal (Golden Globe award for best supporting actor series, miniseries or TV movie, 2005, Emmy award for outstanding supporting actor in a drama series, 2005), 2004-08, $#*! My Dad Says, 2010-11, Weird or what, 2010, Psych, 2011, Comedy Central Roast of Charlie Sheen, 2011, Rookie Blue, 2012, Have I got News for you, 2012, Hot in Cleveland, 2013, 85th Academy Awards, 2013,Kelly Clarksons Cautionary Christmas Music Tale, 2013, The Shatner Project, 2014, Chaos on the Bridge, 2014, Breaking Ground, 2015, Murdoch Mysteries, 2015, Haven, 2015, Clangers, 2015, Cutthroat Kitchen,2016, Better Late than Never, 2016, My Little Pony Friendship is Magic, 2017,Batman The Caped Crusaders vs Two Face, 2017, Private Eyes,2017, The Indian Detective, 2017 (TV spls.) Invasion Iowa, 2005, How William Shatner Changed the World, 2006, William Shatner in Concert, 2006, Comedy Central Roast of William Shatner, 2006; director TV movie TekWar; author: (novels) TekWar, 1989, TekLords, 1991, TekLab, 1991, Tek Vengeance, 1992, Believe (with Michael Tobias), 1992, Tek Secret, 1993, (memoirs) Star Trek Memories, 1993, Star Trek Movie Memories, 1994, Tek Power, 1994, Tek Money, 1995, The Ashes of Eden, 1995, Man O' War, 1996, Tek Kill, 1996, The Return, 1996, Avenger, 1997, Delta Search: Quest for Tomorrow, 1997, Delta Search: In Alien Hands, 1998, Delta Search: Step Into Chaos, 1999, Get A Life, 1999, I'm Working on That, 2002, Captain's Glory, 2006, Star Trek Academy Collision Course, 2007; albums: Transformed Man, 1968, Has Been, 2004, Exodus, 2007, Seeking Major Tom, 2011; Leonard: My Fifty-Year Friendship with a Remarkable Man, 2016 **AW:** Recipient Tyrone Guthrie award, 1956, Theatre World award, 1958, star on Hollywood Walk of Fame, 1983, Golden Globe award for Best Outstanding Actor in a Series, 2006, Governor General of Canada's Performing Arts award for Lifetime Artistic Achievement, 2011; named to Academy TV Arts & Sciences Hall of Fame, 2006; Emmy award nominee for Outstanding Guest Actor in a Comedy Series Emmy (for Third Rock from the Sun), 1999; Emmy award nominee for Best Supporting Actor in a Drama Series (for Boston Legal), 2006 **MEM:** Mem.: American Federation of TV and Radio Artists, Screen Actors Guild, Directors Guild, Actors Equity Association **BA:** 2934 Beverly Glen Circle Suite 715, Bel Air, CA, 90077

SHEA-PORTER, CAROL, T: U.S. Representative from New Hampshire, social worker **I:** Government Administration/Government Relations/Government Services **DOB:** 12/02/1952 **PB:** NYC **PT:** Daughter of William and Peggy Shea; **ED:** MPA, University New Hampshire, 1979; BS in Social Services, University New Hampshire, 1975 **C:** Member, US House Natural Resources Committee, 2013-; Member; Member, US House Armed Services Committee, 2013-; Member, US Congress from 1st New Hampshire District, 2013-; Member, US House Education & Labor Committee, 2007-11; Member, US House Natural Resources Committee, 2007-11; Member, US House Armed Services Committee, 2007-11; Member, US Congress from 1st New

Hampshire District, Washington, 2007-11, 2013-2015, 2017; Director, Multi-Purpose Senior Center,; Director, The Shepard's Center,; History instructor, Prince George's C.C., 1987-89; Instructor, The Charter House, 1987-2001 **CR:** New Hampshire regional coordinator Wesley Clark for Presidential Campaign **PA:** Democrat

SHEEN, MARTIN, **T:** Actor **I:** Media & Entertainment **DOB:** 08/03/1940 **PB:** Dayton **SC:** OH/USA **PT:** Francisco Estevez; Mary Ann (Phelan) Estevez **MS:** Married **SPN:** Janet Sheen (12/23/1961) **CH:** Emilio; Ramon; Carlos; Renee **CW:** Actor, "L.M. Montgomerys Anne of Green Gables" (2016); Actor, "Come Sunday" (2018); Actor, "Popstar, Never Stop Never Stopping" (2016); Actor, "Rules Don't Apply" (2016); Actor, "Grace and Frankie" (2015); Actor, "Last Week Tonight with John Oliver" (2015); Actor, "The Vessel" (2015); Actor, "The Amazing Spider-Man 2" (2014); Actor, "The Whale" (2014); Actor, "Ask Me Anything" (2014); Actor, "Trash" (2014); Actor, "Bhopal: A Prayer for Rain" (2014); Actor, "Selma" (2014); Actor, "Love Letters" (2014); Actor, "Undiscovered Gyrl" (2013); Actor, "Bhopal: A Prayer for Rain" (2013); Featured Actor, "Salinger" (2013); Actor, "Anger Management" (2012-2014); Co-Author, "Along the Way: The Journey of Father and Son" (2012); Actor, "The Amazing Spider-Man" (2012); Actor, "Flatland" (2012); Actor, "The Double" (2011); Actor, "Stella Days" (2011); Actor, "The Kid: Chamaco, The Way" (2011); Actor, "Love Happens" (2009); Actor, "The Departed" (2006); Actor, "Bobby" (2006); Actor, "Celebrity Poker Showdown" (2003); Actor, "Catch Me If You Can" (2002); Actor, "The West Wing" (1999-2006); Actor, "D.R.E.A.M. Team" (1999); Actor, "Letter From Death Row" (1998); Actor, "Storm" (1998); Actor, "Monument Avenue" (1998); Actor, "Free Money" (1998); Actor, "Babylon 5: The River of Souls" (1998); Actor, "Letter From Death Row" (1998); ctor, "Ambrose Chapel" (1998); Actor, "Gunfighter" (1998); Actor, "No Code of Conduct" (1998); Voice Actress, "Shadrach" (1998); Actor, "Stranger in the Kingdom" (1998); Actor, "Talk of the Town" (1998); Actor, "Voyage of Terror" (1998); Narrator, "Tudjman" (1997); Narrator, "Titanic: Anatomy of a Disaster" (1997); Actor, "Medussa's Child" (1997); Actor, "187 Documented" (1997); Actor, "Truth or Consequences" (1997); Actor, "Spawn" (1997); Actor, "The Elevator" (1996); Actor, "The Great War" (1996); Actor, "Project Alf" (1996); Actor, "Marlon Brandon: The Wild One" (1996); Actor, "Entertaining Angels" (1996); Actor, "Spin City" (1996); Actor, "The War At Home" (1996); Actor, "The Break" (1995); Actor, "The American President" (1995); Actor, "Hot Shots, Part Deux!" (1993); Actor, "Hear No Evil" (1993); Actor, "Gettysburg" (1993); Actor, "The Crucible" (1991); Director, "Cadence" (1991); Narrator, "JFK" (1991); Actor, "Night Breaker" (1989); Voice Actress, "The Simpsons" (1989); Actor, "Beverly Hills Brats" (1989); Actor, "Judgement in Berlin" (1988); Actor, "Walking After Midnight" (1988); Executive Producer, Director, "Da" (1988); Actor, "Julius Caesar" (1988); Actor, "Murphy Brown" (1988); Actor, "Conspiracy: The Trial of the Chicago 8" (1987); Actor, "The Believers" (1987); Actor, "Wall Street" (1987); Actor, "Siesta" (1987); Actor, "Shattered Spirits" (1986); Actor, "Samaritan" (1986); Actor, "News at Eleven" (1986); Director, "Babies Having Babies" (1986); Actor, "The Atlanta Child Murders" (1985); Actor, "Consenting Adult" (1985); Actor, "Out of Darkness" (1985); Actor, "Firestarter" (1984); Actor, "No Place to Hide" (1983); Actor, "The Dead Zone" (1983); Actor, "Man, Woman, and Child" (1983); Actor, "Enigma" (1983); Actor, "Eagle's Wing" (1983); Actor, "Choices of the Heart" (1983); Actor, "Kennedy" (1982); Actor, "Gandhi" (1982); Actor, "That Championship Season" (1982); Actor,

"The King of Prussia" (1982); Actor, "Fly Away Home" (1981); Actor, "The Long Road Home" (1980); Actor, "The Final Countdown" (1980); Actor, "Apocalypse Now" (1979); Actor, "Blind Ambition" (1979); Actor, "Taxi!!" (1978); Actor, "The Little Girl Who Lives Down the Lane" (1977); Actor, "The Cassandra Crossing" (1976); Actor, "Death of a Salesman" (1975); Actor, "The Last Survivors" (1975); Actor, "Sweet Hostage" (1975); Actor, "The Legend of Earl Durand" (1974); Actor, "The Execution of Private Slovik" (1974); Actor, "The California Kid" (1974); Actor, "The Story of Pretty Boy Floyd" (1974); Actor, "The Missiles of October" (1974); Actor, "Badlands" (1973); Actor, "Catholics" (1973); Actor, "Welcome Home, Johnny Bristol" (1972); Actor, "The Streets of San Francisco" (1972); Actor, "That Certain Summer" (1972); Actor, "Rage" (1972); Actor, "No Drums, No Bugles" (1971); Actor, "Mongo's Back in Town" (1971); Actor, "Catch-22" (1970); Actor, "The Happiness Cage" (1970); Actor, "Then Came Bronson" (1969); Actor, "The Subject Was Roses" (1969); Actor, "Hello and Goodbye" (1969); Actor, "Romeo and Juliet" (1968); Actor, "The Subject Was Roses" (1968); Actor, "The Incident" (1967); Actor, "The Wicked Crooks" (1967); Actor, "Mannix" (1967); Actor, "Hamlet" (1967); Actor, "The Subject Was Roses" (1964-1966); Actor, "Never Live Over a Pretzel Factory" (1964); Actor, "The Connection," Living Theatre (1959); Actor, "As the World Turns"; Executive Producer, "No Means No"; Actor, "The Edge of Night" **AW:** Recipient, Laetare Medal, University of Notre Dame (2008); Recipient, Screen Actors Guild Award (2001-2002); Recipient, Golden Globe Award (2001); Recipient, Lifetime Achievement Award, Imagen Foundation (1998); Recipient, Emmy Award for Guest Actor in a Comedy Series (1994); Named, Favorite Actor in a New Series, TV Guide Awards

SHEERAN, ED, **T:** Musician **I:** Media & Entertainment **DOB:** 02/17/1991 **PB:** Hebden Bridge **PT:** Son of John Sheeran and Imogen Lock. **ED:** PhD (hon.), University Campus Suffolk, England, 2015 **CW:** Musician: (albums) +, 2011, X, 2014 (Favorite Album, People's Choice Awards, 2015 ./. 2017, (songs) Sing, 2014 (Choice Single Male Artist, Teen Choice Awards, 2014), Thinking Out Loud, 2014 (Song of Year, Best Pop Solo Performance, Grammy Awards) (Movies) Shortland Street, 2014, Undateable, 2015, Home and Away, 2015, Jumpers for Goalposts: Live at Wembley Stadium, 2015, Bridget Jones's Baby, 2016 (Television) The Bastard Executioner, 2015, Game of Thrones, 2017 **AW:** Named Favorite Pop/Rock Male Artist, American Music Awards, 2015, Favorite Male Artist, People's Choice Awards, 2016, 2015, Choice Male Artist, Teen Choice Awards, 2013, Breakout Artist, 2013, Grammy for Song of the Year, 2016, Grammy for Best Pop Solo Performance, 2016, MTV Best Live Performance, 2017, People's Choice Awards Favorite Album and Favorite Male Artist, 2015, Favorite Male Artist, 2016

SHELBY, RICHARD CRAIG, **T:** U.S. Senator from Alabama **I:** Government Administration/Government Relations/Government Services **DOB:** 05/06/1934 **PB:** Birmingham **PT:** Son of Ozie Houston and Alice L. (Skinner) S.; Married Annette Nevin, June 11, 1960; children: Richard Craig, Claude Nevin. **ED:** LLB, University Alabama, 1963; AB, University Alabama, 1957 **CT:** Bar: Alabama 1961, DC 1979 **C:** Chairman, Senate Rules Committee, 2017-,; Chairman, Senate Banking Committee, 2015-2017,; Chairman, Senate Intelligence Committee, 2001,; US Senator from Alabama, 1987-; Chairman, US Senate Banking, Housing & Urban Affairs Committee, 2003-07; Chairman, US Senate Select Committee on Intelli-

gence, 1997-2001; Member, US Congress from 7th Alabama District, 1979-87; Member District 16, Alabama State Senate, 1971-78; Magistrate judge, US District Court (northern district) Alabama, 1966-70; Special assistant attorney general, State of Alabama, 1968-71; Prosecutor, City of Tuscaloosa, 1963-71; Practice law, Tuscaloosa, Alabama, 1963-78; Law clerk, Supreme Court of Alabama, 1961-62 **CIV:** Active Boy Scouts America president Tuscaloosa County Mental Health Association, 1969-70 board governors National Legis. Conference, 1975-78 **AW:** Recipient Congressional Leadership award, Airports Council Internat.-N. Am., 2003, Taxpayer's Friend award, National Taxpayers Union, 1998 **MEM:** Member American Bar Association, Alabama Bar Association, Tuscaloosa County Bar Association, DC Bar Association, American Judiciary Society, Exchange Club, Tuscaloosa County Mental Health Assn.; (former president) **PA:** Republican **BA:** Office of Richard Shelby, 1118 Greensboro Ave Federal Bldg Ste 240, Tuscaloosa, AL, 35401-2816

SHELTON, BLAKE TOLISON, **T:** Musician **I:** Media & Entertainment **DOB:** 06/18/1976 **PB:** Ada **SC:** OK/USA **PT:** Son of Richard and Dorothy Shelton; **CW:** Musician: (albums) Blake Shelton, 2001, The Dreamer, 2003, Blake Shelton's Barn & Grill, 2004, Pure BS, 2007, Startin Fires, 2008, Hillbilly Bone, 2010, Loaded: The Best of Blake Shelton, 2010, Red River Blue, 2011, Cheers, It's Christmas, 2012, Based on a True Story..., 2013 (Album of Year, Country Music Association Awards, 2013), Bringing Back the Sunshine, 2014, If I'm Honest, 2016, Texoma Shore, 2017 (songs) ((with Trace Adkins)) Hillbilly Bone, 2010 (Vocal Event of Year, Academy Country Music Awards, 2010, Collaborative Video of Year, CMT Music Awards, 2010, Vocal Event of Year, Country Music Association Awards, 2010), Who Are You When I'm Not Looking, 2010 (Male Video of Year, CMT Music Awards, 2011), Sure Be Cool if You Did, 2013 (Male Video of Year, CMT Music Awards, 2013), Doin' What She Likes, 2013 (Male Video of Year, CMT Music Awards, 2014); writer (songs) Over You, 2011 (Song of Year, Country Music Association Awards, 2012), vocal coach, judge (TV series) The Voice, 2011- (Gene Weed Special Achievement award, Academy Country Music Awards, 2013), (Film), The Ridiculous 6, Pitch Perfect 2, The Angry Birds Movie, 2016 **AW:** Named Social Superstar of Year, CMT Music Awards, 2016, Favorite Male Country Artist, People's Choice Awards, 2016, Favorite Country Male Artist, American Music Awards, 2011, Male Vocalist of Year, Academy Country Music Awards, 2012, Entertainer of Year, Country Music Association Awards, 2012, Male Vocalist of Year, 2014, 2013, 2012, 2011, 2010, Video of the Year, Academy of Country Music Awards, 2017, American Music Awards Favorite Male Country Artist, 2016

SHEPHERD, BOBBY E., **T:** Federal Judge **I:** Law and Legal Services **DOB:** 11/18/1951 **PB:** Arkadelphia **SC:** AR/USA **ED:** JD, University of Arkansas, 1976; BA, Ouachita Baptist University, 1973 **C:** Judge, US Court Appeals (8th cir.), Little Rock, 2006-; Magistrate Judge, US District Court (we. district) Arkansas, El Dorado, Arkansas, 1993-2006; Circuit Chancery Judge, Arkansas 13th Judicial District, 1991-93; Private Caw Practice, 1984-87; Partner, Landers & Shepherd, 1987-90; Partner, Spencer, Spencer & Shepherd, 1981-84; Partner, Spencer & Spencer, El Dorado, Arkansas, 1976-81 **AW:** Served with US Army Reserve, 1976-81 **BA:** Thomas F. Eagleton Courthouse, 111 South 10th Street, St. Louis, MO, 63102

SHERMAN, BRAD, T: U.S. Representative from California **I:** Government Administration/Government Relations/Government Services **DOB:** 10/24/1954 **PB:** Los Angeles **SC:** CA/USA **PT:** Son of Maurice H. and Lane (Moss) Sherman **ED:** JD magna cum laude, Harvard University, 1979; BA summa cum laude, UCLA, 1974 **CT:** CPA, California **C:** Member, US Congress from 30th California District, 2013-; Member, US Congress from 27th California District, 2003-13; Member, US Congress from 24th California District, Washington, 1997-2003; Member, California Franchise Tax Board, 1991-95; Private practice, L.A., 1980-91 **CR:** Chairman California State Board Equalization, 1991-95, member District 4, 1990-97 **CIV:** Board directors, rep. tax issues, California Common Cause, 1985-89 **CW:** Contributor articles to professional journals; lecturer in field (tax law and policy) **MEM:** Mem.: California Bar Association **BAR:** bar: California 1979 **PA:** Democrat **BA:** 2372 Rayburn House Office Building, Washington, DC, 20515

SHERMAN, CINDY, T: Artist, Photographer **I:** Fine Art **PB:** Glen Ridge **SC:** NJ/USA **ED:** BA, State University College Buffalo, 1976 **C:** Photographer, 1976- **CW:** One-woman exhibitions include Hallwalls Gallery, Buffalo, 1976, 77, Contemporary Arts Museum, Houston, 1980, The Kitchen, New York, 1980, Metro Pictures, New York, 1980, 83, Saman Gallery, Genoa, 1981, Young/Hoffman Gallery, Chicago, 1981, Chantal Crousel Gallery, Paris, 1982, Stedelijk Museum, Amsterdam, 1982, St. Louis Art Museum, 1983, Fine Arts Center Gallery, SUNY-Stony Brook, 1983, Rhona Hoffman Gallery, Chicago, 1983, Douglas Drake Gallery, Kansas City, 1983, 84, Seibu Gallery Contemporary Art, Tokyo, 1984, Akron Art Museum, 1984, Linda Cathcart Gallery, Santa Monica, California, 1992, Museo de Monterrey, Mexico, 1992; retrospective exhibitions include Museum Modern Art, New York, 2012; group exhibitions include Albright-Knox Art Gallery, Buffalo, 1975, Artists Space, New York, 1978, Max Protetch Gallery, New York, 1979, Castelli Graphics, New York, 1980, Lisson Gallery, London, 1980, Centre Pompidou, Paris, 1981; NIT, 1981, Renaissance Society University Chicago, 1982, Metro Pictures, New York, 1982, La Ciennale de Venezia, Venice, Italy, 1982, Documenta 7, Kassel, West Germany, 1982, Chantall Crousel Gallery, Paris, 1982, San Francisco Museum Modern Art, 1982, Institute Contemporary Art, London, 1982, Grey Art Gallery, New York, 1982, Institute Contemporary Art, Philadelphia, 1982, Young Hoffman Gallery, Chicago, 1983, Hirshhorn Gallery, Washington, 1983, Whitney Museum Am. Art, New York, 1983, 85, 91; represented in permanent collections Museum Fine Arts, Houston, Albright/Knox Art Gallery, Buffalo, Dallas Museum Fine Arts, Museum Boymans-van Beuningen, Rotterdam, Akron Art Museum, Ohio, Museum Modern Art, New York City, Walker Art Center, Minneapolis, Tate Gallery, London, Rose Art Museum, Brandeis University, Centre Pompidou, Paris, Stedelijk Museum, Amsterdam, Metropolitan Museum Art, New York, St. Louis Art Museum, San Francisco Museum Modern Art,(- Photography) The Imitation of Life, 2016,(Exhibitions) Serpentine Gallery, 2003, Martin Gropius Bau, 2006, Jeu De Paume,2006-07, Museum of Art, 2009 **AW:** Recipient Roswitha Haftmann Prize, Roswitha Haftmann Foundation, 2012, Time 100 Most Influential, 2017, Member of the Royal Academy of Arts, 2010 **MEM:** Mem.: American Academy of Arts and Letters

SHERWOOD, BILLY, T: Musician **I:** Media & Entertainment **DOB:** 03/14/1965 **PB:** Las Vegas **SC:** NV/USA **CW:** (Solo Album) The Big Peace,1999, No Comment, 2003, At the Speed of Life, 2008, Oneirology, 2010, What Was the Question?, 2011, The Art of Survival, 2012, Divided by One, 2014, Collection, 2015, Archived, 2015, Citizen, 2015(With Yes) Open your Eyes, 1997, The Ladder, 1999, House of Yes: Live from the House of Blues, 2000, Topographic Drama- Live Across America, 2017 **AW:** Rock and Roll Hall of Fame, 2017

SHIFFRIN, MIKAELA, T: Alpine Ski Racer **I:** Athletics **SC:** CO/USA **AW:** 2 Olympic Gold Medals, One Olympic Silver, 2014,18, 3 World Championship Gold Medal, 2013,15,17, One Silver World Championship Medal, 2017, One Bronze Junior World Championship Medal, 2011

SHILLER, ROBERT JAMES, T: Economics Professor, Economist **I:** Education/Educational Services **DOB:** 03/29/1946 **PB:** Detroit **SC:** MI/USA **PT:** Benjamin P. Shiller, Ruth R. (Radzville) Shiller **SPN:** Virginia M. Faulstich, 6/13/1976 **CH:** Two Children **ED:** PhD, Massachusetts Institute of Technology, 1972; MS, Massachusetts Institute of Technology, 1968; BA, University of Michigan, 1967 **C:** Arthur M. Okun Professor of Economics, Yale University, New Haven, CT, 1982-Present; Professor of Finance, Wharton School of Business, University of Pennsylvania, 1981-1982; Professor, University of Pennsylvania, Philadelphia, PA, 1981-1982; Visiting Professor, Massachusetts Institute of Technology, Cambridge, MA, 1981-1982; Associate Professor of Economics, University of Pennsylvania, Philadelphia, PA, 1974-1981; Visiting Scholar, Department of Economics, Massachusetts Institute of Technology, Cambridge, MA, 1974-1975; Research Fellow, National Bureau of Economic Research, Cambridge, MA, 1974-1975; Assistant Professor, University of Minnesota, 1972-1974 **CR:** Fellow, Econometric Society; Guggenheim Fellow; Co-Founder, Chief Economist, Macromarkets, LLC, 1999-Present; Co-Founder, Case, Shiller, Weiss Inc., 1991-2002; Visiting Scholar, Department of Economics, Harvard University, 1980 **CW:** Foreign Editor, Review of Economic Studies, 1981-1984; Associate Editor, Journal of Econometrics, 1980-1983; Author, (Books) Market Volatility, 1989, Macro Markets: Creating Institutions For Managing Society's Largest Economic Risks, 1993, Irrational Exuberance, 2000, New Financial Order: Risk in the 21st Century, 2003, The Subprime Solution: How Today's Global Financial Crisis Happened and What to Do About It, 2008, Finance and the Good Society, 2012; Co-Author, (With George Akerlof) Animal Spirits: How Human Psychology Drives the Economy, and Why It Matters for Global Capitalism, 2009 **AW:** Paul A. Samuelson Award for Macro Markets, 1996, 2010; Commonfund Prize, 2001; The Power 30, Smart Money Magazine, 2008; Deutsche Bank Prize in Financial Economics, 2009; Jamer Vertin Award, Chartered Financial Analyst Institute, 2009; The 50 Most Influential People in Global Finance Bloomberg Markets, 2011; Prize in Innovative Quantitative Applications, Chicago Mercantile Exchange Group, Mathematical Sciences Research Institute, 2012; Nobel Memorial Prize in Economic Sciences (Sveriges Riksbank Prize), Royal Swedish Academy of Sciences, 2013; Grantee, National Science Foundation, 1976-Present **MEM:** American Academy of Arts & Sciences; American Philosophical Society; Vice President, American Economic Association, 2005; President, Eastern Economic Association, 2006-2007

SHIMKUS, JOHN MONDY, T: U.S. Representative from Illinois **I:** Government Administration/Government Relations/Government Services **DOB:** 02/21/1958 **PB:** Collinsville **SC:** IL/USA **PT:** Son of Gene Louis and Kathleen (Mondy) Shimkus; **ED:** MBA, Southern Illinois University, Edwardsville, 1997; BS, US Military Academy, 1980 **C:** Member, US Congress from 15th Illinois District, 2013-; Member, Committee on Energy and Commerce, Republican Study Committee; Member, US Congress from 19th Illinois District, Washington, 1997-2013; Treasurer, Madison County, Edwardsville, 1990-96; Teacher, Metro East Lutheran High School, Edwardsville, Illinois, 1986-90; Stationed at, U.S. Army Base, Monterey, Calif, 1985-86; Served at, U.S. Army Base, Bamberg, Germany, 1981-84; Stationed at, U.S. Army Base, Columbus, Georgia, 1980-81, 85; Advanced through grades to captain, U.S. Army, 1980-86 **CR:** Treasurer Southern Illinois Law Enforcement Commission, 1990-96 liaison officer US Military Academy, 1987-96 **CIV:** Rep. precinct committeeman, Collinsville, 1988- Trustee, Collinsville Township, Illinois, 1989-93 Board directors, Senior Citizen Companion Progressive, Belleville, Illinois, 1991 **MIL:** Lieutenant colonel US Army Reserve, 1985- **MEM:** Mem.: Illinois County Treasurer Association, National Association County Treasurer & Financial Officers (board directors), American Legion Post 365 **PA:** Republican

SHORT, MARTIN, T: Actor **I:** Media & Entertainment **SC:** ON/Canada **PT:** Son of Charles Patrick and Olive Short; Married Nancy Dolman, 1980 (deceased August 21, 2010); children: Katherine, Oliver, Henry. **ED:** Degree in Social Work, McMaster University, 1972 **C:** Actor, 1972- **CW:** Actor: (films) Three Amigos, 1986, Innerspace, 1987, Cross My Heart, 1987, Three Fugitives, 1989, The Big Picture, 1989, Pure Luck, 1991, Father of the Bride, 1991, Captain Ron, 1992, (voice) We're Back! A Dinosaur's Story, 1993, Clifford, 1994, (voice) The Pebble and the Penguin, 1995, Father of the Bride 2, 1995, Mars Attacks!, 1996, Jungle 2 Jungle, 1997, The Fairy Godmother, 1997, A Simple Wish, 1997, Mumford, 1998, Akbar's Adventure Tours, 1998, (voice) Prince of Egypt, 1998, Get Over It, 2001, (voice) Jimmy Neutron: Boy Genius, 2001, (voice) Treasure Planet, 2001, Cinemagique, 2002, (voice) Treasure Planet, 2002, The Santa Clause 3: The Escape Clause, 2006, The Spiderwick Chronicles, 2008, (voice) Hoodwinked Too! Hood VS. Evil, 2010, (voice) Madagascar 2: Europe's Most Wanted, 2012, (voice) Frankenweenie, 2012, (voice) Legends of Oz: Dorothy's Return, 2013, (voice) The Wind Rises, 2013, Inherent Vice, 2014, (TV series) The Associates, 1979, I'm a Big Girl Now, 1980-81, SCTV Network 90, 1982-84 (Emmy award for Outstanding Writing in a Variety or Music Program, 1983), Saturday Night Live, 1984-86, (voice) The Completely Mental Misadventures of Ed Grimley, 1988-89, The Martin Short Show, 1994, (miniseries) Merlin, 1998, Damages, 2010, (voice) The Cat in the Hat Knows a Lot About That!, 2010-12, (TV films) The Family Man, 1979, Sunset Limousine, 1983, Alice in Wonderland, 1999, Prince Charming, 2001, Long Story Short, 2011, (voice) The Cat in the Hat Knows a Lot About Christmas!, 2012; writer: (TV films) Martin Short's Concert for the North Americas, 1985, I, Martin Short Goes Hollywood, 1989, (TV series) Second City TV, 1981, SCTV Network 90, 1981-82, SCTV Channel, 1983, Saturday Night Live, 1984-85; executive prodr.: (TV series) The Martin Short Show, 1994, 99, Primetime Glick, 2001-03; writer, prodr.: (TV films) Martin Short Shorts, 2003; dir.: (TV films) Friends of Gilda, 1993; actor, writer, prodr.: (films) Jiminy Glick in La La Wood, 2004; also numerous revues and cabaret appearances with Second City comedy troupe; 1977-78, Broadway appearances include: The Goodbye Girl, 1993, Little Me, 1999 (Tony award for Best Actor in a Musical), The Producers, 2003, It's Only a Play, 2014; stage appearances Martin Short: Fame Becomes Me, 2006; judge (TV series) Canada's Got Talent, 2012; author (memoir) I Must Say: My

Life As a Humble Comedy Legend, 2014.(Films) Bumblebee, 2018,(Television) Weeds,2011, How I Met Your Mother, 2011, Canada's Got Talent, 2012, Hollywood Game Night, 2013, Working the Engels, 2014, Mulaney, 2014, Unbreakable Kimmy Schmidt, 2015, Difficult People, 2015, May & Marty, 2016, Hairspray Live!, 2016, Modern Family, 2016, BoJack Horseman, 2017, The Simpsons, 2017

SHOWALTER, BUCK, T: Professional Baseball Manager **I:** Athletics **DOB:** 05/23/1956 **PB:** DeFuniak Springs **SC:** FL/USA **ED:** Student, Mississippi State University; Student, Chipola Junior College, Florida **C:** Manager, Baltimore Orioles, 2010-; Senior advisor baseball operations, Cleveland Indians, 2006-07; Manager, Texas Rangers, 2002-06; Studio analyst, ESPN, 2008-10; Studio analyst, ESPN, 2001-02; Manager, Arizona Diamondbacks, 1998-2000; Manager, New York Yankees, 1992-95; Coach, New York Yankees, 1990-92; Manager, Albany-Colonie Yankees, 1989-90; Manager, Fort Lauderdale Yankees, 1987-89; Manager, Oneonta Yankees, 1985-87; Minor league baseball player, 1977-83 **AW:** Named N.Y.-Pa. League Manager of Year, 1985, Eastern League Manager of Year, 1989, American League Manager of Year, 1994, National League Manager of Year, 2004,AL Manager of the Year, 2014

SHULA, DON FRANCIS, T: Retired Professional Football Coach, Professional Sports Team Executive **I:** Professional Training & Coaching **DOB:** 01/04/1930 **PB:** Painesville **PT:** Son of Dan and Mary (Miller) S.; children: David, Donna, Sharon, Anne, Michael; Married Mary Anne Shula **ED:** Sc.D. (hon.), Florida Atlantic University, 1999; Sc.D. (hon.), University Miami, 1992; Sc.D. (hon.), St. Thomas University, 1976; Sc.D. (hon.), Biscayne College, 1974; MA, Case Western Reserve University, 1953; H.H.D. (hon.), John Carroll University, Cleveland, 1972; BS, John Carroll University, Cleveland, 1951 **C:** Vice chairman, Miami Dolphins, 1996-; Owner, president, Shula Enterprises;; Head coach, Miami (Florida) Dolphins, 1970-96; Head coach, Baltimore Colts, 1963-69; Assistant coach, Detroit Lions, 1960-62; Assistant coach, University Kentucky, 1959; Assistant coach, University Virginia, 1958; Professional football player, Washington Redskins, 1957; Professional football player, Baltimore Colts, 1953-56; Professional football player, Cleveland Browns, 1951-52 **CIV:** Florida crusade chairman National Cancer Society, 1975 co-chmn. Jerry Lewis March Against Dystrophy, 1975 national board directors Boy's Hope member national sports committee Multiple Schlerosis Society, Muscular Dystrophy Association board directors Heart Association Greater Miami established Don Shula Foundation, breast cancer research, 1991- sponsor Don Shula Scholarship, 1978- **CW:** Author: The Winning Edge, 1972, (with Ken Blanchard) Everyone's A Coach, 1995 **AW:** Coached 6 Superbowl teams, winning teams 1972, 73; recipient Coach of Year awards 1964, 66, 70, 71, 72, Coach of decade Professional Football Hall of Fame, 1980, Pro Football's All-Time Winningest Coach, 1994, Brotherhood award Florida region National Conference of Christians and Jews, 1977, Light of Flames Leadership award Barry College, 1977, Concern award Cedars Medical Center, 1992, Solheim Lifetime Achievement award, 1992, Jim Thorpe award, 1993, Sportsman of Year Sports Illustrated, 1993, Horrigan award Pro Football Writers,1994, Horatio Alger award, 1995, Vince Lombardi Award of Excellence, 1999; named Baltimore Colts Silver Anniversary Coach, 1977, elected to Pro Football Hall of Fame, 1997, Ellis Island Medal of Honor, 2011

SHUSTER, BILL, T: U.S. Representative from Pennsylvania **I:** Government Administration/Government Relations/Government Services **DOB:** 01/10/1961 **PB:** McKeesport, Pennsylvania **PT:** Son of Elmer Greinart and H. Patricia (Rommel) Shuster; **ED:** MBA, American University, Washington, 1987; BA in Political Sci. & History, Dickinson College, Carlisle, Pennsylvania, 1983 **C:** Chairman, US House Transportation & Infrastructure Committee, 2013-; Member, US House Transportation & Infrastructure Committee, 2001-; Member, US Congress from 9th Pennsylvania District, 2001-; President, General Manager, Shuster Five Star Chrysler, Dodge, and Jeep, 1990-2001; District Manager, Bandag Inc.,; Manager Retail Stores, Goodyear Tire & Rubber Corp. **MEM:** Mem.: National Rifle Association, National Federation Ind. Business, Masons **PA:** Republican **BA:** The Office of Bill Shuster, 2079 Rayburn HOB, Washington, DC, 20515

SHWARTZ, PATTY, T: Federal Judge **I:** Law and Legal Services **DOB:** 07/24/1961 **PB:** Paterson **SC:** NJ/USA **ED:** JD, School of Law, University of Pennsylvania, 1986; BA, Rutgers College, 1983 **C:** Judge, U.S. Court Of Appeals, Third Circuit, Newark, NJ, 2013-Present; Magistrate Judge, U.S. District Court, New Jersey, Newark, NJ, 2003-2013; Executive Assistant U.S. Attorney, U.S. Department of Justice, 2001-2002; Chief, Criminal Division, U.S. Department of Justice, 1999-2003; Deputy Chief, Criminal Division, U.S. Department of Justice, 1995-1999; Assistant U.S. Attorney District, New Jersey, U.S. Department of Justice, Trenton, NJ, 1989-2003; Law Clerk, Hon. Harold Ackerman, U.S. District Court, New Jersey, 1987-1989; Associate, Pepper, Hamilton & Scheetz, Philadelphia, PA, 1986-1987 **CR:** Adjunct Professor of Law, School of Law, Fordham University, 2009-Present **BA:** 601 Market Street, Philadelphia, PA, 19106

SIEBEL, THOMAS M., T: CEO **I:** Technology **CN:** C3 IoT **DOB:** 11/20/1952 **PB:** Chicago **SC:** IL/USA **ED:** MBA, University of Illinois, Urbana-Champaign; MS in Computer Science, University of Illinois, Urbana-Champaign; BA, University of Illinois, Urbana-Champaign **C:** Chairman/Chief Executive Officer, C3 IOT; Founder, Siebel Foundation (1996-Present); Chairman, Siebel Systems, San Mateo, CA (1993-Present); Chief Executive Officer, Siebel Systems, San Mateo, CA (1993-2004); Chief Executive Officer, Gain Technology (Until 1992); Various Positions Including Group Vice President, General Manager, Oracle Corporation **CIV:** Board of Advisors, Stanford University Law School; Board of Advisors, Stanford University Graduate School of Business; Board of Advisors, University of Illinois, College of Engineering **CW:** Author, "Virtual Selling" (2002); Author, "Cyber Rules" (1999); Author, "Taking Care of eBusiness" (2001) **AW:** Named One of Forbes 400 Richest Americans (2006-Present); Named to Top 25 Managers in the World, Business Week Magazine (2000, 2001); Chief Executive Officer of the Year, Industry Week Magazine (2002): David Packard Award, Business Executives for National Security (2002)

SIGNORELLI, AMANDA, T: CEO **I:** Technology **CN:** Techweek **ED:** BS, International Business, Washington University, 2013 **C:** CEO, Techweek, 2015-; Business Analyst, Mckinsey and Company, 2013-15

SILBERMANN, BEN, I: Business Management/ Business Services **PB:** Des Moines **SC:** IA/USA **PT:** Neil Silbermann; Jane (Wang) Silberman **ED:** BA in Political Science, Yale University, 2003 **C:** Co-founder, CEO, Pinterest, Inc., San Francisco 2009-; Product designer, Google Inc., Mountain

View, California, 2002-08 **AW:** Named one of The 35 Under 35, Massachusetts Institute of Technology Technology Review, 2013, The 40 Under 40, Fortune magazine, 2012-14; recipient Tenyck award

SILVER, ADAM, T: National Basketball Association Commissioner **I:** Business Management/Business Services **DOB:** 04/26/1962 **PB:** NYC **SC:** NY/USA **ED:** JD, The University of Chicago Law School, 1988; BA in Political Sci., Duke University, 1984 **C:** Commissioner, NBA, 2014-; COO, deputy commissioner, NBA, 2006-14; COO, NBA Entertainment, 2000-06; President, NBA Entertainment, 1997-2006; Senior vice president, COO, NBA Entertainment, Secaucus, New Jersey, 1995-97; Chief of staff, NBA, 1993-95; Special assistant to commissioner, NBA, 1992-93; Litig. associate, Cravath, Swaine & Moore LLP, New York City, 1989-92; Law clerk to Hon. Kimba Wood, US District Court (southern district) New York, New York City, 1988-89; Legislative aide to Rep. Les AuCoin, US House of Representatives, Washington, 1984-85 **CIV:** Member visiting committee, University Chicago Law School, Member, Special Presidential Council on Campus Life and Culture at Duke University, Board member, New York City Sports Devel. Corp., 2003- Board member, Duke University Libr., Board member, Partnership for a Drug-Free America, Board member, Hands on Network Corp. Service Council, Board member, PENCIL, **CW:** Prodr.: Michael Jordan to the Max, 2000 **AW:** Named one of The Most Influential People in the World of Sports, Business Week, 2008, 2007, 50 Most Influential People in Sports Business, Street & Smith's SportsBus. Journal, 2007-09, The Most Powerful People in Sports, The Sporting News, 2005

SILVERMAN, SARAH, T: Comedian, Actress **I:** Media & Entertainment **PB:** Bedford **PT:** Donald Silverman, Beth Ann Silverman **CW:** Actress, (TV Series) Saturday Night Live, 1993-1994, Mr. Show With Bob And David, 1995-1997, Greg The Bunny, 2002, Crank Yankers (Voice), 2002, The Sarah Silverman Program, 2007-2010, (TV Miniseries) Pilot Season, 2004, (TV Films) Mr. Show And The Incredible, Fantastical News Report, 1998, Smog, 1999, Late Last Night, 1999, Rocky Times, 2000, Saddle Rush (Voice), 2002, (Films) Overnight Delivery, 1998, Bulworth, 1998, There's Something About Mary, 1998, The Bachelor, 1999, The Way Of The Gun, 2000, Black Days, 2001, Say It Isn't So, 2001, Heartbreakers, 2001, Evolution, 2001, Run Ronnie Run, 2002, The School Of Rock, 2003, Nobody's Perfect, 2004, Hair High (Voice), 2004, Rent, 2005, I Want Someone To Eat Cheese With, 2005, School For Scoundrels, 2006, Funny People, 2009, Saint John Of Las Vegas, 2009, Peep World, 2010, Take This Waltz, 2011, The Muppets, 2011, Wreck-It Ralph (Voice), 2012, A Million Ways To Die In The West, 2014, I Smile Back, 2015, Ashby, 2015, Gravy, 2015, Still Punching The Clown, 2015, Popstar: Never Stop Never Stopping, 2016, The Book Of Henry, 2016, (TV Appearances) Star Trek: Voyager, 1996, Seinfeld, 1997, Brotherly Love, 1997, Judge Advocate General, 1997, The Naked Truth, 1997, Futurama, 2000, V.I.P., 2002, Frasier, 2003, Monk, 2004, Entourage, 2004, Aqua Teen Hunger Force (Voice), 2004, Drawn Together (Voice), 2004, American Dad (Voice), 2005, Bob's Burgers (Voice), 2011-2016, Louie, 2012-2014, Masters Of Sex, 2014-2015, Actress, Co-Producer, Who's The Caboose?, 1997; Actress, Writer, Sarah Silverman: Jesus Is Magic, 2005; Actress, Writer, Executive Producer, (TV Films) Susan 313, 2012; Writer, Executive Producer, Sarah Silverman: We Are Miracles, 2013; Author, The Bedwetter: Stories Of Courage, Redemption And Pee, 2010 **AW:** Emmy Award For Outstanding Writing For A Variety Special, Sarah Silverman: We Are Miracles, 2014

SIMPSON, MICHAEL K., T: U.S. Representative from Idaho **I:** Government Administration/Government Relations/Government Services **DOB:** 09/08/1950 **PB:** Burley, Idaho, September 8, 1950 **ED:** DDS, Washington University, St. Louis, 1978; Student, Utah State University **C:** Member, US Congress from 2nd Idaho district, Washington, 1999-; Dentist, Blackfoot, Idaho, 1978-; Member, ho. appropriations committee, agriculture, resources, transportation & infrastructure committee, vet. affairs committee,; Speaker, Idaho House of Representatives, 1991-99; Assistant majority leader, Idaho House of Representatives, 1989; Member, Idaho House of Representatives, 1985-99; Council member, Blackfoot City Council, 1980-84 **CR:** Former speaker majority caucus chairman and assistant majority leader Idaho House Reps. **AW:** Named to Idaho's Rep. Party Hall of Fame; recipient Citizen of Year award, Idaho Family Forum, 1996, Friend of Education award, 1994, Boyd A. Martin award, Association Idaho Cities **MEM:** Mem.: Am. Legis. Exchange Council (state chairman, national board directors, Jefferson award 1994), Idaho State Dental Association (Pres.'s award 1998) **H:** Golf, chess, painting **PA:** Republican

SIMS, CHRISTOPHER ALBERT, T: Economist **I:** Education/Educational Services **CN:** Princeton University **DOB:** 10/21/1942 **PB:** Washington **SC:** DC/USA **PT:** Albert Gladstone Sims, Ruth Bodman (Leiserson) Sims **MS:** Married **SPN:** Catherine Averill Sears, 2/4/1967 **CH:** Benjamin Hayden, Jody Ruth, Nancy Averill **ED:** Postgraduate, University of California, Berkeley, 1963-1964; PhD in Economics, Harvard University, 1968; BA in Mathematics, Harvard University, 1963 **C:** Associate Status, Department Of Operations Research And Financial Engineering, Princeton University, 2012-Present; J.F. Sherrerd '52 University Professor Of Economics, Princeton University, 2012-Present; Harold B. Helms Professor of Economics & Banking, Princeton University, New Jersey, 2004-Present; Professor of Economics, Princeton University, New Jersey, 1999-Present; Henry Ford II Professor of Economics, Yale University, New Haven, CT, 1990-1999; Professor of Economics, University of Minnesota, Minneapolis, MN, 1974-1990; Associate Professor of Economics, University of Minnesota, Minneapolis, MN, 1970-1974; Research Fellow, National Bureau of Economic Research, New York, NY, 1969-1970; Assistant Professor of Economics, Harvard University, Cambridge, MA, 1968-1970; Instructor of Economics, Harvard University, Cambridge, MA, 1967-1968 **CR:** Fellow, Econometric Society, Research Associate, National Bureau of Economic Research, Cambridge, MA, 1970-1971; Graduate Faculty In Statistics, University of Minnesota, 1973-1990; Visiting Professor, Yale University, 1974, Visiting Professor, Massachusetts Institute Of Technology, 1979-1980, Part-Time Consultant, Control Data Business Advisors, 1981-1983, Consultant, Federal Reserve Bank, Minneapolis, MN, 1983, 1986-1987, Director, Institute For Empirical Macroeconomics, Minneapolis, MN, 1987-1991, Director, Graduate Studies, Department of Economics, 1992-1994, Federal National Mortgage Association (Fannie Mae), 1999-2002, Federal Reserve Bank of Philadelphia, 2000-2003, Director, Graduate Studies, Department of Economics, Princeton University, 2003-2008, Federal Reserve Bank of Atlanta, 1995-Present, International Monetary Fund, 2003-Present, Visiting Scholar, Federal Reserve Bank of New York, 1994-1997, 2004-Present **CIV:** Board Member, Barcelona Graduate School of Economics, 2007-Present **AW:** Nobel Prize in Economics, Swedish Royal Academy of Sciences, 2011 **MEM:** American Statistics Association, Institute of Mathematical Statistics, American Academy of Arts & Sciences,

National Academy of Sciences, President, Econometric Society, 1995, President-Elect, American Economic Association, 2011-2012, President, American Economic Association, 2012-2013 **BA:** Yale University, Department of Economics, 37 Hillhouse Avenue, New Haven, CT, USA, 06511-3703

SINEMA, KYRSTEN, T: U.S. Representative from Arizona **I:** Government Administration/Government Relations/Government Services **DOB:** 07/12/1976 **PB:** Tucson, July 12, 1976 **ED:** JD, Arizona State University, 2004; MS in Social Work, Arizona State University, 1999 **C:** Member, US House Financial Services Committee, 2013-; Member, US Congress from 9th Arizona District, Washington, 2013-; Private practice attorney, 2005-; Member District 15, Arizona State Senate, 2011-12; Assistant minority leader, Arizona House of Reps.; Member District 15, Arizona House of Reps., 2005-11; Social worker, Washington Elementary School District, Phoenix, 1995-2002 **CR:** Member Commission Prevent Violence Against Women, 2006- adjunct professor Arizona State University School Social Work, 2003- **CIV:** President board directors, Community Outreach & Advocacy for Refugees (COAR), 2005- Board directors, Arizona Center Progressive Leadership, 2006- Board directors, Girls for a Change, 2005- Board directors, Arizona Death Penalty Forum, 2003- **AW:** Named a Legis. Hero, Arizona League Conservation Voters, 2006; named Legislator of Year, Arizona Pub. Health Association, 2006; named one of The Politics 40 Under 40, TIME Magazine, 2010; recipient CHOICE award, Planned Parenthood, 2006, Stonewall Dem.'s Legislator of Year award, 2005 **MEM:** Mem.: National Organization of Women, Progressive Democrats of America (national board directors 2005-), National Association Social Workers (Legislator of Year 2006), League of Women Voters, Arizona Education Association, Arizona Atty.'s for Criminal Justice, Arizona Advocacy Network, Blue Dog Coalition, Sierra Club (Most Valuable Player 2005, 2006) **PA:** Democrat **BA:** 1725 Longworth House Office Building, Washington, DC, 20515

SINGH, VIJAY, T: Professional Golfer **I:** Athletics **DOB:** 02/22/1963 **PB:** Lautoka, Fiji **C:** Professional Golfer, 1993 **CR:** Player World Cup, 2002 Member International Team The President's Cup, 2009, 2007, 2005, 2003, 2000, 1998, 1996, 1994 **CIV:** Hon. chairperson, National Golf Day, 1999 **AW:** Named Player of Year, PGA Tour, 2004, PGA of America, 2004, PGA European Tour, 2004, Rookie of Year, PGA Tour, 1993; named to World Golf Hall of Fame, 2006; recipient Vardon Trophy, PGA of America, 2004, Byron Nelson award, 2004, Samman award, Pravasi Bharatiya Divas, 2005,PGA Tour Leading Money Winner, 2003, 2004, 2008, Vardon Trophy, 2004, Byron Nelson Award, 2004, European Tour Player of the Year, 2004, FedEx Cup Champion, 2008 **ACH:** Achievements include having 34 career PGA Tour victories and 14 European and Asian Tour victories; winning PGA Tour Major Championships: PGA Championship, 1998, 2004, Masters Tournament, 2002; winning World Golf Championships: Buick Classic, 1993, 1995, Phoenix Open, 1995, 2000, Memorial Tournament, 1997, Buick Open, 1997, 2004, 2005, Spirit International, 1998, Honda Classic, 1999; Shell Houston Open, 2000, 2004, 2005, The Tour Championship, 2000, EDS Byron Nelson Championship, 2003, John Deere Classic, 2003, FUNAI Classic, 2003, AT&T Pebble Beach National Pro-Am, 2004; HP Classic, 2004, Deutsche Bank Championship, 2004, 2008, Bell Canadian Open, 2004, 84 Lumber Classic, 2004, Chrysler Championship, 2004, Sony Open, 2005, Wachovia Championship, 2005; Barclays Classic, 2006, Mercedes Championships, 2007, Arnold

Palmer Invitational, 2007, Bridgestone Invitational, 2008, The Barclays, 2008; ranked number 1 golfer in the world by the Official World Golf Ranking, 2004-05; holds record for: most wins on PGA Tour after the age of 40, most wins by an international player **H:** Snooker, cricket, rugby, soccer

SINISE, GARY, T: Actor **I:** Media & Entertainment **PB:** Blue Island **SC:** IL/USA **PT:** Robert L. Sinise; Mlees S. (Alsip) Sinise **ED:** Honorary LHD, Amherst College (2003) **C:** Bassist, Lieutenant Dan Band **CR:** Co-founder, Artistic Director, Steppenwolf Theatre, Chicago, IL (1974) **CIV:** Member, Advisory Council, Hope for the Warriors; Founder, The Gary Sinise Foundation (2010) **CW:** Actor, Plays, "The Indian Wants the Bronx" (1977), "Getting Out" (1980), "Of Mice and Men" (1980), "Loose Ends" (1982), "True West" (1983), "Balm in Gilead" (1984), "Streamers" (1985), "The Caretaker" (1986), "Grapes of Wrath" (1990), "Buried Child" (1996), "One Flew Over the Cuckoos Nest" (2001); Actor, Films, "A Midnight Clear" (1991), "Jack the Bear" (1991), "Forrest Gump" (1994), "The Quick and the Dead" (1995), "Apollo 13" (1995), "Ransom" (1996), "Albino Alligator" (1996), "Snake Eyes" (1998), "That Championship Season" (1999), "Being John Malkovich" (1999), "Reindeer Games" (1999), "Mission to Mars" (1999), "Bruno" (1999), "All the Rage" (1999), "The Green Mile" (1999), "A Gentleman's Game" (2001), "Made-Up" (2002), "Mission: Space" (2003), "The Human Stain" (2003), "The Big Bounce" (2003), "This Old Cub" (2004), "The Forgotten" (2004), Voice Actor, "Open Season" (2006), "None Less than Heroes, The Honor Flight Story" (2011), "Lt. Dan Band for the Common Good" (2011), "Captain America, The Winter Soldier" (2014), "Beyond Glory" (2016); Actor, TV Films, "True West" (1984), "Family Secrets" (1984), "The Final Days" (1989), "The Grapes of Wrath" (1991), "The Witness" (1992), "My Name is Bill W." (1989), "Truman" (1995), "George Wallace" (1997), "That Championship Season" (1999), "Path to War" (2002), "Fallen Angel" (2003); Actor, TV Miniseries, "The Stand" (1994); Actor, TV Appearances, "Knots Landing" (1980), "Crime Story" (1986-1987), "Hunter" (1990), "Frasier" (1995), "CSI: Miami" (2004-2005), "CSI NY" (2004), "When We Left Earth" (2008), "WWII in HD" (2009), "CSI: Crime Scene Investigation" (2013), Narrator, "Missions That Changed the War" (2012), "Criminal Minds" (2015), "Criminal Minds Beyond Borders" (2016); Actor, Director, Producer, Films, "Of Mice and Men" (1991); Actor, Producer, Films, "Impostor" (2002); Actor, TV Series, "CSI: New York" (2004-2013); Director, Film, "Miles from Home" (1988); Director, Plays, "Landscape of the Body" (1984), "Orphans" (1985-1986); Co-founder, Member, Lieutenant Dan Band (2003-Present) **AW:** Order of Military Medical Merit, Distinguished Service Award, Military Officer's Association; CIMA Humanitarian Award; American Veterans Disabled for Life Award; Presidential Citizen Medal, The White House (2008); Joseph Jefferson Award; Obie Award for Best Director (1982-1983); Joseph Jefferson Award (1996); Disabled American Veterans National Commanders Award (1994); Golden Globe Award for Best Performance by an Actor in a Mini-Series or Motion Picture Made for TV (1996); Screen Actors Guild Award for Outstanding Performance by a Male Actor in a TV Movie or Mini-Series (1996); Emmy Award for Outstanding Lead Actor in a Mini-Series or a Movie (1998); Screen Actors Guild Award for Outstanding Performance by a Male Actor in a TV Movie or Mini-Series (1998) **PA:** Republican **BA:** Gary Sinise Foundation, PO Box 50008, Studio City, CA, 91614

SINONCINI, MATTHEW, **T:** CEO **I:** Manufacturing **CN:** Lear **ED:** BS, Accounting, Wayne State University **C:** President/CEO, Lear Corp., 2011-2018; Senior Vice President/CFO, Lear Corp., 2007-2011; Senior Vice President, Global Finance/CAO, Lear Corp., 2006-2007; Vice President, Global Finance, Lear Corp., 2006-2006; Vice President, Global Finance, Lear Corp., 2004-2006; Vice President, Finance-Europe, Lear Corp., 2001-2004; Director, Lear Corp., 1996-2001

SIRES, ALBIO, **T:** U.S. Representative from New Jersey **I:** Government Administration/Government Relations/Government Services **DOB:** 01/26/1951 **PB:** Bejucal **SC:** Cuba **ED:** MA in Spanish, Middlebury College, Vermont, 1985; BA in Spanish & Marketing, St. Peter's College, Englewood Cliffs, New Jersey, 1974 **C:** Vice Chairman, Democratic Congressional Campaign Committee (DCCC), 2009-; Member, Committee on Foreign Affairs, Committee on Transportation; Member, U.S. Congress from 8th New Jersey District, 2013-; Member, U.S. Congress from 13th New Jersey District, 2006-13; Acting Governor, State of New Jersey, 2005; Acting Governor, State of New Jersey, 2002; Speaker, New Jersey General Assembly, 2002-06; Member District 33, New Jersey General Assembly, 2000-06; Mayor, Town of West New York, New Jersey, 1995-2006; Owner, A.M. Title Agency, Inc.,; Dir Hispanic Outreach Department Community Affairs,, State of New Jersey, 1987-88 **AW:** Named Mayor of Year, New Jersey Conference Mayors, 2004; Recipient William J. Brennan Citation for Justice, New Jersey Bar Association, 2005, Community That Works Award, State of New Jersey **MEM:** Mem.: Legis. Services Commission **PA:** Democrat **BA:** 2342 Rayburn HOB, Washington, DC, 20515

SIRIANO, CHRISTIAN, **T:** Fashion Designer **I:** Apparel & Fashion **DOB:** 11/18/1985 **PB:** Annapolis **SC:** Maryland **PT:** Son of Peter and Joye Siriano; **ED:** Grad., American InterContinental University, London **C:** Designer shoes and handbags, Payless Shoesource, 2009-; Designer, Christian Siriano, 2008-; Launched fragrance line, 2014; Launched clothing line for HSN, Striking by Christian Siriano, 2013; Launched limited edition collection, Christian Siriano for Spiegel, 2011; Launched makeup line for Victoria's Secret, Christian Siriano for VS Makeup, 2009; Collaborated with Starbucks, limited edition gift card, 2009; Designer maternity line, Fierce Mamas, 2008; Designer, Puma, 2008; Freelance make-up artist, Stila, New York City,; Intern, Alexander McQueen, London,; Intern, Vivienne Westwood, London, **CW:** Appeared in (TV reality series) Project Runway, 2007-08 (winner, 2008), appearances in documentaries Christian Siriano: Having a Moment, 2010, Making the Boys, 2011, The Tents, 2011, judge (TV series) Project Runway Junior, 2015-; co-author (with Rennie Dyball): Fierce Style: How To Be Your Most Fabulous Self, 2009 **AW:** Named one of 40 Under 40, Crain's New York Business, 2010; named to Council Fashion Designers of America, 2013, Time 100 Most Influential ,2018 **BA:** Christian Siriano Ltd, 260 W 35th St, New York, NY, 10001-2503

SKARSGÅRD, ALEXANDER, **T:** Actor **I:** Media & Entertainment **PB:** Stockholm **SC:** Sweden **PT:** Stellan Skarsgård; My Skarsgård **ED:** Degree (hon.), Leeds Metropolitan University, 2011; Attended, Leeds Metropolitan University **CW:** Actor: (TV films) Idag röd, 1984, D-dag, 2000, D-dag - Lise, 2000, Judith, 2000, D-dag - Den faerdig film, 2001, Cuppen, 2006; (films) Åke och hans värld, 1984, The Dog That Smiled, 1989, Happy End, 1999, The Diver, 2000, White Water Fury, 2000, Wings of Glass, 2000, Kites Over Helsinki, 2001, Zoolander, 2001, The Dog Trick, 2002, Double Shift, 2005, Om

Sara, 2005, The Last Drop, 2006, Kill Your Darlings, 2006, Exit, 2006, (voice) Metropia, 2009, Beyond the Pole, 2009, 13, 2010, (voice) Moomins and the Comet Chase, 2010, Trust Me, 2010, Melancholia, 2011, Straw Dogs, 2011, Battleship, 2012, Disconnect, 2012, What Maisie Knew, 2012, The East, 2013, The Giver, 2014, The Diary of a Teenage Girl, 2015; actor: (films) Hidden, 2014, Zoolander 2, 2016, War on Everyone, 2016, The Legend of Tarzan, 2016, Mute, 2018, Hold the Dark, 2018, The Aftermath, 2018; (TV miniseries) Golden Brown Eyes, 2007, Generation Kill, 2008; (TV series) True Blood, 2008-14, Eastbound & Down, 2013, Big Little Lies, 2017,(Golden Glove for Best Supporting Actor, Emmy Outstanding Supporting Actor in a Limited Series Drunk History)

SKOLL, JEFFREY S., **T:** Producer, Philanthropist **I:** Media & Entertainment **DOB:** 01/16/1965 **PB:** Montreal **ED:** LLD (hon.), University Toronto, 2003; MBA, Stanford University, 1995; BSEE, University Toronto, 1987; **C:** Chairman/Founder, Participant Media, 2015-; Founder, Skoll Global Threats Fund, 2009-; Founder, chairman, Participant Media, L.A., 2004-; Founder, Capricorn Investment Group, LLC, Palo Alto, 2001-; Founder, chairman, Skoll Foundation, 1999-; Co-founder, president, vice president strategic analysis and planning, eBay Inc., San Jose, California, 1995-99; Manager distribution channels online news information, Knight-Ridder Information; Founder, Micros on the Move Ltd., 1990; Founder, Skoll Engineering, 1987 **CIV:** Board directors, e-Bay Foundation, 1998- Member advisory board, Stanford Grad. School Business, Board directors, Community Foundation Silicon Valley **CW:** Executive prodr.:(-films) House of D, 2004; executive prodr.:(films) Good Night, and Good Luck, 2005, North Country, 2005, Syriana, 2005, American Gun, 2005, Fast Food Nation, 2006, The Visitors, 2007, The Kite Runner, 2007, Charlie Wilson's War, 2007, The Soloist, 2009, The Informant!, 2009, The Crazies, 2010; (documentaries) The World According to Sesame Street, 2006, An Inconvenient Truth, 2006, Chicago 10, 2007, Jimmy Carter: Man from Plains, 2007, Pressure Cooker, 2008, Darfur Now, 2008, Food Inc., 2008, Cane Toads: The Conquest, 2010, Countdown to Zero, 2010, Waiting for Superman, 2010, Casino Jack and the U.S. of Money, 2010, Fair Game, 2010, The Beaver, 2011, The Help, 2011, Contagion, 2011, The Best Exotic Marigold Hotel, 2012, Lincoln, 2012, Promised Land, 2012, Snitch, 2013, A Place at the Table, 2013, Made in America, 2013, The Fifth Estate, 2013, The Hundred-Foot Journey, 2014, Merchants of Doubt, 2014, A Most Violent Year, 2014, The Second Best Exotic Marigold Hotel, 2015, He Named Me Malala, 2015, Bridge of Spies, 2015, Our Brand is Crisis, 2015, Spotlight, 2015, Neruda, 2016, The Light Between Oceans, 2016, Denial, 2016, Deepwater Horizon, 2016, Middle School: The Worst Years of My Life, 2016, A Monster Calls, 2016, An Inconvenient Sequel: Truth to Power, 2017, Shot Caller, 2017, Captive State, 2018 **AW:** Named a WIRED Renegade, WIRED Rave Awards, 2006; named one of The 100 Game Changers, Huffington Post, 2010, The 50 Smartest People in Hollywood, Entertainment Weekly, 2007, The 100 Most Influential People in the World, TIME magazine, 2006, The 50 Most Generous Philanthropists, Fortune magazine, 2005, The Most Innovative Philanthropists of the Past Decade, BusinessWeek, 2003, 2002, The World's Richest People, Forbes magazine, 1999-; recipient Entertainment Industry Environmental Leadership award, Global Green USA, 2009, Visionary award, Producers Guild America, 2009, National Leadership Award, Commonwealth Club Silicon Valley, 2004, Outstanding Philanthropist award, International Association Fundraising Professionals, 2003,

Silicon Valley chapter Association Fundraising Professionals, 2002, Visionary award, Software Development Forum, 2001, Leafy award, 1999

SKORTON, DAVID JAN, **T:** Secretary of the Smithsonian **I:** Museums & Institutions **DOB:** 11/22/1949 **PB:** Milwaukee **SC:** WI/USA **PT:** Son of Samuel and Pauline (Millstein) Skorton; **ED:** MD, Northwestern University, Chicago, 1974; BA in Psychology, Northwestern University, Evanston, Illinois, 1970 **CT:** Cert. in Cardiovascular Disease, Diplomate American Board Internal Medicine, National Board Medical Examiners **C:** Secretary, Smithsonian Institute, 2015-; Professor Medicine & Pediatrics, Weill Cornell Medical College, New York City, 2006-15; President, Professor Biomedical Engineering, Cornell University, Ithaca, New York, 2006-15; President, University Iowa, 2003-06; Vice President External Relations, University Iowa, 2000-03; Professor Biomedical Engineering, University Iowa, Iowa City, 1999-2006; Vice President Research, University Iowa, Iowa City, 1992-2003; Associate Chair Clinical Programs, College Medicine, University Iowa, Iowa City, 1989-92; Professor Internal Medicine, Electrical and Computer Engineering, University Iowa, Iowa City, 1988-2006; Director Division General Internal Medicine, College Medicine, University Iowa, Iowa City, 1985-89; Associate Professor Internal Medicine, Electrical and Computer Engineering, University Iowa, Iowa City, 1984-88; Director Cardiovasc. Image Processing Laboratory, Cardiovasc. Research Center, College Medicine, University Iowa, Iowa City, 1982-96; Assistant Professor Electrical and Computer Engineering, University Iowa, Iowa City, 1982-84; Assistant Professor, University Iowa, Iowa City, 1981-84; Instructor Department Internal Medicine, University Iowa, Iowa City, 1980-81; Adj. Assistant Professor, UCLA, 1978-80; Chief Resident Department Medicine, UCLA, 1978-79; Cardiology Fellowship, UCLA, 1977-79; Intern, Resident, UCLA, 1974-77 **CR:** President New York Racing Association, 2012-14 Past Chair Bus.-Higher Education Forum Co-chair Adv. Board Africa-US Higher Education Initiative, Association Pub. & Land-Grant Universities Member National Adv. Council National Institute Biomedical Imaging & Bioengineering Chairman National Institutes of Health, 1990-92, Member International and Cooperative Projects Fogerty Center Study Section, 1988-92 Co-Founder, Co-dir. Adolescent & Adult Congenital Heart Disease Clinic, University Iowa Hospitals Director Echocardiology Laboratory VA Medical Center, Iowa City, 1980-89 **CIV:** Chair, Task Force Diversifying New York State Economy Through Industry Higher Education Partnerships, 2009 **CW:** Monthly Columnist Cornell Daily Sun, Member Editorial Board American Journal Noninvasive Cardiology, Cardiovasc. Imaging, Echocardiography; Contributor Numerous Articles to Professional Journals, Chapters to Books **AW:** Recipient Alumni Merit award, Feinberg School Medicine, Northwestern University, Distinguished Achievement Award, Roy J. & Lucille A. Carver College Medicine, University Iowa, 2003, Research Career Devel. Award, National Heart Lung & Blood Institute, National Institutes of Health, 1984-89; Regents' Scholar, UCLA, 1967-68,Arts and Sciences Advocacy Award,2015 **MEM:** Fellow: American College of Physicians, American Physiological Society, American Heart Association, American College Cardiology; Mem.: American Association for the Advancement of Science, Institute Medicine, National Institute Biomedical Imaging & Bioengring., Council Foreign Relations (life), Business Higher Education, International Society Adult Congenital Cardiac Disease, Association Univ. Cardiologists **BA:** The Smithsonian, 10th St& Constitution ave, NW, Washington, DC, 20560

SLATER, CHRISTIAN, T: Actor **I:** Media & Entertainment **PB:** New York **SC:** NY/USA **PT:** Michael Hawkins Slater; Mary Jo Slater **CW:** Actor: (films) The Legend of Billie Jean, 1985, The Name of the Rose, 1986, Twisted, 1986, Tucker: The Man and His Dream, 1988, Gleaming the Cube, 1989, Heathers, 1989, Beyond the Stars, 1989, The Wizard, 1989, Tales from the Darkside: The Movie, 1990, Young Guns II, 1990, Pump Up the Volume, 1990, Robin Hood: Prince of Thieves, 1991, Mobsters, 1991, Star Trek VI: The Undiscovered Country, 1991, Kuffs, 1992, FernGully: The Last Rainforest (voice), 1992, Where the Day Takes You, 1992, Untamed Heart, 1993, True Romance, 1993, Jimmy Hollywood, 1994, Interview with the Vampire: Vampire Chronicles, 1994, Murder in the First, 1995, Bed of Roses, 1995, Broken Arrow, 1996, Austin Powers: International Man of Mystery, 1997, The Tears of Julian Po, 1997, Love Stinks, 1999, White Lies, 1999, The Contender, 2000, 3000 Miles to Graceland, 2001, Who Is Cletis Tout?, 2001, Windtalkers, 2002, Run for the Money, 2002, Masked & Anonymous, 2003, Mindhunters, 2004, The Good Shepherd, 2004, Pursued, 2004, Churchill: The Hollywood Years, 2004, Alone in the Dark, 2005, A License to Steal, 2005, Bobby, 2006, Igor (voice), 2008, Dolan's Cadillac, 2009, Lies & Illusions, 2009, Shadows of the White Nights, 2010, Rites of Passage, 2011, Sacrifice, 2011, Without Men, 2011, The River Murders, 2011, Soldiers of Fortune, 2012, Back to the Sea, 2012, Playback, 2012, Guns, Girls and Gambling, 2012, Bullet to the Head, 2012, The Power of Few, 2013, Assassins Run, 2013, Stranded, 2013, Nymphomaniac: Vol. II, 2013, Nymphomanica: Vol I, 2013, Ask Me Anything, 2014, Way of the Wicked, 2014, The Adderall Diaries, 2015, King Cobra, 2016, The Summit,2017, Mune: Guardian of the Moon, 2017, The Wife, 2017, The Public, 2018, Suicide Squad: Hell to Pay, 2018; dir.: Museum of Love, 1996; actor, executive producer (films) Very Bad Things, 1998, The Deal, 2004, actor, co-prodr. Hard Rain, 1998, actor, executive producer Basil, 1998; actor: (TV films) Sherlock Holmes: The Strange Case of Alice Faulkner, 1981, The Hunted Mansion Mystery, 1983, Living Proof: The Hank Williams Junior Story, 1983, Secrets, 1986, Desperate for Love, 1989, Merry Christmas, George Bailey, 1997, Stan Lee's Mighty 7 (voice), 2014, (TV appearances) One Life to Live, 1977, Ryan's Hope, 1985, L.A. Law, 1988, Prehistoric Planet, 2002, The West Wing, 2002, Adventures of Jimmy Neutron: Boy Genius (voice), 2003, Alias, 2003, My Name Is Earl, 2006, Archer (voice), 2014; (TV series) Robot Chicken (voice), 2005-12, My Own Worst Enemy, 2008, The Forgotten, 2009-10, Breaking In, 2011-12, Mind Games, 2014-, Archer (voice), 2014-15, Mr. Robot, 2015- (Golden Globe award for Best Performance by an Actor in a Supporting Role in a Series, Limited Series or Motion Picture Made for TV, 2016, Critics' Choice award for Best Supporting Actor in a Drama Series, 2016)Jake and the Never Land Pirates, 2015, The Lion Guard, 2016, Milo Murphy's Law, 2016, Dawn of the Croods, 2016, Live with Kelly, 2016, Jeff & Some Aliens, 2017, Justice League Action, 2017, Rick and Morty, 2017; (plays) Music Man, 1980, Between Daylight & Boonville, 1980, Copperfield, 1981, Macbeth, 1982, Merlin, 1983, Landscape of the Body, 1984, Dry Land, 1986, One Flew Over the Cuckoo's Nest, 2004-05, The Glass Menagerie, 2005, One Flew Over the Cuckoo's Nest, 2006, Swimming with Sharks, 20007, Spamalot, 2015, Glengarry Glen Rose, 2017 **AW:** Named one of 100 Sexiest Stars in Film History, Empire Magazine, 1995

SLATKIN, LEONARD EDWARD, T: Composer **I:** Media & Entertainment **DOB:** 09/01/1944 **PB:** LA **PT:** Son of Felix and Eleanor (Aller) Slatkin **ED:** Doctorate (hon.), Juilliard School; Studied conducting with Jean Paul Morel, Juilliard School, New York City; Student, LA City College; Student, Ind. University; Conducting study with Felix Slatkin, Amerigo Marino, Ingolf Dahl; Viola study with Sol Schoenbach; Piano study with Victor Aller and Selma Cramer **C:** Music director, Orchestre National de Lyon, France, 2011-; Music Laureate, Detroit Symphony Orchestra, 2018-; Music director, Detroit Symphony Orchestra, 2008-18; Principal guest conductor, Pittsburgh Symphony Orchestra, 2008-; Principal guest conductor, Royal Philharmonic Orchestra, London, 2005-07; Conductor laureate, St. Louis Symphony Orchestra, 1996-; Principal guest conductor, LA Philharmonic, 2004-07; Chief conductor, BBC Symphony Orchestra, 2000-04; Principal guest conductor, Philharmonia Orchestra, London, 1997-2000; Music director, National Symphony Orchestra, Washington, 1996-2008; Music adv., New Orleans Symphony/La. Philharmonic Orchestra, 1977-79; Music director, St. Louis Symphony Orchestra, 1979-96; Assistant conductor, St. Louis Symphony Orchestra, 1968-77; Artistic director, conductor, New York Youth Symphony, 1966 **CR:** Arthur R. Metz Foundation conductor Ind. University Jacobs School Music founder, director National Conducting Institute distinguished artist in residence Am. University, Washington, 2007-08 music adv. Nashville Symphony Orchestra, 2006-09 founder St. Louis Symphony Youth Orchestra, 1969 **CW:** Conducting debut as assistant conductor Youth Symphony of New York, Carnegie Hall, 1966; assistant conductor Juilliard Opera Theater and Dance Department, 1967, St. Louis Symphony Orchestra, 1968-71; associate conductor, 1971-74; guest conductor Concertgebouw, Royal Danish Orchestra, Tivoli, English Chamber Orchestra, BBC Manchester, London Philharmonic, London Symphony Orchestra, Royal Philmarm. Orchestra, 1974, National Orchestra Paris, Scottish National Orchestra, NHK Tokyo, 1986, Vienna State Opera, Lyric Opera Chicago, Stuttgart Opera, Stockholm, Oslo, Israel, Goteborg, Berlin; debut Chicago Symphony Orchestra, 1974, New York Philharmonic, 1974, Philadelphia Orchestra, 1974, USSR Orchestras, 1976-77, Metropolitan Opera, 1991; principal guest conductor Minnesota Orchestra, 1974-; summer artistic director, 1979-89, music director New Orleans Philharmonic Symphony Orchestra, 1977-78; artistic director Great Woods, 1990; artistic administrator, Blossom, 1991; composer: The Raven, Dialogue for Two Cellos and Orchestra, Extension 1, 2, 3, 4; recording artist RCA, Angel EMI, Vox, Telarc, Philips, Warner Brothers; condr.: Arthur R. Metz Foundation, Ind. University **AW:** Decorated Chevalier Legion of Honor, France; recipient 7 Grammy awards, Lifetime Achievement award, Washington DC Mayor's Arts Awards, Gold Baton for service to Am. music, Am. Symphony Orchestra League, National Medal of Arts, US Congress, 2003, Declaration of Honor in Silver, Austrian Government, 1986, Gold Medal Awards, 2005 **MEM:** Mem.: National Academy of Recording Arts and Sciences (board governors Chicago chapter) **BA:** Detroit Symphony Orch, 3711 Woodward Ave, Detroit, MI, 48201

SLAUGHTER, LOUISE MCINTOSH, T: U.S. Representative from New York **I:** Government Administration/Government Relations/Government Services **DOB:** 08/14/1929 **PB:** Lynch **SC:** Kentucky **YOP:** 2018-03-16 **PT:** Daughter of Oscar Lewis and Grace (Byers) McIntosh **ED:** Doctor (hon.), University Kentucky, 2006; MPH, University Kentucky, Lexington, 1953; BS in Microbiol., University Kentucky, Lexington, 1951 **C:** Ranking minority member, US House Rules Committee, 2011-; Member, US Congress from 25th New York District, 2013-; Chair, US House Rules Committee, 2007-11; Ranking minority member, US House Rules Committee, 2005-07; Member, US Congress from 28th New York District, 1993-2013; Member, US Congress from 30th New York District, Washington, 1987-93; Member District 130, New York State Assembly, 1982-86; Regional coordinator to lieutenant governor Mario Cuomo, State of New York, Albany, New York, 1979-82; Regional coordinator to secretary Mario Cuomo, State of New York, Albany, New York, 1976-78; Member, Monroe County Legislature, New York, 1976-79; Market researcher, Procter & Gamble Co., Cincinnati, 1953-56; Bacteriologist, University Kentucky, 1952-53; Bacteriologist, Kentucky Department Health, Louisville, 1951-52 **CIV:** Del., Democratic National Convention, 1972, 1976, 1980, 1988, 1992, 1996 **AW:** Named Lay Educator of Year, Phi Delta Kappa International, Rochester chapter, 1999; recipient Sidney R. Yates National Arts Advocacy award, National Assembly State Arts Agencies, Woman of Vision award, Women in Film & Vision, 2004, Humane Legislator of Year, American Humane Association, 2003, Award for Outstanding Arts Leadership in the US House of Representatives, US Conference Mayors & Americans for the Arts, 1998, Distinguished Public Health Legislator award, Public Health Association, 1997 **MEM:** Mem.: League of Women Voters **PA:** Democrat

SLOAN, TIMOTHY J., T: CEO **I:** Financial Services **CN:** Wells Fargo **ED:** MBA in Fin. and Accounting, University Michigan, Ann Arbor; BA in Economics & History, University Michigan, Ann Arbor **C:** CEO, Wells Fargo, 2016-; Senior executive vice president, CFO, Wells Fargo & Co., San Francisco, 2011-; Senior vice president, chief administrative officer corp. communications, social responsibility & human resources, enterprise marketing, government relations & strategic planning, Wells Fargo & Co., San Francisco, 2010-11; Head commercial bank, real estate and specialized fin. services, Wells Fargo & Co., San Francisco, 2006-10; Group head specialized fin. services, Wells Fargo & Co., San Francisco, 1997-2006; Executive vice president, manager real estate merchant banking division, Wells Fargo & Co., San Francisco, 1994-97; Senior credit officer, group head real estate managed assets group, Wells Fargo & Co., San Francisco, 1991-94; Vice president loan adjustment group, Wells Fargo & Co., San Francisco, 1987-91; Banker, Continental Illinois Bank, Chicago, 1984-87 **CIV:** Board overseers, Huntington Libr.; Board member, Jardin de la Infancia Charter School, Associate trustee, San Marino Schools Foundation, Member corp. adv. board, University Michigan Ross School Business,

SMITH, ADAM, T: Chair of the House Armed Services Committee **I:** Military & Defense Services **DOB:** 06/15/1965 **PB:** Washington, DC **SC:** DC/USA **PT:** Ben Smith; Leila Smith **ED:** Attended, Western Washington University; BA in Political Science, Fordham University, Bronx, NY (1987); JD, University of Washington School of Law (1990) **C:** Chair of the Armed Services Committee (2017-Present); Member, US House Select Committee on the Events Surrounding the 2012 Terrorist Attack in Benghazi (2014—Present); Ranking Member, US House Armed Services Committee, Washington, DC (2011—Present); Member, US Congress from the Ninth Washington District, Washington, DC (1997—Present); Judge Pro Tempore, Seattle City Attorney's Office, Seattle, WA (1996); Prosecutor, Seattle City Attorney's Office, Seattle, WA (1993—1995); Attorney, Cromwell, Mendoza and Belur, Kent, WA (1991—1992); Chair, Law and Justice Committee, Washington State Senate (1993—1997); Member, District 33, Washington State Senate (1990-1996); Driver, United Parcel Service

(UPS) (1985-1987) **CIV:** Member, Kent Drinking Driver Task Force; Highline Citizens for Schools; Kent Meridian HS Site-Based Council; Board of Directors, Judson Park Retirement Home **MEM:** Kiwanis International **PA:** Democrat **BA:** US House of Representatives, 2264 Rayburn House Office Bldg, Washington D.C., DC, 20515

SMITH, ADRIAN M., T: U.S. Representative from Nebraska **I:** Government Administration/ Government Relations/Government Services **DOB:** 12/19/1970 **PB:** Scottsbluff, Nebraska **ED:** Student, Portland State University; BS in Marketing Education, University Nebraska, 1993 **C:** Assistant whip, US Congress from 3rd Nebraska district, 2007-; Member, US Congress from 3rd Nebraska district, 2007-; Member, Committee on Ways and Means; Real estate agent, marketing specialist, Buyers Realty, 1997-; Member, Nebraska Legislature from 48th district, Lincoln, 1998-; Educator, staff devel. project manager, Educational Service Unit 13, 1994-97; Research assistant, University Nebraska Foundation, 1992-93; Staff international, marketing specialist, Nebrs. Gov.'s Office, 1992; Legis. page, Nebraska Legislature, 1992 **CIV:** Board directors, Twin Cities Devel., Chairman land use task force, Vision 2020, Member, Gering City Council, 1994-98 Member, Scotts Bluff County Visitors Adv. Committee, 1995-96 Member, Wyo-Braska Museum Natural Hist., Member, We. Nebraska Regional Airport Operations Board, Member, Calvary Memorial Evangelical Free Church, **MEM:** Mem.: Farm & Ranch Museum Association, Riverside Zoological Society, N. Platte Valley Hist. Society, Scotts Bluff County Board Realtors, Scotts Bluff Kiwanis Club (board directors Camp Kiwanis) **PA:** Republican

SMITH, CHRISTOPHER HENRY, T: U.S. Representative from New Jersey **I:** Government Administration/Government Relations/Government Services **DOB:** 03/04/1953 **PB:** Rahway **SC:** NJ/USA **PT:** Bernard Henry Smith, Katherine Joan (Hall) Smith **ED:** BBA, Trenton State College, New Jersey, 1975; Student, Worcester College, England, 1973-1974 **C:** Congressional-Executive Commission On China, U.S. Congress From Fourth New Jersey District, 1981-Present; Legislative Agent, New Jersey General Assembly, 1979; Director, Institutional Sales, Leisure Unlimited Inc., Woodbridge, NJ, 1978-1980; Executive Director, New Jersey Right To Life Committee, Inc., 1976-1978; Co-Chair, Pro-Life Caucus, U.S. Congress From Fourth New Jersey District; Ranking Member, Security And Cooperation In Europe Commission, U.S. Congress From Fourth New Jersey District; Foreign Affairs And International Relations Committee, U.S. Congress From Fourth New Jersey District **CR:** U.S. Representative to UN International Conference on Immunizing World's Children **CIV:** Co-Chair, Coalition For Autism Research And Education, Past Chair, Commission On Security And Cooperation In Europe, Active In Human Rights Movements, Romania, China, Vietnam, Former Soviet Union **AW:** Blinded American Veterans Foundation, 2003, Leader For Peace Award, Peace Corps, William Wilberforce Award, 2002, Leader of the Year, New Jersey State Postal Workers Union, 2002, Legislator of the Year, JWV Of America, 1996, International Association of Chiropractors, George (Buck) Gillispie Congressional Award for Meritorious Service **MEM:** National Federation of Independent Business **PA:** Republican **BA:** U.S. House of Representatives, 2373 Rayburn House Office Bldg, Washington, DC, USA, 20515

SMITH, D. BROOKS, T: Federal Judge **I:** Law and Legal Services **DOB:** 12/04/1951 **PB:** Altoona **SC:** PA/USA **ED:** JD, Dickinson School Law (1976); BA, Franklin and Marshall College (1973) **C:** Chief Judge, U.S. Court Appeals for the Third Circuit (2016-Present); Judge, U.S. Court of Appeals for the Third Circuit (2002-Present); Chief Judge, U.S. District Court for the Western District of Pennsylvania (2001-2002); Judge, U.S. District Court for the Western District of Pennsylvania (1988-2002); Judge, Court Common Pleas of Blair County, PA (1984-1988); Managing Partner, Jubelirer, Carothers, Krier, Halpern & Smith, Altoona, PA (1981-1983); Private Practice, Jubelirer, Carothers, Krier, Halpern & Smith, Altoona, PA (1976-1984) **CR:** Part-time Assistant District Attorney, Blair County (1977-1979); Special Prosecutor (1981-1983); Part-time District Attorney (1983-1984); Advisory Committee on Criminal Rules, U.S. Judicial Conference (1993-1999); Committee on Space and Facilities, US Judicial Conference (2006-Present) **CIV:** Trustee, Mount Aloysius College (2006-Present); Trustee, Philadelphia University (2005-2006); Trustee, St. Francis College (1992-2004) **MEM:** American Law Institute; Pennsylvania Bar Association; American Judicature Society; Pennsylvania Society; Amen Corner; Blair County Game, Fish and Forestry Association; Board of Directors, Federal Judges Association (1993-1997, 2002); Inns of Court; Allegheny County Bar Association; Pi Gamma Mu **BA:** 601 Market Street, Philadelphia, PA, 19106

SMITH, DONNIE, T: Former Tyson CEO **I:** Business Management/Business Services **ED:** BS in Animal Sci., University Tennessee, Knoxville, 1980 **C:** President, CEO, Tyson Foods, Inc., 2009-16; Group vice president poultry & prepared foods, Tyson Foods, Inc., 2009; Group vice president consumer products, Tyson Foods, Inc., 2008-09; Group vice president logistics & operations services, Tyson Foods, Inc., 2007-08; Senior vice president information systems, purchasing & distribution, Tyson Foods, Inc., 2006-07; Senior vice president, chief information officer, Tyson Foods, Inc., 2005-06; Senior vice president supply chain & management, Tyson Foods, Inc., 2001-05; Executive vice president and general manager supply chain & management, Tyson Foods, Inc., 1999-2001; Various positions including vice president purchasing, Tyson Foods, Inc., 1995; Joined commodities purchasing group, Hdqs. office, Tyson Foods, Inc., Springdale, Arkansas, 1987; Various live poultry production jobs, Tyson Foods, Inc., 1980-87

SMITH, FRED, T: Fedex CEO **I:** Business Management/Business Services **DOB:** 08/11/1944 **PB:** Marks **SC:** Mississippi **PT:** Son of Frederick C. Smith & Sally (Wallace) S. **MS:** Married **SPN:** Diane Avis; Linda Black Grisham, 1969 (div. 1977) **CH:** 8 children **ED:** BS in Econs., Yale University, 1966 **CT:** Cert. commercial pilot. **C:** Chairman board, president, CEO, FedEx Corp., Memphis, 1998-; Chairman board, FedEx Corp., Memphis, 1975-98; CEO, FedEx Corp., Memphis, 1977-98; President, FedEx Corp., Memphis, 1971-75; Founder, FedEx Corp., Memphis, 1971; Owner, Ark Aviation, 1969-71 **CR:** Board of Directors FedEx Corp. (formerly FedEx Express Corp), 1971- **CIV:** Served with U.S. Marine Corps, 1966-70, co-chmn. WWII Memorial Campaign. **AW:** Decorated Purple Heart, Bronze Star, Silver Star; named Person of Year, French-American Chamber of Commerce, 2006, CEO of Year, Chief Executive Magazine, 2004; named one of The Forbes 400: Richest Americans, 2006-; recipient Bower award for Business Leadership, Franklin Institute, 2008, Champion of Work-

place Learning and Performance award, American Society Training & Devel., 2002, Eagle of Aviation award, Embry-Riddle Aeronautical award, 2001, Peter F. Drucker Strategic Leadership award, 1997

SMITH, GEORGE ELWOOD, T: retired physicist, researcher **I:** Sciences **DOB:** 05/10/1930 **PB:** White Plains **PT:** Son of George Francis and Lillian Alfreda (Voorhies) Smith **ED:** PhD in Physics, University Chicago, 1959; MS in Physics, University Chicago, 1956; BS in Physics, University Pennsylvania, 1955 **C:** Retired, Bell Laboratories, 1986; Various positions including head department solid state electronic device devel. and head VLSI (very-large-scale integration) device department, Bell Laboratories; Member tech. staff, Bell Laboratories, Murray Hill, New Jersey, 1959-86 **CW:** Contributor articles to professional journals **AW:** Named to National Inventors Hall of Fame, 2006; recipient Nobel prize in physics, 2009, Edwin H. Land medal, Society Imaging Sci. & Tech., 2001, Computer & Communications prize, NEC Foundation, Tokyo, 1999, Progress medal, Photographic Society America, 1986, Stuart Ballentine medal, Franklin Institute, Philadelphia, 1973, Queen Elizabeth Prize of Engineering, 2017, Draper Prize, 2006 **MEM:** Fellow: IEEE (Morris N. Liebmann Memorial award 1974, Electron Devices Society Distinguished Service award 1997, Device Research Conference Breakthrough award 1999), Am. Physical Society; mem.: NAE (Charles Stark Draper prize 2006), Sigma Xi, Phi Beta Kappa, Pi Mu Epsilon **ACH:** Achievements include co-invention of the charge-coupled device (CCD), a device for the movement of electrical charge, usually from within the device to an area where the charge can be manipulated; CCD technology transforms light into electronic signals, is used in telescopes to probe the universe, underwater cameras to explore the oceans, and for medical diagnostics and microsurgery; patents in field

SMITH, GERRY PARRISH PARRISH, T: CEO of Office Depot **I:** Business Management/Business Services **DOB:** 01/01/1900 **ED:** Bachelor of Business Administration, Pacific Lutheran University, 1986 **C:** CEO, Office Depot, 2017-; CEO/ EVP, Lenovo, 2016-17; SVP/President of the Americas, Lenovo, 2013-15; SVP Global Operations/President of North America, Lenovo, 2012-13; SVP/Global Supply Chain Leader, Lenovo, 2006-12; VP/GM Displays & Singapore Design Center, Dell, 2003-06

SMITH, JAMES "LL COOL J", T: Rap Artist, Actor **I:** Media & Entertainment **PB:** Bay Shore **SC:** NY/ USA **PT:** James Smith, Ondrea Smith **MS:** Married **SPN:** Symone I. Johnson, 8/9/1995 **CH:** Najee Laurent Todd Eugene, Italia Anita Maria, Samaria Leah Wisdom, Nina Simone **C:** Launched, Men's Footwear, Najee; Launched, Clothing Line, Todd Smith **CW:** Rapper, (Albums) Radio, 1984, Bigger And Deffer, 1987, Walking With A Panther, 1989, Mama Said Knock You Out, 1991, 14 Shots To The Dome, 1993, Mr. Smith, 1996, All World-Greatest Hits, 1996, Phenomenon, 1997, The G.O.A.T., 2000, The Definition, 2004, Todd Smith, 2006, Exit 13, 2008, Authentic, 2013, G.O.A.T. 2, 2015; Actor, (Films) Krush Groove, 1984, The Hard Way, 1991, Toys, 1992, The Right To Remain Silent, 1996, Woo, 1997, BAPS, 1997, Caught Up, 1998, Halloween: H20, 1998, Deep Blue Sea, 1999, In Too Deep, 1999, Any Given Sunday, 1999, Kingdom Come, 2001, Rollerball, 2002, Deliver Us From Eva, 2003, Rugrats Go Wild (Voice), 2003, S.W.A.T., 2003, Mindhunters, 2004, Slow Burn, 2005, Last Holiday, 2006, The Deal, 2008, Grudge Match, 2013, (TV Series) In The House, 1995-99, NCIS: Los Angeles, 2009-Present, (TV Appearances) House M.D.,

2005, 30 Rock, 2007, Hawaii Five-0, 2012, American Dad!, 2017, (TV Films) Wildcats, 1986, The Right To Remain Silent, 1996; Host, (TV Series) Lip Sync Battle, 2015-Present; Co-Author, I Make My Own Rules, 1998, The Platinum Workout: Sculpt Your Best Body Ever With Hollywood's Fittest Star, 2006, LL Cool J (Hip-Hop Stars), 2007, (Children's Book) And The Winner Is..., 2002 **AW:** Kennedy Center Honors, 2017, National Association For The Advancement Of Colored People Image Award For Outstanding Actor In A Drama Series, NCIS: Los Angeles, 2013-2014, Grammy Award For Best Rap Solo Performance For Hey Lover, Mr. Smith, 1997, Grammy Award For Best Rap Solo Performance For Mama Said Knock You Out, Mama Said Knock You Out, 1992

SMITH, JASON THOMAS, T: U.S. Representative from Missouri, Former State Legislator **I:** Government Administration/Government Relations/ Government Services **DOB:** 06/16/1980 **PB:** St. Louis **SC:** MO/USA **ED:** Student in international law, Trinity College, Cambridge, England; JD, Oklahoma City University School Law, 2004; BA in Agricultural Economics, University of Missouri, 2001 **C:** Member, U.S. House Natural Resources Committee, 2013-; Secretary, House Republican Conference, Member, Committee on Ways and Means, Republican Study Committee; Member, U.S. Congress from 8th Mo District, Washington, DC 2013-; Member District 120, Missouri House of Reps., 2013; Member District 150, Missouri House of Reps., 2005-13; Attorney, real estate agent, small business owner, farm manager, **CIV:** Member, Sunday school teacher, Grace Community Church Salem, **MEM:** Mem.: National Rifle Association, American Legislative Exchange Council, Missouri Farm Bureau, Missouri Bar Association, Cuba Chamber of Commerce, Steelville Chamber of Commerce, Salem Chamber of Commerce **PA:** Republican **BA:** 1118 Longworth House Office Building, Washington, DC, 20515

SMITH, JERRY EDWIN, T: Federal Judge **I:** Law and Legal Services **DOB:** 11/07/1946 **PB:** Del Rio **SC:** Texas **PT:** Son of Lemuel Edwin and Ruth Irene (Henderson) Smith; **ED:** JD, Yale University, 1972; BA, Yale University, 1969 **CT:** Bar: Texas 1972 **C:** Judge, US Court Appeals (5th cir.), Houston, 1988-; City Attorney, City of Houston, 1984-87; Chairman, Houston Civ. Service Communications, 1982-84; Special Assistant, Office of Attorney General, Texas, 1981-82; Director, Harris County Housing Auth., Texas, 1978-80; Associate then Partner, Fulbright & Jaworski, Houston, 1973-84; Law Clerk to Judge, US District Court (no. district) Texas, Lubbock, 1972-73 **CIV:** Committeeman, State Rep. Executive Committee, Texas, 1976-88 Chairman, Harris County Rep. Party, Houston, 1977-78 **MEM:** Mem.: Houston Bar Association, State Bar Texas **BA:** John Minor Wisdom U.S. Court of Appeals Building Fifth Circuit, 600 Camp St, New Orleans, LA, 70130

SMITH, LAMAR SEELIGSON, T: Chair of the House Science Committee, U.S. Representative from Texas, **I:** Government Administration/Government Relations/Government Services **DOB:** 11/19/1947 **PB:** San Antonio **PT:** Son of Campbell and Eloise Keith (Seeligson) Smith; **ED:** JD, Southern Methodist University School Law, Dallas, 1975; BA, Yale University, New Haven, 1969 **C:** Chairman, US House Sci., Space & Technology Committee, 2013-; Member, US Congress from 21st Texas District, 1987-; Chairman, US House Judiciary Committee, 2011-13; Chairman, US House Standards of Official Conduct Committee, 1999-2001; Bexar County commissioner, 1982-85; Member District 57, Texas House of Reps., 1981-82; Chairman, Bexar County Republican Party, San Antonio, 1978-82; Associate, Maebius & Duncan, Inc., San Antonio, 1975-76; Business writer, Christian Sci. Monitor, Boston, 1970-72; Management intern, Small Business Administration, Washington, 1969-70 **CR:** Partner Lamar Seeligson Ranch, Premont, Texas, 1975- **PA:** Republican **BA:** Office of Lamar Smith, 2409 Rayburn House Office Building, Washington, DC, 20515

SMITH, LAVENSKI ROY, T: Federal Judge **I:** Law and Legal Services **DOB:** 10/31/1958 **PB:** Hope **SC:** AR/USA **MS:** Married **SPN:** Trendle Smith **CH:** 2 Children **ED:** JD, University of Arkansas, 1987; BA, University of Arkansas, 1981 **C:** Chief Judge, U.S. Court of Appeals for the 8th District, 2017-; Judge, US Court Appeals (8th cir.), 2002-; Interim Associate Justice, Arkansas State Supreme Court, 1999-2000; Commissioner, Arkansas Pub. Service Commission, 2001-02; Chairman, Arkansas Pub. Service Commission, 1997-99; Regulatory Liaison to Governor, State of Arkansas, Little Rock, 1996-97; Assistant Professor, John Brown University, 1994-96; Private Practice, Springdale, 1991-94; Staff Lawyer, Ozark Legal Services, 1987-91; Law Clerk, Hall, Wright & Morris, 1985-87 **CIV:** Board of Directors, Northwest Arkansas Christian Justice Center, Trainer, Partners for Family Training, 1993-96, Chairman, Arkansas Pub. Service Commission, 1996-98 **PA:** Republican **BA:** Thomas F. Eagleton Courthouse, 111 South 10th Street, St. Louis, MO, 63102

SMITH, MAGGIE, T: Actress **I:** Fine Art **DOB:** 12/28/1934 **PB:** Ilford **PT:** Daughter of Nathaniel and Margaret Hutton (Little) S. **SPN:** Married Robert Stephens, June 29, 1967 (div. May 1974) **CH:** children: Chris, Toby; Married Beverley Cross, August 23, 1975 (deceased March 1998) **ED:** D.Litt. (hon.), University Cambridge, 1995; D.Litt. (hon.), Oxford University, 1994; D.Litt. (hon.), St. Andrews, 1971 **C:** Assistant stage manager, actor, Oxford Playhouse, 1951-53 **CW:** Stage and film actress, 1952—, stage appearances include New Faces, debut New York City, 1956, Share My Lettuce, 1957, The Stepmother, 1958, Rhinoceros, 1960, Strip the Willow, 1960, The Rehearsal, 1961, The Private Ear and the Public Eye, 1962, Mary, Mary, 1963, Othello, 1964, Twelfth Night, 1952, Hay Fever, 1964, 1977, Master Builder, 1964, Much Ado About Nothing, 1965, 1980, Miss Julie, 1965, Black Comedy, 1965, Hedda Gabler, 1970, Three Sisters, 1970, 1976, Private Lives, 1972, 1974, 1978, Cleopatra, 1976, Way of the World, 1976, 1984—85, A Midsummer Night's Dream, 1977, Richard III, 1977, As You Like It, 1977, Macbeth, 1978, Night and Day, 1979—80, Virginia, 1980, Interpreters, 1985—86, Lettice and Lovage, 1987—88 (Tony award for Best Actress, 1990), 1990, The Importance of Being Earnest, 1993, Three Tall Women, 1994—95, Bed Among the Lentils, 1996, A Delicate Balance, 1997—98, Lady in the Van, 1999—2000, Breath of Life, 2002—03, Talking Heads, 2004, The Lady from Dubuque, 2007, appearances at Old Vic, 1959—60, charter member Royal National Theatre, London, 1963—; actress: (films) Child in the House, 1956, Nowhere to Go, 1958, Go to Blazes, 1962, The VIPs, 1963, The Pumpkin Eater, 1964, Young Cassidy, 1965, Othello, 1965, The Honey Pot, 1967, Oh What a Lovely War, 1968, Hot Millions, 1968, The Prime of Miss Jean Brodie, 1969 (BAFTA award for Best Actress in a Leading Role, 1969, Academy award for Best Actress in a Leading Role, 1970), Travels with My Aunt, 1973, Love and Pain and the Whole Damn Thing, 1973, Murder by Death, 1976, Death on the Nile, 1978, California Suite, 1978 (Golden Globe award for Best Actress - Musical or Comedy, 1979, Academy award for Best Supporting Actress, 1979), Quartet, 1981, Clash of the Titans, 1981, Evil under the Sun, 1981, Better Late Than Never, 1982, The Missionary, 1983, A Private Function, 1984 (BAFTA award for Best Actress, 1984), A Room with a View, 1986 (BAFTA award for Best Supporting Actress, 1986, Golden Globe award for Best Performance by an Actress in a Supporting Role, 1986), The Lonely Passion of Judith Hearn, 1988 (BAFTA award for Best Actress, 1989), Paris by Night, 1988, Hook, 1991, Sister Act, 1992, The Secret Garden, 1993, Sister Act 2: Back in the Habit, 1993, Richard III, 1995, The First Wives Club, 1996, Washington Square, 1997, Tea with Mussolini, 1999 (BAFTA award for Best Supporting Actress, 2000), The Last September, 2000, Harry Potter and the Sorcerer's Stone, 2001, Gosford Park, 2001 (Screen Actors Guild award for Best Ensemble in a Motion Picture, 2002), Divine Secrets of Ya-Ya Sisterhood, 2002, Harry Potter and the Chamber of Secrets, 2002, Harry Potter and the Prisoner of Azkaban, 2004, Ladies in Lavender, 2004, Harry Potter and the Goblet of Fire, 2005, Keeping Mum, 2005, Harry Potter and the Order of the Phoenix, 2007, Becoming Jane, 2007, Harry Potter and the Half-Blood Prince, 2009, From Time to Time, 2009, Nanny McPhee Returns, 2010, (voice) Gnomeo & Juliet, 2011, Harry Potter and the Deathly Hallows: Part 2, 2011, The Best Exotic Marigold Hotel, 2011, Quartet, 2012, My Old Lady, 2014, The Second Best Exotic Marigold Hotel, 2015, The Lady in the Van, 2015, Sherlock Gnomes, 2018; (TV films) Night of the Plague, 1957, Boy Meets Girl, 1957, The Widower, 1958, The Curious Savage, 1958, Sunday Out of Season, 1958, A Phoenix Too Frequent, 1959, For Services Rendered, 1959, Guardian Angel, 1960, The Savages, 1961, Hay Fever, 1965, Penelope, 1965, Much Ado About Nothing, 1967, Home and Beauty, 1967, On Approval, 1968, Man and Superman, 1968, The Merchant of Venice, 1972, The Millionairess, 1972, Mrs. Silly, 1983, Lily in Love, 1983, Bed Among the Lentils, 1988 (BAFTA award for Best Actress, 1987), Memento Mori, 1992, Suddenly Last Summer, 1992, Curtain Call, 1998, David Copperfield, 1999, All the King's Men, 1999, My House in Umbria, 2003 (Emmy award for Best Actress Miniseries or Movie, 2003), Capturing Mary, 2007; (TV series) Downton Abbey, 2010—15 (Screen Actors Guild award for Outstanding Performance by a Female Actor in a Drama Series, 2010, 2014, Emmy award for Best Actress Miniseries or Movie, 2011, Emmy award for Outstanding Supporting Actress in a Drama Series, 2012, 2016, Golden Globe award for Best Performance by an Actress in a Supporting Role in a Series, Mini-series or Motion Picture Made for TV, 2013), Nothing Like a Dame, 2017 **AW:** Recipient Hanbury Shakespeare prize, FVS Foundation 1991, Lifetime Achievement award, BAFTA, 1994, William Shakespeare award for Classical Theatre, Wahington, DC's Shakespeare Theatre, 1999, Special award, Laurence Olivier Theatre, 2010; decorated Commdr. British Empire, 1970, Dame of the British Empire, 1990; named to Theater Hall of Fame, 1994 **MEM:** Fellow: British Film Institute, British Academy Film & Television Arts

SMITH, MILAN DALE JR., T: Federal Judge **I:** Law and Legal Services **DOB:** 05/19/1942 **PB:** Pendleton **SC:** Oregon **ED:** JD, University Chicago, 1969; BA cum laude, Brigham Young University, 1966 **CT:** Bar: California 1970, DC 1972, US Supreme Court 1977, US Tax Court 1978. **C:** Judge, US Court Appeals (9th cir.), 2006-; Partner, Smith Crane Robinson & Parker LLP (formerly Smith & Hilbig LLP), Torrance, California, 1972-2006; Associate, O'Melveny & Myers LLP, L.A., 1969-72 **CIV:** President, Los Angeles State Office Building Authority, 1983-92, Informed Voters League, Torrance, 1975-77 vice chairman, board, Ettie Lee Homes for Youth, 1973-82, California Fair Employment and

Housing Commission, 1987-91 member, Cabinet of the Interfaith Coalition to Heal L.A., head economic devel. subcom., 1992-94 board of trustees, Deseret Trust Co. California, 2000-06 sec.-treas. Criminal Justice Legal Foundation, 1996-2005 chair, board of visitors, School of Religion, Claremont University, 2005-06 **AW:** National Honor scholar, 1966-69, University Chicago **MEM:** Member, Brigham Young University Alumni Association (board of directors (1982-86) **BA:** US Ct Appeals, 125 S Grand Ave, Pasadena, CA, 91105-1510

SMITH, NORMAN RANDY, T: Federal Judge **I:** Law and Legal Services **DOB:** 08/11/1949 **PB:** Logan **SC:** Utah **PT:** Son of Norman Busby and Patricia (Mendenhall) S.; Married La Dean Egbert, January 3, 1984. **ED:** JD, Brigham Young University, 1977; BS magna cum laude, Brigham Young University, 1974 **CT:** Bar: Idaho 1977, U.S. District Court Idaho 1977, U.S. Court Claims 1979, U.S. Tax Court 1978, U.S. Court Appeals (9th cir.) 1979, U.S. Supreme Court 1981. **C:** Judge, US Court Appeals (9th cir.), 2007-; Administrative district judge, Idaho 6th Judicial District, 2004-07; District judge, Idaho 6th Judicial District, 1995-2007; Partner, Merrill & Merrill, Pocatello, Idaho, 1984-95; Associate, Merrill & Merrill, Pocatello, Idaho, 1982-84; Assistant general counsel, J.R. Simplot Co., Boise, Idaho, 1977-82 **CR:** Adjunct professor, Boise St. University, 1979-81, Idaho State University, 1984- **CIV:** Party chairman Idaho Rep. Party, 1993-96 county chairman Bannock County Rep. Party, Pocatello, 1991-93 president Idaho State Civic Symphony, Pocatello, 1992-95, 98-99. **AW:** Named a Teacher of Year, College Business, 2005; named Idaho Statesman of Year, 2005; recipient George G. Granada award, Outstanding judge in Idaho, 2004 **MEM:** Member Idaho District Judges Association (president 1998-2000), Idaho Defense Counsel (president 1992-93), Defense Research Institute (del. Idaho state 1992-94, Exceptional Performance Citation 1993), 6th District Bar Association (president 1994-95), Rotary (Gate City president 1993-94). **H:** Golf, gardening, work **BA:** 95 7th St, Los Angeles, CA, 94103

SMITH, SHEPARD, T: Journalist **I:** Media & Entertainment **DOB:** 01/14/1964 **PB:** Holly Springs **SC:** MS/USA **PT:** David Shepard Smith; Dora Ellen (Anderson) Smith **ED:** Coursework, University of Mississippi **C:** Host, Shepard Smith Reporting, Fox News Channel (2013-Present); General Assignment, Senior Correspondent, Managing Editor, Breaking News Division, Fox News Channel, New York (1996-Present); Host, Studio B with Shepard Smith, Fox News Channel (2002-2013); Anchor, FOX Report, Fox News Channel (1999-2013); Correspondent, A Current Affair, Los Angeles, CA (1995); Reporter, Anchor, WSVN Channel 7, Miami, FL; Reporter, WCPX-TV, Orlando, FL; Reporter, WBBH-TV, Fort Myers, FL; Reporter, WCJB-TV, Gainesville, FL; Reporter, WJHG-TV, Panama City Beach, FL **CW:** Actor, "Volcano" (1977)

SMITH, STEVE, T: Drummer **I:** Media & Entertainment **PB:** Whitman **SC:** MA/USA **CW:** (Albums) (With Journey) Evolution, 1979, Departure, 1980, Dream, After Dream, 1980, Captured, 1981, Escape, 1981, Frontiers, 1983, Raised on Radio, 1986, Trial By Fire, 1996, (With Vital Information) Vital Information, 1983, Orion, 1984, Global Beat, 1987, Fiafiaga, 1988, Vitalive!, 1991, Easier Done than Said, 1992, Ray of Hope, 1996, Where We Come From, 1998, Live Around the World, 2000, Live from Mars, 2001, Show Em Where You Live, 2002, Come on In, 2004, Vitalization, 2007, Live! One Great Night, 2012, Viewpoint, 2015, (Steps Ahead) Live in Tokyo, 1986, NYC, 1989, Yin-Yang, 1992, Steppin Out 2016, (Jazz Legacy) Live on Tour, Vol 1, 2008,

Live on Tour, Vol 2, 2009, (With Others) Ten(Y&T) 1990, The Storm(The Storm), 1990, Cause and Effect, 1998 **AW:** Rock and Roll Hall of Fame, 2017

SMITH, TINA FLINT, T: U.S. Senator from Minnesota **I:** Government Administration/Government Relations/Government Services **DOB:** 03/04/1958 **PB:** Albuquerque **ED:** MBA, Dartmouth College; Bachelor in Political Sci., Stanford University **C:** U.S. Senator from Minnesota, 2018-; Lieutenant governor, State of Minnesota, 2015-; Chief of staff to Mark Dayton, State of Minnesota, 2011-15; Chief of staff to R.T. Ryback, State of Minnesota,; Founder of marketing and communications firm,; Vice president external affairs, Planned Parenthood of Minnesota, North Dakota and South Dakota,; With, Trans-Alaskan Pipeline, Prudhoe Bay, Alaska, **PA:** Dfl

SMITH, TRACY K., T: Poet, Educator **I:** Writing and Editing **DOB:** 04/16/1972 **PB:** Falmouth **ED:** MFA in Creative Writing, Columbia University; BA, Harvard University **C:** Poet Laureate, 2017-Present; Academy Fellowship, 2014; Wallace Stegner Fellow in Poetry, Stanford University, 1997-1999; Assistant Professor, Creative Writing, Lewis Center for the Arts, Richard Stockton Bicentennial Preceptor, Princeton University; Bread Loaf Writers' Conference Fellow **CW:** Author, The Body's Question, 2003, Duende, 2007, Life on Mars, 2011; Contributor, (Book) Ordinary Light, 2015, Several Other Poems **AW:** Image Award for Outstanding Literary Work, National Association for the Advancement of Colored People; Grantee, Ludwig Vogelstein Foundation; Cave Canem Prize for the Best First Book by an African-American Poet, The Body's Question, 2002; Rona Jaffe Foundation Writer's Award, 2004; Whiting Writers' Award for Poetry, 2005; Duende, James Laughlin Award, Academy of American Poets, 2006, Essence Literary Award, 2008; Rolex Mentor and Protégé Arts Initiative, 2009-2011; Pulitzer Prize for Poetry, Life on Mars, 2012; National Book Award for Non-Fiction, 2015

SMITH, VERNON LOMAX, T: Economist, Educator **I:** Education/Educational Services **DOB:** 01/01/1927 **PB:** Wichita **SC:** KS/USA **PT:** Son of Vernon Chessman and Lula Belle Lomax Smith; **ED:** Doctor of Management (hon.), Purdue University, 1990; PhD in Economics, Harvard University, 1955; MA in Economics, University of Kansas, 1952; BSEE, California Institute Tech., 1949 **C:** Professor economics & law, George L. Argyros Endowed chair fin. and economics, Chapman University, Orange, California, 2008-; Professor economics & law, George Mason University, Fairfax, Virginia, 2001-08; McClelland/Regents' professor economics, University of Arizona, Tucson, 1998-2001; Professor economics, University of Arizona, Tucson, 1975-2001; Professor economics, University of Massachusetts, Amherst, 1968-75; Professor economics, Brown University, Providence, 1967-68; Krannert professor, Purdue University, West Lafayette, Ind., 1965-67; Professor, Purdue University, West Lafayette, Ind., 1961-65; Associate professor, Purdue University, West Lafayette, Ind., 1958-61; Assistant professor economics, Purdue University, West Lafayette, Ind., 1955-58 **CR:** Visiting Rasmuson chair economics University Alaska, Anchorage, 2003- board directors Political Economy Research Center, Bozeman, Montana, 2004- Hooker distinguished visiting professor McMaster University, Canada, 1988 visiting professor California Institute Tech., 1974-75, University Southern California, 1974-75, Stanford University, 1961-62 research consultant RAND Corp., Santa Monica, California, 1957-59 **CIV:** President, International Foundation Research

Experimental Economics, 1997- Member selection committee, Frank E. Seidman Distinguished Award in Political Economy, 1993-96 **CW:** Contributing editor Business Scope, 1957-62, member board editors Am. Economic Rev., 1969-72, Sci., 1988-91; associate editor Journal Economic Behavior and Organization, 1985 **AW:** Recipient Nobel prize in economics, 2002, Distinguished Alumni award, California Institute Tech., 1996 **MEM:** Fellow: American Association for the Advancement of Science, Am. Academy Arts & Scis., Econometric Society; mem.: National Academy of Sciences, Pub. Choice Society (president 1988-90), Southern Economic Association (vice president 1985-86), Economic Sci. Association (founding president 1986-87, vice president 1987-89), Association Private Enterprise Education (president 1997, Adam Smith award 1995), Am. Economic Association, Western Economic Association (vice president 1988-89, pres.-elect 1989-90, president 1990-91) **BA:** Chapman University, 1 University Drive, Wilkinson Hall 103, Orange, CA, 92866

SMITH, WAYNE THOMAS, T: Hospital Healthcare Services Company Executive **I:** Medicine & Health Care **DOB:** 01/29/1946 **ED:** Postgrad., King's Fund College Hospital Administration; Master in Hospital Administration, Trinity University; MS, Auburn Univ, 1969; BS, Auburn Univ, 1968 **C:** Chairman board, Community Health Systems, Brentwood, Tennessee, 2001-; President CEO, Community Health Systems, Brentwood, Tennessee, 1996-; Retired, Humana, Inc., 1996; Executive vice president, Humana Health Care Operations, Louisville, 1991-96; Also board directors, Humana Inc, Louisville,; President, COO group health division, Humana Inc, Louisville, 1986-96; Executive vice president, Humana Inc, Louisville, 1985-86; Senior vice president, Humana Inc, Louisville, 1980-85; Vice president central hospital region, Humana Inc, Louisville, 1978-80; With, Humana Inc, Louisville, 1973-96; With, Trinity Univ, 1971-73 **CR:** Executive vice president health plan operations, board directors Humana Health Plan, Inc., Louisville president Humana Health Insurance Nevada, Inc., Humana Health Plan Florida, Inc., Humana Health Plan Ohio, Inc., Humana Health Chicago Insurance Co., Humana Kansas City, Inc. president, COO Humana Health Plan Texas, Prime Health Management Services president, board directors HMPK, Inc. board directors Praxair, Inc. chairman board Federation Am.'s Hospitals **CIV:** Board directors Gov.'s Scholars Program, Kentucky, Actors Theatre of Louisville, Kentucky Center for the Arts, The Louisville Orchestra board overseers University Louisville member executive committee Greater Louisville Fund for the Arts past chair board directors Louisville Collegiate School With U.S. Army, 1969-73, captain, 1973. **AW:** Named America's Top Healthcare CEO, 2010, by Institutional Investor; named a Healthcare Hero, Nashville Business Journal, 2011. **MEM:** Member Group Health Association Am. (board directors), Health Insurance Association Am. (board directors). **BA:** Community Health Sys, 4000 Meridian Blvd, Franklin, TN, 37067

SMITH, WILL, T: Actor, Film Producer, Rapper **I:** Media & Entertainment **DOB:** 09/25/1968 **PB:** Philadelphia **SC:** PA/USA **PT:** Willard Smith, Caroline Smith **SPN:** Jada Koren Pinkett, 12/31/1997; Sheree Zampino, 5/9/1992, Divorced 12/10/1995 **CH:** Trey, Jaden Christopher Syre, Willow Camille Reign **C:** Partner, Overbrook Entertainment **CW:** Rapper, (Albums) (As the Fresh Prince With DJ Jazzy Jeff) And In This Corner..., 1989, Homebase, 1991, Rock the House, 1987, He's the DJ, I'm the Rapper, 1988, Code Red, 1993, Big Willie Style, 1997, Willennium, 1999, Maximum Will Smith, 2000, Born to Reign,

2002, Greatest Hits, 2002, Lost and Found, 2005, (Songs) Just One of Those Days, 1987, Girls Ain't Nothing But Trouble, 1988, Brand New Funk, 1988, A Nightmare on My Street, 1988, Parents Just Don't Understand, 1988, Jazzy's Groove, 1989, I Think I Can Beat Mike Tyson, 1989, The Things That U Do, 1991, Summertime, 1991, Ring My Bell, 1991, I'm Looking for the One (To Be With Me), 1993, Boom! Shake the Room, 1993; Actor, Executive Producer, Writer, (TV Series) All of Us, 2003; Actor, Executive Producer, (Films) I, Robot, 2004; Actor, Producer, Writer, (Films) After Earth, 2013; Actor, Producer, (Films) Hitch, 2005, The Pursuit of Happyness, 2006; Actor, (TV Series) The Fresh Prince of Bel-Air, 1990-1996, (Voice Actor) Happily Ever After: Fairy Tales for Every Child, 1995, (TV Appearances) Blossom, 1991, (Films) Where the Day Takes You, 1992, Made in America, 1993, Six Degrees of Separation, 1993, Bad Boys, 1995, Independence Day, 1996, Men in Black, 1997, Welcome to Hollywood, 1998, Enemy of the State, 1998, Wild Wild West, 1999, The Legend of Bagger Vance, 2000, Ali, 2001, Men in Black II, 2002, Bad Boys II, 2003, (Voice Actor) Shark Tale, 2004, I Am Legend, 2007, Hancock, 2008, Seven Pounds, 2008, Men in Black 3, 2012, Winter's Tale, 2014, Focus, 2015, Concussion, 2015, Suicide Squad, 2016, Collateral Beauty, 2016; Executive Producer, (Films) Showtime, 2002, The Seat Filler, 2004, (Documentaries) Free Angela and All Political Prisoners, 2012, (TV Series) The Fresh Prince of Bel-Air, 1994-1996; Producer, (Films) Saving Face, 2004, ATL, 2006, The Secret Life of Bees, 2008, Lakeview Terrace, 2008, The Karate Kid, 2010, This Means War, 2012, Annie, 2014, Focus, 2015, Concussion, 2015, Suicide Squad, 2016, Collateral Beauty, 2016, Bright, 2017, Aladdin, (TV Series) The Queen Latifah Show, 2013 **AW:** Grammy Award for Best Rap Performance, Parents Just Don't Understand, 1989, Grammy Award for Best Rap Performance By a Duo or Group, Summertime, 1992, Blockbuster Entertainment Award for Favorite Actor - Sci-Fi, Independence Day, 1996, MTV Movie Award for Best Fight, Best Movie Song, Blockbuster Entertainment Award for Favorite Actor - Sci-Fi, Men in Black, 1997, Special International Box Office Achievement Award, 1997, ShoWest Convention Awards Actor of the Year, 1999, BET Award for Best Actor, 2002, 50 Most Powerful People in Hollywood, 2004-2006, American Music Award, Favorite Male Artist, 2005, The 100 Most Influential People, Time Magazine, 2006, Choice Movie Actor: Drama, Teen Choice Awards, The Pursuit of Happyness, 2007, The Top 25 Entertainers of the Year, Entertainment Weekly, 2007, The 50 Smartest People in Hollywood, 2007, The 100 Most Powerful Celebrities, Forbes.com, 2007-2008, Best Male Performance, MTV Movie Awards, 2008, Choice Movie Actor: Horror/Thriller, Teen Choice Awards, I Am Legend, 2008, The Ten Most Fascinating People, Barbara Walters, 2008, Power 150, Ebony Magazine, 2008, People's Choice Award for Favorite Male Action Star, Favorite Male Movie Star, 2009, National Association for the Advancement of Colored People Image Award for Outstanding Actor in a Motion Picture, Seven Pounds, 2009 **BA:** Creative Artists Agency, 2000 Avenue of the Stars, Los Angeles, CA, 90210

SMITHIES, OLIVER, T: Geneticist, Educator **I:** Education/Educational Services **DOB:** 06/23/1925 **PB:** Halifax **SC:** England **ED:** DSc (hon.), University of São Paulo, 2008; DSc (hon.), Duke University, Durham, North Carolina, 2004; DSc (hon.), University of Chicago, 1991; MA, PhD in Biochemistry, Balliol College, Oxford University, England, 1951 **C:** Excellence professor pathology and laboratory medicine, University of North Carolina School of Medicine, Chapel Hill, 1988-; Hilldale professor genetics & medical genetics, University of Wisconsin-Madison, 1980-88; Leon J. Cole professor genetics & medical genetics, University of Wisconsin-Madison, 1971-80; Professor, University of Wisconsin-Madison, 1963-71; Associate professor, University of Wisconsin-Madison, 1961-63; Assistant professor genetics, University of Wisconsin-Madison, 1960-61; Postdoc. fellow in physical chemistry, University of Wisconsin-Madison, 1951-53 **CR:** Member national adv. medical scis. council National Institutes of Health, 1985-90 research assistant, associate Connaught Medical Research Laboratory, Toronto, Canada, 1953-60 **CW:** Contributor, Articles, Professional Journals **AW:** Recipient Nobel prize in physiology/medicine, 2007, Wolf prize in medicine, Israel, 2003, Massry prize, 2002, Oliver Max Gardner award, University North Carolina, 2002, Albert Lasker award for basic medical research, 2001, International Okamoto award, Japan Vascular Disease Research Foundation, 2000, Bristol-Meyers Squibb award for distinguished achievement in cardiovasc./metabolic disease research, 1997, CIBA award, Am. Heart Association, 1996, Alfred P. Sloan award, GM Foundation Cancer Research Foundation, 1994, North Carolina award for sci., 1993, Gairdner Foundation International award, 1993, 1990, Karl Landsteiner Memorial award, Am. Association Blood Banks, 1984, William Allen Memorial award, Am. Society Human Genetics, 1964 **MEM:** Fellow: American Association for the Advancement of Science; mem.: National Academy of Sciences, Royal Society London (foreign), Institute Medicine, Genetics Society America (vice president 1974, president 1975), Am. Academy Arts & Scis. **BA:** U NC Dept Pathology & Lab Medicine, CB #7525 Brinkhous Bullitt Bldg, Chapel Hill, NC, 27599

SMOOT, GEORGE FITZGERALD III, T: Astrophysicist **I:** Sciences **DOB:** 02/20/1945 **PB:** Yukon **SC:** FL/USA **ED:** PhD in Physics, Massachusetts Institute of Technology (1970); BS in Math and Physics, Massachusetts Institute of Technology (1966) **C:** Professor of Physics, University of California, Berkeley (2010-Present); Professor of Physics, Paris Diderot University (2010-Present); Anne Pao Sohmen Professor at Large, IAS Hong Kong University of Science (2016-Present); Research Physicist, Lawrence Berkeley Laboratory (1974-Present); Professor, Physics, University of California, Berkeley, CA (1994-Present); Research Physicist, Space Sciences Laboratory, University of California, Berkeley, CA (1971-Present); Research Physicist, Massachusetts Institute of Technology (1970) **CR:** Team Leader, Differential Microwave Radiometer Experiment, COBE (Cosmic Background Explorer) Satellite; Member, Steering Group on Cosmic Background Explorer Satellite; Principal Investigator on Isotrophy Experiment, NASA (1975, 1980); Member, Management and Operations Working Group for Shuttle Astronomy (1976-1980); Member, Advisory Committee, White Mountain Research Station (1982); Member, Superconducting Magnet Facility for the Space Station Study Team (1985); Member, Center for Particle Astrophysics, University of California, Berkeley (1988); Member, Advisory Committee, Radio Astronomy Laboratory (1990) **CW:** Contributor, Articles to Professional Journals; Co-author, "Wrinkles in Time" (1993) **AW:** Space/Missiles Laurels Award, Aviation Week & Space Technology (1992); Popular Science Award (1992); Distinguished Scientist, ARCS Foundation, Inc. (1993); Kirby Award (1993); Golden Plate Award (1994); Ernesto Orlando Lawrence Award, US Department of Energy (1994); Einstein Medal (2003); Grober Prize with John Mather (2006); Daniel Chalonge Medal (2006); Co-recipient, Nobel Prize in Physics (2006); Oersted Medal (2009); $1 Million Dollar Grand Prize Winner, Game Show Contestant, "Are You Smarter Than a Fifth Grader?" (2009) **MEM:** International Astronomical Union; Committee on the Safety Commercial Nuclear Reactors, American Physical Society (1974-1975); American Astronomical Society; Sigma Xi; American Association for the Advancement of Science **BA:** Lawrence Berkeley Nat Lab 1, Cyclotron Rd 50 5008, Berkeley, CA, 94720

SMUCKER, LLOYD K., T: U.S. Representative from California **I:** Government Administration/Government Relations/Government Services **PT:** Son of Daniel S. and Arie Smucker; **ED:** Attended, Lebanon Valley College, Annville, Pennsylvania; Attended, Franklin and Marshall College, Lancaster, Pennsylvania **C:** U.S. House of Representatives from Pennsylvania's 16th District, 2017-; Member District 13, Pennsylvania State Senate, 2008-16; Member, West Lampeter Township Planning Commission,; Former township supervisor, West Lampeter Township,; Operator for several years, Smucker Co. (family owned construction firm),; Commercial construction business owner,; Former consultant to start-up company **PA:** Republican **BA:** 516 Cannon HOB, Washington, DC, 20515

SNABES, SAMANTHA, T: Co-Founder of Re:3D **I:** Business Management/Business Services **ED:** MBA, Supply Chain Management, University of Michigan; BA, BS, Biology, International Studies, Hispanic Studies, University of Michigan **C:** Co-Founder, Re3d,2013-; Captain, Mississippi Air National Guard, 2010-; Social Entrepreneur in Residence, Open Innovation Program at NASA, 2012-13; Strategist, Wyle Integrated Science and Engineering Group, 2009-12; Vice President, Bioflow Technology, 2006-09 **BA:** Re3d, 1100 Hercules Ave Suite 220, Houston, TX, 77058

SNIPES, WESLEY, T: Actor, Producer **I:** Media & Entertainment **DOB:** 07/31/1962 **PB:** Orlando **SC:** FL/USA **ED:** BFA, Florida, 1985; Student, Southwest College; BFA, State University of New York, Purchase, 1985; Student, High School of Performing Arts, Fiorello H. LaGuardia High School of Music & Art and Performing Arts **CW:** Actor, (Broadway Plays) Boys Of Winter, Execution Of Justice, Death And King's Horsemen, (Films) Wildcats, 1986, Streets Of Gold, 1986, Critical Condition, 1987, Mo'Better Blues, 1989, Major League, 1989, King Of New York, 1990, New Jack City, 1991, Jungle Fever, 1991, The Waterdance, 1992, White Men Can't Jump, 1992, Passenger 57, 1992, Rising Sun, 1993, Demolition Man, 1993, Boiling Point, 1993, Sugar Hill, 1994, Drop Zone, 1994, To Wong Foo, Thanks For Everything, Julie Newmar, 1995, The Money Train, 1995, The Fan, 1996, Murder At 1600, 1997, U.S. Marshals, 1998, One Night Stand, 1998, Play It To The Bone, 1999, Liberty Stands, 2002, Zigzag, 2002, Unstoppable, 2004, Chaos, 2006, The Detonator, 2006, Hard Luck, 2006, The Contractor, 2007, Brooklyn's Finest, 2010, Game Of Death, 2010, Gallowwalkers, 2012, The Expendables 3, 2014, Chi-Raq, 2015, Armed Response, 2017, The Recall, 2017, (TV Series) H.E.L.P., 1990, The Real Malcolm X, 1992, America's Dream, 1996, The Player, 2015, (TV Films) Future Sport, 1998, Disappearing Acts, 2000, (TV Appearances) Miami Vice, 1986, Vietnam War Story, 1987, A Man Called Hawk, 1989, The Days And Nights Of Molly Dodd, 1989, The Bernie Mac Show, 2003; Actor, Producer, (Films) Blade, 1998, Blade II, 2002, Blade: Trinity, 2004; Actor, Executive Producer, (Films) Art Of War, 2000, Undisputed, 2002; Producer, (Films) The Big Hit, 1998, Down In The Delta, 1998, Dr. Ben, 2001; Executive Producer, (Documentaries) Revelations Of The Mayans: 2012 And Beyond,

2012 **AW:** Star, Hollywood Walk of Fame, 1998, National Association For The Advancement Of Colored People Image Award For Best Actor In A TV Movie/Series, America's Dream, 1997, National Association For The Advancement Of Colored People Image Award For Outstanding Lead Actor In A Motion Picture, New Jack City, 1993

SNYDER, RICK, T: Governor of Michigan, Venture Capitalist, Lawyer **I:** Government Administration/Government Relations/Government Services **DOB:** 08/19/1958 **PB:** Battle Creek **SC:** MI/USA **ED:** JD, University of Michigan, 1982; MBA with distinction, University of Michigan, 1979; BA in General Studies with distinction, University of Michigan, 1977 **CT:** CPA; bar: Michigan **C:** Governor, State of Michigan, Lansing, 2011-; Founder, chairman, CEO, Ardesta, LLC, Ann Arbor, Michigan, 2000-10; President, Avalon Investments, 1997-2000; Interim CEO, Gateway, Inc., Irvine, California, 2006; Chairman, Gateway, Inc., Irvine, California, 2005-07; President, COO, Gateway, Inc., Irvine, California, 1996-97; Executive vice president, Gateway, Inc., Irvine, California, 1991-97; Partner, Coopers & Lybrand, 1988-91; Accountant, Coopers & Lybrand, 1982-88 **CR:** Board of Directors Gateway, Inc., 1991-2007 Adjunct Professor, accounting University of Michigan, 1982-84 **CIV:** Member visiting committee, Purdue Univ. School Engineering, Member adv. board, NanoBus. Alliance, Member adv. board, Samuel Zell & Robert H. Lurie Institute for Entrepreneurial Studies, Member, Governor e-Mich. Adv. Council, Member tech. transfer national adv. committee, University Michigan, Board member, University Michigan College Engineering National Adv. Committee, Trustee, The Henry Ford, Member, The Nature Conservancy, Michigan Chapter, Chairman, Ann Arbor SPARK, **MEM:** Mem.: Michigan Bar Association **PA:** Republican **BA:** Office of Rick Snyder, 234 West Baraga Avenue, Marquette, MI, 49855

SODERBERGH, STEVEN ANDREW ANDREW, T: Film Producer, Director, Screenwriter **I:** Media & Entertainment **DOB:** 06/02/1905 **PB:** Atlanta **SC:** Atlanta **PT:** Son of Peter Andrew and Mary Ann (Bernard) S.; **SPN:** Married Elizabeth Jeanne Brantley, December 1, 1989 (div. October 1994), Married Jules Asner, May 10, 2003. **CH:** 1 child, Sarah; **CW:** Writer, director, editor: (films) Sex, Lies, and Videotape, 1989 (Palme d'Or award Cannes Film Festival 1989), King of the Hill, 1993, Schizopolis, 1996, Solaris, 2002; director, editor: (film) Kafka, 1991, Bubble, 2006; executive prodr.: (films) Suture, 1994, Good Night and Good Luck, 2005, The Big Empty, 2005 Syriana, 2005, Rumor Has It..., 2005, PU-239, 2006, I'm Not There, 2007, Wind Chill, 2007, Michael Clayton, 2007, Solitary Man, 2009, Rebecca H. (Return to the Dogs), 2010, We Need to Talk About Kevin, 2011, (documentaries) Roman Polanski: Wanted and Desired, 2008, Playground, 2009, Roman Polanski: Odd Man Out, 2012; prodr.: The Daytrippers, 1997, Pleasantville, 1998; dir.: (films) The Underneath, 1995, Gray's Anatomy, 1996, Out of Sight, 1998, The Limey, 1999, Erin Brokovich, 2000, Traffic, 2000, Ocean's Eleven, 2001, Full Frontal, 2002, The Good German, 2006, Ocean's Thirteen, 2007, The Girlfriend Experience, 2009, The Informant!, 2009, The Last Time I Saw Michael Gregg, 2011, Contagion, 2011, Haywire, 2011, Magic Mike, 2012,The Hunger Games, 2012 Side Effects, 2013, Behind the Candelabra, 2013, Citizenfour, 2014, Da Sweet Blood of Jesus, 2014, Magic Mike XXL, 2015, Logan Lucky, 2017, Ocean's 8, 2018, Unsane, 2018 (TV films) Behind the Candelabra, 2013 (Emmy award for Outstanding Directing for a Miniseries, Movie or Dramatic Special, 2013); director, prodr.: (films):

Ocean's Twelve, 2004, Bubble, 2006, Che, 2008; writer: (film) Nightwatch, 1998; director, prodr.: (TV series) K St., 2003, Unscripted, 2005, Read Oaks, 2014, The Knick, 2014, The Girlfriend Experience, 2016, Godless, 2017, Mosaic, 2018 **AW:** Named a WIRED Renegade, WIRED Rave Awards, 2006 **MEM:** Member AMPAS, Directors Guild Am. (vice president) **PA:** Democrat

SOLOMONOV, MICHAEL, T: Chef and Restaurateur **I:** Food & Restaurant Services **PB:** Savyon **SC:** Israel **C:** Owner/Chef, Zahav, 2008- **CW:** (Book) Zahav: A World of Israeli Cuisine, 2015 **AW:** James Beard Award for Best Chef Mid-Atlantic, 2011, Cookbook of the Year, 2016, Outstanding Chef 2017

SOLOWAY, JILL, T: Comedian **I:** Media & Entertainment **PB:** Chicago **SC:** IL/USA **ED:** Diploma, Communications Arts, University of Wisconsin–Madison **CW:** Producer, Television, "Six Feet Under" (2001-2005); Director, "I Love Dick" (2016); Creator, "Transparent" (2014); Author, Novel, "Jodi K" (2005) **AW:** Named to TIME's 100 Most Influential, TIME Magazine (2015); Golden Globe for Best Comedy (2015)

SORENSON, ARNIE, T: CEO **I:** Leisure, Travel & Tourism **CN:** Marriott **PB:** Tokyo **SC:** Japan **ED:** JD, University of Minnesota, 1983; BA, Luther College, 1980 **C:** President/CEO, Marriott Intl Inc, 2012-; President/COO, Marriott Intl Inc, 2009-2012; VP/Pres:Lodging/CFO, Marriott Intl Inc, 2003-2009; Exec VP/CFO, Marriott Intl Inc, 1998-2003 **MEM:** Board Member, Luther College; Board Member, Microsoft Corp, 2017-

SORKIN, AARON, T: Writer **I:** Writing and Editing **DOB:** 05/31/1905 **PB:** New York City **SC:** New York City **ED:** BFA in Musical Theatre, Syracuse University; Student, State University of New York, Purchase **CW:** Creator, producer (TV series) Sports Nights, 1998-2000 (Humanitas prize, 1999); creator, writer, executive prodr.: TV series The West Wing, 1999-2003 (Emmy award for Best for Outstanding Writing in a Drama Series, 2000, 2001, 2002, 2003, Humanitas prize, 2000, 2002, Writer Guild Am. award, 2001, Television Producer of the Year Producers Guild Am. Golden Laurel award, 2002); creator, writer, executive producer (TV series) Studio 60 on the Sunset Strip, 2006-07, The Newsroom, 2012; writer: screenplays A Few Good Men, 1992, writer: screenplays Malice, 1993, writer: screenplays Charlie Wilson's War, 2007, writer: screenplays Moneyball, 2011 (New York Film Critics Cir. award for Best Screenplay, 2011, Boston Society Film Critics award for Best Screenplay, 2011, Critics' Choice award for Best Adapted Screenplay, 2012); writer (screenplays) Steve Jobs, 2015 (Golden Globe award for Best Screenplay - Motion Picture, 2016), Molly's Game, 2017; (writer): (films) The American President, 1995; (writer, executive producer, actor) The Social Network, 2010 (Golden Globe award for Best Screenplay-Motion Picture, 2011, Academy award for Best Writing (Adapted Screenplay), 2011, National Board Review award for Best Adapted Screenplay, 2010, Boston Society Film Critics award for Best Screenplay, 2010, Writers Guild award for Best Adapted Screenplay, 2011, Critics' Choice award for Best Original Screenplay, 2011); writer: Broadway plays A Few Good Men, 1989 (Outer Critics Circle award as Outstanding American Playwright, 1989), writer: Broadway plays Hidden in this Picture, 1990, writer: Broadway plays Making Movies, 1992, The Farnsworth Invention, 2007

SOROS, GEORGE, T: Hedge Fund Manager, Entrepreneur, Philanthropist **I:** Business Management/Business Services **DOB:** 08/12/1930 **PB:** Budapest **SC:** Hungary **ED:** BS, London School of Economics, 1952; Honorary DCL, University of Oxford, England, 1980; Honorary LLD, New School for Social Research, New York, NY, 1990; Honorary LHD, Yale University, New Haven, CT, 1991; Honorary Degree, University of Bologna, Italy, 1995; Honorary Degree, Corvinus University, Budapest, Hungary **C:** Chairman, Soros Fund Management, LLC, New York, NY, 1996—Present; Co-Founder, Principal Advisor, Quantum Fund, Soros Fund Management, LLC, 1970—Present; Founder, Soros Fund Management, LLC, New York, NY, 1969—Present; Vice President, Arnhold & S. Bleichroeder, New York, NY, 1963-1973; Analyst, Wertheim & Co., New York, NY, 1959-1963; Arbitrage Trader, F.M. Mayer, New York, NY, 1956-1959 **CIV:** Chairman, Open Society Fund, 1981; Chairman, Founding President, Central European University, Budapest, Hungary, 1991; Board of Directors, Center for American Progress, Washington, DC, 2003; Founder, Chairman Open Society Institute, 1993—Present **CW:** Author, (Books) The Alchemy of Finance, 1987, Opening The Soviet System, 1990, Underwriting Democracy, 1991, Soros On Soros: Staying Ahead Of The Curve, 1995, The Crisis Of Global Capitalism: Open Society Endangered, 1998, Open Society: Reforming Global Capitalism, 2000, George Soros On Globalization, 2002, The Bubble Of America Supremacy: Correcting The Misuse Of American Power, 2004, The Age Of Fallibility: Consequences Of The War On Terror, 2006, The New Paradigm For Financial Markets: The Credit Crisis Of 2008 And What It Means, 2008, The Soros Lectures: At The Central European University, 2011, Financial Turmoil In Europe And The U.S.: Essays, 2012; Appearance, (Documentaries) Inside Job, 2010 **AW:** International Center for Finance Award, Yale School of Management, 2000, New York's Influentials, New York Magazine, 2006, The 50 Most Influential People in Global Finance, Bloomberg Markets, 2011, World's Richest People, Forbes Magazine, 1999—Present, The Forbes 400: Richest Americans, 1999—Present **MEM:** Royal Institute of International Affairs, London, England; Council on Foreign Relations **H:** Tennis, Skiing, Chess, Backgammon **PA:** Democrat **BA:** 400 W 59th Street, New York, NY, 10019

SOTO, DARREN, T: U.S. Representative from Florida **I:** Government Administration/Government Relations/Government Services **DOB:** 02/25/1978 **PB:** Ringwood **ED:** JD, George Washington University Law School, 2004; BA in Economic, Rutgers University, 2000 **C:** Member, U.S House of Representatives from Florida's 9th District, 2017; Member, Committee on Agriculture, Committee on Natural Resources; Member District 49, Florida House of Reps., 2007-2017; President, D. Soto Law Offices, 2005-; Member criminal and civil justice appropriations committee, energy and utilities policy committee, Florida House of Reps.,; Ranking member civil justice and courts policy committee, Florida House of Reps.,; Summer associate, L.A. Gonzalez Law Offices, 2002-04; Fin. analyst, Prudential Insurance, 1998-2001 **CIV:** Member, City of Orlando Civil Service Board, 2006- Member, Hispanic C. of C. Metropolitan Orlando, 2006- **MEM:** Mem.: Orange County Democrats (treasurer 2007), Orange County Young Democrats (vice president communications 2007) **PA:** Democrat **BA:** 1429 Longworth House Office Building, Washington, DC, 20515

SOTOMAYOR, SONIA MARIA, **T:** Associate Justice of the U.S. Supreme Court **I:** Law and Legal Services **DOB:** 06/25/1954 **PB:** South Bronx **SC:** New York **PT:** Daughter of Juan and Celina (Baez) Sotomayor; **ED:** LLD (hon.), Yale University, 2013; LLD (hon.), New York University, 2012; LLD (hon.), St. Lawrence University, 2010; LLD (hon.), Howard University, 2010; LLD (hon.), Northeastern University School Law, 2007; LLD (hon.), Hofstra University, 2006; LLD (hon.), Pace University, 2003; LLD (hon.), Princeton University, 2001; LLD (hon.), Brooklyn Law School, 2001; LLD (hon.), Herbert H. Lehman College, 1999; JD, Yale Law School, New Haven, 1979; BA summa cum laude, Princeton University, New Jersey, 1976 **CT:** Bar: US District Court (eastern & southern district) New York 1984, New York 1980 **C:** Associate justice, US Supreme Court, Washington, 2009-; Judge, US Court Appeals (2nd cir.), New York City, 1998-2009; Judge, US District Court (southern district) New York, New York City, 1992-98; Partner, Pavia & Harcourt, New York City, 1988-92; Associate, Pavia & Harcourt, New York City, 1984-87; Assistant district attorney, New York County, New York City, 1979-84 **CR:** Lecturer law Columbia Law School, 1999- adjunct professor New York University School Law, 1998-2007 **CIV:** Board member, Maternity Center Association, New York City, 1985-86 Member, New York State Adv. Panel Inter-Group Relations, 1990-92 Trustee, Princeton University, 2006-11 Board directors, New York City Campaign Fin. Board, New York City, 1988-92 Board directors, State of New York Mortgage Agency, New York City, 1987-92 Board directors, Puerto Rican Legal Defense & Education Fund, New York City, 1980-92 **CW:** Author: My Beloved World: A Memoir, 2013 **AW:** Co-recipient M. Taylor Pyne prize, Princeton University, 1976; named one of The 10 Most Powerful Women in Washington, Fortune magazine, 2010, Washington's Most Influential Women Lawyers, The National Law Journal, 2010, The 100 Most Influential People in the World, TIME magazine, 2010, The 100 Most Powerful Women in DC, Washingtonian magazine, 2011, 2009, The World's 100 Most Powerful Women, Forbes magazine, 2010, 2009; recipient Outstanding Latino Professional award, Latino/a Law Students Association, 2006 **MEM:** Mem.: American Bar Association, American Philosophical Society, Association Hispanic Judges, American Philosophical Society, New York Women's Bar Association, Puerto Rican Bar Association, Hispanic Bar Association, Phi Beta Kappa **ACH:** Achievements include becoming the first Hispanic to serve on the U.S. Supreme Court, 2009 **BA:** US Supreme Court, 1 First St NE, Washington, DC, 20543

SOUTER, DAVID HACKETT, **T:** retired U.S. Supreme Court Justice **I:** Government Administration/Government Relations/Government Services **DOB:** 09/17/1939 **PB:** Melrose **SC:** Massachusetts **PT:** Son of Joseph Alexander and Helen Adams (Hackett) Souter **ED:** BA, MA in Jurisprudence, Oxford University, 1989; LLD (hon.), Harvard University, 2010; LLB, Harvard University, 1966; BA, Harvard University, 1961 **CT:** Bar: New Hampshire 1967 **C:** Associate justice, US Supreme Court, Washington, 1990-2009; Judge, US Court Appeals (1st Cir.), New Hampshire, 1990; Associate justice, New Hampshire Supreme Court, 1983-90; Associate justice, New Hampshire Superior Court, 1978-83; Attorney general, State of New Hampshire, 1976-78; Deputy attorney general, State of New Hampshire, 1971-76; Assistant attorney general, State of New Hampshire, 1968-71; Associate, Orr & Reno, Concord, New Hampshire, 1966-68 **CR:** Member New Hampshire Governor's Commission Crime and Delinquency, 1979-83, 1976-78, New Hampshire

Judicial Council, 1976-78, New Hampshire Police Standards & Training Council, 1976-78, Maine-NH Interstate Boundary Commission, 1971 **CIV:** Overseer, Dartmouth Medical School, 1981-87; Vice president, New Hampshire Hist. Society, 1980-85; Trustee, New Hampshire Hist. Society, 2009-; Trustee, New Hampshire Hist. Society, 1976-85; President, Concord Hospital, 1978-84; Trustee, Concord Hospital, 1972-85 **AW:** Honorary fellow, Magdalen College, Oxford University, Rhodes scholar, 1963 **MEM:** Master: Gray's Inn (London) (hon.); fellow: American Academy Arts & Sciences, Massachusetts Historical Society, American College Trial Lawyers (hon.), American Bar Foundation (hon.); mem.: American Antiquarian Society, American Philosophical Society, New England Hist.-Geneal. Society (hon.), Pilgrim Society (hon.), Merrimack County Bar Association, New Hampshire Bar Association, Phi Beta Kappa **PA:** Republican **BA:** US Supreme Court, 1 First St NE, Washington, DC, 20543

SOUTHWICK, LESLIE H., **T:** Federal Judge **I:** Law and Legal Services **DOB:** 02/10/1950 **PB:** Edinburgh **SC:** Texas **PT:** Son of Lloyd M. and Ruth (Tarpley) S.; **SPN:** Married Sharon E. Polasek, August 18, 1973; **CH:** children: Philip, Catherine **ED:** JD, University Texas, 1975; BA cum laude, Rice University, 1972 **CT:** Bar: Texas 1975, Mississippi 1977 **C:** Judge, US Court Appeals (5th cir.), 2007-; Judge, Mississippi Court Appeals (District 4), 1995-2006; Deputy Assistant Attorney General Civil Division, US Department Justice, Washington, 1989-93; Partner, Brunini, Grantham, Grower & Hewes, Jackson, 1983-89; Associate, Brunini, Grantham, Grower & Hewes, Jackson, 1977-83; Law Clerk to Hon. Charles Clark, US Court Appeals (5th cir.), Jackson, Mississippi, 1976-77; Law Clerk to Hon. John F. Onion Junior, Texas Court Criminal Appeals, Austin, 1975-76 **CR:** Adjunct Professor Mississippi College School Law, Jackson, 1985-89, 98- Member Mississippi Constitution Study Commission, 1985-86. **CIV:** President Hinds County Mental Health Association, Jackson, 1981-82, Jackson Servant Leadership Corp. Mississippi campaign manager George Bush for President, 1980, 88 alternate del. Rep. National Convention, 1984, del., 1988 member State Rep. Executive Committee, 1988 **MIL:** Staff Judge Advocate, 2006, Deputy Staff Judge Advocate US Army, 2004-05 Mississippi Army National Guard, 1997-, Served in US Army Reserve, 1992-97 **CW:** Author: Presidential Also-Rans and Running Mates, 1984, 2nd edit, 1998 (American Library Association Best Reference Book award 1985). **AW:** Named Vol. of Year, Hinds County Mental Health Association, 1981, 85; Recipient Mississippi Bar Judicial Excellence Award, 2004 **MEM:** Member American Bar Association, Mississippi Bar Association Lodges. **BA:** John Minor Wisdom U.S. Court of Appeals Building Fifth Circuit, 600 Camp St, New Orleans, LA, 70130

SPACEK, SISSY, **T:** Actress **I:** Media & Entertainment **PB:** Quitman **SC:** TX/USA **PT:** Edwin Spacek; Virginia Spacek **MS:** Married **SPN:** Jack Fisk (April 12, 1974) **CH:** Schuyler Elizabeth; Virginia Madison **ED:** Attended, Lee Strasberg Theatrical Institute **CW:** Actress: (films) Prime Cut, 1972, Badlands, 1974, Carrie, 1976, Three Women, 1977, Welcome to L.A., 1977, Heartbeat, 1980, Coal Miner's Daughter, 1980 (Academy award Best Actress 1980, Golden Globe Best Actress 1980, LA Film Critics for Best Actress 1980, National Society Film Critics Best Actress 1980), Raggedy Man, 1981, Missing, 1982, The River, 1984, Marie, 1985, Night Mother, 1986, Crimes of the Heart, 1986 (Golden Globe Best Actress 1986), Violets Are Blue, 1986, JFK, 1991, The Long Walk Home,

1990, Hard Promises, 1992, Trading Mom, 1994, The Grass Harp, 1995, Affliction, 1997, Blast From the Past, 1998, Songs in Ordinary Time, 2000, In the Bedroom, 2001 (Best Actress in Drama Golden Globe 2001, Am. Film Institute award, Ind. Spirit award, Broadcast Critics award, Chicago Film Critics award, Florida Film Critics award, Golden Satellite award, Sundance Film Festival award, Southeastern Film award, New York Film Critics award, LA Film Critics award 2001), Last Call, 2002, Tuck Everlasting, 2002, A Home at the End of the World, 2004, Nine Lives, 2005, The Ring Two, 2005, Summer Racing: The Race to Cure Breast Cancer, 2005, North Country, 2005, An American Haunting, 2006, Gray Matters, 2006, Hot Rod, 2007, Lake City, 2008, Four Christmases, 2008, The Help, 2011, Deadfall, 2012, River of Gold, 2016, The Old Man and the Gun, 2018; (TV films) Straight Story, 1999, In the Bedroom, 2001 (Brit. Film Critics Choice award Best Actress 2001, Sundance Film Festival Special prize 2001, Golden Globe Best Actress 2001, Ind. Spirit award Best Female Lead 2001, AFI, Actress of Year 2001, LA Film Critics Best Actress 2001, New York Film Critics Best Actress 2001, Best Actress Academy award 2001), The Migrants, 1973, Katherine, 1975, Verna: United Service Organizations Girl, 1978, A Private Matter, 1992, A Place for Annie, 1994, The Good Old Boys, 1995, Streets of Laredo, 1995, If These Walls Could Talk, 1996, Beyond the Call, 1996, Songs in Ordinary Time, 2000, Midwives, 2001, Last Call, 2002, Appalachia: A History of Mountains and People, 2009, Gimme Shelter, 2010, Big Love, 2010, Bloodline, 2015-2017, Castle Rock, 2018; author: My Extraordinary Ordinary Life, 2012.

SPADE, KATE, **T:** Former Fashion Designer **I:** Apparel & Fashion **DOB:** 12/24/1962 **PB:** Kansas City, Missouri, December 24, 1962 **YOP:** 2018-06-05 **ED:** BA in Journalism and Broadcasting, Arizona State University, 1985 **C:** Co-founder, Kate Spade Home, 2004-; Co-founder, Jack Spade, 1999-; Designer, Kate Spade beauty, 2002-; Designer, Kate Spade shoe collection, 1999-; Designer, Kate Spade paper and social stationary, 1998-; Co-founder, designer, Kate Spade Inc. (formerly Kate Spade Handbags), New York City, 1993-; Designer, Kate Spade glasses, 2001; From assistant to senior fashion editor/head of accessories, Mademoiselle magazine, 1985-92 **CW:** Designer (uniforms) Song Airlines (subsidiary Delta Airlines), 2004 **AW:** Recipient Elle Decor International Design award for bedding, 2004, Am. Food & Entertaining award for Designer of Year, Bon Appetit, 2004, Giants of Design award for Tastemaker, House Beautiful, 2004, FiFi award for Best Fragrance in Ltd. Distribution, UK Fragrance Foundation, 2003, FiFi award for Bath & Body Star of Year, US Fragrance Foundation, 2003, Accessory Designer of Year, Council Fashion Designers of America, 1998, Perry Ellis award, New Fashion Talent, 1996, Entrepreneur Hall of Fame at the University of Missouri, 2017 **MEM:** Mem.: Kappa Kappa Gamma **ACH:** Achievements include stores opening in New York City in 1996, Boston and LA in 1998, and Chicago and San Francisco in 2000

SPADER, JAMES, **T:** Actor **I:** Media & Entertainment **DOB:** 05/24/1905 **PB:** Boston, **SC:** Boston, **PT:** Son of Todd and Jean Spader; **SPN:** Married Victoria Kheel, 1987 (div. 2004); **CH:** children: Sebastian, Elijah; 1 child (with Leslie Stefanson). **ED:** Student, Michael Chekhov Studio; Student, Phillips Academy **CW:** Actor: (films) Team Mates, 1978, Endless Love, 1981, The New Kids, 1985, Tuff Turf, 1985, Pretty in Pink, 1986, Mannequin, 1987, Wall Street, 1987, Less Than Zero, 1987, Baby Boom, 1987, Jack's Back, 1988, The Rachel Papers, 1989, Sex, Lies and Videotape, 1989, Bad Influence,

1990, White Palace, 1990, True Colors, 1991, Storyville, 1992, Bob Roberts, 1992, Music of Chance, 1993, Dream Lover, 1994, Wolf, 1994, Stargate, 1994, Two Days in the Valley, 1996, Crash, 1997, Keys to Tulsa, 1997, Critical Care, 1997, Curtain Call, 1999, Curtain Call, 1999, Supernova, 2000, The Watcher, 2000, Slow Burn, 2000, The Stickup, 2001, Speaking of Sex, 2001, Secretary, 2002, I Witness, 2003, Alien Hunter, 2003, Shadow of Fear, 2004, Shorts, 2009, Lincoln, 2012, The Homesman, 2014, Avengers: Age of Ultron (voice), 2015; (TV films) Cocaine: One Man's Seduction, 1983, Diner, 1983, A Killer in the Family, 1983, Family Secrets, 1984, Starcrossed, 1985, The Pentagon Papers, 2003; (TV series) The Family Tree, 1983, The Practice, 2003-04 (Emmy award for Outstanding Lead Actor in a Drama Series, 2004), Boston Legal, 2004-08 (Emmy award for Outstanding Lead Actor in a Drama Series, 2005, Emmy award for Outstanding Lead Actor in a Drama Series, 2007), The Office, 2011-12; (TV guest appearances) Frasier, 1994, Seinfeld, 1997; (plays) Race, 2009; actor, executive prodr.: (TV series)The Office, 2011, The Blacklist, 2013-

SPEARS, BRITNEY, T: singer **I:** Media & Entertainment **DOB:** 12/02/1981 **PB:** McComb **PT:** Daughter of Jamie and Lynne Spears; **C:** Entertainer, recording artist, 1992 **CR:** Designed limited edition collection for Candie's clothing brand, 2010 released signature fragrance Radiance, 2010, Circus Fantasy, 2009, Hidden Fantasy, 2009, Curious Heart, 2008, Midnight Fantasy, 2007, Curious In Control, 2006, Britney Spears: Fantasy, 2005, Curious Britney Spears, 2004 **CIV:** Founder, supporter, Britney Spears Foundation, 1999- **CW:** Singer: (albums) ...Baby One More Time, 1999 (Guinness World Record for Best-Selling Album by a Teenage Solo Artist 1999-2011), Oops!... I Did It Again, 2000 (Best Song, Kids' Choice Awards, 2001), Britney, 2001, In the Zone, 2003, Britney Spears Greatest Hits: My Prerogative, 2004, B In The Mix, The Remixes, 2005, Blackout, 2007, Circus, 2008 (Best Album, Billboard Awards, 2008), Singles Collection, 2009, Femme Fatale, 2011, Britney Jean, 2013, Glory, 2016, (songs) Baby One More Time, 1998 (Choice Music Single, Teen Choice Awards, 1999), I'm a Slave 4 U, 2001 (Best R&B Dance Track, International Dance Music Awards, 2002), Toxic, 2004 (Choice Music Single, Teen Choice Awards, 2004, Best Dance Recording, Grammy Awards, 2005, Best Song, Kids' Choice Awards, 2005), Womanizer, 2008 (Best Pop Video, MTV Video Music Awards, 2009), Till The World Ends, 2011 (Best Pop Video, MTV Video awards, 2011); performer (TV series) The Mickey Mouse Club, 1993-94; actress: (films)Longshot, 2001, Crossroads, 2002, Austin Powers in Goldmember, 2002, Pauly Shore is Dead, 2003, Fahrenheit 9/11, 2004 (TV appearances) Will & Grace, 2006, How I Met Your Mother, 2008, Glee, 2010, Jane the Virgin, 2015; appeared in (reality TV series) Britney And Kevin: Chaotic, 2005, (documentaries) Britney: For The Record, 2008, judge The X Factor, 2012-13; performer: Planet Hollywood Resort & Casino, 2013- **AW:** Named Favorite Social Media Celebrity, People's Choice Awards, 2016, Best Solo Female Artist, Virgin Media Music Awards, 2009, Sexiest Woman in the World, FHM magazine, 2009, 2008, 2004, Artist of Year, Rolling Stone magazine, 2001, Best Selling Female Dance Artist, World Music Awards, 2001, Best Selling Female Pop Artist, 2001, 2000, Best Female Artist, Kids' Choice Awards, 2001, 2000, Favorite Pop Artist, People's Choice Awards, 2014, Best International Artist, 2000, Favorite Pop/Rock New Artist, American Music Awards, 2000, Album Artist of Year, Billboard Music Awards, 2000, Female Artist of Year, 1999, Best New Artist, 1999, Best Female Artist, Hollywood Reporter, 1999, Best New Artist, 1999;

named one of The World's Most Powerful Celebrities, Forbes magazine, 2010; recipient Billboard Millennium award, Billboard Music Awards, 2016, Candie's Style Icon award, Teen Choice Awards, 2015, Michael Jackson Video Vanguard award, MTV Video Music awards, 2011, Star, Hollywood Walk of Fame, 2003, Fun, Fearless Female of Year award, Cosmopolitan magazine, 2002, Guinness World Record for best-selling teen age artist of all time 1999-2011

SPEIER, JACKIE, T: U.S. Representative from California **I:** Government Administration/Government Relations/Government Services **DOB:** 05/14/1950 **PB:** San Francisco **SC:** CA/USA **ED:** JD, University California Hastings College Law, 1976; BA, University California, Davis, 1972 **CT:** Bar: California **C:** Member, US House Homeland Security Committee, 2011-; Member, Committee on Education and Workforce, Committee on oversight and Government Reform, Committee on Transportation and Infrastructure; Member, US House Oversight & Government Reform Committee, 2008-; Member, US Congress from 14th California District, 2013-; Member, US House Special Committee on Energy Independence & Global Warming, 2008-10; Member, US House Financial Services Committee, 2008-10; Member, US Congress from 12th California District, Washington, 2008-13; Of counsel, Hanson, Bridgett, Marcus, Viahos, & Rudy LLP, San Francisco, 2007-08; Member District 8, California State Senate, 1998-2006; Director governmental & corporate affairs, Poplar ReCare, 1996-98; Vice president governmental & community affairs, Electronic Arts Inc., 1996-98; Chair consumer protection committee, California State Assembly, 1991-95; Majority whip, California State Assembly, 1988-92; Member District 19, California State Assembly, 1986-96; Chair, San Mateo County Board Supervisors, California, 1985-86; Member, San Mateo County Board Supervisors, California, 1980-84; Legal council to Rep. Leo J. Ryan, US Congress, 1973-78 **CW:** Author: This Is Not the Life I Ordered: 50 Ways to Keep Your Head Above Water When Life Keeps Dragging You Down, 2007 **AW:** Named Legis. of Year, Metropolitan Transportation Commission, 2004 **PA:** Democrat **BA:** 115 Cannon House Office Building, Washington, DC, 20515

SPENCE, ANDREW MICHAEL, T: Economist **I:** Financial Services **DOB:** 11/07/1943 **PB:** Montclair **SC:** NJ/USA **ED:** PhD in Economics, with honors, Harvard University, Cambridge, Massachusetts, 1972; BA, MA in Math., Oxford University, 1968; BA in Philosophy, summa cum laude, Princeton University, New Jersey, 1966 **C:** SDA Bocconi School of Management, 2011-; Professor economics, New York University Stern School Business, 2010-; Senior fellow Hoover Institution, Stanford University, California,; Philip H. Knight professor emeritus, professor management, Stanford University, California, 1999-2010; Philip H. Knight professor, dean Grad. School Business, Stanford University, California, 1990-99; Dean Faculty Arts & Scis., Harvard University, 1984-90; George Gund professor economics and business administration, Harvard University, 1983-86; Chairman economics department, Harvard University, 1983-84; Professor business administration, Harvard University, 1979-83; Professor economics, Harvard University, 1977-83; Visiting professor department economics, Harvard University, 1976-77; Hon. research fellow, Harvard University, 1975-76; Assistant professor political economics, Kennedy School Government,, Harvard University, 1971-75 **CR:** Chairman Ind. Commission on Growth & Devel., 2006-10 board directors Nike, Inc., General Mills, Inc. partner, senior advisor Oak Hill Investment Management, Menlo Park, California,

1999- chairman National Research Council Board Sci., Tech. & Economic Policy, 1991-97 member economics adv. committee Sloan Foundation, 1979 member economics adv. panel National Science Foundation, 1977-79 **CW:** Author: Market Signaling: Informational Transfer in Hiring and Related Screening Processes, 1974; co-author: Industrial Organization in an Open Economy, 1980, Competitive Structure in Investment Banking, 1983; contributor articles to professional journals; member editorial board Am. Economics Rev., Bell Journal Economics, Journal Economic Theory and Pub. Policy **AW:** Recipient Golden Plate award, Academy Achievement, 2006, Nobel Prize in Economics, The Nobel Foundation, 2001, John Kenneth Galbraith prize for Excellence in Teaching, Harvard University, 1978; Rhodes scholar, 1966, Danforth fellow, 1966 **MEM:** Fellow: Econometric Society, American Academy Arts & Sciences; mem.: American Economic Association (John Bates Clark medal 1981)

SPENCE, GERRY, T: Lawyer, Writer **I:** Law and Legal Services **DOB:** 01/08/1929 **PB:** Laramie **PT:** Son of Gerald M. and Esther Sophie (Pfleeger) S.; Married Anna Wilson, June 20, 1947; children: Kip, Kerry, Kent, Katy; Married LaNelle Hampton Peterson, November 18, 1969. **ED:** LLD (hon.), University of Wyoming, 1990; LLB, University of Wyoming, 1952; BSL, University of Wyoming, 1949 **CT:** Bar: Wyoming 1952, U.S. Court of Claims 1952, U.S. Supreme Court 1982 **C:** Senior partner, Spence Law Firm, 2004-; Senior partner, Spence, Moriarity & Shockey, 2002-03; Senior partner, Spence, Moriarity & Schuster, Jackson, Wyoming, 1978-2002; Partner, various law firms, Riverton and Casper, Wyoming, 1962-78; County and prosecuting attorney, Fremont County, Wyoming, 1954-62; Sole practice, Riverton, Wyoming, 1952-54 **CR:** Lecturer legal organizations and law schools founder Trial Lawyers College **CW:** Author: (with others) Gunning for Justice, 1982, Of Murder and Madness, 1983, Trial by Fire, 1986, With Justice for None, 1989, From Freedom to Slavery, 1993, How To Argue and Win Every Time, 1995, The Making of a Country Lawyer, 1996, O.J.: The Last Word, 1997, Give Me Liberty, 1998, A Boy's Summer, 2000, Gerry Spence's Wyoming: The Landscapes, 2000, Half Moon and Empty Stars, 2001, Seven Simple Steps to Personal Freedom, 2001, The Smoking Gun, 2003, Win Your Case, 2005, Bloodthirsty Bitches and Pious Pimps of Power: The Rise and Risk of the New Conservative Hate Culture, 2006,(Books) The Lost Frontier: Images and Narrative, 2013, Police State: How America's Cops Get Away with Murder, 2015 **AW:** Recipient Lifetime Achievement award, Consumer Attorneys California (formerly California Trial Lawyers Association), 2008; inducted to, Am. Trial Lawyers Hall of Fame, 2009 **MEM:** Member American Bar Association, Wyoming Bar Association, Wyoming Trial Lawyers Association, Association Trial Lawyers Am., National Association Criminal Defense Lawyers

SPENCER, OCTAVIA, T: Actress **I:** Media & Entertainment **DOB:** 06/26/1905 **PB:** Montgomery **SC:** AL/USA **ED:** BS in Liberal Arts, Auburn University **CW:** Actress: (films) A Time to Kill, 1996, The Sixth Man, 1997, Sparkler, 1997, American Virgin, 1999, Never Been Kissed, 1999, Being John Malkovich, 1999, Blue Streak, 1999, What Planet Are You From?, 2000, Big Momma's House, 2000, Legally Blonde 2: Red, White & Blonde, 2003, S.W.A.T., 2003, Bad Santa, 2003, Win a Date with Tad Hamilton!, 2004, Breakin' All the Rules, 2004, Coach Carter, 2005, Pretty Persuasion, 2005, Beauty Shop, 2005, Pulse, 2006, Next of Kin, 2008, Seven Pounds, 2008, The Soloist, 2009, Halloween II, 2009, Dinner for Schmucks, 2010, Peep World, 2010, Flypaper, 2011,

The Help, 2011 (African American Film Critics Association award for Best Supporting Actress, 2011, Critics' Choice award for Best Supporting Actress, 2012, Golden Globe award for Best Performance by an Actress in a Supporting Role in a Motion Picture, 2012, Screen Actors Guild award for Outstanding Performance by a Female Actor in a Supporting Role, 2012, BAFTA award for Best Supporting Actress, 2012, Academy award for Best Supporting Actress, 2012), Blues for Willadean, 2012, Lost on Purpose, 2013, Paradise, 2013, Get on Up, 2014, Black or White, 2014, Insurgent, 2015, Fathers and Daughters, 2015, The Great Gilly Hopkins, 2015, The Free World, 2016, Zootopia (voice), 2016, The Divergent Series: Allegiant - Part 1, 2016, The Free World,2016, Bad Santa 2, 2016, Hidden Figures, 2016, The Shack, 2017, Small Town Crime, 2017, Gifted, 2017, The Shape of Water, 2017, A Kid Like Jake, 2018; actress: (films) Car Dogs, 2014, Gifted, 2016; (TV series) City of Angels, 2000, The Chronicle, 2001-02, LAX, 2004-05, Ugly Betty, 2007, Halfway Home, 2007, Raising the Bar, 2009, Hawthorne, 2010, 30 Rock, 2013, American Dad!, 2013, Call Me Crazy, 2013, Mom, 2013-15 Red Band Society, 2014-15, Drunk History, 2015,SNL, 2017; (TV films) Call Me Crazy: A Five Film, 2013; actress, co-exec. producer (films) Fruitvale Station, 2013 (National Board Review award for Best Supporting Actress, 2013), guest appearances Chicago Hope, 1999, Just Shoot Me!, 2000, Dharma & Greg, 2001, Presidio Med, 2002, Medium, 2005, The Big Bang Theory, 2008, Mom, 2013-15

SPIEGEL, EVAN THOMAS, T: Entrepreneur; Application Developer **I:** Information Technology and Services **DOB:** 06/04/1990 **PB:** Los Angeles **SC:** California **PT:** Son of John W. and Melissa Ann (Thomas) Spiegel. **ED:** BS in Product Design, Stanford University, 2012; Attended, Art Center College Design, 2007-08 **C:** Co-founder, CEO, Snapchat, Inc., Venice, California, 2012-; Software developer, Intuit, 2010; Intern, Abraxis Bioscience, 2009 **CIV:** Snap Foundation, 2017 **AW:** Named one of The 100 Most Influential People in the World, TIME magazine, 2014, The 40 Under 40, Fortune magazine, 2014, The 30 Under 30 :Technology, Forbes, 2014, The 30 Under 30 Changing the World, TIME magazine, 2013; recipient First Place award for Newspaper Infographics, Columbia Scholastic Press. Association, 2008, Time 100 Most Influential, 2017 **MEM:** Mem.: Kappa Sigma

SPIEGELMAN, ART, T: Cartoonist, Editor **I:** Writing and Editing **DOB:** 02/15/1948 **PB:** Stockholm **SC:** Sweden **PT:** Son of Wladek and Andzia (Zylberberg) S.; **MS:** Married **SPN:** Francoise Mouly, July 12, 1977; **CH:** Nadja, Dashiell **ED:** Student, Harpur College (now State University of New York), Binghamton, New York **C:** Founding editor, Raw, 1980-; Artist, contributing editor, New Yorker, 1992-2003; Contributing editor, Arcade, the Comics Revue, 1975-76; Editor, Douglas Comix, 1972; Creative consultant, artist, designer, editor, writer, Topps Chewing Gum, Inc., Brooklyn, 1966-88 **CR:** Instructor San Francisco Academy Art, 1974-75, New York School Visual Arts, 1979-87. **CW:** Author, illustrator: The Complete Mr. Infinity, 1970, The Viper Vicar of Vice, Villainy, and Vickedness, 1972, Ace Hole, Midge Detective, 1974, The Language of Comics, 1974, Breakdowns: From Maus to Now: An Anthology of Strips, 1977, Work and Turn, 1979, Every Day Has Its Dog, 1979, Two-Fisted Painters Action Adventure, 1980, Maus: A Survivor's Tale, 1986 (Joel M. Cavior award for Jewish Writing 1986, National Book Critics Cir. nomination 1986, Pulitzer prize 1992), Maus, Part Two, 1992 (National Book Critics Cir. nomination 1992, Pulitzer prize 1992, Eisner award, 1992, Harvey award, 1992), Open Me...I'm a Dog!, 1997;

(with J.M. March) The Wild Party, 1994, Kisses from New York; (with F. Mouly) Read Yourself Raw, 1987, In the Shadow of No Towers, 2004 (named one of the 100 Notable Books of 2004, New York Times Book Review), Breakdowns: Portrait of the Artist as a Young %@&*!, 2008; contributor The Apex Treasury of Underground Comics, 1974; compiling editor (with B. Schneider) Whole Grains: A Book of Quotations, 1972; creator (with composer Phillip Johnston) Drawn to Death: A Three Panel Opera, Am. Repertory Theatre Co., Cambridge, Massachusetts; editor (comic series) Little Lit, 2000-03; exhibitions include New York Cultural Center, Institute Contemporary Art, London, Seibu Gallery, Tokyo, Museum Modern Art, New York City, 1991, Galerie St. Etienne, New York City, 1992, Fort Lauderdale Museum Art, 1993, LA Museum Contemporary Art, 2005; creator Wacky Packages, Garbage Pail Kids and other novelties; contributor to numerous underground comics,(Book) Jack and the Box, 2008, Be a Nosem 2009, MetaMaus, 2011, Co-Mix: A Retrospective of Comics, Graphics, and Scraps, 2013 **AW:** Named one of Time Magazine 100 Most Influential People, 2005; named to Will Eisner Award Hall of Fame, 1999, Art Dir.'s Club Hall of Fame, 2006; recipient Playboy Editorial award for best comic strip, 1982, Yellow Kid award for best comic strip author, 1982, Regional Design award, Print magazine, 1983, 1984, 1985, Inkpot award, San Diego Comics Convention, 1987, Stripschappening award for best foreign comics album, 1987, Alpha Art award, Angoulerne, France, 1993, Chevalier de l'Ordre des Arts et des Lettres, France, 2005. **MEM:** Fellow: Am. Academy Arts and Sciences

SPIELBERG, STEVEN ALLAN, T: Film Director, Producer **I:** Media & Entertainment **DOB:** 12/18/1946 **PB:** Cincinnati **SC:** OH/USA **MS:** Married **SPN:** Kate Capshaw, 10/12/1991; Amy Irving, 11/27/1985, Divorced 2/2/1989 **CH:** Max Samuel, Sasha, Sawyer, Destry, Theo, Mikaela, One Stepchild **ED:** Honorary LHD, Boston University, 2009; Honorary DHL, Yale University, 2002; Honorary Doctor of Creative Arts, Brandeis University, 1986; BA, California State University, Long Beach **C:** Founder, Amblin Entertainment, 1984-Present; Co-Founder, (With Jeffrey Katzenberg & David Geffen), Partner, DreamWorks SKG, 1994-2005 **CR:** Fellow, British Academy of Film & TV Arts; Olympic Games, Beijing, China, 2007-2008; Artistic Advisor, 2008; Co-Creator of Concept, Story, and Design of New Game Franchises, EA Games, Los Angeles, CA, 2005-Present **CIV:** Advisory Board, Science Fiction Museum and Hall of Fame **CW:** Director, (Films) The Last Gun, 1959, Jaws, 1975, "1941," 1979, Raiders of the Lost Ark, 1981, Indiana Jones and the Temple of Doom, 1984, Indiana Jones and the Last Crusade, 1989, Hook, 1991, Jurassic Park, 1993, The Lost World: Jurassic Park, 1997, Minority Report, 2002, War of the Worlds, 2005, Indiana Jones and the Kingdom of the Crystal Skull, 2008, Ready Player One, 2018, (TV Films) Duel, 1971, Columbo: Murder By the Book, 1971, Something Evil, 1972, Savage, 1973, (Episodes for TV Series) The Name of the Game, 1968, Marcus Welby, MD, 1969, Night Gallery, 1970, The Psychiatrist, 1971, Owen Marshall: Counselor at Law, 1971; Director, Producer, (Films) E.T. the Extra-Terrestrial, 1982, Twilight Zone: The Movie ("Kick The Can" Segment), 1983, The Color Purple, 1985, Empire of the Sun, 1987, Always, 1989, Schindler's List, 1993, Amistad, 1997, Saving Private Ryan, 1998, Catch Me If You Can, 2002, The Terminal, 2004, Munich, 2005, The Adventures of Tintin, 2011, War Horse, 2011, Lincoln, 2012, Bridge of Spies, 2015, The BFG, 2016, Transformers: The Last Knight, 2017, Jurassic World: Fallen Kingdom, 2018; Director, Writer, (Films) Fighter Squad, 1961, Escape to

Nowhere, 1961, Firelight, 1964, Slipstream, 1967, Amblin', 1968, The Sugarland Express, 1974, Close Encounters of the Third Kind, 1977; Director, Producer, Writer, Artificial Intelligence: AI, 2001; Executive Producer, (Films) I Wanna Hold Your Hand, 1978, Used Cars, 1980, Continental Divide, 1981, Gremlins, 1984, Back to the Future, 1985, Young Sherlock Holmes, 1985, The Money Pit, 1986, An American Tail, 1986, Innerspace, 1987, Batteries Not Included, 1987, Who Framed Roger Rabbit, 1988, The Land Before Time, 1988, Tummy Trouble, 1989, Dad, 1989, Back to the Future: Part II, 1989, Joe Versus the Volcano, 1990, Yume, 1990, Back to the Future: Part III, 1990, Roller Coaster Rabbit, 1990, Gremlins 2: The New Batch, 1990, Arachnophobia, 1990, Trail Mix-Up, 1993, We're Back! A Dinosaur's Story, 1993, I'm Mad, 1994, The Flintstones, 1994, Casper, 1995, Balto, 1995, Twister, 1996, The Lost Children of Berlin, 1997, Men in Black, 1997, Deep Impact, 1998, The Mask of Zorro, 1998, The Last Days, 1998, The Haunting, 1999, Eyes of the Holocaust, 2000, Jurassic Park III, 2001, Price for Peace, 2002, Men in Black II, 2002, The Legend of Zorro, 2005, Monster House, 2006, Disturbia, 2007, Transformers, 2007, Eagle Eye, 2007, Transformers: Revenge of the Fallen, 2009, The Lovely Bones, 2009, (TV Films) Class of '61, 1993, Survivors of the Holocaust, 1996, Shooting War, 2000, Semper Fi, 2001, We Stand Alone Together, 2001, Burma Bridge Busters, 2003, Dan Finnerty & the Dan Band: I Am Women, 2005, All the Way, 2016, (TV Series) The Plucky Duck Show, 1992, Family Dog, 1992, Seaquest DSV, 1993-1996, ER, 1994, Freakazoid!, 1995-1997, Pinky and the Brain, 1995-1998, Pinky, Elmyra & the Brain, 1998, Toonsylvania, 1998-2000, On the Lot, 2007, Terra Nova, 2011, Falling Skies, 2011-2014, Smash, 2012-2013, Under the Dome, 2013-2015, Extant, 2014-2015, (TV Miniseries) Band of Brothers, 2001, Broken Silence, 2002, Taken, 2002, Into the West, 2005, The Pacific, 2010; Executive Producer, Writer, (Films) The Goonies, 1985, (TV Series) Amazing Stories, 1985-1987, Tiny Toon Adventures, 1990-1992, Animaniacs, 1993-1998; Producer, (Films) An American Tail: Fievel Goes West, 1991, Memoirs of a Geisha, 2005, Flags of Our Fathers, 2006, Letters From Iwo Jima, 2006, Real Steel, 2011; Producer, Writer, Poltergeist, 1982; Writer, (Films) Ace Eli and Rodger of the Skies, 1973; Consulting Producer, The Unites States of Tara, 2009-2011 **AW:** Man of the Year Award, Hasty Pudding Theater, Harvard University, 1983, Outstanding Directorial Achievement Award for Feature Films, Directors Guild Of America, 1985, Film Award, British Academy of Film and TV Arts, 1986, Irving Thalberg Member Award, Academy of Motion Picture Arts and Sciences, 1987, Golden Lion Award for Career Achievement, Venice Film Festival, 1993, Schindler's List, Academy Award For Best Director, 1994, Academy Award For Best Picture, 1994, Golden Globe For Best Director, 1994, Life Achievement Award, American Film Institute, 1995, John Huston Award, Artists Rights Foundation, 1995, Entertainment Weekly's Most Powerful Person in Entertainment, 1997, Saving Private Ryan, Academy Award For Best Director, 1999, Golden Globe For Best Director, 1999, Distinguished Pub. Service Award US Navy, 1999, Lifetime Achievement Award, Director Guild of America, 2000, Commander of the Order of the British Empire (CBE), Her Majesty Queen Elizabeth II, 2001, Band of Brothers, Emmy Award for Outstanding Miniseries, 2002, Taken, Emmy Award for Outstanding Miniseries, 2003, The 50 Most Powerful People in Hollywood, Premiere Magazine, 2004-2006, Liberty Kennedy Center Honor, John F. Kennedy Center for Performing Arts, 2006, 50 Smartest People in Hollywood, Entertainment Weekly, 2007, The 100 Most Powerful Celebrities,

Forbes.com, 2007-2008, The French Legion of Honor, 2008, America's Best Leaders, U.S. News & World Report, 2008, Cecil B. Demille Award, Hollywood Foreign Press Association, 2009, Liberty Medal, National Constitution Center, 2009, The Pacific, Emmy Award for Outstanding Miniseries, 2010, David O. Selznick Achievement Award in Theatrical Motion Pictures, Producers Guild of America, 2012, The Adventures of Tintin, Best Animated Feature Film, Golden Globe Award, Hollywood Foreign Press Association, 2012, The 100 Most Influential People in the World, TIME Magazine, 2013, Presidential Medal of Freedom, 2015, Forbes 400: Richest Americans, 1999-Present, World's Richest People, Forbes Magazine 2001-Present, 100 Top Celebrities, Forbes Magazine, 2001-Present **ACH:** Achievements include winning film contest with 40-minute war movie, Escape to Nowhere, at age 13; made film Firelight at age 16, and made 5 films while in college; became TV director at Universal Pictures at age 20. **BA:** DreamWorks SKG, 100 Universal City Plaza, Building 10, Universal City, CA, 91608

SPIETH, JORDAN ALEXANDER, T: Professional Golfer **I:** Athletics **DOB:** 07/27/1993 **PB:** Dallas **PT:** Son of Chris and Shawn Spieth. **ED:** Attended, University Texas **C:** Professional golfer, 2012 **CR:** Winner PGA Tour FedEx Cup Finale, 2015, Masters Tournament, Augusta, Georgia, 2015, Valspar Championship, 2015, Hero World Challenge, 2014, Emirates Australian Open, 2014, John Deere Classic, 2013, US Junior Amateur, 2011, 2009 **CIV:** Founder, Jordan Spieth Charitable Trust, 2013- **AW:** Named PGA Tour Player of Year, 2015, Rolex Junior Player of the Year, American Junior Golf Association, 2009,PGA Tour Rookie of the Year, 2013, PGA Player of the Year, 2015, PGA Tour Player of the Year, 2015, PGA Tour Leading Money Winner, 2015, Fedex Cup Champion, 2015, Vardon Trophy, 2015, 2017, Byron Nelson Award, 2015, 2017, **ACH:** Achievements include ranked first in the world ranking of professional golf in 2015; second youngest (21 years, 8 months) to win the Masters at Augusta, Georgia on April 12, 2015; first player to reach 19 under par at the Masters in 2015; third-youngest player in PGA tour history to win multiple events in 2015; the sixth player in golf history to win the US Open and Masters in the same year, 2015; youngest Player to win the US Open since Bobby Jones in 1923

SPITZ, MARK, T: Professional Swimmer **I:** Athletics **DOB:** 02/10/1950 **PB:** Modesto **SC:** CA/USA **PT:** Son of Arnold and Lenore (Smith); **ED:** BS, Ind. U, 1972 **C:** Commentator, ABC Sports,; Guest TV swimming commentator, Olympic Games,; Member US swimming team, Olympic Games, 1968, 72 **CR:** Former owner Beverly Hills Real Estate Co. **CW:** Author: Mark Spitz: The Extraordinary Life of an Olympic Champion, 2008,Freedom's Fury, 2006 **AW:** Inducted as Honor Swimmer to International Swimming Hall of Fame, 1977; Sullivan award for top athlete in any sport Amateur Athletic Union, 1971; named World Swimmer of Year Swimming World magazine, 1969, 1971, 1972; named to International Swimming Hall of Fame, 1977, International Jewish Hall of Fame, 1979, US Olympic Hall of Fame, 1983, San Jose Sports Hall of Fame, 2007, National Jewish Museum Sports Hall of Fame, 2007, Long Beach City College Hall of Fame, 2007, Ind. University Athletics Hall of Fame. **MEM:** Mem.: Phi Kappa Psi **ACH:** won total of 9 Olympic Gold medals, 4x100m freestyle, 4x200m freestyle, 1968, 1972, 100m freestyle, 200m freestyle, 100m butterfly, 200m butterfly, 4x100m medley, 1972; only Olympian in history to win 7 Gold medals (all World Records) in a single Olympics, Munich Olympic Games, 1972, Silver Medal, 100m but-

terfly, Bronze Medal, 100m freestyle, Mexico City Olympic Games, 1968, 5 Gold medals Pan-Am. Games, 1967, held 32 world records, 1967-1972; 4 times Champion NCAA, 1969-72.

SPOELSTRA, ERIK, T: Professional Basketball Coach **I:** Athletics **DOB:** 11/01/1970 **PB:** Evanston, Illinois, November 1, 1970 **PT:** Son of Jon and Lisa Spoelstra. **ED:** Degree in communications, University Portland, 1992 **C:** Head coach, Miami Heat, 2008-; Assistant coach, director scouting, Miami Heat, 2001-08; Assistant coach, advance scout, Miami Heat, 1999-2001; Assistant coach, video coordinator, Miami Heat, 1997-99; Video coordinator, Miami Heat, 1995-97; Player, coach, Tus Herten, Germany, **CR:** Summer league coach Miami Heat, 2005-07, head, individual player devel. program **AW:** NBA Champion, 2012, 2013, NBA All-Star Game Head Coach, 2013, NBA Champion, 2006 **ACH:** Achievements include head coach of NBA Finals championship winning Miami Heat, 2012, 2013

SPRINGSTEEN, BRUCE (BRUCE FREDERICK JOSEPH SPRINGSTEEN) T: Musician **I:** Media & Entertainment **DOB:** 09/23/1949 **PB:** Freehold **PT:** Son of Douglas Frederick and Adele Ann (Zerilli) Springsteen; **ED:** Student, Ocean County Community College, 1967 **CW:** Musician: (albums with The E Street Band) Greetings from Asbury Park, 1973, The Wild, The Innocent and the E-Street Shuffle, 1973, Born to Run, 1975 (Gold Record award, 1975), Darkness on the Edge of Town, 1978, The River, 1980, Born in the U.S.A., 1984 (Best Pop/Rock Album of Year, Downbeat Readers Poll, 1984), Bruce Springsteen and the E-Street Band Live/1975-85, 1986, Chimes of Freedom, 1988, Bruce Springsteen's Greatest Hits, 1995, Tracks, 1998, 18 Tracks, 1999, Live in New York City, 2001, The Rising, 2002 (Grammy award for Best Male Rock Vocal Performance, 2003, Grammy award for Best Rock Song, 2003, Grammy award for Best Rock Album, 2003), The Essential Bruce Springsteen, 2003, Bruce Springsteen & The E-Street Band: Hammersmith Odeon, London '75, 2006, Magic, 2007, Bruce Springsteen and The E Street Band's Greatest Hits, 2009, Working on a Dream, 2009 (Grammy award for Best Solo Rock Vocal Performance, 2010), The Promise: The Darkness on the Edge of Town Story, 2010, Wrecking Ball, 2012, High Hopes, 2014, The Ties That Bind: The River Collection, 2015, (solo albums) Nebraska, 1982, Tunnel of Love, 1987, Human Touch, 1992, Lucky Town, 1992, The Ghost of Tom Joad, 1995, In Concert/MTV Unplugged, 1997, Devils and Dust, 2005 (Grammy award for Best Solo Rock Vocal Performance, 2006), We Shall Overcome: The Pete Seeger Sessions, 2006 (Grammy award for Best Traditional Folk Album, 2007), (songs) Streets of Philadelphia, 1994 (Golden Globe award for Best Original Song in a Film, 1994, Academy award for Best Original Song in a Film, 1994, MTV Best Video from a Film award, 1994, Grammy award for Song of Year, 1994), Dead Man Walking, 1996, Disorder in the House, 2002 (Grammy award for Best Rock Performance By A Duo Or Group With Vocal, 2003), Once Upon a Time in the West, 2007 (Grammy award for Best Rock Instrumental Performance, 2008), Radio Nowhere, 2007 (Grammy award for Best Rock Song, Best Solo Rock Vocal Peformance, 2008), The Wrestler, 2008 (Critic's Choice award for Best Song, Broadcast Film Critics Association, 2009, Golden Globe award for Best Original Song for Motion Picture, Hollywood Foreign Press Association, 2009), Girls in Their Summer Clothes (Grammy award for Best Rock Song, 2009); appears on: (albums by Rumble Doll) Rumble Doll with Patti Scialfa, 1993, appears on: (albums

by Warren Zevon) The Wind, 2003, appears on: (albums by Ennio Morricone) We All Love Ennio Morricone, 2007; appeared in (concert films) No Nukes, 1980, Bruce Springsteen and the E Street Band: Live in New York City, 2001, Bruce Springsteen and The E Street Band: Live in Barcelona, 2003, Bruce Springsteen & The Sessions Band: Live in Dublin, 2007, London Calling: Live in Hyde Park, 2010, (documentaries) Sun City: Artists United Against Apartheid, 1986, Chuck Berry Hail! Hail! Rock 'n' Roll, 1987, The History of Rock 'N' Roll, 1995, Wings for Wheels: The Making of Born to Run, 2005 (Grammy award for Best Long Form Music Video, 2007), The Promise: The Making of Darkness on the Edge of Town, 2010; author: (memoir) Born to Run, 2016 **AW:** Presidential Medal of Freedom, 2016,Named MusiCares Person of Year, 2013; Grammy for Best Solo Rock Vocal, 2010, named one of The 100 Most Influential People in the World, TIME magazine, 2008, Golden Globe for Best Original Song, 2009; named to New Jersey Hall of Fame, 2008, The Songwriters Hall of Fame, 1999, The Rock & Roll Hall of Fame, 1999; recipient Presidential Medal of Freedom, The White House, 2016, Kennedy Center Honors, John F. Kennedy Center for the Performing Arts, 2009, Grammy award for Best Male Rock Vocalist, 1994, 1987, 1984

SQUERI, STEPHEN J., T: Finance Company Executive **I:** Financial Services **ED:** MBA, Manhattan College; BS, Manhattan College (1981) **C:** Chief Executive Officer, American Express Co., New York, NY (2018-Present); Vice Chairman, American Express Co., New York, NY (2015-2018); Group President, Global Services, American Express Co., New York City, NY (2009-2015); Executive Vice President, Chief Information Officer, American Express Co. (2005-2009); President, Global Commercial Card Group, American Express Co. (2002-2005); President, Establishment Services, American Express Co., U.S. & Canada (2000-2001); Management Positions, American Express Co. (1985-2000); Management Consultant, Arthur Andersen & Co. (1981-1985) **CR:** Board of Directors, J. Crew Group, Inc. (2010-Present); The Guardian Life Insurance Co. of America (2009-Present) **CIV:** Chairperson, The Valerie Fund Golf Tournament; Board of Directors, Raycliff Acquisition Corp.; Board of Trustees, Harlem Children's Zone; Board of Trustees, New York Downtown Hospital; Member, Manhattan College School of Business; Advisory Council, Board of Governors, Monsignor McClancy Memorial High School

SRINIVASAN, SRI, T: Federal Judge, Former Federal Agency Administrator **I:** Law and Legal Services **DOB:** 02/23/1967 **PB:** Chandigarh **SC:** India **SPN:** Carla J. Garrett **ED:** JD, Stanford University Law School, 1995; MBA, Stanford University Business School, 1995; AB with honors, Stanford University, California, 1989 **CT:** Bar: DC **C:** Judge, U.S. Court Appeals (DC Cir.), Washington, 2013-; Principal deputy solicitor general, US Department Justice, Washington, 2011-13; Assistant to solicitor general, US Department Justice, Washington, 2002-07; Partner appellate & complex litigation, hiring partner, O'Melveny & Myers LLP, Washington, DC 2007-11; Associate, O'Melveny & Myers LLP, Washington, DC 1997-2002; Law clerk to Justice Sandra Day O'Connor, Supreme Court of the U.S., Washington, DC 1996-97; Law clerk Hon. J. Harvie Wilkinson III, U.S. Court Appeals (4th cir.), 1995-96 **CR:** Member outside advisory board Georgetown Supreme Court Institute lecturer, Harvard Law School notes editor, Stanford Law Review, 1993-94, associate editor, 1992-93 **CIV:** Board of Directors, Washington Lawyers Committee for Civil Rights & Urban Affairs, Board of Visitors, Stanford Law

School, **CW:** Contributor articles to professional journals **AW:** Named one of The 50 Most Influential Minority Lawyers in America, The National Law Journal, 2008; recipient Award for Excellence, U.S. Department Defense, 2005, Award for Excellence in Furthering the Interests US National Security, US Department Justice, 2003 **MEM:** Mem.: North American South Asian Bar Association (NASABA) (member national advisory council), Order of the Coif **BA:** US Court Appeals, 333 Constitution Ave NW, Washington, DC, 20001

STABENOW, DEBBIE, **T:** U.S. Senator from Michigan **I:** Government Administration/Government Relations/Government Services **DOB:** 04/29/1950 **PB:** Gladwin **SC:** Michigan **PT:** Daughter of Robert Lee and Anna Merle (Hallmark) Greer; **SPN:** Married Dennis Stabenow (div. 1990); Married Tom Athans, February 16, 2003; **CH:** children: Todd Dennis, Michelle Deborah **ED:** BS Magna Cum Laude, Michigan State University, 1972; MSW Magna Cum Laude, Michigan State University, 1975 **C:** Chair, Senate Democratic Policy Committee, 2017-,; Ranking Member, Senate Agriculture Committee, 2015-,; Chair, US Senate Agricultural, Nutrition & Forestry Committee, 2011-2015; Chair, US Senate Agricultural, Nutrition & Forestry Committee, 2011—; Chair, US Senate Democratic Steering & Outreach Committee (DSOC), 2007—; US Senator from Michigan, 2001—; Member, US Congress from 8th Michigan District, Washington, DC, 1997—2001; Member, Michigan State Senate, Lansing, 1991—1994; Member, Michigan House of Reps., Lansing, 1979—1990; County Commissioner, Ingham County, Mason, Michigan, 1975-78; With Special Services, Lansing (Michigan) School District, 1972-73 **CIV:** Founder Ingham County Women's Commission; Co-founder Council Against Domestic Assault **AW:** Recipient Service to Children award Council for Prevention of Child Abuse and Neglect, 1983, Distinguished Service to Michigan Families award Michigan Council Family Relations, 1983, Outstanding Leadership award National Council Community Mental Health Ctrs., 1983, Snyder-Kok Award Mental Health Association Michigan, Awareness Leader of Year Award Awareness Communications Team Developmentally Disabled, 1984, Communicator of Year Award Woman in Communications, 1984, Lawmaker of Year award National Child Support Enforcement Association, 1985, Distinguished Service award Lansing Jaycees, 1985, Distinguished Service in Government award Retarded Citizens of Michigan, 1986, Community award Michigan Mental Health, 1988, Boxing Glove Award National Committee to Preserve Social Security and Medicare, 1999, Home Health Hero National Association for Home Care, 1999, Friend of Farm Bureau Michigan Farm Bureau, 1999, Leadership award National Council of Space Grant Directors, 1998, Outstanding Achievement National Farmers Union, 1998, Legislator of Year Award National Multiple Sclerosis Society, 1992, Association for Children's Mental Health, 1991, Michigan Association of Vol. Administrators, 1989, Citizens Alliance to Uphold Special Education, 1989, Recognition award State 4-H Alumni, 1991, Public. Elected Official award National Association Social Workers, 2004, Congressional Support for Sci. award Institute Food Technologists, 2004, Community Health Defender award National Association Community Health Centers, 2005; named One of Ten Outstanding Young Americans Jaycees, 1986. **MEM:** Member National Association for the Advancement of Colored People, National Association Social Workers, Lansing Regional Chamber of Commerce, Delta Kappa Gamma. **PA:** Democrat **BA:** Office of Debbie Stabenow, US Senate 133 Hart Senate Office Bldg, Washington D.C., DC, 20510

STACHEL, ARI'EL, **T:** Actor **I:** Media & Entertainment **PB:** Berkeley **SC:** CA/USA **ED:** Coursework, New York University Tisch School of the Arts **CW:** Actor, Television, "Blue Bloods" (2015), "Jessica Jones" (2015); Actor, Theatre, "The Band's Visit" (2017) **AW:** Tony Award for Best Featured Actor in a Musical (2018)

STALLONE, SYLVESTER GARDENZIO, **T:** Actor, Film Director, Scriptwriter, Producer **I:** Media & Entertainment **DOB:** 07/06/1946 **PB:** New York City **SC:** NY/USA **PT:** Son of Frank and Jacqueline (Labofish) Stallone **ED:** Student, University Miami, 1967-69; Student, American College of Switzerland, 1965-67 **CW:** Actor: (films) The Party at Kitty and Stud's, 1970, No Place to Hide, 1970, The Prisoner of Second Avenue, 1975, Capone, 1975, Death Race 2000, 1975, Farewell, My Lovely, 1975, Cannonball!, 1976, Nighthawks, 1981, Victory, 1981, Lock Up, 1989, Tango & Cash, 1989, Oscar, 1991, Stop! Or My Mom Will Shoot, 1992, Demolition Man, 1993, The Specialist, 1994, Judge Dredd, 1995, Assassins, 1995, Daylight, 1996, The Good Life, 1997, Cop Land, 1997, An Alan Smithee Film: Burn Hollywood Burn, 1998, Antz (voice), 1998, Get Carter, 2000, D-Tox, 2002, Avenging Angelo, 2002, Shade, 2003, Spy Kids 3-D: Game Over, 2003, Zookeeper (voice), 2011, Bullet to the Head, 2013, Escape Plan, 2013, Grudge Match, 2013, Reach Me, 2014, Ratchet and Clank (voice), 2016, Guardians of the Galaxy Vol 2, 2017, Animal Crackers (voice), 2016, Escape Plan 2: Hades, 2018; writer, actor (films) The Lord's of Flatbush, 1974, Rocky, 1976, F.I.S.T, 1978, First Blood, 1982, Rhinestone, 1984, Rambo: First Blood Part II, 1985, Cobra, 1986, Over the Top, 1987, Rambo III, 1988, Rocky V, 1980, Cliffhanger, 1993, The Expendables 2, 2012, The Expendables 3, 2014, director, writer, actor Paradise Alley, 1978, Rocky II, 1979, Rocky III, 1982, Rocky IV, 1985, Rocky Balboa, 2006, The Expendables, 2010, producer, director, writer, actor Staying Alive, 1983, Rambo, 2008; prodr.: (films) Heart of a Champion: The Ray Mancini Story, 1985; producer, writer, actor (films) Driven, 2001, Creed, 2015 (National Board Review award for Best Supporting Actor, 2015, Golden Globe award for Best Performance by an Actor in a Supporting Role in a Motion Picture, 2016, Critics' Choice award for Best Supporting Actor, 2016), executive producer, writer Father Lefty, 2002, producer, writer Homefront, 2013, TV guest appearances Police Story, 1975, Kojak, 1975, Liberty's Kids: Est. 1776, 2002, Las Vegas, 2005; executive prodr.: (TV series) The Contender, 2006-09; executive prodr.: (TV series) S.T.R.O.N.G., 2016-, Ultimate Beastmaster, 2017, This is Us, 2017; prodr.: The Contender Rematch: Mora versus Manfredo, 2005; author: Sly Moves: My Proven Program to Lose Weight, Build Strength, Gain Will Power, and Live Your Dream, 2005 **AW:** Named Show West Actor of Year, 1979; recipient Caesar award for Career Achievement, 1992, Order of Arts and Letters, French Ministry, 1992, Artistic Achievement award, National Italian Am. Foundation, 1991, Star of Year award, 1977 **MEM:** Mem.: Screen Actors Guild, Directors Guild, Writers Guild, Stuntmen's Association (hon.) **ACH:** Achievements include being nominated for two Oscars (acting and writing) in same year (1976); occurred for only 3d time in history **BA:** International Creative Management, 10250 Constellation Boulevard, Los Angeles, CA, 90067

STANDLEY, JOHN T., **T:** Rite Aid CEO **I:** Business Management/Business Services **ED:** BS in Accounting, Pepperdine University, 1985 **C:** Chairman, CEO, Rite Aid Corp., Camp Hill, Pennsylvania, 2012-; President, CEO, Rite Aid Corp., Camp Hill, Pennsylvania, 2010-13; President, COO, Rite Aid Corp., Camp Hill, Pennsylvania, 2008-10; CEO,

Pathmark Stores, Inc., 2005-08; CFO, Rite Aid Corp., Camp Hill, Pennsylvania, 2003-05; Senior Executive Vice President, Chief Administrative Officer, Rite Aid Corp., Camp Hill, Pennsylvania, 2002; Executive Vice President, CFO, Rite Aid Corp., Camp Hill, Pennsylvania, 1999-2002; Executive Vice President, CFO, Fleming Co. Inc., Oklahoma City, 1999; Senior Vice President, CFO, Fred Meyer, Inc., Portland, Oregon, 1998-99; Senior Vice President, CFO, Ralphs Grocery Co., 1997-98; Senior Vice President Admin., Smith's Food & Drug Stores, Inc., Salt Lake City, 1996-97; CFO, Smitty's Supervalu, Inc., Phoenix, 1994-96; Vice President Fin., Food 4 Less Supermarkets, Inc., Compton, California, 1991-94; Audit Manager Retail and Fin. Industry Groups, Arthur Andersen LLP, LA **CR:** Board Directors Rite Aid Corp., 2009-, Pathmark Stores, Inc., 2005-07 **BA:** Rite Aid HeadQuarters, 30 Hunter Lane, Camp Hill, PA, 17011

STANKEY, JOHN T., **T:** Telecommunications Industry Executive **I:** Media & Entertainment **SC:** California **ED:** MBA, UCLA, 1991; Bachelor in Fin., Loyola Marymount University, LA, 1985 **C:** CEO, Directv, 2015-; Group president, chief strategy officer, AT&T Inc., 2012-; Grp. president telecomm. operations, AT&T Inc., 2007-12; Grp. president operations support, AT&T Inc., 2007; Senior executive vice president, chief tech. officer, AT&T Inc., 2006-07; Senior executive vice president, chief tech. officer, SBC Communications Inc., 2003-06; President, CEO SBC Southwestern Bell, SBC Communications Inc., 2002-03; President industry markets, SBC Communications Inc., 2000-02; Vice president industry markets, SBC Communications Inc., 1998-2000; Executive director advanced communications network, local wholesale operations, Pacific Bell, 1985-98 **AW:** Named one of Top 25 Chief Tech. Officers, InfoWorld magazine, 2006, Premier 100 IT Leaders, Computerworld, 2006

STANTON, GIANCARLO, **T:** Professional Baseball Player **I:** Athletics **PB:** Panorama City **SC:** CA/USA **C:** Right Fielder, New York Yankees, 2018-Present; Right Fielder, Florida Marlins, 2010-2017 **AW:** All-Star, 2012, 2014-2015, 2017, Silver Slugger Award, 2014, 2017, NL Hank Aaron Award, 2014, 2017, NL Home Run Leader, 2014, 2017, NL RBI Leader, 2017, NL MVP, 2017

STANTON, GREG, **T:** Mayor of Phoenix **I:** Government Administration/Government Relations/Government Services **PT:** Fred Stanton; Mary Ann Stanton **ED:** JD, University of Michigan, Ann Arbor, MI; Bachelor, Marquette University, Milwaukee, WI **C:** Mayor, City of Phoenix (2012-Present); Deputy Attorney General, Arizona Attorney General's Office (2009-2011); Member, District 6, Phoenix City Council (2001-2009); Attorney, Quarles & Brady LLP, Phoenix, AZ; Attorney, Jennings Strouss & Salmon, Phoenix, AZ **CIV:** Member, Arizona School of Readiness Board; Member, Flinn Foundation of Arizona Bioscience Steering Committee; Board of Directors, Arizona Theater Co.; Board of Directors, Big Brothers Big Sisters of America, Central Arizona; Arizona Children's Association **AW:** Named Arizona Big Brother of the Year; Named One of Forty Under 40, Phoenix Business Journal; Jacque Steiner Public Leadership Award, Children's Action Alliance **MEM:** Big Brothers Big Sisters of America **PA:** Democrat

STAPLETON, CHRIS, **T:** Musician, Songwriter **I:** Media & Entertainment **DOB:** 04/15/1978 **PB:** Lexington **ED:** Attended, Vanderbilt University **C:** Solo artist, 2013-; Founder, singer, The Jompson Brothers, 2010; Singer, guitarist, The SteelDivers, 2008-10 **CW:** Songwriter for notable songs Never Wanted Nothing More (Kenny Chesney), 2007,

Come Back Song (Darius Rucker), 2010, If it Hadn't Been Love (Adele), 2011, Love's Gonna Make It Alright (George Strait), 2011, Talk is Cheap (Alan Jackson), 2012, Drink a Beer (Luke Bryan), 2013, Crash and Burn (Thomas Rhett), 2015, various others; musician: (albums) Traveller, 2015 (Album of Year, Country Music Association Awards, 2015, Best Country Album, Best Country Solo Performance for Song "Traveller," Grammy Awards, 2016, Album of Year, Song of Year for Song "Nobody to Blame," Academy Country Music Awards, 2016, Top Country Album, Billboard Music Awards, 2016) From A Room:Volume 1,(Grammy for Best Country Album) 2017,From A Room:Volume 2,2017 (songs) Fire Away, 2015 (Breakthrough Video of Year, CMT Music Awards, 2016) **AW:** Named Songwriter of Year, Academy Country Music Awards, 2016, New Male Vocalist of Year, 2016, Male Vocalist of Year, 2016, Country Music Association Awards, 2015, New Artist of Year, 2015, Grammy for Best Country Song, 2018, Grammy for Best Country Solo Performance, 2018

STARR, RINGO, T: Drummer **I:** Media & Entertainment **DOB:** 07/07/1940 **PB:** Liverpool **PT:** Son of Richard and Elsie (Gleave) Starkey; Married Maureen Cox, February 11, 1965 (div. 1975); children: Zak, Jason, Lee; Married Barbara Bach, April 27, 1981. **C:** Solo performer, 1970-; Drummer, singer, The Beatles, 1962-69; Drummer, singer, Rory Storm's Hurricanes, 1959-62; Drummer, Ed Clayton Skiffle Group, 1959 **CR:** Formed Pumpkinhead Records (with Mark Hudson) **CW:** Musician: (albums) (with The Beatles) Please, Please Me, 1963, With the Beatles, 1963, Meet the Beatles, 1964, Beatles for Sale, 1964, A Hard Day's Night, 1964 (Grammy award for Best Performance by a Group, 1964, Grammy award for Best New Artist, 1964), Help!, 1965, Yesterday & Today, 1966, Rubber Soul, 1966, Revolver, 1966, Sergeant Pepper's Lonely Hearts Club Band, 1967 (Grammy award for Album of Year, 1967, Grammy award for Best Contemporary Album, 1967), Magical Mystery Tour, 1967, The Beatles (The White Album), 1968, Yellow Submarine, 1968, Abbey Road, 1969, Let It Be, 1970 (Grammy award for Best Original Score, 1970), Beatles Anthology, 1995 (Grammy award for Best Long Form Music Video, 1996, Grammy awards for Best Pop Performance & Best Short Form Music Video for Free As A Bird single, 1996); film appearances (with The Beatles) A Hard Day's Night, 1964, Help!, 1965, Yellow Submarine (voice), 1968, Let It Be (also co-exec. producer), 1970, TV film appearances Magical Mystery Tour (also co-prodr., co-dir.), 1967; musician: (solo albums) Sentimental Journey, 1970, Beaucoups of Blues, 1970, Ringo, 1973, Goodnight Vienna, 1974, Blast from Your Past, 1975, Ringo's Rotogravure, 1976, Ringo the Fourth, 1977, Scouse the Mouse, 1977, Bad Boy, 1978, Stop and Smell the Roses, 1981, Old Wave, 1983, Starr Struck, 1989, Time Takes Time, 1992, Vertical Man, 1998, I Wanna Be Santa Claus, 1999, Ringo Rama, 2003, Tour 2003, Choose Love, 2005, Liverpool 8, 2008, Y Not, 2010, Ringo 2012, 2012, Postcards from Paradise, 2015, Give More Love, 2017, Ringo Starr & Friends, 2006, Live at Soundstage, 2007, Liverpool 8, 2008, Live on Tour, 2008, Ringo Starr and His All-Starr Band Live 2006, 2008, Y Not, 2010, Ringo 2012, Postcards from Paradise, 2015, (with All-Starr Band) Ringo Starr and His All-Starr Band, 1989, Ringo Starr and His All-Starr Band: Live From Montreux, 1992, Ringo Starr and His Third All-Starr Band, 1997, Ringo & His New All-Starr Band, 2002; musician: (with George Harrison, Ravi Shankar and others) (albums) The Concert For Bangla Desh, 1972 (Grammy award for Album of Year, 1972); actor: (films) Candy, 1968, The Magic Christian, 1969, Commonwealth, 1970, 200 Motels, 1971, Blindman (also known as

Il Cieco and Il Pistolero Cieco), 1972, That'll Be the Day, 1974, Lisztomania, 1975, Sextette, 1978, Caveman, 1981, Give My Regards to Broad Street, 1984, To the North of Katmandu, 1986; actor, producer, director (films) Born to Boogie, 1972, actor, producer Son of Dracula, 1974; actor: (TV films) Ringo, 1978, The Cooler, 1982, Princess Daisy, 1983, Alice in Wonderland, 1985, Shining Time Station Christmas: 'Tis a Gift, 1990; (TV series) Thomas the Tank Engine & Friends (voice), 1985-91, Shining Time Station, 1990-91; featured in documentary Good Ol' Freda, 2013 **AW:** Decorated Order Brit. Empire; recipient Diamond award, World Music Awards, 2008, Star on Hollywood Walk of Fame, 2010, Lifetime Achievement award (as member of The Beatles), Grammy Awards, 2014; named to Roll Hall of Fame (as member of The Beatles), 1998, (as solo musician), 2015, Best Compilation Soundtrack, Grammy's, 2015

STARR, STEPHEN, T: Restaurateur **I:** Food & Restaurant Services **C:** STARR Restaurants, 1995- **AW:** James Beard Award for Outstanding Restaurateur, 2017

STEEL, DANIELLE, T: Writer **I:** Writing and Editing **DOB:** 08/14/1947 **PB:** New York City **SC:** NY/USA **ED:** Attended, Parsons School Design, New York City; Attended, New York University **C:** Blog Host, daniellesteel.net; Owner, Steel Gallery Contemporary Art, San Francisco, California, 2003—2007; Copywriter, Grey Advertising, San Francisco, California, 1973-74; Writer 1973-; Vice President Public Relations and New Business, Supergirls Ltd., New York City, New York, 1968-71 **CW:** Author: (novels) Going Home, 1973, Passion's Promise, 1977, Now And Forever, 1978, The Promise, 1978, Golden Moments, 1979, Season Of Passion, 1980, Summer's End, 1980, The Ring, 1980, Palomino, 1981, To Love Again, 1981, Remembrance, 1981, Loving, 1981, Once In A Lifetime, 1982, Crossings, 1982, A Perfect Stranger, 1983, Thurston House, 1983, Changes, 1983, Full Circle, 1984 (#1 New York Times bestseller), Love: Poems, 1984, Family Album, 1985 (#1 New York Times bestseller), Secrets, 1985, Wanderlust, 1986 (#1 New York Times bestseller), Fine Things, 1987 (#1 New York Times bestseller), Kaleidoscope, 1987 (#1 New York Times bestseller), Zoya, 1988 (#1 New York Times bestseller), Star, 1989 (#1 New York Times bestseller), Daddy, 1989 (#1 New York Times bestseller), Message From Nam, 1990, Heartbeat, 1991 (#1 New York Times bestseller), No Greater Love, 1991, Jewels, 1992 (#1 New York Times bestseller), Mixed Blessings, 1992 (#1 New York Times bestseller), Vanished, 1993, Accident, 1994 (#1 New York Times bestseller), The Gift, 1994 (#1 New York Times bestseller), Wings, 1994, Lightning, 1995, Five Days In Paris, 1995 (#1 New York Times bestseller), Malice, 1996, Silent Honor, 1996, The Ranch, 1997, Special Delivery, 1997 (#1 New York Times bestseller), The Ghost, 1997 (#1 New York Times bestseller), The Long Road Home, 1998 (#1 New York Times bestseller), The Klone and I, 1998 (#1 New York Times bestseller), His Bright Light, 1998, Mirror Image, 1998, Bittersweet, 1999 (#1 New York Times bestseller), Granny Dan, 1999, Irresistible Forces, 1999, The Wedding, 2000 (#1 New York Times bestseller), The House On Hope Street, 2000 (#1 New York Times bestseller), Journey, 2000, Lone Eagle, 2001, Leap Of Faith, 2001 (#1 New York Times bestseller), The Kiss, 2001 (#1 New York Times bestseller), The Cottage, 2002, Sunset in St. Tropez, 2002, Answered Prayers, 2002 (#1 New York Times bestseller), Dating Game, 2003, Johnny Angel, 2003 (#1 New York Times bestseller), Safe Harbour, 2003, Ransom, 2004, Second Chance, 2004, Echoes, 2004, Impossible, 2005, Miracle, 2005, Toxic Bachelors, 2005, The House,

2006 (#1 New York Times bestseller), Coming Out, 2006, H.R.H, 2006, Sisters, 2007, Bungalow 2, 2007, Amazing Grace, 2007, Honor Thyself, 2008, Rogue, 2008, A Good Woman, 2008, One Day at a Time, 2009, Matters of the Heart, 2009, Southern Lights, 2009, Big Girl, 2010, Family Ties, 2010, Legacy, 2010, 44 Charles Street, 2011, Happy Birthday, 2011, Hotel Vendome, 2011, Betrayal, 2012, Friends Forever, 2012, The Sins of the Mother, 2012, A Gift of Hope: Helping the Homeless, 2012, Until the End of Time, 2013, First Sight, 2013, Winners, 2013, Pure Joy, 2013, Power Play, 2014, A Perfect Life, 2014, Pegasus, 2014, Prodigal Son, 2015, Country, 2015, Undercover, 2015, Blue, 2016, Property of a Noblewoman, 2016, (children's books) Martha's New Daddy, 1989, Max and the Babysitter, 1989, Martha's Best Friend, 1989, Max's Daddy Goes to the Hospital, 1989, Max's New Baby, 1989, Martha's New School, 1989, Max Runs Away, 1990, Martha's New Puppy, 1990, Max and Grandma and Grampa Winky, 1991, Martha and Hilary and the Stranger, 1991, Freddie's Trip, 1992, Freddie's First Night Away, 1992, Freddie and the Doctor, 1992, Freddie's Accident, 1992, Pretty Minnie in Paris, 2014; several book titles made into TV films,(Books) The Apartment, 2016, Magic, 2016, Rushing Waters, 2016, The Award, 2016, The Mistress, 2017, Dangerous Games, 2017, Against All Odds, 2017, The Duchess, 2017, The Right Time, 2017, Fairytale, 2017, Past Perfect, 2017, Fall from Grace, 2018, Accidental Heroes, 2018, The Cast, 2018, The Good Fight, 2018 **AW:** Decorated Officier, Order Arts and Lettres France; Named to California Hall of Fame, 2009; Recipient Service to Youth Award, University San Francisco Catholic Youth Orgn./St. Mary's Medical Center, 1999, Outstanding Achievement Award, Larkin St. Youth Services, San Francisco, 2003, Distinguished Service in Mental Health award, New York Presbyn.-Columbia University Medical Ctr./Cornell Medical College, 2009, Outstanding Achievement Award in Mental Health, California Psychiatric Association, Distinguished Service Award, American Psychiatric Association

STEFANIK, ELISE M., T: U.S. Representative from New York **I:** Government Administration/Government Relations/Government Services **DOB:** 07/02/1984 **PB:** Albany **PT:** Daughter of Ken and Melanie Stefanik. **ED:** BA, Harvard. University, 2006 **C:** Mem., US Congress from 21st New York District, Washington, 2015-; Member, Committee on Armed Services, Committee on Education and the Workforce; Marketing management, Premium Plywood Products, Inc., Guilderland Center, New York, 2012-14; Director vice presidential debate prep to Rep. Paul Ryan, US Presidential Election, 2012; Policy director, Foreign Policy Initiative,; Communications director foreign policy initiative, policy director, Tim Pawlenty's Presidential Campaign, 2012; Staff member Domestic Policy Council, The White House, 2006-09 **AW:** Recipient Women's Leadership award, Harvard University **ACH:** Achievements include becoming the youngest woman ever elected to the U.S. Congress, 2014 **PA:** Republican

STEITZ, THOMAS ARTHUR, T: Biophysicist **I:** Sciences **DOB:** 08/23/1940 **PB:** Milw. **ED:** PhD, Harvard University, 1966; DSc (hon.), Lawrence University, Appleton, Wisconsin, 1981; BA, Lawrence University, Appleton, Wisconsin, 1962 **C:** Faculty, Yale University, New Haven, 1970-; Sterling professor molecular biophysics and biochemistry, Yale University, New Haven,; Jane Coffin Childs postdoc. fellow, MRC Laboratory Molecular Biology, Cambridge, England, 1967-70; Postdoc. fellow, Harvard University, 1966-67 **CR:** Visiting professor University Colorado, Boulder, 1992-93 investigator Howard Hughes Medical Institute,

Chevy Chase, Maryland, 1986- **CW:** Contributor articles to professional journals **AW:** Recipient Lucia R. Briggs Distinguished Achievement award, Lawrence University, Nobel prize in chemistry, 2009, Gairdner Foundation International award, 2007, Keio Medical Sci. prize, 2006, Rosenstiel award for distinguished work in basic medical research, 2001, Pfizer award in enzyme chemistry, Am. Chemical Society, 1980; Fairchild Scholar, California Institute Tech., 1984-85, Macy Fellow, Göttingen, Germany, 1976-77,Fellow of the Royal Society, 2011, **MEM:** Fellow: Am. Academy Arts & Scis. (Newcomb Cleveland prize 2001); mem.: National Academy of Sciences

STEPHANOPOULOS, GEORGE ROBERT, T: News Anchor, Political Correspondent **I:** Media & Entertainment **DOB:** 02/10/1961 **PB:** Fall River **PT:** Son of Robert George and Nickolitsa Gloria (Chafos) Stephanopolous; **ED:** LLD (hon.), St. John's University, 2007; MA in Theology, Balliol College, Oxford University, 1986; BA in Political Sci., summa cum laude, Columbia University, New York City, 1982 **C:** Co-anchor Good Morning America, ABC News, 2009-; Chief political corr., ABC News, 2009-; Host This Week with George Stephanopoulos, ABC News, 2012-; Political analyst, corr., ABC News, 1997-; Chief Washington corr., ABC News, 2005-09; Host This Week with George Stephanopoulos, ABC News, 2002-10; Senior adv. to the President for policy and strategy, The White House, Washington, 1993-96; Communications director, The White House, Washington, 1992-96; Communications director, Clinton/Gore Presidential campaign, Little Rock, 1992; Executive floor manager to House Majority leader Dick Gephardt, US House of Representatives, Washington,; Deputy communications director, Dukakis/Bentsen Presidential campaign, 1988; Legis. assistant, chief of staff to Rep. Edward Feighan, US House of Representatives, Washington, **CIV:** Founding member, Next Generation Initiative, 2003 **CW:** Author: All Too Human: A Political Education, 1999 **AW:** Named a Maverick, Details magazine, 2007; named one of 50 Most Powerful People in DC, GQ magazine, 2009; recipient Walter Cronkite award for Excellence in TV Political Journalism, University Southern California Annenberg School Journalism, 2009, 2007, Medal of Excellence, Columbia University, 1993; Rhodes Scholar, Oxford University **MEM:** Mem.: Phi Beta Kappa **PA:** Democrat

STEPHENSON, RANDALL L., T: CEO of AT&T **I:** Business Management/Business Services **CN:** AT&T **DOB:** 04/22/1960 **PB:** Oklahoma City **SC:** OK/USA **ED:** MS in Accounting, University of Oklahoma, Norman; BS in Accounting, Central State University, Edmond, Oklahoma, 1982 **C:** Chairman, president, CEO, AT&T Inc. (merger of SBC Communications & AT&T Corp.), San Antonio, 2007-; COO, AT&T Inc. (merger of SBC Communications & AT&T Corp.), San Antonio, 2005-07; COO, SBC Communications, Inc., 2004-05; Chairman, Cingular Wireless, LLC, 2003-04; Senior executive vice president, CFO, SBC Communications, Inc., 2001-04; Vice president, controller, SBC Communications, Inc., 1997; Controller, SBC Communications, Inc., San Antonio, 1996-97; Director fin. SBC International, SBC Communications, Inc., Mexico City, 1992-96; District manager fin. analysis, Southwestern Bell Telephone Co., 1991-92; Area manager corp. taxes, Southwestern Bell Telephone Co., Oklahoma City, 1986-91; With, Southwestern Bell Telephone Co., Oklahoma City, 1982 **CR:** Chairman Business Roundtable (BRT), 2014- member audit committee H.E. Butt Grocery Co. board directors Emerson Electric, 2006-, AT&T Inc., 2005-, Cingular

Wireless LLC, 2001-06 **CIV:** Member national executive board, Boy Scouts Am., Member, Council on Foreign Relations, Board member, San Antonio Metropolitan Missions Board, Member executive committee, audit committee, United Way San Antonio **AW:** Named one of 50 Who Matter Now, Business 2.0, 2007 **MEM:** Mem.: Oklahoma Society CPAs

STERN, ALAN, T: Planetary Scientist, Engineer **I:** Sciences **DOB:** 11/22/1957 **PB:** New Orleans, November 22, 1957 **PT:** Son of Leonard Arthur and Joel Strauss (Sugar) Stern **ED:** PhD in Astrophysics and Planetary Sci., University Colorado, 1989; MS in Planetary Atmospheres, University Texas, 1981; BA, University Texas, 1981; MS in Aerospace Engineering, University Texas, 1980; BS, University Texas, 1978 **C:** Associate administrator sci. mission directorate, NASA, 2007-2008; Professor adj. Astrophysical and Planetary Scis. Department, University Colorado, Boulder, 2002-; Executive director Space Sci. and Engineering Div., Southwest Research Institute, 2004-07; Department director, Southwest Research Institute, 1998-2005; Section manager, Southwest Research Institute, 1992-97; Principal scientist Space Science Department, Southwest Research Institute, 1991-92; Research associate Center for Astrophysics and Space Astronomy, University Colorado, Boulder, 1990-91; Research fellow Center for Space & Geosciences Policy, University Colorado, Boulder, 1989-91; Assistant to vice president for research, University Colorado, Boulder, 1987-88; Assistant director Office of Space Sci. and Tech., University Colorado, Boulder, 1986-87; Research associate, University Colorado, Boulder, 1989-90; Spacecraft/instrument engineer Laboratory for Atmospheric and Space Physics, University Colorado, Boulder, 1983-86; Systems engineer, Martin Marietta Aerospace, Denver, 1982-83; Engineer, NASA Johnson Space Center, Houston, 1979-80 **CR:** Principal investigator, New Horizons Pluto-Kuiper Belt Mission, Alice UV Spectrometer on New Horizons, Ralph Imager/IR Spectrometer on New Horizons, Lunar Recon Orbiter Lyman-Alpha Mapping (LAMP) Experiment, Alice UV spectrometer in ESA/NASA Rosetta mission project; scientist, Spartan-Halle spacecraft mission, NASA; chairman Neptune/Pluto outer planet sci. working group, 1994-; discovery program sci. working group, 1989-90; member lunar exploration sci. working group, 1992- **CW:** Author: The U.S. Space Program After Challenger, 1987, Pluto and Charon, 1997, The Exploration of Pluto, 1997, The Search for Extra-Solar Earthlike Planet: Techniques and Technology, 1997, Our Worlds, 1998, Our Universe, 2000, Worlds Beyond: The Thrill of Planetary Exploration as told by Leading Experts, 2003; editor: Geophysical Research Letters Special Issues, Pluto and the Moon, 1989, 1991; contributor articles to professional journals **AW:** Named one of The World's Most Influential People, TIME magazine, 2007; recipient Rosetta Grp. Achievement award, NASA, 2005, New Millennium Deep Space-1 Mission Grp. Achievement award, 2002, Hale-Bopp Sounding Rocket Campaign Grp. Achievement award, 1998, Solar Max Repair Mission Recognition award, 1984, Martin Marietta New Design Innovation award, 1983; fellow Colorado Commission Higher Education, 1988-89 **MEM:** Mem.: American Institute of Aeronautics and Astronautics, American Association for the Advancement of Science, Aircraft Owners & Pilots Association; Am. Geophysical Union, Am. Astronomical Society, International Astronomical Union **H:** Flying, scuba diving, photography, skiing, hiking, gardening, writing

STEVENS, JOHN PAUL, T: Retired U.S. Supreme Court Justice **I:** Law and Legal Services **DOB:** 04/20/1920 **PB:** Chicago **SC:** Illinois **PT:** Son of Ernest James and Elizabeth (Street) Stevens; **ED:** LLD (hon.), Princeton University, 2015; JD magna cum laude, Northwestern University, 1947; AB, University Chicago, 1941 **CT:** Bar: Illinois 1949 **C:** Associate justice, US Supreme Court, Washington, 1975-2010; Judge, US Court Appeals (7th Cir.), Chicago, 1970-75; Partner, Rothschild, Stevens, Barry & Myers, 1952-70; Associate counsel, Subcommittee to Study Monopoly Power, US House Judiciary Committee, Washington, 1951-52; Associate, Poppenhusen, Johnston, Thompson & Raymond, 1949-52; Law clerk to Justice Wiley B. Rutledge, US Supreme Court, Washington, 1947-48; Practiced in, Chicago, **CR:** Appellate judge seminar New York University School Law, 1972 chief counsel to commission investigating the judgment of People v. Isaacs Illinois Supreme Court, 1969 member Attorney Gen.'s National Committee to Study Anti-Trust Laws, 1953-55 lecturer anti-trust law University Chicago Law School, 1955-58, Northwestern University School Law, 1953-54 **MIL:** With US Naval Reserve, 1942-45 **CW:** Contributor articles to professional journals; author: Five Chiefs: A Supreme Court Memoir, 2011, Six Amendments: How and Why We Should Change the Constitution, 2014 **AW:** Decorated Bronze Star; recipient Presdl Medal of Freedom, The White House, 2012 **MEM:** Fellow: American Academy Arts & Sciences; mem.: American Law Institute, Federal Bar Association, Illinois Bar Association, American Bar Association, Chicago Bar Association (2d vice president 1970), Order of Coif, Phi Delta Phi, Psi Upsilon, Phi Beta Kappa **BA:** US Supreme Court, 1 First St NE, Washington, DC, 20543

STEVENSON, BRYAN ALLEN, T: Legal Institute Administrator, Law Educator **I:** Education/Educational Services **DOB:** 11/14/1959 **PB:** Milton **SC:** MA/USA **PT:** Son of Howard Carlton and Alice Gertrude (Golden) S. **ED:** JD, Harvard Law School, 1985; MPP, John F. Kennedy School Government, Harvard University, Cambridge, Massachusetts, 1985; BA, Eastern College, St. Davids, Pennsylvania, 1981 **CT:** Bar: Georgia 1985, Alabama 1987. **C:** Professor of clinical law, New York University School Law, New York City, 2003-; Associate professor clinical law, New York University School Law, 2002; Assistant professor clinical law, New York University School Law, 1998; Founder, executive director, Equal Justice Initiative of Alabama, Montgomery, 1995-; Executive director, Alabama Capital Representation Resource Center, Montgomery, 1989-95; Staff Attorney, Southern Prisoners Defense Committee, Atlanta, 1985-89 **CR:** Visiting professor law New York University School of Law, 1997, University of Michigan Law School, 1995. **CW:** Author: Just Mercy, 2014 (Named one of the Best Books of Year, The New York Times, The Washington Post, The Boston Globe, The Seattle Times, Esquire and Time, Carnegie Medal for Nonfiction, National Association for the Advancement of Colored People Image award for Nonfiction, Books for Better Life award, American Library Association Notable Book) **AW:** Recipient National Human Rights award Reebok Human Rights Foundation, 1989, ACLU Medal of Liberty, 1991, American Bar Association Wisdom Award for Pub. Service, 1991, Gleitsman Foundation Citizen Activist award, 200, Olof Palme prize, 2000, Gruber Prize for Justice, Gruber Foundation, 2009, National Pub. Service award Stanfor University Law School, 2010, William Robert Ming Advocacy award National Association for the Advancement of Colored People, 2010, Visionaries award Ford Foundation, 2011; named a MacArthur Fellow, The John D. & Catherine T. MacArthur Foundation, 1995 **H:** Music, piano and keyboards

STEWART, (WILLIAM) PAYNE, T: Professional Golfer **I:** Athletics **PB:** Springfield **SC:** MO/USA **PT:** Married Tracey Stewart; children: Chelsea, Aaron. **AW:** Co-champion Southwest Conference, 1979; winner Indian and Indonesian Opens, 1981, Tweed Head Classic, 1981, Magnolia Classic, 1982, Quad Cities Open, 1982, Walt Disney World Classic, 1983, Hertz Bay Hill Classic, 1987, PGA Championship, 1989, MCI Heritage Classic, 1989, 90, Byron Nelson Golf Classic, 1990, U.S. Open, 1991, 99, Heineken Dutch Open, 1991, Morocco Open, 1992, 93, Houston Open, 1995, AT&T Pebble Beach National Pro-Am, 1999, Skins Game Champion, 1991, 92, 93; member Ryder Cup U.S. team, 1987, 89, 91, 93, World Cup U.S. team, 1987, 90, World Golf Hall of Fame, 2001, Bob Jones Award, 2014

STEWART, CARL E., T: Federal Judge **I:** Law and Legal Services **DOB:** 01/02/1950 **PB:** Shreveport **SC:** Louisiana **PT:** Son of Corine and Richard Stewart; **ED:** JD, Loyola University, New Orleans, 1974; BA magna cum laude, Dillard University, 1971 **C:** Chief judge, US Court Appeals (5th cir.), 2012-; Judge, US Court Appeals (5th cir.), 1994-; Judge, Louisiana Court Appeals (2d cir.), 1991-94; Judge, Louisiana District Court, 1985-91; Special assistant district attorney, assistant prosecutor, City of Shreveport, 1983-85; Principal, Stewart & Dixon, Shreveport, 1983-85; Assistant US attorney (western district) Louisiana, US Department Justice, Shreveport, 1979-83; Staff attorney, Louisiana Attorney General's Office, Shreveport, 1978-79; Attorney, Piper & Brown, Shreveport, Louisiana, 1977-78 **CIV:** Chairman national search committee, Boy Scouts America, Board trustees, American Inns. Court Foundation, Board trustees, Community Foundation Shreveport-Bossier, Shreveport, Louisiana, 1994-2004 **MIL:** Captain Judge Advocate General Corps other, 1974-77, Fort Sam Houston, Texas **AW:** Recipient Times Leadership award, Shreveport Times & Alliance for Education, 2008, A.P. Tureaud Achievement award, Loyola University School Law Black Law Students Association, 2008, American Silver Buffalo award, Boy Scouts America, 2002 **MEM:** Mem.: Louisiana State Bar Association (bench/bar liaison committee), Louisiana Conference Court Appeal Judges, Black Lawyers Association Shreveport-Bossier, American Inns of Court (Harry Booth/Henry Politz chapter Shreveport), National Bar Association, Omega Psi Rhi (Rho Omega chapter) **BA:** John Minor Wisdom U.S. Court of Appeals Building Fifth Circuit, 600 Camp St, New Orleans, LA, 70130

STEWART, CHRIS, T: U.S. Representative from Utah **I:** Government Administration/Government Relations/Government Services **DOB:** 07/15/1960 **PB:** Logan **PT:** Son of Sybil S. Stewart; **ED:** BS in Economics, Utah State University, 1984 **C:** Member, US House Sci., Space & Technology Committee, 2013-; Member, US House Homeland Security Committee, 2013-; Member, US Congress from 2nd Utah District, Washington, 2013-; Member, US House Permanent Select Committee on Intelligence; Member, Republican Study Committee; Member, Committee on Appropriations; Member, US House Natural Resources Committee, 2013; President, CEO, The Shipley Group, 1998-2012 **CW:** Author: (novels) Shattered Bone, 1997, The Kill Box: A Technothriller, 2000, The Third Consequence, 2000, The Great and Terrible: The Brothers, 2003, The Great and Terrible: Where Angels Fall, 2004, The Great and Terrible: The Second Sun, 2005, The Great and Terrible: Fury & Light, 2007, The Fourth War, 2005, The Great and Terrible: From the End of Heaven, 2008, The God of War, 2008, Redefining Joy in the Last Days, 2009, The Great and Terrible: Clear As The Moon, 2010; co-author (with Ted Stewart): Seven Miracles That Saved America, 2009 (National Communications award Freedom Foundation), The Miracle of Freedom: Seven Tipping Points That Saved the World, 2011; co-author: (with Evie Stewart) A Christmas Bell for Anya, 2005 **AW:** Recipient Mackay Trophy for Significant Aerial Achievement, 1995 **H:** Rock climbing, hiking **PA:** Republican

STEWART, JON, T: Television Personality, Comedian **I:** Media & Entertainment **DOB:** 11/28/1962 **PB:** New York City **SC:** NY/USA **PT:** Son of Donald and Marian (Laskin) Leibowitz **ED:** BS in Psychology, College of William & Mary, Williamsburg, Pennsylvania, 1984 **CIV:** Board member, National September 11 Museum & Memorial, 2011- **CW:** Actor: (films) Mixed Nuts, 1994, Wishful Thinking, 1997, Half Baked, 1998, The Faculty, 1998, Playing by Heart, 1998, Big Daddy, 1999, The Office Party, 2000, Jay and Silent Bob Strike Back, 2001, Death to Smoochy, 2002, (voice only) Doogal, 2006, The Adjustment Bureau, 2011, Skum Rocks!, 2013; (TV films) Since You've Been Gone, 1998; (host): (TV series) Short Attention Span Theater, 1991; You Wrote It, You Watch It, 1992; The Jon Stewart Show, 1993-95 (Emmy award for Outstanding Variety, Music or Comedy Program, 2011); The Daily Show (also executive producer, writer), 1999-2015 (Emmy award for Outstanding Writing for a Variety, Music or Comedy Program, 2001, 2003, 2004, 2005, 2006, 2009, 2010-12, 2015); (TV special) The Daily Show with Jon Stewart: Indecision 2000 (Emmy award for Outstanding Writing for a Variety, Music or Comedy Program, 2001, George F. Peabody award, 2001); The Daily Show with Jon Stewart: Indecision 2004 (George F. Peabody award, 2005, 12, 16); writer (TV series) The Sweet Life, 1989; executive prodr.: (TV series) The Colbert Report, 2005-12 (Producers Guild of America award for Producer of Year in Live Entertainment/Competition, 2009, Producers Guild of America award for Outstanding Producer of Live Entertainment & Talk TV, 2013, 2014, Primetime Emmy for Outstanding Variety Series, 2007-10, 2012,14); executive prodr.: (TV series) Important Things with Demetri Martin, 2009-10; (TV films) The Rally to Restore Sanity and/or Fear, 2010; producer, writer, director (films) Rosewater, 2014 (National Board Review award for Freedom of Expression, 2014), creator, executive producer (TV series) The Nightly Show with Larry Wilmore, 2015-; author: Naked Pictures of Famous People, 1998, America (The Book): A Citizen's Guide to Democracy Inaction, 2004 (Publishers Weekly Book of Year, 2004, Quills award for Best Humor Book, Best Audio Book, 2005, Thurber Prize for Am. Humor, 2005, Grammy award for Best Comedy Album, 2005), Earth (The Book): A Visitor's Guide to the Human Race, 2010 (#1 New York Times bestseller, Grammy for Best Spoken Word Album, 2011) **AW:** Named one of The 50 Highest-Earning Political Figures, Newsweek, 2010, The 100 Agents of Change, Rolling Stone magazine, 2009, The 100 Most Powerful Celebrities, Forbes.com, 2008, The 100 Most Influential People, TIME magazine, 2005; named to New Jersey Hall of Fame, 2015

STEWART, PATRICK, T: Actor **I:** Fine Art **DOB:** 05/15/1905 **PB:** Mirfield, **SC:** Mirfield, **PT:** Son of Alfred and Gladys (Barraclough) S.; **SPN:** Married Sunny Ozell, September; Married Wendy Neuss, August 25, 2000 (div. 2003); Married Sheila Falconer, March 3, 1966 (div. 1990); **CH:** children: Daniel, Sophia; **ED:** D. (hon.), University East Anglia, 2011; Trained, Bristol Old Vic Theatre School **CIV:** President, Huddersfield Town Academy, **CW:** Actor: (theatre) Treasure Island (UK, debut), 1959, (US) A Midsummer Night's Dream; (Broadway plays) A Christmas Carol, 1991 (Drama desk award for Outstanding Solo Performance/One Person Show, 1992), 1992-95, 2001, The Tempest, 1995, The Ride Down Mount Morgan, 2000, The Caretaker, 2003-2004, Macbeth, 2008, A Life in Theatre, 2010, Waiting for Godot, 2013, No Man's Land, 2013; Royal Shakespeare Co., 2008 (Laurence Olivier award for Best Supporting Actor, 2009); (TV series) Star Trek: The Next Generation, 1987-94, American Dad! (voice), 2005-15, Family Guy (voice), 2005-14, Eleventh Hour, 2006, Macbeth, 2010, Animal Superpowers, 2012, Richard II, 2012, Futurama, 2012, Robot Chicken, 2012, The Simpsons, 2013, Cosmos A Spacetime Odyssey, 2014, Blunt Talk, 2015 (narrator) Dragons: A Fantasy Made Real, 2004, High Spirits with the Ghostman, 2005, Ted, 2012, Ted 2, 2015; (mini-series) Fall of Eagles, 1974, I, Claudius, 1977, Tinker, Sailor, Soldier, Spy, 1979, Maybury, 1981, Smiley's People, 1982, Playing Shakespeare, 1983, When the Lion Roars, 1992, 500 Nations (voice), 1995, Mysterious Island, 2005, The Hollow Crown, 2012, Oscar's Hotel for Fantastical Creatures (voice), 2015; (TV films) The Gathering Storm, 1974, Anthony and Cleopatra, 1974 (Olivier award for Best Supporting Actor), North and South, 1975, The Madness, 1976, Hamlet, Prince of Denmark, 1980, Little Lord Fauntleroy, 1980, John Paul II, 1984, The Devil's Disciple, 1987, Death Train, 1993, In Search of Dr. Seuss, 1994, Moby Dick, 1997, Safe House, 1998, Animal Farm (voice), 1999, The Snow Queen, 2005, Hamlet, 2009; host on Saturday Night Live, 1994, (films) Hennessy, 1975, Hedda, 1975, Excalibur, 1981, The Plague Dogs (voice), 1982, Dune, 1984, Uindii, 1984, Lifeforce, 1985, Code Name: Emerald, 1985, Wild Geese II, 1985, The Doctor and the Devils, 1985, Lady Jane, 1986, L.A. Story, 1991, Robin Hood: Men in Tights, 1993, Gunmen, 1994, Star Trek: Generations, 1994, The Pagemaster (voice), 1994, Jeffrey, 1995, Let It Me Be (aka Love Dance), 1995, Star Trek: First Contact, 1996, Conspiracy Theory, 1997, Safe House, 1997, Dad Savage, 1997, Master Minds, 1997, Prince of Egypt (voice), 1998, X-Men, 2000, Jimmy Neutron: Boy Genius (voice), 2001, Star Trek: Nemesis, 2002, X-Men 2, 2003, Back to Gaya (voice), 2004, Steamboy, 2004, The Game of Their Lives, 2005, Chicken Little (voice), 2005, X-Men: The Last Stand, 2006, TMNT, 2007, (voice) Earth, 2007, Gnomeo & Juliet (voice), 2011, Ice Age: Continental Drift (voice), 2012, Legends of Oz: Dorothy's Return (voice), 2013, Hunting Elephants, 2013, Sinbad: The Fifth Voyage (voice), 2013, Match, 2014, X-Men: Days of Future Past, 2014, Journey to Space (voice), 2015, Green Room, 2015, Christmas Eve, 2015, Ted 2, 2015, Logan, 2017, Dragonheart Battle for the Heartfire, 2017, The Emoji Movie, 2017, The Wilde Wedding, 2017, The Kid who Would be King, 2018; actor, associate prodr.: (TV films) The Canterville Ghost, 1996; actor, executive prodr.: (TV films) A Christmas Carol, 1999, King of Texas, 2002, The Lion in Winter, 2003; associate prodr.: (films) Star Trek IX: Insurrection, 1998; actor, prodr.: (TV films) Blunt Talk, 2015-; associate artist with Royal Shakespeare Co., 1967-; recording: Prokofiev: Peter and the Wolf (Grammy award for Best spoken Word Album for Children 1996). **AW:** Named a Honorary Knight Commander of the Most Excellent Order of the British Empire, Her Majesty Queen Elizabeth II, 2009; recipient Sir John Gielgud award, National Arts Club, 2008 **ACH:** Achievements include carrying the Olympic torch in the 2012 Summer Olympics

STEYER, THOMAS FAHR, T: Hedge Fund Manager **I:** Financial Services **PT:** Son of Roy H. and Marnie (Fahr) Steyer; **ED:** MBA, Stanford Grad. School of Business, California, 1983; BA in Econs. and Political Sci., summa cum laude, Yale University, 1979 **C:** Creator, NextGen America, 2013-; Managing director, Hellman & Friedman LLC,

San Francisco, 1986-; Founder, senior managing partner, Farallon Capital Management LLC, San Francisco, 1986-2012; Associate risk arbitrage department, Goldman, Sachs & Co.,; Fin. analyst mergers & acquisitions department, Morgan Stanley & Co., **CR:** Board of Directors Capital-Source, Chevy Chase, Maryland **CIV:** Director, Californians for Fair Election Reform, 2007- **MEM:** Fellow: Am. Academy Arts & Scis.; mem.: Phi Beta Kappa **BA:** NextGen America, 72 Baker Rd, Shutebury, MA, 01072

STIGLITZ, JOSEPH, T: Economist **I:** Financial Services **DOB:** 02/09/1943 **PB:** Gary **SC:** IN/USA **PT:** Son of Nathaniel David and Charlotte (Fishman) Stiglitz; **ED:** BA, Amherst College, Massachusetts, 1964; PhD in Economics, Massachusetts Institute of Technology, 1966; DHL (hon.), Amherst College, 1974; LLD (hon.), Northwestern University, 2000; Doctor (hon.), University Leuven, 1996; Doctor (hon.), Ben Gurion University, 1997; Doctor (hon.), Bard College, 2001; Doctor (hon.), University Toronto, 2001; Doctor (hon.), Glasgow University, 2001; Doctor (hon.), University Buenos Aires, 2001; Doctor (hon.), Pomona College, 2002; Doctor (hon.), University Barcelona, 2003; Doctor (hon.), Georgetown University, 2004; Doctor (hon.), Ind. University, 2004; Doctor (hon.), Pace University, 2004; Doctor (hon.), University Oxford, 2004; Doctor (hon.), Drexel University, 2005; Doctor (hon.), Durham University, 2005; Doctor (hon.), Renmin University, 2007; Doctor (hon.), University Venice, 2008; Doctor (hon.), University Manchester, 2008; LLD (hon.), Harvard University, 2014 **C:** Univ. professor, Columbia University, 2003—; Associate professor, Cowles Foundation, Yale University, New Haven, Connecticut, 1968—1970; Assistant professor, Cowles Foundation, Yale University, New Haven, Connecticut, 1967—1968; Assistant professor economics, Massachusetts Institute of Technology, 1966—1967; Professor economics & fin., Grad. School Business and School International & Pub. Affairs, Columbia University, 2001—; Co-founder, co-pres. Initiative Policy Dialogue, Columbia University; Stern visiting professor, Columbia University, New York City, New York, 2000; Professor economics, Princeton University, New Jersey, 1979—1988; Drummond professor political economy, Oxford University, England, 1976—1979; Professor economics, senior fellow Hoover Institution, Stanford University, 1988—2001; Joan Kenney professor economics, Stanford University, California, 1974—1976; Professor economics, Cowles Foundation, Yale University, New Haven, Connecticut, 1970—1974 **CR:** Tapp research fellow Gonville & Caius College, Cambridge, England, 1966—1970; visiting professor department economics University Canterbury, Christchurch, New Zealand, 1967; senior research fellow Institute Devel. Studies, Univ. College Nairobi, 1969—1971; visiting fellow St. Catherine's College, Oxford, 1973—1974; Oskar Morgenstern distinguished fellow & visiting professor Institute Advanced Study, Princeton, 1978—1979; professor economics, senior fellow Hoover Institution, Stanford University, 1988—2001; chairman economic policy committee Organization Economic Co-operation & Devel. (Organization of European Cooperation and Development), 1993—1995; member Council Economic Advisors, The White House, 1993—1995, chairman, 1995—1997; senior vice president, chief economist World Bank, Washington, 1997—2000; senior fellow Brookings Institution, Washington, 2000; chairman Brooks World Poverty Institute, University Manchester, England, 2005— **CIV:** Board trustees Folger Libr., Washington, Amherst College; hon. member board directors Center Global Devel.; board directors Alliance Climate

Protection **CW:** Author: Whither Socialism?, 1996, Frontiers of Development Economics: The Future in Perspective, 2000, New Ideas About Old Age Security: Toward Sustainable Pension Systems in the 21st Century, 2001, Globalization and Its Discontents, 2002, The Rebel Within: Joseph Stiglitz and the World Bank, 2002, The Roaring Nineties: A New History of the World's Most Prosperous Decade, 2003, Freefall: America, Free Markets and the Sinking of the World Economy, 2010, The Price of Inequality: How Today's Divided Society Endangers Our Future, 2012, The Great Divide: Unequal Societies and What We Can Do About Them, 2015; co-author (with C.E. Walsh): Principles of Macroeconomics, 2002, Economics, 2002; co-author: (with R. K. Sah) Peasants Versus City-Dwellers: Taxation and the Burden of Economic Development, 2002; co-author: (with B. Greenwald) Towards a New Paradigm in Monetary Economics, 2003, Creating A Learning Society: A New Approach to Growth, Development, and Social Progress, 2014; co-author: (with Andrew Charlton) Fair Trade For All: How Trade Can Promote Development (Initiative for Policy Dialogue Series), 2006; co-author: (with Linda J. Bilmes) The Three Trillion Dollar War: The True Cost of the Iraq Conflict, 2008; Am. editor Rev. of Economic Studies, 1968—76, associate editor Am. Economic Rev., 1968—76, Energy Econs., Managerial and Decision Econs.; editor: Journal Economic Perspectives, 1986—93; member editorial bd.: World Bank Economic Rev,(Books)The Euro: And its Threat to the Future of Europe, 2016 **AW:** Named one of The 100 Agents of Change, Rolling Stone magazine, 2009, The 100 Most Influential People in the World, TIME magazine, 2011, The 50 Most Influential People in Global Finance, Bloomberg Markets, 2011—12; recipient International Prize of Academia Lincei, 1988, UAP Sci. prize, Paris, 1989, Rechtenwald prize, Germany, 1998, Nobel Prize in Economics, Royal Swedish Academy Sci., 2001, Distinguished Leadership in Government award, Columbia Business School, 2002, John Kenneth Galbraith award, American Agricultural Economics Association, 2004, Benefit award, National Center Law & Economic Justice, 2006; Fellow John Simon Guggenheim Memorial Foundation, 1969—70; grantee Fulbright Fellowship, 1965—66,Legion of Honor,2012, Foreign Member of the Royal Society, 2009 **MEM:** Fellow: National Academy of Sciences, American Philosophical Society, Econometric Society, Brit. Academy (corr.), American Academy Arts & Sciences; mem.: Pontifical Academy Social Sciences, Serbian Sci. Society, Royal Society (foreign), American Economic Association (executive committee 1982-84, vice president 1985, John Bates Clark medal 1979) **BA:** Columbia University, 116th St & Broadway, 212 Uris, New York, NY, 10027

STIVERS, STEVE, T: U.S. Representative from Ohio **I:** Government Administration/Government Relations/Government Services **DOB:** 03/24/1965 **PB:** Cincinnati **ED:** MBA, Ohio State University, Columbus, 1996; BA in Economics and International Relations, Ohio State University, Columbus, 1989 **C:** Member, US House Financial Services Committee, Washington, 2011-; Chair, National Republican Congressional Committee, 2017, Member, Republican Study Committee; Member, US Congress from 15th Ohio District, Washington, 2011-; Member District 16, Ohio State Senate, 2003-09; Lic. securities trader, Ohio Co.,; Vice president government relations, Bank One Corp., **CR:** Member Ohio Public Expenditures Council, 2001-03, Ohio Public Works Commission, 2000-03 **CIV:** Member, Columbus Urban League, 2001-03 Vol., Big Brothers/Big Sisters, 2000- Board directors, trustee, Alvis House, Columbus, 1997- Board directors, Prevent Blindness Ohio, 2004-

Board directors, Contemporary Am. Theatre Co., Columbus, 1997- **MIL:** Active duty Battalion Commander Operation Iraqi Freedom, 2004-05, Iraq, Kuwait, Qatar, Djibouti, lieutenant colonel Ohio Army National Guard, 1985- **AW:** Decorated Bronze Star; recipient Legislator of Year award, Ohio Advocates Mental Health, 2006, Watchdog the Treasury award, United Conservatives Ohio, 2005 **MEM:** Mem.: Ohio National Guard Officers Association, Columbus Athletic Club **PA:** Republican

STODDART, J FRASER, T: Chemist **I:** Sciences **CN:** UCLA **DOB:** 05/24/1942 **PB:** Edinburgh **SC:** Scotland **ED:** DSc, St. Andrews University, 2010; DSc, Trinity College Dublin, 2009; DSc, University Sheffield, 2008; DSc (hon.), University Twente, 2006; DSc (hon.), University Birmingham, 2005; DSc, Edinburgh University, 1980; PhD, Edinburgh University, 1966; BSc, Edinburgh University, Scotland, 1964 **C:** Creator, Mechanostereochemistry Group, 2008-; Professor chemistry, director Center for Chemistry of Integrated Systems, Northwestern University, Evanston, Illinois, 2008-; Director, California NanoSystems Institute, 2003-07; Board director, California NanoSystems Institute, 2000; Acting co-dir., California Nano-Systems Institute, 2002-03; Fred Kavil Chair Nanosystems Sciences, UCLA, 2003-07; Saul Winstein chair, organic chemistry, UCLA, 1997-2003; Head School Chemical, Birmingham University, England, 1993-97; Chair organic chemistry, Birmingham University, England, 1990; Hon. professor chemistry, Birmingham University, England, 1997-2002; Professor Org. Chemical, Birmingham University, England, 1990-97; Researcher, ICI Corp. Laboratory, Runcorn, England, 1978-81; Sci. research council senior visiting fellow, UCLA, 1978; Reader in Chemistry, University Sheffield, England, 1982-91; Lecturer in Chemistry, University Sheffield, England, 1970-82; Imperial Chemical Industries research fellow, University Sheffield, England, 1970; National Research Council postdoctoral fellow, Queen's University, Kingston, Canada, 1967-70; Postgrad. student, University Edinburgh, Scotland, 1964-66 **CR:** Visiting professor Texas Agricultural and Mechanical University, 1980, Messina University, Italy, 1985-87, Ecole Nationale Supérieure de Chemie de Mulhouse, 1987, invited lecturer in supramolecular and macromolecular sci., hon. professor East China University Sci. and Tech. in Shanghai, 2005 Carnegie Centenary visiting professorship, University Scotland, 2005 member scientific adv. board Molecular Foundry, LLNL. **CW:** Member editorial adv. board Crystal Growth and Design, Journal Organic Chemistry, Organic Letters; member international adv. board Collection of Czechoslovak Chemical Communications, Angewandte Chemie; member editorial board Chemistry-A European Journal, Organic Letters; editor Royal Society of Chemistry Series of Monographs on Supramolecular Chemistry; contributor a significant number of articles to professional journals **AW:** Recipient Hope prize 1964, RSC Perkin Division Career award 1980, 81, 82, International Izatt-Christensen award in macrocyclic chemistry, 1993, Chaire Bruylants award, University Louvaine-La-Neuve, Belgium, 1994, Adolf Steinhofer Foundation award, 1995, Nagoya Gold Medal award in organic chemistry, 2004, Mack Memorial award, Ohio State University, 2006, Fusion award, University Nevada, 2006, King Faisal International prize Sci. King Faisal Foundation, 2007, Tetrahedron prize for creativity in organic chemistry, 2007, Feynman prize for nanotech., 2007, Albert Einstein award of sci., 2007, Davy Medal, 2008; Leverhulme research fellow, 1988-89, Humboldt Fellowship, 1998; named Alumnus of Year, University Edinburgh, 2005, Knight Bachelor, 2007. Recipient Nobel Prize in Chemistry 2016

MEM: Fellow Royal Society Edinburgh (hon.) (Royal medal), Royal Society Chemical, German Academy Natural Scis., American Association for the Advancement of Science, Sci. Division Royal Netherlands Academy Arts and Sciences, Royal Society (London) (Davy medal, 2008); member Chemical Soc.(Carbohydrate Chemistry award, 1978), Am. Chemical Society (Arthur C. Cope Scholar award, 1999, Arthur C. Cope award, 2008) **ACH:** Achievements include being co-creator of the world's densest memory circuit in 2007 **BA:** North Western University Department of Chemistry, 2145 Sheridan Road, Evanston, IL, 60208

STONE, EMMA, T: Actress **I:** Media & Entertainment **DOB:** 06/29/1905 **PB:** Scottsdale, **SC:** Scottsdale, **PT:** Daughter of Jeff and Kristen Stone. **CW:** Actress: (TV films) The New Partridge Family, 2005; (TV series) Drive, 2007; (films) Superbad, 2007, The Rocker, 2008, The House Bunny, 2008, Ghosts of Girlfriends Past, 2009, Paper Man, 2009, Zombieland, 2009, (voice) Marmaduke, 2010, Easy A, 2010, Friends With Benefits, 2011, Crazy, Stupid, Love, 2011 (Choice Comedy Actress, Teen Choice Awards, 2012), The Help, 2011 (Choice Movie Actress: Drama, Teen Choice Awards, 2012), The Amazing Spider-Man, 2012, Gangster Squad, 2012, Movie 43, 2013, (voice) The Croods, 2013, The Amazing Spider-Man 2, 2014, Magic in the Moonlight, 2014, Birdman: Or (The Unexpected Virtue of Ignorance), 2014, Irrational Man, 2015, Aloha, 2015, PopStar: Never Stop Never Stopping, 2016, La La Land, 2016, Battle of the Sexes, 2017, The Favourite, 2018 (TV appearances) Medium, 2005, The Suite Life of Zack and Cody, 2006, Malcolm in the Middle, 2006, Lucky Louie, 2006, Drive, 2007, SNL, Robot Chicken, 2011, 30 Rock, 2012, ICarly, 2012, May and Marty, 2016, Maniac, 2018; (Broadway plays) Cabaret, 2014-15 **AW:** Named Favorite Comedic Movie Actress, People's Choice Awards, 2012, Favorite Movie Actress, 2012; recipient Trailblazer award, MTV Movie Awards, 2012, Best Actress, 2017, La La Land, Golden Globes, Best Actress, 2017

STRAIT, GEORGE, T: Musician **I:** Media & Entertainment **DOB:** 05/18/1952 **PB:** Poteet **SC:** TX/USA **PT:** John Byron Strait; Doris Couser Strait **ED:** Honorary PhD, Southwest Texas State University (Now Texas State University), San Marcos, TX (2006); Degree in Agriculture, Southwest Texas State University, San Marcos **CIV:** US Army (1975) **CW:** Musician, "Cold Beer Conversation" (2015); Musician, "Love Is Everything" (2013); Musician, "Pure Country 2: The Gift" (2011); Musician, "Here for a Good Time" (2011); Musician, "Twang" (2009); Musician, "Classic Christmas" (2008); Musician, "Troubadour" (2008); Musician, "I Saw God Today" (2008); Musician, "Live at Texas Stadium" (2007); Musician, "George Strait 22 More Hits" (2007); Musician, "Give It Away" (2006); Musician, "It Just Comes Natural" (2006); Musician, "Good News Bad News" (2005); Musician, "Somewhere Down in Texas" (2005); Musician, "50 Number Ones" (2004); Musician, "Honkytonkville" (2003); Musician, "King of the Hill" (2003); Musician, "20th Century Masters" (2002); Musician, "Grand Champion" (2002); Musician, "The Road Less Traveled" (2001); Musician, "Latest Greatest Strait Greatest Hits" (2000); Musician, "George Strait" (2000); Musician, "Merry Christmas Wherever You Are" (1999); Musician, "Always Never the Same" (1999); Musician, "One Step at a Time" (1998); Musician, "Carrying Your Love With Me" (1997); Musician, "Blue Clear Sky" (1996); Musician, "Strait Out of the Box" (1995); Musician, "Greatest Hits Volume I, II, Lead On" (1994); Musician, "Easy Come, Easy Go" (1993); Actor, "Pure Country" (1992); Musician, "Holding My Own" (1992); Musician, "Pure

Country" (1992); Musician, "Chill of An Early Fall" (1991); Musician, "Ten Strait Hits" (1991); Musician, "Livin' It Up" (1990); Musician, "Beyond the Blue Neon" (1989); Musician, "If You Aint Lovin' (You Aint Livin')" (1988); Musician, "Ocean Front Property" (1987); Musician, "Strait Country" (1985); Musician, "Something Special" (1985); Musician, "Does Fort Worth Ever Cross Your Mind" (1984); Musician, "Right or Wrong" (1983); Musician, "Strait from the Heart" (1982); Actor, "The Soldier" (1982); Musician, "Strait Country" (1981) **AW:** Recipient, Cliffie Stone Icon Award (2017); Named, 50th Anniversary Milestone Award Winner (2015); Recipient, Milestone Award (2015); Named, Entertainer of the Year (2014); Named, Entertainer of the Year, Academy of Country Music (2014); Named, Entertainer of the Year (2013); Recipient, Legend of Live Award, Billboard Touring Awards (2013); Named, Artist of the Decade (2011); Named, #1 in Top 25 Country Singers of the Past 25 Years, Billboard (2010); Recipient, Grammy Award for Best Country Album (2009); Recipient, Award for Album of the Year, Country Music Association (2008); Recipient, Award for Single of the Year, Country Music Association (2008); Recipient, Award for Single Record of the Year, Song of the Year, Country Music Association (2007); Named, Country Music Hall of Fame (2006); Recipient, Album of the Year, Country Music Association (2006); Recipient, Award for Musical Event of Year, Country Music Association (2005); Recipient, Album of the Year, Country Music Association (1996-1998); Recipient, Male Vocalist of the Year, Country Music Association Awards (1996-1997); Recipient, Voice of the Year Award, American Society of Composers (1995); Recipient, Texas Ritter Award for Pure Country (1993); Named, Top Country Vocalist, American Music Awards (1991); Named, Entertainer of the Year (1990); Named, SRO Touring Artist of the Year (1990); Named, Entertainer of the Year (1989-1990); Named, Top Male Vocalist, Academy Country Music Awards (1988); Recipient, Male Vocalist of the Year, Country Music Association Awards (1985-1986); Recipient, Album of the Year, Country Music Association (1985-1986); Named, Top Male Vocalist, Academy Country Music Awards (1984-1985) **BA:** George Strait Productions Inc, PO Box 792063, San Antonio, TX, 78279

STRANCH, JANE BRANSTETTER, T: Federal Judge **I:** Law and Legal Services **DOB:** 09/17/1953 **PB:** Nashville **SC:** TN/USA **ED:** JD, Vanderbilt University Law School, Vanderbilt University (1978); BA, Vanderbilt University, Summa Cum Laude, Nashville, TN (1975) **C:** Judge, U.S. Court of Appeals for the Sixth Circuit (2010-Present); Partner, Branstetter, Stranch & Jennings, PLLC, Nashville, TN (1994-2010); Associate, Branstetter, Stranch & Jennings, PLLC, Nashville, TN (1978-1994); Law Clerk, Branstetter, Stranch & Jennings, PLLC, Nashville, TN (1975-1978) **CR:** Lecturer, Labor Law, Belmont University, Nashville, TN (1981-1983) **MEM:** Fellow, Tennessee Bar Foundation; Fellow, Nashville Bar Foundation; ABA; Lawyers' Association of Women; Tennessee Bar Association; Nashville Bar Association; Phi Alpha Delta; Phi Beta Kappa; Order of the Coif **BAR:** U.S. Court of Appeals for the Ninth Circuit (2008); U.S. District Court for the Western District of Tennessee (2008); U.S. District Court for the Eastern District of Michigan (2005); U.S. District Court for the District of Colorado (2002); Supreme Court of the U.S. (1996); U.S. District Court for the Eastern District of Tennessee (1991); U.S. Court of Appeals for the Sixth Circuit (1982); U.S. Tax Court (1980); U.S. District Court for the Middle District of Tennessee (1979); Tennessee Supreme Court (1978); Tennessee (1978) **BA:** 100 East Fifth Street, Cincinnati, OH, 45202

STRANGE, LUTHER JOHNSON III, T: U.S. Senator from Alabama **I:** Government Administration/Government Relations/Government Services **DOB:** 03/01/1953 **PB:** Birmingham **SC:** AL/USA **ED:** JD, Tulane University Law School, New Orleans, 1979; BA, Tulane University, New Orleans, 1975 **C:** Senator, Alabama, 2017-; Attorney general, State of Alabama, 2011-; Founder, attorney, Strange LLC, Birmingham,; Partner, Bradley Arant Boult Cummings LLP, Birmingham, **CIV:** Eagle scout, Boy Scouts of America, Member adv. board, U.S. Merchant Marine Academy, Kings Point, New York, **AW:** Named one of The Best of the Bar, Birmingham Business Journal, The Best Lawyers in Alabama, Birmingham Magazine **MEM:** Mem.: Rotary **PA:** Republican **BA:** Office of Luther Strange, 326 Russell Senate Office Building, Washington, DC, 20510

STRANGFELD, JOHN R. JR., T: CEO of Prudential Financial **I:** Financial Services **DOB:** 12/27/1953 **ED:** MBA, The University of Virginia; BBA, Susquehanna University, 1975 **C:** Chairman, CEO, Prudential Financial, Inc., 2008-; Vice chairman investments & insurance division, Prudential Financial, Inc., 2002-07; Executive vice president, Prudential Financial, Inc., 2001-02; Chairman, CEO, Prudential Securities, Inc., 2000-01; CEO, Prudential Investment Management, Prudential Insurance Co. Am., 1998-2002; Senior managing director, The Private Asset Management Group, Prudential Financial, Inc., 1995-98; Chairman, PRICOA Capital Group Europe, Prudential Financial, Inc., London, 1989-95; Various management positions., Prudential Financial, Inc., 1977-89 **CR:** Board of Directors Prudential Fin., Inc., 2008- Board of Managers Wachovia Securities Fin. Holdings, LLC, 2003- **CIV:** President Board of Trustees, Darden Foundation, The University of Virginia, Vice Chairman, Board of Trustees, Susquehanna University,

STRAS, DAVID R., T: Federal Judge **I:** Law and Legal Services **DOB:** 07/04/1974 **PB:** Wichita **SC:** KS/USA **ED:** JD, University of Kansas (1999); MBA, University of Kansas (1999); BA, University of Kansas, with Highest Distinction (1995) **C:** Judge, U.S. Court of Appeals for the Eighth Circuit (2018-Present); Associate Justice, Minnesota Supreme Court (2010-2018); Faculty Member, University of Minnesota Law School (2004-2010); Lawyer, Sidley Austin Brown & Wood, Washington, DC (2001-2002); Law Clerk to Honorable J. Michael Luttig, U.S. Court of Appeals for the Fourth Circuit; Law Clerk to Honorable Melvin Brunetti, U.S. Court of Appeals for the Ninth Circuit; Law Clerk to Honorable Clarence Thomas, Supreme Court of the U.S.; Of Counsel, Faegre & Benson LLP; Co-Director, Institute of Law and Politics, University of Minnesota **BA:** Thomas F. Eagleton Courthouse, 111 South 10th Street, St. Louis, MO, 63102

STREEP, MERYL, T: Actress **I:** Media & Entertainment **DOB:** 06/22/1949 **PB:** Summit **PT:** Daughter of Harry, Junior and Mary W. Streep; **ED:** ArtsD (hon.), Harvard University, 2010; DFA (hon.), Dartmouth College, 1981; DFA (hon.), Yale University, 1983; MFA, Yale University, 1975; BA in Drama, Vassar College, 1971 **C:** Co-founder, Mothers & Others for a Livable Planet, **CW:** (appeared with): Green Mountain Guild; actress: (Broadway plays) Trelawny of the Wells, 1975; (plays) 27 Wagons Full of Cotton (Theatre World award), A Memory of Two Mondays, Henry V, Secret Service, The Taming of the Shrew, Measure for Measure, The Cherry Orchard, Happy End, Wonderland, Taken in Marriage, Alice in Concert (Obie award, 1981), Mother Courage, 2006; (films) Julia, 1977, The Deer Hunter, 1978 (National

Society Film Critics award for Best Supporting Actress, 1978), Manhattan, 1979, The Seduction of Joe Tynan, 1979, Kramer versus Kramer, 1979 (New York Film Critics' award for Best Actress, Golden Globe award, Academy award for Best Supporting Actress, 1980), The French Lieutenant's Woman, 1981 (Golden Globe award for Best Actress, 1982), Sophie's Choice, 1982 (Academy award for Best Actress, Golden Globe award for Best Actress, 1983), Still of the Night, 1982, Silkwood, 1983, Falling in Love, 1984, Plenty, 1985, Out of Africa, 1985, Heartburn, 1986, Ironweed, 1987, A Cry in the Dark, 1988 (New York Film Critics' Circle award for Best Actress, 1989), She-Devil, 1989, Postcards From the Edge, 1990, Defending Your Life, 1991, Death Becomes Her, 1992, The House of Spirits, 1993, The River Wild, 1994, The Bridges of Madison County, 1995, Before and After, 1996, Marvin's Room, 1996, Dancing at Lugnasa, 1998, One True Thing, 1998, Music of the Heart, 1999, The Hours, 2002, Adaptation, 2002 (Golden Globe award for Best Supporting Actress, 2003), The Manchurian Candidate, 2004, Lemony Snicket's A Series of Unfortunate Events, 2004, Prime, 2005, A Prairie Home Companion, 2006 (National Society Film Critics award for Best Supporting Actress, 2007), The Devil Wears Prada, 2006 (National Society Film Critics award for Best Supporting Actress, 2007, Golden Globe award for Best Performance by an Actress in a Motion Picture-Musical or Comedy, 2007), Dark Matter, 2007, Evening, 2007, Rendition, 2007, Lions for Lambs, 2007, Mamma Mia!, 2008, Doubt, 2008 (Critics' Choice award for 2008 Best Actress, Broadcast Film Critics Association, 2009, Screen Actors Guild award for Outstanding Performance by a Female Actor in a Leading Role, 2009), Julie & Julia, 2009 (Boston Society Film Critics award for Best Actress, 2009, New York Film Critics Cir. award for Best Actress, 2009, Golden Globe award for Best Performance by an Actress in a Motion Picture-Comedy or Musical, 2010, Critics' Choice award for Best Actress, Broadcast Film Critics Association, 2010), It's Complicated, 2009, The Iron Lady, 2011 (New York Film Critics Cir. award for Best Actress, 2011, Golden Globe award for Best Performance by an Actress in a Motion Picture-Drama, 2012, BAFTA award for Best Leading Actress, 2012, Academy award for Best Actress, 2012), Hope Springs, 2012, August: Osage County, 2013, The Homesman, 2014, The Giver, 2014, Into the Woods, 2014, Ricki and the Flash, 2015, Suffragette, 2015, Florence Foster Jenkins, 2016, We Rise, 2017, The Post, 2017, Mamma Mia! Here We Go Again, 2018, Mary Poppins Returns, 2018; (voice) (films) Rabbit Ears: The Tale of Peter Rabbit, 1987, Rabbit Ears: The Tale of Jeremy Fisher, 1987, The Tailor of Gloucester, 1988, Rabbit Ears: The Fisherman and His Wife, 1989, Chrysanthemum, 1999, Artificial Intelligence: AI, 2001, The Ant Bully, 2006, Fantastic Mr. Fox, 2009, The Guardian Brothers, 2016; actress: (TV films) Secret Service, 1977, The Deadliest Season, 1977, Uncommon Women and Others, 1979, Alice at the Palace, 1982; actress, executive producer (TV films) First Do No Harm, 1997, narrator The Velveteen Rabbit, 1984 (Emmy award for Best Children's Recording), A Vanishing Wilderness, 1990; actress: (TV miniseries) Holocaust, 1978 (Emmy award for Outstanding Lead Actress in a Mini-series, 1978), Angels in America, 2003 (Screen Actors Guild award for Best Actress, Golden Globe award for Best Actress, Emmy award for Outstanding Lead Actress in a Mini-series or a Movie, 2004)Freedom A History of US, 2003, Ocean Voyagers, 2007, Web Therapy, 2010, Makers: Woman Who Maker America, 2013, The Roosevelts, 2014, Five Came Back, 2017; appeared in (documentaries) I Knew It Was You: Rediscovering John Cazale, 2010, narrator To the

Arctic 3D, 2012 **AW:** Named Favorite Movie Icon, People's Choice Awards, 2013, Officer, French Ordre des Arts et des Lettres, 2000; named one of The 100 Most Powerful Women in Entertainment, Hollywood Reporter, 2012, 2009, The 50 Smartest People in Hollywood, Entertainment Weekly, 2007, The 100 Most Influential People in the World, TIME magazine, 2006; named to The New Jersey Hall of Fame, 2008; recipient Presidential Medal of Freedom, The White House, 2014, Lifetime Achievement award-Honorary Golden Bear, Berlin Film Festival, 2012, Kennedy Center Honors, John F. Kennedy Center for the Performing Arts, 2011, National Medal of Arts, National Endowment for the Arts, 2010, Marcos Aurelius Lifetime Achievement award, Rome Film Festival, 2009, Dana Reeve HOPE award, Christopher and Dana Reeve Foundation, 2007, Lifetime Achievement award, American Film Institute, 2004, Bette Davis Lifetime Achievement award, 1999, Gotham award for Lifetime Achievement, 1999, Women in Film Crystal award, 1998, People's Choice award, 1983, 85, 86, 87, 1990, Star of Year award, National Association Theater Owners, 1983, Best Actress award, National Board Review, 1982, Best Supporting Actress award, 1979, Woman of Year award, Hasty Pudding Society, Harvard University, 1980, B'nai Brith, 1979, Mademoiselle award, 1976 **BA:** Creative Artists Agency, 2000 Avenue of the Stars, Los Angeles, CA, 90067

STREISAND, BARBRA JOAN, T: Singer, Actress, Film Director **I:** Media & Entertainment **DOB:** 04/24/1942 **PB:** Bklyn **PT:** Daughter of Emanuel and Diana (Rosen) Streisand; **ED:** LHD (hon.), Brandeis University, 1995 **C:** Founder, Barwood Films, 1972; Co-founder, First Artists Production Co., 1969 **CW:** Performer: (Broadway plays) I Can Get It for You Wholesale, 1961-63; singer: (albums) The Barbra Streisand Album, 1963 (Album of the Year, Grammy Awards, 1963, Best Female Pop Vocal Performance, Grammy Awards, 1963, Grammy Hall of Fame, Grammy Awards, 2006), The Second Barbra Streisand Album, 1963, The Third Album, 1964, People, 1964 (Best Female Pop Vocal Performance, Grammy Awards, 1964), My Name is Barbra, 1965 (Best Female Pop Vocal Performance, Grammy Awards, 1965), My Name is Barbra, Two..., 1965, Color Me Barbra, 1966, Je M'Appelle Barbra, 1966, Simply Streisand, 1967, A Christmas Album, 1967, What About Today, 1969, Stoney End, 1971, Barbra Joan Streisand, 1971, Barbra Streisand... And Other Musical Instruments, 1973, The Way We Were, 1974 (Grammy Hall of Fame, Grammy Awards, 2008), ButterFly, 1974, Lazy Afternoon, 1975, Classical Barbra, 1976, Streisand Superman, 1977, Songbird, 1978, Wet, 1979, Guilty, 1980, Emotion, 1984, The Broadway Album, 1985 (Best Female Pop Vocal Performance, Grammy Awards, 1986), Till I Loved You, 1988, Back to Broadway, 1993, Higher Ground, 1997, A Love Like Ours, 1999, Christmas Memories, 2001, The Movie Album, 2003, Guilty Pleasures, 2005, Love is the Answer, 2009, What Matters Most, 2011, Release Me, 2012, Back to Brooklyn, 2013, Partners, 2014, The Classic Christmas Album, 2014, (songs) Evergreen (Love Theme from A Star is Born), 1976 (Best Original Song, Academy Awards, 1976, Best Original Song, Golden Globe Awards, 1976, Best Pop Vocal Female Performance, Grammy Awards, 1977, Song of the Year, Grammy Awards, 1977), (with Barry Gibb) Guilty, 1981 (Best Pop Vocal Performance, Duo or Group, Grammy Awards, 1980); actress: (films) Funny Girl, 1968 (Best Actress, Academy Awards, 1968, Best Actress Comedy or Musical, Academy Awards, 1968, Best Actress Comedy or Musical, Golden Globe Awards, 1968, Grammy Hall of Fame, Grammy Awards, 2004), Hello, Dolly!, 1969, On a Clear Day You Can See Forever, 1970, The Owl

and the Pussycat, 1970, What's Up, Doc?, 1972, Up the Sandbox, 1972, The Way We Were, 1973, For Pete's Sake, 1974, Funny Lady, 1975, A Star is Born, 1976 (Best Actress Comedy or Musical, Golden Globe Awards, 1976), The Main Event, 1979, All Night Long, 1981, Nuts, 1987, Meet the Fockers, 2004, Little Fockers, 2010, The Guilt Trip, 2012; actress, director, producer (films) Yentl, 1983 (Best Director, Golden Globe Awards, 1984), The Prince of Tides, 1991, The Mirror Has Two Faces, 1996, Meet the Fockers, 2004, Little Fockers, 2010 actress, executive producer The Guilt Trip, 2012; executive prodr.: (TV films) Frankie & Hazel, 2000, What Makes a Family, 2001, Varian's War, 2001; performer: (TV specials) My Name is Barbra, 1965 (Outstanding Individual Achievements in Entertainment, Emmy Awards, 1965), Barbra Streisand: The Concert, 1994 (Outstanding Variety, Music Or Comedy Special, Emmy Awards, 1995, Outstanding Individual Performance in a Variety or Music Program, Emmy Awards, 1995), Barbra Streisand: Timeless, 2001 (Outstanding Individual Performance in a Variety or Music Program, Emmy Awards, 2001)Streisand:Live in Concert, 2009, Babra Streisand: One Night Only at the Village Vanguard, Katie: Barbra is Back, 2012, Encore: Behind the Scenes with Barbra Streisand, 2016; author: My Passion for Design, 2010 **AW:** Named 2011 MusiCares Person of the Year, The Recording Academy and the MusiCares Foundation, Favorite All-Time Musical Performer, People's Choice Awards, 1988, Favorite All-Around Female Entertainer, 1985, Favorite Female Singer of Year, 1975, Singing Star of Year, Am. Guild Variety Artists Georgie Awards, 1980, 1977, 1972, Entertainer of Year, 1970; named to French Legion of Honor, Order of Arts and Letters, 2007; recipient Presidential Medal of Freedom, The White House, 2015, Kennedy Center Honors, John F. Kennedy Center for the Performing Arts, 2008, Humanitarian award, Human Rights Campaign, 2004, Lifetime Achievement award, Am. Film Institute, 2001, National Medal of Arts, National Endowment for the Arts, 2000, Commitment to Life award, AIDS Project Los Angeles, 1992, Lifetime Achievement award, Grammy Awards, 1994, Legend award, 1992, Cecil B. DeMille award for Lifetime Achievement, Golden Globe Awards, 2000, Henrietta World Film Inst award, 1975, 1971, 1970 **BA:** The Streisand Foundation, 1327 Ocean Ave, Santa Monica, CA, 90401

SÜDHOF, THOMAS CHRISTIAN, T: Molecular Genetics Educator **I:** Education/Educational Services **DOB:** 12/22/1955 **PB:** Göttingen **ED:** MD, Georgia Augusta University, Göttingen, Germany, 1982; Degree in Medicine, RWTH, Aachen, Germany, 1977 **C:** Avram Goldstein professor molecular and cellular physiology, Stanford University School Medicine, 2008-; Adjunct professor neurosci., University Texas Southwestern Medical Center, Howard Hughes Medical Institute, Dallas, 2008-; Investigator, University Texas Southwestern Medical Center, Howard Hughes Medical Institute, Dallas, 1991-; Director Center for Neuroscience, University Texas Southwestern Medical Center, Howard Hughes Medical Institute, Dallas, 1997-2006; Gill distinguished chair neurosci. research, University Texas Southwestern Medical Center, Howard Hughes Medical Institute, Dallas, 1995-2008; Professor department molecular genetics, University Texas Southwestern Medical Center, Howard Hughes Medical Institute, Dallas, 1991-2008; Associate professor department molecular genetics, University Texas Southwestern Medical Center, Howard Hughes Medical Institute, Dallas, 1989-91; Assistant investigator, University Texas Southwestern Medical Center, Howard Hughes Medical Institute, Dallas, 1986-89; Assistant professor department molecular genetics, University Texas Southwestern Medical Center, Dallas, 1987-89; Postdoctoral fellow department molecular genetics, University Texas Southwestern Medical Center, Dallas, 1983-85; Postdoctoral fellow, Max-Planck-Inst. Biophysikallsche Chemie, Göttingen, 1982-83 **CR:** Loyd B. Sands distinguished chair in neurosci. member molecular, cellular and devel. neurobiology rev. committee National Institute of Mental Health, 1995-. **CW:** Member editorial board Journal Biological Chemistry and of Neuron; contributor numerous articles to professional publications **AW:** Recipient W. Alden Spencer award Columbia University, 1993, Wilhelm Feldberg award, 1994, MetLife award for Alzheimers Research MetLife Foundation, 2004, Freedom to Discover Achievement award for Neuro-Science, Bristol-Myers Squibb, 2004, Passano Foundation award, 2008; co-recipient Bernhard Katz award, Biophysical Society, 2008, Kavli prize, Norwegian Academy Sci. & Letters, Kavli Foundation and Norway's Ministry of Education and Research, 2010, Albert Lasker Basic Medical Research award, Albert & Mary Lasker Foundation, 2013, Nobel Prize in Physiology or Medicine Karolinska Institute, 2013,Fellow of the Royal Society, 2017,Fellow of the Royal Society, 2017 **MEM:** Fellow: Am. Academy Arts & Sciences; mem.: National Academy of Sciences (Molecular Biology award 1997), Institute Medicine **BA:** Howard Hughes Med Inst Stanford Sch Medicine, 1050 Arastradero Rd B249F, Palo Alto, CA, 94304

SULENTIC, ROBERT E., **T:** CEO of Cbre Group **I:** Business Management/Business Services **ED:** MBA, Harvard University; BA, University Iowa **C:** CEO, Cbre Group Inc, 2012-; President, CB Richard Ellis Group, Inc., 2010-; President, CFO, CB Richard Ellis Group Inc., 2009-10; Group president, devel. services, Asia Pacific and Europe, Middle East and Africa, CB Richard Ellis Group Inc.,; Group president EMEA, Asia Pacific, develop. & investment, CB Richard Ellis Group Inc., LA, 2006-09; Chairman, Trammell Crow Co. (subsidiary CB Richard Ellis Group, Inc.), Dallas, 2002-06; President, CEO, Trammell Crow Co. (subsidiary CB Richard Ellis Group, Inc.), Dallas, 2000-06; Executive vice president, CFO, Trammell Crow Co. (subsidiary CB Richard Ellis Group, Inc.), Dallas, 1998-2000; Executive vice president, national director devel. and investment, Trammell Crow Co. (subsidiary CB Richard Ellis Group, Inc.), Dallas, 1997-98; President Trammell Crow NE, Inc., Trammell Crow Co. (subsidiary CB Richard Ellis Group, Inc.), Dallas, 1995-98; Various positions, Trammell Crow Co. (subsidiary CB Richard Ellis Group, Inc.), Dallas, 1984-94 **CR:** Board directors CB Richard Ellis Group Inc., 2006-09, Trammell Crow Co., 1997-2006, Staples, Inc.

SULLIVAN, DAN, **T:** U.S. Senator from Alaska **I:** Government Administration/Government Relations/Government Services **DOB:** 11/13/1964 **PB:** Fairview Park **SC:** Ohio **ED:** JD, MS in Foreign Service cum laude, Georgetown University, 1993; MA in International Relations, University Birmingham, 1988; BA in Economics, magna cum laude, Harvard University, 1987 **C:** US Senator from Alaska, 2015-; Commissioner, Alaska Department Natural Resources, 2010-13; Attorney general, State of Alaska, Juneau, 2009-10; Assistant secretary for economic, energy & business affairs, US Department State, Washington, 2006-09; Director, acting senior director International Economic Directorate, The White House, Washington, 2002-04; Associate, Perkins Coie, LLP, Anchorage, 2000-02; Law clerk to Chief Justice Warren Matthews, Alaska Supreme Court, 1998-99; Law clerk to Hon. Andrew Kleinfeld, US Court Appeals (9th cir.), Fairbanks, Alaska, 1997-98 **CIV:** Active,

Alaska's Toys for Tots Foundation, 1994- **MIL:** Strategic advisor, special assistant to Commander US Central Command (CENTCOM) US Marine Corps, 2005-06 US Marine Corps Reserve, 1997-, served US Mari **CW:** Co-author: Chosun's Tears, 1999 **AW:** Decorated Defense Meritorious Service Medal; named one of The 10 Outstanding Young Americans, US Junior Chamber of Commerce; recipient Outstanding Service award, National Security Council **MEM:** Mem.: Alaska Bar Association **PA:** Republican

SULLIVAN, JOHN J., **T:** Deputy Secretary of State **I:** Government Administration/Government Relations/Government Services **PB:** Boston **ED:** JD, Columbia University, 1985; BA in History & Political Sci., Brown University, 1981 **C:** Deputy Secretary of State, 2017-; Deputy Secretary, State for Management and Resources, 2017-; Partner, Gibson, Dunn & Crutcher LLP, Washington, 2009-; Deputy secretary, US Department Commerce, Washington, 2008-09; General counsel, US Department Commerce, Washington, 2005-08; Legal counsel, deputy general counsel, US Department Defense, Washington, 2004-05; Partner, Mayer, Brown, Rowe & Maw, LLP, 1993-2004; Deputy general counsel, George H.W. Bush Re-Election Campaign, 1992; Counselor to assistant attorney general Office Legal Counsel, US Department Justice, 1991; Law clerk to Justice David H. Souter, US Supreme Court,; Law clerk to Hon. John Minor Wisdom, US Court Appeals (5th Cir.),

SULZBERGER, ARTHUR OCHS JR., **T:** Chairman of the New York Times **I:** Media & Entertainment **DOB:** 09/22/1951 **PB:** Mount Kisco **SC:** NY/USA **PT:** Son of Arthur Ochs Sulzberger and Barbara Winslow Grant; **ED:** Grad. management devel. program, Harvard Business School, 1985; BA in Political Sci., Tufts University, Medford, Massachusetts, 1974 **C:** Chairman, The New York Times Co., 1997-2018; Pub., The New York Times, 1992-; CEO, The New York Times Co., 2011-12; Deputy pub., The New York Times, 1988-92; Assistant pub., The New York Times, 1987-88; Production coordinator, The New York Times, 1985-87; Senior analyst corp. planning, The New York Times, 1985; Group manager advertising department, The New York Times, 1983-84; Assistant metro editor, The New York Times, 1981-82; Metro reporter, The New York Times, New York City, 1981; Corr. Washington bureau, The New York Times, 1978-81; Corr., Associated Press, London, 1976-78; Reporter, Raleigh Times, North Carolina, 1974-76 **CIV:** Co-founder, chairman, New York City Outward Bound Center, 2002- Former chairman, Times Sq. Business Improvement District **AW:** Recipient Literarian award for Outstanding Service to the American Literary Community, National Book award, 2012, CUNY School of Journalism Journalistic Achievement Award, 2017 **BA:** New York Times, 620 8th Ave #1, New York, NY, 10018

SUNUNU, CHRIS, **T:** Governor of New Hampshire **I:** Government Administration/Government Relations/Government Services **PB:** Salem **SC:** NH/USA **ED:** Thomas Jefferson High School for Science and Technology, 1993; B.S., MIT, 1998 **C:** Governor, New Hampshire, 2017-; Member, New Hampshire Executive Council from the 3rd District, 2011-17

SUOZZI, THOMAS, **T:** U.S. Representative from New York **I:** Government Administration/Government Relations/Government Services **PB:** Glen Cove **SC:** NY/USA **PT:** Joseph A. Suozzi, Marguerite Suozzi **ED:** JD, Fordham University, 1989; BS, Boston College, 1984 **C:** Committee on Foreign Affairs, U.S. Representative from New York's Third District, 2017-Present; Senior Advisor, Lazard,

2010-2012; Executive, Nassau County, New York, 2002-2009; Mayor, Glen Cove, NY, 1994-2001

SUTHERLAND, KIEFER, **T:** Actor **I:** Media & Entertainment **PB:** London **SC:** England **PT:** Donald Sutherland; Shirley Douglas Sutherland **SPN:** Kelly Winn (June 29, 1996) (div. May 16, 2004); Camelia Kath (September 12, 1987) (div. 1990) **CH:** Sarah Jude **C:** Co-owner record label, Ironworks **CW:** Stage appearances include (theater) Throne of Straw, 1977; actor: (films) Max Dugan Returns, 1983, The Bay Boy, 1984, At Close Range, 1986, Crazy Moon, 1986, Stand By Me, 1986, The Lost Boys, 1987, The Killing Time, 1987, Promised Land, 1987, 1969, 1988, Bright Lights, Big City, 1988, Young Guns, 1988, Renegades, 1989, Chicago Joe and the Showgirl, 1990, Flashback, 1990, Flatliners, 1990, (voice) The Nutcracker Prince, 1990, Young Guns II, 1990, Article 99, 1991, Twin Peaks: Fire Walk With Me, 1992, A Few Good Men, 1992, The Vanishing, 1993, The Three Musketeers, 1993, The Cowboy Way, 1994, Eye for an Eye, 1995, A Time to Kill, 1996, The Last Days of Frankie the Fly, 1996, Freeway, 1996, Truth or Consequences N.M, 1997, Dark City, 1997, Sweetheart of the Song Tra Bong, 1998, Ground Control, 1998, (voice) Dinosaur, 1998, The Breakup, 1998, Dark City, 1998, Woman Wanted, 1999, The Red Dove, 1999, Hearts and Bones, 1999, Beat, 2000, Picking Up the Pieces, 2000, Ring of Fire, 2000, The Royal Way, 2000, The Right Temptation, 2000, To End All Wars, 2001, Paradise Found, 2001, Desert Saints, 2002, Dead Heat, 2002, Behind the Red Door, 2002, Phone Booth, 2002, Taking Lives, 2004, Jiminy Glick in La La Wood, 2004, (voice) The Wild, 2006, The Sentinel, 2006, Mirrors, 2008, (voice) Monsters versus Aliens, 2009, (voice) Marmaduke, 2010, Twelve, 2010, Melancholia, 2011, The Reluctant Fundamentalist, 2012, Pompeii, 2014, Forsaken, 2015, Zoolander 2, 2016, Beat-up Little Seagull, 2016, Where is Kyra? ,2017, Flatliners, 2017 (TV films) Trapped in Silence, 1986, Brotherhood of Justice, 1986, Last Light, 1993, Marked, 2014, (TV series) Designated Survivor, 2016; actor, executive prodr.: (TV series) 24, 2001-10, 2014 (Golden Globe award for Best Performance by Actor in TV Series Drama, 2002, Screen Actors Guild award for Best Actor in a Drama Series, 2004, Screen Actors Guild award for Outstanding Performance by a Male Actor in a Drama Series, 2006, Emmy award for Outstanding Lead Actor in a Drama Series, 2006), The Confession, 2011, Touch, 2012-13, 24: Live Another Day, 2014, Playhouse Presents Marked, 2014, Top Gear, 2015, Rammstein in Amerika, 2015, Keeping Canada Alive, 2015; musician: (albums) Down in a Hole, 2016

SUTTON, JEFFREY S., **T:** Federal Judge **I:** Law and Legal Services **DOB:** 10/31/1960 **PB:** Dhahran **SC:** Saudi Arabia **ED:** LLB, Ohio State Univ., 1990; BA, Williams College, 1983 **C:** Judge, U.S. Court Appeals, (6th cir.), Cincinnati, 2003-; Adj. Law Professor, Ohio State Univ., Ohio, 1994-; Partner, Jones, Day, Reavis & Pogue, Columbus, Ohio, 1998-2003; Solicitor, Ohio State, Ohio, 1995-98; Associate, Jones, Day, Reavis & Pogue, Columbus, Ohio, 1992-95; Clerk, Supreme Court for Justice Scalia and Retired Justice Powell, 1991-92; Clerk, Second Circuit Court for Judge Thomas Meskill, 1990-91 **BA:** 100 East Fifth Street, Cincinnati, OH, 45202

SUTTON, MARK STEPHAN, **T:** Paper Company Executive **I:** Manufacturing **ED:** BEE, Louisiana State University, 1983 **C:** Chairman, CEO, International Paper Co., 2015-Present; CEO, International Paper Co., 2014; President, COO, International Paper Co., 2014; Senior Vice President of Industrial Packaging, International Paper Co.,

2011-2014; Senior Vice President of Printing & Commercial Papers in the Americas, International Paper Co., 2010-2011; Senior Vice President of Supply Chain, International Paper Co., 2008-2009; Vice President, Supply Chain, International Paper Co., 2007-2008; Vice President, Strategic Planning, International Paper Co., 2005-2007; Vice President, General Manager, Corrugated Packaging Operations, European, International Paper Co., 2002-2005; Director, European Corrugated Packaging Operations, International Paper Co., 2000-2002; General Manager, Pressure Sensitive Products, International Paper Co., 1998-2000; Mill Manager, Thilmany Mill, International Paper Co., 1994-1998; Engineering Manager, Production Manager, International Paper Co., Nicolet, WI, 1991-1993; Engineer, International Paper Co., Pineville, LA, 1984 **CR:** Board of Directors, International Paper Co., 2014-Present; Business Council and Business Roundtable; Board of Directors, American Forest & Paper Association; International Advisory Board, Moscow School of Management **CIV:** Board of Directors, RISE; Advisory Board, Wang Center for International Business Education; Trustee, New Mexico Institute **BA:** International Paper Company, 6400 Poplar Avenue, Memphis, TN, 38197

SWALWELL, ERIC JR., T: U.S. Representative from California **I:** Government Administration/Government Relations/Government Services **DOB:** 11/16/1980 **PB:** Sac City **SC:** IA/USA **PT:** Eric Swalwell; Vicky Swalwell **ED:** JD, University Maryland School Law, 2006; BA in Government & Politics, University Maryland, 2003 **C:** Member, US House Space, Sci. & Technology Committee, 2013-; Member, US House Homeland Security Committee, 2013-; Member, US Congress from 15th California District, Washington, 2013-; Deputy district attorney, Alameda County, 2006-12; Intern for Rep. Ellen Tauscher, US House of Representatives, 2001-02 **CR:** Member Dublin City Council, 2010-12, Dublin Planning Commission, 2008-10 chairperson Dublin Heritage & Cultural Arts Commission, 2006 **CIV:** Director, San Ramon Soccer Club, 2006-09 **PA:** Democrat

SWANK, HILARY, T: Actress **I:** Media & Entertainment **DOB:** 07/30/1974 **PB:** Lincoln **SC:** NE/USA **PT:** Stephen Swank; Judy Swank **ED:** Attended, Santa Monica College **C:** Co-founder, 2S Films, 2008 **CW:** Actress: (films) Buffy the Vampire Slayer, 1992, The Next Karate Kid, 1994, Sometimes They Come Back...Again, 1996, Kounterfeit, 1996, The Way We Are, 1997, Heartwood, 1998, Boys Don't Cry, 1999 (Golden Globe award for Best Actress, 2000, Academy award for Best Actress, 2000), Affair of the Necklace, 2000, The Gift, 2000, Insomnia, 2002, The Core, 2003, Million Dollar Baby, 2004 (Boston Film Critics award for Best Actress, 2004, Screen Actors Guild award for Outstanding Performance by Female Actor in Leading Role, 2005, Golden Globe award for Best Actress, 2005, Academy award for Best Actress, 2005), The Black Dahlia, 2006, The Reaping, 2007, P.S. I Love You, 2007, Birds of America, 2008, New Year's Eve, 2011, The Homesman, 2014; (TV films) Cries Unheard: The Donna Yaklich Story, 1994, Terror in the Family, 1996, Dying to Belong, 1997, The Sleepwalker Killing, 1997, Iron Jawed Angels, 2004, Mary and Martha, 2013, Trust, 2018; (TV series) Evening Shade, 1991-92, Camp Wilder, 1992, Leaving LA, 1997, Beverly Hills, 90210, 1997-98; actress, executive producer (films) 11:14, 2003, Freedom Writers, 2007, Amelia, 2009, Conviction, 2011, The Resident, 2011, New Years Eve, 2011,The Homesman, 2014, You're Not You, 2014, Lauda: The Untold Story, 2015, Spark, 2017, Logan Lucky, 2017, 55 Steps, 2017, What They Had, 2018,

TV appearances Growing Pains, 1985, Harry and the Hendersons, 1991; prodr.: (films) Something Borrowed, 2011; actress, producer (films) You're Not You, 2014 **AW:** Named one of 100 Most Influential People, TIME magazine, 2005; recipient Star, Hollywood Walk of Fame, 2007, Emery award, Hetrick-Martin Institute, 2006

SWEDISH, JOSEPH R., T: Wellpoint CEO **I:** Business Management/Business Services **PB:** Richmond **SC:** VA/USA **ED:** Master in Health Administration, Duke University, 1979; BS, University of North Carolina, Charlotte, 1973 **C:** CEO, Wellpoint, Inc. (formerly Anthem, Inc.), Indianapolis, 2013-; President, CEO, Trinity Health, Novi, Michigan, 2005-13; President, CEO, Centura Health, Colorado, 1999-2004; President, CEO, Central Florida & East Florida divisions, Hospital Corp. of America, 1994-98 **CR:** Chairman Catholic Health Association, Colorado Hospital Association chairman elect health care system governor council American Hospital Association member National Quality Forum Board chairman Catholic Health Association Board, 2012-13, vice chair/chair elect board directors Health Care Education Trust, National Quality Forum, Loyola University Chicago, Wellpoint, Inc., 2013-, Coventry Health Care, Inc., 2010-13, RehabCare Group Inc., 2003-05, Cross Country Healthcare, Florida, 2002-05 **CIV:** Member board, Metro Denver Boy Scouts, Member economic devel. council, Metro Denver C. of C., Chairman, Colorado Hospital Assn, Member board, Colorado Forum, Member board, Colorado Concern, Board of Directors, Am. Hospital Assn, **AW:** Named Entrepreneur of Year, Rocky Mountain Region, Ernst & Young, 2003; named one of Top 100 Most Powerful Leaders in Healthcare, Modern Healthcare, 2006-; recipient CEO Diversity Leadership award, Diversity Best Practices, 2009, Univ. Medal, Board Regents University Colorado **MEM:** Fellow: American College Healthcare Executives (Career Achievement Regents award 2004) **H:** Fly fishing, golf, skiing **BA:** Wellpoint Headquarters, One Liberty Plaza, New York, NY, 10006

SWIFT, CHRISTOPHER JOHN, T: Insurance Company Executive **I:** Insurance **ED:** BS in Accounting, Marquette University, 1983 **C:** CEO, Hartford Financial Services Group, Inc., Hartford, Connecticut, 2014-; Executive vice president, CFO, Hartford Financial Services Group, Inc., Connecticut, 2010-14; Vice chairman, CFO American Life Insurance Co. (ALICO), American International Group, Inc. (AIG), 2009-10; Vice president, CFO life insurance & retirement services, American International Group, Inc. (AIG), 2005-09; Executive vice president, CFO, head annuity operations AIG AmericanGen. Life Companies, American International Group, Inc. (AIG), 2003-05; Executive vice president, Conning Asset Management,; Head Global Insurance Industry Practice, KPMG LLP, Chicago,; Partner, KPMG LLP, Chicago, 1985-2003 **CR:** Board directors Hartford Financial Services Group, Inc., 2014-; Chairman Board of American Insurance Association; Member Board of Catalyst, Business Council, Committee Encouraging Corporate Philanthropy, Council on Foreign Relations, Geneva Association. **MEM:** Mem.: International Insurance Society

SWIFT, TAYLOR, T: Musician, Singer, Songwriter **I:** Media & Entertainment **DOB:** 12/13/1989 **PB:** Wyomissing **SC:** PA/USA **PT:** Daughter of Scott Kingsley and Andrea Gardner (Finlay) Swift. **C:** Launched fragrance, Wonderstruck,; Spokesmodel, Sony Electronics,; Spokesmodel, American Greetings,; Spokesmodel, Keds,; Spokesmodel,

Diet Coke,; Spokesmodel, CoverGirl, **CW:** Singer: (albums) Taylor Swift, 2006, Songs of the Season, 2007, Fearless, 2008 (Album of Year, Academy Country Music Awards, 2009, Favorite Country Album, American Music Awards, 2009, Album of Year, Country Music Association Awards, 2009, Choice Country Album, Teen Choice Awards, 2009, Top Country Album of Year, Billboard Music Awards, 2009, Album of Year, Best Country Album, Grammy Awards, 2010), Speak Now, 2010 (Top Country Album, Billboard Music Awards, 2011, Favorite Country Album, American Music Awards, 2011), Speak Now: World Tour Live, 2011, Red, 2012 (Top Country Album, Billboard Music Awards, 2013, Favorite Country Album, American Music Awards, 2013), 1989, 2014 (Top Billboard 200 Album, Billboard Music Awards, 2015, Favrite Pop/Rock Album, American Music Awards, 2015, Album of Year, Best Pop Vocal Album, Grammy Awards, 2016), Reputation, 2017, (songs) Tim McGraw, 2006 (Breakthrough Video of Year, CMT Music Awards, 2007), Teardrops On My Guitar, 2006 (Country Song of Year, BMI Awards, 2008), Our Song, 2006 (Video of Year, Female Video of Year, CMT Music Awards, 2008), Love Story, 2008 (Music Video of Year, Country Music Association Awards, 2009, Country Song of Year, BMI Awards, 2009, Video of Year, Female Video of Year, CMT Music Awards, 2009), White Horse, 2008 (Best Female Country Vocal Performance, Best Country Song, Grammy Awards, 2010), Fifteen, 2009 (Choice Country Song, Teen Choice Awards, 2010), You Belong with Me, 2009 (Best Female Video, MTV Video Music Awards, 2009, Country Song of Year, BMI Awards, 2010, Favorite Song, Nickelodeon Kids' Choice Awards, 2010), Mine, 2010 (Video of Year, CMT Music Awards, 2011), Mean, 2010 (Best Country Solo Performance, Best Country Song, Grammy Awards, 2012), Sparks Fly, 2010 (Choice Country Song, Teen Choice Awards, 2012), Eyes Open, 2012 (Choice Single by a Female Artist, Teen Choice Awards, 2012), We Are Never Getting Back Together, 2012 (Top Country Song, Billboard Music Awards, 2013), Shake It Off, 2014 (Favorite Song, People's Choice Awards, 2015, Top Streaming Song-Video, Billboard Music Awards, 2015), Blank Space, 2014 (Best Pop Video, Best Female Video, MTV Video Music Awards, 2015, Song of Year, American Music Awards, 2015), (with Kendrick Lamar) Bad Blood, 2015 (Video of Year, Best Collaboration, MTV Video Music Awards, 2015, Choice Music Collaboration, Teen Choice Awards, 2015, Best Music Video, Grammy Awards, 2016), (with The Civil Wars) Safe & Sound, 2012 (Best Song Written for Visual Media, Grammy Awards, 2013), (featured vocals on Tim McGraw's track) Highway Don't Care, 2013 (Musical Event of Year, Music Video of Year, Country Music Association Awards, 2013, Video of Year, Academy Country Music Awards, 2014); actress: (films) Hannah Montana: The Movie, 2009, Valentine's Day, 2010 (Choice Breakout Female, Teen Choice Awards, 2010), (voice) Dr. Suess' The Lorax, 2012 (Choice Movie Voice, Teen Choice Awards, 2012), The Giver, 2014; guest appearance (TV series) CSI: Crime Scene Investigation, 2009, New Girl, 2013 **AW:** Named Woman of Year, Billboard magazine, 2011, Favorite International Solo Artist of Year, Ind. Music Awards, 2011, Favorite Female Singer, Nickelodeon Kids' Choice Awards, 2010 Favorite Pop Artist, People's Choice Awards, 2016, 2015, Favorite Country Artist, 2014, 2013, 2012, 2011, Favorite Female Artist, 2016, 2015, 2010, Choice Female Country Artist, Teen Choice Awards, 2014, 2013, 2010, Choice Female Artist, 2013, 2012, 2009, Top Touring Artist, Billboard Music Awards, 2016, Top Digital Songs Artist, 2015, Top Hot 100 Artist, 2015, Top Artist, 2015, Top Billboard 200 Artist, 2015, 2013, Top Female Artist, 2015, 2013, Top 100

Greatest Songwriters of All Time, Rolling Stone Magazine, 2015 Top Country Artist, 2013, 2011, Artist of Year, 2013, 2009, Entertainer of Year, Country Music Association Awards, 2011, Entertainment Weekly, 2010, Associated Press, 2009, Female Vocalist of Year, Country Music Association, 2009, Entertainer of Year, Country Music Association Awards, 2009, Favorite Pop/Rock Female Artist, American Music Awards, 2009, Favorite Adult Contemporary Artist, 2015, 2009, Artist of Year, 2013, 2011, 2009, Favorite Country Female Artist, 2013, 2012, 2011, 2010, 2009, 2008, Entertainer of Year, Academy Country Music Awards, 2012, 2011, Top New Female Vocalist, 2008; named one of the 50 Most Powerful Women in Business, Fortune Magazine, 2015, The 10 Most Fascinating People of 2014, Barbara Walters Special, The 100 Most Powerful Women in Entertainment, Hollywood Reporter, 2013, The 100 Most Influential People in the World, TIME magazine, 2010, The 100 Agents of Change, Rolling Stone magazine, 2009, The 25 Most Intriguing People, People magazine, 2009, The 100 Most Beautiful People, 2008-10; recipient Billboard Chart Achievement award, Billboard Music Awards, 2015, Dick Clark award for Excellence, American Music Awards, 2014, Best Female Video for the song I Knew You Were Trouble, MTV Video Music Awards, 2013, Hal David Starlight award, Songwriters Hall of Fame, 2010, Milestone award, Academy Country Music Awards, 2015, Jim Reeves International award, 2011, Crystal Milestone award, 2009, International Artist Achievement award, Country Music Association Awards, 2013, Pinnacle award, 2013, International Artist Achievement award, 2009, Horizon award, 2007 **ACH:** Achievements include recognition as the youngest artist to ever be nominated for and win the Country Music Association Entertainer of the Year award in 2009; the eighth and youngest female artist to win the Academy of Country Music Entertainer of the Year award in 2011

SWINTON, TILDA, I: Medicine & Health Care **DOB:** 05/31/1905 **PB:** London **SC:** London **PT:** Daughter of John Swinton and Judith (Killen) Balfour; **ED:** Degree in England Lit., Cambridge University, England, 1983 **CW:** Actress: (films) Caravaggio, 1986, Egomania - Insel ohne Hoffnung, 1986, Friendship's Death, 1987, Aria, 1987, L' Ispirazione, 1988, Degrees of Blindness, 1988, Das Andere Ende der Welt, 1988, The Last of England, 1988, War Requiem, 1989, Play Me Something, 1989, The Garden, 1990, Edward II, 1991, The Party: Nature Morte, 1991, Man to Man, 1992, Orlando, 1992, Wittgenstein, 1993, Blue, 1993, Remembrance of Things Fast: True Stories Visual Lies, 1994, Female Perversions, 1996, Conceiving Ada, 1997, Love Is the Devil: Study for a Portrait of Francis Bacon, 1998, The War Zone, 1999, The Beach, 2000, Possible Worlds, 2000, The Deep End, 2001 (Boston Society Film Critics award for Best Actress, 2001), Vanilla Sky, 2001, Teknolust, 2002, Adaptation, 2002, Young Adam, 2003 (BAFTA award for Best Actress in Scottish Film, 2004), The Statement, 2003, Absent Presence, 2005, Constantine, 2005, Broken Flowers, 2005, The Chronicles of Narnia: The Lion, the Witch and the Wardrobe, 2005, Sleepwalkers, 2007, The Man from London, 2007, Michael Clayton, 2007 (BAFTA award for Best Supporting Actress, 2008, Academy award for Best Actress in a Supporting Role, 2008), Burn After Reading, 2008, Julia, 2008, The Curious Case of Benjamin Button, 2008, The Limits of Control, 2009, Io sono l'amore, 2010, The Chronicles of Narnia: the Voyage of the Dawn Treader, 2010, Moonrise Kingdom, 2012, Only Lovers Left Alive, 2013, Snowpiercer, 2013, The Zero Theorem, 2013, The Grand Budapest Hotel, 2014, Trainwreck, 2015, A Bigger Splash, 2015, Hail, Caesar!, 2016, Doctor Strange,

2016, Okja, 2017, War Machine, 2017, Suspiria, 2018, Isle of Dogs, 2018; actress, producer (films) Thumbsucker, 2005, Stephanie Daley, 2006, I Am Love, 2009, actress, executive producer We Need to Talk About Kevin, 2011 (National Board Review award for Best Actress, 2011); actress: (TV series) Zastrozzi: A Romance, 1986,The Open Universe, 1986-90 Your Cheatin' Heart, 1990, Shakespeare: The Animated Tales, 1992, Screenplay 1992, Vision of Heaven and Hell, 1994, Love is the Devil, 1998; (TV films) Offene Universum, 1993, The Somme, 2005, Galapagos, 2006; dir.: (documentaries) The Ten Commandments, 2008; writer, executive producer (documentaries) Derek, 2008, writer, director The Seasons in Quincy: Four Portraits of John Berger, 2016 **AW:** Named one of The 100 Most Influential People in the World, TIME magazine, 2012; recipient Bemen Film award, 2001

SWITZER, BARRY, T: Retired Professional Football Coach **I:** Other **DOB:** 10/05/1937 **PB:** Crossett **PT:** Son of Frank and Louise Switzer; Married Kay Switzer, 1963 (div. 1983); children: Greg, Kathy, Dove **ED:** BA, University Arkansas, 1960 **C:** Studio analyst, FOX NFL Sunday, 2007-08; Head coach, Dallas Cowboys, 1994-97; Head coach, University Oklahoma Sooners, 1973-89; Assistant football coach, University Oklahoma Sooners, 1966-72; Assistant football coach, University Arkansas Razorbacks, 1960-65 **CIV:** Served with US Army **CW:** Author: (with Bud Shrake) Bootleggers's Boy, 1990 **AW:** Recipient Jim Thorpe Lifetime Achievement award, 2004, Paul "Bear" Bryant Lifetime Achievement award, 2009; named Walter Camp Coach of Year, 1973; named to College Football Hall of Fame, 2002, Sporting News College Football COY, 1973 **ACH:** Achievements include head coach of the AP/UPI NCAA National Champions University of Oklahoma Sooners, 1974, 75, 85; head coach of Super Bowl XXX Championship winning Dallas Cowboys, 1996

SYKES, DIANE, T: Federal Judge **I:** Law and Legal Services **CN:** US Ct. Appeals (7th cir.) **DOB:** 12/23/1957 **PB:** Milwaukee **SC:** Wisconsin **ED:** JD, Marquette University, 1984; BA, Northwestern University, 1980 **C:** Judge, US Court Appeals (7th cir.), 2004-; Judge, Wisconsin Supreme Court, Madison, 1999-2004; Judge, Milwaukee County Court, 1992-99; Associate, Whyte & Hirschboeck South Carolina, 1985-92; Law clerk to Hon. Terence T. Evans, US District Court (eastern district) WI, 1984-85; Reporter, Milwaukee Journal, **MEM:** Mem.: Am. Law Institute, St. Thomas More Society, Milwaukee Lawyers Chapter, Federalist Society, Seventh Cir. Bar Association, Wisconsin Bar Association **BA:** 219 S. Dearborn Street Room 2722, Chicago, IL, 60604

SZOSTAK, JACK WILLIAM, T: Molecular Biologist, Educator **I:** Sciences **DOB:** 11/09/1952 **PB:** London **PT:** Son of William J. and Viola (Munford) Szostak **ED:** PhD in Biochemistry, Cornell University, Ithaca, New York, 1977; BS in Cell Biology, McGill University, Montreal, Can., 1972 **C:** Professor department genetics, Harvard Medical School, Boston, 1988-; Associate professor department genetics, Harvard Medical School, Boston, 1984-87; Associate professor department biological chemistry, Harvard Medical School, Boston, 1983-84; Assistant professor department biological chemistry, Harvard Medical School, Boston, 1979-83; Research associate in biochemistry, Cornell University, 1977-79 **CR:** Visiting fellow Brasenose College, Oxford University, 2005 Capital Sci. lecturer Carnegie Institution Washington, 2001 investigator Howard Hughes Medical Institute, 1998- Proctor & Gamble lecturer University Illinois, Urbana-Champaign, 1998 Susan

Swerling memorial lecturer Dana Farber Cancer Institute, Boston, 1997 William Rauscher memorial lecturer Rensselaer Poly. Institute, Troy, New York, 1995 Jean Weigle lecturer University Geneva, 1994 Alex Rich distinguished investigator department molecular biology Massachusetts General Hospital, 2000-, molecular biologist, 1988-, associate molecular biologist, 1984-87 **CW:** Member editorial board Chemistry and Biology, 1994-, RNA, 1995-98; contributor articles to professional journals **AW:** Recipient Nobel prize in physiology/medicine, 2009, H.P. Heineken prize, Royal Netherlands Academy Arts & Scis., 2008, Albert Lasker award for basic medical research, 2006, Harrison Howe award, Am. Chemical Society, 2003, Genetics Society of America medal, 2000, Hans Sigrist prize, University Bern, Switzerland, 1997, Louis Vuitton-Moet Hennesey 'Vinci of Excellence' award, 1996,NAS Award in Molecular Biology, 1994 **MEM:** Fellow: New York Academy Scis.; mem.: National Academy of Sciences (Award in molecular biology 1994), Am. Academy Arts & Scis. **ACH:** Achievements include research in origin, early evolution and laboratory synthesis of life; patents in field **BA:** Mass Gen Hosp, Simches Rsch Ctr CPZN 7250 185 Cambridge St, Boston, MA, 02114

TABACKIN, LEWIS BARRY, T: Jazz Musician **I:** Media & Entertainment **DOB:** 03/26/1940 **PB:** Philadelphia **SC:** PA/USA **PT:** Isadore Tabackin, Sarah (Skolnick) Tabackin **MS:** Married **SPN:** Toshiko Akiyoshi, 11/3/1969 **CH:** Michiru Mariano **ED:** Student, Philadelphia Conservatory of Music, 1958-1962 **C:** Advisory Committee, Jazz Foundation of America, 2002-Present **MIL:** U.S. Army, 1963-1965 **CW:** Co-Leader, Toshiko Akiyoshi-Lew Tabackin Big Band, Los Angeles, CA, 1972-Present; (Band Member) Shelly Manne Quartet, 1976-Present, ABC Orchestra, 1970-1972, Doc Severinsen, 1969-1976, NBC Orchestra, 1972-1977, Clark Terry, 1967-1972, Thad Jones & Mel Lewis, 1966-1970, Duke Pearson, 1967-1972, Maynard Ferguson, 1967, Cab Calloway, 1966, Les & Larry Elgart, 1965-1966; Tenor Saxophone and Flute Player, 1956-Present; Musician, Various Albums **AW:** First Place Award, Downbeat Critics Poll, 1976, Album of the Year Award, Stereo Review, 1976, Gold Award, Swing Journal, 1976, First Place, Reader's Poll, Swing Journal, 1977, First Place, Reader's Poll in Big Band Category, Downbeat, 1978, Best Big Band, Downbeat Readers Poll, 1978, Downbeat Critics Poll, 1979 **MEM:** American Federation of Musicians, National Association of Jazz Educators **BA:** The Berkeley Agency, 2490 Channing Way, Suite 406, Berkeley, CA, 94704-2210

TAKANO, MARK ALLAN, T: U.S. Representative from California **I:** Government Administration/Government Relations/Government Services **DOB:** 12/10/1960 **PB:** Riverside **PT:** Son of Williem and Nancy T. **ED:** MFA, University Calif.-Riverside, 2000; BA in Government, Harvard University, 1983 **CT:** Cert. teacher, California **C:** Vice Chair of the House Democratic Conference, 2017, Member, Committee on Ways and Means; Member, US House Veterans' Affairs Committee, 2013-; Member, US House Sci., Space & Technology Committee, 2013-; Member, US Congress from 41st California District, Washington, 2013-; English/History teacher, Rialto Unified School District, Riverside, California, 1988-2012 **CR:** Board trustees Riverside Community College, 1990-2012, president, 1992, '97, '98, '05, '06 **CIV:** Chairman Greater Riverside Urban League, 1989-93 member executive board California Democratic Party, 1988-90. **AW:** Recipient Martin Luther King Visionaries award **PA:** Democrat **BA:** 1507 Longworth House Office Bldg, Washington, DC, 20515

TANZI, RUDOLPH PHD, T: Neuroscientist, Researcher, Educator **I:** Sciences **DOB:** 09/18/1958 **SC:** RI **PT:** Son Of Rudolph Anthony And Anne Marie (Macari) Tanzi; **ED:** PhD in Neurobiology, Harvard University, 1990; BA in History, University Rochester, 1980; BS in Microbiology, University Rochester, 1980; **C:** Director Genetics and Aging Unit, Massachusetts General Hospital, 1999-; Professor Neurology, Massachusetts General Hospital, 1999-; Research Assistant Genetics Unit to Professor, Massachusetts General Hospital, Boston, 1980-99; **CR:** Chairman Sci. Adv. Board Blanchette Rockefeller Neurosciences Institute; Board of Sci. Counselors National Institute Aging; Assistant Professor to Professor Harvard University Medical School, 1992-, Instructor Neurology, 1990-92; **CIV:** Adv. Board, Lifeboat Foundation; **CW:** Editorial Board Neuron, 1994-; co-editor: Molecular Mechanisms of Dementia, 1997, Presenilins and Alzheimer's Disease, 1998, Alzheimer's Disease: Advances in Genetics, Molecular and Cellular Biology, 2006; Co-author: Decoding Darkness: The Search for the Genetic Causes of Alzheimer's Disease, 2001; Contributor Articles to Professional Journals; **AW:** Named Time Magazine's 100 Most Influential, 2015; Recipient Potamkin Prize, 1995, Metropolitan Life Award, 1995, Nathan Shock New Investigator Award, Gerontology Society Am., 1993; Fellow Pew Scholar In Biomed. Scis., 1993, French Foundation, 1991; **MEM:** Fellow: American Association for the Advancement of Science; Mem.: Am. Society Human Genetics, Am. Society for Neurosci; **H:** Skiing, Tennis, Scuba Diving, Piano; **BA:** 3 Oceanside Dr, Hull, MA, 02045-3259

TAPPER, JAKE, T: News Correspondent, Journalist **I:** Writing and Editing **DOB:** 03/12/1969 **PB:** NYC **SC:** NY/USA **PT:** Theodore S. Tapper; Anne Tapper **ED:** Student, University of Southern California School of Cinema-TV; BA in History, Dartmouth College, Magna Cum Laude, Hanover, NH (1991) **C:** Host, State of the Union (2015-Present); Anchor "The Lead," CNN (2013-Present); Chief White House Correspondent, CNN (2013-Present); Chief White House Correspondent, ABC News (2008-2012); National/Senior Political Correspondent, D.C. Bureau, ABC News (2003-2008); Washington Correspondent, Salon.com (1999-2002); Senior Writer, Washington City Paper (1998-1999); With, Handgun Control Inc. (1997); Publicist, Powell Tate, Washington, DC; Press Secretary to Representative Marjorie Margolies-Mezvinsky, U.S. House of Representatives **CR:** Interim Host, "This Week" (2010); Frequent Substitute Host Anchor, "Nightline," "World News," and "Good Morning, America," Weekend Editions; Regular Contributor, ABCNews.com, ABC NewsNOW, "Good Morning America," "Nightline," "World News with Charles Gibson," "This Week with George Stephanopoulos" & "World News with Diane Sawyer"; Substitute Host, "The Spin Room," "Crossfire," "The Point"; Host, Sundance Channel (2003): Correspondent, Series, Entertainment News Specials, VH1 (2002); Host, TV News Show, "Take Five," CNN (2001) **CW:** Author, "Body Slam: The Jesse Ventura Story" (1999); Author, "Down and Dirty: The Plot to Steal the Presidency" (2001); Author, "The Outpost: An Untold Story of American Valor" (2012); Contributor, Political Comic Strip Featured in Roll Call, Capitol Hell (1994-2003); Contributor, Cartoons, American Spectator Magazine, LA Times, Philadelphia Inquirer; Contributing Writer, The New Yorker, New York Times Magazine, Washington Post, LA Times, Weekly Standard; Columnist, TALK Magazine, Frequent Contributor, All Things Considered (NPR) **AW:** Merriman Smith Award, White House Correspondents' Association (2010, 2011, 2012); Walter Cronkite Award for Excellence in Television Political Journalism (2017)

TARANTINO, QUENTIN JEROME, T: Film Director, Scriptwriter **I:** Media & Entertainment **PB:** Knoxville **SC:** TN/USA **PT:** Tony Tarantino; Connie Tarantino **C:** Co-founder (with Lawrence Baker), A Band Apart Records **CW:** Actor: (films) My Best Friend's Birthday, 1987, Eddie Presley, 1993, (voice) The Coriolis Effect, 1994, Sleep With Me, 1994, Somebody to Love, 1994, Destiny Turns on the Radio, 1995, The Anatomy of Horror, 1995, Desperado, 1995, Girl 6, 1996, Steven Spielberg's Director's Chair, 1996, Full Tilt Boogie, 1997, Little Nicky, 2000, Planet of the Pits, 2004, Epreuves d'artistes, 2004, (voice) Diary of the Dead, 2008; actor, writer, producer (films) From Dusk Till Dawn, 1996, writer (story) Natural Born Killers, 1994, writer, director, producer Kill Bill: Vol. 1, 2003, Kill Bill: Vol. 2, 2004, actor, writer, director Reservoir Dogs, 1992, Pulp Fiction, 1994 (Best Original Screenplay, Academy awards, 1995, Best Original Screenplay, British Academy Film and TV Arts, 1995, Best Screenplay, Golden Globe award, Hollywood Foreign Press Association, 1995), actor (voice), writer, director Jackie Brown, 1997; executive prodr.: (films) From Dusk Till Dawn 2: Texas Blood Money, 1999, From Dusk Till Dawn 3: The Hangman's Daughter, 2000; executive prodr.: (films) Hostel, 2005, Daltry Calhoun, 2005, Freedom's Fury, 2006; actor, writer, producer, director (films) Grindhouse, 2007; prodr.: (films) Iron Monkey, 2001; writer, director (films) Inglourious Basterds, 2009 (Best Original Screenplay, Critics Choice Awards, 2010), Django Unchained, 2012 (Best Original Screenplay, Critics Choice Awards, 2013, Best Screenplay, Golden Globe award, Hollywood Foreign Press Association, 2013, Best Original Screenplay, British Academy Film and TV Arts, 2013, Best Original Screenplay, Academy awards, 2013), The Hateful Eight, 2015 (Best Original Screenplay, National Board Review, 2015), Helter Skelter, 2019 writer, producer Curdled, 1996, actor, writer, producer, director ((with Alexandre Rockwell, Robert Rodriguez & Allision Anders)) Four Rooms, 1995; executive prodr.: God Said, 'Ha!, 1998; TV appearances Golden Girls, 1998, 1990, All-American Girl, The Muppets' Wonderful Wizard of Oz, 2005; dir.: (TV episodes) ER, 1994, Jimmy Kimmel Live, 2004, CSI: Crime Scene Investigation, 2005, From Dusk till Dawn The Series, 2014 **AW:** Named one of The 100 Most Influential People in the World, TIME magazine, 2005; recipient Star, Hollywood Walk of Fame, 2015, Critic Choice Music+Film award, 2011, Kirk Douglas award for Excellence in Film, 2009, Building Bridges award, Asian Excellence Awards, 2006

TARTT, DONNA, T: Writer **I:** Writing and Editing **PB:** Greenwood **SC:** MS/USA **ED:** Graduate, Bennington College, 1982 **C:** Writer 1992- **CW:** Author: The Secret History, 1992, The Little Friend, 2002 (WH Smith Literary award, 2003), The Goldfinch, 2013 (Pulitzer Prize in Fiction, 2014); author of several short stories and fiction works,(Short Stories) Tam O Shanter, 1993, A Christmas Pageant, 1993, A Garter Snake, 1995, The Ambush, 2005 (Nonfiction) Basketball Season, 1993, Team Spirit: Memories of Being a Freshman Cheerleader for the Basketball Team, 1944 **AW:** Named one of The 100 Most Influential People in the World, TIME Magazine, 2014, Best Dressed Vanity Fair, 2014, Andrew Carnegie Medal for Excellence for Fiction, 2014, Pulitzer Prize for Fiction, 2014

TATEL, DAVID STEPHEN, T: Federal Judge **I:** Law and Legal Services **DOB:** 03/16/1942 **PB:** Washington **SC:** DC **PT:** Son of Howard Edwin and Molly (Abramowitz) Tatel; **ED:** JD, University Chicago, 1966; BA, University Michigan, 1963 **CT:** Bar: Illinois 1966 **C:** Judge, US Court Appeals (DC cir.), Washington, 1994-; Director Office for Civil Rights, US Department Health Education & Welfare, Washington, 1977-79; Partner, Hogan & Hartson, Washington, 1979-94; Associate, Hogan & Hartson, Washington, 1974-77; Director, National Lawyers Commission for Civil Rights Under Law, Washington, 1972-74; Director, Chicago Lawyer's Committee, 1969-70; Associate, Sidley & Austin, Chicago and Washington, 1970-72; Associate, Sidley & Austin, Chicago and Washington, 1967-69; Instructor, University Michigan, Ann Arbor, 1966-67 **CR:** Chairman, Board Directors Spencer Foundation, Chicago, 1990-97 Co-chmn. National Lawyers Committee for Civil Rights Under Law, Washington, 1989-91 Lecturer Stanford University Law School, 1991-92 **CIV:** Board Directors, Carnegie Foundation for Advancement in Teaching, Stanford, California, 1997- **BA:** US Court of Appeals, 333 Constitution Ave NW, Washington, DC, 20001-2866

TATUM, CHANNING, T: Actor **I:** Media & Entertainment **DOB:** 04/26/1980 **PB:** Cullman **SC:** AL/USA **PT:** Glenn Tatum; Kay (Faust) Tatum **CW:** Voice Actor, "Smallfoot" (2018); Actor, "Logan Lucky" (2017); Actor, "Kingsman: Golden Circle" (2017); Actor, "Hail, Caesar!" (2016); Actor, "Jupiter Ascending" (2015); Actor, Producer, Writer, "Magic Mike XXL" (2015); Actor, "The Hateful Eight" (2015); Guest Voice Actor, "The Simpsons" (2014); Voice Actor, "The Lego Movie" (2014); Actor, "Foxcatcher" (2014); Voice Actor, "The Book of Life" (2014); Actor, "22 Jump Street" (2014); Actor, "White House Down" (2013); Actor, "G.I. Joe: Retaliation" (2013); Actor, "This Is the End" (2013); Actor, "Haywire" (2012); Actor, "The Vow" (2012); Actor, "Side Effects" (2012); Actor, "Magic Mike" (2012); Actor, Executive Producer, "21 Jump Street" (2012); Actor, "The Eagle" (2011); Actor, "The Dilemma" (2011); Actor, "The Son of No One" (2011); Actor, Producer, "10 Years" (2011); Actor, "Dear John" (2010); Executive Producer, "Earth Made of Glass" (2010); Actor, "Fighting" (2009); Actor, "Public Enemies" (2009); Actor, "G.I. Joe: The Rise of Cobra" (2009); Actor, "Step Up 2: The Streets" (2008); Actor, "Stop-Loss" (2008); Actor, "Battle in Seattle" (2007); Actor, "The Trap" (2007); Actor, "She's the Man" (2006); Actor, "Step Up" (2006); Actor, "A Guide to Recognizing Your Saints" (2006); Actor, "Coach Carter" (2005); Actor, "Supercross" (2005); Actor, "Havoc" (2005); Guest Actor, "CSI: Miami" (2004) **AW:** Named, Favorite Movie Actor, People's Choice Awards (2016); Recipient, MTV Movie Award for Best Comedic Performance (2015); Recipient, Trailblazer Award, MTV Movie Awards (2014); Named, Sexiest Man Alive, People Magazine (2012); Recipient, Teen Choice Award for Choice Movie Actor (2009); Recipient, Teen Choice Award for Choice Movie Actor: Drama (2008); Recipient, Teen Choice Award for Choice Breakout Male (2006)

TAYLOR, ANDREW, T: Chef **I:** Food & Restaurant Services **C:** Founder, Big Tree Hospitality, 2015-; Owner, Eventide Oyster Co., 2012-; Owner, Hugos, 2012- **AW:** James Beard Award for Best New Chef Northeast, 2017-

TAYLOR, DAVID S., T: CEO of Procter and Gamble **I:** Consumer Goods and Services **DOB:** 04/20/1958 **PB:** Charlotte **SC:** NC/USA **ED:** BSEE, Duke University (1980) **C:** President, Chief Executive Officer, Procter & Gamble Co. (2015-Present); Group President, Global Beauty, Grooming and Health Care, Procter & Gamble Co. (2015); Group President, Global Health and Grooming, Procter & Gamble Co. (2013-2015); Group President, Global Home Care, Procter & Gamble Co. (2007-2013); President, Global Family Care, Procter & Gamble Co. (2005-2007); Vice President, North America

Family Care, Procter & Gamble Co., Cincinnati, Ohio (2003-2005); Vice President, Western Europe Family Care, Procter & Gamble Co. (2001-2003); General Manager to Vice President, Greater China Hair Care & Anti-counterfeiting, Procter & Gamble Co., Hong Kong (2001); General Manager, Greater China Hair Care and Tissues & Towels, Procter & Gamble Co., Hong Kong (2000-2001); General Manager, Hong Kong & China Hair Care, Procter & Gamble Co., Hong Kong (1998-2000); Marketing Director, Diaper Products, Procter & Gamble Co. (1996-1998); Brand Manager, Pampers, Procter & Gamble Co. (1993-1996); Assistant Brand Manager, Pampers, Procter & Gamble Co., Cincinnati, Ohio (1992-1993); Plant Manager, Procter & Gamble Co., Mehoopany, PA (1989-1992); Operations Manager, Procter & Gamble Co., Albany, GA (1986-1989); Operations Manager, Procter & Gamble Co., Cheboygan, MI (1986-1989; Department Manager, Procter & Gamble Co., Greenville, NC (1983-1985); Production Manager, Procter & Gamble Co., Greenville, NC (1980-1983) **CR:** Board of Directors, TRW Automotive (2010-2015); Vice chairman, China Quality Brand Protection Committee (2000-2001); Board Member, HKANA Retail Association (1998-2001); Regional Development Commission, Mehoopany, PA (1989-1991) **CIV:** Board of Visitors, Duke University Fuqua School of Business (2013-Present); Board of Directors, Cincinnati Freestore Foodbank (2011-Present); Board Member, America's Second Harvest (2006-Present); Board of Directors, Glad Joint Venture (2010); Board Chair, Feeding America (2008-2010); Board of Trustees, Cincinnati Scholarship Foundation (2007); Member, Greater Cincinnati Scholarship Association Advisory Committee (2007); Board of Directors, Feeding America (2006-2013) **BA:** Procter & Gamble Co., 1 Procter & Gamble Plz, Cincinnati, OH, 45202

TAYLOR, LAWRENCE JULIUS, T: Former NFL Player **I:** Athletics **DOB:** 02/04/1959 **PB:** Williamsburg **SC:** VA/USA **PT:** Son of Clarence and Iris Taylor; **ED:** Student, University North Carolina, 1977-80 **C:** Sports commentator The Stadium Show, TNT, 1994-; Owner, All-Pro Products, 1993-; Linebacker, New York Giants, 1981-93 **CR:** Member Superbowl Championship Team, 1990, 1986 **CW:** Co-author (with David Faulkner): LT: Living on the Edge, 1987; co-author: (with Steve Serby) LT: Over the Edge, 2004; author: Taylor, 2006; actor: (TV appearances) Married...with Children, 1994, Coach, 1995, The Jamie Foxx Show, 2000; (films) The Waterboy, 1998, Any Given Sunday, 1999, Shaft, 2000, Mercy Streets, 2000 **AW:** Named NFL All-Pro, 1981-90, National Football Conference Player of Year, United Press International, 1986, 1983, NFL MVP, Associated Press, 1986, NFL Defensive Player of Year, 1986, 1982, 1981; named to NFL's 75th Anniversary All-Time Team, 1994, Pro Football Hall of Fame, Canton, Ohio, 1999, National Football Conference Pro Bowl Team, 1981-90; recipient Humanitarian award, National Black United Fund, Bert Bell award, 1986, NFL Defensive Rookie of Year award, 1981, First-Team All-Pro,1981-90 **ACH:** Achievements include being selected #2 overall in the 1981 NFL Draft

TAYLOR, SCOTT, I: Government Administration/Government Relations/Government Services **DOB:** 07/07/1905 **ED:** A.L.B. ,Harvard University Extension, 2013 **C:** Member, U.S. House of Representatives from Virginias 2nd District, 2017-; Member, Committee on Appropriations; Member, Virginia House of Delegates from the 85th District,2014-17 **MIL:** 1998-2005, U.S. Navy

TAYLOR-JOHNSON, AARON, T: Actor **I:** Media & Entertainment **PB:** High Wycombe **SC:** England **CW:** (Television) Armadillo, 2001, The Bill, 2003, Family Business, 2004, Feather Boy, 2004, I Shouldn't Be Alive, 2006, Casualty, 2006, Talk to Me ,2007, Coming Up, 2007, Nearly Famous, 2007, Sherlock Holmes and the Baker Street Irregulars,2007, Family Guy, 2014,(Films) The Apocalypse, 2000, Tom and Thomas, 2002,Behind Closed Doors, 2003, Shanghai Knights, 2003, Dead Cool, 2004, The Thief Lord, 2006, The Illusionist, 2006,Fast Learners, 2006, The Best Man, 2006, The Magic Door, 2007, Dummy, 2008, Angus, Things and Perfect Snogging, 2008, The Greatest, 2009, Nowhere Boy, 2009,Kick-Ass, 2010, Chatroom, 2010, Albert Nobbs, 2011, Savages, 2012, Anna Karenina, 2012, Kick-Ass 2, 2013, Godzilla, 2014, Captain America: The Winter Soldier, 2014, Avengers: Age of Ultron, 2015, Nocturnal Animals, 2016(Golden Globe for Best Supporting Actor, 2016),The Wall, 2017, Outlaw King, 2018, A Million Little Pieces, 2019

TEAGUE, A. JAMES, T: Energy Executive **I:** Oil & Energy **C:** Chief Executive Officer, Enterprise Products Holdings LLC (2015-Present); Executive Vice President, Chief Operating Officer, Enterprise Products Holdings LLC (2010-2015); Chief Commercial Officer, Enterprise Products GP, LLC (2008-2010); Executive Vice President, Enterprise Products GP, LLC (1999-2010); President, Tejas Natural Gas Liquids, LLC (1998-1999); President, Marketing and Trading, MAPCO, Inc. (1997-1998); Member, Senior Management Teams, MAPCO Inc.; Member, Senior Management Teams, Shell Oil Co. **CR:** Board of Directors, EPE Holdings, LLC (Subsidiary of Dan Duncan LLC) (2009-Present)

TEBOW, TIM, T: Baseball Player, Former Professional Football Player, Former Sports Analyst **I:** Athletics **DOB:** 08/14/1987 **SC:** Philippines **PT:** Son of Robert Ramsey and Pamela Elaine Tebow. **ED:** BA in Family, Youth & Community Sciences, University Florida, Gainesville, 2009 **C:** New York Mets, Outfielder, 2016-; Quarterback, Philadelphia Eagles, 2015-; Contributor, Good Morning America, 2014-15; College football analyst Securities and Exchange Commission Network, ESPN, 2013-15; Quarterback, New York Jets, 2012; Quarterback, Denver Broncos, 2010-12 **CIV:** Active, Goodwill Gators, **CW:** Co-author (with Nathan Whitaker): Through My Eyes, 2011 **AW:** Named Offensive MVP, BCS Championship Game, 2010, Securities and Exchange Commission Offensive MVP, The Sporting News, 2008, 2nd Team All-American, Associated Press, 2009, 1st Team All-American, 2008, 2007, 1st Team All-SEC, 2009, 2008, 2007, Securities and Exchange Commission Offensive Player of Year, 2007; named one of The 100 Most Influential People in the World, TIME magazine, 2012; named to Securities and Exchange Commission All-Freshman Team, 2006; recipient William V. Campbell Trophy, National Football Foundation, 2009, Manning award, Sugar Bowl Committee, 2008, Sports Spirit award, Disney, 2008, ESPY award, Best Male College Athlete, ESPN, 2009, 2008, Chic Harley award, Touchdown Club of Columbus, 2007, James E. Sullivan award, US Amateur Athletic Union, 2007, Davey O'Brien award, Davey O'Brien Foundation, 2007, Maxwell award, Maxwell Football Club, 2008, 2007, Heisman Memorial trophy, Heisman Trophy Trust, 2007 **ACH:** Achievements include member of the BCS National Championship winning University of Florida Gators, 2006, 2008; becoming the first NCAA Division I player with at least 20 rushing and 20 passing touchdowns; becoming the first underclassman to ever win the Heisman Trophy **BA:** Tim Tebow Foundation, 2220 County Road 210 W Suite 108, PMB 317, Jacksonville, FL, 32259

TEMARES, STEVEN H., T: CEO of Bed Bath & Beyond **I:** Business Management/Business Services **PB:** The Bronx **SC:** New York **ED:** JD, University Pennsylvania, 1983; BA, Rutgers University, 1980 **C:** Co-Owner, Sky Blue FC, 2009-; CEO, Bed, Bath & Beyond, Inc., Union, New Jersey, 2006-; President, CEO, Bed, Bath & Beyond Inc., Union, New Jersey, 2003-06; President, COO, Bed, Bath & Beyond Inc., Union, New Jersey, 1999-2003; Executive vice president, COO, Bed, Bath & Beyond Inc., 1997-99; From director real estate, general counsel to executive vice president, Bed, Bath & Beyond Inc., Union, New Jersey, 1992-97; Attorney Real Estate Group, Riker Danzig Scheler Hyland & Perretti, Morristown, New Jersey, 1988-92; Counsel, Universal Maritime Service Corp., New York City, 1986-88; Associate Real Estate Group, Schulte Roth & Zabel LLP, New York City, 1983-85

TENNEY, CLAUDIA, T: U.S. Representative from New York **I:** Government Administration/Government Relations/Government Services **PT:** Daughter of Cynthia and John R. Tenney. **ED:** Grad., University of Cincinnati; Grad., Colgate University **CT:** BAR, New York, Connecticut, Florida **C:** Member, U.S. House of Representatives from New York's 22nd District, 2017-; Member, Republican Study Committee; Member District 115, New York State Assembly, 2011-2017; Co-host, First Look, WIBX 950 Radio, 2010-; Chief of staff, legal counsel to David Townsend, 2003-09; Pub., corp. counsel, Tenney Media Group, 1997; Partner, Groben, Gilroy, Oster and Saunders,; Co-owner, legal counsel, Mid-York Press, Inc.,; Attorney, Claudia Tenney Attorney at Law, Clinton, New York,; Member, Mohawk Valley Community College Foundation Board,; Member, Sitrin Homes Foundation, **PA:** Republican **BA:** 512 Cannon House Office Building, Washington, DC, 20515

TESSIER-LAVIGNE, MARC, T: President of Stanford University **I:** Education/Educational Services **DOB:** 12/18/1959 **PB:** Trenton **SC:** ON/Canada **PT:** Son of Yves Jacques' and Sheila Christine (Midgley) Tessier-L.; **SPN:** Married Mary Alanna Hynes, February 4, 1989; **CH:** Christian, Kyle, Ella **ED:** BSc in Physics, McGill University, 1980; BA in Philosophy & Physiology, Oxford University, 1982; PhD in Neurophysiology, University London, 1986 **C:** President, Stanford University, 2016-; Pres., Carson Family professor and head, Laboratory Brain Devel. and Repair, Rockefeller University, 2011—; Research fellow devel. neurobiology unit, Medical Research Council, London, England, 1986-87; Executive director, Can. Student Pugwash Organization, Ottawa, Ontario, 1982-83; Executive vice president research, chief sci. officer, Genentech Inc., 2009—2011; Executive vice president research drug discovery, Genentech Inc., 2008—2009; Senior vice president research drug discovery, Genentech Inc., 2003—2008; Susan B. Ford professor department biological scis. School Humanities and Scis., Stanford University, 2000—2003; Professor department anatomy and department biochemistry and biophysics, University California, San Francisco, California, 1997—2000; Associate professor department anatomy, University California, San Francisco, California, 1995-97; Assistant professor department anatomy, University California, San Francisco, California, 1991-95; Research fellow Center for Neurobiology,, Columbia University, New York City, New York, 1987-91 **CR:** Assistant investigator Howard Hughes Medical Institute, 1994—1997, investigator, 1997—2003 **CW:** Contributor articles on neurobiology to professional journals **AW:** Recipient McKnight Investigator award, 1994, Karl Judson Herrick award for comparative neurology Am. Association Elected to

American Philosophical Society, 2017, Anatomists, 1994, Ameritec prize for significant contribution in basic research towards cure for paralysis, 1995, Ipsen prize for neuronal plasticity, 1996, Viktor Hamburger award in devel. neurobiology International Journal Devel. Neurosci., Young Investigator award Society Neurosci., 1997, Wakeman award, 1998, Robert Dow award, 2003, Reeve Irvine Research medal, 2007, Gill Distinguished award, University Ind., W. Alden Spencer award, Columbia University, Memorial Sloan-Kettering medal; Hon. fellow, New College, Oxford, W. Maxwell Cowan award for Outstanding Achievement in Developmental Neurosci., Henry G. Friesen International prize, Burke award, The Burke Medical Research Center, NY/NJ CEO Lifetime Achievement award, Rhodes scholar, 1980, Commonwealth scholar, 1983, Markey scholar, 1989, Searle scholar, 1991, McKnight scholar, 1991, Klingenstein fellow, 1992. **MEM:** Fellow: American Association for the Advancement of Science, Royal Society of Canada, Royal Society of London (Ferrier prize 2007); mem.: Institute Medicine, Academy Medical Scis. (UK), National Academy of Sciences, Society for Neuroscience (nominating committee 2000—02) **BA:** Office of the President, Building 10, Stanford University, Stanford, CA, 94305

TESTA, GIULIANO, T: Surgeon **I:** Medicine & Health Care **DOB:** 11/23/1962 **ED:** Attended, University Essen, Germany, 1998-2001; MD, University Padova, Italy, 1988 **CT:** Cert. in general surgeon Am. Board Surgery, 1997 **C:** Director liver transplant hapatobiliary surgery, University Chicago Medical Center, 2005-; Associate professor surgery, University Chicago Medical Center, 2005-; Associate professor surgery, University Illinois, Chicago, 2001-05; Instructor, Southwest Transport Alliance, Dallas, 1997-98; Physician, Croce Verdi, Emergency Service, Padova, 1988-91 **CIV:** MAC chair, Am. Liver Foundation, Chicago, **AW:** Recipient Class Act Winner, University Illinois, 2004, Time 100 Most Influential, 2018 **MEM:** Mem.: American Medical Association, American College of Surgeons, Am. Society Transplantation, International Liver Transplant Society **ACH:** Achievements include first to start the living donor liver transplant **BA:** Univ Chicago Med Ctr, 5841 S Maryland Ave MC5027, Chicago, IL, 60637

TESTER, JON, T: U.S. Senator from Montana **I:** Government Administration/Government Relations/Government Services **DOB:** 08/21/1956 **PB:** Havre, Montana **ED:** BS in Music, University Great Falls, 1978 **C:** Ranking Member, Senate Veterans Affairs Committee, 2017-,; Chairman, Democratic Senatorial Campaign Committee (DSCC), 2015-2017; Chairman, Democratic Senatorial Campaign Committee (DSCC), 2015-; US Senator from Montana, 2007-; Chairman, US Senate Indian Affairs Committee, 2014-15; President, Montana State Senate, 2005-06; Minority leader, Montana State Senate, 2003-05; Minority whip, Montana State Senate, 2001-03; Member, Montana State Senate, 2005-06; Member District 45, Montana State Senate, Helena, 1998-2005; Farmer organic wheat, barley, lentils, peas, millet, buckwheat, alfalfa and hay,; Teacher, Big Sandy School District, 1978-80 **CIV:** Chairman, Big Sandy School Board, 1986-91 Member, Big Sandy School Board, 1983-91 **AW:** Named an Outstanding Agricultural Leader, College Agricultural, Montana State University, 2005 **PA:** Democrat **BA:** Office of Jon Tester, 311 Hart Senate Office Building, Washington, DC, 20510

THALER, RICHARD H., T: Economist **I:** Education/Educational Services **DOB:** 09/12/1945 **PB:** East Orange **SC:** NJ/USA **PT:** Alan M. Thaler; Roslyn (Melnikoff) Thaler **CH:** Gregory Scott;

Maggie Rose; Jessica Lynn **ED:** PhD, University of Rochester (1974); MA, University of Rochester (1970); BA, Case Western Reserve University (1967) **C:** President, American Economic Association (2015-Present); Charles R. Walgreen Distinguished Service Professor of Behavioral Science and Economics, The University of Chicago (1995); H.J.Louis Professor, Cornell University, Ithaca, NY (1988-Present); Professor, Cornell University, Ithaca, NY (1986-Present); Associate Professor, Cornell University, Ithaca, NY (1978-1986); Assistant Professor, University of Rochester, NY (1974-1978) **CR:** Visiting Scholar, National Bureau of Economic Research, Stanford, CA (1977-1978); Russell Sage Foundation, New York City, NY (1991-1992); Visiting Professor, University of British Columbia, Vancouver, Canada (1984-1985) **CW:** Author, "The Winner's Curse" (1992); Contributor, Articles on Psychology and Economics **AW:** Nobel Prize in Economics (2017) **MEM:** American Economics Association **BA:** The University Chicago, 5807 South Woodlawn Ave, Chicago, IL, 60637

THAPAR, AMUL ROGER, T: Federal Judge **I:** Law and Legal Services **DOB:** 04/29/1969 **PB:** Troy **SC:** Michigan **ED:** JD, University California Berkeley, 1994; BS, Boston College, 1991 **C:** Judge, U.S. Court of Appeals for the Sixth Circuit,2017-; Judge, US District Court (eastern district) Kentucky, London, 2008-17; US attorney (eastern district) Kentucky, US Department Justice, Lexington, 2006-07; Assistant US attorney (so. district) Ohio, US Department Justice, Cincinnati, 2002-06; General counsel, Equalfooting.com, 2000-01; Assistant US attorney DC, US Department Justice, Washington, 1999-2000; Associate, Squire, Sanders & Dempsey, Cincinnati, 2001-02; Associate, Williams & Connolly LLP, Washington, 1997-99; Law clerk to Hon. Nathaniel R. Jones, US Court Appeals (6th Cir.), 1996-97; Law clerk to Hon. S. Arthur Spiegel, US District Court (so. district) Ohio, 1994-96 **CR:** Trial advocacy instructor George University Law Center, 1999-2000 adjunct professor law University Cincinnati College Law, 2002-06, 1996-97 founder Street Law Inc., Cincinnati, 1995 **BA:** 100 East Fifth Street, Cincinnati, OH, 45202

THERON, CHARLIZE, T: Actress **I:** Media & Entertainment **DOB:** 08/07/1975 **PB:** Benoni **SC:** South Africa **PT:** Charles Theron; Gerda Theron **ED:** Studied Dance, Joffrey Ballet, New York City, NY **CR:** TV and Print Ad Representative, J'Adore Perfume, Christian Dior (2004-Present) **CIV:** Founder, Charlize Theron Africa Outreach Project (2007-Present); Messenger of Peace, United Nations (2008-Present) **CW:** Actress, Films, "Children of the Corn III" (1995), "2 Days in the Valley" (1996), "That Thing You Do!" (1996), "The Devil's Advocate" (1997), "Trial and Error" (1997), "Celebrity" (1998), "Mighty Joe Young" (1998), "The Astronaut's Wife" (1999), "The Cider House Rules" (1999), "Reindeer Games" (2000), "The Yards" (2000), "Men of Honor" (2000), "The Legend of Bagger Vance" (2000), "Sweet November" (2001), "15 Minutes" (2001), "The Curse of the Jade Scorpion" (2001), "Trapped" (2002), "Waking Up in Reno" (2002), "The Italian Job" (2003), "Head in the Clouds" (2004), "North Country" (2005), "Aeon Flux" (2005), "In the Valley of Elah" (2007), "Battle in Seattle" (2007), "Hancock" (2008), "The Road" (2009), Voice Actor, "Astro Boy" (2009), "Prometheus" (2012), "Snow White and the Huntsman" (2012), "A Million Ways to Die in the West" (2014), "Mad Max: Fury Road" (2015), "The Last Face" (2016), 'The Huntsman: Winter's War" (2016), Voice, Actor, "Kubo and the Two Strings" (2016), "Brain on Fire" (2016), "Atomic Blonde" (2017), "The Fate of the

Furious" (2017), "Gringo" (2018), "Tully" (2018), "Flarsky" (2019); Actress, Producer, Films, "Monster" (2003), "Sleepwalking" (2008), "The Burning Plain" (2009), "Young Adult" (2011), "Dark Places" (2015), "The Coldest City" (2016); Producer, Films, "Brain on Fire" (2016); Actress, TV Films, "Hollywood Confidential" (1997), "The Life and Death of Peter Sellers" (2004); Guest Appearance, TV Series, "Arrested Development" (2005); Executive Producer, TV Films, "Hatfields & McCoys" (2013), "Girlboss" (2017), "The Orville" (2017), "Mindhunter" (2017) **AW:** Named Woman of the Year, Hasty Pudding Theatrical Society (2008); Named One of 50 Most Beautiful People, People Magazine (2000); Best Actress in an Action Movie, "Mad Max: Fury Road," Critics' Choice Award (2016); Best Performance by an Actress in a Motion Picture - Drama, "Monster," Golden Globe Award (2004); Outstanding Performance by a Female Actor in a Leading Role, "Monster," Screen Actors Guild Award (2004); Best Actress in a Leading Role, "Monster," Academy Award (2004)

THIRY, KENT J., T: Healthcare Company Executive **I:** Health, Wellness and Fitness **ED:** MBA, Harvard University, with Honors (1983); BA in Political Science, Stanford University (1978) **C:** Chairman, Chief Executive Officer, Da Vita, Inc., El Segundo, CA (1999-Present); Chairman, Chief Executive Officer, Vivra Holdings Inc. (1997-1999); President, Chief Executive Officer, Vivra, Inc., San Francisco, CA (1992-1997); President, Chief Operating Officer, Vivra, Inc., San Francisco, CA (1991-1992); Partner, Vice President, Bain & Co., Inc. (1983-1991); Senior Consultant, Andersen Consulting (1978-1981) **CR:** Chairman, Oxford Health Plans (2002-2004); Director, Oxford Health Plans (1998-2004); Chairman, Kidney Care Partners; Member, Harvard Business School's Board of Advisors; Member, Board of Directors, Trust for Public Land **CIV:** Board of Directors, Volunteer Center of San Mateo County **MEM:** Phi Beta Kappa

THOMAS, CLARENCE, T: U.S. Supreme Court Justice **I:** Government Administration/Government Relations/Government Services **DOB:** 06/23/1948 **PB:** Pin Point **SC:** GA/USA **PT:** Son of Medical Corps Thomas and Leola Anderson (Williams) **ED:** JD, Yale Law School, 1974; BA cum laude in English Lit., Holy Cross College, 1971; Student, Immaculate Conception Seminary, 1967-68 **C:** Associate justice, US Supreme Court, Washington, 1991-; Judge, US Court Appeals (DC cir.), Washington, 1990-91; Chairman, Equal Employment Opportunity Commission, Washington, 1982-90; Assistant secretary for civil rights, US Department Education, Washington, 1981-82; Legislative assistant to Senator John C. Danforth, US Senate, Washington, 1979-81; Legal counsel, Monsanto Company, St. Louis, 1977-79; Assistant attorney general, State of Missouri, Jefferson City, 1974-77 **CR:** Board advisors DC Cases member board trustees Holy Cross College **CW:** Author: My Grandfather's Son: A Memoir, 2007 **MEM:** Mem.: International Churchill Society **BAR:** Bar: Missouri **PA:** Republican **BA:** Supreme Court of the U.S., 1First St NE, Washington, DC, 20543-0001

THOMAS, MICHAEL TILSON, T: Director **I:** Media & Entertainment **CN:** San Francisco Symphony **DOB:** 12/21/1944 **PB:** Los Angeles **SC:** CA/USA **PT:** Ted Thomas, Roberta Thomas **ED:** Student, University of Southern California **C:** Music Director, San Francisco Symphony, 1995-Present; Principal Conductor, London Symphony Orchestra, 1988-1995; Founder, New World Symphony, Miami Beach, FL, 1987; Principal Guest Conductor, Los Angeles Philharmonic Orchestra, 1981-1985; Music Director, Buffalo Philharmonic Orchestra,

1971-1979; Assistant Conductor, Boston Symphony Orchestra, 1969-1974; Artistic Director, New World Symphony **CR:** Fellow, American Academy of Arts & Sciences **CW:** Conductor, (Performances) Orff: Carmina Burana, Cleveland Orchestra Chorus, 1976, Prokofiev: Romeo and Juliet, San Francisco Symphony, 1997, Stravinsky: The Firebird, Peninsula Boys Choir, 2000, The Rite of Spring, San Francisco Girls Chorus, 2000, Persephone, San Francisco Symphony, 2000, Mahler: Symphony No. 6, 2003, Mahler: Symphony No. 3, 2004, Mahler: Symphony No. 7, 2006, Mahler: Symphony No. 8, 2010, Adams: Harmonielehre & Short Ride in a Fast Machine, 2013; Host, (TV Miniseries) Keeping Score, PBS, 2006, The MTT Files, American Public Media, 2007 **AW:** Koussevitzky Prize, Tanglewood Music Center, 1969, Musician of the Year, Musical America Magazine, 1971, Choral Performance, Orff: Carmina Burana, Cleveland Orchestra Chorus, Grammy Awards, 1976, Ditson Conductor's Award, Columbia University, 1993, Conductor of the Year, Musical America Magazine, 1995, Best Orchestral Performance, Prokofiev: Romeo And Juliet, San Francisco Symphony, Grammy Awards, 1997, Best Orchestral Performance, Mahler: Symphony No. 6, Grammy Awards, 2003, Lifetime Achievement Award, American Symphony Orchestra League, 2003, Best Classical Album, Mahler: Symphony No. 3, Grammy Awards, 2004, Artist of the Year, Gramophone Magazine, 2005, Best Classical Album, Mahler: Symphony No. 7, Grammy Awards, 2006, Best Orchestral Performance, Mahler: Symphony No. 7, Grammy Awards, 2006, Peabody Award, The MTT Files, American Public Media, 2008, National Medal of Arts Award, National Endowment for the Arts, 2010, Best Choral Performance, Best Classical Album, Grammy Awards, Mahler: Symphony No. 8, 2010, Best Orchestral Performance, Adams: Harmonielehre & Short Ride in a Fast Machine, Grammy Awards, 2013, Decorated Chevalier Ordre des Arts et des Lettres of France **BA:** c/o San Francisco Symphony Davies Symphony Hall, 201 Van Ness Avenue, San Francisco, CA, 94102

THOMAS, RAY, T: Musician **I:** Media & Entertainment **DOB:** 06/06/1905 **PB:** Stourport-on-Severn, Worcestershire, England **SC:** Stourport-on-Severn, Worcestershire, England **CW:** (Albums with Moody Blues) The Magnificent Moodies, 1965, Days of Future Passed, 1967, In Search of the Lost Chord, 1968, On the Threshold of a Dream, 1969, To our Children's Children's Children, 1969, A Question of Balance, 1970, Every Good Boy Deserves Favour, 1971, Seventh Sojourn, 1972, Octave, 1978, Long Distance Voyager, 1981, The Present, 1983, The Other Side of Life, 1986, Sur La Mer, 1988, Keys of the Kingdom,1991, Strange Times, 1999 **AW:** Rock and Roll Hall of Fame, 2018

THOMAS, SIDNEY RUNYAN, T: Federal Judge **I:** Law and Legal Services **DOB:** 08/14/1953 **PB:** Bozeman **SC:** Montana **ED:** Doctor (hon.), Rocky Mountain College, 1998; JD Cum Laude, Montana State University, 1978; BA in Speech-Comm., Montana State University, 1975 **CT:** Bar: US Supreme Court 1994, US Court Federal Claims 1986, US District Court (9th Cir.) 1980, US Court Appeals (9th Cir.) 1980, US District Court Montana 1978, Montana 1978 **C:** Chief Judge, US Court Appeals 9th Cir 2014-; Judge, US Court Appeals (9th Cir.), Billings, 1996-; Shareholder, Moulton, Bellimgham, Longo and Mather, Professional Corporation, Billings, Montana, 1978-96 **CR:** Adj. Instructor Rocky Mountain College, Billings, 1982-95 **CW:** Contributor Articles to Professional Journals **AW:** Recipient Outstanding Faculty Award, Rocky Mountain College, 1988, Gov.'s Award for Pub. Service, 1978 **MEM:** Mem.: American Bar Association, Yellowstone County Bar Association, State Bar Montana **BA:** 95 7th St, San Francisco, CA, 94103

THOMPSON, BENNIE G., T: U.S. Representative from Mississippi, Ranking Member of the House Homeland Security Committee **I:** Government Administration/Government Relations/Government Services **DOB:** 01/28/1948 **PB:** Bolton **ED:** Grad., University Southern Mississippi; MS in Educational Administration, Jackson State University, Mississippi, 1972; BA in Political Sci., Tougaloo College, Mississippi, 1968 **C:** Ranking Member, House Homeland Security Committee, 2011-; Member, US Congress from 2nd Mississippi District, 1993-; Chairman, US House Homeland Security Committee, 2007-11; Supervisor, Hinds County, Mississippi, 1980-93; Mayor, Bolton, Mississippi, 1973-79; Alderman, Bolton, Mississippi, 1969-73 **CR:** Presidential appointee National Council Health Planning and Devel. **CIV:** Board directors, Southern Regional Council, Housing Assistance Council, Board trustees, Tougaloo College, **AW:** Named one of 100 Most Influential Black Americans, Ebony magazine, 2006; named to Power 150, 2008 **MEM:** Mem.: Mississippi Association Black Supervisors (founding member), Mississippi Association Black Mayors (founding member) **PA:** Democrat **BA:** Office of Bennie Thompson, 2466 Rayburn HOB, Washington, DC, 20515

THOMPSON, EMMA, T: Actress **I:** Media & Entertainment **PB:** London **SC:** England **PT:** Eric Thompson; Phyllida Law; Married Kenneth Branaugh, August 20, 1989 (div. October 1995) **MS:** Married **SPN:** Greg Wise (July 29, 2003); Kenneth Branaugh, August 20, 1989 (div. October 1995) **CH:** Gaia Romilly Wise **ED:** Student of English, Cambridge University, England **CIV:** Active in Footlights Theatrical Group, Cambridge, England; ambassador ActionAid **CW:** Actress: (films) Henry V, 1989, The Tall Guy, 1989, Dead Again, 1991, Impromptu, 1991, Howard's End, 1992 (Academy award for Best Actress 1993), Peter's Friends, 1992, Much Ado About Nothing, 1993, The Remains of the Day, 1993, In the Name of the Father, 1993, My Father, the Hero, Junior, 1994, Carrington, 1995 (National Board Rev. award for Best Actress, 1995), Sense and Sensibility, 1995, Winter Guest, 1996, Primary Colors, 1998, Judas Kiss, 1998, Maybe Baby, 2000, Treasure Planet (voice), 2002, Love Actually, 2003, Imagining Argentina, 2003, Harry Potter and the Prisoner of Azbakan, 2004, Nanny McPhee, 2005, Stranger Than Fiction, 2006, Harry Potter and the Order of the Phoenix, 2007, Brideshead Revisited, 2008, Last Chance Harvey, 2008, Harry Potter and the Deathly Hallows: Part 2, 2012, Men in Black III, 2012, Brave (voice), 2012, Beautiful Creatures, 2013, Love Punch, 2013, Saving Mr. Banks, 2013 (National Board Review award for Best Actress, 2013), Men, Women & Children (voice), 2014, A Walk in the Woods, 2015, The Legend of Barney Thomson, 2015, Burnt, 2015, Alone in Berlin, 2016, Bridget Jones's Baby, 2016, The Doubt Machine: Inside the Koch Brothers' War on Climate Science, 2016, Beauty and the Beast, 2017, Sea Sorrow, 2017, The Meyerowitz Stories, 2017, The Children Act, 2017; (TV films) Al Fresco, Up For Grabs (a.k.a. Sexually Transmitted), Tutti Frutti, Fortunes of War, 1987, Cheers, 1991, Wit, 2001, The Song of Lunch, 2010, Walking the Dogs, 2012; (miniseries) Angels in America, 2003; actress, executive producer, writer: (films) Nanny McPhee Returns, 2010; (London stage) Me and My Girl, Look Back in Anger; also writer screen adaptation: Sense and Sensibility (Jane Austin), 1995 (New York Film Critics award for Best Screenplay, 1995, LA Film Critics award for Best Screenplay, 1995, Boston Film Critics award for Best Screenplay, 1995, Golden Globe award for Best Adapted Screenplay, 1996, Academy award for Best Adapted Screenplay, 1996, BAFTA award for Best Actress, 1996); actress, writer: (films) Effie

Gray, 2014; executive prodr.: (films) Sold, 2014. **AW:** Recipient Star, Hollywood Walk of Fame, 2010

THOMPSON, GLENN W. JR., T: U.S. Representative from Pennsylvania, Former Health Facility Administrator **I:** Government Administration/Government Relations/Government Services **DOB:** 07/27/1959 **PB:** Bellefonte **SC:** PA/USA **ED:** MEd, Temple University, Philadelphia, 1998; BS in Therapeutic Recreation, The Pennsylvania State University, 1981 **CT:** Lic. nursing home administrator, Marywood University, Scranton, Pennsylvania, 2006 **C:** Member, U.S. Congress from 5th Pennsylvania district, 2009-; Member, Committee on Agriculture,; Committee on Education and the Workforce, Committee on Natural Resources; Rehabilitation services manager, Susquehanna Health Systems, Williamsport, 1995-2009; Recreational therapist, Williamsport Hospital, 1986-95; Residential services aide, Hope Enterprises, Inc., Williamsport, Pennsylvania, 1981-82; Residential services aide, Centre Crest Nursing Home, Bellefonte, 1977-80 **CR:** Director Pennsylvania Head Injury Foundation; director, president Pennsylvania Therapeutic Recreation Society; member international adv. council Commission Accreditation Rehabilitation Facilities, 2006-08; president, Am. Therapeutic Recreation Association, 1998-2003; board of directors, treasurer, 1997-2000; adj. faculty Cambria County Community College, Johnstown, Pennsylvania, 1997-99 **CIV:** President, Juniata Valley Boy Scout Council, 2007-09; Senior vice president, Juniata Valley Boy Scout Council, 2005-07; Member, Bald Eagle Area School Board, 1990-96 Vol., Howard Vol. Fire Co., 1982-2008; Scoutmaster, Howard Boy Scout Troop 353, 1981-2008; Member, Bellefonte Intervally C. of C., 1977-2000; Alternate del., Rep. National Convention, 2004; Chair, Centre County Rep. Party, 2002-08; Vice-chair board of directors, Private Industry Council Central Corridors, 2000-08; Board of directors, Private Industry Council Centre County, 1999-2000 **MEM:** Mem.: Pennsylvania Rural Devel. Council, Pennsylvania Rural Health Association, Rep. Governors Club **PA:** Republican

THOMPSON, MIKE, T: U.S. Representative from California **I:** Government Administration/Government Relations/Government Services **DOB:** 01/24/1951 **PB:** St. Helena, California **PT:** Son of Charles Thompson and Beverly (Forni) Powell; **ED:** MA in Pub. Administration, California State University, Chico, 1996; BA in Political Sci., California State University, Chico, 1982 **C:** Member, US Congress from 5th California District, 2013-; Member, Committee on Armed Services, Committee on Transportation and Infrastructure; Member, US Congress from 1st California District, Washington, 1999-2013; Member District 2, California State Senate, 1991-98; Owner, Maintenance Supervisor, Beringer Winery, **CR:** Instructor Pub. Administration and State Government California State University, Chico, San Francisco State University Instructor Army Airborne School **CIV:** Member, Blue Dog Coalition, Member, New Dem. Coalition, Co-vice Chair, Congl. Sportsmen's Caucus, Co-founder, Co-chair, Congl. Wine Caucus, **MIL:** Staff Sergeant US Army, Vietnam **AW:** Decorated Purple Heart,; Named Outstanding Senator of Year, California Professional Firefighters, 1996, California School Boards Association, 1996, Senator of Year, California Association Homes & Services for Aging, 1995, Legislator of Year, Disabled in State Service, 1994, Police Officers Research Association California, California Association Persons with Handicaps, California Abortion Rights Action League; recipient Outstanding Senator award, Planned Parenthood Affiliates California, 1996, Distinguished Service Award, Aids Project LA,

1995, Legis. Leadership Award, California Association Health Services, 1994, Distinguished Service Award, California Association Hospitals, California State Association Counties **MEM:** Mem.: California Faculty Association, Business & Professional Women's Association, Vietnam Vets. of America, American Legion, Native Sons of Golden West, Sons of Italy **PA:** Democrat

THOMPSON, O. ROGERIEE, T: Federal Judge **I:** Law and Legal Services **DOB:** 08/08/1951 **PB:** Anderson SC: SC/USA **ED:** JD, Boston University Law School, 1976; BA, Brown University, 1973 **C:** Judge, U.S. Court of Appeals, First Circuit, 2010-Present; Associate Justice, Rhode Island Superior Court, 1997-2010; Judge, Rhode Island District Court, 1988-1997; Assistant Solicitor, City of Providence, 1980-1982; Founding Partner, Thompson & Thompson, Providence, RI, 1980-1988; Private Law Practice, Pawtucket, RI, 1979-1980; Staff Attorney, Rhode Island Legal Services, Providence, RI, 1976-1979 **CR:** Chair, Ad Hoc Task Force on Limited English Speaking Litigants, Rhode Island Superior Court **CIV:** Trustee, Bryant University and Brown University **AW:** Dr. Martin Luther King, Junior Hall of Fame of Providence, 2010, Women of Excellence Award, Women's Center of Rhode Island, 2006, One of the Most Distinguished Alumni of the Century, Brown University, National Association for the Advancement of Colored People Judicial Achievement Award, Ada Sawyer Award, Rhode Island Women's Bar Association **PA:** Democrat **BA:** 1 Courthouse Way, Boston, MA, 02210

THORNBERRY, MAC, T: Chair of the House Armed Services Committee **I:** Government Administration/Government Relations/Government Services **DOB:** 07/15/1958 **PB:** Clarendon **SC:** TX/USA **ED:** JD, University Texas Law School, 1983; BA in History, summa cum laude, Texas Tech University, Lubbock, 1980 **C:** Chairman, US House Armed Services Committee, 2015-; Member, US Congress from 13th Texas District, 1995-; Defense attorney, Peterson, Farris, Doores & Jones, Amarillo, Texas, 1989-94; Deputy assistant secretary for legislative affairs, US Department State, 1988-89; Chief of staff to Rep. Larry Combest, US House of Reps., 1985-88; Legislative counsel to Rep. Tom Loeffler, US House of Reps., 1983-85 **MEM:** Mem.: Southwestern Cattle Raisers Association, Texas Cattle Raisers Association **PA:** Republican

THORNE, KIP, T: Physicist, Researcher **I:** Sciences **DOB:** 06/01/1940 **PB:** Logan **SC:** UT/USA **ED:** Honorary DHL, Claremont Graduate University (2002); Honorary DSc, University of Glasgow (2001); Honorary DSc, Utah State University (2000); Honorary Drhc, Moscow University (1981); Honorary DSc, Illinois College (1979); Research Fellow, California Institute of Technology (1966-1967); Postdoctoral Fellow, National Science Foundation (1966); Postdoctoral Fellow in Physics, Princeton University (1965-1966); PhD in Physics, Princeton University (1965); AM in Physics, Princeton University (1963); BS in Physics, California Institute of Technology (1962); Fellow, Danforth Foundation; Fellow, Woodrow Wilson **C:** Feynman Professor of Theoretical Physics Emeritus, California Institute of Technology (2009-Present); Feynman Professor of Theoretical Physics, California Institute of Technology (1991-2009); William R. Kenan, Junior Professor, California Institute of Technology (1981-1991); Professor of Theoretical Physics, California Institute of Technology (1970-1991); Associate Professor of Theoretical Physics, California Institute of Technology (1967-1970) **CR:** Visiting Professor, Moscow University (1998); Member, International Committee on General Relativity and Gravitation (1992-2001); Visiting Professor, Moscow University

(1990); Visiting Professor, Moscow University (1988); Andrew D. White Professor-at-Large, Cornell University (1986-1992); Visiting Professor, Moscow University (1986); Co-Founder, Chair of Steering Committee, LIGO (1984-1987); Visiting Professor, Moscow University (1982-1983); Space Science Board, NASA (1980-1983); Committee on U.S.-USSR Cooperative in Physics (1978-1979); Visiting Professor, Moscow University (1978); Visiting Senior Research Associate, Cornell University (1977); Visiting Professor, Moscow University (1975); Adjunct Professor, University of Utah (1971-1998); Member, International Committee on General Relativity and Gravitation (1971-1980); Visiting Professor, Moscow University (1969); Visiting Professor, Moscow University (1969); Visiting Associate Professor, University of Chicago (1968); Fulbright Lecturer, France (1966) **CW:** Author, "Black Holes and Time Warps: Einstein's Outrageous Legacy" (1994); Author, "Black Holes: The Membrane Paradigm" (1986); Author, "Gravitation" (1973); Co-Author, Gravitation Theory and Gravitational Collapse (1965) **AW:** Recipient, Nobel Prize in Physics (2017); Recipient, Princess of Asturias Award (2017); Recipient, Harvey Prize (2016); Recipient, Kavli Prize (2016); Recipient, Shaw Prize (2016); Recipient, Gruber Prize in Cosmology (2016); Recipient, Special Breakthrough Prize in Fundamental Physics (2016); Named, One of TIME 100 Most Influential People (2016); Recipient, Common Wealth Award, Science Invention (2005); Named, California Scientist of the Year (2004); Recipient, Robinson Prize in Cosmology, University of Newcastle (2002); Recipient, Arthur Holly Compton Memorial Lectureship, Washington University (2001); Recipient, Herzberg Memorial Lectureship, Canada Association of Physicists (2001); Recipient, Charles Darwin Memorial Lectureship, Royal Astronomical Society (2000); Recipient, J. Robert Oppenheimer Memorial Lectureship, University of California (1999); Recipient, Karl Schwarzschild Medal, Astronomical Society of Germany (1996); Recipient, Julius Edgar Lilienfeld Prize, American Physical Society (1996); Recipient, P.A.M. Dirac Memorial Lectureship, Cambridge University (1995); Recipient, Science and Writing Award in Physics and Astronomy, American Institute of Physics (1994); Recipient, Science and Writing Award in Physics and Astronomy, American Institute of Physics (1969); Fellow, John Simon Guggenheim Foundation (1967); Research Fellow, Alfred P. Sloan Foundation (1966-1968) **MEM:** Chair, Topical Group in Gravity (1997-1998); American Philosophical Society; National Academy Sciences; American Academy of Arts and Sciences; American Astronomical Society; International Astronomical Union; American Association for the Advancement of Science; Russian Academy of Sciences; Ligo Science Collaboration; Lisa International Science Team; Sigma Xi; Tau Beta Pi; Fellow, American Physical Society **BA:** California Institute Technology, 130-33 Theoretical Astrophysics 1200 E California Blvd, Pasadena, CA, 91125

THULIN, INGE G., T: 3M CEO **I:** Business Management/Business Services **DOB:** 11/09/1953 **PB:** Malmo **SC:** Sweden **ED:** MBA in Economics & Marketing, Gothenburg University, 1978; DIHM in Marketing & Strategy, Gothenburg University **C:** Chairman, president, CEO, 3M Corp., 2012-; President, CEO, 3M Corp., 2012; Executive vice president, COO, 3M Corp., 2011-12; Executive vice president, international operations, 3M Corp., 2003-11; Area vice president, Asia Pacific, 3M Corp., 2003-04; Vice president, Europe, Central & East Europe and Mid. East, 3M Corp., 2002-03; Vice president, skin health division, 3M Corp., 2000-02; General manager, skin health division, 3M Corp.,

1999-2000; Marketing operations director, 3M Corp., 1998-99; Skin health business unit director, 3M Corp., St. Paul, 1997-98; Managing director, 3M Russia, 1995-97; European business unit manager surgical devices, 3M Europe, 1993-95; Business manager vision care & orthopedic products, 3M Europe, 1991-93; Group manager life sciences sector, 3M Sweden, 1987-91; Various sales & marketing positions, 3M Sweden, 1979-87 **CR:** Board of Directors 3M Corp., 2012-, The Toro Co., 2007- **CIV:** Vice chairman executive committee, U.S. Council for International Business, 2008- Board of Directors, Carlson School of Management University of Minnesota, 2003

THUNE, JOHN RANDOLPH, T: U.S. Senator from South Dakota **I:** Government Administration/Government Relations/Government Services **DOB:** 01/07/1961 **PB:** Murdo, South Dakota **PT:** Son of Harold Thune; **ED:** MBA, University South Dakota, 1984; BBA, Biola University, California, 1983 **C:** Chairman, US Senate Commerce, Sci. & Transportation Committee,, 2015-; Chair, Senate Republican Conference, 2012; US Senator from South Dakota, 2005-; Member, US Congress from South Dakota, 1997-2003; Founder, The Thune Group LLC,; Executive Director, South Dakota Municipal League, 1993-96; Director Railroad Division, State of South Dakota, 1991-93; Executive Director, South Dakota Republican Party, 1989-91; Deputy Staff Director to the Ranking Rep., US Senate Small Business Committee, 1987-89; Legislative Assistant to Senator James Abdnor, US Senate, 1985-87 **CR:** Chairman US Senate Republican Policy Committee (RPC), 2009-12, US Senate Republican Conference, 2012-, Vice Chairman, 2009 **H:** Basketball, Pheasant Hunting **PA:** Republican **BA:** Office of John Thune, U.S. Senate SD-511, Washington, DC, 20510

TIBERI, PATRICK JOSEPH, T: U.S. Representative from Ohio, former state legislator **I:** Government Administration/Government Relations/Government Services **DOB:** 10/21/1962 **PB:** Columbus **ED:** HHD (hon.), Capital University, 2005; BA in Journalism, Ohio State University, 1985 **C:** Member, US Congress from 12th Ohio district, 2001-18; Member, Committee on Ways and Means,; Chair, Joint Economic Committee; Majority leader, Ohio House of Reps.,; Member District 26, Ohio House of Reps., 1993-2000; Realtor, ReMax Achievers, Lewis Center, Ohio, **CIV:** President, co-founder, Windsor Terrace Learning Center, Columbus, Member adv. board, Columbus Italian Cultural Center, **AW:** Recipient Giving from the Heart award, Central Ohio Chapter Alzheimer's Association, Watchdog of Treasury award, United Conservatives Ohio, Pres.'s award, Northland Community Council **MEM:** Mem.: Sons of Italy **PA:** Republican **BA:** 1203 Longworth HOB, Washington, DC, 20515

TILLERSON, REX WAYNE, T: Former U.S. Secretary of State, Former Oil Company Executive **I:** Government Administration/Government Relations/Government Services **DOB:** 03/23/1952 **PB:** Wichita Falls **SC:** TX/USA **PT:** Son of Robert and Patty Tillerson; **ED:** Doctor (hon.), Worcester Polytechnic Institute, 2011; BS in Civil Engineering, The University of Texas at Austin 1975 **C:** Secretary, U.S. Department State, Washington, DC, 2017—2018; Chairman, CEO, president, Exxon Mobil Corp., 2006-2017; President, Exxon Mobil Corp., 2004-06; Senior vice president, Exxon Mobil Corp., 2001-04; Executive vice president, ExxonMobil Development Co., 1999-2001; President, Exxon Neftegas Ltd., 1998-99; Vice president, Exxon Ventures Inc., 1998-99; President, Exxon Yemen Inc., Esso Exploration & Production Khorat Inc., 1995-98; Coordinator, affiliate gas sales, Exxon Co. International, Florham Park, New Jersey, 1992-95; Production adv., Exxon Corp., Dallas, 1992; General manager, central production division, Exxon Co., U.S.A., 1989-92; Business devel. manager, natural gas department, Exxon Co., U.S.A., 1987-89; Various positions, production department, Exxon Co., U.S.A., 1975-87; Joined, Exxon Co., U.S.A., 1975 **CR:** Board of Directors, Exxon Mobil Corp., 2004- **CIV:** National president, Boy Scouts of America, 2010-12 Member executive board, Circle Ten Council, Member, Cockrell School's Friends of Alec Program, Member engineering advisory board, University Texas Austin Cockrell School Engineering, Member development board, University Texas Austin, Hon. trustee, Business Council for International Understanding, Trustee, Center Strategic & International Studies (CSIS), **AW:** Named a Distinguished Alumnus, University Texas, 2007, Distinguished Engineering Grad., 2006; named one of The World's Most Powerful People, Forbes magazine, 2009-15, The Global Elite, Newsweek magazine, 2008, The 25 Most Powerful People in Business, Fortune magazine, 2007; recipient Silver Buffalo award, Boy Scouts of America, 2010, H. Neil Mallon award, World Affairs Council, 2014, Order of Friendship, President Vladimir Putin of Russian Federation, 2013 **MEM:** Mem.: NAE, Emergency Committee for American Trade, Business Council (member executive council 2011-12), Business Roundtable, National Petroleum Council, Boy Scouts of America (national president 2010-12, Silver Buffalo award 2010), U.S.-Russia Business Council, Society Petroleum Engineers, American Petroleum Institute, Ford's Theatre Society (vice chairman), Texas Exes (life), Alpha Phi Omega **H:** Hunting, fishing, golf **BA:** US Department of State, 2201 C St NW, Washington, DC, 20520

TILLIS, THOM, T: U.S. Senator from North Carolina **I:** Government Administration/Government Relations/Government Services **DOB:** 08/30/1960 **PB:** Jacksonville **PT:** Son of Thomas Raymond and Margie Tillis; **ED:** BS in Technology Management, University Maryland, 1996; Attended, Chattanooga State Community College **C:** Member, US Senate Veterans' Affairs Committee, 2015-; Member, US Senate Judiciary Committee, 2015-; Member, US Senate Armed Services Committee, 2015-; Member, US Senate Agricultural, Nutrition & Forestry Committee, 2015-; Member, US Senate Special Committee on Aging, 2015-; US Senator from North Carolina, 2015-; Speaker, North Carolina House of Reps., 2011-15; Member District 98, North Carolina House of Reps., North Carolina, 2007-15; President, Parent Teacher Student Association, Hopewell High School, 2005-06; Commissioner, City of Cornelius, North Carolina, 2003-05; Partner, Pricewaterhousecoopers, **AW:** Named one of The 17 GOP Legislators to Watch, Governing magazine, 2011; recipient Duke Power Citizenship & Service award **PA:** Republican **BA:** Office of Thom Tillis, 185 Dirksen Senate Office Building, Washington, DC, 20510

TIMBERLAKE, JUSTIN RANDALL, T: Singer, Actor **I:** Media & Entertainment **DOB:** 01/31/1981 **PB:** Memphis **PT:** Son of Randy Timberlake and Lynn Harless **C:** Chairman, CEO, Tennman Records, LA, 2007-; Solo vocalist, 2002-; Singer, performer, 'N Sync, 1996-2002 **CR:** Creative, musical, cultural curator Bud Light Platinum, 2013- restaurant co-owner (with Eytan Sugarman) Southern Hospitality, 2007, Destino, 2006, Chi, 2003 launched William Rast clothing line (with Trace Ayala), 2005 **CIV:** Founder, J. Timberlake Foundation, **CW:** Singer ((with 'N Sync)): (albums) NSYNC, 1998, Home for Christmas, 1998, No Strings Attached, 2000, Celebrity, 2001, Essential 'N Sync, 2014; singer: (solo albums) Justified, 2003 (Best Pop Vocal Album, Grammy Awards, 2003),

FutureSex/LoveSounds, 2006 (Favorite Album, Am. Music Awards, 2007), The 20/20 Experience, 2013 (Favorite Album, People's Choice Awards, 2014, Top Billboard 200 Album, Billboar Music Awards, 2014, Top R&B Album, Billboard Music Awards, 2014), The 20/20 Experience (Part 2), 2013 (Favorite Soul/R&B Album, American Music Awards, 2013) Man of the Woods, 2018, (songs) Cry Me a River, 2003 (Best Male Pop Vocal Performance, Grammy Awards, 2003), Sexy Back, 2006 (Favorite R&B Song, People's Choice Awards, 2007, Best Dance Recording, Grammy Awards, 2007), My Love, 2006 (Best Rap/Sung Collaboration, Grammy Awards, 2007, Best Choreography, MTV Video Music Awards, 2007), LoveStoned/I Think She Knows, 2006 (Best Dance Recording, Grammy Awards, 2008), What Goes Around... Comes Around, 2006 (Best Direction, MTV Video Music Awards, 2007, Best Male Pop Vocal Performance, Grammy Awards, 2008), Mirrors, 2013 (Video of Year, Best Editing, MTV Video Music Awards, 2013), Suit and Tie, 2013 (Best Direction, MTV Video Music Awards, 2013, Best Music Video, Grammy Awards, 2014), Holy Grail (with Jay Z), 2013 (Best Rap/Sung Collaboration, Grammy Awards, 2014), Pusher Love Girl, 2013 (Best R&B Song, Grammy Awards, 2014); actor: (films) Longshot, 2000, Edison, 2005, Alpha Dog, 2006, Southland Tales, 2006, Black Snake Moan, 2006, (voice) Shrek the Third, 2007, The Love Guru, 2008, The Social Network, 2010, (voice) Yogi Bear, 2010, Bad Teacher, 2011, Friends with Benefits, 2011, In Time, 2011, Trouble with the Curve, 2012, Runner, Runner, 2013, Inside Llewyn Davis, 2013, Runner Runner, 2013, Justin Timberlake + The Tennessee Kids,2016, Trolls, 2016 , Wonder Wheel, 2017; (TV films) Model Behavior, 2000; (TV series) Saturday Night Live, 2009 (Outstanding Guest Actor in a Comedy Series, Primetime Emmy Awards, 2009) **AW:** Named Top R&B Artist, Billboard Music Awards, 2014, Top Radio Songs Artist, 2014, Top Billboard 200 Artist, 2014, Top Male Artist, 2014, Top Artist, 2014, Man of Year, Hasty Pudding Theatrical Society, 2010, Favorite Male Artist, Favorite Male R&B Artist, People's Choice Awards, 2014, Favorite Male Singer, 2008, Best-Selling Am. Artist, World Music Awards, 2007, Best Male Pop Artist, 2007, Favorite Male Soul/R&B Artist, American Music Awards, 2013, Favorite Male Pop/Rock Artist, 2013, 2007, Male Artist of Year, MTV Video Music Awards, 2007, Quadruple Threat of Year, 2007, International Male Solo Artist, BRIT Awards, 2007, Best Male Artist, MTV Europe Music Awards, 2006, Best Pop Artist, 2006; named one of The 100 Most Powerful Celebrities, Forbes.com, 2008, The 100 Most Influential People in the World, TIME magazine, 2013, 2007; recipient Michael Jackson Video Vanguard award, MTV Video Music Awards, 2013, Futures award, Environmental Media Awards, 2011

TIPSORD, MICHAEL L., T: CEO of State Farm **I:** Insurance **CN:** State Farm **ED:** JD, University of Illinois, Urbana-Champaign; Bachelor in Accounting, Illinois Wesleyan University **CT:** Chartered Property and Casualty Underwriter, 1995, Chartered Life Underwriter, 1991, CPA **C:** Vice Chairman, CFO, State Farm Insurance Companies, 2004-Present; Senior Vice President, CFO, State Farm Insurance Companies, 2002-2004; Vice President, Treasurer, State Farm Insurance Companies, 2001-2002; Vice President, Assistant Treasurer, State Farm Insurance Companies, 1998-2001; Executive Assistant, State Farm Insurance Companies, 1997-1998; Assistant Controller, State Farm Insurance Companies, 1996-1997; Director of Accounting, State Farm Insurance Companies, 1995-1996; Joined, State Farm Insurance Com-

panies, 1988; Assistant Tax Counsel, 1988 **CR:** Board of Directors, Navigant Consulting Inc., 2009-Present; Professor, Department of Accountancy, University of Illinois, Urbana-Champaign; Trustee, State Farm Insurance Co.; Savings and Thrift Trust for U.S. Employees, State Farm Insurance Co.; Employee Retirement Trust, State Farm Association's Funds Trust, State Farm Variable Product Trust, State Farm Mutual Fund Trust; Board of Directors, State Farm Bank, State Farm Vice President Management Corp., State Farm Investment Management Corp., Insurance Placement Service, Inc., State Farm Lloyds, Inc. **CIV:** Board of Trustees, Illinois Wesleyan University **MEM:** Illinois State Bar Association, American Bar Association **BA:** State Farm Headquarters, 1 State Farm Plaza, Bloomington, IL, 61701

TIPTON, SCOTT R., T: U.S. Representative from Colorado, Former State Legislator **I:** Government Administration/Government Relations/Government Services **DOB:** 11/09/1956 **PB:** Espanola **SC:** NM/USA **ED:** BA in Political Sci., Fort Lewis College **C:** Member, U.S. Small Business Committee, 2011-; Member, U.S. House Natural Resources Committee, 2011-; Member, U.S. House Agricultural Committee, 2011-; Member, U.S. Congress from 3rd Colorado District, Washington, DC 2011-; Member District 58, Colorado House of Reps., 2008-10; Chairman, Colorado Republican Party, 1997-2005; Owner, Mesa Indian Trading Co.,; Owner, Mesa Verde Pottery,; President, Tipton Properties,; President, Tipton Ltd., **CR:** Chairman McInnis for Congress, 2002, 1992 **CIV:** Member, Pueblo Community College Adv. Board, Board of Trustees, Mesa Verde National Park, Board member, Mesa Verde Foundation, Board of Trustees, Crow Canyon Archeological Center, **MEM:** Mem.: Montezuma County 100 Club **PA:** Republican

TISCH, JONATHAN MARK, T: CEO of Lowes Hotels & Resorts **I:** Business Management/ Business Services **CN:** Lowes Hotels & Resorts **DOB:** 12/07/1953 **PB:** Atlantic City **SC:** NJ/USA **PT:** Son of Preston Robert and Joan (Hyman) T.; Married Laura Steinberg, 1987 (div.); Married Lizzie Rudnick, 2007 **SPN:** Lizzie Rudnick, 2007; Laura Steinberg, 1987 (div.) **ED:** BA in Political Sci., Tufts University, 1976 **C:** CEO, Lowes Hotels & Resorts, 2016-; Co-chmn., Loews Corp., 2006-; Treasurer, New York Giants, 1991-; Chairman, Loews Hotels, New York City, 2011-; Chairman, CEO, Loews Hotels, New York City, 1989-2011; President, Loews Hotels, New York City, 1986-89; Executive vice president, Loews Hotels, New York City, 1985-86; Vice president, Loews Hotels, New York City, 1982-85; Director devel., Loews Hotels, New York City, 1981-82; Sales manager, Loews Hotels, New York City, 1980-81; Cinematographer, producer, WBZ-TV, Boston, 1976-79 **CR:** Board directors, Loews Corp., 1986-, New York Giants, 1991- chairman New York City & Co., 2002-08 **CIV:** Trustee Robert Steel Foundation, New York City, Gunnery School, Washington, Connecticut, 1983, Tufts University, Medford, Massachusetts, 1986-, Vice Pres.'s Residence Foundation, 1994 chairman New York City host committee for Grammys, 1988, 92, 94 board directors Elizabeth Glaser Pediatric AIDS Foundation, Tribeca Film Institute, Business Council for Museum of Modern Art vice chair economic devel. committee New York City Partnership, 1994- **CW:** Co-author (with Karl Weber): The Power of We: Succeeding Through Partnerships, 2004, Chocolates on the Pillow Aren't Enough: Reinventing The Customer Experience, 2007, Citizen You: Doing Your Part To Change the World, 2010 **AW:** Named CEO of Year, Executive Council of New York, 2006; named one of The Top

Ten Most Influential Business Leaders, Crain's New York Business; recipient Distinguished Alumni award, Tufts University, 1996 **MEM:** Member American Hotel & Motel Association (officer 1994-97), Travel Business Roundtable (chairman 1995-, conference chairman 1995-), Friars Club. **H:** Golf, tennis, skiing

TITUS, DINA, T: U.S. Representative from Nevada **I:** Government Administration/Government Relations/Government Services **DOB:** 05/23/1950 **PB:** Thomasville **PT:** Married Thomas Clayton Wright. **ED:** PhD in Political Sci., Florida State University, 1976; MA, University Georgia, 1973; AB, College William & Mary, 1970 **C:** Member, US Congress from 1st Nevada District, Washington, 2013-; Member, Committee on Foreign Affairs; Member, US House Veterans' Affairs Committee, 2013-; Member, US House Transportation & Infrastructure Committee, Washington, 2013-; Commissioner, US Commission on Civil Rights, Washington, 2011-12; Member, US House Transportation & Infrastructure Committee, Washington, 2009-11; Member, US House Homeland Security Committee, Washington, 2009-11; Member, US House Education & Labor Committee, Washington, 2009-11; Member, US Congress from 3rd Nevada District, Washington, 2009-11; Minority leader, Nevada State Senate, 1993-2008; Member District 7, Nevada State Senate, 1989-2009; Professor political sci., University Nevada, Las Vegas, 2011; Professor political sci., University Nevada, Las Vegas, 1977-2009; Lecturer, North Texas State University, Denton, **CR:** Chairman Nevada Humanities Committee, 1984-86 **CW:** Author: Bombs in the Backyard: Atomic Testing and American Politics, 1986, Battle Born: Federal-State Relations in Nevada during the 20th Century, 1989; appeared in: (TV special) The American Experience: Las Vegas-an Unconventional History, 2006 **AW:** Named Outstanding Democrat of the Year, Paradise Democratic Club Las Vegas, 2009 **MEM:** Member Western Political Sci. Association, Clark County Women's Democratic Club, American Pen Women, Aquavision, PEO. **PA:** Democrat **BA:** 2464 Rayburn House Office Bldg, Washington, DC, 20515

TJOFLAT, GERALD BARD, T: Federal Judge **I:** Law and Legal Services **DOB:** 12/06/1929 **PB:** Pittsburgh **SC:** PA/USA **PT:** Son of Gerald Benjamin and Sarita (Romero-Hermoso) Tjoflat; **ED:** LLD (hon.), William Mitchell College, 1993; DCL (hon.), Jacksonville University, 1978; LLB, Duke University, 1957; Student, University Cincinnati, 1950-52; Student, University Virginia, 1947-50 **CT:** Bar: Florida 1957 **C:** Judge, US Court Appeals (11th cir.), Jacksonville, 1981-; Chief judge, US Court Appeals (11th cir.), Jacksonville, 1989-96; Judge, US Court Appeals (5th cir.), Jacksonville, 1975-81; Judge, US District Court Mid. District, Jacksonville, 1970-75; Judge, 4th Judicial Cir. Court, Florida, 1968-70; Private practice, Jacksonville, Florida, 1957-68 **CR:** U.S. del. 6th and 7th UN Congress for Prevention of Crime and Treatment of Offenders member Federal Judicial Court Committee on Sentencing, Probation and Pretrial Services, 1988-90 chairman Judicial Conference U.S., 1978-87, member committee administration probation system, 1972-87, member, 1989-96, Adv. Corrections Council U.S., 1975-87 **CIV:** Trustee, Episcopalian High School, Jacksonville, 1975-90 Trustee, Jacksonville Marine Institute, 1976-90 Chairman, North Florida council Boy Scouts Am., 1985-90 President, North Florida council Boy Scouts Am., 2000-01 President, North Florida council Boy Scouts Am., 1976-85 Hon. life member, board visitors, Duke University Law School, 2000 Senior warden, St. Johns Cathedral,

Jacksonville, 1992 Senior warden, St. Johns Cathedral, Jacksonville, 1991 Senior warden, St. Johns Cathedral, Jacksonville, 1987 Senior warden, St. Johns Cathedral, Jacksonville, 1983 Senior warden, St. Johns Cathedral, Jacksonville, 1975 Member vestry, St. Johns Cathedral, Jacksonville, 1995-96 Member vestry, St. Johns Cathedral, Jacksonville, 1993 Member vestry, St. Johns Cathedral, Jacksonville, 1985-87 Member vestry, St. Johns Cathedral, Jacksonville, 1981-83 Member vestry, St. Johns Cathedral, Jacksonville, 1977-79 Member vestry, St. Johns Cathedral, Jacksonville, 1973-75 Member vestry, St. Johns Cathedral, Jacksonville, 1969-71 **AW:** Recipient Fordham-Stein prize, 1996, Merit award, Duke University, 1990 **MEM:** Mem.: American Bar Association, Am. Judicature Society, Am. Law Institute, Florida Bar Association **BA:** 56 Forsyth St NW, Atlanta, GA, 30303

TOBIN, JOSEPH WILLIAM, T: Archbishop **I:** Religious **DOB:** 05/03/1952 **PB:** Detroit **SC:** MI/USA **PT:** Joseph Tobin; Marie Terese (Kerwin) Tobin **ED:** MRE, MDiv, Mount St. Alphonsus Seminary Major, New York, NY, 1979; BA, Holy Redeemer College, Waterford, WI, 1977 **C:** Secretary, Congregation for Institutes of Consecrated Life & Societies of Apostolic Life, Rome, Italy, 2010-Present; Titular Archbishop, Archdiocese of Obba, 2010-Present; Ordained Bishop, 2010; Superior General, Congregation of the Most Holy Redeemer, 1997-2010; Consultor General, Congregation of the Most Holy Redeemer, 1991-1997; Pastor, St. Alphonsus Parish, Chicago, IL, 1990-1991; Episcopal Vicar, Archdiocese of Detroit, 1980-1986; Pastor, Holy Redeemer Parish, Detroit, MI, 1984-1990; Parochial Vicar, Holy Redeemer Parish, Detroit, MI, 1979-1984; Ordained Priest, Congregation of the Most Holy Redeemer, 1978; Professed, Congregation of the Most Holy Redeemer, 1972 **BA:** Palazzo della Congregazioni, Piazza Pio XII 3, Rome, Italy, 193-RM **ADD:** Palazzo della Congregazioni, Piazza Pio XII 3, Rome, Italy, 193

TOMJANOVICH, RUDOLPH, T: Retired Professional Basketball Coach **I:** Other **DOB:** 11/24/1948 **PB:** Hamtramck **ED:** Grad., Univ. Michigan, 1970 **C:** Retired, 2005; Head coach, LA Lakers, 2004-05; Personnel consultant, Houston Rockets, 2003-04; Head coach, Houston Rockets, 1992-2003; Assistant coach, Houston Rockets, 1983-92; Scout, Houston Rockets, 1981-83; Player, Houston Rockets, 1970-81 **CR:** Director scouting US Men's Senior National Basketball Team, Beijing, 2008, coach, Sydney, 2000 head coach Western Conference All-Star Team, 1997 **AW:** Named NBA Coach of the Year, Sporting News, 1993; recipient Gold Medal, Sydney Olympic Games, 2000,NBA All-Star , 1974-1977, 1979, First-Team All Big Ten, 1969, 1970, NBA Champion, 1994-95 **ACH:** Achievements include being a member of the NBA Championship winning Houston Rockets, 1994, 1995

TOMLIN, LILY, T: Actress **I:** Media & Entertainment **DOB:** 09/01/1939 **PB:** Detroit **SC:** MI/USA **ED:** Student, Wayne State University; Studied mime with Paul Curtis; Studied acting with Peggy Feury **CR:** Co-founder Lily Tomlin Jane Wagner Cultural Arts Center, LA **CW:** Appearances in concerts and colleges throughout US; actress: (TV series) Rowan & Martin's Laugh-In, 1969-73, The Magic School Bus, 1994-97, (voice), Murphy Brown, 1996-98, The West Wing, 2002-06, Will & Grace, 2005-06, Desperate Housewives, 2008-09, Malibu Country, 2012-13, Grace and Frankie, 2015-, The Magic School Bus Rides Again, 2017 (voice); (TV appearances) The Music Scene, 1969-70, Tomlin, CBS Spls., 1973, 81, 82; 2 ABC Spls., 1974, 1975, Edith Ann Animated Specials,

ABC, 1994, 12 Miles of Bad Road, 2008, Damages, 2010, NCIS, 2011, Web Therapy, 2011-15, Eastbound and Down, 2012; (films) Nashville, 1975 (New York Film Critics award for Best Supporting Actress, 1975), Moment by Moment, 1978, The Incredible Shrinking Woman, 1981, Nine to Five, 1980, All of Me, 1984, Big Business, 1987, Shadows and Fog, 1992, The Player, 1992, Short Cuts, 1993, The Beverly Hillbillies, 1993, And the Band Played On, 1993, Getting Away with Murder, 1995, The Celluloid Closet, 1995, Blue in the Face, 1995, Flirting With Disaster, 1996, Reno Finds Her Mom, 1997, Get Bruce, 1999, Krippendorf's Tribe, 1998, Tea with Mussolini, 1999, Picking Up the Pieces, 2000, The Kid, 2000, Orange County, 2002, I Heart Huckabees, 2004, A Prairie Home Companion, 2006, (voice) The Ant Bully, 2006, The Walker, 2007, The Pink Panther 2, 2009, (voice) Ponyo on the Cliff by the Sea, 2009, Stars in Shorts, 2012, Admission, 2013, Grandma, 2015; executive prodr.: (TV series) Citizen Reno, 2001; one-woman Broadway show Appearing Nitely, 1977 (Special Tony award for Lifetime Achievement, 1977), The Search for Signs of Intelligent Life in the Universe, 1985 (Drama Desk award, Outer Critics Circle award, Tony award for Best Actress, 1986), Not Playing with a Full Deck, 2009; recs: include: This is a Recording, 1972 (Grammy award for Best Comedy Album, 1972), And That's The Truth, 1972, Modern Scream, 1975, On Stage, 1978, 20th Century Masters: The Best of Lily Tomlin, 2003; co-author: Edith Ann: My Life So Far, 1994. **AW:** Recipient 5 Emmy awards for CBS Special 1973, 1981, Emmy award for ABC Special 1975, Emmy award Magic School Bus, 1995, Peabody award Celluloid Closet, 1997, Peabody Edith Ann's Christmas, 1997, Mark Twain Prize for Am. Humor, Kennedy Center, 2003, Kennedy Center Honors, John F. Kennedy Center Performing Arts, Washington, 2014. Screen Actors Guild Lifetime Achievement Award, 2017.

TONKO, PAUL DAVID, T: U.S. Representative from New York, Former State Agency Administrator **I:** Government Administration/Government Relations/Government Services **DOB:** 06/18/1949 **PB:** Amsterdam **ED:** BS in Mechanical and Industrial Engineering, Clarkson College Tech., 1971 **C:** Member, US Congress from 20th New York District, 2013-; Member, US Congress from 21st New York District, Washington, 2009-13; President, CEO, New York State Research & Devel. Authority, Albany, 2007-08; Chairman, New York State Assembly Energy Committee, Albany, 1992-2007; Member District 105, New York State Assembly, Albany, 1983-2007; Chair, Montgomery County Board Supervisors, 1981; Member, Montgomery County Board Supervisors, 1975-83; Senior valuation engineer, New York Department Pub. Service,; Engineer, New York State Department Transportation **CIV:** Member, Schenectady Chamber of Commerce, Member, Montgomery County Chamber of Commerce, Del., Democratic National Convention, 1988 Board directors, American Cancer Society, Montgomery County Unit, Board directors, Montgomery County Red Cross **AW:** Recipient Legis. award, New York State Conference Mayors, 1991 **MEM:** Mem.: Kiwanas, Elks, Lodge 101, K. of C., Council 209 **PA:** Democrat

TOOMEY, PAT, T: U.S. Senator From Pennsylvania **I:** Government Administration/Government Relations/Government Services **DOB:** 11/17/1961 **PB:** Providence **SC:** RI/USA **MS:** Married **SPN:** Kris Ann Duncan, 1997 **CH:** Bridget, Patrick, Jr., Duncan **ED:** BA in Government, Harvard University, Cum Laude, 1984 **C:** U.S. Senate Commerce, Science & Transportation Committee, Washington, DC, 2011-

Present; U.S. Senate Budget Committee, Washington, DC, 2011-Present; U.S. Senate Banking, Housing & Urban Affairs Committee, Washington, DC, 2011-Present; U.S. Senator From Pennsylvania, Washington, DC, 2011-Present; Co-Founder, Toomey Enterprises, Inc., Allentown, PA, 1991-Present; Chairman, U.S. Senate Republican Steering Committee, 2012-2015; Joint Select Committee On Deficit Reduction, Washington, DC, 2011; President, CEO, The Club For Growth, Washington, DC, 2004-2009; U.S. Congress From 15th Pennsylvania District, 1999-2005; Financial Consultant, Hong Kong, 1990-1991; Vice President, Director, U.S. Subsidiary, Morgan Grefell; Investment Banker, Chemical Bank New York, NY **CR:** Board of Directors, Commonwealth Foundation For Public Policy Alternatives, 2007-Present **AW:** Man of the Year, U.S. Marine Corps, 1999, Honor Roll Award, Concord Coalition, 2000 **PA:** Republican **BA:** Office of Pat Toomey, 248 Russell Senate Office Building, Washington, DC, 20510

TORRE, JOE, T: Major League Baseball Executive, Retired Professional Baseball Manager **I:** Athletics **DOB:** 07/18/1940 **PB:** Bklyn. **PT:** Son of Joseph & Margaret Torre; Married Jackie Torre, 1963 (div.); 1 child, Michael; Married Jackie Torre, 1968 (div.); children: Lauren, Christina; Married Alice Wolterman, August 23, 1987; 1 child, **ED:** HHD (hon.), Rider University, 2006 **C:** Executive vice president baseball operations, Major League Baseball, 2012-; Executive vice president baseball operations, Major League Baseball, 2011-12; Manager, L.A. Dodgers, 2008-10; Manager, New York Yankees, 1995-2007; Manager, St. Louis Cardinals, 1990-94; Manager, Atlanta Braves, 1982-84; Player-mgr., New York Mets, 1977-82; Professional baseball player, New York Mets, 1974-77; Professional baseball player, St. Louis Cardinals, 1969-74; Professional baseball player, Milwaukee Braves, 1960-69 **CR:** Member special committee for on-field matters Major League Baseball, 2009-12 co-founder (with Ali Torre) Joe Torre Safe at Home Foundation, 2002- TV broadcaster California Angels, 1984-90 **CW:** Author: Chasing the Dream: My Lifelong Journey to the World Series, 1997, Joe Torre's Ground Rules for Winners: 12 Keys to Managing Team Players, Tough Bosses, Setbacks, and Success, 1999; co-author (with Tom Verducci): The Yankee Years, 2009 (#1 Publishers Weekly bestseller); actor: (films) Taking Care of Business, 1990, Analyze That, 2002, (voice) Everyone's Hero, 2006 **AW:** Named National League MVP, 1971, Player of Year Sporting News, 1971, Manager of Year Associated Press, 1982, American League Manager of Year, 1996, 1998; named to The National League All-Star Team, 1963-67, 70-73; recipient Gold Glove award, 1965, Mgr of Year award, MLB.com, 2007,NL Batting Champion, 1971, NL RBI Leader, 1971, St Louis Cardinals Hall of Fame, 2016, National Baseball Hall of Fame, 2014, Willie, Mickey and Duke Award, 2011, Slocum Award, 2008, Chuck Tanner Major League Baseball Manager of the Year, 2007 **ACH:** Achievements include managing the New York Yankees to 4 World Series Titles 1996, 1998, 1999, 2000

TORRES, NORMA J., T: U.S. Representative from California **I:** Government Administration/ Government Relations/Government Services **C:** Member, U.S. House of Representatives from California's 33rd District, 2015-, Member, Committee on the Judiciary, Committee on Foreign Affairs; Member District 61, California State Assembly, 2008-2015; Member aging and long-term care committee, banking and fin. committee, governmental organization committee, human services committee, insurance committee, select committee on domestic violence, California State Assembly,;

Chair housing and community devel. committee, California State Assembly,; Mayor, City of Pomona, 2006-08; Councilwoman District 6, City of Pomona, 2000-06; Former 911 dispatcher, City of LA Police Department **CR:** Treasurer Executive Committee National Conference Dem. Mayors **CIV:** Vol., Boy Scouts Am., Vol., Am. Youth Soccer Org., Vol., Big Sisters Program, Vol., Suicide Prevention Center, Board member, Fairplex Blue Ribbon Committee, Board member, Tri-City Mental Health, Board member, Pomonoa Valley Transportation Authority, Founder, Neighbors for Pomona Committee, **MEM:** Mem.: American Federation of State Local 3090 **PA:** Democrat **BA:** 236 Cannon House Office Building, Washington, DC, 20515

TORRUELLA, JUAN R., T: Federal Judge **I:** Law and Legal Services **DOB:** 06/07/1933 **PB:** San Juan **SC:** PR/USA **ED:** LLD (hon.), Roger Williams University, 1995; LLD (hon.), St. John's University, 1995; MSt, Oxford University, 2003; MPA, University Puerto Rico, 1984; LLM, University Virginia, 1984; LLB, Boston University, 1957; BS in Business and Fin., University Pennsylvania, 1954 **C:** Chief Judge, U.S. Court of Appeals for the First Circuit,1994-2001; Judge, US Court Appeals (1st cir.), San Juan, 1984-; Chief judge, US Court Appeals (1st cir.), San Juan, 1994-2001; Chief judge, US District Court Puerto Rico, San Juan, 1982-84; Judge, US District Court Puerto Rico, San Juan, 1974-82 **CR:** Former member judicial conference committee International Judicial Relations former member judicial conference executive committee Administration Federal Magistrate Systems, former member judicial conference committee **MEM:** Mem.: Federal Bar Association, American Bar Association, Puerto Rico Bar Association, DC Bar Association, Association Labor Relations Practitioners Puerto Rico and VI **BA:** John J Moakley US Courthouse, 1 Courthouse Ste 2500, Boston, MA, USA, 2210

TOUR, JAMES M., T: Organic Chemist **I:** Sciences **DOB:** 08/18/1959 **PB:** New York **SC:** NY/USA **PT:** Eli Tour; Hedi Tour **ED:** Postdoctoral Fellow in Synthetic Organic Chemistry, National Institutes of Health, Stanford University (1987-1988); Postdoctoral Fellow in Organometallic Chemistry, University of Wisconsin (1986-1987); PhD in Synthetic Organic and Organometallic Chemistry, Purdue University, West Layafette, IN (1986); Graduate Coursework, Department of Chemistry, Purdue University (1981-1986); BS in Chemistry, Syracuse University, Syracuse, NY (1981); Undergraduate Coursework, Department of Chemistry, Syracuse University (1977-1981) **C:** Co-Founder, NanoComposites, Inc. (2004-Present); Co-Founder, Vice President, Molecular Electronics Corp., Houston, TX (1999-Present); Professor of Computer Science, Smalley Institute for Nanoscale Science and Technology, Rice University (1999-Present); Professor of Mechanical Engineering and Materials Science, Smalley Institute for Nanoscale Science and Technology, Rice University (1999-Present); T.T. and W.F. Chao Professor of Chemistry, Smalley Institute for Nanoscale Science and Technology, Rice University (1999-Present); Founder, Principal, NanoJtech Consultants, LLC (2007); Co-Founder, RJAC-10, LLC (2007); Board of Directors, Distinguished Faculty Associate, Hanzen College, Rice University, Houston, TX (1999-2000); Guy F. Lipscomb Professor of Chemistry, University of South Carolina, South Carolina (1996-1999); Professor, Department of Chemistry and Biochemistry, University of South Carolina (1994-1996); Associate Professor, Department of Chemistry and Biochemistry, University of South Carolina (1992-1994); Assistant Professor, Department of Chemistry and Biochemistry, University of South

Carolina, Columbia, SC (1988-1992) **CR:** Member, Department of Commerce, Emerging Technology and Research Advisory Committee (2008-Present); MD Anderson Cancer Research Center, Competitive Grant Renewal Board (2007-Present); Board of Directors, Ariel Ministries (2006-Present); Defense Science Board of Chemistry/Nano Study Section (2007); Director, Carbon Nanotechnology Laboratory (2005-2007); Adjunct Professor, Department of Chemistry, Center for Nanoscale Science and Technology, Rice University, Houston, TX (1999); Member, Technical Advosory Board, California Molecular Electronics Corp. (1998-1999); National Defense Science Study Group (1997-1999); Abbott Distinguished Lecturer, Colorado State University (1997); Member, Advisory Board, Governor's Mathematics and Science, South Carolina (1996-1998); Member, Advisory Committee, Materials Research Center, National Science Foundation (1996-1997); Member, CAREER Program Advisory Committee, National Science Foundation (1995); Weissberger-Williams Lecturer, Eastman Kodak Corp., Rochester, NY (1995); Visiting Scholar, Department of Chemistry, Harvard University (1994); One-Week Visiting Lecturer, Polymer Division, IBM, Almaden Research Center (1988); Consultant in field **CIV:** Member, Defense Science Study Group (2003); Bible Study Teacher, Broad River Maximum Security Prison, Columbia, SC (1989-1999) **CW:** Member, Advisory Board, Chemical Reviews (1999-2002); Author, "Molecular Electronics: Commercial Insights, Chemistry, Devices, Architecture, and Programming"; Contributor, Articles to Professional Journals **AW:** Fellow, National Academy of Inventors (2015); Named, Scientist of the Year, R&D Magazine (2013); Recipient, ACS Nano Lectureship Award (2012); Named, One of Top 10 Chemists in the World Over the Past Decade, Thomson Reuters Citations per Publication Index Survey (2009); Recipient, Houston Technology Center Nanotechnology Award (2009); Recipient, Distinguished Alumni Award, Purdue University (2009); Recipient, Feynman Prize in Experimental Nanotechnology (2008); Recipient, NASA Space Act Award for Development of Carbon Nanotube Reinforced Elastomers (2008); Recipient, George R. Brown Award for Superior Teaching (2007); Recipient, Nanotech Briefs Nano 50 Innovator Award (2006); Recipient, Small Times Magazine Innovator of the Year Award (2006); Recipient, Alan Berman Research Publication Award, Department of the Navy (2006); Recipient, Honda Innovation Award for Nanocars (2005); Recipient, Russell Research Award in Science, Mathematics and Engineering, University of South Carolina (1997); Recipient, Exxon Educational Foundation Research and Training Award (1994); Recipient, Presidential Young Investigator Award in Polymer Chemistry, National Science Foundation (1991-1996); Recipient, Office of Naval Research Young Investigator Award in Polymer Chemistry, Office of Naval Research (1989-1992); Recipient, IBM Corp. Full Graduate Fellowship in Polymer Chemistry, Purdue University (1985-1986); Recipient, Celanese Corp. Graduate Fellowship in Chemistry (1981-1982); Recipient, Award, American Institute of Chemists (1981); Recipient, George Wiley Award in Organic Chemistry (1979) **MEM:** Recipient, Arthur C. Cope Scholar Award (2007); Recipient, Southern Chemist of the Year Award (2005); Member, Editorial Advisory Board, Chemical Reviews (1999-2003); Associate Director, Polymer Division, Materials Research Secretariat (1991-1995); Fellow, American Association for the Advancement of Science; Associate, Materials Research Society; Associate, American Chemical Society **ACH:** Achievements include patents in field; patents pending in field **H:** Bible study; Target shooting **BA:** Rice U Smalley Inst for Nanoscale Science & Technology, 6100 Main St MS 222, Houston, TX, 77005

TOWNES, CHARLES HARD, T: Physics Professor **I:** Education/Educational Services **DOB:** 07/28/1915 **PB:** Greenville SC: SC/USA **PT:** Son of Henry Keith and Ellen Sumter (Hard) Townes; **ED:** PhD, California Institute Tech., 1939; MA in Physics, Duke University, Durham, North Carolina, 1937; BS in Physics, BA in Modern Languages, Furman University, Greenville, 1935 **C:** Professor Grad. School, University of California, Berkeley, 1994; Professor physics emeritus, University of California, Berkeley, 1986-94; Univ. professor physics, University of California, Berkeley, 1967-86; Vice president, director research, Institute Defense Analyses, Washington, 1959-61; Institute professor, Massachusetts Institute of Technology, 1966-67; Professor physics, provost, Massachusetts Institute of Technology, 1961-66; Chairman physics department, Columbia University, 1952-55; Executive director Columbia Radiation Laboratory, Columbia University, 1950-52; Professor physics, Columbia University, 1950-61; Associate professor physics, Columbia University, New York City, 1948-50; Member tech. staff, Bell Telephone Laboratory, 1939-47 **CR:** Member Pres.'s Committee Sci. & Tech., 1976; vice chairman, Pres.'s Sci. Adv. Committee, 1967-69, member, 1966-69; board directors GM, 1973-86, Perkin-Elmer Corp., 1966-69; chairman sci. & tech. adv. committee for manned space flight NASA, 1964-70 Herzberg lecturer University Toronto, 2010; Weinberg lecturer, Oak Ridge National Laboratory, Tennessee, 1997; Centennial lecturer, University Toronto, 1967; Scott lecturer University Cambridge, 1963; director Enrico Fermi International School Physics, Italy, 1963; Fulbright lecturer University Tokyo, 1956, University Paris, 1955-56 **CIV:** Board of directors, Carnegie Institution Washington, Board of directors, Center Theology & Natural Scis., Mount Wilson Institute, **CW:** Author: How the Laser Happened. Adventures of a Scientist, 1999, Making Waves, 1996; co-author (with A. L. Schawlow): Microwave Spectroscopy, 1955; author, co-editor Quantum Electronics, 1960, Quantum Electronics and Coherent Light, 1964, member editorial board Rev. Sci. Instruments, 1950-52, Physical Rev., 1951-53, Journal Molecular Spectroscopy, 1957-60, Proceedings National Academy of Sciences, 1978-84, Can. Journal Physics, 1995-, contributor articles to sci. publications **AW:** Decorated officier Légion d'Honneur, France; named to Engineering & Sci. Hall of Fame, 1983, National Inventors Hall of Fame, 1976; recipient Vannevar Bush medal, 2006, Templeton prize, 2005, Drake award, SETI Institute, Mountain View, California, 2003, Karl Schwarzschild medal, German Astronomical Society, 2002, Rabindranath Tagore Birth Centenary plaque, Asiatic Society, 1999, Frank Annunzio award, Christopher Columbus Fellowship Foundation, 1999, Mendel award, Villanova University, 1999, ADION medal, Nice Observatory, France, 1995, CommonWealth award, 1993, Berkeley citation, University California, 1986, National Medal Sci., 1982, Niels Bohr International Gold medal, 1979, Wilhelm Exner award, Austria, 1970, Distinguished Pub. Service medal, NASA, 1969, Nobel prize for physics, 1964, Thomas Young medal and prize, Institute Physics/Phys. Society England, 1963, Stuart Ballantine medal, Franklin Institute, 1962, Nancy DeLoye Fitzroy and Roland V. Firtzroy Medal, 2012, Golden Goose Award, 2012, SPIE Gold Medal, 2010 **MEM:** Fellow: IEEE (life Medal of Honor 1967), California Academy Scis., Indian National Sci. Academy, Optical Society America (Mees medal 1968), Am. Physical Society (president 1967, Plyler prize 1977, Frederick Ives medal 1996); mem.: NAE (Founders award 2000), National Academy of Sciences (council member 1968-72, chairman space sci. board 1970-73, council member 1978-81, Comstock award 1959, Carty medal 1962), New York

Academy Scis., Max-Planck Institute Physics & Astrophysics (foreign), Pontifical Academy Scis., Russian Academy Scis. (Lomonosov medal 2000), Royal Society, Am. Academy Arts & Scis., Am. Astronomical Society, Am. Philosophical Society **ACH:** Achievements include patents for masers and lasers **BA:** U Calif Dept Physics, 366 Leconte # 7200, Berkeley, CA, 94720

TOWNSHEND, PETE, T: Guitarist, Composer **I:** Media & Entertainment **DOB:** 05/19/1945 **PB:** London **PT:** Son of Cliff and Betty (Dennis) Townshend **C:** Guitarist, The Who (formerly The Detours, The High Numbers), 1964-; Owner, Eel Pie Recording Ltd., 1972-83 **CW:** Guitarist: (albums with The Who) The Who Sings My Generation, 1965, Happy Jack, 1966, The Who Sell Out, 1967, The Magic Bus: The Who on Tour, 1968, Tommy, 1969, Live At Leeds, 1970, Meaty Beaty Big & Bouncy, 1971, Who's Next, 1971, Quadrophenia, 1973, Odds & Sods, 1974, The Who By Numbers, 1975, Who Are You, 1978, Face Dances, 1981, Hooligans, 1981, It's Hard, 1982, Who's Greatest Hits, 1983, Who's Last, 1983, Who's Missing, 1985, Two's Missing, 1987, Who's Better, Who's Best, 1988, Join Together, 1990, Thirty Years of Maximum R&B, 1994, Live at the Isle of Wight Festival 1970, 1996, My Generation: The Very Best of The Who, 1996, The BBC Sessions, 1999, The Blues to the Bush, 1999, The Ultimate Collection, 2002, Live at the Royal Albert Hall, 2003, The Who: Then & Now, 2004, Live from Toronto, 2006, Endless Wire, 2006, Greatest Hits, 2009, Greatest Hits Live, 2010; (soundtracks) The Kids Are Alright, 1979, Quadrophenia, 1979; singer, guitarist: (solo albums) Who Came First, 1972, Secret Policeman's Ball, 1980, Empty Glass, 1980, All the Best Cowboys Have Chinese Eyes, 1982, Scoop, 1983, White City: A Novel, 1985, Another Scoop, 1986, Deep End Live, 1987, The Iron Man: A Musical, 1989, Psychoderelict, 1993, The Best of Pete Townsend, 1996, Cool Walking Smooth Talking, 1996, Pete Townshend Live: A Benefit for Maryville Academy, 1998; (with Ronnie Lane) Rough Mix, 1977; performer: (films) Monterey Pop, 1968, Woodstock, 1970, Tommy, 1975, The Kids Are Alright, 1979, The Who Rocks America 1982, 1982, The Rolling Stones Rock 'N' Roll Circus, 1996, Message to Love: The Isle of Wight Festival, 1997, Amazing Journey: The Story of The Who, 2007; musical dir.: (film and soundtrack) Tommy, 1975; Broadway musical The Who's Tommy, 1993 (Tony award for Best Original Score, 1993, Grammy award for Original Cast Recording, 1993, Dora Mayer Moore award, 1994, Olivier award, 1997); featured in numerous documentaries; author: Horse's Neck, 1985, Who I Am: A Memoir by Pete Townshend, 2012; co-author (with Des McAnuff) Tommy: The Musical, 1993 **AW:** Named to VHI Rock Honor, 2008, Kennedy Center Honors, 2008, Steve Ray Vaughn Award, 2015, The George and Ira Gershwin Award, 2016, The Rock & Roll Hall of Fame (as member of The Who), 1990; recipient Kennedy Center Honors, John F. Kennedy Center for the Performing Arts, 2008, BMI TV Music award, 2004, BMI President award, 2002, Ivor Novello Lifetime Achievement award, 2001, Q Lifetime Achievement award, 1997, International Rock Living Legend award, 1991, BRIT award for Contribution to British Music, 1983, BRIT Lifetime Achievement award, 1983, Lifetime Achievement award, British Phonographic Industry, 1983, Ivor Novello award for Contribution to British Music, 1982

TRAXLER, WILLIAM BYRD JR., T: Federal Judge **I:** Law and Legal Services **DOB:** 05/01/1948 **PB:** Greenville **SC:** South Carolina **PT:** Son of William Byrd and Bettie (Wooten) Traxler; **ED:** JD, University South Carolina, 1973; BA, Davidson College,

1970 **C:** Chief judge, US Court Appeals (4th cir.), 2009-16; Judge, US Court Appeals (4th cir.), Greenville, 1998-; US District judge, District of South Carolina, Greenville, 1992-98; Resident cir. judge, 13th Judicial Court, Greenville, 1998-; Solicitor, 13th Judicial Court, Greenville, 1985-92; Solicitor, 13th Judicial Court, Greenville, 1981-85; Deputy solicitor, 13th Judicial Court, Greenville, 1978-81; Assistant solicitor, 13th Judicial Court, Greenville, 1975-78; Associate, William Byrd Traxler, Greenville, 1973-75 **AW:** Recipient Leadership award, Probation, Parole & Pardon Services, South Carolina, 1990, Outstanding Service award, Solicitors Association, South Carolina, 1987 **BA:** 1100 E Main St #501, Richmond, VA, 23219

TREVINO, LEE BUCK, T: Professional Golfer **I:** Athletics **DOB:** 12/01/1939 **PB:** Dallas **SC:** TX/USA **PT:** Son of Joe and Juanita (Barrett) T. **MS:** Marries **SPN:** Claudia Bove **CH:** Richard Lee, Lesley Ann, Tony Lee, Troy Liana, Olivia Leigh, Daniel Lee **ED:** Student, Public Schools **C:** Chairman, Board, Lee Trevino Enterprises, Inc., 1967-; Joined, PGA Senior Tour, 1989; Joined, PGA Tour, 1967; Assistant Professional, Horizon Hills Country Club, El Paso, Texas, 1966-67; Head Professional, Hardy's Driving Range, Dallas, 1961-65 **CIV:** Honorary Chairman, Christmas Seal Campaign, 1969-72, Sports Ambassador, 1971, Member Pres.'s Conference on Physical Fitness and Sports, Grand Marshal, Sun Carnival Parade, 1969-70, 71-72, Member, Sports Committee, National Multiple Sclerosis Society **AW:** Recipient, Hickok Belt Award, 1971; Named Golf Rookie of Year, 1967, PGA Player of Year, 1971, Texas Pro Athlete of Year, 1970, Gold Tee Award, 1971, Associated Press Pro Athlete of Year, 1971, Player of Year Golf Magazine, 1971, Sportsman of Year Sports Illustrated, 1971, PGA Senior Tour Players of Year, 1990, 92, 94, International Sports Personality of Year Brit. Broadcasting Association, 1971, Rookie and Player of Year, Senior PGA Tour, 1990; Member, Texas Hall of Fame, Am. Gulf Hall of Fame, World Golf Hall of Fame, Jack Nicklaus Trophy, 1990, 1992, 1994, Arnold Palmer Award, 1990, 1992, Byron Nelson Award, 1990, 1991, 1992, Sports Illustrated Sportsman of the Year, 1971 **ACH:** Achievements include Tournament winner Texas Open, 1965, 66, New Mexico Open, 1966, U.S. Open, 1968, 71, Amana Open, 1968, 69, Hawaiian Open, 1968, Tucson Open, 1969, 70, World Cup, 1969, 71, National Airlines Open, 1970, Brit. Open, 1971, 72, Canadian Open 1971, 77, 79, Can. PGA, 1979, Danny Thomas-Memphis Classic, 1971, 72, 80, Tallahassee Open, 1971, Sahara Invitational, 1971, St. Louis Classic, 1972, Hartford Open, 1972, Jackie Gleason Classic, 1973, Doral-Eastern Open, 1973, Mexican Open, 1973, 75, Chrysler Classic, Australia, 1973, PGA Championship, 1974, 84, World Series Golf, 1974, Greater New Orleans Open, 1974, Florida Citrus Open, 1975, Colonial National Invitational, 1976, 78, Colgate Mixed Team Matches, 1979, Brit. Masters, 1985, U.S. Senior Open, 1990; King Hassan Moroccan trophy II, 1977; Lancome trophy Benson & Hedges, 1978, 80; 1st golfer to have scored four sub-par rounds in U.S. Open Competition, 1968; leading Money winner, 1970, 2d pl. money winner 1971, 1972; Vardon trophy winner, 1970 1972, 74, 80; Can. PGA, 1983; PGA Seniors Championship, 1994; captain Ryder Cup Matches, 1985; first golfer to have scored 4 sub-par rounds in PGA competition.

TRIBE, LAURENCE HENRY, T: Law Educator **I:** Law and Legal Services **DOB:** 10/10/1941 **PB:** Shanghai **PT:** Son of George Israel and Paulina (Diatlovitsky) Tribe; Married Carolyn Ricarda Kreye, June 20, 1964; children: Mark Alexander, Kerry Katrina **ED:** LHD (hon.), Hebrew University, 1998; LLD (hon.), Colgate University, 1997; LLD (hon.), Illinois Institute Tech., 1988;

LLD (hon.), American University, 1987; LLD (hon.), University Pacific, 1987; LLD (hon.), Gonzaga University, 1980; JD magna cum laude, Harvard University, 1966; AB summa cum laude in Math., Harvard University, 1962 **CT:** Bar: California 1966, Massachusetts 1978, US Supreme Ct 1978, US Court Appeals DC Cir. 1978, US Court Appeals 9th Cir. 1979, US Court Appeals 1st Cir. 1980, US Court Appeals 2nd Cir. 1982, US Court Appeals 3rd Cir. 1991, US Court Appeals 4th Cir. 1993, US Court Appeals Federal Cir. 1993 **C:** Consultant, Akin Gump Strauss Hauer and Feld LLP, Washington, 2007-; Carl M. Loeb univ. professor, Harvard Law School, Cambridge, Massachusetts, 2004-; Ralph S. Tyler, Junior professor constitutional law, Harvard Law School, Cambridge, Massachusetts, 1982-2004; Professor, Harvard Law School, Cambridge, Massachusetts, 1972-82; Assistant professor law, Harvard Law School, Cambridge, Massachusetts, 1968-71; Executive director tech. assessment panel, National Academy Sciences, Washington, 1968-69; Law clerk to Justice Potter Stewart, US Supreme Court, 1967-68; Law clerk to Justice Matthew O. Tobriner, California Supreme Court, 1966-67 **CR:** Chief appellate counsel California Nuclear Litigation, 1978-83 special deputy attorney general Hawaii, 1983-84 consultant National Science Foundation, National Endowment Humanities, White House, others consultant Marshall Islands for drafting new constitution, 1978-79 chairman Marshall Islands Judicial Service Commission consultant Akin Gump Strauss Hauer & Feld **CW:** Author: Technology: Processes of Assessment and Choice, 1969, Channeling Technology Through Law, 1973, The American Presidency: Its Constitutional Structure, 1974, American Constitutional Law, 1978, 88, 2000, Constitutional Choices, 1985, God Save this Honorable Court, 1985, Abortion: The Clash of Absolutes, 1990, The Invisible Constitution, 2008; co-author: Environmental Protection, 1971, The Supreme Ct.: Trends and Development, 1979, 80, 82, 83, 84, On Reading the Constitution, 1991, Uncertain Justice: The Roberts Court and the Constitution, 2014; To End a Presidency: The Power of Impeachment, 2018; co-editor: When Values Conflict: Essays on Environmental Analysis, Disourse, and Decision, 1976; contributor articles to professional journals **AW:** Recipient Beale prize, 1966, Detur prize, 1969, Coif Triennial Book award, 1980, Scribe award, 1980; national debate champion, 1961; named one of 100 Most Influential Lawyers in America, National Law Journal, 2006; National Science Foundation & Woodrow Wilson Fellow, Harvard University, 1962-63 **MEM:** Fellow Am. Academy Arts and Sciences; member American Bar Association (Silver Gavel Award 1991), ACLU, Phi Beta Kappa

TROTT, DAVE, **T:** U.S. Representative from Michigan, Lawyer **I:** Law and Legal Services **DOB:** 10/16/1960 **PB:** Birmingham **ED:** JD, Duke University School Law, 1985; BA, University Michigan, 1981 **C:** Mem., U.S. Congress from 11th Michigan District, 2014-; Member, Committee on Foreign Affairs, Committee on the Judiciary; Co-owner, Dietz Trott Sports & Entertainment,; Owner, Trott Recovery Services,; Owner, Attorneys Title Agency LLC,; Chairman, CEO, Trott & Trott PC, **CIV:** Chair, Oakland Co. Lincoln Day Dinner, Board, Karmanos Institute, Board, The Community House, Board, Detroit Country Day School, Board, On My Own, Board, University Michigan, **PA:** Republican

TROTZ, BARRY, **T:** Professional Ice Hockey Coach **I:** Professional Training & Coaching **DOB:** 07/15/1962 **PB:** Dauphin, Manitoba **SC:** Canada **C:** Head Coach, Washington Capitals (2014-Present); Head Coach, Nashville Predators (1997-2014);

Head Coach, US Team, American Hockey League All Star Game (1996); Head Coach, Washington Capitals (1992-1995); Assistant Coach, Washington Capitals (1991); Chief Western Scout, Washington Capitals (1988); Head Coach, University of Manitoba (1987); Head Coach, General Manager, Dauphin Kings Junior Hockey Club (1985-1987); Assistant Coach, University of Manitoba (1984) **CR:** Head Coach, NHL All-Star Game (2016) **AW:** Named NHL Coach of the Year, Sporting News (2007); Named to Portland Pirates Hall of Fame (2005); Inductee, University of Manitoba Hall of Fame (2001); Jack Adams Award, NHL (2016); Louis A.R. Pieri Memorial Award (1994); Nashville Community Spirit Award (2005) **BA:** Capital One Arena, 601 F St NW, Washington, DC, 20004

TROUT, MIKE, **T:** Professional Baseball Player **I:** Athletics **DOB:** 08/07/1991 **PB:** Vineland **SC:** NJ/USA **PT:** Son of Jeff and Debbie Trout **C:** Outfielder, LA Angels of Anaheim, 2011 **AW:** Named American League Outstanding Rookie, Major League Baseball Players Association, 2012, American League Rookie of Year, Baseball Writers Association of America, 2012, Minor League Player of Year, Baseball America, 2011; named to American League All-Star Team, Major League Baseball, 2012-14; recipient American League Hank Aaron award, 2014, American League Most Valuable Player Award, Major League Baseball, 2014, American League Silver Slugger award, Major League Baseball, 2012-14, All Star, 2015-17, American League MVP, 2016, AL RBI Leader, 2014, AL Stolen Base Leader, 2012, 30-30 Club, 2012 **ACH:** Achievements include leading the American League in: runs, 2012, 2013; stolen bases, 2012; walks, 2013

TRUMP, DONALD JOHN, **T:** 45th President of the U.S., Real Estate Developer **I:** Government Administration/Government Relations/Government Services **DOB:** 06/14/1946 **PB:** New York **SC:** NY/USA **ED:** BS in Economics, University Pennsylvania, Wharton School, 1968 **C:** President of the U.S., 2017-; Chmn., CEO, The Trump Organization, LLC, New York City, New York, 1980—; Owner, Trump Casino Riverboat, Buffington Harbor, Ind.; Owner, Trump International Hotel and Tower, Chicago, Illinois; Owner, Trump International Hotel and Tower, New York City, New York; Owner, Trump Tower, Trump Park, Trump Palace, Trump Building at 40 Wall St., New York City, New York; Chairman, Trump Entertainment Resorts, Inc., Atlantic City, New Jersey, 2005—2009; Ptnr.-owner, Trump International Hotel and Tower, Chicago, Illinois; Ptnr.-owner, Trump Grande Ocean Resort and Residences, Miami Beach, Florida; Ptnr.-owner, Trump Park Ave. (formerly Delmonico Hotel); Ptnr.-owner, 610 Park Ave. and Trump World Tower, New York City, New York; Owner, Mar-a-Lago Club, Palm Beach, Florida; Owner, Mansion at Seven Springs, Bedford, New York; Owner, W. Side Rail Yards devel. as Trump Pl., New York City, New York; Owner, Trump 29 Casino, Palm Springs, California **CR:** Owner Trump International Golf Club, Palm Beach, Trump National Golf Club, Briarcliff Manor, New York, Ocean Trails Golf Course, Palos Verde, California, Trump National, Bedminster, New Jersey, Trump Management Group Modeling/Talent Agency, Trump Vineyard Estates, Charlottesville, Virginia, 2011, Trump National Golf Club, Charlotte, North Carolina, 2012, Jupiter, Florida, 2012, Trump International Golf Club, Dubai, 2013, International Trump Golf Links, Ireland, 2014, Trump Golf Links, Ferry Point, New York, 2015; president Trump Pageants LP, includes Miss Universe, Miss USA and Miss Teen USA.; launched line of men's suits, 2004; launched signature fragrance, Donald

Trump The Fragrance, 2004; announced launching of Trump University will consist of online courses, CD-ROMS, blogs, consulting services and Learning Annex-type seminars, 2005; Republican nominee for President of the US, 2016; **CIV:** Committee member, Celebration of Nations Commemorating 50th Anniversary UN and UNICEF; Co-chmn. New York Vietnam Vets. Memorial Fund; founding member construction committee Cathedral of St. John the Divine; member New York Citizens Tax Council, Fifth Ave Association, Realty Foundation of New York, Metropolitan Museum of Art's Real Estate Council; member adv. board Lenox Hill Hospital, United Cerebral Palsy; special advisor to Pres.'s Council on Physical Fitness and Sports; member New York Sportsplex Commission; chairman New York citizens committee 78th Ann. National Association for the Advancement of Colored People Convention, 1987; grand marshall Nation's Parade, 1995; board directors Police Athletic League; board overseers Wharton School; founding member adv. board Wharton Real Estate Center; board directors Fred C. Trump Foundation; chairman Donald J. Trump Foundation **CW:** Author: Trump: The Way to the Top: The Best Real Estate Advice I Ever Received: 100 Top Experts Share Their Strategies, 2004, Trump: The Best Golf Advice I Ever Received, 2005, Time to Get Tough: Making America #1 Again, 2011, Crippled America: How to Make America Great Again, 2015; co-author (with Tony Schwartz): Trump: The Art of the Deal, 1987; (with Charles Leerhsen) Surviving at the Top (renamed Trump: The Art of Survival), 1990, (with Kate Bohner) Trump: The Art of the Comeback, 1997, (with Dave Shiflett) The America We Deserve, 2000, (with Meredith McIver) Think Like a Billionaire: Everything You Need to Know About Success, Real Estate, and Life, 2004, Think Like A Champion - An Informal Education in Business and Life, 2009, (with Robert T. Kiyosaki, Sharon Lechter & Meredith McIver) Why We Want You to Be Rich-Two Men-One Message, 2006, (with Bill Zanker) Think Big and Kick Butt - in Business and Life, 2007, (with Robert T. Kiyosaki) Midas Touch: Why Some Entrepreneurs Get Rich-And Why Most Don't, 2011, host, executive producer (TV series) The Apprentice, 2004—15, launched Trump World magazine, 2004, host on syndicated radio program Trumped!, Premiere Radio Networks, 2004 **AW:** Named Developer of Year, Construction Management Association America, 1999, Hotel and Real Estate Visionary of the Century, UTA Federation, 2000; named one of Forbes 400: Richest Americans, 2006—, The 100 Most Powerful Celebrities, Forbes.com, 2008, The 10 Most Fascinating People of 2011, Barbara Walters Special, 2011, The 10 Most Fascinating People of 2015, The 100 Most Influential People in the World, TIME Magazine, 2016; named Time Magazine's Person of the Year, 2016; named to Wharton Hall of Fame, Benefactors board directors, Hist. Society Palm Beach County, 2003; recipient Entrepreneur of Year award, Wharton Entrepreneurial Club, 1984, Ellis Island Medal of Honor, 1986 **ACH:** Achievements include the three-month rebuilding of Wollman Skating Rink in Central Park. **PA:** Republican **BA:** The White House, 1600 Pennsylvania Avenue, Washington, DC, 20500

TRUMP, IVANKA MARIE, **T:** First Daughter and Advisor to the President **I:** Government Administration/Government Relations/Government Services **DOB:** 10/30/1981 **PB:** NYC **PT:** Daughter of Donald John and Ivana (Zelnicek) Trump; **ED:** BS in Economics magna cum laude, U Pennsylvania Wharton School Business, 2004; Attended, Georgetown University, 2000-02 **C:** First Daughter and Advisor to the President, 2017-; Principal, Ivanka Trump Fine Jewelry, 2010-; Executive vice president devel. & acquisitions, The Trump Organization, LLC, 2007-; Launched, Ivanka Trump Lifestyle Collection,; Vice president real estate devel. & acquisition, The Trump Organization, LLC, New York City, 2005-07; Project manager, retail devel. division, Forest City Enterprises, 2004-05; Model, 1997-2007 **CR:** Board directors 100 Women in Hedge Funds, Signature Bank, Inc., 2011-13, Trump Entertainment Resorts Inc., 2007-09 **CW:** Appeared in (documentaries) Born Rich, 2003, (TV series) The Apprentice, 2006-08, Gossip Girl, 2010; author: The Trump Card: Playing to Win in Work and Life, 2009 **AW:** Named one of The 40 Under 40, Fortune magazine, 2014, The 50 Most Powerful Women in New York City, New York Post, 2008, 2007; recipient Joseph Wharton Young Leadership award,Joseph Wharton Award for Young Leadership, 2015, Time 100 Most Influential People, 2017

TRUMP, MELANIA, T: First Lady of the U.S. **I:** Government Administration/Government Relations/Government Services **DOB:** 04/26/1970 **PB:** Novo Mesto, SR Slovenia, SFR **SC:** Yugoslavia **PT:** Viktor Knavs, Amalija Knavs **MS:** Married **SPN:** Donald Trump, 1/22/2005 **CH:** Barron William **ED:** Student, Secondary School of Design and Photography; Student, Architecture and Design, University of Ljubljana **C:** First Lady of the U.S., Washington, DC, 2017-Present; Host, International Women's Day Luncheon, 2017 **CR:** Model, Modeling Agencies; Launched, Melania Timepieces and Jewelry, Melania Skin Care Collection **CIV:** Martha Graham Dance Company, Boys Club of New York, American Red Cross, Make A Wish Foundation, Police Athletic League **CW:** Cover Model, Sports Illustrated Swimsuit Issue, 2000, Interviewee, The Howard Stern Show, 1999, Cover Model, In Style Weddings, New York Magazine, Avenue, Philadelphia Style, Vanity Fair, Vogue **AW:** Runner-Up, Look of the Year Contest, Jana Magazine, 1992

TSONGAS, NIKI, T: U.S. Representative from Massachusetts **I:** Government Administration/Government Relations/Government Services **DOB:** 04/26/1946 **PB:** Chico **SC:** CA/USA **PT:** Daughter of Russell Elmer and Marian Susan (Wyman) Sauvage; **ED:** JD, Boston University, 1988; BA, Smith College, Northampton, Massachusetts, 1968 **C:** Member, U.S. Congress from 3rd Massachusetts District, 2013-; Member, Committee on Armed Services, Committee on Natural Resources; Member, U.S. Congress from 5th Massachusetts District, 2007-13; Dean external affairs, Middlesex Community College, Massachusetts, 1997-2007; Social worker, New York City Department Welfare,; Vol., Eugene McCarthy for U.S. President, 1968 **CIV:** Board directors, The Concord Coalition, Member, Lowell Civic Stadium & Arena Commission, **PA:** Democrat **BA:** 1714 Longworth House Office Building, Washington, DC, 20515

TU, JOHN, T: Co-Founder of Kingston Technologies **I:** Technology **PB:** Chongqing **SC:** China **ED:** B.S., Technische Hochschule Darmstadt **C:** Co-founder, CEO, President, Kingston Tech., Fountain Valley, 1987-; President, Newgen Systems Corp., Fountain Valley, California, 1987-; Vice President, General Manager, AST Research, Irvine, California, 1985-87; President, Camintonn Corp., Santa Ana, California, 1982-85; President, Tu Devel., LA, 1975-82; With, Motorola Co., Wiesbaden, Germany, 1966-74 **AW:** Co-recipient Entrepreneur of Year Award, Asian Business Association, 1997; Named One of Forbes 400: Richest Americans, 2009; Recipient Human Relations Award, Am. Jewish Committee, 1998, Am. Dream Award, Asian Business League, 1996

TURNER, MIKE, T: U.S. Representative from Ohio **I:** Government Administration/Government Rela-

tions/Government Services **DOB:** 01/11/1960 **PB:** Dayton **SC:** OH/USA **PT:** Son of Ray and Vivian Turner **ED:** MBA, University of Dayton, 1992; JD, Case Western Reserve University School of Law, Cleveland, 1985; BS in Political Sci., Ohio Northern University, Ada, 1982 **C:** President of the NATO Parliamentary Assembly, 2014-2016;; Member, Committee on Oversight and Government Reform; Member, US House Armed Services Committee, 2003-; Member, US Representative from 10th Ohio District, 2013-; Member, US Representative from 3rd Ohio District, 2003-13; Mayor, City of Dayton, 1994-2002; President, JMD Devel.; Corporate Counsel, Modern Technologies Corp., Dayton **AW:** Recipient Restore American Hero Award, National Trust Hist. Preservation/HGTV, 2005, National Legislative Leadership Award, US Conference of Mayors, 2005 **MEM:** Mem.: American Bar Association, American Corporate Counsel Association, Ohio Bar Association, Dayton Bar Association **BAR:** Bar: Ohio 1985 **PA:** Republican **BA:** 2368 Rayburn HOB, Washington, DC, 20515

TURNER, SYLVESTER, T: Office of Turner **I:** Government Administration/Government Relations/Government Services **DOB:** 09/27/1954 **ED:** Attended, Harvard University Law School; Attended, University Houston **C:** Mayor, City of Houston, 2016-; Member District 139, Texas House of Representatives, 1988-2016; Member District 139, Texas House of Representatives, 1988-; Founder, attorney, Law Office of Barnes & Turner, 1983-; Former del. chairman, Harris County Legislature, Texas, **CR:** Lecturer South Texas College Law, University Houston Law School adjunct professor Thurgood Marshall School Law **AW:** Named One of Five Outstanding Houstonian, Houston Jaycees, Rookie of Year, Texas Monthly, Legislator of Year, 1995, Houston Police Patrolman's Union; recipient Rising Star award, Harris County Dem. **MEM:** Mem.: Acres Homes Citizens C. of C., Coalition School Improvement, Am. Cancer Society (board member), United Negro College Fund **PA:** Democrat **BA:** Office of Sylvester Turner, PO Box 1562, Houston, TX, 77251

TURNER, TINA, T: Singer **I:** Media & Entertainment **PB:** Brownsville **SC:** TN/USA **PT:** Floyd Richard Bullock; Zelma (Currie) Bullock **CW:** Singer (with): Ike Turner Kings of Rhythm, and Ike and Tina Turner Revue; appeared in (films) Gimme Shelter, 1970, Soul to Soul, 1971, Tommy, 1975, Sergeant Pepper's Lonely Hearts Club Band, 1978, Mad Max Beyond Thunderdome, 1985, Break Every Rule, 1986, Last Action Hero, 1993, (TV series) Ally McBeal, 2000, concert tours of Europe, 1966, Japan and Africa, 1971, Showtime TV concert Wildest Dreams, albums with Ike Turner Hunter, 1970, Ike and Tina Show II, Ike and Tina Show, 1966, Ike and Tina Turner, Bad Dreams, 1973, Ike and Tina Turner Greatest Hits, vol. 1.2 and 3, 1989, Greatest Hits, 1990, Proud Mary, 1991, The Ike and Tina Turner Collection, 1993, solo albums Let Me Touch Your Mind, 1972, Tina Turns the Country On, 1974, Acid Queen, 1975, Love Explosion, 1977, Rough, 1978, Airwaves, 1979, Private Dancer, 1984, Break Every Rule, 1986, Tina Live In Europe, 1988, Foreign Affair, 1989, Simply the Best, 1991, What's Love Got to Do With It? (soundtrack), 1993, Wildest Dreams, 1996, Twenty Four Seven, 2000, All the Best, 2005; solo albums Tina!, 2008; solo albums Tina Live, 2009, recordings Sixties to Nineties, with others, 1994; performer (with USA): for Africa on song We are The World, 1985; author: (autobiography) I, Tina, 1985, I, Tina: My Life Story, 2010; (film of autobiography) What's Love Got To Do With It?, 1993 **AW:** Named to Rock and Roll Hall of Fame, 1991; recipient Kennedy Center Honor, John F.

Kennedy Center for Performing Arts, 2005, 2 MTV Video Music awards, 2 World Music awards, 7 Billboard Music awards, 8 Grammy awards; recipient Grammy Lifetime Achievement Award, 2018;

TURTURRO, JOHN, T: Actor **I:** Media & Entertainment **DOB:** 06/11/1905 **PB:** Brooklyn New York **SC:** Brooklyn New York **PT:** Son of Nicholas and Katherine Turturro; **SPN:** Married Katherine Borowitz, 1985; **CH:** children: Amedeo, Diego **ED:** Student, Yale Drama School; Grad., State University of New York, 1978 **CW:** (Worked in regional theater and off-Broadway productions): Danny and the Deep Blue Sea; Men Without Dates; Tooth of the Crime; La Puta Vida; Chaos and Hard Times; The Bald Soprano; Of Mice and Men; The Resistable Rise of Arturo Ui, 1991; Waiting for Godot; (appeared in Broadway production): Death of a Salesman, 1984; The Cherry Orchard, 2011; actor: (films) The Flamingo Kid, 1984, To Live and Die in L.A., 1985, Desperately Seeking Susan, 1985, Hannah and Her Sisters, 1986, Gung Ho, 1986, Offbeat, 1986, The Color of Money, 1986, The Sicilian, 1987, Five Corners, 1988, Do the Right Thing, 1989, Miller's Crossing, 1990, Men of Respect, 1990, Mo Better Blues, 1990, Jungle Fever, 1991, Barton Fink, 1991, Backtrack, 1991, Brain Donors, 1992, Fearless, 1993, Festival, 1991, Being Human, 1994, Quiz Show, 1994, Grace of My Heart, 1994, Search and Destroy, 1995, Unstrung Heroes, 1995, Clockers, 1995, Box of Moonlight, 1996, Girl 6, 1996, The Big Lebowski, 1997, Animals, 1997, The Truce, 1998, Lesser Prophets, 1998, Rounders, 1998, He Got Game, 1998, The Source, 1999, The Cradle Will Rock, 1999, Company Man, 1999, Two Thousand and None, 1999, Oh Brother, Where Art Thou?, 1999, The Man Who Cried, 1999, The Luzhin Defense, 1999, Anger Management, 2003, Collateral Damage, 2000, Mr. Deeds, 2002, Secret Passage, 2002, Secret Window, 2004, 2BPerfectly Honest, 2004, She Hate Me, 2004, A Few Days in September, 2006, The Good Shepherd, 2006, You Don't Mess with the Zohan, 2008, Miracle at St. Anna, 2008, What Just Happened, 2008, The Taking of Pelham 1 2 3, 2009, Transformers: Revenge of the Fallen, 2009, Cars 2 (voice), 2011, Transformers: Dark of the Moon, 2011, Gods Behaving Badly, 2013, God's Pocket, 2014, Exodus: Gods and Kings, 2014, Partly Cloudy with Sunny Spells, 2015, Mia Madre, 2015, The Ridiculous 6, 2015, Hands of Stone, 2016, Landline, 2017, Hair, 2017, Transformers The Last Knight, 2017,The True Adventures of Woldboy, 2018, Going Places, 2018, Gloria, 2018; (TV films) Monday Night Mayhem, 2002; (TV series) The Night Of, 2016, Difficult People, 2017; director, writer (films) Mac, 1992, director, writer, producer Illuminata, 1998; (actor, director, writer, producer): Romance & Cigarettes, 2005; actor, writer, executive producer (films) Prove per una tragedia siciliana, 2009, actor, director, writer Fading Gigolo, 2013, Rio, I Love You, 2016; dir.: (plays) A Spanish Play, 2007; executive prodr.: (documentaries) Beyond Wiseguys: Italian Americans & the Movies, 2008

TWAIN, SHANIA, T: Singer, Musician **I:** Media & Entertainment **DOB:** 08/28/1965 **PB:** Windsor **SC:** Ontario/Can. **PT:** Daughter of Sharon and Jerry Twain (Stepfather), Clarence Edwards; **CW:** Singer: (Albums) Shania Twain, 1993, The Woman in Me, 1995 (Album of Year, Can. Country Music Association Awards, 1995, Album of Year, Academy Country Music Awards, 1996, Country Album of Year, Billboard Music Awards, 1996, Best Country Album, Grammy Awards, 1996, Top Selling Album Special Achievement Award, Can. Country Music Association Awards, 1997), Come on Over, 1997 (Album of Year, Can. Country Music Association Awards, 1998, Best Selling Country Record of

Year, National Association Record Merchandisers, 1999), Up!, 2002 (Album of Year, Can. Country Music Association Awards, 2003), Greatest Hits, 2004,Now, 2017 (songs) You're Still the One, 1998 (Best Selling Country Single, Billboard Music Awards, 1998, Single of Year, Can. Country Music Association Awards, 1998, VH1 Viewer's Choice award, 1998, Best Country Song, Best Female Country Vocal Performance, Grammy Awards, 1999), From This Moment On, 1998 (Vocal/Instrumental Collaboration of Year, Can. Country Music Association Awards, 1999), That Don't Impress Me Much, 1998, Man! I Feel Like a Woman!, 1999 (Best Female Country Vocal Performance, Grammy Awards, 2000), Come on Over, 1999 (Best Country Song, Grammy Awards, 2000); Author: (autobiography) From This Moment On, 2011; Featured in (reality documentary series) Why Not? With Shania Twain, OWN Network, 2011 **AW:** Named Favorite Country Female Singer, People's Choice Awards, 2005, Favorite Female Musical Performer, 2000, Entertainer of Year, Country Music Association Awards, 1999, Female Artist of Year, Country Music TV (CMT) Awards, 1999, 1998, 1996, Country Artist of Year, Billboard Music Awards, 2003, Female Artist of Year, 1998, Female Country Artist of Year, 1996, Favorite Female Pop/Rock Artist, American Music Awards, 2000, Favorite Female Country Artist, 2000, 1999, 1997, Favorite New Country Artist, 1996, Entertainer of Year, Academy Country Music Awards, 2000, Top New Female Vocalist, 1996, Artist of Year, Juno Awards, Can. Academy Recording Arts & Scis., 2003, Best Songwriter, 2000, Best Country Female Artist, 2000, Best Country Female Vocalist, 1999, Country Female Vocalist of Year, 1998, 1997, 1996, Entertainer of Year, 1996, World's Best Selling Female Country Artist, World Music Awards, 1996, Fan's Choice Entertainer of Year, Can. Country Music Association Awards, 1999, 1998, 1996, Female Vocalist of Year, 2003, 1999, 1998, 1996, 1995, Best Female Artist, Country Music Radio Awards, 1995, Female Video Artist of Year, ABC Radio Networks Country Music Awards, 1995; Named one of 40 Greatest Women in Country Music, Country Music TV, 2002; Named to Canadian Music Hall of Fame, 2011; Recipient Star on the Hollywood Walk of Fame, 2011, Songwriter award, Can. Radio Music Awards, 2004, Star on Canada's Walk of Fame, 2003, International Artist Achievement award, Country Music Association Awards, 1999, Double-Diamond award, Academy Country Music Awards, 1999, Songwriter/Artist of Year award, Nashville Songwriters Association International, 1998, Juno International Achievement award, Can. Academy Recording Arts & Scis., 1997, Outstanding Musical Achievement award, First Americans in the Arts, 1996, Artist a Lifetime, CMT, 2016, Shania Twain Rock this Country Exhibit,Country Music Hall of Fame, 2017 **BA:** Creative Artists Agency, 2000 Avenue of the Stars, Los Angeles, CA, 90067

TWOHEY, MEGAN, T: Investigative Reporter **I:** Writing and Editing **ED:** Georgetown University, 1998 **C:** Investigative Reporter, New York Times,2016-; Reporter, Thomson Reuters, 2012-16; Reporter, Chicago Tribune, 2007-12; Reporter, Milwaukee Journal Sentinel, 2003-07; Reporter, The Moscow Times, 2001-02; Reporter, National Journal, 1999-2001; Editorial Intern, Washington Monthly, 1998-99 **AW:** Time 100 Most Influential, 2018

TYMKOVICH, TIMOTHY MICHAEL, T: Federal Judge **I:** Law and Legal Services **DOB:** 11/02/1956 **PB:** Denver **SC:** CO/USA **ED:** JD, University of Colorado School of Law, 1982; BA, Co. College, 1979 **C:** Chief Judge, U.S. Court of Appeals (10th Cir), 2015-; Judge, U.S. Court of Appeals (10th cir),

2003-; Partner, Hale Hackstaff Tymkovich & Erken-Brack, 1996-2003; Solicitor general, Office of Co. Attorney General, 1991-96; Of counsel, Bradley Campbel Carney & Madsen, 1990-91; Associate, Davis, Graham, & Stubbs, 1983-89; Clerk, Co. Supreme Court, 1982-83 **MEM:** Mem.: ABA, International Society Barristers, Colorado Bar Foundation, Am. Law Institute **BA:** Byron White US Courthouse, 1823 Stout St, Denver, CO, 80257

TYSON, BERNARD J., T: Kaiser CEO **I:** Medicine & Health Care **ED:** MBA in Health Care Administration, Golden Gate University, 1985; BS in Health Services Administration, Golden Gate University, 1982; Advanced Leadership degree, Harvard University **C:** Executive vice president health plan and hospital operations, Kaiser Foundation Health Plan, Inc. and Kaiser Foundation Hospitals, National Georgia, Mid Atlantic CEO, Kaiser Permanente, 2012-, States, Kaiser Permanente, 2007-; Chairman Kaiser Foundation Health Plan, Mid Atlantic States, Kaiser Permanente,; Senior vice president health plan and hospital operations, Kaiser Permanente, 2006-07; Senior vice president brand strategy, Kaiser Permanente,; COO regions outside California, Kaiser Foundation Health Plan, Inc., Kaiser Permanente,; Group president, regions outside California, Kaiser Permanente, 1999; Associate regional manager, No. California, Kaiser Permanente,; President, Central East division, Maryland, Washington DC, Virginia and Ohio, Kaiser Permanente, 1998; Senior vice president, local market leader, East Bay, Kaiser Permanente, California, 1996-98; Vice president, Kaiser Permanente, 1995-96; Administrator, hospital and health plan, Kaiser Permanente, Santa Rosa, California, 1992-95; With San Francisco Medical Center, Kaiser Permanente, 1985-92; Joined, Kaiser Permanente, 1984 **CIV:** Deacon board, Refreshing Springs Church God Christ, Member, United Way, Member, United Negro College Fund, Member executive, Leadership Council Inc., Member, National Association for the Advancement of Colored People, Member, Nat.Assn. Health Services Executives, Board directors, Federal City Council, Board directors, AVMED Health Plan, Gainesville, Florida, Board directors, Alliance Advancing Nonprofit Health, Board directors, United Negro College Fund, San Francisco, Board directors, Executive Leadership Council Foundation, Board directors, National Committee Quality Health Care, Trustee, Alliance Community Health Plans **AW:** Named Sensitizing Corp. America to the Talents of People of Color, National Association for the Advancement of Colored People Freedom Fund, 2001, International Emerging Leaders in Healthcare award, 1998, Time 100 Most Influential, 2017 **MEM:** Mem.: National Managed Health Care Congress (adv. board), Am. Association Health Plans (board directors)

TYSON, CICELY, T: Actress **I:** Media & Entertainment **DOB:** 12/19/1933 **PB:** New York **SC:** NY/USA **ED:** Student, New York University; Student, Actors Studio; Doctorate (hon.), Atlanta University; Doctorate (hon.), Loyola University; Doctorate (hon.), Lincoln University; Doctorate (hon.), Morehouse College **C:** Former secretary, model **CR:** Co-founder Dance Theatre of Harlem; board directors Urban Gateways **CIV:** Recipient Vernon Price award, 1962, Spingarn medal, National Association for the Advancement of Colored People, 2010, Presidential Medal of Freedom, The White House, 2016. **CW:** Actress: (Off-Broadway) The Blacks, 1961-63; (Broadway) The Cool World, 1960, Tiger, Tiger, Burning Bright, 1962, A Hand is on the Gate, 1966, Carry Me Back to Morningside Heights, 1968, Trumpets of the Lord, 1969, The

Corn is Green, 1983, The Trip to Bountiful, 2013 (Drama Desk award for Outstanding Actress in a Play, 2013, Tony award for Best Performance by an Actress in a Leading Role in a Play, 2013), The Gin Game, 2015; (films) Odds Against Tomorrow, 1959, The Last Angry Man, 1959, A Man Called Adam, 1966, The Comedians, 1967, The Heart is a Lonely Hunter, 1968, Sounder, 1972 (National Society Film Critics award for Best Actress, 1972, National Board Review award for Best Actress, 1972), The Blue Bird, 1976, The River Niger, 1976, A Hero Ain't Nothin' But a Sandwich, 1978 (National Association for the Advancement of Colored People Image award for Outstanding Actress in a Motion Picture, 1978), The Concorde-Airport 79, 1979, Bustin' Loose, 1981, Fried Green Tomatoes, 1991, Hoodlum, 1997, Because of Winn-Dixie, 2005, Diary of a Mad Black Woman, 2005 (National Association for the Advancement of Colored People Image award for Outstanding Supporting Actress in a Motion Picture, 2006), Madea's Family Reunion, 2006, Fat Rose and Squeaky, 2006, Idlewild, 2006, Why Did I Get Married Too?, 2010, The Help, 2011, Alex Cross, 2012, The Haunting in Connecticut 2: Ghosts of Georgia, 2013, Showing Roots, 2016, Last Flag Flying, 2017; (TV series) East Side, West Side, 1963-64, The Guiding Light, 1966, Sweet Justice, 1994-95; (TV films) Marriage: Year One, 1971, The Autobiography of Miss Pittman, 1974 (Emmy award for Actress of the Year, 1974, Emmy award for Best Lead Actress in a Drama, 1974), Just an Old Sweet Song, 1976, Wilma, 1977, A Woman Called Moses, 1978, The Marva Collins Story, 1981, Benny's Place, 1982, Playing With Fire, 1985, Samaritan: The Mitch Snyder Story, 1986, Acceptable Risks, 1986, Intimate Encounters, 1986, The Women of Brewster Place, 1989, Heat Wave, 1990, The Kid Who Loved Christmas, 1990, When No One Would Listen, 1992, Duplicates, 1992, House of Secrets, 1993, Oldest Living Confederate Widow Tells All, 1994 (Emmy award for Outstanding Supporting Actress in a Mini-Series or a Special, 1994), Road to Galveston, 1996 (National Association for the Advancement of Colored People Image award for Outstanding Lead Actress in a TV Movie or Mini-Series, 1997), Bridge of Time, 1997, The Prince of Heaven, 1997, Riot, 1997, Ms. Scrooge, 1997, Mama's Flora Family, 1998 (National Association for the Advancement of Colored People Image award for Outstanding Lead Actress in a TV Movie or Mini-Series, 1999), Always Outnumbered, 1998, A Lesson Before Dying, 1999, Aftershock: Earthquake in New York, 1999, Jewel, 2001, The Rosa Parks Story, 2002, Relative Stranger, 2009; (TV miniseries) Roots, 1977, King, 1978; (TV appearances) Frontiers of Faith, 1961, The Nurses, 1962, Naked City, 1963, I Spy, 1965, 66, Cowboy in Africa, 1967, The FBI, 1968, 69, Here Comes the Brides, 1970, Mission Impossible, 1970, Gunsmoke, 1970, Emergency!, 1972, B.L. Stryker, 1990, Touched by an Angel, 2000, The Outer Limits, 2000, House of Cards, 2016, How to Get Away with Murder, 2015-17; music video Willow Smith's 21st Century Girl, 2011; narrator: (documentary) Up from the Bottoms: The Search for the American Dream, 2010; actress, executive prodr.: (TV films) The Trip to Bountiful, 2014 (National Association for the Advancement of Colored People Image award for Outstanding Actress in a TV Movie, Mini-Series or Dramatic Special, 2015). **MEM:** Mem.: Delta Sigma Theta (hon.)

TYSON, NEIL DEGRASSE, T: Astrophysicist **I:** Sciences **DOB:** 10/05/1958 **PB:** New York City, October 5, 1958 **ED:** DS (hon.), Mount Holyoke College, 2012; DS (hon.), Gettysburg College, 2011; DS (hon.), Eastern Connecticut State University, 2010; DS (hon.), Rensselaer Polytechnic

Institute, 2010; DS (hon.), University Alabama, 2010; DS (hon.), University Pennsylvania, 2008; DS (hon.), Worcester Polytechnic University, 2007; DS (hon.), Williams College, 2007; DS (hon.), Pace University, 2006; DS (hon.), College Staten Island, 2004; DS (hon.), Northeastern University, 2003; DS (hon.), Bloomfield College, 2002; DS (hon.), University Richmond, 2001; DS (hon.), Dominican College, 2000; DS (hon.), Ramapo College, 2000; DS (hon.), City University of New York, 1997; PhD in Astrophysics, Columbia University, 1991; MA in Astronomy, University Texas, Austin, 1983; BA in Physics, Harvard University, 1980 **C:** Frederick P. Rose director Hayden Planetarium, American Museum Natural Hist., New York City, 1996-; Research associate, American Museum Natural Hist., New York City, 2003; Chair department astrophysics, American Museum Natural Hist., New York City, 1997-99; Acting director, American Mus.-Hayden Planetarium, New York City, 1995-96; Staff scientist, American Mus.-Hayden Planetarium, New York City, 1994-95; Postdoctoral research associate department astrophysics, Princeton University, 1991-94 **CW:** Author: Merlin's Tour of the Universe, 1989, Universe Down to Earth, 1994, Just Visiting This Planet, 1998, The Sky is Not the Limit: Adventures of an Urban Astrophysicist, 2000, Death by Black Hole: And Other Cosmic Quandaries, 2007, The Pluto Flies: The Rise and Fall of America's Favorite Planet, 2009, Space Chronicles: Facing the Ultimate Frontier, 2012; co-author: One Universe: At Home in the Cosmos, 2000 (Sci. Writing award, Am. Institute Physics, 2001), Origins: Fourteen Billion Years of Cosmic Hist., 2004; co-editor: Cosmic Frontiers: Astronomy at the Cutting Edge, 2001; host (TV series) NOVAscience/NOW, PBS, 2006-, Cosmos: A Spacetime Odyssey, 2014; contributor articles to professional journals, chapters to books,(Books) Welcome to the Universe: An Astrophysical Tour, 2016, Astrophysics for People in a Hurry, 2017 **AW:** Named Sexiest Astrophysicist Alive, People magazine, 2000; named one of The Most Influential People in the World, TIME magazine, 2007, The 25 Leaders Reshaping New York, Crain's New York Business, 2008, The 40 Under 40, 1996; named to The Power 100, Ebony magazine, 2008, 2007; recipient Isaac Asimov award, American Humanist Association, 2009, Douglas S. Morrow Pub. Outreach award, Space Foundation, 2009, Klopsteg Memorial award, American Association Physics Teachers, 2007, Award for Pub. Understanding of Sci. & Tech., American Association for the Advancement of Science, 2007, Distinguished Pub. Service medal, NASA, 2004, Medal of Honor, Columbia University, 2001,Cosmos Award, Planetary Society, 2015, Hubbard Medal, National Geographic Society, 2017, Stephen Hawking medal for Science and Communication, 2017, Grammy for Best Spoken Album, 2017 **MEM:** Fellow: New York Academy Sciences; mem.: National Society Black Physicists, International Planetarium Society, Astronomical Society Pacific, American Physical Society, American Astronomical Society

UDALL, TOM, T: U.S. Senator from New Mexico **I:** Government Administration/Government Relations/Government Services **DOB:** 05/18/1948 **PB:** Tucson **SC:** AZ/USA **PT:** Stewart Lee Udall; Ermalee (Webb) Udall **ED:** JD, University of New Mexico School of Law (1977); LLB in International Law, University of Cambridge, England (1975); BA in Government/Political Science, Prescott College, AZ (1970) **C:** Vice Chair, Senate of Indian Affairs Committee (2017-Present); U.S. Senator from New Mexico, Washington, DC (2009-Present); Member, U.S. Congress from Third Congressional New Mexico District, Washington, DC (1999-2009); Attorney General, State of New Mexico, Santa Fe, NM (1991-1999); Attorney, Miller, Stratvert, Togerson and Schlenker, P.A., Albuquerque, NM (1985-1990); Chief Counsel, New Mexico Department of Health & Environmental, Santa Fe, NM (1983-1984); Private Law Practice, Santa Fe, NM (1981-1983); Assistant U.S. Attorney, Criminal Division, U.S. Department of Justice, Santa Fe, NM (1978-1981); Law Clerk to Chief Judge Oliver Seth, U.S. Court of Appeals for the Tenth Circuit, Santa Fe, NM (1977-1978); Legislative Assistant to Senator Joe Biden, U.S. Senate, Washington, DC (1973) **CIV:** Member, New Mexico Environmental Improvement Board (1986-1987); President, Rio Chama Preservation Trust; Board of Directors, Law Fund (1991-1998); Board of Directors, Santa Fe Chamber Music Festival; Board of Directors, La Compania de Teatro de Albuquerque **AW:** Public Service Award, National Highway Traffic Safety Administration; Legal Impact Award, New Mexico Bar, Prosecution Section; Leadership Award, National Commission Against Drunk Driving **MEM:** President, National Association of Attorney Generals (1996) **BAR:** State Bar of New Mexico (1978) **PA:** Democrat **BA:** Office of Tom Udall, 531 Hart Senate Office Building, Washington, DC, 20510

ULUKAYA, HAMDI, T: Businessman, Philanthropist **I:** Nonprofit & Philanthropy **PB:** Illic **SC:** Turkey **ED:** State University of New York at Albany **C:** CEO/Owner/Founder, Chobani, 2012-; Owner, Founder, Euphrates Inc,2002- **AW:** Time 100, 2017-

UMPLEBY, JIM, T: CEO **I:** Architecture & Construction **CN:** Caterpillar **PB:** Highland **SC:** IN/USA **ED:** B.A., Rose-Hulman Institute of Technology, 1980 **C:** CEO, Caterpillar, 2017-; Group President, Caterpillar, 2013-2017; Vice President, Caterpillar, 2010-2013; Solar Turbines Unit, International Harvester,1980

UNDERWOOD, CARRIE MARIE, T: Singer **I:** Media & Entertainment **DOB:** 03/10/1983 **PB:** Muskogee **SC:** OK/USA **PT:** Daughter of Stephen and Carol Underwood; **ED:** BA, Northeastern State University, Magna Cum Laude, Tahlequah, Oklahoma, 2006 **C:** Founder, Clothing Line, CALIA by Carrie, 2015-; Recording Artist, RCA Music Group, New York City, 2005- **CW:** Singer: (albums) Some Hearts, 2005 (Album of Year, Country Album of Year, Billboard Music Awards, 2006, Album of Year, Academy Country Music Awards, 2007, Favorite Country Album, American Music Awards, 2007, Top Country Album of Decade, Billboard Music Awards, 2009), Carnival Ride, 2007 (Favorite Country Album, American Music Awards, 2008), Play On, 2009 (Favorite Country Album, American Music Awards, 2010, Album of Year, American Country Awards, 2010), Blown Away, 2012 (Favorite Country Album, American Music Awards, 2012), Greatest Hits: Decade #1, 2014, Storyteller, 2015, (songs) Inside Your Heaven, 2005, Jesus, Take the Wheel, 2005 (Country Recorded Song of Year, Gospel Music Association Awards, 2006, Female Video of Year, Breakthrough Video of Year, CMT Music Awards, 2006, Song of Year, Nashville Songwriters Association International Awards, 2006, Single Record of Year, Academy Country Music Awards, 2006, Best Female Country Vocal Performance, Best Country Song, Grammy Awards, 2007), Some Hearts, 2005, Before He Cheats, 2006 (Favorite Country Song, People's Choice Awards, 2007, Video of Year, Female Video of Year, CMT Music Awards, 2007, Video of Year, Academy Country Music Awards, 2007, Single of Year, Country Music Association Awards, 2007, Best Female Country Vocal Performance, Best Country Song, Grammy Awards, 2008), Last Name, 2007 (Favorite Country Song, People's Choice Awards, 2009, Best Female Country Vocal Performance, Grammy Awards, 2009), (with Randy Travis) I Told You So, 2009 (Best Country Collaboration with Vocals, Grammy Awards, 2010), Cowboy Casanova, 2009 (Video of Year, CMT Music Awards, 2010), Temporary Home, 2009, (with Brad Paisley) Remind Me, 2011 (Collaborative Video of Year, CMT Music Awards, 2012), Good Girl, 2012 (Video of Year, CMT Music Awards, 2012), Blown Away, 2012 (Best Country Solo Performance, Best Country Song, Grammy Awards, 2013, Video of Year, CMT Music Awards, 2013), See You Again, 2012 (Video of Year, CMT Music Awards, 2014), Something in the Water, 2014 (Best Country Solo Performance, Grammy Awards, 2015, Video of Year, Female Video of Year, CMT Music Awards, 2015), (with Miranda Lambert) Somethin' Bad, 2014 (Collaborative Vide of Year, CMT Music Awards, 2015), Smoke Break, 2015 (Female Video of Year, Performance of Year, CMT Music Awards, 2016); actress: (films) Soul Surfer, 2011; (TV films) The Sound of Music, 2013; TV appearances How I Met Your Mother, 2010, Blue Bloods, 2011, Soul Surfer, Zendaya: Behind the Scenes, 2012, CMT Crossroads, 2012, The Blown Away Tour: Live, 2013, Nashville, 2013, The Sound of Music Live!, 2013, CMA Country Christmas, 2014, Talking Dead, 2016, The Storyteller Tour: Live from MSG, 2017, Living Every Day: Luke Bryan, 2017; (Movies) Popstar: Never Stop Never Stopping, 2016 **AW:** Choice Country Song, 2017, Teen Choice Awards,- Favorite Female Country Artist, 2017, American Country Countdown Award,Named Favorite Female Country Artist, People's Choice Awards, 2017, 2016, 2015, Favorite Country Artist, 2010, Favorite Star Under 35, 2009, Favorite Female Singer, 2009, 2007, Favorite Female Country Artist, American Music Awards, 2015, 2014, 2007, Favorite New Breakthrough Artist, 2006, Female Vocalist of Year, Country Music Association Awards, 2008, 2007, 2006, Entertainer of Year, Academy Country Music Awards, 2010, 2009, Female Vocalist of Year, 2009, 2008, 2007, Top New Female Vocalist of Year, 2006, Female Country Artist of Year, Billboard Music Awards, 2006, Country Single Sales Artist of Year, 2005, Oklahoman of Year, Oklahoma Today, 2005, Rising Star of Year, Oklahoma Music Hall of Fame, 2005; named one of The 100 Most Influential People in the World, TIME magazine, 2014, The 100 Most Powerful Celebrities, Forbes. com, 2008, The Top 25 Entertainers of Year, Entertainment Weekly, 2007; named to Oklahoma Hall of Fame, 2009; recipient Special Achievement award, Academy Country Music, 2011, Harmony award, Nashville Symphony, 2009, Red Carpet Fashion Icon award, Teen Choice Awards, 2008, Horizon award, Country Music Association, 2006 **ACH:** Achievements include winning the fourth season of American Idol on May 25, 2005; being inducted into the Grand Ole Opry, 2008; becoming the most decorated award winner (13 awards) in the history of the CMT Music Awards, 2015

UNION, GABRIELLE, T: Actress **I:** Education/ Educational Services **PB:** Omaha **SC:** NE/USA **PT:** Sylvester C. Union; Theresa (Glass) Union **ED:** Degree in sociology with honors, UCLA; Student, University Nebraska **CW:** Actress: (films) She's All That, 1999, 10 Things I Hate About You, 1999, Love & Basketball, 2000, Bring It On, 2000, The Brothers, 2001, Two Can Play That Game, 2001, Abandon, 2002, Welcome to Collinwood, 2002, Deliver Us from Eva, 2003, Cradle 2 the Grave, 2003, Bad Boys II, 2003, Breakin' All the Rules, 2004, Constellation, 2005, Neo Ned, 2005, The Honeymooners, 2005, Say Uncle, 2005, Running with Scissors, 2006, Daddy's Little Girls, 2007, The Box, 2007, The Perfect Holiday, 2007, Meet Dave, 2008, Cadillac Records, 2008, Good Deeds, 2012, In Our Nature, 2012,

Think Like a Man, 2012, Miss Dial, 2013, Think Like a Man Too, 2014, Top Five, 2014, With This Ring, 2015, Birth of a Nation, 2016, Almost Christmas, 2016, Sleepless, 2017, Girls Trip, 2017, The Public, 2018, Breaking In, 2018; (TV films) 1973, 1998, H-E Double Hockey Sticks, 1999, Close to Home, 2001, Something the Lord Made, 2004, Football Wives, 2007, Body Politic, 2009, Little in Common, 2011; (TV series) City of Angels, 2000, Night Stalker, 2005-06, FlashForward, 2009-10, Being Mary Jane, 2013- (Outstanding Actress in a TV Movie, Mini-Series or Dramatic Special, National Association for the Advancement of Colored People Image Awards, 2014); TV appearances Moesha, 1996, Goode Behavior, 1996, Sister, Sister, 1997, 7th Heaven, 1996-99, Friends, 2001, The West Wing, 2004, Ugly Betty, 2008, Life, 2009, Army Wives, 2010; executive prodr.: (films) With This Ring, 2015

UNSER, BOBBY, T: Race Car Driver, Commentator **I:** Media & Entertainment **DOB:** 02/20/1934 **PB:** Albuquerque **PT:** Son of Jerry and Mary (Craven) Unser; **C:** Commentator, ABC, 1987-; Former modified stock car race driver; now driver professional racing cars, **CR:** Consultant Expert Accident Reconstructionist, U.S., 1985- **CW:** Co-author: The Unbelievable Unsers, 1970, The Bobby Unser Story, 1978, Unser: An. American Family Portrait, 1988 **AW:** Named U.S. Auto Club National Driving Champion, 1975, 1969; recipient Martini and Rossi Driver of Year, 1974, 1st pl. Pocono 500 award, Championship Auto Racing Taams, Pennsylvania, 1980, 1st pl. California 500 award, U.S. Auto Club, 1980, 1979, 1976, 1974, 1st pl. Indy 500 award, 1981, 1975, 1968,International Motorsports Hall of Fame, 1990, National Sprint Car Hall of Fame, 1997, Colorado Sports Hall of Fame, 1997, Motorsports Hall of Fame, 1994 **ACH:** Achievements include snowmobiling; motorbiking **BA:** Bobby Unser Enterprises, 7700 Central Ave SW, Albuquerque, NM, 87121

UPTON, FREDERICK STEPHEN, T: U.S. Representative from Michigan **I:** Government Administration/Government Relations/Government Services **DOB:** 04/23/1953 **PB:** St. Joseph **PT:** Son of Stephen E. and Elizabeth Brooks (Vial) Upton; **ED:** BA in Journalism, University Michigan, 1975 **C:** Member, U.S. House of Representatives from Michigan's 4th District, 1987-1993, Member, U.S. House of Representatives from Michigan's 6th District, 1993-, Member, Committee on Energy and Commerce, Committee on Deficit Reduction; Chairman, US House Energy & Commerce Committee, Washington, 2011-; Director legis. affairs, Office Management & Budget, Executive Office of the President, Washington, 1984-85; Deputy director legis. affairs, Office Management & Budget, Executive Office of the President, Washington, 1983-84; Legis. assistant, Office Management & Budget, Executive Office of the President, Washington, 1981-83; Staff assistant to Rep. David A. Stockman, US House of Representatives, Washington, 1976-81 **CIV:** Campaign manager, Globensky for Congress, 1981 Field manager, Stockman for Congress, St. Joseph, 1975 **AW:** Named Legislator of Year, American Ambulance Association, 2000; named one of The 10 Members to Watch in the 112th Congress, Roll Call, 2011; recipient Spirit Enterprise award, US Chamber of Commerce, 1988-93 **MEM:** Mem.: Emil Verban Society **PA:** Republican

VALADAO, DAVID G., T: U.S. Representative from California, Former State Legislator, Dairy Farmer **I:** Government Administration/Government Relations/Government Services **DOB:** 04/14/1977 **PB:** Hanford **SC:** CA/USA **PT:** Terra Valadao, 1999; **MS:** Married **CH:** 3 children. **ED:** Attended, College of the Sequoias, 1996-98 **C:** Member, U.S. House

Appropriations Committee, 2013-; Member, U.S. Congress from 21st California District, Washington, 2013-; Member, Committee on House Administration, Committee on the Judiciary, Committee on Science, Space and Technology; Member District 30, California State Assembly, 2011-12; Managing partner, Valadao Dairy,; Chairman, Regional Leadership Council,; Chairman, Land O' Lakes Inc., **PA:** Republican

VALORY, ROSS, T: Bass Player **I:** Media & Entertainment **CW:** (Albums) Journey, 1975, Look into the Future, 1976, Next,1977, Infinity, 1978, Evolution, 1979, Departure, 1980, Captured, 1981, Escape, 1981, Frontiers, 1983, Trial by Fire, 1996, Arrival, 2001, Red 13, 2002, Generations, 2005, Revelation, 2008, Eclipse, 2011; **AW:** Rock and Roll Hall of Fame, 2017

VAN DE PUT, DIRK, T: CEO **I:** Food & Restaurant Services **CN:** Mondelez **PB:** Mechelen **SC:** Belgium **ED:** M.B.A, University of Antwerp; Doctorate, Universiteit Gent **C:** CEO, Mondelez International, 2017-; CEO, Mccain Foods, 2011-17; Director, Mccain Foods, 2010-17; Independent Director, Mattell, 2011-17

VAN DYKE, DICK, T: Actor, Comedian **I:** Media & Entertainment **DOB:** 12/13/1925 **PB:** West Plains **PT:** Son of Loren and Hazel (McCord) Van Dyke; Married Marjorie Willett, February 12, 1948 (div. May 1984); children: Christian, Barry, Stacey, Carrie Beth; Married Arlene Silver, February 29, 2012 **C:** With Wayne Williams, founded advertising agency, Danville, Illinois, 1946 **CIV:** With USAAC, World War II **CW:** Appeared with Philip Erickson in pantomime act The Merry Mutes, Eric and Van, 1947-53; TV master ceremonies The Music Shop, Atlanta, Morning Show, CBS, 1955, Cartoon Show, 1956; TV host Flair, ABC, 1960; (Broadway) The Girls Against the Boys, 1959, Bye Bye Birdie, 1960-61, The Music Man, 1980; (TV series) Dick Van Dyke Show, 1961-66 (Emmy Award for Outstanding Continued Performance by an Actor is a Series, 1964, 1966, Outstanding Individual Achievements in Entertainment-Actors and Performers, 1965), New Dick Van Dyke Show, 1971-74, Van Dyke and Company, 1976; performer weekly comedy program Carol Burnett Show; (TV series) Diagnosis Murder, 1993-2002; (TV films) The Morning After, 1974, Daughters of Privilege, 1991, The House on Sycamore Street, 1992, Diagnosis of Murder, 1992, A Twist of the Knife, 1993, The Dick Van Dyke Show Remembered, 1994; star, executive producer Without Warning, 2002, A Town Without Pity, 2002, Without Warning, 2002, The Gin Game, 2003, The Alan Brady Show, 2003, Scrubs, 2003, The Dick Van Dyke Show Revisited, 2004, Murder 101, 2006, Murder 101: College Can Be Murder, 2007, Murder 101: If Wishes Were Horses, 2007, Murder 101: New Age, 2008, Murder 101: The Locked Room Mystery, 2008, Hollywood Treasure, 2011, The Doctors, 2012, Fun with Dick and Jerry Van Dyke, 2012, Brody Stevens Enjoy It, 2013, Signed Sealed Delivered, 2014, Mickey Mouse Clubhouse, 2014, The Middle, 2015; (films) What a Way To Go, 1964, Mary Poppins, 1965, Divorce American Style, 1967, Chitty, Chitty, Bang, Bang, 1968, The Comic, 1969, Some Kind of Nut, 1969, Cold Turkey, 1971, The Morning After, 1974, The Runner Stumbles, 1979, Drop-Out Father, 1982, Found Money, 1983, Dick Tracy, 1990, Buitenspel, 2005, (voice) Curious George, 2006, Night at the Museum, 2006, Night at the Museum: Secret of the Tomb, 2014, Alexander and the Terrible, Horrible, No good, Very Bad Day, 2014, Merry Xmas 2015, Mary Poppins Returns, 2018; (TV appearances) Golden Girls, 1985, Jake and the Fatman, 1987, Coach, 1989, Sabrina the Teenage Witch, 1996, Becker, 1999, Scrubs, 2004;

author: Altar Egos, 1967, Faith, Hope, and Hilarity, 1970, Those Funny Kids!, 1975, My Lucky Life In and Out of Show Business, 2011, Keep Moving: And Other Tips and Truths About Aging, 2015 **AW:** Recipient Theater World award 1960, Antoinette Perry award for Best Museum Comedy Actor 1961, Emmy award for Comedy National Academy of Television Arts and Sciences, 1962, 1964, 1965, 1977, Life Career award Academy Sci. Fiction, Fantasy and Horror Films, 2000, Lifetime Achievement award in Comedy, 1994, Lifetime Achievement award, Screen Actors Guild, 2013 **BA:** 23215 Mariposa DeOro St., Malibu, CA, 90265

VAN HOLLEN, CHRISTOPHER JR., T: U.S. Senator from Maryland **I:** Government Administration/Government Relations/Government Services **DOB:** 01/10/1959 **PB:** Karachi **PT:** Son of Christopher and Eliza (Farnsworth) Van Hollen; **ED:** JD cum laude, Georgetown University, 1990; MPP, Harvard University, 1985; BA in Philosophy, Swarthmore College, Pennsylvania, 1982 **CT:** Bar: Maryland 1990 **C:** Chairman, Democratic Senatorial Campaign Committee, 2017-,; Member, US Congress from 7th Maryland District (formerly 8th District), Washington, 2003-2017; U.S. Senator from Maryland, 2017-; Ranking member, US House Budget Committee, 2011-; Member, US House Ways & Means Committee, 2007-; Member, US Congress from 7th Maryland District (formerly 8th District), Washington, 2003-; Chairman, Democratic Congressional Campaign Committee (DCCC), 2007-11; Member, Joint Select Committee on Deficit Reduction, 2011; Member, US House Government Reform & Oversight Committee,; Member District 18, Maryland State Senate, Annapolis, 1995-2002; Member, Maryland House Delegates, Annapolis, 1991-95; Associate, Arent, Fox, Kintner, Plotkin & Kahn, Washington, 1991-2002; Senior legis. adv. to Governor William Donald Schaefer, State of Maryland, Washington, 1989-91; Professional staff member Foreign Relations Committee, US Senate, Washington, 1987-89; Legis. assistant for defense & foreign policy to Senator Charles McC. Mathias, US Senate, Maryland, 1985-87 **AW:** Named Oustanding New Member of Year, Committee Education Funding, 2003; recipient Outstanding Service award, Blinded Am. Vets. Foundation, Oustanding Leadership award, Am. Lung Association, Distinguished Superhero award, National Association Community Health Ctrs., 2005, Leadership award, Am. Cancer Society, 2002, Legislator Sponsor award, Maryland Children's Action Network, 2002, Legis. Legacy award, Arc of Maryland, 2002, Conservation Legacy award, 2002, Outstanding Legislator award, Maryland Center Community Devel., 2001, Outstanding Advocacy award, Maryland AIDS Legis. Committee, 2001, Outstanding Legislator award, Advocates Children, Youth & Family, 2000, Environmental Leadership award, Maryland League Conservation Voters, 1992, 1994, 1996, 1998, 2000 **MEM:** Mem.: American Bar Association, Maryland Citizens Association, Kensington Citizens Association, Atlantic Council, Montgomery Bar Association, Maryland Bar Association **PA:** Democrat **BA:** Office of Chris Van Hollen, 110 Hart Senate Office Building, Washington, DC, 20510

VAN ZWEDEN, JAAP, T: Director of the New York Philharmonic **I:** Fine Art **DOB:** 12/12/1960 **PB:** Amsterdam **ED:** Student, Julliard School, New York City **C:** Conductor Laureate, Dallas Symphony, 2018-; Music dir.-designate, New York Philharmonic, 2016-; Music director, Hong Kong Philharmonic Orchestra, 2012-; Music director, Dallas Symphony Orchestra, 2008-; Chief conductor, Royal Flemish Philharmonic, Antwerp, Belgium, 2008-12; Music director designate, Dallas Symphony Orchestra, 2007-08; Chief conductor, artistic director, Netherlands Radio Philharmonic, Hilversum, 2005-12; Chief conductor, Residentie Orchestra, The Hague, Netherlands, 2000-05; Chief conductor, Netherlands Symphony Orchestra, Enschede, 1996-2000; Violinist, concertmaster, Royal Concertgebouw Orchestra, 1979-95 **CR:** Guest conductor Tokyo Philharmonic, Hong Kong Philharmonic, London Philharmonic, City of Birmingham Symphony Orchestra, West German Radio Symphony Orchestra Cologne, Danish Radio Orchestra, St. Louis Symphony Orchestra, Orchestre National de France, Munich Philharmonic, Rotterdam Philharmonic, Oslo Philharmonic, St. Petersburg Philharmonic **CIV:** Co-founder, foundation for autistic children, Papageno Foundation, Netherlands **AW:** Named Conductor of Year, Musical America, 2012 **BA:** New York Philharmonic, 10 Lincoln Center, New York, NY, 10023

VANASKIE, THOMAS IGNATIUS, T: Federal Judge **I:** Law and Legal Services **DOB:** 11/11/1953 **PB:** Shamokin **SC:** Pennsylvania **PT:** Son of John Anthony and Delores (Wesoloski) V.; **SPN:** Married Dorothy Grace Williams, August 12, 1978; **CH:** children: Diane, Laura, Thomas. **ED:** JD cum laude, Dickinson University, 1978; BA magna cum laude, Lycoming College, 1975 **CT:** Bar: U.S. Supreme Court 1983, U.S. Court Appeals (3d cir.) 1982, U.S. District (middle district) Pennsylvania 1980, Pennsylvania 1978 **C:** Judge, US Court Appeals (3rd. District), 2010-; Chief Judge, US District Court (middle district) Pennsylvania, 1999-2006; Judge, US District Court (middle district) Pennsylvania, 1994-2010; Principal, Elliott, Vanaskie & Riley, 1992-94; Partner, Dilworth, Paxson, Kalish & Kauffman, Scranton, 1986-92; Associate, Dilworth, Paxson, Kalish & Kauffman, Scranton, 1980-85; Law Clerk to Chief Judge William Nealon, US District Court (middle district) Pennsylvania, Scranton, 1978-80 **CR:** Counsel Governor Robert P. Casey Committee, Harrisburg, Pennsylvania, 1987-92 Chair Judicial Conference Committee Information Tech. member Third Cir. Judicial Council Chair Automation and Tech. Committee U.S. Cir. Court 3d cir., 2004, Co-chair 3d Cir. Task Force on Information Resources, 1998- Lecturer in Field. **CIV:** Member Scranton Waste Management Committee, 1989 Chair Board Trustee Scranton Preparatory School, 2001-03. **CW:** Contributor Articles to Professional Journal **AW:** Recipient James A. Finnegan Award, Finnegan Foundation **MEM:** Member Judicature, Pennsylvania Bar Association, Federal Judges Association (board directors 1998). **H:** Golf, Reading **PA:** Democrat **BA:** 601 Market St, Philadelphia, PA, 19106

VANDERBILT, GLORIA MORGAN, I: Media & Entertainment **DOB:** 02/20/1924 **PB:** New York **SC:** NY/USA **PT:** Reginald Claypoole Vanderbilt; Gloria (Morgan) Vanderbilt **SPN:** Pasquale di Cicco (div.); Married Sidney Lumet, 1956 (div.); Leopold Stokowski, 1945 (div. 1955) **CH:** Stanislaus; Christopher **ED:** Studied acting with, director Sanford Meisner, beginning 1955; Attended, Mary C. Wheeler, Miss Porter's schools **CW:** Exhibited in one-man shows at Rabun Studio, New York City, 1948, Bertha Shaeffer Gallery, New York City, 1954, Juster Gallery, New York City, 1956, Hammer Gallery, New York City, 1966, 68, Cord Gallery, New York City, 1966, Washington Gallery Art, 1968, Neiman-Marcus, Dallas, 1968, Vestart Gallery, New York City, 1969, Parish Museum, Southampton, New York, also in Nantucket, Massachusetts, Houston, Reading, Pennsylvania, Monterey, California, Nashville; exhibited in group shows, Washington Gallery Art, 1967, Hoover Gallery, San Francisco, 1971, stage career; acted in summer stock production The Swan; made Broadway debut in The Time of

Your Life, 1955; other stage appearances include Picnic, 1955, The Spa, 1956, Peter Pan, 1958, The Green Hat; made TV debut in Tonight At 8:30; other TV appearances include Colgate Comedy Hour, 1955, Flint and Fire on U.S. Steel Hour, 1958, Family Happiness on U.S. Steel Hour, 1959, Very Important People; appeared in film Johnny Concho, 1955; director design film, Riegel Textile Corp., New York City, from 1970; designer stationary and greeting cards, Hallmark Co., fabrics, Bloomcraft Co., bed linens, Martex Co., table linens, Peacock Co., Gloria Vanderbilt jeans; also china, glassware, scarves. Recipient Sylvania award 1959, Fashion award Neiman-Marcus 1969. Author: Love Poems, 1955, (with Alfred Allen Lewis) Gloria Vanderbilt Book of Collage, 1970, Woman to Woman, 1979, Once Upon a Time: A True Story, 1985, novel Never Say Good-Bye, 1989, The Memory Book of Starr Faithfull, 1994; author: (with Alfred Allen Lewis) play Three by Two, early 1960's, Black White, White Knight, 1987; poems and short stories.; author (with Anderson Cooper) The Rainbow Comes and Goes: A Mother and Son on Life, Love, and Loss, 2016 **MEM:** Member Actors Equity, Screen Actors Guild, American Federation of TV and Radio Artists, Authors League Am., Am. Federation Arts

VARGAS, JUAN C., T: U.S. Representative from California **I:** Government Administration/Government Relations/Government Services **DOB:** 03/07/1961 **PB:** National City **SC:** CA/USA **PT:** Son of Tomas and Celina Vargas; **ED:** JD, Harvard Law School; MA in Humanities, Fordham University, Bronx, New York; BA in Political Sci., magna cum laude, University San Diego, 1983 **C:** Member, US House Administration Committee, 2013-; Member, US House Foreign Affairs Committee, 2013-; Member, US House Agricultural Committee, 2013-; Member, US Congress from 51st California District, Washington, 2013-; Member, Committee on the Judiciary, Republican Study Committee; Member District 40, California State Senate, 2010-13; Member District 79, California State Assembly, 2001-06; Councilman District 8, San Diego City Council, 1993-2000 **PA:** Democrat

VARGAS IIOSA, MARIO, T: Writer **I:** Writing and Editing **DOB:** 03/28/1936 **PB:** Arequipa **SC:** Peru **PT:** Ernesto Vargas Maldonaldo; Dora Llosa Ureta **ED:** Honorary DLitt, Princeton University (2015); Honorary Doctorate, University of Paris-Sorbonne (2005); Honorary DLitt, University of Warwick (2004); Honorary Doctorate, Catholic University of Leuven, Belgium (2003); Honorary Doctorate, Skidmore College, New York (2002); Honorary Doctorate, La Trobe University, Australia (2002); Honorary Doctorate, University of Rome (2001); Honorary Doctorate, London University (1998); Honorary Doctorate, Ben-Gurion University, Israel (1998); Honorary Doctorate, University of Lima (1997); Honorary Doctorate, University of Valladolid, Spain (1994); Honorary Doctorate, University of Murcia, Spain (1994); Honorary Doctorate, Yale University (1994); Honorary Doctorate, Francisco Marroquin University, Guatemala (1993); Honorary Doctorate, Dowling College, Oakdale, NY (1993); Honorary Doctorate, Boston University (1992); Honorary Doctorate, University of Genoa, Italy (1992); Honorary LHD, Connecticut College (1991); Honorary Doctorate, Florida International University, Miami, FL (1990); Degree in Literature, National University of San Marcos, Lima, Peru (1958); Coursework, Complutense University, Madrid, Spain **C:** Writer (1959-Present); Spanish Teacher, Berlitz School, Paris, France; Former Journalist, Agence-France Presse, Paris, France; Former Journalist, Radio Panamericana; Former Journalist, El Comercio Magazines, Lima, Peru; Former Journalist of Tourism, Lima, Peru; Former Journalist of Peruvian Culture,

Lima, Peru **CR:** Weidenfeld Visiting Professor and Chair in European Comparative Literature, Oxford University (2004); Chair of Literature and American Culture, Department of Spanish & Portuguese, Georgetown University (2001); Fellow, German Academic Exchange Service, Berlin, Germany (1997-1998); Distinguished Writer in Residence, Georgetown University (1994); Visiting Professor, Princeton University, New Jersey (1993); Visiting Professor, Robert Kennedy Chair, Harvard University (1992-1993); Fellow, Science College, Berlin, Germany (1991-1992); Edna Gene & Jordan Davidson Chair, Florida International University (1991); Writer-in-Residence, Woodrow Wilson International Center for Scholars, Smithsonian Institution, Washington, DC (1980); Visiting Professor, Syracuse University, New York (1980); Simón Bolívar Chair in Latin American Studies, University of Cambridge (1977-1978); Visiting Professor, Edward Larocque Tinker Chair, Columbia University, New York, NY (1975); Lecturer, Latin American Studies, King's College, London, England (1969-1970); Visiting Professor, University of Puerto Rico (1969); Visiting Professor, Washington State University (1968); Lecturer, Queen Mary College, University of London (1967-1968) **CIV:** President, International Freedom Foundation (2002-Present); Presidential Candidate, Peru (1990) **CW:** Author, "The Neighborhood" (2018); Author, "Notes on the Death of Culture" (2015); Author, "The Discreet Hero" (2015); Author, "My Intellectual Journey" (2014); Author, "In Praise of Reading and Fiction: The Nobel Lecture" (2012); Author, "La Civilzacion del Espectaculo" (2012); Author, "Essays on Literature, Art, and Politics" (2011); Author, "Celtic's Dream" (2010); Author, "Journey to Fiction" (2009); Author, "Juan Carlos Onetti" (2009); Author, "The Bad Girl" (2007); Author, "Introduction for LOS TOROS" (2007); Author, "The Temptation of the Impossible" (2004); Author, "The Way to Paradise" (2003); Author, "The Language of Passion" (2001); Author, "The Feast of the Goat" (2000); Author, "Letters to a Young Novelist" (1997); Author, "Notebooks of Don Rigoberto" (1997); Author, "Death in the Andes" (1993); Author, "A Fish in the Water" (1993); Author, "A Writer's Reality" (1990); Author, "In Praise of the Stepmother" (1988); Author, "The Storyteller" (1987); Author, "Who Killed Palomino Molero?" (1986); Author, "The Real Life of Alejandro Mayta" (1984); Author, "The War of the End of the World" (1981); Author, "Aunt Julia and the Scriptwriter" (1977); Author, "The Perpetual Orgy" (1975); Author, "Captain Pantoja and the Special Service" (1973); Author, "García Márquez: Story of a Deicide" (1971); Author, "Conversation in the Cathedral" (1969); Author, "The Green House" (1966); Author, "The Time of the Hero" (1963); Author, "The Cubs and Other Stories" (1959) **AW:** Recipient, Pedro Henriquez Urena International Prize (2016); Recipient, St. Louis Literary Award (2011); Recipient, Nobel Prize in Literature, The Nobel Foundation (2010); Recipient, Harold & Ethel L. Stellfox Visiting Scholar & Writers Award, Dickinson College, Pennsylvania (2008); Recipient, International Medal of Arts, Autonomous Community of Madrid (2005); Recipient, Irving Kristol Award, American Enterprise Institute of Public Policy (2005); Recipient, Medal of Honor, National Institute Culture of Peru (2004); Recipient, Pablo Neruda Centennial Medal, Chile (2004); Recipient, Konex Foundation Award, Buenos Aires, Argentina (2004); Recipient, FCG International Literature Award, Cristóbal Gabarrón Foundation (2003); Recipient, Medal of Honor, City of Trujillo, Peru (2003); Recipient, Bartolome March Award for Excellence in Literature Criticism (2002); Recipient, Nabokov Award, PEN (2002); Recipient, Gold Medal, City of Genoa, Italy (2002); Recipient, Caonabo Gold Award, Dominican Association of

Journalists and Writers (2002); Recipient, Book of the Year Award, Booksellers Guild, Madrid, Spain (2001); Recipient, Award for the Americas, Foundation for the Americas, New York (2001); Recipient, National Book Critics Circle Award (1999); Recipient, University of California, Los Angeles Medal (1999); Recipient, Peace Prize, Frankfurt Book Fair, Germany (1996); Recipient, Jerusalem Prize, Israel (1995); Recipient, Chianti Ruffino Antico Fattore International Literature Prize, Italy (1995); Recipient, Miguel de Cervantes Prize, Ministry of Culture, Spain (1994); Recipient, San Clemente Literature Award, Instituto Rosalia de Castro, Spain (1994); Recipient, Premio Planeta, Barcelona, Spain (1993); Recipient, Golden Palm Award, Hispanic American Arts Center, New York (1992); Recipient, T. S. Eliot Prize, Ingersoll Foundation (1991); Recipient, Scanno Prize, Italy (1989); Recipient, Freedom Award, Max Schmidheiny Foundation, Switzerland (1988); Recipient, Prince of Asturias Prize for Literature, Spain (1986); Recipient, Ritz Paris Hemingway Award, France (1985); Recipient, Church Literature Prize, City Municipal Socialist Group, Madrid, Spain (1982); Recipient, Congressional Medal of Honor, Republic of Peru (1982); Recipient, Journalism Award, La Vanguardia Newspaper, Barcelona (1979); Recipient, Human Rights Award, Latin America Jewish Association (1977); Recipient, Rómulo Gallegos International Literature Prize, Venezuela (1967); Recipient, National Award for Fiction, Peru (1967); Recipient, Spanish Critics Award **MEM:** President, PEN (1976-1979); Fellow, Royal Spanish Academy; Honorary Member, Modern Language Association of America; International Academy of Humanism; Peruvian Academy of Language

VARMUS, HAROLD ELIOT, T: Scientist **I:** Sciences **DOB:** 12/18/1939 **PB:** Oceanside **SC:** NY/USA **PT:** Frank Varmus, Beatrice (Barasch) Varmus **ED:** MD, Columbia University College of Physicians & Surgeons, New York, NY, 1966; MA in English Literature, Harvard University, 1962; BA in English, Amherst College, MA, 1961 **C:** Director, National Cancer Institute, Bethesda, MD, 2010-Present; President, CEO, Memorial Sloan-Kettering Cancer Center, New York, NY, 2000-2010; Director, National Institutes Of Health, Bethesda, MD, 1993-1999; American Cancer Society Professor of Molecular Virology, University of California, San Francisco, 1984-1993; Professor, Department of Biochemistry & Biophysics, University of California, San Francisco, 1982-1993; Professor, Department of Microbiology & Immunology, University of California, San Francisco, 1979-1993; Associate Professor, University of California, San Francisco, 1974-1979; Assistant Professor, University of California, San Francisco, 1972-1974; Lecturer, Department of Microbiology, University of California, San Francisco, 1970-1972; Clinical Associate, National Institute of Arthritis & Metabolic Disease, Bethesda, MD, 1968-1970; Intern, Resident, Columbia-Presbyterian Hospital, 1966-1968 **CR:** Co-Founder, Chairman of the Board, Public Library Of Science (PloS), 2003-Present; Co-Chair, President's Council on Advisors On Science & Technology (PCAST), 2009-2010; World Health Organization Commission on Macroeconomics & Health, 2000-2002; Chairman, Board On Biology, National Research Council, 1991-1993 **CIV:** Chair, Science Board of Grand Challenges In Global Health Initiative, Bill & Melinda Gates Foundation, 2003-2008, Board of Directors, Scientists & Engineers For America, Board Directors, Campaign To Defend The Constitution **MIL:** Surgeon, U.S. Public Health Service, 1968-1970 **CW:** Author, The Art And Politics Of Science, 2009; Contributor, Articles, Professional Journals **AW:** America's Best

Leaders, U.S. News & World Report, 2007, National Medal of Science, The White House, 2002, Vannevar Bush Award, National Science Foundation, 2001, Co-Recipient, Nobel Prize In Physiology/Medicine, The Nobel Foundation, 1989, Alfred P. Sloan Award, GM Cancer Research Foundation, 1984, Gardner Foundation International Award, 1984, Shubitz Cancer Prize, 1984, Passano Foundation Award, 1983, Albert Lasker Award For Basic Medical Research, 1982, Scientist of the Year Award, California Academy of Science, 1982 **MEM:** National Academy Of Sciences, American Society of Biochemistry & Molecular Biology, American Academy of Arts & Sciences, American Society of Cell Biology, American Society of Microbiology, American Society of Virology, Institute of Medicine **PA:** Democrat **BA:** National Cancer Institute, HIH, 6116 Executive Boulevard, Bethesda, MD, 20892

VASOS, TODD J., T: Retail Executive **I:** Retail/Sales **ED:** Bachelor in Marketing, Western Carolina University **C:** CEO, Dollar General Corp., 2015-; COO, Dollar General Corp., 2013-15; Executive vice president, division president & chief merchandising officer, Dollar General Corp., 2008-13; Executive vice president, COO, Longs Drug Stores Corp., 2008; Senior vice president, chief merchandising officer, Longs Drug Stores Corp., 2001-08; Senior vice president, marketing, Longs Drug Stores Corp., 2001-05; Various leadership positions, Phar-Mor Food and Drug Inc., 1994-2001; Various leadership position, Eckerd Drug Corp., 1983-94

VEASEY, MARC, T: U.S. Representative From Texas **I:** Government Administration/Government Relations/Government Services **DOB:** 01/03/1971 **PB:** Tarrant County **SC:** TX/USA **PT:** Joseph Veasey, Corinne Veasey **ED:** BS in Mass Communications, Texas Wesleyan University, 1995 **C:** U.S. House of Science, Space, & Technology Committee, 2013-Present; U.S. House Armed Services Committee, 2013-Present; U.S. Congress from 33rd Texas District, Washington, DC, 2013-Present; District 95, Texas House of Representatives, 2005-2013; Staff Member, U.S. House of Representatives **PA:** Democrat **BA:** Room EXT E2, 806 Capitol Extension, PO Box 2910, Austin, TX, 78768

VEDDER, EDDIE, T: Singer **I:** Media & Entertainment **DOB:** 12/23/1965 **PB:** Evanston, Illinois **PT:** Son of Edward Louis Severson and Karen Lee (Vedder); **C:** Solo Artist, 2007-; Lead Singer, Pearl Jam, 1986 **CW:** Singer: (albums with Pearl Jam) Ten, 1991 (Jeremy - Video of Year, Best Group Video, Best Metal/Hard Rock Video, Best Direction, MTV Music Video Awards, 1993), Alive, 1991, Vs., 1993, Vitalogy, 1994, No Code, 1996, Yield, 1998, Binaural, 2000, Riot Act, 2002, Pearl Jam, 2006, Backspacer, 2009, Lightning Bolt, 2013, (solo albums) Into the Wild (soundtrack), 2007 (Guaranteed - Best Original Song, Golden Globe Awards, 2008), Ukulele Songs, 2011, (soundtracks) Into the Wild, 2007, (songs) Guaranteed, 2007 (Best Original Song-Motion Picture, Golden Globe award, Hollywood Foreign Press Association, 2008); contributor vocals (albums) Temple of the Dog, 1991, Mother Love Bone, 1992, appeared in (films) Singles, 1992, Dead Man Walking, 1995, Walk Hard: The Dewey Cox Story, 2007, Song Sung Blue, 2008, Into the Wild: The Experience, 2008 (documentaries) Hype!, 1996, End of the Century, 2003, Slacker Uprising, 2008, The People Speak, 2009; Song Sung Blue, 2008, Into the Wild: The Experience, 2008, Into the Wild: The Story, The Characters, Kokua 2008: 5 Years of Change, Rock and Roll Hall of Fame Live: Whole Lotta Shakin, 2009, Rock and Roll Hall of Fame Live: Come Together, 2009, The People Speak, 2009, Conan O'Brien Can't Stop,

2011, Water on the Road, 2011, Off the Boulevard, 2011, Pearl Jam Twenty, 2011, Paradise Lost 3: Purgatory, 2011, Cosmic Psychos: Blokes You Can Trust, 2013, Jay-Z: Made in America, 2013 **AW:** Named Favorite Alternative Artist, American Music Awards, 1999, Favorite Heavy Metal/Hard Rock Artist, 1999, Favorite New Heavy Metal/Hard Rock Artist, 1993, Favorite Pop/Rock New Artist, 1993; recipient Environmentalist of Year award, Surf Industry Manufacturers Association, 2007, Rock and Roll Hall of Fame Inductee, 2017

VEGA, DANIELA, T: Actress, Singer **I:** Media & Entertainment **PB:** San Miguel **SC:** Chile **CW:** Actress, Film, "The Guest" (2014), "A Fantastic Woman" (2017) **AW:** Named One of Time's 100 Most Influential People, TIME Magazine (2018)

VELA, FILEMON BARTOLOME, I: Government Administration/Government Relations/Government Services **DOB:** 02/13/1963 **PB:** Harllingen **SC:** TX/USA **PT:** Filemon Bartolome Vela and Blanca Vela **ED:** JD, University Texas School Law, 1987; BA, Georgetown University, 1985 **C:** Member, US House Homeland Security Committee, 2013-; Member, US House Agricultural Committee, 2013-; Member, US Congress from 34th Texas District, Washington, 2013-; Private law practice, 1988-2012 **PA:** Democrat **RE:** Roman Catholic

VELÁZQUEZ, NYDIA MARGARITA, T: U.S. Representative from New York, Ranking Member of the House Small Business Committee **I:** Government Administration/Government Relations/Government Services **DOB:** 03/28/1953 **PB:** Yabucoa **PT:** Daughter of Benito and Carmen (Luisa) Velázquez. **ED:** MA in Political Sci., New York University, 1976; BA in Political Sci., magna cum laude, University Puerto Rico, Rio Piedras, 1974 **C:** Ranking Member, House Small Business Committee, 1993-; Member, US Congress from 7th New York District, 2013-; Chair, US House Small Business Committee, 2007-11; Member, US House Financial Services Committee,; Member, US Congress from 12th New York District, 1993-2013; Director, Department Puerto Rican Community Affairs in the US for the Commonwealth of Puerto Rico, 1989-92; Director Migration Division Office, Puerto Rico Department Labor and Human Resources, 1986-89; Owner, Quick Stop Emporium, 1984-86; City councilwoman District 12, New York City, 1984-86; Special assistant to Rep. Edolphus Towns, US House of Representatives, 1983-84; Adjunct professor Puerto Rican studies, City University of New York Hunter College, 1981-83; Director social sci. department, University Puerto Rico, Humacao, 1977-79; Instructor, University Puerto Rico, Humacao, 1976-81 **CR:** Chair Congressional Hispanic Caucus, 2009-10 **AW:** Named Woman of Year, Hispanic Business Magazine, 2003; recipient Champion of Small Business Devel. award, Association Small Business Devel. Center, 2005, HerMANA award, MANA, 2002, Small Business Beacon award, National Small Business United, 2000 **ACH:** Achievements include being the first Puerto Rican woman elected to the US Congress **PA:** Democrat

VENTER, J. CRAIG, T: Biotechnologist, Biochemist, Geneticist **I:** Sciences **DOB:** 10/14/1946 **PB:** Salt Lake City **ED:** Doctor (hon.), Arizona State University, 2007; PhD in Physiology and Pharmacology, University California, San Diego, 1975; BS in Biochemistry, University California, San Diego, 1972 **C:** Co-Founder/CEO, Human Longevity Inc, 2014-2017,; Executive Chairman of the Board, 2017; Co-founder, President, Institute for Biological Energy Alternatives, 2003-; Co-founder, President, Center for the Advancement Genomics,

2003-; Chairman, Co-founder, President, The J. Craig Venter Sci. Foundation Joint Tech. Center, 2003-; Chairman, Co-founder, President, J. Craig Vetner Institute,; Chairman Sci. Adv. Board, Applera Corp., Norwalk, Connecticut,; Co-founder, CEO, President, Chief Sci. Officer, Celera Genomics Corp., Rockville, Maryland, 1998-2002; Co-founder, Chair, Chief Scientist, The Institute for Genomic Research, 1992-98; Section and Lab Chief National Institute Neurological Disorders and Stroke, National Institutes of Health, Bethesda, Maryland, 1984-92; With, Roswell Park Memorial Institute,; Professor, State University of New York, Buffalo, **CR:** Chairman, Board Trustees The Institute for Genomic Research Member Sci. Adv. Board ValiGene Board Directors High Tech. Council Maryland **MIL:** Served in US Navy, 1967-68, South Vietnam **CW:** Contributor Several Articles to Professional Journals; Author: A Life Decoded, My Genome: My Life, 2007,(Book) Life at the Speed of Light, 2013 **AW:** Named one of The 100 Agents of Change, Rolling Stone magazine, 2009, 10 People Who Mattered, Newsweek, 2008, The 100 Most Influential People in the World, TIME Magazine, 2008, 2007; Recipient National Medal Sci., National Science Foundation, 2009, Eni Award for Research & Environment, 2008, Industrial Application of Sci. Award, National Academy of Sciences, 2002, Gairdner Foundation International Award, 2002, Taylor International Prize in Medicine, Robarts Research Institute, 2001, King Faisal International Award for Sci., 2000, Chiron Corp. Biotech. Research Award, 1999, Beckman Award, 1999, Dickson Prize in Medicine, 2011, Dan David Prize Award, 2012, Leeuwenhoek Medal, 2015 **MEM:** Fellow: Am. Society Microbiology, Am. Academy Arts & Sciences; mem.: National Academy of Sciences **ACH:** Achievements include research in functional and comparative analysis of genome and gene products in viruses, eubacteria, pathogenic bacteria, archea and eukaryotes, both in plants and animals including humans; first to use automated gene sequencers; development of expressed sequence tags (ESTs); discovery of more than half of all human genes

VENTURA, JESSE, T: Former Governor of Minnesota, Retired Professional wrestler **I:** Government Administration/Government Relations/Government Services **DOB:** 07/15/1951 **PB:** Minneapolis, July 15, 1951 **PT:** Son of George and Bernice Janos; **ED:** Attended, North Hennepin Community College, Brooklyn Park, Minnesota **C:** Visiting Fellow, Harvard University, 2004-; Host, Jesse Ventura's America, MSNBC, 2003; Governor, State of Minnesota, St. Paul, 1999-2003; Mayor, City of Brooklyn Park, 1991-95; Commentator, World Championship Wrestling, 1992-94; Co-host, Saturday Night's Main Event, 1985-90; Professional wrestler, World Wrestling Federation, 1973-84 **CIV:** Member, Izaak Walton League America, Vol. football coach, Champlin Park HS, Member advisory board, Make-A-Wish Foundation Minnesota, **MIL:** Served with Underwater Demolition Team 12 US Navy, 1969-75, South Vietnam **CW:** Actor: (films) Predator, 1987, The Running Man, 1989, No Holds Barred, 1989, Thunderground, 1989, Abraxas, Guardian of the Universe, 1991, Ricochet, 1991, Living and Working in Space: The Countdown Has Begun, 1993, Demolition Man, 1993, Batman and Robin, 1997, 20/20 Vision, 1999, Stuck On You, 2003, (voice only) The Ringer, 2005, Borders, 2008, Woodshop, 2009; actor: Hunter, 1985, Zorro, 1991, The X-Files, 1996, Arli$$, 1996; appeared in (documentaries) Beyond the Mat, 1999; author: The Wit and Wisdom of Jesse 'The Body–The Mind' Ventura, 1999, I Ain't Got Time to Bleed: Reworking the Body Politic from the Bottom Up, 1999; co-author (with Julie Mooney): Do I

Stand Alone?: Going to the Mat Against Political Pawns and Media Jackals, 2000; co-author: (with Heron Marquez) Jesse Ventura Tells It Likes It Is: America's Most Outspoken Governor Speaks Out About Government, 2002; co-author: (with Dick Russell) Don't Start the Revolution Without Me!, 2008, American Conspiracies: Lies, Lies, and More Dirty Lies that the Government Tells Us, 2010, 63 Documents the Government Doesn't Want You to Read, 2011, Democrips and Rebloodlicans: No More Gangs in Government, 2012; co-author: (with Dick Russell & David Wayne) They Killed Our President: 63 Reasons to Believe There Was a Conspiracy to Assassinate JFK, 2013, Sh*t Politicians Say:The Funniest,Dumbest Most Outrageous Thing Ever Uttered by Out Leaders, 2016,Jesse Ventura's Marijuana Manifesto, 2016(Television) The World According to Jesse, 2017 **AW:** Decorated Vietnam Service medal, National Defense Service medal; named to The World Wrestling Entertainment (WWE) Hall of Fame, 2004; recipient Frank Gotch award, International Wrestling Institute & Museum, 2003, Iron Mike Mazurki award, California Alley Club, 1999 **MEM:** Mem.: Screen Actors Guild, Am. Federation TV & Radio Announcers **PA:** Independent

VERLANDER, JUSTIN BROOKS, T: Professional Baseball Player **I:** Athletics **DOB:** 02/20/1983 **PB:** Manakin Sabot **PT:** Son of Richard Verlander. **ED:** Student, Vanderbilt University, Nashville **C:** Pitcher, Houston Astros 2017-; Pitcher, Detroit Tigers, 2006-2017; **AW:** Named Player of Year, The Sporting News, 2011, American League MVP, Baseball Writers Association America, 2011, American League Rookie of Year, 2006, Player of Year, Major League Baseball Players Association, 2011, American League Outstanding Pitcher, 2011, American League Outstanding Rookie, 2006; named to American League All-Star Team, Major League Baseball, 2009-13, 2007; recipient American League Cy Young award, Baseball Writers Association America, 2011,Cy Young Award, 2016,2017, All Star, 2013-17, Wins Leader, 2013, 2014, 2016, NL Strikeout Leader, 2016, 2017 **ACH:** Achievements include pitching a no-hitter against the: Milwaukee Brewers, June 12, 2007; Toronto Blue Jays, May 7, 2011; leading the American League in: innings pitched, wins, strikeouts, 2009, 2011; earned run average, 2011; starts, 2011, 2013

VERNICK, GREG, T: Chef **I:** Food & Restaurant Services **ED:** Culinary Degree, Culinary Institute of America; Hospitality Management, Boston University **C:** Head Chef/Owner, Vernick Food & Drink, 2012-Present; Talulas Garden, 2010-2012 **AW:** James Beard Award for Best Chef, 2017

VERONICA, MADONNA, T: Singer, Actress, Producer **I:** Media & Entertainment **DOB:** 08/16/1958 **PB:** Bay City **SC:** Michigan **PT:** Daughter of Sylvio Anthony and Madonna Louise (Fortin) Ciccone; **SPN:** Married Sean Penn, August 16, 1985 (div. September 14, 1989); Married Guy Ritchie, December 22, 2000 (div. 2008); **CH:** 1 child Rocco John; **ED:** Student, University Michigan, 1978 **C:** Designer, Material Girl Clothing Line, 2011—; CEO, Maverick Records, LA, California, 1992—; Dancer, Alvin Ailey Dance Co., New York City, New York, 1979 **CIV:** Co-founder (with Michael Berg) Raising Malawi, 2006—, Raising Malawi Academy for Girls, 2008— **CW:** Singer: (albums) Madonna, 1983, Like a Virgin, 1985, True Blue, 1986, You Can Dance, 1987, Like a Prayer, 1989, The Immaculate Collection, 1990, Erotica, 1992, Bedtime Stories, 1994, Something to Remember, 1995, Ray of Light, 1998 (Grammy award for Best Pop Album 1999), Music, 2000, GHV2: Greatest Hits Volume II, 2002, American Life, 2003, Remixed & Revisited, 2003,

Confessions on a Dancefloor, 2005 (Grammy award for Best Electronic/Dance Album, 2007), I'm Going to Tell You a Secret, 2006, The Confessions Tour, 2007, Hard Candy, 2008, Celebrations, 2009, M.D.N.A., 2012 (Billboard Music award for Top Dance Album, 2013), Rebel Heart, 2015; (soundtracks) Who's That Girl, 1987, I'm Breathless: Music From and Inspired by the Film Dick Tracy, 1990, Evita, 1996; Actress: (films) A Certain Sacrifice, 1980, Vision Quest, 1985, Desperately Seeking Susan, 1985, Shanghai Surprise, 1986, Who's That Girl, 1987, Bloodhounds of Broadway, 1989, Dick Tracy, 1990, Shadows and Fog, 1992, Body of Evidence, 1992, A League of Their Own, 1992, Dangerous Game, 1993, Body of Evidence, 1993, Blue in the Face, 1995, Four Rooms, 1996, Girl 6, 1996, Evita, 1996 (Golden Globe award for Best Actress in Comedy/Musical, 1997), The Next Best Thing, 2000, Swept Away, 2002, (voice) Arthur and the Invisibles, 2006, W.E., 2012; (TV appearances) Will & Grace, 2003; stage appearance: Speed-the-Plow, 1987, Up for Grabs, 2002; Executive Prodr.: (documentaries) Madonna: Truth or Dare, 1991, I'm Going to Tell You a Secret, 2005, Madonna: The Confessions Tour Live from London, 2006; (films) Agent Cody Banks, 2003, Agent Cody Banks 2: Destination London, 2004; (TV films) 30 Days Until I'm Famous, 2004; Writer, Executive Producer, I Am Because We Are, 2008; Director, Executive Prodr.: (films) Filth and Wisdom, 2008; Director, Prodr.: (films) W.E., 2011 (Golden Globe award for Best Original Song-Motion Picture, 2012); Author: Sex, 1992, (children's books) The English Roses, 2003, Mr. Peabody's Apples, 2003, Yakov and the Seven Thieves, 2004, Adventures of Abdi, 2004, Lotsa de Casha, 2005; creator: (dvd workout series) Addicted to Sweat, 2013. **AW:** Greatest Dance Club Songs Artists of All Time,Billboard Music Awards, 2016,Named Top Touring Artist, Billboard Music Awards, 2013, Top Dance Artist, 2013, Favorite Music Icon, People's Choice Awards, 2016; Named one of The 100 Most Powerful Celebrities, Forbes magazine, 2008, The 100 Most Powerful Women, 2010; Named to Rock & Roll Hall of Fame, 2008; Recipient Grammy Award for Best Song Written for Motion Picture, 1999, World's Best Pop Artist Award, World Music Awards, 2007, Best-Selling US Artist, 2007, 2008, Ivor Novello Award for International Hit of Year, Brit. Academy Composers & Songwriters, 2007, Style Icon Award, Elle Magazine, 2007 **BA:** Maverick Records LLC, 9348 Civic Ctr Dr 3rd Fl, Beverly Hills, CA, 90210

VESTAGER, MARGRETHE, T: European Commissioner for Competition **I:** Government Administration/Government Relations/Government Services **DOB:** 04/13/1968 **PB:** Glostrup **SC:** Denmark **PT:** Hans Vestager, Bodil Tybjerg **MS:** Married **SPN:** Thomas Jensen, 6/11/1994 **CH:** Maria, Rebecca, Ella **ED:** Doctorate Honoris Causa, Katholieke Universiteit Leuven, 2017; Degree in Economics, University of Copenhagen, 1993 **C:** Commissioner for Competition, European Commission, 2014-Present; Minister, Economic and Interior Affairs, 2011-2014; Chairman of the Parliamentary Group, Danish Parliament, 2007; Danish Parliament, 2001; Central Board and Executive Committee, SLP, 1989 **CIV:** Trilateral Commission, 2010-2011, Executive Committee, UNICEF, Denmark, 2007-2011, Chairwoman of the Board, Blaagaards Seminarium, Board Member, University College Copenhagen, 2006-2009, Board of Advisors, Royal Greenland, 2004-2007, Chairwoman of the Advisory Board, Institute for Management, Politics, and Philosophy, Copenhagen Business School, 2003-2008 **AW:** TIME 100 Most Influential, 2017

VIGUERIE, RICHARD ART, T: Direct Mail Marketing Executive **I:** Advertising & Marketing **DOB:** 09/23/1933 **PB:** Golden Acres, Texas, September 23, 1933 **PT:** Son of Arthur Camile and Elizabeth Mary (Stoufflet) V. **MS:** Married **SPN:** Elaine Adele O'Leary, February 17, 1962; **CH:** Renee Elaine, Michelle Marie, Richard Ryan **ED:** BS in Political Sci., University Houston, 1958; Student, Texas Agricultural and Industrial University, 1952-56 **C:** Co-founder, Am. Freedom Agenda, 2007; President, chairman, ConservativeHQ.com,; Chairman, Am. Target Advertising, Inc.,; President, Viguerie Co., Falls Church, Virginia, 1965; Executive director, Young Americans for Freedom, 1961-63 **CR:** Chairman board Am. Mailing List Corp., Falls Church, 1972 founder Conservative Digest, Falls Church, 1975-85. **CIV:** With National Guard, 1957. **CW:** Author: The New Right: We're Ready To Lead, 1980, The Establishment versus The People, 1983, America's Right Turn: How Conservatives Used New and Alternative Media to Take Power, 2004, Conservatives Betrayed: How George W. Bush and Other Big Government Republicans Hijacked the Conservative Cause, 2006, Takeover: The 100-Year War for the Soul of the GOP and How Conservatives Can Finally Win it, 2014; **AW:** Named one of 50 Future Leaders of America, Time magazine, 1979, 25 Most Intriguing People of Year, People magazine, 1981, 25 Most Influential Republicans, Newsmax magazine, 2008. **PA:** Republican **BA:** 9625 Surveyor Ct Ste 400, Manassas, VA, 20110-4408

VILLARRUEL, ANTONIA M., T: Dean of Nursing **I:** Education/Educational Services **CN:** University of Pennsylvania **ED:** PhD, Wayne State University, 1993; MSN, University of Pennsylvania, 1982; BSN, Nazareth College, Kalamazoo, MI, 1978 **C:** Dean, Nursing, University of Pennsylvania, 2014-Present **CW:** Co-Author, (Publications) Fidelity After SECOND LIFE Facilitator Training In A Sexual Risk Behavior Intervention, 2016, Estigma Y VIH/SIDA Entre Padres/Madres Y Adolescentes Puertorriquenos/As, 2016, Innovative Nursing Care Models And Culture Of Health: Early Evidence, 2016, Association Of Gender Norms, Relationship And Intrapersonal Variables, And Acculturation With Sexual Communication Among Young Adult Latinos, 2015, The Council For The Advancement Of Nursing Science, Idea Festival Advisory Committee: Good Ideas That Need To Go Further, 2015, A Path Analysis Of Latinoparental, Teenager And Cultural Variables In Teenagers: Sexual Attitudes, Norms, Self-Efficacy, And Sexual Intentions, 2015, Using A Virtual Environment To Deliver Evidence-Based Interventions: The Facilitator's Experience, 2015, Preparing Facilitators From Community-Based Organizations For Evidence-Based Intervention Training In Second Life, 2014, Avatars Travel For Free: Virtual Access To Evidence-Based Intervention Training And Capacity Building, 2014, A Randomized Controlled Trial Testing An HIV Prevention Intervention For Latino Youth, 2006

VISCLOSKY, PETER JOHN, T: U.S. Representative from Indiana **I:** Government Administration/Government Relations/Government Services **DOB:** 08/13/1949 **PB:** Gary **SC:** IN/USA **PT:** John Visclosky, Helen (Kauzlaric) Visclosky **ED:** LLM in International/Comparative Law, Georgetown University, 1983; JD, University of Notre Dame, 1973; BS in Accounting, Indiana University, Indianapolis, IN, 1970 **C:** Appropriations Committee, Subcommittees of Treasury, Postal Service, General Government And Military Construction, U.S. Congress From First Indiana District, 1985-Present; Associate, Greco, Gouveia, Miller, Pera & Bishop, Merrillville, IN, 1982-1984; Associate Staff, Budget Committee, U.S. House Of Representatives, Washington, DC, 1980-1982; Associate Staff, Appropria-

tions Committee, U.S. House Of Representatives, Washington, DC, 1976-1980; Associate, Benjamin, Greco & Gouveia, Merrillville, IN, 1973-1976; Legal Assistant, District Attorney's Office, New York, NY, 1972 **BAR:** U.S. Supreme Court, District of Columbia, Indiana **PA:** Democrat **BA:** Suite 9, 701 E 83d Avenue, Merrillville, IN, USA, 46410

VISENTIN, JOHN, T: CEO **I:** Business Management/Business Services **CN:** Xerox **ED:** Bachelor of Commerce, Concordia University, Montreal **C:** CEO, Xerox, 2018-,; Senior Consultant, Icahn Enterprises, 2018-,; Senior Advisor to the Chairman, Exela Technologies, 2017-,; Operating Partner, Advent International, 2017-,; Founder, Menda Consulting, 2017-,; Chairman of the Board, Presidio, 2015-17,; Advisor, Apollo Global Management, 2013-17,; Advisory Board Member, L2 Think Tank, 2013-14,; Executive VP/GM, HP Enterprise, 2011-12,; SVP Enterprise Services, HP Enterprises, 2011,; General Manager, Integrated Technology Services New York, IBM, 2007-11,; Global Vice President, End-User Services, IBM, 2006-07,; Client Advocacy Executive, Office of the Chairman, IBM, 2004-06,; Vice President, Industrial Sector, East Region, IBM, 2001-04,; Vice President, E-Business Solution Sales, IBM Canada, 2000-01 **BA:** 45 Glover Ave, Norwalk, CT, 06856

VIZGUERRA, JEANETTE, I: Nonprofit & Philanthropy **C:** Advocate for Immigration Reform **AW:** TIME 100 Most Influential, 2017

VOIGHT, JON, T: Actor **I:** Media & Entertainment **PB:** Yonkers **SC:** NY/USA **PT:** Elmer Voight; Barbara (Camp) Voight **ED:** Studied with, Sanford Meisner and Samantha Harper, New York City; BFA, Catholic University, 1960 **CW:** Stage appearances include O Oysters Revue, 1961, The Sound of Music, 1961, A View from the Bridge, 1965, Romeo and Juliet, 1966, The Tempest, 1966, Two Gentlemen of Verona, 1966, That Summer-That Fall, 1967 (Theatre World award 1967), A Streetcar Named Desire, 1973, The Hashish Club, 1975, Hamlet, 1976, The Seagull, 1992; actor: (TV series) Cimarron Strip, 1968, Gunsmoke, 1966-69, 24, 2009, Lone Star, 2010, Ray Donovan, 2013-15 (Golden Globe award for Best Performance by an Actor in a Supporting Role in a Series, Mini-Series or Motion Picture Made for TV, 2014); (films) Fearless Frank, 1967, Hour of the Gun, 1967, Out of It, 1969, Midnight Cowboy, 1969 (New York Critics Circle award for Best Actor, 1969, BAFTA award for Most Promising Newcomer 1969, Golden Globe award for Most Promising Newcomer 1969), Catch-22, 1970, The Revolutionary, 1970, Deliverance, 1972, The All American Boy, 1973, Conrack, 1974, The Odessa File, 1974, End of the Game, 1976, Coming Home, 1978 (Cannes International Film festival award, 1978, New York Film Critics award for Best Actor, 1978, Academy Award for Best Actor in a Leading Role, 1979, Golden Globe award for Best Actor, 1979), The Champ, 1979, Runaway Train, 1985 (Golden Globe award for Best Performance by an Actor in a Motion Picture - Drama, 1996), Desert Bloom, 1986, Eternity, 1990, The Rainbow Warrior, 1992, Heat, 1995, Mission Impossible, 1996, Rosewood, 1997, Anaconda, 1997, Most Wanted, 1997, The Rainmaker, 1997, U Turn, 1997, I Once Had a Life, 1998, Enemy of the State, 1998, Varsity Blues, 1999, A Dog of Flanders, 1999, Pearl Harbor, 2001, Lara Croft: Tomb Raider, 2001, Zoolander, 2001, Ali, 2001, Holes, 2003, Karate Dog, 2004, The Manchurian Candidate, 2004, Superbabies: Baby Geniuses 2, 2004, National Treasure, 2004, September Dawn, 2006, Transformers, 2007, National Treasure: Book of Secrets, 2007, Pride and Glory, 2008, Four Christmases, 2008, Beyond, 2012, Getaway (voice), 2013, The Dark Prince, 2013, Baby Geniuses and the Treasures of Egypt,

2014, Deadly Lessons, 2014, Baby Geniuses and the Space Baby, 2015, Woodlawn, 2015,American Wrestler: The Wizard, 2016, Same Kind of Different as Me, 2017; (TV films) Chernobyl: The Final Warning, 1991, The Last of His Tribe, 1992, Convict Cowboys, 1995, Boys Will Be Boys, 1997, Noah's Ark, 1999, Second string, 2002, Jasper, Texas, 2003, The Five People You Meet in Heaven, 2004, Pope John Paul II, 2005; (mini-series) Return to Lonesome Dove, 1993; actor, producer, co-writer: (films) Lookin' To Get Out, 1982, The Fixer, 1998; dir.: (TV films) The Tin Soldier, 1995; actor, prodr.: (films) Table for Five, 1983, A Tribute to Dustin Hoffman, 1999, Noah's Ark, 1999, Second String, 2000; executive prodr.: (films) The Final Song, 2014

VON FURSTENBERG, DIANE, T: Fashion Designer **I:** Apparel & Fashion **DOB:** 12/31/1946 **PB:** Brussels **PT:** Daughter of Leon L. and Liliane L. (Nahmias) Halfin; **ED:** Student, University Geneva **C:** Spokesperson, Ban Bossy, 2014-; Founder, chairman, DVF Studio (formerly Diane von Furstenberg Studio, L.P.), New York City, 1972-; Founder publication house, Salvy, Paris, 1985; President Diane von Furstenberg Ltd., DVF Studio (formerly Diane von Furstenberg Studio, L.P.), New York City, **CR:** Board directors IAC/InterActiveCorp, 1999-2008 guest judge Project Runway All Stars, 2012, Project Runway, 2008 launched children's collection with GapKids, 2012 launched home collection and signature fragrances, DIANE, 2011 designer Ltd. Edition Sidekick 3 for T-Mobile, DIANE line including signature dresses launched home-shopping business selling Silk Assets collection, 1991 launched cosmetics and fragrance line Tatiana, 1974 **CIV:** Spokesperson, Ban Bossy campaign, 2014 Board member, Vital Voices, Honorary director, Housatonic Valley Association, Director, The Diller-von Furstenberg Family Foundation, **CW:** Author: Diane Von Furstenberg's Book of Beauty, 1977, Beds, 1991, The Bath, 1993, The Table, 1996, Diane: A Signature Life, 1998, The Woman I Wanted to Be, 2014; contributing editor Vanity Fair magazine, 1993; prodr.: (films) Forty Shades of Blue, 2005, Andy Warhol: A Documentary Film, 2006; reality TV personality House of DVF, 2014- **AW:** Named one of The 100 Most Powerful Women, Forbes magazine, 2011-14, The 50 Most Powerful Women in New York City, New York Post, 2007, The 50 Most Powerful Women in New York, Crain's New York Business, 2011, 2009, The 100 Most Influential Women in New York City Business, 2007; named to The Fashion Walk of Fame, 2008; recipient Fashion Icon award, Harper's Bazaar Women of the Year Awards, 2014, Jacqueline Kennedy Onassis medal, Municipal Arts Society, 2011, Lifetime Achievement award, Council Fashion Designers of America, 2005, Ellis Island Medal of Honor, 1986, Gold Medal, Queen Sofia Spanish Institute Medal, 2010 **MEM:** Mem.: Council Fashion Designers of America (president 2006-) **ACH:** Achievements include introducing the knitted jersey wrap dress in 1973, which is in the collection of the Costume Institute of the Metropolitan Museum of Art

VONN, LINDSEY, T: Professional Skier **I:** Athletics **DOB:** 10/18/1984 **PB:** St. Paul **PT:** Daughter of Alan and Linda Kildow **C:** Professional alpine skier, International Ski Federation, 2000-; Member US ski team, Winter Olympic Games, Vancouver, Canada, 2010; Member US ski team, Winter Olympic Games, Turin, Italy, 2006; Member US ski team, Winter Olympic Games, Salt Lake City, 2002 **CW:** Actor: (TV appearances) Law & Order, 2010 **AW:** Named Athlete of Year, Minneapolis Star Tribune, 2008, Female Athlete of Year, Associated Press, 2010, Women's Super G Champion, FIS Alpine Ski World Cup, 2009-12, Women's Downhill

Champion, 2008-12, Women's Overall Champion, 2012, 2008-10; named one of The 100 Most Influential People in the World, TIME magazine, 2013; recipient Women's Combined Champion, FIS Alpine Ski World Cup, 2010-12, Gold medal, women's downhill, Bronze medal, women's super G, Winter Olympic Games, 2010, Gold medal, downhill, super G, FIS Alpine World Ski Championships, Val d'Isere, France, 2009, Silver medal, downhill, super G, FIS Alpine World Ski Championships, Are, Sweden, 2007, Laureus Sportswoman of the Year, 2010, Olympic Spirit Award, 2006, Slieur d'Or Award, 2009 **ACH:** Achievements include becoming the most successful female alpine skier in US history, 2009

VOORHEES, STEVEN C., **T:** Diversified Paper and Packaging Company Executive **I:** Manufacturing **CN:** Westrock **ED:** MBA, University of Virginia; BA in Economics & Mathematics, Northwestern University **C:** CEO, Westrock, 2015-Present; Chief Administrative Officer, Rock-Tenn Co., Norcross, GA, 2008-Present; Executive Vice President, CFO, Rock-Tenn Co., Norcross, GA, 2000-Present; From Chief Administrative Officer To CEO, Rock-Tenn Co., Norcross, GA, 2008-2015; Managing Partner, Kinetic Partners, LLC, Birmingham, AL, 1999-2000; Executive Vice President, Marketing, Sonat Inc., 1980-1999 **BA:** Westrock, 1000 Abernathy Road, Atlanta, GA, 30328

VOUNATSOS, MICHEL, **T:** CEO of Biogen **I:** Biotechnology **CN:** Biogen **ED:** MBA, Hec Paris (1999); Certificate of Clinical and Therapeutic Synthesis in Medicine, Universite de Bordeaux (1988) **C:** Chief Executive Officer, Biogen (2017-Present); Executive Vice President/Chief Commercial OFC, Biogen (2016-2017); President, Primary Care and Customer Centricity, Merck (Now Merck Sharp & Dohme Corp.) (2014-2016); President, Merck Customer Centricity, Merck (Now Merck Sharp & Dohme Corp.) (2012-2013); Chairman and President, MSD China, Merck (Now Merck Sharp & Dohme Corp.) (2011-2012)

WADHWANI, ROMESH, **T:** Application Developer **I:** Technology **SC:** India **ED:** PhD in Electrical Engineering, Carnegie-Mellon Univ.; MS in Electrical Engineering, Carnegie-Mellon Univ.; BS in Electrical Engineering, Indian Institute Tech. **C:** Co-chmn. & director, Lawson Software Inc., 2006-; Managing partner, Symphony Tech. Group, 2002-; Chairman & director, Intentia, 2004-06; Vice chairman, i2 Technologies Inc., 2000-02; Chairman & CEO, Aspect Devel., 1991-2000 **CIV:** Wadhwani Foundation **AW:** Named one of Forbes 400: Richest Americans, 2009 **MEM:** Board of Trustees, John F. Kennedy Center for the Performing Arts

WAGNER, ANN LOUISE, **T:** U.S. Representative from Missouri **I:** Government Administration/Government Relations/Government Services **DOB:** 09/13/1962 **PB:** St. Louis **SC:** MO/USA **MS:** Married **SPN:** Ray Wagner **CH:** Raymond III, Stephen, Mary Ruth **ED:** BSBA, University Missouri, 1984 **C:** Member, US House Financial Services Committee, 2013-; Member, Committee on Oversight and Government Reform; Member, US Congress from 2nd Missouri District, Washington, 2013-; Chairwoman, Roy Blunt's Senatorial Campaign, 2009-10; US ambassador to Luxembourg, US Department State, Luxembourg, 2005-09; Co-chmn., Republican National Committee, Washington, 2001-05; 2nd congressional district chair, Bob Dole Presidential Campaign, 1996; Advisor, Ashcroft for Senate Campaign, 1994; Missouri state executive director, Bush/Quayle Campaign, 1992; Chairman, Missouri Republican Party, Jefferson City, 1999-2001; Director Missouri House & Senate Redistricting

Commission, Missouri Republican Party, 1991; Member, Missouri Federation Republican Women,; Chairman committee, St. Louis County Republican Central Committee,; Member committee, Lafayette Township, **MEM:** Mem.: Republican National Convention Midwestern State Chairman's Association (committee on arrangements 2000, del. 2000, del. chairman 2000) **PA:** Republican **BA:** 435 Cannon House Office Building, Washington, DC, 20515

WAHLBERG, MARK, **T:** Actor **I:** Media & Entertainment **DOB:** 06/06/1905 **PB:** Dorchester, Massachusetts **SC:** Dorchester, Massachusetts **PT:** Son of Donald and Alma Wahlberg; **C:** Co-owner, Wahlburgers, Hingham, Massachusetts, 2011 **CW:** Singer: (albums with Marky Mark and the Funky Bunch) Music for the People, 1991, You Gotta Believe, 1992; actor: (films) Renaissance Man, 1994, The Basketball Diaries, 1995, Fear, 1995, Boogie Nights, 1997, Traveller, 1997, The Big Hit, 1998, Three Kings, 1999, The Corruptor, 1999, The Yards, 1999, The Perfect Storm, 2000, The Planet of the Apes, 2001, Rock Star, 2001, The Truth About Charlie, 2002, The Italian Job, 2003, I Heart Huckabees, 2004, Four Brothers, 2005, Invincible, 2006, The Departed, 2006 (National Society Film Critics award for Best Supporting Actor, 2007), Shooter, 2007, The Happening, 2008, Max Payne, 2008, The Lovely Bones, 2009, Date Night, 2010, The Other Guys, 2010, Ted, 2012, Pain & Gain, 2013, 2 Guns, 2013, Transformers: Age of Extinction, 2014, Mojave, 2015, Ted 2, 2015, Daddy's Home, 2015, (TV films) The Substitute, 1993; actor, prodr.: (films) We Own the Night, 2007, The Fighter, 2010, Contraband, 2012, Broken City, 2013, Lone Survivor, 2013 (Critics' Choice award for Best Actor in an Action Movie, 2014), Transformers: Age of Extinction, 2014, The Gambler, 2014, Entourage, 2015, Ted 2, 2015, Daddy's Home, 2015, Deepwater Horizion, 2016, Patriots Day, 2016 Transformers: The Last Knight, 2017, Daddys Home 2, 2017, All the Money in the World 2017; actor, executive prodr.: (films) Deepwater Horizon, 2016; executive prodr.: (documentaries) Juvvies, 2004, (TV series) Entourage, 2004-11, In Treatment, 2008-10, How to Make It in America, 2010-11, Boardwalk Empire, 2010-14, Ballers, 2014, (TV films) The Missionary, 2013, Teamsters, 2013, Shooter, 2016, (films) Prisoners, 2013, Stealing Cars, 2015; executive prodr., reality TV personality: Wahlburgers, 2014- Shooter, 2016 **AW:** Named one of The 100 Most Influential People in the World, TIME magazine, 2011; recipient Generation award, MTV Movie Awards, 2014

WAITHE, LENA, **T:** Actress **I:** Media & Entertainment **PB:** Chicago **SC:** IL/USA **CW:** Film, "Save Me" (2011), "Dear White People" (2014), "Ladylike" (2014), "Step Sisters" (2018), "Ready Player One" (2018); Television, "Girlfriends" (2007), "Comeback" (2014), "Bones" (2014), "M.O. Diaries" (2012), "How to Rock" (2012), "Hello Cupid" (2013), "Transparent" (2014), "Master of None" (2015), "The Chi" (2018), "This is Us" (2018), "Dear White People" (2018) **AW:** Named One of TIME's 100 Most Influential People, TIME Magazine (2018); Primetime Emmy Award for Outstanding Writing for a Comedy Series

WALBERG, TIM, **T:** U.S. Representative from Michigan **I:** Government Administration/Government Relations/Government Services **DOB:** 04/12/1951 **PB:** Chgo. **PT:** Son of John Andrew and Alice (Wilcox) Walberg **ED:** MA in Communications, Wheaton College Grad. School, 1978; BS in Christian Education, Fort Wayne Bible College, 1975; Attended, Western Illinois University, 1969-70 **C:** Member, US House Oversight & Workforce Committee, Washington, 2011-; Member, US House

Education & Workforce Committee, Washington, 2011-; Member, US House Homeland Security committee, Washington, 2011-; Member, US Congress from 7th Michigan District, Washington, 2011-; Member, US Committee on Energy and Commerce; Member, Republican Study Committee; Member, US Congress from 7th Michigan District, Washington, 2007-09; Division manager, Moody Bible Institute, Chicago, 2001-06; President, Warren Reuther Center for Education & Community Impact, 1999-2001; Member District 57, Michigan House of Reps., 1983-98; Pastor, Union Gospel Church, Tipton, Michigan, 1978-83; Pastor, New Haven Baptist Church, Ind., 1973-77 **CR:** Member Lenawee County Basic Human Needs Task Force **MEM:** Mem.: Lenawee County Riding for Handicapped, Tecumsoh Kiwanis Club **PA:** Republican

WALDEN, DANA, **T:** Fox CEO **I:** Media & Entertainment **ED:** BA in Communications, University Southern California **C:** Chairman, CEO, 20th Century Fox TV, 2014-; President, 20th Century Fox TV, 1999-; Co-chmn., 20th Century Fox TV, 2007-14; Former executive vice president drama devel., 20th Century Fox TV,; Former senior vice president drama, 20th Century Fox TV,; Former vice president drama, 20th Century Fox TV,; Vice president current programming, 20th Century Fox TV, 1994-96; Former senior vice president media and corp. relations, 20th Century Fox TV,; Former vice president marketing, Arsenio Hall Communications, Paramount,; Formerly with, Bender, Goldman & Helper **AW:** Named one of The 100 Most Powerful Women in Entertainment, The Hollywood Reporter, 1999-2014 **MEM:** Mem.: Hollywood Radio and TV Society (vice president 2003-)

WALDEN, GREGORY PAUL, **T:** U.S. Representative from Oregon **I:** Government Administration/Government Relations/Government Services **DOB:** 01/10/1957 **PB:** The Dalles **PT:** Son of Paul Walden **ED:** BS in Journalism, University Oregon, Eugene, 1981 **C:** Chairman, House Energy Committee, 2017-; Chairman, National Republican Congressional Committee (NRCC), 2013-; Member, US Congress from 2nd Oregon District, 1999-; Member District 28, assistant majority leader, Oregon State Senate, 1995-97; Majority leader, Oregon House of Reps., 1991-93; Member District 56, Oregon House of Reps., 1989-95; Owner, Columbia Gorge Broadcasters, Inc., Hood River, Oregon, 1986-2007; Chief of staff to Rep. Denny Smith, US House of Reps., 1984-86; Press secretary to Rep. Denny Smith, US House of Reps., 1981-84 **CIV:** Hon. member board advisors, National Student Leadership Foundation, Board directors, Oregon Health Sciences Foundation, Board directors, member executive committee, Association Oregon Industries **AW:** Named a Friend of Farm Bureau, Oregon Farm Bureau, Hero of Taxpayer, Americans for Tax Reform; named Legislator of Year, Safari Club International, Oregon Rural Electric Cooperative Association, Oregon Association Home Care, National Rural Health Association, National Association Home Care, Central Oregon Visitors Association, Agricultural Retailers Association, National Republican Legislators Association, 1993, Outstanding Young Oregonian, Oregon Jaycees, 1991; recipient Golden Bulldog award, Watchdog of Treasury, Spirit of Enterprise award, US Chamber of Commerce, Senior Legis. Achievement award, Seniors Coalition, Appreciation award, Oregon National Guard, Wheat Adv. award, National Association Wheat Growers, Congl. Champion award, National Association Service Conservation Corps, Champion award, League Private Property Owners, Distinguished Service award, Forest Counties Schools Coalition, Thomas Jefferson award, Food Distributors International, Pub. Service award, American College Nurse-Midwives, Benjamin Franklin award, 60+ Association **MEM:** Mem.: National Federation Ind. Business, Hood River Chamber of Commerce, Elks Club, Rotary Club **PA:** Republican

WALES, JIMMY DONAL, T: Wikipedia CEO **I:** Internet **DOB:** 08/07/1966 **PB:** Huntsville **ED:** Attended PhD programs in finance, Ind. University; Attended PhD programs in finance, University of Alabama; Attended, Auburn University **C:** Founder, Wikia, Inc., 2004-; Founder, Wikimedia Foundation, Inc., St. Petersburg, Florida, 2003-; Founder, Wikipedia (Parent orgn.-Wikimedia Foundation, Inc.), 2001-; Board directors, Wikimedia Foundation, Inc., St. Petersburg, Florida,; Chairman, president, Wikimedia Foundation, Inc., St. Petersburg, Florida, 2005; CEO, Bomis, Inc., San Diego, 2000-01; Founder, Nupedia.com, 1999-2000; Futures and options trader, Chicago Options Associates, Chicago,; Faculty member, Ind. University,; Faculty member, University of Alabama **AW:** Named one of The 50 Most Important People on the Web, PC World, 2007, The Top 25 Web Celebs, Forbes magazine, 2006, The 50 Who Matter Now, Business 2.0, 2007, The 100 Most Influential People in the World, TIME magazine, 2006; named to The Internet Hall of Fame, 2013

WALKEN, CHRISTOPHER, T: Actor **I:** Media & Entertainment **PB:** Astoria **SC:** NY/USA **PT:** Paul Walken **ED:** Studied with Wynn Handman, Actors Studio.; Attended Hofstra University **CW:** Stage appearances include Broadway, off-Broadway and regional theatres throughout US and Can.; Broadway debut in J.B. 1959; other stage appearances include Best Foot Forward, West Side Story, Macbeth, The Lion in Winter (Clarence Derwent award 1966), Hamlet, The Rose Tattoo (Theatre World's Most Promising Personality 1966-67); Romeo and Juliet, The Seagull, 2001, The Night Thoreau Spent in Jail (Joseph Jefferson award 1970-71), Kid Champion (Obie award 1975), Miss Julie, Sweet Bird of Youth, Hurlyburly, 1984, Cinders, 1984, A Bill of Divorcement, 1985, Coriolanus, 1988, Othello, 1992, (also playwright) Him, 1995, Mother Courage, 2006, A Beheading in Spokane, 2010; actor: (films) The Anderson Tapes, 1971, Next Stop Greenwich Village, 1976, The Sentinel, 1977, Roseland, 1977, Annie Hall, 1977, The Deer Hunter, 1978 (New York Film Critics Best Supporting Actor award 1978, Academy award for Best Supporting Actor 1979), Last Embrace, 1979, Dogs of War, 1981, Heavens Gate, 1980, Pennies From Heaven, 1981, The Happiness Cage, 1982, The Dead Zone, 1983, Brainstorm, 1983, A View to a Kill, 1984, At Close Range, 1986, Deadline, 1987, Puss in Boots, 1988, The Milagro Beanfield War, 1988, Biloxi Blues, 1988, Communion, 1989, King of New York, 1990, Homeboy, 1991, The Comfort of Strangers, 1991, McBain, 1991, All American Murder, 1992, Batman Returns, 1992, True Romance, 1993, A Business Affair, 1994, Wayne's World II, 1994, Pulp Fiction, 1994, Search and Destroy, 1995, Nick of Time, 1995, The Addiction, 1995, The Prophecy, 1995, The Funeral, 1996, Basquiat, 1996, The Wild Side, 1996, Things To Do in Denver When You're Dead, 1995, Last Man Standing, 1996, Touch, 1997, Mousehunt, 1997, Excess Baggage, 1997, Suicide Kings, 1997, Antz (voice), 1998, Illuminata, 1998, New Rose Hotel, 1998, The Prophecy II, 1998, Trance, 1998, Sleepy Hollow, 1999, Blast From the Past, 1999, Kiss Toledo Goodbye, 1999, Vendetta, 1999, Scotland PA, 2001, Joe Dirt, 2001, America's Sweethearts, 2001, Chelsea Walls, 2001, The Affair of the Necklace, 2001, Jungle Juice, 2001, Poolhall Junkies, 2002, The Country Bears, 2002, Plots

with a View, 2002, Catch Me If You Can, 2002 (Best Actor in Supporting Role, British Academy Film Award (BAFTA) 2003), Kangaroo Jack, 2003, Gigli, 2003, The Rundown, 2003, Man on Fire, 2004, Envy, 2004, The Stepford Wives, 2004, Around the Bend, 2004, Wedding Crashers, 2005, Domino, 2005, Click, 2006, Man of the Year, 2006, Hairspray, 2007, Balls of Fury, 2007, Evils Calls (voice), 2008, $5 a Day, 2008, The Maiden Heist, 2009, Life's a Beach, 2010, Kill the Irishman, 2011, Dark Horse, 2011, A Late Quartet, 2012, Seven Psychopaths, 2012, Stand Up Guys, 2012, The Power of Few, 2013, Gods Behaving Badly, 2013, Jersey Boys, 2014, One More Time, 2015, The Family Fang, 2015, Eddie the Eagle, 2016, The Jungle Book (voice), 2016, Nine Lives, 2016, Father Figures, 2017, The War with Grandpa, 2018, Irreplaceable You, 2018; (TV films) Sarah, Plain and Tall, 1991, Skylark, 1993, Scam, 1993; The Opportunists, 1999, The Prophecy III: The Ascent, 1999, Sarah, Plain and Tall: 3, 1999, Julius Caesar, 2002, Turks & Caicos, 2014, Peter Pan Live!, 2014; (TV series) Saturday Night Live (Am. Comedy award 2001), Naked City, 1958, Hawaii Five-O, 1968, Kojak, 1973; (TV mini-series) Julius Caesar, 2002, Peter Pan Live, 2014; **AW:** Recipient Man of the Year, Hasty Pudding Theatrical Society, 2008, Best Supporting Male Performance (True Crime: New York City), Spike TV Video Game awards, 2005

WALKER, BILL, T: Governor of Alaska, Lawyer **I:** Law and Legal Services **DOB:** 04/16/1951 **PB:** Fairbanks **SC:** AK/USA **PT:** Ed Walker; Frances Walker **ED:** JD, University of Puget Sound School of Law (1983); BA in Business Administration, Lewis & Clark College (1973) **C:** Governor, State of Alaska, Juneau, AK (2014-Present); Attorney, Owner, Walker Richards LLC (1995-Present); Governor-elect, State of Alaska, Juneau, AK (2014); Attorney, Hughes, Thorsness, Gantz, Powell, & Brundin (1983-1995); Mayor, City of Valdez, Alaska (1979-1980); Councilman, City of Valdez, Alaska (1978-1980); Owner, Bill Walker Construction Co., Valdez, AK (1975-1980); Trans Alaskan Pipeline Construction Worker (1970-1974); Commercial Fisherman (1969); General Counsel, Alaska Gasline Port Authority **CR:** President, Prince William Sound Regional Citizens Advisory Council (1989-2001) **CIV:** Youth Basketball & Soccer Coach, YMCA (1992-1994) **MEM:** Lifetime Member, National Rifle Association **H:** Skiing; Fishing **PA:** Independent

WALKER, DARREN, T: Foundation Administrator **I:** Nonprofit & Philanthropy **PB:** Lafayette **ED:** JD, University Texas School Law, 1986; BA, University Texas, Austin, 1982 **C:** President, Ford Foundation, New York City, 2013-; Vice president for education, creativity & free expression, Ford Foundation, New York City, 2010-13; Vice president for foundation initiatives, Rockefeller Foundation, New York City, 2002-10; Full time vol., The Children's Storefront,; With capital markets division, UBS, 1988-95; COO, Abyssinian Development Corp.,; Associate, Cleary, Gottlieb, Steen & Hamilton, 1986-88 **CR:** Board member Foundation for Arts & Preservation in Embassies, New York City Ballet, Friends of the High Line, Rockefeller Philanthropy Advisors, Arcus Foundation **MEM:** Mem.: Council Foreign Relations

WALKER, GEORGE THEOPHILUS, T: Professor Emeritus **I:** Education/Educational Services **DOB:** 06/27/1922 **PT:** Son of George Theophilus Senior and Rosa (King) W.; **CH:** Gregory, Ian **ED:** DFA (hon.), Spelman College, 2001; MusD (hon.), Bloomfield College, 1997; DHL (hon.), Montclair State University, 1997; MusD (hon.), Curtis Institute Music, 1997; Student of, Nadia

Boulanger; MusD (hon.), Oberlin College, 1983; DFA (hon.), Lafayette College, 1982; Doctor of Museum Arts, University of Rochester, 1957; Artist Diploma, Curtis Institute music, 1945; Student of, Rudolf Serkin, Rosario Scalero; MusB, Oberlin College, 1941 **C:** Professor Emeritus, Rutgers University, Newark, 1992; Distinguished Professor, Rutgers University, Newark, 1976-92; Associate Professor, University Colorado, Boulder, 1968-69; Instructor to Associate Professor, Smith College, Northampton, Massachusetts, 1961-68; Instructor, New School Social Research, New York City, 1961; Instructor, Dalcroze School Music, New York City, 1960-61; Instructor, Dillard University, New Orleans, 1953-54 **CR:** Concert Pianist National Concert Artists, New York City, 1950-53, Columbia Artists, New York City, 1959-60 Adjunct Professor Peabody Institute Johns Hopkins University, Baltimore, 1975-78 Distinguished Professor University Del., Newark, 1975-76 **CIV:** Board of Directors Am. Bach Foundation, 1988 Member Mary Flagler Cary Trust Commission, 1998. **CW:** Composer: Sonata for 2 Pianos (Harvey Gaul Prize 1963), Numerous Sonatas, Cantatas and Concertos, Concerto for Cello and Orchestra, 1982, Sinfonias for Orchestra (Autobiography) Reminiscences of an American Composer and Pianist, 2009 **AW:** Recipient Award Am. Academy and Institute Arts and Letter, 1982, Koussevitsky Award, 1988, Pulitzer Prize, 1996, L.J. Governors Award 1997, Koussevitsky Award 1998, Mary Flagler Cary Charitable Trust Award, 1998, Dorothy Maynor Arts Citizens Award, 2000, A.I. duPont Award Del. Symphony, 2001, Classical Roots Lifetime Achievement Award Detroit Symphony, 2001, Foils for Orchestra Award, Eastman Commission, 2006, Legacy Award, National Opera Association, 2007; Grantee Smith College, University Colorado, Rutger University Research Council, National Education Association, New Jersey State Council for Arts; Fulbright Fellow, 1957, John Hay Whitney Fellow, 1958, Guggenheim Fellow, 1969, 88, Rockefeller Fellow, 1971, 74; Distinguished Scholar University Rochester, 1996; Commissioned New York Philharmonic, Kennedy Center, Cleveland Orchestra, Boston Symphony, New Jersey Symphony, Am. Guild of Organists; Inducted Am. Classical Music Hall of Fame, 2000 **MEM:** Member American Society of Composers, Am. Academy Arts and Letters (Mem.-elect), Am. Bach Foundation (Board of Directors 1988), Am. Symphony League. **BA:** 323 Grove St, Montclair, NJ, 07042

WALKER, MARK HOWARD, T: U.S. House Representative, Pastor **I:** Government Administration/ Government Relations/Government Services **CN:** State of North Carolina **DOB:** 05/20/1969 **PB:** Dothan **SC:** AL/USA **ED:** BA in Biblical Studies, Piedmont Baptist College (Now Piedmont International University) (1999); Coursework, Trinity Baptist College **C:** Member, U.S. Congress from the Sixth North Carolina District, Washington, DC (2015-Present); With, Flow Automotive, North Carolina (1991-1996); Pastor Worship and Music, Lawndale Baptist Church, Greensboro, NC; Pastor, Calvary Baptist Church, Winston-Salem, NC **CIV:** Member, War Memorial Commission, Greensboro City Council, North Carolina (2012-Present) **PA:** Republican

WALKER, SCOTT KEVIN, T: Governor of Wisconsin **I:** Government Administration/Government Relations/Government Services **DOB:** 11/02/1967 **PB:** Colorado Springs **SC:** CO/USA **PT:** Son of Llewellyn Scott and Patricia Ann (Fitch) Walker **ED:** Student, Marquette University, 1990 **C:** Governor, State of Wisconsin, Madison, 2011-; Milwaukee County Executive, City of Milwaukee, Wisconsin, 2002-10; Chairman, Corrections Committee, Wisconsin State Assembly, 1997; Chairman, Committee on Elections and Constitutional Law, Wisconsin State Assembly, 1995; Assemblyman, District 14, Wisconsin State Assembly, 1993-2002; Chairman, 5th Congressional District, Wisconsin State Republican Party, 1991-93; Accountant Administrator, IBM Corp., 1988-90 **CR:** Candidate for the 2016 Republican Party Presidential Nomination; Member, Executive Committee, Wisconsin State Republican Party, 1991- **CIV:** Council Member, Milwaukee County Boy Scouts America, Financial Development Specialist, American Red Cross, 1990-93 **AW:** Named One of The 100 Most Influential People in the World, TIME magazine, 2014 **MEM:** Mem.: Wauwatosa Area Chamber of Commerce, Wauwatosa Historical Society **PA:** Republican

WALLACE, CHRISTOPHER, T: Broadcast Journalist **I:** Media & Entertainment **DOB:** 10/12/1947 **PB:** Chgo. **PT:** Son of Mike and Norma (Kaphan) Wallace, Bill Leonard (Stepfather); **ED:** BA, Harvard University, 1969 **C:** Host FOX News Sunday with Chris Wallace,, FOX News Channel, Washington, 2003-; Substitute host Nightline, ABC News,; Chief corr. 20/20, ABC News, Washington, 1998-2003; Senior corr. Primetime Thursday,, ABC News, 1989-98; Anchor Meet the Press, NBC News, 1987-88; Chief White House corr., NBC News, 1982-89; Anchor Sunday edition NBC Nightly News, NBC News, 1986-87; Anchor Sunday edition NBC Nightly News, NBC News, 1982-84; Washington co-anchor The Today Show, NBC News, 1982; Political reporter, NBC News, Washington, 1978-81; Investigative reporter, NBC News, New York City, 1975-78; Political reporter, Station WBBM-TV, Chicago, 1973-75; National reporter, Boston Globe, 1969-73 **CR:** Covered presidential campaigns and Democratic and Republican conventions, 1988, 1984, 1980 **AW:** Recipient Dupont-Columbia Silver Baton award, Paul White award, Radio, TV Digital News Association, 2013, Sol Taishoff award for Excellence in Broadcast Journalism, 2011, George Polk award, 1992, Emmy award, 1990, 1981, Overseas Press Club award, 1981, George Foster Peabody award, 1978, Founders Award for Excellence in Journalism

WALORSKI, JACKIE, T: U.S. Representative From Indiana **I:** Government Administration/Government Relations/Government Services **DOB:** 08/17/1963 **PB:** South Bend **SC:** IN/USA **ED:** BA in Communications & Public Administration, Taylor University, 1985, Student, Liberty Baptist College, 1981-1983 **C:** U.S. House Veterans' Affairs Committee, 2013-Present; U.S. House Budget Committee, 2013-Present; U.S. House Armed Services Committee, 2013-Present; U.S. Congress from Second Indiana District, Washington, DC, 2013-Present; District 21, Indiana House of Representatives, 2004-2010; Missionary, Romania, 1999-2004; Director of Development, Indiana University, South Bend, IN, 1997-1999; Director of Membership, St. Joseph City Chamber of Commerce, 1996-1997; Director of Institutional Advancement, Ancilla College, 1991-1996; Executive Director, Humane Society, St. Joseph City, 1989-1991; TV Reporter, WSBT-TV, 1985-1989 **CR:** Founder, Impact International, 2000 **PA:** Republican **BA:** 419 Cannon House Office Building, Washington, DC, 20515

WALTERS, MIMI, T: U.S. Representative from California **I:** Government Administration/Government Relations/Government Services **ED:** BA in Political Sci., UCLA, 1984 **C:** Member, US House of Representatives, California's 45th District, 2015-;; Member, Committee on Appropriations, Committee on the Budget; Member District 33, California State Senate, 2009-2015; Member

appropriations committee, judiciary committee, business, professions and economic devel. committee, California State Senate,; Vice chair revenue and taxation committee, California State Senate,; Vice chair elections, reapportionment and constitutional amendments committee, California State Senate,; Chair legis. ethics committee, California State Senate,; Member District 73, California State Assembly, 2004-08; Staff, Kidder Peabody & Co., **PA:** Republican **BA:** Ste 230, 3333 Michelson Dr, Irvine, CA, 92612-8803

WALTRIP, DARRELL LEE, T: Former Professional Racing Driver **I:** Athletics **DOB:** 02/05/1947 **PB:** Owensboro **PT:** Son of Leroy and Margaret Jean (Evans) Waltrip; **ED:** Student, Kentucky Wesleyan College **C:** Owner, Darrell Waltrip Honda Volvo, 1994-; Driver for, Rick Hendrick Motor Sports,; Driver for, Junior Johnson & Associates, **CW:** Author ((with Jade Gurss)): DW: A Lifetime Going Around in Circles, 2004; (with Jay Carty) Darrell Waltrip: One on One: The Faith That Took Him to the Finish Line, 2004; actor(voice): (films) Cars, 2006, Talladega Nights: The Ballad of Ricky Bobby, 2006 **AW:** Named winner, Champion Spark Plug 500, 1991, Daytona 500, 1989, Motorcraft 500, 1989, Goody's 500, 1989, 1988, 1987, Holly Farms 400, 1986, Budweiser 400, 1986, Bisch 500, 1986, Wrangler 500, 1985, Coca Cola 600, 1989, 1988, 1985, Winston Cup Championship, 1985, 1982, 1981, National Association Stock Car Auto Racing Championship, 1985, Winston Cup, 1982, Olsonite Driver of Year, 1979, Driver of Year, National Motorsports Press Association, 1977, Winston Cup Most Popular Driver, 1989-90, Nascar's 50 Greatest Drivers, 1998, International Motorsports Hall of Fame, 2005, Motorsports Hall of Fame of America, 2003, Nascar Hall of Fame, 2012, Fairgrounds Speedway Hall of Fame, 2001 **MEM:** Mem.: National Association Stock Car Auto Racing **ACH:** Achievements include being the top motor sport money winner worldwide with more than 7.5 million dollars **PA:** Republican

WALTZ, CHRISTOPH, T: Actor **I:** Media & Entertainment **PB:** Vienna **SC:** Austria **PT:** Johannes Waltz; Elisabeth Urbancic **CW:** Actor: (TV films) Der Einstand, 1977, Feuer!, 1979, Dr. Margarete Johnsohn, 1982, The Mysterious Stranger, 1982, Der Sandmann, 1983, Das andere Leben, 1987, The Alien Years, 1988, Goldeneye, 1989, Die Angst wird bleiben, 1992, Judgement Day, 1994, Jacob, 1994, Man, 1995, Catherine the Great, 1995, The Tourist, 1996, Einsteins Ende, 1998, Lautlose Jagd, 1998, Vickys Alptraum, 1998, The Final Game, 1998, The Beast, 2000, Riekes Liebe, 2001, Der Flammenmann, 2003, Jennerwein, 2003, Scheidungsopfer Mann, 2004, Die Verzauberung, 2007, Das Geheimnis, 2008, Todsunde, 2008, Das Jungste Gericht, 2008, Die Anwalte, 2008, Tatort, 2008, SNL 2013; (TV series) Parole Chicago, 1979, The Gravy Train, 1990, The Gravy Train Goes East, 1991; (films) Tristan and Isolde, 1982, Wahnfried, 1986, Quicker Than the Eye, 1989, St. Petri Schnee, 1991, Night Time, 1998, Love Scenes From Planet Earth, 1998, Die Braut, 1999, Queen's Messenger, 2000, Ordinary Decent Criminal, 2000, Falling Rocks, 2000, Dorian, 2001, She, 2001, Death, Deceit & Destiny Aboard the Orient Express, 2001, Angst, 2003, Gun-Shy, 2003, Berlin Blues, 2003, Inglourious Basterds, 2009 (Boston Society Film Critics award for Best Supporting Actor, 2009, New York Film Critics Cir. award for Best Supporting Actor, 2009, National Society Film Critics award for Best Supporting Actor, 2010, Golden Globe award for Best Performance by a Actor in a Supporting Role in a Motion Picture, 2010, Screen Actors Guild award for Outstanding Performance by a Male Actor in a Supporting Role, 2010, BAFTA award

for Best Supporting Actor, 2010, Academy award for Best Actor in a Supporting Role, 2010), Water for Elephants, 2011, The Green Hornet, 2011, The Three Musketeers, 2011, Carnage, 2011, Django Unchained, 2012 (Golden Globe award for Best Performance by a Actor in a Supporting Role in a Motion Picture, 2013, BAFTA award for Best Supporting Actor, 2013, Academy award for Best Actor in a Supporting Role, 2013), Epic (voice), 2013, Muppets Most Wanted, 2014, Horrible Bosses 2, 2014, Big Eyes, 2014, Spectre, 2015, The Legend of Tarzan, 2016, Tulip Fever, 2017, Downsizing, 2017, Alita: Battle Angel, 2018, Georgetown, 2018; actor, co-prodr. (films) The Zero Theorem, 2013

WALZ, TIM, T: U.S. Representative from Minnesota **I:** Government Administration/Government Relations/Government Services **DOB:** 04/06/1964 **PB:** West Point **SC:** NE/USA **ED:** MS in Education Leadership, St. Mary's University, Winona, Minnesota, 2001; BS in Social Sci. Education, Chadron State College, Nebraska, 1989 **C:** Member, House Committee on Veterans Affairs, 2007-; Member, US Congress from 1st District Minnesota, 2007-; Teacher, Mankato West High School, Mankato, Minnesota, 1996-2006; Teacher, Alliance Pub. Schools, 1991-96; High school teacher, People's Rep. China, 1989-90 **MIL:** Advanced to Sergeant Major US Army National Guard, 1981-2005, served in Operation Enduring Freedom, 2005 **AW:** Named Minnesota Teacher of Excellence, 2003, Mankato Teacher of Year, 2003, Outstanding Young Nebraskan, Nebraska Junior C. of C., 1993, Neb. Citizen Soldier of Year, 1989; recipient Minnesota Ethics in Education award, 2002 **PA:** Dfl **BA:** Office of Tim Walz, 2313 Rayburn House Office Building, Washington, DC, 20515

WAMBACH, ABBY, T: Retired Professional Soccer Player **I:** Athletics **DOB:** 06/02/1980 **PB:** Rochester **PT:** Daughter of Pete and Judy Wambach; **ED:** Attended, University Florida, Gainesville, 1998-2001 **C:** Forward, head coach, magicJack, Women's Professional Soccer, Boca Raton, Florida, 2011; Forward, Western New York Flash, Women's Professional Soccer, 2013-14; Forward, Washington Freedom, Women's Professional Soccer, 2009-10; Forward, Washington Freedom, Women's United Soccer Association, 2002-03 **CR:** Member US national team Summer Olympic Games, London, 2012, Athens, Greece, 2004, FIFA Women's World Cup, Montreal, 2015, Germany, 2011, China, 2007, U.S., 2003 **CIV:** Ambassador, Athlete Ally, 2013- Devel. champion, US Agency for International Devel. (USAID), 2012- **AW:** Named FIFA Women's Player of Year, 2012, Female Athlete of Year, Associated Press, 2011, US Soccer Federation, 2011, 2010, 2007, 2004, 2003, Founders Cup Champions MVP, 2003, Rookie of Year, Women's United Soccer Association, 2002, All-Star Game MVP, 2002, Southeastern Conference Player of Year, 2001, 2000, 1st Team NCAA All-American, 1999-2001, Southeastern Conference Freshman of Year, 1998; named to University Florida Athletic Hall of Fame, 2012, All-Star Team, Women's Professional Soccer, 2010, 2009, Women's United Soccer Association, 2003, 2002-03; recipient Gold medal, women's soccer, Summer Olympic Games, 2012, 2004 **ACH:** Achievements include member of NCAA Division I national championship winning University of Florida Gators, 1998; member of Women's United Soccer Association's Founders Cup championship winning Washington Freedom, 2003; being a member of the FIFA Women's World Cup champion Team USA, 2015

WANG, ALEXANDER, T: Apparel Designer **I:** Apparel & Fashion **DOB:** 12/26/1983 **PB:** San Francisco **SC:** CA/USA **ED:** Attended, Parsons Design School, New York City **C:** Designer, jewellery line, 2009-; Launched collection for H&M, 2014; Creative director, Balenciaga, 2012-15; Product lines is sold in retailers including Barneys New York, Neiman Marcus, Bergdorf Goodman, Dover Street Market, Browns, Otte and Selfridges,; Launched a footwear line of platform sandals, 2009; Launched line of pre-weathered cotton tees, tanks, and T-shirts dresses, T by Alexander Wang, 2009; Designer, Alexander Wang collection, New York City,; Launched, Alexander Wang womens collection, 2007 **AW:** Nominee Swarovski Womens Wear Designer of Year, Council Fashion Designers of America, 2008; named one of The 100 Most Influential People of 2015, TIME magazine; recipient Swiss Textiles award, 2009, Accessory Designer of Year award, Council Fashion Designers of America, 2011, Swarovski award for Accessory Design, 2010, Emerging Talent award for Womenswear, 2009, Fashion Fund award, 2008 **ADD:** Balenciaga, 40 Rue du Cherche-Midi, Paris, YT, France, 75008

WANG, LISA, T: CEO, Co-Founder, Rhythmic Gymnast **I:** Business Management/Business Services **CN:** SheWorx **DOB:** 09/24/1988 **PB:** Madison **SC:** WI/USA **ED:** Advanced Chinese, Tsinghua University, 2013; BA in American Studies, Yale University, 2012 **C:** CEO, Co-Founder, SheWorx, 2015-Present; Contributing Writer, Forbes, 2017-Present; Entrepreneur Insider, Fortune Magazine, 2016-2017 **CR:** Founder, Fooze, 2015; Hedge Fund Analyst, Wall Street, New York, NY **CW:** Appearance, (Book) Fat Envelope Frenzy, (TV Commercials), Women in Control, Water Company, Netherlands, 2007 **AW:** USA Gymnastics Hall of Fame, 2014, All-Around Title, Athlete of the Year, Five Gold Medals, National Championship, Houston, TX, 2008, All-Around Pan American Games Champion, Rio de Janeiro, Brazil, 2007, Three-Time Senior U.S. National Champion, 2006-2008, First Place All-Around Champion, Leader of First Place U.S. Team, Pacific Alliance Championships, Vancouver, BC, Canada, 2002, Forbes 30 Under 30

WANG, VERA, T: Fashion Designer **I:** Apparel & Fashion **DOB:** 06/27/1949 **PB:** New York **SC:** NY/USA **ED:** BA in Art Hist., Sarah Lawrence College, Bronxville, New York, 1978 **C:** Principal, Vera Wang Bridal House Ltd., New York City, 1990-; Opened first Asian flagship store, Vera Wang Bridal Korea, Seoul, 2012; Expanded to ready-to-wear, fragrance, eyewear, footwear, fine jewelry and home collection, The Vera Wang China and Crystal Collection, Vera Wang Bridal House Ltd.,; Design director, Ralph Lauren Women's Wear, New York City, 1987-89; Various positions including accessories editor, European editor and senior fashion editor Vogue magazine, Condé Nast Pubs., New York City, 1969-85 **CR:** Designer budget label 'Simply Vera' sold exclusively by Kohl's, uniforms currently worn by Philadelphia Eagles cheerleaders, for Olympic figure skaters Nancy Kerrigan and Michelle Kwan **CW:** Author: Vera Wang on Weddings, 2001; costume designer (films) The Parent Trap, 1998, First Daughter, 2004, Sex and the City, 2008, Bride Wars, 2009, TV appearances include Project Runway, 2006, Ugly Betty, 2007, The Apprentice, 2008, Gossip Girl, 2012 **AW:** Named one of The 100 Most Powerful Women, Forbes magazine, 2010; named to US Figure Skating Hall of Fame, 2009; recipient Leadership in the Arts award, Harvard-Radcliffe Asian American Association, 2010, Hall of Fame award, FiFi Awards, 2008, André Leon Talley Lifetime Achievement award, Savannah College Art & Design., 2006, Geoffrey Beene Lifetime Achievement award, Council Fashion Designers of America, 2013, Womenswear Designer of Year award, 2005 **ACH:** Achievements include first in industry to successfully fuse high style and fashion with the tradition and symbolism of the bridal industry; designing wedding and red carpet gowns for Hollywood's elite

WARD, JESMYN, T: Writer, Educator **I:** Writing and Editing **ED:** MFA in Fiction, University of Michigan, 2005; Master's in Media Studies and Communication, Stanford University; Degree in English, Stanford University **C:** Assistant professor creative writing, University of South Alabama, 2011-; John and Renee Grisham Visiting Writer-In-Residence, University Mississippi, 2010-11 **CW:** Author: (novels) Where the Line Bleeds, 2008 (Black Caucus of the American Libr. Association Honor award, Essence Magazine Book Club Selection), Salvage the Bones, 2011 (National Book award (Fiction) Men We Reaped, 2013, (National Book Critics Award 2013) The Fire This Time, 2016, Sing, Unburied, Sing, 2017 (National Book Award 2017), National Book Foundation, 2011, (Oprah.com selected as Book of the Week, 2011), (short stories) Barefoot, 2011 **AW:** Finalist Hurston/Wright Legacy award, Virginia Commonwealth University Cabell First Novelist award; Wallace Stegner Fellow, Stanford University, 2008-10; Time 100 Most Influential, 2018 **BA:** University of South Alabama, HUMB 259, Mobile, AL, 36688

WARDLAW, KIM A. MCLANE, T: Federal Judge **I:** Law and Legal Services **DOB:** 07/02/1954 **PB:** San Francisco **SC:** California **ED:** JD With Honors, UCLA, 1979; AB in Communications Summa Cum Laude, UCLA, 1976; Student, Foothill C.C., Los Altos Hills, California, 1973-74; Student, Santa Clara University, 1972-73 **CT:** Bar: US Supreme Court, US District Court (so. district) Mississippi 1995, US District Court (no. district) Alabama 1994, US District Court Minnesota 1994, US District Court Montana 1993, US District Court (no. district) California 1992, US District Court Nevada 1985, US District Court (so. district) California 1982, US District Court (central district) California 1979, California **C:** Judge, US Court Appeals (9th cir.), 1998-; Judge, US District Court California, LA, 1995-98; Partner, O'Melveny and Myers, 1987-95; Associate O'Melveny and Myers, 1980-87; Law clerk, US District Court Central District California, 1979-80 **CR:** Consultant in Field Vice-Chair UCLA Center for Communications Policy, 1994-, Board Governors, 1994- Mayoral Transition Team City of LA, 1995- Presidential Transition Team Department Justice, Washington, 1993 **CIV:** Active, Blue Ribbon of LA Music Center, 1993- Active Legal Defense and Education Fund, California Leadership Council, 1993- Founding member, LA Chamber Orchestra, 1992- President, Women Lawyers Pub. Action Grant Foundation, 1986-87 Del., Dem. National Convention, 1992 **CW:** Co-author: The Encyclopedia of the American Constitution, 1986; Contributor Articles to Professional Journals **AW:** Named one of Most Prominent Business Attorneys in LA County, LA Business Journal, 1995; Recipient Buddy award, National Organization of Women, 1995 **MEM:** Mem.: National Organization of Women, American Bar Association, Organization Women Executives, Association Business Trial Lawyers (governor 1988-), LA County Bar Association (trustee 1993-94), Women Lawyers Association LA, California Women Lawyers, Mex.-Am. Bar Association LA County, Hollywood Womens Political Committee, Downtown Women Partners, City Club Bunker Hill, Breakfast Club, Chancery Club, Phi Beta Kappa **BA:** 95 7th St, San Francisco, CA, 94103

WARNER, MARK ROBERT, T: Vice Chair of the Senate Intelligence **I:** Government Administration/Government Relations/Government Services **DOB:** 12/15/1954 **PB:** Indianapolis **SC:** IN/USA **PT:** Son of Robert and Margaret Warner; **ED:** JD, Harvard Law School, 1980; BA, The George Washington University, 1977 **C:** Vice Chair, Senate Democratic Caucus, 2017-,; Ranking Member, Senate Intelligence Committee, 2017-,; Policy development adv., Democratic Policy & Communications Center, 2015-; U.S. Senator from Virginia, 2009-; Governor, State of Virginia, Richmond, 2001-06; Founding partner, Columbia Capital Corp., Alexandria, Virginia, 1989 **CR:** Chairman Southern Tech. Council, Education Commission of the States, National Governors Association, 2004-05 member Democratic National Committee, 1993-95 chairman Virginia State Democratic Party, 1993-95 **CIV:** Co-chmn., Virginia Communities in Schools Foundation, Founder, Virginia High-Tech Partnership, Founder, TechRiders, Creator, SeniorNavigator.com, Founding chairman, Virginia Health Care Foundation, Member, Old Presbyterian Meeting House, Past board directors, Virginia Math and Sci. Coalition, Past board directors, Virginia Foundation for Ind. Colleges, Past board directors, Appalachian School Law, Past board directors, George Washington University, Past board directors, Virginia Union University, **MEM:** Mem.: Southern Governors Association (1st vice chairman), Dem. Governors Association (recruitment chairman) **PA:** Democrat **BA:** Office of Mark Warner, 703 Hart Senate Office Building, Washington, DC, 20510

WARREN, ELIZABETH, T: U.S. Senator from Massachusetts **I:** Government Administration/Government Relations/Government Services **DOB:** 06/22/1949 **PB:** Norman **SC:** OK/USA **ED:** BS, University of Houston, 1970; JD, Rutgers University, New Jersey, 1976 **CT:** Bar: New Jersey, Texas; **C:** Vice Chair, Senate Democratic Caucus, 2017-; Member, U.S. Senate Special Committee on Aging, 2013—; Professor Law, University Pennsylvania Law School, Philadelphia, Pennsylvania, 1987—1990; Jay H. Brown Centennial Fellow in Law, University Texas School Law, 1986—1987; Conoco Faculty Fellow in Law, University Texas School Law, 1985—1986; Professor Law, University Texas School Law, 1983—1987; Research Associate Population Research Center,, University Texas, Austin, 1983—1987; Associate Professor of Law, University Houston Law Center, 1981—1983; Associate Dean Academic Affairs, University Houston Law Center, 1980—1981; Assistant Professor Law, University Houston Law Center, 1978—1980; Lecturer, Rutgers School Law, Newark, New Jersey, 1977—1978; Member, U.S. Senate Health, Education, Labor & Pensions Committee, 2013—; Member, U.S. Senate Banking, Housing & Urban Affairs Committee, 2013—; U.S. Senator from Massachusetts, Washington, DC, 2013—; Leo Gottlieb Professor Law, Harvard Law School, Cambridge, Massachusetts, 1995—; Special Adv. to Secretary, US Department Treasury, Washington, DC, 2010—2011; Assistant to President, The White House, Washington, DC, 2010—2011; Chair, Congressional Oversight Panel Overseeing Troubled Asset Relief Program (TARP), Washington, DC, 2008—2010; William A. Schnader Professor Commercial Law, University Pennsylvania Law School, Philadelphia, Pennsylvania, 1990—1995 **CR:** Visiting Associate Professor law University Texas School Law, 1981—1982; Visiting Professor Law University Michigan, 1985; Robert Braucher Visiting Professor Commercial Law Harvard University, 1992—1993; Proposal Reviewer National Science Foundation, 1985—; Board of Editors American Bankruptcy Law Journal, 1989—1992; Editorial Adv. Board Little Brown & Co. Law School Division (now

Aspen Press), 1990—; Committee on Judicial Education Federal Judicial Center, 1990—1999; Board of Trustees American Bankruptcy Board Certification, 1992—1996; Member Executive Committee National Bankruptcy Conference, 1993—1995, 2002—2005; Advisor German Government Task Force on Bankruptcy Reform, 1993; Reporter, Consultant, Senior Advisor National Bankruptcy Rev. Commission, 1995—1997; Honorary Co-chmn. Massachusetts Wisconsin Victory Fund, 2011—2012 **CW:** Co-author: As We Forgive Our Debtors: Consumer Credit and Bankruptcy in America, 1989 (Silver Gavel Award, American Bar Association, 1990), The Law of Debtors and Creditors, 1991, Secured Transactions: A Systems Approach, 1995, Commercial Law: A Systems Approach, 1998, The Fragile Middle Class: Americans in Debt, 2000 (Scholarship Award, American College Consumer Fin. Services Lawyers, 2000); Co-author: (with Amelia Warren Tyagi) The Two-Income Trap: Why Middle-Class Mothers and Fathers Are Going Broke, 2003, All Your Worth: The Ultimate Lifetime Money Plan, 2005; author: A Fighting Chance, 2014 **AW:** Named Bostonian of Year, The Boston Globe, 2009; Named The 100 Most Powerful Women, Forbes magazine, 2010; Named One of The 50 Most Influential Women Lawyers in America, The National Law Journal, 1998, 2007, The Decade's Most Influential Lawyers, 2010, The 100 Most Influential People in the World, TIME Magazine, 2009, 2010, The 50 Most Powerful People in DC, GQ Magazine, 2009, The 10 Most Powerful Women in Washington, Fortune Magazine, 2010, The 50 Most Influential People in Global Finance, Bloomberg Markets, 2011; Named to Who's Who in DC, Crain's New York Business, 2009; Recipient Outstanding Teacher Award, University Houston Law Center, 1981, Frankel Publication Award for Outstanding Writing, 1982, L. Hart Wright Teaching Excellence Award, University Michigan School Law, 1986, Harvey Levin Award for Excellence in Teaching, University Pennsylvania School Law, 1989, 1992, Lindback Award for Distinguished Teaching, University Pennsylvania, 1994, Albert A. Sacks-Paul A. Freund Award for Teaching Excellence, Harvard Law School, 1997, 2009, Commedation for Service, American Bankruptcy Board Certification, 1998, Brown Award for Judicial Scholarship & Education, Federal Judicial Center, 1998, Champion of Consumer Rights Award, National Association Consumer Bankruptcy Attorneys, 2000, Excellence in Education Award, National Conference Bankruptcy Judges, 2001, Lawrence P. King Award, Commercial Law League America, 2002 **MEM:** Fellow: American Association for the Advancement of Science, American College Bankruptcy (Commendation for Outstanding Pub. Service 1998); Mem.: Women's Bar Assn Massachusetts (Leila J. Robinson Award 2009) Association American Law Schools (Chair Commercial and Related Consumer Law Section 1983—84, Chair Commercial Law Workshop 1984, Planning Committee Conference on Teaching Contract Law 1989, Professional Devel. Committee 1988—91, Chair Debtor-creditor Section 1989—90, Chair Legislation Committee Debtor-creditor Section 1990—93), American Law Institute (Executive Committee Council 1994—95, US Adviser, Transnat. Insolvency Project 1995—, Member Nominating Committee 1995—, Executive Committee Council 1998—, 2nd Vice President Council 2000—04) **PA:** Democrat **BA:** Office of Elizabeth Warren, US Senate 317 Hart Senate Office Building, Washington D.C., DC, 20510

WARREN, RICK, T: Pastor **I:** Religious **DOB:** 01/28/1954 **PB:** San Jose **SC:** CA/USA **PT:** Son of James Russell and Dorothy Nell (Armstrong) Warren; **ED:** Doctor in Ministry, Fuller Theological Seminary, 1989; MDiv, Southwestern Baptist Theological Seminary, 1979; BA, California Baptist College, 1977 **C:** Founding pastor, Saddleback Church, Lake Forest, California, 1980-; Founder, pastors.com,; Founder, Purpose Driven Network,; Assistant to president, International Evangelism Association, Fort Worth, 1977-79; Associate pastor, First Baptist Church, Norwalk, California, 1974-76; Youth evangelist, California Southern Baptist Convention, Fresno, 1970-74 **CR:** Keynote speaker Martin Luther King, Junior Ann. Commemorative Service, 2009 host Civil Forum on the Presidency, Lake Forest, California, 2008 **CW:** Author: The Purpose-Driven Church, 1995, Personal Bible Study Methods, 1997, The Power to Change Your Life, 1998, Answers to Life's Difficult Questions, 1999, Planned for God's Pleasure, 2002, The Purpose-Driven Life, 2002 (Gold Medallion award, ECPA Book of Year, 2003), The Emerging Church, 2003, Daily Inspiration for the Purpose-Driven Life, 2004; co-author: The Daniel Plan: 40 Days to a Healthier Life, 2014 **AW:** Named an Outstanding Preacher, McGregor Foundation, 1977; named one of 15 People Who Make America Great, Newsweek, 2006, America's Top 25 Leaders, US News & World Report, 2005, The World's Most Influential People, TIME magazine, 2009, 2008, 2005, 15 World Leaders Who Mattered Most in 2004

WARSHEL, ARIEH, T: Chemistry Professor **I:** Education/Educational Services **DOB:** 11/20/1940 **PB:** Kibbutz Sde Nahum **SC:** Israel **ED:** PhD in Chemical Physics, The Weizmann Institute of Sci., 1969; MS in Chemical Physics, The Weizmann Institute of Sci., 1967; BS Summa Cum Laude in Chemistry, The Technion, Israel Institute of Technology, Haifa, 1966 **C:** Distinguished professor chemistry & biochemistry, University of Southern California, 2011-; Associate professor, The Weizmann Institute of Sci., Rehovot, Israel, 1977-78; Professor chemistry & biochemistry, University of Southern California, 1991; Professor, University of Southern California, 1984; Associate professor, University of Southern California, 1979-84; Assistant professor chemistry, University of Southern California, 1976-78; Visiting scientist, MRC Laboratory of Molecular Biology, Cambridge, England, 1974-76; Senior scientist, The Weizmann Institute of Sci., Rehovot, Israel, 1973-77; Research associate, The Weizmann Institute of Sci., Rehovot, Israel, 1972-73; Research fellow Department Chemistry, Harvard University, Cambridge, Massachusetts, 1970-72 **CR:** Full member University of Southern California Cancer Center, 2004- visiting professor Royal Institute of Technology, 2006 **CW:** Author: Computer Simulation of Chemical Reactions in Enzymes and Solutions, 1991 (University Southern California Faculty Recognition award, 1992); co-editor (with G. Naray-Szabo): Computational Approaches to Biochemical Reactivity, 1997 **AW:** Co-recipient Nobel Prize in Chemistry, Royal Swedish Academy Sciences, 2013; recipient Tolman Medal, 2003, President's Award for Computational Biology, International Society Quantum Biology & Pharmacology, 2006, Annual Award, 1993, Associate's award for Creativity in Research, University Southern California, 1981, Mifal-Hapays prize, 1969, Technion award, 1965; EMBO senior fellowship, The Weizmann Institute of Sci., 1981-82, Alfred P. Sloan Fellow, 1978-80, Israel Chemical Society Gold Medal, 2014, Founders Award of the Biophysical Society, 2014 **MEM:** Fellow: Biophysical Society, Royal Society Chemistry (Soft Matter & Biophysical Chemistry award 2012); mem.: National Academy of Sciences

WASHINGTON, DENZEL, T: Actor **I:** Media & Entertainment **DOB:** 12/28/1954 **PB:** Mount Vernon **SC:** NY/USA **PT:** Denzel Washington; Lynn (Lowe) Washington **MS:** Married **SPN:** Pauletta Pearson (6/25/1983) **CH:** John David; Katia; Malcolm; Olivia **ED:** BA in Drama & Journalism, Fordham University (1977); Student, American Conservatory Theatre, San Francisco, CA **C:** With, New Federal Theatre; With, Manhattan Theatre Club; With, New York Shakespeare Festival **CIV:** Spokesperson, Boys and Girls Clubs of America **CW:** Actor, Stage Appearances, "Coriolanus" (1979), "Spell No. 7," "The Mighty Gents," "Richard III," "One Tiger to a Hill," "Ceremonies in Old Dark Men," "When the Chicken Comes Home to Roost," "A Soldier's Play," "Checkmates" (1988), "Split Second," "Julius Caesar" (2005), "Fences" (2010), "A Raisin in the Sun" (2014); Actor, Films, "Carbon Copy" (1981), "A Soldier's Story" (1981), "Power" (1986), "Cry Freedom" (1987), "For Queen and Country" (1988), "The Mighty Quinn" (1989), "Glory" (1989), "Heart Condition" (1990), "Mo' Better Blues" (1990), "Ricochet" (1991), "Mississippi Masala" (1992), "Malcolm X" (1992), "Much Ado About Nothing" (1993), "Philadelphia" (1993), "The Pelican Brief" (1993), "Crimson Tide" (1995), "Virtuosity" (1995), "Devil in a Blue Dress" (1995), "Courage Under Fire" (1996), "The Preacher's Wife" (1996), "Fallen" (1998), "He Got Game" (1998), "The Siege" (1998), "The Bone Collector" (1999), "The Hurricane" (2000), "Remember the Titans" (2000), "Training Day" (2001), "John Q" (2002), "Out of Time" (2003), "Man on Fire" (2004), "The Manchurian Candidate" (2004), "Inside Man" (2006), "Déjà Vu" (2006), "American Gangster" (2007), "The Taking of Pelham 1 2 3" (2009), "The Book of Eli" (2010), "Unstoppable" (2010), "Flight" (2012), "2 Guns" (2013), "The Magnificent Seven" (2016); Actor, Director, Producer, Films, "Antwone Fisher" (2002); Actor, Director, Films, "The Great Debaters" (2007); Actor, Producer, Films, "The Book of Eli" (2010), "The Equalizer" (2014), "Fences" (2016), "Roman J. Israel" (2017), "The Equalizer 2" (2018); Actor, Executive Producer, Films, "Safe House" (2012); Actor, TV Films, "Wilma" (1977), "License to Kill" (1984), "The George McKenna Story" (1986); Actor, Mini-series, "Flesh and Blood" (1979); Actor, TV Series, "St. Elsewhere" (1982-1988), "License to Kill" (1984), "Hard Lessons: The George McKenna Story" (1986), "Great Performances" (1992), "Liberators: Fighting on Two Fronts in World War II" (1992), "Happily Ever After: Fairy Tales for Every Child" (1995), "Happily Ever After: Fairy Tales for Every Child" (1997), "The March" (2013), "Grey's Anatomy" (2016); Co-author with Daniel Paisner, "A Hand to Guide Me" (2006) **AW:** Harvard Foundation Award (1996); Whitney M. Young Award, LA Urban League (1997); Herbert Hoover Humanitarian Award, The Boys & Girls Clubs of America (2004); Golden Plate Award, Academy Achievement (2005); Stanley Kubrick Britannia Award for Excellence in Film, BAFTA/LA Cunard Britannia Awards (2007); Co-recipient with Wife, Pauletta, Frederick D. Patterson Award, United Negro College Fund (2008); Cecil B. DeMille Award, Hollywood Foreign Press (2016); American Conservatory Theater Scholar; Named One of the 50 Most Powerful People in Hollywood, Premiere Magazine (2002-2006); Named America's Favorite Movie Star, Harris Poll (2007-2008); Named to Power 150, Ebony Magazine (2008); Audelco Award; Obie Award (1981); Tony Award for Best Performance by a Leading Actor in a Play (2010); National Association for the Advancement of Colored People Image Award (1987); Golden Globe Award for Best Performance by an Actor in a Supporting Role in a Motion Picture (1989); Academy Award for Best Supporting Actor (1990); National Association for the Advancement of Colored People Image Award for Outstanding Supporting Actor in a Motion Picture (1992); National Association for the Advancement of Colored People Image Award for Outstanding Lead Actor in a Motion Picture (1997);

Golden Globe Award for Best Performance by Actor in a Motion Picture Drama (2000); Academy Award for Best Actor (2002); National Association for the Advancement of Colored People Image Award for Outstanding Actor in a Motion Picture (2011); African American Film Critics Association Award for Best Actor (2012); National Association for the Advancement of Colored People Image Award for Outstanding Actor in a Motion Picture (2013); National Association for the Advancement of Colored People Image Award for Outstanding Supporting Actor in a Motion Picture (2003); African American Film Critics Association Award for Best Picture (2007); National Association for the Advancement of Colored People Image Award for Outstanding Actor in a Motion Picture (2008) **BA:** William Morris Endeavor Entertainment, 9601 Wilshire Blvd 3rd Fl, Beverly Hills, CA, 90210

WASHINGTON, KERRY, T: Actress **I:** Media & Entertainment **DOB:** 01/31/1977 **PB:** Bronx **SC:** NY/USA **PT:** Daughter of Earl and Valerie Washington; **ED:** Attended, Michael Howard Studios; BS in Anthropology & Sociology, The George Washington University, 1998 **CR:** Member, President Barack Obama's Committee on Arts and Humanities, 2009 **CIV:** Member, President's Committee on the Arts & the Humanities, 2009- **CW:** Actress: (TV films) Magical Make-Over, 1994; (films) Our Song, 2000, Save the Last Dance, 2001, Lift, 2001, Take the A Train, 2002, Bad Company, 2002, U.S. of Lelan, 2003, The Human Stain, 2003, Sin, 2003, Against the Ropes, 2004, Strip Search, 2004, She Hate Me, 2004, Ray, 2004, Sexual Life, 2005, Mr. & Mrs. Smith, 2005, Fantastic Four, 2005, Wait, 2005, Little Man, 2006, The Last King of Scotland, 2006, The Dead Girl, 2006, I Think I Love My Wife, 2007, Miracle at St. Anna, 2008, Lakeview Terrace, 2008, Good Hair, 2009, Life is Hot in Cracktown, 2009, Mother and Child, 2009, For Colored Girls, 2010, Night Catches Us, 2010, The Details, 2011, A Thousand Words, 2012, Django Unchained, 2012 (Outstanding Supporting Actress in a Motion Picture, National Association for the Advancement of Colored People Image Awards, 2013), Peeples, 2013, Cars3, 2017 (voice); (TV series) Scandal, 2012- (Outstanding Actress in a Drama Series, National Association for the Advancement of Colored People Image Awards, 2013, 2014), (TV appearances) Boston Legal, 2005-06, (voice) Black Panther, 2010, How to Get Away with Murder, 2018; actress, executive producer (TV films) Confirmation, 2016 **AW:** Named one of The 100 Most Influential People in the World, TIME magazine, 2014; recipient President's award for Public Service, National Association for the Advancement of Colored People Image Awards, 2013

WASHINGTON, LAUREN, T: CEO **I:** Advertising & Marketing **CN:** Keepup **ED:** MBA in Marketing, Entrepreneurship,Innovation, Northwestern University, 2009-11; BA in Journalism and Mass Communication, University of North Carolina at Chapel Hill, 2001-05 **C:** Co-Founder, Black Women Talk Tech, 2017-; Co-Founder and CEO, Keepup App, 2014-; Director, Brand Planning and Strategy, 2012-14; MBA Resident, Omnicom Group, 2011-12

WASSERMAN-SCHULTZ, DEBBIE, T: U.S. Representative from Florida **I:** Government Administration/Government Relations/Government Services **DOB:** 09/27/1966 **PB:** Forest Hills **SC:** NY/USA **PT:** Daughter of Larry and Ann Wasserman; **ED:** MA in Political Sci., University Florida, 1990; BA in Political Sci., University Florida, 1988 **C:** Member, US House Appropriations Committee, 2006-; Chief deputy whip, 2008-; Member, US Congress from 23rd Florida District, 2013-; Vice chair incumbent retention, Democratic Congressional

Campaign Committee (DCCC), 2009-11; Chair, Democratic National Committee (DNC), 2011-16; Vice chair, Democratic National Committee (DNC), 2009-11; Member, US House Judiciary Committee, 2011; Member, US House Judiciary Committee, 2005-06; Member, US House Budget Committee,; Senior whip, 2005-06; Member, US Congress from 20th Florida District, 2005-13; Member District 34, Florida State Senate, 2003-04; Member District 32, Florida State Senate, 2001-03; Democratic leader pro tempore, Florida House of Reps., 2000; Democratic floor leader, Florida House of Reps., 1998-99; Member District 97, Florida House of Reps., 1993-2001; Legis. aide office to Rep. Peter Deutsch, US House of Representatives, Washington, 1989-92 **CR:** Hon. chair 50-state program Hillary Clinton campaign, 2016 chair South Florida Democratic Caucus, 1998- member legis. adv. council Southern Regional Education Board, 1995- second vice president Gwen Cherry Women's Political Caucus, 1992- member Florida Supreme Court Gender Bias Study Implementation Commission, 1992-, Governor's Commission Education, 1995-97, Florida Education Facilities Study Committee, 1994, Classrooms First Task Force, 1993 **CIV:** Board trustees, Westside Regional Medical Center, Plantation, Florida, 1993- Secretary, vice president, Broward County Young Democrats, 1990-92 Secretary young leadership council, Jewish Federation Greater Fort Lauderdale, 1989-90 Board directors, Southeast Region American Jewish Congress, Board directors, National Jewish Democratic Council, Board directors, South Florida chapter National Safety Council, Board directors, Florida Distance Learning Network, 1995-97 **AW:** Named a Woman of Vision, Weizmann Institute Sci., Quality Floridian, Florida League of Cities, 1994; named Outstanding Legislator of Year, Florida Federation Business & Professional Women, 1994, Woman of Year, AMIT, 1994; named one of The Six Most Unstoppable Women, South Florida Magazine, 1994; recipient Rosemary Barkett award, Academy Florida Trial Lawyers, 1995, Outstanding Family Advocacy award, Dade County Psychological Association, 1993, Giraffe award, Women's Advocacy Majority Minority (WAMM), 1993 **MEM:** Mem.: National Organization of Women, National Council Jewish Women, Hawkes Bluff Panel & Homeowner's Association (secretary), Weston C. of C., Pembroke Pines C. of C., Miramar C. of C., Omicron Delta Kappa **H:** Bowling, golf, politics, old houses **PA:** Democrat **BA:** 1114 Longworth H.O.B., Washington, DC, 20515

WATERS, MAXINE, T: U.S. Representative from California, Ranking member of the House Financial Services Committee **I:** Government Administration/Government Relations/Government Services **DOB:** 08/15/1938 **PB:** St. Louis **SC:** MO/USA **PT:** Daughter of Remus and Velma (Moore) Carr; **ED:** Doctor (hon.), Morgan State University; Doctor (hon.), North Carolina Agrl.& Tech. State University; Doctor (hon.), Spelman College; BA in Sociology, California State University, LA, 1970 **C:** Ranking Member, House Financial Services Committee, 2012-; Member, US Congress from 43rd California District, 2013-; Member, US Congress from 35th California District, 1993-2013; Member, US Congress from 29th California District, Washington, 1991-93; Member District 48, California State Assembly, 1976-91; Vol. coordinator, teacher, Head Start Progressive **CR:** Chair Congressional Black Caucus, 1997-98 member Democratic National Committee, 1980-, National Advisory Committee for Women, 1978- del. Minority AIDS Initiative, 1998, Democratic National Convention, 1972-88 **CIV:** Founder, Project Build, Founder, Free South Africa Movement, Founder, Maxine Waters Employment Preparation Center, Member, Cali-

fornia Peer Counseling Association, National Committee Economic Conversion and Disarmament, Member board, Center Study Sport in Society, LA Women's Foundation **AW:** Named one of The 100 Most Influential Black Americans, Ebony magazine, 2006; named to The Power 150, 2008 **PA:** Democrat **BA:** Office of Maxine Waters, 2221 Rayburn House Office Building, Washington, DC, 20515

WATERSTON, SAM, T: Actor **I:** Media & Entertainment **DOB:** 11/15/1940 **PB:** Cambridge **SC:** MA/USA **ED:** BA, Yale University (1962); Coursework, Paris-Sorbonne University (1961) **CW:** Actor, "Grace and Franki" (2015-Present); Actor, "Anesthesia" (2015); Actor, "Please Be Normal" (2014); Actor, "The Commission" (2013); Actor, "The Newsroom" (2012-2014); Actor, "Hamlet" (2008); Actor, "Le Divorce" (2003); Actor, "The Matthew Shepard Story" (2002); Actor, "A House Divided" (2000); Actor, "Law and Order: Special Victims Unit" (1999); Actor, "Unfinished Journey" (1999); Actor, "Exiled" (1998); Actor, "Miracle at Midnight" (1998); Actor, "Shadow Conspiracy" (1997); Actor, "Thomas Jefferson" (1997); Actor, "The Proprietor" (1996); Actor, "Nixon" (1995); Actor, "Lost Civilizations" (1995); Actor, Producer, "The Journey of August King" (1995); Actor, "Law and Order" (1994-2010); Actor, "Shakespeare & Szekspir" (1994); Actor, "Serial Mom" (1994); Actor, "Abe Lincoln in Illinois" (1993-1994); Actor, "I'll Fly Away: Then and Now" (1993); Actor, "I'll Fly Away" (1991-1993); Actor, "The Man in the Moon" (1991); Actor, "Mindwalk" (1991); Actor, "Crimes and Misdemeanors" (1990); Actor, "Captive in the Land" (1990); Actor, "The Civil War" (1990); Actor, "Welcome Home" (1989); Actor, "Nightmare Years" (1989); Actor, "Terrorist on Trial: The U.S. versus Salim Ajami" (1988); Actor, "A Walk in the Woods" (1988); Actor, "Gore Vidal's Lincoln" (1988); Actor, "September" (1987); Actor, "Hannah and Her Sisters" (1986); Actor, "Just Between Friends" (1986); Actor, "Benefactors" (1986); Actor, "Warning Sign" (1985); Actor, "The Killing Fields" (1984); Actor, "Eagle's Wing" (1983); Actor, "Oppenheimer" (1982); Actor, "Oppenheimer" (1982); Actor, "Q.E.D." (1982); Actor, "Hopscotch" (1980); Actor, "Oppenheimer" (1980); Actor, "Heaven's Gate" (1979); Actor, "Capricorn One" (1978); Actor, "Interiors" (1978); Actor, "Friendly Fire" (1978); Actor, "Sweet William" (1978); Actor, "Rancho Deluxe" (1976); Actor, "The Great Gatsby" (1975); Actor, "The Glass Menagerie" (1975); Actor, "Diabolique" (1975); Actor, "Much Ado About Nothing" (1974); Actor, "Indians," "Oh Dad Poor Dad," "Halfway Up the Tree," "Lunch Hour," "Hamlet," "The Tempest," "Measure for Measure," "Much Ado About Nothing," "Savages," "The Devil's Paradise"; Actor, Crimes and Misdemeanors **AW:** Named, American Theatre Hall of Fame (2012); Inductee, Hollywood Walk of Fame (2010); Recipient, Award for Outstanding Performance by a Male Actor in a Drama Series, Screen Actors Guild (1999); Recipient, Emmy Award for Best Documentary (1996); Recipient, Drama League Award (1994); Recipient, Golden Globe Award for Best Performance by an Actor in a TV Series - Drama (1993); Recipient, Obie Award, Drama Desk Awards **MEM:** Actors' Equity Association; Screen Actors Guild; American Federation of TV and Radio Artists

WATFORD, PAUL JEFFREY, T: Federal Judge **I:** Law and Legal Services **DOB:** 08/25/1967 **PB:** Garden Grove **SC:** California **ED:** JD, UCLA School Law, 1992; BA, University California, Berkeley, 1989 **C:** Judge, US Court Appeals (9th Cir.), 2012-; Partner, Sidley Austin LLP, 2003-12; Associate, Sidley Austin LLP, 2001-03; Assistant US attorney (central district) California, US Department

Justice, L.A., 1997-2000; Associate, Munger, Tolles & Olson, 1996-97; Law clerk to Justice Ruth Bader Ginsburg, US Supreme Court, Washington, 1995-96; Law clerk to Hon. Alex Kozinski, US Court Appeals (9th Cir.), 1994-95 **CR:** Appellate lawyer rep. Ninth Cir. Judicial Conference, 2009-11 lecturer law University of Southern California Gould School Law, 2007-09 **MEM:** Mem.: American Bar Association (co-chair litigation section appellate practice committee 2005-08, member amicus curiae committee 2007-10) **BA:** 95 7th St, San Francisco, CA, 94103

WATSON, EMMA, T: Actress **I:** Media & Entertainment **PB:** Oxford **SC:** England **PT:** Chris Watson; Jacqueline (Luesby) Watson **ED:** BA in English Literature, Brown University, 2014 **CW:** Actress: (films) Harry Potter and the Sorcerer's Stone, 2001, Harry Potter and the Chamber of Secrets, 2002, Harry Potter and the Prisoner of Azkaban, 2004, Harry Potter and the Goblet of Fire, 2005, Harry Potter and the Order of the Phoenix, 2007, Ballet Shoes, 2007, (voice) The Tale of Despereaux, 2008, Harry Potter and the Half-Blood Prince, 2009, Harry Potter and the Deathly Hallows: Part 1, 2010, Harry Potter and the Deathly Hallows: Part 2, 2011, My Week with Marilyn, 2011, The Perks of Being a Wallflower, 2012 (Favorite Drama Movie Actress, People's Choice Awards, 2013), The Bling Ring, 2013, This Is the End, 2013, Noah, 2014, Colonia, The Vicar of Dibley, 2015,Colonia, 2015, 2016, Regression, 2016, The Circle, 2016, Beauty of the Beast, 2017; (TV films) Ballet Shoes, 2007 **AW:** Recipient Trailblazer award, MTV Movie Awards, 2013

WATSON, JAMES D., T: Molecular Biologist, Geneticist, Zoologist **I:** Sciences **DOB:** 04/06/1928 **PB:** Chicago **SC:** Illinois **PT:** Son of James Dewey and Jean (Mitchell) W.;; **SPN:** Married Elizabeth Lewis, 1968; **CH:** children: Rufus Robert, Duncan James. **ED:** MD (hon.), Charles Univ., Prague, 1998; MD (hon.), University Buenos Aires, Argentina, 1986; DSc (hon.), Trinity College, Dublin, 2001; DSc (hon.), Dartmouth, 2001; DSc (hon.), Widener University, 2001; DSc (hon.), Illinois Wesleyan University, 2000; DSc (hon.), University College London, 2000; DSc (hon.), University Judaism, 1999; DSc (hon.), Washington College, 1999; DSc (hon.), University Oxford; DSc (hon.), University Stellenbosch, 1993; DSc (hon.), Fairfield University, 1993; DSc (hon.), University Cambridge, 1993; DSc (hon.), Bard College, 1991; DSc (hon.), Rutgers University, 1988; DSc (hon.), State University of New York, 1983; DSc (hon.), Clarkson College, 1981; DSc (hon.), Rockefeller University, 1980; DSc (hon.), Harvard University, 1978; DSc (hon.), Hofstra University, 1976; DSc (hon.), Albert Einstein College Medicine, 1979; DSc (hon.), Brandeis University, 1973; DSc (hon.), Adelphi University, 1972; DSc (hon.), Long Island University, 1970; LLD (hon.), University Notre Dame, 1965; DSc (hon.), Ind. University, 1963; DSc (hon.), University Chicago, 1961; PhD in Zoology, Ind. University, 1950; BS in Zoology, University Chicago, 1947 **C:** Chancellor Emeritus, Cold Spring Harbor Laboratory, Watson School Biological Sci., New York, 2007-; Director National Center for Human Genome Research,, National Institutes of Health, 1989-92; Associate Director National Center for Human Genome Research,, National Institutes of Health, 1988-89; Chancellor, Cold Spring Harbor Laboratory, Watson School Biological Sci., New York, 2004-07; President, Cold Spring Harbor Laboratory, Watson School Biological Sci., New York, 1994-2004; Director, Cold Spring Harbor Laboratory, Watson School Biological Sci., New York, 1968-94; Professor, Harvard University, 1961-76; Associate Professor, Harvard University, 1958-61; Assistant Professor biology, Harvard University,

1955-58; Senior Research Fellow Biology, California Institute Tech., 1953-55; National Foundation Infantile Paralysis fellow, Cavendish Laboratory, Cambridge University, 1951-52, 55-56; Research Fellow, National Research Council, University Copenhagen, 1950-51 **CR:** Newton-Abraham visiting professor Oxford University, 1994 Institute Advisor Allen Institute for Brain Sci., Seattle, Washington **CW:** Author: Molecular Biology of the Gene, 1965, 4th edition, 1986, The Double Helix, 1968, (with John Tooze) The DNA Story, 1981, (with others) The Molecular Biology of the Cell, 1983, 2nd edition, 1989, 3rd edition 1994, (with John Tooze and David Kurtz) Recombinant DNA, A Short Course, 1983, 2nd edition, 1992, A Passion for DNA, 2000, Genes, Girls and Gamow, 2001, DNA: The Secret of Life, 2003, Avoid Boring People: Lessons From a Life in Science, 2007 **AW:** Named Hon. Fellow Clare College, Cambridge University, Hon. Knight of Brit. Empire, 2002; Recipient (with F.H.C. Crick) John Collins Warren Prize Massachusetts General Hospital, 1959, Eli Lilly Award in biochemistry American Chemical Society, 1959, Albert Lasker prize American Pub. Health Association, 1960, (with F.H.C. Crick) Research Corp. prize, 1962, (with F.H.C. Crick and M.H.F. Wilkins), Nobel Prize in Medicine, 1962, Presidential Medal of Freedom, 1977, Kaul Foundation award for Excellence, 1993, National Biotech. Venture award, 1993, Copley Medal, 1993, Charles A. Dana Award, 1994, Lomonosov medal Russian Academy Sci., 1995, National Medal of Sci., 1997, Liberty medal City of Philadelphia, 2000, Benjamin Franklin medal for Distinguished Achievement in Sciences American Philosophical Society, 2001, Gairdner Foundation award for Merit, 2002, Lotos Club Medal of Merit, 2004, Honorary Knight Commander of the Order of the British Empire, 2002, CSHL Double Helix Medal Honoree, 2008, Mendal Medal, 2008 **MEM:** Member National Academy of Sciences (Carty medal 1971), Am. Philosophical Society, Am. Association Cancer Research, Am. Academy Arts and Scis., Am. Society Biological Chemistry, Royal Society (London), Academy Scis. Russia, Danish Academy Arts and Scis. **ACH:** Achievements include co-discovery of Double-Helix DNA; has become the first person to receive his own personal genome map in 2007.

WATSON, JOHN S., T: CEO of Chevron **I:** Oil & Energy **CN:** Chevron **DOB:** 10/01/1956 **SC:** CA/USA **ED:** MBA, University Chicago, 1980; BA in Agricultural Economics, University California, Davis, 1978 **C:** Chairman, CEO, Chevron Corp., 2010-; Vice chairman, Chevron Corp., 2009; Executive vice president strategy & devel., Chevron Corp., 2008-09; President, Chevron International Exploration and Production, 2005-08; Vice president fin., CFO, ChevronTexaco Corp., 2001-05; Vice president strategic planning, Chevron Corp., 1998-2001; President, Chevron Canada, Ltd., Vancouver, Canada, 1996-98; General manager strategic planning and quality, Chevron USA Products Co., 1995-96; Manager credit card enterprises, Chevron USA Products Co., 1993-95; Manager investor relations, Chevron Corp., 1990-93; Fin. analyst to various fin. and analytical positions including supervisory positions in the comptroller's fin. and profit analysis groups, Chevron Corp., 1980-90 **CR:** Board directors Animal Rescue Foundation, Am. Society Corp. Executives, Business Council, JP Morgan International Council, Business Roundtable, National Petroleum Council, Am. Petroleum Institute, Chevron Corp., 2009- **CIV:** Member chancellor's board advisors, University California Davis, Board directors, Tony LaRussa's Animal Rescue Foundation, **MEM:** Mem.: American Society Corp. Executives

WATSON, THOMAS STURGES, T: Professional Golfer **I:** Athletics **DOB:** 09/04/1949 **PB:** Kansas City **PT:** Son of Raymond Etheridge and Sarah Elizabeth (Ridge) W. **MS:** Married **SPN:** Linda Tova Rubin, July 8, 1973 (div.) **CH:** Margaret Elizabeth, Michael Barrett. **ED:** BS, Stanford University, 1971 **C:** Professional golfer, 1971 **AW:** Winner Western Open, 1974, 1977, 1984; winner Byron Nelson Tournament, 1975, 78, 79, 80; winner Brit. Open, 1975, 77, 80, 82, 83; winner, U.S. Open, 1982; winner World Series, 1975, 80; winner Andy Williams San Diego Open, 1977, 80; winner El Prat, 1977; winner Masters, 1977, 81; winner Bing Crosby National Pro-Am Golf Tournament, 1977, 78; winner Tucson Open, 1978, 84; winner Colgate Hall of Fame Classic, 1978, 79; winner Anheuser Busch Golf Classic, 1978; winner Memorial Tournament, 1979; winner Heritage Classic, 1979, 83; winner Tournament of Champions, 1979, 80, 84; Los Angeles Open, 1980, 82; Greater New Orleans Open, 1980, 81; Dunlop Phoenix, 1980, Atlantic Classic, 1981; Nabisco Championship, 1987, Hong Kong Open, 1992; Recipient Vardon Trophy, 1977, 78, 79, Byron Nelson award, 1977-78, 79-80; named to Ryder Cup Team, 1977, 81, 83, 89 (elected captain 1992-); named Player of Year Professional Golf Association, 1977, 78, 79, 80, 82, 84; elected to PGA World Golf Hall of Fame, 1988, Kansas Golf Hall of Fame, 1991, William H. Richardson award 1990,Bob Jones, 1987, Old Tom Morris Award, 1992, Payne Stewart Award, 2003, Charles Schwab Cup, 2003, 2005 **MEM:** Member U.S. Golf Association, Professional Golfers Association, Golf Course Superintendents Association of Am. (Old Tom Morris award 1992), Butler National Golf Club, Shadow Glen Club, Preston Trails Golf Club, Oakwood Country Club, Par Club, Blue Hills Country Club, Kansas City Country Club, Royal and Ancient Golf Club St. Andrews. **ACH:** Achievements include being the leading money winner PGA, 1977-80, 84.

WATSON COLEMAN, BONNIE M., T: U.S. Representative from New Jersey **I:** Government Administration/Government Relations/Government Services **DOB:** 02/06/1945 **PB:** Camden, New Jersey, February 6, 1945 **ED:** BA, Thomas Edison State College, 1985; Attended, Rutgers University **C:** Member, U.S. House of Representatives from New Jersey's 12th District, 2015-, Member, Committee on Homeland Security, Committee on Oversight and Government Reform; Member District 15, New Jersey General Assembly, 1998-2015; Member, Dem. National Committee, 2002-; President, Watson Co. Inc.,; Chair, New Jersey Dem. State Committee, 2002-06; Majority leader, New Jersey General Assembly, 2006-09; Chair Appropriations Committee, New Jersey General Assembly, 2002-05; Member, Ewing Township Planning Board, 1996-97; Chair, New Jersey Governing Boards Association State Colleges, 1991-93; Member, New Jersey Governing Boards Association State Colleges, 1987-98 **CIV:** Chair board trustees, Richard Stockton College New Jersey, 1990-91 Member board trustees, Richard Stockton College New Jersey, 1981-98 **MEM:** Mem.: Association State Dem. Chairs (executive committee 2002-) **PA:** Democrat **BA:** 1535 Longworth House Office Building, Washington, DC, 20515

WATT, J.J., T: Professional Football Player **I:** Athletics **DOB:** 03/22/1989 **PB:** Pewaukee **SC:** WI/USA **PT:** Son of John and Connie Watt **ED:** Attended, University of Wisconsin, Madison, 2008-11; Attended, Central Michigan University, Mount Pleasant, 2007 **C:** Defensive end, Houston Texans, 2011 **CR:** Founder, president Justin J. Watt Foundation, 2010- **CIV:** Founder, board directors, Justin J. Watt Foundation **AW:** Named Defensive Player of the Year, Associated Press, 2015, 1st

Team All-Pro, 2012-14, Defensive Player of Year, Pro Football Writers America (PFWA), 2012, NFL Defensive Player of Year, Associated Press, 2012; named to The American Football Conference Pro Bowl Team, NFL, 2012-14; recipient Texas Spirit of the Bull Community award, 2014, Bert Bell Award, 2014, Lott IMPACT award, Pacific Club IMPACT Foundation, 2010, Pro Bowl, 2012-15, First-Team All-Pro, 2015, NFL Defensive Player of the Year, 2014-15, Sports Illustrated Sportsperson of the Year, 2017, NFL Sacks Leader, 2012, 2015, First Team All-American, 2010, First-Team All- Big Ten, 2010 **ACH:** Achievements include leading the NFL in: sacks, 2012,2015, 4x Pro Bowl, 2012-2105

WATTERS, JESSE, T: Political Commentator **I:** Media & Entertainment **DOB:** 06/18/1905 **PB:** Philadelphia, Pennsylvania **SC:** Philadelphia, Pennsylvania **C:** Co-Host, The Five, 2017-; Host, Watters World, 2015-; Guest Co-Host,Outnumbered, 2014; Production Staff, OReilly Factor,2004

WATTS, CHARLIE, T: Drummer **I:** Media & Entertainment **DOB:** 05/04/1905 **PB:** Islington, England **SC:** Islington, England **SPN:** Married Shirley Shepherd, October 14, 1964; **CH:** 1 child, Serafina. **ED:** Attended, Harrow Art School, England **C:** Drummer, The Rolling Stones, 1963-; Founder, Charlie Watts Big Band, **CW:** Drummer: (albums with The Rolling Stones) England's Newest Hitmakers: The Rolling Stones, 1964, 12 X 5, 1964, The Rolling Stones, Now!, 1965, Out of Our Heads, 1965, December's Children (And Everybody's), 1965, Big Hits, High Tide, & Green Grass, 1966, Aftermath, 1966, Got Live if You Want It!, 1966, Between the Buttons, 1967, Flowers, 1967, Their Satanic Majesties Request, 1967, Beggars Banquet, 1968, Through the Past, Darkly (Big Hits Vol. 2), 1969, Let It Bleed, 1969, Get Yer Ya-Yas Out!: The Rolling Stones in Concert, 1970, Hot Rocks, 1964-1971, 1971, Sticky Fingers, 1971, More Hot Rocks: Big Hits and Fazed Cookies, 1972, Exile on Main Street, 1972, Goats Head Soup, 1973, It's Only Rock and Roll, 1974, Metamorphosis, 1975, Made in the Shade, 1975,Rolled Gold+: The Very Best of the Rolling Stones, 1975, Black and Blue, 1976, Love You Live, 1977, Some Girls, 1978, Emotional Rescue, 1980, Sucking in the Seventies, 1981, Tattoo You, 1981, Still Life (American Concert, 1981), 1982, Undercover, 1983, Rewind (1971-1984), 1984, Dirty Work, 1986, Singles Collection: The London Years, 1989, Steel Wheels, 1989, Flashpoint, 1990, Jump Back: The Best of the Rolling Stones, 1993, Voodoo Lounge, 1994 (Grammy Award for Best Rock Album, 1994), Stripped, 1995, Bridges to Babylon, 1997, No Security, 1999, Forty Licks, 2002, Singles: 1965-1967, 2004, Live Licks, 2004, A Bigger Bang, 2005, Rarities 1971-2003, 2005, GRRR!, 2012; (soundtracks) Shine a Light, 2008, (albums with The Rolling Stones & other artists) Jamming With Edward, 1972, The Rolling Stones Rock 'N' Roll Circus, 1996; (solo albums) Charlie Watts Orchestra-Live at Fulham Town Hall, 1986, From One Charlie, 1991, Warm and Tender, 1993, One Charlie, 1995, Long Ago and Far Away, 1996,The Charlie Watts-Jim Keltner Project,2000,The Charlie Watts Tentet - Watts at Scott's,2004,The ABC&D of Boogie Woogie - The Magic of Boogie Woogie,2010,The ABC&D of Boogie Woogie Live in Paris,2012,Charlie Watts meets the Danish Radio Big Band, 2017,; performer: (films) Gimme Shelter, 1970, Sympathy for the Devil, 1970, Ladies and Gentlemen: The Rolling Stones, 1974, Let's Spend the Night Together, 1983, Rolling Stones: Live At the Max, 1991, Voodoo Lounge, 1995, The Rolling Stones Rock 'N' Roll Circus, 1996, The Rolling Stones Bridges to Babylon Tour '97-98, 1997, Four Flicks, 2003, The Biggest Bang, 2007, Shine a Light, 2008, Some Girls Live in Texas '78, 2011; appeared in: (documentaries) 25 X 5: The Continuing Adventures of the Rolling Stones, 1989, Stones in Exile, 2010, Crossfire Hurricane, 2012, The Rolling Stones: Charlie Is My Darling, 2012; author: (film) Ode To A High Flying Bird, 1964 **AW:** Named to Rock and Roll Hall of Fame (as member of The Rolling Stones), 1989, 12th on Rolling Stones 100 Greatest Drummers of All Time

WEAVER, SIGOURNEY, T: Actress **I:** Media & Entertainment **DOB:** 10/08/1949 **PB:** New York **SC:** NY/USA **PT:** Sylvester (Pat) Weaver, Elizabeth Inglis **MS:** Married **SPN:** Jim Simpson, 10/1/1984 **CH:** Charlotte **ED:** BA in English, Stanford University, 1971; MA in Drama, Yale University, 1974 **CW:** Actress, (Theatre) Including Watergate Classics, 1973, The Frogs, 1974 The Nature And Purpose Of The Universe, 1974, Daryl And Carol And Kenny And Jenny, The Constant Wife, 1975, Titanic, 1976, Marco Polo Sings A Song, 1977, A Flea In Her Ear, 1978, Conjuring An Event, 1978, Beyond Therapy, 1981, As You Like It, 1981, The Merchant Of Venice, 1986, The Guys, 2002, The Mercy Seat, 2002, Mrs. Farnsworth, 2004, Crazy Mary, 2007, Love Letters, 2007-2008, (Broadway) Hurlyburly, 1984-1985, Sex And Longing, 1996, Vanya And Sonya And Masha And Spike, 2013, (Films) Annie Hall, 1977, Madman, 1978, Alien, 1979, Eyewitness, 1981, The Year Of Living Dangerously, 1982, Deal Of The Century, 1983, Ghostbusters, 1984, Une Femme Ou Deux, 1985, Aliens, 1986, Half Moon Street, 1986, Gorillas In The Mist, 1988, Working Girl, 1988, Ghostbusters II, 1989, 1492: Conquest Of Paradise, 1992, Dave, 1993, Death And The Maiden, 1994, Jeffrey, 1995, Copycat, 1995, Snow White: A Tale Of Terror, 1997, The Ice Storm, 1997, A Map Of The World, 1999, Galaxy Quest, 1999, Airframe, 1999, Company Man, 2000, Speak Truth To Power, 2000, Heartbreakers, 2001, (Voice Actress) Big Bad Love, 2001, Tadpole, 2002, The Guys, 2002, Holes, 2003, The Village, 2004, Imaginary Heroes, 2004, Snow Cake, 2006, The TV Set, 2006, Infamous, 2006, (Voice Actress) Happily N'Ever After, 2007, Vantage Point, 2008, Baby Mama, 2008, (Voice Actress) WALL-E, 2008, Avatar, 2009, Crazy On The Outside, 2010, You Again, 2010, Cedar Rapids, 2011, Paul, 2011, Rampart, 2011, Abduction, 2011, The Cabin In The Woods, 2011, Red Lights, 2012, The Cold Light Of Day, 2012, Vamps, 2012, Exodus: Gods And Kings, 2014, Chappie, 2015, (Voice Actress) Finding Dory, 2016, Ghostbusters, 2016, A Monster Calls, 2016, The Assignment, 2016, The Meyerowitz Stories, 2017, Rakka, 2017, Avatar 2, Avatar 3, (TV Series) Somerset, 1976, (TV Miniseries) The Best Of Families, 1977, Political Animals, 2012, My Depression, 2012, Penn Zero: Part-Time Hero, 2015, Doc Martin, 2015-2017, Years Of Living Dangerously, 2016, The Defenders, 2017, (TV Films) 3 By Cheever: The Sorrows Of Gin, 1979, 3 By Cheever: O Youth And Beauty!, 1979, Prayers For Bobby, 2009, Spring/Fall, 2011; Actress, Co-Writer, Das Lusitania Songspiel, 1976; Co-Producer, Actress, (Films) Alien 3, 1992, Alien: Resurrection, 1997 **AW:** Women in Hollywood Tribute Award, Elle Magazine, 2008, Lifetime Achievement Award, Chicago International Film Festival, 2001, Star, Walk of Fame, 1999, BAFTA Award For Best Supporting Actress, The Ice Storm, 1998, Golden Globe For Best Supporting Actress In A Motion Picture, Working Girl, 1989, Golden Globe Award For Best Actress-Drama, Gorillas in the Mist, 1989 **BA:** United Talent Agency, 9336 Civic Center Drive, Beverly Hills, CA, 90210

WEBER, RANDY, T: U.S. Representative from Texas, Former State Legislator **I:** Government Administration/Government Relations/Government Services **DOB:** 07/02/1953 **PB:** Pearland **ED:** BA in Public Affairs, University Houston, Clear Lake, 1977; Attended, Alvin Community College, Texas, 1971-74 **C:** Member, US House Space, Sci., & Technology Committee, 2013-; Member, US House Foreign Affairs Committee, 2013-; Member, US Congress from 14th Texas District, Washington, 2013-; Owner, Webers Air & Heat Air-Conditioning Co., 1981-; Member District 29, Texas House of Representatives, 2009-13; City councilman, City of Pearland, Texas, 1990-96 **PA:** Republican

WEBSTER, DANIEL ALAN, T: U.S. Representative from Florida **I:** Government Administration/Government Relations/Government Services **DOB:** 04/27/1949 **PB:** Charleston, West Virginia, April 27, 1949 **ED:** BS in Electrical Engineering, Georgia Institute Tech., 1971 **C:** Member, US House Transportation & Infrastructure Committee, 2013-; Member, US Congress from 10th Florida District, 2013-; Member, US House Rules Committee, 2011-14; Member, US Congress from 8th Florida District, Washington, 2011-13; Majority leader, Florida State Senate, 2006-08; Member District 9, Florida State Senate, 2003-08; Member District 12, Florida State Senate, 1999-2002; Republican leader, Florida House of Reps., 1994-96; Republican leader pro tempore, Florida House of Reps., 1992-94; Minority whip, Florida House of Reps., 1988-90; Vice chairman, minority policy committee, Florida House of Reps., 1985-88; Minority fl. leader, Florida House of Reps., 1982-84; Speaker, Florida House of Reps.,; Member District 41, Florida House of Reps.,; Owner, Webster-Air Conditioning & Heating Inc., **AW:** Named Florida Statesman of Year, Florida Republican Party, 1995, Legislator of Year, Florida Chamber of Commerce, 1995; recipient Leadership award, Florida Association State Toppers, 1996, Award, Florida Banking Association, 1995, Special Recognition award, Florida Hotel & Motel Association, 1995, Quality Floridian award, Florida League Cities, 1995, Legislature award, Florida Farm Bureau, 1995, Board Regents, 1995, D.I. Rainey award, Florida Chiropractic Association, 1994, Legislature Leadership award, Florida Medical Society, 1993 **MEM:** Mem.: United Community Action for Israel, Farm Bureau, West Orange & Winter Garden Chamber of Commerce, National Federation Ind. Business, Air Conditioning Contractors Association, Association Building Contractors, Sertoma **PA:** Republican **BA:** 1210 Longworth House Office Building, Washington, DC, 20515

WEI, LU, T: Chairman **I:** Government Administration/Government Relations/Government Services **CN:** CPPCC Shandong Committee **PB:** Tengzhou City **SC:** China **ED:** Bachelor's Degree, Party School of the CPC Central Committee **C:** Chairman, CPPCC Shandong Committee, 2009-; Deputy Secretary,CPC Provincial Committee, 2007-; Delegate, 9th National Peoples Congress ,1998-2003; Mayor, Wuhu City, 1996-98 **AW:** Time 100 Most Influential, 2015

WEINBERG, STEVEN, T: Theoretical Physicist **I:** Sciences **DOB:** 05/03/1933 **PB:** New York **SC:** NY/USA **PT:** Son of Fred and Eva (Israel) Weinberg **ED:** DLitt (hon.), Washington College, 1985; PhD (hon.), Weizman Institute, 1985; Doctor (hon.), University Barcelona, 1996; ScD (hon.), University Waterloo, 2004; ScD (hon.), McGill University, 2003; ScD (hon.), Bates College, 2002; ScD (hon.), University Padua, 1992; ScD (hon.), University Salamanca, 1992; ScD (hon.), Columbia University, 1990; ScD (hon.), Dartmouth College, 1984; ScD (hon.), Clark University, 1982; ScD (hon.), City University of New York, 1980; ScD (hon.), Yale University, 1979; ScD (hon.), University Rochester, 1979; ScD (hon.), University Chicago, 1978; ScD (hon.), Knox College, 1978; AM (hon.), Harvard

University, 1973; PhD, Princeton University, New Jersey, 1957; BA, Cornell University, Ithaca, New York, 1954 **C:** Jack S. Josey-Welch Foundation chair in sci., Regental professor, University Texas, Austin, 1982-; Morris Loeb visiting professor physics, Harvard University, 1983-; Founder Theory Group, department physics, University Texas, Austin,; Higgins professor physics, Harvard University, 1973-82; Professor physics, Massachusetts Institute of Technology, 1969-73; Visiting professor, Massachusetts Institute of Technology, 1967-69; Professor physics, University California, Berkeley, 1964-69; Faculty, University California, Berkeley, 1960-69; Research physicist, Lawrence Radiation Laboratory, Berkeley, California, 1959-60; Research associate, instructor, Columbia University, New York City, 1957-59 **CR:** Board directors Federation Am. Scientists Witherspoon lecturer Washington University, 2001 Sanchez lecturer Texas Agricultural and Mechanical International University, 1998 Bochner lecturer Rice University, 1997 Gibbs lecturer Am. Math. Society, 1996 Sackler lecturer University Copenhagen, 1994 Brittin lecturer University Colorado, 1994 Klein lecturer University Stockholm, 1989 Dirac lecturer University Cambridge, 1986 Clark lecturer University Texas, Dallas, 1986 Hilldale lecturer University Wisconsin, 1985 Einstein lecturer Israel Academy Arts and Sciences, 1984 member Council Scholars, Libr. of Congress, 1983-85 Bampton lecturer Columbia University, 1983 Cherwell-Simon lecturer Oxford University, 1983 member National Research Council Committee International Security & Arms Control, 1981, Pres.'s Committee National Medal Sci., 1979-82 de Shalit lecturer Weizmann Institute, 1979 Bethe lecturer Cornell University, 1979 Lauritsen Memorial lecturer California Institute Tech., 1979 Silliman lecturer Yale University, 1977 Scott lecturer Cavendish Laboratory, Cambridge University, 1975 senior scientist Smithsonian Astrophysical Laboratory, Cambridge, Massachusetts, 1973-82 chair in physics College France, 1971 consultant Institute Defense Analyses, Washington, 1960-73 **CIV:** Board advisors, Santa Barbara Institute Theoretical Physics, 1983-86 **CW:** Author: Principles and Application of the General Theory of Relativity, 1972, The First Three Minutes: A Modern View of the Origin of the Universe, 1977, The Discovery of Subatomic Particles, 1982, Dreams of a Final Theory, 1992, The Quantum Theory of Fields - Vol. I: Foundations, 1995, Modern Applications, Vol. II, 1996, Supersymmetry, Vol. III, 2000, Facing Up: Science and Its Cultural Adversaries, 2001, revised edition, 2003, Glory and Terror: The Growing Nuclear Danger, 2004, Cosmology, 2008, Lake Views: This World and the Universe, 2009; co-author (with R. Feynman): Elementary Particles and the Laws of Physics; member adv. board Issues in Sci. and Tech., 1984-87, member editorial board Journal Math. Physics, 1986-88, member board editors Daedalus, 1990-, Journal Math. Physics, 1998-; contributor articles to professional journals,(Books) To Explain the World: The Discovery of Modern Science, 2015 **AW:** Named an Hon. Citizen, Padua, Italy, 2007; recipient James Joyce award, Literacy & Hist. Society, Univ. College, Dublin, 2009, Trotter prize, Texas Agricultural and Mechanical University, 2008, Lewis Thomas prize, Rockefeller University, 1999, Piazzi prize, Sicily/Palermo, Italy, 1998, Andrew Gemant prize, Am. Institute Physics, 1997, National Medal Sci., 1991, Madison medal, Princeton University, 1991, Elliott Cresson medal, Franklin Institute, 1979, Nobel prize in physics, 1979, Dannie Heineman prize in math. physics, 1977, J. Robert Oppenheimer Memorial prize, 1973,Humanist of the Year, 2002, Benjamin Franklin Medal of the American Philosophical Society, 2004, James Joyce Award, 2009 **MEM:**

Mem.: National Academy of Sciences, Royal Irish Academy (Hamilton lecturer 2005), Texas Institute Letters, Philosophical Society Texas, Royal Society London, Am. Philosophical Society (Benjamin Franklin medal 2004), Council Foreign Relations, International Astronomical Union, Am. Physical Society, Am. Academy Arts & Scis., Cambridge Sci. Society, Headliners Club (Austin), Saturday Club (Boston), Tuesday Club (Austin), Phi Beta Kappa **BA:** U Tex Dept Physics, 1 Univ Station C1600, Austin, TX, 78712

WEISLER, DION J., T: CEO **I:** Technology **CN:** HP Inc. **SC:** Australia **ED:** Bachelor's Degree, Monash University **C:** President/CEO, HP Inc., 2015-Present; Executive Vice President of Printing, Hewlett-Packard Co., 2013-2015; Senior Vice President of Printing, Hewlett-Packard Co., 2012-2013 **MEM:** Thermo Fisher Scientific Inc. Board Member, 2017-Present; HP Inc. Board Member, 2015-Present

WEISS, DANIEL H., T: CEO of the Metropolitan Museum of Art **I:** Museums & Institutions **ED:** MBA, Yale University, 1985; PhD, Johns Hopkins University, 1992; MA, Johns Hopkins University, 1982; BA, The George Washington University, 1979 **C:** CEO, Metropolitan Museum of Art, 2017-; President, Metropolitan Museum of Art, 2015-17; President, Haverford College, Pennsylvania, 2013-15; President, Lafayette College, Easton, Pennsylvania, 2005-13; Dean Zanvyl Krieger School Arts and Scis., Johns Hopkins University, Baltimore, 2002-05; Dean faculty, Johns Hopkins University, Baltimore, 2001-02; Chair Art Hist. Department, Johns Hopkins University, Baltimore, 1998-2001; With, Booz, Allen & Hamilton, **CIV:** Trustee, Park School, Baltimore, Board member, Shriver Hall Concert Series, Board member, Walter Art Museum, John Hopkins,

WEISS, RAINER, T: Physics Educator **I:** Education/Educational Services **DOB:** 09/29/1932 **PB:** Berlin **ED:** PhD, Massachusetts Institute of Technology, 1962; BS, Massachusetts Institute of Technology, 1955 **C:** Professor emeritus, Massachusetts Institute of Technology, 2001-; Professor physics, Massachusetts Institute of Technology, 1973-2001; Chair of COBE, 1976-; Associate professor, Massachusetts Institute of Technology, Cambridge, 1967-73; Assistant professor physics, Massachusetts Institute of Technology, Cambridge, 1964-67; Research associate physics, Princeton University, New Jersey, 1962-64; Assistant professor physics, Tufts University, Medford, Massachusetts, 1961-62; Instructor physics, Tufts University, Medford, Massachusetts, 1960-61 **CR:** Member NASA physical sci. committee, 1970-74, SSSC committee, 1982, infrared detector panel, 1978, others member Panel on Joint Institute of Laboratory Astrophysics, Board on Assessment of NBS Progs., National Academy of Sciences, 1985- coordinator National Science Foundation Panel on Interferometric Observatory for Gravitational Waves, 1986 member National Academy of Sciences space sci. board, 1983-86, others adjunct professor physics, Louisiana State University, 2001-. **AW:** Recipient Massachusetts Institute of Technology Baker award for excellence in teaching, 1968; NASA Achievement Award (Monolithic Bolometers), 1984, Exceptional Sci. Achievement medal, 1991, Group Achievement medal, 1991; NASA/GSFC Group Achievement award, 1990. Nobel prize in Physics 2017,Princess of Asturias Award, 2017, American Ingenuity Award in Physical Science,2016, The Special Breakthrough Prize in Fundamental Physics, 2016, Gruber Prize in Cosmology, 2016, Shaw Prize, 2016, Kavli Prize in Astrophysics, 2016 **MEM:** Fellow American Association for the Advancement of Science, Am. Physical

Society (Einstein prize 2007), Am. Academy Arts & Scis.; member Am. Astronomical Society, New York Academy Scis., National Academy of Sciences, Sigma Xi. **ACH:** Achievements include research in experimental atomic physics, atomic clocks, laser physics, experimental gravitation, millimeter and sub-millimeter astronomy, cosmic background measurements. **BA:** MIT, Office NW22-281, 77 Massachusetts Ave, Cambridge, MA, 02139

WELCH, PETER F., T: U.S. Representative From Vermont, Former State Legislator **I:** Government Administration/Government Relations/Government Services **DOB:** 05/02/1947 **PB:** Springfield **SC:** MA/USA **PT:** Edward Welch; Mart (Tracy) Welch **ED:** LLB, University of California, Berkeley, 1973; AB, College Holy Cross, Worcester, MA, 1969 **C:** U.S. House Oversight & Government Committee, 2007-Present; U.S. House Energy & Commerce Committee, 2007-Present; Chief Deputy Whip, U.S. Congress From Vermont, 2011-Present; Member-at-Large, U.S. Congress From Vermont, 2007-Present; U.S. House Standards of Official Conduct, 2007-2011; President Pro Tempre, Vermont State Senate, 2003-2006; Vermont State Senate, 2002-2007; President Pro Tempre, Vermont State Senate, 1985-1988; Minority Leader, Vermont State Senate, 1982-1984; Vermont State Senate, 1981-1989; Partner, Welch, Graham & Manby, White River Junction, VT; Attorney, Black & Planke, White River Junction, VT **CR:** Rural Working Group, Rural Healthcare Coalition, Northern Border Caucus, Northeast Agricultural Caucus, New England Congressional Caucus, National Guard & Reserve Components Caucus, House Nursing Caucus, House Hunger Caucus, Fire Services Caucus, Congressional Progressive Caucus, Congressional Arts Caucus, Brain Injury Task Force **BAR:** State of Vermont **PA:** Democrat

WELSER-MÖST, FRANZ, T: Director of the Cleveland Orchestra **I:** Media & Entertainment **DOB:** 08/16/1960 **PB:** Linz **SC:** Austria **ED:** LHD (hon.), Cleveland Institute Music; LHD (hon.), Oberlin College; LHD (hon.), Case Western Reserve University, 2003 **C:** Music Director, Cleveland Orchestra, 2002-; General Music Director, Zurich Opera House, 2005-08; Principal Conductor, Zurich Opera House, 2002-05; Music Director, Zurich Opera House, Switzerland, 1995-2000; Principal Conductor, London Philharmonic Orchestra, 1990-96; Chief Conductor, Stadtorchester Winterthur, Switzerland, 1987-90; Chief Conductor, Sinfonieorkester Norrköping, Sweden, 1986-91 **CR:** Guest Conductor Gustav Mahler Youth Orchestra, Bavarian Radio Symphony Orchestra, Vienna Philharmonic, Cleveland Youth Orchestra, Berlin Philharmonic **CW:** Conducting debut Salzburg Festival, Austria, 1985; Am. debut St. Louis, 1989; appearances include Vienna biennial, Lucerne Festical, Carnegie Hall. **AW:** Named Conductor of Year, Musical America International Directory Performing Arts, 2003; named an Academician, Yutse European Academy Foundation, 2006; recipient Silver medal, Region of Upper Austria, 2003, Outstanding Achievement award, Western Law Center Disability Rights, 1995 **MEM:** Mem.: Vienna Singverein (hon.) **BA:** Severance Hall, 11001 Euclid Ave, Cleveland, OH, 44106

WENSTRUP, BRAD ROBERT, T: U.S. Representative From Ohio, Podiatrist **I:** Government Administration/Government Relations/Government Services **DOB:** 06/17/1958 **PB:** Cincinnati **SC:** OH/USA **PT:** Frank John Wenstrup; Joan (Carletti) Wenstrup **ED:** BS, MD, Dr. William M. Scholl College of Podiatric Medicine, 1985; BA in Psychology, University of Cincinnati, 1980 **C:** Permanent Select Committee on Intelligence, Republican Study Committee; U.S. House of Veterans' Affairs, 2013-Present;

U.S. House of Armed Services Committee, 2013-Present; U.S. Congress From Second Ohio District, Washington, DC, 2013-Present; Private Podiatric Surgical Practice, Cincinnati, OH, 1985-2012 **CR:** President, Thank America First Foundation **CIV:** Board Member, Boys Hope/Girls Hope **MIL:** Chief of Surgery, 344th Combat Support Hospital, 2005-2006; Lieutenant Colonel, U.S. Army Reserve, Iraq, 1998-Present **AW:** Decorated Combat Action Badge; Bronze Star **MEM:** Cincinnati Rotary **PA:** Republican **BA:** 7954 Beechmont Avenue, Suite 200, Cincinnati, OH, 45255

WENTWORTH, TIMOTHY C., T: Express Scripts CEO **I:** Business Management/Business Services **ED:** Associate in Business, Monroe Community College; Bachelor in Industrial & Labor Relations, Cornell University **C:** Chief Executive Officer, Express Scripts (2015-Present); Senior Vice President, President of Sales & Account Management, Express-Scripts (2012-Present); Group President, Employer Accountants, Medco Health Solutions, Inc. (2008-2012); President, Chief Executive Officer, Accredo Health Group, Inc. (Subsidiary of Medco Health Solutions Inc.) (2006-2008); Group President, National Accountants, Medco Health Solutions, Inc. (2004-2006); Executive Vice President, Client Strategy & Service, Medco Health Solutions, Inc. (2002-2003); Senior Vice President, Account Management, Medco Health Solutions, Inc. (1998); Senior Vice President, Human Resources; President, Internat, Mary Kay, Inc.; With, PepsiCo, Inc. **BA:** Express Scripts Headquarters, 1 Express Way, St Louis, MO, 63121

WEST, JERRY ALAN, T: Professional Sports Team Executive, Retired Professional Basketball Player **I:** Athletics **DOB:** 05/28/1938 **PB:** Chelyan **PT:** Son of Howard Stewart and Cecil Sue (Creasey) West; **ED:** LHD (hon.), West Virginia University, 2006; LHD (hon.), West Virginia Wesleyan College; BS, West Virginia University, 1960 **C:** Executive Board Member, LA Clippers, 2018-; Advisor to the owners, member executive board, Golden State Warriors, Oakland, 2011-; President basketball operations, Memphis Grizzlies, 2002-07; Executive vice president basketball operations, LA Lakers, 1994-2000; General manager, LA Lakers, 1982-94; Special consultant, LA Lakers, 1979-82; Head coach, LA Lakers, 1976-79; Player, LA Lakers, 1960-74 **CW:** Co-author (with William Libby): Mr. Clutch: The Jerry West Story, 1969; (with Jonathan Coleman) West by West: My Charmed, Tormented Life, 2011 **AW:** Named NBA Executive of Year, Sporting News, 2004, 1995, NBA All-Star Game MVP, 1972, 1st Team All Defense, NBA, 1970-73, NBA Finals MVP, 1969, 1st Team All-NBA, 1970-73, 1962-67, NCAA Final Four Most Outstanding Player, 1959, NCAA 1st Team All-Am., Associated Press, 1960, 1959; named to NBA 50th Anniversary All-Time Team, 1996, NBA 35th Anniversary All-Time Team, 1980, Naismith Memorial Basketball Hall of Fame, 1980, NBA We. Conference All-Star Team, 1961-74; recipient Gold medal, men's basketball, Summer Olympic Games, Rome, 1960,50 Greatest Players in History, 1996, **ACH:** Achievements include leading the NBA in: free throw attempts, free throws made, 1966, 1970; points per game, 1970; assists per game, 1972; member of the NBA Championship winning LA Lakers, 1972

WEST, KANYE OMARI, T: Rap Artist, Music Producer **I:** Media & Entertainment **DOB:** 06/08/1977 **PB:** Atlanta **PT:** Son of Ray and Donda West; **ED:** PhD (hon.), School of Art Institute Chicago, 2015; Attended, Chicago State University; Attended, American Academy Art, Chicago **C:** Designer, DW Kanye West, 2011-; Co-owner, music streaming service, Tidal, 2015-; Founder, producer, G.O.O.D.

(Getting Out Our Dreams) Music, 2004-; Designer, shoe line for Giuseppe Zanotti,; Designer, shoe line for Louis Vitton,; Owner, KW Foods LLC, **CIV:** Founder, Dr, Donda West Foundation (formerly Kanye West Foundation), 2003- **CW:** Singer: (albums) The College Dropout, 2004 (Best Rap Album, Grammy Awards, 2005), Late Registration, 2005 (Top Rap Album, Billboard R&B/Hip-Hop Awards, 2006, Best Rap Album, Grammy Awards, 2006), Graduation, 2007 (Best Rap Album, Grammy Awards, 2008, Favorite Rap/Hip-Hop Album, American Music Awards, 2008), 808s & Heartbreak, 2008, My Beautiful Dark Twisted Fantasy, 2010 (Best Rap Album, Grammy Awards, 2012), (with Jay-Z) Watch the Throne, 2011, Cruel Summer, 2012, Yeezus, 2013, The Life of Pablo, 2016, (songs) Jesus Walks, 2004 (Best Rap Song, Grammy Awards, 2005, Best Male Video, MTV Video Music Awards, 2005), Diamonds from Sierra Leone, 2005 (Best Rap Song, Grammy Awards, 2006), (featuring Jamie Foxx) Gold Digger, 2005 (Hot Rap Track of Year, Billboard R&B/Hip-Hop Awards, 2006, Best Rap Solo Performance, Grammy Awards, 2006), Stronger, 2007 (Best Rap Solo Performance, Grammy Awards, 2008), (featuring T-Pain) Good Life, 2007 (Best Collaboration, BET Awards, 2008, Best Rap Song, Grammy Awards, 2008), (with Common) Southside, 2007 (Best Rap Performance by a Duo or Group, Grammy Awards, 2008), (with Jay-Z, T.I. and Lil Wayne) Swagga Like Us, 2008 (Best Rap Performance by a Duo or Group, Grammy Awards, 2009), (with Estelle) American Boy, 2008 (Best Rap/Song Collaboration, Grammy Awards, 2009), (with Jay-Z and Rihanna) Run This Town, 2009 (Best Rap /Song Collaboration, Best Rap Song, Grammy Awards, 2010), (with Katy Perry) E.T., 2011 (Best Collaboration Video with Katy Perry MTV Video award, 2011), (with Jay-Z) Otis, 2011 (Best Rap Performance, Grammy Awards, 2012, Video of Year, BET Awards, 2012), Niggas in Paris, 2011 (Best Rap Performance, Best Rap Song (with Jay-Z), Grammy Awards, 2013), (with various artists) All of the Lights, 2011 (Best Rap Song, Best Rap/Sung Collaboration, Grammy Awards, 2012), (with Jay-Z, Frank Ocean, The-Dream) No Church in the Wild, 2011 (Best Rap/Sung Collaboration, Grammy Awards, 2013), (with John Legend and Big Sean) One Man Can Change The World, 2015 (Video with a Social Message, MTV Video Music Awards, 2015); writer, producer songs for numerous recording artists including Jermaine Dupri, Foxy Brown, Beanie Sigel, Jay-Z, Nas, Lil Kim, Beyoncé, T.I., Janet Jackson, Common, Rick Ross, others; author: Glow in the Dark, 2009, (Television), The College Dropout Video Anthology, 2004, Entourage, 2007, The Cleveland Show, 2010, VH1 Storytellers, 2010, Keeping up with the Kardashians, 2012, I Am Cait, 2015(Filmography), Fade to Black, 2004, Dave Chappelle's Block Party, 2005, State Property 2, 2005, The Love Guru, 2008, We Were Once a Fairytale, 2009, Runaway, 2010, Cruel Summer, 2012, Anchorman 2: The Legend Continues, 2013 **AW:** Named Choice Rap Artist, Teen Choice Awards, 2009, Favorite Rap/Hip-Hop Male Artist, American Music Awards, 2008, Best Group (The Throne with Jay-Z), BET Awards, 2012, Best Male Hip-Hop Artist, 2011, 2008, 2005, Outstanding New Artist, National Association for the Advancement of Colored People Image Awards, 2005, Rap Artist of Year, Billboard Music Awards, 2004, R&B/Hip-Hop Producer of Year, 2004, Best New R&B/Hip-Hop Artist of Year, 2004, Best Hip-Hop Act, Music of Black Origin (MOBO) Awards, 2008, Best Producer, 2004, Best Hip-Hop Artist, 2004, Best Selling Hip-Hop/Rap Artist, World Music Awards, 2006, Best New Male Artist, 2004; named one of The 100 Agents of Change, Rolling Stone magazine, 2009, Top 25 Entertainers of Year, Entertainment

Weekly, 2007, The 10 Most Fascinating People of 2013, Barbara Walters Special, The 10 Most Fascinating People of 2005, 100 Most Influential People, TIME magazine, 2005; recipient Michael Jackson Video Vanguard award, MTV Video Music Awards, 2015, Artist Achievement award, Billboard Music Awards, 2005, BET Hip Hop Awards, Visionary Award, 2015, Best Hip-Hop Style, 2016

WESTBROOK, RUSSELL, T: Professional Basketball Player **I:** Athletics **DOB:** 11/12/1988 **PB:** Long Beach **SC:** CA/USA **PT:** Son of Russell Westbrook and Shannon Horton; **ED:** Attended, UCLA, 2006-08 **C:** Guard, Oklahoma City Thunder, 2008-Present **CR:** Member US national team Summer Olympic Games, London, 2012, FIBA World Championships, Turkey, 2010 **AW:** Named 1st Team All-Rookie, NBA, 2009; named to Western Conference All-Star Team, 2015, 2011-13; recipient Gold medal, men's basketball, Summer Olympic Games, 2012, Gold medal, FIBA World Championship, 2010,Third- Team All-Pac-10, 2008, Pac-10 Defensive Player of the Year, 2008, NBA Scoring Champion, 2015, 2017, All-NBA Second Team, 2011-13, 2015, All-Nba First Team, 2016-17, NBA All Star Game MVP, 2015-16, NBA All-Star, 2011-13, 2015-2017, NBA Most Valuable Player, 2017 **ACH:** Achievements include being named MVP of the 2015 All-Star Game

WESTERMAN, BRUCE, T: U.S. Representative from Arkansas **I:** Government Administration/Government Relations/Government Services **DOB:** 11/18/1967 **PB:** Hot Springs **PT:** Married Sharon Westerman; children: Eli Westerman, Asa Westerman, Amie Westerman, Ethan Westerman. **ED:** MF, Yale University, 2001; BS in Biological & Agricultural Engineering, University Arkansas, 1990 **C:** Member US House of Representatives from Arkansas's 4th District, 2015-, Member, Committee on the Budget, Committee on Natural Resources, Committee on Science, Space and Technology, Republican Study Committee; Member District 30, Arkansas House of Representatives, 2011-15;; Engineer, forester, Mid-South Engineering Co., 1992-; Plant engineer, Riceland Foods, 1990-92 **PA:** Republican **BA:** 130 Cannon House Office Building, Washington, DC, 20515

WESTON, RANDY, T: Pianist, Composer **I:** Media & Entertainment **DOB:** 04/06/1926 **PB:** Brooklyn **SC:** NY/USA **PT:** Frank Edward Weston; Vivian (Moore) Weston **CH:** Cherryl; Pamela; Niles; Kim **ED:** Coursework, Parkway Music Institute, Brooklyn, NY (1950-1952) **CR:** Lecturer on African Music, United Nations **CW:** Pianist, American Society African Culture Tour, Lagos, Nigeria (1961, 1963); Toured with Randy Weston's Sextet for State Department, North and West Africa (1967); Appearances Include Newport Festival (1958), Monterey Festival (1966), Carnegie Hall (1973), Philharmonic Hall, New York City, NY (1973); Appearances, Major Jazz Clubs, New York City, NY; Numerous United Nations Concerts, Billie Holiday Theatre, New York University; European Tours Include Kingsberg Jazz Festival, Oslo, Norway (1974), Montreux Jazz Festival, Switzerland (1974), Festival de Costa del Sol, Marbella, Spain (1974), Ahus Jazz Festival, Kristianstad, Sweden (1974), Festival at Antibes, France (1974); Tour of Brazil (1981), Festival de Vienne, France (1985), Pompeii Jazz Festival, Italy (1985), International Festival Marrahesh, Marocco (1986), First Festival Gnaoua Culture, Marocco (1987), Lygano Festival Jazz, Switzerland (1988), Jazzaldia, San Sebastian, Spain (1988); Caribbean Cultural Centers Expressions Festival, New York City, NY (1988), Roots Festival, Lagos, Nigeria (1988); Featured Quest Artist, One Hundred Years of Jazz, Amsterdam, The

Netherlands (1989); Lecture-Concerts in Europe Including Bern, Basel, Zurich, Lyons (1975); Records Include "Blue Moses" (1972), "Volcano Blues" (1993), "Monterey '66" (1994); Compositions Include "Pam's Waltz" (1950), "Little Niles" (1950), "Hi Fly" (1958), "Portrait of Vivian" (1959), "Berkshire Blues" (1960), "Uhruru Africa Suite, 4 Movements" (1960), "African Cook Book" (1965), "The Last Day" (1966), "The Ganawa" (1971), "Portrait of F.E. Weston" (1974), "Carnival," "Blues to Africa," "Nuits Americani," "Blue, Trilogy: Portraits of Ellington"; Portraits of Monk; Self-Portrait of Weston, Verve, The Spirits of Our Ancestors (1992), The Splendid Master Gnawa Musicians of Morocco (1995), Saga (1996), Earth Birth (1997), Khepera (1998), Spirit! The Power of Music (1999), Ancient Future (2002), Nuit Africa (2004), Zep Tepi (2006), The Storyteller (2009), The Roots of the Blues (2013), The African Nubian Suite, with Vinshu Bill Wood, Lennie McBrowne (2017), Berkshire Blues (1996); Concert Artist for Radio-TV and Major U.S. Museums Including Smithsonian Institution; Performed Benefit Concerts for Anti-apartheid Committee at United Nations through African-American Musicians Society (1961); Appeared in Film "Jamboree" (1966); Commissioned, The Africans, Spoleto Festival, U.S.A. (1981), The African Queens, Boston Pops (1981), Portrait of Billie Holiday, Orchestra Symphonique de Lyons and Ensemble Instrumental et Big Band de Grenoble, France (1985), African Sunrise, City of Chicago (1985); Spanish TV Films: "Jazz Entre Amigos" (1987), "Randy in Tangier"; Randy Weston, African Rhythms, Boston TV (1989) AW: New Star Pianist Award, Down Beat International Critics Poll (1955); Pianist Most Deserving of Wider Recognition Award (1972); Broadway Award, Hollywood Advertising Club (1965); Premier Prix de L'Academie du Jazz, France (1975); Named World's Best Jazz Pianist, International Roots Festival, Lagos, Nigeria (1988); Randy Weston Week Declared in his Honor, Brooklyn Borough President's Office, Brooklyn Academy of Music (1986); French Office Nationale de Diffusion Artistique Grantee (1976); National Endowment for the Arts Grantee (1974); Number One Record, "Blues Moses," World's Jazz Chart (1972); Composers Awards, American Society of Composers MEM: American Society of Composers; American Federation of Musicians PA: Sufi BA: MM Music Agency, 11 Island Ave #1711, Miami Beach, FL, 33139

WEXNER, LESLIE HERBERT, T: CEO I: Retail/ Sales CN: Victoria's Secret Stores DOB: 09/08/1937 PB: Dayton SC: OH/USA ED: Honorary PhD, Jewish Theological Seminary; Honorary LHD, Brandeis University, 1990; Honorary LLD, Hofstra University, 1987; Honorary HHD, Ohio State University, 1986; BBA, Ohio State University, 1959 C: CEO, Victoria's Secret Megabrand & Intimate Apparel, 2016-Present; Founder, Chairman, CEO, Limited Brands, Inc., Columbus, OH, 1963 CR: Director, Executive Committee, Banc One Corp., Sotheby's Holdings Inc., Visiting Committee, Graduate School of Design, Harvard University, Business Administration Advisory Council, Ohio State University, Chairman, Retail Industry Trade Action Coalition, Fellow, American Academy of Arts & Sciences CIV: Chairman, Columbus Jewish Foundation, Aspen Institute, The Ohio State University, 2009-Present, Columbus Jewish Foundation, Aspen Institute, The Ohio State University, 1988-1997, 2005-Present, Hebrew Immigrant Aid Society, New York, NY, 1982-Present, Board of Directors, Columbus Urban League, 1982-1984, Board of Trustees, Columbus Jewish Federation, 1972, Co-Chairman, International United Jewish Appeal Committee, National Vice Chairman, Treasurer, United Jewish

Appeal, Board of Directors, Executive Committee, American Jewish Joint Distribution Committee, Inc., Columbus Capital Corporation For Civic Improvement, Founding Member, First Chair, The Ohio State University Foundation, Executive Committee, American Israel Public Affairs Committee AW: World's Richest People, Forbes Magazine, 2001-Present, Forbes' Executive Pay, 1999-Present, Forbes 400: Richest Americans, 1999-Present, Top 200 Collectors, Artnews Magazine, 2004-2012, Man of the Year, American Marketing Association, 1974, Decorated Cavaliere, Republic Of Italy MEM: Young Presidents Organization, Sigma Alpha Mu, B'nai B'rith H: Collecting Modern and Contemporary art and British sporting pictures

WHITACRE, ERIC, T: Composer I: Fine Art DOB: 05/28/1905 PB: Reno, Nevada SC: Reno, Nevada ED: BM in Music Composition, University of Nevada; Masters, Juilliard C: Los Angeles Master Chorale, 2016- CW: (Project)Virtual Choir 2.0,2011, Virtual Choir,2012, Virtual Choir,2013, (Album) Light and Gold, 2010, Water Night, 2012 AW: Grammy for Best Choral Performance, 2012

WHITAKER, FOREST, T: Actor I: Media & Entertainment PB: Long View SC: TX/USA ED: Attended, University Southern California; Degree (hon.), Xavier University of Louisiana, 2009 C: Executive director, Nodance Film Festival, 2003; President, Spirit Dance Entertainment CR: Member President Barack Obama's Committee on Arts and Humanities, 2009 CW: Stage appearances (London) Swan, Romeo and Juliet, Hamlet, Ring Around the Moon, Craig's Wife, Whose Life Is It Anyway?, The Greeks, Patchwork Shakespeare, Beggar's Opera, Jesus Christ Superstar; actor: (films) TAG: The Assassination Game, 1982, Fast Times at Ridgemont High, 1982, Vision Quest, 1985, The Color of Money, 1986, Platoon, 1986, Stakeout, 1987, Good Morning, Vietnam, 1987, Bloodsport, 1988, Bird, 1988 (Best Actor, Cannes Film Festival 1988), Johnny Handsome, 1989, Downtown, 1990, Rage in Harlem, 1991, Article 99, 1992, Diary of a Hit Man, 1992, Consenting Adults, 1992, Body Snatchers, 1993, The Crying Game, 1993, Bank Robber, 1993, Blown Away, 1994, Jason's Lyric, 1994, Prêt-à-Porter, 1994, Species, 1995, Smoke, 1995, Phenomenon, 1996, Body Count, 1998, Ghost Dog: The Way of the Samurai, 1999, Light It Up, 1999, Battlefield Earth, 2000, Four Dogs Playing Poker, 2000, Green Dragon, 2001, The Follow, 2001, The Fourth Angel, 2001, Panic Room, 2002, Phone Booth, 2002, Jiminy Glick in La La Wood, 2004, Mary, 2005, A Little Trip to Heaven, 2005, Even Money, 2006, The Marsh, 2006, The Last King of Scotland (Best Actor, New York Film Critics Circle awards, 2006, National Board Review, 2006, African-American Film Critics Association, 2006, National Society Film Critics, 2007, Critics' Choice awards, 2006, Broadcast Film Critics Association, 2007, Best Performance by an Actor in a Motion Picture-Drama, Golden Globe awards, 2007, Outstanding Performance by a Male Actor in a Leading Role, Screen Actors Guild awards, 2007, Best Actor in a Leading Role, British Academy Film and TV Arts, 2007, Best Actor in a Leading Role, Academy Awards, 2007, Outstanding Actor in a Motion Picture, National Association for the Advancement of Colored People Image Awards, 2007), (voice) Everyone's Hero, 2006, Vantage Point, 2008, Street Kings, 2008, (voice) Where the Wild Things Are, 2009, Our Family Wedding, 2010, Repo Men, 2010, My Own Love Song, 2010, The Experiment, 2010, Lullaby for Pi, 2010, Catch .44, 2011, Freelancers, 2012, A Dark Truth, 2012, Pawn 2013, The Last Stand, 2013, Out of the Furnace, 2013, The Butler, 2013 (Outstanding Actor in a Motion Picture, National Association for the Advancement of Colored

People Image Awards, 2014), Zulu, 2013, Black Nativity, 2013, Two Men in Town, 2014, Taken 3, 2015, Southpaw, 2015, Arrival, 2016, Rogue One A Star Wars Story, 2016, Burden, 2018, Finding Steve McQueen, 2018, Labyrinth, 2018, Black Panther, 2018, Sorry to Bother You, 2018; (TV films) Grand Baby, 1985, Hands of a Stranger, 1987, Criminal Justice, 1990, Last Light, 1993, Lush Life, 1993, The Enemy Within, 1994, Rebound: The Legend of Earl The Great Manigault, 1996, The Split, 1998, Witness Protection, 1999, Deacons for Defense, 2003; (TV mini-series) North & South, 1985, North and South Book II, 1986, Roots, 2016; (TV series) The Shield, 2006-07, Criminal Minds, 2011; (TV appearances) Making the Grade, 1982, Cagney & Lacey, 1983, Trapper John, M.D., 1984, Hill Street Blues, 1984, The Fall Guy, 1985, Diff'rent Strokes, 1985, Amazing Stories, 1986, Feast of All Saints, 2001, The Twilight Zone, 2003, ER, 2006, The Shield, 2006, American Dad, 2007, Criminal Minds, 2010, Brick City, 2010, Criminal Minds Suspect Behavior, 2011, Serving Life, 2012, Africa, 2013, Roots, 2016, Star Wars Rebels, 2017, Empire, 2017; actor, director, executive prodr.: (films) First Daughter, 2004; actor, executive prodr.: (films) Green Dragon, 2001, American Gun, 2005; (TV films) Feast of All Saints, 2001; dir.: (films) Waiting to Exhale, 1995, Hope Floats, 1998; (TV films) Strapped, 1993, Black Jaq, 1998; prodr.: (films) Chasing Papi, 2003, Powder Blue, 2009, Fruitvale Station, 2013, Songs My Brothers Taught Me, 2015; actor, prodr.: (films) Vipaka, 2012, Repentance, 2013, Dope (voice), 2015; co-exec. prodr.: (TV films) Door to Door, 2002; executive prodr.: (documentaries) Brick City, 2009-11, Serving Life, 2011, I Am You, 2015, Rising from Ashes, 2012, We Are One, 2016, (films) Monte Carlo, 2011. AW: Recipient Star, Hollywood Walk of Fame, 2007, Joel Siegel award, Critics' Choice Awards, 2014

WHITE, ALAN, T: Drummer I: Media & Entertainment PB: Pelton SC: England CW: (Solo Album) Ramshackled, 1975, (With Chris Squire) Run with the Fox, 1981, (With Alan Price Set) A Price on his Head, 1967, The Amazing Alan Price, 1967, This Price is Right, 1968, (With George Harrison) All Things Must Pass, 1970, Radha Krsna Temple, 1971,(With Yes) Yessongs, 1973, Tales from Topgraphic Oceans, 1973, Relayer, 1974, Going for the One, 1977, Tormato, 1978, Drama, 1980, 90215, 1983, Big Generator, 1987, Union, 1991, Talk, 1994, Keys to Ascension, 1996, Keys to Ascension 2, 1997, Open Your Eyes, 1997, The Ladder, 1999, Magnification, 2001, Fly From Here, 2011, Heaven& Earth, 2014 AW: Rock and Roll Hall of Fame, 2017

WHITE, BETTY, T: Actress, Comedienne I: Media & Entertainment DOB: 01/17/1922 PB: Oak Park PT: Daughter of Horace Loagan and Christine Tess (Cachikis) W.; Married Dyck Barker 1945 (div. 1945), Married Lane Allen 1947 (div. 1949), Married Allen Ludden, 1963 (deceased 1981). ED: Student pub. schools, Beverly Hills, California CIV: Chair, Greater LA Zoo Association, 2010- Zoo commissioner, Greater LA Zoo, 1998- Member, Morris Animal Foundation, 1976- CW: Appearances on radio shows This Is Your FBI, Blondie, The Great Gildersleeve; actress: (TV series) including Hollywood on Television, The Betty White Show, 1954-58, Life With Elizabeth, 1953-55, A Date With The Angels, 1957-58, The Pet Set, 1971, Mary Tyler Moore Show, 1974-77 (Emmy award for Outstanding Continuing Performance by a Supporting Actress in a Comedy Series, 1975, 1976), The Betty White Show, 1977, Mama's Family, 1983-86, The Golden Girls, 1985-92 (Emmy award for Outstanding Lead Actress in a Comedy Series, 1986), Another World, 1988, The Golden

Palace, 1992-93, Maybe This Time, 1995, Hot in Cleveland, 2010- (Screen Actors Guild award for Outstanding Performance by a Female Actor in a Comedy Series, 2011, 2012), (TV films) With This Ring, 1978, The Best Place to Be, 1979, Before and After, 1979, Eunice, 1982, Chance of a Lifetime, 1991, The Story of Santa Claus, 1996, A Weekend in the Country, 1996, The Retrievers, 2001, Annie's Point, 2005, The Lost Valentine, 2011,Betty Whites Off Their Rockers, 2014, The Client List, 2012, Save Me, 2013,Mickey Mouse,2013,The Soul Man, 2014, SNL, 2015, Fireside Chat with Esther,2015, Bones, 2015-17,Smartest Animals in America, 2015, Spongebob Squarepants, 2016, Crowded, 2016, Young and Hungry, 2017, If You're Not in the Obit, Eat Breakfast, 2017 (films) Advise and Consent, 1962, Dennis the Menace 2, 1998, Hard Rain, 1998, The Story of Us, 1999, Bringing Down the House, 2003, The Third Wish, 2004, The Proposal, 2009, You Again, 2010, (voice) Dr. Seuss' The Lorax, 2012, Letter to Jackie Remembering President Kennedy, 2013, Betty White Goes Wild, 2013; (guest appearances) Petticoat Junction, 1969, The Odd Couple, 1972, Fame, 1983, St. Elsewhere, 1985, Who's the Boss, 1985, Matlock, 1987, Empty Nest, 1989, 92, Carol & Company, 1990, Nurses, 1991, Diagnosis Murder, 1994, The Naked Truth, 1995, The John Larroquette Show, 1996 (Emmy award for Outstanding Guest Actress in a Comedy Series, 1996), Suddenly Susan, 1996, (voice) King of the Hill, 1999, 2002, Ally McBeal, 1999, (voice) The Simpsons, 2000, Yes, Dear, 2002, Providence, 2002, That 70s Show, 2002, 03, Everwood, 2003, 2004, The Practice, 2004, My Wife and Kids, 2004, Malcolm in the Middle, 2004, (voice) Father of the Pride, 2004, Boston Legal, 2005; frequent celebrity guest on numerous game shows including Hollywood Squares, Match Game; summer stock appearances Guys and Dolls, Take Me Along, The King and I, Who Was That Lady?, Critic's Choice, Bells are Ringing; host: (reality TV series) Betty White's Off Their Rockers, 2012-13; author: Betty White's Pet-Lovers: How Pets Take Care of Us, 1987, Here We Go Again: My Life in Television, 1995, If You Ask Me (And Of Course You Won't), 2011, (Grammy award for Best Spoken Word Album, 2011). **AW:** Recipient Living Legacy award, Women's International Center, 1988, Star on the Hollywood Walk of Fame, 1995, Lifetime Achievement award, Screen Actors Guild, 2010, inducted into The TV Hall of Fame, 1995, National Association Broadcasters Hall of Fame, 2012; named Honorary Forest Ranger, US Forest Service, 2010; named one of the 10 Most Fascinating People of 2010, Barbara Walters Special; named Entertainer of Year, Associated Press, 2010, Favorite TV Icon, People's Choice Awards, 2015. **MEM:** Member American Federation of TV and Radio Artists, American Humane Association, Greater LA Zoo Association (named an Ambassador to the Animals, 2006). **BA:** Agency for the Performing Arts, 888 Seventh Avenue, New York, NY, 10106

WHITE, DANA, T: Sports Association Executive **I:** Media & Entertainment **PB:** Manchester **ED:** Attended, University Massachusetts **C:** President, Ultimate Fighting Championship (UFC), 2000-; Co-owner, Zuffa LLC,; Manager of boxers and mixed martial arts fighters including Tito Ortiz and Chuck Liddell, Ultimate Fighting Championship (UFC), 2000; Boxing trainer, group exercise instructor,; Founder, Dana White Enterprises, Las Vegas, 1992 **CW:** Prodr.: (TV series) The Ultimate Fighter, 2005- **AW:** Named one of Most Influential People in the World of Sports, Business Week, 2008

WHITE, HELENE NITA, T: Federal Judge **I:** Law and Legal Services **DOB:** 12/02/1954 **PB:** Jackson Heights **SC:** NY/USA **PT:** Daughter of Frank William

and Ruth (Gruber) White **ED:** JD, University Pennsylvania, 1978; AB, Columbia University, 1978 **C:** Judge, US Court Appeals (6th Cir.), 2008-; Judge, Michigan Court Appeals, Detroit, 1993-2008; Judge, Wayne Cir. Court, Detroit, 1983-93; Judge, 36th District Court, Detroit, 1981-83; Judge, Common Pleas Court, Detroit, 1981; Law Clerk to Justice Charles L. Levin, Michigan Supreme Court, Southfield, 1978-80 **CIV:** Chairman, Nominating Committee, Coalition Temporary Shelter, 1988-, Board of Directors, chairman bylaws committee, Coalition Temporary Shelter, 1986-, Board of Directors, Chairman, Bylaws Committee, Metropolitan Detroit YWCA, 1986-87, Program Committee Business and Professional Division, Jewish Welfare Federation, 1987-, Board of Advisors, Detroit Women's Forum, 1988-, Board of Advisors, Sojourner Foundation, 1988 **MEM:** Mem.: American Bar Association, Women Lawyers Association Michigan, National Association Women Judges (chairman publicity 1984, membership committee 1985-), Detroit Bar Association, Pennsylvania Bar Association **BAR:** Bar: Michigan 1979, Pennsylvania 1979 **BA:** 100 East Fifth Street, Cincinnati, OH, 45202

WHITE, MILES D., T: Healthcare Company Executive **I:** Pharmaceuticals **DOB:** 03/10/1955 **PB:** Minneapolis **SC:** MN/USA **ED:** MBA, Stanford University (1980); BS in Mechanical Engineering, Stanford University (1978) **C:** Chairman, Chief Executive Officer, Abbott Labs (1999-Present); Chief Executive Officer, Abbott Labs (1998-1999); Executive Vice President, Abbott Labs (1998-1999); Senior Vice President, Diagnostic Operations, Abbott Labs (1994-1998); Vice President, Diagnostic System & Operations, Abbott Labs (1993-1994); Joined, Abbott Labs (1984); Management Consultant, McKinsey & Co. **CR:** Chairman, Federal Reserve Bank (2005-2007); Chairman, Federal Reserve Bank, Chicago, IL (2002-2004); Board of Directors, Federal Reserve Bank (2002-Present); Board of Directors, McDonald's Corporation (2009-Present); Board of Directors, The Tribune Co. (2005-2006); Board of Directors, Motorola Inc. (2005-2009); Board of Directors, Abbott Laboratories (1998-Present); Board of Directors, Caterpillar Inc. (1998-Present); **CIV:** Board of Trustee, Culver Educational Foundation; Board Trustee, Joffrey Ballet, Chicago, IL; Board Trustee, Northwestern University; Board Trustee, Field Museum, Chicago, IL; Member, Stanford Advisory Council on Interdisciplinary Biosciences; Member, Stanford Graduate School of Business Advisory Council **MEM:** American Academy of Arts & Sciences; Economic Club of Chicago; Chairman, Executives' Club of Chicago

WHITE, SHAUN ROGER, T: Professional Snowboarder, Professional Skateboarder, Olympic Athlete **I:** Athletics **DOB:** 09/03/1986 **PB:** San Diego **PT:** Son of Kathy and Roger White. **C:** Professional skateboarder, 2003-; Professional snowboarder, Burton Snowboarding team, 1999-; Designer, The White Collection,; Skateboarder, Tony Hawk Gigantic Skatepark Tour, 2002 **CR:** Member US snowboarding team Winter Olympic Games, Vancouver, Canada, 2010, Turin, Italy, 2006 **CW:** Actor: (films) The White Album, 2004 **AW:** Named Sports-Choice Action Sports, Teen Choice Awards, 2006; recipient Gold medal, men's halfpipe, Winter Olympic Games, 2018, 2010, 2006, ESPY award, Best US Olympian, ESPN, 2006, ESPY award, Best Male Action Sports Athlete, 2008, 2006, 2003,Chairman of the Board, Spike TV Guys Choice Awards, 2007, 2010, Snowboarder Magazine 9th Best Snowboarder, 2009, Revolver Golden Gods Award, Most Metal Athlete, Transworld Snowboarding Rider of the Year x2, **ACH:**

Achievements include being the youngest snowboarder to win the US Open Slopestyle Championship, 2004; being the first athlete to compete in both Winter and Summer X Games, 2003; winning the gold medal at Winter X Games, Slopestyle, 2003-2006, Halfpipe, 2003, 2006; winning the gold medal at Summer X Games, Vert, 2005; winning all 5 Grand Prix Superpipes, 2005-2006 **BA:** United Talent Agency, 9336 Civic Center Dr, Beverly Hills, CA, 90210

WHITEHEAD, COLSON, T: Novelist **I:** Writing and Editing **PB:** New York City **SC:** NY/USA **ED:** BA, Harvard College, Cambridge, Massachusetts, 1991 **C:** Writer, The New York Times, 2015-; Writer, The Village Voice, New York City, 1991-93 **CW:** Author: (novels) The Intuitionist, 1999 (New Voices Award, Quality Paperback Book Club), John Henry Days, 2001 (Anisfield-Wolf Book Award, 2002, Young Lions Fiction award, New York Pub. Libr., 2002, American Library Association Black Caucus Honor), The Colossus of New York, 2003 (New York Times Notable Book of Year), Apex Hides the Hurt, 2006 (PEN/Oakland Award, New York Times Notable Book of Year), Sag Harbor, 2009; Contributor Works of Non-fiction, Essays and Reviews to Numerous Publications,(Book) Zone One, 2011, The Noble Hustle: Poker, Beef Jerky & Death, 2014,The Underground Railroad, 2016 **AW:** Recipient Whiting Writers' Award for Fiction, 2000; Fellow Cullman Center Scholars & Writers, New York Pub. Libr., John D. & Catherine T. MacArthur Foundation, 2003,Guggenheim Fellowship, 2013 Time 100 Most Influential, 2017, Pulitzer Prize for Fiction, 2017

WHITEHOUSE, SHELDON, T: U.S. Senator from Rhode Island, Former State Attorney General **I:** Government Administration/Government Relations/Government Services **DOB:** 10/20/1955 **PB:** NYC **PT:** Son of Charles Sheldon and Mary (Rand) Whitehouse **ED:** JD, University Virginia, 1982; BA, Yale University, 1978 **CT:** Bar: US Court Appeals (1st cir.) 1984, US Supreme Court 1986, US District Court Rhode Island 1984, Rhode Island 1983, West Virginia 1982 **C:** US Senator from Rhode Island, 2007-; Attorney general, State of Rhode Island, Providence, 1999-2003; US attorney District Rhode Island, US Department Justice, Providence, 1994-98; Director, Department Business Regulation, State of Rhode Island, Providence, 1992-94; Director governor policy office, State of Rhode Island, Providence, 1991-92; Executive counsel to Governor, State of Rhode Island, Providence, 1991; Assistant attorney general, State of Rhode Island, Providence, 1989-90; Chief regulatory unit, State of Rhode Island, Providence, 1988-90; Special assistant attorney general, State of Rhode Island, Providence, 1985-90; Attorney, State of Rhode Island, Providence, 1983-84 **AW:** Recipient Public Achievement award, Common Cause, 1999, Secret Service Honor award, US Department Treasury, 1998, Robert M. Goodrich award for Outstanding Public Employee, Rhode Island Public Expenditure Council, 1993 **PA:** Democrat **BA:** Office of Sheldon Whitehouse, Rm 530 Hart Senate Office Building, Washington, DC, 20510

WHITESIDES, GEORGE M., T: Chemist, Professor **I:** Education/Educational Services **DOB:** 08/03/1939 **PB:** Louisville **SC:** KY/USA **ED:** D Honoris Causa (hon.), University Twente, The Netherlands, 2001; PhD in Chemistry, California Institute Tech., 1964; AB in Chemistry, Harvard University, 1960 **C:** Woodford L. and Ann A. Flowers University Professor, Harvard University, 2004-; Mallinckrodt Professor, Harvard University, Cambridge, 1986-2004; Professor Department Chemistry, Harvard University, Cambridge,

1982-86; Haslam and Dewey Professor, Massachusetts Institute of Technology, Cambridge, 1980-82; Arthur C. Cope Professor, Massachusetts Institute of Technology, Cambridge, 1975-80; Professor, Massachusetts Institute of Technology, Cambridge, 1971-75; Associate Professor, Massachusetts Institute of Technology, Cambridge, 1969-71; Assistant Professor Department Chemistry, Massachusetts Institute of Technology, Cambridge, 1963-69 **CR:** Adv. Position Department Defense Advanced Research Projects Agency, National Science Foundation, National Research Council **AW:** Recipient Benjamin Franklin Medal in Chemistry, Franklin Institute, 2009, Priestley Medal, Am. Chemical Society, 2007, Welch Award, 2005, Linus Pauling Medal Award, 2005, Emanuel Merck Lecture Prize, 2005, Welch Award in Chemistry, 2005, Linus Pauling Medal, 2005, Emanuel Merk Lect. Prize, 2005, Dan David Foundation Prize, 2005, Dickson Prize in Sci., 2005, Jacob Heskel Gabbay Award in Biotech. and Medicine, 2004, Ralph and Helen Oesper Award, Cincinnati Section Am. Chemical Society, 2004, Paracelsus Prize, Swiss Chemical Society, 2004, Kyoto Prize for Advanced Tech., Inamori Foundation, 2003, Pittsburgh Analytical Chemistry Award, Society Analytical Chemists of Pittsburgh, 2003, Researcher of Year Award, Small Times Magazine, 2002, World Tech. Award for Materials, World Tech. Network, 2001, Von Hippel Award, Material Research Society, 2000, Excellence Award in Surface Sci., Surfaces Biomaterials Foundation, 1999, Wallac Oy Innovation Award, Society Biomolecular Screening, 1999, Distinguished Chemist Award, Sierra Nevada Section Am. Chemical Society, 1999, National Medal of Sci., 1998, Madison Marshall Award, Am. Chemical Society, 1996, Defense Advanced Research Projects Agency Award for Significant Technical Achievement, 1996, Arthur C. Cope Award, 1995, James Flack Norris Award, 1994, Arthur C. Cope Scholar Award, 1989, Remsen Award, 1983, Distinguished Alumni Award, California Institute Tech., 1980, Harrison Howe Award, Rochester Section, 1979, Pure Chemistry Award, Am. Chemical Society, 1975; Alfred P. Sloan Fellow, 1968, Othmer Gold Medal, 2010, King Faisal International Prize, 2011, IRI Medal, 2013, R&D Magazine Scientist of the Year, 2007 **MEM:** Fellow: American Association for the Advancement of Science, Indian National Sci. Academy, World Tech. Network, Chemical Research Society India (hon.); Mem.: NAE, National Academy of Sciences, Academia Sinica (Chairman International Sci. Adv. Board Genomics Research Center 2006-), Royal Netherlands Academy Arts and Scis., Materials Research Society India (hon.), Am. Philosophical Society, Am. Academy Arts and Scis. **ACH:** Achievements include patents in field **BA:** Harvard U Dept of Chemistry, 12 Oxford St, Cambridge, MA, 02138

WHITMAN, MEG, T: HP CEO **I:** Information Technology and Services **DOB:** 08/04/1956 **PB:** Long Island, New York, August 4, 1956 **PT:** Daughter of Hendricks Hallett and Margaret (Goodhue) Whitman; **ED:** MBA, Harvard Business School, 1979; BA in Economics, Princeton University, 1977 **C:** Chairman, president, CEO, Hewlett-Packard Co., Palo Alto, 2014-; President, CEO, Hewlett-Packard Co., Palo Alto, 2011-14; Part-time strategic adv., Kleiner Perkins Caulfield & Byers (KPCB), Menlo Park, California, 2011; Republican nominee for Governor of California, 2009-10; Co-chair, Republican Victory '08, 2008; President, CEO, eBay, Inc., San Jose, California, 1998-2008; General manager preschool division, Hasbro Inc., 1997-98; President, CEO, Florists' Transworld Delivery (FTD), 1995-97; President Stride Rite Division, Stride Rite Corp., 1994-95; Executive vice president Keds division, Stride Rite Corp., 1993-94; Corporate

vice president strategic planning, Stride Rite Corp., 1992-93; Senior vice president marketing & consumer products division, The Walt Disney Co, Burbank, California, 1989-92; Vice president, Bain & Co., Inc., 1982-89; Brand assistant, The Procter & Gamble Co., 1979-81 **CR:** Board directors Zaarly, 2011-, ArcSight, Inc., 2011-, Zipcar, Inc., 2011-13, Hewlett-Packard Co., 2011-, DreamWorks Animation SKG, Inc., 2005-08, Gap Inc., 2003-06, The Procter & Gamble Co., 2011-, 2003-08, The Goldman Sachs Group Inc., 2001-02, Staples Inc., 1999-2008, eBay, Inc., 1998-2009 **CIV:** Board directors, The Nature Conservancy, 2011- Trustee, Princeton University, **CW:** Co-author (with Joan O'C Hamilton): The Power of Many: Values for Success in Business and in Life, 2010 **AW:** Named Number One on List of Best CEO's, Worth magazine, 2002; named one of The 50 Most Important People on the Web, PC World, 2007, The 50 Women to Watch, The Wall St. Journal, 2006, 2005, The 100 Most Powerful Women, Forbes magazine, 2012-14, 2010, 2005-07, The 100 Most Influential People in the World, TIME Magazine, 2005, 2004, The 50 Most Powerful Women in Business, Fortune magazine, 2011-15, 1998-2007; recipient Webby Lifetime Achievement award (eBay), 2007 **MEM:** Fellow: American Academy Arts & Sciences **H:** Fly fishing **PA:** Republican **BA:** HP Inc., 1501 Page Mill Road, Palo Alto, CA, 94304

WHITSON, PEGGY ANNETTE, T: Astronaut **I:** Sciences **DOB:** 02/09/1960 **PB:** Mount Ayr **SC:** IA/USA **PT:** Daughter of Earl Keith and Beth Avalee (Walters) S. **MS:** Married **SPN:** Clarence Felton Sams, May 6, 1989 **ED:** PhD in Biochemistry, Rice University, 1985; BS in Biology/Chemistry (summa cum laude), Iowa Wesleyan College, 1981 **C:** International Space Station (ISS) Commander for Expedition-16, launched aboard Soyuz TMA-11 spacecraft, docking with ISS, 2007-17; Crew member, Expedition-5 mission, 2002; Back-up International Space Station Commander for Expedition 14, Johnson Space Center, NASA, Houston, 2005-06; Chief station operations branch, astronaut office, Johnson Space Center, NASA, Houston, 2005; Deputy chief astronaut office, Johnson Space Center, NASA, Houston, 2003-05; Tech. duties, astronaut office operations planning branch, lead Crew Test Support Team in Russia, Johnson Space Center, NASA, Houston, 1998-99; Deputy division chief medical scis. division, Johnson Space Center, NASA, Houston, 1993-96; Project scientist Shuttle-Mir, Johnson Space Center, NASA, Houston, 1993-95; US-USSR Joint Working Group in Space Medicine and Biology, Johnson Space Center, NASA, Houston, 1991-92; Payload element developer, bone cell research experiment (E10) aboard SL-J (STS-47), Johnson Space Center, NASA, Houston, 1991-92; Tech. monitor, biochemistry research lab, biomedical and research branch, Johnson Space Center, NASA, Houston, Utah, 1991-93; Research biochemist, biomedical operations and research branch, Johnson Space Center, NASA, Houston, 1989-93; Supervisor, biochemistry research group, KRUG International, Johnson Space Center, NASA, Houston, 1988-89; National Research Council resident research associate, Johnson Space Center, NASA, Houston, 1986-88; Robert A. Welch Postdoctoral Fellow, Rice University, Houston, 1985-86; Robert A. Welch predoctoral fellow, Rice University, Houston, 1982-85 **CR:** Adj. assistant professor, department internal medicine and department human biological chemistry and genetics, University Texas Medical Branch, Galveston, Texas, 1991-97 adj. assistant professor, Maybee Laboratory for Biochemical and Genetic Engineering, Rice University, 1997 Selected for Space Station Redesign Team, 1993 co-chair U.S./Russian Mission Sci. Working Group, 1995-96 **CW:**

Contributor articles to Biochemistry, Journal Biological Chemistry, Journal Cellular Physiology. **AW:** NASA Outstanding Leadership medal, 2006, 2006, NASA Space Flight medal, 2002, Group Achievement award for Shuttle-Mir Program, 1996, Am. Astronautical Society Randolph Lovelace II award, 1995, NASA Tech Brief award, 1995, NASA Space Act Board award, 1998, 1995, NASA Silver Snoopy award, 1995, NASA Exceptional Service medal, 2006, 2003, 1995, NASA Space Act award for Patent Applications, 1994, NASA Cert. Commendation, 1994, NASA Sustained Superior Performance award, 1990, Krug International Merit award, 1989, Time 100 Most Influential,2018 **MEM:** Member Am. Association Biochemistry and Molecular Biology, New York Academy Scis. **ACH:** Achievements include research in fluid and electrolyte physiology associated with spaceflight, renal stone risk assessments, receptor-ligand interactions, second messenger signaling, and gravitational effects on cytoskeletal structures; patents in field; Aboard International Space Station, first time in the 50 year history of spaceflight that two women (along with Pamela Melroy-flight Commander on Discovery) are in charge of two spacecrafts at the same time; first women to be in charge of the International Space Station, 2007; with Daniel Tani made history, marked the 100th spacewalk at the space station, December, 2007. **BA:** NASA, 300 E St SW, Washington, DC, 20546

WICKER, ROGER FREDERICK, T: U.S. Senator from Mississippi **I:** Government Administration/Government Relations/Government Services **DOB:** 07/05/1951 **PB:** Pontotoc **SC:** MI/USA **PT:** Son of Thomas Frederick and Wordna Glen (Threadgil) Wicker; **ED:** JD, University Miss Law School, 1975; BA in Political Sci. & Journalism, University Mississippi, 1973 **C:** Chairman, National Republican Senatorial Committee (NRSC), 2015-2017; US Senator from Mississippi, 2007-; Member, US House Budget Committee, 2003-07; Member, US House Appropriations Committee, 1995-2007; Member, US Congress from 1st Mississippi District, 1995-2007; Member District 6, Mississippi State Senate, 1988-94; Judge pro tempore Municipal Court, City of Tupelo, 1986-87; Public defender, Lee County, Mississippi, 1984-87; Partner, Sparks, Wicker, & Colburn, 1982-94; Staff member to Rep. Trent Lott, US House of Reps., Washington, 1980-82; Judge adv., US Air Force, 1976-80 **CIV:** Member, Lions Club, Member, Community Devel. Foundation, Member, Tupelo First Baptist Church, Mississippi, **MIL:** Positions up to lieutenant colonel US Air Force Reserve, 1980-2004, with US Air Force, 1976-80 **AW:** Recipient Award, Manufacturing Excellence, National Association of Manufacturers, 2003, Capitol Dome award, American Cancer Society, 2003, National Public Service award, American Heart Association, 1998 **PA:** Republican **BA:** Office of Roger Wicker, 555 dirksen Senate Office Building, Washington, DC, 20510

WIEHOFF, JOHN P., T: CEO of CH Robinson Worldwide **I:** Other **CN:** CH Robinson Worldwide **ED:** Bachelors, St. John's University **CT:** CPA **C:** Chairman, C.H. Robinson Worldwide, Inc. (2007-Present); Chief Executive Officer, C.H. Robinson Worldwide, Inc. (2002-Present); President, C.H. Robinson Worldwide, Inc. (1999-Present); Senior Vice President, Chief Financial Officer, C.H. Robinson Worldwide, Inc. (1998-1999); Treasurer, C.H. Robinson Worldwide, Inc. (1997-1998); Corporate Controller, C.H. Robinson Worldwide, Inc. (1992-1998); With, Arthur Anderson (1984-1992) **CR:** Board of Directors, Donaldson Co., Inc. (2003-Present); Board of Directors, Polaris Industries Inc. (2007-Present); Board of Directors, Donaldson Co., Inc. (2003-Present) **BA:** C H Robinson Worldwide Inc, 14701 Charlson Rd, Eden Prairie, MN, 55347-5088

WIEMAN, CARL EDWIN, T: Physics Professor, Former Federal Official **I:** Education/Educational Services **DOB:** 03/26/1951 **PB:** Corvallis **PT:** Son of N. Orr and Alison W.; **ED:** DSc (hon.), University Chicago, 1997; PhD, Stanford University, 1977; BS, Massachusetts Institute of Technology, 1973 **C:** Professor physics and Grad. School Education, Stanford University, California, 2013-; Associate director for sci., Office Sci. & Tech. Policy (OSTP), Executive Office of the President, Washington, 2010-12; Professor physics, director Carl Wieman Sci. Education Initiative (CWSCI), U British Columbia, Vancouver, 2007; Director Sci. Education Initiative, University Colorado, Boulder, 2006; Distinguished research professor, University Colorado, Boulder, 1997-2006; Professor physics, University Colorado, Boulder, 1987-97; Fellow Joint Institute Laboratory Astrophysics (JILA), University Colorado, Boulder, 1985-2006; Associate professor physics, University Colorado, Boulder, 1984-87; Assistant professor physics, University Michigan, Ann Arbor, 1979-84; Assistant research physicist department physics, University Michigan, Ann Arbor, 1977-79 **CR:** Cherwell-Simon Memorial lecturer Oxford University, 1999 Loeb lecturer Harvard University, 1990-91 Rosenthal Memorial lecturer Columbia University, 1988, Yale University, 1988 **AW:** Named US Professor of Year, Carnegie Foundation Advancement of Teaching/Coun. Advancement & Support of Education, 2004; recipient Vollum award, Reed College, 2009, Nobel Prize in Physics, Nobel Foundation, 2001, Distinguished Teaching Scholar award, National Sci. Foundation, 2001, Benjamin Franklin Medal in Physics, 2000, Lorentz medal, Netherlands Royal Academy Sci., 1998, Sci. award, Bonfils Stanton Foundation, 1998, King Faisal International prize for Sci., 1997, Newcomb Cleveland prize, American Association for the Advancement of Science, 1996, Fritz London prize for low temperature physics, 1996, Einstein medal for laser sci., Society Optical & Quantum Electronics, 1995, E.O. Lawrence Memorial award, US Department Energy, 1993; fellow John Simon Guggenheim Memorial Foundation, 1990-91 **MEM:** Fellow: American Physical Society (Davisson-Germer prize 1994, Schawlow prize in laser sci. 1998); mem.: National Academy of Sciences, American Association for the Advancement of Science, American Association Physics Teachers (Richtmyer lecturer award 1996, Oersted medal 2007), Optical Society America (R.W. Wood prize 1999) **ACH:** Achievements include first to achieve Bose-Einstein condensation, 1995

WIEST, DIANNE, T: Actress **I:** Media & Entertainment **SC:** MO/USA **PT:** Bernard John; Anne (Keddie) Wiest **ED:** Degree in arts and sciences, University Maryland, 1969 **CW:** Appearances in Broadway and off-Broadway plays including Ashes, 1976, Leave It to Beaver is Dead, The Art of Dining (Obie award, 1979, Theatre World award, 1983), Bonjour La Bonjour, Three Sisters, Serenading Louie (Obie award, 1983), After the Fall, Heartbreak House, Our Town, Hunting Cockroaches, 1987, Blue Light, 1994, Memory House, 2005, Third, 2005, The Seagull, 2008, (Broadway plays) Othello, 1982, In the Summer House, 1993, Salome, 2003, All My Sons, 2008, actress (films) It's My Turn, 1980, I'm Dancing as Fast as I Can, 1982, Independence Day, 1982, Footloose, 1984, Falling in Love, 1984, The Purple Rose of Cairo, 1985, Hannah and Her Sisters, 1986 (Academy award for Best Supporting Actress, 1987), Radio Days, 1987, Lost Boys, 1987, September, 1987, Bright Lights, Big City, 1988, Parenthood, 1989, Cookie, 1989, Edward Scissorhands, 1990, Little Man Tate, 1991, Cops and Robbersons, 1994, The Scout, 1994, Bullets Over Broadway, 1994 (Golden Globe award for Best Supporting Actress-Drama, 1995, Academy award for Best Supporting Actress, 1995), Drunks, 1995, The Birdcage, 1996, The Associate, 1996, Practical Magic, 1998, The Horse Whisperer, 1998, Portofino, 1999, I Am Sam, 2001, Dr. Rey!, 2002, Robots (voice only), 2005, A Guide to Recognizing Your Saints, 2006, Dedication, 2007, Dan in Real Life, 2007, Synechdoche, New York, 2008, Passengers, 2008, Rage, 2009, Rabbit Hole, 2010, The Big Year, 2011, Darling Companion, 2012, The Odd Life of Timothy Green, 2012, The Humbling, 2014, Five Nights in Maine, 2015, Sisters, 2015, (TV films) The Wall, 1982, The Face of Rage, 1983, Simple Life of Noah Dearborn, 1999, The Corrections, 2012, (TV miniseries) The 10th Kingdom, 2000, (TV series) Law & Order, 2000-02, The Blackwater Lightship, 2004, Category 6 Day of Destruction, In Treatment, 2008-09 (Emmy award for Outstanding Supporting Actress in a Drama Series, 2008), The Return of Jezebel James,2008, The Blacklist, 2014, Life in Pieces, 2015

WILCZEK, FRANK ANTHONY, T: Physics Professor **I:** Education/Educational Services **DOB:** 05/15/1951 **PB:** Mineola **SC:** NY/USA **PT:** Frank John Wilczek, Mary Rose (Cona) Wilczek **MS:** Married **SPN:** Elizabeth Jordan Devine, 7/3/1973 **CH:** Amity, Mira **ED:** Doctorate Degree, Ohio State University, 2007; Doctorate Degree, Clark University, 2007; Honorary Doctorate Degree, Universitè de Montrèal, 2001; PhD in Physics, Princeton University, 1974; MA in Mathematics, Princeton University, 1972; BS in Mathematics, University of Chicago, 1970 **C:** Herman Feshbach Professor of Physics, Massachusetts Institute of Technology, Cambridge, MA, 2000-Present; Professor, School of Natural Sciences, Institute for Advanced Study, Princeton, NJ, 1989-2000; Professor, Institute for Theoretical Physics, Santa Barbara, CA, 1981-1988; Professor, University of California, Santa Barbara, 1980-1988; Professor, Princeton University, Princeton, NJ, 1980-1981; Associate Professor, Princeton University, Princeton, NJ, 1978-1980; Assistant Professor, Princeton University, Princeton, NJ, 1977-1978; Assistant Professor, Princeton University, New Jersey, 1974-1976; Instructor, Princeton University, New Jersey, 1974 **CR:** Adjunct Professor, Centros Estudios Cientificos, 2002-Present; Visiting Schrodinger-Professor, City of Vienna, Austria, 2002; J. Robert Oppenheimer Professor, Institute for Advanced Study, 1997-2000; Leland J. Haworth Distinguished Scientist, Brookhaven National Laboratory, 1994-1997; Visiting Professor, Harvard University, 1987-1988; Regent's Fellow, Smithsonian Astrophysical Observatory, 1986-1988; Chancellor Robert Huttenback Professor of Physics, University of California, Santa Barbara, 1984-1990; MacArthur Fellow, 1982-1987; Visiting Fellow, Institute for Advanced Study, Princeton, NJ, 1976-1977; A.P. Sloan Fellow, 1975-1977; Lecturer, Several Universities And Societies; Several Advisory Boards; Fellow, American Association for the Advancement of Science; Fellow, American Philosophical Society **CIV:** Trustee, University of Chicago, 1998-2004 **CW:** Editorial Advisor, Daedalus, 2002-Present; Editor-in-Chief, Annals of Physics, 2001-Present; Author, Longing for the Harmonies, 1988, Geometric Phases in Physics, 1989, Fractional Statistics and Anyon Superconductivity, 1990, Fantastic Realities, 2006; Contributor, Articles, Professional Journals **AW:** J.J. Sakurai Prize, American Physical Society, 1986, Dirac Medal, United Nations Educational, 1994, Michelson-Morley Prize, Case Western Reserve University, 2002, Lorentz Medal, 2002, Lilienfeld Prize, American Physics Society, 2003, Europhysics Prize, 2003, Co-Recipient, High Energy and Particle Physics Prize, European Physical Society, 2003, Nobel Prize in Physics, 2004, King Faisal Prize in Science, King Faisal Foundation, 2005 **MEM:** National Academy of Sciences, American Academy of Arts and Sciences, Foreign Member, Royal Netherlands Academy of Arts and Sciences **ACH:** Achievements include discovery of asymptotic freedom in the theory of the strong interaction **H:** Chess, Music, Logic puzzles **BA:** Massachusetts Institute of Technology, Center for Theoretical Physics Building, 6 301 5 Cambridge Center, Cambridge, MA, 02142

WILEY, KEHINDE, T: Portrait Painter **I:** Fine Art **PB:** Los Angeles **SC:** CA/USA **ED:** Coursework, San Francisco Art Institute (1999); MFA, Yale University School of Art (2001) **AW:** Named One of TIME's 100 Most Influential People, TIME Magazine (2018)

WILEY, MIKE, T: Chef **I:** Food & Restaurant Services **C:** Founder, Big Tree Hospitality, 2015-Present; Owner, Eventide Oyster Co., 2012-Present; Owner, Hugos, 2012-Present **AW:** James Beard Award for Best New Chef, Northeast, 2017-Present

WILKENS, LENNY, T: Former Professional Sports Team Executive, Retired Professional Basketball Player **I:** Athletics **DOB:** 10/28/1937 **PB:** Bklyn. **PT:** Son of Leonard Randolph Senior and Henrietta (Cross) W.; Married Marilyn J. Reed, July 28, 1962; children: Leesha Marie, Leonard Randolph III, Jamée McGregor **ED:** HHD (hon.), Providence College, 1980; BS in Econs., Providence College, 1960 **C:** College basketball analyst, FSN,; NBA analyst, FSN, 2005-06; Color analyst Pac-10 men's basketball, FSN, 2004-05; Head coach, New York Knicks, 2004-05; Head coach, Toronto Raptors, 2000-03; Head coach, Atlanta Hawks, 1993-2000; Player/coach, Portland Trail Blazers, 1974-76; Salesman packaging division, Monsanto Co., 1966; Counselor, Jewish Employment Vocational Services, 1962-63; Head coach, Cleveland Cavaliers, 1986-93; Professional basketball player, Cleveland Cavaliers, 1972-74; President basketball operations, Seattle SuperSonics, 2007; Vice chairman, Seattle SuperSonics, 2006-07; General manager, Seattle SuperSonics, 1985-86; Head coach, Seattle SuperSonics, 1977-85; Player, coach, Seattle SuperSonics, 1969-72; Guard, Seattle SuperSonics, 1968-69; Guard, St. Louis Hawks, 1960-68 **CR:** Assistant coach Olympic Basketball Team, 1992, head coach, 1996, World Champion Basketball Team, 1979, 4 NBA All-Star Teams **CIV:** Board regents Gonzaga University, Spokane board directors Seattle Center, Big Brothers Seattle, Bellevue Boys Club, Washington, Seattle Opportunities Industrialization Center, Seattle University co-chmn. UN International Year of Child progressive, 1979, organizer Lenny Wilkens Celebrity Golf Tournament for Special Olympics, founder Lenny Wilken Foundation, Washington **CW:** Author: The Lenny Wilkens Story, 1974 **AW:** Named to NBA All-Star Game, 1963-65, 67-71, 73, NIT-NIKE Hall of Fame, 1988, Naismith Memorial Basketball Hall of Fame, 1989 (as a player), 1998 (as a coach); named NBA All-Star Game MVP, 1971, Man of Year, Boys High Alumni chapter LA, 1979, Sportsman of Year, Seattle chapter City of Hope, 1979, Congl. Black Caucus Coach of Year, 1979, Continental Basketball Association Coach of Year, 1979, Coach of Year, Black Pubs. Association, 1979, NBA Coach of Year, 1994; named one of NBA's 50 Greatest Players, NBA's Top Ten Coaches, 1997; recipient Whitney Young Junior award New York Urban League, 1979, Distinguished Citizens award Boy Scouts Am., 1980,NBA 50th Anniversary All-Time Team, College Basketball Hall of Fame, 2006, Chuck Daly Lifetime Achievement Award, 2010 **BA:** Lenny Wilkins Foundation, P.O. BOX 684, Medina, WA, 98039

WILKIE, ROBERT LEON JR., T: U.S. Secretary of Veterans Affairs **I:** Government Administration/ Government Relations/Government Services **DOB:** 08/06/1962 **PB:** Frankfort, Germany **PT:** Son of Robert Leon and Joy Ann (Somerville) W.; **SPN:** Married Julia Cameron Bullard, May 19, 1990; **CH:** children: Adam, Megan **ED:** Master in Strategic Studies, US Army War College, 2002; LLM in International Law & Legis., Georgetown University, 1992; JD, Loyola of the South, 1988; BA Cum Laude, Wake Forest University, 1985 **C:** U.S. Secretary of Veteran Affairs, 2018–; Undersecretary of Defense, 2017-2018; Vice President, Business Devel. Director, CH2M Hill, Washington, DC, 2010-2017; Assistant Secretary for Legis. Affairs, US Department Defense, Washington, 2006-09; Acting Assistant Secretary for Legis. Affairs, US Department Defense, Washington, 2006; Principal Deputy Assistant Sec for Legis. Affairs, US Department Defense, Washington, 2005-06; Special Assistant to President for National Security Affairs, The White House, Washington, 2003-05; Senior Director, National Security Council, Washington, 2003-05; Counsel & Adv. to Senate Majority Leader Trent Lott, US Senate, 1997-2003; Director, North Carolina Republican Party, 1996-97; Legis. Director to Rep. David Funderburk, US House of Representatives, 1995; Legis. Counsel to Senator Jesse Helms, US Senate, Washington, 1988-95 **CR:** Member Loyola Moot Court Board, 1988. **CIV:** Staff Member Rep. National Convention, 1992. Intelligence Officer US Naval Reserve. **CW:** Author Newspaper Political Editorials, 1990-93. **AW:** Awarded, Defense Distinguished Public Service Medal, 2009, Recipient Bustamonte Award for Outstanding Achievement in International Law The Society Jesus, New Orleans, 1987, Am. Jurisprudence Awards for Excellence in Latin Am. Law International Law and Legislation, 1987-88; Named Junior Intelligence Officer (Reserve) of the Year, Office Naval Intelligence **MEM:** Member American Bar Association, Rep. National Lawyers Association, The Federalist Society **ACH:** Avocations: English history, military history, Southern history and lit., distance running. **PA:** Republican **BA:** U.S. Department of Veterans Affairs, 810 Vermont Avenue, NW, Washington, DC, 20420

WILKINS, ROBERT LEON, T: Federal Judge **I:** Law and Legal Services **DOB:** 10/02/1963 **PB:** Muncie **SC:** IN/USA **ED:** JD, Harvard Law School, 1989; BS, Rose-Hulman Institute of Technology, Cum Laude, 1986 **C:** Judge, U.S. Court of Appeals, District of Columbia Circuit, 2014-Present; Judge, U.S. District Court for the District of Columbia, Washington, DC, 2010-2014; Partner, Venable LLP, Washington, DC, 2000-2010; Contract Attorney, DC Public Defender's Office, Washington, DC, 2000-2002; Chief, Special Litigation, DC Public Defender's Office, Washington, DC, 1996-2000; Staff Attorney, DC Public Defender's Office, Washington, DC, 1990-1996; Law Clerk, Hon. Earl B. Gilliam, U.S. District Court, Southern District, California, 1989 **CR:** DC Access to Justice Commission, 2005-Present; DC Juvenile Justice Advisory Group, 1998-2000; DC Advisory Committee on Sentencing, 1998-2000; DC Truth-in-Sentencing Commission, 1997-1998; Visiting Instructor, Harvard's Law School Trial Advocacy Workshop, 1996, 1999; Lecturer, George Washington University, American University Washington College of Law, Georgetown University Law Center **CIV:** Founder, National African American Museum & Cultural Complex, 1999 **CW:** Contributor, Articles, Professional Journals **AW:** Top Washington Lawyer, Washingtonian Magazine, 2004, Pro Bono Attorney of the Year, American Civil Liberties Union of Maryland, 2001, Henry W. Edgerton Civil Liberties Award, American Civil Liberties Union Fund, National Capital Area, 2001, Practitioner of the Year Award, University of Maryland Black Law Student Association, 1999, The 40 Under 40 Most Successful Young Litigators in America, The National Law Journal **BAR:** U.S. Supreme Court, U.S. District Court of Maryland, U.S. District Court of the District of Columbia, U.S. District Court of Appeals, District of Columbia Circuit, District of Columbia **BA:** 333 Constitution Avenue NW, Washington, DC, 20001

WILKINSON, J. HARVIE III, T: Judge **I:** Law and Legal Services **CN:** U.S. Court of Appeals for the Fourth Circuit **PB:** New York City **SC:** NY/USA **PT:** James Harvie Wilkinson; Letitia (Nelson) Wilkinson **MS:** Married **SPN:** Lossie Grist Noell **CH:** James Nelson; Porter Noell **ED:** Honorary LLD, Christopher Newport University (2003); Honorary JD, University of South Carolina (1998); Honorary JD, University of Richmond (1997); JD, University of Virginia (1972); BA, Yale University (1963-1967) **C:** Judge, U.S. Court of Appeals for the Fourth Circuit (1984-Present); Chief Judge, U.S. Court of Appeals for the Fourth Circuit (1996-2003); Deputy Assistant Attorney General, Civil Rights Division, U.S. Department of Justice (1982-1983); Editor, Norfolk Virginian-Pilot (1978-1981); Professor of Law, University of Virginia (1981-1982, 1983-1984); Associate Professor, University of Virginia (1975-1978); Assistant Professor of Law, University of Virginia (1973-1975); Law Clerk to Honorable Lewis F. Powell, Jr., Supreme Court of the U.S., Washington D.C. (1972-1973) **CIV:** Board of Visitors, University of Virginia (1970-1973); Republican Candidate for Congress from the Third District of Virginia (1970); Board of Directors, Federal Judicial Center (1992-1996); James Madison Memorial Foundation (2003-2005); Board of Trustees, Tuesday Evening Concert Series (2013-2017); Board of Trustees, Virginia Historical Society (2013-Present) **MIL:** Served, U.S. Army (1968-1969) **CW:** Author, "Harry Byrd and the Changing Face of Virginia Politics" (1968); Author, "Serving Justice: A Supreme Court Clerk's View" (1974); Author, "From Brown to Bakke: The Supreme Court and School Integration" (1979); Author, "One Nation Indivisible: How Ethnic Separatism Threatens America" (1997); Author, "Cosmic Constitutional Theory: Why Americans Are Losing Their Inalienable Right to Self-Governance" (2012); Author, "All Falling Faiths: Reflections on the Promise and Failure of the 1960s" (2017) **AW:** Medal, Lawrenceville School (2008); Thomas Jefferson Foundation Medal of Law, University of Virginia (2004); Rule of Law Award, Virginia Holocaust Museum and Virginia Law Foundation (2017) **MEM:** Virginia State Bar; Virginia Bar Association; American Law Institute; American Academy of Arts and Sciences **BAR:** Virginia State Bar (1972) **H:** Hiking; Classical Music; UVA Sports Fan **BA:** 255 W Main St Ste 230, Hon. J. Harvie Wilkinson III, U.S. Courthouse, Charlottesville, VA, 22902

WILL, GEORGE FREDERICK, T: Editor, Journalist, Commentator **I:** Writing and Editing **DOB:** 05/04/1941 **PB:** Champaign **PT:** Son of Frederick L. and Louise (Hendrickson) Will; **ED:** Degree (hon.), University Illinois, 1988; LittD (hon.), Dickinson College, Georgetown University, 1978; LLD (hon.), University San Diego, 1977; MA, PhD in Politics, Princeton University, New Jersey, 1967; BA, Oxford University, England, 1964; BA, Trinity College, Hartford, Connecticut, 1962 **C:** Controller, FOX News Channel, 2013–; Contributing editor, columnist, Newsweek magazine, 1976–; Syndicated columnist, The Washington Post Writers Group, 1974–; Founding panel member, This Week program (formerly This Week with David Brinkley), ABC, 1981-2013; Washington editor, The National Rev., 1973-76; Member staff of Sen. Gordon Allott, US Senate, Washington, 1970-72; Professor political philosophy, University Toronto, 1968-70; Professor political philosophy, Michigan State University, 1967-68 **CIV:** Board governors, Negro Leagues Baseball Museum, **CW:** Author: The Pursuit of Happiness and Other Sobering Thoughts, 1978, The Pursuit of Virtue and Other Tory Notions, 1982, Statecraft as Soulcraft, 1983, The Morning After: American Successes and Excesses 1981-86, 1986, The New Season: A Spectator's Guide to the 1988 Election, 1987, Men at Work: The Craft of Baseball, 1989, Suddenly: The American Idea Abroad and at Home 1986-1990, 1990, Restoration: Congress, Term Limits and the Recovery of Deliberative Democracy, 1992, The Leveling Wind: Politics, the Culture & Other News 1990-94, 1994, The Woven Figure: Conservatism and America's Fabric 1994-97, 1997, Bunts: Curt Flood, Camden Yards, Pete Rose, and Other Reflections on Baseball, 1998, With a Happy Eye But...America and the World 1997-2002, 2002, One Man's America: The Pleasures and Provocations of Our Singular Nation, 2008, A Nice Little Place on the North Side: Wrigley Field at One Hundred, 2014 **AW:** Named Best Writer, Any Subject, Washington Journalism Rev., 1985, Young Leader America, TIME magazine, 1974; named one of The 25 Most Influential Washington Journalists, The National Journal, 1997; recipient Champion of Liberty Award, Goldwater Institute, 2006, Walter B. Wriston Lecture award, Manhattan Institute, 2003, William Allen White award, William Allen White School Journalism, University Kansas, 1993, Madison Medal award, Princeton University, 1992, Cronkite award, Arizona State University, 1991, Silurian Award for Editorial Writing, 1991, 1980, National Headliners Award, 1978, Pulitzer Prize for Commentary, 1977 **H:** Baseball

WILLETT, DON R., T: Federal Judge **I:** Law and Legal Services **DOB:** 07/16/1966 **PB:** Talty **SC:** TX/USA **ED:** MA in Political Sci., Duke University; JD, Duke University; BBA, Baylor University **C:** Judge, U.S. Court of Appeals for the Fifth Circuit,2018-; Justice, Texas Supreme Court, 2005-18; Deputy attorney general for legal counsel, Texas, 2000-04; Legal adv. to governor, Texas, 1996-2000; Attorney, Haynes and Boone, LLP, 1993-96; Law clerk to Honorable Jerre S. Williams, US Court of Appeals (5th cir.), Texas, **CR:** Supreme court liaison Texas Center for Legal Ethics and Professionalism served on Bush-Cheney 2000 Presidential Campaign and Transition Team **CIV:** former member Texas Commission on Volunteerism & Community Service board member National Fatherhood Initiative, Big Brothers Big Sisters Central Texas, SafePlace, Texas Lyceum Association **AW:** Recipient Austin Under 40 award for Govt./Polit. Affairs, 2006 **MEM:** Fellow: Texas Bar Foundation; mem.: Texas Association for Court Administration (judicial adv. board), Am. Law Institute **BA:** John Minor Wisdom U.S. Court of Appeals Building Fifth Circuit, 600 Camp St, New Orleans, LA, 70130

WILLIAMS, BRIAN DOUGLAS, T: News Correspondent, Journalist **I:** Media & Entertainment **DOB:** 05/05/1959 **PB:** Ridgewood **PT:** Son of Gordon L. and Dorothy Williams **ED:** LHD (hon.), Bates College, 2005; LLD (hon.), Villanova University, 2003; Doctor (hon.), Providence College; Doctor (hon.), Elmira College; Doctor (hon.), Catholic University America, 2004; Attended, Catholic University America; Attended, George Washington University **C:** Anchor, breaking news and special events coverage, MSNBC, 2015-; Breaking news anchor, NBC News, 2015-; Anchor, managing editor The News with Brian Williams, CNBC, 2002-04; Anchor, managing editor The News with Brian Williams, MSNBC, 1996-2002; Host Rock Center with Brian Williams, NBC News, 2011-13; Anchor, managing editor NBC Nightly News, NBC News, 2004-15; Chief White House corr., NBC News, 1994-96; Corr., NBC News, 1993-94; Anchor, WCBS-TV, New York City, 1987-93; New Jersey corr., WCAU-TV, Philadelphia, 1985-87; Corr., WTTG-TV, Washington, 1982-84; Reporter, KOAM-TV, Pittsburg, Kansas, 1981; Various lobbying positions, National Association Broadcasters,; Intern, The White House **CIV:** Board directors, Congl. Medal of Honor Foundation, 2006-15 **AW:** Named Best Anchor, USA Today, Man of Year, GQ Magazine, 2001, Father of Year, National Father's Day Committee, 1996; named one of The World's Most Influential People, TIME magazine, 2007; recipient du-Pont Columbia University award, Walter Cronkite award for Excellence in Journalism, Tulane President's Medal, Tulane University, 2006, Sigma Delta Chi award, Society Professional Journalists, 2006, George Foster Peabody award, 2005, 11 National Edward R. Murrow awards, 12 Emmy awards

WILLIAMS, GEISHA, T: CEO of PG&E Corp **I:** Oil & Energy **CN:** PG&E Corp **ED:** B.S., University of Miami; Masters, Business Administration, Nova Southeastern University **C:** President/CEO, PG&E Corp, 2017-; Pres Electric Ops Pacific Gas, PG&E Corp, 2015-2017; President Electric Operations, PG&E Corp, 2015-2017

WILLIAMS, HANK JR., T: Country Music Singer, Songwriter **I:** Media & Entertainment **DOB:** 05/26/1949 **PB:** Shreveport **PT:** Son of Hank and Audrey Williams **CW:** Performer throughout US; recorded song Ain't Misbehavin'; latest albums include: Montana Cafe, 1986, Hank Live, 1987, Born to Boogie, 1987, Wild Streak, 1988, Greatest Hits III, Lone Wolf, 1990, Pure Hank, 1991, (with Clink Black) Maverick, 1992, Out of Left Field, 1993, A Tribute to My Father, 1993, (with Waylon Jennings and Ray Charles) Greatest Hits, vol. 2, 1994, Hog Wild, 1995, High Notes: Original Classic Hits Vol. 8, 1995, American Legends: Best of The Early Years, 1995, 20 Hits Special Collection Vol. 1, 1995, A.K.A. Wham Bam Sam, 1996, The Hits, 1997, The Complete Hank Williams Junior, 1999, Stormy, 1999, I'm One of You, 2003, 127 Rose Avenue, 2009, Old School New Rules, 2012, It's About Time, 2016; composer: All My Roudy Friends, 1993, (TV film) Willa, 1979 (also actor); singer in films The Dangerous Days of Kiowa Jones, 1966, Kelly's Heroes, 1970, The Moonshine War, 1970, actor: (films) A Time to Sing, 1968, Roadie, 1980, (TV series) The Simpsons (voice) 1998-99; author: Living Proof: An Autobiography, 1979 **AW:** Named to Nashville Songwriters Hall of Fame, 2007; recipient Johnny Cash Visionary award, Country Music TV, 2006, Grammy award, 1990, Cliffie Stone Pioneer award, Academy Country Music, 2009, Album of Year, 1989, Video of Year award, 1987-89, Entertainer of Year award, 1989, 1988, 1987, Music Video of Year award, Country Music Association, 1987, Entertainer of Year award, 1988, 1987, 1 Double Platinum album, 5 Platinum albums, 18 Gold albums, No.50 in Rolling Stone's 100 Greatest Country Music Artists of All Time, 2017 **BA:** Webster Public Relations, P.O. Box 23015, Nashville, TN, 37202

WILLIAMS, JODY, T: Political Organization Administrator **I:** Government Administration/Government Relations/Government Services **DOB:** 10/09/1950 **PB:** Brattleboro **SC:** VT/USA **ED:** Honorary PhD, Smith College; Honorary PhD, Lehman College; Honorary PhD, Gustaus Adolphus College; Honorary PhD, Rockhurst University; Honorary PhD, Shensu University; Honorary PhD, Regis University; Honorary PhD, Franklin Pierce College; Honorary PhD, Wesleyan University; Honorary PhD, Royal Military College Canada;

Honorary PhD, Pennsylvania State University; Honorary PhD, Williams College; Honorary PhD, University of Vermont; Honorary PhD, Marlboro College; Honorary PhD, Briar Cliff College; MA in International Relations, Johns Hopkins University, Baltimore, MD (1984); MA in Teaching, School of International Training, VT (1974); BA, University of Vermont, Burlington, VT (1972) **C:** Sam and Cele Keeper Professor in Peace and Social Justice, Graduate College of Social Work, University of Houston (2007-Present); Campaign Ambassador, International Campaign to Ban Landmines (1998-Present); Founding Coordinator, International Campaign to Ban Landmines (1992-1998); Associate Director, Medical Aid for El Salvador, LA (1986-1992); Co-coordinator, Nicaragua-Honduras Education Project, Washington, DC (1984-1986) **CR:** Head, Mission on Darfur, United Nations Human Rights Council (2007); Distinguished Visiting Professor, Social Work & Global Justice (2003-2007) **CIV:** Co-founder, Nobel Women's Initiative (2006); Member, Advisory Committee, Women for World Peace Fund (2003-Present); Member, Human Rights Watch Arms Advisory Committee (1998-Present); Board of Directors, Roots of Peace, CA (2001-Present) **CW:** Author, "Banning Landmines: Disarmament, Citizen Diplomacy and Human Security" (2008); Co-author, "After the Guns Fall: The Enduring Legacy of Landmines" (1995); Senior Editor, "Landmine Monitor Report" (1999-2004); Contributor, Articles to Professional Journals **AW:** Named One of the 100 Most Powerful Women in the World, Forbes Magazine (2004); Fiat Lux Award, Clark University; Hollywood Humanitarian Award (2002); Distinguished Peace Leadership Award, Nuclear Age Peace Foundation (1998); Nobel Peace Prize (1997) **BA:** University of Houston College of Social Work, 4800 Calhoun Rd, Houston, TX, 77004

WILLIAMS, JOHN TOWNER, T: Composer, Conductor **I:** Media & Entertainment **DOB:** 02/08/1932 **PB:** LI **PT:** Son of John and Esther Williams; **ED:** Degree (hon.), Providence College; Degree (hon.), New England Conservatory Music; Degree (hon.), Boston University; Degree (hon.), University Southern California; Degree (hon.), Tufts University; Degree (hon.), Northeastern University, Boston; Degree (hon.), Berklee College Music, Boston; Studied with Madame Rosina Lhevinne, New York City; Student, Juilliard School; Studied with Mario Castelnuovo-Tedesco, Los Angeles; Student, UCLA **C:** Laureate conductor, Boston Pops Orchestra, 1993-; Pianist, Columbia & Twentieth Century-Fox, 1956-; Artist-in-residence, Tanglewood Music Center, Boston, 1993-94; Conductor, Boston Pops Orchestra, 1980-93 **CR:** Guest conductor with orchestras including Cleveland Orchestra, Denver Symphony, Indianapolis Symphony, London Symphony Orchestra, Los Angeles Philharmonic, Montreal Orchestra, Philadelphia Orchestra, and Toronto Orchestra **CIV:** Served with US Air Force, 1952-54. **CW:** Works include: composer (film scores) I Passed for White, 1960, Because They're Young, 1960, The Secret Ways, 1961, Bachelor Flat, 1962, Diamond Head, 1962, Gidget Goes to Rome, 1963, The Killers, 1964, John Goldfarb, Please Come Home, 1964, None But the Brave, 1965, How to Steal a Million, 1966, The Rare Breed, 1966, Not With My Wife, You Don't, 1966, The Plainsman, 1966, Penelope, 1966, A Guide for the Married Man, 1967, Valley of the Dolls, 1967 (Academy award nominee), Fitzwilly, 1968, Sergeant Ryker, 1968, The Reivers, 1969 (Academy award nominee), Daddy's Gone A-Hunting, 1969, Goodbye, Mr. Chips, 1969 (Academy award nominee), The Story of A Woman, 1970, Fiddler on the Roof, 1971 (Academy award for musical adaptation 1971),

The Cowboys, 1972, The Poseidon Adventure, 1972 (Academy award nominee), Images, 1972 (Academy award nominee), Pete 'n' Tillie, 1972, The Paper Chase, 1973, The Long Goodbye, 1973, The Man Who Loved Cat Dancing, 1973, Cinderella Liberty, 1973 (Academy award nominee), Tom Sawyer, 1973 (Academy award nominee), Sugarland Express, 1974, Earthquake, 1974, The Towering Inferno, 1974 (Academy award nominee), Conrack, 1974, Jaws, 1975 (Academy award, Grammy award, Golden Globe award 1976), The Eiger Sanction, 1976, Family Plot, 1976, Midway, 1976, The Missouri Breaks, 1976, Raggedy Ann and Andy, 1977, Black Sunday, 1977, Star Wars, 1977 (Academy award, 3 Grammy awards, Golden Globe award 1977), Close Encounters of the Third Kind, 1977 (2 Grammy awards, Academy award nominee 1978), The Fury, 1978, Jaws II, 1978, Superman, 1978 (2 Grammy awards 1979), Meteor, 1979, Quintet, 1979, Dracula, 1979, "1941", 1979, The Empire Strikes Back, 1980 (2 Grammy awards, Academy award nominee 1980), Raiders of the Lost Ark, 1981 (Grammy award, Academy award nominee 1981), Heartbeeps, 1981, E.T., 1982 (Academy award for best original score, 3 Grammy awards, Golden Globe award 1982), Monsignor, 1982, Yes, Giorgio, 1982 (Academy award nominee), Superman III, 1983, Return of the Jedi, 1983 (Academy award nominee), Indiana Jones and the Temple of Doom, 1984 (Academy award nominee), The River, 1984 (Academy award nominee), Space Camp, 1986, Emma's War, 1986, The Witches of Eastwick, 1987 (Academy award nominee), Empire of the Sun, 1987 (Academy award nominee), Jaws: The Revenge, 1987, Superman IV: The Quest for Peace, 1987, The Secret of My Success, 1987, The Accidental Tourist, 1988 (Academy award nominee, Indiana Jones and the Last Crusade, 1989 (Academy award nominee), Always, 1989, Born On The Fourth of July, 1989 (Academy award nominee), Stanley and Iris, 1990, Presumed Innocent, 1990, Home Alone, 1990 (Academy award nominee), Hook, 1991 (Academy award nominee), JFK, 1991 (Academy award nominee), Far and Away, 1992, Home Alone II, 1992, Jurassic Park, 1993, Schindler's List, 1993 (Academy award 1993, Grammy award 1994), Sabrina, 1995 (Academy award nominee for best original score 1996), Nixon, 1995 (Academy award nominee 1996), Sleepers, 1996, Rosewood, 1997, The Lost World: Jurassic Park, 1997, Seven Years in Tibet, 1997 (Academy award nominee), Amistad, 1997 (Academy award nominee), Saving Private Ryan, 1998 (Academy award nominee, Grammy award 1998), Stepmom, 1998, Star Wars Episode I: The Phantom Menace, 1999, Angela's Ashes, 1999 (Academy award nominee, Grammy award 2000), The Patriot, 2000 (Academy award nominee), Artificial Intelligence, 2001 (Academy award nominee), Harry Potter and The Sorcerer's Stone, 2001 (Academy award nominee), Minority Report, 2002, Star Wars Episode II: Attack Of The Clones, 2002, Harry Potter: The Chamber Of Secrets, 2002, Catch Me If You Can, 2002 (Academy award nominee), Harry Potter: The Prisoner Of Azkaban, 2004, The Terminal, 2004, Star Wars Episode III: The Revenge of the Sith, 2005, War of the Worlds, 2005, Memoirs of a Geisha, 2005 (Broadcast Film Association award, 2006, Best Original Score-Motion Picture, Hollywood Foreign Press Association, Golden Globe award) 2006, Grammy award, 2007), Munich, 2005 (Grammy award, 2007), Indiana Jones and the Kingdom of the Crystal Skull, 2008 (Grammy award, 2009)THE; composer music for songs including:(from Sabrina, lyrics by Alan and Marilyn Bergman) Moonlight, 1995 (Academy award nominee 1996); composer:(TV programs) Heidi, 1969 (Emmy award), Jane

Eyre, 1971 (Emmy award), Masterpiece Theatre, 1971, Malcolm in the Middle, 2000, Smallville, 2001, (main theme) Jack & Bobby, 2004, others; composer numerous concert pieces and symphonies including Jubilee 350 Fanfare for the Boston Pops, 1980, theme to the 1984 Summer Olympic Games, Liberty Fanfare, 1987; recorded numerous albums with Boston Pops Orchestra including Pops in Space, That's Entertainment (Pops on Broadway), Pops on the March, Pops Around the World (Digital Overtures), Aisle Seat, Pops Out of This World, Boston Pops on Stage, America, the Dream Goes On; collaborator: (with Jessye Norman) With A Song in My Heart, Swing, Swing, Swing, Unforgettable; guest conductor major orch **AW:** Recipient several gold and platinum records Recording Industry Association Am., Kennedy Center Honors, John F. Kennedy Center Performing Arts, 2004. **MEM:** Fellow: Am. Academy Arts and Sciences **ACH:** Composer of over seventy-five film scores.

WILLIAMS, MICHELLE, T: Actress **I:** Media & Entertainment **PB:** Kalispell, **SC:** MT/USA **PT:** Larry Richard Williams; Carla (Swenson) Williams **CW:** Actress: (films) Lassie, 1994, Species, 1995, Timemaster, 1995, A Thousand Acres, 1997, Halloween H20: 20 Years Later, 1998, Dick, 1999, But I'm a Cheerleader, 1999, Perfume, 2001, Prozac Nation, 2001, Me Without You, 2001, The U.S. of Leland, 2003, The Station Agent, 2003, A Hole in One, 2004, Imaginary Heroes, 2004, Land of Plenty, 2004, The Baxter, 2005, Brokeback Mountain, 2005 (Broadcast Film Critics Association award for Best Supporting Actress, 2006), The Hawk is Dying, 2006, I'm Not There, 2007, Incendiary, 2008, Deception, 2008, Synecdoche, New York, 2008, Wendy and Lucy, 2008, Mammoth, 2009, Shutter Island, 2010, Meek's Cutoff, 2010, Take This Waltz, 2011, My Week with Marilyn, 2011 (Boston Society Film Critics award for Best Actress, 2011, Golden Globe award for Best Performance by an Actress in a Motion Picture-Comedy or Musical, 2012), Oz the Great and Powerful, 2013, Suite Francaise, 2015, Manchester by the Sea, 2016, Certain Women, 2016, Wonderstruck 2017, The Greatest Showman, 2017, All the Money in the World, 2017, I Feel Pretty, 2018, Venom, 2018; (TV series) Dawson's Creek, 1998-2003; (TV films) My Son Is Innocent, 1996, Killing Mr. Griffin, 1997, If These Walls Could Talk 2, 2000, Cougar Town, 2013; (Broadway plays) Cabaret, 2014, Blackbird, 2016; TV appearances Baywatch, 1993, Raising Caines, 1995, Home Improvement, 1995, Raising Caines, My Son is Innocent, Killing Mr. Griffin, Cougar Town, 2013, actress, executive producer (films) Blue Valentine, 2010 **AW:** Named one of 21 Hottest Stars Under 21, Teen People magazine, 1999

WILLIAMS, ROGER, T: U.S. Representative from Texas, Former State Official **I:** Government Administration/Government Relations/Government Services **DOB:** 09/13/1949 **PB:** Evanston **ED:** Bachelor, Tex Christian University, 1972 **C:** Member, US House Transportation & Infrastructure Committee, 2013-; Member, Committee on Financial Services, Republican Study Committee; Member, US House Budget Committee, 2013-; Member, US Congress from 25th Texas District, Washington, 2013-; Secretary of state, State of Texas, Austin, 2004-07; Baseball coach, Texas Christian University, 1974-76; Professional baseball player, Atlanta Braves farm team, 1971-74; President, CEO, Roger Williams Automall, 1974-95 **CR:** Chair Texas Base Realignment & Closure Response Strike Force, 2005 state finance chair John Cornyn for US Senate, 2002 chairman Texas Republican Victory 2008 Coordinated Campaign, 2007-08, Republican National Committee's Eagles Program, 2001 north

Texas finance chairman, national grassroots fund-raising chairman Bush/Cheney 2004 Campaign, 2004 north Texas chairman Bush/Cheney 2000 Campaign, 2000 regional finance chairman George W. Bush Gubernatorial Campaign, 1998, 1994 **PA:** Republican **BA:** 1122 Longworth House Office Building, Washington, DC, 20515

WILLIAMS, ROY, T: College Basketball Coach **I:** Professional Training & Coaching **DOB:** 08/01/1950 **PB:** Spruce Pine **PT:** Married Wanda; children: Scott, Kimberly. **ED:** MAT, University North Carolina, 1973; BA in Education, University North Carolina, 1972 **C:** Head coach, University North Carolina Tarheels, 2003-; Head coach, University Kansas Jayhawks, 1988-2003; Assistant coach, University North Carolina Tarheels, 1978-88; Basketball & golf coach, Charles D. Owen HS, North Carolina, **CR:** Assistant coach US Olympic Men's Basketball Team, Athens, Greece, 2004, U.S.A. Senior Men's National Basketball Team, 2003 **CW:** Co-author (with Tim Crothers): Hard Work: My Life On and Off the Court, 2009 **AW:** Named National Rookie Coach of Year Basketball Times, 1989, National Coach of Year 1990-92, 1997, 2006, Big 8 Coach of Year (7 times), Coach of Year Associated Press, 1992, 2006, ACC Coach of Year, 2006, 2011, District III Coach of Year US Basketball Writers Association, 2011; recipient John R. Wooden Legends of Coaching award LA Athletic Club, 2003, National Coach of Year award New York Athletic Club, 2005; named to Naismith Memorial Basketball Hall of Fame, 2007,Naismith College Coach of the Year, 1997, Henry Iba Award, 1990, 2006, Big 12 Coach of the Year, 1997, 2002, 2003, Adolph Rupp Cup, 2006 **ACH:** Achievements include head coach of the NCAA Men's Basketball National Championship winning University of North Carolina Tarheels, 2005, 2009

WILLIAMS, SERENA, T: Professional Tennis Player **I:** Athletics **DOB:** 09/26/1981 **PB:** Saginaw, Michigan **PT:** Daughter of Richard and Oracene Williams **C:** Professor tennis player, WTA Tour, 1995-; Designer, Aneres clothing line **CR:** Member US national team Summer Olympic Games, London, 2012, Beijing, 2008, Sydney, 2000, Fed Cup, 2007, 2003, 1999 **CW:** Co-author: Venus & Serena: Serving From The Hip: 10 Rules For Living, Loving and Winning, 2005; co-author: (with Daniel Paisner) On the Line, 2009; (TV appearances include): (voice) The Simpsons, 2001; My Wife and Kids, 2002; Law and Order: Special Victims Unit, 2004; The Division, 2004; appeared in (documentaries) Venus and Serena, 2012 **AW:** Named Sportsperson of the Year, Sports Illustrated, 2015, Female Athlete of Decade, 2000s, Sports Illus., 2009, Sportswoman of the Year, Black Entertainment TV (BET) Awards, 2011, Best Female Athlete, 2007, #1 most marketable female athlete, Sports Business Daily, 2003, WTA Player of Year, 2009, 2008, 2002, Female Athlete of Year, Associated Press, 2013, 2009, 2002, Player of Year, TENNIS Magazine, 1999, WTA Most Improved Player, 1999; named one of The 100 Most Influential People in the World, TIME magazine, 2014, 2010, The Most Influential People in the World of Sports, Business Week, 2008, The 100 Most Powerful Women, Forbes magazine, 2010, The 100 Most Powerful Celebrities, 2008; recipient Women of Year award, Glamour Magazine, 2009, Gold medal, women's singles, women's doubles, Summer Olympic Games, 2012, Gold medal, women's doubles, 2008, 2000, EPSY Award for Best Female Tennis Player, 2015-17, Laureus World Sportswoman of the Year, 2016, ITF Women's Singles World Champion, 2015, WTA Player of the Year, 2015, Associated Press Female Athlete of the Year **ACH:** Achievements include winner of 68 career singles titles, 22 career

doubles titles, and 2 mixed doubles titles, WTA tour; Grand Slam Mixed Doubles Championships (with Max Mirnyi): Wimbledon, US Open, 1998; Grand Slam Championships: US Open, 1999, 2002, 2008, 2012, 2013, 2014; Wimbledon, 2002, 2003, 2009, 2010, 2012, 2015, 2016; French Open, 2002, 2013, 2015; Austalian Open, 2003, 2005, 2007, 2009, 2010, 2015; Grand Slam Doubles Championships (with Venus Williams): French Open, 1999, 2010; US Open, 1999, 2009; Wimbledon, 2000, 2002, 2008, 2009, 2012; Australian Open 2001, 2003, 2009, 2010

WILLIAMS, THOMAS L., T: CEO of Parker Hannifin **I:** Business Management/Business Services **ED:** Bachelors, Bucknell University; MBA, Xavier University **C:** Chairman, Parker Hannifin Corp, 2016-; CEO, Parker Hannifin Corp, 2015-; Exec VP, Parker Hannifin Corp, 2008-15; SVP, Parker Hannifin Corp, 2006-08; VP/Pres:Instrumentation Group, Parker Hannifin Corp, 2005-06; VP:Operations, Parker Hannifin, 2003-05; General Manager of Global Services, GE Transportation Systems, 2002-03; General Manager of Global Services, GE Lighting, 1999-2002 **BA:** 6035 Parkland Blvd, Cleveland, OH, 44124-4141

WILLIAMS, VANESSA L., T: Actress, Recording Artist **I:** Media & Entertainment **DOB:** 03/18/1963 **PB:** Millwood **SC:** NY/USA **PT:** Milton Augustine Williams, Helen L. (Tinch) Williams **SPN:** Rick Fox, 1999, Divorced 2004; Ramon Hervey, Jr., 1988, Divorced 1997 **CH:** Melanie, Jillian, Devin, Sasha Gabriella Fox **ED:** BA in Musical Theater, Syracuse University **C:** Recording Artist, 1988 **CW:** Actress, (Broadway) Kiss of the Spider Woman, 1993-1995, Into The Woods, 2002, Sondheim on Sondheim, 2010, A Trip to Bountiful, 2013, (Films) Pick-Up Artist, 1987, Under the Gun, 1988, Another You, 1991, Harley Davidson and the Marlboro Man, 1991, Eraser, 1996, Hoodlum, 1997, Soul Food, 1997, Dance With Me, 1998, The Adventures of Elmo in Grouchland, 1999, Light It Up, 1999, Shaft, 2000, Johnson Family Vacation, 2004, My Brother, 2006, Hannah Montana: The Movie, 2009, Tyler Perry's Temptation: Confessions of a Marriage Counselor, 2013, (Voice Actress) When Marnie Was There, 2014, (TV Films) Full Exposure: The Sex Tapes Scandal, 1989, The Kid Who Loved Christmas, 1990, Perry Mason: The Case of the Silenced Singer, 1990, Stompin' at the Savoy, 1992, Jacksons: An American Dream, 1992, Nothing Lasts Forever, 1995, Bye Bye Birdie, 1995, The Odyssey, 1997, Futuresport, 1998, Don Quixote, 2000, A Diva's Christmas Carol, 2000, WW3, 2001, Keep the Faith, Baby, 2002, The Trip to Bountiful, 2014, Fantasy Life, 2015, (TV Series) Ugly Betty 2006-2010, Desperate Housewives, 2010-2012, 666 Park Avenue, 2012-2013, (TV Miniseries) Nothing Lasts Forever, 1995, (Guest Appearances) Partners in Crime, 1984, T.J. Hooker, 1986, The Love Boat, 1986, The Fresh Prince of Bel-Air, 1990, Between Brothers, 1997, Vanessa Williams and Friends: Christmas in New York, 1996, Star Trek: Deep Space Nine, 1996, L.A. Doctors, 1999, Ally McBeal, 2002, Boomtown, 2003, South Beach, 2006, Mama Mirabelle's Home Movies, 2007-2008, Actress, Executive Producer, (Films) And Then Came Love, 2007, (TV Films) The Courage to Love, 2000; Singer, (Albums) The Right Stuff, 1988, The Comfort Zone, 1991, The Sweetest Days, 1994, Star Bright, 1996, Next, 1997, Alfie, The Best of Vanessa, 1998, Silver & Gold, 2004, Everlasting Love, 2005, The Real Thing, 2009; #1 Hit Single Save the Best For Last; Vocalist, (Soundtracks) Beverly Hills 90210, 1990, Harley Davidson and the Marlboro Man, 1991, Adventures of Priscilla, Queen of the Desert, 1994, The Mask, 1994, Pocahontas, 1995, Eraser, 1996, Dance With Me, 1998, The Adventures of Elmo in Grouchland, 1999, Isn't She Great, 2000; Host Style World, 2000;

Spokesperson, Proactive Solution; Co-Author, You Don't Know, 2012 **AW:** Outstanding Supporting Actress in a Comedy Series, National Association for the Advancement of Colored People Image Awards, Desperate Housewives, 2013, The 100 Most Powerful Celebrities, Forbes.com, 2008, Outstanding Supporting Actress in a Comedy Series, National Association for the Advancement of Colored People Image Awards, Ugly Betty, 2007-2008, Choice TV: Villain, Teen Choice Awards, Ugly Betty, 2007, Star, Hollywood Walk of Fame, 2007, 50 Most Beautiful People, People Magazine, Top 25 Entertainers of Year, Entertainment Weekly, 2007, Tony Award Best Actress in a Musical, Into the Woods, 2002, Theatre World Award, Kiss of the Spider Woman, 1995, 11 Grammy Award Nominations **ACH:** Achievements include being the first Black to be named Miss America, 1983 (resigned title 1983).

WILLIAMS, VENUS, T: Professional Tennis Player **I:** Athletics **DOB:** 06/17/1980 **PB:** Lynwood **SC:** CA/USA **PT:** Daughter of Richard and Oracene Williams. **C:** Designer, EleVen Fashion Label, 2007-; Professional Tennis Player, WTA Tour, 1994-; Designer Venus Williams Collection, Wilson's Leather Co.,; Owner, V Starr Interiors, **CR:** Member U.S. National Team Summer Olympic Games, London, 2012, Beijing, 2008, Athens, Greece, 2004, Sydney, 2000, Fed Cup, 2007, 2003-05, 1999 **CW:** Appeared in (Documentaries) Venus & Serena, 2012 **AW:** Named one of The 100 Most Powerful Women, Forbes Magazine, 2010; Recipient Gold Medal, Women's Doubles, Summer Olympic Games, 2012, 2008, Gold Medal, Women's Singles, Women's Doubles, 2000, Most Impressive Network Newcomer Award, TENNIS Magazine, 1997,ESPN WTA Player of the Year, 2017, WTA Comeback Player of the Year, 2015, Harris Poll Top 10 Greatest Tennis Player, 2015, US Open Sportsmanship Award, 2015, **MEM:** Mem.: WTA Tour Players' Council **ACH:** Achievements include winner 43 career singles titles, 20 career doubles titles, WTA; Grand Slam Mixed-Doubles Championships (with Justin Gimelstob): Australian Open, French Open, 1998; Grand Slam Doubles Championships (with Serena Williams): French Open, 1999, 2010; US Open, 1999, 2009; Wimbledon, 2000, 2002, 2008, 2009, 2012; Australian Open, 2001, 2003, 2009, 2010; Grand Slam Championships: US Open, 2000, 2001; Wimbledon, 2000, 2001, 2005, 2007, 2008 **H:** Interior Decorating, Fashion Design

WILLIAMSON, OLIVER EATON, T: Economics and Law Professor **I:** Education/Educational Services **DOB:** 09/27/1932 **PB:** Superior **SC:** WI/USA **ED:** PhD (hon.), Shanghai Jiao Tong University, 2010; PhD (hon.), Tsinghva University, 2010; PhD (hon.), Nice University, 2005; PhD (hon.), Valencia University, 2004; PhD (hon.), University of Chile, 2000; PhD (hon.), Copenhagen Business School, 2000; PhD (hon.), HECInternat. Business School, Paris, 1997; PhD (hon.), Turku School Economics & Business Administration, Russia, 1996; PhD (hon.), Groningen University, 1989; PhD (hon.), Norwegian School Economics & Business Administration, 1986; PhD in Economics, Carnegie Mellon University, Pittsburgh, 1963; MBA, Stanford University, California, 1960; BS, Massachusetts Institute of Technology, 1955 **C:** Edgar F. Kaiser Professor Emeritus Business, University California, Berkeley, 2004-; Edgar F. Kaiser Professor Business, University California, Berkeley, 1998-2004; Professor Haas School Business, University California, Berkeley, 1988-98; Professor Economics & Law, University California, Berkeley, California, 1988-2004; Gordon B. Tweedy Professor Economics of Law & Organization, Yale University, New Haven, 1983-88; Charles &

William L. Day Professor Economics & Social Sci., University Pennsylvania, Philadelphia, 1977-83; Director Center Study Organizational Innovation, University Pennsylvania, Philadelphia, 1976-83; Chair Department Economics, University Pennsylvania, Philadelphia, 1976-77; Chair Department Economics, University Pennsylvania, Philadelphia, 1971-72; Professor, University Pennsylvania, Philadelphia, 1968-83; Associate Professor, University Pennsylvania, Philadelphia, 1965-68; Assistant Professor Economics, University California, Berkeley, California, 1963-65 **CR:** Fellow Center Advanced Study in Behavioral Scis., Stanford University, 1977-80 Consultant, Federal Trade Commission, 1978-80, National Science Foundation, 1976-77, US Department Justice, 1967-69, Special Economic Assistant to Assistant Attorney General for Antitrust, 1966-67 Consultant, RAND Corp., Santa Monica, California, 1964-66 **CW:** Author: The Economics of Discretionary Behavior, 1964, Markets and Hierarchies: Analysis and Antitrust Implications, 1975, The Economic Institutions of Capitalism, 1985, The Mechanisms of Governance, 1996; Contributor Articles to Professional Journals **AW:** Recipient Nobel Prize in Economics, 2009, John von Neumann Theory Prize, Institute Operations Research & Management Scis., 1999, Irwin Award for Scholarly Contribution to Management, Academy Management, 1988; Fellow John Simon Guggenheim Memorial Foundation, 1977-78 **MEM:** Fellow: Industrial Organization Society, Am. Economic Association, Econometrics Society, Am. Academy Arts & Scis., Am. Academy Political & Social Sci. (HC Recktenwald Prize in Economics 2004); Mem.: National Academy of Sciences, Am. Law & Economic Association (President 1997-98), International Society New Institutional Economics 1999-2001 **BA:** University of California Haas School of Business, 2220 Piedmont Ave, Berkeley, CA, 94720-0001

WILLIS, BRUCE, T: Actor **I:** Media & Entertainment **DOB:** 03/19/1955 **PB:** Idar-Oberstein **SC:** Germany **PT:** David Willis, Marlene Willis **MS:** Married **SPN:** Emma Hemming, 3/22/2009; Demi Moore, 11/21/1987, Divorced 10/18/2000) **CH:** Rumer Glenn, Scout Larue, Tallulah Belle, Ma **ED:** Student, Stella Adler; Student, Montclair State College **CR:** First Amendment Comedy Theatre **CW:** Actor, (Off-Broadway) Heaven And Earth, 1977, Fool For Love, 1984, Bullpen, The Bayside Boys, The Ballad Of Railroad William, (Broadway) Misery, 2015-2016, (Films) The First Deadly Sin, 1980, The Verdict, 1982, Blind Date, 1987, Sunset, 1988, Die Hard, 1988, In Country, 1989, (Voice Actor) Look Who's Talking, 1989, Die Hard 2: Die Harder, 1990, (Voice Actor) Look Who's Talking Too, 1990, The Bonfire Of The Vanities, 1990, Mortal Thoughts, 1991, Hudson Hawk, 1991, Billy Bathgate, 1991, The Last Boy Scout, 1991, Death Becomes Her, 1992, Striking Distance, 1993, Color Of Night, 1994, North, 1994, Pulp Fiction, 1994, Nobody's Fool, 1994, Die Hard With A Vengeance, 1995, 12 Monkeys, 1995, Four Rooms, 1995, Last Man Standing, 1996, The Jackal, 1997, The Fifth Element, 1997, Mercury Rising, 1998, Armageddon, 1998, The Siege, 1998, Breakfast Of Champions, 1999, The Sixth Sense, 1999, The Story Of Us, 1999, The Kid, 2000, Unbreakable, 2000, Bandits, 2001, Hart's War, 2002, Grand Champion, 2002, True West, 2002, Tears Of The Sun, 2003, (Voice Actor) Rugrats Go Wild!, 2003, Charlie's Angels: Full Throttle, 2003, The Whole Ten Yards, 2004, Sin City, 2005, Alpha Dog, 2006, Lucky Number Slevin, 2006, (Voice Actor) Over The Hedge, 2006, Fast Food Nation, 2006, The Astronaut Farmer, 2007, Grindhouse (Planet Terror Segment), 2007, Perfect Stranger, 2007, Live Free Or Die Hard, 2007, Assassination Of A High School President, 2008, What Just Happened, 2008, Sur-

rogates, 2009, Cop Out, 2010, The Expendables, 2010, Red, 2010, Setup, 2011, Catch .44, 2011, Lay The Favorite, 2012, Fire With Fire, 2012, The Cold Light Of Day, 2012, Moonrise Kingdom, 2012, The Expendables 2, 2012, Fire With Fire, 2012, Looper, 2012, G.I. Joe: Retaliation, 2013, Red 2, 2013, Sin City: A Dame To Kill For, 2014, The Prince, 2014, Vice, 2015, Rock The Kasbah, 2015, Extraction, 2015, Going Under, 2016, Precious Cargo, 2016, Marauders, 2016, Split, 2016, Once Upon A Time In Venice, 2017, First Kill, 2017, The Bombing, 2018, Death Wish, 2018, Acts Of Violence, 2018, Reprisal, 2018, Glass, (TV Appearances) Miami Vice, 1984, The Twilight Zone, 1985, Ally McBeal, 1999, Friends, 2000, Touching Evil, 2004, That 70's Show, 2005, SNL, 2013, (TV Series) Moonlighting, 1985-1989; Actor, Producer, (Films) The Whole Nine Yards, 2000, Hostage, 2005, 16 Blocks, 2006; Executive Producer, (Films) Crocodile Hunter: The Collision Course, 2002, The Hip Hop Project, 2006; Actor, Executive Producer, (Films) A Good Day To Die Hard, 2013, (TV Films) True West, 2002; Singer, (Albums) The Return Of Bruno, 1987, If It Don't Kill You, It Just Makes You Stronger, 1989; Performer, (Concert Film) The Return Of Bruno, 1988 **AW:** Commander, Government of France, 2013, New Jersey Hall of Fame, 2011, The 100 Most Powerful Celebrities, Forbes.com, 2008, Order of Arts & Letters, Government of France, 2005, People's Choice Award, 2000, Star, Walk of Fame, 1998, Emmy Award, Golden Globe Award, Moonlighting, 1987, People's Choice Award, Moonlighting, 1986, International Broadcasting Man of the Year, Hollywood Radio and TV Society **BA:** Ziffren Brittenham Branca Fischer, 1801 Century Park W, Los Angeles, CA, 90067

WILSON, CHARLES REGINALD, T: Federal Judge **I:** Law and Legal Services **DOB:** 10/14/1954 **PB:** Pensacola **SC:** FL/USA **ED:** JD, University of Notre Dame, 1979; BS, University of Notre Dame, 1976 **CT:** Bar: Florida 1979 **C:** Judge, U.S. Court Appeals (11th cir.), Tampa, Florida, 1999-; U.S. Attorney, U.S. District Court (Middle District) Florida, 1994-99; U.S. Magistrate Judge, US District Court (Middle District) Florida, 1990-94; Private Practice, Florida, 1981-86; County Judge, 13th Judicial Cir. of Florida, 1986-90; Assistant County Attorney, Hillsborough County, Florida, 1980-81; Law Clerk to Hon. Joseph W. Hatchett, U.S. Court Appeals (11th cir.), 1979-80 **MEM:** Mem.: Ferguson-White Inn of Am. Inn of Court, Federal Bar Association, Am. Law Institute **BA:** 56 Forsyth St NW, Atlanta, GA, 30303

WILSON, EDWARD O., T: Biologist, Researcher, Theorist **I:** Sciences **DOB:** 06/10/1929 **PB:** Birmingham **SC:** AL/USA **PT:** Son of Edward Osborne and Inez (Freeman) W.; **ED:** DrRerNat, University Würzburg, 2000; DHC, University Montreal, 2004; DHC, University Madrid Complutense, 1995; LLD, University Mississippi Lavelle, 2008; LLD, Grad. Theological Foundation, 2008; LLD, Emory University, 2008; LLD, Simon Fraser University; LHD (hon.), Williams College, 2007; LHD (hon.), Rockefeller University, 2007; LHD (hon.), University Puget Sound, 2006; LHD (hon.), Albion College, 2005; LHD (hon.), University South Alabama, 2003; LHD (hon.), Connecticut College, 2000; LHD (hon.), Bradford College, 1997; LHD (hon.), Pennsylvania State University; LHD (hon.), Yale University, 1998; LHD (hon.), Muhlenburg College, 1998; LHD (hon.), Hofstra University, 1986; DSc (hon.), Clark University, 2005; DSc (hon.), Harvard University, 2004; DSc (hon.), University of the South, 2002; DSc (hon.), Kenyon College, 2002; DSc (hon.), University Portland, 1997; DSc (hon.), University Guelph, 1997; DSc (hon.), College Wooster, 1997; DSc (hon.), Bates College, 1996; DSc (hon.),

Ohio University, 1996; DSc (hon.), University Connecticut, 1995; DSc (hon.), Ripon College, 1994; DSc (hon.), Oxford University, 1993; DSc (hon.), University Massachusetts, 1990; DSc (hon.), Macalester College, 1990; DSc (hon.), Fitchburg State College, 1989; DSc (hon.), Lawrence University, 1979; DSc (hon.), University West Florida, 1979; DSc (hon.), Grinnell College, 1978; DSc (hon.), Duke University, 1978; DPhil, Uppsala University, Sweden; PhD, Harvard University, 1955; LHD (hon.), University Alabama, 1980; MS, University Alabama, 1950; BS, University Alabama, 1949 **C:** Pellegrino University Research Professor Emeritus in Entmology for the Department of Organismic and Evolutionary Biology, Harvard University, 2014-,; Lecturer, Duke University, 2014-; Hon. curator entomology, Society Fellows, Harvard University, 1997-; Faculty, Society Fellows, Harvard University, 1956-; Curator entomology, Society Fellows, Harvard University, 1971-97; Research professor, Society Fellows, Harvard University, 1997-2002; Pellegrino University professor, Society Fellows, Harvard University, 1994-97; Baird professor sci., Society Fellows, Harvard University, 1976-94; Junior fellow, Society Fellows, Harvard University, 1953-56 **CR:** Board directors Conservation International, 1997-, Nature Conservancy, 1994-2002, Am. Academy Liberal Education, 1993-2004, Am. Museum Natural History, 1992-2002, New York Botanical Garden, 1991-95, Organization Tropical Studies, 1984-91, World Wildlife Fund, 1983-94 selection committee Guggenheim Foundation, 1982-89 **CW:** Author: The Insect Societies, 1971, Sociobiology: The New Synthesis, 1975, On Human Nature, 1978 (Pulitzer prize for non-fiction, 1979), Promethean Fire, 1983, Biophilia, 1984, Success and Dominance in Ecosystems, 1990, The Diversity of Life, 1992 (National Wildlife Association award, Deutsche Umweltstiftung Book award, Sir Peter Kent Conservation prize), Naturalist, 1994 (L.A. Times Book prize sci., 1995), In Search of Nature, 1996, Consilience: The Unity of Knowledge, 1998 (Forkosch award International Academy Humanism, 2000), Biological Diversity: The Oldest Human Heritage, 1999, The Future of Life, 2002 (Natural World Book prize, U.K., 2002), Pheidole in the New World: A Dominant, Hyperdiverse Ant Genus, 2003 (Julia Ward Howe prize, 2003), From So Simple A Beginning, 2005, Nature Revealed, 2006, The Creation: An Appeal to Save Life on Earth, 2006; author: (with R.H. MacArthur) The Theory of Island Biogeography, 1967; author: (with C.J. Lumsden) Genes, Mind and Culture, 1981; author: (with Bert Holldobler) The Ants, 1990 (Pulitzer prize for non-fiction, 1991), Journey to the Ants, 1994 (Phi Beta Kappa prize sci., 1995), The Creation, 2006 (Green Book award, Stevens Institute Tech. Center Sci. Writings, 2007), The Superorganism, 2008; others,(Books) Anthill: A Novel, 2010, The Leafcutter Ants: Civilization by Instinct, 2011, The Social Conquest of Earth, 2012, Letters to a Young Scientist, 2014, A Window to Eternity: A Biologist's Walk Through Gorongosa National Park, 2014, The Meaning of Human Existence, 2014, Half-Earth, 2016, The Origins of Creativity, 2017 **AW:** Recipient Pirk award, National PKC Association, 2008, Terceuteram Silver medal, Linnear Society, 2007, Catalonia prize, Spain, 2007, TED Biotech. Prize, 2007, George B. Stibbitz Comms. Pioneer award, Am. Computer Museum, 2006, TED prize, Sampling Foundation, 2006, Prince William of Orange medal, Leiden University, 2006, Rungius medal, Am. Museum Wildlife Art, 2005, Rachel Carson award, International Society Ecotoxicology and Chemistry, 2004, Gov.'s award, Island Alliance, Massachu-

setts, 2004, Frances Hutchinson medal, Chicago Botanical Garden, 2004, Lowell Thomas award, Explorers Club, 2004, Silver Cross of Christopher Columbus, Dominican Republic, 2003, Presidential medal, Republic of Italy, 2002, Busk medal, Royal Geog. Society, 2002, Global Environment Citizens award, Harvard University, 2001, Lifetime Achievement award, Time, 2001, Thoreau medal, Thoreau Society, 2001, Nierenberg prize, Scripps Oceanographic Institute, 2001, Lewis Thomas prize, Rockefeller University, 2001, Phillips Memorial medal, World Conservation Union, 2000, Kistler prize, Foundation for the Future, 2000, King Faisal International prize for sci., 2000, Nonino prize, Letters and Sci., Italy, 2000, Stone award, New England Aquarium, 1999, Hutchinson medal, Garden Club Am., 1997, Washburn medal, Museum Sci., 1996, Schubert prize, Germany, 1996, John Hay award, Orion Society, 1995, Pub. Understanding Sci. award, American Association for the Advancement of Science, 1995, Ecological Society Am. Audubon medal, Audubon Society, 1995, Eminent Ecologist award, Government of Japan, 1994, International prize biology, 1993, Shaw medal, Missouri Botanical Garden, 1993, Achievement award, National Wildlife Federation, 1992, Gold medal, Worldwide Fund for Nature, 1990, Revelle medal, 1990, Prix di'Inst. de la Vie, Paris, 1990, Craford prize in Biosciences, Royal Swedish Academy Sciences, 1990, Weaver award scholarly letters, Ingersoll Foundation, 1989, German Ecological Institute prize, 1987, Silver medal, National Zoological Park, 1987, Tyler Ecology prize, 1984, Leidy medal, Academy Natural Sci., Philadelphia, 1979, Archie Carr medal, University Florida, 1978, Distinguished Service award, Am. Institute Biological Scis., 1976, National Medal Sci., 1976, Mercer award, Ecological Society Am., 1971, Cleve.-AAAS Research prize, 1967; Guggenheim Foundation fellow, 1978,Explorers Club Medal, 2009, BBVA Frontiers of Knowledge Award, 2010, Thomas Jefferson Medal in Architecture, 2010, Heartland Prize, 2010, Earthsky Science Communicator of the Year, 2010 **MEM:** Fellow: Deutsche Akad. Naturforsch., Am. Philosophical Society (Franklin medal 1998), Am. Academy Arts and Scis.; mem.: National Academy of Sciences, Royal Society Sci. Uppsala (Sweden), Russian Academy Sci., Royal Entomological Society (hon. life), Finnish Academy Sci. and Letters, Royal Society London, Netherlands Entomological Society (hon. life), Royal Society Edinburgh (life), Association Tropical Biology (hon. life), Academy Humanism (hon. life), Am. Humanist Association (Distinguished Service award 1982, hon. life, Humanist of Year), Zoological Society London (hon. life), Entomological Society Am. (Founders Memorial award 1972, L.O. Howard award 1985, hon. life), Brit. Ecological Society (hon. life), Am. Genetics Association (hon. life), Explorers Club (life, hon. life, medal) **BA:** Harvard University, Mus Comparative Zoology, Cambridge, MA, 02138

WILSON, FREDERICA SMITH, T: U.S. Representative from Florida **I:** Government Administration/ Government Relations/Government Services **DOB:** 11/05/1942 **PB:** Miami, Florida, November 5, 1942 **PT:** Daughter of Thirlee and Beulah (Finley) Smith; **ED:** LHD (hon.), Florida Memorial University; MA, University Miami, 1972; BS, Fisk University, 1963 **C:** Member, US House Education & the Workforce Committee, 2013-; Member, US House Space, Science, & Tech. Committee, 2011-; Member, US Congress from 24th Florida District, 2013-; Founder, executive director, 5000 Role Models of Excellence Project, 1993-; Member, US House Foreign Affairs Committee, 2011-13; Member, US Con-

gress from 17th Florida District, Washington, 2011-13; Minority whip, Florida State Senate, 2008-10; Minority leader pro tempore, Florida State Senate, 2006-08; Member District 33, Florida State Senate, Tallahassee, 2003-10; Member District 104, Florida House of Reps., Tallahassee, 1998-2002; Executive director, Office Alternative Education & Dropout Prevention, Miami,; Member, Miami-Dade County School Board, Florida, 1992-98 **MEM:** Mem.: National Association Black School Educators, The Links, Inc., Alpha Kappa Alpha **PA:** Democrat

WILSON, JOE, T: U.S. Representative from South Carolina **I:** Government Administration/Government Relations/Government Services **CN:** US Congress from 2nd South Carolina district **PB:** Charleston SC: SC/USA **PT:** Son of Hugh deVeaux and Wray Smart (Graves) Wilson; **ED:** BA, Washington & Lee University, Lexington, Virginia, 1969; JD, University South Carolina, Columbia, 1972 **CT:** Bar: South Carolina 1972 **C:** Member, US Congress from 2nd South Carolina district, 2001-; Partner, Kirkland, Wilson, Moore, Taylor & Thomas, West Columbia, 1972-2001; Staff Member, US Rep. Floyd Spence, Columbia, South Carolina, 1970-72; Staff Member to rep. Strom Thurmond, US Senator Strom Thurmond, Washington, DC, 1967 **CR:** Deputy General Counsel to Secretary Jim Edwards US Department Energy, Washington, 1981-1982; Member South Carolina State Senate, 1984-2001; Presidential Appointee Intergovernmental Adv. Council Education, 1990-1991; Board of Directors Bank of America, Lexington, South Carolina **CIV:** Vice Chairman South Carolina Rep. Party, 1972-1974; Campaign Manager Staff US Rep. Floyd Spence, 1974, 1978, 1980, 1982, 1998, Columbia **MIL:** Served in U.S. Army Reserve, 1972-75, Positions to Colonel South Carolina Army National Guard, 1975-2003 **PA:** Republican

WILSON, THOMAS JOSEPH II, T: CEO of Allstate Corporation **I:** Insurance **CN:** Allstate Corporation **MS:** Married **SPN:** Jill Garling **CH:** Three Children **ED:** Master of Management, Northwestern University, J. L. Kellogg School of Management (1980); BSBA, University of Michigan (1979) **C:** Chairman, President, Chief Executive Officer, Allstate Corporation, Northbrook, IL (2008-Present); President, Allstate Protection (2003-2005); Chairman, President, Allstate Financial (1999-2002); President, Chief Executive Officer, Allstate Corporation (2007-2008); President, Chief Operating Officer, Allstate Corporation, Northbrook, IL (2005-2006); Senior Vice President, Chief Financial Officer, Allstate Corporation, Northbrook, IL (1995-1998); Vice President, Strategy & Analysis, Sears, Roebuck & Co., Chicago, IL (1993-1995); Managing Director, Mergers & Acquisitions, Dean Witter Reynolds, Chicago, IL (1986-1993); Various Financial Positions, Amoco Corp., Chicago, IL (1980-1986) **CR:** Board of Directors, State Street Corporation (2012-Present); Board of Directors, Allstate Corporation (2006-Present) **CIV:** Board of Directors, Rush-Presbyterian-St. Luke's Medical Center and Federal Reserve Bank Chicago

WINELAND, DAVID JEFFREY, T: Physicist **I:** Sciences **DOB:** 02/24/1944 **PB:** Milw. **ED:** PhD in Physics, Harvard University, 1970; Master in Physics, Harvard University; BS in Physics, University California, Berkeley, 1965 **C:** Physicist, National Institute Standards & Technology Lab, Boulder, Colorado, 1975-; Postdoctoral research associate, University Washington, **CR:** Lectureship University Colorado **CW:** Several published articles in Science and Nature **AW:** Co-recipient Nobel Prize in Physics, Royal Swedish Academy Sciences, 2012, Benjamin Franklin medal in Physics, Franklin Institute, 2010; recipient National

Medal Sci., The White House, 2007, International award on Quantum Communications, Silver & Gold medals, US Department Commerce, I. I. Rabi Award of the IEEE, IEEE, 1998, Einstein medal for Laser Sci., Society Optical & Quantum Electronics, 1996, Frederic Ives medal, Optical Society America, 2004, William F. Meggers award, 1990 **MEM:** Fellow: National Institute Standards & Technology, American Physical Society (Davisson-Germer prize 1990, Arthur L. Schawlow prize in Laser Sci. 2001), American Optical Society; mem.: National Academy of Sciences

WINFREY, OPRAH, T: Broadcast Executive **I:** Media & Entertainment **CN:** Harpo Productions **DOB:** 01/29/1954 **PB:** Kosciusko **SC:** Mississippi/USA **PT:** Daughter of Vernon Winfrey and Vernita Lee. **ED:** Doctor (hon.), University of the Free State, 2011; LHD (hon.), Duke University, 2009; BA in Speech Communications and Performing Arts, Tennessee State University, 1987 **C:** Host Oprah's Next Chapter, OWN: The Oprah Winfrey Network, LA, 2012-; Chairman, CEO, chief creative officer, OWN: The Oprah Winfrey Network, LA, 2011-; Owner, producer, chairman, CEO, Harpo Productions, 1986-; Chairman, OWN: The Oprah Winfrey Network, LA, 2011; Host series of celebrity interview spls., Oprah: Behind the Scenes,; Host, Oprah After the Show, Chicago, 2003-06; Host Oprah Winfrey Show,, Harpo Productions Inc., Chicago, 1985-2011; Host talk show A.M. Chicago, Station WLS-TV, 1984; Host morning talk show People Are Talking, Station WJZ-TV, Baltimore, 1978-83; News anchorperson, Station WJZ-TV, Baltimore, 1976-78; Reporter, news anchorperson, Station WTVF-TV, Nashville, 1973-76; News reporter, Station WVOL Radio, Nashville, 1971-72 **CR:** Partner, co-founder Oxygen Media, an Internet and cable TV co., 1998- founder, editorial director O, The Oprah Magazine in conjunction with Hearst Magazines, 2000 launched (magazine) first international edition, O, The Oprah Magazine in South Africa, 2002-, Oprah, After the Show, 2002-, O at Home, 2004-, Oprah Radio (previously Oprah & Friends), XM Satelite Radio Holdings, Inc., 2006- online leader, Oprah.com, launched Live Your Best Life, 2003- started Oprah Book Club creator (TV series) Oprah's Big Give, 2007 board directors Weight Watchers International, Inc., 2015- **CIV:** Established, Seven Fountains Primary Sch, South Africa, 2007 Established, Oprah Winfrey Leadership Academy for Girls, Henley-on-Klip, South Africa, 2006 Established, Oprah Winfrey Scholars Program, Established, ChristmasKindness South Africa, 2002- Established, Oprah's Angel Network, 1997- Established, Oprah Winfrey Foundation, 1987- **CW:** Actress (films) The Color Purple, 1985, Native Son, 1986, Beloved, 1998, Charlotte's Web (voice), 2006, Bee Movie (voice), 2007, The Princess and the Frog (voice), 2009, Jesus Henry Christ, 2012, The Butler, 2013, (TV films) There Are No Children Here, 1993, actress, producer Before Women Had Wings, 1997, (films) Selma, 2014, actress, executive producer, A Wrinkle in Time, 2018 (TV miniseries) The Women of Brewster Place, 1989; executive prodr.: (TV films) Overexposed, 1992, The Wedding, 1998, David and Lisa, 1998, Tuesdays with Morrie, 1999, Amy & Isabelle, 2001, Their Eyes Were Watching God, 2005, Oprah Winfrey Presents: Mitch Albom's For One More Day, 2007; (documentaries) Nine, 1992, Legends Ball, 2006-, Building a Dream: The Oprah Winfrey Leadership Academy, 2007, Oprah Presents: Master Class, 2012-14, (TV spls.) Michael Jackson Talks to... Oprah Live, 1993; executive producer, executive prodr.: The Oprah Winfrey Oscar Special, 2007, Christmas at the White House: An Oprah Primetime Special, 2009, The Star, 2017, The Immortal life of Henrietta

Lacks, 2017; prodr.: (TV series) ABC Afterschool Specials, 1992-93; (films) The Hundred-Foot Journey, 2014; guest appearances include The Fresh Prince of Bel-Air, Ellen, Home Improvement, The Hughleys, Mad TV, 30 Rock, others; author: What I Know For Sure, 2014 **AW:** Time 100 Most Influential, 2018 **ACH:** Initiated a campaign to establish a national database of convicted child abusers, and testified before U.S. Senate Judiciary Committee on behalf of National Child Protection Act in 1991, as a result, President Clinton signed the "Oprah Bill" into Law on December 20, 1993, establishing the national database used by law enforcement agencies around the world; third woman in American entertainment industry to own her own studio; first African-American woman to reach billionaire status; after receiving Lifetime Acheivement Award in 1998, permanently withdrew name from Daytime Emmy Award consideration; Oprah and Oprah Winfrey Show received a total of 39 Daytime Emmy awards: seven for Outstanding Host; nine for Outstanding Talk Show; twenty-one in the Creative Arts categories; and one for supervising producer of the ABC School Special, Shades of Single Protein; celebrated the 20th year anniversary of the Oprah Winfrey Show in November, 2005. **BA:** Harpo Productions, PO Box 909715, Chicago, IL, 60607

WINKLER, HENRY FRANKLIN, T: Actor, Film Producer, Director **I:** Media & Entertainment **DOB:** 10/30/1945 **PB:** NYC **PT:** Son of Harry Irving and Ilse Anna Maria (Hadra) W.; Married Stacey Weitzman, May 5, 1978; children: Zoe Emily, Max Daniel, (stepchildren) Jed Weitzman. **ED:** MFA, Yale School Drama, 1970; DHL (hon.), Emerson College, 1978; BA, Emerson College, 1967 **C:** With, Yale Repertory Theatre, 1970-71 **CR:** Founder New Haven Free Theatre, 1968, Off The Wall New York, improvisation co., 1972 teacher drama UCLA Adult Extension founding member Children's Action Network. **CW:** Actor: Off-Broadway shows, 1972-73, Cincinnati Playhouse, 1973; Broadway shows, The Dinner Party, 2000, The Performers, 2012; London Theatre, Peter Pan, 2006; (films) The Lords of Flatbush, 1972, Crazy Joe, 1974, Heroes, 1977, The One and Only, 1977, Night Shift, 1983, Wes Craven's Scream, 1996, Ground Control, 1998, The Water Boy, 1998, Ugly Naked People, 1999, Elevator Seeking, 1999, Dill Scallion, 1999, P.U.N.K.S., 1999, Down to You, 2000, I Shaved My Legs for This, 2001, Holes, 2003, Fronterz, 2004, Unbeatable Harold, 2005, Berkeley, 2005, The Kid and I, 2005, The King of Central Park, 2006, Click, 2006, A Plumm Summer, 2007, You Don't Mess with the Zohan, 2008, The Most Wonderful Time of the Year, 2008, Group Sex, 2010, Adventures of Serial Buddies, 2011, Beatles Stories, 2012, Running Mates, 2011, Here Comes the Boom, 2012, Serial Buddies, 2013, Larry Gaye Renegade Male Flight Attendant, 2015; (TV series) Happy Days, 1973-84 (Best Actor - TV Series Musical or Comedy, Golden Globe Awards, 1976, 1977), Fonz and the Happy Days Gang (voice), 1980, The Mork & Mindy/Laverne & Shirley with the Fonz Show (voice), 1982, Monty, 1994 (also executive producer), Mr. Sunshine, (voice) Clifford's Puppy Days, 2003 (Performer for an animated program, Daytime Emmy award, Academy TV Arts & Scis., 2005), Out of Practice, 2005-06, Royal Pains, 2010-12, Children's Hospital, 2010-12, Royal Pains, 2010, Parks and Recreation, 2013, Hollywood Game Night, 2014, Hank Zipzer, 2014, Comedy Bang Bang, 2015, Drunk History, 2015, Better Late than Never, 2016, Hank Zipzers Christmas Catastrophe, 2016; (TV films) Katherine, 1975, America Salutes Richard Rodgers: The Sound of His Music, 1976, An American Christmas Carol, 1979, Absolute Strangers, 1991, The Only Way Out, 1994, Truman Capote's One Christmas,

1994, A Child is Missing, 1995 (also executive producer), Dad's Week Off, 1996, National Lampoon's Dad's Week Off, 1997, Detention: The Siege at Johnson High, 1997, Beverly Hills S.U.V., 2006; executive prodr.: (TV) Who Are the Debolts? Where Did They Get Nineteen Kids?, 1977, Starflight:The Plane That Couldn't Land, 1983, Ryan's Four, 1983, When Your Lover Leaves, 1983, Scandal Sheet, 1984, MacGyver, 1985-94, Mr. Sunshine, 1986, A Family Again, 1988, Starting Now, 1989, Sightings, 1992, Dead Man's Gun, 1997, 1999, So Weird, 1999, Sightings: Heartland Ghosts, 2002, WinTuition, 2002, Hollywood Squares, 2002-04, Young MacGyver, 2003, Unexplained Mysteries, 2003, Dallas Reunion: Return to Southfork, 2004, Happy Days: 30th Anniversary Reunion, 2005, Knots Landing Reunion: Together Again, 2005; prodr.: (films) The Sure Thing, 1985; producer, host home video Strong Kids, Safe Kids, 1985, PBS animated special Happy Ever After, 1985, Two Daddies to Love Me, 1988; prodr.: (films) Young Sherlock Holmes, 1985; prodr.: (TV films) Losing a Sister, 1988; president Fair Dinkum Productions, Hollywood, California, 1979-, Winkler-Daniels Productions, Hollywood, 1987-91; prodr.: (TV) Run, Don't Walk for own co. JZM Productions, 1981; dir.: (TV series) Joanie Loves Chachi, 1982; director (TV films) All the Kids Do It, 1984, A Smokey Mountain Christmas, 1986, Memories of Me, 1988, Cop and a Half, 1993, Dave's World, 1993, Too Something, 1995, Clueless, 1996, Sabrina, the Teenage Witch, 1996; (TV appearances) Mary Tyler Moore, 1973, The Bob Newhart Show, 1974, Laverne & Shirley, 1976, 1979, Saturday Night Live, 1977, Mork & Mindy, 1978, Joanie Loves Chachi, 1982, MacGyver, 1990, (voice) Street Sharks, 1995, (voice) South Park, 1998, The Practice, 1999, 2000, (voice) The Simpsons, 1999, The Drew Carey Show, 2001, Law & Order: Special Victims Unit, 2002, Hollywood Squares, 2003, Arrested Development, 2003-05, 2012-, Third Watch, 2004, Crossing Jordon, 2005, Sit Down Shut Up, 2009, Hero Factory, 2010-12; co-author: (with Lin Oliver) (children's book series): Hank Zipzer: The World's Greatest Underachiever, 2003-; author: I've Never Met an Idiot on the River, 2011. **AW:** Recipient Golden Plate award Am. Academy Achievement 1980, Sorrisi e Canzoni Telegatto award (Italian TV award) 1980, Humanitarian award Women in Film, 1988, UN Peace prize, Chevailer de l'Ordre des Arts et des Lettres; named hon. youth chairman Epilepsy Foundation, chairman Toys for Tots, 1977, Best Actor in Comedy Series, Photoplay magazine 1976-77, King of Baccus, Mardi Gras, New Orleans 1977, national spokesperson United Friends of the Children, 1982-; named Office of the Order of the British Empire, 2011. **MEM:** Member American Federation of TV and Radio Artists, Screen Actors Guild, Actors Equity. **BA:** Fair Dinkum Productions, P.O. Box 49914, Los Angeles, CA, 90049

WINSLET, KATE, T: Actress **I:** Media & Entertainment **DOB:** 10/05/1975 **PB:** Reading, Berkshire, England **SC:** Reading Berkshire Eng. **PT:** Daughter of Roger and Sally Bridges Winslet; **CIV:** Founder, Golden Hat Foundation, 2010- **CW:** Actress: (films) Heavenly Creatures, 1994 (London Film Critics' Cir. award for Best Brit. Actress, 1996), Sense and Sensibility, 1995 (BAFTA award for Best Actress in a Supporting Role, 1996, Screen Actors Guild award for Outstanding Performance by a Female Actor in a Supporting Role, 1996), A Kid in King Arthur's Court, 1995, Jude, 1996, Hamlet, 1996, Titanic, 1997, Hideous Kinky, 1998, Holy Smoke, 1999, Faeries (voice), 1999, Quills, 2000, Enigma, 2001, Christmas Carol: The Movie (voice), 2001, Iris: A Memoir of Iris Murdoch, 2001, War Game, 2001, The Life of David Gale, 2003, Plunge: The Movie, 2003, Eternal Sunshine of the Spotless Mind, 2004

(London Film Critics Cir. award for Brit. Actress of Year, 2005), Finding Neverland, 2004, Romance & Cigarettes, 2005, All The King's Men, 2006, Little Children, 2006, Flushed Away (voice), 2006, The Holiday, 2006, The Reader, 2008 (Academy award for Best Performance by an Actress in a Leading Role, 2009, Golden Globe award for Best Supporting Actress, 2009, BAFTA award for Best Actress in a Leading Role, 2009, Screen Actors Guild award for Outstanding Performance by a Female Actor in a Supporting Role, 2009, London Film Critics Cir. award for Best Actress, 2009), Revolutionary Road, 2008 (Golden Globe award for Best Actress, 2009, London Film Critics Cir. award for Best Actress, 2009), Contagion, 2011, Carnage, 2011, Labor Day, 2013, Divergent, 2014, A Little Chaos, 2014, Insurgent, 2015, Steve Jobs, 2015 (Golden Globe award for Best Performance by an Actress in a Supporting Role in a Motion Picture, 2016, BAFTA award for Best Supporting Actress, 2016), The Dressmaker, 2015, Triple 9, 2016; (TV films) Anglo Saxon Attitudes, 1992, Pride (voice), 2004; (TV miniseries) Mildred Pierce, 2011 (Emmy award for Outstanding Lead Actress in a Miniseries or a Movie, 2011, Golden Globe award for Best Performance by an Actress in a Mini-Series or Motion Picture Made for TV, 2012, Screen Actors Guild award for Outstanding Performance by a Female Actor in a TV Movie or Miniseries, 2012); (TV series) Dark Season, 1991, Get Back, 1992; (theater performances include) Peter Pan, What the Butler Saw, A Game of Soldiers, Adrian Mole, (TV appearances) Casualty, 1993, appeared in (documentaries) Being Mick, 2001, co-creator (audio book) Listen to the Storyteller, 2000 (Grammy award for Best Spoken Word Album for Children, 2000), narrator (documentary) A Mother's Courage: Talking Back to Autism, 2010, Author, Creator (public awareness book) The Golden Hat: Talking Back to Autism, 2012 AW: Named a Commander of the Order of the British Empire, Queen Elizabeth II, 2012; named one of The 100 Agents of Change, Rolling Stone magazine, 2009, The World's Most Influential People, TIME magazine, 2009, The 50 Most Powerful Women in New York City, New York Post, 2007; recipient Yo Dona award for Best Humanitarian Work, 2011, Star, Hollywood Walk of Fame, 2014, Britannia award for British Artist of Year, BAFTA/LA Cunard Britannia Awards, 2007 BA: Creative Artists Agency, 2000 Avenue of the Stars, Los Angeles, CA, 90067

WINSTON, JAMEIS, T: Professional Football Player I: Athletics DOB: 01/06/1994 PB: Hueytown PT: Son of Antonor and Loretta Winston. ED: Student in exploratory, Florida State University, Tallahassee, 2012- C: Quarterback, Tampa Bay Buccaneers, 2015-; Quarterback, Florida State University Seminoles, 2013 AW: Named Sporting News Player of Year, 2013, Player of Year, Associated Press, 2013, First Team All-American, 2013, First Team All-Conf., Rookie of Year, Offensive Player of Year & Player of Year, Atlantic Coast Conference, 2013; recipient Heisman Memorial Trophy award, The Heisman Trust, 2013, Walter Camp award, Walter Camp Football Foundation, 2013, Davey O'Brien award, Davey O'Brien Foundation, 2013,PFWA All-Rookie Team, 2015, Pepsi NFL Rookie of the Year, 2015, Pro Bowl, 2015 ACH: Achievements include becoming the youngest recipient of the Heisman Memorial Trophy Award, 2013, a member of the BCS National Championship winning Florida State University Seminoles, 2013 BA: Tampa Bay Buccaneers, One Buccaneer Place, Tampa, FL, 33607

WISE, DAVID, T: Freestyle Skier I: Athletics AW: Four Winter X Games Gold Medals, Superpipe, 2012-2014, 2018, One World Championship Gold Medal, Halfpipe, 2013, Two Olympic Gold Medals, Halfpipe, 2014, 2018

WITHERS, PICK, T: Drummer I: Media & Entertainment PB: Leicester SC: England C: Album with Dire Straits, "Dire Straits" (1978), "Communique" (1979), "Making Movies" (1980), "Money for Nothing" (1988), "Live at the BBC" (1995), "Sultans of Swing: The Very Best of Dire Straits" (1998), "Private Investigations: The Very Best of Dire Straits" (2005); Album with Others, "Spring," "Slow Train Coming," "Giant from the Blue" AW: Inductee, Rock & Roll Hall of Fame (2018)

WITHERSPOON, REESE, T: Actress I: Media & Entertainment DOB: 03/22/1976 PB: New Orleans SC: LA/USA PT: Daughter of John and Betty Witherspoon CR: Launched Lifestyle Website Draper James, 2015-, Global Ambassador, Avon Cosmetics, 2007-, Co-owner, Production Company Type A Films CW: Actress: (films) The Man in the Moon, 1991, A Far Off Place, 1993, Jack the Bear, 1993, S.F.W., 1994, Freeway, 1996, Fear, 1996, Twilight, 1998, Overnight Delivery, 1998, Pleasantville, 1998, Cruel Intentions, 1999, Election, 1999 (National Society Film Critics Award for Best Actress, 2000), Best Laid Plans, 1999, American Psycho, 2000, Little Nicky, 2000, The Trumpet of the Swan (voice), 2001, Legally Blonde, 2001, The Importance of Being Earnest, 2002, Sweet Home Alabama, 2002, Vanity Fair, 2004, Just Like Heaven, 2005, Walk the Line, 2005 (Academy Award for Best Performance by an Actress in a Leading Role, 2006, Golden Globe Award for Best Actress in a Motion Picture-Comedy or Musical, 2006, Screen Actors Guild Award for Best Actress in a Motion Picture, 2006, BAFTA Award for Best Actress in a Leading Role, 2006, Teen Choice award for Choice Actress, 2006), Rendition, 2007, Four Christmases, 2008, Monsters vs. Aliens (voice), 2009, How Do You Know, 2010, Water for Elephants, 2011, This Means War, 2012, Mud, 2012, Devil's Knot, 2013, The Good Lie, 2014, Inherent Vice, 2014, Hot Pursuit, 2015, Sing, 2016, Home Again, 2017, A Wrinkle in Time, 2018; Actress, Executive Producer (films) Legally Blonde 2: Red, White & Blonde, 2003, actress, Producer Penelope, 2006, Wild, 2014, Hot Pursuit, 2015; Producer (films) Gone Girl, 2014; Actress (TV films) Wildflower, 1991, Desperate Choices: To Save My Child, 1992; (TV miniseries) Return to Lonesome Dove, 1993; (TV appearances) Friends, 2000, King of the Hill, 2000, The Simpsons, 2002, Freedom: A History of Us, 2003, Monsters vs. Aliens, Mutant Pumpkins from Outer Space, 2009, The Eric Andre Show, 2012, SNL, 2015, Best Time Ever with Neil Patrick Harris, 2015, The Muppets, 2015, Big Little Lies, 2017, The Mindy Project, 2017 AW: Named Favorite Female Movie Star, People's Choice Awards, 2009, 2008, Favorite Leading Actress, 2006, Favorite Female Film Star, People Magazine, 2004; Named One of The 100 Most Powerful Celebrities, Forbes.com, 2008, The 100 Most Powerful Women in Entertainment, The Hollywood Reporter, 2014, 2007, 50 Most Powerful People in Hollywood, Premiere magazine, 2006, 100 Most Influential People, TIME magazine, 2006, 50 Most Beautiful People, People Magazine, 2002, 25 Most Intriguing People, 2001; Recipient, Star, Hollywood Walk of Fame, 2012, Renaissance Award, Gene Siskel Film Center, 2012

WITT, KATARINA, T: Professional Figure Skater I: Athletics PB: Staaken, Berlin SC: Germany PT: Manfred Witt; Kathe Witt C: Professional figure skater, 1988-; Winner 6 European titles; Winner 4 world titles; Contender Olympic games, 1994; Winner Olympic gold medal, 1984, 88; World class amateur figure skater CR: Creator KW Arts and Entertainment, Frankfurt CW: Appeared in numerous ice shows, TV spls. including Canvas of Ice, 1988; creator TV film Carmen on Ice, 1990 (Emmy award 1990); toured with Katarina Witt

and Brian Boitano-Skating, 1990, Katarina Witt and Brian Boitano-Skating II, 1991; author (with E.M. Swift): Only with Passion: Figure Skating's Most Winning Champion on Competition and Life, 2005 AW: Emmy for Carmen on Ice, 1990, East German Sportswoman of the Year, 1984 PA: Socialist Unity Party

WITTEN, EDWARD, T: Theoretical Physicist I: Sciences DOB: 08/26/1951 PB: Baltimore SC: Maryland ED: PhD (hon.), University Southern California, 2004; PhD (hon.), Columbia University, 1996; PhD (hon.), Hebrew University of Jerusalem, 1993; PhD (hon.), Brandeis University, 1988; PhD, Princeton University, 1976; MA, Princeton University, 1974; BA in history, Brandeis University, 1971 C: Charles Simonyi professor, Princeton University, New Jersey, 1997-; Professor School Natural Scis,, Institute for Advanced Study, Princeton, New Jersey, 1987-; Professor physics, Princeton University, New Jersey, 1980-87; Junior fellow, Harvard University, 1977-80; Postdoctoral fellow, Harvard University, 1976-77 CR: Visiting professor California Institute Tech., 1999-2001 CIV: Board directors, Americans for Peace Now, 1992- CW: Contributor articles to magazines and professional journals; co-author (with M.B. Green and J.H. Schwarz): Superstring Theory, Vol. 1 and 2, Cambridge Univ. Press AW: MacArthur Fellow, 1982; recipient Einstein medal Einstein Society Berne, Switzerland, 1985, Physical and Math. Sci. award New York Academy Sci., 1985, Dirac medal International Center Theoretical Physics, 1985, Alan Waterman award National Science Foundation 1986, Fields Medal, International Math. Union Congress, 1990, Madison medal, Princeton Univ., 1992, New Jersey Pride award, 1996, Award of the Golden Plate, Am. Academy of Achievement, 1997, Klein medal, Stockholm University, 1998, Dannie Heineman prize, Am. Institute of Physics, 1998, Nemmers prize in Math., Northwestern University, 2000, Clay Research award, Clay Math. Institute, 2001, Shalom award, Americans for Peace Now, 2002, National Medal of Science, 2002; co-recipient Crafoord prize in Math., Royal Swedish Academy Scis., 2008, Harvey Prize, 2005, Henri Poincare Prize, 2006, Crafoord Prize, 2008, Lorentz Medal, 2010, Issac Newtown Medal, 2010, Fundamental Physics Prize, 2012, Kyoto Prize, 2014, Albert Einstein award, 2016 MEM: Fellow: Am. Philosophical Society, Am. Physical Society, Am. Academy Arts & Scis., National Academy of Sciences; mem.: Academy Scis. Paris (associate), Pontifical Academy Scis. BA: Inst for Advanced Study Sch Natural Scis, 1 Einstein Dr, Princeton, NJ, 08540

WITTMAN, ROBERT J., T: U.S. Representative from Virginia, Former State Legislator I: Government Administration/Government Relations/Government Services DOB: 02/03/1959 PB: Washington SC: DC/USA ED: PhD in Pub. Policy and Administration, Virginia Commonwealth University, 2002; MPH, University of North Carolina at Chapel Hill, 1990; BS in Biology, Virginia Poly. Institute, 1981 C: Member, U.S. Congress from 1st Virginia district, 2007-; Member, Committee on Armed Services; Member, Committee on Natural Resources; Member, Republican Study Committee; Member District 99, Virginia House of Delegates, 2006-07; Director division shellfish sanitation, Virginia Department Health, 1992-2007; Environmental health specialist, Virginia Department Health, CR: Chairman Westmoreland County Board Supervisors, 2003-05, member, 1996-2005 mayor, Town of Montross Montross Town Council, 1992-96, councilman, 1986-96 CIV: Chairman, Interstate Shellfish Sanitation Conference, Chairman, Rappahannock River Basin

Commission, Chairman, Montross-Westmoreland Sewer Authority, Member, Montross Fall and Spring Festival Committee, Member, Northern Neck Planning District Commission, 2003 Board of Visitors, U.S. Naval Academy, 2009- **MEM:** Mem.: Pi Alpha Alpha **PA:** Republican

WOJCICKI, SUSAN DIANE, T: CEO of Youtube **I:** Business Management/Business Services **CN:** Youtube **DOB:** 07/05/1968 **PB:** Santa Clara **SC:** CA/USA **PT:** Stanley George Wojcicki; Esther Denise (Hochman) Wojcicki **ED:** MBA in Economics, University of California, Los Angeles (1998); MS in Economics, University of California, Santa Cruz (1993); AB in History & Literature, Harvard University, with Honors (1990) **C:** Chief Executive Officer, YouTube, LLC, Google, Inc., Mountain View, CA (2014-Present); Senior Vice President, YouTube, Google, Inc., Mountain View, CA (2014); Senior Vice President of Advertising and Commerce, Google, Inc., Mountain View, CA (2013-2014); Senior Vice President of Advertising, Google, Inc., Mountain View, CA (2011-2013); Senior Vice President of Product Management, Google, Inc., Mountain View, CA (2010-2011); Vice President of Product Management, Google, Inc., Mountain View, CA (2006-2010); Marketing Manager, Google, Inc., Mountain View, CA (1999-2006); Management Consultant, R.B. Webber & Co.; Management Consultant, Bain & Co., Inc.; Former Employee, Intel Corp. **CR:** Board of Directors, HomeAway, Inc. (2011-2012) **AW:** Named, Forbes 100 Most Powerful Women, Forbes Magazine (2017); Named, Forbes Self-Made Women List (2017); Named, One of the 100 Most Powerful Women in Entertainment, The Hollywood Reporter (2014); Named, The Adweek 50, Adweek (2013); Named, One of the 100 Most Powerful Women, The New Establishment, Vanity Fair (2012-2013); Named, One of the 100 Most Powerful Women, Forbes Magazine (2011-2014); Named, One of the 50 Most Powerful Women in Business, Fortune Magazine (2010-2015)

WOLF, NAOMI, T: Writer, Social Critic, Activist **I:** Writing and Editing **DOB:** 11/12/1962 **PB:** San Francisco **PT:** Daughter of Leonard and Deborah W.; Married David Shipley, September 1993. **ED:** BA, Yale University, 1984 **C:** Website co-founder, Daily Cloudt, 2012-; Co-founder, The American Freedom Campaign,; Co-founder, The Woodhull Institute for Ethical Leadership,; Cultural commentary writer, Harper's Bazaar,; Cultural commentary writer, The Washington Post,; Cultural commentary writer, The Guardian,; Frequent blogger on The Huffington Post,; Columnist, Project Syndicate, **CR:** Speaker in the field consultant to Al Gore during presidential campaign on women's issues and social policy **CW:** Author: Vagina: A New Biography, 2012, The Beauty Myth: How Images of Beauty Are Used Against Women, 1990 Fire With Fire: The New Female Power and How It Will Change the 21st Century, 1993, The Treehouse: Eccentric Wisdom from My Father on How to Live, Love and See, 2005, The End of America: A Letter of Warning To A Young Patriot, 2007; contributor to periodicals including The Guardian, New Republic, New York Times, Wall Street Journal,(Book) Give Me Liberty, 2008 **AW:** Rhodes scholar, 1986. **BA:** John Brockman Inc, 5 E 59th St, New York, NY, 10022

WOLF, TOM, T: Governor of Pennsylvania **I:** Government Administration/Government Relations/Government Services **DOB:** 11/17/1948 **PB:** York **PT:** Son of William Trout Wolf and Cornelia (Westerman) Rohlman; **ED:** PhD, Massachusetts Institute of Technology, 1981; MPhil, University London, 1978; BA magna cum laude, Dartmouth College, 1972 **C:** Governor, State of Pennsylvania, Harrisburg, 2015-; Secretary, Pennsylvania

Department Revenue, Harrisburg, Pennsylvania, 2007-08; Chairman, CEO, Wolf Organization, Inc., 2010-13; Co-owner, CEO, Wolf Organization, Inc., 1985-2006; Forklift operator, Wolf Organization, Inc., York, Pennsylvania, **CIV:** Chairman, York County C. of C., Chairman, York College Board Trustees, Chairman, York County Community Foundation, Chairman, York County United Way **PA:** Democrat **BA:** Office of the Governor, 508 Main Capitol Building, Harrisburg, PA, 17120

WOLFE, TOM, T: Writer, Journalist **I:** Writing and Editing **DOB:** 03/02/1931 **PB:** Richmond **YOP:** 2018-05-15 **PT:** Thomas Kennerly Wolfe; Helen (Hughes) Wolfe **MS:** Married **SPN:** Sheila Berger **CH:** Alexandra, Thomas **ED:** Honorary DLitt, University of Richmond, 1993; Honorary DLitt, Johns Hopkins University, 1990; Honorary DLitt, St. Andrews Presbyterian College, 1990; Honorary LHD, Longwood College, 1989; Honorary LHD, Manhattanville College, 1988; Honorary LHD, Randolph-Macon College, 1988; Honorary DFA, School of Visual Arts, 1987; Honorary LHD, Southampton College, New York, 1984; Honorary LHD, Virginia Commonwealth University, 1983; Honorary DLitt, Washington and Lee University, 1974; Honorary DFA, Minneapolis College of Art, 1971; PhD in American Studies, Yale University, 1957; AB, Washington and Lee University, 1951 **C:** Contributing Editor, Esquire Magazine, New York, NY, 1977-Present; Writer, 1965-Present; Contributing Editor, New York Magazine, 1968-1976; Magazine Writer, New York World Journal Tribune, 1966-1967; City Reporter, New York Herald Tribune, 1962-1966; Reporter, Latin American Correspondent, Washington Post, 1959-1962; Reporter, Springfield Union, Springfield, MA, 1956-1959 **CR:** Writer, New York Sunday Magazine, 1962-1966; Contributing Artist, Harper's Magazine, New York, NY, 1978-1981 **CW:** Solo Shows, (Drawings) Maynard Walker Gallery, New York, NY, 1965, Tunnel Gallery, New York, NY, 1974; Author, (Books) The Kandy-Kolored Tangerine-Flake Streamline Baby, 1965, The Electric Kool-Aid Acid Test, 1968, The Pump House Gang, 1968, Radical Chic and Mau-mauing the Flak Catchers, 1970, The Painted Word, 1975, Mauve Gloves and Madmen, Clutter and Vine, 1976, The Right Stuff, 1979, In Our Time, 1980, From Bauhaus to Our House, 1981, The Purple Decades: A Reader, 1982, The Bonfire of the Vanities, 1987, A Man in Full, 1998, (Audio) Ambush at Fort Bragg, 1997, Hooking Up, 2000, I Am Charlotte Simmons, 2004, Back to Blood, 2012; Editor, Contributor, The New Journalism, 1973; Contributor, Articles, Esquire Magazine, Others; Contributor, (Book) The Kingdom of Speech, 2016 **AW:** Front Page Awards for Humor and Foreign News Reporting, Washington Newspaper Guild, 1961; Society of Magazine Writers Award for Excellence, 1970; Frank Luther Mott Research Award, 1973; Virginia Laureate For Literature, 1977; Harold D. Vursell Memorial Award, American Academy and Institute of Arts and Letters, 1980; American Book Award, The Right Stuff, 1980; Columbia Journalism Award, 1980; National Sculpture Society Citation for Art History, 1980; John Dos Passos Award, 1984; Gari Melchers Medal, 1986; Benjamin Pierce Cheney Medal, Eastern Washington University, 1986; Washington Irving Medal, St. Nicholas Society, 1986; Theodore Roosevelt Medal, Theodore Roosevelt Association, 1990; Wilbur Cross Medal, Yale Graduate School Alumni Association, 1990; St. Louis Literary Award, 1990; Quinnipiac College President Award, 1993; Chicago Tribune Literary Prize for Lifetime Achievement, 2003; Golden Plate Award, Academy of Achievement, 2005; Inductee, Academy of Achievement, 2005; Jefferson Lecture in Humanities, 2006; Distinguished Contribution to American Letters, 2010 **BA:** Greenspan Artist Management, 2164 Sunset Plaza Drive, West Hollywood, CA, 90069

WOLLMAN, ROGER LELAND, T: Federal Judge **I:** Law and Legal Services **DOB:** 05/29/1934 **PB:** Frankfort **SC:** SD/USA **PT:** Son of Edwin and Katherine Wollman; **ED:** LLM, Harvard University, 1964; JD magna cum laude, University South Dakota, 1962; BA, Tabor College, Hillsboro, Kansas, 1957 **CT:** Bar: South Dakota 1964 **C:** Judge, US Court Appeals (8th cir.), 1985-; Chief judge, US Court Appeals (8th cir.), 1999-2002; Chief justice, South Dakota Supreme Court, 1978-82; Justice, South Dakota Supreme Court, 1971-85; States attorney, Brown County, Aberdeen, 1967-71; Sole practice, Aberdeen, 1964-71; Law clerk, Hon. George T. Mickleson US District Ct (Southern Dist, South Carolina), 1962-63 **CR:** Member Judicial Conference of US, 1999-2002 **MIL:** With US Army, 1957-59 **MEM:** Mem.: Am. Judicial Society **BA:** Thomas F. Eagleton Courthouse, 111 South 10th Street, Saint Louis, MI, USA, 63102

WOMACK, STEVE, T: U.S. Representative from Arkansas, former mayor **I:** Government Administration/Government Relations/Government Services **DOB:** 02/18/1957 **PB:** Russellville **ED:** Bachelor, Arkansas Tech University, Russelville, 1979 **C:** Chairman of the House Budget Committee, 2018-; Member, US House Appropriations Committee, Washington, 2011-; Member, US Congress from 3rd Arkansas District, Washington, 2011-; Mayor, City of Rogers, 1998-2010; Fin. consultant, Merrill Lynch, Rogers, 1997; Executive officer US Army ROTC program, University Arkansas, Fayetteville, 1990-96; Manager, Station KURM Radio, Rogers, Arkansas, 1979-90 **CR:** Chairman Northwest Arkansas Regional Planning Commission, 2003-05 former councilman Rogers City Council **CIV:** Chairman, Arkansas Commission on National and Community Service, 2001 Appointed member, Arkansas Commission on National and Community Service, 1999 Member, Church at Pinnacle Hills, Rogers, Former member, Rogers Park Commission, Former member, St. Mary's Hospital Foundation, Former member, Northwest Arkansas Community College Task Force, Former president, Rogers-Lowell United Fund, **AW:** Decorated Global War on Terrorism Expeditionary and Service medals, Army Achievement medal, Army Commendation medal, Meritorious Service medal with Oak Leaf Cluster, Legion of Merit; named Citizen of Year, March of Dimes; Paul Harris fellow **MEM:** Mem.: Retired Reserve of Army **PA:** Republican

WOOD, DIANE PAMELA, T: Federal Judge **I:** Law and Legal Services **DOB:** 07/04/1950 **PB:** Plainfield **SC:** NJ/USA **PT:** Daughter of Kenneth Reed and Lucille (Padmore) Wood; **SPN:** Robert L. Sufit **ED:** JD (hon.), Illinois Institute Tech., 2004; JD (hon.), Georgetown University, 2003; JD, University of Texas, 1975; BA, University of Texas, 1971 **CT:** Bar: Illinois 1993, DC 1978, Texas 1975 **C:** Chief judge, U.S. Court Appeals (7th cir.), 2013-; Judge, U.S. Court Appeals (7th cir.), 1995-; Senior lecturer law, University of Chicago Law School, 1995-; Deputy assistant attorney general antitrust division, US Department Justice, 1993-95; Special consultant antitrust division international guide, US Department Justice, 1986-87; Harold J. & Marion F. Green professor international legal studies, University of Chicago Law School, 1990-95; Associate dean, University of Chicago Law School, 1989-92; Professor law, University of Chicago Law School, 1988-95; Assistant professor law, University of Chicago Law School, 1981-88; Assistant professor law, Georgetown University Law Center, Washington, DC 1980-81; Associate, Covington & Burling LLP, Washington, DC 1978-80; Atty.-adv., US Department State, Washington, DC 1977-78; Law clerk to Justice Harry Blackmun, Supreme

Court of the U.S. 1976-77; Law clerk to Hon. Irving Goldberg, U.S. Court of Appeals for the Fifth Circuit 1975-76 **CIV:** Board of directors, Hyde Park-Kenwood Community Health Center, 1983-85 **CW:** Contributor articles to professional journals; board editors: American Journal International Law **MEM:** Fellow: American Academy Arts & Sciences; mem.: American Law Institute (elected council member 2003), American Society International Law, Phi Alpha Delta **PA:** Democrat **BA:** 219 S. Dearborn Street Room 2722, Chicago, IL, 60604

WOOD, RONNIE, T: Guitarist, Painter **I:** Media & Entertainment **DOB:** 06/01/1947 **PB:** London **SC:** England **PT:** Son of Arthur and Mercy Leah Elizabeth (Dyer) Wood; **ED:** Student, Ealing School Art **C:** Guitarist, The Rolling Stones, 1975-; Guitarist, bassist, The New Barbarians, 1979; Guitarist, The Faces, 1969-75; Guitarist, Quiet Melon, 1969; Guitarist, Jeff Beck Group, 1967-69; Guitarist, Creation, 1968; Guitarist, The Birds, 1964-67 **CR:** Host radio show Absolute Radio, 2010- **CW:** Guitarist (albums with The Jeff Beck Group) Truth, 1968, Beck-Ola, 1969, (albums with The Faces) First Step, 1970, Long Player, 1971, A Nod Is as Good as a Wink...To a Blind Horse, 1971, Ooh La La, 1973, Coast to Coast/Overture and Beginners, 1974, Snakes And Ladders: The Best of Faces, 1975, The Best of The Faces, 1977, Good Boys... When they're Asleep, 1999, Five Guys Walk into a Bar..., 2004, (solo albums) I've Got My Own Album To Do, 1974, Now Look, 1976, Gimme Some Neck, 1979, 1234, 1981, Slide on This, 1992, Slide on Live (Plugged in and Standing), 1993, Live and Eclectic, 2000, Live at Electric Ladyland, 2002, Not For Beginners, 2002, Ronnie Wood Anthology: The Essential Crossexion, 2006, The First Barbarians: Live from Kilburn, 2007, I Feel Like Playing, 2010, (albums with The Rolling Stones) Black and Blue, 1976, Love You Live, 1977, Some Girls, 1978, Emotional Rescue, 1980, Sucking in the Seventies, 1981, Tattoo You, 1981, "Still Life" (American Concert, 1981), 1982, Undercover, 1983, Rewind (1971-1984), 1984, Dirty Work, 1986, Steel Wheels, 1989, Flashpoint, 1991, Jump Back: The Best of The Rolling Stones, 1993, Voodoo Lounge, 1994 (Grammy award Best Rock Album), Stripped, 1995, Bridges to Babylon, 1997, No Security, 1999, Forty Licks, 2002, Live Licks, 2004, A Bigger Bang, 2005, Blue and Lonesome,2016, Rarities 1971-2003, 2005, GRRR!, 2012, (albums with Eric Clapton & Others) The Rainbow Concert, 1973, (albums with Ronnie Lane) Mahoney's Last Stand, 1976, (albums with The New Barbarians) Buried Alive: Live in Maryland, 2006, (albums with Bo Diddley) Live at the Ritz, 1988, (soundtrack with The Band & others) The Last Waltz, 1978, (soundtrack with The Rolling Stones) Shine a Light, 2008; performer: (films) The Last Waltz, 1978, Let's Spend the Night Together, 1982, Rolling Stones: Live At the Max, 1991, Bob Dylan 30th Anniversary Concert Celebration, 1993, Voodoo Lounge, 1994, The Rolling Stones Bridges to Babylon Tour '97-98, 1997, Four Flicks, 2003, The Biggest Bang, 2007, Shine a Light, 2008, Some Girls Live in Texas '78, 2011; appeared in (documentaries) 25 X 5: The Continuing Adventures of the Rolling Stones, 1989, Being Mick, 2001, Stones in Exile, 2010, Crossfire Hurricane, 2012, BB King: The Life of Riley, 2012; author: (limited edition art book) Wood on Canvas: Every Picture Tells a Story, 1998; co-author: Ronnie: The Autobiography, 2007 **AW:** Named Greatest Touring Band of All Time, World Music Awards, 2006, Small Breeder of Year, Irish Throroughbred Breeders Association, 1998; named to The Rock and Roll Hall of Fame, (as member of The Faces), 2012, (as member of The Rolling Stones), 1989; recipient Sony Radio Personality of Year award, 2011, Outstanding Contribution award, Classic Rock & Roll of Honor, 2009, Ivor Novello award for Outstanding Contribution to British Music, 1991, Grammy LIfetime Achievement award, 1986, Nordoff-Robbins Silver Clef, 1982

WOOD, ROY, T: Singer, Songwriter **I:** Media & Entertainment **PB:** Kitts Green **SC:** England **CW:** (Solo Albums) Boulders, 1973, Mustard, 1975, On the Road Again, 1979, Starting Up, 1987(The Move) The Move, 1968, Shazam, 1970, Looking On, 1970, Message from the Country, 1971,(With ELO) The Electric Light Orchestra, 1971, ELO 2, 1973(With Wizzard) Wizzard Brew, 1973, Introducing Eddy and the Falcons, 1974, Main Street, 2000, (With Solo) Boulders, 1973, Mustard, 1975, On The Road Again, Starting Up, 1987, (With Wizzo Band) Super Active Wizzo, 1979 **AW:** Rock and Roll Hall of Fame, 2017

WOODALL, ROBERT, T: U.S. Representative from Georgia **I:** Government Administration/Government Relations/Government Services **DOB:** 02/11/1970 **PB:** Athens **ED:** JD, University Georgia, Athens, 1998; BA, Furman University, Greenville, South Carolina, 1992 **C:** Member, Transportation & Infrastructure Committee; Member, US House Government Oversight & ReformCom., 2011-; Member, US House Budget Committee, 2011-; Member, US House Rules Committee, Washington, 2011-; Member, US Congress from 7th Georgia District, Washington, 2011-; Chairman, Republican Study Committee, 2014-15; Chief of staff, to Rep John Linder, US House of Reps., Washington, 2000-10; Legislative corr., legislative assistant, legislative director, to Rep John Linder, US House of Reps., Washington, 1994-2000; Law clerk, Balch & Bingham, 1993-94 **CW:** Co-author: FairTax: The Truth, 2008 **PA:** Republican

WOODARD, ALFRE, T: Actress **I:** Media & Entertainment **DOB:** 05/27/1905 **PB:** Tulsa Oklahoma **SC:** Tulsa Oklahoma **PT:** Daughter of Marion H. and Constance W.; Married Roderick Spencer, October 21, 1983; children: Mavis, Duncan. **ED:** Student, Boston University **CR:** Member President Barack Obama's Committee on Arts and Humanities, 2009 **CW:** Actress: (films) Remember My Name, 1976, Health, Cross Creek, 1983, Extremities, 1986, Scrooged, 1988, Mandela, 1988, Miss Firecracker, 1989, Grand Canyon, 1991, The Gun in Betty Lou's Handbag, 1992, Passion Fish, 1992, Heart and Souls, 1993, Rich in Love, 1993, Bopha!, 1993, Blue Chips, 1994, Crooklyn, 1994, How to Make an American Quilt, 1995, Statistically Speaking, 1995, Primal Fear, 1996, A Step Toward Tomorrow, 1996, Stat Trek: First Contact, 1996, Follow Me Home, 1996, Down in the Delta, 1998, Brown Sugar, 1998, Mumford, 1999, What's Cooking, 2000, Love and Basketball, 2000, K-PAX, 2001, Baby of the Family, 2002, (voice) The Wild Thornberrys Movie, 2002, The Singing Detective, 2003, The Core, 2003, Radio, 2003, The Forgotten, 2004, Beauty Shop, 2005, Something New, 2006, The Family That Preys, 2008, Reach for Me, 2008, AmericanEast, 2008, 12 Years a Slave, 2013, Annabelle, 2014, Captain America: Civil War, 2016, So B. It, 2016, Burning Sands, 2017,(TV series) Tucker's Witch, 1982-83, Sara, 1985, St. Elsewhere, 1985-87, Hill Street Blues (Emmy award for Guest Appearance in Drama Series 1984), L.A. Law (Emmy award for Guest Appearance in a Drama Series 1987), Desperate Housewives (Screen Actors Guild Award for Outstanding Performance by an Ensemble in a Comedy Series, 2006), 2005-06, My Own Worst Enemy, 2008, Three Rivers, 2009-10, True Blood, 2010-12, Memphis Beat, 2010-11, Copper, 2013, State of Affairs, 2014-15, Luke Cage, 2016-; (TV spls.) For Colored Girls Who Have Considered Suicide/When the Rainbow is Enuf, Trial of the Moke, Words by Heart, (TV films) A Mother's Courage: The Mary Thomas Story, Child Saver, Ambush Murder, Freedom Road, 1979, Sophisticated Gents, 1981, The Killing Floor, Unnatural Causes, 1986, Mandela, 1987, The Child Saver, Sweet Revenge, 1990, Blue Bayou, 1990, Race to Freedom: The Underground Railroad, 1994, Wizard of Oz in Concert, 1995, The Piano Lesson, 1995, Journey to Mars, 1996, Gulliver's Travels, 1996, Member of the Wedding, 1997, Miss Evers' Boys, 1997, (Golden Globe for Best Actress, Mini Series) Cadillac Desert (miniseries), 1997, Holiday Heart, 2000, A Wrinkle in Time (miniseries), 2003, The Water is Wide, 2005, Maggie Hill, 2009, Steel Magnolias, 2012 (Outstanding Actress in a TV Movie, Mini-Series or Dramatic Special, National Association for the Advancement of Colored People Image Awards, 2013), others, (plays) For Colored Girls Who Have Considered Suicide, When the Rainbow is Enuf, (off-Broadway plays) A Map of the World, 1985, A Winter's Tale 1989, So Nice They Named Twice, Horatio, What's Cookin', 2000, Love and Basketball, 2000, Dinosaur, 2000; actress, executive prodr.: (films) Funny Valentines, 1999; executive prodr.: (documentaries) Soft Vengeance: Albie Sachs and the New South Africa, 2014. **AW:** Recipient Josephine Premice award for Sustained Excellence, Classical Theatre of Harlem, 2006.

WOODS, DARREN, T: CEO of ExxonMobil **I:** Oil & Energy **CN:** ExxonMobil **PB:** Wichita **SC:** KS/USA **ED:** B.A., Texas A&M University, M.B.A, Kellogg School of Management **C:** CEO, ExxonMobil, 2017-

WOODS, TIGER, T: Professional Golfer **I:** Athletics **DOB:** 12/30/1975 **PB:** Cypress **SC:** CA/USA **PT:** Earl Dennison Woods, Kultida Woods **SPN:** Elin Nordegren, 10/5/2004, Divorced 8/23/2010 **CH:** Sam Alexis, Charlie Axel **ED:** Student, Stanford University, California, 1994-1996 **C:** Professional Golfer, 1996—Present **CR:** Founder, Chairman, Tiger Woods Design, 2006-Present; U.S. Team, Presidents Cup, 2011, 2009, 2007, 2005, 2003, 2000, 1998, Dunhill Cup, 1998, Ryder Cup, 2012, 2010, 2006, 2004, 2002, 1999, 1997, Walker Cup Match, Porthcawl, Wales, 1995, World Amateur Team Championships, Versailles, France, 1994 **CIV:** Co-Founder, (With Father) Tiger Woods Foundation 1996-Present, (With The Tiger Woods Foundation) Start Something (Partners With Target Corporation), 2000, Tiger Woods Learning Center, Southern California, 2006, Tiger Woods Foundation National Junior Golf Team, Target World Challenge (Also Host), Tiger Jam (AT&T-Sponsored Event) (Also Host), And Various Grant/Scholarship Programs **AW:** Winner, Optimist International Junior World Championship, 1984-1985, 1988-1991, Winner, Insurance Youth Golf Classic, 1990, 1992, Winner, CIF-Southern California HS Invitational Championship, 1991, Winner, Southern California Junior Championship, 1991, Winner, Edgewood Tahoe Junior Classic, 1991, Winner, Los Angeles City Junior Championship, 1991, Winner, Orange Bowl Junior International Championship, 1991, American Junior Golf Association, 1991, Winner, U.S. Junior Amateur Championship, 1991, Winner, PING/Phoenix Junior Championship, 1991-1992, First Team Rolex Junior All American, 1991-1992, National Amateur of the Year, Titleist-Golfweek, 1991-1992, Golf Digest, 1991-1992, Southern California Player of the Year, 1991-1993, Winner, Pro Gear San Antonio Shootout, 1992, Winner, Nabisco Mission Hills Desert Junior Championship, 1992, Winner, U.S. Junior Amateur Championship, 1992-1993, Winner, Southern California Junior Best Ball Championship, 1993, Dial Award, 1993, Golf World, 1993-1994, Player of the Year, Orange County, 1994, L.A. Times, 1994, Orange County

League MVP, 1994, Winner, Jerry Pate Invitational, 1994, Winner, William Tucker Invitational, 1994, Winner, Southern California Golf Association Amateur Championship, 1994, Winner, Western Amateur Championship, 1994, Winner, Pacific Northwest Amateur Championship, 1994, Winner, U.S. Amateur Championship, 1994-1996, Winner, Stanford Invitational, 1995, First Team All-American, 1995-1996, PAC-10 Player of the Year, 1995-1996, Jack Nicklaus College Player of the Year, 1996, Winner, Tri-Match Championship (Stanford University, Arizona State University, University of Arizona), 1996, Winner, Cleveland Golf Championship, 1996, Winner, PAC-10 Championship, 1996, Fred Haskins College Player of the Year, 1996, PGA Tour Rookie of the Year, 1996, Winner, Cougar Classic, 1996, Winner, Walt Disney World/Oldsmobile Classic, 1996, Winner, Las Vegas Invitational, 1996, Winner, NCAA Championship, 1996, Winner, John A. Burns Invitational, 1996, Sports Illustrated, 1996, 2000, Winner, Masters Tournament, 1996-1997, 2001-2002, 2005, Winner, Asian Honda Classic, 1997, Winner, GTE Byron Nelson Classic, 1997, Winner, Motorola Western Open, 1997, 1999, Winner, Mercedes Championships, 1997, 2000, Associated Press, 1997, 1999, 2000, 2006, Jack Nicklaus Trophy, PGA America, Golf Writers Association America, 1997, 1999-2003, 2005-2006, PGA Tour Player of the Year, 1997, 1999-2003, 2005-2007, 2009, 2013, Winner, BellSouth Classic, 1998, Winner, Johnnie Walker Classic, 1998, 2000, Winner, PGA Grand Slam, 1998-2002, 2005-2006, ESPY Award, Best Male Athlete, 1998, 2000-2002, 2008, Mark H. McCormack Award As No. 1 Player On World Ranking, 1998-2010, World Sportsman of the Year, World Sports Academy, 1999, Winner, Tour Championship, 1999, Winner, World Cup Individual and Team Titles (with Mark O'Meara), 1999, Winner, National Car Rental Classic, 1999, Winner, Deutsche Bank-SAP Open, 1999, 2001-2002, Winner, WGC NEC Invitational, 1999-2001, 2005, Winner, WGC American Express Championship, 1999, 2002-2003, 2005-2006, Winner, PGA Championship, 1999-2000, 2006-2007, Winner, Buick Invitational, 1999, 2003, 2005-2008, Byron Nelson Award, PGA Tour, 1999-2003, 2005-2007, 2009, Winner, Memorial Tournament, 1999-2001, 2009, 2012, Vardon Trophy, PGA Of America, 1999, 2000-2003, 2005, 2007, 2009, 2013, World Champion Of Champions, L'Equipe, France, 2000, Winner, AT&T Pebble Beach Pro-Am, 2000, Most Powerful Person In Sports, Sporting News, 2000, Winner, Bell Canadian Open, 2000, Winner, World Cup (With David Duval), 2000, Male Athlete of the Year, Sportsman of the Year, Reuters, 2000, Winner, Bay Hill Invitational, 2000-2003, Winner, British Open Championship, 2000, 2005-2006, Winner, U.S. Open Championship, 2000, 2002, 2008, Winner, Williams World Challenge, 2001, Winner, The Players Championship, 2001, 2013, Winner, Buick Open, 2002, 2006, 2009, Winner, Western Open, 2003, Winner, WGC Accenture Match Play Championship, 2003-2004, 2008, Winner, Ford Championship, 2005-2006, ESPY Award, Best Golfer, 2005-2008, Player of the Year, Golf Writers Association America, 2006, Winner, Deutsche Bank Championship, 2006, Winner, Target World Challenge, 2006, Winner, WGC Bridgestone Invitational, 2006-2007, The California Hall Of Fame, 2007, Winner, Wachovia Championship, 2007, Winner, WGC American CA Championship, 2007, Winner, Target World Challenge, 2007, Charlie Bartlett Award, Golf Writers Association America, 2007, The Most Influential People In The World Of Sports, Business Week, 2007-2008, FedEx Cup, PGA, 2007, 2009, Winner, BMW Championship, 2007, 2009, The 100 Most Powerful Celebrities, Forbes.com, 2008, Winner, Dubai Desert Classic, 2008, Power 150, Ebony Magazine, 2008, ESPY Award, Best Champi-

onship Performance, ESPN, 2008, Winner, Arnold Palmer Invitational, 2008-2009, 2012-2013, Athlete of the Decade, Associated Press, 2009, Winner, WGC Bridgestone Invitational, 2009, The 40 Under 40 Rising Stars, Fortune Magazine, 2009, Winner, AT&T National, 2009, The World's Most Influential People, TIME Magazine, 2009, Stanford University Athletics Hall Of Fame, 2009, Winner, AT&T National, 2012, Winner, WGC Bridgestone Invitational, 2013, Winner, Farmers Insurance Open, 2013, Winner, WGC-Cadillac Championship, 2013 **ACH:** Achievements include winning 14 major PGA Tour events including Masters Tournament, 1997, 2001, 2002, 2005, PGA Championship, 1999, 2000, 2006, 2007; US Open Championship, 2000, 2002, 2008, Brit. Open Championship, 2000, 2005, 2006; youngest player, first African Am., first Asian Am., and having largest margin of victory (12 strokes) to win Masters Tournament, 1997; first player ever to win US Open, Brit. Open and PGA Championship in same year, 2000; first player ever to hold all 4 major golf championships at the same time, 2001; ranked number 1 by the Official World Golf Ranking for a record 281 consecutive weeks, 2005-2010; youngest to win 50 PGA Tour titles with victory at Buick Open, 2006; winner for the 7th time of the Farmers Insurance Open at Torrey Pines, also marked the milestone of the 75th time winning a PGA Tour event in 2013 **BA:** PGA PO Box 109601, 186 Atlantis Boulevard, Lake Worth, FL, 33462-1111

WOODWARD, BOB, T: Editor, Writer **I:** Writing and Editing **DOB:** 03/26/1943 **PB:** Geneva, Ill. **PT:** Son of Alfred E. and Jane (Upshur) Woodward; **ED:** BA, Yale University, 1965 **C:** Associate editor, The Washington Post, 2008-; Assistant managing editor, The Washington Post, 1981-2008; Metropolitan editor, The Washington Post, 1979-81; Reporter, The Washington Post, 1971-78; Reporter, Montgomery County Sentinel, Maryland, 1970-71 **CW:** Author: Wired: The Short Life and Fast Times of John Belushi, 1984, Veil: The Secret Wars of the CIA, 1981-1987, 1987, The Commanders: The Pentagon and the First Gulf War, 1989-1991, 1991, The Agenda: Inside the Clinton White House, 1994, The Choice: How Bill Clinton Won, 1996, Shadow: Five Presidents and the Legacy of Watergate, 1974-1999, 1999, Maestro: Greenspan's Fed and the American Boom, 2000, Bush At War: Inside the Bush White House, 2002, Plan of Attack, 2004, The Secret Man: The Story of Watergate's Deep Throat, 2005, State of Denial: Bush at War, Part III, 2006, The War Within: A Secret White House History 2006-2008, 2008, Obama's Wars, 2010 (#1 New York Times bestseller), The Price of Politics, 2012, The Last of the President's Men, 2015; co-author: (with Carl Bernstein) All the President's Men, 1974, The Final Days, 1976, (with Scott Armstrong) The Brethren: Inside the Supreme Court, 1979; Fear: Trump in the White House 2018 **AW:** Co-recipient two Pulitzer Prizes (Public Service, 1973 and National Reporting, 2002) through contributions to articles with the Washington Post; recipient Gerald R. Ford prize for Reporting on the Presidency, 2002, William Allen White medal, 2000, George Polk award, 1972, Sigma Delta Chi award, 1973, Worth Bingham prize foe Investigative Reporting, 1986, 1972, Heywood Broun award, 1972

WOODWARD, JOANNE, T: Actress **I:** Media & Entertainment **DOB:** 02/27/1930 **PB:** Thomasville **SC:** GA/USA **PT:** Wade Woodward; Elinor (Trimmier) Woodward **MS:** Widowed **SPN:** Paul Newman (1/29/1958, Deceased 9/2008) **CH:** Elinor Terese; Melissa Stewart; Clea Olivia **ED:** Degree, Sarah Lawrence College, New York (1990); Coursework, Louisiana State University (1947-1949); Diploma, Neighborhood Playhouse Dra-

matic School, New York, NY **CIV:** Co-Founder, Hole in the Wall Gang Camp (1988); Artistic Director, Westport Country Playhouse **CW:** Actress, "Lucky Them" (2013); Actress, "Empire Falls" (2005); Executive Producer, "Blind Spot" (2003); Voice Actress, "My Knees Were Jumping: Remembering the Kindertransports" (1998); Actress, "James Dean: A Portrait" (1996); Actress, "Breathing Lessons" (1994); Actress, "Philadelphia" (1993); Voice Actress, "The Age of Innocence" (1993); Actress, "Foreign Affairs" (1993); Actress, "Blind Spot" (1993); Actress, "Mr. & Mrs. Bridge" (1990); Narrator, Film Documentary, "Angel Dust" (1989); Actress, "Sweet Bird of Youth," Toronto, Canada (1988); Actress, "Glass Menagerie" (1987); Actress, "The Glass Menagerie," Williamstown Theatré Festival (1985); Actress, "Do You Remember Love?" (1985); Actress, "Harry and Son" (1984); Actress, "Candida" (1982); Actress, "Crisis at Central High" (1981); Actress, "The Shadow Box" (1980); Actress, "Streets of L.A." (1979); Actress, "See How She Runs" (1978); Actress, "The End" (1978); Actress, "Come Back, Little Sheba" (1977); Actress, "Sybil" (1976); Actress, "The Drowning Pool" (1975); Actress, "Summer Wishes, Winter Dreams" (1973); Actress, "The Effect of Gamma Rays on Man-in-the-Moon Marigolds" (1972); Actress, "They Might Be Giants" (1971); Actress, "All the Way Home" (1971); Actress, "WUSA" (1970); Actress, "Winning" (1969); Actress, "Rachel, Rachel," (1968); Actress, "A Big Hand for the Little Lady" (1965); Actress, "A Fine Madness" (1965); Actress, "Baby Want a Kiss" (1964); Actress, "The Stripper" (1963); Actress, "A New Kind of Love" (1963); Actress, "Paris Blues" (1961); Actress, "The Fugitive Kind" (1960); Actress, "Sound and the Fury" (1959); Actress, "Long Hot Summer" (1958); Actress, "Rally Round the Flag Boys" (1958); Actress, "No Down Payment" (1957); Actress, "Three Faces of Eve" (1957); Actress, "A Kiss Before Dying" (1956); Actress, "Count Three and Pray" (1955); Understudy, "Picnic" (1953); TV Appearance, "Penny," Robert Montgomery Presents (1952) **AW:** Recipient, Emmy Award (1985); Recipient, Emmy Award (1978); Recipient, Star, Hollywood Walk of Fame (1960); Recipient, Academy Award for Best Actress; Recipient, National Board of Review Award; Recipient, Foreign Press Award; Recipient, Cannes Film Festival Award; Recipient, New York Film Critics Award; Co-Recipient, Kennedy Center Honors for Lifetime Achievement in the Performing Arts; Recipient, Golden Globe Award for Best Actress **PA:** Democrat **ADD:** ICM, 40 W 57th St Fl 16, New York, NY, 10019-4098

WRAY, CHRISTOPHER ASHER, T: Director of the FBI **I:** Government Administration/Government Relations/Government Services **ED:** JD, Yale University, 1989; Grad. cum laude, Yale University, 1989 **C:** 8th Director of the FBI, Washington, 2017-; Partner, King & Spalding LLP, Washington, 2005-; Assistant attorney general criminal division, US Department Justice, Washington, 2003-05; Acting assistant attorney general criminal division, US Department Justice, Washington, 2003; Principal associate attorney general criminal division, US Department Justice, Washington, 2001-03; Associate deputy attorney general, US Department Justice, Washington, 2001; Assistant US attorney (northern district) Georgia, US Department Justice, Atlanta, 1997-2001; Associate, King & Spalding, LLP, Atlanta, 1993-97; Law clerk to Hon. J. Michael Luttig, U.S. Court Appeals (4th Cir.), 1992-93 **BA:** Federal Bureau of Investigation, 935 Pennsylvania Avenue, NW, Washington, DC, 20535

WREN, JOHN D., T: Chairman, CEO, Marketing and Corporate Communications Holding Company Executive **I:** Advertising & Marketing

DOB: 07/22/1952 **ED:** MBA, Adelphi University, 1975; BA, Adelphi University, 1975 **CT:** CPA **C:** Chairman, CEO, Omnicom Group Inc., 2018-; President, CEO, Omnicom Group, Inc., New York City, 1997-2018; President, Omnicom Group, Inc., New York City, 1995-97; Chairman, CEO, Diversified Agency Services (subsidiary Omnicom Group, Inc.), 1993-95; President, Diversified Agency Services (subsidiary Omnicom Group, Inc.), 1990-93; CFO, Diversified Agency Services (subsidiary Omnicom Group, Inc.), 1986-90; With, Needham Harper Worldwide, 1984-86; With, Norton Simon Inc., 1981-84; Management Consultant, Arthur Anderson & Co., 1975-81 **CR:** Board of Directors Omnicom Group, Inc., 1993-; Member, International Business Council, World Economic Forum; Member, Board of Directors, Lincoln Center for the Performing Arts; Trustee, Arthur Ashe Foundation **AW:** Named Agency Executive of the Year, Advertising Age, 2006 **PA:** Republican **BA:** Omnicom Group Inc, 437 Madison Ave, New York, NY, 10022

WRIGHT, LAWRENCE GEORGE, T: Author **I:** Writing and Editing **DOB:** 08/02/1947 **PB:** Oklahoma City **SC:** OK/USA **PT:** John Donald Wright; Dorothy (Peacock) Wright **MS:** Married **SPN:** Roberta Murphy (1/22/1970) **CH:** Gordon; Caroline **ED:** MA in Linguistics, American University, Cairo, Egypt (1971); BA, Tulane University (1969) **C:** Founder, Texas Writers' Month; Writer, Texas Monthly Magazine, Austin, Texas (1980); Writer, Southern Voices, Southern Regional Council, Atlanta, GA (1973-1980); English Teacher, American University, Cairo, Egypt **CR:** Member, Council on Foreign Relations **CW:** Author, "Saints & Sinners" (1993), "Remembering Satan" (1994), "Twins: Genes, Environment, and the Mystery of Identity" (1997), "The Looming Tower" (2006), Novels, "God's Favorite" (2000), Children's Book, "City Children, Country Summer" (1979), Memoir, "In the New World" (1988), Screenplay, "Noriega: God's Favorite" (2000), Co-author with Ed Zwick, Menno Meyjes, "The Siege" (1998), Plays, "Sonny's Last Shot"; Contributing Writer, The New Yorker (1992-Present); Author, Book, "Going Clear: Scientology, Hollywood, and the Prison of Belief" (2013), "Thirteen Days in September: Carter, Begin and Sadat at Camp David" (2014), "The Terror Years: From Al-Qaeda to the Islamic State" (2016) **AW:** O'Henry Award for Best Work of Magazine Journalism, Texas Institute of Letters (2005); Overseas Press Club's Ed Cunningham Award for Best Magazine Reporting; John Bartlow Martin Award for Public Interest Magazine Journalism; National Magazine Award for Reporting; New York University Olive Branch Award for International Reporting; Pulitzer Prize (2007); PEN Center USA Literary Award (2007); Named to 50 Books for Our Time, Newsweek (2009); National Book Critics Circle Award (2013); Primetime Emmy for Outstanding Documentary (2015); Pulitzer Prize for General Nonfiction (2007); Helen Bernstein Book Award, New York Public Library (2007); J. Anthony Lukas Book Prize (2007) **ACH:** Fluent in Arabic. **BA:** Penguin Random House Speakers Bureau, 1745 Broadway, New York, NY, 10019

WRIGHT, ROBIN, T: Actress **I:** Media & Entertainment **PB:** Dallas **SC:** TX/USA **PT:** Fred Wright; Gayle (Gaston) Wright **CW:** Actress: (films) Hollywood Vice Squad, 1986, The Princess Bride, 1987, Denial, 1990, State of Grace, 1990, The Playboys, 1992, Toys, 1992, Forrest Gump, 1995, The Crossing Guard, 1995, Moll Flanders, 1996, Loved, 1997, She's So Lovely, 1997, Hurlyburly, 1998, Message in a Bottle, 1999, How to Kill Your Neighbor's Dog, 2000, Unbreakable, 2000, The

Pledge, 2001, The Last Castle, 2001, White Oleander, 2002, The Singing Detective, 2003, A Home at the End of the World, 2004, Nine Lives, 2005, Sorry, Haters, 2005, Max, 2005, Breaking and Entering, 2006, Room 10, 2006, Beowulf, 2007, What Just Happened, 2008, The Private Lives of Pippa Lee, 2009, State of Play, 2009, A Christmas Carol, 2009, The Conspirator, 2010, Moneyball, 2011, Rampart, 2011, The Girl with the Dragon Tattoo, 2011, Two Mothers, 2013, A Most Wanted Man, 2014, Everest, 2015, Wonder Woman,2017, Blade Runner 2049, Justice League, 2017; (documentaries) Searching for Debra Winger, 2002; (TV series) The Yellow Rose, 1983-84; actress: (TV series) Santa Barbara, 1984, House of Cards, 2013- (Golden Globe award for Best Performance by an Actress in a TV Series - Drama, 2014); actress, executive producer (films) Virgin, 2003, Hounddog, 2007, actress, producer The Congress, 2013 **AW:** Named one of The 100 Most Influential People in the World, TIME magazine, 2014

WU, CONSTANCE TIANMIN, T: Actress **I:** Media & Entertainment **DOB:** 03/22/1982 **PB:** Richmond **SC:** VA/USA **ED:** BFA in Acting, Conservatory of Theatre Arts, State University of New York at Purchase, 2005; Student, Lee Strasberg Theatre and Film Institute; Postgraduate Work, Psycholinguistics **C:** Actress, (Films) Stephanie Daley, 2006, The Architect, 2006, Year Of The Fish, 2007, Sound Of My Voice, 2011, Watching TV With The Red Chinese, 2012, Best Friends Forever, 2013, Ties, 2013, Taylor Manifest, 2013, Deadly Revenge, 2013, Electric Slide, 2014, My Mother Is Not A Fish, 2013, Parallels, 2015, Low Budget Ethnic Movie, 2015, Nine Minutes, 2017, All The Creatures Were Stirring, 2017, The Feels, 2017, Crazy Rich Asíans, 2018, (Voice Actress) Next Gen, 2018 (TV Shows) Law And Order: SVU, 2006, One Life To Live, 2007, Torchwood, 2011, EastSiders, 2012, Browsers, 2013, Covert Affairs, 2013, Franklin And Bash, 2014, High Moon, 2014, Children's Hospital, 2015, Fresh Off The Boat, 2015, Royal Pains, 2016, Dimension 404, 2017 **CIV:** Sundance Screenwriters' Lab, 2014 **AW:** Time 100, 2017, Nominee, Critics' Choice Television Award for Best Actress in a Comedy Series, Television Critics Association TCA Award for Individual Achievement in Comedy, Fresh Off the Boat, 2015 **BA:** Generate Management, 8750 Wilshire Boulevard, Suite 200, Beverly Hills, CA, 90211

WUERL, DONALD WILLIAM, T: Cardinal **I:** Religious **DOB:** 11/12/1940 **PB:** Pittsburgh **SC:** PA/USA **ED:** ThD, Pontifical University of Saint Thomas Aquinas (Angelicum), 1974; ThM, Pontifical Gregorian University, 1967; MA in Philosophy, Catholic University America, Rome, 1963; BA, Catholic University America, 1962 **C:** Archbishop, of Washington, DC 2006-; Appointed Cardinal-priest, of San Pietro in Vincoli (Saint Peter in Chains), 2010; Elevated to Cardinal, 2010; Bishop, of Pittsburgh, 1988-2006; Auxiliary Bishop, of Seattle, Washington, 1985-87; Appointed Titular Bishop, of Rossmarkaeum (Rosemarkie), 1985; Ordained Bishop, 1986; Rector, Saint Paul Seminary, Pittsburgh, 1981-85; Vice-rector, Saint Paul Seminary, Pittsburgh, 1980-81; Secretary to Cardinal John Wright, Congregation for Clergy, Rome, 1969-79; Assistant Pastor, Parochial Vicar, Saint Rosalia Church, Pittsburgh, 1967-69; Ordained Priest, of Pittsburgh, Pennsylvania, 1966 **CR:** Official Congregation for Clergy, Rome, 1969-79 Member Alumni Board of Governors Catholic University America, 1977-84 Executive Secretary to Papal Representative for Study of Seminaries in U.S., 1982-85 Board Governor, Pontifical North American College, Rome, 1994-2003, Chairman 1998-1999 Chaplain, Order of Malta,

1999- Serves on Various Committees within the U.S. Conference of Catholic Bishops Member Congregation for the Clergy, 2010-, Pontifical Council for Promoting Christian Unity, 2010-, Pontifical Council for Culture, 2011-, Congregation for the Doctrine of the Faith, 2012-, Congregation for Bishops, 2013- Relator General XIII Ordinary General Assembly of the Synod of Bishops, 2012 Member American Catholic Historical Association, Catholic Theological Society America, Fellowship Catholic Scholars. **CW:** Author: The Forty Martyrs, 1971, Fathers of the Church, 1975, The Catholic Priesthood Today, 1976, The Teaching of Christ: A Catholic Catechism for Adults, 1976, A Visit to the Vatican, 1981, The Church and Her Sacraments: Making Christ Visible, 1990, The Gift of Faith: A Question and Answer Version of the Teaching of Christ, 2001, The Catholic Way: Faith for Living Today, 2001, The Sacraments: A Continuing Encounter with Christ, 2010, The Mass: The Glory, the Mystery, the Tradition, 2011, The Gift of Blessed John Paul II, 2011, Seek First the Kingdom: Challenging the Culture by Living Our Faith, 2012, Faith That Transforms Us: Reflections on the Creed, 2013, New Evangelization: Passing on the Catholic Faith Today, 2013; co-author: The Teaching of Christ: A Catholic Catechism for Adults, 1976, revised, 1984, 1991, abridged, 1979, study guide, 1977, A Catholic Catechism, 1986; Contributing Author: New Catholic Encyclopedia; Contributor Articles to Religion Publications; Author Religious Cassette Programs; Host (TV program) The Teaching of Christ **BA:** Archdiocesan Pastoral Center, 5001 Eastern Ave, Hyattsville, MD, 20782

WYDEN, RON, T: U.S. Senator from Oregon **I:** Government Administration/Government Relations/Government Services **DOB:** 05/03/1949 **PB:** Wichita **SC:** KS/USA **ED:** JD, University of Oregon School of Law (1974); AB in Political Science, Stanford University, with Distinction (1971); Coursework, University of Santa Barbara (1969) **C:** U.S. Senator from Oregon (1996-Present); Ranking Member, Senate Finance Committee (2015); Chairman, U.S. Senate Finance Committee (2014-2015); Chairman, U.S. Senate Energy & Natural Resources Committee (2013-2014); Member, U.S. Congress from Third Oregon District, Washington, DC (1981-1996); Instructor of Gerontology, University of Portland (1980); Instructor of Gerontology, Portland State University (1979); Director, Oregon Legal Services for Elderly (1977-1979); Instructor of Gerontology, University of Oregon (1976); Co-Founder, Co-Director, Oregon Gray Panthers (1974-1980); Campaign Aide to Senator Wayne Morse, U.S. Senate (1974, 1972) **CIV:** Oregon Environmental Council **CW:** Contributor, Articles to Professional Journals **AW:** Named, One of the 50 Most Important People on the Web, PC World (2007); Recipient, Champion of Science Award, University of Oregon/The Science Coalition (2003); Named, Legislator of the Year, Information of Technology Council (2000); Recipient, Philip A. Hart Public Service Award, Consumer Federation of America (1999); Listee, People of the Year, PC Computing Magazine (1999); Named, Senator of the Year, National Association Police Organization (1997); Recipient, Significant Service Award, Multnomah County Area Agency on Aging (1980); Named, Young Man of the Year, Oregon Junior Chamber of Commerce (1980); Recipient, Citizen of the Year Award, Oregon Association of Social Workers (1979); Recipient, Service to Oregon Consumers Award, Oregon Consumers League (1978); Named, Legislators Hall of Fame, American Electronics Association **MEM:** ABA; Iowa Bar Association; Oregon Bar Association

BAR: Oregon (1975) **PA:** Democrat **BA:** Office of Ron Wyden, US Senate 221 Dirksen Senate Office Bldg, Washington D.C., DC, 20510

WYLIE, CHRISTOPHER, T: Activist **I:** Nonprofit & Philanthropy **PB:** Victoria, British Columbia **SC:** Canada **C:** Director of Research, Cambridge Analytica Ltd. **AW:** Named One of TIME's 100 Most Influential People, TIME Magazine (2018)

WYNN, JAMES ANDREW JR., T: Federal Judge **I:** Law and Legal Services **DOB:** 03/17/1954 **PB:** Robersonville **SC:** NC/USA **ED:** LLM, University of Virginia (1995); JD, Marquette University (1979); BA in Journalism, University of North Carolina (1975) **C:** Judge, U.S. Court of Appeals for the Fourth Circuit (2010-Present); Associate Justice, North Carolina Supreme Court (1998-1999); Judge, North Carolina Court of Appeals (1990-1998, 1999-2010); Partner, Fitch, Wynn & Associates (1984-1990); Assistant Appellate Defender, State of North Carolina (1983-1984); Reserve Captain, Judge Advocate General Corporation, U.S. Navy (1983-2009); Captain, Judge Advocate General Corporation, U.S. Navy, Norfolk, VA (1979-1983) **BA:** 1100 E Main St #501, Richmond, VA, 23219

YARBOROUGH, WILLIAM CALEB, T: Retired Race Car Driver **I:** Athletics **DOB:** 03/27/1939 **PB:** Timmonsville **AW:** Named Grand National Champion, Champion National Association Stock Car Auto Racing, 1976, champion, Winston Cup, 1976-78, winner, Winston-Salem 500, 1974, Wilkes 400, 1974, Virginia 500, 1977, 1974, Southern 500, 1978, 1974, 1973, 1968, National 500, 1973, Mazon-Dixon 500, 1969, Daytona 500, 1984, 1983, 1977, 1968, Carolina 500, 1975, Capital City 400, 1976, Cam 2 Moto Oil 400, 1977, Atlanta 500, 1974, 1968, 1967,NASCAR Hall of Fame, 2012, NASCAR's 50 Greatest Drivers, 1998, Talladega Walk of Fame Inductee, 1996, South Carolina Athletic Hall of Fame Inductee, 1978 **BA:** Cale Yarborough Motors of SC Inc., 2723 West Palmetto Street, Florence, SC, 29501

YARMUTH, JOHN ALLAN, T: Ranking Democrat of the House Budget Committee **I:** Government Administration/Government Relations/Government Services **DOB:** 11/04/1947 **PB:** Louisville **SC:** KY/USA **PT:** Son of Stanley Robert and Edna Elaine (Klein) Yarmuth; **ED:** Student, Georgetown University School of Law; BA in Am. Studies, Yale University, 1969 **C:** Ranking Democrat of the U.S. House Committee of Budget, 2017-; Member, U.S. House Ethics Committee, 2011-; Member, U.S. Congress from 3rd Kentucky District, 2007-; Founder, Executive Editor, Louisville Eccentric Observer Newsweekly, 1990-2003; Worked in Public Relations and Marketing, Caretenders Healthcorp, 1986-90; Assistant Vice President Univ. Relations, University of Louisville, 1983-86; Pub., Louisville Today magazine, 1976-82; Legis. Assistant to Senator Marlow Cook, U.S. Senate, Washington, 1971-75; Stockbroker, Stein Brothers & Boyce, Louisville, 1969-70 **CR:** Founder, President Center Kentucky Progress **CIV:** Board of Directors, Station WKPC-TV, Louisville, 1983-88 Board of Directors, Louisville School Art, 1980-83 Board of Directors, Better Business Bureau, Louisville, 1979-85 Board of Regents, Planned Parenthood Louisville Forum, Board of Regents, Jewish Community Center, Board of Regents, No. Kentucky University, Highland Heights, 1980-83 **CW:** Host (radio talk shows) Yarmuth & Ziegler, WAVE 3 TV, 2003, Guest Appearances Hot Button, 2004-05, Editor, Owner (publications) Kentucky Golfer **AW:** Named Person of Year, Louisville Chapter Alzheimer's Association, 2004; Named to Atherton High School Hall of Fame, 2002; Recipient Editorial and

Column Writing Awards, Metro Louisville Journalism **MEM:** Mem.: Society Professional Journalists, Kentucky Golf Association, South Carolina Melrose Club, Valhalla Golf Club **H:** Golf **PA:** Democrat

YEAGER, CHUCK, T: Retired Air Force General **I:** Military & Defense Services **DOB:** 02/13/1923 **PB:** Myra, West Virginia **PT:** Son of Albert Hal and Susie May (Sizemore) Yeager **SPN:** Married Glennis Faye Dickhouse (deceased 1990), February 26, 1945; Married Victoria Scott D'Angelo, 2003 **ED:** Doctor in Aeronautical Sci., Salem College, West Virginia, 1975; DSc (hon.), Marshall University, Huntington, West Virginia, 1969; DSc (hon.), West Virginia University, 1948; Grad., Air War College, 1961; Grad., Air Command and Staff School, 1952 **C:** Retired, 1975; Director Aerospace Safety, Air Force Inspection and Safety Center, Norton AFB, California, 1973-75; Special Assistant to Commander, Air Force Inspection and Safety Center, Norton AFB, California, 1973; U.S. Defense rep. to Pakistan, 1971-73; Vice Commander, 17th Air Force, Ramstein Air Base, Federal Republic Germany, 1969-71; Commander, 405th Fighter Wing, Seymour Johnson AFB, North Carolina, 1968-69; Director, Space School, Edwards AFB, 1960; Commander, Astronaut Training, Air Force Aerospace Research Pilots School,; Various Command Assignments, U.S. Air Force, U.S., Germany, France and Spain, 1954-62; Experimental Flight Test Pilot, U.S. Air Force, 1945-54; Fighter Pilot, ETO, U.S. Air Force, 1943-46; Advanced Through Grades to Brigadier General, U.S. Air Force, 1969; Enlisted in, US Army Air Force, 1941 **CR:** Speaker in Field Hon. Chairman Duncan Hunter Presidential Campaign, 2006 Presidential Commission to Investigate Challenger Accident, 1986 Consultant to Commander Test Pilot School, Edwards AFB, 1975-97 **CIV:** Founder, Chairman, General Chuck Yeager Foundation, California, 2002- **CW:** Actor: (films) Smokey and the Bandit II, 1980, The Right Stuff, 1983; (TV movies) Flying Without Fear, 1985; (TV appearances) Goodyear Television Playhouse, 1953, I Dream of Jeannie, 1964; Co-author: (with Leo Janos) Yeager: An Autobiography, 1985, (with Charles Leerhsen) Press On!, 1988, The Quest for Mach One: A First-Person Account of Breaking the Sound Barrier, 1998; featured in: Spaceflight, 1985, Looney Tunes 50th Anniversary, 1986, Realizing 'The Right Stuff,' 2003, The Real Men with 'The Right Stuff,' 2003, Pancho Barnes! A Documentary Film, 2008 **AW:** Decorated Distinguished Service Medal with Oak Leaf Cluster, Silver Star with Oak Leaf Cluster, Legion of Merit with Oak Leaf Cluster, Distinguished Flying Cross with 2 Oak Leaf Clusters, Bronze Star with V Device, Air Medal with 10 Oak Leaf Clusters, Air Force Commendation Medal, Purple Heart; Recipient Collier Trophy, 1948, Harmon Internat Trophy, 1958, Congl. Medal of Honor, 1976, Presidential Medal of Freedom, 1985; **ACH:** Achievements include flying in 64 combat missions in World War II, over 120 combat missions in Vietnam; being the first man to fly faster than the speed of sound, October 14, 1947 **BA:** General Chuck Yeager Foundation, 13393 Grass Valley Ave, Grass Velley, CA, 0

YEARWOOD, TRISHA, T: Country Music Singer, Songwriter **I:** Media & Entertainment **DOB:** 09/19/1964 **PB:** Monticello **PT:** Daughter of Jack Howard and Gwendolyn (Paulk) Y.; Married Chris Latham, 1987 (div. 1991); Married Robert Reynolds, May 21, 1994 (div. 1999); Married Garth Brooks, December 10, 2005; 3 stepchildren. **ED:** BA Business Administration, Belmont University, 1987 **C:** Recording artist, MCA Records,; Demo singer, commercial jingles singer, MTM Records,; Intern, MTM Records, **CW:** Singer: (albums)

Trisha Yearwood, 1991, Hearts in Armor, 1992, The Song Remembers When, 1993, Thinkin' About You, 1995, Everybody Knows, 1996, (songbook) A Collection of Hits, 1997, Where Your Road Leads, 1998, Real Live Woman, 2000, Inside Out, 2001, Jasper County, 2005, Live in Concert, 2007, Heaven, Heartache & the Power of Love, 2007, PrizeFighter, 2014, Christmas Together, 2016; back-up vocalist Garth Brooks albums; opening act Garth Brooks Tour, 1991; author: (cookbooks) Georgia Cooking in an Oklahoma Kitchen: Recipes from My Family to Yours, 2008, Home Cooking with Trisha Yearwood: Stories and Recipes to Share with Family and Friends, 2010, Trisha's Table: My Feel-Good Favorites for a Balanced Life, 2015; host: (Television) Trisha's Southern Cooking, 2012-(Emmy award for Outstanding Culinary Program, 2012),Nashville, 2015, The Passion, 2016 **AW:** Named Best New Country Artist Am. Music Awards, 1992, Top New Female Vocalist Academy Country Music, 1992, Top Female Vocalist of Year, 1998; Top Female Vocalist of Year, Country Museum Association, 1997, 1998; first female in country music history to have debut single reach #1 on charts with She's in Love with the Boy, 1991; recipient Grammy awards for Best Female Country Vocal, 1998, Best Country Vocal Collaboration (with Aaron Neville) 1994, (with Garth Brooks), 1998; named to Georgia Music Hall of Fame, 2000.

YELLEN, JANET LOUISE, T: Former Chairman of the Board of Governors of the Federal Reserve System **I:** Financial Services **DOB:** 08/13/1946 **PB:** Bklyn. **PT:** Daughter of Julius and Anna Ruth (Blumenthal) Yellen; **ED:** LHD (hon.), Bard College, 2000; LLD (hon.), Brown University, 1998; PhD in Economics, Yale University, New Haven, 1971; BA in Economics summa cum laude, Brown University, Providence, 1967 **C:** Eugene E. & Catherine M. Trefethem professor emeritus business administration, University California Berkeley Haas School Business, 1999-; Chair, Federal Reserve Systems, Washington, 2014-; President, CEO, Federal Reserve Bank San Francisco, 2004-10; Chair, Council Economic Advisors, Executive Office of the President, Washington, 1997-99; Bernard T. Rocca Junior professor international business & trade, University California Berkeley Haas School Business, 1992-94; Professor, University California Berkeley Haas School Business, 1985-92; Associate professor, University California Berkeley Haas School Business, 1982-85; Assistant professor economics, University California Berkeley Haas School Business, 1980-82; Lecturer, London School Economics & Political Sci., Washington, 1978-80; Vice chair, Federal Reserve Systems, Washington, 2010-14; Member board governors, Federal Reserve Systems, Washington, 1994-97; Economist trade & financial studies section, Federal Reserve Systems, Washington, 1977-78; Consultant division international finance, Federal Reserve Systems, Washington, 1974-75; Assistant professor economics, Harvard University, Cambridge, Massachusetts, 1971-76 **CR:** Member Council on Foreign Rels, 1976-81 Yrjö Jahnsson Foundation lecturer on macroecon. theory, Helsinki, 1977-78 adv. board Brookings Panel on Economic Activity, 1999-, senior adviser, 1989-94, member, 1990-91, 1987-88 senior adviser Macroeconomic Advisers, 2003- principal investigator Russell Sage Foundation Grant on Sustainable Employment, 2000 research associate National Bureau Economic Research, 1999- fellow Yale Corp., 2000- research affiliate Yale University, 1976 member panel economic advisers Congressional Budget Office, 1993-94, consultant, 1975-76 research fellow Massachusetts Institute of Technology, Cambridge,

1974 chair Economic Policy Committee Organization for Economic Cooperative and Devel., 1997-99, President Interagency Committee on Women's Business Enterprise, 1997-99 member National Academy of Sciences Panel, Ensuring Best Presidential Sci. and Tech. Appointments, 2000, Organization of European Cooperation and Development, High-Level Sustainable Devel. Group, 1999-2001, ambassador adv. council for Marshall Scholarships, 1996- board directors Delta Dental California, 2003-, Economists Allied for Arms Reduction, 2002- adv. board California Assembly Select Committee on Asian Trade, 2003, Jerome Levy Economics Institute, 2002-, Center International Political Economy, 1999-, Women's Economic Round Table, 1999- committee visitors, economics progressive National Science Foundation, 2004, 1996, member advisory panel in economics, 1991-92, 1977-78 **CW:** Co-author (with Arrow and Shavell): The Limits of the Market in Resource Allocation, 1977; co-author: (with Alan Blinder) The Fabulous Decade: Macroeconomics Lessons from the 1990's, 2001; associate editor Journal Economic Perspectives, 1987-91; contributor articles to professional journals **AW:** Named one of The 100 Most Influential People in the World, TIME magazine, 2014, The 100 Most Powerful Women, Forbes magazine, 2014, The World's Most Powerful People, 2013-14, The 50 Most Influential People in Global Finance, Bloomberg Markets, 2012-14, The 50 Women to Watch, The Wall St. Journal, 2005; recipient Adam Smith award, National Association Business Economics (NABE), 2010, Wilbur Lucius Cross Medal, Yale University, 1997, Maria & Sidney Rolfe award for National Economic Service, Women's Economic Round Table, 1997; fellow National Science Foundation, 1967-71; grantee, 1990-94, 1975-77; Guggenheim fellow, 1986-87, Hon. Woodrow Wilson fellow, 1967,Time 100 Most Influential, 2017, Sovereign Wealth Fund #1 Public Investor, 2015, Bloomberg Market #1 Most Influential Economists and Policymakers, 2015 **MEM:** Fellow: American Academy Arts & Sciences; mem.: Western Economic Association (president 2003-04), American Economic Association (adv. committee to president 1986-87, nominating committee 1988-90), Phi Beta Kappa **ACH:** Achievements include the first woman to become chair of the Federal Reserve System, 2013 **PA:** Democrat **BA:** Federal Reserve Building, 2051 Constitution Ave NW, Washington, DC, 20418

YOAKAM, DWIGHT, **T:** Musician **I:** Media & Entertainment **PB:** Pikeville **SC:** KY/USA **PT:** David Yoakam; Ruth Ann (Tibbs) Yoakam **ED:** Ph.D (hon.), Ohio Valley College, 2005 **C:** Solo artist, 2013-; Founder, singer, The Jompson Brothers, 2010; Singer, guitarist, The SteelDivers, 2008-10 **CR:** Founder Bakersfield Biscuits **CW:** Songwriter for notable songs Never Wanted Nothing More (Kenny Chesney), 2007, Come Back Song (Darius Rucker), 2010, If it Hadn't Been Love (Adele), 2011, Love's Gonna Make It Alright (George Strait), 2011, Talk is Cheap (Alan Jackson), 2012, Drink a Beer (Luke Bryan), 2013, Crash and Burn (Thomas Rhett), 2015, various others; musician: (albums) Traveller, 2015 (Album of Year, Country Music Association Awards, 2015, Best Country Album, Best Country Solo Performance for Song ""Traveller,"" Grammy Awards, 2016, Album of Year, Song of Year for Song ""Nobody to Blame,"" Academy Country Music Awards, 2016, Top Country Album, Billboard Music Awards, 2016), (songs) Fire Away, 2015 (Breakthrough Video of Year, CMT Music Awards, 2016)(Albums)Guitars, Cadillacs, Etc., Etc,1986,Hillbilly Deluxe,1987, Buenas Noches From a Lonely Room,1988,If There Was a Way ,1990,This Time,1993,Gone,1995,A

Long Way Home,1998,dwightyoakamacoustic.net ,2000,Tomorrow's Sounds Today,2000,-South of Heaven, West of Hell,2001,Population Me,2003,Blame the Vain,2005,3 Pears ,2012,Second Hand Heart,2015, Swimmin' Pools, Movie Stars,2016,(Film)Red Rock West, 1992, The Little Death, 1995, Sling Blade, 1996, Painted Hero, 1997, The Newtown Boys, 1998, The Minus Man, 1999, South of Heaven, West of Hell,2001, Panic Room, 2002, Hollywood Homicide, 2003, Three Way, 2004, Wedding Crashers, 2005, The Three Burials of Melquiades Estrada, 2005, Bandidas, 2006, Crank, 2006, Two:Thirteen, 2008, Four Christmases, 2008, Crank: High Voltage, 2009, Dirty Girl, 2010, The Last Rite of Ransom Pride, 2010, Bloodworth, 2010, 90 Minutes in Heaven, 2015, Logan Lucky, 2017 **AW:** Named Songwriter of Year, Academy Country Music Awards, 2016, New Male Vocalist of Year, 2016, Male Vocalist of Year, 2016, Country Music Association Awards, 2015, New Artist of Year, 2015

YODER, KEVIN W., **T:** U.S. Representative from Kansas, former state legislator **I:** Government Administration/Government Relations/Government Services **DOB:** 01/18/1976 **PB:** Hutchinson **ED:** JD, University Kansas, 2002; BA in Political Sci. and English, University Kansas, 1999 **C:** Member, US House Appropriations Committee, Washington, 2011-; Member, US Congress from 3rd Kansas District, Washington, 2011-; Member, Republican Study Committee; Member District 20, Kansas House of Reps., 2003-10; Special assistant Office Counternarcotics, US Department Defense, 2001; Partner, Speer & Holliday, Olathe, Kansas, 2005-10; Associate, Speer & Holliday LLP, Olathe, Kansas, 2003-05; Law clerk, Payne & Jones, Overland Park, Kansas, 2000-01 **PA:** Republican

YOHO, TED, **T:** U.S. Representative from Florida, Veterinarian **I:** Government Administration/Government Relations/Government Services **DOB:** 04/13/1955 **PB:** Minneapolis **SC:** MN/USA **ED:** Doctor in Veterinary Medicine, Florida College Veterinary Medicine, 1983; BS in Animal Sci., University Florida, 1979; AA, Broward Community College, 1977 **C:** Member, US House Foreign Affairs Com, 2013-; Member, US House Agricultural Com, 2013-; Member, US Congress from 3rd Florida District, Washington, 2013-; Private veterinary practice, 1983-2010 **MEM:** Mem.: National Rifle Association, Florida Cattlemen's Association, Florida Association of Equine Practitioners, Florida Veterinary Medical Association, American Veterinary Medical Association **PA:** Republican

YOUNG, ANDRE (DR DRE), **T:** Entrepreneur, Record Producer, Rap Musician **I:** Media & Entertainment **DOB:** 02/18/1965 **PB:** LA **PT:** Son of Theodore and Verna Young; Married Nicole Threatt, 1996; children: Truice, Truly; children from previous relationships: Curtis, Andre Junior (deceased), Marcel. **C:** Co-founder, Beats Electronics, LLC, Santa Monica, California, 2006-; Founder, CEO, Aftermath Entertainment, Santa Monica, 1996-; Co-founder, Death Row Records, 1992-95; Musician, NWA, 1986-91 **CW:** Singer: (albums with N.W.A.) Straight Outta Compton, 1989, 100 Miles and Runnin', 1990, Efil4zaggin, 1991, NWA Greatest Hits, 1996; (solo albums) The Chronic, 1993, 2001, 1999 (Grammy award for Best Rap Album, 2001), Compton: A Soundtrack by Dr. Dre, 2015; prodr.: (albums) Doggy Style, 1993, Murder Was the Case, 1994, U Can't Cee Me and California Love singles, 1996, Wild Wild West, 1999, The SLim SHady Lp, 1999, The Marshall Mathers LP, 2000, Death Row: Snoop Doggy Dogg at His Best, 2001, The Eminem Show, 2002;

(soundtracks) Above the Rim, 1994; (songs) Let Me Ride, 1993 (Grammy award for Best Rap Solo Performance, 1994), Forgot About Dre (with Eminem, 2000, (MTV Video Music award for Best Rap Video, 2000, Grammy award for Best Rap Performance by a Duo or Group, 2001), Crack a Bottle, 2009 (Grammy award for Best Rap Performance by a Duo or Group, 2010), actor: (films) Who's The Man, 1993, Ride, 1998, Whiteboyz, 1999, The Wash, 2001, Training Day, 2001, Unity, 2015.(Television) The Defiant Ones, 2017 **AW:** MTV Best Video Award, 2000, Grammy for Best Rap Performance, 2010, Best Rap Album, 2010,Named to Rock and Roll Hall of Fame (as member of N.W.A) 2016; recipient Founder's award, American Society Composers, Authors & Publishers, 2010

YOUNG, ANDREW JACKSON JR., **T:** Consulting Firm Executive, Former Mayor, Former U.S. Representative from Georgia **I:** Government Administration/Government Relations/Government Services **DOB:** 03/12/1932 **PB:** New Orleans **SC:** Louisiana **PT:** Son of Andrew J. and Daisy (Fuller) Y.; **MS:** Married **SPN:** Carolyn M. (1996); Jean Childs, June 7, 1954 (deceased 1994); **CH:** Andrea, Lisa Dru, Paula Jean, Andrew J. III; **ED:** Numerous other hon. degrees; LL.D. (hon.), Dartmouth University, 2005; LL.D. (hon.), Atlanta University; LL.D. (hon.), Swarthmore College; LL.D. (hon.), Yale University, 1973; LL.D. (hon.), Clark College, 1973; LL.D. (hon.), Wilberforce University, 1971; D.D. (hon.), United Theological Seminary Twin Cities, 1970; D.D. (hon.), Wesleyan University, 1970; B.D., Hartford Theological Seminary, 1955; BS, Howard University, 1951; Student, Dillard University, 1947-48 **C:** Founder, Andrew Young Foundation, 2003-; President, National Council of Churches, 2000-2001; Founding principal, co-chmn., Goodworks International LLC, 1996-; Professor pub. affairs, Georgia State University, Atlanta,; Co-chmn., Atlanta Committee for the Olympic Games, 1996; Mayor, City of Atlanta, 1982-90; Permanent US rep., UN, New York City, 1977-79; Member, US Congress from 5th Georgia District, 1973-77; Executive vice president, Southern Christian Leadership Conference, 1967-70; Executive director, Southern Christian Leadership Conference, 1964-70; Administrator citizen education program, Southern Christian Leadership Conference, 1961-64; Member staff, Southern Christian Leadership Conference, 1961-70; Associate director department youth work, National Council Churches, 1957-61; Pastor, Thomasville, Georgia, 1955-57; Ordained to ministry, Congl. Church, 1955 **CR:** Chairman national steering committee Working Families for Wal-Mart, 2006 president National Council Churches, 2000-01 **CIV:** Chairman Atlanta Community Relations Commission, 1970-72 chairman board Delta Ministry of Mississippi board directors Martin Luther King, Junior Center for Social Change, Robert F. Kennedy Memorial Foundation, Field Foundation, Southern Christian Leadership Conference **CW:** Author: A Way Out of No Way: The Spiritual Memoirs of Andrew Young, 1994, An Easy Burden: The Civil Rights Movement and the Transformation of America, 1996,Andrew Young at the United Nations, 1978, Andrew Young, Remembrance & Homage, 1978,; The History of the Civil Rights Movement, 1990,; Trespassing Ghost: A Critical Study of Andrew Young ,1978,; Walk in My Shoes: Conversations between a Civil Rights Legend and his Godson on the Journey Ahead with Kabir Sehgal, 2010, The Politician, 2010 **AW:** Recipient Pax-Christi award St. John's University, 1970; Springarn medal.; Presidential Medal of Freedom, 1980, French Legion of Honor medal, 1982; co-recipient, Martin Luther King, Junior, Award for Public

Service (Ebony magazine), 1990. **MEM:** Member Ams. Dem. Action, Alpha Phi Alpha **PA:** Democrat

YOUNG, DAVID, **T:** U.S. Representative from Iowa **I:** Government Administration/Government Relations/Government Services **DOB:** 05/11/1968 **PB:** Van Meter **SC:** IA/USA **ED:** BA, Drake University, 1991 **C:** Committee on Appropriations, U.S. Representative from Iowa's Third District, 2015-Present; Chief of Staff, U.S. Sen. Charles Grassley of Iowa, 2006-2013; Campaign Manager, U.S. Sen. James Bunning of Kentucky, 1998-2006; Staff, U.S. Sen. Hank Brown of Colorado, 1993-1996 **BA:** 240 Cannon HOB, Washington, DC, 20515

YOUNG, DONALD EDWIN, **T:** U.S. Representative from Alaska **I:** Government Administration/Government Relations/Government Services **DOB:** 06/09/1933 **PB:** Meridian **SC:** CA/USA **ED:** BA, Chico State College, California, 1958; AA, Yuba Junior College, 1952 **C:** Member at-large, U.S. Congress from Alaska, 1973-; Chairman, US House Transportation & Infrastructure Committee, 2001-07; Chairman, US House National Resources Committee, 1995-2001; Member, Alaska State Senate, 1970-73; Member, Alaska House of Reps., 1966-70; Mayor, Fort Yukon City Council, 1960-68; Member, Fort Yukon City Council, 1960-68 **MIL:** Served in 41st Tank Battalion US Army, 1955-57 **PA:** Republican

YOUNG, MICHAEL WARREN PHD, **T:** Geneticist, Educator **I:** Sciences **PB:** Miami **SC:** Florida **PT:** Son of Lloyd George and Mildred (Tillery) Y.; **SPN:** Married Laurel Ann Eckhardt, December 27, 1978; **CH:** children: Natalie, Arissa. **ED:** PhD in Genetics, University Texas, Austin, 1975; BA in Biology, University Texas, Austin, 1971 **C:** Richard and Jeanne Fisher Professor, Rockefeller University, 2004-; Professor, Rockefeller University, 1988-; Head Laboratory Genetics, Rockefeller University,; Associate Professor, Rockefeller University, 1984-88; Assistant Professor Genetics, Rockefeller University, New York City, 1978-83; National Institutes of Health Postdoctoral Fellow, Stanford (California) University Medical School, 1975-77 **CR:** Investigator Howard Hughes Medical Institute, New York City, 1987-96 Adv. Panel on Genetic Biology National Science Foundation, Washington, 1983-87 Special Advisor Am. Cancer Society, New York City, 1985- Special Reviewer Genetics Study Section National Institutes of Health, Bethesda, Maryland, 1990-, Cell Biology Study Section, 1993-97 Head Rockefeller Unit National Science Foundation Sci. and Tech. Center Biological Timing, 1991-2001 Vice President Academic Affairs, 2004-. **CW:** Contributor Articles to Professional Journals **AW:** Meyer Foundation Fellow, New York City, 1978-83; Co-recipient Peter and Patricia Gruber Foundation Neuroscience Prize, 2009, Louisa Gross Horwitz Prize, Columbia University, 2011, Canada Gairdner International Award, 2012, Massry Prize, 2012, Wiley Arize, 2013, The Shaw Prize in Life Science and Medicine, 2013 **MEM:** Fellow New York Society Fellows, American Academy Microbiology; member American Association for the Advancement of Science, Genetics Society America, American Society Microbiologists, New York Academy Sciences, Harvey Society, National Academy of Sciences, American Chemical Society **ACH:** Achievements include research on transposable DNA elements, molecular genetics of nerve and muscle development, biological clocks, molecular control of circadian rhythms. **BA:** 51 Greenwoods Rd Old, Tappan , NJ, 07675-7018

YOUNG, NEIL, **T:** Guitarist, Songwriter **I:** Media & Entertainment **DOB:** 11/12/1945 **PB:** Toronto **SC:** Ont. Can. **PT:** Son of Scott Alexander and Edna Blow (Ragland) Young; **ED:** LHD (hon.), San Francisco State University, 2006; MusD (hon.), Lakehead University, Thunder Bay, Ontario, 1992 **C:** Singer, guitarist, Crosby, Stills, Nash & Young, 1969-70, 74-75; Singer, guitarist, Buffalo Springfield, 1967-68 **CIV:** Co-founder, host, Bridge School Benefit, Mountain View, California, 1986-; Co-founder, board directors, Farm Aid, 1985- **CW:** Singer, guitarist (albums with Buffalo Springfield) Buffalo Springfield, 1966, Buffalo Springfield Again, 1967, Last Time Around, 1968, The Best of Retrospective, 1969; (albums with Crosby, Stills, Nash & Young) Déjà Vu, 1970, 4 Way Street, 1971, So Far, 1974, American Dream, 1988, Looking Forward, 1999; (solo albums) Neil Young, 1968, Harvest, 1972, Time Fades Away, 1973, On the Beach, 1974, Hawks & Doves, 1980, Everybody's Rockin', 1983, Old Ways, 1985, Landing on Water, 1986, This Note's for You, 1988, Eldorado, 1989, Freedom, 1989, Harvest Moon, 1992, Mirror Ball, 1995, Silver & Gold, 2000, Prairie Wind, 2005, Living with War, 2006, Living with War: In the Beginning, 2006, Chrome Dreams II, 2007, Fork in the Road, 2009, Le Noise, 2010, A Treasure, 2011, A Letter Home, 2014, Storytone, 2014, The Monsanto Years,2015, Peace Trail, 2016, Hitchhiker, 2017, The Visitor, 2017; (albums with Crazy Horse) Everybody Knows This is Nowhere, 1969, After the Gold Rush, 1970, Tonight's the Night, 1975, Zuma, 1975, American Stars 'N Bars, 1977, Comes a Time, 1978, Rust Never Sleeps, 1979, Re-ac-tor, 1981, Trans, 1982, Life, 1987, Ragged Glory, 1990, Sleeps with Angels, 1994, Broken Arrow, 1996, Are You Passionate?, 2002, Greendale, 2003, Americana, 2012, Psychedelic Pill, 2012; (with Stills-Young Band) Long May You Run, 1976; (live albums) Live Rust, 1979, Weld, 1991, Arc, 1991, Unplugged, 1993, Year of the Horse, 1997, Road Rock Vol. 1, 2000, Live at the Fillmore East, 2006, Live at Massey Hall 1971, 2007, Sugar Mountain - Live At Canterbury House 1968, 2008, The Archives Vol. 1 1963-1972, 2009 (Best Art Direction On A Boxed/Spl. Ltd. Edition Package, Grammy Awards, 2010), Dreamin' Man Live '92, 2009, (compilations) Decade, 1977, Lucky Thirteen, 1983, Decade - The Very Best of Neil Young (1966-1976), 2002, Greatest Hits, 2004; composer (soundtracks) Journey Through the Past, 1972, 'Where the Buffalo Roam', 1980, Philadelphia, 1994, Dead Man, 1996; dir.(under pseudonym Bernard Shakey):(films) Journey Through the Past, 1973, Rust Never Sleeps, 1979, Human Highway, 1982, Greendale, 2003, CSNY Déjà Vu, 2008; appeared in (documentaries) The Last Waltz, 1978; director, performer (short films) Americana, 2012; author: Waging Heavy Peace, 2012 **AW:** Named Person of Year, MusiCares Foundation, Inc., 2010; named one of The Top 50 Guitarists of All Time, Gibson.com, 2010, The Greatest Living Songwriters, Paste Magazine, 2006, The 100 Greatest Artists of Hard Rock, VH1, 2000, The 100 Agents of Change, Rolling Stone magazine, 2009, The 100 Greatest Singers of All-Time, 2008, The 100 Greatest Artists of All Time, 2004, The 100 Greatest Guitarists of All Time, 2003, Mojo magazine, 1996; named to Canada's Walk of Fame, 2000, The Rock & Roll Hall of Fame, (as a member of Buffalo Springfield), 1997, (as a solo artist), 1995, The Canadian Music Hall of Fame, 1992; recipient Allan Waters Humanitarian award, Can. Academy Recording Arts & Scis., 2011, Grammy award for Best Rock Song, National Academy Recording Arts & Scis., 2011, Spirit of Liberty award, People for American Way, 2001 **BA:** ICM Partners, 10250 Constellation Boulevard,9th Blvd, Los Angeles, CA, 90067

YOUNG, TODD C., **T:** U.S. Senator from Indiana **I:** Government Administration/Government Relations/Government Services **DOB:** 08/24/1972 **PB:** Marion County **PT:** Son of Bruce and Nancy Young **ED:** JD, Indiana Univ., 2006; MA, Univ. London, 2001; MBA, Univ. Chicago; BS cum laude, US Naval Academy, Annapolis, 1995 **C:** Member, US Congress from 9th Ind. District, Washington, 2011-2017; U.S. Senator from Indiana, 2017-; Member, US House Armed Services Committee, Washington, 2011-; Member, US House Budget Committee, Washington, 2011-; Member, US Congress from 9th Ind. District, Washington, 2011-; Deputy prosecutor, Orange County, Ind., 2007-; Attorney, Tucker & Tucker PC, Paoli, Ind., 2006-; Management consultant, Crowe Chizek & Co.; Legis. assistant for energy policy to US Senator Richard Lugar, US Senate, Washington; Policy analyst, Heritage Foundation, Washington; Advanced to captain, US Marine Corps, 1995-2000 **CIV:** Pro bono mediator, Ind. Civil Rights Commission, Board director, HVAF Indiana, Board director, Crisis Pregnancy Center **MEM:** Mem.: Orange County Bar Association (president 2008) **PA:** Republican **BA:** Office of Todd Young, 400 Russell Senate Office Building, Washington, DC, 20510

YZERMAN, STEVE, **T:** Retired Professional Hockey Player **I:** Athletics **DOB:** 05/09/1965 **PB:** Cranbrook, British Columbia **SC:** Canada **C:** Vice President, General Manager, Tampa Bay Lightning (2010-Present); Vice President, Alternate Governor, Detroit Red Wings (2006-2010); Captain, Detroit Red Wings (1986-2006); Center, Detroit Red Wings (1983-2006) **CR:** General Manager, Team Canada, IIHF World Championship, Moscow, Russia (2007); Executive Director, Team Canada, Olympic Games, Vancouver, Canada (2008-2010); Member, Team Canada, Olympic Games, Salt Lake City, Utah (2002); Member, Team Canada, Olympic Games, Nagano, Japan (1998) **AW:** Named GM of the Year (2015); Named NHL Rookie of the Year, Sporting News (1984); Named to NHL All-Star Game (1984, 1988-1993, 1997, 1999, 2000); Named to First All-Star Team, NHL (2000); Named to All-Rookie Team (1984); Frank J. Selke Trophy (2000); Bill Masterton Trophy (2003); Conn Smythe Trophy (1998); Lester Patrick Trophy (2006); Lester B. Pearson Award (1989); Named One of the 100 Greatest NHL Players (2017); Stanley Cup Champion (2002); Stanley Cup Champion, (As Executive) (2008); Bill Masterton Memorial Trophy (2003); Lester Patrick Award (2006); Inductee, Ottawa Sports Hall of Fame (2008); Inductee, Michigan Sports Hall of Fame (2008); Inductee, Canada Sports Hall of Fame (2008); Inductee, Hockey Hall of Fame (2009); Inductee, IIHF Hall of Fame (2014); Order of Hockey in Canada (2014); NHL General Manager of the Year Award (2015) **ACH:** Achievements include being the youngest person ever to play in the NHL All-Star game, 1984; being a member of Stanley Cup Champion Detroit Red Wings, 1997, 1998, 2002; being a member of gold medal winning Canadian Hockey Team, Salt Lake City Olympics, 2002; being the longest serving captain in NHL history; having his number, 19, retired by Detroit Red Wings, 2007; being inducted into the Canadian Sports Hall of Fame, 2008; being inducted into the Hockey Hall of Fame, 2009; being inducted into the International Ice Hockey Hall of Fame, 2014

ZAKARIA, FAREED RAFIQ, **T:** Journalist, Author **I:** Writing and Editing **DOB:** 01/20/1964 **PB:** Mumbai **PT:** Son of Rafiq Ahmed and Fatma Rafiq Zakaria **ED:** PhD in Political Sci., Harvard University, 1993; BA, Yale University, 1986 **C:** Editor-at-large, Columnist, TIME magazine, 2010-;

Editor, Newsweek International, 2000-10; Host, Fareed Zakaria GPS, CNN, 2008-; Managing Editor, Foreign Affairs, New York City, 1993-2000; Executive Coordinator, Changing Security Environmental Project, Olin Institute, Harvard University, Cambridge, Massachusetts, 1991-92; Reporter, Researcher, The New Republic, Washington, 1987 **CR:** Columnist Washington Post, Newsweek, Host, Foreign Exchange with Fareed Zakaria, PBS, 2005-07; News Analyst, This Week with George Stephanopoulos, 2002-07 **CIV:** Trustee, Shakespeare & Co. Inc., Trustee, Yale University, 2006- **CW:** Author: From Wealth to Power: The Unusual Origins of America's World Role, 1998, The Future of Freedom: Illiberal Democracy at Home and Abroad, 2003 (New York Times bestseller), The Post-American World, 2008 (New York Times bestseller), The Post American World, Release 2.0, 2011, In Defense of a Liberal Education, 2015; Co-editor (with James F. Hoge): The American Encounter: The U.S. and the Making of the Modern World: Essays from 75 Years of Foreign Affairs, 1997 **AW:** Padma Bhushan Award, 2010, Named One of The 50 Highest-Earning Political Figures, Newsweek, 2010, The Top 100 Public Intellectuals, Foreign Policy & Prospect magazine, 2007, The 21 Most Important People of the 21st Century, Esquire magazine, 1999; Recipient Overseas Press Club award, 1998 **MEM:** Mem.: Council on Foreign Relations (board directors), Century Association

ZARIF, MOHAMMAD JAVAD, T: Diplomat **I:** International Affairs/International Business **PB:** Tehran **SC:** Iran **C:** Minister, Foreign Affairs (2013-Present); Chief Negotiator, Iran Nuclear Issue (2013-2015); Ambassador to Iran, United Nations (2002-2007) **AW:** Named One of TIME's 100 Most Influential People, TIME Magazine (2015)

ZELDIN, LEE M., T: U.S. Representative from New York **I:** Government Administration/Government Relations/Government Services **DOB:** 01/30/1980 **PB:** East Meadow **ED:** JD, Albany Law School, 2003; BA in Political Sci., cum laude, State University of New York, Albany, 2001 **CT:** Bar: New York 2004 **C:** Member, U.S. House of Representatives from New York's 1st District, 2015-, Committee on Foreign Affairs, Committee on Financial Services; Member District 3, New York State Senate, 2011-2015; Private practice attorney, Smithtown, New York, 2008-; Attorney, Raiser & Kenniff, PC, New York City, 2007-08; Counsel, Port Authority New York & New Jersey, 2007; Retired as captain, US Army, 2007; Military magistrate, 18th Airborne Corps, US Army, Fort Bragg, 2006-07; Judge Advocate General Corps attorney, Operation Iraqi Freedom, US Army, Iraq, 2006; Assigned Judge Advocate General Corps, 82nd Airborne Division, US Army, Fort Bragg, North Carolina, 2004-06; 2nd lieutenant, military intelligence corps, US Army, Fort Huachuca, Arizona, 2003-04; Legis. aide, Office Senator Kenneth P. Lavalle, New York, 1998-2000 **CIV:** Candidate New York Congl. district 1, US House of Reps., 2008 **MIL:** Serves with US Army Reserve, 2007- **MEM:** Mem.: VFW, New York State Bar Association, Jewish War Vets., American Legion **H:** Piano, Tae Kwon Do, boating **PA:** Republican **BA:** 1517 Longworth House Office Building, Washington, DC, 20515

ZELLWEGER, RENÉE, T: Actress **I:** Media & Entertainment **DOB:** 04/25/1969 **PB:** Katy **SC:** TX/USA **PT:** Emil Erich Zellweger; Kjellfrid Irene Andreassen **ED:** BA in English, University of Texas, Austin (1991) **CW:** Actress (films) Reality Bites, 1994, 8 Seconds, 1994, Love and a .45, 1994, Texas Chainsaw Massacre: The Next Generation,

1994, Empire Records, 1995, The Low Life, 1995, The Whole Wide World, 1996, Jerry Maguire, 1996 (Broadcast Film Critics Association award for Breakthrough Artist, 1997, National Board Rev. award for Breakthrough Performance, 1996), Deceiver, 1997, A Price Above Rubies, 1998, One True Thing, 1998, The Bachelor, 1999, Nurse Betty, 2000 (Golden Globe award for Best Actress, 2001), Me, Myself & Irene, 2000, Bridget Jones's Diary, 2001, White Oleander, 2002, Chicago, 2002 (Golden Globe award for Best Actress, 2003, Screen Actors Guild award for Outstanding Performance by a Female Actor in a Leading Role, 2003), Down with Love, 2003, Cold Mountain, 2003 (Academy award for Best Supporting Actress, 2004, Golden Globe award for Best Supporting Actress, 2004, Screen Actors Guild award for Outstanding Performance by a Female Actor in a Supporting Role, 2004, BAFTA award for Best Actress in a Supporting Role, 2004), Shark Tale (voice), 2004, Bridget Jones: The Edge of Reason, 2004, Cinderella Man, 2005, Bee Movie (voice), 2007, Leatherheads, 2008, Appaloosa, 2008, New in Town, 2009, Monsters versus Aliens (voice), 2009, My One and Only, 2009, Case 39, 2009, My Own Love Song, 2010, The Whole Truth, 2016, Bridget Jones's Baby, 2016, Same Kind of Different as Me, 2017, Best Day of my Life,2018 (TV films) A Taste for Killing, 1992, Murder in the Heartland, 1993, Shake, Rattle and Rock!, 1994, actress, executive producer (films) Miss Potter, 2006; executive prodr.: (TV films) Living Proof, 2008; producer, writer (TV films) Cinnamon Girl, 2013 **AW:** Named Woman of Year, Hasty Pudding Theatrical Society, 2009; recipient Crystal award, Women in Film Crystal + Lucy awards, 2007

ZETA-JONES, CATHERINE, T: Actress **I:** Media & Entertainment **DOB:** 09/25/1969 **PB:** Swansea **SC:** Wales **PT:** David Jones; Patricia (Fair) Jones **MS:** Married **SPN:** Michael Douglas (2000) **CW:** Actress, Films, "Les 1001 Nuits (Italy)" (1990), "Christopher Columbus: The Discovery" (1992), "Splitting Heirs" (1993), "Blue Juice" (1995), "The Phantom" (1996), "The Mask of Zorro" (1998), "Entrapment" (1999), "The Haunting" (1999), "High Fidelity" (2000), "Traffic" (2000), "America's Sweethearts" (2001), "Chicago" (2002), Voice Actor, "Sinbad: Legend of the Seven Seas" (2003), "Intolerable Cruelty" (2003), "The Terminal" (2004), "Ocean's Twelve" (2004), "The Legend of Zorro" (2005), "No Reservations" (2007), "Death Defying Acts" (2008), "The Rebound" (2009), "Lay the Favorite" (2012), "Rock of Ages" (2012), "Playing for Keeps" (2012), "Broken City" (2013), "Side Effects" (2013), "Red 2" (2013), "Dad's Army" (2016); Actress, TV Films, "Out of the Blue" (1991), "The Cinder Path" (1994), "The Return of the Native" (1994), "Catherine the Great" (1995); Actress, TV Series, "The Darling Buds of May" (1991-1993), "The Young Indiana Jones Chronicles" (1992-1993); Actress, TV Miniseries, "Titanic" (1996), "Feud: Bette and Joan" (2017), "Cocaine Grandmother" (2018); Actress, Broadway Plays, "A Little Night Music" (2009), "The Children's Monologues" (2017) **AW:** Blockbuster Entertainment Award for Favorite Female Newcomer, "The Mask of Zorro" (1998); European Film Award/Jameson People's Choice Award for Best European Actress, "Entrapment" (1999); Best Supporting Actress, "Chicago," Academy Award; Best Actress in a Supporting Role, "Chicago," BAFTA Award; Outstanding Performance by a Female Actor in a Supporting Role, "Chicago," Screen Actors Guild Award; Best Supporting Actress, "Chicago," Broadcast Film Critics Association Award; Best Supporting Actress, "Chicago," Phoenix Film Critics Society Award; Best Performance by a Leading Actress in a Musical, "A Little

Night Music," Tony Awards (2010) **BA:** William Morris Endeavor Entertainment, One William Morris Place, Beverly Hills, CA, 90212

ZIMMER, ROBERT JEFFREY, T: President of the University of Chicago **I:** Education/Educational Services **DOB:** 11/05/1947 **PB:** New York **SC:** NY/USA **PT:** Son of Max S. and Harriet (Brokaw) Zimmer; **ED:** PhD, Harvard University, 1975; AB summa cum laude, Brandeis University, 1968 **C:** President, University Chgo, 2006-; Professor math, University Chicago, 1980-; Provost, Ford Foundation professor math., Brown University, Providence, 2002-06; Professor math., University Calif.-Berkeley, 1981-83; Deputy provost, University Chicago, 2000-01; Deputy provost for research, University Chicago, 1998-2000; Associate provost for research & education, University Chicago, 1995-98; Chairman math department, University Chicago, 1991-95; Associate professor, University Chicago, 1979-80; Instructor, University Chicago, 1977-79; Assistant professor, US Naval Academy, Annapolis, Maryland, 1975-77 **CR:** Vice president research Argonne National Laboratory, 2000-02 **CW:** Author: Ergodic Theory and Semisimple Groups, 1984, Essential Results of Functional Analysis; contributor articles to professional journals **AW:** Sloan Foundation fellow, 1979-83 **MEM:** Fellow: American Association for the Advancement of Science, Am. Academy Arts & Scis. **BA:** The University of Chicago, 5801 South Ellis ave, Suite 501, Chicago, IL, 60637

ZINKE, RYAN K., T: Secretary of the Interior, Former State Legislator **I:** Government Administration/Government Relations/Government Services **DOB:** 11/01/1961 **PB:** Bozeman **ED:** MS in Global Leadership, University San Diego, 2004; MBA in Fin., National University, 1991; BS in Geology, University Oregon, 1984 **C:** Member, U.S. House of Representatives from Montana's at-large district, 2015-2017; Secretary, US Department of the Interior, Washington, DC, 2017—; Member District 2, Montana State Senate, 2009-2017; President, Great Northern Peace Park Foundation, 2008; Pres./CEO, CDI, 2008; Director, Naval Special Warfare Tech., 2006; Deputy Commander, CJSOTF-AP Special Forces, Iraq, 2004; Executive officer, SEAL Training Center, 2003; Commander, Joint Task Force, Kosovo, 2001; Commander, Joint Task Force, Bosnia, 1999; Ground force Commander, Joint Special Operations Command, 1996; Mission Commander, SEAL Team Six, 1992 **PA:** Republican **BA:** Department of the Interior, 1849 C Street N.W., Washington, DC, 20240

ZUBRETSKY, JOSEPH M., T: Insurance Company Executive **I:** Insurance **ED:** BSBA, Univ. of Hartford **C:** President, CEO, Molina Healthcare, 2017-; Senior executive vice president, CFO, Aetna, Inc., Hartford, Connecticut, from 2010; Executive vice president, CFO, chief risk officer, Aetna, Inc., Hartford, Connecticut, 2007-10; Senior vice president fin., investments & corp. develop., UnumProvident Corp., 2005-07; President, CEO, GAB Robins Group, 1999-2005; Executive vice president business develop., CFO, MassMutual Financial Group, 1997-99; Executive vice president, CFO, Healthsource Inc., 1996-97; Partner, Coopers & Lybrand, 1990-96 **BA:** Molina Healthcare, 200 Oceangate, Ste. 100, Long Beach, CA, 90820

ZUCKER, JEFFREY A., T: Broadcast Executive **I:** Media & Entertainment **CN:** CNN Worldwide **DOB:** 04/09/1965 **PB:** Homestead **SC:** FL/USA **ED:** BA in American History, Harvard College, 1986 **C:** President, CNN Worldwide, 2013-Present; President, CEO, NBC Universal, Inc., 2007-2010; CEO,

NBC Universal TV, 2005-2007; President, NBC Entertainment, News And Cable Group, 2003-2005; President, NBC Entertainment, 2000-2003; Executive Producer, Today, 1994-2000; Executive Producer, NBC Nightly News With Tom Brokaw, 1993; Executive Producer, Today, 1992-1993; Field Producer, NBC News, 1989; Researcher, 1988 Olympic Games, Seoul, Korea, NBC Sports, 1986-1988; Executive Producer, Now With Tom Brokaw And Katie Couric **CW:** Executive Producer, "California Fire," Now With Tom Brokaw And Katie Couric, "Tragedy In Rwanda," Now With Tom Brokaw And Katie Couric, "The Brain," Now With Tom Brokaw And Katie Couric, (News Segments) Russian Coup, 1991, Persian Gulf War, 1991, 1993, 1997, Presidential Inaugurations, The Bombing Of Centennial Olympic Park, 1996, 1996, 2000, Political Conventions, Decision, 2000, (Daytime Talk Show) Katie, 2011-2012; Writer, The Games Of The XXIV Olympiad; Supervising Producer, "Senator Edward Kennedy," Today **AW:** Emmy Award For Outstanding Informational Or Cultural Program, "The Brain," Now With Tom Brokaw And Katie Couric, 1994, Emmy Award For Outstanding Background/Analysis Of A Single Current Story, "Tragedy In Rwanda," Now With Tom Brokaw And Katie Couric, 1994, Emmy Award For Outstanding Coverage Of A Single Breaking News Story, "California Fire," Now With Tom Brokaw And Katie Couric, 1993, Emmy Award For Outstanding Interview, "Senator Edward Kennedy," Today, 1991, Emmy Award For Outstanding Writing, The Games Of The XXIV Olympiad, 1988

ZUCKERBERG, MARK ELLIOT, T: Facebook CEO, Entrepreneur **I:** Technology **DOB:** 05/14/1984 **PB:** Dobbs Ferry **PT:** Son of Edward and Karen (Kempner) Zuckerberg; **ED:** Attended, Harvard University, 2002-04 **C:** Chairman, CEO, Facebook, Inc., Menlo Park, California, 2012-; CEO, Facebook, Inc., Palo Alto, California, 2004-12; Co-founder, Facebook, Inc., Palo Alto, California, 2004 **CR:** Board directors Facebook, Inc., 2004- **CW:** Appeared on (TV series) Saturday Night Live, 2011 **AW:** Named Person of the Year, TIME magazine, 2010, Best Start-up CEO, CrunchBase, 2007, Most Influential Person in High Tech. Industry, Agenda Setters, 2007, Media Achiever of Year, Campaign Media Awards, 2007; named one of The 50 Most Influential People in Global Finance, Bloomberg Markets, 2012, The 10 Most Fascinating People of 2010, Barbara Walters Special, The Most Influential Jews in the World, The Jerusalem Post, 2011-13, The World's Most Powerful People, Forbes magazine, 2010-14, The World's Richest People, 2009-, The Forbes 400: Richest Americans, 2009-, The 100 Agents of Change, Rolling Stone magazine, 2009, The 40 Under 40, Fortune magazine, 2009-14, The 50 Most Interesting, Creativity magazine, 2008, The 100 Most Influential People in the World, TIME magazine, 2016, 2011, 2008, The Ten Smartest People in Tech, Forbes magazine, 2010, The Top 25 Web Celebs, 2007, The 50 Who Matter Now, Business 2.0, 2006 **ACH:** Achievements include development of one of the most widely used networking websites among college and high school students throughout the US, Canada and Europe; recognition as the youngest ever self-made billionaire

ALPHABETICAL INDEX

71st Edition

ALPHABETICAL INDEX

71st Edition

BANAAD-OMIOTEK, Maria Lourdes Geraldine — Medical Doctor P. 55
BANDERAS, Antonio — Actor P.2034
BANDURSKI, Bruce Lord — Ecologist, Ecomanagement Advisor,
Environmental Diplomat P. 56
BANERJEE, Ashis — Assistant Professor P.1655
BANIS, Robert J. — Pharmaceutical Company Executive, Educator,
Publisher P. 57
BANKS, Jim — U.S. Representative from Indiana P.2034
BANKS, Richard Charles — Ornithologist (Retired) P.1655
BANNON, Steve — Former Senior Counselor to the President P.2034
BAQUET, Dean Paul — Journalist P.2035
BARABASH, Claire — Lawyer, Special Education Services
Professional, Psychologist P.1369
BARAJAS-LOPEZ, Carlos — Professor P.1370
BARBE, Betty Catherine — Marketing Professional P.1655
BARBE, David O. — President of the American Medical Association P.2035
BARBER, Edward Bruce — Medical Products Executive P. 58
BARBER, James William — Theology Studies Educator,
Director P.1656
BARBER, Patricia Louise — Adult Nurse Practitioner P.1370
BARCHAS, Jack David — Psychiatrist, Chief P. 59
BARCUS, Michael Harland — Author P. 60
BARD, Allen Joseph — Chemist, Educator P.2035
BARDEM, Javier — Actor P.2036
BARDEN, George V. — Municipal Official P.1656
BARISH, Barry C. — Physics Professor, Researcher P.2036
BARKER, Barbara Ann — Ophthalmologist P.1656
BARKER, Robert Osborne — Mediator, Educator (Retired) P.1656
BARKER, Verlyn Lloyd — Educator, Minister (Retired) P.1371
BARKLEY, Charles Wade — Former NBA Player P.2036
BARLETTA, Joseph Francis — Newspaper Executive, Lawyer P.1657
BARLETTA, Lou James — U.S. Representative From Pennsylvania,
former Mayor P.2036
BARLOW, William P. Jr — Accountant P. 61
BARNES, Harris H. III — President P.1657
BARNES, Robert Vincent — Art Educator (Retired) P.1657
BARNETT, Mary L. — Teacher P.1371
BARNETT, William Arnold — Oswald Distinguished Professor
of Macroeconomics P.1657
BARON, Marty — Newspaper Editor P.2036
BARR, Andy — U.S. Representative from Kentucky P.2036
BARR, John B. — Consultant, Chemist P.1658
BARR, Roseanne — Actress, Comedienne, Television Producer P.2036
BARRA, Mary — CEO P.2037
BARRACANO, Henry Ralph — Oil Industry Executive P.1658
BARRAGAN, Nanette — U.S. Representative from California P.2037
BARRANGER, Milly Slater — Theater Educator, Author P. 62
BARRASSO, John Anthony — U.S. Senator From Wyoming P.2037
BARREDO, Rita M. — Auditor (Retired) P.1658
BARRETT, Amy C. — Federal Judge P.2037
BARRETT, Evelyn Carol — Secondary Education Teacher (Retired) P.1372
BARRETT, George S. — Chairman of Cardinal Health P.2037
BARRINGTON, Martin J. — Tobacco Products Company Executive P.2037
BARRON, David Jeremiah — Federal Judge, Law Educator P.2037
BARRY, Herbert III — Psychologist P. 63
BARTHEL, William Frederick Jr. — Engineer, Electronics Company
Executive P.1372
BARTO, Susan Carol — Writer P.1658
BARTON, David — Religious Studies Educator, Writer, Historian P. 64, 1373
BARTON, Joe — U.S. Representative from Texas P.2038
BARTOSHUK, Linda May — Psychologist, Educator, Researcher P.1373

BARTSCH, Joel A. — President of the Houston Museum of
Natural Science P.2038
BARYSHNIKOV, Mikhail — Ballet Dancer, Actor P.2038
BASAERI, Hamid — Research Assistant P.1658
BASINGER, Kim — Actress P.2038
BASQUIN, Kit Smyth — Writer, Art Historian (Retired) P.1374
BASS, Aaron C. Jr. — School System Administrator P. 65
BASS, Hilarie — Lawyer P.2038
BASS, Jack — Communications Educator P.1374
BASS, Karen Ruth — U.S. Representative from California, former
State Legislator P.2038
BASSETT, Angela Evelyn — Actress P.2038
BASTIAN, Edward H. — CEO P.2038
BATALHA, Natalie Marie — Astronomer P.2039
BATCHELDER, Alice Moore — Federal Judge P.2039
BATCHELLER, Joe Ann — Entrepreneur P. 66
BATES, Charles Walter — Attorney, Youth Development Volunteer,
Writer P.1658
BATES, Kathy — Actress P.2039
BATES, Mason — Composer P.2039
BATTEY, Bonnie W. — Nursing Educator P. 67
BAUM, Herbert Merrill — Consumer Products Company Executive P.1659
BAYAN, Nami — Internist P. 68
BEA, Carlos Tiburcio — Federal Judge P.2039
BEAL, Robert Lawrence — President P. 69
BEALS, L. Alan — CEO and President (Retired) P.1659
BEAMON, Bob — Retired Professional Track and Field Athlete P.2039
BEAN-WATERS, Francena — Community Liaison (Freelance) P.1659
BEAR, Larry Alan — Lawyer, Educator (Retired) P. 70
BEATON, Albert E. — Professor Emeritus P.1659
BEATTY, Joyce — U.S. Representative from Ohio P.2039
BEAUCHAMP, John L. — Senior Vice President of Wealth
Management, Senior Consultant P.1660
BEAUPRE, Elaine Marcia Kenow — Retired Chamber of Commerce
Executive P.1660
BEAVERS, Roy L. — Utilities Executive, Volunteer, Writer (Retired) P. 71
BECK, Eva Carol — Musician P.1660
BECKER, Boris — Retired Professional Tennis Player P.2039
BECKER, Charles — Adult Education Educator (Retired) P. 72
BECKER, Philip Scott — Neurologist P. 73
BECKHAM, Odell Cornelius — Professional Football Player P.2040
BECKWITH, Mary Ann — Art Educator P.1375
BEDENBAUGH, Angela O. — Chemistry Educator P. 74
BEE, Samantha — Comedian, Actress P.2040
BEER, James R. — Circuit Judge P. 75
BEERY, Arthur — Artist P.1660
BEESON, Craig Cano — Pharmacologist P. 76
BEETHAM STARK, Nellie May — Author, Painter, Forest Ecologist P.1660
BEETON, Alfred Merle — Lab Administrator P.1661
BEHM, Mark Edward — Academic Administrator P.1661
BELAFONTE, Harry — Singer, Concert Artist, Actor P.2040
BELEW, Barbara Jeanne — Music Educator P. 77
BELICHICK, Bill — Professional Football Coach P.2040
BELL, Leveon — Professional Football Player P.2040
BELLEW, Carole K. — Owner P.1661
BELLOTTI-CLARK, Ann Marie J. — Chief Financial Officer P. 78
BELLOVIN, Sabra M. — Doctor P.1661
BELLOWS, Thomas J. — Political Scientist, Educator P.1375
BELT, David Levin — Lawyer P.1661
BELTRAN, Elio F. — Artist, Author P.1661

BLANCHETT, Cate — Actress P. 2047
BLAND, Bob — Activist and Fashion Designer P. 2048
BLANK, Arthur M. — Professional Sports Team Executive,
    Retired Retail Executive P. 2048
BLANKENSHIP, Charles P. Jr. — CEO P. 2048
BLANKFEIN, Lloyd Craig — Goldman Sachs CEO P. 2048
BLASER, Martin Jack — Professor P. 2048
BLAVAT, Jerry — Television Personality P. 1383
BLEAM, Laura Jane — Pediatric Nurse P. 1669
BLECHARCZYK, Nathan — Chief Strategy Officer of Airbnb P. 2048
BLEVINS, Ernest Everett — Genealogist, Researcher, Historian P. 1383
BLIGE, Mary Jay — Singer, Actress P. 2049
BLISS, Corwin "Corry" Albert — Campaign Manager P. 2049
BLOBEL, Günter — Cell Biologist, Educator P. 2049
BLOCK, John Robinson — Newspaper Publisher P. 100
BLODGETT-GRIFFIN, Cynthia — President, Lead Educator P. 101
BLOUNT, Sally E. — Dean P. 2049
BLUM, Jason — CEO P. 2049
BLUM, Kenneth — Pharmaceutical Executive, Educator (Retired),
    Neuroscientist P. 1384
BLUM, Rod — U.S. Representative from Iowa P. 2049
BLUMENAUER, Earl — U.S. Representative from Oregon P. 2049
BLUMENTHAL, Richard — U.S. Senator from Connecticut P. 2050
BLUNT, Emily — Actress P. 2050
BLUNT, Roy Dean — U.S. Senator from Missouri P. 2050
BLUNT ROCHESTER, Lisa — U.S. Representative from Delaware P. 2050
BOARDMAN, John Michael — Mathematician, Professor Emeritus P. 102
BOCHCO, Steven — Screenwriter, Television Producer P. 2050
BOCHY, Bruce Douglas — Professional Baseball Manager P. 2050
BOCK, Philip E. — Retired P. 1669
BOCZKO, Ian — Partner P. 1669
BODNAR, Peter O. — Managing Partner P. 1669
BOEHEIM, Jim — College Basketball Coach P. 2051
BOGART, Danya — Partner P. 103
BOISVERT, Therese A. — Credentialing Compliance Coordinator P. 1384
BOITANO, Brian — Olympic Iceskater, Athlete P. 2051
BOLAND, Winnifred Joan — Librarian (Retired) P. 1669
BOLLENDORF, Robert F. — Professor (Retired) P. 1670
BOLLINGER, Lee Carroll — President of Columbia University P. 2051
BOLT, Usain — Professional Runner P. 2051
BOLTON, John R. — Director P. 2051
BONAMICI, Suzanne Marie — U.S. Representative from Oregon P. 2052
BONBON, Bernard Saturnin — Associate Professor, Researcher,
    Specialist in Mathematical Problems of Visual Space P. 104
BONDS, Barry Lamar — Professional Baseball Player P. 2052
BONFIGLIO, Joseph — Proprietor P. 105
BON-JOVI, Jon — Musician, Actor, former Sports Team Executive P. 2052
BONNER, John Tyler — College Professor P. 2052
BOOKER, Cory Anthony — U.S. Senator from New Jersey P. 2052
BOOMERSHINE, Donald Eugene — Municipal Official (Retired) P. 1670
BOORSTEIN, Laurence — Project Manager, Engineer P. 1385
BOOTH, Charles Edward — Pastor P. 1385
BOOZMAN, John Nichols — U.S. Senator from Arkansas P. 2053
BORAS, Scott D. — Professional Sports Agent P. 2053
BORENE, Scott M. — Founder, Managing Attorney P. 1670
BORENSTEIN, David G. — Rheumatologist P. 106
BORER, Jeffrey Stephen — Professor of Medicine, Cell Biology,
    Radiology P. 107
BORG, Bjorn — Retired Professional Tennis Player P. 2053
BOROWSKY, Philip — Lawyer P. 108
BORTHWICK, Douglas M. — Attorney P. 109
BOSE, Sandip — Principal Research Scientist P. 1670

BOSEMAN, Chadwick — Actor P. 2053
BOSKIN, Joseph — History Professor, Director of Urban Studies P. 1670
BOSKIN, Michael Jay, Jay, — Economics Professor P. 109
BOSLEY, Karen L. — Professor of Humanities P. 111
BOSSY, Michael — Retired Professional Hockey Player P. 2053
BOST, Mike — U.S. Representative from Illinois P. 2053
BOSWELL, James Aurthur Jr — Professor P. 1670
BOSWORTH, Thomas Lawrence — Architect, Educator (Retired) P. 112
BOTKIN, Daniel B. — Professor Emeritus of Biology P. 113
BOURDAIN, Anthony Michael — Chef, Writer, Television Personality P. 2053
BOURKE-FAUSTINA, Marlene F. — Music Educator P. 114
BOURNE, Charles Percy — Information Scientist, Educator P. 115
BOURQUE, Ray — Retired Professional Hockey Player P. 2053
BOUTWELL, Anne — Associate Director P. 1671
BOVERIE, Patricia — Professor, Director P. 1671
BOWEN, Wayne Darrell — Upjohn Professor of Pharmacology P. 1671
BOWLES, Barbara Landers — Investment Executive (Retired) P. 1672
BOWLT, John Ellis — Professor Emeritus, Director P. 1386
BOWMAN, Scotty — Former Professional Hockey Coach P. 2053
BOXER, Barbara — U.S. Senator from California P. 2054
BOYD, Edward Lee — Physicist, Computer Scientist P. 1386
BOYLE, Brendan F. — U.S. Represenive from Pennsylvania P. 2054
BRADBURY, Michelle S. — Co-Director, Radiologist, Professor P. 116
BRADEN, Everette Arnold — Attorney, Judge (Retired) P. 117
BRADFORD, Sam — Professional Football Player P. 2054
BRADLEY, Laurence Alan — Psychologist P. 118
BRADWAY, Robert — President, CEO P. 2054
BRADY, James Joseph — Labor Arbitrator P. 1387
BRADY, Kevin Patrick — U.S. Representative from Texas P. 2054
BRADY, Mary Rolfres — Music Educator P. 1672
BRADY, Robert A. — U.S. Representative from Pennsylvania P. 2054
BRADY, Stephen Kalani — Associate Professor, Physician P. 119
BRADY, Tom — Professional Football Player P. 2054
BRAMBLE, Ronald Lee — President & CEO, Principal P. 120
BRANAGH, Kenneth — Actor, Film Director P. 2055
BRANCA, John — Lawyer P. 1672
BRANCH, Elizabeth L. — Federal Judge P. 2055
BRANDES, David W. — Neurologist, Educator, Multiple Sclerosis
    and Sleep Specialist P. 121
BRANDON, Raymond Wilson — CEO P. 1672
BRANDOW, Stephen Jon — Catholic Priest, Diocesan Scout Chaplain P. 122
BRANDT, William A. Jr. — Executive Chairman P. 123
BRANNON, Jean — Education Educator P. 1672
BRANSCOMB, Lewis LHD — Physicist P. 124
BRANSON, Harley Kenneth — Finance Company Executive P. 1672
BRASWELL, Jackie Boyd — State Agency Administrator P. 1672
BRAT, Dave — U.S. Representative from Virginia P. 2055
BRAUER, Stephen Franklin — Diplomat, Manufacturing Company
    Executive P. 1673
BRAULT, Lorain — Healthcare Executive P. 1673
BRAULT, Rose M. — Advanced Registered Nurse Practitioner, Educator P. 125
BRAXTON, Kerry E. Esq. — Assistant General Counsel P. 1674
BREEDIN, B. Brent — Historian P. 1387
BREEN, Edward Deveaux — Chemical Company Executive P. 2055
BRENES, Jeremy — Homeopath, Researcher, President P. 1388
BRENNAN, Stephan Y. — Managing Shareholder P. 1674
BRENNECKE, Allen Eugene — Attorney at Law P. 1388
BRENNECKE, Allen Eugene — Lawyer (Retired) P. 1674
BRENNER, Fred James — Biology Professor P. 126
BRENNER, M. Harvey — Professor P. 1674
BREYER, James William — Venture Capitalist P. 2055

BURSON, Thomas Daniel — Retired Aerospace Company Executive P.1682
BURSTEIN, Stephen D. — Neurosurgeon P.1682
BURSTYN, Ellen — Actress P.2063
BURTI, Christopher L. Sr — Vice President, Senior Legal Counsel P.1682
BURTON, J. Bryan — Music Educator P.1395
BURTON, Richard J. — Partner P. 149
BURTON, Tim — Director P.2063
BUSCH, Douglas Dale — Principal P. 150
BUSER, Carolyn Elizabeth — Adult Education Educator P. 151
BUSER, Stephen — Emeritus Professor of Finance P.1682
BUSH, Barbara — Former First Lady P.2064
BUSH, George Herbert Walker — 41st President of the U.S. P.2064
BUSH, George Walker — 43rd President of the U.S. P.2064
BUSH, Jeb — President P.2064
BUSH, John K. — Federal Judge P.2064
BUSH, Laura Welch — Former First Lady P.2064
BUSH, Wesley G. — Aerospace Transportation Executive P.2064
BUSSEL, James B. — Pediatrician P.1683
BUSTOS, Cherie — U.S. Representative from Illinois P.2065
BUSWELL, Arthur — Physician, Surgeon P. 152
BUTHIAU, Didier Nicolas — Physician P.1683
BUTKUS, Dick — Former NFL Player P.2065
BUTLER, William T. — Academic Administrator P. 153
BUTTERFIELD, Alexander — Aviation Executive (Retired),
    Former Military Officer, Presidential Appointee P. 154
BUTTERFIELD, George Kenneth Jr. — U.S. Representative from
    North Carolina P.2065
BUTTERFIELD, Stephen A. — Education Educator P. 155
BUTZ, Norbert Leo — Actor P.2065
BUZZELLI, Charlotte Grace — Special Education Educator P. 156
BYRNE, Bradley — U.S. Representative from Alabama P.2065
BYRNE, Granville Bland III — Attorney P.1683
BYTHEWOOD, David A. — Attorney, Owner P. 157
CABRANES, Jose Alberto — Federal Judge P.2065
CACCIATORE, S. Sammy — Lawyer P. 158
CAFORIO, Giovanni — CEO P.2065
CAGE, Nicolas — Actor P.2066
CAHILLANE, Steven A A. — CEO of Kellogg Co P.2066
CAIN, Jonathan — Singer, Songwriter P.2066
CAIN BLANCHARD, Mary Josie — Director P. 159
CAINE, Clifford J. — Educational Administrator, Consultant P.1683
CAINE, Michael — Actor P.2066
CALAGIONE, Sam — Owner P.2066
CALANTZOPOULOS, André — Tobacco Company Executive P.2066
CALATRAVA, Santiago — Architect P.2066
CALDWELL, Billy R. — Geologist P.1683
CALDWELL, Mark Donald — Educational Sales Executive P.1683
CALDWELL, Zoe — Actress, Film Director P.2067
CALIFANO, Joseph Anthony Jr. — Chairman of the National Center
    on Addiction and Substance Abuse P.2067
CALIPARI, John Vincent — College Basketball Coach P.2067
CALKINS, Evan — Physician P.1396
CALLAHAN, Consuelo Maria — Federal Judge P.2067
CALLAHAN, Daniel John — President P.1684
CALLAWAY BRABANT, Sarah — Sociologist, Educator P.1684
CALLENDER, Deborah J. — Physical Scientist, Lieutenant
    Commander P. 160
CALVERT, Ken — U.S. Representative from California P.2068
CAMERON, James — Film Director, Screenwriter, Producer P.2068
CAMERON, Matthew David — Musician P.2068
CAMERY, John William — Computer Engineer P. 161
CAMP, Charles Henry — Lawyer P. 162

CAMPBELL, Joan Virginia Loweke — Language Educator P.1685
CAMPBELL, Magda — Psychiatrist, Child Psychiatrist P.1396
CAMPBELL, William W. — Medical Educator, Clinical Neurologist P. 163
CAMPION, Jane — Film Director P.2068
CAMPOS, Luís, — Writer P.1397
CANAHUATI, Judy — Senior Nutrition, Maternal Child Health
    Advisor, Lactation Consultant P. 164
CANNON, Kim — Lawyer P.1685
CANNON, Mark Wilcox — Federal Government Official (Retired),
    Venture Capitalist P. 165
CANORA, Marco — Chef, Restaurateur P.2068
CANTILLI, Edmund Joseph — Professor Emeritus P.1685
CANTILO, Patrick Herrera — Partner P.1686
CANTWELL, Maria E. — U.S. Senator from Washington P.2068
CAPECCHI, Mario Renato — Geneticist, Educator P.2069
CAPITO, Shelley Moore — U.S. Senator from West Virginia P.2069
CAPRARO, Franz — Accountant P.1686
CAPRITTO, Anthony Joseph III — Lawyer P. 166
CAPUANO, Michael Everett — U.S. Representatives from
    Massachusetts P.2069
CARALEY, Demetrios James — Political Science Professor, Writer,
    Publisher P.1686
CARANGELO, Robert F. — Partner P.1686
CARASSO, Alfred Samuel — Mathematician P.1686
CARBAJAL, Salud — U.S. Representative from California P.2069
CARD, Ann M, — Advocate P. 167
CÁRDENAS, Tony — U.S. Representative from California, former
    City Councilman P.2069
CARDER, Dan — Director for Center for Alternative Fuels Engines
    and Emissions P.2069
CARDIN, Ben — U.S. Senator from Maryland P.2069
CARELL, Steve — Actor, Comedian P.2070
CAREY, Mariah — Singer P.2070
CARLILE, Christopher Blake — Corporate Executive, Military Officer
    (Retired), Command Pilot P. 168
CARLISLE, Rick — Professional Basketball Coach P.2070
CARLOS, Wendy — Composer P.2070
CARLSON, Erik — CEO P.2070
CARLSON, Gretchen Elizabeth — Television Personality P.2070
CARLSON, Herbert Christian Jr — Physicist, Consultant P. 169
CARLSON, Robert — Financial Planner P.1397
CARLSON, Tucker — News Correspondent P.2070
CARLTON, Steven Norman — Former Professional Baseball Player P.2071
CARMANY, George Walter III — Finance Company Executive,
    Consultant P.1687
CARMI, Shlomo — Engineering Educator P.1687
CARMICHAEL, William D. — Consultant, Educator P. 170
CARNAHAN, Caroline — Owner, Operator P. 171
CARNES, Edward Earl — Federal Judge P.2071
CARNES, Julie Elizabeth — Federal Judge P.2071
CARNEY, John C. Jr. — Governor of Delaware P.2071
CARNEY, Susan Laura — Federal Judge P.2071
CARO, Robert Allan — Historian, Writer P.2071
CARO, William Allan — Physician, Professor P.1398
CAROL, Joy Haupt — Author, Educator, Retreat Leader P.1687
CARPENTER, John Howard Howard — Film Director, Producer,
    Writer P.2071
CARPENTER, Pamela Prisco — Bank Executive P.1687
CARPER, Tom — U.S. Senator from Delaware P.2071
CARR, Edward — Lawyer P.1688
CARRERAS, Jose — Tenor P.2072
CARRERE, Charles Scott — Judge P.1688

COOK, Grant — Senior Counsel, Commercial Trial Lawyer P.1700
COOK, Hardy Merrill III — Literature and Language Professor P. 211
COOK, Ian M. — Chairman, CEO P.2090
COOK, Jay D. MD, FAAM — Neurology Consultant P.1700
COOK, Michael H. — Lawyer, Partner, and Co-chair P. 212
COOK, Paul J. Jr. — U.S. Representative from California P.2090
COOK, Quentin — Church Administrator P.1700
COOK, Scott David — Co-Founder of Intuit P.2090
COOK, Tim — CEO of Apple, Inc. P.2091
COOK WIGGINS, Cynthia — Founder, Owner P.1700
COOKE, Sara Mullin — Daycare Administrator P.1700
COOL, Donald A. — Technical Executive P.1412
COONS, Christopher Andrew — U.S. Senator from Delaware P.2091
COOPER, Alan S. — Of Counsel P.1701
COOPER, Anderson Hays — Broadcast Journalist, News
    Correspondent P.2091
COOPER, Bradley — Actor P.2091
COOPER, Byron Stanley — Internist P.1701
COOPER, Fred M. — Physicist P.1412
COOPER, James Hayes Shofner — U.S. Representative from
    Tennessee P.2091
COOPER, Roy Asberry III — Governor of North Carolina P.2091
COOPER, Thomas David — Metallurgical Engineer, Consultant P.1701
COOPER MCCALL, Maxine — Publisher, Minister, Educator P.1701
COPELAND, Elaine Johnson — Academic Administrator P. 213
COPELAND, Misty Danielle — Dancer P.2091
COPELAND, Robert G. — Lawyer P.1702
COPENHAVER, John Barns — CEO, Attorney P. 214
COPPOLA, Francis — Film Producer, Director, Screenwriter P.2092
COPPOLA, Sofia Carmina — Film Director, Film Producer,
    Scriptwriter P.2092
CORBAT, Michael Louis — CEO P.2092
CORBETT, Patricia — Social Worker P. 215
CORDANI, David M. — President and CEO P.2092
CORDEN, James — Actor, Television Personality P.2092
CORDON-CARDO, Carlos — Professor, Chair P. 216
COREA, Chick — Musician, Composer P.2092
CORIGLIANO, John Paul — Composer P.2093
CORINTHIOS, Michael Jean Georges — Electrical Engineer P.1702
CORKER, Bob — U.S. Senator from Tennessee P.2093
CORMIER, Jason L. — Neurosurgeon P.1702
CORNELL, Brian Christian — CEO of Target P.2093
CORNELL, Eric Allin — Physics Professor P.2093
CORNISH, Nancy Lee Latham — Music Educator P. 217
CORNYN, John — U.S. Senator from Texas P.2093
CORPUZ, Laura Balatbat — Interlibrary Loan Coordinator, Writer P.1702
CORREA, Lou — U.S. Representative from California P.2094
CORROTHERS, Helen Gladys — Criminal Justice Consultant P.1703
CORYELL, May M. — Language Educator P.1413
COSS, Richard G. — Psychology Professor P. 218
COSTA, Gregg Jeffrey — Federal Judge P.2094
COSTA, Jim — U.S. Representative from California P.2094
COSTELLO, Ryan A. — U.S. Representative from Pennsylvania,
    County Commissioner P.2094
COSTNER, Kevin — Actor P.2094
COTA, Harold Maurice — Professor Emeritus P.1703
COTILLARD, Marion — Actress P.2094
COTTON, Tom — U.S. Senator from Arkansas P.2094
COTTRELL, Mary-Patricia Tross — Bank Executive P.1413
COUGHLAN, Patrick Campbell — Lawyer, Mediator P.1414
COULTER, Ann Hart — Writer, Political Columnist, Lawyer P.2095
COURIC, Katie — Broadcast Journalist P.2095

COURTNEY, Joe — U.S. Representative from Connecticut P.2095
COWLES, Jim — Lawyer P. 219
COX, Barbara — Physical Therapist P.1703
COX, Bobby — Retired Professional Baseball Manager P.2095
COX, Joyce Wellborn — Secondary School Educator P. 220
COX, Laverne — Actress P.2095
COX, Margaret PhD — Educator P.1703
CRACCHIOLO, James M. — CEO of Ameriprise Financial P.2095
CRAFT, Edmund Coleman Jr. — Automotive Parts Manufacturing
    Executive (Retired) P.1704
CRAGG, Gordon Mitchell — Special Volunteer P.1704
CRAIGMYLE, Nancy Alker — Researcher P. 221
CRAKES, Gary — Professor Emeritus P.1704
CRAMER, John Sanderson — Healthcare Executive P. 222
CRAMER, Kevin — U.S. Representative from North Dakota P.2095
CRANDALL, Roger W. — Massachusetts Mutual CEO P.2096
CRANE, Christopher Mark — President and CEO of Exelon Corp. P.2096
CRANSTON, Bryan Lee Lee — Actor P.2096
CRAPO, Michael — U.S. Senator from Idaho P.2096
CRAWFORD, Fred — Public Information Officer P. 223
CRAWFORD, Rick — U.S. Representative from Arkansas P.2096
CRAWLEY, Cheryl — Educational Leadership Consultant,
    Superintendent (Retired) P.1704
CREEL, Gavin — Actor and Singer P.2096
CREININ, Arnie — President, CEO P. 224
CRENN, Dominique — Chef P.2096
CRENSHAW, Ben — Professional Golfer P.2096
CRETAN, Donna — Critical Care and Neonatal Nurse P.1414
CREW, Debra Ann — Farmers Group CEO P.2097
CRISCI, Mathew G. — Author/Screenwriter, Social Commentator,
    Fortune 500 Executive P. 225
CRISPO, Richard — Coordinator P.1705
CRIST, Charlie — U.S. Representative from Florida P.2097
CRITES, Richard D. — Lawyer, Deputy Sheriff P. 226
CRIVARO, Alan J. — Attorney at Law P.1705
CROFT, Vicki Faye — Librarian Emeritus P.1705
CROPPER, Andre D. — EO/IR Engineering Fellow & Chief Engineer P.1705
CROSBY, David S. — Statistics Educator, Consultant P. 227
CROSBY, Marena L. — Academic Administrator P. 228
CROSBY, Sidney — Professional Hockey Player P.2097
CROSS, Eugene "Gene" W. — Engineer P.1415
CROSSLEY, Frank Alphonso — Metallurgical Engineer P. 229
CROSSLEY, Nancy Ruth — Federal Agency Administrator P.1415
CROW, Mary Lynn — Educator, Psychologist P. 230
CROW, Rita Jane — Secondary School Educator P.1706
CROWE, John T. — Lawyer P. 231
CROWE, Russell — Actor P.2097
CROWLEY, Joseph — U.S. Representative from New York P.2097
CROYLE, Barbara Ann — Executive Director P. 232
CRUISE, Tom — Actor P.2097
CRUM, Albert B. — Psychiatrist P.1706
CRUSE, Julius M. Jr. — Professor P. 233
CRUTCHER, Brian — CEO P.2098
CRUTCHFIELD, C. Barry — Lawyer P. 234
CRUTCHFIELD, William Gayle — Retail Executive P. 235
CRUZ, Jose Bejar Jr — Professor Emeritus P.1707
CRUZ, Penélope — Actress P.2098
CRUZ, Ted — U.S. Senator from Texas P.2098
CRYSTAL, Billy — Actor P.2098
CUBAN, Mark — President and Chairman P.2098
CUELLAR, Henry Roberto — U.S. Representative From Texas, Lawyer P.2099
CULBERSON, John Abney — U.S. Representative from Texas P.2099

FRENCH, Elizabeth Irene — Retired Biology Professor, Musician,
    Violin Teacher   P. 385
FRENCH, John III — Lawyer, Director   P. 386
FRIEDBERG, Ahron — Psychiatrist   P.1755
FRIEDEN, Thomas R. — Federal Agency Administrator   P.2143
FRIEDENTHAL-ROOS, Sybil — Elementary School Educator   P. 387
FRIEDLAND, Michelle — Federal Judge   P.2143
FRIEDMAN, C. Marshall — Owner, Attorney   P.1755
FRIEDMAN, Richard Charles MD — Psychiatrist, Adjunct Research
    Professor of Psychology, Clinical Professor   P. 388
FRIEDMAN, Sonia — Theatre Producer   P.2143
FRIESE, Robert Charles — Lawyer   P. 389
FRISCH, Sidney Jr. — Lawyer, Real Estate Broker, Insurance Broker   P.1446
FRITZ, Lance M. — Rail Transportation Company Executive   P.2143
FROST, Barry Warren — Attorney   P.1755
FROST, Glen E. — Attorney at Law   P.1755
FUCCILLO, Ralph — Foundation Administrator, Consultant   P. 390
FUDGE, Marcia Louise — U.S. Representative from Ohio,
    former Mayor   P.2143
FUENTES, Yvonne — Associate Professor of Spanish   P.1756
FUJIMURA, Robert Kanji — Biochemist, Molecular Biologist   P. 391
FUKUCHI, Ken-ichiro — Medical Educator, Researcher   P.1756
FUKUSHIMA, Glen S. — Senior Fellow   P.1756
FUKUYAMA, Francis — Political Scientist, Author   P.2143
FULKERSON, Catherine — CEO Reston Association   P. 392
FULLER, David Otis Jr. — Lawyer/Judge   P.1756
FULLER, Edwin — Hotel Executive   P. 393
FULLER, James W. — Financial Planner   P.1756
FULLER, Robert — Architect   P.1757
FUNDERBURK, Raymond — Circuit Court Judge   P.1757
FUNK, William H. — Engineering Educator (Retired)   P. 394
FURLOTTI, Alexander Amato — Real Estate and Investment
    Company Executive, Philanthropist   P.1757
FURNAS, David William — Plastic Surgeon   P. 395
FURRER, John R. — Manufacturing Executive (Retired)   P. 396
FURST, Daniel Eric — Medical Educator   P. 397
FUTTER, Ellen Victoria — President   P.2144
GAAR, Marilyn — Manager   P.1757
GABBARD, Tulsi — U.S. Representative from Hawaii   P.2144
GABLE, Robert Elledy — Real Estate Company Executive   P. 398
GABRICK, Robert William — Archival and Educational Consultant,
    Writer, Researcher   P. 399
GABRIEL, Michael — Retired Psychology Professor   P.1757
GADUS, Peg — Pastoral Associate/Business Manager   P.1758
GAETA, Rosemarie — Psychotherapist   P.1758
GAETZ, Matt — U.S. Representative from Florida   P.2144
GAGEL, Robert Francis — Endocrinologist, Educator   P.1758
GAGELMAN, Rita — Parish Ministry Associate   P.1758
GAGLIARDI, Ugo Oscar — Application Developer   P. 400
GAIMAN, Neil Richard — Novelist, Comics Writer, Screenwriter   P.2144
GALATIANOS, Gus A. — Computer Company Executive   P.1758
GALESI, Deborah Lee — Artist   P. 401
GALLAGHER, Mike — U.S. Representative from Wisconsin   P.2145
GALLAGHER, Thomas C. — Chairman and CEO   P.2145
GALLAND, Leo — Director, Researcher   P. 402
GALLEGO, Ruben — U.S. Representative from Arizona   P.2145
GALLUP, John Gardiner — Paper Company Executive (Retired)   P. 403
GALVIN, Matthew Reppert — Psychiatrist   P. 404
GAMACHE, Bernadette — Vice President of Finance   P.1758
GAMPEL, Elaine Susan — Investment Company Executive   P.1759
GAMST, Frederick C. — Professor Emeritus   P. 405
GANLEY, James — Professor (Retired)   P. 406

GANT, Donald — Investment Banker   P.1759
GARAMENDI, John Raymond — U.S. Representative from California   P.2145
GARCETTI, Eric Michael — Mayor of Los Angeles   P.2145
GARDNER, Cory Scott — U.S. Senator from Colorado   P.2145
GARDNER, Mary Frances — Doctor   P. 407
GARDNER, Stephen David — Lawyer   P.1759
GARFIELD, Andrew Russell — Actor   P.2145
GARFIELD, Ernest — President   P.1759
GARFIELD-WOODBRIDGE, Nancy — Children's Book Author   P. 408
GARG, Ooshma — CEO   P.2145
GARLAND, Cedric Frank — Epidemiologist, Educator   P.1759
GARLAND, Gregory Cyril — Chairman, CEO   P.2145
GARLAND, Merrick Brian — Federal Judge   P.2145
GARNER, Shirley Imogene — Music Educator   P.1759
GARNETT, Kevin Maurice — Professional Basketball Player   P.2146
GARRAHAN-MASTERS, Mary Patricia — Social Worker (Retired),
    Writer   P.1447
GARRETT, Geoffrey PhD — Dean   P.2146
GARRETT, Thomas A. — U.S. Representative from Virginia   P.2146
GARRICK, B. John — Research Scientist   P. 409
GARRIGUES, Gretchen — Global Chief Marketing Officer   P. 410
GARRIS, Charles Alexander Jr — Professor of Engineering   P.1760
GARTEN, Ina — Cookbook Author, Televison Show Host   P.2146
GARTZ, Rolf — Foundation Administrator   P.1760
GATCH, Milton McCormick — Library Director, Clergyman,
    Educator   P. 411
GATES, Bill — Software Company Executive, Philanthropist   P.2146
GATES, Melinda French — Charitable Foundation Administrator   P.2147
GATES, Thomas Edward — Attorney, Civil Engineer   P. 412
GAVIN, Mary Jane — Medical/Surgical Nurse (Retired)   P.1447
GEBBIA, Joe — Co-founder   P.2147
GEER CLEMENT, Evelyn — Librarian, Educator (Retired)   P.1448
GEHRY, Frank — Architect   P.2147
GEISS, Roger William — Pathologist, Medical Educator   P. 413
GELLER, Margaret Joan — Astrophysicist, Educator   P.2147
GELLER, Robert James — Advertising Executive   P.1760
GENEL, Myron — Pediatrician, Educator   P. 414
GENEROUS, William Thomas Jr. — Coach, Educator   P.1760
GENINI, Ronald Walter — History Educator   P.1448
GENNETTE, Jeffrey — Chairman and CEO of Macy's Inc.   P.2147
GEORGE, John S. — Research Scientist, Deputy Group Leader   P.1760
GEORGE, Paul — Professional Basketball Player   P.2148
GERARD, Red — Olympic Snowboarder   P.2148
GERARD-SHARP, Monica F. — President   P. 415
GERDNER, Linda Ann — Consulting Assistant Professor   P. 416
GERE, Richard — Actor   P.2148
GERKEN, Heather K. — Law Educator   P.2148
GERMAIN, Pamela — Health Facility Administrator (Retired),
    Educator   P.1760
GERMANOTTA, Stefani (Lady Gaga) — Singer, Songwriter   P.2148
GERO, Anthony George — Securities and Commodities Trader   P.1761
GERVAIS, Ricky — Actor   P.2148
GERWIG, Greta — Actress   P.2149
GEWEKE, John Frederick — Economics Professor   P. 417
GEYMAN, John Payne — Physician, Educator   P.1761
GHANI, Rula — First Lady of Afghanistan   P.2149
GHIRARDI, GianCarlo — Professor (Retired)   P.1762
GIACONA, Corrado Anthony II — President, CEO   P. 418
GIAMBENE, Giovanni — Engineering Educator   P.1762
GIANFORTE, Greg R. — U.S. Representative from Montana, former
    Information Technology Executive   P.2149

GIANNOTTA, Steven L. — Neurosurgery Professor, Chairman of
    Neurological Surgery   P. 419
GIBBONS, Dona Alden Coe — Senior System Analyst   P.1449
GIBBONS, Julia Smith — Federal Judge   P.2149
GIBBS, Bob — U.S. Representative from Ohio   P.2149
GIBBS, Joe Jackson — Former NFL Coach   P.2149
GIBBS, Lawrence Blair — Lawyer   P.1762
GIBSON, Bob — Former Professional Baseball Player   P.2149
GIBSON, John R. — Software Engineer   P.1449
GIBSON, Mel — Actor, Film Director and Producer   P.2149
GIBSON PEVEAR, Roberta C. — State Legislator   P. 420
GIGLIOTTI, Joanne Marie — Artist, Arts Administrator   P.1450
GILBERT, Martha Jane — Literature and Language Educator
    (Retired)   P.1762
GILBERT, O.L. — Attorney   P.1450
GILES, Melva Theresa — Nursing Professor, Researcher, Clinical
    Specialist   P.1451
GILKESON, Robert — Vice Chairman of Radiology   P. 421
GILL, Anne Whalen — Lawyer   P. 422
GILL, Joan Cox — Professor   P.1762
GILL, Stephen — Physicist (Retired)   P.1451
GILL, Vince — Country Musician, Singer   P.2150
GILLIBRAND, Kirsten Elizabeth Rutnick — U.S. Senator from New
    York   P.2150
GILLMAN, Joan Ava — Elementary School Educator, Musician   P.1763
GILLON, Michael — Astronomer   P.2150
GILMAN, Sid — Neurologist   P. 423
GINGOLD, Dennis M. — Chairman of the Board   P.1452
GINGRICH, (NEWTON LEROY GINGRICH), Newt — Writer, former
    U. S. Representative from Georgia   P.2150
GINSBURG, Ruth Bader — Associate Justice of the U.S. States
    Supreme Court   P.2150
GINTHER, Donna — Professor   P.1763
GIOVANELLI, John — Research Chemist (Retired)   P.1763
GIROLO, Nella Sue — Voice Educator (Retired)   P. 424
GIROTTI, Albert W. — Biochemist   P.1763
GIRVIGIAN, Raymond — Architect (Retired)   P.1452
GIUFFRIDA, Nadja — Founder, CEO   P.1763
GIULIANI, Rudy — Lawyer, Former Mayor of NYC   P.2151
GLAHN, Harry R. — Scientist Emeritus (Retired)   P.1763
GLASER, Daniel S. — CEO of Marsh & McLennon   P.2151
GLASS, David L. — Division Director   P. 425
GLASS, Dennis Robert — CEO and President of Lincoln National Group   P.2151
GLASS, Glenda June — Clinical Microbiologist (Retired)   P.1764
GLASS, Milton Louis — Former Chief Financial Officer   P. 426
GLASS, Philip — Composer, Musician   P.2151
GLASS, Renèe, — President, Co-Founder   P. 427
GLASS, Ronald Bernhard Jacob — Attending Radiologist   P.1764
GLASSER, Joseph — Founder and President Emeritus   P. 428
GLAUBER, Roy J. — Theoretical Physicist   P.2152
GLAVINE, Tom — Former Professional Baseball Player   P.2152
GLENN, Guy C. — Pathologist   P. 429
GLOR, Jeff — News Correspondent   P.2152
GLOVER, Danny — Actor   P.2152
GLOVER, Donald — Actor, Writer, Director   P.2153
GLUSKER, Jenny — Professor Emeritus   P. 430
GLUSKI, Andrés R. — Power Distribution Company Executive   P.2153
GODARD, Jean-Luc — Film Director   P.2153
GOERGER, Virginia Frances — Owner, Photographer, Designer   P.1764
GOFF, Gregory J. — Oil & Gas company Executive   P.2153
GOHMERT, Louie — U.S. Representative from Texas   P.2153
GOINES, Leonard — Freelance Musician   P.1764

GOLD, Daryl — Attorney   P. 431
GOLDBERG, Susan — Magazine Editor   P.2153
GOLDBERG, Whoopi — Actress, Comedienne   P.2154
GOLDBLATT, Hal Michael — Chief Financial Officer, Photographer,
    Author   P.1765
GOLDEN, Leon — Classicist, Educator   P.1765
GOLDFARB, Helene Diane — Counseling Administrator (Retired)   P.1765
GOLDING, Gregory S. — Senior Vice President   P.1765
GOLDMAN, Lee — Dean, Cardiologist, Educator   P.2154
GOLDMAN, Peter Louis — Writer   P. 432
GOLDMAN, Stanford M. — Medical Educator   P.1765
GOLDSTEIN, Jack C. — Attorney   P. 433
GOLDSTEIN, Margaret Ann — Professor Emeritus, Life Member   P.1766
GOLDSTEIN, Norman — Clinical Professor of Dermatology   P.1453
GOLUB, Lorne M. — SUNY Distinguished Professor   P.1767
GOMEZ, Jimmy — U.S. Representative from California   P.2154
GOMEZ, Selena Marie Marie — Actress, Singer   P.2154
GOMILLION-WILLIAMS, Bridgette L. — Senior Silicon Chemist   P. 434
GOMOLL, Andreas H. — Associate Professor Of Orthopedic Surgery   P.1767
GONZALEZ, Richard A. — Pharmaceutical Executive   P.2154
GONZALEZ, Vincente — U.S. Representative from Texas   P.2155
GONZÁLEZ COLÓN, Jennifer — Resident Commission of Puerto Rico   P.2155
GONZALEZ-GERTH, Miguel — Literature Educator, Language
    Educator   P. 435,1453
GOOD, Lynn Jones — Electrical Power Company Executive   P.2155
GOODELL, Roger Stokoe — National Football League Commissioner   P.2155
GOODING, Charles Thomas "Tom" — Psychologist   P. 436
GOODING, Cuba — Actor   P.2155
GOODLATTE, Robert William — Chairman of the House Judiciary
    Committee,U.S. Representative from Virginia, Lawyer   P.2155
GOODMAN, John — Actor   P.2155
GOODMAN, Marcia Louisa — Medical Resident (Retired)   P. 437
GOODMAN, Martin D. — Surgeon   P.1767
GOODMAN, Shira D. — Retail Office and Business Products Executive   P.2156
GOODMAN, Willa Louise — Women's Federal Program Manager
    (Retired)   P.1767
GOODMAN-MILONE, Constance (Connie) — Writer   P. 438
GOODNIGHT, James H. — CEO of SAS   P.2156
GOOSTREE, Tricia D. — Managing Partner   P. 439
GORDER, Joe — Valero CEO   P.2156
GORDON, Ella — Women's Health Nurse (Retired)   P. 440
GORDON, Helen H. — Author, Game Publisher   P. 441
GORDON, Jeff — Former Professional Stock Car Racer   P.2156
GORDON, John C. — Laboratory Fellow   P.1767
GORDON, Malcolm S. — Professor of Biology   P.1767
GORDON, Martin Eli — Physician, Educator   P.1454
GORDON, Sharon Ann — Mathematics Educator (Retired),
    Preschool Educator (Retired)   P. 442
GORDON-LEVITT, Joseph — Actor   P.2156
GORDY, Berry — Entrepreneur, Film Producer, Recording Industry
    Executive   P.2156
GORE, Al — Enviormental Activist, 45th Vice President of the U.S.   P.2157
GORE, Steven Lowell — Accountant   P. 443
GORELICK, Kenneth J. — Managing Director   P.1768
GORMAN, James P. — Morgan Stanley CEO   P.2157
GORN, Janet Marie — Senior Foreign Affairs Officer   P. 444
GORSKY, Alex — Chairman & CEO of Johnson & Johnson   P.2157
GORSUCH, Neil McGill — Associate Justice of the U.S. Supreme
    Court   P.2157
GOSAR, Paul Anthony — U.S. Representative From Arizona, Dentist   P.2157
GOSLING, Ryan — Actor   P.2157
GOSSARD, Stone Carpenter — Musician   P.2157

NASH, William D. — Retail Executive P.2278
NASHAN, Kevin — Chef P.2278
NASKY, H. Gregory — Lawyer .... P. 869
NASSTROM, Roy Richard — Educational Consultant P.1875
NASTASI-SCRIPA, Rosalia Josephine — Engineering Professor
    (Retired), Distinguished Professor Emeritus .... P. 870
NASUTA, Nickolas E. — Sole Proprietor .... P. 871
NATALICIO, Diana Siedhoff — Academic Administrator P.2278
NATANI, Kirmach — Psychologist .... P. 872
NAUGHTON, James — Actor P.2278
NAUGLE, Ronald Clinton — Historian, Professor Emeritus .... P. 873
NAUMAN, St. Elmo Jr — Minister, University Professor (Retired) .... P. 874
NAUMANN, Jens RSSW — Administrator .... P. 875
NAVARRA, Tova — Writer P.1876
NAVRATILOVA, Martina — Former Professional Tennis Player P.2278
NAYEF, Mohammed Bin Bin — Crown Prince of Saudia Arabia P.2278
NEAL, Durwood E. Jr — Professor P.1876
NEAL, Michael B. — Attorney at Law P.1876
NEAL, Richard Edmund — U.S. Representatives from Massachusetts P.2278
NEAL SIAMIS, Janet — Painter .... P. 876
NEEDLES, Belverd Earl Jr — Distinguished Professor at DePaul
    University School of Accountancy, Educator .... P. 877
NEESON, Liam — Actor P.2279
NEFF, Thomas — Executive Recruiter .... P. 878
NEGISHI, Ei-ichi — Chemistry Professor .... P. 879
NEIDORFF, Michael F. — CEO P.2279
NEILL, Darryl Boyd — Professor P.1542
NELLIS, William — Associate P.1876
NELLOR WICKWIRE, Patricia Joanne — Psychologist, Educator .... P. 880
NELSON, Bill — U.S. Senator From Florida P.2279
NELSON, Edith E. — Consultant Dietitian P.1877
NELSON, Kevin A. — Public Health Analyst P.1877
NELSON, Larry Gene — Professional Golfer P.2279
NELSON, Willie Hugh — Musician P.2279
NELSON PITTMAN, Amanda — Music Educator .... P. 881
NELSONS, Andris — Conductor P.2280
NEMEC, Michael Lee — Lawyer .... P. 882
NEMIR, Donald Philip — Lawyer P.1877
NERA, Nena M. — President P.1877
NEUBAUER, Dean V. — Engineering Fellow, Chief Statistician, Data
    Analytics Leader P.1877
NEUMAN, Clifford — Computer Scientist, Educator P.1877
NEUSTADT, David Harold — Physician (Retired) P.1543
NEUSTEIN, Amy PhD — CEO and Founder P.1878
NEWELL, Gabe — Computer Game Development Company Executive P.2280
NEWHOUSE, Daniel — U.S. Representative from Washington P.2280
NEWLAN BOWER, Janet Esther — Freelance Writer, Educator
    (Retired) P.1878
NEWMAN, Michael Rodney — Lawyer P.1878
NEWMAN, Rachel N. — Editor (Retired) .... P. 883
NEWSOM, Kevin — Federal Judge P.2280
NEWTON, Cam — Professional Football Player P.2280
NEWTON, Wayne — Entertainer, Actor, Recording Industry Executive P.2280
NEWTON, William A. Jr — Pediatrician P.1543
NÉZET-SÉGUIN, Yannick — Director of the Philadelphia Orchestra P.2281
NGUYEN, Jacqueline Hong-Ngoc — Federal Judge P.2281
NGUYEN, San Duy — Psychiatrist, Educator .... P. 884
NIAKAN, Kathy — Developmental Biologist P.2281
NIBLOCK, Robert A. — CEO P.2281
NICHOLAS, Henry Thompson III — Philanthropist P.2281
NICHOLAS, Nickie Lee — Industrial Hygienist (Retired) P.1878
NICHOLSON, Jack — Actor P.2281

NICKLAUS, Jack William — Sports Apparel Executive, Professional
    Golfer (Retired) P.2281
NIELSEN, George Lee — Senior Principal Architect P.1878
NIELSEN, Kirstjen M. — U.S. Secretary of Homeland Security P.2282
NIELSEN, Michael Edward — Professor, Chairman P.1879
NIEMEYER, Paul Victor — Federal Judge P.2282
NIEMONEN, Jack Edwin — Sociologist P.1879
NIMBLEY, Thomas — CEO P.2282
NIMETZ, Matthew — Lawyer & Investment Company Executive,
    Diplomat P.1879
NIRAJ, Ashutosh — Cardiologist .... P. 885
NITZE, William A. — Entrepreneur, Not-for-Profit Developer,
    Government Official .... P. 886
NIXON, Cynthia — Actress P.2282
NIXON, Daniel Walker — Adjunct Professor of Medicine .... P. 887
NOAH, Trevor — Television Personality, Comedian P.2282
NOEM, Kristi Lynn — U.S. Representative from South Dakota P.2282
NOHRIA, Nitin — Dean P.2282
NOLAN, Christopher — Film Director, Producer, Writer P.2283
NOLAN, Peter — Physics Professor .... P. 888
NOLAN, Richard Thomas — Episcopal Minister, Professor,
    Writer (Retired) .... P. 889
NOLAN, Rick — U.S. Representative from Minnesota P.2283
NOLAN, Stanton Peelle — Surgeon, Educator .... P. 890
NONNA, John — Lawyer P.1544
NOOYI, Indra Krishnamurthy — CEO P.2283
NORA, James Jackson — Physician, Writer, Educator .... P. 891
NORBECK, Jack Carl — President P.1880
NORCROSS, Donald — U.S. Representative from New Jersey P.2283
NORDBY, Eugene Jorgen — Orthopedic Surgeon .... P. 892
NORDSTRAND, Nathalie — Artist P.1880
NORMAN, Gregory John — Professional Golfer P.2283
NORMAN, Ralph W. — U.S. Representative from South Carolina P.2283
NORQUIST, Grover Glenn — Founder and President of Americans
    for Tax Reform P.2283
NORRIS, Charles Richard Jr. — Physician, Psychiatrist P.1880
NORRIS, Jo Anne W. — Curriculum Leader, School Counselor P.1544
NORTHAM, Ralph Shearer — Governor of Virginia, former
    Lieutenant Governor of Virginia, former State Legislator P.2283
NORTON, Edward — Actor P.2283
NORTON, Eleanor Holmes — Delegate to the U.S. House of
    Representatives P.2284
NORTON, Jenny — Director P.1880
NORTON, Mary Beth — History Professor, Writer .... P. 893
NORVILLE, H. Scott — Professor of Civil Engineering .... P. 894
NOTTER, Robert H. — Biomedical Researcher P.1881
NOVAKOVIC, Phebe N. — General Dynamics CEO P.2284
NOVALES, Ronald Richards — Zoologist, Educator P.1881
NOWITZKI, Dirk Werner — Professional Basketball Player P.2284
NUNES, Devin Gerald — U.S. Congressman from California P.2284
NUNN, Patarica Dian — Poet .... P. 895
NUSBAUM, Geoffrey D. — Psychotherapist .... P. 896
NUSKIND, Jeffrey M. — Senior Medical Physicist .... P. 897
NUTTER, David George — Principal .... P. 898
NUWER, Henry — Journalist P.1881
NYDEGGER, Rick D. — Lawyer .... P. 899
NYENHUIS, Jacob Eugene — Interim Director P.1545
OATES, Joyce Carol — Writer, Retired Educator P.2284
OBAMA, Barack Hussein Jr. — 44th President of the U.S. P.2284
OBAMA, Michelle LaVaughn Robinson — Former First Lady P.2285
OBERBILLIG, Molly — Utilities Executive .... P. 900
O'BLOCK, Robert L. — Executive Director .... P. 901

PETTIT, Ghery St. John — President   P.1555
PETTY, Elizabeth D. — Numeracy Coach, Data Coach   P. 954
PETTY, Richard — Retired Professional Racing Driving   P.2301
PETZ, Lawrence D. — Medical Director   P.1895
PFISTER, Alfred Karl — Educator, Internist   P. 955
PHELPS, Edmund Strother Jr. — Economics Professor   P.2301
PHELPS, Michael — Professional Swimmer   P.2301
PHILBIN, Gary M. — Retail Executive   P.2301
PHILIPP, Karla Ann — Musician, Educator, Conductor   P.1896
PHILLIPS, Gail Susan — Teacher   P.1556
PHILLIPS, Gregory Alan — Federal Judge, Former State Attorney
    General, former Federal Prosecutor   P.2301
PHILLIPS, Ted — Advertising Executive   P.1897
PHILLIS, Marilyn Hughey — Artist   P.1896
PHOCAS, George J. — International Lawyer   P. 956
PHOENIX, Joaquin Raphael — Actor   P.2302
PICHAI, Sundar — Internet Company Executive   P.2302
PICKEL, Grover Lee — Immunochemist   P. 957
PICKETT, Stephen Wesley — Independent Consultant   P.1897
PIECUCH, Jim — History Professor, Writer   P.1897
PIERARD, Richard Victor — History Educator   P.1898
PIERCE, David Hyde Hyde — Actor   P.2302
PIERCE, Michael Norman — Medical Director   P.1898
PIERSON, Deirdre, K. — Partner, Attorney   P.1556
PIESCHE, Antoinette — Owner   P.1899
PIIRTO, Douglas Donald — Owner, Consulting Forester   P.1899
PIKETTY, Thomas — Economist   P.2302
PIKUS, David H. — A Principal   P.1899
PILLARD, Nina — Federal Judge, Law Educator   P.2302
PILLERS, De-Ann — Professor   P.1900
PILLINGER, Marc H. — Partner   P. 958
PILLSBURY-GREDZENS, Sandra May — Sole Proprietor, Art Educator   P. 959
PINDER, Mike — Musician and Keyboardist   P.2302
PINE, Chris Whitelaw Whitelaw — Actor   P.2302
PINEDA, Arnel — Singer   P.2302
PINGREE, Chellie M. — U.S. Representative from Maine   P.2302
PINKETT-SMITH, Jada — Actress   P.2303
PINSKY, Robert Neal — Poet, Educator   P.2303
PIRODSKY, Donald Max — Psychiatrist, Educator   P.1900
PISANI, Anthony Michael — Architect   P. 960
PITINO, Rick — College Basketball Coach   P.2303
PITT, Brad — Actor, Film Producer   P.2303
PITTENGER, Robert — U.S. Representative from North Carolina   P.2303
PIZARRO, Pedro — CEO of Edison Intl   P.2303
PIZZAMIGLIO, Albert Theodore — Conductor, Band Leader   P.1900
PLANT, Jackson Vaughn — Bishop   P.1900
PLANT, Robert Anthony — Musician   P.2304
PLATSOUCAS, Chris Dimitrios — Immunologist   P. 961
PLATT, Ben — Actor   P.2304
PLAYER, Gary Jim — Professional Golfer, Businessman, Golf Course
    Designer   P.2304
PLOTKIN, Irving H. — Economist, Consultant   P.1900
PLOTTEL, Jeanine Parisier — Foreign Language Educator   P. 962
PLUMMER, Anita Ellescas — Artist   P.1557
PLUMMER, Christopher — Actor   P.2304
POCAN, Mark — U.S. Representative from Wisconsin, former State
    Legislator   P.2305
PODESTA, Tony — Lobbyist   P.2305
POE, Ted — U.S. Representative from Texas, former Judge   P.2305
POEHLER, Amy — Comedienne, Actress   P.2305
POGUE, John Marshall — President   P.1901
POGUE, Richard Welch — Lawyer   P. 963

POHOST, Gerald Michael — Cardiologist, Medical Educator   P.1901
POITIER, Sidney — Actor   P.2305
POLICINSKI, Chris — CEO   P.2306
POLIQUIN, Bruce Lee — U.S. Representative from Maine   P.2306
POLIS, Jared Schutz — U.S. Representative from Colorado,
    Entrepreneur, Philanthropist   P.2306
POLISI, Joseph William — President of The Juilliard School   P.2306
POLITZER, Hugh David — Physicist, Educator   P.2306
POLK, Hiram Carey Jr — Professor of Surgery   P.1902
POLK, Michael B. — CEO   P.2306
POLLACK, Marsha — Secondary School Educator   P.1902
POLLAN, Michael — Author, Journalist, Professor   P.2306
POLLARA, Joanne — Elementary School Principal   P. 964
POLLOCK, Richard A. — Surgeon   P.1903
POMFRET, David B. — Physician   P.1903
POMPEO, Mike — U.S. Secretary of State   P.2307
PONDER, Catherine — Founding Minister   P.1903
PONSKY, Jeffrey — Surgeon   P.1903
POOCHIGIAN, Donald Vaughn — Professor   P.1903
POOLER, Rosemary S. — Federal Judge   P.2307
POON, Peter — Engineer   P.1903
POPE, Bob — Lawyer   P.1904
POPOVICH, Gregg Charles — Professional Basketball Coach   P.2307
PORTE, Michael Sheldon — Communications Educator (Retired)   P.1904
PORTER, Wayne — Executive Director   P. 965
PORTMAN, Natalie — Actress   P.2307
PORTMAN, Rob — U.S. Senator from Ohio   P.2307
PORTWAY, Patrick Stephen — Founder, President, Executive   P. 966
POSEN, Zac — Apparel Designer   P.2308
POSEY, Bill — U.S. Representative from Florida   P.2308
POST , Glenn F. III — CEO   P.2308
POSTELL, Cindy Deborah — English Teacher   P.1557
POTVIN, Denis Charles — Professional Hockey Player   P.2308
POULSON, Robert J. Jr. — Attorney   P. 967
POULTON, Roberta Doris — Nurse, Consultant   P.1904
POWELL, Colin Luther — Former U.S. Secretary of State, former
    Chairman of the Joint Chiefs of Staff   P.2308
POWELL, Dina Habib — Former National Security Advisor for
    Strategy   P.2308
POWELL, Jerome H. — Federal Official, Political Scientist   P.2308
POWELL, Jonathan Patrick — Owner, President   P. 968
POWELL, Raymond William — Financial Planner,
    School Administrator (Retired)   P.1904
POWELL, William C. — Consumer Products Company Executive   P.1558
POWER, Samantha J. — U.S. Representative to the U.N.   P.2309
POYDASHEFF, Robert Stephen — Lawyer   P.1904
PRADHAN, Basant K. — Associate Professor, Physician   P.1905
PRADO, Edward Charles — Federal Judge   P.2309
PRATT, Chris — Actor   P.2309
PRATT, Gregory Carl — President   P.1905
PREMA, Nitya — Psychotherapist   P.1905
PRESCOTT, Edward Christian — Economist   P.2309
PRICE, David Eugene — U.S. Representative from North Carolina,
    Education Educator   P.2309
PRICE, Nick — Professional Golfer   P.2309
PRIEBUS, Reince R. — Political Organization Administrator, Lawyer   P.2310
PRIGMORE, Jay — Senior Engineer   P.1905
PRINGLE, Robert — Lawyer   P. 969
PRISCO, Frank J. — Psychotherapist   P.1905
PRISING, Jonus — CEO   P.2310
PRITYCHENKO, Boris — Scientist   P.1906
PROBSTEIN, Ronald — Engineering Educator   P. 970

PROCHASKA, Charles — Aerospace Engineer — P. 971
PROCTOR, Conrad Arnold — Member — P. 1906
PROKASY, William Frederick — Vice President (Retired) — P. 1906
PROSSER, David Thomas Jr — State Supreme Court Justice, State Legislator — P. 972
PRUITT, Scott — Former Administrator of the Environmental Protection Agency — P. 2310
PRUSINER, Stanley — Neurologist — P. 2310
PRUTER, Margaret — Editor — P. 1906
PRYOR, Jill Anne — Federal Judge — P. 2310
PRYOR, William Holcombe Jr. — Federal Judge, former State Attorney General, Educator — P. 2311
PUASCHUNDER, Julia Margarete — Teaching Fellow — P. 1907
PUCK, Wolfgang — Chef — P. 2311
PUGH, Revella Booker — Senior Pastor and Business Owner — P. 1907
PUJJI, Payal — Executive Chairman — P. 2311
PUJOLS, Albert — Professional Baseball Player — P. 2311
PULLING, Thomas Leffingwell — Investment Advisor (Retired) — P. 973
PURDY, William Richard — Lawyer — P. 974
PURIS, Martin Ford — Chairman, CEO — P. 1558
PURSEL WILLIAMS, Cecilia — Optometrist — P. 975
PUTO, Anne Marie — Reading Specialist — P. 1559
PUTTLITZ, Karl J. Sr — Metallurgist — P. 1907
PYLE, Walter K. — Lawyer — P. 1907
PYNCHON, Thomas Ruggles Jr. — Writer — P. 2311
PYSHER, Zane Kermit — Counselor — P. 1908
QUAKKELAAR, Arnold J. — Ministry Executive — P. 1559
QUARLES, Steven P. — Lawyer — P. 1908
QUAYLE, Dan — Former Vice President of the U.S. — P. 2311
QUENNEVILLE, Joel — Head Coach — P. 2312
QUIGLEY, Mike — U.S. Representative from Illinois, former County Commissioner — P. 2312
QUINCEY, James Robert — Coca-Cola CEO — P. 2312
QURAESHI, Zahir — G.W. Haworth Chair of Global Business — P. 1908
RABB, David — Co-Owner, Executive Vice President — P. 1908
RABIN, Jill M. — Obstetrician, Gynecologist, Urogynecologist — P. 1560
RABUN, John Brewton Jr — Criminal Justice Agency Administrator — P. 976
RACHAMIM, Rubin — Chemist — P. 977
RADER, Jan — Fire Chief — P. 2312
RADFORD, Diane M. MD, FACS, FRCSEd — Surgeon, Oncologist, Medical Director — P. 1560
RAE, Issa — Actress, Writer, Director — P. 2312
RAGAUSKAS, Arthur Jonas — Professor, Chair — P. 1908
RAGGI, Reena — Federal Judge — P. 2312
RAGSDALE, Dick Elliot — Health Company Executive (Retired) — P. 978
RAGUTHU, Manjula — Physician, Director — P. 1561
RAIMONDO, Gina Marie — Governor of Rhode Island, former State Treasurer — P. 2312
RAINERI, Fernando O. — Senior Lecturer — P. 979
RAINES, Edgar Frank Jr. — Contract Historian — P. 980
RAINEY KING, Joy — Poet, Executive Secretary — P. 1561
RAJADHYAKSHA, Vikram — Civil Engineering Consultant, Engineering Company Executive — P. 981
RAJAN, Madhav V. — Professor, Academic Administrator — P. 2312
RAJAN, Raghuram G. — Bank Executive, Economics Professor — P. 2312
RALPH, NancyJo — Music Educator (Retired) — P. 982
RAMAKRISHNAN, Venkatraman — Structural Biologist — P. 2312
RAMOS, Jorge — Newscaster — P. 2312
RAMOS-CANO, Hazel Balatero — Caterer (Retired), Chef, Innkeeper (Retired) — P. 1909
RANCK, James Byrne Jr. — Neuroscience Researcher, Educator — P. 983
RANDALL, Kikkan — Cross-Country Skier — P. 2313

RANDALL, R. Lor — LB & OLIVE S. Young Presidential Endowed Chair in Cancer Research, Director of Sarcoma Services — P. 984
RANDOLPH, Leonard McElroy Jr — Military Officer — P. 985
RANGASWAMI, Arun A. — Associate Professor of Pediatrics — P. 1909
RANSOM, Linwood H. Jr. — CEO — P. 1909
RANTZE-BYRD, Betty — Actor, Writer, Photographer — P. 1562
RAO, Rama K. — Pharmaceutical Executive, BlockChain Entrepreneur — P. 986
RARDIN, Ronald L. — Engineering Educator — P. 1562
RASH, Wayne Jr. — Journalist — P. 1909
RASKA, Karel MD, PhD — Pathologist — P. 1909
RASKIN, Jamin B. — U.S. Representative from Maryland — P. 2313
RASMUSSEN, Stephen Scott — Nationwide CEO — P. 2313
RATCLIFFE, John Lee — U.S. Representative from Texas — P. 2313
RATNER, Mark A. — Emeritus Professor of Chemistry — P. 1910
RAU, R. Ronald — Physicist (Retired) — P. 987
RAUB, Donald Wilmer — Minister, Author — P. 1910
RAUNER, Bruce Vincent — Governor of Illinois, Investment Company Executive (Retired) — P. 2313
RAVEN, Ronald J. — Education Educator — P. 1910
RAWLINSON, Johnnie Blakeney — Federal Judge — P. 2313
RAY, Marilyn A. — Professor Emeritus — P. 988
RAY, Rachael Domenica — Cookbook Author, Television Personality — P. 2313
RAYBURN, Carole Ann — Psychologist, Researcher, Writer — P. 1910
RAYMER, John David — Teacher, Founding Member, Participant — P. 1563
READ, Ian C. — CEO and Chairman at Pfizer Inc. — P. 2313
REAGAN, Gary — State Legislator, Lawyer — P. 1911
REBEIZ, Constantin Anis — Biochemist — P. 989
REBUELTA, Avelino Luis — Public Administration Educator — P. 990
RECKER, Robert R. — Medical Educator, Internist — P. 991
REDDITT, Paul Lewis — Religious Studies Educator (Retired) — P. 1911
REDFORD (CHARLES ROBERT REDFORD), Robert — Actor, Film Director and Producer — P. 2314
REDMAYNE, Eddie — Actor, Model — P. 2314
REDSTONE, Sumner Murray — Retired Founder of Viacom — P. 2314
REECE, John — Electrical Engineer, Educator, Researcher — P. 1040
REED, Jack — U.S. Senator from Rhode Island — P. 2315
REED, Robert R. III — Professor — P. 992
REED, Thomas James — Law Educator — P. 1911
REED, Tom — U.S. Representative from New York, Lawyer — P. 2315
REEDER, Robert H. — Lawyer (Retired) — P. 993
REETZ, Ruth — Artist — P. 1912
REEVES, Keanu — Actor — P. 2315
REGENSTREIF, Herbert — Lawyer — P. 1912
REGES, Marianna — Marketing Executive (Retired) — P. 1912
REGUEIRO, Miguel — Professor of Medicine — P. 1912
REICH, Steve — Composer — P. 2315
REICHERT, David George — U.S. Representative from Washington — P. 2315
REID, Edward — Senior Counsel — P. 994
REID, Harry Mason — Former U.S. Representative from Nevada — P. 2315
REID, Karen — Associate Professor of Psychology — P. 1563
REIDENBERG, Daniel Jay — Executive Director — P. 995
REIF, L. Rafael — President — P. 2316
REIFF, Daniel Drake — Art Historian (Retired), Educator — P. 1912
REIFFEL, Robert Siskind — Plastic Surgeon — P. 1913
REILLY, George Augustine — Attorney — P. 1913
REINERTSEN, Norman — Air Transportation Executive (Retired) — P. 996
REINHARDT, Stephen D. — Federal Judge — P. 2316
REININGHAUS, Ruth — Artist (Retired) — P. 1564
REINISCH, June Machover — Psychologist — P. 1913
REMINGER, Richard Thomas — Lawyer, Artist — P. 997
REMPFER-SMITH, Roberta I. — Educator (Retired) — P. 998
RENACCI, Jim — U.S. Representative from Ohio — P. 2316

SULENTIC, Robert E. — CEO of Cbre Group   P.2369
SULLIVAN, Dan — U.S. Senator from Alaska   P.2369
SULLIVAN, James Gerald — Small Business Owner   P.1188
SULLIVAN, John Dominic — Theater Producer   P.1595
SULLIVAN, John J. — Deputy Secretary of State   P.2369
SULZBERGER, Arthur Ochs Jr. — Chairman of the New York Times   P.2369
SUMIDA, Gerald Aquinas — Partner   P.1965
SUMMERS, Stanley Eugene — Mechanical Engineer   P.1189
SUNUNU, Chris — Governor of New Hampshire   P.2369
SUOMI, Rory E. — Physical Education Educator   P.1596
SUOZZI, Thomas — U.S. Representative from New York   P.2369
SUPINO, Phyllis — Medical Researcher   P.1596
SUPPA-FRIEDMAN, Janice — Secondary School Educator   P.1966
SUPPES, Christine Johnson — Writer, Online Publishing Executive   P.1190
SUSSMAN, Laureen — Real Estate Agent   P.1966
SUTHERLAND, Kiefer — Actor   P.2369
SUTTENFIELD, Diana — Co-Founder   P.1191
SUTTON, Jeffrey S. — Federal Judge   P.2369
SUTTON, Kerry Peter — Graphics Designer   P.1597
SUTTON, Mark Stephan — Paper Company Executive   P.2369
SUTTON, Paul J. — Lawyer   P.1192
SWABY, Cleveland — Founder, CEO   P.1966
SWALWELL, Eric Jr. — U.S. Representative from California   P.2370
SWAN, George Steven — Associate Professor   P.1966
SWANEY WEHN, Karen — Assistant Professor   P.1966
SWANK, Hilary — Actress   P.2370
SWANN, Richard Rockwell — Lawyer, Banker   P.1193
SWARTZ, Benjamin Kinsell Jr — Archaeologist, Educator   P.1597
SWEDISH, Joseph R. — Wellpoint CEO   P.2370
SWEIGART, Linda Inez — Nursing Educator   P.1966
SWIFT, Christopher John — Insurance Company Executive   P.2370
SWIFT, Taylor — Musician, Singer, Songwriter   P.2370
SWINDLE, Jason W. Sr. — Senior Partner   P.1194
SWINTON, Tilda — Actress   P.2371
SWISHER, Michael Scott — CEO, President   P.1967
SWITZER, Barry — Retired Professional Football Coach   P.2371
SWITZER, Carolyn — Artist   P.1967
SYDOW, Michael David Sr. — Attorney   P.1967
SYED, Ibrahim Bijli — Professor, Medical Educator, Medical Physicist   P.1967
SYKES, Diane — Federal Judge   P.2371
SYPHER, Francis J. — Writer, Editor, Educator   P.1968
SZOSTAK, Jack William — Molecular Biologist, Educator   P.2371
TABACKIN, Lewis Barry — Jazz Musician   P.2371
TABAKU, Florian — Principal   P.1968
TACK, Theresa Rose — Women's Health Nurse   P.1598
TACKETT, Natalie J. — State Agency Administrator   P.1598
TAHA, Assad — Acute Care Surgeon   P.1195
TAKANO, Mark Allan — U.S. Representative from California   P.2371
TALBOT, Martha H. — Secretary-Treasurer   P.1599
TALBOTT, Ben Johnson Jr. — Lawyer   P.1196
TALPE, Fernand P. — CEO   P.1969
TAMBOLI, Akbar R. — Consultant   P.1969
TAMBURRO, Peter J. Jr — Teacher   P.1197
TAMERLER, Candan — Wesley G. Cramer Professor   P.1969
TANDBERG, Gerilyn — Associate Professor   P.1599
TANESI, Jussara — Concrete Materials Researcher   P.1970
TANGHERLINI, Frank Robert — Physics Professor   P.1970
TANNER, Jimmie Eugene — Dean (Retired)   P.1971
TANNIS, Winston — Founding Executive Chair, Lawyer, Mediator   P.1198
TANZI, Rudolph PhD — Neuroscientist, Researcher, Educator   P.2372
TAPLEY, Byron D. — Professor of Aerospace Engineering   P.1199
TAPPER, Jake — News Correspondent, Journalist   P.2372

TARANTINO, Quentin Jerome — Film Director, Scriptwriter   P.2372
TARDIFF-KOZLOWSKI, Jill A. — Professional Cheesemonger, Customer-Service Specialist   P.1971
TARNOW, Herman, H., — Attorney   P.1200
TARRO, Giulio — Virologist   P.1201
TARTT, Donna — Writer   P.2372
TATEL, David Stephen — Federal Judge   P.2372
TATUM, Channing — Actor   P.2372
TAUB, Theodore Calvin — Attorney (Retired)   P.1600
TAYLOR, Andrew — Chef   P.2372
TAYLOR, Cora Hodge — Coordinator of Contract Programs   P.1202
TAYLOR, David S. — CEO of Procter & Gamble   P.2372
TAYLOR, Estelle Wormley — Language Educator, Dean   P.1203
TAYLOR, Lawrence Julius — Former NFL Player   P.2373
TAYLOR, Scott — U.S. Representative from Virginia   P.2373
TAYLOR, Stephen Marl — Psychiatrist, Medical Director   P.1971
TAYLOR-JOHNSON, Aaron — Actor   P.2373
TEAGUE, A. James — Energy Executive   P.2373
TEBOW, Tim — Baseball Player, former Professional Football Player, former Sports Analyst   P.2373
TEEM, Paul Lloyd Jr. — Bank Executive (Retired)   P.1971
TEMAM, Roger M. — Distinguished Professor, Mathematician   P.1972
TEMARES, Steven H. — CEO of Bed Bath & Beyond   P.2373
TEN EYCK, Dorothea F. — Real Estate Agent   P.1600
TENNEY, Claudia — U.S. Representative from New York   P.2373
TERRY, Frances — Psychiatric Nurse Practitioner   P.1601
TESSIER-LAVIGNE, Marc — President of Stanford University   P.2373
TESTA, Giuliano — Surgeon   P.2374
TESTER, Jon — U.S. Senator from Montana   P.2374
TETTERTON, Holli Y. — Director of Human Resources and Accounts Payable   P.1972
THALER, Richard H. — Economist   P.2374
THAPAR, Amul Roger — Federal Judge   P.2374
THEIS, Pol — Founder   P.1972
THEON, John S. — Meteorologist   P.1972
THERON, Charlize — Actress   P.2374
THEURER, Byron W. — Aerospace Engineer, Business Owner   P.1972
THIRY, Kent J. — Healthcare Company Executive   P.2374
THOMAS, Clarence — U.S. Supreme Court Justice   P.2374
THOMAS, Joyce Marie Marie — Nurse Manager   P.1973
THOMAS, Laurence — Professor   P.1204
THOMAS, Lindsey Kay Jr. — Research Ecology Biologist, Educator, Consultant   P.1973
THOMAS, Michael Tilson — Director   P.2374
THOMAS, Paul — Science Educator   P.1205
THOMAS, Priscilla D. — County Commissioner (Retired)   P.1601
THOMAS, Ray — Musician   P.2375
THOMAS, Sarah Elaine — Music Educator   P.1602
THOMAS, Sidney Runyan — Federal Judge   P.2375
THOMAS, Tom — Manufacturing Executive   P.1973
THOMAS-JOHN, Yvonne Maree — Artist   P.1602
THOMASSEN, Pauline Frances — Medical and Surgical Nurse (Retired)   P.1206
THOMASSON, Dan — Publishing Executive   P.1973
THOMPSON, Bennie G. — U.S. Representative from Mississippi, Ranking Member of the House Homeland Security Committee   P.2375
THOMPSON, Emma — Actress   P.2375
THOMPSON, Glenn W. Jr. — U.S. Representative from Pennsylvania, Former Health Facility Administrator   P.2375
THOMPSON, Howard Elliott — Professor Emeritus   P.1973
THOMPSON, James W. — Partner   P.1207

WELCH, Jasper A. Jr — Security Company Executive, Consultant   P.1620
WELCH, Oliver Wendell — Pharmaceutical Executive   P.1994
WELCH, Peter F. — U.S. Representative From Vermont, former State
     Legislator   P.2398
WELLS, Nancy — Director   P.1995
WELLS, Roger Stanley — Software Engineer (Retired)   P.1289
WELLS-BURTON, Eva Ella Mary — Insurance Salesperson,
     Primary School Educator   P.1620
WELSER-MÖST, Franz — Director of the Cleveland Orchestra   P.2398
WELSH, John Beresford — Lawyer   P.1995
WENSTRUP, Brad Robert — U.S. Representative From Ohio, Podiatrist   P.2398
WENTWORTH, Timothy C. — Express Scripts CEO   P.2399
WERNER, Felix-Martin — Neuroscientist   P.1995
WERTIME, Timothy Ray — Music Educator   P.1621
WEST, Allen Bernard — Executive Director, Retired Lieutenant
     Colonel   P.1995
WEST, Jerry Alan — Professional Sports Team Executive, Retired
     Professional Basketball Player   P.2399
WEST, Kanye Omari — Rap Artist, Music Producer   P.2399
WESTBERRY, Jory EdD — Principal   P.1995
WESTBIE, Barbara J. — Painter, Poet, Retired Graphic Designer   P.1995
WESTBROOK, Russell — Professional Basketball Player   P.2399
WESTERMAN, Bruce — U.S. Representative from Arkansas   P.2399
WESTON, Francine Evans — Secondary School Educator (Retired)   P.1290
WESTON, Randy — Pianist, Composer   P.2399
WETHERELL, Albert A. — Secondary School Educator (Retired)   P.1621
WEXNER, Leslie Herbert — CEO   P.2400
WEYLAND, Jack — Physics Educator (Retired), Author   P.1996
WHAM, David Buffington — Secondary School Educator   P.1996
WHAYNE, Thomas French — Professor, Cardiologist, Educator   P.1291
WHEALEY, Lois Deimel — Humanities Scholar (Retired)   P.1292
WHEELER, John W. — Lawyer   P.1996
WHEELER, Thomas Beardsley — Insurance Company Executive   P.1293
WHELTLE, Margaret Maie — Chairman   P.1996
WHIPPS, Edward F. — Principal   P.1294
WHISNAND, Rex — Association Housing Executive   P.1997
WHITACRE, Eric — Composer   P.2400
WHITAKER, Forest — Actor   P.2400
WHITAKER, Thomas Russell — English Literature Educator,
     Professor Emeritus   P.1295
WHITE, Alan — Drummer   P.2400
WHITE, Arthur L. — Education Educator   P.1997
WHITE, Betty — Actress, Comedienne   P.2400
WHITE, Dana — Sports Association Executive   P.2401
WHITE, George — Founder   P.1296
WHITE, Helen Lou — School Nurse Practitioner (Retired)   P.1622
WHITE, Helene Nita — Federal Judge   P.2401
WHITE, Joe Ellis Jr. — President   P.1997
WHITE, Letitia H. — Assistant General Council (Retired)   P.1997
WHITE, Miles D. — Healthcare Company Executive   P.2401
WHITE, Polly Sears — Religious Organization Administrator
     (Retired)   P.1622
WHITE, R. Stephen — Physics Professor   P.1297
WHITE, Ralph Paul — Automotive Executive, Consultant   P.1623
WHITE, Robert — Board of Directors   P.1298
WHITE, Sarah Elizabeth — Lawyer   P.1998
WHITE, Shaun Roger — Professional Snowboarder, Professional
     Skateboarder, Olympic Athlete   P.2401
WHITE, William Fredrick — Lawyer   P.1299
WHITEHAWK, Ann S. — Secondary School Educator (Retired)   P.1998
WHITEHEAD, Colson — Novelist   P.2401
WHITEHEAD, Jane K. — Archaeologist   P.1623

WHITEHOUSE, Sheldon — U.S. Senator from Rhode Island,
     former State Attorney General   P.2401
WHITEHURST, Brooks M. — President, Chemical Engineer   P.1300
WHITENER, Carolyn Raye — Artist, Commercial Artist, Interior
     Designer   P.1301
WHITESIDES, George M. — Chemist, Professor   P.2401
WHITHAM, Michele A. — Owner   P.1303
WHITMAN, Daniel — Government Agency Administrator   P.1302
WHITMAN, Meg — HP CEO   P.2402
WHITNEY, Lori — Legislative Staff Member   P.1998
WHITSON, Peggy Annette — Astronaut   P.2402
WHITTINGTON, Lorin Dale — Music Educator (Retired)   P.1998
WHITTINGTON, Ralph E. — Consultant, Curator (Retired)   P.1304
WICKER, Roger Frederick — U.S. Senator from Mississippi   P.2402
WICKLUND, David Wayne — Lawyer   P.1624
WIDMAN, Gary L. — President Emeritus   P.1624
WIEHOFF, John P. — CEO   P.2402
WIEMAN, Carl Edwin — Physics Professor, former Federal Official   P.2403
WIERNIK, Peter — Oncologist   P.1998
WIESE, Wolfgang Lothar — Physicist (Retired)   P.1305
WIEST, Dianne — Actress   P.2403
WIGINTON, Jay Spencer — Independent Industrial Consultant   P.1306
WIJEMANNE, Subhashie — Assistant Professor of Neurology   P.1307
WILCOX, David Eric — Electrical Engineer, Educator, Consultant   P.1308
WILCOX, Helena Marguerita — Music Educator   P.1999
WILCZEK, Frank Anthony — Physics Professor   P.2403
WILDER, Janet — Performing Company Executive   P.1309
WILDNAUER, Richard H. PhD, MBA — Life Science Executive,
     Independent Board Director   P.1625
WILEY, Kehinde — Portrait Painter   P.2403
WILEY, Mike — Chef   P.2403
WILKENS, Lenny — Former Professional Sports Team Executive,
     Retired Professional Basketball Player   P.2403
WILKEY, Elmira Smith — Illustrator, Artist, Writer   P.1999
WILKIE, Robert Leon Jr. — U.S. Secretary of Veterans Affairs   P.2404
WILKINS, Robert Leon — Federal Judge   P.2404
WILKINSON, J. Harvie III — Judge   P.2404
WILL, George Frederick — Editor, Journalist, Commentator   P.2404
WILLARD, Louis Charles — Licensed Tax Preparer, Librarian   P.1625
WILLAUER, George Jacob — American Literature Educator   P.1626
WILLETT, Don R. — Federal Judge   P.2404
WILLETT, James Delos — Science Educator   P.2000
WILLIAMS, Ann Meagher — Hospital Administrator (Retired)   P.1310
WILLIAMS, Brian Douglas — News Correspondent, Journalist   P.2404
WILLIAMS, Geisha — CEO   P.2405
WILLIAMS, Hank Jr. — Country Music Singer, Songwriter   P.2405
WILLIAMS, Janet L. — Environmental Research Technician   P.1311
WILLIAMS, Jody — Political Organization Administrator   P.2405
WILLIAMS, John P. — Professor   P.2000
WILLIAMS, John Towner — Composer, Conductor   P.2405
WILLIAMS, Jonathan H. — Senior Research Scientist (Retired)   P.1312
WILLIAMS, Mark Leon — Professor   P.1313
WILLIAMS, Michelle — Actress   P.2406
WILLIAMS, Roger — U.S. Representative from Texas, former
     State Official   P.2406
WILLIAMS, Roy — College Basketball Coach   P.2406
WILLIAMS, Serena — Professional Tennis Player   P.2406
WILLIAMS, Thomas E. — President   P.2001
WILLIAMS, Thomas L. — CEO of Parker Hannifin   P.2406
WILLIAMS, Una Joyce — Social Worker (Retired), Clinical Social
     Worker   P.1314
WILLIAMS, Vanessa L. — Actress, Recording Artist   P.2406